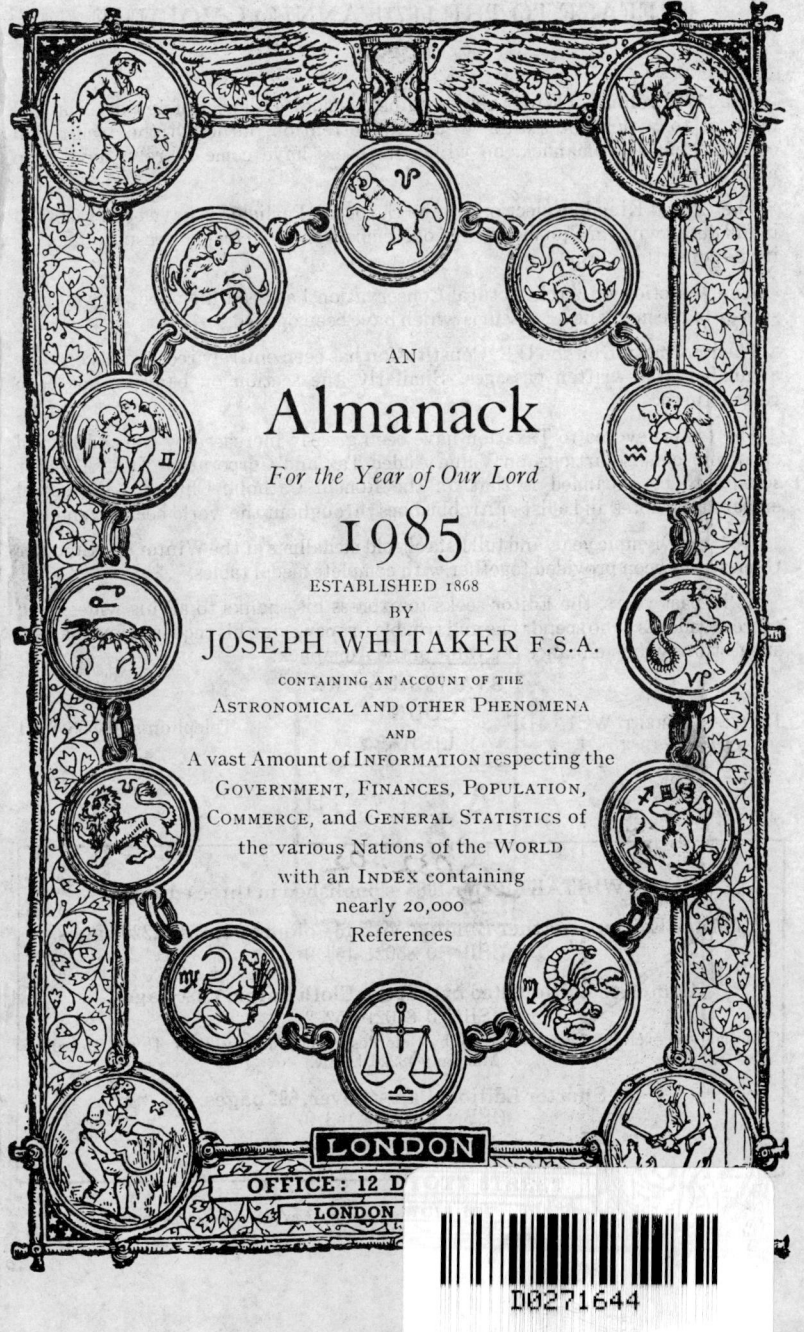

AN

Almanack

For the Year of Our Lord

1985

ESTABLISHED 1868

BY

JOSEPH WHITAKER F.S.A.

CONTAINING AN ACCOUNT OF THE
ASTRONOMICAL AND OTHER PHENOMENA

AND

A vast Amount of INFORMATION respecting the
GOVERNMENT, FINANCES, POPULATION,
COMMERCE, and GENERAL STATISTICS of
the various Nations of the WORLD
with an INDEX containing
nearly 20,000
References

LONDON

OFFICE: 12 D

LONDON

PREFACE TO THE 117TH ANNUAL VOLUME
(1985)

The 117th volume of WHITAKER contains, as usual, a number of new or expanded features to which the Editor would call attention, although the traditional contents of the Almanack, on which its users have come to rely, have been maintained.

The United Kingdom elections to the European Parliament have been recorded in full detail with an alphabetical list of Members and the complete results of voting in the constituencies.

A new section on Architectural Conservation has been included, as well as a survey of the many new Museums which have been opened.

The information on the U.K. Constitution has been entirely recast and contains a number of rewritten passages. Similarly, the section on banking has been restructured.

The pages devoted to Taxation have been greatly increased by the addition of clear and concise articles on Value Added Tax and Corporation Tax. Another section to be expanded is that on the Roman Catholic Church with useful explanatory notes and a list of Archbishops throughout the world been given.

1984 was Olympic year, and full lists of gold medallists at the Winter and Summer Games have been provided together with complete medal tables.

As in past years, the Editor seeks to express his thanks to all his widespread correspondents, who spend time and trouble in answering his requests, and making suggestions which enhance the value of the Almanack.

12 DYOTT STREET, WC1A 1DF
October, 1984

Telephone: 01-836 8911

Note—"WHITAKER" for 1985 is published in three editions:

Library Edition, Leather Binding with 16 Coloured Maps, 1,220 pages.
(ISBN 0 85021 154 9)

Complete Edition, Red and Green Cloth Cover, 1,220 pages.
(ISBN 0 85021 152 2)

(Distributed exclusively in the U.S.A. by Gale Research Company, Book Tower, Detroit, Michigan 48226, U.S.A.)

Shorter Edition, Paper Cover, 692 pages.
(ISBN 0 85021 153 0)

© 1984 J. Whitaker & Sons, Ltd.

TYPESET BY CCC, PRINTED AND BOUND IN GREAT BRITAIN BY WILLIAM CLOWES LIMITED
BECCLES AND LONDON

TABLE OF CONTENTS

And in "Complete Edition" and "Library Edition"

AA

AI

Pages 693–1236 *are omitted from the* Shorter Edition

Pages 693–1236 are omitted from the Shorter Edition

2

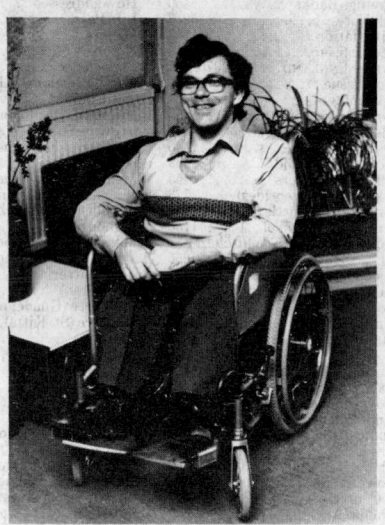

Pages 693–1236 *are omitted from the* Shorter Edition

Pages 693–1236 are omitted from the Shorter Edition

Pages 693–1236 are omitted from the Shorter Edition

Pages 693-1236 are omitted from the Shorter Edition

Pages 693–1236 *are omitted from the* Shorter Edition

14

16

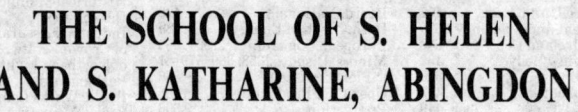

Pages 693–1236 are omitted from the Shorter Edition

The Book Trade Benevolent Society

The Book Trade can take pride in its own charity, the Book Trade Benevolent Society: pride in its generous support of the Society and in the fine work done by the Society since it began well over 100 years ago.

The support which is offered by the Society is twofold. Some 40 people live at The Retreat, at Kings Langley in Hertfordshire, where the executive secretary, Mrs Ann Brown is permanently based. And, through its relief committee, the Society finds and helps, with advice and finance, retired book trade people with a wide range of worries.

Much valuable time is given by active members of the trade to the Society, under its president, Mr Thomas Joy, MVO, FRSA, but there is a continuing need to raise more money; The Retreat alone has running costs of over £50,000 a year.

Bookrest, the fund-raising and publicity arm of the BTBS under the chairmanship of Viscount Macmillan of Ovenden, offers events to suit all tastes, as an important addition to the donations and covenants which help to finance the Society. In 1984, Bookrest's activities include the Book Ball, the Bookrest Walk, a Book Sale, a Pro-Am Golf Tournament, the publication by Collins of *Gluttony, Pride and Lust* (with all profits going to the BTBS) and a Christmas Carol Service at St. Martin-in-the-Fields. But whilst Bookrest works hard to raise funds, and the Society receives so much generous help, more is always welcomed – and needed.

The Book Trade Benevolent Society, Dillon Lodge, the Bookseller's Retreat, Kings Langley, Herts WD4 8LT.

Pages 693–1236 *are omitted from the* Shorter Edition

Pages 693–1236 are omitted from the Shorter Edition

Pages 693–1236 *are omitted from the* Shorter Edition

Pages 693-1236 *are omitted from the* Shorter Edition

Pages 693–1236 are omitted from the Shorter Edition

Pages 693–1236 *are omitted from the* Shorter Edition

Pages 693–1236 are omitted from the Shorter Edition

Pages 693–1236 *are omitted from the* Shorter Edition

Pages 693–1236 *are omitted from the* Shorter Edition

Pages 693–1236 *are omitted from the* Shorter Edition

Pages 693–1236 *are omitted from the* Shorter Edition

Pages 693–1236 *are omitted from the* Shorter Edition

Pages 693–1236 *are omitted from the* Shorter Edition

Pages 693–1236 *are omitted from the* Shorter Edition

Pages 693–1236 *are omitted from the* Shorter Edition

Pages 693–1236 *are omitted from the* Shorter Edition

Pages 693–1236 *are omitted from the* Shorter Edition

Pages 693–1236 *are omitted from the* Shorter Edition

Pages 693–1236 *are omitted from the* Shorter Edition

Pages 693–1236 are omitted from the Shorter Edition

Pages 693–1236 are omitted from the Shorter Edition

Pages 693–1236 are omitted from the Shorter Edition

Pages 693–1236 are omitted from the Shorter Edition

Pages 693–1236 are omitted from the Shorter Edition

Pages 693–1236 are omitted from the Shorter Edition

Pages 693–1236 *are omitted from the* Shorter Edition

Pages 693–1236 *are omitted from the* Shorter Edition

Pages 693–1236 *are omitted from the* Shorter Edition

Pages 693–1236 are omitted from the Shorter Edition

Pages 693–1236 *are omitted from the* Shorter Edition

Pages 693–1236 *are omitted from the* Shorter Edition

Pages 693–1236 *are omitted from the* Shorter Edition

Pages 693–1236 are omitted from the Shorter Edition

Pages 693–1236 *are omitted from the* Shorter Edition

Pages 693–1236 *are omitted from the* Shorter Edition

Pages 693–1236 are omitted from the Shorter Edition

OCCURRENCES DURING PRINTING
CURRENT AFFAIRS

Sept. 1. Unemployment rose in August to 3,115,088. **3.** T.U.C. conference opened in Brighton and the National Union of Mineworkers won a massive majority for "total support". **7.** It was reported that more than 20 people had died in a food poisoning outbreak at a psychiatric hospital in Wakefield. **9.** Talks between the miners' union and the Coal Board began in Edinburgh; the talks collapsed on Sept. 14 after a series of meetings. SDP conference opened in Buxton. **10.** In Cabinet reshuffle, Mr. Douglas Hurd became the new Northern Ireland Secretary. **13.** It was announced that Pan American Airways had agreed to buy a fleet of European Airbus jets. **15.** The Princess of Wales gave birth to a baby boy to be known as Prince Harry. **17.** The Liberal Assembly opened in Bournemouth. **18.** The dock strike was called off. **20.** In East Beirut, a suicide car bomb explosion wrecked the new U.S. Embassy, killing a number of people. **21.** Steel unions rejected miners' appeal to stop production. **25.** Walter Pidgeon, the film actor, died at the age of 86. **26.** In Peking, Britain and China initialled their agreement for the return of Hong Kong to China in 1997. **29.** Arms and ammunition destined for the I.R.A. were seized on a fishing trawler off the west coast of Ireland.

Oct. 1. Labour Party conference opened in Blackpool. Mr. Alan Traill was elected next Lord Mayor of London. **5.** Leonard Rossiter, the actor, died, aged 57. **8.** Coal Board and miners' union accepted an invitation by ACAS to talks on the pit strike. **9.** Conservative Party conference opened in Brighton. **10.** A High Court judge imposed fines of £200,000 on the N.U.M. and £1,000 on its president, Mr. Arthur Scargill, for contempt of court.

THE ARMED FORCES

The following is a list of senior appointments in the Ministry of Defence reorganization from January 2, 1985:—

Defence Staff
Vice-Chief of the Defence Staff: Air Marshal Sir Peter Harding (as Air Chief Marshal).
Deputy Chief of Defence Staff (Commitments): Rear-Admiral Sir John Woodward (as Vice-Admiral).
Deputy Chief of Defence Staff (Systems): Air Marshal Sir Donald Hall.
Deputy Under-Secretary of State (Policy): Mr. D. A. Nicholls.
Deputy Chief of Defence Staff (Programmes and Personnel): Major-General J. L. Chapple (as Lieutenant-General).
Chief of Defence Intelligence: Air Marshal Sir Michael Armitage.

Office of Management and Budget
Second Permanent Under-Secretary: Mr. J. N. H. Blelloch.
Deputy Under-Secretary of State (Resources and Programmes): Mr. K. C. Macdonald.
Deputy Under-Secretary of State (Finance): Mr. J. D. Bryars.
Deputy Under-Secretary of State (Administration): Mr. B. E. Robson.
Deputy Under-Secretary of State (Civilian Management): Mr. R. M. Hastie-Smith.

Company Liquidations

	1975	1976	1977	1978	1979	1980	1981	1982
England and Wales								
Compulsory liquidations	2,287	2,511	2,425	2,265	2,064	2,935	2,771	3,745
Voluntary liquidations:								
Creditors'	3,111	3,428	3,406	2,821	2,473	3,955	5,825	8,322
Members'	3,917	4,173	3,650	3,615	4,030	3,970	3,638	3,908
Total liquidations notified (all types)	9,315	10,112	9,481	8,701	8,567	10,860	12,234	15,975
Scotland								
Compulsory liquidations	53	84	67	78	56	135	158	177
Voluntary liquidations:								
Creditors'	151	145	204	196	182	244	280	326
Members'	276	299	222	230	214	242	248	253
Total liquidations notified (all types)	480	528	493	504	452	621	686	756
Northern Ireland								
Compulsory liquidations	3	7	1	8	7	8	16	10
Voluntary liquidations:								
Creditors'	15	42	31	45	27	66	83	111
Members'	36	38	42	36	37	39	39	41
Total liquidations notified (all types)	54	87	74	89	71	113	138	162

U.K. TRADE OVERSEAS (£'000)

	1982		1983	
	Imports	Exports	Imports	Exports
Benelux*	7,336,472	6,951,534	8,231,668	8,013,374
Denmark	1,335,640	1,096,642	1,512,620	1,159,184
Faroe Islands	8,925	2,397	15,932	2,332
France	4,269,103	4,486,458	5,043,118	5,651,521
W. Germany	7,414,073	5,414,733	9,667,444	6,063,989
Greece	151,688	255,281	164,917	280,204
Rep. of Ireland	2,000,033	2,890,497	2,290,067	3,055,275
Italy	2,745,094	2,022,711	3,188,219	2,292,788
E.E.C.—Total	25,252,103	23,117,856	30,098,053	26,516,335
Afghanistan	20,855	9,344	19,837	10,310
Albania	45	4,453	240	2,983
Algeria	176,304	199,234	157,645	233,426
Andorra....................	220	7,635	381	6,533
Angola	7,368	25,781	45,732	22,847
Antigua	6,245	12,606	1,718	10,465
Argentina	58,728	37,349	194	4,472
Australia	493,196	1,043,615	552,642	940,279
Austria	404,318	251,032	438,446	273,702
Bahamas	18,273	26,364	24,013	17,815
Bahrain	35,459	152,272	37,488	150,264
Bangladesh	25,558	58,179	25,189	50,979
Barbados	14,887	26,886	11,899	31,938
Belize	13,326	10,455	11,565	8,726
Benin	1,227	14,941	2,887	10,577
Bermuda	5,128	18,222	4,019	24,924
Bhutan	1	89	—	99
Bolivia	20,899	4,943	14,834	4,711
Botswana	19,140	5,163	21,713	3,250
Brazil	443,956	158,837	560,277	157,758
Brit. Indian Ocean Terr.	186	1,240	7	714
Brunei	2,434	41,804	27,154	106,477
Bulgaria	21,009	46,104	12,355	44,577
Burma	5,342	44,242	4,726	21,927
Burundi...................	8,737	1,522	3,485	3,155
Cameroon	9,108	22,462	52,481	26,445
Canada....................	1,439,619	851,703	1,552,187	968,269
Cape Verde	49	2,068	122	1,246
Cayman Is.	613	6,717	610	4,046
Central African Rep.	878	576	902	536
Chad	3	1,082	8	2,244
Chile.....................	111,206	56,897	107,644	43,520
China	193,231	103,051	231,417	159,722
Colombia	34,502	50,328	56,458	51,023
The Comoros	108	258	278	597
Congo....................	2,393	9,766	4,335	9,560
Cook Is.	80	109	144	197
Costa Rica	15,068	5,455	22,299	11,041
Cuba	17,688	64,835	14,010	45,737
Cyprus	89,908	111,882	87,436	127,837
Czechoslovakia	82,007	70,105	101,302	69,456
Djibouti	53	6,521	184	7,712
Dominica..................	11,376	7,423	12,251	7,653
Dominican Rep.	5,752	10,161	6,662	11,594
Ecuador	9,288	60,792	11,022	35,008
Egypt	412,802	338,645	79,826	370,489
El Salvador	2,017	5,244	425	7,653
Equatorial Guinea	156	633	13	10
Ethiopia...................	10,833	27,584	12,071	34,092
Falkland Is.................	2,568	4,150	4,022	7,269
Fiji	39,826	9,088	46,943	12,184
Finland	849,933	513,558	996,017	539,721
French Guyana	35	1,200	853	897
French Polynesia	2	1,962	93	2,601
Gabon.....................	27,634	14,179	66,135	18,798
Gambia	2,031	10,087	3,781	13,261
German Dem. Rep.	133,921	63,665	167,625	50,997
Ghana	78,438	66,709	58,192	82,234
Gibraltar	4,229	29,712	4,266	26,495
Greenland..................	1,095	288	3,114	140

* Belgium, Luxembourg and the Netherlands

	1982		1983	
	Imports	Exports	Imports	Exports
Grenada	4,704	3,687	5,387	7,293
Guadeloupe	93	3,245	587	2,124
Guatemala	13,476	8,127	9,764	7,440
Guinea	1,956	6,840	668	7,190
Guinea-Bissau	—	431	94	477
Guyana	50,495	13,145	42,810	13,685
Haiti	2,615	3,704	1,646	4,171
Honduras	4,693	4,659	7,082	9,539
Hong Kong	872,545	732,489	1,178,343	726,711
Hungary	44,051	77,446	53,834	91,845
Iceland	72,721	102,714	66,505	65,176
India	379,169	805,321	366,928	804,779
Indonesia	91,704	212,066	169,454	193,642
Iran	225,971	333,715	100,545	629,980
Iraq	79,764	875,179	30,334	400,259
Israel	275,139	224,362	314,148	354,860
Ivory Coast	56,097	28,238	79,255	25,591
Jamaica	92,760	56,025	94,036	116,188
Japan	2,657,977	681,463	3,355,450	797,848
Jordan	17,487	295,274	28,680	262,503
Kampuchea	92	479	184	826
Kenya	104,312	153,858	128,464	111,249
Kiribati	79	321	42	371
Korea, North	235	3,857	362	2,527
Korea, South	321,691	167,752	440,354	168,942
Kuwait	104,793	333,247	67,281	333,273
Laos	355	880	56	626
Lebanon	24,237	67,640	11,521	81,435
Lesotho	682	1,260	216	2,080
Liberia	8,213	14,069	7,181	13,877
Libya	342,476	260,937	224,050	274,169
Macao	19,349	2,551	24,220	1,039
Madagascar	3,355	3,548	3,731	4,907
Malawi	42,478	20,893	42,060	18,183
Malaysia	185,239	210,805	222,673	248,239
Maldives	57	615	44	840
Mali	3,385	4,403	3,833	15,856
Malta	42,792	71,823	40,852	71,895
Martinique	34	2,400	35	3,029
Mauritania	5,462	1,943	6,044	1,719
Mauritius	119,450	20,857	128,437	22,499
Mayotte	5	795	26	771
Mexico	106,067	162,946	160,978	95,674
Mongolia	3,861	64	1,350	242
Montserrat	193	1,786	164	2,159
Morocco	60,219	95,487	75,602	99,727
Mozambique	10,611	14,473	9,176	28,618
Namibia	45,413	3,973	62,437	3,425
Nauru	32	1,843	1,421	1,715
Nepal	3,844	4,650	6,115	5,011
Netherlands Antilles	76,421	59,359	97,486	84,489
New Caledonia	255	2,141	73	1,965
New Zealand	539,137	323,201	486,305	286,054
Nicaragua	3,282	4,940	1,810	2,367
Niger	574	17,346	6,854	9,660
Nigeria	356,802	1,225,164	387,975	798,276
Niue & Tokelau	14	364	50	198
Norway	2,023,441	924,651	2,820,760	828,612
Oceania, Australian	171	1,584	69	1,011
Oceania, U.S.	255	2,141	418	3,418
Oman	46,425	265,283	91,216	448,900
Pakistan	81,531	199,178	80,277	191,647
Panama	9,521	83,250	5,341	42,276
Papua New Guinea	28,031	15,911	28,142	18,236
Paraguay	2,790	16,915	3,129	15,263
Peru	92,120	39,370	118,414	32,947
Philippines	127,061	97,908	160,701	102,949
Pitcairn	25	453	14	760
Poland	151,737	133,340	177,067	151,727
Polar Regions	296	782	4,864	901
Portugal	379,949	430,684	475,902	396,988
Puerto Rico	33,445	25,735	58,804	35,936
Qatar	33,984	245,390	10,063	216,385

	1982		1983	
	Imports	Exports	Imports	Exports
La Réunion	74	2,889	73	3,684
Romania	51,515	115,244	58,865	82,160
Rwanda	510	2,079	2,919	2,326
St. Helena	754	7,049	457	10,343
St. Kitts etc.	5,656	3,996	1,798	4,498
St. Lucia	15,530	6,273	21,960	6,276
St. Pierre & Miquelon	254	363	578	250
St. Vincent	10,891	3,265	12,496	4,357
Sao Tomé & Principé	494	1,510	218	597
Saudi Arabia	1,447,775	1,361,665	897,702	1,478,587
Senegal	14,196	22,349	22,333	13,212
Seychelles	696	10,086	615	7,502
Sierra Leone	14,438	19,110	17,710	13,735
Singapore	245,453	406,172	404,122	469,155
Solomon Is.	4,212	1,035	5,486	1,463
Somalia	883	12,095	681	18,987
South Africa	745,803	1,192,891	764,909	1,109,039
Spain	956,935	870,416	1,110,029	1,128,439
Canary Is.	44,574	83,508	56,305	98,603
Ceuta & Melilla	—	4,679	24	8,190
Sri Lanka	42,000	60,211	39,784	70,136
Sudan	9,929	136,636	18,693	133,432
Surinam	7,593	10,586	11,584	8,914
Swaziland	40,049	7,654	23,966	3,536
Sweden	1,673,165	1,935,264	2,051,931	2,397,464
Switzerland	1,669,922	1,196,203	2,154,085	1,385,894
Syria	25,644	89,535	18,859	72,320
Taiwan	335,537	125,183	458,307	128,467
Tanzania	19,521	71,985	46,525	62,056
Thailand	76,529	104,825	87,823	131,833
Tonga	38	764	25	648
Togo	1,827	21,881	2,161	12,212
Trinidad & Tobago	65,154	158,436	52,748	148,811
Tunisia	12,628	38,632	18,126	44,659
Turkey	207,763	218,116	184,976	244
Turks & Caicos Is.	5	405	18	902
Tuvalu	7	48	35	55
Uganda	23,107	31,272	29,645	21,092
U.A.E.	266,959	558,968	309,806	567,765
U.S.A.	6,638,250	7,457,114	7,442,671	8,836,979
U.S.S.R.	645,135	355,678	728,491	445,008
Upper Volta	1,289	2,166	1,514	3,048
Uruguay	23,107	13,926	33,361	10,763
Vanuatu	21	294	28	811
Vatican City	174	776	289	615
Venezuela	141,892	148,666	183,731	87,937
Vietnam	133	876	603	951
Virgin Is., British	460	2,348	172	3,455
Virgin Is., U.S.	137	27,450	9,706	4,981
Wallis & Futuna	—	—	—	5
Western Samoa	107	285	156	468
Yemen, North	1,340	52,593	1,857	56,315
Yemen, South	26,631	35,577	10,627	36,673
Yugoslavia	52,115	158,881	83,951	148,646
Zaire	15,801	20,557	11,192	21,129
Zambia	39,957	61,248	50,242	55,501
Zimbabwe	62,584	95,019	68,446	64,734

THE ANTARCTIC

THE ANTARCTIC is generally defined as the area lying within the Antarctic Convergence—the zone where cold northward-flowing Antarctic sea water sinks below warmer southward-flowing water. This zone is at about lat. 50° S. in the Atlantic Ocean and lat. 55°–62° S. in the Pacific Ocean. The continent itself lies almost entirely within the Antarctic Circle, an area of about 5·5 million square miles, 99 per cent of which is permanently ice-covered. The average thickness of the ice is 7,100 ft. but in places exceeds 14,500 ft., submerging entire mountain ranges; some mountains protrude—the highest being Vinson Massif, 16,066 ft. The ice amounts to some 7·2 million cubic miles and represents 91 per cent of the world's fresh water.

Along one-third of the Antarctic coastline, land-ice flowing outwards forms extensive ice shelves, fragments of which break off to form tabular icebergs, leaving ice cliffs up to 150 ft. high. Much of the sea freezes in winter, forming fast ice which breaks up in summer and drifts north as pack ice. The presence of ice and continuous darkness in winter restrict access to the coastline by sea in the summer months.

The most conspicuous physical features of the continent are its high inland plateau (much of it over 10,000 ft.), the Transantarctic Mountains (which together with the large embayments of the Weddell Sea and Ross Sea mark the approximate boundary between Greater and Lesser Antarctica), and the mountainous Antarctic Peninsula and off-lying islands (which extend northwards towards South America). The continental shelf averages about 20 miles in width (half the global mean, and in places it is non-existent) and reaches exceptional depths (1,300–2,600 ft., which is 3–6 times the global mean).

Climate.—On land, summer temperatures range from just below freezing around the coast to −30° F. (about −34° C.) on the plateau, and in winter −5° F. (−20° C.) on the coast to −85° F. (−65° C.) inland. Over a large area the maxima do not exceed +5° F. (−15° C.).

Precipitation is scanty over the plateau but amounts to 10–30 in. (water equivalent) along the coast and some scientific stations are permanently buried by snow. Some rain falls over the more northerly areas in summer. Gravity winds on the plateau slopes and cyclonic storms further north can both exceed 100 m.p.h. and gusts have been known to reach 150 m.p.h. Visibility can be reduced to zero in blizzards.

Flora and Fauna.—Although a small number of flowering plants, ferns and clubmosses occur on the sub-Antarctic islands, only two (a grass and a pearlwort) extend south of 60° S. Antarctic vegetation is dominated by lichens and mosses, with a few liverworts, algae, and fungi. Most of these occur around the coast or on islands, but lichens and some mosses also occur inland.

The only land animals are tiny insects and mites with nematodes, rotifers, and tardigrades in the mosses, but large numbers of seals, penguins, and other sea-birds go ashore to breed in the summer. The emperor penguin is the only species which breeds ashore throughout the winter. In contrast, the Antarctic seas abound with life—a wide variety of invertebrates (including krill) and fish providing food for the seals, penguins, and other birds and a residual population of whales.

Exploration and Antarctic Treaty.—In the 180 years from Captain James Cook's circumnavigation of the Antarctic in 1772–75 to the mid-1950's, about half of all expeditions to the Antarctic were British and a number of these made major contributions to geographical and scientific knowledge of the area. Notable, were the expeditions of Sir James Clark Ross, Captain Robert Scott, and Sir Ernest Shackleton.

Apart from four years during World War II, British Antarctic research has been continuous since 1925, and most of it is now organized and carried out by the British Antarctic Survey (a component of the Natural Environment Research Council).

The world-wide International Geophysical Year, 1957–58, gave great impetus to Antarctic research. Prior to the mid-1950's, only 17 stations were operated in the Antarctic by four nations and vast areas of the continent were still unknown. By 1957, 44 stations had been established by 12 nations. The co-operative scientific effort proved so fruitful that the 12 nations involved pledged themselves to continue to promote scientific and technical co-operation unhampered by politics (territorial claims being left in abeyance) and agreed that the continent should be used for peaceful purposes only. These aims were embodied in the Antarctic Treaty (covering the area south of lat. 60° S., excluding the high seas but including the ice shelves), which came into force in 1961. It has since been signed by a further 20 acceding nations, four of which are active in the Antarctic and have therefore been accorded consultative status.

Potential resources.—Increasing pressure on the world's food and mineral supplies has stimulated the search for new sources even in the extremely hostile polar environment. Minerals have been found in great variety but not in commercially exploitable concentrations in accessible localities. (For example, coal seams occur in the Theron Mountains and Horlick Mountains.)

There are indications that off-shore hydrocarbons could be present but mostly below great depths of stormy, ice-infested seas. However, the Antarctic Treaty nations and their scientific advisors are already considering the environmental implications of possible mineral exploration and exploitation.

Currently, the chief interest is in marine protein, including the shrimp-like krill already fished commercially by Japan, Poland and U.S.S.R. Basic research to ensure rational management of stocks of this key organism is being continued by international groups, but it is estimated that they could sustain a yield equal to the present total annual world fish catch.

Scientific research.—At present, five British stations are maintained in the British Antarctic Territory and at South Georgia. Two are biological stations, two geophysical observatories, and one is the centre for airborne earth sciences. One other smaller station is open in the summer only.

There are a further 35 stations operated by 12 other nations including a station maintained at the South Pole by the U.S.A

The staff of these stations and summer field-workers are the only people present on the continent and off-lying islands. There are no indigenous inhabitants.

(British Antarctic Survey, *see* entry on p. 425).

CONVERSION TABLES FOR WEIGHTS AND MEASURES

NOTE.—The central figures in heavy type represent either of the two columns beside them, as the case may be. *Examples:*—1 centimetre=0·394 inch and 1 inch=2·540 centimetres. 1 metre=1·094 yards and 1 yard=0·914 metre. 1 kilometre=0·621 mile and 1 mile=1·609 kilometres.

Length			Area			Volume			Weight (Mass.)					
Centimetres		Inches	Square Centimetres		Square Inches	Cubic Centimetres		Cubic Inches	Long Tons		Short Tons	Metric Tonnes		Short Tons
2·540	1	0·394	6·452	1	0·155	16·387	1	0·061	0·893	1	1·120	0·907	1	1·102
5·080	2	0·787	12·903	2	0·310	32·774	2	0·122	1·786	2	2·240	1·814	2	2·205
7·620	3	1·181	19·355	3	0·465	49·161	3	0·183	2·679	3	3·360	2·722	3	3·305
10·160	4	1·575	25·806	4	0·620	65·548	4	0·244	3·571	4	4·480	3·629	4	4·409
12·700	5	1·969	32·258	5	0·775	81·936	5	0·305	4·464	5	5·600	4·536	5	5·512
15·240	6	2·362	38·710	6	0·930	98·323	6	0·366	5·357	6	6·720	5·443	6	6·614
17·780	7	2·756	45·161	7	1·085	114·710	7	0·427	6·250	7	7·840	6·350	7	7·716
20·320	8	3·150	51·613	8	1·240	131·097	8	0·488	7·143	8	8·960	7·257	8	8·818
22·860	9	3·543	58·064	9	1·395	147·484	9	0·549	8·036	9	10·080	8·165	9	9·921
25·400	10	3·937	64·516	10	1·550	163·871	10	0·610	8·929	10	11·200	9·072	10	11·023
50·800	20	7·874	129·032	20	3·100	327·742	20	1·220	17·857	20	22·400	18·144	20	22·046
76·200	30	11·811	193·548	30	4·650	491·613	30	1·831	26·786	30	33·600	27·216	30	33·069
101·600	40	15·748	258·064	40	6·200	655·484	40	2·441	35·714	40	44·800	36·287	40	44·092
127·000	50	19·685	322·580	50	7·750	819·355	50	3·051	44·643	50	56·000	45·359	50	55·116
152·400	60	23·622	387·096	60	9·300	983·226	60	3·661	53·571	60	67·200	54·431	60	66·139
177·800	70	27·559	451·612	70	10·850	1147·097	70	4·272	62·500	70	78·400	63·503	70	77·162
203·200	80	31·496	516·128	80	12·400	1310·968	80	4·882	71·429	80	89·600	72·575	80	88·185
228·600	90	35·433	580·644	90	13·950	1474·839	90	5·492	80·357	90	100·800	81·647	90	99·208
254·000	100	39·370	645·160	100	15·500	1638·710	100	6·102	89·286	100	112·000	90·719	100	110·231

Metres		Yards	Square Metres		Square Yards	Cubic Metres		Cubic Yards	Metric Tonnes		Long Tons	Kilograms		Av. Pounds
0·914	1	1·094	0·836	1	1·196	0·765	1	1·308	1·016	1	0·984	0·454	1	2·205
1·829	2	2·187	1·672	2	2·392	1·529	2	2·616	2·032	2	1·968	0·907	2	4·409
2·743	3	3·281	2·508	3	3·588	2·294	3	3·924	3·048	3	2·953	1·361	3	6·614
3·658	4	4·374	3·345	4	4·784	3·058	4	5·232	4·064	4	3·937	1·814	4	8·819
4·572	5	5·468	4·181	5	5·980	3·823	5	6·540	5·080	5	4·921	2·268	5	11·023
5·486	6	6·562	5·017	6	7·176	4·587	6	7·848	6·096	6	5·905	2·722	6	13·228
6·401	7	7·655	5·853	7	8·372	5·352	7	9·156	7·112	7	6·889	3·175	7	15·432
7·315	8	8·749	6·689	8	9·568	6·116	8	10·464	8·128	8	7·874	3·629	8	17·637
8·230	9	9·843	7·525	9	10·764	6·881	9	11·772	9·144	9	8·858	4·082	9	19·842
9·144	10	10·936	8·361	10	11·960	7·646	10	13·080	10·161	10	9·842	4·536	10	22·046
18·288	20	21·872	16·723	20	23·920	15·291	20	26·159	20·321	20	19·684	9·072	20	44·092
27·432	30	32·808	25·084	30	35·880	22·937	30	39·239	30·481	30	29·526	13·608	30	66·139
36·576	40	43·745	33·445	40	47·840	30·582	40	52·318	40·642	40	39·368	18·144	40	88·185
45·720	50	54·681	41·806	50	59·799	38·228	50	65·398	50·802	50	49·210	22·680	50	110·231
54·864	60	65·617	50·168	60	71·759	45·873	60	78·477	60·963	60	59·052	27·216	60	132·277
64·008	70	76·553	58·529	70	83·719	53·519	70	91·557	71·123	70	68·894	31·752	70	154·324
73·152	80	87·489	66·890	80	95·679	61·164	80	104·636	81·284	80	78·737	36·287	80	176·370
82·296	90	98·425	75·251	90	107·639	68·810	90	117·716	91·444	90	88·579	40·823	90	198·416
91·440	100	109·361	83·613	100	119·599	76·455	100	130·795	101·605	100	98·421	45·359	100	220·464

Kilometres		Miles	Square Kilometres		Square Miles	Litres		Gallons	Bushels U.S.		Bushels U.K.	Hectares		Acres
1·609	1	0·621	2·590	1	0·386	4·546	1	0·220	1·032	1	0·969	0·405	1	2·471
3·219	2	1·243	5·180	2	0·772	9·092	2	0·440	2·064	2	1·938	0·809	2	4·942
4·828	3	1·864	7·770	3	1·158	13·638	3	0·660	3·096	3	2·907	1·214	3	7·413
6·437	4	2·485	10·360	4	1·544	18·184	4	0·880	4·128	4	3·876	1·619	4	9·884
8·047	5	3·107	12·950	5	1·931	22·730	5	1·100	5·160	5	4·845	2·023	5	12·355
9·656	6	3·728	15·540	6	2·317	27·276	6	1·320	6·192	6	5·814	2·428	6	14·826
11·265	7	4·350	18·130	7	2·703	31·822	7	1·540	7·224	7	6·783	2·833	7	17·297
12·875	8	4·971	20·720	8	3·089	36·368	8	1·760	8·256	8	7·752	3·237	8	19·769
14·484	9	5·592	23·310	9	3·475	40·914	9	1·980	9·288	9	8·721	3·642	9	22·240
16·093	10	6·214	25·900	10	3·861	45·460	10	2·200	10·321	10	9·689	4·047	10	24·711
32·187	20	12·427	51·800	20	7·722	90·919	20	4·400	20·641	20	19·379	8·094	20	49·421
48·280	30	18·641	77·700	30	11·583	136·379	30	6·599	30·962	30	29·068	12·140	30	74·132
64·374	40	24·855	103·600	40	15·444	181·839	40	8·799	41·282	40	38·758	16·187	40	98·842
80·467	50	31·069	129·499	50	19·305	227·298	50	10·999	51·603	50	48·447	20·234	50	123·555
96·561	60	37·282	153·399	60	23·166	272·758	60	13·199	61·923	60	58·137	24·281	60	148·266
112·654	70	43·496	181·299	70	27·027	318·217	70	15·398	72·244	70	67·826	28·328	70	172·974
128·748	80	49·710	207·199	80	30·888	363·677	80	17·598	82·564	80	77·516	32·375	80	197·685
144·841	90	55·923	233·099	90	34·749	409·137	90	19·798	92·885	90	87·205	36·422	90	222·395
160·934	100	62·137	258·999	100	38·610	454·596	100	21·998	103·205	100	96·695	40·469	100	247·105

SYMBOLS FOR CORRECTING PROOFS

Supplied by WILLIAM CLOWES LTD, Beccles, Suffolk, Printers of "WHITAKER"

Letter(s) or word(s) requiring alteration should be struck through IN INK in the text and the substitution should be written in the nearest margin followed by / (the symbol used to denote that the marginal mark is concluded). Insertions should be indicated by / or /\ at the conclusion of the marginal mark *and* at the desired place in the text.

Alteration required	Mark in margin	Mark in text	Alteration required	Mark in margin	Mark in text
Delete (take out)	ℐ or ℐ	/ or —— Vertical stroke to delete one or two letters; horizontal line to delete more	Take letter(s) or word(s) from beginning of one line to end of preceding line	*back* or *take back*	⅂
Delete and close up	ℐ̶ or ℐ̶	⊤ Strike out letter(s) not required and add "close up" mark above and below	Begin a new paragraph	*n. p.*	[before first word of new paragraph
Close up: delete space between letters	◡	◡ linking letters or words	No new para. here or run on previous matter with later matter	*run on*	between paras. or other matter
Use ligature (fi, fl, ffl, etc.) or diphthong (æ, œ)	*enclosing ligature or diphthong required*	◡ enclosing letters to be altered	Spell out in full the abbreviation, contraction, or figure	*spell out*	Encircle, words, etc., or figures concerned
Insert space between letters or words	#		Insert omitted portion of copy	*out - see copy*	Attach the relevant copy to the proof, indicating omitted portion
Leave as printed (i.e. a cancellation of previous marking)	*stet*	•••• under letter(s) or word(s) crossed out but to be retained	Inserted or substituted letter(s), figure(s), or sign(s) under which this is placed to be superscript (i.e. high alignment)[1]	⌐ (see footnote)	for insertions For substitutions encircle letter(s). figure(s). or sign(s) to be altered
Invert type (of letter(s) upside down)	☊	Encircle letter(s) to be altered	Inserted or substituted letter(s), figure(s), or sign(s) over which this is placed to be subscript (low alignment)[2]	⌐ (see footnote)	for insertions For substitutions encircle letter(s), figure(s), etc., to be altered
"Battered" letter(s) to be replaced by similar but undamaged characters	×	Encircle letter(s) or word(s) to be replaced and write the correct letter(s) in the margin	Change to lower case	*l. c.*	Encircle letter(s) to be altered
Push down space or "high" letter(s) or word(s)	⊥	Encircle space, letter(s), or word(s) affected	Replace "wrong fount" by letter(s) of correct fount	*w. f.*	Encircle letter(s) or word(s) to be altered
Transpose	*tr.* or *trs.*	between letters or words, numbered when necessary	Change to capital letters	*caps.*	≡ under letter(s) or word(s) to be altered
Take letter(s) or word(s) from end of one line to beginning of next line	*take over* or *over*	⌐	Change to small capitals	*s. c.*	═ under letter(s) or word(s) to be altered

indicates a superior (superscript) figure one   indicates an inferior (subscript) figure two

Alteration required	Mark in margin	Mark in text	Alteration required	Mark in margin	Mark in text
Use capital letters for initial letter(s) (as desired) and small capitals for rest of word(s)	*caps* & *s.c.*	≡ under initial letter(s) and = under the remainder of the word(s)	Move lines to the left		at right side of group of lines to be moved (indicating approx. position)
Change to bold type	*bold*	∿ Draw wavy line under letter(s) or word(s) to be altered	Move portion of matter so that it is positioned as indicated	[ ]	[ ] at limits of required position
Change to roman type	*rom.*	Encircle letter(s) or word(s) to be altered	Raise lines	*raise*	⊤ over lines to be raised
Change to italic type	*italic*	── Draw this straight line under letter(s) or word(s) to be altered	Lower lines	*lower*	⊥ under lines to be lowered
Letter(s) or word(s) to be underlined	*underline*	under letter(s), word(s), etc., to be underlined	Correct the vertical alignment	‖	‖
			Straighten lines	══	══ through lines to be straightened
Equalize space between words	*eq. #*	⌐ between words	Insert parentheses (round-shaped brackets)	(/) or (/)/	⋏ ⋏⋏
Reduce space	*less #*	⌐ between words	Insert [square] brackets	[/] or [/]/	⋏ ⋏⋏
Space to be inserted between lines or paragraphs	#>	*Amount of space should be indicated*	Insert hyphen	/-/	⋏
To be placed in centre of line, etc.	*centre*	Position to be indicated by ⌐ ⌐	Insert en (= half-em) rule (*see above*)	*en*/	⋏
Indent one en (approx. space occupied by n of type in use)	*en* □⋏	indicating approximate position	Insert one-em rule (*see above*)	*em*/	⋏
Indent one em (approx. space occupied by M of type in use)	*em* □⋏	Ditto	Insert two-em rule (*see above*)	*2 em*/	⋏
Indent two ems (approx. space occupied by MM of type in use)	□□⋏	Ditto	Insert apostrophe	⸝	⋏
Move to the left	⌐	⌐ Ditto	Insert single quotation marks	⸜ ⸝	⋏ ⋏
Move to the right	⌐	⌐ Ditto	Insert double quotation marks	⸜⸜ ⸝⸝	⋏ ⋏
Move lines to the right		at left side of group of lines to be moved (indicating approx. position)	Insert ellipsis	···/	⋏
			Insert leader (*visual guide to alignment in contents pages, etc.*)	⦿⦿⦿	⋏ (*three, two, or one dot*)
			Insert shilling stroke (oblique)	(/)	⋏

Punctuation	⸴⋏	⸴/	⸵⋏	⸵/	⨀	⨀	?⋏	?/	!⋏	!/

FOREIGN EXCHANGE RATES

Country	Denomination	1939 Average Rate to £ (approx.)	15 September, 1984 Middle Rate
A. London Market Rates			
Austria	*Schilling*	—	26·9050
Belgium	*Franc*	26·49 *Belgas*	77·05
Canada	*Canadian Dollar*	4·545	1·6500
Denmark	*Krone*	22·26	13·8800
Finland	*Markka*	217¼	7·9090
France	*Franc*	176·10	11·7430
Germany (West)	*Deutsche Mark*	—	3·8300
Greece	*Drachma*	545	149·45
Italy	*Lira*	85	2,357·0
Japan	*Yen*	½d	308·30
Netherlands	*Guilder*	8·34	4·3150
Netherlands (Antilles)	*Antillian Guilder*	8·34	2·2230
Norway	*Krone*	19·45	10·7830
Portugal	*Escudo*	110·07	197·75
Spain	*Peseta*	42·45	214·50
Sweden	*Krona*	18·59	10·7975
Switzerland	*Franc*	19·87	3·1525
U.S.A.	*Dollar*	4·485	1·2490
B. Former Scheduled Territories			
Australia	*Australian Dollar*	A£1·2525	1·5125
Bahamas	*Bahamas Dollar*	—	1·2490
Barbados	*Barbados Dollar*	—	2·4840
Belize	*Belize Dollar*	—	2·4840
Bermuda	*Bermuda Dollar*	—	1·2490
Cyprus	*Cyprus £*	—	0·7775
Ghana	*New Cedi*	—	48·4660
Hong Kong	*Hong Kong Dollar*	—	9·8125
Iceland	*Krona*	—	41·7550
India	*Rupee*	13·38	14·80
Jamaica	*Jamaica Dollar*	—	5·13
Jordan	*Dinar*	Par	0·500
Kenya	*Shilling*	—	18·78
Kuwait	*Dinar*	—	0·4650
Libya	*Dinar*	—	0·3675
Malawi	*Kwacha*	—	1·87
Malaysia	*Ringitt*	8·571	2·9420
Malta	*Maltese £*	—	0·6010
New Zealand	*New Zealand Dollar*	£1·2425	2·5460
Nigeria	*Naira*	—	1·0615
Pakistan	*Rupee*	—	16·30
South Africa	*Rand*	S.A.£1	2·0930
Sri Lanka	*Rupee*	13·38 (Ceylon Rs.)	31·43
Tanzania	*Shilling*	—	21·95
Trinidad	*Trinidad and Tobago $*	—	2·9810
Uganda	*Shilling*	—	532·50
Yemen	*Riyal*	—	7·18
Zambia	*Kwacha*	—	2·40
C. Other Rates			
Algeria	*Dinar*	—	6·3655
Argentina	*Peso*	19	102·76
Bolivia	*Peso*	141·50	6,210·00
Brazil	*Cruzeiro*	82	2,698·00
Bulgaria	*Lev*	375	1·3388
Burma	*Kyat*	13·38	10·9506
Chile	*Peso*	116½	115·9150
China	*Renminbi Yuan*	4½	3·1063
Colombia	*Peso*	7·59	129·6550
Costa Rica	*Colon*	25·16	56·90
Cuba	*Peso*	4·386	0·7775
Czechoslovakia	*Koruna*	—	8·90
Ecuador	*Sucre*	66	83·40
Egypt	*Egyptian £*	97½ (per £100 London)	1·0312
Ethiopia	*Ethiopian Dollar*	—	2·58
Germany (East)	*Ostmark*	—	3·8300

Country	Denomination	1939 Average Rate to £ (approx.)	15 September, 1984 Middle Rate
Guatemala	*Quetzel*	4·386	1·2490
Guinea Republic	*Syli*	—	30·80
Haiti	*Gourde*	22·4	6·21
Honduras Republic	*Lempira*	8¼	2·50
Hungary	*Forint*	20¾	64·12
Indonesia	*Rupiah*	—	1,324·95
Iran	*Rial*	80·50 (Persian)	116·90
Iraq	*Dinar*	Par	0·3928
Israel	*Israel £*	Par	444·00
Lebanon	*Lebanese £*	9·65	8·7035
Malagasy Republic	*M. G. Franc*	17 (F. Fr.)	790·90
Mexico	*Peso*	—	243·5350
Morocco	*Dirham*	176·10 (F. Fr.)	11·40
Nicaragua	*Cordoba*	24	12·4250
Paraguay	*Guarani*	—	298·20
Peoples Democratic Republic of Vietnam	*Dong*	—	12·95
Peru	*Sol*	24¼	4,899·92
Philippines	*Peso*	—	22·01
Poland	*Zloty*	23½	159·20
Rumania	*Leu*	655	6·43
Salvador, El	*Colon*	11·20	3·1110
Saudi Arabia	*Riyal*	—	4·4210
Sudan	*Sudan £*	97¼ (per 100)	1·6340
Syria	*Syrian £*	—	6·20
Thailand	*Baht*	10·91	28·42
Tunisia	*Tunisian Dinar*	—	1·02
Turkey	*Turkish Lira*	—	507·33
Uruguay	*New Peso*	9	70·0450
U.S.S.R.	*Rouble*	23·75	1·0746
Venezuela	*Bolivar*	14·15	15·1250
Yugoslavia	*New Y Dinar*	197½ (YD)	217·4110
Zaire Republic	*Zaire*	—	48·54

BUCHAN'S WEATHER PERIODS OR RECURRENCES OF WEATHER

Dr. Alexander Buchan, F.R.S., Secretary of the Scottish Meteorological Society, published in 1867 a paper in the Journal of that Society entitled "Interruptions in the regular rise and fall of temperature in the course of the year". Buchan gave six cold periods and three warm periods, based on his examination of the mean daily temperature as recorded at stations in Scotland covering long periods. The cold periods were February 7–14, April 11–14, May 9–14, June 29–July 4, August 6–11, November 6–13, and the warm periods July 12–15, August 12–15, and December 3–14. This early work aroused considerable interest later. It should be noted, however, that Buchan claimed no more than the existence of tendencies for short spells of relatively cold and warm weather to occur at certain times of the year.

In recent years these smaller fluctuations of weather super-imposed on the normal seasonal changes have been examined from the aspect of tendencies to stormy or anticyclonic spells over the British Isles and have been referred to as "singularities". Stormy periods are relatively warm in winter and cool in summer. The following tendencies have been given:—Jan. 5–17 stormy; Jan. 18–24 anticyclonic; Jan. 24–Feb. 1 stormy; Feb. 8–16 anticyclonic; Feb. 21–25 cold; Feb. 26–Mar. 9 stormy; Mar. 12–19 anticyclonic; Mar. 24–31 stormy; April 10–15 stormy; April 23–26 unsettled; June 1–21 summer monsoon; July 10–24 warm; Aug. 20–30 stormy; Sept. 1–17 anticyclonic; Sept. 17–24 stormy; Sept. 24–Oct. 4 anticyclonic; Oct. 5–12 stormy; Oct. 16–20 anticyclonic; Oct. 24–Nov. 13 stormy; Nov. 15–21 anticyclonic; Nov. 24–Dec. 14 stormy; Dec. 18–24 anticyclonic; Dec. 25–Jan. 1 stormy.

ABBREVIATIONS

Ψ = Seaport.

A

A.—Associate of.
A.A.—Automobile Association; Anti-Aircraft.
A.A.A.—Amateur Athletic Association.
A. and M.—(Hymns) Ancient and Modern.
A.B.—Able-bodied seaman.
A.B.A.—Amateur Boxing Association.
abbrev.—abbreviation.
A.B.M.—Anti-ballistic missile defence system.
Abr.—abridged.
a.c.—alternating current.
a/c.—accounts.
A.C.—Companion, Order of Australia; Aircraftman.
A.C.A.S.—Advisory, Conciliation and Arbitration Service.
A.C.T.—Australian Capital Territory.
A.C.T.T.—Association of Cinematograph, Television and Allied Technicians.
A.C.U.—Association of Commonwealth Universities.
ad(vert)—advertisement.
A.D.—(Anno Domini) In the year of our Lord.
A.D.C.—Aide-de-Camp.
A.D.C. (P).—Personal A.D.C. to The Queen.
adj.—adjective.
Adjt.—Adjutant.
Ad lib.—(ad libitum) at pleasure.
Adm.—Admiral; Admission.
adv.—adverb.
A.E.—Air Efficiency Award.
A.E.A.—Atomic Energy Authority.
A.E.M.—Air Efficiency Medal.
A.E.R.E.—Atomic Energy Research Establishment.
A.F.C.—Air Force Cross; Association Football Club.
A.F.M.—Air Force Medal.
A.F.V.—Armoured fighting vehicle.
A.G.—Adjutant-General.
A.H.—(Anno Hegirae) In the year of the Hegira.
alt.—altitude.
a.m.—(ante meridiem) before noon.
A.M.—(Anno mundi) In the year of the world.
A.M.D.G.—(Ad majorem Dei gloriam) To the greater glory of God.
amp.—ampere.
A.N.C.—African National Congress.
anon.—anonymous.
A.N.Z.A.C.—Australian and New Zealand Army Corps.
A.O.—Officer, Order of Australia.
A.O.C.—Air Officer Commanding.
A.P.T.—Advanced Passenger Train.
A.R.C.—Agricultural Research Council.
A.S.—Anglo-Saxon.
A.S.A.—Amateur Swimming Association.

A.S.B.—Alternative Service Book.
A.S.E.A.N.—Association of South East Asia Nations.
A.S.H.—Action on Smoking and Health.
A.S.L.E.F.—Associated Society of Locomotive Engineers and Firemen.
A.S.L.I.B.—Association of Special Libraries and Information Bureaux.
A.S.T.M.S.—Association of Scientific, Technical and Managerial Staffs.
A.T.C.—Air Training Corps.
A.U.C.—(ab urbe condita) In the year from the foundation of Rome; (anno urbis conditae) In the year of the founding of the city.
A.U.E.W.—Amalgamated Union of Engineering Workers.
A.U.T.—Association of University Teachers.
A.V.—Authorized Version.
A.V.R.—Army Volunteer Reserve.
A.W.O.L.—Absent without leave.

B

b.—born; bowled.
B.A.—Bachelor of Arts.
B.A.A.—British Astronomical Association; British Airports Authority.
B. Acc.—Bachelor of Accountancy.
B.A.F.—British Athletic Federation.
B.A.F.T.A.—British Academy of Film and Television Arts.
B.A.O.R.—British Army of the Rhine.
B. Arch.—Bachelor of Architecture.
B.A.S.—British Antarctic Survey.
B.B.—Boys' Brigade.
B.B.C.—British Broadcasting Corporation.
B.C.—Before Christ; British Columbia.
B. Ch. (or Ch.B.)—Bachelor of Surgery.
B.C.L.—do, of Civil Law.
B.Com.—do, of Commerce.
B.D.—do, of Divinity.
B.D.A.—British Dental Association.
B.D.S. (or B.Ch.D.)—Bachelor of Dental Surgery.
B. Ed.—do, of Education.
B.E.M.—British Empire Medal.
B. Eng.—Bachelor of Engineering.
B.F.I.—British Film Institute.
B.F.P.O.—British Forces Post Office.
B.I.M.—British Institute of Management.
B.L.A.I.S.E.—British Library Automated Information Service.
B. Litt.—Bachelor of Literature or of Letters.
B.M.—do, of Medicine; British Museum.
B.M.A.—British Medical Association.

B.M.C.—British Motor Corporation.
B. Mus.—Bachelor of Music.
B.O.T.B.—British Overseas Trade Board.
Bp.—Bishop.
B. Pharm.—Bachelor of Pharmacy.
B. Phil.—do, of Philosophy.
Br. (or Brit.)—British.
B.R.—British Rail.
B.R.C.S.—British Red Cross Society.
Brig.—Brigadier.
B.Sc.—Bachelor of Science.
B.S.C.—British Steel Corporation.
B.S.I.—British Standards Institution.
B.S.T.—British Summer Time.
Bt. (or Bart.)—Baronet.
B.T.G.—British Technology Group.
B. Th.—Bachelor of Theology.
B.t.u.—British thermal unit.
B.U.P.A.—British United Provident Association.
B.V.M.—Blessed Virgin Mary.
B.V.M.S.—Bachelor of Veterinary Medicine and Surgery.
B.W.B.—British Waterways Board.

C

c.—(circa) about.
C.—Celsius; Centigrade.
C. (or Con.)—Conservative.
C.A.—Chartered Accountant (Scottish Institute).
C.A.A.—Civil Aviation Authority.
C.A.B.—Citizens' Advice Bureau.
Cantab.—(of) Cambridge.
Cantuar.—of Canterbury (Archbishop).
C.A.P.—Common Agricultural Policy.
Capt.—Captain.
Caricom—Caribbean Community and Common Market.
Carliol.—of Carlisle (Bishop).
C.A.S.—Chief of Air Staff.
C.B.—Companion, Order of the Bath.
C.B.E.—Commander, Order of the British Empire.
C.B.I.—Confederation of British Industry.
cc.—cubic centimetres.
C.C.—County Council; County Councillor; Chamber of Commerce.
C.C.C.—County Cricket Club.
C. Chem.—Chartered Chemist.
C.D.—Civil Defence.
Cdr.—Commander.
Cdre.—Commodore.
C.E.—Civil Engineer.
C.E.G.B.—Central Electricity Generating Board.
C. Eng.—Chartered Engineer.
C.E.N.T.O.—Central Treaty Organization.
C.E.T.—Common External Tariff; Central European Time.
Cestr.—of Chester (Bishop).

cf.—confer; compare.

C.F.—Chaplain to the Forces.

C.G.M.—Conspicuous Gallantry Medal.

C.G.S.—Chief of General Staff; Centimetre-gramme-second (system).

C.H.—Companion of Honour.

Ch.B./M.—Bachelor/Master of Surgery.

C.I.—The Imperial Order of the Crown of India; Channel Islands.

C.I.A.—Central Intelligence Agency.

C.I.D.—Criminal Investigation Department.

C.I.E.—Companion, Order of the Indian Empire.

c.i.f.—cost, insurance and freight.

C.-in-C.—Commander-in-Chief.

C.I.P.F.A.—Chartered Institute of Public Finance and Accountancy.

Cicestr.—of Chichester (*Bishop*).

C.L. (*or* C. Litt.)—Companion of Literature.

C.M.—(*Chirurgiae Magister*) Master of Surgery.

C.M.G.—Companion, Order of St. Michael and St. George.

C.M.S.—Church Missionary Society.

C.N.A.A.—Council for National Academic Awards.

C.N.D.—Campaign for Nuclear Disarmament.

c/o—care of.

C.O.—Commanding Officer; Conscientious Objector.

C.O.D.—Cash on delivery.

C. of E.—Church of England.

C.O.H.S.E.—Confederation of Health Service Employees.

C.O.I.—Central Office of Information.

Col.—Colonel.

Comecon.—Council for Mutual Economic Assistance (East European).

C.P.—Communist Party.

Cpl.—Corporal.

C.P.R.E.—Council for the Protection of Rural England.

C.R.E.—Council for Racial Equality.

C.S.C.—Conspicuous Service Cross.

C.S.E.—Certificate of Secondary Education.

C.S.I.—Companion, Order of the Star of India.

C.T.—Civic Trust.

C.T.C.—Cyclists' Touring Club.

C.V.O.—Commander, Royal Victorian Order.

cwt.—hundredweight.

D

d.—(*denarius*) penny.

D.B.E.—Dame Commander, Order of the British Empire.

d.c.—direct current.

D.C.—District of Columbia.

D.C.B.—Dame Commander, Order of the Bath.

D. Ch.—(*Doctor Chirurgiae*) Doctor of Surgery.

D.C.L.—Doctor of Civil Law.

D.C.M.—Distinguished Conduct Medal.

D.C.M.G.—Dame Commander, Order of St. Michael and St. George.

D.C.V.O.—Dame Commander, Royal Victorian Order.

D.D.—Doctor of Divinity.

D.D.S.—*do*, of Dental Surgery.

D.D.T.—dichlorodiphenyl-trichloroethane (insecticide).

del.—(*delineavit*) he/she drew it.

D.E.S.—Department of Education and Science.

D.F.C.—Distinguished Flying Cross.

D.F.M.—Distinguished Flying Medal.

D.G.—(*Dei gratia*) By the grace of God; Director-General.

D.H.Q.—District Headquarters.

D.H.S.S.—Department of Health and Social Security.

Dip. Ed.—Diploma in Education.

Dip. H. E.—Diploma in Higher Education.

Dip. Tech.—Diploma in Technology.

D.J.—Disc jockey.

D.L.—Deputy-Lieutenant.

D. Litt.—Doctor of Letters *or* of Literature.

D. Mus.—*do*, of Music.

D.N.A.—deoxyribonucleic acid.

D.N.B.—Dictionary of National Biography.

Do.—(*ditto*) the same.

D.o.E.—Department of the Environment.

D.O.M.—(*Dominus Omnium Magister*) God the Master of All.

D. Phil.—Doctor of Philosophy.

D.P.P.—Director of Public Prosecutions.

Dr.—Doctor.

D.Sc.—Doctor of Science.

D.S.C.—Distinguished Service Cross.

D.S.M.—Distinguished Service Medal.

D.S.O.—Companion, Distinguished Service Order.

D.Th.—Doctor of Theology.

Dunelm.—of Durham.

D.V.—(*Deo volente*) God willing.

E

E. (*or* O.E.)—Errors and omissions excepted.

Ebor.—of York (*Archbishop*).

E.C.—European Community; Electricity Council.

E.C.G.—Electrocardiograph.

E.C.S.C.—European Coal and Steel Community.

E.C.T.U.—European Confederation of Trade Unions.

E.D.—Efficiency Decoration.

E.E.C.—European Economic Community.

E.E.G.—Electroencephalograph.

E.F.T.A.—European Free Trade Association.

e.g.—(*exempli gratia*) for the sake of example.

Elien.—of Ely (*Bishop*).

E.M.S.—European Monetary System.

E.N.E.A.—European Nuclear Energy Agency.

E.R.—Elizabeth Regina.

E.R.D.—Emergency Reserve Decoration.

E.R.N.I.E.—Electronic random number indicator equipment.

E.S.A.—European Space Agency.

E.S.P.—Extra-sensory perception.

E.S.R.C.—Economic and Social Research Council.

et al.—(*et alibi*) and elsewhere; (*et alii*) and others.

etc.—(*et cetera*) and the other things.

et seq.—(*et sequentia*) and the following.

Euratom—European Atomic Energy Commission.

ex lib.—(*ex libris*) from the books of.

Exon.—of Exeter (*Bishop*).

F

f (ff)—and the following page(s).

F.—Fahrenheit; Fellow of.

F.A.—Football Association.

F.A.N.Y.—First Aid Nursing Yeomanry.

F.A.O.—Food and Agriculture Organization.

F.B.A.—Fellow of British Academy.

F.B.A.A.—*do*, of the British Association of Accountants.

F.B.I.—Federal Bureau of Investigation.

F.B.I.M.—Fellow of the British Institute of Management.

F.B.S.—*do*, of Botanical Society.

F.C.A.—*do*, of Institute of Chartered Accountants (of England and Wales).

F.C.C.A.—*do*, of Association of Certified Accountants.

F.C.G.I.—*do*, of City and Guilds Institute.

F.C.I.A.—*do*, of Corporation of Insurance Agents.

F.C.I.B.—*do*, of Corporation of Insurance Brokers.

F.C.I.B.S.—*do*, of Chartered Institution of Building-Services Engineers.

F.C.I.I.—*do*, of Chartered Insurance Institute.

F.C.I.S.—*do*, of Chartered Institute of Secretaries and Administrators.

F.C.I.T.—*do*, of Chartered Institute of Transport.

F.C.M.A.—*do*, of Institute of Cost and Management Accountants.

F.C.O.—Foreign and Commonwealth Office.

fcp.—foolscap.

F.C.P.—Fellow of the College of Preceptors.

F.D.—(*Fidei Defensor*) Defender of the Faith.

F.D.R.—Federal Republic of Germany.

fec.—(*fecit*) he did it/made it.

F.F.A.S.—Fellow of the Faculty of Architects and Surveyors.

F.F.R.—*do*, of Faculty of Radiologists.

F.G.S.—*do*, of Geological Society.

F.H.—Fire hydrant.

F.H.S.—Fellow of the Heraldry Society.

F.I.A.—*do*, of Institute of Actuaries.

F.I.Arb.—*do*, of Institute of Arbitrators.

F.I.B.—*do*, of Institute of Bankers.

F.I.C.E.—*do*, of Institution of Civil Engineers.

F.I.C.S.—*do*, of Institution of Chartered Shipbrokers.

F.I.E.E.—*do*, of Institution of Electrical Engineers.

F.I.M.—*do*, of Institution of Metallurgists.

F.Inst.F.—*do*, of the Institute of Fuel.

F.Inst.P.—*do*, of Institute of Physics.

F.I.Q.S.—*do*, of Institute of Quantity Surveyors.

F.I.R.E.—*do*, of Institute of Radio Engineers.

F.I.S.—*do*, of Institute of Statisticians; Family Income Supplement.

F.J.I.—*do*, of Institute of Journalists.

fl.—*(floruit)* he/she flourished.

F.L.A.—Fellow of the Library Association.

F.L.S.—*do*, of Linnean Society.

F.M.—Field Marshal.

fo.—folio.

F.O.—Flying Officer.

f.o.b.—free on board.

F.P.A.—Family Planning Association.

F.Ph.S.—Fellow of the Philosophical Society.

F.P.S.—*do*, of Pharmaceutical Society.

F.R.A.D.—*do*, of Royal Academy of Dancing.

F.R.A.I.—*do*, of Royal Anthropological Institute.

F.R.A.M.—*do*, of Royal Academy of Music.

F.R.A.S.—*do*, of Royal Astronomical Society.

F.R.Ae.S.—*do*, of Royal Aeronautical Society.

F.R.B.S.—*do*, of Royal Society of British Sculptors.

F.R.C.M.—*do*, of Royal College of Music.

F.R.C.O.—*do*, of Royal College of Organists.

F.R.C.O.G.—*do*, of Royal College of Obstetricians and Gynaecologists.

F.R.C.P., (Ed.), (I.)—*do*, of Royal College of Physicians (in Edinburgh), (of Ireland).

F.R.C.P.S.G.—*do*, of Royal College of Physicians and Surgeons of Glasgow.

F.R.C.S., (Ed.), (I.)—*do*, of Royal College of Surgeons (in Edinburgh), (of Ireland).

F.R.C.V.S.—*do*, of Royal College of Veterinary Surgeons.

F.R.Econ.S.—*do*, of Royal Economic Society.

F.R.G.S.—*do*, of Royal Geographical Society.

F.R.H.S.—*do*, of Royal Horticultural Society.

F.R.Hist.S.—*do*, of the Royal Historical Society.

F.R.I.B.A.—*do*, of Royal Institute of British Architects.

F.R.I.C.S.—*do*, of Royal Institution of Chartered Surveyors.

F.R.M.S.—*do*, of Royal Microscopical Society.

F.R.Met.S.—*do*, of Royal Meteorological Society.

F.R.N.S.—*do*, of Royal Numismatic Society.

F.R.P.S.—*do*, of Royal Photographic Society.

F.R.S.—*do*, of Royal Society.

F.R.S.A.—*do*, of Royal Society of Arts.

F.R.S.C.—*do*, of Royal Society of Chemistry.

F.R.S.E.—*do*, of Royal Society of Edinburgh.

F.R.S.L.—*do*, of Royal Society of Literature.

F.R.T.P.I.—*do*, of Royal Town Planning Institute.

F.S.A.—*do*, of Society of Antiquaries.

F.S.S.—*do*, of Statistical Society.

F.S.V.A.—*do*, of Society of Valuers and Auctioneers.

F.T.—*Financial Times*.

F.T.I.—Fellow of the Textile Institute.

F.T.I.I.—*do*, of the Taxation Institute Inc.

F.Z.S.—*do*, of the Zoological Society.

G

G.A.T.T.—General Agreement on Tariffs and Trade.

G.B.E.—Knight/Dame Grand Cross, Order of the British Empire.

G.C.—George Cross.

G.C.B.—Knight/Dame Grand Cross, Order of the Bath.

G.C.E.—General Certificate of Education.

G.C.H.Q.—Government Communications Headquarters.

G.C.I.E.—Knight Grand Commander, Order of the Indian Empire.

G.C.M.G.—Knight/Dame Grand Cross, Order of St. Michael and St. George.

G.C.S.I.—Knight Grand Commander, Order of the Star of India.

G.C.V.O.—Knight/Dame Grand Cross, Royal Victorian Order.

G.D.I.—Gross domestic income.

G.D.P.—Gross domestic product.

G.D.R.—German Democratic Republic (E. Germany).

Gen.—General.

G.H.Q.—General Headquarters.

Gib.—Gibraltar.

G.L.C.—Greater London Council.

G.M.—George Medal.

G.M.T.—Greenwich Mean Time.

G.N.P.—Gross national product.

G.O.C.—General Officer Commanding.

G.P.—General Practitioner.

Gp. Capt.—Group Captain.

G.S.O.—General Staff Officer.

H

H.A.C.—Honourable Artillery Company.

H.B.M.—Her Britannic Majesty('s).

H.C.F.—Highest common factor.

H.E.—His Excellency; His Eminence; high explosive.

H.H.—His/Her Highness.

H.I.M.—His/Her Imperial Majesty.

H.J.S.—*(hic jacet sepultus)* here lies buried.

H.M.—His/Her Majesty.

H.M.A.S.—Her Majesty's Australian Ship.

H.M.C.—Headmasters' Conference.

H.M.I.—Her Majesty's Inspector.

H.M.L.—Her Majesty's Lieutenant.

H.M.S.—Her Majesty's Ship.

H.M.S.O.—Her Majesty's Stationery Office.

H.N.C.—Higher National Certificate.

H.N.D.—Higher National Diploma.

Hon.—Honourable; Honorary.

h.p.—horse power.

H.P.—Hire purchase.

H.Q.—Headquarters.

H.R.H.—His/Her Royal Highness.

H.S.E.—*(hic sepultus est)* here lies buried. *cf.* H.J.S.

H.T.R.—High temperature reactor.

H.W.M.—High water mark.

I

I.A.A.S.—Incorporated Association of Architects and Surveyors.

I.A.E.A.—International Atomic Energy Agency.

I.A.T.A.—International Air Transport Association.

I.B.A.—Independent Broadcasting Authority.

Ibid.—*(ibidem)* in the same place.

I.B.R.D.—International Bank for Reconstruction and Development.

I.C.A.O.—International Civil Aviation Organization.

I.C.B.M.—Inter-continental ballistic missile.

I.C.I.—Imperial Chemical Industries.

I.C.J.—International Court of Justice.

I.C.R.C.—International Committee of the Red Cross.

I.C.T.—International Computers and Tabulators.

Id.—*(idem)* the same.

i.e.—*(id est)* that is.

I.E.A.—International Energy Agency.

I.F.C.—International Finance Corporation.

I.H.S.—*(Iesus Hominum Salvator)* Jesus the Saviour of Mankind; originally, these were the Greek capital letters, I H Σ.

I.L.E.A.—Inner London Education Authority.

I.L.O.—International Labour Organization.

I.M.C.O.—Inter-Governmental Maritime Consultative Organization.

I.M.F.—International Monetary Fund.

Inc.—Incorporated.

Incog.—(*incognito*) unknown, unrecognized.

I.N.L.A.—Irish National Liberation Army.

In loc.—(*in loco*) in its place.

I.N.R.I.—(*Iesus Nazarenus Rex Iudaeorum*) Jesus of Nazareth, King of the Jews.

Inst.—(*instant*) current month.

Intelsat—International Telecommunications Satellite Consortium.

Interpol—International Criminal Police Commission.

I.O.M.—Isle of Man.

I.O.U.—I owe you.

I.O.W.—Isle of Wight.

I.Q.—Intelligence quotient.

I.R.A.—Irish Republican Army.

I.R.B.M.—Intermediate-range ballistic missile.

I.R.C.—International Red Cross.

I.S.O.—Imperial Service Order.

I.T.U.—International Telecommunication Union.

I.T.V.—Independent Television.

I.W.A.—Inland Waterways Association.

J

J.—Judge.

J.P.—Justice of the Peace.

K

K.—Köchel numeration (of Mozart's works).

K.A.N.U.—Kenyan African National Union.

K.B.E.—Knight Commander, Order of the British Empire.

K.C.B.—*do*, Order of the Bath.

K.C.I.E.—*do*, Order of the Indian Empire.

K.C.M.G.—*do*, Order of St. Michael and St. George.

K.C.S.I.—*do*, Order of the Star of India.

K.C.V.O.—*do*, Royal Victorian Order.

K.G.—Knight of the Garter.

K.G.B.—Soviet State Security Service.

K.K.K.—Ku Klux Klan.

k.o.—knock out (boxing).

K.P.—Knight, Order of St. Patrick.

K.St.J.—Knight, Order of St. John of Jerusalem.

Kt.—Knight.

K.T.—Knight, Order of the Thistle.

K.V.—Kilovolt.

K.W.—Kilowatt.

K.W.h.—Kilowatt hour.

L

L. (*or* Lib.)—Liberal.

Lab.—Labour.

Lat.—Latitude.

L.A.M.D.A.—London Academy of Music and Dramatic Art.

lb.—(*libra*) pound weight.

l.b.w.—leg before wicket.

l.c.—lower case (*printing*).

L.C.J.—Lord Chief Justice.

L.C.M.—Least common multiple.

L.C.P.—Licentiate of College of Preceptors.

L.D.S.—*do*, in Dental Surgery.

L.E.A.—Local Education Authority.

L.H.D.—(*Litterarum Humaniorum Doctor*) Doctor of Humane Letters.

Lic. Med.—Licentiate in Medicine.

Lic. S.—*do*, in Surgery.

Lit.—Literary.

Lit. Hum.—(*Litterae Humaniores*) study of the classics.

Litt. D.—Doctor of Letters.

L.J.—Lord Justice.

LL.B.—Bachelor of Laws; LL.D.—Doctor of Laws; LL.M.—Master of Laws.

L.M.—Licentiate in Midwifery.

L.M.S.S.A.—*do*, in Medicine and Surgery, Society of Apothecaries.

loc. cit.—(*loco citato*) in the place cited.

log.—logarithm.

Londin.—of London (*Bishop*).

L.R.A.D.—Licentiate of the Royal Academy of Dancing.

L.R.A.M.—*do*, of the Royal Academy of Music.

L.R.C.P., (Ed.)—*do*, of the Royal College of Physicians, (of Edinburgh).

L.R.C.S., (Ed.)—*do*, of the Royal College of Surgeons, (of Edinburgh).

L.R.C.P.S.G.—*do*, of the Royal College of Physicians and Surgeons of Glasgow.

L.R.C.V.S.—*do*, of Royal College of Veterinary Surgeons.

L.S.—(*loco sigilli*) place of the seal.

L.S.A.—Licentiate of Society of Apothecaries.

L.s.d.—(*Librae, solidi, denarii*) £, shillings and pence.

L.S.E.—London School of Economics.

L.S.O.—London Symphony Orchestra.

Lt.—Lieutenant.

L.T.A.—Lawn Tennis Association.

Ltd.—Limited liability.

L.Th.—Licentiate in Theology.

L.T.M.—*do*, of Tropical Medicine.

L.W.M.—Low water mark.

M

M.—Member of; Monsieur.

M.A.—Master of Arts.

M.A.F.F.—Ministry of Agriculture, Fisheries and Food.

Maj.—Major.

max.—maximum.

M.B./D.—Bachelor/Doctor of Medicine.

M.B.E.—Member, Order of the British Empire.

M.C.—Master of Ceremonies; Military Cross.

M.C.C.—Marylebone Cricket Club.

M.Ch.(D.)—Master of (Dental) Surgery.

M.D.S.—*do*, of Dental Surgery.

M.E.—Middle English.

M.E.C.—Member of Executive Council.

M.Ed.—Master of Education.

mega—one million times.

M.E.P.—Member of the European Parliament.

M.F.H.—Master of Foxhounds.

Mgr.—Monsignor.

M.I.—Military Intelligence.

micro—one-millionth part.

milli—one-thousandth part.

min.—minimum.

M.L.A.—Member of Legislative Assembly.

M.L.C.—Member of Legislative Council.

Mlle.—Mademoiselle.

M.L.R.—Minimum lending rate.

M.M.—Military Medal.

Mme.—Madame.

M.N.—Merchant Navy.

M.O.—Medical Officer/Orderly.

M.O.D.—Ministry of Defence.

M.O.T.—Ministry of Transport.

M.P.—Member of Parliament; Military Police.

m.p.h.—miles per hour.

M.R.—Master of the Rolls.

M.R.C.—Medical Research Council.

M.S.—Master of Surgery; Manuscript (pl. MSS).

M.Sc.—*do*, of Science.

M.T.B.—Motor Torpedo Boat.

M.Th.—Master of Theology.

Mus. B./D.—Bachelor/Doctor of Music.

M.V.—million volts (*or* megavolts); Merchant Vessel; Motor Vessel.

M.V.O.—Member, Royal Victorian Order.

M.W.—million watts (*or* megawatts).

N

N.A.A.F.I.—Navy Army and Air Force Institutes.

N.A.B.M.—National Association of British Manufacturers.

N.A.L.G.O.—National and Local Government Officers Association.

N.A.S.A.—National Aeronautics and Space Administration.

N.A.T.O.—North Atlantic Treaty Organization.

N.B.—(*Nota bene*) note well; New Brunswick.

N.C.B.—National Coal Board.

N.C.O.—Non-commissioned Officer.

n.d.—no date (*of books*).

N.E.B.—New English Bible.

N.E.D.C.—National Economic Development Council.

Nem. con.—(*Nemine contradicente*) no one contradicting.

N.E.R.C.—Natural Environment Research Council.

N.F.T.—National Film Theatre.

N.G.A.—National Graphical Association.

N.H.S.—National Health Service.

N.I.—Northern Ireland.

No.—(*numero*) number.

Non seq.—(*Non sequitur*) it does not follow.

Norvic.—of Norwich (*Bishop*).

N.P.—Notary Public.

N.R.A.—National Rifle Association.

N.S.—New Style (calendar); Nova Scotia.

N.S.P.C.C.—National Society for the Prevention of Cruelty to Children.

N.S.W.—New South Wales.

N.T.—National Theatre; New Testament.

N.U.J.—National Union of Journalists.

N.U.M.—*do*, of Mineworkers.

N.U.P.E.—*do*, of Public Employees.

N.U.R.—*do*, of Railwaymen.

N.U.S.—*do*, of Seamen; *do*, of Students.

N.U.T.—*do*, of Teachers.

N.W.T.—Northwest Territory.

N.Y.—New York.

N.Z.—New Zealand.

O

O. and M.—Organization and method.

O.A.P.E.C.—Organization of Arab Petroleum Exporting Countries.

O.A.S.—Organization of American States.

O.A.U.—Organization of African Unity.

Ob. (*or* obit.)—died.

O.B.E.—Officer, Order of the British Empire.

O.C.—Officer Commanding.

O.E.—Old English.

O.E.C.D.—Organization for Economic Co-operation and Development.

O.E.D.—Oxford English Dictionary.

O.F.M.—Order of Friars Minor (Franciscans).

O.H.M.S.—On Her Majesty's Service.

O.M.—Order of Merit.

O.P.—Order of Preachers (Dominicans); opposite prompt side (of theatre); out of print (of books).

op.—(*opus*) work.

op. cit.—(*opere citato*) in the work cited.

O.P.C.S.—Office of Population Censuses and Surveys.

O.P.E.C.—Organization of Petroleum Exporting Countries.

O.S.—Old Style (calendar).

O.S.A.—Order of St. Augustine.

O.S.B.—Order of St. Benedict.

O. St. J.—Officer, Order of St. John of Jerusalem.

O.T.—Old Testament.

O.T.C.—Officer Training Corps.

Oxon.—(of) Oxford; Oxfordshire.

Oz.—ounce.

P

P.A.—Press Association.

p.c.—per cent.

P.C.—Privy Counsellor; Police Constable.

P.C.C.—Parochial Church Council.

P.D.S.A.—People's Dispensary for Sick Animals.

P.E.—Physical Education.

Petriburg—of Peterborough (*Bishop*).

Ph.D.—Doctor of Philosophy.

pinx(it)—he/she painted it.

P.L.A.—Port of London Authority.

P.L.C.—Public Limited Company.

P.L.O.—Palestine Liberation Organization.

p.m.—(*post meridiem*) afternoon.

P.M.—Prime Minister.

P.M.R.A.F.N.S.—Princess Mary's Royal Air Force Nursing Service.

P.O.—Post Office; Postal Order; Petty Officer; Pilot Officer.

P. & O.—Peninsular and Oriental Steamship Co.

P.O.U.N.C.—Post Office Users' National Council.

P.O.W.—Prisoner of War.

p.p. (*or* per pro)—(*per procurationem*) by proxy.

P.P.S.—Parliamentary Private Secretary.

P.R.—Proportional Representation; Public Relations.

P.R.A.—President of the Royal Academy.

Pro tem.—(*pro tempore*) for the time being.

P.R.S.—President of the Royal Society.

P.R.S.E.—*do*, of Edinburgh.

Prox.—(*proximo*) next month.

Ps.—Psalm.

P.S.—(*Post scriptum*) postscript.

P.S.B.R.—Public sector borrowing requirement.

Pte.—Private.

P.T.O.—Please turn over.

Q

Q.A.R.(A.)N.C.—Queen Alexandra's Royal (Army) Nursing Corps.

Q.A.R.N.N.S.—Queen Alexandra's Royal Naval Nursing Service.

Q.B.—Queen's Bench.

Q.C.—Queen's Counsel.

Q.e.d.—(*quod erat demonstrandum*) which was to be proved.

Q.G.M.—Queen's Gallantry Medal.

Q.H.C.—Honorary Chaplain to the Queen.

Q.H.D.S.—Honorary Dental Surgeon to the Queen.

Q.H.N.S.—Honorary Nursing Sister to the Queen.

Q.H.P.—Honorary Physician to the Queen.

Q.H.S.—Honorary Surgeon to the Queen.

Q.M.G.—Quartermaster General.

Q.P.M.—Queen's Police Medal.

Q.S.—Quarter Sessions.

Q.S.O.—Quasi-stellar object (quasar).

Q.S.S.s—Quasi-stellar radio sources (quasar).

q.v.—(*quod vide*) which see.

R

R.—(*Rex*) King; (*Regina*) Queen.

R.A.—Royal Artillery; Royal Academy/Academician.

R.A.C.—Royal Armoured Corps; Royal Automobile Club.

R.A.D.A.—Royal Academy of Dramatic Art.

R.A.D.C.—Royal Army Dental Corps.

R.A.E.—Royal Aircraft Establishment.

R.A.E.C.—Royal Army Education Corps.

R.Ae.S.—Royal Aeronautical Society.

R.A.F.—Royal Air Force.

R.A.M.—Royal Academy of Music.

R.A.M.C.—Royal Army Medical Corps.

R.A.N.—Royal Australian Navy.

R. and D.—Research and Development.

R.A.O.C.—Royal Army Ordnance Corps.

R.A.P.C.—Royal Army Pay Corps.

R.A.V.C.—Royal Army Veterinary Corps.

R.B.A.—Royal Society of British Artists.

R.B.S.—Royal Society of British Sculptors.

R.C.—Roman Catholic; Red Cross.

R.C.M.—Royal College of Music.

R.C.N.—Royal Canadian Navy.

R.C.N.C.—Royal Corps of Naval Constructors.

R.C.T.—Royal Corps of Transport.

R.D.—Naval Reserve Decoration; Rural Dean; refer to drawer (*banking*).

R.D.I.—Designer for Industry of the Royal Society of Arts.

R.E.—Royal Engineers.

R.E.M.E.—Royal Electrical and Mechanical Engineers.

Rep.—Republican; Representative.

Rev.—Reverend.

R.G.N.—Registered General Nurse.

R.G.S.—Royal Geographical Society.

R.H.S.—Royal Horticultural Society; Royal Humane Society.

R.I.—Royal Institution; Royal Institute of Painters in Watercolours; Rhode Island.

R.I.A.—Royal Irish Academy.

R.I.B.A.—Royal Institute of British Architects.

R.I.P.—(*Requiescat in pace*) May he/she rest in peace.

R.L.—Rugby League.

R.M.—Royal Marines.

R.M.A.—Royal Military Academy.

R.M.S.—Royal Mail Steamer.

R.N.—Royal Navy.

R.N.I.B.—Royal National Institute for the Blind.

R.N.L.I.—Royal National Lifeboat Institution.

R.N.R.—Royal Naval Reserve.

R.N.V.R.—Royal Naval Volunteer Reserve.

R.N.Z.N.—Royal New Zealand Navy.

Ro.—(*Recto*) on the right-hand page.

R.O.C.—Royal Observer Corps.

Roffen.—of Rochester (*Bishop*).

R.O.I.—Royal Institute of Oil Painters.

Ro. S.P.A.—Royal Society for the Prevention of Accidents.

R.P.—Royal Society of Portrait Painters.

r.p.m.—revolutions per minute.

R.R.C.—Lady of Royal Red Cross.

R.R.E.—Royal Radar Establishment.

R.S.A.—Royal Society of Arts; Royal Scottish Academician; Republic of South Africa.

R.S.C.—Royal Shakespeare Company.

R.S.E.—Royal Society of Edinburgh.

R.S.M.—Regimental Sergeant Major.

R.S.P.B.—Royal Society for the Protection of Birds.

R.S.P.C.A.—Royal Society for the Prevention of Cruelty to Animals.

R.S.V.P.—(*Respondez s'il vous plaît*) Answer, if you please.

R.S.W.—Royal Scottish Society of Painters in Watercolours.

R.T.P.I.—Royal Town Planning Institute.

R.U.—Rugby Union.

R.U.C.—Royal Ulster Constabulary.

R.V.—Revised Version (of Bible).

R.W.S.—Royal Water Colour Society.

R.Y.S.—Royal Yacht Squadron.

S

s.—(*solidus*) shilling.

S.A.—Salvation Army; Sex Appeal; South Africa; South America; South Australia.

Salop.—Shropshire.

S.A.L.T.—Strategic Arms Limitation Treaty.

Sarum.—of Salisbury (*Bishop*).

S.A.S.—Special Air Service Regiment.

S.B.S.—Special Boat Squadron.

Sc.D.—Doctor of Science.

S.C.M.—State Certified Midwife.

S.D.P.—Social Democratic Party.

S.D.L.P.—Social Democratic and Labour Party (N. Ireland).

S.E.A.T.O.—South East Asia Treaty Organization.

S.E.N.—State Enrolled Nurse.

S.E.R.C.—Science and Engineering Research Council.

S.H.A.P.E.—Supreme Headquarters, Allied Powers, Europe.

S.I.—(*Système International d'Unités*) International System of Units; Statutory Instruments.

Sic.—So written.

Sig.—Signalman.

S.J.—Society of Jesus (Jesuits).

S.N.P.—Scottish National Party.

S.O.G.A.T.—Society of Graphical and Allied Trades.

S.O.S.—Save Our Souls (distress signal).

s.p.—(*sine prole*) without issue.

S.P.C.K.—Society for the Promotion of Christian Knowledge.

sp.gr.—specific gravity.

S.P.Q.R.—(*Senatus Propulusque Romanus*) The Senate and People of Rome.

Sqn. Ldr.—Squadron Leader.

S.R.N.—State Registered Nurse.

SS.—Saints.

S.S.—Steamship.

S.S.A.F.A.—Soldiers', Sailors', and Airmen's Families Association.

S.S.C.—Solicitor before Supreme Court (Scotland).

S.S.F.—Society of St. Francis.

St.—Saint; Street.

S.T.A.R.—Satellites for Telecommunications, Applications and Research.

Stet.—Let it stand.

S.T.D.—Subscriber Trunk Dialling.

s.t.p.—Standard temperature and pressure.

S.T.P.—(*Sacrae Theologiae Professor*) Doctor of Divinity.

Sub Lt.—Sub-Lieutenant.

S.W.A.P.O.—South West Africa People's Organization.

T

T.A.—Territorial Army.

T.B.—Tuberculosis.

T.C.C.B.—Test and County Cricket Board.

T.D.—Territorial Decoration.

temp.—temperature; temporary employee.

T.E.S.—*Times Education Supplement.*

T.G.W.U.—Transport and General Workers Union.

T.L.S.—*Times Literary Supplement.*

T.N.T.—trinitrotoluene (explosive).

Toc. H.—Talbot House.

tr.—transpose (*printing*).

Truron—of Truro (*Bishop*).

T.T.—Teetotal; Tubercular tested.

T.U.C.—Trades Union Congress.

T.V.—Television.

U

U.—Unionist.

U.A.E.—United Arab Emirates.

u.c.—upper case (*printing*).

U.C.C.A.—University Central Council on Admissions.

U.C.L.—University College, London.

U.D.I.—Unilateral Declaration of Independence.

U.D.R.—Ulster Defence Regiment.

U.F.O.—Unidentified flying object.

U.G.C.—University Grants Committee.

u.h.f.—ultra-high frequency.

U.K.—United Kingdom.

U.K.A.E.A.—United Kingdom Atomic Energy Authority.

Ult.—(*ultimo*) in the preceding month.

U.N.E.S.C.O.—United Nations Educational, Scientific and Cultural Organization.

U.N.I.C.E.F.—United Nations International Children's Emergency Fund.

Unita.—National Union for the Total Independence of Angola.

U.N.O.—United Nations Organization.

U.P.U.—Universal Postal Union.

U.S. (*or* U.S.A.)—United States (of America).

U.S.P.G.—United Society for the Propagation of the Gospel.

U.S.S.R.—Union of Soviet Socialist Republics.

U.U.—Ulster Unionist.

V

v.—(*versus*) against.

V.—Volt.

V.A.—Vicar Apostolic; Victoria and Albert Order.

V. and A.—Victoria and Albert Museum.

V.A.D.—Voluntary Aid Detachment.

V.A.T.—Value added tax.

V.C.—Victoria Cross.

V.D.—Volunteer Officers' Decoration; venereal disease.

V.D.U.—Visual display unit.

Ven.—Venerable.

Verb. sap.—(*Verbum sapienti satis est*) A word to the wise is enough.

v.h.f.—very high frequency.

V.I.P.—Very important person.

Viz.—(*videlicet*) namely.

Vo.—(*Verso*) on the left-hand page.

V.R.D.—Volunteer Reserve Decoration.

V.S.O.—Voluntary Service Overseas.

V.T.O.L.—Vertical take-off and landing (*aircraft*).

W

W.A.S.P.—White, Anglo-Saxon Protestant.

W.C.C.—World Council of Churches.

W.E.A.—Workers' Educational Association.

W.E.U.—Western European Union.

W.H.O.—World Health Organization.

W.I.—West Indies; Women's Institutes.

Winton.—of Winchester (*Bishop*).

W.M.O.—World Meteorological Organization.

W.O.—Warrant Officer.

W.R.A.C.—Women's Royal Army Corps.

W.R.A.F.—Women's Royal Air Force.

W.R.N.S.—Women's Royal Naval Service.

W.R.V.S.—Women's Royal Voluntary Service.

W.S.—Writer to the Signet.

Y

Y.H.A.—Youth Hostels Association.

Y.M.C.A.—Young Men's Christian Association.

Y.W.C.A.—Young Women's Christian Association.

Z

Z.A.N.U.—Zimbabwe African National Union.

Z.A.P.U.—Zimbabwe African People's Union.

BEING THE FIRST YEAR AFTER BISSEXTILE OR LEAP YEAR

Golden Number	X	St. George's Day	,, 23
Epact	8	Ascension Day	May 16
Dominical Letter	F	Whit Sunday	,, 26
Solar Cycle	6	Trinity Sunday	June 2
Roman Indiction	8	Corpus Christi	,, 6
Julian Period	6698	Duke of Edinburgh's Birthday (1921)	June 10
Julian Day, Jan. 1 (begins at noon)	2,446,067	Queen's Official Birthday	,, 15
New Year's Day (Tuesday)	Jan. 1	Prince William of Wales's Birthday	
Australia Day	,, 26	(1982)	,, 21
Septuagesima Sunday	Feb. 3	Princess of Wales's Birthday (1961)	July 1
Accession of Queen Elizabeth II	,, 6	National Day Canada (1867)	,, 1
New Zealand Day	,, 6	The Queen Mother's Birthday (1900)	Aug. 4
Prince Andrew's Birthday (1960)	,, 19	Princess Anne's Birthday (1950)	,, 15
Ash Wednesday	,, 20	Jewish New Year (5746)	Sept. 16
St. David's Day	Mar. 1	Islamic New Year (1406)	,, 16
Prince Edward's Birthday (1964)	,, 10	Remembrance Sunday	Nov. 10
St. Patrick's Day	,, 17	Prince of Wales's Birthday (1948)	,, 14
Good Friday	Apr. 5	St. Andrew's Day	,, 30
Easter Day	,, 7	First Sunday in Advent	Dec. 1
Birthday of Queen Elizabeth II	,, 21	Christmas Day	,, 25

Spring Equinox	Sun enters Sign Aries	March 20d 16h	
Summer Solstice	,, ,, ,, Cancer	June 21d 10h	G.M.T.
Autumn Equinox	,, ,, ,, Libra	Sept. 23d 02h	
Winter Solstice	,, ,, ,, Capricornus	Dec. 21d 22h	

CALENDAR FOR THE YEAR 1985

January
Su.		—	6	13	20	27
M.	—	7	14	21	28	
Tu.	1	8	15	22	29	
W.	2	9	16	23	30	
Th.	3	10	17	24	31	
F.	4	11	18	25	—	
S.	5	12	19	26	—	

April
Su.		—	7	14	21	28
M.	1	8	15	22	29	
Tu.	2	9	16	23	30	
W.	3	10	17	24	—	
Th.	4	11	18	25	—	
F.	5	12	19	26	—	
S.	6	13	20	27	—	

July
Su.		—	7	14	21	28
M.	1	8	15	22	29	
Tu.	2	9	16	23	30	
W.	3	10	17	24	31	
Th.	4	11	18	25	—	
F.	5	12	19	26	—	
S.	6	13	20	27	—	

October
Su.		—	6	13	20	27
M.	—	7	14	21	28	
Tu.	1	8	15	22	29	
W.	2	9	16	23	30	
Th.	3	10	17	24	31	
F.	4	11	18	25	—	
S.	5	12	19	26	—	

February
Su.		—	3	10	17	24
M.	—	4	11	18	25	
Tu.	—	5	12	19	26	
W.	—	6	13	20	27	
Th.	—	7	14	21	28	
F.	1	8	15	22	—	
S.	2	9	16	23	—	

May
Su.		—	5	12	19	26
M.	—	6	13	20	27	
Tu.	—	7	14	21	28	
W.	1	8	15	22	29	
Th.	2	9	16	23	30	
F.	3	10	17	24	31	
S.	4	11	18	25	—	

August
Su.		—	4	11	18	25
M.	—	5	12	19	26	
Tu.	—	6	13	20	27	
W.	—	7	14	21	28	
Th.	1	8	15	22	29	
F.	2	9	16	23	30	
S.	3	10	17	24	31	

November
Su.		—	3	10	17	24
M.	—	4	11	18	25	
Tu.	—	5	12	19	26	
W.	—	6	13	20	27	
Th.	—	7	14	21	28	
F.	1	8	15	22	29	
S.	2	9	16	23	30	

March
Su.		—	3	10	17	24	31
M.	—	4	11	18	25	—	
Tu.	—	5	12	19	26	—	
W.	—	6	13	20	27	—	
Th.	—	7	14	21	28	—	
F.	1	8	15	22	29	—	
S.	2	9	16	23	30	—	

June
Su.		—	2	9	16	23	30
M.	—	3	10	17	24	—	
Tu.	—	4	11	18	25	—	
W.	—	5	12	19	26	—	
Th.	—	6	13	20	27	—	
F.	—	7	14	21	28	—	
S.	1	8	15	22	29	—	

September
Su.		1	8	15	22	29
M.	2	9	16	23	30	
Tu.	3	10	17	24	—	
W.	4	11	18	25	—	
Th.	5	12	19	26	—	
F.	6	13	20	27	—	
S.	7	14	21	28	—	

December
Su.		1	8	15	22	29
M.	2	9	16	23	30	
Tu.	3	10	17	24	31	
W.	4	11	18	25	—	
Th.	5	12	19	26	—	
F.	6	13	20	27	—	
S.	7	14	21	28	—	

CALENDAR FOR THE YEAR 1986

January
Su.		—	5	12	19	26
M.	—	6	13	20	27	
Tu.	—	7	14	21	28	
W.	1	8	15	22	29	
Th.	2	9	16	23	30	
F.	3	10	17	24	31	
S.	4	11	18	25	—	

April
Su.		—	6	13	20	27
M.	—	7	14	21	28	
Tu.	1	8	15	22	29	
W.	2	9	16	23	30	
Th.	3	10	17	24	—	
F.	4	11	18	25	—	
S.	5	12	19	26	—	

July
Su.		—	6	13	20	27
M.	—	7	14	21	28	
Tu.	1	8	15	22	29	
W.	2	9	16	23	30	
Th.	3	10	17	24	31	
F.	4	11	18	25	—	
S.	5	12	19	26	—	

October
Su.		—	5	12	19	26
M.	—	6	13	20	27	
Tu.	—	7	14	21	28	
W.	1	8	15	22	29	
Th.	2	9	16	23	30	
F.	3	10	17	24	31	
S.	4	11	18	25	—	

February
Su.		—	2	9	16	23
M.	—	3	10	17	24	
Tu.	—	4	11	18	25	
W.	—	5	12	19	26	
Th.	—	6	13	20	27	
F.	—	7	14	21	28	
S.	1	8	15	22	—	

May
Su.		—	4	11	18	25
M.	—	5	12	19	26	
Tu.	—	6	13	20	27	
W.	—	7	14	21	28	
Th.	1	8	15	22	29	
F.	2	9	16	23	30	
S.	3	10	17	24	31	

August
Su.		—	3	10	17	24	31
M.	—	4	11	18	25	—	
Tu.	—	5	12	19	26	—	
W.	—	6	13	20	27	—	
Th.	—	7	14	21	28	—	
F.	1	8	15	22	29	—	
S.	2	9	16	23	30	—	

November
Su.		—	2	9	16	23	30
M.	—	3	10	17	24	—	
Tu.	—	4	11	18	25	—	
W.	—	5	12	19	26	—	
Th.	—	6	13	20	27	—	
F.	—	7	14	21	28	—	
S.	1	8	15	22	29	—	

March
Su.		—	2	9	16	23	30
M.	—	3	10	17	24	31	
Tu.	—	4	11	18	25	—	
W.	—	5	12	19	26	—	
Th.	—	6	13	20	27	—	
F.	—	7	14	21	28	—	
S.	1	8	15	22	29	—	

June
Su.		1	8	15	22	29
M.	2	9	16	23	30	
Tu.	3	10	17	24	—	
W.	4	11	18	25	—	
Th.	5	12	19	26	—	
F.	6	13	20	27	—	
S.	7	14	21	28	—	

September
Su.		—	7	14	21	28
M.	1	8	15	22	29	
Tu.	2	9	16	23	30	
W.	3	10	17	24	—	
Th.	4	11	18	25	—	
F.	5	12	19	26	—	
S.	6	13	20	27	—	

December
Su.		—	7	14	21	28
M.	1	8	15	22	29	
Tu.	2	9	16	23	30	
W.	3	10	17	24	31	
Th.	4	11	18	25	—	
F.	5	12	19	26	—	
S.	6	13	20	27	—	

DAY OF			
Month	Week		

Janus, god of the portal, facing two ways, past and future.

Sun's Longitude 300° ≈ 20ᵈ 03ᵃ

1	Tu.	**Circumcision.**
2	W.	Gen. James Wolfe b. 1727.
3	Th.	Cicero b. 106 B.C. Clement Attlee b. 1883.
4	F.	Louis Braille b. 1809. Augustus John b. 1879.
5	S.	Edward the Confessor d. 1066.
6	♒	**Epiphany.** Twelfth Day.
7	M.	First Balloon Crossing of English Channel 1785.
8	Tu.	Galileo d. 1642. Wilkie Collins b. 1824.
9	W.	Napoleon III d. 1873.
10	Th.	Archbp. Laud beheaded 1645.
11	F.	HILARY LAW SITTINGS BEGIN.
12	S.	Edmund Burke b. 1729. J. Singer Sargent b. 1856.
13	♒	**1st S. after Epiphany.** Edmund Spenser d. 1599.
14	M.	Edmund Halley d. 1742. Lewis Carroll d. 1898.
15	Tu.	Martin Luther King b. 1929.
16	W.	Coruña 1809. Amilcare Ponchielli d. 1886.
17	Th.	Anton Chekov b. 1860. Lloyd George b. 1863.
18	F.	Scott reached S. Pole 1912.
19	S.	James Watt b. 1736. Paul Cezanne b. 1839.
20	♒	**2nd S. after Epiphany.**
21	M.	Louis XVI guillotined 1793.
22	Tu.	Francis Bacon b. 1561. Lord Byron b. 1788.
23	W.	Edouard Manet b. 1832. Anna Pavlova d. 1931.
24	Th.	Sir Winston Churchill d. 1965.
25	F.	**Conversion of St. Paul.** Robert Burns b. 1759.
26	S.	Gen. Charles Gordon killed 1885.**
27	♒	**3rd S. after Epiphany.** Mozart b. 1756.
28	M.	Charlemagne d. 814. Henry VIII d. 1547.
29	Tu.	Thomas Paine b. 1737. Frederick Delius b. 1862.
30	W.	Charles I exec. 1649. Gandhi killed 1948.
31	Th.	Franz Schubert b. 1797. Anna Pavlova b. 1885.**

PHENOMENA

January 3ᵈ 15ʰ Mercury at greatest western elongation (23°).

3ᵈ 20ʰ Earth at Perihelion (147,000,000 kilometres).

14ᵈ 22ʰ Jupiter in conjunction with the Sun.

16ᵈ 08ʰ Saturn in conjunction with the Moon. Saturn 2° N.

19ᵈ 13ʰ Mercury in conjunction with the Moon. Mercury 3° N.

22ᵈ 02ʰ Venus at greatest eastern elongation (47°).

25ᵈ 00ʰ Venus in conjunction with the Moon. Venus 5° N.

25ᵈ 04ʰ Mars in conjunction with the Moon. Mars 4° N.

31ᵈ 05ʰ Mercury in conjunction with Jupiter. Mercury 1°·3 S.

CONSTELLATIONS

The following constellations are near the meridian at

	d	h		d	h
Dec.	1	24	Dec.	16	23
Jan.	1	22	Jan.	16	21
Feb.	1	20	Feb.	15	19

Draco (below the Pole), Ursa Minor (below the Pole), Camelopardus, Perseus, Auriga, Taurus, Orion, Eridanus and Lepus.

MINIMA OF ALGOL

d	h	d	h
3	5	20	10
6	2	23	7
8	23	26	4
11	20	29	1
14	17	31	22
17	14		

PHASES OF THE MOON

	d	h	m
○ Full Moon	7	02	16
☾ Last Quarter	13	23	27
● New Moon	21	02	28
☽ First Quarter	29	03	29

	d	h
Perigee (369,590 kilometres)	12	03
Apogee (404,640 ,,)	27	10

Mean Longitude of Ascending Node on January 1, 55°.

MONTHLY NOTES

Jan. 1. Bank Holiday in England, Scotland, Wales and Northern Ireland.

2. Bank Holiday, Scotland.

26. Australia Day. Republic Day, India.

**Centenary

Day	Right Ascension	Dec. −	Equation of Time	Rise 52°	Rise 56°	Transit	Set 52°	Set 56°	Sidereal Time	Transit of First Point of Aries
	h m s	° ′	m s	h m	h m	h m	h m	h m	h m s	h m s
1	18 45 45	23 02	− 3 24	8 08	8 32	12 04	15 59	15 36	6 42 21	17 14 48
2	18 50 10	22 57	− 3 52	8 08	8 31	12 04	16 00	15 37	6 46 18	17 10 52
3	18 54 34	22 51	− 4 20	8 08	8 31	12 05	16 01	15 38	6 50 14	17 06 56
4	18 58 58	22 45	− 4 48	8 08	8 31	12 05	16 02	15 40	6 54 11	17 03 00
5	19 03 22	22 39	− 5 15	8 07	8 30	12 05	16 04	15 41	6 58 07	16 59 04
6	19 07 45	22 32	− 5 41	8 07	8 30	12 06	16 05	15 42	7 02 04	16 55 08
7	19 12 08	22 24	− 6 08	8 06	8 29	12 06	16 06	15 44	7 06 00	16 51 13
8	19 16 30	22 17	− 6 33	8 06	8 28	12 07	16 08	15 46	7 09 57	16 47 17
9	19 20 52	22 08	− 6 59	8 05	8 28	12 07	16 09	15 48	7 13 54	16 43 21
10	19 25 13	22 00	− 7 23	8 05	8 27	12 08	16 10	15 49	7 17 50	16 39 25
11	19 29 34	21 51	− 7 47	8 04	8 26	12 08	16 12	15 51	7 21 47	16 35 29
12	19 33 54	21 41	− 8 11	8 03	8 25	12 08	16 13	15 53	7 25 43	16 31 33
13	19 38 13	21 31	− 8 34	8 03	8 24	12 09	16 14	15 54	7 29 40	16 27 37
14	19 42 32	21 21	− 8 56	8 02	8 23	12 09	16 16	15 56	7 33 36	16 23 41
15	19 46 51	21 10	− 9 18	8 01	8 22	12 09	16 18	15 58	7 37 33	16 19 45
16	19 51 08	20 59	− 9 39	8 00	8 21	12 10	16 19	16 00	7 41 29	16 15 49
17	19 55 25	20 48	− 9 59	7 59	8 19	12 10	16 21	16 02	7 45 26	16 11 53
18	19 59 42	20 36	−10 19	7 58	8 17	12 10	16 22	16 04	7 49 23	16 07 58
19	20 03 57	20 24	−10 38	7 57	8 16	12 11	16 24	16 05	7 53 19	16 04 02
20	20 08 12	20 11	−10 57	7 56	8 15	12 11	16 26	16 07	7 57 16	16 00 06
21	20 12 26	19 58	−11 14	7 55	8 14	12 11	16 27	16 09	8 01 12	15 56 10
22	20 16 40	19 44	−11 31	7 54	8 13	12 12	16 29	16 11	8 05 09	15 52 14
23	20 20 52	19 30	−11 47	7 53	8 11	12 12	16 31	16 13	8 09 05	15 48 18
24	20 25 04	19 16	−12 02	7 51	8 09	12 12	16 33	16 15	8 13 02	15 44 22
25	20 29 15	19 02	−12 17	7 50	8 07	12 12	16 35	16 17	8 16 58	15 40 26
26	20 33 25	18 47	−12 30	7 49	8 06	12 13	16 37	16 20	8 20 55	15 36 30
27	20 37 35	18 32	−12 43	7 47	8 04	12 13	16 39	16 22	8 24 52	15 32 34
28	20 41 43	18 16	−12 55	7 46	8 03	12 13	16 40	16 24	8 28 48	15 28 38
29	20 45 51	18 00	−13 06	7 45	8 01	12 13	16 42	16 26	8 32 45	15 24 43
30	20 49 58	17 44	−13 17	7 44	8 00	12 13	16 43	16 28	8 36 41	15 20 47
31	20 54 04	17 27	−13 26	7 42	7 58	12 14	16 45	16 30	8 40 38	15 16 51

THE SUN　　s.d. 16″·3

Duration of Civil (C), Nautical (N), and Astronomical (A), Twilight (in minutes)

Lat. °	Jan. 1 C	N	A	Jan. 11 C	N	A	Jan. 21 C	N	A	Jan. 31 C	N	A
52	41	84	125	40	82	123	38	80	120	37	78	117
56	47	96	141	45	93	138	43	90	134	41	87	130

ASTRONOMICAL NOTES

MERCURY, magnitude −0·1, is a morning object for the first ten days of the month, visible for a short while above the south-east horizon around the time of beginning of morning civil twilight. For the remainder of the month it is unsuitably placed for observation

VENUS is a brilliant evening object, magnitude −4·0, visible in the south-western sky for several hours after sunset. On the evening of the 24th the crescent Moon will be seen approaching the planet.

MARS, magnitude +1·2, is visible low in the south-western sky in the evenings until shortly after 20ʰ. Towards the end of the month Mars moves from Aquarius into Pisces.

JUPITER is unsuitably placed for observation, conjunction occurring on the 14th.

SATURN, magnitude +0·8, is a morning object in the constellation of Libra. It is visible low in the south-eastern sky before dawn. On the morning of the 16th the old crescent Moon will be seen approaching the planet.

THE MOON

Day	R.A.	Dec.	Hor. Par.	Semi-diam.	Sun's Co-long.	P.A. of Bright Limb	Phase	Age	Rise 52°	Rise 56°	Tran-sit	Set 52°	Set 56°
	h m	° ′	′	′	°	°		d	h m	h m	h m	h m	h m
1	1 54	+ 9·2	54·4	14·8	21	249	67	9·5	12 31	12 21	19 45	2 04	2 13
2	2 39	+14·1	54·8	14·9	33	251	75	10·5	12 47	12 32	20 29	3 16	3 30
3	3 26	+18·5	55·2	15·1	45	255	83	11·5	13 07	12 46	21 17	4 30	4 49
4	4 17	+22·2	55·8	15·2	57	261	90	12·5	13 34	13 07	22 09	5 45	6 10
5	5 11	+24·9	56·5	15·4	70	269	95	13·5	14 12	13 40	23 05	6 58	7 29
6	6 09	+26·4	57·1	15·6	82	283	99	14·5	15 04	14 31	. .	8 04	8 37
7	7 09	+26·4	57·8	15·7	94	350	100	15·5	16 12	15 41	0 03	8 57	9 28
8	8 09	+24·8	58·3	15·9	106	81	99	16·5	17 32	17 07	1 02	9 37	10 03
9	9 08	+21·6	58·8	16·0	118	96	95	17·5	18 58	18 40	1 59	10 06	10 26
10	10 05	+17·2	59·1	16·1	130	104	90	18·5	20 24	20 13	2 53	10 28	10 42
11	10 59	+11·8	59·3	16·1	142	109	82	19·5	21 50	21 44	3 45	10 46	10 53
12	11 51	+ 5·8	59·3	16·2	155	111	72	20·5	23 14	23 14	4 35	11 01	11 03
13	12 42	− 0·6	59·3	16·2	167	112	61	21·5	. .	. .	5 23	11 15	11 12
14	13 33	− 6·8	59·2	16·1	179	112	50	22·5	0 38	0 44	6 12	11 31	11 22
15	14 25	−12·7	59·0	16·1	191	109	39	23·5	2 03	2 15	7 02	11 48	11 34
16	15 19	−18·0	58·7	16·0	203	105	28	24·5	3 28	3 47	7 54	12 10	11 49
17	16 15	−22·2	58·4	15·9	215	99	19	25·5	4 53	5 19	8 50	12 39	12 12
18	17 14	−25·1	58·1	15·8	228	92	11	26·5	6 11	6 43	9 47	13 19	12 47
19	18 14	−26·5	57·6	15·7	240	82	5	27·5	7 18	7 52	10 46	14 13	13 39
20	19 14	−26·3	57·1	15·6	252	67	1	28·5	8 10	8 42	11 43	15 20	14 49
21	20 11	−24·7	56·6	15·4	264	3	0	29·5	8 47	9 14	12 37	16 35	16 09
22	21 06	−21·7	56·1	15·3	276	278	1	0·9	9 14	9 34	13 28	17 52	17 32
23	21 57	−17·8	55·5	15·1	288	262	4	1·9	9 33	9 48	14 15	19 07	18 54
24	22 45	−13·2	55·0	14·8	301	255	9	2·9	9 49	9 58	14 58	20 20	20 12
25	23 30	− 8·2	54·6	14·9	313	251	15	3·9	10 01	10 06	15 39	21 30	21 27
26	0 13	− 2·9	54·3	14·8	325	249	22	4·9	10 13	10 13	16 19	22 39	22 41
27	0 56	+ 2·4	54·2	14·8	337	249	30	5·9	10 24	10 20	16 58	23 48	23 55
28	1 39	+ 7·6	54·2	14·8	349	249	39	6·9	10 36	10 28	17 39	. .	. .
29	2 22	+12·6	54·4	14·8	2	251	49	7·9	10 50	10 37	18 21	0 58	1 10
30	3 08	+17·2	54·8	14·9	14	254	58	8·9	11 08	10 49	19 07	2 10	2 27
31	3 57	+21·1	55·3	15·1	26	259	68	9·9	11 31	11 07	19 56	3 24	3 47

MERCURY ☿

Day	R.A.	Dec. −	Diam.	Phase	Tran-sit	5° high. 52°	5° high. 56°	Day	R.A.	Dec. −	Diam.	Phase	Tran-sit	
	h m	°	″		h m	h m	h m		h m	°	″		h m	
1	17 09	20·7	7	57	10 26	7 04	7 33	16	18 25	23·3	5	83	10 44	
4	17 20	21·4	7	65	10 26	7 10	7 41	19	18 43	23·4	5	86	10 51	Mercury is too
7	17 35	22·0	6	71	10 29	7 18	7 50	22	19 02	23·4	5	88	10 58	close to the
10	17 50	22·5	6	76	10 33	7 26	8 00	25	19 22	23·1	5	90	11 06	Sun for
13	18 07	23·0	6	80	10 38	7 35	8 10	28	19 41	22·7	5	92	11 14	observation
16	18 25	23·3	5	83	10 44	7 43	8 19	31	20 01	22·1	5	94	11 22	

VENUS ♀   MARS ♂

Day	R.A.	Dec. −	Diam.	Phase	Tran-sit	5° high. 52°	5° high. 56°	Day	R.A.	Dec. −	Diam.	Phase	Tran-sit	5° high. 52°	5° high. 56°
	h m	°	″		h m	h m	h m		h m	°	″		h m	h m	h m
1	21 57	14·2	20	61	15 14	19 24	19 07	1	22 29	10·5	5	91	15 46	20 18	20 05
6	22 18	12·0	21	60	15 16	19 39	19 24	6	22 44	9·0	5	91	15 41	20 21	20 10
11	22 38	9·7	22	57	15 16	19 53	19 40	11	22 58	7·5	5	92	15 35	20 24	20 15
16	22 57	7·3	23	54	15 15	20 05	19 56	16	23 12	6·0	5	92	15 30	20 27	20 19
21	23 16	4·8	24	52	15 14	20 17	20 10	21	23 26	4·4	5	92	15 24	20 29	20 23
26	23 33	2·4	26	49	15 12	20 28	20 23	26	23 39	2·8	5	93	15 18	20 32	20 27
31	23 50	0·1	27	46	15 09	20 38	20 35	31	23 53	1·3	5	93	15 12	20 34	20 30

SUNRISE AND SUNSET

Day	London a.m. h m	London p.m. h m	Bristol a.m. h m	Bristol p.m. h m	Birmingham a.m. h m	Birmingham p.m. h m	Manchester a.m. h m	Manchester p.m. h m	Newcastle a.m. h m	Newcastle p.m. h m	Glasgow a.m. h m	Glasgow p.m. h m	Belfast a.m. h m	Belfast p.m. h m
1	8 06	4 02	8 16	4 12	8 18	4 03	8 25	4 00	8 31	3 48	8 48	3 54	8 47	4 08
2	8 06	4 03	8 16	4 13	8 18	4 04	8 25	4 01	8 31	3 49	8 47	3 55	8 47	4 09
3	8 06	4 04	8 16	4 14	8 18	4 05	8 25	4 02	8 31	3 50	8 47	3 56	8 47	4 10
4	8 06	4 05	8 15	4 15	8 18	4 07	8 25	4 04	8 31	3 52	8 47	3 58	8 47	4 12
5	8 06	4 06	8 15	4 16	8 17	4 08	8 24	4 05	8 30	3 53	8 46	3 59	8 46	4 13
6	8 06	4 07	8 15	4 17	8 17	4 09	8 24	4 06	8 30	3 54	8 46	4 00	8 46	4 14
7	8 05	4 08	8 15	4 19	8 16	4 11	8 23	4 08	8 29	3 56	8 45	4 02	8 45	4 16
8	8 04	4 09	8 14	4 20	8 16	4 12	8 23	4 09	8 28	3 57	8 44	4 03	8 44	4 17
9	8 04	4 11	8 14	4 22	8 15	4 14	8 22	4 11	8 28	3 59	8 44	4 05	8 44	4 19
10	8 04	4 12	8 13	4 23	8 15	4 15	8 22	4 12	8 27	4 01	8 43	4 07	8 43	4 21
11	8 03	4 14	8 13	4 24	8 14	4 17	8 21	4 14	8 26	4 02	8 42	4 08	8 42	4 22
12	8 02	4 15	8 12	4 26	8 13	4 18	8 20	4 15	8 25	4 04	8 41	4 10	8 41	4 24
13	8 02	4 16	8 12	4 27	8 13	4 19	8 20	4 16	8 24	4 06	8 40	4 12	8 40	4 26
14	8 01	4 18	8 11	4 29	8 12	4 21	8 19	4 18	8 23	4 07	8 39	4 14	8 39	4 27
15	8 00	4 20	8 10	4 30	8 11	4 23	8 18	4 20	8 22	4 09	8 38	4 15	8 38	4 29
16	7 59	4 21	8 09	4 32	8 10	4 24	8 17	4 21	8 21	4 11	8 37	4 17	8 37	4 31
17	7 58	4 23	8 08	4 33	8 09	4 26	8 16	4 23	8 20	4 13	8 36	4 19	8 36	4 33
18	7 57	4 24	8 07	4 35	8 08	4 27	8 15	4 24	8 19	4 14	8 35	4 21	8 35	4 34
19	7 56	4 26	8 06	4 36	8 07	4 29	8 14	4 26	8 18	4 16	8 33	4 23	8 34	4 36
20	7 55	4 28	8 05	4 38	8 06	4 31	8 13	4 28	8 17	4 18	8 32	4 25	8 33	4 38
21	7 54	4 29	8 04	4 39	8 05	4 32	8 12	4 30	8 16	4 20	8 31	4 27	8 32	4 40
22	7 53	4 31	8 03	4 41	8 04	4 34	8 10	4 32	8 14	4 22	8 29	4 29	8 30	4 42
23	7 52	4 33	8 02	4 43	8 03	4 36	8 09	4 33	8 13	4 24	8 28	4 31	8 29	4 43
24	7 50	4 35	8 00	4 45	8 01	4 38	8 08	4 35	8 11	4 26	8 26	4 33	8 28	4 45
25	7 49	4 36	7 59	4 46	8 00	4 39	8 06	4 37	8 09	4 28	8 24	4 35	8 26	4 47
26	7 48	4 38	7 58	4 48	7 59	4 41	8 05	4 39	8 08	4 30	8 23	4 37	8 25	4 49
27	7 46	4 40	7 56	4 50	7 57	4 43	8 03	4 41	8 06	4 32	8 21	4 39	8 23	4 51
28	7 45	4 42	7 55	4 52	7 56	4 45	8 02	4 43	8 05	4 34	8 20	4 42	8 22	4 54
29	7 44	4 44	7 54	4 54	7 55	4 47	8 00	4 45	8 03	4 36	8 18	4 44	8 20	4 56
30	7 42	4 45	7 52	4 55	7 53	4 48	7 59	4 47	8 02	4 38	8 16	4 46	8 18	4 58
31	7 41	4 47	7 51	4 57	7 52	4 50	7 57	4 49	8 00	4 40	8 14	4 48	8 16	5 00

JUPITER ♃   SATURN ♄

Day	R.A. h m	Dec. – °	Transit h m		R.A. h m	Dec. – °	Transit h m	5° high 52° h m	5° high 56° h m
1	19 33	22·0	12 49	Jupiter is	15 32	16·9	8 48	4 59	5 20
11	19 43	21·6	12 20	too close to	15 35	17·1	8 12	4 26	4 47
21	19 53	21·2	11 50	the Sun for	15 38	17·3	7 36	3 50	4 12
31	20 03	20·8	11 21	observation	15 41	17·4	6 59	3 14	3 36

Equatorial diameter of Jupiter 32″; of Saturn 16″.   Diameters of Saturn's rings 36″ and 14″.

URANUS ♅   NEPTUNE ♆

Day	R.A. h m	Dec. – ° ′	Transit h m		R.A. h m	Dec. – ° ′	Transit h m	
1	16 56·4	22 38	10 13	Uranus is too	18 06·4	22 19	11 22	Neptune is too
11	16 58·8	22 42	9 36	close to the Sun	18 08·0	22 19	10 45	close to the Sun
21	17 01·0	22 45	8 58	for observation	18 09·6	22 19	10 07	for observation
31	17 02·9	22 48	8 21		18 11·0	22 18	9 29	

Diameter 4″   Diameter 2″

Month	Week		

Februa, Roman festival
of Purification

Sun's Longitude 330°)(18ᵈ 17ʰ

1	F.	Mary Shelley d. 1851. Dame Clara Butt b. 1873.
2	S.	**Purification.** James Joyce b. 1882.
3	☉	**9th S. before Easter.** Mendelssohn b. 1809.
4	M.	Charles Lindbergh b. 1902.
5	Tu.	Sir Robert Peel b. 1788.
6	W.	QUEEN'S ACCESSION 1952. Charles II d. 1685.**
7	Th.	Sir Thomas More b. 1478. Charles Dickens b. 1812.
8	F.	Mary, Queen of Scots exec. 1587.
9	S.	Lord Darnley killed 1567. Alban Berg b. 1885.**
10	☉	**8th S. before Easter.** Charles Lamb b. 1775.
11	M.	Thomas Edison b. 1847. Sir Vivian Fuchs b. 1908.
12	Tu.	Charles Darwin b. 1809. Abraham Lincoln b. 1809.
13	W.	Massacre of Glencoe 1692.
14	Th.	VALENTINE'S DAY. Capt. Cook killed 1779.
15	F.	Galileo b. 1564. Sir Ernest Shackleton b. 1874.
16	S.	Admiral Coligny b. 1519.
17	☉	**7th S. before Easter.**
18	M.	Mary I b. 1516. Martin Luther d. 1546.
19	Tu.	SHROVE TUESDAY. PRINCE ANDREW b. 1960.
20	W.	**Ash Wednesday.**
21	Th.	Card. Newman b. 1801. W. H. Auden b. 1907.
22	F.	George Washington b. 1732. Schopenhauer b. 1788.
23	S.	Samuel Pepys b. 1633. George F. Handel b. 1685.**
24	☉.	**1st S. in Lent.** Wilhelm Grimm b. 1786.
25	M.	Pierre Renoir b. 1841. Enrico Caruso b. 1873.
26	Tu.	Victor Hugo b. 1802.
27	W.	Longfellow b. 1807. Sir Hubert Parry b. 1848.
28	Th.	Montaigne b. 1533. Henry James d. 1916.

PHENOMENA

February 8ᵈ 02ʰ Venus in conjunction with Mars. Venus 3° N.

12ᵈ 16ʰ Saturn in conjunction with the Moon. Saturn 3° N.

15ᵈ 19ʰ Venus in conjunction with the Moon. Venus 4° N.

17ᵈ 10ʰ Jupiter in conjunction with the Moon. Jupiter 4° N.

19ᵈ 08ʰ Mercury in superior conjunction.

23ᵈ 06ʰ Venus in conjunction with the Moon. Venus 8° N.

23ᵈ 08ʰ Mars in conjunction with the Moon. Mars 3° N.

26ᵈ 18ʰ Venus at greatest brilliancy.

CONSTELLATIONS

The following constellations are near the meridian at

	d	h		d	h
Jan.	1	24	Jan.	16	23
Feb.	1	22	Feb.	15	21
Mar.	1	20	Mar.	16	19

Draco (below the Pole), Camelopardus, Auriga, Taurus, Gemini, Orion, Canis Minor, Monoceros, Lepus, Canis Major and Puppis.

MINIMA OF ALGOL

d	h	d	h
3	18	18	3
6	15	20	23
9	12	23	20
12	9	26	17
15	6		

MONTHLY NOTES

Feb.   1. Pheasant and partridge shooting ends.
       6. National Day, New Zealand.
     20. First Day of Lent.

PHASES OF THE MOON

	d	h	m
○ Full Moon	5	15	19
☽ Last Quarter	12	07	57
● New Moon.........	19	18	43
☽ First Quarter	27	23	41

	d	h
Perigee (364,270 kilometres)	8	04
Apogee (405,510 ,,)	24	04

Mean Longitude of Ascending Node on February 1, 53°.

QUARTER DAYS (England, Wales and Northern Ireland)

Lady Day.....March 25	*Michaelmas* ..September 29
Midsummer ..June 24	*Christmas* ....December 25

SCOTTISH TERM DAYS

Candlemas ...February 2	*Lammas*......August 1
Whitsunday ..May 15	*Martinmas* ...November 11

Removal Terms are May 28 and November 28.

**Centenary

	THE SUN					s.d. 16·2			Sidereal Time	Transit of First Point of Aries
Day	Right Ascension	Dec. −	Equation of Time	Rise		Transit	Set			
				52°	56°		52°	56°		
	h m s	° ′	m s	h m	h m	h m	h m	h m	h m s	h m s
1	20 58 09	17 11	− 13 35	7 40	7 55	12 14	16 48	16 33	8 44 34	15 12 55
2	21 02 13	16 53	− 13 43	7 39	7 53	12 14	16 50	16 35	8 48 31	15 08 59
3	21 06 17	16 36	− 13 50	7 37	7 51	12 14	16 51	16 37	8 52 27	15 05 03
4	21 10 20	16 18	− 13 56	7 36	7 49	12 14	16 53	16 39	8 56 24	15 01 07
5	21 14 22	16 00	− 14 01	7 34	7 47	12 14	16 55	16 41	9 00 21	14 57 11
6	21 18 23	15 42	− 14 06	7 32	7 45	12 14	16 57	16 43	9 04 17	14 53 15
7	21 22 23	15 23	− 14 09	7 30	7 43	12 14	16 59	16 46	9 08 14	14 49 19
8	21 26 22	15 05	− 14 12	7 28	7 41	12 14	17 00	16 48	9 12 10	14 45 23
9	21 30 21	14 46	− 14 15	7 26	7 39	12 14	17 02	16 50	9 16 07	14 41 28
10	21 34 19	14 26	− 14 16	7 25	7 37	12 14	17 04	16 52	9 20 03	14 37 32
11	21 38 16	14 07	− 14 17	7 23	7 35	12 14	17 06	16 54	9 24 00	14 33 36
12	21 42 13	13 47	− 14 16	7 21	7 33	12 14	17 08	16 56	9 27 56	14 29 40
13	21 46 08	13 27	− 14 16	7 19	7 30	12 14	17 10	16 59	9 31 53	14 25 44
14	21 50 03	13 07	− 14 14	7 17	7 28	12 14	17 12	17 01	9 35 50	14 21 48
15	21 58 58	12 46	− 14 12	7 15	7 26	12 14	17 14	17 04	9 39 46	14 17 52
16	21 57 51	12 25	− 14 09	7 14	7 24	12 14	17 15	17 06	9 43 43	14 13 56
17	22 01 44	12 05	− 14 05	7 12	7 22	12 14	17 17	17 08	9 47 39	14 10 00
18	22 05 36	11 44	− 14 01	7 10	7 19	12 14	17 19	17 10	9 51 36	14 06 04
19	22 09 28	11 23	− 13 55	7 08	7 17	12 14	17 21	17 12	9 55 32	14 02 08
20	22 13 18	11 01	− 13 50	7 06	7 14	12 14	17 23	17 14	9 59 29	13 58 13
21	22 17 09	10 39	− 13 43	7 03	7 12	12 14	17 25	17 16	10 03 25	13 54 17
22	22 20 58	10 18	− 13 36	7 01	7 09	12 14	17 27	17 19	10 07 22	13 50 21
23	22 24 47	9 56	− 13 28	6 59	7 06	12 13	17 29	17 21	10 11 19	13 46 25
24	22 28 35	9 34	− 13 20	6 57	7 04	12 13	17 31	17 23	10 15 15	13 42 29
25	22 32 23	9 11	− 13 11	6 55	7 02	12 13	17 32	17 25	10 19 12	13 38 33
26	22 36 10	8 49	− 13 02	6 53	7 00	12 13	17 34	17 27	10 23 08	13 34 37
27	22 39 56	8 27	− 12 51	6 51	6 58	12 13	17 36	17 29	10 27 05	13 30 41
28	22 43 42	8 04	− 12 41	6 49	6 55	12 13	17 37	17 32	10 31 01	13 26 45

Duration of Civil (C), Nautical (N), and Astronomical (A), Twilight (in minutes)

Lat. °	Feb. 1			Feb. 11			Feb. 21			Feb. 28		
	C	N	A	C	N	A	C	N	A	C	N	A
52	37	77	117	35	75	114	34	74	113	34	73	112
56	41	86	130	39	83	126	38	81	125	38	81	124

ASTRONOMICAL NOTES

MERCURY is unsuitably placed for observation, superior conjunction occurring on the 19th.

VENUS is a magnificent evening star, magnitude −4·3, dominating the western sky for several hours after sunset. Keen sighted observers may be able to detect the planet before sunset, especially if they know exactly where to look and can shield themselves from direct sunlight. Venus and Mars are within a few degrees of each other throughout the month.

MARS, magnitude +1·4, continues to be visible as an evening object, low in the western sky. The crescent Moon will be seen near Mars on the evenings of the 22nd and 23rd.

JUPITER is unsuitably placed for observation.

SATURN, magnitude +0·7, is visible in the mornings, low above the south-eastern horizon. By the end of the month it is above the horizon by 01ʰ. The Last Quarter Moon will be seen near the planet on the mornings of the 12th and 13th.

ZODIACAL LIGHT. The evening cone may be observed in the western sky after the end of twilight between the 7th and the 21st. This faint phenomenon is only visible under good conditions, in the absence of both moonlight and artificial lighting.

THE MOON

Day	R.A.	Dec.	Hor. Par.	Semi-diam.	Sun's Co-long.	P.A. of Bright Limb	Phase	Age	Rise 52°	Rise 56°	Transit	Set 52°	Set 56°
	h m	°	′	′	°	°		d	h m	h m	h m	h m	h m
1	4 49	+24.2	56.0	15.3	38	264	76	10.9	12 03	11 33	20 50	4 38	5 06
2	5 45	+26.1	56.8	15.5	50	271	85	11.9	12 48	12 15	21 47	5 47	6 20
3	6 44	+26.7	57.6	15.7	62	280	91	12.9	13 49	13 16	22 46	6 46	7 19
4	7 45	+25.6	58.4	15.9	74	291	96	13.9	15 05	14 37	23 45	7 32	8 00
5	8 45	+23.0	59.1	16.1	87	315	99	14.9	16 31	16 10	..	8 06	8 28
6	9 44	+18.9	59.7	16.3	99	64	100	15.9	18 01	17 46	0 42	8 31	8 47
7	10 41	+13.6	60.0	16.4	111	98	97	16.9	19 30	19 22	1 36	8 50	9 00
8	11 35	+ 7.5	60.2	16.4	123	106	92	17.9	20 57	20 56	2 28	9 07	9 11
9	12 28	+ 1.0	60.1	16.4	135	110	85	18.9	22 24	22 28	3 18	9 21	9 20
10	13 20	− 5.5	59.9	16.3	147	110	76	19.9	23 50	..	4 08	9 36	9 30
11	14 12	−11.7	59.5	16.2	159	109	65	20.9	..	0 01	4 59	9 53	9 41
12	15 06	−17.1	59.0	16.1	171	106	54	21.9	1 17	1 34	5 51	10 13	9 55
13	16 02	−21.6	58.4	15.9	184	101	43	22.9	2 42	3 06	6 45	10 40	10 15
14	17 00	−24.8	57.9	15.8	196	95	32	23.9	4 02	4 33	7 42	11 16	10 45
15	17 59	−26.5	57.4	15.6	208	88	23	24.9	5 12	5 46	8 39	12 05	11 31
16	18 58	−26.7	56.8	15.5	220	80	14	25.9	6 07	6 41	9 36	13 07	12 34
17	19 55	−25.4	56.3	15.4	232	72	8	26.9	6 48	7 17	10 30	14 19	13 51
18	20 50	−22.8	55.9	15.2	245	62	3	27.9	7 17	7 40	11 22	15 35	15 13
19	21 42	−19.1	55.4	15.1	257	42	1	28.9	7 38	7 55	12 09	16 50	16 35
20	22 30	−14.7	55.0	15.0	269	311	0	0.2	7 55	8 06	12 53	18 04	17 54
21	23 16	− 9.7	54.6	14.9	281	265	2	1.2	8 08	8 15	13 35	19 16	19 11
22	24 00	− 4.4	54.4	14.8	293	255	5	2.2	8 20	8 22	14 15	20 25	20 25
23	0 42	+ 0.9	54.2	14.8	306	252	10	3.2	8 31	8 28	14 55	21 34	21 39
24	1 25	+ 6.2	54.1	14.7	318	251	16	4.2	8 42	8 35	15 35	22 44	22 54
25	2 08	+11.3	54.1	14.7	330	251	23	5.2	8 55	8 43	16 16	23 55	..
26	2 53	+16.0	54.3	14.8	342	253	32	6.2	9 10	8 54	17 00	..	0 10
27	3 40	+20.1	54.7	14.9	354	257	41	7.2	9 30	9 08	17 47	1 07	1 28
28	4 30	+23.5	55.2	15.0	6	261	50	8.2	9 57	9 29	18 38	2 20	2 47

MERCURY ☿

Day	R.A.	Dec. −	Diam.	Phase	Transit		Day	R.A.	Dec. −	Diam.	Phase	Transit	
	h m	°	″		h m			h m	°	″		h m	
1	20 08	21.9	5	94	11 25		16	21 51	15.3	5	99	12 08	
4	20 28	21.0	5	96	11 33	Mercury is too	19	22 11	13.3	5	100	12 17	Mercury is too
7	20 49	19.9	5	97	11 42	close to the	22	22 32	11.1	5	100	12 26	close to the
10	21 09	18.5	5	98	11 51	Sun for	25	22 53	8.8	5	99	12 35	Sun for
13	21 30	17.0	5	99	11 59	observation	28	23 14	6.3	5	97	12 44	observation
16	21 51	15.3	5	99	12 08		31	23 34	3.6	5	92	12 53	

VENUS ♀

Day	R.A.	Dec. +	Diam.	Phase	Transit	5° high 52°	5° high 56°
	h m	°	″		h m	h m	h m
1	23 54	0.6	27	46	15 09	20 41	20 38
6	0 09	3.0	29	43	15 04	20 48	20 48
11	0 24	5.3	31	39	14 59	20 54	20 56
16	0 37	7.5	33	36	14 52	20 58	21 02
21	0 49	9.5	36	32	14 44	21 01	21 06
26	0 58	11.4	39	28	14 34	21 02	21 07
31	1 06	13.0	42	24	14 21	21 00	21 06

MARS ♂

Day	R.A.	Dec.	Diam.	Phase	Transit	5° high 52°	5° high 56°
	h m	°	″		h m	h m	h m
1	23 56	−1.0	5	93	15 11	20 34	20 30
6	0 10	+0.6	5	94	15 05	20 36	20 34
11	0 23	+2.2	5	94	14 59	20 38	20 37
16	0 37	+3.7	5	94	14 53	20 40	20 40
21	0 51	+5.2	5	95	14 46	20 42	20 43
26	1 04	+6.7	5	95	14 40	20 44	20 45
31	1 18	+8.2	4	95	14 34	20 45	20 48

SUNRISE AND SUNSET

Day	London a.m. h m	London p.m. h m	Bristol a.m. h m	Bristol p.m. h m	Birmingham a.m. h m	Birmingham p.m. h m	Manchester a.m. h m	Manchester p.m. h m	Newcastle a.m. h m	Newcastle p.m. h m	Glasgow a.m. h m	Glasgow p.m. h m	Belfast a.m. h m	Belfast p.m. h m
1	7 40	4 49	7 49	4 59	7 50	4 52	7 55	4 51	7 58	4 42	8 12	4 50	8 14	5 02
2	7 38	4 51	7 48	5 01	7 48	4 54	7 53	4 53	7 56	4 44	8 10	4 52	8 12	5 04
3	7 37	4 53	7 46	5 03	7 47	4 56	7 52	4 55	7 54	4 46	8 08	4 54	8 11	5 06
4	7 35	4 55	7 44	5 05	7 45	4 58	7 50	4 57	7 52	4 49	8 06	4 57	8 09	5 08
5	7 34	4 56	7 43	5 06	7 43	5 00	7 48	4 59	7 50	4 51	8 04	4 59	8 07	5 10
6	7 32	4 58	7 41	5 08	7 41	5 02	7 46	5 01	7 48	4 53	8 02	5 01	8 05	5 12
7	7 30	5 00	7 40	5 10	7 39	5 04	7 44	5 03	7 46	4 55	8 00	5 03	8 03	5 14
8	7 29	5 01	7 38	5 11	7 38	5 06	7 43	5 05	7 45	4 57	7 59	5 05	8 02	5 16
9	7 27	5 03	7 36	5 13	7 36	5 08	7 41	5 07	7 43	4 59	7 57	5 07	8 00	5 18
10	7 25	5 05	7 35	5 15	7 34	5 10	7 39	5 09	7 41	5 01	7 55	5 09	7 58	5 20
11	7 23	5 07	7 33	5 17	7 32	5 12	7 37	5 11	7 39	5 03	7 53	5 11	7 56	5 22
12	7 21	5 09	7 31	5 19	7 30	5 14	7 35	5 13	7 37	5 05	7 51	5 13	7 54	5 24
13	7 19	5 10	7 29	5 21	7 28	5 15	7 33	5 14	7 34	5 07	7 48	5 15	7 52	5 26
14	7 17	5 12	7 27	5 22	7 26	5 17	7 31	5 16	7 32	5 09	7 46	5 17	7 50	5 28
15	7 15	5 14	7 25	5 24	7 24	5 19	7 29	5 18	7 30	5 12	7 44	5 20	7 47	5 30
16	7 13	5 16	7 23	5 26	7 22	5 21	7 27	5 20	7 28	5 14	7 42	5 22	7 45	5 32
17	7 11	5 18	7 21	5 28	7 20	5 23	7 25	5 22	7 25	5 16	7 39	5 24	7 43	5 34
18	7 09	5 20	7 19	5 30	7 18	5 25	7 23	5 24	7 23	5 18	7 37	5 26	7 41	5 36
19	7 07	5 21	7 17	5 31	7 16	5 26	7 21	5 26	7 21	5 20	7 35	5 28	7 39	5 38
20	7 05	5 23	7 15	5 33	7 14	5 28	7 19	5 28	7 19	5 22	7 32	5 31	7 36	5 41
21	7 03	5 25	7 13	5 35	7 12	5 30	7 16	5 30	7 17	5 24	7 30	5 33	7 34	5 43
22	7 01	5 27	7 11	5 37	7 10	5 32	7 14	5 32	7 14	5 26	7 27	5 35	7 31	5 45
23	6 59	5 29	7 09	5 39	7 08	5 34	7 12	5 34	7 12	5 28	7 25	5 37	7 29	5 47
24	6 57	5 31	7 07	5 41	7 06	5 36	7 10	5 36	7 10	5 30	7 23	5 39	7 27	5 49
25	6 55	5 33	7 05	5 43	7 04	5 38	7 07	5 38	7 07	5 32	7 20	5 41	7 24	5 51
26	6 53	5 34	7 03	5 44	7 02	5 39	7 05	5 40	7 05	5 35	7 18	5 44	7 22	5 53
27	6 51	5 36	7 01	5 46	7 00	5 41	7 03	5 42	7 02	5 37	7 15	5 46	7 20	5 55
28	6 49	5 38	6 59	5 48	6 57	5 43	7 00	5 44	7 00	5 39	7 13	5 48	7 17	5 57

JUPITER ♃   SATURN ♄

Day	R.A. h m	Dec. − °	Transit h m		R.A. h m	Dec. − °	Transit h m	5° high. 52° h m	5° high. 56° h m
1	20 04	20·7	11 18	Jupiter is	15 41	17·4	6 56	3 10	3 32
11	20 13	20·3	10 48	too close to	15 43	17·5	6 18	2 33	2 55
21	20 22	19·8	10 18	the Sun for	15 45	17·6	5 40	1 55	2 17
31	20 31	19·3	9 47	observation	15 46	17·6	5 02	1 17	1 39

Equatorial diameter of Jupiter 33″; of Saturn 17″. Diameters of Saturn's rings 38″ and 15″.

URANUS ♅   NEPTUNE ♆

Day	R.A. h m	Dec. − ° ′	Transit h m	10° high. 52° h m	10° high. 56° h m	R.A. h m	Dec. − ° ′	Transit h m	10° high. 52° h m	10° high. 56° h m
1	17 03·1	22 48	8 17	6 06	7 08	18 11·1	22 18	9 25	7 09	8 07
11	17 04·7	22 51	7 40	5 31	6 34	18 12·4	22 18	8 47	6 32	7 30
21	17 06·0	22 52	7 02	4 54	5 59	18 13·4	22 17	8 09	5 54	6 52
31	17 07·0	22 54	6 23	4 15	5 21	18 14·3	22 16	7 30	5 16	6 14

Diameter 4″   Diameter 2″

DAY OF		
Month	Week	

Mars, Roman god of

battle

Sun's Longitude 0° ♈ 20ᵈ 16ᵂ

1	F.	**St. David.** Frederick Chopin b. 1810.
2	S.	Bedrich Smetana b. 1824. Cardinal Hume b. 1923.
3	♋.	**2nd S. in Lent.** Sir Henry Wood b. 1869.
4	M.	Antonio Vivaldi b. 1678.
5	Tu.	Henry II b. 1133. Gerardus Mercator b. 1512.
6	W.	Michaelangelo b. 1475. Elizabeth Barrett Browning b. 1806.
7	Th.	Sir John Herschel b. 1792. Maurice Ravel b. 1875.
8	F.	Outbreak of Russian Revolution 1917.
9	S.	William Cobbett b. 1763. Mussorgsky b. 1839.
10	♋.	**3rd S. in Lent.** PRINCE EDWARD b. 1964.
11	M.	William Huskisson b. 1770.
12	Tu.	Bishop Berkeley b. 1685**. Nijinsky b. 1890 N.S.
13	W.	Joseph Priestley b. 1733. Sir Hugh Walpole b. 1884.
14	Th.	Johann Strauss b. 1804. Albert Einstein b. 1879.
15	F.	Julius Caesar d. 44 B.C. Lord Melbourne b. 1779.
16	S.	Georg Simon Ohm b. 1787.
17	♋	**4th S. in Lent. St. Patrick.**
18	M.	Rimsky-Korsakov b. 1844. Wilfred Owen b. 1893.
19	Tu.	**St. Joseph of Nazareth.** Livingstone b. 1813.
20	W.	Henry IV d. 1413. Henrik Ibsen b. 1828.
21	Th.	Archbp Cranmer exec. 1556. J. S. Bach b. 1685.
22	F.	Sir Anthony van Dyck b. 1599.
23	S.	Donald Campbell b. 1921. Sir Roger Bannister b. 1929.
24	♋.	**5th S. in Lent.** Elizabeth I d. 1603.
25	M.	**Annunciation.** Arturo Toscanini b. 1867.
26	Tu.	A. E. Housman b. 1859. Tennessee Williams b. 1911.
27	W.	James I d. 1625. Capt. Scott d. 1912.
28	Th.	Raphael b. 1483. Neil Kinnock b. 1942.
29	F.	Towton 1461. Sir William Walton b. 1902.
30	S.	Goya b. 1746. Vincent van Gogh b. 1853.
31	♋.	**Palm Sunday.** Franz Joseph Haydn b. 1732.

PHENOMENA

March 11ᵈ 23ʰ Saturn in conjunction with the Moon. Saturn 3° N.

17ᵈ 02ʰ Jupiter in conjunction with the Moon. Jupiter 5° N.

17ᵈ 07ʰ Mercury at greatest eastern elongation. (18°).

20ᵈ 16ʰ Equinox.

22ᵈ 18ʰ Mercury in conjunction with the Moon. Mercury 6° N.

22ᵈ 19ʰ Venus in conjunction with the Moon. Venus 12° N.

23ᵈ 02ʰ Mercury in conjunction with Venus. Mercury 5° S.

24ᵈ 12ʰ Mars in conjunction with the Moon. Mars 1°·4 N.

CONSTELLATIONS

The following are near the meridian at

	d	h		d	h
Feb.	1	24	Feb.	15	23
Mar.	1	22	Mar.	16	21
Apr.	1	20	Apr.	15	19

Cepheus (below the Pole), Camelopardus, Lynx, Gemini, Cancer, Leo, Canis Minor, Hydra, Monoceros, Canis Major and Puppis.

MINIMA OF ALGOL

d	h	d	h
1	14	18	19
4	11	21	15
7	7	24	12
10	4	27	9
13	1	30	6
15	22		

PHASES OF THE MOON

	d	h	m
○ Full Moon	7	02	13
☾ Last Quarter.......	13	17	34
● New Moon	21	11	59
☽ First Quarter	29	16	11

	d	h
Perigee (359,350 kilometres)	8	08
Apogee (406,290　　,,　　)	23	15

Mean Longitude of Ascending Node on March 1, 52°.

Summer Time in 1985 (*see* p. 142).—Begins: March 31ᵈ at 01ʰ G.M.T. Ends: October 27ᵈ 01ʰ G.M.T.

MONTHLY NOTES

Mar.
11. Commonwealth Day.

18. Bank Holiday in Northern Ireland.

25. Lady Day. Quarter Day.

31. Financial Year 1984–85 ends.

**Centenary

Day	Right Ascension	Dec.	Equation of Time	Rise 52°	Rise 56°	Transit	Set 52°	Set 56°	Sidereal Time	Transit of First Point of Aries
	h m s	° ′	m s	h m	h m	h m	h m	h m	h m s	h m s
1	22 47 27	−7 41	−12 29	6 46	6 52	12 12	17 39	17 34	10 34 58	13 22 49
2	22 51 12	−7 18	−12 18	6 44	6 49	12 12	17 41	17 36	10 38 54	13 18 53
3	22 54 56	−6 55	−12 05	6 42	6 47	12 12	17 43	17 38	10 42 51	13 14 58
4	22 58 40	−6 32	−11 53	6 40	6 44	12 12	17 45	17 40	10 46 48	13 11 02
5	23 02 23	−6 09	−11 39	6 37	6 41	12 12	17 46	17 42	10 50 44	13 07 06
6	23 06 06	−5 46	−11 26	6 35	6 39	12 11	17 48	17 44	10 54 41	13 03 10
7	23 09 49	−5 23	−11 11	6 33	6 36	12 11	17 50	17 46	10 58 37	12 59 14
8	23 13 31	−5 00	−10 57	6 31	6 34	12 11	17 52	17 48	11 02 34	12 55 18
9	23 17 12	−4 36	−10 42	6 29	6 32	12 11	17 54	17 51	11 06 30	12 51 22
10	23 20 53	−4 13	−10 27	6 27	6 29	12 10	17 56	17 53	11 10 27	12 47 26
11	23 24 34	−3 49	−10 11	6 25	6 27	12 10	17 58	17 55	11 14 23	12 43 30
12	23 28 15	−3 26	− 9 55	6 22	6 24	12 10	17 59	17 57	11 18 20	12 39 34
13	23 31 55	−3 02	− 9 39	6 20	6 21	12 10	18 01	17 59	11 22 17	12 35 38
14	23 35 36	−2 38	− 9 23	6 18	6 19	12 09	18 03	18 01	11 26 13	12 31 43
15	23 39 15	−2 15	− 9 06	6 15	6 16	12 09	18 04	18 03	11 30 10	12 27 47
16	23 42 55	−1 51	− 8 49	6 12	6 14	12 09	18 06	18 05	11 34 06	12 23 51
17	23 46 35	−1 27	− 8 32	6 10	6 11	12 08	18 08	18 07	11 38 03	12 19 55
18	23 50 14	−1 04	− 8 15	6 08	6 08	12 08	18 09	18 09	11 41 59	12 15 59
19	23 53 53	−0 40	− 7 57	6 06	6 05	12 08	18 11	18 11	11 45 56	12 12 03
20	23 57 32	−0 16	− 7 40	6 03	6 03	12 08	18 13	18 13	11 49 52	12 08 07
21	00 01 11	+0 08	− 7 22	6 01	6 00	12 07	18 15	18 15	11 53 49	12 04 11
22	00 04 49	+0 31	− 7 04	5 59	5 57	12 07	18 17	18 17	11 57 46	12 00 15
23	00 08 28	+0 55	− 6 46	5 56	5 55	12 07	18 19	18 19	12 01 42	11 56 19
24	00 12 06	+1 19	− 6 28	5 54	5 52	12 06	18 20	18 22	12 05 39	11 52 23
25	00 15 45	+1 42	− 6 10	5 52	5 50	12 06	18 22	18 24	12 09 35	11 48 28
26	00 19 23	+2 06	− 5 52	5 50	5 48	12 06	18 24	18 26	12 13 32	11 44 32
27	00 23 02	+2 29	− 5 34	5 47	5 45	12 05	18 25	18 28	12 17 28	11 40 36
28	00 26 40	+2 53	− 5 15	5 45	5 42	12 05	18 27	18 30	12 21 25	11 36 40
29	00 30 18	+3 16	− 4 57	5 43	5 40	12 05	18 29	18 32	12 25 21	11 32 44
30	00 33 57	+3 40	− 4 39	5 40	5 37	12 04	18 30	18 34	12 29 18	11 28 48
31	00 37 35	+4 03	− 4 21	5 38	5 35	12 04	18 32	18 36	12 33 15	11 24 52

THE SUN   s.d. 16′·1

Duration of Civil (C), Nautical (N), and Astronomical (A), Twilight (in minutes)

Lat. °	Mar. 1 C	N	A	Mar. 11 C	N	A	Mar. 21 C	N	A	Mar. 31 C	N	A
52	34	73	112	34	73	113	34	74	116	34	76	120
56	38	81	124	37	80	125	37	82	129	38	84	136

ASTRONOMICAL NOTES

MERCURY, magnitude −1·1 to +2·0, becomes visible as an evening object after the first few days of March and remains so until almost the end of the month. It may be seen above the western horizon around the end of evening civil twilight. On the evening of the 22nd, at sunset, Mercury will be seen passing 6° N. of the thin crescent Moon, then only about 30 hours old. At the same time Mercury will also be passing about 6° S. of Venus. For observers in the British Isles this appearance of Mercury is the only evening one during the year.

VENUS is a brilliant object in the early evening skies, in the west. However the period available for observation is shortening and by the end of the month the planet sets only about an hour after the Sun.

MARS, magnitude +1·6, is still visible in the early evening sky, low above the western horizon.

JUPITER is too close to the Sun for observation at first but by the middle of the month it should be possible to see it as a morning object, low above the south-eastern horizon for a short while before dawn. Its magnitude is −1·6.

SATURN is a morning object, magnitude +0·6, low above the south-eastern horizon.

ZODIACAL LIGHT. The evening cone may be observed in the western sky after the end of twilight between the 8th and the 22nd.

THE MOON

Day	R.A.	Dec.	Hor. Par.	Semi-diam.	Sun's Co-long.	P.A. of Bright Limb	Phase	Age	Rise 52°	Rise 56°	Transit	Set 52°	Set 56°
	h m	°	'	'	°	°		d	h m	h m	h m	h m	h m
1	5 24	+25·8	55·9	15·2	19	267	60	9·2	10 35	10 02	19 32	3 30	4 02
2	6 21	+26·9	56·7	15·5	31	274	70	10·2	11 27	10 53	20 29	4 33	5 07
3	7 20	+26·5	57·6	15·7	43	281	79	11·2	12 36	12 05	21 27	5 24	5 56
4	8 19	+24·5	58·6	16·0	55	289	87	12·2	13 57	13 32	22 24	6 02	6 28
5	9 19	+21·0	59·5	16·2	67	297	94	13·2	15 26	15 08	23 20	6 31	6 50
6	10 16	+16·1	60·2	16·4	79	309	98	14·2	16 57	16 46	..	6 53	7 05
7	11 12	+10·1	60·8	16·6	92	187	100	15·2	18 28	18 23	0 14	7 10	7 17
8	12 07	+ 3·5	61·0	16·6	104	97	99	16·2	19 58	20 00	1 06	7 26	7 27
9	13 00	− 3·3	61·0	16·6	116	107	95	17·2	21 28	21 36	1 58	7 41	7 36
10	13 55	− 9·9	60·6	16·5	128	108	88	18·2	22 58	23 13	2 50	7 57	7 46
11	14 50	−15·8	60·1	16·4	140	107	79	19·2	..	..	3 44	8 16	7 59
12	15 47	−20·8	59·4	16·2	152	103	69	20·2	0 27	0 50	4 39	8 41	8 17
13	16 46	−24·4	58·6	16·0	164	98	58	21·2	1 52	2 22	5 36	9 14	8 44
14	17 45	−26·5	57·8	15·8	177	91	47	22·2	3 07	3 41	6 34	9 59	9 25
15	18 45	−27·0	57·1	15·6	189	85	37	23·2	4 07	4 42	7 32	10 58	10 24
16	19 43	−26·0	56·4	15·4	201	78	27	24·2	4 51	5 22	8 27	12 08	11 37
17	20 38	−23·6	55·8	15·2	213	71	18	25·2	5 23	5 48	9 19	13 22	12 58
18	21 29	−20·2	55·3	15·1	225	65	11	26·2	5 45	6 04	10 07	14 38	14 20
19	22 18	−15·9	54·9	15·0	238	60	6	27·2	6 02	6 16	10 51	15 52	15 40
20	23 04	−11·1	54·5	14·9	250	52	2	28·2	6 16	6 24	11 33	17 04	16 57
21	23 48	− 5·9	54·3	14·8	262	30	0	29·2	6 28	6 31	12 14	18 14	18 12
22	0 30	− 0·5	54·1	14·7	274	279	0	0·5	6 39	6 38	12 53	19 23	19 26
23	1 13	+ 4·9	54·0	14·7	286	257	2	1·5	6 50	6 44	13 33	20 32	20 41
24	1 56	+10·1	54·0	14·7	299	253	6	2·5	7 02	6 52	14 14	21 43	21 57
25	2 40	+14·9	54·1	14·7	311	253	11	3·5	7 16	7 01	14 56	22 55	23 14
26	3 26	+19·2	54·3	14·8	323	255	17	4·5	7 33	7 13	15 42	..	..
27	4 15	+22·8	54·6	14·9	335	259	25	5·5	7 57	7 31	16 30	0 07	0 33
28	5 07	+25·4	55·1	15·0	347	264	34	6·5	8 29	7 58	17 22	1 18	1 49
29	6 02	+26·9	55·8	15·2	360	270	43	7·5	9 14	8 39	18 17	2 23	2 58
30	6 59	+27·0	56·5	15·4	12	276	53	8·5	10 14	9 41	19 13	3 18	3 51
31	7 57	+25·6	57·4	15·6	24	283	64	9·5	11 28	11 00	20 09	4 00	4 29

MERCURY

Day	R.A.	Dec.	Diam.	Phase	Transit	5° high 52°	5° high 56°	Day	R.A.	Dec. +	Diam.	Phase	Transit	5° high 52°	5° high 56°
	h m	°	"		h m	h m	h m		h m	°			h m	h m	h m
1	23 20	− 5·4	5	95	12 47	17 50	17 43	16	0 47	7·2	7	50	13 13	19 19	19 22
4	23 41	− 2·7	5	90	12 55	18 13	18 08	19	0 57	8·8	8	37	13 10	19 24	19 28
7	24 00	0·0	6	83	13 03	18 34	18 31	22	1 02	9·9	9	25	13 03	19 21	19 26
10	0 18	+ 2·6	6	74	13 08	18 53	18 53	25	1 04	10·4	9	15	12 52	19 11	19 17
13	0 34	+ 5·1	6	62	13 12	19 09	19 10	28	1 01	10·2	10	8	12 37	18 49	18 54
16	0 47	+ 7·2	7	50	13 13	19 19	19 22	31	0 56	9·5	11	2	12 19	18 26	18 30

VENUS ♀

Day	R.A.	Dec. +	Diam.	Phase	Transit	5° high 52°	5° high 56°
	h m	°	"		h m	h m	h m
1	1 03	12·4	40	26	14 27	20 59	21 06
6	1 09	13·8	44	21	14 22	20 52	20 59
11	1 12	14·9	47	16	13 55	20 40	20 47
16	1 11	15·5	51	12	13 34	20 23	20 31
21	1 06	15·6	54	7	13 10	19 59	20 07
26	0 58	15·0	57	4	12 42	19 29	19 37
31	0 48	13·9	59	2	12 12	18 49	18 57

MARS ♂

Day	R.A.	Dec. +	Diam.	Phase	Transit	5° high 52°	5° high 56°
	h m	°	"		h m	h m	h m
1	1 12	7·6	4	95	14 37	20 44	20 47
6	1 26	9·0	4	95	14 31	20 46	20 50
11	1 40	10·4	4	96	14 25	20 47	20 52
16	1 54	11·8	4	96	14 19	20 48	20 55
21	2 08	13·1	4	96	14 13	20 49	20 57
26	2 21	14·3	4	97	14 07	20 50	20 59
31	2 35	15·5	4	97	14 02	20 51	21 01

SUNRISE AND SUNSET

Day	London a.m. h m	London p.m. h m	Bristol a.m. h m	Bristol p.m. h m	Birmingham a.m. h m	Birmingham p.m. h m	Manchester a.m. h m	Manchester p.m. h m	Newcastle a.m. h m	Newcastle p.m. h m	Glasgow a.m. h m	Glasgow p.m. h m	Belfast a.m. h m	Belfast p.m. h m
1	6 47	5 40	6 56	5 50	6 55	5 45	6 58	5 46	6 57	5 41	7 10	5 50	7 15	5 59
2	6 45	5 42	6 54	5 52	6 53	5 47	6 56	5 48	6 55	5 43	7 08	5 52	7 13	6 01
3	6 43	5 43	6 52	5 53	6 50	5 49	6 53	5 50	6 52	5 45	7 05	5 54	7 10	6 03
4	6 41	5 45	6 50	5 55	6 48	5 51	6 51	5 52	6 50	5 47	7 03	5 56	7 08	6 05
5	6 38	5 47	6 48	5 57	6 46	5 53	6 49	5 54	6 48	5 49	7 00	5 59	7 06	6 07
6	6 36	5 48	6 45	5 58	6 43	5 55	6 46	5 56	6 45	5 51	6 57	6 01	7 03	6 09
7	6 34	5 50	6 43	6 00	6 41	5 57	6 44	5 58	6 43	5 53	6 55	6 03	7 01	6 11
8	6 32	5 52	6 41	6 02	6 39	5 58	6 42	5 59	6 40	5 55	6 52	6 05	6 58	6 13
9	6 29	5 53	6 39	6 03	6 36	6 00	6 39	6 01	6 38	5 57	6 50	6 07	6 56	6 15
10	6 27	5 55	6 37	6 05	6 34	6 02	6 37	6 03	6 35	5 59	6 47	6 09	6 53	6 17
11	6 25	5 57	6 35	6 07	6 32	6 03	6 35	6 04	6 33	6 01	6 45	6 11	6 51	6 19
12	6 23	5 58	6 33	6 08	6 30	6 05	6 33	6 06	6 30	6 03	6 42	6 13	6 48	6 21
13	6 20	6 00	6 30	6 10	6 27	6 07	6 30	6 08	6 27	6 05	6 39	6 15	6 45	6 23
14	6 18	6 02	6 28	6 12	6 25	6 09	6 28	6 10	6 25	6 07	6 37	6 17	6 43	6 25
15	6 16	6 04	6 26	6 14	6 23	6 11	6 25	6 12	6 22	6 09	6 34	6 19	6 40	6 27
16	6 13	6 05	6 23	6 15	6 20	6 12	6 23	6 14	6 20	6 11	6 31	6 21	6 38	6 29
17	6 11	6 07	6 21	6 17	6 18	6 14	6 21	6 16	6 18	6 13	6 29	6 23	6 36	6 31
18	6 09	6 09	6 19	6 19	6 16	6 16	6 18	6 18	6 15	6 15	6 26	6 25	6 33	6 33
19	6 06	6 10	6 16	6 20	6 13	6 17	6 15	6 19	6 12	6 16	6 24	6 27	6 30	6 34
20	6 04	6 12	6 14	6 22	6 11	6 19	6 13	6 21	6 10	6 18	6 21	6 29	6 28	6 36
21	6 02	6 14	6 12	6 24	6 09	6 21	6 11	6 23	6 08	6 20	6 18	6 31	6 25	6 38
22	6 00	6 16	6 10	6 26	6 07	6 23	6 08	6 25	6 05	6 22	6 16	6 34	6 23	6 40
23	5 58	6 17	6 08	6 27	6 05	6 24	6 06	6 27	6 03	6 24	6 13	6 36	6 20	6 42
24	5 55	6 19	6 05	6 29	6 02	6 26	6 03	6 29	6 00	6 26	6 10	6 38	6 17	6 44
25	5 53	6 21	6 03	6 31	6 00	6 28	6 01	6 31	5 58	6 28	6 08	6 40	6 15	6 46
26	5 50	6 22	6 00	6 32	5 57	6 29	5 58	6 32	5 55	6 30	6 05	6 42	6 12	6 48
27	5 48	6 24	5 58	6 34	5 55	6 31	5 56	6 34	5 52	6 32	6 02	6 44	6 09	6 50
28	5 46	6 26	5 56	6 36	5 53	6 33	5 54	6 36	5 50	6 34	6 00	6 46	6 06	6 52
29	5 44	6 28	5 54	6 37	5 50	6 35	5 51	6 38	5 47	6 36	5 57	6 48	6 03	6 54
30	5 42	6 29	5 52	6 39	5 48	6 36	5 49	6 39	5 45	6 38	5 55	6 50	6 01	6 56
31	5 39	6 31	5 49	6 40	5 46	6 38	5 47	6 41	5 42	6 40	5 42	6 52	5 58	6 58

JUPITER ♃ / SATURN ♄

Day	JUPITER R.A. h m	Dec. − °	Transit h m	5° high. 52° h m	5° high. 56° h m	SATURN R.A. h m	Dec. − °	Transit h m	5° high. 52° h m	5° high. 56° h m
1	20 30	19·4	9 53	6 21	6 47	15 45	17·6	5 10	1 25	1 47
11	20 38	18·9	9 23	5 46	6 11	15 46	17·5	4 30	0 45	1 07
21	20 46	18·4	8 51	5 12	5 36	15 45	17·5	3 51	0 05	0 27
31	20 53	17·9	8 19	4 37	5 00	15 44	17·4	3 10	23 20	23 42

Equatorial diameter of Jupiter 34″; of Saturn 18″. Diameters of Saturn's rings 39″ and 16″.

URANUS ♅ / NEPTUNE ♆

Day	URANUS R.A. h m	Dec. − ° ′	Transit h m	10° high. 52° h m	10° high. 56° h m	NEPTUNE R.A. h m	Dec. − ° ′	Transit h m	10° high. 52° h m	10° high. 56° h m
1	17 06·8	22 53	6 31	4 23	5 29	18 14·2	22 17	7 38	5 23	6 21
11	17 07·5	22 54	5 52	3 44	4 50	18 14·9	22 16	6 59	4 45	5 43
21	17 07·7	22 55	5 13	3 05	4 11	18 15·4	22 16	6 21	4 06	5 04
31	17 07·6	22 55	4 34	2 26	3 32	18 15·6	22 15	5 41	3 26	4 24

Diameter 4″   Diameter 2″

Aperire, to open. Earth opens to receive seed.
Sun's Longitude 30° ♉ 20^{d} 03^{h}

Day of Month	Day of Week	
1	M.	William Harvey b. 1578. Bismark b. 1815
2	Tu.	Charlemagne b. 742. Copenhagen 1801.
3	W.	HILARY LAW SITTINGS END.
4	Th.	MAUNDY THURSDAY.
5	F.	**Good Friday.** Joseph Lister b. 1827.
6	S.	Badajoz 1812. Peary reached N. Pole 1909.
7	S̶.	**Easter Day.** William Wordsworth b. 1770.
8	M.	Sir Adrian Boult b. 1889.
9	Tu.	Isambard Kingdom Brunel b. 1806. Lenin b. 1870.
10	W.	William Hazlitt b. 1778. Gen. William Booth b. 1829.
11	Th.	Treaty of Utrecht 1713. U.S. Civil War starts 1861.
12	F.	First manned space flight 1961.
13	S.	Edict of Nantes 1598. Samuel Beckett b. 1906.
14	S̶.	**1st S. after Easter.** Low Sunday.
15	M.	Henry James b. 1843. Loss of *Titanic* 1912.
16	Tu.	EASTER LAW SITTINGS BEGIN. Culloden 1746.
17	W.	Diet of Worms 1521. Edward Gibbon b. 1737.
18	Th.	San Francisco earthquake 1906.
19	F.	David Ricardo b. 1772. Lexington 1775.
20	S.	Napoleon III b. 1808. Adolf Hitler b. 1889.
21	S̶.	**2nd S. after Easter.** QUEEN ELIZABETH II b. 1926.
22	M.	Henry Fielding b. 1707. Immanuel Kant b. 1724.
23	Tu.	**St George.** Shakespeare b. 1564; d. 1616.
24	W.	Edmund Cartwright b. 1743. Anthony Trollope b. 1815.
25	Th.	**St. Mark.** Oliver Cromwell b. 1599.
26	F.	David Hume b. 1711. Alfred Krupp b. 1812.
27	S.	Samuel Morse b. 1791. Gen. Ulysses Grant b. 1822.
28	S̶.	**3rd S. after Easter.** Mutiny on the *Bounty* 1789.
29	M.	Sir Thomas Beecham b. 1879. Sir Malcolm Sargent b. 1895.
30	Tu.	Mary II b. 1662. Franz Lehar b. 1870.

PHENOMENA

April 3^{d} 14^{h} Mercury in inferior conjunction.

3^{d} 22^{h} Venus in inferior conjunction.

8^{d} 07^{h} Saturn in conjunction with the Moon. Saturn 3° N.

13^{d} 17^{h} Jupiter in conjunction with the Moon. Jupiter 5° N.

17^{d} 23^{h} Venus in conjunction with the Moon. Venus 10° N.

18^{d} 04^{h} Mercury in conjunction with the Moon. Mercury 3°N.

22^{d} 13^{h} Mars in conjunction with the Moon. Mars 0°·4 S.

CONSTELLATIONS

The following constellations are near the meridian at

	d	h		d	h
Mar.	1	24	Mar.	16	23
Apr.	1	22	Apr.	15	21
May	1	20	May	16	19

Cepheus (below the Pole), Cassiopeia (below the Pole), Ursa Major, Leo Minor, Leo, Sextans, Hydra and Crater.

MINIMA OF ALGOL

d	h	d	h
2	3	19	8
4	24	22	4
7	20	25	1
10	17	27	22
13	14	30	19
16	11		

PHASES OF THE MOON

	d	h	m
○ Full Moon	5	11	32
☾ Last Quarter	12	04	41
● New Moon	20	05	22
☽ First Quarter	28	04	25

	d	h
Perigee (356,970 kilometres)	5	18
Apogee (406,540 „)	19	17

Mean Longitude of Ascending Node on April 1, 50°.

See note on *Summer Time*, p. 98.

MONTHLY NOTES

April 5. Income Tax Year (1984–85) ends.
6. First day of Passover.
6. Lent ends at midnight.
8. Bank Holiday, England, Wales and N. Ireland.
14. Greek Orthodox Easter.

	THE SUN					s.d. 16'·0			Sidereal Time	Transit of First Point of Aries
Day	Right Ascension	Dec. +	Equation of Time	Rise 52°	Rise 56°	Transit	Set 52°	Set 56°		
	h m s	° '	m s	h m	h m	h m	h m	h m	h m s	h m s
1	0 41 14	4 26	− 4 03	5 35	5 32	12 04	18 34	18 38	12 37 11	11 20 56
2	0 44 52	4 49	− 3 45	5 33	5 29	12 04	18 35	18 40	12 41 08	11 17 00
3	0 48 31	5 12	− 3 27	5 31	5 27	12 03	18 37	18 42	12 45 04	11 13 04
4	0 52 10	5 35	− 3 09	5 28	5 24	12 03	18 39	18 44	12 49 01	11 09 08
5	0 55 49	5 58	− 2 52	5 26	5 21	12 03	18 40	18 46	12 52 57	11 05 13
6	0 59 28	6 21	− 2 34	5 24	5 19	12 02	18 42	18 48	12 56 54	11 01 17
7	1 03 08	6 44	− 2 17	5 22	5 16	12 02	18 44	18 50	13 00 50	10 57 21
8	1 06 47	7 06	− 2 00	5 20	5 13	12 02	18 45	18 52	13 04 47	10 53 25
9	1 10 27	7 28	− 1 44	5 17	5 10	12 02	18 47	18 54	13 08 43	10 49 29
10	1 14 07	7 51	− 1 27	5 15	5 08	12 01	18 49	18 56	13 12 40	10 45 33
11	1 17 47	8 13	− 1 11	5 13	5 05	12 01	18 50	18 58	13 16 37	10 41 37
12	1 21 28	8 35	− 0 55	5 10	5 03	12 01	18 52	19 00	13 20 33	10 37 41
13	1 25 09	8 57	− 0 40	5 08	5 01	12 01	18 54	19 02	13 24 30	10 33 45
14	1 28 50	9 19	− 0 24	5 06	4 58	12 00	18 56	19 04	13 28 26	10 29 49
15	1 32 32	9 40	− 0 09	5 04	4 56	12 00	18 58	19 06	13 32 23	10 25 53
16	1 36 14	10 02	+ 0 05	5 02	4 53	12 00	19 00	19 08	13 36 19	10 21 58
17	1 39 57	10 23	+ 0 19	5 00	4 50	12 00	19 01	19 10	13 40 16	10 18 02
18	1 43 39	10 44	+ 0 33	4 57	4 47	11 59	19 03	19 12	13 44 12	10 14 06
19	1 47 23	11 05	+ 0 46	4 55	4 45	11 59	19 04	19 14	13 48 09	10 10 10
20	1 51 06	11 25	+ 0 59	4 53	4 43	11 59	19 06	19 17	13 52 06	10 06 14
21	1 54 50	11 46	+ 1 12	4 51	4 40	11 59	19 08	19 19	13 56 02	10 02 18
22	1 58 35	12 06	+ 1 24	4 49	4 38	11 58	19 09	19 21	13 59 59	9 58 22
23	2 02 20	12 26	+ 1 35	4 47	4 35	11 58	19 11	19 23	14 03 55	9 54 26
24	2 06 05	12 46	+ 1 47	4 45	4 32	11 58	19 13	19 25	14 07 52	9 50 30
25	2 09 51	13 06	+ 1 57	4 43	4 30	11 58	19 14	19 27	14 11 48	9 46 34
26	2 13 37	13 26	+ 2 08	4 41	4 28	11 58	19 16	19 29	14 15 45	9 42 38
27	2 17 24	13 45	+ 2 17	4 39	4 26	11 58	19 18	19 31	14 19 41	9 38 43
28	2 21 11	14 04	+ 2 27	4 37	4 23	11 57	19 19	19 33	14 23 38	9 34 47
29	2 24 59	14 23	+ 2 36	4 35	4 21	11 57	19 21	19 35	14 27 35	9 30 51
30	2 28 47	14 41	+ 2 44	4 33	4 19	11 57	19 23	19 37	14 31 31	9 26 55

Duration of Civil (C), Nautical (N), and Astronomical (A), Twilight (in minutes)

Lat. °	Apr. 1			Apr. 11			Apr. 21			Apr. 30		
	C	N	A	C	N	A	C	N	A	C	N	A
52	34	76	121	35	79	128	37	84	138	39	89	152
56	38	85	137	40	90	148	42	96	167	44	105	200

ASTRONOMICAL NOTES

MERCURY is unsuitably placed for observation, inferior conjunction occurring on the 3rd.

VENUS is a brilliant morning object, visible low above the east-north-east horizon just before sunrise. During the month its magnitude varies from − 3·3 on the 1st to − 4·2 on the 30th. Although inferior conjunction occurs on the 3rd it is an interesting fact that Venus is over 5° high at both sunrise and sunset in England on the 1st, giving the assiduous observer the rare opportunity of seeing Venus in the mornings *and* the evenings for a few days around inferior conjunction. Intending observers should be aware that since Venus is just under 8° N. of the Sun at this conjunction then it will be much fainter than normal since only an extremely thin crescent of the planet will be illuminated by the Sun, as seen from the Earth.

MARS, magnitude + 1·7, is still visible for a short while in the evening sky, low above the western horizon. On the evening of the 22nd Mars will be seen a few degrees below and to the right of the thin crescent Moon, then only 2½ days old.

JUPITER is a brilliant object in the south-eastern sky in the mornings, magnitude − 1·7.

SATURN, magnitude + 0·4, is now visible for the greater part of the night, crossing the meridian well before dawn. The gibbous Moon will be seen approaching Saturn on the morning of the 8th.

THE MOON

Day	R.A.	Dec.	Hor. Par.	Semi-diam.	Sun's Co-long.	P.A. of Bright Limb	Phase	Age	Rise 52°	Rise 56°	Transit	Set 52°	Set 56°
	h m	°	′	′	°	°		d	h m	h m	h m	h m	h m
1	8 55	+22.8	58.4	15.9	36	289	74	10.5	12 52	12 30	21 04	4 31	4 54
2	9 51	+18.5	59.3	16.2	48	294	83	11.5	14 20	14 06	21 58	4 55	5 11
3	10 47	+13.0	60.2	16.4	61	299	91	12.5	15 50	15 43	22 50	5 13	5 23
4	11 42	+6.7	60.9	16.6	73	304	97	13.5	17 21	17 20	23 42	5 29	5 33
5	12 36	-0.2	61.3	16.7	85	319	100	14.5	18 53	18 58	..	5 44	5 43
6	13 30	-7.1	61.4	16.7	97	95	100	15.5	20 26	20 38	0 35	6 00	5 52
7	14 27	-13.6	61.2	16.7	109	106	97	16.5	22 00	22 19	1 29	6 17	6 04
8	15 25	-19.2	60.6	16.5	121	105	91	17.5	23 31	23 58	2 26	6 40	6 19
9	16 25	-23.5	59.9	16.3	134	101	83	18.5	..	..	3 24	7 10	6 42
10	17 27	-26.2	59.0	16.1	146	95	73	19.5	0 54	1 27	4 25	7 51	7 18
11	18 28	-27.2	58.0	15.8	158	88	63	20.5	2 02	2 38	5 24	8 47	8 12
12	19 28	-26.5	57.1	15.6	170	82	52	21.5	2 53	3 26	6 22	9 55	9 23
13	20 25	-24.5	56.3	15.3	182	76	42	22.5	3 28	3 55	7 15	11 10	10 44
14	21 18	-21.2	55.6	15.2	194	70	32	23.5	3 53	4 14	8 05	12 26	12 07
15	22 07	-17.1	55.1	15.0	207	66	23	24.5	4 11	4 26	8 50	13 41	13 28
16	22 53	-12.4	54.6	14.9	219	63	16	25.5	4 25	4 35	9 33	14 53	14 45
17	23 37	-7.2	54.3	14.8	231	60	9	26.5	4 37	4 42	10 14	16 04	16 00
18	0 20	-1.9	54.1	14.7	243	58	4	27.5	4 48	4 49	10 53	17 13	17 14
19	1 02	+3.5	54.0	14.7	256	56	1	28.5	4 58	4 55	11 32	18 22	18 29
20	1 45	+8.8	53.9	14.7	268	32	0	29.5	5 10	5 01	12 13	19 32	19 44
21	2 28	+13.8	54.0	14.7	280	257	1	0.8	5 23	5 10	12 55	20 44	21 02
22	3 14	+18.3	54.2	14.8	292	254	3	1.8	5 39	5 20	13 39	21 57	22 21
23	4 03	+22.1	54.4	14.8	304	256	7	2.8	6 00	5 36	14 27	23 09	23 38
24	4 54	+25.0	54.8	14.9	317	261	12	3.8	6 29	5 59	15 17	..	..
25	5 47	+26.7	55.2	15.0	329	266	20	4.8	7 09	6 35	16 10	0 16	0 50
26	6 43	+27.2	55.8	15.2	341	272	28	5.8	8 03	7 28	17 05	1 14	1 49
27	7 40	+26.3	56.5	15.4	353	279	38	6.8	9 11	8 40	18 00	1 59	2 31
28	8 36	+23.9	57.2	15.6	6	284	48	7.8	10 29	10 04	18 54	2 33	2 59
29	9 32	+20.2	58.1	15.8	18	290	59	8.8	11 53	11 35	19 46	2 58	3 18
30	10 26	+15.3	59.0	16.1	30	294	70	9.8	13 19	13 08	20 37	3 18	3 31

MERCURY ☿

Day	R.A.	Dec. +	Diam.	Phase	Transit		Day	R.A.	Dec. +	Diam.	Phase	Transit	
	h m	°	″		h m			h m	°	″		h m	
1	0 53	9.1	11	1	12 13		16	0 26	2.3	11	15	10 48	
4	0 45	7.7	11	0	11 53	Mercury is too close to the Sun for observation	19	0 27	1.7	10	21	10 38	Mercury is too close to the Sun for observation
7	0 37	6.2	11	2	11 34		22	0 31	1.5	10	27	10 30	
10	0 31	4.6	11	5	11 16		25	0 37	1.6	9	32	10 25	
13	0 27	3.3	11	10	11 00		28	0 45	2.1	9	37	10 21	
16	0 26	2.3	11	15	10 48		31	0 55	2.8	8	42	10 20	

VENUS ♀   MARS ♂

Day	R.A.	Dec. +	Diam.	Phase	Transit	5° high. 52°	5° high. 56°	Day	R.A.	Dec. +	Diam.	Phase	Transit	5° high. 52°	5° high. 56°
	h m	°	″		h m	h m	h m		h m	°	″		h m	h m	h m
1	0 46	13.6	59	1	12 06	5 30	5 22	1	2 38	15.7	4	97	14 00	20 51	21 01
6	0 35	11.9	59	1	11 35	5 09	5 02	6	2 52	16.8	4	97	13 55	20 51	21 01
11	0 26	9.9	58	2	11 07	4 49	4 43	11	3 07	17.9	4	97	13 49	20 51	21 02
16	0 19	8.1	55	6	10 41	4 31	4 29	16	3 21	18.9	4	98	13 44	20 50	21 03
21	0 16	6.5	52	10	10 18	4 19	4 15	21	3 35	19.8	4	98	13 39	20 50	21 04
26	0 17	5.3	48	14	10 00	4 06	4 04	26	3 50	20.6	4	98	13 33	20 50	21 05
31	0 21	4.6	44	18	9 45	3 54	3 54	31	4 04	21.3	4	98	13 28	20 50	21 06

SUNRISE AND SUNSET

	London		Bristol		Birmingham		Manchester		Newcastle		Glasgow		Belfast	
	a.m.	p.m.	a.m.	p.m.	a.m.	p.m.	a.m.	p.m.	a.m.	p.m.	a.m.	p.m.	a.m.	p.m.
	h m	h m	h m	h m	h m	h m	h m	h m	h m	h m	h m	h m	h m	h m
1	5 37	6 33	5 47	6 42	5 43	6 40	5 44	6 43	5 39	6 42	5 49	6 54	5 57	7 00
2	5 35	6 34	5 45	6 43	5 41	6 42	5 42	6 45	5 37	6 44	5 47	6 56	5 55	7 02
3	5 33	6 36	5 43	6 45	5 39	6 43	5 40	6 46	5 35	6 45	5 44	6 58	5 53	7 03
4	5 31	6 38	5 41	6 47	5 36	6 45	5 37	6 48	5 32	6 47	5 41	7 00	5 50	7 05
5	5 28	6 39	5 38	6 49	5 34	6 47	5 35	6 50	5 30	6 49	5 39	7 02	5 48	7 07
6	5 26	6 41	5 36	6 50	5 31	6 49	5 32	6 52	5 27	6 51	5 36	7 04	5 45	7 09
7	5 24	6 42	5 34	6 52	5 29	6 51	5 30	6 54	5 24	6 53	5 33	7 06	5 43	7 11
8	5 21	6 44	5 31	6 54	5 26	6 53	5 27	6 56	5 22	6 55	5 31	7 08	5 40	7 13
9	5 19	6 45	5 29	6 55	5 24	6 54	5 25	6 58	5 19	6 57	5 28	7 10	5 38	7 15
10	5 17	6 47	5 27	6 57	5 22	6 56	5 22	6 59	5 17	6 59	5 26	7 12	5 35	7 17
11	5 15	6 49	5 25	6 59	5 20	6 58	5 20	7 01	5 14	7 01	5 23	7 14	5 33	7 18
12	5 12	6 50	5 22	7 00	5 17	6 59	5 18	7 03	5 12	7 03	5 21	7 16	5 31	7 20
13	5 10	6 52	5 20	7 02	5 15	7 01	5 15	7 05	5 09	7 05	5 18	7 18	5 28	7 22
14	5 08	6 54	5 18	7 04	5 13	7 03	5 13	7 07	5 07	7 07	5 16	7 20	5 26	7 24
15	5 06	6 56	5 16	7 06	5 11	7 05	5 11	7 09	5 05	7 09	5 13	7 22	5 23	7 26
16	5 03	6 57	5 13	7 07	5 08	7 06	5 08	7 11	5 02	7 11	5 11	7 24	5 21	7 28
17	5 01	6 59	5 11	7 09	5 06	7 08	5 06	7 12	5 00	7 13	5 08	7 26	5 18	7 30
18	4 59	7 01	5 09	7 11	5 04	7 10	5 04	7 14	4 57	7 15	5 05	7 29	5 16	7 32
19	4 57	7 02	5 07	7 12	5 02	7 11	5 01	7 16	4 55	7 17	5 03	7 31	5 13	7 34
20	4 55	7 04	5 05	7 14	5 00	7 13	4 59	7 18	4 53	7 19	5 01	7 33	5 11	7 36
21	4 53	7 06	5 03	7 16	4 58	7 15	4 57	7 20	4 50	7 21	4 58	7 35	5 09	7 38
22	4 51	7 07	5 01	7 17	4 56	7 16	4 55	7 21	4 48	7 23	4 56	7 37	5 06	7 40
23	4 49	7 09	4 59	7 19	4 54	7 18	4 53	7 23	4 45	7 25	4 53	7 39	5 04	7 42
24	4 47	7 11	4 57	7 21	4 52	7 20	4 51	7 25	4 43	7 27	4 51	7 41	5 02	7 44
25	4 45	7 13	4 55	7 22	4 49	7 22	4 48	7 27	4 41	7 28	4 49	7 42	5 00	7 45
26	4 43	7 14	4 53	7 24	4 47	7 23	4 46	7 28	4 38	7 30	4 46	7 44	4 57	7 47
27	4 41	7 16	4 51	7 25	4 45	7 25	4 44	7 30	4 36	7 32	4 44	7 46	4 55	7 49
28	4 39	7 18	4 49	7 27	4 43	7 27	4 42	7 32	4 34	7 34	4 42	7 48	4 53	7 51
29	4 37	7 19	4 47	7 28	4 41	7 29	4 40	7 34	4 32	7 36	4 40	7 50	4 51	7 53
30	4 35	7 21	4 45	7 30	4 39	7 31	4 38	7 36	4 30	7 38	4 38	7 52	4 48	7 55

JUPITER ♃ / SATURN ♄

	JUPITER ♃					SATURN ♄				
Day	R.A.	Dec. −	Transit	5° high.		R.A.	Dec. −	Transit	5° high.	
				52°	56°				52°	56°
	h m	°	h m	h m	h m	h m	°	h m	h m	h m
1	20 54	17·9	8 16	4 33	4 56	15 44	17·4	3 06	23 16	23 38
11	21 01	17·5	7 43	3 57	4 20	15 42	17·2	2 25	22 34	22 56
21	21 06	17·1	7 09	3 21	3 43	15 39	17·1	1 43	21 51	22 13
31	21 11	16·8	6 34	2 44	3 06	15 37	16·9	1 01	21 08	21 29

Equatorial diameter of Jupiter 37″; of Saturn 18″. Diameters of Saturn's rings 41″ and 17″.

URANUS ♅ / NEPTUNE ♆

	URANUS ♅					NEPTUNE ♆				
Day	R.A.	Dec. −	Transit	10° high.		R.A.	Dec. −	Transit	10° high.	
				52°	56°				52°	56°
	h m	° ′	h m	h m	h m	h m	° ′	h m	h m	h m
1	17 07·6	22 55	4 30	2 22	3 28	18 15·6	22 15	5 38	3 22	4 20
11	17 07·1	22 54	3 50	1 42	2 48	18 15·6	22 15	4 58	2 42	3 40
21	17 06·2	22 53	3 10	1 01	2 07	18 15·3	22 15	4 19	2 02	3 00
31	17 05·1	22 52	2 29	0 21	1 27	18 14·9	22 15	3 39	1 22	2 20

Diameter 4″　　　　Diameter 2″

Maia, goddess of growth and increase.

Sun's Longitude 60° II 21^d 03^h

Month	Week	
1	W.	**SS. Philip and James.**
2	Th.	Catherine the Great b. 1729. Von Richthofen b. 1892.
3	F.	Nicolo Machiavelli b. 1469. D'Oyly Carte b. 1844.
4	S.	Start of General Strike 1926.
5	☗.	**4th S. after Easter.** Kierkegaard b. 1813.
6	M.	Sigmund Freud b. 1856. Edward VII d. 1910.
7	Tu.	Johannes Brahms b. 1833. Peter Tchaikovsky b. 1840.
8	W.	Pres. Harry S. Truman b. 1884. V.E. Day 1945.
9	Th.	Sir James Barrie b. 1860.
10	F.	Sir Henry Morton Stanley d. 1904.
11	S.	Fontenoy 1745. Spencer Perceval assass. 1812.
12	☗.	**5th S. after Easter. Rogation Sunday.**
13	M.	Sir Arthur Sullivan b. 1842.
14	Tu.	**St. Matthias.** Gabriel Fahrenheit b. 1686.
15	W.	Metternich b. 1773. Emily Dickinson d. 1886.
16	Th.	**Ascension Day.** H. E. Bates b. 1905.
17	F.	Edward Jenner b. 1749. Relief of Mafeking 1900.
18	S.	Bertrand Russell b. 1872. Pope John Paul II b. 1920.
19	☗.	**S. after Ascension.** Anne Boleyn exec. 1536.
20	M.	Balzac b. 1799. G. K. Chesterton b. 1874.
21	Tu.	Albrecht Dürer b. 1471. Alexander Pope b. 1688.
22	W.	Richard Wagner b. 1813. Victor Hugo d. 1885.**
23	Th.	Ramillies 1706. Leopold von Ranke d. 1886.
24	F.	Easter Law Sittings End.
25	S.	Ralph Waldo Emerson b. 1803.
26	☗.	**Pentecost. Whit Sunday.**
27	M.	Arnold Bennett b. 1867. Isadora Duncan b. 1878.
28	Tu.	William Pitt the Younger b. 1759.
29	W.	Charles II b. 1630. Restoration Day 1660.
30	Th.	Joan of Arc burned 1431.
31	F.	Walt Whitman b. 1819. Jutland 1916.

PHENOMENA

May 1^d 15^h Mercury at greatest western elongation (27°).

9^d 13^h Venus at greatest brilliancy.

11^d 05^h Jupiter in conjunction with the Moon. Jupiter 5° N.

15^d 18^h Saturn at opposition.

15^d 23^h Venus in conjunction with the Moon. Venus 3° N.

18^d 01^h Mercury in conjunction with the Moon. Mercury 1°·5 S.

21^d 10^h Mars in conjunction with the Moon. Mars 1°·9 S.

CONSTELLATIONS

The following constellations are near the meridian at

	d h		d h
Apr. 1	24	Apr. 15	23
May 1	22	May 16	21
June 1	20	June 15	19

Cepheus (below the Pole), Cassiopeia (below the Pole), Ursa Minor, Ursa Major, Canes Venatici, Coma Berenices, Bootes, Leo, Virgo, Crater, Corvus, and Hydra.

ALGOL

ALGOL is inconveniently situated for observation during May.

PHASES OF THE MOON

	d	h	m
○ Full Moon	4	19	53
☾ Last Quarter	11	17	34
● New Moon	19	21	41
☽ First Quarter	27	12	56

	d	h
Perigee (357,620 kilometres)	4	05
Apogee (406,100 „)	17	00

Mean Longitude of Ascending Node on May 1, 49°.

See note on *Summer Time*, p. 98.

MONTHLY NOTES

May 6. Bank Holiday, England, Wales, N. Ireland and Scotland.
        9. Liberation Day, Channel Islands.
     15. Whitsunday (Scotland). Scottish Term Day.
     21. First Day of Ramadân.
     26. Jewish Feast of Weeks begins.
     27. Bank Holiday, England, Wales, N. Ireland and Scotland.
     28. Removal Day, Scotland.
            ** Centenary.

Day	Right Ascension	Dec. +	Equation of Time	Rise 52°	Rise 56°	Transit	Set 52°	Set 56°	Sidereal Time	Transit of First Point of Aries
	h m s	° ′	m s	h m	h m	h m	h m	h m	h m s	h m s
1	2 32 36	15 00	+ 2 52	4 31	4 16	11 57	19 25	19 39	14 35 28	9 22 59
2	2 36 25	15 18	+ 2 59	4 29	4 14	11 57	19 26	19 41	14 39 24	9 19 03
3	2 40 15	15 36	+ 3 06	4 27	4 12	11 57	19 28	19 43	14 43 21	9 15 07
4	2 44 05	15 53	+ 3 12	4 25	4 10	11 57	19 29	19 45	14 47 17	9 11 11
5	2 47 56	16 11	+ 3 18	4 23	4 08	11 57	19 31	19 47	14 51 14	9 07 15
6	2 51 48	16 28	+ 3 23	4 21	4 06	11 57	19 33	19 49	14 55 10	9 03 19
7	2 55 40	16 44	+ 3 27	4 20	4 04	11 56	19 35	19 51	14 59 07	8 59 23
8	2 59 32	17 01	+ 3 31	4 18	4 01	11 56	19 36	19 53	15 03 04	8 55 28
9	3 03 25	17 17	+ 3 35	4 16	3 59	11 56	19 38	19 55	15 07 00	8 51 32
10	3 07 19	17 33	+ 3 37	4 14	3 57	11 56	19 40	19 57	15 10 57	8 47 36
11	3 11 13	17 49	+ 3 40	4 13	3 55	11 56	19 41	19 59	15 14 53	8 43 40
12	3 15 08	18 04	+ 3 41	4 11	3 53	11 56	19 43	20 01	15 18 50	8 39 44
13	3 19 04	18 19	+ 3 42	4 09	3 51	11 56	19 44	20 02	15 22 46	8 35 48
14	3 23 00	18 34	+ 3 43	4 08	3 49	11 56	19 45	20 04	15 26 43	8 31 52
15	3 26 57	18 48	+ 3 43	4 06	3 48	11 56	19 47	20 06	15 30 39	8 27 56
16	3 30 54	19 02	+ 3 42	4 05	3 46	11 56	19 49	20 08	15 34 36	8 24 00
17	3 34 52	19 16	+ 3 41	4 04	3 44	11 56	19 50	20 10	15 38 33	8 20 04
18	3 38 50	19 29	+ 3 39	4 02	3 42	11 56	19 52	20 12	15 42 29	8 16 08
19	3 42 49	19 43	+ 3 36	4 01	3 40	11 56	19 54	20 13	15 46 26	8 12 13
20	3 46 49	19 55	+ 3 33	3 59	3 39	11 56	19 55	20 15	15 50 22	8 08 17
21	3 50 49	20 08	+ 3 30	3 58	3 37	11 57	19 56	20 17	15 54 19	8 04 21
22	3 54 50	20 20	+ 3 26	3 57	3 35	11 57	19 58	20 18	15 58 15	8 00 25
23	3 58 51	20 32	+ 3 21	3 55	3 34	11 57	19 59	20 20	16 02 12	7 56 29
24	4 02 52	20 43	+ 3 16	3 54	3 32	11 57	20 00	20 21	16 06 09	7 52 33
25	4 06 55	20 54	+ 3 10	3 53	3 31	11 57	20 02	20 23	16 10 05	7 48 37
26	4 10 57	21 05	+ 3 04	3 52	3 30	11 57	20 03	20 25	16 14 02	7 44 41
27	4 15 00	21 15	+ 2 58	3 51	3 29	11 57	20 04	20 27	16 17 58	7 40 45
28	4 19 04	21 25	+ 2 51	3 50	3 27	11 57	20 05	20 29	16 21 55	7 36 49
29	4 23 08	21 35	+ 2 43	3 49	3 26	11 57	20 06	20 30	16 25 51	7 32 53
30	4 27 12	21 44	+ 2 35	3 48	3 25	11 57	20 07	20 31	16 29 48	7 28 58
31	4 31 17	21 53	+ 2 27	3 47	3 24	11 58	20 08	20 33	16 33 44	7 25 02

Duration of Civil (C), Nautical (N), and Astronomical (A), Twilight (in minutes)

Lat. °	May 1 C	N	A	May 11 C	N	A	May 21 C	N	A	May 31 C	N	A
52	39	90	154	41	97	179	44	106	T.A.N.	46	116	T.A.N.
56	45	106	209	49	121	T.A.N.	53	143	T.A.N.	57	T.A.N.	T.A.N.

ASTRONOMICAL NOTES

MERCURY is unsuitably placed for observation.

VENUS is a magnificent morning object, attaining its greatest brilliancy, magnitude −4·2, on the 9th. However it is never visible for more than an hour before sunrise. As seen through a telescope the apparent diameter shrinks from 44″ to 28″ during May as the distance from the Earth increases. At the same time the phase increases from a thin crescent to a 42% illuminated disk by the end of the month.

MARS is gradually disappearing from view in the lengthening evening twilight and will not be seen again until September.

JUPITER, magnitude −2·0, is a brilliant object in the south-eastern sky in the mornings. Jupiter is in Capricornus. On the morning of the 11th the Moon, near Last Quarter, passes 5° south of the planet.

SATURN, magnitude +0·2, is at opposition on the 15th, and thus visible throughout the hours of darkness.

ECLIPSE. A total eclipse of the Moon occurs on the 4th. See page 148 for details.

ECLIPSE. A partial eclipse of the Sun occurs on the 19th. See page 148 for details.

THE MOON

Day	R.A.	Dec.	Hor. Par.	Semi-diam.	Sun's Co-long.	P.A. of Bright Limb	Phase	Age	Rise 52°	Rise 56°	Transit	Set 52°	Set 56°
	h m	°	′	′	°	°		d	h m	h m	h m	h m	h m
1	11 19	+ 9·4	59·8	16·3	42	297	80	10·8	14 47	14 42	21 27	3 34	3 41
2	12 12	+ 2·9	60·6	16·5	54	298	88	11·8	16 16	16 18	22 19	3 49	3 50
3	13 05	− 3·9	61·1	16·6	67	298	95	12·8	17 47	17 56	23 11	4 03	3 59
4	14 00	−10·7	61·3	16·7	79	297	99	13·8	19 21	19 37	..	4 19	4 09
5	14 58	−16·8	61·2	16·7	91	104	100	14·8	20 56	21 19	0 07	4 39	4 22
6	15 58	−21·8	60·8	16·6	103	106	98	15·8	22 27	22 58	1 06	5 05	4 40
7	17 01	−25·3	60·1	16·4	115	100	93	16·8	23 46	..	2 07	5 41	5 10
8	18 05	−27·0	59·3	16·1	127	93	86	17·8	..	0 21	3 10	6 32	5 56
9	19 07	−27·0	58·3	15·9	140	86	77	18·8	0 46	1 21	4 10	7 38	7 03
10	20 07	−25·3	57·4	15·6	152	80	68	19·8	1 29	1 58	5 08	8 53	8 24
11	21 03	−22·4	56·5	15·4	164	74	58	20·8	1 58	2 21	6 00	10 11	9 49
12	21 54	−18·4	55·7	15·2	176	70	47	21·8	2 18	2 35	6 48	11 28	11 12
13	22 41	−13·7	55·1	15·0	188	67	38	22·8	2 34	2 45	7 32	12 42	12 32
14	23 26	− 8·6	54·6	14·9	201	65	29	23·8	2 46	2 53	8 13	13 53	13 48
15	0 09	− 3·3	54·2	14·8	213	64	20	24·8	2 57	2 59	8 53	15 02	15 02
16	0 51	+ 2·1	54·1	14·7	225	64	13	25·8	3 08	3 05	9 32	16 12	16 16
17	1 34	+ 7·5	54·0	14·7	237	65	7	26·8	3 19	3 12	10 12	17 21	17 31
18	2 17	+12·5	54·0	14·7	250	68	3	27·8	3 31	3 19	10 53	18 33	18 48
19	3 02	+17·2	54·2	14·8	262	74	1	28·8	3 46	3 29	11 37	19 46	20 07
20	3 50	+21·2	54·4	14·8	274	212	0	0·1	4 05	3 43	12 24	20 59	21 26
21	4 41	+24·4	54·7	14·9	286	253	1	1·1	4 31	4 03	13 14	22 08	22 41
22	5 35	+26·4	55·1	15·0	299	260	4	2·1	5 08	4 35	14 06	23 10	23 45
23	6 30	+27·2	55·6	15·1	311	267	9	3·1	5 57	5 22	15 01	23 59	..
24	7 27	+26·6	56·1	15·3	323	274	16	4·1	7 01	6 29	15 55	..	0 32
25	8 23	+24·6	56·7	15·4	335	280	24	5·1	8 16	7 49	16 49	0 36	1 04
26	9 18	+21·3	57·3	15·6	347	286	34	6·1	9 37	9 17	17 40	1 03	1 25
27	10 11	+16·7	58·0	15·8	360	290	44	7·1	11 00	10 47	18 30	1 24	1 39
28	11 03	+11·3	58·7	16·0	12	293	55	8·1	12 24	12 17	19 19	1 40	1 50
29	11 54	+ 5·1	59·4	16·2	24	295	66	9·1	13 49	13 48	20 08	1 55	1 58
30	12 45	− 1·4	60·0	16·3	36	295	77	10·1	15 16	15 22	20 58	2 09	2 07
31	13 38	− 8·0	60·5	16·5	49	293	86	11·1	16 46	16 58	21 51	2 23	2 16

MERCURY ☿

Day	R.A.	Dec. +	Diam.	Phase	Transit		Day	R.A.	Dec. +	Diam.	Phase	Transit	
	h m	°	″		h m			h m	°	″		h m	
1	0 55	2·8	8	42	10 20		16	2 07	10·0	6	66	10 33	
4	0 59	3·9	8	47	10 20	Mercury is too	19	2 25	11·9	6	72	10 39	Mercury is too
7	1 20	5·1	7	52	10 21	close to the	22	2 44	13·8	6	77	10 48	close to the
10	1 34	6·6	7	57	10 24	Sun for	25	3 06	15·8	6	83	10 57	Sun for
13	1 50	8·2	7	61	10 28	observation	28	3 29	17·8	5	88	11 09	observation
16	2 07	10·0	6	66	10 33		31	3 53	19·7	5	93	11 22	

VENUS ♀   MARS ♂

Day	R.A.	Dec. +	Diam.	Phase	Transit	5° high. 52°	5° high. 56°	Day	R.A.	Dec. +	Diam.	Phase	Transit	
	h m	°	″		h m	h m	h m		h m	°	″		h m	
1	0 21	4·6	44	18	9 45	3 54	3 54	1	4 04	21·3	4	98	13 28	
6	0 28	4·3	41	23	9 32	3 43	3 43	6	4 19	22·0	4	99	13 23	
11	0 38	4·4	38	27	9 22	3 32	3 32	11	4 33	22·6	4	99	13 18	Mars is too
16	0 50	4·8	35	31	9 14	3 22	3 21	16	4 48	23·1	4	99	13 13	close to the
21	1 03	5·6	32	35	9 08	3 12	3 10	21	5 03	23·5	4	99	13 08	Sun for
26	1 18	6·5	30	39	9 03	3 02	3 00	26	5 18	23·8	4	99	13 03	observation
31	1 33	7·6	28	42	8 59	2 53	2 50	31	5 32	24·1	4	99	12 58	

SUNRISE AND SUNSET

Day	London a.m.	London p.m.	Bristol a.m.	Bristol p.m.	Birmingham a.m.	Birmingham p.m.	Manchester a.m.	Manchester p.m.	Newcastle a.m.	Newcastle p.m.	Glasgow a.m.	Glasgow p.m.	Belfast a.m.	Belfast p.m.
	h m	h m	h m	h m	h m	h m	h m	h m	h m	h m	h m	h m	h m	h m
1	4 33	7 23	4 43	7 32	4 37	7 32	4 36	7 37	4 27	7 40	4 35	7 54	4 47	7 56
2	4 32	7 25	4 42	7 33	4 35	7 34	4 34	7 39	4 25	7 42	4 33	7 56	4 45	7 58
3	4 30	7 26	4 40	7 35	4 33	7 36	4 32	7 41	4 23	7 44	4 31	7 58	4 43	8 00
4	4 28	7 27	4 38	7 37	4 31	7 38	4 30	7 43	4 21	7 46	4 29	8 00	4 41	8 02
5	4 26	7 29	4 36	7 38	4 29	7 39	4 28	7 45	4 19	7 48	4 26	8 02	4 38	8 04
6	4 24	7 30	4 34	7 40	4 27	7 41	4 26	7 47	4 17	7 50	4 24	8 04	4 36	8 06
7	4 22	7 32	4 32	7 42	4 25	7 43	4 24	7 48	4 15	7 51	4 22	8 06	4 34	8 08
8	4 20	7 33	4 30	7 43	4 23	7 44	4 22	7 50	4 13	7 53	4 20	8 08	4 32	8 10
9	4 19	7 35	4 29	7 45	4 22	7 46	4 20	7 52	4 11	7 55	4 18	8 10	4 30	8 12
10	4 17	7 36	4 27	7 46	4 20	7 47	4 18	7 54	4 09	7 57	4 16	8 12	4 28	8 14
11	4 16	7 38	4 26	7 48	4 18	7 49	4 16	7 55	4 07	7 59	4 14	8 14	4 26	8 15
12	4 14	7 40	4 24	7 50	4 17	7 51	4 14	7 57	4 05	8 01	4 12	8 16	4 24	8 17
13	4 12	7 41	4 22	7 51	4 15	7 52	4 13	7 59	4 03	8 03	4 10	8 18	4 23	8 19
14	4 10	7 43	4 20	7 53	4 13	7 54	4 11	8 01	4 01	8 04	4 08	8 19	4 21	8 21
15	4 09	7 44	4 19	7 54	4 12	7 55	4 09	8 02	3 59	8 06	4 06	8 21	4 19	8 22
16	4 07	7 46	4 17	7 56	4 10	7 57	4 07	8 04	3 57	8 08	4 04	8 23	4 17	8 24
17	4 06	7 47	4 16	7 57	4 09	7 58	4 06	8 05	3 56	8 09	4 02	8 25	4 16	8 25
18	4 04	7 49	4 15	7 59	4 07	8 00	4 04	8 07	3 54	8 11	4 01	8 27	4 14	8 27
19	4 03	7 50	4 14	8 00	4 06	8 02	4 03	8 08	3 53	8 13	3 59	8 29	4 13	8 29
20	4 02	7 52	4 12	8 02	4 05	8 03	4 02	8 10	3 51	8 14	3 57	8 30	4 11	8 30
21	4 00	7 53	4 11	8 03	4 03	8 05	4 00	8 11	3 50	8 16	3 56	8 32	4 10	8 32
22	3 59	7 55	4 10	8 05	4 02	8 06	3 59	8 13	3 48	8 18	3 54	8 34	4 08	8 34
23	3 58	7 56	4 09	8 06	4 01	8 08	3 58	8 14	3 46	8 20	3 52	8 36	4 06	8 36
24	3 57	7 57	4 07	8 07	3 59	8 09	3 56	8 16	3 45	8 21	3 51	8 37	4 05	8 37
25	3 55	7 59	4 06	8 09	3 58	8 10	3 55	8 17	3 43	8 23	3 49	8 39	4 03	8 39
26	3 54	8 00	4 05	8 10	3 57	8 11	3 54	8 18	3 42	8 24	3 48	8 40	4 02	8 40
27	3 53	8 01	4 04	8 11	3 56	8 13	3 53	8 20	3 41	8 26	3 46	8 42	4 01	8 42
28	3 53	8 03	4 03	8 12	3 55	8 14	3 52	8 21	3 40	8 27	3 45	8 44	4 00	8 43
29	3 52	8 04	4 02	8 13	3 53	8 16	3 50	8 23	3 38	8 29	3 44	8 45	3 58	8 45
30	3 51	8 05	4 01	8 14	3 52	8 17	3 49	8 24	3 37	8 30	3 43	8 47	3 57	8 46
31	3 50	8 06	4 00	8 15	3 51	8 18	3 48	8 25	3 36	8 31	3 42	8 48	3 56	8 47

	JUPITER ♃					SATURN ♄				
Day	R.A.	Dec. −	Transit	5° high. 52°	5° high. 56°	R.A.	Dec. −	Transit	5° high. 52°	5° high. 56°
	h m	°	h m	h m	h m	h m	°	h m	h m	h m
1	21 11	16·8	6 34	2 44	3 06	15 37	16·9	1 01	4 50	4 29
11	21 15	16·6	5 59	2 07	2 28	15 34	16·8	0 19	4 09	3 48
21	21 17	16·4	5 22	1 29	1 50	15 31	16·6	23 32	3 28	3 07
31	21 18	16·4	4 44	0 51	1 11	15 28	16·4	22 50	2 47	2 26

Equatorial diameter of Jupiter 41″; of Saturn 19″.   Diameters of Saturn's rings 42″ and 17″.

	URANUS ♅					NEPTUNE ♆				
Day	R.A.	Dec. −	Transit	10° high. 52°	10° high. 56°	R.A.	Dec. −	Transit	10° high. 52°	10° high. 56°
	h m	° ′	h m	h m	h m	h m	° ′	h m	h m	h m
1	17 05·1	22 52	2 29	0 21	1 27	18 14·9	22 15	3 39	1 22	2 20
11	17 03·7	22 50	1 48	23 35	0 46	18 14·2	22 15	2 59	0 42	1 40
21	17 02·1	22 48	1 08	22 54	0 05	18 13·4	22 15	2 19	23 59	1 00
31	17 00·3	22 46	0 27	22 13	23 21	18 12·4	22 15	1 38	23 19	0 20

Diameter 4″   Diameter 2″

Month	Week		

Junius, Roman *gens*
(family).
Sun's Longitude 90° ♋ 21ᵈ 11ʰ

1	S.	Glorious First of June 1794.
2	♋.	**Trinity Sunday.** CORONATION DAY 1953.
3	M.	George V b. 1865. Evacuation of Dunkirk 1940.
4	Tu.	TRINITY LAW SITTINGS BEGIN.
5	W.	Adam Smith b. 1723. Maynard Keynes b. 1883.
6	Th.	Capt. Scott b. 1868. D-Day 1944.
7	F.	Beau Brummell b. 1778. Paul Gauguin b. 1848.
8	S.	Robert Schumann b. 1810. Sir John Millais b. 1829.
9	♋.	**1st S. after Trinity.** George Stephenson b. 1781.
10	M.	DUKE OF EDINBURGH b. 1921.
11	Tu.	**St. Barnabas.** John Constable b. 1776.
12	W.	Charles Kingsley b. 1819.
13	Th.	Thomas Arnold b. 1795. W. B. Yeats b. 1865.
14	F.	Naseby 1645. Nicholas Clerihew Bentley b. 1907.
15	S.	Magna Carta signed 1215.
16	♋.	**2nd S. after Trinity.** Quatre Bras 1815.
17	M.	Edward I b. 1239. John Wesley b. 1703.
18	Tu.	Waterloo 1815. Capt. M. Webb b. 1848.
19	W.	James I b. 1566. Blaise Pascal b. 1623.
20	Th.	Black Hole of Calcutta 1756.
21	F.	PRINCE WILLIAM OF WALES b. 1982.
22	S.	Puccini b. 1858. Anzio landings 1944.
23	♋.	**3rd S. after Trinity.** Plassey 1757.
24	M.	**St. John Baptist.** Bannockburn 1314.
25	Tu.	Little Big Horn 1876. George Orwell b. 1903.
26	W.	George IV d. 1830. U.N. Charter signed 1945.
27	Th.	Charles Parnell b. 1846. Helen Keller b. 1880.
28	F.	Henry VIII b. 1491. Rousseau b. 1712.
29	S.	**St. Peter.** Peter Paul Rubens b. 1577.
30	♋.	**4th S. after Trinity.** John Gay b. 1685.**

PHENOMENA

June 1ᵈ 22ʰ Saturn in conjunction with the Moon. Saturn 3° N.

6ᵈ 19ʰ Uranus at opposition.

7ᵈ 14ʰ Mercury in superior conjunction.

7ᵈ 16ʰ Jupiter in conjunction with the Moon. Jupiter 5° N.

12ᵈ 22ʰ Venus at greatest western elongation. (46°).

14ᵈ 11ʰ Venus in conjunction with the Moon. Venus 1°·9 S.

21ᵈ 11ʰ Summer Solstice.

23ᵈ 19ʰ Neptune at opposition.

29ᵈ 05ʰ Saturn in conjunction with the Moon. Saturn 3° N.

CONSTELLATIONS

The following constellations are near the meridian at

	d	h		d	h
May	1	24	May	16	23
June	1	22	June	15	21
July	1	20	July	16	19

Cassiopeia (below the Pole), Ursa Minor, Draco, Ursa Major, Canes Venatici, Bootes, Corona, Serpens, Virgo and Libra.

ALGOL

ALGOL is inconveniently situated for observation during June.

PHASES OF THE MOON

		d	h	m
○	Full Moon	3	03	50
☾	Last Quarter.......	10	08	19
●	New Moon.........	18	11	58
☽	First Quarter	25	18	53

		d	h
Perigee (360,920 kilometres)		1	13
Apogee (405,130 ,,)		13	14
Perigee (365,770 ,,)		29	09

Mean Longitude of Ascending Node on June 1, 47°.

See note on *Summer Time*, p. 98.

MONTHLY NOTES

June 15. Queen's Official Birthday.

21. Longest day.

24. Midsummer Day. Quarter Day.

**Centenary.

Day	THE SUN s.d. 15'·8									Sidereal Time	Transit of First Point of Aries
	Right Ascension	Dec. +	Equation of Time	Rise		Transit	Set				
				52°	56°		52°	56°			
	h m s	° '	m s	h m	h m	h m	h m	h m		h m s	h m s
1	4 35 22	22 01	+ 2 18	3 46	3 22	11 58	20 10	20 34		16 37 41	7 21 06
2	4 39 28	22 09	+ 2 09	3 45	3 21	11 58	20 11	20 35		16 41 38	7 17 10
3	4 43 34	22 17	+ 2 00	3 45	3 20	11 58	20 12	20 36		16 45 34	7 13 14
4	4 47 40	22 24	+ 1 50	3 44	3 19	11 58	20 13	20 38		16 49 31	7 09 18
5	4 51 47	22 31	+ 1 40	3 44	3 18	11 58	20 14	20 39		16 53 27	7 05 22
6	4 55 54	22 38	+ 1 29	3 43	3 18	11 59	20 15	20 40		16 57 24	7 01 26
7	5 00 02	22 44	+ 1 18	3 42	3 17	11 59	20 16	20 41		17 01 20	6 57 30
8	5 04 09	22 49	+ 1 07	3 42	3 16	11 59	20 17	20 42		17 05 17	6 53 34
9	5 08 17	22 55	+ 0 56	3 41	3 16	11 59	20 17	20 43		17 09 13	6 49 38
10	5 12 26	23 00	+ 0 44	3 41	3 15	11 59	20 18	20 44		17 13 10	6 45 43
11	5 16 34	23 04	+ 0 32	3 41	3 15	12 00	20 18	20 45		17 17 07	6 41 47
12	5 20 43	23 08	+ 0 20	3 40	3 14	12 00	20 19	20 46		17 21 03	6 37 51
13	5 24 52	23 12	+ 0 08	3 40	3 14	12 00	20 20	20 47		17 25 00	6 33 55
14	5 29 01	23 15	− 0 05	3 40	3 14	12 00	20 20	20 47		17 28 56	6 29 59
15	5 33 10	23 18	− 0 18	3 39	3 13	12 00	20 21	20 48		17 32 53	6 26 03
16	5 37 20	23 20	− 0 31	3 39	3 13	12 01	20 22	20 48		17 36 49	6 22 07
17	5 41 29	23 22	− 0 44	3 39	3 13	12 01	20 22	20 49		17 40 46	6 18 11
18	5 45 39	23 24	− 0 57	3 39	3 13	12 01	20 23	20 49		17 44 42	6 14 15
19	5 49 49	23 25	− 1 10	3 39	3 13	12 01	20 23	20 50		17 48 39	6 10 19
20	5 53 58	23 26	− 1 23	3 39	3 13	12 01	20 23	20 50		17 52 36	6 06 23
21	5 58 08	23 27	− 1 36	3 40	3 13	12 02	20 24	20 50		17 56 32	6 02 28
22	6 02 18	23 27	− 1 49	3 40	3 13	12 02	20 24	20 50		18 00 29	5 58 32
23	6 06 27	23 26	− 2 02	3 40	3 13	12 02	20 24	20 50		18 04 25	5 54 36
24	6 10 37	23 25	− 2 15	3 40	3 14	12 02	20 24	20 51		18 08 22	5 50 40
25	6 14 46	23 24	− 2 28	3 41	3 14	12 03	20 24	20 51		18 12 18	5 46 44
26	6 18 56	23 22	− 2 41	3 41	3 14	12 03	20 24	20 50		18 16 15	5 42 48
27	6 23 05	23 20	− 2 53	3 41	3 15	12 03	20 24	20 50		18 20 11	5 38 52
28	6 27 14	23 18	− 3 06	3 42	3 16	12 03	20 24	20 50		18 24 08	5 34 56
29	6 31 22	23 15	− 3 18	3 42	3 16	12 03	20 24	20 50		18 28 05	5 31 00
30	6 35 31	23 11	− 3 30	3 43	3 17	12 04	20 23	20 49		18 32 01	5 27 04

Duration of Civil (C), Nautical (N), and Astronomical (A), Twilight (in minutes)

Lat. °	June 1			June 11			June 21			June 30		
	C	N	A	C	N	A	C	N	A	C	N	A
52	47	117	T.A.N.	48	125	T.A.N.	49	128	T.A.N.	49	125	T.A.N.
56	58	T.A.N.	T.A.N.	61	T.A.N.	T.A.N.	63	T.A.N.	T.A.N.	62	T.A.N.	T.A.N.

ASTRONOMICAL NOTES

MERCURY is unsuitably placed for observation, superior conjunction occurring on the 7th.

VENUS is a brilliant morning object, magnitude −3·9, reaching greatest western elongation on the 12th. On the morning of the 14th the old crescent Moon will be seen approaching the planet.

MARS is unsuitably placed for observation.

JUPITER, magnitude −2·2, is a brilliant object in the south-eastern sky in the mornings though never at any great altitude since it is well south of the equator.

SATURN, magnitude +0·3, is visible for the greater part of the night low in the southern sky. Saturn is in Libra. The gibbous Moon passes near the planet on the night of the 1st-2nd and again on the morning of the 29th.

URANUS is at opposition on the 6th in the south-western part of Ophiuchus. Uranus is barely visible to the naked-eye since its magnitude is only +5·8 but it is readily located with only small optical aid.

NEPTUNE is at opposition on the 23rd, in the eastern part of Sagittarius. It is not visible to the naked-eye since its magnitude is +7·7.

THE MOON

Day	R.A.	Dec.	Hor. Par.	Semi-diam.	Sun's Co-long.	P.A. of Bright Limb	Phase	Age	Rise 52°	Rise 56°	Transit	Set 52°	Set 56°
	h m	°	′	′	°	°		d	h m	h m	h m	h m	h m
1	14 33	−14·3	60·7	16·5	61	289	93	12·1	18 19	18 38	22 47	2 40	2 26
2	15 31	−19·7	60·7	16·5	73	282	98	13·1	19 53	20 19	23 47	3 02	2 42
3	16 33	−23·9	60·5	16·5	85	237	100	14·1	21 19	21 53	..	3 33	3 05
4	17 37	−26·5	59·9	16·3	97	107	99	15·1	22 30	23 06	0 49	4 16	3 42
5	18 41	−27·2	59·2	16·1	109	95	95	16·1	23 22	23 55	1 53	5 16	4 40
6	19 44	−26·1	58·4	15·9	122	86	89	17·1	23 58	..	2 53	6 29	5 58
7	20 42	−23·5	57·5	15·7	134	79	82	18·1	..	0 24	3 49	7 49	7 25
8	21 37	−19·8	56·6	15·4	146	74	73	19·1	0 22	0 42	4 41	9 09	8 51
9	22 26	−15·2	55·8	15·2	158	70	63	20·1	0 40	0 53	5 27	10 26	10 14
10	23 13	−10·1	55·1	15·0	170	67	54	21·1	0 53	1 02	6 10	11 39	11 33
11	23 56	− 4·8	54·7	14·9	183	66	44	22·1	1 05	1 09	6 50	12 50	12 48
12	0 39	+ 0·7	54·3	14·8	195	66	34	23·1	1 16	1 15	7 30	13 59	14 03
13	1 21	+ 6·0	54·2	14·8	207	67	26	24·1	1 27	1 21	8 10	15 09	15 17
14	2 04	+11·2	54·1	14·8	219	69	18	25·1	1 38	1 28	8 50	16 20	16 33
15	2 49	+16·0	54·3	14·8	232	73	11	26·1	1 52	1 37	9 33	17 32	17 52
16	3 36	+20·2	54·5	14·9	244	78	6	27·1	2 10	1 50	10 19	18 46	19 11
17	4 27	+23·6	54·8	14·9	256	87	2	28·1	2 34	2 07	11 08	19 57	20 29
18	5 20	+26·0	55·2	15·1	268	102	0	29·1	3 07	2 35	12 01	21 03	21 37
19	6 16	+27·1	55·7	15·2	281	239	0	0·5	3 52	3 18	12 55	21 57	22 30
20	7 13	+26·8	56·2	15·3	293	264	2	1·5	4 53	4 19	13 51	22 38	23 07
21	8 10	+25·1	56·7	15·4	305	274	7	2·5	6 05	5 37	14 45	23 08	23 31
22	9 05	+22·0	57·2	15·6	317	281	13	3·5	7 25	7 03	15 38	23 30	23 47
23	9 59	+17·7	57·7	15·7	330	287	21	4·5	8 48	8 33	16 28	23 47	23 58
24	10 51	+12·5	58·2	15·9	342	290	31	5·5	10 11	10 02	17 16	..	..
25	11 41	+ 6·6	58·7	16·0	354	293	41	6·5	11 31	11 31	18 04	0 02	0 07
26	12 31	+ 0·2	59·1	16·1	6	293	53	7·5	12 58	13 01	18 52	0 15	0 15
27	13 22	− 6·2	59·5	16·2	19	293	64	8·5	14 24	14 33	19 42	0 29	0 24
28	14 15	−12·4	59·8	16·3	31	290	75	9·5	15 53	16 09	20 34	0 44	0 33
29	15 10	−18·0	59·9	16·3	43	285	84	10·5	17 23	17 47	21 31	1 03	0 46
30	16 09	−22·6	59·9	16·3	55	278	92	11·5	18 52	19 23	22 32	1 29	1 04

MERCURY ☿

Day	R.A.	Dec. +	Diam.	Phase	Transit		Day	R.A.	Dec. +	Diam.	Phase	Transit	
	h m	°	″		h m			h m	°	″		h m	
1	4 02	20·3	5	95	11 26	Mercury is too close to the Sun for observation	16	6 22	25·1	5	92	12 47	Mercury is too close to the Sun for observation
4	4 29	22·0	5	98	11 42		19	6 48	24·9	5	86	13 02	
7	4 57	23·3	5	100	11 58		22	7 13	24·4	6	81	13 15	
10	5 25	24·3	5	99	12 15		25	7 37	23·5	6	75	13 26	
13	5 54	24·9	5	96	12 32		28	7 58	22·4	6	70	13 36	
16	6 22	25·1	5	92	12 47		31	8 18	21·2	6	64	13 43	

VENUS ♀

Day	R.A.	Dec. +	Diam.	Phase	Transit	5° high 52°	5° high 56°
	h m	°	″		h m	h m	h m
1	1 37	7·9	28	43	8 59	2 51	2 48
6	1 54	9·1	26	46	8 56	2 42	2 37
11	2 12	10·5	25	49	8 54	2 33	2 27
16	2 30	11·9	23	51	8 54	2 25	2 18
21	2 50	13·3	22	54	8 53	2 17	2 09
26	3 10	14·7	21	56	8 54	2 10	2 01
31	3 31	16·1	20	59	8 55	2 03	1 53

MARS ♂

Day	R.A.	Dec. +	Diam.	Phase	Transit	
	h m	°	″		h m	
1	5 35	24·1	4	99	12 57	
6	5 50	24·2	4	99	12 52	Mars is too close to the Sun for observation
11	6 05	24·3	4	100	12 47	
16	6 19	24·3	4	100	12 42	
21	6 34	24·1	4	100	12 37	
26	6 48	23·9	4	100	12 31	
31	7 02	23·6	4	100	12 26	

SUNRISE AND SUNSET

Day	London a.m.	London p.m.	Bristol a.m.	Bristol p.m.	Birmingham a.m.	Birmingham p.m.	Manchester a.m.	Manchester p.m.	Newcastle a.m.	Newcastle p.m.	Glasgow a.m.	Glasgow p.m.	Belfast a.m.	Belfast p.m.
	h m	h m	h m	h m	h m	h m	h m	h m	h m	h m	h m	h m	h m	h m
1	3 49	8 07	3 59	8 16	3 50	8 19	3 47	8 26	3 35	8 33	3 40	8 50	3 55	8 48
2	3 48	8 08	3 58	8 17	3 49	8 20	3 46	8 28	3 34	8 34	3 39	8 51	3 54	8 50
3	3 48	8 09	3 58	8 19	3 49	8 22	3 45	8 29	3 33	8 35	3 38	8 52	3 53	8 51
4	3 47	8 10	3 57	8 20	3 48	8 23	3 44	8 30	3 32	8 36	3 37	8 53	3 52	8 52
5	3 46	8 11	3 56	8 21	3 47	8 24	3 44	8 31	3 31	8 38	3 36	8 55	3 52	8 53
6	3 45	8 12	3 55	8 22	3 46	8 25	3 43	8 32	3 31	8 39	3 36	8 56	3 51	8 54
7	3 45	8 13	3 55	8 23	3 46	8 26	3 42	8 33	3 30	8 40	3 35	8 57	3 50	8 55
8	3 44	8 14	3 54	8 23	3 45	8 26	3 42	8 34	3 29	8 41	3 34	8 58	3 50	8 56
9	3 44	8 15	3 54	8 24	3 45	8 27	3 41	8 35	3 28	8 42	3 33	8 59	3 49	8 57
10	3 43	8 15	3 53	8 25	3 44	8 28	3 41	8 36	3 28	8 43	3 33	9 00	3 49	8 58
11	3 43	8 16	3 53	8 26	3 44	8 29	3 40	8 37	3 27	8 44	3 32	9 01	3 48	8 59
12	3 43	8 17	3 53	8 26	3 44	8 29	3 40	8 38	3 27	8 45	3 32	9 02	3 48	9 00
13	3 43	8 17	3 53	8 27	3 44	8 30	3 39	8 38	3 26	8 45	3 31	9 02	3 47	9 00
14	3 42	8 18	3 52	8 28	3 43	8 31	3 39	8 39	3 26	8 46	3 31	9 03	3 47	9 01
15	3 42	8 18	3 52	8 28	3 43	8 31	3 39	8 40	3 26	8 47	3 31	9 04	3 47	9 02
16	3 42	8 19	3 52	8 29	3 43	8 32	3 39	8 40	3 26	8 47	3 31	9 04	3 47	9 02
17	3 42	8 19	3 52	8 29	3 43	8 32	3 39	8 40	3 26	8 47	3 30	9 05	3 47	9 02
18	3 42	8 20	3 52	8 30	3 43	8 33	3 39	8 41	3 26	8 48	3 30	9 05	3 47	9 03
19	3 42	8 20	3 52	8 30	3 43	8 33	3 39	8 41	3 26	8 48	3 30	9 06	3 47	9 03
20	3 42	8 20	3 52	8 30	3 43	8 33	3 39	8 42	3 26	8 49	3 30	9 06	3 47	9 04
21	3 42	8 21	3 52	8 31	3 43	8 34	3 39	8 42	3 26	8 49	3 31	9 06	3 47	9 04
22	3 43	8 21	3 53	8 31	3 44	8 34	3 39	8 42	3 26	8 49	3 31	9 06	3 47	9 04
23	3 43	8 21	3 53	8 31	3 44	8 34	3 39	8 42	3 26	8 49	3 31	9 07	3 47	9 04
24	3 43	8 21	3 53	8 31	3 44	8 34	3 40	8 42	3 27	8 49	3 32	9 07	3 48	9 04
25	3 43	8 21	3 53	8 31	3 44	8 34	3 40	8 42	3 27	8 49	3 32	9 07	3 48	9 04
26	3 44	8 21	3 54	8 31	3 45	8 34	3 41	8 42	3 28	8 49	3 32	9 07	3 49	9 04
27	3 44	8 21	3 54	8 31	3 45	8 34	3 41	8 42	3 28	8 49	3 33	9 06	3 49	9 04
28	3 45	8 21	3 55	8 31	3 46	8 34	3 42	8 42	3 29	8 49	3 33	9 06	3 50	9 04
29	3 45	8 21	3 55	8 31	3 46	8 34	3 42	8 42	3 29	8 49	3 34	9 06	3 50	9 04
30	3 46	8 21	3 56	8 31	3 47	8 34	3 43	8 42	3 30	8 49	3 35	9 06	3 51	9 04

JUPITER ♃ · SATURN ♄

Day	Jupiter R.A.	Jupiter Dec. −	Jupiter Transit	Jupiter 5° high. 52°	Jupiter 5° high. 56°	Saturn R.A.	Saturn Dec. −	Saturn Transit	Saturn 5° high. 52°	Saturn 5° high. 56°
	h m	°	h m	h m	h m	h m	°	h m	h m	h m
1	21 18	16·4	4 40	0 47	1 08	15 27	16·4	22 46	2 43	2 22
11	21 18	16·4	4 01	0 08	0 29	15 25	16·3	22 04	2 02	1 41
21	21 17	16·6	3 20	23 24	23 45	15 22	16·2	21 22	1 21	1 00
31	21 14	16·8	2 38	22 44	23 05	15 21	16·1	20 40	0 40	0 20

Equatorial diameter of Jupiter 45″; of Saturn 18″.   Diameters of Saturn's rings 41″ and 16″.

URANUS ♅ · NEPTUNE ♆

Day	Uranus R.A.	Uranus Dec. −	Uranus Transit	Uranus 10° high. 52°	Uranus 10° high. 56°	Neptune R.A.	Neptune Dec. −	Neptune Transit	Neptune 10° high. 52°	Neptune 10° high. 56°
	h m	° ′	h m	h m	h m	h m	° ′	h m	h m	h m
1	17 00·2	22 45	0 22	2 32	1 28	18 12·3	22 15	1 34	3 50	2 52
11	16 58·4	22 43	23 37	1 52	0 48	18 11·2	22 15	0 54	3 09	2 11
21	16 56·6	22 40	22 56	1 11	0 08	18 10·0	22 16	0 13	2 30	1 31
31	16 55·0	22 38	22 15	0 31	23 24	18 08·9	22 16	23 29	1 49	0 50

Diameter 4″   Diameter 2″

Month	Week	Julius Caesar, formerly *Quintilis*, 5th month (from March). Sun's Longitude 120° ♌ 22ᵈ 22ʰ
1	M.	PRINCESS OF WALES b. 1961.
2	Tu.	Archbp. Cranmer b. 1489. Marston Moor 1644.
3	W.	**St. Thomas.** Franz Kafka b. 1883.
4	Th.	INDEPENDENCE DAY, U.S.A., 1776.
5	F.	Sir Stamford Raffles b. 1781; d. 1826. Rhodes b. 1853.
6	S.	Sir Thomas More exec. 1535. Sedgemoor 1685.
7	♋.	**5th S. after Trinity.** Gustave Mahler b. 1860.
8	M.	Percy Bysshe Shelley drowned 1822.
9	Tu.	Mrs. Ann Radcliffe b. 1764.
10	W.	John Calvin b. 1509. Marcel Proust b. 1871.
11	Th.	Robert the Bruce b. 1274. Courtrai 1302.
12	F.	Julius Caesar b. 102 B.C.
13	S.	John Clare b. 1793. Jean Paul Marat d. 1793.
14	♋.	**6th S. after Trinity.** FÊTE NATIONALE, FRANCE.
15	M.	ST. SWITHIN'S DAY. Duke of Monmouth d. 1685.**
16	Tu.	Sir Joshua Reynolds b. 1723. Amundsen b. 1872.
17	W.	Isaac Watts b. 1674. Charlotte Corday d. 1793.
18	Th.	William Thackeray b. 1811. W. G . Grace b. 1848.
19	F.	*Mary Rose* sank 1545. Edgar Degas b. 1834.
20	S.	Petrarch b. 1304. Sir Edmund Hillary b. 1919.
21	♋.	**7th S. after Trinity.** First Men on Moon 1969.
22	M.	**St. Mary Magdalene.** Gregor Mendel b. 1822.
23	Tu.	Gen. Ulysses Grant d. 1885.**
24	W.	Simón Bolivár b. 1783. Dumas (père) b. 1802.
25	Th.	**St. James.** First Cross Channel Flight 1909.
26	F.	G. B. Shaw b. 1856. C. G. Jung b. 1875.
27	S.	A. Dumas (fils) b. 1824. Hilaire Belloc b. 1870.
28	♋.	**8th S. after Trinity.** Robespierre exec. 1794.
29	M.	Defeat of Spanish Armada 1588.
30	Tu.	Emily Brontë b. 1818. Henry Moore b. 1898.
31	W.	TRINITY LAW SITTINGS END. Franz Liszt d. 1886.

PHENOMENA

July 4ᵈ 23ʰ Jupiter in conjunction with the Moon. Jupiter 5° N.

5ᵈ 10ʰ Earth at aphelion (152,000,000 kilometres).

14ᵈ 01ʰ Mercury at greatest eastern elongation (27°).

14ᵈ 09ʰ Venus in conjunction with the Moon. Venus 5° S.

18ᵈ 03ʰ Mars in conjunction with the Sun.

19ᵈ 21ʰ Mercury in conjunction with the Moon. Mercury 7° S.

26ᵈ 10ʰ Saturn in conjunction with the Moon. Saturn 3° N.

CONSTELLATIONS

The following constellations are near the meridian at

	d	h		d	h
June 1	24		June 15	23
July 1	22		July 16	21
Aug. 1	20		Aug. 16	19

Ursa Minor, Draco, Corona, Hercules, Lyra, Serpens, Ophiuchus, Libra, Scorpius and Sagittarius.

MINIMA OF ALGOL

d	h	d	h
2	21	20	2
5	18	22	23
8	14	25	19
11	11	28	16
14	8	31	13
17	5		

PHASES OF THE MOON

		d	h	m
○	Full Moon	2	12	08
☾	Last Quarter	10	00	49
●	New Moon	17	23	56
☽	First Quarter	24	23	39
○	Full Moon	31	21	41

	d	h
Apogee (404,250 kilometres)	11	08
Perigee (369,640 „)	25	18

Mean Longitude of Ascending Node on July 1, 46°.

See note on *Summer Time*, p. 98.

MONTHLY NOTES

July 1. National Day, Canada.

3. Dog Days begin (end Aug. 15).

5. Tynwald Day, Isle of Man.

12. Bank holiday, Northern Ireland.

** Centenary.

Day	Right Ascension	Dec. +	Equation of Time	Rise 52°	Rise 56°	Transit	Set 52°	Set 56°	Sidereal Time	Transit of First Point of Aries
	h m s	° ′	m s	h m	h m	h m	h m	h m	h m s	h m s
1	6 39 39	23 08	−3 42	3 44	3 18	12 04	20 23	20 49	18 35 58	5 23 08
2	6 43 47	23 04	−3 53	3 44	3 19	12 04	20 23	20 48	18 39 54	5 19 13
3	6 47 55	22 59	−4 04	3 45	3 20	12 04	20 22	20 48	18 43 51	5 15 17
4	6 52 03	22 54	−4 15	3 46	3 21	12 04	20 22	20 47	18 47 47	5 11 21
5	6 56 10	22 49	−4 26	3 47	3 22	12 04	20 21	20 47	18 51 44	5 07 25
6	7 00 16	22 43	−4 36	3 48	3 23	12 05	20 21	20 46	18 55 41	5 03 29
7	7 04 23	22 37	−4 46	3 49	3 24	12 05	20 20	20 45	18 59 37	4 59 33
8	7 08 29	22 31	−4 56	3 50	3 25	12 05	20 19	20 44	19 03 34	4 55 37
9	7 12 35	22 24	−5 05	3 51	3 26	12 05	20 18	20 43	19 07 30	4 51 41
10	7 16 40	22 16	−5 14	3 52	3 27	12 05	20 18	20 42	19 11 27	4 47 45
11	7 20 45	22 09	−5 22	3 53	3 28	12 05	20 17	20 41	19 15 23	4 43 49
12	7 24 50	22 01	−5 30	3 54	3 29	12 06	20 16	20 40	19 19 20	4 39 53
13	7 28 54	21 52	−5 38	3 55	3 31	12 06	20 15	20 39	19 23 16	4 35 58
14	7 32 58	21 43	−5 45	3 56	3 32	12 06	20 14	20 38	19 27 13	4 32 02
15	7 37 01	21 34	−5 51	3 57	3 34	12 06	20 13	20 37	19 31 10	4 28 06
16	7 41 03	21 25	−5 57	3 59	3 36	12 06	20 12	20 35	19 35 06	4 24 10
17	7 45 06	21 15	−6 03	4 00	3 37	12 06	20 11	20 34	19 39 03	4 20 14
18	7 49 07	21 05	−6 08	4 01	3 39	12 06	20 10	20 33	19 42 59	4 16 18
19	7 53 08	20 54	−6 13	4 03	3 40	12 06	20 09	20 31	19 46 56	4 12 22
20	7 57 09	20 43	−6 17	4 05	3 42	12 06	20 08	20 30	19 50 52	4 08 26
21	8 01 09	20 32	−6 20	4 06	3 44	12 06	20 07	20 28	19 54 49	4 04 30
22	8 05 08	20 20	−6 23	4 07	3 45	12 06	20 05	20 26	19 58 45	4 00 34
23	8 09 07	20 08	−6 25	4 08	3 47	12 06	20 04	20 24	20 02 42	3 56 38
24	8 13 06	19 56	−6 27	4 09	3 49	12 06	20 02	20 22	20 06 39	3 52 43
25	8 17 03	19 43	−6 28	4 11	3 50	12 06	20 01	20 21	20 10 35	3 48 47
26	8 21 00	19 30	−6 29	4 12	3 52	12 06	20 00	20 19	20 14 32	3 44 51
27	8 24 57	19 17	−6 29	4 14	3 54	12 06	19 59	20 17	20 18 28	3 40 55
28	8 28 52	19 03	−6 28	4 15	3 56	12 06	19 57	20 16	20 22 25	3 36 59
29	8 32 48	18 49	−6 26	4 17	3 58	12 06	19 56	20 14	20 26 21	3 33 03
30	8 36 42	18 35	−6 24	4 19	4 00	12 06	19 54	20 12	20 30 18	3 29 07
31	8 40 36	18 20	−6 22	4 20	4 01	12 06	19 52	20 10	20 34 14	3 25 11

THE SUN   s.d. 15′·8

Duration of Civil (C), Nautical (N), and Astronomical (A), Twilight (in minutes)

Lat. °	July 1 C	N	A	July 11 C	N	A	July 21 C	N	A	July 31 C	N	A
52	48	124	T.A.N.	46	116	T.A.N.	44	107	T.A.N.	41	98	180
56	61	T.A.N.	T.A.N.	58	T.A.N.	T.A.N.	53	144	T.A.N.	49	122	T.A.N.

ASTRONOMICAL NOTES

MERCURY is unsuitably placed for observation.

VENUS continues to be observable as a brilliant morning object, magnitude −3·7. During the second half of the month observers with a good east-north-east horizon should be able to see it shortly before 02ʰ. On the morning of the 14th the old crescent Moon will be seen approaching the planet. On the morning of the 15th Venus passes 3° N. of Aldebaran.

MARS is unsuitably placed for observation, conjunction occurring on the 18th.

JUPITER, magnitude −2·3, is now visible low above the south-eastern horizon well before midnight.

SATURN is visible in the south-western sky, magnitude +0·6. By the end of the month it will be too low for observation long before midnight.

TWILIGHT. Reference to the section just above these notes shows that astronomical twilight last all night for some time around the summer solstice (i.e. in June and July), even in southern England. Under these conditions the sky never gets completely dark since the Sun is always less than 18° below the horizon.

THE MOON

Day	R.A.	Dec.	Hor. Par.	Semi-diam.	Sun's Co-long.	P.A. of Bright Limb	Phase	Age	Rise 52°	Rise 56°	Transit	Set 52°	Set 56°
	h m	°	′	′	°	°		d	h m	h m	h m	h m	h m
1	17 11	−25·7	59·7	16·3	67	268	97	12·5	20 10	20 45	23 34	2 05	1 34
2	18 15	−27·1	59·3	16·2	79	240	100	13·5	21 11	21 45	..	2 57	2 21
3	19 18	−26·7	58·7	16·0	92	117	100	14·5	21 53	22 22	0 36	4 05	3 31
4	20 19	−24·6	58·0	15·8	104	91	97	15·5	22 23	22 45	1 35	5 24	4 56
5	21 16	−21·2	57·3	15·6	116	81	92	16·5	22 43	22 59	2 29	6 46	6 24
6	22 08	−16·8	56·5	15·4	128	75	86	17·5	22 59	23 09	3 19	8 05	7 51
7	22 56	−11·8	55·8	15·2	140	71	78	18·5	23 12	23 17	4 04	9 22	9 13
8	23 42	− 6·4	55·2	15·0	153	68	69	19·5	23 23	23 24	4 46	10 34	10 31
9	0 25	− 0·9	54·7	14·9	165	67	60	20·5	23 33	23 30	5 26	11 45	11 46
10	1 08	+ 4·5	54·4	14·8	177	68	50	21·5	23 45	23 37	6 06	12 55	13 01
11	1 51	+ 9·8	54·2	14·8	189	69	41	22·5	23 58	23 45	6 46	14 05	14 16
12	2 35	+14·7	54·3	14·8	202	72	32	23·5	..	23 55	7 28	15 17	15 34
13	3 21	+19·0	54·5	14·8	214	76	23	24·5	0 14	..	8 13	16 30	16 53
14	4 10	+22·7	54·8	14·9	226	81	16	25·5	0 35	0 11	9 01	17 43	18 12
15	5 03	+25·4	55·2	15·1	238	88	9	26·5	1 04	0 34	9 52	18 51	19 25
16	5 58	+26·9	55·8	15·2	251	98	4	27·5	1 45	1 11	10 47	19 50	20 24
17	6 55	+27·1	56·3	15·4	263	114	1	28·5	2 41	2 06	11 42	20 36	21 07
18	7 53	+25·7	56·9	15·5	275	11	0	0·0	3 50	3 20	12 38	21 10	21 35
19	8 50	+22·9	57·5	15·7	287	264	1	1·0	5 10	4 46	13 32	21 35	21 53
20	9 45	+18·8	58·0	15·8	300	279	5	2·0	6 34	6 17	14 24	21 54	22 06
21	10 38	+13·7	58·4	15·9	312	286	11	3·0	7 59	7 48	15 14	22 09	22 16
22	11 30	+ 7·8	58·8	16·0	324	290	19	4·0	9 23	9 18	16 02	22 23	22 24
23	12 20	+ 1·5	59·0	16·1	336	292	28	5·0	10 46	10 48	16 50	22 36	22 32
24	13 10	− 5·0	59·2	16·1	348	292	39	6·0	12 11	12 18	17 38	22 51	22 41
25	14 02	−11·2	59·3	16·2	71	290	50	7·0	13 37	13 51	18 29	23 08	22 52
26	14 55	−16·8	59·3	16·2	13	287	62	8·0	15 06	15 27	19 23	23 30	23 08
27	15 52	−21·6	59·2	16·1	25	282	72	9·0	16 33	17 01	20 21	..	23 32
28	16 52	−25·0	59·1	16·1	37	275	82	10·0	17 53	18 28	21 21	0 01	..
29	17 54	−26·9	58·8	16·0	50	266	90	11·0	19 00	19 36	22 22	0 46	0 11
30	18 56	−27·1	58·4	15·9	62	255	95	12·0	19 49	20 20	23 22	1 46	1 10
31	19 57	−25·6	57·9	15·8	74	236	99	13·0	20 23	20 48	..	3 00	2 29

MERCURY ☿

Day	R.A.	Dec. +	Diam.	Phase	Transit		Day	R.A.	Dec. +	Diam.	Phase	Transit	
	h m	°	″		h m			h m	°	″		h m	
1	8 18	21·2	6	64	13 43		16	9 28	9·28	8	40	13 52	
4	8 35	19·8	7	59	13 49	Mercury is too	19	9 36	12·7	9	35	13 48	Mercury is too
7	8 51	18·4	7	54	13 52	close to the	22	9 42	11·5	9	30	13 41	close to the
10	9 06	16·9	7	50	13 54	Sun for	25	9 45	10·5	10	24	13 32	Sun for
13	9 18	15·4	8	45	13 54	observation	28	9 46	9·7	10	19	13 21	observation
16	9 28	14·0	8	40	13 52		31	9 43	9·3	11	13	13 06	

VENUS ♀

Day	R.A.	Dec. +	Diam.	Phase	Transit	5° high 52°	5° high 56°
	h m	°	″		h m	h m	h m
1	3 31	16·1	20	59	8 55	2 03	1 53
6	3 52	17·4	19	61	8 57	1 57	1 46
11	4 14	18·5	18	63	8 59	1 53	1 41
16	4 37	19·5	17	65	9 02	1 50	1 37
21	5 00	20·4	17	67	9 06	1 47	1 33
26	5 24	21·1	16	69	9 10	1 49	1 34
31	5 48	21·5	16	71	9 14	1 51	1 35

MARS ♂

Day	R.A.	Dec. +	Diam.	Phase	Transit	
	h m	°	″		h m	
1	7 02	23·6	4	100	12 26	
6	7 17	23·3	4	100	12 20	
11	7 31	22·8	4	100	12 15	Mars is too
16	7 45	22·3	4	100	12 09	close to the
21	7 58	21·7	4	100	12 03	Sun for
26	8 12	21·1	4	100	11 57	observation
31	8 25	20·4	4	100	11 51	

SUNRISE AND SUNSET

Day	London a.m. h m	London p.m. h m	Bristol a.m. h m	Bristol p.m. h m	Birmingham a.m. h m	Birmingham p.m. h m	Manchester a.m. h m	Manchester p.m. h m	Newcastle a.m. h m	Newcastle p.m. h m	Glasgow a.m. h m	Glasgow p.m. h m	Belfast a.m. h m	Belfast p.m. h m
1	3 47	8 21	3 57	8 30	3 48	8 33	3 44	8 41	3 31	8 48	3 36	9 05	3 52	9 03
2	3 47	8 20	3 57	8 30	3 48	8 33	3 44	8 41	3 31	8 48	3 36	9 05	3 52	9 03
3	3 48	8 20	3 58	8 29	3 49	8 32	3 45	8 40	3 32	8 47	3 37	9 04	3 53	9 02
4	3 49	8 20	3 59	8 29	3 50	8 32	3 46	8 40	3 33	8 47	3 38	9 04	3 54	9 02
5	3 50	8 19	4 00	8 29	3 51	8 32	3 47	8 39	3 34	8 46	3 39	9 03	3 55	9 01
6	3 50	8 19	4 00	8 28	3 51	8 31	3 48	8 39	3 35	8 45	3 40	9 02	3 56	9 01
7	3 51	8 18	4 01	8 27	3 52	8 30	3 49	8 38	3 36	8 45	3 41	9 02	3 57	9 00
8	3 52	8 18	4 02	8 27	3 53	8 30	3 50	8 37	3 37	8 44	3 42	9 01	3 58	8 59
9	3 53	8 17	4 03	8 26	3 54	8 29	3 51	8 36	3 39	8 43	3 44	9 00	3 59	8 58
10	3 54	8 16	4 04	8 25	3 55	8 28	3 52	8 36	3 40	8 42	3 45	8 59	4 00	8 58
11	3 55	8 16	4 05	8 25	3 56	8 28	3 53	8 35	3 41	8 41	3 46	8 58	4 01	8 57
12	3 56	8 15	4 06	8 24	3 57	8 27	3 54	8 34	3 42	8 40	3 48	8 57	4 02	8 56
13	3 57	8 14	4 08	8 23	3 59	8 26	3 56	8 33	3 44	8 39	3 49	8 55	4 04	8 55
14	3 58	8 13	4 09	8 22	4 00	8 25	3 57	8 32	3 45	8 38	3 50	8 54	4 05	8 54
15	3 59	8 12	4 10	8 21	4 01	8 24	3 58	8 31	3 46	8 37	3 52	8 53	4 06	8 53
16	4 01	8 11	4 11	8 20	4 02	8 23	3 59	8 30	3 47	8 36	3 53	8 52	4 07	8 52
17	4 02	8 10	4 12	8 19	4 04	8 21	4 01	8 28	3 49	8 34	3 55	8 50	4 09	8 50
18	4 03	8 09	4 13	8 18	4 05	8 20	4 02	8 27	3 50	8 33	3 56	8 49	4 10	8 49
19	4 04	8 08	4 15	8 17	4 07	8 19	4 04	8 26	3 52	8 32	3 58	8 48	4 12	8 48
20	4 05	8 06	4 16	8 16	4 08	8 17	4 05	8 24	3 53	8 30	3 59	8 46	4 13	8 46
21	4 07	8 05	4 17	8 15	4 09	8 16	4 06	8 23	3 55	8 28	4 01	8 44	4 15	8 44
22	4 08	8 04	4 19	8 14	4 11	8 15	4 08	8 22	3 57	8 27	4 03	8 43	4 17	8 43
23	4 09	8 03	4 20	8 13	4 12	8 14	4 09	8 21	3 58	8 25	4 04	8 41	4 18	8 41
24	4 11	8 01	4 21	8 11	4 14	8 12	4 11	8 19	4 00	8 24	4 06	8 40	4 20	8 40
25	4 12	8 00	4 23	8 10	4 15	8 11	4 12	8 18	4 02	8 22	4 08	8 38	4 22	8 38
26	4 14	7 58	4 24	8 08	4 17	8 09	4 14	8 16	4 03	8 21	4 10	8 36	4 23	8 37
27	4 15	7 57	4 25	8 07	4 18	8 08	4 15	8 15	4 05	8 19	4 11	8 34	4 25	8 35
28	4 16	7 55	4 26	8 05	4 19	8 06	4 16	8 13	4 06	8 17	4 13	8 33	4 26	8 33
29	4 18	7 54	4 28	8 04	4 21	8 05	4 18	8 12	4 08	8 16	4 15	8 31	4 28	8 32
30	4 19	7 52	4 29	8 02	4 22	8 03	4 20	8 10	4 10	8 14	4 16	8 29	4 30	8 30
31	4 21	7 51	4 31	8 01	4 24	8 02	4 21	8 08	4 11	8 12	4 18	8 27	4 31	8 28

JUPITER ♃ / SATURN ♄

Day	Jupiter R.A. h m	Jupiter Dec. − °	Jupiter Transit h m	Jupiter 5° high 52° h m	Jupiter 5° high 56° h m	Saturn R.A. h m	Saturn Dec. − °	Saturn Transit h m	Saturn 5° high 52° h m	Saturn 5° high 56° h m
1	21 14	16·8	2 38	22 44	23 05	15 21	16·1	20 41	0 40	0 20
11	21 11	17·1	1 55	22 02	22 24	15 19	16·0	20 01	0 00	23 36
21	21 06	17·5	1 11	21 21	21 43	15 19	16·0	19 21	23 16	22 56
31	21 01	17·8	0 27	20 40	21 03	15 19	16·1	18 41	22 36	22 16

Equatorial diameter of Jupiter 48″; of Saturn 18″. Diameters of Saturn's rings 40″ and 15″.

URANUS ♅ / NEPTUNE ♆

Day	Uranus R.A. h m	Uranus Dec. − ° ′	Uranus Transit h m	Uranus 10° high 52° h m	Uranus 10° high 56° h m	Neptune R.A. h m	Neptune Dec. − ° ′	Neptune Transit h m	Neptune 10° high 52° h m	Neptune 10° high 56° h m
1	16 55·0	22 38	22 15	0 31	23 24	18 08·9	22 16	23 29	1 49	0 50
11	16 53·5	22 36	21 34	23 47	22 45	18 07·7	22 16	22 48	1 08	0 09
21	16 52·3	22 34	20 54	23 07	22 05	18 06·7	22 17	22 08	0 24	23 24
31	16 51·3	22 33	20 14	22 27	21 26	18 05·7	22 17	21 28	23 44	22 44

Diameter 4″   Diameter 2″

DAY OF		Julius Caesar *Augustus*, formerly *Sextilis*, 6th month (from March). *Sun's Longitude* 150° ♏ 23ᵈ 05ʰ
Month	**Week**	

1	Th.	Minden 1754. The Nile 1798.
2	F.	William II (Rufus) d. 1100. Sir Arthur Bliss b. 1891.
3	S.	Stanley Baldwin b. 1876. Rupert Brooke b. 1887.
4	♅.	**9th S. after Trinity.** QUEEN ELIZABETH THE QUEEN MOTHER b. 1900.
5	M.	Maupassant b. 1850.
6	Tu.	**Transfiguration.** First atomic bomb 1945.
7	W.	Admiral Robert Blake d. 1657.
8	Th.	Great Train Robbery 1963.
9	F.	Izaac Walton b. 1593. Thomas Telford b. 1757.
10	S.	Otterburn 1388. Sir Charles Napier b. 1782.
11	♅.	**10th S. after Trinity.** Battle of Britain began 1940.
12	M.	George IV b. 1762. Robert Southey b. 1774.
13	Tu.	Blenheim 1704. Sir Basil Spence b. 1907.
14	W.	John Galsworthy b. 1867. Japan surrenders 1945.
15	Th.	PRINCESS ANNE b. 1950. Thomas De Quincy b. 1785.**
16	F.	Peterloo Massacre 1819.
17	S.	Frederick the Great d. 1786. Davy Crockett b. 1786.
18	♅	**11th S. after Trinity.**
19	M.	John Dryden b 1631. John Flamsteed b. 1646.
20	Tu.	Gen. William Booth d. 1912. Trotsky assass. 1940.
21	W.	PRINCESS MARGARET b. 1930.
22	Th.	Bosworth Field 1485. Richard III d. 1485.**
23	F.	William Wallace exec. 1305.
24	S.	**St. Bartholomew.** Vesuvius erupts A.D. 79.
25	♅.	**12th S. after Trinity.** Paris liberated 1944.
26	M.	Crecy 1346. Prince Albert b. 1819.
27	T.	Earl Mountbatten of Burma assass. 1979.
28	W.	von Goethe b. 1749. Count Tolstoy b. 1828.
29	Th.	John Locke b. 1632. Sir Charles Napier d. 1853.
30	F.	Mary Shelley b. 1797. Lord Rutherford b. 1871.
31	S.	Henry V d. 1422. John Bunyan d. 1688.

PHENOMENA

August 1ᵈ 02ʰ Jupiter in conjunction with the Moon. Jupiter 4° N.

4ᵈ 12ʰ Jupiter at opposition.

10ᵈ 22ʰ Mercury in inferior conjunction.

13ᵈ 08ʰ Venus in conjunction with the Moon. Venus 5° S.

22ᵈ 16ʰ Saturn in conjunction with the Moon. Saturn 3° N.

28ᵈ 04ʰ Jupiter in conjunction with the Moon. Jupiter 4° N.

28ᵈ 12ʰ Mercury at greatest western elongation (18°).

CONSTELLATIONS

The following constellations are near the meridian at

	d	h		d	h
July	1	24	July 16	23	
Aug.	1	22	Aug. 16	21	
Sept.	1	20	Sept. 15	19	

Draco, Hercules, Lyra, Cygnus, Sagitta, Ophiuchus, Serpens, Aquila and Sagittarius.

MINIMA OF ALGOL

d	h	d	h
3	10	17	18
6	7	20	15
9	3	23	12
12	0	26	8
14	21	29	5

PHASES OF THE MOON

	d	h	m
☾ Last Quarter	8	18	29
● New Moon	16	10	06
☽ First Quarter	23	04	36
○ Full Moon	30	09	27

		d	h
Apogee (404,120 kilometres)		8	02
Perigee (367,360 „)	)	20	04
Mean Longitude of Ascending Node on August 1, 44°.

See note on *Summer Time*, p. 98.

MONTHLY NOTES

Aug. 1. Lammas. Scottish Term Day.

5. Bank Holiday, Scotland.

12. Grouse shooting begins.

26. Bank and General Holiday, England, Wales and N. Ireland.

**Centenary.

Day	Right Ascension	Dec. +	Equation of Time	Rise 52°	Rise 56°	Transit	Set 52°	Set 56°	Sidereal Time	Transit of First Point of Aries
	h m s	° ′	m s	h m	h m	h m	h m	h m	h m s	h m s
1	8 44 30	18 05	− 6 19	4 21	4 03	12 06	19 50	20 08	20 38 11	3 21 15
2	8 48 22	17 50	− 6 15	4 23	4 05	12 06	19 48	20 06	20 42 08	3 17 19
3	8 52 14	17 35	− 6 10	4 24	4 07	12 06	19 47	20 04	20 46 04	3 13 23
4	8 56 06	17 19	− 6 05	4 25	4 09	12 06	19 46	20 02	20 50 01	3 09 28
5	8 59 57	17 03	− 6 00	4 27	4 11	12 06	19 44	20 00	20 53 57	3 05 32
6	9 03 47	16 47	− 5 54	4 29	4 13	12 06	19 42	19 58	20 57 54	3 01 36
7	9 07 37	16 30	− 5 47	4 31	4 14	12 06	19 40	19 56	21 01 50	2 57 40
8	9 11 26	16 13	− 5 39	4 33	4 16	12 06	19 38	19 54	21 05 47	2 53 44
9	9 15 15	15 56	− 5 32	4 34	4 18	12 05	19 36	19 51	21 09 43	2 49 48
10	9 19 03	15 39	− 5 23	4 36	4 20	12 05	19 34	19 49	21 13 40	2 45 52
11	9 22 50	15 21	− 5 14	4 38	4 22	12 05	19 32	19 47	21 17 37	2 41 56
12	9 26 37	15 03	− 5 04	4 39	4 24	12 05	19 30	19 44	21 21 33	2 38 00
13	9 30 24	14 45	− 4 54	4 41	4 26	12 05	19 28	19 41	21 25 30	2 34 04
14	9 34 10	14 27	− 4 44	4 42	4 28	12 05	19 26	19 39	21 29 26	2 30 08
15	9 37 55	14 08	− 4 32	4 43	4 30	12 04	19 24	19 37	21 33 23	2 26 13
16	9 41 40	13 50	− 4 21	4 45	4 32	12 04	19 22	19 35	21 37 19	2 22 17
17	9 45 24	13 31	− 4 08	4 47	4 34	12 04	19 20	19 33	21 41 16	2 18 21
18	9 49 08	13 11	− 3 56	4 48	4 36	12 04	19 18	19 30	21 45 12	2 14 25
19	9 52 51	12 52	− 3 42	4 50	4 38	12 04	19 16	19 28	21 49 09	2 10 29
20	9 56 34	12 32	− 3 28	4 51	4 40	12 03	19 14	19 26	21 53 06	2 06 33
21	10 00 16	12 13	− 3 14	4 53	4 42	12 03	19 12	19 23	21 57 02	2 02 37
22	10 03 58	11 53	− 2 59	4 55	4 44	12 03	19 10	19 20	22 00 59	1 58 41
23	10 07 39	11 32	− 2 44	4 57	4 46	12 03	19 08	19 18	22 04 55	1 54 45
24	10 11 20	11 12	− 2 28	4 58	4 48	12 02	19 05	19 15	22 08 52	1 50 49
25	10 15 00	10 51	− 2 12	4 59	4 50	12 02	19 03	19 12	22 12 48	1 46 53
26	10 18 40	10 31	− 1 56	5 01	4 52	12 02	19 01	19 10	22 16 45	1 42 57
27	10 22 20	10 10	− 1 39	5 03	4 54	12 02	18 59	19 08	22 20 41	1 39 02
28	10 25 59	9 49	− 1 21	5 05	4 56	12 01	18 57	19 05	22 24 38	1 35 06
29	10 29 38	9 27	− 1 03	5 07	4 58	12 01	18 55	19 03	22 28 35	1 31 10
30	10 33 16	9 06	− 0 45	5 08	5 00	12 01	18 52	19 00	22 32 31	1 27 14
31	10 36 54	8 45	− 0 27	5 09	5 02	12 00	18 50	18 58	22 36 28	1 23 18

THE SUN   s.d. 15′·8

Duration of Civil (C), Nautical (N), and Astronomical (A), Twilight (in minutes)

Lat. °	Aug. 1 C	N	A	Aug. 11 C	N	A	Aug. 21 C	N	A	Aug. 31 C	N	A
52	41	97	177	39	89	153	37	83	138	35	79	127
56	48	120	T.A.N.	45	106	205	42	96	166	40	89	147

ASTRONOMICAL NOTES

MERCURY is unsuitably placed for observation during the first three weeks of the month, inferior conjunction occurring on the 10th. Afterwards Mercury is visible in the mornings, magnitude +0·6 to −0·3, when it may be seen low above the eastern horizon around the time of beginning of morning civil twilight.

VENUS is a brilliant morning object, magnitude −3·5, visible in the east for several hours before sunrise. On the morning of the 13th the old crescent Moon wil be seen approaching Venus. Around the 23rd of the month Venus will be passing south of the twins, Castor and Pollux.

MARS is unsuitably placed for observation.

JUPITER, magnitude −2·4, is at opposition on the 4th, and thus visible throughout the hours of darkness. Jupiter is in Capricornus. On the morning of the 28th the gibbous Moon passes 4°S. of the planet.

SATURN, magnitude +0·7, is an evening object, visible low in the south-western sky for several hours after sunset. Even in a small telescope the Rings of Saturn are a beautiful sight and they are now well open after the Earth's last passage through the ring plane early in 1980.

METEORS. The maximum of the famous Perseid meteor shower occurs on the 12th, and observers should expect to see most meteors during the early hours of the morning on that day.

THE MOON

Day	R.A.	Dec.	Hor. Par.	Semi-diam.	Sun's Co-long.	P.A. of Bright Limb	Phase	Age	Rise 52°	Rise 56°	Transit	Set 52°	Set 56°
	h m	°	′	′	°	°		d	h m	h m	h m	h m	h m
1	20 55	−22·6	57·4	15·6	86	151	100	14·0	20 46	21 05	00 18	4 21	3 57
2	21 49	−18·5	56·8	15·5	98	90	98	15·0	21 04	21 16	01 09	5 43	5 26
3	22 39	−13·6	56·1	15·3	110	78	95	16·0	21 17	21 25	01 56	7 01	6 50
4	23 25	− 8·2	55·5	15·1	123	72	90	17·0	21 29	21 32	02 40	8 16	8 11
5	0 10	− 2·7	55·0	15·0	135	70	83	18·0	21 40	21 38	03 21	9 28	9 28
6	0 53	+ 2·9	54·6	14·9	147	69	75	19·0	21 51	21 44	04 01	10 39	10 44
7	1 36	+ 8·3	54·4	14·8	159	69	67	20·0	22 03	21 51	04 42	11 49	11 59
8	2 20	+13·3	54·3	14·8	171	71	57	21·0	22 17	22 01	05 23	13 01	13 16
9	3 05	+17·9	54·3	14·8	184	74	48	22·0	22 36	22 14	06 06	14 13	14 34
10	3 53	+21·8	54·6	14·9	196	78	39	23·0	23 01	22 33	06 52	15 26	15 53
11	4 44	+24·8	55·0	15·0	208	84	29	24·0	23 36	23 03	07 42	16 36	17 09
12	5 38	+26·7	55·5	15·1	220	90	21	25·0	. .	23 50	08 35	17 39	18 14
13	6 34	+27·3	56·2	15·3	233	98	13	26·0	0 26	. .	09 30	18 30	19 04
14	7 32	+26·4	56·9	15·5	245	107	7	27·0	1 30	0 57	10 26	19 09	19 37
15	8 30	+24·1	57·6	15·7	257	119	3	28·0	2 47	2 20	11 22	19 37	19 58
16	9 27	+20·3	58·3	15·9	269	151	0	29·0	4 12	3 52	12 16	19 58	20 13
17	10 21	+15·3	58·9	16·0	282	259	1	0·6	5 38	5 25	13 07	20 15	20 24
18	11 14	+ 9·5	59·3	16·2	294	282	3	1·6	7 05	6 58	13 57	20 29	20 33
19	12 06	+ 3·0	59·6	16·2	306	289	9	2·6	8 31	8 31	14 46	20 43	20 41
20	12 57	− 3·6	59·7	16·3	318	291	16	3·6	9 57	10 03	15 35	20 57	20 49
21	13 49	−10·0	59·6	16·3	331	290	26	4·6	11 25	11 37	16 26	21 13	20 59
22	14 43	−15·9	59·5	16·2	343	288	37	5·6	12 53	13 12	17 19	21 34	21 13
23	15 39	−20·9	59·2	16·1	355	283	48	6·6	14 21	14 48	18 15	22 01	21 34
24	16 38	−24·6	58·9	16·0	7	278	59	7·6	15 44	16 17	19 14	22 40	22 07
25	17 38	−26·8	58·5	15·9	19	271	70	8·6	16 54	17 30	20 14	23 35	22 58
26	18 40	−27·4	58·0	15·8	32	263	80	9·6	17 47	18 21	21 13	. .	. .
27	19 40	−26·3	57·6	15·7	44	255	88	10·6	18 24	18 52	22 09	0 44	0 11
28	20 38	−23·7	57·1	15·6	56	246	94	11·6	18 50	19 12	23 02	2 02	1 35
29	21 32	−19·9	56·6	15·4	68	235	98	12·6	19 09	19 24	23 50	3 23	3 03
30	22 23	−15·2	56·1	15·3	80	203	100	13·6	19 24	19 33	. .	4 42	4 29
31	23 10	−10·0	55·6	15·1	93	98	99	14·6	19 36	19 40	00 34	5 59	5 51

MERCURY ☿

Day	R.A.	Dec. +	Diam.	Phase	Transit		Day	R.A.	Dec. +	Diam.	Phase	Transit	5° high. 52°	5° high. 56°
	h m	°	″		h m			h m	°	″		h m	h m	h m
1	9 42	9·3	11	12	13 01		16	9 04	12·7	10	5	11 24	4 52	4 45
4	9 36	9·3	11	7	12 43	Mercury is too	19	9 00	13·8	10	11	11 09	4 31	4 23
7	9 28	9·8	11	3	12 23	close to the	22	9 00	14·7	9	19	10 58	4 15	4 06
10	9 19	10·6	11	1	12 02	Sun for	25	9 05	15·3	8	30	10 52	4 06	3 56
13	9 11	11·6	11	2	11 42	observation	28	9 15	15·4	7	42	10 50	4 03	3 53
16	9 04	12·7	10	5	11 24		31	9 28	15·2	7	54	10 53	4 06	3 57

VENUS ♀   MARS ♂

Day	R.A.	Dec. +	Diam.	Phase	Transit	5° high. 52°	5° high. 56°	Day	R.A.	Dec. +	Diam.	Phase	Transit	
	h m	°	″		h m	h m	h m		h m	°	″		h m	
1	5 53	21·6	16	71	9 15	1 52	1 36	1	8 28	20·2	4	100	11 49	
6	6 18	21·8	15	73	9 20	1 45	1 39	6	8 41	19·4	4	100	11 43	
11	6 43	21·8	15	75	9 26	2 01	1 46	11	8 54	18·6	4	100	11 36	Mars is too
16	7 08	21·5	14	76	9 31	2 08	1 53	16	9 07	17·7	4	100	11 29	close to the
21	7 33	21·0	14	78	9 36	2 15	2 01	21	9 20	16·8	4	100	11 22	Sun for
26	7 58	20·2	13	79	9 41	2 26	2 13	26	9 33	15·8	4	100	11 15	observation
31	8 23	19·2	13	81	9 47	2 38	2 25	31	9 45	14·8	4	100	11 08	

SUNRISE AND SUNSET

Day	London a.m.	London p.m.	Bristol a.m.	Bristol p.m.	Birmingham a.m.	Birmingham p.m.	Manchester a.m.	Manchester p.m.	Newcastle a.m.	Newcastle p.m.	Glasgow a.m.	Glasgow p.m.	Belfast a.m.	Belfast p.m.
	h m	h m	h m	h m	h m	h m	h m	h m	h m	h m	h m	h m	h m	h m
1	4 22	7 49	4 32	7 59	4 25	8 00	4 23	8 06	4 13	8 10	4 20	8 25	4 33	8 26
2	4 24	7 47	4 34	7 57	4 27	7 58	4 25	8 05	4 15	8 08	4 22	8 23	4 35	8 25
3	4 26	7 46	4 36	7 56	4 29	7 57	4 26	8 03	4 17	8 06	4 24	8 21	4 36	8 23
4	4 27	7 44	4 37	7 54	4 30	7 55	4 28	8 01	4 19	8 04	4 26	8 19	4 38	8 21
5	4 29	7 42	4 39	7 52	4 32	7 53	4 30	7 59	4 21	8 02	4 28	8 17	4 40	8 19
6	4 30	7 41	4 40	7 50	4 33	7 51	4 31	7 57	4 22	8 00	4 30	8 15	4 42	8 17
7	4 32	7 39	4 42	7 48	4 35	7 49	4 33	7 55	4 24	7 58	4 32	8 12	4 44	8 14
8	4 33	7 37	4 43	7 47	4 36	7 48	4 35	7 53	4 26	7 56	4 34	8 10	4 46	8 12
9	4 35	7 35	4 45	7 45	4 38	7 46	4 37	7 51	4 28	7 54	4 36	8 08	4 48	8 10
10	4 37	7 33	4 47	7 43	4 40	7 44	4 39	7 49	4 30	7 52	4 38	8 06	4 50	8 08
11	4 38	7 32	4 48	7 41	4 41	7 42	4 40	7 47	4 32	7 50	4 40	8 04	4 51	8 06
12	4 40	7 30	4 50	7 39	4 43	7 40	4 42	7 45	4 34	7 47	4 42	8 01	4 53	8 04
13	4 41	7 28	4 51	7 37	4 45	7 38	4 44	7 43	4 36	7 45	4 44	7 59	4 55	8 02
14	4 43	7 26	4 53	7 35	4 47	7 36	4 46	7 41	4 37	7 43	4 45	7 57	4 57	8 00
15	4 44	7 24	4 54	7 34	4 48	7 33	4 47	7 38	4 39	7 40	4 47	7 54	4 58	7 57
16	4 46	7 22	4 56	7 32	4 50	7 31	4 49	7 36	4 41	7 38	4 49	7 52	5 00	7 55
17	4 47	7 20	4 57	7 30	4 52	7 29	4 51	7 34	4 43	7 36	4 51	7 50	5 02	7 53
18	4 49	7 18	4 59	7 28	4 54	7 27	4 53	7 32	4 45	7 34	4 53	7 48	5 04	7 51
19	4 50	7 16	5 00	7 26	4 55	7 25	4 54	7 30	4 47	7 32	4 55	7 46	5 06	7 49
20	4 52	7 14	5 02	7 24	4 57	7 23	4 56	7 28	4 48	7 29	4 56	7 43	5 07	7 46
21	4 53	7 12	5 03	7 22	4 58	7 21	4 57	7 26	4 50	7 27	4 58	7 41	5 09	7 44
22	4 55	7 10	5 05	7 20	5 00	7 19	4 59	7 24	4 52	7 25	5 00	7 39	5 11	7 42
23	4 57	7 07	5 07	7 17	5 02	7 16	5 01	7 21	4 54	7 22	5 02	7 36	5 13	7 40
24	4 58	7 05	5 08	7 15	5 03	7 14	5 02	7 19	4 56	7 19	5 04	7 33	5 14	7 37
25	5 00	7 03	5 10	7 13	5 05	7 12	5 04	7 17	4 58	7 17	5 06	7 31	5 16	7 35
26	5 02	7 01	5 12	7 11	5 07	7 10	5 06	7 14	5 00	7 15	5 08	7 29	5 18	7 32
27	5 03	6 59	5 13	7 09	5 08	7 08	5 08	7 12	5 02	7 12	5 10	7 26	5 20	7 30
28	5 05	6 57	5 15	7 07	5 10	7 06	5 10	7 10	5 04	7 10	5 12	7 23	5 22	7 27
29	5 07	6 54	5 17	7 04	5 12	7 03	5 11	7 07	5 05	7 07	5 14	7 21	5 24	7 25
30	5 08	6 52	5 18	7 02	5 13	7 01	5 13	7 05	5 07	7 05	5 16	7 18	5 26	7 22
31	5 10	6 50	5 20	7 00	5 15	6 59	5 15	7 03	5 09	7 03	5 18	7 16	5 28	7 20

JUPITER ♃ / SATURN ♄

Day	R.A.	Dec. −	Transit	5° high. 52°	5° high. 56°	R.A.	Dec. −	Transit	5° high. 52°	5° high. 56°
	h m	°	h m	h m	h m	h m	°	h m	h m	h m
1	21 01	17·9	0 23	4 05	3 42	15 19	16·1	18 37	22 32	22 12
11	20 56	18·3	23 34	3 17	2 53	15 19	16·2	17 59	21 53	21 33
21	20 51	18·6	22 49	2 30	2 06	15 21	16·3	17 21	21 14	20 54
31	20 46	18·9	22 06	1 45	1 20	15 23	16·5	16 43	20 36	20 15

Equatorial diameter of Jupiter 48″; of Saturn 17″.   Diameters of Saturn's rings 38″ and 15″.

URANUS ♅ / NEPTUNE ♆

Day	R.A.	Dec. −	Transit	10° high. 52°	10° high. 56°	R.A.	Dec. −	Transit	10° high. 52°	10° high. 56°
	h m	° ′	h m	h m	h m	h m	° ′	h m	h m	h m
1	16 51·3	22 32	20 10	22 22	21 22	18 05·6	22 17	21 24	23 40	22 40
11	16 50·7	22 31	19 30	21 43	20 42	18 04·8	22 18	20 44	23 00	22 00
21	16 50·4	22 31	18 50	21 03	20 03	18 04·2	22 18	20 04	22 20	21 21
31	16 50·5	22 31	18 11	20 24	19 23	18 03·9	22 19	19 24	21 40	20 41

Diameter 4″   Diameter 2″

DAY OF		*Septem* (seven), 7th month of Roman (pre-Julian) Calendar. *Sun's Longitude* 180° ♎ 23ᵈ 02ʰ
Month	Week	

1	♋.	**13th S. after Trinity.** Louis XIV d. 1715.
2	M.	Fire of London starts 1666. Omdurman 1898.
3	Tu.	Worcester 1651. World War II begins 1939.
4	W.	Anton Bruckner b. 1824. Albert Schweitzer d. 1965.
5	Th.	Louis XIV b. 1638.
6	F.	Sailing of *Mayflower* 1620.
7	S.	Elizabeth I b. 1533. Borodino 1812.
8	♋.	**14th S. after Trinity.** Richard I b. 1157.
9	M.	Flodden 1513. Cardinal Richelieu b. 1585.**
10	Tu.	Treaty of St. Germain 1919.
11	W.	Malplaquet 1709. D. H. Lawrence b. 1885.**
12	Th.	H. H. Asquith b. 1852. Maurice Chevalier b. 1888.
13	F.	William Cecil b. 1520. Quebec 1759.
14	S.	Dante d. 1321. Duke of Wellington d. 1852.
15	♋.	**15th S. after Trinity.** BATTLE OF BRITAIN DAY.
16	M.	Henry V b. 1387. Fire of Moscow 1812.
17	Tu.	James II d. 1701. W. Savage Landor d. 1864.
18	W.	Dr. Samuel Johnson b. 1709.
19	Th.	Poitiers 1356. Sir Francis Chichester b. 1901.
20	F.	Mungo Park b. 1771. Valmy 1792.
21	S.	**St. Matthew.** Gustav Holst b. 1874.
22	♋.	**16th S. after Trinity.** Zutphen 1586.
23	M.	Wilkie Collins d. 1889. Sigmund Freud d. 1939.
24	Tu.	Horace Walpole b. 1717.
25	W.	Stamford Bridge 1066. Shostakovich b. 1906.
26	Th.	Sir Barnes Wallis b. 1887. T. S. Eliot b. 1888.
27	F.	Edward II d. 1327. Bossuet b. 1627.
28	S.	Caravaggio b. 1573. Clemenceau b. 1841.
29	♋.	**17th S. after Trinity. St. Michael and All Angels.**
30	M.	Pierre Corneille d. 1684. Lord Raglan b. 1788.

PHENOMENA

September 4ᵈ 21ʰ Mercury in conjunction with Mars. Mercury 0°·01 S.

12ᵈ 08ʰ Venus in conjunction with the Moon. Venus 5° S.

13ᵈ 08ʰ Mars in conjunction with the Moon. Mars 4° S.

19ᵈ 02ʰ Saturn in conjunction with the Moon. Saturn 3° N.

22ᵈ 20ʰ Mercury in superior conjunction.

23ᵈ 02ʰ Equinox.

24ᵈ 06ʰ Jupiter in conjunction with the Moon. Jupiter 4° N.

CONSTELLATIONS

The following constellations are near the meridian at

	d	h		d	h
Aug. 1	24		Aug. 16	23	
Sept. 1	22		Sept. 15	21	
Oct. 1	20		Oct. 16	19	

Draco, Cepheus, Lyra, Cygnus, Vulpecula, Sagitta, Delphinus, Equuleus, Aquila, Aquarius and Capricornus.

MINIMA OF ALGOL

d	h	d	h
1	2	18	7
3	23	21	4
6	20	24	0
9	16	26	21
12	13	29	18
15	10		

PHASES OF THE MOON

	d	h	m
☾ Last Quarter	7	12	16
● New Moon	14	19	20
☽ First Quarter	21	11	03
○ Full Moon	29	00	08

	d	h
Apogee (404,790 kilometres)	4	21
Perigee (362,300 ")	16	19

Mean Longitude of Ascending Node on September 1, 42°.

See note on *Summer Time*, p. 98.

MONTHLY NOTES

Sept.   2. Partridge shooting begins.

16. Jewish New Year (A.M. 5746).

16. Moslem New Year (A.H. 1406).

25. Jewish Day of Atonement (Yom Kippur).

29. Michaelmas. Quarter day.

30. First Day of Tabernacles.

    ** Centenary.

Day	Right Ascension	Dec.	Equation of Time	Rise 52°	Rise 56°	Transit	Set 52°	Set 56°	Sidereal Time	Transit of First Point of Aries
	h m s	° ′	m s	h m	h m	h m	h m	h m	h m s	h m s
1	10 40 32	+8 23	− 0 08	5 11	5 04	12 00	18 48	18 55	22 40 24	1 19 22
2	10 44 10	+8 01	+ 0 11	5 13	5 06	12 00	18 46	18 53	22 44 21	1 15 26
3	10 47 47	+7 39	+ 0 30	5 15	5 08	11 59	18 43	18 50	22 48 17	1 11 30
4	10 51 24	+7 17	+ 0 50	5 17	5 10	11 59	18 41	18 48	22 52 14	1 07 34
5	10 55 00	+6 55	+ 1 10	5 18	5 11	11 59	18 39	18 45	22 56 10	1 03 38
6	10 58 37	+6 33	+ 1 30	5 20	5 13	11 58	18 37	18 43	23 00 07	0 59 42
7	11 02 13	+6 10	+ 1 50	5 21	5 15	11 58	18 35	18 40	23 04 04	0 55 47
8	11 05 49	+5 48	+ 2 11	5 22	5 17	11 58	18 32	18 37	23 08 00	0 51 51
9	11 09 25	+5 25	+ 2 31	5 24	5 19	11 57	18 30	18 34	23 11 57	0 47 55
10	11 13 01	+5 03	+ 2 52	5 26	5 21	11 57	18 28	18 32	23 15 53	0 43 59
11	11 16 37	+4 40	+ 3 13	5 27	5 23	11 57	18 25	18 29	23 19 50	0 40 03
12	11 20 12	+4 17	+ 3 34	5 29	5 25	11 56	18 23	18 27	23 23 46	0 36 07
13	11 23 48	+3 54	+ 3 55	5 31	5 27	11 56	18 20	18 24	23 27 43	0 32 11
14	11 27 23	+3 31	+ 4 16	5 32	5 29	11 56	18 18	18 21	23 31 40	0 28 15
15	11 30 58	+3 08	+ 4 37	5 34	5 31	11 55	18 16	18 18	23 35 36	0 24 19
16	11 34 34	+2 45	+ 4 59	5 36	5 33	11 55	18 13	18 15	23 39 33	0 20 23
17	11 38 09	+2 22	+ 5 20	5 37	5 35	11 55	18 11	18 13	23 43 29	0 16 27
18	11 41 44	+1 59	+ 5 41	5 39	5 37	11 54	18 09	18 10	23 47 26	0 12 32
19	11 45 19	+1 35	+ 6 03	5 41	5 39	11 54	18 07	18 08	23 51 22	0 08 36
20	11 48 55	+1 12	+ 6 24	5 42	5 41	11 53	18 04	18 05	23 55 19	0 04 40
21	11 52 30	+0 49	+ 6 45	5 43	5 43	11 53	18 02	18 02	23 59 15 { 0 00 44 / 23 56 48	
22	11 56 05	+0 25	+ 7 06	5 45	5 44	11 53	18 00	18 00	0 03 12	23 52 52
23	11 59 41	+0 02	+ 7 28	5 47	5 46	11 52	17 57	17 57	0 07 08	23 48 56
24	12 03 16	−0 21	+ 7 49	5 49	5 48	11 52	17 55	17 55	0 11 05	23 45 00
25	12 06 52	−0 45	+ 8 09	5 51	5 50	11 52	17 53	17 52	0 15 02	23 41 04
26	12 10 28	−1 08	+ 8 30	5 52	5 52	11 51	17 50	17 49	0 18 58	23 37 08
27	12 14 04	−1 31	+ 8 51	5 54	5 54	11 51	17 48	17 46	0 22 55	23 33 12
28	12 17 40	−1 55	+ 9 11	5 56	5 56	11 51	17 45	17 44	0 26 51	23 29 17
29	12 21 16	−2 18	+ 9 31	5 57	5 58	11 50	17 43	17 41	0 30 48	23 25 21
30	12 24 53	−2 41	+ 9 51	5 59	6 00	11 50	17 41	17 39	0 34 44	23 21 25

Duration of Civil (C), Nautical (N), and Astronomical (A), Twilight (in minutes)

Lat. °	Sept. 1 C	N	A	Sept. 11 C	N	A	Sept. 21 C	N	A	Sept. 30 C	N	A
52	35	79	127	34	76	120	34	74	115	34	73	113
56	39	89	146	38	84	135	37	82	129	37	80	126

ASTRONOMICAL NOTES

MERCURY, magnitude −0·3 to −1·1, is visible as a morning object for the first ten days of the month, when it may be seen low above the eastern horizon at the time of beginning of morning civil twilight. For the remainder of the month Mercury is too close to the Sun for observation. On the morning of the 6th Mercury will be seen approaching Regulus, passing 1° N. of that star after sunrise. Mercury will be seen near Mars on the mornings of the 4th and 5th. There should be no problem of identification, however, since Mercury is then nearly 3 magnitudes brighter than Mars.

VENUS is a brilliant morning object, magnitude −3·4. By the end of September it is still visible for two hours before sunrise. On the morning of the 12th the old crescent Moon will be seen approaching Venus, while on the 21st Venus will be seen approaching Regulus.

MARS gradually becomes visible as a morning object, magnitude +2·0, low above the eastern horizon for a short while before twilight inhibits observation.

JUPITER, magnitude −2·3, is a brilliant object in the night sky though by the end of the month it is no longer visible after midnight.

SATURN, magnitude +0·8, is an evening object, visible low in the south-western sky.

ZODIACAL LIGHT. The morning cone may be seen stretching up from the eastern horizon before the beginning of twilight from the 14th to the 27th.

THE MOON

Day	R.A.	Dec.	Hor. Par.	Semi-diam.	Sun's Co-long.	P.A. of Bright Limb	Phase	Age	Rise 52°	Rise 56°	Tran-sit	Set 52°	Set 56°
	h m	° ′	′	′	°	°		d	h m	h m	h m	h m	h m
1	23 55	− 4·4	55·1	15·0	105	77	97	15·6	19 47	19 46	1 17	7 12	7 10
2	0 38	+ 1·2	54·7	14·9	117	72	93	16·6	19 57	19 52	1 57	8 23	8 26
3	1 21	+ 6·7	54·4	14·8	129	70	88	17·6	20 08	19 59	2 37	9 34	9 24
4	2 05	+12·0	54·2	14·8	141	71	81	18·6	20 22	20 07	3 18	10 46	10 59
5	2 50	+16·7	54·2	14·8	153	73	73	19·6	20 38	20 18	4 01	11 58	12 17
6	3 37	+20·8	54·3	14·8	166	76	64	20·6	21 00	20 34	4 45	13 10	13 35
7	4 26	+24·1	54·5	14·9	178	81	55	21·6	21 30	20 58	5 33	14 21	14 53
8	5 19	+26·4	55·0	15·0	190	86	45	22·6	22 12	21 37	6 24	15 27	16 02
9	6 14	+27·5	55·6	15·1	202	93	36	23·6	23 09	22 34	7 17	16 23	16 58
10	7 10	+27·1	56·3	15·3	214	99	26	24·6	. .	23 50	8 13	17 06	17 37
11	8 08	+25·3	57·1	15·6	227	106	18	25·6	0 21	. .	9 08	17 38	18 02
12	9 04	+22·1	58·0	15·8	239	113	10	26·6	1 42	1 19	10 02	18 01	18 19
13	10 00	+17·5	58·8	16·0	251	121	5	27·6	3 09	2 52	10 55	18 20	18 31
14	10 54	+11·9	59·6	16·2	263	134	1	28·6	4 37	4 27	11 46	18 35	18 40
15	11 47	+ 5·4	60·1	16·4	276	239	0	0·2	6 05	6 02	12 36	18 49	18 49
16	12 39	− 1·3	60·4	16·5	288	284	2	1·2	7 34	7 37	13 27	19 02	18 57
17	13 32	− 8·1	60·5	16·5	300	289	7	2·2	9 04	9 14	14 18	19 18	19 06
18	14 27	−14·4	60·3	16·4	312	289	14	3·2	10 35	10 52	15 12	19 37	19 18
19	15 23	−19·9	60·0	16·3	325	285	23	4·2	12 07	12 31	16 09	20 02	19 36
20	16 23	−24·0	59·5	16·2	337	280	34	5·2	13 34	14 06	17 08	20 38	20 05
21	17 24	−26·7	58·8	16·0	349	274	45	6·2	14 49	15 26	18 09	21 28	20 51
22	18 26	−27·6	58·2	15·9	1	267	56	7·2	15 47	16 23	19 08	22 33	21 58
23	19 27	−26·8	57·6	15·7	13	260	67	8·2	16 28	16 58	20 05	23 49	23 19
24	20 25	−24·6	57·0	15·5	26	253	76	9·2	16 57	17 20	20 58	. .	. .
25	21 19	−21·1	56·4	15·4	38	247	85	10·2	17 17	17 34	21 47	1 09	0 46
26	22 10	−16·6	55·9	15·2	50	242	91	11·2	17 32	17 43	22 32	2 28	2 12
27	22 57	−11·5	55·4	15·1	62	237	96	12·2	17 44	17 50	23 14	3 44	3 35
28	23 42	− 6·0	55·0	15·0	74	229	99	13·2	17 55	17 56	23 55	4 58	4 54
29	0 26	− 0·4	54·7	14·9	86	338	100	14·2	18 05	18 02	. .	6 10	6 11
30	1 09	+ 5·2	54·4	14·8	99	77	99	15·2	18 16	18 08	0 35	7 21	7 27

MERCURY ☿

Day	R.A.	Dec. +	Diam.	Phase	Tran-sit	5° high. 52°	5° high. 56°	Day	R.A.	Dec.	Diam.	Phase	Tran-sit	
	h m	°	″		h m	h m	h m		h m	°	″		h m	
1	9 34	15·0	7	59	10 54	4 09	4 00	16	11 15	+6·8	5	97	11 37	
4	9 52	14·1	6	70	11 01	4 20	4 12	19	11 36	+4·5	5	99	11 46	Mercury is too
7	10 12	12·7	6	81	11 09	4 36	4 29	22	11 56	+2·1	5	100	11 54	close to the
10	10 33	11·0	5	88	11 18	4 54	4 49	25	12 15	−0·3	5	100	12 02	Sun for
13	10 54	9·0	5	94	11 28	5 14	5 10	28	12 34	−2·6	5	99	12 09	observation
16	11 15	6·8	5	97	11 37	5 35	5 33	31	12 53	−4·9	5	98	12 15	

VENUS ♀   MARS ♂

Day	R.A.	Dec. +	Diam.	Phase	Tran-sit	5° high. 52°	5° high. 56°	Day	R.A.	Dec. +	Diam.	Phase	Tran-sit	5° high. 52°	5° high. 56°
	h m	°	″		h m	h m	h m		h m	°	″		h m	h m	h m
1	8 28	9·0	13	81	9 48	2 40	2 26	1	9 48	14·5	4	99	11 07	4 25	4 16
6	8 52	17·7	13	83	9 52	2 52	2 39	6	10 00	13·5	4	99	10 59	4 23	4 15
11	9 16	16·3	13	84	9 57	3 05	2 54	11	10 12	12·4	4	99	10 52	4 21	4 15
16	9 41	14·6	12	85	10 01	3 18	3 09	16	10 24	11·2	4	99	10 44	4 20	4 14
21	10 04	12·7	12	86	10 05	3 32	3 24	21	10 36	10·1	4	99	10 36	4 18	4 13
26	10 28	10·7	12	88	10 09	3 46	3 41	26	10 48	8·9	4	99	10 29	4 17	4 12
31	10 51	8·6	12	89	10 13	4 01	3 58	31	11 00	7·7	4	98	10 21	4 15	4 12

SUNRISE AND SUNSET

Day	London a.m. h m	London p.m. h m	Bristol a.m. h m	Bristol p.m. h m	Birmingham a.m. h m	Birmingham p.m. h m	Manchester a.m. h m	Manchester p.m. h m	Newcastle a.m. h m	Newcastle p.m. h m	Glasgow a.m. h m	Glasgow p.m. h m	Belfast a.m. h m	Belfast p.m. h m
1	5 11	6 48	5 21	6 58	5 16	6 57	5 17	7 00	5 11	7 00	5 20	7 13	5 30	7 17
2	5 13	6 45	5 23	6 55	5 18	6 54	5 18	6 58	5 13	6 58	5 22	7 11	5 31	7 15
3	5 15	6 43	5 25	6 53	5 20	6 52	5 20	6 55	5 15	6 55	5 24	7 08	5 33	7 12
4	5 16	6 41	5 26	6 51	5 21	6 50	5 22	6 53	5 17	6 52	5 26	7 05	5 35	7 10
5	5 18	6 39	5 28	6 49	5 23	6 48	5 24	6 51	5 18	6 50	5 27	7 03	5 37	7 08
6	5 20	6 37	5 30	6 46	5 25	6 45	5 26	6 48	5 20	6 47	5 29	7 00	5 39	7 05
7	5 21	6 34	5 31	6 44	5 27	6 43	5 28	6 46	5 22	6 45	5 31	6 58	5 41	7 03
8	5 23	6 32	5 33	6 42	5 28	6 41	5 29	6 43	5 24	6 42	5 33	6 55	5 42	7 00
9	5 25	6 30	5 35	6 39	5 30	6 38	5 31	6 41	5 26	6 40	5 35	6 52	5 44	6 58
10	5 26	6 28	5 36	6 37	5 32	6 36	5 33	6 38	5 28	6 37	5 37	6 50	5 46	6 55
11	5 28	6 26	5 38	6 35	5 34	6 34	5 35	6 36	5 30	6 35	5 39	6 47	5 48	6 53
12	5 29	6 23	5 39	6 33	5 35	6 33	5 36	6 33	5 31	6 32	5 41	6 44	5 49	6 50
13	5 31	6 21	5 41	6 31	5 37	6 29	5 38	6 31	5 33	6 30	5 43	6 42	5 51	6 48
14	5 33	6 19	5 43	6 28	5 39	6 26	5 40	6 29	5 35	6 27	5 45	6 39	5 53	6 45
15	5 34	6 16	5 44	6 26	5 40	6 24	5 41	6 26	5 37	6 24	5 47	6 36	5 55	6 42
16	5 35	6 14	5 45	6 23	5 42	6 21	5 43	6 24	5 39	6 22	5 49	6 34	5 57	6 40
17	5 37	6 12	5 47	6 21	5 44	6 19	5 45	6 22	5 41	6 19	5 51	6 31	5 59	6 37
18	5 38	6 09	5 48	6 18	5 45	6 16	5 46	6 19	5 43	6 16	5 53	6 28	6 01	6 35
19	5 40	6 07	5 50	6 16	5 47	6 14	5 48	6 17	5 45	6 14	5 55	6 26	6 03	6 32
20	5 42	6 05	5 52	6 14	5 49	6 12	5 50	6 14	5 47	6 11	5 57	6 23	6 05	6 29
21	5 43	6 02	5 53	6 12	5 50	6 09	5 51	6 12	5 48	6 09	5 59	6 20	6 06	6 27
22	5 45	6 00	5 55	6 10	5 52	6 07	5 53	6 09	5 50	6 06	6 01	6 18	6 08	6 24
23	5 46	5 58	5 56	6 07	5 53	6 05	5 55	6 07	5 52	6 04	6 03	6 15	6 10	6 22
24	5 48	5 55	5 58	6 05	5 55	6 02	5 57	6 04	5 54	6 01	6 05	6 12	6 12	6 19
25	5 50	5 53	6 00	6 03	5 57	6 00	5 59	6 02	5 56	5 59	6 07	6 10	6 14	6 17
26	5 51	5 51	6 01	6 01	5 58	5 58	6 01	5 59	5 58	5 56	6 09	6 07	6 16	6 14
27	5 53	5 48	6 03	5 58	6 00	5 55	6 02	5 57	5 59	5 54	6 11	6 04	6 17	6 12
28	5 54	5 46	6 04	5 56	6 01	5 53	6 04	5 54	6 01	5 51	6 13	6 02	6 19	6 09
29	5 56	5 44	6 06	5 54	6 03	5 51	6 06	5 52	6 03	5 49	6 15	5 59	6 21	6 07
30	5 58	5 41	6 08	5 51	6 05	5 48	6 08	5 49	6 05	5 46	6 17	5 57	6 23	6 04

JUPITER ♃　　　　　SATURN ♄

Day	Jup. R.A. h m	Jup. Dec. − °	Jup. Transit h m	Jup. 5° high 52° h m	Jup. 5° high 56° h m	Sat. R.A. h m	Sat. Dec. − °	Sat. Transit h m	Sat. 5° high 52° h m	Sat. 5° high 56° h m
1	20 46	18·9	22 01	1 41	1 16	15 23	16·5	16 40	20 32	20 11
11	20 42	19·1	21 19	0 57	0 32	15 25	16·7	16 03	19 54	19 33
21	20 40	19·3	20 37	0 10	23 45	15 28	16·9	15 27	19 16	18 55
31	20 39	19·3	19 57	23 29	23 03	15 32	17·1	14 51	18 38	18 17

Equatorial diameter of Jupiter 46″; of Saturn 16″. Diameters of Saturn's rings 36″ and 14″.

URANUS ♅　　　　　NEPTUNE ♆

Day	Ura. R.A. h m	Ura. Dec. − ° ′	Ura. Transit h m		Nep. R.A. h m	Nep. Dec. − ° ′	Nep. Transit h m	Nep. 10° high 52° h m	Nep. 10° high 56° h m
1	16 50·5	22 31	18 07	Uranus is	18 03·8	22 19	19 20	21 36	20 37
11	16 51·0	22 32	17 28	too close to	18 03·7	22 19	18 41	20 57	19 58
21	16 51·9	22 34	16 50	the Sun for	18 03·8	22 20	18 02	20 17	19 18
31	16 53·1	22 36	16 12	observation	18 04·1	22 20	17 23	19 38	18 39

Diameter 4″　　　　　Diameter 2″

DAY OF		
Month	Week	

Octo (eight), 8th month
of Roman (pre-Julian)
Calendar.

Sun's Longitude 210° ♏ 23ᵈ 11ʰ

1	Tu.	MICHAELMAS LAW SITTINGS BEGIN.
2	W.	Mahatma Gandhi b. 1869. Archbp. Runcie b. 1921.
3	Th.	William Morris d. 1896. Sir Malcolm Sargent d.
4	F.	Rembrandt d. 1669. [1967.
5	S.	Denis Diderot b. 1713. R101 disaster 1930.
6	☉.	**18th S. after Trinity.** William Tyndale exec. 1536.
7	M.	Archbp. Laud b. 1573. Edgar Allen Poe d. 1849.
8	Tu.	Henry Fielding d. 1754. Earl Attlee d. 1967.
9	W.	Saint-Saëns b. 1835. Alfred Dreyfus b. 1859.
10	Th.	Giuseppe Verdi b. 1813. Fridtjof Nansen b. 1861.
11	F.	Camperdown 1797. Jean Cocteau d. 1963.
12	S.	Edward VI b. 1537. Ramsey MacDonald b. 1866.
13	☉.	**19th S. after Trinity.** Margaret Thatcher b. 1925.
14	M.	Hastings 1066. Dwight Eisenhower b. 1890.
15	Tu.	Friedrich Nietzche b. 1844. P. G. Wodehouse b. 1882.
16	W.	Marie Antoinette exec. 1793. Ben Gurion b. 1886.
17	Th.	Sir Philip Sidney d. 1586. Saratoga 1777.
18	F.	**St. Luke.** Thomas Love Peacock b. 1785.**
19	S.	John I d. 1216. Leigh Hunt b. 1784.
20	☉.	**20th S. after Trinity.** Lord Palmerston b. 1784.
21	M.	S. T. Coleridge b. 1772. Trafalgar 1805.
22	Tu.	Franz Liszt b. 1811. Sarah Bernhardt b. 1844.
23	W.	Edgehill 1642. El Alamein 1942.
24	Th.	Peace of Westphalia 1648.
25	F.	Agincourt 1415. Balaclava 1854.
26	S.	Domenico Scarlatti b. 1685.** Trotsky b. 1879.
27	☉.	**21st S. after Trinity.** Capt. Cook b. 1728.
28	M.	**SS. Simon and Jude.** John Locke d. 1704.
29	Tu.	Sir Walter Raleigh exec. 1618.
30	W.	R. B. Sheridan b. 1751. Ezra Pound b. 1885.**
31	Th.	Hallowmass Eve. John Keats b. 1795.

PHENOMENA

October 4ᵈ 23ʰ Venus in conjunction with Mars. Venus 0°·1 N.

12ᵈ 01ʰ Mars in conjunction with the Moon. Mars 3° S.

12ᵈ 09ʰ Venus in conjunction with the Moon. Venus 3° S.

15ᵈ 05ʰ Mercury in conjunction with the Moon. Mercury 1°·3 S.

16ᵈ 15ʰ Saturn in conjunction with the Moon. Saturn 4° N.

21ᵈ 13ʰ Jupiter in conjunction with the Moon. Jupiter 5° N.

30ᵈ 21ʰ Mercury in conjunction with Saturn. Mercury 4° S.

CONSTELLATIONS

The following constellations are near the meridian at

	d	h		d	h
Sept.	1	24	Sept.	15	23
Oct.	1	22	Oct.	16	21
Nov.	1	20	Nov.	15	19

Ursa Major (below the Pole), Cepheus, Cassiopeia, Cygnus, Lacerta, Andromeda, Pegasus, Capricornus, Aquarius and Piscis Austrinus.

MINIMA OF ALGOL

d	h	d	h
2	15	19	20
5	12	22	17
8	9	25	13
11	5	28	10
14	2	31	7
16	23		

PHASES OF THE MOON

	d	h	m
☾ Last Quarter.......	7	05	04
● New Moon.........	14	04	33
☽ First Quarter	20	20	13
○ Full Moon	28	17	38

	d	h
Apogee (405,760 kilometres)	2	13
Perigee (358,280 ,,)	15	01
Apogee (406,310 ,,)	29	22

Mean Longitude of Ascending Node on October 1, 41°.

MONTHLY NOTES

Oct.   1. Pheasant shooting begins.

      27. *Summer Time* ends at 01ʰ G.M.T.

        **Centenary.

Day	THE SUN									Sidereal Time	Transit of First Point of Aries
	Right Ascension	Dec. −	Equation of Time	Rise		Transit	Set				
				52°	56°		52°	56°			
	h m s	° ′	m s	h m	h m	h m	h m	h m	h m s	h m s	
1	12 28 30	3 05	+10 11	6 01	6 02	11 50	17 38	17 37	0 38 41	23 17 29
2	12 32 07	3 28	+10 30	6 02	6 04	11 49	17 36	17 34	0 42 37	23 13 33
3	12 35 45	3 51	+10 49	6 04	6 06	11 49	17 33	17 32	0 46 34	23 09 37
4	12 39 22	4 14	+11 08	6 06	6 08	11 49	17 31	17 29	0 50 30	23 05 41
5	12 43 01	4 38	+11 26	6 07	6 10	11 48	17 29	17 26	0 54 27	23 01 45
6	12 46 39	5 01	+11 44	6 09	6 12	11 48	17 26	17 23	0 58 24	22 57 49
7	12 50 18	5 24	+12 02	6 11	6 14	11 48	17 24	17 20	1 02 20	22 53 53
8	12 53 58	5 47	+12 19	6 12	6 16	11 48	17 22	17 18	1 06 17	22 49 57
9	12 57 37	6 09	+12 36	6 14	6 18	11 47	17 19	17 16	1 10 13	22 46 02
10	13 01 18	6 32	+12 52	6 16	6 20	11 47	17 17	17 13	1 14 10	22 42 06
11	13 04 58	6 55	+13 08	6 17	6 22	11 47	17 15	17 10	1 18 06	22 38 10
12	13 08 40	7 18	+13 23	6 19	6 24	11 47	17 13	17 07	1 22 03	22 34 14
13	13 12 21	7 40	+13 38	6 21	6 27	11 46	17 11	17 04	1 25 59	22 30 18
14	13 16 04	8 03	+13 52	6 23	6 29	11 46	17 09	17 02	1 29 56	22 26 22
15	13 19 47	8 25	+14 06	6 25	6 31	11 46	17 06	16 59	1 33 53	22 22 26
16	13 23 30	8 47	+14 19	6 27	6 33	11 46	17 04	16 57	1 37 49	22 18 30
17	13 27 14	9 09	+14 32	6 28	6 35	11 45	17 02	16 55	1 41 46	22 14 34
18	13 30 58	9 31	+14 44	6 30	6 37	11 45	17 00	16 53	1 45 42	22 10 38
19	13 34 44	9 53	+14 55	6 31	6 39	11 45	16 58	16 51	1 49 39	22 06 42
20	13 38 29	10 14	+15 06	6 33	6 41	11 45	16 56	16 48	1 53 35	22 02 47
21	13 42 16	10 36	+15 16	6 35	6 43	11 45	16 54	16 46	1 57 32	21 58 51
22	13 46 03	10 57	+15 26	6 37	6 45	11 45	16 52	16 43	2 01 28	21 54 55
23	13 49 50	11 18	+15 35	6 38	6 47	11 44	16 50	16 41	2 05 25	21 50 59
24	13 53 38	11 39	+15 43	6 40	6 49	11 44	16 48	16 39	2 09 22	21 47 03
25	13 57 27	12 00	+15 51	6 42	6 51	11 44	16 46	16 36	2 13 18	21 43 07
26	14 01 17	12 21	+15 57	6 44	6 54	11 44	16 44	16 33	2 17 15	21 39 11
27	14 05 07	12 41	+16 04	6 46	6 56	11 44	16 42	16 31	2 21 11	21 35 15
28	14 08 59	13 02	+16 09	6 48	6 58	11 44	16 40	16 29	2 25 08	21 31 19
29	14 12 50	13 22	+16 14	6 49	7 00	11 44	16 38	16 27	2 29 04	21 27 23
30	14 16 43	13 41	+16 18	6 50	7 02	11 44	16 36	16 25	2 33 01	21 23 27
31	14 20 37	14 01	+16 21	6 52	7 04	11 44	16 34	16 23	2 36 57	21 19 32

s.d. 16′·1

Duration of Civil (C), Nautical (N), and Astronomical (A), Twilight (in minutes)

Lat. °	Oct. 1			Oct. 11			Oct. 21			Oct. 31		
	C	N	A	C	N	A	C	N	A	C	N	A
52	34	73	113	34	73	112	34	74	113	36	75	114
56	37	80	125	37	80	124	38	81	124	40	83	126

ASTRONOMICAL NOTES

MERCURY is unsuitably placed for observation.

VENUS is a brilliant morning object, magnitude − 3·4, though gradually drawing closer to the Sun. Venus is near Mars on the 4th–5th while on the morning of the 12th the old crescent Moon will be seen approaching Venus.

MARS, magnitude +2·0, is a morning object, low above the east-south-eastern horizon. Its slightly reddish colour should assist in identification. During the month Mars moves from Leo into Virgo. On the morning of the 12th Mars will be seen near the old crescent Moon.

JUPITER, magnitude −2·1, is a splendid evening object, visible in the south-western sky in the constellation of Capricornus. The four Galilean satellites are readily observable with almost any small telescope or good pair of binoculars provided that the mounting is rigid. Eclipses and shadow-transits of these satellites are given on page 147.

SATURN is lost in the evening twilight and will not be visible again this year.

ECLIPSE. A total eclipse of the Moon occurs on the 28th. See page 148 for details.

THE MOON

Day	R.A.	Dec.	Hor. Par.	Semi-diam.	Sun's Co-long.	P.A. of Bright Limb	Phase	Age	Rise 52°	Rise 56°	Transit	Set 52°	Set 56°
	h m	°	′	′	°	°		d	h m	h m	h m	h m	h m
1	1 52	+10·5	54·2	14·8	111	72	96	16·2	18 28	18 15	1 15	8 32	8 43
2	2 36	+15·5	54·1	14·7	123	72	92	17·2	18 43	18 25	1 57	9 44	10 01
3	3 22	+19·8	54·1	14·7	135	74	86	18·2	19 02	18 38	2 41	10 57	11 20
4	4 11	+23·4	54·2	14·8	147	78	79	19·2	19 28	18 58	3 27	12 09	12 38
5	5 02	+26·0	54·4	14·8	159	83	71	20·2	20 05	19 30	4 16	13 16	13 51
6	5 55	+27·4	54·9	15·0	172	89	62	21·2	20 54	20 18	5 08	14 15	14 52
7	6 51	+27·6	55·5	15·1	184	95	52	22·2	21 59	21 25	6 01	15 02	15 36
8	7 47	+26·3	56·2	15·3	196	101	42	23·2	23 14	22 47	6 55	15 38	16 06
9	8 42	+23·7	57·1	15·5	208	107	32	24·2	..	..	7 49	16 04	16 25
10	9 37	+19·7	58·0	15·8	220	112	23	25·2	0 37	0 17	8 41	16 24	16 38
11	10 31	+14·5	58·9	16·1	233	117	14	26·2	2 03	1 50	9 32	16 39	16 48
12	11 23	+ 8·4	59·8	16·3	245	120	7	27·2	3 31	3 25	10 22	16 53	16 56
13	12 16	+ 1·7	60·6	16·5	257	124	2	28·2	5 00	5 00	11 13	17 07	17 04
14	13 09	− 5·3	61·0	16·6	269	148	0	29·2	6 31	6 37	12 04	17 21	17 13
15	14 04	−12·0	61·2	16·7	281	287	1	0·8	8 04	8 18	12 59	17 39	17 23
16	15 02	−18·0	61·1	16·6	294	288	5	1·8	9 40	10 01	13 56	18 02	17 39
17	16 02	−22·9	60·6	16·5	306	284	11	2·8	11 13	11 43	14 57	18 33	18 03
18	17 05	−26·2	60·0	16·3	318	278	20	3·8	12 37	13 13	15 59	19 19	18 43
19	18 09	−27·6	59·2	16·1	330	271	30	4·8	13 43	14 21	17 01	20 21	19 44
20	19 12	−27·3	58·3	15·9	342	264	41	5·8	14 31	15 03	18 00	21 36	21 04
21	20 11	−25·4	57·5	15·7	355	257	52	6·8	15 03	15 28	18 55	22 56	22 32
22	21 07	−22·1	56·7	15·5	7	252	62	7·8	15 25	15 44	19 45	..	23 58
23	21 58	−17·8	56·1	15·3	19	247	72	8·8	15 41	15 54	20 31	0 16	..
24	22 46	−12·8	55·5	15·1	31	244	80	9·8	15 53	16 01	21 13	1 33	1 21
25	23 31	− 7·4	55·0	15·0	43	242	88	10·8	16 04	16 07	21 54	2 47	2 41
26	0 15	− 1·9	54·6	14·9	56	241	93	11·8	16 14	16 13	22 34	3 59	3 58
27	0 57	+ 3·7	54·3	14·8	68	241	97	12·8	16 25	16 18	23 14	5 09	5 13
28	1 40	+ 9·2	54·1	14·7	80	241	100	13·8	16 36	16 25	23 55	6 20	6 29
29	2 24	+14·2	54·0	14·7	92	73	100	14·8	16 50	16 33	..	7 32	7 47
30	3 10	+18·8	54·0	14·7	104	70	99	15·8	17 07	16 45	0 38	8 45	9 05
31	3 58	+22·6	54·0	14·7	116	74	96	16·8	17 30	17 02	1 23	9 57	10 24

MERCURY ☿

Day	R.A.	Dec. −	Diam.	Phase	Transit		Day	R.A.	Dec. −	Diam.	Phase	Transit	
	h m	°	″		h m			h m	°	″		h m	
1	12 53	4·9	5	98	12 15		16	14 21	15·1	5	91	12 44	
4	13 11	7·1	5	97	12 22	Mercury is too	19	14 38	16·9	5	89	12 50	Mercury is too
7	13 29	9·3	5	96	12 29	close to the	22	14 55	18·5	5	87	12 55	close to the
10	13 46	11·3	5	94	12 33	Sun for	25	15 13	19·9	5	84	13 00	Sun for
13	14 04	13·3	5	93	12 39	observation	28	15 29	21·2	6	81	13 05	observation
16	14 21	15·1	5	91	12 44		31	15 45	22·3	6	78	13 09	

VENUS ♀

Day	R.A.	Dec.	Diam.	Phase	Transit	5° high 52°	5° high 56°
	h m	°	″		h m	h m	h m
1	10 51	+8·6	12	89	10 13	4 01	3 58
6	11 14	+6·4	11	90	10 16	4 16	4 14
11	11 37	+4·0	11	91	10 19	4 31	4 31
16	12 00	+1·7	11	92	10 22	4 47	4 49
21	12 23	−0·8	11	93	10 26	5 02	5 07
26	12 46	−3·2	11	94	10 29	5 19	5 26
31	13 09	−5·6	11	94	10 32	5 35	5 44

MARS ♂

Day	R.A.	Dec. +	Diam.	Phase	Transit	5° high 52°	5° high 56°
	h m	°	″		h m	h m	h m
1	11 00	7·7	4	98	10 21	4 15	4 12
6	11 12	6·5	4	98	10 13	4 13	4 11
11	11 23	5·3	4	98	10 05	4 11	4 10
16	11 35	4·0	4	98	9 57	4 09	4 09
21	11 47	2·8	4	98	9 48	4 07	4 08
26	11 58	1·5	4	97	9 40	4 06	4 08
31	12 10	0·3	4	97	9 32	4 04	4 07

Day	SUNRISE AND SUNSET													
	London		Bristol		Birmingham		Manchester		Newcastle		Glasgow		Belfast	
	a.m.	p.m.	a.m.	p.m.	a.m.	p.m.	a.m.	p.m.	a.m.	p.m.	a.m.	p.m.	a.m.	p.m.
	h m	h m	h m	h m	h m	h m	h m	h m	h m	h m	h m	h m	h m	h m
1	6 00	5 39	6 10	5 49	6 07	5 46	6 10	5 47	6 07	5 44	6 19	5 54	6 25	6 02
2	6 01	5 37	6 11	5 47	6 08	5 44	6 11	5 45	6 09	5 41	6 21	5 51	6 27	5 59
3	6 03	5 34	6 13	5 44	6 10	5 41	6 13	5 42	6 11	5 39	6 23	5 49	6 29	5 57
4	6 05	5 32	6 15	5 42	6 12	5 39	6 15	5 40	6 13	5 36	6 25	5 46	6 31	5 54
5	6 06	5 30	6 16	5 40	6 13	5 37	6 16	5 38	6 15	5 33	6 27	5 43	6 33	5 51
6	6 08	5 28	6 18	5 38	6 15	5 35	6 18	5 36	6 17	5 31	6 29	5 41	6 35	5 49
7	6 10	5 26	6 19	5 36	6 17	5 32	6 20	5 33	6 19	5 28	6 31	5 38	6 37	5 46
8	6 12	5 24	6 21	5 34	6 19	5 30	6 22	5 31	6 21	5 26	6 33	5 36	6 39	5 44
9	6 13	5 22	6 22	5 32	6 20	5 27	6 23	5 28	6 22	5 23	6 35	5 33	6 40	5 41
10	6 15	5 19	6 24	5 29	6 22	5 25	6 25	5 26	6 24	5 21	6 37	5 31	6 42	5 39
11	6 16	5 17	6 26	5 27	6 24	5 23	6 27	5 24	6 26	5 19	6 39	5 28	6 44	5 37
12	6 18	5 15	6 27	5 25	6 26	5 20	6 29	5 21	6 28	5 16	6 41	5 25	6 46	5 34
13	6 20	5 13	6 29	5 23	6 28	5 18	6 31	5 19	6 30	5 14	6 43	5 23	6 48	5 32
14	6 21	5 11	6 31	5 21	6 30	5 16	6 33	5 17	6 32	5 11	6 45	5 20	6 50	5 30
15	6 23	5 08	6 33	5 18	6 32	5 13	6 35	5 14	6 34	5 09	6 47	5 18	6 52	5 27
16	6 25	5 06	6 35	5 16	6 33	5 11	6 36	5 12	6 36	5 06	6 49	5 15	6 53	5 25
17	6 26	5 04	6 36	5 14	6 35	5 09	6 38	5 10	6 38	5 04	6 51	5 13	6 55	5 23
18	6 28	5 02	6 38	5 12	6 37	5 07	6 40	5 07	6 40	5 01	6 53	5 10	6 57	5 20
19	6 30	5 00	6 40	5 10	6 39	5 05	6 42	5 05	6 42	4 59	6 55	5 08	6 59	5 18
20	6 31	4 58	6 41	5 08	6 40	5 03	6 44	5 03	6 44	4 57	6 57	5 05	7 01	5 15
21	6 33	4 55	6 43	5 05	6 42	5 00	6 46	5 00	6 46	4 54	6 59	5 03	7 03	5 13
22	6 35	4 53	6 45	5 03	6 44	4 58	6 48	4 58	6 48	4 52	7 01	5 01	7 05	5 11
23	6 37	4 51	6 47	5 01	6 46	4 56	6 50	4 56	6 50	4 50	7 04	4 58	7 08	5 08
24	6 38	4 49	6 48	4 59	6 47	4 54	6 52	4 54	6 52	4 48	7 06	4 56	7 10	5 06
25	6 40	4 47	6 50	4 57	6 49	4 52	6 54	4 52	6 54	4 46	7 08	4 54	7 12	5 04
26	6 42	4 45	6 52	4 55	6 51	4 50	6 56	4 50	6 56	4 43	7 10	4 51	7 14	5 02
27	6 44	4 43	6 54	4 53	6 53	4 48	6 58	4 47	6 58	4 41	7 12	4 49	7 16	4 59
28	6 46	4 41	6 56	4 51	6 55	4 46	7 00	4 45	7 00	4 39	7 14	4 47	7 18	4 57
29	6 47	4 39	6 57	4 49	6 56	4 44	7 01	4 43	7 02	4 36	7 16	4 44	7 20	4 55
30	6 49	4 38	6 59	4 47	6 58	4 43	7 03	4 42	7 04	4 34	7 18	4 42	7 22	4 53
31	6 51	4 36	7 01	4 46	7 00	4 41	7 05	4 40	7 06	4 32	7 20	4 40	7 24	4 51

	JUPITER ♃					SATURN ♄			
Day	R.A.	Dec. −	Transit	5° high		R.A.	Dec. −	Transit	
				52°	56°				
	h m	°	h m	h m	h m	h m	°	h m	
1	20 39	19·3	19 57	23 29	23 03	15 32	17·1	14 51	Saturn is too close to the Sun for observation
11	20 39	19·3	19 18	22 50	22 24	15 36	17·4	14 16	
21	20 41	19·2	18 41	22 13	21 48	15 40	17·7	13 41	
31	20 44	19·0	18 04	21 40	21 15	15 45	17·9	13 06	

Equatorial diameter of Jupiter 42″; of Saturn 15″. Diameters of Saturn's rings 35″ and 14″.

	URANUS ♅				NEPTUNE ♆			
Day	R.A.	Dec. −	Transit		R.A.	Dec. −	Transit	
	h m	° ′	h m		h m	° ′	h m	
1	16 53·1	22 36	16 12	Uranus is too close to the Sun for observation	18 04·1	22 20	17 23	Neptune is too close to the Sun for observation
11	16 54·7	22 38	15 34		18 04·6	22 20	16 44	
21	16 56·5	22 41	14 57		18 05·4	22 21	16 05	
31	16 58·6	22 45	14 19		18 06·4	22 21	15 27	

Diameter 4″   Diameter 2″

Novem (nine), 9th month of Roman (pre-Julian) Calendar.

Sun's Longitude 240° ♐ 22^d 09^h

Day of Month	Day of Week	
1	F.	**All Saints.** L. S. Lowry b. 1887.
2	S.	**All Souls.** Marie Antoinette b. 1755.
3	𝕾.	**22nd S. after Trinity.** Henri Matisse d. 1954.
4	M.	Mendelssohn d. 1847. Wilfred Owen d. 1918.
5	Tu.	Guy Fawkes Night (1605). Inkerman 1854.
6	W.	Peter Tchaikovsky d. 1893.
7	Th.	Marie Curie b. 1867. October Revolution 1917.
8	F.	Edmund Halley b. 1656. Fred Archer d. 1886.
9	S.	Ivan Turgenev b. 1818. Edward VII b. 1841.
10	𝕾.	**23rd S. after Trinity.** Martin Luther b. 1483.
11	M.	ARMISTICE DAY, 1918. Prince of Condé d. 1686.
12	Tu.	Mrs. Gaskell d. 1865. *Tirpitz* sunk 1944.
13	W.	Edward III b. 1312. R. L. Stevenson b. 1850.
14	Th.	PRINCE OF WALES b. 1948.
15	F.	William Pitt the Elder b. 1708.
16	S.	Henry III d. 1272. Opening of Suez Canal 1869.
17	𝕾.	**24th S. after Trinity.** Mary I d. 1558.
18	M.	Carl von Weber b. 1786. Chester A. Arthur d. 1886.
19	Tu.	Charles I b. 1600. Franz Schubert d. 1828.
20	W.	QUEEN'S WEDDING DAY 1947. Chatterton b. 1752.
21	Th.	Voltaire b. 1694. André Gide b. 1869.
22	F.	George Eliot b. 1819. J. F. Kennedy assass. 1963.
23	S.	Perkin Warbeck d. 1499. Thomas Tallis d. 1585.**
24	𝕾.	**25th S. after Trinity.** Laurence Sterne b. 1713.
25	M.	Charles Kemble b. 1775. Andrew Carnegie b. 1835.
26	Tu.	William Cowper b. 1731. Coventry Patmore d. 1896.
27	W.	Anders Celsius b. 1701. Fanny Kemble b. 1809.
28	Th.	William Blake b. 1757. Friedrich Engels b. 1820.
29	F.	Donizetti b. 1798. C. S. Lewis b. 1898.
30	S.	**St. Andrew.** Jonathan Swift b. 1667.

PHENOMENA

November 8^d 09^h Mercury at greatest eastern elongation (23°).

9^d 18^h Mars in conjunction with the Moon. Mars 1°·7 S.

11^d 11^h Venus in conjunction with the Moon. Venus 0°·8 N.

14^d 04^h Mercury in conjunction with the Moon. Mercury 0°·5 N.

18^d 01^h Jupiter in conjunction with the Moon. Jupiter 5° N.

23^d 02^h Saturn in conjunction with the Sun.

28^d 22^h Mercury in inferior conjunction.

CONSTELLATIONS

The following constellations are near the meridian at

	d	h		d	h
Oct.	1	24	Oct.	16	23
Nov.	1	22	Nov.	15	21
Dec.	1	20	Dec.	16	19

Ursa Major (below the Pole), Cepheus Cassiopeia, Andromeda, Pegasus, Pisces, Aquarius and Cetus.

MINIMA OF ALGOL

d	h	d	h
3	4	17	12
6	1	20	9
8	22	23	6
11	18	26	2
14	15	28	23

PHASES OF THE MOON

	d	h	m
☾ Last Quarter	5	20	07
● New Moon	12	14	20
☽ First Quarter	19	09	04
○ Full Moon	27	12	42

	d	h
Perigee (356,870 kilometres)	12	13
Apogee (406,230 „)	25	22

Mean Longitude of Ascending Node on November 1, 39°.

MONTHLY NOTES

Nov. 1. Fox-hunting begins.
9. Lord Mayor's Show.
10. Remembrance Sunday.
11. Martinmas. Scottish Term Day.
28. Removal Day, Scotland.

** Centenary.

Day	Right Ascension	Dec. −	Equation of Time	Rise 52°	Rise 56°	Transit	Set 52°	Set 56°	Sidereal Time	Transit of First Point of Aries
	THE SUN					s.d. 16'·2				
	h m s	° '	m s	h m	h m	h m	h m	h m	h m s	h m s
1	14 24 31	14 20	+16 23	6 54	7 06	11 44	16 32	16 20	2 40 54	21 15 36
2	14 28 26	14 40	+16 25	6 56	7 08	11 44	16 30	16 18	2 44 51	21 11 40
3	14 32 22	14 59	+16 25	6 58	7 10	11 44	16 29	16 16	2 48 47	21 07 44
4	14 36 18	15 17	+16 25	7 00	7 13	11 44	16 27	16 14	2 52 44	21 03 48
5	14 40 16	15 36	+16 24	7 02	7 15	11 44	16 25	16 12	2 56 40	20 59 52
6	14 44 14	15 54	+16 22	7 04	7 17	11 44	16 23	16 09	3 00 37	20 55 56
7	14 48 13	16 12	+16 20	7 05	7 19	11 44	16 22	16 07	3 04 33	20 52 00
8	14 52 13	16 29	+16 16	7 07	7 22	11 44	16 20	16 05	3 08 30	20 48 04
9	14 56 14	16 47	+16 12	7 09	7 24	11 44	16 19	16 03	3 12 26	20 44 08
10	15 00 16	17 04	+16 07	7 11	7 26	11 44	16 17	16 02	3 16 23	20 40 12
11	15 04 19	17 21	+16 01	7 13	7 28	11 44	16 16	16 00	3 20 20	20 36 17
12	15 08 22	17 37	+15 54	7 14	7 30	11 44	16 14	15 58	3 24 16	20 32 21
13	15 12 27	17 53	+15 46	7 16	7 32	11 44	16 12	15 56	3 28 13	20 28 25
14	15 16 32	18 09	+15 37	7 18	7 34	11 44	16 10	15 54	3 32 09	20 24 29
15	15 20 38	18 25	+15 28	7 20	7 36	11 45	16 09	15 52	3 36 06	20 20 33
16	15 24 45	18 40	+15 17	7 21	7 38	11 45	16 08	15 51	3 40 02	20 16 37
17	15 28 52	18 55	+15 06	7 23	7 40	11 45	16 07	15 49	3 43 59	20 12 41
18	15 33 01	19 10	+14 54	7 25	7 42	11 45	16 05	15 48	3 47 55	20 08 45
19	15 37 10	19 24	+14 42	7 26	7 44	11 45	16 04	15 46	3 51 52	20 04 49
20	15 41 20	19 38	+14 28	7 28	7 46	11 46	16 03	15 45	3 55 49	20 00 53
21	15 45 31	19 51	+14 14	7 29	7 48	11 46	16 02	15 44	3 59 45	19 56 57
22	15 49 43	20 04	+13 58	7 31	7 50	11 46	16 00	15 42	4 03 42	19 53 02
23	15 53 56	20 17	+13 42	7 33	7 52	11 46	15 59	15 40	4 07 38	19 49 06
24	15 58 09	20 30	+13 26	7 35	7 54	11 47	15 58	15 39	4 11 35	19 45 10
25	16 02 23	20 42	+13 08	7 36	7 56	11 47	15 57	15 38	4 15 31	19 41 14
26	16 06 38	20 53	+12 50	7 38	7 58	11 47	15 56	15 37	4 19 28	19 37 18
27	16 10 53	21 05	+12 31	7 40	8 00	11 48	15 56	15 36	4 23 24	19 33 22
28	16 15 09	21 15	+12 11	7 41	8 01	11 48	15 55	15 34	4 27 21	19 29 26
29	16 19 26	21 26	+11 51	7 42	8 02	11 48	15 54	15 33	4 31 18	19 25 30
30	16 23 44	21 36	+11 30	7 44	8 04	11 49	15 54	15 32	4 35 14	19 21 34

Duration of Civil (C), Nautical (N), and Astronomical (A), Twilight (in minutes)

Lat. °	Nov. 1 C	N	A	Nov. 11 C	N	A	Nov. 21 C	N	A	Nov. 30 C	N	A
52	36	75	115	37	78	117	38	80	120	39	82	123
56	40	84	127	41	87	130	43	90	134	45	93	137

ASTRONOMICAL NOTES

MERCURY is unsuitably placed for observation, inferior conjunction occurring on the 28th.

VENUS is a bright morning star, magnitude −3·4. It is drawing towards the Sun, the period available for observation shortening noticeably during the month. Venus is near Spica on the 3rd, while the old crescent Moon will be seen approaching the planet on the morning of the 11th.

MARS, magnitude +1·9, is visible in the south-eastern sky for about two hours before fading in the morning twilight. The Moon is in the vicinity of Mars on the mornings of the 9th and 10th.

JUPITER, magnitude −1·9, continues to be visible as a splendid evening object, low in the south-western sky. By the end of the month it is not visible after 20ʰ.

SATURN is unsuitably placed for observation, conjunction occurring on the 23rd.

ECLIPSE. A total eclipse of the Sun occurs on the 12th. See page 148 for details.

HALLEY'S COMET. Last seen in 1910, this comet returns to perihelion in 1986 and should be visible in small telescopes or binoculars during the last two months of 1985, in the evenings. Positions are given in the table below:

Date	R.A. h m	Dec. ° '	Date	R.A. h m	Dec. ° '
Nov. 11	4 29·4	+22 14	Dec. 11	23 39·6	+6 00
Nov. 21	2 58·0	+20 19	Dec. 21	22 48·5	+0 51
Dec. 1	1 05·4	+13 39	Dec. 31	22 17·5	−2 18

If these positions are plotted on a map it will be noted that the comet will pass very close to Kappa Tauri on Nov. 12·0, Tau Arietis on Nov. 19·1 and Zeta Arietis on Nov. 19·7. Even with optical aid the comet is unlikely to exhibit more than a very short tail.

THE MOON

Day	R.A.	Dec.	Hor. Par.	Semi-diam.	Sun's Co-long.	P.A. of Bright Limb	Phase	Age	Rise 52°	Rise 56°	Transit	Set 52°	Set 56°
	h m	°	'	'	°	°		d	h m	h m	h m	h m	h m
1	4 48	+25.5	54.2	14.8	128	79	91	17.8	18 03	17 29	2 12	11 07	11 40
2	5 41	+27.2	54.4	14.8	141	84	85	18.8	18 47	18 11	3 02	12 09	12 45
3	6 35	+27.7	54.8	14.9	153	91	77	19.8	19 45	19 10	3 55	13 00	13 35
4	7 30	+26.9	55.4	15.1	165	97	68	20.8	20 56	20 26	4 48	13 38	14 09
5	8 25	+24.7	56.0	15.3	177	103	59	21.8	22 14	21 51	5 40	14 07	14 31
6	9 18	+21.2	56.8	15.5	189	108	48	22.8	23 36	23 20	6 31	14 28	14 46
7	10 11	+16.6	57.7	15.7	201	112	38	23.8	..	..	7 21	14 45	14 56
8	11 02	+11.0	58.7	16.0	214	115	28	24.8	1 00	0 50	8 09	14 59	15 04
9	11 53	+ 4.7	59.6	16.2	226	117	18	25.8	2 26	2 22	8 58	15 12	15 12
10	12 44	− 2.1	60.4	16.5	238	116	10	26.8	3 53	3 56	9 48	15 25	15 20
11	13 38	− 8.9	61.1	16.6	250	114	4	27.8	5 24	5 34	10 40	15 41	15 29
12	14 34	−15.3	61.4	16.7	262	107	1	28.8	7 00	7 17	11 37	16 00	15 41
13	15 34	−20.8	61.4	16.7	275	299	0	0.4	8 37	9 02	12 37	16 27	16 01
14	16 38	−25.0	61.1	16.6	287	286	3	1.4	10 09	10 43	13 41	17 07	16 33
15	17 44	−27.3	60.5	16.5	299	277	9	2.4	11 28	12 05	14 46	18 04	17 26
16	18 49	−27.6	59.6	16.2	311	269	16	3.4	12 25	13 00	15 49	19 17	18 42
17	19 52	−26.1	58.7	16.0	323	262	26	4.4	13 04	13 33	16 47	20 38	20 11
18	20 51	−23.1	57.7	15.7	336	256	36	5.4	13 30	13 51	17 40	22 01	21 41
19	21 45	−19.0	56.8	15.5	348	251	46	6.4	13 48	14 03	18 28	23 20	23 07
20	22 34	−14.1	56.0	15.3	360	248	56	7.4	14 02	14 11	19 12	..	..
21	23 20	− 8.8	55.4	15.1	372	246	66	8.4	14 13	14 18	19 54	0 36	0 28
22	0 04	− 3.2	54.8	14.9	384	245	75	9.4	14 24	14 23	20 34	1 48	1 46
23	0 47	+ 2.4	54.4	14.8	36	245	83	10.4	14 34	14 29	21 13	2 59	3 01
24	1 29	+ 7.8	54.2	14.8	49	247	89	11.4	14 45	14 35	21 54	4 09	4 17
25	2 13	+13.0	54.0	14.7	61	250	94	12.4	14 57	14 43	22 36	5 20	5 33
26	2 58	+17.7	54.0	14.7	73	256	98	13.4	15 13	14 53	23 21	6 33	6 52
27	3 45	+21.7	54.0	14.7	85	274	100	14.4	15 35	15 09	..	7 46	8 11
28	4 35	+24.8	54.2	14.8	97	54	100	15.4	16 04	15 32	0 08	8 57	9 28
29	5 28	+26.9	54.4	14.8	109	74	98	16.4	16 45	16 09	0 58	10 02	10 38
30	6 22	+27.7	54.7	14.9	121	84	94	17.4	17 39	17 03	1 51	10 57	11 33

MERCURY ☿

Day	R.A.	Dec. −	Diam.	Phase	Transit	Day	R.A.	Dec. −	Diam.	Phase	Transit
	h m	°	"		h m		h m	°	"		h m
1	15 51	22.7	6	76	13 10	16	16 51	24.9	8	41	13 10
4	16 06	23.6	6	72	13 14	19	16 54	24.5	8	29	13 00
7	16 21	24.3	6	66	13 16	22	16 50	23.7	9	17	12 43
10	16 34	24.7	7	59	13 17	25	16 40	22.5	10	7	12 20
13	16 44	24.9	7	51	13 15	28	16 25	20.9	10	0	11 53
16	16 51	24.9	8	41	13 10	31	16 09	19.3	10	2	11 25

Mercury is too close to the Sun for observation (both columns)

VENUS ♀ · MARS ♂

	VENUS ♀							MARS ♂						
Day	R.A.	Dec. −	Diam.	Phase	Transit	5° high 52°	5° high 56°	Day	R.A.	Dec. −	Diam.	Phase	Transit	5° high 52°	56°
	h m	°	"		h m	h m	h m		h m	°	"		h m	h m	h m
1	13 13	6.1	11	94	10 33	5 38	5 47	1	12 12	0.0	4	97	9 30	4 03	4 07
6	13 37	8.5	11	95	10 36	5 54	6 06	6	12 23	1.2	4	97	9 22	4 01	4 06
11	14 00	10.7	10	96	10 40	6 11	6 25	11	12 35	2.5	4	96	9 14	4 00	4 06
16	14 24	12.9	10	96	10 45	6 29	6 45	16	12 46	3.7	4	96	9 06	3 58	4 05
21	14 49	15.0	10	97	10 49	6 46	7 05	21	12 58	4.9	4	96	8 58	3 56	4 04
26	15 13	16.9	10	97	10 55	7 04	7 26	26	13 09	6.1	4	95	8 49	3 55	4 04
31	15 39	18.6	10	98	11 00	7 22	7 47	31	13 21	7.3	4	95	8 41	3 53	4 03

SUNRISE AND SUNSET

Day	London a.m. h m	London p.m. h m	Bristol a.m. h m	Bristol p.m. h m	Birmingham a.m. h m	Birmingham p.m. h m	Manchester a.m. h m	Manchester p.m. h m	Newcastle a.m. h m	Newcastle p.m. h m	Glasgow a.m. h m	Glasgow p.m. h m	Belfast a.m. h m	Belfast p.m. h m
1	6 53	4 34	7 03	4 44	7 02	4 39	7 07	4 38	7 08	4 30	7 22	4 38	7 25	4 49
2	6 55	4 32	7 04	4 42	7 04	4 37	7 09	4 36	7 10	4 28	7 24	4 36	7 27	4 47
3	6 56	4 30	7 06	4 40	7 05	4 35	7 10	4 34	7 12	4 26	7 26	4 34	7 29	4 45
4	6 58	4 29	7 08	4 39	7 07	4 33	7 12	4 32	7 14	4 24	7 28	4 32	7 31	4 43
5	7 00	4 27	7 09	4 37	7 09	4 31	7 14	4 30	7 16	4 22	7 30	4 30	7 33	4 41
6	7 02	4 26	7 11	4 36	7 11	4 29	7 16	4 28	7 18	4 20	7 32	4 28	7 35	4 39
7	7 03	4 24	7 13	4 34	7 13	4 28	7 18	4 27	7 20	4 18	7 34	4 26	7 37	4 38
8	7 05	4 22	7 14	4 32	7 15	4 26	7 20	4 25	7 22	4 16	7 36	4 24	7 39	4 36
9	7 07	4 21	7 16	4 31	7 17	4 24	7 22	4 23	7 25	4 14	7 39	4 22	7 41	4 34
10	7 09	4 19	7 18	4 29	7 19	4 22	7 24	4 21	7 27	4 12	7 41	4 20	7 43	4 32
11	7 10	4 18	7 20	4 28	7 21	4 21	7 26	4 19	7 29	4 10	7 43	4 18	7 45	4 30
12	7 12	4 16	7 22	4 26	7 23	4 19	7 28	4 18	7 31	4 09	7 45	4 16	7 47	4 28
13	7 14	4 15	7 23	4 25	7 24	4 18	7 30	4 16	7 33	4 07	7 47	4 15	7 49	4 27
14	7 15	4 13	7 25	4 23	7 26	4 16	7 32	4 15	7 35	4 06	7 49	4 13	7 51	4 25
15	7 17	4 12	7 27	4 22	7 28	4 15	7 33	4 13	7 36	4 04	7 51	4 11	7 53	4 23
16	7 19	4 10	7 29	4 20	7 30	4 13	7 35	4 11	7 38	4 02	7 53	4 10	7 55	4 22
17	7 20	4 09	7 30	4 19	7 31	4 12	7 37	4 10	7 40	4 01	7 55	4 08	7 57	4 20
18	7 22	4 08	7 32	4 18	7 33	4 11	7 39	4 08	7 43	3 59	7 58	4 06	7 59	4 18
19	7 24	4 06	7 34	4 16	7 35	4 09	7 41	4 07	7 45	3 58	8 00	4 05	8 01	4 17
20	7 26	4 05	7 36	4 15	7 37	4 08	7 43	4 06	7 47	3 56	8 02	4 03	8 03	4 16
21	7 27	4 04	7 37	4 14	7 38	4 07	7 45	4 04	7 49	3 55	8 04	4 02	8 05	4 14
22	7 29	4 03	7 39	4 13	7 40	4 06	7 47	4 03	7 50	3 53	8 05	4 00	8 07	4 13
23	7 31	4 02	7 41	4 12	7 42	4 05	7 48	4 02	7 52	3 52	8 07	3 59	8 08	4 12
24	7 32	4 01	7 42	4 11	7 43	4 04	7 50	4 01	7 54	3 51	8 09	3 57	8 10	4 11
25	7 34	4 00	7 44	4 10	7 45	4 03	7 52	4 00	7 56	3 49	8 11	3 56	8 12	4 09
26	7 35	3 59	7 45	4 09	7 46	4 02	7 53	3 59	7 58	3 48	8 13	3 55	8 14	4 08
27	7 37	3 58	7 47	4 08	7 48	4 01	7 55	3 58	7 59	3 47	8 15	3 54	8 15	4 07
28	7 38	3 57	7 48	4 08	7 49	4 00	7 56	3 57	8 01	3 46	8 17	3 53	8 17	4 06
29	7 40	3 56	7 50	4 07	7 51	3 59	7 58	3 56	8 03	3 45	8 18	3 52	8 19	4 05
30	7 41	3 55	7 51	4 06	7 52	3 58	7 59	3 55	8 04	3 45	8 20	3 51	8 20	4 05

JUPITER ♃ / SATURN ♄

Day	R.A. h m	Dec. − °	Transit h m	5° high. 52° h m	5° high. 56° h m	R.A. h m	Dec. − °	Transit h m	
1	20 44	19·0	18 01	21 36	21 11	15 45	18·0	13 02	Saturn is
11	20 49	18·7	17 26	21 04	20 39	15 50	18·2	12 28	too close to
21	20 54	18·3	16 52	20 33	20 09	15 55	18·5	11 53	the Sun for
31	21 00	17·9	16 19	20 02	19 39	16 00	18·7	11 19	observation

Equatorial diameter of Jupiter 38″; of Saturn 15″. Diameters of Saturn's rings 34″ and 14″.

URANUS ♅ / NEPTUNE ♆

Day	R.A. h m	Dec. − ° ′	Transit h m		R.A. h m	Dec. − ° ′	Transit h m	
1	16 58·8	22 45	14 16	Uranus is too	18 06·5	22 21	15 23	Neptune is too
11	17 01·1	22 48	13 39	close to the Sun	18 07·7	22 21	14 45	close to the Sun
21	17 03·6	22 52	13 02	for observation	18 09·1	22 21	14 03	for observation
31	17 06·2	22 55	12 25		18 10·5	22 21	13 29	

Diameter 4″ Diameter 2″

DAY OF		
Month	Week	*Decem* (ten), 10th month of Roman (pre-Julian) Calendar. *Sun's Longitude* 27° ♑ 21ᵈ 22ʰ

Sun's Longitude 27° ♑ 21ᵈ 22ʰ

1	♐.	**Advent Sunday.** Edmund Campion exec. 1581.
2	M.	Austerlitz 1805. John Brown exec. 1859.
3	Tu.	Joseph Conrad b. 1857. Anton Webern b. 1883.
4	W.	Thomas Carlyle b. 1795. Edith Cavell b. 1865.
5	Th.	Mozart d. 1791. Christina Rossetti b. 1830.
6	F.	Henry VI b. 1421. Warren Hastings b. 1732.
7	S.	Lord Darnley b. 1545. Pearl Harbour 1941.
8	♐.	**2nd S. in Advent.** Mary, Queen of Scots b. 1542.
9	M.	John Milton b. 1608. Joseph Stalin b. 1879.
10	Tu.	Abdication of Edward VIII 1936.
11	W.	Llywelyn ap Gruffydd d. 1282. Berlioz b. 1803.
12	Th.	Gustave Flaubert b. 1821. Edvard Munch b. 1863.
13	F.	Dr. Samuel Johnson d. 1784.
14	S.	Prince Albert d. 1861. George VI b. 1895.
15	♐.	**3rd S. in Advent.** Rasputin d. 1916.
16	M.	Beethoven b. 1770. Jane Austen b. 1775.
17	Tu.	First flight by Wright brothers 1903.
18	W.	Charles Wesley b. 1707.
19	Th.	Emily Brontë d. 1848. J. M. W. Turner d. 1851.
20	F.	Leopold von Ranke b. 1795. Gen. Ludendorff d. 1937.
21	S.	Michaelmas Law Sittings End.
22	♐.	**4th S. in Advent.** Giacomo Puccini b. 1858.
23	M.	Roger Ascham d. 1568. Richard Arkwright b. 1732.
24	Tu.	Christmas Eve. John I b. 1167.
25	W.	**Christmas Day.**
26	Th.	**St. Stephen.** Thomas Gray b. 1716.
27	F.	**St. John.** Louis Pasteur b. 1822.
28	S.	**Holy Innocents Day.**
29	♐.	**1st S. after Christmas.** Thomas à Beckett d. 1170.
30	M.	Rudyard Kipling b. 1865. Pablo Casals b. 1876.
31	Tu.	The Young Pretender b. 1720. Matisse b. 1869.

PHENOMENA

December 4ᵈ 04ʰ Mercury in conjunction with Venus. Mercury 1°·6 N.

5ᵈ 11ʰ Venus in conjunction with Saturn. Venus 1°·1 S.

8ᵈ 10ʰ Mars in conjunction with the Moon. Mars 0°·01 S.

10ᵈ 18ʰ Mercury in conjunction with the Moon. Mercury 5° N.

10ᵈ 23ʰ Saturn in conjunction with the Moon. Saturn 4° N.

15ᵈ 18ʰ Jupiter in conjunction with the Moon. Jupiter 5° N.

16ᵈ 17ʰ Mercury in conjunction with Saturn. Mercury 0°·5 N.

17ᵈ 05ʰ Mercury at greatest western elongation (21°).

21ᵈ 22ʰ Winter Solstice.

CONSTELLATIONS

The following constellations are near the meridian at

	d	h		d	h
Nov.	1	24	Nov.	15	23
Dec.	1	22	Dec.	16	21
Jan.	1	20	Jan.	16	19

Ursa Major (below the Pole), Ursa Minor (below the Pole), Cassiopeia, Andromeda, Perseus, Triangulum, Aries, Taurus, Cetus and Eridanus.

MINIMA OF ALGOL

d	h	d	h
1	20	19	1
4	17	21	22
7	14	24	19
10	11	27	15
13	7	30	12
16	4		

PHASES OF THE MOON

	d	h	m
☾ Last Quarter	5	09	01
● New Moon	12	00	54
☽ First Quarter	19	01	58
○ Full Moon	27	07	30

	d	h
Perigee (358,680 kilometres)	11	01
Apogee (405,600 ,,)	23	07

Mean Longitude of Ascending Node on December 1, 37°.

MONTHLY NOTES

Dec. 10. Grouse shooting ends.

21. Shortest day.

25. Quarter day.

26. General Holiday, England, Wales, N. Ireland and Scotland.

31. Various licences expire.

Day	Right Ascension	Dec. −	Equation of Time	Rise 52°	Rise 56°	Transit	Set 52°	Set 56°	Sidereal Time	Transit of First Point of Aries
		THE SUN					s.d. 16′·3			
	h m s	° ′	m s	h m	h m	h m	h m	h m	h m s	h m s
1	16 28 02	21 46	+11 08	7 45	8 06	11 49	15 53	15 31	4 39 11	19 17 38
2	16 32 21	21 55	+10 46	7 47	8 08	11 49	15 53	15 30	4 43 07	19 13 42
3	16 36 41	22 04	+10 23	7 48	8 09	11 50	15 52	15 30	4 47 04	19 09 47
4	16 41 01	22 12	+ 9 59	7 49	8 11	11 50	15 51	15 29	4 51 00	19 05 51
5	16 45 22	22 20	+ 9 35	7 50	8 12	11 51	15 50	15 29	4 54 57	19 01 55
6	16 49 44	22 28	+ 9 10	7 51	8 14	11 51	15 50	15 28	4 58 54	18 57 59
7	16 54 06	22 35	+ 8 44	7 53	8 16	11 51	15 50	15 27	5 02 50	18 54 03
8	16 58 28	22 41	+ 8 18	7 54	8 17	11 52	15 49	15 27	5 06 47	18 50 07
9	17 02 51	22 48	+ 7 52	7 55	8 19	11 52	15 49	15 26	5 10 43	18 46 11
10	17 07 15	22 53	+ 7 25	7 56	8 20	11 53	15 49	15 26	5 14 40	18 42 15
11	17 11 39	22 59	+ 6 57	7 58	8 21	11 53	15 49	15 26	5 18 36	18 38 19
12	17 16 03	23 04	+ 6 30	7 59	8 22	11 54	15 48	15 25	5 22 33	18 34 23
13	17 20 28	23 08	+ 6 01	8 00	8 23	11 54	15 48	15 25	5 26 29	18 30 27
14	17 24 53	23 12	+ 5 33	8 00	8 24	11 55	15 48	15 25	5 30 26	18 26 32
15	17 29 18	23 15	+ 5 04	8 01	8 25	11 55	15 48	15 25	5 34 23	18 22 36
16	17 33 44	23 18	+ 4 35	8 02	8 26	11 56	15 49	15 25	5 38 19	18 18 40
17	17 38 10	23 21	+ 4 06	8 02	8 27	11 56	15 49	15 25	5 42 16	18 14 44
18	17 42 36	23 23	+ 3 37	8 03	8 27	11 57	15 49	15 26	5 46 12	18 10 48
19	17 47 02	23 25	+ 3 07	8 04	8 28	11 57	15 50	15 26	5 50 09	18 06 52
20	17 51 28	23 26	+ 2 37	8 04	8 28	11 58	15 50	15 26	5 54 05	18 02 56
21	17 55 54	23 26	+ 2 08	8 05	8 29	11 58	15 51	15 26	5 58 02	17 59 00
22	18 00 21	23 27	+ 1 38	8 06	8 30	11 59	15 51	15 27	6 01 58	17 55 04
23	18 04 47	23 26	+ 1 08	8 06	8 30	11 59	15 52	15 27	6 05 55	17 51 08
24	18 09 13	23 26	+ 0 38	8 07	8 31	12 00	15 52	15 28	6 09 52	17 47 12
25	18 13 40	23 24	+ 0 08	8 07	8 31	12 00	15 53	15 29	6 13 48	17 43 17
26	18 18 06	23 23	− 0 21	8 07	8 31	12 01	15 53	15 30	6 17 45	17 39 21
27	18 22 32	23 21	− 0 51	8 08	8 32	12 01	15 54	15 31	6 21 41	17 35 25
28	18 26 58	23 18	− 1 20	8 08	8 32	12 02	15 55	15 32	6 25 38	17 31 29
29	18 31 24	23 15	− 1 50	8 08	8 32	12 02	15 56	15 33	6 29 34	17 27 33
30	18 35 49	23 11	− 2 19	8 08	8 32	12 03	15 57	15 34	6 33 31	17 23 37
31	18 40 15	23 07	− 2 48	8 08	8 32	12 03	15 58	15 35	6 37 27	17 19 41

Duration of Civil (C), Nautical (N), and Astronomical (A), Twilight (in minutes)

Lat. °	Dec. 1 C	N	A	Dec. 11 C	N	A	Dec. 21 C	N	A	Dec. 31 C	N	A
52	40	82	123	41	84	125	41	85	126	41	84	125
56	45	93	138	47	96	141	47	97	142	41	96	141

ASTRONOMICAL NOTES

MERCURY is visible low above the E.S.E. horizon around the time of beginning of morning civil twilight, for all except the first and last few days of the month. During this period its magnitude increases from +1·5 to −0·3. On the morning of the 4th Mercury passes 1°·6 N. of Venus, and on the 16th and 17th will be seen close to Saturn: on the morning of the 21st it will be seen near Antares, passing 6°N. of the star after sunrise.

VENUS is a morning object, magnitude −3·4, for the first two weeks of the month, visible low in the south east for a short while before sunrise. Thereafter it is lost in the morning twilight. Venus will be seen approaching Saturn on the morning of the 5th, though some optical aid will be required since Saturn is then 4 magnitudes fainter than Venus.

MARS continues to be visible in the mornings in the south-eastern sky. Its magnitude is +1·7. At the beginning of the month Mars is in Virgo, passing 3°N. of Spica on the 2nd: late in December it moves into Libra. The old crescent Moon will be seen approaching the planet on the morning of the 8th.

JUPITER continues to be visible as a splendid evening object, low in the south-western sky, magnitude −1·7. The crescent Moon, just under 4 days old, passes 5°S. of Jupiter on the evening of the 15th.

SATURN is unsuitably placed for observation.

METEORS. The maximum of the well-known Geminid meteor shower occurs on the 14th, most meteors being seen before dawn on that day.

THE MOON

Day	R.A.	Dec.	Hor. Par.	Semi-diam.	Sun's Co-long.	P.A. of Bright Limb	Phase	Age	Rise 52°	Rise 56°	Transit	Set 52°	Set 56°
	h m	°	′	′	°	°		d	h m	h m	h m	h m	h m
1	7 17	+27·2	55·0	15·0	134	92	89	18·4	18 45	18 14	2 43	11 39	12 11
2	8 11	+25·3	55·5	15·1	146	98	82	19·4	20 00	19 35	3 36	12 10	12 36
3	9 04	+22·2	56·1	15·3	158	104	74	20·4	21 20	21 01	4 26	12 33	12 53
4	9 56	+17·9	56·7	15·5	170	109	65	21·4	22 41	22 29	5 15	12 51	13 04
5	10 46	+12·7	57·5	15·7	182	112	54	22·4	..	23 56	6 03	13 05	13 13
6	11 35	+ 6·8	58·3	15·9	194	114	43	23·4	0 02	..	6 49	13 18	13 20
7	12 25	+ 0·4	59·1	16·1	206	114	32	24·4	1 25	1 25	7 36	13 30	13 27
8	13 15	− 6·1	59·9	16·3	219	113	22	25·4	2 51	2 57	8 26	13 44	13 35
9	14 09	−12·6	60·5	16·5	231	110	13	26·4	4 21	4 34	9 18	14 01	13 46
10	15 06	−18·4	61·0	16·6	243	104	6	27·4	5 56	6 17	10 15	14 23	14 01
11	16 07	−23·2	61·1	16·7	255	92	2	28·4	7 31	8 00	11 17	14 55	14 25
12	17 13	−26·4	61·0	16·6	267	14	0	29·4	8 59	9 35	12 22	15 43	15 07
13	18 20	−27·6	60·5	16·5	280	285	2	1·0	10 09	10 46	13 28	16 50	16 13
14	19 26	−26·9	59·8	16·3	292	271	6	2·0	10 58	11 30	14 31	18 11	17 40
15	20 28	−24·4	59·0	16·1	304	262	12	3·0	11 30	11 55	15 29	19 37	19 14
16	21 25	−20·5	58·0	15·8	316	256	20	4·0	11 52	12 10	16 21	21 01	20 45
17	22 18	−15·7	57·1	15·5	328	251	30	5·0	12 08	12 20	17 07	22 20	22 10
18	23 06	−10·3	56·2	15·3	340	248	39	6·0	12 21	12 27	17 51	23 35	23 31
19	23 51	− 4·7	55·5	15·1	353	247	49	7·0	12 31	12 33	18 32	..	..
20	0 35	+ 0·9	54·9	15·0	5	246	59	8·0	12 42	12 39	19 12	0 47	0 48
21	1 17	+ 6·5	54·4	14·8	17	247	68	9·0	12 52	12 44	19 52	1 58	2 04
22	2 01	+11·7	54·2	14·8	29	250	77	10·0	13 04	12 52	20 33	3 08	3 20
23	2 45	+16·5	54·1	14·7	41	253	84	11·0	13 19	13 01	21 17	4 20	4 37
24	3 32	+20·7	54·1	14·7	53	258	90	12·0	13 39	13 15	22 04	5 33	5 56
25	4 21	+24·1	54·2	14·8	66	266	95	13·0	14 05	13 35	22 53	6 45	7 14
26	5 13	+26·4	54·5	14·8	78	285	98	14·0	14 42	14 07	23 45	7 53	8 28
27	6 07	+27·5	54·8	14·9	90	320	100	15·0	15 32	14 56	..	8 52	9 28
28	7 03	+27·3	55·1	15·0	102	66	99	16·0	16 36	16 03	0 39	9 39	10 12
29	7 58	+25·7	55·6	15·1	114	87	97	17·0	17 50	17 23	1 32	10 13	10 41
30	8 52	+22·8	56·0	15·3	126	97	93	18·0	19 09	18 49	2 23	10 38	11 00
31	9 44	+18·8	56·5	15·4	138	104	87	19·0	20 29	20 16	3 13	10 57	11 12

MERCURY ☿

Day	R.A.	Dec. −	Diam.	Phase	Transit	5° high 52°	5° high 56°	Day	R.A.	Dec. −	Diam.	Phase	Transit	5° high 52°	5° high 56°
	h m	°	″		h m	h m	h m		h m	°	″		h m	h m	h m
1	16 09	19·3	10	2	11 25	7 55	8 21	16	16 04	18·4	7	60	10 26	6 47	7 11
4	15 56	18·0	9	11	11 02	7 20	7 43	19	16 17	19·3	6	68	10 27	6 55	7 21
7	15 49	17·3	9	24	10 44	6 58	7 20	22	16 32	20·3	6	74	10 30	7 05	7 33
10	15 49	17·3	8	37	10 34	6 46	7 08	25	16 48	21·2	6	79	10 35	7 16	7 47
13	15 55	17·7	7	49	10 28	6 44	7 07	28	17 05	22·0	6	83	10 40	7 29	8 01
16	16 04	18·4	7	60	10 26	6 47	7 11	31	17 23	22·8	5	87	10 46	7 41	8 16

VENUS ♀ / MARS ♂

Day	R.A.	Dec. −	Diam.	Phase	Transit	5° high 52°	5° high 56°	Day	R.A.	Dec. −	Diam.	Phase	Transit	5° high 52°	5° high 56°
	h m	°	″		h m	h m	h m		h m	°	″		h m	h m	h m
1	15 39	18·6	10	98	11 00	7 22	7 47	1	13 21	7·3	4	95	8 41	3 53	4 03
6	16 05	20·1	10	98	11 06	7 39	8 07	6	13 33	8·5	4	95	8 33	3 52	4 03
11	16 31	21·4	10	99	11 13	7 57	8 28	11	13 44	9·6	5	94	8 25	3 50	4 02
16	16 58	22·4	10	99	11 20	8 13	8 45	16	13 56	10·7	5	94	8 17	3 48	4 02
21	17 25	23·1	10	99	11 28	8 27	9 03	21	14 08	11·8	5	94	8 09	3 46	4 01
26	17 52	23·5	10	100	11 35	8 40	9 16	26	14 20	12·8	5	93	8 01	3 44	4 01
31	18 20	23·7	10	100	11 43	8 50	9 27	31	14 32	13·8	5	93	7 54	3 44	4 01

Day	London		Bristol		Birmingham		Manchester		Newcastle		Glasgow		Belfast	
	a.m.	p.m.	a.m.	p.m.	a.m.	p.m.	a.m.	p.m.	a.m.	p.m.	a.m.	p.m.	a.m.	p.m.
	h m	h m	h m	h m	h m	h m	h m	h m	h m	h m	h m	h m	h m	h m
1	7 43	3 55	7 53	4 06	7 54	3 58	8 01	3 55	8 06	3 44	8 22	3 50	8 22	4 04
2	7 44	3 54	7 54	4 05	7 55	3 57	8 02	3 54	8 08	3 43	8 24	3 49	8 24	4 03
3	7 46	3 53	7 56	4 04	7 57	3 56	8 04	3 53	8 09	3 42	8 25	3 48	8 25	4 02
4	7 47	3 53	7 57	4 04	7 58	3 56	8 05	3 53	8 11	3 41	8 27	3 47	8 27	4 01
5	7 48	3 53	7 58	4 04	8 00	3 55	8 07	3 52	8 12	3 40	8 28	3 46	8 28	4 00
6	7 50	3 52	7 59	4 03	8 01	3 55	8 08	3 52	8 14	3 40	8 30	3 46	8 30	4 00
7	7 51	3 52	8 01	4 03	8 02	3 54	8 09	3 51	8 15	3 39	8 31	3 45	8 31	3 59
8	7 52	3 51	8 02	4 02	8 04	3 54	8 11	3 51	8 17	3 39	8 33	3 44	8 33	3 59
9	7 53	3 51	8 03	4 02	8 05	3 53	8 12	3 50	8 18	3 38	8 34	3 43	8 34	3 58
10	7 54	3 51	8 04	4 02	8 06	3 53	8 13	3 50	8 19	3 38	8 35	3 43	8 35	3 58
11	7 56	3 51	8 05	4 01	8 07	3 53	8 14	3 50	8 20	3 38	8 36	3 43	8 36	3 58
12	7 57	3 51	8 06	4 01	8 08	3 53	8 15	3 50	8 21	3 38	8 38	3 43	8 37	3 58
13	7 58	3 51	8 07	4 01	8 09	3 53	8 16	3 50	8 22	3 38	8 39	3 43	8 38	3 58
14	7 58	3 51	8 08	4 01	8 10	3 53	8 17	3 50	8 23	3 38	8 40	3 43	8 39	3 58
15	7 59	3 58	8 09	4 01	8 11	3 53	8 18	3 50	8 24	3 38	8 41	3 43	8 40	3 58
16	8 00	3 51	8 09	4 02	8 12	3 53	8 19	3 50	8 25	3 38	8 42	3 43	8 41	3 58
17	8 01	3 52	8 10	4 02	8 13	3 53	8 20	3 50	8 26	3 38	8 43	3 43	8 42	3 58
18	8 02	3 52	8 11	4 02	8 14	3 53	8 21	3 50	8 27	3 38	8 44	3 43	8 43	3 58
19	8 03	3 52	8 12	4 02	8 15	3 53	8 22	3 50	8 28	3 38	8 44	3 44	8 44	3 58
20	8 03	3 53	8 12	4 03	8 15	3 54	8 22	3 50	8 28	3 38	8 45	3 44	8 44	3 58
21	8 04	3 53	8 13	4 03	8 16	3 54	8 23	3 51	8 29	3 39	8 46	3 44	8 45	3 59
22	8 04	3 54	8 13	4 04	8 16	3 55	8 24	3 52	8 30	3 40	8 46	3 45	8 46	4 00
23	8 05	3 54	8 14	4 04	8 17	3 55	8 24	3 52	8 30	3 40	8 47	3 45	8 46	4 00
24	8 05	3 55	8 14	4 05	8 17	3 56	8 24	3 53	8 30	3 41	8 47	3 46	8 46	4 01
25	8 06	3 55	8 15	4 05	8 18	3 57	8 25	3 54	8 31	3 42	8 47	3 47	8 47	4 02
26	8 06	3 56	8 15	4 06	8 18	3 57	8 25	3 54	8 31	3 42	8 48	3 48	8 47	4 02
27	8 06	3 57	8 15	4 07	8 18	3 58	8 25	3 55	8 31	3 43	8 48	3 48	8 47	4 03
28	8 06	3 58	8 15	4 08	8 18	3 59	8 25	3 56	8 31	3 44	8 48	3 49	8 47	4 04
29	8 06	3 59	8 16	4 09	8 18	4 00	8 25	3 57	8 31	3 45	8 48	3 50	8 47	4 05
30	8 06	3 49	8 16	4 10	8 18	4 01	8 25	3 58	8 31	3 46	8 48	3 51	8 47	4 06
31	8 06	4 00	8 16	4 11	8 18	4 02	8 25	3 59	8 31	3 47	8 48	3 52	8 47	4 07

JUPITER ♃

Day	R.A.	Dec. −	Transit	5° high.		R.A.	Dec. −	Transit	
				52°	56°				SATURN ♄
	h m	°	h m	h m	h m	h m	°	h m	
1	21 00	17·9	16 19	20 02	19 39	16 00	18·7	11 19	Saturn is
11	21 07	17·4	15 46	19 33	19 11	16 05	19·0	10 44	too close to
21	21 15	16·8	15 15	19 04	18 43	16 09	19·2	10 10	the Sun for
31	21 23	16·2	14 44	18 36	18 16	16 14	19·4	9 35	observation

Equatorial diameter of Jupiter 35″; of Saturn 15″. Diameters of Saturn's rings 34″ and 15″.

	URANUS ♅					NEPTUNE ♆			
Day	R.A.	Dec. −	Transit			R.A.	Dec. −	Transit	
	h m	° ′	h m			h m	° ′	h m	
1	17 06·2	22 55	12 25	Uranus is too close to the Sun for observation		18 10·5	22 21	13 29	Neptune is too close to the Sun for observation
11	17 08·8	22 59	11 48			18 12·1	22 21	12 51	
21	17 11·5	23 02	11 12			18 13·7	22 20	12 14	
31	17 14·0	23 05	10 35			18 15·4	22 20	11 36	

Diameter 4″   Diameter 2″

INTRODUCTION TO ASTRONOMICAL SECTION

GENERAL

The astronomical data are given in a form suitable for those who practise naked-eye astronomy or use small telescopes. No attempt has been made to replace the *Astronomical Almanac* for professional astronomers. Positions of the heavenly bodies are given only to the degree of accuracy required by amateur astronomers for setting telescopes, or for plotting on celestial globes or star atlases. Where intermediate positions are required, linear interpolation may be employed.

All data are, unless otherwise stated, for 0^h G.M.T., *i.e.* at the midnight at the beginning of the day named.

(*See notes on British Summer Time, p. 142*).

Definitions of the terms used cannot be given in an ephemeris of this nature. They must be sought in astronomical literature and text-books. Probably the best source for the amateur is Norton's *Star Atlas* (Gall and Inglis, 16th edition, 1973; £4·50), which contains an excellent introduction to observational astronomy, and the finest series of star maps yet produced for showing stars visible to the naked eye. Certain more extended ephemerides are available in the British Astronomical Association Handbook, an annual very popular among amateur astronomers. (Secretary: Burlington House, Piccadilly, London, W.1.)

A special feature has been made of the times when the various heavenly bodies are visible in the British Isles. Since two columns, calculated for latitudes 52° and 56°, are devoted to risings and settings, the range 50° to 58° can be covered by interpolation and extrapolation. The times given in these columns are G.M.T.'s for the meridian of Greenwich. An observer west of this meridian must add his longitude (in time) and vice versa.

In accordance with the usual convention in astronomy, + and − indicate respectively north and south latitudes or declinations.

FIRST PAGE OF EACH MONTH

The Zodiacal signs through which the Sun is passing during each month are illustrated. The date of transition from one sign to the next, to the nearest hour, is also given.

The FASTS AND FESTIVALS in black-letter type are those so given in the Prayer Book.

Under the heading PHENOMENA will be found particulars of the more important conjunctions of the Sun, Moon and planets with each other, and also the dates of eclipses and other astronomical phenomena of special interest.

The CONSTELLATIONS listed each month are those that are near the meridian at the beginning of the month at 22^h local mean time. Allowance must be made for Summer Time if necessary. The fact that any star crosses the meridian 4^m earlier each night or 2^h earlier each month may be used, in conjunction with the lists given each month, to find what constellations are favourably placed at any moment. The table preceding the list of constellations may be extended indefinitely at the rate just quoted.

Times of MINIMA OF ALGOL are approximate times of the middle of the period of diminished light.

The Principal PHASES OF THE MOON are the G.M.T.'s when the difference between the longitude of the Moon and that of the Sun is 0°, 90°, 180° or 270°. The times of perigee and apogee are those when the Moon is nearest to, and farthest from, the Earth, respectively. The nodes or points of intersection of the Moon's orbit and the ecliptic make a complete retrograde circuit of the ecliptic in about 19 years. From a knowledge of the longitude of the ascending node and the inclination, whose value does not vary much from 5°, the path of the Moon among the stars may be plotted on a celestial globe or star atlas.

The MONTHLY NOTES are self-explanatory.

SECOND PAGE OF EACH MONTH

The Sun's semi-diameter, in arc, is given once a month.

The right ascension given is that of the true Sun. The right ascension of the mean Sun is obtained by applying the equation of time, with the sign given, to the right ascension of the true Sun, or, more easily, by applying 12^h to the column Sidereal Time. The direction in which the equation of time has to be applied in different problems is a frequent source of confusion and error. Apparent Solar Time is equal to the Mean Solar Time plus the Equation of Time. For example at noon on Aug. 8 the Equation of Time is $-5^m\ 36^s$ and thus at 12^h Mean Time on that day the Apparent Time is $12^h - 5^m\ 36^s = 11^h\ 54^m\ 24^s$.

The Greenwich Sidereal Time at 0^h and the Transit of the First Point of Aries (which is really the mean time when the sidereal time is 0^h) are used for converting mean time to sidereal time and vice versa.

The G.M.T. of transit of the Sun at Greenwich may also be taken as the L.M.T. of transit in any longitude. It is independent of latitude. The G.M.T. of transit in any longitude is obtained by adding the longitude to the time given if west, and vice versa.

The legal importance of SUNRISE and SUNSET is that the Road Traffic Act, 1956, defines Lighting-up Time for vehicles as being from half an hour after sunset to half an hour before sunrise throughout the year. In all laws and regulations "sunset" refers to the local sunset, i.e. the time at which the Sun sets at the place in question. This common-sense interpretation has been upheld by legal tribunals. Thus the necessity for providing for different latitudes and longitudes, as already described, is evident.

The times of SUNRISE and SUNSET are those when the Sun's upper limb, as affected by refraction is on the true horizon of an observer at sea-level. Assuming the mean refraction to be 34′, and the Sun's semi-diameter to be 16′, the time given is that when the true zenith distance of the Sun's centre is $90° + 34′ + 16′$ or $90°\ 50′$, or, in other words, when the depression of the Sun's centre below the true horizon is 50′. The upper limb is then 34′ below the true horizon, but is brought there by refraction. It is true, of course, that an observer on a ship might see the Sun for a minute or so longer, because of the dip of the horizon, while another viewing the sunset over hills or mountains would record an earlier time. Nevertheless, the moment when the true zenith distance of the Sun's centre is 90° 50′ is a precise time dependent only on the latitude and longitude of the place, and independent of its altitude above sea-level, the contour of its horizon, the vagaries of refraction or the small seasonal change in the Sun's semi-diameter; this moment is suitable in every way as a definition of sunset (or sunrise) for all statutory purposes.

It is well known that light reaches us before sunrise and also continues to reach us for some time after sunset. The interval between darkness and sunrise or sunset and darkness is called twilight. Astronomically speaking, twilight is considered to begin or end when the Sun's centre is 18° below the horizon, as no light from the Sun can then reach the observer. As thus defined twilight may last several hours; in high latitudes at the summer solstice the depression of 18° is not reached, and twilight lasts from sunset to sunrise.

The need for some sub-division of twilight was met some years ago by dividing the gathering darkness into four steps.

(1) *Sunrise or Sunset*, defined as above.
(2) *Civil twilight*, which begins or ends when the Sun's centre is 6° below the horizon. This marks the time when operations requiring daylight may commence or must cease. In England it varies from about 30 to 60 minutes after sunset and the same interval before sunrise.
(3) *Nautical twilight*, which begins or ends when the Sun's centre is 12° below the horizon. This marks the time when it is, to all intent and purposes, completely dark.
(4) *Astronomical twilight*, which begins or ends when the Sun's centre is 18° below the horizon. This marks theoretical perfect darkness. It is of little practical importance, especially if nautical twilight is tabulated.

To assist observers the durations of civil, nautical and astronomical twilights are given at intervals of ten days. The beginning of a particular twilight is found by subtracting the duration from the time of sunrise, while the end is found by adding the duration to the time of sunset. Thus the beginning of astronomical twilight in latitude 52°, on the Greenwich meridian, on March 11 is found as 06ʰ 25ᵐ − 113ᵐ = 04ʰ 32ᵐ and similarly the end of civil twilight as 17ʰ 58ᵐ + 34ᵐ = 18ʰ 32ᵐ.

The letters T.A.N. are printed when twilight lasts all night.

Lighting-up time is a crude attempt to approximate to civil twilight over the British Isles.

Under the heading ASTRONOMICAL NOTES will be found notes describing the position and visibility of all the planets and also of other phenomena; these are intended to guide naked-eye observers, or those using small telescopes.

THIRD PAGE OF EACH MONTH

The Moon moves so rapidly among the stars that its position is given only to the degree of accuracy that permits linear interpolation. The right ascension and declination are geocentric, i.e. for an imaginary observer at the centre of the Earth. To an observer on the surface of the Earth the position is always different, as the altitude is always less on account of parallax which may reach 1°.

The lunar terminator is the line separating the bright from the dark part of the Moon's disk. Apart from irregularities of the lunar surface, the terminator is elliptical, because it is a circle seen in projection. It becomes the full circle forming the limb, or edge, of the Moon at New and Full Moon. The selenographic longitude of the terminator is measured from the mean centre of the visible disk, which may differ from the visible centre by as much as 8°, because of libration.

Instead of the longitude of the terminator the Sun's selenographic colongitude is tabulated. It is numerically equal to the selenographic longitude of the morning terminator, measured eastward from the mean centre of the disk. Thus its value is approximately 270° at New Moon, 360° at First Quarter, 90° at Full Moon and 180° at Last Quarter.

The Position Angle of the Bright Limb is the position angle of the midpoint of the illuminated limb, measured eastward from the north point on the disk. The column PHASE shows the percentage of the area of the Moon's disk illuminated; this is also the illuminated percentage of the diameter at right angles to the line of cusps. The terminator is a semi-ellipse whose major axis is the line of cusps, and whose semi-minor axis is determined by the tabulated percentage; from New Moon to Full Moon the east limb is dark, and vice versa.

The times given as moonrise and moonset are those when the upper limb of the Moon is on the horizon of an observer at sea-level. The Sun's horizontal parallax is about 9″, and is negligible when considering sunrise and sunset, but that of the Moon averages about 57′. Hence the computed time represents the moment when the true zenith distance of the Moon is 90° 50′ (as for the Sun) minus the horizontal parallax. The time required for the Sun or Moon to rise or set is about four minutes (except in high latitudes).

The tables have been constructed for the meridian of Greenwich, and for latitudes 52° and 56°. They give Greenwich Mean Time (G.M.T.) throughout the year. To obtain the G.M.T. of the phenomenon as seen from any other latitude and longitude, first interpolate or extrapolate for latitude by the usual rules of proportion. To the time thus found the longitude (expressed in time) is to be *added* if west (as it usually is in Great Britain) or *subtracted* if east. If the longitude is expressed in degrees and minutes of arc, it must be converted to time at the rate of 1° = 4ᵐ and 15′ = 1ᵐ.

The G.M.T. of transit of the Moon over the meridian of Greenwich is given: these times are independent of latitude, but must be corrected for longitude. For places in the British Isles it suffices to add the longitude if west, and vice versa. For more remote places a further correction is necessary because of the rapid movement of the Moon relative to the stars. The entire correction is conveniently determined by first finding the west longitude λ of the place. If the place is in west longitude, λ is the ordinary west longitude; if the place is in east longitude λ is the complement to 24^h (or 360°) of the longitude and will be greater than 12^h (or 180°). The correction then consists of two positive portions, namely λ and the fraction λ/24 (or λ°/360) multiplied by the difference between consecutive transits. Thus for Sydney, N.S.W., the longitude is 10^h 05^m east, so λ = 13^h 55^m and the fraction λ/24 is 0·58. The transit on the local date 1985 January 11 is found as follows:

	d	h	m
G.M.T. of transit at Greenwich . . . . . Jan	10	02	53
λ		13	55
0·58 × (3^h 45^m − 2^h 53^m)			30
G.M.T. of transit at Sydney		10	17	18
Corr. to N.S.W. Standard Time			10	00
Local standard time of transit		11	03	18

It is evident of course, that for any given place the quantities λ and the correction to local standard time may be combined permanently, being here 23^h 55^m.

Positions of Mercury are given for every third day, and those of Venus and Mars for every fifth day; they may be interpolated linearly. The column PHASE shows the illuminated percentage of the disk. In the case of the inner planets this approaches 100 at superior conjunction and 0 at inferior conjunction. When the phase is less than 50 the planet is crescent-shaped or horned; for greater phases it is gibbous. In the case of the exterior planet Mars, the phase approaches 100 at conjunction and opposition, and is a minimum at the quadratures.

Since the planets cannot be seen when on the horizon, the actual times of rising and setting are not given; instead, the time when the planet has an apparent altitude of 5° has been tabulated. If the time of transit is between 00^h and 12^h the time refers to an altitude of 5° above the eastern horizon: if between 12^h and 24^h, to the western horizon. The phenomenon tabulated is the one that occurs between sunset and sunrise; unimportant exceptions to these rules may occur because changes are not made during a month, except in the case of Mercury. The times given may be interpolated for latitude and corrected for longitude as in the case of the Sun and Moon.

The G.M.T. at which the planet transits the Greenwich meridian is also given. The times of transit are to be corrected to local meridians in the usual way, as already described.

PAGE FOUR OF EACH MONTH

The G.M.T.'s of Sunrise and Sunset may be used not only for these phenomena, but also for Lighting-up Times, which, under the Road Traffic Act, 1956, are from half an hour after sunset to half an hour before sunrise throughout the year.

The particulars for the four outer planets resemble those for the planets on Page III of each month, except that, under Uranus and Neptune, times when the planet is 10° high instead of 5° high are given;

this is because of the inferior brightness of these planets. The polar diameter of Jupiter is about 3″ less than the equatorial diameter, while that of Saturn is about 2″ less. The diameters given for the rings of Saturn are those of the major axis (in the plane of the planet's equator) and the minor axis respectively. The former has a small seasonal change due to the slightly varying distance of the Earth from Saturn, but the latter varies from zero when the Earth passes through the ring plane every 15 years to its maximum opening half-way between these periods. The rings were open at their widest extent in the middle of 1973.

TIME

From the earliest ages, the natural division of time into recurring periods of day and night has provided the practical time scale for the everyday activities of mankind. Indeed, if any alternative means of time measurement is adopted, it must be capable of adjustment so as to remain in general agreement with the natural time scale defined by the diurnal rotation of the Earth on its axis. Ideally the rotation should be measured against a fixed frame of reference; in practice it must be measured against the background provided by the celestial bodies. If the Sun is chosen as the reference point, we obtain Apparent Solar Time, which is the time indicated by a sundial. It is not a uniform time, but is subject to variations which amount to as much as a quarter of an hour in each direction. Such wide variations cannot be tolerated in a practical time scale, and this has led to the concept of Mean Solar Time in which all the days are exactly the same length and equal to the average length of the Apparent Solar Day.

The positions of the stars in the sky are specified in relation to a fictitious reference point in the sky known as the First Point of Aries (or the Vernal Equinox). It is therefore convenient to adopt this same reference point when considering the rotation of the Earth against the background of the stars. The time scale so obtained is known as Apparent Sidereal Time.

Greenwich Mean Time

The daily rotation of the Earth on its axis causes the Sun and the other heavenly bodies to appear to cross the sky from East to West. It is convenient to represent this relative motion as if the Sun really performed a daily circuit around a fixed Earth. Noon in Apparent Solar Time may then be defined as the time at which the Sun transits across the observer's meridian. In Mean Solar Time, noon is similarly defined by the meridian transit of a fictitious Mean Sun moving uniformly in the sky with the same average speed as the true Sun. Mean Solar Time observed on the meridian of the transit circle telescope of the Royal Observatory at Greenwich is called Greenwich Mean Time (G.M.T.). The mean solar day is divided into 24 hours and, for astronomical and other scientific purposes, these are numbered 0 to 23, commencing at midnight. Civil time is usually reckoned in two periods of 12 hours, designated a.m. (before noon) and p.m. (after noon).

Universal Time

Before 1925 January 1 G.M.T. was reckoned in 24 hours commencing at noon: since that date it has been reckoned from midnight. In view of the risk of confusion in the use of the designation G.M.T. before and after 1925, the International Astronomical Union recommended in 1928 that astronomers should, for the present, employ the term Universal Time, U.T. (or Weltzeit, W.Z.) to denote G.M.T. measured from Greenwich Mean Midnight.

In precision work it has now become necessary to take account of small variations, hitherto negligible, in Universal Time. These arise from small irregularities in the rotation of the Earth. Observed astronomical time is designated U.T.0. Observed time corrected for the effects of the motion of the poles (giving rise to a "wandering" in longitude) is designated U.T.1. There is also a seasonal fluctuation in the rate of rotation of the Earth arising from meteorological causes, often called the annual fluctuation. U.T.1 corrected for this effect is designated U.T.2 and provides a time scale free from short-period fluctuations. It is still subject to small secular and irregular changes.

Apparent Solar Time

As has been mentioned, the time shown by a sundial is called Apparent Solar Time. It differs from Mean Solar Time by an amount known as the Equation of Time, which is the total effect of two causes which make the length of the apparent solar day non-uniform. One cause of variation is that the orbit of the Earth is not a circle, but an ellipse, having the Sun at one focus. As a consequence, the angular speed of the Earth in its orbit is not constant; it is greatest at the beginning of January when the Earth is nearest the Sun. The other cause is due to the obliquity of the ecliptic; the plane of the equator (which is at right-angles to the axis of rotation of the Earth) does not coincide with the ecliptic (the plane defined by the apparent annual motion of the Sun around the celestial sphere) but is inclined to it at an angle of 23° 26'. As a result, the apparent solar day is shorter than average at the equinoxes and longer at the solstices. From the combined effects of the components due to obliquity and eccentricity, the equation of time reaches its maximum values in February (−14 mins.) and early November (+16 mins.). It has a zero value on four dates during the year, and it is only on these dates (approx. April 15, June 14, Sept. 1, and Dec. 25) that a sundial shows Mean Solar Time.

Sidereal Time

A sidereal day is the duration of a complete rotation of the Earth with reference to the First Point of Aries. The term sidereal (or "star") time is perhaps a little misleading since the time scale so defined is not exactly the same as that which would be defined by successive transits of a selected star, as there is a small progressive motion between the stars and the First Point of Aries due to the precession of the Earth's axis. This makes the length of the sidereal day shorter than the true period of rotation by 0·008 seconds. Superimposed on this steady precessional motion are small oscillations called nutation, giving rise to fluctuations in apparent sidereal time amounting to as much as 1·2 seconds. It is therefore customary to employ Mean Sidereal Time, from which these fluctuations have been removed. The conversion of G.M.T. to Greenwich sidereal time (G.S.T.) may be performed by adding the value of the G.S.T. at 0^h on the day in question (page II of each month) to the G.M.T. converted to sidereal time using the table on p. 146.

Example. To find the G.S.T. at August $8^d\ 02^h\ 41^m\ 11^s$ G.M.T.

				h	m	s
G.S.T. at 0^h ..	..	..	..	21	05	47
G.M.T. ..	..	..	..	2	41	11
Acceleration for 2^h ..	..	..				20
,, ,, $41^m\ 11^s$ ..	..	..				7
Sum = G.S.T. = ..	..	..		23	47	25

If the observer is not on the Greenwich meridian then his longitude, measured positively westwards from Greenwich, must be subtracted from the G.S.T. to obtain Local Sidereal Time (L.S.T.). Thus, in the above example, an observer 5^h east of Greenwich, or 19^h west, would find his L.S.T. as $4^h\ 47^m\ 25^s$.

Ephemeris Time

In the study of the motions of the Sun, Moon and planets, observations taken over an extended period are used in the preparation of tables giving the apparent position of the body each day. A table of this sort is known as an ephemeris, and may be used in the comparison of current observations with tabulated positions. A detailed examination of the observations made over the past 300 years shows that the Sun, Moon and planets appear to depart from their predicted positions by amounts proportional to their mean motions. The only satisfactory explanation is that the time scale to which the observations were referred was not uniform as had been supposed. Since the time scale was based on the rotation of the Earth, it follows that this rotation is subject to irregularities. The fact that the discrepancies between the observed and ephemeris positions were proportional to the mean motions of the bodies made it possible to secure agreement by substituting a revised time scale and recomputing the ephemeris positions. The time scale which brings the ephemeris into agreement with the observations has been named Ephemeris Time (E.T.).

The new unit of time has been defined in terms of the apparent annual motion of the Sun. Thus the second is now defined in terms of the annual motion of the Earth in its orbit around the Sun (1/31556925·9747 of the Tropical Year for 1900 January $0^d\ 12^h$ E.T.) instead of in terms of the diurnal rotation of the Earth on its axis (1/86 400 of the Mean Solar Day). In many branches of scientific work other than astronomy there has been a demand for a unit of time that is invariable, and the second of Ephemeris time was adopted by the Comité International des Poids et Mésures in 1956. The length of the unit has been chosen to provide general agreement with U.T. throughout the 19th and 20th centuries. During 1985 the estimated difference E.T. − U.T. is 55 seconds. The precise determination of E.T. from astronomical observations is a lengthy process, as the accuracy with which a single observation of the Sun can be made is far less than that obtainable in, for instance, a comparison between clocks. It is therefore necessary to average the observations over an extended period. Largely on account of its faster motion, the position of the Moon may be observed with greater accuracy, and a close approximation to Ephemeris Time may be obtained by comparing observations of the moon with its ephemeris position. Even in this case, however, the requisite standard of accuracy can only be achieved by averaging over a number of years.

Atomic Time

The fundamental standards of time and frequency must be defined in terms of a periodic motion adequately uniform, enduring and susceptible of measurement. This has led in the past to the adoption of standards based on the observed motions in the Solar System. Recent progress has made it possible to consider the use of other natural standards, such as atomic or molecular oscillations. The oscillations so far employed are not in fact continuous periodic motions such as the revolution of the electrons in their orbits around the nuclei. The continuous oscillations are generated in an electrical circuit, the frequency of which is then compared or brought into coincidence with the frequency characteristic of the absorption or emission by the atoms or molecules when they change between two selected energy levels. At the National Physical Laboratory regular comparisons have been made since the middle of 1955 between quartz clocks of high stability and a frequency defined by atoms of caesium. The standard has proved of great value in the precise calibration of frequencies and time intervals: it has also been possible to build up a scale of "atomic time" by using continuously-running quartz clocks calibrated in terms of the caesium frequency standard.

Radio Time Signals

The establishment of a uniform time system by the assessment of the performance of standard clocks in terms of astronomical observations is the work of a national observatory, and standard time is then made generally available by means of radio time signals. In the United Kingdom, the Royal Greenwich Observatory is responsible for the legal standard of time, and controls the "6-pips" radio signals emitted by the British Broadcasting Corporation. Signals by land line from the Observatory correct the Post Office Speaking Clock, TIM.

For survey and scientific purposes in which the highest accuracy is required, special signals are transmitted from the Post Office Radio Station at Rugby. The International Signals, consisting of a five-minute series of pips, one-tenth of a second long, with the pips at the minutes lengthened for identification, are radiated at 02.54–03.00, 08.54–09.00, 14.54–15.00, 20.54–21.00 from GBR (16 kHz) and associated H.F. transmitters. The seconds pulses superposed on the MSF standard frequency transmissions, which consists of five cycles of a 1,000 c.p.s. tone, are derived from the same master control at the transmitting

station, and are radiated for ten minutes in each quarter-hour on 2½, 5, and 10 MHz for 24 hours per day, and continuously on 60 kHz. The carrier frequencies of all the MSF transmissions, and of GBR, are closely controlled, and measured regularly at the National Physical Laboratory in terms of the caesium atomic resonance.

The new Coordinated Universal Time (U.T.C.) system standard frequency emissions and radio time signals are broadcast on MSF, GBR, and by other national transmitters, eg. by WWV and WWVH in the U.S.A. in conformity with the International Atomic Time Scale in which the time intervals between pips correspond exactly to the seconds defined as follows: "The second is the duration of 9 192 631 770 periods of the radiation corresponding to the transition between the 2 hyperfine levels of the ground state of the caesium 133 atom."

As the rate of rotation of the Earth is variable the time signals will be adjusted by the introduction of a leap second when necessary in order that UTC shall not depart from UT by more than $0^s\cdot9$. For convenience it has been decided to introduce leap seconds, when necessary, on the last second of a month preferably on 31 Dec. and/or 30 June. In the case of a positive leap second $23^h 59^m 60^s$ will be followed one second later by $0^h 00^m 00^s$ of the first day of the month. In the case of a negative leap second (required if the Earth were to make a sudden change of rate and begin to gain relative to UTC) $23^h 59^m 58^s$ will be followed one second later by $0^h 00^m 00^s$ of the first day of the month.

From 1972 Jan. 1 the six pips on the BBC have consisted of 5 short pips from second 55 to second 59 followed by one lengthened pip, the start of which indicates the exact minute.

SUMMER TIME

In the United Kingdom, Summer Time, one hour in advance of G.M.T. will be kept between 01^h G.M.T. on the last Sunday in March and 01^h G.M.T. on the day following the fourth Saturday in October. Thus, in 1985, Summer Time will be in force between March 31 and October 27.

Variations from the standard time of some countries occurs during part of the year: they are decided annually and are usually referred to as Summer Time or Daylight Saving Time. These variations occur in:

The Commonwealth.—Parts of Australia; Bahamas; Canada; Channel Islands; Gibraltar; Hong Kong; New Zealand; Bermuda; Malta.

Foreign Countries.—Albania; Argentina; Austria; Brazil; Bulgaria; Canary Is.; Chile; parts of China; Corsica; Costa Rica; Cuba; Cyprus Ercan; Cyprus Larnaca; Czechoslovakia; Denmark; Dominican Republic; Egypt; Faroe; Finland; France; Germany; Greece; Guatemala; Haiti; Hungary; Iceland; Iraq; Israel; Italy; Libya; Macau; Madeira; Mexico; Mongolia; Morocco; Norway; Pescadores Is.; Poland; Portugal; Romania; Sicily; Sudan; Sweden; Switzerland; Syria; Taiwan; Turkey; Uruguay; parts of U.S.A.; U.S.S.R; Yugoslavia.

In the Dominican Republic, the Irish Republic, and Paraguay, the variation occurs in winter and is called Winter Time.

STANDARD TIME

In the year 1880 it was enacted by statute that the word "time", when it occurred in any legal document relating to Great Britain, was to be interpreted, unless otherwise specifically stated, as the Mean Time of the Greenwich meridian.* Since the year 1883 the system of Standard Time by Zones has been gradually accepted, and now almost throughout the world a Standard Time which differs from that of Greenwich by an integral number of hours, either fast or slow, is used.

The large territories of the United States, Canada and U.S.S.R. are divided into zones approximately $7\frac{1}{2}°$ on either side of central meridians. The important ones are given below; there are in addition zones from 5 to 13 hours fast in the U.S.S.R. centred at 60° E. to 180° E.

Central-European	Hungary, Switzerland, Italy, Czechoslovakia, Yugoslavia, Albania, Tunisia, Nigeria, Malta, Sicily, Central African Republic, Cameroon Republic, Zaire, Angola, Spitsbergen, Benin, Corsica, Sardinia, Portugal, Niger, Irish Republic, Gibraltar.
Greenwich Time	The United Kingdom, Faroe, Channel Is., Morocco, Iceland, Mauritania, Sierra Leone, Ivory Coast, Ifni, Ghana, Principe I., St. Helena, Gambia, Canary Is., Ascension I., Tangier, São Tomé, Rio de Oro, Madeira, Mali, Senegal, Liberia, Guinea Bissau, Algeria.

Fast on Greenwich Time

12 hrs. F ...	Fiji, Kiribati Republic, New Zealand, Marshall Is., Caroline Is. (east of 160° E.), Nauru I.
$11\frac{1}{2}$,, F ...	Norfolk I.
11 ,, F ...	New Caledonia, Santa Cruz and Solomon Is., Ponape, Sakhalin, Republic of Vanuatu, Caroline Is. (150°E. to 160°E.).
10 ,, F ...	Victoria, N.S.W. (except Broken Hill Area), Queensland, Tasmania, Admiralty Islds., Australian Capital Territory, Mariana Islds., Caroline Is., Truk. (135°E. to 150°E.).
$9\frac{1}{2}$,, F ...	South Australia, Northern Territory of Australia, N.S.W. (Broken Hill Area).
9 ,, F ...	Japan, Schouten Islds., Kurile Islds., Manchuria, Korea, Irian Jaya, Caroline Is. (west of 135°E.).
$8\frac{1}{4}$,, F ...	Molucca Islds.
8 ,, F ...	China (coast), Hong Kong, Philippine Is., Macau, Timor, Western Australia, Sulawesi (Celebes), Kalimantan†, Taiwan, Pescadores Islds, Malaysia.
7 ,, F ...	Sumatra, Java, Christmas I. (Indian Ocean), Thailand, Cambodia, Laos, Vietnam.
$6\frac{1}{2}$,, F ...	Burma, Cocos-Keeling Islds.
6 ,, F ...	Bangladesh, Chagos Archipelago.
$5\frac{1}{2}$,, F ...	India, Sri Lanka, Laccadive Islds., Andaman and Nicobar Islds.
5 ,, F ...	Pakistan.
4 ,, F ...	Mauritius, Seychelles, Réunion, U.S.S.R., 40° E. to 52° 30′ E, United Arab Emirates.
$3\frac{1}{2}$,, F ...	Iran.
3 ,, F ...	U.S.S.R. west of 40° E., Iraq, Ethiopia, Yemen (Dem. Repub.), Socotra I., Somali Republic, Comoro Islds., Madagascar, Uganda, Kenya, Tanzania, Turkey, Cyprus, Bahrain.
2 ,, F ...	Greece, Bulgaria, Romania, Finland, Israel, Jordan, Egypt, Syria, Zimbabwe, Malawi, South Africa, Mozambique, Sudan, Burundi, Rwanda, Crete, Lebanon, Libya, Zambia, Botswana, Lesotho.
E. European	
1 hr. F ...	Sweden, Norway, Denmark, Netherlands, Belgium, Germany, France, Luxemburg, Spain, Monaco, Balearic Islds., Poland, Austria.

Slow on Greenwich time

1 hr. S ...	Azores, Cape Verde Is.
2 hrs. S ...	Fernando Noronha I., South Georgia.
3 ,, S ...	Greenland (excluding Thule), Eastern Brazil, Argentina, Uruguay, French Guiana, Guyana.
$3\frac{1}{2}$,, S ...	Newfoundland, Suriname.
4 ,, S ...	Canada east of 68° W., Greenland (Thule Area), Puerto Rico, Lesser Antilles, Central Brazil, Falkland Islds., Paraguay, Bermuda, Bolivia, Chile, Curaçao I., Venezuela, Labrador, Dominican Republic.
Atlantic	
5 hrs. S ...	Canada from 68° W. to 85° W. (north) or 90° W. (south), Eastern States of U.S.A., Jamaica, Bahama Islds., Haiti, Peru, Panama, W. Brazil, Colombia, Cayman Is., Ecuador, Cuba.
Eastern	
6 hrs. S ...	Central parts of U.S.A., Canada from 85° W. to 102° W., Costa Rica, Salvador, Honduras, part of Mexico, Guatemala, Nicaragua.
Central	
7 hrs. S ...	Canada from 102° W. to 120° W., Mountain States of U.S.A., part of Mexico.
Mountain	
8 hrs. S ...	Canada west of 120° W., Alaska (southeast coast), Western States of U.S.A., part of Mexico, Yukon (east of 138° W.).
Pacific	
9 hrs. S ...	Alaska E. of W. 169°·5, Yukon (west of 138° W.).
10 ,, S ...	Low Archipelago, Austral and Society Islds., Hawaii, Fanning I., Christmas Islds. (Pacific Ocean), Aleutian Islds. (W. of W. 169°·5).
11 ,, S ...	Alaska (west coast), Samoa, Midway Islds.

In the Tonga Islands the time $13h$ fast and in Chatham Is. $12h\ 45m$ fast on Greenwich is used, as the Date line is to the East of them.

THE DATE OR CALENDAR LINE

The line where the change of date occurs is a modification of the 180th meridian, and is drawn so as to include islands of any one group on the same side of the line, or for political reasons. It is indicated by joining up the following nine points:

Lat.	Long.	Lat.	Long.	Lat.	Long.
60° S.	180°	15° S.	$172\frac{1}{2}°$ W.	53° N.	170° E.
51° S.	180°	5° S.	180°	$65\frac{1}{4}°$ N.	169° W.
45° S.	$172\frac{1}{2}°$ W.	48° N.	180°	75° N.	180°

---

* Summer Time is the "legal" time during the period in which its use is ordained. † *Formerly* Indonesian Borneo.

RISING AND SETTING TIMES

Table 1. Hour Angle

Dec.	Latitude and Declination of Opposite Signs						0°	Latitude and Declination of Same Signs					
	50°	45°	40°	30°	20°	10°	0°	10°	20°	30°	40°	45°	50°
°	h m	h m	h m	h m	h m	h m	h m	h m	h m	h m	h m	h m	h m
0	6 00	6 00	6 00	6 00	6 00	6 00	6 00	6 00	6 00	6 00	6 00	6 00	6 00
1	5 55	5 56	5 57	5 58	5 59	5 59	6 00	6 01	6 01	6 02	6 03	6 04	6 05
2	5 50	5 52	5 53	5 55	5 57	5 58	6 00	6 02	6 03	6 05	6 07	6 08	6 10
3	5 45	5 48	5 50	5 53	5 56	5 58	6 00	6 02	6 04	6 07	6 10	6 12	6 15
4	5 40	5 44	5 46	5 51	5 54	5 57	6 00	6 03	6 06	6 09	6 14	6 16	6 20
5	5 36	5 40	5 43	5 48	5 52	5 56	6 00	6 04	6 08	6 12	6 17	6 20	6 24
6	5 31	5 36	5 39	5 46	5 51	5 56	6 00	6 04	6 09	6 14	6 21	6 24	6 29
7	5 26	5 32	5 36	5 44	5 50	5 55	6 00	6 05	6 10	6 16	6 24	6 28	6 34
8	5 21	5 27	5 33	5 41	5 48	5 54	6 00	6 06	6 12	6 19	6 27	6 33	6 39
9	5 16	5 23	5 29	5 39	5 47	5 53	6 00	6 07	6 13	6 21	6 31	6 37	6 44
10	5 11	5 19	5 26	5 37	5 45	5 53	6 00	6 07	6 15	6 23	6 34	6 41	6 49
11	5 06	5 15	5 22	5 34	5 44	5 52	6 00	6 08	6 16	6 26	6 38	6 45	6 54
12	5 01	5 11	5 19	5 32	5 42	5 51	6 00	6 09	6 18	6 28	6 41	6 49	6 59
13	4 56	5 06	5 15	5 29	5 40	5 51	6 00	6 09	6 20	6 31	6 45	6 54	7 04
14	4 51	5 02	5 12	5 27	5 39	5 50	6 00	6 10	6 21	6 33	6 48	6 58	7 09
15	4 46	4 58	5 08	5 24	5 38	5 49	6 00	6 11	6 22	6 36	6 52	7 02	7 14
16	4 40	4 53	5 04	5 22	5 36	5 48	6 00	6 12	6 24	6 38	6 56	7 07	7 20
17	4 35	4 49	5 00	5 19	5 35	5 48	6 00	6 12	6 25	6 41	7 00	7 11	7 25
18	4 29	4 44	4 57	5 17	5 33	5 47	6 00	6 13	6 27	6 43	7 03	7 16	7 31
19	4 23	4 39	4 53	5 14	5 31	5 46	6 00	6 14	6 29	6 46	7 07	7 21	7 37
20	4 17	4 35	4 49	5 11	5 30	5 45	6 00	6 15	6 30	6 49	7 11	7 25	7 43
21	4 11	4 30	4 44	5 09	5 28	5 44	6 00	6 16	6 32	6 51	7 16	7 30	7 49
22	4 04	4 25	4 40	5 06	5 26	5 44	6 00	6 16	6 34	6 54	7 20	7 35	7 56
23	3 58	4 19	4 36	5 03	5 24	5 43	6 00	6 17	6 36	6 57	7 24	7 41	8 02
24	3 52	4 14	4 32	5 00	5 23	5 42	6 00	6 18	6 37	7 00	7 28	7 46	8 08
25	3 45	4 09	4 28	4 58	5 21	5 41	6 00	6 19	6 39	7 02	7 32	7 51	8 15
26	3 38	4 03	4 24	4 55	5 19	5 40	6 00	6 20	6 41	7 05	7 36	7 57	8 22
27	3 30	3 57	4 19	4 52	5 17	5 39	6 00	6 21	6 43	7 08	7 41	8 03	8 30
28	3 23	3 51	4 14	4 48	5 15	5 38	6 00	6 22	6 45	7 12	7 46	8 09	8 37
29	3 15	3 45	4 09	4 45	5 14	5 38	6 00	6 22	6 46	7 15	7 51	8 15	8 45

SUNRISE AND SUNSET

The local mean time of sunrise or sunset (as defined on page 138) may be found by determining the appropriate hour angle from the table above and applying it to the time of transit given in the ephemeris for each month. The hour angle is negative for sunrise and positive for sunset. A small correction to the hour angle, which always has the effect of increasing it numerically, is necessary to allow for the Sun's semi-diameter (16′) and for refraction (34′). This correction may be obtained from Table 2. The resulting local mean time may be converted into the standard time of the country by taking the difference between the longitude of the standard meridian of the country and that of the place, and adding it to the local mean time if the place is west of the standard meridian, and subtracting it if the place is east of the standard meridian.

Example.—Required the N.Z. Mean Time (12ʰ fast on G.M.T.) of sunset on May 24 at Auckland. The latitude is 36° 50′ south (or minus) and the longitude 11ʰ 39ᵐ east. Taking the declination as +20°·7, we find

	h	m
Tabular entry for 30° Lat. and Dec. 20°, opposite signs	+	5 11
Proportional part for 6° 50′ of Lat.	−	15
Proportional part for 0°·7 of Dec.	−	3
Correction (Table 2)	+	6
Hour angle		4 59
Sun transits		11 57
Longitudinal correction	+	21
N.Z. Mean Time		17 17

Table 2. Correction for Refraction and Semi-Diameter

Latitude	Declination			
	0°	10°	20°	29°
°	m	m	m	m
0	4	4	4	5
20	4	4	5	5
30	5	5	5	6
40	5	6	6	7
50	6	6	7	9

MOONRISE AND MOONSET

It is possible to calculate the times of moonrise and moonset using Table 1 though the method is more complicated because the apparent motion of the Moon is much more rapid than that of the Sun.

The parallax of the Moon, about 57′, is near to the sum of the semi-diameter and refraction but has the opposite effect on these times. It is thus convenient to neglect all three quantities in the method outlined below.

Table 3. Longitude Correction

A \ X	40^m	45^m	50^m	55^m	60^m	65^m	70^m
h	m	m	m	m	m	m	m
1	2	2	2	2	3	3	3
2	3	4	4	5	5	5	6
3	5	6	6	7	8	8	9
4	7	8	8	9	10	11	12
5	8	9	10	11	13	14	15
6	10	11	13	14	15	16	18
7	12	13	15	16	18	19	20
8	13	15	17	18	20	22	23
9	15	17	19	21	23	24	26
10	17	19	21	23	25	27	29
11	18	21	23	25	28	30	32
12	20	23	25	28	30	33	35
13	22	24	27	30	33	35	38
14	23	26	29	32	35	38	41
15	25	28	31	34	38	41	44
16	27	30	33	37	40	43	47
17	28	32	35	39	43	46	50
18	30	34	38	41	45	49	53
19	32	36	40	44	48	51	55
20	33	38	42	46	50	54	58
21	35	39	44	48	53	57	61
22	37	41	46	50	55	60	64
23	38	43	48	53	58	62	67
24	40	45	50	55	60	65	70

Method

1. With arguments φ, δ_0 enter Table 1 on p. 144 to determine h_0 where h_0 is negative for moonrise and positive for moonset.

2. Form approximate times from
$$t_R = T_0 + \lambda + h_0$$
$$t_S = T_0 + \lambda + h_0$$

3. Determine δ_R, δ_S for times t_R, t_S respectively.

4. Re-enter Table 1 on p. 144 with—
   (a) arguments φ, δ_R to determine h_R
   (b) arguments φ, δ_S to determine h_S

5. Form $t_R = T_0 + \lambda + h_R + AX$
   $$t_S = T_0 + \lambda + h_S + AX$$

   where $A = (\lambda + h)$

   and $\begin{aligned} X &= (T_0 - T_{-1}) \quad \text{if } (\lambda + h) \text{ is negative} \\ X &= (T_1 - T_0) \quad \text{if } (\lambda + h) \text{ is positive} \end{aligned}$

   AX is the respondent in Table 3.

Example.—To find the times of moonrise and moonset at Vancouver ($\varphi = +49°$, $\lambda = +8^h\ 12^m$) on 1985 January 10. The starting data (from p. 128) are

$$\begin{array}{ll} & \text{h\quad m} \\ T_{-1} = & 1\quad 59 \\ T_0 = & 2\quad 53 \\ T_1 = & 3\quad 45 \\ \delta = & +17° \end{array}$$

1. $h_0 = 4^h\ 38^m$
2. Approximate values
$$\begin{aligned} t_R &= 10^d\ 02^h\ 53^m + 8^h\ 12^m + (-4^h\ 38^m) \\ &= 10^d\ 06^h\ 27^m \\ t_S &= 10^d\ 02^h\ 53^m + 8^h\ 12^m + (+4^h\ 38^m) \\ &= 10^d\ 15^h\ 43^m \end{aligned}$$
3. $\delta_R = +15°\cdot7$
   $\delta_S = +13°\cdot7$
4. $h_R = -4^h\ 45^m$
   $h_S = +4^h\ 55^m$
5. $t_R = 10^d\ 02^h\ 53^m + 8^h\ 12^m + (-4^h\ 45^m) + 8^m$
   $= 10^d\ 06^h\ 28^m$
   $t_S = 10^d\ 02^h\ 53^m + 8^h\ 12^m + (+4^h\ 55^m) + 28^m$
   $= 10^d\ 16^h\ 28^m$

To get the L.M.T. of the phenomenon the longitude is subtracted from the G.M.T. thus
Moonrise $= 10^d\ 06^h\ 28^m - 8^h\ 12^m = 9^d\ 22^h\ 16^m$
Moonset $= 10^d\ 16^h\ 28^m - 8^h\ 12^m = 10^d\ 08^h\ 16^m$

Notation

φ = latitude of observer
λ = longitude of observer (measured positively towards the west)
T_{-1} = time of transit of Moon on previous day
T_0 = time of transit of Moon on day in question
T_1 = time of transit of Moon on following day
δ_0 = approximate declination of Moon
δ_R = declination of Moon at moonrise
δ_S = declination of Moon at moonset
h_0 = approximate hour angle of Moon
h_R = hour angle of Moon at moonrise
h_S = hour angle of Moon at moonset
t_R = time of moonrise
t_S = time of moonset

ASTRONOMICAL CONSTANTS

Solar Parallax	$8''\cdot794$
Precession for the year 1985	$50''\cdot275$
,, in R.A.	$3\cdot074$
,, in Declination	$20''\cdot040$
Constant of Nutation	$9''\cdot211$
Constant of Aberration	$20''\cdot496$
Mean Obliquity of Ecliptic (1985)	$23°\ 26'\ 28''$
Moon's Equatorial Hor. Parallax	$57'\ 02''\cdot70$
Velocity of Light *in vacuper sec*	$299792\cdot5$ km.
Solar motion *per sec*	$20\cdot0$ km.
Equatorial radius of the Earth	$6378\cdot140$ km.
Polar radius of the Earth	$6356\cdot755$ km.

North Galactic Pole {R.A. $12^h\ 49^m$ (1950·0).
(I.A.U. *Standard*). {Dec. 27°·4 N.
Solar Apex .... R.A. $18^h\ 06^m$ Dec. $+30°$
Length of Year ... Tropical .... $365\cdot24220$

(*In Mean Solar Days*)		
	Sidereal	$365\cdot25636$
	Anomalistic	$365\cdot25964$
	(*Perihelion to Perihelion*)	
	Eclipse	$346\cdot6200$

		d h m s
Length of Month	New Moon to New	29 12 44 02·9
(*Mean Values*)	Sidereal	27 07 43 11·5
	Anomalistic	27 13 18 33·2
	(*Perigee to Perigee*)	

MEAN AND SIDEREAL TIME

	Acceleration							Retardation					MEAN REFRACTION	
h	m s	h	m s	m s	s		h	m s	h	m s	m s	s	Alt. Ref.	Alt. Ref.
1	0 10	13	2 08	0 00	0		1	0 10	13	2 08	0 00	0		
2	0 20	14	2 18	3 02	1		2	0 20	14	2 18	3 03	1	1 20 — 21	4 30 — 10
3	0 30	15	2 28	9 07	2		3	0 29	15	2 27	9 09	2	1 30 — 20	5 06 — 9
				15 13	3						15 15	3	1 41 — 19	5 50 — 8
4	0 39	16	2 38	21 18	4		4	0 39	16	2 37	21 21	4	1 52 — 18	6 44 — 7
5	0 49	17	2 48	27 23	5		5	0 49	17	2 47	27 28	5	2 05 — 17	7 54 — 6
6	0 59	18	2 57	33 28			6	0 59	18	2 57	33 34		2 19 — 16	9 27 — 5
				39 34	6						39 40	6	2 35 — 15	11 39 — 4
7	1 09	19	3 07	45 39	7		7	1 09	19	3 07	45 46	7	2 52 — 14	15 00 — 3
8	1 19	20	3 17	51 44	8		8	1 19	20	3 17	51 53	8	3 12 — 13	20 42 — 2
9	1 29	21	3 27	57 49	9		9	1 28	21	3 26	57 59	9	3 34 — 12	32 20 — 1
10	1 39	22	3 37	60 00	10		10	1 38	22	3 36	60 00	10	4 00 — 11	62 17 — 0
11	1 48	23	3 47				11	1 48	23	3 46			4 30	90 00
12	1 58	24	3 57				12	1 58	24	3 56				

The length of a sidereal day in mean time is $23^h 56^m 04^s\cdot09$. Hence 1^h M.T. $= 1^h + 9^s\cdot86$ S.T. and 1^h S.T. $= 1^h - 9^s\cdot83$ M.T.

To convert an interval of mean time to the corresponding interval of sidereal time, enter the acceleration table with the given mean time (taking the hours and the minutes and seconds separately) and add the acceleration obtained to the given mean time. To convert an interval of sidereal time to the corresponding interval of mean time, take out the retardation for the given sidereal time and subtract.

The columns for the minutes and seconds of the argument are in the form known as Critical Tables. To use these tables, find in the appropriate left-hand column the two entries between which the given number of minutes and seconds lies; the quantity in the right-hand column between these two entries is the required acceleration or retardation. Thus the acceleration for $11^m 26^s$ (which lies between the entries $9^m 07^s$ and $15^m 13^s$) is 2^s. If the given number of minutes and seconds is a tabular entry, the required acceleration or retardation is the entry in the right-hand column *above* the given tabular entry; e.g. the retardation for $45^m 46^s$ is 7^s.

Example.—Convert $14^h 27^m 35^s$ from S.T. to M.T.

	h	m	s
Given S.T.	14	27	35
Retardation for 14^h		2	18
Retardation for $27^m 35^s$			5
Corresponding M.T.	14	25	12

For further explanation, see p. 141.
The refraction table is also in the form of a critical table.

THE SUMMER TIME ACTS

In 1916 an Act ordained that during a defined period of that year the legal time for general purposes in Great Britain should be one hour in advance of Greenwich Mean Time. The practice was stabilized (until the war) by the *Summer Time Acts*, 1922 to 1925, which enacted that "For the purposes of this Act, the period of summer time shall be taken to be the period beginning at two o'clock, Greenwich Mean Time, in the morning of the next day following the third Saturday in April, or, if that day is Easter Day, the day next following the second Saturday in April and ending at two o'clock, Greenwich Mean Time, in the morning of the day next following the first Saturday in October."

During the Second World War the duration of Summer Time was extended and in the years 1941–45 and in 1947, Double Summer Time (2 hrs. in advance of Greenwich Mean Time) was in force. Summer Time was extended in each year from 1948 to 1952 and again in 1961–1964, by Order in Council.

The duration of Summer Time during the last few years is given in the following table.

1960 Apr. 10—Oct. 2	1974 Mar. 17—Oct. 27
1961 Mar. 26—Oct. 29	1975 Mar. 16—Oct. 26
1962 Mar. 25—Oct. 28	1976 Mar. 21—Oct. 24
1963 Mar. 31—Oct. 27	1977 Mar. 20—Oct. 23
1964 Mar. 22—Oct. 25	1978 Mar. 19—Oct. 29
1965 Mar. 21—Oct. 24	1979 Mar. 18—Oct. 28
1966 Mar. 20—Oct. 23	1980 Mar. 16—Oct. 26
1967 Mar. 19—Oct. 29	1981 Mar. 29—Oct. 25
1968 Feb. 18—Oct. 27	1982 Mar. 28—Oct. 24
1972 Mar. 19—Oct. 29	1983 Mar. 27—Oct. 23
1973 Mar. 18—Oct. 28	1984 Mar. 25—Oct. 28

(British Standard Time, also one hour ahead of G.M.T., was kept between 1968 Oct. 27–1971 Oct. 31.)
In 1985 Summer Time will be in force from March 31 to October 27.

ASTRONOMERS ROYAL

John Flamsteed, first Astronomer Royal	1675–1719
Edmund Halley	1720–1742
James Bradley	1742–1762
Nathaniel Bliss	1762–1764
Nevil Maskelyne	1765–1811
John Pond	1811–1835
Sir George Biddell Airy	1835–1881
Sir William Henry Mahoney Christie	1881–1910
Sir Frank Watson Dyson	1910–1933
Sir Harold Spencer Jones	1933–1955
Sir Richard van der Riet Woolley	1955–1971
Sir Martin Ryle	1972–1982
Prof. F. Graham Smith	1982–

PHENOMENA OF JUPITER'S SATELLITES, 1985

G.M.T. Sat. Phen.

March

d	h	m		
15	05	54	IV	Sh.E.
24	05	40	I	Ec.D.
25	05	07	I	Sh.E.

April

d	h	m		
1	04	45	I	Sh.I.
3	04	48	II	Ec.D.
18	04	20	III	Ec.R.
26	04	30	IV	Ec.R.

May

d	h	m		
2	04	06	I	Ec.D.
3	03	32	I	Sh.E.
10	03	09	I	Sh.I.
13	02	48	III	Sh.I.
14	02	09	II	Sh.I.
18	02	22	I	Ec.D.
19	01	47	I	Sh.E.
21	01	53	IV	Sh.I.
26	01	25	I	Sh.I.
26	03	41	I	Sh.E.
30	01	25	II	Ec.D.

June

d	h	m		
2	03	18	I	Sh.I.
7	00	40	IV	Sh.E.
8	02	01	II	Sh.E.
10	02	31	I	Ec.D.
11	01	57	I	Sh.E.
15	01	46	II	Sh.E.
18	01	34	I	Sh.I.
18	02	19	III	Sh.E.
25	02	43	III	Sh.I.
25	03	28	I	Sh.I.
26	00	47	I	Ec.D.
27	00	14	I	Sh.E.

July

d	h	m		
1	01	05	II	Ec.D.
2	00	12	IV	Ec.D.
2	23	03	II	Sh.E.
3	02	41	I	Ec.D.
3	23	50	I	Sh.I.
4	02	08	I	Sh.E.
8	03	42	II	Ec.D.
9	22	46	II	Sh.I.
10	01	37	II	Sh.E.
11	01	44	I	Sh.I.
11	23	03	I	Ec.D.
12	22	31	I	Sh.E.

G.M.T. Sat. Phen.

July

d	h	m		
13	00	37	III	Ec.D.
17	01	21	II	Sh.I.
18	03	39	I	Sh.I.
19	00	57	I	Ec.D.
19	22	07	I	Sh.I.
20	00	25	I	Sh.E.
23	22	19	III	Sh.E.
24	03	55	II	Sh.I.
25	22	14	II	Ec.D.
26	02	51	I	Ec.D.
27	00	02	I	Sh.I.
27	02	20	IV	Sh.I.
27	02	20	I	Sh.E.
30	22	41	III	Sh.I.
31	02	19	III	Sh.E.

August

d	h	m		
2	00	52	II	Ec.D.
3	01	56	I	Sh.I.
3	04	15	I	Sh.E.
3	22	39	I	Ec.D.
3	23	14	I	Ec.D.
4	22	44	I	Sh.E.
7	02	42	III	Sh.I.
10	03	51	I	Sh.I.
10	22	22	II	Sh.I.
11	01	14	II	Sh.E.
11	03	26	I	Ec.R.
11	22	20	I	Sh.I.
12	00	38	I	Sh.E.
12	20	29	IV	Sh.I.
12	21	55	I	Ec.R.
13	01	21	IV	Sh.E.
18	00	15	III	Ec.R.
18	00	57	II	Sh.I.
19	00	15	I	Sh.I.
19	02	34	I	Sh.E.
19	22	20	II	Ec.R.
19	23	49	I	Ec.R.
20	21	02	I	Sh.E.
26	02	10	I	Sh.I.
27	00	58	II	Sh.E.
27	01	44	I	Ec.R.
27	20	39	I	Sh.I.
27	22	58	I	Sh.E.
28	19	41	II	Sh.E.
28	20	12	I	Ec.R.

G.M.T. Sat. Phen.

September

d	h	m		
3	22	35	I	Sh.I.
4	00	53	I	Sh.E.
4	19	25	II	Sh.I.
4	22	07	I	Ec.R.
4	22	16	II	Sh.E.
4	22	23	III	Sh.E.
5	19	22	I	Sh.E.
7	00	43	IV	Ec.D.
11	00	30	I	Sh.I.
11	22	00	I	Sh.I.
11	22	46	III	Sh.I.
12	00	02	I	Ec.R.
12	00	51	II	Sh.E.
12	21	17	I	Sh.E.
13	19	34	II	Ec.R.
19	00	35	II	Sh.I.
19	20	55	I	Sh.I.
19	23	12	I	Sh.E.
20	20	26	I	Ec.R.
20	22	13	II	Ec.R.
22	20	19	III	Ec.R.
23	18	53	IV	Ec.D.
23	23	43	IV	Ec.R.
26	22	50	I	Sh.I.
27	22	21	I	Ec.R.
28	19	37	I	Sh.E.
29	19	19	II	Sh.E.
29	20	41	III	Ec.D.

October

d	h	m		
5	19	15	I	Sh.I.
5	21	32	I	Sh.E.
6	18	45	I	Ec.R.
6	19	04	II	Sh.I.
6	21	54	II	Sh.E.
10	18	29	III	Sh.E.
12	21	11	I	Sh.I.
12	23	28	I	Sh.E.
13	20	40	I	Ec.R.
13	21	39	II	Sh.I.
14	17	57	I	Sh.E.
15	19	27	II	Ec.R.
17	18	53	III	Sh.I.
17	22	30	III	Sh.E.
18	21	20	IV	Sh.I.
19	23	07	I	Sh.I.
20	22	35	I	Ec.R.

G.M.T. Sat. Phen.

October

d	h	m		
21	17	36	I	Sh.I.
21	19	53	I	Sh.E.
22	22	06	II	Ec.R.
24	22	55	III	Sh.I.
28	19	31	I	Sh.I.
28	21	48	I	Sh.E.
29	18	59	I	Ec.R.
31	19	00	II	Sh.E.

November

d	h	m		
4	20	23	IV	Sh.E.
4	20	27	III	Ec.R.
4	21	27	I	Sh.I.
5	20	54	I	Ec.R.
6	18	13	I	Sh.E.
7	18	45	II	Sh.I.
7	21	36	II	Sh.E.
11	20	48	III	Ec.D.
13	17	52	I	Sh.I.
13	20	09	I	Sh.E.
14	21	21	I	Sh.I.
16	19	19	II	Ec.R.
20	19	48	I	Sh.I.
21	19	14	I	Ec.R.
22	18	39	III	Sh.E.
23	21	57	II	Ec.R.
28	21	09	I	Ec.R.
29	18	29	I	Sh.E.
29	19	03	III	Sh.I.
29	19	39	IV	Ec.D.

December

d	h	m		
2	18	44	II	Sh.E.
6	18	08	I	Sh.I.
6	20	25	I	Sh.E.
7	17	34	I	Ec.R.
9	18	29	II	Sh.I.
14	19	29	I	Ec.R.
15	16	49	I	Sh.E.
16	18	36	IV	Ec.R.
17	16	56	III	Ec.D.
18	19	08	II	Ec.R.
22	18	45	I	Sh.E.
29	18	23	I	Sh.I.
30	17	48	I	Ec.R.

Jupiter's satellites transit across the disk from east to west, and pass behind the disk from west to east. The shadows that they cast also transit across the disk. With the exception at times of Satellite IV, the satellites also pass through the shadow of the planet, i.e. they are eclipsed. Just before opposition the satellite disappears in the shadow to the west of the planet, and reappears from occultation on the east limb. Immediately after opposition the satellite is occulted at the west limb, and reappears from eclipse to the east of the planet. At times approximately two to four months before and after opposition, both phases of eclipses of Satellite III may be seen. When Satellite IV is eclipsed, both phases may be seen.

The list of phenomena gives most of the eclipses and shadow transits visible in the British Isles under favourable conditions.

Ec. = Eclipse	R = Reappearance
Sh. = Shadow transit	I = Ingress
D = Disappearance	E = Egress

Owing to the inclination of the plane of the orbits of Jupiter's satellites to the direction of the Sun there are no phenomena of Satellite IV during the year.

CELESTIAL PHENOMENA FOR OBSERVATION IN 1985

ECLIPSES, 1985

There will be four eclipses during 1985, two of the Sun and two of the Moon. *Penumbral eclipses are not mentioned in this section as they are difficult to observe.*

1. A total eclipse of the Moon on May 4 is visible from Australasia, Indonesia, the Philippine Islands, Japan, Asia except the extreme northern and north-eastern parts, the Indian Ocean, the Southern Ocean, part of Antarctica, Africa, Europe except northern Scandinavia (but including the British Isles), the South Atlantic Ocean and the extreme eastern part of South America. The eclipse begins at $18^h 17^m$ and ends at $21^h 35^m$. Totality lasts from $19^h 22^m$ to $20^h 30^m$. As seen from the British Isles the Moon will rise partly or totally eclipsed (depending on the exact location of the observer).

2. A partial eclipse of the Sun on May 19 is visible from north-eastern Asia, Japan, the North Pacific Ocean, the northern part of North America, the arctic regions, Greenland, Iceland and the extreme north-west of Europe. The eclipse begins at $19^h 15^m$ and ends at $23^h 42^m$. At the time of maximum eclipse 0·84 of the Sun's diameter is obscured. It is not visible from the British Isles.

3. A total eclipse of the Moon on October 28 is visible from the extreme west of Alaska, the western part of the Pacific Ocean, Australasia, Indonesia, the Philippine Islands, Japan, Asia, the arctic regions, the Indian Ocean, Africa, Europe (including the British Isles), Iceland and the extreme east of Greenland. The eclipse begins at $15^h 55^m$ and ends at $19^h 29^m$. Totality lasts from $17^h 20^m$ to $18^h 04^m$. As seen from the British Isles the Moon will rise partly eclipsed, but before totality commences.

4. A total eclipse of the Sun on November 12. The path of totality begins in the South Pacific Ocean and ends in Victoria Land in Antarctica. The partial phase is visible from the South Pacific Ocean, the southern part of South America, the Southern Ocean and most of Antarctica. The eclipse begins at $12^h 09^m$ and ends at $16^h 12^m$; the total phase begins at $13^h 51^m$ and ends at $14^h 30^m$. The maximum duration of totality is $1^m 59^s$.

LUNAR OCCULTATIONS

Observations of the times of these occultations are made by both amateur and professional astronomers. Such observations are later analysed to yield accurate positions of the Moon: this is one method of determining the difference between ephemeris time and universal time.

Many of the observations made by amateurs are obtained with the use of a stop-watch which is compared with a time signal immediately after the observation. Thus an accuracy of about one-fifth of a second is obtainable, though the observer's personal equation may amount to one-third or one-half of a second.

The list on the opposite page includes most of the occultations visible under favourable conditions in the British Isles. No occultation is included unless the star is at least $10°$ above the horizon and the Sun sufficiently far below the horizon to permit the star to be seen with the naked eye or in a small telescope. The altitude limit is reduced from $10°$ to $2°$ for stars and planets brighter than magnitude 2·0 and such occultations are also predicted in daylight.

The column Phase shows whether a disappearance (1) or reappearance (2) is to be observed. The column headed "El. of Moon" gives the elongation of the Moon from the Sun, in degrees. The elongation increases from $0°$ at New Moon to $180°$ at Full Moon and on to $360°$ (or $0°$) at New Moon again. Times and position angles (P), reckoned from the north point in the direction north, east, south, west, are given for Greenwich (Lat. $51° 30'$, Long. $0°$) and Edinburgh (Lat. $56° 00'$, Long. $3° 12'$ west).

The coefficients a and b are the variations in the G.M.T. for each degree of longitude (positive to the west) and latitude (positive to the north) respectively: they enable approximate times (to within about 1^m generally) to be found for any point in the British Isles. If the point of observation is $\Delta\lambda$ degrees west and $\Delta\phi$ degrees north, the approximate time is found by adding $a.\Delta\lambda + b.\Delta\phi$ to the given G.M.T.

As an illustration the disappearance of Mars on April 22 at Liverpool will be found from both Greenwich and Edinburgh.

	Greenwich	Edinburgh
	°	°
Longitude	0·0	+3·2
Long. of Liverpool	+3·0	+3·0
$\Delta\lambda$	+3·0	−0·2
Latitude	+51·5	+56·0
Lat. of Liverpool	+53·4	+53·4
$\Delta\phi$	+1·9	−2·6
	h m	h m
G.M.T.	12 01·2	12 15·0
$a.\Delta\lambda$	−1·8	0·0
$b.\Delta\phi$	+5·5	−9·6
	12 04·9	12 05·4

If the occultation is given for one station but not the other, the reason for the suppression is given by the following code.

N = star not occulted.
A = star's altitude less than $10°$ ($2°$ for bright stars and planets).
S = Sun not sufficiently below the horizon.
G = occultation is of very short duration.

It will be noticed that in some cases the coefficients a and b are not given: this is because the occultation is so short that prediction for other places by means of these coefficients would not be reliable.

LUNAR OCCULTATIONS, 1985

Date		Z.C. No.	Mag.	Phase	El. of Moon	GREENWICH				EDINBURGH			
						U.T.	a	b	P	U.T.	a	b	P
					°	h m	m	m	°	h m	m	m	°
Jan.	4	631	5·6	D.D.	143	..				0 39·6	−0·8	−3·7	131
	4	634	5·3	D.D.	143	1 22·1	−0·6	−2·3	109	1 11·0	−0·7	−1·7	96
	4	657	5·4	D.D.	145	4 10·0	−0·0	−0·8	61	4 06·1	−0·2	−0·8	53
	4	656	4·4	D.D.	145	4 17·1	−0·3	−0·1	35	4 16·3	−0·5	0·3	24
	4	767	5·5	D.D.	153	21 35·9	−1·7	−0·1	99	21 32·6	−1·3	0·7	83
	9	1484	3·6	R.D.	218	24 05·3	−0·9	−1·5	336	23 51·4	..	..	3
	14	1962	5·2	R.D.	272	3 16·9	−1·8	3·0	244	3 22·8	−1·2	1·9	257
	16	2217	5·5	R.D.	299	5 08·8	−0·4	−0·1	325	A			
	27	219	5·1	D.D.	75	19 01·2	−1·2	0·1	58	18 59·4	−0·9	0·6	42
	31	716	6·2	D.D.	121	22 02·5	−1·4	−0·1	67	21 59·4	−1·2	0·6	51
Feb.	1	742	6·0	D.D.	124	A				3 47·8	0·1	−0·8	57
	1	867	6·9	D.D.	133	23 05·9	−1·0	−3·3	136	22 50·7	−1·1	−2·0	119
	2	877	6·6	D.D.	134	0 57·3	−0·5	−1·9	106	0 47·5	−0·7	−1·6	96
	11	2053	4·6	R.D.	254	..				2 21·0	..	..	233
	27	660	4·4	D.D.	89	22 20·2	−0·7	−1·0	70	22 14·2	−0·8	−0·6	58
	27	664	5·4	D.D.	90	23 05·0	−0·9	0·6	30	23 07·6	..	..	10
Mar.	1	822	5·9	D.D.	103	2 28·3	0·5	−1·4	105	2 23·4	0·4	−1·5	101
	2	1089	6·8	D.D.	123	19 52·4	−1·6	3·2	41	..			
	4	1251	5·9	D.D.	138	0 26·5	−1·7	0·0	55	0 22·6	..	..	44
	8	1866	5·9	R.D.	206	22 57·8	−0·8	0·6	292	22 57·9	−0·6	0·5	302
	9	1891	4·4	R.D.	210	5 08·3	−0·8	−1·6	296	4 58·9	−0·8	−1·4	297
	12	2290	2·5	D.B.	250	4 44·5	−1·5	−0·2	100	4 39·8	−1·3	0·0	99
	12	2290	2·5	R.D.	251	5 57·4	−1·3	−0·9	302	5 49·9	−1·1	−0·7	303
	30	1061	6·1	D.D.	94	0 29·0	0·6	−2·4	147	0 19·9	0·4	−2·4	142
Apr.	1	1334	7·0	D.D.	119	1 15·3	−0·3	−1·5	90	1 07·2	−0·4	−1·5	87
	1	1435	6·6	D.D.	129	20 02·9	..	..	42	..			
	1	1436	6·9	D.D.	130	20 45·4	..	..	55				
	22	MARS	1·7	D.D.	25	12 01·2	−0·6	2·9	26	12 15·0	0·1	3·7	7
	22	MARS	1·7	R.B.	25	13 10·9	−2·1	−0·1	277	13 01·5	−2·4	−1·1	298
	24	852	5·0	D.D.	51	20 49·6	−0·0	−2·0	111	20 40·5	−0·2	−1·9	103
	29	1514	6·1	D.D.	112	21 48·7	−1·0	−1·6	119	21 39·0	−1·0	−1·4	115
May	2	1866	5·9	D.D.	152	20 00·6	−1·0	0·4	110	S			
	3	1891	4·4	D.D.	155	2 08·8	−0·7	−1·6	105	1 59·4	−0·7	−1·5	105
	5	2290	2·5	D.B.	196	23 42·5	−1·8	1·2	68	23 42·5	−1·6	1·3	64
	6	2290	2·5	R.D.	197	0 30·6	−0·6	−0·7	340	0 26·3	−0·4	−0·5	342
	24	1251	5·9	D.D.	58	23 13·0	0·1	−1·0	62	23 08·1	−0·0	−1·2	60
Jun.	24	1684	7·0	D.D.	79	21 57·2	−0·3	−1·9	125	S			
	29	2290	2·5	D.D.	144	19 08·7	−1·5	1·4	74	A			
	29	2290	2·5	R.B.	144	20 00·3	−0·5	−0·4	335	19 57·6	−0·3	−0·2	339
	29	2305	5·9	D.D.	146	22 44·6	..	..	169	22 36·7	−0·7	−1·0	167
	29	2314	5·8	D.D.	146	23 48·7	−1·2	−1·4	137	23 39·6	−1·1	−1·1	135
July	25	2111	7·0	D.D.	102	21 02·9	−1·0	−1·5	140	S			
	27	2411	6·6	D.D.	128	21 49·8	..	..	35	A			
	28	2554	4·4	D.D.	141	20 37·3	−1·3	0·1	115	A			
Aug.	23	2371	4·9	D.D.	99	20 53·6	−1·1	−1·1	90	A			
Sep.	11	1251	5·9	R.D.	312	4 23·0	0·0	3·3	225	4 34·9	−0·2	2·3	245
	24	3102	6·9	D.D.	132	20 57·1	−1·2	0·5	45	20 56·1	−1·0	0·5	38
Nov.	4	1169	5·4	R.D.	252	S				6 31·4	−1·7	0·6	239
	5	1274	5·7	R.D.	261	2 00·5	−1·2	−0·5	320	1 50·9	..	..	346
	20	3428	5·2	D.D.	109	23 28·5	−0·8	−2·1	98	23 18·7	−0·6	−1·3	79
	30	1088	5·6	R.D.	217	20 23·3	..	..	328	..			
Dec.	24	525	6·4	D.D.	145	A				4 10·6	..	..	6

MEAN PLACES OF STARS, 1985.0

Name	Mag.	R.A.	Dec.	Spectrum
		h m	° ′	
α Andromedæ *Alpheratz*	2·1	0 07·6	+ 29 00	A0p
β Cassiopeiæ *Caph*	2·3	0 08·4	+ 59 04	F5
γ Pegasi *Algenib*	2·8	0 12·5	+ 15 06	B2
α Phœnicis	2·4	0 25·5	− 42 23	K0
α Cassiopeiæ *Schedar*	2·2	0 39·6	+ 56 27	K0
β Ceti *Diphda*	2·0	0 42·8	− 18 04	K0
γ Cassiopeiæ*	Var.	0 55·8	+ 60 38	B0p
β Andromedæ *Mirach*	2·1	1 08·9	+ 35 32	M0
δ Cassiopeiæ	2·7	1 24·8	+ 60 09	A5
α Eridani *Achernar*	0·5	1 37·2	− 57 19	B5
β Arietis *Sheratan*	2·6	1 53·8	+ 20 44	A5
γ Andromedæ *Almak*	2·3	2 03·0	+ 42 15	K0
α Arietis *Hamal*	2·0	2 06·3	+ 23 24	K2
α Ursæ Minoris *Polaris*	2·0	2 16·4	+ 89 12	F8
β Persei *Algol**	Var.	3 07·2	+ 40 54	B8
α Persei *Mirfak*	1·8	3 23·2	+ 49 49	F5
η Tauri *Alcyone*	2·9	3 46·6	+ 24 04	B5p
α Tauri *Aldebaran*	0·9	4 35·1	+ 16 29	K5
β Orionis *Rigel*	0·1	5 13·8	− 8 13	B8p
α Aurigæ *Capella*	0·1	5 15·6	+ 45 59	G0
γ Orionis *Bellatrix*	1·6	5 24·3	+ 6 20	B2
β Tauri *Elnath*	1·7	5 25·3	+ 28 36	B8
δ Orionis	2·2	5 31·2	− 0 19	B0
α Leporis	2·6	5 32·1	− 17 50	F0
ε Orionis	1·7	5 35·5	− 1 13	B0
ζ Orionis	1·8	5 40·1	− 1 57	B0
κ Orionis	2·1	5 47·0	− 9 40	B0
α Orionis *Betelgeuse**	Var.	5 54·4	+ 7 24	M0
β Aurigæ *Menkalinan*	1·9	5 58·4	+ 44 57	A0p
β Canis Majoris *Mirzam*	2·0	6 22·0	− 17 57	B1
α Carinæ *Canopus*	− 0·7	6 23·6	− 52 41	F0
γ Geminorum *Alhena*	1·9	6 36·8	+ 16 25	A0
α Canis Majoris *Sirius*	− 1·5	6 44·5	− 16 42	A0
ε Canis Majoris	1·5	6 58·0	− 28 57	B1
δ Canis Majoris	1·9	7 07·8	− 26 22	F8p
α Geminorum *Castor*	1·6	7 33·6	+ 31 55	A0
α Canis Minoris *Procyon*	0·4	7 38·5	+ 5 16	F5
β Geminorum *Pollux*	1·1	7 44·4	+ 28 04	K0
ζ Puppis	2·3	8 03·1	− 39 58	Od
γ Velorum	1·8	8 09·1	− 47 18	Oap
ε Carinæ	1·9	8 22·2	− 59 28	K0
δ Velorum	2·0	8 44·3	− 54 39	A0
λ Velorum *Suhail*	2·2	9 07·4	− 43 22	K5
β Carinæ	1·7	9 13·0	− 69 39	A0
ι Carinæ	2·2	9 16·7	− 59 13	F0
α Hydræ *Alphard*	2·0	9 26·8	− 8 36	K2
α Leonis *Regulus*	1·3	10 07·6	+ 12 02	B8
γ Leonis *Algeiba*	1·9	10 19·1	+ 19 55	K0
β Ursæ Majoris *Merak*	2·4	11 00·9	+ 56 28	A0
α Ursæ Majoris *Dubhe*	1·8	11 02·8	+ 61 50	K0

* γ Cassiopeiæ, 1984 mag. 2·6.   β Persei, mag. 2·2 to 3·2.
    α Orionis, mag. 0·1 to 1·2.

The positions of heavenly bodies on the celestial sphere are defined by two co-ordinates, right ascension and declination, which are analogous to longitude and latitude on the surface of the Earth. If we imagine the plane of the terrestrial equator extended indefinitely, it will cut the celestial sphere in a great circle known as the celestial equator. Similarly the plane of the Earth's orbit, when extended, cuts in the great circle called the ecliptic. The two intersections of these circles are known as the First Point of Aries and the First Point of Libra. If from any star a perpendicular be drawn to the celestial equator, the length of this perpendicular is the star's declination. The arc, measured eastwards along the equator from the First Point of Aries to the foot of this perpendicular, is the right ascension. An alternative definition of right ascension is that it is the angle at the celestial pole (where the Earth's axis, if prolonged, would meet the sphere) between the great circles to the First Point of Aries and to the star.

The plane of the Earth's equator has a slow movement, so that our reference system for right ascension and declination is not fixed. The consequent alteration in these quantities from year to year is called precession. In right ascension it is an increase of about 3ˢ a year for equatorial stars, and larger or smaller changes in either direction for stars near the poles, depending on the right ascension of the star. In declination it varies between + 20″ and − 20″ according to the right ascension of the star.

A star or other body crosses the meridian when the sidereal time is equal to its right ascension. The altitude is then a maximum, and may be deduced by remembering that the altitude of the elevated pole is numerically equal to the latitude, while that of the equator at its intersection with the meridian is equal to the co-latitude, or complement of the latitude.

MEAN PLACES OF STARS, 1985.0

Name	Mag.	R.A.	Dec.	Spectrum
		h m	° '	
δ Leonis	2·6	11 13·3	+20 36	A3
β Leonis *Denebola*	2·1	11 48·3	+14 39	A2
γ Ursæ Majoris *Phecda*	2·4	11 53·0	+53 47	A0
γ Corvi	2·6	12 15·0	−17 28	B8
α Crucis	1·0	12 25·8	−63 01	B1
γ Crucis	1·6	12 30·3	−57 02	M3
γ Centauri	2·2	12 40·7	−48 53	A0
γ Virginis	2·7	12 40·9	− 1 22	F0
β Crucis	1·3	12 46·8	−59 36	B1
ε Ursæ Majoris *Alioth*	1·8	12 53·4	+56 02	A0*p*
α Canum Venaticorum	2·9	12 55·3	+38 24	A0*p*
ζ Ursæ Majoris *Mizar*	2·1	13 23·3	+55 00	A2*p*
α Virginis *Spica*	1·0	13 24·4	−11 05	B2
η Ursæ Majoris *Alkaid*	1·9	13 46·9	+49 23	B3
β Centauri *Hadar*	0·6	14 02·8	−60 18	B1
θ Centauri	2·1	14 05·8	−36 18	K0
α Bootis *Arcturus*	0·0	14 15·0	+19 16	K0
α Centauri *Rigil Kent*	0·1	14 38·6	−60 46	G0
ε Bootis	2·4	14 44·3	+27 08	K0
β Ursæ Minoris *Kochab*	2·1	14 50·7	+74 13	K5
α Coronæ Borealis *Alphecca* ..	2·2	15 34·1	+26 46	A0
δ Scorpii	2·3	15 59·4	−22 35	B0
β Scorpii	2·6	16 04·6	−19 46	B1
α Scorpii *Antares*	1·0	16 28·5	−26 24	M0
α Trianguli Australis........	1·9	16 47·1	−69 00	K2
ε Scorpii	2·3	16 49·2	−34 16	K0
α Herculis*	Var.	17 14·0	+14 24	M3
λ Scorpii	1·6	17 32·6	−37 06	B2
α Ophiuchi *Rasalhague*	2·1	17 34·2	+12 34	A5
θ Scorpii	1·9	17 36·2	−42 59	F0
κ Scorpii	2·4	17 41·4	−39 01	B2
γ Draconis	2·2	17 56·3	+51 29	K5
ε Sagittarii *Kaus Australis* ...	1·9	18 23·2	−34 24	A0
α Lyræ *Vega*	0·0	18 36·4	+38 46	A0
σ Sagittarii................	2·0	18 54·3	−26 19	B3
β Cygni *Albireo*	3·1	19 30·1	+27 56	K0
α Aquilæ *Altair*	0·8	19 50·1	+ 8 50	A5
β Capricorni	3·1	20 20·2	−14 50	G0
γ Cygni	2·2	20 21·7	+40 12	F8*p*
α Pavonis	1·9	20 24·5	−56 47	B3
α Cygni *Deneb*.............	1·3	20 40·9	+45 14	A2*p*
α Cephei *Alderamin*	2·4	21 18·2	+62 31	A5
ε Pegasi...................	2·4	21 43·4	+ 9 48	K0
δ Capricorni	2·9	21 46·2	−16 12	A5
α Gruis	1·7	22 07·3	−47 02	B5
δ Cephei*	3·7	22 28·6	+58 20	*
β Gruis	2·1	22 41·8	−46 58	M3
α Piscis Austrini *Fomalhaut* ..	1·2	22 56·8	−29 42	A3
β Pegasi *Scheat*	2·4	23 03·0	+28 00	M0
α Pegasi *Markab*............	2·5	23 04·0	+15 07	A0

* α Herculis, mag. 3·1 to 3·9.
  δ Cephei, mag. 3·7 to 4·4, Spectrum F5 to G0.

Thus in London (Lat. 51° 30′) the meridian altitude of *Sirius* is found as follows:

	°	′
Altitude of equator	38	30
Declination south	16	42
Difference	21	48

The altitude of *Capella* (Dec. +45° 59′) at lower transit is:

	°	′
Altitude of pole	51	30
Polar distance of star	44	01
Difference	7	29

The brightness of a heavenly body is denoted by its magnitude. Omitting the exceptionally bright stars *Sirius* and *Canopus*, the twenty brightest stars are of the first magnitude, while the faintest stars visible to the naked eye are of the sixth magnitude. The magnitude scale is a precise one, as a difference of five magnitudes represents a ratio of 100 to 1 in brightness. Typical second magnitude stars are *Polaris* and the stars in the Belt of Orion. The scale is most easily fixed in memory by comparing the stars with Norton's *Star Atlas* (see page 138). The stars *Sirius* and *Canopus* and the planets Venus and Jupiter are so bright that their magnitudes are expressed by negative numbers. A small telescope will show stars down to the ninth or tenth magnitude, while stars fainter than the twentieth magnitude may be photographed by long exposures with the largest telescopes.

Some of the astronomical information in this ALMANACK has been taken from *Astronomical Phenomena*, and is published here by arrangement with, and with the permission of, the Controller of H.M. Stationery Office.

ELEMENTS OF THE SOLAR SYSTEM

Orb	Mean Distance from Sun		Sidereal Period	Synodic Period	Inclination of Orbit to Ecliptic	Diameter	Mass compared with Earth	Period of Rotation on Axis
	Radii of Earth's Orbit	Millions of kilometres						
			y d	Days	° ′	km.		d h m
Sun	...	...	...	...	...	1,392,000	332,948	25 09
Mercury	0·39	58	88	116	7 00	4,880	0·055	59
Venus	0·72	108	225	584	3 24	12,100	0·815	243
Earth	1·00	150	1 0	...	...	12,756eq.	1·00	23 56
Mars	1·52	228	1 322	780	1 51	6,790	0·107	24 37
Jupiter	5·20	778	11 315	399	1 18	142,800eq. 134,200p.	318	9 50 / 9 56
Saturn	9·54	1427	29 167	378	2 29	120,000eq. 108,000p.	95	10 14 / 10 38
Uranus	19·19	2870	84 6	370	0 46	52,000	14·6	16–28
Neptune	30·07	4497	164 288	367	1 46	48,400	17·2	18–20
Pluto	39·46	5950	247 255	367	17 09	3,000?	0·01	6 09

THE SATELLITES

Name	Star Mag.	Mean distance from Primary	Sidereal Period of Revolution	Name	Star mag.	Mean distance from Primary	Sidereal Period of Revolution
Earth		km.	d h m	*Saturn*		km.	d h m
Moon	—	384,400	27 07 43	Mimas	12	186,000	22 37
				Enceladus	12	238,000	1 08 53
Mars				Tethys	11	295,000	1 21 18
Phobos	11	9,400	7 39	Dione	11	378,000	2 17 41
Deimos	12	23,500	1 06 18	Rhea	10	527,000	4 12 25
				Titan	8½	1,222,000	15 22 42
Jupiter				Hyperion	14	1,483,000	21 06 38
V. Amalthea	13	181,000	11 57	Iapetus	11	3,560,000	79 07 56
I. Io	5½	422,000	1 18 28	Phoebe	16	12,950,000	550
II. Europa	5½	671,000	3 13 14				
III. Ganymede	5	1,070,000	7 03 43	*Uranus*			
IV. Callisto	6	1,883,000	16 16 32	Miranda	17	130,000	1 10 00
XIII. Leda	20	11,000,000	240	Ariel	14	192,000	2 12 29
VI. Himalia	14	11,480,000	251	Umbriel	15	267,000	4 03 28
X. Lysithea	19	11,720,000	259	Titania	14	438,000	8 16 56
VII. Elara	16	11,740,000	260	Oberon	14	586,000	13 11 07
XII. Ananke	19	21,200,000	631	*Neptune*			
XI. Carme	18	22,600,000	692	Triton	13½	355,000	5 21 03
VIII. Pasiphae	19	23,500,000	744	Nereid	19	5,562,000	359 10 00
IX. Sinope	18	23,600,000	758	*Pluto*			
				Charon	17	20,000	6 09 22

THE EARTH

The shape of the Earth is that of an oblate spheroid or solid of revolution whose meridian sections are ellipses not differing much from circles, whilst the sections at right angles are circles. The length of the equatorial axis is about 12,756 kilometres, and that of the polar axis is 12,714 kilometres. The mean density of the Earth is 5·5 times that of water, although that of the surface layer is less. The Earth and Moon revolve about their common centre of gravity in a lunar month; this centre in turn revolves round the Sun in a plane known as the ecliptic, that passes through the Sun's centre. The Earth's equator is inclined to this plane at an angle of 23½°. This tilt is the cause of the seasons. In mid-latitudes, and when the Sun is high above the Equator, not only does the high noon altitude make the days longer, but the Sun's rays fall more directly on the Earth's surface; these effects combine to produce summer. In equatorial regions the noon altitude is large throughout the year, and there is little variation in the length of the day. In higher latitudes the noon altitude is lower, and the days in summer are appreciably longer than those in winter.

The average velocity of the Earth in its orbit is 30 kilometres a second. It makes a complete rotation on its axis in about 23h 56m of mean time, which is the sidereal day. Because of its annual revolution round the Sun, the rotation with respect to the Sun, or the solar day, is more than this by about four minutes (*see* p. 140). The extremity of the axis of rotation, or the North Pole of the Earth, is not rigidly fixed, but wanders over an area roughly 20 metres in diameter.

TERRESTRIAL MAGNETISM

A magnetic compass points along the horizontal component of a magnetic line of force. These directions converge on the "magnetic dip-poles". At these poles a freely suspended magnetized needle would become vertical. Not only do the positions of these poles change with time, but their exact location is ill-defined, particularly so in the case of the north dip-pole where the lines of force, on the north side of it, instead of converging radially, tend to bunch into a channel. Although it is therefore unrealistic to attempt to specify the locations of the dip-poles exactly, the present adopted positions are 77°·3 N., 101°·8 W. and 65°·6 S., 139°·4 E. The two magnetic dip-poles are thus not antipodal, the line joining them passing the centre of the Earth at a distance of about 1,200 kilometres. The distances of the magnetic dip-poles from the north and south geographical poles are about 1,300 and 2,700 kilometres respectively.

There is also a "magnetic equator", at all points of which the vertical force is zero and a magnetized needle remains horizontal. This line runs between 2° and 10° north of the geographical equator in the eastern hemisphere, turns sharply south off the West African coast, and crosses South America through Brazil, Bolivia and Peru; it recrosses the geographical equator in mid-Pacific.

Reference has already been made to secular changes in the Earth's field. The following table indicates the changes in magnetic declination (or variation of the compass). Similar, though much smaller, changes have occurred in "dip" or magnetic inclination. Secular changes differ throughout the world. Although the London observations strongly suggest a cycle of several hundred years, an exact repetition is unlikely.

London		Greenwich	
1580	11° 15′ E.	1850	22° 24′ W.
1622	5 56 E.	1900	16 29 W.
1665	1 22 W.	1925	13 10 W.
1730	13 00 W.	1950	9 07 W.
1773	21 09 W.	1975	6 39 W.

In order that up-to-date information on the variation of the compass may be available, many governments publish magnetic charts on which there are lines (called isogonic) passing through all places at which specified values of declination will be found at the date of the chart.

In the British Isles, isogonic lines now run approximately north-east to south-west. Though there are considerable local deviations due to geographical causes, a rough value of magnetic declination may be obtained by assuming that at 50° N. on the meridian of Greenwich, the value in 1985 is 4° 35′ west and allowing an increase of 14′ for each degree of latitude northwards and one of 31′ for each degree of longitude westwards. For example, at 53° N., 5° W., declination will be about 4° 35′ + 42′ + 155′, i.e. 7° 52′ west. The average annual change at the present time is about 9½′ decrease.

The number of magnetic observatories now approaches 200—widely scattered over the globe. There are three in Great Britain maintained by the Government: at Hartland, North Devon, and at Eskdalemuir in Dumfriesshire, Scotland, and at Lerwick, Shetland Islands. Some recent annual mean values of the magnetic elements for Hartland are given below.

The normal worldwide terrestrial magnetic field corresponds approximately to that of a very strong small bar magnet near the centre of the Earth but with appreciable smooth spatial departures. The origin and slow secular change of the normal field is not yet fully understood but is generally ascribed to electric currents associated with fluid motions within the Earth's core. Superposed on the normal field are local and regional anomalies whose magnitudes may in places exceed that of the normal field; these are due to the influence of mineral deposits in the Earth's crust. A small proportion of the field is of external origin, mostly associated with electric currents in the ionosphere. The configuration of the external field and the ionization of the atmosphere depend on the incident particle and radiation flux. There are, therefore, short-term and non-periodic as well as diurnal, 27-day, seasonal and 11-year periodic changes in the magnetic field, dependent upon the position of the Sun and the degree of solar activity.

Year	Declination West	Dip or Inclination	Horizontal Force	Vertical Force
	° ′	° ′	oersted	oersted
1950	11 06	66 54	0·1848	0·4334
1955	10 30	66 49	0·1859	0·4340
1960	9 59	66 44	0·1871	0·4350
1965	9 30	66 34	0·1887	0·4354
1970	9 06	66 26	0·1903	0·4364
1975	8 32	66 17	0·1921	0·4373
1980	7 44	66 10	0·1933	0·4377
1983	7 15	66 09	0·1934	0·4379

Magnetic Storms. Occasionally—sometimes with great suddenness—the Earth's magnetic field is subject for several hours to marked disturbance. In extreme cases, departures in field intensity as much as one tenth the normal value are experienced. In many instances, such disturbances are accompanied by widespread displays of aurorae, marked changes in the incidence of cosmic rays, an increase in the reception of "noise" from the Sun at radio frequencies together with rapid changes in the ionosphere and induced electric currents within the earth which adversely affect radio and telegraphic communications. The disturbances are generally ascribed to flux changes in the stream of neutral and ionized particles which emanates from the Sun and through which the Earth is continuously passing. Some of these changes are associated with visible eruptions on the Sun, usually in the region of sun-spots. There is a marked tendency for disturbances to recur after intervals of about 27 days, the apparent period of rotation of the Sun on its axis, which is consistent with the sources being located on particular areas of the Sun.

Artificial Satellites Launched in 1982–3

Desig-nation	Satellite	Launch date	i	P	e	Perigee height (km)
1982–		1982	°	m		
116	Meteor 2-09, rocket	December 14	81·2	102·0	0·006	812
117	*Cosmos 1424, rocket*	December 16	64·9	89·7	0·013	171
118	DMSP 2-01, rocket	December 21	98·7	101·4	0·001	816
119	*Cosmos 1425, rocket,* engine	December 23	70·0	92·1	0·005	347
120	Cosmos 1426, *rocket*	December 28	50·5	90·1	0·011	209
121	Cosmos 1427, rocket	December 29	65·8	94·0	0·004	445
1983–		1983				
01	Cosmos 1428, rocket	January 12	82·9	104·7	0·003	957
02	Cosmos 1429–1436, rocket	January 19	74·0	115·9	0·003	1,468
03	Cosmos 1437, rocket	January 20	81·2	97·6	0·002	628
04	IRAS, PIX2	January 26	99·1	103·1	0·001	896
05	*Cosmos 1438, rocket,* engine	January 27	70·4	88·9	0·002	209
06	Sakura 2A, rocket	February 4	0·3	1,444·7	0·019	35,145
07	*Cosmos 1439, rocket*	February 6	70·4	88·7	0·006	170
08	NOSS 4, SSU-D, SSU-A, SSU-B, SSU-C	February 9	63·4	107·8	0·008	1,063
09	*Cosmos 1440, rocket,* engine	February 10	82·3	89·9	0·001	260
10	Cosmos 1441, rocket	February 18	81·1	97·5	0·001	631
11	Tenma, rocket,	February 20	31·5	94·4	0·001	487
12	*Cosmos 1442, rocket*	February 25	67·2	89·9	0·015	170
13	Cosmos 1443, rocket	March 2	51·6	88·9	0·005	191
14	*Cosmos 1444, rocket,* engine	March 2	72·8	92·3	0·004	358
15	Molniya 3V, *launcher, launcher rocket,* rocket	March 11	62·8	735·3	0·748	419
16	Ekran 10, *launcher rocket, launcher,* rocket	March 12	0·1	1,427·5	0·000	35,613
17	*Cosmos 1445, rocket*	March 15	50·7	88·4	0·003	176
18	*Cosmos 1446, rocket,* engine	March 16	69·9	89·1	0·001	222
19	Molniya 1BH, *launcher rocket, launcher,* rocket	March 16	62·8	736·5	0·747	453
20	Astron 1, launcher rocket, launcher, rocket	March 23	51·1	5,879·2	0·923	1,950
21	Cosmos 1447, rocket	March 24	82·9	104·9	0·004	961
22	NOAA 8, rocket	March 28	98·7	101·3	0·002	808
23	Cosmos 1448, rocket	March 30	83·0	104·8	0·003	963
24	*Cosmos 1449, rocket,* engine	March 31	72·9	90·1	0·013	195
25	Molniya 1BJ, *launcher rocket, launcher,* rocket	April 2	62·9	700·0	0·738	470
26	*STS 6*, TDRS 1	April 4	28·5	90·0	0·001	278
27	Cosmos 1450, rocket	April 6	65·9	94·4	0·003	472
28	Raduga 12, *launcher, launcher rocket,* rocket	April 8	1·3	1,443·0	0·001	35,873
29	*Cosmos 1451, rocket,* engine	April 8	82·3	90·0	0·007	227
30	RCA Satcom 6	April 11	0·1	1,435·9	0·001	35,746
31	Cosmos 1452, rocket	April 12	74·0	100·8	0·002	785
32	?	April 15	96·5	88·5	0·012	136
33	Rohini 3, rocket	April 17	46·6	97·0	0·033	388
34	Cosmos 1453, rocket	April 19	74·0	94·5	0·003	471
35	Soyuz T-8, rocket, module	April 20	51·6	90·4	0·001	287
36	*Cosmos 1454, rocket*	April 22	67·1	89·6	0·013	171
37	Cosmos 1455, rocket	April 23	82·5	97·8	0·002	637
38	Cosmos 1456, launcher rocket, launcher, rocket	April 25	62·9	710·7	0·735	620
39	*Cosmos 1457, rocket*	April 26	70·4	89·7	0·013	171
40	*Cosmos 1458, rocket,* capsule	April 28	82·3	89·1	0·003	212
41	GOES 6	April 28	0·5	1,703·9	0·159	33,367
42	Cosmos 1459, rocket	May 6	83·0	104·8	0·005	947
43	*Cosmos 1460, rocket,* engine	May 6	70·3	92·2	0·005	349
44	Cosmos 1461, *rocket*	May 7	65·0	93·3	0·001	429
45	*Cosmos 1462, rocket,* engine	May 17	82·3	89·9	0·001	259

Artificial Satellites Launched in 1983—(cont.)

Desig-nation	Satellite	Launch date	i	P	e	Perigee height (km)
1983–		1983	°	m		
46	Cosmos 1463, rocket	May 19	82·9	103·6	0·086	301
47	Intelsat 5F-6, rocket	May 19	0·2	1,436·0	0·000	35,767
48	Cosmos 1464, rocket	May 24	82·9	104·9	0·004	968
49	Cosmos 1465, rocket	May 26	50·7	93·4	0·014	349
50	Cosmos 1466, rocket	May 26	64·9	89·7	0·013	174
51	Exosat	May 26	72·5	5,431·3	0·934	356
52	Cosmos 1467, rocket, engine	May 31	72·9	90·2	0·012	199
53	Venus 15, launcher rocket, launcher	June 2		(space probe)		
54	Venus 16, launcher rocket, launcher	June 7				
55	Cosmos 1468, rocket, engine	June 7	82·3	89·9	0·002	255
56	NOSS 5, rocket, GB 1, GB 2	June 10	63·3	107·4	0·008	1,048
57	Cosmos 1469, rocket, engine	June 14	72·8	90·3	0·008	232
58	EGS 1, Oscar 10	June 16	0·0	1,427·6	0·004	35,464
59	STS 7, Telesat 7, Palapa 3, SPAS-01	June 18	28·5	90·5	0·002	295
60	?, rocket, capsule	June 20	96·4	88·5	0·005	169
61	Cosmos 1470, rocket	June 23	82·5	97·8	0·002	635
62	Soyuz T-9, rocket	June 27	51·6	91·1	0·001	325
63	Hilat 1, rocket	June 27	82·0	101·0	0·005	772
64	Cosmos 1471, rocket	June 28	67·1	89·8	0·012	185
65	Galaxy 1	June 28	0·1	1,437·3	0·015	35,194
66	Gorizont 7, launcher rocket, launcher, rocket	July 1	1·3	1,478·1	0·001	36,566
67	Prognoz 9, launcher rocket, launcher, rocket	July 1	64·9	91·4	0·017	229
68	Cosmos 1472, rocket, engine	July 5	82·3	91·6	0·002	338
69	Cosmos 1473–1480, rocket	July 6	74·0	114·5	0·004	1,397
70	Cosmos 1481, launcher rocket, launcher, rocket	July 8	62·9	707·4	0·733	643
71	Cosmos 1482, rocket, engine	July 13	70·0	92·2	0·004	352
72	Navstar 8, rocket	July 14	62·8	725·8	0·016	19,952
73	Molniya 1BK, launcher rocket, launcher, rocket	July 19	62·9	700·0	0·738	459
74	Cosmos 1483, rocket, engine	July 20	82·3	89·9	0·001	260
75	Cosmos 1484, rocket	July 24	98·0	97·3	0·005	594
76	Cosmos 1485, rocket, engine	July 26	72·8	92·3	0·004	358
77	Telstar 3A	July 28	0·2	1,435·9	0·008	35,436
78	SDS 8, rocket	July 31				
79	Cosmos 1486, rocket	August 3	74·0	100·8	0·002	784
80	Cosmos 1487, rocket, engine	August 5	82·3	89·9	0·001	261
81	Sakura 28	August 5	0·3	1,450·7	0·013	35,535
82	Cosmos 1488, rocket, engine	August 9	72·9	92·3	0·004	358
83	Cosmos 1489, rocket	August 10	64·7	89·8	0·015	171
84	Cosmos 1490–1492, launcher, launcher rocket	August 10	64·8	678·3	0·001	19,157
85	Progress 17, rocket	August 17	51·6	90·2	0·006	257
86	China 11, rocket	August 19	63·3	90·0	0·016	173
87	Cosmos 1493, rocket, engine	August 23	72·9	92·3	0·004	360
88	Raduga 13, launcher rocket, launcher, rocket	August 25	1·3	1,476·7	0·001	36,522
89	STS 8, Insat 1B, rocket	August 30	28·5	90·3	0·000	294
90	Molniya 3W, launcher, launcher rocket, rocket	August 30	62·9	735·7	0·748	430
91	Cosmos 1494, rocket	August 31	50·7	93·5	0·015	345
92	Cosmos 1495, rocket, engine	September 3	82·3	89·0	0·002	215
93	Cosmos 1496, rocket	September 7	67·2	89·6	0·013	170
94	RCA Satcom 7	September 8	0·1	1,436·0	0·001	35,725
95	Cosmos 1497, rocket, engine	September 9	72·8	92·3	0·004	357

SATELLITE ORBITS

To consider the orbit of an artificial satellite it is best to imagine that one is looking at the Earth from a distant point in space. The Earth would then be seen to be rotating about its axis inside the orbit described by the rapidly revolving satellite. The inclination of a satellite orbit to the Earth's equator (which generally remains almost constant throughout the satellite's lifetime) gives at once the maximum range of latitudes over which the satellite passes. Thus a satellite whose orbit has an inclination of 53° will pass overhead all latitudes between S. 53° and N. 53°, but would never be seen in the zenith of any place nearer the poles than these latitudes. If we consider a particular place on the earth, whose latitude is less than the inclination of the satellite's orbit then the Earth's rotation carries this place under first the northbound part of the orbit and then, later on, under the southbound position of the orbit, these two occurrences being always less than 12 hours apart for satellites moving in direct orbits (*i.e.* to the east). For satellites in retrograde orbits the words "northbound" and "southbound" should be interchanged in the preceding statement. As the value of the latitude of the observer increases and approaches the value of the inclination of the orbit, so this interval gets shorter until (when the latitude is equal to the inclination) only one overhead passage occurs each day.

SATELLITE LAUNCHINGS

Apart from their names, *e.g.* Cosmos 6 Rocket or Injun 3, the satellites are also classified according to their date of launch. Thus 1961 α refers to the launching of Samos 2. The next satellite launching was 1961 β and so on. A number following the Greek letter is intended to indicate the relative brightness of the satellites put in orbit. From the beginning of 1963 the Greek letters are replaced by numbers and the numbers by roman letters *e.g.* 1963–01A. In this table are given the designation and names of the main objects in orbit (in the order A, B, C . . . etc.), the launch date and some initial orbital data. These are the inclination to the equator (*i*), the nodal period of revolution (*P*), the eccentricity, *e*, and the perigee height. The names of those satellites which have already disintegrated in the Earth's atmosphere or returned to the Earth's surface are printed in *italics*.

OBSERVATION OF SATELLITES

The regression of the orbit around the Earth causes alternate periods of visibility and invisibility, though this is of little concern to the radio or radar observer. To the visual observer the following cycle of events normally occurs (though the cycle may start in any position): invisibility, morning observations before dawn, invisibility, evening observations after dusk, invisibility, morning observations before dawn, and so on. With reasonably high satellites and for observers in high latitudes around the summer solstice the evening observations follow the morning observations without interruption as sunlight passing over the polar regions can still illuminate satellites which are passing over temperate latitudes at local midnight. At the moment all satellites rely on sunlight to make them visible though a satellite with a flashing light has been suggested for a future launching. The observer must be in darkness or twilight in order to make any useful observations and the durations of twilight and the sunrise, sunset times given on page II of each month will be a useful guide.

Some of the satellites are visible to the naked eye and much interest has been aroused by the spectacle of a bright satellite disappearing into the Earth's shadow. The event is even more fascinating telescopically as the disappearance occurs gradually as the satellite traverses the Earth's penumbral shadow, and during the last few seconds before the eclipse is complete the satellite may change colour (under suitable atmospheric conditions) from yellow to red. This is because the last rays of sunlight are refracted through the denser layers of our atmosphere before striking the satellite.

Some satellites rotate about one or more axes so that a periodic variation in brightness is observed. This was particularly noticeable in several of the U.S.S.R. satellites.

Satellite research has already provided some interesting results. Among them may be mentioned a revised value of the Earth's oblateness, 1/298·2, and the discovery of the Van Allen radiation belts.

ROYAL OBSERVATORIES

Royal Greenwich Observatory
Herstmonceux, East Sussex, BN27 1RP
[0323 833171]

The Royal Observatory was founded at Greenwich by Charles II in 1675 "for the advancement of navigation and nautical astronomy". Because of smog and light pollution, the Observatory was moved to Herstmonceux in East Sussex after the Second World War. (The old site at Greenwich is now part of the National Maritime Museum). The traditional work in positional astronomy and the determination of time remain as important activities of the Observatory. The well-known "Greenwich 6 pips" are sent from Herstmonceux to the B.B.C. by land line. The rate of rotation of the Earth and other geophysical parameters are monitored by the satellite laser ranging telescope. Various almanacs and other astronomical data are prepared by H.M. Nautical Almanac Office, which is part of the Royal Greenwich Observatory. However, as an establishment of the Science and Engineering Research Council, the main task of the Observatory now is the provision of facilities for research in optical astronomy for astronomers in the universities. In particular, this involves the provision and running of the British telescopes and instrumentation at the Roque de los Muchachos Observatory on the island of La Palma in the Canary Islands (including the 4·2 metre William Herschel telescope). At Herstmonceux, there are facilities for the processing of astronomical data obtained from the telescopes on La Palma and elsewhere; these include a node of the STARLINK computing network. *Director*, Prof. A. Boksenberg, F.R.S.

Royal Observatory
Blackford Hill, Edinburgh

The Observatory was founded by the Astronomical Institution in 1818 and its Royal Charter dates from 1822. Its endowments include the Crawford Library of historical books and manuscripts. It is now responsible for some major national astronomical facilities funded by the Science and Engineering Research Council, including a 1·2 m Schmidt telescope in Australia, a 3·8 m infrared telescope in Hawaii and COSMOS, a fast automatic plate measuring machine. The Observatory is also part of the U.K. Starlink network for astronomical image and data processing. The Observatory specializes in the development of advanced technologies and the application of these to studies of the properties of matter in extreme environments in space. The Astronomy Department of Edinburgh University is housed in the Observatory. *Director and Astronomer Royal for Scotland*, Prof. M. S. Longair.

WEATHER IN THE UNITED KINGDOM, 1983–1984

(1983) July—Rainfall totals were below normal except in a few isolated parts of the United Kingdom and less than half the normal amount fell in most places with less than ten per cent in a few places in eastern Scotland, southern Wales and southwest England. Generally it was the driest July since 1919 in Northern Ireland and since 1955 in Scotland. In Tynemouth it was the driest July since 1871. In spite of this there were many thunderstorms and 87·1 mm. (3·4 ins.) of rain fell at Croydon (Greater London) on the 6th whilst 112·2 mm. (4·4 ins.) fell on Honister Pass (Cumbria) and 104·8 mm. (4·1 ins.) at Ireshopeburn (Durham) on the 17th. Severe flooding occurred locally on several occasions including Lampeter (Dyfed) on the 11th when 66·3 mm. (2·6 ins.) of rain fell in 50 minutes. Four men were killed by lightning at Barnes (Greater London) on the 6th, at Grasmere (Cumbria) on the 17th and at Donnington (Shropshire) and Boston (Lincolnshire) on the 18th. Hailstones the size of golfballs fell at Lampeter (Dyfed) on the 17th and some the size of marbles broke car windscreens at Okehampton (Devon) on the 23rd. Monthly mean temperatures were above normal everywhere and were more than 4°C. (7°F.) above normal in parts of southern England. It was the hottest calendar month for 325 years of record in central England. It was also the hottest month in more than 100 years of record in Greater London, Plymouth and Durham. In Northern Ireland, Armagh had its hottest month since July 1868 and in Scotland it was the hottest month since July 1976. The temperature reached 33·7°C. (92·7°F.) at Liphook (Hampshire) on the 16th and 31·5°C. (88·7°F.) at Coatbridge (Strathclyde) on the 12th. A temperature of 30·8°C. (87·4°F.) at Belfast on the 12th equalled the highest value on record in Northern Ireland. The heat, often with high humidity, caused many problems. Operating theatres had to be closed in Cardiff and the death rate of elderly people was up by 50 per cent. Several people were drowned when swimming. Railway engines overheated and there were huge traffic jams to the coast. Freshwater fish died in some areas and Judges and counsel removed their wigs in the High Court. Monthly sunshine totals were above normal almost everywhere with more than 140 per cent. of average being recorded in areas mainly in the northwest and south. It was mainly dull in eastern coastal areas during the second week and in Shetland during the second half of the month. Fog occurred frequently, particularly during the second and fourth weeks and persisted over coastal areas at times. Tornadoes caused severe damage to a stone building at Allenheads (Northumberland) on the 17th and to a house in Ivybridge (Devon) on the 31st.

August—Rainfall totals were mostly below normal and much of the United Kingdom had less than half the normal amount with parts of East Anglia, east Scotland, the Midlands, central southern and southeast England having less than 10 per cent of normal. Rather more rain fell elsewhere and some scattered areas in Wales had above average rainfall. In general it was the driest August since 1976. In the Midlands it was the driest since 1955 and in eastern England it was the driest since 1947. There were a few heavy falls of rain with 85 mm. (3·3 ins.) at Llwynon (Gwynedd) on the 16th and 73·8 mm. (2·9 ins.) at Swyddffynnon (Dyfed) on the 19th. Thunderstorms, heavy at times, occurred widely on the 1st and 2nd especially in southeast England. On the 2nd a small tornado knocked a child off his feet at Thorpe (Surrey) and funnel clouds were observed over the sea off Brighton (Sussex) and near Jersey airport. Gales occurred in a few exposed areas in the north on the 3rd and 4th and again around mid-month.

Thunderstorms were again widespread in all districts from the 19th to 23rd, and over Wales and western England on the 31st. Flooding occurred locally in southeast England on the 22nd. There were further gales in the north on the 29th and 30th. Fog patches occurred frequently over coasts and hills in the northeast and Shetland between the 19th and 24th and fog was widespread in central and southern areas on the 18th and 23rd. Monthly mean temperatures were above average nearly everywhere and generally it was the warmest August since 1975 in Great Britain and since 1955 in Northern Ireland. The temperature reached 30°C. (86°F.) at Hull and Aldenham (Hertfordshire) on the 14th and 32·1°C. (89·8°F.) at Yeovilton (Somerset) on the 19th. A slight frost occurred in a few isolated places and the temperature fell to −1·2°C. (29·8°F.) at Stonehaugh (Northumberland) on the 29th and to −1·5°C. (29·3°F.) at St. Harmon (Powys) on the 30th. The fine weather resulted in an early and rapid cereal harvest but root crops failed through lack of rain. Several hundred water fowl died at various places in central and southern England as a result of low water levels and high temperatures. Sunshine totals were above average except in the far north and west of Scotland, parts of Northern Ireland and parts of the Essex and Kent coasts. More than 125 per cent of average was recorded in much of southern Scotland, the north and.south of England, the Midlands and Wales and scattered places elsewhere. Parts of Greater Manchester and Shropshire received more than 150 per cent of average. Northern Ireland was frequently cloudy between the 15th and 27th.

September—Rainfall totals were above average in most areas. Below average totals were recorded mainly in parts of southeastern and northwestern England, the west of Scotland and Northern Ireland. For the first three and a half weeks all districts had showers or periods of rain and it was heavy in places on several occasions. On the 1st, thunderstorms were widespread over England and Wales. On the 2nd and 3rd gales reached storm force particularly in the south: a gust of 73 kts. (84 mph) was recorded at Dover (Kent) and 75 kts. (86 mph) was recorded at Gwennap Head (Cornwall). Two anglers were drowned off St. Agnes (Cornwall), a yachtsman was drowned off the Isles of Scilly, a lorry driver was killed by a falling tree at Chippenham (Wiltshire), the Q.E.2 was delayed from docking at Southampton and much of the bumper apple crop was destroyed. Power lines were brought down and ferries delayed or cancelled. On the 2nd 154·9 mm. (6·1 ins.) of rain fell at Capel Curig (Gwynedd) and flooding and landslips occurred in north Wales on the 3rd. On the 4th and 5th there were severe gales over Northern Ireland, the south of Scotland and northern England when a gust of 74 kts. (85 mph) was recorded at Machrihanish (Strathclyde) and one of 92 kts. (106 mph) was recorded at Lowther Hill (Strathclyde). Extensive damage was caused to boats in the Firth of Clyde, power lines were brought down and ferries delayed or cancelled. There was further flooding with landslips in north Wales on the 10th. On the 15th a tornado damaged four buildings at Quernmore Hill Farm near Hazelrigg (Lancashire) and trees were stripped of their branches along a 1·2 km. (0·75 miles) track. Fog formed widely over central and southern districts between the 26th and 29th and coastal fog was rather persistent in places in the southwest between the 25th and 30th. There were further gales locally in the north on the 29th and 30th. Monthly mean temperatures were generally below average except in parts of southern England, the Midlands, East Anglia and locally in Lincolnshire where they were slightly above normal. The period 10th to 13th was particularly cool. On the 24th temperatures rose to 27·1°C. (80·8°F.) at Rumleigh (Devon) and to 26·2°C. (79·2°F.) at St. Helier (Channel Islands) and on the 26th, 23·6°C. (74·5°F.) was recorded at Culterty (Grampian). Temperatures fell to −3·5°C. (25·7°F.) at Grantown-on-Spey (Highland), Bonchester Bridge (Borders) and Carnwath (Strathclyde) on the 25th. Sunshine totals were below normal almost everywhere with many places having less than 75 per cent of the normal amount. In some parts it was one of the dullest Septembers this century while at Armagh the total was the lowest since records began there in 1880. Only at a few scattered locations in the Grampian Region, Tyne and Wear, South Yorkshire and Shropshire were sunshine totals slightly above normal.

October—Rainfall totals were very varied ranging from more than twice the normal amount in parts of north and west Scotland to about half the average at a few places in the eastern half of England and the Channel Islands. All districts had frequent showers or periods of rain until the 18th. In the west rainfall was often heavy especially over western Scotland. Scattered thunderstorms occurred at times especially between the 3rd and 16th. On the 4th 82·6 mm. (3·3 ins.) of rain fell at Kinlochleven House (Highland) and on the 6th 90·1 mm. (3·5 ins.) was recorded at Blaenau Ffestiniog (Gwynedd) where 96·5 mm. (3·8 ins.) fell on the 9th. Also until the 18th winds were frequently strong with gales in exposed places especially in the north and west. The gales were severe at times and on the 15th ferries from Ramsgate (Kent) and Douglas (Isle of Man) were cancelled and boats were unable to enter harbour at Bridlington (Humberside). Trains between Waterloo (London) and Guildford (Surrey) were delayed by fallen trees. A gust of 80 kts. (92 mph) was recorded at The Needles (Isle of Wight) on the 15th and trains in south Wales were delayed by flooding. On the 16th a lady was killed at Alnwick (Northumberland) when a tree fell on her car and the roof was ripped off an hotel at Blackpool (Lancashire) and off the village hall at Mickleby (North Yorkshire). A gust of 95 kts. (109 mph) was recorded at Lowther Hill (Strathclyde). On the 17th snow fell on High Peak (Derbyshire). Gales were again severe over northern Scotland during the last week and a gust of 95 kts. (109 mph) was recorded at Cairngorm (Highland) on the 25th and one of 83 kts. (96 mph) at Fair Isle (Shetland) on the 30th. There was heavy rain at times in the northwest and far north of Scotland during this week. Fog was fairly widespread in southern England on the 23rd, 26th and 27th. Monthly mean temperatures were near but mostly below normal. The month started warm and in much of East Anglia and southeast England it was very warm and the temperature exceeded 24°C. (75°F.) in places on the 4th. The temperature fell to −7·5°C. (18·5°F.) at Balmoral (Grampian) on the 21st and to −9·0°C. (15·8°F.) at St. Harmon (Powys) on the 29th. On the 30th the temperature at Bournemouth (Dorset) was the lowest for October since 1895 and at Penzance (Cornwall) it was the lowest since 1894. Sunshine totals were below average over Scotland except in parts of the east, the western half of Northern Ireland, much of northwest England and Wales and places in the south from Sussex to Cornwall. Fort Augustus (Highland) had its second lowest total for 100 years. Elsewhere sunshine totals were above normal with more than 125 per cent of average being recorded in parts of the Midlands, east and northeast England, Greater London and the Grampian Region.

November—Rainfall totals were well below average everywhere except for parts of Norfolk and northern

Suffolk and many places recorded well under 50 per cent of the normal amount. The highest daily fall during the month was 51·6 mm. (2·0 ins.) at Cilfynydd (Mid-Glamorgan). There was rain over much of the Kingdom on the 2nd. The north of Scotland had periods of rain during the first few days and on the 7th and 8th this unsettled weather extended south into England and Wales. On the 14th winds increased to gale force along the Channel coasts and a gust of 60 knots (69 mph) was reported from the Lizard (Cornwall). On the 19th the wind reached gale force in northern Scotland and rain showers turned to snow in Orkney and Shetland and later over central Scotland. 5 cms. (2 ins.) of snow was reported on roads near Aberdeen early on the 21st and sleet showers spread down the east coast of England. During the 24th rain fell over much of England and Wales with most places recording at least 19 mm. (0·75 ins.). On the 26th and early on the 27th gusts of over 60 knots (69 mph) were reported widely over southern England and at Langdon Bay (Kent) a gust of 77 knots (89 mph) was recorded. Scotland had further snow and hail showers. Fog occurred over wide areas on the mornings of the 3rd to 6th and 8th to 11th when it tended to persist in the east Midlands and parts of Lincolnshire and Yorkshire. Monthly mean temperatures were above normal everywhere in spite of the second half of the month being cold. On the 1st the temperature at Colwyn Bay (Clwyd) was 6°C. (11°F.) above normal and the maximum temperature there was 18·9°C. (66·0°F.). On the 10th the temperature reached 18·2°C. (64·8°F.) at Eskmeals (Cumbria). On the night of the 14th there was heavy frost over much of Wales and southern England with a minimum air temperature of −9°C. (15·8°F.). On the 22nd and 23rd the temperature fell to −11·5°C. (11·3°F.) at St. Harmon (Powys). Sunshine totals were below normal everywhere except southern Scotland, a small area of the coast of southwest Wales and isolated places on the coasts of Sussex and Kent and parts of Lancashire and Cheshire. 8·0 hours of sunshine were recorded at Jersey Airport on the 3rd and 8·3 hours were recorded at St. Mawgan (Cornwall) on the 15th. The autumn period (September, October, November) as a whole was generally rather dry except in parts of Scotland. The seasonal temperature was near normal and the sunshine totals were below normal especially in northern Scotland.

December—Rainfall totals were generally above average with places in the north of England having twice the normal amount. East Anglia, parts of southern England and south Wales and the Channel Islands had less than normal. The month started with some heavy rain and strong winds in Scotland and Northern Ireland. Rain moved south across all of the Kingdom on the 5th. The 9th was a very wet and stormy day. Winds gusted to over 60 knots (69 mph) and 75 knots (86 mph) was recorded at Tynemouth. At Holyhead (Anglesey) an oil rig was torn from its moorings and in central London the wind reached 58 knots (67 mph) and the Christmas Tree in Trafalgar Square was blown over to a dangerous angle for a time. On the 8th 66 mm. (2·6 ins.) of rain fell at Nantmor (Gwynedd) and on the 10th there was sleet and snow. In northern England and high ground in Wales roads were blocked by the first real snowfall of the winter. On the 11th there was rain in Devon and Cornwall and snow over the Pennines, Wales and central Scotland. On the 13th and 14th there were strong winds and heavy rain over Scotland which moved south into England and Wales. 50·7 mm. (2·0 ins.) of rain fell at Bastreet (Cornwall) on the 14th and a gust of 65 knots (75 mph) was recorded at The Lizard. The 18th to 20th were very stormy and gales caused structural damage to the Plymouth Polytechnic. High tides, heavy rain and gales brought floods to the south and southwest coasts of England. Okehampton (Devon) had 60 mm. (2·4 ins.) of rain on the 18th and on the 20th gusts of 78 knots (90 mph) were reported from Brixham (Devon) and The Lizard. On the 21st a tornado was reported at Shoreham (West Sussex) and thunder and hail occurred in southern England. Scotland had a very wet and windy end to the month and 64·3 mm. (2·5 ins.) of rain fell at Fort William (Highland) on the 27th. By the 31st gales had extended into England and become severe over Scotland. Monthly mean temperatures were above normal everywhere but there were some cold days and widespread frost at times. On the 2nd the temperature rose to 15·2°C. (59·4°F.) at Aberdovey (Gwynedd) which was 6°C. (11°F.) above normal. From the 2nd to 5th central southern England had night temperatures of −4°C. to −6°C. (24·8°F. to 21·2°F.). On the 13th the temperature fell to −8·4°C. (16·9°F.) at Linton-on-Ouse (North Yorkshire) while on the 27th a temperature of 16°C. (60·8°F.) at St. Abbs Head (Borders), Newcastle-on-Tyne and Aberdeen was 10°C. (18°F.) above normal. The Christmas holiday was generally very mild. Sunshine totals were above normal over most of England and Wales but below normal in Scotland, Northern Ireland, coastal Wales and northern England. On the 2nd St. Helier (Channel Islands) had 8·0 hrs. of sunshine.

Year (1983)—January was one of the windiest months for many years with above average rainfall in most western areas. Gales caused considerable damage and four people died in heavy seas in a rescue attempt at Blackpool (Lancashire) on the 5th. A gust of 78 knots (90 mph) was recorded at Lerwick (Shetland) on the 6th and 80 knots (92 mph) occurred at several places in Scotland on the 9th. Heavy snow fell in the Midlands on the 13th. In Dumfries it was the mildest January since 1916. February was mainly cold and dry but with frequent snow in the north and east in the first half of the month. A gust of 106 knots (122 mph) was recorded at Lowther Hill (Dumfries and Galloway) on the 1st. At least six people were killed, many injured and widespread damage occurred in the gales. Vehicles were blown over and vessels were stormbound. The Thames Barrier was raised for the first time and there was coastal flooding at Oban and from Whitby to Great Yarmouth. March was mild for the first three weeks then turned cold. The 21st was the worst day with heavy showers, snow, hail and thunder. Violent squalls and lightning caused considerable damage. On the 25th a violent thundersquall caused much damage in Stratton Strawless (Norfolk) and on the 29th a caravan was blown over near Stockport (Cheshire). Lightning badly damaged a row of houses in Walthamstow (London) on the 31st. April was cold and very wet in England and Wales with a few places having three times the normal amount. On the 3rd snow blocked roads near Dover and on the 10th a freighter capsized in gales near the Scilly Isles, a trawler was abandoned and two yachtsmen lost overboard in the Channel. Tornadoes caused damage in Derby on the 22nd, and at Wirksworth, Cromford and Birchover (Derbyshire) on the 26th. May was another very wet month and Finningley (West Yorkshire) had 345 per cent of the normal rainfall. Thunder was frequent and on the 21st hail was 10 cms. (4 ins.) deep on the M.40 in Buckinghamshire. Waterlogged land delayed crop planting, particularly potatoes and beet. There was flooding in places. Tornadoes caused damage in Romsey (Hampshire) and Gloucester on the 16th, Kirkheaton (West Yorkshire) on the 17th and Oakham (Leicestershire) on the 20th. Lightning destroyed a bungalow at Ferring (West Sussex) on the 27th. June was rather changeable but on the 1st storms were widespread with flooding in the Mid-

lands and East Anglia. There were unusually severe storms on the 5th and 7th when hail nearly 3 inches in diameter fell at Winfrith (Dorset) and in Greater Manchester and hail 2 inches in diameter fell in many places. Considerable damage was caused and on the 5th the weight of hail sank yachts at Christchurch and squalls capsized others off the Isle of Wight. There was local flooding. Thunderstorms were severe causing flooding in the south from the 22nd to 24th. Greenwich had its driest June since 1925. July was generally dry and was the driest in Northern Ireland since 1919 and in Tynemouth since 1871. There were thunderstorms and severe floods. At Lampeter (Dyfed) 66·3 mm. (2·6 ins.) of rain fell in 50 minutes on the 11th. Lightning killed men at Barnes on the 6th, Grasmere on the 17th and at Donnington and Boston on the 18th. Golfball sized hail fell at Lampeter on the 17th. It was the hottest month for over 100 years in Greater London, Plymouth and Durham and since 1868 in Armagh. The heat caused many problems and many elderly people died. Tornadoes caused damage in Allenheads (Northumberland) on the 17th and Ivybridge (Devon) on the 31st. August was a warm dry month. In general it was the driest August since 1976 and the warmest since 1975. The cereal harvest was early and rapid but root crops failed because of the weather. There was flooding in southeast England on the 22nd. September was another wet and stormy month. On the 2nd and 3rd two men drowned off St. Agnes (Cornwall), a yachtsman drowned off Scilly, a lorry driver was killed by a falling tree at Chippenham, much of the apple crop was destroyed and the Q.E.2 was delayed. Heavy rain caused floods and landslips in north Wales. On the 4th there was extensive damage to boats in the Firth of Clyde and on the 10th more floods and landslips in north Wales. A tornado caused damage near Hazelrigg (Lancashire) on the 15th. The sunshine total at Armagh was the lowest since 1880. October brought variable weather over the Kingdom but gales on the 15th halted ferries from Ramsgate and Douglas and closed the harbour at Bridlington. Trees fell across railway lines between Waterloo and Guildford. On the 15th floods occurred in south Wales and a falling tree killed a lady in a car at Alnwick on the 16th when roofs were blown off buildings at Blackpool and Mickleby (North Yorkshire). Bournemouth and Penzance had their lowest October temperatures since 1895 and 1894 respectively on the 30th. November was a quieter month with low rainfall and above average temperatures. 5 cms. (2 ins.) of snow fell near Aberdeen on the 21st. December was another wet month with stormy periods. On the 9th an oil rig was torn from its moorings at Anglesey and the Christmas Tree in Trafalgar Square was blown to a dangerous angle. Storms on the 18th to 20th caused damage in Plymouth and flooding on the south and southwest coasts of England. The Christmas Holiday was very mild.

(1984) January—Rainfall totals were well above normal everywhere except for a small area in southwest Wales. Several places had twice the normal amount and it was the wettest January since 1948 over England and Wales and the 5th was the wettest day this century. On the 1st there were showers of hail, sleet and snow over Scotland and this was the start of a month when snow fell somewhere in the United Kingdom on 30 days, the 10th being the day without any. On the 2nd, gusts of over 80 knots (92 mph) were reported along the south coast of England and at Benbecula (Hebrides) a gust of 90 knots (104 mph) was recorded. The strong winds and snow showers brought blizzards to the north. During the next week snow affected many areas. On the 10th 59·4 mm. (2·3 ins.) of rain fell at Nantmor (Gwynedd) and on the 11th violent winds caused considerable damage in Northern Ireland and Scotland. The night of the 12th/13th was again stormy and many places had heavy rain. On the 13th a gust of 90 knots (104 mph) was recorded at St. Abbs Head (Borders). The night of the 13th was very wet over most of England and Wales but Northern Ireland, Scotland and northern England had heavy snow. On the 14th there was further snow and in the east of England there were thunderstorms in which a tornado damaged 100 houses near Doncaster (South Yorkshire). Further snow, often heavy and drifting in gale force winds, continued over northern areas for the next four days. There was freezing rain and snow in the extreme south of England on the 18th. Strong winds returned on the 21st to give a further three days of blizzards. On the 24th a gust of 70 knots (81 mph) was reported near Lands End and a cargo ship sank near Guernsey with the loss of 17 lives. Further periods of snow affected much of the United Kingdom until the 26th when a tornado caused damage in Teignmouth (Devon). On the 25th 37·2 mm. (1·5 ins.) of rain fell at Okehampton (Devon). The last five days of the month brought milder weather and much of the accumulated snow melted. There was some rain in the south. Monthly mean temperatures were generally above average in the southern half of the United Kingdom and below average in the northern half. On the 2nd and 16th the temperature rose to 14°C. (57·2°F.) at Colwyn Bay (Clwyd) while on the 20th it fell to −20·6°C. (−5·1°F.) at Aviemore (Highland). Sunshine totals were mostly above average except for north and west Scotland, south-west Wales, the northern coasts of Devon and Cornwall and the Channel Islands. In central London it was the sunniest January since 1929 and on the 19th 7·5 hours of sunshine were recorded at Tenby (Dyfed). On the 21st Jubilee Corner (Kent) had 7·2 hours of sunshine while 7·3 hours were recorded at Shoeburyness (Essex) on the 31st.

February—Rainfall amounts were very variable, being above normal in scattered areas and well below in others but in general the east and south were the driest areas with the Midlands, the north and Northern Ireland being the wettest. On the 4th sleet and snow moved south and there was hail and thunder in the north. A gust of 78 knots (90 mph) was recorded at Collarfirth Hill (Shetlands) and there was drifting snow in the extreme north. There was thunder in East Anglia and gusts of over 60 knots (69 mph) inland. Much structural damage was done to buildings and travel was badly disrupted. On the 5th 33 mm. (1·3 ins.) of rain fell at Bastreet (Cornwall). It was dry but very cloudy from the 8th to 12th then overnight fog became dense in parts of the Midlands and northwest England. During the next few days fog and frost became more widespread and by the 15th the south and west coasts of England and the Moray Firth were the only clear areas. By the 16th only the Hebrides had more than 1 hour of sunshine. On the 19th there was rain in western areas turning to sleet and snow which was heavy for a time in Northern Ireland, Wales and southwest England. On the 20th there was heavy snow in northern England and southern Scotland while on the 21st and 22nd there were snow and hail showers and a thunderstorm in the Channel Islands. The rest of the month was fairly dry but cloudy. Monthly mean temperatures were near normal except in northern Scotland where they were above average. The temperature fell to −9·2°C. (15·4°F.) at Eskdalemuir (Dumfries and Galloway) on the 1st but rose to 13·5°C. (56·3°F.) at Malvern (Hereford and Worcester) on the 4th. On the 16th the temperature never rose above −2·0°C. (28·4°F.) at Fylingdales (North Yorkshire). On the 29th the temperature rose to 12·3°C. (54·1°F.) at Kilkeel (Co. Down). Sunshine totals were above

average in much of southeast England and the Channel Islands but below average elsewhere. It was very dull in the north of Scotland. On the 13th 9·1 hours of sunshine were recorded at East Hoathly (Sussex) and 8·8 hours were recorded at Portland Bill (Dorset) on the 24th. The winter period (December, January, February) was wet or very wet in most areas with near or just above normal temperatures. The north and west of the United Kingdom were dull or very dull but much of England and Wales had above average sunshine especially in the southeast of England where central London had its sunniest winter since records began there in 1929.

March—Rainfall totals were mainly above normal and more than twice the normal amount fell in parts of southeast Scotland and northeast England. Western areas had less than normal amounts with parts of south Wales and southeast England recording less than 50 per cent of normal. There was rain on the 1st of the month when Lerwick (Shetland) had 33·1 mm. (1·3 ins.). Many places had sleet or snow showers, heavy in the north and east, on the 2nd which was also a very windy day. Gales swept over much of the United Kingdom with storm force winds over many coastal areas. The gales died down on the 3rd and there was further rain on the 4th to be followed by five mostly dry but cloudy days with some fog and frost overnight. Most places had a wet day on the 11th with wintry showers and some thunderstorms. There was some light rain and sleet at times during the next seven days with overnight fog and frost. On the 21st there was rain and snow in Scotland and Northern Ireland and winds became strong again. This was the start of an unsettled period with strong winds and heavy rain moving slowly eastwards across the United Kingdom. Many places had heavy rain on the 23rd which was the wettest day of the year up to that date. 50·6 mm. (2·0 ins.) fell at Long Kesh (Co. Down). The 24th saw further rain and strong winds over much of England and Scotland. The heaviest and most persistent rain fell in south Scotland and central and eastern parts of England where it turned to sleet and snow at times especially over high ground. In southern England there were some temporary accumulations of snow. The weather during the last few days of the month was very unsettled with periods of rain and snow and sometimes accompanied by hail and thunder. There was fog and frost overnight. Monthly mean temperatures were below normal everywhere making March a rather cold month. On the 1st the temperature at Lerwick (Shetland) never rose above 0·9°C. (33·6°F.). The temperature rose to 16·1°C. (61°F.) at the Lizard (Cornwall) on the 5th but fell to −8·4°C. (16·9°F.) at Tummel Bridge (Tayside) on the 18th. Sunshine totals were below normal everywhere except in the southwestern half of Cornwall where they were near or a little above normal. Many places received less than 50 per cent of the normal amount and it was especially dull over central England and East Anglia where some places had less than 40 per cent of normal. On the 31st 11·2 hours of sunshine were recorded at Benbecula (Hebrides).

April—Rainfall totals were generally very low with some areas of southern England receiving less than 5 per cent of the normal amount, even none at all at scattered places. The only area to have near or above normal amounts was northwest Scotland. Generally it was the driest April for 27 years. The month started with snow showers everywhere but most places become dry on the 2nd. On the 3rd there was a little rain in extreme western areas which moved to eastern parts on the 4th. On the 10th 28 mm. (1·1 ins.) of rain fell at Prabost (Isle of Skye) and there were wintry showers over northern England, Scotland and Northern Ireland on the 11th. On the 13th 46 mm. (1·8 ins.) of rain fell at Prabost. There were hail and snow showers in Scotland on the 14th which gradually moved south to give a few wintry showers in southeast England on the 16th. The rest of the month was dry except in Scotland where showers continued until the 22nd. On the 18th 29·7 mm. (1·2 ins.) fell at Sloy (Strathclyde). Monthly mean temperatures were near normal everywhere but the month started very cold. The afternoon temperatures on the 1st were 3 to 4°C. (5·4 to 7·2°F.) below normal and the warmest place, with a maximum temperature of 9°C. (48·2°F.) was Newquay (Cornwall). On the 2nd the temperature fell to −7·3°C. (18·9°F.) at Tummel Bridge (Tayside) and on the 4th the maximum temperature at Exton (Somerset) was only 2·8°C. (37·0°F.). The last 10 days of the month were very warm and in parts of Wales new extreme low temperatures for April were recorded during the first week and new extreme high ones during the last week. On the 22nd the temperature reached 26·2°C. (79·2°F.) at St. Helier (Channel Islands) while 24·1°C. (75·4°F.) was recorded at Glasgow on the 25th. On the 26th 25·3°C. (77·5°F.) at Fort William (Highland) was 2°C. (3·6°F.) higher than the temperature at Cairo. Sunshine totals were well above normal except in the extreme north of Scotland where a few places had a little below normal amounts. The really outstanding feature of the month was the sunshine enjoyed by most of the United Kingdom during the last 10 days. Much of the country basked in over 12 hours of sunshine per day and on the 27th 14·3 hours were recorded at Bastreet (Cornwall). London had 90 per cent. of the maximum possible sunshine during the last week which gave it the sunniest April since records were kept there in 1881. The coasts of north and east Scotland and eastern England had much low cloud and little or no sunshine during this period.

May—Rainfall totals were above normal in England south and east of a line from Bristol to Scarborough and well below normal everywhere else. Eskdalemuir (Dumfries and Galloway) had only 4 mm. (0·16 ins.) during the whole month. Some places in central southern England had as much rain on the 1st May as they had received during the whole of April. Thunder was reported from Swindon (Wiltshire). Thundery outbreaks affected southern England on the 2nd and there was thunder in central Scotland on the 4th. On the 10th there was snow for a time in parts of northeast England. On the 15th showers spread over Wales and central and southern England and spread north during the next few days with north Norfolk and north Scotland remaining dry until the 20th. On the 21st and 22nd there was a lot of heavy rain over much of England and Wales. Most places had at least 20 mm. (0·8 ins.) of rain and it was the first significant fall in many places for over seven weeks. At Penzance (Cornwall) 47·5 mm. (1·9 ins.) of rain fell on this day. The Spring Bank Holiday weekend of 26/27th was wet over most of southern and eastern England. The last three days of the month were generally dry in the south but there was some rain in places in Scotland. Monthly mean temperatures were mostly near or a little below normal. A warm day in central Scotland on the 4th gave Tummel Bridge (Tayside) a temperature of 21·9°C. (71·4°F.) but by the 6th the maximum temperature at the same place was only 10°C. (50°F.) and the maximum at Lerwick (Shetland) was 5°C. (41·0°F.).

Air frosts were reported widely in northern areas on the 7th and 8th while on the 9th air frost was reported over much of England and Wales with a minimum temperature of −4°C. (24·8°F.) at Bastreet (Cornwall). On the 14th the temperature fell to −6·1°C. (21·0°F.) at St. Harmon (Powys). Southern England had its warmest day of the month on the 24th when the temperature rose to 24·6°C. (76·3°F.) at Weymouth (Dorset). Sunshine totals were below normal in south and southeast England, East Anglia and the Midlands but mainly above normal elsewhere. At Prabost (Isle of Skye) 15·7 hours of sunshine were recorded on the 27th. The Spring (March, April, May) period was generally rather cold with near average sunshine. Rainfall was above average in southeast England but well below average in the west, especially in southwest Scotland. Glasgow (Strathclyde) had its driest Spring since 1869 and the Dumfries and Galloway Region had its driest this century.

June—Rainfall totals were very variable but generally below normal with only parts of East Anglia and small areas of north Scotland, north Wales and around Edinburgh having above average amounts. It was especially dry in southwest England where Penzance (Cornwall) had a total of only 3·6 mm. (0·14 ins.) for the whole month. The month began with showers and scattered thunderstorms and on the 1st Clacton-on-Sea (Essex) had 36 mm. (1·4 ins.) of rain. By the 7th most of the United Kingdom had become dry but many coastal areas were affected by fog. On the 8th and 9th there was overnight fog inland. A few places in southeast England had thundery showers on the 10th. The 12th brought rain to all areas except the extreme south and it was heavy in places especially in north and west Scotland. This rain moved into southern Scotland and northern England on the 13th. On the 16th there were isolated thunderstorms in central England and on the 17th thunder affected southern and eastern England. The heaviest falls were along the Thames Valley and over the Chilterns. 59·9 mm. (2·4 ins.) fell at Luton (Bedfordshire) on the 17th. There were reports that hail and lightning killed two young boys in St. Albans (Hertfordshire). Further thunderstorms affected central and eastern England on the 20th and Honnington (Suffolk) had 36 mm. (1·4 ins.) of rain in less than 1 hour. Generally in East Anglia there was considerable flooding and damage from lightning. On the 21st and 22nd there was rain in most areas but amounts were small in the south. During the last week rain continued in the north. Monthly mean temperatures were near normal almost everywhere. The month began cold but many places in Scotland became warm on the 5th and by the 7th most areas were warm. On the 9th the temperature at Cape Wrath (Highland) did not rise above 9°C. (48·2°F.). Temperatures fell generally on the 11th and were well below those of the previous day. This was especially true in the southeast of England where temperatures fell by 8°C. (14·4°F.). On the 16th most places became very warm and on the 18th the temperature rose to 28·7°C. (83·7°F.) at Yeovilton (Somerset). The last week became generally cool and the temperature fell to −0·7°C. (30·7°F.) at Eskdalemuir (Dumfries and Galloway) on the 30th. Sunshine totals were a little above average in England and Wales, near average in Northern Ireland and below average in Scotland. On the 8th Prestwick (Strathclyde) and Dhu Loch (Isle of Bute) recorded 15·8 hours of sunshine.

AVERAGE AND GENERAL VALUES, 1982–1984 (June)

Month	Rainfall (mm.)				Temperature (°C.)				Bright Sunshine (hrs. per day)			
	Aver. 1941–1970	1982	1983	1984	Aver. 1941–1970	1982	1983	1984	Aver. 1941–1970	1982	1983	1984
England and Wales												
January........	86	72	92	144	4·0	3·6	7·0	4·3	1·6	1·9	1·6	2·2
February.......	65	44	42	55	4·2	5·5	2·6	4·2	2·4	2·0	2·7	2·2
March	59	101	67	66	6·2	6·6	7·0	5·3	3·7	4·9	2·8	2·1
April..........	58	23	108	12	8·8	8·9	7·3	8·4	5·3	5·9	4·7	7·3
May	67	46	117	58	11·6	11·9	10·6	10·1	6·3	7·3	4·3	5·5
June	61	129	37	43	14·7	15·7	14·6	14·7	6·8	5·4	5·8	6·9
July	73	39	40	—	16·3	16·8	19·2	—	5·9	5·6	7·4	—
August.........	90	90	33	—	16·1	16·4	17·6	—	5·5	5·4	6·9	—
September	83	78	101	—	14·3	14·8	14·2	—	4·4	4·9	3·7	—
October	83	125	78	—	11·2	10·7	11·0	—	3·3	2·3	3·6	—
November	97	126	53	—	7·2	8·5	8·1	—	1·9	2·0	1·5	—
December	90	100	111	—	5·1	4·9	6·3	—	1·5	1·5	1·6	—
YEAR	912	973	879	—	10·0	10·4	10·4	—	4·0	4·1	3·9	—
Scotland												
January........	137	154	220	223	3·5	2·9	5·6	2·2	1·4	1·2	1·0	1·3
February.......	104	107	59	104	3·7	5·5	2·7	4·5	2·5	2·2	2·4	1·6
March	92	153	149	119	5·4	5·6	6·2	4·8	3·4	3·7	2·2	2·3
April..........	90	46	74	54	7·5	8·2	5·8	7·8	5·0	4·8	4·4	5·9
May	91	92	115	23	9·9	9·9	9·0	9·6	5·7	6·9	3·7	6·7
June	92	72	86	66	12·7	12·8	12·2	12·9	5·8	5·3	5·5	4·9
July	112	57	43	—	14·1	15·1	16·0	—	4·8	6·0	5·9	—
August.........	129	156	51	—	14·0	14·3	15·5	—	4·5	4·4	5·0	—
September	137	200	172	—	12·5	12·2	13·3	—	3·7	3·3	2·9	—
October	149	196	230	—	9·9	9·6	9·4	—	2·7	2·1	2·4	—
November	142	229	49	—	6·3	6·6	7·3	—	1·7	1·5	1·5	—
December	156	213	208	—	4·6	3·9	6·1	—	1·1	1·0	0·8	—
YEAR	1431	1675	1456	—	8·7	8·9	9·1	—	3·5	3·4	3·1	—

TEMPERATURE AND RAINFALL RECORDS

WORLD: The maximum air temperature recorded is 57·8°C. (136°F.) at San Louis, Mexico on August 11, 1933; the minimum air temperature recorded is −88·3°C. (−127°F.) at Vostok, Antarctica on August 24, 1960. The greatest rainfall recorded in one day is 1870 mm. (73·62 ins.) at Cilaos, Isle de Réunion on March 16, 1952; the greatest rainfall in one calendar month is 9,300 mm. (366·14 ins.) at Cherrapunji, Assam in July 1861, the greatest annual total being 22,990 mm. (905·12 ins.) also at Cherrapunji in 1861.

UNITED KINGDOM: The maximum air temperature recorded is 38·1°C. (100·5°F.) at Tonbridge, Kent on July 22 1868; the minimum air temperature recorded is −27·2°C. (−17°F.) at Braemar (Grampian) on February 11, 1895 and 10th January 1982. The greatest rainfall recorded in one day is 280 mm. (11 ins.) at Martinstown, Dorset on July 18, 1955. The greatest annual total is 6,528 mm. (257 ins.) at Sprinkling Tarn, Cumbria in 1954.

WIND FORCE MEASURES

The *Beaufort Scale* of wind force has been accepted internationally and is used in communicating weather conditions. Devised originally by Admiral Sir Francis Beaufort in 1805, it now consists of the numbers 0–17, each representing a certain strength or velocity of wind at 10 m. (33 ft.) above ground in the open.

Scale No.	Wind Force	M.p.h.	Knots	Scale No.	Wind Force	M.p.h.	Knots
0	Calm	1	1	9	Strong gale	47–54	41–47
1	Light air	1–3	1–3	10	Whole gale	55–63	48–55
2	Slight breeze	4–7	4–6	11	Storm	64–72	56–63
3	Gentle breeze	8–12	7–10	12	Hurricane	73–82	64–71
4	Moderate breeze	13–18	11–16	13	—	83–92	72–80
5	Fresh breeze	19–24	17–21	14	—	93–103	81–89
6	Strong breeze	25–31	22–27	15	—	104–114	90–99
7	High wind	32–38	28–33	16	—	115–125	100–108
8	Gale	39–46	34–40	17	—	126–136	109–118

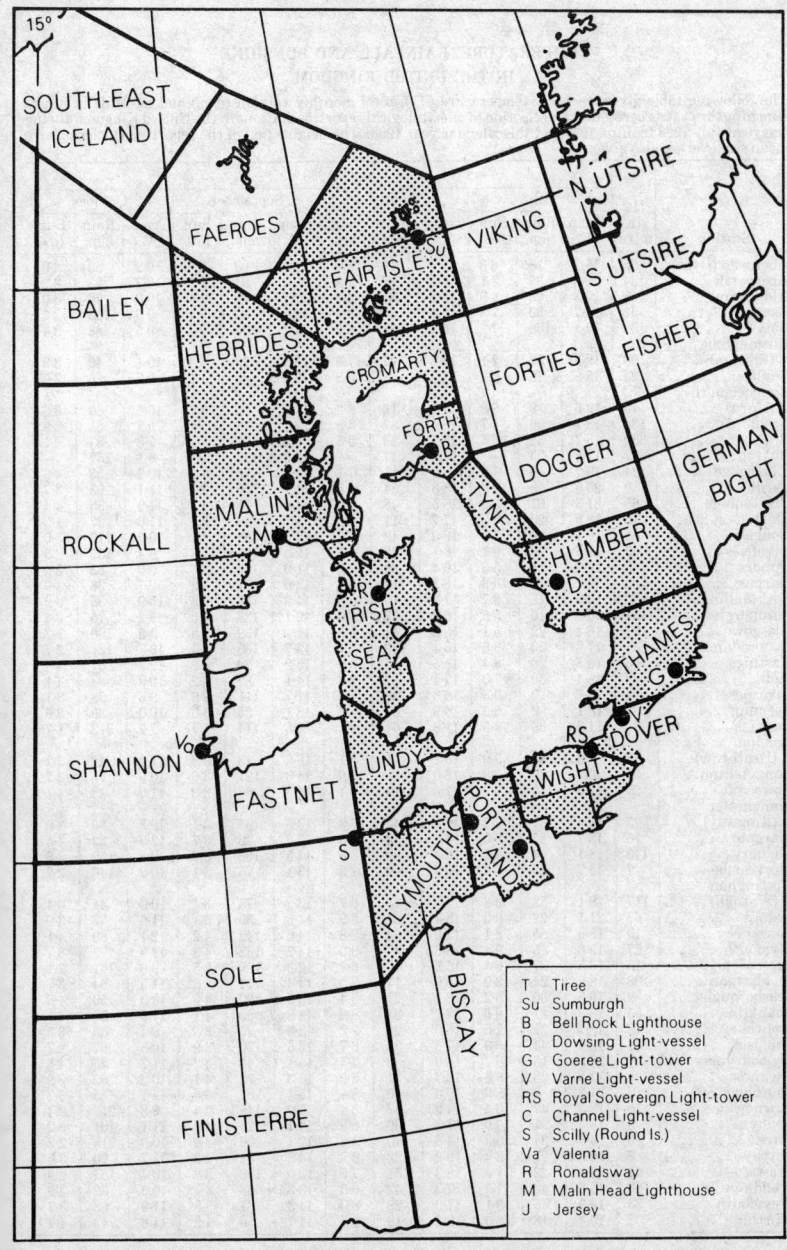

T   Tiree
Su Sumburgh
B   Bell Rock Lighthouse
D   Dowsing Light-vessel
G   Goeree Light-tower
V   Varne Light-vessel
RS Royal Sovereign Light-tower
C   Channel Light-vessel
S   Scilly (Round Is.)
Va Valentia
R   Ronaldsway
M   Malin Head Lighthouse
J   Jersey

TEMPERATURE, RAINFALL AND SUNSHINE
IN THE UNITED KINGDOM

The following table gives mean air temperature (°C.), total monthly rainfall (mm.) and mean daily bright sunshine (hrs.) at a representative selection of climatological reporting stations in the United Kingdom during the year July 1983 to June 1984 and the calendar year 1983. The heights (m.) of the reporting stations above mean sea level are also given.

	Ht. in mtrs.	July			August			September			October		
Station		Temp. °C.	Rain mm.	Sun hrs.	Temp. °C.	Rain mm.	Sun hrs.	Temp. °C.	Rain mm.	Sun hrs.	Temp. °C.	Rain mm.	Sun hrs.
Aberdeen (Dyce) .	65	15·7	18	6·3	15·6	13	5·8	11·7	98	3·8	9·2	59	4·0
Aberporth	134	17·3	39	8·1	16·3	57	7·2	13·4	94	3·9	10·7	82	3·2
Aldergrove	68	17·3	29	6·0	16·7	31	4·6	12·7	96	2·4	10·0	76	3·0
Aspatria	61	17·7	39	7·3	16·3	38	8·1	12·5	90	3·4	9·9	153	2·6
Bala	163	17·4	168	7·1	15·4	38	6·5	12·4	193	2·7	9·5	188	2·4
Birmingham (Elmdon)	98	19·3	52	7·1	17·2	27	7·3	13·5	76	3·6	10·1	48	3·8
Boulmer	23	15·5	28	5·3	14·9	31	5·8	12·5	85	4·1	9·7	26	3·9
Bournemouth (Hurn)	10	19·6	9	8·8	17·7	14	8·2	14·3	66	3·7	10·8	80	3·6
Bradford	134	18·1	96	4·7	16·8	47	5·8	12·7	72	3·1	9·7	81	2·9
Braemar	339	15·7	34	6·6	15·1	23	5·5	9·5	92	3·1	7·3	87	2·1
Buxton	307	17·5	35	—	15·3	47	—	11·5	183	—	8·1	157	—
Cambridge.......	24	19·7	49	7·8	18·0	11	7·1	14·5	70	4·2	10·9	33	4·3
Cardiff	9	20·5	18	8·0	18·3	34	7·5	14·1	186	3·1	11·1	93	3·7
Cheltenham	65	21·3	61	8·5	18·5	18	7·9	14·0	76	4·1	11·2	53	4·4
Clacton-on-Sea...	16	18·5	20	7·7	17·7	11	6·3	14·7	46	3·7	11·6	37	4·5
Douglas	85	17·1	29	7·8	16·0	42	7·2	12·6	138	3·1	10·3	117	3·0
Dumfries	49	17·5	29	6·1	16·1	33	6·5	12·0	105	2·6	9·4	152	2·5
Dundee	45	16·7	11	5·3	16·4	36	5·2	11·9	104	3·6	9·3	52	3·0
Durham	102	17·7	20	6·3	16·3	42	6·1	12·6	61	3·9	9·7	36	4·0
East Malling	33	19·9	11	8·7	17·7	15	6·6	14·5	35	3·8	10·9	58	3·9
Edinburgh.......	134	16·5	10	5·5	16·3	37	6·0	12·1	123	3·8	9·2	75	3·4
Glasgow.........	107	16·4	22	5·1	15·8	41	5·5	11·1	139	2·5	8·5	196	1·7
Gogerddan	31	17·7	30	8·6	16·4	139	7·7	13·7	138	3·4	10·7	121	2·7
Hastings	45	19·3	20	8·4	18·5	15	8·8	15·2	79	4·2	12·2	61	4·4
Hull	2	18·4	39	7·0	17·4	17	6·7	14·1	89	4·2	10·9	38	4·1
Inverness	4	16·7	9	5·5	16·3	28	5·2	11·7	111	2·9	9·6	78	3·1
Leeming.........	32	18·1	9	6·3	16·9	30	6·7	13·1	58	3·6	10·0	39	3·6
Lerwick	82	11·7	69	4·5	11·8	64	2·1	9·8	114	1·7	7·7	212	1·7
London (Heathrow)	25	21·8	50	8·0	19·1	11	7·1	15·3	43	3·8	11·4	42	3·7
Long Ashton.....	51	20·4	26	8·8	18·0	18	7·6	14·3	121	3·6	10·9	75	3·7
Lowestoft	25	17·6	15	7·7	17·3	11	6·1	14·3	83	3·6	11·0	43	4·1
Manchester (Ringway)	75	19·4	67	7·3	17·3	45	7·3	13·5	95	3·1	10·3	89	3·0
Margate.........	16	18·7	25	8·0	18·1	13	5·3	15·3	23	3·7	12·3	32	4·4
Melbury.........	143	18·1	4	9·7	16·4	29	8·5	13·5	163	3·7	10·3	152	3·6
Morecambe	7	18·7	25	6·7	16·9	76	7·3	13·1	75	3·1	10·3	146	2·7
Nottingham (Watnall)......	117	19·1	52	6·8	17·3	13	6·7	13·2	75	3·4	10·0	41	3·4
Oxford	63	21·1	22	8·3	18·4	24	6·9	14·5	59	3·1	11·0	53	3·9
Penzance	19	18·9	85	8·1	17·9	32	7·8	14·6	142	4·2	12·1	89	4·1
Plymouth	27	19·8	15	9·4	18·3	37	9·0	14·7	132	4·3	11·9	72	3·7
Prestwick	16	16·5	27	6·4	15·9	40	6·7	12·3	126	2·5	9·9	161	2·1
St. Mawgan......	103	18·9	24	8·9	18·0	17	8·5	14·4	111	3·8	11·5	84	3·7
Scarborough.....	52	16·5	30	5·2	16·1	27	5·4	13·5	90	4·0	10·5	50	4·0
Shanklin	55	19·3	21	9·6	17·7	23	8·8	14·8	69	4·1	11·9	50	4·1
Shawbury	72	18·7	22	7·5	16·9	29	7·2	13·3	75	3·5	9·7	35	3·5
Sheffield........	131	19·4	44	6·0	17·3	31	6·7	13·5	120	3·9	10·5	67	2·7
Shoeburyness	2	18·9	15	8·7	17·0	9	7·3	15·1	41	4·2	11·7	45	4·5
Skegness	5	17·3	26	6·0	16·7	11	5·0	14·3	72	4·1	10·2	32	3·9
Southampton	3	21·3	9	8·9	19·3	40	8·4	15·1	82	3·8	11·7	55	3·7
Stornoway	15	13·9	47	6·4	14·0	53	3·4	10·9	148	2·4	8·8	219	2·4
Tenby...........	5	18·7	7	10·0	17·3	36	8·3	14·1	125	4·0	11·1	101	3·2
Tiree............	9	14·6	37	5·3	14·6	70	4·7	12·1	106	3·2	10·0	215	2·3
Torbay..........	8	19·7	27	9·4	18·2	23	8·7	14·8	81	4·2	11·7	70	3·6
Trawscoed.......	61	17·8	22	7·4	16·3	151	7·5	13·5	158	3·8	10·4	154	2·9
Waddington	68	18·8	42	7·9	17·2	42	6·6	13·5	63	4·1	10·3	32	3·9
Weymouth	23	19·3	5	9·1	17·9	29	8·0	14·8	61	3·8	11·9	68	3·7
Worthing	2	19·4	18	8·6	18·2	19	8·5	14·7	56	4·2	11·6	43	4·2

TEMPERATURE, RAINFALL AND SUNSHINE IN THE UNITED KINGDOM—*contd.*

Mean Temperature of the air (°C.), Rainfall (mm.) and Bright Sunshine (as mean hours per day) at a representative selection of reporting stations during the year July 1983 to June 1984. Fuller details of the weather are given in the *Monthly Weather Report* published by the Meteorological Office.

	1983									1984					
	November			December			Year			January			February		
Station	Temp. °C.	Rain mm.	Sun hrs.	Temp. °C.	Rain mm.	Sun hrs.	Temp. °C.	Rain mm.	Sun hrs.	Temp. °C.	Rain mm.	Sun hrs.	Temp. °C.	Rain mm.	Sun hrs.
Aberdeen (Dyce)	6·4	21	1·6	5·5	73	0·8	—	—	—	0·6	155	1·7	3·5	47	1·9
Aberporth	8·4	45	2·0	7·1	122	1·6	9·9	822	4·1	4·9	81	1·4	4·7	52	2·0
Aldergrove	7·7	33	1·4	6·5	110	0·9	9·0	622	3·1	2·5	150	1·5	4·6	88	1·8
Aspatria	6·9	45	2·1	6·0	129	1·1	—	—	—	2·9	125	1·5	3·7	39	2·4
Bala	6·5	45	1·3	5·8	183	0·9	—	—	—	3·5	213	0·9	3·5	98	1·6
Birmingham (Elmdon)	7·3	34	1·1	5·3	67	1·7	9·6	635	3·6	3·5	89	2·5	2·9	53	1·8
Boulmer	7·1	24	1·8	5·8	83	1·2	—	—	—	2·5	97	2·7	3·7	28	2·0
Bournemouth (Hurn)	7·9	46	1·3	6·4	117	2·3	10·5	744	4·4	4·9	154	2·7	4·5	37	2·8
Bradford	6·7	36	1·3	5·3	167	1·1	—	—	—	2·5	180	1·4	2·9	65	1·3
Braemar	4·7	18	1·3	3·4	159	0·4	7·1	946	3·0	−1·7	226	0·8	1·6	97	1·4
Buxton	5·9	91	—	4·3	237	—	8·1	1460	—	1·7	217	—	1·7	128	—
Cambridge	7·6	45	1·3	5·5	36	2·0	—	580	—	3·8	57	3·1	3·4	42	2·3
Cardiff	8·4	64	1·2	6·7	122	1·9	10·9	1062	3·7	4·9	206	2·3	4·9	67	2·1
Cheltenham	7·9	25	1·2	6·5	59	1·8	10·8	655	4·1	4·3	70	2·6	3·5	47	1·5
Clacton-on-Sea	7·9	33	1·9	5·6	43	2·1	10·4	459	4·3	4·2	80	3·3	4·1	29	2·8
Douglas	8·3	41	1·7	7·1	217	0·9	9·6	1113	4·0	4·1	169	1·8	4·7	85	1·9
Dumfries	6·8	17	1·4	5·5	141	0·9	—	965	3·1	2·5	167	1·4	3·7	79	1·7
Dundee	6·7	16	2·1	5·5	99	0·9	9·0	639	3·3	1·7	111	1·8	3·6	47	2·0
Durham	6·7	33	1·8	5·1	98	1·6	9·0	674	3·8	2·1	84	1·9	3·0	28	1·9
East Malling	7·9	34	1·7	5·7	75	2·0	10·6	581	4·3	4·9	110	2·9	4·1	27	2·7
Edinburgh	6·9	11	2·4	5·4	60	1·1	8·8	694	3·5	1·7	94	2·1	3·4	42	1·9
Glasgow	6·4	22	1·6	5·1	98	0·9	8·5	992	2·8	1·4	144	1·0	3·3	91	1·7
Gogerddan	7·9	69	1·7	7·0	127	1·5	9·9	—	3·9	5·0	121	1·1	4·5	48	1·8
Hastings	8·7	42	2·6	6·9	88	2·3	10·9	693	4·9	5·3	141	3·0	4·8	37	3·0
Hull	7·9	46	—	5·7	121	—	10·1	729	—	3·4	98	—	3·8	34	—
Inverness	7·5	23	1·3	5·8	100	0·7	9·1	650	2·9	1·3	58	0·8	4·9	31	1·6
Leeming	7·2	28	1·5	5·7	98	1·4	9·5	611	3·6	2·6	108	1·8	3·3	25	1·7
Lerwick	6·1	90	0·3	4·5	187	0·3	—	—	—	1·7	142	0·9	4·1	90	0·9
London (Heathrow)	8·7	39	1·4	6·1	51	1·9	11·0	534	4·1	4·9	73	2·8	4·5	33	2·5
Long Ashton	7·9	46	1·3	6·4	96	1·9	10·6	877	4·2	4·7	157	2·1	4·1	53	1·9
Lowestoft	7·9	63	1·2	5·6	41	1·4	10·0	528	4·0	3·5	77	2·1	3·6	34	2·1
Manchester (Ringway)	7·7	53	1·7	5·9	122	1·5	10·0	894	3·6	3·6	112	1·8	3·7	52	2·1
Margate	9·1	24	—	6·7	54	—	11·0	476	—	4·9	91	—	4·3	20	—
Melbury	7·9	84	1·3	6·6	200	1·9	—	—	—	4·7	268	1·5	4·4	112	1·9
Morecambe	7·6	60	1·8	5·9	197	1·1	9·9	1059	3·6	3·8	143	1·5	3·9	64	2·1
Nottingham (Watnall)	7·2	39	1·1	5·1	76	1·4	9·6	669	3·4	2·9	109	2·2	2·9	49	1·6
Oxford	7·7	43	1·5	5·9	50	2·0	10·8	578	4·0	4·5	81	2·8	3·7	35	2·3
Penzance	10·5	68	1·5	8·7	147	2·2	11·5	1043	—	6·5	223	2·3	7·1	76	3·2
Plymouth	9·9	62	1·0	8·1	135	2·0	11·3	880	4·6	6·5	215	2·2	5·9	51	2·7
Prestwick	7·5	26	2·0	6·3	110	1·1	9·3	939	3·6	3·1	124	1·4	4·3	78	1·8
St. Mawgan	9·3	60	1·5	7·9	114	2·2	10·8	872	4·4	6·1	170	1·7	5·7	67	2·2
Scarborough	7·8	52	1·4	5·8	119	1·2	9·4	673	—	3·5	101	1·9	3·8	28	2·4
Shanklin	8·7	49	1·4	7·1	85	2·3	—	—	—	5·3	145	2·8	5·5	43	2·8
Shawbury	6·7	38	1·0	5·7	69	1·7	—	—	—	3·5	69	2·1	3·3	34	1·5
Sheffield	7·7	41	1·0	5·8	142	1·2	9·9	906	3·3	3·2	160	1·2	3·2	80	1·5
Shoeburyness	7·9	30	2·0	5·9	47	2·3	—	—	—	4·9	65	3·3	4·2	24	2·7
Skegness	8·1	55	1·2	5·3	60	1·8	9·8	551	3·6	3·5	82	1·2	3·5	38	1·5
Southampton	8·9	41	1·8	6·9	94	1·7	11·4	652	4·4	5·7	125	2·5	5·3	32	2·6
Stornoway	7·5	56	1·4	6·4	196	0·7	8·3	1258	3·1	2·3	154	0·9	5·6	63	1·6
Tenby	8·8	50	1·6	7·9	122	1·9	—	—	—	5·1	162	2·5	5·2	65	2·2
Tiree	8·5	44	1·3	7·3	163	0·7	9·2	1074	3·6	3·7	208	1·0	5·6	85	1·1
Torbay	9·5	53	1·5	7·7	114	2·6	11·3	795	4·7	6·1	191	2·7	5·8	48	2·5
Trawscoed	7·9	77	1·9	6·7	141	1·4	9·9	1298	—	4·7	156	1·2	4·5	87	1·8
Waddington	7·3	43	1·6	5·0	40	1·9	—	—	—	2·5	91	2·4	2·8	41	2·3
Weymouth	8·8	39	1·8	7·7	85	2·4	11·0	685	—	6·1	122	2·7	5·4	42	2·6
Worthing	8·7	41	2·7	6·8	94	2·2	10·8	619	4·9	5·3	125	3·0	4·7	31	2·8

TEMPERATURE, RAINFALL AND SUNSHINE IN THE UNITED KINGDOM—*contd.*

Mean Temperature of the air (°C.), Rainfall (mm.) and Bright Sunshine (as mean hours per day) at a representative selection of reporting stations during the year July 1983 to June 1984. Fuller details of the weather are given in the *Monthly Weather Report* published by the Meteorological Office.

	1984											
	March			April			May			June		
Station	Temp. °C.	Rain mm.	Sun hrs.	Temp. °C.	Rain mm.	Sun hrs.	Temp. °C.	Rain mm.	Sun hrs.	Temp. °C.	Rain mm.	Sun hrs.
Aberdeen (Dyce)	3·9	98	2·2	7·0	17	5·9	8·5	16	6·9	12·5	43	5·0
Aberporth	4·7	35	3·2	8·9	8	7·2	9·3	45	7·6	12·7	25	6·7
Aldergrove	4·7	58	2·2	8·4	21	6·0	9·9	25	8·4	14·0	53	5·6
Aspatria	4·7	53	2·3	7·7	15	7·0	9·9	19	8·0	13·4	74	6·2
Bala	4·1	48	1·2	7·2	9	6·9	8·7	44	6·2	13·1	40	5·6
Birmingham (Elmdon)	4·4	47	1·4	7·7	2	7·4	9·6	67	4·9	14·7	33	6·3
Boulmer.............	4·7	74	2·1	6·2	12	6·1	7·7	19	6·7	12·2	31	5·9
Bournemouth (Hurn)	5·1	73	2·8	8·0	1	8·2	10·3	80	5·1	14·9	27	9·8
Bradford	4·4	53	1·5	7·6	12	6·1	9·5	33	—	13·9	39	5·6
Braemar	1·9	143	1·8	5·7	11	6·4	7·7	21	5·9	12·3	47	5·5
Buxton..............	2·9	81	—	6·4	15	—	8·6	41	—	12·8	65	—
Cambridge..........	4·9	31	1·5	7·7	14	7·7	9·5	76	4·2	14·7	49	7·0
Cardiff	6·1	31	2·4	9·3	9	7·7	11·6	60	5·5	15·7	28	8·2
Cheltenham	5·0	52	2·2	8·7	11	8·0	10·7	67	5·3	15·7	47	8·3
Clacton-on-Sea......	4·9	56	2·3	7·5	15	7·6	9·4	54	4·1	14·3	62	7·2
Douglas	5·0	34	1·9	8·1	36	6·7	10·2	13	8·9	13·3	60	6·7
Dumfries	4·7	33	1·6	7·8	13	6·0	10·3	14	7·1	13·9	39	5·5
Dundee	4·7	101	2·5	7·4	6	5·3	10·0	18	7·1	14·5	41	6·3
Durham	4·4	52	1·7	7·5	13	6·9	9·1	31	6·0	13·5	37	5·3
East Malling	5·3	59	1·9	7·9	7	7·5	10·1	58	4·5	15·1	60	7·5
Edinburgh..........	4·1	91	2·5	7·3	11	6·1	9·6	36	7·0	13·7	50	6·2
Glasgow............	4·5	58	2·0	8·1	13	5·0	10·9	18	6·6	13·7	37	4·5
Gogerddan	4·9	26	2·7	8·7	11	7·5	9·7	47	6·9	13·5	40	6·0
Hastings	5·5	90	3·0	8·8	3	8·5	10·4	60	5·1	14·7	23	8·9
Hull	4·8	66	—	7·9	19	—	9·7	67	—	14·7	48	—
Inverness	5·1	36	2·1	8·1	12	6·2	10·1	8	5·6	13·2	26	4·7
Leeming	4·7	57	1·9	7·7	11	6·6	9·3	32	6·1	14·1	28	6·4
Lerwick	3·1	81	2·4	5·6	75	4·6	7·5	27	4·3	10·2	52	3·8
London (Heathrow)	5·7	73	1·7	9·3	5	7·7	10·9	91	4·7	16·3	36	7·9
Long Ashton........	5·1	39	2·3	8·9	3	8·0	10·5	97	5·9	15·3	25	8·7
Lowestoft	4·7	66	1·9	7·1	21	7·2	9·1	73	3·6	13·6	24	5·7
Manchester (Ringway)	4·9	41	2·0	8·7	14	7·2	10·7	31	6·2	14·3	30	5·4
Margate.............	5·1	51	—	7·9	23	7·9	9·1	57	3·7	14·7	32	7·7
Melbury............	4·5	43	3·2	8·1	8	8·4	8·9	46	6·6	13·3	27	8·0
Morecambe	5·1	40	2·1	8·7	9	7·2	10·9	35	7·2	13·9	55	5·9
Nottingham (Watnall)..........	4·3	61	1·5	7·9	7	7·3	9·8	72	5·2	14·5	36	7·6
Oxford	5·3	50	1·6	8·6	2	7·9	10·4	72	4·6	15·8	30	8·1
Penzance	6·7	54	4·5	9·6	26	8·9	11·1	76	7·0	14·9	4	9·0
Plymouth	6·2	46	3·9	9·4	10	8·7	11·1	73	6·1	15·1	8	10·1
Prestwick	4·9	35	2·0	8·2	24	6·6	10·0	16	8·0	13·1	40	5·5
St. Mawgan	5·5	55	4·3	9·5	3	8·9	9·9	64	6·5	13·8	9	7·3
Scarborough........	4·8	55	2·1	6·0	13	6·6	8·5	47	5·9	13·5	22	6·2
Shanklin	5·9	77	3·3	8·1	1	8·3	10·1	81	5·1	14·7	9	10·1
Shawbury	4·5	35	1·5	7·5	7	6·9	9·5	44	6·1	13·8	47	5·6
Sheffield	4·8	52	1·5	8·4	10	6·9	10·4	55	5·1	14·8	41	7·3
Shoeburyness	4·9	38	2·1	7·5	10	8·0	9·4	63	4·3	14·5	25	7·8
Skegness	4·9	43	1·4	7·3	20	7·3	9·1	77	4·0	13·9	27	5·3
Southampton	6·0	80	2·5	9·7	2	7·9	11·5	93	5·1	16·5	20	9·1
Stornoway	5·0	81	2·3	7·5	70	6·2	8·5	20	7·7	11·3	44	4·1
Tenby..............	5·5	34	3·6	8·5	5	8·2	10·5	31	7·1	14·3	19	8·4
Tiree...............	5·5	58	3·1	8·3	64	6·8	9·3	16	8·8	12·2	50	4·2
Torbay.............	6·1	58	3·1	9·1	8	8·9	11·1	45	5·5	15·8	6	10·8
Trawscoed..........	4·9	33	2·6	8·2	12	7·6	8·9	35	6·6	13·5	46	6·0
Waddington	4·5	52	1·7	7·5	15	7·1	9·3	70	5·6	14·3	27	6·9
Weymouth	5·7	52	2·7	8·9	2	8·1	10·7	58	5·1	15·1	27	10·1
Worthing	5·7	82	3·0	8·3	3	8·2	10·4	70	5·3	14·6	9	8·8

Weather Record, July, 1983 / Weather Record, August, 1983

Day	Max. °C.	Min. °C.	Wind Speed knots	Rainfall mm.	Sunshine hrs.	Max. °C.	Min. °C.	Wind Speed knots	Rainfall mm.	Sunshine hrs.	Day
1	22.3	8.6	5.2	0.1	8.8	20.0	14.2	7.2	0.0	3.1	1
2	25.3	13.8	5.9	0.0	6.2	19.4	9.2	5.0	0.2	6.3	2
3	26.2	11.0	3.2	0.0	14.5	22.5	7.1	3.7	0.0	13.6	3
4	28.4	14.9	3.6	0.0	11.4	23.9	10.3	4.9	0.0	2.4	4
5	28.8	15.4	6.3	0.0	13.8	24.6	12.3	5.1	0.0	12.0	5
6	26.6	17.0	3.5	20.4	2.0	21.2	13.7	5.0	0.0	4.9	6
7	26.1	15.4	2.8	0.0	5.5	22.7	12.9	5.7	0.0	4.9	7
8	28.2	16.4	3.5	0.0	3.9	26.4	14.7	8.3	0.0	9.7	8
9	27.2	16.9	6.2	0.0	8.4	28.0	15.2	10.7	0.0	7.6	9
10	27.5	15.9	6.5	0.0	8.4	25.3	15.7	9.4	0.0	9.7	10
11	30.6	16.3	6.2	0.0	12.6	21.5	15.7	4.6	0.0	4.1	11
12	30.6	17.7	5.4	0.0	13.6	25.3	11.8	6.1	0.0	9.8	12
13	31.6	17.6	5.3	0.0	11.6	23.7	12.3	4.5	0.0	12.9	13
14	31.4	15.4	4.3	0.0	8.3	28.8	13.6	3.7	0.0	8.1	14
15	32.6	17.9	5.5	0.0	11.7	27.2	16.3	6.3	0.0	10.2	15
16	32.8	19.1	3.7	0.0	11.7	25.6	14.1	7.0	0.0	6.6	16
17	28.5	18.6	7.3	0.0	8.8	25.9	17.9	6.0	0.0	1.7	17
18	28.5	17.7	4.5	0.0	7.5	26.9	13.1	4.0	0.0	12.1	18
19	25.6	16.7	5.2	0.0	4.3	30.2	17.5	9.4	0.0	11.0	19
20	21.2	15.9	6.5	0.0	0.6	24.2	17.9	7.3	0.0	3.5	20
21	23.8	11.6	7.2	0.0	14.0	24.2	14.9	5.5	3.4	6.1	21
22	27.3	14.3	9.0	7.4	5.6	26.3	16.8	3.6	7.7	3.0	22
23	24.6	16.7	5.2	0.1	4.2	26.1	14.9	2.8	0.0	4.0	23
24	22.7	15.9	6.0	0.9	3.5	22.4	16.0	6.8	0.0	0.4	24
25	25.3	16.8	3.5	0.0	2.5	26.1	13.6	7.9	0.0	11.6	25
26	28.2	16.7	4.1	0.0	5.3	26.7	15.3	6.6	0.0	9.6	26
27	27.0	18.0	6.9	0.0	6.4	25.9	13.2	3.8	0.0	10.0	27
28	26.8	16.1	8.3	0.0	9.6	21.0	14.2	8.2	0.0	4.4	28
29	31.4	15.1	4.0	0.0	13.4	19.4	13.7	6.8	0.0	4.9	29
30	30.0	17.6	3.9	0.0	8.9	21.7	7.9	3.7	0.0	5.4	30
31	28.9	17.9	4.3	21.4	0.8	26.9	13.0	2.6	0.1	5.5	31
Total ..	—	—	—	50.3	247.8	—	—	—	11.4	219.1	.. Total
Mean ..	27.6	16.0	5.3	—	8.0	24.5	13.8	5.9	—	7.1	.. Mean
Temp. °F.	81.7	60.8	—	—	—	76.1	56.8	—	—	—	Temp. °F.
Average	22.0	12.8	8.2	58.0	181.0	21.5	12.5	8.0	65.0	170.0	Average

Weather Record, September, 1983 / Weather Record, October, 1983

Day	Max. °C.	Min. °C.	Wind Speed knots	Rainfall mm.	Sunshine hrs.	Max. °C.	Min. °C.	Wind Speed knots	Rainfall mm.	Sunshine hrs.	Day
1	22.4	15.2	4.0	0.2	0.4	16.7	14.4	5.6	1.0	0.0	1
2	20.6	11.4	14.5	1.9	4.9	19.2	13.8	5.9	0.0	1.7	2
3	19.3	13.3	16.0	0.0	1.4	20.0	15.4	7.7	0.0	0.0	3
4	23.4	12.5	12.7	0.0	3.8	23.8	13.9	8.7	0.0	5.9	4
5	21.6	12.6	8.9	0.0	10.3	18.8	12.0	9.5	0.0	6.0	5
6	21.0	8.0	5.6	0.0	6.8	17.9	8.7	5.5	0.0	3.0	6
7	21.2	7.0	4.7	0.0	7.8	16.5	11.6	7.6	0.4	0.0	7
8	19.5	12.0	8.3	0.8	0.1	13.5	6.0	8.6	6.6	0.1	8
9	18.7	13.0	8.0	3.2	0.2	16.2	12.5	7.9	1.5	0.0	9
10	18.1	11.4	6.9	3.5	4.6	16.1	13.4	10.4	3.3	4.1	10
11	14.1	9.2	9.3	0.6	0.0	14.3	7.7	8.6	0.8	6.3	11
12	15.9	8.9	6.9	0.0	4.7	15.6	8.2	9.7	0.0	0.1	12
13	16.0	9.5	5.2	11.1	0.0	18.1	13.7	8.2	7.3	1.3	13
14	19.0	14.3	7.6	5.1	0.9	15.6	8.8	7.5	2.1	6.2	14
15	18.2	13.5	11.8	3.5	5.8	13.8	8.5	13.3	17.3	0.0	15
16	17.8	11.5	11.0	0.0	4.1	13.8	9.5	14.7	0.2	6.9	16
17	19.0	11.0	8.0	3.0	4.8	13.3	8.3	9.5	0.0	6.1	17
18	17.6	12.1	10.9	0.4	1.2	16.1	10.5	13.1	1.2	1.6	18
19	19.1	11.0	9.6	3.3	7.8	14.6	9.8	7.4	0.0	8.4	19
20	17.0	8.5	6.5	2.9	3.0	12.6	2.5	2.4	0.0	5.3	20
21	14.9	10.8	7.3	3.2	0.0	13.2	4.5	5.3	0.0	6.1	21
22	17.6	5.6	4.5	0.0	6.7	12.8	3.3	4.3	0.0	8.9	22
23	23.0	9.6	7.1	0.0	8.9	15.1	-1.0	2.7	0.0	8.1	23
24	22.4	12.9	5.1	0.2	2.8	12.2	2.8	4.9	0.0	2.1	24
25	20.4	10.3	4.7	0.0	10.2	13.4	3.2	4.3	0.0	0.5	25
26	24.4	10.3	4.5	0.0	9.6	14.2	4.6	3.1	0.0	2.9	26
27	19.3	15.2	3.8	0.0	0.1	13.8	7.9	4.1	0.0	6.2	27
28	19.6	14.7	7.5	0.0	2.7	11.0	4.6	5.7	0.0	7.9	28
29	19.7	12.9	5.1	0.0	0.1	9.5	1.8	4.7	0.0	8.3	29
30	18.6	13.6	6.9	0.0	0.0	10.1	-2.3	5.0	0.0	0.0	30
31						11.6	5.8	3.7	0.0	0.0	31
Total ..	—	—	—	42.9	113.7	—	—	—	41.7	114.0	.. Total
Mean ..	19.3	11.4	7.8	—	3.8	14.9	7.9	7.1	—	3.7	.. Mean
Temp. °F.	66.7	52.5	—	—	—	58.8	46.2	—	—	—	Temp. °F.
Average	19.1	10.8	7.9	52.0	142.0	15.1	7.8	7.8	57.0	105.0	Average

Entries of Maximum Temperature cover the day period 9–21 h.; Minimum Temperature the night period 21–9 h. entered to the day of reading; Rainfall is for the 24 hours commencing at 9 h. on the day of entry; Sunshine is for the 24 hours 0–24 h.; Mean Wind Speed is 10 metres above the ground. 100 knots = 115.1 m.p.h.; 100 mm. = 3.94 ins.; °F. = 9/5°C. + 32.
Averages are for the period 1941–1970 except for mean wind speed which is for 1961–1980.

Weather Record, November, 1983

Day	Temperature Max. °C.	Min. °C.	Wind Speed knots	Rain-fall mm.	Sun-shine hrs.
1	15.6	6.6	5.3	0.0	0.0
2	15.0	13.3	2.8	1.6	0.0
3	14.4	11.2	3.6	0.0	4.3
4	13.3	6.2	2.2	0.0	3.3
5	12.6	8.5	2.3	0.0	0.0
6	14.8	10.4	3.5	0.0	0.0
7	14.7	10.8	5.6	1.0	0.2
8	17.0	11.6	5.2	0.0	1.5
9	16.7	9.4	3.8	0.0	1.7
10	16.2	9.7	4.3	0.0	5.7
11	12.6	7.5	4.9	0.0	0.0
12	9.6	8.3	5.9	0.0	0.3
13	9.6	6.8	7.0	0.0	2.9
14	6.1	2.6	11.2	0.0	7.2
15	7.4	-2.8	6.0	0.0	1.3
16	9.2	4.5	8.1	0.3	0.1
17	9.3	7.1	8.5	0.0	0.0
18	9.2	7.0	5.1	0.0	0.0
19	7.8	5.4	3.0	0.0	0.0
20	9.6	4.5	4.8	0.0	0.0
21	5.5	0.6	6.0	0.0	6.5
22	5.6	-3.2	2.4	0.0	5.2
23	4.5	-7.0	2.0	0.0	1.3
24	10.1	-1.3	5.6	3.6	0.0
25	14.8	9.1	12.8	4.3	0.0
26	14.0	13.0	14.0	26.9	0.0
27	11.6	10.0	12.5	1.8	0.0
28	10.0	7.0	9.0	0.0	0.6
29	9.7	2.2	4.1	0.0	0.8
30	8.4	4.4	4.5	0.0	0.0
31	—				
Total	—	—	—	39.5	42.9
Mean	11.2	6.1	5.9	—	1.4
Temp. °F.	52.2	43.0	—	—	—
Average	9.9	4.5	8.9	63.0	61.0

Weather Record, December, 1983

Temperature Max. °C.	Min. °C.	Wind Speed knots	Rain-fall mm.	Sun-shine hrs.	Day
7.0	1.5	6.3	0.0	6.5	1
7.7	-0.8	4.5	0.0	6.3	2
7.6	-3.0	1.9	0.0	5.3	3
9.5	-4.9	2.7	0.0	5.8	4
10.5	1.4	3.0	2.0	3.6	5
6.1	-0.3	4.0	0.0	5.1	6
4.9	-3.6	3.1	0.0	4.4	7
11.1	3.4	11.1	7.8	0.0	8
10.0	8.9	16.4	5.8	0.8	9
4.1	3.1	11.0	0.0	4.9	10
2.6	-4.4	3.3	1.3	1.1	11
3.7	0.9	3.7	0.1	0.1	12
8.6	-2.9	7.9	0.0	0.5	13
6.1	5.5	14.7	0.8	0.0	14
8.8	4.2	8.7	0.6	0.2	15
7.0	2.5	8.0	3.9	0.0	16
9.2	5.6	4.0	2.7	1.1	17
6.8	3.5	12.0	5.2	0.0	18
10.2	5.3	9.2	6.0	0.1	19
10.7	7.4	13.8	7.6	0.4	20
8.9	6.5	8.5	2.8	1.9	21
11.8	5.3	8.1	1.5	0.1	22
12.2	7.2	6.9	2.1	1.0	23
13.7	9.6	10.4	0.7	0.0	24
12.7	10.3	8.5	0.0	0.2	25
10.0	6.5	9.8	0.0	1.9	26
13.0	3.8	11.8	0.0	0.0	27
12.2	10.1	7.4	0.0	2.0	28
8.1	6.9	4.2	0.0	0.0	29
8.8	2.6	4.5	0.0	5.2	30
9.6	1.0	11.1	0.0	0.0	31
—	—	—	50.9	58.5	Total
8.8	3.3	7.8	—	1.9	Mean
47.8	37.9	—	—	—	Temp. °F.
7.1	2.5	7.0	54.0	45.0	Average

Weather Record, January, 1984

Day	Temperature Max. °C.	Min. °C.	Wind Speed knots	Rain-fall mm.	Sun-shine hrs.
1	11.9	8.2	14.1	1.0	0.2
2	11.7	4.1	12.8	9.4	0.0
3	6.8	2.8	15.0	0.3	2.6
4	6.5	1.9	7.9	0.0	5.5
5	9.4	-1.4	6.4	2.9	0.0
6	7.9	1.0	4.8	0.6	2.3
7	7.9	7.0	9.0	0.0	3.8
8	5.8	1.0	7.4	0.0	4.6
9	3.6	-1.5	3.9	0.0	1.7
10	11.0	1.9	7.5	0.1	0.0
11	12.1	10.1	13.6	0.7	0.4
12	6.0	1.1	11.1	3.9	5.1
13	13.0	4.2	16.7	4.0	1.6
14	8.6	6.9	13.8	0.2	4.5
15	5.1	0.7	12.7	0.0	6.3
16	11.4	0.4	13.2	9.6	0.0
17	6.4	2.9	13.1	0.0	5.5
18	5.8	0.0	6.1	0.2	6.6
19	3.9	-0.5	6.5	0.0	3.8
20	5.4	-1.8	4.6	0.0	5.3
21	4.5	-0.3	7.3	4.8	6.9
22	6.4	0.2	7.2	7.2	0.5
23	5.7	-0.4	8.3	8.5	1.0
24	3.1	0.8	7.2	0.1	0.0
25	6.2	-2.9	5.4	12.3	5.4
26	9.0	2.2	9.9	2.1	3.2
27	8.2	5.4	7.5	0.4	0.1
28	7.7	4.5	5.4	1.1	1.5
29	9.2	5.3	6.2	0.0	3.9
30	7.9	1.5	7.6	3.3	1.0
31	7.0	0.5	4.7	0.6	4.8
Total	—	—	—	73.3	88.1
Mean	7.6	2.1	8.9	—	2.8
Temp. °F.	45.7	35.8	—	—	—
Average	6.1	1.4	8.6	52.0	48.0

Weather Record, February, 1984

Temperature Max. °C.	Min. °C.	Wind Speed knots	Rain-fall mm.	Sun-shine hrs.	Day
9.5	0.6	6.8	2.3	0.0	1
9.3	3.8	10.5	0.4	3.0	2
12.4	5.0	10.3	3.2	3.0	3
12.2	4.0	10.3	1.9	0.1	4
8.0	2.2	10.7	0.3	5.1	5
11.0	5.5	19.5	0.8	0.0	6
7.6	5.5	12.7	0.6	2.4	7
8.4	4.5	15.3	0.4	4.7	8
8.7	2.4	5.6	0.0	8.3	9
8.2	-1.3	2.4	0.0	1.4	10
9.9	6.9	2.7	0.0	0.0	11
9.5	5.7	6.5	0.0	4.5	12
7.4	-1.7	3.3	0.0	8.7	13
9.0	-2.5	3.6	0.0	7.5	14
1.8	-2.3	2.8	0.0	0.1	15
2.2	-0.8	2.5	0.0	0.0	16
7.0	-0.7	2.7	0.0	0.1	17
7.5	-1.6	5.8	0.0	8.1	18
4.7	-3.0	8.5	0.0	7.8	19
5.6	-2.0	7.9	5.3	2.9	20
8.4	3.8	10.7	4.0	2.2	21
5.9	5.0	10.3	12.3	0.0	22
4.8	2.4	9.5	0.0	0.1	23
4.9	1.7	7.6	0.0	0.0	24
4.1	1.5	9.9	0.0	0.1	25
3.5	0.5	7.9	0.4	0.0	26
4.9	2.8	7.2	0.7	0.0	27
4.8	2.9	6.1	0.3	0.0	28
6.1	2.5	2.5	0.0	1.5	29
					30
					31
—	—	—	32.9	71.6	Total
7.1	1.8	7.7	—	2.5	Mean
44.8	35.2	—	—	—	Temp. °F.
7.0	1.5	9.3	39.0	65.0	Average

Weather Record, March, 1984

Day	Max. °C.	Min. °C.	Wind Speed knots	Rain-fall mm.	Sun-shine hrs.
1	12.5	3.5	4.5	1.6	2.9
2	6.6	2.5	15.7	0.0	6.7
3	8.0	2.0	10.7	0.0	4.5
4	7.3	−0.1	3.9	0.0	0.0
5	11.0	4.1	2.9	0.0	0.0
6	13.8	6.5	2.6	0.0	0.8
7	11.1	6.9	5.3	0.0	0.1
8	6.2	1.2	6.5	0.0	0.0
9	7.0	3.0	5.3	0.2	0.6
10	8.1	2.8	4.1	0.0	0.0
11	10.5	3.9	4.0	13.5	0.3
12	8.6	3.3	8.7	0.0	1.8
13	6.4	2.5	8.2	0.0	0.5
14	10.2	1.5	6.3	0.0	8.0
15	6.3	1.0	9.0	0.0	0.0
16	5.5	1.2	9.0	0.0	0.1
17	5.8	1.6	7.7	0.0	0.1
18	5.8	2.4	5.5	0.0	0.0
19	7.6	0.9	6.1	0.0	0.5
20	10.6	1.6	6.2	0.0	2.2
21	8.8	1.5	2.6	0.0	4.3
22	11.4	3.1	2.5	0.0	0.3
23	12.6	2.4	10.9	21.3	3.5
24	7.9	5.6	8.9	10.1	1.4
25	7.8	2.6	8.8	11.6	0.1
26	10.4	5.6	5.7	0.4	1.3
27	10.2	3.5	5.8	4.5	0.4
28	7.7	0.5	3.6	6.0	0.0
29	11.0	2.6	3.6	0.1	5.5
30	11.8	−0.3	3.3	2.6	5.5
31	7.0	2.5	9.9	1.5	0.0
Total ..	—	—	—	73.4	51.4
Mean ..	8.9	2.6	6.4	—	1.7
Temp. °F.	48.0	36.7	—	—	—
Average	10.3	2.7	9.5	39.0	117.0

Weather Record, April, 1984

Max. °C.	Min. °C.	Wind Speed knots	Rain-fall mm.	Sun-shine hrs.	Day
7.0	1.4	11.6	0.3	3.4	1
8.7	−0.2	7.0	0.0	8.9	2
9.2	−3.1	3.1	0.0	10.9	3
10.5	−0.4	6.7	0.0	7.6	4
7.9	−0.4	4.3	2.0	0.4	5
7.0	4.2	5.4	1.5	0.0	6
9.5	4.6	3.9	0.0	3.3	7
10.0	5.0	2.7	0.0	0.1	8
12.2	5.4	2.7	0.2	2.4	9
9.1	5.1	3.5	0.3	0.1	10
13.0	5.5	5.5	1.1	0.8	11
12.7	1.6	2.9	0.0	12.5	12
14.8	2.2	4.5	0.0	12.3	13
17.2	1.4	4.6	0.0	10.9	14
13.9	3.6	6.0	0.0	4.9	15
12.3	−0.5	5.3	0.0	9.7	16
14.0	0.3	2.9	0.0	9.6	17
16.4	5.8	4.9	0.0	2.1	18
18.4	8.0	6.0	0.0	6.3	19
19.8	5.6	4.2	0.0	7.2	20
23.7	5.8	4.5	0.0	10.8	21
18.8	10.4	6.2	0.0	3.4	22
18.4	5.8	7.9	0.0	12.5	23
21.2	3.8	7.9	0.0	13.1	24
22.2	8.0	7.9	0.0	12.7	25
21.4	7.7	7.1	0.0	12.9	26
19.2	5.3	7.4	0.0	13.3	27
17.4	3.9	8.4	0.0	13.1	28
15.0	5.2	8.7	0.0	12.6	29
17.7	5.0	8.7	0.0	12.7	30
					31
—	—	—	5.4	230.5	.. Total
14.6	3.9	5.7	—	7.7	.. Mean
58.3	39.0	—	—	—	Temp. °F.
13.8	5.0	8.3	40.0	136.0	Average

Weather Record, May, 1984

Day	Max. °C.	Min. °C.	Wind Speed knots	Rain-fall mm.	Sun-shine hrs.
1	18.5	6.5	8.0	0.0	9.4
2	17.1	6.0	6.8	14.6	4.4
3	13.5	7.1	3.8	0.0	0.2
4	17.1	7.0	5.1	0.0	6.0
5	14.8	7.7	7.0	0.1	4.8
6	12.6	7.5	10.0	0.0	0.1
7	12.7	3.9	12.0	0.0	7.2
8	11.1	3.9	8.2	0.0	4.7
9	16.2	1.6	3.4	0.0	9.2
10	12.5	8.0	4.4	2.5	2.6
11	13.9	3.8	10.0	0.0	9.3
12	14.4	5.5	11.5	0.0	12.5
13	16.6	4.2	10.7	0.0	10.2
14	16.5	6.1	4.7	0.0	0.1
15	13.1	6.8	3.4	1.9	0.0
16	17.0	8.5	3.7	1.3	0.2
17	12.9	9.1	4.3	0.8	0.1
18	14.4	8.9	5.0	0.0	1.1
19	16.0	5.2	3.2	0.0	0.0
20	11.9	7.2	4.1	3.4	0.0
21	13.7	6.5	4.3	19.7	0.5
22	12.1	9.2	8.3	4.0	0.0
23	18.3	7.5	6.2	0.5	9.6
24	23.0	10.2	6.3	0.0	12.7
25	12.5	8.8	3.9	13.1	0.0
26	10.9	8.8	9.4	21.5	0.0
27	10.1	5.0	8.3	1.1	0.0
28	10.9	9.1	6.7	0.2	0.0
29	17.2	7.9	6.3	0.0	8.9
30	20.3	7.9	3.1	0.0	11.8
31	19.4	9.3	5.0	6.2	13.1
Total ..	—	—	—	90.9	144.7
Mean ..	14.9	6.9	6.4	—	4.7
Temp. °F.	58.8	44.4	—	—	—
Average	17.2	7.7	8.5	50.0	191.0

Weather Record, June, 1984

Max. °C.	Min. °C.	Wind Speed knots	Rain-fall mm.	Sun-shine hrs.	Day
15.0	9.4	5.6	1.7	3.1	1
16.7	8.8	9.3	8.0	8.9	2
16.5	10.9	7.7	0.0	6.6	3
18.0	6.6	4.3	5.1	4.2	4
16.1	8.9	6.6	0.0	1.5	5
18.1	9.8	4.1	8.2	6.0	6
21.8	12.0	9.0	0.0	4.6	7
21.9	10.0	5.6	0.0	11.0	8
23.3	8.0	3.2	0.0	12.0	9
24.6	11.5	4.2	0.0	11.4	10
18.7	11.9	4.8	0.0	2.6	11
18.8	12.3	7.3	0.0	2.1	12
21.5	14.5	9.6	0.0	6.7	13
23.7	14.9	6.6	0.0	7.9	14
23.3	10.5	3.3	0.0	14.4	15
23.2	11.7	2.8	0.0	5.8	16
25.3	13.6	3.1	12.4	7.0	17
26.0	13.9	3.0	0.0	13.8	18
26.2	16.1	2.8	0.0	7.7	19
27.0	17.5	3.8	0.0	10.2	20
21.8	15.2	4.9	0.0	10.4	21
20.9	11.2	11.0	0.1	2.5	22
19.7	7.8	6.4	0.6	8.8	23
18.3	9.0	5.2	0.0	11.1	24
22.9	12.7	8.8	0.0	9.2	25
25.8	12.8	5.2	0.0	14.8	26
24.4	12.3	6.6	0.0	11.7	27
17.4	10.3	5.0	0.0	2.2	28
18.8	7.3	4.7	0.0	8.4	29
19.4	8.5	3.8	0.0	10.4	30
					31
—	—	—	36.1	237.0	.. Total
21.2	11.3	5.6	—	7.9	.. Mean
70.2	52.3	—	—	—	Temp. °F.
20.7	10.9	8.4	48.0	216.0	Average

TIDAL CONSTANTS

THE TIME OF HIGH WATER *at the undermentioned Ports and Places may be* approximately *found by taking the appropriate Time of High Water at the Standard Port (as shown on pp. 172, 173, etc.) and adding thereto the quantities annexed. The columns headed "Springs" and "Neaps" show the height of the tide above datum for Mean High Water Springs and Mean High Water Neaps respectively.*

Tidal data is no longer available for a number of places which formerly appeared in the list below. These places (with the name of the substitute now recorded) are: *Air Point* (Mostyn Quay); *Ardrishaig* (East Loch Tarbert); *Arisaig* (Loch Moidart); *Ayr Pt., I.o.M.* (Peel), *Beachy Head* (Eastbourne); *Beaumaris* (Menai Bridge); *Brieile* (Scheveningen); *Broughty Ferry* (Newburgh); *Burryport* (Whiteford Lighthouse); *Caen* (Cayeux); *Caernarvon* (Llanddwyn Isld.); *Dumbarton* (Bowling); *Fareham* (Itchenor); *Fifeness* (Anstruther Easter); *Glasson Dock* (Tarn Pt.); *Gravesend* (Tilbury); *Greenwich* (R. Albert Dock); *Hythe* (Totland Bay); *Lancaster* (Duddon Bar); *Lynmouth* (Porlock Bay); *Nash Pt.* (Chepstow); *Needles Pt.* (Freshwater Bay); *Neath* (Porthcawl); *Nore Lt.* (Chatham); *Port Harrington* (Hestan Islet); *Portishead* (Avonmouth); *St. Agnes* (Coverack); *St. Mary's* (Sennen Cove); *Start Pt.* (Lulworth Cove); *Stockton* (Seaham); *Sutton Bridge* (Blacktoft); *Torbay* (Torquay); *Worms Head* (Ferryside); *Honfleur Harbour* (Duclair).

Port	Diff.	Springs	Neaps	Port	Diff.	Springs	Neaps
	h.m.	metres	metres		h.m.	metres	metres
Aberdeen.........Leith	−1 19	4·3	3·4	Coverack .... Avonmouth	−2 02	5·3	4·2
Aberdovey..... Liverpool	−3 00	5·0	3·5	Cowes.......... London	−2 23	4·2	3·5
Aberystwyth .. Liverpool	−3 30	5·0	3·5	Cromarty........ Leith	−2 56	4·3	3·4
Aldeburgh...... London	−3 05	2·8	2·7	Cromer........... Hull	+0 35	5·3	4·2
Alderney .... London	+5 33	6·3	4·7	Dartmouth ..... London	+4 32	4·8	3·6
Alloa..............Leith	+0 47	5·6	4·2	Deal .... London	−2 37	6·1	5·0
Amlwch....... Liverpool	−0 33	7·3	5·8	Devonport (see Plymouth)			
Anstruther Easter . Leith	−0 22	5·5	4·4	Dieppe .... London	−3 03	9·3	7·2
Antwerp .... London	+0 50	5·6	4·3	Dingle Hbr..... Liverpool	+5 33	3·8	2·9
Appledore ... Avonmouth	−1 15	7·5	5·2	Donegal Hbr. .. Liverpool	−5 24	3·9	3·0
Arbroath..........Leith	−0 33	5·0	4·1	Douglas .... Liverpool	−0 04	6·9	5·4
Ardrossan ..... Greenock	−0 15	3·2	2·7	Dover .... London	−2 52	6·7	5·3
†Arundel........ London	−1 43	3·1	2·2	Duclair......... London	−1 35	7·1	6·4
Avonmouth ....A'mouth	0 00	13·2	10·0	Duddon Bar ... Liverpool	+0 03	8·5	6·6
Ayr .... Greenock	−0 25	3·0	2·6	Dunbar ....Leith	−0 07	5·2	4·2
Ballycotton.. Avonmouth	−1 47	4·1	3·3	Dundalk (Sldr's Pt) L'pool	+0 22	5·1	4·2
Banff..............Leith	−2 44	3·5	2·8	Dundee ....Leith	+0 11	5·3	4·3
Bantry .... Liverpool	+5 54	3·4	2·6	Dungeness ...... London	−3 04	7·7	5·8
Bardsey Island . Liverpool	−3 18	4·5	3·3	Dunkirk .... London	−1 54	5·8	4·8
Barmouth ..... Liverpool	−2 57	5·0	3·5	Eastbourne ..... London	−2 50	7·3	5·6
Barnstaple .. Avonmouth	−1 00	4·1	1·4	East Loch Tarbert G'nock	+0 05	3·4	2·9
Barrow .... Liverpool	+0 15	9·1	7·1	Exmouth Dock .. London	+4 55	4·0	2·8
Barry .... Avonmouth	−0 22	11·4	8·7	Eyemouth ....Leith	−0 20	4·7	3·7
Belfast .... London	−2 45	3·5	3·0	Falmouth ...... London	+3 35	5·3	4·2
Berwick..........Leith	−0 02	4·7	3·8	Ferryside.... Avonmouth	−0 58	6·7	4·5
Bideford..... Avonmouth	−1 15	5·9	3·6	Filey Bay.........Leith	+1 50	5·8	4·9
Blacktoft.......... Hull	+0 31	5·7	3·9	Fishguard ..... Liverpool	−4 00	4·8	3·4
Blakeney .... Hull	+0 29	3·1	2·1	Flushing .... London	−0 40	4·9	4·0
Blyth ....Leith	+0 50	5·0	3·9	Folkestone ..... London	−3 04	7·1	5·7
Boscastle .... Avonmouth	−1 20	7·3	5·6	Formby .... Liverpool	−0 21	9·0	7·3
Boulogne....... London	−2 44	8·9	7·2	Fowey .... London	+3 53	5·4	4·3
Bovisand Pier... London	+3 55	5·3	4·3	Fraserburgh ....Leith	−2 19	3·9	3·1
Bowling....... Greenock	+0 15	4·0	3·4	*Freshwater Bay London	−4 33	2·6	2·3
Brest........... London	+2 28	7·5	5·9	Galway .... Liverpool	−6 08	5·1	3·9
Bridgewater . Avonmouth	−0 22	4·6	1·9	Glasgow .... Greenock	+0 30	4·7	4·1
Bridlington........Leith	+2 03	6·1	4·7	Goole .... Hull	+0 59	5·7	3·7
Bridport .... London	+4 37	4·1	3·0	Gorleston ...... London	−5 00	2·4	2·0
Brighton .... London	−2 50	6·5	5·1	Granton..........Leith	0 00	5·6	4·5
Buckie ....Leith	−2 56	4·1	3·2	Granville ...... London	+5 32	12·8	9·6
Bude Haven . Avonmouth	−1 33	7·7	5·8	Grimsby.......... Hull	−0 28	7·0	5·6
Bull Sand Fort ..... Hull	−0 46	6·9	5·5	Hartlepool.........Leith	+0 58	5·1	4·0
Burntisland ....Leith	0 00	5·6	4·5	Harwich .... London	−2 02	4·0	3·4
Calais .... London	−2 04	7·2	6·0	Hastings .... London	−2 57	7·5	5·8
Campbeltown .. Greenock	+0 07	2·9	2·6	Haverfordwest . Liverpool	−4 50	2·2	0·3
Cape Cornwall ..A'mouth	−2 30	6·0	4·3	Hestan Islet ... Liverpool	+0 25	8·3	6·3
Cardiff ..... Avonmouth	−0 15	12·2	9·4	Hilbre Island... Liverpool	−0 16	9·0	7·2
Cardigan, Port . Liverpool	−3 37	4·7	3·4	Holyhead...... Liverpool	−0 48	5·7	4·5
Carmarthen . Avonmouth	−0 48	2·6	0·4	Hook of Holland . London	−0 01	2·3	1·8
Cayeux......... London	−2 55	10·2	7·8	*Hurst Point ... London	−3 38	2·7	2·3
Chatham (N.Lock) London	−1 10	6·0	4·9	Ijmuiden .... London	+1 09	2·0	1·7
Chepstow... Avonmouth	+0 20	No Data		Ilfracombe... Avonmouth	−1 10	9·2	6·9
Cherbourg...... London	−6 00	6·3	5·0	Inveraray ..... Greenock	+0 11	3·3	3·0
Chester ..... Liverpool	+1 05	4·0	2·0	Invergordon.......Leith	−2 49	4·4	3·5
Chichester Hbr. . London	−2 25	4·9	4·0	Ipswich .... London	−1 42	4·2	3·4
*Christchurch Hbr. L'don	−4 53	1·8	1·4	Itchenor .... London	−2 16	5·1	4·0
Cobh .... Liverpool	−5 56	4·1	3·3	Kinsale .... Liverpool	−6 08	4·0	3·2

† Very Approximate.   * 1st H.W. (Springs).

Port	Diff. h.m.	Springs metres	Neaps metres	Port	Diff. h.m.	Springs metres	Neaps metres
Kirkcudbright . *Liverpool*	+0 15	7·5	5·9	†Rosslare...... *Liverpool*	−5 23	1·9	1·4
Kirkwall ....*Leith*	−4 15	2·9	2·2	Rosyth ....*Leith*	+0 07	5·8	4·7
Lamlash.......*Greenock*	−0 26	3·2	2·7	Ryde .... *London*	−2 23	4·5	3·7
Le Havre .... *London*	−3 55	7·8	6·5	St. Anne's ..... *London*	−0 04	9·3	7·1
Lerwick ....*Leith*	−3 49	2·2	1·6	St. Helier ...... *London*	+4 48	11·1	8·1
Limerick Dock . *Liverpool*	−4 24	5·9	4·5	St. Ives ...... *Avonmouth*	−1 55	6·6	4·9
Littlehampton .. *London*	−2 33	5·7	4·6	St. Malo .... *London*	+5 27	12·1	9·1
Lizard Point . *Avonmouth*	−2 17	5·3	4·2	St. Peter Port ... *London*	+4 54	9·0	6·7
Llanddwyn Island *L'pool*	−1 53	5·0	4·0	Salcombe .... *London*	+4 10	5·3	4·1
Llanelli .....*Avonmouth*	−0 56	7·8	5·8	Saltash .... *London*	+4 14	5·6	4·4
Loch Long ..... *Greenock*	−0 05	3·4	2·9	Scarborough ....*Leith*	+1 33	5·7	4·6
Loch Moidart .. *Greenock*	+6 02	4·8	3·5	Scheveningen... *London*	+0 29	2·1	1·8
Londonderry ... *London*	−5 37	2·7	2·0	Scrabster ....*Leith*	+6 04	5·0	3·7
Looe ....*London*	+3 55	5·4	4·2	Seaham ....*Leith*	+0 53	5·2	4·1
Lossiemouth ....*Leith*	−3 01	4·1	3·2	Selsey Bill ...... *London*	−2 28	5·3	4·4
Lowestoft .....*London*	−4 25	2·4	2·1	Sennen Cove. *Avonmouth*	−2 30	6·1	4·8
Lulworth Cove.. *London*	+5 00	2·3	1·5	Sharpness Dock . *A'mouth*	+0 42	9·3	5·8
Lundy Island *Avonmouth*	−1 23	8·0	5·9	Sheerness ...... *London*	−1 16	5·7	4·8
Lyme Regis ..... *London*	+4 55	4·3	3·1	Shoreham ...... *London*	−2 43	6·2	5·0
*Lymington .... *London*	−3 33	3·0	2·6	Silloth ...... *Liverpool*	+0 35	9·2	6·9
Margate........ *London*	−1 52	4·8	3·9	Southampton ... *London*	−2 52	4·5	3·7
Maryport....... *Liverpool*	+0 24	8·6	6·6	Southend ...... *London*	−1 22	5·7	4·8
Menai Bridge .. *Liverpool*	−0 28	7·4	5·9	Southwold ...... *London*	−3 50	2·5	2·2
Mevagissey ..... *London*	+3 53	5·4	4·3	Spurn Head (see Bull Sand Fort)			
Middlesbrough .....*Leith*	+1 09	5·6	4·5	Stirling ....*Leith*	+1 13	2·9	1·6
Milford Haven . *Liverpool*	−5 07	7·0	5·2	Stonehaven........*Leith*	−1 09	4·5	3·6
Minehead ... *Avonmouth*	−0 40	10·6	8·1	Stornoway ..... *Liverpool*	−4 15	4·8	3·7
Montrose..........*Leith*	−0 19	4·8	3·9	Stranraer ..... *Greenock*	−0 20	3·0	2·5
Morecambe .... *Liverpool*	+0 01	9·5	7·6	Stromness ....*Leith*	−5 24	3·4	2·6
Mostyn Quay .. *Liverpool*	−0 10	8·7	6·9	Sunderland........*Leith*	+0 51	5·2	4·2
Newburgh.........*Leith*	+0 48	4·1	3·0	*Swanage ...... *London*	−5 13	2·0	1·4
Newcastle on Tyne . *Leith*	+0 54	5·3	4·1	Swansea......... *Bristol*	−0 49	9·6	7·3
Newhaven...... *London*	−2 48	6·6	5·2	Tarn Point .... *Liverpool*	+0 05	8·3	6·4
Newport (Gwent)*A'mouth*	−0 15	12·1	9·0	Tay River (Bar) ....*Leith*	−0 21	5·2	4·2
Newquay ..... *Avonmouth*	−1 58	7·0	5·3	Tees R. (Ent.) ....*Leith*	+1 08	5·5	4·3
New Quay (Card.) . *L'pool*	−3 30	4·9	3·4	Teignmouth .... *London*	+4 37	4·8	3·6
North Shields...... *Leith*	+0 51	5·0	3·9	Tenby .... *Avonmouth*	−1 05	8·4	6·3
North Sunderland .. *Leith*	+0 05	4·8	3·7	Tilbury.......... *London*	−0 49	6·5	5·4
Oban.......... *Greenock*	+5 47	4·0	2·9	Tobermory .... *Liverpool*	−5 12	4·4	3·3
Old Lynn Road ..... *Hull*	+0 05	7·3	5·8	Torquay........ *London*	+4 40	4·9	3·7
Orfordness ..... *London*	−2 50	2·8	2·7	*Totland Bay ... *London*	−3 53	2·7	2·3
Ostend .... *London*	−1 32	5·1	4·2	Troon .... *Greenock*	−0 25	3·2	2·7
Padstow ..... *Avonmouth*	−1 45	7·3	5·6	Truro .... *Avonmouth*	+3 43	5·3	4·2
Peel........... *Liverpool*	−0 02	5·3	4·2	Tyne River (Ent.)... *Leith*	+0 56	5·1	3·9
Pembroke Dock *Liverpool*	−5 07	7·0	5·2	Ushant.......... *London*	+2 30	7·5	5·8
Penzance .... *Avonmouth*	−2 24	5·6	4·4	Valentia Hbr... *Liverpool*	+5 31	3·8	3·0
Peterhead ....*Leith*	−1 59	3·8	3·1	Walton-on-Naze. *London*	−2 10	4·2	3·4
Plymouth ...... *London*	+4 05	5·5	4·4	Waterford Hbr . *Liverpool*	−5 34	4·5	3·5
Plymouth Breakwater (see Bovisand Pier)				Weston S. Mare . *A'mouth*	−0 25	12·0	9·0
*Poole (Entrance) *London*	−5 03	2·0	1·6	†Wexford Hbr .. *Liverpool*	−5 03	1·7	1·4
Porlock Bay . *Avonmouth*	−0 50	10·2	7·8	Whitby ....*Leith*	+1 22	5·4	4·3
Porthcawl .. *Avonmouth*	−0 53	9·9	7·5	Whiteford Lt. Hse. *Bristol*	−0 59	8·7	6·7
Portmadoc..... *Liverpool*	−2 45	5·1	3·4	Whitehaven ... *Liverpool*	+0 10	8·0	6·3
Portland .... *London*	+5 10	2·1	1·4	Wick ....*Leith*	−3 26	3·4	2·7
Portpatrick... *Liverpool*	+0 22	3·8	3·0	Wisbech Cut .... *Hull*	+0 01	7·0	5·1
Portsmouth..... *London*	−2 23	4·7	3·8	Woolwich ...... *London*	−0 22	7·0	5·9
Port Talbot .. *Avonmouth*	−0 53	9·6	7·3	Workington ... *Liverpool*	+0 20	8·2	6·4
Preston .... *Liverpool*	0 00	5·4	3·5	Worthing ..... *London*	−2 36	6·1	4·8
Pwllheli ...... *Liverpool*	−3 07	5·0	3·4	Yarmouth Roads *London* (see Gorleston)			
R.A. Dock (see Woolwich)				*Yarmth.(I.O.W.) *London*	−3 28	3·1	2·5
Ramsey (I.O.M.) *Liverpool*	+0 04	7·3	5·8	Youghal....... *Liverpool*	−5 50	4·1	3·3
Ramsgate....... *London*	−2 32	4·9	3·8				

† Very Approximate. * 1st H.W. (Springs).

EXAMPLE.—Required times of high water at Stranraer on *January* 2, 1985:—

(a) *Morning Tide.*
Appropriate time of high
water at *Greenock* .... 0834 hrs. *(Jan.* 2)
Tidal difference .... −0020 hrs.

(b) *Afternoon Tide.*
Appropriate time of high
water at *Greenock* .... 2106 hrs. *(Jan* 2).
Tidal difference .... −0020 hrs.

H.W at *Stranraer* ... 0814 hrs.   H.W. at *Stranraer* ... 2046 hrs.

Tidal predictions (pp. 172–183) for London Bridge, Liverpool, Avonmouth, Hull, Dún Laoghaire and Leith are computed by the Institute of Oceanographic Sciences, copyright reserved. Those for Greenock have been supplied by the Hydrographer of the Navy and are crown copyright.

JANUARY, 1985

High Water at the undermentioned Places (G.M.T.*)—

Day of Month	Day of Week	London Bridge †3·20 m. below Mn. h.m.	Ht. m.	Aft. h.m.	Ht.	Liverpool †4·93 m. below Mn. h.m.	Ht.	Aft. h.m.	Ht.	Avonmouth †6·50 m. below Mn. h.m.	Ht.	Aft. h.m.	Ht.	Hull (Albert Dock) †3·90 m. below Mn. h.m.	Ht.	Aft. h.m.	Ht.	Greenock †1·62 m. below Mn. h.m.	Ht.	Aft. h.m.	Ht.	Leith and Granton †2·90 m. below Mn. h.m.	Ht.	Aft. h.m.	Ht.	Dun Laoghaire ‡0·20 m. above Mn. h.m.	Ht.	Aft. h.m.	Ht.
1	Tu	0842	5·6	2128	5·7	622	7·1	1845	7·4	145	9·8	1425	10·2	049	6·0	1345	5·6	725	2·9	20 2	2·9	10 3	4·4	22 9	4·5	725	3·2	1926	3·4
2	W	946	5·6	2227	5·9	727	7·3	1948	7·6	253	10·0	1528	10·4	2 1	6·0	1454	5·8	834	2·9	21 6	3·0	11 2	4·5	23 9	4·6	814	3·4	2018	3·5
3	Th	1045	6·0	2320	6·1	823	7·6	2043	7·9	355	10·4	1626	10·9	3 7	6·1	1549	6·1	928	3·1	22 0	3·1	1155	4·7	—	—	858	3·5	21 5	3·6
4	F	1139	6·0	—	—	911	8·0	2131	8·2	451	11·0	1720	11·4	4 3	6·4	1635	6·4	1013	3·2	2247	3·1	0 6	4·7	1246	4·8	937	3·7	2149	3·7
5	Sa	1 0	6·3	1229	6·3	955	8·4	2214	8·5	543	11·6	1810	11·9	452	6·4	1718	6·7	1053	3·3	2331	3·2	057	4·9	1332	5·0	1015	3·8	2230	3·7
6	Su	5 7	6·6	1317	6·5	1035	8·7	2257	8·8	629	12·1	1856	12·3	539	6·8	1753	6·9	1132	3·4	—	—	147	5·1	1415	5·2	1053	3·9	2310	3·8
7	M	142	6·8	1404	6·8	1116	9·0	2339	9·0	714	12·5	1941	12·5	621	6·9	1838	7·1	016	3·3	1213	3·5	231	5·3	1456	5·3	1131	4·0	2352	3·8
8	Tu	227	6·9	1449	7·0	1157	9·2	—	—	757	12·7	2023	12·7	7 3	7·1	1916	7·2	1 1	3·5	1255	3·6	314	5·5	1535	5·4	036	3·9	1212	4·1
9	W	310	7·0	1532	7·2	021	9·1	1239	9·3	839	12·9	21 5	12·8	745	7·2	1955	7·2	148	3·6	1338	3·7	355	5·5	1615	5·4	122	3·8	1254	4·1
10	Th	350	7·0	1616	7·2	1·4	9·1	1324	9·3	921	13·1	2148	12·8	827	7·2	2034	7·1	234	3·8	1423	3·8	437	5·4	1659	5·4	2 8	3·7	1339	4·2
11	F	430	6·8	1659	7·0	149	9·0	14 8	9·0	10 4	13·0	2231	12·8	911	7·0	2117	7·0	320	3·9	15 8	3·8	524	5·3	1747	5·3	3 0	3·7	1427	4·1
12	Sa	512	6·8	1746	6·8	237	8·8	1456	8·8	1049	12·8	2318	12·2	956	6·9	22 0	6·7	4·5	3·9	1555	3·8	614	5·2	1838	5·3	356	3·6	1518	4·0
13	Su	556	6·6	1836	6·6	327	8·5	1548	8·8	1137	12·3	—	—	1045	6·8	2251	6·5	450	3·8	1644	3·5	7 5	5·1	1931	5·0	5 0	3·5	1616	3·8
14	M	645	6·5	1934	6·4	423	8·2	1645	8·4	0 7	11·7	1231	11·8	1142	6·5	2350	6·3	538	3·7	1738	3·5	8 5	4·9	2027	5·0	610	3·5	1723	3·7
15	Tu	745	6·3	2040	6·3	526	8·0	1751	8·1	1 6	11·2	1334	11·3	1 3	6·6	1252	6·3	637	3·6	1842	3·4	9 7	4·9	2131	5·0	720	3·6	1837	3·7
16	W	858	6·3	2152	6·3	638	7·9	19 7	8·1	218	11·0	1450	11·2	220	6·6	14 5	6·5	758	3·5	1959	3·4	1013	4·8	2242	5·0	824	3·7	1948	3·8
17	Th	1016	6·3	23 2	6·3	749	8·0	2019	8·3	334	11·0	16 4	11·0	338	6·6	1517	6·6	913	3·5	2116	3·4	1123	4·8	2351	5·0	919	3·6	2053	3·8
18	F	1130	6·3	—	—	854	8·3	2124	8·4	442	11·4	1712	11·5	448	6·9	1620	6·7	1012	3·4	2221	3·3	055	5·3	1225	5·1	10 7	3·5	2151	3·8
19	Sa	0 7	6·5	1234	6·4	950	8·6	2219	8·6	543	11·9	1811	11·9	544	6·9	1715	6·9	11 2	3·4	2318	3·3	150	5·3	1321	5·2	1052	3·5	2242	4·1
20	Su	1 2	6·5	1328	6·6	1040	8·8	23 8	8·6	635	12·3	1905	12·4	634	6·9	18 1	6·9	1148	3·3	—	—	240	5·3	1411	5·2	1134	3·5	2327	4·1
21	M	149	6·6	1415	6·8	1125	9·2	2350	8·9	721	12·6	2025	12·5	716	6·9	1842	6·9	011	3·3	1234	3·6	325	5·4	1455	5·4	0 9	4·1	1215	4·0
22	Tu	232	6·7	1457	7·0	029	8·9	1243	9·2	8 4	12·8	211	12·4	754	6·9	1919	6·9	1 6	3·2	1316	3·6	4 4	5·4	1536	5·4	050	3·8	1254	3·7
23	W	310	6·8	1536	7·1	138	8·8	1319	9·1	842	12·8	2135	12·2	827	6·8	1954	6·8	147	3·3	1356	3·6	442	5·3	1614	5·3	129	3·7	1335	3·7
24	Th	346	6·9	1613	7·1	154	8·8	1352	8·9	917	12·7	22 4	12·1	9 0	6·7	2026	6·6	228	3·2	1433	3·6	517	5·0	1649	5·3	2 7	3·6	1413	3·6
25	F	420	6·8	1649	6·9	211	8·4	1427	8·6	950	12·4	2234	11·6	931	6·6	21 0	6·5	3 5	3·2	1543	3·5	555	4·8	1726	5·1	246	3·4	1452	3·5
26	Sa	452	6·7	1723	6·8	246	8·1	15 4	8·3	1020	12·1	23 5	11·1	1042	6·6	2134	6·6	338	3·3	1620	3·2	634	4·6	18 4	4·9	325	3·3	1532	3·6
27	Su	526	6·5	1800	6·4	322	7·8	1543	7·9	1052	11·7	2339	10·6	10 4	6·5	2212	6·1	411	3·3	17 1	3·7	715	4·6	1842	4·8	410	3·3	1617	3·5
28	M	6 1	6·2	1839	6·1	4 6	7·4	1631	7·5	1126	11·1	12 7	10·5	1126	6·2	2254	5·9	445	3·1	17 1	3·5	8 0	4·4	1922	4·8	5 4	3·1	1711	3·5
29	Tu	642	5·9	1926	5·8	457	7·1	1734	7·2	022	10·0	12 7	9·9	1042	5·9	2346	6·1	524	3·0	1749	3·7	20 8	4·4	20 8	4·5	5 4	3·1	1820	3·3
30	W	733	5·6	2020	5·6	5 1	7·1	1734	7·1	128	9·5	1420	9·7	1126	5·9	1345	—	6 9	3·0	1849	3·2	21 5	4·3	21 5	4·4	610	3·1	1820	3·3
31	Th	837	5·4	2122	5·6	614	7·0	1850	7·1	—	—	—	—	057	5·6	1345	—	9 7	3·0	20 0	2·9	959	4·3	2215	4·4	718	3·2	1932	3·2

*All times shown are Greenwich Mean Time.   †Difference of height in metres from Ordnance Datum (Newlyn).   ‡Difference of height in metres from Ordnance Datum (Dublin).

FEBRUARY, 1985

High Water at the undermentioned Places (G.M.T.*)—

Day of Month	Day of Week	London Bridge (†Datum 3·20 m. below) Mn. h.m.	Ht. m.	Aft. h.m.	Ht. m.	Liverpool (†Datum 4·93 m. below) Mn. h.m.	Ht. m.	Aft. h.m.	Ht. m.	Avonmouth (†Datum 6·50 m. below) Mn. h.m.	Ht. m.	Aft. h.m.	Ht. m.	Hull (Albert Dock) (†Datum 3·90 m. below) Mn. h.m.	Ht. m.	Aft. h.m.	Ht. m.	Greenock (†Datum 1·62 m. below) Mn. h.m.	Ht. m.	Aft. h.m.	Ht. m.	Leith and Granton (†Datum 2·90 m. below) Mn. h.m.	Ht. m.	Aft. h.m.	Ht. m.	Dun Laoghaire (‡Datum 0·20 m. above) Mn. h.m.	Ht. m.	Aft. h.m.	Ht. m.
1	F	946	5·4	2226	5·7	733	7·1	20 5	7·4	254	9·6	1536	9·9	218	5·8	15 0	5·8	818	3·0	2117	3·0	1111	4·4	2331	4·5	817	3·3	2034	3·4
2	Sa	1054	5·6	2330	5·9	839	7·6	21 5	7·8	4 7	10·2	1645	10·6	329	6·0	16 4	6·4	928	3·1	2220	3·1	038	4·7	1216	4·6	9 8	3·5	2127	3·5
3	Su	—	—	12 1	6·0	932	8·1	2157	8·3	513	11·0	1747	11·4	431	6·3	1657	6·8	1023	3·1	2314	3·1	133	4·9	1311	4·8	953	3·7	2214	3·7
4	M	034	6·3	13 0	6·5	1019	8·6	2242	8·8	610	11·8	1841	12·1	523	6·6	1740	7·2	1111	3·2	—	—	220	5·2	1359	5·1	1035	3·9	2256	3·8
5	Tu	127	6·7	1351	7·0	11 4	9·1	2326	9·2	659	12·5	1927	12·7	6 8	7·0	1821	7·5	0 4	3·1	1157	3·5	3 1	5·6	1440	5·4	1114	4·1	2338	3·9
6	W	213	7·0	1437	7·3	1146	9·5	—	—	742	13·1	2011	13·2	650	7·3	19 0	7·7	053	3·2	1244	3·8	340	5·6	1518	5·6	1155	4·2	1237	4·3
7	Th	256	7·2	1519	7·5	010	9·4	1228	9·7	826	13·6	2053	13·6	731	7·6	1938	7·9	140	3·2	1330	3·8	420	5·6	1558	5·7	021	4·0	1322	4·3
8	F	336	7·3	16 2	7·6	062	9·6	1310	9·8	9 7	13·9	2134	13·7	812	7·7	2018	7·9	225	3·3	1415	3·9	5 4	5·6	1640	5·7	1 3	4·0	14 7	4·3
9	Sa	416	7·3	1644	7·4	135	9·5	1352	9·7	949	13·9	2214	13·5	853	7·6	2103	7·6	3 8	3·3	1458	4·0	551	5·2	1727	5·7	147	4·0	1456	4·2
10	Su	455	7·2	1727	7·1	218	9·3	1436	9·5	1031	13·5	2257	12·9	934	7·4	2141	7·4	347	3·3	1541	3·9	642	5·2	1815	5·5	236	3·9	1552	4·0
11	M	536	6·9	1812	6·7	3 1	8·9	1521	9·0	1115	12·8	2339	12·0	1019	7·0	2228	7·2	426	3·3	1626	3·9	735	4·7	19 5	5·3	328	3·6	1656	3·8
12	Tu	621	6·7	19 3	6·4	350	8·4	1613	8·5	—	—	1256	11·8	11 9	6·6	2325	6·9	5 7	3·3	1715	3·6	835	4·6	20 0	5·1	426	3·4	1813	3·6
13	W	716	6·4	20 2	6·2	449	7·9	1720	7·9	029	11·1	1413	10·2	—	—	1212	6·0	554	3·3	1813	3·3	946	4·6	21 6	4·7	535	3·4	1934	3·6
14	Th	826	6·3	2112	6·0	6 4	7·5	1846	7·5	135	10·3	1541	10·1	036	6·4	1328	6·2	659	3·2	1927	3·2	11 8	5·0	2227	4·8	652	3·6	2048	3·6
15	F	948	6·0	2233	6·1	728	7·5	2012	7·6	3 1	10·5	17 1	10·7	2 5	6·2	1453	6·3	840	3·1	21 0	2·9	053	5·1	2348	5·0	8 4	3·7	2151	3·7
16	Sa	1115	6·1	2349	6·2	844	8·0	2122	8·0	423	11·2	18 1	11·4	339	6·2	16 7	6·7	10 2	3·0	2221	3·0	148	5·3	1219	5·2	9 8	3·9	2240	3·7
17	Su	—	—	1224	6·4	945	8·4	2216	8·4	530	12·0	1849	12·4	449	6·4	1747	6·9	1057	3·3	2321	3·1	234	5·3	1317	5·3	10 2	4·0	2321	3·9
18	M	049	6·4	1319	6·6	1033	8·8	2259	8·7	624	12·5	1930	12·8	542	6·8	1825	7·2	011	3·2	—	—	313	5·2	14 6	5·3	1047	3·7	2358	4·0
19	Tu	137	6·6	14 4	6·7	1113	9·1	2336	8·9	747	12·8	20 6	12·6	624	6·9	1859	7·5	054	3·3	1226	3·5	345	5·1	1445	5·2	1126	3·6	12 1	3·7
20	W	216	6·7	1442	7·0	1150	9·3	—	—	822	12·9	2039	12·8	659	6·9	1930	7·6	2 9	3·3	13 5	3·6	446	4·9	1550	5·1	030	3·5	13 7	3·6
21	Th	253	6·9	1517	7·1	010	9·0	1222	9·3	854	13·0	21 8	12·8	8 1	6·9	2032	7·5	239	3·3	1343	3·6	518	4·8	1621	5·0	1 1	3·4	1340	3·5
22	F	325	6·9	1549	7·1	041	8·9	1255	9·3	922	12·9	2136	12·5	829	6·9	2114	7·3	3 6	3·2	1417	3·7	552	4·6	1653	4·9	133	3·4	1413	3·4
23	Sa	355	6·9	1620	7·0	110	8·8	1324	9·1	950	12·7	22 2	12·3	857	6·7	2133	7·0	332	3·2	1446	3·5	626	4·4	1726	4·7	2 4	3·2	1449	3·5
24	Su	424	6·8	1649	6·8	138	8·7	1354	8·9	1019	12·2	2223	11·7	928	6·4	2213	6·6	4 2	3·1	1515	3·4	7 6	4·3	18 0	4·5	238	3·1	1529	3·3
25	M	454	6·8	1720	6·6	2 6	8·4	1425	8·5	1045	11·4	2252	10·9	959	6·1	2255	6·2	437	3·2	1546	3·3	756		1836	4·3	315		1618	3·2
26	Tu	526	6·5	1754	6·4	237	8·1	1457	8·1	1113	10·6	2322	10·2	1035	5·8	2354	5·8	519	3·1	1622	3·3	—	—	1919		4 1		1724	
27	W	6 3	6·2	1831	6·1	311	7·7	1536	7·7	1151	9·9	—	—	1119		—	—	—	—	17 4	3·1	—	—	2017		5 3		—	—
28	Th	643	5·8	1916	5·7	356	7·3	1631	7·2	—	—	—	—	—	—	—	—	—	—	1756	3·0	—	—	—	—	—	—	—	—

*All times shown are Greenwich Mean Time.   †Difference of height in metres from Ordnance Datum (Newlyn).
‡Difference of height in metres from Ordnance Datum (Dublin).
†Difference of height in metres from Ordnance Datum.

MARCH, 1985

High Water at the undermentioned Places (G.M.T.*)—

Datum of Predictions (†difference below, except Dun Laoghaire which is ‡0·20 m. above):
London Bridge 3·20 m. below · Liverpool 4·93 m. below · Avonmouth 6·50 m. below · Hull (Albert Dock) 3·90 m. below · Greenock 1·62 m. below · Leith and Granton 2·90 m. below · Dun Laoghaire 0·20 m. above

Day of Month	Day of Week	London Bridge Mn (h.m.)	Ht (m.)	Aft (h.m.)	Ht (m.)	Liverpool Mn	Ht	Aft	Ht	Avonmouth Mn	Ht	Aft	Ht	Hull (Albert Dock) Mn	Ht	Aft	Ht	Greenock Mn	Ht	Aft	Ht	Leith and Granton Mn	Ht	Aft	Ht	Dun Laoghaire Mn	Ht	Aft	Ht
1	F	737	5·5	2015	5·5	5 5	6·9	1756	6·9	010	9·5	1257	9·3	—	—	1231	5·5	610	3·0	1859	2·9	9 3	4·1	2136	4·2	618	3·1	1848	3·1
2	Sa	851	5·3	2132	5·4	642	7·0	1930	7·0	135	9·1	1440	9·2	133	5·6	1416	5·5	713	3·0	2031	2·9	1028	4·2	23 5	4·3	734	3·2	20 6	3·2
3	Su	1014	5·5	2257	5·6	8 8	7·3	2043	7·3	321	9·5	1612	10·0	3 1	5·8	1532	5·8	840	3·0	22 3	2·9	1148	4·4	—	—	838	3·4	21 8	3·4
4	M	1139	5·9	—	—	910	8·0	2138	8·3	444	10·6	1723	11·1	412	6·2	1631	6·3	956	3·2	23 2	3·0	018	4·6	1249	4·7	928	3·7	2158	3·7
5	Tu	011	6·1	1242	6·6	10 0	8·7	2226	8·9	546	11·8	1819	12·1	5 6	6·6	1718	6·8	1052	3·4	2352	3·1	114	4·9	1337	5·1	1014	3·9	2240	3·8
6	W	1 6	6·7	1333	7·1	1044	9·3	23 9	9·4	638	12·8	19 7	13·1	550	7·1	1758	7·3	1141	3·5	—	—	2 1	5·3	1418	5·4	1053	4·1	2320	4·0
7	Th	152	7·1	1418	7·5	1127	9·7	2351	9·8	723	13·4	1951	13·8	631	7·5	1838	7·8	038	3·3	1229	3·7	239	5·6	1456	5·7	1134	4·3	2359	4·1
8	F	234	7·4	15 0	7·7	—	—	12 8	10·1	8 6	14·1	2032	14·2	710	7·8	1916	8·1	123	3·3	1316	3·8	317	5·7	1535	5·9	—	—	1216	4·3
9	Sa	314	7·6	1542	7·7	032	9·9	1250	10·0	847	14·3	2112	14·4	743	7·9	1955	8·3	2 6	3·3	14 0	4·0	357	5·8	1617	6·0	039	4·1	1258	4·4
10	Su	353	7·6	1623	7·6	113	9·8	1331	10·0	928	14·3	2152	14·3	829	7·8	2037	8·2	245	3·4	1442	4·0	440	5·7	17 3	5·9	122	4·1	1344	4·4
11	M	433	7·4	17 4	7·1	154	9·5	1412	9·6	10 9	14·1	2231	13·9	910	7·5	2121	7·8	321	3·5	1524	3·9	527	5·5	1751	5·6	2 7	4·0	1435	4·4
12	Tu	515	7·1	1747	6·7	236	9·1	1452	9·0	1051	13·7	2312	13·1	952	7·1	22 9	7·3	357	3·5	16 6	3·8	618	5·3	1841	5·3	257	3·9	1529	4·0
13	W	6 0	6·8	1832	6·3	322	8·5	1549	8·3	1132	12·7	2356	11·9	1041	6·6	23 6	6·6	435	3·4	1654	3·5	7 8	4·9	1939	5·0	354	3·6	1635	3·7
14	Th	653	6·4	1927	6·0	419	7·8	1658	7·5	—	—	1224	10·3	1140	6·1	—	—	519	3·2	1749	3·2	8 8	4·6	2049	4·7	5 3	3·4	1756	3·5
15	F	8 2	6·1	2036	5·8	537	7·3	1834	7·1	1 0	10·3	1342	9·5	022	6·1	1257	5·8	614	3·0	1859	2·9	924	4·4	2218	4·6	626	3·3	1926	3·4
16	Sa	924	5·9	22 0	5·8	713	7·3	20 6	7·3	232	9·5	1519	9·5	2 5	5·9	1433	5·8	757	2·8	2059	2·9	1055	4·5	2342	4·7	748	3·4	2044	3·6
17	Su	1058	6·1	2327	6·0	833	7·6	2114	7·8	4 4	10·0	1644	10·3	339	5·9	1552	6·1	952	2·9	2227	2·8	—	—	12 9	4·9	855	3·5	2144	3·7
18	M	—	—	13 0	6·4	931	8·1	2213	8·7	513	11·0	1743	11·8	441	6·2	1645	6·5	1048	3·0	2318	2·8	045	4·9	1349	5·1	949	3·8	2229	3·7
19	Tu	029	6·4	1344	6·7	1032	9·0	2313	8·9	6 5	11·8	1829	11·9	526	6·5	1726	6·9	1131	3·2	—	—	135	5·1	1425	5·2	1032	3·9	23 5	3·7
20	W	116	6·7	1420	6·9	1052	9·2	2344	9·0	646	12·4	19 7	12·7	6 3	6·7	1834	7·2	034	3·1	1246	3·4	216	5·2	1455	5·3	11 7	4·0	2336	3·7
21	Th	155	6·8	1453	7·1	1156	9·3	—	—	723	12·8	1941	13·0	635	7·1	19 3	7·6	139	3·1	1351	3·4	249	5·2	1523	5·4	—	—	1237	3·7
22	F	229	6·9	1521	7·0	012	9·0	1225	9·2	757	13·1	2012	13·0	7 3	7·1	1934	7·6	1 8	3·1	1444	3·4	319	5·3	1550	5·4	030	3·7	13 7	3·6
23	Sa	258	6·9	1548	7·0	039	9·0	1255	8·9	826	13·1	2040	13·0	730	7·2	20 5	7·5	2 5	3·1	1513	3·3	345	5·2	1619	5·3	057	3·6	1340	3·6
24	Su	325	6·9	1616	6·9	1 6	8·9	1323	8·9	854	13·1	21 5	12·9	757	7·2	2036	7·2	229	3·2	1549	3·2	412	5·1	1651	5·2	126	3·6	1414	3·5
25	M	353	6·9	1644	6·8	133	8·6	1351	8·6	921	12·8	2132	12·4	825	6·8	21 5	6·9	253	3·3	1631	3·1	441	5·0	1724	5·0	159	3·5	1456	3·5
26	Tu	423	6·8	1716	6·6	2 1	8·4	1422	8·2	948	12·4	2155	11·8	853	6·5	2142	6·5	322	3·3	1721	3·0	512	4·9	18 0	4·8	236	3·5	1546	3·3
27	W	455	6·6	1753	6·3	234	8·0	15 1	7·8	1013	11·4	2217	11·0	922	6·2	2221	6·1	358	3·3	1820	3·0	546	4·7	1846	4·5	321	3·3	1652	3·3
28	Th	532	6·4	1834	6·0	318	7·6	1555	7·3	1038	11·0	2245	10·4	953	6·2	2318	5·7	440	3·2	1952	2·8	625	4·5	1948	4·3	418	3·2	1817	3·2
29	F	612	6·0	1928	5·7	421	7·1	1716	6·9	1112	10·6	2329	9·9	1034	5·8	—	—	531	3·1	—	—	714	4·3	2110	4·2	531	3·2	1941	3·2
30	Sa	7 3	5·7	2047	5·5	558	6·9	1857	7·0	—	—	1214	9·3	1136	5·5	—	—	630	3·0	—	—	824	4·1	2239	4·3	654	3·1	—	—
31	Su	813	5·5	—	—	—	—	—	—	050	9·2	1354	9·1	050	5·5	1331	5·4	—	—	1952	2·8	952	4·1	—	—	—	—	—	—

*All times shown are Greenwich Mean Time.   †Difference of height in metres from Ordnance Datum (Newlyn).   ‡Difference of height in metres from Ordnance Datum (Dublin).

APRIL, 1985

High Water at the undermentioned Places (G.M.T.*)—

Day of Month	Day of Week	LONDON BRIDGE †Datum of Predictions 3·20 m. below				LIVERPOOL †Datum of Predictions 4·93 m. below				AVONMOUTH †Datum of Predictions 6·50 m. below				HULL (Albert Dock) †Datum of Predictions 3·90 m. below				GREENOCK †Datum of Predictions 1·62 m. below				LEITH AND GRANTON †Datum of Predictions 2·90 m. below				DUN LAOGHAIRE †Datum of Predictions 0·20 m. above			
		Mn. h.m.	Ht. m.	Aft. h.m.	Ht. m.	Mn. h.m.	Ht. m.	Aft. h.m.	Ht. m.	Mn. h.m.	Ht. m.	Aft. h.m.	Ht. m.	Mn. h.m.	Ht. m.	Aft. h.m.	Ht. m.	Mn. h.m.	Ht. m.	Aft. h.m.	Ht. m.	Mn. h.m.	Ht. m.	Aft. h.m.	Ht. m.	Mn. h.m.	Ht. m.	Aft. h.m.	Ht. m.
1	M	945	5·6	2224		733	7·3	2016	7·7	239	9·5	1536	9·9	234	5·7	1458	5·8	755	3·0	2148	2·9	1114	4·4	2350	4·6	8 4	3·4	2045	3·5
2	Tu	1113	6·1	2343		840	8·1	2112	8·4	410	10·6	1654	11·2	346	6·2	16 0	6·3	927	3·1	2243	3·0	046	5·0	1218	4·7	9 0	3·7	2134	3·7
3	W		6·7	1218		932	8·8	22 0	9·1	518	11·9	1753	12·5	441	6·8	1648	7·4	1028	3·3	2329	3·1	132	5·3	13 7	5·1	946	4·2	2216	3·9
4	Th	039	7·2	13 9		1019	9·4	2244	9·6	611	13·0	1842	13·4	526	7·6	1730	7·4	1118	3·5	12 7	3·7	212	5·6	1349	5·5	1029	4·2	2255	4·1
5	F	126	7·5	1354		11 2	9·9	2326	9·9	659	14·0	1927	14·3	6 7	7·6	1811	8·1	012	3·4	1255	3·8	251	5·8	1429	5·8	1110	4·3	2333	4·2
6	Sa	2 8	7·6	1436		1144	10·2			744	14·4	20 9	14·3	645	7·9	1850	8·2	055	3·4	1340	3·9	331	5·8	15 9	6·0	1152	4·4		
7	Su	249	7·6	1518		0 8	10·0	1227	10·2	826	14·4	2050	13·7	724	7·9	1934	8·3	137	3·4	1423	3·9	415	5·7	1553	5·9	013	4·4	1237	4·4
8	M	329	7·4	1559		049	9·9	13 9	9·9	9 7	14·2	2129	13·8	8 4	7·8	2018	8·1	215	3·5	15 4	3·8	5 2	5·5	1640	5·9	056	4·2	1325	4·3
9	Tu	412	7·1	1640		130	9·6	1352	9·5	948	13·4	2210	13·4	846	7·5	21 5	7·6	252	3·6	1548	3·6	552	5·2	1729	5·7	143	4·1	1414	4·1
10	W	457	7·5	1723		212	9·1	1437	8·8	1030	12·2	2249	12·2	929	7·1	2156	7·0	328	3·6	1635	3·3	645	4·9	1824	5·5	233	3·9	1511	3·9
11	Th	544	7·2	18 8		3 0	8·5	1531	8·0	1112	11·0	2334		1019	6·6	2258	6·3	4 7	3·6	1729	3·0	746	4·6	1924	5·3	331	3·7	1618	3·7
12	F	639	6·8	20 4		357	7·8	1642	7·3	038	12·4	1319	9·3	1116	6·1			450	3·3	1838	2·7	9 2	4·6	2035	4·9	439	3·5	1742	3·5
13	Sa	744	6·4	2124		516	7·3	1817	7·0	2 4	9·2	1613	10·0	015	5·8	1229	4·4	7 9	2·7	2053	2·6	1029	4·6	22 1	4·6	6 2	3·4	1913	3·4
14	Su	9 0	6·0	2258		645	7·1	1945	7·3	334	10·8	1712	11·0	159	6·0	14 4	5·7	923	2·8	2211	2·7	1144	4·6	2320	4·6	725	3·4	2027	3·6
15	M	1030	6·5			8 1	8·2	2047	8·2	444	11·7	1758	11·8	322	6·3	1524	6·0	1020	3·1	2255	3·0	1238	4·8			832	3·5	2122	3·7
16	Tu	0 1	6·3	1234		945	8·6	2134	8·7	534	12·3	1836	12·6	419	6·6	1616	6·4	11 2	3·1	2329	3·3	1 5	4·6	1319	5·0	925	3·7	2237	3·7
17	W	048	6·5	1316		1021	8·8	2210	8·7	617	12·8	1910	12·7	5 1	6·9	1657	6·7	1140	3·1			144	4·6	1353	5·2	10 5	3·8	23 5	3·7
18	Th	127	6·3	1351		1054	9·0	2242	8·9	653	12·8	1941	12·8	534	6·9	1732	7·3	0 2	3·1	1215	3·3	216	5·2	1423	5·3	1040	3·8	2331	3·8
19	F	2 1	6·8	1422		1156	9·1	2312	9·0	726	12·9	20 9	12·8	6 4	7·1	18 4	7·4	033	3·1	1249	3·3	245	5·2	1451	5·3	1110	3·9	2357	3·9
20	Sa	229	6·9	1449		010	9·0	2342		757	12·9	2037	12·3	632	7·2	19 7	7·4	1 2	3·2	1320	3·2	311	5·2	1519	5·2	1138	3·9		
21	Su	256	6·9	1515		036	8·9	1225	9·0	826	12·5	21 4	12·7	659	7·1	1940	7·2	127	3·2	1348	3·1	339	5·1	1549	5·2	025	3·7	1237	3·8
22	M	324	6·9	1543		1 6	8·7	1255	8·8	854	12·5	2129	11·7	727	7·1	2012	7·0	152	3·2	1416	3·1	441	4·9	1622	4·8	054	3·7	1311	3·7
23	Tu	356	6·8	1614		137	8·5	1326	8·6	922	12·3	2156	11·2	755	6·8	2046	6·7	218	3·3	1447	3·0	517	4·6	1657	4·8	130	3·6	1350	3·6
24	W	431	6·7	1648		213	7·8	14 1	8·2	950	11·9	2230	10·6	825	6·5	2121	6·5	249	3·3	1525	2·9	559	4·4	1738	4·8	210	3·5	1435	3·6
25	Th	5 9	6·5	1725		258	7·4	1443	7·8	1020	11·2	2320	10·0	853	6·2	2146	6·1	327	3·4	16 8	2·8	652	4·3	1829	4·6	256	3·5	1528	3·5
26	F	553	6·3	18 7		4 3	7·3	1538	7·4	11 1	10·0	12 5	9·6	925	5·9	22 2	5·8	411	3·4	1658	2·7	8 0	4·3	1933	4·4	352	3·4	1632	3·4
27	Sa	645	6·0	19 2		530	7·6	1657	7·1			1331	9·7	10 9	5·7	23 2	5·6	5 1	3·3	1756	2·8	1034	4·3	2048	4·3	459	3·3	1752	3·3
28	Su	754	5·7	2018		656	7·3	1827	7·3	039	9·7	15 4	10·1	1112	5·9	1249	5·9	559	2·9	1926	5·6			22 7	4·3	616	3·3	1912	3·3
29	M	2018		2152		530	7·3	1827	7·6	211	10·1			027	5·7	1249		559	2·9	1926	5·6	8 0	4·3	2048	4·3	616	3·3	1912	3·3
30	Tu	921	5·9	2152		656	7·6	1942	7·9	211	10·1	15 4	10·3	2 2	5·9	1418		718	3·0	2120	2·8	1034	4·5	2314	4·7	729	3·5	2016	3·5

* All times shown are Greenwich Mean Time.   †Difference of height in metres from Ordnance Datum (Newlyn).
‡Difference of height in metres from Ordnance Datum (Dublin).

MAY, 1985

High Water at the undermentioned Places (G.M.T.*)—

Day of Month	Day of Week	London Bridge †Datum of Predictions 3·20 m. below Mn.	Ht.	Aft.	Ht.	Liverpool †Datum of Predictions 4·93 m. below Mn.	Ht.	Aft.	Ht.	Avonmouth †Datum of Predictions 6·50 m. below Mn.	Ht.	Aft.	Ht.	Hull (Albert Dock) †Datum of Predictions 3·90 m. below Mn.	Ht.	Aft.	Ht.	Greenock †Datum of Predictions 1·62 m. below Mn.	Ht.	Aft.	Ht.	Leith and Granton †Datum of Predictions 2·90 m. below Mn.	Ht.	Aft.	Ht.	Dun Laoghaire ‡Datum of Predictions 0·20 m. above Mn.	Ht.	Aft.	Ht.
1	W	1044	6·3	23 9	6·2	8 4	8·2	2040	8·5	336	11·0	1621	11·5	312	6·4	1521	6·4	852	3·1	2213	3·0	1138	4·8			828	3·7	21 5	3·7
2	Th	1149	6·9			9 0	8·9	2131	9·1	445	12·2	1722	12·5	410	6·8	1614	7·0	956	3·3	2257	3·1	010	5·0	1230	5·2	918	4·0	2149	3·9
3	F	0 8	6·7	1242	7·2	949	9·4	2217	9·5	543	13·1	1815	13·3	457	7·2	17 1	7·5	1049	3·4	2339	3·1	057	5·3	1316	5·5	10 3	4·1	2228	4·1
4	Sa	057	7·1	1328	7·4	1035	9·8	23 1	9·8	634	13·6	19 2	13·6	539	7·5	1746	7·8	1140	3·4	1229	3·7	140	5·6	14 0	5·8	1047	4·2	23 7	4·2
5	Su	141	7·3	1412	7·4	1120	10·0	2344	9·8	720	13·9	1945	13·9	619	7·7	1831	7·9	023	3·5	1316	3·7	223	5·7	1531	5·9	1130	4·3	2348	4·3
6	M	225	7·4	1454	7·4			12 5	9·9	8 5	13·6	2029	13·6	7 0	7·7	1917	7·7	1 5	3·6	14 1	3·6	3 6	5·7	1622	5·8	032	4·3	1216	4·3
7	Tu	3 8	7·5	1536	7·3	027	9·7	1250	9·6	849	12·8	2110	12·8	742	7·3	20 5	7·2	146	3·6	1445	3·4	351	5·5	1713	5·5	120	4·2	13 6	4·2
8	W	355	7·4	1620	7·0	110	9·4	1335	9·2	931	11·8	2152	11·7	826	7·0	2056	6·7	224	3·6	1531	3·2	440	5·2	18 9	5·2	213	4·1	14 0	4·0
9	Th	444	7·2	17 5	6·7	155	9·0	1423	8·6	1014	10·7	2235	10·7	912	6·6	2149	6·1	3 2	3·5	1619	2·9	531	4·9	19 8	4·8	310	4·0	1459	3·7
10	F	533	6·8	1750	6·3	244	8·5	1518	7·9	1150	9·8	2322	9·8	10 0	6·2	2248	5·7	343	3·5	1712	2·9	626	4·6	2015	4·6	416	3·8	1721	3·5
11	Sa	627	6·4	1838	6·0	341	8·0	1624	7·4	131	9·6	1253	9·6	1054	5·9	2357	5·7	428	3·3	1818	2·7	725	4·4	2128	4·5	531	3·6	1845	3·4
12	Su	724	6·1	1935	5·8	449	7·6	1742	7·1	355	10·0	14 5	10·0	1157	5·5			521	2·7	20 7	2·6	832	4·6	2239	4·5	649	3·5	1954	3·4
13	M	830	5·9	2044	5·6	6 7	7·5	19 2	7·2	452	11·3	1519	11·3	014	5·8	1313	5·8	634	2·7	2127	2·7	947	4·7	2337	4·5	848	3·6	2047	3·5
14	Tu	949	5·9	2210	5·6	720	7·6	2053	7·6	537	11·9	1626	11·9	126	5·8	1436	6·2	827	2·7	2212	2·8	1057	4·7			930	3·6	2127	3·6
15	W	11 4	6·0	2322	6·1	818	7·9	2153	7·9	618	12·2	1716	12·2	224	5·8	1536	6·6	934	3·0	2248	2·8	025	4·9	1237	4·9	10 5	3·6	2230	3·6
16	Th	1158	6·3			9 4	8·2	2232	8·2	653	12·4	1758	12·4	342	5·8	1621	7·1	1021	3·1	2321	3·0	1 3	4·9	1314	5·1	1037	3·7	2258	3·7
17	F	012	6·4	1242	6·8	943	8·5	22 7	8·5	727	12·4	1835	12·4	459	6·5	1659	7·0	11 1	3·1	2353	3·1	137	5·0	1347	5·2	11 7	3·7	2327	3·7
18	Sa	053	6·6	1317	6·8	1020	8·7	2311	8·7	759	11·9	19 9	11·9	532	6·9	1734	6·9	1138	3·1			2 9	5·1	1419	5·2	1140	3·7	2358	3·8
19	Su	127	6·7	1348	6·8	1054	8·8	2342	8·8	833	11·7	1941	11·7	6 1	7·0	1810	6·8	022	3·1	1214	3·1	239	5·1	1453	5·2	032	3·8	1213	3·7
20	M	157	6·7	1418	6·8	1127	8·8	12 0	8·8	913	12·5	2012	12·5	631	7·0	1845	6·5	051	3·2	1319	3·0	312	5·1	1527	5·2	1 8	3·8	1251	3·6
21	Tu	227	6·7	1447	6·8	014	8·8	1234	8·9	938	12·4	2043	12·4	733	6·8	1919	6·2	119	3·3	1429	2·9	344	5·1	16 5	5·2	152	3·9	1335	3·5
22	W	3 1	6·7	1519	6·8	046	8·6	1310	8·7	989	11·7	2115	11·7	8 4	6·7	1955	6·1	149	3·3	1510	2·9	421	5·0	1645	4·9	239	3·6	1421	3·5
23	Th	338	6·7	1553	6·6	123	8·3	1349	8·7	989	10·9	2150	10·9	839	6·5	2032	6·0	225	3·4	1556	2·9	5 0	4·9	1730	4·7	332	3·6	1514	3·4
24	F	416	6·6	1630	6·5	2 4	8·1	1434	8·0	1019	10·9	2233	10·9	917	6·3	2112	6·0	3 5	3·4	1646	2·9	546	4·7	1821	4·6	433	3·5	1614	3·3
25	Sa	457	6·6	17 9	6·3	253	7·8	1531	7·7	11 6	10·5	2327	10·4	10 3	6·1	2159	6·0	351	3·4	1742	2·8	640	4·6	1920	4·5	542	3·5	1724	3·3
26	Su	542	6·5	1753	6·2	353	7·8	1640	7·6			12 5	10·4	11 2	6·0	2255	6·0	440	3·4	1859	2·8	740	4·5	2024	4·5	652	3·5	1837	3·3
27	M	635	6·3	1846	5·9	5 5	7·8	1754	7·7	032	10·6	1314	10·6	0 5	6·0			537	3·2	2036	2·9	847	4·6	2131	4·7	756	3·8	1941	3·5
28	Tu	740	6·1	1955	6·0	619	8·4	19 4	8·9	148	10·9	1434	10·9	126	6·0	1217	6·0	648	3·2	2135	3·0	954	4·7	2234	4·7	850	3·9	2035	3·7
29	W	856	6·1	2117	6·3	727	8·8	20 6	8·9	3 5	11·4	1549	11·4	234	6·4	1335	6·4	813	3·2	2223	3·1	1057	4·8	2333	4·8			2122	3·9
30	Th	1012	6·5	2233	6·6	826	8·8	21 0	8·9	414	12·1	1652	12·1	335	6·8	1442	6·8	922	3·3	2223	3·1	1154	5·2						
31	F	1118	6·8	2336													1541	7·0												

JUNE, 1985

High Water at the undermentioned Places (G.M.T.*)—

Day of Week	Day of Month	London Bridge †Datum of Predictions 3·20 m. below				Liverpool †Datum of Predictions 4·93 m. below				Avonmouth †Datum of Predictions 6·50 m. below				Hull (Albert Dock) †Datum of Predictions 3·90 m. below				Greenock †Datum of Predictions 1·62 m. below				Leith and Granton †Datum of Predictions 2·90 m. below				Dun Laoghaire ‡Datum of Predictions 0·20 m. above			
		Mn. h.m.	Ht. m.	Aft. h.m.	Ht. m.	Mn. h.m.	Ht. m.	Aft. h.m.	Ht. m.	Mn. h.m.	Ht. m.	Aft. h.m.	Ht. m.	Mn. h.m.	Ht. m.	Aft. h.m.	Ht. m.	Mn. h.m.	Ht. m.	Aft. h.m.	Ht. m.	Mn. h.m.	Ht. m.	Aft. h.m.	Ht. m.	Mn. h.m.	Ht. m.	Aft. h.m.	Ht. m.
Sa	1	031	6·8	1215	7·0	921	9·2	2150	9·2	516	12·7	1749	12·9	427	7·1	1634	7·3	1019	3·4	23 8	3·2	025	5·3	1247	5·4	939	4·0	22 3	4·0
Su	2	120	6·9	13 4	7·0	1012	9·4	2238	9·4	610	13·0	1839	13·3	515	7·3	1727	7·5	1112	3·5	2353	3·3	112	5·4	1336	5·6	1026	4·1	2246	4·1
M	3	2 8	7·0	1351	7·0	11 1	9·5	2325	9·5	7 0	13·2	1926	13·3	6 0	7·4	1818	7·6	038	3·5	12 5	3·5	2 0	5·4	1428	5·7	1113	4·1	2327	4·1
Tu	4	256	7·1	1436	7·0	1149	9·5			748	13·1	2011	13·2	645	7·4	19 9	7·5	120	3·6	1255	3·5	246	5·6	1518	5·7			12 2	4·1
W	5	343	7·2	1519	6·9	010	9·5	1236	9·2	834	12·9	2056	12·9	728	7·3	1959	6·9	2 2	3·6	1344	3·4	334	5·5	16 9	5·6	013	4·1	1254	4·1
Th	6	433	7·2	16 4	6·7	056	9·5	1324	8·9	919	12·4	2139	12·3	813	7·2	2050	6·5	243	3·6	1432	3·3	423	5·4	17 2	5·5	1 3	4·1	1347	3·9
F	7	520	6·9	1648	6·7	141	9·3	1412	8·5	10 3	11·6	2223	11·5	857	7·0	2139	6·5	326	3·5	1519	3·2	514	5·2	1755	5·4	156	4·0	1445	3·8
Sa	8	6 8	6·6	1732	6·4	229	9·0	15 1	8·0	1047	10·9	23 6	10·9	942	6·8	2230	5·8	410	3·4	16 6	3·0	6 6	5·0	1848	5·2	252	3·9	1543	3·6
Su	9	657	6·2	1815	6·1	319	8·6	1555	7·6	1130	10·3	2354	10·4	1028	6·5	2322		5 0	3·1	1655	2·9	659	4·7	1944	5·1	350	3·7	1650	3·5
M	10	752	6·0	19 4	5·9	414	8·3	1654	7·2			1219	10·0	1119	6·3			6 0	2·9	1750	2·7	755	4·6	2043	4·9	453	3·6	18 0	3·3
Tu	11	856	5·9	20 2	5·7	515	7·7	18 0	7·3	049	10·2	1316	9·9	024	5·6	1219	6·1	718	2·8	1857	2·6	854	4·6	2144	4·7	6 2	3·5	19 6	3·3
W	12	10 6	5·9	2111	5·7	619	7·6	19 0	7·6	151	10·2	1419	10·0	137	5·5	1328	6·3	835	2·8	2016	2·6	955	4·6	2241	4·6	7 6	3·5	20 0	3·2
Th	13	11 8	6·1	2223	5·8	721	7·6	20 2	7·9	256	10·5	1524	10·4	244	5·7	1439	6·3	932	2·9	2116	2·7	1053	4·6	2333	4·5	8 2	3·4	2045	3·5
F	14	1157	6·3	2325	6·1	816	7·8	2049	7·8	356	10·9	1621	10·9	336	5·9	1536	6·5	1019	2·9	22 1	2·9	1144	4·7			848	3·5	2122	3·6
Sa	15	011	6·3	1236	6·3	9 4	8·1	2129	8·2	451	11·7	1713	11·3	419	6·2	1624	6·7	111	3·0	2238	3·0	017	4·7	1230	4·5	928	3·5	2156	3·7
Su	16	050	6·4	1313	6·6	946	8·3	2244	8·6	539	11·9	1758	11·7	457	6·5	17 8	6·7	1141	3·0	2313	3·1	059	4·8	1314	4·8	10 5	3·6	2228	3·8
M	17	127	6·5	1349	6·7	1026	8·5	2320	8·8	622	12·0	1839	11·9	532	6·7	1747	6·8	020	3·2	2347	3·1	137	4·9	1354	4·9	1042	3·6	23 0	3·8
Tu	18	2 6	6·6	1426	6·7	11 4	8·6	2357	8·7	7 3	12·0	1917	12·0	6 5	6·8	1825	6·8	054	3·3	1220	3·0	216	5·0	1435	5·0	1117	3·6	2336	3·8
W	19	247	6·7	15 5	6·8	1142	8·7	1219	8·7	741	12·0	1954	12·1	641	6·8	19 4	6·8	130	3·4	1259	2·9	252	5·0	1515	5·1	1155	3·6	1237	3·6
Th	20	327	6·8	1543	6·7			1259	8·6	819	11·9	2032	11·9	716	6·8	1944	6·8	253	3·5	15 4	2·9	329	5·1	1555	5·2	013	3·8	1320	3·6
F	21	4 9	6·8	1621	6·6	035	8·9	1342	8·5	857	11·9	2110	11·9	752	6·8	2025	6·7	337	3·5	1420	2·9	4 8	5·0	1636	5·2	053	3·8	14 7	3·6
Sa	22	449	6·8	17 1	6·4	116	8·8	1429	8·4	936	11·7	2150	11·7	830	6·7	21 7	6·7	426	3·5	1549	2·9	450	4·9	1722	5·1	137	3·9	1457	3·6
Su	23	534	6·7	1743	6·3	159	8·7	1519	8·2	11 4	11·5	2235	11·5	911	6·7	2152	6·6	518	3·4	1637	2·9	535	4·9	18 9	4·9	222	3·8	1553	3·5
M	24	622	6·5	1831	6·2	246	8·5	1616	8·0	1154	11·3	2323	11·3	956	6·6	2242	6·5	621	3·2	1726	2·9	626	4·8	19 1	4·8	313	3·8	1655	3·5
Tu	25	719	6·4	1930	6·2	339	8·4	1720	8·0	018	11·5	1253	11·1	1047	6·5	2339	6·4	735	3·2	1825	2·9	719	4·9	1957	4·8	510	3·7	18 2	3·5
W	26	826	6·3	2042	6·3	438	8·3	1828	8·2	121	11·5	14 4	11·4	048	6·4	1256	6·5	849	3·2	1942	2·9	816	4·9	2056	4·8	618	3·7	1906	3·4
Th	27	939	6·3	2156	6·3	543	8·3	1933	8·2	234	11·4	1518	11·4	157	6·4	14 6	6·6	953	3·2	2065	2·8	917	4·9	2158	4·8	726	3·7	20 6	3·5
F	28	1048	6·5	23 8	6·5	650	8·3	2034	8·5	346	11·6	1626	11·6	3 1	6·6	1514	7·0			2153	3·0	1021	4·9	23 0	4·9	828	3·8	2058	3·6
Sa	29	1150	6·6			758	8·5	2131	8·7	452	11·9	1726	12·2	4 2	6·8	1620	6·8			2243	3·1	1126	5·1	2359	4·9	925	3·9	2145	3·9
Su	30					9 0	8·7																	1228	5·2				

*All times shown are Greenwich Mean Time. †Difference of height in metres from Ordnance Datum (Newlyn).
‡Difference of height in metres from Ordnance Datum (Dublin).

JULY, 1985

High Water at the undermentioned Places (G.M.T.*)—

Datum of Predictions: London Bridge 3·20 m. below · Liverpool 4·93 m. below · Avonmouth 6·50 m. below · Hull (Albert Dock) 3·90 m. below · Greenock 1·62 m. below · Leith and Granton 2·90 m. below · Dun Laoghaire 0·20 m. above

Day of Month	Day of Week	LONDON BRIDGE Mn. h.m.	Ht. m.	Aft. h.m.	Ht. m.	LIVERPOOL Mn. h.m.	Ht. m.	Aft. h.m.	Ht. m.	AVONMOUTH Mn. h.m.	Ht. m.	Aft. h.m.	Ht. m.	HULL (Albert Dock) Mn. h.m.	Ht. m.	Aft. h.m.	Ht. m.	GREENOCK Mn. h.m.	Ht. m.	Aft. h.m.	Ht. m.	LEITH AND GRANTON Mn. h.m.	Ht. m.	Aft. h.m.	Ht. m.	DUN LAOGHAIRE Mn. h.m.	Ht. m.	Aft. h.m.	Ht. m.
1	M	011	6·5	1246	6·6	957	8·9	2223	9·1	553	12·2	1822	12·5	458	7·0	1720	7·1	1052	3·2	2332	3·3	054	5·2	1327	5·4	1016	3·9	2230	4·0
2	Tu	1 9	6·6	1337	6·6	1051	9·0	2312	9·3	648	12·4	1912	12·7	547	7·1	1817	7·2	1148	3·2			146	5·3	1421	5·5	11 6	3·9	2316	4·1
3	W	159	6·7	1423	6·8	1140	9·1			738	12·4	1959	12·8	634	7·2	19 7	7·1	020	3·4	1242	3·2	236	5·4	1514	5·5	1155	3·9		
4	Th	249	6·9	15 8	6·8	0 0	9·3	1228	9·0	825	12·4	2043	12·7	717	7·2	1954	7·0	1 6	3·5	1334	3·1	324	5·4	16 3	5·5	0 2	4·1	1244	3·8
5	F	334	7·1	1550	6·9	045	9·3	1312	8·8	9 7	12·4	2125	12·4	759	7·2	2039	6·8	150	3·6	1423	3·1	410	5·4	1649	5·3	050	4·1	1335	3·7
6	Sa	419	7·1	1631	6·8	127	9·1	1354	8·6	948	11·9	22 6	12·0	839	7·1	2119	6·6	232	3·6	15 8	3·1	455	5·3	1735	5·1	140	4·1	1422	3·6
7	Su	5 1	7·0	17 9	6·6	2 9	8·9	1434	8·3	1026	11·5	2242	11·5	918	7·1	2159	6·3	312	3·5	1550	3·0	541	5·1	1821	4·9	228	4·0	1513	3·5
8	M	543	6·7	1747	6·4	250	8·6	1515	7·9	11 2	11·0	2320	11·2	957	6·9	2238	6·1	353	3·4	1631	3·0	627	4·9	19 7	4·8	317	3·8	16 6	3·3
9	Tu	624	6·4	1828	6·1	334	8·2	16 0	7·6	1139	10·7			1040	6·6	2322	5·9	435	3·2	1712	2·8	713	4·6	1954	4·5	4 9	3·7	17 2	3·3
10	W	710	6·1	1917	5·9	421	7·8	1652	7·3	0 3	10·8	1222	10·4	1129	6·4			522	3·0	1757	2·8	759	4·8	2043	4·4	4 9	3·7	1757	3·2
11	Th	8 2	5·9	2016	5·7	515	7·6	1753	7·2	055	10·5	1317	10·1	015	5·6	1228	6·1	618	2·8	1851	2·7	849	4·6	2136	4·4	5 3	3·5	1851	3·2
12	F	9 1	5·7	2119	5·5	618	7·4	19 0	7·2	155	10·3	1422	10·0	120	5·6	1338	5·9	725	2·7	1956	2·7	945	4·6	2234	4·4	6 4	3·3	1956	3·3
13	Sa	10·0	5·8	2231	5·7	724	7·4	20 2	7·4	3 0	10·3	1528	10·2	227	5·7	1449	6·0	835	2·7	21 0	2·8	1046	4·4	2332	4·5	8 3	3·4	2041	3·3
14	Su	1057	5·9	2319	5·8	825	7·6	2056	7·8	4 3	10·5	1629	10·6	329	5·9	1552	6·1	935	2·8	2153	3·0	1148	4·6			937	3·5	2122	3·4
15	M	1150	6·0			918	7·9	2142	8·2	5 2	10·9	1725	11·1	421	6·2	1644	6·3	1028	2·9	2237	3·0	024	4·6	1245	4·7	1019	3·5	22 2	3·5
16	Tu	014	6·0	1241	6·3	10 3	8·3	2224	8·5	556	11·3	1814	11·6	5 6	6·4	1730	6·5	1114	2·9	2318	3·1	114	4·9	1336	4·8	1059	3·6	2239	3·7
17	W	1 4	6·3	1327	6·4	1047	8·5	23 5	8·8	643	11·7	1859	11·9	546	6·6	1812	6·6	12 1	2·9	2357	3·2	159	5·1	1424	4·9	1140	3·7	2337	3·8
18	Th	151	6·5	1412	6·7	1127	8·7	2344	9·0	726	11·9	1940	12·2	625	6·8	1853	6·8	037	3·3	1245	2·8	238	5·3	15 5	5·1	036	3·5	13 4	3·7
19	F	234	6·8	1454	6·9			12 8	8·9	8 8	12·2	2020	12·5	7 2	7·0	1933	7·0	119	3·5	1414	2·9	316	5·4	1545	5·2	118	3·6	1349	3·8
20	Sa	318	7·0	1535	6·9	025	9·2	1249	9·0	847	12·4	21 1	12·8	740	7·1	2013	7·2	2 0	3·5	1457	2·9	355	5·3	1624	5·4	2 3	3·7	1435	3·8
21	Su	359	7·1	1613	6·9	1 6	9·2	1331	9·0	928	12·6	2142	12·8	819	7·2	2054	7·2	243	3·6	1540	3·0	435	5·4	17 6	5·4	250	3·7	1525	3·7
22	M	438	7·1	1649	6·9	148	9·1	1413	8·9	10 9	12·7	2224	12·8	858	7·2	2135	7·1	326	3·6	1621	3·1	6 7	5·3	1751	5·2	343	3·6	1621	3·6
23	Tu	520	6·9	1727	6·7	230	9·1	1458	8·6	1049	12·4	23 8	12·0	939	7·1	2220	6·9	412	3·5	17 4	3·0	656	5·3	1840	5·1	442	3·9	1724	3·5
24	W	6 4	6·7	1811	6·4	317	8·9	1548	8·4	1134	11·9	2356	11·9	1024	7·0	23 9	6·6	5 0	3·5	1751	3·0	749	5·1	1931	4·9	550	3·8	1834	3·6
25	Th	653	6·4	19 2	6·1	4 7	8·6	1645	8·1			1225	11·3	010	6·4	1224	6·4	556	3·3	1852	2·9	847	5·0	2025	4·8			1941	3·7
26	F	754	6·2	20 8	6·3	5 8	8·3	1753	7·9	052	11·3	1330	10·9	120	6·3	1340	6·4	7 3	3·1	2015	2·9	936	4·9	2127	4·8	816	3·7	2042	3·7
27	Sa	9 4	6·2	2125	6·2	621	8·0	19 7	7·9	2 2	10·9	1449	11·0	234	6·3	15 3	6·4	823	3·0	2131	3·0			2237	4·9	919	3·7	2135	3·8
28	Su	1017	6·2	2245	6·2	740	8·0	2019	8·1	321	10·8	16 3	11·4	346	6·5	1621	6·5	941	3·0	2233	3·2	1113		2347	4·9	1015	3·8	2225	3·9
29	M	1130	6·3			851	8·3	2122	8·5	437	11·0	1712	11·9	448	6·7	1725	6·8	1046	3·0	2324	3·2			1225	5·0	11 5	3·8	2310	4·1
30	Tu	0 1	6·3	1234	6·3	955	8·5	2217	8·9	544	11·3	1812	11·9	539	6·9	1817	6·9	1145	3·0			049	5·0	1327	5·0				
31	W	1 3	6·5	1328	6·4	1047	8·8	23 5	9·2	641	11·9	1903	11·9									144	5·2	1422	5·3				

*All times shown are Greenwich Mean Time.   †Difference of height in metres from Ordnance Datum (Newlyn).   ‡Difference of height in metres from Ordnance Datum (Dublin).

AUGUST, 1985

High Water at the undermentioned Places (G.M.T.*)—

Day of Month	Day of Week	London Bridge †Datum 3·20 m. below Mn. (h.m.)	Ht. (m.)	Aft. (h.m.)	Ht. (m.)	Liverpool †Datum 4·93 m. below Mn. (h.m.)	Ht. (m.)	Aft. (h.m.)	Ht. (m.)	Avonmouth †Datum 6·50 m. below Mn. (h.m.)	Ht. (m.)	Aft. (h.m.)	Ht. (m.)	Hull (Albert Dock) †Datum 3·90 m. below Mn. (h.m.)	Ht. (m.)	Aft. (h.m.)	Ht. (m.)	Greenock †Datum 1·62 m. below Mn. (h.m.)	Ht. (m.)	Aft. (h.m.)	Ht. (m.)	Leith and Granton †Datum 2·90 m. below Mn. (h.m.)	Ht. (m.)	Aft. (h.m.)	Ht. (m.)	Dun Laoghaire ‡Datum 0·20 m. above Mn. (h.m.)	Ht. (m.)	Aft. (h.m.)	Ht. (m.)
1	Th	155	6·7	1413	6·6	1133	8·9	2349	9·4	730	12·2	1948	12·7	622	7·1	19 2	7·0	013	3·3	1239	3·0	232	5·3	1510	5·4	1151	3·8	2354	4·1
2	F	240	6·9	1456	6·7	029	9·4	1215	9·0	812	12·4	2029	12·8	740	7·3	1941	6·9	058	3·4	1329	3·0	315	5·4	1553	5·4	036	4·1	1233	3·8
3	Sa	321	7·1	1534	6·9	1 6	9·3	1253	8·9	850	12·5	21 5	12·7	815	7·4	2018	6·9	142	3·5	1413	3·0	354	5·4	1632	5·3	118	4·1	1314	3·7
4	Su	4 0	7·1	16 9	6·9	141	9·1	1327	8·8	925	12·5	2141	12·6	849	7·4	2051	6·8	220	3·5	1451	3·0	433	5·3	17 9	5·2	2 0	4·0	1354	3·7
5	M	437	7·0	1642	6·8	216	8·8	1434	8·5	957	12·1	2213	12·3	924	7·2	2124	6·7	256	3·5	1526	3·0	551	5·2	1748	4·9	240	3·9	1435	3·6
6	Tu	512	6·7	1715	6·6	251	8·5	1510	8·3	1028	11·8	2244	11·9	10 0	6·9	2156	6·5	331	3·4	1558	3·0	629	5·0	1826	4·7	321	3·7	1515	3·5
7	We	546	6·5	1750	6·4	329	8·0	1550	7·5	1058	11·4	2318	11·3	1041	6·5	2231	6·5	4 6	3·1	1631	2·9	7 9	4·7	1946	4·5	4 6	3·5	1559	3·3
8	Th	624	6·2	1831	6·1	414	7·6	1642	7·2	1130	10·8	2356	10·6	1132	6·1	2313	6·0	445	3·1	17 8	2·9	753	4·5	2034	4·3	457	3·3	1650	3·3
9	F	7 7	5·9	1920	5·8	513	7·2	1753	6·9	1210	10·1	—	—	0 8	5·7	1242	5·7	529	3·0	1750	2·9	846	4·4	2134	4·3	6 3	3·2	1752	3·2
10	Sa	759	5·7	2020	5·7	631	7·0	1916	6·9	045	9·9	13 6	9·6	126	5·6	14 5	5·6	624	2·8	1843	2·8	956	4·4	2236	4·3	716	3·2	1858	3·2
11	Su	9 0 0	5·5	2127	5·5	751	7·2	2026	7·5	155	9·5	1427	9·4	243	5·6	1521	5·9	731	2·8	1947	2·8	1115	4·4	2356	4·4	821	3·3	20 0	3·3
12	M	10 0	5·5	2233	5·5	856	7·6	2121	8·0	315	9·5	1548	9·7	349	5·9	1624	6·0	850	2·7	21 1	2·8	—	—	1225	4·4	915	3·4	2051	3·5
13	Tu	11 8	5·7	2344	5·7	946	8·1	2121	8·5	431	10·1	1658	10·5	442	6·3	1715	6·6	10 2	2·8	22 4	3·0	054	4·7	1322	4·8	10 0	3·6	2137	3·7
14	W	045	6·2	13 9	6·2	1030	8·6	2248	8·9	533	10·8	1753	11·4	526	6·6	1753	6·7	1058	2·8	2340	3·2	140	4·9	14 9	5·1	1043	3·8	2218	4·0
15	Th	134	6·7	1355	6·8	1115	9·0	2327	9·3	624	11·7	1839	12·1	6 5	7·0	1836	7·3	1147	2·8	—	—	221	5·1	1449	5·1	1121	3·9	2256	4·0
16	F	218	7·1	1437	7·1	1151	9·3	2327	9·4	7 7	12·2	1923	12·7	643	7·3	1914	7·5	024	3·4	1318	3·2	258	5·5	1526	5·5	12 1	—	2336	4·2
17	Sa	3 0	7·3	1515	7·3	1231	9·6	—	—	749	12·6	20 4	13·0	720	7·7	1954	7·6	1 7	3·4	14 1	3·2	336	5·6	16 4	5·6	015	4·3	12 1	4·0
18	Su	341	7·3	1553	7·3	3 0	9·6	1312	9·3	830	13·2	2044	13·6	757	7·7	2032	7·6	150	3·6	1442	3·1	414	5·7	1645	5·6	056	4·3	1242	4·0
19	M	420	7·4	1630	7·2	341	9·7	1352	9·3	910	13·5	2124	13·6	836	7·7	2111	7·7	233	3·7	1521	3·1	457	5·7	1728	5·3	140	4·4	1323	4·0
20	Tu	459	7·0	17 8	7·0	420	9·5	1433	9·0	949	13·4	22 4	13·5	917	7·2	2153	7·2	314	3·8	1558	3·2	544	5·6	1816	5·3	225	4·2	1456	3·9
21	W	540	6·7	1749	6·7	2 8	9·5	1518	8·6	1028	12·9	2245	12·8	357	7·2	2240	7·1	357	3·5	1638	3·2	632	5·1	19 6	5·0	317	4·3	1549	3·8
22	Th	627	6·3	1836	6·4	251	9·1	16 8	8·1	11 9	12·1	2329	11·9	10 2	6·8	2336	6·3	443	3·5	1721	3·1	725	5·1	20 0	4·8	417	3·9	1652	3·6
23	F	721	6·1	1941	6·2	339	8·6	16 8	7·7	1156	11·2	—	—	1054	6·1	—	—	536	3·5	1810	3·1	827	4·9	21 5	4·6	528	3·7	18 6	3·5
24	Sa	830	6·1	21 4	6·1	441	8·1	1723	7·3	021	10·3	1256	10·3	024	6·3	1330	6·4	640	3·3	19 5	3·1	945	4·8	2225	4·6	652	3·6	1923	3·5
25	Su	949	5·9	2233	5·9	735	7·6	2012	7·5	133	10·1	1423	10·0	1 7	6·4	1511	6·4	813	3·3	1933	3·0	1113	4·7	2345	4·7	813	3·6	2032	3·7
26	M	1112	5·9	2353	5·9	854	7·9	2118	8·4	3 3	9·9	1549	10·4	150	6·6	1627	6·9	9 8	3·3	2121	2·8	—	—	1227	4·9	915	3·6	2131	3·8
27	Tu	—	—	1221	6·3	953	8·4	2210	9·0	430	10·4	17 5	11·0	233	6·6	1723	7·1	946	2·8	2231	3·1	048	4·9	1327	5·1	1015	3·8	2219	4·0
28	W	055	6·7	1314	6·7	1040	8·8	2234	9·3	539	11·9	18 3	12·5	314	7·2	1845	7·0	1054	2·8	2321	2·9	140	5·2	1416	5·3	11 0	3·9	23 2	4·1
29	Th	144	6·9	1359	6·9	1119	9·3	2334	9·3	631	11·9	1850	12·5	357	7·2	1917	7·1	1147	3·3	—	—	223	5·3	1459	5·3	1140	3·9	23 2	4·2
30	F	225	7·1	1437	7·1	1040	8·8	2332	9·3	714	12·3	1931	12·8	443	7·2	1845	7·2	0 6	3·3	1232	3·3	1459	5·3	1459	5·3	11 0	3·9	2341	4·2
31	Sa	—	—	—	—	1154	9·1	—	—	752	12·6	20 6	13·0	641	7·1	1917	7·1	049	3·4	1313	3·0	3 0	5·4	1534	5·4	1213	3·9	—	—

* All times shown are Greenwich Mean Time.   †Difference of height in metres from Ordnance Datum (Newlyn).

‡Difference of height in metres from Ordnance Datum (Dublin).

†Difference of height in metres from Ordnance Datum.

‡Difference of height in metres from Ordnance Datum (Dublin).

SEPTEMBER, 1985

High Water at the undermentioned Places (G.M.T.*)—

Day of Month	Day of Week	LONDON BRIDGE †Datum of Predictions 3·20 m. below Mn. h.m.	Ht.	Aft. h.m.	Ht.	LIVERPOOL †Datum of Predictions 4·93 m. below Mn. h.m.	Ht.	Aft. h.m.	Ht.	AVONMOUTH †Datum of Predictions 6·50 m. below Mn. h.m.	Ht.	Aft. h.m.	Ht.	HULL (Albert Dock) †Datum of Predictions 3·90 m. below Mn. h.m.	Ht.	Aft. h.m.	Ht.	GREENOCK †Datum of Predictions 1·62 m. below Mn. h.m.	Ht.	Aft. h.m.	Ht.	LEITH AND GRANTON †Datum of Predictions 2·90 m. below Mn. h.m.	Ht.	Aft. h.m.	Ht.	DUN LAOGHAIRE ‡Datum of Predictions 0·20 m. above Mn. h.m.	Ht.	Aft. h.m.	Ht.
1	Su	3 1	7.1	1511	7.0	0 7	9.1	1227	9.1	826	12.8	2040	13.1	714	7.6	1948	7.1	127	3.0	1351	3.0	332	5.5	16 7	5.3	016	4.2	1246	3.8
2	M	335	7.1	1542	7.0	039	9.5	1256	9.5	857	12.8	2111	13.0	747	7.6	2018	7.1	2 3	3.1	1424	3.1	4 5	5.4	1639	5.4	051	4.2	1318	3.8
3	Tu	4 6	6.9	1610	6.9	110	9.2	1326	9.2	927	12.7	2141	12.7	819	7.5	2047	6.9	234	3.1	1452	3.1	437	5.3	1711	5.3	126	4.1	1352	3.7
4	W	435	6.8	1640	6.7	140	9.0	1354	8.8	953	12.3	22 9	12.2	851	7.3	2115	6.7	3 4	3.1	1520	3.1	512	5.2	1744	5.0	2 1	3.9	1425	3.6
5	Th	5 5	6.6	1712	6.5	211	8.6	1425	8.2	1019	11.7	2235	11.4	925	6.9	2146	6.4	334	3.1	1549	3.0	547	5.0	1819	4.7	238	3.8	15 4	3.5
6	F	539	6.3	1749	6.2	243	8.2	1458	7.8	1044	10.9	23 4	10.5	10 0	6.5	2220	6.1	4 8	3.1	1623	3.0	624	4.7	1856	4.3	317	3.6	1550	3.3
7	Sa	615	6.0	1832	5.9	321	7.6	1541	7.3	1111	10.1	2337	9.7	1041	6.0	23 1	5.7	450	3.0	17 4	2.9	7 6	4.5	1943	4.1	4 6	3.4	1647	3.3
8	Su	659	5.7	1924	5.5	414	7.1	1647	6.9	1151	9.4			1137	5.5			538	2.8	1753	2.8	8 2	4.3	2045	4.2	510	3.2	18 0	3.2
9	M	755	5.4	2032	5.3	537	6.7	1827	6.7	034	8.9	13 4	8.8	0 8	5.4	1323	5.3	638	2.7	1852	2.7	919	4.2	22 6	4.3	633	3.1	1916	3.5
10	Tu	9 8	5.2	2153	5.3	719	6.9	1957	6.9	212	8.7	1458	9.1	159	5.5	1453	5.5	8 4	2.7	20 9	2.7	1047	4.2	2327	4.3	753	3.5	2018	3.5
11	W	1033	5.4	2318	5.7	833	7.5	2056	7.9	356	9.4	1627	10.1	317	5.7	16 2	6.0	945	3.0	2133	3.0	029	4.6	1259	4.6	853	3.7	21 9	3.8
12	Th	1150	5.4			924	8.1	2142	8.6	5 5	10.6	1726	11.4	414	6.2	1654	6.5	1129	2.9	2231	2.8	116	5.0	1346	5.3	939	3.7	2153	4.0
13	F	021	6.3	1245	5.7	10 7	8.8	2224	9.1	557	11.8	1814	12.4	5 1	6.7	1734	6.9			2319	3.3	156	5.3	1425	5.5	1021	3.9	2232	4.4
14	Sa	110	6.9	1330	6.3	1048	9.3	23 4	9.6	643	13.4	1859	13.8	540	7.2	1814	7.3	0 6	3.5	1212	3.0	233	5.6	15 7	5.7	1058	4.1	2310	4.5
15	Su	155	7.4	1411	6.9	1127	9.6	2343	10.0	726	13.8	1941	13.8	617	7.6	1850	7.6	050	3.6	1254	3.0	3 9	5.7	1538	5.8	1136	4.2	2350	4.5
16	M	236	7.6	1449	7.5			12 7	9.8	8 8	13.8	2022	14.2	653	7.9	1927	7.8	135	3.8	1337	3.1	348	5.9	1620	5.7			1213	4.3
17	Tu	315	7.6	1527	7.6	024	10.1	1246	9.8	847	14.0	21 3	14.2	731	8.1	20 5	7.8	216	3.8	1417	3.2	433	5.9	17 5	5.6	030	4.5	1254	4.3
18	W	355	7.1	1605	7.6	1 3	10.0	1327	9.6	927	13.8	2142	13.8	812	8.0	2044	7.6	257	3.8	1454	3.4	520	5.4	1753	5.3	114	4.5	1337	4.4
19	Th	435	7.1	1645	7.5	144	9.4	1408	9.2	10 6	13.1	2224	12.8	854	7.7	2125	7.2	341	3.7	1532	3.4	612	5.1	1843	5.1	2 3	4.4	1425	4.1
20	F	518	6.8	1730	7.2	227	8.7	1453	8.7	1045	12.0	23 6	11.6	942	7.3	2213	6.7	427	3.5	1610	3.4	7 8	5.0	1940	4.8	256	4.2	1521	3.9
21	Sa	6 1	6.2	1821	6.4	317	8.5	1548	8.1	1130	10.8	2357	10.3	1037	6.6	23 8	6.1	519	3.2	1653	3.2	816	4.8	2051	4.5	357	3.9	1625	3.7
22	Su	655	5.9	1928	6.1	423	7.7	17 4	7.7			1232	9.9	1150	6.1			624	2.9	1744	3.0	943	4.6	2218	4.6	514	3.6	1745	3.6
23	M	8 4	5.7	2049	5.9	557	7.5	1839	7.5	113	9.5	14 2	9.4	025	5.9	1337	5.9	812	2.7	1859	2.8	1112	4.5	2338	4.5	647	3.6	19 9	3.7
24	Tu	924	5.7	2219	6.0	735	7.4	20 4	7.9	249	9.4	1535	10.0	327	5.9	1515	6.3	10 4	2.7	2115	2.8	1112	4.5	2218	4.5	811	3.6	2023	3.7
25	W	1052	5.9	2337	6.5	849	7.9	2152	8.5	419	10.1	1651	11.0	423	6.6	1621	6.6	1054	2.9	2224	2.7	1220	5.0	2338	5.0	916	3.9	2121	4.1
26	Th	036	6.9	1255	6.8	939	8.8	2231	8.9	523	11.2	1746	12.0	5 6	6.6	1711	6.8	1135	3.0	2310	3.1	039	5.0	1314	5.2	10 5	3.9	22 7	4.2
27	F	123	7.0	1337	7.1	1020	9.3	23 6	9.4	611	12.6	1829	12.6	543	7.3	1749	7.3	028	3.3	1212	3.1	126	5.2	1357	5.3	1044	3.9	2246	4.2
28	Sa	2 2	7.2	1413	7.3	1055	9.0	2339	9.5	650	12.5	19 7	13.0	615	7.5	1819	7.0	028	3.4	1212	3.1	2 4	5.4	1435	5.4	1117	4.2	2320	4.2
29	Su	237	7.2	1444	7.2	1127	9.1			726	12.8	1941	13.2	543	7.3	1849	7.1	1 4	3.4	1246	3.0	236	5.4	15 7	5.4	1147	4.0	2351	3.9
30	M					1156	9.1			758	13.0	2012	13.3	648	7.6	1917	7.6			1320	3.1	3 5	5.5	1536	5.3			1215	

OCTOBER, 1985

High Water at the undermentioned Places (G.M.T.*)—

Day of Month	Day of Week	London Bridge †Datum 3·20 m. below Mn.	Ht.	Aft.	Ht.	Liverpool †Datum 4·93 m. below Mn.	Ht.	Aft.	Ht.	Avonmouth †Datum 6·50 m. below Mn.	Ht.	Aft.	Ht.	Hull (Albert Dock) †Datum 3·90 m. below Mn.	Ht.	Aft.	Ht.	Greenock †Datum 1·62 m. below Mn.	Ht.	Aft.	Ht.	Leith and Granton †Datum 2·90 m. below Mn.	Ht.	Aft.	Ht.	Dun Laoghaire ‡Datum 0·20 m. above Mn.	Ht.	Aft.	Ht.
1	Tu	3 7	7·0	1512	7·0	0 8	9·4	1224	9·1	827	13·1	2042	13·2	719	7·6	1944	7·2	138	3·4	1349	3·1	334	5·4	16 4	5·2	021	4·1	1242	3·9
2	W	334	6·9	1538	6·9	038	9·2	1252	8·9	854	12·8	2110	12·8	751	7·4	2012	7·2	2 7	3·3	1416	3·2	4 4	5·3	1633	5·1	051	4·0	1311	3·8
3	Th	359	6·8	16 7	6·8	1 6	9·0	1319	8·7	919	12·5	2136	12·2	822	7·2	2039	6·8	234	3·2	1441	3·2	435	5·2	1736	5·0	125	3·7	1344	3·8
4	F	427	6·7	1640	6·6	135	8·6	1347	8·4	943	11·8	22 0	12·0	853	6·8	21 7	6·5	3 3	3·1	1510	3·3	5 8	5·0	1814	4·8	2 0	3·6	1421	3·7
5	Sa	459	6·5	1716	6·4	243	8·2	1419	8·0	1028	10·9	2224	10·4	925	6·2	2135	6·2	337	3·1	1545	3·2	547	4·8	1736	4·8	240	3·4	15 6	3·5
6	Su	534	6·2	1757	6·1	2 6	7·7	1458	7·6	11 5	9·5	2346	9·6	1055	5·9	2210	5·8	417	3·0	1627	3·2	632	4·4	20 7	4·4	331	3·4	16 1	3·4
7	M	615	5·8	1846	5·4	334	7·2	1559	7·1	1055	10·3	23 6	9·0	10 3	5·3	2210	5·3	5 4	2·9	1716	3·1	733	4·2	2128	3·9	435	3·2	1711	3·3
8	Tu	7 6	5·5	1949	5·4	454	6·7	1737	6·9	1 6	8·7	1232	8·9	1 6	5·7	1232	6·0	6 1	2·8	1812	3·0	852	4·2	2250	4·4	557	3·3	1831	3·4
9	W	818	5·5	2118	5·4	639	6·9	1914	7·3	237	9·1	1418	9·1	237	6·2	1418	6·6	722	2·7	1926	2·8	1017	4·3	2353	4·7	722	3·6	1943	3·6
10	Th	956	5·4	2247	5·9	759	7·5	2020	8·0	338	10·2	1528	10·2	338	6·8	1528	7·1	924	2·9	2058	2·7	1131	4·6	----	----	825	3·8	2038	3·8
11	F	1118	5·9	2351	6·5	853	8·2	2110	8·7	428	11·6	1621	11·6	427	7·3	1621	7·5	1019	2·9	2253	2·9	043	5·1	1227	4·9	914	4·1	2124	4·1
12	Sa	----	----	1214	6·6	938	8·9	2153	9·3	525	12·8	1744	12·8	547	7·8	1744	7·9	11 1	3·1	2341	3·5	124	5·4	1312	5·3	953	4·3	22 5	4·3
13	Su	043	7·1	1304	7·1	1019	9·6	2235	9·8	615	13·6	1822	13·6	627	8·0	1822	7·9	1142	3·1	1224	3·6	2 2	5·8	1354	5·6	1030	4·3	2243	4·5
14	M	127	7·5	1341	7·4	1059	9·8	2316	10·1	742	14·1	19 0	14·1	823	8·0	19 0	7·6	028	3·8	13 7	3·3	242	5·8	1431	5·8	11 7	4·4	2323	4·6
15	Tu	2 9	7·6	1420	7·4	1140	10·0	2357	10·2	823	14·3	1938	14·3	945	7·9	1938	7·3	114	3·8	1347	3·6	324	5·7	1510	5·8	1145	4·4	----	----
16	W	250	7·6	15 1	7·7	----	----	12 0	9·9	9 4	14·1	2019	14·1	9 4	7·6	2019	6·3	157	3·9	1426	3·6	410	5·4	1553	5·7	0 6	4·5	1226	4·4
17	Th	331	7·4	1543	7·6	041	10·0	13 3	9·7	929	14·0	2122	14·1	929	6·9	21 3	5·6	241	3·8	15 5	3·5	5 1	5·1	1640	5·4	051	4·3	1311	4·3
18	F	413	7·1	1628	7·3	124	9·6	1345	9·3	1028	13·0	2252	12·4	1028	6·4	2150	5·8	325	3·6	1545	3·4	554	5·4	1729	5·1	143	4·1	14 1	4·2
19	Sa	457	6·7	1719	6·9	2 9	8·9	1433	8·7	1146	12·5	2252	13·0	1146	5·9	2248	6·2	413	3·4	1630	3·1	554	5·4	1822	5·1	239	3·8	1457	4·0
20	Su	544	6·3	1814	6·4	3 4	8·3	1531	8·1	1028	10·2	2346	10·0	0 0	5·9	2248	6·5	5 6	3·1	1723	3·1	656	4·7	1924	4·6	345	3·6	16 4	3·8
21	M	636	5·9	1919	6·1	413	7·6	1647	7·6	057	9·3	1219	9·8	135	6·5	1333	6·7	612	3·1	1836	2·8	8 8	4·6	2036	4·7	637	3·5	1723	3·7
22	Tu	741	5·7	2030	5·9	544	7·4	1817	7·6	222	9·3	1340	9·5	258	6·9	1458	7·1	817	2·8	2049	2·7	931	4·6	2159	5·1	757	3·7	1849	3·8
23	W	856	5·6	2155	6·0	716	7·4	1937	7·9	452	10·1	15 7	10·0	356	7·4	1559	7·2	947	2·7	2158	3·0	1052	5·0	2315	5·3	857	3·9	20 2	3·9
24	Th	1024	5·9	2313	6·4	823	7·9	2037	8·4	540	11·1	1621	11·9	438	7·5	1719	7·0	1032	2·9	2243	3·3	1157	5·2	1246	5·3	1019	3·9	2144	4·0
25	F	1136	6·4	----	----	912	8·3	2124	9·0	619	12·5	1716	12·6	515	7·4	1750	7·5	11 7	3·0	2321	3·2	013	5·2	1327	5·3	1050	4·0	2222	4·1
26	Sa	011	6·9	1228	6·8	952	8·7	2202	9·2	655	12·9	1838	12·9	549	7·3	1818	7·4	1139	3·1	2359	3·3	058	5·3	1353	5·3	1117	4·0	2253	4·1
27	Su	056	7·2	13 9	7·1	1026	9·0	2235	9·2	727	13·1	1944	13·1	621	7·4	1845	7·4	034	3·4	1213	3·4	134	5·3	1434	5·3	1144	4·0	2323	4·1
28	M	134	7·1	1344	7·1	1057	9·2	23 8	9·1	757	13·1	2013	13·1	653	7·2	1913	7·2	1 8	3·4	1243	3·3	2 6	5·3	15 3	5·2	1211	4·0	2352	4·1
29	Tu	2 8	7·1	1415	7·0	1125	9·2	2339	9·1	757	13·0	2013	13·0	726	7·3	1940	7·0	138	3·3	1312	3·3	234	5·4	1530	5·2	1211	4·0	1211	4·0
30	W	236	7·0	1442	7·0	1154	9·1	----	----	825	13·0	2042	13·0	726	7·3	1940	7·0	1 8	3·4	1338	3·3	3 3	5·4	16 0	5·3	1144	3·9	1211	4·0
31	Th	3 1	6·9	1510	6·9	0 8	9·1	1221	9·0	825	12·6	2042	12·6	726	7·3	1940	7·0	138	3·3	1338	3·3	334	5·3	16 0	5·3	022	3·9	1240	3·9

* All times shown are Greenwich Mean Time.   †Difference of height in metres from Ordnance Datum (Newlyn).

‡Difference of height in metres from Ordnance Datum (Dublin).

NOVEMBER, 1985

High Water at the undermentioned Places (G.M.T.*)—

Day of Month	Day of Week	LONDON BRIDGE †Datum of Predictions 3·20 m. below				LIVERPOOL †Datum of Predictions 4·93 m. below				AVONMOUTH †Datum of Predictions 6·50 m. below				HULL (*Albert Dock*) †Datum of Predictions 3·90 m. below				GREENOCK †Datum of Predictions 1·62 m. below				LEITH AND GRANTON †Datum of Predictions 2·90 m. below				DUN LAOGHAIRE ‡Datum of Predictions 0·20 m. above			
		Mn.	Ht.	Aft.	Ht.	Mn.	Ht.	Aft.	Ht.	Mn.	Ht.	Aft.	Ht.	Mn.	Ht.	Aft.	Ht.	Mn.	Ht.	Aft.	Ht.	Mn.	Ht.	Aft.	Ht.	Mn.	Ht.	Aft.	Ht.
		h.m.	m.	h.m.	m.	h.m.	m.	h.m.	m.	h.m.	m.	h.m.	m.	h.m.	m.	h.m.	m.	h.m.	m.	h.m.	m.	h.m.	m.	h.m.	m.	h.m.	m.	h.m.	m.
1	F	327	6·8	1541	6·8	038	8·9	1250	8·8	850	12·4	2110	12·0	757	7·0	20 8	6·8	2 6	3·2	14 6	3·3	4 6	5·2	1631	5·1	054	3·8	1314	3·9
2	Sa	356	6·7	1614	6·7	1 9	8·6	1320	8·5	917	11·7	2136	11·2	829	6·7	2036	6·6	237	3·1	1436	3·4	442	5·1	17 6	4·9	133	3·7	1353	3·8
3	Su	430	6·6	1652	6·5	142	8·2	1354	8·2	942	11·0	22 3	10·5	9 3	6·3	21 4	6·3	312	3·1	1513	3·4	522	4·8	1746	4·7	215	3·6	1439	3·7
4	M	5 5	6·3	1734	6·3	222	7·8	1437	7·8	1010	10·4	2238	9·9	943	6·0	2142	6·0	354	3·0	1556	3·3	612	4·6	1836	4·5	3 6	3·4	1532	3·6
5	Tu	546	6·0	1824	6·0	312	7·4	1535	7·4	1052	9·9	2333	9·4	1035	5·7	2238	5·7	441	2·9	1645	3·3	714	4·4	1939	4·4	4 9	3·3	1635	3·5
6	W	636	5·7	1924	5·7	426	7·0	1635	7·3	1153	9·6	—	—	1153	5·5	—	—	536	2·8	1741	3·2	825	4·3	2052	4·4	6 5	3·3	1748	3·5
7	Th	744	5·5	2046	5·5	556	7·1	1825	7·5	052	9·3	1331	10·6	0 8	5·5	1333	5·7	650	2·9	1850	3·1	940	4·4	22 4	4·5	644	3·4	1859	3·7
8	F	915	5·6	2210	6·0	713	7·6	1934	8·1	227	9·8	1614	11·8	147	5·8	1444	6·1	845	2·9	2018	3·2	1049	4·7	23 8	4·8	750	3·6	20 0	3·9
9	Sa	1037	6·0	2318	6·6	813	8·3	2030	8·7	349	11·0	1712	12·8	253	6·3	1542	6·6	943	3·0	2128	3·4	1146	5·0	—	—	841	3·8	2051	4·1
10	Su	1137	6·1	—	—	903	8·9	2119	9·3	451	12·1	18 4	13·5	346	6·8	1631	7·1	1027	3·0	2223	3·6	0 1	5·2	1235	5·3	925	4·0	2135	4·3
11	M	012	7·1	1228	7·0	949	9·4	22 6	9·7	544	13·1	1853	13·9	435	7·3	1715	7·4	11 9	3·3	2313	3·7	048	5·5	1319	5·6	10 3	4·2	2218	4·4
12	Tu	1 0	7·3	1313	7·3	1033	9·7	2251	10·0	634	13·9	1938	14·0	520	7·7	1756	7·7	0 3	3·8	1236	3·5	132	5·7	14 1	5·7	1042	4·3	23 0	4·5
13	W	144	7·4	1357	7·5	1116	9·9	2336	10·0	8 4	13·5	2023	13·7	6 5	7·9	1836	7·7	051	3·8	1319	3·6	216	5·8	1441	5·8	1120	4·4	2347	4·4
14	Th	226	7·3	1440	7·5	12 0	9·9	—	—	847	13·8	2155	13·1	652	8·0	1919	7·7	139	3·8	1442	3·7	3 3	6·0	1531	5·8	—	—	12 4	4·4
15	F	310	7·3	1528	7·3	022	9·8	1245	9·7	931	13·8	2242	13·1	738	7·8	20 2	7·5	225	3·5	1526	3·7	353	5·9	1610	5·6	035	4·3	1250	4·3
16	Sa	355	7·1	1619	7·0	1 9	9·4	1330	9·3	1017	12·8	2334	12·2	830	7·5	2047	7·2	313	3·3	1612	3·5	446	5·7	1710	5·6	129	4·2	1343	4·1
17	Su	441	6·8	1711	6·8	159	8·8	1420	8·8	11 6	10·9	—	—	924	6·9	2135	6·9	4 2	3·1	17 5	3·5	542	5·4	18 6	5·1	225	4·0	1440	4·1
18	M	530	6·4	18 5	6·6	254	8·2	1517	8·3	034	9·7	13 7	9·9	1021	6·3	2227	6·5	455	2·9	1813	3·0	643	4·9	19 5	4·7	332	3·8	1545	3·9
19	Tu	621	6·1	19 2	6·2	359	7·6	1624	7·9	141	9·6	1419	10·1	1129	6·2	2329	6·2	558	2·7	1955	3·1	749	4·8	2011	4·7	432	3·7	1657	3·8
20	W	716	5·8	20 5	6·0	513	7·3	1739	7·7	254	10·0	1532	10·8	—	—	1257	5·9	735	2·8	2113	3·0	9 1	4·7	2122	4·6	611	3·5	1817	3·7
21	Th	822	5·7	2118	5·9	634	7·4	1852	7·8	458	11·5	1633	11·5	043	6·0	1419	5·9	9 1	2·9	2246	3·1	1014	4·7	2233	4·7	726	3·5	1929	3·7
22	F	939	5·8	2235	6·2	741	7·6	1955	8·1	543	12·1	1722	12·1	141	6·1	1521	5·9	1029	3·2	2326	3·3	1116	4·8	2331	4·9	824	3·6	2027	3·8
23	Sa	1057	6·1	2336	6·6	833	8·0	2044	8·4	622	12·4	18 4	12·7	314	6·3	1645	6·7	11 3	3·3	—	—	—	—	12 7	4·9	9 9	3·7	2114	3·9
24	Su	1153	6·5	—	—	915	8·3	2127	8·6	657	12·6	1842	12·7	444	6·8	1718	6·9	1136	3·3	12 8	3·3	019	5·0	1250	5·0	948	3·8	2152	3·9
25	M	024	6·8	1236	6·8	952	8·6	22 4	8·8	730	12·7	1916	12·5	520	7·1	1749	7·0	0 4	3·3	1238	3·3	058	5·1	1327	5·1	1019	3·9	2226	3·9
26	Tu	1 3	6·9	1313	6·8	1026	8·8	2238	8·9	8 1	12·5	1949	12·2	557	7·1	1818	7·1	039	3·3	13 7	3·4	133	5·2	1359	5·2	1049	3·9	2256	3·9
27	W	135	6·9	1345	6·8	1057	8·9	2312	8·9	830	12·2	2020	11·8	631	7·1	1846	7·0	112	3·2	1337	3·4	2 6	5·3	1433	5·2	1116	3·9	2327	3·9
28	Th	2 4	6·9	1415	6·8	1127	8·9	2346	8·9	—	—	2051	11·8	7 4	7·0	1916	7·0	145	3·1	—	—	240	5·3	15 4	5·2	1145	3·9	2359	3·9
29	F	233	6·9	1447	6·8	—	—	12 0	8·9	—	—	—	—	740	6·8	1947	6·8	—	—	—	—	314	5·3	1537	5·3	—	—	1219	3·9
30	Sa	3 4	6·8	1522	6·7	018	8·7	1231	8·8	—	—	—	—	—	—	—	—	—	—	—	—	350	5·2	1611	5·1	036	3·7	1254	3·9

* All times shown are Greenwich Mean Time.   † Difference of height in metres from Ordnance Datum (Newlyn).   ‡ Difference of height in metres from Ordnance Datum (Dublin).   † Difference of height in metres from Ordnance Datum.   ‡ Difference of height in metres from Ordnance Datum.

DECEMBER, 1985

High Water at the undermentioned Places (G.M.T.*)—

Day of Month	Day of Week	LONDON BRIDGE †Datum of Predictions 3·20 m. below Mn.	Ht.	Aft.	Ht.	LIVERPOOL †Datum of Predictions 4·93 m. below Mn.	Ht.	Aft.	Ht.	AVONMOUTH †Datum of Predictions 6·50 m. below Mn.	Ht.	Aft.	Ht.	HULL (Albert Dock) †Datum of Predictions 3·90 m. below Mn.	Ht.	Aft.	Ht.	GREENOCK †Datum of Predictions 1·62 m. below Mn.	Ht.	Aft.	Ht.	LEITH AND GRANTON †Datum of Predictions 2·90 m. below Mn.	Ht.	Aft.	Ht.	DUN LAOGHAIRE †Datum of Predictions 0·20 m. above Mn.	Ht.	Aft.	Ht.
		h.m.	m.	h.m.	m.	h.m.	m.	h.m.	m.	h.m.	m.	h.m.	m.	h.m.	m.	h.m.	m.	h.m.	m.	h.m.	m.	h.m.	m.	h.m.	m.	h.m.	m.	h.m.	m.
1	Su	338	6·7	16 0	6·7	053	8·5	13 6	8·6	9 0	11·8	2124	11·4	815	6·7	2019	6·7	219	3·1	1412	3·5	428	5·1	1649	5·0	115	3·6	1335	3·9
2	M	413	6·6	1640	6·6	130	8·3	1342	8·4	932	11·4	2159	11·0	853	6·5	2054	6·5	257	3·0	1451	3·5	511	4·9	1731	4·9	159	3·6	1418	3·8
3	Tu	449	6·4	1722	6·5	212	8·0	1427	8·2	1010	11·1	2240	10·6	936	6·3	2135	6·3	340	3·0	1534	3·5	558	4·8	1819	4·7	249	3·5	15 7	3·8
4	W	529	6·2	18 8	6·3	3 1	7·8	1521	7·9	1057	10·8	2330	10·6	1026	6·1	2227	6·1	425	3·0	1622	3·5	653	4·6	1915	4·7	345	3·4	16 3	3·7
5	Th	617	6·0	19 4	6·1	4 2	7·5	1626	7·8	1156	10·6			1126	6·0	2333	6·0	517	3·0	1716	3·4	754	4·6	2015	4·7	449	3·4	17 6	3·7
6	F	716	5·8	2015	6·0	513	7·5	1737	7·9	032	10·3	13 4	10·7	050	6·1	1241	6·0	617	2·9	1818	3·3	858	4·6	2119	4·7	6 0	3·4	1816	3·7
7	Sa	833	5·8	2132	6·0	625	7·8	1848	8·6	149	10·5	1423	11·0	2 4	6·4	1355	6·1	746	3·0	1935	3·3	10 2	4·7	2221	5·1	7 8	3·5	1922	3·8
8	Su	953	6·1	2242	6·5	731	8·2	1951	8·6	310	11·1	1538	11·7	3 7	6·7	1458	6·4	9 0	3·1	2050	3·4	11 3	5·0	2320	5·1	8 6	3·7	2020	4·0
9	M	11 1	6·5	2343	6·8	829	8·7	2049	9·0	417	11·9	1642	12·4	4 4	7·2	1558	6·6	951	3·2	2151	3·4	1158	5·2			854	3·9	2112	4·1
10	Tu	1158	6·8			921	9·1	2142	9·3	518	12·6	1740	12·9	459	7·4	1647	6·9	1039	3·4	2247	3·5	016	5·4	1249	5·4	938	4·1	22 0	4·2
11	W	036	6·8	1252	6·9	1010	9·4	2233	9·6	611	13·1	1834	13·2	554	7·6	1736	7·2	1125	3·5	2341	3·5	1 9	5·6	1338	5·6	1021	4·2	2247	4·2
12	Th	124	6·9	1341	6·9	1058	9·6	2323	9·6	7 2	13·4	1924	13·2	646	7·6	1821	7·5			1212	3·6	2 0	5·7	1427	5·7	11 3	4·3	2334	4·2
13	F	211	6·9	1430	7·2	1146	9·7			749	13·4	2013	13·2	737	7·4	19 6	7·5	034	3·6	1258	3·7	253	5·7	1515	5·7	1148	4·3		
14	Sa	256	7·0	1521	7·3	012	9·5	1234	9·6	836	13·2	2100	12·8	826	6·8	1951	7·4	126	3·6	1343	3·8	343	5·7	16 5	5·6	025	4·1	1237	4·3
15	Su	342	6·9	1610	7·1	1 2	9·2	1321	9·4	921	12·8	2146	12·2	915	6·4	2034	7·3	215	3·5	1428	3·8	437	5·6	1655	5·5	118	4·0	1330	4·2
16	M	428	6·9	17 1	7·1	149	8·8	14 9	9·0	10 6	12·2	2230	11·5	10 4	6·1	2118	7·1	3 4	3·3	1513	3·8	528	5·4	1748	5·3	214	3·8	1424	4·1
17	Tu	515	6·7	1749	6·8	239	8·4	1458	8·7	1051	11·5	2315	10·9	1055	5·8	22 3	6·9	352	3·2	1558	3·6	623	5·1	1841	5·0	313	3·7	1521	4·0
18	W	6 0	6·4	1838	6·4	331	7·9	1551	8·3	1137	11·0			1153	5·7	2252	6·4	440	3·1	1646	3·4	719	4·8	1936	4·8	417	3·5	1625	3·8
19	Th	646	6·1	1930	6·1	427	7·6	1648	7·9	0 0	10·6	1228	10·6					531	3·0	1743	3·2	817	4·6	2033	4·6	527	3·4	1733	3·7
20	F	740	5·8	2030	5·9	530	7·3	1751	7·7	052	10·2	1324	10·5			13 4	5·7	632	2·9	1854	3·0	919	4·6	2133	4·6	638	3·3	1842	3·6
21	Sa	844	5·7	2139	5·9	638	7·3	1856	7·6	152	10·1	1429	10·4	056	6·1	1418	6·1	746	2·8	2012	3·0	1021	4·6	2233	4·6	740	3·5	1944	3·6
22	Su	959	5·8	2248	6·1	741	7·5	1958	7·8	258	10·4	1534	10·9	211	6·2	1515	6·2	853	2·9	2117	3·0	1117	4·7	2330	4·7	830	3·5	2037	3·6
23	M	11 6	6·0	2342	6·3	833	7·7	2049	8·0	4 3	10·9	1635	11·3	317	6·2	16 4	6·2	943	3·0	22 9	3·1			12 7	4·8	912	3·6	2121	3·6
24	Tu	1158	6·2			918	8·1	2135	8·2	550	11·3	1729	11·7	410	6·2	1645	6·6	1025	3·2	2253	3·2	018	4·8	1251	4·9	949	3·7	2159	3·7
25	W	025	6·4	1241	6·4	957	8·3	2216	8·4	631	11·8	1814	12·0	455	6·6	1722	6·7	11 2	3·3	2336	3·2	1 3	4·9	1333	5·0	1022	3·8	2235	3·7
26	Th	1 3	6·6	1319	6·5	1035	8·6	2252	8·6	712	12·2	1855	12·1	537	6·7	1756	6·8	1137	3·3			145	5·0	1412	5·1	1055	3·9	23 9	3·7
27	F	138	6·7	1357	6·6	1111	8·8	2329	8·6	744	12·2	20 8	12·1	615	6·8	1828	6·9	016	3·3	1210	3·4	224	5·1	1447	5·2	1128	3·9	2344	3·7
28	Sa	213	6·8	1434	6·7	1146	8·8			818	12·2	2043	12·0	652	6·8	19 2	6·9	054	3·2	1244	3·4	3 2	5·2	1523	5·2			12 2	3·9
29	Su	251	6·8	1514	6·8	0 5	8·7	1221	8·9	853	12·2	2118	12·0	727	6·9	1935	7·0	132	3·1	1319	3·5	339	5·2	1558	5·2	022	3·7	1239	3·9
30	M	329	6·8	1553	6·8	042	8·7	1257	8·9	929	12·2	2155	11·9	8 5	7·0	2011	6·9	210	3·0	1356	3·5	418	5·2	1635	5·2	1 1	3·7	1318	4·0
31	Tu	4 6	6·7	1633	6·7	121	8·6	1337	8·8					844	6·8	2049	6·8	250	3·0	1436	3·6	458	5·1	1716	5·1	144	3·6	14 0	4·0

*All times shown are Greenwich Mean Time.   †Difference of height in metres from Ordnance Datum (Newlyn).
‡Difference of height in metres from Ordnance Datum (Dublin).

NAUTICAL MEASURES

Distance is measured in nautical (or sea) miles. The nautical mile is traditionally defined as the length of a minute of arc of a great circle of the earth; but as this length varies in different latitudes (owing to the fact that the earth is not a perfect sphere), 6,080 feet, a "rounded off value" of the mean length, has been adopted in British practice as the standard length of the nautical mile. On this basis 33 nautical miles exactly equal 38 statute miles; the statute (land) mile contains 5,280 feet. A *cable*, as a measure used by seamen, is 600 feet (100 fathoms) approximately one-tenth of a nautical mile. *Soundings at sea* are recorded in fathoms (6 feet); 100 fathoms = 1 cable length; 10 cables = 1 nautical mile.

NOTE.—The British standard nautical mile of 6,080 feet is now obsolete. The international nautical mile of 1,852 metres was adopted in the Hydrographic Department in 1970. Also, the cable and the fathom are obsolescent. Distances are tending to be expressed in decimal parts of a sea mile, or in metres, rather than cables. Depths are expressed in metres on all new Admiralty charts.

Speed is measured in *nautical miles per hour*, called *knots*. A knot is a measure of speed and is not used to express distance. A ship moving at the rate of 30 nautical miles per hour is said to be "doing 30 knots"

and as the nautical mile is longer than the land or statute mile this represents a land speed of over 34¼ miles per hour.

Knots	m.p.h.	Knots	m.p.h.	Knots	m.p.h.
1	1·1515	15	17·2727	29	33·3939
2	2·3030	16	18·4242	30	34·5454
3	3·4545	17	19·5757	31	35·6969
4	4·6060	18	20·7272	32	36·8484
5	5·7575	19	21·8787	33	38·0000
6	6·9090	20	23·0303	34	39·1515
7	8·0606	21	24·1818	35	40·3030
8	9·2121	22	25·3333	36	41·4545
9	10·3636	23	26·4848	37	42·6060
10	11·5151	24	27·6363	38	43·7575
11	12·6666	25	28·7878	39	44·9090
12	13·8180	26	29·9393	40	46·0606
13	14·9696	27	31·0908	41	47·2121
14	16·1212	28	32·2424	42	48·3636

Net tonnage.—The gross tonnage less certain deductions for crew space, engine room, water ballast and other spaces not used for passengers or cargo.
Gross tonnage.—The total volume of all the enclosed spaces of a vessel, the unit of measurement being a ton of 100 cubic feet.

CHRONOLOGICAL NOTES

TIME MEASURES

Kelvin (1883) estimated the age of the earth's crust at 20–400 million years. Study of radio-activity has since shown cooling to have been slower. Holmes and others gave 1,500–2,000 million years as the age of the oldest known rocks. Jeffreys suggests an age not exceeding 8,000 million years for the separate existence of the earth, which, probably with other related planets, separated from the sun after a star-collision. Very early rocks, almost without traces of fossils, are variously named in North America and Europe and account for a period down to about 5,000 million years ago.

PALÆOZOIC (Old Animal Life) PERIODS include:—
Cambrian, Ordovician and Silurian rocks, all named from Wales (Cambria, Ordovices, Silures, the two latter ancient Celtic peoples). These rocks account for about 200 million years and there then followed a major phase of mountain-building, called *Caledonian* because studied early in Scotland, characterized by N.E.–S.W. lines of hills and valleys in several areas.
Devonian, including the Old Red Sandstone.
Carboniferous, including Mountain Limestone, Millstone Grit and Coal Measures.
These rocks account for about 100 million years and then there followed a major phase of mountain-building called *Hercyian* because widespread in W. Germany and adjacent areas. In Britain there are E.–W. lines of hills and valleys, and some N.–S.

MESOZOIC (Middle Forms of Life) PERIODS include:—
Permian rocks, widespread in Perm district, U.S.S.R. *Triassic,* including New Red Sandstone. *Jurassic,* important in the Jura Mts. *Cretaceous,* including the Greensands and the Chalk of England. In the Mesozoic, modern large land groups of animals, reptiles, birds and mammals first appear, but almost no modern genera or species of animals are known.

CAINOZOIC or CENOZOIC (Recent forms of Life) PERIODS include:—

Eocene. A few existing genera or species. *Oligocene.* A minority of existing forms. *Miocene.* Approach to a balance of existing and extinct forms. *Pliocene.* A majority of existing forms. *Pleistocene.* A very large majority of existing forms. *Holocene.* Existing forms only, save for a few exterminated by man. In the last 50 million years, from the Miocene through the Pliocene, the Alpine-Himalayan and the circum-Pacific phases of mountain building reached their climax.

During the Pleistocene period ice sheets repeatedly locked up masses of water as land ice, its weight depressed the land, but the locking up of water lowered sea-level by 100–200 metres. Milankovitch has worked out variations of radiation theoretically receivable from the sun and has reached conclusions not very markedly different as to the dates from those of Penck who studied sediments, and both can fit into Deperet's scheme based on study of river terraces. Milankovitch gives 600,000 years for the Pleistocene.

Phases of the Pleistocene:—
(a) Early Glaciations (probably 2), Gunz glaciations of Penck's Alpine series. About 600 to 500 thousand years ago.
(b) An interglacial phase with high sea level, Milazzian terraces (of Deperet's series) around the Mediterranean. About 500,000 years ago.
(c) A second pair of Glaciations, the Mindel of Penck's series. About 500 to rather before 400 thousand years ago.
(d) A long interglacial phase with high sea level, but less high than during (b). Tyrrhenian terraces around the Mediterranean. From about 400 to about 200 thousand years ago.
(e) The penultimate series of glaciations (probably 3), the Riss of Penck's series. About 200 to 150 thousand years ago.
(f) An interglacial phase with fairly high sea level, less high than during (d). Monastirian terraces

around the Mediterranean. From about 150 to about 120 thousand years ago.

(g) The ultimate series of glaciations (probably 3, preceded perhaps by a cool phase), the Wurm of Penck's series. From about 115 to rather more than 20 thousand years ago.

(h) The last glacial retreat merging into the Holocene period about 10,000 or 8,000 years ago.

MAN IN THE PLEISTOCENE

In the East African Miocene fragmentary remains of apes with possible human links in thigh bone characters have been found by Hopwood and Leakey.

In S. Africa at Taungs, Sterkfontein and Kroomdraai have been found remains of *Australopithecus, Plesianthropus* and *Paranthropus*, possibly linked with early man in limb characters and some features of skull and teeth though the brains are small and rather ape-like. The cave deposits in which they occur are supposed to be late Pliocene or early Pleistocene.

Java and Peking finds began with Dubois' discovery (1892) of an imperfect skull cap, some teeth and a possibly related femur indicating the erect posture. Later finds by von Koenigswald and by Weidenreich (1937–41) have emphasized the human relationship of the Java specimens, and also give evidence of gigantism (the name *Meganthropus* has been used). The specimens are usually given a Middle Pleistocene age. Oppenoorth (1932) discovered robust skulls and human Pleistocene bones on a terrace of the Solo river, Java. Twelve specimens from Chou Kou Tien near Peking studied by Black and Weidenreich and called *Sinanthropus* are broadly like the Java finds; the name *Pithecanthropus* had better be used for all.

A jaw from Mauer, Heidelberg, found 1902, and dated to the mid Pleistocene is very large but human in form. A skull cap from Neanderthal near Düsseldorf, Germany, has been under discussion for 100 years. It and later found congeners belong to the onset of the 4th series of Glaciations (Penck's Wurm). The best preserved of these skulls is that of La Chapelle aux Saints (France) with very strong brow-ridges. Related skulls of rather earlier date from Steinheim, Ehringsdorf, Krapina and elsewhere are less specialized and more akin to modern man. Skulls from Sacco Pastore and Circeo in Italy are related to the Neanderthal group.

Mt. Carmel has yielded to Professor Dorothy Garrod and Dr. McCown several mid- or late-Pleistocene specimens apparently related both to modern types and to the Neanderthal group.

A skull from Galilee, and a skull from Kabwe (formerly Broken Hill), Zambia, are related to the Neanderthal group.

Oakley has estimated the age of Pleistocene fossil bones from their fluorine content. The back part of a skull from Swanscombe, N. Kent, has in this way been dated to the mid Pleistocene. Its discoverer, Marston, has won widespread support for his view linking it with modern types.

Controversy over the Piltdown skull and jaw is ended. The skull was dated by Oakley's method as late Pleistocene, or later, so the old name *Eoanthropus* is inappropriate. The ape-like jaw was found to be modern and to have nothing to do with the skull.

With the last retreat of the ice sheets it seems that the Neanderthal group, and probably the Pithecanthropus group, became extinct. Well-known specimens of man of modern type with diversity of form have been found at Combe Capelle, Cro-Magnon,

Chancelade and elsewhere in the later Pleistocene in France and others in Czechoslovakia.

HUMAN CULTURAL STAGES

Until about 8 or 7 thousand years ago men lived by hunting and collecting. In the middle of the Pleistocene they already made finely shaped hand axes (Abbevillean and Acheulian) from stone cores by chipping off flakes, using flint, chert, obsidian, rhyolite, quartzite, etc. in many regions, and these cultures spread from Africa to Spain, France and Britain during some interglacial periods. Apparently the men hunted and made pitfalls for animals as Leakey has shown at Olorgesailie in Kenya, while women and children collected. Fire was used very early. In the continental interior of Eurasia rough stone flakes were long used rather than shaped stone cores and apparently in cold periods at any rate this culture spread west to Britain. In the later part of the Riss-Wurm interglacial, stone flakes became finer especially in regions where contact was made with makers of core-tools, and in some groups both cores and flakes were used.

With the last retreat of the ice-sheets stone flakes became the dominant tools, with diverse types suited to scraping, boring, sawing, etc.—Aurignacian, followed in France by Solutrian, in which long leaf-like flakes were treated as cores and shaped very skilfully by pressing off flakes. The Magdalenian stage next following used flakes but specialized in implements of bone, horn and ivory. In some areas the Aurignacian grades into the Magdalenian and this seems to be largely the case in parts of Britain. All the above cultures are often grouped as Palæolithic.

About 8 or 7 thousand years ago people in S.W. Asia began to cultivate cereals on river mud laid down by annual floods, thus keeping the soil fertile and allowing durable settlement with concomitant advances in mud brick construction, pot-making, stone grinding, which had begun earlier and gave an improved control of shape, carpentering, weaving and other inventions. In all this development the Nile valley was early concerned and its regular floods from summer rains in Abyssinia could be managed to give such an advantage that Egypt gained a unique primacy in early history. Domestication of animals was added very early to cultivation of crops, most probably as a source of milk, flesh, leather, sinews, etc. Neolithic Culture was thus characterized by stone axes shaped by grinding or rubbing, by cultivation usually by domestic animals, often by durable settlements and a variety of arts and crafts.

Especially after the practice of castration of surplus male animals was introduced, domestic beasts were used for work, notably for pulling a modified hoe to scratch the drying surface of river-mud and so keep it from caking too hard. This is the early plough, valuable in lands where plant food in the soil is drawn up nearly to the surface as moisture rises and evaporates. Animals were also used as porters and tractors.

Heating stones in fires, probably for water-heating, led to the discovery of impure copper and the invention of bronze (standardized at about 10 per cent. tin and 90 per cent. copper) at the beginning of the Bronze Age in S.W. Asia and/or Egypt. By that time, about 5,000 years ago, cities and trade were developing and the basic arts were spreading to the Indus basin, the Mediterranean and the loess areas of Central Europe. Western Europe on the one hand and N. China on the other were affected somewhat later but more than 4,000 years ago; and China rapidly advanced to a high skill in pottery and bronze. Over 3,000 years ago in Anatolia the smelting of iron was developed, and it spread thence in the next centuries, beginning the Iron Age. Iron nails and tools made possible larger boats, houses, furniture and especially larger ploughs, working deeper into the earth and so suited to cooler lands, where plant food was often deep in the soil because evaporation was not very strong and rain might occur at every season. So the farmer needed to bring up the deeper layers to the surface in north-west Europe. With the spread of iron, especially about 2,000 to 1,000 years ago, northwest Europe emerged from its former low status and went ahead, still more after houses were improved with more privacy, chimneys and beds.

The evolution of culture in the Americas is much discussed. Early drifts of hunters viâ Alaska may have occurred in the late Pleistocene. Probably a good deal of Neolithic culture (stone implements, pottery, etc.) spread by the same route to America about or after 5,000 years ago but did not take Asiatic cereals or domestic animals. America also received contributions to its life by maritime routes especially following the North Pacific currents.

TIME MEASUREMENT AND CALENDARS

MEASUREMENTS OF TIME

Measurements of Time.—These are based on the time taken by the earth to rotate on its axis (*Day*); by the moon to revolve round the earth (*Month*); and by the earth to revolve round the sun (*Year*). From these, which are not commensurable, certain average or mean intervals have been adopted for ordinary use.

The Day begins at midnight and is divided into 24 hours of 60 minutes, each of 60 seconds. The hours are counted from midnight up to 12 noon (when the sun crosses the meridian), and these hours are designated A.M. (*ante meridiem*); and again from noon up to 12 at midnight, which hours are designated P.M. (*post meridiem*), except when the *Twenty-four Hour* reckoning is employed. The 24-hour reckoning ignores A.M. and P.M., and the hours are numbered 0 to 23 from midnight to midnight.

Colloquially the 24 hours are divided into *day* and *night*, day being the time while the sun is above the horizon (including the four stages of twilight defined on p. 139). Day is subdivided further into *morning*, the early part of daytime, ending at noon; *afternoon* from noon to 6 p.m. and *evening*, which may be said to extend from 6 p.m. until midnight. *Night*, the dark period between day and day, begins at the close of Astronomical Twilight (*see* p. 139) and extends beyond midnight to sunrise the next day.

The names of the Days—Sunday, Monday, Tuesday (Tiw = God of War), Wednesday (Woden or Odin), Thursday (Thor), Friday (Frig = wife of Odin), and Saturday—are derived from Old English translations or adaptions of the Roman titles (Sol, Luna, Mars, Mercurius, Jupiter, Venus and Saturnius).

The Week is a period of 7 days.

The Month in the ordinary calendar is approximately the twelfth part of a year, but the lengths of the different months vary from 28 (or 29) days to 31.

The Year.—The *Equinoctial or Tropical Year* is the time that the earth takes to revolve round the sun from equinox to equinox, or 365·2422 mean solar days. The *Calendar Year* consists of 365 days, but a year the date of which is divisible by 4, without remainder, is called *bissextile* (see Roman Calendar) or *Leap Year* and consists of 366 days, one day being added to the month February, so that a date "leaps over" a day of the week. The last year of a century is not a leap year unless its number is divisable by 400 (*e.g.* the years 1800 and 1900 had only 365 days).

The Solstice.—A Solstice is the point in the Tropical Year at which the Sun attains its greatest distance, north or south, from the Equator. In the northern hemisphere the greatest distance north of the Equator is the Summer Solstice and the greatest distance south is the Winter Solstice.

The Summer Solstice is also the *Longest Day*, measured from sunrise to sunset. At the Solstice the Sun, reaching its greatest northern declination, appears to stand still, the times of sunrise and sunset and the consequent length of the day showing no variation for several days together, before and after the longest day (June 21 or 22). For the remainder of this century the longest day will fall each year on June 21.

The date of the Solstice varies according to locality. If the Solstice falls on June 21 late in the day by Greenwich time, that day will be the longest of the year at Greenwich even though it may be by only a second of time or a fraction thereof, but it will be on June 22, local date, in Japan, and so June 22 will be the longest day there and at places in Eastern longitudes.

Leaving aside the question of locality, the date of the Solstice is also affected by the length of the Tropical Year, which is 365¼ days less about 11 minutes. If a Solstice happens late on June 21 in one year, it will be nearly six hours later in the next, *i.e.* early on June 22, and that will be the longest day. This delay of the Solstice is not permitted to continue because the extra day in Leap Year brings it back a day in the Calendar.

However, because of the 11 minutes above mentioned the additional day in Leap Year brings the Solstice back too far by 44 minutes, and the time of the Solstice in the Calendar is earlier as the century progresses. (In the year 2000 the Summer Solstice reaches its earliest date for 100 years, *i.e.*, June 21^d 02^h.) To remedy this the last year of a century is in most cases not a Leap Year, and the omission of the extra day puts the date of the Solstice later by about six hours too much, compensation for which is made by making the fourth centennial year a Leap Year.

Similar considerations apply to the day of the Winter Solstice, or the *Shortest Day* of the year. For the remainder of this century the shortest day will fall on Dec. 21 in two years of four and on Dec. 22 in the remaining two years. In the year 2000 the Winter Solstice reaches its earliest date, *i.e.*, Dec. 21^d 13^h. The difference due to locality also prevails in the same sense as for the longest day.

At Greenwich the Sun sets at its earliest by the clock about ten days before the shortest day, which is a circumstance that may require explanation. The daily change in the time of sunset is due in the first place to the Sun's movement southwards at this time of the year, which diminishes the interval between the Sun's transit, and its setting, and, secondly, because of the daily decrease of the Equation of Time which causes the time of Apparent noon to be continuously later, day by day, and so in a measure counteracts the first effect. The rates of the change of these two quantities are not equal, nor are they uniform, but are such that their combination causes the date of earliest sunset to be Dec. 12 or 13 at Greenwich. In more southerly latitudes the effect of the movement of the Sun is less, and the change in the time of sunset depends on that of the Equation of Time to a greater degree, and the date of earliest sunset is earlier than it is at Greenwich.

The Equinox is the point at which the Sun crosses the Equator and day and night are of equal length all over the world. This occurs in March (Vernal

Equinox—about March 21) and September (Autumnal Equinox—about September 21).

The Historical Year.—Before the year 1752, two Calendar systems were in use in England. The Civil or Legal Year began on March 25, while the Historical Year began on January 1. Thus the Civil or Legal date 1658 March 24, was the same day as 1659 March 24 Historical; and a date in that portion of the year is written as: March 24 165⅞, the lower figure showing the Historical year.

The New Year.—In England in the seventh century, and as late as the thirteenth, the year was reckoned from Christmas Day, but in the twelfth century the Anglican Church began the year with the Feast of The Annunciation of the Blessed Virgin (Lady Day) on March 25 and this practice was adopted generally in the fourteenth century. The Civil or Legal year in the British Dominions (exclusive of Scotland) began with "Lady Day" until 1751. But in and since 1752 the civil year has begun with Jan. 1. Certain dividends are still paid by the Bank of England on dates based on Old Style. New Year's Day in *Scotland* was changed from March 25 to Jan. 1 in 1600.

On the Continent of Europe Jan. 1 was adopted as the first day of the year by Venice in 1522, Germany in 1544, Spain, Portugal, and the Roman Catholic Netherlands in 1556, Prussia, Denmark and Sweden in 1559, France 1564, Lorraine 1579, Protestant Netherlands 1583, Russia 1725, and Tuscany 1751.

The Masonic Year.—Two dates are quoted in warrants, dispensations etc., issued by the United Grand Lodge of England, those for the current year being expressed as *Anno Domini* 1985—*Anno Lucis* 5985. This *Year of Light* is based on the Book of Genesis I: 3, the 4000 year difference being derived from *Ussher's Notation*, published in 1654, which place the Creation of the World in 4,000 B.C.

Regnal Years.—These are the years of a sovereign's reign, and each begins on the anniversary of his or her accession: *e.g.* Regnal year 33 of the present Queen began on Feb. 6, 1984. The system was used for dating Acts of Parliament until 1962. Since 1962 Acts of Parliament have been dated by the calendar year. The *Summer Time Act* of 1925, for example, is quoted as 15 and 16 Geo. V. c. 64, because it became law in the session which extended over part of both of these regnal years. The regnal years of Edward VII began on January 22, which was the day of Queen Victoria's death in 1901, so that Acts passed in that reign are, in general, quoted with only one year number, but year 10 of the series ended on May 6, 1910, being the day on which King Edward died, and Acts of the Parliamentary Session 1910 are headed 10 Edw. VII. and 1 Geo. V.; Acts passed in 1936 were dated 1 Edw. VIII. and 1 Geo. VI.; Acts passed in 1952 were dated 16 Geo. VI. and 1 Elizabeth II.

Lord Mayor's Day.—The Lord Mayor of London was previously elected on the Feast of St. Simon and St. Jude (Oct. 28), and from the time of Edward I, at least, was presented to the King or to the Barons of the Exchequer on the following day, except that day be a Sunday. The day of election was altered to Oct. 16 in 1346, and after some further changes was fixed for Michaelmas Day in 1546, but the ceremonies of admittance and swearing-in of the Lord Mayor continued to take place on Oct. 28 and 29 respectively until 1751. In 1752, at the reform of the Calendar (*see* page 188), the Lord Mayor was continued in office until Nov. 8, the "New Style" equivalent of Oct. 28. The Lord Mayor is now presented to the Lord Chief Justice at the Royal Courts of Justice on the second Saturday in November to make the final declaration

of office, having been sworn in at Guildhall on the preceding day.

Dog Days.—The days about the heliacal rising of the Dog Star, noted from ancient times as the hottest and most unwholesome period of the year in the Northern Hemisphere. Their incidence has been variously calculated as depending on the Greater or Lesser Dog Star (Sirius or Procyon) and their duration has been reckoned as from 30 to 54 days. A generally accepted period is from July 3 to Aug. 15.

Metonic (Lunar, or Minor) **Cycle.**—In the year 432 B.C. Meton, an Athenian astronomer, found that 235 Lunations are very nearly, though not exactly equal in duration to 19 Solar Years, and, hence, after 19 years the Phases of the Moon recur on the same days of the month (nearly). The dates of Full Moon in a cycle of nineteen years were inscribed in *figures of gold* on public monuments in Athens, and the number showing the position of a year in the Cycle is called the **Golden Number** of that year.

Solar (or Major) **Cycle.**—A period of twenty-eight years, in any corresponding year of which the days of the week recur on the same day of the month.

Julian Period.—Proposed by Joseph Scaliger in 1582. The period is 7980 Julian years, and its first year coincides with the year 4713 B.C. 7980 is the product of the number of years in the Solar Cycle, the Metonic Cycle and the cycle of the Roman Indication (28 × 19 × 15).

Roman Indication.—A period of fifteen years, instituted for fiscal purposes about A.D. 300.

Epact.—The age of the calendar Moon, diminished by one day, on January 1, in the ecclesiastical lunar calendar.

THE FOUR SEASONS

Spring, the first season of the year, is defined astronomically to begin in the *Northern Hemisphere* at the Vernal Equinox when the Sun enters the sign Aries and to terminate at the Summer Solstice. In *Great Britain,* Spring in popular parlance comprises the months of February, March and April. In the *Southern Hemisphere* Spring corresponds with Autumn in the Northern Hemisphere.

Summer, the second and warmest season, begins astronomically at the Summer Solstice when the Sun enters the sign of Cancer. Summer terminates at the Autumnal Equinox. In popular parlance Summer in *Great Britain* includes the months of May, June, July and August, Midsummer Day being June 24.

Autumn, the third season, begins astronomically at the Autumnal Equinox when the Sun enters the sign Libra and ends at the Winter Solstice. In *Great Britain* it is popularly held to include the months of September and October. A warm period sometimes occurs round about St. Luke's Day (Oct. 18) and is known as "St. Luke's Summer." In the *Southern Hemisphere* it corresponds with Spring of the Northern.

Winter, the fourth and coldest season, begins astronomically at the Winter Solstice when the Sun enters the sign of Capricornus, and ends at the Vernal Equinox. In *Great Britain* the season is popularly held to comprise the months of November, December and January, mid-winter being marked by the Shortest Day. A warm period sometimes occurs round about Martinmas (Nov. 11) and is known as "St. Martin's Summer." In the *Southern Hemisphere* it corresponds with Summer of the Northern.

THE CHRISTIAN CALENDAR

In the Christian chronological system the years are distinguished by cardinal numbers before or after the Incarnation, the period being denoted by the letters B.C. (Before Christ) or, more rarely, A.C. (*Ante Christum*), and A.D. (*Annus Domini*). The correlative dates of the epoch are the 4th year of the 194th Olympiad, the 753rd year from the Foundation of Rome, A.M. 3761 (Jewish Chronology), and the 4714th year of the Julian Period.

The system was introduced into Italy in the sixth century, and though first used in France in the seventh it was not universally established there until about the eighth century. It has been said that the system was introduced into England by St. Augustine (A.D. 596), but was probably not generally used until some centuries later. It was ordered to be used by the Bishops at the Council of Chelsea, A.D. 816. The actual date of the birth of Christ is somewhat uncertain.

The Julian Calendar.—In the Julian Calendar all the centennial years were Leap Years, and for this reason towards the close of the sixteenth century there was a difference of 10 days between the tropical and calendar years; the equinox fell on March 11 of the Calendar, whereas at the time of the Council of Nicaea, A.D. 325, it had fallen on March 21. In 1582 Pope Gregory ordained that Oct. 5th should be called Oct. 15th and that of the end-century years only the fourth should be a Leap Year (*see* p. 186).

The Gregorian Calendar was adopted by Italy, France, Spain, and Portugal in 1582; by Prussia, the German Roman Catholic States, Switzerland, Holland, and Flanders on Jan. 1, 1583, Poland 1586, Hungary 1587, the German and Netherland Protestant States and Denmark 1700, Sweden (gradually) by the omission of eleven leap days, 1700–1740; Great Britain and her Dominions (including the North American Colonies) in 1752, by the omission of eleven days (Sept. 3 being reckoned as Sept. 14). Japan adopted the calendar in 1872, China in 1912, Bulgaria in 1915, Turkey and Soviet Russia in 1918, Yugoslavia and Rumania in 1919, and Greece in February, 1923.

In the same year that the change was made in England from the Julian to the Gregorian Calendar, the beginning of the new year was also changed from March 25 to January 1 (*see* p. 187).

The Orthodox Churches.—Some Orthodox Churches still use the Julian reckoning, but the majority of Greek Churches and the Rumanian Orthodox Church have adopted a modified "New Calendar", observing the Gregorian Calendar for fixed feasts and the Julian for movable feasts.

The Orthodox Church year begins on September 1. There are four fast periods, and in addition to Pascha (Easter), twelve great feasts, as well as numerous commemorations of the Saints of the Old and New Testaments throughout the year.

The Dominical Letter is one of the letters A–G which are used to denote the Sundays in successive years. If the first day of the year is a Sunday the letter is A; if the second, B; the third, C; and so on. Leap year requires two letters, the first for Jan. 1—Feb. 29, the second for March 1—Dec. 31.

Epiphany.—The Feast of the Epiphany, commemorating the manifestation of Christ, later became associated with the offering of gifts by the Magi. The day was of exceptional importance from the time of the Council of Nicaea (A.D. 325) as the primate of Alexandria was charged at every Epiphany Feast with the announcement in a letter to the Churches of the date of the forthcoming Easter. The day was of considerable importance in Britain as it influenced dates, ecclesiastical and lay, *e.g.* **Plow Monday**, when work was resumed in the fields, falls upon the Monday in the first full week after the Epiphany.

Lent.—The Teutonic word *Lent*, which denotes the Fast preceding Easter, originally meant no more than the Spring season; but from Anglo-Saxon times, at least, it has been used as the equivalent of the more significant Latin term **Quadragesima**, meaning the "Forty Days" or, more literally, the fortieth day. As early as the fifth century some of the Fathers of the Church put forward the view that the forty days Fast is of Apostolic origin, but this is not supported or believed by modern scholars; and it appears to some that it dates from the early years of the fourth century. There is some suggestion that the Fast was kept originally for only forty hours. **Ash Wednesday** is the first day of Lent, which ends at midnight before Easter Day.

Sexagesima and Septuagesima.—It has been suggested that the unmeaning application of the names *Sexagesima* and *Septuagesima* to the second and third Sundays before Lent was made by analogy with the names *Quadragesima* and *Quinquagesima*. Another less likely conjecture is that *Septuagesima* means the seventh day before the Octave of Easter. It is not certain whether the name *Quinquagesima* is due to the fact that the Sunday in question is the fiftieth day before Easter (reckoned inclusive) or was simply formed on the analogy of *Quadragesima* (*New English Dictionary*).

Palm Sunday, the Sunday before Easter and the beginning of Holy Week, commemorates the triumphal entry of Christ into Jerusalem and is celebrated in Britain (when palm is not available) by branches of willow gathered for use in the decoration of churches on that day.

Maundy Thursday, the day before Good Friday, the name itself being a corruption of *dies mandati* (day of the mandate) when Christ washed the feet of the disciples and gave them the mandate to love one another.

Easter-Day is the first Sunday after the full moon which happens upon, or next after, the 21st day of March; and if the full moon happens upon a Sunday, Easter-Day is the Sunday after. This definition is contained in an Act of Parliament (24 Geo. II., cap. 23), and explanation is given in the preamble to the Act that the day of Full Moon depends on certain tables that have been prepared. These are the tables whose essential points are given in the early pages of the Book of Common Prayer. The Moon referred to is not the real Moon of the heavens, but a hypothetical Moon on whose "Full" the date of Easter depends, and the lunations of this "Calendar" Moon consist of twenty-nine and thirty days alternately with certain necessary modifications to make the date of its Full agree as nearly as possible with that of the real Moon, which is known as the **Paschal Full Moon**. As at present ordained, Easter falls on one of 35 days—(March 22–April 25).

A Fixed Easter.—On June 15, 1928, the House of Commons agreed to a motion for the third reading of the Bill that Easter Day shall, in the Calendar year next but one after the commencement of the Act and in all subsequent years, be *the first Sunday after the second Saturday in April*. Easter would thus fall between April 9 and 15, both inclusive—that is, on the second or third Sunday in April. A clause in the Bill provided that before it shall come into operation regard shall be had to any opinion expressed officially by the various Christian Churches. Efforts by the World Council of Churches to secure a unanimous choice of date for Easter by its 239 member Churches have so far been unsuccessful.

Holy Days and Saints Days were the normal factors in early times for settling the dates of future and recurrent appointments, *e.g.* the **Quarter Days** in England and Wales are the Feast of the Nativity, the Feast of the Annunciation, the Feast of St. John the Baptist and the Feast of St. Michael and All the Holy Angels, while **Term Days** in Scotland are Candlemas (Feast of the Purification), Whitsunday (a fixed date), Lammas (Loaf Mass) and Martinmas (St. Martin's Day). **Law Sittings** in England and Wales commence on the Feast of St. Hilary and the term which begins on Old Michaelmas Day ends on the former feast of St. Thomas the Apostle.

The number of Saints commemorated in the Calendar of the Book of Common Prayer is 73, but (with the exception of All Saint's Day) "days" are appointed only for those whose names are mentioned in the Bible. **Red Letter Days** (*see also* p. 225) were Holy Days and Saints Days indicated in early ecclesiastical calendars by letters printed in red ink. The days to be distinguished in this way were finally approved at the Council of Nicaea, A.D. 325, and special services are set apart for them in the Book of Common Prayer.

Rogation Days.—These are the Monday, Tuesday and Wednesday preceding Ascension Day, "Holy Thursday", and in the fifth century were ordered by the Church to be observed as Public Fasts with solemn processions and supplications. The processions were discontinued as religious observances at the Reformation, but survive in the ceremony known as "Beating the Parish Bounds".

Ascension Day is forty days after Easter Day.

Ember Days.—The Ember Days at the Four Seasons are the Wednesday, Friday and Saturday before (1) the Third Sunday in Advent, (2) the Second Sunday in Lent, and (3) the Sundays nearest to the Festivals of St. Peter, and St. Michael and All Angels.

Whit Sunday (or Pentecost) is seven weeks after Easter Day. It is generally said that this name is a variant of White Sunday, and was so called from the albs or white robes of the newly baptized, but other derivations have been suggested. In the Roman Catholic Church Sundays are reckoned "after Pentecost".

Trinity Sunday is eight weeks after Easter Day, on the Sunday following Whit Sunday, and subsequent Sundays are reckoned in the Church of England as "after Trinity".

Thomas Becket (1118–1170) was consecrated Archbishop of Canterbury on the Sunday after Whit Sunday and his first act was to ordain that the day of his consecration should be held as a new festival in honour of the Holy Trinity. The observance thus originated spread from Canterbury throughout the whole of Christendom.

Advent Sunday is the Sunday nearest to St. Andrew's Day, Nov. 30, which allows three Sundays between Advent and Christmas Day in all cases. The Sunday preceding Advent is the 27th after Trinity if Easter falls on one of the days, March 22–26 inclusive. It is the 22nd after Trinity when Easter Day is on April 24 or 25. If the date of Easter were determined as proposed (*see Fixed Easter*) there would generally be 24 Sundays after Trinity, the number being 25 only in the years when Easter fell on April 9. With a Fixed Easter there would never be a sixth Sunday after Epiphany. There would be a fifth Sunday when Easter Day fell on April 15 or April 14, the year being a leap year.

A TABLE OF THE MOVABLE FEASTS TO THE YEAR 2000

Year	Ash Wednesday	Easter	Ascension	Whit Sunday	Sundays after Trinity	Advent
1980	Feb. 20	April 6	May 15	May 25	xxv	Nov. 30
1981	March 4	April 19	May 28	June 7	xxiii	Nov. 29
1982	Feb. 24	April 11	May 20	May 30	xxiv	Nov. 28
1983	Feb. 16	April 3	May 12	May 22	xxv	Nov. 27
1984	March 7	April 22	May 31	June 10	xxiii	Dec. 2
1985	Feb. 20	April 7	May 16	May 26	xxv	Dec. 1
1986	Feb. 12	March 30	May 8	May 18	xxvi	Nov. 30
1987	March 4	April 19	May 28	June 7	xxiii	Nov. 29
1988	Feb. 17	April 3	May 12	May 22	xxv	Nov. 27
1989	Feb. 8	March 26	May 4	May 14	xxvii	Dec. 3
1990	Feb. 28	April 15	May 24	June 3	xxiv	Dec. 2
1991	Feb. 13	March 31	May 9	May 19	xxvi	Dec. 1
1992	March 4	April 19	May 28	June 7	xxiii	Nov. 29
1993	Feb. 24	April 11	May 20	May 30	xxiv	Nov. 28
1994	Feb. 16	April 3	May 12	May 22	xxv	Nov. 27
1995	March 1	April 16	May 25	June 4	xxiv	Dec. 3
1996	Feb. 21	April 7	May 16	May 26	xxv	Dec. 1
1997	Feb. 12	March 30	May 8	May 18	xxvi	Nov. 30
1998	Feb. 25	April 12	May 21	May 31	xxiv	Nov. 29
1999	Feb. 17	April 4	May 13	May 23	xxv	Nov. 28
2000	March 8	April 23	June 1	June 11	xxiii	Dec. 3

NOTES CONCERNING TABLE OF MOVABLE FEASTS

Ash Wednesday (first day in *Lent*) can fall at earliest on February 4 and at latest on March 10.
Easter Day can fall at earliest on March 22 and at latest on April 25.
Ascension Day can fall at earliest on April 30 and at latest on June 3.
Whit Sunday can fall at earliest on May 10 and at latest on June 13.
Rogation Sunday is the Sunday next before *Holy Thursday* (Ascension Day).
Trinity Sunday is the Sunday next after *Whit Sunday*.
Corpus Christi falls on the Thursday next after *Trinity Sunday*.
There are not less than xxii and not more than xxvii *Sundays after Trinity*.
Advent Sunday is the Sunday nearest to November 30.

A TABLE OF EASTER DAYS AND SUNDAY LETTERS, 1500 TO 2025

		1500—1599	1600—1699	1700—1799	1800—1899	1900—1999	2000—2025
d	Mar. 22	1573	1668	1761	1818		
e	„ 23	1505-16	1600	1788	1845-56	1913	2008
f	„ 24		1611-95	1706-99		1940	
g	„ 25	1543-54	1627-38-49	1722-33-44	1883-94	1951	
A	„ 26	1559-70-81-92	1654-65-76	1749-58-69-80	1815-26-37	1967-78-89	
b	Mar. 27	1502-13-24-97	1608-87-92	1785-96	1842-53-64	1910-21-32	2005-16
c	„ 28	1529-35-40	1619-24-30	1703-14-25	1869-75-80	1937-48	
d	„ 29	1551-62	1635-46-57	1719-30-41-52	1807-12-91	1959-64-70	
e	„ 30	1567-78-89	1651-62-73-84	1746-55-66-77	1823-34	1902-75-86-97	
f	„ 31	1510-21-32-83-94	1605-16-78-89	1700-71-82-93	1839-50-61-72	1907-18-29-91	2002-13-24
g	April 1	1526-37-48	1621-32	1711-16	1804-66-77-88	1923-34-45-56	2018
A	„ 2	1553-64	1643-48	1727-38-52(NS)	1809-20-93-99	1961-72	
b	„ 3	1575-80-86	1659-70-81	1743-63-68-74	1825-31-36	1904-83-88-94	
c	„ 4	1507-18-91	1602-13-75-86-97	1708-79-90	1847-58	1915-20-26-99	2010-21
d	„ 5	1523-34-45-56	1607-18-29-40	1702-13-24-95	1801-63-74-85-96	1931-42-53	2015
e	April 6	1539-50-61-72	1634-45-56	1729-35-40-60	1806-17-28-90	1947-58-69-80	
f	„ 7	1504-77-88	1667-72	1751-65-76	1822-33-44	1901-12-85-96	
g	„ 8	1509-15-20-99	1604-10-83-94	1705-87-92-98	1849-55-60	1917-28	2007-12
A	„ 9	1531-42	1615-26-37-99	1710-21-32	1871-82	1939-44-50	2023
b	„ 10	1547-58-69	1631-42-53-64	1726-37-48-57	1803-14-87-98	1955-66-77	
c	April 11	1501-12-63-74-85-96	1658-69-80	1762-73-84	1819-30-41-52	1909-71-82-93	2004
d	„ 12	1506-17-28	1601-12-91-96	1789	1846-57-68	1903-14-25-36-98	2009-20
e	„ 13	1533-44	1623-28	1707-18	1800-73-79-84	1941-52	
f	„ 14	1555-60-66	1639-50-61	1723-34-45-54	1805-11-16-95	1963-68-74	
g	„ 15	1571-82-93	1655-66-77-88	1750-59-70-81	1827-38	1900-06-79-90	2001
A	April 16	1503-14-25-36-87-98	1609-20-82-93	1704-75-86-97	1843-54-65-76	1911-22-33-95	2006-17
b	„ 17	1530-41-52	1625-36	1715-20	1808-70-81-92	1927-38-49-60	2022
c	„ 18	1557-68	1647-52	1731-42-56	1802-13-24-97	1954-65-76	
d	„ 19	1500-79-84-90	1663-74-85	1747-67-72-78	1829-35-40	1908-81-87-92	
e	„ 20	1511-22-95	1606-17-79-90	1701-12-83-94	1851-62	1919-24-30	2003-14-25
f	April 21	1527-38-49	1622-33-44	1717-28	1867-78-89	1935-46-57	2019
g	„ 22	1565-76	1660	1739-53-64	1810-21-32	1962-73-84	
A	„ 23	1508	1671		1848	1905-16	2000
b	„ 24	1519	1603-14-98	1709-91	1859		2011
c	„ 25	1546	1641	1736	1886	1943	

PUBLIC HOLIDAYS

BANK HOLIDAYS IN ENGLAND, WALES, NORTHERN IRELAND AND THE CHANNEL ISLANDS ARE (1985):—Jan. 1; April 8; May 6; May 27; Aug. 26 and Dec. 26.

Liberation Day (May 9) is a bank and public holiday in the Channel Islands.

Banks are also closed on Good Friday and Christmas Day and on all Saturdays.

The Stock Exchange is closed on Bank Holidays, Good Friday, Christmas Day and New Year's Day; and on Saturdays throughout the year.

Custom House and Docks, as Banks; with the Queen's Birthday (when decreed).

Excise and Stamp Offices, as Banks; with Whit Tuesday and Coronation Day, if and when decreed.

Law Offices.—Good Friday, Easter Monday and Tuesday, Spring Bank Holiday (*see* col. 1), Christmas Day, and first week-day after Christmas.

BANK HOLIDAYS IN SCOTLAND ARE (1985):—Jan. 1 and 2; May 6 and 27; Aug. 5; Dec. 26.

Banks in Scotland are also closed on Good Friday, Christmas Day and on Saturdays.

Scotland has special Term (*Quarter*) *Days:*—Candlemas, Feb. 2; Whitsunday, May 15 (fixed date); Lammas, Aug. 1; and Martinmas, Nov. 11; the *Removal Terms* are May 28 and Nov. 28.

THE JEWISH CALENDAR

Origin.—The story in the Book of Genesis that the Flood began on the seventeenth day of the second month; that after the end of 150 days the waters were abated; and that on the seventeenth day of the seventh month the Ark rested on Mount Ararat, indicates a calendar of some kind and that the writers recognized 30 days as the length of a lunation. There is other mention of months by their original numbers in the Book of Genesis and in establishing the rite of the Passover Moses spoke of *Abib* as the month when

the Israelites came out from Egypt and Abib was to be the first month of the year. In the first Book of Kings three months are mentioned by name, Zif the second month, Ethanim the seventh and Bul the eighth, but these are not names now in use. After the Dispersion, Jewish communities were left in considerable doubt as to the times of Fasts and Festivals, and this led to the formation of the Jewish Calendar as used to-day, which, it is said, was done in A.D. 358 by Rabbi Hillel II, a descendant of

Gamaliel—though some assert that it did not happen until much later. This calendar is luni-solar, and is based on the lengths of the lunation and of the tropical year as found by Hipparchus (*Circ.* 120 B.C.) which differ little from those adopted at the present day. The year 5745 A.D. (1984–85) is the 7th year of the 303rd *Metonic* (Minor or Lunar) *Cycle* of 19 years and the 5th year of the 206th *Solar* (or Major) *Cycle* of 28 years since the Era of the Creation, which the Jews hold to have occurred at the time of the Autumnal Equinox in the year known in the Christian Calendar as 3760 B.C. (954 of the Julian Period) and the epoch or starting point of Jewish Chronology corresponds to Oct. 7, 3761 B.C. At the beginning of each Solar Cycle the *Teku ah* of Nisar. (the vernal equinox) returns to the same day and to the same hour.

The hour is divided into 1080 *minims* and the month between one new moon and the next is reckoned as 29 days, 12 hours, 793 minims. The normal calendar year, called a Common Regular year, consists of 12 months of 30 days and 29 days alternately. Since 12 months such as these comprise only 354 days, in order that each of them shall not diverge greatly from an average place in the solar year, a thirteenth month is occasionally added after the fifth month of the Civil year (which commences on the first day of the month Tishri), or as the penultimate month of the Ecclesiastical (which commences on the first day of month Nisan), the years when this happens being called Embolismic. Of the 19 years that form a Metonic cycle, 7 are embolismic; they occur at places in the cycle indicated by the numbers 3, 6, 8, 11, 14, 17, 19, these places being chosen so that the accumulated excesses of the solar years should be as small as possible. The first of each month is called the day of New Moon, though it is not necessarily the day of astronomical New Moon, that being the day on which conjunction of Sun and Moon occurs, but there is generally a difference of a day or two. In practice, in a month which follows one of 30 days, the day preceding its first day is also observed as a day of New Moon. The dates in the Christian calendar of the first days of the months depend on that of the first of Tishri, which therefore controls the dates of fasts and festivals in the Jewish year. For certain ceremonial reasons connected with these, the first of Tishri must not fall on a Sunday, Wednesday or Friday, and if this should happen as the result of the computation it is postponed to the next day in the Christian calendar. Also, if the New Moon of Tishri falls on any day of the week at noon or later than noon, then the following day is to be taken for the celebration of that New Moon and is Tishri 1, provided that it is not one of the forbidden days, in which case there is a further postponement of a day. These rules and others have been considered in detail, and finally a calendar scheme has been drawn up in which a Jewish year is of one of the following six types: Common Deficient (353 days), Common Regular (354 days), Common Abundant (355 days), Embolismic Deficient (383 days), Embolismic Regular (384 days), or Embolismic Abundant (385 days).

The Regular year has an alternation of 30 and 29 days. In an Abundant year, whether Common or Embolismic, Marcheshvan, the second month of the Civil year, has 30 days instead of 29; in Deficient years Kislev, the third month, has 29 instead of 30. The additional month in Embolismic years which is called Adar I., and precedes the month called Adar in Common years and Adar II., or Ve-Adar, in Embolismic, always has 30 days, but neither this, nor the other variations mentioned, is allowed to change the number of days in the other months which still follow the alternation of the normal twelve. In Embolismic years the month intercalated precedes Adar and usurps its name, but the usual Adar festivals are kept in Ve-Adar.

These are then the main features of the Jewish Calendar which must be considered permanent, because as a Jewish law it cannot be altered except by a great Synhedrion.

The Jewish day begins between sunset and nightfall. The time used is that of the meridian of Jerusalem, which is $2h. 21m.$ in advance of Greenwich Mean Time. Rules for the beginning of Sabbaths and Festivals were laid down for the latitude of London in the eighteenth century and hours for nightfall are now fixed annually by the Chief Rabbi.

Jewish Calendar 5745–46

Jewish Month				A.M. 5745				A.M. 5746	
Tishri	1 ..	..	..	1984 September	27	..	..	1985 September	16
Marcheshvan	1 ..	..	..	October	27	..	..	October	16
Kislev	1 ..	..	..	November	25	..	..	November	14
Tebet	1 ..	..	..	December	25	..	..	December	13
Shebat	1 ..	..	..	1985 January	23	..	..	1986 January	11
Adar	1 ..	..	..	February	22	..	..	February	10
Ve-Adar	1 ..	..	..			..	..	March	12
Nisan	1 ..	..	..	March	23	..	..	April	10
Iyar	1 ..	..	..	April	22	..	..	May	10
Sivan	1 ..	..	..	May	21	..	..	June	8
Tammuz	1 ..	..	..	June	20	..	..	July	8
Ab	1 ..	..	..	July	19	..	..	August	6
Elul	1 ..	..	..	August	18	..	..	September	5

A.M. 5745 (745) is a Common Regular Year of 12 months, 51 Sabbaths and 354 days. A.M. 5746 (746) is an Embolismic Deficient Year of 13 months, 52 Sabbaths and 383 days.

Jewish Fasts and Festivals

Tishri	1	Rosh Hoshanah (New Year).	Tebet	10	Fast of Tebet.
,,	3	*Fast of Gedaliah.	Adar	13	§Fast of Esther.
,,	10	Yom Kippur (Day of Atonement).	,,	14	Purim.
,,	15–22	Succoth (Feast of Tabernacles).	,,	15	Shushan Purim.
,,	21	Hoshana Rabba.	Nisan	15–21	Passover.
,,	22	Solemn Assembly.	Sivan	6 and 7	Shavuot (Pentecost or Feast of Weeks).
,,	23	Rejoicing of the Law.	Tammuz	17	*Fast of Tammuz.
Kislev	25	Dedication of the Temple	Ab	9	*Fast of Ab.

NOTES.—* If these dates fall on the Sabbath the Fast is kept on the following day.

§ This fast is observed on Adar 11 (or Ve-Adar 11 in Embolismic years) if Adar 13 falls on a Sabbath.

THE ROMAN CALENDAR

Roman historians adopted as an epoch the Foundation of Rome, which is believed to have happened in the year 753 B.C., and the ordinal number of the years in Roman reckoning is followed by the letters A.U.C. (*Ab Urbe Condita*), so that the year 1985 is 2738 A.U.C. (MMDCCXXXVIII). The Calendar that we know has developed from one established by Romulus, who is said to have used a year of 304 days divided into ten months, beginning with March, to which Numa added January and February, making the year consist of 12 months of 30 and 29 days alternately, with an additional day so that the total was 355. It is also said that Numa ordered an intercalary month of 22 or 23 days in alternate years, making 90 days in eight years, to be inserted after Feb. 23, but there is some doubt as to the origination and the details of the intercalation in the Roman Calendar, though it is certain that some scheme of this kind was inaugurated and not fully carried out, for in the year 46 B.C. Julius Cæsar, who was then Pontifex Maximus,

found that the Calendar had been allowed to fall into some confusion. He therefore sought the help of the Egyptian astronomer Sosigenes, which led to the construction and adoption (45 B.C.) of the Julian Calendar, and, by a slight alteration, to the Gregorian now in use. The year 46 B.C. was made to consist of 445 days, and is called the *Year of Confusion*. In the Roman (Julian) Calendar the days of the month were counted backwards from three fixed points, or days, and an intervening day was said to be so many days *before* the next coming point, the first *and* last being counted. These three points were (1) the Kalends; (2) the Nones; and (3) the Ides. Their positions in the months and the method of counting from them will be seen in the table below. The year containing 366 days was called *bissextillis annus*, as it had a doubled sixth day (*bissextus dies*) before the March Kalends on Feb. 24—*ante diem sextum Kalendas Martias*, or VI Kal. Mart.

Present Days of the Month	March, May, July, October have thirty-one days	January, August, December have thirty-one days	April, June, September, November have thirty days	February has twenty-eight days, and in Leap Year twenty-nine
1	Kalendis.	Kalendis.	Kalendis.	Kalendis.
2	VI. ⎫	IV. ⎫ Ante	IV. ⎫ Ante	IV. ⎫ Ante
3	V. ⎬ Ante	III. ⎭ Nonas.	III. ⎭ Nonas.	III. ⎭ Nonas.
4	IV. ⎬ Nonas.	Pridie Nonas.	Pridie Nonas.	Pridie Nonas.
5	III. ⎭	Nonis.	Nonis.	Nonis.
6	Pridie Nonas.	VIII. ⎫	VIII. ⎫	VIII. ⎫
7	Nonis.	VII. ⎬	VII. ⎬	VII. ⎬
8	VIII. ⎫	VI. ⎬ Ante	VI. ⎬ Ante.	VI. ⎬ Ante
9	VII. ⎬	V. ⎭ Idus.	V. ⎭ Idus.	V. ⎭ Idus.
10	VI. ⎬ Ante	IV. ⎬	IV. ⎬	IV. ⎬
11	V. ⎭ Idus.	III. ⎭	III. ⎭	III. ⎭
12	IV. ⎬	Pridie Idus.	Pridie Idus.	Pridie Idus.
13	III. ⎭	Idibus.	Idibus.	Idibus.
14	Pridie Idus.	XIX. ⎫	XVIII. ⎫	XVI. ⎫
15	Idibus.	XVIII. ⎬	XVII. ⎬	XV. ⎬
16	XVII. ⎫	XVII. ⎬	XVI. ⎬	XIV. ⎬
17	XVI. ⎬	XVI. ⎬	XV. ⎬	XIII. ⎬
18	XV. ⎬	XV. ⎬	XIV. ⎬	XII. ⎬
19	XIV. ⎬	XIV. ⎬	XIII. ⎬	XI. ⎬
20	XIII. ⎬	XIII. ⎬	XII. ⎬	X. ⎬
21	XII. ⎬ Ante Kalendas (of the month following).	XII. ⎬ Ante Kalendas (of the month following).	XI. ⎬ Ante Kalendas (of the Month following).	IX. ⎬ Ante Kalendas Martias.
22	XI. ⎬	XI. ⎬	X. ⎬	VIII. ⎬
23	X. ⎬	X. ⎬	IX. ⎬	VII. ⎬
24	IX. ⎬	IX. ⎬	VIII. ⎬	VI. ⎬
25	VIII. ⎬	VIII. ⎬	VII. ⎬	V. ⎬
26	VII. ⎬	VII. ⎬	VI. ⎬	IV. ⎬
27	VI. ⎬	VI. ⎬	V. ⎬	III. ⎭
28	V. ⎬	V. ⎬	IV. ⎬	Pridie Kalendas Martias.
29	IV. ⎬	IV. ⎬	III. ⎭	
30	III. ⎭	III. ⎭	Pridie Kalendas (of the month following).	
31	Pridie Kalendas (of the month following).	Pridie Kalendas (of the month following).		

ROMAN NUMERALS

1	I	9	IX	17	XVII	70	LXX	600	DC
2	II	10	X	18	XVIII	80	LXXX	700	DCC
3	III	11	XI	19	XIX	90	XC	800	DCCC
4	IV	12	XII	20	XX	100	C	900	CM
5	V	13	XIII	30	XXX	200	CC	1000	M
6	VI	14	XIV	40	XL	300	CCC	1500	MD
7	VII	15	XV	50	L	400	CD	1900	MCM
8	VIII	16	XVI	60	LX	500	D	2000	MM

Other Examples: 43 = XLIII; 66 = LXVI; 98 = XCVIII.

339 = CCCXXXIX; 619 = DCXIX; 988 = CMLXXXVIII; 996 = CMXCVI.

1674 = MDCLXXIV; 1962 = MCMLXII.

A bar placed over a numeral has the effect of multiplying the number by 1,000, *e.g.*:

6,000 = $\overline{\text{VI}}$; 16,000 = $\overline{\text{XVI}}$; 160,000 = $\overline{\text{CLX}}$; 666,000 = $\overline{\text{DCLXVI}}$.

THE MOSLEM CALENDAR

The basic date of the Moslem Calendar is the *Hejira*, or Flight of Muhammad from Mecca to Medina, the corresponding date of which is A.D. 622, July 16, in the Julian Calendar. Hejira years are used principally in Iran, Turkey, Arabia, Egypt, in certain parts of India and in Malaya. The system was adopted about A.D. 632, commencing from the first day of the month preceding the Hejira. The years are purely lunar and consist of 12 months containing in alternate sequence 30 or 29 days, with the intercalation of one day at the end of the 12th month at stated intervals in each cycle of 30 years, the object of the intercalation being to reconcile the date of the first of the month with the date of the actual New Moon. Some adherents still take the date of the evening of the first visibility of the crescent as that of the first of the month. In each cycle of 30 years 19 are common and contain 354 days and 11 are intercalary (355 days), the latter being called *kabishah*.

The mean length of the Hejira year is 354 days, 8 hours, 48 minutes and the period of mean lunation is 29 days, 12 hours, 44 minutes.

To ascertain if a Hejira year is common or *kabishah* divide it by 30; the quotient gives the number of completed cycles and the remainder shows the place of the year in the current cycle. If the remainder is 2, 5, 7, 10, 13, 16, 18, 21, 24, 26 or 29 the year is *kabishah* and consists of 355 days.

Hejira year A.H. 1405 (remainder 25) is a common year; A.H. 1406 (remainder 26) is a *Kabishah* year.

Hejira Years 1405 and 1406

Name and Length of Month	A.H. 1405		A.H. 1406	
Muharram (30)	1984	Sept. 27	1985	Sept. 16
Safar (29)		Oct. 27		Oct. 16
Rabîa I (30)		Nov. 25		Nov. 14
Rabîa II (29)		Dec. 25		Dec. 14
Jumâda I (30)	1985	Jan. 23	1986	Jan. 12
Jumâda II (29)		Feb. 22		Feb. 11
Rajab (30)		Mar. 23		Mar. 12
Shaabân (29)		April 22		April 11
Ramadân (30)		May 21		May 10
Shawwâl (29)		June 20		June 9
Dhû'l-Qa'da (30)		July 19		July 8
Dhû'l-Hijja (29 or 30)		Aug. 18		Aug. 7

OTHER EPOCHS AND CALENDARS

China.—Until the year A.D. 1911 a Lunar Calendar was in force in China, but with the establishment of the Republic the Government adopted the Gregorian Calendar, and the new and old systems were used simultaneously by the people for several years. Since 1930 the publication and use of the old Lunar Calendar have been banned by the Government, and an official Chinese Calendar, corresponding with the European or Western system, is compiled, but the old Lunar Calendar is still in use to some extent in China. The old Chinese Calendar, with a cycle of 60 years, is still in use in Tibet, Hong Kong, Singapore, Malaysia and elsewhere in South-East Asia.

Ethiopia.—In the Coptic Calendar, which is used by part of the population of Egypt and Ethiopia, the year is made up of 12 months of 30 days each, followed, in general, by 5 complementary days. Every fourth year is an Intercalary or Leap year and in these years there are 6 complementary days. The Intercalary year of the Coptic Calendar immediately precedes the Leap year of the Julian Calendar. The Era is that of Diocletian or the Martyrs, the origin of which is fixed at A.D. 284, Aug. 29 (Julian date).

Greece.—Ancient Greek chronology was reckoned in *Olympiads*, cycles of 4 years corresponding with the periodic Olympic Games held on the plain of Olympia in Elis once in 4 years, the intervening years being the first, second, etc., of the Olympiad which received the name of the victor at the Games. The first recorded Olympiad is that of Choroebus, 776 B.C.

India.—In addition to the Moslem reckoning there are six eras used in India. The principal astronomical system was the *Kaliyuga Era*, which appears to have been adopted in the fourth century A.D. It began on Feb. 18, 3102 B.C. The chronological system of Northern India, known as the *Vikrama Samvat Era*, prevalent in Western India, began on Feb. 23, 57 B.C. The year A.D. 1985 is, therefore, the year 2042 of the Vikrama Era.

The *Saka Era* of Southern India dating from March 3, A.D. 78, was declared the uniform national calendar of the Republic of India with effect from March 22, 1957, to be used concurrently with the Gregorian Calendar. As revised, the year of the new *Saka Era*

begins at the spring equinox, with five successive months of 31 days and seven of 30 days in ordinary years; six months of each length in leap years. The year A.D. 1985 is 1907 of the revised *Saka Era*.

In the Hills, the *Saptarshi Era* dates from the moment when the Saptarshi, or saints, were translated and became the stars of the Great Bear in 3076 B.C.

The *Buddhists* reckoned from the death of Buddha in 543 B.C. (the actual date being 487 B.C.); and the epoch of the *Jains* was the death of Vardhamana, the founder of their faith, in 527 B.C.

Iran.—The chronology of Iran (Persia) is the Era of Hejira, which began on A.D. 622, July 16. The *Zoroastrian Calendar* was used in pre-Moslem days and is still employed by Zoroastrians in Iran and India (Parsees) with era beginning A.D. 632, June 16.

Japan.—The Japanese Calendar is the Gregorian, and is essentially the same as that in use by Western nations, the years, months and weeks being of the same length and beginning on the same days as those of the Western Calendar. The numeration of the years is different, for Japanese chronology is based on a system of epochs or periods, each of which begins at the accession of an Emperor or other important occurrence, the method being not unlike the former British system of Regnal years, but differing from it in the particular that each year of a period closes on Dec. 31. The Japanese scheme begins about A.D. 650 and the three latest epochs are defined by the reigns of Emperors, whose actual names are not necessarily used:

Epoch Meiji from 1868 Oct. 13 to 1912 July 31

,, Taishô ,, 1912 Aug. 1 to 1926 Dec. 25

,, Shôwa ,, 1926 Dec. 26

Hence the year Shôwa 60 begins 1985 Jan. 1. The months are not named. They are known as First Month, Second Month, etc., first month being the equivalent to January. The days of the week are Nichiyôbi (Sun-day), Getsuyôbi (Moon-day), Kayôbi (Fire-day), Suiyôbi (Water-day), Mokuyôbi (Wood-day), Kinyôbi (Metal-day), Doyôbi (Earth-day).

EASY REFERENCE CALENDAR

for any year between 1770 and 2025 together with the dates of Easter in each of those years
TO SELECT THE CORRECT CALENDAR FOR ANY YEAR consult the INDEX below

INDEX TO CALENDARS

Year		Year		Year		Year		Year		Year	
1770	C	1813	K	1856	F*	1899	A	1942	I	1984	B*
1771	E	1814	M	1857	I	1900	C	1943	K	1985	E
1772	H*	1815	A	1858	K	1901	E	1944	N*	1986	G
1773	K	1816	D*	1859	M	1902	G	1945	C	1987	I
1774	M	1817	G	1860	B*	1903	I	1946	E	1988	L*
1775	A	1818	I	1861	E	1904	L*	1947	G	1989	A
1776	D*	1819	K	1862	G	1905	A	1948	J*	1990	C
1777	G	1820	N*	1863	I	1906	C	1949	M	1991	E
1778	I	1821	C	1864	L*	1907	E	1950	A	1992	H*
1779	K	1822	E	1865	A	1908	H*	1951	C	1993	K
1780	N*	1823	G	1866	C	1909	K	1952	F*	1994	M
1781	C	1824	J*	1867	E	1910	M	1953	I	1995	A
1782	E	1825	M	1868	H*	1911	A	1954	K	1996	D*
1783	G	1826	A	1869	K	1912	D*	1955	M	1997	G
1784	J*	1827	C	1870	M	1913	G	1956	B*	1998	I
1785	M	1828	F*	1871	A	1914	I	1957	E	1999	K
1786	A	1829	I	1872	D*	1915	K	1958	G	2000	N*
1787	C	1830	K	1873	G	1916	N*	1959	I	2001	C
1788	F*	1831	M	1874	I	1917	C	1960	L*	2002	E
1789	I	1832	B*	1875	K	1918	E	1961	A	2003	G
1790	K	1833	E	1876	N*	1919	G	1962	C	2004	J*
1791	M	1834	G	1877	C	1920	J*	1963	E	2005	M
1792	B*	1835	I	1878	E	1921	M	1964	H*	2006	A
1793	E	1836	L*	1879	G	1922	A	1965	K	2007	C
1794	G	1837	A	1880	J*	1923	C	1966	M	2008	F*
1795	I	1838	C	1881	M	1924	F*	1967	A	2009	I
1796	L*	1839	E	1882	A	1925	I	1968	D*	2010	K
1797	A	1840	H*	1883	C	1926	K	1969	G	2011	M
1798	C	1841	K	1884	F*	1927	M	1970	I	2012	B*
1799	E	1842	M	1885	I	1928	B*	1971	K	2013	E
1800	G	1843	A	1886	K	1929	E	1972	N*	2014	G
1801	I	1844	D*	1887	M	1930	G	1973	C	2015	I
1802	K	1845	G	1888	B*	1931	I	1974	E	2016	L*
1803	M	1846	I	1889	E	1932	L*	1975	G	2017	A
1804	B*	1847	K	1890	G	1933	A	1976	J*	2018	C
1805	E	1848	N*	1891	I	1934	C	1977	M	2019	E
1806	G	1849	C	1892	L*	1935	E	1978	A	2020	H*
1807	I	1850	E	1893	A	1936	H*	1979	C	2021	K
1808	L*	1851	G	1894	C	1937	K	1980	F*	2022	M
1809	A	1852	J*	1895	E	1938	M	1981	I	2023	A
1810	C	1853	M	1896	H*	1939	A	1982	K	2024	D*
1811	E	1854	A	1897	K	1940	D*	1983	M	2025	G
1812	H*	1855	C	1898	M	1941	G				

* Leap Year

A

```
        January                  May                   September
Su. ..  1  8 15 22 29         7 14 21 28          3 10 17 24
M. ..   2  9 16 23 30      1  8 15 22 29          4 11 18 25
Tu. ..  3 10 17 24 31      2  9 16 23 30          5 12 19 26
W. ..   4 11 18 25         3 10 17 24 31          6 13 20 27
Th. ..  5 12 19 26         4 11 18 25             7 14 21 28
F. ..   6 13 20 27         5 12 19 26          1  8 15 22 29
S. ..   7 14 21 28         6 13 20 27          2  9 16 23 30

        February                 June                  October
Su. ..  5 12 19 26         4 11 18 25          1  8 15 22 29
M. ..   6 13 20 27         5 12 19 26          2  9 16 23 30
Tu. ..  7 14 21 28         6 13 20 27          3 10 17 24 31
W. ..   1  8 15 22         7 14 21 28          4 11 18 25
Th. ..  2  9 16 23      1  8 15 22 29          5 12 19 26
F. ..   3 10 17 24      2  9 16 23 30          6 13 20 27
S. ..   4 11 18 25      3 10 17 24             7 14 21 28

        March                    July                  November
Su. ..  5 12 19 26         2  9 16 23 30          5 12 19 26
M. ..   6 13 20 27         3 10 17 24 31          6 13 20 27
Tu. ..  7 14 21 28         4 11 18 25             7 14 21 28
W. ..   1  8 15 22 29      5 12 19 26          1  8 15 22 29
Th. ..  2  9 16 23 30      6 13 20 27          2  9 16 23 30
F. ..   3 10 17 24 31      7 14 21 28          3 10 17 24
S. ..   4 11 18 25      1  8 15 22 29          4 11 18 25

        April                    August                December
Su. ..  2  9 16 23 30      6 13 20 27          3 10 17 24 31
M. ..   3 10 17 24         7 14 21 28          4 11 18 25
Tu. ..  4 11 18 25      1  8 15 22 29          5 12 19 26
W. ..   5 12 19 26      2  9 16 23 30          6 13 20 27
Th. ..  6 13 20 27      3 10 17 24 31          7 14 21 28
F. ..   7 14 21 28      4 11 18 25          1  8 15 22 29
S. ..   1  8 15 22 29   5 12 19 26          2  9 16 23 30
```

B (Leap year)

```
        January                  May                   September
Su. ..  1  8 15 22 29      6 13 20 27          2  9 16 23 30
M. ..   2  9 16 23 30         7 14 21 28          3 10 17 24
Tu. ..  3 10 17 24 31      1  8 15 22 29          4 11 18 25
W. ..   4 11 18 25         2  9 16 23 30          5 12 19 26
Th. ..  5 12 19 26         3 10 17 24 31          6 13 20 27
F. ..   6 13 20 27         4 11 18 25             7 14 21 28
S. ..   7 14 21 28         5 12 19 26          1  8 15 22 29

        February                 June                  October
Su. ..  5 12 19 26         3 10 17 24             7 14 21 28
M. ..   6 13 20 27         4 11 18 25          1  8 15 22 29
Tu. ..  7 14 21 28         5 12 19 26          2  9 16 23 30
W. ..   1  8 15 22 29      6 13 20 27          3 10 17 24 31
Th. ..  2  9 16 23         7 14 21 28          4 11 18 25
F. ..   3 10 17 24      1  8 15 22 29          5 12 19 26
S. ..   4 11 18 25      2  9 16 23 30          6 13 20 27

        March                    July                  November
Su. ..  4 11 18 25      1  8 15 22 29          4 11 18 25
M. ..   5 12 19 26      2  9 16 23 30          5 12 19 26
Tu. ..  6 13 20 27      3 10 17 24 31          6 13 20 27
W. ..   7 14 21 28      4 11 18 25             7 14 21 28
Th. ..  1  8 15 22 29   5 12 19 26          1  8 15 22 29
F. ..   2  9 16 23 30   6 13 20 27          2  9 16 23 30
S. ..   3 10 17 24 31   7 14 21 28          3 10 17 24

        April                    August                December
Su. ..  1  8 15 22 29      5 12 19 26          2  9 16 23 30
M. ..   2  9 16 23 30      6 13 20 27          3 10 17 24 31
Tu. ..  3 10 17 24         7 14 21 28          4 11 18 25
W. ..   4 11 18 25      1  8 15 22 29          5 12 19 26
Th. ..  5 12 19 26      2  9 16 23 30          6 13 20 27
F. ..   6 13 20 27      3 10 17 24 31          7 14 21 28
S. ..   7 14 21 28      4 11 18 25          1  8 15 22 29
```

Easter Days

March 26.	1815	1826	1837	1967	1978	1989.
April 2.	1809	1893	1899	1961.		
April 9.	1871	1882	1939	1950	2023.	
April 16.	1775	1786	1797	1843	1854	1865 1911
April 23.	1905.	[1922	1933	1995	2006	2017.

Easter Days

April 1.	1804	1888	1956.	
April 8.	1792	1860	1928	2012.
April 22.	1832	1984.		

C

January					May					September			
Su.		7	14	21	28		6	13	20	27		2	9	16	23	30
M.	1	8	15	22	29		7	14	21	28		3	10	17	24
Tu.	2	9	16	23	30	1	8	15	22	29		4	11	18	25
W.	3	10	17	24	31	2	9	16	23	30		5	12	19	26
Th.	4	11	18	25		3	10	17	24	31		6	13	20	27
F.	5	12	19	26		4	11	18	25		7	14	21	28
S.	6	13	20	27		5	12	19	26	1	8	15	22	29

February				June				October				
Su.	4 11 18 25	3 10 17 24	7 14 21 28
M.	5 12 19 26	4 11 18 25	1 8 15 22 29
Tu.	6 13 20 27	5 12 19 26	2 9 16 23 30
W.	7 14 21 28	6 13 20 27	3 10 17 24 31
Th.	1 8 15 22	7 14 21 28	4 11 18 25
F.	2 9 16 23	1 8 15 22 29	5 12 19 26
S.	3 10 17 24	2 9 16 23 30	6 13 20 27

March				July				November				
Su.	4 11 18 25	1 8 15 22 29	4 11 18 25
M.	5 12 19 26	2 9 16 23 30	5 12 19 26
Tu.	6 13 20 27	3 10 17 24 31	6 13 20 27
W.	7 14 21 28	4 11 18 25	7 14 21 28
Th.	1 8 15 22 29	5 12 19 26	1 8 15 22 29
F.	2 9 16 23 30	6 13 20 27	2 9 16 23 30
S.	3 10 17 24 31	7 14 21 28	3 10 17 24

April				August				December				
Su.	1 8 15 22 29	5 12 19 26	2 9 16 23 30
M.	2 9 16 23 30	6 13 20 27	3 10 17 24 31
Tu.	3 10 17 24	7 14 21 28	4 11 18 25
W.	4 11 18 25	1 8 15 22 29	5 12 19 26
Th.	5 12 19 26	2 9 16 23 30	6 13 20 27
F.	6 13 20 27	3 10 17 24 31	7 14 21 28
S.	7 14 21 28	4 11 18 25	1 8 15 22 29

Easter Days

March 25.	1883	1894	1951.			
April 1.	1866	1877	1923	1934	1945	2018.
April 8.	1787	1798	1849	1855	1917	2007.
April 15.	1770	1781	1827	1838	1900	1906 1979
April 22.	1810	1821	1962	1973.	[1990	2001.

D (Leap year)

January				May				September				
Su.	7 14 21 28	5 12 19 26	1 8 15 22 29
M.	1 8 15 22 29	6 13 20 27	2 9 16 23 30
Tu.	2 9 16 23 30	7 14 21 28	3 10 17 24
W.	3 10 17 24 31	1 8 15 22 29	4 11 18 25
Th.	4 11 18 25	2 9 16 23 30	5 12 19 26
F.	5 12 19 26	3 10 17 24 31	6 13 20 27
S.	6 13 20 27	4 11 18 25	7 14 21 28

February				June				October				
Su.	4 11 18 25	2 9 16 23 30	6 13 20 27
M.	5 12 19 26	3 10 17 24	7 14 21 28
Tu.	6 13 20 27	4 11 18 25	1 8 15 22 29
W.	7 14 21 28	5 12 19 26	2 9 16 23 30
Th.	1 8 15 22 29	6 13 20 27	3 10 17 24 31
F.	2 9 16 23	7 14 21 28	4 11 18 25
S.	3 10 17 24	1 8 15 22 29	5 12 19 26

March				July				November				
Su.	3 10 17 24 31	7 14 21 28	3 10 17 24
M.	4 11 18 25	1 8 15 22 29	4 11 18 25
Tu.	5 12 19 26	2 9 16 23 30	5 12 19 26
W.	6 13 20 27	3 10 17 24 31	6 13 20 27
Th.	7 14 21 28	4 11 18 25	7 14 21 28
F.	1 8 15 22 29	5 12 19 26	1 8 15 22 29
S.	2 9 16 23 30	6 13 20 27	2 9 16 23 30

April				August				December				
Su.	7 14 21 28	4 11 18 25	1 8 15 22 29
M.	1 8 15 22 29	5 12 19 26	2 9 16 23 30
Tu.	2 9 16 23 30	6 13 20 27	3 10 17 24 31
W.	3 10 17 24	7 14 21 28	4 11 18 25
Th.	4 11 18 25	1 8 15 22 29	5 12 19 26
F.	5 12 19 26	2 9 16 23 30	6 13 20 27
S.	6 13 20 27	3 10 17 24 31	7 14 21 28

Easter Days

March 24	1940.		
March 31.	1872	2024.	
April 7.	1776	1844	1912 1996.
April 14.	1816	1968.	

E

January				May				September				
Su.	6 13 20 27	5 12 19 26	1 8 15 22 29
M.	7 14 21 28	6 13 20 27	2 9 16 23 30
Tu.	1 8 15 22 29	7 14 21 28	3 10 17 24
W.	2 9 16 23 30	1 8 15 22 29	4 11 18 25
Th.	3 10 17 24 31	2 9 16 23 30	5 12 19 26
F.	4 11 18 25	3 10 17 24 31	6 13 20 27
S.	5 12 19 26	4 11 18 25	7 14 21 28

February				June				October				
Su.	3 10 17 24	2 9 16 23 30	6 13 20 27
M.	4 11 18 25	3 10 17 24	7 14 21 28
Tu.	5 12 19 26	4 11 18 25	1 8 15 22 29
W.	6 13 20 27	5 12 19 26	2 9 16 23 30
Th.	7 14 21 28	6 13 20 27	3 10 17 24 31
F.	1 8 15 22	7 14 21 28	4 11 18 25
S.	2 9 16 23	1 8 15 22 29	5 12 19 26

March				July				November				
Su.	3 10 17 24 31	7 14 21 28	3 10 17 24
M.	4 11 18 25	1 8 15 22 29	4 11 18 25
Tu.	5 12 19 26	2 9 16 23 30	5 12 19 26
W.	6 13 20 27	3 10 17 24 31	6 13 20 27
Th.	7 14 21 28	4 11 18 25	7 14 21 28
F.	1 8 15 22 29	5 12 19 26	1 8 15 22 29
S.	2 9 16 23 30	6 13 20 27	2 9 16 23 30

April				August				December				
Su.	7 14 21 28	4 11 18 25	1 8 15 22 29
M.	1 8 15 22 29	5 12 19 26	2 9 16 23 30
Tu.	2 9 16 23 30	6 13 20 27	3 10 17 24 31
W.	3 10 17 24	7 14 21 28	4 11 18 25
Th.	4 11 18 25	1 8 15 22 29	5 12 19 26
F.	5 12 19 26	2 9 16 23 30	6 13 20 27
S.	6 13 20 27	3 10 17 24 31	7 14 21 28

Easter Days

March 24.	1799.	[1918	1929	1991	2002	2013.
March 31.	1771	1782	1793	1839	1850	1861 1907
April 7.	1822	1833	1901	1985.		
April 14.	1805	1811	1895	1963	1974.	
April 21.	1867	1878	1889	1935	1946	1957 2019.

F (Leap year)

January				May				September				
Su.	6 13 20 27	4 11 18 25	7 14 21 28
M.	7 14 21 28	5 12 19 26	1 8 15 22 29
Tu.	1 8 15 22 29	6 13 20 27	2 9 16 23 30
W.	2 9 16 23 30	7 14 21 28	3 10 17 24
Th.	3 10 17 24 31	1 8 15 22 29	4 11 18 25
F.	4 11 18 25	2 9 16 23 30	5 12 19 26
S.	5 12 19 26	3 10 17 24 31	6 13 20 27

February				June				October				
Su.	3 10 17 24	1 8 15 22 29	5 12 19 26
M.	4 11 18 25	2 9 16 23 30	6 13 20 27
Tu.	5 12 19 26	3 10 17 24	7 14 21 28
W.	6 13 20 27	4 11 18 25	1 8 15 22 29
Th.	7 14 21 28	5 12 19 26	2 9 16 23 30
F.	1 8 15 22	6 13 20 27	3 10 17 24 31
S.	2 9 16 23	7 14 21 28	4 11 18 25

March				July				November				
Su.	2 9 16 23 30	6 13 20 27	2 9 16 23 30
M.	3 10 17 24 31	7 14 21 28	3 10 17 24
Tu.	4 11 18 25	1 8 15 22 29	4 11 18 25
W.	5 12 19 26	2 9 16 23 30	5 12 19 26
Th.	6 13 20 27	3 10 17 24 31	6 13 20 27
F.	7 14 21 28	4 11 18 25	7 14 21 28
S.	1 8 15 22 29	5 12 19 26	1 8 15 22 29

April				August				December				
Su.	6 13 20 27	3 10 17 24 31	7 14 21 28
M.	7 14 21 28	4 11 18 25	1 8 15 22 29
Tu.	1 8 15 22 29	5 12 19 26	2 9 16 23 30
W.	2 9 16 23 30	6 13 20 27	3 10 17 24 31
Th.	3 10 17 24	7 14 21 28	4 11 18 25
F.	4 11 18 25	1 8 15 22 29	5 12 19 26
S.	5 12 19 26	2 9 16 23 30	6 13 20 27

Easter Days

March 23.	1788	1856	2008.
April 6.	1828	1980.	
April 13.	1884	1952.	
April 20.	1924.		

G

	January	May	September
Su.	.. 5 12 19 26	4 11 18 25	7 14 21 28
M.	.. 6 13 20 27	5 12 19 26	1 8 15 22 29
Tu.	.. 7 14 21 28	6 13 20 27	2 9 16 23 30
W.	.. 1 8 15 22 29	7 14 21 28	3 10 17 24
Th.	.. 2 9 16 23 30	1 8 15 22 29	4 11 18 25
F.	.. 3 10 17 24 31	2 9 16 23 30	5 12 19 26
S.	.. 4 11 18 25	3 10 17 24 31	6 13 20 27

	February	June	October
Su.	.. 2 9 16 23	1 8 15 22 29	5 12 19 26
M.	.. 3 10 17 24	2 9 16 23 30	6 13 20 27
Tu.	.. 4 11 18 25	3 10 17 24	7 14 21 28
W.	.. 5 12 19 26	4 11 18 25	1 8 15 22 29
Th.	.. 6 13 20 27	5 12 19 26	2 9 16 23 30
F.	.. 7 14 21 28	6 13 20 27	3 10 17 24 31
S.	.. 1 8 15 22	7 14 21 28	4 11 18 25

	March	July	November
Su.	.. 2 9 16 23 30	6 13 20 27	2 9 16 23 30
M.	.. 3 10 17 24 31	7 14 21 28	3 10 17 24
Tu.	.. 4 11 18 25	1 8 15 22 29	4 11 18 25
W.	.. 5 12 19 26	2 9 16 23 30	5 12 19 26
Th.	.. 6 13 20 27	3 10 17 24 31	6 13 20 27
F.	.. 7 14 21 28	4 11 18 25	7 14 21 28
S.	1 8 15 22 29	5 12 19 26	1 8 15 22 29

	April	August	December
Su.	.. 6 13 20 27	3 10 17 24 31	7 14 21 28
M.	.. 7 14 21 28	4 11 18 25	1 8 15 22 29
Tu.	.. 1 8 15 22 29	5 12 19 26	2 9 16 23 30
W.	.. 2 9 16 23 30	6 13 20 27	3 10 17 24 31
Th.	.. 3 10 17 24	7 14 21 28	4 11 18 25
F.	.. 4 11 18 25	1 8 15 22 29	5 12 19 26
S.	.. 5 12 19 26	2 9 16 23 30	6 13 20 27

Easter Days

March 23.	1845	1913.				
March 30.	1777	1823	1834	1902	1975	1986 1997.
April 6	1806	1817	1890	1947	1958	1969.
April 13.	1800	1873	1879	1941.	[2014	2025.
April 20.	1783	1794	1851	1862	1919	1930 2003

H (Leap year)

	January	May	September
Su.	.. 5 12 19 26	3 10 17 24 31	6 13 20 27
M.	.. 6 13 20 27	4 11 18 25	7 14 21 28
Tu.	.. 7 14 21 28	5 12 19 26	1 8 15 22 29
W.	.. 1 8 15 22 29	6 13 20 27	2 9 16 23 30
Th.	.. 2 9 16 23 30	7 14 21 28	3 10 17 24
F.	.. 3 10 17 24 31	1 8 15 22 29	4 11 18 25
S.	.. 4 11 18 25	2 9 16 23 30	5 12 19 26

	February	June	October
Su.	.. 2 9 16 23	7 14 21 28	4 11 18 25
M.	.. 3 10 17 24	1 8 15 22 29	5 12 19 26
Tu.	.. 4 11 18 25	2 9 16 23 30	6 13 20 27
W.	.. 5 12 19 26	3 10 17 24	7 14 21 28
Th.	.. 6 13 20 27	4 11 18 25	1 8 15 22 29
F.	.. 7 14 21 28	5 12 19 26	2 9 16 23 30
S.	.. 1 8 15 22 29	6 13 20 27	3 10 17 24 31

	March	July	November
Su.	.. 1 8 15 22 29	5 12 19 26	1 8 15 22 29
M.	.. 2 9 16 23 30	6 13 20 27	2 9 16 23 30
Tu.	.. 3 10 17 24 31	7 14 21 28	3 10 17 24
W.	.. 4 11 18 25	1 8 15 22 29	4 11 18 25
Th.	.. 5 12 19 26	2 9 16 23 30	5 12 19 26
F.	.. 6 13 20 27	3 10 17 24 31	6 13 20 27
S.	.. 7 14 21 28	4 11 18 25	7 14 21 28

	April	August	December
Su.	.. 5 12 19 26	2 9 16 23 30	6 13 20 27
M.	.. 6 13 20 27	3 10 17 24 31	7 14 21 28
Tu.	.. 7 14 21 28	4 11 18 25	1 8 15 22 29
W.	.. 1 8 15 22 29	5 12 19 26	2 9 16 23 30
Th.	.. 2 9 16 23 30	6 13 20 27	3 10 17 24 31
F.	.. 3 10 17 24	7 14 21 28	4 11 18 25
S.	.. 4 11 18 25	1 8 15 22 29	5 12 19 26

Easter Days

March 29.	1812	1964.	
April 5.	1896.		
April 12.	1868	1936	2020.
April 19.	1772	1840	1908 1992.

I

	January	May	September
Su.	.. 4 11 18 25	3 10 17 24 31	6 13 20 27
M.	.. 5 12 19 26	4 11 18 25	7 14 21 28
Tu.	.. 6 13 20 27	5 12 19 26	1 8 15 22 29
W.	.. 7 14 21 28	6 13 20 27	2 9 16 23 30
Th.	.. 1 8 15 22 29	7 14 21 28	3 10 17 24
F.	.. 2 9 16 23 30	1 8 15 22 29	4 11 18 25
S.	.. 3 10 17 24 31	2 9 16 23 30	5 12 19 26

	February	June	October
Su.	.. 1 8 15 22	7 14 21 28	4 11 18 25
M.	.. 2 9 16 23	1 8 15 22 29	5 12 19 26
Tu.	.. 3 10 17 24	2 9 16 23 30	6 13 20 27
W.	.. 4 11 18 25	3 10 17 24	7 14 21 28
Th.	.. 5 12 19 26	4 11 18 25	1 8 15 22 29
F.	.. 6 13 20 27	5 12 19 26	2 9 16 23 30
S.	.. 7 14 21 28	6 13 20 27	3 10 17 24 31

	March	July	November
Su.	.. 1 8 15 22 29	5 12 19 26	1 8 15 22 29
M.	.. 2 9 16 23 30	6 13 20 27	2 9 16 23 30
Tu.	.. 3 10 17 24 31	7 14 21 28	3 10 17 24
W.	.. 4 11 18 25	1 8 15 22 29	4 11 18 25
Th.	.. 5 12 19 26	2 9 16 23 30	5 12 19 26
F.	.. 6 13 20 27	3 10 17 24 31	6 13 20 27
S.	.. 7 14 21 28	4 11 18 25	7 14 21 28

	April	August	December
Su.	.. 5 12 19 26	2 9 16 23 30	6 13 20 27
M.	.. 6 13 20 27	3 10 17 24 31	7 14 21 28
Tu.	.. 7 14 21 28	4 11 18 25	1 8 15 22 29
W.	.. 1 8 15 22 29	5 12 19 26	2 9 16 23 30
Th.	.. 2 9 16 23 30	6 13 20 27	3 10 17 24 31
F.	.. 3 10 17 24	7 14 21 28	4 11 18 25
S.	.. 4 11 18 25	1 8 15 22 29	5 12 19 26

Easter Days

March 22.	1818.					
March 29.	1807	1891	1959	1970.	[1953	2015.
April 5.	1795	1801	1863	1874	1885	1931 1942
April 12.	1789	1846	1857	1903	1914	1925 1998
April 19.	1778	1829	1835	1981	1987.	[2009.

J (Leap year)

	January	May	September
Su.	.. 4 11 18 25	2 9 16 23 30	5 12 19 26
M.	.. 5 12 19 26	3 10 17 24 31	6 13 20 27
Tu.	.. 6 13 20 27	4 11 18 25	7 14 21 28
W.	.. 7 14 21 28	5 12 19 26	1 8 15 22 29
Th.	.. 1 8 15 22 29	6 13 20 27	2 9 16 23 30
F.	.. 2 9 16 23 30	7 14 21 28	3 10 17 24
S.	.. 3 10 17 24 31	1 8 15 22 29	4 11 18 25

	February	June	October
Su.	.. 1 8 15 22	6 13 20 27	3 10 17 24 31
M.	.. 2 9 16 23	7 14 21 28	4 11 18 25
Tu.	.. 3 10 17 24	1 8 15 22 29	5 12 19 26
W.	.. 4 11 18 25	2 9 16 23 30	6 13 20 27
Th.	.. 5 12 19 26	3 10 17 24	7 14 21 28
F.	.. 6 13 20 27	4 11 18 25	1 8 15 22 29
S.	.. 7 14 21 28	5 12 19 26	2 9 16 23 30

	March	July	November
Su.	.. 7 14 21 28	4 11 18 25	7 14 21 28
M.	.. 1 8 15 22 29	5 12 19 26	1 8 15 22 29
Tu.	.. 2 9 16 23 30	6 13 20 27	2 9 16 23 30
W.	.. 3 10 17 24 31	7 14 21 28	3 10 17 24
Th.	.. 4 11 18 25	1 8 15 22 29	4 11 18 25
F.	.. 5 12 19 26	2 9 16 23 30	5 12 19 26
S.	.. 6 13 20 27	3 10 17 24 31	6 13 20 27

	April	August	December
Su.	.. 4 11 18 25	1 8 15 22 29	5 12 19 26
M.	.. 5 12 19 26	2 9 16 23 30	6 13 20 27
Tu.	.. 6 13 20 27	3 10 17 24 31	7 14 21 28
W.	.. 7 14 21 28	4 11 18 25	1 8 15 22 29
Th.	.. 1 8 15 22 29	5 12 19 26	2 9 16 23 30
F.	.. 2 9 16 23 30	6 13 20 27	3 10 17 24 31
S.	.. 3 10 17 24	7 14 21 28	4 11 18 25

Easter Days

March 28.	1880	1948.
April 4.	1920.	
April 11.	1784	1852 2004.
April 18.	1824	1976.

K

	January	May	September
Su.	. . 3 10 17 24 31	2 9 16 23 30	5 12 19 26
M.	. . 4 11 18 25	3 10 17 24 31	6 13 20 27
Tu.	. . 5 12 19 26	4 11 18 25	7 14 21 28
W.	. . 6 13 20 27	5 12 19 26	1 8 15 22 29
Th.	. . 7 14 21 28	6 13 20 27	2 9 16 23 30
F.	1 8 15 22 29	7 14 21 28	3 10 17 24
S.	2 9 16 23 30	1 8 15 22 29	4 11 18 25

	February	June	October
Su.	. . 7 14 21 28	6 13 20 27	3 10 17 24 31
M.	. 1 8 15 22	7 14 21 28	4 11 18 25
Tu.	. 2 9 16 23	1 8 15 22 29	5 12 19 26
W.	. 3 10 17 24	2 9 16 23 30	6 13 20 27
Th.	. 4 11 18 25	3 10 17 24	7 14 21 28
F.	. 5 12 19 26	4 11 18 25	1 8 15 22 29
S.	. 6 13 20 27	5 12 19 26	2 9 16 23 30

	March	July	November
Su.	. . 7 14 21 28	4 11 18 25	7 14 21 28
M.	. 1 8 15 22 29	5 12 19 26	1 8 15 22 29
Tu.	. 2 9 16 23 30	6 13 20 27	2 9 16 23 30
W.	. 3 10 17 24 31	7 14 21 28	3 10 17 24
Th.	. 4 11 18 25	1 8 15 22 29	4 11 18 25
F.	. 5 12 19 26	2 9 16 23 30	5 12 19 26
S.	. 6 13 20 27	3 10 17 24 31	6 13 20 27

	April	August	December
Su.	. . 4 11 18 25	1 8 15 22 29	5 12 19 26
M.	. . 5 12 19 26	2 9 16 23 30	6 13 20 27
Tu.	. . 6 13 20 27	3 10 17 24 31	7 14 21 28
W.	. . 7 14 21 28	4 11 18 25	1 8 15 22 29
Th.	. 1 8 15 22 29	5 12 19 26	2 9 16 23 30
F.	. 2 9 16 23 30	6 13 20 27	3 10 17 24 31
S.	. 3 10 17 24	7 14 21 28	4 11 18 25

Easter Days

March 28.	1869 1875 1937.		[2010 2021.
April 4.	1779 1790 1847 1858 1915	1926 1999	
April 11.	1773 1819 1830 1841 1909	1971 1982	
April 18.	1802 1813 1897 1954 1965.		[1993.
April 25.	1886 1943.		

L (Leap year)

	January	May	September
Su.	. . 3 10 17 24 31	1 8 15 22 29	4 11 18 25
M.	. . 4 11 18 25	2 9 16 23 30	5 12 19 26
Tu.	. . 5 12 19 26	3 10 17 24 31	6 13 20 27
W.	. . 6 13 20 27	4 11 18 25	7 14 21 28
Th.	. . 7 14 21 28	5 12 19 26	1 8 15 22 29
F.	1 8 15 22 29	6 13 20 27	2 9 16 23 30
S.	2 9 16 23 30	7 14 21 28	3 10 17 24

	February	June	October
Su.	. . 7 14 21 28	5 12 19 26	2 9 16 23 30
M.	. 1 8 15 22 29	6 13 20 27	3 10 17 24 31
Tu.	. 2 9 16 23	7 14 21 28	4 11 18 25
W.	. 3 10 17 24	1 8 15 22 29	5 12 19 26
Th.	. 4 11 18 25	2 9 16 23 30	6 13 20 27
F.	. 5 12 19 26	3 10 17 24	7 14 21 28
S.	. 6 13 20 27	4 11 18 25	1 8 15 22 29

	March	July	November
Su.	. . 6 13 20 27	3 10 17 24 31	6 13 20 27
M.	. . 7 14 21 28	4 11 18 25	7 14 21 28
Tu.	. 1 8 15 22 29	5 12 19 26	1 8 15 22 29
W.	. 2 9 16 23 30	6 13 20 27	2 9 16 23 30
Th.	. 3 10 17 24 31	7 14 21 28	3 10 17 24
F.	. 4 11 18 25	1 8 15 22 29	4 11 18 25
S.	. 5 12 19 26	2 9 16 23 30	5 12 19 26

	April	August	December
Su.	. . 3 10 17 24	7 14 21 28	4 11 18 25
M.	. . 4 11 18 25	1 8 15 22 29	5 12 19 26
Tu.	. . 5 12 19 26	2 9 16 23 30	6 13 20 27
W.	. . 6 13 20 27	3 10 17 24 31	7 14 21 28
Th.	. 7 14 21 28	4 11 18 25	1 8 15 22 29
F.	1 8 15 22 29	5 12 19 26	2 9 16 23 30
S.	2 9 16 23 30	6 13 20 27	3 10 17 24 31

Easter Days

March 27.	1796 1864 1932 2016.
April 3.	1836 1904 1988.
April 17.	1808 1892 1960.

M

	January	May	September
Su.	. . 2 9 16 23 30	1 8 15 22 29	4 11 18 25
M.	. . 3 10 17 24 31	2 9 16 23 30	5 12 19 26
Tu.	. . 4 11 18 25	3 10 17 24 31	6 13 20 27
W.	. . 5 12 19 26	4 11 18 25	7 14 21 28
Th.	. . 6 13 20 27	5 12 19 26	1 8 15 22 29
F.	. 7 14 21 28	6 13 20 27	2 9 16 23 30
S.	1 8 15 22 29	7 14 21 28	3 10 17 24

	February	June	October
Su.	. . 6 13 20 27	5 12 19 26	2 9 16 23 30
M.	. . 7 14 21 28	6 13 20 27	3 10 17 24 31
Tu.	. 1 8 15 22	7 14 21 28	4 11 18 25
W.	. 2 9 16 23	1 8 15 22 29	5 12 19 26
Th.	. 3 10 17 24	2 9 16 23 30	6 13 20 27
F.	. 4 11 18 25	3 10 17 24	7 14 21 28
S.	. 5 12 19 26	4 11 18 25	1 8 15 22 29

	March	July	November
Su.	. . 6 13 20 27	3 10 17 24 31	6 13 20 27
M.	. . 7 14 21 28	4 11 18 25	7 14 21 28
Tu.	. 1 8 15 22 29	5 12 19 26	1 8 15 22 29
W.	. 2 9 16 23 30	6 13 20 27	2 9 16 23 30
Th.	. 3 10 17 24 31	7 14 21 28	3 10 17 24
F.	. 4 11 18 25	1 8 15 22 29	4 11 18 25
S.	. 5 12 19 26	2 9 16 23 30	5 12 19 26

	April	August	December
Su.	. . 3 10 17 24	7 14 21 28	4 11 18 25
M.	. . 4 11 18 25	1 8 15 22 29	5 12 19 26
Tu.	. . 5 12 19 26	2 9 16 23 30	6 13 20 27
W.	. . 6 13 20 27	3 10 17 24 31	7 14 21 28
Th.	. . 7 14 21 28	4 11 18 25	1 8 15 22 29
F.	. 1 8 15 22 29	5 12 19 26	2 9 16 23 30
S.	. 2 9 16 23 30	6 13 20 27	3 10 17 24 31

Easter Days

March 27.	1785 1842 1853 1910 1921	2005.
April 3.	1774 1825 1831 1983 1994.	
April 10.	1803 1814 1887 1898 1955	1966 1977.
April 17.	1870 1881 1927 1938 1949	2022.
April 24.	1791 1859 2011.	

N (Leap year)

	January	May	September
Su.	. . 2 9 16 23 30	7 14 21 28	3 10 17 24
M.	. . 3 10 17 24 31	1 8 15 22 29	4 11 18 25
Tu.	. . 4 11 18 25	2 9 16 23 30	5 12 19 26
W.	. . 5 12 19 26	3 10 17 24 31	6 13 20 27
Th.	. . 6 13 20 27	4 11 18 25	7 14 21 28
F.	. 7 14 21 28	5 12 19 26	1 8 15 22 29
S.	1 8 15 22 29	6 13 20 27	2 9 16 23 30

	February	June	October
Su.	. . 6 13 20 27	4 11 18 25	1 8 15 22 29
M.	. . 7 14 21 28	5 12 19 26	2 9 16 23 30
Tu.	. 1 8 15 22 29	6 13 20 27	3 10 17 24 31
W.	. 2 9 16 23	7 14 21 28	4 11 18 25
Th.	. 3 10 17 24	1 8 15 22 29	5 12 19 26
F.	. 4 11 18 25	2 9 16 23 30	6 13 20 27
S.	. 5 12 19 26	3 10 17 24	7 14 21 28

	March	July	November
Su.	. . 5 12 19 26	2 9 16 23 30	5 12 19 26
M.	. . 6 13 20 27	3 10 17 24 31	6 13 20 27
Tu.	. . 7 14 21 28	4 11 18 25	7 14 21 28
W.	. 1 8 15 22 29	5 12 19 26	1 8 15 22 29
Th.	. 2 9 16 23 30	6 13 20 27	2 9 16 23 30
F.	. 3 10 17 24 31	7 14 21 28	3 10 17 24
S.	. 4 11 18 25	1 8 15 22 29	4 11 18 25

	April	August	December
Su.	. . 2 9 16 23 30	6 13 20 27	3 10 17 24 31
M.	. . 3 10 17 24	7 14 21 28	4 11 18 25
Tu.	. . 4 11 18 25	1 8 15 22 29	5 12 19 26
W.	. . 5 12 19 26	2 9 16 23 30	6 13 20 27
Th.	. . 6 13 20 27	3 10 17 24 31	7 14 21 28
F.	. 7 14 21 28	4 11 18 25	1 8 15 22 29
S.	1 8 15 22 29	5 12 19 26	2 9 16 23 30

Easter Days

March 26.	1780.
April 2.	1820 1972.
April 9.	1944.
April 16.	1876.
April 23.	1848 1916 2000.

The World

The **Superficial Area** of the Earth is estimated to be 196,836,000 square miles, of which 55,786,000 square miles are Land and 141,050,000 square miles Water. The **Diameter** of the Earth at the Equator is 7,926½ English miles, and at the Poles 7,900 English miles. The Equatorial **Circumference** is 24,901·8 English miles, divided into 360 Degrees of Longitude, each of 69·17 English (or 60 Geographical) miles; these Degrees are measured from the Meridian of Greenwich, and numbered East and West of that point to meet in the Antipodes at the 180th Degree. Distance North and South of the Equator is marked by Parai.els of Latitude, which proceed from zero (at the Equator) to 90° at the Poles.

The velocity of a given point of the Earth's surface at the Equator exceeds 1,000 miles an hour (24,901·8 miles in 24 hours); the Earth's velocity in its orbit round the Sun is about 66,600 miles an hour (584,000,000 miles in 365¼ days). The Earth is distant from the Sun 93,000,000 miles, on the average.

AREA AND POPULATION

The total population of the world in mid-1975, was estimated by the *United Nations Statistical Office* at 3,967,000,000 compared with 3,003,000,000 in 1960 and 2,070,000,000 in 1930. Figures of areas in the following table are of land area and inland water, but exclude uninhabited polar regions and some uninhabited islands. Figures for Europe and Asia exclude U.S.S.R. which is shown separately. Figures for Oceania exclude Hawaii which is included with North America, being the 50th State of U.S.A.

Continent, etc.	Area		Estimated Population, 1975
	Sq. miles '000	Sq. km. '000	
Europe	1,903	4,929	473,000,000
Asia*	10,661	27,611	2,256,000,000
U.S.S.R. ...	8,649	22,402	255,000,000
Africa.....	11,683	30,258	401,000,000
America...	16,241	42,063	561,000,000
Oceania ...	3,286	8,510	21,000,000
Total....	52,422	135,773	3,967,000,000

* Excludes U.S.S.R. (shown separately); includes European and Asiatic Turkey.

A United Nations report (*The Future Growth of World Population*) in 1958, pointed out that the population of the world had increased since the beginning of the 20th Century at an unprecedented rate: in 1850 it was estimated at 1,094,000,000 and in 1900 at 1,550,000,000, an increase of 42 per cent in 50 years. By 1925 it had risen to 1,907,000,000—23 per cent in 25 years—and by 1950 it had reached 2,500,000,000, an increase of 31 per cent in 25 years. Levels of population and the trend in distribution of the population by continents as forecast for the year 2000 were:—

Continent, etc.	[millions]	
	2000	
	Estimated Population	Per cent
Europe (including U.S.S.R.)	947	15·1
Asia (excluding U.S.S.R.)...	3,870	61·8
Africa	517	8·2
N. America	312	5·0
Latin America†	592	9·4
Oceania	29	0·5
World	6,267	100

† Mexico and the remainder of America south of U.S.A.

THE CONTINENTS

Europe (including European Russia) forms about one-fourteenth of the land surface of the globe. Its length from the North Cape, 71° 12' N., to Cape Matapan, in the south of Greece, 36° 23' N., is about 2,400 miles, and its breadth from Cape St. Vincent to the Urals is about 3,300 miles. The boundary between Europe and Asia is the Urals in the north, while in the south-east it follows the valley of the Manych, north of the Caucasus.

Asia (including Asiatic Russia) extends over nearly one-third of the land surface of the globe. The distance between its extreme longitudes, the west coast of Asia Minor (26° E.) and the East Cape (170° W.), is 6,000 miles. The extreme latitudes, Cape Chelyuskin (78° 30″ N.) and Cape Bulus (76 miles north of the Equator), are 5,350 miles apart. Asia is bounded by the ocean on all sides except the west, where the isthmus of Suez connects it with Africa. The land boundary between Europe and Asia is formed on the west mainly by the Ural Mountains, the Ural River and in the south-west the valley of the Manych, which stretches from the Caspian Sea to the mouth of the Don. The islands of the archipelago which lie in the south-east between the continents of Asia and Australia may be divided into two groups by a line passing east of Timor, Timor Laut, the Kei Islands and the Moluccas.

Africa is about three times the area of Europe. Its extreme longitudes are 17° W. at Cape Verde and 51° 27′ 52″ E. at Ras Hafun. The extreme latitudes are Cape Blanco in 37° N. and Cape Agulhas in 35° S., at a distance of about 5,000 miles. It is surrounded by seas on all sides, except in the narrow isthmus of Suez, through which is cut the Suez Canal.

North America, including Mexico, is a little less than twice the size of Europe. Its extreme longitudes extend from a little west of 170° W. to 52¼° W. in the east of Newfoundland, and its extreme latitudes from about 80° N. lat. to 15° N. lat. in the south of Mexico. It is surrounded by seas on all sides except in the south, where it joins the isthmian States of *Central America*, which have an area of about 200,000 square miles. The area of the *West Indies* is about 65,000 square miles, a little more than half that of the United Kingdom. They extend from about 27° N. latitude to 10° N. latitude.

South America is a little more than 1¾ times the size of Europe. The extreme longitudes are Cape Branco 35° W. and Punta Parina 81° W., and the extreme latitudes, Punta Gallinas, 12¼° N. and Cape Horn 56° S. South America is surrounded by the ocean, except where it is joined to Central America by the narrow isthmus through which is cut the Panama Canal.

Oceania extends over an area 1⅓ times the size of Europe, from Australia (in the West) to the most easterly islands of Polynesia, and from New Zealand (in the south) to the Sandwich Islands (Hawaii) in the north.

Countries and Their Capitals

The appended tables of area and population are based on such information as is immediately available.

With regard to areas it will be realized that no complete survey of many countries has yet been either achieved or even undertaken and that consequently accurate area figures are not available.

The populations given hereunder are derived from various sources; some have as their basis an authenticated census; some are official and some are unofficial estimates. In certain cases where later information becomes available during printing the new figures are given in the overseas sections of the ALMANACK. What has been said about the survey of many of the world's countries applies equally to the question of census.

AFRICA

COUNTRY	Area Sq. Miles	Population	Capital	Population of Capital
Algeria	855,200	20,200,000	Algiers	3,250,000
Angola	488,000	7,100,000	Ψ Luanda	1,000,000
Benin	47,000	3,338,240*	Ψ Porto Novo	104,000
Botswana	220,000	937,000	Gaborone	60,000
Burundi	10,747	4,480,000	Bujumbura	150,000
Cameroon	475,400†	8,320,000	Yaoundé	337,000
Cape Verde Islands	1,516	296,093	Ψ Praia	6,000
Central African Republic	234,000	2,379,000	Bangui	350,000
Chad	488,000	4,000,000	Ndjaména	150,000
Comoros	800	385,000	Moroni	..
Congo	129,960	2,100,000	Brazzaville	156,000
Djibouti	9,000	350,000	Ψ Djibouti	150,000
Egypt	385,110	47,000,000	Cairo	11,000,000
Equatorial Guinea	28,000†	150,000	Ψ Malabo	9,000
Ethiopia	400,000	31,000,000	Addis Ababa	1,300,000
Gabon	101,400	1,200,000	Ψ Libreville	251,000
Gambia	4,003	700,000*	Ψ Banjul	45,000*
Ghana	92,100	14,000,000	Ψ Accra	851,614
Guinea	96,865	6,412,000	Ψ Conakry	655,000
Guinea-Bissau	14,000	760,000	Ψ Bissau	..
Ivory Coast	127,000	7,000,000	Ψ Abidjan	1,700,000
Kenya	224,960	17,000,000	Nairobi	1,000,000
Lesotho	11,716	1,204,000	Maseru	240,081
Liberia	43,000	1,481,524	Ψ Monrovia	300,000
Libya	810,000	3,100,000	Ψ Tripoli	1,000,000
Madagascar	228,000	9,000,000	Antananarivo	700,000
Malawi	45,747	5,547,460*	Lilongwe	102,924*
Mali	465,000	7,160,000	Bamako	600,000
Mauritania	419,000	1,634,000	Nouakchott	500,000
Mayotte	144	50,400	Dzaoudzi	4,147
Mauritius, etc.	805	983,685	Ψ Port Louis	147,599
Morocco	180,000	20,419,555	Ψ Rabat	518,616
Western Sahara	125,000	63,000	Villa Cisneros	250
Mozambique	297,657	12,000,000	Ψ Maputo	850,000
Namibia	318,261	1,039,400	Windhoek	61,260
Niger	459,000	5,310,000	Niamey	100,000
Nigeria	356,669	85,000,000	Ψ Lagos	3,000,000
Réunion	969	515,814	St. Denis	109,072
Rwanda	10,169	5,100,000	Kigali	7,000
St. Helena	47	5,499	Ψ Jamestown	1,516
Ascension	38	1,438	Ψ Georgetown	..
Tristan da Cunha	45	298	Ψ Edinburgh	..
Sao Tomé & Principé	372	113,000	Ψ São Tomé	3,187
Senegal	77,814	5,661,000	Ψ Dakar	1,000,000
Seychelles	171	65,000	Ψ Victoria	24,733
Sierra Leone	27,925	3,123,000*	Ψ Freetown	274,000*
Somalia	246,000	5,000,000	Ψ Mogadishu	600,000
South Africa	1,130,422†	29,290,000	{ Pretoria	528,407
			{ Ψ Cape Town	1,107,764
Spanish Presidios:—				
Ceuta	5	67,187	..	..
Melilla	72	64,942	..	..
Sudan	967,500	19,500,000	Khartoum	194,000
Swaziland	6,782	600,000	Mbabane	30,000
Tanzania	362,820	17,551,925*	Ψ Dar-es-Salaam	757,346
Togo	21,000	2,470,000	Lomé	247,000
Tunisia	63,380	6,520,000	Ψ Tunis	1,133,000
Uganda	91,000	12,600,000	Kampala	400,000
Upper Volta	100,000	6,600,000	Ouagadougou	200,000
Zaire	905,582	29,400,000	Kinshasa	2,500,000
Zambia	290,587	6,050,000	Lusaka	641,000
Zimbabwe	150,820	7,539,000	Harare	656,000

* Latest census result.   † Sq. km.   Ψ Seaport.

AMERICA

Country	Area Sq. Miles	Population	Capital	Population of Capital
North America				
Canada.................	3,851,809	24,889,800	Ottawa	710,000*
Alberta...............	255,000	2,361,000	Edmonton.........	682,000
British Columbia......	366,000	2,823,900	Ψ Victoria	236,400
Manitoba.............	251,000	1,051,500	Winnipeg	584,842
New Brunswick	28,000	710,500	Ψ Fredericton	64,439
Newfoundland	156,000	567,681*	Ψ St. John's	154,820
Nova Scotia...........	21,425	866,100	Ψ Halifax	176,871
Ontario...............	412,000	8,625,107*	Toronto..........	2,131,159
Prince Edward Island .	2,184	123,700	Ψ Charlottetown....	15,282*
Quebec...............	594,860	6,470,300	Ψ Quebec	166,474*
Saskatchewan	251,700	992,700	Regina............	167,900
Yukon Territory.......	207,000	23,153*	Whitehorse	14,814
Northwest Territories ..	1,305,000	45,741*	Yellowknife	9,483
Mexico...............	761,604	67,383,000*	Mexico City	16,000,000
St. Pierre and Miquelon..	93	6,041	Ψ St. Pierre	..
United States	3,536,855	231,106,727	Washington, D.C. ..	633,425
Central America and the West Indies				
Anguilla	35	7,000	The Valley	500
Antigua and Barbuda....	170	78,000	Ψ St. John's	22,000
Bahamas	5,380	237,090*	Ψ Nassau...........	135,437*
Barbados	166	248,983*	Ψ Bridgetown	17,552
Belize	8,867	148,300	Belmopan	4,000
Bermuda	21	57,237	Ψ Hamilton	1,617
Cayman Islands	100	18,750	Ψ George Town	8,200
Costa Rica	19,653	2,276,676	San José	808,919
Cuba..................	44,178	9,700,000	Ψ Havana	1,924,886
Dominica..............	290	74,069*	Ψ Roseau...........	8,346*
Dominican Republic	19,322	5,647,977*	Ψ Santo Domingo ...	1,550,739*
Grenada...............	133	110,410	Ψ St. George's	7,500
Guadeloupe............	657	328,400	Ψ Basse-Terre	15,778
Guatemala	42,042	7,500,000	Guatemala	1,500,000
Haiti..................	10,700	6,009,000	Ψ Port au Prince	506,525
Honduras	43,278	3,600,000	Tegucigalpa	533,600
Jamaica	4,244	265,400	Ψ Kingston.........	662,501
Martinique	427	328,566	Ψ Fort de France	100,576
Montserrat	39	12,073	Ψ Plymouth	1,623
Netherlands Antilles	394	253,234	Ψ Willemstad	154,928
Nicaragua	57,145	2,700,000	Managua	615,000
Panama	32,537	1,940,000	Ψ Panama City	418,000
Puerto Rico............	3,459	3,196,520	Ψ San Juan........	518,700
St. Kitts-Nevis	101	44,404*	Ψ Basseterre	15,000
St. Lucia	238	124,000	Ψ Castries	50,282
St. Vincent	133	127,883	Ψ Kingstown	33,694
El Salvador	8,200	4,939,400	San Salvador	425,119
Trinidad and Tobago	1,980	1,055,800	Ψ Port of Spain	55,800
Turks and Caicos Islds ...	192	7,436	Ψ Grand Turk	3,146
Virgin Islands:—				
British	59	12,034*	Ψ Road Town	2,479
U.S..................	133	96,569	Ψ Charlotte Amalie ..	11,000
South America				
Argentina..............	1,079,965	27,862,771*	Ψ Buenos Aires	9,677,200*
Bolivia	415,000	6,000,000	La Paz	654,700
Brazil.................	3,289,440	119,098,922*	Brasilia	1,176,748*
Chile..................	290,000	11,000,000	Santiago	4,000,000
Colombia	440,000	28,100,000	Bogotá	5,000,000
Ecuador	226,000	8,000,000	Quito	800,000
Falkland Islands	4,700	1,813	Ψ Stanley	1,050
Guiana, *French*	35,135	73,022	Ψ Cayenne	38,135
Guyana	83,000	793,000	Ψ Georgetown	185,000
Paraguay	157,000	3,026,165*	Ψ Asunción	720,000*
Peru	531,000	14,121,564	Lima	3,595,000
Surinam	63,250	390,000	Ψ Paramaribo	110,000
Uruguay	72,172	2,886,187	Ψ Montevideo	1,345,858
Venezuela	353,894	14,516,735*	Caracas	3,507,800

* Latest census result.   Ψ Seaport.

ASIA

The expressions "The Near East," "The Middle East" and "The Far East" often appear in the Press of English-speaking countries, but have no definite boundaries. The following limits have been suggested:— *Near East* (Turkey to Iran) 25°–60° E. long., *Middle East* (Baluchistan to Burma) 60°–100° E. long., *Far East* (Thailand to Japan) 100°–160° E. long.

COUNTRY	Area Sq. Miles	Population	Capital	Population of Capital
Afghanistan	250,000	15,500,000	Kabul	1,500,000
Bahrain	231	350,798*	Ψ Manama	121,986*
Bangladesh	55,126	89,940,000*	Dhaka	3,458,602
Bhutan	18,000	1,300,000	Thimphu	
Brunei	2,226	200,000	Ψ Bandar Seri Begawan	58,000
Burma	262,000	35,313,905*	Ψ Rangoon	2,458,712*
Cambodia	70,000	6,000,000	Ψ Phnom Penh	
China (inc. *Tibet*)	3,700,000	1,008,175,288*	Peking	9,230,687*
Taiwan	13,800	18,270,749*	Taipei	2,196,237
Macau	5	248,316	Ψ Macau	157,175
Hong Kong	404	5,344,400	Ψ Victoria	767,000
India	1,261,816	683,880,051*	Delhi	6,196,414
Indonesia	735,000	157,000,000	Ψ Jakarta	6,503,449
Iran (Persia)	628,000	39,190,000	Tehran	6,200,000
Iraq	172,000	13,500,000	Baghdad	3,205,645
Israel	7,992	3,921,700	Jerusalem	448,200
Japan	142,812	118,390,000	Tokyo	11,806,729
Jordan	37,700	2,400,000	Amman	750,000
Korea:—				
North Korea	48,000	18,000,000	Pyongyang	1,500,000
South Korea	38,500	39,000,000	Seoul	8,367,000
Kuwait	7,500	1,786,616	Ψ Kuwait	400,000
Laos	90,000	3,000,000	Vientiane	90,000
Lebanon	4,300	2,780,000	Ψ Beirut	702,000
Malaysia	130,000	13,435,588*	Kuala Lumpur	937,875*
Johore	7,330	1,601,504*	Johore Bahru	..
Kedah	3,640	1,102,200*	Alor Star	..
Kelantan	5,765	877,575	Koto Bahru	..
Malacca	640	453,153*	Ψ Malacca	..
Negri Sembilan	2,570	563,955*	Seremban	..
Pahang	13,900	770,644*	Kuantan	..
Penang	400	911,586*	Ψ George Town	234,930
Perak	8,100	1,762,288*	Ipoh	125,776
Perlis	310	147,726*	Kangar	..
Sabah	29,000	1,002,608*	Kota Kinabalu	41,830
Sarawak	48,000	1,294,753*	Ψ Kuching	63,491
Selangor	3,166	1,467,441*	Shah Alam	451,810
Trengganu	5,000	406,000	Kuala Trengganu	..
Maldive Islands	115	160,200	Ψ Malé	37,000
Mongolia	600,000	1,820,400	Ulan Bator	435,000
Nepal	54,362	16,000,000	Kathmandu	235,000
Oman	120,000	850,000	Ψ Muscat	30,000
Pakistan	310,403	83,780,000	Islamabad	250,000
Philippines	114,834	48,098,460*	Ψ Manila	5,925,884
Qatar	4,000	250,000	Doha	200,000
Saudi Arabia	927,000	9,160,000	Riyadh	1,000,000
Singapore	226	2,502,400	..	..
Sri Lanka	25,332	14,800,001*	Ψ Colombo	585,776
Syria	70,800	10,400,000	Damascus	2,250,000
Thailand (Siam)	198,247	49,459,000	Ψ Bangkok	5,733,000
Turkey	285,000	45,217,556	Ankara	3,196,460
United Arab Emirates	32,000	1,300,000	..	..
U.S.S.R. (Asia)		59,446,000		
R.S.F.S.R. (Asia)	*See* Europe			
Armenia (Hyastan)	11,300	3,263,000	Erevan	1,114,000
Azerbaidjan	33,436	6,498,000	Ψ Baku	1,661,000
Georgia	27,000	5,171,000	Tbilisi	1,140,000
Turkmenistan	188,400	3,123,000	Ashkhabad	347,000
Uzbekistan	157,000	17,496,000	Tashkent	1,985,000
Tadjikstan	54,000	4,366,000	Dushanbe	539,000
Kazakhstan	1,065,000	15,654,000	Alma Ata	1,046,000
Kirghizia	77,000	3,875,000	Frunze	590,000
Vietnam	129,000	60,000,000	Hanoi	925,000
Yemen A.R.	75,000	8,556,974	Sana'a	277,817
Yemen P.D.R.	112,000	1,800,000	Ψ Aden	270,000

Ψ Seaport.　　* Latest census report.

EUROPE AND THE MEDITERRANEAN

Country	Area Sq. Miles	Population	Capital	Population of Capital
Albania	10,700	2,752,300	Tirana	200,000
Andorra	190	41,600	Andorra La Vella	16,000
Austria	32,376	7,551,300	Vienna	1,531,346
Belgium	11,781	9,863,374	Brussels	1,000,221
Bulgaria	43,000	8,929,000	Sofia	1,082,315
Cyprus	3,572	618,300	Nicosia	233,500
Czechoslovakia	49,400	15,280,148	Prague	1,191,125
Denmark	17,000	5,116,464	Ψ Copenhagen	575,217
Finland	130,165	4,844,000	Ψ Helsinki	482,800
France	213,000	54,334,871	Paris	10,073,059
Germany:—				
Federal Republic of Germany‡	96,011	61,333,000	Bonn	292,200
German Democratic Republic	41,768	16,740,000	East Berlin	1,166,641
Gibraltar	2	28,719*	Ψ Gibraltar	
Greece	51,182	9,740,417*	Athens	3,027,331*
Hungary	36,000	10,710,000	Budapest	2,093,000
Iceland	40,500	237,894	Ψ Reykjavik	87,106
Irish Republic	26,600	3,443,405*	Ψ Dublin	525,882*
Italy	131,000	56,830,000	Rome	2,830,569
Liechtenstein	62	26,512	Vaduz	4,896
Luxemburg	999	365,500	Luxemburg	78,900
Malta and Gozo	121	341,000	Ψ Valletta	14,042
Monaco	½	28,000	Monaco-ville	1,443
Netherlands	13,500	14,394,589	Amsterdam	687,397
Norway	°386,308	4,106,651	Ψ Oslo	448,747
Poland	121,000	36,400,000*	Warsaw	1,572,000
Portugal§	34,000	9,862,700	Ψ Lisbon	1,707,500
Romania	°237,500	22,480,000	Bucharest	1,960,097
San Marino	23	22,053	San Marino	..
Spain	196,700	37,682,355	Madrid	3,158,818
Sweden	173,436	8,327,484	Ψ Stockholm	1,535,539
Switzerland	15,950	6,365,960	Berne	145,700
The United Kingdom†	93,026	55,776,422*	Ψ London	6,696,008*
England	50,053	46,362,836*		
Wales	7,969	2,791,851*	Ψ Cardiff	281,300
Scotland	29,798	5,130,735*	Ψ Edinburgh	446,361
Northern Ireland	5,206	1,491,000*	Ψ Belfast	297,862*
U.S.S.R. (Europe)		214,397,000		
R.S.F.S.R.	6,593,391	142,108,000	Moscow	8,546,000
Ukraine	252,046	50,681,000	Kiev	2,355,000
Belorussia	80,300	9,878,000	Minsk	1,442,000
Moldavia	13,912	4,083,000	Kishinev	605,000
Estonia	17,413	1,519,000	Ψ Tallinn	458,000
Latvia	24,695	2,589,000	Ψ Riga	875,000
Lithuania	26,173	3,539,000	Vilnius	535,000
Vatican City State	109 *acres*	731	Vatican City	..
Yugoslavia	98,725	22,420,000	Belgrade	1,455,000

† *Land* areas are shown for U.K. and parts (*total* area of U.K., 94,216 sq. miles). ‡ Data include West Berlin. § Data include Madeira (314 sq. miles) and the Azores (922 sq. miles). Ψ Seaport. ° sq. kilometres. * Latest census report.

THE SEVEN WONDERS OF THE WORLD

I. THE PYRAMIDS OF EGYPT.—From Gizeh (near Cairo) to a southern limit 60 miles distant. The oldest is that of Zoser, at Saqqara, built about 2,700 B.C. The Great Pyramid of Cheops covers more than 12 acres and was originally 481 ft. in height and 756 × 756 ft. at the base.

II. THE HANGING GARDENS OF BABYLON.—Adjoining Nebuchadnezzar's palace, 60 miles south of Baghdad. Terraced gardens, ranging from 75 to 300 ft. above ground level, watered from storage tanks on the highest terrace.

III. THE TOMB OF MAUSOLUS.—At Halicarnassus, in Asia Minor. Built by the widowed Queen Artemisia about 350 B.C. The memorial originated the term mausoleum.

IV. THE TEMPLE OF DIANA AT EPHESUS.—Ionic temple erected about 350 B.C. in honour of the goddess and burned by the Goths in A.D. 262.

V. THE COLOSSUS OF RHODES.—A bronze statue of Apollo, set up about 280 B.C. According to legend it stood at the harbour entrance of the seaport of Rhodes.

VI. THE STATUE OF JUPITER OLYMPUS.—At Olympia in the plain of Ellis, constructed of marble inlaid with ivory and gold by the sculptor Phidias, about 430 B.C.

VII. THE PHAROS OF ALEXANDRIA.—A marble watch tower and lighthouse on the island of Pharos in the harbour of Alexandria.

OCEANIA

Country	Area Sq. Miles	Population	Capital	Population of Capital
Australia	2,968,000	15,451,900	Canberra	230,800
New South Wales	309,000	5,360,400	Ψ Sydney	3,332,550
Queensland	667,000	2,471,600	Ψ Brisbane	1,138,370
South Australia	380,070	1,340,400	Adelaide	969,160
Tasmania	26,383	433,300	Ψ Hobart	128,603*
Victoria	87,884	4,034,600	Ψ Melbourne	2,836,800
Western Australia	975,920	1,363,239	Perth	948,850
Northern Territory	520,280	126,300*	Ψ Darwin	46,655
Norfolk Island	13	1,849	Ψ Kingston	. .
Fiji	7,072	671,712	Ψ Suva	71,000
French Polynesia	1,522	148,372	Ψ Papeete	15,220
Kiribati	264	60,000	Tarawa	20,000
Guam	209	105,979	Agaña	. .
Mariana, Caroline and Marshall Islands†	687	133,442	Saipan	. .
Nauru	8	7,254*	Ψ Nauru	. .
New Caledonia	7,374	139,600	Ψ Noumea	12,000
New Zealand	103,736	3,230,000	Ψ Wellington	342,500
Cook Islands . . . . }	200	{ 17,400	Avarua	. .
Niue . . . . }		{ 3,002	Alofi	956
Ross Dependency	175,000	. .	. .	. .
Papua New Guinea	178,260	3,160,000	Ψ Port Moresby	138,500
Pitcairn Islands	1·75	61	. .	. .
Samoa:—				
Eastern	76	32,297	Ψ Fagatogo	. .
Western	1,097	158,130*	Ψ Apia	33,100*
Solomon Islands	11,500	244,000	Ψ Honiara	18,346
Tonga, etc.	288	98,000	Ψ Nuku'alofa	21,000
Tuvalu	10	9,000	Ψ Funafuti	2,120
Vanuatu	6,050	112,596*	Ψ Vila	14,801*
Wallis and Futuna Is.	106	11,943	Mata-Utu	. .

† Trust Territory of the Pacific Islands.   Ψ Seaport.   * Latest census result.

THE LARGEST CITIES OF THE WORLD

Ψ = Seaport	Population	Ψ = Seaport	Population
Mexico City, Mexico	16,000,000	Bogotá, Colombia	5,000,000
Ψ Shanghai, China	11,859,000	Ψ Guangzhou, China	5,000,000
Tokyo, Japan	11,806,729	Ψ Istanbul, Turkey	4,870,747
Cairo, Egypt	11,000,000	Ψ Leningrad, U.S.S.R.	4,832,000
Paris, France	10,073,059	Shenyang, China	4,400,000
Ψ Buenos Aires, Argentina	9,677,200	Ψ Madras, India	4,300,000
Peking, China	9,230,687	Luda, China	4,200,000
Ψ Calcutta, India	9,200,000	Alexandria, Egypt	4,000,000
Moscow, U.S.S.R.	8,546,000	Santiago, Chile	4,000,000
São Paulo, Brazil	8,490,763	Ψ Rangoon, Burma	3,973,782
Seoul, Korea	8,367,000	Lima, Peru	3,595,000
Ψ Bombay, India	8,300,000	Caracas, Venezuela	3,507,800
Tianjin, China	7,390,000	Ψ Ho Chi Minh City, Vietnam	3,500,000
Ψ New York, U.S.A.	7,071,030	Wuhan, China	3,500,000
Ψ Surabaya, Indonesia	7,027,913	Dhaka, Bangladesh	3,458,602
Ψ London, U.K.	6,776,000	Ψ Sydney, Australia	3,332,550
Ψ Jakarta, Indonesia	6,503,449	Ψ Algiers, Algeria	3,250,000
Chiongqing, China	6,200,000	Baghdad, Iraq	3,205,645
Tehran, Iran	6,200,000	Ankara, Turkey	3,196,460
Delhi, India	6,196,414	Pusan, Korea	3,160,000
Manila, Philippines	5,925,884	Madrid, Spain	3,158,818
Ψ Bangkok, Thailand	5,733,000	Chicago, U.S.A.	3,005,072
Ψ Karachi, Pakistan	5,500,000	Ψ Lagos, Nigeria	3,000,000
Ψ Rio de Janeiro, Brazil	5,094,396		

OCEAN AREAS AND DEPTHS

The greatest known Ocean Depth (in the Pacific, off the Philippines, 36,198 feet) is not much greater than the greatest land height (in the Himalayas); but the mean depth of the Ocean floor exceeds 12,000 feet, while the mean height of the surface of the land area of the Earth above sea level is only 2,300 feet. The following table gives the areas of the principal oceans and seas, with the greatest known depth of each:—

Oceans

Name	Area of Basin (sq. miles)	Greatest Depth (feet)
Pacific	63,986,000	Mariana Trench, 36,198
Atlantic	31,530,000	Puerto Rico Trench, 27,498
Indian	28,350,000	Diamantina, 26,400
Arctic	5,541,600	17,850

Seas

Name	Area of Basin (sq. miles)	Greatest Depth (feet)
Malay	3,137,000	Kei Trench, 21,342
Caribbean	1,770,170	Cayman, 23,000
Mediterranean	1,145,000	Matapan, 14,435
Bering	878,000	Buldir Trough, 13,422
Okhotsk	582,000	Kurile Trough, 11,154
East China	480,000	*about* 10,500
Hudson Bay	472,000	*about* 1,500
Japan	405,000	*about* 10,200
Andaman	305,000	*about* 11,000
North Sea	221,000	Skaggerak, 1,998
Red Sea	178,000	20° N., 7,254
Baltic	158,000	*about* 1,300

PRINCIPAL LAND AREAS OF THE WORLD BELOW SEA LEVEL
(With approx. greatest depth in feet below Mean Sea Level.)

Europe: Netherlands coastal areas (15).
Asia: Jordan Valley, Dead Sea (1290)*.
China: Sinkiang, Turfan Basin (980).
U.S.S.R.–Iran: Caspian Sea (85)*.
Arabia: Trucial Oman–U.A.E. (70).
Africa: Libyan Desert Depressions:—
Qattara (440), Faiyum (150).
Wadi Ryan (140), Sittra (110).

Africa: Libyan Desert Depressions (*continued*)—
Areg (80), Wadi Natrun (75).
Melfa (60), Siwa (55), Bahrain (50).
Eritrea: Salt Plains depression (385).
Algeria-Tunisia: Shott Melghir and El Gharsa (90)*.
America: Death Valley (275), Salton Sea (245)*.
Australia: Lake Eyre (40).

* Water surface

PRINCIPAL HEIGHTS ABOVE SEA LEVEL

	Feet
Europe: Alps—Mont Blanc	15,782
England: Scafell Pike	3,210
Wales: Snowdon	3,560
Scotland: Ben Nevis	4,406
Ireland: Carrantuohill	3,414
Asia: Everest	29,028
Africa: Kilimanjaro	19,340

North America: McKinley	20,320
South America: Aconcagua	22,834
Australia: Kosciusko	7,316
New Zealand: Cook	12,349
Oceania: Jayakusumu, Indonesia	16,500
Antarctica: Vinson Massif	16,863

THE ARCTIC OCEAN

The Arctic Ocean consists of a deep sea over 2,000 fathoms, on the southern margin of which there is a broad continental shelf with numerous islands. Into this deeper sea there is only one broad channel, about 700 miles, between Greenland and Scandinavia. Bering Strait is only 49 miles wide and 27 fathoms deep. The southern boundary of the Arctic Ocean is the Wyville-Thomson and Faeroe-Icelandic submarine ridge, which separates the North Atlantic from the Norwegian and Greenland Seas. The Norwegian Deep lies between Norway and Jan Mayen and Iceland; it exceeds 1,500 fathoms. The Greenland Deep, of similar depth, lies between Spitsbergen and Greenland. These two depressions are separated by a somewhat deeply submerged ridge from the east of Jan Mayen to Bear Island, south of Spitsbergen. A shallow ridge from the north-west of Spitsbergen to Greenland separates the Greenland Sea from the deep North Polar Basin. This extends from the north of Spitsbergen and Franz Josef Land to the north of the New Siberia Islands and of the North American Arctic Archipelago. Another more shallow depression is Baffin Bay, less than 1,000 fathoms. This is separated from the North Atlantic by a submarine ridge. Barent's Sea, between Spitsbergen, Norway and Novaya Zemlya, and the Kara Sea, between Novaya Zemlya and the Siberian coast, are respectively below 200 and 100 fathoms. The total area of the Arctic Sea is about 5·5 million square miles, of which 2·3 million square miles are probably covered with floating ice.

THE WORLD'S LAKES
The areas of some of these lakes are subject to seasonal variation.

Name	Country	Length (Miles)	Area (Sq. Miles)	Name	Country	Length (Miles)	Area (Sq. Miles)
Caspian Sea	Asia	750	170,000	Amadjuak	Baffin Island	75	4,000
Superior	North America	350	31,820	Onega	U.S.S.R.	145	3,800
	Africa	200	26,828	Eyre	Australia	130	3,700
Aral	U.S.S.R.	265	26,000	Turkana			
Huron	North America	206	23,010	(Rudolph)	Africa	185	3,500
Michigan	North America	307	22,400	Titicaca	South America	110	3,200
Tanganyika	Africa	420	12,700	Athabasca	Canada	100	3,058
Great Bear	Canada	175	12,200	Nicaragua	Central America	100	3,000
Baikal	U.S.S.R.	330	12,150	Gairdner	Australia	100	3,000
Great Slave	Canada	300	11,170	Reindeer	Canada	160	2,444
Malawi	Africa	360	11,000	Torrens	Australia	130	2,200
Erie	North America	241	9,940	Koko-Nor	China	68	2,300
Winnipeg	Canada	260	9,398	Issyk-Kul	U.S.S.R.	115	2,250
Maracaibo	South America	130	8,296	Vänern	Sweden	93	2,140
Ontario	North America	193	7,540	Winnipegosis	Canada	122	2,086
Balkhash	U.S.S.R.	323	7,050	Bangweolo	Africa	150	2,000
Ladoga	U.S.S.R.	130	7,000	Nipigon	Canada	70	1,870
Chad	Africa	175	6,000	Manitoba	Canada	130	1,817
Nettilling	Baffin Island	120	5,000	Van	Turkey	80	1,450

VOLCANOES OF THE WORLD

Volcano	Locality	Height in Feet	Volcano	Locality	Height in Feet
Cotopaxi	Ecuador	19,344	Nyamuragira	Zaire	10,150
Kluchevskaya	U.S.S.R.	15,584	Villarica	Chile	9,325
Mount Wrangell	Alaska	14,000	Ruapehu	New Zealand	9,175
Mauna Loa	Hawaii	13,680	Paricutin	Mexico	9,100
Cameroon	Cameroon	13,350	Asama	Japan	8,340
Erebus	Antarctica	12,200	Mt. St. Helens	Washington, U.S.A.	8,300
Nyiragongo	Zaire	11,560	Ngauruhoe	New Zealand	7,515
Iliamna	Aleutian Range, U.S.A.	11,000	Hecla	Iceland	4,892
Etna	Sicily	10,958	Vesuvius	Italy	4,190
Baker	Cascades, U.S.A.	10,778	Kilauea	Hawaii	4,090
Chillan	Chile	10,500	Stromboli	Lipari Islands, Italy	3,034

QUIESCENT

Llullaillaco	Chile	22,057	Tristan da Cunha	South Atlantic	6,700
Demavend	Iran	18,384	Pelée	Martinique, W. Indies	4,430
Pico de Teyde	Tenerife	12,198	Tarawera	New Zealand	3,646
Semerou	Indonesia	12,060	Soufrière	St. Vincent Is., W.I.	3,000
Haleakala	Hawaii	10,022	Krakatoa	Sunda Strait	2,600
Tongariro	New Zealand	6,458			

BELIEVED EXTINCT

Aconcagua	Andes	22,834	Elbruz	Caucasus	18,480
Chimborazo	Ecuador	20,560	Popocatepetl	Mexico	17,887
Kilimanjaro	Tanzania	19,340	Karisimbi	Rwanda and Zaire	14,786
Antisana	Ecuador	18,713	Fujiyama	Japan	12,388
Citlaltepetl	Mexico	18,700			

THE HIGHEST MOUNTAINS
The following list contains some of the principal peaks of such ranges as the Himalayas and the Andes, and the highest mountains in other ranges.

Name	Range or Country	Height in Feet	Name	Range or Country	Height in Feet
EVEREST	Himalayas	29,028	Sajama	Andes	21,390
K2	Karakoram	28,250	Chimborazo	Andes	20,560
Kanchenjunga	Himalayas	28,208	McKinley	Alaska	20,320
Makalu	Himalayas	27,824	Mount Logan	Yukon	19,850
Dhaulagiri	Himalayas	26,810	Cotopaxi	Andes	19,344
Nanga Parbat	Himalayas	26,660	Kilimanjaro	Tanzania	19,340
Annapurna	Himalayas	26,502	Antisana	Andes	18,713
Nanda Devi	Himalayas	25,645	Citlaltepetl	S. Madre	18,700
Kamet	Himalayas	25,447	Elbruz	Caucasus	18,480
Namcha Barwa	China	25,445	Demavend	Elburz	18,384
Minya Konka	China	24,900	Mount St. Elias	Alaska	18,008
Pik Kommunizma	Pamirs	24,590	Popocatepetl	Mexico	17,887
Pik Pobedy	Tian Shan	24,406	Foraker	Alaska	17,395
Aconcagua	Andes	22,834	Mount Lucania	Yukon	17,150
Bonete	Andes	22,545	Tolima	Andes	17,109
Ojos del Salado	Andes	22,516	Kenya	Kenya	17,058
Huascaran	Andes	22,204	Ararat	Armenia	16,945
Llullaillaco	Andes	22,057	Vinson Massif	Antarctica	16,863

THE LONGEST RIVERS

River	Outflow	Length in Miles
Nile	Mediterranean	4,150
Amazon	Atlantic	3,900
Mississippi-Missouri–Red Rock	Gulf of Mexico	3,800
Yangtze	North Pacific	3,400
Ob-Irtysh	Arctic	3,200
Hwang-ho	North Pacific	2,900
Congo	Atlantic	2,900
Amur	North Pacific	2,800
Lena	Arctic	2,800
Mekong	China Sea	2,800
Niger	Gulf of Guinea	2,600
Mackenzie	Beaufort Sea	2,500
Paraná	Atlantic	2,450
Volga	Caspian Sea	2,300
Yenisei	Arctic	2,300
Madeira	Amazon	2,100
Yukon	Bering Sea	2,000
Arkansas	Mississippi	2,000
Colorado	Gulf of California	2,000
St. Lawrence	Gulf of St. Lawrence	1,800
Rio Grande del Norte	Gulf of Mexico	1,800
São Francisco	Atlantic	1,800
Salween	Gulf of Martaban	1,800
Danube	Black Sea	1,725
Euphrates	Persian Gulf	1,700
Indus	Arabian Sea	1,700
Brahmaputra	Bay of Bengal	1,680
Zambesi	Indian Ocean	1,630
Murray-Darling	Southern Ocean	1,600
Severn	Bristol Channel	220
Thames	North Sea (Thames Head to Nore)	215

SOME FAMOUS BRIDGES

Among the outstanding *suspension bridges* of the World are the Verrazano Narrows Bridge, New York (main span, 4,260 ft.); the Golden Gate Bridge, San Francisco (4,200 ft.); Mackinac Bridge, Michigan (3,800 ft.); Bosporus, Turkey (3,523 ft.); George Washington Bridge, New York (3,500 ft.); the Ponte Salazar (Tagus Bridge), Portugal (3,323 ft.); Forth Road Bridge, Scotland (3,300 ft.); Severn Bridge, England (3,240 ft.); Tacoma Bridge, Washington, U.S.A. (2,800 ft.); Orinoco Bridge, Venezuela (2,336 ft.) and the Kanmon Bridge, Japan (2,336 ft.). Lengths shown above are all those of the main or longest span. The Humber Bridge was opened in 1981 and has the longest single central span, 4,626 ft., of any suspension bridge in the world.

The Transbay Bridge (*suspension and cantilever*), crossing San Francisco Bay from Oakland to San Francisco is 7½ miles long, with spans of 2,310 ft. each.

Among important *steel arch* bridges are the Bayonne Bridge, from New Jersey to Staten Island, U.S.A. (1,652 ft.); Sydney Harbour Bridge, Australia (1,650 ft.); the Runcorn-Widnes Bridge, England (1,082 ft.); and the Glen Canyon Bridge over the Colorado River, U.S.A. (1,028 ft.). Major *concrete trestle* bridges include the Lake Pontchartrain Causeway, U.S.A. of 2,170 spans extending 24 miles and the Oosterscheldebrug, Netherlands, 3¼ miles long. Gladesville Bridge, Sydney, Australia, is a *concrete arch* bridge of 1,000 ft. span. The Tay Bridge in Scotland is a *steel box girder* bridge supported on twin piers (42 spans), 7,365 ft long.

The Chesapeake Bay Bridge-Tunnel (17·6 miles long) joining Cape Charles, Virginia, to Chesapeake Beach has 12·5 miles of *concrete trestle* bridge.

THE LARGEST ISLANDS

Name of Island	Ocean	Area in Sq. Miles	Name of Island	Ocean	Area in Sq. Miles
Greenland (Denmark)	Arctic	840,000	Sulawesi (Indonesia)	Indian	69,000
New Guinea	Pacific	305,000	South Island, N.Z.	Pacific	58,093
Borneo (various)	„	290,000	Java (Indonesia)	Indian	48,800
Madagascar	Indian	228,000	North Island, N.Z.	Pacific	44,281
Baffin Land (Canada)	Arctic	190,000	Cuba	Atlantic	44,000
Sumatra (Indonesia)	Indian	163,000	Newfoundland (Canada)	Atlantic	42,750
Honshū (Japan)	Pacific	88,839	Luzon (Philippines)	Pacific	40,400
Great Britain	Atlantic	88,745	Iceland	Atlantic	40,000
Victoria (Canada)	Arctic	80,000	Mindanao (Philippines)	Pacific	36,500
Ellesmere (Canada)	Arctic	77,000	Ireland	Atlantic	32,600

GREAT SHIP CANALS OF THE WORLD

Canal	Opened	Length, miles	Depth (ft.)†	Width (ft.)†
North Sea (Netherlands)	1876	14½	43	148
Corinth (Greece)	1893	4	26	72
Kiel (Germany)	1895	61	31	132
Manchester (England)	1894	35½	30	120
Panama	1914	50½	45	300
Suez (Egypt)	1869	100	42	197
Terneuzen-Ghent (Netherlands–Belgium)	1895	18½	38	102
St. Lawrence Seaway (Canada)	1959	378*	27	200

† Of largest vessels permitted.   * Includes Lake Ontario and Welland Canal.

INLAND WATERWAYS.—The British Waterways Board are the navigational authority for nearly 2,000 miles of canals and river navigations in England, Scotland and Wales. Some 340 miles are maintained and are being developed as commercial waterways for use by freight-carrying vessels, and another 1,200 miles are being developed for boating, fishing and other amenities. Over a third has now been restored to full navigational use and other stretches are available to small boats. The Manchester Ship Canal, Bridgewater Canal, Rochdale Canal, River Thames and Fenland Waterways are among those which are the responsibility of other authorities.

WATERFALLS OF THE WORLD

In order of height

Fall	Locality	Height in Feet
Angel Falls	Venezuela	3,212
Ribbon Fall	Yosemite, U.S.A.	1,612
Upper Yosemite	Yosemite, U.S.A.	(a) 1,430
Gavarnie	Pyrenees	1,385
Wollomombie	New South Wales	(b) 1,100
Staubbach	Switzerland	980
Seward	Peru	887
Vettisfoss	Norway	856
King Edward VIII	Guyana	840
Gersoppa	Mysore, India	(c) 830
Sutherland	New Zealand	(d) 815
Kaieteur (Köituök)	Guyana	741
Kalambo	Tanzania	(e) 704
Maletsunyane	Lesotho	630
Bridalveil	Yosemite, U.S.A.	620
Nevada	Yosemite, U.S.A.	594
Skjeggedalsfoss	Norway	525
Eas-Coul-Aulin	Scotland	(f) 511

In order of volume

Fall	Locality	Width in Yards
Khon Cataracts (1)	Indo-China	15,840
Guayra (2)	Brazil	5,300
Victoria (3)	Zimbabwe Rhodesia—Zambia	1,760
Niagara (4)	Canada–U.S.A.	1,200

On the basis of annual flow the Guayra Falls in Brazil are the most spectacular, with a flow of 470,000 cubic feet per second (annual average).

Notes.—(a) Out of a total fall of 2,565 ft.; (b) 1,700 ft.; (c) 960 ft.; (d) 1,904 ft.; (e) 3,000 ft.; (f) 658 ft.

(1) Height, 50–70 ft.; (2) 90–130 ft.; (3) 236–354 ft.; (4) 158–175 ft.

LONGEST RAILWAY TUNNELS

E.R. = Eastern Region; L.M.R. = London Midland Region; S.R. = Southern Region; W.R. = Western Region

United Kingdom

		Miles	Yards
Severn	W.R.	4	628
Totley	L.M.R.	3	950
Standedge	E.R.	3	66
Woodhead	L.M.R.	3	66
Sodbury	W.R.	2	924
Disley	L.M.R.	2	346
Bramhope	E.R.	2	241
Ffestiniog	L.M.R.	2	338
Cowburn	L.M.R.	2	182
Sevenoaks	S.R.	1	1693
Rhondda	W.R.	1	1683
Morley	E.R.	1	1609
Box	W.R.	1	1452
Catesby	L.M.R.	1	1240
Dove Holes	L.M.R.	1	1224
Littleborough (Summit)	L.M.R.	1	1125
Vict. Waterloo (Liverpool)	L.M.R.	1	946
Ponsbourne	E.R.	1	924
Polhill	S.R.	1	851
Queensbury	E.R.	1	741
Merthyr	W.R.	1	737
Kilsby	L.M.R.	1	666
Bleamoor	L.M.R.	1	869
Shepherd's Well	S.R.	1	609
Gildersome	E.R.	1	571
Strood	S.R.	1	569
Clayton	S.R.	1	499
Oxted	S.R.	1	501
Sydenham	S.R.	1	381
Drewton	E.R.	1	354

		Miles	Yards
Merstham New (Quarry)	S.R.	1	353
Wapping	L.M.R.	1	351
Mersey	Mersey	1	350
Greenock	Scottish Region	1	351
Bradway	E.R.	1	267
Slough	L.M.R.	1	255
Watford, New	L.M.R.	1	230
Caerphilly	W.R.	1	173
Llangyfelach	W.R.	1	192
Abbot's Cliff	S.R.	1	182
Corby	L.M.R.	1	166
Halton	L.M.R.	1	176
Wenvoe	W.R.	1	107
Sapperton	W.R.	1	100
Sharnbrook	L.M.R.	1	100

The London Underground *Northern Line* between Morden and East Finchley by the City Branch serves 25 stations and uses tunnels totalling 17½ miles in length).

The World

		Miles	Yards
Simplon	Switzerland–Italy	12	560
Apennine	Italy	11	880
St. Gotthard	Switzerland	9	550
Lötschberg	Switzerland	9	130
Mont Cenis	Italy	8	870
Cascade	United States	7	1410
Arlberg	Austria	6	650
Moffat	United States	6	200
Shimizu	Japan	6	70

DISTANCE OF THE HORIZON

The limit of distance to which one can see varies with the height of the spectator. The greatest distance at which an object on the surface of the sea, or of a level plain, can be seen by a person whose eyes are at a height of five feet from the same level is nearly three miles. At a height of 20 feet the range is increased to nearly six miles, and an approximate rule for finding the range of vision for small heights is to increase the square root of the number of feet that the eye is above the level surface by a third of itself, the result being the distance of the horizon in miles, but is slightly in excess of that in the table below, which is computed by a more precise formula. The table may be used conversely to show the distance of an object of given height that is just visible from a point in the surface of the earth or sea. Refraction is taken into account both in the approximate rule and in the Table.

At a height of	the range is	At a height of	the range is	At a height of	the range is
5 ft.	2·9 miles	500 ft.	29·5 miles	4,000 ft	83·3 miles
20 ft.	5·9 „	1,000 ft.	41·6 „	5,000 „	93·1 „
50 „	9·3 „	2,000 „	58·9 „	20,000 „	186·2 „
100 „	13·2 „	3,000 „	72·1 „		

CONTROL OF IMMIGRATION STATISTICS 1983

The following table shows the statistics of people accepted for settlement, the main measure of immigration of persons subject to immigration control. They comprise people accepted for settlement on arrival at the ports, and people accepted for settlement on removal of time limit. The latter are people initially admitted to the country subject to a time limit which was subsequently removed on application to the Home Office.

ACCEPTANCES FOR SETTLEMENT BY NATIONALITY 1983

Geographical region and nationality	Total	Men	Women	Children
All Nationalities	53,460	15,620	25,100	12,740
Europe				
European Community				
Belgium	70	30	40	†
Denmark	140	40	80	20
France	520	150	320	40
Germany (Federal Rep.)	680	180	420	90
Greece	200	120	60	20
Italy	600	350	200	50
Luxembourg	†	†	†	—
Netherlands	460	160	250	60
European Community	2,680	1,020	1,380	280
Other Western Europe				
Austria	110	20	70	20
Cyprus	560	300	220	40
Finland	130	10	100	20
Malta	200	90	90	20
Norway	230	60	120	50
Portugal	390	120	190	80
Spain	480	150	260	70
Sweden	330	90	160	70
Switzerland	170	40	100	20
Turkey	580	250	200	130
Yugoslavia	140	40	70	30
Other Western Europe	3,310	1,150	1,590	550
Eastern Europe				
Bulgaria	10	—	10	†
Czechoslavakia	30	†	20	10
German Democratic Republic	10	—	10	†
Hungary	20	†	20	†
Poland	390	60	290	40
Romania	20	10	10	†
USSR	40	†	30	10
Eastern Europe	520	80	380	60
Europe	6,520	2,260	3,360	890
Americas				
Argentina	80	30	30	20
Barbados	40	10	20	†
Brazil	140	20	100	20
Canada	1,140	420	540	170
Chile	120	40	50	30
Colombia	180	20	120	40
Cuba	—	—	—	—
Guyana	190	40	120	40
Jamaica	310	70	160	80
Mexico	70	10	50	10
Peru	50	10	30	10
Trinidad and Tobago	170	30	110	40
U.S.A.	3,940	1,100	1,770	1,060
Uruguay	†	†	†	—
Venezuela	70	10	40	10
West Indies Associated States	40	10	20	10
Americas	6,530	1,810	3,180	1,540
Africa				
Algeria	100	70	20	10
Egypt	380	230	120	30
Ethiopia	50	20	30	†
Ghana	560	160	300	100
Kenya	640	130	280	230
Libya	100	60	20	30

† Negligible.

ACCEPTANCES FOR SETTLEMENT BY NATIONALITY 1983—*Continued*

Geographical region and nationality	Total	Men	Women	Children
Mauritius	520	200	280	30
Morocco	150	50	80	20
Nigeria	360	140	160	60
Sierra Leone	60	20	30	10
Somalia	20	†	10	†
South Africa	840	240	360	230
Sudan	50	30	20	10
Tanzania	320	80	150	90
Tunisia	50	30	20	†
Uganda	100	40	40	20
Zambia	90	30	40	30
Zimbabwe	280	90	100	90
Africa	4,670	1,620	2,040	1,000
Asia				
Indian sub-continent				
Bangladesh	4,870	230	1,640	3,010
India	5,380	1,430	3,180	760
Pakistan	6,440	890	3,240	2,300
Indian sub-continent	16,690	2,550	8,060	6,080
Middle East				
Iran	1,980	1,210	480	300
Iraq	430	240	120	70
Israel	310	110	130	70
Jordan	150	100	30	20
Kuwait	†	†	†	—
Lebanon	260	120	80	60
Saudi Arabia	30	20	10	10
Syria	100	50	30	20
Middle East	3,280	1,850	870	550
Remainder of Asia				
China	160	20	120	20
Indonesia	60	10	40	10
Japan	1,010	290	400	320
Malaysia	780	260	480	40
Philippines	680	60	450	170
Singapore	140	40	90	10
Sri Lanka	920	370	400	140
Thailand	260	30	200	40
BDTC Hong Kong	1,050	340	390	330
Remainder of Asia	5,070	1,420	2,560	1,080
Asia	25,040	5,820	11,490	7,710
Australasia				
Australia	2,680	990	1,480	210
New Zealand	1,980	830	1,050	100
Australasia	4,660	1,830	2,530	300
British Overseas citizens	3,280	1,410	1,300	570
Other countries not elsewhere specified*	820	240	390	190
Stateless*	1,930	620	790	530
All Nationalities	53,460	15,620	25,110	12,740
Foreign	26,560	7,820	12,300	6,440
Commonwealth	26,910	7,800	12,810	6,300
Old Commonwealth	5,800	2,250	3,070	470
New Commonwealth and Pakistan	27,550	6,430	12,980	8,130
Foreign excluding Pakistan	20,120	6,930	9,060	4,130

*Includes refugees from south-east Asia.   † Negligible.

EMIGRANTS FROM THE UNITED KINGDOM (Thousands)

	Total			Professional			Manual and Clerical			Not gainfully employed†		
	Persons	Males	Females	Persons	Males	Females	Persons	Males	Females	Persons	Males	Females
1976	210	118	93	70	50	20	56	36	20	84	31	53
1977	209	117	91	66	49	17	62	39	23	81	30	51
1978	192	108	85	56	39	16	56	36	20	81	33	48
1979	189	106	82	58	43	15	52	30	22	79	34	45
1980	229	134	95	65	49	16	62	42	20	102	43	59
1981	233	133	100	67	50	17	60	38	22	105	44	61
1982	259	135	124	67	48	19	66	37	29	126	50	76

† Includes housewives, students, children and retired persons.

ENGLISH KINGS AND QUEENS A.D. 827 TO 1603

Name	DYNASTY	MARRIED	Access.	Died	Age	Rgnd. Yrs.
	Saxons and Danes					
EGBERT	King of Wessex and all England		827	839	—	12
ETHELWULF	Son of Egbert		839	858	—	19
ETHELBALD	Son of Ethelwulf		858	860	—	2
ETHELBERT	Son of Ethelwulf		858	866	—	8
ETHELRED	Son of Ethelwulf		866	871	—	5
ALFRED THE GREAT	Son of Ethelwulf	Ealhswith of Gaini	871	899	52	28
EDWARD THE ELDER	Son of Alfred the Great	1. Egwyn; 2. Elfled; 3. Eadgifu	899	925	55	26
ATHELSTAN	Eldest son of Edward the Elder (by 1)		925	940	45	15
EDMUND	Third son of Edward the Elder (by 3)	1. Elgifu; 2. Ethelfled	940	946	25	6
EDRED	Fourth son of Edward the Elder (by 3)		946	955	32	9
EDWY	Son of Edmund (by 1)	1. Ethelfled; 2. Elfthryth	955	959	18	3
EDGAR	Second son of Edmund (by 1)		959	975	32	17
EDWARD THE MARTYR	Son of Edgar (by 1)		975	978	17	4
ETHELRED II	Younger son of Edgar (by 2)	1. Elgifu; 2. Emma, dau. of Richard, Duke of Normandy	978	1016	48	37
EDMUND IRONSIDE	Eldest son of Ethelred II (by 1)	1. Elgifu of Deira; 2. Emma, widow of Ethelred II	1016	1016	27	0
CANUTE THE DANE	By conquest and election		1017	1035	40	18
HAROLD I	Son of Canute (by 1)		1035	1040	—	5
HARDICANUTE	Son of Canute (by 2)		1040	1042	24	2
EDWARD THE CONFESSOR	Son of Ethelred II (by 2)	Edith, dau. of Earl Godwin	1042	1066	62	24
HAROLD II	Son of Earl Godwin		1066	1066	44	0
	The House of Normandy					
WILLIAM I	Obtained the Crown by Conquest	Matilda, dau. of Baldwin, Count of Flanders	1066	1087	60	21
WILLIAM II	Third son of William I	(Died unmarried)	1087	1100	43	13
HENRY I	Youngest son of William I	1st Matilda, dau. of Malcolm Canmore, K. of Scotland; 2nd Adelicia, dau. of Godfrey, D. of Louvaine	1100	1135	67	35
STEPHEN	Third son of Stephen, Count of Blois, by Adela, fourth dau. of William I.	Matilda, dau. of Eustace, Count of Boulogne	1135	1154	50	19
	The House of Plantagenet					
HENRY II	Son of Geoffrey Plantagenet by Matilda, only dau. of Henry I; his grandmother, Matilda of Scotland, was a lineal descendant of Alfred and Egbert.	Eleanor, dau. of Guienne and divorced Queen of Louis VII of France	1154	1189	56	35
RICHARD I	Eldest surviving son of Henry II	Berengaria, dau. of Sancho VI, K. of Navarre	1189	1199	42	10
JOHN	Sixth and youngest son of Henry II	1st Avisa, dau. of E. of Gloucester, divorced upon grounds of consanguinity; 2nd Isabella dau. of Aymer, count of Angoulême	1199	1216	50	17
HENRY III	Elder son of John	Eleanor, dau. of Raymond, Count of Provence	1216	1272	65	56
EDWARD I	Eldest surviving son of Henry III	1st Eleanor, dau. of Ferdinand III, K. of Castile; 2nd Margaret, dau. of Philip III, the Hardy, K. of France	1272	1307	68	35
EDWARD II	Eldest surviving son of Edward I	Isabella, dau. of Philip IV, the Fair, K. of France	1307	1327	43	20

Name	DYNASTY	MARRIED	Access.	Died	Age	Rgnd.
						Yrs.
EDWARD III	Eldest son of Edward II	Philippa, dau. of William, Count of Holland and Hainault.	1327	1377	65	50
RICHARD II	Son of the Black Prince, eldest son of Edward III	1st Anne, dau. of Emp. Charles IV; 2nd Isabel, dau. of Charles VI of France.	1377	dep. 1399 (d. 1400)	34	22
	The House of Lancaster					
HENRY IV	Son of John of Gaunt, 4th son of Edward III	1st Mary de Bohun, dau. of the E. of Hereford; 2nd Joanna of Navarre, widow of John de Montfort, D. of Brittany.	1399	1413	47	13
HENRY V	Eldest surviving son of Henry IV	Katherine, dau. of Charles VI, K. of France	1413	1422	34	9
HENRY VI	Only son of Henry V (died 1471)	Margaret of Anjou, dau. of René, D. of Anjou	1422	dep. 1461	49	39
	The House of York					
EDWARD IV	Son of Richard, grandson of Edmund, fifth son of Edward III; and of Anne, great-grand-daughter of Lionel, third son of Edward III	Elizabeth Widvile (or Woodville), dau. of Sir Richard Widvile and widow of Sir John Grey of Groby.	1461	1483	41	22
EDWARD V	Eldest son of Edward IV	(Died unmarried)	1483	1483	13	75 days
RICHARD III	Younger brother of Edward IV	Anne, dau. of the E. of Warwick, and widow of Edward, Prince of Wales, s. of Henry VI	1483	1485	32	2
	The House of Tudor					
HENRY VII	Son of Edmund, eldest son of Owen Tudor, by Katherine, widow of Henry V; his mother, Margaret Beaufort, was great-grand-daughter of John of Gaunt	Elizabeth, dau. of Edward IV	1485	1509	53	24
HENRY VIII	Only surviving son of Henry VII	1st Katherine of Aragon, widow of his elder brother Arthur, (divorced); 2nd Anne, dau. of Sir Thomas Boleyn, (beheaded); 3rd Jane, dau. of Sir John Seymour, (died in childbirth of a son, aft. Edward VI); 4th Anne, sister of William, D. of Cleves, (divorced); 5th Catherine Howard, niece of the Duke of Norfolk, (beheaded); 6th Catherine, dau. of Sir Thomas Parr and widow of Edward Nevill, Lord Latimer.	1509	1547	56	38
EDWARD VI	Son of Henry VIII by Jane Seymour	(Died unmarried)	1547	1553	16	6
JANE	Grand-daughter of Mary, younger sister of Henry VIII, (beheaded Feb. 12, 1554).	Lord Guildford Dudley	1553	1554	17	14 days
MARY I	Daughter of Henry VIII by Katherine of Aragon	Philip II of Spain	1553	1558	43	5
ELIZABETH I	Daughter of Henry VIII by Anne Boleyn	(Died unmarried)	1558	1603	69	44

BRITISH KINGS AND QUEENS FROM 1603

Name	DYNASTY	MARRIED	Access.	Died	Age	Rgnd. Yrs.
JAMES I (VI OR SCOT.)	*The House of Stuart* Son of Mary, Queen of Scots, grand-daughter of James IV and Margaret, daughter of Henry VII.	Anne, dau. of Frederick II of Denmark	1603	1625	59	22
CHARLES I	Only surviving son of James I	Henrietta-Maria, dau. of Henry IV of France	1625	Beh. 1649	48	24
	Commonwealth declared May 19, 1649 *Oliver Cromwell, Lord Protector, 1653–8; Richard Cromwell, Lord Protector, 1658–9*					
CHARLES II	Eldest son of Charles I (restored 1660)	The Infanta Catharine of Portugal, dau. of John IV and sister of Alphonso VI	1649	1685	55	36
JAMES II (VII OR SCOT.)	Second son of Charles I (Interregnum, Dec. 11, 1688—Feb. 13, 1689)	1st Lady Anne Hyde, dau. of Edward, E. of Clarendon, who died before James ascended the throne; 2nd Mary Beatrice Eleanor d'Este, dau. of Alphonso, D. of Modena.	1685	Dep. 1688 Dec. 1701	68	3
WILLIAM III and MARY II	Son of William Prince of Orange and grandson of Charles I / Eldest Daughter of James II		1689	{ 1702 / 1694	51 / 33	13 / 6
ANNE	Second daughter of James II	Prince George of Denmark	1702	1714	49	12
GEORGE I	*The House of Hanover* Son of Elector of Hanover, by Sophia, daughter of Elizabeth, daughter of James I	Sophia, dau. of George William, D. of Celle.	1714	1727	67	13
GEORGE II	Only son of George I	Wilhelmina Caroline, dau. of John Frederick, Margrave of Brandenburg-Anspach.	1727	1760	77	33
GEORGE III	Grandson of George II	Charlotte Sophia, dau. of Charles Lewis Frederick, D. of Mecklenburg-Strelitz	1760	1820	81	59
GEORGE IV	Eldest son of George III (Regent from February 5, 1811)	Caroline, dau. of Charles William Ferdinand, D. of Brunswick-Wolfenbuttel.	1820	1830	67	10
WILLIAM IV	Third son of George III	Adelaide, dau. of George Frederick Charles, D. of Saxe-Meiningen.	1830	1837	71	7
VICTORIA	Daughter of Edward, 4th son of George III	Francis Albert Augustus Charles Emmanuel, D. of Saxe, Pr. of Saxe-Cobourg and Gotha.	1837	1901	81	63
EDWARD VII	*The House of Saxe-Coburg* Eldest son of Victoria	Princess Alexandra of Denmark	1901	1910	68	9
GEORGE V	*The House of Windsor* Surviving son of Edward VII	H.S.H. Princess Victoria Mary of Teck	1910	1936	70	25
EDWARD VIII	Eldest son of George V (abdicated 1936)	(Mrs. Wallis Warfield, June 3, 1937.)	1936	1972	77	325 days
GEORGE VI	Second son of George V	The Lady Elizabeth Angela Marguerite, dau. of the 14th Earl of Strathmore and Kinghorne (HER MAJESTY QUEEN ELIZABETH THE QUEEN MOTHER).	1936	1952	56	15
ELIZABETH II	Elder daughter of George VI	Philip, son of Prince Andrew of Greece (H.R.H. THE DUKE OF EDINBURGH).	1952	WHOM GOD PRESERVE.		

SCOTTISH KINGS AND QUEENS A.D. 1057 to 1603

SOVEREIGN	MARRIED	Access.	Died
MALCOLM III (CANMORE) ...	Son of Duncan I	1057	1093
	1st Ingibiorg, widow of Thorfinn, Earl of Orkney; 2nd Margaret, sister of Edgar the Atheling.		
DONALD BÁN	Brother of Malcolm Canmore	1093	—
DUNCAN II	Son of Malcolm Canmore, by first marriage ...	1094	1094
DONALD BÁN	(Restored)	1094	1097
EDGAR	Son of Malcolm Canmore, by second marriage ...	1097	1107
	Sybilla, natural daughter of Henry I of England ...		
ALEXANDER I	Son of Malcolm Canmore	1107	1124
	Matilda, daughter of Waltheof, Earl of Northumbria		
DAVID I	Son of Malcolm Canmore	1124	1153
	widow of Simon, Earl of Northampton		
MALCOLM IV ('THE MAIDEN')	Son of Henry, eldest son of David I	1153	1165
	Died unmarried		
WILLIAM I ('THE LION')	Brother of Malcolm the Maiden	1165	1214
	Ermengarde, daughter of Richard, Viscount of Beaumont.		
ALEXANDER II	Son of William the Lion	1214	1249
	1st Joanna, daughter of King John; 2nd Mary, daughter of Ingelram de Coucy (*Picardy*)		
ALEXANDER III	Son of Alexander II, by second marriage ...	1249	1286
	1st Margaret, daughter of Henry III of England; 2nd Joleta, daughter of the Count de Dreux		
MARGARET, MAID OF NORWAY	Daughter of Eric II of Norway, grand-daughter of Alexander III.	1286	1290
	Died unmarried		
JOHN BALIOL		1292	1296
ROBERT I (BRUCE)	Grandson of eldest daughter of David, Earl of Huntingdon, brother of William the Lion	1306	1329
	1st Isabella, daughter of Donald, Earl of Mar; 2nd Elizabeth de Burgh, sister of Earl of Ulster.		
DAVID II	Great-grandson of 2nd daughter of David, Earl of Huntingdon, brother of William the Lion	1329	1371
	1st Joanna, daughter of Edward II of England; 2nd Margaret, widow of Sir John Logie (divorced, 1369).		
ROBERT II (STEWART)	Son of Robert I, by second marriage	1371	1390
	1st Elizabeth, dau. of Sir Robert. Mure (or More) of Rowallan; 2nd Euphemia, dau., of Hugh, Earl of Ross,		
ROBERT III	Son of Marjorie, daughter of Robert I by first marriage, and Walter the Steward.	1390	1406
	widow of John, Earl of Moray.		
	Annabella, daughter of Sir John Drummond of Stobhall, niece of Margaret Logie.		
JAMES I	(John, Earl of Carrick) son of Robert II	1406	1437
	Jane Beaufort, daughter of John, Earl of Somerset, 4th son of John of Gaunt and grandson of Edward III of England.		
JAMES II	Son of Robert III	1437	1460
	Mary, daughter of Arnold, Duke of Gueldres		
JAMES III	Son of James I	1460	1488
	Margaret, daughter of Christian I of Denmark, Norway and Sweden.		
JAMES IV	Eldest son of James II	1488	1513
	Margaret Tudor, daughter of Henry VII		
JAMES V	Eldest son of James III	1513	1542
	1st Madeleine, daughter of Francis I of France; 2nd Mary of Lorraine, daughter of Duc de Guise, widow of Duc de Longueville.		
MARY	Daughter of James V, by second marriage	1542	1587
	1st Francis, Dauphin of France; 2nd Henry, Lord Darnley; 3rd James, Earl of Bothwell		
JAMES VI (Ascended the Throne of England 1603)	Son of Mary, by second marriage	1567	1625
	Anne, daughter of Frederick II of Denmark		

WELSH SOVEREIGNS AND PRINCES

WALES was ruled by Sovereign Princes from the "earliest times" until the death of Llywelyn in 1282. The first English Prince of Wales was the son of Edward I, and was born in Caernarvon town on April 25, 1284. According to a discredited legend, he was presented to the Welsh chieftains as their Prince, in fulfilment of a promise that they should have a Prince who "could not speak a word of English" and should be native born. This son, who afterwards became Edward II, was created "Prince of Wales and Earl of Chester" at the famous Lincoln Parliament on February 7, 1301. The title Prince of Wales is borne after individual conferment and is not inherited at birth; it was conferred on Prince Charles by Her Majesty the Queen on July 26, 1958. He was invested at Caernarvon on July 1, 1969.

Independent Princes, A.D. 844 to 1282

Rhodri the Great	844–878
Anarawd, son of Rhodri	878–916
Hywel Dda, the Good	916–950
Iago ab Idwal (or Ieuaf)	950–979
Hywel ab Ieuaf, the Bad	979–985
Cadwallon, his brother	985–986
Maredudd ab Owain ap Hywel Dda	986–999
Cynan ap Hywel ab Ieuaf	999–1008
Llywelyn ap Seisyll	1018–1023
Iago ab Idwal ap Meurig	1023–1039
Gruffydd ap Llywelyn ap Seisyll	1039–1063
Bleddyn ap Cynfyn	1063–1075
Trahaern ap Caradog	1075–1081
Gruffydd ap Cynan ab Iago	1081–1137
Owain Gwynedd	1137–1170
Dafydd ab Owain Gwynedd	1170–1194
Llywelyn Fawr, the Great	1194–1240
Dafydd ap Llywelyn	1240–1246
Llywelyn ap Gruffydd ap Llywelyn	1246–1282

English Princes, since A.D. 1301

Edward, b. 1284 (Edwd. II), cr. Pr. of Wales	1301
Edward the Black Prince, s. of Edward III	1343
Richard (Richard II), s. of the Black Prince	1377
Henry of Monmouth (Henry V)	1399
Edward of Westminster, son of Henry VI	1454
Edward of Westminster (Edward V)	1472
Edward, son of Richard III (d. 1484)	1483
Arthur Tudor, son of Henry VII	1489
Henry Tudor (Hen. VIII), s. of Henry VII	1503
Henry Stuart, son of James I (d. 1612)	1610
Charles Stuart (Charles I), s. of James I	1616
Charles (Charles II), son of Charles I	1630
James Francis Edward, "The Old Pretender" (d. 1766)	1688
George Augustus (Geo. II), s. of George I	1714
Frederick Lewis, s. of George II (d. 1751)	1727
George William Frederick (George III)	1751
George Augustus Frederick (George IV)	1762
Albert Edward (Edward VII)	1841
George (George V)	1901
Edward (Edward VIII)	1910
Charles Philip Arthur George	1958

THE FAMILY OF QUEEN VICTORIA

QUEEN VICTORIA *was born* May 24, 1819; *succeeded* to the Throne June 20, 1837; *married* Feb. 10, 1840 Albert, PRINCE CONSORT (*born* Aug. 26, 1819, *died* Dec. 14, 1861); *died* Jan. 22, 1901. Her Majesty had issue:—

1. H.R.H. Princess Victoria (*Princess Royal*) (1840–1901), married, 1858, Frederick, German Emperor; had issue:—

(1) H.I.M. William II (1859–1941), *German Emperor* 1888–1918, married Princess Augusta Victoria of Schleswig-Holstein-Sonderburg-Augustenburg (1858–1921), and secondly, Princess Hermine of Reuss (1887–1947). Had issue:—

(a) Prince William (1882–1951), (*Crown Prince* 1888–1918), married Duchess Cecilia of Mecklenburg-Schwerin (died 1954). (The Crown Prince's children:—Prince Wilhelm (1906–1940); Prince Louis Ferdinand, born 1907, married (1938) Grand Duchess Kira (died 1967), daughter of Grand Duke Cyril of Russia (and has issue four sons and two daughters); Prince Hubertus (1909–1950); Prince Frederick George (1911–1966); Princess Alexandrine Irene, born 1915; Princess Cecilia (1917–1975).

(b) Prince Eitel Frederick (1883–1942), married Duchess Sophie of Oldenburg (marriage dissolved 1926).

(c) Prince Adalbert (1884–1948), married Duchess Adelaide of Saxe-Meiningen. (Prince Adalbert's children:—Princess Victoria Marina, born 1917; Prince William Victor, born 1919.)

(d) Prince Augustus William (1887–1949), married Princess Alexandra of Schleswig-Glucksburg (marriage dissolved 1920). (Prince Augustus's son is Prince Alexander, born 1912.)

(e) Prince Oscar (1888–1958), married Countess von Ruppin. (Prince Oscar's children:—Prince Oscar (1915–1939); Prince Burchard, born 1917; Princess Herzeleide, born 1918; Prince William, born 1922.)

(f) Prince Joachim (1890–1920), married Princess Marie of Anhalt.

(g) Princess Victoria (1892–1980), married (1913)

the Duke of Brunswick. (Princess Victoria's children:—Prince Ernest, born 1914, married Princess Ortrud von Glucksburg, 1951; Prince George, born 1915; Princess Frederica (1917–1981), married Paul I, King of the Hellenes (*see* below); Prince Christian Oskar, born 1919; Prince Welf Heinrich born 1923, married Princess Alexandra of Ysemburg, 1960).

(2) Princess Charlotte (1860–1919), married (1878) the Duke of Saxe-Meiningen. (Princess Charlotte's daughter, Princess Feodora (1879–1945), married (1898) the Prince Henry XXX. of Reuss.

(3) Prince Henry (1862–1929), married (1888) Princess Irene of Hesse (issue, Prince Waldemar (1889–1945); Prince Sigismund (1896–1978)).

(4) Princess Victoria (1866–1929), married firstly (1890) Prince Adolphus of Schaumburg-Lippe, secondly (1927) Alexander Zubkov.

(5) Prince Waldemar (1868–1879).

(6) Princess Sophia (1870–1932), married (1889) Constantine, *King of the Hellenes*, having issue:—

(a) George II. (1890–1947), *King of the Hellenes* 1922–24 and 1935–47, married Princess Elisabeth of Romania (marriage dissolved 1935).

(b) Alexander (1893–1920), *King of the Hellenes* 1917–1920, married (1919) Aspasia Manos; had issue Princess Alexandra (born 1921), who married, March 20, 1944, King Petar II. of Yugoslavia.

(c) Princess Helena (1896–1982), married (1921) King Carol of Romania, (marriage dissolved 1928) having issue, King Michael, G.C.V.O., born 1921, married (1948) Princess Anne of Bourbon Parma, and has issue, Princess Marguerite, born 1949, Princess Helene, born 1950, and Princess Irina, born 1953.

(d) Paul (1901–1964), *King of the Hellenes* 1947–1964, married 1938, Princess Frederica of Brunswick (*see* above); had issue Constantine (*Constantine XIII*.), born 1940, married 1964, H.R.H. Princess

Anne-Marie of Denmark, and has issue; Sophia, born 1938, married (1962) Don Juan Carlos, Prince of Spain (Juan Carlos I), and has issue; and Irene, born 1942.

(e) Princess Eirene (1904–1974), married (1939) the Duke of Aosta; had issue.

(f) Princess Catherine, born 1913, married (1947) Major R. C. A. Brandram and has issue.

(7) Princess Margarete (1872–1954), married Prince Frederick Charles of Hesse (issue Prince Frederick William (1893–1916); Prince Maximilian (1894–1914); Prince Philipp (1896–1980), married (1925) Princess Mafalda, daughter of King Victor Emmanuel III. of Italy (and has issue, Prince Maurice, born 1926, and Prince Henry, born 1927); Prince Wolfgang, born 1896; Prince Richard, born 1901.

2. H.M. KING EDWARD VII (*see* p. 216).

3. H.R.H. Princess Alice (1843–1878), married Prince Louis (afterwards reigning Grand Duke) of Hesse. Issue:—

(i) Victoria Alberta (1863–1950), married Admiral of the Fleet the Marquess of Milford Haven, having issue:—

(a) Alice (*H.R.H. Princess Andrew of Greece*) (1885–1969), married Prince Andrew of Greece; having issue (*see* p. 216).

(b) Lady Louise Mountbatten (*Queen of Sweden*) (1889–1965), married Nov. 3, 1923, H.R.H. The Crown Prince of Sweden, later King Gustaf VI. Adolf (died 1973).

(c) George, Marquess of Milford Haven, G.C.V.O., (1892–1938), Capt. R.N., married (1916) Countess Nadejda (died 1963), daughter of Grand Duke Michael of Russia; had issue:—Lady Elizabeth, born 1917; David Michael, Marquess of Milford Haven, O.B.E., D.S.O., Lieutenant, R.N. (ret.) (1919–1970), having issue, George Ivar Louis, *Marquess of Milford Haven, b.* 1961; Lord Ivar Mountbatten, *b.* 1963.

(d) Louis, Admiral of the Fleet Earl Mountbatten of Burma, K.G., P.C., G.C.B., O.M., G.C.S.I., G.C.I.E., G.C.V.O., D.S.O. (1900–1979), married 1922, Edwina Cynthia Annette (died 1960), daughter of Lord Mount Temple; having issue two daughters, Patricia (Countess Mountbatten of Burma), born 1924 and the Lady Pamela Hicks, born 1929.

(ii) Elizabeth Fedorovna (1864–1918), (*Grand Duchess Sergius of Russia*).

(iii) Irene (1866–1953), (*Princess Henry of Prussia*), married Prince Henry of Prussia (*see* p. 214).

(iv) Ernest Ludwig, Grand Duke of Hesse (1868–1937), having married (1905) Princess Eleonore of Solms-Hohensolmslich, with issue (a) George, Grand Duke of Hesse, born 1906, married Princess Cecilie of Greece and Denmark (*see* p. 216); *accidentally killed* (with mother, wife and two sons) Nov. 16, 1937; (b) Ludwig, Grand Duke of Hesse (1908–1968), married (Nov. 17, 1937) Margaret, daughter of 1st Lord Geddes.

(v) Frederick William (1870–1873).

(vi) Alix (*Tsaritsa of Russia*) (1872–1918), married (1894) Nicholas II. (*Tsar of All the Russias*), assassinated July 16, 1918, with the Tsar and their issue (Grand Duchess Olga; Grand Duchess Tatiana; Grand Duchess Marie; Grand Duchess Anastasia, and the Tsarevitch).

(vii) Mary (1874–1878).

4. Admiral of the Fleet H.R.H. Prince Alfred, *Duke of Edinburgh* (1844–1900), married 1874, Marie Alexandrovna (died 1920), only daughter of Alexander II, Emperor of Russia; succeeded as *Duke of Saxe-Coburg and Gotha* Aug. 22, 1893; had issue:—

(1) Alfred (*Prince of Saxe-Coburg*) (1874–1899).

(2) Marie (*Queen of Romania*) (1875–1938), married (1893), King Ferdinand of Romania; having issue:—

(a) King Carol II. of Romania (1893–1953), married (1921) Princess Helena of Greece (*see* p. 214).

(b) Elizabeth (*Queen of the Hellenes*) (1894–1956), married (1921) King George II of the Hellenes.

(c) Marie (1900–1961), married (1922) King Alexander of Yugoslavia, having issue:—Petar, King of Yugoslavia (1923–1970), married (1944) Princess Alexandra of Greece, having issue, Prince Alexander, born 1945; Prince Tomislav, born 1928, married (1957) Princess Margarita of Baden (*see* p. 216) and has issue, Prince Nicholas, born 1958; Prince Andrej, born 1929, married 1956, Princess Christina of Hesse).

(d) Prince Nicolas, born 1903.

(e) Princess Ileana, born 1909; married (1), Archduke Anton of Austria (having issue:— Stephen, born 1932); and, (2), Dr. Stefan Issarescu.

(f) Prince Mircea (1913–1916).

(3) Victoria (1876–1936), married (1894) Grand Duke of Hesse and (1905) the Grand Duke Cyril of Russia; having issue:—

(a) Marie (1907–1951), married (1925) Prince Friedrich Carl of Leiningen.

(b) Kira Cyrillovna (1909–1967), married (1938) Prince Ludwig of Germany.

(c) Vladimir Cyrillovitch, born 1917, married (1948) Princess Leonida Bagration-Moukhransky, and has issue, a daughter.

(4) Alexandra (1878–1942), married (1896) Prince of Hohenlohe Langenburg; had issue:—

(a) Gottfried (1897–1960).

(b) Maria (*Princess Friedrich of Holstein-Glucksburg*) (1899–1967).

(c) Princess Alexandra (1901–1963).

(d) Princess Irma, born 1902.

(5) Princess Beatrice (1884–1966), married (1909) Infante Alfonso Maria of Orleans (died 1975), and had issue.

5. H.R.H. Princess Helena Augusta Victoria (1846–1923), married 1866, General H.R.H. *Prince Christian of Schleswig-Holstein* (died 1917). Issue:—

(i) H.H. Prince Christian Victor (1867–1900).

(ii) H.H. Prince Albert (1869–1931).

(iii) H.H. Princess Helena Victoria (1870–1948).

(iv) H.H. Princess Marie Louise (1872–1956).

(v) H.H. Prince Harold (May 12–20, 1876).

6. H.R.H. Princess Louise (1848–1939), married 1871, the Marquess of Lorne, afterwards the 9th Duke of Argyll; without issue.

7. Field Marshal H.R.H. Prince Arthur, *Duke of Connaught* (1850–1942), married 1879, H.R.H. Princess Louisa of Prussia (died 1917). Issue:—

(i) H.R.H. Princess Margaret (1882–1920), married H.R.H. the Crown Prince of Sweden, later KING GUSTAV VI. ADOLF (died 1973) having issue:—

(a) Duke of Westerbotten (1906–1947), married (1932) Princess Sybil of Saxe-Coburg-Gotha (died 1972), having issue one son, now King Carl XVI Gustaf of Sweden, and 4 daughters.

(b) Duke of Upland (Count Sigvard Bernadotte), born 1907.

(c) Princess Ingrid (*Queen Mother of Denmark*), born 1910, married (1935) King Frederick IX. of Denmark (died 1972) and has issue 3 daughters.

(d) Duke of Halland, born 1912.

(e) Duke of Dalecarlia, born 1916.

(ii) Major-Gen. H.R.H. Prince Arthur (1883–1938), married 1913, H.H. the Duchess of Fife; had issue (see below).

(iii) H.R.H. Princess Patricia (*Lady Patricia Ramsay*) (1886–1974), married 1919, Adm. Hon. Sir Alexander Ramsay (died 1972), having issue Alexander Arthur Alfonso David, born 1919.

8. H.R.H. Prince Leopold, *Duke of Albany* (1853–1884), married Princess Helena of Waldeck (died 1922). Issue:—

(i) H.R.H. Princess Alice (*Countess of Athlone*)

(1883–1981), married 1904, Maj.-Gen. the Earl of Athlone (died 1957), having issue—

(*a*) Lady May Helen Emma, born 1906, married (1931) Sir Henry Abel-Smith, K.C.M.G., K.C.V.O., D.S.O., and has issue a son and 2 daughters.

(*b*) *Viscount Trematon* (1907–1928).

(ii) Charles Edward (1884–1954), *Duke of Saxe-Coburg-Gotha* (1900–1918), married (1905) Princess Victoria of Schleswig-Holstein; surviving issue 2 sons and 2 daughters.

9. **H.R.H. Princess Beatrice** (1857–1944), married

1885, H.R.H. Prince Henry of Battenberg (1858–1896); having issue:— (i) Alexander, *Marquess of Carisbrooke* (1886–1960), married Lady Irene Denison (died 1956); having issue a daughter, Lady Iris Mountbatten (1920–1982).

(ii) Victoria Eugénie (1887–1969), married 1906, His Majesty Alfonso XIII. (*King of Spain* 1886–1931; born 1886, died 1941), having issue.

(iii) Major Lord Leopold Mountbatten (1889–1922).

(iv) Maurice (1891–1914), died of wounds received in action.

THE FAMILY OF KING EDWARD VII

KING EDWARD VII, eldest son of Queen Victoria, *born* Nov. 9, 1841; *married* March 10, 1863, Her Royal Highness Princess Alexandra, eldest daughter of King Christian IX. of Denmark; *succeeded* to the Throne Jan. 22, 1901; *died* May 6, 1910.

1. H.R.H. PRINCE ALBERT VICTOR, *Duke of Clarence and Avondale and Earl of Athlone* (1864–1892).

2. H.M. KING GEORGE V (*see* below). Assumed by Royal Proclamation (June 17, 1917) for his House and Family as well as for all descendants in the male line of Queen Victoria who are subjects of these Realms, the name of WINDSOR; (*see* p. 217).

3. H.R.H. LOUISE, *Princess Royal* (1867–1931), married July 27, 1889, 1st *Duke of Fife* (died 1912). Issue:—

(i) H.H. Princess Alexandra, Duchess of Fife (*H.R.H. Princess Arthur of Connaught*) (1891–1959), married 1913, H.R.H. Prince Arthur. Issue:—

Alastair Arthur, Duke of Connaught (1914–1943).

(ii) H.H. Princess Maud (1893–1945), married 1923, 11th Earl of Southesk. Issue:—

The Duke of Fife, born 1929; married (1956) Hon. Caroline Dewar (marriage dissolved, 1966) and has issue.

4. H.R.H. PRINCESS VICTORIA (1868–1935).

5. H.R.H. PRINCESS MAUD (1869–1938), married 1896, Haakon VII., King of Norway (died 1957). Issue:—

H.M. Olav V., K.G., K.T., G.C.B., G.C.V.O., KING OF NORWAY, born 1903, *married* 1929, H.R.H. Princess Marthe of Sweden (died 1954). Issue:—

(*a*) H.R.H. Princess Ragnhild, born 1930.

(*b*) H.R.H. Princess Astrid, born 1932.

(*c*) H.R.H. Harald, Crown Prince of Norway, G.C.V.O., born 1937.

6. H.R.H. PRINCE ALEXANDER JOHN CHARLES ALBERT (April 6–7, 1871).

THE FAMILY OF PRINCE ANDREW OF GREECE

Prince Andrew of Greece (1882–1944), *married* Princess Alice of Battenberg (*H.R.H. Princess Andrew of Greece*), who *died* 1969; had issue:—

(1) Princess Margarita (1905–1981), *married* Prince Gottfried of Hohenlohe-Langenburg (*see* p. 215); issue, Prince Kraft, *born* 1935, Princess Beatrix, *born* 1936, Prince George, *born* 1938; Prince Ruprecht and Prince Albrecht, *born* 1944.

(2) Princess Theodora (1906–1969), *married* Prince Berthold of Baden (*died* 1963); issue, Princess Margarita, *born* 1932 (married, 1957, Prince Tomislav of Yugoslavia (see p. 215)), Prince Max, *born* 1933, Prince Louis, *born* 1937.

(3) Princess Cecilie, *born* 1911, *married* George, Grand Duke of Hesse, accidentally killed with husband and two sons, 1937 (*see* p. 215).

(4) Princess Sophie, born 1914, *married* (i) Prince Christopher of Hesse (died, 1944), having issue, Princess Christina, *born* 1933, Princess Dorothea, *born* 1934, Prince Charles, *born* 1937, Prince Rainer, *born* 1939, Princess Clarissa, *born* 1944); *married* (ii) Prince George of Hanover, and has further issue.

(5) Prince Philip (*H.R.H. the Prince Philip, Duke of Edinburgh*), *born* June 10, 1921 (*see* p. 218).

THE FAMILY OF KING GEORGE V

KING GEORGE V., second son of King Edward VII., *born* June 3, 1865; *married* July 6, 1893, Her Serene Highness Princess Victoria Mary Augusta Louise Olga Pauline Claudine Agnes (Queen Mary), *succeeded* to the throne May 6, 1910; *died* Jan. 20, 1936. Queen Mary died March 24, 1953. Issue:—

H.R.H. THE DUKE OF WINDSOR (EDWARD Albert Christian George Andrew Patrick David), *born* June 23, 1894, *succeeded* to the Throne as KING EDWARD VIII., Jan. 20, 1936; *abdicated* Dec. 11, 1936; *married* June 3, 1937, Mrs. Wallis Warfield (The Duchess of Windsor), *died* May 28, 1972.

H.M. KING GEORGE VI. (Albert Frederick Arthur George) *born* at York Cottage, Sandringham, Dec. 14, 1895; *married* April 26, 1923, to Lady Elizabeth Angela Marguerite (HER MAJESTY QUEEN ELIZABETH THE QUEEN MOTHER), daughter of the 14th Earl of Strathmore and Kinghorne, *succeeded* to the throne Dec. 11, 1936; *died* Feb. 6, 1952, having had issue (*see* pp. 218 and 219).

H.R.H. THE PRINCESS ROYAL (Victoria Alexandra Alice MARY), *born* April 25, 1897, *married* Feb. 28, 1922, the 6th Earl of Harewood (*born* Sept. 9, 1882; *died* May 24, 1947), *died* at Harewood House, Yorks., March 28, 1965, leaving issue:—

(1) George Henry Hubert Lascelles, *7th Earl of Harewood, born* Feb. 7, 1923; *married*, firstly, Sept. 29, 1949, Maria Donata (Marion), daughter of the late Erwin Stein (marriage dissolved 1967), and has issue,

(i) David Henry George, Viscount Lascelles, *born* Oct. 21, 1950; (ii) James Edward, *born* Oct. 5, 1953,

married, April 4, 1973, Fredericka Duhrrson; (iii) Robert Jeremy Hugh, *born* Feb. 14, 1955; secondly, July 31, 1967, Mrs. Patricia Elizabeth Tuckwell, and has issue, Mark Hubert, *born* July 5, 1964.
  (2) Gerald David Lascelles, *born* Aug. 21, 1924, *married* July 15, 1952, Miss Angela Dowding (marriage dissolved, 1978), and has issue, Henry Ulick, *born* May 19, 1953; secondly, Nov. 17, 1978, Mrs. Elizabeth Evelyn Colvin.

H.R.H. THE DUKE OF GLOUCESTER (Henry William Frederick Albert), Duke of Gloucester, Earl of Ulster and Baron Culloden, *born* March 31, 1900, *married* Nov. 6, 1935, Lady Alice Montagu-Douglas-Scott, daughter of the 7th Duke of Buccleuch (H.R.H. Princess Alice, Duchess of Gloucester, C.I., G.C.B., G.C.V.O., G.B.E., Grand Cordon of Al Kamal, Colonel-in-Chief of the Royal Hussars (Prince of Wales's Own), the King's Own Scottish Borderers, the Royal Corps of Transport, Deputy Colonel-in-Chief, Royal Anglian Regt., Air Chief Commandant W.R.A.F., *born* Dec. 25, 1901); *died* June 10, 1974, leaving issue:
  (1) H.R.H. Prince William Henry Andrew Frederick, *born* Dec. 18, 1941; *accidentally killed* Aug. 28, 1972
  (2) H.R.H. Prince Richard Alexander Walter George, *Duke of Gloucester*, G.C.V.O., Colonel-in-Chief, Gloucestershire Regiment, Grand Prior of the Order of St. John of Jerusalem, *born* Aug. 26, 1944, *married* July 8, 1972, Brigitte von Deurs and has issue, (i) Alexander Patrick George Richard, Earl of Ulster, *born* Oct. 24, 1974, (ii) Davina Elizabeth Alice Benedikte (Lady Davina Windsor), *born* Nov. 19, 1977 and (iii) Rose Victoria Brigitte Louise (Lady Rose Windsor), *born* March 1, 1980.

H.R.H. THE DUKE OF KENT (George Edward Alexander Edmund), Duke of Kent, Earl of St. Andrews and Baron Downpatrick, *born* Dec. 20, 1902, *married* Nov. 29, 1934, H.R.H. Princess Marina of Greece and Denmark (*born* Nov. 30, O.S., 1906; *died* Aug. 27, 1968). *Killed on Active Service,* Aug. 25, 1942 leaving issue:—
  (1) H.R.H. Prince EDWARD George Nicholas Paul Patrick, *Duke of Kent*, G.C.M.G., G.C.V.O., *born* Oct. 9, 1935. Lt.-Col. The Royal Scots Dragoon Guards, Personal A.D.C. to the Queen, Colonel, Scots Guards, Colonel-in-Chief, Royal Regiment of Fusiliers, *married* June 8, 1961, Katharine Lucy Mary, G.C.V.O., Controller Commandant, Women's Royal Army Corps, Hon. Major-General, Colonel-in-Chief Army Catering Corps, daughter of Sir William Worsley, Bt., and has issue, (i) George Philip Nicholas, Earl of St. Andrews, *born* June 26, 1962; (ii) Helen Marina Lucy (Lady Helen Windsor), *born* April 28, 1964; (iii) Nicholas Charles Edward Jonathan (Lord Nicholas Windsor), *born* July 25, 1970. *Residences*—Anmer Hall, Norfolk; York House, St. James's Palace, S.W.1.
  (2) H.R.H. Princess ALEXANDRA Helen Elizabeth Olga Christabel, G.C.V.O., *born* Dec. 25, 1936, Colonel-in-Chief, 17th/21st Lancers, The King's Own Border Regiment, Deputy Colonel-in-Chief, The Light Infantry, Hon. Colonel North Irish Horse, Air Chief Commandant, Princess Mary's Royal Air Force Nursing Service, *married* April 24, 1963, Hon. Angus Ogilvy, son of the 12th Earl of Airlie, *born* Sept. 14, 1928, and has issue, (i) James Robert Bruce, *born* Feb. 29, 1964 and (ii) Marina Victoria Alexandra, *born* July 31, 1966. *Residence of Princess Alexandra*—22 Friary Court, St. James's Palace, S.W.1.
  (3) H.R.H. Prince MICHAEL George Charles Franklin, *born* July 4, 1942, Major, Royal Hussars, *married* June 30, 1978, Baroness Marie-Christine von Reibnitz, and has issue, (i) Frederick Michael George David Louis (Lord Frederick Windsor), *born* April 6, 1979 and (ii) Gabriella Marina Alexandra Ophelia (Lady Ella), born April 23, 1981.

H.R.H. PRINCE JOHN, *born* July 12, 1905; *died* Jan. 18, 1919.

Order of Succession to the Throne
(as at Oct. 1984)

1. H.R.H. Prince of Wales; 2. H.R.H. Prince William of Wales; 3. H.R.H. Prince Henry of Wales; 4. H.R.H. Prince Andrew; 5. H.R.H. Prince Edward; 6. H.R.H. Princess Anne, Mrs Mark Phillips; 7. Master Peter Phillips; 8. Miss Zara Phillips; 9. H.R.H. Princess Margaret, Countess of Snowden; 10. Viscount Linley; 11. Lady Sarah Armstrong-Jones; 12. H.R.H. Duke of Gloucester; 13. Earl of Ulster; 14. Lady Davina Windsor; 15. Lady Rose Windsor; 16. H.R.H. Duke of Kent; 17. Earl of St. Andrews; 18. Lord Nicholas Windsor; 19. Lady Helen Windsor; 20. Lord Frederick Windsor; 21. Lady Gabriella Windsor; 22. H.R.H. Princess Alexandra, Hon. Mrs Angus Ogilvy; 23. Mr James Ogilvy; 24. Miss Marina Ogilvy.

THE HOUSE OF WINDSOR

Her Most Excellent Majesty ELIZABETH THE SECOND (Elizabeth Alexandra Mary of Windsor) by the Grace of God, of the United Kingdom of Great Britain and Northern Ireland and of Her other Realms and Territories Queen, Head of the Commonwealth, Defender of the Faith, Sovereign of the British Orders of Knighthood and Sovereign Head of the Order of St. John, Lord High Admiral of the United Kingdom, Colonel-in-Chief of The Life Guards, The Blues and Royals (Royal Horse Guards and 1st Dragoons), The Royal Scots Dragoon Guards (Carabiniers and Greys), 16th/5th The Queen's Royal Lancers, Royal Tank Regiment, Corps of Royal Engineers, Grenadier Guards, Coldstream Guards, Scots Guards, Irish Guards, Welsh Guards, The Royal Welch Fusiliers, The Queen's Lancashire Regiment, The Argyll and Sutherland Highlanders (Princess Louise's), The Royal Green Jackets, Royal Army Ordnance Corps, Corps of Royal Military Police, The Queen's Own Mercian Yeomanry, The Duke of Lancaster's Own Yeomanry, Canadian Forces Military Engineers Branch, The King's Own Calgary Regiment, Royal 22e Regiment, Governor-General's Foot Guards, The Canadian Grenadier Guards, Le Régiment de la Chaudière, 2nd Bn. Royal New Brunswick Regt. (North Shore), The 48th Highlanders of Canada, The Argyll and Sutherland Highlanders of Canada (Princess Louise's), The Calgary Highlanders, Royal Australian Engineers, Royal Australian Infantry Corps, Royal Australian Army Ordnance Corps, Royal Australian Army Nursing Corps, The Corps of Royal New Zealand Engineers, Royal New Zealand Infantry Regiment, Royal New Zealand Army Ordnance Corps, Royal Malta Artillery, Malawi Rifles, Captain-General of Royal Regiment of Artillery, The Honourable Artillery Company, Combined Cadet Force, Royal Canadian Artillery, Royal Regiment of Australian Artillery, Royal Regiment of New Zealand Artillery, Royal New Zealand Armoured Corps, Air-Commodore-in-Chief, R. Aux.A.F., R.A.F.

Regiment, Royal Observer Corps, Royal Canadian Air Force Auxiliary, Australian Citizen Air Force, Commandant-in-Chief, Royal Air Force College, Cranwell, Hon. Air Commodore, R.A.F. Marham, Hon. Commissioner, Royal Canadian Mounted Police, Master of the Merchant Navy and Fishing Fleets, Head of the Civil Defence Corps.

Elder daughter of His late Majesty King George VI and of Her Majesty Queen Elizabeth the Queen Mother; *born* at 17 Bruton Street, London, W.1, April 21, 1926, *succec led* to the throne February 6, 1952, *crowned* June 2, 1953; having *married*, November 20, 1947, in Westminster Abbey, Philip, Duke of Edinburgh, Earl of Merioneth and Baron Greenwich (H.R.H. The Prince Philip, Duke of Edinburgh), K.G., P.C., K.T., O.M., G.B.E., Admiral of the Fleet, Field Marshal, Marshal of the Royal Air Force, Admiral of the Fleet, Royal Australian Navy, Field Marshal, Australian Military Forces, Marshal of the Royal Australian Air Force, Admiral of the Fleet, Royal New Zealand Navy, Field Marshal New Zealand Army, Marshal of the Royal New Zealand Air Force, Captain General, Royal Marines, Colonel-in-Chief, The Queen's Royal Irish Hussars, The Duke of Edinburgh's Royal Regiment (Berkshire and Wiltshire), The Queen's Own Highlanders (Seaforth and Camerons), Corps of Royal Electrical and Mechanical Engineers, Intelligence Corps, Army Cadet Force, The Royal Canadian Regiment, The Royal Hamilton Light Infantry (Wentworth Regt.), The Cameron Highlanders of Ottawa, The Queen's Own Cameron Highlanders of Canada, The Seaforth Highlanders of Canada, The Royal Canadian Army Cadets, The Royal Australian Electrical and Mechanical Engineers, The Australian Cadet Corps, Corps of Royal New Zealand Electrical and Mechanical Engineers, Colonel of Grenadier Guards, Hon. Colonel, Edinburgh and Heriot-Watt Universities Officers' Training Corps, The Trinidad and Tobago Regiment, Admiral, Royal Canadian Sea Cadets, Air Commodore-in-Chief, Royal New Zealand Air Force, Air Training Corps, Royal Canadian Air Cadets, Colonel-in-Chief, Air Reserve Group of Air Command (Canada), Hon. Air Commodore, R.A.F. Kinloss, Master of the Corporation of Trinity House, Ranger of Windsor Park. *See* p. 216.

CHILDREN OF HER MAJESTY

H.R.H. THE PRINCE OF WALES (CHARLES Philip Arthur George), K.G., K.T., G.C.B, A.D.C., Prince of Wales and Earl of Chester, Duke of Cornwall and Duke of Rothesay, Earl of Carrick and Baron Renfrew, Lord of the Isles and Great Steward of Scotland, Personal A.D.C. to the Queen, Great Master of the Order of the Bath, Commander Royal Navy, Wing Commander Royal Air Force, Colonel-in-Chief The Cheshire Regiment, The Royal Regiment of Wales (24th/41st Foot), The Gordon Highlanders, The Parachute Regiment, 2nd King Edward VII's Own Gurkha Rifles (The Sirmoor Rifles), Lord Strathcona's Horse (Royal Canadians), Royal Regiment of Canada, Royal Winnipeg Rifles, Royal Australian Armoured Corps, The Royal Pacific Islands Regiment, Air Reserve Group of Air Command (Canada), Air Commodore-in-Chief Royal New Zealand Air Force, Colonel Welsh Guards, Hon. Air Commodore, R.A.F. Brawdy, *born* November 14, 1948, *married* July 29, 1981, Lady Diana Frances Spencer (H.R.H. The Princess of Wales, *born* July 1, 1961), youngest daughter of the 8th Earl Spencer and the Hon. Mrs. Shand Kydd; and has issue, (i) William Arthur Philip Louis (H.R.H. Prince William of Wales), *born* June 21, 1982, and (ii) Henry Charles Albert David (H.R.H. Prince Henry of Wales), *born* Sept. 15, 1984.

H.R.H. PRINCESS ANNE ELIZABETH ALICE LOUISE, G.C.V.O. Chief Commandant Women's Royal Naval Service, Colonel-in-Chief 14th/20th King's Hussars, Royal Corps of Signals, The Royal Scots (The Royal Regiment), The Worcestershire and Sherwood Foresters Regiment, 8th Canadian Hussars (Princess Louise's), Canadian Forces Communications and Electronics Branch, Grey and Simcoe Foresters, The Regina Rifle Regiment, Royal Australian Corps of Signals, Royal New Zealand Corps of Signals, Royal New Zealand Nursing Corps, Hon. Air Commodore, R.A.F. Lyneham, Commandant-in-Chief, Ambulance and Nursing Cadets, Commandant-in-Chief, Women's Transport Service (FANY), *born* August 15, 1950, *married* Nov. 14, 1973, Capt. Mark Anthony Peter Phillips, C.V.O., Personal A.D.C. to the Queen, and has issue, (i) Peter Mark Andrew, *born* Nov. 15, 1977, and (ii) Zara Anne Elizabeth, *born* May 15, 1981.

H.R.H. PRINCE ANDREW ALBERT CHRISTIAN EDWARD, C.V.O., *born* Feb. 19, 1960. Lieutenant, Royal Navy.

H.R.H. PRINCE EDWARD ANTONY RICHARD LOUIS, *born* March 10, 1964.

MOTHER OF HER MAJESTY

H.M. QUEEN ELIZABETH THE QUEEN MOTHER (Elizabeth Angela Marguerite) (daughter of the 14th Earl of Strathmore and Kinghorne), Lady of the Garter, Lady of the Thistle, Order of the Crown of India, Grand Master of the Royal Victorian Order, Dame Grand Cross of the Order of the British Empire, Royal Victorian Chain, Doctor of Civil Law, Doctor of Literature, Colonel-in-Chief 1st the Queen's Dragoon Guards, The Queen's Own Hussars, 9th/12th Royal Lancers (Prince of Wales's) The King's Regiment, The Royal Anglian Regiment, The Light Infantry, The Black Watch (Royal Highland Regiment), Royal Army Medical Corps, The Black Watch (Royal Highland Regiment) of Canada, The Toronto Scottish Regiment, Canadian Forces Medical Services, Royal Australian Army Medical Corps, Royal New Zealand Army Medical Corps, Hon. Colonel The Royal Yeomanry, The London Scottish, University of London Officers' Training Corps, Commandant-in-Chief R.A.F. Central Flying School, W.R.N.S., W.R.A.C., W.R.A.F., Air Chief Commandant, Women's Royal Australian Air Force, Patron St. Andrew's Ambulance Association, Commandant-in-Chief Nursing Corps and Divisions. *Born* August 4, 1900, *married* April 26, 1923, Prince Albert Frederick Arthur George of Windsor, Duke of York (*see* King GEORGE VI).

Residences.—Clarence House, St. James's, S.W.1.; Castle of Mey, Caithness, Scotland.

SISTER OF HER MAJESTY

H.R.H. PRINCESS MARGARET ROSE (The Princess Margaret, Countess of Snowdon), C.I., G.C.V.O., Colonel-in-Chief, 15th/19th The King's Royal Hussars, The Royal Highland Fusiliers (Princess Margaret's Own Glasgow and Ayrshire Regiment), Queen Alexandra's Royal Army Nursing Corps, The Highland Fusiliers of Canada, The Princess Louise Fusiliers, Women's Royal Australian Army Corps, Deputy Colonel-in-Chief, The

Royal Anglian Regiment, Hon. Air Commodore, R.A.F. Coningsby, Commandant-in-Chief, St. John Ambulance Brigade Cadets, Grand President, St. John Ambulance Association and Brigade, Dame Grand Cross of the Order of St. John of Jerusalem, President of the Girl Guides Association; *born* Aug. 21, 1930; *married* May 6, 1960 Anthony Charles Robert Armstrong-Jones, G.C.V.O. (*born* March 7, 1930, son of the late Ronald Armstrong-Jones, Q.C. and the Countess of Rosse, *created* Earl of Snowdon, 1961, Constable of Caernarvon Castle, *marriage dissolved*, 1978); and has issue, (i) David Albert Charles, Viscount Linley, *born* Nov. 3, 1961, and (ii) Sarah Frances Elizabeth (Lady Sarah Armstrong-Jones), *born* May 1, 1964.

Residence.—Kensington Palace, W.8.

Precedence in England

The Sovereign
The Prince Philip, Duke of
Edinburgh.
The Prince of Wales, The Prince
Andrew, The Prince Edward.
Princes of the Blood Royal.
Archbishop of Canterbury.
Lord High Chancellor.
Archbishop of York.
The Prime Minister.
Lord President of the Council.
Speaker of the House of Commons.
Lord Privy Seal.
High Commissioners of
Commonwealth Countries and
Ambassadors of Foreign States.
Dukes, according to their Patents
of Creation:
(1) Of England; (2) of Scotland;
(3) of Great Britain; (4) of Ireland;
(5) those created since the Union.
Ministers and Envoys.
Eldest sons of Dukes of Blood
Royal.
Marquesses, in same order as
Dukes.
Dukes' eldest Sons.
Earls, in same order as Dukes.
Younger sons of Dukes of Blood
Royal.
Marquesses' eldest Sons.
Dukes' younger Sons.
Viscounts, in same order as Dukes.
Earls' eldest Sons.
Marquesses' younger Sons.
Bishops of London, Durham and
Winchester.
All other English Bishops,
according to their seniority of
Consecration.
Secretaries of State, if of the
degree of a Baron.
Barons, in same order as Dukes.
Treasurer of H.M.'s Household.
Comptroller of H.M.'s Household.
Vice-Chamberlain of H.M.'s
Household.
Secretaries of State under the
degree of Baron.
Viscounts' eldest Sons.
Earls' younger Sons.
Barons' eldest Sons.

Knights of the Garter if
Commoners.
Privy Councillors if of no higher
rank.
Chancellor of the Exchequer.
Chancellor of the Duchy of
Lancaster.
Lord Chief Justice of England.
Master of the Rolls.
President of the Family Division.
Vice-Chancellor.
The Lords Justices of Appeal.
Judges of the High Court.
Vice-Chancellor of County
Palatine of Lancaster.
Viscounts' younger Sons.
Barons' younger Sons.
Sons of Life Peers.
Baronets of either Kingdom,
according to date of Patents.
Knights of the Thistle if
Commoners.
Knights Grand Cross of the Bath.
Members of the Order of Merit.
Knights Grand Commanders of the
Star of India.
Knights Grand Cross of St.
Michael and St. George.
Knights Grand Commanders of the
Indian Empire.
Knights Grand Cross of the Royal
Victorian Order.
Knights Grand Cross of Order of
the British Empire.
Companions of Honour.
Knights Commanders of the above
Orders.
Knights Bachelor.
Official Referees of The Supreme
Court.
Circuit judges and judges of the
Mayor's and City of London
Court.
Companions and Commanders *e.g.*
C.B.; C.S.I.; C.M.G.; C.I.E.; C.V.O.;
C.B.E.; D.S.O.; M.V.O. (4th); O.B.E.;
I.S.O.
Eldest Sons of younger Sons of
Peers.
Baronets' eldest Sons.
Eldest Sons of Knights in the same
order as their Fathers.

M.V.O. (5th); M.B.E.
Younger Sons of the younger Sons
of Peers.
Baronets' younger Sons.
Younger Sons of Knights in the
same order as their Fathers.
Naval, Military, Air, and other
Esquires by Office.

WOMEN

Women take the same rank as
their husbands or as their brothers;
but the daughter of a Peer marrying
a Commoner retains her title as
Lady or Honourable. Daughters of
Peers rank next immediately after
the wives of their elder brothers,
and before their younger brothers'
wives. Daughters of Peers marrying Peers of lower degree take the
same order of precedence as that of
their husbands; thus the daughter
of a Duke marrying a Baron becomes of the rank of Baroness only
while her sisters married to commoners retain their rank and take
precedence of the Baroness. Merely
official rank on the husband's part
does not give any similar precedence to the wife.

Peeresses in their own right take
the same Precedence as Peers of the
same rank, i.e. from their date of
creation.

LOCAL PRECEDENCE

ENGLAND AND WALES.—No written code of county or city order of
precedence has been promulgated,
but in Counties the Lord Lieutenant stands first, and secondly (normally) the Sheriff, and therefore in
Cities and Boroughs the Lord Lieutenant has social precedence over
the Mayor; but at City or Borough
functions the Lord Mayor or Mayor
will preside. At Oxford and Cambridge the High Sheriff takes precedence of the Vice-Chancellor.
SCOTLAND.—*See* Index.

THE QUEEN'S HOUSEHOLD

Lord Chamberlain, The Earl of Airlie.
Lord Steward, The Duke of Northumberland, K.G., P.C., G.C.V.O., T.D., F.R.S.
Master of the Horse, The Earl of Westmorland, K.C.V.O.
Treasurer of the Household, J. Cope, M.P.
Comptroller of the Household, Carol Mather, M.C., M.P.
Vice-Chamberlain, The Hon. Robert Boscawen, M.C., M.P.

Gold Stick, Maj.-Gen. Lord Michael Fitzalan Howard, G.C.V.O., C.B., C.B.E., M.C.; General Sir Desmond Fitzpatrick, G.C.B., D.S.O., M.B.E., M.C.
Vice-Admiral of the United Kingdom, Admiral Sir John Bush, G.C.B., D.S.C.
Rear-Admiral of the United Kingdom, Admiral Sir William O'Brien, K.C.B., D.S.C.
First and Principal Naval Aide-de-Camp, Admiral Sir John Fieldhouse, G.C.B., G.B.E.
Flag Aide de Camp, Admiral Sir Desmond Cassidi, G.C.B.
Aides-de-Camp General, General Sir John Stanier, G.C.B., M.B.E.; General Sir Thomas Morony, K.C.B., O.B.E.; General Sir Roland Guy, K.C.B., C.B.E., D.S.O.; General Sir Frank Kitson, K.C.B., C.B.E., M.C.
Air Aides-de-Camp, Air Chief Marshal Sir Keith Williamson, G.C.B., A.F.C.; Air Chief Marshal Sir Thomas Kennedy, K.C.B., A.F.C.

Mistress of the Robes, The Duchess of Grafton, G.C.V.O.
Ladies of the Bedchamber, The Marchioness of Abergavenny, D.C.V.O.; The Countess of Airlie, C.V.O.
Extra Lady of the Bedchamber, The Countess of Cromer, C.V.O.
Women of the Bedchamber, Hon. Mary Morrison, D.C.V.O.; Lady Susan Hussey, D.C.V.O.; Lady Abel Smith, D.C.V.O.; Mrs. John Dugdale, D.C.V.O.
Extra Women of the Bedchamber, Mrs. John Woodroffe, C.V.O.; Lady Rose Baring, D.C.V.O., Mrs. Michael Wall, D.C.V.O.
Extra Equerries, Vice-Admiral Sir Conolly Abel-Smith, G.C.V.O., C.B.; Vice-Adm. Sir Peter Ashmore, K.C.B., K.C.V.O., D.S.C.; Rear-Adm. the Earl Cairns, G.C.V.O., C.B.; Lt.-Col. The Lord Charteris of Amisfield, P.C., G.C.B., G.C.V.O., O.B.E., Q.S.O.; Vice-Adm. Sir Peter Dawnay, K.C.V.O., C.B., D.S.C.; Sir Edward Ford, K.C.B., K.C.V.O.; Rear Adm. P. Greening; Brig. Sir Geoffrey Hardy-Roberts, K.C.V.O., C.B., C.B.E.; Sir William Heseltine, K.C.V.O., C.B.; Rear-Admiral Sir Hugh Janion, K.C.V.O.; Lt.-Col. Sir John Johnston, K.C.V.O., M.C.; Major Sir Rennie Maudslay, G.C.V.O., K.C.B., M.B.E.; Air Commodore Sir Dennis Mitchell, K.B.E., C.V.O., D.F.C., A.F.C.; The Rt. Hon Sir Philip Moore, K.C.B., K.C.V.O., C.M.G.; Rear-Adm. Sir Patrick Morgan, K.C.V.O., C.B., D.S.C.; Lt.-Col. Ririd Myddleton, M.V.O.; Lt.-Col. Sir Eric Penn, G.C.V.O., O.B.E., M.C.; Cdr. Sir Philip Row, K.C.V.O., O.B.E., R.N.; Maj.-Gen. Sir Guy Salisbury-Jones, G.C.V.O., C.M.G., C.B.E., M.C.; Air Vice-Marshal John Severne, M.V.O., O.B.E., A.F.C.; Group Capt. Peter Townsend, C.V.O., D.S.O., D.F.C.; Rear-Admiral Sir Richard John Trowbridge, K.C.V.O.; Lt.-Col. G. West; Air Commodore Sir Archie Little Winskill, K.C.V.O., C.B.E., D.F.C.

THE PRIVATE SECRETARY'S OFFICE
Buckingham Palace, S.W.1

Private Secretary to The Queen, The Rt. Hon. Sir Philip Moore, G.C.V.O., K.C.B., C.M.G.
Deputy Private Secretary, Sir William Heseltine, K.C.V.O., C.B.
Assistant Private Secretary, R. Fellowes, M.V.O..
Defence Services Secretary, Major General Michael Palmer.
Press Secretary, M. S. McA. Shea.
Assistant Press Secretaries, J. Haslam; V. Chapman (*temp.*).
Chief Clerk, Miss A. Bowlby, M.V.O., M.B.E.
Secretary to the Private Secretary, Miss E. Pearce.
Clerks, Miss J. M. Damrel; Miss A. C. Bailey, M.V.O.; Miss J. A. Adams, M.V.O.; Miss A. K. Nicholson; Mrs. J. Bean, M.V.O.; Mrs. W. I. Eldridge; Mrs. A. Crooks; Mrs. J. Rose; Miss V. Walker; Mrs. A. M. Neal, M.V.O. (*Press*); Miss F. M. Simpson, M.V.O. (*Press*); Miss S. P. Brennan (*Press*); Miss J. Simpson (*Press*).
Lady in Waiting's Office, Miss A. Carritt.

The Queen's Archives
Round Tower, Windsor Castle.

Keeper of The Queen's Archives, The Rt. Hon. Sir Philip Moore, G.C.V.O., K.C.B., C.M.G.
Assistant Keeper, Sir Robin Mackworth-Young, K.C.V.O., F.S.A.
Registrar, Miss J. Langton, M.V.O.
Assistant Registrars, Miss E. Cuthbert, M.V.O.; Miss F. Dimond, M.V.O.; Mrs. G. de Bellaigue.

DEPARTMENT OF THE KEEPER OF THE PRIVY PURSE AND TREASURER TO THE QUEEN
Buckingham Palace, S.W.1.

Keeper of the Privy Purse and Treasurer to The Queen, P. T. Miles.

Privy Purse Office

Assistant Keeper of the Privy Purse, Major S. G. B. Blewitt, M.V.O.
Chief Accountant, G. H. Franklin, M.V.O.
Chief Clerk, D. Waters, M.V.O.
Accountant, Mrs. E. Smith.
Clerks, Miss C. Hall, Miss S. Ram.
Land Agent, Sandringham, J. Loyd, C.V.O.
Resident Factor, Balmoral, M. Leslie.

Treasurer's Office

Deputy Treasurer to The Queen, R. D. Wood, C.V.O., V.R.D.
Chief Accountant and Paymaster, F. R. Mintram, M.V.O.
Assistant Chief Accountant and Paymaster, D. Walker, M.V.O.
Accountant, Mrs. J. Maitland, M.V.O.
Establishment Officer, P. Wright, C.V.O.
Clerks, Mrs. C. Auton; Miss G. Wickham; Mrs. D. C. Mowbray; Miss C. Mackenzie; Miss C. McCartney.
Print Unit, Mrs. N. Phelps, M.V.O.; Miss I. Hoaen.

Royal Almonry

Lord High Almoner, The Rt. Rev. the Lord Bishop of Rochester.
Hereditary Grand Almoner, The Marquess of Exeter.
Sub-Almoner, Rev. Canon A. D. Caesar, M.A., MUS.B., F.R.C.O.
Secretary, P. Wright, C.V.O.
Assistant Secretary, D. Waters, M.V.O.

THE LORD CHAMBERLAIN'S OFFICE
St. James's Palace, S.W.1.

Comptroller, Lt.-Col. Sir John Johnston, K.C.V.O., M.C.
Assistant Comptroller, Lt.-Col. G. West.
Secretary, J. E. P. Titman, C.V.O.
Assistant Secretary, P. D. Hartley, M.V.O.
Registrar, M. E. Bishop, M.V.O.

State Invitations Assistant, Major J. C. Leech.

Clerks, D. Rankin-Hunt; Miss S. Hay; Miss A. Thomas; Mrs. S. Taylor; Mrs. P. Dymoke; Mrs J. Anderson; Miss J. Hockley; Miss S. Bowring.

Permanent Lords in Waiting, The Lord Cobbold, K.G., G.C.V.O.; Lt.-Col. The Lord Charteris of Amisfield, P.C., G.C.B., G.C.V.O., O.B.E., Q.S.O.

Lords in Waiting, The Lord Somerleyton; The Viscount Boyne; The Viscount Long; The Lord Skelmersdale; The Lord Lucas of Chilworth; The Earl of Caithness; The Baroness Trumpington (*Baroness in Waiting*).

Gentlemen Ushers, Carron Greig, C.V.O.; Lt.-Cmdr. John Holdsworth, C.V.O., O.B.E., R.N.; Col. Gerard Leigh, C.B.E., C.V.O.; Lt.-Col. Sir Julian Paget, Bt., C.V.O.; Air Chief Marshal Sir Neville Stack, K.C.B., C.V.O., C.B.E., A.F.C.; Group-Capt. John Slessor; Major Nigel Chamberlayne-Macdonald, O.B.E., M.V.O.; Air Chief Marshall Sir Roy Austen-Smith, K.B.E., C.B., D.F.C.; Vice-Admiral Sir David Loram, K.C.B., M.V.O.; Capt. Michael Barrow, D.S.O., R.N.

Extra Gentlemen Ushers, Capt. Andrew Yates, M.V.O., R.N.; Major Thomas Harvey, C.V.O., D.S.O.; Brig. Charles Britten, O.B.E., M.C.; Air Vice-Marshal Sir Ranald Reid, K.C.B., D.S.O., M.C.; Esmond Butler, C.V.O.; Maj.-Gen. Sir Cyril Colquhoun, K.C.V.O., C.B., O.B.E.; Lt.-Col. Sir John Hugo, K.C.V.O., O.B.E.; General Sir Rodney Moore, G.C.V.O., K.C.B., C.B.E., D.S.O.; Vice-Admiral Sir Ronald Brockman, K.C.B., C.S.I., C.I.E., C.V.O., C.B.E.; Air Marshal Sir Maurice Heath, K.B.E., C.B., C.V.O.; Maj.-Gen. Sir Peter Gillett, K.C.V.O., C.B., O.B.E.; Sir James Scholtens, K.C.V.O.; Sir Patrick O'Dea, K.C.V.O.; Brig.-Gen. Stewart Cooper, C.V.O., O.B.E., C.D.; Capt. Robert Whitten, O.B.E., R.A.N.; Admiral Sir David Williams, G.C.B.; Capt. Michael Tufnell, C.V.O., D.S.C., R.N.

Gentleman Usher to the Sword of State, Air Chief Marshal Sir John Barraclough, K.C.B., C.B.E., D.F.C., A.F.C.

Gentleman Usher of the Black Rod, Lt.-Gen. Sir David House, G.C.B., C.B.E., M.C.

Serjeants at Arms, P. A. Wright, C.V.O.; G. A. Harris, M.V.O., M.B.E.; J. E. P. Titman, C.V.O.

Marshal of the Diplomatic Corps, Lt.-Gen. Sir John Richards, K.C.B.

Vice-Marshal, The Hon. Eustace Gibbs.

Constable & Governor of Windsor Castle, Marshal of the Royal Air Force Sir John Grandy, G.C.B., K.B.E., D.S.O.

Keeper of the Jewel House, Tower of London, vacant.

Surveyor of The Queen's Pictures, Sir Oliver Millar, K.C.V.O., F.B.A., F.S.A.

Assistant, Miss C. Crichton-Stuart.

Librarian, Sir Robin Mackworth-Young, K.C.V.O., F.S.A.

Curator of the Print Room, The Hon. Mrs. Roberts.

Adviser for The Queen's Works of Art, Sir Francis Watson, K.C.V.O., F.S.A.

Surveyor of The Queen's Works of Art, Geoffrey de Bellaigue, C.V.O., F.S.A.

Assistant, Mrs D. Harland.

Master of The Queen's Music, Malcolm Williamson, C.B.E.

Poet Laureate, vacant.

Bargemaster, E. Hunt.

Keeper of the Swans, F. J. Turk, M.V.O.

Superintendent of the State Apartments, St. James's Palace, C. H. Philips, M.B.E.

ASCOT OFFICE
St. James's Palace, S.W.1.

Her Majesty's Representative at Ascot, Col. P. Bengough, O.B.E.

Secretary, Miss L. Thompson-Royd.

ECCLESIASTICAL HOUSEHOLD
The College of Chaplains.

Clerk of the Closet, The Bishop of Bath and Wells.

Deputy Clerk of the Closet, Rev. Canon A. D. Caesar, M.A., MUS.B., F.R.C.O.

Chaplains to the Queen, Ven. E. J. G. Ward, M.V.O., M.A.; Rev. J. R. W. Stott, M.A.; Canon P. T. Ashton, M.V.O., M.A.; Rev. A. H. H. Harbottle, M.V.O., M.A.; Canon E. M. Pilkington, M.A.; Ven. J. R. Youens, C.B., O.B.E., M.C.; Ven. T. Barfett, M.A.; Prof. Canon G. R. Dunstan, M.A., D.D., F.S.A.; Canon S. H. Hoffman, M.A.; Rev. D. N. Griffiths, M.A.; Canon D. R. Vicary, M.A., B.SC.; Canon A. Glendining, M.V.O.; Ven. C. W. Borrett, M.A.; Canon J. G. Grimwade, M.A.; Canon J. S. Robertson, M.A.; Canon D. Landreth, T.D., M.A.; Canon J. V. Bean, M.A.; Ven. B. A. O'Ferrall, C.B., M.A.; Canon C. M. Rushton, M.A.; Canon P. A. Welsby, M.A., PH.D.; Canon P. W. Miller; Canon G. Carnell, M.A.; Rev. K. Huxley, M.A.; Ven. R. Simpson, M.V.O., M.A.; Ven. P. Ashford; Canon G. A. Elcoat; Canon D. C. Gray, T.D., M.PHIL., A.K.C.; Canon S. Wilkinson, A.K.C.; Canon J. Treadgold, B.A.; Ven. D. Scott, M.A.; Canon A. Russell, D.PHIL.; Canon S. Barrington-Ward, M.A.; Canon E. James, M.A., A.K.C.; Canon J. Hester, M.A.

Extra Chaplains, Rev. E. S. Abbott, K.C.V.O., D.D., M.A.; Canon J. S. D. Mansel, K.C.V.O., M.A., F.S.A.; Preb. S. A. Williams, C.V.O.; M.A.

Chapels Royal

Dean of the Chapels Royal, The Bishop of London.

Sub-Dean of Chapels Royal, Rev. Canon A. D. Caesar, M.A., MUS.B., F.R.C.O.

Priests in Ordinary, Rev. W. Booth, M.A.; Rev. J. H. Williams, B.A.

Organist, Choirmaster and Composer, R. J. Popplewell, F.R.C.O., F.R.C.M.

Domestic Chaplain—Buckingham Palace, Rev. Canon A. D. Caesar, M.A., MUS.B., F.R.C.O.

Domestic Chaplain—Windsor Castle, The Dean of Windsor.

Domestic Chaplain—Sandringham, Rev. J. G. M. W. Murphy, M.A.

Chaplain—Royal Chapel, Windsor Great Park, Canon J. Treadgold, B.A.

Chaplain—Hampton Court Palace, Canon M. Moore, M.A.

Chaplain—Tower of London, Rev. J. F. M. Llewellyn, M.V.O., M.A.

Organist and Choirmaster—Hampton Court Palace, Gordon Reynolds, M.V.O., A.R.C.M.

MEDICAL HOUSEHOLD

Head of the Medical Household and Physician, J. C. Batten, M.D., F.R.C.P.

Physicians, A. M. Dawson, M.D., F.R.C.P.; C. Elliot, M.R.C.G.P.

Serjeant Surgeon, W. Slack, M.CH., F.R.C.S.

Surgeon Oculist, P. Holmes Sellors, M.A., B.M., B.CH., F.R.C.S.

Surgeon Gynaecologist, G. D. Pinker, C.V.O., F.R.C.S.(Edin.), F.R.C.O.G.

Surgeon Dentist, N. A. Sturridge, L.D.S., B.D.S., D.D.S.

Physician to the Household, R. Thompson, D.M., F.R.C.P.

Surgeon to the Household, B. Jackson, M.S., F.R.C.S.

Surgeon Oculist to the Household, T. J. ffytche, F.R.C.S., L.R.C.P.

Apothecary to The Queen and to the Household, N. R. Southward, M.A., M.B., B.CHIR., M.R.C.P.

Apothecary to the Household at Windsor, J. P. Clayton, M.V.O., M.A., M.B., B.CHIR., M.R.C.S., L.R.C.P.

Apothecary to the Household at Sandringham, H. K. Ford, M.V.O., M.B., F.R.C.G.P.

Coroner of The Queen's Household, Lt.-Col. G. McEwan, M.B., CH.B.

CENTRAL CHANCERY
OF THE ORDERS OF KNIGHTHOOD
St. James's Palace, S.W.1.

Secretary, Maj.-Gen. D. H. G. Rice, C.B.E.
Assistant Secretary, G. A. Harris, C.V.O., M.B.E.
Insignia Clerk, M. G. P. Kelly, M.V.O.
Clerks, J. McGurk, M.V.O.; Mrs. E. Searle; Miss S. Koller; Miss R. A. Wells; Miss T. Perfect.

The Honorable Corps of Gentlemen at Arms
St. James's Palace, S.W.1.

Captain, The Lord Denham, P.C.; *Lieutenant*, Col. R. J. V. Crichton, M.C.; *Standard Bearer*, Major The Marquess of Donegall; *Clerk of the Cheque & Adjutant*, Major D. Jamieson, V.C.; *Harbinger*, Lt. Col. J. Eagles.

Gentlemen of the Corps

Brigadier, A. N. Breitmeyer.
Colonels, P. Pardoe; A. G. Way, M.C.; T. Hall, O.B.E.; P. Gengough, O.B.E.; Hon. N. Crossley, T.D.; T. Wilson.
Lieutenant-Colonels, N. H. R. Speke, M.C.; D. A. St. G. Laurie, O.B.E., M.C.; P. Hodgson; R. Steele, M.B.E.; W. S. P. Lithgow; Sir James Scott, Bt.; R. Mayfield, D.S.O.
Majors, Sir Richard Carne Rasch, Bt.; J. D. Dillon, D.S.C., R.M.; The Lord Suffield, M.C.; T. St. Aubyn; Sir Torquhil Matheson of Matheson, Bt.; F. J. H. Matheson; J. A. J. Nunn; Sir Philip Duncombe, Bt.; I. B. Ramsden, M.B.E.; M. J. Drummond-Brady; A. Arkwright; G. M. B. Colenso-Jones.
Captain, The Lord Monteagle of Brandon.

The Queen's Bodyguard of the Yeoman of the Guard
St. James's Palace, S.W.1.

Captain, The Earl of Swinton; *Lieutenant*, Col. H. T. Brassey, O.B.E., M.C.; *Clerk of the Cheque and Adjutant*, Col. A. B. Pemberton, M.B.E.; *Ensign*, Major B. M. H. Shand, M.C.; *Exons.*, Capt. Sir Charles McGrigor, Bt.; Col. G. W. Tufnell.

MASTER OF THE HOUSEHOLD'S DEPARTMENT
Board of Green Cloth
Buckingham Palace, S.W.1.

Master of the Household, Vice-Admiral Sir Peter Ashmore, K.C.B., K.C.V.O., D.S.C.
Deputy Master of the Household, Lt.-Col. B. A. Stewart-Wilson, M.V.O.
Assistants to the Master of the Household, M. D. Tims, C.V.O.; M. Parker.
Chief Clerk, A. Hancock.
Deputy to Assistant, M. Jephson.
Senior Clerks, J. S. Cowdery; A. Bell.
Clerks, Miss S. Derry, M.V.O.; Miss D. Graham; Mrs. A. Wise; Mrs. T. King; Miss A. Perkins; R. Smith.
Superintendent, Windsor Castle, Major Barrie Eastwood, M.B.E.
Assistant to Superintendent, Capt. R. McClosky.
Palace Steward, C. S. Dickman, R.V.M..
Chief Housekeeper, Miss A. de Trey-White.

ROYAL MEWS DEPARTMENT
Buckingham Palace, S.W.1.

Crown Equerry, Lt.-Col. Sir John Miller, K.C.V.O., D.S.O., M.C.
Equerries, Lt.-Col. B. A. Stewart-Wilson, M.B.E.; Major Hugh Lindsay; Capt. A. Matheson (*temp.*).

Veterinary Surgeon, Peter Scott Dunn, M.V.O., M.R.C.V.S.
Supt. Royal Mews, Buckingham Palace, Lt.-Col. William Marsh.
Comptroller of Stores, Major L. Marsham.
Chief Clerk, P. Almond.
Deputy Chief Clerk, A. J. W. Scovell, M.V.O.
Office Keeper, P. M. Goodman.

HER MAJESTY'S HOUSEHOLD IN SCOTLAND

Hereditary Lord High Constable, The Earl of Erroll.
Hereditary Master of the Household, The Duke of Argyll.
Lord Lyon King of Arms, Malcolm R. Innes of Edinight, C.V.O., W.S.
Hereditary Bearer of the Royal Banner of Scotland, The Earl of Dundee, P.C.
Hereditary Bearer of the Scottish National Flag, The Earl of Lauderdale.
Hereditary Keepers:—
Holyrood, The Duke of Hamilton and Brandon.
Falkland, N. J. Crichton-Stuart.
Stirling, The Earl of Mar and Kellie.
Dunstaffnage, The Duke of Argyll.
Keeper of Dumbarton Castle, Brig. A. S. Pearson, C.B., D.S.O., O.B.E., M.C., T.D.
Governor of Edinburgh Castle, Lieut.-Gen. Sir Alexander Boswell, K.C.B., C.B.E.
Dean of the Order of the Thistle, The Very Rev. Prof. J. McIntyre, M.A., B.D., D.Litt., D.D.
Dean of the Chapel Royal, Very Rev. Prof. R. A. S. Barbour, M.C., M.A., D.D.
Chaplains in Ordinary, Rev. R. A. S. Barbour, M.C., M.A., D.D.; Rev. W. J. Morris, D.D., LL.D., Ph.D.; Rev. H. W. McP. Cant, M.A., B.D.; Rev. K. MacVicar, M.B.E., D.F.C., T.D., M.A.; Very Rev. Prof. J. McIntyre, M.A., D.D., D.Litt.; Rev. A. J. C. Macfarlane, M.A.; Rev. J. McLeod, M.A.; Rev. G. I. Macmillan, M.A., B.D.; Very Rev. W. B. Johnston, M.A., B.D., D.D.; Rev. C. Forrester-Paton, M.A., B.D.
Extra Chaplains, Very Rev. J. A. Fraser, M.B.E., T.D., D.D.; Very Rev. the Lord MacLeod of Fuinary, M.C., D.D.; Very Rev. Prof. J. S. Stewart, M.A., D.D.; Rev. Prof. E. P. Dickie, M.C., D.D.; Very Rev. R. L. Small, C.B.E., D.D.; Very Rev. W. R. Sanderson, D.D.; Rev. W. H. Rogan, D.D.; Very Rev. R. W. V. Selby Wright, C.V.O., T.D., M.A., D.D., F.R.S.E., F.S.A.(scot.); Rev. T. J. T. Nicol, M.V.O., M.B.E., M.C., T.D.; Very Rev. G. T. H. Reid, M.C., M.A., D.D.; Very Rev. H. Douglas, K.C.V.O., C.B.E., M.A., D.D.
Domestic Chaplain, Balmoral, Rev. J. A. K. Angus, T.D., M.A.
Historiographer, Prof. G. Donaldson, M.A., Ph.D., F.B.A., F.R.S.E.
Botanist, (vacant).
Painter and Limner, D. A. Donaldson, R.S.A., R.P.
Sculptor, Benno Schotz, R.S.A.
Astronomer, Prof. M. S. Longair, B.SC., Ph.D., M.A.
Physicians in Scotland, R. F. Robertson, C.B.E., M.D., P.R.C.P. (Ed.), F.R.C.P.; P. Brunt, M.D., F.R.C.P.
Surgeons in Scotland, P. F. Jones, M.A., M.Chir., F.R.C.S.; T. J. McNair, M.D., F.R.C.S.
Extra Surgeons in Scotland, Prof. Sir Charles Illingworth, C.B.E., M.D., F.R.C.S.Ed.; Prof. Sir Donald Douglas, M.B.E., Ch.M., M.S., D.SC., F.R.C.S.
Apothecary to the Household at Balmoral, P. Crawford, M.B., Ch.B., D.Obst., R.C.O.G.
Apothecary to the Household at the Palace of Holyroodhouse, D. G. Illingworth, M.V.O., M.D., F.R.C.P., F.R.C.G.P.
Heralds & Pursuivants of Arms, (see pages 373–74).

THE QUEEN'S BODYGUARD FOR SCOTLAND

The Royal Company of Archers.
Archers' Hall, Edinburgh.

Captain General and Gold Stick for Scotland, Col. The Earl of Stair, K.C.V.O., M.B.E.
Captains, Major The Lord Home of the Hirsel, P.C., K.T.; The Duke of Buccleuch and Queensberry, K.T., V.R.D.; Lt.-Col. Sir John Gilmour, Bt., D.S.O., T.D.; Major Sir Alastair Blair, K.C.V.O., T.D.
Lieutenants, Col. The Lord Clydesmuir, K.T., C.B., M.B.E., T.D.; Major The Lord Maclean, P.C., K.T., G.C.V.O., K.B.E.; Major Sir Hew Hamilton-Dalrymple, Bt., C.V.O.; Major The Earl of Wemyss and March, K.T.
Ensigns, The Earl of Airlie; Lt.-Gen. Sir William Turner, K.B.E., C.B., D.S.O.; The Earl of Dalhousie, K.T., G.C.V.O., G.B.E., M.C. Capt. I. M. Tennant.
Brigadiers, Maj.-Gen. The Earl Cathcart, C.B., D.S.O., M.C.; Capt. N. E. F. Dalrymple-Hamilton, C.V.O., M.B.E., D.S.C., R.N.; The Marquess of Lothian, K.C.V.O.; Col. the Hon John Warrender, O.B.E., M.C.; Commodore Sir John Clerk of Penicuik, Bt., C.B.E., V.R.D., R.N.R.; The Earl of Elgin and Kincardine, K.T.; Col. G. R. Simpson, D.S.O., M.V.O., T.D.; Major D. H. Butter, M.C.; The Earl of Minto, M.B.E.; Maj.-Gen. Sir John Swinton, K.C.V.O., O.B.E.; General Sir Michael Gow, G.C.B.; The Hon. Lord Elliott, M.C.; Maj. The Hon. L. H. C. Maclean.
Adjutant, Major Sir Hew Hamilton-Dalrymple, Bt., C.V.O.
Surgeon, Col. G. M. Warrack, C.B.E., D.S.O., T.D.
Chaplain, Very Rev. R. W. V. Selby Wright, C.V.O., D.D., T.D., F.R.S.E.
President of the Council and Silver Stick for Scotland, Col. the Lord Clydesmuir, K.T., C.B., M.B.E., T.D.
Vice-President, Major Sir Hew Hamilton-Dalrymple, Bt., C.V.O.
Secretary, Col. H. F. O. Bewsher, O.B.E..
Treasurer, R. A. G. Douglas-Miller.

HOUSEHOLD OF THE PRINCE PHILIP, DUKE OF EDINBURGH

Private Secretary and Treasurer, B. H. McGrath.
Assistant Private Secretary, Brig. C. Robertson.
Equerry, Sqn. Ldr. T. J. Finneron.
Extra Equerry, J. B. V. Orr, C.V.O.
Temporary Equerries, Major The Hon. A. Wigram, Grenadier Guards; Capt. A. Milton, R.M.
Chief Clerk and Accountant, V. G. Jewell.

HOUSEHOLD OF QUEEN ELIZABETH THE QUEEN MOTHER

Lord Chamberlain, Major the Earl of Dalhousie, K.T., G.C.V.O., G.B.E., M.C.
Comptroller and Extra Equerry, Capt. Sir Alastair S. Aird, K.C.V.O.
Private Secretary and Equerry, Lt.-Col. Sir Martin Gilliat, G.C.V.O., M.B.E.
Treasurer and Equerry, Major Sir Ralph Anstruther, Bt., K.C.V.O., M.C.
Equerry, Major the Hon. Sir Francis Legh, K.C.V.O.
Press Secretary and Extra Equerry, Major Arthur J. S. Griffin, C.V.O.
Extra Equerries, The Lord Sinclair, M.V.O.; Maj. Raymond Seymour, M.V.O.
Equerry (Temp.), Capt. J. Lowther-Pinkerton.
Apothecary to the Household, Sir Ralph Southward, K.C.V.O., M.B., Ch.B., F.R.C.P.
Surgeon-Apothecary to the Household (Royal Lodge, Windsor), J. P. Clayton, M.V.O., M.A., M.B., B.Chir., M.R.C.S., L.R.C.P.

Mistress of the Robes, The Dowager Duchess of Abercorn, G.C.V.O.
Ladies of the Bedchamber, The Dowager Viscountess Hambleden, D.C.V.O.; The Lady Grimthorpe, C.V.O.
Women of the Bedchamber, Ruth, Lady Fermoy, D.C.V.O., O.B.E.; Mrs Patrick Campbell-Preston, C.V.O.; Lady Elizabeth Basset, C.V.O; Lady Angela Oswald.
Extra Women of the Bedchamber, Lady Victoria Wemyss, C.V.O.; The Hon. Mrs. Geoffrey Bowlby, C.V.O.; Lady Katharine Seymour, D.C.V.O.; Lady Jean Rankin, D.C.V.O.; The Hon. Mrs. John Mulholland, D.C.V.O.
Clerk Comptroller, M. Blanch, M.V.O.
Chief Accountant, J. P. Kyle, M.V.O.
Clerks, Mrs. R. Murphy, M.V.O.; Miss F. Fletcher, M.V.O.

HOUSEHOLD OF THE PRINCE AND PRINCESS OF WALES

Private Secretary and Treasurer to The Prince and Princess of Wales, The Hon. Edward Adeane.
Assistant Private Secretary, D. Roycroft.
Comptroller, Lt.-Col. P. Creasey.
Equerry to The Prince of Wales, Maj. J. M. W. Stenhouse, Gordon Highlanders.
Equerry to The Princess of Wales, Lt.-Cdr. P. Eberle, R.N.
Extra Equerry, Sqn.-Ldr. Sir David Checketts, K.C.V.O.
Temporary Equerry, Capt. S. Stephenson, Welsh Guards.
Lady in Waiting, Miss Anne Beckwith-Smith.
Extra Ladies in Waiting, The Hon. Mrs. Vivian Baring; Mrs. George West.
Secretary, M. M. Colborne.

HOUSEHOLD OF THE PRINCESS ANNE, MRS. MARK PHILLIPS

Private Secretary, Lt.-Col. P. Gibbs.
Ladies in Waiting, Mrs. Andrew Feilden, M.V.O.; Miss Victoria Legge-Bourke; Mrs. Malcolm Innes; The Hon. Mrs. Legge-Bourke.
Extra Ladies in Waiting, Mrs. Richard Carew Pole, M.V.O.; The Countess of Lichfield.
Personal Secretary, Mrs. David Hodgson, M.V.O.
Secretary, Mrs. E. Barrington Haynes.

HOUSEHOLD OF THE PRINCESS MARGARET, COUNTESS OF SNOWDON

Treasurer, Major The Hon. Sir Francis Legh, K.C.V.O.
Private Secretary and Comptroller, The Lord Napier and Ettrick, M.V.O.
Personal Secretary, Miss M. Murray Brown, C.V.O.
Extra Ladies in Waiting, The Lady Elizabeth Cavendish, M.V.O.; Mrs. Alastair Aird, M.V.O.; Mrs. Robin Benson, M.V.O.; The Lady Juliet Townsend, M.V.O.; Mrs. Jane Stevens; The Hon. Mrs. Wills, M.V.O.; The Lady Glenconner; The Hon. Mrs. Whitehead; The Countess Alexander of Tunis; Mrs. Angus Blair.

THE DUKE AND DUCHESS OF GLOUCESTER'S HOUSEHOLD

Comptroller, Private Secretary and Equerry, Lt.-Col. Sir Simon Bland, K.C.V.O.
Ladies in Waiting, Mrs. Michael Wigley, M.V.O.; Mrs. Euan McCorquodale; Mrs. Howard Page.
Extra Lady in Waiting, Miss Jennifer Thomson.

PRINCESS ALICE, DUCHESS OF GLOUCESTER'S HOUSEHOLD

Comptroller, Private Secretary and Equerry, Lt.-Col. Sir Simon Bland, K.C.V.O.
Ladies in Waiting, Dame Jean Maxwell-Scott, D.C.V.O.; Mrs. Michael Harvey.
Extra Ladies in Waiting, Miss Dorothy Meynell, C.V.O.; Mrs. Cedric Holland, C.V.O.; Miss Diana Harrison; The Hon. Jane Walsh; Miss Jane Egerton Warburton.

THE DUKE AND DUCHESS OF KENT'S HOUSEHOLD

Treasurer, Sir Philip Hay, K.C.V.O., T.D.
Private Secretary, Lieut.-Cdr. Sir Richard Buckley, K.C.V.O., R.N.
Ladies in Waiting, Mrs. Alan Henderson, M.V.O.; Mrs. David Napier, M.V.O.; Miss Sarah Partridge.
Extra Lady in Waiting, Mrs. Peter Wilmot-Sitwell.

HOUSEHOLD OF PRINCESS ALEXANDRA

Lady in Waiting, The Lady Mary Fitzalan-Howard, C.V.O.
Private Secretary and Extra Lady in Waiting, Miss Mona Mitchell, M.V.O.
Extra Ladies in Waiting, The Hon. Lady Rowley; The Lady Mary Colman.
Extra Equerry, Maj. P. C. Clarke, C.V.O.

HOUSEHOLD OF PRINCE MICHAEL OF KENT

Treasurer, Sir Peter Scott, K.B.E., C.M.G.

HONORARY PHYSICIANS TO THE QUEEN (CIVIL)

(Appointed for three years from Feb. 1, 1984)

G. Crompton, *Chief Medical Officer, Welsh Office*; G. D. Duncan, *Regional Medical Officer, East Anglian Regional Health Authority*; I. Smith McDonald, *Deputy Chief Medical Officer, Scottish Office*; Miss P. G. Walsh Mason, *Senior Principal Medical Officer, Department of Health and Social Security*; P. C. Moore, *District Medical Officer, Shropshire*; T. K. Sweeney, *Senior Principal Medical Officer, Department of Health and Social Security*.

THE QUEEN'S BIRTHDAY, 1985

The date for the observance of the Queen's Birthday in 1985 both at home and abroad will be Saturday, June 15.

ROYAL SALUTES

On the Anniversaries of the Birth, Accession and Coronation of the Sovereign and on the Anniversaries of the birth of H.M. the Queen Mother and H.R.H. the Duke of Edinburgh a salute of 62 guns is fired on the wharf at the Tower of London.

On extraordinary and triumphal occasions, such as on the occasion of the Sovereign opening, proroguing or dissolving Parliament in Person, or when passing through London in procession, except when otherwise ordered, 41 guns only are fired.

On the occasion of the birth of a Royal infant a salute of 41 guns is fired from the two Saluting Stations in London, *i.e.* Hyde Park and the Tower of London.

Constable of the Royal Palace and Fortress of London, General Sir Peter Hunt, G.C.B., D.S.O., O.B.E.
Lieutenant of the Tower of London, Lt.-Gen. Sir Hugh Cunningham, K.B.E.
Resident Governor and Keeper of the Jewel House, Maj.-Gen. A. P. W. MacLellan, M.B.E.
Master Gunner of St. James's Park, Lt.-Gen. Sir Thomas Morony, K.C.B., O.B.E.
Master Gunner within the Tower, Col. R. A. Burford, T.D.

THE ROYAL ARMS

QUARTERLY.—1st and 4th *gules*, three lions passant guardant in pale *or* (*England*); 2nd *or*, a lion rampant within a double tressure flory counterflory *gules* (*Scotland*); 3rd *azure*, a harp *or*, stringed *argent* (*Ireland*); the whole encircled with the Garter.

SUPPORTERS.—*Dexter*: a lion rampant guardant *or*, imperially crowned. *Sinister*: a unicorn *argent*, armed crined and unguled *or*, gorged with a coronet composed of crosses patées and fleurs de lis, a chain affixed passing between the forelegs and reflexed over the back.

BADGES.—The red and white rose united (*England*), a thistle (*Scotland*); a harp *or*, the strings *argent*, with a shamrock leaf *vert* (*Ireland*); upon a mount *vert*, a dragon passant wings elevated *gules* (*Wales*).

THE UNION JACK

The national flag of the United Kingdom is the Union Flag, generally known as the Union Jack, the name deriving from the use of the Union Flag on the jack-staff of naval vessels. It is a combination of the cross of the patron saint of England, St. George (*cross gules in a field argent*), the cross of the patron saint of Scotland, St. Andrew (*saltire argent in a field azure*) and a cross similar to that of St. Patrick, patron saint of Ireland (*saltire gules in a field argent*). The Union Flag was first introduced in 1606 after the union of England and Scotland, the cross of St. Patrick being added in 1801.

ANNUITIES TO THE ROYAL FAMILY

The annuity payable to Her Majesty is known as the Civil List, and is payable out of the Consolidated Fund under the authority of a Civil List Act following the recommendation of a Parliamentary Select Committee. The amount of the Civil List was fixed in the Civil List Act 1952 at £475,000, was increased from January 1, 1972, under the Civil List Act 1972 to £980,000, and has been variously increased since.

The allocation for the calendar year 1984 was as follows:—

The Queen	£3,850,000
Queen Elizabeth The Queen Mother	334,400
The Duke of Edinburgh	186,500
Prince Andrew	20,000
Prince Edward	20,000
The Princess Anne	116,200
The Princess Margaret	113,100
Princess Alice, Duchess of Gloucester	45,800
*Duke of Gloucester *Duke of Kent } To share *Princess Alexandra	331,000
	5,017,000
*Refunded by The Queen	331,000
Total	4,686,000

These figures combine the sums payable directly from the Consolidated Fund with the supplements provided by the Royal Trustees from the grant made to them in the vote for economic and financial administration in the Estimates.

THE FLYING OF FLAGS

Days for hoisting the Union Flag on Government Buildings (from 8 A.M. to sunset).

February 6 (1952).—Her Majesty's Accession.
February 19 (1960).—Birthday of The Prince Andrew.
March 1.—St. David's Day (in Wales only).
March 10 (1964).—Birthday of The Prince Edward.
March 11.—Commonwealth Day 1985.
April 21 (1926).—Birthday of Her Majesty the Queen.
April 23.—St. George's Day (in England only). Where a building has two or more flagstaffs the Cross of St. George may be flown in addition to the Union Jack but not in a superior position.
June 2 (1953).—Coronation Day.
June 10 (1921).—Birthday of The Duke of Edinburgh.
June 15.—Queen's Official Birthday, 1985.
July 1 (1961).—Birthday of The Princess of Wales.
Aug. 4 (1900).—Birthday of Her Majesty Queen Elizabeth the Queen Mother.
Aug. 15 (1950).—Birthday of The Princess Anne.
Aug. 21 (1930).—Birthday of The Princess Margaret.
Nov. 10.—Remembrance Sunday, 1985.
Nov. 14 (1948).—Birthday of The Prince of Wales.
Nov. 20 (1947).—Her Majesty's Wedding Day.
Nov. 30.—St. Andrew's Day (in Scotland only).
And on the occasion of the opening and closing of Parliament by the Queen, flags should be flown on Government buildings in the Greater London area, whether or not Her Majesty performs the ceremony in person.

The only additions to the above list will be those notified to the Department of the Environment by Her Majesty's command and communicated by the Ministry to the other Departments. The list applies to all Government Buildings in London and elsewhere in the United Kingdom. In cases where it has been the practice to fly the Union Jack daily, *e.g.* on some Custom Houses, that practice may continue.

Flags will be flown at half-mast on the following occasions:...

(*a*) From the announcement of the death up to the funeral of the Sovereign, except on Proclamation Day, when they are hoisted right up from 11 A.M. to sunset.

(*b*) The funerals of members of the Royal Family, subject to special commands from Her Majesty in each case.

(*c*) The funerals of Foreign Rulers, subject to special commands from Her Majesty in each case.

(*d*) The funerals of Prime Ministers and ex-Prime Ministers of the United Kingdom.

(*e*) Other occasions by special command of Her Majesty.

On occasions when days for flying flags coincide with days for flying flags at half mast the following rules will be observed. Flags will be flown: (*a*) although a member of the Royal Family, or a near relative of the Royal Family, may be lying dead, unless special commands be received from Her Majesty to the contrary, and (*b*) although it may be the day of the funeral of a Foreign Ruler. If the body of a very distinguished subject is lying at a Government Office the flag may fly at half mast on that office until the body has left (provided it is a day on which the flag would fly) and then the flag is to be hoisted right up. On all other Government Buildings the flag will fly as usual.

The *Royal Standard* is only to be hoisted when the Queen is actually present in the building, and never when Her Majesty is passing in procession.

RED-LETTER DAYS

Scarlet Robes are worn by the Judges of the Queen's Bench Division on *Red-Letter Days* at the sittings of a Criminal Court and on all State Occasions.

RED-LETTER DAYS AND STATE OCCASIONS, 1985.

Jan. 25. Conversion of St. Paul.	*May* 16. Ascension Day.	*July* 25. St. James.
Feb. 2. Purification.	*June* 2. Coronation Day.	*Aug.* 4. Birthday of Queen Elizabeth the Queen Mother.
„ 6. Queen's Accession.	„ 10. Birthday of The Duke of Edinburgh.	*Oct.* 18. St. Luke.
„ 20. Ash Wednesday.	„ 11. St. Barnabas.	„ 28. St. Simon and St. Jude.
Mar. 25. Annunciation.	„ 15. Queen's Official Birthday (1985).	*Nov.* 1. All Saints.
Apr. 21. Queen's Birthday.	„ 24. St. John the Baptist.	„ 9. Lord Mayor's Day.
„ 25. St. Mark.	„ 29. St. Peter.	„ 14. Birthday of The Prince of Wales.
May 1. St. Philip and St. James.	*July* 3. St. Thomas.	„ 30. St. Andrew.
„ 14. St. Matthias.		

THE MILITARY KNIGHTS OF WINDSOR

Founded in 1348 after the Wars in France to assist English Knights, who, having been prisoners in the hands of the French, had become impoverished by the payments of heavy ransoms. They received a pension and quarters in Windsor Castle. Edward III founded the Order of the Garter later in the same year, incorporating the Knights of Windsor and the College of St. George into its foundation and raising the number of Knights to 26 to correspond with the number of the Knights of the Garter. Known later as the Alms Knights or Poor Knights of Windsor, their establishment was reduced under the will of King Henry VIII to 13 and Statutes were drawn up by Queen Elizabeth I.

In 1833 King William IV changed their designation to The Military Knights and granted them their present uniform which consists of a scarlet tail-coat with white cross sword-belt, crimson sash and cocked hat with plume. The badges are the Shield of St. George and the Star of the Order of the Garter. The Knights receive a small stipend in addition to their Army pensions and quarters in Windsor Castle. They take part in all ceremonies of the Noble Order of the Garter and attend Sunday morning service in St. George's Chapel as representatives of the Knights of the Garter.

Applications for appointment should be made to The Military Secretary, Ministry of Defence, Army Dept.

Governor, Maj.-Gen. Sir Peter Gillett, K.C.V.O., C.B., O.B.E.

Military Knights, Lt.-Colonel R. W. Dobbin, O.B.E.; Major H. Smith, M.B.E., R.V.M.; Lt.-Colonel A. R. Clark, M.C.; Lt.-Colonel C. A. Harvey; Major A. E. Wollaston, M.V.O.; Brigadier A. L. Atkinson, O.B.E.; Brigadier J. F. Linders, O.B.E., M.C; Brigadier A. C. Tyler, C.B.E., M.C., D.L.; Major W. L. Thompson, M.V.O., M.B.E., D.C.M.; Major L. W. Dickerson; Major J. C. Cowley, D.C.M.; Brigadier C. J. Codner, C.B.E., M.C.

THE PEERAGE

The rules which govern the creation and succession of Peerages are extremely complicated. There are, technically, five separate Peerages, the Peerage of England, of Scotland, of Ireland, of Great Britain, and of the United Kingdom. The Peerage of Great Britain dates from 1707 when an Act of Union combined the two Kingdoms of England and Scotland and separate Peerages were discontinued; and the Peerage of the United Kingdom from 1801 when Great Britain and Ireland were combined under an Act of Union. Some Scottish Peers have received additional Peerages of Great Britain or of the United Kingdom since 1707, and some Irish Peers additional Peerages of the United Kingdom since 1801. The Peerage of Ireland was not entirely discontinued from 1801 but holders of Irish Peerages, whether pre-dating or created subsequent to the Union of 1801, are not entitled to sit in the House of Lords if they have no additional English, Scottish, Great Britain or United Kingdom Peerage. (However, they are eligible for election to the House of Commons and to vote in Parliamentary elections, which other Peers are not.) An Irish Peer holding a Peerage of a lower grade which enables him to sit in the House of Lords is introduced there by the title which enables him to sit, though for all other purposes he is known by his higher title. In the Peerage of Scotland there is no rank of Baron; the equivalent rank is Lord of Parliament, abbreviated to 'Lord'. All Peers of England, Scotland, Great Britain or the United Kingdom who are of full age (21 years) and of British nationality are entitled to sit in the House of Lords. Certain ancient Peerages pass on death to the nearest heir, male or female, and several are now held by women (see also p. 247). Since the Peerages Act, 1963, Peeresses in their own Right have been entitled to sit in the House of Lords, subject to the qualifications applying to Peers.

The Peerages Act, 1963, enables Peers or Peeresses to disclaim their Peerages for life: living Peers, within 12 months after the passing of the Act (July 31, 1963); a person subsequently succeeding to a Peerage, within 12 months (one month if an M.P.) after the date of succession, or of attaining his or her majority, if later. The disclaimer is irrevocable but does not affect the descent of the Peerage after the disclaimant's death, and children of a disclaimed Peer may, if they wish, retain their precedence and any courtesy titles and styles borne as children of a Peer. Non-hereditary or Life Peerages, in the degree of Baron or Baroness, have been conferred by the Crown since 1876 on eminent judges, the Lords of Appeal or Law Lords, to enable them to carry out the judicial functions of the House of Lords, and since 1958 on men and women of distinction in public life, giving them seats in the House of Lords. Life Peers and Peeresses are addressed identically as an hereditary Peer or Peeress, and their children have the same courtesy style as the children of an hereditary Peer or Peeress.

No fees for Dignities have been payable since 1937. The House of Lords surrendered the ancient right of peers to be tried for treason or felons by their peers in 1948.

PEERAGES EXTINCT SINCE THE LAST ISSUE

EARLDOM.—Fingall (cr. 1628). BARONIES.—Amulree (cr. 1929); Glenavy (cr. 1921); Henderson (cr. 1945); Ormathwaite (cr. 1868); Pentland (cr. 1909).

DISCLAIMER OF PEERAGES

Earl of Durham; Earl of Home; Earl of Sandwich; Viscount Hailsham; Viscount Stansgate; Lord Altrincham; Lord Archibald; Lord Beaverbrook; Lord Fraser of Allander; Lord Merthyr; Lord Monkswell; Lord Reith; Lord Sanderson of Ayot; Lord Silkin; Lord Southampton.

PEERS WHO ARE MINORS

EARLS (2): Albemarle (b. 1965); Hardwicke (b. 1971).   BARONS (3): Fermoy (b. 1967); Inverforth (b. 1966);
VISCOUNTS (2): Goschen (b. 1965); Dillon (b. 1973).   Wrottesley (b. 1968).

COMPOSITION OF THE HOUSE OF LORDS (At Aug. 4, 1984)

Archbishops and Bishops	25	
Peers by Succession	763	(18 Women)
Hereditary Peers of first creation (including the Prince of Wales)	31	
Life Peers under the Appellate Jurisdiction Act 1876	20	
Life Peers under the Life Peerages Act 1958	364	(46 Women)
TOTAL	1185	
Of whom:		
Peers without Writs of Summons	100	(7 Minors)
Peers on Leave of Absence from the House	155	

Contractions and Symbols.—S. or I. appended to the date of creation denotes a *Scottish* or *Irish* title, the further addition of a * implies that the Peer in question holds also an *Imperial* title, which is specified (after the name) by its more definite description as *Engl., Brit.,* or *U.K.* When both titles are alike, as in the case of Argyll, this star is appended to the conjoined date below, and it then denotes that such date is that of the imperial creation. The mark ° signifies that there is no "of" in the Marquessate or Earldom so designated; *b.* signifies born; *s.*, succeeded; *m.*, married; *w.*, widower or widow; *M.*, minor; † Information on *Eldest Son or Heir* not ascertained at time of going to press.

ROYAL DUKES

Style, His Royal Highness the Duke of ——.
Addressed as, Sir, or more formally, May it please your Royal Highness.

1947 *Edinburgh,* The Prince Philip, Duke of Edinburgh, K.G., P.C., K.T., O.M., G.B.E., *b.* 1921, *m.* (*see* pp. 218 and 219).

1337 *Cornwall,* Charles, Prince of Wales, Duke of Cornwall (*Scottish Duke, Rothesay,* 1398). K.G., P.C., K.T., G.C.B., *b.* 1948, (*see* p. 218).

1928 *Gloucester* (2nd), Richard, Duke of Gloucester, G.C.V.O., *b.* 1944, *s.* 1974, *m.* (see p. 217.)

1934 *Kent* (2nd), Edward Duke of Kent, G.C.M.G., G.C.V.O., *b.* 1935, *s.* 1942, *m.* (*see* p. 217).

ARCHBISHOPS

Style, The Most Rev. His Grace the Lord Archbishop of——.
Addressed as, My Lord Archbishop; or, Your Grace.

Trans.

1980   *Canterbury* (102nd), Robert Alexander Kennedy Runcie. P.C., M.C., D.D., *b.* 1921, *m. Consecrated Bishop of St. Albans,* 1970.

1983   *York* (95th), John Stapylton Habgood, P.C., PH.D. *b.* 1927, *m. Consecrated Bishop of Durham,* 1973.

DUKES

Style, His Grace the Duke of——. *Addressed as,* My Lord Duke; or, Your Grace. The eldest sons of Dukes and Marquesses take, by courtesy, their father's second title. The other sons and the daughters are styled Lord Edward, Lady Caroline. etc.

Created.	*Title, Order of Succession, Name, etc.*	*Eldest Son or Heir.*
1868 I.*	*Abercorn* (5th), James Hamilton (6th *Brit. Marq.,* 1790, and 14th *Scott. Earl,* 1606 both *Abercorn*), *b.* 1934, *s.* 1979, *m.*	Marquess of Hamilton, *b.* 1969.
1701 s. } 1892* }	*Argyll,* Ian Campbell (12th *Scottish* and 5th *U.K. Duke, Argyll*), *b.* 1937, *s.* 1973, *m.*	Marquess of Lorne, *b.* 1968.
1703 s.	*Atholl* (10th), George Iain Murray, *b.* 1931, *s.* 1957.	Godfrey P. *M.*, D.S.O., *b.* 1901.
1682	*Beaufort* (11th), David Robert Somerset, *b.* 1928, *s.* 1984, *m.*	Henry J. F. *S., b.* 1952.
1694	*Bedford* (13th), John Robert Russell, *b.* 1917, *s.* 1953, *m.*	Marquess of Tavistock, *b.* 1940.
1663 s.*	*Buccleuch* (9th) & (11th) *Queensberry* (1684), Walter Francis John Montagu-Douglas-Scott, K.T., V.R.D. (8th *Engl. Earl, Doncaster,* 1662), *b.* 1923, *s.* 1973, *m.*	Earl of Dalkeith, *b.* 1954.
1694	*Devonshire* (11th), Andrew Robert Buxton Cavendish, P.C., M.C., *b.* 1920, *s.* 1950, *m.*	Marquess of Hartington, *b.* 1944.
1900	*Fife* (3rd), James George Alexander Bannerman Carnegie, *b.* 1929, *s.* 1959. (see p. 216).	Earl of Macduff, *b.* 1961.
1675	*Grafton* (11th), Hugh Denis Charles FitzRoy, K.G., *b.* 1919, *s.* 1970, *m.*	Earl of Euston, *b.* 1947.
1643 s.*	*Hamilton* (15th), Angus Alan Douglas Douglas-Hamilton (*Premier Peer of Scotland;* 12th *Brit. Duke, Brandon,* 1711), *b.* 1938, *s.* 1973, *m.*	Marquess of Douglas and Clydesdale, *b.* 1978.
1766 I.*	*Leinster* (8th), Gerald FitzGerald (*Premier Duke, Marquess and Earl of Ireland;* 8th *Brit. Visct., Leinster,* 1747) *b.* 1914, *s.* 1976, *m.*	Marquess of Kildare, *b.* 1948.
1719	*Manchester* (11th), Sidney Arthur Robin George Drogo Montagu, *b.* 1929, *s.* 1977, *m.*	Lord Angus C. D. *M., b.* 1938.
1702	*Marlborough* (11th), John George Vanderbilt Henry Spencer-Churchill, *b.* 1926, *s.* 1972, *m.*	Marquess of Blandford, *b.* 1955.
1707 s.*	*Montrose* (7th), James Angus Graham (5th *Brit. Earl, Graham,* 1722), *b.* 1907, *s.* 1954, *m.*	Marquess of Graham, *b.* 1935.
1756	*Newcastle* (*under Lyme*) (9th), Henry Edward Hugh Pelham-Clinton-Hope, O.B.E., *b.* 1907, *s.* 1941, *m.*	Edward C. *Pelham-Clinton, b.* 1920
1483	*Norfolk* (17th), Miles Francis Stapleton Fitzalan-Howard, K.G., C.B., C.B.E., M.C. (*Premier Duke and Earl;* 12th *Eng. Baron Beaumont,* 1309; 4th *U.K. Baron Howard of Glossop,* 1869), *b.* 1915, *s.* 1975, *m.* (*Earl Marshal*).	Earl of Arundel and Surrey, *b.* 1956.
1766	*Northumberland* (10th), Hugh Algernon Percy, K.G., P.C., G.C.V.O., T.D., F.R.S., *b.* 1914, *s.* 1940, *m.* (*Lord Steward*).	Earl Percy, *b.* 1953.
1716	*Portland* (9th), Victor Frederick William Cavendish-Bentinck, C.M.G. (5th *U.K. Baron, Bolsover,* 1880) *b.* 1897, *s.* 1980, *m.*	(None to Dukedom), to Earldom of Portland, Henry N. Aldenburg-*B., b.* 1919.
1675	*Richmond* (9th) & *Gordon* (4th, 1876), Frederick Charles Gordon-Lennox (9th *Scott. Duke, Lennox.* 1675), *b.* 1904, *s.* 1935, *m.*	Earl of March and Kinrara, *b.* 1929.
1707 s.*	*Roxburghe* (10th), Guy David Innes-Ker (5th *U.K. Earl, Innes,* 1837), *b.* 1954, *s.* 1974, *m.* (*Premier Baronet of Scotland*).	Marquess of Bowmont, *b.* 1981.
1703	*Rutland* (10th), Charles John Robert Manners, C.B.E., *b.* 1919, *s.* 1940, *m.*	Marquess of Granby, *b.* 1959.
1684	*St. Albans* (13th), Charles Frederick Aubrey de Vere Beauclerk, O.B.E., *b.* 1915, *s.* 1964, *m.*	Earl of Burford, *b.* 1939.
1547	*Somerset* (18th), Percy Hamilton Seymour, *b.* 1910, *s.* 1954, *m.*	Lord Seymour, *b.* 1952.
1833	*Sutherland* (6th), John Sutherland Egerton, T.D. (5th *U.K. Earl Ellesmere,* 1846), *b.* 1915, *s.* 1963, *m.*	Cyril R. *E., b.* 1905.
1814	*Wellington* (8th), Arthur Valerian Wellesley, M.V.O., O.B.E., M.C. (9th *Irish Earl, Mornington,* 1760), *b.* 1915, *s.* 1972, *m.*	Marquess of Douro, *b.* 1945.
1874	*Westminster* (6th), Gerald Cavendish Grosvenor, *b.* 1951, *s.* 1979, *m.*	†

MARQUESSES

Style, The Most Hon. the Marquess of——. *Addressed as,* My Lord Marquess.
In titles marked ° the "of" is *not* used. For the style of Marquesses' sons and daughters, *see* under "DUKES,"above.

1916   *Aberdeen and Temair* (5th), Archibald Victor Dudley Gordon, (11th *Scott. Earl, Aberdeen,* 1682), *b.* 1913, *s.* 1974.   Lord Alastair N. J. *G., b.* 1920.

Created.	Title, Order of Succession, Name, etc.	Eldest Son or Heir.
1876	`Abergavenny (5th), John Henry Guy Nevill, K.G., O.B.E., b. 1914, s. 1954, m.`	Guy R. G. N., b. 1945.
1821	*Ailesbury* (8th), Michael Sidney Cedric Brudenell-Bruce, b. 1926, s. 1974, m.	Earl of Cardigan, b. 1952.
1831	*Ailsa* (7th), Archibald David Kennedy, O.B.E., (19th *Scott. Earl, Cassillis,* 1509), b. 1925, s. 1957, m.	Earl of Cassillis, b. 1956.
1815	*Anglesey* (7th), George Charles Henry Victor Paget, b. 1922, s. 1947, m.	Earl of Uxbridge, b. 1950.
1789	*Bath* (6th), Henry Frederick Thynne, b. 1905, s. 1946, m.	Viscount Weymouth, b. 1932.
1826	*Bristol* (6th), Victor Frederick Cochrane Hervey, b. 1915, s. 1960, m.	Earl Jermyn, b. 1954.
1796	*Bute* (6th), John Crichton-Stuart (11th *Scott. Earl, Dumfries,* 1633), b. 1933, s. 1956, m.	Earl of Dumfries, b. 1958.
1812	°*Camden* (6th), David George Edward Henry Pratt, b. 1930, s. 1983, m.	Earl of Brecknock, b. 1965.
1815	*Cholmondeley* (6th), George Hugh Cholmondeley, G.C.V.O., M.C. (10th *Irish Viscount, Cholmondeley,* 1661), b. 1919, s. 1968, m. (*Lord Great Chamberlain*).	Earl of Rocksavage, b. 1960.
1816 I.*	°*Conyngham* (7th), Frederick William Henry Francis Conyngham (7th *U.K. Baron, Minster, U.K.* 1821), b. 1924, s. 1974, m.	Earl of Mount Charles, b. 1951.
1791 I.*	*Donegall* (7th), Dermot Richard Claud Chichester (7th *Brit. Baron, Fisherwick,* 1790, 6th *Brit. Baron, Templemore,* 1831), b. 1916, s. to Marquessate, 1975: to Templemore Barony, 1953, m.	Earl of Belfast, b. 1952.
1789 I.*	*Downshire* (7th), Arthur Wills Percy Wellington Blundell Trumbull Sandys Hill (7th *Brit. Earl, Hillsborough,* 1772), b. 1894, s. 1918, w.	A. Robin I. H., b. 1929.
1888	*Dufferin & Ava* (5th), Sheridan Frederick Terence Hamilton-Temple-Blackwood (11th *Irish Baron, Dufferin & Clandeboye,* 1800), b. 1938, s. 1945, m.	(None to Marquessate), to Irish Barony, Sir Francis G. *Blackwood,* Bt., b. 1916.
1801 I.*	*Ely* (8th) Charles John Tottenham (8th *U.K. Baron, Loftus,* 1801), b. 1913, s. 1969, m.	Viscount Loftus, b. 1943.
1801	*Exeter* (7th), William Martin Alleyne Cecil, b. 1909, s. 1981, m.	Lord Burghley, b. 1935.
1800 I.*	*Headfort* (6th), Thomas Geoffrey Charles Michael Taylour (4th *U.K. Baron, Kenlis,* 1831), b. 1932, s. 1960, m.	Earl of Bective, b. 1959.
1793	*Hertford* (8th), Hugh Edward Conway Seymour (9th *Irish Baron, Conway,* 1712), b. 1930, s. 1940, m.	Earl of Yarmouth, b. 1958.
1599 S.*	*Huntly* (12th), Douglas Charles Lindsay Gordon (*Premier Marquess of Scotland*) (4th *U.K. Baron, Meldrum,* 1815), b. 1908, s. 1937, m.	Earl of Aboyne, b. 1944.
1784	*Lansdowne* (8th), George John Charles Mercer Nairne Petty-Fitzmaurice, P.C. (8th *Irish Earl. Kerry,* 1723), b. 1912, s. 1944, m.	Earl of Shelburne, b. 1941.
1902	*Linlithgow* (3rd), Charles William Frederick Hope, M.C., T.D. (9th *Scott. Earl, Hopetoun* 1703), b. 1912, s. 1952, m.	Earl of Hopetoun, b. 1946.
1816 I.*	*Londonderry* (9th), Alexander Charles Robert Vane-Tempest-Stewart (6th *U.K. Earl, Vane,* 1823), b. 1937, s. 1955, m.	Viscount Castlereagh, b. 1972.
1701 S.*	*Lothian* (12th), Peter Francis Walter Kerr, K.C.V.O. (6th *U.K. Baron, Kerr,* 1821), b. 1922, s. 1940, m.	Earl of Ancram, M.P., b. 1945.
1917	*Milford Haven* (4th), George Ivar Louis Mountbatten, b. 1961, s. 1970.	Lord Ivar A. M. M., b. 1963.
1838	*Normanby* (4th), Oswald Constantine John Phipps, C.B.E. (8th *Irish Baron, Mulgrave,* 1767), b. 1912, s. 1932, m.	Earl of Mulgrave, b. 1954.
1812	*Northampton* (7th), Spencer Douglas David Compton, b. 1946, s. 1978.	Earl Compton, b. 1973.
1825 I.*	*Ormonde* (7th), James Hubert Theobald Charles Butler, M.B.E. (7th *U.K. Baron, Ormonde,* 1821), b. 1899, s. 1971, w.	(None to Marquessate), to Earldoms of Ormonde and Ossory, Viscount Mountgarret, b. 1936.
1682 S.	*Queensberry* (12th), David Harrington Angus Douglas, b. 1929, s. 1954, m.	Viscount Drumlanrig, b. 1967.
1926	*Reading* (4th), Simon Charles Henry Rufus Isaacs, b. 1942, s. 1980, m.	Lord Anthony M. R. I., b. 1943.
1789	*Salisbury* (6th), Robert Edward Peter Gascoyne-Cecil, b. 1916, s. 1972, m.	Viscount Cranborne, M.P., b. 1946.
1800 I.*	*Sligo* (10th), Denis Edward Browne (10th *U.K. Baron, Monteagle,* 1806), b. 1908, s. 1952, m.	Earl of Altamont, b. 1939.
1787	°*Townshend* (7th), George John Patrick Dominic Townshend, b. 1916, s. 1921, m.	Viscount Raynham, b. 1945.
1694 S.*	*Tweeddale* (13th), Edward Douglas John Hay (4th *U.K. Baron, Tweeddale,* 1881), b. 1947, s. 1979.	Lord Charles D. M. H., b. 1947.
1789 I.*	*Waterford* (8th), John Hubert de la Poer Beresford (8th *Brit. Baron, Tyrone,* 1786), b. 1933, s. 1934, m.	Earl of Tyrone, b. 1958.
1551	*Winchester* (18th), Nigel George Paulet (*Premier Marquess of England*), b. 1941, s. 1968, m.	Earl of Wiltshire, b. 1969.
1892	*Zetland* (3rd), Lawrence Aldred Mervyn Dundas (5th *U.K. Earl of Zetland,* 1838, 6th *Brit. Baron Dundas,* 1794), b. 1908, s. 1961, m.	Earl of Ronaldshay, b. 1937.

EARLS

Style (see also note, p. 247). The Right Hon. the Earl of ——. *Addressed as,* My Lord.
The eldest sons of Earls take, by courtesy, their father's second title, the younger sons
being styled the Hon., *e.g.* the Hon. John ——, but the daughters Lady Elizabeth ——,
etc. Where marked ° the "of" is not used.

Created.	*Title, Order of Succession, Name, etc.*	*Eldest Son or Heir.*
1639 s.	*Airlie* (13th), David George Coke Patrick Ogilvy, *b.* 1926, *s.* 1968, *m.*	Lord Ogilvy, *b.* 1958.
1696	*Albemarle* (10th), Rufus Arnold Alexis Keppel, *b.* 1965, *s.* 1979, *M.*	Hon. Walter A. C. *K.*, D.S.C., *b.* 1914.
1952	°*Alexander of Tunis* (2nd), Shane William Desmond Alexander, *b.* 1935, *s.* 1969, *m.*	Hon. Brian J. *A.*, *b.* 1939.
1826	°*Amherst* (5th), Jeffery John Archer Amherst, M.C., *b.* 1896, *s.* 1927.	(None.)
1789 I.	°*Annesley* (10th), Patrick Annesley, *b.* 1924, *s.* 1979, *m.*	Hon. Philip H.*A.*, *b.* 1927.
1785 I.	*Antrim* (9th), Alexander Randal Mark McDonnell, *b.* 1935, *s.* 1977, *m.* (*Viscount Dunluce.*)	Hon. Randal A. *M.*, *b.* 1967.
1762 I.*	*Arran* (9th), Arthur Desmond Colquhoun Gore (5th *U.K. Baron Sudley,* 1884), *b.* 1938, *s.* 1983, *m.*	Paul A. *G.*, C.M.G., C.V.O., *b.* 1921.
1955	°*Attlee* (2nd), Martin Richard Attlee, *b.* 1927, *s.* 1967, *m.*	Viscount Prestwood, *b.* 1956.
1961	*Avon* (2nd), Nicholas Eden, O.B.E., T.D., *b.* 1930, *s.* 1977.	(None.)
1714	*Aylesford* (11th), Charles Ian Finch-Knightley, *b.* 1918, *s.* 1958, *m.*	Lord Guernsey, *b.* 1947.
1937	°*Baldwin of Bewdley* (4th), Edward Alfred Alexander Baldwin, *b.* 1938, *s.* 1976, *m.*	Viscount Corvedale, *b.* 1973.
1922	*Balfour* (4th) Gerald Arthur James Balfour, *b.* 1925, *s.* 1968, *m.*	Eustace A. G. *B.*, *b.* 1921.
1772	°*Bathurst* (8th), Henry Allen John Bathurst, *b.* 1927, *s.* 1943, *m.*	Lord Apsley, *b.* 1961.
1919	°*Beatty* (3rd), David Beatty, *b.* 1946, *s.* 1972, *m.*	Viscount Borodale, *b.* 1973.
1797 I.	*Belmore* (8th), John Armar Lowry-Corry, *b.* 1951, *s.* 1960.	Frederick H. L.-*C.*, *b.* 1926.
1739 I.* ⎫	*Bessborough* (2nd), Frederick Edward Neuflize Ponsonby (10th *Irish*	Arthur M. L. *P.*, *b.* 1912 (to
1937 ⎭	*Earl Bessborough*), *b.* 1913, *s.* 1956, *m.*	Irish Earldom only).
1922	*Birkenhead* (3rd), Frederick William Robin Smith, *b.* 1936, *s.* 1975.	(None.)
1815	*Bradford* (7th), Richard Thomas Orlando Bridgeman, *b.* 1947, *s.* 1981, *m.*	Viscount Newport, *b.*1980.
1677 s.	*Breadalbane and Holland* (10th), John Romer Boreland Campbell, *b.* 1919, *s.* 1959.	(None.)
1469 s.*	*Buchan* (17th), Malcolm Harry Erskine, (8th *U.K. Baron Erskine* 1806), *b.* 1930, *s.* 1984, *m.*	Lord Cardross, *b.* 1960.
1746	*Buckinghamshire* (10th), (George) Miles Hobart-Hampden, *b.* 1944, *s.* 1983, *m.*	Sir Robert Hobart, Bt., *b.* 1915.
1800	°*Cadogan* (7th), William Gerald Charles Cadogan, M.C., *b.* 1914, *s.* 1933, *m.*	Viscount Chelsea, *b.* 1937.
1878	°*Cairns* (5th), David Charles Cairns, G.C.V.O., C.B., *b.* 1909, *s.* 1946, *m.*	Viscount Garmoyle, *b.* 1939.
1455 s.	*Caithness* (20th), Malcolm Ian Sinclair, *b.* 1948, *s.* 1965, *m.*	Lord Berriedale, *b.* 1981.
1800 I.	*Caledon* (7th), Nicholas James Alexander, *b.* 1955, *s.* 1980, *m.*	Earl Alexander of Tunis (*see* above.)
1661	*Carlisle* (12th), Charles James Ruthven Howard, M.C. (*Scott. Baron, Ruthven of Freeland,* 1651), *b.* 1923, *s.* 1963, *m.*	Viscount Morpeth, *b.* 1949.
1793	*Carnarvon* (6th), Henry George Alfred Marius Victor Francis Herbert, *b.* 1898, *s.* 1923.	Lord Porchester, K.C.V.O., K.B.E., *b.* 1924.
1748 I.*	*Carrick* (9th), Brian Stuart Theobald Somerset Caher Butler (3rd *U.K. Baron, Butler,* 1912), *b.* 1931, *s.* 1957.	Viscount Ikerrin, *b.* 1953.
1800 I.	°*Castle Stewart* (8th), Arthur Patrick Avondale Stuart, *b.* 1928, *s.* 1961, *m.*	Viscount Stuart, *b.* 1953.
1814	°*Cathcart* (6th), Alan Cathcart, C.B., D.S.O., M.C. (15th *Scott. Baron, Cathcart,* 1447), *b.* 1919, *s.* 1927, *m.*	Lord Greenock, *b.* 1952.
1647 I.	*Cavan* (12th), Michael Edward Oliver Lambart, T.D., *b.* 1911, *s.* 1950, *m.*	Roger C. *L.*, *b.* 1944.
1827	°*Cawdor* (6th), Hugh John Vaughan Campbell, *b.* 1932, *s.* 1970, *m.*	Viscount Emlyn, *b.* 1962.
1801	*Chichester* (9th), John Nicholas Pelham, *b.* 1944, *s.* 1944, *m.*	Richard A. H. *P.*, *b.* 1952.
1803 I.*	*Clancarty* (8th), William Francis Brinsley Le Poer Trench (7th *U.K. Visct. Clancarty,* 1823), *b.* 1911, *s.* 1975, *m.*	Nicholas P. R. *Le P. T.*, *b.* 1952.
1776 I.*	*Clanwilliam* (6th), John Charles Edmund Carson Meade (4th *U.K. Baron Clanwilliam,* 1828), *b.* 1914, *s.* 1953, *m.*	John H. *M.*, *b.* 1919.
1776	*Clarendon* (7th), George Frederick Laurence Hyde Villiers, *b.* 1933, *s.* 1955, *m.*	Lord Hyde, *b.* 1976.
1620 I.*	*Cork & Orrery* (1660), Patrick Reginald Boyle (13th *Irish Earl* and 9th *Brit. Baron, Boyle of Marston,* 1711), *b.* 1910, *s.* 1967, *m.*	Hon. John W. *B.*, D.S.C., *b.* 1916.
1850	*Cottenham* (8th), Kenelm Charles Everard Digby Pepys, *b.* 1948, *s.* 1968, *m.*	Hon. Mark J. *P.*, *b.* 1983.
1762 I.*	*Courtown* (9th), James Patrick Montagu Burgoyne Winthrop Stopford (8th *Brit. Baron, Saltersford,* 1796), *b.* 1954, *s.* 1975.	Hon. Jeremy N. *S.*, *b.* 1958.
1697	*Coventry* (11th), George William Coventry, *b.* 1934, *s.* 1940, *m.*	Viscount Deerhurst, *b.* 1957.
1857	°*Cowley* (7th), Garret Graham Wellesley, *b.* 1934, *s.* 1975, *m.*	Viscount Dangan, *b.* 1965.
1892	*Cranbrook* (5th), Gathorne Gathorne-Hardy, *b.* 1933, *s.* 1978, *m.*	Lord Medway, *b.* 1968.
1801	*Craven* (8th), Simon George Craven, *b.* 1961, *s.* 1983.	†
1398 s.*	*Crawford* (29th) *and Balcarres* (12th), Robert Alexander Lindsay, P.C., (*Premier Earl on Union Roll and* 5th *U.K. Baron, Wigan,* 1826), *b.* 1927, *s.* 1975, *m.*	Lord Balniel, *b.* 1958.

Created.	Title, Order of Succession, Name, etc.	Eldest Son or Heir.
1861	*Cromartie* (4th), Roderick Grant Francis, Mackenzie, M.C., T.D., *b.* 1904, *s.* 1962, *m.*	Viscount Tarbat, *b.* 1948.
1901	*Cromer* (3rd), George Rowland Stanley Baring, K.G., G.C.M.G., M.B.E., P.C., *b.* 1918, *s.* 1953, *m.*	Viscount Errington, *b.* 1946.
1633 s.*	*Dalhousie* (16th), Simon Ramsay, K.T., G.C.V.O., G.B.E., M.C. (4th *U.K. Baron, Ramsay*, 1875), *b.* 1914, *s.* 1950, *m.*	Lord Ramsay, *b.* 1948.
1725 I.*	*Darnley* (11th), Adam Ivo Stuart Bligh (20th *English Baron, Clifton of Leighton Bromswold*, 1608), *b.* 1941, *s.* 1980, *m.*	Lord Clifton, *b.* 1968.
1711	*Dartmouth* (9th), Gerald Humphry Legge, *b.* 1924, *s.* 1962, *m.*	Viscount Lewisham, *b.* 1949.
1761	°*De La Warr* (10th), William Herbrand Sackville, *b.* 1921, *s.* 1976, *m.*	Lord Buckhurst, *b.* 1948.
1622	*Denbigh* (11th) *and Desmond* (10th), William Rudolph Michael Feilding (10th *Irish Earl, Desmond*, 1622), *b.* 1943, *s.* 1966, *m.*	Viscount Feilding, *b.* 1970.
1485	*Derby* (18th), Edward John Stanley, M.C., *b.* 1918, *s.* 1948, *m.*	Hon. Edward R. W. S., *b.* 1962.
1553	*Devon* (17th), Charles Christopher Courtenay, *b.* 1916, *s.* 1935, *m.*	Lord Courtenay, *b.* 1942.
1800 I.*	*Donoughmore* (8th), Richard Michael John Hely-Hutchinson, (8th *U.K. Visct., Hutchinson*, 1821), *b.* 1927, *s.* 1981, *m.*	Viscount Suirdale, *b.* 1952.
1661 I.*	*Drogheda* (11th), Charles Garrett Ponsonby Moore, K.G., K.B.E. (2nd *U.K. Baron. Moore*, 1954), *b.* 1910, *s.* 1957, *m.*	Viscount Moore, *b.* 1937.
1837	*Ducie* (6th), Basil Howard Moreton, *b.* 1917, *s.* 1952, *m.*	Lord Moreton, *b.* 1951.
1860	*Dudley* (4th), William Humble David Ward, *b.* 1920, *s.* 1969, *m.*	Viscount Ednam, *b.* 1947.
1660 s.*	*Dundee* (12th), Alexander Henry Scrymgeour, (2nd *U.K. Baron, Glassary*, 1954), *b.* 1949, *s.* 1983, *m.*	Lord Scrymgeour, *b.* 1982.
1669 s.	*Dundonald* (14th), Ian Douglas Leonard Cochrane, *b.* 1918, *s.* 1958, *m.*	Lord Cochrane, *b.* 1961.
1686 s.*	*Dunmore* (11th), Kenneth Randolph Murray, *b.* 1913, *s.* 1981, *m.*	Viscount Fincastle, *b.* 1946.
1822 I.	*Dunraven and Mount Earl* (7th), Thady Windham Thomas Wyndham-Quin, *b.* 1939, *s.* 1965, *m.*	(None).
1837	*Effingham* (6th), Mowbray Henry Gordon Howard (16th *E. Baron, Howard of Effingham*, 1554), *b.* 1905, *s.* 1946, *m.*	Lt.-Cmdr. David P. M. A. *H.*, *b.* 1939.
1507 s. } 1859*	*Eglinton* (18th) *&* (9th) *Winton* (1600), Archibald George Montgomerie (6th *U.K. Earl Winton*, 1859), *b.* 1939, *s.* 1966, *m.*	Lord Montgomerie, *b.* 1966.
1733 I.*	*Egmont* (11th), Frederick George Moore Perceval (9th *Brit. Baron, Lovel & Holland*, 1762), *b.* 1914, *s.* 1932, *m.*	Viscount Perceval, *b.* 1934.
1821	*Eldon* (5th), John Joseph Nicholas Scott, *b.* 1937, *s.* 1976, *m.*	Viscount Encombe, *b.* 1962.
1633 s.*	*Elgin* (11th), *& Kincardine* (15th) (1647), Andrew Douglas Alexander Thomas Bruce, (4th *U.K. Baron, Elgin*, 1849), K.T., *b.* 1924, *s.* 1968, *m.*	Lord Bruce, *b.* 1961.
1789 I.*	*Enniskillen* (6th), David Lowry Cole, M.B.E., (4th *U.K. Baron, Grinstead*, 1815) *b.* 1918, *s.* 1963, *m.*	Viscount Cole, *b.* 1942.
1789 I.*	*Erne* (6th). Henry George Victor John Crichton (3rd *U.K. Baron, Fermanagh*, 1876), *b.* 1937, *s.* 1940, *m.*	Viscount Crichton, *b.* 1971.
1452 s.	*Erroll* (24th), Merlin Sereld Victor Gilbert Hay (*Hereditary Lord High Constable and Knight Marischal of Scotland*), *b.* 1948, *s.* 1978, *m.*	Son, *b.* 1984.
1661	*Essex* (10th), Robert Edward de Vere Capell, *b.* 1920, *s.* 1981, *m.*	Visct. Malden, *b.* 1944.
1711	°*Ferrers* (13th), Robert Washington Shirley, P.C., *b.* 1929, *s.* 1954, *m.*	Viscount Tamworth, *b.* 1952.
1789	°*Fortescue* (7th), Richard Archibald Fortescue, *b.* 1922, *s.* 1977, *m.*	Viscount Ebrington, *b.* 1951.
1841	*Gainsborough* (5th), Anthony Gerard Edward Noel, *b.* 1923, *s.* 1927, *m.*	Viscount Campden, *b.* 1950.
1623 s.*	*Galloway* (13th), Randolph Keith Reginald Stewart (6th *Brit. Baron, Stewart of Garlies*, 1796), *b.* 1928, *s.* 1978, *m.*	Alexander D. *S.*, M.B.E., T.D., *b.* 1914.
1703 s.*	*Glasgow* (10th), Patrick Robin Archibald Boyle (4th *U.K. Baron, Fairlie*, 1897), *b.* 1939, *s.* 1984, *m.*	Viscount of Kelburn, *b.* 1978.
1806 I.*	*Gosford* (7th), Charles David Nicholas Alexander John Sparrow Acheson (5th *U.K. Baron, Worlingham*, 1835), *b.* 1942, *s.* 1966.	Hon. Patrick B. V. M. *A.*, *b.* 1915.
1945	*Gowrie* (2nd), Alexander Patric Greysteil Hore-Ruthven, P.C. (3rd *U.K. Baron, Ruthven of Gowrie*, 1919), *b.* 1939, *s.* 1955, *m.*	Viscount Ruthven of Canberra, *b.* 1964.
1684 I.*	*Granard* (9th), Arthur Patrick Hastings Forbes, A.F.C. (4th *U.K. Baron, Granard*, 1806), *b.* 1915, *s.* 1948, *m.*	Peter A. E. H. *F.*, *b.* 1957.
1833	°*Granville* (5th), Granville James Leveson-Gower, M.C., *b.* 1918, *s.* 1953, *m.*	Lord Leveson, *b.* 1959.
1806	°*Grey* (6th), Richard Fleming George Charles Grey, *b.* 1939, *s.* 1963, *m.*	Philip K. *G.*, *b.* 1940.
1752	*Guilford* (9th), Edward Francis North, *b.* 1933, *s.* 1949, *m.*	Lord North, *b.* 1971.
1619 s.	*Haddington* (12th), George Baillie-Hamilton, K.T., M.C., T.D., *b.*1894, *s.* 1917, *m.*	Lord Binning, *b.* 1941.
1919	°*Haig* (2nd), George Alexander Eugene Douglas Haig, O.B.E., *b.* 1918, *s.* 1928, *m.*	Viscount Dawick, *b.* 1961.
1944	*Halifax* (3rd), Charles Edward Peter Neil Wood (5th *U.K. Viscount, Halifax*, 1866), *b.* 1944, *s.* 1980, *m.*	Lord Irwin, *b.* 1977.
1898	*Halsbury* (3rd), John Anthony Hardinge Giffard, F.R.S., *b.* 1908, *s.* 1943, *w.*	Adam E. *G.*, *b.* 1934.
1754	*Hardwicke* (10th), Joseph Philip Sebastian Yorke, *b.* 1971, *s.* 1974, *M.*	Richard C. J. *Y.*, *b.* 1916.
1812	*Harewood* (7th), George Henry Hubert Lascelles, *b.* 1923, *s.* 1947, *m.* (*See also* p. 217).	Viscount Lascelles, *b.* 1950.

Created.	Title, Order of Succession, Name, etc.	Eldest Son or Heir.
1742	*Harrington* (11th), William Henry Leicester Stanhope (8th *Brit. Viscount, Stanhope of Mahon*, 1717), *b.* 1922, *s.* 1929, *m.*	Viscount Petersham, *b.* 1945.
1809	*Harrowby* (6th), Dudley Ryder, *b.* 1892, *s.* 1956, *w.*	Viscount Sandon, *b.* 1922.
1821	°*Howe* (7th), Frederick Richard Penn Curzon, *b.* 1951, *s.* 1984, *m.*	†
1529	*Huntingdon* (15th), Francis John Clarence Westenra Plantagenet Hastings, *b.* 1901, *s.* 1939, *m.*	Lt. Col. R. H. W. S. *H.*, D.S.O., O.B.E., M.C., *b.* 1917.
1885	*Iddesleigh* (4th), Stafford Henry Northcote, *b.* 1932, *s.* 1970, *m.*	Viscount St. Cyres, *b.* 1957.
1756	*Ilchester* (9th), Maurice Vivian de Touffreville Fox-Strangways, *b.* 1920, *s.* 1970, *m.*	Hon. Raymond G. *F.-S.*, *b.* 1921.
1929	*Inchcape* (3rd), Kenneth James William Mackay, *b.* 1917, *s.* 1939, *m.*	Viscount Glenapp, *b.* 1943.
1919	*Iveagh* (3rd), Arthur Francis Benjamin Guinness, *b.* 1937, *s.* 1967, *m.*	Viscount Elveden, *b.* 1969.
1925	°*Jellicoe* (2nd), George Patrick John Rushworth Jellicoe, P.C., D.S.O., M.C., *b.* 1918, *s.* 1935, *m.*	Viscount Brocas, *b.* 1950.
1697	*Jersey* (9th), George Francis Child-Villiers (12th *Irish Visct., Grandison*, 1620), *b.* 1910, *s.* 1923, *m.*	Viscount Villiers, *b.* 1948.
1822 I.	*Kilmorey* (6th), Richard Francis Needham, M.P., *b.* 1942, *s.* 1977, *m.*	Viscount Newry and Morne, *b.* 1966.
1866	*Kimberley* (4th), John Wodehouse, *b.* 1924, *s.* 1941, *m.*	Lord Wodehouse, *b.* 1951.
1768 I.	*Kingston* (11th), Barclay Robert Edwin King-Tenison, *b.* 1943, *s.* 1948.	Viscount Kingsborough, *b.* 1969.
1633 S.*	*Kinnoull* (15th), Arthur William George Patrick Hay (9th *Brit. Baron, Hay of Pedwardine*, 1711), *b.* 1935, *s.* 1938, *m.*	Viscount Dupplin, *b.* 1962.
1677 S.*	*Kintore* (12th), (James) Ian Keith (2nd *U.K. Visct., Stonehaven*, 1938), *b.* 1908, *s.* to Viscountcy, 1941, to Earldom, 1974, *m.*	Lord Inverurie, *b.* 1939.
1914	°*Kitchener of Khartoum* (3rd), Henry Herbert Kitchener, T.D., *b.* 1919, *s.* 1937.	Henry H. *K.*, *b.* 1890.
1756 I.	*Lanesborough* (9th), Denis Anthony Brian Butler, T.D., *b.* 1918, *s.* 1950.	Cdr. T. B. J. D. *B.*, *b.* 1913.
1624 S.	*Lauderdale* (17th), Patrick Francis Maitland, *b.* 1911, *s.* 1968, *m.*	Viscount Maitland, *b.* 1937.
1837	*Leicester* (6th), Anthony Louis Lovel Coke, *b.* 1909, *s.* 1976, *m.*	Viscount Coke, *b.* 1936.
1641 S.	*Leven* (14th) & (13th) *Melville* (1690), Alexander Robert Leslie-Melville, *b.* 1924, *s.* 1947, *m.*	Lord Balgonie, *b.* 1954.
1831	*Lichfield* (5th), Thomas Patrick John Anson, *b.* 1939, *s.* 1960, *m.*	Viscount Anson, *b.* 1978.
1803 I.*	*Limerick* (6th), Patrick Edmund Pery, K.B.E. (6th *U.K. Baron, Foxford*, 1815), *b.* 1930, *s.* 1967, *m.*	Viscount Glentworth, *b.* 1963.
1633 S.	*Lindsay* (14th), William Tucker Lindesay-Bethune, *b.* 1901, *s.* 1943, *m.*	Viscount Garnock, *b.* 1926.
1626	*Lindsey* (14th) *and Abingdon* (9th) (1682), Richard Henry Rupert Bertie, *b.* 1931, *s.* 1963, *m.*	Lord Norreys, *b.* 1958.
1776 I.	*Lisburne* (8th), John David Malet Vaughan, *b.* 1918, *s.* 1965, *m.*	Viscount Vaughan, *b.* 1945.
1822 I.*	*Listowel* (5th), William Francis Hare, P.C., G.C.M.G. (3rd *U.K. Baron, Hare*, 1869), *b.* 1906, *s.* 1931, *m.*	Viscount Ennismore, *b.* 1964.
1905	*Liverpool* (5th), Edward Peter Bertram Savile Foljambe, *b.* 1944, *s.* 1969, *m.*	Viscount Hawkesbury, *b.* 1972.
1945	°*Lloyd George of Dwyfor* (3rd), Owen Lloyd George, *b.* 1924, *s.* 1968, *m.*	Viscount Gwynedd, *b.* 1951.
1785 I.*	*Longford* (7th), Francis Aungier Pakenham, K.G., P.C. (6th *U.K. Baron, Silchester*, 1821; 1st *U.K. Baron, Pakenham*, 1945), *b.* 1905, *s.* 1961, *m.*	Thomas F. D. *P.*, *b.* 1933.
1807	*Lonsdale* (7th), James Hugh William Lowther, *b.* 1922, *s.* 1953, *m.*	Viscount Lowther, *b.* 1949.
1838	*Lovelace* (5th), Peter Axel William Locke King (12th *British Baron, King*, 1725), *b.* 1951, *s.* 1964.	(None.)
1795 I.*	*Lucan* (7th), Richard John Bingham (3rd *U.K. Baron, Bingham*, 1934), *b.* 1934, *s.* 1964, *m.*	Lord Bingham, *b.* 1967.
1880	*Lytton* (4th), Noel Anthony Scawen Lytton, O.B.E. (17th *English Baron, Wentworth*, 1529), *b.* 1900, *s.* 1951, *m.*	Viscount Knebworth, *b.* 1950.
1721	*Macclesfield* (8th), George Roger Alexander Thomas Parker, *b.* 1914, *s.* 1975, *m.*	Viscount Parker, *b.* 1943.
1800	*Malmesbury* (6th), William James Harris, T.D., *b.* 1907, *s.* 1950, *m.*	Viscount FitzHarris, *b.* 1946.
1776 & 1792	*Mansfield and Mansfield* (8th), William David Mungo James Murray (14th *Scott. Visct., Stormont*, 1621), *b.* 1930, *s.* 1971, *m.*	Viscount Stormont, *b.* 1956.
1565 S.	*Mar* (13th) & (15th) *Kellie* (1616), John Francis Hervey Erskine, *b.* 1921, *s.* 1955, *m.*	Lord Erskine, *b.* 1949.
1785 I.	*Mayo* (10th), Terence Patrick Bourke, *b.* 1929, *s.* 1962, *m.*	Lord Naas, *b.* 1953.
1627 I.*	*Meath* (14th), Anthony Windham Normand Brabazon (5th *U.K. Baron, Chaworth*, 1831), *b.* 1910, *s.* 1949, *m.*	Lord Ardee, *b.* 1941.
1766 I.	*Mexborough* (8th), John Christopher George Savile, *b.* 1931, *s.* 1980, *m.*	Viscount Pollington, *b.* 1959.
1813	*Minto* (6th), Gilbert Edward George Lariston Garnet Elliot-Murray-Kynynmound, M.B.E., *b.* 1928, *s.* 1975, *w.*	Viscount Melgund, *b.* 1953.
1562 S.*	*Moray* (20th) Douglas John Moray Stuart (12th *Brit. Baron, Stuart of Castle Stuart*, 1796), *b.* 1928, *s.* 1974, *m.*	Lord Doune, *b.* 1966.
1815	*Morley* (6th), John St. Aubyn Parker, *b.* 1923, *s.* 1962, *m.*	Visct. Boringdon, *b.* 1956.
1458 S.	*Morton* (22nd), John Charles Sholto Douglas, *b.* 1927, *s.* 1976, *m.*	Lord Aberdour, *b.* 1952.
1789	*Mount Edgcumbe* (8th), Robert Charles Edgcumbe, *b.* 1939, *s.* 1982, *m.*	Piers V. *E.*, *b.* 1946.
1831	*Munster* (7th), Anthony Charles FitzClarence, *b.* 1926, *s.* 1983, *m.*	†

Created.	Title, Order of Succession, Name, etc.	Eldest Son or Heir.
1805	°*Nelson* (9th), Peter John Horatio Nelson, b. 1941, s. 1981, m.	Viscount Merton, b. 1971.
1660 s.	*Newburgh* (11th), Prince Giulio Cesare Taddeo Cosimo Rospigliosi, b. 1907, s. 1977, m.	Viscount Kynnaird, b. 1942.
1827 I.	*Norbury* (6th), Noel Terence Graham-Toler, b. 1939, s. 1955, m.	Viscount Glandine, b. 1967.
1806 I.*	*Normanton* (6th), Shaun James Christian Welbore Ellis Agar (9th Brit. Baron, Mendip, 1791) (4th U.K. Baron, Somerton, 1873), b. 1945, s. 1967, m.	Viscount Somerton, b. 1982.
1647 s.	*Northesk* (13th), Robert Andrew Carnegie, b. 1926, s. 1975, m.	Lord Rosehill, b. 1954.
1801	*Onslow* (7th), Michael William Coplestone Dillon Onslow, b. 1938, s. 1971, m.	Viscount Cranley, b. 1967.
1696	*Orkney* (8th), Cecil O'Bryen Fitz-Maurice, b. 1919, s. 1951, m.	O, Peter St. J. F-M., b. 1938
1925	*Oxford & Asquith* (2nd), Julian Edward George Asquith, K.C.M.G., b. 1916, s. 1928, m.	Viscount Asquith, b. 1952.
1929	°*Peel* (3rd), William James Robert Peel (4th U.K. Viscount Peel, 1895), b. 1947, s. 1969, m.	Viscount Clanfield, b. 1976.
1551	*Pembroke* (17th) & (14th) *Montgomery* (1605), Henry George Charles Alexander Herbert, b. 1939, s. 1969.	Lord Herbert, b. 1978.
1605 s.	*Perth* (17th), John David Drummond, P.C., b. 1907, s. 1951, m.	Viscount Strathallan, b. 1935.
1905	*Plymouth* (3rd), Other Robert Ivor Windsor-Clive (15th English Baron, Windsor, 1529), b. 1923, s. 1943, m.	Viscount Windsor, b. 1951.
1785 I.	*Portarlington* (7th), George Lionel Yuill Seymour Dawson-Damer, b. 1938, s. 1959, m.	Viscount Carlow, b. 1965.
1743	*Portsmouth* (9th), Gerard Vernon Wallop, b. 1898, s. 1943, w.	Visct. Lymington, b. 1954.
1804	*Powis* (6th), Christian Victor Charles Herbert (7th Irish Baron, Clive, 1762), b. 1904, s. 1974.	George W. H., b. 1925.
1765	*Radnor* (8th) Jacob Pleydell-Bouverie, b. 1927, s. 1968, m.	Viscount Folkestone, b. 1955.
1831 I.*	*Ranfurly* (6th), Thomas Daniel Knox, K.C.M.G. (7th U.K. Baron, Ranfurly, 1826), b. 1913, s. 1933, m.	Gerald F. N. K., b. 1929.
1771 I.	*Roden* (9th), Robert William Jocelyn, b. 1909, s. 1956, m.	Viscount Jocelyn, b. 1938.
1801	*Romney* (7th), Michael Henry Marsham, b. 1910, s. 1975, m.	Julian C. M., b. 1948.
1703 s.*	*Rosebery* (7th), Neil Archibald Primrose (3rd U.K. Earl, Midlothian, 1911), b. 1929, s. 1974, m.	Lord Dalmeny, b. 1967.
1806 I.	*Rosse* (7th), William Brendan Parsons, b. 1936, s. 1979, m.	Lord Oxmantown, b. 1969.
1801	*Rosslyn* (7th), Peter St. Clair-Erskine, b. 1958, s. 1977, m.	Hon. David S. St. C.-E., b. 1917.
1457 s.	*Rothes* (21st), Ian Lionel Malcolm Leslie, b. 1932, s. 1975, m.	Lord Leslie, b. 1958.
1861	°*Russell* (4th), John Conrad Russell, b. 1921, s. 1970.	Hon. Conrad S. R. R., b. 1937.
1915	°*St. Aldwyn* (2nd), Michael John Hicks-Beach, P.C., G.B.E., T.D., b. 1912, s. 1916, m.	Viscount Quenington, b. 1950.
1815	*St. Germans* (9th), Nicholas Richard Michael Eliot, b. 1914, s. 1960, m.	Lord Eliot, b. 1941.
1690	*Scarbrough* (12th), Richard Aldred Lumley (13th Irish Visct., Lumley, 1628), b. 1932, s. 1969, m.	Viscount Lumley, b. 1973.
1701 s.	*Seafield* (13th), Ian Derek Francis Ogilvie-Grant, b. 1939, s. 1969, m.	Visct. Reidhaven, b. 1963.
1882	*Selborne* (4th), John Roundell Palmer, b. 1940, s. 1971, m.	Viscount Wolmer, b. 1971.
1646 s.	*Selkirk* (10th) (George) Nigel Douglas-Hamilton, P.C., K.T., G.C.M.G., G.B.E., A.F.C., Q.C., b. 1906, s. 1940, m.	The Master of Selkirk, b. 1939.
1672	*Shaftesbury* (10th), Anthony Ashley-Cooper, b. 1938, s. 1961, m.	Lord Ashley, b. 1977.
1756 I.*	*Shannon* (9th), Richard Bentinck Boyle (8th Brit. Bn., Carleton 1786), b. 1924, s. 1963.	Viscount Boyle, b. 1960.
1442	*Shrewsbury* (22nd) & *Waterford* (I. 1446), Charles Henry John Benedict Crofton Chetwynd Chetwynd-Talbot (Premier Earl of England and Ireland; Earl Talbot, 1784), b. 1952, s. 1980, m.	Viscount Ingestre, b. 1978.
1961	*Snowdon* (1st), Antony Charles Robert Armstrong-Jones, G.C.V.O., b. 1930, m. (See also p. 219).	Viscount Linley, b. 1961 (see also p. 219).
1880	°*Sondes* (5th), Henry George Herbert Milles-Lade, b. 1940, s. 1970.	(None.)
1633 s.*	*Southesk* (11th), Charles Alexander Carnegie, K.C.V.O. (3rd U.K. Baron, Balinhard, 1869), b. 1893, s. 1941, m.	The Duke of Fife, b. 1929 (see pp. 216 and 227).
1765	°*Spencer* (8th), Edward John Spencer, M.V.O., b. 1924, s. 1975, m.	Viscount Althorp, b. 1964.
1703 s.*	*Stair* (13th), John Aymer Dalrymple, K.C.V.O., M.B.E (6th U.K. Baron, Oxenfoord, 1841), b. 1906, s. 1961, m.	Viscount Dalrymple, b. 1961.
1984	*Stockton* (1st), (Maurice) Harold Macmillan, P.C., O.M., F.R.S., b. 1894.	Viscount Macmillan of Ovenden, b. 1943.
1821	*Stradbroke* (6th), Robert Keith Rous, b. 1937, s. 1983, m.	Hon. Robert K. R., b. 1961.
1847	*Strafford* (8th), Thomas Edmund Byng, b. 1936, s. 1984, m.	Viscount Enfield, b. 1964.
1937	*Strathmore* (4th), Fergus Michael Claude Bowes-Lyon (17th Scottish Earl, Strathmore & Kinghorne 1606), b. 1928, s. 1957.	Lord Glamis, b. 1957.
1603	*Suffolk* (21st) & (14th) *Berkshire* (1626), Michael John James George Robert Howard, b. 1935, s. 1941, m.	Viscount Andover, b. 1974.
1955	*Swinton* (2nd), David Yarburgh Cunliffe-Lister, b. 1937, s. 1972, m.	Hon. Nicholas J. C.-L., b. 1939.
1714	*Tankerville* (10th), Peter Grey Bennet, b. 1956, s. 1980.	Rev. the Hon. George A. G. B., b. 1925.
1822	°*Temple of Stowe* (7th), Ronald Stephen Brydges Temple-Gore-Langton, b. 1910, s. 1966.	W. Grenville A. T.-G.-L., b. 1924.

Created.	Title, Order of Succession, Name, etc.	Eldest Son or Heir.
1815	*Verulam* (7th), John Duncan Grimston (11th *Irish Visct., Grimston,* 1719; 16th *Scott. Baron, Forrester of Corstorphine,* 1633), *b.* 1951, *s.* 1973, *m.*	Viscount Grimston, *b.* 1978.
1729	°*Waldegrave* (12th), Geoffrey Noel Waldegrave, K.G., G.C.V.O., T.D., *b.* 1905, *s.* 1936, *m.*	Viscount Chewton, *b.* 1940.
1759	*Warwick &* °*Brooke* (1746), David Robin Francis Guy Greville (8th *Earl Brooke* and 8th *Earl of Warwick*), *b.* 1934, *s.* 1984.	Lord Brooke, *b.* 1957.
1633 s.*	*Wemyss* (12th) *&* (8th) *March* (1697), Francis David Charteris, K.T. (5th *U.K. Baron, Wemyss,* 1821), *b.* 1912, *s.* 1937, *m.*	Lord Neidpath, *b.* 1948.
1621 I.	*Westmeath* (13th), William Anthony Nugent, *b.* 1928, *s.* 1971, *m.*	Hon. Sean C. W. N., *b.* 1965.
1624	*Westmorland* (15th), David Anthony Thomas Fane, K.C.V.O., *b.* 1924, *s.* 1948, *m.* (*Master of the Horse*).	Lord Burghersh, *b.* 1951.
1876	*Wharncliffe* (4th), Alan James Montagu-Stuart-Wortley-Mackenzie, *b.* 1935, *s.* 1953, *m.*	Alan R. *Montagu-Stuart-Wortley, b.* 1927.
1801	*Wilton* (7th), Seymour William Arthur John Egerton, *b.* 1921, *s.* 1927, *m.*	Lord Ebury, *b.* 1934 (*see* p. 239).
1628	*Winchilsea* (16th) *&* (11th) *Nottingham* (1681), Christopher Denys Stormont Finch-Hatton, *b.* 1936, *s.* 1950, *m.*	Viscount Maidstone, *b.* 1967.
1766 I.	°*Winterton* (7th), Robert Chad Turnour, *b.* 1915, *s.* 1962, *m.*	N. Cecil *T.,* D.F.M., C.D., *b.* 1919.
1956	*Woolton* (3rd), Simon Frederick Marquis, *b.* 1958, *s.* 1969.	(None.)
1837	*Yarborough* (7th), John Edward Pelham, *b.* 1920, *s.* 1966, *m.*	Lord Worsley, *b.* 1963.
1922	*Ypres* (3rd), John Richard Charles Lambart French, *b.* 1921, *s.* 1948, *m.*	(None.)

VISCOUNTS

Style (*see also* note, p. 247), The Right Hon. the Viscount ——. *Addressed as,* My Lord. The eldest sons of Viscounts and Barons have no distinctive title; they, as well as their brothers and sisters, are styled the Hon. Robert, Hon. Mary, &c.

Created.	Title, Order of Succession, Name, etc.	Eldest Son or Heir.
1945	*Addison* (3rd), Michael Addison, *b.* 1914, *s.* 1976, *m.*	Hon. William M. W. *A., b.* 1945.
1946	*Alanbrooke* (3rd), Alan Victor Harold Brooke, *b.* 1932, *s.* 1972.	(None).
1919	*Allenby* (3rd), Lt.-Col. Michael Jaffray Hynman Allenby, *b.* 1931, *s.* 1984, *m.*	Hon. Henry J. H. *A., b.* 1968.
1911	*Allendale* (3rd), Wentworth Hubert Charles Beaumont, *b.* 1922, *s.* 1956, *m.*	Hon. Wentworth P. I. *B., b.* 1948.
1642 s.	*Arbuthnott* (16th *Viscount of Arbuthnott*), John Campbell Arbuthnott, D.S.C., *b.* 1924, *s.* 1966, *m.*	Master of Arbuthnott, *b.* 1950.
1751 I.	*Ashbrook* (10th), Desmond Llowarch Edward Flower, K.C.V.O., M.B.E., *b.* 1905. *s.* 1936, *m.*	Hon. Michael L. W. *F., b.* 1935.
1917	*Astor* (4th), William Waldorf Astor, *b.* 1951, *s.* 1966, *m.*	Hon. William W. *A., b.* 1979.
1781 I.	*Bangor* (7th), Edward Henry Harold Ward, *b.* 1905, *s.* 1950, *m.*	Hon. William M. D. *W., b.* 1948.
1720 I.*	*Barrington* (11th), Patrick William Daines Barrington (5th *U.K. Baron Shute,* 1880), *b.* 1908, *s.* 1960.	(None.)
1925	*Bearsted* (3rd), Marcus Richard Samuel, T.D., *b.* 1909, *s.* 1948, *w.*	Hon. Peter M. *S.,* M.C., T.D., *b.* 1911.
1963	*Blakenham* (2nd), Michael John Hare, *b.* 1938, *s.* 1982, *m.*	Hon. Caspar J. *H., b.* 1972.
1935	*Bledisloe* (3rd), Christopher Hiley Ludlow Bathurst, Q.C., *b.* 1934, *s.* 1979, *m.*	Hon. Rupert E. L. *B., b.* 1964.
1712	*Bolingbroke & St. John* (7th), Kenneth Oliver Musgrave St. John, *b.* 1927, *s.* 1974, *m.*	Hon. Henry F. *St. J., b.* 1957.
1960	*Boyd of Merton* (2nd), Simon Donald Rupert Neville Lennox-Boyd, *b.* 1939, *s.* 1983, *m.*	Hon. Benjamin A. *L.-B., b.* 1964.
1717 I.*	*Boyne* (10th), Gustavus Michael George Hamilton-Russell (4th *U.K. Baron, Brancepeth,* 1866), *b.* 1931, *s.* 1942, *m.*	Hon. Gustavus M. S. *H.-R., b.* 1965.
1929	*Brentford* (4th), Crispin William Joynson-Hicks, *b.* 1933, *s.* 1983, *m.*	Hon. Paul W. *J.-H., b.* 1971.
1929	*Bridgeman* (3rd), Robin John Orlando Bridgeman, *b.* 1930, *s.* 1982, *m.*	Hon. William O. C. *B., b.* 1968.
1868	*Bridport* (4th), Alexander Nelson Hood (7th *Duke of Brontë in Sicily,* 1799, and 6th *Irish Baron, Bridport* 1794), *b.* 1948, *s.* 1969, *m.*	Hon. Peregrine A. N. *H., b.* 1974.
1952	*Brookeborough* (2nd), John Warden Brooke, P.C. (N.I.), *b.* 1922, *s.* 1973, *m.*	Hon. Alan H. *B., b.* 1952.
1933	*Buckmaster* (3rd), Martin Stanley Buckmaster, O.B.E., *b.* 1921, *s.* 1974.	Hon. Colin J. *B., b.* 1923.
1939	*Caldecote* (2nd), Robert Andrew Inskip, D.S.C., *b.* 1917, *s.* 1947, *m.*	Hon. Piers J. H. *I., b.* 1947.
1941	*Camrose* (2nd), (John) Seymour Berry, T.D., *b.* 1909, *s.* 1954.	Lord Hartwell, M.B.E., T.D., *b.* 1911 (*see* p. 249).
1952	*Chandos* (3rd), Thomas Orlando Lyttelton, *b.* 1953, *s.* 1980.	Hon. Matthew P. A. *L., b.* 1956.

Created.	*Title, Order of Succession, Name, etc.*	*Eldest Son or Heir.*
1665 I.	*Charlemont* (13th), Charles Wilberforce Caulfeild (17th *Irish Baron, Caulfeild of Charlemont*, 1620), *b.* 1899, *s.* 1979, *m.*	John D. C., *b.* 1934.
1921	*Chelmsford* (3rd), Frederic Jan Thesiger, *b.* 1931, *s.* 1970, *m.*	Hon. Frederic C. P. T., *b.* 1962.
1717 I.	*Chetwynd* (10th), Adam Richard John Casson Chetwynd, *b.* 1935, *s.* 1965, *m.*	Hon. Adam D. C., *b.* 1969.
1911	*Chilston* (4th), Alastair George Akers-Douglas, *b.* 1946, *s.* 1982, *m.*	Hon. Oliver I. A.-D., *b.* 1973.
1902	*Churchill* (3rd), Victor George Spencer (5th *U.K. Baron Churchill*, 1815), *b.* 1934, *s.* 1973.	None to Viscountcy; to Barony, R. Harry R. S., *b.* 1926.
1718	*Cobham* (11th), John William Leonard Lyttelton (8th *Irish Baron, Westcote*, 1776), *b.* 1943, *s.* 1977, *m.*	Hon. Christopher C. L., *b.* 1947.
1902	*Colville of Culross* (4th), John Mark Alexander Colville, Q.C. (13th *Scott. Baron, Colville of Culross*, 1604), *b.* 1933, *s.* 1945, *m.*	Master of Colville, *b.* 1959.
1826	*Combermere* (5th), Michael Wellington Stapleton-Cotton, *b.* 1929, *s.* 1969, *m.*	Hon. Thomas R. W. S.-C., *b.* 1969.
1917	*Cowdray* (3rd), Weetman John Churchill Pearson, T.D. (3rd *U.K. Baron, Cowdray*, 1910), *b.* 1910, *s.* 1933, *m.*	Hon. Michael O. W. P., *b.* 1944.
1927	*Craigavon* (3rd), Janric Fraser Craig, *b.* 1944, *s.* 1974.	(None).
1886	*Cross* (3rd), Assheton Henry Cross, *b.* 1920, *s.* 1932, *m.*	(None).
1943	*Daventry* (2nd), Robert Oliver FitzRoy, *b.* 1893, *s.* 1962, *w.*	Francis H. M. *FitzRoy-Newdegate*, *b.* 1921.
1937	*Davidson* (2nd), John Andrew Davidson, *b.* 1928, *s.* 1970, *m.*	Hon. Malcolm W. M. D., *b.* 1934.
1956	*De L'Isle* (1st), William Philip Sidney, V.C., K.G., P.C., G.C.M.G., G.C.V.O., (6th *Baron De L'Isle and Dudley*, 1835), *b.* 1909, *m.*	Maj. Hon. Philip J. A. S., M.B.E., *b.* 1945.
1776 I.	*De Vesci* (7th), Thomas Eustace Vesey (8th *Irish Baron, Knapton*, 1750), *b.* 1955, *s.* 1983.	†
1917	*Devonport* (3rd), Terence Kearley, *b.* 1944, *s.* 1973.	Chester D. H. K., *b.* 1932.
1964	*Dilhorne* (3rd), John Mervyn Manningham-Buller, *b.* 1932, *s.* 1980, *m.*	Hon. James E.*M.-B.*, *b.* 1956.
1622 I.	*Dillon* (22nd), Henry Benedict Dillon, *b.* 1973, *s.* 1982, *M.*	Hon. Richard A. L. D., *b.* 1948.
1785 I.	*Doneraile* (9th), Richard St. John St. Leger, *b.* 1923, *s.* 1957, *m.*	Hon. Richard A. *St. L.*, *b.* 1946.
1680 I.*	*Downe* (11th), John Christian George Dawnay (4th *U.K. Baron, Dawnay*, 1897), *b.* 1935, *s.* 1965, *m.*	Hon. Richard H. D., *b.* 1967.
1959	*Dunrossil* (2nd), John William Morrison, C.M.G., *b.* 1926, *s.* 1961, *m.*	Hon. Andrew W. R. M., *b.* 1953.
1964	*Eccles* (1st), David McAdam Eccles, C.H., P.C., K.C.V.O., *b.* 1904, *w.*	Hon. John D. E., *b.* 1931.
1897	*Esher* (4th), Lionel Gordon Baliol Brett, C.B.E., *b.* 1913, *s.* 1963, *m.*	Hon. Christopher L. B. B., *b.* 1936.
1816	*Exmouth* (10th), Paul Edward Pellew, *b.* 1940, *s.* 1970, *m.*	Hon. Edward F. P., *b.* 1978.
1620 S.	*Falkland* (15th), Lucius Edward William Plantagenet Cary (*Premier Scottish Viscount on the Roll*), *b.* 1935, *s.* 1984, *m.*	Master of Falkland, *b.* 1963
1720	*Falmouth* (9th), George Hugh Boscawen (26th *Eng. Baron, Le Despencer*, 1264), *b.* 1919, *s.* 1962, *m.*	Hon. Evelyn A. H. B., *b.* 1955.
1918	*Furness* (2nd), William Anthony Furness, *b.* 1929, *s.* 1940.	(None.)
1720 I.*	*Gage* (7th), George John St. Clere Gage, (6th *Brit. Baron, Gage*, 1790), *b.* 1932, *s.* 1982, *m.*	Hon. Henry N G., *b.* 1934.
1727 I.	*Galway* (12th), George Rupert Monckton-Arundell, *b.* 1922, *s.* 1980, *m.*	Hon. John P. *M.-A.*, *b.* 1952.
1478 I.*	*Gormanston* (17th), Jenico Nicholas Dudley Preston (*Premier Viscount of Ireland*; 5th *U.K. Baron, Gormanston*, 1868), *b.* 1939, *s.* 1940, *m.*	Hon. Jenico F. T. P., *b.* 1974.
1816 I.	*Gort* (8th), Colin Leopold Prendergast Vereker, *b.* 1916, *s.* 1975, *m.*	Hon. Foley R.S.P.*V.*, *b.* 1951.
1900	*Goschen* (4th), Giles John Harry Goschen, *b.* 1965, *s.* 1977, *M.*	(None.)
1849	*Gough* (5th), Shane Hugh Maryon Gough, *b.* 1941, *s.* 1951.	(None.)
1937	*Greenwood* (2nd), David Henry Hamar Greenwood, *b.* 1914, *s.* 1948.	Hon. Michael G. H. G., *b.* 1923.
1946	*Hall* (2nd), (William George) Leonard Hall, *b.* 1913, *s.* 1965, *m.*	(None.)
1891	*Hambleden* (4th), William Herbert Smith, *b.* 1930, *s.* 1948, *m.*	Hon. William H. B. S., *b.* 1955.
1884	*Hampden* (6th), Anthony David Brand, *b.* 1937, *s.* 1975, *m.*	Hon. Francis, A. B., *b.* 1970.
1936	*Hanworth* (2nd), David Bertram Pollock, *b.* 1916, *s.* 1936, *m.*	Hon. David S. G. P., *b.* 1946.
1791 I.	*Harberton* (10th), Thomas de Vautetort Pomeroy, *b.* 1910, *s.* 1980, *m.*	Hon. Robert W. P., *b.* 1916.
1846	*Hardinge* (6th), Charles Henry Nicholas Hardinge, *b.* 1956, *s.* 1984.	*Hon.* Andrew H. *H.*, *b.* 1960.
1791 I.	*Hawarden* (8th), Robert Leslie Eustace Maude, *b.* 1926, *s.* 1958, *m.*	Hon. Robert C. W. L. *M.*, *b.* 1961.
1960	*Head* (2nd), Richard Antony Head, *b.* 1937, *s.* 1983, *m.*	Hon. Henry J. *H.*, *b.* 1980.
1550	*Hereford* (18th), Robert Milo Leicester Devereux (*Premier Viscount of England*), *b.* 1932, *s.* 1952.	Hon. Charles R. de B. *D.*, *b.* 1975.
1842	*Hill* (8th), Antony Rowland Clegg-Hill, *b.* 1931, *s.* 1974, *m.*	Peter D. R. C. *C.-H.*, *b.* 1945.
1796	*Hood* (7th), Alexander Lambert Hood (*Irish Baron, Hood*, 1782), *b.* 1914, *s.* 1981, *m.*	Hon. Henry L. A. *H.*, *b.* 1958.

Created.	Title, Order of Succession, Name, etc.	Eldest Son or Heir.
1956	*Ingleby* (2nd), Martin Raymond Peake, b. 1926, s. 1966, m.	(None.)
1945	*Kemsley* (2nd), (Geoffrey) Lionel Berry, b. 1909, s. 1968, m.	Richard G. B., b. 1951.
1911	*Knollys* (3rd) David Francis Dudley Knollys, b. 1931, s. 1966, m.	Hon. Patrick N. M. K., b. 1962.
1895	*Knutsford* (5th), Julian Thurston Holland-Hibbert, C.B.E., b. 1920, s. 1976.	Michael H.-H., b. 1926.
1945	*Lambert* (2nd), George Lambert, T.D., b. 1909, s. 1958, m.	Hon. Michael J. L., b. 1912.
1954	*Leathers* (2nd), Frederick Alan Leathers, b. 1908, s. 1965, m.	Hon. Christopher G. L., b. 1941.
1922	*Leverhulme* (3rd), Philip William Bryce Lever, T.D., b. 1915, s. 1949, w.	(None.)
1781 I.	*Lifford* (8th), Alan William Wingfield Hewitt, b. 1900, s. 1954, m.	Hon. Edward J. W. H., b. 1949.
1921	*Long* (4th), Richard Gerard Long, b. 1929, s. 1967, m.	Hon. James R. L., b. 1960.
1957	*Mackintosh of Halifax* (3rd), (John) Clive Mackintosh, b. 1958, s. 1980, m.	Hon. Graham C. M., b. 1964.
1955	*Malvern* (3rd), Ashley Kevin Godfrey Huggins, b. 1949, s. 1978.	Hon. M. James H., b. 1928.
1945	*Marchwood* (3rd), David George Staveley Penny, b. 1936, s. 1979, m.	Hon. Peter G. W. P., b. 1965.
1942	*Margesson* (2nd), Francis Vere Hampden Margesson, b. 1922, s. 1965, m.	Hon. Richard F. D. M., b. 1960.
1660 I.*	*Massereene* (13th) & (6th) *Ferrard* (1797), John Clotworthy Talbot Foster Whyte-Melville Skeffington (6th *U.K. Baron, Oriel*, 1821), b. 1914, s. 1956, m.	Hon. John D. C. W.-M. F. S., b. 1940.
1802	*Melville* (9th), Robert David Ross Dundas, b. 1937, s. 1971, m.	Hon. Robert H. K. D., b. 1984.
1916	*Mersey* (4th), Richard Maurice Clive Bigham, b. 1934, s. 1979, m.	Hon. Edward J. H. B., b. 1966.
1717 I.	*Midleton* (11th), Trevor Lowther Brodrick (*Brit. Baron, Brodrick, Peper Harow*, 1796), b. 1903, s. 1979, m.	Alan H. B., b. 1949.
1962	*Mills* (2nd), Roger Clinton Mills, b. 1919, s. 1968, m.	Hon. Christopher P. R. M., b. 1956.
1716 I.	*Molesworth* (11th), Richard Gosset Molesworth, b. 1907, s. 1961, w.	Hon. Robert B. K. M., b. 1959.
1801 I.*	*Monck* (7th), Charles Stanley Monck (4th *U.K. Baron, Monck*, 1866), b. 1953, s. 1982.	Hon. George S. M., b. 1957.
1957	*Monckton of Brenchley* (2nd), Gilbert Walter Riversdale Monckton, C.B., O.B.E., M.C., b. 1915, s. 1965, m.	Hon Christopher W. M., b. 1952.
1935	*Monsell* (2nd), Henry Bolton Graham Eyres-Monsell, b. 1905, s. 1969.	(None.)
1946	*Montgomery of Alamein* (2nd), David Bernard Montgomery, C.B.E, b. 1928, s. 1976, m.	Hon. Henry D. M., b. 1954.
1550 I.*	*Mountgarret* (17th), Richard Henry Piers Butler (4th *U.K. Baron, Mountgarret*, 1911), b. 1936, s. 1966, m.	Hon. Piers J. R. B., b. 1961.
1964	*Muirshiel* (1st), John Scott Maclay, P.C., K.T., C.H., C.M.G., b. 1905, w.	(None.)
1952	*Norwich* (2nd), John Julius Cooper, b. 1929, s. 1954, m.	Hon. Jason C. D. B. C., b. 1959.
1651 S.	*Oxfuird* (12th), John Donald Alexander Arthur Makgill, claim established 1977, b. 1899, m.	George H. M., b. 1934.
1873	*Portman*, (9th), Edward Henry Berkeley Portman, b. 1934, s. 1967, m.	Hon. Christopher E. B. P., b. 1958.
1743 I.*	*Powerscourt* (10th), Mervyn Niall Wingfield (4th *U.K. Baron, Powerscourt*, 1885), b. 1935, s. 1973, m.	Hon. Mervyn A. W., b. 1963.
1900	*Ridley* (4th), Matthew White Ridley, T.D., b. 1925, s. 1964, m.	Hon. Matthew W. R., b. 1958.
1960	*Rochdale* (1st), John Durival Kemp, O.B.E., T.D. (2nd *U.K. Baron, Rochdale*, 1913), b. 1906, m.	Hon. St. John D. K., b. 1938.
1919	*Rothermere* (3rd), Vere Harold Esmond Harmsworth, b. 1925, s. 1978, m.	Hon. Harold J. E. V. H., b. 1967.
1937	*Runciman of Doxford* (2nd), Walter Leslie Runciman, O.B.E., A.F.C. (3rd *U.K. Baron, Runciman*, 1933), b. 1900, s. 1949, m.	Hon. Walter G. R., F.B.A., b. 1934.
1918	*St. Davids* (2nd), Jestyn Reginald Austen Plantagenet Philipps (19th *English Baron, Strange of Knokin* 1299, 7th *English Baron, Hungerford*, 1426 *and De Moleyns*, 1445), b. 1917, s. 1938, m.	Hon. Colwyn J. J. P., b. 1939.
1801	*St. Vincent* (7th), Ronald George James Jervis, b. 1905, s. 1940, m.	Hon. Edward R. J. J., b. 1951.
1937	*Samuel* (3rd), David Herbert Samuel, PH.D., b. 1922, s. 1978, m.	Hon. Dan J. S., b. 1925.
1911	*Scarsdale* (3rd), Francis John Nathaniel Curzon (7th *Brit. Baron, Scarsdale*, 1761), b. 1924, s. 1977, m.	Hon. Peter G. N. C., b. 1949.
1905	*Selby* (4th), Michael Guy John Gully, b. 1942, s. 1959, m.	Hon. Edward T. W. G., b. 1967.
1805	*Sidmouth* (7th), John Tonge Anthony Pellew Addington, b. 1914, s. 1976, m.	Hon. Christopher J. A., b. 1941.
1940	*Simon* (2nd), John Gilbert Simon, C.M.G., b. 1902, s. 1954, m.	Hon. Jan D. S., b. 1940.
1960	*Slim* (2nd), John Douglas Slim, O.B.E., b. 1927, s. 1970, m.	Hon. Mark W. R. S., b. 1960.
1954	*Soulbury* (2nd), James Herwald Ramsbotham, b. 1915, s. 1971, w.	Hon. Sir Peter E. R., G.C.M.G., G.C.V.O., b. 1919.

Created.	Title, Order of Succession, Name, etc.	Eldest Son or Heir.
1776 I.	*Southwell* (7th), Pyers Anthony Joseph Southwell, *b.* 1930, *s.* 1960, *m.*	Hon. Richard A. P. S., *b.* 1956.
1959	*Stuart of Findhorn* (2nd), David Randolph Moray Stuart, *b.* 1924, *s.* 1971, *m.*	Hon. James D. S., *b.* 1948.
1957	*Tenby* (3rd), William Lloyd George, *b.* 1927, *s.* 1983, *m.*	Hon. Timothy H. G. *L. G.*, *b.* 1962.
1952	*Thurso* (2nd), Robin Macdonald Sinclair, *b.* 1922, *s.* 1970, *m.*	Hon. John A. *S.*, *b.* 1953.
1983	*Tonypandy* (1st), (Thomas) George Thomas, P.C., *b.* 1909.	(None).
1721	*Torrington* (11th), Timothy Howard St. George Byng, *b.* 1943, *s.* 1961, *m.*	John L. *B.*, M.C., *b.* 1919.
1936	*Trenchard* (2nd), Thomas Trenchard, M.C., *b.* 1923, *s.* 1956, *m.*	Hon. Hugh *T.*, *b.* 1951.
1921	*Ullswater* (2nd), Nicholas James Christopher Lowther, *b.* 1942, *s.* 1949, *m.*	Hon. Benjamin J. *L.*, *b.* 1975.
1621 I.	*Valentia* (15th), Richard John Dighton Annesley, *b.* 1929, *s.* 1983, *m.*	Hon. Francis W. D. *A.*, *b.* 1959.
1960	*Ward of Witley* (1st), George Reginald Ward, P.C., *b.* 1907, *w.*	(None).
1964	*Watkinson* (1st), Harold Arthur Watkinson, P.C., C.H., *b.* 1910, *m.*	(None.)
1952	*Waverley* (2nd), David Alastair Pearson Anderson, *b.* 1911, *s.* 1958, *m.*	Hon. John D. F. *A.*, *b.* 1949.
1938	*Weir* (3rd), William Kenneth James Weir, *b.* 1933, *s.* 1975, *m.*	Hon. James W. H. *W.*, *b.* 1965.
1983	*Whitelaw* (1st), William Stephen Ian Whitelaw, P.C., C.H., M.C., *b.* 1918, *m.*	(None).
1918	*Wimborne* (3rd), Ivor Fox-Strangways Guest (4th *U.K. Baron, Wimborne*, 1880), *b.* 1939, *s.* 1967, *m.*	Hon. Ivor M.V.*G.*, *b.* 1968.
1923	*Younger of Leckie* (3rd), Edward George Younger, O.B.E., T.D., *b.* 1906, *s.* 1946, *w.*	Rt. Hon. George K. H. *Y.*, T.D., M.P., *b.* 1931.

BISHOPS

Style, The Right Rev. the Lord Bishop of ——. *Addressed as,* My Lord.

Apptd.		
1981	*London* (130th), Graham Douglas Leonard, P.C., D.D., *b.* 1921, *cons.* 1964, *trans.* 1973 and 1981, *m.*
1984	*Durham* (92nd), Prof. David Edward Jenkins, M.A., *b.* 1925, *cons.* 1984, *m.*
1974	*Winchester* (94th), John Vernon Taylor, M.A., *b.* 1914, *cons.* 1974, *m.*
1975	*Bath and Wells* (74th), John Monier Bickersteth, M.A., *b.* 1921, *cons.* 1970, *trans.* 1975, *m.*
1977	*Birmingham* (6th), Hugh William Montefiore, D.D., *b.* 1920, *cons.* 1970, *m.*
1982	*Blackburn* (6th), David Stewart Cross, M.A., *b.* 1928, *cons.* 1976, *trans.* 1982, *m.*
1984	*Bradford* (7th), Robert Kerr Williamson, *b.* 1932, *cons.* 1984, *m.*
1975	*Bristol* (53rd), Ernest John Tinsley, M.A., B.D., *b.* 1919, *cons.* 1975.
1972	*Carlisle* (64th), Henry David Halsey, B.A., *b.* 1919, *cons.* 1968, *trans.* 1972, *m.*
1971	*Chelmsford* (6th), Albert John Trillo, M.TH., B.D., F.K.C., *b.* 1915, *cons.* 1963, *trans.* 1968 and 1971, *m.*
1982	*Chester* (39th), Michael Alfred Baughen, *b.* 1930, *cons.* 1982, *m.*
1974	*Chichester* (99th), Eric Waldram Kemp, D.D., *b.* 1915, *m.*
1976	*Coventry* (6th), John Gibbs, B.A., B.D., *b.* 1917, *cons.* 1973, *trans.* 1976, *m.*
1969	*Derby* (4th), Cyril William Johnston Bowles, M.A., *b.* 1916, *cons.* 1969, *m.*
1977	*Ely* (66th), Peter Knight Walker, D.D., *b.* 1919, *cons.* 1972, *trans.* 1977, *m.*
1973	*Exeter* (68th), Eric Arthur John Mercer, *b.* 1917, *cons.* 1965, *m.*
1975	*Gloucester* (37th), John Yates, M.A., *b.* 1925, *cons.* 1972, *trans.* 1975, *m.*
1983	*Guildford* (7th), Michael Edgar Adie, M.A. *b.* 1929, *cons.* 1983, *m.*
1973	*Hereford* (103rd), John Richard Gordon Eastaugh, *b.* 1920, *cons.* 1973, *m.*
1978	*Leicester* (4th), Cecil Richard Rutt, C.B.E., M.A., *b.* 1925, *cons,* 1966, *m.*
1984	*Lichfield* (97th), Keith Norman Sutton, M.A., *b.* 1934, *cons.* 1978, *m.*
1974	*Lincoln* (69th), Simon Wilton Phipps, M.C., M.A., *b.* 1921, *cons.* 1968, *trans.* 1974, *m.*
1975	*Liverpool* (6th), David Stuart Sheppard, M.A., *b.* 1929, *cons.* 1969, *m.*
1979	*Manchester* (9th), Stanley Eric Francis Booth-Clibborn, M.A., *b.* 1924, *m.*
1981	*Newcastle* (10th), Andrew Alexander Kenny Graham, *b.* 1929, *cons.* 1977.
1971	*Norwich* (69th), Maurice Arthur Ponsonby Wood, D.S.C., M.A., *b.* 1916, *cons.* 1971, *m.*
1978	*Oxford* (40th), Patrick Campbell Rodger, M.A., *b.* 1920, *cons.* 1970, *trans.* 1978, *m.*
1984	*Peterborough* (36th), William John Westwood, M.A., *b.* 1925, *cons.* 1975, *m.*
1984	*Portsmouth* (7th), Timothy John Bavin, M.A., *b.* 1935, *cons.* 1974.
1977	*Ripon* (11th), David Nigel de Lorentz Young, M.A., *b.* 1931, *cons.* 1977, *m.*
1961	*Rochester* (104th), Richard David Say, D.D., *b.* 1914, *cons.* 1961, *m.*
1980	*St. Albans* (8th), John Bernard Taylor, M.A., *b.* 1929, *cons.* 1980, *m.*
1978	*St. Edmundsbury & Ipswich* (7th), John Waine, M.A., *b.* 1930, *cons.* 1975, *m.*
1981	*Salisbury* (76th), John Austin Baker, M.A., *b.* 1928, *cons.* 1982, *m.*
1980	*Sheffield* (5th), David Ramsay Lunn, M.A., *b.* 1930, *cons.* 1980.
1983	*Sodor & Man* (78th), Arthur Henry Attwell, B.D., M.A., *b.* 1920, *cons.* 1983.
1980	*Southwark* (7th), Ronald Oliver Bowlby, M.A., *b.* 1926, *cons.* 1972, *trans.* 1980, *m.*
1970	*Southwell* (7th), John Denis Wakeling, M.C., M.A., *b.* 1918, *cons.* 1970, *m.*
1981	*Truro* (12th), Peter Mumford, M.A., *b.* 1922, *cons.* 1974, *trans.* 1981, *m.*
1976	*Wakefield* (9th), Colin Clement Walter James, M.A., *b.* 1926, *cons.* 1973, *m.*
1982	*Worcester* (111th), Philip Harold Ernest Goodrich, M.A., *b.* 1929, *cons.* 1973, *trans.* 1982, *m.*

BARONS

Style (see *also* note, p. 247), The Right Hon. the Lord ——.
Addressed as, My Lord.

Created.	Title, Order of Succession, Name, etc.	Eldest Son or Heir.
1911	*Aberconway* (3rd), Charles Melville McLaren, *b.* 1913, *s.* 1953, *m.*	Hon. Henry C. *McL.*, *b.* 1948.
1873	*Aberdare* (4th), Morys George Lyndhurst Bruce, P.C., K.B.E., *b.* 1919, *s.* 1957, *m.*	Hon. Alastair J. L. *B.*, *b.* 1947.
1835	*Abinger* (8th), James Richard Scarlett, *b.* 1914, *s.* 1943, *m.*	Hon. James H. *S.*, *b.* 1959.
1869	*Acton* (3rd), John Emerich Henry Lyon-Dalberg-Acton, C.M.G., M.B.E., T.D., *b.* 1907, *s.* 1924, *m.*	Hon. Richard G. *L.-D.-A.*, *b.* 1941.
1887	*Addington* (6th), Dominic Bryce Hubbard, *b.* 1963, *s.* 1982, *M.*	Hon. Michael W. L. *H.*, *b.* 1965.
1955	*Adrian* (2nd), Richard Hume Adrian, F.R.S., *b.* 1927, *s.* 1977, *m.*	(None.)
1921	*Ailwyn* (4th), Carol Arthur Fellowes, T.D., *b.* 1896, *s.* 1976, *m.*	(None.)
1907	*Airedale* (4th), Oliver James Vandeleur Kitson, *b.* 1915, *s.* 1958.	(None.)
1896	*Aldenham* (5th), and (3rd) *Hunsdon of Hunsdon* (1923), Antony Durant Gibbs, *b.* 1922, *s.* 1969, *m.*	Hon. Vicary T. *G.*, *b.* 1948.
1962	*Aldington* (1st), Toby Austin Richard William Low, P.C., K.C.M.G., C.B.E., D.S.O., T.D., *b.* 1914, *m.*	Hon Charles H. S. *L.*, *b.* 1948.
1902	*Allerton* (3rd), George William Lawies Jackson, *b.* 1903, *s.* 1925, *m.*	(None.)
1929	*Alvingham* (2nd), Maj.-Gen. Robert Guy Eardley Yerburgh, C.B.E., *b.* 1926, *s.* 1955, *m.*	Capt. Hon. Robert R. G. *Y.*, *b.* 1956.
1892	*Amherst of Hackney* (4th), William Hugh Amherst Cecil, *b.* 1940, *s.* 1980, *m.*	Hon. Hugh W. A. *C.*, *b.* 1968.
1881	*Ampthill* (4th), Geoffrey Denis Erskine Russell, *b.* 1921, *s.* 1973, *m.*	Hon. David W. E. *R.*, *b.* 1947.
1947	*Amwell* (2nd), Frederick Norman Montague, *b.* 1912, *s.* 1966, *m.*	Hon. Keith N. *M.*, *b.* 1943.
1863	*Annaly* (5th), Luke Robert White, *b.* 1927, *s.* 1970, *m.*	Hon. Luke R. *W.*, *b.* 1954.
1903	*Armstrong* (3rd), William Henry Cecil John Robin Watson-Armstrong, *b.* 1919, *s.* 1972, *m.*	(None.)
1885	*Ashbourne* (4th), Edward Barry Greynville Gibson, *b.* 1933, *s.* 1983, *m.*	Hon. Edward C. D'O. *G.*, *b.* 1967.
1835	*Ashburton* (6th), Alexander Francis St. Vincent Baring, K.G., K.C.V.O., *b.* 1898, *s.* 1938, *w.*	Hon. Sir John F. H. B., C.V.O., *b.* 1928.
1892	*Ashcombe* (4th), Henry Edward Cubitt, *b.* 1924, *s.* 1962, *m.*	M. Robin *C.*, *b.* 1936.
1911	*Ashton of Hyde* (3rd), Thomas John Ashton, T.D., *b.* 1926, *s.* 1983, *m.*	Hon. Thomas H. *A.*, *b.* 1958.
1800 I.	*Ashtown* (6th), Christopher Oliver Trench, *b.* 1931, *s.* 1979, *m.*	Sir Nigel C. C. *T.*, K.C.M.G., *b.* 1916.
1956	*Astor of Hever* (3rd), John Jacob Astor, *b.* 1946, *s.* 1984, *m.*	Hon. Philip D. P. *A.*, *b.* 1959.
1789 I. 1793* }	*Auckland* (9th), Ian George Eden (9th *Brit. Baron, Auckland*), *b.* 1926, *s.* 1957, *m.*	Hon. Robert I. B. *E.*, *b.* 1962.
1313	*Audley* (25th), Richard Michael Thomas Souter, *b.* 1914, *s.* 1973, *m.*	Three co-heiresses.
1900	*Avebury* (4th), Eric Reginald Lubbock, *b.* 1928, *s.* 1971.	Hon. Lyulph A. J. *L.*, *b.* 1954.
1718 I.	*Aylmer* (13th), Michael Anthony Aylmer, *b.* 1923, *s.* 1982, *m.*	Hon. A. Julian *A.*, *b.* 1951.
1929	*Baden-Powell* (3rd), Robert Crause Baden-Powell, *b.* 1936, *s.* 1962, *m.*	Hon. David M. *B.-P.*, *b.* 1940.
1780	*Bagot* (9th), Heneage Charles Bagot, *b.* 1914, *s.* 1979, *m.*	Hon. Charles H. S. *B.*, *b.* 1944.
1953	*Baillieu* (3rd), James William Latham Baillieu, *b.* 1950, *s.* 1973, *m.*	Hon. Robert L. *B.*, *b.* 1979.
1607 S.	*Balfour of Burleigh* (8th), Robert Bruce, *b.* 1927, *s.* 1967, *m.*	Hon. Victoria B., *b.* 1973.
1945	*Balfour of Inchrye* (1st), Harold Harington Balfour, P.C., M.C., *b.* 1897, *m.*	Hon. Ian *B.*, *b.* 1924.
1924	*Banbury of Southam* (3rd), Charles William Banbury, *b.* 1953, *s.* 1981, *m.*	(None.)
1698	*Barnard* (11th), Harry John Neville Vane, T.D., *b.* 1923, *s.* 1964, *m.*	Hon. Henry F. C. *V.*, *b.* 1959.
1887	*Basing* (5th), Neil Lutley Sclater-Booth, *b.* 1939, *s.* 1983, *m.*	Hon. Stuart W. *S.-C.*, *b.* 1969.
1647 S.	*Belhaven & Stenton* (13th), Robert Anthony Carmichael Hamilton, *b.* 1927, *s.* 1961, *m.*	Master of Belhaven, *b.* 1953.
1848 I.	*Bellew* (7th), James Bryan Bellew, *b.* 1920, *s.* 1981, *m.*	Hon. Bryan E. *B.*, *b.* 1943.
1856	*Belper* (4th), (Alexander) Ronald George Strutt, *b.* 1912, *s.* 1956.	Hon. Richard H. *S.*, *b.* 1941.
1938	*Belstead* (2nd), John Julian Ganzoni, P.C., *b.* 1932, *s.* 1958.	(None.)
1922	*Bethell* (4th), Nicholas William Bethell, *b.* 1938, *s.* 1967.	Hon. James N. *B.*, *b.* 1967.
1938	*Bicester* (3rd), Angus Edward Vivian Smith, *b.* 1932, *s.* 1968.	Hugh C. V. *S.*, *b.* 1934.
1903	*Biddulph* (4th), Robert Michael Christian Biddulph, *b.* 1931, *s.* 1972, *m.*	Hon. Anthony N. C. M.*B.*, *b.* 1959.
1938	*Birdwood* (3rd), Mark William Ogilvie Birdwood, *b.* 1938, *s.* 1962, *m.*	(None.)
1958	*Birkett* (2nd), Michael Birkett, *b.* 1929, *s.* 1962, *m.*	Hon. Thomas *B.*, *b.* 1982.
1935	*Blackford* (4th), William Keith Mason, *b.* 1962, *s.* 1977.	(None.)
1907	*Blyth* (4th), Anthony Audley Rupert Blyth, *b.* 1931, *s.* 1977, *m.*	Hon. Riley A. J. *B.*, *b.* 1955.
1797	*Bolton* (7th), Richard William Algar Orde-Powlett, *b.* 1929, *s.* 1963, *m.*	Hon. Harry A. N. *O.-P.*, *b.* 1954.
1922	*Borwick* (4th), James Hugh Myles Borwick, M.C., *b.* 1917, *s.* 1961, *m.*	Hon. George S. *B.*, *b.* 1922.
1761	*Boston* (10th), Timothy George Frank Boteler Irby, *b.* 1939, *s.* 1978, *m.*	Hon. George W. E. B. *I.*, *b.* 1971.
1942	*Brabazon of Tara* (3rd), Ivon Anthony Moore-Brabazon, *b.* 1946, *s.* 1974, *m.*	Hon. Benjamin R. *M.-B.*, *b.* 1983.
1880	*Brabourne* (7th), John Ulick Knatchbull, *b.* 1924, *s.* 1943, *m.*	Lord Romsey, *b.* 1947, *see* p. 247.

Created.	Title, Order of Succession, Name, etc.	Eldest Son or Heir.
1925	*Bradbury* (2nd), John Bradbury, b. 1914, s. 1950, m.	Hon. John B., b. 1940.
1962	*Brain* (2nd), Christopher Langdon Brain, b. 1926. s. 1966, m.	Hon. Michael C. B., D.M., b. 1928.
1981	*Brandon of Oakbrook*, Henry Vivian Brandon, P.C., M.C., b. 1920, m. (*Lord of Appeal*).	(Law Life Peerage.)
1938	*Brassey of Apethorpe* (3rd), David Henry Brassey, b. 1932, s. 1967, m.	Hon. Edward B., b. 1964.
1788	*Braybrooke* (9th), Henry Seymour Neville, b. 1897, s. 1943, m.	Hon. Robin H. C. N., b. 1932.
1529	*Braye* (7th), Thomas Adrian Verney-Cave, b. 1902, s. 1952, m.	Hon. Penelope M., b. 1941.
1980	*Bridge of Harwich*, Nigel Cyprian Bridge, P.C., b. 1917, m. (*Lord of Appeal*).	(Law Life Peerage.)
1957	*Bridges* (2nd), Thomas Edward Bridges, K.C.M.G., b. 1927, s. 1969, m.	Hon. Mark T. B., b. 1954.
1982	*Brightman*, John (Anson) Brightman, P.C., b. 1911, m. (*Lord of Appeal*).	(Law Life Peerage.)
1945	*Broadbridge* (3rd), Peter Hewett Broadbridge, b. 1938, s. 1972, m.	Hon. Hugh T. B., b. 1903.
1933	*Brocket* (3rd), Charles Ronald George Nall-Cain, b. 1952, s. 1967, m.	Hon. Richard P. C. N.-C., b. 1953.
1860	*Brougham and Vaux* (5th), Michael John Brougham, b. 1938, s. 1967.	Hon. Charles W. B., b. 1971.
1945	*Broughshane* (2nd), Patrick Owen Alexander Davison, b. 1903, s. 1953, m.	Hon. Alexander D., b. 1936.
1776	*Brownlow* (7th), Edward John Peregrine Cust, b. 1936, s. 1978, m.	Hon. Peregrine E. Q. C., b. 1974.
1942	*Bruntisfield* (1st), Victor Alexander George Anthony Warrender, M.C., b. 1899, m.	Col. Hon. John R. W., O.B.E., M.C., T.D., b. 1927.
1950	*Burden* (2nd), Philip William Burden, b. 1916, s. 1970, m.	Hon. Andrew P. B., b. 1959.
1529	*Burgh* (7th), Alexander Peter Willoughby Leith, b. 1935, s. 1959, m.	Hon. Alexander G. D. L., b. 1958.
1903	*Burnham* (5th), William Edward Harry Lawson, b. 1920, s. 1963, m.	Hon. Hugh J. F. L., b. 1931.
1897	*Burton* (3rd), Michael Evan Victor Baillie, b. 1924, s. 1962, m.	Hon. Evan M. R. B., b. 1949.
1643	*Byron* (12th), Richard Geoffrey Gordon Byron, D.S.O., b. 1899, s. 1983, m.	Hon. Richard N. B., b. 1948.
1937	*Cadman* (3rd), John Anthony Cadman, b. 1938, s. 1966, m.	Hon. Nicholas A. J. C., b. 1977.
1796	*Calthorpe* (10th), Peter Waldo Somerset Gough-Calthorpe, b. 1927, s. 1945, m.	(None.)
1945	*Calverley* (3rd), Charles Rodney Muff, b. 1946, s. 1971, m.	Hon. Jonathan E. M., b.1975.
1383	*Camoys* (7th), (Ralph) Thomas (Campion George Sherman) Stonor, b. 1940, s. 1976, m.	Hon. William S., b. 1974.
1715 I.	*Carbery* (11th), Peter Ralfe Harrington Evans-Freke, b. 1920, s. 1970, m.	Hon. Michael P. E.-F., b. 1942.
1834 I. 1838* }	*Carew* (6th), William Francis Conolly-Carew, C.B.E. (6th *U.K. Baron*, *Carew*, 1838), b. 1905, s. 1927, m.	Hon. Patrick T. C.-C., b. 1938.
1916	*Carnock* (4th), David Henry Arthur Nicolson, b. 1920, s. 1982.	Nigel N., M.B.E., b. 1917.
1796 I. 1797* }	*Carrington* (6th), Peter Alexander Rupert Carington, P.C., C.H., K.C.M.G., M.C. (6th *Brit. Baron*, *Carrington*, 1797), b. 1919, s. 1938, m.	Hon. Rupert F. J. C., b. 1948.
1812 I.	*Castlemaine* (8th), Roland Thomas John Handcock, b. 1943, s. 1973, m.	Terence R. H., b. 1902.
1936	*Catto* (2nd), Stephen Gordon Catto, b. 1923, s. 1959, m.	Hon. Innes G. C., b. 1950.
1918	*Cawley* (3rd), Frederick Lee Cawley, b. 1913, s. 1954, m.	Hon. John F. C., b. 1946.
1937	*Chatfield* (2nd), Ernle David Lewis Chatfield, b. 1917, s. 1967, m.	(None.)
1858	*Chesham* (5th), John Charles Compton Cavendish, P.C., b. 1916, s. 1952, m.	Hon. Nicholas C. C., b. 1941.
1945	*Chetwode* (2nd), Philip Chetwode, b. 1937, s. 1950.	Hon. Roger C., b. 1968.
1945	*Chorley* (2nd), Roger Richard Edward Chorley, b. 1930, s. 1978, m.	Hon. Nicholas R. D. C., b. 1966.
1858	*Churston* (4th), Richard Francis Roger Yarde-Buller, V.R.D., b. 1910, s. 1930, m.	Hon. John F. Y.-B., b. 1934.
1946	*Citrine* (2nd), Norman Arthur Citrine, b. 1914, s. 1983, m.	Hon. Ronald E. C., b. 1919.
1800 I.	*Clanmorris* (7th), John Michael Ward Bingham, b. 1908, s. 1960, m.	Hon. Simon J. W. B., b. 1937.
1672	*Clifford of Chudleigh* (13th) (Lewis) Hugh Clifford, O.B.E., b. 1916, s. 1964, m.	Hon. Thomas H. C., b. 1948.
1299	*Clinton* (22nd), Gerard Neville Mark Fane Trefusis, b. 1934, *title called out of abeyance* 1965, m.	Hon. Charles P. R. F. T., b. 1962.
1955	*Clitheroe* (1st), Ralph Assheton, P.C., K.C.V.O., b. 1901, m.	Hon. Ralph J. A., b. 1929.
1919	*Clwyd* (2nd), (John) Trevor Roberts, b. 1900, s. 1955, m.	Hon. J. Anthony R., b. 1935.
1948	*Clydesmuir* (2nd), Ronald John Bilsland Colville, K.T., C.B., M.B.E., T.D., b. 1917, s. 1954, m.	Hon. David R. C., b. 1949.
1960	*Cobbold* (1st), Cameron Fromanteel Cobbold, K.G., P.C., G.C.V.O., b. 1904, m.	Hon. David A. F. Lytton-Cobbold, b. 1937.
1919	*Cochrane of Cults* (3rd), Thomas Charles Anthony Cochrane, b. 1922, s. 1968.	Hon. R. H. Vere C., b. 1926.
1954	*Coleraine* (2nd), (James) Martin (Bonar) Law, b. 1931, s. 1980, m.	Hon. James P. B. L., b. 1975.
1873	*Coleridge* (5th), William Duke Coleridge, b. 1937, s. 1984.	Hon. James D. C., b. 1967.
1946	*Colgrain* (3rd), David Colin Campbell, b. 1920, s. 1973, m.	Hon. Alastair C. L. C., b. 1951.
1917	*Colwyn* (3rd), (Ian) Anthony Hamilton-Smith, b. 1942, s. 1966, m.	Hon. Craig P. H.-S., b. 1968.
1956	*Colyton* (1st), Henry Lennox D'Aubigné Hopkinson, P.C., C.M.G., b. 1902, m.	Hon. Nicholas H. E. H., b. 1932.
1841	*Congleton* (8th), Christopher Patrick Parnell, b. 1930, s. 1967, m.	Hon. John P. C. P., b. 1959.

Created.	Title, Order of Succession, Name, etc.	Eldest Son or Heir.
1927	*Cornwallis* (3rd), Fiennes Neil Wykeham Cornwallis, O.B.E., b. 1921, s. 1982, m.	Hon. Fiennes W. J. C., b. 1946.
1874	*Cottesloe* (4th), John Walgrave Halford Fremantle, G.B.E., T.D., b. 1900, s. 1956, m.	Hon. John T. F., b. 1927.
1929	*Craigmyle* (3rd), Thomas Donald Mackay Shaw, b. 1923, s. 1944, m.	Hon. Thomas C. S., b. 1960.
1899	*Cranworth* (3rd), Philip Bertram Gurdon, b. 1940, s. 1964, m.	Hon. Sacha W. R. G., b. 1970.
1959	*Crathorne* (2nd), Charles James Dugdale, b. 1939, s. 1977, m.	Hon. Thomas A. J. D., b. 1977.
1892	*Crawshaw* (4th), William Michael Clifton Brooks, b. 1933, s. 1946.	Hon. David G. B., b. 1934.
1940	*Croft* (2nd), Michael Henry Glendower Page Croft, b. 1916, s. 1947, w.	Hon. Bernard W. H. P. C., b. 1949.
1797 I.	*Crofton* (6th), Charles Edward Piers Crofton, b. 1949, s. 1974, m.	Hon. Guy P. G. C., b. 1951.
1375	*Cromwell* (7th), Godfrey John Bewicke-Copley, b. 1960, s. 1982.	Hon. Thomas D. B.-C., b. 1964.
1947	*Crook* (1st), Reginald Douglas Crook, b. 1901, m.	Hon. Douglas E. C., b. 1926.
1971	*Cross of Chelsea*, (Arthur) Geoffrey (Neale) Cross, P.C., b. 1904, m. (*Lord of Appeal, retired*).	(Law Life Peerage.)
1920	*Cullen of Ashbourne* (2nd), Charles Borlase Marsham Cokayne, M.B.E., b. 1912, s. 1932, m.	Hon. Edmund W. M. C., b. 1916.
1914	*Cunliffe* (3rd), Roger Cunliffe, b. 1932, s. 1963, m.	Hon. Henry C., b. 1962.
1927	*Daresbury* (2nd), Edward Greenall, b. 1902, s. 1938, w.	Hon. Edward G. G., b. 1928.
1924	*Darling* (2nd), Robert Charles Henry Darling, b. 1919, s. 1936, m.	Hon. Robert J. H. D., b. 1944.
1946	*Darwen* (2nd), Cedric Percival Davies, b. 1915, s. 1950, m.	Hon. Roger M. D., b. 1938.
1923	*Daryngton* (2nd), Jocelyn Arthur Pike Pease, b. 1908, s. 1949.	(None.)
1932	*Davies* (3rd), David Davies, b. 1940, s. 1944, m.	Hon. David D. D., b. 1975.
1812 I.	*Decies* (6th), Arthur George Marcus Douglas de la Poer Beresford, b. 1915, s. 1944, m.	Hon. Marcus H. T. *de la P.B.*, b. 1948.
1299	*de Clifford* (27th), John Edward Southwell Russell, b. 1928, s. 1982, m.	Hon. William S. R., b. 1930.
1851	*De Freyne* (7th), Francis Arthur John French, b. 1927, s. 1935, m.	Hon. Fulke C. A. J. F., b. 1957.
1821	*Delamere* (5th), Hugh George Cholmondeley, b. 1934, s. 1979, m.	Hon. Thomas P. G. C., b. 1968.
1838	*de Mauley* (6th), Gerald John Ponsonby, b. 1921, s. 1962, m.	Col. Hon. Thomas M. P., T.D., b. 1930.
1937	*Denham* (2nd), Bertram Stanley Mitford Bowyer, P.C., b. 1927, s. 1948, m.	Hon. Richard G. B., b. 1959.
1834	*Denman* (5th), Charles Spencer Denman, C.B.E., M.C., T.D., b. 1916, s. 1971, m.	Hon. Richard T. S. D., b. 1946.
1957	*Denning*, Alfred Thompson Denning, P.C., b. 1899, m. (*Master of the Rolls, retired*).	(Law Life Peerage.)
1885	*Deramore* (6th), Richard Arthur de Yarburgh-Bateson, b. 1911, s. 1964, m.	(None.)
1887	*De Ramsey* (3rd), Ailwyn Edward Fellowes, K.B.E., T.D., b. 1910, s. 1925, m.	Hon. John A. F., b. 1942.
1264	*de Ros* (28th), Peter Trevor Maxwell, b. 1958, s. 1983 (*Premier Barony of England*).	Hon. Diana E. M., b. 1957.
1881	*Derwent* (4th), Patrick Robin Gilbert Vanden-Bempde-Johnstone, C.B.E., b. 1901, s. 1949, m.	Hon. Robin E. L. V.-B.-J., M.V.O., b. 1930.
1831	*De Saumarez* (6th), James Victor Broke Saumarez, b. 1924, s. 1969, m.	Hon. Eric D. S., b. 1956.
1910	*de Villiers* (3rd), Arthur Percy de Villiers, b. 1911, s. 1934.	Hon. Alexander C. *de V.*, b. 1940.
1961	*Devlin*, Patrick Arthur Devlin, P.C., F.B.A., b. 1905, m. (*Lord of Appeal retired*).	(Law Life Peerage.)
1930	*Dickinson* (2nd), Richard Clavering Hyett Dickinson, b. 1926, s. 1943, m.	Hon. Martin H. D., b. 1961.
1620 I. 1765* }	*Digby* (12th), Edward Henry Kenelm Digby, (6th *Brit. Baron, Digby*), b. 1924, s. 1964, m.	Hon. Henry N. K. D., b. 1954.
1968	*Diplock*, (William John) Kenneth Diplock, P.C., b. 1907, m. (*Lord of Appeal*).	(Law Life Peerage.)
1615	*Dormer* (16th), Joseph Spencer Philip Dormer, b. 1914, s. 1975.	Geoffrey H. D., b. 1920.
1943	*Dowding* (2nd), Derek Hugh Tremenheere Dowding, b. 1919, s. 1970, m.	Hon. Piers H. T. D., b. 1948.
1963	*Drumalbyn* (1st), Niall Malcolm Stewart Macpherson, P.C., K.B.E., b. 1908, w.	(None.)
1929	*Dulverton* (2nd), (Frederick) Anthony Hamilton Wills, C.B.E., T.D., b. 1915, s. 1956, m.	Hon. Gilbert M. H. W., b. 1944.
1800 I.	*Dunalley* (6th), Henry Desmond Graham Prittie, b. 1912, s. 1948, m.	Hon. Henry F. C. P., b. 1948.
1324 I.	*Dunboyne* (28th), Patrick Theobald Tower Butler, b. 1917, s. 1945, m.	Hon. John F. B., b. 1951.
1802	*Dunleath* (4th), Charles Edward Henry John Mulholland, T.D., b. 1933, s. 1956, m.	Sir Michael H. M., Bt., b. 1915.
1439 I.	*Dunsany* (19th), Randal Arthur Henry Plunkett (20th *I.*, *Baron*, *Killean*, 1449), b. 1906, s. 1957, m.	Hon. Edward J. C. P., b. 1939.
1780	*Dynevor* (9th), Richard Charles Uryan Rhys, b. 1935, s. 1962.	Hon. Hugo G. U. R., b. 1966.
1928	*Ebbisham* (2nd), Rowland Roberts Blades, T.D., b. 1912, s. 1953, m.	(None.)
1857	*Ebury* (6th), Francis Egerton Grosvenor, b. 1934, s. 1957, m.	Hon. Julian F. M. G., b. 1959.
1974	*Edmund-Davies* (Herbert) Edmund Edmund-Davies, P.C., b. 1906, m. (*Lord of Appeal, retired*).	(Law Life Peerage.)

Created.	Title, Order of Succession, Name, etc.	Eldest Son or Heir.
1643	*Elibank* (14th), Alan d'Ardis Erskine-Murray, b. 1923, s. 1973, m.	Master of Elibank, b. 1964.
1802	*Ellenborough* (8th), Richard Edward Cecil Law, b. 1926, s. 1945, m.	Capt. Hon. Rupert E. H. L., b. 1955.
1509 s.*	*Elphinstone* (18th), James Alexander Elphinstone (4th *U.K. Baron Elphinstone*, 1885), b. 1953, s. 1975, m.	Master of Elphinstone, b. 1980.
1934	*Elton* (2nd), Rodney Elton, T.D., b. 1930, s. 1973, m.	Hon. Edward P. E., b. 1966.
1964	*Erroll of Hale* (1st), Frederick James Erroll, P.C., T.D., b. 1914, m.	(None.)
1964	*Erskine of Rerrick* (2nd), Iain Maxwell Erskine, b. 1926, s. 1980, m.	(None.)
1627 s.	*Fairfax of Cameron* (14th), Nicholas John Albert Fairfax, b. 1956, s. 1964, m.	Hon. Hugh N. T. F., b. 1958.
1961	*Fairhaven* (3rd), Ailwyn Henry George Broughton, b. 1936, s. 1973, m.	Hon. James H. A. B., b. 1963.
1916	*Faringdon* (3rd), Charles Michael Henderson, b. 1937, s. 1977, m.	Hon. James H. H., b. 1961.
1756 I.	*Farnham* (12th), Barry Owen Somerset Maxwell, b. 1931, s. 1957, m.	Hon. Simon K. M., b. 1933.
1856 I.	*Fermoy* (6th), Patrick Maurice Burke Roche, b. 1967, s. 1984, M.	Hon. E. Hugh B. R., b. 1972.
1826	*Feversham* (6th), Charles Anthony Peter Duncombe, b. 1945, s. 1963, m.	Hon. Jasper O. S. D., b. 1968.
1798 I.	*ffrench* (7th), Peter Martin Joseph Charles John ffrench, b. 1926, s. 1955 m.	Hon Robuck J. P. C. M. ff., b. 1956.
1909	*Fisher* (3rd), John Vavasseur Fisher, D.S.C., b. 1921, s. 1955, m.	Hon. Patrick V. F., b. 1953.
1295	*Fitzwalter* (21st), Fitzwalter Brook Plumptre, b. 1914 *called out of abeyance*, 1953, m.	Hon. Julian B. P., b. 1952.
1776	*Foley* (8th), Adrian Gerald Foley, b. 1923, s. 1927, m.	Hon. Thomas H. F., b. 1961.
1445 s.	*Forbes* (22nd), Nigel Ivan Forbes, K.B.E. (*Premier Baron of Scotland*), b. 1918, s. 1953, m.	Master of Forbes, b. 1946.
1821	*Forester* (8th), (George Cecil) Brooke Weld-Forester, b. 1938, s. 1977, m.	Hon Charles R. G., W.-F., b. 1975.
1922	*Forres* (4th), Alastair Stephen Grant Williamson, b. 1946, s. 1978, m.	Hon George A. M. W., b. 1972.
1917	*Forteviot* (3rd), Henry Evelyn Alexander Dewar, M.B.E., b. 1906, s. 1947, m.	Hon. John J. E. D., b. 1938.
1975	*Fraser of Tullybelton*, Walter Ian Reid Fraser, P.C., b. 1911, m. (*Lord of Appeal*).	(Law Life Peerage.)
1951	*Freyberg* (2nd), Paul Richard Freyberg, O.B.E., M.C., b. 1923, s. 1963, m.	Hon. Valerian B. F., b. 1970.
1917	*Gainford* (3rd), Joseph Edward Pease, b. 1921, s. 1971, m.	Hon. George P., b. 1926.
1818 I.	*Garvagh* (5th), (Alexander Leopold Ivor) George Canning, b. 1920, s. 1956, m.	Hon. Spencer G. S. de R. C., b. 1953.
1942	*Geddes* (3rd), Euan Michael Ross Geddes, b. 1937, s. 1975, m.	Hon. James G. N. G., b. 1969.
1876	*Gerard* (4th), Robert William Frederick Alwyn Gerard, b. 1918, s. 1953.	Anthony R. H. G., b. 1949.
1824	*Gifford* (6th), Anthony Maurice Gifford, Q.C., b. 1940, s. 1961, m.	Hon. Thomas A. G., b. 1967.
1917	*Gisborough* (3rd), Thomas Richard John Long Chaloner, b. 1927, s. 1951, m.	Hon. Thomas P. L. C., b. 1961.
1960	*Gladwyn* (1st), (Hubert Miles) Gladwyn Jebb, G.C.M.G., G.C.V.O., C.B., b. 1900, m.	Hon. Miles A. G. J., b. 1930.
1899	*Glanusk* (4th), David Russell Bailey, b. 1917, s. 1948, m.	Hon. Christopher R. B., b. 1942.
1918	*Glenarthur* (4th), Simon Mark Arthur, b. 1944, s. 1976, m.	Hon. Edward A. A., b. 1973.
1911	*Glenconner* (3rd), Colin Christopher Paget Tennant, b. 1926, s. 1983, m.	Hon. Charles E. P. T., b. 1957.
1964	*Glendevon* (1st), John Adrian Hope, P.C., b. 1912, m.	Hon. Julian J. S. H., b. 1950.
1922	*Glendyne* (3rd), Robert Nivison, b. 1926, s. 1967, m.	Hon. John N., b. 1960.
1939	*Glentoran* (2nd), Daniel Stewart Thomas Bingham Dixon, P.C., (N.I.), K.B.E., b. 1912, s. 1950, w.	Hon. Thomas R. V. D., M.B.E., b. 1935.
1909	*Gorell* (4th), Timothy John Radcliffe Barnes, b. 1927, s. 1963, m.	Hon. Ronald A. H. B., b. 1931.
1953	*Grantchester* (2nd), Kenneth Bent Suenson-Taylor, Q.C., b. 1921, s. 1976, m.	Hon. Christopher J. S-.T., b. 1951.
1782	*Grantley* (7th), John Richard Brinsley Norton, M.C., b. 1923, s. 1954, m.	Hon. Richard W. B. N., b. 1956.
1794 I.	*Graves* (8th), Peter George Wellesley Graves, b. 1911, s. 1963, m.	Evelyn P. G., b. 1926.
1445 s.	*Gray* (22nd), Angus Diarmid Ian Campbell-Gray, b. 1931, s. 1946, m.	Master of Gray, b. 1964.
1950	*Greenhill* (2nd), Stanley Ernest Greenhill, M.D., b. 1917, s. 1967, m.	Hon. Malcolm G., b. 1924.
1927	*Greenway* (4th), Ambrose Charles Drexel Greenway, b. 1941, s. 1975.	Hon. Mervyn S. K. G., b. 1942.
1902	*Grenfell* (3rd), Julian Pascoe Francis St. Leger Grenfell, b. 1935, m. 1976, m.	Francis P. J. G., b. 1938.
1944	*Gretton* (3rd), John Henrik Gretton, b. 1941, s. 1982, m.	Hon. John L. G., b. 1975.
1869	*Greville* (4th), Ronald Charles Fulke Greville, b. 1912, s. 1952.	(None.)
1955	*Gridley* (2nd), Arnold Hudson Gridley, b. 1906, s. 1965, m.	Hon. Richard D. A. G., b. 1956.
1964	*Grimston of Westbury* (2nd), Robert Walter Sigismund Grimston, b. 1925, s. 1979, m.	Hon. Robert J. S. G., b. 1951.
1886	*Grimthorpe* (4th), Christopher John Beckett, O.B.E., b. 1915, s. 1963, m.	Hon. Edward J. B., b. 1954.
1961	*Guest*, Christopher William Graham Guest, P.C., b. 1901, m. (*Lord of Appeal, retired*).	(Law Life Peerage.)
1945	*Hacking* (3rd), Douglas David Hacking, b. 1938, s. 1971, m.	Hon. Douglas F. H., b. 1968.
1950	*Haden-Guest* (3rd), Richard Haden Haden-Guest, b. 1904, s. 1974, m.	Hon. Peter H. H.-G., b. 1913.

Created.	Title, Order of Succession, Name, etc.	Eldest Son or Heir.
1886	*Hamilton of Dalzell* (3rd), John d'Henin Hamilton, K.C.V.O., M.C., b. 1911, s. 1952, m.	Hon. James L. H., b. 1938.
1874	*Hampton* (6th), Richard Humphrey Russell Pakington, b. 1925, s. 1974, m.	Hon. John H. A. P., b. 1964.
1939	*Hankey* (2nd), Robert Maurice Alers Hankey, K.C.M.G., K.C.V.O., b. 1905, s. 1963, m.	Hon. Donald R. A. H., b. 1938.
1958	*Harding of Petherton* (1st), John Harding, G.C.B., C.B.E., D.S.O., M.C., Field Marshal, b. 1896, w.	Hon. John C. H., b. 1928.
1910	*Hardinge of Penshurst* (3rd), George Edward Charles Hardinge, b. 1921, s. 1960, m.	Hon. Julian A. H., b. 1945.
1876	*Harlech* (5th), (William) David Ormsby-Gore, P.C., K.C.M.G., b. 1918, s. 1964, m.	Hon. Francis D. O.-G., b. 1954.
1939	*Harmsworth* (2nd), Cecil Desmond Bernard Harmsworth, b. 1903, s. 1948, m.	Hon. Eric B. N. H., b. 1905.
1815	*Harris* (5th), George St. Vincent Harris, C.B.E., M.C., b. 1889, s. 1932, w.	Hon. George R. J. H., b. 1920.
1954	*Harvey of Tasburgh* (2nd), Peter Charles Oliver Harvey, b. 1921, s. 1968, m.	Hon. John W. H., b. 1923.
1295	*Hastings* (22nd), Edward Delaval Henry Astley, b. 1912, s. 1956, m.	Hon. Delaval T. H. A., b. 1960.
1835	*Hatherton* (7th), Thomas Charles Tasman Littleton, T.D., b. 1907, s. 1973, m.	Edward C. L., b. 1950.
1776	*Hawke* (9th), Bladen Wilmer Hawke, b. 1901, s. 1939, m.	Hon. Theodore H., b. 1904.
1927	*Hayter* (3rd), George Charles Hayter Chubb, K.C.V.O., C.B.E., b. 1911, s. 1967, m.	Hon. George W. M. C., b. 1943.
1945	*Hazlerigg* (2nd), Arthur Grey Hazlerigg, M.C., b. 1910, s. 1949, w.	Hon. Arthur G. H., b. 1951.
1797 I.	*Headley* (7th), Charles Rowland Allanson-Winn, b. 1902, s. 1969, m.	Hon, John R. A.-W., b. 1934.
1943	*Hemingford* (3rd), Dennis Nicholas Herbert, b. 1934, s. 1982, m.	Hon. Christopher D. C. H., b. 1973.
1906	*Hemphill* (5th), Peter Patrick Fitzroy Martyn Martyn-Hemphill, b. 1928, s. 1957, m.	Hon. Charles A. M. M.-H., b. 1954.
1799 I.*	*Henley* (8th), Oliver Michael Robert Eden (6th *U.K. Baron, Northington*, 1885), b. 1953, s. 1977.	Hon. Andrew F. E., b. 1955.
1800 I.*	*Henniker* (8th), John Patrick Edward Chandos Henniker-Major, K.C.M.G., C.V.O., M.C. (4th *U.K. Baron, Hartismere*, 1866), b. 1916, s. 1980, m.	Hon. Mark I. P. C. H.-M., b. 1947.
1886	*Herschell* (3rd), Rognvald Richard Farrer Herschell, b. 1923, s. 1929, m.	(None.)
1935	*Hesketh* (3rd), Thomas Alexander Fermor-Hesketh, b. 1950, s. 1955, m.	Hon. Robert F.-H., b.1951.
1828	*Heytesbury* (6th), Francis William Holmes à Court, b. 1931, s. 1971, m.	Hon. James W. H. à C., b. 1967.
1886	*Hindlip* (5th), Henry Richard Allsopp, b. 1912, s. 1966, m.	Hon. Charles H. A., b. 1940.
1950	*Hives* (2nd), John Warwick Hives, b. 1913, s. 1965, m.	Matthew P. H., b. 1971.
1912	*Hollenden* (3rd), Gordon Hope Hope-Morley, b. 1914, s. 1977, m.	Hon. Ian H. H.-M., b. 1946.
1897	*Holm Patrick* (3rd), James Hans Hamilton, b. 1928, s. 1942, m.	Hon. Hans. J. D. H., b. 1955.
1933	*Horder* (2nd), Thomas Mervyn Horder, b. 1911, s. 1955.	(None.)
1797 I.	*Hotham* (8th), Henry Durand Hotham, b. 1940, s. 1967, m.	Hon. William B. H., b. 1972.
1881	*Hothfield* (4th), Thomas Sackville Tufton, b. 1916, s. 1961.	George W. A. T., T.D., b. 1904.
1597	*Howard de Walden* (9th), John Osmael Scott-Ellis (5th *U.K. Baron, Seaford*, 1826), b. 1912, s. 1946, m.	Co-heiresses. To U.K. Barony, Colin H. F. Ellis, b. 1946.
1930	*Howard of Penrith* (2nd), Francis Philip Howard, b. 1905, s. 1939, m.	Hon. Philip E. H., b. 1945.
1960	*Howick of Glendale* (2nd), Charles Evelyn Baring, b. 1937, s. 1973, m.	Hon. David E. C. B., b. 1975.
1796 I.	*Huntingfield* (6th), Gerard Charles Arcedeckne Vanneck, b. 1915, s. 1969, m.	Hon. Joshua C. V., b. 1954.
1866	*Hylton* (5th), Raymond Hervey Jolliffe, b. 1932, s. 1967, m.	Hon. William H. M. J., b. 1967.
1933	*Iliffe* (2nd), Edward Langton Iliffe, b. 1908, s. 1960, m.	Robert P. R. I., b. 1944.
1543 I.	*Inchiquin* (18th), Conor Myles John O'Brien, b. 1943, s. 1982.	Murrough R. O'B., b. 1910.
1962	*Inchyra* (1st), Frederick Robert Hoyer Millar, G.C.M.G., C.V.O., b. 1900, m.	Hon. Robert C. R. H. M., b. 1935.
1964	*Inglewood* (1st), William Morgan Fletcher-Vane, T.D., b. 1909, w.	Hon. W. Richard F.-V., b. 1951.
1919	*Inverforth* (4th), Andrew Peter Weir, b. 1966, s. 1982, M.	Hon. John V. W., b. 1935.
1941	*Ironside* (2nd), Edmund Oslac Ironside, b. 1924, s. 1959, m.	Hon. Charles E. G. I., b. 1956.
1952	*Jeffreys* (2nd), Mark George Christopher Jeffreys, b. 1932, s. 1960, m.	Hon. Christopher H. M. J., b. 1957.
1924	*Jessel* (2nd), Edward Herbert Jessel, C.B.E., b. 1904, s. 1950, m.	(None.)
1906	*Joicey* (4th), Michael Edward Joicey, b. 1925, s. 1966, m.	Hon. James M. J., b. 1953.
1976	*Keith of Kinkel*, Henry Shanks Keith, b. 1922, m. (*Lord of Appeal*).	(Law Life Peerage.)
1937	*Kenilworth* (4th), John Randle Siddeley, b. 1954, s. 1981, m.	(None).
1935	*Kennet* (2nd), Wayland Hilton Young, b. 1923, s. 1960, m.	Hon. William A. T. Y., b. 1957.
1776 I. 1886*	} *Kensington* (8th), Hugh Ivor Edwardes (*U.K. Baron, Kensington*), b. 1933, s. 1981, m.	Hon. William O. A. E., b. 1964.
1951	*Kenswood* (2nd), John Michael Howard Whitfield, b. 1930, s. 1963, m.	Hon. Michael C. W., b. 1955.
1788	*Kenyon* (5th), Lloyd Tyrell-Kenyon, C.B.E., b. 1917, s. 1927, m.	Hon. Lloyd T.-K., b. 1947.

Created.	Title, Order of Succession, Name, etc.	Eldest Son or Heir.
1947	*Kershaw* (4th), Edward John Kershaw, *b.* 1936, *s.* 1962, *m.*	Hon. John C. E. *K., b.* 1971.
1943	*Keyes* (2nd), Roger George Bowlby Keyes, *b.* 1919, *s.* 1945, *m.*	Hon. Charles W. P. *K., b.* 1951.
1909	*Kilbracken* (3rd), John Raymond Godley, D.S.C., *b.* 1920, *s.* 1950, *m.*	Hon. Christopher J. *G., b.* 1945.
1971	*Kilbrandon*, Charles James Dalrymple Shaw, P.C., *b.* 1906, *m.* (*Lord of Appeal, retired*).	(Law Life Peerage.)
1900	*Killanin* (3rd), Michael Morris, M.B.E., T.D., *b.* 1914, *s.* 1927, *m.*	Hon. G. Redmond F. *M., b.* 1947.
1943	*Killearn* (2nd), Graham Curtis Lampson, *b.* 1919, *s.* 1964, *m.*	Hon. Victor M. G. A. *L., b.* 1941.
1789 I.	*Kilmaine* (7th), John David Henry Browne, *b.* 1948, *s.* 1978, *m.*	Hon. John F. S. *B., b.* 1983.
1831	*Kilmarnock* (7th), Alastair Ivor Gilbert Boyd, *b.* 1927, *s.* 1975, *m.*	Hon. Robin J. *B., b.* 1941.
1941	*Kindersley* (3rd), Robert Hugh Molesworth Kindersley, *b.* 1929, *s.* 1976, *m.*	Hon. Rupert J. M. *K., b.* 1955.
1223 I.	*Kingsale* (35th), John de Courcy (*Premier Baron of Ireland*), *b.* 1941, *s.* 1969.	Nevinson R. *de C., b.* 1920.
1682 s. ⎱ 1860* ⎰	*Kinnaird* (13th), Graham Charles Kinnaird (5th *U.K. Baron, Kinnaird*), *b.* 1912, *s.* 1972, *m.*	(None.)
1902	*Kinross* (4th), David Andrew Balfour, O.B.E., T.D., *b.* 1906, *s.* 1976, *m.*	Hon. Christopher P. *B.,* 1949.
1951	*Kirkwood* (3rd), David Harvie Kirkwood, PH.D., *b.* 1931, *s.* 1970, *m.*	Hon. James S. *K., b.* 1937.
1979	*Lane*, Geoffrey Dawson Lane, P.C., A.F.C., *b.* 1918, *m.* (*Lord Chief Justice of England*).	(Law Life Peerage.)
1800 I	*Langford* (9th), Geoffrey Alexander Rowley-Conwy, O.B.E., *b.* 1912, *s.* 1953, *m.*	Hon. Owen G. *R.-C., b.* 1958.
1942	*Latham* (2nd), Dominic Charles Latham, *b.* 1954, *s.* 1970.	Anthony M. *L., b.* 1954.
1431	*Latymer* (7th), Thomas Burdett Money-Coutts, *b.* 1901, *s.* 1949, *w.*	Hon. Hugo N. *M.-C., b.* 1926.
1869	*Lawrence* (5th), David John Downer Lawrence, *b.* 1937, *s.* 1968.	(None.)
1947	*Layton* (2nd), Michael John Layton, *b.* 1912, *s.* 1966, *m.*	Hon. Geoffrey M. *L., b.* 1947.
1859	*Leconfield* (7th), John Max Henry Scawen Wyndham (2nd *U.K. Baron, Egremont*, 1963), *b.* 1948, *s.* 1972, *m.*	Hon. George R. V. *W., b.* 1983.
1839	*Leigh* (5th), John Piers Leigh, *b.* 1935, *s.* 1979, *m.*	Hon. Christopher D. P. *L., b.* 1960.
1962	*Leighton of St. Mellons* (2nd), (John) Leighton Seager, *b.* 1922, *s.* 1963, *m.*	Hon. Robert W. H. L. *S., b.* 1955.
1797	*Lilford* (7th), George Vernon Powys, *b.* 1931, *s.* 1949, *m.*	Hon. Mark V. *P., b.,* 1975.
1945	*Lindsay of Birker* (2nd), Michael Francis Morris Lindsay, *b.* 1909, *s.* 1952, *m.*	Hon. James F. *L., b.* 1945.
1758 I.	*Lisle* (7th), John Nicholas Horace Lysaght, *b.* 1903, *s.* 1919, *m.*	Patrick J. *L., b.* 1931.
1925	*Lloyd* (2nd), Alexander David Frederick Lloyd, M.B.E., *b.* 1912, *s.* 1941, *m.*	(None.)
1895	*Loch* (4th), Spencer Douglas Loch, M.C., *b.* 1920, *s.* 1982, *m.*	(None.)
1850	*Londesborough* (9th), Richard John Denison, *b.* 1959, *s.* 1968.	(None.)
1541 I.	*Louth* (16th), Otway Michael James Oliver Plunkett, *b.* 1929, *s.* 1950, *m.*	Hon. Jonathan O. *P., b.* 1952.
1458 s. ⎱ 1837* ⎰	*Lovat* (15th), Simon Christopher Joseph Fraser. D.S.O., M.C., T.D. (4th *U.K. Baron, Lovat*), *b.* 1911, *s.* 1933, *m.*	Master of Lovat, *b.* 1939.
1946	*Lucas of Chilworth* (2nd), Michael William George Lucas, *b.* 1926, *s.* 1967, *m.*	Capt. Hon. Simon W. *L., b.* 1957.
1929	*Luke* (2nd), Ian St. John Lawson-Johnston, K.C.V.O., T.D., *b.* 1905, *s.* 1943, *m.*	Hon. Arthur C. St. J. *L.-J., b.* 1933.
1839	*Lurgan* (5th), John Desmond Cavendish Brownlow, O.B.E., *b.* 1911, *s.* 1984.	†
1914	*Lyell* (3rd), Charles Lyell, *b.* 1939, *s.* 1943.	(None.)
1859	*Lyveden* (6th), Ronald Cecil Vernon, *b.* 1915, *s.* 1973, *m.*	Hon. Jack L. *V., b.* 1938.
1959	*MacAndrew* (2nd), Colin Nevil Glen MacAndrew, *b.* 1919, *s.* 1979, *m.*	Hon. Christopher A. C. *MacA., b.* 1945.
1776 I.	*Macdonald* (8th), Godfrey James Macdonald, *b.* 1947, *s.* 1970, *m.*	Hon. Godfrey E. H. T. *M., b.* 1982.
1949	*Macdonald of Gwaenysgor* (2nd), Gordon Ramsay Macdonald, *b.* 1915, *s.* 1966, *m.*	Hon. Kenneth L. *M., b.* 1921.
1937	*McGowan* (3rd), Harry Duncan Cory McGowan, *b.* 1938, *s.* 1966, *m.*	Hon. Harry J. C. *Mc. G., b.* 1971.
1922	*Maclay* (3rd), Joseph Paton Maclay, *b.* 1942, *s.* 1969, *m.*	Hon. Joseph P. *M., b.* 1977.
1955	*McNair* (2nd), (Clement) John McNair, *b.* 1915, *s.* 1975, *m.*	Hon. Duncan J. *McN., b.* 1947.
1951	*Macpherson of Drumochter* (2nd), James Gordon Macpherson, *b.* 1924, *s.* 1965, *m.*	Hon. James A. *M., b.* 1979.
1937	*Mancroft* (2nd), Stormont Mancroft Samuel Mancroft, K.B.E., T.D., *b.* 1914, *s.* 1942, *m.*	Hon. Benjamin L. S. *M., b.* 1957.
1807	*Manners* (5th), John Robert Cecil Manners, *b.* 1923, *s.* 1972, *m.*	Hon. John H. R. *M., b.* 1956.
1922	*Manton* (3rd), Joseph Rupert Eric Robert Watson, *b.* 1924, *s.* 1968, *m.*	Lieut. Hon. Miles R. M. *W., b.* 1958.
1908	*Marchamley* (3rd), John William Tattersall Whiteley, *b.* 1922, *s.* 1949, *m.*	Hon. William F. *W., b.* 1968.

Created.	Title, Order of Succession, Name, etc.	Eldest Son or Heir.
1964	*Margadale* (1st), John Granville Morrison, T.D., *b.* 1906, *w.*	Hon. James I. *M.*, T.D., *b.* 1930.
1961	*Marks of Broughton* (2nd), Michael Marks, *b.* 1920, *s.* 1964, *m.*	Hon. Simon R. *M.*, *b.* 1950.
1930	*Marley* (2nd), Godfrey Pelham Leigh Aman, *b.* 1913, *s.* 1952, *m.*	(None.)
1964	*Martonmere* (1st), (John) Roland Robinson, P.C., G.B.E., K.C.M.G., *b.* 1907, *m.*	John S. *R.*, *b.* 1963.
1776 I.	*Massy* (9th), Hugh Hamon John Somerset Massy, *b.* 1921, *s.* 1958, *m.*	Hon. David H. S. *M.*, *b.* 1947.
1935	*May* (3rd), Michael St. John May, *b.* 1931, *s.* 1950, *m.*	Hon. Jasper B. St. J. *M.*, *b.* 1965.
1928	*Melchett* (4th), Peter Robert Henry Mond, *b.* 1948, *s.* 1973.	(None.)
1925	*Merrivale* (3rd), Jack Henry Edmond Duke, *b.* 1917, *s.* 1951, *m.*	Hon. Derek J. P. *D.*, *b.* 1948.
1919	*Meston* (3rd), James Meston, *b.* 1950, *s.* 1984, *m.*	Son (*no details*).
1838	*Methuen* (6th), Anthony John Methuen, *b.* 1925, *s.* 1975.	Hon. Robert A. H. *M.*, *b.* 1931.
1905	*Michelham* (2nd), Herman Alfred Stern, *b.* 1900, *s.* 1919, *m.*	Hon. Jack *Michelham*, *b.* 1903.
1711	*Middleton* (12th), (Digby) Michael Godfrey John Willoughby, M.C., *b.* 1921, *s.* 1970, *m.*	Hon. Michael C. J. *W.*, *b.* 1948.
1939	*Milford* (2nd), Wogan Philipps, *b.* 1902, *s.* 1962, *m.*	Hon. Hugo J. L. *P.*, *b.* 1929.
1933	*Milne* (2nd), George Douglass Milne, T.D., *b.* 1909, *s.* 1948, *m.*	Hon. George A. *M.*, *b.* 1941.
1951	*Milner of Leeds* (2nd), Arthur James Michael Milner, *b.* 1923, *s.* 1967, *m.*	Hon. Richard J. *M.*, *b.* 1959.
1947	*Milverton* (2nd), Rev. Fraser Arthur Richard Richards, *b.* 1930, *s.* 1978, *m.*	Hon. Michael H. *R.*, *b.* 1936.
1873	*Moncreiff* (5th), Harry Robert Wellwood Moncreiff, *b.* 1915, *s.* 1942, *m.*	Hon. Rhoderick H. W. *M.*, *b.* 1954.
1884	*Monk Bretton* (3rd), John Charles Dodson, *b.* 1924, *s.* 1933, *m.*	Hon. Christopher M. *D.*, *b.* 1958.
1728	*Monson* (11th), John Monson, *b.* 1932, *s.* 1958, *m.*	Hon. Nicholas J. *M.*, *b.* 1955.
1885	*Montagu of Beaulieu* (3rd), Edward John Barrington Douglas-Scott-Montagu, *b.* 1926, *s.* 1929, *m.*	Hon. Ralph *D.-S.-M.*, *b.* 1961
1839	*Monteagle of Brandon* (6th), Gerald Spring Rice, *b.* 1926, *s.* 1946, *m.*	Hon. Charles J. S. *R.*, *b.* 1953.
1943	*Moran* (2nd), (Richard) John (McMoran) Wilson, K.C.M.G., *b.* 1924, *s.* 1977, *m.*	Hon. James McM. *W.*, *b.* 1952.
1918	*Morris* (3rd), Michael David Morris, *b.* 1937, *s.* 1975, *m.*	Hon. Thomas A. S. *M.*, *b.* 1982.
1950	*Morris of Kenwood* (2nd), Philip Geoffrey Morris, *b.* 1928, *s.* 1954, *m.*	Hon. Jonathan D. *M.*, *b.* 1968.
1945	*Morrison* (2nd), Dennis Morrison, *b.* 1914, *s.* 1953.	(None.)
1831	*Mostyn* (5th), Roger Edward Lloyd Lloyd-Mostyn, M.C., *b.* 1920, *s.* 1965, *m.*	Hon. Llewellyn R. L. *L.-M.*, *b.* 1948.
1933	*Mottistone* (4th), David Peter Seely, C.B.E., *b.* 1920, *s.* 1966, *m.*	Hon. Peter J. P. *S.*, *b.* 1949.
1945	*Mountevans* (3rd), Edward Patrick Broke Evans, *b.* 1943, *s.* 1974, *m.*	Hon. Jeffrey de C. R. *E.*, *b.* 1948.
1283	*Mowbray* (26th), *Segrave* (27th) (1283), & *Stourton* (23rd) (1448), Charles Edward Stourton, C.B.E., *b.* 1923, *s.* 1965, *m.*	Hon. Edward W. S. *S.*, *b.* 1953.
1932	*Moyne* (2nd), Bryan Walter Guinness, *b.* 1905, *s.* 1944, *m.*	Hon. Jonathan B. *G.*, *b.* 1930.
1929	*Moynihan* (3rd), Antony Patrick Andrew Cairnes Berkeley Moynihan, *b.* 1936, *s.* 1965.	Hon. Colin B. *M.*, M.P., *b.* 1955.
1781 I.	*Muskerry* (8th), Hastings Fitzmaurice Tilson Deane, *b.* 1907, *s.* 1966, *m.*	Hon. Robert F. *D.*, *b.* 1948.
1627 S.*	*Napier and Ettrick* (14th), Francis Nigel Napier, M.V.O. (5th *U.K.* Baron, *Ettrick*, 1872), *b.* 1930, *s.* 1954, *m.*	Master of Napier, *b.* 1962.
1868	*Napier of Magdala* (5th), (Robert) John Napier, O.B.E., *b.* 1904, *s.* 1948, *m.*	Hon. Robert A. *N.*, *b.* 1940.
1940	*Nathan* (2nd), Roger Carol Michael Nathan, *b.* 1922, *s.* 1963, *m.*	Hon. Rupert H. B. *N.*, *b.* 1957.
1960	*Nelson of Stafford* (2nd), Henry George Nelson, *b.* 1917, *s.* 1962, *m.*	Hon. Henry R. G. *N.*, *b.* 1943.
1959	*Netherthorpe* (3rd), James Frederick Turner, *b.* 1964, *s.* 1982.	Hon. Patrick A. *T.*, *b.* 1971.
1946	*Newall* (2nd), Francis Storer Eaton Newall, *b.* 1930, *s.* 1963, *m.*	Hon. Richard H. E. *N.*, *b.* 1961.
1776 I.	*Newborough* (7th), Robert Charles Michael Vaughan Wynn, D.S.C., *b.* 1917, *s.* 1965, *m.*	Hon. Robert V. *W.*, *b.* 1949.
1892	*Newton* (4th), Peter Richard Legh, *b.* 1915, *s.* 1960, *m.*	Hon. Richard T. *L.*, *b.* 1950.
1930	*Noel-Buxton* (3rd), Martin Connal Noel-Buxton, *b.* 1940, *s.* 1980.	Hon. Charles C. *N.-B.*, *b.* 1975.
1957	*Norrie* (2nd), (George) Willoughby Moke Norrie, *b.* 1936, *s.* 1977, *m.*	Hon. Mark W. J. *N.*, *b.* 1972.
1884	*Northbourne* (5th), Christopher George Walter James, *b.* 1926, *s.* 1982, *m.*	Hon. Charles W. H. *J.*, *b.* 1960.
1866	*Northbrook* (5th), Francis John Baring, *b.* 1915, *s.* 1947, *m.*	Hon. Francis T. *B.*, *b.* 1954.
1878	*Norton* (7th), John Arden Adderley, O.B.E., *b.* 1915, *s.* 1961, *m.*	Hon. James N. A. *A.*, *b.* 1947.
1906	*Nunburnholme* (4th), Ben Charles Wilson, *b.* 1928, *s.* 1974, *m.*	Hon. Charles T. *W.*, *b.* 1935.
1950	*Ogmore* (2nd), Gwilym Rees Rees-Williams, *b.* 1931, *s.* 1976, *m.*	Hon. Morgan R.-*W.*, *b.* 1937.
1870	*O'Hagan* (4th), Charles Towneley Strachey, *b.* 1945, *s.* 1961, *m.*	Hon. Richard T. *S.*, *b.* 1950.
1868	*O'Neill* (4th), Raymond Arthur Clanaboy O'Neill, T.D., *b.* 1933, *s.* 1944, *m.*	Hon. Shane S. C. *O'N.*, *b.* 1965.
1836 I.*	*Oranmore and Browne* (4th), Dominick Geoffrey Edward Browne (2nd *U.K. Baron Mereworth*, 1926), *b.* 1901, *s.* 1927, *m.*	Hon. Dominick G. T. *B.*, *b.* 1929.

Created.	*Title, Order of Succession, Name, etc.*	*Eldest Son or Heir.*
1933	*Palmer* (3rd), Raymond Cecil Palmer, O.B.E., *b.* 1916, *s.* 1950, *m.*	Hon. Gordon W. N. *P.*, O.B.E., T.D., *b.* 1918.
1914	*Parmoor* (4th), (Frederick Alfred) Milo Cripps, *b.* 1929, *s.* 1977.	M. Anthony L. *C.*, C.B.E., D.S.O., T.D., Q.C., *b.* 1913.
1962	*Pearce,* Edward Holroyd Pearce, P.C., *b.* 1901, *m.* (*Lord of Appeal, retired*).	(Law Life Peerage.)
1937	*Pender* (3rd), John Willoughby Denison-Pender, *b.* 1933, *s.* 1965, *m.*	Hon. Henry J. R. *D.-P.*, *b.* 1968.
1866	*Penrhyn* (6th), Malcolm Frank Douglas-Pennant, D.S.O., M.B.E., *b.* 1908, *s.* 1967, *m.*	Hon. Nigel *D.-P.*, *b.* 1909.
1603	*Petre* (17th), Joseph William Lionel Petre, *b.* 1914, *s.* 1915, *m.*	Hon. John P. L. *P.*, *b.* 1942.
1918	*Phillimore* (3rd), Robert Godfrey Phillimore, *b.* 1939, *s.* 1947.	Hon. Claud S. *P.*, *b.* 1911.
1945	*Piercy* (3rd), James William Piercy, *b.* 1946, *s.* 1981.	Hon. Mark E. P. *P.*, *b.* 1953.
1827	*Plunket* (8th), Robin Rathmore Plunket, *b.* 1925, *s.* 1975, *m.*	Hon. Shaun A. F. S. *P.*, *b.* 1931.
1831	*Poltimore* (7th), Mark Coplestone Bampfylde, *b.* 1957, *s.* 1978, *m.*	Hon. David C. W. *B.*, *b.* 1924.
1690 s.	*Polwarth* (10th), Henry Alexander Hepburne-Scott, T.D., *b.* 1916, *s.* 1944, *m.*	Master of Polwarth, *b.* 1947.
1930	*Ponsonby of Shulbrede* (3rd), Thomas Arthur Ponsonby, *b.* 1930, *s.* 1976, *m.*	Hon. Frederick M. T. *P.*, *b.* 1958.
1958	*Poole* (1st), Oliver Brian Sanderson Poole, P.C., C.B.E., T.D., *b.* 1911, *m.*	Hon. David C. *P.*, *b.* 1945.
1852	*Raglan* (5th), FitzRoy John Somerset, *b.* 1927, *s.* 1964, *m.*	Hon. Geoffrey S., *b.* 1932.
1932	*Rankeillour* (4th), Peter St. Thomas More Henry Hope, *b.* 1935, *s.* 1967.	Michael R. *H.*, *b.* 1940.
1953	*Rathcavan* (2nd), Phelim Robert Hugh O'Neill, P.C. (N.I.), *b.* 1909, *s.* 1982, *m.*	Hon. Hugh D. T. *O'N.*, *b.* 1939.
1916	*Rathcreedan* (2nd), Charles Patrick Norton, T.D., *b.* 1905, *s.* 1930, *m.*	Hon. Christopher J. *N.*, *b.* 1949.
1868 I.	*Rathdonnell* (5th), Thomas Benjamin McClintock Bunbury, *b.* 1938, *s.* 1959, *m.*	Hon. William L. McC *B.*, *b.* 1966.
1911	*Ravensdale* (3rd), Nicholas Mosley, M.C., *b.* 1923, *s.* 1966, *m.*	Hon. Shaun N. *M.*, *b.* 1949.
1821	*Ravensworth* (8th), Arthur Waller Liddell, *b.* 1924, *s.* 1950, *m.*	Hon. Thomas A. H. *L.*, *b.* 1954.
1821	*Rayleigh* (5th), John Arthur Strutt, *b.* 1908, *s.* 1947, *w.*	John G. *S.*, *b.* 1960.
1937	*Rea* (3rd), John Nicolas, Rea, M.D., *b.* 1928, *s.* 1981, *m.*	Hon. Matthew J. *R.*, *b.* 1956.
1628 s.	*Reay* (14th), Hugh William Mackay, *b.* 1937, *s.* 1963, *m.*	Master of Reay, *b.* 1965.
1902	*Redesdale* (5th), Clement Napier Bertram Mitford, *b.* 1932, *s.* 1963, *m.*	Hon. Rupert B. *M.*, *b.* 1967.
1928	*Remnant* (3rd), James Wogan Remnant, C.V.O., *b.* 1930, *s.* 1967, *m.*	Hon. Philip J. *R.*, *b.* 1954.
1806 I.	*Rendlesham* (8th), Charles Anthony Hugh Thellusson, *b.* 1915, *s.* 1943, *m.*	Hon. Charles W. B. *T.*, *b.* 1954.
1933	*Rennell* (3rd), (John Adrian) Tremayne Rodd, *b.* 1935, *s.* 1978, *m.*	Hon. James R. D. T. *R.*, *b.* 1978.
1964	*Renwick* (2nd), Harry Andrew Renwick, *b.* 1935, *s.* 1973, *m.*	Hon. Robert J. *R.*, *b.* 1966.
1885	*Revelstoke* (4th), Rupert Baring, *b.* 1911, *s.* 1934.	Hon. John *B.*, *b.* 1934.
1905	*Ritchie of Dundee* (5th), (Harold) Malcolm Ritchie, *b.* 1919, *s.* 1978, *m.*	Hon. Charles R. R. *R.*, *b.* 1958.
1935	*Riverdale* (2nd), Robert Arthur Balfour, *b.* 1901, *s.* 1957, *m.*	Hon. Mark R. *B.*, *b.* 1927.
1961	*Robertson of Oakridge* (2nd), William Ronald Robertson, *b.* 1930, *s.* 1974, *m.*	Hon. William B. E. *R.*, *b.* 1975.
1938	*Roborough* (2nd), Massey Henry Edgcumbe Lopes, *b.* 1903, *s.* 1938, *m.*	Hon. Henry M. *L.*, *b.* 1940.
1931	*Rochester* (2nd), Foster Charles Lowry Lamb, *b.* 1916, *s.* 1955, *m.*	Hon. David C. *L.*, *b.* 1944.
1934	*Rockley* (3rd), James Hugh Cecil, *b.* 1934, *s.* 1976, *m.*	Hon. Anthony R. *C.*, *b.* 1961.
1782	*Rodney* (9th), John Francis Rodney, *b.* 1920, *s.* 1973, *m.*	Hon. George B. *R.*, *b.* 1953.
1651 s.*	*Rollo* (13th), Eric John Stapylton Rollo (4th *U.K. Baron, Dunning,* 1869), *b.* 1915, *s.* 1947, *m.*	Master of Rollo, *b.* 1943.
1959	*Rootes* (2nd), William Geoffrey Rootes, *b.* 1917, *s.* 1964, *m.*	Hon. Nicholas G. *R.*, *b.* 1951.
1980	*Roskill,* Eustace Wentworth Roskill, P.C., *b.* 1911, *m.* (*Lord of Appeal*).	(Law Life Peerage.)
1796 I. 1838* }	*Rossmore* (7th), William Warner Westenra (6th *U.K. Baron, Rossmore*), *b.* 1931, *s.* 1958.	(None.)
1939	*Rotherwick* (2nd), (Herbert) Robin Cayzer, *b.* 1912, *s.* 1958, *w.*	Hon. H. Robin *C.*, *b.* 1954.
1885	*Rothschild* (3rd), Nathanial Mayer Victor Rothschild, G.B.E., G.M., F.R.S., *b.* 1910, *s.* 1937, *m.*	Hon. N. C. Jacob *R.*, *b.* 1936.
1911	*Rowallan* (3rd), Arthur Cameron Corbett, *b.* 1919, *s.* 1977.	Hon. John P. C. *C.*, *b.* 1947.
1947	*Rugby* (2nd), Alan Loader Maffey, *b.* 1913, *s.* 1969, *m.*	Hon. Robert C. *M.*, *b.* 1951.
1975	*Russell of Killowen,* Charles Ritchie Russell, P.C., *b.* 1908, *m.* (*Lord of Appeal, retired*).	(Law Life Peerage.)
1919	*Russell of Liverpool* (3rd), Simon Gordon Jared Russell, *b.* 1952, *s.* 1981, *m.*	Hon. Adam M. H. *R.*, *b.* 1957.
1876	*Sackville* (6th), Lionel Bertrand Sackville-West, *b.* 1913, *s.* 1965, *m.*	Hugh R. I. *S.-W.*, M.C., *b.* 1919.
1964	*St. Helens* (2nd), Richard Francis Hughes-Young, *b.* 1945, *s.* 1980, *m.*	(None.)
1559	*St. John of Bletso* (21st), Anthony Tudor St. John, *b.* 1957, *s.* 1978.	Edmund O. *St. J.*, *b.* 1927.
1935	*St. Just* (2nd), Peter George Grenfell, *b.* 1922, *s.* 1941, *m.*	(None.)
1852	*St. Leonards* (4th), John Gerard Sugden, *b.* 1950, *s.* 1972.	Edward C. *S.*, *b.* 1902.
1887	*St. Levan* (4th), John Francis Arthur St. Aubyn, D.S.C., *b.* 1919, *s.* 1978, *m.*	Hon. O. Piers *St. A.*, M.C., *b.* 1920.
1885	*St. Oswald* (4th), Rowland Denys Guy Winn, M.C., *b.* 1916, *s.* 1957, *w.*	Hon. Derek E. A. *W.*, *b.* 1919.
1972	*Salmon,* Cyril Barnet Salmon, P.C., *b.* 1903, *m.* (*Lord of Appeal, retired*).	(Law Life Peerage.)
1945	*Sandford* (2nd), Rev. John Cyril Edmondson, D.S.C., *b.* 1920, *s.* 1959, *m.*	Hon. James J. M. *E.*, *b.* 1949.

Created.	Title, Order of Succession, Name, etc.	Eldest Son or Heir.
1871	*Sandhurst* (5th), (John Edward) Terence Mansfield, D.F.C., b. 1920, s. 1964, m.	Hon. Guy R. J. M., b. 1949.
1802	*Sandys* (7th), Richard Michael Oliver Hill, b. 1931, s. 1961, m.	Marcus T. H., b. 1931.
1888	*Savile* (3rd), George Halifax Lumley-Savile, b. 1919, s. 1931.	Hon. Henry L. T. L.-S., b. 1923.
1447	*Saye and Sele* (21st), Nathaniel Thomas Allen Fiennes, b. 1920, s. 1968, m.	Hon. Richard I. F., b. 1959.
1977	*Scarman*, Leslie George Scarman, P.C., O.B.E., b. 1911, m. (*Lord of Appeal*).	(Law Life Peerage.)
1932	*Selsdon* (3rd), Malcolm McEacharn Mitchell-Thomson, b. 1937, s. 1963, m.	Hon. Callum M. M. M.-T., b. 1969.
1916	*Shaughnessy* (3rd), William Graham Shaughnessy, b. 1922, s. 1938, m.	Hon. Michael J. S., b. 1946.
1783 I.	*Sheffield* (8th), Thomas Henry Oliver Stanley (8th *U.K. Baron, Stanley*	Hon. Richard O. S., b. 1956.
1839*	*of Alderley and* 7th *U.K. Baron Eddisbury*, 1848), b. 1927, s. 1971, m.	
1946	*Shepherd* (2nd), Malcolm Newton Shepherd, P.C., b. 1918, s. 1954, m.	Hon. Graeme G. S., b. 1949.
1784	*Sherborne* (8th), Ralph Stawell Dutton, F.S.A., b. 1898, s. 1982.	(None).
1964	*Sherfield* (1st), Roger Mellor Makins, G.C.B., G.C.M.G., b. 1904, m.	Hon. Christopher J. M., b. 1942.
1902	*Shuttleworth* (5th), Charles Geoffrey Nicholas Kay-Shuttleworth, b. 1948, s. 1975, m.	Hon. Thomas E. K.-S., b. 1976.
1963	*Silsoe* (2nd), David Malcolm Trustram Eve, Q.C., b. 1930, s. 1976, m.	Hon. Simon R. T. E., b. 1966.
1947	*Simon of Wythenshawe* (2nd), Roger Simon, b. 1913, s. 1960, m.	Hon. Matthew S., b. 1955.
1449 S.	*Sinclair* (17th), Charles Murray Kennedy St. Clair, M.V.O., b. 1914, s. 1957, m.	Master of Sinclair, b. 1968.
1957	*Sinclair of Cleeve* (2nd), John Robert Kilgour Sinclair, O.B.E., b. 1919, s. 1979, m.	Hon. John L. R. S., b. 1953.
1919	*Sinha* (3rd), Sudhindro Prosanno Sinha, b. 1920, s. 1967, m.	Hon. Sushanto S., b. 1953.
1828	*Skelmersdale* (7th), Roger Bootle-Wilbraham, b. 1945, s. 1973, m.	Hon. Andrew B.-W., b. 1977.
1916	*Somerleyton* (3rd), Savile William Francis Crossley, b. 1928, s. 1959, m.	Hon. Hugh F. S. C., b. 1971.
1784	*Somers* (8th), John Patrick Somers Cocks, b. 1907, s. 1953, m.	Philip S. S. C., b. 1948.
1917	*Southborough* (4th), Francis Michael Hopwood, b. 1922, s. 1982, m.	(None.)
1959	*Spens* (2nd), William George Michael Spens, b. 1914, s. 1973, m.	Hon. Patrick M. R. S., b. 1942.
1640	*Stafford* (14th), Basil Francis Nicholas Fitzherbert, b. 1926, s. 1941, m.	Hon. Francis M. W. F., b. 1954.
1938	*Stamp* (3rd), Trevor Charles Stamp, M.D., b. 1907, s. 1941, m.	Hon. Trevor C. B. S., M.D., b. 1935.
1318	*Strabolgi* (11th), David Montague de Burgh Kenworthy, b. 1914, s. 1953, m.	Rev. the Hon. Jonathan M. A. K., b. 1916.
1954	*Strang* (2nd), Colin Strang, b. 1922, s. 1978, w.	(None.)
1955	*Strathalmond* (3rd), William Roberton Fraser, b. 1947, s. 1976, m.	Hon. William G. F., b. 1976.
1936	*Strathcarron* (2nd), David William Anthony Blyth Macpherson, b. 1924, s. 1937, m.	Hon. Ian D. P. M., b. 1949.
1955	*Strathclyde* (1st), Thomas Dunlop Galbraith, P.C., b. 1891, m.	Thomas G. D. du R. de B. G., b. 1960.
1900	*Strathcona and Mount Royal* (4th), Donald Euan Palmer Howard, b. 1923, s. 1959, m.	Hon. Donald A. S. H., b. 1961.
1836	*Stratheden & Campbell* (1841) (5th), Gavin Campbell, b. 1901, s. 1981, m.	Hon. Donald C., b. 1934.
1884	*Strathspey* (5th), Donald Patrick Trevor Grant, b. 1912, s. 1948, m.	Hon. James P. G., b. 1943.
1838	*Sudeley* (7th), Merlin Charles Sainthill Hanbury-Tracy, b. 1939, s. 1941, m.	Claud E. F. Hanbury-Tracy-Domvile, T.D., b. 1904.
1786	*Suffield* (11th), Anthony Philip Harbord-Hamond, M.C., b. 1922, s. 1951, m.	Hon. Charles A. A. H.-H., b. 1953.
1893	*Swansea* (4th), John Hussey Hamilton Vivian, b. 1925, s. 1934, m.	Hon. Richard A. H. V., b. 1957.
1907	*Swaythling* (3rd), Stuart Albert Samuel Montagu, O.B.E., b. 1898, s. 1927, m.	Hon. David C. S. M., b. 1928.
1919	*Swinfen* (3rd), Roger Mynors Swinfen Eady, b. 1938, s. 1977, m.	Hon. Charles R. P. S. E., b. 1971.
1935	*Sysonby* (3rd), John Frederick Ponsonby, b. 1945, s. 1956.	(None.)
1831 I	*Talbot of Malahide* (9th), Joseph Hubert George Talbot, b. 1899, s. 1975.	Reginald J. R. Arundell, b. 1931.
1946	*Tedder* (2nd), John Michael Tedder, SC.D., PH.D., D.SC., b. 1926, s. 1967, m.	Hon. Robin J. T., b. 1955.
1982	*Templeman*, Sydney (William) Templeman, P.C., M.B.E., b. 1920, m. (*Lord of Appeal*).	(Law Life Peerage).
1884	*Tennyson* (4th), Harold Christopher Tennyson, b. 1919, s. 1951.	Hon. Mark A. T., D.S.C., b. 1920.
1918	*Terrington* (4th), (James Allen) David Woodhouse, b. 1915, s. 1961, m.	Hon. C. Montague W., D.S.O., O.B.E., b. 1917.
1940	*Teviot* (2nd), Charles John Kerr, b. 1934, s. 1968, m.	Hon. Charles R. K., b. 1971.
1616	*Teynham* (20th), John Christopher Ingham Roper-Curzon, b. 1928, s. 1972, m.	Hon. David J. H. I. R.-C., b. 1965.
1964	*Thomson of Fleet* (2nd), Kenneth Roy Thomson, b. 1923, s. 1976, m.	Hon. David K. R. T., b. 1957.

Created.	Title, Order of Succession, Name, etc.	Eldest Son or Heir.
1792	*Thurlow* (8th), Francis Edward Hovell-Thurlow-Cumming-Bruce, K.C.M.G., *b.* 1912, *s.* 1971, *m.*	Hon. Roualeyn R. *H.-T.-C.-B.*, *b.* 1952.
1876	*Tollemache* (5th), Timothy John Edward Tollemache, *b.* 1939, *s.* 1975, *m.*	Hon. Edward J. H. *T.*, *b.* 1976.
1564 s.	*Torphichen* (15th), James Andrew Douglas Sandilands, *b.* 1946, *s.* 1975, *m.*	Douglas R. A. *S.*, *b.* 1926.
1947	*Trefgarne* (2nd), David Garro Trefgarne, *b.* 1941, *s.* 1960, *m.*	Hon. George G. *T.*, *b.* 1970.
1921	*Trevethin* (4th), *and Oaksey* (2nd), John Geoffrey Tristram Lawrence (2nd *U.K. Baron, Oaksey*, 1947), *b.* 1929, *s.* 1971, *m.*	Hon. Patrick J. T. *L.*, *b.* 1960.
1880	*Trevor* (4th), Charles Edwin Hill-Trevor, *b.* 1928, *s.* 1950, *m.*	Hon. Marke C. *H.-T.*, *b.* 1970.
1461 I.	*Trimlestown* (19th), Charles Aloysius Barnewall, *b.* 1899, *s.* 1937, *m.*	Hon. Anthony E. *B.*, *b.* 1928.
1940	*Tryon* (3rd), Anthony George Merrik Tryon, *b.* 1940, *s.* 1976, *m.*	Hon. Charles G. B. *T.*, *b.* 1976.
1935	*Tweedsmuir* (2nd), John Norman Stuart Buchan, C.B.E., C.D., *b.* 1911, *s.* 1940, *m.*	Hon. William *B.*, *b.* 1916.
1523	*Vaux of Harrowden* (10th), John Hugh Philip Gilbey, *b.* 1915, *s.* 1977, *m.*	Hon. Anthony W. *G.*, *b.* 1940.
1800 I.	*Ventry* (7th), Arthur Frederick Daubeney Olav Eveleigh-de-Moleyns, *b.* 1898, *s.* 1936.	Andrew W. *Daubeny-De M.*, *b.* 1943.
1762	*Vernon* (10th), John Lawrance Vernon, *b.* 1923, *s.* 1963, *m.*	Robert V. *Harcourt*, *b.* 1918.
1922	*Vestey* (3rd), Samuel George Armstrong Vestey, *b.* 1941, *s.* 1954, *m.*	Hon. William G. *V.*, *b.* 1983.
1841	*Vivian* (5th), Anthony Crespigny Claude Vivian, *b.* 1906, *s.* 1940, *m.*	Hon. Nicholas *V.*, *b.* 1935.
1934	*Wakehurst* (3rd), (John) Christopher Loder, *b.* 1925, *s.* 1970, *m.*	Hon. Timothy W. *L.*, *b.* 1958.
1723	*Walpole* (9th), Robert Henry Montgomerie Walpole, T.D., *b.* 1913, *s.* 1931, *m.*	Hon. Robert H. *W.*, *b.* 1938.
1780	*Walsingham* (9th), John de Grey, M.C., *b.* 1925, *s.* 1965, *m.*	Hon. Robert *de G.*, *b.* 1969.
1936	*Wardington* (2nd), Christopher Henry Beaumont Pease, *b.* 1924, *s.* 1950, *m.*	Hon. William S. *P.*, *b.* 1925.
1792 I.	*Waterpark* (7th), Frederick Caryll Philip Cavendish, *b.* 1926, *s.* 1948, *m.*	Hon. Roderick A. *C.*, *b.* 1959.
1942	*Wedgwood* (4th), Piers Anthony Weymouth Wedgwood, *b.* 1954, *s.* 1970.	John *W.*, M.D., *b.* 1919.
1861	*Westbury* (5th), David Alan Bethell, M.C., *b.* 1922, *s.* 1961, *m.*	Hon. Richard N. *B.*, M.B.E., *b.* 1950.
1944	*Westwood* (2nd), William Westwood, *b.* 1907, *s.* 1953, *m.*	Hon. William G. *W.*, *b.* 1944.
1935	*Wigram* (2nd), (George) Neville (Clive) Wigram, M.C., *b.* 1915, *s.* 1960, *m.*	Maj. Hon. Andrew F. C. *W.*, *b.* 1949.
1964	*Wilberforce*, Richard Orme Wilberforce, P.C., C.M.G., O.B.E., *b.* 1907, *m.* (*Lord of Appeal, retired*).	(Law Life Peerage.)
1491	*Willoughby de Broke* (20th), John Henry Peyto Verney, M.C., A.F.C., *b.* 1896, *s.* 1923, *m.*	Hon. Leopold D. *V.*, *b.* 1938.
1946	*Wilson* (2nd), Patrick Maitland Wilson, *b.* 1915, *s.* 1964, *m.*	(None.)
1937	*Windlesham* (3rd), David James George Hennessy, P.C., C.V.O., *b.* 1932, *s.* 1962, *m.*	Hon. James *H.*, *b.* 1968.
1951	*Wise* (2nd), John Clayton Wise, *b.* 1923, *s.* 1968, *m.*	Hon. Christopher J. C. *W.*, PH.D., *b.* 1949.
1869	*Wolverton* (5th), Nigel Reginald Victor Glyn, *b.* 1904, *s.* 1932.	Jeremy C. *G.*, *b.* 1930.
1928	*Wraxall* (2nd), George Richard Lawley Gibbs, *b.* 1928, *s.* 1931.	Hon. Eustace H. B. *G.*, C.M.G., *b.* 1929.
1915	*Wrenbury* (3rd), John Burton Buckley, *b.* 1927, *s.* 1940, *m.*	Hon. William E. *B.*, *b.* 1966.
1838	*Wrottesley* (6th), Clifton Hugh Lancelot de Verdon Wrottesley, *b.* 1968, *s.* 1977, *M.*	Hon. Mark *W.*, *b.* 1951.
1919	*Wyfold* (3rd), Hermon Robert Fleming Hermon-Hodge, *b.* 1915, *s.* 1942.	(None.)
1829	*Wynford* (8th), Robert Samuel Best, M.B.E., *b.* 1917, *s.* 1943, *m.*	Hon. John P. *B.*, *b.* 1950.
1308	*Zouche* (18th), James Assheton Frankland, *b.* 1943, *s.* 1965, *m.*	Hon. Roger N. *F.*, *b.* 1909.

PEERESSES IN THEIR OWN RIGHT

Peerages are occasionally granted immediately to ladies of distinction or the widows of distinguished men; but frequently the instances falling under this heading are the result of regular inheritance in lines which are open to females in default of males. A Peeress in her Own Right retains her title after marriage, and if her husband's rank is the superior she is designated by the two titles jointly, the inferior one last: her hereditary claim still holds good in spite of any marriage whether higher or lower. No rank held by a woman can confer any title or even precedence upon her husband but the rank of a Peeress in her Own Right is inherited by her eldest son (or perhaps daughter), to whomsoever she may have been married.

COUNTESSES IN THEIR OWN RIGHT

Style, The Countess of —— *Addressed as,* My Lady.

Created.	Title, Name, etc.	Eldest Son or Heir.
1643 s.	*Dysart,* Rosamund Agnes Greaves, *b.* 1914, *s.* 1975.	Lady Katherine *Grant, b.* 1918.
1633 s.	*Loudoun,* Barbara Huddleston Abney-Hastings, *b.* 1919, *s.* 1960, *m.*	Lord Mauchline, *b.* 1942.
c. 1115 s.	*Mar,* Margaret of Mar (*Premier Earldom of Scotland*), *b.* 1940, *s.* 1975, *m.*	The Mistress of Mar, *b.* 1963.
1947	*Mountbatten of Burma,* Patricia Edwina Victoria Knatchbull, *b.* 1924, *s.* 1979, *m.*	Lord Romsey, *b.* 1947.
1235 s.	*Sutherland,* Elizabeth Millicent Sutherland, *b.* 1921, *s.* 1963, *m.*	Lord Strathnaver, *b.* 1947.

BARONESSES IN THEIR OWN RIGHT

Style, The Baroness —— *Addressed as,* My Lady.

Created.	Title, Name, etc.	Eldest Son or Heir.
1421	*Berkeley,* Mary Lalle Foley-Berkeley, *b.* 1905, *title called out of abeyance,* 1967.	Hon. Cynthia E. *Gueterbock, b.* 1909.
1455	*Berners,* Vera Ruby Williams, *b.* 1901, *s.* 1950, *m.*	Two co-heiresses.
1321	*Dacre,* Rachel Leila Douglas-Home, *b.* 1929, *title called out of abeyance,* 1970, *m.*	Hon. James T. A. *D.-H., b.* 1952.
1332	*Darcy de Knayth,* Davina Marcia Ingrams, *b.* 1938, *s.* 1943, *w.*	Hon. Caspar D. *I., b.* 1962.
1439	*Dudley,* Barbara Amy Felicity Wallace, *b.* 1907, *s.* 1972, *w.*	Hon. Jim. A. H. *W., b.* 1930.
1490 s.	*Herries,* Anne Elizabeth Fitzalan-Howard, *b.* 1938, *s.* 1975.	Lady Mary *F.-H.,* c.v.o., *b.* 1940.
1602 s.	*Kinloss,* Beatrice Mary Grenville Freeman-Grenville, *b.* 1922, *s.* 1944, *m.*	Master of Kinloss, *b.* 1953.
1663	*Lucas of Crudwell* (*Scottish Baroness, Dingwall* 1609), Anne Rosemary Palmer, *b.* 1919, *s.* 1958, *m.*	Hon. Ralph M. *P., b.* 1951.
1681 s.	*Nairne,* Katherine Evelyn Constance Bigham (*Katherine, Viscountess Mersey*), *b.* 1912, *s.* 1944, *m.*	Visct. Mersey, *b.* 1934 (*see* p. 235).
1945	*Portal of Hungerford,* Rosemary Ann Portal, *b.* 1923, *s.* 1971.	Hon. Mavis E. A. *P., b.* 1926.
1445 s.	*Saltoun,* Flora Marjory Fraser, *b.* 1930, *s.* 1979, *m.*	Hon. Katharine I. M. I. *F., b.* 1957.
1489 s.	*Sempill,* Ann Moira Sempill, *b.* 1920, *s.* 1965, *m.*	Master of Sempill, *b.* 1949.
1313	*Willoughby de Eresby,* Nancy Jane Marie Heathcote-Drummond-Willoughby, *b.* 1934, *s.* 1983.	Two co-heiresses.

THE PREFIX RIGHT HONOURABLE

"Right Honourable."—By long established custom, or courtesy, members of her Majesty's Most Honourable Privy Council are entitled to be designated "The Right Honourable," but, in practice, this prefix is sometimes absorbed in other designations; for example, a Prince of the Blood admitted a Privy Counsellor remains "His Royal Highness"; a Duke remains "His Grace"; a Marquess is still styled "Most Honourable". The style of all other Peers whether Privy Counsellors or not, is "Right Honourable", although it is more usual to describe them with the prefix "The", omitting the more elaborate styles. A Privy Counsellor who is not a Peer should be addressed as The Right (or Rt.) Hon.——. A Peer below the rank of Marquess who is a Privy Counsellor should be addressed as The Right (or Rt). Hon. the Lord (or Earl or Viscount)——, p.c., or, less elaborately, The Lord (or Earl or Viscount)——p.c.

LIFE PEERS
Created under Life Peerages Act, 1958

BARONS

1974 *Alexander of Potterhill*, William Picken Alexander, PH.D., *b.* 1905, *m.*
1976 *Allen of Abbeydale*, Philip Allen, G.C.B., *b.* 1912, *m.*
1974 *Allen of Fallowfield*, Alfred Walter Henry Allen, C.B.E., *b.* 1914, *m.*
1961 *Alport*, Cuthbert James McCall Alport, P.C., T.D., *b.* 1912, *w.*
1965 *Annan*, Noel Gilroy Annan, O.B.E., *b.* 1916, *m.*
1970 *Ardwick*, John Cowburn Beavan, *b.* 1910, *m.*
1973 *Ashby*, Eric Ashby, D.SC., F.R.S., *b.* 1904, *m.*
1967 *Aylestone*, Herbert William Bowden, P.C., C.H., C.B.E., *b.* 1905, *m.*
1977 *Baker*, John Fleetwood Baker, O.B.E., SC.D., F.R.S., *b.* 1901, *w.*
1968 *Balogh*, Thomas Balogh, *b.* 1905, *m.*
1982 *Bancroft*, Ian Powell Bancroft, G.C.B., *b.* 1922, *m.*
1974 *Banks*, Desmond Anderson Harvie Banks, C.B.E., *b.* 1918, *m.*
1974 *Barber*, Anthony Perrinott Lysberg Barber, P.C., T.D., *b.* 1920, *w.*
1983 *Barnett*, Joel Barnett, P.C., *b.* 1923, *m.*
1982 *Bauer*, Prof. Peter Thomas Bauer, *b.* 1915.
1967 *Beaumont of Whitley*, Timothy Wentworth Beaumont, *b.* 1928, *m.*
1965 *Beeching*, Richard Beeching, PH.D., *b.* 1913, *m.*
1979 *Bellwin*, Irwin Norman Bellow, *b.* 1923, *m.*
1981 *Beloff*, Max Beloff, *b.* 1913, *m.*
1981 *Benson*, Henry Alexander Benson, G.B.E., *b.* 1909, *m.*
1969 *Bernstein*, Sidney Lewis Bernstein, *b.* 1899, *m.*
1964 *Beswick*, Frank Beswick, P.C., *b.* 1912, *m.*
1968 *Black*, William Rushton Black, *b.* 1893, *w.*
1971 *Blake*, Robert Norman William Blake, F.B.A., *b.* 1916, *m.*
1983 *Blanch*, Rt. Rev. Stuart Yarworth Blanch, P.C., *b.* 1918, *m.*
1978 *Blease*, William John Blease, *b.* 1914, *m.*
1964 *Blyton*, William Reid Blyton, *b.* 1899, *m.*
1980 *Boardman*, Thomas Gray Boardman, M.C., T.D., *b.* 1919, *m.*
1958 *Boothby*, Robert John Graham Boothby, K.B.E., *b.* 1900, *m.*
1976 *Boston of Faversham*, Terence George Boston, Q.C.,*b.* 1930, *m.*
1983 *Bottomley*, Arthur George Bottomley, P.C., O.B.E., *b.* 1907, *m.*
1963 *Bowden*, Bertram Vivian Bowden, PH.D., *b.* 1910.
1972 *Boyd-Carpenter*, John Archibald Boyd-Carpenter, P.C., *b.* 1908, *m.*
1976 *Briggs*, Asa Briggs, *b.* 1921, *m.*
1974 *Briginshaw*, Richard William Briginshaw, *m.*
1976 *Brimelow*, Thomas Brimelow, G.C.M.G., *b.* 1915, *m.*
1964 *Brockway*, (Archibald) Fenner Brockway, *b.* 1888, *m.*
1975 *Brookes*, Raymond Percival Brookes, *b.* 1909, *m.*
1979 *Brooks of Tremorfa*, John Edward Brooks, *b.* 1927, *m.*
1964 *Brown*, Wilfred Banks Duncan Brown, P.C., M.B.E., *b.* 1908, *m.*
1983 *Broxbourne*, Derek Colclough Walker-Smith, P.C., T.D., Q.C., *b.* 1910, *m.*
1974 *Bruce of Donington*, Donald William Trevor Bruce, *b.* 1912, *m.*
1983 *Bruce-Gardyne*, John, (Jock), Bruce-Gardyne, *b.* 1930, *m.*
1976 *Bullock*, Alan Louis Charles Bullock, F.B.A., *b.* 1914, *m.*
1978 *Buxton of Alsa*, Aubrey Leland Oakes Buxton, M.C., *b.* 1918, *w.*
1965 *Caccia*, Harold Anthony Caccia, G.C.M.G., G.C.V.O., *b.* 1905, *m.*
1983 *Cameron of Balhousie*, Neil Cameron, K.T., G.C.B., C.B.E., D.S.O., D.F.C., *Marshal of the Royal Air Force.*, *b.* 1920, *m.*
1984 *Cameron of Lochbroom*, Kenneth John Cameron, Q.C.
1981 *Campbell of Alloway*, Alan Robertson Campbell, Q.C., *b.* 1917, *m.*
1974 *Campbell of Croy*, Gordon Thomas Calthrop Campbell, P.C., M.C., *b.* 1921, *m.*
1966 *Campbell of Eskan*, John Middleton Campbell, *b.* 1912, *w.*
1964 *Caradon*, Hugh Mackintosh Foot, P.C., G.C.M.G., K.C.V.O., O.B.E., *b.* 1907, *m.*
1983 *Carmichael of Kelvingrove*, Neil George Carmichael, *b.* 1921, *m.*
1975 *Carr of Hadley*, (Leonard) Robert Carr, P.C., *b.* 1916, *m.*
1977 *Carver*, (Richard) Michael (Power) Carver, G.C.B., C.B.E., D.S.O., M.C., *Field Marshal*, *b.* 1915, *m.*
1982 *Cayzer*, (William) Nicholas Cayzer, *b.* 1910, *m.*
1964 *Chalfont*, (Alun) Arthur Gwynne Jones, P.C., O.B.E., M.C., *b.* 1919, *m.*
1962 *Champion*, Arthur Joseph Champion, P.C., *b.* 1897, *m.*
1978 *Charteris of Amisfield*, Martin Michael Charles Charteris, P.C., G.C.B., G.C.V.O., O.B.E., *b.* 1913, *m.*
1963 *Chelmer*, Eric Cyril Boyd Edwards, M.C., T.D., *b.* 1914, *m.*
1974 *Chelwood*, Tufton Victor Hamilton Beamish, M.C., *b.* 1917, *m.*
1977 *Chitnis*, Pratap Chidamber Chitnis, *b.* 1936, *m.*
1979 *Cledwyn of Penrhos*, Cledwyn Hughes, P.C., C.H., *b.* 1916, *m.*
1978 *Cockfield*, (Francis) Arthur Cockfield, P.C., *b.* 1916, *m.*
1980 *Coggan*, Rt. Rev. (Frederick) Donald Coggan, P.C., D.D., Royal Victorian Chain, *b.* 1909, *m.*
1964 *Collison*, Harold Francis Collison, C.B.E., *b.* 1909, *m.*
1981 *Constantine of Stanmore*, Theodore Constantine, C.B.E., *b.* 1910, *m.*
1966 *Cooper of Stockton Heath*, John Cooper, *b.* 1908, *m.*
1959 *Craigton*, Jack Nixon Browne, P.C., C.B.E., *b.* 1904, *m.*
1978 *Croham*, Douglas Albert Vivian Allen, G.C.B., *b.* 1917, *m.*
1973 *Crowther-Hunt*, Norman Crowther Crowther-Hunt, PH.D, *b.* 1920, *m.*

1974 *Cudlipp*, Hugh Cudlipp, O.B.E., *b.* 1913, *m.*
1979 *Dacre of Glanton*, Hugh Redwald Trevor-Roper, *b.* 1914, *m.*
1974 *Darling of Hillsborough*, George Darling, P.C., *b.* 1905, *m.*
1970 *Davies of Leek*, Harold Davies, P.C., *b.* 1904, *w.*
1974 *Davies of Penrhys*, Gwilym Elfed Davies, *b.* 1913, *m.*
1983 *Dean of Beswick*, Joseph Jabez Dean, *b.* 1923.
1976 *Delfont*, Bernard Delfont, *b.* 1909, *m.*
1970 *Diamond*, John Diamond, P.C., *b.* 1907, *m.*
1967 *Donaldson of Kingsbridge*, John George Stuart Donaldson, O.B.E., *b.* 1907, *m.*
1978 *Donnet of Balgay*, Alexander Mitchell Donnet, C.B.E., *b.* 1916, *m.*
1974 *Duncan-Sandys*, Duncan Edwin Duncan-Sandys, P.C., C.H., *b.* 1908, *m.*
1983 *Eden of Winton*, John Benedict Eden, P.C., *b.* 1925, *m.*
1972 *Elworthy*, (Samuel) Charles Elworthy, K.G., G.C.B., C.B.E., D.S.O., M.V.O., D.F.C., A.F.C., *Marshal of the Royal Air Force, b.* 1911, *m.*
1974 *Elwyn-Jones*, Frederick Elwyn-Jones, P.C., C.H., *b.* 1909, *m.*
1981 *Elystan-Morgan*, Dafydd Elystan Elystan-Morgan, *b.* 1932, *m.*
1980 *Emslie*, George Carlyle Emslie, P.C., M.B.E., *b.* 1919, *m.* (*Lord Justice-General of Scotland*).
1968 *Energlyn*, William David Evans, D.SC., PH.D., *b.* 1912, *m.*
1983 *Ennals*, David Hedley Ennals, P.C., *b.* 1922, *m.*
1978 *Evans of Claughton*, (David Thomas) Gruffydd Evans, *b.* 1928, *m.*
1983 *Ezra*, Derek Ezra, M.B.E., *b.* 1919, *m.*
1983 *Fanshawe of Richmond*, Anthony Henry Fanshawe Royle, K.C.M.G., *b.*, 1927, *m.*
1958 *Ferrier*, Victor Ferrier Noel-Paton, E.D., *b.* 1900, *m.*
1983 *Fitt*, Gerard Fitt, *b.* 1926, *m.*
1970 *Fletcher*, Eric George Molyneux Fletcher, P.C., LL.D., *b.* 1903, *m.*
1979 *Flowers*, Brian Hilton Flowers, F.R.S., *b.* 1924, *m.*
1967 *Foot*, John Mackintosh Foot, *b.* 1909, *m.*
1982 *Forte*, Charles Forte, *b.* 1908, *m.*
1962 *Franks*, Oliver Shewell Franks, P.C., O.M., G.C.M.G., K.C.B., C.B.E., F.B.A., *b.* 1905, *m.*
1974 *Fraser of Kilmorack*, (Richard) Michael Fraser, C.B.E., *b.* 1915, *m.*
1966 *Fulton*, John Scott Fulton, *b.* 1902, *m.*
1982 *Gallacher*, John Gallacher, *b.* 1920, *m.*
1979 *Galpern*, Myer Galpern, *b.* 1903.
1963 *Gardiner*, Gerald Austin Gardiner, P.C., C.H., *b.* 1900, *m.*
1974 *Geoffrey-Lloyd*, Geoffrey William Geoffrey-Lloyd, P.C., *b.* 1902.
1970 *George-Brown*, George Alfred George-Brown, P.C., *b.* 1914, *m.*
1975 *Gibson*, (Richard) Patrick (Tallentyre) Gibson, *b.* 1916, *m.*
1979 *Gibson-Watt*, (James) David Gibson-Watt, P.C., M.C., *b.* 1918, *m.*
1977 *Glenamara*, Edward Watson Short, P.C., C.H., *b.* 1912, *m.*
1965 *Goodman*, Arnold Abraham Goodman, C.H., *b.* 1913.
1982 *Gormley*, Joseph Gormley, O.B.E., *b.* 1917, *m.*
1976 *Grade*, Lew Grade, *b.* 1906, *m.*
1983 *Graham of Edmonton*, (Thomas) Edward Graham, *b.*1925, *m.*
1967 *Granville of Eye*, Edgar Louis Granville, *b.* 1899, *m.*
1958 *Granville-West*, Daniel Granville West, *b.* 1904, *m.*
1983 *Gray of Contin*, James, (Hamish), Hector Northey Gray, P.C., *b.* 1927, *m.*
1974 *Greene of Harrow Weald*, Sidney Francis Greene, C.B.E., *b.* 1910, *m.*
1974 *Greenhill of Harrow*, Denis Arthur Greenhill, G.C.M.G., O.B.E., *b.* 1913, *m.*
1975 *Gregson*, John Gregson, *b.* 1924.
1968 *Grey of Naunton*, Ralph Francis Alnwick Grey, G.C.M.G., G.C.V.O., O.B.E., *b.* 1910, *m.*
1983 *Grimond*, Joseph Grimond, P.C., T.D., *b.* 1913, *m.*
1970 *Hailsham of St. Marylebone*, Quintin McGarel Hogg, P.C., C.H., *b.* 1907, *w.* (*Lord High Chancellor*).
1972 *Hale*, (Charles) Leslie Hale, *b.* 1902, *w.*
1983 *Hanson*, James Edward Hanson, *b.* 1922, *m.*
1974 *Harmar-Nicholls*, Harmar Harmar-Nicholls, *b.* 1912, *m.*
1974 *Harris of Greenwich*, John Henry Harris, *b.* 1930, *m.*
1979 *Harris of High Cross*, Ralph Harris, *b.* 1924, *m.*
1968 *Hartwell*, (William) Michael Berry, M.B.E., T.D., *b.* 1911, *w.*
1971 *Harvey of Prestbury*, Arthur Vere Harvey, C.B.E., *b.* 1906, *m.*
1974 *Harvington*, Robert Grant Grant-Ferris, P.C., *b.* 1907, *m.*
1978 *Hatch of Lusby*, John Charles Hatch, *b.* 1917.
1983 *Henderson of Brompton*, Peter Gordon Henderson, K.C.B., *b.* 1922, *m.*
1967 *Heycock*, Llewellyn Heycock, C.B.E., *b.* 1905, *m.*
1963 *Hill of Luton*, Charles Hill, P.C., M.D., *b.* 1904, *m.*
1979 *Hill-Norton*, Peter John Hill-Norton, G.C.B., *Admiral of the Fleet, b.* 1915, *m.*
1967 *Hirshfield*, Desmond Barel Hirshfield, *b.* 1913, *m.*
1979 *Holderness*, Richard Frederick Wood, P.C., *b.* 1920, *m.*
1974 *Home of the Hirsel*, Alexander Frederick Douglas-Home, P.C., K.T., *b.* 1903, *m.*
1979 *Hooson*, (Hugh) Emlyn Hooson, Q.C., *b.* 1925, *m.*
1974 *Houghton of Sowerby*, (Arthur Leslie Noel) Douglas Houghton, P.C., C.H., *b.* 1898, *m.*
1983 *Howard of Henderskelfe*, George Anthony Geoffrey Howard, *b.* 1920, *w.*
1978 *Howie of Troon*, William Howie, *b.* 1924, *m.*
1961 *Hughes*, William Hughes, P.C., C.B.E., *b.* 1911, *m.*
1966 *Hunt*, (Henry Cecil) John Hunt, K.G., C.B.E., D.S.O., *b.* 1910, *m.*
1973 *Hunt of Fawley*, John Henderson Hunt, C.B.E., D.M., *b.* 1905, *m.*
1980 *Hunt of Tanworth*, John Joseph Benedict Hunt, G.C.B., *b.* 1919, *m.*
1978 *Hunter of Newington*, Robert Brockie Hunter, M.B.E., F.R.C.P., *b.* 1915, *m.*

1978 *Hutchinson of Lullington*, Jeremy Nicolas Hutchinson, Q.C., *b.* 1915, *m.*
1982 *Ingrow*, John Aked Taylor, O.B.E., T.D., *b.* 1917, *m.*
1979 *Irving of Dartford*, Sydney Irving, P.C., *b.* 1918, *m.*
1975 *Jacobson*, Sydney Jacobson, M.C., *b.* 1908, *m.*
1968 *Jacques*, John Henry Jacques, *b.* 1905, *m.*
1959 *James of Rusholme*, Eric John Francis James, *b.* 1909, *m.*
1981 *Jenkins of Putney*, Hugh Gater Jenkins, *b.* 1908, *m.*
1981 *John-Mackie*, John John-Mackie, *b.* 1909, *m.*
1983 *Kaberry of Adel*, Donald Kaberry, T.D., *b.* 1907, *m.*
1981 *Kadoorie*, Lawrence Kadoorie, C.B.E., *b.* 1899, *m.*
1976 *Kagan*, Joseph Kagan, *b.* 1915, *m.*
1965 *Kahn*, Richard Ferdinand Kahn, C.B.E., F.B.A., *b.* 1905.
1974 *Kaldor*, Nicholas Kaldor, F.B.A., *b.* 1908, *m.*
1970 *Kearton*, (Christopher) Frank Kearton, O.B.E., F.R.S., *b.* 1911, *m.*
1980 *Keith of Castleacre*, Kenneth Alexander Keith, *b.* 1916, *m.*
1966 *Kilmany*, William John St. Clair Anstruther-Gray, P.C., M.C., *b.* 1905, *m.*
1983 *King of Wartnaby*, John Leonard King, *m.*
1965 *Kings Norton*, Harold Roxbee Cox, PH.D., *b.* 1902, *m.*
1975 *Kirkhill*, John Farquharson Smith, *b.* 1930, *m.*
1974 *Kissin*, Harry Kissin, *b.* 1912, *m.*
1964 *Leatherland*, Charles Edward Leatherland, O.B.E., *b.* 1898, *m.*
1979 *Lever of Manchester*, Harold Lever, P.C., *b.* 1914, *m.*
1982 *Lewin*, Terence Thornton Lewin, K.G., G.C.B., M.V.O., D.S.C., *Admiral of the Fleet, b.* 1920, *m.*
1965 *Lloyd of Hampstead*, Dennis Lloyd, Q.C., LL.D., *b.* 1915, *m.*
1973 *Lloyd of Kilgerran*, Rhys Gerran Lloyd, C.B.E., Q.C., *b.* 1907, *m.*
1974 *Lovell-Davis*, Peter Lovell Lovell-Davis, *b.* 1924, *m.*
1979 *Lowry*, Robert Lynd Erskine Lowry, P.C., *b.* 1919, *m.* (*Lord Chief Justice of Northern Ireland*).
1980 *McAlpine of Moffat*, (Robert) Edwin McAlpine, *b.* 1907, *m.*
1983 *McAlpine of West Green*, (Robert) Alistair McAlpine, *b.* 1942, *m.*
1975 *McCarthy*, William Edward John McCarthy, *b.* 1925, *m.*
1976 *McCluskey*, John Herbert McCluskey, Q.C., *b.* 1929, *m.*
1966 *McFadzean*, William Hunter McFadzean, K.T., *b.* 1903, *m.*
1980 *McFadzean of Kelvinside*, Francis Scott McFadzean, *b.* 1915, *m.*
1978 *McGregor of Durris*, Oliver Ross McGregor, *b.* 1921, *m.*
1982 *McIntosh of Haringey*, Andrew Robert McIntosh, *b.* 1933, *m.*
1979 *Mackay of Clashfern*, James Peter Hymers Mackay, P.C., Q.C., *b.* 1927, *m.*
1974 *Mackie of Benshie*, George Yull Mackie, C.B.E., D.S.O., D.F.C., *b.* 1919, *m.*
1971 *Maclean*, Charles Hector Fitzroy Maclean, P.C., K.T., G.C.V.O., K.B.E., *b.* 1916, *m.*
1982 *MacLehose of Beoch*, (Crawford) Murray MacLehose, K.T., G.B.E., K.C.M.G., K.C.V.O., *b.* 1917, *m.*
1967 *MacLeod of Fuinary*, Very Rev. George Fielden MacLeod, M.C., D.D., *b.* 1895, *m.*
1966 *Maelor*, Thomas William Jones, *b.* 1898, *m.*
1967 *Mais*, Alan Raymond Mais, G.B.E., T.D., E.R.D., *b.* 1911, *m.*
1981 *Marsh*, Richard William Marsh, P.C., *b.* 1928, *m.*
1980 *Marshall of Leeds*, Frank Shaw Marshall, *b.* 1915, *m.*
1980 *Matthews*, Victor Collin Matthews, *b.* 1919, *m.*
1983 *Maude of Stratford-upon-Avon*, Angus Edmund Upton Maude, P.C., T.D, *b.* 1912, *m.*
1971 *Maybray-King*, Horace Maybray Maybray-King, P.C., PH.D., *b.* 1901, *m.*
1981 *Mayhew*, Christopher Paget Mayhew, *b.* 1915, *m.*
1979 *Miles*, Bernard James Miles, C.B.E., *b.* 1907, *m.*
1978 *Mishcon*, Victor Mishcon, *b.* 1915, *m.*
1981 *Molloy*, William John Molloy, *b.* 1918, *m.*
1961 *Molson*, (Arthur) Hugh (Elsdale) Molson, P.C., *b.* 1903, *m.*
1967 *Morris of Grasmere*, Charles Richard Morris, K.C.M.G., *b.* 1898, *m.*
1971 *Moyola*, James Dawson Chichester-Clark, P.C. (N.I.), *b.* 1923, *m.*
1983 *Mulley*, Frederick William Mulley, P.C., *b.* 1918, *m.*
1964 *Murray of Newhaven*, Keith Anderson Hope Murray, K.C.B., PH.D., *b.* 1903.
1979 *Murton of Lindisfarne*, (Henry) Oscar Murton, P.C., O.B.E., T.D., *b.* 1914, *m.*
1975 *Northfield*, (William) Donald Chapman, *b.* 1923.
1966 *Nugent of Guildford*, (George) Richard (Hodges) Nugent, P.C., *b.* 1907, *m.*
1973 *O'Brien of Lothbury*, Leslie Kenneth O'Brien, P.C., G.B.E., *b.* 1908, *m.*
1970 *Olivier*, Laurence Kerr Olivier, O.M., *b.* 1907, *m.*
1970 *O'Neill of the Maine*, Terence Marne O'Neill, P.C. (N.I.), *b.* 1914, *m.*
1976 *Oram*, Albert Edward Oram, *b.* 1913, *m.*
1971 *Orr-Ewing*, (Charles) Ian Orr-Ewing, O.B.E., *b.* 1912, *m.*
1974 *Paget of Northampton*, Reginald Thomas Paget, Q.C., *b.* 1908, *m.*
1975 *Parry*, Gordon Samuel David Parry, *b.* 1925, *m.*
1976 *Peart*, (Thomas) Frederick Peart, P.C., *b.* 1914, *m.*
1967 *Penney*, William George Penney, O.M., K.B.E., PH.D., D.SC., F.R.S., *b.* 1909, *m.*
1982 *Pennock*, Raymond (William) Pennock, *b.* 1920, *m.*
1979 *Perry of Walton*, Walter Laing Macdonald Perry, O.B.E., M.D., D.SC., F.R.S.E., F.R.C.P., *b.* 1921, *m.*
1983 *Peyton of Yeovil*, John Wynne William Peyton, P.C., *b.* 1919, *m.*
1975 *Pitt of Hampstead*, David Thomas Pitt, *b.* 1913, *m.*
1978 *Plant*, Cyril Thomas Howe Plant, C.B.E., *b.* 1910, *m.*
1959 *Plowden*, Edwin Noel Plowden, K.C.B., K.B.E., *b.* 1907, *m.*
1981 *Plummer of St. Marylebone*, (Arthur) Desmond (Herne) Plummer, T.D., *b.* 1914, *m.*
1973 *Porritt*, Arthur Espie Porritt, G.C.M.G., G.C.V.O., C.B.E., *b.* 1900, *m.*
1975 *Pritchard*, Derek Wilbraham Pritchard, *b.* 1910, *m.*

1982 *Prys-Davies*, Gwilym Prys Prys-Davies, *b.* 1923, *m.*
1982 *Quinton*, Anthony Meredith Quinton, *b.* 1925, *m.*
1974 *Ramsey of Canterbury*, Rt. Rev. Arthur Michael Ramsey, P.C., D.D., Royal Victorian Chain, *b.* 1904, *m.*
1978 *Rawlinson of Ewell*, Peter Anthony Grayson Rawlinson, P.C., Q.C., *b.* 1919, *m.*
1976 *Rayne*, Max Rayne, *b.* 1918, *m.*
1983 *Rayner*, Derek George Rayner, *b.* 1926.
1970 *Reigate*, John Kenyon Vaughan-Morgan, P.C., *b.* 1905, *m.*
1978 *Reilly*, Paul Reilly, *b.* 1912, *m.*
1979 *Renton*, David Lockhart-Mure Renton, P.C., K.B.E., T.D., Q.C., *b.* 1908, *m.*
1964 *Rhodes*, Hervey Rhodes, K.G., P.C., D.F.C., *b.* 1895, *w.*
1979 *Richardson*, John Samuel Richardson, M.V.O., M.D., F.R.C.P., *b.* 1910, *m.*
1983 *Richardson of Duntisbourne*, Gordon William Humphreys Richardson, K.G., P.C., M.B.E., T.D, *b.* 1915, *m.*
1961 *Robens of Woldingham*, Alfred Robens, P.C., *b.* 1910, *m.*
1969 *Roberthall*, Robert Lowe Roberthall, K.C.M.G., C.B., *b.* 1901, *m.*
1977 *Roll of Ipsden*, Eric Roll, K.C.M.G., C.B., *b.* 1907, *m.*
1979 *Ross of Marnock*, William Ross, P.C., M.B.E., *b.* 1911, *m.*
1975 *Ryder of Eaton Hastings*, Sydney Thomas Franklin (Don) Ryder, *b.* 1916, *m.*
1962 *Sainsbury*, Alan John Sainsbury, *b.* 1902, *m.*
1977 *Saint Brides*, John Morrice Cairns James, P.C., G.C.M.G., C.V.O., M.B.E., *b.* 1916, *m.*
1972 *Samuel of Wych Cross*, Harold Samuel, *b.* 1912, *m.*
1979 *Scanlon*, Hugh Parr Scanlon, *b.* 1913, *m.*
1976 *Schon*, Frank Schon, *b.* 1912, *m.*
1972 *Seebohm*, Frederic Seebohm, T.D., *b.* 1909, *m.*
1978 *Sefton of Garston*, William Henry Sefton, *b.* 1915, *m.*
1964 *Segal*, Samuel Segal, *b.* 1902, *m.*
1958 *Shackleton*, Edward Arthur Alexander Shackleton, K.G., P.C., O.B.E., *b.* 1911, *m.*
1959 *Shawcross*, Hartley William Shawcross, P.C., G.B.E., Q.C., *b.* 1902, *w.*
1970 *Shinwell*, Emanuel Shinwell, P.C., C.H., *b.* 1884, *w.*
1980 *Sieff of Brimpton*, Marcus Joseph Sieff, O.B.E., *b.* 1913, *m.*
1971 *Simon of Glaisdale*, Jocelyn Edward Salis Simon, P.C., *b.* 1911, *m.* (*Lord of Appeal, retired*).
1978 *Smith*, Rodney Smith, K.B.E., F.R.C.S., *b.* 1914, *m.*
1978 *Soames*, (Arthur) Christopher (John) Soames, P.C., C.H., G.C.M.G., G.C.V.O., C.B.E., *b.* 1920, *m.*
1965 *Soper*, Rev. Donald Oliver Soper, PH.D., *b.* 1903, *m.*
1983 *Stallard*, Albert William Stallard, *b.* 1921, *m.*
1979 *Stewart of Fulham*, Robert Michael Maitland Stewart, P.C., C.H., *b.* 1906, *m.*
1981 *Stodart of Leaston*, James Anthony Stodart, P.C., *b.* 1916, *m.*
1983 *Stoddart of Swindon*, David Leonard Stoddart, *b.* 1926, *m.*
1969 *Stokes*, Donald Gresham Stokes, T.D., *b.* 1914, *m.*
1976 *Stone*, Joseph Ellis Stone, *b.* 1903, *m.*
1979 *Strauss*, George Russell Strauss, P.C., *b.* 1901, *m.*
1981 *Swann*, Michael Meredith Swann, PH.D., F.R.S., *b.* 1920, *m.*
1971 *Tanlaw*, Simon Brooke Mackay, *b.* 1934, *m.*
1958 *Taylor*, Stephen James Lake Taylor, M.D., *b.* 1910, *m.*
1978 *Taylor of Blackburn*, Thomas Taylor, C.B.E., *b.* 1929, *m.*
1968 *Taylor of Gryfe*, Thomas Johnston Taylor, *b.* 1912, *m.*
1982 *Taylor of Hadfield*, Francis Taylor, *b.* 1905, *m.*
1966 *Taylor of Mansfield*, Harry Bernard Taylor, C.B.E., *b.* 1895, *w.*
1981 *Thomas of Swynnerton*, Hugh Swynnerton Thomas, *b.* 1931, *m.*
1977 *Thomson of Monifieth*, George Morgan Thomson, P.C., K.T., *b.* 1921, *m.*
1967 *Thorneycroft*, (George Edward) Peter Thorneycroft, P.C., C.H., *b.* 1909, *m.*
1962 *Todd*, Alexander Robertus Todd, O.M., D.SC., D.Phil., F.R.S., *b.* 1907, *m.*
1981 *Tordoff*, Geoffrey Johnson Tordoff, *b.* 1928, *m.*
1974 *Tranmire*, Robert Hugh Turton, P.C., K.B.E., M.C., *b.* 1903, *m.*
1974 *Trend*, Burke St. John Trend, P.C., G.C.B., C.V.O., *b.* 1914, *m.*
1968 *Trevelyan*, Humphrey Trevelyan, K.G., G.C.M.G., C.I.E., O.B.E., *b.* 1905, *m.*
1979 *Underhill*, (Henry) Reginall Underhill, C.B.E., *b.* 1914, *m.*
1964 *Wade*, Donald William Wade, *b.* 1904, *m.*
1974 *Wallace of Campsie*, George Wallace, *b.* 1915, *m.*
1974 *Wallace of Coslany*, George Douglas Wallace, *b.* 1906, *m.*
1961 *Walston*, Henry David Leonard George Walston, C.V.O., *b.* 1912, *m.*
1972 *Watkins*, Tudor Elwyn Watkins, *b.* 1903, *m.*
1977 *Wedderburn of Charlton*, Kenneth William Wedderburn, *b.* 1927, *m.*
1976 *Weidenfeld*, (Arthur) George Weidenfeld, *b.* 1919.
1980 *Weinstock*, Arnold Weinstock, *b.* 1924, *m.*
1965 *Wells-Pestell*, Reginald Alfred Wells-Pestell, *b.* 1910, *m.*
1978 *Whaddon*, John Derek Page, *b.* 1927, *m.*
1970 *Wheatley*, John Wheatley, P.C., *b.* 1908, *m.*
1974 *Wigoder*, Basil Thomas Wigoder, Q.C., *b.* 1921, *m.*
1963 *Willis*, Edward Henry Willis, *b.* 1918, *m.*
1969 *Wilson of Langside*, Henry Stephen Wilson, P.C., Q.C., *b.* 1916, *m.*
1983 *Wilson of Rievaulx*, (James) Harold Wilson, K.G., P.C., O.B.E., F.R.S., *b.* 1916, *m.*
1975 *Winstanley*, Michael Platt Winstanley, *b.* 1918, *m.*
1965 *Winterbottom*, Ian Winterbottom, *b.* 1913, *m.*
1974 *Wolfenden*, John Frederick Wolfenden, C.B.E., *b.* 1906, *m.*
1967 *Woolley*, Harold Woolley, C.B.E., *b.* 1905, *w.*
1978 *Young of Dartington*, Michael Young, PH.D., *b.* 1915, *m.*
1971 *Zuckerman*, Solly Zuckerman, O.M., K.C.B., F.R.S., M.D., D.SC., *b.* 1904, *m.*

BARONESSES

1979 *Airey of Abingdon*, Diana Josceline Barbara Neave Airey, b. 1919, w.
1970 *Bacon*, Alice Martha Bacon, P.C., C.B.E., b. 1911.
1967 *Birk*, Alma Birk, b. 1921, m.
1964 *Brooke of Ystradfellte*, Barbara Muriel Brooke, D.B.E., b. 1908, w.
1962 *Burton of Coventry*, Elaine Frances Burton, b. 1904.
1982 *Carnegy of Lour*, Elizabeth Patricia Carnegy of Lour, b. 1925.
1982 *Cox*, Caroline Anne Cox, b. 1937, m.
1978 *David*, Nora Ratcliff David, b. 1913, m.
1974 *Delacourt-Smith of Alteryn*, Margaret Rosalind Delacourt-Smith, b. 1916, m.
1978 *Denington*, Evelyn Joyce Denington, D.B.E., b. 1907, m.
1972 *Elles*, Diana Louie Elles, b. 1921, m.
1958 *Elliot of Harwood*, Katharine Elliot, D.B.E., b. 1903, w.
1981 *Ewart-Biggs*, (Felicity) Jane Ewart-Biggs, b. 1929, w.
1975 *Faithfull*, Lucy Faithfull, O.B.E., b. 1910.
1974 *Falkender*, Marcia Matilda Falkender, C.B.E., b. 1932.
1974 *Fisher of Rednal*, Doris Mary Gertrude Fisher, b. 1919, w.
1963 *Gaitskell*, Anna Dora Gaitskell, w.
1981 *Gardner of Parkes*, (Rachel) Trixie (Anne) Gardner, b. 1927, m.
1974 *Hornsby-Smith*, (Margaret) Patricia Hornsby-Smith, P.C., D.B.E., b. 1914.
1965 *Hylton-Foster*, Audrey Pellew Hylton-Foster, b. 1908, w.
1979 *Jeger*, Lena May Jeger, b. 1915, w.
1981 *Lane-Fox*, Felicity Lane-Fox, O.B.E., b. 1918.
1970 *Lee of Asheridge*, Janet Bevan, P.C., b. 1904, w.
1967 *Llewelyn-Davies of Hastoe*, Annie Patricia Llewelyn-Davies, P.C., b. 1915, w.
1978 *Lockwood*, Betty Lockwood, b. 1924, m.
1979 *McFarlane of Llandaff*, Jean Kennedy McFarlane, b. 1926.
1971 *Macleod of Borve*, Evelyn Hester Macleod, b. 1915, w.
1970 *Masham of Ilton*, Susan Lilian Primrose Cunliffe-Lister, b. 1935, m. (*Countess of Swinton*).
1982 *Nicol*, Olive Mary Wendy Nicol, b. 1923, m.
1963 *Northchurch*, Frances Joan Davidson, D.B.E. (*Dowager Viscountess Davidson*), b. 1894, w.
1964 *Phillips*, Norah Phillips, b. 1910, w.
1974 *Pike*, (Irene) Mervyn (Parnicott) Pike, D.B.E., b. 1918.
1981 *Platt of Writtle*, Beryl Catherine Platt, C.B.E., b. 1923, m.
1974 *Robson of Kiddington*, Inga-Stina Robson, b. 1919, w.
1979 *Ryder of Warsaw*, (Sue Ryder), C.M.G., O.B.E., b. 1924, m.
1971 *Seear*, (Beatrice) Nancy Seear, b. 1913.
1967 *Serota*, Beatrice Serota, b. 1919, m.
1966 *Sharp*, Evelyn Adelaide Sharp, G.B.E., b. 1903.
1973 *Sharples*, Pamela Sharples, b. 1923, m.
1974 *Stedman*, Phyllis Stedman, O.B.E., b. 1916, m.
1974 *Stewart of Alvechurch*, Mary Elizabeth Henderson Stewart, m.
1980 *Trumpington*, Jean Alys Barker, m.
1974 *Vickers*, Joan Helen Vickers, D.B.E., b. 1907.
1970 *White*, Eirene Lloyd White, b. 1909, w.
1958 *Wootton of Abinger*, Barbara Frances Wright, C.H., b. 1897, w.
1971 *Young*, Janet Mary Young, b. 1926, m.

THE ORDER OF ST. JOHN

The Most Venerable Order of the Hospital of St. John of Jerusalem

St. John's Gate, Clerkenwell, EC1M 4DA

Grand Prior, H.R.H. The Duke of Gloucester, G.C.V.O.

Lord Prior, Sir Maurice Dorman, G.C.M.G., G.C.V.O.   *Chancellor*, The Earl St. Aldwyn, P.C., G.B.E., T.D.

Surnames of Peers and Peeresses differing from their Titles

Abney Hastings—*Loudoun*
Acheson—*Gosford*
Adderley—*Norton*
Addington—*Sidmouth*
Agar—*Normanton*
Akers Douglas—*Chilston*
Alexander—*Alexander of Potterhill**
Alexander—*Alexander of Tunis*
Alexander—*Caledon*
Allen—*Allen of Abbeydale**
Allen—*Allen of Fallowfield**
Allen—*Croham**
Allanson Winn—*Headley*
Allsopp—*Hindlip*
Aman—*Marley*
Anderson—*Waverley*
Annesley—*Valentia*
Anson—*Lichfield*
Anstruther-Gray—*Kilmany**
Armstrong Jones—*Snowdon*
Arthur—*Glenarthur*
Ashley Cooper—*Shaftesbury*
Ashton—*Ashton of Hyde*
Asquith—*Oxford & A.*
Assheton—*Clitheroe*
Astley—*Hastings*
Astor—*Astor of Hever*
Bailey—*Glanusk*
Baillie—*Burton*
Baille Hamilton—*Haddington*
Baldwin—*Baldwin of Bewdley*
Balfour—*Kinross*
Balfour—*Riverdale*
Balfour—*Balfour of Inchrye*
Bampfylde—*Poltimore*
Banbury—*Banbury of Southam*
Baring—*Ashburton*
Baring—*Cromer*
Baring—*Howick of Glendale*
Baring—*Northbrook*
Baring—*Revelstoke*
Barker—*Trumpington**
Barnes—*Gorell*
Barnewall—*Trimlestown*
Bathurst—*Bledisloe*
Beamish—*Chelwood**
Beauclerk—*St. Albans*
Beaumont—*Allendale*
Beaumont—*Beaumont of Whitley**
Beavan—*Ardwick**
Beckett—*Grimthorpe*
Bellow—*Bellwin**
Bennet—*Tankerville*
Beresford—*Decies*
Beresford—*Waterford*
Berry—*Camrose*
Berry—*Hartwell**
Berry—*Kemsley*
Bertie—*Lindsey*

Best—*Wynford*
Bethell—*Westbury*
Bevan—*Lee of Asheridge**
Bewicke Copley—*Cromwell*
Bigham—*Mersey*
Bigham—*Nairne*
Bingham—*Clanmorris*
Bingham—*Lucan*
Bishop—*Bishopston**
Blades—*Ebbisham*
Bligh—*Darnley*
Bootle Wilbraham—*Skelmersdale*
Boscawen—*Falmouth*
Boston—*Boston of Faversham**
Bourke—*Mayo*
Bowden—*Aylestone**
Bowes Lyon—*Strathmore*
Bowyer—*Denham*
Boyd—*Kilmarnock*
Boyle—*Cork and Orrery*
Boyle—*Glasgow*
Boyle—*Shannon*
Brabazon—Meath
Brand—*Hampden*
Brassey—*Brassey of Apethorpe*
Brett—*Esher*
Bridgeman—*Bradford*
Brodrick—*Midleton*
Brooke—*Alanbrooke*
Brooke—*Brooke of Ystradfellte**
Brooke—*Brookeborough*
Brooks—*Brooks of Tremorfa**
Brooks—*Crawshaw*
Brougham—*Brougham and Vaux*
Broughton—*Fairhaven*
Browne—*Craigton**
Browne—*Kilmaine*
Browne—*Oranmore and Browne*
Browne—*Sligo*
Brownlow—*Lurgan*
Bruce—*Aberdare*
Bruce—*Balfour of Burleigh*
Bruce—*Bruce of Donington**
Bruce—*Elgin and Kincardine*
Brudenell Bruce—*Ailesbury*
Buchan—*Tweedsmuir*
Buchanan-Smith—*Balerno**
Buckley—*Wrenbury*
Burton—*Burton of Coventry**
Butler—*Carrick*
Butler—*Dunboyne*
Butler—*Lanseborough*
Butler—*Mountgarret*
Butler—*Ormonde*
Buxton—*Buxton of Alsa**
Buxton—*Noel-Buxton*
Byng—*Strafford*
Byng—*Torrington*

Cameron—*Cameron of Balhousie**
Cameron—*Cameron of Lochbroom**
Campbell—*Argyll*
Campbell—*Breadalbane and Holland*
Campbell—*Campbell of Alloway**
Campbell—*Campbell of Croy**
Campbell—*Campbell of Eskan**
Campbell—*Cawdor*
Campbell—*Colgrain*
Campbell—*Stratheden and Campbell*
Campbell Gray—*Gray*
Canning—*Garvagh*
Capell—*Essex*
Carington—*Carrington*
Carmichael—*Carmichael of Kelvingrove**
Carnegie—*Fife*
Carnegie—*Northesk*
Carnegie—*Southesk*
Carr—*Carr of Hadley**
Cary—*Falkland*
Caulfeild—*Charlemont*
Cavendish—*Chesham*
Cavendish—*Devonshire*
Cavendish—*Waterpark*
Cavendish Bentinck—*Portland*
Cayzer—*Rotherwick*
Cecil—*Amherst of Hackney*
Cecil—*Exeter*
Cecil—*Rockley*
Chaloner—*Gisborough*
Chapman—*Northfield**
Charteris—*Charteris of Amisfield**
Charteris—*Wemyss and March*
Cheshire—*Ryder of Warsaw**
Chetwynd Talbot—*Shrewsbury*
Chichester—*Donegall*
Chichester Clark—*Moyola**
Child Villiers—*Jersey*
Cholmondeley—*Delamere*
Chubb—*Hayter*
Clegg Hill—*Hill*
Clifford—*Clifford of Chudleigh*
Clifton of Mar—*Mar*
Cochrane—*Cochrane of Cults*
Cochrane—*Dundonald*
Cocks—*Somers*
Cokayne—*Cullen of Ashbourne*
Coke—*Leicester*
Cole—*Enniskillen*
Colville—*Clydesmuir*
Colville—*Colville of Culross*
Compton—*Northampton*
Conolly Carew—*Carew*

Constantine—*Constantine of Stanmore**
Cooper—*Norwich*
Cooper—*Cooper of Stockton Heath**
Corbett—*Rowallan*
Courtenay—*Devon*
Cox—*Kings Norton**
Craig—*Craigavon*
Crichton—*Erne*
Crichton Stuart—*Bute*
Cripps—*Parmoor*
Cross—*Cross of Chelsea*
Crossley—*Somerleyton*
Cubitt—*Ashcombe*
Cunliffe Lister—*Masham of Ilton**
Cunliffe Lister—*Swinton*
Curzon—*Howe*
Curzon—*Scarsdale*
Cust—*Brownlow*
Dalrymple—*Stair*
Darling—*Darling of Hillsborough**
Davidson—*Northchurch**
Davies—*Darwen*
Davies—*Davies of Leek**
Davies—*Davies of Penrhys**
Davison—*Broughshane*
Dawnay—*Downe*
Dawson Damer—*Portarlington*
De Courcy—*Kingsale*
De Grey—*Walsingham*
Delacourt Smith—*Delacourt Smith of Alteryn**
De Yarburgh Bateson—*Deramore*
Dean—*Dean of Beswick**
Deane—*Muskerry*
Denison—*Londesborough*
Denison Pender—*Pender*
Devereux—*Hereford*
Dewar—*Forteviot*
Dixon—*Glentoran*
Dodson—*Monk Bretton*
Donaldson—*Donaldson of Kingsbridge**
Donnet—*Donnet of Balgay*
Douglas—*Morton*
Douglas—*Queensberry*
Douglas Hamilton—*Hamilton*
Douglas Hamilton—*Selkirk*
Douglas Home—*Dacre*
Douglas-Home—*Home of the Hirsel**
Douglas Pennant—*Penrhyn*
Douglas Scott Montagu—*Montagu of Beaulieu*
Drummond—*Perth*
Dugdale—*Crathorne*
Duke—*Merrivale*
Duncombe—*Feversham*
Dundas—*Melville*
Dundas—*Zetland*
Dutton—*Sherborne*

* Life Peer created under Life Peerages Act, 1958

Eady—Swinfen
Eden—Auckland
Eden—Avon
Eden—Henley
Eden—Eden of Winton*
Edgcumbe—Mount Edgcumbe
Edmondson—Sandford
Edwardes—Kensington
Edwards—Chelmer*
Egerton—Sutherland
Egerton—Wilton
Eliot—St. Germans
Elliot—Elliot of Harwood*
Elliot-Murray-Kynynmound—Minto
Erroll—Errol of Hale
Erskine—Buchan
Erskine—Erskine of Rerrick
Erskine—Mar & Kellie
Erskine Murray—Elibank
Evans—Energlyn*
Evans—Evans of Claughton*
Evans—Mountevans
Evans Freke—Carbery
Eve—Silsoe
Eveleigh de Moleyns—Ventry
Eyres Monsell—Monsell
Fairfax—Fairfax of Cameron
Fane—Westmorland
Feilding—Denbigh
Fellowes—Ailwyn
Fellowes—De Ramsey
Fermor Hesketh—Hesketh
Fiennes—Saye & Sele
Finch Hatton—Winchilsea
Finch Knightley—Aylesford
Fisher —Fisher of Rednal*
Fitzalan Howard—Herries
Fitzalan Howard—Norfolk
FitzClarence—Munster
FitzGerald—Leinster
Fitzherbert—Stafford
FitzRoy—Daventry
FitzRoy—Grafton
Fletcher Vane—Inglewood
Flower—Ashbrooke
Foley Berkeley—Berkeley
Foljambe—Liverpool
Foot—Caradon*
Forbes—Granard
Fox Strangways—Ilchester
Frankland—Zouche
Fraser—Fraser of Kilmorack*
Fraser—Fraser of Tullybelton
Fraser—Lovat
Fraser—Saltoun
Fraser—Strathalmond
Freeman Grenville—Kinloss

Freeman Mitford—Redesdale
Fremantle—Cottesloe
French—De Freyne
French—Ypres
Galbraith—Strathclyde
Ganzoni—Belstead
Gardner—Gardner of Parkes*
Gascoyne Cecil—Salisbury
Gathorne Hardy—Cranbrook
Gibbs—Alderham
Gibbs—Wraxall
Gibson—Ashbourne
Giffard—Halsbury
Gilbey—Vaux of Harrowden
Glyn—Wolverton
Godley—Kilbracken
Gordon—Aberdeen
Gordon—Huntly
Gordon Lennox—Richmond
Gore—Arran
Gough Calthorpe—Calthorpe
Graham—Graham of Edmonton*
Graham—Montrose
Graham Toler—Norbury
Grant—Strathspey
Grant Ferris—Harvington*
Granville—Granville of Eye*
Gray—Gray of Contin*
Greaves—Dysart
Greenall—Daresbury
Greene—Greene of Harrow Weald*
Greenhill—Greenhill of Harrow*
Grenfell—St. Just
Greville—Warwick
Grey—Grey of Naunton*
Grimston—Grimston of Westbury
Grimston—Verulam
Grosvenor—Ebury
Grosvenor—Westminster
Guest—Wimborne
Guinness—Iveagh
Guinness—Moyne
Gully—Selby
Gurdon—Cranworth
Gwynne Jones—Chalfont*
Hall—Lockwood*
Hamilton—Abercorn
Hamilton—Belhaven and Stenton
Hamilton—Hamilton of Dalzell
Hamilton—Holm Patrick
Hamilton Russel—Boyne
Hamilton Temple Blackwood—Dufferin
Hanbury Tracy—Sudeley
Handcock—Castlemaine
Harbord Hamond—Suffield

Harding—Harding of Petherton
Hardinge—Hardinge of Penshurst
Hare—Blakenham
Hare—Listowel
Harmsworth—Rothermere
Harris—Harris of Greenwich*
Harris—Harris of High Cross*
Harris—Malmesbury
Harvey—Harvey of Prestbury
Harvey—Harvey of Tasburgh
Hastings—Huntingdon
Hatch—Hatch of Lusby*
Hay—Erroll
Hay—Kinnoull
Hay—Tweeddale
Heathcote-Drummond-Willoughby—Willoughby de Eresby
Hely Hutchinson—Donoughmore
Henderson—Henderson of Brompton*
Henderson—Faringdon
Hennessy—Windlesham
Henniker Major—Henniker
Hepburne Scott—Polwarth
Herbert—Carnarvon
Herbert—Hemingford
Herbert—Pembroke
Herbert—Powis
Hermon Hodge—Wyfold
Hicks Beach—St. Aldwyn
Hervey—Bristol
Hewitt—Lifford
Hill—Downshire
Hill—Hill of Luton*
Hill—Sandys
Hill Trevor—Trevor
Hobart Hampden—Buckinghamshire
Hogg—Hailsham of St. Marylebone*
Holland Hibbert—Knutsford
Holms à Court—Heytesbury
Hood—Bridport
Hope—Glendevon
Hope—Linlithgow
Hope—Rankeillour
Hope Morley—Hollenden
Hopkinson—Colyton
Hopwood—Southborough
Hore Ruthven—Gowrie
Houghton—Houghton of Sowerby*
Hovell Thurlow Cumming Bruce—Thurlow
Howard—Carlisle
Howard—Effingham
Howard—Howard of Henderskelfe*
Howard—Howard of Penrith
Howard—Strathcona
Howard—Suffolk and Berkshire

Howie—Howie of Troon*
Hoyer Millar—Inchyra
Hubbard—Addington
Huggins—Malvern
Hughes—Cledwyn of Penrhos*
Hughes Young—St. Helens
Hunt—Hunt of Fawley*
Hunt—Hunt of Tanworth*
Hunter—Hunter of Newington*
Hutchinson—Hutchinson of Lullington*
Ingrams—Darcy de Knayth
Innes Ker—Roxburghe
Inskip—Caldecote
Irby—Boston
Irving—Irving of Dartford*
Isaacs—Reading
Jackson—Allerton
James—James of Rusholme*
James—Saint Brides*
James—Northbourne
Jebb—Gladwyn
Jervis—St. Vincent
Jocelyn—Roden
Jolliffe—Hylton
Jones—Maelor*
Joynson Hicks—Brentford
Kaberry—Kaberry of Adel*
Kay Shuttleworth—Shuttleworth
Kearley—Devonport
Keith—Keith of Castleacre*
Keith—Keith of Kinkel
Keith—Kintore
Kemp—Rochdale
Kennedy—Ailsa
Kenworthy—Strabolgi
Keppel—Albemarle
Kerr—Lothian
Kerr—Teviot
King—Lovelace
King—Maybray King*
King—King of Wartnaby*
King Tenison—Kingston
Kitchener—Kitchener of Khartoum
Kitson—Airedale
Knatchbull—Brabourne
Knatchbull,—Knatchbull, Mountbatten of Burma
Knox—Ranfurly
Lamb—Rochester
Lambart—Cavan
Lampson—Killearn
Larnach Nevill—Abergavenny
Lascelles—Harewood
Law—Coleraine
Law—Ellenborough
Lawrence—Trevethin and Oaksey
Lawson—Burnham
Lawson Johnston—Luke
Lee—Lee of Asheridge*

* Life Peer created under Life Peerages Act, 1958

Le Poer Trench—*Clancarty*
Legge—*Dartmouth*
Legh—*Newton*
Leith—*Burgh*
Lennox Boyd—*Boyd of Merton*
Leslie—*Rothes*
Leslie Melville—*Leven*
Lever—*Lever of Manchester*
Lever—*Leverhulme*
Leveson Gower—*Granville*
Liddell—*Ravensworth*
Lindesay Bethune—*Lindsay*
Lindsay—*Crawford*
Lindsay—*Lindsay of Birker*
Littleton—*Hatherton*
Llewelyn-Davies—*Llewelyn-Davies of Hastoe**
Lloyd—*Lloyd of Hampstead**
Lloyd—*Lloyd of Kilgerran**
Lloyd George—*Lloyd George of Dwyfor*
Lloyd George—*Tenby*
Lloyd Mostyn—*Mostyn*
Loder—*Wakehurst*
Lopes—*Roborough*
Low—*Aldington*
Lowry Corry—*Belmore*
Lowther—*Lonsdale*
Lowther—*Ullswater*
Lubbock—*Avebury*
Lucas—*Lucas of Chilworth*
Lumley—*Scarbrough*
Lumley Savile—*Savile*
Lyon Dalberg Acton—*Acton*
Lysaght—*Lisle*
Lyttelton—*Chandos*
Lyttelton—*Cobham (Viscountcy)*
McAlpine—*McAlpine of Moffat**
McAlpine—*McAlpine of West Green**
McClintock Bunbury—*Rathdonnell*
Macdonald—*Macdonald of Gwaenysgor*
McDonnell—*Antrim*
McFadzean—*McFadzean of Kelvinside**
McFarlane—*McFarlane of Llandaff**
McGregor—*McGregor of Durris*
McIntosh—*McIntosh of Haringey**
Mackay—*Inchcape*
Mackay—*Mackay of Clashfern*
Mackay—*Reay*
Mackay—*Tanlaw*
Mackie—*John-Mackie**
Mackie—*Mackie of Benshie**
Mackintosh—*Mackintosh of Halifax*

McLaren—*Aberconway*
MacLehose—*MacLehose of Beoch**
Macleod—*Macleod of Borve**
MacLeod—*Macleod of Fuinary**
Maclay—*Muirshiel*
Macmillan—*Stockton*
Macpherson—*Drumalbyn*
Macpherson—*Macpherson of Drumochter*
Macpherson—*Strathcarron*
Maffey—*Rugby*
Maitland—*Lauderdale*
Makgill—*Oxfuird*
Makins—*Sherfield*
Manners—*Rutland*
Manningham Buller—*Dilhorne*
Mansfield—*Sandhurst*
Marks—*Marks of Broughton*
Marquis—*Woolton*
Marshall—*Marshall of Leeds**
Marsham—*Romney*
Martyn Hemphill—*Hemphill*
Mason—*Blackford*
Maude—*Hawarden*
Maude—*Maude of Stratford-upon-Avon**
Maxwell—*De Ros*
Maxwell—*Farnham*
Meade—*Clanwilliam*
Milles Lade—*Sondes*
Milner—*Milner of Leeds*
Mitchell Thomson—*Selsdon*
Monckton—*Galway*
Monckton—*Monckton of Brenchley*
Monckton—*Ruthven of Freeland*
Mond—*Melchett*
Money-Coutts—*Latymer*
Montagu—*Manchester*
Montagu—*Swaythling*
Montagu Douglas Scott—*Buccleuch*
Montagu Stuart Wortley Mackenzie—*Wharncliffe*
Montague—*Amwell*
Montgomerie—*Eglinton*
Montgomery—*Montgomery of Alamein*
Moore—*Drogheda*
Moore Brabazon—*Brabazon of Tara*
Moreton—*Ducie*
Morris—*Killanin*
Morris—*Morris of Grasmere**
Morris—*Morris of Kenwood*
Morrison—*Dunrossil*
Morrison—*Margadale*
Mosley—*Ravensdale*
Mountbatten—*Edinburgh*
Mountbatten—*Milford Haven*

Mountbatten—*Mountbatten of Burma*
Muff—*Calverley*
Mulholland—*Dunleath*
Murray—*Atholl*
Murray—*Dunmore*
Murray—*Mansfield and Mansfield*
Murray—*Murray of Newhaven**
Murton—*Murton of Lindisfarne**
Nall Cain—*Brocket*
Napier—*Napier and Ettrick*
Napier—*Napier of Magdala*
Neave—*Airey of Abingdon**
Needham—*Kilmorey*
Nelson—*Nelson of Stafford*
Neville—*Braybrooke*
Nicolson—*Carnock*
Nivison—*Glendyne*
Noble—*Glenkinglas**
Noel—*Gainsborough*
Noel Paton—*Ferrier**
North—*Guilford*
Northcote—*Iddesleigh*
Norton—*Grantley*
Norton—*Rathcreedan*
Nugent—*Nugent of Guildford**
Nugent—*Westmeath*
O'Brien—*Inchiquin*
O'Brien—*O'Brien of Lothbury**
Ogilvie Grant—*Seafield*
Ogilvy—*Airlie*
O'Neill—*O'Neill of the Maine**
O'Neill—*Rathcavan*
Orde Powlett—*Bolton*
Ormsby Gore—*Harlech*
Page—*Whaddon**
Paget—*Anglesey*
Paget—*Paget of Northampton**
Pakenham—*Lonford*
Pakington—*Hampton*
Palmer—*Lucas of Crudwell*
Palmer—*Selborne*
Parker—*Macclesfield*
Parker—*Morley*
Parnell—*Congleton*
Parsons—*Rosse*
Paulet—*Winchester*
Peake—*Ingleby*
Pearson—*Cowdray*
Pease—*Daryngton*
Pease—*Gainford*
Pease—*Wardington*
Pelham—*Chichester*
Pelham—*Yarborough*
Pelham Clinton Hope—*Newcastle*
Pellew—*Exmouth*
Penny—*Marchwood*
Pepys—*Cottenham*
Perceval—*Egmont*
Percy—*Northumberland*
Perry—*Perry of Walton**
Pery—*Limerick*

Petty Fitzmaurice—*Lansdowne*
Peyton—*Peyton of Yeovil**
Philipps—*Milford*
Philipps—*St. Davids*
Phipps—*Normanby*
Pitt—*Pitt of Hampstead**
Platt—*Platt of Writtle**
Pleydell Bouverie—*Radnor*
Plummer—*Plummer of St. Marylebone**
Plumptre—*Fitzwalter*
Pluckett—*Dunsany*
Plunkett—*Fingall*
Plunkett—*Louth*
Pollock—*Hanworth*
Pomeroy—*Harberton*
Ponsonby—*Bessborough*
Ponsonby—*De Mauley*
Ponsonby—*P. of Shulbrede*
Ponsonby—*Sysonby*
Portal—*Portal of Hungerford*
Powys—*Lilford*
Pratt—*Camden*
Preston—*Gormanston*
Primrose—*Rosebery*
Prittie—*Dunalley*
Ramsay—*Dalhousie*
Ramsey—*Ramsey of Canterbury*
Ramsbotham—*Soulbury*
Rawlinson—*Rawlinson of Ewell**
Rees Williams—*Ogmore*
Rhys—*Dynevor*
Richards—*Milverton*
Richardson—*Richardson of Duntisbourne**
Ritchie—*Ritchie of Dundee*
Robens—*Robens of Woldingham*
Roberts—*Clwyd*
Robertson—*Robertson of Oakridge*
Robinson—*Martonmere*
Robson—*Robson of Kiddington**
Roche—*Fermoy*
Rodd—*Rennell*
Roll—*Roll of Ipsden**
Roper Curzon—*Teynham*
Rospigliosi—*Newburgh*
Ross—*Ross of Marnock**
Rous—*Stradbroke*
Rowley Conwy—*Langford*
Royle—*Fanshawe of Richmond**
Runciman—*Runciman of Doxford*
Russell—*Ampthill*
Russell—*Bedford*
Russell—*De Clifford*
Russell—*Russell of Killowen*
Russell—*R. of Liverpool*
Ryder—*Harrowby*
Ryder—*Ryder of Eaton Hastings**
Sackville—*De La Warr*
Sackville West—*Sackville*

* Life Peer created under Life Peerages Act, 1958

St. Aubyn—*St. Levan*
St. Clair—*Sinclair*
St. Clair Erskine—
  Rosslyn
St. John—*St. J. of Blesto*
St. John—*Bolingbroke
  and St. John*
St. Leger—*Doneraile*
Samuel—*Bearsted*
Samuel—*Samuel of Wych
  Cross*
Sandilands—*Torphichen*
Saumarez—*De Saumarez*
Savile—*Mexborough*
Scarlett—*Abinger*
Sclater Booth—*Basing*
Scott—*Eldon*
Scott Ellis—*Howard de
  Walden*
Scrymgeour
  Wedderburn—*Dundee*
Seager—*Leighton of St.
  Mellons*
Seely—*Mottistone*
Sefton—*Sefton of
  Garston**
Seymour—*Hertford*
Seymour—*Somerset*
Shaw—*Craigmyle*
Shaw—*Kilbrandon*
Shirley—*Ferrers*
Short—*Glenamara**
Siddeley—*Kenilworth*
Sidney—*De L'Isle*
Sieff—*Sieff of Brimpton**
Simon—*Simon of
  Glaisdale**
Simon—*Simon of
  Wythenshawe*
Sinclair—*Caithness*
Sinclair—*Sinclair of
  Cleeve*
Sinclair—*Thurso*
Skeffington—*Massereene*
Smith—*Bicester*
Smith—*Birkenhead*
Smith—*Colwyn*
Smith—*Hambleden*
Smith—*Kirkhill**
Somerset—*Beaufort*

Somerset—*Raglan*
Souter—*Audley*
Spencer—*Churchill*
Spencer Churchill—
  Marlborough
Spring Rice—*Monteagle
  of Brandon*
Stanhope—*Harrington*
Stanley—*Derby*
Stanley—*Sheffield*
Stapleton Cotton—
  Combermere
Stern—*Michelham*
Stewart—*Galloway*
Stewart—*Stewart of
  Alvechurch**
Stewart—*Stewart of
  Fulham**
Stodart—*Stodart of
  Leaston**
Stoddart—*Stoddart of
  Swindon**
Stonor—*Camoys*
Stopford—*Courtown*
Stourton—*Mowbray*
Strachey—*O'Hagan*
Strutt—*Belper*
Strutt—*Rayleigh*
Stuart—*Castle Stewart*
Stuart—*Moray*
Stuart—*Stuart of
  Findhorn*
Suenson Taylor—
  Grantchester
Sugden—*St. Leonards*
Talbot—*T. of Malahide*
Taylor—*Taylor of
  Blackburn**
Taylor—*Taylor of Gryfe**
Taylor—*Taylor of
  Hadfield**
Taylor—*Taylor of
  Mansfield**
Taylour—*Headfort*
Temple Gore Langton—
  Temple of Stowe
Tennant—*Glenconner*
Thellusson—*Rendlesham*
Thesiger—*Chelmsford*
Thomas—*Thomas of
  Swynnerton**

Thomas—*Tonypandy*
Thomson—*Thomson of
  Fleet*
Thomson—*Thomson of
  Monifieth**
Thynne—*Bath*
Tottenham—*Ely*
Trefusis—*Clinton*
Trench—*Ashtown*
Trevor Roper—*Dacre of
  Glanton**
Tufton—*Hothfield*
Turner—*Netherthorpe*
Turnour—*Winterton*
Turton—*Tranmire**
Tyrell Kenyon—*Kenyon*
Vanden Bempde
  Johnstone—*Derwent*
Vane—*Barnard*
Vane Tempest Stewart—
  Londonderry
Vanneck—*Huntingfield*
Vaughan—*Lisburne*
Vaughan Morgan—
  Reigate*
Vavasseur Fisher—
  Fisher
Vereker—*Gort*
Verney—*Willoughby de
  Broke*
Verney Cave—*Braye*
Vernon—*Lyveden*
Vesey—*De Vesci*
Villiers—*Clarendon*
Vintcent—*Wharton*
Vivian—*Swansea*
Walker-Smith—
  Broxbourne*
Wallace—*Dudley
  (Barony)*
Wallace—*Wallace of
  Campsie**
Wallace—*Wallace of
  Coslany**
Wallop—*Portsmouth*
Ward—*Bangor*
Ward—*Dudley (Earldom)*
Ward—*Ward of Witley*
Warrender—*Bruntisfield*
Watson—*Manton*

Watson Armstrong—
  Armstrong
Wedderburn—
  *Wedderburn of
  Charlton**
Weir—*Inverforth*
Weld Forester—*Forester*
Wellesley—*Cowley*
Wellesley—*Wellington*
West—*Granville-West**
Westenra—*Rossmore*
White—*Annaly*
Whiteley—*Marchamley*
Whitfield—*Kenswood*
Willey—*Barnby*
Williams—*Berners*
Williamson—*Forres*
Willoughby—*Middleton*
Wills—*Dulverton*
Wilson—*Moran*
Wilson—*Nunburnholme*
Wilson—*Wilson of
  Langside**
Wilson—*Wilson of
  Rievaulx**
Windsor—*Cornwall*
Windsor—*Gloucester*
Windsor—*Kent*
Windsor Clive—
  Plymouth
Wingfield—*Powerscourt*
Winn—*St. Oswald*
Winn—*Headley*
Wodehouse—*Kimberley*
Wood—*Halifax*
Wood—*Holderness**
Woodhouse—*Terrington*
Wright—*Wootton of
  Abinger**
Wyndham—*Leconfield*
Wyndham Quin—
  Dunraven
Wynn—*Newborough*
Yarde Buller—*Churston*
Yerburgh—*Alvingham*
Yorke—*Hardwicke*
Young—*Kennet*
Young—*Young of
  Dartington**
Younger—*Y. of Leckie*

* Life Peer created under Life Peerages Act, 1958

COURTESY TITLES

Holders of Courtesy Titles are addressed in the same manner as holders of substantive titles.

From this list it will be seen that, for example, the "Marquess of Blandford" is heir to the Dukedom of Marlborough, and "Viscount Althorp" to the Earldom of Spencer. Titles of second heirs are also given, and the Courtesy Title of the father of a second heir is indicated by *; e.g., Earl of Burlington, eldest son of *Marquess of Hartington.

Marquesses

Blandford—*Marlborough*
Bowmont—*Roxburghe*
Douglas and Clydesdale—*Hamilton*
*Douro—*Wellington*
*Graham—*Montrose*
Granby—*Rutland*
Hamilton—*Abercorn*
*Hartington—*Devonshire*
*Kildare—*Leinster*
Lorne—*Argyll*
*Tavistock—*Bedford*

Earls

*Aboyne—*Huntly*
Altamont—*Sligo*
Ancram—*Lothian*
Arundel and Surrey—*Norfolk*
Bective—*Headfort*
Belfast—*Donegall*
*Brecknock—*Camden*
*Burford—*St. Albans*
Burlington—**Hartington*
Cardigan—*Ailesbury*
Cassillis—*Ailsa*
Compton—*Northampton*
Dalkeith—*Buccleuch*
*Euston—*Grafton*
*Hopetoun—*Linlithgow*
Jermyn—*Bristol*
Macduff—*Fife*
*March and Kinrara—*Richmond*
*Mount Charles—*Conyngham*
Mornington—**Douro*
Mulgrave—*Normanby*
Offaly—**Kildare*
Percy—*Northumberland*
Rocksavage—*Cholmondeley*
*Ronaldshay—*Zetland*
St. Andrews—*Kent*
*Shelburne—*Lansdowne*
Tyrone—*Waterford*
Ulster—*Gloucester*
Uxbridge—*Anglesey*
Wiltshire—*Winchester*
Yarmouth—*Hertford*

Viscounts

Aithrie—**Hopetoun*
Althorp—*Spencer*
Andover—*Suffolk and Berkshire*
Anson—*Lichfield*
Asquith—*Oxford & Asquith*
Bayham—**Brecknock*
Boringdon—*Morley*
Borodale—*Beatty*
Boyle—*Shannon*
Brocas—*Jellicoe*
Calne and Calstone—**Shelburne*
Campden—*Gainsborough*
Carlow—*Portarlington*
Castlereagh—*Londonderry*
Chelsea—*Cadogan*
Chewton—*Waldegrave*
Clanfield—*Peel*
Coke—*Leicester*
Cole—*Enniskillen*
Corvedale—*Baldwin of Bewdley*
Cranborne—*Salisbury*
Cranley—*Onslow*
Crichton—*Erne*
Dalrymple—*Stair*
Dawick—*Haig*
Deerhurst—*Coventry*
Drumlanrig—*Queensberry*
Dupplin—*Kinnoull*
Ebrington—*Fortescue*
Ednam—*Dudley*
Elveden—*Iveagh*
Emlyn—*Cawdor*
Encombe—*Eldon*
Ennismore—*Listowel*
Enfield—*Strafford*
Errington—*Cromer*
Feilding—*Denbigh*
FitzClarence—*Munster*
FitzHarris—*Malmesbury*
Folkestone—*Radnor*
Garmoyle—*Cairns*
Garnock—*Lindsay*
Glandine—*Norbury*
Glenapp—*Inchcape*
Glentworth—*Limerick*
Grimston—*Verulam*
Gwynedd—*Lloyd George of Dwyfor*
Hawkesbury—*Liverpool*
Ikerrin—*Carrick*
Ingestre—*Shrewsbury*
Ipswich—**Euston*
Jocelyn—*Roden*
Kelburn—*Glasgow*
Kingsborough—*Kingston*
Knebworth—*Lytton*
Kynnaird—*Newburgh*
Lascelles—*Harewood*
Lewisham—*Dartmouth*
Linley—*Snowdon*
Loftus—*Ely*
Lowther—*Lonsdale*
Lumley—*Scarbrough*
Lymington—*Portsmouth*
Macmillan of Ovenden—*Stockton*
Maidstone — *Winchilsea and Nottingham*
Maitland—*Lauderdale*
Melgund—*Minto*
Merton—*Nelson*
Moore—*Drogheda*
Morpeth—*Carlisle*
Newport—*Bradford*
Newry and Mourne—*Kilmorey*
Parker—*Macclesfield*
Perceval—*Egmont*
Petersham—*Harrington*
Pollington—*Mexborough*
Prestwood—*Attlee*
Quenington—*St. Aldwyn*
Raynham—*Townshend*
Reidhaven—*Seafield*
Ruthven of Canberra and Dirleton—*Gowrie*
St. Cyres—*Iddesleigh*
Sandon—*Harrowby*
Slane—**Mount Charles*
Stormont—*Mansfield*
Strathallan—*Perth*
Stuart—*Castle Stewart*
Sudley—*Arran*
Suirdale—*Donoughmore*
Tamworth—*Ferrers*
Tarbat—*Cromartie*
Tiverton—*Halsbury*
Vaughan—*Lisburne*
Villiers—*Jersey*
Weymouth—*Bath*
Windsor—*Plymouth*
Wolmer—*Selborne*

Barons (Lord—)

Aberdour—*Morton*
Apsley—*Bathurst*
Ardee—*Meath*
Ashley—*Shaftesbury*
Balgonie—*Leven & Melville*
Berriedale—*Caithness*
Bingham—*Lucan*
Binning—*Haddington*
Brooke—*Warwick*
Bruce—*Elgin*
Buckhurst—*De La Warr*
Burghersh—*Westmorland*
Cardross—*Buchan*
Clifton—*Darnley*
Cochrane—*Dundonald*
Courtenay—*Devon*
Dalmeny—*Rosebery*
Delvin—*Westmeath*
Doune—*Moray*
Dundas—**Ronaldshay*
Eliot—*St. Germans*
Erskine—*Mar & Kellie*
Fintrie—**Graham*
Glamis—*Strathmore*
Greenock—*Cathcart*
Guernsey—*Aylesford*
Herbert—*Pembroke*
Howland—**Tavistock*
Hyde—*Clarendon*
Inverurie—*Kintore*
Irwin—*Halifax*
Leslie—*Rothes*
Leveson—*Granville*
Mauchline—*Loudoun*
Medway—*Cranbrook*
Montgomerie—*Eglinton and Winton*
Moreton—*Ducie*
Naas—*Mayo*
Neidpath—*Wemyss & March*
Norreys—*Lindsey & Abingdon*
North—*Guilford*
Ogilvy—*Airlie*
Oxmantown—*Rosse*
Porchester—*Carnarvon*
Ramsay—*Dalhousie*
Romsey—*Mountbatten of Burma*
Rosehill—*Northesk*
Scrymgeour—*Dundee*
Settrington—**March and Kinrara*
Seymour—*Somerset*
Silchester—*Longford*
Strathavon and Glenlivet—**Aboyne*
Strathnaver—*Sutherland*
Vere of Hanworth—**Burford*
Wodehouse—*Kimberley*
Worsley—*Yarborough*

THE PRIVY COUNCIL

Apart from Cabinet Ministers, who must be Privy Counsellors and are sworn in on first assuming office, membership of the Council (retained for life) is accorded by the Sovereign on the recommendation of the Prime Minister to eminent people in independent monarchical countries of the Commonwealth. Cabinet Ministers principally form the active Privy Council.

Name	Year	Name	Year	Name	Year
Jenkins, Roy Harris	1964	Nairne, Sir Patrick	1982	Shore, Peter	1967
Jones, Aubrey	1955	Northumberland, Duke of	1973	Silkin, John	1966
Jones, Sir Edward Warburton	1979	Nott, Sir John	1979	Silkin, Samuel	1974
Jopling, Michael	1979	Nugent of Guildford, Lord	1962	Simon of Glaisdale, Lord	1961
Joseph, Sir Keith, Bt	1962	Nutting, Sir Anthony, Bt.	1954	Sinclair, Ian	1977
Kaufman, Gerald	1978	Oakes, Gordon	1979	Slade, Sir Christopher	1982
Keith of Kinkel, Lord	1976	O'Brien of Lothbury, Lord	1970	Smith, John	1978
Kelly, Sir Basil	1984	O'Connor, Sir Patrick	1980	Snedden, Sir Billy	1972
Kenilorea, Sir Peter	1979	O'Donnell, Turlough	1979	Soames, Lord	1958
Kerr, Sir Michael	1981	Oliver, Sir Peter	1980	Somare, Michael	1977
Kerr, Sir Robert	1977	Oppenheim, Mrs. Sally	1979	Somers, Edward	1981
Kilbrandon, Lord	1971	Orme, Stanley	1974	Stanley, John	1984
Kilmany, Lord	1962	Ormrod, Sir Roger	1974	Steel, David	1977
King, Thomas	1979	Orr, Sir Alan	1971	Stephen, Sir Ninian	1979
Kinnock, Neil	1983	Owen, David	1976	Stephenson, Sir John	1971
Kitto, Sir Frank	1963	Palliser, Sir Michael	1983	Stevas, Norman St. John-	1979
Lane, Lord	1975	Parker, Sir Roger	1983	Stevenson, Sir Melford	1973
Lange, David	1984	Parkinson, Cecil	1981	Stewart, Donald	1977
Lansdowne, Marquess of	1964	Pearce, Lord	1957	Stewart of Fulham, Lord	1964
Lauti, Toaripi	1979	Peart, Lord	1964	Stockton, Earl of	1942
Lawson, Nigel	1981	Percival, Sir Ian	1983	Stodart of Leaston, Lord	1974
Lawton, Sir Frederick	1972	Perth, Earl of	1957	Stott, Lord	1964
Lee of Asheridge, Baroness	1966	Peyton of Yeovil, Lord	1970	Strathclyde, Lord	1953
Lever of Manchester, Lord	1969	Pindling, Sir Lynden	1976	Strauss, Lord	1947
Listowel, Earl of	1946	Poole, Lord	1963	Talboys, Brian	1977
Llewelyn-Davies of Hastoe, Baroness	1975	Powell, Enoch	1960	Tebbit, Norman	1981
		Prentice, Reginald	1966	Templeman, Lord	1978
London, The Bishop of	1981	Price, George	1982	Thatcher, Mrs. Margaret	1970
Longford, Earl of	1948	Prior, James	1970	Thomas, Peter	1964
Louisy, Allan	1981	Puapua, Tomasi	1982	Thomson of Monifieth,	
Lowry, Lord	1974	Purchas, Sir Francis	1982	Lord	1966
Mabon, Dickson	1977	Pym, Francis	1970	Thomson, David	1981
McCarthy, Sir Thaddeus	1968	Raison, Timothy	1982	Thorneycroft, Lord	1951
MacIntyre, Duncan	1980	Ramgoolam, Sir		Thorpe, Jeremy	1967
Mackay of Clashfern, Lord	1979	Seewoosagur	1971	Tonypandy, Viscount	1968
McKell, Sir William	1948	Ramsden, James	1963	Tranmire, Lord	1955
MacKenzie, Gregor	1977	Ramsey of Canterbury, Rt.		Trend, Lord	1972
Maclean, Lord	1971	Rev. Lord	1956	Turner, Sir Alexander	1968
McMahon, Sir William	1966	Rawlinson of Ewell, Lord	1964	Urwin, Thomas	1979
McMullin, Duncan	1980	Rees, Merlyn	1966	Varley, Eric	1974
McTiernan, Sir Edward	1963	Rees, Peter	1983	Wakeham, John	1983
Mara, Sir Kamisese	1973	Reigate, Lord	1961	Walker, Harold	1979
Marsh, Lord	1966	Renton, Lord	1962	Walker, Peter	1970
Marshall, Sir John Ross	1966	Rhodes, Lord	1969	Waller, Sir George	1976
Marten, Sir Neil	1981	Richardson of Duntisbourne, Lord	1976	Ward of Witley, Viscount	1957
Martonmere, Lord	1962	Richardson, Ivor	1978	Watkins, Sir Tasker	1980
Mason, Roy	1968	Richmond, Sir Clifford	1973	Watkinson, Viscount	1955
Maude of Stratford-upon-Avon, Lord	1979	Ridley, Nicholas	1983	Weatherill, Bernard	1980
		Rippon, Geoffrey	1962	Welensky, Sir Roy	1960
May, Sir John	1982	Robens of Woldingham, Lord	1951	Wheatley, Lord	1947
Maybray-King, Lord	1965	Robinson, Sir Kenneth	1964	Whitelaw, Viscount (*Lord President*)	1967
Megarry, Sir Robert	1978	Rodgers, William	1975	Wilberforce, Lord	1964
Megaw, Sir John	1969	Roskill, Lord	1971	Willey, Frederick Thomas	1964
Mellish, Robert	1967	Ross of Marnock, Lord	1964	Williams, Alan	1977
Millan, Bruce	1975	Rowling, Sir Wallace	1974	Williams, Shirley	1974
Molson, Lord	1956	Russell of Killowen, Lord	1962	Willis, Eustace George	1967
Molyneaux, James	1983	St. Aldwyn, Earl	1959	Wilson of Rievaulx, Lord	1947
Moore, Sir Philip	1977	Saint Brides, Lord	1968	Wilson of Langside, Lord	1967
Morris, Alfred	1979	Salmon, Lord	1964	Windeyer, Sir Victor	1963
Morris, Charles	1978	Scarman, Lord	1973	Windlesham, Lord	1973
Morris, John	1970	Seaga, Edward	1981	Withers, Reginald	1977
Moyle, Roland	1978	Selkirk, Earl of	1955	Woodhouse, Sir Owen	1974
Muirshiel, Viscount	1952	Shackleton, Lord	1966	Wylie, Lord	1970
Muldoon, Sir Robert	1976	Shawcross, Lord	1946	York, The Archbishop of	1983
Mulley, Lord	1964	Shearer, Hugh	1969	Young, Baroness	1981
Murray, Lionel	1976	Sheldon, Robert	1977	Younger, George	1979
Murray, Lord	1974	Shepherd, Lord	1965		
Murton of Lindisfarne, Lord	1976	Shinwell, Lord	1945		

ORDERS OF CHIVALRY

The Most Noble Order of the Garter (1348)—K.G.

Ribbon, Garter Blue. *Motto*, Honi soit qui mal y pense (*Shame on him who thinks evil of it*).
The number of Knights Companions is limited to 24.

SOVEREIGN OF THE ORDER—THE QUEEN

Lady of the Garter—H.M. QUEEN ELIZABETH THE QUEEN MOTHER, 1936.
Extra Ladies of the Garter—H.M. JULIANA, QUEEN OF THE NETHERLANDS, 1958
H.M. THE QUEEN OF DENMARK, 1979

Royal Knights

H.R.H. the Duke of Edinburgh, 1947.
H.R.H. the Prince of Wales, 1958.

Extra Knights

H.M. the King of Norway, 1959.
H.M. the King of the Belgians, 1963.
H.I.M. the Emperor of Japan, 1971.
H.R.H. the Grand Duke of Luxemburg, 1972.
H.M. the King of Sweden, 1983

Knights Companions

The Duke of Northumberland, 1959.
The Viscount De L'Isle, 1968.

The Lord Ashburton, 1969.
The Lord Cobbold, 1970.
Sir Cennydd Traherne, 1970.
The Earl Waldegrave, 1971.
The Earl of Longford, 1971.
The Lord Rhodes, 1972.
The Earl of Drogheda, 1972.
The Lord Shackleton, 1974.
The Lord Trevelyan, 1974.
The Marquess of Abergavenny, 1974.
The Lord Wilson of Rievaulx, 1976.
The Duke of Grafton, 1976.
The Earl of Cromer, 1977.
The Lord Elworthy, 1977.
The Lord Hunt, 1979.
Sir Paul Hasluck, 1979.

Sir Richard Hull, 1980
The Duke of Norfolk, 1983
The Lord Lewin, 1983
The Lord Richardson of Duntisbourne, 1983
Prelate, The Bishop of Winchester.
Chancellor, The Marquess of Abergavenny, K.G., O.B.E.
Register, The Dean of Windsor.
Garter King of Arms, Lt.-Col. Sir Colin Cole, K.C.V.O., T.D.
Gentleman Usher of the Black Rod, Lt.-General Sir David House, G.C.B., C.B.E., M.C.
Secretary, Sir Walter Verco, K.C.V.O.

The Most Ancient and Most Noble Order of the Thistle—K.T.

Ribbon, Green. *Motto*, Nemo me impune lacessit (*No one provokes me with impunity*).
The number of Knights is limited to 16.

SOVEREIGN OF THE ORDER—THE QUEEN

Lady of the Thistle—H.M. QUEEN ELIZABETH THE QUEEN MOTHER, 1937

Royal Knights

H.R.H. the Duke of Edinburgh, 1952.
H.R.H. the Prince of Wales (*Duke of Rothesay*), 1977.

Extra Knight

H.M. the King of Norway, 1962.

Knights

The Earl of Haddington, 1951.
The Lord Home of the Hirsel, 1962.

The Earl of Wemyss and March, 1966.
The Lord Maclean, 1969.
The Earl of Dalhousie, 1971.
The Lord Clydesmuir, 1972.
The Viscount Muirshiel, 1973.
Sir Donald Cameron of Lochiel, 1973.
The Earl of Selkirk, 1976.
The Lord McFadzean, 1976.
The Hon. Lord Cameron, 1978.
The Duke of Buccleuch and Queensberry, 1978.
The Earl of Elgin and Kincardine, 1981.

The Lord Thomson of Monifieth, 1981.
The Lord MacLehose of Beoch, 1983.
The Lord Cameron of Balhousie, 1983.
Chancellor, The Lord Home of the Hirsel.
Dean, The Very Rev. Prof. J. McIntyre, M.A., B.D., D.Litt., D.D.
Secretary and Lord Lyon King of Arms, Malcolm R. Innes of Edingight, C.V.O., W.S.
Usher of the Green Rod, Rear-Admiral D.A. Dunbar-Nasmith, C.B., D.S.C.

The Most Honourable Order of the Bath (1725)

Ribbon, Crimson. *Motto*, Tria juncta in uno (*Three joined in one*). (Remodelled 1815, and enlarged many times since. The Order is divided into civil and military divisions.)

G.C.B. Mil.   G.C.B. Civ.   K.C.B. Mil.   K.C.B. Civ.   C.B. Mil.

THE SOVEREIGN; *Great Master and First or Principal Knight Grand Cross*, H.R.H. The Prince of Wales, K.G., K.T., G.C.B.; *Dean of the Order*, The Dean of Westminster; *Bath King of Arms*, Admiral of the Fleet Sir Michael Pollock, G.C.B., M.V.O., D.S.C.; *Registrar and Secretary*, Rear-Admiral C. D. Madden, C.B., C.B.E., M.V.O., D.S.C.; *Genealogist*, Dr. C. Swan, M.V.O., PH.D.; *Gentleman Usher of the Scarlet Rod*, Air Marshal Sir Denis Crowley-Milling, K.C.B., C.B.E., D.S.O., D.F.C.; *Deputy Secretary*, Maj.-Gen. D. H. G. Rice, C.B.E.; *Chancery*, Central Chancery of the Orders of Knighthood, St. James's Palace, S.W.1.—G.C.B., Knight (or Dame) Grand Cross; K.C.B., Knight Commander; D.C.B., Dame Commander; C.B., Companion. Women became eligible for the Order from Jan. 1, 1971.

The Order of Merit (1902)—O.M.
Ribbon, Blue and Crimson.

O.M.Mil. This Order is designed as a special distinction for eminent men and women—without conferring a knighthood upon them. The Order is limited in numbers to 24, with the addition of foreign honorary members. Membership is of two kinds, Military and Civil, the badge of the former having crossed swords, and the latter oak leaves. Membership is denoted by the suffix O.M., which follows the first class of the Order of the Bath and precedes the letters designating membership of the inferior classes of the Bath and all classes of the lesser Orders of Knighthood. O.M.Civ.

THE SOVEREIGN
H.R.H. THE DUKE OF EDINBURGH (1968)

Sir (Frank) Macfarlane Burnet, 1958.
Henry Spencer Moore, 1963.
Dorothy Hodgkin, 1965.
The Lord Zuckerman, 1968.
The Lord Penney, 1969.
Dame Veronica Wedgwood, 1969.
Sir Isaiah Berlin, 1971.

Sir George Edwards, 1971.
Sir Alan Hodgkin, 1973.
Paul Adriaen Maurice Dirac, 1973.
The Earl of Stockton, 1976.
Sir Ronald Syme, 1976.
The Lord Todd, 1977.
The Lord Franks, 1977.
Sir Frederick Ashton, 1977.

The Lord Olivier, 1981.
Sir Peter Medawar, 1981.
Gp. Capt. L. Cheshire, V.C., 1981.
Sir Andrew Huxley, 1983.
Sir Sidney Nolan, 1983.
Sir Michael Tippett, 1983.
Rev. Prof. Owen Chadwick, K.B.E., 1983.

Secretary and Registrar, Sir Edward Ford, K.C.B., K.C.V.O.
Chancery, Central Chancery of the Orders of Knighthood, St. James's Palace, S.W.1.

The Most Exalted Order of the Star of India (1861)

Ribbon, Light Blue, with White Edges. *Motto*, Heaven's Light our Guide.
G.C.S.I. THE SOVEREIGN; *Registrar*, Maj.-Gen. D. H. G. Rice, C.B.E.; G.C.S.I. Knight Grand Commander; K.C.S.I., Knight Commander; C.S.I., Companion. No conferments since 1947.

The Most Distinguished Order of St. Michael and St. George (1818)

Ribbon, Saxon Blue, with Scarlet centre. *Motto*, Auspicium melioris ævi (Token of a better age)
THE SOVEREIGN; *Grand Master*, H.R.H. The Duke of Kent, G.C.M.G., G.C.V.O., A.D.C.; *Prelate*, The Rt. Rev. R. Woods, K.C.V.O.; *Chancellor*, The Lord Carrington, P.C., C.H., K.C.M.G., M.C.; *Secretary*, Sir Antony Acland, K.C.M.G., K.C.V.O.; *Registrar*, Sir Charles Johnston, G.C.M.G.; *King of Arms*, The Lord Saint Brides, P.C., G.C.M.G., C.V.O., M.B.E.; *Gentleman Usher of the Blue Rod*, Sir John Moreton, K.C.M.G., K.C.V.O., M.C.; *Dean*, The Dean of St. Paul's; *Deputy Secretary*, Maj.-Gen. D. H. G. Rice, C.B.E. *Chancery*, Central Chancery of the Orders of Knighthood, St. James's Palace, S.W.1.—G.C.M.G., Knight (or Dame) Grand Cross; K.C.M.G., Knight Commander; D.C.M.G., Dame Commander; C.M.G., Companion.

The Most Eminent Order of the Indian Empire (1868)

Ribbon, Imperial Purple. *Motto*, Imperatricis auspiciis (*Under the auspices of the Empress*).
G.C.I.E. THE SOVEREIGN; *Registrar*, Maj.-Gen. D. H. G. Rice, C.B.E.; G.C.I.E., Knight Grand Commander; K.C.I.E., Knight Commander; C.I.E., Companion. No conferments since 1947.

The Royal Victorian Order (1896)

Ribbon, Blue, with Red and White Edges. *Motto*, Victoria.
THE SOVEREIGN; *Grand Master*, H.M. Queen Elizabeth the Queen Mother; *Chancellor*, The Lord Chamberlain; *Secretary*, The Keeper of the Privy Purse; *Registrar*, The Secretary of the Central Chancery of the Orders of Knighthood; *Chaplain*, The Rev. J. H. Williams. *Hon. Genealogist*, Sir Walter Verco, K.C.V.O., G.C.V.O., Knight or Dame Grand Cross; K.C.V.O., Knight Commander; D.C.V.O., Dame Commander; C.V.O., M.V.O., Member, 4th or 5th Class.

The Royal Victorian Chain (1902)

Founded by King Edward VII, in 1902. It confers no precedence on its holders.
H.M. THE QUEEN
H.M. QUEEN ELIZABETH THE QUEEN MOTHER (1937).

H.M. Juliana, Queen of the Netherlands (1950).
H.M. the King of Norway (1955).
H.M. the King of Thailand (1960).
H.I.H. the Crown Prince of Ethiopia (1965).
H.M. the King of Jordan (1966).

H.M. King Zahir Shah of Afghanistan (1971).
Rt. Hon. Roland Michener (1973).
H.M. the Queen of Denmark (1974).
The Right Rev. the Lord Ramsey of Canterbury (1974).
H.M. the King of Nepal (1975).

H.M. the King of Sweden (1975).
The Right Rev. the Lord Coggan (1980).
Ratu Sir George Cakobau (1982).
H.M. Queen Beatrix of the Netherlands (1982).

The Most Excellent Order of the British Empire (1917)

Ribbon, Rose pink edged with pearl grey with vertical pearl stripe in centre (Military Division); without vertical pearl stripe (Civil Division). *Motto,* For God and the Empire.

G.B.E.   K.B.E.

THE SOVEREIGN: *Grand Master,* H.R.H. the Prince Philip, Duke of Edinburgh, K.G., P.C., K.T., O.M., G.B.E.; *Prelate,* The Bishop of London; *King of Arms,* Admiral Sir Anthony Morton, G.B.E., K.C.B.; *Registrar,* Maj.-Gen. D. H. G. Rice, C.B.E.; *Secretary,* Sir Robert Armstrong, G.C.B., C.V.O.; *Dean,* The Dean of St. Paul's; *Gentleman Usher of the Purple Rod,* Sir Robert Bellinger, G.B.E.; *Chancery,* Central Chancery of the Orders of Knighthood, St. James's Palace, S.W.1. G.B.E., Knight or Dame Grand Cross; K.B.E. Knight Commander; D.B.E., Dame Commander; C.B.E., Commander; O.B.E., Officer; M.B.E., Member. The Order was divided into *Military* and *Civil* divisions in Dec. 1918.

Order of the Companions of Honour (June 4, 1917)—C.H.

Ribbon, Carmine, with Gold Edges.

This Order consists of one Class only and carries with it no title. It ranks after the 1st Class of the Order of the British Empire, *i.e.,* Knights and Dames Grand Cross (Mil. and Civ. Div.). The number of awards is limited to 65 (excluding honorary members) and the Order is open to both sexes. *Secretary and Registrar,* The Secretary of the Central Chancery of the Orders of Knighthood.

Anthony, Rt. Hon. John Douglas, 1982.
Ashley, Rt. Hon. Jack, 1975.
Ashton, Sir Frederick, 1970.
Aylestone, The Lord, 1975.
Bryant, Sir Arthur, 1967.
Carrington, The Lord, 1983.
Cecil, Lord David Gascoyne, 1949.
Cledwyn of Penrhos, The Lord, 1977.
de Valois, Dame Ninette, 1982.
Duncan-Sandys, The Lord, 1973.
Eccles, The Viscount, 1984.
Elwyn-Jones, The Lord, 1976.
Fraser, Rt. Hon. Malcolm, 1977.
Freud, Lucian, 1983.
Gardiner, The Lord, 1975.
Gielgud, Sir John, 1977.
Glenamara, The Lord, 1976.
Goodman, The Lord, 1972.
Gorton, Rt. Hon. Sir John Grey, 1971.
Greene, Graham, 1966.

Hailsham of St. Marylebone, The Lord, 1974.
von Hayek, *Prof.* Friedrich, 1984.
Healey, Rt. Hon. Denis, 1979.
Houghton of Sowerby, The Lord, 1967.
Jones, James Larkin, 1978.
McMahon, Rt. Hon. Sir William, 1972.
Marshall, Rt. Hon. Sir John Ross, 1973.
Mayer, Sir Robert, 1973.
Medawar, Sir Peter, 1972.
Moore, Henry Spencer, 1955.
Muirshiel, TheViscount, 1962.
Muldoon, Rt. Hon. Sir Robert, 1977.
Pasmore, Victor, 1981.
Perutz, *Prof.* Max Ferdinand, 1975.
Piper, John Egerton Christmas, 1972.
Popper, *Prof.* Sir Karl, 1982.
Powell, Sir Philip, 1984.
Rahman, Tunku Abdul, 1960.

Runciman, *Hon.* Sir Steven, 1984.
Sanger, Frederick, 1981.
Shinwell, The Lord, 1965.
Sitwell, Sir Sacheverell, Bt., 1984.
Smith, Arnold Cantwell, 1975.
Soames, The Lord, 1980.
Somare, Rt. Hon. Michael Thomas, 1978.
Stewart of Fulham, The Lord, 1969.
Talboys, Rt. Hon. Brian Edward, 1981.
Thorneycroft, The Lord, 1980
Tippett, Sir Michael, 1979.
Trudeau, Rt. Hon. Pierre Elliot, 1984.
Watkinson, The Viscount, 1962.
Whitelaw, The Viscount, 1974.
Wootton of Abinger, The Baroness, 1977.
Honorary Members, M. René Massigli, 1954; Lee Kuan Yew, 1970; Dr. Joseph Luns, 1971.

The Royal Victoria and Albert (for Ladies)—V.A.

Instituted in 1862, and enlarged in 1864, 1865, and 1880. Badge, a medallion of Queen Victoria and the Prince Consort, surmounted by a crown, which was attached to a bow of white moiré ribbon. The honour did not confer any rank or title upon the recipient. The last holder of the honour, H.R.H. the Princess Alice, Countess of Athlone, died in 1981.

The Imperial Order of the Crown of India (for Ladies)—C.I.

Instituted Dec. 31, 1877. Badge, the royal cipher in jewels within an oval, surmounted by an Heraldic Crown and attached to a bow of light blue watered ribbon, edged white. The honour does not confer any rank or title upon the recipient. No conferments have been made since 1947.

H.M. THE QUEEN, 1947.
H.M. Queen Elizabeth the Queen Mother, 1931.

H.R.H. the Princess Margaret, Countess of Snowdon, 1947.
H.R.H. the Princess Alice, Duchess of Gloucester, 1937.

H.H. Maharani of Travancore, 1929.
Eugenie Marie, Countess Wavell, 1943.

The Imperial Service Order (1902)—I.S.O.

Ribbon, Crimson, with Blue Centre.

Appointment of Companion of this Order shall be open to those members of the Civil Services whose eligibility shall be determined by the grade held by such persons. The Order consists of The SOVEREIGN and Companions (not exclusively male) to a number not exceeding 1475 of whom 875 may belong to the Home Civil Services and 600 to Overseas Civil Services. *Secretary,* Sir Robert Armstrong, G.C.B., C.V.O. *Registrar,* Maj.-Gen. D. H. G. Rice, C.B.E., St. James's Palace, S.W.1.

BARONETS, KNIGHTS GRAND CROSS, KNIGHTS GRAND COMMANDERS, KNIGHTS COMMANDERS AND KNIGHTS BACHELOR

Badge of Baronets
of England, Great Britain, U.K.,
(and Ireland marked I.).

Badge of Baronets
of Scotland or Nova Scotia
(marked S. or N.S.).

NOTES CONCERNING BARONETS

Clause II. of the Royal Warrant of February 8, 1910, ordains as follows:—"That no person whose name is not entered upon the Official Roll shall be received as a Baronet, or shall be addressed or mentioned by that title in any Civil or Military Commission, Letters Patent or other official document." When an obelisk (†) precedes a name it indicates that, *at the time of going to press*, the Baronet concerned has not been registered on the Official Roll of the Baronetage. The date of creation of the Baronetcy is given in parenthesis ( ).

Baronets are addressed as "Sir" (with Christian name) and in writing as "Sir Robert A—, Bt." Baronet's wives are addressed (formally) as "Your Ladyship" or "Lady A—," without any Christian name unless a daughter of a Duke, Marquess or Earl, in which case "The Lady Mary A—"; if daughter of a Viscount or Baron "The Hon. Lady A—."

NOTES CONCERNING KNIGHTS GRAND CROSS, ETC.

Knights Grand Cross, Knights Grand Commanders and Knights Commanders are addressed in the same manner as Baronets (*q.v.*), but in writing the appropriate initials (G.C.B., K.C.B., &c.) are appended to surname after "Bt." if they are also baronets or in place of "Bt." if they are not. Knights Bachelor are addressed as "Sir —— (first or Christian name)" and in writing as "Sir —— B ——." The wife of a Knight Grand Cross, Knight Grand Commander, Knight Commander or Knight Bachelor is addressed as stated for the wife of a Baronet.

NOTES CONCERNING KNIGHTS BACHELOR

The Knights Bachelor do not constitute a Royal Order, but comprise the surviving representation of the ancient State Orders of Knighthood. The Register of Knights Bachelor, instituted by James I. in the 17th century, lapsed, and in 1908 a voluntary Association under the title of "The Society of Knights" (now "The Imperial Society of Knights Bachelor" by Royal command) was formed with the primary objects of continuing the various registers dating from 1257 and obtaining the uniform registration of every created Knight Bachelor. In 1926 a design for a badge to be worn by Knights Bachelor was approved and adopted, a miniature reproduction being shown above; in 1974 a neck badge and miniature were added. The Officers of the Society are:—*Knight Principal,* Sir Colin Cole, K.C.V.O.; *Deputy Knight Principal,* Sir Gilbert Inglefield, G.B.E., T.D.; *Prelate,* Rt. Rev. G. A. Ellison, P.C., K.C.V.O.; *Hon. Registrar,* Sir Arthur Driver; *Hon. Treasurer,* Sir John Howard; *Office,* 21 Old Buildings, Lincoln's Inn, W.C.2.

BARONETAGE AND KNIGHTAGE
(Revised to Sept. 1, 1984)
Peers are not included in this list

A full entry in italic type indicates that the recipient of a Knighthood died during the year in which the honour was conferred. The name is included for purposes of record.

Aarons, Sir Daniel Sidney, Kt., O.B.E., M.C.

Aarvold, *His Hon.* Sir Carl Douglas, Kt., O.B.E., T.D.

Abal, Sir Tei, Kt., C.B.E.

Abbott, Sir Albert Francis, Kt., C.B.E.

Abdy, Sir Valentine Robert Duff, Bt. (1850).

Abel, Sir Seselo (Cecil) Charles Geoffrey, Kt., O.B.E.

Abeles, Sir (Emil Herbert) Peter, Kt.

Abell, Sir Anthony Foster, K.C.M.G.

Abell, Sir George Edmond Brackenbury, K.C.I.E., O.B.E.

Abercromby, Sir Ian George, Bt. (s. 1636).

Abraham, Sir Edward Penley, Kt., C.B.E., F.R.S.

Abrahams, Sir Charles, K.C.V.O.

Ackner, *Rt. Hon.* Sir Desmond James Conrad, Kt.

Ackroyd, Sir John Robert Whyte, Bt. (1956).

Acland, Sir Antony Arthur, K.C.M.G., K.C.V.O.

Acland, *Maj.* Sir Christopher Guy Dyke, Bt. (1890).

Acland, *Maj.-Gen.* Sir John Hugh Bevil, K.C.B., C.B.E.

Acland, Sir Richard Thomas Dyke, Bt. (1644).

Acton, Sir Harold Mario Mitchell, Kt., C.B.E.

Acutt, Sir Keith Courtney, K.B.E.

Adair, *Maj.-Gen.* Sir Allan Henry Shafto, Bt., G.C.V.O., C.B., D.S.O., M.C. (1838).

Adam, *Hon.* Sir Alistair Duncan Grant, Kt.

Adam, Sir Christopher Eric Forbes, Bt. (1917).

Adams, Sir Philip George Doyne, K.C.M.G.

Adams-Schneider, *Rt. Hon.* Sir Lancelot Raymond, K.C.M.G.

Adamson, Sir (William Owen) Campbell, Kt.

Adcock, Sir Robert Henry, Kt., C.B.E.

Addison, Sir William Wilkinson, Kt.

Ademola, *Rt. Hon.* Sir Adetokunbo Adegboyega, K.B.E.

Adrien, *Hon.* Sir Maurice Latour-, Kt.

Agnew, Sir Crispin Hamlyn, Bt. (s. 1629).

Agnew, Sir Geoffrey William Gerald, Kt.

Agnew, Sir (John) Anthony Stuart, Bt. (1895).

Agnew, *Cdr.* Sir Peter Garnett, Bt. (1957).

Agnew, Sir Robert David Garrick, Kt., C.B.E.

Agnew, Sir (William) Godfrey, K.C.V.O., C.B.

Ah-Chuen, Sir Jean Etienne Moi-Lin, Kt.

Aiken, *Air Chief Marshal* Sir John Alexander Carlisle, K.C.B.

Ainley, Sir (Alfred) John, Kt., M.C.

Ainsworth, Sir (Thomas) David, Bt. (1916).

Aird, *Capt.* Sir Alastair Sturgis, K.C.V.O.

Aird, Sir (George) John, Bt. (1901).

Airey, Sir Lawrence, K.C.B.

Aisher, Sir Owen Arthur, Kt.

Aitchison, Sir Charles Walter de Lancey, Bt. (1938).

Aitken, Sir (John William) Maxwell, Bt., D.S.O., D.F.C. (1916).

Aitken, Sir Robert Stevenson, Kt., M.D., D.Phil.

Akehurst, *Lt.-Gen.* Sir John Bryan, K.C.B., C.B.E.

Albert, Sir Alexis François, Kt., C.M.G., V.R.D.

Albery, Sir Donald Arthur Rolleston, Kt.

Albu, Sir George, Bt. (1912).

Aldington, Sir Geoffrey William, K.B.E., C.M.G.

Alexander, Sir Alexander Sandor, Kt.

Alexander, Sir Charles Gundry, Bt. (1945).

Alexander, Sir Claud Hagart-, Bt. (1886).

Alexander, *Hon.* Sir Darnley Arthur Raymond, Kt., C.B.E.

Alexander, Sir Desmond William Lionel Cable, Bt. (1809).

Alexander, Sir Douglas Hamilton, Bt. (1921).

Alexander, Sir (John) Lindsay, Kt.

Alexander, *Prof.* Sir Kenneth John Wilson, Kt.

Alexander, Sir Norman Stanley, Kt., C.B.E.

Allan, Sir Anthony James Allan Havelock-, Bt. (1858).

Allan, Sir Colin Hamilton, K.C.M.G., O.B.E.

Allard, Sir Gordon Laidlaw, Kt.

Allcroft, Sir Philip Magnus-, Bt., C.B.E. (1917).

Allen, *Prof.* Sir Geoffrey, Kt., Ph.D., F.R.S.

Allen, Sir Peter Christopher, Kt.

Allen, Sir Richard Hugh Sedley, K.C.M.G.

Allen, Sir (William) Denis, G.C.M.G., C.B.

Allen, Sir William Guilford, Kt.

Allen, Sir (William) Kenneth Gwynne, Kt.

Alleyne, *Rev.* John Olpherts Campbell, Bt., (1769).

Allinson, Sir (Walter) Leonard, K.C.V.O., C.M.G.

Alment, Sir (Edward) Anthony John, Kt.

Anderson, *Prof.* Sir (James) Norman (Dalrymple), Kt., O.B.E., Q.C., F.B.A.

Anderson, *General* Sir John D'Arcy, G.B.E., K.C.B., D.S.O.

Anderson, *Maj.-Gen.* Sir John Evelyn, Kt.

Anderson, Sir John Muir, Kt., C.M.G.

Anderson, Sir Kenneth, K.B.E., C.B.

Anderson, *Hon.* Sir Kenneth Mc-Coll, K.B.E.

Anderson, *Hon.* Sir Kevin Victor, Kt.

Anderson, *Vice-Adm.* Sir Neil Dudley, K.B.E., C.B.

Anderson, *Prof.* Sir (William) Ferguson, Kt., O.B.E.

Andrew, *Rev.* Sir (George) Herbert, K.C.M.G., C.B.

Andrewes, Sir Christopher Howard, Kt., M.D., F.R.S.

Andrews, *Rt. Hon.* Sir John Lawson Ormrod, K.B.E.

Annamunthodo, *Prof.* Sir Harry, Kt., F.R.C.S.

Ansell, *Col.* Sir Michael Picton Kt., C.B.E., D.S.O.

Anson, *Vice-Adm.* Sir Edward Rosebery, K.C.B.

Anson, *Rear-Admiral* Sir Peter, Bt., C.B. (1831).

Anstey, *Brig.* Sir John, Kt., C.B.E., T.D.

Anstruther, Sir Ralph Hugo, Bt. K.C.V.O., M.C. (s. 1694).

Anthony, Sir (Michael) Mobolaji Bank-, K.B.E.

Antico, Sir Tristan Venus, Kt.

Antrobus, Sir Philip Coutts, Bt. (1815).

Arbuthnot, Sir Keith Robert Charles, Bt. (1823).

Arbuthnot, Sir John Sinclair-Wemyss, Bt., M.B.E., T.D. (1964).

Archdale, *Comdr.* Sir Edward Folmer, Bt., D.S.C., R.N. (1928).

Archer, Sir Archibald, Kt., C.M.G.

Archer, *General* Sir (Arthur) John, K.C.B., O.B.E.

Archer, Sir Clyde Vernon Harcourt, Kt.

Arculus, Sir Ronald, K.C.M.G., K.C.V.O.

Armitage, *Air Marshal* Sir Michael John, K.C.B., C.B.E.

Armitage, Sir Robert Perceval, K.C.M.G., M.B.E.

Armstrong, Sir Andrew St. Clare, Bt. (1841).

Armstrong, Sir Robert Temple, G.C.B., C.V.O.

Armstrong, Sir Thomas Henry Wait, Kt., D.MUS.

Armytage, Sir John Martin, Bt. (1738).

Arnold, *Rt. Hon.* Sir John Lewis, Kt.

Arnott, Sir Alexander John Maxwell, Bt. (1896).

Arnott, *Prof.* Sir (William) Melville, Kt., T.D., M.D.

Arrindell, Sir Clement Athelston, G.C.M.G.

Arrowsmith, Sir Edwin Porter, K.C.M.G.

Arthur, Sir Basil Malcolm, Bt. (1841).

Arundell, *Brig.* Sir Robert Duncan Harris, K.C.M.G., O.B.E.

Arup, Sir Ove Nyquist, Kt., C.B.E.

Ashburnham, Sir Denny Reginald, Bt. (1661).

Ashe, Sir Derick Rosslyn, K.C.M.G.

Ashenheim, Sir Neville Noel, Kt., C.B.E.

Ashmore, *Admiral of the Fleet* Sir Edward Beckwith, G.C.B., D.S.C.

Ashmore, *Vice-Adm.* Sir Peter William Beckwith, K.C.B., K.C.V.O., D.S.C.

Ashton, Sir Frederick William Mallandaine, Kt., O.M., C.H., C.B.E.

Ashworth, Sir Herbert, Kt.

Aske, *Rev.* Sir Conan, Bt. (1922).

Astbury, Sir George, Kt.

Astley, Sir Francis Jacob Dugdale, Bt. (1821).

Aston, Sir Harold George, Kt., C.B.E.

Aston, *Hon.* Sir William John, K.C.M.G.

Astor, *Hon.* Sir John Jacob, Kt., M.B.E.

Astwood, *Hon.* Sir James Rufus, Kt.

Astwood, *Lt.-Col.* Sir Jeffrey Carlton, Kt., C.B.E., E.D.

Atcherley, Sir Harold Winter, Kt.

Atiyah, Sir Michael Francis, Kt., Ph.D., F.R.S.

Atkins, *Rt. Hon.* Sir Humphrey Edward Gregory, K.C.M.G., M.P.

Atkins, Sir William Sydney Albert, Kt., C.B.E.

Atkinson, *Air Marshal* Sir David William, K.B.E., Q.H.P.

Atkinson, Sir Frederick John, K.C.B.

Atkinson, Sir John Alexander, K.C.B., D.F.C.

Atkinson, Sir (John) Kenneth, Kt.

Atkinson, *Maj.-Gen.* Sir Leonard Henry, K.B.E.

Atkinson, Sir Robert, Kt., D.S.C.

Attenborough, Sir Richard Samuel, Kt., C.B.E.

Atwell, Sir John William, Kt., C.B.E., F.R.S.E.

Atwill, Sir (Milton) John (Napier), Kt.

Austin, Sir William Ronald, Bt. (1894).

Austin, *Vice-Admiral* Sir Peter Murray, K.C.B.

Auswild, Sir James Frederick John, Kt., C.B.E.

Ayer, *Prof.* Sir Alfred Jules, Kt., F.B.A.

Aykroyd, Sir William Miles, Bt., M.C. (1920).

Aykroyd, Sir Cecil William, Bt. (1929).

Aylmer, Sir Fenton Gerald, Bt. (I 1622).

Backhouse, Sir Jonathan Roger, Bt. (1901).

Bacon, Sir Nicholas Hickman Ponsonby, Bt. *Premier Baronet of England* (1611 and 1627).

Bacon, Sir Ranulph Robert Maunsell, Kt.

Bacon, Sir Sidney Charles, Kt., C.B.

Baddeley, Sir John Wolsey Beresford, Bt. (1922).

Baddiley, *Prof.* Sir James, Kt., Ph.D., D.SC., F.R.S., F.R.S.E.

Badenoch, Sir John, Kt., D.M., F.R.C.P.

Badger, *Prof.* Sir Geoffrey Malcolm, Kt.

Bagge, Sir John Alfred Picton, Bt. (1867).

Bagnall, *Gen.* Sir Nigel Thomas, K.C.B., C.V.O., M.C.

Bailey, Sir Brian Harry, Kt., O.B.E.

Bailey, Sir Derrick Thomas Louis, Bt., D.F.C. (1919).

Bailey, Sir Donald Coleman, Kt., O.B.E.

Bailey, *Prof.* Sir Harold Walter, Kt., D.Phil., F.B.A.

Bailey, Sir Richard John, Kt., C.B.E.

Baillie, Sir Gawaine George Hope, Bt. (1823).

Baines, *Prof.* Sir George Grenfell-, Kt., O.B.E.

Baird, Sir David Charles, Bt. (1809).

Baird, *Prof.* Sir Dugald, Kt., M.D.

Baird, *Lt.-Gen.* Sir James Parlane, K.B.E., M.D.

Baird, Sir James Richard Gardiner, Bt., M.C. (s. 1695).

Baird, *Vice-Adm.* Sir Thomas Henry Eustace, K.C.B.

Bairsto, *Air Marshal* Sir Peter Edward, K.B.E.

Baker, Sir (Allan) Ivor, Kt., C.B.E.

Baker, Sir Humphrey Dodington Benedict Sherston-, Bt. (1796).

Baker, Sir (Stanislaus) Joseph, Kt., C.B.

Balcombe, *Hon.* Sir (Alfred) John, Kt.

Balderstone, Sir James Schofield, Kt.

Baldwin, Sir Peter Robert, K.C.B.

Balfour, *General* Sir (Robert George) Victor FitzGeorge-, K.C.B., C.B.E., D.S.O., M.C.

Ball, *Air Marshal* Sir Alfred Henry Wynne, K.C.B., D.S.O., D.F.C.

Ball, Sir Charles Irwin, Bt. (1911).

Ball, *Prof.* Sir Robert James, Kt., Ph.D.

Balmer, Sir Joseph Reginald, Kt.

Banks, Sir Maurice Alfred Lister, Kt.

Banner, Sir George Knowles Harmood-, Bt. (1924).

Bannerman, *Lt.-Col.* Sir Donald Arthur Gordon, Bt. (s. 1682).

Bannister, Sir Roger Gilbert, Kt., C.B.E., D.M., F.R.C.P.

Barber, Sir Derek Coates, Kt.

Barber, *Hon.* Sir (Edward Hamilton) Esler, Kt.

Barber, *Lt.-Col.* Sir William Francis, Bt., T.D. (1960).

Barclay, Sir Colville Herbert Sanford, Bt. (s. 1668).

Barclay, Sir Roderick Edward, G.C.V.O., K.C.M.G.

Barford, Sir Leonard, Kt.

Baring, Sir Charles Christian, Bt. (1911).

Baring, *Hon.* Sir John Francis Harcourt, Kt., C.V.O.

Baring, Sir Mark, K.C.V.O.

Barker, Sir Alwyn Bowman, Kt., C.M.G.

Barker, Sir Harry Heaton, Kt., K.B.E.

Barker, Sir William, K.C.M.G., O.B.E.

Barlow, Sir Christopher Hilaro, Bt. (1803).

Barlow, Sir (George) William, Kt.

Barlow, Sir John Denman, Bt. (1907).

Barlow, Sir Thomas Erasmus, Bt., D.S.C. (1902).

Barnard, Sir (Arthur) Thomas, Kt., C.B., O.B.E.

Barnard, *Capt.* Sir George Edward, Kt.

Barnes, Sir Denis Charles, K.C.B.

Barnes, Sir (Ernest) John (Ward), K.C.M.G., M.B.E.

Barnes, Sir James George, Kt., M.B.E.

Barnes, Sir Kenneth, K.C.B.

Barnes, Sir William Lethbridge Gorell-, K.C.M.G., C.B.

Barnett, *Air Chief Marshal* Sir Denis Hensley Fulton, G.C.B., C.R.E., D.F.C.

Barnett, Sir Oliver Charles, Kt., C.B.E., Q.C.

Barnewall, Sir Reginald Robert, Bt. (I 1623).

Barraclough, *Air Chief Marshal* Sir John, K.C.B., C.B.E., D.F.C., A.F.C.

Barraclough, Sir Kenneth James Priestley, Kt., C.B.E., T.D.

Barran, Sir David Haven, Kt.

Barran, Sir John Napoleon Ruthven, Bt. (1895).

Barratt, Sir Lawrence Arthur, Kt.

Barrett, Sir Arthur George, Kt.

Barrett, *Lt.-Gen.* Sir David William Scott-, K.B.E., M.C.

Barrett, *Lt.-Col.* Sir Dennis Charles Titchener, Kt., T.D.

Barrie, Sir Walter, Kt.

Barrington, Sir Alexander (Fitzwilliam Croker), Bt. (1831).

Barrington, Sir Kenneth Charles Peto, Kt.

Barritt, Sir David Thurlow, Kt.

Barron, Sir Donald James, Kt.

Barrow, *Capt.* Sir Richard John Uniacke, Bt. (1835).

Barry, Sir (Lawrence) Edward (Anthony Tress), Bt. (1899).

Barry, Sir (Philip) Stuart Milner-, K.C.V.O., C.B., O.B.E.

Bartlett, *Lt.-Col.* Sir Basil Hardington, Bt. (1913).

Barton, Sir Charles Newton, Kt., O.B.E., E.D.

Barton, *Prof.* Sir Derek Harold Richard, Kt., F.R.S., F.R.S.E.

Barttelot, Sir Brian Walter de Stopham, Bt. (1875).

Barwick, *Rt. Hon.* Sir Garfield Edward John, G.C.M.G.

Basten, Sir Henry Bolton, Kt., C.M.G.

Batchelor, Sir Ivor Ralph Campbell, Kt., C.B.E.

Bate, Sir David Lindsay, K.B.E.

Bate, Sir (Walter) Edwin, Kt., O.B.E.

Bateman, Sir Cecil Joseph, K.B.E.

Bateman, Sir Charles Harold, K.C.M.G., M.C.

Bateman, Sir Geoffrey Hirst, Kt., F.R.C.S.

Bateman, Sir Ralph Melton, K.B.E.

Bates, *Prof.* Sir David Robert, Kt., D.Sc., F.R.S.

Bates, *Maj.-Gen.* Sir (Edward) John (Hunter), K.B.E., C.B., M.C.

Bates, Sir Geoffrey Voltelin, Bt., M.C. (1880).

Bates, Sir John David, Kt., C.B.E., V.R.D.

Bates, Sir (John) Dawson, Bt., M.C. (1937).

Bates, Sir (Julian) Darrell, Kt., C.M.G., C.V.O.

Batho, Sir Maurice Benjamin, Bt. (1928).

Bathurst, Sir Frederick Peter Methuen Hervey-, Bt. (1818).

Bathurst, Sir Maurice Edward, Kt., C.M.G., C.B.E., Q.C.

Batsford, Sir Brian Caldwell Cook, Kt.

Batty, Sir William Bradshaw, Kt., T.D.

Baxendell, Sir Peter Brian, Kt., C.B.E.

Baxter, *Prof.* Sir (John) Philip, K.B.E., C.M.G.

Bayliss, *Prof.* Sir Noel Stanley, Kt., C.B.E.

Bayliss, Sir Richard Ian Samuel, K.C.V.O., M.D., F.R.C.P.

Bayly, *Vice-Adm.* Sir Patrick Uniacke, K.B.E., C.B., D.S.C.

Baynes, Sir John Christopher Malcolm, Bt. (1801).

Bazley, Sir Thomas Stafford, Bt. (1869).

Beach, *General* Sir (William Gerald) Hugh, G.B.E., K.C.B., M.C.

Beale, Sir William Francis, Kt., O.B.E.

Beament, Sir James William Longman, Kt., Sc.D., F.R.S.

Beattie, *Hon.* Sir Alexander Craig, Kt.

Beattie, *Hon.* Sir David Stuart, G.C.M.G., G.C.V.O.

Beauchamp, Sir Christopher Radstock Proctor-, Bt. (1745).

Beaumont, Sir George (Howland Francis), Bt. (1661).

Beaumont, Sir Richard Ashton, K.C.M.G., O.B.E.

Beavis, *Air Chief Marshal* Sir Michael Gordon, K.C.B., C.B.E., A.F.C.

Becher, Sir William Fane Wrixon, Bt., M.C. (1831).

Beck, Sir Edgar Charles, Kt., C.B.E.

Beckett, *Capt.* Sir (Martyn) Gervase, Bt., M.C. (1921).

Beckett, Sir Terence Norman, Kt., C.B.E.

Bedbrook, Sir George Montario, Kt., O.B.E.

Bedingfeld, *Capt.* Sir Edmund George Felix Paston-, Bt. (1661).

Beecham, John Stratford Roland, Bt. (1914).

Beeck, Sir Marcus Truby, Kt.

Beeley, Sir Harold, K.C.M.G., C.B.E.

Beetham, *Marshal of the Royal Air Force* Sir Michael James, G.C.B., C.B.E., D.F.C., A.F.C.

Beevor, Sir Thomas Agnew, Bt. (1784).

Begg, *Admiral of the Fleet* Sir Varyl Cargill, G.C.B., D.S.O., D.S.C.

Beit, Sir Alfred Lane, Bt. (1924).

Beith, Sir John Greville Stanley, K.C.M.G.

Beldam, *Hon.* Sir (Alexander) Roy (Asplan), Kt., Q.C.

Bell, Sir Charles William, Kt., C.B.E.

Bell, Sir Gawain Westray, K.C.M.G., C.B.E.

Bell, Sir (George) Raymond, K.C.M.G., C.B.

Bell, Sir John Lowthian, Bt. (1885).

Bell, Sir (William) Ewart, K.C.B.

Bell, Sir William Hollin Dayrell Morrison-, Bt. (1905).

Bellew, Sir Arthur John Grattan-, Kt., C.M.G., Q.C.

Bellew, Hon. Sir George Rothe, K.C.B., K.C.V.O., F.S.A.

Bellew, Sir Henry Charles Gratton-, Bt. (1838).

Bellinger, Sir Robert Ian, G.B.E.

Bellingham, Sir Noel Peter Roger, Bt. (1796).

Bemrose, Sir (John) Maxwell, Kt.

Benn, *Capt.* Sir (Patrick Ion) Hamilton, Bt. (1920).

Benn, Sir John Andrews, Bt. (1914).

Bennett, Sir Charles Moihi Te Arawaka, Kt., D.S.O.

Bennett, Sir Frederic Mackarness, Kt., M.P.

Bennett, Sir Hubert, Kt.

Bennett, *Lt.-Gen.* Sir Phillip Harvey, K.B.E.

Bennett, Sir Reginald Frederick Brittain, Kt., V.R.D.

Bennett, Sir Ronald Wilfrid Murdoch, Bt. (1929).

Bennett, Sir William Gordon, Kt.

Benson, Sir Arthur Edward Trevor, G.C.M.G.

Benson, *Rev.* Sir (Clarence) Irving, Kt., C.B.E.

Benthall, Sir (Arthur) Paul, K.B.E.

Berger, *Vice-Adm.* Sir Peter Egerton Capel, K.C.B., M.V.O., D.S.C.

Berkeley, Sir Lennox Randal Francis, Kt., C.B.E.

Berlin, Sir Isaiah, Kt., O.M., C.B.E.

Bernard, Sir Dallas Edmund, Bt. (1954).

Berney, Sir Julian Reedham Stuart, Bt. (1620).

Berrill, Sir Kenneth Ernest, K.C.B.

Berry, *Hon.* Sir Anthony George, Kt., M.P.

Berthon, *Vice-Adm.* Sir Stephen Ferrier, K.C.B.

Berthoud, Sir Eric Alfred, K.C.M.G.

Bethune, Sir Alexander Maitland Sharp, Bt. (s. 1683).

Bethune, *Hon.* Sir (Walter) Angus, Kt.

Bevan, Sir Martyn Evan Evans, Bt. (1958).

Bevan, Sir Timothy Hugh, Kt.

Beynon, *Prof.* Sir (William John) Granville, Kt., C.B.E., PH.D., D.SC., F.R.S.

Bibby, *Maj.* Sir (Arthur) Harold, Bt., D.S.O. (1959).

Biddulph, Sir Stuart Royden, Bt. (1664).

Bide, Sir Austin Ernest, Kt.

Biggs, Sir Lionel William, Kt.

Biggs, Sir Norman Paris, Kt.

Biggs-Davison, Sir John Alec, Kt., M.P.

Bing, Sir Rudolf Franz Josef, K.B.E.

Bingham, *Hon.* Sir Thomas Henry, Kt.

Bird, *Lt.-Gen.* Sir Clarence August, K.C.I.E., C.B., D.S.O.

Bird, Sir Cyril Pangbourne, Kt.

Bird, Sir Richard Geoffrey Chapman, Bt. (1922).

Bird, *Col.* Sir Richard Dawnay Martin-, Kt., C.B.E., T.D.

Birkin, Sir Charles Lloyd, Bt. (1905).

Birkmyre, Sir Henry, Bt. (1921).

Birsay, Lord, *see* Leslie, Sir Harald.

Bishop, Sir Frederick Arthur, Kt., C.B., C.V.O.

Bishop, Sir George Sidney, Kt., C.B., O.B.E.

Bishop, *Instructor Rear-Adm.,* Sir William, K.B.E., C.B.

Bjelke-Petersen, *Hon.* Sir Johannes, K.C.M.G.

Black, Sir Cyril Wilson, Kt.

Black, *Prof.* Sir Douglas Andrew Kilgour, Kt., M.D., F.R.C.P.

Black, Sir Hermann David, Kt.

Black, Sir James Whyte, Kt., F.R.C.P., F.R.S..

Black, Sir Robert Brown, G.C.M.G., O.B.E.

Black, Sir Robert David, Bt. (1922).

Blackburn, *Hon.* Sir Richard Arthur, Kt., O.B.E.

Blacker, *General* Sir Cecil Hugh, G.C.B., O.B.E., M.C.

Blackett, Sir George William, Bt. (1673).

Blackwell, Sir Basil Davenport, Kt.

Blackwood, Sir Francis (George), Bt. (1814).

Blagden, Sir John Ramsay, Kt., O.B.E., T.D.

Blair, *Maj.* Sir Alastair Campbell, K.C.V.O., T.D.

Blair, *Lt.-Gen.* Sir Chandos, K.C.V.O., O.B.E., M.C.

Blair, Sir James Hunter-, Bt. (1786).

Blake, Sir Alfred Lapthorn, K.C.V.O., M.C.

Blake, Sir (Francis) Michael, Bt. (1907).

Blake, Sir (Thomas) Richard (Valentine), Bt. (I 1622).

Blaker, Sir John, Bt. (1919).

Blaker, *Rt. Hon.* Sir Peter Allan Renshaw, K.C.M.G., M.P.

Blakiston, Sir Ferguson Arthur James, Bt. (1763).

Bland, Sir Henry Armand, Kt., C.B.E.

Bland, *Lt.-Col.* Sir Simon Claud Michael, K.C.V.O.

Blaxter, Sir Kenneth Lyon, Kt., F.R.S., F.R.S.E.

Blennerhassett, Sir (Marmaduke) Adrian Francis William, Bt. (1809).

Blois, Sir Charles Nicholas Gervase, Bt. (1686).

Blomefield, Sir Thomas Charles Peregrine, Bt. (1807).

Bloomfield, *Hon.* Sir John Stoughton, Kt., Q.C.

Blosse, *Capt.* Sir Richard Hely Lynch-, Bt. (1622).

Blount, Sir Walter Edward Alpin, Bt., D.S.C. (1642).

Blundell, Sir (Edward) Denis, G.C.M.G., G.C.V.O., K.B.E.

Blundell, Sir Michael, K.B.E.

Blunden, Sir William, Bt. (I 1766).

Blunt, Sir David Richard Reginald Harvey, Bt. (1720).

Blyde, Sir Henry Ernest, K.B.E.

Boardman, Sir Kenneth Ormrod, Kt.

Bodilly, *Hon.* Sir Jocelyn, Kt., V.R.D.

Boevey, Sir Thomas Michael Blake Crawley-, Bt. (1784).

Boileau, Sir Guy (Francis), Bt. (1838).

Boles, Sir Jeremy John Fortescue, Bt. (1922).

Boles, Sir John Dennis, Kt., M.B.E.

Bolland, Sir Edwin, K.C.M.G.

Bollers, *Hon.* Sir Harold Brodie Smith, Kt.

Bolte, *Hon.* Sir Henry Edward, G.C.M.G.

Bolton, Sir Frederic Bernard, Kt., M.C.

Bonallack, Sir Richard Frank, Kt., C.B.E.

Bonar, Sir Herbert Vernon, Kt., C.B.E.

Bond, Sir Kenneth Raymond Boyden, Kt.

Bondi, *Prof.* Sir Hermann, K.C.B., F.R.S.

Bonham, *Maj.* Sir Antony Lionel Thomas, Bt. (1852).

Bonsall, Sir Arthur Wilfred, K.C.M.G., C.B.E.

Bonsor, Sir Nicholas Cosmo, Bt., M.P. (1925).

Boolell, Sir Satcam, Kt.

Boon, Sir Peter Coleman, Kt.

Boord, Sir Nicolas John Charles, Bt. (1896).

Booth, Sir Christopher Charles, Kt., M.D., F.R.C.P.

Booth, Sir Douglas Allen, Bt. (1916).

Booth, Sir Gordon, K.C.M.G., C.V.O.

Booth, Sir Michael Savile Gore-, Bt. (I 1760).

Booth, Sir Robert Camm, Kt., C.B.E., T.D.

Boothby, Sir Hugo Robert Brooke, Bt. (1660).

Boreel, Sir Francis David, Bt. (1645).

Boreham, Sir (Arthur) John, K.C.B.

Boreham, *Hon.* Sir Leslie Kenneth Edward, Kt.

Bornu, The Waziri of, K.C.M.G., C.B.E.

Borrie, Sir Gordon Johnson, Kt.

Borthwick, Sir John Thomas, Bt. M.B.E. (1908).

Bossom, *Hon.* Sir Clive, Bt. (1953).

Boswall, Sir (Thomas) Alford Houstoun-, Bt. (1836).

Boswell, *Lt.-Gen.* Sir Alexander Crawford Simpson, K.C.B., C.B.E.

Bottomley, Sir James Reginald Alfred, K.C.M.G.

Boughey, Sir John George Fletcher, Bt. (1798). .

Boulton, Sir (Harold Hugh) Christian, Bt. (1905).

Boulton, Sir William Whytehead, Bt., C.B.E., T.D. (1944).

Bourne, Sir (John) Wilfrid, K.C.B.

Bovell, *Hon.* Sir (William) Stewart, Kt.

Bowater, Sir (John) Vansittart, Bt. (1914).

Bowater, Sir Euan David Vansittart, Bt. (1939).

Bowden, Sir Frank, Bt. (1915).

Bowen, Sir Geoffrey Fraser, Kt.

Bowen, *Hon.* Sir Nigel Hubert, K.B.E.

Bowen, Sir Thomas Frederic Charles, Bt. (1921).

Bower, *Air Marshal* Sir Leslie William Clement, K.C.B., D.S.O., D.F.C.

Bower, *Lt.-Gen.* Sir Roger Herbert, K.C.B., K.B.E.

Bowes, Sir (Harold) Leslie, K.C.M.G., C.B.E.

Bowlby, Sir Anthony Hugh Mostyn, Bt. (1923).

Bowman, Sir George, Bt. (1961).

Bowman, Sir John Paget, Bt. (1884).

Bowman-Shaw, Sir (George) Neville, Kt.

Bowmar, Sir Charles Erskine, Kt.

Boxer, *Air Vice-Marshal* Sir Alan Hunter Cachemaille, K.C.V.O., C.B., D.S.O., D.F.C.

Boyce, Sir Robert Charles Leslie, Bt. (1952).

Boyd, Sir Alexander Walter, Bt. (1916).

Boyd, Sir John McFarlane, Kt., C.B.E.

Boyd, *Prof.* Sir Robert Lewis Fullarton, Kt., C.B.E., D.SC., F.R.S.

Boyes, Sir Brian Gerald Barratt-, K.B.E.

Boyle, *Marshal of the Royal Air Force* Sir Dermot Alexander, G.C.B., K.C.V.O., K.B.E., A.F.C.

Boyle, Sir Lawrence, Kt., PH.D.

Boyle, Sir Stephen Gurney, Bt. (1904).

Boyne, Sir Henry Brian, Kt., C.B.E.

Boynton, Sir John Keyworth, Kt., M.C.

Brabham, Sir John Arthur, Kt., O.B.E.

Bradbury, *Surgeon Vice-Adm.* Sir Eric Blackburn, K.B.E., C.B.

Bradford, Sir Edward Alexander Slade, Bt. (1902).

Bradlaw, *Prof.* Sir Robert Vivian, Kt., C.B.E.

Bradman, Sir Donald George, Kt.

Bradshaw, *Lt.-Gen.* Sir Richard Phillip, K.B.E.

Brain, Sir (Henry) Norman, K.B.E., C.M.G.

Braine, Sir Bernard Richard, Kt., M.P..

Braithwaite, Sir (Joseph) Franklin Madders, Kt.

Bramall, *Field Marshal* Sir Edwin Noel Westby, G.C.B., O.B.E., M.C.

Bramall, Sir (Ernest) Ashley, Kt.

Bramley, *Prof.* Sir Paul Anthony, Kt.

Branch, Sir William Allan Patrick, Kt.

Brancker, Sir (John Eustace) Theodore, Kt., Q.C.

Branigan, Sir Patrick Francis, Kt., Q.C.

Bray, Sir Theodor Charles, Kt., C.B.E.

Braynen, Sir Alvin Rudolph, Kt.

Brearley, Sir Norman, Kt., C.B.E., D.S.O., M.C., A.F.C.

Bremridge, Sir John Henry, K.B.E.

Brennan, *Hon.* Sir (Francis) Gerard, K.B.E.

Brett, Sir Lionel, Kt.

Brickwood, Sir Basil Greame, Bt. (1927).

Bridges, *Hon.* Sir Phillip Rodney, Kt., C.M.G.

Briggs, *Hon.* Sir Geoffrey Gould, Kt.

Bright, *Hon.* Sir Charles Hart, K.B.E., Q.C.

Brinckman, *Col.* Sir Roderick Napoleon, Bt., D.S.O., M.C. (1831).

Brinton, *Maj.* Sir (Esme) Tatton (Cecil), Kt.

Brisco, Sir Donald Gilfrid, Bt. (1782).

Briscoe, Sir John Leigh Charlton, Bt., D.F.C. (1910).

Brise, Sir John Archibald Ruggles-, Bt., C.B., O.B.E., T.D. (1935).

Bristow, *Hon.* Sir Peter Henry Rowley, Kt.

Britton, Sir Edward Louis, Kt., C.B.E.

Broackes, Sir Nigel, Kt.

Broadbent, Sir Ewen, K.C.B., C.M.G.

Broadbent, Sir William Francis, Bt. (1893).

Broadhurst, *Air Chief Marshal* Sir Harry, G.C.B., K.B.E., D.S.O., D.F.C., A.F.C.

Brockhoff, Sir Jack Stuart, Kt.

Brocklebank, Sir Aubrey Thomas, Bt. (1885).

Brockman, *Vice-Adm.* Sir Ronald Vernon, K.C.B., C.V.O., C.S.I., C.I.E., C.B.E.

Brockman, *Hon.* Sir Thomas Charles Drake-, Kt., D.F.C.

Brodie, Sir Benjamin David Ross, Bt. (1834).

Brogan, *Lt.-Gen.* Sir Mervyn Francis, K.B.E., C.B.

Bromhead, Sir John Desmond Gonville, Bt. (1806).

Bromley, Sir Rupert Charles, Bt. (1757).

Bromley, Sir Thomas Eardley, K.C.M.G.

Brook, Sir Robin, Kt., C.M.G., O.B.E.

Brooke, Sir Francis George Windham, Bt. (1903).

Brooke, Sir Alistair Weston, Bt. (1919).

Brooke, Sir (Norman) Richard (Rowley), Kt., C.B.E.

Brooke, Sir Richard Neville, Bt. (1662).

Brookes, Sir Wilfred Deakin, Kt., C.B.E., D.S.O.

Brooksbank, Sir Edward Nicholas, Bt. (1919).

Broom, *Air Marshal* Sir Ivor Gordon, K.C.B., C.B.E., D.S.O., D.F.C., A.F.C.

Brotherston, Sir John Howie Flint, Kt., M.D., F.R.C.P.

Broughton, *Air Marshal* Sir Charles, K.B.E., C.B.

Broughton, Sir Evelyn Delves, Bt. (1661).

Broun, Sir Lionel John Law, Bt. (s. 1686).

Brown, Sir Allen Stanley, Kt., C.B.E.

Brown, Sir (Arthur James) Stephen, K.B.E.

Brown, *Lt.-Col.* Sir Charles Frederick Richmond, Bt. (1863).

Brown, Sir (Charles) James Officer, Kt., M.D

Brown, Sir (Cyril) Maxwell Palmer, K.C.B., C.M.G.

Brown, Sir David, Kt.

Brown, *Vice-Adm.* Sir David Worthington, K.C.B.

Brown, Sir Derrick Holden-, Kt.

Brown, Sir Douglas Denison, Kt.

Brown, Sir Edward Joseph, Kt., M.B.E.

Brown, *Prof.* Sir (Ernest) Henry Phelps, Kt., M.B.E., F.B.A.

Brown, Sir (Frederick Herbert) Stanley, Kt., C.B.E.

Brown, Sir John Douglas Keith, Kt.

Brown, Sir John Gilbert Newton, Kt., C.B.E.

Brown, Sir Mervyn, K.C.M.G., O.B.E..

Brown, *Hon.* Sir Ralph Kilner, Kt., O.B.E., T.D.

Brown, Sir Raymond Frederick, Kt., O.B.E.

Brown, Sir Robert Crichton-, K.C.M.G., C.B.E., T.D.

Brown, *Rt. Hon.* Sir Stephen, Kt.

Brown, Sir Thomas, Kt.

Brown, *Air Commodore* Sir Vernon Sydney, Kt., C.B., O.B.E.

Brown, Sir William Brian Piggott-, Bt. (1903).

Browne, Sir (Edward) Humphrey, Kt., C.B.E.

Browne, *Rt. Hon.* Sir Patrick Reginald Evelyn, Kt., O.B.E., T.D.

Browne, Sir Thomas Anthony Gore, Kt.

Brownrigg, Sir Nicholas (Gawen), Bt. (1816).

Bruce, Sir Arthur Atkinson, K.B.E., M.C.

Bruce, Sir (Francis) Michael Ian, Bt. (s. 1628).

Bruce, Sir Hervey James Hugh, Bt. (1804).

Bruce, *Rt. Hon.* Sir (James) Roualeyn Hovell-Thurlow-Cumming-, Kt.

Brunner, Sir John Henry Kilian, Bt. (1895).

Brunton, Sir (Edward Francis) Lauder, Bt. (1908).

Bryan, Sir Andrew Meikle, Kt.

Bryan, Sir Arthur, Kt.

Bryan, Sir Paul Elmore Oliver, Kt., D.S.O., M.C., M.P.

Bryant, Sir Arthur Wynne Morgan, Kt., C.H., C.B.E.

Bryce, *Hon.* Sir (William) Gordon, Kt., C.B.E.

Bryden, Sir William James, Kt., C.B.E., Q.C.

Bryson, *Vice-Adm.* Sir Lindsay Sutherland, K.C.B.

Buchan, Sir John, Kt., C.M.G.

Buchanan, Sir Charles Alexander James Leith-, Bt. (1775).

Buchanan, Sir Andrew George, Bt. (1878).

Buchanan, *Prof.* Sir Colin Douglas, Kt., C.B.E.

Buchanan, *Vice-Adm.* Sir Peter William, K.B.E.

Buck, Sir (Philip) Antony (Fyson), Kt., Q.C., M.P.

Buckley, *Rt. Hon.* Sir Denys Burton, Kt., M.B.E.

Buckley, Sir John William, Kt.

Buckley, *Rear-Adm.* Sir Kenneth Robertson, K.B.E.

Buckley, *Lt.-Comdr.* Sir (Peter) Richard, K.C.V.O.

Bulkeley, Sir Richard Harry David Williams-, Bt., T.D. (1661).

Bull, Sir George, Bt. (1922).

Bull, Sir Graham MacGregor, Kt., M.D., F.R.C.P.

Bull, Sir Walter Edward Avenon, K.C.V.O.

Bullard, Sir Julian Leonard, K.C.M.G.

Bullus, Sir Eric Edward, Kt.

Bulmer, Sir William Peter, Kt.

Bunbury, Sir (John) William Napier, Bt. (1681).

Bunbury, Sir (Richard David) Michael Richardson-, Bt. (I 1787).

Bunch, Sir Austin Wyeth, Kt., C.B.E.

Bunting, Sir (Edward) John, K.B.E.

Burbidge, Sir Herbert Dudley, Bt. (1916).

Burbury, *Hon.* Sir Stanley Charles, K.C.M.G., K.C.V.O., K.B.E.

Burden, Sir Frederick Frank Arthur, Kt.

Burder, Sir John Henry, Kt.

Burdett, Sir Savile Aylmer, Bt. (1665).

Burgen, Sir Arnold Stanley Vincent, Kt., F.R.S.

Burgess, *General* Sir Edward Arthur, K.C.B., O.B.E.

Burgess, Sir John Lawie, Kt., O.B.E., T.D.

Burgh, Sir John Charles, K.C.M.G., C.B.

Burke, Sir Aubrey Francis, Kt., O.B.E.

Burke, *Prof.* Sir Joseph Terence, K.B.E.

Burke, Sir Thomas Stanley, Bt. (I 1797).

Burley, Sir Victor George, Kt., C.B.E.

Burman, Sir (John) Charles, Kt.

Burman, Sir Stephen France, Kt., C.B.E.

Burnet, Sir (Frank) Macfarlane, O.M., K.B.E., M.D., F.R.S.

Burnet, Sir James William Alexander (Sir Alastair Burnet), Kt.

Burnett, *Air Chief Marshal* Sir Brian Kenyon, G.C.B., D.F.C., A.F.C.

Burnett, Sir David Humphery, Bt., M.B.E., T.D. (1913).

Burney, Sir Anthony George Bernard, Kt., O.B.E.

Burney, Sir Cecil Denniston, Bt. (1921).

Burns, Sir Charles Ritchie, K.B.E., M.D.

Burns, Sir John Crawford, Kt.

Burns, Sir Malcolm McRae, K.B.E.

Burns, Sir Terence, Kt.

Burns, *Maj.-Gen.* Sir (Walter Arthur) George, K.C.V.O., C.B., D.S.O., O.B.E., M.C.

Burrell, *Vice-Adm.* Sir Henry Mackay, K.B.E., C.B.

Burrell, Sir Walter Raymond, Bt., C.B.E., T.D. (1774).

Burrenchobay, Sir Dayendranath, K.B.E., C.M.G., C.V.O.

Burrows, Sir Bernard Alexander Brocas, G.C.M.G.

Burrows, Sir (Robert) John (Formby), Kt.

Burston, Sir Samuel Gerald Wood, Kt., O.B.E.

Burt, *Hon.* Sir Francis Theodore Page, K.C.M.G.

Burton, Sir Carlisle Archibald, Kt., O.B.E.

Burton, Sir George Vernon Kennedy, Kt., C.B.E.

Burton, *Air Marshal* Sir Harry, K.C.B., C.B.E., D.S.O.

Burton-Chadwick, Sir Joshua Kenneth, Bt. (1935).

Busby, Sir Matthew, Kt., C.B.E.

Bush, *Hon.* Sir Brian Drex, Kt.

Bush, *Admiral* Sir John Fitzroy Duyland, G.C.B., D.S.C.

Busk, Sir Douglas Laird, K.C.M.G.

Butler, Sir Clifford Charles, Kt., Ph.D., F.R.S.

Butler, Sir Michael Dacres, G.C.M.G.

Butler, Sir (Reginald) Michael (Thomas), Bt. (1922).

Butler, *Hon.* Sir Richard Clive, Kt.

Butler, *Col.* Sir Thomas Pierce, Bt., C.V.O., D.S.O., O.B.E. (1628).

Butt, Sir (Alfred) Kenneth Dudley, Bt. (1929).

Butterfield, *Prof.* Sir (William) John (Hughes), Kt., O.B.E., D.M., F.R.C.P.

Butterworth, Sir (George) Neville, Kt.

Buxton, Sir Thomas Fowell Victor, Bt. (1840).

Buzzard, Sir Anthony Farquhar, Bt. (1929).

Byers, Sir Maurice Hearne, Kt., C.B.E., Q.C.

Byford, Sir Lawrence, Kt., C.B.E., Q.P.M.

Byrne, Sir Clarence Askew, Kt., O.B.E., D.S.C.

Cable, Sir James Eric, K.C.V.O., C.M.G.

Cadbury, Sir (George) Adrian (Hayhurst), Kt.

Cadell, *Vice-Adm.* Sir John Frederick, K.B.E.

Cadwallader, Sir John, Kt.

Caffyn, *Brig.* Sir Edward Roy, K.B.E., C.B., T.D.

Cahn, Sir Albert Jonas, Bt. (1934).

Cain, Sir Edward Thomas, Kt., C.B.E.

Caine, Sir Sydney, K.C.M.G.

Cairncross, Sir Alexander Kirkland, K.C.M.G.

Cairns, *Rt. Hon.* Sir David Arnold Scott, Kt.

Cakobau, *Ratu* Sir George, G.C.M.G., G.C.V.O., O.B.E., Royal Victorian Chain.

Caldicott, *Hon.* Sir John Moore, K.B.E., C.M.G.

Caldwell, *Surgeon Vice-Adm.* Sir (Eric) Dick, K.B.E., C.B.

Callaghan, Sir Allan Robert, Kt., C.M.G.

Callaghan, Sir Bede Bertrand, Kt., C.B.E.

Callard, Sir Eric John, Kt.

Callaway, *Prof.* Sir Frank Adams, Kt., C.M.G., O.B.E.

Calley, Sir Henry Algernon, Kt., D.S.O., D.F.C.

Callinan, Sir Bernard James, Kt., C.B.E., D.S.O., M.C.

Calthorpe, *Brig.* Sir Richard Hamilton Anstruther-Gough-, Bt., C.B.E. (1929).

Cameron, *Lt.-Gen.* Sir Alexander Maurice, K.B.E., C.B., M.C.

Cameron of Lochiel, Sir Donald Hamish, K.T., C.V.O., T.D.

Cameron, Sir (Eustace) John, Kt., C.B.E.

Cameron, Sir James Clark, Kt., C.B.E., T.D.

Cameron, *Hon.* Sir John, Kt., D.S.C., Q.C. (Lord Cameron).

Cameron, Sir John Watson, Kt., O.B.E.

Camilleri, *His Hon.* Sir Luigi Antonio, Kt, LL.D.

Campbell, Sir Alan Hugh, G.C.M.G.

Campbell, Sir Clifford Clarence, G.C.M.G., G.C.V.O.

Campbell, Sir Colin Moffat, Bt., M.C. (s. 1668).

Campbell, *Col.* Sir Guy Theophilus Halswell, Bt., O.B.E., M.C. (1815).

Campbell, *Maj.-Gen.* Sir Hamish Manus, K.B.E., C.B.

Campbell, Sir Ilay Mark, Bt. (1808).

Campbell, Sir (James) Keith, Kt., C.B.E.

Campbell, Sir Matthew, K.B.E., C.B., F.R.S.E.

Campbell, Sir Niall Alexander Hamilton, Bt. (1831).

Campbell, Sir Ralph Abercromby, Kt.

Campbell, Sir Robin Auchinbreck, Bt. (S. 1628).

Campbell, Sir Thomas Cockburn-, Bt. (1821).

Campbell, *Hon.* Sir Walter Benjamin, Kt.

Campion, Sir Harry, Kt., C.B., C.B.E.

Cantley, *Hon.* Sir Joseph Donaldson, Kt., O.B.E.

Carberry, Sir John Edward Doston, Kt.

Carden, *Lt.-Col.* Sir Henry Christopher, Bt., O.B.E. (1887).

Carden, Sir John Craven, Bt. (I 1787).

Carew, Sir Rivers Verain, Bt. (1661).

Carey, Sir Peter Willoughby, G.C.B.

Carlill, *Vice-Adm.* Sir Stephen Hope, K.B.E., C.B., D.S.O.

Carmichael, Sir David Peter William Gibson-Craig-, Bt. (s. 1702 and 1831).

Carmichael, Sir John, K.B.E.

Carnac, *Rev. Canon* Sir (Thomas) Nicholas Rivett-, Bt. (1836).

Carnegie, *Lt.-Gen.* Sir Robin Macdonald, K.C.B., O.B.E.

Carnegie, Sir Roderick Howard, Kt.

Carnwath, Sir Andrew Hunter, K.C.V.O.

Caröe, Sir (Einar) Athelstan (Gordon), Kt., C.B.E.

Carr, Sir James Henry Brownlow, Kt.

Carr, *Air Marshal* Sir John Darcy Baker-, K.B.E., C.B., A.F.C.

Carreras, *Lt.-Col.* Sir James, K.C.V.O., M.B.E.

Carrick, *Hon.* Sir John Leslie, K.C.M.G.

Carter, Sir (Arthur) Desmond Bonham-, Kt., T.D.

Carter, Sir Charles Frederick, Kt., F.B.A.

Carter, Sir Derrick Hunton, Kt., T.D.

Carter, *Hon.* Sir Douglas Julian, K.C.M.G.

Carter, Sir John, Kt., Q.C.

Carter, *His Hon.* Sir Walker Kelly, Kt., Q.C.

Carter, Sir William Oscar, Kt.

Cartland, Sir George Barrington, Kt., C.M.G.

Cary, Sir Roger Hugh, Bt. (1955).

Cash, Sir Gerald Christopher, G.C.M.G., K.C.V.O., O.B.E.

Cass, Sir John Patrick, Kt., O.B.E.

Cassel, Sir Harold Felix, Bt., T.D., Q.C. (1920).

Cassels, *Field Marshal* Sir (Archibald) James Halkett, G.C.B., K.B.E., D.S.O.

Cassels, *Vice-Adm.* Sir Simon Alastair Cassillis, K.C.B., C.B.E.

Cassidi, *Admiral* Sir (Arthur) Desmond, G.C.B.

Casson, Sir Hugh Maxwell, K.C.V.O., P.R.A., F.R.I.B.A.

Cater, Sir Jack, K.B.E.

Cater, Sir John Robert, Kt.

Catherwood, Sir (Henry) Frederick (Ross), Kt.

Catling, Sir Richard Charles, Kt., C.M.G., O.B.E.

Cato, *Hon.* Sir Arnott Samuel, K.C.M.G.

Caughey, Sir Thomas Harcourt Clarke, K.B.E.

Caulfield, *Hon.* Sir Bernard, Kt.

Cave, Sir Charles Edward Coleridge, Bt. (1896).

Cave, Sir (Charles) Philip Haddon-, K.B.E., C.M.G.

Cave, Sir Richard Guy, Kt., M.C.

Cave, Sir Richard Phillip, K.C.V.O., C.B.

Cave, Sir Robert Cave-Browne-, Bt. (1641).

Cawley, Sir Charles Mills, Kt., C.B.E., Ph.D.

Cayley, Sir Digby William David, Bt. (1661).

Cayzer, Sir James Arthur, Bt. (1904).

Cecil, *Rear-Adm.* Sir (Oswald) Nigel Amherst, K.B.E., C.B.

Chacksfield, *Air Vice-Marshal* Sir Bernard Albert, K.B.E., C.B.

Chadwick, Sir Albert Edward, Kt., C.M.G., M.S.M.

Chadwick, Sir John Edward, K.C.M.G.

Chadwick, *Rev. Prof.* (William) Owen, O.M., K.B.E., F.B.A.

Chalk, *Hon.* Sir Gordon William Wesley, K.B.E.

Chamberlain, *Hon.* Sir Reginald Roderic St. Clair, Kt.

Chan, *Rt. Hon.* Sir Julius, K.B.E.

Chance, Sir Roger James Ferguson, Bt., M.C. (1900).

Chancellor, Sir Christopher John, Kt., C.M.G.

Chandler, Sir Geoffrey, Kt., C.B.E.

Chaney, *Hon.* Sir Frederick Charles, K.B.E., A.F.C.

Chapman, Sir George Alan, Kt.

Chapman, Sir Robert Macgowan, Bt., C.B.E., T.D. (1958).

Chapman, *Hon.* Sir Stephen, Kt.

Charles, Sir Joseph Quentin, Kt.

Charnley, Sir (William) John, Kt., C.B.

Chatterton, *Rev.* Percy, K.B.E., C.M.G.

Chau, *Hon.* Sir Sik-Nin, Kt., C.B.E.

Chaytor, Sir George Reginald, Bt. (1831).

Cheadle, Sir Eric Wallers, Kt., C.B.E.

Cheeketts, *Sqn. Ldr.* Sir David John, K.C.V.O.

Cheetham, Sir Nicolas John Alexander, K.C.M.G.

Chegwidden, Sir Thomas Sidney, Kt., C.B., C.V.O.

Chester, Sir (Daniel) Norman, Kt., C.B.E.

Chesterman, Sir (Dudley) Ross, Kt., Ph.D.

Chesterton, Sir Oliver Sidney, Kt., M.C.

Chetwynd, Sir Arthur Ralph Talbot, Bt. (1795).

Cheyne, Sir Joseph Lister Watson, Bt., O.B.E. (1908).

Chichester, Sir (Edward) John, Bt. (1641).

Child, Sir (Coles John) Jeremy, Bt. (1919).

Chilton, *Air Marshal* Sir (Charles) Edward, K.B.E., C.B.

Chilton, *Brig.* Sir Frederick Oliver, Kt., C.B.E., D.S.O.

Chilver, Sir (Amos) Henry, Kt., D.S.C., F.R.S.

Chitty, Sir Thomas Willes, Bt. (1924).

Cholmeley, Sir Montague John, Bt. (1806).

Christie, Sir George William Langham, Kt.

Christie, *Hon.* Sir Vernon Howard Colville, Kt.

Christie, Sir William, Kt., M.B.E.

Christison, *Gen.* Sir (Alexander Frank) Philip, Bt., G.B.E., C.B., D.S.O., M.C. (1871).

Christofas, Sir Kenneth Cavendish, K.C.M.G., M.B.E.

Christopherson, Sir Derman Guy, Kt., O.B.E., D.Phil., F.R.S.

Chung, Sir Sze-yuen, Kt., C.B.E.

Cilento, Sir Raphael West, Kt., M.D.

Clapham, Sir Michael John Sinclair, K.B.E.

Claringbull, Sir (Gordon) Frank, Kt., Ph.D.

Clark, Sir George Anthony, Bt. (1917).

Clark, Sir (Gordon Colvin) Lindesay, K.B.E., C.M.G., M.C.

Clark, Sir John Allen, Kt.

Clark, Sir John Douglas, Bt. (1886).

Clark, Sir John Stewart-, Bt. (1918).

Clark, Sir Robert Anthony, Kt., D.S.C.

Clark, Sir Robin Chichester-, Kt.

Clark, Sir (Thomas) Fife, Kt., C.B.E.

Clark, Sir William Gibson, Kt., M.P.

Clarke, Sir (Charles Mansfield) Tobias, Bt. (1831).

Clarke, *Prof.* Sir Cyril Astley, K.B.E., M.D., Sc.D., F.R.S., F.R.C.P.

Clarke, Sir Ellis Emmanuel Innocent, G.C.M.G.

Clarke, Sir (Henry) Ashley, G.C.M.G., G.C.V.O.

Clarke, Sir Henry Osmond Osmond-, K.C.V.O., C.B.E.

Clarke, Sir Jonathan Dennis, Kt.

Clarke, Sir Rupert William John, Bt., M.B.E. (1882).

Clay, Sir Henry Felix, Bt. (1841).

Clayden, *Rt. Hon.* Sir (Henry) John Kt.

Clayson, Sir Eric Maurice, Kt.

Clayton, Sir Arthur Harold, Bt., D.S.C. (1732).

Clayton, *Air Marshal* Sir Gareth Thomas Butler, K.C.B., D.F.C.

Clayton, *Admiral* Sir Richard Pilkington, G.C.B.

Clayton, Sir Robert James, Kt., C.B.E.

Clayton, *Prof.* Sir Stanley George, Kt., M.D.

Cleary, Sir Joseph Jackson, Kt.

Clegg, Sir Alexander Bradshaw, Kt.

Clegg, Sir Cuthbert Barwick, Kt.

Clegg, Sir Walter, Kt., M.P.

Clements, Sir John Selby, Kt., C.B.E.

Cleminson, Sir James Arnold Stacey, Kt., M.C.

Clerk, Sir John Dutton, Bt., C.B.E., V.R.D. (s. 1679).

Clerke, Sir John Edward Longueville, Bt. (1660).

Clifford, Sir (Geoffrey) Miles, K.B.E., C.M.G., E.D.

Clifford, Sir Roger Charles Joseph Gerrard, Bt. (1887).

Clothier, Sir Cecil Montacute, K.C.B., Q.C.

Clowes, *Col.* Sir Henry Nelson, K.C.V.O., D.S.O., O.B.E.

Clucas, Sir Kenneth Henry, K.C.B.

Clutterbuck, *Vice-Adm.* Sir David Granville, K.B.E., C.B.

Coates, Sir Ernest William, Kt., C.M.G.

Coates, Sir Frederick Gregory Lindsay, Bt. (1921).

Coats, Sir Alastair Francis Stuart, Bt. (1905).

Cobban, Sir James Macdonald, Kt., C.B.E., T.D.

Cochrane, Sir (Henry) Marc (Sursock), Bt. (1903).

Cockburn, Sir John Elliot, Bt. (s. 1671).

Cockburn, Sir Robert, K.B.E., C.B., Ph.D.

Cockcroft, Sir Wilfred Halliday, Kt., D.Phil.

Cockerell, Sir Christopher Sydney, Kt., C.B.E., F.R.S.

Cockram, Sir John, Kt.

Cocks, Sir (Thomas George) Barnett, K.C.B., O.B.E.

Codrington, Sir Simon Francis Bethell, Bt. (1876).

Codrington, Sir William Alexander, Bt. (1721).

Coghill, Sir Egerton James Nevill Tobias, Bt. (1778).

Cohen, Sir Bernard Nathaniel Waley-, Bt. (1961).

Cohen, Sir Edward, Kt.

Cohen, Sir Rex Arthur Louis, K.B.E.

Coldstream, Sir George Phillips, K.C.B., K.C.V.O., Q.C.

Coldstream, *Prof.* Sir William Menzies, Kt., C.B.E.

Cole, Sir (Alexander) Colin, K.C.V.O., T.D.

Cole, Sir David Lee, K.C.M.G., M.C.

Cole, Sir (Robert) William, Kt.

Coles, Sir Kenneth Frank, Kt.

Coles, Sir Norman Cameron, Kt.

Colfox, Sir (William) John, Bt. (1939).

Collett, Sir Ian Seymour, Bt. (1934).

Collett, Sir (Thomas) Kingsley, Kt., C.B.E.

Collier, *Air Vice-Marshal* Sir (Alfred) Conrad, K.C.B., C.B.E.

Colingwood, *Lt.-Gen.* Sir (Richard) George, K.B.E., C.B., D.S.O.

Collins, Sir Arthur James Robert, K.C.V.O.

Collins, Sir Geoffrey Abdy, Kt.

Collins, *Vice-Adm.* Sir John Augustine, K.B.E., C.B.

Colman, Sir Michael Jeremiah, Bt. (1907).

Colquhoun, *Maj.-Gen.* Sir Cyril Harry, K.C.V.O., C.B., O.B.E.

Colquhoun of Luss, Sir Ivar Iain, Bt. (1786).

Colt, Sir Edward William Dutton Bt. (1694).

Colthurst, Sir Richard La Touche, Bt. (1744).

Colville, Sir (Henry) Cecil, Kt.

Colville, Sir John Rupert, Kt., C.B., C.V.O.

Combs, Sir Willis Ide, K.C.V.O., C.M.G.

Compston, *Vice-Adm.* Sir Peter Maxwell, K.C.B.

Compton, Sir Edmund Gerald, G.C.B., K.B.E.

Compton Miller, Sir John (Francis), Kt., M.B.E., T.D.

Comyn, *Hon.* Sir James, Kt.

Conant, Sir John Ernest Michael, Bt. (1954).

Connell, Sir Charles Gibson, Kt.

Conran, Sir Terence Orby, Kt.

Constable, Sir Robert Frederick Strickland-, Bt. (1641).

Constantine, *Air Chief Marshal* Sir Hugh Alex, K.B.E., C.B., D.S.O.

Cook, Sir Christopher Wymondham Rayner Herbert, Bt. (1886).

Cook, Sir (Philip) Halford, Kt., O.B.E.

Cook, Sir William Richard Joseph, K.C.B., F.R.S.

Cooke, Sir Charles Fletcher-, Kt., Q.C.

Cooke, *Lt.-Col.* Sir David William Perceval, Bt. (1661).

Cooke, Sir John Fletcher-, Kt., C.M.G.

Cooke, Sir Robert Gordon, Kt.

Cooke, *Rt. Hon.* Sir Robin Brunskill, Kt.

Cooley, Sir Alan Sydenham, Kt., C.B.E.

Coop, Sir Maurice Fletcher, Kt.

Cooper, Sir William Daniel Charles, Bt. (1863).

Cooper, Sir Francis Ashmole, Bt., Ph.D. (1905).

Cooper, *Rt. Hon.* Sir Frank, G.C.B., C.M.G.

Cooper, *General* Sir George Leslie Conroy, G.C.B., M.C.

Cooper, Sir Gilbert Alexander, Kt., C.B.E., E.D.

Cooper, Sir Patrick Graham Astley, Bt. (1821).

Cooper, *Prof.* Sir (William) Mansfield, Kt.

Coote, Sir Christopher John, Bt., *Premier Baronet of Ireland* (I 1621).

Copas, *Most Rev.* Virgil, K.B.E., D.D.

Corbet, Sir John Vincent, Bt., M.B.E. (1808).

Corfield, *Rt. Hon.* Sir Frederick Vernon, Kt., Q.C.

Corfield, Sir Kenneth George, Kt.

Cork, Sir Kenneth Russell, G.B.E.

Corley, Sir Kenneth Sholl Ferrand, Kt.

Cormack, Sir Magnus Cameron, K.B.E.

Cornford, Sir (Edward) Clifford, K.C.B.

Cornforth, Sir John Warcup, Kt., C.B.E., D.Phil., F.R.S.

Cornwall, *General* Sir James Handyside Marshall-, K.C.B., C.B.E., D.S.O., M.C.

Corry, Sir James Perowne Ivo Myles, Bt. (1885).

Cortazzi, Sir (Henry Arthur) Hugh, G.C.M.G.

Cory, Sir Clinton James Donald, Bt. (1919).

Coslett, *Air Marshal* Sir (Thomas) Norman, K.C.B., O.B.E.

Costain, Sir Albert Percy, Kt.

Costar, Sir Norman Edgar, K.C.M.G.

Cotter, *Lt.-Col.* Sir Delaval James Alfred, Bt., D.S.O. (I. 1763).

Cotterell, Sir John Henry Geers, Bt. (1805).

Cotton, Sir John Richard, K.C.M.G., O.B.E.

Cotton, *Hon.* Sir Robert Carrington, K.C.M.G.

Cottrell, Sir Alan Howard, Kt., Ph.D., F.R.S.

Cotts, Sir (Robert) Crichton Mitchell, Bt. (1921).

Coulson, Sir John Eltringham, K.C.M.G.

Couper, Sir (Robert) Nicholas (Oliver), Bt. (1841).

Court, *Hon.* Sir Charles Walter Michael, K.C.M.G., O.B.E.

Courtenay, *Hon.* Sir (Woldrich) Harrison, K.B.E.

Coutts, Sir Walter Fleming, G.C.M.G., M.B.E.

Couzens, Sir Kenneth Edward, K.C.B.

Covacevich, Sir (Anthony) Thomas, Kt., D.F.C.

Cowen, *Rt. Hon. Prof.* Sir Zelman, G.C.M.G., G.C.V.O., Q.C.

Cowley, *Lt.-Gen.* Sir John Guise, K.B.E., C.B.

Cowper, Sir Norman Lethbridge, Kt., C.B.E.

Cowperthwaite, Sir John James, K.B.E., C.M.G.

Cox, Sir Anthony Wakefield, Kt., C.B.E., F.R.I.B.A.

Cox, Sir (Ernest) Gordon, K.B.E., T.D., D.S.C., F.R.S.

Cox, Sir Geoffrey Sandford, Kt., C.B.E.

Cox, Sir (George) Trenchard, Kt., C.B.E., F.S.A.

Cox, *Vice-Adm.* Sir John Michael Holland, K.C.B.

Cox, Sir John William, Kt., C.B.E.

Cox, Sir Mencea Ethereal, Kt.,

Cradock, Sir Percy, G.C.M.G.

Craig, Sir (Albert) James (Macqueen), G.C.M.G.

Craig, *Air Chief Marshal* Sir David Brownrigg, G.C.B., O.B.E.

Cramer, *Hon.* Sir John Oscar, Kt.

Crane, Sir Harry Walter Victor, Kt., O.B.E.

Crane, Sir James William Donald, Kt., C.B.E.

Craufurd, Sir Robert James, Bt. (1781).

Craven, *Air Marshal* Sir Robert Edward, K.B.E., C.B., D.F.C.

Crawford, *Hon.* Sir George Hunter, Kt.

Crawford, Sir John Grenfell, Kt., C.B.E.

Crawford, Sir (Robert) Stewart, G.C.M.G., C.V.O

Crawford, *Prof.* Sir Theodore, Kt.

Crawford, *Vice-Adm.* Sir William Godfrey, K.B.E., C.B., D.S.C.

Crawshaw, *Hon.* Sir (Edward) Daniel (Weston), Kt.

Crawshay, *Col.* Sir William Robert, Kt., D.S.O., E.R.D., T.D.

Creagh, *Maj.-Gen.* Sir (Kilner) Rupert Brazier-, K.B.E., C.B., D.S.O.

Creasey, *General* Sir Timothy May, K.C.B., O.B.E.

Creswell, Sir Michel Justin, K.C.M.G.

Creswick, Sir Alexander Reid, Kt.

Crichton, Sir Andrew James Maitland-Makgill-, Kt.

Crichton, Sir (John) Robertson (Dunn), Kt.

Cripps, Sir John Stafford, Kt., C.B.E.

Crisp, Sir (John) Peter, Bt. (1913).

Crisp, *Hon.* Sir (Malcolm) Peter, Kt.

Critchett, Sir Ian (George Lorraine), Bt. (1908).

Croft, Sir Bernard Hugh Denman, Bt. (1671).

Croft, Sir John Archibald Radcliffe, Bt. (1818).

Crofton, Sir (Hugh) Patrick Simon, Bt. (1801).

Crofton, *Prof.* Sir John Wenman, Kt.

Crofton, Sir Malby Sturges, Bt. (1838).

Croker, Sir Walter Russell, K.B.E.

Crookenden, *Lt.-Gen.* Sir Napier, K.C.B., D.S.O., O.B.E.

Croom, Sir John Halliday, Kt., T.D.

Cross, Sir Cecil Lancelot Stewart, Kt., C.B.E.

Cross, *Air Chief Marshal* Sir Kenneth Brian Boyd, K.C.B., C.B.E., D.S.O., D.F.C.

Crossland, Sir Leonard, Kt.

Crossley, Sir Christopher John, Bt. (1909).

Crossman, Sir Douglas Peter, Kt., T.D.

Crosthwaite, Sir (Ponsonby) Moore, K.C.M.G.

Crowe, Sir Colin Tradescant, G.C.M.G.

Crowley, Sir Brian Hurtle, Kt., M.M.

Crutchley, *Admiral* Sir Victor Alexander Charles, V.C., K.C.B., D.S.C.

Cruthers, Sir James Winter, Kt.

Cubbon, Sir Brian Crossland, G.C.B.

Cubitt, Sir Hugh Guy, Kt., C.B.E.

Cuckney, Sir John Graham, Kt.

Cumming, Sir William Gordon Gordon-, Bt. (1804).

Cunard, Sir Guy Alick, Bt. (1859).

Cuninghame, Sir John Christopher Foggo Montgomery-, Bt. (N.S. 1672).

Cuninghame, Sir William Henry Fairlie-, Bt. (s. 1630).

Cunliffe, Sir David Ellis, Bt.

Cunningham, Sir Charles Craik, G.C.B., K.B.E., C.V.O.

Cunningham, *Lt.-Gen.* Sir Hugh Patrick, K.B.E.

Cunynghame, Sir Andrew David Francis, Bt. (s. 1702).

Cunynghame, Sir James Ogilvy Blair-, Kt., O.B.E.

Curle, Sir John Noel Ormiston, K.C.V.O., C.M.G.

Curlewis, *His Hon.* Sir Adrian Herbert, Kt., C.V.O., C.B.E.

Curran, *Rt. Hon.* Sir Lancelot Ernest, Kt.

Curran, Sir Samuel Crowe, Kt., D.SC., Ph.D., F.R.S., F.R.S.E.

Currie, *Prof.* Sir Alastair Robert, Kt., F.R.C.P., F.R.C.P.E., F.R.S.E.

Currie, Sir George Alexander, Kt.

Currie, Sir Neil Smith, Kt., C.B.E.

Currie, Sir William George Cubitt, Bt. (1847).

Curtis, Sir (Edward) Leo, Kt.

Curtis, Sir William Peter, Bt. (1802).

Curtiss, *Air Marshal* Sir John Bagot, K.C.B., K.B.E.

Cuthbert, *Vice-Adm.* Sir John Wilson, K.B.E., C.B.

Cuthbertson, Sir David Paton, Kt., C.B.E., M.D., D.SC.

Cuthbertson, Sir Harold Alexander, Kt.

Cutler, Sir (Arthur) Roden, V.C., K.C.M.G., K.C.V.O., C.B.E.

Cutler, Sir Charles Benjamin, K.B.E., E.D.

Cutler, Sir Horace Walter, Kt., O.B.E.

Dacie, *Prof.* Sir John Vivian, Kt., M.D., F.R.S.

Dainton, *Prof.* Sir Frederick Sydney, Kt., Ph.D., D.SC., F.R.S

Daldry, Sir Leonard Charles, K.B.E.

Dale, Sir William Leonard, K.C.M.G.

Dalrymple, Sir Hew Fleetwood Hamilton-, Bt., C.V.O. (s. 1697).

Dalton, Sir Alan Nugent Goring, Kt., C.B.E.

Dalton, *Maj.-Gen.* Sir Charles James George, Kt., C.B., C.B.E.

Dalton, *Vice-Adm.* Sir Norman Eric, K.C.B., O.B.E.

Daly, *Lt.-Gen.* Sir Thomas Joseph, K.B.E., C.B., D.S.O.

Dalyell, Sir Tam, Bt., M.P. (N.S. 1685).

Daniel, Sir Goronwy Hopkin, K.C.V.O., C.B., D.Phil.

Daniell, Sir Peter Averell, Kt., T.D.

Danks, Sir Alan John, K.B.E.

Darell, Sir Jeffrey Lionel, Bt., M.C. (1795).

Dargie, Sir William Alexander, Kt., C.B.E.

Darling, Sir Clifford, Kt.

Darling, Sir James Ralph, Kt., C.M.G., O.B.E.

Darling, *General* Sir Kenneth Thomas, G.B.E., K.C.B., D.S.O.

Darlington, *Rear-Adm.* Sir Charles Roy, K.B.E.

Darvall, Sir (Charles) Roger, Kt., C.B.E.

Dashwood, Sir Francis John Vernon Hereward, Bt., *Premier Baronet of Great Britain* (1707).

Dashwood, Sir Richard James, Bt. (1684).

Davenport, *Lt.-Col.* Sir Walter Henry Bromley-, Kt., T.D.

Davidson, *Hon.* Sir Charles William, K.B.E.

Davie, *Rev.* Sir Arthur Patrick Ferguson-, Bt. (1847).

Davie, Sir Paul Christopher, Kt.

Davies, *Air Marshal* Sir Alan Cyril, K.C.B., C.B.E.

Davies, *Hon.* Sir (Alfred William) Michael, Kt.

Davies, Sir Alun Talfan, Kt., Q.C.

Davies, Sir (David) Arthur, K.B.E.

Davies, Sir David Henry, Kt.

Davies, *Hon.* Sir (David Herbert) Mervyn, Kt., M.C., T.D.

Davies, Sir David Joseph, Kt.

Davies, *Vice-Adm.* Sir Lancelot Richard Bell, K.B.E.

Davies, Sir Oswald, Kt., C.B.E.

Davies, Sir Richard Harries, K.C.V.O., C.B.E.

Davies, Sir Victor Caddy, Kt., O.B.E.

Davis, Sir Charles Sigmund, Kt., C.B.

Davis, Sir Colin Rex, Kt., C.B.E.

Davis, *Hon.* Sir (Dermot) Renn, Kt., O.B.E.

Davis, Sir (Ernest) Howard, Kt., C.M.G., O.B.E.

Davis, Sir John Gilbert, Bt. (1946).

Davis, *Air Chief Marshal* Sir John Gilbert, G.C.B., O.B.E.

Davis, Sir John Henry Harris, Kt.

Davis, Sir Maurice Herbert, Kt., O.B.E.

Davis, Sir Rupert Charles Hart-, Kt.

Davis, *Hon.* Sir Thomas Robert Alexander Harries, K.B.E.

Davis, *Admiral* Sir William Wellclose, G.C.B., D.S.O.

Davison, *Rt. Hon.* Sir Ronald Keith, G.B.E., C.M.G.

Dawbarn, Sir Simon Yelverton, K.C.V.O., C.M.G.

Dawnay, *Vice-Adm.* Sir Peter, K.C.V.O., C.B., D.S.C.

Dawson, *Hon.* Sir Daryl Michael, K.B.E., C.B.

Dawson, Sir Hugh Michael Trevor, Bt. (1920).

Dawson, *Air Chief Marshal* Sir Walter Lloyd, K.C.B., C.B.E., D.S.O.

Dawtry, Sir Alan (Graham), Kt., C.B.E., T.D.

Day, Sir Derek Malcolm, K.C.M.G.

Day, Sir Robin, Kt.

Deacon, Sir George Edward Raven, Kt., C.B.E., F.R.S., F.R.S.E.

Deakin, Sir (Frederick) William (Dampier), Kt., D.S.O.

Dean, Sir John Norman, Kt.

Dean, Sir Patrick Henry, G.C.M.G.

Deane, *Hon.* Sir William Patrick, K.B.E.

Dearing, Sir Ronald Ernest, Kt., C.B.

Debenham, Sir Gilbert Ridley, Bt. (1931).

De Bunsen, Sir Bernard, Kt., C.M.G.

Deer, Sir (Arthur) Frederick, Kt., C.M.G.

de Gale, Sir Leo Victor, G.C.M.G., C.B.E.

de Hoghton, Sir (Richard) Bernard (Cuthbert), Bt. (1611).

De la Bère, Sir Cameron, Bt. (1953).

Delacombe, *Maj.-Gen.* Sir Rohan, K.C.M.G., K.C.V.O., K.B.E., C.B., D.S.O.

de la Mare, Sir Arthur James, K.C.M.G., K.C.V.O.

de la Rue, Sir Eric Vincent, Bt. (1898).

De Lestang, Sir Marie Charles Emmanuel Clement Nageon, Kt.

de Lotbinière, *Lt.-Col.* Sir Edmond Joly, Kt.

Delve, Sir Frederick William, Kt., C.B.E.

de Montmorency, Sir Arnold Geoffroy, Bt. (I 1631).

Denby, Sir Richard Kenneth, Kt.

Denholm, *Col.* Sir William Lang, Kt., T.D.

Denman, Sir (George) Roy, K.C.B., C.M.G.

Denning, *Lt.-Gen.* Sir Reginald Francis Stewart, K.C.V.O., K.B.E., C.B.

Denny, Sir Alistair Maurice Archibald, Bt. (1913).

Denny, Sir Anthony Coningham de Waltham, Bt. (I 1782).

Denny, Sir (Jonathan) Lionel (Percy), G.B.E., M.C.

Derham, *Prof.* Sir David Plumley, K.B.E., C.M.G.

Derham, Sir Peter John, Kt.

de Trafford, Sir Dermot Humphrey, Bt. (1841).

Deverell, Sir Colville Montgomery, G.B.E., K.C.M.G., C.V.O.

Devesi, Sir Baddeley, G.C.M.G., G.C.V.O.

Devitt, Sir Thomas Gordon, Bt. (1916).

Dewes, Sir Herbert John Salisbury, Kt., C.B.E.

Dewey, Sir Anthony Hugh, Bt. (1917).

Dewhurst, *Prof.* Sir (Christopher) John, Kt.

D'Eyncourt, Sir (John) Jeremy (Eustace) Tennyson-, Bt. (1930).

de Zulueta, Sir Philip Francis, Kt.

Dhenin, *Air Marshal* Sir Geoffrey Howard, K.B.E., A.F.C., G.M., M.D.

Dhrangadhra, H.H. the Maharaja Raj Saheb of, K.C.I.E.

Dibela, *Hon.* Sir Kingsford, G.C.M.G.

Dickens, Sir Louis Walter, Kt., D.F.C., A.F.C.

Dickinson, Sir Harold Herbert, Kt.

Dickinson, Sir Samuel Benson, Kt.

Dickson, *Marshal of the Royal Air Force* Sir William Forster, G.C.B., K.B.E., D.S.O., A.F.C.

Dilbertson, Sir Geoffrey, C.B.E.

Dilke, Sir John Fisher Wentworth, Bt. (1862).

Dill, Sir Nicholas Bayard, Kt., C.B.E.

Dillon, *Rt. Hon.* Sir (George) Brian (Hugh), Kt.

Dillon, Sir John Vincent, Kt., C.M.G.

Dillon, Sir Max, Kt.

Diver, *Hon.* Sir Leslie Charles, Kt.

Dixon, *Air Vice-Marshal* Sir (Francis Wilfred) Peter, K.B.E.

Dixon, Sir John George, Bt. (1919).

Dobson, Sir Denis William, K.C.B., O.B.E., Q.C.

Dobson, *General* Sir Patrick John Howard-, G.C.B.

Dobson, Sir Richard Portway, Kt.

Dodds, Sir Ralph Jordan, Bt. (1964).

Dodson, Sir Derek Sherborne Lindsell, K.C.M.G., M.C.

Dodsworth, Sir John Christopher Smith-, Bt. (1784).

Doig, Sir James Nimmo Crawford, Kt.

Doll, *Prof.* Sir (William) Richard (Shaboe), Kt., O.B.E., F.R.S., D.M., M.D., D.SC.

Donaldson, Sir Dawson, K.C.M.G.

Donaldson, *Rt. Hon.* Sir John Francis, Kt.

Donne, *Hon.* Sir Gaven John, K.B.E.

Donne, Sir John Christopher, Kt.

Donner, Sir Patrick William, Kt.

Dookun, Sir Dewoonarain, Kt.

Dorman, *Lt.-Col.* Sir Charles Geoffrey, Bt., M.C. (1923).

Dorman, Sir Maurice Henry, G.C.M.G., G.C.V.O.

Dos Santos, Sir Errol Lionel, Kt., C.B.E.

Dougherty, *Maj.-Gen.* Sir Ivan Noel, Kt., C.B.E., D.S.O., E.D.

Douglas, *Prof.* Sir Donald Macleod, Kt., M.B.E.

Douglas, Sir (Edward) Sholto, Kt.

Douglas, *Very Rev.* Sir Hugh Osborne, K.C.V.O., C.B.E.

Douglas, Sir Robert McCallum, Kt., O.B.E.

Douglas, Sir Sholto Courtenay Mackenzie, Bt., M.C. (1831).

Douglas, *Rt. Hon.* Sir William Randolph, K.C.M.G.

Dove, Sir Clifford Alfred, Kt., C.B.E., E.R.D.

Dover, *Prof.* Sir Kenneth James, Kt., D.Litt., F.B.A., F.R.S.E.

Down, Sir Alastair Frederick, Kt., O.B.E., M.C., T.D.

Downey, Sir Gordon Stanley, K.C.B.

Downward, Sir William Atkinson, Kt.

Dowse, *Maj.-Gen.* Sir Maurice Brian, K.C.V.O., C.B., C.B.E.

Dowson, Sir Philip Manning, Kt., C.B.E., A.R.A.

Doyle, Sir John Francis Reginald William Hastings, Bt. (1828).

D'Oyly, *Cdr.* Sir John Rochfort, Bt., R.N. (1663).

Drake, Sir (Arthur) Eric (Courtney), Kt., C.B.E.

Drake, *Hon.* Sir (Frederick) Maurice, Kt., D.F.C.

Drake, Sir James, Kt., C.B.E.

Drew, Sir Arthur Charles Walter, K.C.B.

Drew, Sir Ferdinand Caire, Kt., C.M.G.

Drew, *Lt.-Gen.* Sir (William) Robert (Macfarlane), K.C.B., C.B.E., Q.H.P.

Dreyer, *Admiral* Sir Desmond Parry, G.C.B., C.B.E., D.S.C.

Dring, *Lt.-Col.* Sir Arthur John, K.B.E., C.I.E.

Driver, Sir Arthur John, Kt.

Driver, Sir Eric William, Kt.

Drummond, *Lieut.-Gen.* Sir (William) Alexander (Duncan), K.B.E., C.B.

Dryden, Sir John Stephen Gyles, Bt. (1733 and 1795).

Duckmanton, Sir Talbot Sydney, Kt., C.B.E.

Duckworth, *Maj.* Sir Richard Dyce, Bt. (1909).

du Cros, Sir Claude Philip Arthur Mallet, Bt. (1916).

Dudding, Sir John Scarborough, Kt.

Duff, *Rt. Hon.* Sir (Arthur) Antony, G.C.M.G., C.V.O., D.S.O., D.S.C.

Duffus, *Hon.* Sir William Algernon Holwell, Kt.

Dugdale, Sir William Stratford, Bt., M.C. (1936).

du Heaume, Sir Francis Herbert, Kt., C.I.E., O.B.E.

Duke, *Maj.-Gen.* Sir Gerald William, K.B.E., C.B., D.S.O.

Dunbar, Sir Archibald Ranulph, Bt. (s 1700).

Dunbar, Sir David Hope-, Bt. (s 1664).

Dunbar, Sir Drummond Cospatrick Ninian, Bt., M.C. (s 1698).

Dunbar, Sir Jean Ivor, Bt. (s 1694).

Dunbar of Hempriggs, Dame Maureen Daisy Helen, Bt. (s 1706).

Duncan, Sir Arthur Bryce, Kt.

Duncan, Sir James Blair, Kt.

Duncan, Sir William Barr McKinnon, Kt., C.B.E.

Duncombe, Sir Philip Digby Pauncefort-, Bt. (1859).

Dungarpur, H.H. the Maharawal of, G.C.I.E., K.C.S.I.

Dunham, *Prof.* Sir Kingsley Charles, Kt., Ph.D., F.R.S., F.R.S.E.

Dunk, Sir William Ernest, Kt., C.B.E.

Dunlop, Sir Ernest Edward, Kt., C.M.G., O.B.E.

Dunlop, Sir John Wallace, K.B.E.

Dunlop, Sir Thomas, Bt. (1916).

Dunlop, Sir William Norman Gough, Kt.

Dunn, *Air Marshal* Sir Eric Clive, K.B.E., C.B., B.E.M.

Dunn, *Lt.-Col.* Sir Francis Vivian, K.C.V.O., O.B.E.

Dunn, *Air Marshal* Sir Patrick Hunter, K.B.E., C.B., D.F.C.

Dunn, *Rt. Hon.* Sir Robin Horace Walford, Kt., M.C.

Dunnett, Sir (Ludovic) James, G.C.B., C.M.G.

Dunning, Sir Simon William Patrick, Bt. (1930).

Dunphie, *Maj.-Gen.* Sir Charles Anderson Lane, Kt., C.B., C.B.E., D.S.O.

Dunstan, *Lt.-Gen.* Sir Donald Beaumont, K.B.E., C.B.

Duntze, Sir George Edwin Douglas, Bt., C.M.G. (1774).

Dupree, Sir Peter, Bt. (1921).

Dupuch, Sir (Alfred) Etienne (Jerome), Kt., O.B.E.

Durand, *Rev.* Sir (Henry Mortimer) Dickon, Bt. (1892).

Durie, Sir Alexander Charles, Kt., C.B.E.

Durkin, *Air Marshal* Sir Herbert, K.B.E., C.B.

Durlacher, *Admiral* Sir Laurence George, K.C.B., O.B.E., D.S.C.

Durrant, Sir William Henry Estridge, Bt. (1784).

Duval, Sir Charles Gaetan, Kt.

Duval, Sir Francis John, Kt., C.B.E.

Dyer, *Prof.* Sir (Henry) Peter (Francis) Swinnerton, Bt., F.R.S. (1678).

Dyke, Sir Derek William Hart, Bt. (1677).

Earle, *Air Chief Marshal* Sir Alfred, G.B.E., C.B.

Earle, Sir (Hardman) George (Algernon), Bt. (1869).

East, Sir (Lewis) Ronald, Kt., C.B.E.

Eastham, *Hon.* Sir (Thomas) Michael, Kt.

Eastick, *Brig.* Sir Thomas Charles, Kt., C.M.G., D.S.O., E.D.

Easton, *Admiral* Sir Ian, K.C.B., D.S.C.

Easton, *Air Commodore* Sir James Alfred, K.C.M.G., C.B., C.B.E.

Eastwood, Sir John Bealby, Kt.

Eberle, *Admiral* Sir James Henry Fuller, G.C.B.

Ebrahim, Sir (Mahomed) Currimbhoy, Bt. (1910).

Eburne, Sir Sidney Alfred William, Kt., M.C.

Eccles, *Prof.* Sir John Carew, Kt., D.Phil., F.R.S.

Echlin, Sir Norman David Fenton, Bt. (t 1721).

Eckersley, Sir Donald Payze, Kt., O.B.E.

Edden, *Vice-Adm.* Sir (William) Kaye, K.B.E., C.B.

Edge, Sir William, Bt. (1937).

Edmenson, Sir Walter Alexander, Kt., C.B.E.

Edmonstone, Sir Archibald Bruce Charles, Bt. (1774).

Edwardes, Sir Michael Owen, Kt.

Edwards, Sir Christopher John Churchill, Bt. (1866).

Edwards, Sir George Robert, Kt., O.M., C.B.E., F.R.S.

Edwards, Sir John Clive Leighton, Bt. (1921).

Edwards, Sir Llewellyn Roy, Kt.

Edwards, Sir Martin Llewellyn, Kt.

Edwards, *Prof.* Sir Samuel Frederick, Kt., F.R.S.

Egerton, Sir John Alfred Roy, Kt.

Egerton, Sir (Philip) John (Caledon) Grey-, Bt. (1617).

Egerton, Sir Seymour John Louis, G.C.V.O.

Eggleston, *Hon.* Sir Richard Moulton, Kt.

Eldridge, *Lt.-Gen.* Sir (William) John, K.B.E., C.B., D.S.O., M.C.

Eley, Sir Geoffrey Cecil Ryves, Kt., C.B.E.

Eliott, Sir Arthur Francis Augustus Boswell, Bt. (s 1666).

Elkins, *Vice-Adm.* Sir Robert Francis, K.C.B., C.V.O., O.B.E.

Elliot, Sir John Blumenfeld, Kt.

Elliott, Sir Hugh Francis Ivo, Bt., O.B.E. (1917).

Elliott, Sir Norman Randall, Kt., C.B.E.

Elliott, Sir Randal Forbes, K.B.E.

Elliott, Sir (Robert) William, Kt.

Elliott, Sir Ronald Stuart, Kt.

Ellis, Sir John Rogers, Kt., M.B.E., M.D., F.R.C.P.

Ellis, Sir Ronald, Kt.

Ellison, *Rt. Rev.* and *Rt. Hon.* Gerald Alexander, K.C.V.O.

Ellison, *Col.* Sir Ralph Harry Carr-, Kt., T.D.

Ellwood, *Air Marshal* Sir Aubrey Beauclerk, K.C.B., D.S.C.

Elphinstone, Sir John, Bt. (s 1701).

Elphinstone, Sir (Maurice) Douglas (Warburton), Bt., T.D. (1816).

Elstub, Sir St. John de Holt, Kt., C.B.E.

Elton, Sir Charles Abraham Grierson, Bt. (1717).

Elyan, Sir (Isadore) Victor, Kt.

Emery, Sir (James) Frederick, Kt.

Emery, Sir Peter Frank Hannibal, Kt., M.P.

Empson, *Admiral* Sir (Leslie) Derek, G.B.E., K.C.B.

Emson, *Air Marshal* Sir Reginald Herbert, K.B.E., C.B., A.F.C.

Engholm, Sir Basil Charles, K.C.B.

Engineer, Sir Noshirwan Phirozshah, Kt.

Engle, Sir George Lawrence Jose, K.C.B., Q.C.

Engledow, *Prof.* Sir Frank Leonard, Kt., C.M.G., F.R.S.

English, Sir Cyril Rupert, Kt.

English, Sir David, Kt.

Entwistle, Sir (John Nuttall) Maxwell, Kt.

Ereaut, Sir Herbert Frank Cobbold, Kt.

Errington, *Col.* Sir Geoffrey Frederick, Bt. (1963).

Errington, Sir Lancelot, K.C.B.

Erskine, Sir (Thomas) David, Bt. (1821).

Esmonde, Sir John Henry Grattan, Bt. (i 1629).

Espie, Sir Frank Fletcher, Kt., O.B.E.

Esplen, Sir William Graham, Bt. (1921).

Evans, Sir Anthony Adney, Bt. (1920).

Evans, Sir Athol Donald, K.B.E.

Evans, *Air Chief Marshal* Sir David George, G.C.B., C.B.E.

Evans, Sir David Lewis, Kt., O.B.E., D.Litt.

Evans, *Lt.-Gen.* Sir Geoffrey Charles, K.B.E., C.B., D.S.O.

Evans, Sir Geraint Llewellyn, Kt., C.B.E.

Evans, *Hon.* Sir Haydn Tudor, Kt.

Evans, Sir Hywel Wynn, K.C.B.

Evans, Sir Ian William Gwynne-, Bt. (1913).

Evans, Sir Richard Mark, K.C.M.G.

Evans, Sir (Robert) Charles, Kt.

Evans, Sir (William) Vincent (John), G.C.M.G., M.B.E., Q.C.

Eveleigh, *Rt. Hon.* Sir Edward Walter, Kt., E.R.D.

Everard, *Maj.-Gen.* Sir Christopher Earle Welby-, K.B.E., C.B.

Everard, Sir Nugent Henry, Bt. (1911).

Everson, Sir Frederick Charles, K.C.M.G.

Every, Sir John Simon, Bt. (1641).

Evetts, *Lt.-Gen.* Sir John Fullerton, Kt., C.B., C.B.E., M.C.

Ewart, Sir (William) Ivan (Cecil), Bt., D.S.C. (1887).

Ewbank, *Hon.* Sir Anthony Bruce, Kt.

Ewin, Sir (David) Ernest Thomas Floyd, Kt., O.B.E., M.V.O.

Ewing, *Vice-Adm.* Sir (Robert) Alastair, K.B.E., C.B., D.S.C.

Ewing, Sir Ronald Archibald Orr-, Bt. (1886).

Eyre, Sir Reginald Edwin, Kt., M.P.

Faber, Sir Richard Stanley, K.C.V.O., C.M.G.

Fadahunsi, Sir Joseph Odeleye, K.C.M.G.

Fagge, Sir John William Frederick, Bt. (1660).

Fairbairn, *Hon.* Sir David Eric, K.B.E., D.F.C.

Fairbairn, Sir (James) Brooke, Bt. (1869).

Fairbairn, Sir Robert Duncan, Kt.

Fairfax, Sir Vincent Charles, Kt., C.M.G.

Fairfax, Sir Warwick Oswald, Kt.

Fairgrieve, Sir (Thomas) Russell, Kt., C.B.E., T.D.

Fairhall, *Hon.* Sir Allen, K.B.E.

Falconer, *Hon.* Sir Douglas William, Kt., M.B.E.

Falconer, Sir James Fyfe, Kt., M.B.E.

Falk, Sir Roger Salis, Kt., O.B.E.

Falkiner, *Lt.-Col.* Sir Terence Edmond Patrick, Bt. (i 1778).

Falkner, Sir (Donald) Keith, Kt.

Falle, Sir Samuel, K.C.M.G., K.C.V.O., D.S.C.

Falshaw, Sir Donald, Kt.

Falvey, *Hon.* Sir John Neil, K.B.E., Q.C.

Faridkot, *Col.* H.H. the Raja of, K.C.S.I.

Farmer, Sir Lovedin George Thomas, Kt.

Farndale, *Lt.-Gen.* Sir Martin Baker, K.C.B.

Farquhar, *Lt.-Col.* Sir Peter (Walter), Bt., D.S.O. (1796).

Farquharson, *Hon.* Sir Donald Henry, Kt.

Farquharson, Sir James Robbie, K.B.E.

Farr, Sir John Arnold, Kt., M.P.

Farrar-Hockley, *General* Sir Anthony Heritage, G.B.E., K.C.B., D.S.O., M.C.

Farrer, Sir Charles Matthew, K.C.V.O.

Farrington, *Maj.* Sir Henry Francis Colden, Bt. (1818).

Faulkner, Sir Eric Odin, Kt., M.B.E.

Faulkner, Sir Percy, K.B.E., C.B.

Faulks, Sir Neville Major Ginner, Kt., M.B.E., T.D.

Fawkes, Sir Randol Francis, Kt.

Fawcett, Sir James Edmund Sandford, Kt., D.S.C.

Fawcus, Sir (Robert) Peter, K.B.E., C.M.G.

Fayrer, Sir John Lang Macpherson, Bt., (1896).

Feilden, Sir Henry Wemyss, Bt., (1846).

Feldman, Sir Basil Samuel, Kt.

Fell, Sir Anthony, Kt.

Fellowes, Sir William Albemarle, K.C.V.O.

Fennessy, Sir Edward, Kt., C.B.E.

Ferens, Sir Thomas Robinson, Kt., C.B.E.

Ferguson, *Lt.-Col.* Sir Neil Edward Johnson-, Bt., T.D. (1906).

Fergusson of Kilkerran, Sir Charles, Bt. (s. 1703).

Fergusson, Sir James Herbert Hamilton Colyer-, Bt. (1866).

Feroze, Sir Rustam Moolan, Kt., F.R.C.S.

ffolkes, Sir Robert Francis Alexander, Bt. (1774).

fforde, Sir Arthur Frederic Brownlow, G.B.E.

Field, Sir John Osbaldiston, K.B.E., C.M.G.

Fieldhouse, Sir Harold, K.B.E., C.B.

Fieldhouse, *Admiral* Sir John David Elliott, G.C.B., G.B.E.

Fiennes, Sir John Saye Wingfield Twisleton-Wykeham-, K.C.B., Q.C.

Fiennes, Sir Maurice Alberic Twisleton-Wykeham-, Kt.

Fiennes, Sir Ranulph Twisleton-Wykeham-, Bt. (1916).

Figg, Sir Leonard Clifford William, K.C.M.G.

Figgess, Sir John George, K.B.E., C.M.G.

Figgures, Sir Frank Edward, K.C.B., C.M.G.

Figures, Sir Colin Frederick, K.C.M.G., O.B.E.

Fingland, Sir Stanley James Gunn, K.C.M.G.

Finlay, Sir Graeme Bell, Bt., E.R.D. (1964).

Finlay, *Prof.* Sir Moses, Kt., PH.D., F.B.A.

Finley, Sir Peter Hamilton, Kt., O.B.E., D.F.C.

Finniston, Sir (Harold) Montague, Kt., PH.D., F.R.S.

Finsberg, Sir Geoffrey, Kt., M.B.E., M.P.

Firth, *Prof.* Sir Raymond William, Kt., PH.D., F.B.A.

Fisher, Sir George Read, Kt., C.M.G.

Fisher, *Hon.* Sir Henry Arthur Pears, Kt.

Fisher, Sir Nigel Thomas Loveridge, Kt., M.C.

Fison, Sir (Frank Guy) Clavering, Kt.

Fison, Sir Richard Guy, Bt., D.S.C. (1905).

Fitzgerald, *Rev.* Sir Edward Thomas, Bt. (1903).

FitzGerald, Sir George Peter Maurice, Bt., M.C., *The Knight of Kerry* (1880).

Fitzgerald, Sir William James, Kt., M.C., Q.C.

FitzHerbert, Sir John Richard Frederick, Bt. (1784).

Fitzmaurice, *Lt.-Col.* Sir Desmond FitzJohn, Kt., C.I.E.

Fitzpatrick, *General* Sir (Geoffrey Richard) Desmond, G.C.B., D.S.O., M.B.E., M.C.

Fitzpatrick, *Air Marshal* Sir John Bernard, K.B.E., C.B.

Flanagan, Sir James Bernard, Kt., C.B.E.

Flavelle, Sir (Joseph David) Ellsworth, Bt. (1917).

Fleming, Sir Charles Alexander, K.B.E., F.R.S.

Fleming, *Instr. Rear-Adm.* Sir John, K.B.E., D.S.C.

Fleming, *Rt. Rev.* William Launcelot Scott, K.C.V.O., D.D.

Fletcher, *Hon.* Sir Alan Roy, Kt.

Fletcher, Sir James Muir Cameron, Kt.

Fletcher, Sir John Henry Lancelot Aubrey-, Bt. (1782).

Fletcher, Sir Leslie, Kt., D.S.C.

Fletcher, Sir Norman Seymour, Kt.

Fletcher, *Air Chief Marshal* Sir Peter Carteret, K.C.B., O.B.E., D.F.C., A.F.C.

Floyd, Sir Giles Henry Charles, Bt. (1816).

Foley, Sir (Thomas John) Noel, Kt., C.B.E.

Foot, Sir Geoffrey James, Kt.

Foots, Sir James William, Kt.

Forbes, *Hon.* Sir Alastair Granville, Kt.

Forbes, Sir Archibald Finlayson, G.B.E.

Forbes of Pitsligo, Sir Charles Edward Stuart-, Bt. (s 1626).

Forbes of Brux, *Hon.* Sir Ewan, Bt. (s 1630).

Forbes, *Hon.* Sir Hugh Henry Valentine, Kt.

Forbes, *Vice-Adm.* Sir John Morrison, K.C.B.

Forbes, *Maj.* Sir Hamish Stewart, Bt., M.B.E., M.C. (1823).

Ford, *Capt.* Sir Aubrey St. Clair-, Bt., D.S.O., R.N. (1793).

Ford, *Prof.* Sir Edward, Kt., O.B.E., M.D.

Ford, *Maj.* Sir Edward William Spencer, K.C.B., K.C.V.O.

Ford, *Air Marshal* Sir Geoffrey Harold, K.B.E., C.B.

Ford, Sir Henry Russell, Bt. (1929).

Ford, *Prof.* Sir Hugh, Kt., F.R.S.

Ford, Sir John Archibald, K.C.M.G., M.C.

Ford, *Maj.-Gen.* Sir Peter St. Clair-, K.B.E., C.B., D.S.O.

Ford, Sir Richard Brinsley, Kt., C.B.E.

Ford, *General* Sir Robert Cyril, G.C.B., C.B.E.

Ford, Sir Sidney William George, Kt., M.B.E.

Foreman, Sir Philip Frank, Kt., C.B.E.

Forman, Sir John Denis, Kt., O.B.E.

Forrest, Sir James Alexander, Kt.

Forrest, *Rear Adm.* Sir Ronald Stephen, K.C.V.O.

Forster, Sir Oliver Grantham, K.C.M.G., M.V.O.

Forwood, Sir Dudley Richard, Bt. (1895).

Foster, Sir John Gregory, Bt. (1930).

Foster, *Hon.* Sir Peter Harry Batson Woodroffe, Kt., M.B.E., T.D.

Foster, Sir Robert Sidney, G.C.M.G., K.C.V.O.

Foulis, Sir Ian Primrose Liston-, Bt. (s 1634).

Foulkes, Sir Nigel Gordon, Kt.

Fowden, Sir Leslie, Kt., F.R.S.

Fowke, Sir Frederick (Woollaston Rawdon), Bt. (1814).

Fowler, Sir (Edward) Michael Coulson, Kt.

Fowler, Sir Robert William Doughty, K.C.M.G.

Fox, Sir (Henry) Murray, G.B.E.

Fox, *Rt. Hon.* Sir Michael John, Kt.

Fox, Sir (Robert) David (John) Scott, K.C.M.G.

Fox, Sir Theodore Fortescue, Kt., M.D., Ll.D.

Frame, Sir Alistair Gilchrist, Kt.

France, Sir Arnold William, G.C.B.

Francis, Sir Frank Chalton, K.C.B., F.S.A.

Frank, Sir Douglas George Horace, Kt., Q.C.

Frank, *Prof.* Sir (Frederick) Charles, Kt., O.B.E., F.R.S.

Frank, Sir Robert John, Bt. (1920).

Frankel, Sir Otto Herzberg, Kt., D.SC., F.R.S.

Franklin, Sir Eric Alexander, Kt., C.B.E.

Franklin, Sir Michael David Milroy, K.C.B., C.M.G.

Franks, Sir Arthur Temple, K.C.M.G.

Fraser, Sir Basil Malcolm, Bt. (1921).

Fraser, Sir Bruce Donald, K.C.B.

Fraser, *General* Sir David William, G.C.B., O.B.E.

Fraser, Sir Douglas Were, Kt., I.S.O.

Fraser, *Air Marshal* Sir (Henry) Paterson, K.B.E., C.B., A.F.C.

Fraser, Sir Hugh, Bt. (1961).

Fraser, Sir Ian, Kt., D.S.O., O.B.E.

Fraser, Sir (James) Campbell, Kt.

Fraser, Sir James David, Bt. (1943).

Fraser, Sir Robert Brown, Kt., O.B.E.

Fraser, Sir (William) Kerr, G.C.B.

Fraser, Sir (William) Robert, K.C.B., K.B.E.

Frederick, *Maj.* Sir Charles Boscawen, Bt. (1723).

Freeland, Sir John Redvers, K.C.M.G.

Freeman, *His Eminence* James Darcy, K.B.E.

Freeman, Sir James Robin, Bt. (1945).

Freeman, Sir (Nathaniel) Bernard, Kt., C.B.E.

Freeman, Sir Ralph, Kt., C.V.O., C.B.E.

Freer, *Air Chief Marshal* Sir Robert William George, G.B.E., K.C.B.

Freeth, *Hon.* Sir Gordon, K.B.E.

French, *Hon.* Sir Christopher James Saunders, Kt.

Fretwell, Sir George Herbert, K.B.E., C.B.

Fretwell, *Maj.* Sir John Emsley, K.C.M.G.

Frew, Sir John Lewtas, Kt., O.B.E.

Froggatt, Sir Leslie Trevor, Kt.

Frossard, Sir Charles Keith, Kt.

Frost, *Hon.* Sir (Thomas) Sydney, Kt.

Fry, Sir John Nicholas Pease, Bt. (1894).

Fry, *Hon.* Sir William Gordon, Kt.

Fryberg, Sir Abraham, Kt., M.B.E.

Fuchs, Sir Vivian Ernest, Kt., PH.D.

Fuller, *Hon.* Sir John Bryan Munro, Kt.

Fuller, Sir John William Fleetwood, Bt. (1910).

Fung Ping-Fan, *Hon.* Sir Kenneth Kt., C.B.E.

Furness, Sir Stephen Roberts, Bt. (1913).

Gadsden, Sir Peter Drury Haggerston, G.B.E.

Gage, Sir Berkeley Everard Foley, K.C.M.G.

Gairy, *Rt. Hon.* Sir Eric Matthew, Kt.

Gaitskell, Sir Arthur, Kt., C.M.G.

Gallwey, Sir Philip Frankland-Payne-, Bt. (1812).

Galsworthy, Sir Arthur Norman, K.C.M.G.

Galsworthy, Sir John Edgar, K.C.V.O., C.M.G.

Gamble, Sir David, Bt. (1897).

Gandell, Sir Alan Thomas, Kt., C.B.E.

Ganilau, *Ratu* Sir Penaia Kanatabatu, G.C.M.G., K.C.V.O., K.B.E., D.S.O.

Gardener, Sir Alfred John, K.C.M.G., C.B.E.

Gardner, Sir Douglas Bruce Bruce-, Bt. (1945).

Gardner, Sir Edward Lucas, Kt., Q.C., M.P.

Gardner-Thorpe, *Col.* Sir Ronald, G.B.E., T.D.

Garland, *Hon.* Sir Ransley Victor, K.B.E.

Garlick, Sir John, K.C.B.

Garner, Sir Anthony Stuart, Kt.

Garran, Sir (Isham) Peter, K.C.M.G.

Garrett, *Hon.* Sir Raymond William, Kt., A.F.C.

Garrioch, Sir William Henry, Kt.

Garrow, Sir Nicholas, Kt., O.B.E.

Garthwaite, Sir William Francis Cuthbert, Bt., D.S.C. (1919).

Garvey, Sir Ronald Herbert, K.C.M.G., K.C.V.O., M.B.E.

Garvey, Sir Terence Willcocks, K.C.M.G.

Gascoigne, *Maj.-Gen.* Sir Julian Alvery, K.C.M.G., K.C.V.O., C.B., D.S.O.

Geddes, Sir (Anthony) Reay (Mackay), K.B.E.

Gentry, *Maj.-Gen.* Sir William George, K.B.E., C.B., D.S.O.

George, Sir Arthur Thomas, Kt.

Gethin, *Lt.-Col.* Sir Richard Patrick St. Lawrence, Bt. (I 1665).

Ghurburrun, Sir Rabindrah, Kt.

Gibbon, *General* Sir John Houghton, G.C.B., O.B.E.

Gibbons, Sir William Edward Doran, Bt. (1752).

Gibbs, *Air Marshal* Sir Gerald Ernest, K.B.E., C.I.E., M.C.

Gibbs, *Rt. Hon.* Sir Harry Talbot, G.C.M.G., K.B.E.

Gibbs, *Rt. Hon.* Sir Humphrey Vicary, G.C.V.O., K.C.M.G., O.B.E.

Gibbs, *Field-Marshal* Sir Roland Christopher, G.C.B., C.B.E., D.S.O., M.C.

Gibson, Sir Alexander Drummond, Kt., C.B.E.

Gibson, Sir Christopher Herbert, Bt. (1931).

Gibson, *Rev.* Sir David, Bt. (1926).

Gibson, *Vice-Adm.* Sir Donald Cameron Ernest Forbes, K.C.B., D.S.C.

Gibson, Sir Donald Edward Evelyn, Kt., C.B.E.

Gibson, Sir John Hinshelwood, Kt., C.B., T.D., Q.C.

Gibson, *Hon.* Sir Marcus George, Kt.

Gibson, *Rt. Hon.* Sir Maurice White, Kt.

Gibson, Sir Peter Leslie, Kt.

Gibson, *Hon.* Sir Ralph Brian, Kt.

Gibson, Sir Ronald George, Kt., C.B.E., F.R.C.S.

Giddings, *Air Marshal* Sir (Kenneth Charles) Michael, K.C.B., O.B.E., D.F.C., A.F.C.

Gielgud, Sir (Arthur) John, Kt., C.H.

Giffard, Sir (Charles) Sydney (Rycroft), K.C.M.G.

Gilbert, *Brig.* Sir Herbert Ellery, K.B.E., D.S.O.

Gilbertson, Sir Geoffrey, Kt., C.B.E.

Gilbey, Sir (Walter) Derek, Bt. (1893).

Gilchrist, Sir Andrew Graham, K.C.M.G.

Gilchrist, Sir (James) Finlay (Elder), Kt., O.B.E.

Giles, Sir Alexander Falconer, K.B.E., C.M.G.

Giles, Sir (Henry) Norman, Kt., O.B.E.

Gilkison, Sir Alan Fleming, Kt., C.B.E.

Gillard, *Hon.* Sir Oliver James, Kt.

Gillett, *Maj.-Gen.* Sir Peter Bernard, K.C.V.O., C.B., O.B.E.

Gillett, Sir Robin Danvers Penrose, Bt., G.B.E., R.D. (1959).

Gilliat, *Lt.-Col.* Sir Martin John, G.C.V.O., M.B.E.

Gillies, Sir Alexander, Kt.

Gilmour, *Rt. Hon.* Sir Ian Hedworth John Little, Bt., M.P. (1926).

Gilmour, Sir John Edward, Bt., D.S.O., T.D. (1897).

Gingell, *Air Chief Marshal* Sir John, G.B.E., K.C.B.

Gladstone, Sir (Erskine) William, Bt. (1846).

Glass, Sir Leslie Charles, K.C.M.G.

Glasspole, Sir Florizel Augustus, G.C.M.G, G.C.V.O.

Glen, Sir Alexander Richard, K.B.E., D.S.C.

Glenn, Sir (Joseph Robert) Archibald, Kt., O.B.E.

Glidewell, *Hon.* Sir Iain Derek Laing, Kt.

Glock, Sir William Frederick, Kt., C.B.E.

Glover, Sir Gerald Alfred, Kt.

Glover, *Lt.-Gen.* Sir James Malcolm, K.C.B., M.B.E.

Glubb, *Lt.-Gen.* Sir John Bagot, K.C.B., C.M.G., D.S.O., O.B.E., M.C.

Glyn, Sir Anthony Geoffrey Leo Simon, Bt. (1927).

Glyn, Sir Richard Lindsay, Bt., (1759 and 1800).

Goad, Sir (Edward) Colin (Viner), K.C.M.G.

Godber, Sir George Edward, G.C.B., D.M.

Goddard, *Air Marshal* Sir (Robert) Victor, K.C.B., C.B.E.

Godwin, *Prof.* Sir Harry, Kt., F.R.S.

Goff, *Rt. Hon.* Sir Robert Lionel Archibald, Kt.

Goff, Sir Robert (William) Davis-, Bt. (1905).

Goffin, Sir (John) Dean, Kt.

Gold, Sir Arthur Abraham, Kt., C.R.E.

Gold, Sir Joseph, Kt.

Goldberg, *Prof.* Sir Abraham, Kt., M.D., D.S.C., F.R.C.P.

Goldman, Sir Samuel, K.C.B.

Goldsmid, *Maj.-Gen.* Sir James Arthur d'Avigdor-, Bt., C.B., O.B.E., M.C. (1934).

Goldsmith, Sir James Michael, Kt.

Gombrich, *Prof.* Sir Ernst Hans Josef, Kt., C.B.E., Ph.D., F.B.A., F.S.A.

Gomes, Sir Stanley Eugene, Kt.

Gooch, Sir Richard John Sherlock, Bt. (1746).

Gooch, Sir Robert Douglas, Bt. (1866).

Goodale, Sir Ernest William, Kt., C.B.E., M.C.

Goode, Sir William Allmond Codrington, G.C.M.G.

Goodenough, Sir Richard Edmund, Bt. (1943).

Goodhart, Sir Philip Carter, Kt., M.P.

Goodhart, Sir Robert Anthony Gordon, Bt. (1911).

Goodhew, Sir Victor Henry, Kt.

Goodison, Sir Nicholas Proctor, Kt.

Goodsell, Sir John William, Kt., C.M.G.

Goodson, *Lt.-Col.* Sir Alfred Lassam, Bt. (1922).

Goodwin, Sir Reginald Eustace, Kt., C.B.E.

Goodwin, *Lt.-Gen.* Sir Richard Elton, K.C.B., C.B.E., D.S.O.

Goody, *Most Rev.* Launcelot John, K.B.E.

Goold, Sir George Leonard, Bt. (1801).

Goold, Sir James Duncan, Kt.

Gordon, Sir Andrew Cosmo Lewis Duff-, Bt. (1813).

Gordon, Sir Charles Addison Somerville Snowden, K.C.B.

Gordon, Sir John Charles, Bt. (s 1706).

Gordon, Sir Keith Lyndell, Kt., C.M.G.

Gordon, Sir (Lionel) Eldred (Peter) Smith-, Bt. (1838).

Gordon, *Hon.* Sir Sidney Samuel, Kt., C.B.E.

Gore, Sir Richard Ralph St. George, Bt. (I 1622).

Goring, Sir William Burton Nigel, Bt. (1627).

Gorton, *Rt. Hon.* Sir John Grey, G.C.M.G., C.H.

Goschen, Sir Edward Christian, Bt., D.S.O. (1916).

Gosling, Sir Frederick Donald, Kt.

Gould, *Hon.* Sir Trevor Jack, Kt.

Goulding, *Hon.* Sir (Ernest) Irvine, Kt.

Goulding, Sir William Lingard Walter, Bt. (1904).

Gourlay, *General* Sir (Basil) Ian (Spencer), K.C.B., O.B.E., M.C., R.M.

Govan, Sir Lawrence Herbert, Kt.

Gow, *Gen.* Sir (James) Michael, G.C.B.

Gowans, *Hon.* Sir (Urban) Gregory, Kt.

Gowans, Sir James Learmonth, Kt., C.B.E., F.R.C.P., F.R.S.

Gower, Sir (Herbert) Raymond, Kt., M.P.

Gowing, *Prof.* Sir Lawrence Burnett, Kt., C.B.E.

Graaff, Sir de Villiers, Bt., M.B.E. (1911).

Grace, Sir John Te Herekiekie, K.B.E., M.V.O.

Graesser, *Col.* Sir Alastair Stewart Durward, Kt., D.S.O., O.B.E., M.C., T.D.

Graham, Sir Charles Spencer Richard, Bt. (1783).

Graham, Sir James Bellingham, Bt. (1662).

Graham, Sir John Alexander Noble, Bt., K.C.M.G. (1906).

Graham, Sir John Moodie, Bt. (1964).

Graham, Sir (John) Patrick, Kt.

Graham, Sir Norman William, Kt., C.B.

Graham, Sir Ralph Wolfe, Bt. (1629).

Grandy, *Marshal of the Royal Air Force* Sir John, G.C.B., K.B.E., D.S.O.

Grant, Sir Archibald, Bt. (s 1705).

Grant, *Hon.* Sir Clifford, Kt.

Grant, Sir (John) Anthony, Kt., M.P.

Grant, Sir Kenneth Lindsay, Kt., O.B.E.

Grant, Sir Patrick Alexander Benedict, Bt. (s 1688).

Grantham, *Admiral* Sir Guy, G.C.B., C.B.E., D.S.O.

Granville, Sir Keith, Kt., C.B.E.

Gray, Sir John Archibald Browne, Kt., SC.D., F.R.S.

Gray, *Vice-Adm.* Sir John Michael Dudgeon, K.B.E., C.B.

Gray, Sir William Hume, Bt. (1917).

Gray, Sir William Stevenson, Kt.

Grayson, Sir Ronald Henry Rudyard, Bt. (1922).

Greatbatch, Sir Bruce, Kt., K.C.V.O., C.M.G., M.B.E.

Green, Sir (Edward) Stephen (Lycett), Bt., C.B.E. (1886).

Green, Sir George Ernest, Kt.

Green, *Hon.* Sir Guy Stephen Montague, K.B.E.

Green, Sir Owen Whitley, Kt.

Green, Sir Peter James Frederick, Kt.

Greenaway, Sir Derek Burdick, Bt., C.B.E. (1933).

Greenborough, Sir John, K.B.E.

Greene, Sir Hugh Carleton, K.C.M.G., O.B.E.

Greene, Sir (John) Brian Massy-, Kt.

Greenwell, Sir Edward Bernard, Bt. (1906).

Greeves, *Maj.-Gen.* Sir Stuart, K.B.E., C.B., D.S.O., M.C.

Grenside, Sir John Peter, Kt., C.B.E.

Gretton, *Vice-Adm.* Sir Peter William, K.C.B., D.S.O., O.B.E., D.S.C.

Grey, Sir Anthony Dysart, Bt. (1814).

Grey, Sir Paul Francis, K.C.M.G.

Grierson, Sir Richard Douglas, Bt. (s 1685).

Grieve, Sir (Herbert) Ronald (Robinson), Kt.

Grieve, *Prof.* Sir Robert, Kt.

Griffin, *Admiral* Sir Anthony Templer Frederick Griffith, G.C.B.

Griffin, Sir Charles David, Kt., C.B.E.

Griffin, Sir John Bowes, Kt., Q.C.

Griffiths, Sir Percival Joseph, K.B.E., C.I.E.

Griffiths, Sir John Norton-, Bt. (1922).

Griffiths, Sir Reginald Ernest, Kt.

Griffiths, *Rt. Hon.* Sir (William) Hugh, Kt., M.C.

Grimwade, Sir Andrew Sheppard, Kt., C.B.E.

Grindrod, *Most Rev.* John Basil Rowland, K.B.E.

Groom, Sir Thomas Reginald, Kt.

Groom, *Air Marshal* Sir Victor Emmanuel, K.C.V.O., K.B.E., C.B., D.F.C.

Grotrian, Sir Philip Christian Brent, Bt. (1934).

Grove, Sir Charles Gerald, Bt. (1874).

Grove, Sir Edmund Frank, K.C.V.O.

Groves, Sir Charles Barnard, Kt., C.B.E.

Grugeon, Sir John Drury, Kt.

Grundy, *Air Marshal* Sir Edouard Michael FitzFrederick, K.B.E., C.B.

Guinness, Sir Alec, Kt., C.B.E.

Guinness, Sir Howard Christian Sheldon, Kt., V.R.D.

Guinness, Sir Kenelm Ernest Lee, Bt. (1867).

Guise, Sir John, G.C.M.G., K.B.E.

Guise, Sir John Grant, Bt. (1783).

Gujadhur, Sir Radhamohun, Kt., C.M.G.

Gull, Sir Michael Swinnerton Cameron, Bt. (1872).

Gunn, *Prof.* Sir John Currie, Kt., C.B.E.

Gunn, Sir William Archer, K.B.E., C.M.G.

Gunning, Sir Robert Charles, Bt. (1778).

Gunston, *Maj.* Sir Derrick Wellesley, Bt., M.C. (1938).

Gunther, Sir John Thomson, Kt., C.M.G., O.B.E.

Gurden, Sir Harold Edward, Kt.

Gutch, Sir John, K.C.M.G., O.B.E.

Guthrie, Sir Malcolm Connop, Bt., (1936)

Guthrie, *Hon.* Sir Rutherford Campbell, Kt., C.M.G.

Guy, *General* Sir Roland Kelvin, K.C.B., C.B.E., D.S.O.

Habakkuk, Sir (Hrothgur) John, Kt., F.B.A.

Hackett, *General* Sir John Winthrop, G.C.B., C.B.E., D.S.O., M.C.

Haddow, Sir (Thomas) Douglas, K.C.B.

Hadley, Sir Leonard Albert, Kt.

Hadow, Sir Gordon, Kt., C.M.G., O.B.E.

Hadow, Sir Reginald Michael, K.C.M.G.

Hague, *Prof.* Sir Douglas Chalmers, Kt., C.B.E.

Haines, Sir Cyril Henry, K.B.E.

Hale, *Prof.* Sir John Rigby, Kt.

Haley, Sir William John, K.C.M.G.

Hall, Sir Arnold Alexander, Kt., F.R.S.

Hall, Sir Basil Brodribb, K.C.B., M.C., T.D.

Hall, *Air Marshal* Sir Donald Percy, K.C.B., C.B.E., A.F.C.

Hall, Sir Douglas Basil, Bt., K.C.M.G. (s 1687)

Hall, Sir (Frederick) John (Frank), Bt. (1923).

Hall, Sir John Bernard, Bt. (1919).

Hall, Sir Peter Reginald Frederick, Kt., C.B.E.

Hall, Sir Robert de Zouche, K.C.M.G.

Hall, *Brig.* Sir William Henry, K.B.E., D.S.O., E.D.

Hallett, *Vice-Adm.* Sir Cecil Charles Hughes-, K.C.B., C.B.E.

Halliday, Sir George Clifton, Kt.

Halliday, *Vice-Adm.* Sir Roy William, K.B.E., D.S.C.

Hallifax, *Vice-Adm.* Sir David John, K.C.B., K.B.E.

Hallinan, Sir (Adrian) Lincoln, Kt.

Hallinan, Sir Eric, Kt.

Halsey, *Rev.* Sir John Walter Brooke, Bt. (1920).

Hambling, Sir (Herbert) Hugh, Bt. (1924).

Hamburger, Sir Sidney Cyril, Kt., C.B.E.

Hamer, *Hon.* Sir Rupert James, K.C.M.G., E.D.

Hamill, Sir Patrick, Kt., Q.P.M.

Hamilton, Sir (Charles) Denis, Kt., D.S.O.

Hamilton, Sir Edward Sydney, Bt. (1776 and 1819).

Hamilton, Sir James Arnott, K.C.B., M.B.E.

Hamilton, *Admiral* Sir John Graham, G.B.E., C.B.

Hamilton, Sir Michael Aubrey, Kt.

Hamilton, Sir Patrick George, Bt. (1937).

Hamilton, Sir (Robert Charles) Richard Caradoc, Bt. (s 1646).

Hamilton, Sir Bruce Stirling-, Bt. (s 1673)

Hammett, *Hon.* Sir Clifford James, Kt.

Hammick, Sir Stephen George, Bt. (1834).

Hampshire, Sir Stuart Newton, Kt., F.B.A.

Hanbury, Sir John Capel, Kt., C.B.E.

Hancock, *Lt.-Col.* Sir Cyril Percy, K.C.I.E., O.B.E., M.C.

Hancock, *Air Marshal* Sir Valston Eldridge, K.B.E., C.B., D.F.C.

Hancock, *Prof.* Sir (William) Keith, K.B.E., F.B.A.

Hand, *Most Rev.* Geoffrey David, K.B.E.

Handley, Sir David John Davenport-, Kt., O.B.E.

Hanham, Sir Michael William, Bt., D.F.C. (1667).

Hanley, Sir Michael Bowen, K.C.B.

Hanmer, Sir John Wyndham Edward, Bt. (1774).

Hanson, Sir Anthony Leslie Oswald, Bt. (1887).

Hanson, Sir (Charles) John, Bt. (1918).

Harcourt-Smith, *Air Marshal* Sir David, K.C.B., D.F.C.

Harders, Sir Clarence Waldemar, Kt., O.B.E.

Hardie, Sir Charles Edgar Mathewes, Kt., C.B.E.

Harding, Sir George William, K.C.M.G., C.V.O.

Harding, Sir Harold John Boyer, Kt.

Harding, *Air Marshal* Sir Peter Robin, K.C.B.

Hardinge, Sir Robert Arnold, Bt. (1801).

Hardingham, Sir Robert Ernest, Kt., C.M.G., O.B.E.

Hardman, Sir Henry, K.C.B.

Hardy, *Prof.* Sir Alister Clavering, Kt., D.SC., F.R.S.

Hardy, Sir Harry, Kt.

Hardy, Sir James Dundas, Kt., C.B.E.

Hardy, Sir James Gilbert, Kt., O.B.E.

Hardy, Sir Rupert John, Bt., (1876).

Hare, Sir Thomas, Bt. (1818).

Harford, Sir James Dundas, K.B.E., C.M.G.

Harford, Sir (John) Timothy, Bt. (1934).

Harington, *General* Sir Charles Henry Pepys, G.C.B., C.B.E., D.S.O., M.C.

Harington, Sir Nicholas John, Bt. (1611).

Harland, *Air Marshal* Sir Reginald Edward Wynyard, K.B.E., C.B.

Harley, Sir Thomas Winlack, Kt., M.B.E., M.C.

Harman, Sir Cecil William Francis Stafford-King-, Bt. (1914).

Harman, *General* Sir Jack Wentworth, G.C.B., O.B.E., M.C.

Harman, *Hon.* Sir Jeremiah LeRoy, Kt.

Harmer, Sir Frederic Evelyn, Kt., C.M.G.

Harmer, Sir (John) Dudley, Kt., O.B.E.

Harmsworth, Sir Hildebrand Harold, Bt. (1922).

Harpham, Sir William, K.B.E., C.M.G.

Harris, *Prof.* Sir Alan James, Kt., C.B.E.

Harris, Sir Anthony Kyrle Travers, Bt. (1953).

Harris, *Prof.* Sir Charles Herbert Stuart-, Kt., C.B.E., M.D.

Harris, Sir Charles Joseph William, K.B.E.

Harris, *Lt.-Gen.* Sir Ian Cecil, K.B.E., C.B., D.S.O.

Harris, *Maj.-Gen.* Sir Jack Alexander Sutherland-, K.C.V.O., C.B.

Harris, Sir Jack Wolfred Ashford, Bt. (1932).

Harris, Sir Lewis Edward, Kt., O.B.E.

Harris, Sir Ronald Montague Joseph, K.C.V.O., C.B.

Harris, Sir William Gordon, K.B.E., C.B.

Harris, Sir William Woolf, Kt., O.B.E.

Harrison, Sir Ernest Thomas, Kt.

Harrison, Sir Francis Alexander Lyle, Kt., M.B.E., Q.C.

Harrison, Sir Geoffrey Wedgwood, G.C.M.G., K.C.V.O.

Harrison, *Surgeon Vice-Adm.* Sir John Albert Bews, K.B.E.

Harrison, *Hon.* Sir John Richard, Kt., E.D.

Harrison, Sir Michael James Harwood, Bt. (1961).

Harrison, *Prof.* Sir Richard John, Kt., F.R.S.

Harrison, Sir Robert Colin, Bt. (1922).

Harrop, Sir Peter John, K.C.B.

Hart, Sir Byrne, Kt., C.B.E., M.C.

Hart, Sir Francis Edmund Turton-, K.B.E.

Hartley, *Air Marshal* Sir Christopher Harold, K.C.B., C.B.E., D.F.C., A.F.C.

Hartley, Sir Frank, Kt., C.B.E., Ph.D.

Hartnett, Sir Laurence John, Kt., C.B.E.

Hartopp, Sir John Edmund Cradock-, Bt. (1796).

Hartwell, Sir Brodrick William Charles Elwin, Bt. (1805).

Harvey, Sir Charles Richard Musgrave, Bt. (1933).

Haskard, Sir Cosmo Dugal Patrick Thomas, K.C.M.G., M.B.E.

Haslam, *Hon.* Sir Alec Leslie, Kt.

Haslam, *Rear-Adm.* Sir David William, K.B.E., C.B.

Hasluck, *Rt. Hon.* Sir Paul Meernaa Caedwalla, K.G., G.C.M.G., G.C.V.O.

Hassan, Sir Joshua Abraham, Kt., C.B.E., M.V.O., Q.C.

Hassett, *General* Sir Francis George, K.B.E., C.B., D.S.O., M.V.O.

Hastings, Sir Stephen Lewis Edmonstone, Kt., M.C.

Hatty, Sir Cyril James, Kt.

Haughton, Sir James, Kt., C.B.E., Q.P.M.

Havelock, Sir Wilfrid Bowen, Kt.

Havers, *Rt. Hon.* Sir (Robert) Michael (Oldfield), Kt., Q.C., M.P.

Hawker, Sir (Frank) Cyril, Kt.

Hawkings, Sir Francis Geoffrey, Kt.

Hawkins, Sir Arthur Ernest, Kt.

Hawkins, Sir Humphry Villiers Caesar, Bt. (1778).

Hawkins, Sir Paul Lancelot, Kt., T.D., M.P.

Hawkins, *Vice-Adm.* Sir Raymond Shayle, K.C.B.

Hawley, *Maj.* Sir David Henry, Bt. (1795).

Hawley, Sir Donald Frederick, K.C.M.G., M.B.E.

Haworth, Sir (Arthur) Geoffrey, Bt. (1911).

Haworth, *Hon.* Sir William Crawford, Kt.

Hawthorne, *Prof.* Sir William Rede, Kt., C.B.E., SC.D., F.R.S.

Hay, Sir (Alan) Philip, K.C.V.O., T.D.

Hay, Sir Arthur Thomas Erroll, Bt., I.S.O. (s 1663).

Hay, Sir David Osborne, Kt., C.B.E., D.S.O.

Hay, Sir Frederick Baden-Powell, Bt. (s 1703).

Hay, Sir James Brian Dalrymple-, Bt. (1798).

Hayday, Sir Frederick, Kt., C.B.E.

Haydon, Sir Walter Robert, K.C.M.G.

Hayes, Sir Brian David, K.C.B.

Hayes, Sir Claude James, K.C.M.G.

Hayes, *Vice-Adm.* Sir John Osier Chattock, K.C.B., O.B.E.

Hayman, Sir Peter Telford, K.C.M.G., C.V.O., M.B.E.

Hayter, Sir William Goodenough, K.C.M.G.

Hayward, Sir Alfred, K.B.E.

Hayward, Sir Anthony William Byrd, Kt.

Hayward, Sir Edward Waterfield, Kt.

Hayward, Sir Richard Arthur, Kt., C.B.E.

Head, Sir Francis David Somerville, Bt. (1838).

Healey, Sir Charles Arthur Chadwyck-, Bt., O.B.E., T.D. (1919).

Heap, Sir Desmond, Kt.

Heath, Sir Barrie, Kt., D.F.C.

Heath, Sir Mark Evelyn, K.C.V.O., C.M.G.

Heath, *Air Marshal* Sir Maurice Lionel, K.B.E., C.B., C.V.O.

Heathcoat Amory, Sir Ian, Bt. (1874).

Heathcote, Sir Michael Perryman, Bt. (1733).

Heaton, Sir Yvo Robert Henniker-, Bt. (1912).

Hedstrom, Sir John Maynard, K.B.E.

Hein, Sir (Charles Henri) Raymond, Kt., Q.C.

Hele, Sir Ivor Thomas Henry, Kt., C.B.E.

Hellaby, Sir Frederick Reed Alan, Kt.

Hellings, *General* Sir Peter William Cradock, K.C.B., D.S.C., M.C., R.M.

Helpmann, Sir Robert Murray, Kt., C.B.E.

Henare, Sir James Clendon Tau, K.B.E., D.S.O.

Henderson, Sir Guy Wilmot McLintock, Kt., Q.C.

Henderson, Sir James Thyne, K.B.E., C.M.G.

Henderson, Sir (John) Nicholas, G.C.M.G.

Henderson, Sir Neville Vicars, Kt., C.B.E.

Henderson, *Admiral* Sir Nigel Stuart, G.B.E., K.C.B.

Henderson, Sir William MacGregor, Kt., D.SC., F.R.S.

Henley, Sir Douglas Owen, K.C.B.

Henley, *Rear-Adm.* Sir Joseph Charles Cameron, K.C.V.O., C.B.

Hennessy, Sir James Patrick Ivan, K.B.E., C.M.G.

Hennessy, Sir John Wyndham Pope-, Kt., C.B.E., F.B.A., F.S.A.

Henniker, *Brig.* Sir Mark Chandos Auberon, Bt., C.B.E., D.S.O., M.C. (1813).

Henry, Sir Denis Aynsley, Kt., O.B.E., Q.C.

Henry, Sir James Holmes, Bt., C.M.G., M.C., T.D., Q.C. (1923).

Henry, *Hon.* Sir Trevor Ernest, Kt.

Hepburn, Sir Ninian Buchan Archibald John Buchan-, Bt. (1815).

Herbecq, Sir John Edward, K.C.B.

Herbert, *Admiral* Sir Peter Geoffrey Marshall, K.C.B., O.B.E.

Hermon, Sir John Charles, Kt., O.B.E.

Heron, Sir Conrad Frederick, K.C.B., O.B.E.

Herries, Sir Michael Alexander Robert Young-, Kt., O.B.E., M.C.

Heseltine, Sir William Frederick Payne, K.C.V.O., C.B.

Hetherington, Sir Arthur Ford, Kt., D.S.C.

Howie, Sir James William, Kt., M.D.

Howlett, *Lt.-Gen.* Sir Geoffrey Hugh Whitby, K.B.E., M.C.

Hoyle, *Prof.* Sir Fred, Kt., F.R.S.

Hoyos, *Hon.* Sir Fabriciano Alexander, Kt.

Huckle, Sir (Henry) George, Kt., O.B.E.

Huddie, Sir David Patrick, Kt.

Hudleston, *Air Chief Marshal* Sir Edmund Cuthbert, G.C.B., C.B.E.

Hudson, Sir Havelock Henry Trevor, Kt.

Hudson, *Lt.-Gen.* Sir Peter, K.C.B., C.B.E.

Huggins, *Hon.* Sir Alan Armstrong, Kt.

Hugh-Jones, Sir Wynn Normington, Kt., M.V.O.

Hughes, Sir David Collingwood, Bt. (1773).

Hughes, *Prof.* Sir Edward Stuart Reginald, Kt., C.B.E.

Hughes, Sir Jack William, Kt.

Hughes, *Air Marshal* Sir (Sidney Weetman) Rochford, K.C.B., C.B.E., A.F.C.

Hughes, Sir Trevor Poulton, K.C.B.

Hughes, Sir Trevor Denby Lloyd-, Kt.

Hugo, *Lt.-Col.* Sir John Mandeville, K.C.V.O., O.B.E.

Hull, *Field Marshal* Sir Richard Amyatt, K.G., G.C.B., D.S.O.

Hulme, *Hon.* Sir Alan Shallcross, K.B.E.

Hulse, Sir (Hamilton) Westrow, Bt. (1739).

Hulton, Sir Edward George Warris, Kt.

Hulton, Sir Geoffrey Alan, Bt. (1905).

Hume, Sir Alan Blyth, Kt., C.B.

Humphreys, Sir Olliver William, Kt., C.B.E.

Humphreys, Sir (Raymond Evelyn) Myles, Kt.

Hunn, Sir Jack Kent, Kt., C.M.G.

Hunt, Sir David Wathen Stather, K.C.M.G., O.B.E.

Hunt, *General* Sir Peter Mervyn, G.C.B., D.S.O., O.B.E.

Hunt, Sir Rex Masterman, Kt., C.M.G.

Hunt, Sir Robert Frederick, Kt., C.B.E.

Hunter, *Hon.* Sir Alexander Albert, K.B.E.

Hunter, Sir Ian Bruce Hope, Kt., M.B.E.

Hurley, Sir John Garling, Kt., C.B.E.

Hutchinson, Sir Joseph Burtt, Kt., C.M.G., SC.D., F.R.S.

Hutchinson, *Hon.* Sir Ross, Kt., D.F.C.

Hutchinson, *Lt.-Cdr.* Sir (George) Ian Clark, Kt., R.N.

Hutchinson, *Hon.* Sir Michael, Kt., Q.C.

Hutchison, Sir Peter, Bt. (1939).

Hutchison, Sir Peter Craft, Bt. (1956).

Hutchison, Sir (William) Kenneth, Kt., C.B.E., F.R.S.

Hutson, Sir Francis Challenor, Kt., C.B.E.

Hutton, Sir Leonard, Kt.

Huxley, *Prof.* Sir Andrew Fielding, Kt., O.M., F.R.S.

Huxley, Sir Leonard George Holden, K.B.E., D.Phil., Ph.D.

Huxtable, *Lt.-Gen.* Sir Charles Richard, K.C.B., C.B.E.

Hyatali, *Hon.* Sir Isaac Emanuel, Kt.

Ibbs, Sir John Robin, Kt.

Illingworth, *Prof.* Sir Charles Frederick William, Kt., C.B.E.

Inch, Sir John Ritchie, Kt., C.V.O., C.B.E.

Ingilby, Sir Thomas Colvin William, Bt. (1866).

Inglefield, Sir Gilbert Samuel, G.B.E., T.D.

Inglefield, *Col.* Sir John Frederick Crompton-, Kt., T.D.

Inglis, Sir Brian Scott, Kt.

Inglis, *Maj.Gen.* Sir Drummond, K.B.E., C.B., M.C.

Inglis of Glencorse, Sir Roderick John, Bt. (s 1703).

Ingram, Sir James Herbert Charles, Bt. (1893).

Innes, Sir Charles Kenneth Gordon, Bt. (N.S. 1686).

Innes, Sir Ronald Gordon Berowald, Bt., O.B.E. (s 1628).

Inniss, *Hon.* Sir Clifford de Lisle, Kt.

Irish, Sir Ronald Arthur, Kt., O.B.E.

Ironmonger, Sir (Charles) Ronald, Kt.

Irving, *Rear-Adm.* Sir Edmund George, K.B.E., C.B.

Irwin, Sir James Campbell, Kt., O.B.E., E.D.

Isham, Sir Ian Vere Gyles, Bt. (1627).

Issigonis, Sir Alec Arnold Constantine, Kt., C.B.E., F.R.S.

Jack, *Hon.* Sir Alieu Sulayman, Kt.

Jack, Sir Daniel Thomson, Kt., C.B.E.

Jackling, Sir Roger William, G.C.M.G.

Jackman, *Air Marshal* Sir (Harold) Douglas, K.B.E., C.B.

Jackson, Sir William Mather, Bt. (1869).

Jackson, Sir Geoffrey Holt Seymour, K.C.M.G.

Jackson, Sir (John) Edward, K.C.M.G.

Jackson, *Hon.* Sir Lawrence Walter, K.C.M.G.

Jackson, Sir Michael Roland, Bt. (1902).

Jackson, Sir Nicholas Fane St. George, Bt. (1913).

Jackson, *Air Vice-Marshal* Sir Ralph Coburn, K.B.E., C.B.

Jackson, Sir Robert, Bt. (1815).

Jackson, Sir Robert Gillman Allen, K.C.V.O., C.M.G., O.B.E.

Jackson, *General* Sir William Godfrey Fothergill, G.B.E., K.C.B., M.C.

Jacob, *Lt.-Gen.* Sir (Edward) Ian (Claud), G.B.E., C.B.

Jacob, Sir Isaac Hai, Kt., Q.C.

Jacobs, *Hon.* Sir Kenneth Sydney, K.B.E.

Jacobs, Sir Wilfred Ebenezer, G.C.M.G., K.C.V.O., O.B.E., Q.C.

Jaffray, Sir William Otho, Bt. (1892).

Jagatsingh, *Hon.* Sir Kher, Kt.

Jakeway, Sir (Francis) Derek, K.C.M.G., O.B.E.

Jakobovits, Rabbi Immanuel, Kt.

James, Sir Gerard Bowes Kingston, Bt. (1823).

Janion, *Rear-Adm.* Sir Hugh Penderel, K.C.V.O.

Janvrin, *Vice-Adm.* Sir (Hugh) Richard (Benest), K.C.B., D.S.C.

Jardine, *Maj.* Sir (Andrew) Rupert (John) Buchanan-, Bt., M.C. (1885).

Jardine, Sir Andrew Colin Douglas, Bt. (1916).

Jardine, Sir William Edward, Bt., O.B.E., T.D. (s 1672).

Jarratt, Sir Alexander Anthony, Kt., C.B.

Jarrett, Sir Clifford George, K.B.E., C.B.

Jawara, *Hon.* Sir Dawda Kairaba, Kt.

Jeewoolall, Sir Ramesh, Kt.

Jeffcoate, *Prof.* Sir (Thomas) Norman (Arthur), Kt., F.R.C.S.

Jefferson, Sir George Rowland, Kt., C.B.E.

Jefferson, Sir Mervyn Stewart Dunnington-, Bt. (1958).

Jeffreys, *Prof.* Sir Harold, Kt., D.SC., F.R.S.

Jehangir, Sir Hirjee Cowasjee, Bt. (1908).

Jejeebhoy, Sir Rustom, Bt. (1857).

Jellicoe, Sir Geoffrey Alan, Kt., C.B.E., F.R.I.B.A.

Jenkins, Sir Evan Meredith, G.C.I.E., K.C.S.I.

Jenkins, Sir Owain Trevor, Kt.

Jenkinson, Sir Anthony Banks, Bt. (1661).

Jenks, Sir Richard Atherley, Bt. (1932).

Jennings, Sir Albert Victor, Kt.

Jennings, Sir Raymond Winter, Kt., Q.C.

Jennings, *Prof.* Sir Robert Yewdall, Kt., Q.C.

Jenour, Sir (Arthur) Maynard (Chesterfield), Kt., T.D.

Jephcott, *Hon.* Sir Bruce Reginald, Kt., C.B.E.

Jephcott, Sir (John) Anthony, Bt. (1962).

Jessel, Sir Charles John, Bt. (1883).

Joel, *Hon.* Sir Asher Alexander, K.B.E.

John, Sir Rupert Godfrey, Kt.

Johnson, *Hon.* Sir David Powell Croom-, Kt., D.S.C., V.R.D.

Johnson, Sir Henry Cecil, K.B.E.

Johnson, Sir Peter Colpoys Paley, Bt. (1755).

Johnson, Sir Ronald Ernest Charles, Kt., C.B.

Johnson, Sir Victor Philipse Hill, Bt. (1818).

Johnson Smith, Sir Geoffrey, Kt., M.P.

Johnston, Sir Alexander, G.C.B., K.B.E.

Johnston, Sir Charles Collier, Kt., T.D.

Johnston, Sir Charles Hepburn, G.C.M.G.

Johnston, Sir John Baines, G.C.M.G., K.C.V.O.

Johnston, *Lt.-Gen.* Sir Maurice Robert, K.C.B., O.B.E.

Johnston, Sir Thomas Alexander, Bt. (s 1626).

Johnstone, Sir Frederic Allan George, Bt. (s 1700).

Jolliffe, Sir Anthony Stuart, G.B.E.

Jones, *Maj.-Gen.* Sir (Arthur) Guy Salisbury-, G.C.V.O., C.M.G., C.B.E., M.C.

Jones, Sir Brynmor, Kt., Ph.D., SC.D.

Jones, *General* Sir Charles Phibbs, G.C.B., C.B.E., M.C.

Jones, Sir Christopher Lawrence-, Bt. (1831).

Jones, *Air Marshal* Sir Edward Gordon, K.C.B., C.B.E., D.S.O., D.F.C.

Jones, *Rt. Hon.* Sir Edward Warburton, Kt.

Jones, Sir Edwin Martin Furnival, Kt., C.B.E.

Jones, Sir Eric Malcolm, K.C.M.G., C.B., C.B.E.

Jones, *Prof.* Sir Ewart Ray Herbert, Kt., D.SC., Ph.D., F.R.S.

Jones, Sir Francis Avery, Kt., C.B.E., F.R.C.P.

Jones, *Air Marshal* Sir George, K.B.E., C.B., D.F.C.

Jones, Sir Glyn Smallwood, G.C.M.G., M.B.E.

Jones, Sir Harry Ernest, Kt., C.B.E.

Jones, Sir Harry Vincent Lloyd-, Kt.

Jones, Sir Henry Frank Harding, G.B.E.

Jones, Sir James Duncan, K.C.B.

Jones, *Air Marshal* Sir (John) Humphrey Edwardes, K.C.B., C.B.E., D.F.C., A.F.C.

Jones, Sir (John) Kenneth (Trevor), Kt., C.B.E., Q.C.

Jones, Sir John Lewis, K.C.B., C.M.G.

Jones, Sir John Prichard-, Bt. (1910).

Jones, Sir Keith Stephen, Kt.

Jones, *Hon.* Sir Kenneth George Illtyd, Kt.

Jones, Sir (Owen) Trevor, Kt.

Jones, Sir Samuel Owen, Kt.

Jones, Sir Simon Warley Frederick Benton, Bt. (1919).

Jones, Sir (William) Elwyn (Edwards), Kt.

Jones, Sir (William) Emrys, Kt.

Jones, *Hon.* Sir William Lloyd Mars-, Kt., M.B.E.

Jordan, *Air Marshal* Sir Richard Bowen, K.C.B., D.F.C.

Joseph, *Maj.* Sir (Herbert) Leslie, Kt.

Joseph, *Rt. Hon.* Sir Keith Sinjohn, Bt., M.P. (1943).

Jungius, *Vice-Adm.*, Sir James George, K.B.E.

Junor, Sir John Donald Brown, Kt.

Jupp, *Hon.* Sir Kenneth Graham, Kt., M.C.

Kalo, Sir Kwamala, Kt., M.B.E.

Kan Yuet-Keung, *Hon.* Sir, G.B.E.

Karimjee, Sir Tayabali Hassanali Alibhoy, Kt.

Katsina, The Emir of, K.B.E., C.M.G.

Katz, *Prof.* Sir Bernard, Kt., F.R.S.

Kavali, Sir Thomas, Kt., O.B.E.

Kay, *Prof.* Sir Andrew Watt, Kt.

Kaye, Sir Emmanuel, Kt., C.B.E.

Kaye, Sir John Phillip Lister Lister-, Bt. (1812).

Kaye, Sir David Alexander Gordon, Bt. (1923).

Keane, Sir Richard Michael, Bt. (1801).

Keatinge, Sir Edgar Mayne, Kt., C.B.E.

Keeble, Sir (Herbert Ben) Curtis, G.C.M.G.

Kellett, Sir Brian Smith, Kt.

Kellett, Sir Stanley Everard, Bt. (1801).

Kelliher, Sir Henry Joseph, Kt.

Kelly, *Rt. Hon.* Sir (John William) Basil, Kt.

Kelly, Sir William Theodore, Kt., O.B.E.

Kemp, Sir Leslie Charles, K.B.E.

Kemsley, *Col.* Sir Alfred Newcombe, K.B.E., C.M.G., E.D.

Kendrew, *Maj.-Gen.* Sir Douglas Anthony, K.C.M.G., C.B., C.B.E., D.S.O.

Kendrew, Sir John Cowdery, Kt., C.B.E., SC.D., F.R.S.

Kenilorea, *Rt. Hon.* Sir Peter, K.B.E.

Kennard, *Lt.-Col.* Sir George Arnold Ford, Bt. (1891).

Kennaway, Sir John Lawrence, Bt. (1791).

Kennedy, Sir Albert Henry, Kt.

Kennedy, Sir Clyde David Allen, Kt.

Kennedy, Sir George Ronald Derrick, Bt., O.B.E. (1836).

Kennedy, *Hon.* Sir Paul Joseph Morrow, Kt., Q.C.

Kennedy, *Air Chief Marshal* Sir Thomas Lawrie, K.C.B., A.F.C.

Kennedy-Good, Sir John, K.B.E.

Kennon, *Vice-Adm.* Sir James Edward Campbell, K.C.B., C.B.E.

Kenny, Sir Patrick John, Kt.

Kent, Sir Harold Simcox, G.C.B., Q.C.

Kent, Sir Percy Edward (Peter), Kt., D.SC., Ph.D., F.R.S.

Kenyon, Sir George Henry, Kt.

Kerr, *Rt. Hon.* Sir John Robert, G.C.M.G., G.C.V.O.

Kerr, *Rt. Hon.* Sir Michael Robert Emanuel, Kt.

Kerr, *Hon.* Sir Alastair Blair-, Kt.

Kerruish, Sir Henry Charles, Kt., O.B.E.

Kerry, Sir Michael James, K.C.B., Q.C.

Kershaw, Sir (John) Anthony, Kt., M.C., M.P.

Keswick, Sir William Johnston, Kt.

Keville, Sir (William) Errington, Kt., C.B.E.

Kidd, Sir Robert Hill, K.B.E., C.B.

Kidu, *Hon.* Sir Buri (William), Kt.

Kikau, *Ratu* Sir Jone Latianara, K.B.E.

Kiki, *Hon.* Sir (Albert) Maori, K.B.E.

Killen, *Hon.* Denis James, K.C.M.G.

Killick, Sir John Edward, G.C.M.G.

Kilpatrick, Sir William John, K.B.E.

Kimball, Sir Marcus Richard, Kt.

Kimber, Sir Charles Dixon, Bt. (1904).

Kinahan, Sir Robert George Caldwell, Kt., E.R.D.

King, Sir Albert, Kt., O.B.E.

King, *General* Sir Frank Douglas, G.C.B., M.B.E.

King, Sir James Granville Le Neve, Bt., T.D. (1888).

King, Sir Richard Brian Meredith, K.C.B., M.C.

King, Sir Sydney Percy, Kt., O.B.E.

King, Sir Wayne Alexander, Bt. (1815).

Kingsland, Sir Richard, Kt., C.B.E., D.F.C.

Kingsley, Sir Patrick Graham Toler, K.C.V.O.

Kininmonth, Sir William Hardie, Kt., F.R.S.A., F.R.I.B.A.

Kinloch, Sir David, Bt. (s 1686).

Kinloch, Sir John, Bt. (1873).

Kirby, *Hon.* Sir Richard Clarence, Kt.

Kirkley, Sir (Howard) Leslie, Kt., C.B.E.

Kirkpatrick, Sir Ivone Elliott, Bt. (s 1685).

Kirwan, Sir (Archibald) Laurence Patrick, K.C.M.G., T.D.

Kitson, *General* Sir Frank Edward, K.C.B., C.B.E., M.C.

Kitson, Sir Timothy Peter Geoffrey, Kt.

Kitto, *Rt. Hon.* Sir Frank Walters, K.B.E.

Kleinwort, Sir Kenneth Drake, Bt. (1909).

Knight, Sir Allan Walton, Kt., C.M.G.

Knight, Sir Arthur William, Kt.

Knight, Sir Harold Murray, K.B.E., D.S.C.

Knight, *Air Marshal* Sir Michael William Patrick, K.C.B., A.F.C.

Knights, Sir Philip Douglas, Kt., C.B.E., Q.P.M.

Knill, Sir John Kenelm Stuart, Bt. (1893).

Knipe, Sir Leslie Francis, Kt., M.B.E.

Knott, Sir John Laurence, Kt., C.B.E.

Knowles, Sir Charles Francis, Bt. (1765).

Knowles, Sir Leonard Joseph, Kt., C.B.E.

Knox, *Hon.* Sir William Edward, Kt.

Kornberg, *Prof.* Sir Hans Leo, Kt., D.SC., SC.D., Ph.D., F.R.S.

Krusin, Sir Stanley Marks, Kt., C.B.

Kyle, *Air Chief Marshal* Sir Wallace Hart, G.C.B., K.C.V.O., C.B.E., D.S.O., D.F.C.

Labouchere, Sir George Peter, G.B.E., K.C.M.G.

Lacon, Sir Edmund Vere, Bt. (1818).

Lacy, Sir Hugh Maurice Pierce, Bt. (1921).

Lagesen, *Air Marshal* Sir Philip Jacobus, K.C.B., D.F.C., A.F.C.

Laidlaw, Sir Christophor Charles Fraser, Kt.

Laing, Sir Hector, Kt.

Laing, Sir (John) Maurice, Kt.

Laing, Sir (William) Kirby, Kt.

Laithwaite, Sir (John) Gilbert, G.C.M.G., K.C.B., K.C.I.E., C.S.I.

Lake, Sir (Atwell) Graham, Bt. (1711).

Laker, Sir Frederick Alfred, Kt.

Lakin, Sir Michael, Bt. (1909).

Lamb, Sir Albert (Larry), Kt.

Lamb, Sir Albert Thomas, K.B.E., C.M.G., D.F.C.

Lamb, Sir Lionel Henry, K.C.M.G., O.B.E.

Lambart, Sir Oliver Francis, Bt. (1911).

Lambert, Sir Anthony Edward, K.C.M.G.

Lambert, Sir Edward Thomas, K.B.E., C.V.O.

Lambert, Sir Greville Foley, Bt. (1711).

Lambert, Sir John Henry, K.C.V.O., C.M.G.

Lancaster, *Vice-Adm.* Sir John Strike, K.B.E., C.B.

Lancaster, Sir Osbert, Kt., C.B.E.

Lane, Sir David William Stennis Stuart, Kt.

Lane, Sir Peter Stewart, Kt.

Lang, *Lt.-Gen.* Sir Derek Boileau, K.C.B., D.S.O., M.C.

Lang, Sir John Gerald, G.C.B.

Langham, Sir James Michael, Bt. (1660).

Langley, *Maj.-Gen.* Sir Henry Desmond Allen, K.C.V.O., M.B.E.

Langman, Sir John Lyell, Bt. (1906).

Langrishe, Sir Hercules Ralph Hume, Bt. (1 1777).

Lapsley, *Air Marshal* Sir John Hugh, K.B.E., C.B., D.F.C., A.F.C.

Lapun, *Hon.* Sir Paul, Kt.

Larcom, Sir (Charles) Christopher Royden, Bt. (1868).

Larmour, Sir Edward Noel, K.C.M.G.

Lartigue, Sir Louis Cools-, Kt., O.B.E.

Lasdun, Sir Denys Louis, Kt., C.B.E., F.R.I.B.A.

Laskey, Sir Denis Seward, K.C.M.G., C.V.O.

Latey, *Hon.* Sir John Brinsmead, Kt., M.B.E.

Latham, Sir Joseph, Kt., C.B.E.

Latham, Sir Richard Thomas Paul, Bt. (1919).

Latimer, Sir Courtenay Robert, Kt., C.B.E.

Latimer, Sir Graham Stanley, K.B.E.

Laucke, *Hon.* Sir Condor Louis, K.C.M.G.

Lauder, Sir Piers Robert Dick-, Bt. (s 1690).

Laurantus, Sir Nicholas, Kt., M.B.E.

Laurence, Sir Peter Harold, K.C.M.G., M.C.

Laurie, Sir Robert Bayley Emilius, Bt. (1834).

Lavan, *Hon.* Sir John Martin, Kt.

Law, *Hon.* Sir Eric John Ewan, Kt.

Law, *Admiral* Sir Horace Rochfort, G.C.B., O.B.E., D.S.C.

Lawes, Sir (John) Michael Bennet, Bt. (1882).

Lawler, Sir Peter James, Kt., O.B.E.

Lawrence, Sir David Roland Walter, Bt. (1906).

Lawrence, Sir Guy Kempton, Kt., D.S.O., O.B.E., D.F.C.

Lawrence, Sir John Waldemar, Bt., O.B.E. (1858).

Lawrence, Sir Robert Leslie Edward, Kt., C.B.E., F.R.S.

Lawrence, Sir William, Bt. (1867).

Lawson, Sir Christopher Donald, Kt.

Lawson, *Lt.-Col.* Sir John Charles Arthur Digby, Bt., D.S.O., M.C. (1900).

Lawson, *Hon.* Sir Neil, Kt.

Lawson, *Gen.* Sir Richard George, K.C.B., D.S.O., O.B.E.

Lawson, Sir William Howard, Bt. (1841).

Lawton, *Prof.* Sir Frank Ewart, Kt.

Lawton, *Rt. Hon.* Sir Frederick Horace, Kt.

Layfield, Sir Frank Henry Burland Willoughby, Kt., Q.C.

Lea, *Lt.-Gen.* Sir George Harris, K.C.B., D.S.O., M.B.E.

Lea, *Vice-Adm.,* Sir John Stuart Crosbie, K.B.E.

Lea, Sir Thomas Claude Harris, Bt. (1892).

Leach, *Prof.* Sir Edmund Ronald, Kt., Ph.D., F.B.A.

Leach, *Admiral of the Fleet* Sir Henry Conyers, G.C.B.

Leach, Sir Ronald George, G.B.E.

Leahy, Sir John Henry Gladstone, K.C.M.G.

Lean, Sir David, Kt., C.B.E.

Leask, *Lt.-Gen.* Sir Henry Lowther Ewart Clark, K.C.B., D.S.O., O.B.E.

Leather, Sir Edwin Hartley Cameron, K.C.M.G., K.C.V.O.

Leaver, Sir Christopher, G.B.E.

Le Bailly, *Vice-Adm.* Sir Louis Edward Stewart Holland, K.B.E., C.B.

Le Cheminant, *Air Chief Marshal* Sir Peter de Lacey, G.B.E., K.C.B., D.F.C.

Lechmere, Sir Berwick Hungerford, Bt. (1818).

Ledger, Sir Joseph Francis, Kt.

Ledwidge, Sir (William) Bernard (John), K.C.M.G.

Lee, Sir Arthur James, K.B.E., M.C.

Lee, *Air Chief Marshal* Sir David John Pryer, G.B.E., C.B.

Lee, Sir (George) Wilton, Kt.

Lee Hau Shik, *Col.* Sir, K.B.E.

Lee, Sir (Henry) Desmond (Pritchard), Kt.

Lee, *Brig.* Sir Leonard Henry, Kt., C.B.E.

Lee, *Col.* Sir William Allison, Kt., O.B.E., T.D.

Leeds, Sir Christopher Anthony, Bt. (1812).

Lees, *Air Marshal* Sir (Ronald) Beresford, K.C.B., C.B.E., D.F.C.

Lees, Sir Thomas Edward, Bt. (1897).

Lees, Sir Thomas Harcourt Ivor, Bt. (1804).

Lees, Sir William Antony Clare, Bt. (1937).

Leese, Sir John Henry Vernon, Bt. (1908).

Le Fleming, Sir William Kelland, Bt. (1705).

Legard, Sir Charles Thomas, Bt. (1660).

Leggatt, *Hon.* Sir Andrew Peter, Kt.

Leggett, Sir Clarence Arthur Campbell, Kt., M.B.E.

Leggo, Sir Jack Frederick, Kt., D.F.C.

Legh, *Major* Hon. Sir Francis Michael, K.C.V.O.

Leigh, Sir John, Bt. (1918).

Leigh, Sir Neville Egerton, K.C.V.O.

Leighton, Sir Michael John Bryan, Bt. (1693).

Leitch, Sir George, K.C.B., O.B.E.

Leith, Sir Andrew George Forbes-, Bt. (1923).

Le Marchant, Sir Denis, Bt. (1841).

Le Marchant, Sir Spencer, Kt.

Le Masurier, Sir Robert Hugh, Kt., D.S.C.

Lemon, Sir (Richard) Dawnay, Kt., C.B.E.

Leng, *General* Sir Peter John Hall, K.C.B., M.B.E., M.C.

Lennard, *Rev.* Sir Hugh Dacre Barrett-, Bt. (1801).

Lennox, *Rear Adm.* Sir Alexander Henry Charles, K.C.V.O., C.B., D.S.O.

Lennox, *Lt.-Gen.* Sir George Charles Gordon, K.B.E., C.B., C.V.O., D.S.O.

Leon, Sir John Ronald, Bt. (1911).

Leonard, *Hon.* Sir (Hamilton) John, Kt., Q.C.

Leonard, Sir Reginald Byron, Kt., C.M.G., O.B.E.

Leonard, Sir Walter McEllister, Kt., D.F.C.

Le Quesne, Sir (Charles) Martin, K.C.M.G.

Le Quesne, Sir (John) Godfray, Kt., Q.C.

Leslie, Sir John Norman Ide, Bt. (1876).

†Leslie, Sir (Percy) Theodore, Bt. (s 1625).

Lethbridge, Sir Thomas Periam Hector Noel, Bt. (1804).

Leuchars, Sir William Douglas, K.B.E.

Leuchars, Sir William Douglas, K.B.E.

Lever, Sir (Tresham) Christopher Arthur Lindsay, Bt. (1911).

Levey, Sir Michael Vincent, Kt., M.V.O.

Levine, Sir Montague Bernard, Kt.

Levinge, *Maj.* Sir Richard Vere Henry, Bt., M.B.E. (1 1704).

Levy, Sir (Enoch) Bruce, Kt., O.B.E.

Levy, Sir Ewart Maurice, Bt. (1913).

Lewando, Sir Jan Alfred, Kt., C.B.E.

Lewis, Sir Allen Montgomery, G.C.M.G., Q.C.

Lewis, *Admiral* Sir Andrew Mackenzie, K.C.B.

Lewis, Sir Ian Malcolm, Kt.

Lewis, *Prof.* Sir Jack, Kt., F.R.S.

Lewis, Sir Kenneth, Kt., M.P.

Lewis, Sir William Arthur, Kt.

Lewthwaite, Sir William Anthony, Bt. (1927).

Ley, Sir Francis Douglas, Bt., M.B.E., T.D. (1905).

Leyland, Sir Vivyan Edward Naylor-, Bt. (1895).

Lickley, Sir Robert Lang, Kt., C.B.E.

Lidbury, Sir John Towersey, Kt.

Lidderdale, Sir David William Shuckburgh, K.C.B.

Liddle, Sir Donald Ross, Kt.

Liggins, Sir Edmund Naylor, Kt., T.D.

Lighthill, *Prof.* Sir (Michael) James, Kt., F.R.S.

Lighton, Sir Christopher Robert, Bt., M.B.E. (I 1791).

Lim, Sir Han Hoe, Kt., C.B.E.

Lincoln, Sir Anthony Handley, K.C.M.G., C.V.O.

Lincoln, *Hon.* Sir Anthony Leslie Julian, Kt.

Lindley, Sir Arnold Lewis George, Kt.

Lindop, Sir Norman, Kt.

Lindsay, Sir James Harvey Kincaid Stewart, Kt.

Lindsay, Sir Ronald Alexander, Bt., (1962).

Lindsay, Sir William, Kt., C.B.E.

Lindsay-Fynn, Sir Basil Mortimer, Kt.

Linstead, Sir Hugh Nicholas, Kt., O.B.E.

Lintott, Sir Henry John Bevis, K.C.M.G.

Lithgow, Sir William James, Bt. (1925).

Little, *Hon.* Sir Douglas Macfarlane, Kt.

Little, *Most Rev.* Thomas Francis, K.B.E.

Littler, Sir Emile, Kt.

Livermore, Sir Harry, Kt.

Llewellyn, Sir David Treharne, Kt.

Llewellyn, Sir (Frederick) John, K.C.M.G.

Llewellyn, *Lt.-Col.* Sir Henry Morton, Bt., C.B.E. (1922).

Llewellyn, *Col.* Sir (Robert) Godfrey, Bt., C.B., C.B.E., M.C., T.D. (1959).

Llewelyn, Sir John Michael Dillwyn-Venables-, Bt. (1890).

Lloyd, *Hon.* Sir Anthony John Leslie, Kt.

Lloyd, *Maj.* Sir (Ernest) Guy (Richard), Bt., D.S.O. (1960).

Lloyd, Sir (John) Peter (Daniel), Kt.

Loane, *Most Rev.* Marcus Lawrence, K.B.E.

Lock, *Comdr.* Sir (John) Duncan, Kt.

Lockhart, Sir Muir Edward Sinclair-, Bt. (s 1636).

Lockspeiser, Sir Ben, K.C.B., F.R.S.

Lockwood, Sir Joseph Flawith, Kt.

Loder, Sir Giles Rolls, Bt. (1887).

Lodge, Sir Thomas, Kt.

Loehnis, Sir Clive, K.C.M.G.

Loewen, *General* Sir Charles Falkland, G.C.B., K.B.E., D.S.O.

Logan, Sir Donald Arthur, K.C.M.G.

Logan, Sir Douglas William, Kt., D.Phil.

Logan, Sir Raymond Douglas, Kt.

Lokoloko, Sir Tore, G.C.M.G., G.C.V.O., O.B.E.

Lomax, Sir John Garnett, K.B.E., C.M.G., M.C.

Long, Sir Ronald, Kt.

Longden, Sir Gilbert James Morley, M.B.E.

Longland, Sir David Walter, Kt., C.M.G.

Longland, Sir John Laurence, Kt.

Longley, Sir Norman, Kt., C.B.E.

Looker, Sir Cecil Thomas, Kt.

Loram, *Vice-Adm.* Sir David Anning, K.C.B., M.V.O.

Lorimer, Sir (Thomas) Desmond, Kt.

Lousada, Sir Anthony Baruh, Kt.

Lovell, *Prof.* Sir (Alfred Charles) Bernard, Kt., O.B.E., F.R.S.

Lovelock, Sir Douglas Arthur, K.C.B.

Loveridge, Sir John Henry, Kt., C.B.E.

Low, Sir Alan Roberts, Kt.

Low, Sir James Richard Morrison-, Bt. (1908).

Lowe, *Air Chief Marshal* Sir Douglas Charles, G.C.B., D.F.C., A.F.C.

Lowe, *Air Vice-Marshal* Sir Edgar Noel, K.B.E., C.B.

Lowe, Sir Francis Reginald Gordon, Bt. (1918).

Lowson, Sir Ian Patrick, Bt. (1951).

Lowther, *Maj.* Sir Charles Douglas, Bt. (1824).

Loyd, Sir Francis Alfred, K.C.M.G., O.B.E.

Lubbock, Sir Alan, Kt., F.S.A.

Lucas, Sir Cyril Edward, Kt., C.M.G., F.R.S.

Lucas, Sir Thomas Edward, Bt. (1887).

Luckhoo, *Hon.* Sir Joseph Alexander, Kt.

Luckhoo, Sir Lionel Alfred, K.C.M.G., C.B.E., Q.C.

Lucy, Sir Edmund John William Hugh Cameron-Ramsay-Fairfax, Bt. (1836).

Luddington, Sir Donald Collin Cumyn, K.B.E., C.M.G., C.V.O.

Luke, *Hon.* Sir Emile Fashole, K.B.E.

Luke, Sir Stephen Elliot Vyvyan, K.C.M.G.

Lumby, Sir Henry, Kt., C.B.E.

Lus, *Hon.* Sir Pita, Kt., O.B.E.

Lush, *Hon.* Sir George Hermann, Kt.

Lushington, Sir Henry Edmund Castleman, Bt. (1791).

Lusty, Sir Robert Frith, Kt.

Luyt, Sir Richard Edmonds, G.C.M.G., K.C.V.O., D.C.M.

Lygo, *Admiral* Sir Raymond Derek, K.C.B.

Lyle, Sir Gavin Archibald, Bt. (1929).

Lyons, Sir Edward Houghton, Kt.

Lyons, Sir (Isidore) Jack, Kt., C.B.E.

Lyons, Sir James Reginald, Kt.

Lyons, *His Hon.* Sir Rudolph, Kt., Q.C.

Lyons, Sir William, Kt.

McAdam, Sir Ian William James, Kt., O.B.E.

Macadam, Sir Peter, Kt.

McAllister, Sir Reginald Basil, Kt., C.M.G., C.V.O.

McAlpine, *Hon.* Sir (John) Kenneth, K.C.M.G.

McAlpine, Sir Robin, Kt., C.B.E.

Macara, Sir (Charles) Douglas, Bt. (1911).

McArthur, *Col.* Sir Malcolm Hugh, Kt., O.B.E.

Macartney, Sir John Barrington, Bt. (I 1799).

Macaulay, Sir Hamilton, Kt., C.B.E.

McAvoy, Sir (Francis) Joseph, Kt., C.B.E.

McCaffrey, Sir Thomas Daniel, Kt.

McCall, Sir Charles Patrick Home, Kt., M.B.E., T.D.

McCarthy, *Rt. Hon.* Sir Thaddeus Pearcey, K.B.E.

McCauley, *Air Marshal* Sir John Patrick Joseph, K.B.E., C.B.

McCaw, *Hon.* Sir Kenneth Malcolm, Kt., Q.C.

McClintock, Sir Eric Paul, Kt.

McConnell, *Cdr.* Sir Robert Melville Terence, Bt., V.R.D. (1900).

McCowan, *Hon.* Sir Anthony James Denys, Kt., Q.C.

McCowan, Sir Hew Cargill, Bt. (1934).

McCray, Sir Lionel Joseph, Kt.

McCullough, *Hon.* Sir (Iain) Charles (Robert), Kt.

McCusker, Sir James Alexander, Kt.

MacDermot, Sir Dermot Francis, K.C.M.G., C.B.E.

McDermott, Sir (Lawrence) Emmet, K.B.E.

MacDonald, *General* Sir Arthur Leslie, K.B.E., C.B.

McDonald, *Air Chief Marshal* Sir Arthur William Baynes, K.C.B., A.F.C.

McDonald, Sir Duncan, Kt., C.B.E.

Macdonald, Sir Herbert George deLorme, K.B.E.

Macdonald of Sleat, Sir Ian Godfrey Bosville, Bt. (s 1625).

McDonald, Sir James, K.B.E.

Macdonald, *Vice-Adm.* Sir Roderick Douglas, K.B.E.

McDonald, *Hon.* Sir William John Farquhar, Kt.

MacDonald, *Air Chief Marshal* Sir William Laurence Mary, G.C.B., C.B.E., D.F.C.

MacDougall, Sir (George) Donald (Alastair), Kt., C.B.E., F.B.A.

McDowell, Sir Frank Schofield, Kt.

McDowell, Sir Henry McLorinan, K.B.E.

McEvoy, *Air Chief Marshal* Sir Theodore Newman, K.C.B., C.B.E.

McEwen, Sir John Roderick Hugh, Bt. (1953).

McEwin, *Hon.* Sir (Alexander) Lyell, K.B.E.

McFarland, Sir Basil (Alexander Talbot), Bt., C.B.E. (1914).
McFarlane, Sir Ian, Kt.
Macfarlane, Sir George Gray, Kt., C.B.
Macfarlane, Sir James Wright, Kt.
Macfarlane, Sir Norman Somerville, Kt.
MacFarquhar, Sir Alexander, K.B.E., C.I.E.
McGeoch, *Vice-Adm.* Sir Ian Lachlan Mackay, K.C.B., D.S.O., D.S.C.
Macgregor, Sir Edwin Robert, Bt. (1828).
MacGregor of MacGregor, Sir Gregor, Bt. (1795).
McGregor, Sir Ian Alexander, Kt., C.B.E., F.R.S.
McGrigor, *Capt.* Sir Charles Edward, Bt. (1831).
McInerney, *Hon.* Sir Murray Vincent, Kt.
McIntosh, *Vice-Adm.* Sir Ian Stewart, K.B.E., C.B., D.S.O., D.S.C.
Macintosh, *Prof.* Sir Robert Reynolds, Kt., M.D.
McIntosh, Sir Ronald Robert Duncan, K.C.B.
Mack, *Hon.* Sir William George Albert, K.B.E.
McKaig, *Admiral* Sir (John) Rae, K.C.B., C.B.E.
McKay, *Hon.* Sir Donald Norman, K.C.M.G.
Mackay, Sir George Patrick Gordon, Kt., C.B.E.
Mackay, Sir James Mackerron, K.B.E., C.B.
McKay, Sir James Wilson, Kt.
Mackay, Sir John Andrew, Kt., C.B.E.
Mackay, Sir William Calder, Kt., O.B.E., M.C.
McKee, *Air Marshal* Sir Andrew, K.C.B., C.B.E., D.S.O., D.F.C., A.F.C.
McKee, *Maj.* Sir William Cecil, Kt., E.R.D.
McKell, *Rt. Hon.* Sir William John, G.C.M.G., Q.C.
MacKenna, Sir Bernard Joseph Maxwell, Kt.
McKenzie, Sir Alexander, K.B.E.
Mackenzie, Sir Alexander Alwyne Brinton Muir-, Bt. (1805).
Mackenzie, Sir (Alexander George Anthony) Allan, Bt. (1890).
Mackenzie, *Vice-Adm.* Sir Hugh Stirling, K.C.B., D.S.O., D.S.C.
Mackenzie, Sir Robert Evelyn, Bt. (s 1673)
Mackenzie, *Capt.* Sir Roderick (Edward François McQuhae), Bt. (s 1703).
Mackeson, Sir Rupert Henry, Bt. (1954).
Mackie, Sir Maitland, Kt., C.B.E.
McKie, Sir William Neil, Kt., M.V.O., D.Mus.
MacKinlay, Sir Bruce, Kt., C.B.E.
MacKintosh, Sir Angus Mackay, K.C.V.O., C.M.G.
McKissock, Sir Wylie, Kt., O.B.E., F.R.C.S.
Mackworth, *Cdr.* Sir David Arthur Geoffrey, Bt. (1776).

Maclaren, Sir Hamish Duncan, K.B.E., C.B., D.F.C.
Maclean, Sir Fitzroy Hew Royle, Bt., C.B.E. (1957).
McLean, Sir Francis Charles, Kt., C.B.E.
MacLean, *Vice-Adm.* Sir Hector Charles Donald, K.B.E., C.B., D.S.C.
McLean, *Lt.-Gen.* Sir Kenneth Graeme, K.C.B., K.B.E.
Maclean, Sir Robert Alexander, K.B.E.
MacLellan, Sir (George) Robin (Perronet), Kt., C.B.E.
Maclennan, Sir Ian Morrison Ross, K.C.M.G.
McLennan, Sir Ian Munro, K.C.M.G., K.B.E.
McLeod, Sir Charles Henry, Bt. (1925).
McLeod, Sir Ian George, Kt.
Macklin, Sir Bruce Roy, Kt., O.B.E.
McLintock, Sir William Traven, Bt. (1934).
Maclure, Sir John Robert Spencer, Bt. (1898).
McMahon, Sir Brian Patrick, Bt. (1817).
McMahon, *Rt. Hon.* Sir William, G.C.M.G., C.H.
McMichael, *Prof.* Sir John, Kt., M.D., F.R.S.
MacMillan, Sir Kenneth, Kt.
MacMillan, *General* Sir Gordon Holmes Alexander, K.C.B., K.C.V.O., C.B.E., D.S.O., M.C.
Macmillan, Sir Alexander McGregor Graham, Kt.
Macmillan, Sir (James) Wilson, K.B.E.
McMullin, *Hon.* Sir Alister Maxwell, K.C.M.G.
Macnab, *Brig.* Sir Geoffrey Alex Colin, K.C.M.G., C.B.
Macnaghten, Sir Patrick Alexander, Bt. (1836).
McNamara, *Air Marshal* Sir Neville Patrick, K.B.E., D.F.C.
McNee, Sir David Blackstock, Kt., Q.P.M.
McNeice, Sir (Thomas) Percy (Fergus), Kt., C.M.G., O.B.E.
McNeill, *Hon.* Sir David Bruce, Kt.
McNicoll, *Vice-Adm.* Sir Alan Wedel Ramsay, K.B.E., C.B., G.M.
McPetrie, Sir James Carnegie, K.C.M.G., O.B.E.
MacPherson, Sir Keith Duncan, Kt.
Macpherson, *Hon.* Sir William Alan, Kt., T.D.
Macready, Sir Nevil John Wilfrid, Bt. (1923).
Macrory, Sir Patrick Arthur, Kt.
McShine, *Hon.* Sir Arthur Hugh, Kt.
Mactaggart, Sir Ian Auld, Bt. (1938).
MacTier, Sir (Reginald) Stewart, Kt., C.B.E.
McTiernan, *Rt. Hon.* Sir Edward Aloysius, K.B.E.
Madden, *Admiral* Sir Charles Edward, Bt., G.C.B. (1919).
Maddock, Sir Ieuan, Kt., C.B., O.B.E., F.R.S.

Maddocks, Sir Kenneth Phipson, K.C.M.G., K.C.V.O.
Maddox, Sir (John) Kempson, Kt., V.R.D., M.D.
Madhorao Genesh Deshpande *Rao Bahadur* Sir, K.B.E.
Madigan, Sir Russell Tullie, Kt., O.B.E.
Magarey, Sir James Rupert, Kt.
Magill, Sir Ivan Whiteside, K.C.V.O.
Maguire, *Air Marshal* Sir Harold John, K.C.B., D.S.O., O.B.E.
Mahon, Sir George Edward John, Bt. (1819).
Maihar, The Maharaja of, K.C.I.E.
Maini, Sir Amar Nath, Kt., C.B.E.
Mais, *Hon.* Sir (Robert) Hugh, Kt.
Maitland, Sir Donald James Dundas, G.C.M.G., O.B.E.
Maitland, Sir Richard John, Bt. (1818).
Makins, Sir Paul Vivian, Bt. (1903).
Malcolm, Sir David Peter Michael, Bt. (s. 1665).
Malet, *Col.* Sir Edward William St. Lo, Bt., O.B.E. (1791).
Mallabar, Sir John Frederick, Kt.
Mallet, Sir (William) Ivo, G.B.E., K.C.M.G.
Mallinson, Sir (William) Paul, Bt. (1935).
Malone, *Hon.* Sir Denis Eustace Gilbert, Kt.
Mamo, Sir Anthony Joseph, Kt., O.B.E.
Mander, Sir Charles Marcus, Bt. (1911).
Mandi, *Col.* H.H. the Raja of, K.C.S.I.
Mann, *Hon.* Sir Michael, Kt.
Mann, Sir Rupert Edward, Bt. (1905).
Mansel, *Rev. Canon* James Seymour Denis, K.C.V.O.
Mansel, Sir Philip, Bt. (1622).
Mansergh, *Vice-Adm.* Sir (Cecil) Aubrey (Lawson), K.B.E., C.B., D.S.C.
Mansfield, *Vice-Adm.* Sir (Edward) Gerard (Napier), K.B.E., C.V.O.
Mansfield, Sir Philip(Robert Aked), K.C.M.G.
Mant, Sir Cecil George, Kt., C.B.E.
Mara, *Rt. Hon. Ratu* Sir Kamisese Kapaiwai Tuimacilai, G.C.M.G., K.B.E.
Marchant, Sir Herbert Stanley, K.C.M.G., O.B.E.
Margetson, *Maj.* Sir Philip Reginald, K.C.V.O., M.C.
Marjoribanks, Sir James Alexander Milne, K.C.M.G.
Mark, Sir Robert, G.B.E.
Markham, Sir Charles John, Bt. (1911).
Marking, Sir Henry Ernest, K.C.V.O., C.B.E., M.C.
Marks, Sir John Hedley Douglas, Kt., C.B.E.
Marling, Sir Charles William Somerset, Bt., (1882).
Marnham, Sir Ralph, K.C.V.O.
Marr, Sir Leslie Lynn, Bt. (1919).
Marre, Sir Alan Samuel, K.C.B.
Marriott, Sir Ralph George Cavendish Smith-, Bt. (1774).
Marsack, Sir Charles Croft, K.B.E.

Marsden, Sir John Dentŏn, Bt., (1924).

Marsh, *Rt. Hon.* Sir Richard William, Kt.

Marshall, Sir Arthur Gregory George, Kt., O.B.E.

Marshall, Sir Denis Alfred, Kt.

Marshall, Sir Hugo Frank, K.B.E, C.M.G.

Marshall, *Rt. Hon.* Sir John Ross, G.B.E., C.H.

Marshall, *Prof.* Sir (Oshley) Roy, Kt., C.B.E.

Marshall, Sir Peter Harold Reginald, K.C.M.G.

Marshall, Sir Robert Braithwaite, K.C.B., M.B.E.

Marshall, Sir Walter Charles, Kt., C.B.E., F.R.S.

Martell, *Vice-Adm.* Sir Hugh Colenso, K.B.E., C.B.

Marten, *Rt. Hon.* Sir Neil, Kt.

Martin, *Air Marshal* Sir Harold Brownlow, K.C.B., D.S.O., D.F.C., A.F.C.

Martin, *Vice-Adm.* Sir John Edward Ludgate, K.C.B., D.S.C.

Martin, *Prof.* Sir (John) Leslie, Kt., PH.D.

Martin, Sir John Miller, K.C.M.G., C.B., C.V.O.

Martin, Sir Sidney Launcelot, Kt.

Marwick, Sir Brian Allan, K.B.E., C.M.G.

Masefield, Sir Peter Gordon, Kt.

Mason, *Hon.* Sir Anthony Frank, K.B.E.

Mason, Sir (Basil) John, Kt., C.B., D.SC., F.R.S.

Mason, *Vice-Adm.* Sir Frank Trowbridge, K.C.B.

Mason, Sir Frederick Cecil, K.C.V.O., C.M.G.

Mason, Sir John Charles Moir, K.C.M.G.

Mason, *Prof.* Sir Ronald, K.C.B., F.R.S.

Mather, *Prof.* Sir Kenneth, C.B.E., D.SC., F.R.S.

Mather, Sir William Loris, Kt., O.B.E., M.C., T.D.

Mathers, Sir Robert William, Kt.

Matheson, Sir James Adam Louis, K.B.E., C.M.G.

Matheson, *Major* Sir Torquhil Alexander, Bt. (1882).

Mathias, Sir Richard Hughes, Bt. (1917).

Matthews, Sir Bryan Harold Cabot, Kt., C.B.E., SC.D., F.R.S.

Matthews, Sir Peter Alec, Kt.

Matthews, Sir Peter Jack, Kt., C.V.O., O.B.E., Q.P.M.

Matthews, Sir Russell, Kt., O.B.E.

Matthews, Sir Stanley, Kt., C.B.E.

Maudslay, *Major* Sir (James) Rennie, G.C.V.O., K.C.B., M.B.E.

Mavor, *Air Marshal* Sir Leslie Deane, K.C.B., A.F.C.

Maxwell, Sir Aymer, Bt. (s 1681).

Maxwell, Sir Nigel Mellor Heron-, Bt. (s 1683).

Maxwell, Sir Robert Hugh, K.B.E.

May, *Rt. Hon.* Sir John Douglas, Kt.

May, Sir Kenneth Spencer, Kt., C.B.E.

Mayall, Sir (Alexander) Lees, K.C.V.O., C.M.G.

Maycock, Sir William d'Auvergne, Kt., C.B.E., M.V.O., M.D., F.R.C.P.

Mayer, Sir Robert, K.C.V.O., C.H.

Mayhew, Sir Patrick Barnabas Burke, Kt., Q.C., M.P.

Mayhew-Sanders, Sir John Reynolds, Kt.

Maynard, *Air Chief Marshal* Sir Nigel Martin, K.C.B., C.B.E., D.F.C., A.F.C.

Meade, Sir (Richard) Geoffrey (Austin), K.B.E., C.M.G., C.V.O.

Meaney, Sir Patrick Michael, Kt.

Medawar, Sir Peter Brian, Kt., O.M., C.H., C.B.E., D.SC., F.R.S.

Medlycott, Sir (James) Christopher, Bt. (1808).

Meere, Sir Francis Anthony, Kt., C.B.E.

Megarry, *Rt. Hon.* Sir Robert Edgar, Kt., F.B.A.

Megaw, *Rt. Hon.* Sir John, Kt., C.B.E., T.D.

Meinertzhagen, Sir Peter, Kt., C.M.G.

Mellor, Sir John Serocold Paget, Bt. (1924).

Melville, Sir Eugene, K.C.M.G.

Melville, Sir Harry Work, K.C.B., PH.D., D.SC., F.R.S.

Melville, Sir Leslie Galfreid, K.B.E.

Melville, Sir Ronald Henry, K.C.B.

Mensforth, Sir Eric, Kt., C.B.E.

Menter, Sir James Woodham, Kt., PH.D., SC.D., F.R.S.

Menteth, Sir James Wallace Stuart-, Bt. (1838).

Menzies, Sir Peter Thomson, Kt.

Merrison, Sir Alexander Walter, Kt., F.R.S.

Merton, *Air Chief Marshal* Sir Walter Hugh, G.B.E., K.C.B.

Meyer, Sir Anthony John Charles, Bt., M.P. (1910).

Meyjes, Sir Richard Anthony, Kt.

Meyrick, *Lt.-Col.* Sir George David Elliott Tapps-Gervis-, Bt., M.C. (1791).

Meyrick, Sir David John Charlton, Bt. (1880).

Michelmore, Sir Walter Harold Strachan, Kt., M.B.E.

Micklethwait, Sir Robert Gore, Kt., Q.C.

Middlemore, Sir William Hawkslow, Bt. (1919).

Middleton, Sir George Humphrey, K.C.M.G.

Middleton, Sir George Proctor, K.C.V.O.

Middleton, Sir Peter Edward, K.C.B.

Middleton, Sir Stephen Hugh, Bt. (1662).

Miers, *Rear-Adm.* Sir Anthony Cecil Capel, V.C., K.B.E., C.B., D.S.O.

Milbank, Sir Anthony Frederick, Bt. (1882).

Milburn, Sir John Nigel, Bt. (1905).

Miles, *Prof.* Sir (Arnold) Ashley, Kt., C.B.E., M.D., F.R.S.

Miles, Sir William Napier Maurice, Bt. (1859).

Millais, Sir Ralph Regnault, Bt. (1885).

Millar, Sir Oliver Nicholas, K.C.V.O., F.B.A.

Millar, Sir Ronald Graeme, Kt.

Millard, Sir Guy Elwin, K.C.M.G., C.V.O.

Miller, Sir Douglas Sinclair, K.C.V.O., C.B.E.

Miller, *Lt.-Gen.* Sir Euan Alfred Bews, K.C.B., K.B.E., D.S.O., M.C.

Miller, Sir (Ian) Douglas, Kt.

Miller, Sir John Holmes, Bt. (1705).

Miller, *Lt.-Col.* Sir John Mansel, K.C.V.O., D.S.O., M.C.

Miller, Sir Joseph Holmes, Kt., O.B.E.

Miller, Sir (Oswald) Bernard, Kt.

Miller, Sir Richard Hope, Kt.

Miller, Sir Stephen James Hamilton, K.C.V.O., M.D., F.R.C.S.

Miller of Glenlee, Sir Frederick William Macdonald, Bt. (1788).

Milling, *Air Marshal* Sir Denis Crowley-, K.C.B., C.B.E., D.S.O., D.F.C.

Millis, Sir Leonard William Francis, Kt., C.B.E.

Mills, *Vice-Adm.* Sir Charles Piercy, K.C.B., C.B.E., D.S.C.

Mills, Sir Frank, K.C.V.O., C.M.G.

Mills, Sir John Lewis Ernest Watts, Kt., C.B.E.

Mills, Sir Peter Frederick Leighton, Bt. (1921).

Mills, Sir Peter McLay, Kt., M.P.

Milman, Sir Dermot Lionel Kennedy, Bt. (1800).

Milmo, *Hon.* Sir Helenus Patrick Joseph, Kt.

Milner, Sir (George Edward) Mordaunt, Bt. (1717).

Milnes Coates, Sir Anthony Robert, Bt. (1911).

Minhinnick, Sir Gordon Edward George, K.B.E.

Minogue, *Hon.* Sir John Patrick, Kt.

Miskin, *Hon.* Sir James William, Kt., Q.C.

Mitchell, *Air Cdre.* Sir Arthur Dennis, K.B.E., C.V.O., D.F.C., A.F.C.

Mitchell, Sir Derek Jack, K.C.B., C.V.O.

Mitchell, Sir Hamilton, K.B.E.

Mitchell, Sir (Seton) Steuart Crichton, K.B.E., C.B.

Moberly, Sir John Campbell, K.B.E., C.M.G.

Mocatta, *Hon.* Sir Alan Abraham, Kt., O.B.E.

Moffat, Sir John Smith, Kt., O.B.E.

Mogg, *General* Sir (Herbert) John, G.C.B., C.B.E., D.S.O.

Moir, Sir Ernest Ian Royds, Bt. (1916).

†Molony, Sir Thomas Desmond, Bt. (1925).

Moncreiffe, Sir (Rupert) Iain (Kay), Bt., C.V.O., Q.C. (s 1685).

Monro, Sir Hector Seymour Peter, Kt., M.P.

Monson, Sir (William Bonnar) Leslie, K.C.M.G., C.B.

Montgomery, Sir (Basil Henry) David, Bt. (1801).

Mookerjee, Sir Birendra Nath, Kt.

Moon, Sir Edward, Bt., M.C. (1887).

Moon, Sir Edward Penderel, Kt., O.B.E.

Moon, Sir Peter James Scott, K.C.V.O., C.M.G.

Moon, Sir (Peter) Wilfred Giles, Bt. (1855).

Moore, Sir Edward Stanton, Bt., O.B.E. (1923).

Moore, Sir Francis Thomas, Kt.

Moore, Sir Henry Roderick, Kt., C.B.E.

Moore, *General* Sir (James Newton) Rodney, G.C.V.O., K.C.B., C.B.E., D.S.O.

Moore, *Hon.* Sir John Cochrane, Kt.

Moore, *Maj.-Gen.* Sir (John) Jeremy, K.C.B., O.B.E., M.C.

Moore, Sir John Michael, K.C.V.O., C.B., D.S.C.

Moore, Sir Norman Winfrid, Bt. (1919).

Moore, *Rt. Hon.* Sir Philip Brian Cecil, G.C.V.O., K.C.B., C.M.G.

Moore, Sir William Roger Clotworthy, Bt., T.D. (1932).

Moores, Sir John, Kt., C.B.E.

Mootham, Sir Orby Howell, Kt.

Mordaunt, Sir Richard Nigel Charles, Bt. (1611).

Mordecai, Sir John Stanley, Kt., C.M.G.

More, Sir Jasper, Kt.

Moreton, Sir John Oscar, K.C.M.G., K.C.V.O., M.C.

Morgan, Sir (Clifford) Naunton, Kt.

Morgan, *Maj.-Gen.* Sir David John Hughes, Bt., C.B., C.B.E. (1925).

Morgan, Sir Ernest Dunstan, K.B.E.

Morgan, *Rear-Adm.* Sir Patrick John, K.C.V.O., C.B., D.S.C.

Morley, Sir Godfrey William Rowland, Kt., O.B.E., T.D.

Morony, *Gen.* Sir Thomas Lovett, K.C.B., O.B.E.

Morpeth, Sir Douglas Spottiswoode, Kt., T.D.

Morris, *Air Marshal* Sir Arnold Alec, K.B.E., C.B.

Morris, Sir Robert Byng, Bt. (1806).

Morris, *Air Marshal* Sir Douglas Griffith, K.C.B., C.B.E., D.S.O., D.F.C.

Morris, *His Hon.* Sir Owen Temple Temple-, Kt., Q.C.

Morrow, Sir Ian Thomas, Kt.

Morse, Sir Christopher Jeremy, K.C.M.G.

Morton, *Admiral* Sir Anthony Storrs, G.B.E., K.C.B.

Morton, Sir Brian, Kt.

Morton, Sir Ralph John, Kt., C.M.G., O.B.E., M.C.

Moseley, Sir George Walker, K.C.B.

Moser, *Prof.* Sir Claus Adolf, K.C.B., C.B.E., F.B.A.

Moses, Sir Charles Joseph Alfred, Kt., C.B.E.

Moss, Sir John Herbert Theodore Edwards-, Bt. (1868).

Mostyn, Sir Jeremy John Antony, Bt. (1670).

Mostyn, *Lt.-Gen.* Sir Joseph David Frederick, K.C.B., C.B.E.

Mott, Sir John Harmer, Bt. (1930).

Mott, *Prof.* Sir Nevill Francis, Kt., F.R.S.

Mount, Sir James William Spencer, Kt., C.B.E., B.E.M.

Mount, Sir William Malcolm, Bt. (1921).

Mountain, Sir Denis Mortimer, Bt. (1922).

Mowbray, Sir John, Kt.

Mowbray, Sir John Robert, Bt. (1880).

Moynihan, Sir Noel Henry, Kt.

Muir, Sir David John, Kt., C.M.G.

Muir, Sir John Harling, Bt. (1892).

Muir, Sir Laurence Macdonald, Kt.

Muir Wood, Sir Alan Marshall, Kt., F.R.S.

Muirhead, Sir David Francis, K.C.M.G., C.V.O.

Muldoon, *Rt. Hon.* Sir Robert David, G.C.M.G., C.H.

Mulholland, Sir Michael Henry, Bt. (1945).

Mumford, Sir Albert Henry, K.B.E.

Mummery, Sir Hugh Evelyn, K.C.V.O., M.D., F.R.C.S.

Munro, Sir Ian Talbot, Bt. (s 1634).

Munro, Sir Robert Lindsay, Kt., C.B.E.

Munro, Sir Sydney Douglas Gun-, G.C.M.G., M.B.E.

Munro, Sir (Thomas) Torquil (Alfonso), Bt. (1825).

Murdoch, *Air Marshal* Sir Alister Murray, K.B.E., C.B.

Murless, Sir (Charles Francis) Noel, Kt.

Murley, Sir Reginald Sydney, K.B.E., T.D., F.R.C.S.

Murphy, Sir Leslie Frederick, Kt.

Murray, *Rear-Adm.* Sir Brian Stewart, K.C.M.G.

Murray, Sir Donald Frederick, K.C.V.O., C.M.G.

Murray, *General* Sir Horatius, G.C.B., K.B.E., D.S.O.

Murray, Sir James, K.C.M.G.

Murray, Sir Nigel Andrew Digby, Bt. (s 1628).

Murray, Sir Patrick Ian Keith, Bt. (s 1673).

Murray, Sir Rowland William Patrick, Bt. (s 1630).

Murrie, Sir William Stuart, G.C.B., K.B.E.

Mursell, Sir Peter, Kt., M.B.E.

Musgrave, Sir Christopher Patrick Charles, Bt. (1611).

Musgrave, Sir (Frank) Cyril, K.C.B.

Musgrave, Sir Richard James, Bt. (1782).

Musker, Sir John, Kt.

Musson, *General* Sir Geoffrey Randolph Dixon, G.C.B., C.B.E., D.S.O.

Mustill, *Hon.* Sir Michael John, Kt.

Myers, Sir Kenneth Ben, Kt., M.B.E.

Myers, *Prof.* Sir Rupert Horace, K.B.E.

Mynors, Sir Humphrey Charles Baskerville, Bt. (1964).

Mynors, *Prof.* Sir Roger Aubrey Baskerville, Kt., F.B.A.

Nabarro, Sir John David Nunes, Kt., M.D., F.R.C.P.

Nairn, Sir (Michael) George, Bt. (1904).

Nairn, Sir Robert Arnold Spencer-, Bt. (1933).

Nairne, *Rt. Hon.* Sir Patrick Dalmahoy, G.C.B., M.C.

Nalder, *Hon.* Sir Crawford David, Kt.

Nall, *Lt.-Cdr.* Sir Michael Joseph, Bt., R.N. (1954).

Napier, Sir Joseph William Lennox, Bt., O.B.E. (1867).

Napier, Sir William Archibald, Bt. (s 1627).

Napley, Sir David, Kt.

Narain, Sir Sathi, K.B.E.

Neal, Sir Eric James, Kt.

Neal, Sir Leonard Francis, Kt., C.B.E.

Neale, Sir Alan Derrett, K.C.B., M.B.E.

Neave, Sir Arundell Thomas Clifton, Bt. (1795).

Neill, *Hon.* Sir Brian Thomas, Kt.

Neill, Sir Francis Patrick, Kt., Q.C.

Neill, *Rt. Hon.* Sir Ivan, Kt.

Nelson, *Maj.-Gen.* Sir (Eustace) John (Blois), K.C.V.O., C.B., D.S.O., O.B.E., M.C.

Nelson, *Air Marshal* Sir (Sidney) Richard (Carlyle), K.C.B., O.B.E., M.D.

Nelson, *Maj.* Sir William Vernon Hope, Bt., O.B.E. (1912).

Nepean, *Lt.-Col.* Sir Evan Yorke, Bt. (1802).

Ness, *Air Marshal* Sir Charles Ernest, K.C.B., C.B.E.

Nevill, *Air Vice-Marshal* Sir Arthur de Terrotte, K.B.E., C.B.

Neville, Sir Richard Lionel John Baines, Bt. (1927).

Neville, *Maj.-Gen.* Sir Robert Arthur Ross, K.C.M.G., C.B.E., R.M.

Newbold, Sir Charles Demorée, K.B.E., C.M.G., Q.C.

Newman, Sir Geoffrey Robert, Bt. (1836).

Newman, Sir Gerard Robert Henry Sigismund, Bt. (1912).

Newman, Sir Jack, Kt., C.B.E.

Newman, Sir Kenneth Leslie, Kt.

Newns, Sir (Alfred) Foley (Francis Polden), K.C.M.G., C.V.O.

Newton, Sir (Harry) Michael (Rex), Bt. (1900).

Newton, Sir Hubert, Kt.

Newton, Sir Kenneth Garnar, Bt., O.B.E., T.D. (1924).

Newton, Sir (Leslie) Gordon, Kt.

Ngata, Sir Henare Kohere, K.B.E.

Niall, Sir Horace Lionel Richard, Kt., C.B.E.

Nicholas, Sir Herbert Richard, Kt., O.B.E.

Nicholas, Sir John William, K.C.V.O., C.M.G.

Nicholls, *Hon.* Sir Donald James, Kt., Q.C.

Nicholls, Sir Douglas Ralph, K.C.V.O., O.B.E.

Nicholls, *Air Marshal* Sir John Moreton, K.C.B., C.B.E., D.F.C., A.F.C.

Nichols, Sir Edward Henry, Kt., T.D.

Nicholson, *Hon.* Sir David Eric, Kt.

Nicholson, Sir Godfrey, Bt. (1958).

Nicholson, Sir John Charles, Bt. (1859).

Nicholson, Sir John Norris, Bt., K.B.E., C.I.E. (1912).

Nickerson, Sir Joseph, Kt.

Nicolson, Sir David Lancaster, Kt.

Nield, Sir Basil Edward, Kt., C.B.E., Q.C.

Nield, Sir William Alan, G.C.M.G., K.C.B.

Nightingale, Sir Charles Manners Gamaliel, Bt. (1628).

Nightingale, Sir John Cyprian, Kt., C.B.E., B.E.M., Q.P.M.

Nimmo, *Hon.* Sir John Angus, Kt., C.B.E.

Niven, Sir (Cecil) Rex, Kt., C.M.G., M.C.

Nixon, Sir Edwin Ronald, Kt., C.B.E.

Nixon, *Rev.* Sir Kenneth Michael John Basil, Bt. (1906).

Noad, Sir Kenneth Beeson, Kt., M.D.

Noble, Sir Andrew Napier, Bt., K.C.M.G. (1923).

Noble, Sir Marc Brunel, Bt. (1902).

Noble, Sir Peter Scott, Kt.

Noble, Sir (Thomas Alexander) Fraser, Kt., M.B.E.

Nock, Sir Norman Lindfield, Kt.

Noel, Sir Claude, Kt., C.M.G.

Nolan, *Hon.* Sir Michael Patrick, Kt.

Nolan, Sir Sidney Robert, Kt., O.M., C.B.E.

Nordmeyer, *Hon.* Sir Arnold Henry, K.C.M.G.

Norman, Sir Arthur Gordon, K.B.E., D.F.C.

Norman, *Rt. Rev.* Edward Kinsella, K.B.E., D.S.O., M.C.

Norman, *Vice-Adm.* Sir (Horace) Geoffrey, K.C.V.O., C.B., C.B.E.

Norman, Sir Mark Annesley, Bt. (1915).

Norman, Sir Robert Wentworth, Kt.

Norris, Sir Alfred Henry, K.B.E.

Norris, *Vice-Adm.* Sir Charles Fred Wivell, K.B.E., C.B., D.S.O.

Norris, *Air Chief Marshal* Sir Christopher Neil Foxley-, G.C.B., D.S.O., O.B.E.

Norris, Sir Eric George, K.C.M.G.

Norris, *Maj.-Gen.* Sir Frank Kingsley, K.B.E., C.B., D.S.O., E.D.

Norris, *Hon.* Sir John Gerald, Kt., E.D., Q.C.

North, Sir Thomas Lindsay, Kt.

North, Sir (William) Jonathan (Frederick), Bt. (1920).

Northam, Sir William Herbert, Kt., C.B.E.

Norton, Sir Clifford John, K.C.M.G., C.V.O.

Norwood, Sir Walter Neville, Kt.

Nossal, Sir Gustav Joseph Victor, Kt., C.B.E.

Nott, *Rt. Hon.* Sir John William Frederic, K.C.B.

Nourse, *Hon.* Sir Martin Charles, Kt.

Nugent, Sir John Edwin Lavallin, Bt. (I 1795).

Nugent, *Maj.* Sir Peter Walter James, Bt. (1831).

Nugent, Sir Robin George Colborne, Bt. (1806).

Nuttall, Sir Nicholas Keith Lillington, Bt. (1922).

Nutting, *Rt. Hon.* Sir (Harold) Anthony, Bt. (1903).

Oakeley, Sir (Edward) Atholl, Bt. (1790).

Oakes, Sir Christopher, Bt. (1939).

Oakeshott, Sir Walter Fraser, Kt., F.B.A., F.S.A.

Oakshott, Hon. Sir Anthony Hendrie, Bt. (1959).

Oates, Sir Thomas, Kt., C.M.G., O.B.E.

Oatley, Sir Charles William, Kt., O.B.E., F.R.S.

Obolensky, *Prof.* Sir Dimitri, Kt.

O'Brien, Sir Frederick William Fitzgerald, Kt.

O'Brien, Sir Timothy John, Bt. (1849).

O'Brien, Sir Richard, Kt., D.S.O., M.C.

O'Brien, *Admiral* Sir William Donough, K.C.B., D.S.C.

O'Collins, *Most Rev.* James Patrick, K.B.E., D.D.

O'Connell, Sir Morgan Donal Conail, Bt. (1869).

O'Connor, *Lt.-Gen.* Sir Denis Stuart Scott, K.B.E., C.B.

O'Connor, Sir Kenneth Kennedy, K.B.E., M.C., Q.C.

O'Connor, *Rt. Hon.* Sir Patrick McCarthy, Kt.

O'Dea, Sir Patrick Jerad, K.C.V.O.

Ogilvie, Sir Alec Drummond, Kt.

Ogilvy, Sir David John Wilfrid, Bt. (s 1626).

O'Halloran, Sir Charles Ernest, Kt.

Ohlson, Sir Brian Eric Christopher, Bt. (1920).

Okeover, *Capt.* Sir Peter Ralph Leopold Walker-, Bt. (1886).

Oldman, *Col.* Sir Hugh Richard Deare, K.B.E., M.C.

Olewale, *Hon.* Sir Niwia Ebia, Kt.

Oliphant, Sir Mark Laurence Elwin, K.B.E., F.R.S.

Oliver, Sir (Frederick) Ernest, Kt., C.B.E., T.D.

Oliver, *Rt. Hon.* Sir Peter Raymond, Kt.

O'Loghlen, Sir Coleman Michael, Bt. (1838).

Olver, Sir Stephen John Linley, K.B.E., C.M.G.

O'Neil, *Hon.* Sir Desmond Henry, Kt.

O'Neill, *Hon.* Sir Con Douglas Walter, G.C.M.G.

Onslow, *Maj.-Gen.* Sir Denzil Macarthur-, Kt., C.B.E., D.S.O., E.D.

Onslow, Sir John Roger Wilmot, Bt. (1797).

Oppenheim, Sir Alexander, Kt., O.B.E., D.SC., F.R.S.E.

Oppenheim, Sir Duncan Morris, Kt.

Oppenheimer, Sir Michael Bernard Grenville, Bt. (1921).

Oppenheimer, Sir Philip Jack, Kt.

Opperman, *Hon.* Sir Hubert Ferdinand, Kt., O.B.E.

Orde, Sir John Alexander Campbell-, Bt. (1790).

O'Regan, *Hon.* Sir John Barry, Kt.

Organe, *Prof.* Sir Geoffrey Stephen William, Kt., M.D.

Ormond, Sir John Davies Wilder, Kt., B.E.M.

Ormrod, *Rt. Hon.* Sir Roger Fray Greenwood, Kt.

Orr, *Rt. Hon.* Sir Alan Stewart, Kt., O.B.E.

Orr, Sir David Alexander, Kt., M.C.

Orr, Sir John Henry, Kt., O.B.E., Q.P.M.

Osborn, Sir Richard Henry Danvers, Bt. (1662).

Osborn, Sir John Holbrook, Kt, M.P.

Osborne, Sir Basil, Kt., C.B.E.

Osborne, Sir Peter George, Bt. (I 1629).

Osifelo, Sir Frederick Aubarua, Kt., M.B.E.

Osman, Sir Abdul Raman Mahomed, G.C.M.G., C.B.E.

Osmond, Sir Douglas, Kt., C.B.E.

Osmond, Sir (Stanley) Paul, Kt., C.B.

Otton, Sir Geoffrey John, K.C.B.

Otton, *Hon.* Sir Philip Howard, Kt., Q.C.

Oulton, Sir Antony Derek Maxwell, K.C.B.

Outerbridge, *Col. Hon.* Sir Leonard Cecil, Kt., C.B.E., D.S.O.

Outram, Sir Alan James, Bt. (1858).

Overall, Sir John Wallace, Kt., C.B.E., M.C.

Overton, Sir Hugh Thomas Arnold, K.C.M.G.

Owen, Sir Hugo Dudley Cunliffe-, Bt. (1920).

Owen, Sir Hugh Bernard Pilkington, Bt. (1813).

Owen, Sir Ronald Hugh, Kt.

Owo, The Olowo of, Kt.

Packard, *Lieut.-Gen.* Sir (Charles) Douglas, K.B.E., C.B., D.S.O.

Padmore, Sir Thomas, G.C.B.

Pagan, *Brig.* Sir John Ernest, Kt., C.M.G., M.B.E., E.D.

Page, Sir Alexander Warren, Kt., M.B.E.

Page, Sir (Arthur) John, Kt., M.P.

Page, Sir Frederick William, Kt., C.B.E.

Page, Sir Harry Robertson, Kt.

Page, Sir John Joseph Joffre, Kt., O.B.E.

Paget, Sir John Starr, Bt. (1886).

Paget, Sir Julian Tolver, Bt., C.V.O. (1871).

Pain, *Lt.-Gen.* Sir (Horace) Rollo (Squarey), K.C.B., M.C.

Pain, *Hon.* Sir Peter Richard, Kt.

Palliser, *Rt. Hon.* Sir (Arthur) Michael, G.C.M.G.

Palmer, Sir Charles Mark, Bt. (1886).

Palmer, Sir Geoffrey Christopher John, Bt. (1660).

Palmer, Sir John Chance, Kt.

Palmer, Sir John Edward Somerset, Bt. (1791).

Palmer, *Brig.* Sir Otho Leslie Prior-, Kt., D.S.O.

Panckridge, *Surgeon Vice-Adm.* Sir (William) Robert (Silvester), K.B.E., C.B.

Pao, Sir Yue-Kong, Kt., C.B.E.

Pape, *Hon.* Sir George Augustus, Kt.

Pararajasingam, Sir Sangarapillai, Kt.

Parbo, Sir Arvi Hillar, Kt.

Parham, *Admiral* Sir Frederick Robertson, G.B.E., K.C.B., D.S.O.

Paris, Sir Edward Talbot, Kt., C.B., D.SC.

Parish, Sir David Elmer Woodbine, Kt., C.B.E.

Park, *Hon.* Sir Hugh Eames, Kt.

Parker, Sir (Arthur) Douglas Dodds-, Kt.

Parker, Sir Douglas William Leigh, Kt., O.B.E.

Parker, Sir John Edward, Kt.

Parker, Sir Karl Theodore, Kt., C.B.E., Ph.D., F.B.A.

Parker, Sir Peter, Kt., M.V.O.

Parker, Sir Richard (William) Hyde, Bt. (1681).

Parker, *Rt. Hon.* Sir Roger Jocelyn, Kt.

Parker, *Vice-Adm.* Sir (Wilfred) John, K.B.E., C.B., D.S.C.

Parker, Sir (William) Alan, Bt. (1844).

Parkes, Sir Alan Sterling, Kt., C.B.E., Ph.D., D.SC., SC.D., F.R.S.

Parkes, Sir Basil Arthur, Kt., O.B.E.

Parkes, Sir Edward Walter, Kt., SC.D.

Parkinson, Sir Nicholas Fancourt, Kt.

Parry, Sir Ernest Jones-, Kt.

Parry, Sir (Frank) Hugh (Nigel), Kt., C.B.E.

Parry, Sir Thomas, Kt., F.B.A.

Parsons, Sir Anthony Derrick, G.C.M.G., M.V.O., M.C.

Parsons, Sir (John) Michael, Kt.

Parsons, Sir Richard Edmund (Clement Fownes), K.C.M.G.

Part, Sir Antony Alexander, Kt., G.C.B., M.B.E.

Partabgarh, H.H. the Maharawab of, K.C.S.I.

Pasley, Sir John Malcolm Sabine, Bt. (1794).

Patch, *Air Chief Marshal* Sir Hubert Leonard, K.C.B., C.B.E.

Paterson, Sir Dennis Craig, Kt.

Paterson, Sir George Mutlow, Kt., O.B.E., Q.C.

Paterson, Sir John Valentine Jardine, Kt.

Paton, *Prof.* Sir George Whitecross, Kt.

Paton, Sir Leonard Cecil, Kt., C.B.E., M.C.

Paton, *Capt.* Sir Stuart Henry, K.C.V.O., C.B.E., R.N. (*ret.*).

Paton, Sir (Thomas) Angus (Lyall), Kt., C.M.G., F.R.S.

Paton, *Prof.* Sir William Drummond Macdonald, Kt., C.B.E., D.M., F.R.S., F.R.C.P.

Pattinson, *Hon.* Sir Baden, K.B.E.

Paul, Sir John Warburton, G.C.M.G., O.B.E., M.C.

Paull, Sir Gilbert James, Kt.

Payne, Sir Robert Frederick, Kt.

Peacock, Sir Geoffrey Arden, Kt., C.V.O.

Peake, Sir Francis Harold, Kt.

Pearce, Sir Austin William, Kt., C.B.E., Ph.D.

Pearce, Sir Eric Herbert, Kt., O.B.E.

Peard, *Rear-Adm.* Sir Kenyon Harry Terrell, K.B.E.

Pearman, *Hon.* Sir James Eugene, Kt., C.B.E.

Pears, Sir Peter Neville Luard, Kt., C.B.E.

Pearson, Sir Francis Fenwick, Bt., M.B.E. (1964).

Pearson, Sir (James) Denning, Kt.

Pearson, *General* Sir Thomas Cecil Hook, K.C.B., C.B.E., D.S.O.

Pease, Sir (Alfred) Vincent, Bt. (1882).

Pease, Sir Richard Thorn, Bt. (1920).

Peat, Sir Henry, K.C.V.O., D.F.C.

Peck, Sir Edward Heywood, G.C.M.G.

Peck, Sir John Howard, K.C.M.G.

Pedder, *Vice-Adm.* Sir Arthur Reid, K.B.E., C.B.

Pedder, *Air Marshal* Sir Ian Maurice, K.C.B., O.B.E., D.F.C.

Pedler, Sir Frederick Johnson, Kt.

Peek, Sir Francis Henry Grenville, Bt. (1874).

Peek, *Vice-Adm.* Sir Richard Innes, K.B.E., C.B., D.S.C.

Peel, Sir John Harold, K.C.V.O.

Peel, Sir (William) John, Kt.

Peierls, Sir Rudolf Ernst, Kt., C.B.E., D.SC., D.Phil., F.R.S.

Peile, *Vice-Adm.* Sir Lancelot Arthur Babington, K.B.E., C.B., D.S.O., M.V.O.

Peirse, Sir Henry Grant de la Poer Beresford-, Bt. (1814).

Pelly, Sir John Alwyne, Bt. (1840).

Pemberton, Sir Francis Wingate William, Kt., C.B.E.

Pendred, *Air Marshal* Sir Lawrence Fleming, K.B.E., C.B., D.F.C.

Penn, *Lt.-Col.* Sir Eric Charles William Mackenzie, G.C.V.O., O.B.E., M.C.

Penruddock, Sir Clement Frederick, Kt., C.B.E.

Percival, Sir Anthony Edward, Kt., C.B.

Percival, *Rt. Hon.* Sir (Walter) Ian, Kt., Q.C., M.P.

Pereira, Sir (Herbert) Charles, Kt., D.SC., F.R.S.

Perkins, *Surgeon Vice-Adm.* Sir Derek Duncombe Steele-, K.C.B., K.C.V.O.

Perkins, Sir (Walter) Robert Dempster, Kt.

Perrin, Sir Michael Willcox, Kt., C.B.E.

Perring, Sir Ralph Edgar, Bt. (1963).

Perris, Sir David (Arthur), Kt., M.B.E.

Perrott, Sir Donald Cyril Vincent, K.B.E.

Perry, Sir (David) Norman, Kt., M.B.E.

Pestell, Sir John Richard, K.C.V.O.

Peterkin, Sir Neville, Kt.

Petersen, Sir Jeffrey Charles, K.C.M.G.

Peterson, Sir Arthur William, K.C.B., M.V.O.

Petit, Sir Dinshaw Manockjee, Bt. (1890).

Peto, Sir Henry George Morton, Bt. (1855).

Peto, Sir Michael Henry Basil, Bt. (1927).

Petrie, Sir (Charles) Richard (Borthwick), Bt., T.D. (1918).

Pettigrew, Sir Russell Hilton, Kt.

Pettingel, Sir William Walter, Kt., C.B.E.

Pettit, Sir Daniel Eric Arthur, Kt.

Petty, *Hon.* Sir Horace Rostill, Kt.

Phaltan, *Maj.* the Raja of, K.C.I.E.

Philip, Sir William Shearer, Kt., C.M.G., M.C.

Philips, *Prof.* Sir Cyril Henry, Kt.

Philipson, Sir Robert James, Kt., P.R.S.A., A.R.A.

Phillips, *Prof.* Sir David Chilton, Kt., Ph.D., F.R.S.

Phillips, Sir Fred Albert, Kt., C.V.O.

Phillips, Sir Henry Ellis Isidore, Kt., C.M.G., M.B.E.

Phillips, Sir Horace, K.C.M.G.

Phillips, Sir John Grant, K.B.E.

Phillips, Sir Robin Francis, Bt. (1912).

Phipps, *Vice-Adm.* Sir Peter, K.B.E., D.S.C., V.R.D.

Pickard, Sir Cyril Stanley, K.C.M.G.

Pickering, Sir Edward Davies, Kt.

Pickthorn, Sir Charles William Richards, Bt. (1959).

Pierre, Sir Joseph Henry, Kt.

Piers, Sir Charles Robert Fitzmaurice, Bt. (1661).

Pigot, *Maj.-Gen.* Sir Robert Anthony, Bt., C.B., O.B.E. (1764).

Pigott, Sir Berkeley Henry Sebastian, Bt. (1808).

Pike, Sir Philip Ernest Housden, Kt., Q.C.

Pike, Sir Theodore Ouseley, K.C.M.G.

Pike, *Lt.-Gen.* Sir William Gregory Huddleston, K.C.B., C.B.E., D.S.O.

Pilcher, Sir (Charlie) Dennis, Kt., C.B.E.

Pilcher, Sir John Arthur, G.C.M.G.

Pilditch, Sir Richard Edward, Bt. (1929).

Pile, Sir Frederick Devereux, Bt. M.C. (1900).

Pile, Sir William Denis, G.C.B., M.B.E.

Pilkington, Sir Lionel Alexander Bethune (Alastair), Kt.

Pilkington, Sir Thomas Henry Milborne-Swinnerton-, Bt. (s 1635).

Pillar, *Admiral* Sir William Thomas, G.B.E, K.C.B.

Pim, *Capt.* Sir Richard Pike, K.B.E., V.R.D., R.N.V.R.

Pindling, *Rt. Hon.* Sir Lynden Oscar, K.C.M.G.

Pinsent, Sir Christopher Roy, Bt. (1938).

Piper, Sir David Towry, Kt., C.B.E.

Pippard, *Prof.* Sir (Alfred) Brian, Kt., F.R.S.

Pirbhai, Sir Eboo, Kt., O.B.E.

Pirie, *Gp. Capt.* Sir Gordon Hamish, Kt., C.B.E.

Pitblado, Sir David Bruce, K.C.B., C.V.O.

Pitman, Sir Hubert Percival Lancaster, Kt., O.B.E.

Pitman, Sir (Isaac) James, K.B.E.

Pitoi, Sir Sere, Kt., C.B.E.

Pitt, *Prof.* Sir Harry Raymond, Kt., Ph.D., F.R.S.

Pitts, Sir Cyril Alfred, Kt.

Pixley, Sir Neville Drake, Kt., M.B.E., V.R.D.

Pizey, *Admiral* Sir (Charles Thomas) Mark, G.B.E., C.B., D.S.O.

Plaister, Sir Sydney, Kt., C.B.E.

Platt, Sir Harry, Bt., M.D. (1958).

Platt, *Prof.* Hon. Sir Peter, Bt. (1959).

Playfair, Sir Edward Wilder, K.C.B.

Pleass, Sir Clement John, K.C.M.G., K.C.V.O., K.B.E.

Pliatzky, Sir Leo, K.C.B.

Plimmer, Sir Clifford Ulric, K.B.E.

Plimsoll, Sir James, Kt., C.B.E.

Plowman, Sir (John) Anthony, Kt.

Plowman, Sir John Robin, Kt., C.B.E.

Plumb, Sir (Charles) Henry, Kt.

Plumb, *Prof.* Sir John Harold, Kt.

Pochin, Sir Edward Eric, Kt., C.B.E., M.D., F.R.C.P.

Poett, *General* Sir (Joseph Howard) Nigel, K.C.B., D.S.O.

Pole, *Col.* Sir John Gawen Carew, Bt., D.S.O., T.D. (1628).

Pole, Sir Peter Van Not en–, Bt. (1791).

Pollard, Sir Charles Herbert, Kt., C.B.E.

Pollen, Sir John Michael Hungerford, Bt. (1795).

Pollock, Sir George, Kt., Q.C.

Pollock, Sir George Frederick, Bt. (1866).

Pollock, Sir George Seymour Montagu-, Bt. (1872).

Pollock, *Admiral of the Fleet* Sir Michael Patrick, G.C.B., M.V.O., D.S.C.

Pollock, Sir William Horace Montagu-, K.C.M.G.

Pond, *Prof.* Sir Desmond Arthur, Kt., M.D., F.R.C.P.

Ponsonby, Sir Ashley Charles Gibbs, Bt., M.C. (1956).

Pontin, Sir Frederick William, Kt.

Poore, Sir Herbert Edward, Bt. (1795).

Pope, *Vice-Adm.* Sir (John) Ernle, K.C.B.

Pope, Sir Joseph Albert, Kt., D.Sc., Ph.D.

Pope, Sir Sidney Barton, Kt.

Popper, *Prof.* Sir Karl Raimund, Kt., C.H., Ph.D., F.R.S.

Popplewell, *Hon.* Sir Oliver Bury, Kt., Q.C.

Portal, Sir Francis Spencer, Bt. (1901).

Porter, Sir Andrew Marshall Horsbrugh-, Bt., D.S.O. (1902).

Porter, *Prof.* Sir George, Kt., F.R.S., Ph.D., Sc.D.

Porter, Sir Leslie, Kt.

Porter, *Air Marshal* Sir (Melvin) Kenneth (Drowley), K.C.B., C.B.E.

Porter, *Hon.* Sir Murray Victor, Kt.

Porter, Sir Robert Evelyn, Kt.

Porter, *Rt. Hon.* Sir Robert Wilson, Kt., Q.C.

Posnett, Sir Richard Neil, K.B.E., C.M.G.

Pott, Sir Leslie, K.B.E.

Potter, Sir (Joseph) Raymond (Lynden), Kt.

Potter, *Maj.-Gen.* Sir (Wilfrid) John, K.B.E., C.B.

Potter, Sir (William) Ian, Kt.

Pound, Sir John David, Bt. (1905).

Powell, Sir (Arnold Joseph) Philip, Kt., C.H., O.B.E., R.A., F.R.I.B.A.

Powell, Sir Nicholas Folliott Douglas, Bt. (1897).

Powell, Sir Richard Royle, G.C.B., K.B.E., C.M.G.

Power, *Vice-Adm.* Sir Arthur Mackenzie, K.C.B., M.B.E.

Power, Sir Alastair John Cecil, Bt. (1924).

Powles, Sir Guy Richardson, K.B.E., C.M.G., E.D.

Powlett, *Vice-Adm.* Sir Peveril Barton Reibey Wallop William-, K.C.B., K.C.M.G., C.B.E., D.S.O.

Poynton, Sir (Arthur) Hilton, G.C.M.G.

Prain, Sir Ronald Lindsay, Kt., O.B.E.

Prendergast, Sir John Vincent, K.B.E., C.M.G., G.M.

Prentice, *Hon.* Sir William Thomas, Kt., M.B.E.

Prescott, Sir Mark, Bt. (1938).

Preston, Sir Kenneth Huson, Kt.

Preston, Sir Peter Sansome, K.C.B.

Preston, Sir Ronald Douglas Hildebrand, Bt. (1815).

Pretyman, Sir Walter Frederick, K.B.E.

Prevost, *Capt.* Sir George James Augustine, Bt. (1805).

Price, Sir Charles Keith Napier Rugge-, Bt. (1804).

Price, Sir David Ernest Campbell, Kt., M.P.

Price, Sir Francis Caradoc Rose, Bt. (1815).

Price, Sir Frank Leslie, Kt.

Price, Sir (James) Robert, K.B.E.

Price, Sir Leslie Victor, Kt., O.B.E.

Price, Sir Norman Charles, K.C.B.

Price, Sir Robert John Green-, Bt. (1874).

Prichard, Sir Montague Illtyd, Kt., C.B.E., M.C.

Prickett, *Air Chief Marshal* Sir Thomas Other, K.C.B., D.S.O., D.F.C.

Prideaux, Sir Humphrey Povah Treverbian, Kt., O.B.E.

Prideaux, Sir John Francis, Kt., O.B.E.

Primrose, Sir John Ure, Bt. (1903).

Pringle, *Air Marshal* Sir Charles Norman Seton, K.B.E.

Pringle, *Lt.-Gen.* Sir Steuart (Robert), Bt., K.C.B., R.M. (s 1683).

Pritchard, Sir Asa Hubert, Kt.

Pritchard, Sir John Michael, Kt., C.B.E.

Pritchard, Sir Neil, K.C.M.G.

Pritchett, Sir Victor Sawdon, Kt., C.B.E.

Proby, Sir Peter, Bt. (1952).

Proctor, Sir (George) Philip, K.B.E.

Proctor, Sir Roderick Consett, Kt., M.B.E.

Proud, Sir John Seymour, Kt.

Pryke, Sir David Dudley, Bt. (1926).

Pugh, Sir Idwal Vaughan, K.C.B.

Pugsley, *Prof.* Sir Alfred Grenvile, Kt., O.B.E., D.SC., F.R.S.

Pullinger, Sir (Francis) Alan, Kt., C.B.E.

Pumphrey, Sir (John) Laurence, K.C.M.G.

Purchas, *Rt. Hon.* Sir Francis Brooks, Kt.

Pyke, Sir Louis Frederick, Kt., E.D.

Quilter, Sir Anthony Raymond Leopold Cuthbert, Bt. (1897).

Rabukawaqa, Sir Josua Rasilau, K.B.E., M.V.O.

Raby, Sir Victor Harry, K.B.E., C.B., M.C.

Radcliffe, Sir Sebastian Everard, Bt. (1813).

Radclyffe, Sir Charles Edward Mott-, Kt.

Radford, Sir Ronald Walter, K.C.B., M.B.E.

Radzinowicz, *Prof.* Sir Leon, Kt., LL.D.

Rae, *Hon.* Sir Wallace Alexander Ramsay, Kt.

Raeburn, Sir Michael Edward Norman, Bt. (1923).

Raeburn, *Maj.-Gen.* Sir (William) Digby (Manifold), K.C.V.O., C.B., D.S.O., M.B.E.

Raikes, Sir (Henry) Victor (Alpin MacKinnon), K.B.E.

Raikes, *Vice-Adm.* Sir Iwan Geoffrey, K.C.B., C.B.E., D.S.C.

Ralli, Sir Godfrey Victor, Bt., T.D. (1912).

Ramgoolam, *Rt. Hon.* Sir Seewoosagur, G.C.M.G.

Rampton, Sir Jack Leslie, K.C.B.

Ramsay, Sir Alexander William Burnett, Bt. (1806).

Ramsay, *Cdre.* Sir James Maxwell, K.C.M.G., K.C.V.O., C.B.E., D.S.C.

Ramsay, Sir Neis Alexander, Bt. (s 1666)

Ramsay, Sir Thomas Meek, Kt., C.M.G.

Ramsbotham, *Hon.* Sir Peter Edward, G.C.M.G., G.C.V.O.

Ramsden, Sir Geoffrey Charles Frescheville, Kt., C.I.E.

Ramsden, Sir (Geoffrey) William Pennington-, Bt. (1689).

Ramsey, Sir Alfred Ernest, Kt.

Ranger, Sir Douglas, Kt., F.R.C.S.

Rank, Sir Benjamin Keith, Kt., C.M.G.

Rankin, Sir Hugh (Charles Rhys), Bt. (1898).

Rankine, Sir John Dalziel, K.C.M.G., K.C.V.O.

Raper, *Vice-Adm.* Sir (Robert) George, K.C.B.

Rapp, Sir Thomas Cecil, K.B.E., C.M.G., M.C.

Rasch, *Maj.* Sir Richard Guy Carne, Bt. (1903).

Rashleigh, Sir Harry Evelyn Battie, Bt. (1831).

Rault, Sir Louis Joseph Maurice, Kt.

Rawlins, *Surgeon Vice-Adm.* Sir John Stuart Pepys, K.B.E.

Rawlinson, Sir Anthony Henry John, Bt. (1891).

Rawlinson, Sir Anthony Keith, K.C.B.

Raymond, Sir Stanley Edward, Kt.

Read, *Air Marshal* Sir Charles Frederick, K.B.E., C.B., D.F.C., A.F.C.

Read, *General* Sir (John) Antony (Jervis), G.C.B., C.B.E., D.S.O., M.C.

Read, Sir John Emms, Kt.

Read, *Lt.-Gen.* Sir John Hugh Sherlock, K.C.B., O.B.E.

Reade, Sir Clyde Nixon, Bt. (1661).

Readhead, Sir James Templeman, Bt. (1922).

Reay, *Lt.-Gen.* Sir Hubert Alan John, K.B.E.

Redfearn, Sir Herbert, Kt.

Redfern, Sir (Arthur) Shuldham, K.C.V.O., C.M.G.

Redgrave, Sir Michael Scudamore, Kt., C.B.E.

Redgrave, *Maj.-Gen.* Sir Roy Michael Frederick, K.B.E., M.C.

Redman, *Lt.-Gen.* Sir Harold, K.C.B., C.B.E.

Redmayne, Sir Nicholas, Bt. (1964).

Redmond, Sir James, Kt.

Redshaw, Sir Leonard, Kt., T.D.

Redwood, Sir Peter Boverton, Bt. (1911).

Reece, Sir Gerald, K.C.M.G., C.B.E.

Reece, Sir (Louis) Alan, Kt., C.M.G.

Reed, *Hon.* Sir Nigel Vernon, Kt., C.B.E.

Rees, Sir (Charles William) Stanley, Kt., T.D.

Rees-Mogg, Sir William, Kt.

Reeve, *Hon.* Sir (Charles) Trevor, Kt.

Reffell, *Vice-Adm.* Sir Derek Roy, K.C.B.

Refshauge, *Maj-Gen.* Sir William Dudley, Kt., C.B.E.

Reid, Sir Alexander James, Bt. (1897).

Reid, *Hon.* Sir George Oswald, Kt., Q.C.

Reid, *Air Vice-Marshal* Sir (George) Ranald Macfarlane, K.C.B., D.S.O., M.C.

Reid, Sir Hugh, Bt. (1922).

Reid, Sir John Thyne, Kt., C.M.G.

Reid, Sir Norman Robert, Kt.

Reid, Sir William, Kt., C.B.E., Ph.D.

Reilly, Sir (D'Arcy) Patrick, G.C.M.G., O.B.E.

Reiss, Sir John Anthony Ewart, Kt., B.E.M.

Renals, Sir Stanley, Bt. (1895).

Rendell, Sir William, Kt.

Rennie, *Hon.* Sir Alfred Baillie, Kt.

Rennie, Sir John Shaw, G.C.M.G., O.B.E.

Renshaw, Sir Charles Maurice Bine, Bt. (1903).

Renwick, Sir Richard Eustace, Bt. (1921).

Reporter, Sir Shapoor Ardeshirji, K.B.E.

Revans, Sir John, Kt., C.B.E.

Rex, *Hon.* Sir Robert Richmond, K.B.E., C.M.G.

Reynolds, Sir David James, Bt. (1923).

Rhodes, Sir John Christopher Douglas, Bt. (1919).

Rhodes, Sir Peregrine Alexander, K.C.M.G.

Richards, *Hon.* Sir Edward Trenton, Kt., C.B.E.

Richards, Sir (Francis) Brooks, K.C.M.G., D.S.O.

Richards, Sir Gordon, Kt.

Richards, Sir James Maude, Kt., C.B.E.

Richards, *Lt.-Gen.* Sir John Charles Chisholm, K.C.B., R.M.

Richards, Sir Rex Edward, Kt., D.SC., F.R.S.

Richardson, *General* Sir Charles Leslie, G.C.B., C.B.E., D.S.O.

Richardson, Sir Egerton Rudolf, Kt., C.M.G.

Richardson, Sir (Horace) Frank, Kt.

Richardson, Sir (John) Eric, Kt., C.B.E.

Richardson, Sir Leslie Lewis, Bt. (1924).

Richardson, *Lt.-Gen.* Sir Robert Francis, K.C.B., C.V.O., C.B.E.

Richardson, Sir Simon Alaisdair Stewart-, Bt. (s 1630).

Richardson, Sir William Robert, Kt.

Riches, Sir Derek Martin Hurry, K.C.M.G.

Riches, Sir Eric William, Kt., M.C.

Riches, *General* Sir Ian Hurry, K.C.B., D.S.O.

Richmond, Sir Alan James, Kt.

Richmond, *Rt. Hon.* Sir Clifford Parris, K.B.E.

Richmond, Sir John Christopher Blake, K.C.M.G.

Richmond, Sir John Frederick, Bt. (1929).

Richmond, *Vice-Adm.* Sir Maxwell, K.B.E., C.B., D.S.O.

Rickett, Sir Denis Hubert Fletcher, K.C.M.G., C.B.

Ricketts, Sir Robert Cornwallis Gerald St. Leger, Bt. (1828).

Ricks, Sir John Plowman, Kt.

Riddell, Sir John Charles Buchanan-, Bt. (s 1628).

Ridley, Sir Sydney, Kt.

Ridsdale, Sir Julian Errington, Kt., C.B.E., M.P.

Rigby, *Lt.-Col.* Sir (Hugh) John (Macbeth), Bt. (1929).

Rigby, *Hon.* Sir Ivo Charles Clayton, Kt.

Riley, Sir Ralph, Kt., F.R.S.

Ring, Sir Lindsay Roberts, G.B.E.

Ringadoo, *Hon.* Sir Veerasamy, Kt.

Ripley, Sir Hugh, Bt. (1880).

Risk, Sir Thomas Neilson, Kt.

Risson, *Maj.-Gen.* Sir Robert Joseph Henry, Kt., C.B., C.B.E., D.S.O., E.D.

Ritchie, Sir James Edward Thomson, Bt. (1918).

Rix, Sir John, Kt., M.B.E.

Roberts, Sir Bryan Clieve, K.C.M.G., Q.C.

Roberts, Sir David Arthur, K.B.E., C.M.G., C.V.O.

Roberts, *Hon.* Sir Denys Tudor Emil, K.B.E., Q.C.

Roberts, Sir Edward Fergus Sidney, Kt., C.B.E.

Roberts, Sir Frank Kenyon, G.C.M.G., G.C.V.O.

Roberts, Sir Geoffrey Newland, Kt., C.B.E., A.F.C.

Roberts, *Brig.* Sir Geoffrey Paul Hardy-, K.C.V.O., C.B., C.B.E.

Roberts, Sir Gilbert Howland Rookehurst, Bt. (1809).

Roberts, Sir Gordon James, Kt., C.B.E.

Roberts, *General* Sir Ouvry Lindfield, G.C.B., K.B.E., D.S.O.

Roberts, Sir Peter Geoffrey, Bt. (1919).

Roberts, Sir Stephen James Leake, Kt.

Roberts, Sir William James Denby, Bt. (1909).

Robertson, *Prof.* Sir Alexander, Kt., C.B.E.

Robertson, Sir James Anderson, Kt., C.B.E.

Robertson, *Prof.* Sir Rutherford Ness, Kt., C.M.G.

Robinson, Sir Albert Edward Phineas, Kt.

Robinson, Sir Dove Myer, Kt.

Robinson, *Prof.* Sir (Edward) Austin (Gossage), Kt., C.M.G., O.B.E., F.B.A.

Robinson, Sir George Gilmour, Kt.

Robinson, Sir John Beverley, Bt. (1854).

Robinson, Sir John James Michael Laud, Bt. (1660).

Robinson, *Rt. Hon.* Sir Kenneth, Kt.

Robinson, Sir Niall Bryan Lynch-, Bt., D.S.C. (1920).

Robinson, Sir (Wilfred Henry) Frederick, Bt. (1908).

Robson, *Prof.* Sir James Gordon, Kt., C.B.E.

Robson, Sir Thomas Buston, Kt., M.B.E.

Robson, *Vice-Adm.* Sir (William) Geoffrey (Arthur), K.B.E., C.B., D.S.O., D.S.C.

Roche, Sir David O'Grady, Bt. (1838).

Rodger, Sir William Glendinning, Kt., O.B.E.

Rodgers, Sir John Charles, Bt. (1964).

Rodrigues, Sir Alberto Maria, Kt., C.B.E., E.D.

Roe, *Air Chief Marshal* Sir Rex David, G.C.B., A.F.C.

Rogers, *Air Chief Marshal* Sir John Robson, K.C.B., C.B.E.

Rogers, Sir Philip, G.C.B., C.M.G.

Rogers, Sir Philip James, Kt., C.B.E.

Roll, *Rev.* Sir James William Cecil, Bt. (1921).

Rooke, Sir Denis Eric, Kt., C.B.E.

Ropner, Sir John Bruce Woollacott, Bt. (1952).

Ropner, Sir Robert Douglas, Bt. (1904).

Roscoe, Sir Robert Bell, K.B.E.

Rose, Sir Alec Richard, Kt.

Rose, Sir Clive Martin, G.C.M.G.

Rose, Sir Julian Day, Bt. (1872 and 1909).

Rose, Sir David Lancaster, Bt. (1874).

Roseveare, Sir Martin Pearson, Kt.

Rosier, *Air Chief Marshal* Sir Frederick Ernest, G.C.B., C.B.E., D.S.O.

Roskill, Sir Ashton Wentworth, Kt., Q.C.

Ross, Sir Alexander, Kt.

Ross, Sir Archibald David Manisty, K.C.M.G.

Ross, *Hon.* Sir Dudley Bruce, Kt.

Ross, Sir James Keith, Bt., R.D., F.R.C.S. (1960).

Ross, Sir Lewis Nathan, Kt., C.M.G.

Rosser, Sir Melvyn Wynne, Kt.

Rossi, Sir Hugh Alexis Louis, Kt., M.P.

Rossiter, *Hon.* Sir John Frederick, K.B.E.

Rostron, Sir Frank, Kt., M.B.E.

Roth, *Prof.* Sir Martin, Kt., M.D., F.R.C.P.

Rothenstein, Sir John Knewstub Maurice, Kt., C.B.E., Ph.D.

Rothnie, Sir Alan Keir, K.C.V.O., C.M.G.

Rous, Sir Stanley Ford, Kt., C.B.E.

Rous, Sir Anthony Gerald Roderick, K.C.M.G., O.B.E.

Row, *Hon.* Sir John Alfred, Kt.

Row, *Cdr.*, Sir Philip John, K.C.V.O., O.B.E., R.N.

Rowe, Sir Henry Peter, K.C.B.

Rowell, Sir John Joseph, Kt., C.B.E.

Rowland, *Air Marshal* Sir James Anthony, K.B.E., D.F.C., A.F.C.

Rowlands, *Air Marshal* Sir John Samuel, K.B.E., G.C.

Rowlandson, Sir (Stanley) Graham, Kt., M.B.E.

Rowley, Sir Charles Robert, Bt. (1836).

Rowley, Sir Joshua Francis, Bt. (1786).

Rowling, *Rt. Hon.* Sir Wallace Edward, K.C.M.G.

Rowntree, Sir Norman Andrew Forster, Kt.

Roxburgh, *Vice-Adm.* Sir John Charles Young, K.C.B., C.B.E., D.S.O., D.S.C.

Royden, Sir Christopher John, Bt. (1905).

Rucker, Sir Arthur Nevil, K.C.M.G., C.B., C.B.E.

Rugg, Sir (Edward) Percy, Kt.

Rumbold, Sir (Horace) Algernon (Fraser), K.C.M.G., C.I.E.

Rumbold, Sir Henry John Sebastian, Bt. (1779).

Rumbold, Sir Jack Seddon, Kt.

Runciman, *Hon.* Sir Steven; (James Cochran Stevenson), Kt., C.H.

Rundall, Sir Francis Brian Anthony, G.C.M.G., O.B.E.

Rusby, *Vice-Adm.* Sir Cameron, K.C.B., M.V.O.

Russell, Sir Archibald Edward, Kt., C.B.E., F.R.S.

Russell, Sir Charles Ian, Bt. (1916).

Russell, *Rt. Hon.* Sir Charles Ritchie, Kt.

Russell, Sir Evelyn Charles Sackville, Kt.

Russell, Sir George Michael, Bt. (1812).

Russell, *Hon.* Sir Thomas Patrick, Kt.

Russo, Sir Peter George, Kt., C.B.E.

Ryan, Sir Derek Gerald, Bt. (1919).

Rycroft, Sir (Richard) Newton, Bt. (1784).

Ryland, Sir (Albert) William (Cecil), Kt., C.B.

Ryle, *Prof.* Sir Martin, Kt., F.R.S.

Rymill, Sir Arthur Campbell, Kt.

Ryrie, Sir William Sinclair, K.C.B.

Sainsbury, *Hon.* Sir John Davan, Kt.

Sainsbury, Sir Robert James, Kt.

Saint, Sir (Sidney) John, Kt., C.M.G., O.B.E.

St. Aubyn, Sir John Molesworth-, Bt., C.B.E. (1689).

St. George, Sir Denis Howard, Bt. (1 1766).

St. Johnston, *Col.* Sir (Thomas) Eric, Kt., C.B.E.

Sakzewski, Sir Albert, Kt.

Salmon, *Air Vice-Marshal* Sir (Cyril John) Roderic, K.B.E., C.B.

Salomon, Sir Walter Hans, Kt.

Salt, Sir Anthony Houlton, Bt. (1869).

Salt, Sir (Thomas) Michael John, Bt. (1899).

Samuel, Sir Jon Michael Glen, Bt. (1898).

Samuels, Sir Alexander, Kt., C.B.E.

Samuelson, Sir (Bernard) Michael (Francis), Bt. (1884).

Sanders, Sir Harold George, Kt., Ph.D.

Sanders, Sir Robert Tait, K.B.E., C.M.G.

Sanderson, Sir (Charles) Russell, Kt.

Sanderson, Sir (Frank Philip) Bryan, Bt. (1920).

Sandford, Sir Folliott Herbert, K.B.E., C.M.G.

Sandilands, Sir Francis Edwin Prescott, Kt., C.B.E.

Sandover, Sir (Alfred) Eric, Kt., M.C.

Sarell, Sir Roderick Francis Gisbert, K.C.M.G., K.C.V.O.

Sargant, Sir (Henry) Edmund, Kt.

Saunders, *Air Chief Marshal* Sir Hugh William Lumsden, G.C.B., K.B.E., M.C., D.F.C., M.M.

Saunders, *Hon.* Sir John Anthony Holt, Kt., C.B.E., D.S.O., M.C.

Saunders, *Prof.* Sir Owen Alfred, Kt., D.S.C., F.R.S.

Saunders, Sir Peter, Kt.

Sauzier, Sir (André) Guy, Kt., C.B.E., E.D.

Savage, Sir Ernest Walter, Kt.

Savory, Sir Reginald Charles Frank, Kt., C.B.E.

Sayer, *Vice-Adm.* Sir Guy Bourchier, K.B.E., C.B., D.S.C.

Sayers, *Prof.* Sir Edward George, Kt., C.M.G., M.D.

Scarlett, Sir Peter William Shelley Yorke, K.C.M.G., K.C.V.O.

Scherger, *Air Chief Marshal* Sir Frederick Rudolph William, K.B.E., C.B., D.S.O., A.F.C.

Scholtens, Sir James Henry, K.C.V.O.

Schultz, Sir (Joseph) Leopold, Kt., O.B.E.

Schuster, Sir (Felix) James Moncrieff, Bt., O.B.E. (1906).

Scoon, Sir Paul, G.C.M.G., O.B.E.

Scoones, *Maj.-Gen.* Sir Reginald Laurence, K.B.E., C.B., D.S.O.

Scopes, Sir Leonard Arthur, K.C.V.O., C.M.G., O.B.E.

Scott, Sir Bernard Francis William, Kt., C.B.E., T.D.

Scott, Sir (Charles) Hilary, Kt.

Scott, Sir (Charles) Peter, K.B.E., C.M.G.

Scott, Sir David Aubrey, G.C.M.G.

Scott, Sir David John Montagu-Douglas-, K.C.M.G., O.B.E.

Scott, Sir Anthony Percy, Bt. (1913).

Scott, Sir Edward Arthur Dolman, Bt. (1806).

Scott, Sir Eric, Kt., O.B.E.

Scott, Sir George Edward, Kt., C.B.E.

Scott, Sir Ian Dixon, K.C.M.G., K.C.V.O., C.I.E.

Scott, *Lt.-Col.* Sir James Walter, Bt. (1962).

Scott, Sir Michael, K.C.V.O., C.M.G.

Scott, Sir Michael Fergus Maxwell, Bt. (*E* 1642).

Scott, Sir Oliver Christopher Anderson, Bt. (1909).

Scott, Sir Peter Markham, Kt., C.B.E., D.S.C.

Scott, *Hon.* Sir Richard Rashleigh Folliott, Kt., Q.C.

Scott, Sir Ronald Stewart, Kt.

Scott, Sir Terence Charles Stuart Morrison-, Kt., D.S.C., D.SC.

Scott, Sir Walter, Bt. (1907).

Scott, *Rear-Adm.* Sir (William) David (Stewart), K.B.E., C.B.

Scowen, *Prof.* Sir Eric Frank, Kt., M.D., D.SC.

Scragg, *Air Vice-Marshal* Sir Colin, K.B.E., C.B., A.F.C.

Scrivenor, Sir Thomas Vaisey, Kt., C.M.G.

Seale, Sir John Henry, Bt. (1838).

Seaman, Sir Keith David, K.C.V.O., O.B.E.

Sebright, Sir Hugo Giles Edmund, Bt. (1626).

Secombe, Sir Harry Donald, Kt., C.B.E.

Seconde, Sir Reginald Louis, K.C.M.G., C.V.O.

Seely, Sir Nigel Edward, Bt. (1896).

Selby, Sir Kenneth, Kt.

Seligman, Sir Peter Wendel, Kt., C.B.E.

Sellors, Sir Thomas Holmes, Kt., D.M.

Sells, Sir David Perronet, Kt.

Senior, Sir Edward Walters, Kt., C.M.G.

Sergeant, Sir Patrick, Kt.

Series, Sir (Joseph Michel) Emile, Kt., C.B.E.

Serpell, Sir David Radford, K.C.B., C.M.G., O.B.E.

Seton, Sir (Christopher) Bruce, Bt. (s 1663)

Seton, Sir Robert James, Bt. (s 1683)

Sewell, Sir John Allan, Kt., I.S.O.

Seymour, *Cdr.* Sir Michael Culme-Bt., R.N. (1809).

Shakerley, Sir Geoffrey Adam, Bt. (1838).

Shakespeare, Sir William Geoffrey, Bt. (1942).

Shankland, Sir Thomas Murray, Kt., C.M.G.

Shann, Sir Keith Charles Owen, Kt., C.B.E.

Shapland, Sir William Arthur, Kt.

Sharp, Sir Edward Harold Wilfred, Bt. (1922).

Sharp, Sir Eric, C.B.E.

Sharp, Sir George, Kt., O.B.E.

Sharp, Sir Kenneth Johnston, Kt., T.D.

Sharp, Sir Milton Reginald, Bt. (1920).

Sharp, Sir Richard Lyall, K.C.V.O., C.B.

Sharp, Sir (William Harold) Angus, K.B.E., Q.P.M.

Sharpe, Sir Frank Victor, Kt., C.M.G., O.B.E., E.D.

Sharpe, *Hon.* Sir John Henry, Kt., C.B.E.

Sharpe, Sir Reginald Taaffe, Kt., Q.C.

Shaw, Sir (Charles) Barry, Kt., C.B., Q.C.

Shaw, Sir John Michael Robert Best-, Bt. (1665).

Shaw, Sir Michael Norman, Kt., M.P.

Shaw, Sir Robert, Bt. (1821).

Shaw, Sir Roy, Kt.

Shaw, Sir Run Run, Kt., C.B.E.

Sheen, *Hon.* Sir Barry Cross, Kt.

Sheffield, Sir Reginald Adrian Berkeley, Bt. (1755).

Shehadie, Sir Nicholas Michael, Kt., O.B.E.

Shelbourne, Sir Philip, Kt.

Sheldon, *Hon.* Sir (John) Gervase (Kensington), Kt.

Shelley, Sir John Richard, Bt. (1611).

Shepheard, Sir Peter Faulkner, Kt., C.B.E.

Shepheard, Sir Victor George, K.C.B.

Shepherd, Sir Peter Malcolm, Kt., C.B.E.

Sherlock, Sir Philip Manderson, K.B.E.

Sherman, Sir Alfred, Kt.

Sherman, Sir Louis, Kt., O.B.E.

Shields, Sir Neil Stanley, Kt., M.C.

Shiffner, Sir Henry David, Bt. (1818).

Shillington, Sir (Robert Edward) Graham, Kt., C.B.E.

Sholl, *Hon.* Sir Reginald Richard, Kt.

Shone, Sir Robert Minshull, Kt., C.B.E.

Short, *Brig.* Sir Noel Edward Vivian, Kt., M.B.E., M.C.

Shuckburgh, Sir (Charles Arthur) Evelyn, G.C.M.G., C.B.

Shuckburgh, Sir Charles Gerald Stewkley, Bt. (1660).

Sich, Sir Rupert Leigh, Kt., C.B.

Siddall, Sir Norman, Kt., C.B.E.

Sidey, *Air Marshal* Sir Ernest Shaw, K.B.E., C.B., M.D.

Sie, Sir Banja Tejan-, G.C.M.G.

Simeon, Sir John Edmund Barrington, Bt. (1815).

Simmonds, Sir Oliver Edwin, Kt.

Simogun, Sir Petar, Kt., M.B.E., B.E.M.

Simpson, *General* Sir Frank Ernest Wallace, G.B.E., K.C.B., D.S.O.

Simpson, Sir William James, Kt.

Sinclair, Sir Clive Marles, Kt.

Sinclair, Sir George Evelyn, Kt., C.M.G., O.B.E.

Sinclair, Sir Ian McTaggart, K.C.M.G., Q.C.

Sinclair, Sir John Rollo Norman Blair, Bt. (s 1704).

Sinclair, *Air Vice-Marshal* Sir Laurence Frank, K.C.B., G.C., C.B.E., D.S.O.

Sinclair, Sir Ronald Ormiston, K.B.E.

Singh, *Hon.* Sir Vijay Raghubir, Kt.

Singhania, Sir Padampat, Kt.

Singhateh, *Alhaj'i* Sir Farimang, G.C.M.G.

Singleton, Sir Edward Henry Sibbald, Kt.

Sisson, Sir Roy, Kt.

Sitwell, Sir Sacheverell, Bt., C.H. (1808).

Skelhorn, Sir Norman John, K.B.E., Q.C.

Skellerup, Sir Valdemar Reid, Kt., C.B.E.

Skinner, *Hon.* Sir Henry Albert, Kt.

Skinner, Sir Thomas Edward, K.B.E.

Skinner, Sir (Thomas) Keith (Hewitt), Bt. (1912).

Skipwith, Sir Patrick Alexander D'Estoteville, Bt. (1622).

Skyrme, Sir William Thomas Charles, K.C.V.O., C.B., C.B.E.,T.D.

Slade, Sir Benjamin Julian Alfred, Bt. (1831).

Slade, *Rt. Hon.* Sir Christopher John, Kt.

Slaney, *Prof.* Sir Geoffrey, K.B.E.

Slattery, *Rear-Adm.* Sir Matthew Sausse, K.B.E., C.B.

Sleight, Sir John Frederick, Bt. (1920).

Slimmings, Sir William Kenneth MacLeod, Kt., C.B.E.

Slynn, *Hon.* Sir Gordon, Kt.

Smallpeice, Sir Basil, K.C.V.O.

Smallwood, *Air Chief Marshal* Sir Denis Graham, G.B.E., K.C.B., D.S.O., D.F.C.

Smart, *Prof.* Sir George Algernon, Kt., M.D., F.R.C.P.

Smart, Sir Jack, Kt., C.B.E.

Smedley, Sir Harold, K.C.M.G., M.B.E.

Smeeton, *Vice-Adm.* Sir Richard Michael, K.C.B., M.B.E.

Smiley, Sir Hugh Houston, Bt. (1903).

Smirk, *Prof.* Sir (Frederick) Horace, K.B.E., M.D.

Smith, Sir Alan, Kt., C.B.E., D.F.C.

Smith, Sir Alexander Mair, Kt., Ph.D.

Smith, Sir (Alexander) Rowland, Kt.

Smith, Sir Arthur Henry, Kt.

Smith, *Maj.-Gen.* Sir Cecil Miller, K.B.E., C.B., M.C.

Smith, Sir Christopher Sydney Winwood, Bt. (1809).

Smith, Sir Dudley (Gordon), Kt., M.P.

Smith, *Maj.-Gen.* Sir Edmund Hakewill, K.C.V.O., C.B., C.B.E., M.C.

Smith, *Vice-Adm.* Sir (Edward Michael) Conolly Abel, G.C.V.O., C.B.

Smith, *Maj.-Gen.* Sir Francis Brian Wyldbore-, Kt., C.B., D.S.O., O.B.E.

Smith, Sir (Frank) Ewart, Kt.

Smith, *Vice-Adm.* Sir Geoffrey Thistleton-, K.B.E., C.B., G.M.

Smith, Sir Charles Bracewell-, Bt. (1947).

Smith, *Col.* Sir Henry Abel, K.C.M.G., K.C.V.O., D.S.O.

Smith, Sir Henry Thompson, K.B.E., C.B.

Smith, Sir Howard Frank Trayton, G.C.M.G.

Smith, *Hon.* Sir James Alfred, Kt., C.B.E., T.D.

Smith, Sir (James) Eric., Kt., C.B.E., Sc.D., F.R.S.

Smith, Sir John Hamilton-Spencer-, Bt. (1804).

Smith, Sir John Kenneth Newson-, Bt. (1944).

Smith, Sir Laurence Barton Grafftey-, K.C.M.G., K.B.E.

Smith, Sir Leonard Herbert, Kt., C.B.E.

Smith, Sir Leslie Edward George, Kt.

Smith, *Hon.* Sir Murray Stuart-, Kt.

Smith, Sir Raymond Horace, K.B.E.

Smith, Sir Reginald Beaumont, Kt.

Smith, Sir Richard Rathbone Vassar-, Bt., T.D. (1917).

Smith, Sir Richard Robert Law-, Kt., C.B.E., A.F.C.

Smith, Sir Robert Hill, Bt., (1945).

Smith, *Air Marshal* Sir Roy Dudley Austen-, K.B.E., C.B.

Smith, *Prof.* Sir Thomas Broun, Kt., Q.C.

Smith, Sir Thomas Gilbert, Bt. (1897).

Smith, *Admiral* Sir Victor Alfred Trumper, K.B.E., C.B., D.S.C.

Smith, Sir William Reardon Reardon-, Bt. (1920).

Smith, Sir (William) Reginald Verdon, Kt.

Smith, Sir (William) Richard Prince-, Bt. (1911).

Smithers, *Prof.* Sir David Waldron, Kt., M.D.

Smithers, Sir Peter Henry Berry Otway, Kt., V.R.D., D.Phil.

Smithers, *Hon.* Sir Reginald All-free, Kt.

Smyth, Sir Thomas Bowyer, Bt., (1661).

Smyth, Sir Timothy John, Bt. (1955).

Snedden, *Rt. Hon.* Sir Billy Mackie, K.C.M.G., Q.C.

Snelling, Sir Arthur Wendell, K.C.M.G., K.C.V.O.

Snelson, Sir Edward Alec Abbott, K.B.E.

Soame, Sir Charles John Buckworth-Herne-, Bt. (1697).

Sobell, Sir Michael, Kt.

Sobers, Sir Garfield St. Auburn, Kt.

Solomon, Sir David Arnold, Kt., M.B.E.

Solomons, *Hon.* Sir Louis Adrian, Kt.

Solti, Sir Georg, K.B.E.

Somerset, Sir Henry Beaufort, Kt., C.B.E.

Somerville, Sir Robert, K.C.V.O.

Sopwith, Sir Charles Ronald, Kt.

Sopwith, Sir Thomas Octave Murdoch, Kt., C.B.E.

Sorsbie, Sir Malin, Kt., C.B.E.

Soutar, *Air Marshal* Sir Charles John Williamson, K.B.E.

South, Sir Arthur, Kt.

Southby, *Lt.-Col.* Sir (Archibald) Richard (Charles), Bt., O.B.E., (1937).

Southern, Sir Richard William, Kt., F.B.A.

Southern, Sir Robert, Kt., C.B.E.

Southey, Sir Robert John, Kt., C.M.G.

Southward, Sir Ralph, K.C.V.O., F.R.C.P.

Southwood, *Prof.* Sir (Thomas) Richard (Edmund), Kt., F.R.S.

Southworth, *Hon.* Sir Frederick, Kt.

Souyave, *Hon.* Sir (Louis) Georges, Kt.

Sowrey, *Air Marshal* Sir Frederick Beresford, K.C.B., C.B.E.

Soysa, Sir Warusahennedige Abraham Bastian, Kt., C.B.E.

Sparkes, Sir Robert Lyndley, Kt.

Sparrow, Sir John, Kt.

Spearman, Sir Alexander Young Richard Mainwaring, Bt. (1840).

Speed, Sir Robert William Arney, Kt., C.B., Q.C.

Speelman, *Jonkheer* Sir Cornelis Jacob, Bt. (1686).

Speight, *Hon.* Sir Graham Davies, Kt.

Speir, Sir Rupert Malise, Kt.

Spencer, Sir Kelvin Tallent, Kt., C.B.E., M.C.

Spender, *Hon.* Sir Percy Claude, K.C.V.O., K.B.E., Q.C.

Spender, *Prof.* Sir Stephen Harold, Kt., C.B.E.

Spicer, Sir Peter James, Bt. (1906).

Spooner, Sir James Douglas, Kt.

Spotswood, *Marshal of the Royal Air Force* Sir Denis Frank, G.C.B., C.B.E., D.S.O., D.F.C.

Springer, Sir Hugh Worrell, G.C.M.G., C.B.E.

Spry, *Brig.* Sir Charles Chambers Fowell, Kt., C.B.E., D.S.O.

Spry, *Hon.* Sir John Farley, Kt.

Spurling, *Hon.* Sir (Arthur) Dudley, Kt., C.B.E.

Stabb, *Hon.* Sir William Walter, Kt., Q.C.

Stack, *Air Chief Marshal* Sir (Thomas) Neville, K.C.B., C.V.O., C.B.E., A.F.C.

Staine, *Hon.* Sir Albert Llewellyn, Kt., C.B.E.

Stainton, Sir Anthony Nathaniel, K.C.B., Q.C.

Stainton, Sir John Ross, Kt., C.B.E.

Stallard, Sir Peter Hyla Gawne, K.C.M.G., C.V.O., M.B.E.

Stallworthy, *Prof.* Sir John Arthur, Kt., F.R.C.S.

Stamer, Sir (Lovelace) Anthony, Bt. (1809).

Stanbridge, *Air Vice-Marshal* Sir Brian Gerald Tivy, K.C.V.O., C.B.E., A.F.C.

Stanford, *Vice-Adm.* Sir Peter Maxwell, K.C.B., M.V.O.

Stanier, *Brig.* Sir Alexander Beville Gibbons, Bt., D.S.O., M.C. (1917).

Stanier, *General* Sir John Wilfred, G.C.B., M.B.E.

Stansfield, Sir Walter, Kt., C.B.E., M.C., Q.P.M.

Staples, Sir John Richard, Bt. (I. 1628).

Stapleton, Sir Henry Alfred, Bt. (1679).

Stark, Sir Andrew Alexander Steel, K.C.M.G., C.V.O.

Starke, *Hon.* Sir John Erskine, Kt.

Starkey, Sir John Philip, Bt. (1935).

Starrit, Sir James, K.C.V.O.

Statham, Sir Norman, K.C.M.G., C.V.O.

Staughton, *Hon.* Sir Christopher Stephen Thomas Jonathan Thayer, Kt.

Staveley, Sir John Malfroy, K.B.E., M.C.

Staveley, *Admiral* Sir William Doveton Minet, G.C.B.

Stebbings, Sir John Chalmer, Kt.

Stedman, Sir George Foster, K.B.E., C.B., M.C.

Steedman, *Air Chief Marshal* Sir Alasdair (Alexander McKay Sinclair), G.C.B., C.B.E., D.F.C.

Steel, Sir David Edward Charles, Kt., D.S.O., M.C., T.D.

Steel, *Maj.* Sir (Fiennes) William Strang, Bt. (1938).

Steel, Sir James, Kt., C.B.E.

Steel, Sir (Joseph) Lincoln (Spedding), Kt.

Steele, Sir Kenneth Charles, Kt., D.F.C.

Steele, Sir Philip John Rupert, Kt.

Steere, Sir Ernest Henry Lee-, K.B.E.

Stenhouse, Sir Nicol, Kt.

Stening, *Col.* Sir George Grafton Lees, Kt., E.D.

Stephen, Sir James Alexander, Bt. (1891).

Stephen, *Rt. Hon.* Sir Ninian Martin, G.C.M.G., G.C.V.O., K.B.E.

Stephens, Sir David, K.C.B., C.V.O.

Stephenson, Sir Henry Upton, Bt. (1936).

Stephenson, *Rt. Hon.* Sir John Frederick Eustace, Kt.

Stephenson, Sir William Samuel, Kt., M.C., D.F.C.

Sternberg, Sir Sigmund, Kt.

Stevens, *Air Marshal* Sir Alick Charles, K.B.E., C.B.

Stevens, *Vice-Adm.* Sir John Felgate, K.B.E., C.B.

Stevens, Sir Laurence Houghton, Kt., C.B.E.

Stevenson, *Rt. Hon.* Sir (Aubrey) Melford (Steed), Kt.

Stevenson, *Vice-Adm.* Sir Hugh David, K.B.E.

Stevenson, Sir Simpson, Kt.

Stevenson, Sir William Alfred, K.B.E.

Steward, Sir William Arthur, Kt.

Stewart, Sir Alan, K.B.E.

Stewart, Sir David Brodribb, Bt., T.D. (1960).

Stewart, Sir David James Henderson-, Bt. (1957).

Stewart, Sir Dugald Leslie Lorn, K.C.V.O., C.M.G.

Stewart, Sir Edward Jackson, Kt.

Stewart, *Prof.* Sir Frederick Henry, Kt., Ph.D., F.R.S., F.R.S.E.

Stewart, Sir Hector Hamilton, K.B.E.

Stewart, Sir Herbert Ray, Kt., C.I.E.

Stewart, Sir Houston Mark Shaw-, Kt., M.C. (S. 1667).

Stewart, Sir Hugh Charlie Godfray, Bt. (1803).

Stewart, Sir Iain Maxwell, Kt.

Stewart, Sir James Douglas, Kt.

Stewart, Sir James Watson, Bt. (1920).

Stewart, Sir Alan d'Arcy, Bt. (I 1623).

Stewart, Sir Michael Norman Francis, K.C.M.G., O.B.E.

Stewart, Sir Robertson Huntly, Kt., C.B.E.

Stewart, Sir Ronald Compton, Bt. (1937).

Stinson, Sir Charles Alexander, K.B.E.

Stirling, Sir Alexander John Dickson, K.B.E., C.M.G.

Stirling, Sir Charles Norman, K.C.M.G., K.C.V.O.

Stoby, Sir Kenneth Sievewright, Kt.

Stockdale, Sir Edmund Villiers Minshull, Bt. (1960).

Stocker, *Hon.* Sir John Dexter, Kt., M.C., T.D.

Stockil, Sir Raymond Osborne, K.B.E.

Stockwell, *General* Sir Hugh Charles, G.C.B., K.B.E., D.S.O.

Stoker, *Prof.* Sir Michael George Parke, Kt., C.B.E., F.R.C.P., F.R.S., F.R.S.E.

Stone, *Prof.* Sir (John) Richard (Nicholas), Kt., C.B.E.

Stonhouse, Sir Philip Allan, Bt. (1628).

Storey, *Hon.* Sir Richard, Bt. (1960).

Stormonth Darling, Sir James Carlisle, Kt., C.B.E., M.C., T.D.

Storrar, Sir John, Kt., C.B.E., M.C.

Stott, Sir Adrian George Ellingham, Bt. (1920).

Stourton, Sir Ivo Herbert Evelyn Joseph, Kt., C.M.G., O.B.E.

Stow, Sir Christopher Philipson-, Bt., D.F.C. (1907).

Stow, Sir John Montague, G.C.M.G., K.C.V.O.

Stowe, Sir Kenneth Ronald, K.C.B., C.V.O.

Stracey, Sir John Simon, Bt. (1818).

Strachey, Sir Charles, Bt. (1801).

Straker, Sir Michael Ian Bowstead, Kt., C.B.E.

Strasser, Sir Paul, Kt.

Stratton, Sir Richard James, K.C.M.G.

Stratton, *Lt.-Gen.* Sir William Henry, K.C.B., C.V.O., C.B.E., D.S.O.

Straubenzee, Sir William Radcliffe van, Kt., M.P., M.B.E.

Strawson, *Prof.* Sir Peter Frederick, Kt.

Street, *Hon.* Sir Laurence Whistler, K.C.M.G.

Strong, Sir Charles Lorz, K.C.V.O.

Strong, Sir Roy Colin, Kt., Ph.D., F.S.A.

Stronge, Sir James Anselan Maxwell, Bt. (1803).

Strutt, Sir Nigel Edward, Kt., T.D.

Stuart, Sir Kenneth Lamonte, Kt.

†Stuart, Sir Phillip Luttrell, Bt. (1660).

Stuart-Smith, *Hon.* Sir Murray, Kt.

Stubblefield, Sir (Cyril) James, Kt., D.SC., Ph.D., F.R.S.

Stubbs, Sir James Wilfrid, K.C.V.O., T.D.

Stucley, *Lt.* Sir Hugh George Coplestone Bampfylde, Bt. (1859).

Studd, Sir Edward Fairfax, Bt. (1929).

Studd, Sir Peter Malden, G.B.E., K.C.V.O.

Studholme, Sir Henry Gray, Bt., C.V.O. (1956).

Style, *Lt. Cdr.* Sir Godfrey William, Kt., C.B.E., D.S.C., R.N.

Style, Sir William Montague, Bt. (1627).

Suffield, Sir (Henry John) Lester, Kt.

Sugden, Sir Arthur, Kt.

Sullivan, Sir Richard Arthur, Bt. (1804).

Summerfield, *Hon.* Sir John Crampton, Kt., C.B.E.

Summerhayes, Sir Christopher Henry, K.B.E., C.M.G.

Summers, Sir Felix Roland Brattan, Bt. (1952).

Summerson, Sir John Newenham, Kt., C.B.E., F.B.A., F.S.A.

Sunderland, *Prof.* Sir Sydney, Kt., C.M.G., M.D.

Surridge, Sir (Ernest) Rex (Edward), Kt., C.M.G.

Sutherland, Sir (Frederick) Neil, Kt., C.B.E.

Sutherland, Sir Iain Johnstone Macbeth, K.C.M.G.

Sutherland, Sir John Brewer, Bt. (1921).

Sutherland, Sir Maurice, Kt.

Suttie, Sir George Philip Grant-, Bt. (s 1702).

Sutton, Sir Frederick Walter, Kt., O.B.E.

Sutton, Sir Richard Lexington, Bt. (1772).

Sutton, Sir Stafford William Powell Foster-, K.B.E., C.M.G., Q.C.

Swaffield, Sir James Chesebrough, Kt., C.B.E., R.D.

Swallow, Sir William, Kt.

Swann, Sir Anthony Charles Christopher, Bt., C.M.G., O.B.E., (1906).

Swanwick, Sir Graham Russell, Kt., M.B.E.

Swartz, *Hon.* Sir Reginald William Colin, K.B.E., E.D.

Swayne, Sir Ronald Oliver Carless, Kt., M.C.

Swinson, Sir John Henry Alan, Kt., O.B.E.

Swinton, *Maj.-Gen.* Sir John, K.C.V.O., O.B.E.

Swire, Sir Adrian Christopher, Kt.

Swiss, Sir Rodney Geoffrey, Kt., O.B.E.

Swynnerton, Sir Roger John Massy, Kt., C.M.G., O.B.E., M.C.

Sykes, Sir Francis Godfrey, Bt. (1781).

Sykes, Sir John Charles Anthony le Gallais, Bt. (1921).

Sykes, Sir Tatton Christopher Mark, Bt. (1783).

Syme, Sir Colin Yorke, Kt.

Syme, *Prof.* Sir Ronald, Kt., O.M., F.B.A.

Symington, *Prof.* Sir Thomas, Kt., M.D., F.R.S.E.

Synge, Sir Robert Carson, Bt. (1801).

Tait, *Admiral* Sir (Allan) Gordon, K.C.B., D.S.C.

Tait, Sir James Sharp, Kt., Ph.D.

Tait, Sir Peter, K.B.E.

Tait, *Air Vice-Marshal* Sir Victor Hubert, K.B.E., C.B.

Talbot, *Vice-Adm.* Sir (Arthur Allison) FitzRoy, K.B.E., C.B., D.S.O.

Talbot, *Hon.* Sir Hilary Gwynne, Kt.

Tallack, Sir Hugh Mackay, Kt.

Tancred, Sir Henry Lawson-, Bt. (1662).

Tang, Sir Shiu-kin, Kt., C.B.E.

Tange, Sir Arthur Harold, Kt., C.B.E.

Tansley, Sir Eric Crawford, Kt., C.M.G.

Tapp, *Maj.-Gen.* Sir Nigel Prior Hanson, K.B.E., C.B., D.S.O.

Tate, *Lt.-Col.* Sir Henry, Bt. (1898).

Taylor, *Lt.-Gen.* Sir Allan Macnab, K.B.E., M.C.

Taylor, Sir Alvin Burton, Kt.

Taylor, Sir (Arthur) Godfrey, Kt.

Taylor, Sir Charles Stuart, Kt., T.D.

Taylor, Sir George, Kt., D.SC., F.R.S., F.R.S.E.

Taylor, Sir Henry Milton, Kt.

Taylor, Sir James, Kt., M.B.E., D.SC.

Taylor, Sir John Lang, K.C.M.G.

Taylor, Sir Nicholas Richard Stuart, Bt. (1917).

Taylor, *Hon.* Sir Peter Murray, Kt.

Taylor, Sir Robert Mackinlay, Kt., C.B.E.

Tebbit, Sir Donald Claude, G.C.M.G.

Te Heu Heu, Sir Hepi Hoani, K.B.E.

Telford, Sir Robert, Kt., C.B.E.

Temple, Sir John Meredith, Kt.

Temple, Sir Rawden John Afamado, Kt. C.B.E., Q.C.

Temple, *Maj.* Sir Richard Anthony Purbeck, Bt., M.C. (1876).

Tennant, Sir Mark Dalcour, K.C.M.G., C.B.

Tennant, Sir Peter Frank Dalrymple, Kt., C.M.G., O.B.E.

Teo, Sir Fiatau Penitala, G.C.M.G., G.C.V.O., I.S.O., M.B.E.

Terry, Sir Andrew Henry Bouhier Imbert-, Bt. (1917).

Terry, Sir George Walter Roberts, Kt., C.B.E., Q.P.M.

Terry, Sir John Elliott, Kt.

Terry, *Air Chief Marshal* Sir Peter David George, G.C.B., A.F.C.

Tetley, Sir Herbert, K.B.E., C.B.

Tett, Sir Hugh Charles, Kt.

Thalben-Ball, Sir George Thomas, Kt., C.B.E.

Thiess, Sir Leslie Charles, Kt., C.B.E.

Thomas, Sir Frederick William, Kt.

Thomas, Sir (Godfrey) Michael (David) Bt. (1694).

Thomas, Sir John Maldwyn, Kt.

Thomas, Sir Patrick Muirhead, Kt., D.S.O., T.D.

Thomas, Sir Robert Evan, Kt.

Thomas, Sir William James Cooper, Bt. (1919).

Thomas, Sir (William) Michael (Marsh), Bt. (1918).

Thompson, Sir Edward Hugh Dudley, Kt., M.B.E., T.D.

Thompson, Sir Edward Walter, Kt.

Thompson, Sir (Humphrey) Simon Meysey-, Bt. (1874).

Thompson, *Hon.* Sir John, Kt.

Thompson, Sir Paul Anthony, Bt. (1963).

Thompson, *Lt.-Col.* Sir Peile Beaumont, Bt., O.B.E. (1890).

Thompson, Sir Peter Anthony, Kt.

Thompson, Sir Ralph Patrick, Kt.

Thompson, Sir Richard Hilton Marler, Bt. (1963).

Thompson, Sir Robert Grainger Ker, K.B.E., C.M.G., D.S.O., M.C.

Thompson, Sir (Thomas) Lionel Tennyson, Bt. (1806).

Thomson, Sir Adam, Kt., C.B.E.

Thomson, Sir Evan Rees Whitaker, Kt.

Thomson, Sir (Frederick) Douglas David, Bt. (1929).

Thomson, Sir Ivo Wilfrid Home, Bt. (1925).

Thomson, *Lt.-Col.* Sir John, K.B.E., T.D.

Thomson, Sir John Adam, K.C.M.G.

Thorley, Sir Gerald Bowers, Kt., T.D.

Thorn, Sir John Samuel, Kt., O.B.E.

Thorne, *Maj.-Gen.* Sir David Calthrop, K.B.E.

Thorne, *Lt.-Col.* Sir Peter Francis, K.C.V.O., C.B.E.

Thornton, *Lt.-Gen.* Sir Leonard Whitmore, K.C.B., C.B.E.

Thornton, Sir Peter Eustace, K.C.B.

Thorold, Sir Anthony Henry, Bt., O.B.E., D.S.C. (1642).

Thouron, Sir John Rupert Hunt, K.B.E.

Throckmorton, Sir Robert George Maxwell, Bt. (1642).

Thwin, Sir U, Kt.

Tibbits, *Capt.* Sir David Stanley, Kt., D.S.C., R.N.(*ret*).

Tickell, Sir Crispin Charles Cervantes, K.C.V.O.

Tikaram, Sir Moti, K.B.E.

Tilney, Sir John Dudley Robert Tarleton, Kt., T.D.

Tippet, *Vice-Adm.* Sir Anthony Sanders, K.C.B.

Tippett, Sir Michael Kemp, Kt., O.M., C.H., C.B.E.

Titterton, *Prof.* Sir Ernest William, Kt., C.M.G.

Tizard, Sir John Peter Mills, Kt.

Tod, *Air Marshal* Sir John Hunter Hunter-, K.B.E., C.B.

Todd, Sir Bryan James, Kt.

Todd, Sir Geoffrey Sydney, K.C.V.O., O.B.E.

Todd, Sir Herbert John, Kt., C.I.E.

Tollemache, *Maj.-Gen.* Sir Humphry Thomas, Bt., C.B., C.B.E., R.M. (1793).

Tombs, Sir Francis Leonard, Kt.

Tomkins, Sir Alfred George, Kt., C.B.E.

Tomkins, Sir Edward Emile, G.C.M.G., C.V.O.

Tomlinson, Sir Frank Stanley, K.C.M.G.

Tooley, Sir John, Kt.

Tooth, Sir Hugh Vere Huntly Duff Munro-Lucas-, Bt. (1920).

Tooth, *Hon.* Sir Seymour Douglas, Kt.

Toothill, Sir John Norman, Kt., C.B.E.

ToRobert, Sir Henry Thomas, K.B.E.

Tory, Sir Geofroy William, K.C.M.G.

Touche, Sir Anthony George, Bt. (1920).

Touche, Sir Rodney Gordon, Bt. (1962).

Tovey, Sir Brian John Maynard, K.C.M.G.

Townley, Sir John Barton, Kt.

Townsend, *Rear-Adm.* Sir Leslie William, K.C.V.O., C.B.E.

Townsing, Sir Kenneth Joseph, Kt., C.M.G.

Traherne, *Col.* Sir Cennydd George, K.G., T.D.

Trant, *General* Sir Richard Brooking, K.C.B.

Travancore, *Maj.-Gen.* H.H. the Maharajah of, G.C.S.I., G.C.I.E.

Travers, Sir Thomas A'Beckett, Kt.

Treacher, *Admiral* Sir John Devereux, K.C.B.

Treatt, *Hon.* Sir Vernon Haddon, K.B.E., M.M., Q.C.

Trehane, Sir Walter Richard, Kt.

Trelawny, Sir John Barry Salusbury-, Bt. (1628).

Trench, Sir David Clive Crosbie, G.C.M.G., M.C.

Trench, Sir Nigel Clive Cosby, K.C.M.G.

Trench, Sir Peter Edward, Kt., C.B.E., T.D.

Trescowthick, Sir Donald Henry, K.B.E.

Trethowan, Sir (James) Ian (Raley), Kt.

Trethowan, *Prof.* Sir William Henry, Kt. C.B.E., F.R.C.P.

Trevaskis, Sir (Gerald) Kennedy (Nicholas), K.C.M.G., O.B.E.

Trevelyan, Sir George Lowthian, Bt. (1874).

Trevelyan, Sir Norman Irving, Bt. (1662).

Trewby, *Vice-Adm.* Sir (George Francis) Allan, K.C.B.

Trinder, Sir (Arnold) Charles, G.B.E.

Tritton, Sir Anthony John Ernest, Bt. (1905).

Trollope, Sir Anthony Owen Clavering, Bt. (1642).

Troubridge, *Lt.-Cdr.* Sir Peter, Bt., R.N. (1799).

Troughton, Sir Charles Hugh Willis, Kt., C.B.E., M.C., T.D.

Troup, *Vice-Adm.* Sir (John) Anthony (Rose), K.C.B., D.S.C.

Trowbridge, *Rear-Adm.* Sir Richard John, K.C.V.O.

Truscott, Sir Denis Henry, G.B.E., T.D.

Truscott, Sir George James Irving, Bt. (1909).

Trusted, Sir Harry Herbert, Kt., Q.C.

Tuck, Sir Bruce Adolph Reginald, Bt. (1910).

Tucker, Sir Henry James, K.B.E.

Tuckwell, Sir Edward George, K.C.V.O., F.R.C.S.

Tuke, Sir Anthony Favill, Kt.

Tuite, Sir Christopher Hugh, Bt., Ph.D. (1622).

Tuivaga, Sir Timoci Uluiburotu, Kt.

Tupper, Sir Charles Hibbert, Bt. (1888).

Turbott, Sir Ian Graham, Kt., C.M.G., C.V.O.

Turing, Sir John Leslie, Bt., M.C. (s 1638).

Turnbull, Sir Francis Fearon, K.B.E., C.B., C.I.E.

Turnbull, Sir Richard Gordon, G.C.M.G.

Turner, *Rt. Hon.* Sir Alexander Kingcome, K.B.E.

Turner, *Admiral* Sir (Arthur) Francis, K.C.B., D.S.C.

Turner, Sir Harvey, Kt., C.B.E.

Turner, *Lt.-Gen.* Sir William Francis Robert, K.B.E., C.B., D.S.O.

Tuttle, *Air Marshal* Sir Geoffrey William, K.B.E., C.B., D.F.C.

Tuzo, *General* Sir Harry Craufurd, G.C.B., O.B.E., M.C.

Twiss, *Admiral* Sir Frank Roddam, K.C.B., K.C.V.O., D.S.C.

Tyler, *Maj.-Gen.* Sir Leslie Norman, K.B.E., C.B.

Tymms, Sir Frederick, K.C.I.E., M.C.

Tyree, Sir (Alfred) William, Kt., O.B.E.

Tyrrell, Sir Murray Louis, K.C.V.O., C.B.E.

Tyrwhitt, Sir Reginald Thomas Newman, Bt. (1919).

Udoma, Sir Ethelbert Udo, Kt.

Unsworth, Hon. Sir Edgar Ignatius Godfrey, Kt., C.M.G.

Unwin, Sir Keith, K.B.E., C.M.G.

Urquhart, Sir Andrew, K.C.M.G., M.B.E.

Urwick, Sir Alan Bedford, K.C.V.O., C.M.G.

Usher, Sir Peter Lionel, Bt. (1899).

Vallat, Sir Francis Aimé, G.B.E., K.C.M.G., Q.C.

Vanderfelt, Sir Robin Victor, K.B.E.

van der Post, Sir Laurens Jan, Kt., C.B.E.

Vane, Sir John Robert, Kt., D.Phil., D.SC., F.R.S.

Vangeke, *Most Rev.* Louis, K.B.E.

Vanneck, *Air Commodore* Hon. Sir Peter Beckford Rutgers, G.B.E., C.B., A.F.C.

Vaughan, Sir (George) Edgar, K.B.E.

Vaughan, Sir Gerard Folliott, Kt., M.P., F.R.C.P.

Vavasour, *Cdr.* Sir Geoffrey William, Bt., D.S.C., R.N. (1828).

Veale, Sir Alan John Ralph, Kt.

Verco, Sir Walter John George, K.C.V.O.

Verney, Sir John, Bt., M.C. (1946).

Verney, Sir Ralph Bruce, Bt., K.B.E. (1818).

Vernon, Sir James, Kt., C.B.E.

Vernon, Sir Nigel John Douglas, Bt. (1914).

Vesey, Sir (Nathaniel) Henry (Peniston), Kt., C.B.E.

Vestey, Sir (John) Derek, Bt. (1921).

Vial, Sir Kenneth Harold, Kt., C.B.E.

Vick, Sir (Francis) Arthur, Kt., O.B.E., D.SC., Ph.D.

Vickers, *Lt.-Gen.* Sir Richard Maurice Hilton, K.C.B., M.V.O., O.B.E.

Vickery, Sir Philip Crawford, Kt., C.I.E., O.B.E.

Victoria, Sir (Joseph Aloysius) Donatus, Kt., C.B.E.

Villiers, Sir Charles Hyde, Kt., M.C.

Villiers, *Vice-Adm.* Sir (John) Michael, K.C.B., O.B.E.

Vincent, *Lt.-Gen.* Sir Richard Frederick, K.C.B., D.S.O.

Vincent, Sir William Percy Maxwell, Bt. (1936).

Vinelott, *Hon.* Sir John Evelyn, Kt.

Vines, Sir William Joshua, Kt., C.M.G.

Virtue, *Hon.* Sir John Evenden, K.B.E.

Vyse, *Lt.-Gen.* Sir Edward Dacre-Howard-, K.B.E., C.B., M.C.

Vyvyan, Sir John Stanley, Bt. (1645).

Waddell, Sir Alexander Nicol Anton, K.C.M.G., D.S.C.

Waddell, Sir James Henderson, Kt., C.B.

Wade, *Col.* Sir George Albert, Kt., M.C.

Wade, *Air Chief Marshal* Sir Ruthven Lowry, K.C.B., D.F.C.

Wade, Sir (William) Oulton, Kt.

Wade-Gery, Sir Robert Lucian, K.C.M.G., K.C.V.O.

Wadley, Sir Douglas, Kt.

Waechter, Sir Harry Leonard D'Arcy, Bt. (1911).

Wagner, Sir Anthony Richard, K.C.B., K.C.V.O.

Waite, *Hon.* Sir John Douglas, Kt.

Wake, Sir Hereward, Bt., M.C., (1621).

Wakefield, Sir (Edward) Humphry (Tyrell), Bt. (1962).

Wakefield, Sir Peter George Arthur, K.B.E., C.M.G.

Wakeford, *Air Marshal* Sir Richard Gordon, K.C.B., M.V.O., O.B.E., A.F.C.

Wakeley, Sir John Cecil Nicholson, Bt., F.R.C.S. (1952).

Wakeman, Sir (Offley) David, Bt. (1828).

Walker, *Rev.* Alan Edgar, Kt., O.B.E.

Walker, Sir Allan Grierson, Kt., Q.C.

Walker, Sir Baldwin Patrick, Bt. (1856).

Walker, Sir (Charles) Michael, G.C.M.G.

Walker, *Vice-Adm.* Sir (Charles) Peter (Graham), K.B.E., C.B., D.S.C.

Walker, Sir Michael Leolin Forestier-, Bt. (1835).

Walker, Sir Edward Ronald, Kt., C.B.E.

Walker, *Air Chief Marshal* Sir (George) Augustus, G.C.B., C.B.E., D.S.O., D.F.C., A.F.C.

Walker, Sir Gervas George, Kt.

Walker, *Maj.* Sir Hugh Ronald, Bt. (1906).

Walker, Sir Hugh Selby Norman-, K.C.M.G., O.B.E.

Walker, Sir James Graham, Kt., M.B.E.

Walker, Sir James Heron, Bt. (1868).

Walker, Sir John, K.C.M.G., O.B.E.

Walker, *General* Sir Walter Colyear, K.C.B., C.B.E., D.S.O.

Walker, Sir William Giles Newsom, Kt., T.D.

Wall, Sir Patrick Henry Bligh, Kt., M.C., M.P.

Wallace, *Hon.* Sir Gordon, Kt.

Wallace, Sir Ian James, Kt., C.B.E.

Waller, *Rt. Hon.* Sir George Stanley, Kt., O.B.E.

Waller, Sir (John) Keith, Kt., C.B.E.

Waller, Sir John Stainer, Bt. (1815).

Waller, Sir Robert William, Bt. (1780).

Walley, Sir John, K.B.E., C.B.

Walmsley, *Air Marshal* Sir Hugh Sydney Porter, K.C.B., K.C.I.E., C.B.E., M.C., D.F.C.

Walsh, Sir Alan, Kt., D.SC., F.R.S.

Walsh, Sir David Philip, K.B.E., C.B.

Walsh, Prof. Sir John Patrick, K.B.E.

Walsham, *Rear-Adm.* Sir John Scarlett Warren, Bt., C.B., O.B.E. (1831).

Walter, Sir Harold Edward, Kt.

Walters, *Prof.* Sir Alan Arthur, Kt.

Walters, Sir Frederick Donald, Kt.

Walters, Sir Peter Ingram, Kt.

Walters, Sir Roger Talbot, K.B.E., F.R.I.B.A.

Walton, *Prof.* Sir John Nicholas, Kt., T.D., F.R.C.P.

Walton, Sir John Robert, Kt.

Walton, *Hon.* Sir Raymond Henry, Kt.

Wan, Sir Wamp, Kt., M.B.E.

Wanstall, *Hon.* Sir Charles Gray, Kt.

Ward, Sir Arthur Hugh, K.B.E.

Ward, *General* Sir (Alfred) Dudley, G.C.B., K.B.E., D.S.O.

Ward, Sir Aubrey Ernest, Kt.

Ward, Sir John Guthrie, G.C.M.G.

Ward, Sir Joseph James Laffey, Bt. (1911).

Ward, *Maj.-Gen.* Sir Philip John Newling, K.C.V.O., C.B.E.

Ward, *General* Sir Richard Erskine, G.B.E., K.C.B., D.S.O., M.C.

Ward, Sir Terence George, Kt., C.B.E.

Wardale, Sir Geoffrey Charles, K.C.B.

Wardlaw, Sir Henry (John), Bt. (s 1631).

Wardle, Sir Thomas Edward Jewell, Kt.

Ware, Sir Henry Gabriel, K.C.B.

Waring, Sir Alfred Holburt, Bt. (1935).

Wark, Sir Ian William, Kt., C.M.G., C.B.E., Ph.D., D.SC.

Warmington, *Lt.-Cdr.* Sir Marshall George Clitheroe, Bt., R.N. (1908).

Warner, Sir Edward Courtenay Henry, Bt. (1910).

Warner, Sir Edward Redston, K.C.M.G., O.B.E.

Warner, Sir Frederick Archibald, G.C.V.O., K.C.M.G.

Warner, Sir Frederick Edward, Kt., F.R.S.

Warner, *Hon.* Sir Jean-Pierre Frank Eugene, Kt.

Warren, Sir Alfred Henry, Kt., C.B.E.

Warren, Sir (Harold) Brian (Seymour), Kt.

Warren, Sir Brian Charles Pennefather, Bt. (1784).

Warren, *Hon.* Sir Edward Emerton, K.C.M.G., K.B.E.

Wass, Sir Douglas William Gretton, G.C.B.

Waterhouse, Sir Ellis Kirkham, Kt., C.B.E.

Waterhouse, *Hon.* Sir Ronald Gough, Kt.

Waterlow, Sir Christopher Rupert, Bt. (1873).

Waterlow, Sir (James) Gerard, Bt. (1930).

Wates, Sir Ronald Wallace, Kt.

Watkins, *Rt. Hon.* Sir Tasker, Kt., V.C.

Watson, *Capt.* Sir Derrick William Inglefield Inglefield-, Bt., T.D. (1895).

Watson, Sir Francis John Bagott, K.C.V.O., F.B.A., F.S.A.

Watson, Sir James Andrew, Bt. (1866).

Watson, Sir Michael Milne-, Bt., C.B.E. (1937).

Watson, Sir Noel Duncan, K.C.M.G.

Watson, *Vice-Admiral* Sir Philip Alexander, K.B.E., M.V.O.

Watson, *Vice-Adm.* Sir (Robert) Dymock, K.C.B., C.B.E.

Watt, Sir Alan Stewart, Kt., C.B.E.

Watt, *Brig.* Sir George Steven Harvie-, Bt., T.D., Q.C. (1945).

Watt, *Surgeon Vice-Adm.* Sir James, K.B.E., F.R.C.S.

Wauchope, Sir Patrick George Don-, Bt. (s 1667).

Way, Sir Richard George Kitchener, K.C.B., C.B.E.

Wayne, *Prof.* Sir Edward Johnson, Kt., M.D., Ph.D.

Weatherhead, Sir Arthur Trenham, Kt., C.M.G.

Weaver, Sir Tobias Rushton, Kt., C.B.

Webb, *Lt.-Gen.* Sir Richard James Holden, K.B.E., C.B.

Webb, Sir Thomas Langley, Kt.

Webster, *Hon.* Sir Peter Edlin, Kt.

Webster, Sir Richard James, Kt., D.S.O.

Wedderburn, Sir Andrew John Alexander Ogilvy-, Bt. (1803).

Wedderspoon, Sir Thomas Adam, Kt.

Wedgwood, Sir John Hamilton, Bt., T.D. (1942).

Weeks, Sir Hugh Thomas, Kt., C.M.G.

Weipers, *Prof.* Sir William Lee, Kt.

Weir, Sir Michael Scott, K.C.M.G.

Weir, Sir Roderick Bignell, Kt.

Weiss, Sir Eric, Kt.

Welby, Sir (Richard) Bruno Gregory, Bt. (1801).

Welch, Sir John Reader, Bt. (1957).

Weld, *Col.* Sir Joseph William, Kt., O.B.E., T.D.

Weldon, Sir Anthony William, Bt. (i. 1723).

Welensky, *Rt. Hon.* Sir Roy (Roland), K.C.M.G.

Wellings, Sir Jack Alfred, Kt., C.B.E.

Wellington, Sir (Reginald Everard) Lindsay, Kt., C.B.E.

Wells, Sir Charles Maltby, Bt. (1944).

Wells, Sir John Julius, Kt., M.P.

Westall, *General* Sir John Chaddesley, K.C.B., C.B.E., R.M.

Westerman, Sir (Wilfred) Alan, Kt., C.B.E.

Wheatley, Sir (George) Andrew, Kt., C.B.E.

Wheeler, Sir Ernest Richard, K.C.V.O., M.B.E.

Wheeler, Sir Frederick Henry, Kt., C.B.E.

Wheeler, *Air Chief Marshal* Sir (Henry) Neil (George), G.C.B., C.B.E., D.S.O., D.F.C., A.F.C.

Wheeler, Sir John Hieron, Bt. (1920).

Wheeler, *Hon.* Sir Kenneth Henry, Kt.

Wheldon, Sir Huw Pyrs, Kt., O.B.E., M.C.

Wheler, *Capt.* Sir Trevor Wood, Bt. (1660).

Whishaw, Sir Charles Percival Law, Kt.

Whitaker, *Maj.* Sir James Herbert Ingham, Bt. (1936).

White, *Hon.* Sir Alfred John, Kt.

White, Sir Christopher Robert Meadows, Bt. (1937).

White, Sir Dick Goldsmith, K.C.M.G., K.B.E.

White, Sir Ernest Keith, Kt., C.B.E., M.C.

White, Sir Frederick William George, K.B.E., Ph.D., F.R.S.

White, Sir George Stanley James, Bt. (1904).

White, Sir Harold Leslie, Kt., C.B.E.

White, *Wing-Cdr.* Sir Henry Arthur Dalrymple-, Bt., D.F.C. (1926).

White, *Hon.* Sir John Charles, Kt., M.B.E.

White, Sir John Woolmer, Bt. (1922).

White, *Admiral* Sir Peter, G.B.E.

White, Sir Thomas Astley Woollaston, Bt. (1802).

White, Sir (Vincent) Gordon (Lindsay), K.B.E.

Whitehead, Sir Rowland John Rathbone, Bt. (1889).

Whiteley, Sir Hugo Baldwin Huntington-, Bt. (1918).

Whiteley, *General* Sir Peter John Frederick, G.C.B., O.B.E., R.M.

Whitford, *Hon.* Sir John Norman Keates, Kt.

Whitley, *Air Marshal* Sir John René, K.B.E., C.B., D.S.O., A.F.C.

Whitmore, Sir Clive Anthony, K.C.B., C.V.O.

Whitmore, Sir John Henry Douglas, Bt. (1954).

Whittaker, (Sir) Joseph Meredith, Kt., T.D.

Whitteridge, Sir Gordon Coligny, K.C.M.G., O.B.E.

Whittle, *Air Commodore* Sir Frank, K.B.E., C.B.

Wicks, *Hon.* Sir James, Kt.

Wicks, Sir James Albert, Kt.

Wigan, Sir Alan Lewis, Bt. (1898).

Wiggin, Sir John Henry, Bt., M.C. (1892).

Wigglesworth, *Prof.* Sir Vincent Brian, Kt., C.B.E., M.D., F.R.S.

Wigram, *Rev. Canon* Sir Clifford Woolmore, Bt. (1805).

Wilbraham, Sir Richard Baker, Bt. (1776).

Wilcox, Sir Malcolm George, Kt., C.B.E.

Wilford, Sir (Kenneth) Michael, G.C.M.G.

Wilkins, Sir Graham John, Kt.

Wilkinson, Sir (David) Graham (Brook) Bt. (1941).

Wilkinson, *Prof.* Sir Denys Haigh, Kt., F.R.S.

Wilkinson, *Prof.* Sir Geoffrey, Kt., F.R.S.

Wilkinson, *Rt. Hon.* Sir Nicolas Christopher Henry Browne-, Kt.

Wilkinson, Sir Harold, Kt., C.M.G.

Wilkinson, Sir Peter Allix, K.C.M.G., D.S.O., O.B.E.

Wilkinson, Sir (Robert Francis) Martin, Kt.

Willatt, Sir (Robert) Hugh, Kt.

Willcocks, Sir David Valentine, Kt., C.B.E., M.C.

Williams, Sir Alwyn, Kt., Ph.D., F.R.S.

Williams, Sir Anthony James, K.C.M.G.

Williams, Sir Brandon Meredith Rhys-, Bt., M.P. (1918).

Williams, *Prof.* Sir Bruce Rodda, K.B.E.

Williams, *Admiral* Sir David, G.C.B.

Williams, Sir Donald Mark, Bt. (1866).

Williams, Sir Edgar Trevor, Kt., C.B., C.B.E., D.S.O.

Williams, *Hon.* Sir Edward Stratten, K.C.M.G., K.B.E.

Williams, Sir Francis John Watkin, Bt., Q.C. (1798).

Williams, Sir Gwilym Tecwyn, Kt., C.B.E.

Williams, Sir Henry Morton Leech, Kt., M.B.E.

Williams, Sir Henry Sydney, Kt., O.B.E.

Williams, Sir (John) Leslie, Kt., C.B.E.

Williams, *Capt.* Sir John Protheroe, Kt., C.M.G., O.B.E.

Williams, Sir John Robert, K.C.M.G.

Williams, Sir Leonard, K.B.E., C.B.

Williams, Sir Osmond, Bt., M.C. (1909).

Williams, Sir Peter Watkin, Kt.

Williams, *Prof.* Sir Robert Evan Owen, Kt., M.D., F.R.C.P.

Williams, Sir (Robert) Philip Nathaniel, Bt. (1915).

Williams, Sir Robin Philip, Bt. (1953).

Williams, Sir Rolf Dudley-, Bt. (1964).

Williams, Sir (William) Maxwell (Harries), Kt.

Williams, Sir (William) Thomas, Kt., Q.C.

Williamson, *Air Chief Marshal* Sir Keith Alec, G.C.B., A.F.C.

Williamson, Sir (Nicholas Frederick) Hedworth, Bt. (1642).

Willink, Sir Charles William, Bt. (1957).

Willis, *Hon.* Sir Eric Archibald, K.B.E., C.M.G.

Willis, *Vice-Adm.* Sir (Guido) James, K.B.E.

Willis, Sir John Ramsay, Kt.

Willison, *Lt.-Gen.* Sir David John, K.C.B., O.B.E., M.C.

Willison, Sir John Alexander, Kt., O.B.E.

Willoughby, *Maj.-Gen.* Sir John Edward Francis, K.B.E., C.B.

Wills, Sir David Seton, Bt. (1904).

Wills, Sir Hugh David Hamilton, Kt., C.B.E., T.D.

Wills, Sir John Spencer, Kt.

Wills, Sir John Vernon, Bt. (1923).

Wilmot, Sir Henry Robert, Bt. (1759).

Wilmot, *Cdr.* Sir John Assheton Eardley-, Bt., M.V.O., D.S.C., R.N. (1821).

Wilson, Sir Alan Herries, Kt., F.R.S.

Wilson, *Lt.-Gen.* Sir (Alexander) James, K.B.E., M.C.

Wilson, Sir Angus Frank Johnstone, Kt., C.B.E.

Wilson, Sir Austin George, Kt., O.B.E.

Wilson, Sir Charles Haynes, Kt.

Wilson, Sir David, Bt. (1920).

Wilson, Sir David Mackenzie, Kt.

Wilson, Sir Geoffrey Masterman, K.C.B., C.M.G.

Wilson, *Prof.* Sir Graham Selby, Kt., M.D.

Wilson, Sir John Foster, Kt., C.B.E.

Wilson, Sir John Gardiner, Kt., C.B.E.

Wilson, Sir John Martindale, K.C.B.

Wilson, Sir Keith Cameron, Kt.

Wilson, Sir (Leslie) Hugh, Kt., O.B.E.

Wilson, Sir Mathew Martin, Bt. (1874).

Wilson, Sir Reginald Holmes, Kt.

Wilson, *Rt. Rev.* Roger Plumpton, K.C.V.O., D.D.

Wilson, Sir Roland, K.B.E.

Wilson, *Hon.* Sir Ronald Darling, K.B.E., C.M.G.

Wilson, Sir Thomas Douglas, Bt., M.C. (1906).

Wilton, Sir (Arthur) John, K.C.M.G., K.C.V.O., M.C.

Wiltshire, Sir Frederick Munro, Kt., C.B.E.

Windeyer, *Prof.* Sir Brian Wellingham, Kt.

Windeyer, *Rt. Hon.* Sir (William John) Victor, K.B.E., C.B., D.S.O., E.D.

Wingate, *Capt.* Sir Miles Buckley, K.C.V.O.

Winneke, *Hon.* Sir Henry Arthur, K.C.M.G., K.C.V.O., O.B.E.

Winnifrith, Sir (Alfred) John (Digby), K.C.B.

Winnington, Sir Francis Salwey William, Bt. (1755).

Winskill, *Air Commodore* Sir Archie Little, K.C.V.O., C.B.E., D.F.C.

Winterbottom, Sir Walter, Kt., C.B.E.

Winterton, *Maj.-Gen.* Sir (Thomas) John (Willoughby), K.C.B., K.C.M.G., C.B.E.

Wise, Sir John Humphrey, K.C.M.G., C.B.E.

Wiseman, Sir John William, Bt. (1628).

Wolfson, Sir David, Kt.

Wolfson, Sir Isaac, Bt., F.R.S. (1962).

Wolfson, Sir Leonard Gordon, Kt.

Wollen, Sir (Ernest) Russell (Storey), K.B.E.

Wolseley, Sir Charles Garnet Mark Richard, Bt. (1628).

Wolseley, Sir Garnet, Bt. (I 1745).

Wolstenholme, Sir Gordon Ethelbert Ward, Kt., O.B.E.

Wombwell, Sir George Philip Frederick, Bt. (1778).

Womersley, Sir Peter John Walter, Bt. (1945).

Wontner, Sir Hugh Walter Kingwell, G.B.E., C.V.O.

Wood, Sir Anthony John Page, Bt. (1837).

Wood, Sir David Basil Hill-, Bt. (1921).

Wood, Sir Frederick Ambrose Stuart, Kt.

Wood, Sir George Ernest Francis, K.B.E., I.S.O.

Wood, Sir Henry Peart, Kt., C.B.E.

Wood, Sir Ian Jeffreys, Kt., M.B.E.

Wood, *Prof.* Sir John Crossley, Kt., C.B.E.

Wood, *Hon.* Sir John Kember, Kt., M.C.

Wood, Sir Kenneth Millns, Kt.

Wood, Sir William Alan, K.C.V.O., C.B.

Woodall, *Lt.-Gen.* Sir John Dane, K.C.M.G., K.B.E., C.B., M.C.

Woodfield, Sir Philip John, K.C.B., C.B.E.

Woodhouse, *Rt. Hon.* Sir (Arthur) Owen, K.B.E., D.S.C.

Woodroffe, *Most Rev.* George Cuthbert Manning, K.B.E.

Woodroofe, Sir Ernest George, Kt., Ph.D.

Woodruff, *Prof.* Sir Michael Francis Addison, Kt., D.SC.

Woods, Sir Colin Philip Joseph, K.C.V.O., C.B.E.

Woods, *Most Rev.* Frank, K.B.E., D.D.

Woods, *Rt. Rev.* Robert Wilmer, K.C.V.O.

Woodward, *Hon.* Sir Albert Edward. Kt., O.B.E.

Woodward, *Vice-Adm.* Sir John Forster, K.C.B.

Woolf, *Hon.* Sir Harry Kenneth, Kt.

Woolf, Sir John, Kt.

Woollaston, Sir (Mountford) Tosswill, Kt.

Woolley, Sir Richard van der Riet, Kt., O.B.E., F.R.S.

Wordie, Sir John Stewart, Kt., C.B.E., V.R.D.

Worsley, *General* Sir John Francis, K.B.E., C.B., M.C.

Worsley, *General* Sir Richard Edward, G.C.B., O.B.E.

Worsley, Sir (William) Marcus (John), Bt. (1838).

Worthington, *Air Vice Marshal* Sir Geoffrey Luis, K.B.E., C.B.

Wraight, Sir John Richard, K.B.E., C.M.G.

Wrangham, Sir Geoffrey Walter, Kt.

Wraxall, Sir Charles Frederick Lascelles, Bt. (1813).

Wrey, Sir (Castel) Richard Bourchier, Bt. (1628).

Wright, Sir Allan Frederick, K.B.E.

Wright, Sir Denis Arthur Hepworth, G.C.M.G.

Wright, Sir Edward Maitland, Kt., D.Phil., F.R.S.E.

Wright, Sir (John) Oliver, G.C.M.G., G.C.V.O., D.S.C.

Wright, Sir Patrick Richard Henry, K.C.M.G.

Wright, Sir Paul Hervé Giraud, K.C.M.G., O.B.E.

Wright, *Hon.* Sir Reginald Charles, Kt.

Wright, Sir Richard Michael Cory-, Bt. (1903).

Wright, Sir Rowland Sydney, Kt., C.B.E.

Wrightson, Sir Charles Mark Garmondsway, Bt. (1900).

Wyatt, Sir Woodrow Lyle, Kt.

Wykeham, *Air Marshal* Sir Peter Guy, K.C.B., D.S.O., O.B.E., D.F.C., A.F.C.

Wylie, Sir Campbell, Kt., E.D., Q.C.

Wyndham, Sir Harold Stanley, Kt., C.B.E.

Wynn, *Lt.-Col.* Sir Owen Watkin Williams-, Bt., C.B.E. (1688).

Wynter, Sir Luther Reginald, Kt., C.B.E.

Yapp, Sir Stanley Graham, Kt.

Yarrow, Sir Eric Grant, Bt., M.B.E. (1916).

Yeend, Sir Geoffrey John, Kt., C.B.E.

Yellowlees, Sir Henry, K.C.B.

Yocklunn, Sir (Soong Chung) John, K.C.V.O.

Yonge, Sir (Charles) Maurice, Kt., C.B.E., D.SC., F.R.S., F.R.S.E.

Yorston, Sir (Robert) Keith, Kt., C.B.E.

Youde, Sir Edward, G.C.M.G., M.B.E.

Youens, Sir Peter William, Kt., C.M.G., O.B.E.

Young, Sir Brian Walter Mark, Kt.

Young, *Lt.-Gen.* Sir David Tod, K.B.E., C.B., D.F.C.

Young, *Prof.* Sir Frank George, Kt., D.SC., Ph.D., F.R.S.

Young, Sir George Samuel Knatchbull, Bt., M.P. (1813).

Young, *Most Rev.* Guilford Clyde, K.B.E.

Young, *Hon.* Sir Harold William, K.C.M.G.

Young, *Hon.* Sir John McIntosh, K.C.M.G.

Young, Sir John Kenyon Roe, Bt. (1821).

Young, Sir Leslie Clarence, Kt., C.B.E.

Young, Sir Norman Smith, Kt.

Young, Sir Richard Dilworth, Kt.

Young, Sir Robert Christopher Mackworth-, K.C.V.O.

Young, Sir Roger William, Kt.

Young, Sir Stephen Stewart Templeton, Bt. (1945).

Young, Sir William Neil, Bt. (1769).

Younger, *Maj.-Gen.* Sir John William, Bt., C.B.E. (1911).

Younger, Sir William McEwan, Bt., D.S.O. (1964).

Zeidler, Sir David Ronald, Kt. C.B.E.

Zoleveke, Sir Gideon Pitabose, K.B.E.

Zurenuo, *Rt. Rev.* Zurewe Kamong, Kt., O.B.E.

Baronetcies Extinct (Since last issue).—Campbell of Glenavy (U.K., 1917); Dillon (U.K., 1801); Pechell (G.B., 1797); Walsh (U.K., 1804).

Dames Grand Cross and Dames Commanders of the Order of the Bath, the Order of St. Michael and St. George, the Royal Victorian Order and the Order of the British Empire

NOTE.—Dames Grand Cross (G.C.B., G.C.M.G., G.C.V.O. or G.B.E.) and Dames Commanders (D.C.B., D.C.M.G., D.C.V.O. or D.B.E.) are addressed in a manner similar to that of Knights Grand Cross or Knights Commanders, *e.g.* "Miss Florence Smith" after receiving the honour would be addressed as "Dame Florence", and in writing as "Dame Florence Smith, G. (or D.) C.B., G. (or D.) C.M.G., G. (or D.) C.V.O., OR G. (or D.) B.E." Where such award is made to a lady already in enjoyment of a higher title the appropriate letters are appended to her name, *e.g.* "The Countess of —— G.C.V.O." Peeresses in their own right, and Life Peeresses, are not included in this list. Dames Grand Cross rank after wives of Baronets and before wives of Knights Grand Cross. Dames Commanders rank after the wives of Knights Grand Cross and before the wives of Knights Commanders.

DAMES GRAND CROSS AND DAMES COMMANDERS

H.M. Queen Elizabeth The Queen Mother, K.G., K.T., C.I., G.M.V.O.

H.R.H. The Princess Margaret, Countess of Snowdon, C.I., G.C.V.O.

H.R.H. The Princess Alice, Duchess of Gloucester, G.C.B., C.I., G.C.V.O., G.B.E.

H.R.H. The Princess Alexandra of Kent, G.C.V.O.

H.R.H. The Princess Anne, G.C.V.O.

H.R.H. The Duchess of Kent, G.C.V.O.

Abercorn, Mary, Duchess of, G.C.V.O.

Ackroyd, Dame (Dorothy) Elizabeth, D.B.E.

Albemarle, The Countess of, D.B.E.

Alexander of Tunis, Margaret Diana, Countess, G.B.E.

Anderson, Dame Judith, D.B.E.

Norris, Dame Ada May, D.B.E., C.M.G.

Ollerenshaw, Dame Kathleen Mary, D.B.E., D.Phil.

Origo, *Marchesa* Iris, D.B.E.

Parker, Dame Marjorie Alice Collett, D.B.E.

Paterson, Dame Betty Fraser Ross, D.B.E.

Pepys, Lady (Mary) Rachel, D.C.V.O.

Pickerill, Dame Cecily Mary Wise, D.B.E.

Plowden, The Lady, D.B.E.

Prentice, Dame Winifred Eva, D.B.E.

Purves, Dame Daphne Helen, D.B.E.

Pyke, The Lady, D.B.E.

Railton, *Brig.* Dame Mary, D.B.E.

Railton, Dame Ruth (Mrs. Cecil Harmsworth King), D.B.E.

Rankin, Dame Annabelle Jane Mary, D.B.E.

Rankin, Lady Jean Margaret Florence, D.C.V.O.

Raven, Dame Kathleen Annie (Mrs. J. T. Ingram), D.B.E.

Reader, Dame Audrey Tattie Hinchcliff, D.B.E.

Rees, Dame Dorothy Mary, D.B.E.

Riddelsdell, Dame Mildred, D.C.B., C.B.E.

Ridley, Dame (Mildred) Betty, D.B.E.

Roberts, Dame Jean, D.B.E.

Roberts, Dame Joan Howard, D.B.E.

Roberts, Dame Shelagh Marjorie, D.B.E.

Robertson, *Commandant* Dame Nancy Margaret, D.B.E.

Roe, Dame Raigh Edith, D.B.E.

Rosebery, Eva, Countess of, D.B.E.

Saunders, Dame Cicely Mary Strode, D.B.E., F.R.C.P.

Scott, Dame Catherine Campbell, D.B.E.

Scott, Dame Catherine Margaret Mary (Mrs. Denton), D.B.E.

Seccombe, Dame Joan Anna Dalziel, D.B.E.

Seymour, Lady Katharine, D.C.V.O.

Shepherd, Dame Margaret Alice, D.B.E.

Sherlock, Dame Sheila Patricia Violet, D.B.E., M.D., F.R.C.P., F.R.C.P.E.

Sloss, Hon. Dame (Ann) Elizabeth (Oldfield) Butler-, D.B.E.

Smieton, Dame Mary Guillan, D.B.E.

Smith, Lady Abel, D.C.V.O.

Smith, Dame Enid Mary Russell Russell-, D.B.E.

Smith, Dame Margot, D.B.E.

Snagge, *Air Commandant* Dame Nancy Marion, D.B.E.

Soames, The Lady, D.B.E.

Springman, Dame Ann Marcella, D.B.E.

Stark, Dame Freya (Mrs. Perowne), D.B.E.

Stephens, *Air Commandant* Dame Anne, D.B.E.

Stevenson, Dame Hilda Mabel, D.B.E.

Stewart, Dame Muriel Acadia, D.B.E.

Sutherland, Dame Joan (Mrs. Bonynge), D.B.E.

Tangney, Dame Dorothy Margaret, D.B.E.

Taylor, Dame Jean Elizabeth, D.C.V.O.

Te Ata-I-Rangikaahu, Dame Ariki nui, D.B.E.

Te Kanawa, Dame Kiri Janette (Mrs. Park), D.B.E.

Tilney, Guinevere, Lady, D.B.E.

Turner, Dame Eva, D.B.E.

Turner, *Brig.* Dame Margot, D.B.E., R.R.C.

Tylecote, Dame Mabel, D.B.E.

Tyrwhitt, *Brigadier*, Dame Mary Joan Caroline, D.B.E.

Uatioa, Dame Mere, D.B.E.

Uvarov, Dame Olga, D.B.E.

Van Praagh, Dame Margaret (Peggy), D.B.E.

Vaughan, Dame Janet Maria, (Mrs. Gourlay), D.B.E., F.R.S.

Wakehurst, Margaret, Lady, D.B.E.

Walker, Dame Susan Armour, D.B.E.

Wall, (Alice) Anne (Mrs. Michael Wall), D.C.V.O.

Warburton, Dame Anne Marion, D.C.V.O., C.M.G.

Warnock, Dame (Helen) Mary, D.B.E.

Wedega, Dame Alice, D.B.E.

Wedgwood, Dame (Cicely) Veronica, O.M., D.B.E.

Welsh, *Air Chief Commandant* Ruth Mary, Lady, D.B.E.

Weston, Dame Margaret Kate, D.B.E.

Whateley, *Chief Controller* Dame Leslie Violet, D.B.E.

Williamson, Dame (Elsie) Marjorie, D.B.E., Ph.D.

Winner, Dame Albertine Louise, D.B.E., M.D.

Woollcombe, Dame Jocelyn May, D.B.E.

Wormald, Dame Ethel May, D.B.E.

Yarwood, Dame Elizabeth Ann, D.B.E.

Yonge, Dame Ida Felicity Ann, D.B.E.

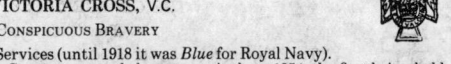

THE VICTORIA CROSS, V.C.

FOR CONSPICUOUS BRAVERY

The ribbon *is Crimson* for all Services (until 1918 it was *Blue* for Royal Navy).

Instituted on January 29, 1856, the Victoria Cross was awarded retrospectively to 1854, the first being held by Lieut. C. D. Lucas, R.N. for bravery in the Baltic Sea on June 21, 1854 (gazetted Feb. 24, 1857). The first 62 Crosses were presented by Queen Victoria in Hyde Park, London, on June 26, 1857.

The V.C. is worn before all other decorations, on the left breast, and consists of a cross-pattée of bronze, 1½ inches in diameter, with the Royal Crown surmounted by a lion in the centre, and beneath there is the inscription "For Valour." Holders of the V.C. receive a tax-free annuity of £100, irrespective of need or other conditions. In 1911, the right to receive the Cross was extended to Indian soldiers, and in 1920 a Royal Warrant extended the right to Matrons, Sisters and Nurses, and the Staff of the Nursing Services and other services pertaining to Hospitals and Nursing, and to Civilians of either sex regularly or temporarily under the orders, direction or supervision of the Naval, Military, or Air Forces of the Crown.

Surviving Recipients of the Victoria Cross

Agansing Rai, *Havildar* (Gurkha Rifles), *World War* 1944

Ali Haidar, *Jemadar* (Frontier Force Rifles), *World War* 1945

Anderson, *Lt.-Col.* C. G. W., M.C. (Australian M.F.), *World War* 1942

Annand, *Capt.* R. W. (Durham L.I.), *World War* 1940

Bhanbhagta Gurung, *Capt.* (2nd Gurkha Rifles), *World War* 1945

Bhandari Ram, *Capt.* (Baluch R.), *World War* .. 1944

Burton, *Corpl.* R. H. (Duke of Wellington's R.), *World War* 1944

Campbell, *Brigadier* L. M., D.S.O., O.B.E., T.D. (A. & S. Highrs.), *World War* 1943

Carne, *Col.* J. P., D.S.O. (Glos. R.), *Korea* 1951

Chapman, *Sergt.* E. T., B.E.M. (Monmouthshire R.), *World War* 1945

Cheshire, *Group Capt.* G. L., D.S.O., D.F.C. (R.A.F.), *World War* 1944

Cooper, *Lt.* E. (K.R.R.C.), *Gt. War* 1917

Cruickshank, *Fl. Lt.* J. A. (R.A.F.V.R.), *World War* 1944

Crutchley, *Admiral* Sir Victor Alexander, K.C.B., D.S.C. (R.N.), *Gt. War* 1918

Currie, *Maj.* D. V., C.B.E. (S. Alberta R., Canada), *World War* 1944

Cutler, Sir A. R., K.C.M.G., K.C.V.O., C.B.E. (Australia), *World War* 1941

Dean, *Col.* D. J., O.B.E. (R. W. Kent R.), *Gt. War*..............................1918

De L'Isle, *Maj.* The Viscount, K.G., P.C., G.C.M.G., G.C.V.O. (*Hon.* W. P. Sidney) (Gren. Gds.), *World War* 1944

Eardley, *Sergt.* G. H., M.M. (K.S.L.I.), *World War*..................................1944

Elliott, *Lt.* the Rev. K. (N.Z.M.F.), *World War* ..1942

Ervine-Andrews, *Lt.-Col.* H. M. (E. Lancs. R.), *World War* 1940

Foote, *Maj.-Gen.* H. R. B., C.B., D.S.O. (R. Tank R.), *World War* 1942

Foote, *Rev.* J. W. (Canada), *World War* 1942

Fraser, *Cdr.* I. E., D.S.C. (R.N.R.), *World War* ...1945

Ganju Lama, *Jemadar,* M.M. (Gurkha Rifles), *World War*..........................1944

Gardner, *Capt.* P. J., M.C. (R.T.R.), *World War* ..1941

Ghale, *Subedar* Gaje (Gurkha Rifles), *World War* 1943

Gian Singh, *Jemadar* (Punjab R.), *World War* ..1945

Gordon, *W.O. II* J. H. (Australia), *World War* 1941

Gould, *Lt.* T. W. (R.N.), *World War* 1942

Hinton, *Sergt.* J. D. (N.Z.M.F.), *World War* 1941

Jackson, *W.O.* N. C. (R.A.F.V.R.), *World War* ..1944

Jamieson, *Maj.* D. A. (R. Norfolk R.), *World War*................................1944

Joynt, *Lt.-Col.* W. D. (Aust. I. F.), *Gt. War* 1918

Kamal Ram, *Havildar,* (Punjab R.), *World War*................................1944

Kenna, *Pte.* E. (Australian M.F.), *World War* ...1945

Kenneally, *C.-Q.-M.-S.* J. P. (Irish Gds.), *World War*................................1943

Lachiman Gurung, *Rifleman* (Gurkha Rifles), *World War* 1945

Laurent, *Lt.* H. J. (N.Z. Rif. Bgde.), *Gt. War* 1918

Learoyd, *Wing-Cmdr.* R. A. B. (R.A.F.), *World War*................................1940

Magennis, *L/S* J. J. (R.N.), *World War* 1945

Mahony, *Lt.-Col.* J. K., C.D. (Westminster R., Canada), *World War* 1944

Merritt, *Lt.-Col.* C. C. I., C.D. (S. Saskatchewan R.), *World War* 1942

Miers, *Rear-Adm.* Sir A. C. C., K.B.E., C.B., D.S.O. (R.N.), *World War* 1942

Moon, *Lt.* Rupert V. (Aust. Inf.), *Gt. War* 1917

Norton, *Capt.* G. R., M.M. (S.A.M.F.), *World War*................................1944

Parkash Singh, *Maj.* (Punjab R.), *World War* ...1943

Payne, *W.O.* K. (Australian Army), *Vietnam* ...1969

Place, *Rear-Adm.* B. C. G., C.B., D.S.C. (R.N.), *World War* 1943

Porteous, *Brig.* P. A. (R.A.), *World War* 1942

Rambahadur Limbu, *Lt.* (Gurkha Rifles), *Sarawak* 1965

Rattey, *Sergt.* R. R. (Australia), *World War* 1945

Reid, *Fl.-Lt.* W. (R.A.F.V.R.), *World War* 1943

Rutherford, *Capt.* C. S., M.C., M.M. (Quebec R.), *Gt. War* 1918

Ryder, *Capt.* R. E. D. (R.N.), *World War* 1942

Smith, *Sergt.* E. A., C.D. (Seaforth Highrs. of Canada), *World War* 1944

Smythe, *Capt.* Q. G. M. (S.A.M.F.), *World War* ..1942

Speakman, *Sergt.* W. (Black Watch), *Korea* 1951

Starcevich, *Pte.* L. T. (Australia), *World War*................................1945

Tilston, *Col.* F. A. (Essex Scottish, Canada), *World War* 1945

Trent, *Group Capt.* L. H., D.F.C. (R.N.Z.A.F.), *World War* 1943

Tulbahadur Pun, *W.O. I.* (Gurkha Rifles), *World War* 1944

Umrao Singh, *Sub-Major* (I.A.), *World War* 1944

Upham, *Capt.* C. H. (and Bar, 1942), (N.Z.M.F.), *World War* 1941

Watkins, *Maj. Rt. Hon.* Sir Tasker (Welch R.), *World War* 1944

West, *Air Commodore* Ferdinand M. F., C.B.E., M.C. (R.A.F.), *Gt. War* 1918

Wilson, *Lt.-Col.* E. C. T. (E. Surrey R.), *World War*................................1940

Wright, *C.S.M.* P. H. (Coldstream Gds.), *World War*................................1943

THE GEORGE CROSS, G.C. (1940)

For Gallantry

The ribbon is *dark blue* threaded through a bar adorned with laurel leaves.

Instituted *September, 24th,* 1940 (with amendments, *November 3rd,* 1942).

The George Cross is worn before all other decorations (except the V.C.) on the left breast § and consists of a plain silver cross with four equal limbs, the cross having in the centre a circular medallion bearing a design showing St. George and the Dragon. The inscription "For Gallantry" appears round the medallion and in the angle of each limb of the cross is the Royal cypher "G VI" forming a circle concentric with the medallion. The reverse is plain and bears the name of the recipient and the date of the award. The cross is suspended by a ring from a bar adorned with laurel leaves on dark blue ribbon 1½ inches wide.

The cross is intended primarily for civilians and awards to the fighting services are confined to actions for which purely military honours are not normally granted. It is awarded only for acts of the greatest heroism or of the most conspicuous courage in circumstances of extreme danger. From April 1, 1965, holders of the Cross have received a tax-free annuity of £100.

§ When worn by a woman it may be worn on the left shoulder from a ribbon of the same width and colour fashioned into a bow.

Empire Gallantry Medal.—The Royal Warrant which ordained that the grant of the Empire Gallantry Medal should cease authorized holders of that medal to return it to the Central Chancery of the Orders of Knighthood and to receive in exchange the George Cross. A similar provision applied to posthumous awards of the Empire Gallantry Medal made after the outbreak of war in 1939.

In October 1971 all surviving holders of the Albert Medal and the Edward Medal exchanged those decorations for the George Cross.

THE DISTINGUISHED SERVICE ORDER (1886)—D.S.O.

Ribbon, Red, with Blue Edges.

Bestowed in recognition of especial services in action of commissioned officers in the Navy, Army and Royal Air Force and (1942) Mercantile Marine. The members are Companions only and rank immediately before the 4th Class of the Royal Victorian Order. A Bar may be awarded for any additional act of service.

PRINCIPAL DECORATIONS AND MEDALS (in order of Precedence)

Victoria Cross.—1856.—V.C.

George Cross.—1940.—G.C.

British Orders of Knighthood, Etc. (For D.S.O. *see* p. 300).

Royal Red Cross.—1883—R.R.C. (Class I).—For ladies.

Distinguished Service Cross.—1914.—D.S.C.—In substitution for the Conspicuous Service Cross, 1901; is for officers of R.N. below the rank of Captain, and Warrant Officers.

Military Cross.—Dec. 1914.—M.C.—Awarded to Captains, Lieutenants, and Warrant Officers (Cl I. and II.) in the Army and Indian and Colonial Forces.

Distinguished Flying Cross.—1918.—D.F.C.—For Bestowal upon Officers and Warrant Officers in the Royal Air Force (and Fleet Air Arm from April 9, 1941) for acts of gallantry when flying in active operations against the enemy.

Air Force Cross.—1918.—A.F.C.—Instituted as preceding but for acts of courage or devotion to duty when flying, although not in active operations against the enemy (extended to Fleet Air Arm since April 9, 1941).

Royal Red Cross (Class II—A.R.R.C.).

Order of British India.

Kaisar-i-Hind Medal.

Order of St. John.

Albert Medal.—1866.—A.M.—"For Gallantry in Saving Life at Sea" or "on Land." (Holders receive £100 tax-free annuity).

Union of South Africa Queen's Medal for Bravery, in Gold.

Medal for Distinguished Conduct in the Field.—1854.—D.C.M.—Awarded to warrant officers, non-commissioned officers and men of the Army and R.A.F.

Conspicuous Gallantry Medal.—1874.—C.G.M.—Is bestowed upon warrant officers and men of the R.N. and since 1942 of Mercantile Marine and R.A.F.

The George Medal.—G.M.—Established by King George VI in 1940 is a recognition of acts of gallantry.

The Edward Medal.—1907.—In recognition of heroic acts by miners or quarrymen, or of others who have endangered their lives in rescuing those so employed. (Holders receive £100 tax-free annuity).

Royal West African Frontier Force Distinguished Conduct Medal.

King's African Rifles Distinguished Conduct Medal.

Union of South Africa Queen's Medal for Bravery in Silver.

Distinguished Service Medal.—1914.—D.S.M.—For chief petty officers, petty officers, men, and boys of all branches of the Royal Navy, and since 1942 of Mercantile Marine, to non-commissioned officers and men of the Royal Marines, and to all other persons holding corresponding positions in Her Majesty's Service afloat.

Military Medal.—1916.—M.M.—For warrant and non-commissioned officers and men and serving women.

Distinguished Flying Medal.—1918.—D.F.M.—and the Air Force Medal.—A.F.M.—For warrant and non-commissioned officers and men for equivalent services as for D.F.C. and A.F.C. (extended to Fleet Air Arm, April 9, 1941).

Constabulary Medal (Ireland).

Medal for Saving Life at Sea.

Colonial Police Medal for Gallantry (C.P.M.)

Queen's Gallantry Medal.—1974.

British Empire Medal.—B.E.M.—(formerly the Medal of the Order of the British Empire, for Meritorious Service; also includes the Medal of the Order awarded before Dec. 29, 1922).

Queen's Police (Q.P.M.) and Fire Services Medals for Distinguished Service, (Q.F.S.M.).

Queen's Medal for Chiefs.

War Medals and Stars (in order of date).

Polar Medals (in order of date).

Royal Victorian Medal (Gold, Silver and Bronze).

Imperial Service Medal.

Police Medals for Valuable Service.

Badge of Honour.

Jubilee, Coronation and Durbar Medals.

King George V, King George VI and Queen Elizabeth II Long and Faithful Service Medals.

Medal for Meritorious Service.

Long Service and Good Conduct Medal.

Naval Long Service and Good Conduct Medal.

Royal Marine Meritorious Service Medal.

Royal Air Force Meritorious Service Medal.

Royal Air Force Long Service and Good Conduct Medal.

Royal West African Frontier Force Long Service and Good Conduct Medal.

King's African Rifles Long Service and Good Conduct Medal.

Police and Fire Brigade Long Service and Good Conduct Medal.

Colonial Police and Fire Brigades Long Service Medal.

Colonial Prison Service Medal.

Army Emergency Reserve Decoration.—E.R.D.

Volunteer Officer's Decoration.—V.D.

Volunteer Long Service Medal.

Volunteer Officer's Decoration (for India and the Colonies).

Volunteer Long Service Medal (for India and the Colonies).

Colonial Auxiliary Forces Long Service Medal.

Medal for Good Shooting (Naval).

Militia Long Service Medal.

Imperial Yeomanry Long Service Medal.

Territorial Decoration.—1908.—T.D.

Efficiency Decoration.—E.D.

Territorial Efficiency Medal.

Efficiency Medal.

Special Reserve Long Service and Good Conduct Medal.

Decoration for Officers, Royal Navy Reserve.—1910.—R.D.

Decoration for Officers, R.N.V.R.—V.R.D.

Royal Naval Reserve Long Service and Good Conduct Medal.

R.N.V.R. Long Service and Good Conduct Medal.

Royal Naval Auxiliary Sick Berth Reserve Long Service and Good Conduct Medal.

Royal Fleet Reserve Long Service and Good Conduct Medal.

Royal Naval Wireless Auxiliary Reserve Long Service and Good Conduct Medal.

Air Efficiency Award.—1942.—A.E.

The Queen's Medal.—(For Champion Shots in the Army, T.A. and R.A.F.).

Cadet Forces Medal.—1950.

Coast Life Saving Corps Long Service Medal.—1911.

Special Constabulary Long Service Medal.

Royal Observer Corps Medal.

Civil Defence Long Service Medal.

Service Medal of the Order of St. John.

Badge of the Order of the League of Mercy.

Voluntary Medical Service Medal.—1932.

Women's Royal Voluntary Service Medal.

Colonial Special Constabulary Medal.

Foreign Orders, Decorations and Medals (in order of date).

THE UNITED KINGDOM CONSTITUTION

The United Kingdom constitution is not contained in any single document but has evolved in the course of time, formed partly by statute, partly by common law and partly by convention. A constitutional monarchy, the United Kingdom is governed by Ministers of the Crown in the name of the Sovereign, who is head both of the state and the government.

The organs of government are the *legislature* (Parliament), the *executive* and the *judiciary*. The executive consists of Her Majesty's Government (Cabinet and other Ministers), government departments (*see* pp. 369–449), local authorities (*see* pp. 619–622), and public corporations operating nationalised industries or social or cultural services (*see* pp. 369–449). The judiciary, *i.e.* judges, pronounce on the law, both written and unwritten, interpret statutes and are responsible for the enforcement of the law; the judiciary is independent of both the legislature and the executive (*see* Law Courts and Offices).

THE MONARCHY

The Sovereign personifies the state and is, in law, an integral part of the legislature, head of the executive, head of the judiciary, the Commander-in-Chief of all armed forces of the Crown and the 'Supreme Governor' of the Church of England. The seat of the monarchy is in the United Kingdom. In the Channel Islands and the Isle of Man, which are Crown dependencies, the Sovereign is represented by a Lieutenant-Governor: in the member states of the Commonwealth of which the Sovereign is head of state, her representative is a Governor-General (*see also* p. 693): in United Kingdom dependencies the Sovereign is usually represented by a Governor, who is responsible to the British Government.

Although the powers of the monarchy are now very limited, restricted mainly to the advisory and ceremonial, there are important acts of government which require the participation of the Sovereign. These include summoning, proroguing and dissolving Parliament, giving Royal Assent to Bills passed by Parliament, appointing important office-holders, *e.g.* government ministers, judges, bishops, and governors, conferring peerages, knighthoods and other honours, and granting pardon to a person wrongly convicted of a crime. An important function is appointing a Prime Minister, by convention the leader of the political party which enjoys, or can secure, a majority of votes in the House of Commons. In international affairs the Sovereign as head of State has the power to declare war and make peace, to recognise foreign states and governments, to conclude treaties and to annex or cede territory. However, as the Sovereign entrusts executive power to Ministers of the Crown and acts on the advice of her Ministers, which she cannot ignore, in practice royal prerogative powers are exercised by Ministers, who are responsible to Parliament.

Ministerial responsibility does not diminish the Sovereign's importance to the smooth working of government. She holds meetings of the Privy Council, gives audiences to her Ministers and other officials at home and overseas, receives accounts of Cabinet decisions, reads dispatches and signs state papers; she must be informed and consulted on every aspect of national life; and she must show complete impartiality.

In the event of the Sovereign's absence abroad, it is necessary to appoint *Counsellors of State* under Letters Patent to carry out the chief functions of the Monarch, including the holding of Privy Councils and giving Royal Assent to Acts passed by Parliament. The normal procedure is to appoint as Counsellors three or four members of the Royal Family among those remaining in the United Kingdom. In the event of the Sovereign on accession being under the age of eighteen years, or at any time unavailable or incapacitated by infirmity of mind or body for the performance of the royal functions, provision is made for a Regency.

THE PRIVY COUNCIL

The Sovereign in Council, or Privy Council, was the chief source of executive power until the system of Cabinet government developed. Now its main function is to advise the Sovereign to approve Orders in Council and to advise on the issue of royal proclamations. The Council's own statutory responsibilities (independent of the powers of the Sovereign in Council) include powers of supervision over the registering bodies for the medical and allied professions. A full Council is summoned only on the death of the Sovereign or when the Sovereign announces his or her intention to marry (for full list of Counsellors, *see* pp. 258–259).

There are a number of advisory Privy Council committees, whose meetings the Sovereign does not attend. Some are prerogative committees, such as those dealing with legislative matters submitted by the legislatures of the Channel Islands and the Isle of Man or with applications for charters of incorporation; and some are provided for by statute, *e.g.* those for the universities of Oxford and Cambridge and the Scottish universities.

The Judicial Committee of the Privy Council is the final court of appeal from courts of the United Kingdom dependencies, courts of independent Commonwealth countries which have retained the right of appeal, courts of the Channel Islands and the Isle of Man, some professional and disciplinary committees and church sources. The Committee is composed of all Privy Counsellors who hold, or have held, high judicial office, although usually only three or five hear each case.

Administrative work is carried out by the Privy Council Office under the direction of the Lord President of the Council, a Cabinet Minister.

PARLIAMENT

Parliament is the supreme law-making authority and can legislate for the United Kingdom as a whole or for any parts of it separately (the Channel Islands and the Isle of Man are Crown dependencies and not part of the United Kingdom). The main functions of Parliament are to pass laws, to provide (by voting taxation) the means of carrying on the work of government and to scrutinise government policy and administration, particularly proposals for expenditure. By custom, Parliament is also consulted before the ratification of international treaties and agreements.

Parliament emerged during the late thirteenth and early fourteenth centuries. The nucleus of early Parliaments were the officers of the King's household and the King's judges, joined by such ecclesiastical and lay magnates as the King might summon, and occasionally by the knights of the shires, burgesses and proctors of the lower clergy. By the end of Edward III's reign a "House of Commons" was beginning to appear: the first known Speaker was elected in 1377.

Parliamentary procedure is based on custom and precedent, partly formulated in the Standing Orders of both Houses (*see* p. 308), and each House has the right to control its own internal proceedings and to commit for contempt. The system of debate in the two Houses is similar; when a subject has been moved and seconded, the Speaker proposes the question as the subject of a debate. Members speak from wherever they have been sitting. Questions are decided by a vote on a simple majority. Draft legislation is introduced, in either House, as a public Bill. Public Bills can be introduced by a Government Minister or a private Member, but in practice the majority of Bills which become law are introduced by the Government. To become law, a Bill must be passed by each House (for parliamentary stages, *see* Bill, p. 306) and then sent to the Sovereign for the Royal Assent, after receipt of which it becomes an Act of Parliament.

Proceedings of both Houses are public, except on extremely rare occasions. The minutes (called Votes and Proceedings in the Commons, and Minutes of Proceedings in the Lords) and the speeches (The Official Report of Parliamentary Debates, *Hansard*) are published daily. Proceedings are also recorded for sound transmission on radio and television; a Parliamentary Sound Archive has been established.

By the Parliament Act of 1911, the maximum duration of a Parliament is five years, if not previously dissolved, the term being reckoned from the date given on the writs for the new Parliament. The maximum life has been prolonged by legislation in such rare circumstances as the two world wars (Jan. 31, 1911–Nov. 25, 1918: Nov. 26, 1935–June 15, 1945). Dissolution and writs for a general election are ordered by the Queen on the advice of the Prime Minister. The life of a Parliament is divided into *sessions*, usually of one year in length, beginning and ending most often in October or November.

THE HOUSE OF LORDS

The House of Lords consists of the Lords Spiritual and Temporal. The Lords Spiritual are the Archbishops of Canterbury and York, the Bishops of London, Durham and Winchester, and the 21 senior diocesan Bishops of the Church of England. The Lords Temporal consist of all hereditary Peers and Peeresses of England, Scotland, Great Britain and the United Kingdom who have not disclaimed their Peerages, Life Peers and Peeresses, and those Lords of Appeal in Ordinary created Life Peers (Law Lords). Disclaimants of an hereditary Peerage lose their right to sit in the House of Lords but gain the right to vote at Parliamentary elections and to offer themselves for election to the House of Commons. (*See also* p. 226). Peers who do not wish to attend sittings of the House of Lords may apply for leave of absence for the duration of a Parliament.

Until the beginning of this century the House of Lords had considerable power, being able to vote any Bill submitted to it by the House of Commons, but those powers were greatly reduced by the Parliament Act of 1911 and subsequently by the Parliament Act of 1949 (*see* **Parliament Acts 1911 and 1949**, p. 307).

Combined with its legislative role, the House of Lords has judicial powers as the ultimate Court of Appeal for Courts in Great Britain and Northern Ireland, except for criminal cases in Scotland. These powers are exercised by the Lord Chancellor and the Law Lords.

Members of the House of Lords are unpaid. However, they are entitled to reimbursement of travelling expenses on parliamentary business within the U.K. and certain other expenses incurred for the purpose of attendence at sittings of the House, within a maximum for each day of £43·00 for overnight subsistence, £18·00 for day subsistence and incidental travel, and £17·00 for secretarial costs, postage and certain additional expenses.

The House is presided over by the Lord Chancellor, who is *ex officio* Speaker of the House. A panel of deputy Speakers is appointed by Royal Commission. The first deputy Speaker is the Lord Chairman of Committees, appointed at the beginning of each session, a salaried officer of the House who takes the chair in Committee of the whole House and in some Select Committees. He is assisted by a panel of Deputy Chairmen, headed by the salaried Principal Deputy Chairman of Committees, who is also Chairman of the European Communities Committee of the House. The permanent officers include the Clerk of the Parliament and other Clerks who, with other officers of the House, are collectively known as the Parliament Office; the Gentleman-Usher of the Black Rod, who is also Serjeant at Arms in attendence upon the Lord Chancellor and is responsible for security and for accommodation and services in the House of Lords; and the Yeoman Usher who is Deputy Serjeant at Arms and assists Black Rod in his duties.

OFFICERS OF THE HOUSE OF LORDS

Speaker, The Rt. Hon. Quintin McGarel Hogg, c.h., Lord Hailsham of St. Marylebone.
  Private Secretary, M. H. Collon.
Chairman of Committees, The Rt. Hon. Lord Aberdare, k.b.e. £28,000
Principal Deputy Chairman of Committees, The Rt. Hon. Baroness Llewelyn-Davies of Hastoe £25,160

Clerk of the Parliaments, J. C. Sainty £45,500

Clerk Assistant and Principal Clerk, Public Bills, J. E. Grey, c.b. £36,500

Reading Clerk and Clerk of the Journals, M. A. J. Wheeler-Booth £30,750

Counsel to Chairman of Committees, D. Rippengal, c.b., q.c. £36,500
Second Counsel, K. Newman, c.b. £30,750
Assistant Counsel, G. A. Preston ... £20,493–£24,409

Principal Clerks, E. D. Graham (*Private Bills and Committees*); J. A. Vallance White (*Judicial Office and Fourth Clerk at the Table*); J. M. Davies (*Overseas and European Office*) £30,750

Chief Clerks, P. D. G. Hayter; C. A. J. Mitchell; M. G. Pownall .... £20,493–£24,409
Senior Clerks, B. P. Keith; D. R. Beamish (*Seconded as Secretary to the Leader of the House and Chief Whip*); R. H. Walters, D.Phil.; D. F. Slater; Miss F. M. MacLeod
  £13,649–£17,906
Clerk of the Records, H. S. Cobb, F.S.A.
  £20,493–£24,409

Deputy Clerk of the Records, D. J. Johnson, F.S.A. .... £16,902–£20,567
Assistant Clerks of the Records, J. C. Morgan (*Sound Archives*); S. K. Ellison .. £12,326–£17,906
Accountant, E. W. Field .... £13,649–£22,044
Assistant Accountant, C. Preece ... £11,329–£13,768
Judicial Taxing Clerk, C. G. Osborne
  £11,329–£13,768
Librarian, R. H. V. C. Morgan ... £20,493–£24,409
Deputy Librarian, D. L. Jones...... £16,902–£20,567
Library Clerks, P. G. Davis, ph.d.; Miss E. M. McInnes....................... £12,326–£17,906
Examiners of Petitions for Private Bills, E. D. Graham; H. M. Barclay.
Gentleman-Usher of the Black Rod and Serjeant-at-Arms, Lt.-General Sir David House, g.c.b., c.b.e., m.c. £28,980
Yeoman Usher of the Black Rod and Deputy Serjeant-at-Arms, Brigadier D. M. Stileman, o.b.e. .... £12,905–£16,907
Staff Superintendent, Maj. F. P. Horsfall, m.b.e.
Shorthand Writer, Mrs. E. M. C. Holland   fees
Editor, Official Report (Hansard), D. A. Dumbreck £19,697
Asst. do. Mrs. M. E. E. C. Villiers £15,544

THE HOUSE OF COMMONS

The Members of the House of Commons are elected by universal adult suffrage. For electoral purposes, the United Kingdom is divided into constituencies, each of which returns one Member to the House of Commons, the Member being the candidate who obtains the largest number of votes cast in the constituency. To ensure equitable representation the four Boundary Commissions keep constituency boundaries under review and recommend any redistribution of seats which may seem necessary due to population movements, etc. The number of seats was raised to 640 in 1945, then reduced to 625 in 1948, and subsequently rose to 630 in 1955, 635 in 1970 and 650 in 1983. Of the present 650 seats there are 523 for England, 38 for Wales, 72 for Scotland and 17 for Northern Ireland. Elections are by secret ballot, each elector casting one vote: voting is not compulsory. When a seat becomes vacant between General Elections, a by-election is held.

British subjects and citizens of the Irish Republic can stand for election as Members of Parliament (M.P.s) provided they are 21 or over and not subject to disqualification. Those disqualified from sitting in the House include undischarged bankrupts, people sentenced to more than one year's imprisonment, clergy of the Church of England, Church of Scotland, Church of Ireland and Roman Catholic Church, peers, and holders of certain offices listed in the House of Commons Disqualification Act 1975 (*e.g.* members of the judiciary, Civil Service, regular armed forces, police forces, some local government officers and some members of public corporations and government commissions). A candidate does not require any party backing but his or her nomination for election must be supported by the signatures of ten people registered in the constituency. A candidate must also deposit with the returning officer £150, which is forfeit if the candidate does not receive more than 12·5 per cent of the votes cast. All election expenses, except the candidate's personal expenses, are subject to a statutory limit of £2,700, plus 2·3 pence for each elector in a borough constituency or 3·1 pence for each elector in a county constituency. (*See* pp. 312–319 for an alphabetical list of M.P.s, pp. 320–345 for the results of the last General Election and subsequent by-elections).

The week's business of the House is outlined each Thursday by the Leader of the House, after consultation between the Chief Government Whips and the Chief Opposition Whips. About the half of the time will be taken up by the Government's legislative programme, and the rest by other business, e.g. question time. As a rule Bills likely to raise political controversy are introduced in the Commons before going on to the Lords, and the Commons claims exclusive control in respect of national taxation and expenditure, and in respect of local rates and charges upon them. Bills such as the Finance Bill, which imposes taxation, and the Consolidated Fund Bills, which authorise expenditure, must begin in the Commons. A Bill of which the financial provisions are subsidiary may begin in the Lords; and the Commons may waive their rights in regard to Lords' amendments affecting finance.

The Commons has a public register of M.P.s financial interests. Members must also disclose any relevant financial interest or benefit in a matter before the House when taking part in a debate, in any other proceedings of the House or in consultations with other Members, with Ministers or civil servants.

Since 1911 Members of the House of Commons have received payments and travelling facilities; they are entitled to claim income tax relief on expenses incurred in the course of their Parliamentary duties.

Salary rates since 1911 as follows:

	p.a.		p.a.
1911	£400	1977 July	£6,270
1937	600	1978 June	6,897
1946	1,000	1979 June	9,450
1957	1,750	1980 June	11,750
1964	3,250	1981 June	13,950
1972 Jan	4,500	1982 June	14,510
1975 June	5,750	1983 June	15,308
1976 June	6,062	1984 Jan	16,106

In October 1969 Members were granted an allowance for secretarial and research expenses.

	p.a.		p.a.
1969 Oct	£500	1979 June	£4,600
1972 Jan	1,000	1980 Feb	6,750
1974 Aug	1,750	1980 Aug	8,000
1975 June	3,200	1981 June	8,480
1976 June	3,512	1982 June	8,820
1977 June	3,687	1983 June	11,364
1978 June	4,200		

Also, since January 1972, Members can claim reimbursement for the additional cost of staying overnight away from their main residence while on Parliamentary business.

	p.a.		p.a.
1972	£750	1978 July	£3,046
1974 Aug	1,050	1979 July	3,866
1975 July	1,814	1980 Aug	4,903
1976 July	2,038	1981 Aug	5,206
1977 July	2,534	1982 Aug	6,000

From March 1980 provision was made enabling each Member in receipt of Secretarial and Research Allowance to contribute sums to an approved pension scheme for the provision of a pension, or other benefits, for or in respect of persons whose salary is met by him.

To 31 March 1981	£786 p.a.
1982	838
1983	875
1984	1,136

The cost of travel allowances for 1983/84 was stated in July 1983 to be £3,127,700 (car mileage claims £2,172,150, rail travel £584,850 and air travel £370,700).

The Ministerial Salaries and Members' Pensions Act 1965 established a contributory pension fund providing pensions for former Members of Parliament and for dependents of deceased former Members. The Fund was reconstituted and the scheme restructured to bring it into line with pension schemes in the public sector by the Parliamentary and Other Pensions Acts 1972: further Acts modifying the arrangements for Members, Ministers and certain officeholders are the Parliamentary and Other Pensions and Salaries Act 1976; the Parliamentary Pensions Act 1978; the House of Commons Members' Fund and Parliamentary Pensions Act 1981 and the Parliamentary Pensions. etc., Act 1984. The arrangements now provide a pension of one-fiftieth of salary for each year of pensionable service with a maximum of 2/3rds of salary at age 65. Pension is normally payable at age 65, for men and women, or on later retirement. Pensions may be paid earlier e.g. on ill-health retirement. The widow of a former Member receives a pension of one-half her late husband's pension. Pensions are index-linked. Members contribute 9 per cent of salary to the pension fund: there is an Exchequer contribution, currently just over three times the amount contributed by Members, but under review.

The House of Commons Members' Fund provides

for annual or lump sum grants to ex-Members, their widows and children whose incomes are below certain limits. Alternatively, payments of £1,218 per annum to ex-Members with at least ten years service and who left the House of Commons before October 1964 and £609 per annum to their widows are made as of right. Members contribute £24 per annum and the Exchequer £115,000 per annum to the Fund. The income of the Fund in 1982–83 was £249,788 and estimated expenditure on grants and payments was £161,807. The net assets of the Fund as at September 30, 1983 amounted to £852,034.

The House of Commons is presided over by the Speaker, who has considerable powers to maintain order in the House. His deputy, the Chairman of Ways and Means, and two Deputy Chairmen, all of whom may preside over sittings of the House of Commons, are elected by the House; they, like the Speaker, neither speak nor vote other than in their official capacity. The staff of the House are employed by a Commission chaired by the Speaker. The Clerk of the House of Commons, the Serjeant at Arms and the other Heads of Departments (*see* below) are permanent officers of the House, not M.P.s. The Clerk of the House is the principal adviser to the Speaker on the privileges and procedures of the House and his department's responsibilities relate to the conduct of the business of the House and its Committees. The Serjeant at Arms, who attends upon the Speaker on ceremonial occasions, is responsible for security and for accommodation and services in the Commons part of the building.

OFFICERS OF THE HOUSE OF COMMONS

Speaker, The Rt. Hon. Bernard Weatherill, M.P. for Croydon North East £40,340
Chairman of Ways and Means, The Rt. Hon. Harold Walker, M.P. for Doncaster Central £30,410
First Deputy Chairman of Ways and Means, The Rt. Hon. Ernest Armstrong, M.P. for Durham North
West.. £27,920
Second Deputy Chairman of Ways and Means, Paul Dean, M.P. for Woodspring £27,920

Offices of the Speaker and Chairman of Ways and Means

Speaker's Secretary, W. A. Beaumont, O.B.E., A.E.
£20,493–£24,409
Speaker's Counsel, T. R. F. Skemp, C.B., Q.C.;
G. E. Gammie, C.B. £29,833
Chaplain to the Speaker, The Rev. Canon T. Beeson.
Staff Inspector, H. W. Bunkell ..... £13,649–£17,906

Department of the Clerk of the House

Clerk of the House of Commons, K. A.
Bradshaw, C.B. £45,500
Clerk Asst., C. J. Boulton £36,500
Clerk of Committees, D. A. M. Pring, C.B., M.C. £36,250
Principal Clerks—
  Public Bills, J. H. Willcox £30,750
  Select Committees, R. S. Lankester £30,750
  Table Office, D. W. Limon £30,750
  Private Bills, H. M. Barclay £30,750
  Journals, M. T. Ryle £30,750
  Overseas Office, J. F. Sweetman, T.D. £30,750
  Standing Committees, A. A. Barrett £26,705
  Second Clerk, Select Committees, C. B.
  Winnifrith £26,705
  Financial Committees, W. R. McKay £26,705
Deputy Principal Clerks, J. R. Rose; A. J.
Hastings; R. J. Willoughby; S. A. L.
Panton; R. B. Sands; G. Cubie; M. R. Jack,
PH.D.; D. G. Millar; Mrs. J. Sharpe; R. W. G.
Wilson; W. A. Proctor; F. A. Cranmer;
C. R. M. Ward, PH.D.; Mrs. H. E. Irwin
£20,493–£24,409
Senior Clerks, Ms. A. Milner-Barry; R. J.
Rogers; D. W. N. Doig; A. Sandall; M. Litt;
M. H. Cooper, PH.D.; D. L. Natzler; D. J.
Cairncross; E. P. Silk; Mrs. S. A. de Ste.
Croix; A. R. Kennon; D. W. Robson; L. C.
Laurence Smyth; A. R. Green; D. F.
Harrison; S. J. Priestley; C. P. R. Bennett;
A. H. Doherty; P. A. Evans; P. D. Brittain
(*acting*); F. W. Clark (*acting*); R. F. Giles
(*acting*); J. C. McDowell (*acting*) . £13,649–£17,906
Examiners of Private Bills, E. D. Graham;
H. M. Barclay.
Taxing Officer, H. M. Barclay.

Department of the Serjeant at Arms

Serjeant at Arms, Major G. V. S. Le Fanu ... £30,750
Deputy Serjeant at Arms, Major P. N. W.
Jennings...................... £20,493–£24,409
Assistant Serjeant at Arms, M. J. A.
Cummins .... £17,593–£20,862
Deputy Assistant Serjeant at Arms, P. A. J.
Wright .... £14,519–£17,906

Department of the Library

Librarian, D. Menhennet, D.PHIL £30,750
Deputy Librarian, D. J. T. Englefield
£20,493–£24,409

Library and Information Service

Assistant Librarians, H. J. Palmer; G. F.
Lock........................... £20,493–£22,928
Deputy Assistant Librarians, M. A. Griffith-
Jones; J. B. Poole, PH.D.; Miss J. B.
Tanfield; S. Z. Young; Mrs. H. R. Coates;
Miss P. J. Baines; K. G. Cuninghame; Mrs.
J. M. Wainwright.............. £16,902–£20,567
Senior Library Clerks, Miss E. K. Andrews,
D.PHIL.; Mrs. B. L. Miller; Mrs. J. M. Lourie;
Mrs. F. Poole; Mrs. C. B. Andrews; Mrs. J.
M. Fiddick; C. C. Pond, PH.D.; C. R. Barclay;
P. Nealon; Mrs. C. M. Gillie; Miss C. E.
Nield; R. C. Clements; Mrs R. E. Grogan;
R. J. Ware, D.PHIL; Ms. D. Gore, PH.D; R. J.
Twigger; B. K. Winetrobe; Mrs. J. V. Lee
£10,720–£17,906

Vote Office

Deliverer of the Vote, G. R. Russell . £16,201–£22,044
Deputy Deliverer of the Vote, H. C. Foster
£11,329–£14,773

Administration Department

Head of Administration Department, H. McE.
Allen £30,750
Accountant, J. L. G. Dobson .... £20,493–£24,409
Deputy Accountant, A. J. Lewis..... £17,593–£22,044
Assistant Accountants, G. P. Brown; F. W.
Brewer; A. R. Marskell; M. J. Barram
£11,329–£15,926

Head of Establishments Office, A. C. J. Poole
£20,493–£23,818
Deputy Head of Establishments Office, J. A.
Robb .... £17,593–£22,044
Assistant Head of Establishments Office, D. J.
Mouat .... £11,329–£15,364
Computer Development Officer, R. S. Morgan
£18,754–£23,818

Department of the Official Report

Editor, K. S. Morgan .... £23,393–£24,409
Deputy Editor, L. R. Johns £18,963
Principal Assistant Editors, R. V. Hadlow; J.
Gourley................................ £17,789

Senior Assistant Editors, F. G. Brotherston;
C. R. G. Watson........................ £17,789
Assistant Editor, P. Walker .... £16,201–£17,197
Deputy Assistant Editors, E. Holland; I.
Church £16,380

Refreshment Department

General Manager, W. J. J. Smillie.......... £21,898
Deputy General Manager, E. J. Nash
£13,649–£17,906
Catering Accountant, D. R. W. Wood
£13,649–£17,906

PARLIAMENTARY INFORMATION
The following is a short glossary of aspects of work of Parliament:
(*Unless otherwise stated, references are to* House of Commons *procedures.*)

Adjournment Debate.—Usually a half-hour debate introduced by a backbencher at the end of business for the day. The subjects raised are often local or personal issues.

Bill.—Proposed legislation is termed a *Bill*. The stages of a Public Bill in the House of Commons are as follows:
First Reading: There is no debate at this stage, which nowadays merely constitutes an order to have the Bill printed.
Second Reading: The debate on the principle of the Bill.
Committee Stage: The detailed examination of a Bill, clause by clause. In most cases this takes place in a *Standing Committee*, or the whole House may act as a Committee. Rarely, a Bill may be examined by a *Select Committee* (*see* below).
Report Stage: Detailed review of a Bill as amended in Committee.
Third Reading: Final debate on a Bill.
Public Bills go through the same stages in the House of Lords, except that in almost all cases the Committee Stage is taken in the Committee of the Whole House.
Some Public Bills may start in the House of Lords, in which case the Lords stages are taken first.
Both Houses have to agree the same text of a Bill, so that the *Amendments* made by the second House are then considered in the originating House and if not agreed, sent back or themselves amended, until agreement is reached.

Chiltern Hundreds.—A legal fiction, a nominal office of profit under the Crown, the acceptance of which requires a Member to vacate his seat. The Manor of Northstead is similar. These are the only means by which an M.P. may resign.

Closure & Guillotine.—To prevent deliberate waste of time of either house, a motion may be made that the question be now put. In the House of Commons, if the Speaker decides that the rights of a minority are not being prejudiced and 100 members support the motion, it is put to the vote immediately; and, if carried, the original motion is put to the House, without further debate. The *Guillotine* represents a more rigorous and systematic application of the Closure. Under this system, a Bill proceeds in accordance with a rigid timetable and discussion is limited to the time allotted to each group of clauses. The Closure is possible in the House of Lords, but is hardly ever used. There is, however, no procedure for a guillotine. The completion of business in the Lords is traditionally ensured by mutual agreement from all sides of the House.

Consolidated Fund Bill.—A Bill to authorize issue of sums to maintain Government service. The Bill is dealt with without debate, but afterwards members may raise topics of public or local importance.

Delegated Legislation.—This consists, principally, of Statutory Instruments within the meaning of the Statutory Instruments Act 1946. These fall into three broad categories:—(i) "Affirmative Instruments", which are subject to approval by resolutions of both Houses before they can come into or remain in force; (ii) "Negative Instruments", which are subject to annulment by resolution of either House; and (iii) "General Instruments", which include those not required to be laid before Parliament and those which are required to be so laid but are not subject to approval or annulment. There are in addition Special Procedure Orders, which are another form of delegated legislation, subject to procedures which allow time for petitions to be lodged against them.

Dissolution.—Parliament comes to an end either by Dissolution by the Sovereign or the expiration of the term of five years for which the House of Commons was elected. Dissolution is normally effected by a Royal Proclamation.

Early Day Motion.—A motion put on the Order Paper by an M.P. without in general the real prospect of its being debated. Such motions are expressions of backbench opinion.

Emergency Debate.—In the Commons a method of obtaining prompt discussion of a matter of urgency is by moving the adjournment under Standing Order No. 10 for the purpose of discussing a specific and important matter that should have urgent consideration. A member may ask leave to make this motion by giving written notice to the Speaker, usually before 12 noon, and if the Speaker considers the matter of sufficient importance and it obtains the support of 40 members, it is discussed usually at 7 p.m. on the following day.

Father of the House.—The Member whose service in the House of Commons, in aggregate, is the longest. The present Father of the House is the Rt. Hon. James Callaghan, elected first in 1945.

General Synod Measure.—A measure passed by the national assembly of the Church of England under the Church of England Assembly (Powers) Act 1919. These measures are considered by the Ecclesiastical Committee, who make a report, and are then considered by both Houses, and if approved, sent for the Royal Assent.

Hansard.—The official report of debates in both Houses (and in Standing Committees) published by H.M.S.O., normally on the day after the sitting concerned.

Hours of Meeting.—The House of Commons meets on Monday, Tuesday, Wednesday and Thursday at 2.30 p.m., and on Friday at 9.30 a.m. The House of Lords normally meets during the Session at 2.30 p.m. on Tuesday and Wednesday and on most Mondays; and at 3 p.m. on Thursday. In the latter part of the Session, the House usually sits also on Mondays at 2.30 p.m., and occasionally on Fridays at 11 a.m.

Hybridity.—A Public Bill which is considered to affect specific private or local interests, as distinct from *all* such interests of a single category, is called a Hybrid Bill and is subject to a special form of scrutiny.

Leader of the Opposition.—In 1937 the office of Leader of the Opposition was recognized and a salary of £2,000 per annum was assigned to the post, thus following a practice which had prevailed in the Dominion of Canada since 1906. In July 1983 the salary was £36,490. The present Leader of the Opposition is the Rt. Hon. Neil Kinnock.

The Lord Chancellor.—The Lord High Chancellor of Great Britain is (*ex officio*) the Speaker of the House of Lords. Unlike the Speaker of the House of Commons, he is a member of the Government, and takes part in debates and votes in divisions. He has none of the powers to maintain order that the Speaker in the Commons has, these powers being exercised in the Lords by the House as a whole. The Lord Chancellor sits in the Lords on one of the *Woolsacks*, couches covered with red cloth and stuffed with wool. If he wishes to address the House in any way except formally as Speaker, he leaves the Woolsack and steps towards his place as a peer.

Naming.—When a member has been named, *i.e.* contrary to the practice of the House called by surname and not addressed as the "Hon. Member for ... (his constituency)", the Leader of the House moves that he "be suspended from the service of the House" for (in the case of a first offence) a period of a week. The period of suspension is increased, should the member offend again.

Opposition Day.—A day on which the topic for debate is chosen by the Opposition. There are 19 such days in a normal session.

Parliament Acts 1911 and 1949.—Under these Acts certain Bills may become law without the consent of the Lords.

Since at least the 18th century the Commons have had the privilege of having bills concerned with supply (*i.e.* taxation and money matters) passed without amendment by the Lords; though until 1911 the Lords retained the right to reject such bills outright.

By the Parliament Act 1911 a Bill which has been endorsed by the Speaker of the House of Commons as a Money Bill and has been passed by the Commons and sent up to the Lords at least one month before the end of a session can become law without the consent of the Lords if it is not passed by them without amendment within a month.

Under the Parliament Act 1911 and 1949, if the Lords reject any other Public Bill (except those dealing with certain subjects such as the prolongation of Parliament) which has been passed by the Commons in two successive sessions then that Bill shall (unless the Commons direct to the contrary) become law without the consent of the Lords.

The effect of the Parliament Acts is therefore that the Lords have power to delay a Public Bill for thirteen months from its first Second Reading in the House of Commons.

Prime Minister's Questions.—The Prime Minister answers questions from 3.15 to 3.30 pm on Tuesdays and Thursdays. Nowadays the "open question" predominates. Members ask the Prime Minister what are his or her official engagements for the day or whether an official visit will be made to such and such a place. A supplementary question on virtually any topic can then be put.

Private Bill.—A Bill promoted by a body or an individual to give powers additional to, or in conflict with, the general law, and to which a separate procedure applies.

Private Members' Bill.—A Public Bill promoted by a Member who is not a member of H.M. Government.

Private Notice Question.—A question adjudged of urgent importance on submission to Mr. Speaker, answered at the end of oral questions—usually at 3.30 p.m.

Privilege.—The following are covered by the privilege of Parliament: (i) freedom from interference in going to, attending at, and going from, Parliament; (ii) freedom of speech; (iii) the printing and publishing of anything relating to the proceedings of the two Houses is subject to privilege; (iv) each House is the guardian of its dignity and may punish any insult to the House as a whole.

Prorogation.—The bringing to an end, by the Sovereign on the advice of the Government, of a Session of Parliament. All Public Bills which have not completed their stages lapse on Prorogation.

Queen's Speech.—The Speech delivered by H.M. The Queen at the State Opening of Parliament, in which the Government's programme for the year is set forth. The Speech is, of course, drafted for and approved by the Cabinet.

Question Time.—Oral questions are answered in the Commons from 2.30 to 3.30 pm every day except Friday. They are also taken at the start of the Lords sittings, with a daily limit of four oral questions.

Royal Assent.—The Royal Assent is signified by Letters Patent to such Bills and Measures as have passed both Houses of Parliament (or Bills which have been passed under the Parliament Acts 1911 and 1949). The Sovereign has not given Royal Assent in person since 1854. On occasion, for instance in the Prorogation of Parliament, Royal Assent may be pronounced to the two Houses by Lords Commissioners; but more usually Royal Assent is notified to each House sitting separately in accordance with the Royal Assent Act 1967. The Norman formulae for Royal Assent are then endorsed on the Acts by the Clerk of the Parliaments.

The power to withold assent (colloquially known as the Royal Veto) resides with the Sovereign, but has not been exercised in the United Kingdom since 1707, in the reign of Queen Anne.

Select Committees consisting usually of 10–15 members of all parties are a means used by both Houses in order to investigate certain matters.

Most Select Committees in the House of Commons are now tied to Departments—each Committee investigates subjects within a Government Department's remit. At the time of going to press these were: Agriculture, Defence, Education Science and Arts, Employment, Energy, Environment, Foreign Affairs, Home Affairs, Scottish Affairs, Social Services, Trade and Industry, Transport, Treasury and Civil Service, Welsh Affairs.

There are other House of Commons Select Committees dealing with Public Accounts (*i.e.* the spending by H.M. Government of money voted by Parliament), European Legislation and Statutory Instruments, and also domestic committees dealing, for example, with Privilege and Services. Public Select Committees usually take evidence in public: their evidence and reports are published by H.M. Stationery Office.

The principal Select Committee in the House of Lords is that on the European Communities, which has, at present, seven sub-committees dealing with all areas of community policy. The House of Lords also has a Select Committee on Science and Technology, which appoints sub-committees to deal with specific subjects. In addition, *ad hoc* Select Committees have been set up from time to time to investigate specific subjects, *e.g.* Unemployment.

The Speaker.—The Speaker of the House of Commons is the spokesman and president of the Chamber. He is elected by the House at the beginning of each Parliament or when the previous Speaker retires or dies. He neither speaks in debates nor votes in divisions except when the voting is equal. His position in the precedence of the Kingdom is high, only the Prime Minister and the Lord President of the Council (when not peers) among Commoners going before him. He takes precedence of all Lords, except the two Archbishops and the Lord Chancellor, and Speakers are almost invariably raised to the Peerage on vacating their office.

Standing Orders.—Rules which have from time to time been agreed by each House of Parliament to regulate the conduct of its business. These orders are not irrevocable, may be revised, amended or repealed, and are from time to time suspended or dispensed with.

State Opening.—This marks the start of each new Parliament or new session of Parliament. Parliament is normally opened, in the presence of both Houses, by the Queen in person, who makes the Speech from the Throne which outlines the Government's policies for the coming session (*see* **Queen's Speech**). In the absence of the Queen, Parliament is opened by Royal Commission, and the Queen's Speech is read by one of the Lords Commissioner specially appointed by Letters Patent for the occasion.

Strangers.—Anyone who is not a Member or Officer of the House is a *stranger*. Visitors are generally admitted to debates of both Houses but may be excluded if the House so decides. In practice this happens only in time of war.

Ten Minute Rule.—A colloquial term for Standing Order No. 15, under which backbenchers have an opportunity on Tuesdays and Wednesdays to introduce a bill and speak in its favour for about ten minutes. Time is also available for a short opposing speech.

Vacant Seats.—When a vacancy occurs in the House of Commons during a session of Parliament the Writ for the by-election is moved, by a Whip of the party to whom the member whose seat has been vacated belonged. If the House is in recess, the Speaker can issue a writ, should two members certify to him that a seat is vacant.

Whips.—In order to secure the attendance of Members of a particular party in Parliament on all occasions, and particularly on the occasion of an important division, Whips (originally known as "Whippers-in") are appointed for the purpose. The written appeal or circular letter issued by them is also known as a "whip", its urgency being denoted by the number of times it is underlined. Neglect to respond to a three-lined whip, headed "Most important", is tantamount in the Commons to secession (at any rate temporarily) from the party. Whips are officially recognized by Parliament and are provided with office accommodation in both Houses. In the House of Commons, Government and some Opposition Whips receive salaries from public funds.

Public Information Service.—Enquiries from the general public and organizations of all kinds about the work, composition and history of the House of Commons are answered by the Public Information Office, House of Commons, S.W.1 (01-219 4272). This office also edits the House of Commons Weekly Information Bulletin (published by H.M. Stationery Office). The Journal and Information Office, House of Lords, S.W.1 (01-219 3107) answers queries relating to the procedure and practice of the Lords.

HER MAJESTY'S GOVERNMENT

Her Majesty's Government is the body of Ministers responsible for the administration of national affairs, determining policy and introducing into Parliament any legislation necessary to give effect to government policy. The majority of Ministers are members of the House of Commons but members of the House of Lords may also hold Ministerial responsibility, and certain offices, *e.g.* Lord Chancellor, are always held by members of the House of Lords. The Prime Minister is, by recent convention, always a member of the House of Commons.

THE PRIME MINISTER

The office of Prime Minister, which had been in existence for nearly 200 years, was officially recognised in 1905 and its holder was granted a place in the Table of Precedence. The Prime Minister, by tradition also First Lord of the Treasury and Minister for the Civil Service, is appointed by the Sovereign and is usually the leader of the party which enjoys, or can secure, a majority in the House of Commons. Other Ministers are appointed by the Sovereign on the recommendation of the Prime Minister, who also allocates functions amongst Ministers and has the power to obtain their resignation or dismissal individually.

The Prime Minister informs the Sovereign of state and political matters, advises on the dissolution of Parliament, and makes recommendations for important Crown appointments, the award of honours, etc.

As the chairman of Cabinet meetings and leader of a political party, the Prime Minister is responsible for translating party policy into government activity: and as leader of the Government the Prime Minister is responsible to Parliament and to the electorate for the policies and their implementation.

The Prime Minister also represents the nation in international affairs, *e.g.* summit conferences.

THE CABINET

The Cabinet developed during the 18th century as an inner committee of the Privy Council, which was the chief source of executive power until that time. It is composed of about 20 Ministers chosen by the Prime Minister, usually the heads of government departments (known as Secretaries of State or Ministers unless they have a special title, *e.g.* Chancellor of the Exchequer) and the holders of various traditional offices. Ministers of State can be given a seat in the Cabinet.

The Cabinet's functions are the final determination of policy, control of government and co-ordination of government departments. The exercise of its functions is dependent upon enjoying majority support in the House of Commons. Cabinet meetings are held in private, taking place once or twice a week during parliamentary sittings and less often during a recess. Proceedings are confidential, the members being bound by their oath as Privy Counsellors not to disclose information about the proceedings.

The convention of collective responsibility means that the Cabinet acts unanimously even when Cabinet Ministers do not all agree on a subject. The policies of departmental Ministers must be consistent with the policies of the Government as a whole, and once the Government's policy has been decided, each Minister is expected to support it or resign.

The convention of Ministerial responsibility holds a Minister, as the political head of his or her department, accountable to Parliament for the department's work. Departmental Ministers usually decide all matters within their responsibility, although on matters of political importance they normally consult their colleagues collectively. A decision by a departmental Minister is binding on the Government as a whole.

HER MAJESTY'S MINISTRY

THE CABINET

Prime Minister, First Lord of the Treasury and Minister for the Civil Service, THE RT. HON. MARGARET HILDA THATCHER, M.P., F.R.S, *born* Oct. 13, 1925.
Secretary of State for the Home Department, The Rt. Hon. Leon Brittan, Q.C., M.P., *born* Sept. 25, 1939.
Lord High Chancellor, The Rt. Hon. Lord Hailsham of St. Marylebone, C.H., *born* Oct. 9, 1907.
Secretary of State for Foreign and Commonwealth Affairs, The Rt. Hon. Sir Richard Edward Geoffrey Howe, Q.C., M.P., *born* Dec. 20, 1926.
Chancellor of the Exchequer, The Rt. Hon. Nigel Lawson, M.P., *born* March 11, 1932.
Secretary of State for Trade and Industry and President of the Board of Trade, The Rt. Hon. Norman Beresford Tebbit, M.P., *born* March 29, 1931.
Secretary of State for Defence, The Rt. Hon. Michael Ray Dibdin Heseltine, M.P., *born* March 21, 1933.
Lord Privy Seal and Leader of the House of Commons, The Rt. Hon. (William) John Biffen, M.P., *born* Nov. 3, 1930.
Secretary of State for Employment, The Rt. Hon. Thomas Jeremy King, M.P., *born* June 13, 1933.
Lord President of the Council and Leader of the House of Lords, The Viscount Whitelaw, P.C., C.H., M.C., *born* June 28, 1918.
Minister of Agriculture, Fisheries and Food, The Rt. Hon. Thomas Michael Jopling, M.P., *born* Dec. 10, 1930.
Secretary of State for the Environment, The Rt. Hon. Charles Patrick Fleeming Jenkin, M.P., *born* Sept. 7, 1926.
Secretary of State for Scotland, The Rt. Hon. George Kenneth Hotson Younger, T.D., M.P., *born* Sept. 22, 1931.
Secretary of State for Wales, The Rt. Hon. Roger Nicholas Edwards, M.P., *born* Feb. 25, 1934.
Secretary of State for Northern Ireland, The Rt. Hon. Douglas Richard Hurd, C.B.E., M.P., *born* March 8, 1930.
Secretary of State for Social Services, The Rt. Hon. Peter Norman Fowler, M.P., *born* Feb. 2, 1938.
Secretary of State for Energy, The Rt. Hon. Peter Edward Walker, M.B.E., M.P., *born* March 25, 1932.
Secretary of State for Education and Science, The Rt. Hon. Sir Keith Sinjohn Joseph, Bt., M.P., *born* Jan. 17, 1918.
Chief Secretary to the Treasury, The Rt. Hon. Peter Wynford Innes Rees, Q.C., M.P., *born* Dec. 9, 1926.
Secretary of State for Transport, The Rt. Hon. Nicholas Ridley, M.P., *born* Feb 17, 1929.
Chancellor of the Duchy of Lancaster, The Earl of Gowrie, P.C., *born* Nov. 26, 1939 (*Minister for the Arts*).
Minister Without Portfolio, David Ivor Young (to be a Life Peer and P.C.), *born* Feb. 27, 1932.

LAW OFFICERS

Attorney-General, The Rt. Hon. Sir Robert Michael Oldfield Havers, Q.C., M.P., *born* 1923.
Lord Advocate, The Lord Cameron of Lochbroom, P.C., Q.C.
Solicitor-General, Sir Patrick Barnabas Burke Mayhew, Q.C., M.P., *born* 1929.
Solicitor-General for Scotland, Peter Lovat Fraser, Q.C., M.P., *born* 1945.

MINISTERS NOT IN THE CABINET

Parliamentary Secretary to the Treasury, The Rt. Hon. John Wakeham, M.P., *born* 1932.
Economic Secretary to the Treasury, Ian Stewart, M.P., *born* 1935.
Financial Secretary to the Treasury, John Edward Michael Moore, M.P., *born* 1937.
Paymaster General, John Selwyn Gummer, M.P., *born* 1939.
Ministers of State:
  Agriculture, Fisheries and Food, John Roddick Russell MacGregor, M.P., O.B.E., *born* 1937; The Lord Belstead, P.C., *born* 1932.
  Defence, John Paul Stanley, M.P., *born* 1942 (*Armed Forces*); The Rt. Hon. Adam Courtauld Butler, M.P., *born* 1931 (*Procurement*).
  Employment, Hon. Peter Hugh Morrison, M.P., *born* 1944.
  Energy, The Rt. Hon. Alick Laidlaw Buchanan-Smith, M.P., *born* 1932.
  Foreign and Commonwealth Office, The Baroness Young, P.C., *born* 1926; Malcolm Leslie Rifkind, M.P., *born* 1946; Richard Napier Luce, M.P., *born* 1936; The Rt. Hon. Timothy Hugh Francis Raison, M.P., *born* 1929 (*Minister for Overseas Development*).
  Health, Rt. Hon. Kenneth Harry Clarke, Q.C., M.P., *born* 1940.
  Home Office, Giles Shaw, M.P., *born* 1931; The Lord Elton, T.D., *born* 1930.
  Housing and Construction, Ian Gow, M.P., T.D., *born* 1937.
  Industry, Norman Stewart Hughson Lamont, M.P., *born* 1942.
  Information Technology, Geoffrey Edwin Pattie, M.P., *born* 1936.
  Local Government, Rt. Hon. Kenneth Wilfred Baker, M.P., *born* 1934.

Northern Ireland Office, Dr. Rhodes Boyson, M.P., *born* 1925.
Scottish Office, The Lord Gray of Contin, P.C., *born* 1927.
Social Security, Anthony Harold Newton, O.B.E., M.P., *born* 1937.
Trade, The Rt. Hon. Paul Channon, M.P., *born* 1935.
Transport, Mrs. Lynda Chalker, M.P., *born* 1942.
Treasury, Barney Hayhoe, M.P., *born* 1925.
Welsh Office, John Stradling Thomas, *born* 1925.

PARLIAMENTARY UNDER SECRETARIES, ETC.

Agriculture, Fisheries and Food, Mrs. P. Fenner, M.P.
Defence, The Lord Trefgarne; J. Lee, M.P.
Education and Science, R. Dunn, M.P.; Hon. P. Brooke, M.P.
Employment, P. Bottomley, M.P.; Hon. A. Clark, M.P.
Energy, A. Goodlad, M.P.; D. Hunt, M.P.
Environment, Sir George Young, Bt., M.P.; N. Mac-Farlane, M.P.; Hon. W. Waldegrave, M.P.; The Earl of Avon.
Foreign and Commonwealth Affairs, T. Renton, M.P.
Health and Social Security, R. Whitney, O.B.E., M.P.; J. Patten, M.P.; The Lord Glenarthur.
Home Office, D. Mellor, M.P.
Northern Ireland Office, N. P. Scott, M.B.E., M.P.; C. Patten, M.P; The Lord Lyell.
Scottish Office, M. Ancram, M.P.; J. A. Stewart, M.P.; J. MacKay, M.P.
Trade and Industry, A. Fletcher, M.P.; J. Butcher, M.P.; D. Trippier, M.P.; The Lord Lucas of Chilworth.
Transport, D. Mitchell, M.P.; M. Spicer.
Treasury, Lords Commissioners, The Hon. D. Thompson, M.P.; The Hon. I. Lang, M.P.; The Hon. T. Garel-Jones, M.P.
Welsh Office, I. W. P. Roberts, M.P.

GOVERNMENT WHIPS

The Government Whips in the House of Lords are: The Captain of the Honourable Corps of the Gentlemen at Arms (Lord Denham), the Captain of the Queen's Bodyguard of the Yeoman of the Guard (Earl of Swinton), the political Lords in Waiting (Viscount Long, Lord Skelmersdale, The Lord Brabazon of Tara, Earl of Caithness) and the Lady in Waiting (Baroness Trumpington).

The Government Whips in the House of Commons are: *Chief Whip*, the Parliamentary Secretary to the Treasury (Rt. Hon. J. Wakeham): *Deputy Chief Whip*, the Treasurer, H.M. Household (J. Cope); the Comptroller, H.M. Household (C. Mather); the Vice-Chamberlain, H.M. Household (R. Boscawen); Lords Commissioners (D. Thompson, I. Lang, T. Garel-Jones): *Assistant Whips*, Hon. A. Hamilton, J. Major, Hon. D. Hogg, Hon. T. Sainsbury, M. Neubert.

GOVERNMENT BY PARTY

Before the reign of William and Mary the principal Officers of State were chosen by and were responsible to the Sovereign alone and not to Parliament or the nation at large. Such officers acted sometimes in concert with one another, but more often independently, and the fall of one did not, of necessity, involve that of others, although all were liable to be dismissed at any moment.

In 1693 the Earl of Sunderland recommended to William III the advisability of selecting a Ministry from the political party which enjoyed a majority in the House of Commons and the first united Ministry was drawn in 1696 from the Whigs, to which party the King owed his throne, the principal members being Russell (the Admiral), Somers (the Advocate), Lord Wharton and Charles Montague (afterwards Chancellor of the Exchequer). This group became known as the *Junto* and was regarded with suspicion as a novelty in the political life of the nation, being a small section meeting in secret apart from the main body of Ministers. It may be regarded as the forerunner of the *Cabinet* and in course of time it led to the establishment of the principle of joint responsibility of Ministers, so that internal disagreement caused a change of personnel or resignation of the whole body of Ministers.

The accession of George I, who was unfamiliar with the English language, led to a disinclination on the part of the Sovereign to preside at meetings of his Ministers and caused the appearance of a *Prime Minister*, a position first acquired by Robert Walpole in 1721 and retained without interruption for 20 years and 326 days.

In 1828 the old party of the Whigs became known as *Liberals*, a name originally given to it by its opponents to imply laxity of principles, but gradually accepted by the party to indicate its claim to be pioneers and champions of political reform and progressive legislation. In 1861 a Liberal Registration Association was founded and Liberal Associations became widespread. As the outcome of a

conference at Birmingham in 1877 a National Liberal Federation was formed, with headquarters in London. The Liberal Party was in power for long periods during the second half of the nineteenth century in spite of the set-back during the Home Rule crisis of 1886, which resulted in the secession of the Liberal Unionists, and for several years during the first quarter of the twentieth century, but after a further split into National and Independent Liberals it numbered only 59 in all after the General Election of 1929, with a further fall to 12 (excluding National Liberals) after the 1945 Election.

Soon after the change from Whig to Liberal the Tory Party became known as *Conservative*, a name traditionally believed to have been invented by John Wilson Croker in 1830 and to have been generally adopted about the time of the passing of the Reform Act of 1832 to indicate that the preservation of national institutions was the leading principle of the party. After the Home Rule crisis of 1886 the dissentient Liberals entered into a compact with the Conservatives, under which the latter undertook not to contest their seats, but a separate *Liberal Unionist* organization was maintained until 1912, when it was united with the Conservatives.

The Labour Party.—Labour candidates for Parliament made their first appearance at the General Election of 1892, when there were 27 standing as "Labour" or "Liberal-Labour."

In 1900 the *Labour Representative Committee* was set up in order to establish a distinct Labour Group in Parliament, with its own whips, its own policy, and a readiness to co-operate with any party which might be engaged in promoting legislation in the direct interest of labour. In 1906 the L.R.C. became known as *The Labour Party*.

Social Democratic Party.—The Council for Social Democracy was announced by four former Labour Cabinet Ministers—Roy Jenkins, David Owen, William Rodgers and Mrs. Shirley Williams—on Jan. 25, 1981. Subsequently a number of sitting Labour

Members of Parliament, together with one Conservative, crossed the floor of the Commons to join the new group, and on March 26, 1981 the Social Democratic Party was launched in London, followed by eight regional launches. Later in the year the S.D.P. and the Liberal Party formed an electoral *Alliance*, though each party decides its own policy and maintains its own party organisation.

The government of the day is formed by the party which wins the largest number of seats in the House of Commons at a General Election, or which has the support of a majority of members in the House of Commons. By tradition, the leader of the majority party is asked by the Sovereign to form a government, while the largest minority party becomes the official Opposition with its own leader and own "Shadow Cabinet". Leaders of the Government and Opposition sit on the front benches of the Commons with their supporters (the back-benchers) sitting behind them.

When a party is in Opposition and its leadership becomes vacant, it makes its free choice among the various personalities available; but if the party is in office, the Sovereign's choice may anticipate, and in a certain sense forestall, the decision of the party.

POLITICAL PARTIES

CONSERVATIVE AND UNIONIST PARTY, Central Office, 32 Smith Square, SW1P 3HH.—*Party Chairman*, J. S. Gummer, M.P.; *Deputy Chairman*, M. Spicer, M.P.; *Hon. Treasurers*, Lord McAlpine of West Green, Sir Oulton Wade; *Dir. of Organisation*, Sir Anthony Garner.

SCOTTISH CONSERVATIVE AND UNIONIST PARTY, Central Office, 3 Chester Street, Edinburgh, EH3 7RF.—*Chairman*, Sir James Good; *Deputy Chairman*, Dr. A. Smith, C.B.E.; *Dir.*, W. Henderson.

LABOUR PARTY, 150 Walworth Road, SE17.—*Chairman*, E. Heffer, M.P.; *Vice-Chairman*, A. Hadden; *Treasurer*, Rt. Hon. A. Booth; *Gen. Sec.*, J. E. Mortimer; *Parliamentary Party Leader*, Rt. Hon. N. Kinnock, M.P.; *Deputy Leader*, Rt. Hon. R. Hattersley, M.P.; *Leader of the Labour Peers*, Lord Ponsonby of Shulbrede.

SHADOW CABINET.—Rt. Hon N. Kinnock, M.P. (*Leader of the Opposition*); Rt. Hon. R. Hattersley, M.P. (*Treasury and Economic Affairs*); Rt. Hon. D. Healey, M.P. (*Foreign and Commonwealth Affairs*); Rt. Hon. G. Kaufman, M.P. (*Home Affairs*); Rt. Hon. P. Shore, M.P. (*Leader of the House; Trade and Industry*); Rt. Hon. J. Smith, M.P. (*Employment*); Dr. J. Cunningham, M.P. (*Environment*); J. Prescott, M.P. (*Transport*); Rt. Hon. J. Silkin, M.P. (*Defence and Disarmament*); Rt. Hon. P. Archer, M.P. (*Northern Ireland*); B. Jones, M.P. (*Wales*); R. Cook, M.P. (*European and Community Affairs*); E. Heffer, M.P. (*Housing and Construction*); M. Meacher, M.P. (*Health and Social Security*); G. Radice, M.P.(*Education*); Rt. Hon. S. Orme, M.P. (*Energy*).

Labour Whips in the House of Lords are: *Chief Whip*, Lord Ponsonby of Shulbrede; *Deputy Chief Whip*, Baroness David; Lord John-Mackie, Lord Graham of Edmonton, Lord Stoddart of Swindon, Lord Dean of Beswick, Baroness Nicol. Labour Whips in the House of Commons are: *Chief Whip*, Rt. Hon M. F. L. Cocks; *Deputy Chief Whip*, N. Hogg, M.P.; R. Corbett, L. Cunliffe, D. Dixon, J. Hamilton, F. Haynes, J. Home-Robertson, A. McKay, J. McWilliam, A. Mitchell, Dr. R. Thomas.

LIBERAL PARTY, Headquarters, 1 Whitehall Place, SW1A 2HE.—*Chairman*, P. Tyler; *Deputy Chairmen*, S. Mole, O.B.E., A. Ellis, O.B.E.; *Hon. Treasurers*, Sir Hugh Jones, M.V.O., A. Jacobs; *Sec. Gen.*, J. Spiller, M.B.E.; *Parliamentary Party Leader*, Rt. Hon. D. Steel, M.P.; *Leader of the Liberal Peers*, Lady Seear.

The Liberal Whip in the House of Lords is Lord Wigoder. Liberal Whips in the House of Commons are: *Chief Whip*, A. Beith; *Deputy Chief Whip*, M. Meadowcroft.

SCOTTISH LIBERAL PARTY, 4 Clifton Terrace, Edinburgh, EH12 5DR.—*Chairman*, R. Finnie; *Deputy Chairmen*, M. Bruce, M.P., R. Waddell, J. Wallace, M.P.; *Hon. Treasurer*, D. King; *Gen. Sec.*, D. Miller.

WELSH LIBERAL PARTY, 15/17 Dumfries Chambers, 91 St. Mary's Street, Cardiff, CF1 1DW.—*Chairman*, W. Roddick; *Deputy Chairman*, G. Griffiths; *Hon. Treasurers*, P. Davies, Dr. G. Morrison; *Sec.*, Mrs. L. Scharer.

PLAID CYMRU, 51 Cathedral Road, Cardiff, CF1 9HD.—*Chairman*, D. Iwan; *Deputy Chairman*, S. Morgan; *Hon. Treasurer*, J. Dixon; *Sec.*, D. Williams; *Parliamentary Party Leader*, D. Wigley; *Vice-President*, P. Williams.

SCOTTISH NATIONAL PARTY, 6 North Charlotte Street, Edinburgh, EH2 4JH.—*Chairman*, G. Wilson, M.P.; *Senior Vice-Chairman*, J. Fairlie; *Hon. Treasurer*, A. Morgan; *National Sec.*, N. R. McCallum; *Parliamentary Party Leader*, Rt. Hon. D. Stewart, M.P.

SOCIAL DEMOCRATIC PARTY, 4 Cowley Street, SW1P 3NB.—*President*, Rt. Hon. Mrs. S. Williams; *Vice-President*, Rt. Hon. W. Rodgers; *National Sec.*, R. Newby; *Parliamentary Party Leader*, Rt. Hon. Dr. D. Owen, M.P.

The S.D.P. Whip in the House of Lords is Lord Diamond. The S.D.P. Whip in the House of Commons is J. Cartwright, M.P.

NORTHERN IRELAND

SOCIAL DEMOCRATIC AND LABOUR PARTY, 38 University Street, Belfast, BT7 1FZ.—*Chairman*, S. Farren; *Deputy Chairmen*, B. Caraher, A. Maginness; *Hon. Treasurer*, B. McIvor; *Gen. Sec.*, E. Hanna; *Parliamentary Party Leader*, J. Hume, M.P.; *Deputy Leader*, S. Mallon.

ULSTER DEMOCRATIC UNIONIST PARTY, 296 Albertbridge Road, Belfast, BT5 4GW.—*Chairman*, J. McClure; *Deputy Chairman*, S. Gibson; *Hon. Treasurer*, D. Herron; *Sec.*, A. Kane; *Parliamentary Party Leader*, Dr. I. Paisley, M.P.; *Deputy Leader*, P. Robinson, M.P.

ULSTER UNIONIST PARTY, Council Headquarters, 3 Glangall Street, Belfast, BT12 5AE.—*Chairman*, Mrs. H. Bradford; *Hon. Treasurer*, J. Cunningham; *Sec.*, F. Millar; *Parliamentary Party Leader*, Rt. Hon. J. H. Molyneaux, M.P.

ALPHABETICAL LIST OF MEMBERS OF THE HOUSE OF COMMONS

For abbreviations, *see* page 320.

Maj.

Nellist, David J. (b. 1952), Lab., Coventry, S.E. 2,682
*Nelson, R. Anthony (b. 1948), C., Chichester 20,117
*Neubert, Michael J. (b. 1933), C., Romford 10,574
*Newton, Antony H. (b. 1937), C., Braintree 13,441
Nicholls, Patrick C. M. (b. 1948), C., Teignbridge 8,218
Nicholson, James F. (b. 1945), O.U.P., Newry and Armagh 1,554
*Normanton, Tom (b. 1917), C., Cheadle .. 9,380
Norris, Steven J. (b. 1945), C., Oxford, E. .. 1,267
*Oakes, Rt. Hon. Gordon J. (b. 1931), Lab., Halton 6,829
O'Brien, William (b. 1929), Lab., Normanton 4,183
*O'Neill, Martin J. (b. 1945), Lab., Clackmannan 9,639
*Onslow, Cranley G. D. (b. 1926), C., Woking 16,237
Oppenheim, Phillip A. C. L. (b. 1956), C., Amber Valley 3,318
*Oppenheim, Rt. Hon. Mrs. Sally (b. 1930), C., Gloucester 12,537
*Orme, Rt. Hon. Stanley (b. 1923), Lab., Salford, E. 9,541
*Osborn, Sir John H. (b. 1922), C., Sheffield, Hallam 11,774
Ottaway, Richard G. J. (b. 1945), C., Nottingham, N. 362
*Owen, Rt. Hon. Dr. David A. L. (b. 1938), S.D.P./All., Plymouth, Devonport 4,936
*Page, Sir A. John (b. 1919), C., Harrow, W. 11,021
*Page, Richard L. (b. 1941), C., Hertfordshire, S.W. 12,194
*Paisley, Rev. Ian R. K. (b. 1926), D.U.P., Antrim, N. 13,173
*Park, George M. (b. 1914), Lab., Coventry, N.E. 8,775
*Parkinson, Rt. Hon. Cecil E. (b. 1931), C., Hertsmere 14,870
*Parris, Matthew F. (b. 1940), C., Derbyshire, W. 15,325
*Parry, Robert (b. 1933), Lab., Liverpool, Riverside 17,378
Patchett, Terry (b. 1940), Lab., Barnsley, E. 17,492
*Patten, Christopher F. (b. 1944), C., Bath . 5,304
*Patten, John H. C. (b. 1945), C., Oxford, W. and Abingdon 7,151
*Pattie, Geoffrey E. (b. 1936), C., Chertsey and Walton 15,699
*Pavitt, Laurence A. (b. 1914), Lab., Brent, S. 10,519
*Pawsey, James F. (b. 1933), C., Rugby and Kenilworth 14,241
Peacock, Mrs. Elizabeth J. (b. 1937), C., Batley and Spen 870
*Pendry, Thomas (b. 1934), Lab., Stalybridge and Hyde 4,362
*Penhaligon, David C. (b. 1944), L./All., Truro 10,480
*Percival, Rt. Hon. Sir W. Ian (b. 1921), C., Southport 5,039
Pike, Peter L. (b. 1937), Lab., Burnley 770
*Pollock, Alexander (b. 1944), C., Moray ... 1,713
*Porter, George B. (b. 1939), C., Wirral, S. . 13,838
*Powell, Rt. Hon. J. Enoch (b. 1912), O.U.P., Down, S. 548
*Powell, Raymond (b. 1928), Lab., Ogmore . 17,364
Powell, William R. (b. 1948), C., Corby ... 3,168
Powley, John A. (b. 1936), C., Norwich, S. . 1,712
*Prentice, Rt. Hon. Reginald E. (b. 1923), C., Daventry 13,136
*Prescott, John L. (b. 1938), Lab., Hull, E. . 10,074
*Price, Sir David E. C. (b. 1924), C., Eastleigh 13,008
Prior, Rt. Hon. James M. L. (b. 1927), C., Waveney 14,298
Proctor, K. Harvey (b. 1947), C., Billericay 14,615

Maj.

*Pym, Rt. Hon. Francis L. (b. 1922), C., Cambridgeshire, S.E. 13,764
*Radice, Giles H. (b. 1936), Lab., Durham, N. 13,437
Raffan, Keith W. (b. 1947), C., Delyn 5,944
*Raison, Rt. Hon. Timothy H. F. (b. 1929), C., Aylesbury 14,920
Randall, Stuart J. (b. 1938), Lab., Hull, W. 3,654
*Rathbone, J. R. (Tim) (b. 1933), C., Lewes . 13,904
Redmond, Martin (b. 1937), Lab., Don Valley 6,466
*Rees, Rt. Hon. Merlyn (b. 1920), Lab., Morley and Leeds South 5,854
*Rees, Rt. Hon. Peter W. I. (b. 1926), C., Dover 9,220
*Renton, Ronald T. (b. 1932), C., Mid Sussex 16,744
*Rhodes James, Robert V. R. (b. 1933), C., Cambridge 5,968
*Rhys Williams, Sir Brandon M., Bt. (b. 1927), C., Kensington 5,101
*Richardson, Ms. Jo (b. 1923), Lab., Barking 4,026
*Ridley, Rt. Hon. Nicholas (b. 1929), C., Cirencester and Tewkesbury 13,827
*Ridsdale, Sir Julian E. (b. 1915), C., Harwich 12,502
*Rifkind, Malcolm L. (b. 1946), C., Edinburgh, Pentlands 4,309
*Rippon, Rt. Hon. A. Geoffrey F. (b. 1924), C., Hexham 8,308
*Roberts, Allan (b. 1943), Lab., Bootle 15,139
*Roberts, Ernest A. C. (b. 1912), Lab., Hackney, N. and Stoke Newington 8,545
*Roberts, I. Wyn P. (b. 1930), C., Conwy ... 4,268
*Robertson, George I. M. (b. 1946), Lab., Hamilton 15,019
*Robinson, Geoffrey (b. 1938), Lab., Coventry, N.W. 3,038
Robinson, Mark N. F. (b. 1948), C., Newport, W. 581
*Robinson, Peter D. (b. 1949), D.U.P., Belfast, E. 7,989
Roe, Mrs. Marion A. (b. 1936), C., Broxbourne 17,466
Rogers, Allan R. (b. 1932), Lab., Rhondda . 21,370
*Rooker, Jeffrey W. (b. 1941), Lab., Birmingham, Perry Bar 7,402
*Ross, Ernest (b. 1942), Lab., Dundee, W. .. 10,150
*Ross, Stephen S. (b. 1926), L./All., Isle of Wight 3,503
*Ross, William (b. 1936), O.U.P., East Londonderry 7,262
*Rossi, Sir Hugh A. L. (b. 1927), C., Hornsey and Wood Green 3,899
*Rost, Peter L. (b. 1930), C., Erewash 11,319
Rowe, Andrew (b. 1935), C., Mid Kent 12,543
*Rowlands, Edward (b. 1940), Lab., Merthyr Tydfil and Rhymney 22,730
*Rumbold, Mrs. Angela C. R. (b. 1932), C., Mitcham and Morden 6,451
Ryder, Richard A. (b. 1949), C., Norfolk, Mid 15,515
*Ryman, John (b. 1931), Lab., Blyth Valley 3,243
Sackville, Hon. Thomas G. (b. 1950), C., Bolton, W. 7,152
*Sainsbury, Hon. Timothy A. D. (b. 1932), C., Hove 17,219
*St. John-Stevas, Rt. Hon. Norman A. F. (b. 1929), C., Chelmsford 378
Sayeed, Jonathan (b. 1948), C., Bristol, E. . 1,789
*Scott, Nicholas P. (b. 1933), C., Chelsea ... 12,021
Sedgemore, Brian C. J. (b. 1937), Lab., Hackney, S. and Shoreditch 7,691
*Shaw, J. Giles D. (b. 1931), C., Pudsey 5,314
*Shaw, Sir Michael N. (b. 1920), C., Scarborough 13,929
*Sheerman, Barry J. (b. 1940), Lab., Huddersfield 3,955

	Maj.
*Weetch, Kenneth T. (*b.* 1933), *Lab., Ipswich*	1,077
*Wells, Sir John J. (*b.* 1925), *C., Maidstone* .	7,226
*Wells, P. Bowen (*b.* 1935), *C., Hertford and Stortford*	12,929
*Welsh, Michael C. (*b.* 1926), *Lab., Doncaster, N.*	12,711
*Wheeler, John D. (*b.* 1940), *C., Westminster, N.*	1,710
*White, James (*b.* 1922), *Lab., Glasgow, Pollok*	11,532
Whitfield, John (*b.* 1941), *C., Dewsbury* ...	2,086
*Whitney, Raymond W. (*b.* 1930), *C., Wycombe*	13,197
*Wiggin, A. W. (Jerry) (*b.* 1937), *C., Weston-Super-Mare*	9,491
*Wigley, Dafydd W. (*b.* 1944), *P.C., Caernarfon*	10,989
*Wilkinson, John A. D. (*b.* 1940), *C., Ruislip-Northwood*	12,982
*Williams, Rt. Hon. Alan J. (*b.* 1930), *Lab., Swansea, W.*	2,350
*Wilson, R. Gordon (*b.* 1938), *S.N.P., Dundee, E.*	5,016

	Maj.
*Winnick, David J. (*b.* 1933), *Lab., Walsall, N.*	2,824
Winterton, Mrs. J. Ann (*b.* 1941), *C., Congleton*	8,459
*Winterton, Nicholas R. (*b.* 1938), *C., Macclesfield*	20,679
*Wolfson, Geoffrey M. (*b.* 1934), *C., Sevenoaks*	15,706
Wood, Timothy J. R. (*b.* 1940), *C., Stevenage*	1,755
*Woodall, Alec (*b.* 1918), *Lab., Hemsworth* .	14,190
Woodcock, Michael (*b.* 1943), *C., Ellesmere Port and Neston*	7,087
*Wrigglesworth, Ian W. (*b.* 1939), *S.D.P./All., Stockton, S.*	102
Yeo, Timothy S. K. (*b.* 1945), *C., Suffolk, S.*	11,269
*Young, David W. (*b.* 1930), *Lab., Bolton, S.E.*	8,753
*Young, Sir George S. K., Bt. (*b.* 1941), *C., Ealing, Acton*	10,092
*Younger, Rt. Hon. George K. H. (*b.* 1931), *C., Ayr*	7,987

SMALL MAJORITIES

The following M.P.s were returned in June 1983 with majorities of fewer than 500 votes.

D. H. Spencer (*C., Leicester, S.*)	7
J. K. Hargreaves (*C., Hyndburn*)	21
R. H. Lewis (*Lab., Carlisle*)	71
J. J. Hanley (*C., Richmond and Barnes*)	74
Rev. R. T. W. McCrea (*D.U.P., Ulster, Mid*)	78
I. W. Wrigglesworth (*S.D.P./All., Stockton, S.*)	102
T. W. Torney (*Lab., Bradford, S.*)	110
Mrs. R. Short (*Lab., Wolverhampton, N.E.*)	214
R. Corbett (*Lab., Birmingham, Erdington*)	231
Hon. Mrs. G. P. Dunwoody (*Lab., Crewe and Nantwich*)	290
P. C. Snape (*Lab., West Bromwich, E.*)	298
Rt. Hon. W. Harrison (*Lab., Wakefield*)	360
R. G. J. Ottaway (*C., Nottingham, N.*)	362
C. R. Smith (*Lab., Islington, S. and Finsbury*) .	363
R. Beggs (*O.U.P., Antrim, E.*)	367
Rt. Hon. N. A. F. St. John Stevas (*C., Chelmsford*)	378
Mrs. M. M. Beckett (*Lab., Derby, S.*)	421
J. Marek (*Lab., Wrexham*)	424
Lord James Douglas-Hamilton (*C., Edinburgh, W.*)	498

THE PRINCIPAL PARTIES IN PARLIAMENT (1931–1983)

General Election	Conservative	Liberal	Labour
1931	471	72 (a)	65 (b)
1935	387	54 (c)	166 (d)
1945	189	25 (e)	396 (f)
1950	298 (g)	9	315 (h)
1951	320 (i)	6	296 (h)
1955	344 (i)	6	277 (j)
1959	365 (i)	6	258 (k)
1964	303 (i)	9	317
1966	253 (i)	12	363 (l)
1970	330 (m)	6	287 (n)
1974 (February)	296	14	301 (o)
1974 (October)	276	13	319 (p)
1979	339	11	268 (q)
1983	397	23 (r)	209 (s)

NOTES.—(a) Liberal National 35 (Simon); Liberal 33 (Samuel); 4 (Lloyd George). (b) National Labour 13 (MacDonald); Labour 52 (Henderson). (c) Liberal National 33; Liberal 21. (d) National Labour 8; Labour 154; I.L.P. 4. (e) Liberal National 13; Liberal

12. (f) Labour 393; I.L.P. 3. (g) Incl. Nat. Liberal. (h) Irish Nationalists (2) and Speaker make total of 625. (i) Including associates. (j) Sinn Fein (2) and Speaker make total of 630. (k) Independent (1) makes total of 630. (l) Republican Labour (1) makes total of 630. (m) Including Ulster Unionists. (n) Scottish Nationalists (1); Independent (5) and Speaker make total of 630. (o) United Ulster Unionist Council (11), Scottish Nationalists (7), Plaid Cymru (2); Social Democratic and Labour Party (1); Social Democrat (1); Independent Labour (1); and Speaker make total of 635. (p) Scottish Nationalists (11); United Ulster Unionist (10); Plaid Cymru (3); Social Democratic and Labour Party (1); Independent (1) and Speaker make a total of 635. (q) Ulster Unionist (5); Democratic Unionist (3); Plaid Cymru (2); Scottish Nationalists (2); Social Democratic and Labour (1); United Ulster Unionist (1); Independent (2) and Speaker make a total of 635. (r) Liberal 17; S.D.P. 6. (s) Official Unionist (11); Democratic Unionist (3); Scottish Nationalists (2); Plaid Cymru (2); Ulster Popular Unionist (1); Social Democratic and Labour Party (1) and Provisional Sinn Fein (1) make a total of 650.

THE HOUSE OF COMMONS BY CONSTITUENCIES, JUNE 1983

The figures following the name of the Constituency denote the total number of *Electors* in the Parliamentary Division at the General Election of June 1983.

ABBREVIATIONS — *C.* = Conservative; *D.U.P.* = Democratic Unionist Party; *Ind.* = Independent; *L./All. S.D.P./ All.* = Liberal and Social Democratic Alliance; *Lab.* = Labour; *O.U.P.* = Official Unionist Party; *P.C.* = Plaid Cymru; *S.D.L.P.* = Social Democratic and Labour Party; *S.F.* = Sinn Fein; *S.N.P.* = Scottish National Party; *U.P.U.P* = Ulster Popular Unionist Party.

A.B. = Assassin's Bullet; *A.C.I.E.* = Against Cuts In Education; *A.C.M.* = Anti-Common Market; *A.Corr.* = Anti-Corruption; *All.* = Alliance (N.I.); *A.V.* = Anti-Vivisection; *B.B.H.* = Belgrano, Blood, Hunger; *B.E.L.L.S.* = Ban Every Licensing Law Society; *B.N.P.* = British National Party; *C.A.C.M.* = Conservative Against Common Market; *C.B.W.U.* = Campaign for Black and White Unity; *C.D.* = Christian Democrat; *C.F.C.P.* = Conservative For Capital Punishment; *C.M.P.* = Common Market Party; *Com.* = Community; *Comm.* = Communist; *Corn Nat.* = Cornish Nationalist; *C.U.I.* = Council for United Ireland; *Eco.* = Ecology; *Eth. Min.* = Ethnic Minority; *F.A.M.P.* = Freddie's Alternative Medicine Party; *F.D.P.* = Fancy Dress Party; *F.P.* = Feudal Party; *F.W.D.* = Freedom from World Domination; *I.F.P.* = Islington and Finsbury Party; *Ind. Pow.* = Independent Powellite; *I.N.P.* = Irish National Party; *I.W.R.P.* = Isle of White Resident's Party; *J.A.H.C.* = Jesus And His Cross; *J.D.F.* = Justice for Divorced Fathers; *L.A.O.* = Law And Order; *L.I.L.* = Local Independent Labour; *L.M.* = Loony Monster; *Loony Soc.* = Loony Society; *L.T.U.* = Labour and Trade Union; *M.D.P.* = Modern Democratic Party; *M.K.* = Mebyon Kernow; *M.P.P.* = Multiracial Political Party; *N.A.* = Noise Abatement; *Nat. Lab.* = National Labour Party; *N.F.* = National Front; *O.N.C.* = One Nation Conservative; *P.A.L.* = Party of Associates with Licensees; *P.F.A.* = Prosperity For All; *P.R.* = Proportional Representation; *R.A.P.* = Radical and Anti-Parliamentarian; *R.C.C.P.* = Restoration of Capital and Corporal Punishment; *Rev. Comm.* = Revolutionary Communist; *R.H.C.P.* = Reintroduction of Hanging and Corporal Punishment; *S.A.C.A.* = Servicemen's and Citizen's Association; *S.B.I.L.P.* = Southport Back In Lancashire Party; *S.D.B.P.* = Stop Deportation of Black People; *S.E.E.* = Spare the Earth Ecology; *S.P.G.B.* = Socialist Party of Great Britain; *T.E.F.* = Traditional English Food; *T.V.C.A.B.L.* = Tactically Vote Conservative Annihilate Bennites Livingstoneites; *U.P.* = Unemployed Party; *W.C.P.P.P.* = Workers' Charter with Pensioners' Political Power; *W.F.L.O.E.* = Women For Life On Earth; *W.P.* = Workers' Party; *W.P.W.S.* = Workers' Party for a Workers' State; *W.Reg.* = Wessex Regionalist; *Wrld Gv.* = World Government; *W.R.P.* = Workers' Revolutionary Party.

An asterisk * denotes membership of the last House. In the seats where there has been either a minor change or no change at all to the boundary, the 1979 majorities are shown below the 1983 result.

ENGLAND

Aldershot (Hants)
E. 77,593

*J. M. G. Critchley, C.		31,288
N. Westbrook, L/All.		19,070
A. Crawford, Lab.		6,070
C. maj.		12,218

Aldridge-Brownhills
(W. Midlands)
E. 60,803

*R. C. S. Shepherd C.		24,148
R. T. Burford, Lab.		11,864
P. Gunn, S.D.P./All.		11,599
C. maj.		12,284

Altrincham and Sale
(Gtr. Manchester)
E. 65,984

*W. F. Montgomery C.		25,321
B. Clancy, L/All.		14,410
A. Erwin, Lab.		7,684
Mrs. C. Marsh, Eco.		629
L. J. Wolstenholme, Ind.		152
C. Maj.		10,911

Amber Valley (Derbys)
E. 66,720

P. A. C. L. Oppenheim, C.		21,502
D. M. Bookbinder, Lab.		18,184
B. Johnson, L/All.		10,989
P. Griffiths, Ind.		856
C. maj.		3,318

Arundel (W. Sussex)
E. 74,849

*R. M. Marshall, C.		31,096
J. Walsh, L/All.		15,391
G. C. Rees, Lab.		4,302
J. Wadman, C.F.C.P.		1,399
C. maj.		15,705

Ashfield (Notts)
E. 68,791

*D. F. Haynes, Lab.		21,859
R. Seligman, C.		15,772
Mrs. F. Stein, L/All.		13,812
Lab. maj.		6,087

Ashford (Kent)
E. 65,442

*H. K. Speed, R.D., C.		27,230
Mrs. J. Hawkes, S.D.P./All.		13,319
P. Lewis, Lab.		6,167
Dr. C. A. Porter, Eco.		569
J. W. King, Nat. Lab.		456
R. E. Lockwood, B.N.P.		195
C. maj.		13,911
(May '79, C. maj. 13,638)		

Ashton-under-Lyne
(Gtr. Manchester)
E. 58,963

*Rt. Hon. R. E. Sheldon, Lab.		20,987
R. Spring, C.		13,290
J. Adler, S.D.P./All.		7,521
D. Hallsworth, Rev. Comm.		407
Lab. maj.		7,697
(May '79, Lab. maj. 8,379)		

Aylesbury (Bucks)
E. 72,792

*Rt. Hon. T. H. F. Raison, C.		30,230
M. Soole, S.D.P./All.		15,310
M. P. Moran, Lab.		6,364
T. Chapman, Ind.		166
C. maj.		14,920

Banbury (Oxon)
E. 65,324

A. B. Baldry, C.		26,225
K. Fitchett, S.D.P./All.		13,200
J. B. Hodgson, Lab.		9,343
D. N. Brough, Loony Soc.		383
C. maj.		13,025

Barking (Gtr. London)
E. 52,362

*Ms. J. Richardson, Lab.		14,415
H. Summerson, C.		10,389
J. Gibb, L/All.		8,770
I. Newport, N.F.		646
Lab. maj.		4,026

Barnsley (S. Yorks)

CENTRAL E. 55,115

*Rt. Hon. R. Mason, Lab.		21,847
H. Oldfield, C.		7,674
Rev. G. Reid, L./All.		7,011
Lab. maj.		14,173

EAST E. 53,611

T. Patchett, Lab.		23,905
P. Tomlinson, L./All.		6,413
G. England, C.		5,749
Lab. maj.		17,492

WEST AND PENISTONE E. 60,648

*A. McKay, Lab.		22,560
T. Hartley, C.		12,218
J. Evans, S.D.P./All.		9,624
Lab. maj.		10,342

Barrow and Furness (Cumbria)
E. 67,896

C. S. Franks, C.		22,284
*Rt. Hon. A. E. Booth, Lab.		17,707
D. Cottier, S.D.P./All.		11,079
C. maj.		4,577

Basildon (Essex)
E. 69,604

D. A. A. Amess, C.	......	17,516
J. G. H. Fullbrook, *Lab.*	..	16,137
Miss S. Slipman, *S.D.P./*		
All.	....	11,634
C. maj.	....	1,379

Basingstoke (Hants)
E. 71,975

A. R. F. Hunter, C.	....	28,381
*G. E. Hudson Davies,		
S.D.P./All.	....	15,931
J. McAllister, *Lab.*	......	10,646
I. Wilson, *B.N.P.*	....	344
C. maj.	....	12,450

Bassetlaw (Notts)
E. 65,721

*J. W. Ashton, *Lab.*	....	22,231
M. Cleasby, *C.*	....	18,400
B. Withnall, *S.D.P./All.*	..	8,124
Lab. maj.	....	3,831

Bath (Avon)
E. 64,325

*C. F. Patten, C.	....	22,544
J. M. Dean, *S.D.P./All.*	...	17,240
A. J. Pott, *Lab.*	....	7,259
D. Grimes, *Eco.*	....	441
R. S. Wardle, *Prog. L.*	...	319
G. S. Young, *Wrld. Gv.*	...	67
C. maj.	....	5,304
(May '79, C. maj. 9,112)		

Batley and Spen (W. Yorks)
E. 73,798

Mrs. E. J. Peacock, C.	....	21,433
*K. J. Woolmer, *Lab.*	.....	20,563
D. S. Woollery, *S.D.P./All.*	11,678
R. Lord, *Eco.*	....	493
C. maj.	....	870

Battersea (Gtr. London)
E. 65,938

*A. Dubs, *Lab.*	....	19,248
R. Allason, *C.*	....	15,972
M. Harris, *S.D.P./All.*	....	7,675
M. J. Salt, *N.F.*	....	539
Mrs. S. Wilmington, *Eco.*	.	377
T. Jackson, *C.B.W.U.*	....	86
Mrs. K. Purie-Harwell,		
Com.	....	22
Lab. maj.	....	3,276

Beaconsfield (Bucks)
E. 66,168

*T. J. Smith, C.	....	30,552
D. Ive, *L./All.*	....	12,252
J. S. Smith, *Lab.*	....	5,107
C. maj.	....	18,300

Beckenham (Gtr. London)
E. 58,719

*Sir P. C. Goodhart, C.	.....	23,606
Mrs. C. Forrest, *L./All.*	...	10,936
J. P. Dowd, *Lab.*	....	6,386
G. W. Younger, *B.N.P.*	...	203
C. maj.	....	12,670
(May '79, C. maj. 13,751)		

Bedfordshire

MID. *E.* 75,558

*N. W. Lyell, q.c., C.	......	33,042
Mrs. M. Howes, *L./All.*	...	15,661
J. Tizard, *Lab.*	....	9,420
C. maj.	....	17,381

NORTH *E.* 71,491

*T. H. H. Skeet, C.	....	27,969
Miss P. Healy, *Lab.*	......	11,323
N. J. Hughes, *Ind.*	......	344
C. maj.	....	13,849

SOUTH WEST *E.* 76,298

*W. D. Madel, C.	....	31,767
R. Byfield, *S.D.P./All.*	...	16,036
W. Cochrane, *Lab.*	....	9,899
C. maj.	....	15,731

Berwick-upon-Tweed (Nthmb)
E. 53,585

*A. J. Beith, *L./All.*	....	21,958
J. Brazier, *C.*	....	13,743
Mrs. V. Baird, *Lab.*	......	5,975
L./All. maj.	....	8,215

Bethnal Green and Stepney
(Gtr. London)
E. 55,333

*Rt. Hon. P. D. Shore, *Lab.*	15,740
S. Charters, *L./All.*	......	9,382
D. Argyropulo, *C.*	....	4,323
V. J. Clark, *N.F.*	....	800
J. Rees, *Comm.*	....	243
B. Chadhuri, *Ind.*	....	214
P. Mahoney, *R.A.P.*	......	136
Lab. maj.	....	6,358

Beverley (Humberside)
E. 75,813

*Sir P. H. B. Wall, M.C.,		
V.R.D., C.	....	31,233
M. Pitts, *L./All.*	....	17,364
E. M. Morley, *Lab.*	....	6,921
C. maj.	....	13,869

Bexhill and Battle
(E. Sussex)
E. 61,785

C. F. Wardle, *C.*	....	30,329
P. Smith, *L./All.*	....	10,583
I. Pearson, *Lab.*	....	3,587
Miss A. Rix, *Eco.*	....	538
C. maj.	....	19,746

Bexleyheath
(Gtr. London)
E. 59,263

*C. D. Townsend, C.	......	23,411
B. Standen, *L./All.*	....	13,153
A. Erlam, *Lab.*	....	7,560
C. maj.	....	10,258

Billericay (Essex)
E. 74,779

*K. H. Proctor, C.	....	29,635
E. Bonner, *L./All.*	....	15,020
S. Sewell, *Lab.*	....	10,528
C. maj.	....	14,615

Birkenhead (Merseyside)
E. 67,293

*F. Field, *Lab.*	....	23,249
T. Peet, *C.*	....	13,535
G. Lindsay, *L./All.*	......	9,782
Miss H. Clarke, *Eco.*	.....	337
Lab. maj.	....	9,714

Birmingham (W. Midlands)

EDGBASTON *E.* 55,063

*Mrs. J. C. J. Knight, M.B.E.,		
C.	....	19,585
J. Binns, *S.D.P./All.*	.....	8,167
P. A. Bilson, *Lab.*	....	7,647
J. Hurdley, *Eco.*	....	516
S. T. Hardwick, *Ind. C.*	...	293
Ms. P. A. Davies, *Comm.*	..	169
Miss. D. C. Howlett,		
J.A.H.C.	....	97
C. maj.	....	11,418

ERDINGTON *E.* 56,019

R. Corbett, *Lab.*	....	14,930
D. Moylan, *C.*	....	14,699
C. Barber, *S.D.P./All.*	....	7,915
Lab. maj.	....	231

HALL GREEN *E.* 61,023

*Sir R. E. Eyre, C.	....	21,142
M. H. Willis, *Lab.*	....	11,769
J. Hemming, *L./All.*	......	10,175
C. maj.	....	9,373

HODGE HILL *E.* 61,234

*T. A. G. Davis, *Lab.*	......	19,692
P. Roe, *C.*	....	14,600
G. A. Gospill, *L./All.*	.....	6,557
N. Tomkinson, *N.F.*	......	529
Lab. maj.	....	5,092

LADYWOOD *E.* 60,441

Ms. C. Short, *Lab.*	....	19,278
Mrs. P. Le Hunte, *C.*	......	10,248
K. Hardeman, *L./All.*	.....	7,758
B. Bakhtaura, *S.D.B.P.*	...	355
R. W. Atkinson, *W.R.P.*	...	198
Lab. maj.	....	9,030

NORTHFIELD *E.* 74,326

R. D. King, *C.*	....	22,596
*J. Spellar, *Lab.*	....	19,836
D. Webb, *L./All.*	....	10,045
P. Sheppard, *Comm.*	.....	420
C. maj.	....	2,760

PERRY BARR *E.* 74,371

*J. W. Rooker, *Lab.*	....	27,061
M. D. Portillo, *C.*	....	19,659
C. E. G. Williams, *L./All.*	.	4,773
Lab. maj.	....	7,402

SELLY OAK *E.* 71,671

*A. M. Beaumont-Dark, C.		23,008
J. Turner, *Lab.*	....	17,612
K. Wheldall, *S.D.P./All.*	..	10,613
C. maj.	....	5,396

SMALL HEATH *E.* 59,376

*Rt. Hon. D. H. Howell,		
Lab.	....	22,874
P. Nischal, *C.*	....	7,622
A. Bostock, *S.D.P./All.*	...	5,722
Lab. maj.	....	15,252

SPARKBROOK E. 53,612
*Rt. Hon. R. S. G. Hattersley,
  Lab. 19,757
P. Douglas-Osborn, C. ... 9,209
O. S. Parmar, S.D.P./All. 3,416
Ms. F. Eden, Rev. Comm. 305
C. S. A. Chinn, Ind. 281
  Lab. maj. 10,548

YARDLEY E. 57,707
*A. D. G. Bevan, C. 17,986
R. D. Godsiff, Lab. 15,121
D. Bennett, S.D.P./All. ... 8,109
R. Jones, N.F. 415
  C. maj. 2,865

Bishop Auckland (Durham)
E. 71,142
*D. Foster, Lab. 22,750
B. Legg, C. 18,444
A. Collinge, L./All. 10,070
  Lab. maj. 4,306

Blaby (Leics)
E. 71,930
*Rt. Hon. N. Lawson, C. ... 32,689
R. Lustig, L./All. 15,573
C. Wrigley, Lab. 6,838
P. Gegan, N.F. 568
  C. maj. 17,116
  (May '79, C. maj. 20,640)

Blackburn (Lancs)
E. 76,078
*J. W. Straw, Lab. 25,400
G. Mather, C. 22,345
E. Fairbrother, S.D.P./All. 8,174
D. A. Riley, N.F. 864
  Lab. maj. 3,055

Blackpool (Lancs)
NORTH E. 57,576
*N. A. Miscampbell, Q.C.,
  C. 20,592
C. Heyworth, L./All. 10,440
M. J. Hindley, Lab. 8,730
A. S. Hanson, N.F. 514
  C. maj. 10,152
  (May '79, C. maj. 10,229)

SOUTH E. 56,201
*Rt. Hon. Sir P. A. R. Blaker,
  C. 19,852
F. J. Jackson, Lab. 9,714
A. Cox, S.D.P./All. 9,417
W. Smith, N.F. 263
  C. maj. 10,138
  (May '79, C. maj. 8,848)

Blaydon (Tyne & Wear)
E. 65,481
*J. D. McWilliam, Lab. ... 21,285
A. Williams, C. 14,063
M. Carr, S.D.P./All. 12,607
  Lab. maj. 7,222

Blyth Valley (Nthmb)
E. 57,639
*J. Ryman, Lab. 16,583
Ms. R. Brownlow, S.D.P./
  All. 13,340
A. Hargreaves, C. 11,657
S. Robinson, Ind. 406
  Lab. maj. 3,243

Bolsover (Derbys)
E. 64,769
*D. E. Skinner, Lab. 26,514
S. Roberts, C. 12,666
S. Reddish, S.D.P./All. ... 7,886
  Lab. maj. 13,848

Bolton (Gtr. Manchester)
NORTH EAST E. 58,918
P. G. Thurnham, C. 19,632
*Mrs. W. A. Taylor, Lab. ... 17,189
J. Alcock, S.D.P./All. 8,311
D. P. Ball, B.N.P. 186
T. L. Keen, Ind. 104
  C. maj. 2,443

SOUTH EAST E. 67,527
*D. W. Young, Lab. 23,984
J. Walsh, C. 15,231
Mrs. M. Rothwell, L./All. . 10,157
T. L. Keen, P.R. 296
  Lab. maj. 8,753

WEST E. 67,354
Hon. T. G. Sackville, C. ... 23,731
D. Green, Lab. 16,579
R. Baker, S.D.P./All. 12,321
  C. maj. 7,152

Boothferry (Humberside)
E. 72,370
*Sir P. E. O. Bryan, D.S.O.,
  M.C., C. 30,536
A. Ellis, L./All. 13,116
T. Geraghty, Lab. 9,271
  C. maj. 17,420

Bootle (Merseyside)
E. 75,354
*A. Roberts, Lab. 27,282
R. Watson, C. 12,143
J. Wall, S.D.P./All. 12,068
  Lab. maj. 15,139

Bosworth (Leics)
E. 73,097
*Rt. Hon. A. C. Butler, C. .. 31,663
M. Fox, S.D.P./All. 14,369
D. J. M. Janner, Lab. 11,120
  C. maj. 17,294

Bournemouth (Dorset)
EAST E. 70,711
*D. A. Atkinson, C. 25,176
Dr. J. Millward, L./All. ... 13,760
M. J. Shutler, Lab. 4,026
Mrs. M. Hogarth, Ind. C. . 3,644
T. Dykes, Eco. 273
J. Stooks, L.M. 225
  C. maj. 11,416

WEST E. 72,297
J. V. Butterfill, C. 28,466
M. James, L./All. 15,135
K. Horrocks, Lab. 6,243
J. H. Morse, B.N.P. 180
  C. maj. 13,331

Bow and Poplar (Gtr. London)
E. 57,768
*I. Mikardo, Lab. 15,878
E. Flounders, L./All. 10,017
S. Eyres, C. 5,129
Miss S. Bartlett, N.F. 596
A. J. Snooks, Lab. Ind. ... 266
K. R. Scotcher, W.R.P. ... 117
  Lab. maj. 5,861

Bradford (W. Yorks)
NORTH E. 66,439
G. J. Lawler, C. 16,094
C. P. Wall, Lab. 14,492
P. Birkby, S.D.P./All. 11,962
*B. T. Ford, Ind. Lab. 4,018
A. Howarth, Loony Soc. .. 194
M. Easter, B.N.P. 193
  1,602

SOUTH E. 69,588
*T. W. Torney, Lab. 18,542
G. T. Hall, C. 18,432
D. A. Pearl, S.D.P./All. ... 12,143
R. Adsett, Eco. 308
  Lab. maj. 110

WEST E. 71,296
M. F. Madden, Lab. 19,499
S. Day, C. 16,162
*E. Lyons, S.D.P./All. 13,301
Ms. B. Slaughter, W.R.P. . 139
  Lab. maj. 3,337

Braintree (Essex)
E. 73,548
*A. H. Newton, O.B.E., C. ... 29,462
I. Bing, S.D.P./All. 16,021
Mrs. J. M. Dyson, Lab. ... 10,551
  C. maj. 13,441
  (May '79, C. maj. 12,518)

Brent (Gtr. London)
EAST E. 61,489
*Rt. Hon. R. Freeson, Lab. . 18,363
R. Lacey, C. 13,529
M. Rosen, S.D.P./All. 6,598
J. O'Leary, I.N.P. 289
G. Downing, W.R.P. 222
K. Radclyffe, Ind. 88
  Lab. maj. 4,834

NORTH E. 62,679
*Dr. R. R. Boyson, C. 24,842
Mrs. S. Jackson, Lab. 10,191
T. Mann, S.D.P./All. 9,082
  C. maj. 14,651

SOUTH E. 62,783
*L. A. Pavitt, Lab. 21,259
C. Smedley, C. 10,740
R. Billins, L./All. 7,557
R. Sawh, Eth. Min. 356
  Lab. maj. 10,519

Brentford and Isleworth
(Gtr. London)
E. 69,170

*B. J. Hayhoe, C.		24,515
P. Rowlands, Lab.		15,128
M. Wilks, S.D.P./All.		11,438
P. Andrews, N.F.		427
R. Simmerson, C.A.C.M.		179
C. maj.		9,387

(May '79, C. maj. 4,994)

Brentwood and Ongar (Essex)
E. 65,976

*R. A. McCrindle, C.		29,484
N. Amor, L./All.		15,282
J. W. Orpe, Lab.		5,739
C. maj.		14,202

Bridgwater (Somerset)
E. 64,224

*Rt. Hon. T. J. King, C.		25,107
Mrs. R. Farley, S.D.P./All.		14,410
A. J. May, Lab.		8,524
C. maj.		10,697

Bridlington (Humberside)
E. 76,718

*J. E. Townend, C.		31,284
Mrs. E. Martin, S.D.P./All.		14,675
M. Craven, Lab.		7,370
S. Tooke, Eco.		803
C. maj.		16,609

Brigg and Cleethorpes
(Humberside)
E. 77,471

*M. R. Brown, C.		28,893
G. Wigginton, L./All.		16,704
J. D. Hough, Lab.		11,404
C. maj.		12,189

Brighton (E. Sussex)
KEMPTOWN E. 60,877

*A. Bowden, M.B.E., C.		22,265
R. Fitch, Lab.		12,887
D. T. Burke, S.D.P./All.		8,098
E. Budden, N.F.		290
C. maj.		9,378

PAVILION E. 59,761

*Rt. Hon. H. J. Amery, C.		21,323
M. Neves, S.D.P./All.		10,191
H. Spillman, Lab.		9,879
C. maj.		11,132

Bristol (Avon)
EAST E. 66,296

J. Sayeed, C.		19,844
*Rt. Hon. A. N. W. Benn, Lab.		18,055
P. Tyrer, L./All.		10,404
E. Andrews, N.F.		343
G. Dorey, Eco.		311
C. maj.		1,789

NORTH WEST E. 72,996

M. C. Stern, C.		24,617
Dr. Sarah Palmer, Lab.		18,290
Mrs. H. Long, S.D.P./All.		13,228
C. maj.		6,327

SOUTH E. 72,067

*Rt. Hon. M. F. L. Cocks, Lab.		21,824
A. Gammell, C.		17,405
D. Stanbury, S.D.P./All.		9,674
G. Collard, Eco.		352
A. Chester, Comm.		224
Mrs. L. Byrne, W.R.P.		113
Lab. maj.		4,419

WEST E. 73,190

*Hon. W. A. Waldegrave, C.		25,400
G. Ferguson, L./All.		15,222
Mrs. P. Tatlow, Lab.		10,094
J. Scott, Eco.		872
S. Boyle, Ind.		142
C. maj.		10,178

Bromsgrove (H & W)
E. 66,146

*H. D. Miller, C.		27,911
A. J. Milligan, S.D.P./All.		10,736
G. Titley, Lab.		10,280
J. Churchman, Eco.		716
C. maj.		17,175

Broxbourne (Herts)
E. 67,387

Mrs. M. A. Roe, C.		29,328
B. Pollock, L./All.		11,862
M. J. Stears, Lab.		8,159
J. R. Smith, B.N.P.		502
C. maj.		17,466

Broxtowe (Notts)
E. 69,760

*J. T. Lester, C.		28,522
K. Melton, L./All.		13,444
M. Warner, Lab.		11,368
C. maj.		15,078

Buckingham
E. 62,758

G. G. H. Walden, C.M.G., C.		27,552
R. Ryder, L./All.		13,584
M. Groucutt, Lab.		7,272
C. maj.		13,968

Burnley (Lancs)
E. 66,542

P. L. Pike, Lab.		20,178
I. Bruce, C.		19,408
M. Steed, L./All.		11,195
Lab. maj.		770

Burton (Staffs)
E. 71,849

*I. J. Lawrence, Q.C., C.		27,874
R. E. G. Slater, Lab.		16,227
Mrs. J. Garner, L./All.		10,420
C. maj.		11,647

(May '79, C. maj. 9,801)

Bury (Gtr. Manchester)
NORTH E. 66,065

A. J. H. Burt, C.		23,923
*F. R. White, Lab.		21,131
Mrs. E. Wilson, L./All.		7,550
C. maj.		2,792

SOUTH E. 64,827

D. A. G. Sumberg, C.		21,718
D. Boden, Lab.		17,998
K. Evans, S.D.P./All.		9,628
C. maj.		3,720

Bury St. Edmunds (Suffolk)
E. 72,875

*E. W. Griffiths, C.		31,081
Sir R. Harland, S.D.P./All.		14,959
W. Moszczynski, Lab.		6,666
C. maj.		16,122

Calder Valley (W. Yorks)
E. 71,309

*D. Thompson, C.		24,439
D. Shutt, L./All.		16,440
Ms. A. Holmes, Lab.		15,108
C. maj.		7,999

Cambridge
E. 67,018

*R. V. R. Rhodes James, C.		20,931
M. Oakeshott, S.D.P./All.		14,963
Ms. J. Jones, Lab.		14,240
J. Dougrez-Lewis, Loony Soc.		286
C. maj.		5,968

Cambridgeshire
NORTH EAST E. 69,894

*C. R. Freud, L./All.		26,936
N. Duval, C.		21,741
R. J. Harris, Lab.		4,625
L./All. maj.		5,195

SOUTH EAST E. 66,885

*Rt. Hon. F. L. Pym, M.C., C.		28,555
C. Slee, S.D.P./All.		14,791
Ms. M. Jackson, Lab.		6,261
C. maj.		13,764

SOUTH WEST E. 76,228

*Sir J. A. Grant, C.		32,521
D. Nicholls, L./All.		18,654
J. Gluza, Lab.		6,703
C. maj.		13,867

Cannock and Burntwood (Staffs)
E. 66,188

J. G. D. Howarth, C.		20,976
*G. E. Roberts, Lab.		18,931
J. W. Withnall, S.D.P./All.		11,336
C. maj.		2,045

Canterbury (Kent)
E. 73,464

*D. L. Crouch, C.		29,029
J. Purchese, L./All.		13,287
Ms. J. Gould, Lab.		7,906
D. Conder, Eco.		962
J. White, Ind.		226
C. maj.		15,742

Carlisle (Cumbria)
E. 54,515

*R. H. Lewis, Lab.		15,618
R. Sowler, C.		15,547
R. Hunt, S.D.P./All.		10,471
Lab. maj.		71

(May '79, Lab. maj. 4,556)

Carshalton and Wallington
(Gtr. London)
E. 68,682

*F. N. Forman, C.	25,396
J. Ensor, S.D.P./All.	14,641
Mrs. J. Baker, Lab.	8,655
R. Steel, Eco.	784
C. maj.	10,755
(May '79, C. maj. 10,371)	

Castle Point (Essex)
E. 64,023

*Sir B. R. Braine, C.	26,730
Ms. A. Bastow, S.D.P./All.	11,313
Ms. L. Cunningham, Lab.	7,621
C. maj.	15,417

Cheadle
(Gtr. Manchester)
E. 66,474

*T. Normanton, T.D., C.	28,452
P. Clark, L./All.	19,072
K. Parker, Lab.	3,553
C. maj.	9,380

Chelmsford (Essex)
E. 78,849

*Rt. Hon. N. A. F. St. John-Stevas, C.	29,824
S. Mole, L./All.	29,446
C. Playford, Lab.	3,208
P. D. P. Waite, Ind.	127
C. maj.	378

Chelsea (Gtr. London)
E. 53,864

*N. P. Scott, M.B.E., C.	19,122
J. Fryer, L./All.	7,101
N. Palmer, Lab.	3,876
Ms. A. Fielding, Ind.	139
C. maj.	12,021
(May '79, C. maj. 15,690)	

Cheltenham (Glos.)
E. 76,068

*C. G. Irving, C.	29,187
R. Holme, L./All.	23,669
Mrs. J. M. James, Lab.	4,390
D. Swindley, Eco.	479
C. maj.	5,518

Chertsey and Walton (Surrey)
E. 70,210

*G. E. Pattie, C.	29,679
R. de St. Croix, S.D.P./All.	13,980
D. Green, Lab.	6,902
F. Barrett, F.A.M.P.	318
C. maj.	15,699
(May '79, C. maj. 12,024)	

Chesham and Amersham
(Bucks)
E. 69,980

*Rt. Hon. Sir I. H. J. L. Gilmour, BT., C.	32,435
R. Bradnock, L./All.	16,556
C. Duncan, Lab.	4,150
C. maj.	15,879

Chesterfield (Derbys)
E. 68,486

*Rt. Hon. E. G. Varley, Lab.	23,881
N. Bourne, C.	16,118
M. Payne, L./All.	9,705
Lab. maj.	7,763
(see by-election on p. 345)	

Chichester (W. Sussex)
E. 77,259

*R. A. Nelson, C.	35,482
H. Gibson, S.D.P./All.	15,365
R. H. Rhodes, Lab.	3,995
J. Sherlock, Eco.	838
C. maj.	20,117
(May '79, C. maj. 23,776)	

Chingford (Gtr. London)
E. 56,228

*Rt. Hon. N. B. Tebbit, C.	22,541
R. Hoskins, L./All.	10,127
W. D. Shepherd, Lab.	7,239
J. Morgan, Eco.	479
B. Cheetham, N.F.	380
J. Neighbour, Ind.	104
S. Barklem, Ind.	34
C. maj.	12,414
(May '79, C. maj. 12,383)	

Chipping Barnet (Gtr. London)
E. 58,423

*S. B. Chapman, C.	23,164
C. Perkin, L./All.	10,771
N. J. M. Smith, Lab.	6,599
E. Parry, Eco.	552
J. Hopkins, Ind.	195
C. maj.	12,393
(May '79, C. maj. 14,007)	

Chislehurst (Gtr. London)
E. 54,567

*R. E. Sims, C.	22,108
P. Lingard, L./All.	10,047
A. H. McDonald, Lab.	7,320
A. Waite, B.N.P.	201
C. maj.	12,061
(Maj. '79, C. maj. 9,765)	

Chorley (Lancs)
E. 72,841

*D. R. Dover, C.	27,861
I. Taylor, Lab.	17,586
P. O'Neill, S.D.P./All.	11,691
A. S. Holgate, Eco.	451
Mrs. E. Rokas, Ind.	114
C. maj.	10,275

Christchurch (Dorset)
E. 65,489

*R. J. Adley, C.	31,722
S. Alexander, S.D.P./All.	11,984
J. R. Mitchell, Lab.	3,590
C. maj.	19,738

Cirencester and Tewkesbury
(Glos)
E. 80,067

*Rt. Hon. N. Ridley, C.	34,282
P. Beckerlegge, L./All.	20,455
T. J. R. Penny, Lab.	5,243
C. maj.	13,827

City of Chester
E. 64,508

*Hon. P. H. Morrison, C.	22,645
D. E. Robertson, Lab.	13,546
A. Stunell, L./All.	11,874
C. maj.	9,099

The City of London and Westminster South
E. 67,773

*Hon. P. L. Brooke, C.	20,754
A. Walker-Smith, L./All.	7,367
S. Jones, Lab.	6,013
R. Shorter, Eco.	419
A. Reeve, N.F.	248
A. Spence, Comm.	161
W. Litvin, Ind.	147
C. maj.	13,387

Colchester (Essex)
NORTH   E. 77,292

*Sir P. A. F. Buck, Q.C., C.	29,921
R. Montgomerie, L./All.	14,873
R. C. Allen, Lab.	10,397
D. Wilkinson, Ind. C.	784
R. Davies, Ind.	510
C. maj.	15,048

SOUTH, AND MALDON   E. 79,582

*Rt. Hon. J. Wakeham, C.	31,296
J. Stevens, S.D.P./All.	19,131
H. J. Barnard, Lab.	7,932
C. maj.	12,165

Colne Valley (W. Yorks)
E. 69,634

*R. S. Wainwright, L./All.	21,139
J. Holt, C.	17,993
A. Williams, Lab.	13,668
T. L. Keen, Ind.	260
L./All. maj.	3,146

Congleton (Cheshire)
E. 63,897

Mrs. J. A. Winterton, C.	23,895
C. Smedley, L./All.	15,436
E. Gill, Lab.	9,783
C. maj.	8,459

Copeland (Cumbria)
E. 54,216

*Dr. J. A. Cunningham, Lab.	18,756
Mrs. V. Wilson, C.	16,919
J. Beasley, S.D.P./All.	6,722
Lab. maj.	1,837
(May '79, Lab. maj. 5,455)	

Corby (Northants)
E. 63,067

W. R. Powell, C.	20,827
*W. D. Homewood, Lab.	17,659
T. G. Whittington, L./All.	9,905
Miss R. Stanning, Eco.	505
C. maj.	3,168

Cornwall
NORTH   E. 66,813

*G. A. Neale, C.	28,146
D. Chambers, L./All.	23,087
J. Hayday, Lab.	2,096
J. C. A. Whetter, Corn. Nat.	364
C. maj.	5,059

SOUTH EAST *E.* 65,166

*R. A. Hicks, *C.*	28,326
D. Blunt, *L./All.*	19,972
A. J. Bebb, *Lab.*	2,507
J. Chadwick, *Eco.*	337
Mrs. J. Dent, *Ind.*	94
C. maj.	8,354

Coventry (W. Midlands)

NORTH EAST *E.* 67,037

*G. M. Park, *Lab.*	22,190
D. Weeks, *C.*	13,415
D. Simmons, *S.D.P./All.*	10,251
R. Prince, *W.R.P.*	342
J. Meacham, *Comm.*	193
Lab. maj.	8,775

NORTH WEST *E.* 52,072

*G. Robinson, *Lab.*	17,239
A. Coombs, *C.*	14,201
W. Talbot, *L./All.*	7,479
Lab. maj.	3,038

SOUTH EAST *E.* 52,538

D. J. Nellist, *Lab.*	15,307
J. Arnold, *C.*	12,625
G. Kilby, *L./All.*	9,323
Lab. maj.	2,682

SOUTH WEST *E.* 65,077

*J. P. Butcher, *C.*	22,223
D. Edwards, *Lab.*	15,776
Mrs. M. Lyle, *S.D.P./All.*	11,174
Mrs. W. Williamson, *Nat. Party*	214
C. maj.	6,447

Crawley (W. Sussex)
E. 70,713

Hon. A. N. W. Soames, *C.*	25,963
L. Allan, *Lab.*	14,149
T. Forester, *S.D.P./All.*	13,900
C. maj.	11,814

Crewe and Nantwich (Cheshire)
E. 71,787

*Hon. Mrs. G. P. Dunwoody, *Lab.*	22,031
P. Rock, *C.*	21,741
J. Pollard, *S.D.P./All.*	9,820
Lab. maj.	290

Crosby (Merseyside)
E. 83,274

*G. M. Thornton, *C.*	30,604
*Mrs. S. V. Williams, *S.D.P./All.*	27,203
R. Waring, *Lab.*	6,611
P. Hussey, *Eco.*	415
C. maj.	3,401

Croydon (Gtr. London)

CENTRAL *E.* 56,531

*J. E. M. Moore, *C.*	20,866
A. S. McKinley, *Lab.*	9,045
T. Burgess, *S.D.P./All.*	8,864
C. maj.	11,821

NORTH EAST *E.* 62,923

*Rt. Hon. B. B. Weatherill, *C.*	22,292
J. Goldie, *S.D.P./All.*	10,665
Ms. K. Riley, *Lab.*	9,503
C. maj.	11,627

NORTH WEST *E.* 58,333

H. J. Malins, *C.*	16,674
*W. H. Pitt, *L./All.*	12,582
I. Smedley, *Lab.*	9,561
N. Griffin, *N.F.*	336
R. Rowe, *Eco.*	286
C. maj.	4,092

SOUTH *E.* 64,482

*Sir W. G. Clark, *C.*	29,842
J. Forrest, *L./All.*	12,402
R. C. E. Brooks, *Lab.*	3,568
C. maj.	17,440
(May '79, C. maj. 20,868)	

Dagenham (Gtr. London)
E. 62,960

B. C. Gould, *Lab.*	15,665
R. Neill, *C.*	12,668
Mrs. J. Horne, *S.D.P./All.*	10,769
J. A. Pearce, *N.F.*	645
D. Walshe, *Comm.*	141
Lab. maj.	2,997

Darlington (Durham)
E. 65,233

M. C. Fallon, *C.*	22,434
*O. O'Brien, *Lab.*	18,996
R. Dutton, *S.D.P./All.*	8,737
A. Clark, *C.D.*	108
C. maj.	3,438
(May '79, Lab. maj. 1,052)	

Dartford (Kent)
E. 71,622

*R. J. Dunn, *C.*	28,199
D. Townsend, *Lab.*	14,636
J. Mills, *L./All.*	11,204
A. H. Crockford, *F.D.P.*	374
G. E. Nye, *N.F.*	282
C. maj.	13,563

Daventry (Northants)
E. 64,314

*Rt. Hon. R. E. Prentice, *C.*	26,357
D. Collins, *S.D.P./All.*	13,221
D. Middleton, *Lab.*	9,840
C. maj.	13,136

Davyhulme (Gtr. Manchester)
E. 64,363

*W. S. Churchill, *C.*	22,055
D. Wrigley, *L./All.*	13,041
S. Rogers, *Lab.*	12,887
C. maj.	9,014

Denton and Reddish
(Gtr. Manchester)
E. 68,661

*A. F. Bennett, *Lab.*	22,123
J. Snadden, *C.*	16,998
J. Begg, *S.D.P./All.*	10,869
Lab. maj.	5,125

Derby

NORTH *E.* 70,374

G. Knight, *C.*	22,303
*P. Whitehead, *Lab.*	18,797
S. Connolly, *L./All.*	9,924
C. maj.	3,506

SOUTH *E.* 68,578

Mrs. M. M. Beckett, *Lab.*	18,169
G. Hales, *C.*	17,748
I. Smith, *S.D.P./All.*	9,976
E. Wall, *Eco.*	297
Lab. maj.	421

Derbyshire

NORTH EAST *E.* 68,273

*R. J. Ellis, *Lab.*	21,094
I. Bridge, *C.*	19,088
S. Hardy, *S.D.P./All.*	11,494
Lab. maj.	2,006

SOUTH *E.* 75,391

Mrs. E. Currie, *C.*	25,909
P. Kent, *Lab.*	17,296
R. MacFarquhar, *S.D.P./All.*	15,959
C. maj.	8,613

WEST *E.* 68,668

*M. F. Parris, *C.*	29,695
V. Bingham, *L./All.*	14,370
J. S. March, *Lab.*	9,060
C. maj.	15,325

Devizes (Wilts)
E. 83,211

*Hon. C. A. Morrison, *C.*	33,644
Mrs. E. Palmer, *S.D.P./All.*	18,020
D. Hulme, *Lab.*	10,468
Mrs. G. Ewen, *W. Reg.*	234
C. maj.	15,624
(May '79, C. maj. 16,088)	

Dewsbury (W. Yorks)
E. 83,211

J. Whitfield, *C.*	20,297
D. Ripley, *Lab.*	18,211
*D. Ginsburg, *S.D.P./All.*	13,065
C. maj.	2,086

Doncaster (S. Yorks)

CENTRAL *E.* 71,039

*Rt. Hon. H. Walker, *Lab.*	21,154
J. Somers, *C.*	18,646
T. Stables, *S.D.P./All.*	10,524
Lab. maj.	2,508

NORTH *E.* 72,184

*M. C. Welsh, *Lab.*	26,626
B. M. L. Stephen, *C.*	13,915
D. Orford, *S.D.P./All.*	9,916
Lab. maj.	12,711

Don Valley (S. Yorks)
E. 73,112

M. Redmond, *Lab.*	23,036
Mrs. B. Utting, *C.*	16,570
D. Lange, *L./All.*	11,482
Lab. maj.	6,466

Dorset

NORTH *E.* 67,524

*N. B. Baker, *C.*	30,058
Dr. G. Tapper, *L./All.*	18,678
Ms. J. Fox, *Lab.*	2,710
D. C. T. Fox, *W. Reg.*	294
C. maj.	11,380

SOUTH E. 68,998
*Viscount Cranborne, C. .. 28,631
S. Head, S.D.P./All. 13,533
D. Hewitt, Lab. 7,831
Mrs. B. Smith, Ind. 151
  C. maj. 15,098

WEST E. 60,997
*J. W. Spicer, C. 27,030
T. Jones, L./All. 13,078
D. Cash, Lab. 5,168
  C. maj. 13,952

Dover (Kent)
E. 67,922

*Rt. Hon. P. W. I. Rees, Q.C.,
  C. 25,454
S. Love, Lab. 16,234
G. Nice, S.D.P./All. 10,601
M. Potter, Eco. 404
  C. maj. 9,220

Dudley (W. Midlands)
EAST E. 74,765
*Rt. Hon. Dr. J. W. Gilbert,
  Lab. 24,441
Mrs. S. Gillies, C. 18,625
C. Simon, S.D.P./All. 10,272
  Lab. maj. 5,816

WEST E. 77,795
*J. G. Blackburn, C. 27,250
W. Price, Lab. 18,527
G. Lewis, L./All. 13,251
  C. maj. 8,723

Dulwich (Gtr. London)
E. 56,596

G. F. Bowden, C. 15,424
Ms. C. Huey, Lab. 13,565
D. Taverne, S.D.P./All. .. 8,376
R. Barker, N.F. 338
R. Baker, Eco. 237
R. W. Vero, Loony Soc. ... 99
  C. maj. 1,859

Durham
CITY OF E. 66,925
*W. M. Hughes, Lab. 18,163
D. Stoker, S.D.P./All. 16,190
M. Lavis, C. 15,438
  Lab. maj. 1,973

NORTH E. 71,256
*G. H. Radice, Lab. 26,404
D. Howarth, L./All. 12,967
S. Popat, C. 12,418
  Lab. maj. 13,437

NORTH WEST E. 60,747
*Rt. Hon. E. Armstrong,
  Lab. 19,135
J. T. Middleton, C. 12,779
C. Foote Wood, L./All. ... 11,008
  Lab. maj. 6,356

Ealing (Gtr. London)
ACTON E. 62,078
*Sir G. S. K. Young, BT., C. .. 22,051
G. J. Daniel, Lab. 11,959
P. Mitchell, S.D.P./All. .. 10,593
S. Pulley, Comm. 192
  C. maj. 10,092

NORTH E. 68,538
*H. Greenway, C. 23,128
H. J. Benn, Lab. 16,837
A. Miller, L./All. 11,021
J. Shore, B.N.P. 306
  C. maj. 6,291

SOUTHALL E. 71,441
*S. J. Bidwell, Lab. 26,664
N. Linacre, C. 15,548
M. Nadeen, L./All. 8,059
E. Pendrous, N.F. 555
S. Paul, Ind. 150
  Lab. maj. 11,116
  (May '79, Lab. maj. 11,278)

Easington (Durham)
E. 65,732

*J. D. Dormand, Lab. 25,912
F. Patterson, L./All. 11,120
C. J. Coulson-Thomas, C. . 7,342
  Lab. maj. 14,792

East Berkshire
E. 81,512

A. J. MacKay, C. 33,967
K. O'Sullivan, S.D.P./All. 17,868
Ms. E. Rogers, Lab. 7,953
  C. maj. 16,099

Eastbourne (E. Sussex)
E. 72,980

*I. R. E. Gow, T.D., C. 31,501
P. Driver, L./All. 18,015
C. Clark, Lab. 3,790
  C. maj. 13,486

Eastleigh (Hants)
E. 82,447

*Sir D. E. C. Price, C. 32,393
M. Kyrle, L./All. 19,385
P. Hallman, Lab. 13,008
  C. maj. 13,008

East Lindsey (Lincs)
E. 69,715

*P. H. B. Tapsell, C. 27,151
J. Sellick, L./All. 19,634
G. R. Lowis, Lab. 4,299
  C. maj. 7,517

Eccles (Gtr. Manchester)
E. 67,230

*L. Carter-Jones, Lab. 21,644
D. Philp, C. 15,639
K. A. Hemsley, L./All. 9,392
B. Cottam, Comm. 485
  Lab. maj. 6,005

Eddisbury (Cheshire)
E. 71,056

*A. R. Goodlad, C. 28,407
R. Fletcher, L./All. 13,561
D. G. Hanson, Lab. 11,169
  C. maj. 14,846

Edmonton (Gtr. London)
E. 64,809

I. D. Twinn, C. 18,968
*T. E. Graham, Lab. 17,775
L. Brass, L./All. 7,523
D. J. Bruce, B.N.P. 372
  C. maj. 1,193

Ellesmere Port and Neston
(Cheshire)
E. 69,992

M. Woodcock, C. 24,371
A. Davies, Lab. 17,284
L. George, S.D.P./All. 11,413
  C. maj. 7,087

Elmet (W. Yorks)
E. 67,008

S. L. Batiste, C. 23,909
R. Wilson, Lab. 16,053
Mrs. G. Paterson, S.D.P./
  All. 10,589
  C. maj. 7,856

Eltham (Gtr. London)
E. 55,062

*P. J. Bottomley, C. 19,530
C. P. Moore, Lab. 11,938
E. Randall, L./All. 9,030
P. Banks, B.N.P. 276
  C. maj. 7,592

Enfield (Gtr. London)
NORTH E. 67,980
*T. J. C. Eggar, C. 25,456
B. G. Grayson, Lab. 13,740
J. Daly, S.D.P./All. 9,452
Miss T. Persighetti, Eco. . 320
J. Billingham, B.N.P. 268
  C. maj. 11,716

SOUTHGATE E. 65,438
*Hon. Sir A. G. Berry, C. .. 26,451
D. Morgan, L./All. 10,632
Ms. M. Honeyball, Lab. ... 8,132
M. Braithwaite, B.N.P. ... 318
  C. maj. 15,819

Epping Forest (Essex)
E. 66,578

*Sir J. A. Biggs-Davison, C. 27,373
M. Pettman, S.D.P./All. .. 11,995
Ms. H. J. Bryan, Lab. 8,289
R. Boenke, Eco. 452
S. Smith, B.N.P. 330
  C. maj. 15,378
  (May '79, C. maj. 15,453)

Epsom and Ewell (Surrey)
E. 70,630

*Hon. A. G. Hamilton, C. .. 30,737
M. Anderson, L./All. 13,542
W. R. Carpenter, Lab. 6,587
  C. maj. 17,195

Erewash (Derbys)
E. 73,335

*P. L. Rost, C. 25,167
W. Moore, Lab. 13,848
J. Corbett, S.D.P./All. 12,331
W. G. Camm, Ind. Lab. ... 4,158
  C. maj. 11,319

Erith and Crayford
(Gtr. London)
E. 56,066

D. A. Evennett, C. 15,289
*A. J. Wellbeloved, S.D.P./
  All. 14,369
M. G. Smart, Lab. 11,260
O. Hawke, B.N.P. 272
  C. maj. 920

Esher (Surrey)
E. 61,745

*D. C. M. Mather, M.C., C.	.	28,577
C. Wheatley, L./All.	.....	12,665
Ms. D. D. Plaskow, Lab.	..	3,250
W. Wellie, Loony Soc.	....	664
C. maj.	....	15,912

Exeter (Devon)
E. 73,441

*J. G. Hannam, C.	....	26,660
S. Mennell, S.D.P./All.	..	16,780
R. Evans, Lab.	....	13,088
P. Frings, Eco.	....	779
C. maj.	....	9,880
(May '79, C. maj. 8,027)		

Falmouth and Camborne
(Cornwall)
E. 65,624

*W. D. Mudd, C.	....	24,614
D. Fieldsend, S.D.P./All.	.	13,589
A. Bunt, Lab.	....	10,446
R. Jenkin, M.K.		582
C. maj.	....	11,025

Fareham (Hants)
E. 71,901

*P. R. C. Lloyd, C.	......	32,762
S. Yolland, L./All.	....	16,446
D. Sommerville, Lab.	....	3,808
C. maj.	....	16,316

Faversham (Kent)
E. 76,467

*R. D. Moate, C.	....	29,849
M. Goyder, S.D.P./All.	..	15,252
C. M. Bromley, Lab.	.....	11,130
C. maj.	....	14,597

Feltham and Heston
(Gtr. London)
E. 78,366

*R. P. Ground, Q.C., C.	....	23,724
R. W. Kerr, Lab.	....	21,576
A. Alagappa, L./All.	......	8,706
S. Glass, N.F.	....	696
C. maj.	....	2,148
(May '79, Lab. maj. 4,105)		

Finchley (Gtr. London)
E. 55,638

*Rt. Hon. Mrs. M. H. Thatcher, C.	.....	19,616
L. G. Spigel, Lab.	....	10,302
Dr. Margaret Joachim, L./All.	....	7,763
Ms. S. Wilkinson, W.F.L.O.E.	....	279
D. Sutch, Loony Soc.	....	235
A. J. Noonan, B.E.L.L.S.	.	75
Miss H. M. Anscomb, Ind.		42
A. P. Whitehead, L.A.O.	.	37
D. A. Webb, Anti-Censor	.	28
B. C. Wareham, P.A.L.	...	27
B. C. Wedmore, B.B.H.	...	13
C. maj.	....	9,314
(May '79, C. maj. 7,878)		

Folkestone and Hythe (Kent)
E. 67,802

M. Howard, C.	....	27,261
J. MacDonald, L./All.	....	15,591
L. Lawrie, Lab.	....	4,700
P. A. Todd, Ind.	....	318
C. maj.	....	11,670
(May '79, C. maj. 16,020)		

Fulham (Gtr. London)
E. 51,833

*M. Stevens, C.	....	18,204
A. Powell, Lab.	....	13,415
D. Rendel, L./All.	....	7,194
Ms. J. Grimes, Eco.	......	277
R. Pearce, N.F.	....	229
J. Keats, Ind. L.	....	102
C. maj.	....	4,789
(May '79, C. maj. 1,499)		

Fylde (Lancs)
E. 62,238

*Sir E. L. Gardner, Q.C., C.	.	27,879
Mrs. E. A. Smith, L./All.	..	10,777
D. J. King, Lab.	....	4,821
H. Fowler, Ind.	....	863
C. maj.	....	17,012

Gainsborough and Horncastle
(Lincs)
E. 67,115

E. J. E. Leigh, C.	....	25,625
A. Phillips, L./All.	....	20,558
C. James, Lab.	....	3,886
G. Dixon, Eco.	....	279
C. maj.	....	5,067

Gateshead East (Tyne & Wear)
E. 68,364

*B. Conlan, Lab.	....	22,981
F. Rogers, C.	....	12,659
P. Nunn, S.D.P./All.	.....	11,920
Lab. maj.	....	10,322

Gedling (Notts)
E. 66,656

*Sir P. W. Holland, C.	....	27,207
A. Berkeley, S.D.P./All.	..	12,543
J. Peck, Lab.	....	10,330
J. Szatter, Ind.	....	186
C. maj.	....	14,664

Gillingham (Kent)
E. 69,256

J. R. Couchman, C.	......	26,381
C. Lewcock, L./All.	......	15,538
A. S. West, Lab.	....	9,084
C. maj.	....	10,843
(May '79, C. maj. 10,499)		

Glanford and Scunthorpe
(Humberside)
E. 71,962

R. S. Hickmet, C.	....	20,356
J. Ellis, Lab.	....	19,719
C. Nottingham, S.D.P./All.		12,819
C. maj.	....	637

Gloucester
E. 74,268

*Rt. Hon. Mrs. S. Oppenheim, C.	....	27,235
C. W. V. Hinds, Lab.	.....	14,698
M. Golder, S.D.P./All.	...	13,499
J. Waters, Eco.	....	479
R. Rhodes, B.N.P.	....	260
C. maj.	....	12,537

Gosport (Hants)
E. 64,877

*P. J. Viggers, C.	....	28,179
P. Chegwyn, L./All.	......	13,728
B. B. Bond, Lab.	....	4,319
R. A. McMillan, Ind.	.....	241
C. maj.	....	14,451

Grantham (Lincs)
E. 75,047

*Hon. D. M. Hogg, C.	.....	31,692
S. Titley, L./All.	....	12,781
T. E. Savage, Lab.	....	10,677
C. maj.	....	18,911

Gravesham (Kent)
E. 71,150

*T. D. Brinton, C.	....	25,968
J. F. Ovenden, Lab.	......	17,505
M. Horton, S.D.P./All.	...	10,826
P. Johnson, N.F.	....	420
M. Sewell, Eco.	....	103
C. maj.	....	8,463

Great Grimsby (Humberside)
E. 68,388

*A. V. Mitchell, Lab.	......	18,330
C. Hancock, C.	....	17,599
P. Genney, S.D.P./All.	...	14,552
Lab. maj.	....	731
(May '79, Lab. maj. 6,241)		

Great Yarmouth
(Norfolk)
E. 62,809

M. R. H. Carttiss, C.	.....	22,423
O. Lloyd, Lab.	....	11,223
E. Minett, L./All.	....	10,803
C. maj.	....	11,200

Greenwich (Gtr. London)
E. 51,586

*N. G. Barnett, Lab.	......	13,361
A. Rolfe, C.	....	12,150
T. Ford, S.D.P./All.	......	8,783
I. Dell, B.N.P.	....	259
R. Mallone, Fellowship	...	242
Ms. F. Hook, Comm.	.....	149
Lab. maj.	....	1,211

Guildford (Surrey)
E. 75,134

*Rt. Hon. D. A. R. Howell, C.		30,016
Mrs. M. Sharp, S.D.P./All.		18,192
K. Chesterton, Lab.	......	5,853
A. Farrell, P.A.L.	....	425
C. maj.	....	11,824

Hackney (Gtr. London)
NORTH AND STOKE NEWINGTON
E. 66,754

*E. A. C. Roberts, *Lab.*	....	18,989
E. Hartley-Booth, *C.*	.....	10,444
D. Ash, *L./All.*	....	5,746
D. Fitzpatrick, *Eco.*		492
M. Goldman, *Comm.*	.....	426
J. Field, *N.F.*	....	396
Lab. maj.	....	8,545

SOUTH AND SHOREDITCH E. 71,304

B. C. J. Sedgemore, *Lab.*	..	16,621
P. Croft, *C.*	....	8,930
*R. W. Brown, *S.D.P./All.*		7,025
J. Roberts, *Ind.L.*	....	3,724
S. Quilty, *L.I.L.*	....	704
R. Ashton, *N.F.*	....	593
Mrs. V. Tyndall, *B.N.P.*	..	374
D. Green, *Comm.*	....	246
R. Goldstein, *W.R.P.*	.....	141
Lab. maj.	....	7,691

Halesowen and Stourbridge
(W. Midlands)
E. 76,403

*J. H. R. Stokes, *C.*	......	28,250
T. Clitheroe, *S.D.P./All.*	..	14,934
C. Ellison, *Lab.*	....	14,611
D. Rudd, *Eco.*	....	582
C. maj.	....	13,316

Halifax (W. Yorks)
E. 72,747

R. Galley, *C.*	....	22,321
*Dr. Shirley Summerskill,		
Lab.	....	20,452
F. Cockroft, *S.D.P./All.*	..	11,868
C. maj.	....	1,869

Halton (Cheshire)
E. 72,743

*Rt. Hon. G. J. Oakes, *Lab.*		24,752
P. Pedley, *C.*	....	17,923
R. Tilling, *S.D.P./All.*	....	10,649
Lab. maj.	....	6,829

Hammersmith (Gtr. London)
E. 46,718

*C. S. Soley, *Lab.*	....	13,645
N. Mansfield, *C.*	....	11,691
M. Starks, *S.D.P./All.*	....	4,925
S. Knott, *Ind. L.*	....	1,912
Ms. D. Sutherland, *Eco.*	..	325
Mrs. L. Bennett, *N.F.*	....	250
Ms. C. Dixon, *W.R.P.*	....	81
P. Dick, *Ind.*	....	73
Lab. maj.	....	1,954
(May '79, Lab. maj. 3,506)		

Hampshire
EAST E. 79,303

*M. J. Mates, *C.*	....	36,968
Ms. R. Bryan, *L./All.*	....	18,641
S. J. Cowan, *Lab.*	....	3,247
C. maj.	....	18,327

NORTH WEST E. 65,780

*D. B. Mitchell, *C.*	....	28,044
I. Willis, *L./All.*	....	15,922
M. J. Davis, *Lab.*	....	4,957
C. maj.	....	12,122

Hampstead and Highgate
(Gtr. London)
E. 66,554

*Sir G. Finsberg, *M.B.E.*, *C.*	.	18,366
J. McDonnell, *Lab.*	......	14,996
Mrs. A. Sofer, *S.D.P./All.*	.	11,030
J. Stevenson, *Poet*	....	156
C. maj.	....	3,370

Harborough (Leics)
E. 72,177

*Sir J. A. Farr, *C.*	....	32,957
T. Swift, *L./All.*	....	14,472
M. Upham, *Lab.*	....	6,285
B. Fewster, *Eco.*	....	802
J. Taylor, *B.N.P.*	....	280
C. maj.	....	18,485
(May '79, C. maj. 21,978)		

Harlow (Essex)
E. 69,715

J. J. J. Hayes, *C.*	....	21,924
*A. S. Newens, *Lab.*	......	18,250
J. Bastick, *L./All.*	....	12,891
J. Ward, *Ind.*	....	256
C. maj.	....	3,674
(May '79, Lab. maj. 1,392)		

Harrogate (N. Yorks)
E. 72,815

*R. G. Banks, *C.*	....	30,269
J. Burney, *S.D.P./All.*	....	14,381
J. Dixon, *Lab.*	....	5,128
D. Kelly, *R.H.C.P.*	....	316
P. Vessey, *N.F.*	....	163
C. maj.	....	15,888

Harrow (Gtr. London)
EAST E. 79,926

*H. J. Dykes, *C.*	....	28,834
R. Hains, *L./All.*	....	16,166
D. Brough, *Lab.*	....	12,941
C. maj.	....	12,668

WEST E. 73,151

*Sir A. J. Page, *C.*	....	28,056
S. Bayliss, *S.D.P./All.*	....	17,035
K. A. Toms, *Lab.*	....	7,811
C. maj.	....	11,021

Hartlepool (Cleveland)
E. 69,346

*E. L. Leadbitter, *Lab.*	....	22,048
F. Rodgers, *C.*	....	18,958
N. Bertram, *S.D.P./All.*	...	7,422
Lab. maj.	....	3,090
(May '79, Lab. maj. 8,162)		

Harwich (Essex)
E. 72,179

*Sir J. E. Ridsdale, *C.B.E.*, *C.*	27,422
R. Goodenough, *L./All.*	...	14,920
R. Knight, *Lab.*	....	8,302
C. maj.	....	12,502

Hastings and Rye (E. Sussex)
E. 69,747

*K. R. Warren, *C.*	....	25,626
D. Amies, *L./All.*	....	14,646
N. Knowles, *Lab.*	....	7,304
G. McNally, *Ind.*	....	503
C. maj.	....	10,980

Havant (Hants)
E. 73,096

*I. S. Lloyd, *C.*	....	29,148
Mrs. E. Cleaver, *S.D.P./All.*	17,192
R. J. Norris. *Lab.*	....	6,335
C. maj.	....	11,956

Hayes and Harlington
(Gtr. London)
E. 57,620

T. P. Dicks, *C.*	....	16,451
P. Fagan, *Lab.*	....	12,217
*N. D. Sandelson, *S.D.P./All.*	11,842
F. Hill, *Freedom*	....	324
C. maj.	....	4,234
(May '79, Lab. maj. 3,302)		

Hazel Grove (Gtr. Manchester)
E. 63,630

*T. R. Arnold, *C.*	....	22,627
A. Vos, *L./All.*	....	20,605
J. Comyn-Platt, *Lab.*	.....	5,895
C. maj.	....	2,022

Hemsworth (W. Yorks)
E. 54,323

*A. Woodall, *Lab.*	....	22,081
J. Woofindin, *L./All.*	.....	7,891
D. Williamson, *C.*	....	7,291
Lab. maj.	....	14,190

Hendon (Gtr. London)
NORTH E. 54,505

*J. M. Gorst, *C.*	....	18,499
K. Craig, *S.D.P./All.*	.....	9,474
A. M. Williams, *Lab.*	.....	8,786
B. Franklin, *Nat.*	....	194
R. Clayton, *Ind. Dem.*	....	116
C. maj.	....	9,025
(May '79, C. maj. 6,392)		

SOUTH E. 53,929

*Rt. Hon. P. J. M. Thomas,		
Q.C., *C.*	....	17,115
M. Palmer, *L./All.*	....	10,682
Mrs. D. N. Neall, *Lab.*	...	7,415
C. maj.	....	6,433
(May '79, C. maj. 8,750)		

Henley (Oxon)
E. 62,120

*Rt. Hon. M. R. D. Heseltine,		
C.	....	27,039
I. Brook, *L./All.*	....	13,258
I. Roxburgh, *Lab.*	....	4,282
Ms. R. Johnson,		
W.F.L.O.E.	....	517
T. Rogers, *O.N.C.*	....	213
C. maj.	....	13,781

Hereford
E. 64,051

*C. R. Shepherd, *C.*	......	23,334
C. Green, *L./All.*	....	21,057
J. Evans, *Lab.*	....	3,690
Ms. V. Murray, *Eco.*	......	463
C. maj.	....	2,277
(May '79, C. maj. 4,970)		

Hertford and Stortford
E. 68,615

*P. B. Wells, C.	29,039
R. Wotherspoon, S.D.P./	
All.	16,110
J. Carr, Lab.	6,203
G. Wiles, B.N.P.	304
P. Cullen, P.F.A.	221
C. maj.	12,929

Hertfordshire

NORTH E. 75,439

*B. H. I. H. Stewart, C.	29,302
G. Binney, L./All.	19,359
J. Reilly, Lab.	11,104
C. maj.	9,943

SOUTH WEST E. 74,371

*R. L. Page, C.	30,217
I. Blair, L./All.	18,023
E. Playfair, Lab.	7,818
M. Lupton, Ind.	307
C. maj.	12,194

WEST E. 76,597

R. B. Jones, C.	28,436
N. Hollinghurst, S.D.P./	
All.	18,860
P. Boateng, Lab.	13,583
C. maj.	9,576

Hertsmere (Herts)
E. 72,997

*Rt. Hon. C. E. Parkinson,	
C.	28,628
Mrs. Z. Gifford, L./All.	13,758
I. D. D. Reed, Lab.	10,315
R. Parkinson, Ind. Comm.	1,116
C. maj.	14,870

Hexham (Nthmb)
E. 54,341

*Rt. Hon. A. G. F. Rippon,	
Q.C., C.	21,374
E. Robson, L./All.	13,066
S. J. Byers, Lab.	7,056
C. maj.	8,308

Heywood and Middleton
(Gtr. Manchester)
E. 59,870

*J. Callaghan, Lab.	18,111
Mrs. C. Hodgson, C.	14,137
A. Rumbelow, S.D.P./All.	9,262
K. Henderson, B.N.P.	316
Lab. maj.	3,974

High Peak (Derbys)
E. 67,358

C. J. Hawkins, C.	24,534
D. Marquand, S.D.P./All.	14,594
D. J. Wilcox, Lab.	13,755
C. maj.	9,940

Holborn and St. Pancras
(Gtr. London)
E. 71,604

*F. G. Dobson, Lab.	20,486
A. Kerpel, C.	13,227
W. Jones, L./All.	9,242
R. Price, W.R.P.	155
Lab. maj.	7,259

Holland with Boston (Lincs)
E. 63,562

*R. B. Body, C.	24,962
Mrs. C. Le Brun, L./All.	13,226
J. A. Moore, Lab.	6,970
C. maj.	11,736

Honiton (Devon)
E. 72,232

*Sir P. F H. Emery, C.	32,602
A. Sampson, S.D.P./All.	17,833
R. A. C. Sharpe, Lab.	3,377
C. maj.	14,769

Hornchurch (Gtr. London)
E. 61,741

*R. C. Squire, C.	21,393
A. R. Williams, Lab.	12,209
J. Martin, S.D.P./All.	11,251
Mrs. A. Joyce, N.F.	402
M. Crowson, Eco.	219
C. maj.	9,184
(May '79, C. maj. 769)	

Hornsey and Wood Green
(Gtr. London)
E. 73,870

*Sir H. A. L. Rossi, C.	22,323
Mrs. V. Veness, Lab.	18,424
M. Burrell, S.D.P./All.	10,995
P. Lang, Eco.	854
C. maj.	3,899

Horsham (W. Sussex)
E. 80,407

*P. M. Hordern, C.	37,897
G. Archibald, S.D.P./All.	16,112
G. R. Ward, Lab.	4,999
P. Spurrier, Eco.	925
C. maj.	21,785

Houghton and Washington
(Tyne & Wear)
E. 75,686

R. Boyes, Lab.	26,168
R. Kenyon, S.D.P./All.	12,347
R. Vane, C.	12,104
Lab. maj.	13,821

Hove (E. Sussex)
E. 71,918

*Hon. T. A. D. Sainsbury, C.	28,628
Mrs. T. Beamish, L./All.	11,409
C. Wright, Lab.	6,550
T. Layton, S.E.E.	524
K. Lillie, M.D.P.	189
C. maj.	17,219
(May '79, C. maj. 19,449)	

Huddersfield (W. Yorks)
E. 68,174

*B. J. Sheerman, Lab.	20,051
J. Tweddle, C.	16,096
Mrs. K. J. L. Hasler, L./All.	12,027
H. Hirst, Ind.	271
Lab. maj.	3,955

Hull (Humberside)

EAST E. 70,037

*J. L. Prescott, Lab.	23,615
D. Bunting-Leng, C.	13,541
Mrs. C. Gurevitch, L./All.	10,172
Lab. maj.	10,074

NORTH E. 74,543

*J. K. McNamara, Lab.	21,365
C. Hayward, C.	15,337
T. A. Smith, S.D.P./All.	13,381
R. Tenney, Nat.	222
Lab. maj.	6,028

WEST E. 57,702

S. J. Randall, Lab.	15,361
M. Humphreys, C.	11,707
W. Unwin, S.D.P./All.	9,575
Lab. maj.	3,654

Huntingdon (Cambs)
E. 76,668

*J. Major, C.	34,254
Mrs. S. Gatiss, L./All.	13,906
M. Slater, Lab.	6,317
T. Eiloart, Eco.	444
C. maj.	20,348

Hyndburn (Lancs)
E. 59,341

J. K. Hargreaves, C.	19,405
*A. Davidson, Lab.	19,384
J. Bridgen, S.D.P./All.	6,716
F. Smith, Eco.	226
P. Gateson, Ind.	169
C. maj.	21

Ilford (Gtr. London)

NORTH E. 60,248

*V. W. H. Bendall, C.	22,042
M. J. Gapes, Lab.	10,841
I. Roxburgh, S.D.P./All.	10,052
C. maj.	11,201

SOUTH E. 58,208

*N. G. Thorne, O.B.E., T.D., C.	18,672
J. H. Hogben, Lab.	14,106
R. Scott, L./All.	7,999
R. A. Martin, B.N.P.	316
C. maj.	4,566

Ipswich (Suffolk)
E. 67,292

*K. T. Weetch, Lab.	22,191
Dr. Elizabeth Cottrell, C.	21,114
Mrs. P. Miernik, L./All.	7,220
A. Pearson, B.N.P.	235
Lab. maj.	1,077

Isle of Wight
E. 94,226

*S. S. Ross, L./All.	38,407
Mrs. V. Bottomley, C.	34,904
Mrs. C. Wilson, Lab.	1,828
B. McDermott, I.W.R.P.	208
L./All. maj.	3,503
(May '79, L. maj. 352)	

Islington (Gtr. London)

NORTH E. 59,984
J. B. Corbyn, *Lab.*		14,951
D. Coleman, *C.*		9,344
*J. Grant, *S.D.P./All.*		8,268
*M. O'Halloran, *Ind. Lab.*		4,091
L. Bearsford-Walker, *B.N.P.*		176
R. Lincoln, *C.U.I.*		134
Lab. maj.		5,607

SOUTH AND FINSBURY E. 59,795
C. R. Smith, *Lab.*		13,460
*G. Cunningham, *S.D.P./All.*		13,097
A. Johnston, *C.*		9,894
J. Donegan, *N.F.*		341
J. Murphy, *I.F.P.*		102
D. Stentiford, *B.N.P.*		94
C. Slapper, *S.P.G.B.*		85
Lab. maj.		363

Jarrow (Tyne & Wear)
E. 63,770
*D. Dixon, *Lab.*		25,151
Miss S. Copland, *C.*		11,274
J. A. Lennox, *L./All.*		9,094
Lab. maj.		13,877

Keighley (W. Yorks)
E. 63,678
*G. P. A. Waller, *C.*		21,370
*R. Cryer, *Lab.*		18,596
J. Wells, *L./All.*		9,951
M. Penney, *Eco.*		302
C. maj.		2,774

Kensington (Gtr. London)
E. 49,584
*Sir B. M. Rhys Williams, BL., *C.*		14,274
B. T. Bousquet, *Lab.*		9,173
W. Goodhart, *S.D.P./All.*		6,873
J. Porritt, *Eco.*		649
T. Knight, *Ind.*		86
C. maj.		5,101
(May '79, C. maj. 5,463)		

Kettering (Northants)
E. 62,819
R. N. Freeman, *C.*		23,223
Mrs. C. Goodhart, *S.D.P./All.*		14,637
A. Gordon, *Lab.*		10,119
C. maj.		8,586

Kingston upon Thames
(Gtr. London)
E. 56,794
*N. S. H. Lamont, *C.*		22,094
R. Hayes, *L./All.*		13,222
P. J. Smith, *Lab.*		4,977
Miss A. Presant-Collins, *Eco.*		290
P. Dodd, *Loony Soc.*		259
C. maj.		8,872
(May '79, C. maj. 13,544)		

Kingswood (Avon)
E. 72,159
R. A. Hayward, *C.*		22,573
T. Walker, *Lab.*		20,776
M. Gilbert, *S.D.P./All.*		12,591
C. maj.		1,797

Knowsley (Merseyside)

NORTH E. 55,606
*R. Kilroy-Silk, *Lab.*		24,949
A. Birch, *C.*		7,758
B. McColgan, *S.D.P./All.*		5,715
J. Simons, *W.R.P.*		246
Lab. maj.		17,191

SOUTH E. 68,114
S. F. Hughes, *Lab.*		25,727
Miss E. Lamont, *C.*		13,958
I. Smith, *L./All.*		8,173
Lab. maj.		11,769

Lancaster (Lancs)
E. 56,040
*Mrs. M. E. Kellett-Bowman, *C.*		21,050
C. Harkins, *Lab.*		10,414
W. Booth, *L./All.*		10,214
S. R. Leach, *Ind.*		179
C. maj.		10,636

Langbaurgh (Cleveland)
E. 77,387
J. R. Holt, *C.*		24,239
Mrs. G. Johnson, *Lab.*		18,215
R. Ashby, *L./All.*		15,615
C. maj.		6,024

Leeds (W. Yorks)

CENTRAL E. 63,299
D. J. Fatchett, *Lab.*		18,706
P. Wrigley, *L./All.*		10,484
M. Ashley-Brown, *C.*		9,192
G. Cummins, *B.N.P.*		331
J. M. Rogers, *Comm.*		314
Lab. maj.		8,222

EAST E. 63,611
*Rt. Hon. D. W. Healey, C.H., M.B.E., *Lab.*		18,450
A. Bell, *C.*		12,355
Mrs. M. Clay, *L./All.*		10,884
A. H. Brons, *N.F.*		475
Lab. maj.		6,095

NORTH EAST E. 65,226
*Rt. Hon. Sir K. S. Joseph, BT., *C.*		21,940
P. Crystal, *S.D.P./All.*		12,945
R. Sedler, *Lab.*		10,951
E. Tibbitts, *A. Corr.*		128
P. Holton, *A.C.I.E.*		123
C. maj.		8,995

NORTH WEST E. 68,004
*Dr. K. Hampson, *C.*		22,579
N. Jones, *S.D.P./All.*		14,042
J. Battle, *Lab.*		10,757
A. Laurence, *Eco.*		673
C. G. Haygreen, *Ind. C.*		437
C. maj.		8,537

WEST E. 67,538
M. J. Meadowcroft, *L./All.*		17,908
*J. Dean, *Lab.*		15,860
Miss J. Keeble, *C.*		12,515
A. Braithwaite, *B.N.P.*		334
L./All. maj.		2,048

Leicester

EAST E. 67,071
P. N. E. Bruinvels, *C.*		19,117
Ms. P. Hewitt, *Lab.*		18,184
*T. Bradley, *S.D.P./All.*		10,362
R. V. Ganatra, *Ind.*		970
R. L. Sutton, *B.N.P.*		459
C. maj.		933
(May '79, Lab. maj. 2,856)		

SOUTH E. 73,573
D. H. Spencer, Q.C., *C.*		21,424
*J. Marshall, *Lab.*		21,417
R. Renold, *L./All.*		9,410
C. Davis, *Eco.*		495
C. Pickard, *B.N.P.*		280
D. P. Roberts, *W.P.W.S.*		161
C. maj.		7
(May '79, Lab. maj. 1,998)		

WEST E. 67,691
*Hon. G. E. Janner, *Lab.*		20,837
R. Meacham, *C.*		19,125
S. Fernando, *S.D.P./All.*		5,935
R. Hill, *B.N.P.*		469
B. J. Prangle, *W.R.P.*		176
Lab. maj.		1,712
(May '79, Lab. maj. 8,838)		

Leigh (Gtr. Manchester)
E. 68,063
*L. F. Cunliffe, *Lab.*		25,477
P. Johnston, *C.*		13,163
D. Eccles, *S.D.P./All.*		10,468
Lab. maj.		12,314

Leominster (H & W)
E. 66,286
*P. Temple-Morris, *C.*		29,276
R. Pincham, *L./All.*		19,490
D. Wilcox, *Lab.*		1,932
Miss F. M. Norman, *Eco.*		668
C. maj.		9,786

Lewes (E. Sussex)
E. 67,366
*J. R. Rathbone, *C.*		29,261
D. Bellotti, *L./All.*		15,357
Ms. S. Sander, *Lab.*		4,244
R. Mutter, *Eco.*		1,221
C. maj.		13,904

Lewisham (Gtr. London)

DEPTFORD E. 58,663
*Rt. Hon. J. E. Silkin, *Lab.*		17,360
R. Wheatley, *C.*		11,328
Miss D. Abbott, *S.D.P./All.*		6,734
P. Wilson, *B.N.P.*		317
S. B. Housego, *A.B.*		173
Lab. maj.		6,032

EAST E. 61,216
Hon. C. B. Moynihan, *C.*		17,168
*R. Moyle, *Lab.*		15,259
Ms. P. Toynbee, *S.D.P./All.*		9,351
R. C. Edmonds, *B.N.P.*		288
A. Hassard, *Eco.*		270
G. Roberts, *Comm.*		135
P. Gibson, *W.R.P.*		71
C. maj.		1,909

WEST *E.* 63,043

J. C. Maples, *C.*		19,521
*C. Price, *Lab.*		17,015
H. Mooney, *L./All.*		7,470
R. F. Hoy, *B.N.P.*		336
C. maj.		2,506

Leyton (Gtr. London)
E. 57,770

H. M. Cohen, *Lab.*		16,504
W. Neilson-Hansen, *C.*		11,988
*B. Magee, *S.D.P./All.*		9,448
Lab. maj.		4,516
(May '79, Lab. maj. 5,734)		

Lincoln
E. 72,887

*K. M. Carlisle, *C.*		25,244
M. Withers, *Lab.*		14,958
F. Stockdale, *S.D.P./All.*		13,631
G. Blades, *Ind.*		523
C. maj.		10,286

Littleborough and Saddleworth
(Gtr. Manchester)
E. 64,018

*G. K. Dickens, *C.*		20,510
R. Knowles, *L./All.*		14,644
S. Moore, *Lab.*		12,106
R. Barry, *R.C.C.P.*		398
C. maj.		5,650

Liverpool

BROADGREEN *E.* 63,826

T. Fields, *Lab.*		18,802
D. Dougherty, *C.*		15,002
R. Pine, *Ind. L.*		7,021
*Lt. Col. R. Crawshaw,		
o.b.e., t.d., *S.D.P./All.*		5,169
Lab. maj.		3,800

GARSTON *E.* 64,326

E. Loyden, *Lab.*		21,450
J. Ross, *C.*		17,448
Miss R. Cooper, *L./All.*		7,153
Lab. maj.		4,002

MOSSLEY HILL *E.* 62,789

*D. P. Alton, *L./All.*		18,845
B. Keefe, *C.*		14,650
A. C. Snowden, *Lab.*		12,352
M. Erikson-Rohrer, *N.F.*		212
L./All. maj.		4,195

RIVERSIDE *E.* 61,638

*R. Parry, *Lab.*		24,978
T. Morrison, *C.*		7,600
P. Zentner, *S.D.P./All.*		5,381
J. Blevin, *Comm.*		261
D. Latchford, *W.R.P.*		234
Lab. maj.		17,378

WALTON *E.* 73,532

*E. S. Heffer, *Lab.*		26,980
A. Maddox, *C.*		12,865
D. Croft, *L./All.*		10,970
D. J. M. McKechnie,		
B.N.P.		343
Lab. maj.		14,115

WEST DERBY *E.* 63,088

R. N. Wareing, *Lab.*		23,905
W. Trelawney, *C.*		12,062
*E. Ogden, *S.D.P./All.*		7,871
Lab. maj.		11,843

Loughborough (Leics)
E. 70,668

*S. J. Dorrell, *C.*		29,056
M. Jones, *Lab.*		12,876
J. Frears, *S.D.P./All.*		12,189
D. Whitebread, *Eco.*		591
J. A. Peacock, *B.N.P.*		228
C. maj.		16,180

Ludlow (Salop)
E. 63,256

*E. P. Cockeram, *C.*		26,278
D. Lane, *S.D.P./All.*		14,975
P. M. Davis, *Lab.*		5,949
C. maj.		11,303

Luton (Beds)
E. 69,805

NORTH *E.* 69,805

*J. R. Carlisle, *C.*		26,115
K. Hopkins, *Lab.*		14,134
D. Stephen, *S.D.P./All.*		13,769
C. maj.		11,981

SOUTH *E.* 71,015

*G. F. J. Bright, *C.*		22,531
I. M. Clemitson, *Lab.*		17,910
D. Franks, *L./All.*		13,395
C. maj.		4,621

Macclesfield (Cheshire)
E. 73,082

*N. R. Winterton, *C.*		32,538
Mrs. R. Coleman, *L./All.*		11,859
P. B. Kelly, *Lab.*		9,923
M. Reeman, *Ind.*		488
C. maj.		20,679

Maidstone (Kent)
E. 70,357

*Sir J. J. Wells, *C.*		26,420
J. Burnett, *L./All.*		19,194
G. T. Carey, *Lab.*		6,280
C. maj.		7,226

Makerfield (Gtr. Manchester)
E. 69,176

*M. T. F. McGuire, *Lab.*		25,114
E. Hay, *C.*		14,238
R. Grayson, *L./All.*		11,633
Lab. maj.		10,876

Manchester

BLACKLEY *E.* 60,106

*K. Eastham, *Lab.*		20,132
P. Ridgway, *C.*		13,676
J. Cookson, *L./All.*		8,081
Lab. maj.		6,456

CENTRAL *E.* 69,188

*R. K. Litherland, *Lab.*		27,353
D. Eager, *C.*		8,868
A. Ahmed, *S.D.P./All.*		4,956
A. Coles, *N.F.*		729
Lab. maj.		18,485

GORTON *E.* 64,645

*Rt. Hon. G. B. Kaufman,		
Lab.		22,460
J. Kershaw, *C.*		12,495
K. Whitmore, *L./All.*		8,348
M. Cowle, *Comm.*		333
L. C. Andrews, *B.N.P.*		231
Lab. maj.		9,965

WITHINGTON *E.* 64,606

*F. J. Silvester, *C.*		18,329
Mrs. F. W. Done, *Lab.*		15,956
B. Lever, *S.D.P./All.*		12,231
M. G. Gibson, *F.P.*		184
C. maj.		2,373

WYTHENSHAWE *E.* 60,995

*Rt. Hon. A. Morris, *Lab.*		23,172
Mrs. J. Jacobs, *C.*		12,488
D. Sandiford, *L./All.*		6,766
Lab. maj.		10,684
(May '79, Lab. maj. 12,113)		

Mansfield (Notts)
E. 65,277

*Rt. Hon. J. D. Concannon,		
Lab.		18,670
R. Wrenn, *C.*		16,454
S. Taylor, *S.D.P./All.*		11,036
Lab. maj.		2,216

Medway (Kent)
E. 63,387

*Mrs. P. E. Fenner, *C.*		22,507
R. E. Bean, *Lab.*		13,851
F. Winckless, *S.D.P./All.*		9,658
C. maj.		8,656

Meriden (W. Midlands)
E. 74,161

*I. C. Mills, *C.*		28,474
*E. J. Sever, *Lab.*		13,456
Mrs. P. M. Dunbar, *S.D.P./		
All.*		10,674
C. L. Collins, *N.F.*		460
C. maj.		15,018

Middlesbrough (Cleveland)
E. 62,950

S. Bell, *Lab.*		21,220
Mrs. L. Campey, *C.*		11,551
D. Sanders, *L./All.*		8,871
M. Simpson, *W.R.P.*		207
Lab. maj.		9,669

Mid Kent
E. 66,510

A. Rowe, *C.*		25,400
Mrs. A. Wainman, *L./All.*		12,857
V. Hull, *Lab.*		8,928
D. Delderfield, *New Brit.*		324
C. maj.		12,543

Mid Sussex
E. 77,005

*R. T. Renton, *C.*		35,310
J. Campbell, *L./All.*		18,566
Mrs. P. A. Hawkes, *Lab.*		3,470
J. Bray, *Ind.*		196
C. maj.		16,744

Milton Keynes (Bucks)
E. 79,229

*W. R. Benyon, *C.*		28,181
Mrs. J. Nightingale,		
S.D.P./All.		16,659
J. Thakoordin, *Lab.*		13,045
A. Francis, *Eco.*		494
R. G. W. Rickord, *B.N.P.*		290
C. maj.		11,522

Mitcham and Morden
(Gtr. London)
E. 63,535

*Mrs. A. C. R. Rumbold, C.B.E., C.	19,827
D. Nicholas, Lab.	13,376
B. Douglas-Mann, S.D.P./All.	12,720
J. Perryman, N.F.	539
C. maj.	6,451
(May '79, Lab. maj. 618)	

Mole Valley (Surrey)
E. 65,067

*Rt. Hon. K. W. Baker, C.	29,691
Ms. S. Thomas, L./All.	14,973
Ms. F. Lines, Lab.	4,147
C. maj.	14,718

Morecambe and Lunesdale
(Lancs)
E. 53,238

*Hon. M. A. Lennox-Boyd, C.	21,968
T. Clare, S.D.P./All.	9,774
A. C. Bryning, Lab.	6,882
Mrs. I. Woods, Ind.	208
C. maj.	12,194

Morley and Leeds South
(W. Yorks)
E. 60,864

*Rt. Hon. M. Rees, Lab.	18,995
W. Hyde, C.	13,141
P. Burley, S.D.P./All.	9,216
Lab. maj.	5,854

Newark (Notts)
E. 64,008

*R. T. Alexander, C.	26,334
J. McGuigan, Lab.	12,051
S. Thompstone, S.D.P./All.	10,076
Mrs. P. Hewis, Eco.	463
C. maj.	14,283

Newbury (Berks)
E. 71,343

*R. M. C. McNair-Wilson, C.	31,836
A. Richards, L./All.	18,798
R. C. Knight, Lab.	3,027
C. maj.	13,038

Newcastle-under-Lyme (Staffs)
E. 65,400

*J. Golding, Lab.	21,210
L. Lawrence, C.	18,406
A. Thomas, L./All.	10,916
Lab. maj.	2,804

Newcastle upon Tyne

CENTRAL E. 62,687

P. R. G. Merchant, C.	18,161
N. Todd, Lab.	15,933
*J. Horam, S.D.P./All.	9,923
D. N. Jacques, Eco.	478
C. maj.	2,228

EAST E. 59,587

N. H. Brown, Lab.	19,247
A. Barnes, C.	11,755
*M. Thomas, S.D.P./All.	11,293
Lab. maj.	7,492

NORTH E. 69,432

*R. C. Brown, Lab.	18,985
P. Straw, C.	16,429
J. Shipley, L./All.	15,136
Lab. maj.	2,556

New Forest (Hants)
E. 70,033

*P. M. E. D. McNair-Wilson, C.	34,157
R. Harrison, L./All.	13,232
D. T. James, Lab.	4,075
C. maj.	20,925

Newham (Gtr. London)

NORTH EAST E. 62,463

*R. Leighton, Lab.	19,282
Mrs. H. Gardener, C.	10,773
Mrs. A. Winfield, L./All.	7,943
F. Adams, N.F.	794
Lab. maj.	8,509
(May '79, Lab. maj. 10,040)	

NORTH WEST E. 49,814

T. Banks, Lab.	13,042
K. D. Irons, C.	6,124
A. Kellaway, S.D.P./All.	5,204
*A. Lewis, Ind. Lab.	3,074
M. Hipperson, N.F.	525
Lab. maj.	6,918
(May '79, Lab. maj. 10,455)	

SOUTH E. 50,362

*N. J. Spearing, Lab.	13,561
A. Reilly, S.D.P./All.	6,250
N. Thompson, C.	6,212
I. H. M. Anderson, N.F.	993
Lab. maj.	7,311
(May '79, Lab. maj. 12,773)	

Norfolk

MID E. 68,953

R. A. Ryder, O.B.E., C.	29,032
D. Cargill, S.D.P./All.	13,517
L. J. Potter, Lab.	8,950
M. McNee, Ind. Pow.	405
C. maj.	15,515

NORTH E. 65,101

*R. F. Howell, C.	26,230
J. Elworthy, S.D.P./All.	13,007
E. A. Barber, Lab.	9,317
C. maj.	13,223

NORTH WEST E. 69,181

H. C. Bellingham, C.	23,358
*C. Brocklebank-Fowler, S.D.P./All.	20,211
M. Tilbury, Lab.	10,139
C. maj.	3,147

SOUTH E. 73,523

*J. R. R. MacGregor, O.B.E., C.	30,747
R. Carden, L./All.	18,612
H. A. Holzer, Lab.	7,408
C. maj.	12,135

SOUTH WEST E. 70,398

*Sir P. L. Hawkins, T.D., C.	28,632
B. Baxter, L./All.	13,722
A. L. Rosenberg, Lab.	9,072
C. maj.	14,910

Normanton (W. Yorks)
E. 61,249

W. O'Brien, Lab.	18,782
A. Paul, C.	14,599
P. Pantelli, S.D.P./All.	9,741
Lab. maj.	4,183

Northampton

NORTH E. 68,370

*A. R. Marlow, C.	23,129
D. Offenbach, Lab.	13,269
A. Rounthwaite, L./All.	12,829
C. maj.	9,860

SOUTH E. 68,910

*M. W. L. Morris, C.	26,824
K. Kyle, S.D.P./All.	11,698
M. Coleman, Lab.	11,533
C. maj.	15,126

Northavon (Avon)
E. 73,553

*J. A. Cope, C.	30,790
Dr. G. Conrad, L./All.	17,807
Mrs. N. P. J. Norris, Lab.	8,243
K. Radmall, Eco.	499
C. maj.	12,983

North Devon
E. 63,638

*A. Speller, C.	28,066
R. Blackmore, L./All.	19,339
P. E. James, Lab.	2,893
R. Joanes, Eco.	669
C. maj.	8,727

North Shropshire
E. 73,333

*Rt. Hon. W. J. Biffen, C.	28,496
D. Evans, L./All.	16,829
Miss H. Jones, Lab.	7,860
J. L. Phillimore, Ref.	135
C. maj.	11,667

North Warwickshire
E. 68,625

Hon. F. A. A. Maude, C.	22,452
J. E. Tomlinson, Lab.	19,867
H. Kerry, S.D.P./All.	11,207
C. maj.	2,585

North West Leicestershire
E. 68,510

D. G. Ashby, C.	24,760
Mrs. I. Read, Lab.	18,098
G. Cort, L./All.	12,043
Mrs. D. Freer, Eco.	637
C. maj.	6,662

North Wiltshire
E. 76,150

*R. F. Needham, C.	30,924
C. S. M. Graham, L./All.	23,692
S. R. Allsop, Lab.	2,888
E. Barnham, Eco.	678
H. Baile de la Perrière, J.D.F.	113
C. maj.	7,232
(May '79, C. maj. 4,697)	

Norwich (Norfolk)

NORTH *E.* 62,781

H. P. Thompson, *C.*	21,355
*Rt. Hon. D. Ennals, *Lab.*	15,476
G. Jones, *L./All.*	10,796
Ms. F. Cairns, *W.R.P.*	194
C. maj.	5,879

SOUTH *E.* 64,100

J. A. Powley, *C.*	18,998
*J. Garrett, *Lab.*	18,286
J. Hardie, *S.D.P./All.*	11,968
A. Carter, *Eco.*	468
P. Williams, *N.F.*	145
J. Ward, *Ind.*	91
C. maj.	1,712

Norwood (Gtr. London)
E. 55,663

*J. D. Fraser, *Lab.*	16,280
J. P. Parfitt, *C.*	13,397
M. Noble, *S.D.P./All.*	6,371
Miss C. M. Williams, *N.F.*	343
J. Sanderson, *Ind.*	123
Lab. maj.	2,883

Nottingham

EAST *E.* 63,638

M. Knowles, *C.*	17,641
M. Sloman, *Lab.*	16,177
M. Bird, *S.D.P./All.*	8,385
D. S. Merrick, *Ind. C.*	1,421
C. maj.	1,464

NORTH *E.* 71,807

R. G. J. Ottaway, *C.*	18,730
*W. Whitlock, *Lab.*	18,368
L. Williams, *S.D.P./All.*	9,200
J. Peck, *Comm.*	1,184
C. maj.	362

SOUTH *E.* 65,059

M. M. Brandon-Bravo, *C.*	22,238
K. S. Coates, *Lab.*	16,523
R. Poynter, *L./All.*	9,697
C. maj.	5,715

Nuneaton (Warwicks)
E. 66,072

L. D. Stevens, *C.*	20,666
J. Haynes, *Lab.*	15,605
Ms. R. Levitt, *S.D.P./All.*	14,264
G. E. Davis, *Ind. Lab.*	504
C. maj.	5,061

Old Bexley and Sidcup
(Gtr. London)
E. 50,255

*Rt. Hon. E. R. G. Heath, M.B.E., *C.*	22,422
P. Vickers, *L./All.*	9,704
C. A. Kiff, *Lab.*	5,116
C. maj.	12,718
(May '79, C. maj. 13,456)	

Oldham (Gtr. Manchester)

CENTRAL AND ROYTON
E. 67,177

*J. A. Lamond, *Lab.*	18,611
J. Farquahar, *C.*	15,299
M. Jackson, *S.D.P./All.*	11,022
Lab. maj.	3,312

WEST *E.* 57,445

*M. H. Meacher, *Lab.*	17,690
D. Dickinson, *C.*	14,510
R. A. M. Smith, *L./All.*	7,745
J. Street, *W.C.P.P.P.*	180
Lab. maj.	3,180

Orpington (Gtr. London)
E. 58,759

*I. R. Stanbrook, *C.*	25,569
J. W. Cook, *L./All.*	15,418
D. M. Bean, *Lab.*	3,439
L. T. Taylor, *B.N.P.*	215
C. maj.	10,151

Oxford

EAST *E.* 63,613

S. J. Norris, *C.*	18,808
A. D. Smith, *Lab.*	17,541
Mrs. M. Godden, *L./All.*	10,690
C. maj.	1,267

WEST AND ABINGDON *E.* 67,413

*J. H. C. Patten, *C.*	23,778
D. E. T. Luard, *S.D.P./All.*	16,627
J. Jacottet, *Lab.*	8,440
Ms. S. Starmer, *Eco.*	544
R. Jones, *Loony Soc.*	267
C. N. Smith, *U.P.*	95
P. Doubleday, *Ind.*	86
Ms. R. Pinder, *Ind.*	26
C. maj.	7,151

Peckham (Gtr. London)
E. 59,128

*Ms. H. Harman, *Lab.*	16,616
T. Eckersley, *C.*	7,792
A. Sawdon, *S.D.P./All.*	7,006
Mrs. M. Bailey, *N.F.*	800
Lab. maj.	8,824

Pendle (Lancs)
E. 64,483

*J. R. L. Lee, *C.*	22,739
G. Rogers, *Lab.*	16,604
G. Lishman, *L./All.*	12,056
C. maj.	6,135

Penrith and The Border
(Cumbria)
E. 68,164

*Rt. Hon. W. S. I. Whitelaw, C.H., M.C., *C.*	29,304
M. Young, *L./All.*	13,883
A. L. Williams, *Lab.*	6,612
C. maj.	15,421
(see p. 344 for by-election result)	

Peterborough (Cambs.)
E. 78,957

*Dr. B. S. Mawhinney, *C.*	27,270
B. Fish, *Lab.*	16,831
The Lady Walston, *S.D.P./All.*	13,142
N. Callaghan, *Eco.*	511
D. Hyland, *W.R.P.*	155
P. Gallagher, *Ind. Lab.*	0
C. maj.	10,439

Plymouth (Devon)

DEVONPORT *E.* 61,813

Rt. Hon. Dr. D. A. L. Owen, S.D.P./All.	20,843
Miss. A. Widdecombe, *C.*	15,907
J. Priestley, *Lab.*	9,845
J. E. Sullivan, *Ind. C.*	292
R. Bearsford-Walker, *B.N.P.*	72
Mrs. F. Hill, *C.D.*	21
S.D.P./All. maj.	4,936

DRAKE *E.* 52,383

*Miss J. E. Fookes, *C.*	19,718
W. Fitzgerald, *S.D.P./All.*	11,133
Ms. S. A. Cresswell, *Lab.*	7,921
C. W. Bradbury, *B.N.P.*	163
C. maj.	8,585

SUTTON *E.* 59,890

*Hon. A. K. M. Clark, *C.*	25,203
A. Puttick, *L./All.*	13,516
Ms. F. Holland, *Lab.*	6,538
S. Shaw, *Eco.*	470
C. maj.	11,687

Pontefract and Castleford
(W. Yorks)
E. 64,878

*G. Lofthouse, *Lab.*	24,990
B. Howell, *C.*	11,299
D. Dale, *L./All.*	7,452
Lab. maj.	13,691

Poole (Dorset)
E. 70,731

*J. D. Ward, C.B.E., *C.*	30,358
B. Clements, *L./All.*	15,929
M. V. Castle, *Lab.*	5,595
A. Foster, *S.A.C.A.*	177
C. maj.	14,429

Portsmouth (Hants)

NORTH *E.* 77,923

*P. H. S. Griffiths, *C.*	31,413
S. Luxon, *S.D.P./All.*	13,414
N. Beard, *Lab.*	12,013
C. maj.	17,999

SOUTH *E.* 74,357

*R. B. Pink, C.B.E., V.R.D., *C.*	25,101
M. Hancock, *S.D.P./All.*	12,766
Mrs. S. T. Thomas, *Lab.*	11,324
A. J. Evens, *Ind. L.*	554
G. A. Knight, *N.F.*	279
D. W. Fry, *T.E.F.*	172
C. maj.	12,335
(see by-election on p. 345)	

Preston (Lancs)
E. 64,969

*S. G. Thorne, *Lab.*	21,810
T. Huntley, *C.*	14,832
M. Connolly, *S.D.P./All.*	10,039
Lab. maj.	6,978

Pudsey (W. Yorks)
E. 70,583

*J. G. D. Shaw, *C.*	24,455
J. Cummins, *L./All.*	19,141
Ms. S. M. Price, *Lab.*	9,542
R. Smith, *Ind.*	387
C. maj.	5,314

Putney (Gtr. London)
E. 68,853

*D. J. Mellor, C.	21,863
P. Hain, *Lab.*	16,844
C. Welchman, *L./All.*	7,668
M. Connolly, *N.F.*	290
Mrs. R. Baillie-Grohman, *Eco.*	190
L. Chalk, *Soc.*	88
W. Williams, *Ind.*	41
C. maj.	5,019
(May '79, C. maj. 2,634)	

Ravensbourne (Gtr. London)
E. 58,811

*J. L. Hunt, C.	27,143
Mrs. C. M. Boston, *S.D.P./All.*	11,631
J. R. Holbrook, *Lab.*	4,037
A. T. Shotton, *B.N.P.*	242
C. maj.	15,512

Reading (Berks)
EAST E. 67,511

*Sir G. F. Vaughan, C.	24,516
C. Huhne, *S.D.P./All.*	13,008
K. Boyle, *Lab.*	9,218
G. Darnton, *Eco.*	519
P. Baker, *B.N.P.*	147
B. Shone, *C.M.P.*	113
C. maj.	11,508

WEST E. 66,080

*R. A. B. Durant, C.	24,948
R. J. Day, *L./All.*	13,549
R. Evans, *Lab.*	9,220
E. Lilley, *Ind.*	161
C. maj.	11,399

Redcar (Cleveland)
E. 63,447

*J. Tinn, *Lab.*	18,348
P. Bassett, *C.*	15,244
G. Nightingale, *S.D.P./All.*	11,614
Lab. maj.	3,104
(May '79, Lab. maj. 8,053)	

Reigate (Surrey)
E. 70,320

*G. A. Gardiner, C.	29,932
Mrs. E. Pamplin, *S.D.P./All.*	13,625
B. A. Symons, *Lab.*	6,114
D. Newell, *Eco.*	1,029
C. maj.	16,307

Ribble Valley (Lancs)
E. 59,982

*D. C. Waddington, Q.C., C.	29,223
M. Carr, *S.D.P./All.*	10,632
E. A. Saville, *Lab.*	6,214
C. maj.	18,591

Richmond and Barnes
(Gtr. London)
E. 55,845

J. J. Hanley, *C.*	20,695
A. J. Watson, *L./All.*	20,621
K. Vaz, *Lab.*	3,156
C. maj.	74

Richmond (N. Yorks)
E. 75,196

*Rt. Hon. L. Brittan, Q.C., C.	32,373
D. Raw, *L./All.*	14,307
Mrs. B. L. M. Hawkins, *Lab.*	4,997
C. maj.	18,066

Rochdale (Gtr. Manchester)
E. 66,976

*C. Smith, M.B.E., L./All.	21,858
Ms. V. Broon, *Lab.*	14,271
A. Fearn, *C.*	10,616
P. Barker, *N.F.*	463
P. Courtney, *U.P.*	204
L./All. maj.	7,587
(May '79, L. maj. 5,294)	

Rochford (Essex)
E. 69,392

Dr. M. Clark, C.	29,495
R. Boyd, *L./All.*	16,393
M. Witzer, *Lab.*	5,105
C. maj.	13,102

Romford (Gtr. London)
E. 55,758

*M. J. Neubert, C.	20,771
J. Bates, *L./All.*	10,197
J. Hoepelman, *Lab.*	7,494
Mrs. M. P. Caine, *N.F.*	432
C. maj.	10,574
(May '79, C. maj. 8,812)	

Romsey and Waterside (Hants)
E. 70,782

*M. K. B. Colvin, C.	30,361
A. Bloss, *S.D.P./All.*	16,671
M. Knight, *Lab.*	6,604
C. maj.	13,690

Rossendale and Darwen (Lancs)
E. 74,401

*D. A. Trippier, C.	27,214
C. Robinson, *Lab.*	18,393
M. Taylor, *L./All.*	12,246
C. maj.	8,821

Rotherham (S. Yorks)
E. 61,165

*J. S. Crowther, Lab.	22,236
C. Middleton, *C.*	10,527
P. Bowler, *L./All.*	8,192
Lab. maj.	11,709
(May '79, Lab. maj. 13,445)	

Rother Valley (S. Yorks)
E. 65,127

K. J. Barron, *Lab.*	21,781
J. Derrick, *C.*	13,156
J. Boddy, *S.D.P./All.*	11,903
Lab. maj.	8,625

Rugby and Kenilworth
(Warwicks)
E. 74,501

*J. F. Pawsey, C.	29,622
D. Owen-Jones, *L./All.*	15,381
P. Blundell, *Lab.*	13,180
C. maj.	14,241

Ruislip-Northwood
(Gtr. London)
E. 56,378

*J. A. D. Wilkinson, C.	24,498
R. Stephenson, *L./All.*	11,516
M. O'Brien, *Lab.*	5,105
C. maj.	12,982
(May '79, C. maj. 17,207)	

Rushcliffe (Notts)
E. 70,333

*R. Hon. K. H. Clarke, Q.C., C.	33,253
J. Hamilton, *L./All.*	13,033
V. R. Coaker, *Lab.*	7,290
Mrs. M. Pooks, *Eco.*	518
C. maj.	20,220
(May '79, C. maj. 22,484)	

Rutland and Melton (Leics)
E. 75,180

*M. A. Latham, C.	33,262
D. J. Farrer, *L./All.*	14,909
J. Whitby, *Lab.*	6,414
Ms. H. A. Goddard, *Eco.*	532
C. maj.	18,353

Ryedale (N. Yorks)
E. 78,388

*J. D. Spence, C.	33,312
Mrs. E. Shields, *L./All.*	17,170
P. Bloom, *Lab.*	5,816
C. maj.	16,142

Saffron Walden (Essex)
E. 69,385

*A. G. B. Haselhurst, C.	30,869
J. Torode, *S.D.P./All.*	15,620
R. P. Trory, *Lab.*	6,078
W. D. Smedley, *A.C.M.*	797
C. maj.	15,249
(May '79, C. maj. 15,363)	

St. Albans (Herts)
E. 72,849

P. B. Lilley, *C.*	29,676
A. S. B. Walkington, *L./All.*	21,115
Mrs. R. Austin, *Lab.*	6,213
C. maj.	8,561

St. Helens (Merseyside)
NORTH E. 71,059

*J. Evans, Lab.	25,334
A. Rhodes, *C.*	16,075
N. Derbyshire, *L./All.*	11,525
Lab. maj.	9,259

SOUTH E. 69,172

G. E. Bermingham, *Lab.*	22,906
R. Bull, *C.*	13,244
P. Briers, *S.D.P./All.*	10,939
M. Davies, *Ind.*	1,780
Lab. maj.	9,662

St. Ives (Cornwall)
E. 64,012

D. A. Harris, *C.*	24,297
H. Carter, *S.D.P./All.*	16,438
Ms. M. Crowley, *Lab.*	5,310
P. Prior, *M.K.*	569
H. Hoptrough, *Eco.*	439
N. Horner, *Ind.*	219
C. maj.	7,859

Salford East
(Gtr. Manchester)
E. 63,946

*Rt. Hon. S. Orme, *Lab.* ...	21,373
S. Cole, *C.*	11,832
A. Williams, *S.D.P./All.* ..	6,190
S. Carter, *W.R.P.*	417
Lab. maj.	9,541

Salisbury (Wilts)
E. 74,189

S. R. Key, *C.*	28,876
J. Lakeman, *L./All.*	21,702
Mrs. C. K. Lamberth, *Lab.*	3,139
Miss M. Kemp, *W. Reg.* ...	182
T. Abbott, *Ind.*	86
C. maj.	7,174

Scarborough (N. Yorks)
E. 72,362

*Sir M. N. Shaw, *C.*	27,977
Mrs. R. Jordan, *S.D.P./All.*	14,048
J. Battersby, *Lab.*	9,545
C. maj.	13,929

Sedgefield (Durham)
E. 61,702

A. C. L. Blair, *Lab.*	21,401
T. Horton, *C.*	13,120
D. Shand, *S.D.P./All.*	10,183
M. Logan-Salton, *Ind.*	298
Lab. maj.	8,281

Selby (N. Yorks)
E. 65,365

*Rt. Hon. M. J. H. Alison, *C.*	26,712
W. Whitaker, *L./All.*	10,747
Mrs. S. Haines, *Lab.*	9,687
C. maj.	15,965

Sevenoaks (Kent)
E. 71,327

*G. M. Wolfson, *C.*	30,722
S. Jakobi, *L./All.*	15,016
R. Gooding, *Lab.*	6,439
G. L. Burnett, *N.F.*	416
C. maj.	15,706

Sheffield (S. Yorks)
ATTERCLIFFE E. 64,204

*A. E. P. Duffy, *Lab.*	23,067
G. Millward, *C.*	11,455
Ms. I. Addison, *S.D.P./All.*	10,241
Lab. maj.	11,612

BRIGHTSIDE E. 67,260

*Miss V. J. Maynard, *Lab.*	25,531
F. Butler, *L./All.*	10,322
D. Grayson, *C.*	7,888
P. A. Spinks, *N.F.*	286
Lab. maj.	15,209

CENTRAL E. 66,769

R. G. Caborn, *Lab.*	24,759
Miss P. Major, *S.D.P./All.*	7,969
Miss P. Rawlings, *C.*	7,908
Miss V. Gill, *Comm.*	296
C. Barrett, *Rev. Comm.* ...	222
Lab. maj.	16,790

HALLAM E. 78,878

*Sir J. H. Osborn, *C.*	26,851
M. Johnson, *L./All.*	15,077
Ms. J. McCrindle, *Lab.* ...	10,463
P. Booler, *Ind. C.*	656
C. maj.	11,774

HEELEY E. 74,659

W. Michie, *Lab.*	24,111
S. Cordle, *C.*	15,743
J. M. Day, *S.D.P./All.*	12,813
Lab. maj.	8,368

HILLSBOROUGH E. 74,422

*M. H. Flannery, *Lab.*	20,901
D. Chadwick, *L./All.*	19,355
Mrs. C. Smith, *C.*	15,881
Lab. maj.	1,546

Sherwood (Notts)
E. 69,091

A. S. Stewart, *C.*	21,595
W. Bach, *Lab.*	20,937
Mrs. M. E. Cooper, *S.D.P./All.*	10,172
C. maj.	658

Shipley (W. Yorks)
E. 67,584

*J. M. Fox, M.B.E., *C.*	25,866
W. Wallace, *L./All.*	14,421
M. A. Leathley, *Lab.*	11,218
S. Shepherd, *Eco.*	521
C. maj.	11,445

Shoreham (W Sussex)
E. 69,720

*R. N. Luce, *C.*	31,679
J. Ingram, *L./All.*	15,913
Mrs. S. J. Hurcombe, *Lab.*	3,794
C. maj.	15,766

Shrewsbury and Atcham (Salop)
E. 66,554

D. L. Conway, *C.*	24,397
A. Bowen, *L./All.*	15,773
A. Mosley, *Lab.*	9,080
C. maj.	8,624
(May '79, C. maj. 10,184)	

Skipton and Ripon
(N. Yorks)
E. 69,421

*J. G. B. Watson, *C.*	31,509
Mrs. K. C. Brooks, *L./All.*	16,463
Ms. M. A. Billing, *Lab.* ...	4,044
C. maj.	15,046

Slough (Berks)
E. 71,907

J. A. Watts, *C.*	22,064
*Miss J. Lestor, *Lab.*	18,958
N. Bosanquet, *S.D.P./All.*	9,519
G. John, *N.F.*	528
I. Flindall, *Eco.*	325
C. maj.	3,106

Solihull (W. Midlands)
E. 73,677

J. M. Taylor, *C.*	31,947
I. Gillett, *L./All.*	14,553
I. Jamieson, *Lab.*	6,075
C. maj.	17,394

Somerton and Frome
(Somerset)
E. 64,695

*Hon. R. T. Boscawen, *C.* ..	26,988
N. Hinton, *S.D.P./All.* ...	17,761
J. B. Osborn, *Lab.*	4,867
C. maj.	9,227

Southampton (Hants)
ITCHEN E. 72,233

C. R. Chope, *C.*	21,937
*R. Mitchell, *S.D.P./All.* ...	16,647
J. Denham, *Lab.*	14,324
C. maj.	5,290

TEST E. 74,668

*S. J. A. Hill, *C.*	24,657
A. P. V. Whitehead, *Lab.* .	15,311
A. Vinson, *S.D.P./All.* ...	14,592
C. maj.	9,346

Southend (Essex)
EAST E. 57,690

*E. M. Taylor, *C.*	21,743
C. George, *S.D.P./All.*	11,052
C. O. O'Brien, *Lab.*	6,188
C. maj.	10,691
(May '79, C. maj. 10,774)	

WEST E. 67,486

*Rt. Hon. H. P. G. Channon, *C.*	26,360
G. Grant, *L./All.*	18,327
Mrs. J. Nisbet, *Lab.*	3,675
C. maj.	8,033
(May '79, C. maj. 16,864)	

South Hams (Devon)
E. 74,276

*A. D. Steen, *C.*	31,855
A. Rogers, *L./All.*	19,454
G. J. Morris, *Lab.*	3,824
Ms. W. Morgan, *Eco.*	518
C. maj.	12,401

Southport (Merseyside)
E. 70,089

*Sir W. I. Percival, Q.C., *C.* .	25,612
I. B. Brodie-Brown, *L./All.*	20,573
F. P. Brady, *Lab.*	4,233
K. L. Wood, *S.B.I.L.P.* ...	374
C. maj.	5,039
(May '79, C. maj. 6,527)	

South Ribble (Lancs)
E. 72,401

*R. J. Atkins, *C.*	27,625
F. Duffy, *Lab.*	14,966
R. Walker, *L./All.*	13,690
C. maj.	12,659

South Shields (Tyne & Wear)
E. 61,924

*D. G. Clark, *Lab.*	19,055
P. Groves, *C.*	12,653
P. Angus, *S.D.P./All.*	9,288
Lab. maj.	6,402

Southwark and Bermondsey
(Gtr. London)
E. 55,839

*S. H. W. Hughes, *L./All.*	..	17,185
*J. Tilley, *Lab.*	....	12,021
R. Hughes, *C.*	....	4,481
J. S. Sneath, *N.F.*	....	474
K. T. Mason, *New Brit.*	....	154
A. Farehk, *Rev. Comm.*	...	54
S. C. McKenzie, *Nat.*	.....	50
T. L. Keen, *Ind.*	....	50
L./All. maj.	....	5,164

Spelthorne (Surrey)
E. 72,236

Rt. Hon. Sir H. E. G. Atkins,		
C.	....	26,863
A. Layton, *S.D.P./All.*	....	13,357
M. C. Rowlands, *Lab.*	.....	7,926
R. Adams, *Ind. C.*	....	2,816
E. Butterfield, *A.C.M.*	....	325
C. maj.	....	13,506
(May '79, C. maj. 16,153)		

Stafford
E. 70,570

Rt. Hon. Sir H. C. P. J.		
Fraser, M.B.E., *C.*	......	27,639
D. Dunn, *S.D.P./All.*	.....	13,362
M. J. D. Poulter, *Lab.*	.....	12,789
J. Caruso, *Gizza Job*	...	212
C. maj.	....	14,277
(see by-election on p. 345)		

Staffordshire

MID E. 67,425

*B. J. Heddle, *C.*	....	27,210
T. Jones, *L./All.*	....	13,330
P. Lane, *Lab.*	....	11,720
C. maj.	....	13,880

MOORLANDS E. 72,466

*D. L. Knox, *C.*	....	30,079
B. Campbell, *Lab.*	....	13,513
P. Gubbins, *S.D.P./All.*	...	12,370
C. maj.	....	16,566

SOUTH E. 73,038

*P. T. Cormack, *C.*	....	32,764
J. Chambers, *L./All.*	.....	13,004
M. J. Cartwright, *Lab.*	...	9,568
C. maj.	....	19,760
(May '79, C. maj. 17,433)		

SOUTH EAST E. 63,324

D. L. Lightbown, *C.*	......	24,556
Mrs. C. M. Crawley, *Lab.*	.	13,658
M. Lynch, *S.D.P./All.*	....	10,220
C. maj.	....	10,898

Stalybridge and Hyde
(Gtr. Manchester)
E. 67,916

*T. Pendry, *Lab.*	....	21,798
B. Silvester, *C.*	....	17,436
J. Hughes, *L./All.*	....	8,339
B. Nylan, *N.F.*	....	294
Lab. maj.	....	4,362
(May '79, Lab. maj. 6,580)		

Stamford and Spalding (Lincs)
E. 65,955

*Sir K. Lewis, *C.*	....	27,728
P. Lee, *S.D.P./All.*	......	15,972
Ms. A. Mullender, *Lab.*	...	5,354
C. maj.	....	11,756

Stevenage (Herts)
E. 67,706

T. J. R. Wood, *C.*	....	20,787
B. R. M. Stoneham, *S.D.P./*		
All.	....	19,032
Mrs. S. Reeves, *Lab.*	.....	12,673
D. R. Bowmaker, *B.N.P.*	...	236
C. maj.	....	1,755

Stockport (Gtr. Manchester)
E. 58,908

A. R. Favell, *C.*	....	18,517
P. R. Ward, *Lab.*	....	12,731
*T. McNally, *S.D.P./All.*	...	12,129
M. Shipley, *Eco.*	....	369
K. Walker, *Nat.*	....	194
C. maj.	....	5,786

Stockton (Cleveland)

NORTH E. 70,277

F. Cook, *Lab.*	....	18,339
H. Davies, *C.*	....	16,469
Rt. Hon. W. Rodgers,		
S.D.P./All.	....	14,630
Lab. maj.	....	1,870

SOUTH E. 73,790

I. W. Wrigglesworth,		
S.D.P./All.	....	19,550
T. Finnegan, *C.*	....	19,448
F. Griffiths, *Lab.*	....	13,998
D. Fern, *Ind.*	....	205
S.D.P./All. maj.	....	102

Stoke-on-Trent (Staffs)

CENTRAL E. 66,934

M. Fisher, *Lab.*	....	21,194
K. Mans, *C.*	....	12,944
Ms. V. Freeman, *S.D.P./*		
All.	....	9,458
C. S. Cook, *Loony Soc.*	....	504
Lab. maj.	....	8,250

NORTH E. 75,251

*J. S. Forrester, *Lab.*	......	24,721
R. Ibbs, *C.*	....	16,518
T. Beswick, *S.D.P./All.*	...	12,186
Lab. maj.	....	8,203

SOUTH E. 70,600

*Rt. Hon. J. Ashley, *C.H.,*		
Lab.	....	23,611
P. Maxwell, *C.*	....	16,506
W. Walley, *L./All.*	....	9,050
Lab. maj.	....	7,105

Stratford-on-Avon (Warwicks)
E. 76,649

A. T. Howarth, C.B.E., *C.*	..	34,041
W. J. B. Taylor, *L./All.*	...	16,124
*F. O. Hooley, *Lab.*	......	5,731
C. maj.	....	17,917

Streatham (Gtr. London)
E. 60,032

*W. J. M. Shelton, *C.*	......	18,264
Mrs. M. Long, *Lab.*	......	12,362
P. Billenness, *L./All.*	.....	8,321
K. Handy, *N.F.*	....	321
C. maj.	....	5,902

Stretford (Gtr. Manchester)
E. 57,448

A. J. Lloyd, *Lab.*	....	18,028
W. Sweeney, *C.*	....	13,686
D. Wilks, *S.D.P./All.*	.....	8,141
S. A. Ud-Din, *Ind. Lab.*	...	336
Lab. maj.	....	4,342

Stroud (Glos)
E. 77,528

Sir J. A. Kershaw, M.C.,		
C.	....	30,896
G. Fallon, *L./All.*	....	19,182
D. R. Parsons, *Lab.*	......	10,141
C. maj.	....	11,714

Suffolk

CENTRAL E. 75,641

M. Lord, *C.*	....	30,096
N. Baldwin, *L./All.*	......	15,365
Mrs. M. Sierakowski, *Lab.*	.	10,828
C. maj.	....	14,731

COASTAL E. 71,521

*J. S. Gummer, *C.*	....	31,240
D. Houseley, *S.D.P./All.*	..	15,618
D. Ballantyne, *Lab.*	......	6,780
C. maj.	....	15,622

SOUTH E. 76,209

T. S. K. Yeo, *C.*	....	29,469
R. Kemp, *L./All.*	....	18,200
S. Billcliffe, *Lab.*	....	10,516
C. maj.	....	11,269

Sunderland
(Tyne & Wear)

NORTH E. 78,520

R. A. Clay, *Lab.*	....	24,179
C. Lewis, *C.*	....	16,983
D. McCourt, *L./All.*	......	11,090
Lab. maj.	....	7,196

SOUTH E. 75,124

*G. A. T. Bagier, *Lab.*	.....	22,869
A. Mitchell, *C.*	....	17,321
J. Anderson, *S.D.P./All.*	..	9,865
Lab. maj.	....	5,548

Surbiton (Gtr. London)
E. 46,949

R. P. Tracey, *C.*	....	18,245
C. Nowakowski, *S.D.P./*		
All.	....	9,496
N. D. Waskett, *Lab.*	......	5,173
J. Maclellan, *Eco.*	....	551
C. maj.	....	8,749
(May '79, C. maj. 10,802)		

Surrey

EAST E. 58,485

Rt. Hon. Sir R. E. G. Howe,		
Q.C., *C.*	....	27,272
Mrs. S. Liddell, *L./All.*	..	11,836
H. Pincott, *Lab.*	....	4,249
C. maj.	....	15,436
(May '79, C. maj. 19,400)		

NORTH WEST E. 78,377

*W. M. J. Grylls, *C.*	......	35,297
J. Weedon, *L./All.*	....	14,279
J. Burrow, *Lab.*	....	5,452
C. maj.	....	21,018
(May '79, C. maj. 25,456)		

SOUTH WEST   *E.* 69,875
*Rt. Hon. M. V. Macmillan,
  C. 31,067
G. Scott, *L./All.* 16,716
S. E. D. Williams, *Lab.* 4,239
  C. maj. 14,351
  (*see* by-election on p 345)

Sutton and Cheam
(Gtr. London)
E. 63,099

*D. N. Macfarlane, C. 26,782
C. Caswill, *L./All.* 16,518
G. S. Dixon, *Lab.* 3,568
  C. maj. 10,264
  (May '79, C. maj. 15,706)

Sutton Coldfield (W. Midlands)
E. 67,695

*Rt. Hon. P. N. Fowler, C. .. 31,753
A. Jones, *L./All.* 12,769
C. C. Gibbons, *Lab.* 4,066
  C. maj. 18,984
  (May '79, C. maj. 26,107)

Swindon (Wilts)
E. 76,833

S. C. Coombs, *C.* 22,310
*D. Stoddart, Lab. 20,915
D. J. Scott, *S.D.P./All.* 13,743
  C. maj. 1,395
  (May '79, Lab. maj. 5,899)

Tatton (Cheshire)
E. 68,747

M. N. Hamilton, C. 27,877
D. Levy, *S.D.P./All.* 13,917
D. W. Davies, *Lab.* 9,295
  C. maj. 13,960

Taunton (Somerset)
E. 70,359

*Rt. Hon. E. D. L. du Cann,
  C. 28,112
M. Cocks, *S.D.P./All.* 15,545
J. Gray, *Lab.* 9,498
  C. maj. 12,567
  (May '79, C. maj. 12,724)

Teignbridge (Devon)
E. 67,515

P. C. M. Nicholls, *C.* 28,265
J. Alderson, *L./All.* 20,047
M. Loughlin, *Lab.* 3,749
A. Hope, *Loony Soc.* 241
  C. maj. 8,218

Thanet (Kent)

NORTH   *E.* 66,678
R. J. Gale, *C.* 26,801
W. MacMillan, *S.D.P./All.* 12,256
Ms. C. Booth, *Lab.* 6,482
B. Dobing, *B.N.P.* 324
  C. maj. 14,545

SOUTH   *E.* 61,989
*J. W. P. Aitken, C. 24,512
I. Josephs, *L./All.* 10,461
M. Clark, *Lab.* 8,429
  C. maj. 14,051

Thurrock (Essex)
E. 66,300

*Dr. Oonagh McDonald,
  Lab. 17,600
Miss J. Tallon, *C.* 15,878
D. Benson, *S.D.P./All.* ... 9,761
M. J. Bibby, *Ind.* 1,220
R. W. Sinclair, *B.N.P.* 252
J. Paul, *Comm.* 199
  Lab. maj. 1,722

Tiverton (Devon)
E. 63,828

*R. J. Maxwell-Hyslop, C. .. 27,101
D. Morrish, *L./All.* 19,215
D. A. Gorbutt, *Lab.* 3,154
  C. maj. 7,886

Tonbridge and Malling (Kent)
E. 72,549

*Rt. Hon. J. P. Stanley, C. .. 30,417
F. Freeman, *S.D.P./All.* .. 16,897
D. J. Bishop, *Lab.* 6,896
  C. maj. 13,520
  (May '79, C. maj. 16,252)

Tooting (Gtr. London)
E. 68,083

*T. M. Cox, Lab. 19,640
R. Harris, *C.* 16,981
Mrs. J. Neuberger, *S.D.P./*
  All. 8,317
P. Berbridge, *N.F.* 355
Ms. E. Shaw, *Eco.* 255
R. E. Lewis, *Comm.* 181
H. Patel, *Eth. Min.* 146
C. Redgrave, *W.R.P.* 72
  Lab. maj. 2,659

Torbay (Devon)
E. 67,337

*Sir F. M. Bennett, C. 25,721
M. Mitchell, *L./All.* 19,166
P. W. Rackley, *Lab.* 3,521
Mrs. A. M. L. Murray,
  Ratepayer 500
  C. maj. 6,555

Torridge and West Devon
E. 70,648

*Sir P. M. Mills, C. 31,156
V. Howell, *L./All.* 18,805
W. A. Tupman, *Lab.* 3,531
M. J. Beale, *Ind.* 116
Miss H. E. Rous, *W. Reg.* .. 113
  C. maj. 12,351

Tottenham (Gtr. London)
E. 67,944

*N. Atkinson, Lab. 22,423
P. Murphy, *C.* 13,027
A. L'Estrange, *L./All.* 6,990
W. G. Hurry, *Ind. C.* 652
  Lab. maj. 9,396

Truro (Cornwall)
E. 68,514

*D. C. Penhaligon, L./All. .. 31,279
P. Buddell, *C.* 20,799
Ms. J. M. Beecroft, *Lab.* .. 2,479
  L./All. maj. 10,480

Tunbridge Wells (Kent)
E. 73,700

*Sir P. B. B. Mayhew, Q.C.,
  C. 31,199
P. Blaine, *L./All.* 16,073
S. J. Casely, *Lab.* 6,042
D. Smith, *N.F.* 236
  C. maj. 15,126
  (May '79, C. maj. 20,536)

Twickenham (Gtr. London)
E. 64,116

*T. F. H. Jessel, C. 25,110
J. Waller, *L./All.* 20,318
Ms. P. A. Nicholas, *Lab.* .. 3,732
J. Clarke, *Eco.* 424
T. Denville-Faulkner, *N.F.* 234
R. W. Kenyon, *Ind.* 40
  C. maj. 4,792

Tyne Bridge
(Tyne & Wear)
E. 60,808

*H. L. Cowans, Lab. 21,127
R. Crawley, *C.* 9,434
A. Dawson, *L./All.* 6,852
  Lab. maj. 11,693

Tynemouth
(Tyne & Wear)
E. 74,549

*N. G. Trotter, C. 27,029
P. J. Cosgrove, *Lab.* 17,420
D. Mayhew, *L./All.* 11,153
  C. maj. 9,609

Upminster (Gtr. London)
E. 66,445

*Sir N. C. Bonsor, BT., C. .. 25,153
D. Osman, *S.D.P./All.* 12,339
A. Hughes, *Lab.* 9,829
G. Nobes-Pride, *N.F.* 566
  C. maj. 12,814
  (May '79, C. maj. 9,065)

Uxbridge (Gtr. London)
E. 61,615

*J. M. Shersby, C. 23,875
P. Russell, *S.D.P./All.* 11,038
P. J. Magee, *Lab.* 9,611
  C. maj. 12,837
  (May '79, C. maj. 7,995)

Vauxhall (Gtr. London)
E. 64,867

*S. K. Holland, Lab. 18,234
K. Manning, *C.* 10,454
R. Liddle, *S.D.P./All.* 9,515
J. Wright, *N.F.* 508
P. J. Lingard, *Loony Soc.* .. 266
D. Cook, *Comm.* 199
G. B. Shorter, *W.P.* 38
  Lab. maj. 7,780

Wakefield (W. Yorks)
E. 68,416

*Rt. Hon. W. Harrison,
  Lab. 19,166
N. Hazell, *C.* 18,806
Dr. D. Carlton, *S.D.P./All.* 9,166
Mrs. V. Parker, *B.N.P.* ... 295
  Lab. maj. 360

Wallasey (Merseyside)
E. 68,462

*Mrs. L. Chalker, C.	......	22,854
J. A. Robertson, Lab.	.....	16,146
J. Richardson, S.D.P./All.		10,717
C. maj.	....	6,708
(May '79, C. maj. 5,381)		

Wallsend (Tyne & Wear)
E. 76,268

*W. E. Garrett, Lab.	....	26,615
Miss M. Leigh, C.	....	14,101
Mrs. J. Phylactou, S.D.P./		
All.	....	13,522
Lab. maj.	....	12,514

Walsall (W. Midlands)
E. 68,868

NORTH E. 67,257

*D. J. Winnick, Lab.	......	20,782
N. Stephens, C.	....	17,958
A. Bentley, L./All.	....	10,141
Lab. maj.	....	2,824

SOUTH E. 67,257

*B. T. George, Lab.	......	21,735
D. Nicholson, C.	....	21,033
B. Silver, S.D.P./All.	.....	6,586
J. Parker, B.N.P.	....	632
Lab. maj.	....	702

Walthamstow (Gtr. London)
E. 48,324

*E. P. Deakins, Lab.	......	13,241
A. Amos, C.	....	11,936
P. Leighton, S.D.P./All.	..	7,192
P. Mitchell, N.F.		444
S. Lambert, Eco.	....	424
Lab. maj.	....	1,305
(May '79, Lab. maj. 4,403)		

Wansbeck (Nthmb)
E. 63,398

J. Thompson, Lab.	....	21,732
J. A. Thompson, L./All.		13,901
C. Michell, C.	....	10,563
Lab. maj.	....	7,831

Wansdyke (Avon)
E. 71,094

*J. H. Aspinwall, C.	......	28,434
R. Denton-White, L./All.		15,368
L. Williams, Lab.	....	12,168
A. Stout, W. Reg.	....	213
C. maj.	....	13,066

Wanstead and Woodford
(Gtr. London)
E. 57,705

*Rt. Hon. C. P. F. Jenkin,		
C.	....	23,765
K. Crawford, L./All.	.....	9,411
Mrs. L. S. Hilton, Lab.	...	5,334
Mrs. C. Warth, Eco.	......	476
H. Marshall, N.F.	....	456
C. maj.	....	14,354
(May '79, C. maj. 17,750)		

Wantage (Oxon)
E. 63,950

R. V. Jackson, C.	....	25,992
Mrs. W. Tumin, S.D.P./All.	15,867
A. J. D. Popper, Lab.	.....	7,115
A. P. Barrett Mockler, W.		
Reg.	....	183
C. maj.	....	10,125

Warley (W. Midlands)
EAST E. 57,439

*A. M. W. Faulds, Lab.	...	18,036
M. Whitby, C.	....	14,645
B. Hamer, S.D.P./All.	....	6,697
H. Singh Randhawa,		
Comm.	....	217
Lab. maj.	....	3,391

WEST E. 57,165

*Rt. Hon. P. K. Archer, Q.C.,		
Lab.	....	18,272
Miss A. McIntyre, C.	.....	13,004
A. G. Baines, L./All.	.....	7,485
Lab. maj.	....	5,268

Warrington (Cheshire)
NORTH E. 69,850

*E. D. H. Hoyle, Lab.	......	20,873
S. Sexton, C.	....	15,596
D. Harrison, S.D.P./All.	..	13,951
I. Sloan, B.N.P.	....	267
Lab. maj.	....	5,277

SOUTH E. 72,803

*Rt. Hon. M. Carlisle, Q.C.,		
C.	....	22,740
Dr. D. Colin-Thome, Lab.	.	16,275
I. Marks, L./All.	....	14,827
N. Chantrell, Eco.	....	403
C. maj.	....	6,465

Warwick and Leamington
E. 70,858

*Sir D. G. Smith, C.	....	26,512
R. Behrens, S.D.P./All.	...	13,480
R. Chessum, Lab.	....	11,463
N. Charlton, Eco.	....	685
C. maj.	....	13,032

Watford (Herts)
E. 71,992

*W. A. T. T. Garel-Jones,		
C.	....	26,273
P. Burton, S.D.P./All.	....	14,267
I. Wilson, Lab.	....	14,247
C. maj.	....	12,006

Waveney (Suffolk)
E. 77,960

*Rt. Hon. J. M. L. Prior, C.		30,371
J. A. Lark, Lab.	....	16,073
Ms. G. Artis, S.D.P./All.	..	12,234
C. maj.	....	14,298

Wealden (E. Sussex)
E. 69,244

*Sir G. J. Johnson Smith,		
C.	....	31,926
D. Pace, S.D.P./All.	......	14,741
Mrs. P. Knight, Lab.	.....	3,060
C. maj.	....	17,185

Wellingborough (Northants)
E. 67,598

*P. D. Fry, C.	....	25,715
J. Mann, Lab.	....	13,659
L. Stringer, L./All.	......	12,994
Miss D. M. P. Garnett,		
Ind.	....	228
C. maj.	....	12,056

Wells (Somerset)
E. 62,159

D. P. Heathcoat-Amory, C.		25,385
A. Butt-Philip, L./All.	....	18,810
A. M. Leigh, Lab.	....	3,747
G. Livings, Ind.	....	273
C. maj.	....	6,575

Welwyn Hatfield (Herts)
E. 72,644

*C. P. Y. Murphy, C.	......	27,498
Dr. L. Granshaw, S.D.P./		
All.	....	15,252
J. France, Lab.	....	14,898
C. maj.	....	12,246

Wentworth (S. Yorks)
E. 62,057

*P. Hardy, Lab.	....	25,538
R. Norton, C.	....	9,603
M. Tildsley, S.D.P./All.	..	8,082
Lab. maj.	....	15,935

West Bromwich (W. Midlands)
EAST E. 59,391

*P. C. Snape, Lab.	....	15,894
C. Cole, C.	....	15,596
M. Smith, L./All.	....	10,200
Lab. maj.	....	298

WEST E. 58,341

*Miss B. Boothroyd, Lab.	...	18,896
D. Harman, C.	....	12,257
A. Collingbourne, S.D.P./		
All.	....	6,094
Lab. maj.	....	6,639
(May '79, Lab. maj. 9,468)		

Westbury (Wilts)
E. 80,244

*D. Walters, M.B.E., C.	.....	31,133
D. Hughes, L./All.	....	22,627
H. W. Thomas, Lab.	......	6,058
P. Ekins, Eco.	....	609
J. C. Banks, W. Reg.	.....	131
C. maj.	....	8,506

West Gloucestershire
E. 74,266

*P. Marland, C.	....	27,092
J. Watkinson, S.D.P./All.		17,440
M. J. Hodkinson, Lab.	...	14,572
C. maj.	....	9,652
(May '79, C. maj. 4,174)		

West Lancashire

K. H. Hind, C.	....	25,458
Ms. J. Farrington, Lab.	..	18,600
A. Sackville, S.D.P./All.	..	10,983
C. maj.	....	6,858

Westminster North
(Gtr. London)
E. 68,988

**J. D. Wheeler, C.	19,134
A. Latham, *Lab.*	17,424
G. Halliwell, *S.D.P./All.*	6,956
T. Cooper, *Eco.*	527
T. L. Keen, *T.V.C.A.B.L.*	148
B. Fisher, *Ind.*	73
C. maj.	1,710

Westmorland and Lonsdale
(Cumbria)
E. 67,161

*Rt. Hon. T. M. Jopling, C.	29,775
K. Hulls, *L./All.*	13,188
C. Stott, *Lab.*	4,798
R. Gibson, *Eco.*	805
C. maj.	16,587

Weston-Super-Mare (Avon)
E. 71,439

*A. W. Wiggin, T.D., C.	27,948
J. Marks, *S.D.P./All.*	18,457
R. L. Berry, *Lab.*	5,781
C. maj.	9,491

Wigan (Gtr. Manchester)
E. 72,390

*R. Stott, C.B.E., Lab.	29,859
J. Piggott, *L./All.*	12,554
H. Cadman, *C.*	12,320
Lab. maj.	17,305

Wimbledon (Gtr. London)
E. 64,132

*Rt. Hon. Sir R. M. O. Havers, Q.C., C.	24,169
D. Twigg, *L./All.*	12,623
R. B. Tansey, *Lab.*	8,806
A. Jones, *Eco.*	717
E. Weakner, *P.A.L.*	114
C. maj.	11,546
(May '79, C. maj. 13,315)	

Winchester (Hants)
E. 72,792

*J. E. D. D. Browne, C.	31,908
J. MacDonald, *S.D.P./All.*	18,861
W. H. Allchin, *Lab.*	4,512
S. Winkworth, *W. Reg.*	155
C. maj.	13,047

Windsor and Maidenhead
(Berks)
E. 78,619

*Dr. A. Glyn, E.R.D., C.	32,191
P. Winner, *L./All.*	13,988
Mrs. V. I. Price, *Lab.*	6,383
W. O. Board, *Ind. C.*	1,842
G. F. C. Gillmore, *N.F.*	511
P. B. Illesley, *Ind.*	300
C. R. Bex, *W. Reg.*	68
C. ma	18,203

Wirral (Merseyside)
SOUTH *E.* 60,864

*G. B. Porter, C.	24,766
P. Hollingsworth, *S.D.P./All.*	10,928
K. J. S. Rimmer, *Lab.*	10,411
C. maj.	13,838

WEST *E.* 61,646

*D. J. F. Hunt, M.B.E., C.	25,276
S. Mulholland, *L./All.*	10,125
J. McCabe, *Lab.*	9,855
C. maj.	15,151

Witney (Oxon)
E. 69,362

*Rt. Hon. D. R. Hurd, C.B.E., C.	28,695
P. J. Baston, *L./All.*	15,983
Mrs. C. B. Douse, *Lab.*	7,145
C. maj.	12,712

Woking (Surrey)
E. 78,327

*C. G. D. Onslow, C.	32,748
P. Goldenberg, *L./All.*	16,511
Mrs. D. B. Broer, *Lab.*	6,566
D. Comens, *P.A.L.*	368
C. maj.	16,237
(May '79, C. maj. 18,392)	

Wokingham (Berks)
E. 71,725

*Sir W. R. van Straubenzee, M.B.E., C.	32,925
J. Leston, *L./All.*	17,227
M. Orton, *Lab.*	4,362
C. maj.	15,698

Wolverhampton (W. Midlands)
NORTH EAST *E.* 63,716

*Mrs. R. Short, Lab.	17,941
A. Burnside, *C.*	17,727
R. Yarnell, *L./All.*	8,524
C. Baugh, *N.F.*	585
Lab. maj.	214

SOUTH EAST *E.* 56,428

*R. Edwards, Lab.	17,440
P. McLoughlin, *C.*	12,428
J. Wernick, *L./All.*	9,112
Lab. maj.	5,012

SOUTH WEST *E.* 68,847

*N. W. Budgen, C.	25,214
R. M. Jones, *Lab.*	13,694
E. Harwood, *S.D.P./All.*	10,724
J. Deary, *A.C.M.*	201
C. maj.	11,520

Woodspring (Avon)
E. 71,280

*A. P. Dean, C.	31,932
R. Morgan, *L./All.*	16,800
D. H. White, *Lab.*	6,536
D. M. Robyns, *W. Reg.*	177
C. maj.	15,132

Woolwich (Gtr. London)
E. 56,297

*J. C. Cartwright, S.D.P./All.	15,492
Mrs. A. Wise, *Lab.*	12,767
Mrs. P. Drummond-Brown, *C.*	9,616
T. C. Fitz-Gerald, *B.N.P.*	384
S.D.P./All. maj.	2,725
(May '79, Lab. maj. 10,460)	

Worcester
E. 66,531

*Rt. Hon. P. E. Walker, M.B.E., C.	24,381
C. Phipps, *S.D.P./All.*	13,510
J. Rudd, *Lab.*	11,208
K. A. Axon, *B.N.P.*	208
C. maj.	10,871

Worcestershire
MID *E.* 74,254

*E. Forth, C.	28,159
R. E. Maher, *Lab.*	13,954
Mrs. M. Fairhead, *S.D.P./All.*	12,866
D. W. Fletcher, *N.P.*	386
C. maj.	14,205

SOUTH *E.* 73,278

*W. M. H. Spicer, C.	30,095
D. Phillips, *L./All.*	18,706
P. Sandland-Nielson, *Lab.*	4,183
G. Woodford, *Eco.*	866
G. R. G. Pass, *Ind.*	113
C. maj.	11,389

Workington (Cumbria)
E. 56,119

*D. N. Campbell-Savours, Lab.	23,239
M. Smith, *C.*	16,111
N. Blackshaw, *L./All.*	5,311
Lab. maj.	7,128
(May '79, Lab. maj. 5,756)	

Worsley (Gtr. Manchester)
E. 71,987

T. Lewis, *Lab.*	21,675
S. Windle, *C.*	17,536
*J. F. Roper, S.D.P./All.	14,545
Lab. maj.	4,139

Worthing (W. Sussex)
E. 75,772

*Rt. Hon. T. L. Higgins, C.	32,807
A. Clare, *L./All.*	17,554
A. Minto, *Lab.*	3,158
M. Wingfield, *N.F.*	292
D. Monks, *B.N.P.*	103
C. maj.	15,253
(May '79, C. maj. 20,380)	

The Wrekin (Salop)
E. 77,226

*P. W. Hawksley, C.	22,710
B. Grocott, *Lab.*	21,379
M. Biltcliffe, *S.D.P./All.*	14,208
C. maj.	1,331

Wycombe (Bucks)
E. 70,065

*R. W. Whitney, O.B.E., C.	27,221
A. Page, *S.D.P./All.*	14,024
C. Bastin, *Lab.*	8,636
M. Amin, *M.P.P.*	327
C. maj.	13,197

Wyre (Lancs)
E. 65,934

*Sir W. Clegg, C.	26,559
I. Murdoch, *S.D.P./All.*	11,748
W. Goldsmith, *Lab.*	8,743
C. maj.	14,811

Wyre Forest (H & W)
E. 68,298

*J. E. Bulmer, C.	....	24,809
A. Batchelor, L./All.	......	16,632
R. B. Williams, Lab.	......	9,850
C. maj.	....	8,177

Yeovil (Somerset)
E. 66,102

J. J. D. Ashdown, L./All.	.	26,608
D. Martin, C.	....	23,202
P. J. Brushett, Lab.	......	2,928
L./All. maj.	....	3,406

York (N. Yorks)
E. 78,311

C. R. Gregory, C.	......	24,309
*A. W. Lyon, Lab.	....	20,662
J. V. Cable, S.D.P./All.	...	13,523
A. J. Lister, Ind.	......	204
T. G. Brattan, B.N.P.	....	148
C. maj.	....	3,647
(May '79, Lab. maj. 1,250)		

WALES

Aberavon (W. Glam.)

*Rt. Hon. J. Morris, Q.C.,		
Lab.	....	23,745
Mrs. S. Cutts, L./All.	.....	8,206
G. Bailey, C.	....	6,605
G. Phillips, P.C.	....	1,859
Lab. maj.	....	15,539

Alyn and Deeside (Clwyd)
E. 56,618

*S. B. Jones, Lab.	....	17,806
S. Burns, C.	....	16,438
E. C. H. Owen, S.D.P./All.		9,535
A. Shore, P.C.	....	413
Lab. maj.	....	1,368

Blaenau Gwent
E. 55,948

*Rt. Hon. M. M. Foot, Lab.		30,113
G. Atkinson, L./All.	......	6,408
T. Morgan, C.	....	4,816
S. Morgan, P.C.	....	1,624
Lab. maj.	....	23,705

Brecon and Radnor (Powys)
E. 47,277

*T. E. Hooson, C.	......	18,255
D. Morris, Lab.	....	9,471
R. Livsey, L./All.	....	9,226
Ms. S. Meredudd, P.C.	.....	640
R. Booth, Ind.	....	278
C. maj.	....	8,784

Bridgend (Mid Glam)
E. 53,918

P. C. Hubbard-Miles, C.	..	15,950
J. A. Fellows, Lab.	......	14,623
R. Smart, S.D.P./All.	.....	9,630
K. Bush, P.C.	....	1,312
C. maj.	....	1,327

Caernarfon (Gwynedd)
E. 44,147

*D. W. Wigley, P.C.	....	18,308
D. Jones, C.	....	7,319
Mrs. B. H. Williams, Lab. .		6,736
O. G. Griffiths, L./All.	....	2,356
P.C. maj.	....	10,989
(May '79, P.C. maj. 8,724)		

Caerphilly (Mid Glam)
E. 63,479

R. Davies, Lab.	....	21,570
A. Lambert, L./All.	......	10,017
C. Welby, C.	....	9,295
L. Whittle, P.C.	....	6,414
Lab. maj.	....	11,553

Cardiff (S. Glam)
E. 53,815

CENTRAL   E. 53,815

*I. Grist, C.	....	16,090
M. German, L./All.	......	12,638
R. T. Davies, Lab.	....	9,387
P. Morgan, P.C.	....	704
C. maj.	....	3,452

NORTH   E. 53,377

G. H. Jones, C.	....	19,433
A. W. Jeremy, S.D.P./All.		12,585
Ms. J. Hutt, Lab.	....	8,256
Dr. D. Huws, P.C.	....	974
C. maj.	....	6,848

SOUTH AND PENARTH   E. 59,520

*Rt. Hon. L. J. Callaghan,		
Lab.	....	17,448
D. Tredinnick, C.	....	15,172
W. Roddick, L./All.	......	8,816
Ms. S. Edwards, P.C.	.....	673
B. T. Lewis, F.W.D.	......	165
Lab. maj.	....	2,276

WEST   E. 58,538

S. Terlezki, C.	....	15,472
D. Seligman, Lab.	....	13,698
*J. Thomas, S.D.P./All.	...	10,388
M. Parri, P.C.	....	848
G. Jones, Eco.	....	352
C. maj.	....	1,774

Carmarthen (Dyfed)
E. 63,468

*Dr. R. G. Thomas, Lab. ...		16,459
N. M. Thomas, C.	....	15,305
G. Evans, P.C.	....	14,099
Mrs. J. Colin, S.D.P./All.		5,737
B. Kingzett, Eco.	....	374
C. Grice, B.N.P.	....	154
Lab. maj.	....	1,154

Ceredigion and Pembroke North
(Dyfed)
E. 60,523

*G. W. Howells, L./All.	....	19,677
T. Raw-Rees, C.	....	14,038
G. E. Hughes, Lab.	....	6,840
C. Dafis, P.C.	....	6,072
Miss M. Smith, Eco.	......	431
L./All. maj.	....	5,639

Clwyd

NORTH WEST   E. 62,503

*Sir A. J. C. Meyer, BT., C.	.	23,283
J. Lewis, L./All.	....	13,294
I. Campbell, Lab.	....	7,433
Mrs. M. Rhys, P.C.	....	1,669
C. maj.	....	9,989

SOUTH WEST   E. 55,792

R. L. Harvey, C.	....	14,575
*R. T. Ellis, S.D.P./All.	...	13,024
D. B. Carter, Lab.	....	11,829
T. Schiavone, P.C.	....	3,684
C. maj.	....	1,551

Conwy (Gwynedd)
E. 51,567

*I. W. P. Roberts, C.	......	16,413
Rev. J. R. Roberts, L./All.		12,145
I. Walters, Lab.	....	6,731
D. Iwan, P.C.	....	4,105
C. maj.	....	4,268

Cynon Valley (Mid Glam)
E. 50,284

*I. L. Evans, Lab.	....	20,668
F. Aubel, S.D.P./All.	.....	7,594
J. Arbuthnot, C.	....	5,240
Mrs. P. Jarman, P.C.	.....	3,421
Lab. maj.	....	13,074
(see by-election on p. 345)		

Delyn (Clwyd)
E. 62,483

K. W. Raffan, C.	....	20,242
J. Colbert, Lab.	....	14,298
J. H. Parry, L./All.	......	12,545
H. Huws, P.C.	....	1,558
C. maj.	....	5,944

Gower (W. Glam.)
E. 56,693

*G. L. Wardell, Lab.	......	16,972
Dr. A. R. T. Kenyon, C. ...		15,767
G. Jones, S.D.P./All.	.....	10,450
N. Williams, P.C.	....	1,444
Lab. maj.	....	1,205

Islwyn (Gwent)
E. 50,259

*N. G. Kinnock, Lab.	.....	23,183
D. Johnson, S.D.P./All.	..	8,803
M. Bevan, C.	....	5,511
A. Richards, P.C.	....	1,574
Lab. maj.	....	14,380

Llanelli (Dyfed)
E. 63,826

*Rt. Hon. D. J. D. Davies,		
Lab.	....	23,207
N. Kennedy, C.	....	9,601
K. Rees, L./All.	....	9,076
H. T. Edwards, P.C.	......	5,880
R. E. Hitchon, Comm.	.....	371
Lab. maj.	....	13,606

Meirionnydd Nant Conwy
(Gwynedd)
E. 30,459

*D. E. Thomas, P.C.	......	9,709
D. Lloyd, C.	....	7,066
D. Roberts, S.D.P./All.	..	4,254
G. Williams, Lab.	....	3,735
P.C. maj.	....	2,643

Merthyr Tydfil and Rhymney
(Mid Glam)
E. 59,486

*E. Rowlands, Lab.	....	29,053
P. Owen, L./All.	....	6,323
R. Blauston, C.	....	5,449
G. Howells, P.C.	....	2,058
T. Gould, W.R.P.	....	256
Lab. maj.	....	22,730

Monmouth (Gwent)
E. 56,112

*J. Stradling-Thomas, C.		21,746
C. Lindley, *S.D.P./All.*		12,403
C. Short, *Lab.*		9,593
G. Williams, *P.C.*		493
C. maj.		9,343

Montgomery (Powys)
E. 37,474

A. C. Carlile, *L./All.*		12,863
*D. Williams, C.		12,195
J. Wilson, *Lab.*		2,550
C. Clowes, *P.C.*		1,585
D. W. Rowlands, *Ind.*		487
L./All. maj.		668
(May '79, C. maj. 1,593)		

Neath (W. Glam)
E. 55,272

*D. R. Coleman, C.B.E., Lab.		22,670
K. Davies, *S.D.P./All.*		9,066
R. Buckley, *C.*		7,350
D. I. Owen, *P.C.*		3,046
J. Donovan, *Comp. Dem.*		150
Lab. maj.		13,604

Newport (Gwent)

EAST *E.* 52,503

*R. J. Hughes, Lab.		15,931
R. Thomason, *C.*		13,301
Ms. F. David, *S.D.P./All.*		10,293
D. Thomas, *P.C.*		697
Lab. maj.		2,630

WEST *E.* 54,125

M. N. F. Robinson, *C.*		15,948
B. Davies, *Lab.*		15,367
Dr. W. Jones, *L./All.*		10,163
D. Watkins, *P.C.*		477
C. maj.		581

Ogmore (Mid Glam)
E. 51,378

*R. Powell, Lab.		23,390
J. Parsons, *L./All.*		6,026
R. O'Sullivan, *C.*		5,806
E. J. Merriman, *P.C.*		3,124
Dr. N. Thomas, *Eco.*		1,161
Lab. maj.		17,364

Pembroke (Dyfed)
E. 67,885

*Rt. Hon. R. N. Edwards, C.		24,860
A. P. Griffiths, *Lab.*		15,504
Rev. J. Pullin, *S.D.P./All.*		10,983
O. Osmond, *P.C.*		1,073
D. Hoffmann, *Eco.*		478
G. S. Phillips, *Ind.*		136
C. maj.		9,356

Pontypridd (Mid Glam)
E. 60,883

*B. T. John, Lab.		20,188
R. Langridge, *S.D.P./All.*		11,444
R. Evans, *C.*		10,139
Mrs. J. Davies, *P.C.*		2,065
A. K. Jones, *Eco.*		449
Lab. maj.		8,744

Rhondda (Mid Glam)
E. 62,587

A. R. Rogers, *Lab.*		29,448
A. Lloyd, *S.D.P./All.*		8,078
G. Davies, *P.C.*		4,845
P. Meyer, *C.*		3,973
A. True, *Comm.*		1,350
Lab. maj.		21,370
(May '79, Lab. maj. 31,481)		

Swansea (W. Glam)

EAST *E.* 57,285

*D. Anderson, Lab.		22,297
M. Shrewsbury, *L./All.*		8,762
N. O'Shaughnessy, *C.*		8,080
C. Reid, *P.C.*		1,531
W. R. Jones, *Comm.*		294
Lab. maj.		13,535

WEST *E.* 58,237

*Rt. Hon. A. J. Williams, Lab.		18,042
Dr. J. Lewis, *C.*		15,692
P. Berry, *S.D.P./All.*		8,036
Mrs. M. Pennar, *P.C.*		795
G. E. Oubridge, *Eco.*		265
Lab. maj.		2,350

Torfaen (Gwent)
E. 58,739

*L. Abse, Lab.		20,678
G. Blackburn, *L./All.*		12,393
P. Martin, *C.*		9,751
Mrs. P. Cox, *P.C.*		896
Lab. maj.		8,285
(May '79, Lab. maj. 17,368)		

Vale of Glamorgan (S. Glam)
E. 62,885

*Sir H. R. Gower, C.		22,421
M. E. Sharp, *Lab.*		12,028
A. Evans, *S.D.P./All.*		11,154
J. Dixon, *P.C.*		1,068
C. maj.		10,393

Wrexham (Clwyd)
E. 60,707

J. Marek, *Lab.*		16,120
Mrs. K. Wood, *C.*		15,696
M. Thomas, *L./All.*		13,974
J. Thomas, *P.C.*		1,239
Lab. maj.		424

Ynys Môn/Anglesey
(Gwynedd)
E. 50,359

*K. L. Best, T.D., *C.*		15,017
I. W. Jones, *P.C.*		13,333
T. Williams, *Lab.*		6,791
D. Thomas, *S.D.P./All.*		4,947
C. maj.		1,684
(May '79, C. maj. 2,817)		

SCOTLAND

Aberdeen (Grampian)

NORTH *E.* 63,049

*R. Hughes, Lab.		19,262
C. S. Deans, *S.D.P./All.*		10,118
Mrs. G. Scanlan, *C.*		7,426
J. McGugan, *S.N.P.*		3,790
Ms. M. Harty, *Eco.*		367
Lab. maj.		9,144

SOUTH *E.* 57,540

P. G. Malone, *C.*		15,393
R. Middleton, *Lab.*		11,812
I. G. Philip, *S.D.P./All.*		10,372
S. Coull, *S.N.P.*		1,974
C. maj.		3,581

Angus East (Tayside)
E. 59,359

*P. L. Fraser, Q.C., *C.*		19,218
A. Welsh, *S.N.P.*		15,691
Miss P. Hammond, *S.D.P./All.*		4,978
C. McConnell, *Lab.*		3,497
Mrs. P. Ross, *Eco.*		239
C. maj.		3,527

Argyll and Bute (S'clyde)
E. 47,497

*J. J. MacKay, C.		13,380
Mrs. J. R. Michie, *L./All.*		9,536
I. Smith, *S.N.P.*		8,514
C. McCafferty, *Lab.*		3,204
C. maj.		3,844

Ayr (S'clyde)
E. 65,010

*Rt. Hon. G. K. H. Younger, T.D., *C.*		21,325
K. MacDonald, *Lab.*		13,338
C. Brodie, *L./All.*		12,740
I. Goldie, *S.N.P.*		2,431
C. maj.		7,987

Banff and Buchan (Grampian)
E. 60,403

*A. McQuarrie, C.		16,072
D. Henderson, *S.N.P.*		15,135
E. Needham, *S.D.P./All.*		6,084
I. F. R. Lloyd, *Lab.*		3,150
C. maj.		937

Caithness and Sutherland
(H'land)
E. 30,871

*R. A. R. Maclennan, S.D.P./All.		12,119
A. Scouller, *C.*		5,276
D. Carrigan, *Lab.*		3,325
J. Ingram, *S.N.P.*		2,568
S.D.P./All. maj.		6,843
(May '79, Lab. maj. 2,539)		

Carrick, Cumnock and Doon Valley (S'clyde)
E. 55,925

*G. Foulkes, Lab.		21,394
J. McInnes, *C.*		10,024
R. Logan, *S.D.P./All.*		7,421
R. Wyllie, *S.N.P.*		2,694
Lab. maj.		11,370

Clackmannan (Central)
E. 47,642

*M. J. O'Neill, Lab.		16,478
Mrs. J. Jones, *S.N.P.*		6,839
C. Hendry, *C.*		6,490
Mrs. H. Campbell, *S.D.P./All.*		6,205
Lab. maj.		9,639

Clydebank and Milngavie
(S'clyde)
E. 50,831

*H. McCartney, Lab.		17,288
J. Gourlay, *S.D.P./All.*		9,573
R. Graham, *C.*		7,852
A. Aitken, *S.N.P.*		3,566
J. Bollan, *Comm.*		308
Lab. maj.		7,715
((May '79, Lab. maj. 12,003))		

Clydesdale (S'clyde)
E. 60,240

*Rt. Hon. Dame Judith Hart,		
D.B.E., *Lab.*		17,873
P. Bainbridge, *C.*		13,007
Miss M. Craig, *S.D.P./All.*		9,908
T. McAlpine, *S.N.P.*		5,271
Lab. maj.		4,866

Cumbernauld and Kilsyth
(S'clyde)
E. 44,190

*N. Hogg, Lab.		16,629
D. Herbison, *S.D.P./All.*		6,701
G. Murray, *S.N.P.*		5,875
Mrs. A. Thompson, *C.*		4,590
Lab. maj.		9,928

Cunninghame (S'clyde)

NORTH *E.* 53,126

*J. A. Corrie, C.		15,557
J. N. Carson, *Lab.*		13,920
R. Leishman, *S.D.P./All.*		7,268
C. Cameron, *S.N.P.*		3,460
C. maj.		1,637

SOUTH *E.* 48,552

*D. Lambie, Lab.		19,344
P. Gallie, *C.*		7,576
J, Boss, *L./All.*		6,370
Mrs. K. Ullrich, *S.N.P.*		2,451
Lab. maj.		11,768

Dumbarton (S'clyde)
E. 57,373

*I. Campbell, Lab.		15,810
I. Lawson, *C.*		13,695
R. Sawyer, *S.D.P./All.*		9,813
I. Bayne, *S.N.P.*		3,768
Lab. maj.		2,115
(May '79, Lab. maj. 6,457)		

Dumfries (D & G)
E. 57,594

*Sir H. S. P. Monro, C.		18,730
J. McCall, *S.D.P./All.*		10,036
T. McAughtrie, *Lab.*		8,764
E. Gibson, *S.N.P.*		4,527
C. maj.		8,694

Dundee (Tayside)

EAST *E.* 62,752

*R. G. Wilson, S.N.P.		20,276
C. Bowman, *Lab.*		15,260
Mrs. B. Vaughan, *C.*		7,172
S. Rottger, *L./All.*		3,546
S.N.P. maj.		5,016
(May '79, S.N.P. maj. 2,519)		

WEST *E.* 62,703

*E. Ross, Lab.		20,288
D. Senior, *C.*		10,138
Mrs. E. Dick, *S.D.P./All.*		7,976
J. Lynch, *S.N.P.*		7,973
P. Marks, *Eco.*		302
Lab. maj.		10,150
(May '79, Lab. maj. 10,457)		

Dunfermline (Fife)

EAST *E.* 49,881

J. G. Brown, Lab.		18,515
D. Harcus, *L./All.*		7,214
C. Shenton, *C.*		6,764
G. Hunter, *S.N.P.*		2,573
A. Maxwell, *Comm.*		864
Lab. maj.		11,301

WEST *E.* 49,075

*R. G. Douglas, Lab.		12,998
Dr. P. Davison, *C.*		10,524
F. Moyes, *S.D.P./All.*		9,434
J. Fairlie, *S.N.P.*		2,798
S. Dobson, *Eco.*		321
Lab. maj.		2,474

East Kilbride (S'clyde)
E. 61,420

*Dr. M. S. Miller, Lab.		17,535
D. Sullivan, *S.D.P./All.*		13,199
R. Dalkeith, (Earl of Dalk-		
eith) *C.*		11,483
D. Urquhart, *S.N.P.*		4,795
W. Doolan, *Comm.*		256
Lab. maj.		4,336

East Lothian
E. 62,351

*J. D. Home Robertson,		
Lab.		20,934
M. Fry, *C.*		14,693
M. Kibby, *L./All.*		9,950
R. Knox, *S.N.P.*		2,083
Lab. maj.		6,241

Eastwood (S'clyde)
E. 59,378

*J. A. Stewart, C.		21,072
J. Pickett, *S.D.P./All.*		12,477
J. McGuire, *Lab.*		9,083
Ms. J. Herriot, *S.N.P.*		2,618
C. maj.		8,595

Edinburgh (Lothian)

CENTRAL *E.* 57,064

*A. M. Fletcher, C.		14,095
R. Kelley, *Lab.*		11,529
Dr. Marion Macleod,		
S.D.P./All.		9,498
R. Halliday, *S.N.P.*		1,810
D. Carson, *Comm.*		119
C. maj.		2,566

EAST *E.* 51,156

*G. S. Strang, Lab.		16,169
P. Martin, *C.*		10,303
R. Mcleod, *L./All.*		7,570
P. Scott, *S.N.P.*		1,976
Lab. maj.		5,866

LEITH *E.* 60,562

*R. D. M. Brown, Lab.		16,177
D. Graham, *S.D.P./All.*		11,204
B. Cooklin, *C.*		10,706
J. Young, *S.N.P.*		2,646
Lab. maj.		4,973

PENTLANDS *E.* 59,295

*M. L. Rifkind, C.		17,051
K. Smith, *S.D.P./All.*		12,742
E. Milligan, *Lab.*		10,390
N. MacCormick, *S.N.P.*		2,642
A. Nicol-Smith, *Eco.*		687
C. maj.		4,309

SOUTH *E.* 62,517

*M. A. F. J. Ancram (Earl of		
Ancram), C.		16,485
J. Godfrey, *S.D.P./All.*		12,830
R. A. McCreadie, *Lab.*		12,824
N. MacCallum, *S.N.P.*		2,256
Mrs. L. Hendry, *Eco.*		450
C. maj.		3,655

WEST *E.* 61,050

*Lord James Douglas-Ham-		
ilton, C.		17,646
D. King, *L./All.*		17,148
A. Wood, *Lab.*		9,313
J. Nicoll, *S.N.P.*		2,126
C. maj.		498

Falkirk (Central)

EAST *E.* 52,045

*H. Ewing, Lab.		17,956
D. Masterton, *C.*		7,895
A. Wedderburn, *S.D.P./*		
All.		6,967
J. MacGregor, *S.N.P.*		4,490
Miss F. McGregor, *Comm.*		334
Lab. maj.		10,061

WEST *E.* 49,402

*D. A. Canavan, Lab.		16,668
I. Mitchell, *C.*		7,690
M. Harris, *L./All.*		7,477
B. Cochrane, *S.N.P.*		4,739
Lab. maj.		8,978

Fife

CENTRAL *E.* 54,389

*W. W. Hamilton, Lab.		17,008
Mrs. T. Little, *L./All.*		9,214
D. Mason, *C.*		8,863
J. Taggart, *S.N.P.*		4,039
D. Allison, *Eco.*		297
Lab. maj.		7,794

NORTH EAST *E.* 50,476

*J. S. B. Henderson, C.		17,129
M. Campbell, *L./All.*		14,944
Dr. J. K. M. Hulbert,		
S.N.P.		2,442
D. Caldwell, *Lab.*		2,429
T. G. Flinn, *Eco.*		242
		2,185

Galloway and Upper Nithsdale
(D & G)
E. 51,831

*I. B. Lang, C.		17,579
G. Thompson, *S.N.P.*		12,118
G. Douglas, *L./All.*		5,129
M. B. Miller, *Lab.*		4,464
C. maj.		5,461

Glasgow (S'clyde)

CATHCART *E.* 51,055

*J. A. Maxton, Lab.		16,037
D. May, *C.*		11,807
K. Bloomer, *S.D.P./All.*		8,710
W. Steven, *S.N.P.*		2,151
Lab. maj.		4,230

CENTRAL *E.* 51,217
R. McTaggart, Lab.	17,066
W. Harvey, *C.*	6,104
Mrs. I. Nelson, *L./All.*	5,366
P. Mallan, *S.N.P.*	3,300
J. McGoldrick, *Comm.*	347
Lab. maj.	10,962

GARSCADDEN *E.* 50,589
D. C. Dewar, Lab.	19,635
W. Lyden, *S.D.P./All.*	6,161
K. Macleod, *C.*	5,368
N. MacLeod, *S.N.P.*	3,566
S. A. Barr, *Comm.*	218
Lab. maj.	13,474
(May '79, Lab. maj.	15,198

GOVAN *E.* 51,754
Rt. Hon. B. Millan, Lab.	20,370
I. McDonald, *S.D.P./All.*	7,313
A. Mackenzie, *C.*	7,180
P. Kindlen, *S.N.P.*	2,207
Lab. maj.	13,057

HILLHEAD *E.* 57,016
Rt. Hon. R. H. Jenkins, S.D.P./All.	14,856
N. Carmichael, Lab.	13,692
M. Tosh, *C.*	9,638
G. Leslie, *S.N.P.*	2,203
J. Davidson, *Ind. C.*	249
A. Whitelaw, *Eco.*	239
J. Robins, *A.V.*	139
S.D.P./All. maj.	1,164

MARYHILL *E.* 51,847
J. M. Craigen, Lab.	18,724
Ms. E. Attwooll, *L./All.*	7,521
J. Gibbs, *C.*	5,014
I. Morrison, *S.N.P.*	2,408
P. Smith, *Comm.*	274
Lab. maj.	11,203

POLLOK *E.* 53,217
J. White, Lab.	18,973
J. Carlaw, *C.*	7,441
G. McKell, *L./All.*	6,308
F. Hannigan, *S.N.P.*	3,585
Lab. maj.	11,532

PROVAN *E.* 47,706
H. D. Brown, Lab.	20,040
A. Heron, *S.D.P./All.*	4,655
Miss S. Gordon, *C.*	3,374
Mrs. P. Kennedy, *S.N.P.*	2,737
J. Jackson, *Comm.*	294
Lab. maj.	15,385
(May '79, Lab. maj. 18,844)	

RUTHERGLEN *E.* 59,209
Rt. Hon. J. G. Mackenzie, Lab.	21,510
R. Brown, *L./All.*	12,384
Mrs. H. Hodgins, *C.*	8,017
K. Fee, *S.N.P.*	2,438
C. Corrigan, *W.R.P.*	148
Lab. maj.	9,126

SHETTLESTON *E.* 51,955
D. Marshall, Lab.	19,203
I. Henderson, *C.*	6,787
S. Strachen, *L./All.*	6,568
D. Hood, *S.N.P.*	2,801
K. Hill, *B.N.P.*	103
Lab. maj.	12,416

SPRINGBURN *E.* 53,373
M. J. Martin, Lab.	22,481
J. Kelly, *L./All.*	4,882
D. Tweedie, *C.*	4,565
J. McLaughlin, *S.N.P.*	2,804
Lab. maj.	17,599

Gordon (Grampian)
E. 65,537
M. G. Bruce, L./All.	20,134
J. Cran, *C.*	19,284
G. Grant, *Lab.*	3,899
K. Guild, *S.N.P.*	2,636
L./All. maj.	850

Greenock and Port Glasgow
(S'clyde)
E. 59,437
N. A. Godman, Lab.	20,650
A. Blair, *L./All.*	16,025
C. Chrichton, *C.*	4,314
A. Clayton, *S.N.P.*	2,989
G. McKinlay, *W.R.P.*	114
Lab. maj.	4,625
(May '79, Lab. maj. 11,282)	

Hamilton (S'clyde)
E. 61,430
G. I. M. Robertson, Lab.	24,384
S. Donaldson, *L./All.*	9,365
Mrs. M. Scott, *C.*	8,940
Mrs. M. Whitehead, *S.N.P.*	3,816
Lab. maj.	15,019

Inverness, Nairn and Lochaber
(H'land)
E. 63,645
D. R. Johnston, L./All.	20,671
D. G. Maclean, *C.*	13,373
D. McMillan, *Lab.*	6,448
H. Vernal, *S.N.P.*	4,395
L./All. maj.	7,298

Kilmarnock and Loudoun
(S'clyde)
E. 61,394
W. McKelvey, Lab.	20,250
R. Leckie, *C.*	11,450
A. Ross, *S.D.P./All.*	10,545
C. Calman, *S.N.P.*	4,165
Lab. maj.	8,800
(May '79, Lab. maj. 11,467)	

Kincardine and Deeside
(Grampian)
E. 59,552
Rt. Hon. A. L. Buchanan-Smith, C.	20,293
S. Waugh, *L./All.*	12,497
Mrs. M. Morell, *Lab.*	6,472
A. Tuttle, *S.N.P.*	3,297
C. maj.	7,796

Kirkcaldy (Fife)
E. 53,078
H. P. H. Gourlay, Lab.	15,380
I. Walker, *C.*	10,049
M. Black, *S.D.P./All.*	9,274
D. Wood, *S.N.P.*	3,452
Lab. maj.	5,331

Linlithgow (Lothian)
E. 58,111
T. Dalyell, Lab.	19,694
C. Jones, *C.*	8,333
D. Ramsey, *S.N.P.*	8,026
P. Cockcroft, *S.D.P./All.*	7,432
Dr. Morag Parnell, *Comm.*	199
Lab. maj.	11,361

Livingston (Lothian)
E. 53,284
R. F. Cook, Lab.	14,255
A. Henderson, *L./All.*	9,304
J. Campbell, *C.*	9,129
K. MacAskill, *S.N.P.*	5,090
Lab. maj.	4,951

Midlothian
E. 60,496
A. Eadie, B.E.M., Lab.	19,401
A. Dewar, *S.D.P./All.*	13,245
D. Menzies, *C.*	9,922
Mrs. M. Hird, *S.N.P.*	2,826
Lab. maj.	6,156

Monklands (S'clyde)
EAST *E.* 49,030
Rt. Hon. J. Smith, Lab.	18,358
J. Love, *C.*	8,559
A. Rennie, *L./All.*	5,721
T. Johnston, *S.N.P.*	3,185
Lab. maj.	9,799

WEST *E.* 50,345
T. Clarke, C.B.E., Lab.	20,642
L. Cameron, *C.*	8,378
R. Ackland, *S.D.P./All.*	6,605
A. Lyon, *S.N.P.*	2,473
Lab. maj.	12,264

Moray (Grampian)
E. 60,804
A. Pollock, C.	16,944
H. Watt, *S.N.P.*	15,231
M. Burnett, *L./All.*	7,901
J. Kiddie, *Lab.*	3,139
C. maj.	1,713

Motherwell (S'clyde)
NORTH *E.* 56,512
J. Hamilton, C.B.E., Lab.	24,483
R. Hargrave, *C.*	6,589
G. Whitelaw, *L./All.*	5,970
R. Lyle, *S.N.P.*	5,333
Lab. maj.	17,894

SOUTH *E.* 52,183
Dr. J. W. Bray, Lab.	19,939
P. Walker, *C.*	7,590
B. Ashley, *S.D.P./All.*	6,754
J. Wright, *S.N.P.*	3,743
Lab. maj.	12,349
(May '79, Lab. maj. 10,937)	

North Tayside
E. 51,972
W. C. Walker, C.	19,269
A. Morgan, *S.N.P.*	9,170
D. Skene, *L./All.*	7,255
N. Wylie, *Lab.*	2,057
C. maj.	10,099

Orkney and Shetland (Islands)
E. 30,087

J. R. Wallace, L./All.	.....	9,374
D. Myles, C.	....	5,224
Mrs. W. Ewing, *S.N.P.*	...	3,147
Ms. R. Goodlad, *Lab.*	....	2,665
L./All. maj.	....	4,150
(May '79, L. maj. 6,810)		

Paisley (S'clyde)

NORTH *E.* 50,464

A. Adams, Lab.	....	15,782
Miss A. McCartin, *S.D.P./*		
All.	....	8,195
B. Townsend, *C.*	....	7,425
H. Morrell, *S.N.P.*	......	2,783
Dr. Nicolette Carlaw, *Eco.*		439
Lab. maj.	....	7,587

SOUTH *E.* 52,031

N. F. Buchan, Lab.	......	15,633
Mrs. E. Buchanan, *L./All.*		9,104
J. Knox, *C.*	....	7,819
J. Mitchell, *S.N.P.*	....	4,918
D. Mellor, *Eco.*	....	271
Lab. maj.	....	6,529

Perth and Kinross (Tayside)
E. 61,478

N. H. Fairbairn, Q.C., C.	..	17,888
G. D. Crawford, *S.N.P.*	...	11,155
B. Coutts, *L./All.*	....	10,997
A. J. Stuart, *Lab.*	....	4,414
C. maj.	....	6,733

Renfrew West and Inverclyde
(S'clyde)
E. 53,510

Mrs. A. A. McCurley, *C.*	..	13,669
Dr. J. D. Mabon, S.D.P./		
All.	....	12,347
G. Doherty, *Lab.*	....	12,139
W. Taylor, *S.N.P.*	....	3,653
C. maj.	....	1,322

Ross, Cromarty and Skye
(H'land)
E. 48,401

C. P. Kennedy, S.D.P./All.		13,528
Rt. Hon. H. Gray, C.	....	11,824
M. Elder, *Lab.*	....	4,901
Miss K. Matheson, *S.N.P.*		4,863
S.D.P./All. maj.	....	1,704

Roxburgh and Berwickshire
(Borders)
E. 41,702

A. J. Kirkwood, L./All.	...	15,920
I. Sproat, C.	....	12,524
D. Briggs, *Lab.*	....	2,326
R. Shirley, *S.N.P.*	....	852
L./All. maj.	....	3,396

Stirling (Central)
E. 56,302

M. B. Forsyth, C.	....	17,039
M. Connarty, *Lab.*	....	11,906
R. Finnie, *L./All.*	....	10,174
W. Houston, *S.N.P.*	......	3,488
C. maj.	....	5,133

Strathkelvin and Bearsden
(S'clyde)
E. 60,500

M. W. Hirst, C.	....	17,501
R. Waddell, *L./All.*	....	13,801
A. P. Ingram, *Lab.*	....	12,308
Mrs. M. Bain, *S.N.P.*	....	4,408
C. maj.	....	3,700

Tweeddale, Ettrick and Lauderdale (Borders)
E. 37,075

Rt. Hon. D. M. S. Steel, L./		
All.	....	16,868
A. Ballentine, *C.*	....	8,329
M. Saren, *Lab.*	....	2,200
A. Macartney, *S.N.P.*	....	1,455
L./All. maj.	....	8,539

Western Isles (Islands)
E. 22,822

Rt. Hon. D. J. Stewart,		
S.N.P.	....	8,272
B. D. H. Wilson, *Lab.*	.....	4,560
M. Morrison, *C.*	....	1,460
N. McLeod, *L./All.*	......	876
S.N.P. maj.	....	3,712
(May '79, S.N.P. maj. 3,063)		

NORTHERN IRELAND

Antrim

EAST *E.* 58,863

R. Beggs, *O.U.P.*	....	14,293
J. Allister, *D.U.P.*	....	13,926
S. Neeson, *All.*	....	7,620
M. O'Cleary, *S.D.L.P.*	....	1,047
W. Cunning, *Ind.*	....	741
A. Kelly, *W.P.*	....	581
O.U.P. maj.	....	367

NORTH *E.* 63,254

Rev. I. R. K. Paisley,		
D.U.P.	....	23,922
Rev. R. Coulter, *O.U.P.*	..	10,749
S. Farren, *S.D.L.P.*	......	6,193
P. McMahon, *S.F.*	....	2,860
M. H. Samuel, *Eco.*	....	451
D.U.P. maj.	....	13,173

SOUTH *E.* 59,321

C. Forsythe, *O.U.P.*	......	17,727
R. Thompson, *D.U.P.*	.....	10,935
G. Mawhinney, *All.*	......	4,612
A. Maginness, *S.D.L.P.*	....	3,377
S. Laverty, *S.F.*	....	1,629
K. Smyth, *W.P.*	....	549
O.U.P. maj.	....	6,792

Belfast

EAST *E.* 55,581

P. D. Robinson, D.U.P.	...	17,631
D. J. M. Burchill, *O.U.P.*	..	9,642
O. Napier, *All.*	....	9,373
D. Donaldson, *S.F.*	....	682
Mrs. M. Tang, *L.T.U.*	....	584
P. Prendiville, *S.D.L.P.*	...	519
F. Cullen, *W.P.*	....	421
H. Boyd, *N.A.*	....	59
D.U.P. maj.	....	7,989

NORTH *E.* 61,128

A. C. Walker, O.U.P.	.....	15,339
G. Searight, *D.U.P.*	......	8,260
B. Feeney, *S.D.L.P.*	......	5,944
J. Austin, *S.F.*	....	5,451
P. Maguire, *All.*	....	3,879
S. Lynch, *W.P.*	....	2,412
W. Gault, *Ind. D.U.P.*	....	1,134
O.U.P. maj.	....	7,079

SOUTH *E.* 53,694

Rev. W. M. Smyth, O.U.P.		18,669
D. Cook, *All.*	....	8,945
R. S. McRae, *D.U.P.*	......	4,565
Dr. A. McDonnell, *S.D.L.P.*		3,216
S. McKnight, *S.F.*	....	1,107
G. Carr, *W.P.*	....	856
O.U.P. maj.	....	9,724

WEST *E.* 59,750

G. Adams, S.F.	....	16,379
Dr. J. Hendron, *S.D.L.P.*	.	10,934
G. Fitt, Ind.	....	10,326
T. Passmore, *O.U.P.*	.....	2,435
G. A. Haffey, *D.U.P.*	.....	2,399
Ms. M. McMahon, *W.P.*	..	1,893
S.F. maj.	....	5,445

Down

NORTH *E.* 61,574

J. A. Kilfedder, U.P.U.P.	.	22,861
J. Cushnahan, *All.*	....	9,015
R. McCartney, *O.U.P.*	.....	8,261
C. O'Baoill, *S.D.L.P.*	.....	645
U.P.U.P. maj.	....	13,846

SOUTH *E.* 66,968

Rt. Hon. J. E. Powell, M.B.E.,		
O.U.P.	....	20,693
E. McGrady, *S.D.L.P.*	....	20,145
P. Fitzsimmons, *S.F.*	.....	4,074
C. Harvey, *D.U.P.*	....	3,743
P. M. D. Forde, *All.*	.....	1,823
Ms. M. Magee, *W.P.*	.....	851
O.U.P. maj.	....	548

East Londonderry
E. 67,365

W. Ross, O.U.P.	....	19,469
J. McClure, *D.U.P.*	....	12,207
A. Doherty, *S.D.L.P.*	.....	9,397
J. Davey, *S.F.*	....	7,073
Mrs. M. McGrath, *All.*	....	2,401
F. Donnelly, *W.P.*	....	819
O.U.P. maj.	....	7,262

Fermanagh and South Tyrone
E. 67,880

K. Maginnis, O.U.P.	.....	28,630
O. Carron, S.F.	....	20,954
Mrs. R. Flanaghan,		
S.D.L.P.	....	9,923
D. Kettyles, *W.P.*	....	649
O.U.P. maj.	....	7,676

Foyle
E. 67,432

J. Hume, S.D.L.P.	....	24,071
G. Campbell, *D.U.P.*	.....	15,923
M. McGuiness, *S.F.*	......	10,607
G. O'Grady, *All.*	....	1,108
E. Melaugh, *W.P.*	....	582
S.D.L.P. maj.	....	8,148

Lagan Valley
E. 60,099

Rt. Hon. J. H. Molyneaux,		
O.U.P.		24,017
Rev. W. Beattie, *D.U.P.*		6,801
S. Close, *All.*		4,593
C. Boomer, *S.D.L.P.*		2,603
R. McAuley, *S.F.*		1,751
G. Loughlin, *W.P.*		809
O.U.P. maj.		17,216

Newry and Armagh
E. 62,387

J. F. Nicholson, *O.U.P.*		18,988
S. Mallon, *S.D.L.P.*		17,434
J. McAllister, *S.F.*		9,928

T. Moore, *W.P.*		1,070
O.U.P. maj.		1,554

Strangford
E. 60,232

Rt. Hon. J. D. Taylor,		
O.U.P.		19,086
S. Gibson, *D.U.P.*		11,716
A. Morrow, *All.*		6,171
J. Curry, *S.D.L.P.*		1,713
R. Heath, *Ind. L.*		430
O.U.P. maj.		7,370

Ulster, Mid-
E. 63,899

Rev. R. T. W. McCrea,		
D.U.P.		16,174

D. G. Morrison, *S.F.*		16,096
P. D. Haughey, *S.D.L.P.*		12,044
W. J. Thompson, *O.U.P.*		7,066
Dr. J. A. Lagan, *All.*		1,735
T. A. Owens, *W.P.*		766
D.U.P. maj.		78

Upper Bann
E. 60,795

J. H. McCusker, O.U.P.		24,888
J. McDonald, *S.D.L.P.*		7,807
J. Wells, *D.U.P.*		4,547
B. Curran, *S.F.*		4,110
T. French, *W.P.*		2,392
O.U.P. maj.		17,081

BY-ELECTIONS (Since 1983 General Election)

Penrith and The Border
(July 28, 1983)

D. Maclean, *C.*	17,530
M. Young, *L./All.*	16,978
L. Williams, *Lab.*	2,834
D. Sutch, *Ind.*	412
E. Morgan, *Ind.*	150
H. Anscomb, *Ind.*	72
J. Connell, *Ind.*	69
P. Smith, *Ind.*	35
C. maj.	552

Chesterfield
(March 1, 1984)

Rt. Hon. T. Benn, *Lab.*	24,633
M. Payne, *Lib./All.*	18,369
N. Bourne, *C.*	8,028
B. Maynard, *Ind.*	1,355
D. Sutch, *Ind.*	178
D. Bentley, *Ind.*	116
J. Davey, *Ind.*	83
T. A. Layton, *Ind.*	46
Helen Anscomb, *Ind.*	34
J. Bardwaj, *Ind.*	33
D. Butler, *Ind.*	24
P. Nicholls-Jones, *Ind.*	22
S. Shaw, *Ind.*	20
C. Hill, *Ind.*	17
G. R. Piccaro, *Ind.*	15
D. Cahill, *Ind.*	12
J. Connell, *Ind.*	7
Lab. maj.	6,264

Cynon Valley
(May 3, 1984)

Ann Clwyd, *Lab.*	19,389
F. Aubel, *S.D.P./All.*	6,554
C. Jones, *P.C.*	3,619

J. Arbuthnot, *C.*	2,441
Mary Winter, *Comm.*	642
N. Recontre, *Ind.*	215
P. Nicholls-Jones, *Ind.*	122
Lab. maj.	12,835

Stafford
(May 3, 1984)

W. Cash, *C.*	18,713
D. Dunn, *S.D.P./All.*	14,733
M. Poulter, *Lab.*	12,677
C. Teasdale, *Ind.*	210
C. maj.	3,980

Surrey South West
(May 3, 1984)

Virginia Bottomley, *C.*	21,545
G. Scott, *L./All.*	18,946
Barbara Roche, *Lab.*	2,949
V. Litvin, *Ind.*	117
Helen Anscomb, *Ind.*	82
P. Smith, *Ind.*	29
C. maj.	2,599

Portsmouth South
(June 14, 1984)

M. T. Hancock, *S.D.P./All.*	15,358
P. R. J. Rock, *C.*	14,017
Sally Thomas, *Lab.*	10,846
G. A. Knight, *N.F.*	226
T. A. F. Mitchell, *Ecology*	190
A. J. Evans, *Ind.*	113
T. A. Layton, *Ind.*	50
A. N. Andrews, *Ind.*	42
P. R. Smith, *Ind.*	41
S.D.P./All. maj.	1,341

EUROPEAN PARLIAMENT (U.K. MEMBERS AND ELECTIONS)

UNITED KINGDOM MEMBERS OF THE EUROPEAN PARLIAMENT

An asterisk* denotes membership of the previous parliament.

*Gordon J. Adam (*Lab.*), Northumbria; *Richard A. Balfe (*Lab.*), London, South Inner; *Robert C. Battersby (*C.*), Humberside; Christopher J. P. Beazley (*C.*), Cornwall and Plymouth; *Peter G. Beazley (*C.*), Bedfordshire, S.; *The Lord Bethell (*C.*), London, N.W.; *Miss Beata A. Brookes (*C.*), Wales, N.; *Mrs. Janey Buchan (*Lab.*), Glasgow; Bryan M. D. Cassidy (*C.*), Dorset E. and Hampshire W.; *Rt. Hon. Mrs. Barbara A. Castle (*Lab.*), Greater Manchester, W.; *Sir Frederick Catherwood (*C.*), Cambridge and Bedfordshire N.; *Kenneth D. Collins (*Lab.*), Strathclyde, E.; *Richard J. Cottrell (*C.*), Bristol; Mrs. Christine M. Crawley (*Lab.*), Birmingham, E.; G. Robert Cryer (*Lab.*), Sheffield; *David M. Curry (*C.*), Essex, N.E.; Mrs. Margaret M. Daly (*C.*), Somerset and Dorset W.; *John de Courcy Ling (*C.*), Midlands, Central; *Basil R. V. Z. de Ferranti (*C.*), Hampshire, Central; *The Marquess of Douro (*C.*), Surrey, W.

*The Baroness Elles (*C.*), Thames Valley; James E. M. Elles (*C.*), Oxford and Buckinghamshire; Michael N. Elliott (*Lab.*), London, W.; *Mrs. Winifred M. Ewing (*S.N.P.*), Highlands and Islands; Mrs. I. Sheila Faith (*C.*), Cumbria and Lancashire, N.; Alec Falconer (*Lab.*), Scotland Mid and Fife; J. Glyn Ford (*Lab.*), Greater Manchester, W.; *Winston J. Griffiths (*Lab.*), Wales, S.; Michael J. Hindley (*Lab.*), Lancashire, E.; Geoffrey W. Hoon (*Lab.*), Derbyshire; *Paul F. Howell (*C.*), Norfolk; Leslie J. Huckfield (*Lab.*), Merseyside, E.; Stephen S. Hughes (*Lab.*), Durham; *John Hume (*S.D.L.P.*), N. Ireland; *Alasdair H. Hutton (*C.*), Scotland, S.; Mrs. Caroline F. Jackson (*C.*), Wiltshire; *Christopher M. Jackson (*C.*), Kent, E.; Michael L. Kilby (*C.*), Nottingham.

*Alfred Lomas (*Lab.*), London, N.E.; Michael McGowan (*Lab.*), Leeds; Hugh McMahon (*Lab.*), Strathclyde, W.; Edward H. C. Macmillan Scott (*C.*), York; *John L. Marshall (*C.*), London, N.; David W. Martin (*Lab.*), Lothians; *Thomas Megahy (*Lab.*), Yorkshire, S.W.; C. James O. Moorhouse (*C.*), London S. and Surrey E.; D. Richard Morris (*Lab.*), Wales, Mid and W.; A. Stanley Newens (*Lab.*), London, Central; Edward Newman (*Lab.*), Greater Manchester, Central; *William F. Newton Dunn (*C.*), Lincolnshire; *Tom Normanton (*C.*), Cheshire, E.; *The Lord O'Hagan (*C.*), Devon; *Rev. Ian R. K. Paisley (*D.U.P.*), N. Ireland; *George B. Patterson (*C.*), Kent, W.; *Andrew Pearce (*C.*), Cheshire, W.; Terence J. Pitt (*Lab.*), Midlands, W.; *Sir Henry Plumb (*C.*), The Cotswolds; *Derek Prag (*C.*), Hertfordshire; *Peter N. Price (*C.*), London, S.E.; *Christopher J. Prout (*C.*), Shropshire and Stafford; *James L. C. Provan (*C.*), Scotland, N.E.; *Miss Joyce C. Quin (*Lab.*), Tyne and Wear; *Dame Shelagh M. Roberts (*C.*), London, S.W.

*Sir James Scott-Hopkins (*C.*), Hereford and Worcester; *Barry H. Seal (*Lab.*), Yorkshire, W.; *R. Madron Seligman (*C.*), Sussex, W.; *Dr. Alexander Sherlock (*C.*), Essex, S.W.; *Richard J. Simmonds (*C.*), Wight and Hampshire, E.; *Anthony. M. H. Simpson (*C.*), Northamptonshire; Llewellyn Smith (*Lab.*), Wales, S.E.; George W. Stevenson (*Lab.*), Staffordshire, E.; Kenneth Stewart (*Lab.*), Merseyside, W.; *Sir John Stewart-Clark, Bt. (*C.*), Sussex, E.; *Rt. Hon. John Taylor (*O.U.P.*), N. Ireland; John E. Tomlinson (*Lab.*), Birmingham, W.; Mrs. Carol Tongue (*Lab.*), London, E.; *Frederick A. Tuckman (*C.*), Leicester; *Amédée E. Turner (*C.*), Suffolk; *Hon. Sir Peter B. R. Vanneck (*C.*), Cleveland and Yorkshire N.; *Michael J. Welsh (*C.*), Lancashire, Central; Norman West (*Lab.*), Yorkshire, South.

UNITED KINGDOM ELECTIONS TO EUROPEAN PARLIAMENT

(June 14, 1984)

An asterisk * denotes membership of the previous Parliament. For abbreviations, *see* p. 320

Bedfordshire, South
E. 524,974

*P. G. Beazley, C.		72,088
W. Cochrane, *Lab.*		57,106
P. A. Dixon, *L./All.*		36,444
C. maj.		*14,982*

Birmingham, East
E. 548,899

Mrs. C. M. Crawley, *Lab.*		76,377
*Miss N. E. Forster, *C.*		54,994
D. A. Bennett *S.D.P./All.*		21,927
Miss D. Howell, *Ind.*		1,440
Lab. maj.		*21,383*

Birmingham, West
E. 518,707

J. E. Tomlinson, *Lab.*		61,946
C. Hart, *C.*		55,702
J. C. Binns, *S.D.P./All.*		19,422
Lab. maj.		*6,244*

Bristol
E. 569,765

*R. J. Cottrell, *C.*		94,652
R. L. Berry, *Lab.*		77,008
P. J. Farley, *S.D.P./All.*		33,698
C. maj.		*17,644*

Cambridge and Bedfordshire North
E. 523,899

*Sir Frederick Catherwood, *C.*		86,117
H. G. Bottomley, *Lab.*		38,901
A. N. Duff, *L./All.*		36,341
C. maj.		*47,216*

Cheshire, East
E. 498,568

*T. Normanton, *C.*		71,182
A. Stephenson, *Lab.*		52,806
J. P. Corbett, *S.D.P./All.*		31,374
C. maj.		*18,376*

Cheshire, West
E. 539,761

*A. Pearce, *C.*		74,579
D. G. Hanson, *Lab.*		64,887
E. C. H. Owen, *S.D.P./All.*		30,470
C. maj.		*9,692*

Cleveland and Yorkshire North
E. 566,083

*Hon. Sir P. Vanneck,, C.		73,217
P. F. Tinnion, *Lab.*		70,592
C. Beever, *S.D.P./All.*		35,916
C. maj.		*2,625*

Cornwall and Plymouth
E. 506,004

C. J. P. Beazley, *C.*		81,627
J. C. Marks, *S.D.P./All.*		63,876
J. D. Cosgrove, *Lab.*		35,952
A. I. Parkin, *Ind.*		5,645
R. J. Trevallion, *Ind.*		2,981
J. Whetter, *Ind.*		1,892
C. maj.		*17,751*

The Cotswolds
E. 527,081

*Sir H. Plumb, *C.*		94,740
Miss M. E. Burton, *L./All.*		45,798
Miss J. A. Royall, *Lab.*		36,738
C. maj.		*48,942*

Cumbria and Lancashire North
E. 547,433

Mrs. I. S. Faith, *C.*		86,127
J. R. Atkinson, *Lab.*		62,332
Mrs. K. C. Brooks, *L./All.*		39,622
C. maj.		*23,795*

Derbyshire
E. 553,020

G. W. Hoon, *Lab.*		79,466
*T. N. B. Spencer, *C.*		72,613
Miss J. M. Elles, *S.D.P./All.*		30,824
Lab. maj.		*6,853*

Devon
E. 560,807

*Lord O'Hagan, C.	110,129
P. G. Driver, *L./All.*	53,519
D. A. Gorbutt, *Lab.*	30,017
P. S. Christie, *Eco.*	6,919
Lady Rous, *Ind.*	659
C. maj.	*56,610*

Dorset East and Hampshire West
E. 565,709

B. M. D. Cassidy, *C.*	109,072
J. M. Goss, *L./All.*	49,181
D. T. James, *Lab.*	31,223
C. maj.	*59,891*

Durham
E. 530,104

S. S. Hughes, *Lab.*	106,073
Hon. W. R. Fletcher-Vane, C.	44,846
C. Foote Wood, *L./All.*	32,307
Lab. maj.	*61,227*

Essex, N.E.
E. 574,022

*D. M. Curry, C.	97,138
B. L. Stapleton, *Lab.*	42,836
A. E. Ross, *S.D.P./All.*	34,769
C. maj.	*54,302*

Essex, S.W.
E. 557,704

*Dr. A. Sherlock, C.	72,190
C. O'Brien, *Lab.*	56,169
A. F. C. Morris, *L./All.*	29,385
C. maj.	*16,021*

Glasgow
E. 518,178

*Mrs. J. Buchan, Lab.	91,015
Miss S. Chadd, *C.*	25,282
C. Mason, *L./All.*	20,867
N. MacLeod, *S.N.P.*	16,456
Lab. maj.	*65,733*

Greater Manchester, Central
E. 507,941

E. Newman, *Lab.*	76,830
T. R. M. Sewell, *C.*	48,753
G. E. A. O. Weddell, *L./All.*	24,192
K. J. Martin, *Ind.*	1,430
Lab. maj.	*28,077*

Greater Manchester, East
E. 510,586

J. G. Ford, *Lab.*	65,101
T. K. Thornber, *C.*	56,450
Mrs. B. Gaskin, *S.D.P./All.*	27,801
M. J. Shipley, *Eco.*	3,158
Lab. maj.	*8,651*

Greater Manchester, West
E. 528,896

*Rt. Hon. Mrs. B. A. Castle, Lab.	93,740
*W. J. Hopper, C.	56,042
J. R. Boddy, *S.D.P./All.*	17,894
Lab. maj.	*37,698*

Hampshire, Central
E. 524,649

*B. R. V. Z. de Ferranti, C.	84,086
F. B. Jacobs, *S.D.P./All.*	39,265
M. V. Castle, *Lab.*	39,228
C. maj.	*44,821*

Hereford and Worcester
E. 560,654

*Sir J. Scott-Hopkins, C.	84,077
P. E. S. Nielson, *Lab.*	44,143
I. D. Phillips, *L./All.*	37,854
Mrs. F. M. Norman, *Eco.*	8,179
C. maj.	*39,934*

Hertfordshire
E. 505,206

*D. Prag, C.	87,603
A. McWalter, *Lab.*	41,671
Mrs. F. M. Beckett, *S.D.P./All.*	40,877
C. maj.	*45,932*

Highlands and Islands
E. 307,265

*Mrs. W. M. Ewing, S.N.P.	49,410
D. R. Johnston, *L./All.*	33,133
D. Webster, *C.*	18,847
Rev. J. McArthur, *Lab.*	16,644
S.N.P. maj.	*16,277*

Humberside
E. 503,080

*R. C. Battersby, C.	61,952
P. D. Crampton, *Lab.*	53,937
S. W. Unwin, *S.D.P./All.*	27,318
C. maj.	*8,015*

Kent, East
E. 554,808

*C. M. Jackson, C.	92,340
D. A. Enright, *Lab.*	43,473
A. Kinch, *S.D.P./All.*	34,601
S. Dawe, *Eco.*	5,405
C. maj.	*48,867*

Kent, West
E. 565,693

*G. B. Patterson, C.	85,414
A. Woodhams, *Lab.*	50,784
P. H. Billenness, *L. All.*	33,306
Mrs. C. A. Bunyan, *Eco.*	4,991
C. maj.	*34,630*

Lancashire, Central
E. 524,132

*M. J. Welsh, C.	82,370
Miss H. M. Jones, *Lab.*	56,175
*M. Gallagher, *S.D.P./All.*	24,936
C. maj.	*26,195*

Lancashire, East
E. 534,542

M. J. Hindley, *Lab.*	75,711
*E. T. Kellett-Bowman, C.	67,806
A. G. Lishman, *L./All.*	26,320
Lab. maj.	*7,905*

Leeds
E. 527,653

M. McGowan, *Lab.*	70,535
J. G. Holt, *C.*	60,178
S. J. Cooksey, *L./All.*	36,097
Lab. maj.	*10,357*

Leicester
E. 564,350

*F. A. Tuckman, C.	72,508
P. A. Soulsby, *Lab.*	69,616
D. N. Simmonds, *S.D.P./All.*	29,656
A. G. Barrett, *Ind.*	3,249
C. maj.	*2,892*

Lincolnshire
E. 551,904

*W. F. Newton Dunn, C.	92,606
C. W. Sewell, *Lab.*	47,161
G. Purves, *L./All.*	37,244
C. maj.	*45,445*

London, Central
E. 543,825

A. S. Newens, *Lab.*	77,842
*A. D. Fergusson, C.	64,545
E. Wistrich, *S.D.P./All.*	30,269
J. E. Porritt, *Eco.*	5,945
R. J. Maynard, *Ind.*	1,569
Lab. maj.	*13,297*

London, East
E. 537,831

Miss C. Tongue, *Lab.*	73,870
*A. R. Tyrrell, C.	61,711
Mrs. J. Horne, *S.D.P./All.*	26,379
Lab. maj.	*12,159*

London, North
E. 564,359

*J. L. Marshall, C.	74,846
E. Large, *Lab.*	69,993
J. Skinner, *L./All.*	31,344
P. S. J. Lang, *Eco.*	4,682
C. maj.	*4,853*

London, N.E.
E. 513,781

*A. Lomas, Lab.	79,907
M. Batchelor, *C.*	27,242
J. P. Heppell, *L./All.*	17,344
Mrs. J. Lambert, *Eco.*	4,797
Lab. maj.	*52,665*

London, N.W.
E. 518,365

*The Lord Bethell, C.	69,803
Ms. P. Healy, *Lab.*	62,381
A. Ketteringham, *L./All.*	29,609
C. maj.	*7,422*

London, S.E.
E. 561,984

*P. N. Price, C.	81,508
S. J. Cowan, *Lab.*	61,493
J. H. Fryer, *L./All.*	38,614
W. E. Turner, *Ind.*	989
C. maj.	*20,015*

London, S.W.
E. 499,273

*Dame Shelagh M. Roberts, C.	70,490
Miss A. J. Pollack, *Lab.*	63,623
D. J. Twigg, *L/All.*	32,268
Mrs. S. G. Willington, *Eco.*	3,066
C. maj.	*6,867*

London South and Surrey East
E.505,393

*C.J.O.Moorhouse, C.	....	82,122
A.S.MacKinlay, Lab.	....	37,465
J.G.Parry, L./All.	......	34,522
C.maj.	*...............*	*44,657*

London, South Inner
E.530,672

*R.A.Balfe, Lab.	....	77,661
Mrs.D.Miller, C.	....	46,180
J.Daly, S.D.P./All.	......	25,391
Mrs.J.Owens, Eco.	....	3,281
Lab.maj.	*..............*	*31,481*

London, West
E.516,661

M.N.Elliot, Lab.	....	79,554
*B.H.Hord, C.	....	74,325
C.Layton, S.D.P./All.	.....	36,687
Mrs. D. M. Sutherland, Eco.	....	4,361
Lab.maj.	*..............*	*5,229*

Lothians
E.516,068

D.W.Martin, Lab.	....	74,989
I.J.Henderson, C.	....	49,065
Dr.J.D.Mabon, S.D.P./All.	....	36,636
Dr.D.Stevenson, S.N.P.	..	22,331
Miss L. Hendry, Eco.	......	2,560
Lab.maj.	*..............*	*25,924*

Merseyside, East
E.537,285

L.J.Huckfield, Lab.	.....	87,086
T.G.D.R.B.Galbraith, C.	.	38,047
T.Bishop, S.D.P./All.	....	17,259
Lab.maj.	*..............*	*49,039*

Merseyside, West
E.551,532

K.Stewart, Lab.	....	65,915
*Miss G.D.Hooper, C.	......	52,718
P.R.Clark, L./All.	....	37,303
Lab.maj.	*..............*	*13,197*

Midlands, Central
E.533,798

*J.de Courcy Ling, C.	.....	67,884
D.J.Blackman, Lab.	......	55,155
P.Langmead, S.D.P./All.	..	27,912
A.Enstone, Ind.	....	1,494
C.maj.	*...............*	*12,729*

Midlands, West
E.533,796

T.J.Pitt, Lab.	....	74,091
A.T.Burnside, C.	....	54,406
C.Carter, L./All.	....	17,709
Lab.maj.	*..............*	*19,685*

Norfolk
E.543,214

*P.F.Howell, C.	....	95,459
A.E.B.Heading, Lab.	....	58,602
L.Williams, S.D.P./All.	..	37,703
C.maj.	*................*	*36,857*

Northamptonshire
E.547,188

*A.M.H.Simpson, C.	.....	88,668
J.Dickie, Lab.	....	48,809
Mrs. C. M. Goodhart, S.D.P./All.	....	37,421
Mrs.A.Bryant, Ind.	......	3,330
C.maj.	*................*	*39,859*

Northumbria
E.512,979

*G.J.Adam, Lab.	....	78,417
C.M.M.Crichton, C.	......	62,717
G.Scott, L./All.	....	42,946
Lab.maj.	*..............*	*15,700*

Nottingham
E.554,473

M.L.Kilby, C.	....	82,500
K.Coates, Lab.	....	66,374
K.M.Melton, L./All.	.....	33,169
Lab.maj.	*..............*	*16,126*

Oxford and Buckinghamshire
E.542,343

J.E.M.Elles, C.	....	94,136
R.J.Liddle, S.D.P./All.	...	45,055
J.G.Power, Lab.	....	39,164
C.maj.	*...............*	*49,081*

Scotland, Mid. and Fife
E.528,529

A.Falconer, Lab.	....	80,038
*J.R.Purvis, C.	....	52,872
Mrs.J.T.Jones, S.N.P.	...	30,511
A. A. I. Wedderburn, S.D.P./All.	....	24,220
Lab.maj.	*..............*	*27,166*

Scotland, North-East
E.548,711

*J.L.C.Provan, C.	....	53,809
F.Doran, Lab.	....	44,638
D.Hood, S.N.P.	....	33,448
I.G.Philip, S.D.P./All.	...	25,490
C.maj.	*................*	*9,171*

Scotland, South
E.484,760

*A.H.Hutton, C.	....	60,843
R.Stewart, Lab.	....	57,706
Mrs. E. M. Buchanan, L./All.	....	23,598
I.R.Goldie, S.N.P.	....	22,242
C.maj.	*................*	*3,137*

Sheffield
E.558,984

G.R.Cryer, Lab.	....	93,530
D.R.Grayson, C.	....	47,247
Miss M.Holmstedt, L./All.	.	23,935
Lab.maj.	*..............*	*46,283*

Shropshire and Stafford
E.562,823

*C.J.Prout, C.	....	82,291
D.J.A.Hallam, Lab.	.....	57,359
R.M.Burman, L./All.	....	37,209
C.maj.	*................*	*24,932*

Somerset and Dorset West
E.540,393

Mrs.M.Daly, C.	....	98,928
R.G.Moore, L./All.	.....	58,677
Mrs.J.Linden, Lab.	.....	36,836
C.maj.	*................*	*40,251*

Staffordshire, East
E.563,376

G.W.Stevenson, Lab.	....	76,753
*R.J.Moreland, C.	....	68,886
R.Fox, S.D.P./All.	....	26,093
Lab.maj.	*..............*	*7,867*

Strathclyde, East
E.498,458

*K. D.Collins, Lab.	....	90,792
G.Leslie, S.N.P.	....	27,330
P.R.Leckie, C.	....	24,857
Ms.P.de Seume, L./All.	....	11,883
Lab.maj.	*..............*	*63,462*

Strathclyde, West
E.499,162

H.McMahon, Lab.	......	70,234
Miss J. Lait, C.	....	47,196
Mrs.J.Herriot, S.N.P.	...	28,866
D.J.Herbison, S.D.P./All.	.	25,955
Lab.maj.	*..............*	*23,038*

Suffolk
E.516,050

*A.E.Turner, C.	....	88,243
W.Moszczynski, Lab.	....	41,145
C.Leakey, L./All.	....	34,084
C.maj.	*................*	*47,098*

Surrey, West
E.504,923

*The Marquess of Douro, C.	.	96,675
E.Mortimer, S.D.P./All.	.	44,087
N.K.A.S.Vaz, Lab.	......	22,531
C.maj.	*................*	*52,588*

Sussex, East
E.537,397

*Sir J.Stewart-Clark, Bt., C.	....	102,287
J.Busby, S.D.P./All.	....	36,666
H.Spillman, Lab.	....	32,213
Mrs.E.Evelyn, Eco.	....	5,401
C.maj.	*................*	*65,621*

Sussex, West
E.531,934

*R.M.Seligman, C.	......	104,257
Dr.J.M.M.Walsh, L./All.	.	46,755
G.C.Rees, Lab.	....	22,857
D.Aherne, Eco.	....	3,842
C.maj.	*................*	*57,502*

Thames Valley
E.519,564

*The Baroness Elles, C.	.....	74,928
R.B.Bastin, Lab.	....	36,123
R.W.Bradnock, L./All.	....	32,704
C.maj.	*................*	*38,805*

Tyne and Wear
E.543,955

*Miss J.G.Quin, Lab.	......	89,024
R.R.Cook, C.	....	39,610
B.P.Carroll, S.D.P./All.	...	19,081
Lab.maj.	*..............*	*49,414*

Wales, Mid and West
E.533,644

D.R.Morris, Lab.	....	89,362
D.Lewis, C.	....	52,910
D.Lloyd, L./All.	....	35,168
Dr.P.Williams, P.C.	....	32,880
Miss M.A.Smith, Eco.	.....	4,266
Lab.maj.	*..............*	*36,452*

Wales, North
E. 516,153

*Miss B. A. Brooks, C.	69,139
R. T. Ellis, S.D.P./All.	56,861
C. I. Campbell, Lab.	54,768
D. Iwan, P.C.	38,117
C. maj.	*12,278*

Wales, South
E. 509,434

*W. J. Griffiths, Lab.	99,936
Miss J. R. Pattman, C.	55,678
Mrs. J. Davis, L./All.	26,588
Dr D. Huws, P.C.	13,201
Lab. maj.	*44,258*

Wales, S.E.
E. 565,739

L. Smith, Lab.	131,916
R. Whyatt, C.	36,359
C. D. Lindley, S.D.P./All.	28,330
S. Morgan, P.C.	18,833
Lab. maj.	*95,557*

Wight and Hampshire, East
E. 544,189

*R. J. Simmonds, C.	96,666
Mrs. S. Ludford, L./All.	53,738
J. A. Phillips, Lab.	36,445
C. maj.	*42,928*

Wiltshire
E. 531,501

Mrs. C. F. Jackson, C.	86,873
J. B. Ainslie, L./All.	60,404
P. Whiteside, Lab.	35,457
C. maj.	*26,469*

York
E. 517,592

E. H. C. McMillan-Scott, C.	80,636
Mrs. S. Haines, Lab.	44,234
M. G. Howard, S.D.P./All.	33,356
C. maj.	*36,402*

Yorkshire, South
E. 516,431

N. West, Lab.	98,020
Mrs. R. P. N. Pockley, C.	30,271
D. Eden, S.D.P./All.	19,306
Lab. maj.	*67,749*

Yorkshire, S.W.
E. 518,423

*T. Megahy, Lab.	88,464
A. J. A. Lodge, C.	44,291
J. F. Crossley, L./All.	26,964
Lab. maj.	*44,173*

Yorkshire, West
E. 560,190

*B. H. Seal, Lab.	86,259
I. C. Bruce, C.	65,405
E. Lyons, S.D.P./All.	28,709
Lab. maj.	*20,854*

Northern Ireland
E. 1,077,605

	First Preference
*Rev. I. R. K. Paisley, D.U.P.	230,251
*J. Hume, S.D.L.P.	151,399
*Rt. Hon. J. D. Taylor, O.U.P.	147,169
D. Morrison, S.F.	91,476
D. Cook, All.	34,046
J. Kilfedder, U.P.U.P.	20,092
S. Lynch, W.P.	8,712
C. McGuigan, Eco.	2,172

Rev. I. R. K. Paisley, J. Hume, and Rt. Hon. J. D. Taylor were elected by the single transferable voting system.

VOTES CAST AT U.K. GENERAL ELECTIONS, 1974–83

General Election, February 1974*

Conservative	11,868,906
Labour	11,639,243
Liberal	6,063,470
Scottish Nationalist	632,032
Plaid Cymru	171,634
Communist	32,741
Others	207,884

General Election, October, 1974*

Labour	11,456,597
Conservative	10,464,675
Liberal	5,346,800
Scottish Nationalist	839,628
Plaid Cymru	166,321
Others	195,065

General Election, 1979*

Conservative	13,697,753
Labour	11,506,741
Liberal	4,305,324
Scottish Nationalist	504,259
National Front	191,706
Plaid Cymru	132,544
Others	188,063

General Election, 1983*

Conservative	13,012,602
Labour	8,457,124
Liberal/S.D.P. Alliance	7,780,587
Scottish Nationalist	331,975
Plaid Cymru	125,309
Others	198,383

*Excluding Northern Ireland

MAJORITIES IN THE HOUSE OF COMMONS SINCE 1945

Year	Party	Majority	Year	Party	Majority
1945	Labour	146	1966	Labour	99
1950	Labour	8	1970	Conservative	31
1951	Conservative	16	1974 (Feb.)	No Majority	
1955	Conservative	59	1974 (Oct.)	Labour	5
1959	Conservative	100	1979	Conservative	43
1964	Labour	5	1983	Conservative	144

PARLIAMENTARY SUMMARY, LORDS AND COMMONS, 1983–84

There was no prorogation of Parliament in the autumn and so the current session's programme continued when both Houses re-assembled on Oct. 24 following upon the summer recess.

When the second reading of the Prevention of Terrorism Bill was debated in the Commons on Oct. 24, Mr. Roy Hattersley, deputy leader of the Labour Party, described the measure as "an unacceptable erosion of civil liberties". Labour's amendment seeking to deny a second reading to the Bill was defeated by 302 to 144 votes.

In the Lords on Oct. 25, Admiral of the Fleet Lord Lewin, former Chief of the Defence Staff, made his maiden speech during the debate on the Defence Estimates and urged the Government and N.A.T.O. to extend their commitment to a three per cent increase in defence spending beyond 1985–86.

Grenada

In the Commons on Oct. 25, Mrs. Thatcher said she had told President Reagan in a telephone call some hours before the U.S. invasion of Grenada of her very considerable doubts about a military intervention, of which she made plain her disapproval. The Foreign Secretary (Sir Geoffrey Howe) was later at the centre of a row when he declined to condemn the U.S. action and received calls to resign when he repeatedly refused to approve or disapprove the invasion. Sir Geoffrey stated that early that morning the U.S.A. informed the British Government of their conclusion that for them and those Caribbean States which had proposed it, intervention was the right course to pursue. Mr. Healey, Labour's Foreign Affairs spokesman, condemned the invasion and declared it was a serious matter when a Commonwealth country subject to the Queen was invaded by a foreign State. It appeared the Government had been deceived by its American ally and by some of its Commonwealth partners. Sir Geoffrey replied that President Reagan had made clear that the foremost reason for his decisive action was the protection of innocent lives, including a thousand Americans. An emergency debate on the invasion was held on Oct. 26 when the Foreign Secretary admitted that the U.S. Government should have consulted more fully with the British before their action but said the affair should not be allowed to damage relations between the two old allies. For Labour, Mr. Healey accused the Foreign Secretary of having misled the House over the imminence of an invasion and described Mrs. Thatcher as President Reagan's "obedient poodle". Finally the Opposition's attack on the Government's handling of the crisis was defeated when a procedural motion to adjourn was rejected by 336 to 211 votes.

Cuts in the N.H.S.

In his first speech in the Commons as Labour leader on Oct. 27, Mr. Neil Kinnock initiated a debate on cuts in the National Health Service and moved a motion pledging Labour to maintain and improve the standards of health care "free for all at time of use and need", and calling on the Government to reverse its stated policy of cuts in hospital and medical services. Mr. Fowler, Social Services Secretary, moved an amendment which reaffirmed the Government's commitment to the N.H.S. and the maintenance and improvement of standards of patient care and which endorsed its efforts to ensure the best value for money spent on patient care. Dr. David Owen, S.D.P. leader, said that for the first time in the history of the N.H.S. not only would there be an absolute reduction this year in the numbers of staff employed, there was also a real chance of no growth in real terms in health resources. Labour's motion was defeated by 338 to 205 votes and the Government's amendment was carried by 331 to 204.

Cruise Missiles

Oct. 31, Mr. Heseltine, Defence Secretary, moved a motion in the Commons reaffirming support for the 1979 N.A.T.O. decision on intermediate-range nuclear forces and which also supported the West's efforts "to achieve a balanced and verifiable agreement at the Geneva negotiations" although confirming that without agreement on the zero option, Cruise missiles must be operationally deployed in the U.K. at the end of 1983. Mr. Healey, Labour's main spokesman, said the deployment of Cruise missiles would weaken the N.A.T.O. alliance and heighten the danger of nuclear war. Mr. Steel, Liberal leader, moved a Liberal/S.D.P. amendment, supporting multilateral disarmament and arms control efforts. The motion urged the Government to negotiate immediately on the basis of the U.S. offer for installation at British expense of a dual-key system for any Cruise missiles based in the U.K., but Mr. Heseltine rejected dual-key control. When M.P.s entered the lobbies to vote, peace demonstrators caused a noisy disruption in the Strangers' Gallery. The Alliance motion was defeated by 360 to 22 votes, and the Government's own motion was carried by 362 to 218.

The Commons gave a second reading on Nov. 7 to the Police and Criminal Evidence Bill by 339 to 188 votes. The Home Secretary announced that criminal suspects were to have their rights increased by having access to duty solicitors. Mr. Kaufman, Labour's spokesman on home affairs, said the Bill would undermine civil liberties in ways which were unprecedented in modern history and Mr. Alex Carlisle, for the Liberals, called it a "blunderbuss approach".

Mr. John Smith, Labour's employment spokesman, pledged that a Labour Government would repeal the Trade Union Bill when it was discussed on second reading on Nov. 8, but in the end the measure was given a comfortable passage by 362 to 189 votes. Mr. Tom King, Employment Secretary, said the Government was giving the unions back to their members but Mr. Smith forecast an increase in unofficial strikes would result from the imposition of secret ballots.

A Private Member's Bill which introduced a system of certification for video cassettes was given an unopposed second reading in the Commons on Nov. 11. Mr. David Mellor, Home Office Under-Secretary, pledged the Government's support and said the most extreme videos would not get a certificate and that anyone selling uncertificated material would be liable to a fine up to £10,000.

On Nov. 14, the Defence Secretary (Mr. Heseltine) announced the arrival of Cruise missiles at Greenham Common and emphasized the Government remained committed to arms control despite their deployment, but faced fierce criticism from the Opposition benches. Peers had a wide-ranging and analytical debate on ways to reduce crimes of violence on Nov. 15.

A Labour motion attacking the Government's plan to cut householders' renovation grants from 90 per cent to 75 per cent was defeated in the Commons on Nov. 16 by 342 to 196 votes. In the Lords on the same day, Viscount Tonypandy, former Speaker of the Commons, made his maiden speech during a debate on Cyprus.

Economic Statement

The Chancellor of the Exchequer (Mr. Nigel Lawson) delivered his autumn economic statement in the Commons on Nov. 17 and said: "For the first time in many years we are now enjoying low inflation combined with steady growth.

"This is a winning combination. Our task is to keep that winning combination by sticking to—and indeed reinforcing—the policies which have brought it about."

Mr. Lawson said that firm monetary policies had led in the past year to falling inflation, renewed growth and solid evidence of Britain's continuing recovery from world recession.

"Progress both on inflation and growth this year has been better than expected at the time of the Budget", he added.

Mr. Lawson cited a growth in output of about five per cent since the low point of the recession early in 1981, a fall in inflation to around five per cent and significant gains in productivity, competitiveness and profitability. Employment appeared to be rising and unemployment levelling off.

Output this year was expected to be about three per cent higher than in 1982, and the Industry Act forecast pointed to continuing growth next year.

Recovery in the rest of the world, so far hesitant outside North America, was now widely expected to show some improvement.

With higher exports offsetting some slow-down in the growth of domestic demand, overall United Kingdom output was forecast to rise by a further three per cent in 1984.

With inflationary pressures remaining weak, inflation was likely to edge down again next year to a rate of around 4½ per cent by the fourth quarter.

Mr. Lawson said downward pressure would continue to be exerted on public borrowing.

"Despite the measures I announced on July 7 it is clear that this year's public sector borrowing requirement is likely to be above the £8·2 billion expected at the time of the Budget.

"The out-turn is, of course, still uncertain but is now forecast to be £10 billion, mainly as a result of public expenditure running higher than expected."

The forecast for 1984–85 made the conventional assumptions that direct taxes and excise duties were both revalorized in line with prices, and that the public sector borrowing requirement was held next year to the £8 billion assumed at the time of the last Budget in accordance with the medium term financial strategy.

"On this basis the forecast implies the need for some net increase in taxes in next year's Budget.

"This is, of course, at this stage, subject to a wide margin of uncertainty, and will need to be reviewed, with other relevant factors, in the light of more up-to-date information, before I come to make my Budget judgment."

Following this year's public expenditure review, the public expenditure planning total for next year, 1984–85, would remain at £126·4 billion.

That was the provisional figure for 1984–85 published in the Public Expenditure White Paper in February this year. It was also broadly the same in real terms as the likely out-turn for this year, 1983–84.

"So, with the economy expanding, public expenditure should continue to fall as a percentage of gross domestic product next year."

The Chancellor said that within the unchanged total for 1984–85 there had inevitably been changes in both directions in individual programmes.

"In broad terms, the autumn statement shows increases in spending for health and personal social services, education, law and order, agricultural support, arts and libraries, and for a number of other programmes.

"Social security spending will also increase, although there will be reductions in the coverage of help with housing costs, particularly housing benefit."

The Social Security programme provided for an uprating in November 1984 based on the rise in prices in the 12 months to May 1984.

"These increases are offset by higher receipts from the sale of council houses and the like, and by a reduction in planned spending on home improvement grants, defence, employment, trade and industry, and several other programmes—including the aggregate external financing limits of the nationalised industries.

"Net receipts from special sales of assets are forecast to increase by some £400 million reflecting, among other things, the fact that the privatisation of Enterprise Oil is now expected not this year but in 1984–85."

The February White Paper provided for a provisional contingency reserve of £3 billion and that figure remained intact.

Turning to the Government's review of manpower requirements up to 1988, Mr. Lawson said the new plans provided for a continued steady reduction in the size of the Civil Service.

"Numbers will come down to 593,000 by 1988, a fall of six per cent below the existing target of 630,000, which we expect to be achieved on or before April 1, 1984."

National insurance contributions were reviewed each autumn in the light of advice from the Government Actuary on the prospects for the National Insurance Fund in the coming financial year, Mr. Lawson said.

"As usual, the earnings limits will need to be increased.

"The lower earnings limit will rise to £34 a week, in line with the single rate retirement pension, and the upper earnings limit will rise to £250 a week, broadly in line with the increase in prices and earnings.

"The taxpayers' contribution to the fund—the so-called Treasury Supplement—will be reduced from 13 per cent to 11 per cent.

"In each of the last four years we have had to increase the Class 1 National Insurance Contribution rate itself.

"I am glad to say that we shall not need to do so for 1984–85. So the full Class 1 rate will remain unchanged at 9 per cent for employees and 10·45 per cent for employers.

Debate on the Economic Statement

Mr. Hattersley, Labour's economic spokesman, said today's improvements stemmed from the temporary reversal—not from long-term success—of Government policy and denounced the predicted increase in gas and electricity prices as a badly disguised fuel tax. The prospect of growth and the prophecy of recovery were as bogus as the Chancellor was complacent. Mr. Roy Jenkins (S.D.P., Hillhead) said in the circumstances it was dogmatic nonsense and not sound finance to continue to drive down the public spending borrowing requirement. Mr. Richard Wainwright (Lib., Colne Valley) thought the Chancellor had painted a false dawn and then obscured it with heavy clouds of higher taxation, including fuel taxes. A full-scale debate on the economic statement took place on Nov. 24.

On Nov. 21, the Lords gave a second reading to the Matrimonial and Family Proceedings Bill which the Lord Chancellor (Lord Hailsham) said had been widely misunderstood and distorted. Lord Elwyn-

Jones, a former Labour Lord Chancellor, spoke of concern about the bill's so-called "clean-break provisions" to end financial liability between spouses after divorce. The Bishop of Rochester said they should consider maintaining the three-year rule before a couple could file for divorce.

The Stock Exchange

Mr. Shore, Labour spokesman on trade and industry, told M.P.s on Nov. 22 that the Bill to exempt the Stock Exchange from the provisions of the 1976 Restrictive Trade Practices Act would provide a precedent and an encouragement for any other organized interest group to seek exemption from legislative scrutiny and accused Ministers of flagrantly intervening to frustrate judicial proceedings. The Trade Secretary (Mr. Tebbit), who moved the second reading of the Bill, refuted charges that by reaching agreement with the Stock Exchange the Government had sold out the interests of investors or the country to those of the City. On Nov. 30, when remaining stages of the Bill were considered, an amendment moved by Mr. Bryan Gould, a Labour spokesman on trade and industry, which would have nullified the legislation at the end of 1986 unless Parliament decided otherwise in the preceding three months, was eventually withdrawn and the Bill was given a third reading by 190 to 130 votes.

On Nov. 23 during a debate in which the Government's pensions record suffered heavy criticism from Labour, the Social Services Secretary (Mr. Fowler) announced that a comprehensive inquiry into the future of occupational and state pensions was to be held.

Mr. Austin Mitchell (Lab., Great Grimsby) was unsuccessful on Dec. 6 in obtaining leave to introduce a Bill which would, he said, bring the whole matter of company donations into the open and put it on a democratic and accountable basis. He demanded an independent inquiry into possible links between company donations to the Conservative Party and the Honours system. Mr. Cranley Onslow (Con., Woking) attacked the Bill's "sordid little proposals" and described it as a "shabby and scurrilous attack" on the integrity of the members of the Honours Scrutiny Committee.

Televizing of the Lords

On a free vote in the Lords on Dec. 8, peers passed a motion by 74 to 24 votes, instructing the House's Sound Broadcasting Committee to report on how to implement the public televising of some of the Lords' proceedings. Viscount Whitelaw, Lord President of the Council, supported the proposal to allow television cameras into the Chamber. Lord Hill of Luton, ex-chairman of both the B.B.C. and I.T.A., said that since television had largely displaced the Press as a source of information for most people it inevitably followed that the doors should be opened to it. The Earl of Selkirk (Con.) doubted if the Lords were sufficiently newsworthy for the broadcasters and Lord Howard of Henderskelfe, also an ex-chairman of the B.B.C., said Parliamentary proceedings were important but extremely dull at times; Parliament was not telegenic but it ought to be available.

On Dec. 15 the Telecommunications Bill to convert British Telecom into a private company completed all its stages in the Commons. The Bill received a third reading by 313 to 187 votes, after a total of 520 hours had been consumed in debating it and its predecessor which was lost because of the calling of the General Election.

M.P.s voted 96 to 76 on Dec. 16 to give a second reading to a private member's Bill, sponsored by Mr. Austin Mitchell (Lab., Great Grimsby), to break the solicitors' monopoly on conveyancing although there was opposition on behalf of the Government by Sir Patrick Mayhew, Solicitor General, who put forward proposals to allow conveyancing by solicitors working for banks and building societies.

The Commons rose at 9.30 a.m. on Dec. 20 after sitting all night discussing the Consolidated Fund Bill which allows M.P.s to raise a wide ranging list of topics; the sitting lasted 19 hours and later in the day when meeting at the normal starting time, M.P.s gave a second reading by 298 to 188 votes, to the Health and Social Security Bill to allow non-opticians to sell spectacles. On Dec. 22 the Housing Minister (Mr. Ian Gow) announced proposals to help elderly tenants take up their right to buy the special local authority accommodation in which they lived. A new clause, approved by 257 to 165 votes, provided that tenants in non-sheltered accommodation for the elderly would have an unqualified right to buy. The Bill was also given a third reading by 238 to 152 votes.

Ordnance Privatization

Both the Lords and the Commons reassembled on Jan. 16 following the Christmas recess. Two Tory back-benchers, Mrs. Ann Winterton (Congleton) and Mr. Ben Dover (Chorley), who had two of the 13 ordnance factories in their constituencies, twice voted against the Government on a Bill paving the way for the privatization of the Royal Ordnance factories. A third Conservative, Sir Ian Gilmour, an ex-Cabinet Minister, abstained. The Bill was savaged by Mr. Denzil Davies, a Labour spokesman on defence, who described it as probably the most irresponsible and most damaging and most indefensible privatization measure "even this Government had introduced". However, the Bill received a second reading by 354 to 206 votes, after an Opposition amendment declining to give it a second reading was defeated by 355 to 188 votes.

The Rates Bill

On Jan. 17, the Rates Bill, which introduced proposals for capping the rates of high-spending local authorities, was given its second reading in the Commons after a fierce and critical debate and despite opposition from Mr. Edward Heath, former Tory Prime Minister, and other Tories. Mr. Heath was among 13 Conservatives who voted with Labour, Liberal, and S.D.P. M.P.s against the second reading which was successful by 347 to 247 votes. The Tory rebels also included former Ministers in Sir Ian Gilmour, Mr. Maurice Macmillan, Mr. Reginald Prentice, Mr. Keith Speed, and Mr. Geoffrey Rippon. Mr. Francis Pym, former Foreign Secretary, was among some 20 Tories who also abstained. A move by Mr. Rippon to have the committee stage of the Bill discussed on the floor of the House was defeated by 346 to 255 votes. Mr. Jenkin, Environment Secretary, moving the Bill's second reading, said the Government had a duty to protect ratepayers and to ensure all parts of the public sector worked within national economic policy. Dr. Cunningham, Shadow Environment Secretary, termed the measure as economically, democratically and morally indefensible and called it the "Abolition of Local Democracy Bill". Mr. Heath declared the Bill conferred Draconian powers "such as we have never taken before". Mr. Rippon, a former Tory Environment Secretary, condemned the Bill as one of the most deplorable brought before the Commons in all the time he had been an M.P. In a third vote on the issue, a resolution authorizing expenditure to implement the measure was carried by 333 to 98 votes.

On Jan. 19 three Conservative M.P.s voted against the Government on a Labour motion criticizing cuts in housing benefits by £230 million. Less than 10 Tories abstained and the motion was rejected by 330 to 198 votes. Numbers of restive Conservatives were assuaged with assurances that changes to the regulations would be made before they were laid before the House and by a promise from Mr. Fowler, Social Services Secretary, that he would have another look at the proposals for the cuts.

Rate Support Grant

When the rate support grant for 1984–85 was heatedly discussed in the Commons on Jan. 23, Tory M.P.s, including Mr. Pym, withdrew their threats to vote against the Government after Mr. Waldegrave, Environment Under-Secretary, gave an assurance that low-spending local councils would receive fairer treatment from whatever constraints there might be from 1985–86 onwards. The rate support grant was then approved by 332 to 203 votes, but four Conservatives voted against the proposals with about a dozen others abstaining. Mr. Jenkin, Environment Secretary, accepted the sense of unfairness felt by councils which still found themselves faced with demanding targets in spite of having made great efforts to make savings and cut staff costs. Dr. Cunningham, for Labour, said the grant involved further massive cuts in cash the Government were willing to give to councils to support services needed by the community; it was a disgraceful assault on local government and local democracy.

G.C.H.Q.

On Jan. 25, the Foreign Secretary (Sir Geoffrey Howe) announced the decision to ban workers at the Government Communications Headquarters at Cheltenham from union membership because of the special nature of the work there. He assured M.P.s it was not the intention to introduce similar measures outside the field of security and intelligence. Staff would be allowed to belong only to a departmental staff association approved by their director and those who decided to remain would each get £1,000 for withdrawal of certain rights in the interests of national security. The statement produced anger and resentment especially from the Labour benches, but the Tory M.P. for Cheltenham, Mr. Charles Irving, classified it as the removal of a democratic right, criticizing the Government for failing to consult workers' representatives at the Headquarters before reaching its decision. Dr. David Owen, S.D.P. leader, said it would have been preferable to have negotiated no-strike agreements with the staff. Mr. Healey, Shadow Foreign Secretary, accused the Government of indulging in a shabby affair. The unabated anger among Labour M.P.s spilled over into Prime Minister's question hour on the next day, when Mr. Kinnock, Labour leader, called the action dictatorial and a shameful and shame-faced decision. Mrs. Thatcher denied there had been any American intervention of any kind and as Labour M.P.s raucously pursued the issue throughout the whole 15 minutes of the Prime Minister's allotted question time she stressed the need to protect the Headquarters from the risk of industrial action which could interfere with operations essential to security.

After a running series of attacks against the G.C.H.Q. decision, a full debate on the issue opened in the Commons on Feb. 27. Mr. Healey, the Labour main speaker, rejected the Government's claim that they were only concerned with national security and suggested that the real reason was fear about the reaction of G.C.H.Q. staff to the introduction of lie detectors as a condition of service. It might be there had also been American pressure. The Foreign Secretary (Sir Geoffrey Howe) said that despite the

trade unions' no-strike assurance the conflict of loyalty involved in trade union membership could lead to future disruption. Mr. James Callaghan, the former Labour Prime Minister, prompted the Government to ask the Security Commission to consider the union proposals to see if they adequately safeguarded security requirements. Liberals and Social Democrats forced a division on an adjournment motion which, with Labour abstaining, resulted in a Government win by 201 to 25 votes. A dozen Tory M.P.s abstained, including Mr. Edward Heath, and seven Labour M.P.s, including two Front-Bench spokesmen, voted with the Alliance.

On Jan. 25, after the G.C.H.Q. announcement, M.P.s completed the remaining stages of the Prevention of Terrorism Bill, which was given a third reading by 184 to 84 votes.

On Jan. 26, Mr. Prior, Northern Ireland Secretary, rejected demands for his own resignation and that of Mr. Nicholas Scott, his Under-Secretary with responsibility for Ulster prisons, when he reported that the governor of the Maze prison had resigned following the publication of the Hennessy Report into the security failure which led to the mass break-out by I.R.A. prisoners last Sept. On Feb. 9, M.P.s discussed the Hennesssy Report and the debate ended in a vote won by the Government by 154 to 13 votes.

On Jan. 30, the Data Protection Bill was given a second reading by M.P.s by 226 to 104 votes, but a Labour motion to refer the Bill to a special committee which could take evidence from outside experts was defeated by 215 to 111 votes.

Mr. Peter Shore, Shadow Industry Secretary, moved a motion on Feb. 1 calling on the Government to help in the formation of a new corporate plan for shipbuilding and said a new relationship between British shipowners and shipbuilders would be brought about only with a strong Government lead. Mr. Tebbit, Industry Secretary, turned down Labour's demands for more Government assistance for the industry and said about £1 billion of public money had been consumed by it since nationalization by way of losses and intervention fund subsidy. The Opposition motion was defeated by 285 to 198 votes.

M.P.s ordered out

Mr. Dennis Skinner, Labour M.P. for Bolsover, was ordered out of the Chamber on Feb. 3 by the Deputy Speaker, after accusing Mr. Selwyn Gummer, Minister of State, Employment, of being a hypocrite, and refusing to withdraw the charge. Another Labour M.P., Mr. David Nellist (Coventry S.E.) was ordered out of the Commons on Feb. 29 after refusing to withdraw a remark that a Tory M.P. was "well paid" to support the South African Government.

Defeat for Government in the Lords

The Government was defeated by 12 votes in the Lords on Feb. 12 during the committee stage of the Telecommunications Bill. An Opposition amendment charging the Trade and Industry Secretary and the new Director-General of Telecommunications with seeing there was no financial discrimination between customers based on geographical location was successful by 118 to 106 votes. On Feb. 22, peers voted 129 to 112 in favour of an Opposition amendment setting out circumstances in which the Home Secretary could authorize telephone tapping.

Low Pay

The Opposition opened a debate on the problems of low pay in the Commons on Feb. 26 when Mr. John Smith, Shadow Employment Secretary, moved a motion accusing the Government of deliberately fostering low rates and calling on it to abandon its threat to abolish wages councils. Mr. David Penhaligon, for the Liberals, also said wages councils were the only form of protection offered to the low paid and they should be extended. Mr. Selwyn Gummer, Minister of State, Employment, replied the Government proposed to examine if the activities of wage councils increased unemployment. Labour's motion was defeated by 289 to 196 votes, and a Government amendment declaring that the most important step towards any improvement in pay levels was a general improvement in the economy was carried by 286 to 196 votes.

The Matrimonial and Family Proceedings Bill was given a second reading in the Commons on Feb. 16 by 186 to 68 votes.

There was a debate on the Government's spending plans for the next three years on Mar. 6 when the proposals contained in the White Paper were considered, and a Labour amendment deploring them was defeated by 301 to 199 votes.

THE BUDGET

The Chancellor of the Exchequer (Mr. Lawson) presented his first Budget on March 13. He said:

"As a result of our determined efforts, inflation is at its lowest level since the 'sixties. Economic recovery is well under way. Employment is growing.

"Across the economy, total money incomes grew in 1983 by about 8 per cent, of which 3 per cent represented real growth in output.

"Output in the second half of 1983 is now reckoned to have exceeded the previous peak, before the world recession set in, and is still rising strongly.

"Our rate of economic growth last year was the highest in the European Community.

"The balance of payments on current account last year is estimated to have been in surplus by about £2 billion.

"Recovery is set to continue throughout this year at an annual rate of 3 per cent. Inflation is expected to remain low, edging back down to 4½ per cent by the end of this year.

"With rising incomes and low inflation, consumption will continue to grow, and, encouraged by improved profitability and better long-term growth prospects, investment is expected to rise by a good 6 per cent this year.

"Looking abroad, too, economic prospects are more favourable than for some time.

"But despite the risks there is a growing sense throughout the industrialised world that the recovery this time is one which can be sustained. The essential requirement is the continued pursuit of prudent monetary and fiscal policies.

"So far as funding is concerned, the Public Sector's Borrowing Requirement will be significantly lower in the coming year.

"In financing it, the role of National Savings will remain important. This year's National Savings' target of £3 billion is likely to be achieved : the target for the coming year will again be £3 billion.

BORROWING

"The Medium Term Financial Strategy has always envisaged that the Public Sector Borrowing Requirement would fall as a percentage of Gross Domestic Product over the medium term. By 1981–82 we had brought it down to 3½ per cent of G.D.P.

"Since then there has been little further fall. The latest estimate of the P.S.B.R. for the current year, 1983–84, remains what it was in November: around £10 billion, equivalent to 3¼ per cent of G.D.P.

"This is significantly above what was intended at the time of last year's Budget, and would have been higher still had it not been for the July measures.

"We now need a further substantial reduction in borrowing to help bring interest rates down further as monetary growth slows down.

"Last year's Medium Term Financial Strategy showed an illustrative P.S.B.R. for 1984–85 of 2½ per cent of G.D.P., equivalent to around £8 billion, but I believe that it is possible, and indeed prudent, to aim for a somewhat lower figure. I am therefore providing for a P.S.B.R. next year of 2¼ per cent of G.D.P. or £7¼ billion.

While the measures I announce will, after indexation, be broadly neutral in their effects on revenue in 1984–85, they will reduce taxation in 1985–86 by well over £1¾ billion.

"And the medium term financial strategy published today shows that there should be room for further tax cuts not only in 1985–86, but throughout the remainder of this Parliament, provided that we stick firmly to our published plans for public expenditure to 1986–87, and maintain an equally firm control of public spending thereafter."

EXPENDITURE

The Green Paper on the prospects for public spending and taxation over the next 10 years concludes that, without firm control over public spending, there can be no prospect of bringing the burden of tax back to more reasonable levels.

"On the assumptions made in the Green Paper, the burden of taxation will be reduced to the levels of the early 1970s only if public spending is kept broadly stable in real terms over the next ten years."

Mr. Lawson said that in contrast to previous years, he had no package of public expenditure measures to announce. The Social Services Secretary would be announcing the new rates of Social Security benefits, including child benefit, when the May retail price index was known.

Mr. Lawson said: "At the beginning of the last Parliament, the Government set itself the target of reducing the size of the Civil Service from 732,000 in April, 1979, to 630,000 by April this year.

"That target will be achieved. We have now set outselves the further target of 593,000 by April 1988.

"The tax changes I shall announce will reduce manpower requirements by at least 1,000 in my own departments, which will help towards meeting the 1988 target.

TAX REFORM

Mr. Lawson said the Budget would significantly reduce the overall burden of tax over the next two years taken together, and he hoped to have scope for further reductions in future Budgets.

"The changes I shall be proposing are the taxation of savings and investment, business taxation, and the taxation of personal income and spending."

Mr. Lawson said the proposals on the taxation of savings and investment should improve the direction and quality of both.

"They will contribute further to the creation of a property-owning and share-owning democracy, in which more decisions are made by individuals rather than by institutions.

"I propose to halve the rate of Stamp Duty to one per cent. The new rate will apply straight away to Stock Exchange deals.

"For the home buyer, the new flat rate one per cent Stamp Duty will start at £30,000. Below this level no duty will be payable.

"As a result of this £5,000 increase in the threshold 90 per cent of first-time home buyers will not have to pay stamp duty at all.

"Reducing the rate of duty on share transfers will remove an important disincentive to investment in equities, and increase the international competitiveness of our stock market. It should also help British companies to raise equity finance."

He had four proposals to encourage the issue of corporate bonds.

"I shall go ahead with the new arrangements for deep discount stock and the reliefs for companies issuing Eurobonds, and for convertible loan stock, which were announced but not enacted last year.

"I propose to exempt from Capital Gains Tax most corporate fixed interest securities provided they are held for more than a year. Since such securities are already exempt from Stamp Duty this means that the tax concessions for private sector borrowing in the corporate bond market will now be virtually the same as for Government borrowing in the gilt-edged market.

"The reductions in Stamp Duty will cost £450 million in 1984–85, of which £160 million is the cost of the relief on share transfers, and £290 million the cost of the relief on transfers of houses and other buildings and land."

LIFE ASSURANCE

The Chancellor said the main effect of life assurance premium relief was unduly to favour institutional rather than direct investment.

"I therefore propose to withdraw the relief on all new contracts made after today. This change will apply only to new (or newly enhanced) policies, taken out after today.

"Existing policies will not be affected at all. The change is estimated to yield about £90 million in 1984–85.

"I am also proposing to curtail the special—but unfortunately widely abused—privileges for what are known as 'tax exempt' Friendly Societies, and bring them into line with the normal rules for Friendly Societies doing 'mixed' business.

"However, the limits within which in future all Friendly Societies will be able to write assurance on a tax exempt basis will be increased from £500 to £750.

"The Investment Income Surcharge was an unfair and anomalous tax on savings and on the rewards of successful enterprise.

"In the vast majority of cases it is a tax on savings made out of hard-earned and fully-taxed income. More than half of those who pay the Investment Income Surcharge are over 65, and of these half would otherwise be liable to tax at only the basic rate.

"I have therefore decided that the investment income surcharge should be abolished. The cost in 1984–85 will be some £25 million, building up to around £350 million in a full year.

"I propose to draw more closely together the tax treatment of depositors in banks and building societies. These institutions compete in the same market for personal deposits. I believe that they should be able to do so on more equal terms as far as tax is concerned.

"The major source of unequal treatment, against which the banks in particular have frequently complained, is the special arrangement for interest paid by building societies."

COMPOSITE RATE

"The societies pay tax at a special rate—the 'composite rate'—on the interest paid to the depositor, who receives credit for income tax at the full basic rate.

"I am satisfied that the advantage of the composite rate arrangement outweighs the disadvantage.

"It follows that equal treatment of building societies and banks should be achieved, not by removing the composite rate from the societies, but by extending it to the banks and other licensed deposit takers.

"Non-taxpayers will continue to be able to receive interest gross, should they wish to do so, by putting their money into appropriate National Savings facilities.

"I propose to extend the composite rate arrangements to interest received by U.K. resident individuals from banks and other licensed deposit takers with effect from 1985–86.

"The composite rate will not apply either to non-residents or to the corporate sector. Arrangements will also be made to exclude from the scheme certificates of deposit and time deposits of £50,000 or more."

BUSINESS TAXATION

"The measures I am announcing today will, taking the next two years together, result in a substantial reduction in the burden of taxation on British business. In addition, I shall be proposing a far-reaching reform of company taxation.

"The current rates of Corporation Tax are far too high, penalising profit and success, and blunting the cutting edge of enterprise.

"I propose to restructure the capital allowances in three annual stages.

"In the case of plant and machinery, and assets whose allowances are linked with them, the first year allowance will be reduced from 100 per cent to 75 per cent for all such expenditure incurred after today, and to 50 per cent for expenditure incurred after March 31 next year.

"After March 31, 1986, there will be no first year allowances and all expenditure on plant and machinery will qualify for annual allowances on a 25 per cent reducing balance basis.

"In addition, from next year annual allowances will be given as soon as the expenditure is incurred, and not, as they are today, when the asset comes into use.

"This will bring forward the entitlement to annual allowances for those assets, such as ships and oil rigs, for which some payment is normally made well before they are brought into use.

"For industrial buildings, I propose that the initial allowance should fall from 75 per cent to 50 per cent from tonight, and be further reduced to 25 per cent from March 31 next year. After March 31, 1986, the initial allowance will be abolished, and expenditure will be written off on an annual four per cent straight line basis.

"When these changes have all taken place, tax allowances for both plant and machinery and industrial buildings will still on average be rather more generous than would be provided by a strict system of commercial depreciation.

"I propose not to allow Stock Relief for increases in prices after this month.

"The changes I have announced, in capital allowances and stock relief, enable me to embark on a major programme of progressive reductions in the main rate of Corporation Tax.

"In the year just ending, on which tax is generally payable in 1984–85, the rate will be cut from 52 per cent to 50 per cent.

"For profits earned in 1984–85 the rate will be further cut to 45 per cent. Looking further ahead to profits earned in 1985–86, the rate will go down to 40 per cent; and for profits earned in 1986–87 the main rate of Corporation Tax will be 35 per cent—no less than 17 percentage points below the current rate.

"The majority of companies are not liable to pay the main rate of Corporation Tax at all. For them it is the small companies' rate, at present 38 per cent, which applies.

"I propose to reduce this rate forthwith to 30 per cent for profits earned in 1983–84 and thereafter.

"These corporation tax measures will cost £280 million in 1984–85, in 1985–86 the cost will be £450 million—made up of £1,100 million by way of reductions in the rates, only partially offset by a £650 million reduction in the value of the reliefs.

"During the whole transitional period these measures should have a broadly neutral effect on the financial position of companies.

"But when the changes have fully worked through, companies will enjoy very substantial reductions on the tax they paid."

He said that the Business Expansion Scheme, introduced last year as a successor to the Business Start Up Scheme, was designed to offer generous incentives for investment by new or expanding companies in high risk areas.

"The ownership of farmland cannot be said to fall within this category, and I therefore propose that from tomorrow farming should cease to be treated as a qualifying trade under the scheme. I propose to abolish two reliefs in the personal tax field which were introduced at a time when this country suffered from excessively high rates of income tax.

"As we have reduced those rates, the reliefs are no longer justified.

"The first is the 50 per cent tax relief (falling after 9 years to 25 per cent) applied to the emoluments of foreign-domiciled employees working here for foreign employers.

"These employees are often paying much less tax here than they would either in their own country or in most other European countries.

"At present income tax rates the need for this relief has clearly disappeared. Moreover, it is open to widespread abuse.

"I therefore propose to withdraw the relief for all new cases from today. For existing beneficiaries, the 25 per cent relief will cease on April 6, and the 50 per cent relief will be phased out over the next five years.

"I also propose to withdraw the foreign earnings relief for United Kingdom residents who work at least 30 days abroad in a tax year.

"I propose to withdraw the matching relief for the self-employed who spend 30 days abroad, and for those resident in the United Kingdom who have separate employments or separate trades carried on wholly abroad.

"The relief will be halved to 12½ per cent in 1984–85 and removed entirely from April 6, 1985.

"However, I am not making any change to the 100 per cent deduction given for absences abroad of 365 days or more.

"In addition, I have authorised consultations by the Inland Revenue about a possible relaxation in the rules governing the taxation of expenses reimbursed to employees for travel overseas.

"The abolition of these reliefs will eventually yield revenue savings of over £150 million: and represents another useful step in the removal of complexity and distortions in the tax system.

"I need to set the car benefit scales for 1985–86 for those provided with the use of a car by their employer.

"I am proposing an increase of 10 per cent in both the car and car fuel scales with effect from April 1985."

Transfer Tax Changes

"I propose in addition to statutory indexation to reduce the highest rate of Capital Transfer Tax from 75 per cent to 60 per cent, for lifetime gifts I propose to simplify the scale so that the rate is always one-half of that on death.

"For Capital Gains Tax I will bring forward in the Finance Bill proposals to double the limit for retirement relief to a figure of £100,000, backdated to April 1983.

"I am proposing no other changes this year in Capital Gains Tax beyond the statutory indexation of the exempt amount from £5,300 to £5,600. We have done much to improve the Development Land Tax.

Early in the last Parliament, my predecessor increased the threshold from £10,000 to £50,000. I now propose a further increase to £75,000, which will reduce the number of cases liable to the tax by more than one-third.

"Next share options. The measures introduced in the last Parliament to improve employee involvement through profit-sharing and savings-related share options schemes have been a notable success. To maintain and build on this progress I propose to increase the monthly limit on contributions to savings-related share option schemes from £50 to £100. I have also authorised the Inland Revenue to double the tax-free limits under the concession on long service awards, and to include within these limits the gift of shares in the employee's company.

"I propose that, subject to certain necessary limits and conditions, share options generally be taken out of income tax altogether, leaving any gain to be charged to capital gains tax on ultimate disposals of the shares.

"The new rules will apply to options meeting the necessary conditions which are granted from April 6.

"I am taking two measures to prevent an unjustified loss of tax in the North Sea. First, in addition to the P.R.T. measures on farmouts which I announced last September, I am limiting the potential Corporation Tax cost of such deals.

"Second, I propose to repeal the provision which allows Advance Corporation Tax to be repaid where Corporation Tax is reduced by P.R.T.

"Ever since V.A.T. was introduced in this country, we have treated imports differently from the way our main European competitors treat them.

"I propose to move to the system used by our European competitors. We shall provide the same facilities for payment of V.A.T. on imports as apply to Customs duties. That means that most importers will be able to defer payment of V.A.T. by on average one month from the date of importation.

"This change will apply from October 1. By bringing forward V.A.T. receipts, it will bring an extra £1·2 billion in 1984–85, some of which will be borne by foreign producers and manufacturers. There will, of course, be no increased revenue in subsequent years."

Abolition of Surcharge

"The second change I propose to make on Oct. 1 concerns the National Insurance Surcharge.

"This tax on jobs was introduced by the Labour Government in 1977 at the rate of two per cent, and further increased in 1979 to 3½ per cent. During the last Parliament, this Government reduced it to one per cent, and we are pledged to abolish it during the lifetime of this Parliament.

"Given the impact that this tax has, not only on industrial costs but also—at a time of high unemployment—on jobs, I have decided to take the opportunity of this, my first Budget, to fulfil that pledge.

"Abolition of the National Insurance Surcharge from October will reduce private sector employers' costs by almost £350 million in 1984–85, and over £850 million in a full year. As before, the benefit will be confined to the private sector."

Indirect Taxation

Turning to the taxation of personal income and spending, the Chancellor said:

"Having regard to the representations I have received on health grounds, I propose an increase in the tobacco duty which, including V.A.T., will put 10p on the price of a packet of cigarettes, with corresponding increases for hand-rolling tobacco and cigars. I do not, however, propose any increase in the duty on pipe tobacco.

"I propose to raise most of the other Excise duties

broadly in line with inflation, so as to maintain their real value.

"I propose to increase the duties on petrol and derv by amounts which, including V.A.T., will raise the price at the pumps by 4½p and 3½p a gallon respectively.

"This does no more than keep pace with inflation.

"I do not propose to increase the duty on heavy fuel oil, which is of particular importance to industrial costs.

"There is one Excise duty which I propose to do away with altogether. Many of those who find it hardest to make ends meet, including in particular many pensioners, use paraffin stoves to heat their homes. I propose to abolish the duty on kerosene. The various rates of Vehicle Excise Duty will, once again, go up roughly in line with prices. Thus the duty for cars and light vans will be increased by £5, from £85 to £90 a year. However, I propose to exempt from Vehicle Excise Duty all recipients of the war pensioners' Mobility Supplement. In addition, the existing V.A.T. relief for motor vehicles designed or adapted for use by the handicapped will be extended, and matched by a new car tax relief.

"The effect will be that neither V.A.T. nor car tax will apply to family cars designed for disabled people or substantially adapted for their use.

"The rules of the European Community, so far as alcoholic drinks are concerned, are designed to prevent a member state from protecting its own domestic product by imposing a significantly higher duty on competing imports.

"In pursuit of this, the Commission has taken a number of countries to the European Court of Justice.

"In our case, the Commission contended that we were protecting beer by under-taxing it in relation to wine. I am now implementing the judgment handed down by the court last year.

"Accordingly I propose to increase the duty on beer by the minimum amount needed to comply with the judgment and maintain revenue: 2p on a typical pint of beer, including V.A.T.

"At the same time, the duty on table wine will be reduced by the equivalent of about 18p a bottle, again including V.A.T.

"As for the rest of the alcoholic drinks, cider will go up by 3p a pint. I propose to increase the duty on sparkling wine, fortified wine and spirits by about 10p a bottle, including V.A.T.

"These changes in Excise duties will, all told, bring in some £840 million in 1984–85, some £200 million more than is required to keep pace with inflation. The addition is due to the increase in tobacco duty."

The remainder of the extra revenue needed to enable a substantial switch this year from taxes on earnings to taxes on spending must come from V.A.T.

He proposed no change in the rate of V.A.T. but instead, intended to broaden the base of the tax by extending the 15 per cent rate to two areas of expenditure that had hitherto been zero-rated.

At present repairs and maintenance to buildings were taxed, but alterations were not.

"The borderline between these two categories is the most confused in the whole field of V.A.T. I propose to end this confusion and illogicality by bringing all alterations into tax.

"£290 million of the cost of the reduction in stamp duty in 1984–85 relates to transfers of land and buildings, and of that £290 million some 90 per cent relates to buildings and building land.

"Nevertheless, to allow a reasonable time for existing commitments to be completed or adjusted, the V.A.T. change will be deferred until June 1."

Most food was zero-rated, but food served in restaurants was taxed, together with a miscellaneous range of items including ice-cream, confectionery, soft drinks and crisps, which were brought into tax by Mr. Healey, the former Labour Chancellor.

"Take-away food clearly competes with other forms of catering, and I therefore intend to bring into tax hot take-away food and drinks, with effect from May 1.

"The total effect of the extensions of the V.A.T. coverage I have proposed will be to increase the yield of the tax by £375 million in 1984–85 and by £650 million in a full year.

"The total impact on the retail price index of the V.A.T. changes and Excise Duty changes taken together would be less than three-quarters of one per cent."

PERSONAL TAXATION

Since taking office in 1979, the Government had cut the basic rate of income tax from 33 per cent to 30 per cent and sharply reduced the confiscatory higher rates inherited from the last Labour Government.

"But as a result of the changes to taxes on spending which I have announced, I can take a further step in this Budget.

"So far as the allowances and thresholds are concerned, I must clearly increase these by the amounts set out in the statutory indexation formula, based on the 5·3 per cent increase in the retail price index to December.

"I have decided that this year, the right course is to use every penny I have in hand, within the framework of a revenue neutral budget, to lift the level of the basic tax thresholds, for the married and single alike.

"I propose to increase the other thresholds in line with the statutory indexation requirement, but by no more.

"The first higher rate of 40 per cent will apply when taxable income reaches £15,400 a year and the top rate of 60 per cent to taxable income over £38,100.

"The single age allowance will rise from £2,360 to £2,490 and the married age allowance from £3,755 to £3,955.

"For the basic thresholds, statutory indexation would mean putting the single and married allowances up by £100 and £150 respectively.

"I propose to increase the basic thresholds by well over double what is required by indexation.

"The single person's allowance will be increased by £220 from £1,785 to £2,005; and the married man's allowance by £360, from £2,795 to £3,155.

"This is an increase of around 12½ per cent, or some 7 per cent in real terms, and it brings the married man's tax allowance for 1984–85 to its highest level in real terms since the war.

"It means that the great majority of married couples will enjoy an income tax cut of at least £2 a week, and it means that a large number of people, those with the smallest incomes of all, are taken out of income tax altogether.

"Some 850,000 people—over 100,000 of them widows—who would have paid tax if threshholds had not been increased, will pay no tax in 1984–85. That is 400,000 more taken out of tax than if the allowances had merely been indexed."

All these changes would take effect under P.A.Y.E. on the first pay day after May 10.

Their cost was considerable—some £1·8 billion in 1984–85 of which roughly half represented the cost of indexation.

Mr. Lawson concluded: "This is as far as I can go on income tax this year, within a broadly revenue-neutral Budget for 1984–85."

The Debate on the Budget

The Labour leader, Mr. Kinnock, making his first response to a Budget statement, observed: "This is a Budget which does more for the City of London than it does for the country." He denied claims it would be a broadly neutral budget; it was not neutral to relieve the obligations of the rich while maintaining the obligations of the modestly well-off and the poor. What they had witnessed in the last four years was a conspiracy against the basic interests of the British people, their needs for development, employment, and for care and opportunity. A four-day debate on the Budget statement ended on Mar. 19, when the Chancellor, replying, declared the Budget had set a clear strategy for defeating inflation and creating a more dynamic and efficient economy. A strong recovery now under way was accompanied by low and declining rates of inflation. Earlier in winding-up for the Opposition, Mr. Jeffrey Rooker said the Budget ignored the unemployed and made the rich richer. The Government carried its Budget resolutions after six divisions in which the majority ranged between 324 and 136 votes.

On Mar. 16, the Video Recordings Bill passed its final stage in the Commons although some M.P.s had reservations that it had gone too far in the direction of censorship, but it was unopposed.

On Mar. 21 Mrs. Thatcher, reporting on the recent Brussels summit, made it clear she was prepared to withhold some payments from the European Community as a result of the failure to reach agreement on Britain's budgetary contribution. Mr. Heath and Mr. Pym joined in urging the Prime Minister not to act illegally by withholding payments but other Tory M.P.s supported vociferously her declared intent to act to safeguard British interests. Mrs. Thatcher said the U.K. would be prepared to consider an increase in the Community's financial resources but only on condition there was effective control of agricultural and other spending with a fair sharing of the budget burden. An Opposition motion attacking the Government over energy price rises was defeated by 289 to 202 votes. On Mar. 26 during the report stage of the Trade Union Bill, the Labour amendment giving individual unions the opportunity to declare on whether they wanted the change to secret ballots being imposed on them was rejected by 272 to 174 votes.

Several Tory back-benchers voted against the Government on Mar. 27 during the report stage of the Rates Bill. Mr. Geoffrey Rippon and Mr. Reg Prentice were among those who supported a new clause proposed by Dr. John Cunningham, Opposition Environment spokesman, in a move to lessen the Bill's impact on local authorities. The clause was nonetheless defeated easily by 301 to 193 votes. Next day, when the report stage was completed, Mr. Jenkin, Environment Secretary, promised to seek to limit the blanket curb on rate increases during its consideration in the Lords, thus exempting those authorities which had kept to Government spending guidelines over a period of years. This relaxation seemed to satisfy many Tory back-benchers threatening another vote against the Government and a mere handful rebelled ultimately and supported an amendment seeking to delete the general power of rate-capping, voting being 404 to 202 votes against the amendment. The Government later had a 125-vote majority on the third reading of the Bill.

Tory rebellion

Conservative back-benchers again rebelled on April 2 but in considerable strength on this occasion after they protested during the report stage about the Government's refusal to change its Trade Union Bill to make it compulsory for union members to contract-in to the political levy if they wished to. About 80 Tories supported an amendment calling for an end to the system under which union members could contract-out of paying the levy, but in the event only 40 of them actually voted for it in the

lobby although a fair number also abstained. But with Labour M.P.s marching through the same lobby as the Government, the amendment was crushed by 415 to 57 votes. However, Mr. King, Employment Secretary, promised new legislation if the unions failed to keep their side of an agreement made between him and the T.U.C. by which the Government abandoned plans to introduce a contracting-in system in return for a new code of conduct.

Mr. Giles Radice, Shadow Education Secretary, moved a motion on April 3 deploring the Government's curbs on local authority educational expenditure but this was defeated by 302 to 206 votes. Sir Keith Joseph, Education Secretary, said Labour was still living in a make-believe world where there were no restraints on spending.

The Rates Bill arrived in the Lords for its second reading on April 9 when Baroness Birk moved an Opposition amendment which while not denying a second reading to the measure expressed a belief it would bring damaging constitutional changes in relations between central and local government, undermine the authority and responsibility of local councillors, and gravely weaken local democracy. The amendment also asked the Government to embark on thorough reform of local government finance. Lord Bellwin, Local Government Minister, declared the Bill was neither unconstitutional nor authoritarian and that if anything was unconstitutional it was the behaviour of the minority of councils at whom it was directed. The Opposition amendment was defeated by 235 to 153 votes, and the Bill was read a second time without a division.

Policing of the Miner's Dispute

There was plenty of hard-hitting debate in the Commons on April 10 in an emergency debate, initiated by a Labour M.P., on the implications for civil liberties and the rule of law of policing operations connected with the mining dispute. Mr. Brittan, Home Secretary, said the police had been subjected to a campaign of denigration when militant miners' leaders found they could not close the coalfields by violence; their purpose had been to avoid a national ballot at all costs and bring about the closure of coalfields by picketing. Mr. Gerald Kaufman, Shadow Home Secretary, said the police had exceeded their powers because of the intolerable dilemma in which they had been placed. On a formal motion to adjourn, on which the debate took place, the Government had a majority of 157.

Later the Government had a majority of 97 on the second reading of the Finance Bill, the debate on which overspilled into the early hours of April 11. Labour efforts to keep the discussion going throughout the night were countered by the Government Chief Whip (Mr. John Wakeham) moving the closure which was carried by 220 to 108 votes.

Tories revolt on G.L.C.

Another Commons revolt by Tory M.P.s emerged on April 11 when Mr. Heath protested about legislation for which he said the Government had no General Election mandate and Mr. Pym, Mr. Rippon, and Sir Ian Gilmour, all former Cabinet ministers, supported a Conservative amendment to the Bill paving the way for abolition of the G.L.C. and six metropolitan authorities, but this was not selected for a vote. The rumpus erupted on the second reading of the Local Government (Interim Provisions) Bill, which cancelled next year's elections to the G.L.C. and metropolitan councils in preparation for a measure in the next session to abolish these authorities. Mr. Heath claimed there was no justification for proposals which would change political control in the affected cities by "Parliamentary diktat". It immediately put the Conservative Party open to the charge of the greatest piece of gerrymandering in the last 150 years of British history. Mr. Jenkin, Environment Secretary, moving the second reading, promised that the Order beginning abolition would not be made unless and until a second reading had been given to the main Bill. Dr. John Cunningham, Labour's chief spokesman, moved an amendment asking the House not to give the Bill a second reading in the absence of Parliamentary approval of alternative arrangements for administering services which were now the responsibility of the G.L.C. and the metropolitan councils. Mr. Pym described the Bill as a thoroughly bad precedent and said it should be withdrawn. At the conclusion of a tense debate, the Bill was given a second reading by 301 to 208 votes. Nineteen Tories joined Labour in voting against the measure and about 20 others abstained, the rebel Tories including Mr. Heath, Sir Ian Gilmour, Mr. Pym, and Mr. Rippon.

On April 25, there was an Opposition attack on Government transport policy and during the exchanges, Mr. Ridley, Transport Secretary, observed the Government would have further plans for taking State-owned transport industries out of the public sector. The Labour motion accused the Government of basing its transport policy on an "ideological obsession" with competition, profit and privatization and was defeated by 247 to 168 votes. In the early hours of April 26, the Trade Union Bill received a third reading in the Commons by 231 to 149 votes.

The Libyan Embassy Siege

The Home Secretary announced on May 1 a number of measures to prevent a repetition of the Libyan Embassy siege. As well as the review of his powers to ban demonstrations by foreigners, stronger action was to be taken to prevent Libyans coming to this country to harass their own dissidents. Mr. Brittan said the police believed that the murder of the policewoman was committed by one of two people who were in the Embassy, both of whom had diplomatic immunity. Apart from this bar to a prosecution, the police were of the view that there was not sufficient evidence to sustain a prosecution. Mr. Kaufman, Labour's spokesman, said we had suffered a national humiliation—a woman police constable having been shot down in cold blood and colleagues obliged to escort her murderer in safety out of the country. He accused the Government of complacency in the face of obvious dangers arising from the activities of the former "Libyan People's Bureau". Dr. Owen, S.D.P. leader, said the Home Secretary was locking the stable door after the horse had bolted, or rather had been escorted out of the country. At question time earlier, Mrs. Thatcher refused to set up an external inquiry into the circumstances leading to the murder of the policewoman but said an internal inquiry would be held under the Cabinet Office although the conclusions would not be made public. The Foreign Secretary made it clear also that foreign missions which indulged in terrorist and other unacceptable activities as had the "Bureau" would be expelled in future. In a statement, he told M.P.s that while the review of diplomatic rules was to go ahead, he was taking immediate unilateral action to strengthen control over the operations of foreign missions.

M.P. suspended

Mr. Tam Dalyell, Labour M.P. for Linlithgow, was ordered from the Commons on May 2 for persistently failing to withdraw an allegation that Mrs. Thatcher had lied over the sinking of the Argentine warship,

the *General Belgrano*, during the Falklands campaign. He was "named" after being asked 10 times to withdraw the remark made during question time exchanges about trade initiatives with the new civilian government in Argentina. Some Labour M.P.s objected to the formal motion moved by the Leader of the House (Mr. Biffen) to suspend Mr. Dalyell for five working days, but it was carried by 196 to 33 votes.

In the Lords on May 8, the Government beat off an all-party attack to remove the clause in the Rates Bill which gave the Environment Secretary rate-capping powers over any local authority if both Houses of Parliament endorsed the necessary order. The Labour amendment was supported by Tory peers but the Government threw it out by 140 to 130 votes.

Tory rebels renew attack

The Tory rebels on the second reading of the Local Government (Interim Provisions) Bill returned to the fray when the committee stage opened on May 9 with Mr. Geoffrey Rippon (Con., Hexham) leading the onslaught in calling the proposals abject, squalid, and shameful. Sir Ian Gilmour spoke in aid of a Labour amendment that there should be an independent inquiry into the financial and other effects before the Government moved to abolish the councils. The Environment Secretary said that to have held the elections when the abolition proposals were before the Commons would have been a recipe for confusion and chaos. The amendment was defeated by 319 to 184 votes. On the next day, Mr. Heath was one of the 12 Conservatives who voted against proposals for the interim government of London and six other cities once next year's elections for the seven councils had been cancelled. Mr. Heath castigated the Government for "completely immoral" proposals for the reform of local government which were likely to transfer control of the G.L.C. from Labour to the Conservatives through the proposed temporary bodies nominated by lower tier councils. The Tory rebels supported a Labour amendment seeking to delete the arrangements for the nominated bodies but it was defeated by 271 to 168. There was more trouble for the Government in the Lords on the same day when two defeats were inflicted on them during consideration of Commons' amendments to the Housing and Building Control Bill.

The Police and Criminal Evidence Bill was given a third reading in the Commons on May 16 by 286 to 190 votes, with a demonstration in the Strangers' Gallery shortly before the division when a dozen protestors were ejected. Mr. Kaufman, Labour's main spokesman, maintained the Bill remained profoundly obnoxious and promised the next Labour Government would repeal it. His main objections were to the police power to detain without charge for 96 hours and the provisions on stop and search. But the Home Secretary said the Bill struck a fair balance between necessary powers for the police and appropriate safeguards.

Longest sitting since the war

The Commons had its longest sitting since the war on May 22/23 after an all-night performance by the Liberal/S.D.P. Alliance who talked throughout the night of May 22 and into the morning of May 23 to delay progress of the Bill paving the way for the abolition of the G.L.C. and six metropolitan councils. Having prolonged the committee stage, the Alliance M.P.s began moving and speaking on amendments tabled by Labour M.P.s. About mid-morning, Mr. Simon Hughes (Lib., Southwark and Bermondsey) moved to the empty Labour Front Bench and remained there addressing the Chamber for over an hour before a group of Labour M.P.s reappeared to sit on both sides of Mr. Hughes and another Liberal M.P. However, the Alliance tactics backfired as the hours ticked away and Tory M.P.s voted down all Labour and Liberal moves to end the proceedings. The outcome of this marathon sitting was that the Government took tactical advantage of the circumstances by moving straight on from the committee stage to the third reading planned for May 24 with the abandonment of May 23's scheduled business. Consequently the Government obtained a third reading for its Bill a day earlier than planned.

Debate on the miners' strike

The first full-scale debate on the miners' strike took place on June 7, when Mr. Michael Foot, the former Labour leader, alleged that the Prime Minister had misled both the Commons and the country when she said the Government had not intervened. He added that the bitterness in mining areas would be increased when miners read how Mrs. Thatcher had lied to the House. Conservatives immediately shouted "Withdraw" which later Mr. Foot did, as he put it, on the instructions of the Speaker. Mr. Stan Orme, Shadow Energy Secretary, put the Labour motion condemning the Government's mishandling of the dispute and attacked the unilateral decision of the N.C.B. to lose 20,000 jobs and close over 20 pits in the coming year. The Energy Secretary (Mr. Peter Walker) said the Government had exceeded the investment proposals in the "Plan for Coal" by a substantial amount. The Opposition motion was defeated by 272 to 179 votes and a Government amendment was carried by 273 to 178.

Heavy defeat for Government in Lords

On June 11 the Local Government (Interim Provisions) Bill reached the Lords for second reading debate after its stormy passage through the Commons. Lord Hooson (Lib.) moved an amendment which asserted the Bill was a dangerous precedent which sought to give non-elected bodies the powers of properly constituted councils, but it was defeated by 237 to 217 votes and the second reading was approved unopposed. There was a serious shock for the Government on June 28 when their plans to abolish the G.L.C. and metropolitan councils suffered a humiliating setback in the Lords. Peers voted to insert a new clause into the Bill which stopped the proposed suspension of elections until Royal Assent was given to another Bill which the Government planned to introduce in the next session. Effectively it prevented the Environment Secretary from setting up interim councils composed of nominated councillors from the boroughs to take over county functions next May. Lord Elwyn-Jones (Lab.) moved the new clause which was widely supported in all parts of the House and was carried by 191 to 143 votes, a majority against the Government of 48. In the Commons on June 29, the Environment Secretary was confronted with a barrage of questions about his intentions after the Lords defeat and there were calls for his resignation. Mr. Jenkin repeated the determination to abolish the G.L.C. and metropolitan councils but said he would consider the options. On July 5, Mrs. Thatcher announced that the Government was determined to cancel next year's elections for the authorities concerned but would extend the term of office of the councillors for another year. On July 16 in the Lords, Viscount Whitelaw, Leader of the House, urged peers to support new proposals extending the life of the present councils until April 1, 1986. Baroness Birk (Lab.) countered that peers should complement their decision of June 28 when the Government suffered a 48-vote defeat by ensuring

that council elections did take place. However, Lord Whitelaw's appeals to amend the measure by extending the life of the G.L.C. and other councils affected were successful. An amendment requiring elections to be held next May was rejected by 248 to 155 votes. Lord Molson, who led Conservative supporters into the Opposition lobby in June, said the Government amendments established an important constitutional principle. They had accepted the Lords' considered opinion.

The Duke of Gloucester made his maiden speech in the Lords on May 13 during a debate on smoking and health and urged a complete phasing out of tobacco advertizing and a ban on sponsorship by the industry. Lord Glenarthur, Under-Secretary, Health and Social Security, said the Government preferred to rely on voluntary agreements with the tobacco industry.

Another defeat for Government in the Lords

There was another defeat for the Government in the Lords on June 19 when peers voted that trade union executives should be elected by postal ballot. Voting was 85 to 65 on a Tory backbench amendment supported by Alliance and independent peers to the Trade Union Bill, an anti-Government majority of 20.

E.E.C. milk quotas

At the end of the debate in the Commons on July 3 on the new Common Market milk quotas introduced to curb the growing surpluses the Government won the vote by 333 to 212, but not without sharp criticism from both sides of the House. Mr. Edward du Cann, chairman of the Tory 1922 Committee, described as economic madness a system which discouraged exports and warned it would cause unemployment in the British dairy industry. Labour's spokesman, Mr. Robert Hughes, blamed the hardship of dairy farmers on the Government which had failed to protect British interests. The Agriculture Minister (Mr. Jopling) stressed the need to curb the "frightening spiral" of costs for the Common Agricultural Policy.

The Opposition launched an attack on the Government on July 5, on the National Health Service, but lost the vote by 297 to 174.

M.P.s had another all-night sitting on July 11/12 lasting almost 22 hours, most of it taken up with the report stage of the Finance No. 2 Bill which received its third reading on July 12 by 331 to 168 votes. The Chancellor of the Exchequer declared there was no question whatsoever of the Government changing course in its economic strategy and that the present industrial unrest would not undermine the soundness of the British economy. In the Lords new Government amendments to the Trade Union Bill recast those parts with a presumption that ballots for elections would be postal unless a union was satisfied that in their particular circumstances workplace ballots met all requirements for secrecy, voting convenience, and freedom from interference or constraint. By 142 to 44 votes, peers inserted a "freedom to vote without interference" provision but a Liberal amendment permitting a modified voting system was rejected by 134 to 39 votes.

Mr. Skinner suspended

Mr. Dennis Skinner (Lab., Bolsover) was suspended from the Commons for five days on July 17 after refusing to withdraw an allegation that Mrs. Thatcher was capable of "bribing" the Appeal Court judges who would hear the G.C.H.Q. appeal case on trade union membership. The episode arose when M.P.s were quizzing the Prime Minister after she had made a statement about the High Court ruling that the Government's ban on unions at Cheltenham was invalid. Mr. Skinner did not respond when asked to withdraw by the Speaker and then an angry Prime Minister demanded that the allegation be "totally and unreservedly withdrawn". The Speaker "named" Mr. Skinner and the motion that he be suspended was carried by 218 to 84 votes. Mrs. Thatcher told M.P.s that in view of the implications for national security of this judgment, the Government was appealing against it. Mr. Kinnock maintained the Government had been found guilty of breaking the law but Mrs. Thatcher replied that the word used in the judgment was "invalid". Mrs. Thatcher said the Government must and would accept the court's final ruling.

More Tory rebels

When the Commons dealt with the Lords' amendments to the Trade Union Bill on July 24, thirty-five Tories voted with Liberals and S.D.P., and two more acted as tellers for a proposal to make postal votes compulsory for the election of senior union officials rather than placing an onus on unions to hold them. They were defeated nonetheless by 467 to 52 votes. On the same day Mr. Jenkin, Environment Secretary, named the 18 local authorities selected for rate-capping legislation. Dr. John Cunningham, Labour's spokesman, said it was "an unprecedented stride along an authoritarian path to central control in Britain."

On July 25, M.P.s started to discuss the Consolidated Fund (Appropriation No. 2) Bill, on which a range of subjects was debated, and this did not conclude until 9 a.m. on July 26 after which there was the normal adjournment motion which meant the House rose at 9.25 a.m. after sitting nearly 19 hours non-stop. On July 26, when considering a Government motion on the period of the summer recess, a Labour amendment proposing a recall of Parliament on Aug. 13 because of the continuing miners' dispute was defeated by 261 to 155 votes; the motion for the summer adjournment from Aug. 1 to Oct. 22 was then approved.

Opposition censure motion

The last big debate before the summer adjournment occurred on July 31 on an Opposition motion on "the shambles of the Government's economic, employment, and industrial policies", presented in a forthright speech by Mr. Kinnock. The Prime Minister made a robust reply and Labour's critical motion was defeated by 353 votes to 184. Earlier on the same day, Mr. Martin Flannery, Labour M.P. for Sheffield Hillsborough, was suspended for refusing to withdraw a claim that "tame Tory judges" were being used by the Government against striking miners; after being "named" by the Speaker, Mr. Flannery was suspended for five sitting days by 260 to 80 votes.

PUBLIC ACTS OF PARLIAMENT 1983–84

This list of Public Acts commences with 7 Public Acts which received the Royal Assent before September 1983 and which were mentioned briefly in the last summary. Those Public Acts which follow received the Royal Assent after August 1983. The date stated after each Act is the date on which it came into operation.

Appropriation (No. 2) Act 1983 (July 26, 1983) applies a sum out of the Consolidated Fund to the service of the year ending March 31, 1984 and appropriates the supplies granted in this session of Parliament.

Companies (Beneficial Interests) Act 1983 (July 26, 1983) makes provision for disregarding certain interests and rights (such as residual interests under pension and employees' share schemes) in determining for the purposes of provisions of the Companies Acts 1948 and 1980 whether a company is beneficially interested under a trust or has a beneficial interest in shares.

International Monetary Arrangements Act 1983 (various dates) substitutes a new limit for the limit on lending to the International Monetary Fund imposed by s. 2(1) of the 1979 Act and provides for the Bank of England to be indemnified in respect of certain financial assistance.

Local Authorities (Expenditure Powers) Act 1983 (July 26, 1983) removes certain restrictions on the powers of local authorities under s. 137 of the Local Government Act 1972 and s. 83 of the Local Government (Scotland) Act 1973.

Car Tax Act 1983 (October 26, 1983) consolidates the enactments relating to car tax.

Medical Act 1983 (October 26, 1983) consolidates the Medical Acts 1956 to 1978 and certain related provisions, with amendments to give effect to recommendations of the Law Commission and the Scottish Law Commission.

Value Added Tax Act 1983 (October 26, 1983) consolidates the enactments relating to VAT.

Oil Taxation Act 1983 (December 1, 1983) amongst other things this Act varies the reliefs available for certain expenditure incurred in connexion with assets used or to be used in connexion with oil fields; brings into charge to petroleum revenue tax certain sums received or receivable in respect of such assets and of certain other assets situated in the U.K., the territorial sea thereof or a designated area, within the meaning of the Continental Shelf Act 1964. In the main the Act relaxes the rules relating to petroleum revenue tax relief for expenditure on assets with shared use (e.g. pipelines) and as corollary charges related receipts (e.g. pipeline tariffs) to PRT subject to an exempt allowance. The Act clears up major uncertainties for the industry under existing law, as a result of detailed consultation with the industry.

Consolidated Fund (No. 3) Act 1983 (December 21, 1983) applies certain sums out of the Consolidated Fund to the service of the years ending on March 31, 1984 and 1985.

British Shipbuilders (Borrowing Powers) Act 1983 (December 21, 1983) amends the limit on borrowing etc. of British Shipbuilders laid down in the Aircraft and Shipbuilding Industries Act 1977.

Petroleum Royalties (Relief) Act 1983 (February 21, 1984) confers on holders of petroleum production licences an exemption from royalties (including royalties in kind) in respect of petroleum from certain new fields off the coast of Great Britain.

Coal Industry Act 1983 (December 21, 1983) increases the limits on the borrowing powers of the N.C.B. and makes further provision with respect to grants and payments by the Secretary of State in connexion with the coal industry.

Consolidated Fund Act 1984 (March 13, 1984) applies certain sums out of the Consolidated Fund to the service of the years ending on March 31, 1983 and 1984.

Restrictive Trade Practices (Stock Exchange) Act 1984 (March 13, 1984) exempts certain agreements relating to the Stock Exchange from the Restrictive Trade Practices Act 1976.

Occupiers' Liability Act 1984 (May 13, 1984) amends the law of England and Wales as to the liability of persons as occupiers of premises for injury suffered by persons other than their visitors; and amends the Unfair Contract Terms Act 1977 as it applies to England and Wales in relation to persons obtaining access to premises for recreational or educational purposes.

Tourism (Overseas Promotion) (Scotland) Act 1984 (May 13, 1984) enables the Scottish Tourist Board to carry on abroad activities to promote tourism to and within Scotland.

Merchant Shipping Act 1984 (May 13, 1984) makes provision for the service of improvement notices and prohibition notices in connexion with statutory provisions relating to the safety of ships and other matters; makes further provision with respect to the ascertainment of ships' tonnages for the purposes of s. 503 of the Merchant Shipping (Oil Pollution) Act 1894 and s. 4 of the Merchant Shipping (Oil Pollution) Act 1971; and for connected purposes.

Education (Amendment) (Scotland) Act 1984 (May 13, 1984) enables the Secretary of State to control the use of dangerous materials or apparatus in educational establishments in Scotland.

Pensions Commutation Act 1984 (day to be appointed) dissolves the Pensions Commutation Board and amends the Pensions Commutation Act 1871.

Prevention of Terrorism (Temporary Provisions) Act 1984 (March 22, 1984) repeals and re-enacts with amendments the provisions of the Prevention of Terrorism (Temporary Provisions) Act 1976.

Lotteries (Amendment) Act 1984 (June 12, 1984) amends the Lotteries and Amusements Act 1976 so as to abolish certain offences respecting foreign lotteries.

Town and Country Planning Act 1984 (August 12, 1984) makes further provision with respect to the application to Crown land of the enactments relating to town and country planning and enables persons in occupation of land by virtue of a licence in writing to appeal against certain enforcement notices issued under those enactments.

Education (Grants and Awards) Act 1984 (June 12, 1984) makes provision for the payment of education support grants to local education authorities in England and Wales; and amends Education Act 1962 s. 1(3) so as to refer to the higher national diploma of the Business and Technician Education Council instead of the corresponding diplomas of the Councils there mentioned.

Telecommunications Act 1984 (day or days to be appointed) provides for the appointment and functions of a Director General of Telecommunications; abolishes British Telecommunications' exclusive privilege with respect to telecommunications and deals with related areas.

Road Traffic (Driving Instruction) Act 1984 (day or days to be appointed) amends part V of the Road Traffic Act 1972 which contains provisions concerning driving instruction.

Anatomy Act 1984 (day or days to be appointed) makes provision about the use of bodies of deceased persons, and parts of such bodies, for anatomical examination and about the possession and disposal of bodies of deceased persons, and parts of such bodies, authorised to be used for anatomical examination.

Law Reform (Husband and Wife) (Scotland) Act 1984 (July 24, 1984) abolishes actions for breach of promise of marriage, adherence and enticement and other miscellaneous rules relating to husband and wife.

Foreign Limitation Periods Act 1984 (day to be appointed) provides for any law relating to the limitation of actions to be treated, for the purposes of cases in which effect is given to foreign law or to determinations by foreign courts as a matter of substance rather than as a matter of procedure.

Fosdyke Bridge Act 1984 (May 24, 1984) repeals Fosdyke Bridge Transfer Act 1870 ss. 25, 29, 30 and 32.

Tenants' Rights, etc. (Scotland) Amendment Act 1984 (July 24, 1984) amends Parts I and II of the 1980 Act with respect to the disposal of, and the rights of secure tenants of, dwelling-houses held by local authorities and certain other bodies in Scotland; and deals with related areas.

Trade Marks (Amendment) Act 1984 (October 1, 1987 or such earlier date as may be appointed) amends the Trade Marks Act 1938 to afford registration for service marks.

Agriculture (Amendment) Act 1984 (July 24, 1984) enables grants under s. 64 of the Agriculture Act 1967 towards fulfilling guarantees of bank loans to be made in relation to a wider range of co-operative marketing businesses; extends the powers of obtaining information conferred by s. 1(1) of the Agricultural Statistics Act 1979 and repeals s. 1(5) of that Act (which deals with application of provisions as to entry and inspection).

Somerset House Act 1984 (June 26, 1984) confers leasing powers on the Crown in respect of the Fine Rooms and other parts of Somerset House with a view to their use for artistic, cultural or other purposes.

Public Health (Control of Diseases) Act 1984 (September 26, 1984) consolidates certain enactments relating to the control of disease and to the establishment and functions of port health authorities, including enactments relating to burial and cremation and to the regulation of common lodging-houses and canal boats; with amendments to give effect to recommendations of the Law Commission.

Registered Homes Act 1984 (day or days to be appointed) consolidates certain enactments relating to residential care homes and nursing homes and

Registered Homes Tribunals; with amendments to give effect to recommendations of the Law Commission.

Dentists Act 1984 (part on July 26, the rest on October 1, 1984) consolidates the Acts 1957 to 1983 and gives effect to a recommendation of the Law Commission and the Scottish Law Commission.

Betting, Gaming and Lotteries (Amendment) Act 1984 (August 26, 1984) amends the provisions of the 1963 Act in relation to the conduct and advertisement of licensed betting offices and makes provision for the alteration of fees payable under para 20, Sched. 1 to that Act.

Inshore Fishing (Scotland) Act 1984 (day or days to be appointed) makes fresh provision as regards the regulation of inshore sea fishing—for example, the Secretary of State is given a general power to prohibit sea fishing in specified areas—and for connected purposes.

County Courts Act 1984 (August 1, 1984) consolidates certain enactments relating to county courts.

Housing and Building Control Act 1984 (part on August 26, 1984 the rest on a day or days to be appointed) makes further provision with respect to the disposal of, and the rights of secure tenants of, dwelling-houses held by local authorities and other bodies (e.g. governors of an aided school) in England and Wales; and amends the law relating to the supervision of building work, the building regulations, sanitation and buildings and building control by providing for such work to be supervised otherwise than by local authorities.

Food Act 1984 (September 26, 1984) consolidates various enactments relating to food and drugs.

Rating and Valuation (Amendment) (Scotland) Act 1984 (various dates) amends the law of Scotland as regards rating, valuation and local government finance and for connected purposes. For example, it gives powers to the Secretary of State to control rates determined by local authorities.

London Regional Transport Act 1984 (various dates, one to be appointed) makes provision with respect to transport in and around Greater London.

Rates Act 1984 (various dates) enables the Secretary of State to limit the rates made and precepts issued by local authorities; requires local authorities to consult representatives of industrial and commercial ratepayers before reaching decisions on expenditure and the means of financing it; makes provision for requiring additional information to be given to ratepayers; requires notice of the rates payable in respect of a dwelling-house to be given to any occupier not in receipt of a demand note; and for connected purposes.

Juries (Disqualification) Act 1984 (day to be appointed) disqualifies certain persons (e.g. those who have been placed on probation in the last five years in the U.K., Isle of Man or Channel Isles) from jury service who have served or had imposed on them certain sentences.

Data Protection Act 1984 (various dates) regulates the use of automatically processed information relating to individuals and the provision of services in respect of such information. For instance, it requires data users who hold, and computer bureaux providing services in respect of personal data to be registered.

Mental Health (Scotland) Act 1984 (September 30, 1984) consolidates the 1960 Act.

Child Abduction Act 1984 (October 12, 1984) amends the criminal law relating to the abduction of children, such as the abduction of children by their parents.

Cycle Tracks Act 1984 (September 12, 1984) amends the definition of cycle track in the Highways Act 1980 and makes further provision in relation to cycle tracks within the meaning of that Act.

Video Recordings Act 1984 (day or days to be appointed) provides for regulation of the distribution of video recordings.

Animal Health and Welfare Act 1984 (various dates some to be appointed) amends the provisions of the Animal Health Act 1981 relating to the seizure of things for the purpose of preventing the spread of disease and to powers of entry and declarations as to places infected with a disease, and enables certain orders under that Act to operate in or over territorial waters. It also makes further provision with respect to slaughter of poultry, artificial breeding of livestock, feeding stuffs and veterinary drugs and repeals the Improvement of Live Stock (Licensing of Bulls) Act 1931 and the Horse Breeding Act 1958.

Agricultural Holdings Act 1984 (various dates) amends the law with respect to agricultural holdings by, *inter alia*, changing the formula for fixing rent by arbitration and abolishing statutory succession in the case of agricultural tenancies granted on or after July 12, 1984.

Matrimonial and Family Proceedings Act 1984 (various dates some to be appointed) amends the Matrimonial Causes Act 1973 by allowing petitions for divorce or nullity to be presented without leave of the court after one year of marriage; amends that Act and other Acts so far as they relate to the exercise of the jurisdiction of courts in England and Wales to make provision for financial relief or to exercise related powers in matrimonial and certain other family proceedings; and makes various other provisions and amendments relating to family and inheritance law.

Finance Act 1984 (July 26, 1984) grants certain duties, alters others and amends the law relating to the National Debt and the Public Revenue and makes further provision with respect to Finance. For example, the Act imposes VAT on takeaway food and building alterations; removes first year and initial capital allowances and life assurance relief; and reduces stamp duty on conveyances and transfers.

Appropriation Act 1984 (July 26, 1984) appropriates a sum out of the Consolidated Fund to the service of the year ending on March 31, 1985, appropriates the supplies granted in this Session of Parliament and repeals certain Consolidated Fund and Appropriation Acts.

Prescription and Limitation (Scotland) Act (September 26, 1984) makes new provision for Scotland with respect to the extinction of obligations to make contributions between wrongdoers; amends the law relating to time-limits for bringing actions which consist of or include a claim for damages in respect of personal injuries or a person's death; makes provision relating to the application of the rules of law of a country other than Scotland in respect of the extinction of obligations or the limitation of time within which proceedings may be brought to enforce obligations; and for connected purposes.

Cable and Broadcasting Act 1984 (day or days to be appointed) provides for the establishment and functions of a Cable Authority and makes other provision with respect to cable programme services; amends the Broadcasting Act 1981 to provide for the establishment and functions of a Satellite Broadcasting Board and to make other provision with respect to broadcasting services and for connected purposes.

Repatriation of Prisoners Act (day to be appointed) makes provision for facilitating the transfer between the U.K. and places outside the British Isles of persons for the time being detained in prisons, hospitals or other institutions by virtue of orders made in the course of the exercise by courts and tribunals of their criminal jurisdiction.

Health and Social Security Act (day or days to be appointed) amends the Opticians Act 1958; and the National Health Service Act 1977 and the National Health Service (Scotland) Act 1978 in relation to general ophthalmic services, finance in the N.H.S. and certain functions of the Secretary of State; amends the N.H.S. (Amendment) Act 1977 in relation to Family Practitioner Committees; provides for the reimbursement of the cost of certain treatment in the E.E.C. (medical and maternity costs if the patient is ordinarily resident in Great Britain and a national of a member state or dependent of such national); and amends the law relating to social security, statutory sick pay and contracted out occupational pension schemes; and for connected purposes.

Trade Union Act 1984 (various dates, some to be appointed) makes provision for election to certain positions in trade unions and with respect to ballots held in connexion with strikes or other forms of industrial action; requires trade unions to compile and maintain registers of members' names and addresses, amends the law relating to expenditure by trade unions and unincorporated employers' associations on political objectives and amends the Employment Act 1980.

Capital Transfer Tax Act 1984 (January 1, 1985) consolidates the provisions relating to CTT.

Local Government (Interim Provisions) Act (various dates) makes provision for the composition of the G.L.C. and metropolitan county councils pending a decision by Parliament on their continued existence; establishes a commission for safeguarding the interests of local government staff employed by or in the areas of those authorities; requires those authorities to furnish information in connexion with proposals for the abolition of those authorities and for the transfer of their functions; postpones the exercise of certain functions by or in relation to those authorities; and makes various other related provisions in connexion with those authorities, London borough councils, the Common Council and metropolitan district councils.

Road Traffic Regulation Act 1984
Housing Defects Act 1984
Parliamentary Pensions Etc. Act 1984

PARLIAMENTARY ASSOCIATIONS

COMMONWEALTH PARLIAMENTARY ASSOCIATION (1911)

The Commonwealth Parliamentary Association consists of 127 branches in the national, state, provincial or territorial parliaments in the countries of the Commonwealth. Commonwealth Parliamentary conferences and general assemblies are held every year in different countries of the Commonwealth.

President (1984–85), Hon. H. Swan, M.L.A., Speaker of the Legislative Assembly of Saskatchewan (*Canada*).

Secretary-General, Sir Robin Vanderfelt, K.B.E., Palace of Westminster, S.W.1.

Secretary, United Kingdom Branch, P. Cobb, Westminster Hall, Houses of Parliament, S.W.1.

THE INTER-PARLIAMENTARY UNION (1889)

To facilitate personal contact between Members of all Parliaments in the promotion of representative institutions, peace and international co-operation. *Secretary General*, Pio Carlo Terenzio (*Italy*).

BRITISH GROUP

Palace of Westminster, SW1

Hon. President, The Lord Chancellor; Mr. Speaker. *President*, The Rt. Hon. Margaret Thatcher, M.P. *Secretary*, Capt. P. J. Shaw, R.N.

PRIME MINISTERS AND SPEAKERS

PRIME MINISTERS SINCE 1782

Marquess of Rockingham, *Whig,* March 27, 1782.
Earl of Shelburne, *Whig,* July 13, 1782.
Duke of Portland, *Coalition,* April 4, 1783.
William Pitt, *Tory,* Dec. 7, 1783.
Henry Addington, *Tory,* March 21, 1801.
William Pitt, *Tory,* May 16, 1804.
Lord Grenville, *Whig,* Feb. 10, 1806.
Duke of Portland, *Tory,* March 31, 1807.
Spencer Perceval, *Tory,* Dec. 6, 1809.
Earl of Liverpool, *Tory,* June 16, 1812.
George Canning, *Tory,* April 30, 1827.
Viscount Goderich, *Tory,* Sept. 8, 1827.
Duke of Wellington, *Tory,* Jan. 26, 1828.
Earl Grey, *Whig,* Nov. 24, 1830.
Viscount Melbourne, *Whig,* July 13, 1834.
Sir Robert Peel, *Tory,* Dec. 26, 1834.
Viscount Melbourne, *Whig,* March 18, 1835.
Sir Robert Peel, *Tory,* Sept., 6, 1841.
Lord John Russell, *Whig,* July 6, 1846.
Earl of Derby, *Tory,* Feb. 28, 1852.
Earl of Aberdeen, *Peelite,* Dec. 28, 1852.
Viscount Palmerston, *Liberal,* Feb. 10, 1855.
Earl of Derby, *Conservative,* Feb. 25, 1858.
Viscount Palmerston, *Liberal,* June 18, 1859.
Earl Russell, *Liberal,* Nov. 6, 1865.
Earl of Derby, *Conservative,* July 6, 1866.
Benjamin Disraeli, *Conservative,* Feb. 27, 1868.
W. E. Gladstone, *Liberal,* Dec. 9, 1868.
Benjamin Disraeli, *Conservative,* Feb. 21, 1874.
W. E. Gladstone, *Liberal,* April 28, 1880.
Marquess of Salisbury, *Conservative,* June 24, 1885.
W. E. Gladstone, *Liberal,* Feb. 6, 1886.
Marquess of Salisbury, *Conservative,* Aug. 3, 1886.
W. E. Gladstone, *Liberal,* Aug. 18, 1892.
Earl of Rosebery, *Liberal,* March 3, 1894.
Marquess of Salisbury, *Conservative,* July 2, 1895.
A. J. Balfour, *Conservative,* July 12, 1902.
Sir H. Campbell-Bannerman, *Liberal,* Dec. 5, 1905.
H. H. Asquith, *Liberal,* April 8, 1908.
H. H. Asquith, *Coalition,* May 26, 1915.
D. Lloyd-George, *Coalition,* Dec. 7, 1916.
A. Bonar Law, *Conservative,* Oct. 23, 1922.
S. Baldwin, *Conservative,* May 22, 1923.
J. R. MacDonald, *Labour,* Jan. 22, 1924.
S. Baldwin, *Conservative,* Nov. 4, 1924.
J. R. MacDonald, *Labour,* June 8, 1929.
J. R. MacDonald, *Coalition,* Aug. 25, 1931.
S. Baldwin, *Coalition,* June 7, 1935.
N. Chamberlain, *Coalition,* May 28, 1937.
W. S. Churchill, *Coalition,* May 11, 1940.
W. S. Churchill, *Conservative,* May 23, 1945.
C. R. Attlee, *Labour,* July 26, 1945.
Sir W. S. Churchill, *Conservative,* Oct. 26, 1951.
Sir A. Eden, *Conservative,* April 6, 1955.
H. Macmillan, *Conservative,* Jan. 13, 1957.
Sir A. Douglas-Home, *Conservative,* Oct. 19, 1963.
J. H. Wilson, *Labour,* Oct. 16, 1964.
J. H. Wilson, *Labour,* March 31, 1966.
E. R. G. Heath, *Conservative,* June 19, 1970.

J. H. Wilson, *Labour,* March 4, 1974.
L. J. Callaghan, *Labour,* April 5, 1976.
Mrs. M. H. Thatcher, *Conservative,* May 4, 1979.
Mrs. M. H. Thatcher, *Conservative,* June 9, 1983.

SPEAKERS OF THE COMMONS SINCE 1660

PARLIAMENT OF ENGLAND

1660 Sir Harbottle Grimston.
1661 Sir Edward Turner.
1673 Sir Job Charlton.
1673 Sir Edward Seymour.
1678 Sir Robert Sawyer.
1679 Sir William Gregory.
1680 Sir William Williams.
1685 Sir John Trevor.
1688 Henry Powle.
1694 Paul Foley.
1698 Sir Thomas Lyttelton.
1700 Robert Harley (*Earl of Oxford and Mortimer*).
1702 John Smith.

PARLIAMENT OF GREAT BRITAIN

1708 Sir Richard Onslow (*Lord Onslow*).
1710 William Bromley.
1713 Sir Thomas Hanmer.
1715 Spencer Compton (*Earl of Wilmington*).
1727 Arthur Onslow.
1761 Sir John Cust.
1770 Sir Fletcher Norton.
1780 Charles Cornwall.
1788 Hon. William Grenvill (*Lord Grenville*).
1789 Henry Addington (*Viscount Sidmouth*).

PARLIAMENT OF UNITED KINGDOM

1801 Sir John Mitford (*Lord Redesdale*).
1802 Charles Abbot (*Lord Colchester*).
1817 Charles M. Sutton (*Viscount Canterbury*).
1835 James Abercromby (*Lord Dunfermline*).
1839 Charles Shaw-Lefevre (*Viscount Eversley*).
1857 J. Evelyn Denison (*Viscount Ossington*).
1872 Sir Henry Brand (*Viscount Hampden*).
1884 Arthur Wellesley Peel (*Viscount Peel*).
1895 William Court Gully (*Viscount Selby*).
1905 James W. Lowther (*Viscount Ullswater*).
1921 John Henry Whitley.
1928 Hon. Edward Algernon FitzRoy.
1943 Col. D. Clifton Brown (*Viscount Ruffside*).
1951 William Shepherd Morrison (*Viscount Dunrossil*).
1959 Sir Harry Hylton-Foster.
1965 Horace Maybray King, PH.D. (*Lord Maybray-King*).
1971 (John) Selwyn (Brooke) Lloyd (*Lord Selwyn-Lloyd*).
1976 (Thomas) George Thomas (*Viscount Tonypandy*).
1983 (Bruce) Bernard Weatherill.

THE QUEEN'S AWARDS FOR EXPORT AND TECHNOLOGY

The Queen's Award for Export Achievement and The Queen's Award for Technological Achievement were instituted by Royal Warrant in 1976, the two separate Awards taking the place of The Queen's Award to Industry which had been instituted in 1965. This was the major change made as a result of a number of recommendations by a committee chaired by the Duke of Edinburgh that reviewed all aspects of the Award scheme in 1975 after its second 5-year period of operation; all the recommendations were accepted by the Government. The reports of the 3 committees that have considered the scheme, in 1965, 1970, and 1975—under the chairmanship of the Duke of Edinburgh, Lord McFadzean and the Duke of Edinburgh respectively—are available on loan from The Queen's Awards Office.

The Awards are designed to recognize and encourage outstanding achievements in exporting goods or services from the United Kingdom and in advancing process or product technology. They differ from a personal Royal honour in that they are given to a unit as a whole—management and employees working as a team.

They may be applied for by any organization within the United Kingdom, the Channel Islands or the Isle of Man producing goods or services which meet the criteria for the Awards. Eligibility is not influenced in any way by the particular activities of the unit applying, its location, or size. Units or agencies of central and local government with industrial functions, as well as research associations, educational institutions and bodies of a similar character, are also eligible, provided that they can show they have contributed to industrial efficiency.

The criteria on which recommendations for the Awards are based are:

1. Export Achievement
A substantial and sustained increase in export earnings to a level which is outstanding for the products or services concerned and for the size of the applicant unit's operations. Account will be taken of any special market factors described in the application. Applicants for the Award will be expected to explain the basis of the achievement (e.g. improved marketing organization or new initiative to cater for export markets) and this will be taken into consideration. Export earnings considered will include receipts by the applicant unit in this country from the export of goods produced in this country, and the provision of services to non-residents. Account will be taken of the overseas expenses incurred other than marketing expenses. Income from profits (after overseas tax) remitted to this country from the applicant unit's direct investments in its overseas branches, subsidiaries or associates in the same general line of business will be taken into account, but not receipts from profits on other overseas investments or by interest on overseas loans or credits.

2. Technological Achievement
A significant advance, leading to increased efficiency, in the application of technology to a production or development process in British industry or the production for sale of goods which incorporate new and advanced technological qualities.

Each award is formally conferred by a Grant of Appointment and is symbolized by a representation of its emblem cast in stainless steel and encapsulated in a transparent acrylic block. Presentations are usually made on behalf of The Queen by Her Majesty's Lord Lieutenants at the principal place of business or production of the unit. A reception is given annually by The Queen at Buckingham Palace for representatives of the winners of the Awards.

Awards are held for five years and holders are entitled to fly the appropriate Award flag and to display the emblem on the packaging of goods produced in this country, on the goods themselves, on the unit's stationery, in advertising and on certain articles used by employees: units may also display the emblem of any previous current Awards during the 5 years.

Awards are announced on April 21—the actual birthday of Her Majesty the Queen—and published formally in a special supplement to the London Gazette. All enquires about the scheme and requests for application forms—completed forms must be returned by October 31—should be made to: The Secretary, The Queen's Awards Office, Dean Bradley House, 52 Horseferry Road, London S.W.1. Telephone: 01–222 2277.

Export Achievement Awards

In 1984, the Queen's Award was conferred on the following concerns for export achievement:

ACF (Great Britain) Ltd., Cumbernauld, Glasgow; The Aluminium Powder Company Ltd., Sutton Coldfield, West Midlands; Amchem Company Ltd., Loughborough, Leicestershire; Ove Arup Partnership, London, W.1; Aston Martin Lagonda Ltd., Newport Pagnell, Buckinghamshire; The Beecham Products Overseas Branch of Beecham Group PLC, Slough, Berkshire; Binnie and Partners, London, S.W.1; Biwater Treatment Ltd., Dorking, Surrey; Bovis International Ltd., London, W.4; The Dynamics Group of British Aerospace PLC, Stevenage, Hertfordshire; British Airways Engine Overhaul Ltd., Cardiff; British Electricity International Ltd., London, S.W.1; M. Brody Ltd., London, E.1; Bronx Engineering Holdings PLC, Stourbridge, West Midlands; Brymor Ltd., Tonbridge, Kent; Burlington Slate Ltd., Coniston, Cumbria; Caledonian Airmotive Ltd., Prestwick, Ayrshire; Camtex Fabrics Ltd., Workington, Cumbria; Cherry Valley Farms Ltd., Rothwell, Lincolnshire; Church & Co. (Footwear) Ltd., Northampton; The Cummins Daventry Division of Cummins Engine Co. Ltd., Daventry, Northamptonshire; The Royal Ordnance Factories of the Ministry of Defence, London, W.C.2; John Dewar & Sons Ltd., Perth; Alan Dick & Company Ltd., Cheltenham, Gloucestershire; Dunsford Wesley Ltd., Castleford, West Yorkshire; Edendeck Ltd., Burnley, Lancashire; Elco Power Plant Ltd., Sherburn in Elmet, West Yorkshire; Environmental Resources Ltd., London, W.1; The Financial Times Ltd., London, E.C.4; GB Textiles Ltd., Nottingham; Glenfrome Engineering Ltd., Bristol; Goddard & Gibbs Studios, London, E.2; Harper & Tunstall Ltd., Wellingborough, Northamptonshire; Hepco Slide Systems Ltd., Greenford, Middlesex; Hestair Eagle Ltd., Warwick; Horsell Graphic Industries Ltd., Leeds, West Yorkshire; IML Air Couriers Ltd., Feltham, Middlesex; Impalloy Ltd., Bloxwich, Walsall; The Mond Division of Imperial Chemical Industries PLC., Runcorn, Cheshire; The Petrochemicals & Plastics Division of Imperial Chemical Industries PLC., Welwyn Garden City, Hertfordshire; The Pharmaceuticals Division of Imperial Chemical Industries PLC., Macclesfield, Cheshire; International Aeradio PLC., Southall, Middlesex; Invertron Simulated Systems Ltd., Burgess Hill, West Sussex; JCB Materials Handling Ltd.,

Uttoxeter, Staffordshire; Jaguar Cars Ltd., Coventry, West Midlands; Jenner Fenton Slade Ltd., London, E.C.3; James Keiller & Son Ltd., Dundee; King, Taudevin & Gregson (Holdings) Ltd., Sheffield; Lasgo Exports Ltd., London, N.W.10; Littelfuse Olvis Ltd., Washington, Tyne & Wear; John Lobb Ltd., London, S.W.1; A. M. Lock & Co. Ltd., Oldham, Lancashire; The Frimley Unit of Marconi Space & Defence Systems Ltd., Camberley, Surrey; Marks & Spencer PLC., London, W.1; Marshall Cavendish Services Ltd., Brighton, East Sussex; Jim Marshall (Products) Ltd., Bletchley, Milton Keynes; Merrol Fire Protection Engineers Ltd., Bilston, West Midlands; The Neath Industrial Components Unit of Metal Box PLC., Neath, West Glamorgan; Micro Focus Ltd., Newbury, Berkshire; L. G. Mouchel & Partners, West Byfleet, Surrey; Needle Industries (Sheffield) Ltd., Sheffield; The Equipment Division of Pafra Ltd., Basildon, Essex; Pirelli Construction Company Ltd., Eastleigh, Hampshire; Plessey Radar Ltd., Weybridge, Surrey; Portex Ltd., Hythe, Kent; Prescot Rod Rollers Ltd., Prescot, Merseyside; Purification Products Ltd., Otley, West Yorkshire; Ruston Diesels Ltd., Newton-le-Willows, Merseyside; The Weston Simfire Division of Schlumberger Electronics (UK) Ltd., Enfield, Middlesex; Schwitzer Household Manufacturing Ltd., Bradford; James Scott (Electrical Transmission) Ltd., Darlington, County Durham; The Missile Systems Division of Short Brothers Ltd., Belfast; Skeltonhall Ltd., Sheffield; The McEvoy Division of Smith International (North Sea) Ltd., Stroud, Gloucestershire; Soundout Laboratories Ltd., Surbiton, Surrey; Spritebrand Ltd., Pickering, North Yorkshire; Stelmo Ltd., Charing, Kent; Stroud Riley Drummond PLC., Bradford; Tenneco Organics Ltd., Avonmouth, Bristol; Thames Television International, London, W.1; Tileman & Company Ltd., London, S.W.15; Titus International Ltd., Iver, Buckinghamshire; ULG Consultants Ltd., Warwick; United Scientific Instruments Ltd., London, W.1; Vetco Offshore Ltd., Hayes, Middlesex; Vosper Hovermarine Ltd., Southampton; Joseph Walker, Aberlour, Scotland; Wimpol Ltd., Swindon, Wiltshire.

Awards for Technological Achievement 1984

In 1984, the following concerns received the Queen's Award for technological achievement:

A.P.V. Hall Products Ltd., Dartford, Kent (*"Hall-screw" single screw refrigeration compressor*); Acorn Computers Ltd., Cambridge (*BBC micro-computer system*); The Bentley Engineering Co. Ltd., Leicester (*Electronic pattern preparation system for sock production*); The Stevenage Division of The Dynamics Group of British Aerospace PLC., Stevenage, Hertfordshire (*Sea Skua missile*); British Communications Corporation Ltd., and Racal Research Ltd., of Racal Electronics Ltd., Bracknell, Berkshire (*Development of the Jaguar V frequency hopping radio and associated electronic counter measure (ECCM) module*); The Videotex Section of BT Research Department and the Prestel Executive of British Telecommunications, Martlesham Heath, Ipswich and London, E.C.4 (*"Prestel" viewdata system*); G. Clancey Ltd., Halesowen, West Midlands (*Shell moulded, chilled camshafts process*); Dowty Rotol Ltd., Gloucester (*Aircraft propellers*); The Gas Tube Division of the English Electric Valve Company Ltd., Chelmsford, Essex (*Hydrogen thyratons*); The Magnetron Department of the English Electric Valve Company Ltd., Lincoln (*Magnetrons for medical and industrial application*); FBC Ltd., Hauxton, Cambridgeshire (*"Sportak" fungicide for agricultural use*); Leslie Hartridge Ltd., Buckingham (*Video display fuel metering system*); The Research and Development Department of The Hepworth Iron Co. Ltd., Sheffield (*Roller kiln process*); Instrumental Colour Systems Ltd., Newbury, Berkshire (*Colour assessment of fabric using micro-processor based instrumentation (jointly with The Textile Technology Departments of Marks and Spencer PLC*)); Kaldair Ltd., Feltham, Middlesex (*Oilfield flare installations*); The Central Textile Technology Department and the Textile Groups' Technology Departments of Marks and Spencer PLC., London, W.1 (*Colour assessment of fabrics using micro-processor based instrumentation (jointly with Instrumental Colour Systems Ltd.*)); Matthew Hall Mechanical and Electrical Engineers Ltd., London, S.E.1 (*Fire engineering for the Statfjord "A" offshore oil platform*); Microvitec Ltd., Bradford (*Low complexity colour display system for micro-computer use*); The National Institute of Agricultural Engineering, Silsoe, Bedfordshire (*Forage conditioning machinery*); The Tensar Division of Netlon Ltd., Blackburn (*Strengthening of plastic materials through molecular orientation of the polymer chains*); Planer Products Ltd., Sunbury-on-Thames, Middlesex (*Animal embryo freezer*); Racal Defence Electronics (Radar) Ltd., Walton-on-Thames, Surrey (*"Cutlass" radar processor*); The Link Miles Division of The Singer Company (UK) Ltd., Lancing, Sussex (*"Image" computer generated visual system for flight simulators*).

BRITISH OIL STATISTICS (million tonnes)

	1975	1979	1980	1981	1982
Oil production†					
Land	0·1	0·1	0·2	0·2	0·3
Offshore	1·5	77·8	80·2	89·2	103·1
Refinery output	86·6	90·6	79·2	72·0	70·7
Deliveries of petroleum products for inland consumption	82·8	84·6	71·2	66·3	67·2
Exports (including re-exports):					
Crude petroleum	0·8	38·8	38·5	51·4	60·4
Refined petroleum products and process oils	14·3	14·4	16·1	13·1	14·5
Imports:					
Crude petroleum	87·2	57·9	44·8	33·1	28·3
Refined petroleum products and process oils	16·0	16·0	14·1	14·1	17·2

† Crude oil plus condensates and petroleum gases derived at onshore treatment plants.

CIVIL SERVICE STAFF

Analysis by ministerial responsibility at 1 April in each year

† Full-time equivalents (thousands)

	1977	1978	1979	1980	1981	1982	1983
Total civil and defence departments	745·6	735·7	732·3	704·9	689·6	666·4	648·9
of which Non-industrials	*571·1*	*567·3*	*565·8*	*547·5*	*539·9*	*528·0*	518·5
Industrials	*174·4*	*168·4*	*166·5*	*157·4*	*149·7*	*138·4*	130·4
Total civil departments	486·9	485·3	484·6	465·1	460·0	449·4	440·0
Agriculture, Fisheries and Food	15·5	14·6	14·5	14·3	13·6	13·1	12·7
Chancellor of the Exchequer's	129·3	128·9	128·2	119·0	114·9	121·0	117·4
Departments:							
Customs and Excise	29·3	28·8	28·8	27·2	26·8	26·2	25·4
Inland Revenue	83·9	85·2	84·6	78·3	75·6	74·0	73·1
Department for National Savings	12·2	10·9	10·8	10·4	10·0	9·1	8·3
Treasury and others	3·9	4·0	4·0	3·1	2·5	11·7	10·6
Education and Science	4·0	3·7	3·7	3·7	3·6	3·5	3·5
Employment	52·5	53·7	53·6	50·7	53·8	58·7	57·9
Energy	1·3	1·3	1·3	1·3	1·2	1·1	1·1
Environment	61·5	57·3	56·0	51·7	47·0	42·1	39·4
Foreign and Commonwealth	12·4	12·1	12·1	11·6	11·4	11·1	11·1
Home	32·6	33·2	33·5	34·1	35·4	34·6	35·1
Industry	9·7	9·5	9·5	9·1	8·8	8·3	7·7
Scotland	13·0	13·5	13·7	13·6	13·6	13·4	13·1
Social Services	98·3	99·5	100·9	98·9	100·1	98·0	96·4
Trade	10·0	9·7	9·6	9·4	9·3	8·9	8·9
Transport	13·6	14·5	13·9	13·5	13·7	13·0	13·0
Wales	1·6	2·5	2·6	2·5	2·3	2·3	2·2
Other civil departments	31·5	31·3	31·4	31·7	31·3	20·2	20·5
Total Ministry of Defence	258·7	250·4	247·7	239·8	229·6	216·9	208·9

† Part-time employees are counted as half units.

POLICE FORCE STRENGTHS

Number

	1976	1977	1978	1979	1980	1981	1982
England and Wales							
Regular police							
Authorised establishment	116,880	116,980	117,668	118,322	118,930	120,008	120,125
Strength:							
Men	101,042	98,935	99,134	102,360	105,563	107,379	108,517
Women....................	6,997	7,789	8,477	9,394	10,355	10,702	10,935
Seconded:							
Men	1,368	1,400	1,386	1,477	1,430	1,424	1,419
Women....................	69	77	78	78	75	70	80
Additional constables:							
Men	144	97	85	114	96	90	89
Women....................	–	–	1	2	1	1	1
Scotland							
Regular police							
Authorised establishment:							
Men	13,163	13,144	13,162	13,148	13,187	13,195	13,205
Women....................							
Strength:							
Men	11,442	11,069	11,477	12,280	12,419	12,379	12,433
Women....................	737	763	746	786	771	749	719
Central service:							
Men	55	52	51	56	60	54	55
Women....................	2	3	4	4	5	2	2
Seconded:							
Men	99	78	72	72	69	78	73
Women....................	7	8	5	3	2	5	4
Additional regular police:							
Authorised establishment ..	157	174	179	126	72	67	62
Strength	138	174	176	148	71	66	62
Northern Ireland							
Royal Ulster Constabulary							
Strength:							
Men	4,811	5,140	5,495	5,938	6,224	6,622	7,017
Women....................	442	552	615	676	711	712	701

GOVERNMENT AND PUBLIC OFFICES

All salaries throughout the section were supplied by individual Offices and are subject to variation. At the time of going to press, it was not possible to confirm the information required.

ADVISORY, CONCILIATION AND ARBITRATION SERVICE
11–12 St. James's Square, SW1Y 4LA
[01–214 6000]

The Advisory, Conciliation and Arbitration Service (ACAS) is an independent organisation set up under the Employment Protection Act, 1975, under the management of a Council appointed by the Secretary of State for Employment. The functions of the Service are to provide facilities for conciliation, mediation and arbitration as a means of avoiding and resolving industrial disputes; and to provide advisory services to industry on industrial relations matters.
Chairman, J. P. Lowry, C.B.E.
Chief Conciliation Officer, D. G. Boyd.
Director of Resources and General Policy Branch, E. Norcross.

MINISTRY OF AGRICULTURE, FISHERIES AND FOOD
Whitehall Place, London, S.W.1†
[01–233 3000]

The Ministry of Agriculture, Fisheries and Food is responsible for administering government policy for agriculture, horticulture and fishing in England and for many food matters in the United Kingdom. Some of the Ministry's responsibilities for animal health extend to Great Britain. In association with the Intervention Board for Agricultural Produce and the other Agricultural Departments in the United Kingdom it is responsible for the administration of the EEC common agricultural and fisheries policy and for various national support schemes. It also administers schemes for the control and eradication of animal and plant diseases and for assistance to capital investment in farm and horticultural businesses and land drainage; it exercises responsibilities relating to applied research and development. The Agricultural Development and Advisory Service (ADAS) is part of the Ministry. The Ministry sponsors the food and drink manufacturing industries and distribution trades. It is concerned with the supply and quality of food, food compositional standards, hygiene, labelling and advertising of food and has certain responsibilities for ensuring public health standards in the manufacture, preparation and distribution of basic foods.
†Unless otherwise stated, this is the main address of Divisions of the Ministry.

Salary List
Minister	£31,271
Minister of State (Commons)	£21,881
Minister of State (Lords)	£28,000
Parliamentary Secretary	£16,411
Permanent Secretary (Grade 1)	£45,500
Deputy Secretary (Grade 2)	£36,500
Under Secretary (Grade 3)	£29,500
Assistant Secretary (Grade 4)	£19,243 to £23,159
Senior Principal (Grade 6)	£15,605 to £20,794
Principal	£12,399 to £16,656
Senior Executive Officer	£10,079 to £12,518
HEO (D)	£ 8,166 to £10,218
Assistant Solicitor (Grade 5)	£20,051 to £23,159
Chief Scientific Officer (Grade 4)	£24,077
Deputy Chief Scientific Officer (Grade 5)	£19,243 to £23,159
Senior Principal Scientific Officer (Grade 6)	£15,605 to £20,794
Chief Statistician (Grade 5)	£19,243 to £23,159

Minister, THE RT. HON. MICHAEL JOPLING, M.P.
Private Secretary (*Principal*), C. I. Llewelyn.
Assistant Private Secretary, D. L. Dawson.
Parliamentary Private Secretary, P. Marland, M.P.;
Ministers of State, JOHN MACGREGOR, M.P., O.B.E.;
THE LORD BELSTEAD, P.C.
Private Secretaries, (*to Mr. MacGregor*), D. W. Harbourne; (*to Lord Belstead*), R. Scrutton.
Parliamentary Private Secretary (*to Mr. MacGregor*), M. Lord, M.P.
Parliamentary Secretary, Mrs. P. Fenner, M.P.
Private Secretary, A. A. D. McKerrell.
Parliamentary Clerk (*Senior Executive Officer*), T. A. Buchan.
Permanent Secretary, Sir Michael Franklin, K.C.B., C.M.G.
Private Secretary, T. J. Osmond.

ESTABLISHMENT DEPARTMENT
Director of Establishments (*Under Secretary*), J. H. Holroyd.

Manpower Division
Victory House, 30–34 Kingsway, W.C. 2.
[01–405 4310]
Assistant Secretary, Mrs. A. M. Blackburn.

Establishments (General) Division
Victory House, 30–34 Kingsway, W.C.2
[01–405 4310]
Assistant Secretary, R. D. Rider.

Staff Training Branch*
Principal, J. M. Lynes.

Welfare Branch
Victory House, 30–34 Kingsway, W.C.2.
[01–405 4310]
Chief Welfare Officer (*Senior Executive Officer*), R. R. J. Huckins.

Personnel Division
Victory House, 30–34 Kingsway, W.C.2
[01–405 4310]
Assistant Secretary, C. J. A. Barnes.

FINANCE DEPARTMENT
Principal Finance Officer (*Under Secretary*), G. W. Wilson.

Finance Division I*
Assistant Secretary, B. H. B. Dickinson.

Finance Division II*
Assistant Secretary, J. A. Brown.

Financial Management
Assistant Secretary, D. J. Coates.

Audit Division*
Director of Audit, S. T. K. Hester.
Assistant Director of Audit, F. W. Martin.

LEGAL DEPARTMENT
55 Whitehall, S.W.1
[01–217 3000]

Legal Adviser and Solicitor (*Deputy Secretary*), G. J. Jenkins.
Principal Assistant Solicitors (*Under Secretaries*), A. E. Munir; J. McElheran.

*At Great Westminster House, Horseferry Road, S.W.1 [01–216 6311].

Legal Division A1
Assistant Solicitor, J. O. Stansfield.

Legal Division A2
Assistant Solicitor, A. Yavash.

Legal Division A3
Assistant Solicitor, J. H. Jordan.

Legal Division B1
Assistant Solicitor, J. F. McCleary.

Legal Division B2
Assistant Solicitor, G. R. J. Robertson.

Legal Division B3
Assistant Solicitor, Miss E. A. Stephens.

Legal Division B4
Assistant Solicitor, B. T. Atwood.

MANAGEMENT SERVICES

Under Secretary, C. R. Cann.

Office Services Division
Senior Principal, J. E. Nunn, D.F.C.

Management Services Division
Victory House, 30–34 Kingsway, W.C.2.
[01-405 4310]
Assistant Secretary, C. R. Bodrell.

Information Division
Chief Information Officer-A (Assistant Secretary),
J. A. Colmer.
Chief Press Officer, G. Shepherd.
Principal Librarian, T. C. J. Norton.

**Information Technology and Procedures
Division**
Victory House, 30–34 Kingsway, W.C.2.
[01-405 4310]
Assistant Secretary, W. J. Willis.

CHIEF SCIENTIST'S GROUP

Chief Scientist (Fisheries and Food), G. A. H. Elton,
C.B., D.SC., Ph.D. *(Under Secretary).**
Chief Scientist (Agriculture and Horticulture), G. H.
O. Burgess, Ph.D. *(Under Secretary).**

RESEARCH AND DEVELOPMENT
REQUIREMENTS DIVISION*

Assistant Secretary, A. V. Vickery.

FOOD SCIENCE DIVISION
65 Romney Street, S.W.1
[01–212 7676]

Deputy Chief Scientific Officer, R. N. Crossett, D.Phil.

AGRICULTURAL COMMODITIES

Deputy Secretary, D. H. Andrews, C.B., C.B.E.

EUROPEAN COMMUNITY

Under Secretary, Mrs. E. A. J. Attridge.

European Community Division I
Assistant Secretary, R. J. Packer.

European Community Division II
Assistant Secretary, R. E. Melville.

CEREALS, SUGAR AND EXTERNAL
RELATIONS

Under Secretary, D. A. Hadley.

*At Great Westminster House, Horseferry Road,
S.W.1 [01–216 6311].

Cereals Division
Assistant Secretary, R. C. Lowson.

Sugar, Oils and Fats Division
Assistant Secretary, D. F. Roberts.

External Relations
Assistant Secretary, P. A. Cocking.

MEAT, POULTRY AND EGGS

Under Secretary, Mrs. J. M. Archer.

Pigs, Eggs and Poultry Division
Assistant Secretary, M. Ring.

Beef Division
Assistant Secretary, G. R. Waters.

Sheep and Livestock Subsidies Division
Assistant Secretary, Mrs. A. M. Pickering.

MILK, POTATOES AND
AGRICULTURAL MARKETING

Under Secretary, J. E. Dixon, C.M.G.

Milk and Milk Products Division I
Assistant Secretary, S. Wentworth.

Milk and Milk Products Division II
Assistant Secretary, I. C. Redfern.

Milk and Milk Products Division III
Assistant Secretary, A. R. Cruickshank.

Marketing Policy and Potatoes Division*
Assistant Secretary, G. P. McLachlan.

FISHERIES AND FOOD

Deputy Secretary, W. E. Mason, C.B.

FISHERIES DEPARTMENT*

Fisheries Secretary (Under Secretary), D. H. Griffiths.

Fisheries Division I
Assistant Secretary, H. R. Neilson.

Fisheries Division II
Assistant Secretary, R. W. Holmwood.

Fisheries Division III
Assistant Secretary, M. T. Haddon.

Fisheries Division IV
Assistant Secretary, J. C. Edwards.

Sea Fisheries Inspectorate
Chief Inspector, P. J. Derham, O.B.E.

Fisheries Research
*Director of Fisheries Research and Development for
Great Britain*, A. Preston.
Deputy Directors of Fisheries Research , H. W. Hill;
D. J. Garrod.

Fisheries Laboratory
Pakefield Road, Lowestoft, Suffolk NR33 0HT
[0502 62244]

Fisheries Laboratory
Remembrance Avenue, Burnham-on-Crouch,
Essex CM0 8HA
[0621 782658]

Fisheries Experiment Station
Benarth Road, Conwy, Gwynedd LL32 8UB
[049 263 3883]
Inspector of Salmon and Freshwater Fisheries, B.
Stott.

*At Great Westminster House, Horseferry Road,
S.W.1 [01–216 6311].

Fish Diseases Laboratory
The Nothe, Weymouth, Dorset DT4 8UB
[03057 72137]
Officer-in-charge (*Principal Scientific Officer*), B. J. Hill.

Torry Research Station
P.O. Box 31, 135 Abbey Road,
Aberdeen AB9 8DG
[0224 877071]
Director, Dr. J. J. Connell.

Humber Laboratory
Wassand Street, Hull HU3 4AR
[0482 27879]
Officer-in-charge, Dr. J. R. Burt.

FOOD POLICY
Under Secretary, G. E. Myers.

Food Policy and Exports Promotion Division
Assistant Secretary, B. E. Camp.

Alcoholic Drinks Division
Assistant Secretary, G. A. Hollis.

Tropical Foods*
Assistant Secretary, R. S. Thomas.

STANDARDS (FOOD, FERTILISERS AND
FEEDING STUFFS)*
Under Secretary, G. P. Jupe.

Standards Division*
Assistant Secretary, C. A. Cockbill.

Emergencies Division
Assistant Secretary, A. Jeffrey Smith.

Environmental Pollution, Pesticides and Infestation Control*
Assistant Secretary, G. M. Trevelyan.

LAND AND RESOURCES
Deputy Secretary, E. J. G. Smith, C.B.

LAND
Under Secretary, B. Peart.

Land Improvement Division*
Assistant Secretary, M. Madden.

Land Use and Tenure Division*
Assistant Secretary, P. W. Murphy.

Land Drainage Division*
Assistant Secretary, R. C. McIvor.

ANIMAL HEALTH
Under Secretary, J. W. Hepburn.

Animal Health Division I
Government Buildings, Hook Rise South,
Tolworth, Surbiton, Surrey
[01–337 6611]
Assistant Secretary, W. R. Small.

Animal Health Division II
Government Buildings, Hook Rise South,
Tolworth, Surbiton, Surrey.
[01–337 6611]
Assistant Secretary, A. R. Burne.

Animal Health Division III
Tolworth Tower, Surbiton, Surrey
[01–399 5191]
Assistant Secretary, K. W. Wilkes.

* At Great Westminster House, Horseferry Road,
S.W.1 [01–216 6311].

Meat Hygiene Division
Tolworth Tower, Surbiton, Surrey
[01–399 5191]
Assistant Secretary, P. M. Boyling (*temporary*).

HORTICULTURE AND AGRICULTURAL
RESOURCES POLICY
Under Secretary, P. Parkhouse.

Horticulture Division*
Assistant Secretary, R. E. Mordue.

Agricultural Resources Policy Division
Eagle House, 90/96 Cannon Street, E.C.4
[01–623 4266]
Assistant Secretary, G. K. Bruce.

Plant Variety, Rights Office and Seeds
White House Lane, Huntingdon Road, Cambridge
[0223 277151]
Assistant Secretary, F. H. Goodwin.

ECONOMICS AND STATISTICS
Director of Economics and Statistics (*Under Secretary*), C. W. Capstick, C.M.G.

Economics (Farm Business) Division
Senior Economic Adviser, Mrs. S. M. Dickinson.

Economics (International) Division
Senior Economic Adviser, R. W. Irving.

Economics (Resource Use) Division
55 Whitehall, S.W.1.
[01–233 3000]
Senior Economic Adviser, A. P. Power, Ph.D.

Statistics (Agricultural Commodities) Division
Chief Statistician, P. Roberts.

Statistics (Census and Prices) Division
Chief Statistician, D. E. Bradbury.

Economics and Statistics (Food)
Senior Economic Adviser, J. M. Slater, Ph.D.

REGIONAL ORGANIZATION
Deputy Secretary, E. J. G. Smith, C.B.

Eastern Region
Block C, Government Buildings,
Brooklands Avenue, Cambridge CB2 2DR
[0223 358911]
Chief Regional Officer, T. W. Nicol.

Northern Region
Block 2, Government Buildings, Lawnswood,
Leeds S16 5PY
[0532 674411]
Chief Regional Officer, A. F. Baines.

South Eastern Region
Block A, Government Offices,
Coley Park, Reading RG1 6DT
[0734 581222]
Chief Regional Officer, J. A. Bamford.

South Western Region
Block 3, Government Bldgs., Burghill Road,
Westbury-on-Trym, Bristol BS10 6NJ
[0272 500000]
Chief Regional Officer, B. F. Shorney.

Midlands and Western Region
Woodthorne, Wolverhampton WV6 8TQ
[0902 754190]
Chief Regional Officer, R. J. D. Carden.

*At Great Westminster House, Horseferry Road,
S.W.1 [01–216 6311].

AGRICULTURAL DEVELOPMENT AND ADVISORY SERVICE (A.D.A.S.)

Director General and Chief Scientific Advisor, Prof. R. L. Bell.

AGRICULTURE*

Chief Agricultural Officer (Under Secretary), J. J. North.
Senior Agricultural Officers, M. Barker; P. Ingram.
Senior Horticultural Officer, D. J. Fuller.
Superintending Horticultural Marketing Inspector, J. P. Blakey.

AGRICULTURAL SCIENCE

Head of Service (Under Secretary), P. J. Bunyan, D.SC., PH.D.*

Pest Infestation Control Laboratory
London Road, Slough, Berks. SL3 7HJ
[75 34626]
Head of Biology Division and Officer in Charge of Slough Laboratory, D. C. Drummond.

Plant Pathology Laboratory and Plant Health and Seeds Inspectorate
Hatching Green, Harpenden, Herts. AL5 2BD
[0582 75241/46]
Deputy Head of Biology Division and Officer in Charge of Harpenden Laboratory, R. A. Lelliott.
Chief Plant Health and Seeds Inspector, J. J. Baker
£15,605 to £20,794

Great Westminster House, Horseferry Road, S.W.1.
[01–216 6311]
Staff Officer, Science Services, K. G. Gostick
£15,605 to £20,794

LAND AND WATER SERVICE*

Director (Under Secretary), D. B. S. Fitch.
Assistant Director, B. D. Trafford.

VETERINARY
Government Buildings, Hook Rise South, Tolworth, Surbiton, Surrey KT6 7NF
[01–337 6611]

Chief Veterinary Officer, W. H. G. Rees.
Director of Veterinary Field Services (Under Secretary), J. G. Loxam.

Central Veterinary Laboratory, New Haw, Weybridge, Surrey KT15 3NB
[91 41111]
Director of Veterinary Laboratories (Under Secretary), A. J. Stevens.

Lasswade Veterinary Laboratory, Eskgrove, Lasswade, Midlothian EH18 1HU
[031–663 6525]

Cattle Breeding Centre, Shinfield, Reading, Berks. RG2 9BZ
[0734 883157]

ADAS ADMINISTRATION*

Senior A.D.A.S. Officer (Wales), T. M. K. Evans.

Agricultural Development and Advice Division
Assistant Secretary, Mrs. E. Buttle.

*At Great Westminster House, Horseferry Road, S.W.1 [01-216 6311].

AGRICULTURAL AND FOOD RESEARCH COUNCIL
160 Great Portland Street, W1N 6DT
[01-580 6655]

The former Agricultural Research Council was incorporated by Royal Charter on July 23, 1931. The *Science and Technology Act,* 1965, transferred responsibility for the Research Council to the Secretary of State for Education and Science and a new Charter received Royal approval in 1967. The Council is charged with the organization and development of agricultural and food research and may, in particular, establish or develop institutions or departments of institutions and make grants for investigation and research relating to the advancement of agriculture. In 1983, the Council formally adopted the title Agricultural and Food Research Council in recognition of the increasing importance of food research and the expanding contribution the Council expects to make to it. The Council is financed jointly from the Parliamentary vote of the Department of Education and Science and the Ministry of Agriculture, Fisheries and Food.

Chairman, The Earl of Selborne; (*Members*), Prof. R. L. Bell, PH.D.; Dr. G. H. O. Burgess, F.R.S.E.; J. E. Cross; Prof. B. Crossland, C.B.E., F.R.S.; G. A. H. Elton, C.B., PH.D.; Prof. B. K. Follett, F.R.S.; Prof. I. M. Glynn, F.R.S.; A. C. Green; R. Halstead, C.B.; L. P. Hamilton; Prof. J. L. Harper, F.R.S.; Prof. J. L. Jinks, F.R.S.; Prof. Sir Hans Kornberg, F.R.S.; C. Mackey; M. Mackie; J. A. Parry; B. C. Read, C.B.E.; Prof. D. C. Smith, F.R.S.; E. J. G. Smith, C.B.; Prof. E. J. L. Soulsby, PH.D.
Assessors, Dr. W. O. Brown, D.SC.; Prof. J. R. Quayle, F.R.S.; W. H. G. Rees.
Deputy Chairman and Secretary, Sir Ralph Riley, F.R.S.
Second Secretary, J. A. F. Rook, D.SC., F.R.S.E.
Under-Secretary, G. M. P. Myers.
Heads of Divisions, R. Prideaux; J. Dickens; Prof. R. F. Curtis, PH.D.; R. J. Harris; B. G. Jamieson, PH.D.
Policy Group, W. S. Wise.
Principal Information Officer, M. F. Goodwin.
For the Research Institutes under the control of the Council, *see* Index.

EXECUTIVE COUNCIL OF THE COMMONWEALTH AGRICULTURAL BUREAUX
Farnham House, Farnham Royal, Slough, Berks.
[Farnham Common: 2281]

The Commonwealth Agricultural Bureaux, founded in 1929, consist of four Institutes and ten Bureaux, under the control of an Executive Council, comprising representatives of the Commonwealth countries which contribute to its funds. Each Institute and Bureau is concerned with its own particular branch of agricultural science and acts as a clearing house for the dissemination of information of value to research workers throughout the world. They deal respectively with entomology, mycology, helminthology and nematology, biological control, agricultural economics, animal breeding and genetics, animal health, nutrition, dairy science and technology, forestry, horticulture and plantation crops, pastures and field crops, plant breeding and genetics, and soils and fertilizers. The information is published in journals which have a monthly circulation of 32,000 in 150 countries. The abstract journals are produced by computer-assisted processes, and the whole data base has been consolidated and is available in machine-readable form. Review articles, books, maps, monographs and annotated bibliographies on particular subjects are also issued.

Chairman, Dr. D. G. Crosby (*Canada*).
Vice-Chairman, Dr. M. Moore (*Australia*).
Executive Director, N. G. Jones, D.F.C.

Institutes

Commonwealth Institute of Entomology, 56 Queen's Gate, S.W.7. *Director*, N. C. Pant, Ph.D.

Commonwealth Mycological Institute, Ferry Lane, Kew, Richmond, Surrey. *Director*, D. L. Hawksworth, Ph.D.

Commonwealth Institute of Biological Control, Gordon Street, Curepe, Trinidad. *Director*, F. D. Bennett, Ph.D.

Commonwealth Institute of Parasitology, 395A Hatfield Road, St. Albans, Herts. *Director*, R. L. J. Muller, Ph.D.

Bureaux

Agricultural Economics, Dartington House, Little Clarendon Street, Oxford.—*Director*, (vacant).

Animal Breeding and Genetics, Animal Breeding Research Organization, The King's Buildings, West Mains Road, Edinburgh, Scotland.—*Director*, J. D. Turton.

Animal Health, Central Veterinary Laboratory, New Haw, Weybridge, Surrey.—*Director*, R. M. Mack.

Dairy Science and Technology, Lane End House, Shinfield, Reading.—*Director*, E. J. Mann.

Forestry, Commonwealth Forestry Institute, South Parks Road, Oxford.—*Director*, W. Finlayson.

Horticulture and Plantation Crops, East Malling Research Station, Maidstone, Kent.—*Director*, D. O'D. Bourke.

Nutrition, Rowett Research Institute, Bucksburn, Aberdeen, Scotland.—*Director*, A. A. Woodham, Ph.D.

Pastures and Field Crops, Hurley, Maidenhead, Berks.—*Director*, P. J. Boyle.

Plant Breeding and Genetics, Department of Applied Biology, Pembroke Street, Cambridge.—*Director*, Miss O. Holbeck.

Soils, Rothamsted Experimental Station, Harpenden, Herts.—*Director*, B. Butters.

COLLEGE OF ARMS OR HERALDS COLLEGE
Queen Victoria Street, E.C.4
[01–248 2762]

The College of Arms is open daily from 10–4 (Mondays to Fridays) when an Officer of Arms is in attendance to deal with enquiries by the public, though such enquiries may also be directed to any of the Officers of Arms, either personally or by letter.

There are 13 officers of the College, 3 Kings of Arms, 6 Heralds and 4 Pursuivants, who specialize in genealogical and heraldic work for their respective clients. The College possesses the finest records on these subjects in the world. It is the official repository of the Arms and pedigrees of English, Northern Irish, and Commonwealth families and their descendants, and its records include official copies of the records of Ulster King of Arms, the originals of which remain in Dublin.

Arms have been and still are granted by Letters Patent from the Kings of Arms under Authority delegated to them by the Sovereign, such authority having been expressly conferred on them since at least the fifteenth century. A right to Arms can only be established by the registration in the official records of the College of Arms of a pedigree showing direct male line descent from an ancestor already appearing therein as being entitled to Arms, or by making application through the College of Arms for a Grant of Arms.

Earl Marshal, His Grace the Duke of Norfolk, K.G., C.B., C.B.E., M.C.

Kings of Arms

Garter, Sir Colin Cole, K.C.V.O., T.D., F.S.A.

Clarenceux, Sir Anthony Richard Wagner, K.C.B., K.C.V.O., D.Litt., F.S.A.

Norroy and Ulster, John Phillip Brooke Brooke-Little, C.V.O., F.S.A.

Heralds

York (*and Registrar*), Conrad Marshall John Fisher Swan, M.V.O., Ph.D., F.S.A.

Chester, David Hubert Boothby Chesshyre, F.S.A.

Windsor, Theobald David Mathew.

Richmond, Michael Maclagan, F.S.A.

Lancaster, Peter Llewellyn Gwynn-Jones.

Somerset, Thomas Woodcock.

Earl Marshal's Secretary, Sir Walter John George Verco, K.C.V.O., Surrey Herald Extraordinary.

Pursuivants

Rouge Dragon, Patric Laurence Dickinson.

Portcullis, Peter Brotherton Spurrier.

Bluemantle, Terence David McCarthy.

Rouge Croix, Henry Edgar Paston-Bedingfeld.

COURT OF THE LORD LYON
H.M. New Register House, Edinburgh
[031–556 7255]

The Scottish Court of Chivalry, including the genealogical jurisdiction of the *Ri-Sennachie* of Scotland's Celtic Kings, adjudicates rights to arms and administration of *The Scottish Public Register of All Arms and Bearings* (under 1672 cap. 47) and *Public Register of All Genealogies*. The Lord Lyon presides and judicially establishes rights to existing arms or succession to Chiefship, or for cadets with scientific "differences" showing position in clan or family. Pedigrees are also established by decrees of Lyon Court, and by Letters Patent. As *Royal Commissioner in Armory*, he grants Patents of Arms (which constitute the grantee and heirs noble in the Noblesse of Scotland) to "virtuous and well-deserving" Scotsmen, and petitioners (personal or corporate) in Her Majesty's overseas realms of Scottish connection, and issues birthbrieves. In Scots Law, Arms are protected by Statute; their usurpation is punishable, and the Registration Fees of Honour on patents and matriculations are payable to H.M. Exchequer.

Lord Lyon King of Arms, Malcolm Rognvald Innes of Edinght, C.V.O., W.S., F.S.A. *Scot.*

Heralds

Albany, Sir Iain Moncreiffe of that Ilk, Bt., C.V.O., Q.C., Ph.D.

Islay, John I. D. Pottinger, M.V.O.

Marchmont, Major David Maitland Maitland-Titterton, T.D., F.S.A. *Scot.*

Rothesay Extraordinary, Lt.-Col. Harold Andrew Balvaird Lawson, C.V.O.

Pursuivants

Carrick, John A. Spens, R.D., W.S.
Unicorn, Sir Crispin Agnew of Lochnaw, Bt.
Dingwall, Charles J. Burnett.

Lyon Clerk and Keeper of Records, John I. D. Pottinger, M.V.O.
Procurator-Fiscal, Ivor Reginald Guild, W.S.
Herald Painter, Mrs. J. Phillips.
Macer, Thomas C. Gray.

ART GALLERIES, ETC.

ARTS COUNCIL OF GREAT BRITAIN
105 Piccadilly, W1V 0AU
[01-629 9495]

The Arts Council is Great Britain's principal channel for public financial support of the arts. It funds the major arts organizations in England, the Regional Arts Associations and the Scottish and Welsh Arts Councils. It also provides a service of advice, information and help to artists, arts organizations and the general public. In addition, the Council runs the Hayward and Serpentine Galleries, the Wigmore Hall and the Poetry Library in London, organizes art exhibitions and co-ordinates tours of drama, opera, dance and contemporary music.

It is an independent body established by Royal Charter in 1946. Its aims are: (a) to develop and improve the knowledge, understanding and practice of the arts; (b) to increase the accessibility of the arts to the public throughout Great Britain; (c) to advise and co-operate with government departments, local authorities and other bodies on any matters concerned whether directly or indirectly with these aims. The arts with which the Council is mainly concerned are dance and mime, drama, literature, music and opera, and the visual arts, including photography and arts films.

The Council receives a grant-in-aid from the Government, and for the year 1984–85 the amount is £100,500,000.

Chairman, Sir William Rees-Mogg.
Secretary-General, L. Rittner.

ROYAL FINE ART COMMISSION
2 Carlton Gardens, SW1Y 5AA
[01–930 3935]

Appointed in May, 1924, "to enquire into such questions of public amenity or of artistic importance as may be referred to them from time to time by any of our Departments of State, and to report thereon to such Department; and, furthermore, to give advice on similar questions when so requested by public or quasi-public bodies, where it appears to the said Commission that their assistance would be advantageous." In August, 1933, a Royal Warrant extended the Terms of Reference of the Commission—"so that it shall also be open to the said Commission, if they so desire, to call the attention of any of Our Departments of State, or of the appropriate public or quasi-public bodies, to any project or development which in the opinion of the said Commission may appear to affect amenities of a national or public character"; in May, 1946, a Royal Warrant further extended the Terms of Reference of the Commission as follows:—

We Do give and grant unto you, or any three or more of you, full power to call before you such persons as you shall judge likely to afford you any information upon the subject of this Our Commission; and also to call for, have access to and examine all such books, documents, registers and records as may afford you the fullest information on the subject, and to inquire of and concerning the premises by all other lawful ways and means whatsoever: We Do authorize and empower you, or any three or more of you, to visit and personally inspect such places as you may deem it expedient so to inspect for the more effectual carrying out of the purposes aforesaid:

Chairman, Sir Derman Christopherson, O.B.E., D.Phil. F.R.S.
Commissioners, The Countess of Airlie, C.V.O.; Miss Elizabeth Chesterton, O.B.E.; Sir Anthony Cox, C.B.E., F.R.I.B.A.; Sir Philip Dowson, C.B.E.; Sir Ralph Freeman, C.V.O., C.B.E.; Mark Girouard, Ph.D.; A. J. Gordon, C.B.E.; The Duke of Grafton, K.G., F.S.A.; R. MacCormac; P. Nuttgens, C.B.E., Ph.D.; Sir David Piper, C.B.E.; Sir Philip Powell, O.B.E., A.R.A.; Miss W. Taylor; W. Whitfield, C.B.E.; Sir Hugh Wilson, O.B.E.
Secretary, S. Cantacuzino, F.R.I.B.A.

ROYAL FINE ART COMMISSION FOR SCOTLAND
9 Atholl Crescent,
Edinburgh EH3 8HA
[031–229 1109]

Commissioners, Prof. A. J. Youngson, D.Litt. (*Chairman*); Miss Louise G. Annand, M.B.E.; J. P. Boys, A.R.S.A., F.R.I.B.A.; B. Klein, C.B.E.; W. K. Mackay; I. Metzstein, A.R.S.A.; Prof. F. N. Morcos-Asaad, Ph.D.; A. Morrocco, LL.D., R.S.A.; J. D. Richards, C.B.E., A.R.S.A.; R. R. Steedman, R.S.A.; Mrs. F. M. E. Walker; H. A. Wheeler, O.B.E., P.R.S.A., F.R.I.B.A.
Secretary, C. Prosser.

NATIONAL GALLERY
Trafalgar Square, WC2N 5DN
[01–839 3321]

Hours of opening.—Weekdays 10 to 6, Sundays 2 to 6. Closed on Good Friday, Christmas Eve, Christmas Day, Boxing Day, New Year's Day and May Day Bank Holiday.

The National Gallery was founded in 1824, following a Parliamentary grant of £60,000 for the purchase and exhibition of the Angerstein collection of pictures. The present site was first occupied in 1838 and enlarged and improved at various times throughout the years. A substantial extension to the north of the building with a public entrance in Orange Street was opened in 1975. Expenses for 1984–85 are estimated at £7,024,000.

Trustees

The Lord Annan, O.B.E. (*Chairman*); H. Hodgkin, C.B.E.; S. Young; Miss Bridget Riley, C.B.E.; Hon. Sir John Baring, C.V.O.; The Marquess of Dufferin and Ava; Sir Isaiah Berlin, O.M., C.B.E., F.B.A.; Sir Rex Richards, F.R.S., D.Phil,; M. Sacher; Mrs. C. Hubbard; Hon. J. Rothschild.

Officers

Director, Sir Michael Levey, M.V.O., F.B.A. . . . £30,375
Keeper and Deputy Director, A. J. W. Braham
£19,243 to £21,678
Keeper, Education and Exhibitions, A. J. W. Smith
£19,243 to £21,678
Deputy Keepers, C. P. H. Brown; M. J. Wilson
£15,652 to £19,317
Assistant Keepers, Dr. D. R. Gordon; M. J. C. Helston . . . . £9,470 to £16,656
Scientific Adviser to the Trustees, R. H. G. Thomson, C.B.E. . . . . £19,243 to £21,678
Chief Restorer, M. H. Wyld . . . . . . £19,243 to £21,678
Finance and Establishments, D. C. E. Gunn
£10,079 to £12,518

NATIONAL PORTRAIT GALLERY
St. Martin's Place, WC2H 0HE
[01–930 1552]

Open Monday to Friday 10 to 5. Saturday 10 to 6. Sunday 2 to 6.

The first grant was made in 1856 to form a gallery of the portraits of the most eminent persons in British history, the collections being successively housed in Great George Street, Westminster, in South Kensington, and in Bethnal Green. The present building was opened in 1896, £80,000 being contributed to its cost by Mr. W. H. Alexander; an extension erected at the expense of Lord Duveen was opened in 1933.

Chairman, The Lord Kenyon, C.B.E., F.S.A.

Trustees, The Lord President of the Council (*ex officio*); The President of the Royal Academy of Arts (*ex officio*); Prof. Sir Lawrence Gowing, K.B.E.; The Duke of Grafton, K.G., F.S.A.; J. P. Ehrman, F.B.A., F.S.A.; Sir Oliver Millar, K.C.V.O., F.B.A., F.S.A.; Prof. J. Roberts; Prof. B. R. Morris; The Rev. Prof. W. O. Chadwick, K.B.E., D.D., F.B.A.; Mrs. Susan Crosland; Prof. M. Gowing, C.B.E., F.B.A.; Sir Huw Wheldon, O.B.E., M.C.; The Marquess of Anglesey, F.S.A; The Lord Rockley; H. Keswick.

Director, J. T. Hayes, PH.D., F.S.A £22,201
Deputy Keeper, M. Rogers, D.Phil. £15,652 to £19,317

TATE GALLERY
Millbank, SW1P 4RG
[01–821 1313]

Hours of opening.—Weekdays 10 to 5.50. Sundays 2 to 5.50. Closed on New Year's Day, Good Friday, May Day Holiday, Christmas Eve, Christmas Day and Boxing Day.

The Tate Gallery comprises three national collections: (a) British painting of all periods; (b) modern foreign painting; (c) modern sculpture. Works are displayed at the Gallery as two collections: The British Collection, in which Hogarth, Blake, Turner, Constable and the Pre-Raphaelites are particularly well represented and the Modern Collection, which includes major works by virtually all leading artists and a fine collection of contemporary prints. There is an almost continuous programme of major loan exhibitions, and free lectures, films and guided tours are offered nearly every day throughout the year. The Gallery was opened in 1897, the cost of erection (£80,000) being defrayed by Sir Henry Tate, who also contributed the nucleus of the present collection. The Turner Wing, built at the expense of Sir Joseph Duveen was opened in 1920. Lord Duveen defrayed the cost of galleries to contain the collection of modern foreign painting, completed in 1926, and a new sculpture hall, completed in 1937. The latest and largest extension to the Tate Gallery was opened by Her Majesty Queen Elizabeth II on May 24, 1979. This extension, costing £3,200,000, has increased the public areas of the Gallery 50 per cent and also includes purpose-built accommodation for the Conservation Department and the Photographic Department, and extra accommodation for the reserve collection. The Clore Gallery for the Turner Collection is being built adjoining the Tate Gallery and is due to open in 1986. Nearly £6,000,000 is being donated from the Clore Foundation. Expenses for 1984–85 are estimated at £5,595,000.

Director, A. Bowness, C.B.E. £26,087
Trustees, The Lord Hutchinson, Q.C. (*Chairman*); P. Heron, C.B.E.; P. Moores; P. Palumbo; R. Rogers; Sir Rex Richards, D.SC., F.R.S.; A. Caro, C.B.E.; The Countess of Airlie, C.V.O.; Mrs. C. Hubbard; Dr. J. Golding.

Keeper of the British Collection, M. R. F. Butlin
£20,493 to £22,928

Keeper of the Modern Collection, R. E. Alley
£20,493 to £22,928
Keeper of Museum Services, M. G. Compton
£20,493 to £22,928
Keeper of Conservation, The Viscount Dunluce
£20,493 to £22,928
Deputy Keepers, R. E. Morphet; L. A. Parris; Miss R. Rattenbury; R. Perry .... £16,902 to £20,567
Administration Officer, R. Aylward
£13,649 to £17,906

WALLACE COLLECTION
Hertford House, Manchester Square, W.1
[01–935 0687]

Admission free. Open on weekdays 10 a.m. to 5 p.m.: Sundays 2 p.m. to 5 p.m. Closed on Good Friday, December 24–26, January 1 and May Day.

The Wallace Collection was bequeathed to the nation by the widow of Sir Richard Wallace, Bt., K.C.B., M.P., on her death in 1897, and Hertford House was subsequently acquired by the Government. The collection includes pictures, drawings and miniatures, French furniture, sculpture, bronzes, porcelain, armour and miscellaneous *objets d'art*. The total net expenses were estimated at £823,000 in 1984–85.

Director, J. A. S. Ingamells.
Assistants to Director, P. Hughes; Miss R. J. Savill.
Establishment and Finance Officer, A. W. Houldershaw.

NATIONAL GALLERIES OF SCOTLAND
The Mound, Edinburgh EH2 2EL
[031–556 8921]

Director, C. E. Thompson £22,044
Trustees, R. W. Begg, C.B.E., (*Chairman*); The Marquess of Bute; Prof. H. A. D. Miles; J. Notman; Prof. M. Kemp; C. J. Risk; J. Knox.
Restorer, J. P. Dick .... £15,652 to £19,317
Curator of Education and Information, C. J. M. Johnstone .... £11,076 to £16,656
Secretary, J. Gordon .... £10,079 to £12,518

Comprising:

National Gallery of Scotland
The Mound, Edinburgh
[031–556 8921]

Open: Monday to Saturday 10 to 5; Sunday 2 to 5; Closed 25, 26, 27, 31 December; 1, 2, 3 January.
Keeper, H. Macandrew .... £15,652 to £19,317
Assistant Keepers, H. N. A. Brigstocke, PH.D. (£11,076 to £16,656); Miss L. M. Errington, PH.D. (£9,470 to £12,518).
Keeper of Prints and Drawings, K. K. Andrews
£15,652 to £19,317

Scottish National Portrait Gallery
1 Queen Street, Edinburgh
[031–556 8921]

Hours—as for National Gallery of Scotland.
Keeper, D. Thomson, PH.D. .... £15,652 to £19,317
Assistant Keepers, Miss R. K. Marshall, PH.D.; J. E. Holloway .... £11,076 to £16,656

Scottish National Gallery of Modern Art
Inverleith House, Royal Botanic Garden,
Edinburgh
[031–332 3754]

(During 1984 the gallery will move to Belford Road, Edinburgh.)

Open: Monday to Saturday 10 to 5 (or dusk, if earlier); Sunday 2 to 5 (or dusk if earlier); Closed 25, 26, 27, 31 December, 1, 2, 3 January.
Keeper, W. D. Hall .... £15,652 to £19,317
Assistant Keeper, K. S. Hartley ... £9,470 to £12,518

(For other British Art Galleries, *see* Index.)

ASSOCIATED BRITISH PORTS
150 Holborn, EC1N 2LR
[01-430 1177]

Constituted under the *Transport Act*, 1981. A.B.P. owns and operates 19 active ports and traffic through them in 1983 totalled 82,631,000 tonnes. Net registered tonnage of shipping entering and leaving the ports in 1983 totalled 134,600,000 tons and passengers in transit totalled 2,939,000. Net profit, before tax, 1983, £14,470,000.
Chairman, J. K. Stuart £47,944
Deputy Chairman, Sir Charles Ball, Bt.
Deputy Chairman and Joint Managing Director, D. Stringer, O.B.E.
Joint Managing Director, J. Williams.

UNITED KINGDOM ATOMIC ENERGY AUTHORITY
11 Charles II Street, SW1Y 4QP
[01-930 5454]

Established by the Atomic Energy Authority Act, 1954, the Authority is responsible for providing research and development support for the U.K. nuclear power programme. It also undertakes work on other civil applications of nuclear energy and on various projects outside the nuclear field on repayment. The UKAEA has eight laboratories and a London headquarters employing some 14,000 people. The annual turnover is some £300m.
Chairman, A. Allen, C.B.E. £52,000
    Deputy Chairman and Chief Executive, (vacant).
Members (Full-time), Dr. T. N. Marsham, C.B.E.; Dr. L. E. J. Roberts, C.B.E., F.R.S. £38,500
(Part-time) Sir Peter Hirsch, F.R.S.; Sir John McFarlane Boyd, C.B.E.; Dr. N. L. Franklin, C.B.E., F.R.S.; J. Bullock; R. E. J. Roberts; C. Allday, C.B.E.; Sir Alan Cottrell, F.R.S. *(each £4,473)*; F. E. Bonner, C.B.E.; I. T. Manley, C.B. *(each unpaid)*.
Secretary, P. J. Searby, C.B.E.

THE BANK OF ENGLAND
Threadneedle Street, EC2R 8AH

The Bank of England was incorporated in 1694 under Royal Charter. It is the banker of the Government on whose behalf it manages the Note Issue and the National Debt. As central reserve bank of the country, the Bank keeps the accounts of British banks, who maintain with it a proportion of their cash resources, and of most overseas central banks.
Governor, R. Leigh-Pemberton.
Deputy Governor, C. W. McMahon.
Directors, Dr. D. V. Atterton, C.B.E.; Hon. Sir John Baring, C.V.O.; G. Blunden; Sir Adrian Cadbury; Sir Robert Clark, D.S.C.; G. A. Drain, C.B.E.; R. D. Galpin; E. A. J. George; Prof. B. Griffiths; Sir Hector Laing; A. D. Loehnis; A. Lord, C.B.; The Lord Nelson of Stafford; D. G. Scholey, C.B.E.; Sir David Steel, D.S.O., M.C.; D. A. Walker.
Associate Director, Banking Supervision, W. P. Cooke.
Assistant Directors, M. J. Balfour; A. L. Coleby; D. A. Dawkins; B. Quinn; C. J. Farrow.
Chief Advisers, J. S. Flemming *(Economic)*; C. A. E. Goodhart; D. G. Holland, C.M.G.

Chief of Banking Department (*Chief Cashier*), D. H. F. Somerset.
Chief Registrar, J. G. Drake.
General Manager, Printing Works, G. L. Wheatley.
Secretary, P. E. Towndrow.
Head of Information Division, P. H. Kent.
The Auditor, J. A. Penny.

(For list of Principal Banks *see* Index.)

BOUNDARY COMMISSIONS

The Commissions are constituted under the House of Commons (Redistribution of Seats) Act 1949 as amended by the House of Commons (Redistribution of Seats) Act 1958. The Speaker of the House of Commons is ex-officio chairman of all four Commissions in the United Kingdom. Each of the four Commissions is required by law to keep the parliamentary constituencies in their part of the United Kingdom under review. Each of the three Commissions in Great Britain is required by law to keep the European Assembly constituencies in their part of Great Britain under review.

England
St. Catherines House, 10 Kingsway, WC2B 6JP
[01–242 0262]

Deputy Chairman, The Hon. Mr. Justice Walton.
Joint Secretaries, G. P. Barnes and A. N. Pickersgill.

Wales
St. Catherines House, 10 Kingsway, WC2B 6JP
[01–242 0262]

Deputy Chairman, The Hon. Mr. Justice Kenneth Jones.
Joint Secretaries, G. P. Barnes and A. N. Pickersgill.

Scotland
St. Andrew's House, Edinburgh
[031–556 8501]

Deputy Chairman, The Hon. Lord Ross.
Secretary, A. Simmen.

Northern Ireland
c/o Northern Ireland Office,
Whitehall, SW1A 2AZ
[01–273 5480]

Deputy Chairman, The Hon. Mr. Justice Murray.
Secretary, B. A. Blackwell.

BRITISH AEROSPACE p.l.c.
Headquarters: Brooklands Road, Weybridge, Surrey.
[0932 53444]

British Aerospace is primarily engaged, either on its own or in collaboration with other companies, in the design, development and production of military and civil aircraft, guided weapons and space systems, and in the provision of defence support services. Nationalisation in 1977 brought together in British Aerospace the former companies of British Aircraft Corporation (Holdings) Ltd., Hawker Siddeley Aviation Ltd., Hawker Siddeley Dynamics Ltd. and Scottish Aviation Ltd. On January 1, 1981, under the British Aerospace Act 1980, all the property, rights, liabilities and obligations of the former nationalised corporation were vested in British Aerospace Public Limited Company. In February 1981, H.M. Government offered for sale up to 100 million Ordinary Shares, representing approximately half of the issued share capital of the company. The

resultant ownership of British Aerospace has become: H.M. Government 48·43%, ordinary shareholders 48·43% and employee shareholders 3·14%. Employing some 77,980 people in the U.K. and overseas, British Aerospace functions through two major operating groups—Aircraft and Dynamics.
Chairman, Sir Austin W. Pearce, C.B.E., PH.D. £87,260
Managing Director, Admiral Sir Raymond Lygo, K.C.B.
Secretary and Legal Adviser, B. Cookson.

BRITISH AIRPORTS AUTHORITY
Head Office: Gatwick Airport, W. Sussex.

Set up under the *Airports Authority Acts*, 1965 and 1975, the Authority owns and manages seven major airports—Heathrow, Gatwick, Stansted, Glasgow, Prestwick, Edinburgh and Aberdeen. The Authority's total assets are £1,027,171,000.
Chairman, N. J. Payne, C.B.E. £36,750
Managing Director, J. Mulkern.

BRITISH AIRWAYS p.l.c.
Speedbird House, London Airport, Heathrow, Middlesex [01–759 5511]

Pursuant to the Civil Aviation Act, 1980 and the Orders made thereunder, the undertaking of British Airways Board became vested in British Airways p.l.c. as from April 1, 1984. British Airways has seven main subsidiary companies: British Airways Helicopters, British Airways Associated Companies, British Airways Engine Overhaul, British Airtours, British Airways Tour Operations Ltd., Alta Holidays and Martin Rooks & Co.

British Airways has 183 aircraft in service (150 fixed wing and 33 helicopters), and at the operating level, made a surplus before interest and other charges of £313,000,000 for the year to March 31, 1984, compared with a surplus of £190,000,000 in the previous year.
Chairman, The Lord King of Wartnaby, C.B.E.
Chief Executive, C. Marshall.

BRITISH BROADCASTING CORPORATION
Broadcasting House, W1A 1AA   [01–580 4468]

The BBC was incorporated under Royal Charter as successor to the British Broadcasting Company, Ltd., whose licence expired Dec. 31, 1926. Its present Charter came into force Aug. 1, 1981, for 15 years. The Chairman, Vice-Chairman and other Governors are appointed by the Queen in Council. The BBC is financed by revenue from receiving licences for the Home services and by a Grant in Aid from Parliament for the External services. The total number of receiving licences in the U.K. at March 31, 1984 was 18,631,753, of which 3,261,272 were for monochrome receivers and 15,370,481 for colour receivers. Annual television fees are: monochrome £15; colour £46.

Board of Governors

Chairman, S. Young. £26,673
Vice-Chairman, Sir William Rees-Mogg. £6,790
Governors, The Lady Faulkner of Downpatrick (*N. Ireland*) (£6,790); W. Peat, C.B.E. (*Scotland*) (£6,790); A. Roberts (*Wales*) (£6,790); Miss D. M. S. D. Park, C.M.G., O.B.E.; Sir John Johnston, G.C.M.G., K.C.V.O.; Miss J. Barrow, O.B.E.; Sir John Boyd, C.B.E.; M. McAlpine; The Lady Parkes; The Earl of Harewood .... (*each*) £3,395

Board of Management

Director-General, A. D. G. Milne.
Managing Directors, D. T. Muggeridge (*External Services*); R. T. L. Francis (*Radio*); W. F. Cotton, O.B.E. (*Television*).
Assistant Director-General, A. Protheroe, M.B.E., T.D.
Directors, G. Buck (*Finance*); D. J. Webster (*United States*); T. B. McCrirrick (*Engineering*); J. F. Wilkinson (*Public Affairs*); M. Checkland (*Resources, Television*); B. G. Wenham (*Programmes, Television*).

Other Senior Staff

Deputy Managing Director, Radio, C. J. McLelland.
Deputy Managing Director, External Services, A. S. Kark.
Deputy Director of Engineering, G. Cook.
Deputy Director of Personnel, R. Chase.
General Manager, Publications, J. G. Holmes.
Legal Adviser, A. Jennings.
Chief Assistant to Director-General, Margaret Douglas.
Secretary, D. Holmes.
Managing Director, B.B.C. Enterprises, B. Parkin.
Controller BBC-1, M. Grade.
Controller BBC-2, G. McDonald.
Controller Radio 1, D. Chinnery.
Controller Radio 2, B. Marriot.
Controller Radio 3, I. McIntyre.
Controller Radio 4, D. Hatch.
Controller Information Services, M. Bunce.
Deputy Secretary, Patricia Hodgson.

Controllers of Regional Offices

English Regions, M. Alder, Broadcasting Centre, Pebble Mill Road, Birmingham.
Scotland, P. E. B. Chalmers, Broadcasting House, Queen Margaret Drive, Glasgow.
Wales, G. S. Jones, Broadcasting House, Llantrisant Road, Llandaff, Cardiff.
Northern Ireland, J. S. Hawthorne, C.B.E., Broadcasting House, 25–27 Ormeau Avenue, Belfast.

THE BRITISH COUNCIL
10 Spring Gardens, SW1A 2BN

The British Council was established in 1934 and incorporated by Royal Charter in 1940. Its principal aims and functions are: to promote a wider knowledge of Britain and the English language abroad, to develop closer cultural relations between Britain and other countries and to administer educational aid programmes. The Council receives grants from the Foreign and Commonwealth Office and the Overseas Development Administration (estimated for 1984/85 at £82,700,000); acts as the agent of the Overseas Development Administration in specific aid programmes (totalling £63,200,000); and gains, from sources other than the British taxpayer, earnings from English language teaching, paid educational services, and acting for international organizations, including U.N. agencies (£35,900,000).
Chairman, Sir David Orr, M.C.
Director-General, Sir John Burgh, K.C.M.G., C.B.

BRITISH RAILWAYS BOARD
Euston Square, P.O. Box 100, NW1 2DZ
[01–262 3232]

The British Railways Board came into being on Jan. 1, 1963 under the terms of the *Transport Act*, 1962. The Board became responsible for the provision of railway services in Great Britain and for associated shipping, hotel, catering and other services formerly carried on by the British Transport Commission.
Chairman, R. B. Reid, C.B.E. £60,948
Deputy Chairman, Sir Richard Cave, M.C. (part-time).
Vice-Chairman, D. Fowler, C.B.E.

Members, The Viscount Caldecote, D.S.O.*; S. D. Jenkins*; Prudence Leith*; H. R. Macleod*; G. Myers; M. V. Posner*; J. G. Urquhart, C.V.O.
* Part-time members, paid *pro rata.*
Secretary, J. Batley.

BRITISH SHIPBUILDERS
Headquarters: Benton House, 136 Sandyford Road, Newcastle upon Tyne.
[0632 326772]

Established under the Aircraft and Shipbuilding Industries Act of 1977, British Shipbuilders is a national corporation responsible for all publicly-owned shipyards, etc. in England and Scotland.
Chairman and Chief Executive, J. G. Day.
Corporation Secretary, P. C. M. Thompson.

BRITISH STANDARDS INSTITUTION
British Standards House, 2 Park Street, W.1
[Enquiry Section: B.S.I., Linford Wood, Milton Keynes, MK14 6LE. Tel. 0908 320066]

The British Standards Institution is the recognized authority in the U.K. for the preparation and publication of national standards for industrial and consumer products. The Institution originated in 1901, when the Institutions of Civil, Mechanical and Electrical Engineers, together with the Iron and Steel Institute and the Institution of Naval Architects, formed a joint Engineering Standards Committee—which subsequently became the British Engineering Standards Association. A Royal Charter was granted in 1929 and with the extension of the scope of the organization to include the building, chemical and textile industries its title was later changed to "British Standards Institution".

The Institution, in consultation with the interests concerned, now prepares standards relating to nearly every sector of the nation's industry and trade. There are over 8,500 British Standards covering specifications of quality, construction dimensions, performance or safety; methods of test and analysis; glossaries of terms; and codes of practice. Over 600 new and revised British Standards are published each year.

British Standards are issued for voluntary adoption though in a number of cases compliance with a British Standard is required by legislation. The Institution operates certification schemes under which industrial and consumer products are certified as complying with the relevant British Standard and manufacturers satisfying the requirements of such schemes may use the Institution's certification trade marks known as the "Kitemark" and the "Safety Mark". Other testing and certification services, together with information services, are available to industry, including help in meeting technical requirements in export markets.

The Institution is financed by voluntary subscriptions, an annual Government grant, the sale of its publications and fees for testing and certification. There are more than 15,000 subscribing members of B.S.I.
Director General, D. G. Spickernell, C.B.

BRITISH STEEL CORPORATION
9 Albert Embankment, SE1 7SN
[01-735 7654]

The British Steel Corporation was established under the Iron and Steel Act 1967 which vested in the Corporation the shares of the fourteen major steel companies. The Corporation's main duty is to supply such iron and steel products as it thinks fit in sufficient quantities and at such prices as will meet reasonable demand.

Chairman, R. Haslam.
Deputy Chairman and Chief Executive, R. Scholey, C.B.E.
Members (full-time), Dr. D. Grieves; G. H. Sambrook; J. G. Stewart.
Members (part-time), Sir John Boyd, C.B.E.; The Lord Gregson; S. J. Gross, C.M.G.; R. Halstead, C.B.E.; I. K. MacGregor.
Secretary, I. M. P. Evans.

BRITISH TECHNOLOGY GROUP
101 Newington Causeway, SE1 6BU
[01-403 6666]

British Technology Group (BTG) is the name under which the National Research Development Corporation and the National Enterprise Board have been co-operating since 1981. BTG's primary function is to promote the development and commercialization of technology derived from U.K. public sector sources, i.e. universities, polytechnics, research councils, government research establishments and other public bodies. BTG takes responsibility for protecting and licensing inventions from these sources, provides funds for development, seeks licensees and negotiates licence agreements with industry. The general aim is to ensure that maximum advantage is taken of the commercial potential of successful U.K. research and development.
Chairman, C. Barker.

BRITISH TELECOM
2-12 Gresham Street, E.C.2
[01-357 3000]

British Telecom, formerly part of the Post Office, was established as a separate public corporation on 1 October, 1981. Consequent upon the Telecommunications Act 1984, it became a public limited company on 6 August, 1984. British Telecom's Board remit is to provide telecommunications and data processing services.

British Telecom Board

Members, Sir George Jefferson, C.B.E. (*Chairman*); D. Vander Weyer (*Deputy Chairman*); J. Hodgson, C.B.E. (*Vice-Chairman*); M. Bett (*Personnel and Corporate Services*); F. D. Perryman (*Finance*); I. D. T. Vallance (*Managing Director, Local Communications Services*); J. Alvey, C.B. (*Managing Director for Development and Procurement and Engineer-in-Chief*); R. E. G. Back (*Managing Director, National Networks*); C. Crook (*Managing Director, BT Enterprises*); J. A. C. King (*Marketing and Corporate Strategy*); *Part-time Directors,* G. D. W. Odgers; J. F. Goble; Sir George Macfarlane, C.B.
Secretary to the Board, M. Argent.

BRITISH TOURIST AUTHORITY
Queen's House, 64 St. James's Street, S.W.1
[01-629 9191]

Under the Development of Tourism Act, 1969, four co-equal statutory Tourist Boards were established: the British Tourist Authority, the English Tourist Board, the Scottish Tourist Board and the Wales Tourist Board. Each is financed mainly by direct grant-in-aid from Government and is an independent statutory body. The British Tourist Authority has specific responsibility for promoting tourism to Great Britain from overseas. It also has a general responsibility for tourism within Great Britain as a whole.
Chairman, D. R. Y. Bluck, O.B.E. (*part-time*), £25,000.
Director General, L. J. Lickorish, C.B.E.

English Tourist Board
4, Grosvenor Gardens, S.W.1

Scottish Tourist Board
23, Ravelston Terrace, Edinburgh

Wales Tourist Board
3 Castle Street, Cardiff

BRITISH WATERWAYS BOARD
Melbury House, Melbury Terrace, NW1 6JX
[01–262 6711]

Chairman, Sir Leslie Young, C.B.E. (*part-time*).
Vice-Chairman, Dr. A. Robertson.
Members (all part-time), P. R. Lisle, O.B.E.; J. Weston;
　Rear Admiral D. A. Dunbar-Nasmith; M. Everard;
　H. G. C. Aldous.
Chief Executive, D. G. McCance.
Secretary and Deputy Chief Executive, T. T. Luckcuck.

BRITOIL p.l.c.
150 St. Vincent Street, Glasgow
[041–204 2525]

Chairman, Sir Philip Shelbourne.
Joint Managing Directors, I. Clark; M. Ford.
Executive Directors, J. Evans; M. Kelly; R. Speirs;
　Sir Archie Lamb, K.B.E.

CABINET OFFICE

The Cabinet Office comprises the Secretariat, who
support Ministers collectively in the conduct of
Cabinet business; the Management and Personnel
Office (M.P.O.) which is responsible for the management and organization of the Civil Service and
recruitment into it, training, efficiency, personnel
management and senior appointments; the Central
Statistical Office; and the Historical Section. Other
functions are from time to time laid on the Office,
some ephemerally and some permanently. Non-
departmental Ministers may be attached to the Office.
The functions of the Cabinet Office (M.P.O.) are in
support of the Prime Minister in her capacity as
Minister for the Civil Service, with responsibility for
day-to-day supervision delegated to the Minister of
State, Privy Council Office.
The Prime Minister.
Principal Private Secretary to the Prime Minister,
　F. E. R. Butler.
Private Secretaries to the Prime Minister, C. Powell
　(*Overseas Affairs*); A. Turnbull (*Economic Affairs*);
　T. J. Flesher (*Parliamentary Affairs*); D. M. Barclay
　(*Home Affairs*).
Personal Assistant to the Prime Minister, Mrs. C. M.
　Ryder.
Secretary for Appointments, J. R. Catford.
Political Secretary, S. Sherbourne.
Economic Adviser, Sir Alan Walters.
Foreign Affairs Adviser, Sir Percy Cradock, G.C.M.G.
Adviser on Efficiency, Sir Robin Ibbs.
Policy Unit, J. Redwood; Hon. C. Monckton; N. C.
　Owen; P. Shipley; D. Pascall; R. Young; D. Willets.
Chief Press Secretary, B. Ingham.
Deputy Chief Press Secretary, Miss J. Caines.
Assistant Private Secretary to Prime Minister, Miss J.
　Drever.
Parliamentary Private Secretary, The Rt. Hon. M.
　Alison, M.P.
*Secretary to the Cabinet and Head of Home Civil Ser-
　vice*, Sir Robert Armstrong, G.C.B., C.V.O.　£45,000

SECRETARIAT
70 Whitehall, SW1A 2AS
[01–233 3000]

Second Permanent Secretary, The Rt. Hon. Sir
　Antony Duff, G.C.M.G., C.V.O., D.S.O., D.S.C. . £37,500
Deputy Secretaries, B. G. Cartledge, C.M.G.; P. L.
　Gregson, C.B.; Dr. R. B. Nicholson (*Chief Scientific
　Adviser*); D. F. Williamson, C.B. £32,500
Under Secretaries, C. J. S. Brearley; M. S. Buckley;
　G. Stapleton; D. E. J. Jago; M. R. Morland
　　　　　　　　　　　　　　　　　　　　£26,750
Assistant Secretaries, Brig. J. A. J. Budd; H. Burke;
　D. H. Colvin; R. G. Courtney; D. R. C. Durie; J. R.
　Fonblanque; Brig. A. B. D. Gurdon, C.B.E.; J. R.
　James; Miss S. J. Lambert; J. M. Mackintosh,
　C.M.G.; D. K. Reynolds; M. Townley; R. Watson
　　　　　　　　　　　　　　　£19,243 to £23,159
Senior Principals, J. L. Wright, O.B.E.; Dr. A. V.
　Harrison . . . . £16,343 to £20,794

MANAGEMENT AND PERSONNEL OFFICE
Great George Street, SW1P 3AL
[01–233 3000]
Second Permanent Secretary, Miss A. E. Mueller, C.B.
　　　　　　　　　　　　　　　　　　　　£37,500
*Director, Top Management Programme (Deputy Sec-
　retary*), J. F. Mayne £32,500
Security Adviser, Air Vice Marshal B. G. Lock, C.B.,
　C.B.E., A.F.C.

**Senior and Public Appointment, Conduct,
Machinery of Government**

*Director, Public Appointments Unit (Under Secre-
　tary*), C. V. Peterson, C.V.O. £26,750
Assistant Secretaries, Mrs. E. C. Flanagan; G. T.
　Morgan; A. Phillips . . . . £19,243 to £23,159

Security Division

Assistant Secretary, S. R. Davie

MPO/Treasury Financial Management Unit

Under Secretary, A. W. Russell £26,750
Assistant Secretary, D. Northrop . £19,243 to £23,159
Senior Principal, D. Jamieson . . . £16,343 to £20,794

Management and Efficiency

Under Secretary, I. B. Beesley £26,750
Assistant Secretaries, R. B. Brown; Miss K. Jenkins
　　　　　　　　　　　　　　　£19,243 to £23,159
Senior Principal, E. Brown . . . . . . £16,343 to £20,794

Personnel Management

Under Secretary, J. A. Chilcot £26,750
Assistant Secretaries, D. P. Laughrin; J. R. Merchant;
　C. D. Stevens . . . . £19,243 to £23,159

Training and Civil Service College

Deputy Secretary, D. J. Trevelyan, C.B.
*Under Secretary, Training and Principal, Civil Serv-
　ice College*, N. E. A. Moore £26,750
Head of Training Division (Assistant Secretary), P. R.
　Coster . . . . £19,243 to £23,159
College Secretary (Assistant Secretary), J. Buckley
　　　　　　　　　　　　　　　£19,243 to £23,159
Directors (Assistant Secretaries), P. Hearson; E. J.
　Henstridge; R. J. Eason; G. H. Mungeam; Dr. P.
　Lund . . . . £19,243 to £23,159

Civil Service Commission
Alencon Link, Basingstoke, Hants. RG21 1JB
[0256 29222]

First Commissioner (Deputy Secretary), D. J. Trevelyan, C.B. £32,500
Commissioners (Under Secretaries), E. J. Morgan (*Director, Civil Service Selection Board*), N. B. J. Gurney £26,750
Commissioners (part-time), N. Johnson; Dr. J. S. MacFarlane.
Assistant Secretary, A. W. Duncan

£19,243 to £23,159
Senior Principals, G. J. Court; J. D. Diston; Dr. D. B. Macdonald; B. G. Sharp .... £16,343 to £20,794

Civil Service Selection Board

Director (Under Secretary), E. J. Morgan £26,750
Assistant Secretaries, G. H. Wollen; M. H. G. Rogers
£19,243 to £23,159
Chief Psychologist (Senior Principal Psychologist), D. J. McLeod.

Medical Advisory Service
Tilbury House, Petty France, SW1H 9EU
[01-213 3000]

Medical Adviser, Dr. A. M. Semmence.
Principal Medical Officers, Dr. P. J. Constable; Dr. M. L. E. Espir.

CENTRAL STATISTICAL OFFICE
Great George Street, SW1P 3AQ
[01-233 3000]

Director and Head of the Government Statistical Service, Sir John Boreham, K.C.B. £37,500
Private Secretary, Mrs. C. D. Bates.
Under Secretaries, D. W. Flaxen; K. G. Forecast; J. D. Wells £26,750
Assistant Secretaries, P. Altobell; Miss S. P. Carter; A. A. Croxford; T. J. Griffin; P. B. Kenny; K. Mansell; D. Ramprakash; R. G. Ward; Dr. J. H. Ludley.

HISTORICAL SECTION
Hepburn House, Marsham Street, SW1P 4HW
[01-211 6605]

Departmental Records Adviser (Senior Principal), Mrs. H. E. Forbes.

ESTABLISHMENT OFFICER'S GROUP

Principal Establishment and Finance Officer, Under Secretary, J. W. Stevens .... £19,243 to £23,159

Personnel Services

Senior Principal, A. L. Thomas .. £16,343 to £20,794

Office Services and Organization

Senior Principal, J. W. Bridle .... £16,343 to £20,794

Finance

Senior Finance Officer (Senior Principal), C. J. Parry .... £12,399 to £16,656

Information Services

Chief Press Officer (Senior Principal), J. Stubbs
£12,399 to £16,656

Internal Audit

Principal, A. Holman.

CHARITY COMMISSION
Ryder Street, St. James's, SW1Y 6AH
[01-214 6000]

Northern Office:
Graeme House, Derby Square, Liverpool L2 7SB
[051-227 3191]

Central Register of Charities,
St. Alban's House, Haymarket, SW1Y 4QX
[01-214 6000]

The Charity Commission was constituted under Act of Parliament in 1853 and reconstituted under the Charities Act, 1960, with the general function of promoting the effective use of charitable monies and a duty to keep a register of charities in England and Wales. The Official Custodian for Charities holds investments for charities and remits the income, free of income tax, to trustees.

Chief Commissioner, D. A. Peach £26,826
Commissioners, C. A. H. Parsons; F. W. Trinder.
Deputy Commissioners, R. W. Groves; J. Farquharson; M. A. Rao; J. F. Claricoat; Mrs. J. F. R. Quint .... £20,051 to £23,159
Assist. Commissioners, Mrs. F. E. Middleton; G. S. Goodchild; H. K. Udvadia; Mrs. H. M. Phillips; Miss D. F. Taylor; S. K. Sen; J. A. Dutton; K. M. Dibble; P. P. White; N. M. Mackenzie; Mrs. L. Gabriel; Mrs. V. D. Roscoe; S. Slack ... £14,401 to
£19,317
Secretary and Asst. Commissioner, D. Forrest
£19,243 to £23,159
Principals, P. C. A. Pyman (*Asst. Commissioner*); D. McNaught (*Asst. Commissioner*); Miss S. M. St. C. Smith (*Asst. Commissioner*); J. H. Vining
£12,399 to £16,656
Official Custodian for Charities, S. H. Way
£16,343 to £20,794
Deputy Official Custodian, R. J. Crick
£12,399 to £16,656
Establishment Officer, J. M. Samuels
£12,399 to £16,656
Deputy Establishment Officer, Mrs. D. F. M. Blacksell
£10,079 to £12,518
Senior Executive Officers, R. E. Hatton; R. E. Edwards; B. W. Pyle; B. J. Reeve; G. B. Ward; M. C. T. Seymour; Miss S. A. Davies; M. J. McManus; Mrs. B. Nixon; E. K. W. Norbury; J. M. Mooney; Ms. K. Byra; Mrs. S. E. Gillingham; Mrs. M. E. Whittaker; A. M. Billam .... £10,079 to £12,518

CHURCH COMMISSIONERS
1 Millbank, SW1P 3JZ
[01-222 7010]

The Church Commissioners were established on April 1, 1948, by the amalgamation of *Queen Anne's Bounty* (established 1704) and the *Ecclesiastical Commissioners* (established 1836).

The Commissioners' main task is to improve the stipends and housing of the Church of England clergy and to provide them and their widows with adequate pensions and assistance with housing in retirement. They also carry out administrative duties in connection with pastoral reorganization and redundant churches, and have been designated by the General Synod as the Central Stipends Authority of the Church of England.

The Commissioners' income for the year ended Dec. 31, 1983, was derived from the following sources:—

	£'s million
Stock exchange investments	32·3
Land and property	37·9
Mortgages, loans, etc.	5·8
Trust income, and diocesan/parish contributions for stipends	38·4
	£114·4

This income was applied as follows:—	
Clergy stipends	68·8
Clergy and widows' pensions	24·7
Clergy houses	8·3
Episcopal administration and payments to Chapters	3·9
Church buildings	1·5
Administrative expenses of the Commissioners	6·1
Administrative expenses of other bodies	0·8
	£114·1
Plus added to reserves	0·3
	£114·4

Constitution

The 2 Archbishops, the 41 diocesan Bishops, 5 deans or provosts, 10 other clergy and 10 laymen appointed by the General Synod; 4 laymen nominated by the Queen; 4 persons nominated by the Archbishop of Canterbury; The Lord Chancellor; The Lord President of the Council; the First Lord of the Treasury; The Chancellor of the Exchequer; The Secretary of State for the Home Dept; The Speaker of the House of Commons; The Lord Chief Justice; The Master of the Rolls; The Attorney-General; The Solicitor-General; The Lord Mayor and two Aldermen of the City of London; The Lord Mayor of York and one representative from each of the Universities of Oxford and Cambridge.

Church Estates Commissioners

First, Sir Douglas Lovelock, K.C.B.
Second, Sir William van Straubenzee, M.B.E., M.P.
Third, Mrs. B. E. Haworth.

Officers

Secretary, The Hon. Kenneth Lamb.
Assets Secretary, J. E. Shelley.
General Purposes Secretary, P. Locke.
Assistant Secretaries, D. I. Archer (*Chief Accountant*); J. R. Beard (*Estates*); J. M. Davies (*Redundant Churches*); D. J. Day (*Pastoral*); M. D. Elengorn (*Stipends*); J. W. D. McIntyre (*Houses*); W. J. Pennel (*Bishoprics*); A. P. Thomas (*Investments*).
Deputy Accountant and Trust Officer, G. C. Baines.
Deputy Estates Secretary, P. H. P. Shaw, M.V.O.
Establishment Officer, C. P. Canton.
Computer Manager, J. W. Ferguson.
Press & Information Officer, J. C. Reddington.
Principals, D. N. Goodwin; J. Cheesman; Mrs. B. A. Bartlett; W. R. Herbert; M. J. Symon; R. M. Hutchings; E. G. Peacock; Miss A. M. Mackie.
Senior Executive Officers, A. W. Atkins; R. J. Bishop; C. R. Bullen; P. D. Chadwick; Mrs. D. Christmas; G. Duckworth; J. A. W. Elloy; M. G. S. Farrell; K. Higgins; D. E. Jarrett; D. W. H. Lewis; D. J. B. Long; R. V. Leavey; G. Pincott; K. A. Reading; P. S. D. Reeve; J. M. Shirley; N. M. Waring; G. Wills.

Legal Department

Official Solicitor, J. W. Cook, C.B.E.
Deputy Solicitor, A. J. L. Campbell.

Assistant Solicitor, J. P. Guy.
Senior Legal Assistants, Miss J. M. Bland; J. D. Carter; Rev. B. G. Hall; Miss S. M. S. Jones; R. D. C. Murray; Mrs. S. E. Prosser; Miss I. E. Slaughter.

Main Agents

Messrs. Cluttons, 5 Great College Street, Westminster, S.W.1; Messrs. Smiths Gore, The King's Lodgings, Minster Precincts, Peterborough; Messrs. Chestertons, 40 Connaught Street, W.2. and 26 Clifton Road, W.9.

CIVIL AVIATION AUTHORITY
C.A.A. House, 45–59 Kingsway, WC2B 6TE
[01–379 7311]

Chairman, J. Dent, C.B.E. (*part-time*) £35,000
Managing Director, J. L. Curle.
Secretary, G. M. E. White.

COMMONWEALTH DEVELOPMENT CORPORATION
33 Hill Street, W1A 3AR
[01–629 8484]

The Corporation's area of operations covers Commonwealth countries which have achieved independence since 1948, the remaining territories dependent upon Britain and, with Ministerial approval, any other developing country. The Corporation is authorized to borrow up to £750,000,000.
Chairman (*part-time*), The Lord Kindersley.
Deputy Chairman (*part-time*), Sir Colin Campbell, Bt., M.C.
Members (*part-time*), H.R.H. The Prince of Wales; J. M. Clay; Hon. J. D. Eccles; The Lord Lovell-Davis; V. Robertson, O.B.E.; D. Warburton.
General Manager, Sir Peter Meinertzhagen, C.M.G.

COMMONWEALTH OFFICE
See Foreign and Commonwealth Office

COMMONWEALTH SECRETARIAT
Marlborough House,
Pall Mall, SW1Y 5HX
[01–839 3411]

Secretary-General, His Excellency Shridath S. Ramphal, Kt., C.M.G., Q.C.
(*See also* p. 694)

COUNTRYSIDE COMMISSION
John Dower House, Crescent Place,
Cheltenham, Glos. GL50 3RA
[0242 521381]

The Countryside Commission is an independent agency set up in 1968 to promote the conservation and enhancement of landscape beauty in England and Wales, to encourage the provision and improvement of facilities in the countryside for enjoyment, including the need to secure access for open air recreation. Since April 1982 the Commission has been funded by annual grant from the Department of the Environment. Its executive powers and responsibilities are defined under the Countryside Act, 1949, the Local Government Act, 1974 and the Wildlife & Countryside Act, 1981. Members of the Commission are appointed by the Secretary of State for the Environment and the Secretary of State for Wales acting jointly.
Chairman, Sir Derek Barber £14,015
Deputy Chairman, (vacant).
Director, A. A. C. Phillips £28,583

Assistant Directors, D. E. Coleman (*acting*) (*Regions*);
P. L. Leonard (*Policy*) .... £19,243 to £23,159
National Heritage Adviser, Mrs. M. D. Laverack
£15,605 to £20,794
Secretary, G. H. Taylor .... £12,399 to £16,656
Head of Conservation Branch, M. E. Taylor
£12,399 to £16,656
Head of Recreation & Access Branch, M. J. Kirby
£12,399 to £16,656
Head of Communications Branch, M. H. Glen
£12,399 to £16,656
Regional Officers, C. G. Coggins (*Newcastle*); B.
Walbank (*Cambridge*); Dr. S. A. Bucknall (*Leeds*);
R. J. Lloyd (*Bristol*); R. T. Thomas (*Manchester*); I.
P. Mitchell (*acting*) (*London*); F. S. Walmsley
(*Birmingham*) .. *various scales between* £12,399 to
£16,656

Office for Wales
8 Broad Street, Newtown, Powys
[0686 26799]

Chairman, R. E. M. Rees £7,913
Principal Officer, A. M. H. Fitton £12,399 to £16,656

COUNTRYSIDE COMMISSION FOR SCOTLAND
Battleby, Redgorton, Perth
[0738 27921]

Established under the Countryside (Scotland) Act,
1967, with functions for the provision, development
and improvement of facilities for the enjoyment of
the Scottish countryside, and for the conservation
and enhancement of the natural beauty and amenity
thereof.
Chairman, D. W. Nickson, C.B.E. (*part-time*).
Commissioners, J. M. S. Arnott; Mrs. F. Ballantyne;
Dr. D. J. Bennet; J. R. Carr (*Vice-Chairman*); I. R.
Thomson; A. W. Driver; Prof. C. H. Gimingham;
G. R. Marwick; D. Ross; R. R. Steedman; G. G.
Stewart.
Director, J. Foster.
Deputy Director, T. Huxley.
Secretary, W. B. Prior.
Asst. Directors. D. Aldridge (*Conservation Educa-
tion*); J. M. Fladmark (*Research and Development*);
J. R. Turner (*Planning*).

COVENT GARDEN MARKET AUTHORITY
Market Towers, New Covent Garden Market,
1 Nine Elms Lane, SW8 5NX
[01–720 2211]

The Covent Garden Market Authority is constituted under the Covent Garden Market Acts, 1961 to
1977, the members being appointed by the Minister of
Agriculture, Fisheries and Food. The Authority
owns a 60-acre site comprising a fruit and vegetable
market, a flower market and an administration
building. The Authority is empowered to borrow
capital up to £45,000,000.
Chairman, P. Firmston-Williams, O.B.E. (*part-time*)
£17,575
Members (*part-time*), Sir Adrian Cadbury; P. J. Hunt;
E. I. Kingston; R. Pierson; J. A. Harvey ... £3,400
General Manager, C. M. G. Allen, C.B.E.
Secretary, P. M. Liggins.

CRIMINAL INJURIES COMPENSATION BOARD
10–12 Russell Square, WC1B 5EN
[01–636 2812 and 01–636 4201]

The Board was constituted in 1964 to administer
the Government scheme for *ex gratia* payments of
compensation to victims of crimes of violence.

Chairman, M. Ogden, Q.C.
Members, I. J. Black, Q.C.; D. Calcutt, Q.C.; H. Carlisle,
Q.C.; W. Chedlow, Q.C.; Miss B. Cooper, Q.C.; Sir
Alun Davies, Q.C.; Sir Richard Denby; C. Fawcett,
Q.C.; J. Law, Q.C.; E. Lewis, Q.C.; Sir Denis Marshall;
M. Morland, Q.C.; H. Morton, Q.C.; Sir John Palmer;
I. M. S. Park, C.B.E.; Miss S. Ritchie, Q.C.; L. Stuart
Shields, Q.C.; R. I. Sutherland, Q.C.; C. H. Whitby,
Q.C.
Secretary and Solicitor, R. H. Johnstone.
Chief Executive, T. F. Corbett.

CROWN AGENTS FOR OVERSEA GOVERNMENTS AND ADMINISTRATIONS
4 Millbank, S.W.1
[01–222 7730]

The Crown Agents act as financial, commercial
and professional agents for almost 100 governments
and over 300 public authorities and international
bodies. Their services are available to any government and to any organization in the public sector.
They are a public service and do not act for individuals
or for commercial concerns in the private sector.
The Crown Agents also act for the United Nations
and as authorised agents for projects financed by the
International Bank for Reconstruction and Development (The World Bank), the International Development Association and the Asian Development
Bank.
Chairman, P. A. Graham, O.B.E.

CROWN ESTATE COMMISSIONERS
13/15 Carlton House Terrace, SW1Y 5AH
[01–214 6000]
78 Pall Mall, SW1Y 5ES

THE CROWN ESTATE (formerly The Crown
Lands).—The Land Revenues of the Crown in
England and Wales have been collected on the public
account since 1760, when George III surrendered
them and received a fixed annual payment or *Civil
List*. At the time of the surrender the gross revenues
amounted to about £89,000 and the net return to
about £11,000.

In the year ended March 31, 1984, the total Receipts
by the Commissioners were £39,112,000. The Expenditure was £17,897,000. The sum of £19,000,000 was
paid to the Exchequer in 1983–84 as *Surplus Revenue*,
being a net sum from which no deductions have been
made for administration.
The Land Revenues in *Ireland* have been carried
to the Consolidated Fund since 1820; from April 1,
1923, as regards Southern Ireland, they have been
collected and administered by the Irish Free State
(Republic of Ireland).
The Land Revenues in *Scotland* were transferred
to the Commissioners in 1833.
First Commissioner and Chairman (*part-time*), The
Earl of Crawford and Balcarres.
Second Commissioner (*and Secretary*), Dr. K. Dexter,
C.B. £34,250
Commissioners (*part-time*), R. B. Caws, C.B.E.; P.
Sober; O. H. Colburn; G. D. Lillingston; Capt. I. M.
Tennant; J. N. C. James.
Deputy Commissioners, D. J. Chapman; R. G. L.
Osborne .... £19,243 to £23,159
Crown Estate Surveyor, C. F. Hynes
£18,374 to £20,794
Crown Estate Receiver for Scotland, D. B. Cooke
£10,079 to £12,518
Principals, A. Barker; J. Stumbke £12,399 to £16,656
*Organization and Establishments Officer and Clerk to
the Board*, J. L. Isom .... £12,399 to £16,656

Accountant and Receiver-General, R. G. Bell
$£12,399$ to $£16,656$
Senior Executive Officers, J. S. Ellingford; M. J.
Gravestock; R. Parnell; A. H. Woodhouse; M. W.
Dillon; I. M. L. Gorwyn .... $£10,079$ to $£12,518$
Legal Adviser and Assistant Solicitor, M. A. Jaffe
$£20,051$ to $£23,159$
Senior Legal Assistants, M. R. Brocklehurst; I. R.
Colquhoun; M. A. J. Cordingley; J. B. Postgate; H.
Turnsek; A. M. Spratt .... $£14,401$ to $£19,317$
Solicitor, Scotland, D. F. Stewart.

Windsor Estate

Surveyor and Deputy Ranger, A. R. Wiseman, M.V.O.

BOARD OF CUSTOMS AND EXCISE
King's Beam House, Mark Lane, EC3R 7HE
[01–626 1515]

Commissioners of Customs were first appointed in
1671 and housed by the King in London, the present
"Long Room" in the Custom House, Lower Thames
Street, E.C.3, replaced that built by Charles II and
was rebuilt after destruction by fire in 1718 and 1814.
The Excise Department was formerly under the
Inland Revenue Department and was amalgamated
with the Customs Department on April 1, 1909.

The Board

Chairman, A. M. Fraser, C.B., T.D. .... $£44,033$
Private Sec., J. R. Lester.
Deputy Chairmen, B. H. Knox; L. D. Hawken, C.B.
$£35,278$
Commissioners, D. L. Bryars; C. Freedman, C.B.; N.
E. Godfrey; L. J. Harris; P. Jefferson Smith; Mrs.
V. P. M. Strachan; R. Weston .... $£28,583$

Headquarters Office

Assistant Secretaries, J. C. Barnes; R. S. Bielby; O. A.
Brown, M.M., B.E.M.; B. J. Cockerell; N. J. Collings;
C. C. Finlinson; R. D. Goddard; P. Hammond; P.
Hogg; D. J. Howard; P. S. Jenkins; T. M. Jenkins;
J. Kelly; P. B. Kent; R. N. Lewis; V. Matthews; W.
F. McGuigan; R. A. Mechem; A. C. Morrow; P.
Nash; C. J. Packman; B. E. M. Prophet, T.D.; R. H.
Stiff; G. F. Taylor; J. W. Tracey; J. Vaughan; D.
A. Walton; P. J. Webb; W. D. Whitmore; P. G.
Wilmott .... $£19,243$ to $£23,159$

Chief Statistician, B. F. Middleton
$£19,243$ to $£23,159$
Head of Press and Information Division, J. E. L. Dahn
$£12,399$ to $£16,656$

V.A.T. Central Unit

Controller, R. A. Huband .... $£19,243$ to $£23,159$
Deputy Controller, M. J. Wardle .. $£16,343$ to $£20,794$

Solicitor's Office

Solicitor, A. J. Jeddere-Fisher .... $£35,278$
Principal Assistant Solicitors, W. S. Hill; P. V. H.
Smith .... $£28,583$
Assistant Solicitors, P. Breur; G. F. Butt; M. A.
Cooper; P. J. C. Ellis; I. W. Gardner; D. E. T. S.
Keefe; R. G. C. King; D. V. Levette-Yeats; G. W.
M. McFarlane; M. Michael; D. E. J. Nissen; J.
Sellers; Miss E. S. Thomas .... $£20,051$ to $£23,159$

Accountant and Comptroller-General's Office

Accountant and Comptroller-General, B. Halliwell
$£26,236$
Deputy Accountant-General, C. A. Bray
$£19,243$ to $£23,159$

Statistical Office

Controller, N. Harvey .... $£19,243$ to $£23,159$

Investigation Division
Chief Investigation Officer, P. D. Cutting
$£19,243$ to $£23,159$

Collectors of Customs and Excise
England and Wales

Birmingham: H. L. Hellier.
Bristol: R. E. Grimstead.
Dover: A. Collie.
East Anglia: W. K. Herbert.
East Midlands: E. N. Taylor.
Leeds: I. MacLeod.
Liverpool: W. H. Hargreaves.
London Airports: R. Craggs.
London City and South: W. Crawford.
London Port: D. J. Fellingham.
London North and West: A. G. Smith.
Manchester: P. J. Little.
Northampton: G. D. Town.
Northern England: D. Smith.
Reading: J. H. Tee.
Southampton: S. J. C. Jones.
South Wales and the Borders: A. Ferguson.
South West England: G. H. Clayton.

Scotland

Aberdeen: D. F. W. Fryett.
Edinburgh: T. Riccalton.
Glasgow & Clyde: D. R. Inglis.

Northern Ireland

Belfast: B. E. Barclay.
Salaries:
All $£19,243$ to $£23,159$.

MINISTRY OF DEFENCE
See Armed Forces Section

DESIGN COUNCIL
28 Haymarket, S.W.1

The Design Council's aim is to improve the design
of British products by: advising companies on up-to-
date practice in engineering and industrial design;
selecting well designed British goods for The Design
Centre and for the annual Design Council Awards;
publishing information to help manufacturers, designers, and others professionally involved in design;
and promoting improvements in design education at
all levels. The Design Centres in London and Glasgow
mount exhibitions showing new developments in
design and include shops selling selected British
products. There is a smaller Design Centre in Cardiff
and offices in Belfast and Wolverhampton. Publications include the monthly *Design* and *Engineering*
magazines, the termly *Designing* magazine for
schools, as well as books and other periodicals. There
is a comprehensive design bookshop in the London
Design Centre. The Design Council is funded partly
by a Government grant-in-aid and partly by earned
revenues.
Chairman, Sir William Barlow.
Director, K. Grant.

DEVELOPMENT COMMISSION
11 Cowley Street, SW1P 3NA
[01–222 9134]

The Development Commission, England's rural
development agency, is a statutory body funded by
Government grant-in-aid which undertakes economic and social problems in rural areas and advises
the Government on related rural matters in England.
It concentrates its resources in priority areas—Rural
Development Areas—but some assistance, particularly through its main agency, the Council for Small

Industries in Rural Areas, is available both within and outside the RDAs.

Chairman, N. Vinson, M.V.O.

Other Commissioners, Mrs. P. Batty Shaw, C.B.E.; Prof. M. D. I. Chisholm; D. J. C. Davenport; W. E. G. Humphrey, O.B.E., D.F.C.; The Lord Montagu of Beaulieu; C. V. Wilkinson; A. Leavett.

Chief Executive, J. V. Williams ... £20,493 to £24,409

THE DUCHY OF CORNWALL
10 Buckingham Gate, SW1E 6LA
[Telephone: 01–834 .7346]

The Duchy of Cornwall was instituted by Edward III in 1337 for the support of his eldest son, Edward, the Black Prince, and since 1503 the eldest surviving son of the Sovereign has, as heir apparent, succeeded to the Dukedom by inheritance. As the oldest of the English Duchies, it has enjoyed a long association with the Crown. Before elevation to a dukedom, it was an earldom from 1227, when Richard, King of the Romans and younger brother of Henry III, was created Earl of Cornwall.

The Prince's Council

H.R.H. The Prince of Wales, K.G., K.T., G.C.B.; The Lord Franks, O.M., P.C., G.C.M.G., K.C.B., C.B.E., F.B.A. (*Lord Warden of the Stannaries*); Hon. Sir John Baring, C.V.O. (*Receiver General*); P. T. Miles; R. A. Morritt, Q.C. (*Attorney-General to the Prince of Wales*); F. J. Williams; J. E. Pugsley; J. W. Y. Higgs (*Secretary and Keeper of the Records*).

Other Officers of the Duchy of Cornwall

Auditors, J. H. Bowman; P. L. Ainger; H. Hughes.
Solicitor, M. H. Boyd-Carpenter.
Administrator, K. J. S. Knott.
Deputy Receiver, J. H. Roberts.
Sheriff (1984–85), R. Lyle.

THE DUCHY OF LANCASTER
Lancaster Place, Strand, WC2E 7ED
[01–836 8277]

The estates and jurisdiction known as the Duchy and County Palatine of Lancaster have been attached to the Crown since 1399, when John of Gaunt's son came to the throne as Henry IV. As the Lancaster inheritance it goes back to 1265. Edward III erected Lancashire into a County Palatine in 1351.

Chancellor of the Duchy of Lancaster, THE EARL OF GOWRIE, P.C. (*Minister for the Arts*).

Private Secretary, A. K. Galloway.

Attorney-General and Attorney and Serjeant within the County Palatine of Lancaster, J. L. Knox, Q.C.

Receiver-General, P. T. Miles.

Vice-Chancellor, His Hon. A. J. Blackett-Ord.

Clerk of the Council and Keeper of Records, M. K. Ridley.

Solicitor, W. O. Farrer.

Asst. Solicitor, I. J. Dicker.

Chief Clerk, P. C. Clarke, C.V.O.

ECONOMIC AND SOCIAL RESEARCH COUNCIL

1 Temple Avenue, EC4Y 0BD
[01–353 5252]

The E.S.R.C. was set up by Royal Charter in 1965 for the promotion of social science research. The Council carries out its role by awarding research grants, by initiating research and research contracts, by awarding postgraduate studentships and bursaries, and through its research units. In addition the Council provides advice and disseminates knowl-edge on the social sciences. A list of publications is available from the E.S.R.C. Information Office.

Chairman, Prof. Sir Douglas Hague, C.B.E.

Secretary, Dr. C. S. Smith.

DEPARTMENT OF EDUCATION AND SCIENCE
Elizabeth House, York Road, SE1 7PH
[01–928 9222]

The Government Department of Education was, until the establishment of a separate office, a Committee of the Privy Council appointed in 1839 to supervise the distribution of certain grants which had been made by Parliament since 1834. The Act of 1899 established the Board of Education, with a President and Parliamentary Secretary, and created a Consultative Committee. The Education Act of 1944 established the Ministry of Education. In April 1964 the office of the Minister of Science was combined with the Ministry to form the Department of Education and Science. The cost of administration for the financial year 1984–85 was estimated at £48,382,000.

Salary List

Secretary of State	£40,930
Parliamentary Under Secretaries	£26,780
Permanent Secretary (Grade 1)	£44,033
Deputy Secretaries (Grade 2)	£35,278
Under Secretaries (Grade 3)	£28,583
Chief Inspectors (Grade 4)	£25,176

Assistant Secretaries
Chief Information Officer (A)
Senior Economic Adviser
Chief Statisticians
Professional and Technical Directing Grade B } (Grade 5) £19,243 to £23,159
Staff Inspectors
Divisional Inspectors
Chief Architect

Senior Principals
Professional and Technological } (Grade 6) £15,605 to £20,794
Superintendents
Senior Principal Scientific Officers

H.M. Inspectors (Grade 6)	£15,605 to £20,801
Principals	£12,399 to £16,656
Economic Advisers	£12,399 to £16,656
Principal Catering Officer	£12,399 to £16,656
Statisticians	£12,399 to £16,656
Principal Research Officers	£12,399 to £16,656
Principal Scientific Officers	£11,343 to £14,931
Senior Executive Officers	£10,079 to £12,518
Senior Librarian	£10,079 to £12,518
Principal Professional and Technological Officers	£10,079 to £12,163

Secretary of State for Education and Science, THE RT. HON. SIR KEITH JOSEPH, BT., M.P.

Private Sec., Miss C. E. Hodkinson.

Parliamentary Private Secretary, P. Lloyd, M.P.

Parliamentary Under Secretaries of State, R. Dunn, M.P.; Hon. P. Brooke, M.P.

Permanent Secretary, D. J. S. Hancock.

Deputy Secretaries, R. H. Bird, C.B.; W. O. Ulrich; P. H. Halsey, M.V.O.

Under Secretaries, A. E. D. Chamier (*Director of Establishments*); C. A. Clark; N. W. Stuart (*Accountant General*); J. I. Langtry; D. G. Libby; B. M. Norbury; N. Summers; D. W. Tanner; J. H. Thompson; N. B. W. Thompson; W. B. Wakefield (*Director of Statistics*); C. R. Walker.

Architects, Building and Schools II Branch

Assistant Secretaries, B. L. Baish; A. S. Gann; G. J. Mungeam; B. C. Peatey.

Principals, Miss N. Bartman; Miss A. F. Brown; W. M. Caldow; Miss M. d' Armenia; S. F. Denning; D. G. Halladay; R. D. Hull; P. S. Lewis; P. J. Middleton; J. K. Santell; G. R. E. Stewart; M. J. P. Vann; J. N. Walmsley.

Chief Architect, J. D. Kay.

Superintending Architects, R. Clynes; D. H. Griffin; M. S. Hacker; G. E. Hughes; R. L. Thompson.

Superintending Engineer (Mechanical and Electrical), L. E. J. Piper.

Superintending Quantity Surveyor, B. G. Whitehouse.

Principal Architects, R. W. U. Alcock; J. W. Boon; A. J. Branton; A. M. Cutler; Miss C. G. Edwards; Miss R. Hall; Miss E. J. Lloyd-Jones; P. Marriott; D. S. Nightingale; G. J. Parker; T. W. Prosser; O. M. Stepan; D. F. Wicks; J. J. Wilson.

Principal Quantity Surveyors, G. C. Battersby; T. W. A. Carden; W. P. Horsnell; D. W. Revell; J. L. S. Sinclair; D. E. Strachan.

Architects, Grade I, A. J. Benson-Wilson; E. C. Bissell; J. R. C. Brooke; S. Cassels; L. S. Curtis; P. Lenssen; Miss K. M. S. Livingston; Miss B. M. T. Sanders; A. C. Thompson.

Quantity Surveyor, Grade I, A. A. Jones.

Engineer (Mechanical and Electrical), Grade I, M. J. Patel.

Establishments and Organization Branch

Assistant Secretaries, Mrs. H. M. Williams; Miss D. C. Fordham.

Senior Principals, G. J. Aylett; E. B. Granshaw; R. E. Judd.

Principals, J. A. C. Cooke; K. W. Cawdron; G. H. N. Evans; Mrs. S. G. Evans; J. Melbourne.

Senior Executive Officers, C. H. Boxall; Miss P. I. Cartwright; D. Fielding; A. J. Hall; L. A. Hartigan; G. A. Holley; A. A. J. Howling; S. N. Jardine; K. M. Jones; R. C. Knight; M. L. Lyons; Mrs. N. A. T. Malt; Miss P. E. V. McCarthy; Mrs. J. D. Nisbet; Miss M. P. Osborne; A. G. Short; B. C. Willett; Miss J. D. Worsfold.

Library

Librarian, D. N. Allum.

Finance Branch

Assistant Secretaries, P. A. Shaw; Miss J. A. Gilbey *(Deputy Accountant General).*

Senior Principal, W. Gamble.

Principals, E. A. Alcock; P. J. Edwards; W. A. Irvine; D. J. Jones; K. Robinson; A. J. Stewart; C. E. Treen; A. J. Wye.

Senior Executive Officers, M. J. Bidgood; A. L. Haines; D. J. Noble; C. Walker; J. J. Watson.

Further and Higher Education Branch 1

Assistant Secretaries, D. M. Forrester; C. H. Saville; M. J. G. Smith.

Senior Principal, E. J. Herbert.

Principals, Miss B. S. Gilbert; Miss N. M. Hill; D. R. Pollard; Mrs. S. L. Scales; R. L. Smith; D. K. Timms; A. R. Williams.

Senior Executive Officers, Miss J. Y. Alexander; Miss L. M. Clarke; Miss S. A. Clarke; Mrs. S. Jetha; A. D. Petty; D. A. Robins.

Further and Higher Education Branch 2

Assistant Secretaries, J. C. Hedger; R. P. Ritzema; A. G. B. Woollard.

Principals, B. Bekhradnia; P. F. Curran; K. L. R. English; P. L. Jones; M. McBride; W. H. Miller.

Further and Higher Education Branch 3

Assistant Secretaries, G. Etheridge; D. W. R. Lewis; D. V. Stafford.

Principals, R. J. Yelland; A. Callaghan; P. W. Fulford-Jones; J. S. Harris; Mrs. K. H. Jameson; J. Nicholls.

Senior Executive Officers, W. A. Smyth; Miss G. G. Beauchamp; M. Bleach.

Legal Branch

Assistant Legal Adviser, D. H. Ingham.

Senior Legal Assistant, R. C. Perkins; D. J. Aries.

Senior Executive Officer, M. P. Black.

Pensions Branch
Mowden Hall, Staindrop Road,
Darlington, Co. Durham
[Darlington: 460155]

Assistant Secretary, F. M. Scott.

Principals, A. F. Cowan; P. Ramsden; K. M. Miles.

Senior Executive Officers, M. Barker; K. I. Dixon; R. S. Evans; J. Ford; O. N. Thomason.

Teachers 2, External Relations and General Branch

Assistant Secretaries, Mrs. C. M. Chattaway; R. W. Chattaway; R. D. Horne.

Senior Economic Adviser, B. D. Cullen.

Principals, D. H. Allen; D. H. Griffiths; Mrs. C. K. Saville; D. K. Timms; C. J. Dowe; Miss J. P. Partington.

Chief Information Officer, N. S. Gaffin.

Principal Scientific Officer, R. B. Ladley.

Economic Advisers, R. A. B. Parsons; K. J. Sear.

Staff Inspector, I. B. Butterworth.

Schools Branch I

Assistant Secretaries, M. M. Capey; E. R. Morgan; J. W. Whitaker.

Principals, H. H. Barrick; Miss A. M. J. Benham; Mrs. G. W. Dishart; Miss P. I. Laidlaw; M. Williams; A. N. Brown; Miss J. F. Cramphorn; J. S. Street; A. Wilshaw.

Senior Executive Officer, A. R. Faish.

Senior Catering Adviser, T. A. Ball.

Schools Branch III

Assistant Secretaries, Miss D. J. Dawson; A. J. C. Edwards; N. J. Sanders.

Staff Inspector, A. Clegg.

Principals, S. W. Cosser; Miss B. M. Ellington; B. D. Glickman; Miss R. M. King; R. J. Green; Mrs. P. Masters.

Senior Executive Officer, M. E. Mait.

Science Branch

Assistant Secretaries, R. P. Norton; I. R. M. Thom.

Principals, S. F. Denning; K. C. Humphrey; L. B. Webb; A. B. McClean; K. D. J. Root.

Statistics Branch

Assistant Secretary, L. R. F. Wiggins.

Chief Statisticians, J. A. McGinnety; J. W. Gardner.

Senior Principal, A. J. Harley.

Principals, K. Baxter; J. K. Bushnell; A. M. Cooper.

Statisticians, R. E. Dew; R. K. Jain; Mrs. S. Keith; T. C. Knight; B. O. Longman; Mrs. A. E. Mellor; C. J. Spiller; M. S. Stock.

Principal Research Officer, D. J. Hodges.

Senior Executive Officers, A. Allison; J. R. Bayles; Miss M. A. Bellamy; D. Craggs; Miss J. C. Esnouf; A. D. R. Gray; Mrs. J. Jarvis; B. Lillburn; M. Midwood; B. Robinson; E. S. Simpson; J. B. Taylor; P. J. Uren; R. Woodward.

Teachers 1 Branch (Salaries and Qualification)

Assistant Secretaries, Mrs. I. Wilde; D. A. Wilkinson.

Senior Principal, (vacant).

Principals, Mrs. H. K. Douglas; S.T. Crowne; R. S. Darvwalla; E. W. Grogan.

Senior Executive Officers, Miss B. P. Lincoln; M. J. F. Rabaets; J. Wilde.

H.M. Inspectorate (England)

Chief Inspectors, B. C. Arthur; G. W. Elsmore; J. A. Everson; E. Lord; E. Norris; Mrs. P. Perry.

Divisional Inspectors, B. A. Chaplin; E. C. Cordell; J. T. G. Chugg; Miss V. J. Evans; W. S. Fowler; W. G. Hamflett; D. T. E. Marjoram.

Staff Inspectors, T. W. F. Allan; R. Arnold; B. C. Arthur; A. Ashbrook; G. Benfield; T. H. Bennetts; J. K. Brierley; P. Brown; I. B. Butterworth; T. Carroll; A. G. Clegg; Miss S. Crisp; J. Dalglish; D. A. Denegri; D. Flanagan; A. Gibson; G. Goldstein; F. H. Green; V. Green; B. W. V. Hawes; R. A. S. Hennessy; G. A. Hicks; W. H. Himsworth; D. Hollingsworth; B. W. Howes; L. J. Jackson; H. C. H. Jones; D. G. Lambert; J. G. Lavender; M. Le Guillou; A. G. Loosemore; D. W. McAllister; P. F. Marlow; A. R. Marshall; T. P. Melia; R. F. Mildon; A. C. Millett; C. P. Parsons; Mrs. R. W. Peacocke; G. T. Peaker; Miss S. A. Polak; D. L. Rees; A. J. Rose; C. W. Rowland; I. P. Salisbury; P. Samuel; E. Scott; J. G. Slater; M. E. Sprinks; M. J. Tomlinson; D. G. Toose; A. F. Turberfield; G. W. Verow; W. H. Wainwright; D. E. Walker; R. C. Williams; M. Wylie.

H. M. Inspectors, Mrs. C. A. Agambar; Miss J. A. Aldwinckle; Mrs. G. M. V. Alexander; D. J. Allen; Mrs. M. I. Ambrose; T. I. Ambrose; K. J. Anglesey; P. T. Armitstead; Miss J. L. Atkin; D. Baillie; W. G. Bakehouse; Mrs. C. A. Baker; A. M. Barnes; J. M. Barnes; G. Barratt; R. E. Barrett; E. A. Bassett; Mrs. E. P. Baxell; P. E. B. Belshaw; S. G. L. Bignell; D. B. F. Billimore; Miss V. Blackburn; A. J. Boddington; Mrs. C. M. Bond; Miss J. M. Bonner; P. R. Booth; R. G. Booth; Mrs. B. K. Bottomley; D. M. W. Boulton; Miss E. Bourne; C. B. Bowring-Carr; G. R. H. Boys; D. J. Bradbury; P. L. Bradbury; R. J. Brake; T. E. Brand; Mrs. H. S. Bridge; E. F. H. Brittain; J. Broadbent; Miss M. I. Brogden; F. Brook; D. G. Buckland; M. J. Buckley; T. A. Burdett; K. R. Burford; J. M. Burgess; J. W. Butler; P. Cadenhead; Miss M. E. Caistor; R. A. Callender; M. J. Campbell; Mrs. J. Carswell; Mrs. E. Cave; R. B. Chalmers; M. G. C. Channon; B. J. Chopping; Miss D. H. Chorley; D. Clare; P. R. Clarke; G. Clay; D. G. Close; M. J. Collier; M. J. Convey; Miss M. Corlett; D. A. Cormican; A. T. Cox; P. Cradock; G. Cranmer; J. Creedy; L. S. Crickmore; Mrs. M. E. Crisp; R. J. Crowcroft; R. Daniels; C. M. Davies; B. Denton; T. Dickinson; T. Dillon; A. Dobson; Mrs. G. Dolden; Mrs. C. R. Donoughue; J. A. S. Dossett; S. R. G. Downs; P. S. Edwards; P. D. Edwards; D. L. Elliott; J. A. Elliott; Mrs. V. E. Emmett; J. M. Evans; K. J. Evans; Mrs. G. Everson; J. H. Fairhurst; V. A. Farthing; Miss R. R. Feldmeier; Mrs. B. R. D. Fisher; B. P. Fitzgerald; J. Fitzpatrick; D. H. M. Foster; R. S. Fowler; R. C. Fox; W. H. Francis; G. R. Frater; P. S. Friend; R. C. Frost; J. P. Fulton; P. Gannon; P. H. W. Garwood; I. Gera; G. D. Gibbs; J. E. A. Gifford; G. A. Gill; M. D. Gill; C. R. Gillings; M. S. Girling; C. Goodhead; Mrs. K. N. Gosling; J. G. Goulding; Miss S. Gracey; D. I. Grant; V. Green; R. M. Griffiths; Mrs. P. E. Guest-Jones; E. E. J. Haidon; D. S. Hale; D. J. Halligan; N. J. Hallmark; J. A. Hamer; R. A. Hargreaves; B. R. Harris; D. J. Hart; M. Hart; K. N. Hastings; F. W. Hawkins; G. H. Haworth; B. P. Hayes; G. M. Hearnshaw; M. L. Hening; R. A. S. Hennessey; J. F. Herbert; J. A. Hertrich; P. M. Hesketh; P. Highfield; J. A. Hill; Mrs. G. A. Hindhaugh; D. J. House; M. J. Howarth; B. A. F. Hubbard; A. J. Hughes; J. B. Hurn; W. E. Husband; J. B. Huskins; A. J. Hymans; E. S. Ingledew; P. F. J. Irvine; A. R. Ivatts; M. J. Ive; B. Jelly; J. C. Jennings; D. W. John; Miss S. H. Johns; P. W. R. Johnson; D. A. Jones; Mrs. M. E. Jones; Mrs. A. C. K. Keelan-Towner; M. Kerrigan; M. A.

Khan; B. L. King; J. B. Knox; D. G. Labon; G. N. E. Lageard; B. M. Lane; J. P. Leigh; Miss B. J. Lewis; D. F. Lewis; D. J. Lewis; T. L. Lilley; E. R. B. Little; Miss B. M. Lockwood; A. B. Lomax; Mrs. E. M. Lowe; W. G. Lowe; T. L. Lusty; J. A. Mabey; C. McCall; M. E. Madden; E. McDonald; J. McGinn; Mrs. J. C. McGinty; J. McGuire; G. W. S. Mackay; D. M. McIntosh; Mrs. P. R. Maclay; Mrs. J. McLean; D. J. Marjoram; Miss R. J. Marlor; G. D. Marrow; C. P. Marshall; J. G. Marshall; T. W. Martin; J. H. Mayhew; M. R. E. Mealing; Miss B. E. Megson; T. G. Melling; Miss A. C. Millett; H. Millington; J. K. Millington; D. Mills; Miss H. A. Moffat; A. R. H. Monk; R. W. Mycock; H. Myers; R. Nicholls; A. J. Nisbett; P. M. Nixon; J. P. O'Connor; Miss K. M. O'Leary; P. J. H. Oliver; P. I. Orr; Miss M. Osborn; A. Owen; W. E. Owen; Miss P. Park; K. Parker; D. J. Parks; F. Parrott; J. M. Parsons; I. M. Paterson; P. J. Pearson; Mrs. D. M. Penn; Miss I. Perlmutter; Miss J. M. Phillips; K. Pinder; M. W. A. Pitts; C. Potts; Mrs. J. H. Paraskeva-Hunt; H. A. Price; B. H. Proctor; M. E. Pullee; Mrs. P. E. Pulver; J. Reynolds; C. Richards; J. D. Richards; J. C. Richardson; G. Robson; S. J. A. Rogers; C. Rowe; R. Roundhill; D. H. Rutt; M. V. Salter; Mrs. J. Sartain; Mrs. K. J. Saunders; C. H. Selby; E. L. Sewell; D. T. V. Sharman; J. R. Shirtcliff; B. D. Short; Mrs. V. M. Sida; T. A. G. Silk; P. J. Silvester; P. Singh; G. Sleightholme; Mrs. M. M. Smart; P. J. C. Smith; P. R. Smith; R. T. Smith; D. E. Soulsby; M. E. Sprakes; Mrs. B. Staniland; J. Stanyer; J. W. Steel; J. M. Steels; J. B. Stevenson; Mrs. M. T. Stiles; R. W. Stockdale; C. F. Stoneman; Miss M. E. Stride; R. Summersby; D. W. Sylvester; D. W. Taylor; J. A. Taylor; Miss P. M. M. Taylor; R. S. Taylor; J. D. Thomas; K. W. Thomas; D. L. Thorburn; R. M. Thorpe; J. Tierney; M. J. Todd; D. R. Trainor; J. E. Trickey; A. D. J. Turner; Mrs. J. W. Turner; Mrs. S. P. Twite; J. R. Ungoed-Thomas; D. G. Vallis; A. Walmsley; Miss P. Walters; M. Wardlow; Mrs. A. P. Warren; R. K. Warren; D. H. Watts; Mr. R. Webb; R. R. Weir; D. J. Wells; D. L. West; P. E. Weston; D. J. Whitaker; C. G. White; F. Whiteman; Mrs. O. Whittingham; Miss S. Whitworth; C. C. B. Wightwick; J. Wilkinson; J. B. Willcock; D. G. Williams; H. G. Williams; J. R. Williams; K. G. Williams; D. P. T. Woodgate; Mrs. S. A. Woodroffe; J. A. Woodrow; J. I. Wragg; Miss B. M. Wright; E. H. Wright; J. L. Wright; T. Wylie; F. P. Young; R. E. Young.

H.M. Inspectorate Support Services

Principal, P. J. Thorpe.
Senior Executive Officer, P. A. Clarke.

H.M. Inspectorate (Wales)

Chief Inspector, I. R. Lloyd.

Staff Inspectors, L. M. Evans; G. L. L. Jones; R. E. Jones; P. Thomas; R. Thomas; P. C. Webb; M. J. F. Wynn.

H.M. Inspectors, S. J. Adams; Miss M. Anthony; H. W. Davies; R. G. Dayies; G. Evans; K. M. Evans; N. B. Evans; W. A. Evans; Mrs L. Gainsbury; J. Garrett, O.B.E.; Mrs. K. P. Godfrey; A. Higgins; G. E. Humphreys; E. H. Hutton; I. Huws-Roberts; R. L. James; W. R. Jenkins; T. W. John; A. H. Jones; G. D. Jones; L. Jones; O. E. Jones; J. M. Laugharne; M. J. Law; I. M. Lewis; R. A. Lowe; I. G. Morgan; J. Nicholas; Miss P. A. Nicholas; P. E. Owen; T. E. Parry; T. G. Prosser; G. O. Roberts; Miss D. Selleck; M. W. Stone; R. S. Taylor; Gavin Thomas; Glyndwr Thomas; W. E. Thomas; P. B. Walker; G. Warren; B. Wigley; R. Williams.

ELECTRICITY AUTHORITIES

THE ELECTRICITY COUNCIL
30 Millbank, SW1P 4RD
[01–834 2333]

Chairman, T. P. Jones, C.B. ...... £55,000 to £60,000
Deputy Chairman, A. Plumpton, C.B.E.
£37,325 to £47,240
Deputy Chairman, O. Brooks (*part-time*)
£20,000 to £25,000
Members, R. W. Orson; R. A. Farrance
£35,000 to £40,000
Members from the Central Electricity Generating Board, Sir Walter Marshall, C.B.E., F.R.S.; F. E. Bonner, C.B.E.; G. A. W. Blackman, C.B.E.
Secretary, R. Savinson.

CENTRAL ELECTRICITY GENERATING BOARD
Sudbury House, 15 Newgate Street, EC1A 7AU
[01–634 5111]

Chairman, Sir Walter Marshall, C.B.E., F.R.S.
£55,000 to £60,000
Deputy Chairman, F. E. Bonner, C.B.E.
£45,000 to £50,000
Members, G. A. W. Blackman, C.B.E.; J. W. Baker
£35,000 to £40,000
Part-time Members, A. G. Derbyshire, F.R.I.B.A.; Sir Eric Sharp, C.B.E.; R. V. Giordano (*each*) ... £4,270
Secretary, G. H. Hadley.

ELECTRICITY BOARDS
The 12 Area Electricity Boards

(The Chairmen of Area Boards receive a salary of £30,000 to £35,000).
London, Templar House, 81–87 High Holborn, WC1V 6NU. *Chairman*, D. G. Jefferies. *Sec.*, D. G. Rees.
South Eastern, Grand Avenue, Hove, East Sussex BN3 2LS. *Chairman*, G. A. Squair. *Sec.*, S. M. Wide.
Southern, Southern Electricity House, Littlewick Green, Maidenhead, Berks. *Chairman*, D. A. Ross. *Sec.*, R. C. Collier.
South Western, Electricity House, Colston Avenue, Bristol BS1 4TS. *Chairman*, K. F. Whittle. *Sec. and Solicitor*, S. G. Marshall.
Eastern, P.O. Box 40, Wherstead, Ipswich, Suffolk 1P9 2AQ. *Chairman*, J. C. Smith. *Sec.*, W. L. M. French.
East Midlands, P.O. Box 4, North P.D.O., 398 Coppice Road, Arnold, Nottingham NG5 7HX. *Chairman*, J. F. Harris. *Sec.*, T. F. C. Walker.
Midlands, P. O. Box 8 Mucklow Hill, Halesowen, West Midlands B62 8BP. *Chairman*, J. J. Wilson. *Sec.*, R. K. Young.
South Wales, St. Mellons, Cardiff CF3 9XW. *Chairman*, J. Wynford Evans. *Sec.*, C. K. Powell.
Merseyside and North Wales, Sealand Road, Chester. *Chairman*, B. R. Hastings, *Sec.*, C. W. Leonard.
Yorkshire, Wetherby Road, Scarcroft, Leeds LS14 3HS. *Chairman*, W. J. Prior, C.B.E. *Sec. and Solicitor*, R. Dickinson.
North Eastern, Carliol House, Newcastle upon Tyne NE99 1SE. *Chairman*, T. Rutherford, C.B.E., *Sec.*, J. W. Dalgleish.
North Western, Cheetwood Road, Manchester M8 8BA. *Chairman*, J. D. M. Bell. *Sec.*, B. Benson.

NORTH OF SCOTLAND HYDRO-ELECTRIC BOARD
16 Rothesay Terrace, Edinburgh EH3 7SE
[031–225 1361]

Chairman, M. Joughin, C.B.E. (*part-time*) £16,050
Deputy Chairman and Chief Executive, K. R. Vernon, C.B.E.

Members (*part-time*), A. T. H. Tulloch; C. A. MacLeod; Mrs. C. A. M. Davis (*Chairman of Consultative Council*).; M. G. N. Walker; Rear-Admiral D. A. Dunbar-Nasmith, C.B., D.S.C.; D. J. Miller; C. S. Macphie (*each* £2,675).
Secretary, J. E. M. Watts.

SOUTH OF SCOTLAND ELECTRICITY BOARD
Spean Street, Glasgow G44 4BE
[041–637 7177]

Chairman, D. J. Miller £40,660
Deputy Chairman, I. M. H. Preston £35,300
Part-time Members, A. Barr; D. McLean; N. C. Kuenssberg; Prof. D. I. MacKay; Mrs. J. A. Thomson (£3,250); M. Joughin, C.B.E. (*unpaid*); G. B. Whyte (*unpaid*).
Secretary, D. A. S. MacLaren.

DEPARTMENT OF EMPLOYMENT
Caxton House, Tothill Street, SW1H 9NF
[01–213 3000]

The Department of Employment is responsible for Government policies affecting the working life of the country's population and the needs of potential workers.

These policies include the promotion of good industrial relations, pay, special measures to deal with unemployment and redundancy and regional employment problems.

The Department is also responsible for producing and publishing a wide range of statistics, including the figures for retail prices, earnings, employment and unemployment and industrial disputes.

Many of the Department's executive functions and services have been transferred to a number of new bodies, operating independently, but reporting to the Secretary of State for Employment.

Secretary of State for Employment, THE RT. HON. THOMAS KING, M.P. £30,304
Private Secretary, D. J. Norrington.
Assistant Private Secretaries, P. R. Smith; Ms. J. Rutherford.
Parliamentary Private Secretary, T. Durant, M.P.
Minister of State, HON. P. MORRISON, M.P. ... £21,364
Under Secretaries of State, P. Bottomley, M.P.; Hon. A. Clark, M.P. £16,154
Permanent Secretary, M. E. Quinlan, C.B. £44,033
Deputy Secretaries, D. J. Derx, C.B.; D. B. Smith, C.B. £35,278
Solicitor, G. E. McClelland £35,278

Industrial Relations

Under Secretaries, J. H. Galbraith; M. Wake £28,583
Assistant Secretaries, D. G. Talintyre; N. Covington; E. G. Whybrew .... £19,243 to £23,159
Chief Wages Inspector, J. A. Dyble
£15,605 to £20,794
Secretary of Wages Councils, S. Cottingham
£12,399 to £16,656

Manpower Policy

Under Secretary (*Division 1*), G. A. Brand ... £28,583
Under Secretary (*Division 2*), M. E. G. Fogden
£28,583
Assistant Secretaries, R. A. David; D. W. Brown; P. Tansley; R. T. B. Dykes; M. J. Brimmer; I. A. W. Fair........................ £19,243 to £23,159

Overseas Divisions

Under-Secretary, W. R. B. Robinson £28,583
Assistant Secretaries, Miss M.E. Green; M. W. Smart
£19,243 to £23,159

Economic and Social Division

Under Secretary, G. L. Reid £28,583
Assistant Secretaries, A. G. Johnson; P. Brannen
£19,243 to £23,159

Establishments Division

Director of Establishments, R. S. Allison £28,583
Assistant Secretary, S. Torson . . . £19,243 to £23,159
Assistant Secretary (Group Personnel Unit), J. W.
Cooper . . . . £19,243 to £23,159
Head of Information, A. E. Moorey
£19,243 to £23,159
Deputy Head of Information, S. Reardon
£15,605 to £20,794

Finance Division

Accountant-General, F. J. Bayliss £28,583
Director of Accounts and Financial Management, R.
H. Chambers . . . . £19,243 to £23,159
Assistant Secretary (Policy), G. Kahan
£19,243 to £23,159

Solicitor's Division

Solicitor, G. E. McClelland £35,278

Statistics Division

Director of Statistics, P. D. Dworkin £28,583
Chief Statisticians, B. J. Buckingham; Mrs. A. V.
Wheatcroft; D. J. Sellwood; D. E. Allnutt
£19,243 to £23,159
Director of Computing, B. P. White.

Health and Safety Commission

Chairman, Dr. J. Cullen £44,033
Members of the Commission, D. Mason; Dr. M. C.
Shannon; Dr. C. M. Thomas; R. F. Eberlie; P.
Jacques; G. Lloyd; R. W. Buckton; Dr. A. H. Raper.
Secretary, Miss C. Johnson . . . . . . £15,605 to £20,794

Health and Safety Executive

Director General, J. D. Rimington £37,982
Deputy Director General , Dr. K. P. Duncan . £35,278

Hazardous Substances Division

Director, C. D. Burgess £28,583

Safety and Policy Division

Director, D. J. Hodgkins £28,583

H.M. Industrial Air Pollution Inspectorate

H.M. Chief Alkali Inspector, Dr. L. Reed £28,583

H.M. Mines and Quarries Inspectorate

H.M. Chief Inspector of Mines and Quarries, A.
Harley £33,407

Employment Medical Advisory Service

Director of Medical Services, (vacant).

H.M. Factory Inspectorate

H.M. Chief Inspector of Factories, J. D. G. Hammer
£28,583

H.M. Nuclear Installations Inspectorate

H.M. Chief Inspector of Nuclear Installations, R. D.
Anthony £28,583

Research and Laboratory Services Division

Director, Dr. A. G. Johnston £28,583

H.M. Agriculture Inspectorate

H.M. Chief Agricultural Inspector, J. R. Whitaker.
£19,243 to £23,159

DEPARTMENT OF ENERGY
Thames House South,
Millbank, SW1P 4QJ (unless otherwise stated)
[01–211 3000]

The Department of Energy is responsible within the Government for the development of policies in relation to all forms of energy. It also discharges governmental functions connected with the publicly-owned coal, gas and electricity industries. It is responsible for the Atomic Energy Authority; is the sponsoring Department for the nuclear power industry and is responsible for the development of oil and gas resources on the British sector of the Continental Shelf. It is the sponsoring Department for the oil industry and is responsible for international aspects of energy problems, including relations and co-operation with oil producing countries. The Department is the co-ordinating body for energy conservation policy and for encouraging the development of new sources of energy.

Salary List

Secretary of State	£31,271
Minister of State	£21,881
Parliamentary Under-Secretary of State	£22,520 (Lords)
	£16,411 (Commons)
Permanent Under-Secretary of State	£45,500
Deputy Secretary	£36,500
Director of P.E.D.	£39,484
Head of Information	£23,159
Under Secretary	£29,500
Reservoir Evaluation Specialist I	£35,758
Assistant Secretary	£23,159
Reservoir Evaluation Specialist II	£33,629
Senior Principal	£20,794
Chief Electrical Engineering Inspector	£23,159
Deputy Chief Scientific Officer .	£23,159
Senior Principal Scientific Officer	£19,317
Chief Statistician	£23,159
Senior Economic Adviser	£23,159
Director (Gas and Oil Measurement Branch)	£23,159
Petroleum Specialist II	£29,390
A.D./Accounts	£21,406
Director of Engineering	£23,159
Assistant Director of Engineering	£20,794

Secretary of State for Energy, THE RT. HON. PETER
WALKER, M.B.E., M.P.
Principal Private Secretary, M.F. Reidy.
Parliamentary Private Secretary, S. Dorrell, M.P.
Assistant Private Secretaries, J. S. Neilson; E. G.
Huke; K. R. Loader.
Minister of State for Energy, THE RT. HON. ALICK
BUCHANAN-SMITH, M.P.
Private Secretary, Miss S. A. Killen.
Parliamentary Private Secretary, J. Watson, M.P.
Assistant Private Secretary, Miss J. A. Bennington.
Parliamentary Under-Secretaries of State, A. Goodlad,
M.P.; D. Hunt, M.P.
Permanent Under Secretary of State, Sir Kenneth
Couzens, K.C.B.
Private Secretary, M. J. Wilshire.
Deputy Secretaries, J. R. S. Guinness; I. T. Manley.
Chief Scientific Adviser, Sir Sam Edwards.
Parliamentary Clerk, G. L. Davey.

Establishment and Finance Division

*Principal Establishment and Finance Officer (Under
Secretary)*, R. T. J. Wilson.

Assistant Secretaries, K. C. Price; R. Beasley; G. W. Thynne; C. C. Wilcock.

Electricity Division

Under Secretary, A. W. Brown.
Assistant Secretaries, P. G. P. D. Fullerton; Dr. D. H. Metz.
Chief Electrical Engineering Inspector, A. T. Baldock.

Coal Division

Under Secretary, R. J. Priddle.
Assistant Secretaries, Ms. A. Beaton; C. P. Carter.

Atomic Energy Division

Under Secretary, C. E. Henderson.
Assistant Secretaries, G. H. Stevens; J. R. Bretherton; N. A. C. Hirst.

Energy Technology Division

Chief Scientist (Under Secretary), Dr. D. Pooley.
Deputy Chief Scientific Officers, D. C. Gore; Dr. R. G. S. Skipper.
Assistant Secretary, Dr. W. J. Burroughs.
Senior Principal Scientific Officers, H. F. Ferguson; G. S. Dearnley; Dr. G. Preston; E. G. Bevan; W. Macpherson; Dr. D. Fairmaner.

Energy Policy

Under Secretary, D. I. Morphet.
Assistant Secretaries, Miss P. A. Boys; E. Pash; J. Whaley; P. H. Agrell.

Energy Efficiency Office

Director General, W. I. MacIntyre.
Directors, Miss S. M. Cohen; Dr. E. G. Finer; G. G. Bevan; J. R. Wakely.

Economics and Statistics Division

Under Secretary, E. H. M. Price.
Chief Statistician, J. J. M. Harris.
Senior Economic Advisers, A. J. Meyrick; S. A. Price; Dr. K. J. Wigley.

Oil Division

Under Secretary, A. J. Wiggins.
Assistant Secretaries, Dr. C. J. Myerscough; S. W. Fremantle; A. J. Dorken; L. F. Barclay; H. L. Ross.

Gas Division

Under Secretary, G. G. Campbell.
Assistant Secretaries, Dr. F. R. Heathcote; P. T. Harding; Dr. J. G. Wright; D. R. Davis.

Gas and Oil Measurement Branch
Government Buildings, Saffron Road, Wigston, Leicester
[0533 785354]

Director, J. Plant.

Petroleum Engineering Division

Director of P.E.D., P. J. Walmsley, M.B.E..
Reservoir Evaluation Specialist I, K. R. J. Trott.
Reservoir Evaluation Specialists II, J. R. V. Brooks; D. W. Mann.
Petroleum Specialists II, S. A. Warner; D. R. Clementson; J. R. Petrie.
Senior Principal, P. D. Atkinson.
Senior Principal Scientific Officer, J. N. Mansfield.
Assistant Director Engineer, G. N. Marriott.

Offshore Supplies Office
Headquarters Office:
Alhambra House, 45 Waterloo Street, Glasgow G2 6AS
[041–221 8777]

Director General, J. E. d'Ancona.
Director Industry, W. E. Allison.

Director Policy and Administration, A. E. Maule.
Director Research and Development, Dr. J. E. P. Miles.
Director China Unit, Dr. K. P. Forrest.
Senior Principal Business Development, H. Holden.
Senior Principal Scientific Officers, C. J. Hughes; D. W. Partridge.
Assistant Director Engineers, H. M. Whiteside; P. R. Taylor.

Information Division

Head of Information, Miss R. C. A. Christopherson.
Chief Information Officer, G. D. Meredith.

DEPARTMENT OF THE ENVIRONMENT
2 Marsham Street, SW1P 3EB
[01–212 3434]

The Department of the Environment is responsible for planning and land use; local government; housing, construction; inner city areas; new towns; environmental protection; conservation areas and countryside affairs; royal parks and palaces; historic buildings and ancient monuments; sport and recreation. The Property Services Agency is responsible for all construction activities, supplies and transport at home and abroad for all Government departments including the Ministry of Defence and some repayment clients including British Telecom.

Salary List

Secretary of State		£30,304
Minister of State (Local Govt. & Environmental Services)		£26,670
Minister of State (Housing & Construction)		£21,364
Parliamentary Under Secretary of State		£16,154
Permanent Secretary (Grade 1)		£45,500
Second Permanent Secretary (1A)		£42,000
Chief Executive (1A)		£42,000
Deputy Secretary (2)		£36,500
Director General (2)		£36,500
Solicitor and Legal Adviser (2)		£36,500
Chief Economic Adviser (2)		£36,500
Director, B.R.S., U.I.P.P.L. (3)		£30,375
Under Secretary (3)		£29,500
Director, Information (4)		£25,455
Director, Regional Office (3)		£29,500
Director Works, P.S.A. London (3)		£29,500
Chief Planning Inspector (3)		£29,500
Principal Establishment Officer (3)		£29,500
Principal Finance Officer (Under Sec.) (3)		£29,500
Principal Assistant Solicitor (3)		£29,500
Chief Scientific Officer (B) (4)		£25,455
Director Contracts (P.S.A.) (4)		£25,455
Deputy Director Research (B.R.E.) (4)		£25,455
Deputy Chief Planner (4)		£25,455
Director, P.S.A. Regions (4)		£25,455
Deputy Chief Scientific Officer (5)		£19,243 to £23,159
Assistant Director/Director "B" (5)	£19,243	to £23,159
Assistant Chief Planner (5)	£19,243	to £23,159
Assistant Secretary (5)	£19,243	to £23,159
Controller, Regional Office (5)	£19,243	to £23,159
Chief Statistician (5)	£19,243	to £23,159
Senior Economic Adviser (5)	£19,243	to £23,159
Controller of Accounts (5)	£19,243	to £23,159

Secretary of State for the Environment, THE RT. HON.
PATRICK JENKIN, M.P.
  Private Secretary, J. F. Ballard.
  Special Advisers, Sir Robert Cooke; C. Mockler.
  Parliamentary Private Secretary, M. Thornton, M.P.

Minister for Local Government, THE RT. HON. KEN-
NETH WILFRED BAKER, M.P.
  Private Secretary, M. J. Bailey.

Minister for Housing and Construction, IAN GOW, M.P.
  Private Secretary, P. J. J. Britton.
Parliamentary Under-Secretaries of State:—
  N. MacFarlane, M.P.; Sir George Young, Bt., M.P.;
  Hon. W. Waldegrave, M.P.; The Earl of Avon.
  Private Secretaries, Miss S. Faulkner (to Mr. Mac-
  Farlane); T. Beattie (to Sir George Young); Mrs.
  J. M. Dunn (to Mr. Waldegrave).
  Parliamentary Clerk, L. Peacock.
Permanent Secretary, Sir George Moseley, K.C.B.
  Private Secretary, R. G. Wakeford.
Lord in Waiting, The Lord Skelmersdale.
  Private Secretary, G. Davies.
Second Permanent Secretary, Sir Peter Harrop, K.C.B.
  Private Secretary, W. Hills.
Chief Executive, Second Permanent Secretary, Prop-
  erty Services Agency, A. G. Manzie, C.B..

Information

Director, D. A. McDonald.

Merseyside Task Force

Under Secretary, K. E. C. Sorensen.
Grade 5, R. W. Bunce; D. J. Morrison; M. A. R. Lunn.

PROPERTY SERVICES AGENCY

Chief Executive, A. G. Manzie, C.B..
  Private Secretary, J. Cunliffe.

DEPUTY CHIEF EXECUTIVE 1

Deputy Secretary, G. H. Chipperfield.

Estate Surveying Services

Director, (vacant).
Grade 5, K. T. Garland; J. M. Phillips; P. J. M. Butter.

Home Regional Services

Director, A. J. Aveling.
Grade 5, D. W. Royle; M. Clayton.

Property Services Agency Regions (Home)

Directors:
  London, G. Hopkinson.
  Eastern, P. S. Draper.
  Midland, K. H. A. Allen.
  North East, S. P. Singh.
  North West, H. Rogers.
  South East, B. E. G. Clark.
  South West, J. M. Rex.
  Southern, A. R. Cruttenden.
  Central Office for Wales, H. S. Pearce.

Scottish Services

Director, A. G. Gosling.
Grade 5, D. R. Smith; M. J. Mannings.

DEPUTY CHIEF EXECUTIVE 2

Grade 2, H. P. Johnston, C.B.

Defence Services I

Director, R. A. Gomme.
Grade 5, R. A. Munday; G. J. Skinner; R. T. Turner;
  J. H. Clemits; C. D. Boylan.

Defence Services II

Director, B. G. Skeates.
Grade 5, J. S. Stevens; P. Kitchen; A. Levy; R. M.
  Hutson; A. S. Kennedy; S. C. D. Duguid.

Civil Accommodation

Director, R. G. S. Johnston.
Grade 5, R. J. Dorrington; B. E. Fensome; A. K. W.
  Morgan; E. A. Spencer; M. G. Stuart.

DIRECTOR GENERAL OF DESIGN SERVICES

Grade 2, J. B. Jefferson, C.B.E.

Architectural and Quantity Surveying Services

Director, E. J. Bowman.
Grade 5, K. A. Miles; G. F. Jones.

Civil Engineering Services

Director, R. F. Hughes.
Grade 5, H. B. Gould; G. H. Sowden.

Mechanical and Electrical Engineering Services

Director, A. W. Loten.
Grade 5, R. C. Cracknell.

Design Standards Office

Director, J. P. Lynch.

Establishments, Property Services Agency

Principal Establishment Officer, A. R. Atherton.
Grade 5, G. N. Bendon; G. Flanagan; R. A. Stead; L.
  W. Culver.

Finance, Property Services Agency

Principal Finance Officer, M. V. Hawtin.
Director of Contracts, C. Pink.
Grade 5, A. E. Coules.
Comptroller of Accounts, J. A. Pearson.
Director Accountant, P. L. Jones.

THE CROWN SUPPLIERS

Controller, J. A. Dole.
Assistant Controllers, E. L. Pinfold; A. H. Pollington;
  J. P. Plowman.
Financial Controller, N. L. Gregory.

PLANNING, INNER CITIES, NEW TOWNS AND LONDON

Deputy Secretary, J. Delafons, C.B.

Inner Cities

Under Secretary, (vacant).
Grade 5, N. Sanders; J. S. Parker; M. B. Gahagan.

Regional Policy and Development

Under Secretary, D. C. L. Wroe.
Grade 5, S. T. Garrish; W. B. Solesbury.

Greater London Housing and Planning

Under Secretary, T. L. Jones.
Grade 5, R. Williams; W. Grevatt; A. Buchanan.

Planning Land Use Policy

Under Secretary, R. D. Jefferies.
Grade 5, D. N. Donaldson; G. I. Fuller; I. H. Nicol; R.
  C. Mabey; C. K. Howes.

Planning Practice, Minerals and New Towns

Under Secretary and Chief Planner, Dr. M. R.
  Richardson.
Grade 5, R. A. Bird; A. J. C. Simcock; P. F. Everall;
  J. H. H. Baxter.

HOUSING AND CONSTRUCTION

Deputy Secretary, W. I. McIndoe.
Under Secretaries, B. D. Ponsford; R. J. A. Sharp; R. G. Brown; D. T. Routh.
Chief Architect (Grade 4), Miss P. R. Tindale.
Grade 5, L. B. Hicks; N. W. Summerton; P. J. Wilde; P. F. Emms; A. H. Corner; D. J. Phillips; J. J. Rendell; J. A. Penfold; R. J. Gibson; A. G. Watson; J. M. Hope; I. G. Urquhart; J. P. Henry; D. T. I. G. Davies; I. C. MacPherson; A. E. Holmans; B. C. Isherwood.

WATER DIRECTORATE

Under Secretary, J. A. L. Gunn.
Grade 5, P. T. McIntosh; Mrs. L. A. C. Simcock; M. G. Healey; H. Wenban-Smith.

FINANCE AND LOCAL GOVERNMENT

Deputy Secretary, Principal Finance Officer, T. M. Heiser, C.B.

Local Government Finance Policy

Under Secretary, P. F. Owen.
Grade 5, R. A. J. Mayer; P. J. Fletcher; R. U. Young; J. Hobson; J. Kidgell; J. W. Smith.

Housing, Water and Central Finance

Under Secretary, F. A. Osborn.
Grade 5, J. A. Owen; D. R. Bradley; D. A. C. Heigham.
Director Accountant (Grade 5), B. Redfern.

Local Government

Under Secretary, D. C. Pickup.
Grade 5, H. G. Dormer; R. Brown; D. O. McCreadie.

Local Government Reorganisation

Under Secretary, J. P. G. Rowcliffe.
Grade 5, Mrs. D. S. Phillips; D. P. Walley.

ENVIRONMENTAL PROTECTION, RURAL AFFAIRS AND SPORT

Deputy Secretary, Dr. M. W. Holdgate, C.B.

Central Directorate on Environmental Pollution

Under Secretary, D. Gruffydd Jones.
Grade 4, Dr. D. A. Everest.
Grade 5, F. Kendall; Miss F. McConnell; L. F. Rutterford; Dr. N. J. King; P. S. MacCormack.

Directorate of Waste Disposal

Under Secretary, P. Critchley.
Grade 5, D. R. Lewis; Dr. F. S. Feates; R. G. D. Osmond.

Directorate of Rural Affairs

Under Secretary, T. R. Hornsby.
Grade 5, A. Flexman; G. D. Edmonds.

Sports and Recreation

Grade 5, D. V. Teasdale.

ANCIENT MONUMENTS AND HISTORIC BUILDINGS DIRECTORATE

Director (Under Secretary), T. R. Hornsby.
Grade 5, B. Strong; R. Jones.

DEPARTMENTS OF THE ENVIRONMENT AND TRANSPORT REGIONAL OFFICES

West Midlands (Birmingham)

Chairman, Regional Board and Regional Director, H. F. Ellis-Rees.
Regional Controllers, S. Jones; D. L. Saunders; N. H. Perry.

Yorkshire and Humberside (Leeds)

Chairman, Regional Board and Regional Director, R. J. Green.
Regional Controllers, J. B. Wilson; M. Roberts.

North West (Manchester)

Chairman, Regional Board and Regional Director, D. C. Renshaw.
Regional Controllers, D. R. Ritchie; P. W. Peck; D. J. Morrison.

Northern (Newcastle upon Tyne)

Chairman, Regional Board and Regional Director, A. G. Balls.
Regional Controllers, J. A. M. Hastings; R. G. Bell.

South West (Bristol)

Chairman, Regional Board and Regional Director, G. M. Wedd.
Regional Controller, J. Ashbridge.

East Midlands (Nottingham)

Chairman, Regional Board and Regional Director, P. M. Hewitt, O.B.E.

South East

Chairman, Regional Board and Regional Director, J. Peeler.
Regional Controllers, N. Thompson; M. W. McD. Cairns.
Assistant Chief Planner, J. A. Colley.

Eastern

Chairman, East Anglia Regional Board and Regional Director, W. J. S. Batho.
Regional Controllers, Miss K. B. Pailing; J. J. Parsons.

STATISTICS (ENVIRONMENT)

Under Secretary, D. C. L. Wroe.
Grade 5, R. F. Sellwood; F. D. Sando; W. H. Stott; J. E. Kidgell; P. S. MacCormack.

CHIEF ECONOMIC ADVISER (ENVIRONMENT)

Deputy Secretary, H. J. D. Cole.
Grade 5, B. C. Isherwood; A. A. E. Holmans; J. W. Smith; D. A. C. Heigham; H. B. Wenban-Smith.

CHIEF SCIENTIST (ENVIRONMENT)

Deputy Secretary, Dr. M. W. Holdgate, C.B.

Environment Science Policy Unit

Director, Dr. D. Everest.
Grade 5, C. L. Robson.

Building Research Establishment

Director, Dr. R. G. H. Watson.
Deputy Director, R. E. Jeanes.
Grade 5, T. J. Griffiths; Dr. S. J. Leach; Dr. J. B. Menzies; K. N. Palmer; J. M. Baker.

LEGAL

Solicitor and Legal Adviser, M. J. Ware.
Principal Assistant Solicitor, Mrs. A. S. Granham.

DEPARTMENTS OF THE ENVIRONMENT AND TRANSPORT—COMMON SERVICES
2 Marsham Street, SW1P 3EB
(01–212 3434)

ORGANIZATION AND ESTABLISHMENTS
Director General, Organization and Establishments,
(Deputy Secretary), K. F. J. Ennals, c.b.

Senior Staff Management
Under Secretary, F. W. Girling
Grade 5, B. Taylor; H. D. Hallett.
Chief Librarian, P. Kirwan

Personnel, Management and Training
Under Secretary, G. D. Crane
Grade 5, S. T. McQuillin; C. R. Grimsey; P. Stringfellow; Mrs. M. McDonald.

Administrative Resources
Under Secretary, D. J. Burr
Grade 5, A. Z. Levy; L. S. Moyle; Ms. E. A. Hopkins; Mrs. L. A. Thomas.

Establishments Organization Division
Grade 5, Miss M. Prest

PLANNING INSPECTORATE
Chief Planning Inspector, Miss E. B. Haran.
Grade 4, J. D. Adshead; R. J. Amblin.
Grade 5, R. D. Compton.
Assistant Chief Planning Inspectors, M. M. Cross; A. S. Barnes; F. E. Booth; P. J. Roberts; N. E. Heijne; K. G. Robbins; T. M. Millington.

ROYAL COMMISSION ON ENVIRONMENTAL POLLUTION
Church House, Great Smith Street, SW1P 3BL
[01–212 8620]

Set up on Feb. 20, 1970, "to advise on matters, both national and international, concerning the pollution of the environment; on the adequacy of research in this field; and the future possibilities of danger to the environment."
Chairman, Prof. Sir Richard Southwood, f.r.s.
Members, A. Archer; Prof. C. Blake; Prof. B. E. Clayton; Prof. G. R. Conway; The Earl of Cranbrook; Dr. R. H. Cummings; J. W. Edmonds; Prof. G. E. Fogg, c.b.e., f.r.s.; The Lord Nathan; Prof. D. E. Newland; J. J. R. Pope; Dr. C. W. Suckling, f.r.s.; Prof. M. P. Vessey.
Secretary, T. E. Radice.

EQUAL OPPORTUNITIES COMMISSION
Overseas House, Quay Street, Manchester M3 3HN
[061–833 9244]

Press Office: 1 Bedford Street. W.C.2
[01–379 6323]

Regional Offices: 249 West George Street,
Glasgow [041–226 4591]

Caerwys House, Windsor Place, Cardiff
[0222–43552]

Chairman, The Baroness Platt of Writtle ... £20,356
Deputy Chairman, Mrs. J. Finlay £17,800
Members, Prof. Angela Bowey; Mrs. R. Brown; J. Dunlop; D. Guereca; B. Marks; Mrs. T. Marsland; Mrs. M. Patterson, c.b.e.; Ann Robinson; Miss D. Rookledge; R. Skelton; Miss M. Sproat; Muriel Turner.
Chief Executive, Miss M. Sindell.

EXCHEQUER AND AUDIT DEPARTMENT
See National Audit Office

EXPORT CREDITS GUARANTEE DEPARTMENT
P.O. Box 272, Aldermanbury House,
Aldermanbury, EC2P 2EL
[01–382 7000]

The Export Credits Guarantee Department is responsible to the Secretary of State for Trade. The Export Guarantees and Overseas Investment Act 1978 enables E.C.G.D. to encourage U.K. exports by making available export credit insurance to British firms engaged in selling overseas and to guarantee repayment to banks in Britain providing finance for export credit. Guarantees under Section 1 of the Act are given after consultation with an Advisory Council of bankers and businessmen.

The Act also empowers E.C.G.D. to insure British private investment overseas against political risks, such as war, expropriation and restrictions on remittances.

Secretary, J. Gill c.b. £35,278
Deputy to the Secretary, (vacant).
Under Secretaries, R. T. Kemp; D. C. Smith; D. H. Twyford; F. J. Chapman £28,583
Assistant Secretaries, K. G. Lockwood; G. Bromley; C. E. Breach; P. Henley; J. H. Hall; A. C. Elston; R. Wild; J. W. Coggins; R. A. Ranson; J. K. Sedman; W. J. C. Pinnell; A. J. Bray; C. Foxall; B. J. Davison; Miss S. E. Harding; J. R. Weiss .... £19,243 to £23,159
Senior Principals, A. P. Fowell; G. C. Bird; F. Wilmot; P. C. B. Duncan; M. J. Long; H. C. Cunningham; J. G. M. Cochrane
  £15,605 to £20,794
Principals, H. E. Allen; J. S. Anderson; P. Armstrong; D. D. Baird; R. Bennett; T. R. Black; G. Blackburn; C. M. Bossom; P. J. Callaghan; J. D. Cameron; A. P. C. Carcas; A. L. Childs; D. R. Coombe; D. C. Cooper; A. B. Coyne; M. J. Crane; Ms. R. Q. Davies; T. W. Denyer; R. A. Dew; K. Dixey; C. L. W. Durning; R. I. Fear; R. X. Fear; P. A. F. Field; G. C. Fisher; J. M. Foster; R. R. Fryatt; P. C. Gaudoin; R. Gotts; D. A. Green; G. H. Hill; R. Holloway; K. I. Humphrey; T. M. Jaffray; P. F. Jennings; G. G. Jones; R. Jones; N. A. Lambert; R. F. Lethbridge; G. J. A. Link; V. P. Lunn-Rockliffe; Miss R. M. Martin; D. W. Miller; D. Miner; J. Moon; A. J. E. Muckersie; P. L. Neal; D. W. Overy; E. R. Packer; M. D. Pentecost; R. J. Pomeroy; S. C. Pond; Mrs. V. A. Randall; I. L. S. L. Robertson; S. Rosenthal; J. R. Savage; R. Scott; D. Shannon; B. M. Sidwell, t.d.; K. Smith; J. Snowden; C. T. Spillane; R. W. Stears; R. M. Sutton; C. M. Thorogood; D. A. H. Tickner; D. L. Townley; J. A. Tyler; P. M. Walker; E. J. Walsby; A. R. Watt; R. A. Watt; Miss J.West; T. D. Wright; D. L. Wyatt; G. A. Young
  £12,399 to £16,656
Principal Information Officer, M. J. Ricketts
  £12,399 to £16,656
Senior Executive Officers, Mrs. C. Adivihalli; Miss J. Allbutt; J. S. Astruc; J. E. Atkinson; R. G. Bamber; T. L. Barry; R. H.Bayliff; D. M. Beaton; A. B. Bennett; B. Blades; R. A. Bounds; R. G. Bowden; Mrs. S. D. Bowden; J. S. Brown; D. Q. Bryars; A. R. Burrows; D. F. Cannon; L. D. N. Charman; Mrs. H. V. Cieslik; P. G. Coles; D. Collins; Mrs. A. C. Cowie; W. S. Cowie; W. R. Cox; R. P. D. Crick; J. C. W. Croall; J. Currie; Miss P. A. Currin; J. R. Cutmore; A. F. Danson; M. F. Demaine; R. R. Dick; L. D. Easterbrook; A. C. Faulkner; N. F. George; J. H. E. Gibbs; J. E. F. Grafton; W. Graham; R. T. Griffiths; P. Hambleton; P. Handovsky; R. A. Hardy; K. R. Harvey; J. Hawkins; F. H. Hogben; Mrs. J. R. Hurst; K. Illingworth; P. J. Jackson; A.

E. Jenkinson; K. H. Jones; Miss S. J. Johnson; R.
W. Kee; B. D. Kennard; C. King; J. R. King; A. B.
Lane; A. R. Lane; Mrs. F. M. Lewis; I. Mackay;
Mrs. M. E. Maddox; K. A. Marshall; R. A. J. de C.
Mayer; R. K. McGowan; J. S. McKibbin; S.
Merchack; D. J. Morris; G. A. Newhouse; R. G. B.
Palmer; E. T. A. Parsons; T. O. Parry; C. H. G.
Pearse; P. Petrides; S. S. Pillai; Miss N. A. M.
Preedy; C. G. Purdy; T. Roberts; P. Roderick; F.
Rossington; M. Russell; R. P. R. Russell; M. Scales;
I. C. Scott; J. Silberston; A. C. M. Simpson; J. P.
Smith; K. R. Smith; R. G. Smith; M. L. Snell; B. C.
Southwell; R. J. Stafford; R. S. Summers; J.
Sweeney; Miss V. M. Taylor; C. D. M. Thomas; P.
D. Vivash; J. A. Walsh; T. J. M. West; R. F.
Whinnett; J. Whitehouse; M. D. Wiggett; J. M.
Willis; R. W. Willis; R. A. Wilson; D. Wood; J. A.
Youd; P. W. Youngs .... £10,079 to £12,518
Principal Scientific Officer, A. P. G. Hare
£11,343 to £14,931
Senior Information Officer, J. W. Pilbeam
£10,079 to £12,518

Regional Offices

Belfast: Windsor House, 9–15 Bedford Street,
Belfast (0232 231743); *Birmingham:* Colmore Centre,
115 Colmore Row, Birmingham (021–233 1771); *Bristol:* 1 Redcliffe Street, Bristol (0272–299971); *Cambridge:* 72–80 Hills Road, Cambridge (0223–68801);
City of London: Clements House, 14–18 Gresham
Street, E.C.2 (01–726 4050); *Croydon:* Sunley House,
Bedford Park, Croydon (01–680 5030); *Glasgow:* Fleming House, 134 Renfrew Street, Glasgow (041–
332 8707); *Leeds:* West Riding House, 67 Albion
Street, Leeds (0532–450631); *Manchester:* Townbury
House, Blackfriars Street, Salford (061–834 8181).

Export Guarantees Advisory Council

Chairman, W. J. Benson.
Deputy Chairman, R. J. Dent.
Other Members, J. N. Scott; Miss M. Neville-Rolfe;
W. A. J. Dacombe; M. D. McWilliam; W. G. Barrett;
R. H. George; W. Hogbin.

OFFICE OF FAIR TRADING
Field House, Bream's Buildings, EC4A 1PR
[01–242 2858]

The Office of Fair Trading is a government
department responsible for the administration of the
Fair Trading Act, 1973, the Consumer Credit Act,
1974, the Restrictive Trade Practices Act, 1976, the
Estate Agents Act, 1979, and the Competition Act,
1980. Under the supervision of the Director General
of Fair Trading the office keeps under review
commercial activities in the United Kingdom and
aims to protect the consumer against unfair practices
and is divided between five main areas: consumer
affairs, consumer credit, monopolies and mergers,
restrictive trade practices and anti-competitive practices.
Director General, Sir Gordon Borrie £42,750
Deputy Director General, Miss E. M. Llewellyn-
Smith £35,278

Consumer Affairs Division

Director, C. T. Newton £28,583
Assistant Directors, D. G. Hyde; M. D. C. Johnson; S.
G. Linstead .... £19,243 to £23,159

Competition Policy Division

Director, L. Lightman £28,583
Assistant Directors, Mrs. E. C. Jones; D. W. Lightfoot;
Lady O. M. Wood
£19,243 to £23,159

Legal Division

Director, T. J. G. Pratt £28,583

Chief Information Officer, J. E. Perry
£15,605 to £20,794
Senior Economic Adviser, A. G. Atkinson
£19,243 to £23,159
Establishment and Finance Officer, J. F. H. Craven
£12,399 to £16,656

FOREIGN AND COMMONWEALTH
OFFICE
Downing Street, SW1A 2AL
[01-233 3000]

On the recommendations of the Committee on
Representational Services Overseas appointed by the
Prime Minister under the Chairmanship of Lord
Plowden in 1962, H.M. Diplomatic Service was created
on Jan. 1, 1965, by the amalgamation of the Foreign
Service, the Commonwealth Service, and the Trade
Commission Service, and is now responsible for the
manning of the overseas posts of these three former
services. On Aug. 1, 1966, the Colonial Office was
merged into the Commonwealth Relations Office to
form the Commonwealth Office. The Foreign Office
and Commonwealth Office combined on Oct. 1, 1968.
In November 1970 overseas development became
the ultimate responsibility of the Secretary of State
for Foreign and Commonwealth Affairs, although it
remained in the day-to-day charge of the Minister
for Overseas Development (now the Overseas Development Administration), except for the period from
March 1974 to June 1975 when the Ministry of
Overseas Development reverted to its independent
status.
Secretary of State, THE RT. HON. SIR GEOFFREY HOWE,
Q.C., M.P..................................£38,910
  Private Secretary, L. V. Appleyard.
  Assistant Private Secretaries, Mrs. A. J. Walters;
   C. R. Budd; P. F. Ricketts; J. Houston.
  Social Secretary, Miss D. F. Lothian.
*Ministers of State for Foreign and Commonwealth
Affairs,* THE BARONESS YOUNG, P.C. (£25,350);
MALCOLM RIFKIND, M.P.; RICHARD LUCE, M.P. (*each*
£30,410).
*Minister of State for Foreign and Commonwealth
Affairs (Minister for Overseas Development),* RT.
HON. TIMOTHY RAISON, M.P...............£30,410
Parliamentary Under Secretary of State, T. Renton,
M.P.......................................£25,460
*Permanent Under Secretary of State and Head of the
Diplomatic Service,* Sir Antony Acland, K.C.M.G.,
K.C.V.O...................................£45,000
  Private Secretary, M. H. Jay.
Deputy Under Secretaries, J. S. Whitehead, C.M.G.,
C.V.O. (*Chief Clerk*); Sir William Harding, K.C.M.G.,
C.V.O.; E. A. J. Fergusson; Sir Percy Cradock,
G.C.M.G.; A. D. S. Goodall, C.M.G.; Sir Crispin Tickell,
K.C.V.O.; D. M. D. Thomas, C.M.G. (*and Political
Director*)................................£32,500
Assistant Under Secretaries, S. J. Barrett, C.M.G.
(*Director of Communications*); N. J. Barrington,
C.M.G., C.V.O.; S. L. Egerton, C.M.G.; M. R. H.
Jenkins, C.M.G.; C. H. Imray, C.M.G. (*Chief Inspector
and Deputy Chief Clerk*); J. R. Johnson, C.M.G.; K.
G. MacInnes, C.M.G. (*Principal Finance Officer*); R.
J. O'Neill, C.M.G.; R. W. Renwick, C.M.G.; D. C.
Thomas, C.M.G.; J. C. Thomas, C.M.G.; P. J. Weston;
D. C. Wilson £26,087
Inspectors, (vacant) (*Head of Home Inspectorate*); A.
J. Pover; J. R. Leeland; P. A. McLean; R.
Westbrook..................£20,493 to £24,409
Legal Adviser, Sir John Freeland, K.C.M.G.
Second Legal Adviser, H. G. Darwin, C.M.G.

Deputy Legal Advisers, A. D. Watts, C.M.G.; P. R. N. Fifoot, C.M.G.

Legal Counsellors, D. H. Anderson; F. Burrows, C.M.G.; D. M. Edwards; Mrs. E. M. Denza, C.M.G.; A. I. Aust; J. D. P. Bickford; M. R. Eaton £24,409

Senior Economic Advisers, Miss P. I. J. Harvey; J. M. C. Rollo . . . . £20,493 to £24,409

International Labour Adviser, A. E. Smith
£20,493 to £24,409

Overseas Police Adviser, R. P. Bryan, O.B.E.
£20,493 to £24,409

Signals Department (Government Communications Headquarters)
Priors Road, Cheltenham, Gloucestershire
[0242–21491]

Director, Sir Brian Tovey, K.C.M.G. £32,500

Principal Establishment Officer, P. H. Marychurch
£26,750

Heads of Departments
(£20,493 to £24,409. Assistant Heads of Dept.,
£19,257 or £13,649 to £17,906; except where stated)

Aid Policy Dept., B. Ireton; *Asst.*, M. Elliott.

Arms Control and Disarmament Dept., Hon. M. Pakenham; *Asst.*, S. I. Soutar.

Central African Dept., Miss T. A. H. Solesby; *Asst.*, D. I. Lewty.

Claims Dept., D. M. Kerr, O.B.E.

Commonwealth Co-ordination Dept., A. C. Watson, C.M.G.; *Asst.*, J. Illman.

Communications Administration Dept., B. B. Bushell; *Assts.*, V. A. Lister, M.B.E.; A. Riches.

Communication Engineering Dept., R. Castle-Smith, M.B.E. *Deputy Head of Dept.*, P. J. Rothery.

Communications Operations Dept., B. P. Austin; *Assts.*, H. McQuade; E. G. B. Jarman.

Communications Planning Staff, C. K. Davies.

Communications Technical Services Dept., P. Mason; *Assts.*, C. Higham; N. L. Allen; D. L. Houghton.

Consular Dept., M. W. Atkinson, M.B.E.; *Assts.*, Miss D. Symes; T. Abbott.

Cultural Relations Dept., J. E. C. Macrae; *Assts.*, W. T. Hull, M.B.E.; L. W. Boyes.

Defence Dept., R. J. Alston; *Assts.*, C. D. Crabbie; R. D. Hart.

East African Dept., W. N. Wenban-Smith; *Asst.*, D. H. Doble.

Eastern European Dept., J. A. Birch; *Asst.*, A. Carter.

Economic Relations Dept., M. L. Tait, M.V.O.; *Asst.*, G. Stegmann.

Economic Advisers, S. H. Broadbent; *Deputy Head*, J. M. C. Rollo.

Energy Science and Space Dept., D. E. S. Blatherwick, O.B.E.; *Asst.*, S. J. L. Wright.

European Community Dept. (External), B. L. Crowe; *Asst.*, F. Richards.

European Community Dept. (Internal), P. S. Fairweather; *Asst.*, J. S. Wall, M.V.O.

Falkland Islands Dept., A. E. Palmer, C.V.O.; *Deputy Head*, N. R. Jarrold.

Far Eastern Dept., M. Elliott; *Asst.*, I. C. Orr.

Finance Dept., M. A. Marshall; *Deputy Head of Dept.*, G. F. Griffiths (£20,493 to £24,409); *Assts.*, R. J. Beveridge; A. H. Ellis.

Govt. Hospitality Fund, Brig. A. Cowan, M.B.E. (*Secretary*) £20,493 to £24,409.

Hong Kong Dept., A. C. Galsworthy.

Information Dept., T. J. Clark; *Assts.* P. J. W. Le Breton; B. J. Everett.

Information Technology Dept., A. C. Thorpe; *Asst.*, J. Duffy.

Library and Records Dept., Miss E. C. Blayney; H. Hannam.

Maritime, Aviation and Environment Dept., J. W. D. Gray; *Asst.*, R. J. Chase.

Mexico and Caribbean Dept., C. D. Sanderson; *Asst.*, Miss M. L. Croll.

Middle East Dept., D. K. Haskell, C.V.O.; *Asst.*, R. A. M. Hendrie.

Migration and Visa Dept., A. J. Cambridge; *Asst.*, D. O. Amy, O.B.E.

Nationality and Treaty Dept., D. W. Partridge; *Asst.*, Miss Y. J. E. Veale, O.B.E.

Near East and North Africa Dept., C. W. Long; *Asst.*, P. M. Nixon, O.B.E.

News Dept., (vacant); *Deputy Head*, I. A. Roberts.

North America Dept., N. H. Marshall; *Asst.*, D. R. MacLennan.

Nuclear Energy Dept., I. R. Kenyon; *Asst.*, P. C. F. Gregory-Hood.

Office Services and Transport Unit, D. M. Harrison, O.B.E. (£19,257)

Overseas Estate Dept., R. J. Carrick, C.M.G., M.V.O.; *Deputy Head*, M. H. R. Bertram.

Permanent Under Secretary's Dept., P. G. Wallis; *Deputy Head*, G. J. B. Williams.

Personnel Operations Dept., A. M. Wood; *Deputy Head*, S. W. J. Fuller; *Assts.*, R. R. Best, M.B.E.; J. B. Horrocks, M.B.E.; E. Clay.

Personnel Policy Dept., K. E. H. Morris; *Asst.*, J. B. Donnelly.

Personnel Services Dept., J. T. Masefield; *Assts.*, B. E. Bowley; A. F. Blake-Pauley.

Planning Staff, Miss L. P. Neville-Jones.

Protocol Dept., Hon. E. Gibbs, C.M.G. (*H.M. Vice-Marshal of the Diplomatic Corps*) £24,409; S. W. F. Martin, M.V.O. (*First Assistant Marshal of the Diplomatic Corps*). *Assts.*, R. D. Gordon; D. K. Sprague.

Republic of Ireland Dept., G. Clark.

Research Dept., P. E. Hall (*Director*).

Security Dept., Mrs. V. E. Sutherland; *Asst.*, P. S. Astley, M.V.O.

South America Dept., A. J. Sindall; *Asst.*, D. Coates.

South Asian Dept., T. C. Wood; *Asst.*, B. E. Cleghorn.

South-East Asian Dept., J. D. Hartland-Swann; *Asst.*, D. J. Carter.

Southern African Dept., A. Reeve; *Asst.*, N. J. Thorpe.

Southern-European Dept., R. A. Neilson, M.V.O.; *Asst.*, H. N. H. Synott.

South Pacific Dept., J. S. Chick; *Asst.*, D. Pragnell, M.V.O., O.B.E.

Soviet Dept., N. H. R. A. Broomfield; *Asst.*, J. M. Macgregor.

Trade Relations and Exports Dept., A. White, O.B.E.; *Assts.*, A. A. Joy; G. Feast.

Training Dept., Mrs. J. J. Campbell.

Director of Language Centre, F. M. A. Cargill.

United Nations Dept., N. C. R. Williams; *Assts.*, R. B. Janvrin; T. N. Byrne.

West African Dept., M. Daly; *Asst.*, P. J. Priestley.

West Indian and Atlantic Dept., J. C. Edwards; *Asst.*, Dr. C. Brown.

Western European Dept., M. Llewelyn-Smith; *Asst.*, D. R. C. Christopher.

CORPS OF QUEEN'S MESSENGERS

Superintendent of the Queen's Messenger Service, Lt.-Col. E. M. T. Crump.

Queen's Diplomatic Service Messengers, R. J. Angel; Col. B. C. F. Arkle, M.B.E., T.D.; Maj. I. G. M. Bamber; Cdr. R. D. D. Bamford; Sqn.-Ldr. L. C. Bazalgette; Maj. G. M. Benson; Lt.-Cdr. B. R. Bezance; Lt.-Col. G. P. Blaker; Capt. D. F. A. Bloom, G.M.; Lt.-Col. J. B. B. Clee; Major F. C. W. Courtenay-Thompson; Col. J. M. Deans; Maj. P. T. Dunn; Maj. A. M. Farmer; Lt.-Col. J. W. A. Fleming; J. W. Hannah, M.B.E.; Lt.-Col. K. Hitchcock; J. O. Hollis; Cdr. R. G. E. Howe; Lt.-Col. P. S. Kerr-Smiley; Lt.-Col. J. M. C. Kimmins; Maj. D. B. Metcalfe; G. F. Miller; Maj. J. K. Nairne; Wg.-Cdr.

R. A. Nash; Maj. L. M. Phillips; Lt.-Col. H. M. L. Smith; Col. W. H. F. Stevens, O.B.E., A.D.C.; Col. D. W. F. Taylor; Sqn.-Ldr. J. A. Watson; Flt.-Lt. C. J. D. Willoughby; Lt.-Cdr. R. N. J. Wright.

FOREIGN COMPENSATION COMMISSION
Alexandra House, Kingsway, WC2B 6TT
[01-438 7045]

The Commission was set up by the Foreign Compensation Act 1950, primarily to distribute under Orders in Council funds received from other governments in accordance with agreements to pay compensation for expropriated British property and other losses sustained by British nationals. Amending Acts followed, the Foreign Compensation Act 1962 dealt with Egyptian compensation and the Foreign Compensation Act 1969 with claims for losses in the Baltic States and ceded territories of the USSR. The Commission has since 1950 completed the determination of claims and distribution of funds in respect of Egypt (1962), Yugoslavia, Czechoslovakia, Bulgaria, Poland, Hungary, Romania (1961), and moneys received from the Board of Trade under the USSR Order in Council 1969, dealing with the Baltic States and ceded territories. The Commission has also completed the determination of claims in respect of Egypt (1971) and Romania (1976) and made a final payment from each Fund. The Commission has the further duty of registering claims for British-owned property in contemplation of agreements with other countries, and it has done so in seven instances since 1950, the most recent being under the German Democratic Republic (Registration) Order, 1975, and the People's Republic of China (Registration) Order, 1980. The latter Order came into operation on January 5, 1981, and enabled certain claims of United Kingdom nationals relating to property in, and debts or pensions owing from persons in the territory controlled by the People's Republic of China to be registered and reported on by the Commission.

An Agreement was made on January 29, 1982, between the United Kingdom and Czechoslovakia on the settlement of certain outstanding claims and financial issues. The Czechoslovakia Order in Council 1982, came into operation on September 1, 1982, and provides for payments to the Commission by H.M. Government of compensation received under this Agreement, and for the determination of claims to such compensation and its distribution by the Commission.

Chairman, A. W. E. Wheeler, C.B.E.
Commissioner, J. A. S. Hall, D.F.C., Q.C.
Secretary and Chief Examiner, D. H. Wright.

FORESTRY COMMISSION
231 Corstorphine Road, Edinburgh
[031-334 0303]

The Forestry Commissioners are charged with the general duty of promoting the interests of forestry, the development of afforestation, the production and supply of timber and the maintenance of reserves of growing trees in Great Britain. Including the former Crown Woods, transferred to it in 1924, the Commission has acquired about 3,000,000 acres of land (75 per cent being plantable), of which about 2,000,000 acres are under plantations. Under various grant schemes, financial assistance is given to private owners and local authorities in respect of approved works of afforestation.

Chairman, Sir David Montgomery, Bt. (*part-time*) £16,160
Director-General and Deputy Chairman, G. D. Holmes, C.B. £34,250
Head of Forest and Estate Management, J. N. Kennedy £27,750

Head of Administration and Finance, G. S. Murray £27,750
Head of Harvesting and Marketing, G. J. Francis £27,750
Senior Officer, Wales (Victoria House, Aberystwyth), R. T. Bradley £23,159

REGISTRY OF FRIENDLY SOCIETIES (CENTRAL OFFICE) AND OFFICE OF THE INDUSTRIAL ASSURANCE COMMISSIONER
15-17 Great Marlborough Street, W1V 2AX
[01-437 9992]

The Department acts as a public registry for mutual organizations registered under, mainly, the Building Societies Act 1962, Friendly Societies Act 1974 and the Industrial and Provident Societies Act 1965. This function includes certifying that the rules are within the law, receiving and checking annual returns and putting both rules and annual returns on the public record files which are open to search by the public.

The Department's main responsibility, however, is the prudential supervision of those mutual organizations which hold investors' money, particularly the building societies and larger friendly societies, to protect the money placed with those societies by investors. The Department acts as the main channel of communication between the Government and building societies and friendly societies, and is responsible for offering advice to Ministers on policy issues affecting those societies.

The Chief Registrar has certain powers to arbitrate in disputes between members and registered societies.
Chief Registrar and Industrial Assurance Commissioner, J. M. Bridgeman £30,375
Asst. Registrar and Deputy Head of Department, A. Wilson £25,455
Asst. Registrar, R. L. Devlin ..... £19,243 to £23,159
Senior Principal, S. Whitehead .. £15,605 to £20,794
Establishment and Finance Officer and Head of Establishments & Records Branch, G. S. Royston .... £15,605 to £20,794
Senior Legal Assistants, C. B. E. White; Mrs. S. Hay; A. Lawton .... £14,401 to £19,317
Registrations Branch (*Head*), R. E. Merrick .... £12,399 to £16,656
Returns Branch A (*Head*), T. R. Richards .... £12,399 to £16,656
Returns Branch B (*Head*), F. da Rocha .... £12,399 to £16,656
Inspections Branch (*Head*), C. Bell .... £12,399 to £16,656
Head, Financial Appraisal Group (*Statistician*), A. G. Tebbutt .... £12,399 to £16,656

Registry of Friendly Societies, Scotland
58 Frederick Street, Edinburgh, EH2 1AB
[031-226 3224]

Assistant Registrar, J. L. J. Craig, W.S.

GAMING BOARD FOR GREAT BRITAIN
Berkshire House, 168-173 High Holborn, WC1V 7AA
[01-240 0821]

Established on October 25, 1968, to maintain a broad oversight of developments in gaming in Great Britain, to check prospective gaming licensees management and staff, and to advise the Home Secretary on making regulations which may be needed for the further control of gaming.

Chairman, The Lord Allen of Abbeydale, G.C.B. (*part-time*) £11,298
Members, Mrs. E. B. Y. Hunter-Jones; P. B. Kavanagh, C.B.E., Q.P.M.; N. A. Ward-Jones (*part-time*) £6,790
Secretary, M. H. Hogan.

BRITISH GAS CORPORATION
152 Grosvenor Road, SW1V 3JL
[01–821 1444]

British Gas was established in 1973. It explores for, purchases and transmits gas, and through its 12 Regions supplies gas to over 16 million customers throughout Great Britain.
Chairman, Sir Denis Rooke, C.B.E., F.R.S. £58,100
Chief Executive, R. Evans.
Secretary, G. C. Hogg.

GAS REGIONS

Scottish, Granton House, 4 Marine Drive, Edinburgh EH5 1YB. *Chairman,* R. W. Hill.
Northern, Norgas House, P.O. Box 1GB, Killingworth, Newcastle-upon-Tyne NE99 1GB. *Chairman,* K. Summersgill.
North Western, Welman House, Altrincham, Cheshire WA15 8AE. *Chairman,* G. B. Scott.
North Eastern, New York Road, Leeds LS2 7PE. *Chairman,* R. H. Greenfield.
East Midlands, P.O. Box 145, De Montfort Street, Leicester LE1 9DB. *Chairman,* E. A. Haynes.
West Midlands, Wharf Lane, Solihull, West Midlands B91 2JP. *Chairman,* H. V. Keating.
Wales, Helmont House, Churchill Way, Cardiff CF1 4NB. *Chairman,* D. H. Fisher.
Eastern, Star House, Potters Bar, Herts. EN6 2PD. *Chairman,* D. H. Griffiths, O.B.E.
North Thames, North Thames House, London Road, Staines, Middx. TW18 4AE. *Chairman,* J. Gadd.
South Eastern, Segas House, Katherine Street, Croydon CR9 1JU. *Chairman,* A. A. Dove.
Southern, 80 St. Mary's Road, Southampton SO9 5AT. *Chairman,* D. A. Young.
South Western, Riverside, Temple Street, Keynsham, Bristol BS18 1EQ. *Chairman,* A. I. D. Frith.

THE GOVERNMENT ACTUARY
22 Kingsway, WC2B 6LE
[01–242 6828]

Government Actuary, E. A. Johnston, C.B. . . . £39,250
Directing Actuaries, D. H. Loades; G. G. Newton; C. M. Stewart, C.B. £30,750
Chief Actuaries, D. G. Ballantine; C. L. Cannon; C. D. Daykin; J. L. Field; R. T. Foster; M. A. Pickford £25,878
Senior Actuaries, C. A. Harris; T. W. Hewitson; P. H. Hinton; P. M. Hodgett; Mrs. I. W. Lane; C. F. Morrison; A. P. Pavelin; R. D. Senior; D. F. Renn; A. G. Young . . . . £16,987 to £24,409

GOVERNMENT HOSPITALITY FUND
2 Carlton Gardens, SW1Y 5AA
[01–214 6000]

Instituted in 1908 for the purpose of organizing official hospitality on a regular basis, with a view to the promotion of international goodwill.
Minister in Charge, R. Luce, M.P.
Secretary, Brig. A. Cowan, M.B.E.

DEPARTMENT OF HEALTH AND SOCIAL SECURITY
Alexander Fleming House, Elephant and Castle, SE1 6BY
[01–407 5522]

The Department of Health and Social Security was created on November 1, 1968, from the Ministry of Health and Ministry of Social Security. The Department performs the functions of the two former Ministries.

The Department is responsible for the administration of the National Health Service in England and for the personal social services run by local authorities in England for children, the elderly, infirm, handicapped and other persons in need. It has functions relating to food hygiene and welfare foods. The Department is also concerned with the medical and surgical treatment of war pensioners in England, the Channel Isles, Isle of Man or living in the Irish Republic, and is responsible for the ambulance and first aid services in emergency, under the Civil Defence Act, 1948. The Department represents the United Kingdom on the World Health Organization of the United Nations. Responsibility for the administration of the Health Services in Wales was transferred to the Welsh Office on April 1, 1969. The Department is responsible for the social security services in England, Scotland and Wales. These services comprise schemes for war pensions, national insurance, child benefit, industrial injuries, attendance allowances, mobility allowances and supplementary benefits.

Secretary of State for Social Services, THE RT. HON. (PETER) NORMAN FOWLER, M.P. £38,910
   Private Secretary, S. A. Godber . £19,243 to £23,159
   Assistant Private Secretaries, S. H. F. Hickey; Miss E. Roberts.
   Parliamentary Private Secretary, (vacant).
   Special Adviser to the Secretary of State, N. True.
Minister of State for Social Security, ANTONY HAROLD NEWTON, O.B.E., M.P. £30,410
Minister of State (Health), THE RT. HON. KENNETH HARRY CLARKE, Q.C., M.P. £30,410
Parliamentary Under Secretaries of State, R. Whitney, O.B.E., M.P.; J. Patten, M.P. (*Health and Personal Social Services*) £25,460; The Lord Glenarthur (*Health and Social Security*) £21,450
Permanent Secretary, Sir Kenneth Stowe, K.C.B., C.V.O. £42,750
   Private Secretary, J. A. Doran.
Second Permanent Secretary, Sir Geoffrey Otton, K.C.B.
   Private Secretary, Mrs. M. Kirk.
Deputy Secretaries, B. R. Rayner; G. G. Hulme; G. W. France; G. A. Hart; J. S. Heppell; (one vacancy) £34,250
Chief Medical Officer, Dr. E. D. Acheson £39,500
Chief Works Officer, J. Bolton £27,750
Librarian, J. Wormald . . . . £12,399 to £16,656
Chief Scientist, Prof. Sir Desmond Pond, M.D., F.R.C.P. £34,250
Assistant Chief Scientist, Prof. R. J. Cole, PH.D. £26,236

Solicitors Office

Solicitor, H. Knorpel, C.B. £34,250
Principal Assistant Solicitors, J. St. L. Brockman; P. K. J. Thompson; R. J. Butcher £27,750

Establishment and Personnel Division I

Director of Establishment and Personnel (Departmental) Under Secretary, B. W. Taylor £27,750
Assistant Secretaries, B. H. Street; J. R. Simpson; G. R. West . . . . £19,243 to £23,159

Establishment and Personnel Division II

Director of Establishment and Personnel (Headquarters) Under Secretary, M. C. Malone-Lee . . . £27,750
Assistant Secretaries, P. V. Foster; J. F. Shaw £19,243 to £23,159

Regional Directorate

Under Secretary, E. Caines £27,750
Assistant Secretaries, R. A. Wallace; B. Bridges; R. Tilney . . . . £19,243 to £23,159

Statistics and Research Division

Director of Statistics and Research, A. R. Smith
£27,750
Chief Statisticians, B. Mahon; Ms. P. A. Stewart; J. A. Rowntree; M. V. Wilde; D. Wallage; R. J. Scott; C. P. Hogan .... £19,243 to £23,159

International Relations Division

Under Secretary, I. G. Gilbert £27,750
Assistant Secretaries, Miss K. E. W. Blunt; G. C. M. Lupton .... £19,243 to £23,159

Information Division

Director of Information, Mrs. J. Hewlett-Davies
£27,750
Deputy Director, J. M. Bolitho ... £19,243 to £23,159

Economic Advisers Office

Chief Economic Adviser, C. Smee £27,750
Senior Economic Advisers, C. H. Smee; N. J. Glass; J. W. Hurst; (one vacancy) ...... £19,243 to £23,159

Social Security Division A

Under Secretary, B. J. Ellis £27,750
Assistant Secretaries, M. E. H. Platt; D. R. Armatage
£19,243 to £23,159

Social Security Division B

Under Secretary, C. M. Regan £27,750
Assistant Secretaries, F. Sutton; T. Whiteley; J. W. White .... £19,243 to £23,159

Social Security Division C

Under Secretary, J. H. Ward £27,750
Assistant Secretaries, N. L. J. Montagu; S. E. Reeve
£19,243 to £23,159

Social Security Supplementary Benefits Division

Under Secretary, Mrs. A. E. Bowtell £27,750
Assistant Secretaries, R. M. Orton; W. A. Healey; A. G. Turner .... £19,243 to £23,159

Finance Divisions

Under Secretaries (Health), T. S. Heppell; Mrs. G. T. Banks £27,750
Assistant Secretaries, P. J. Fletcher; M. G. Lillywhite; R. A. Cubitt; R. Smith; T. Luce £19,243 to £23,159 *(Social Security)*
Under Secretary, E. B. McGinnis £27,750
Assistant Secretaries, K. Bird; B. Walmsley; M. W. Whippman .... £19,243 to £23,159

Medical Divisions (Health)

Deputy Chief Medical Officers, Gillian R. Ford, C.B.; E. L. Harris, C.B.; Elizabeth C. Shore, C.B. . £34,250
Senior Principal Medical Officers, M. E. Abrams; I. T. Field; Barbara MacGibbon; N. P. Halliday; Pamela Mason; R. M. Oliver; D. C. Ower, T.D.; Diana M. Walford; G. Jones £27,750
Chief Scientific Officer, C. Gregory.
Principal Medical Officers, A. W. G. English; J. Heckford; J. S. Hetters; J. L. Hunt; R. D. Mann; G. K. Matthew, M.B.E.; R. G. Penn; G. C. Rivett; A. H. Sippert; R. H. Smith; J. H. Steadman; R. Wilkins £25,176
Medical Staff Officers, Alison Smithies; Dr. T. K. Sweeney.

Medical Division (Social Security)

Chief Medical Adviser, Dr. P. R. Greenfield . £27,750
Principal Medical Officers, B. Purdy; W. R. Eggington; D. F. Rice; T. J. G. Phillips £25,176

N.H.S. PERSONNEL DIVISIONS
Division P1

Under Secretary, P. J. Wormald £27,750
Assistant Secretaries, Mrs. P. Petrie; Mrs. C. Palmer; R. W. Benning; Miss M. E. Stuart
£19,243 to £23,159

Division P2

Under Secretary, P. G. Perry £27,750
Assistant Secretaries, R. M. Drury; B. A. R. Smith; J. H. James .... £19,243 to £23,159

Division P3

Under Secretary, R. B. Mayoh £27,750
Assistant Secretaries, R. K. Alder; Ms. K. M. Higgs
£19,243 to £23,159

Division P4

Assistant Secretary, W. F. Farrant
£19,243 to £23,159

Superannuation Branch

Deputy Secretary, N. E. Clarke £34,250
Assistant Secretary, J. M. Bankier
£19,243 to £23,159

Supply Division

Controller of Supply, F. R. Higson £28,583
Assistant Secretaries, J. F. Sharpe; V. J. Hartley
£19,243 to £23,159
Director of Scientific and Technical Branch, R. T. Rogers £26,236
Superintendents, R. W. B. Allen; Miss M. N. Duncan; Dr. D. C. Potter; Dr. N. A. Slark; A. D. C. Shipley
£15,605 to £20,794

Industry and Exports Division

Under Secretary, D. de Peyer £27,750
Assistant Secretaries, J. F. Sharpe; J. R. Long
£19,243 to £23,159

Community Services Division

Under Secretary, J. S. Scott-Whyte £27,750
Assistant Secretaries, J. Knight; D. Brereton; Mrs. M. A. J. Pearson; Miss P. Winterton; C. E. Stone
£19,243 to £23,159

Mental Health Division

Under Secretary, E. B. McGinnis £27,750
Assistant Secretaries, Mrs. V. M. Demmery; B. A. Harrison; Mrs. P. M. Williamson
£19,243 to £23,159

Regional Liaison Division

Under Secretary, B. R. Rayner £27,750
Assistant Secretaries, D. J. Morris; S. Thorpe-Tracey; Mrs. E. A. Woods; A. D. Bacon . £19,243 to £23,159

Management Support and Computers Division

Under Secretary, M. E. G. Fogden £27,750
Assistant Secretaries, J. W. E. Clutterbuck; T. A. Howell; M. J. Pinches; J. Y. Marshall; J. M. Wray
£19,243 to £23,159

Children's Division

Under Secretary, Mrs. J. M. Firth £27,750
Assistant Secretaries, A. B. Barton; R. Toulmin; N. Teller; Miss M. R. Edwards; R. J. Petch
£19,243 to £23,159

Social Work Service

Chief Social Work Officer (Deputy Secretary), W. B. Utting £34,250
Deputy Directors of Social Work Service, Miss A. M. Sheridan; M. Phillips £24,308

Principal Social Work Service Officers (HQ), Miss
P. M. Baker; J. H. Barnes; D. E. Gregory; D. G.
Gilroy; Miss M. I. Denham; J. Hodder; Mrs. I.
Midforth; Miss P. P. Thayer ... £17,504 to £21,676
Principal Social Work Officers (Regions), Miss C. M.
Clark; H. J. Devey; Miss M. I. Ellis; A. B. Hannan;
J. F. Corcoran; W. A. Hollingberry; Miss C. F.
Jayne; Miss M. S. Markham; Mrs. E. I. Tate.

Medicines Division

Under Secretary, N. M. Hale £27,750
Assistant Secretary, J. B. Brown . £19,243 to £23,159

Health Service Division

Under Secretary, J. P. Cashman £27,750
Assistant Secretaries, J. A. Parker; A. B. Barton; I.
Jewsbury; J. B. Sharp .... £19,243 to £23,159

Catering and Dietetics Branch

Chief Officer on Catering and Dietetics, A. R. Horton
£16,343 to £20,794
Deputy Chief Officer, Miss E. J. Young (*acting*)
£12,399 to £16,656

Domestic Services Management Branch

Chief Officer, Miss M. Mawson ... £16,343 to £20,794
Deputy Chief Officer, Miss I. D. Oliver
£12,399 to £16,656

Works Group

Chief Works Officer (Director-General of Works), J.
Bolton £34,250

Directorate of Works Development

Director or Works Development and Chief Architect,
R. H. Goodman £27,750
Assistant Chief Architects, M. A. Meager; P. L. Ward
£19,243 to £23,159
Superintending Architects, B. Hitchcox; G. Mayers;
G. Miles; A. J. Noakes; J. Ward £15,605 to £20,794
Assistant Chief Engineer, S. Ratcliffe
£19,243 to £23,159
Superintending Engineers, B. C. Oliver; M. Rundle
£15,605 to £20,794
Assistant Chief Surveyor, J. M. Singh £22,996
Superintending Surveyor, A. F. Millington
£15,605 to £20,794

Directorate of Works Operations

Director of Works Operations and Chief Engineer,
T. A. Nicholls £27,750
Assistant Chief Architect, C. Davies
£19,243 to £23,159
Superintending Architects, J. D. Twells; M. F. Kemp
£15,605 to £20,794
Assistant Chief Engineers, I. E. G. Mahon; Dr. K. I.
Murray .... £19,243 to £23,159
Superintending Engineers, R. S. Body; T. Wagstaff;
R. J. Tuthill .... £15,605 to £20,794
Superintending Surveyor, B. K. Gilbert
£15,605 to £20,794

Directorate of Works Construction and Cost Intelligence

Director of Works Construction and Chief Surveyor,
K. W. Hudson £27,750
Assistant Chief Architect, M. J. Bench
£19,243 to £23,159
Superintending Architect, D. J. Burnett
£15,605 to £20,794
Superintending Engineer, (vacant)
£15,605 to £20,794
Assistant Chief Surveyor, D. A. Butler
£19,243 to £23,159

Superintending Surveyors, N. J. M. Barton; D. W.
Luscombe .... £15,605 to £20,794

Administrative Support and Land Branch

Assistant Secretary, N. Illingworth
£19,243 to £23,159

Dental Division

Chief Dental Officer, M. C. Downer £27,750
Deputy Chief Dental Officer, D. R. Whittington
£25,176
Senior Dental Officers, W. G. Everett; Dr. A. M.
Milne; W. N. McL. Niven; J. Rodgers,
D.F.M.; C. Howard £23,159

Nursing Division

Chief Nursing Officer, Mrs. A. A. B. Poole ... £27,750
Deputy Chief Nursing Officer, Miss S. P. C. Wright-
Warren £24,178
Principal Nursing Officers, M. A. Clark; Miss M. E.
Fraser; Dr. S. LeLean; Mrs. D. A. Patey; Mrs. E. B.
Rivett; J. Tait; Miss J. Wheeler; Miss J. Wood-
ward £21,273

Pharmaceutical Division

Chief Pharmaceutical Officer, Dr. B. A. Wills £27,750
Deputy Chief Pharmaceutical Officer, C. A. Johnson
£19,243 to £23,159
Superintending Pharmaceutical Officers, R. Baker;
Dr. J. M. Calderwood; A. G. Stewart; B. H.
Hartley .... £15,605 to £20,794
Principal Pharmaceutical Officers, K. J. Ayling; D. I.
R. Begg; A. C. Cartwright; Miss R. Coulson; B. A.
Curran; Mrs. M. A. Dow; A. T. Gray; D. Haythorn
Thwaite; Miss D. Hepburn; W. J. Hewlett; Mrs. S.
Kelly; Dr. B. R. Mathews; J. R. V. Merrills; A. J.
Middleton; Miss M. J. E. Millar; Dr. J. Purves;
Miss M. L. Rabouhans; A. R. Rogers; J. R. Sharp;
Miss R. J. Smith; R. L. Smith; R. B. Trigg; J. L.
Turner; J. A. Wandless .... £13,907 to £16,537

North Fylde Central Office

Controller, J. M. Bankier .... £19,243 to £23,159

Newcastle upon Tyne Central Office

Controller, D. V. Chislett £27,750
Assistant Secretaries, E. H. W. Luxton; J. Wailes; J.
W. W. Nairn .... £19,243 to £23,159

Scotland

Argyle House, 2 Lady Lawson Street, Edinburgh

Controller, F. S. Clark .... £19,243 to £23,159

Regional Organization [England and Wales]

North Eastern, Government Buildings, Lawnswood,
Leeds and Arden House, Regent Centre, Regent
Farm Road, Gosforth, Newcastle upon Tyne.
Regional Controller, R. Walton.
London North, Olympic House, Olympic Way, Wem-
bley, Middx. *Regional Controller*, J. F. Jones.
London South, Sutherland House, 29–37 Brighton
Road, Sutton, Surrey and Grosvenor House, Basing
View, Basingstoke, Hants. *Regional Controller*,
Mrs. S. P. Maunsell.
Wales and South Western, Gabalfa, Cardiff and
Flowers Hill, Bristol. *Regional Controller*, T. Grif-
fighs.
West Midlands, Five Ways Tower, Frederick Road,
Edgbaston, Birmingham. *Regional Controller*, J. T.
Green.
North Western, St. Martin's House, Stanley Precinct,
Bootle, Merseyside. *Regional Controller*, E. Stuf-
fins.

INDUSTRIAL INJURIES ADVISORY COUNCIL
Friars House, 157–168 Blackfriars Road,
SE1 8EU
[01–703 6380]

The Industrial Injuries Advisory Council is a statutory body under the Social Security Act, 1975, which considers and advises the Secretary of State for Social Services on Regulations and other questions relating to industrial injuries benefit or its administration.

Chairman, Prof. C. R. Lowe, C.B.E.

Members, J. R. Boddy, M.B.E.; D. W. Boydell; R. W. Buckton; B. L. Cawley; Prof. D. M. Conning; Dr. R. J. Donaldson, O.B.E.; Prof. J. M. Harrington; Dr. P. C. Elmes; P. R. A. Jacques; J. Ll. McQuitty, O.B.E., Q.C.; T. W. Mawer; Dr. M. L. Newhouse; Dr. A. J. Newman Taylor; Dr. P. W. Reynolds; S. J. Stanbrook; D. W. Vallis.

Secretary, B. O'Gorman.

NATIONAL INSURANCE JOINT AUTHORITY
151 Great Titchfield Street, W.1.
[01–636 1696]

Members, The Secretary of State for Social Services; the Head of the Department of Health and Social Services for Northern Ireland.

Deputies for the Secretary of State for Social Services, Sir Kenneth Stowe, K.C.B., C.V.O., I. G. Gilbert; for the Head of the Department of Health and Social Services for Northern Ireland, N. Dugdale; R. F. Mills.

Joint Financial Advisers, E. A. Johnston; T. S. Heppell; F. A. Elliott.

Secretary, J. D. Leach.

SOCIAL SECURITY—OFFICE OF THE CHIEF INSURANCE OFFICER
Cumberland House,
15/17 Cumberland Place, Southampton
[0703–34541]

Chief Insurance Officer, P. A. Parsons.

SOCIAL SECURITY ADVISORY COMMITTEE
New Court, Carey Street, W.C.2
[01–831 6111]

The Social Security Advisory Committee (SSAC) was established by the Social Security Act 1980 to advise the Secretary of State for Social Services and the Department of Health and Social Services for Northern Ireland on all Social Security matters except those relating to benefits for industrial injuries and diseases and occupational pensions. The Social Security Housing Benefit Act 1982 added housing benefit to the Committee's responsibilities.

Chairman, (vacant) £9,520

Members, Mrs. J. Browning; Mrs. J. Cheetham; Dr. R. J. Donaldson, O.B.E.; Rev. G. H. Good, M.B.E.; H. Hodge; P. Jacques; Mrs. J. L. Lysaght, C.B.E.; T. S. McLeod; Dr. D. Ray; Dr. A. V. Stokes, O.B.E.; Prof. Olive Stevenson; H. G. Simpson, C.B.E.; R. G. Wendt.

Secretary, Miss G. Moore.

NATIONAL HEALTH SERVICE REGIONAL HEALTH AUTHORITIES

England is divided between 14 Regional Health Authorities, each with at least one university medical school within its boundaries. Each Region contains a number of district health authorities (which are the operational NHS authorities, responsible for assessing needs in their areas, for planning, organizing and administering district health services to meet them). The district health authorities are generally coterminous with the local authorities which provide complementary personal social services. Four of the postgraduate teaching hospitals are now managed by district health authorities and eight are now managed by special health authorities. The Chairmen, and members of Regional Health Authorities and special health authorities, and the Chairmen of district health authorities are appointed by the Secretary of State for Social Services.

Regions

Northern, Benfield Road, Walker Gate, Newcastle upon Tyne. *Chairman*, Prof. B. E. Tomlinson, C.B.E., M.D. *Regional Administrator*, D. Hague.

Yorkshire, Park Parade, Harrogate. *Chairman*, B. Askew. *Regional Administrator*, W. A. H. Holroyd.

Trent, Fulwood House, Old Fulwood Road, Sheffield. *Chairman*, J. M. Carlisle. *Regional Administrator*, B. Edwards.

East Anglia, Union Lane, Chesterton, Cambridge. *Chairman*, Sir Arthur South. *Regional Administrator*, J. H. Stewart.

North East Thames, 40 Eastbourne Terrace, W2. *Chairman*, D. Berniman. *Regional Administrator*, M. J. Fairey.

North West Thames, 40 Eastbourne Terrace, W2. *Chairman*, Dame Betty Paterson, D.B.E. *Regional Administrator*, D. J. Kenny.

South East Thames, Thrift House, Collington Avenue, Bexhill-on-Sea, E. Sussex. *Chairman*, Sir Peter Baldwin. *Regional Administrator*, P. H. J. Le Fleming.

South West Thames, 40 Eastbourne Terrace, W2. *Chairman*, A. V. Driver. *Regional Administrator*, A. J. Kember.

Wessex, Highcroft, Romsey Road, Winchester, Hants. *Chairman*, B. Thwaites, PH.D. *Regional Administrator*, J. Hoare.

Oxford, Old Road, Headington, Oxford. *Chairman*, Sir Gordon Roberts, C.B.E. *Regional Administrator*, P. M. Cooke.

South Western, King Square House, 26–27 King Square, Bristol. *Chairman*, W. V. S. Seccombe. *Regional Administrator*, R. Nicholls.

West Midlands, Arthur Thompson House, 146–150 Hagley Road, Birmingham. *Chairman*, J. Ackers. *Regional Administrator*, K. F. Bales.

Mersey, Wilberforce House, The Strand, Liverpool. *Chairman*, R. D. Wilson. *Regional Administrator*, D. Nichol.

North Western, Gateway House, Piccadilly South, Manchester. *Chairman*, Sir John Page. *Regional Administrator*, Dr. J. L. Roberts.

SCOTTISH HOME AND HEALTH DEPARTMENT
and
NATIONAL HEALTH SERVICE, SCOTLAND
See Scottish Office

HIGHLANDS AND ISLANDS DEVELOPMENT BOARD
Bridge House, 27 Bank Street,
Inverness IV1 1QR
[0463 234171]

The Board, a grant-aided body, responsible to the Secretary of State for Scotland, has two broad objectives. These are (1) to assist the people of the Highlands and Islands to improve their economic and social conditions; (2) to enable the Highlands and

Islands to play a more effective part in the economic and social development of the nation. To this end the Board will concert, promote, assist or undertake measures for economic and social development.
Chairman, R. Cowan.
Secretary, J. A. MacAskill.

HISTORIC BUILDINGS AND MONUMENTS COMMISSION FOR ENGLAND
Fortress House,
23 Savile Row, W.1.
[01–734 6010]

Under the National Heritage Act, 1983, the duties of the Commission are: (i) to secure the preservation of ancient monuments and historic buildings situated in England; (ii) to promote the preservation and enhancement of the character and appearance of conservation areas situated in England; (iii) to promote the public's enjoyment of, and advance their knowledge of, ancient monuments and historic buildings situated in England and their preservation. The Commission has two statutory advisory committees (*see below*).
Chairman, The Lord Montagu of Beaulieu.
Deputy Chairman, H.R.H. the Duke of Gloucester, G.C.V.O.
Commissioners, J. Beecham; J. Benson; P. M. Burnham; H. M. Colvin; Prof. R. Cramp; Sir Arthur Drew, K.C.B.; A. H. Emery; D. W. Insall; Mrs. J. Jenkins; Prof. A. C. Renfrew; The Earl of Shelburne.
Chief Executive, P. W. Rumble.

Historic Buildings Advisory Committee
25 Savile Row, W.1.
[01–734 6010]
Chairman, Mrs. J. Jenkins.
Secretary, Mrs. E. J. Sharman.

Ancient Monuments Advisory Committee
23 Savile Row, W.1.
[01–734 6010]
Chairman, Sir Arthur Drew, K.C.B.
Secretary, A. F. W. Swift.

HISTORIC BUILDINGS COUNCIL (WALES)
Welsh Office, Cathays Park, Cardiff CF1 3NQ
[0222–825111]

Chairman, The Marquess of Anglesey, F.S.A.
Members, W. Lindsay Evans; Prof. J. Eynon, F.R.I.B.A., F.S.A.; The Earl Lloyd George of Dwyfor; J. B. Hilling; Prof. Glanmor Williams, C.B.E., D.Litt., F.S.A.; R. Haslam.
Secretary, R. J. Bolus.

HISTORIC BUILDINGS COUNCIL (SCOTLAND)
25 Drumsheugh Gardens, Edinburgh EH3 7RN
[031–226 3611–4]

Chairman, The Marquess of Bute.
Members, I. Begg; R. G. Cant; Mrs. K. Dalyell; Prof. J. D. Dunbar-Nasmith, C.B.E., F.R.I.B.A.; M. Ellington; I. Hutchison; The Hon. Lord Jauncey, Q.C.; Dr. M. Lindsay, C.B.E., T.D.; C. McWilliam; K. Newis, C.B., C.V.O.; H. F. Smith.
Secretary, D. J. Christie.

HISTORICAL MANUSCRIPTS COMMISSION
See page 431

ROYAL COMMISSION ON HISTORICAL MONUMENTS [ENGLAND]
Fortress House, 23 Savile Row, W1X 1AB
[01–734 6010]

The Royal Commission on Historical Monuments (England) was appointed in 1908 to survey and publish accounts of historically significant buildings, earthworks and stone constructions up to the year 1714. A new Royal Warrant in 1963 allowed the Commissioners to extend this date limit at their discretion; for practical purposes 1850 is normally taken as the limit. The Commission has published up to the present inventories covering in whole or in part eleven counties and five cities and has also published numerous other works including national and local surveys of types of monument. It is primarily a recording body though the Commissioners recommend that certain structures should be preserved. A part of the Commission is the National Monuments Record, the public archive of information, documents and photographs of archaeological sites and historic buildings.
Chairman, (vacant).
Commissioners, P. Ashbee, F.S.A.; Prof. R. J. C. Atkinson, C.B.E., F.S.A.; Prof. M. W. Beresford; R. A. Buchanan, Ph.D.; A. R. Dufty, C.B.E., F.S.A.; P. Kidson, Ph.D., F.S.A.; Prof. C. Renfrew, Ph.D., F.B.A., F.S.A.; Prof. A. L. F. Rivet, F.B.A., F.S.A.; J. Thirsk, Ph.D., F.B.A.; Sir Harry Hookway; Prof. J. K. Downes, Ph.D., F.S.A.; Prof. A. C. Thomas, Ph.D., F.S.A.; Prof. M. Biddle, F.S.A.; Prof. P. E. Lasko, C.B.E., F.B.A., F.S.A.
Secretary, P. J. Fowler, Ph.D., F.S.A.

ROYAL COMMISSION ON ANCIENT AND HISTORICAL MONUMENTS IN WALES
Edleston House, Queens Road,
Aberystwyth SY23 2HP
[Aberystwyth: 4381]

The Commission was appointed in 1908 to make an inventory of the Ancient and Historical Monuments in Wales and Monmouthshire. The Commission now includes the National Monuments Record for Wales.
Chairman, Prof. R. J. C. Atkinson, C.B.E., F.S.A.
Commissioners, M. R. Apted, Ph.D.; G. C. Boon, F.S.A.; R. W. Brunskill, Ph.D.; Prof. D. Ellis Evans, D.Phil., F.B.A.; G. Jenkins, F.S.A.; Prof. E. M. Jope, F.B.A., F.S.A.; J. B. Smith; Prof. Dewi-Prys Thomas; Prof. Glanmor Williams, Litt.D., F.S.A.; Prof. J. G. Williams.
Secretary, P. Smith, F.S.A.

ROYAL COMMISSION ON ANCIENT AND HISTORICAL MONUMENTS OF SCOTLAND
54 Melville Street, Edinburgh EH3 7HF
[031–225 5994]

The Commission was appointed in 1908 to make an inventory of the Ancient and Historical Monuments of Scotland and to specify those that seem most worthy of preservation. It also has a responsibility to record monuments threatened with destruction, including a statutory duty to record historic buildings for which Listed Building Consent for demolition has been granted. The National Monuments Record of Scotland, a branch of the Commission, contains an extensive collection of pictorial and documentary material relating to Scottish ancient monuments and historic buildings and is open daily for public reference. It also supplies archaeological information to the Ordnance Survey for mapping purposes.
Chairman, The Earl of Wemyss and March, K.T.

Commissioners, Prof. K. H. Jackson, F.B.A.; Prof. A. A. M. Duncan; Prof. J. D. Dunbar-Nasmith, C.B.E., F.R.I.B.A.; Prof. Rosemary Cramp, F.S.A.; H. M. Colvin, C.B.E., F.B.A.; Prof. L. Alcock, F.S.A., F.R.S.E.; Prof. G. Jobey, D.S.O., F.S.A; Prof. J. Butt.
Secretary, J. G. Dunbar, F.S.A.

ANCIENT MONUMENTS BOARD (WALES)
Crown Offices, Cathays Park, Cardiff

Chairman, Prof. G. Williams, C.B.E., D.Litt., F.S.A.
Members, Prof. R. J. C. Atkinson, C.B.E., F.S.A.; G. C. Boon, V.P.S.A.; R. B. Heaton; The Lord Kenyon, C.B.E., F.S.A.; Prof. R. R. Davies, D.Phil.; D. Moore, F.S.A.
Secretary, R. J. Bolus.

ANCIENT MONUMENTS BOARD (SCOTLAND)
3–11, Melville Street, Edinburgh EH3 7QD
[031 226 2570]

Chairman, M. Magnusson, F.R.S.E., F.S.A.Scot.
Members, J. G. Dunbar, F.S.A., F.S.A.Scot.; Prof. G. Jobey, D.S.O., F.S.A., F.S.A.Scot.; Dr. G. G. Simpson, F.S.A., F.S.A.Scot; Dr. A. Fenton, F.S.A., F.S.A.Scot.; Mrs. M. M. Paterson, F.S.A.Scot.; H. J. Smith, M.B.E.; The Rt. Hon. Lady Grimond; Prof. L. Alcock, F.S.A., F.R.S.E., F.S.A.Scot.; J. Simpson; Sir Jamie Stormonth Darling, C.B.E., M.C., T.D., W.S.; Prof. J. J. Wilkes, Ph.D., F.S.A.

HOME-GROWN CEREALS AUTHORITY
Hamlyn House, Highgate Hill, N19 5PR

Constituted under the Cereals Marketing Act, 1965, the Authority consists of 9 members representing U.K. cereal growers, 9 representing dealers in, or processors of, grain and 3 independent members. The purpose of the Authority is to improve the marketing of U.K. grain, production of which was about 21·4 million tonnes in 1983. One of the major functions of the Authority is to provide a market information service. It also supports research related to improving the marketing of cereals and has initiated other developments with the same aim. The Authority also acts as the agent of the Intervention Board for Agricultural Produce in respect of intervention buying, storage and disposal of cereals and oilseed rape within the U.K. under the Common Agricultural Policy and for certain other aspects of the E.E.C. arrangements for cereals in the U.K.
Chairman, A. Laing, C.B.E.
General Manager, C. J. Ames.

HOME OFFICE
50 Queen Anne's Gate, SW1H 9AT
[01–213 3000]

The Home Office deals with those internal affairs in England and Wales which have not been assigned to other Departments. The Home Secretary is particularly concerned with the administration of justice; criminal law; the treatment of offenders including probation and the prison service; the police; immigration and nationality; passport department; community relations; certain public safety matters; fire and civil defence services and also with broad questions of national broadcasting policy. He personally is the link between The Queen and the public and exercises certain powers on Her behalf including that of the Royal Pardon.

Other subjects dealt with include electoral arrangements; addresses and petitions to The Queen; ceremonial and formal business connected with honours;

requests for extradition of criminals; scrutiny of local authority byelaws; grant of licences for scientific experiments on animals; cremations, burials and exhumations; firearms; dangerous drugs and poisons, general policy on laws relating to shops, liquor licensing, gaming and lotteries, charitable collections and marriage; theatre and cinema licensing; coordination of government action in relation to the voluntary social services; and sex discrimination policy.

Salary List

Secretary of State	£38,910
Ministers of State	£30,410
Permanent Under Secretary of State	£45,500
Deputy Under Secretary of State	£36,500
Assistant Under Secretary of State	£29,500
Assistant Secretary	£19,243 to £23,159
Senior Principal	£16,343 to £20,794
Principal and Deputy Director	£12,399 to £16,656
Senior Executive Officer and Senior Librarian	£10,079 to £12,518
Principal Psychologist	£12,399 to £16,656
Principal Scientific Officer	£11,343 to £14,931
Senior Scientific Officer	£8,970 to £11,476
Principal Professional and Technology Officers	£13,211 to £15,711
Professional and Technology Officers I	£10,079 to £12,518

Secretary of State for the Home Department, THE RT. HON. LEON BRITTAN, Q.C., M.P.
Principal Private Secretary, H. H. Taylor.
Private Secretaries, Ms. C. J. Heald; N. Pantling.
Parliamentary Private Secretaries, K. Carlisle, M.P.; T. Smith, M.P.
Parliamentary Clerk, T. C. Morris.
Ministers of State, GILES SHAW, M.P.; THE LORD ELTON, T.D.; DAVID WADDINGTON, Q.C., M.P.
Parliamentary Under-Secretary of State, D. Mellor, M.P. £25,460
Permanent Under Secretary of State, Sir Brian Cubbon, G.C.B.
Private Secretary, H. S. Webber.
Deputy Under Secretaries of State, D. E. R. Faulkner; W. N. Hyde; J. Nursaw, C.B. (*Legal Adviser*); M. J. A. Partridge, C.B.; R. F. D. Shuffrey, C.B., C.V.O. (*Principal Establishment Officer*); C. J. Train (*Director-General of the Prison Service*).
Chief Medical Officer (at Department of Health and Social Security), Sir Henry Yellowlees, K.C.B.

Broadcasting Department
Assistant Under-Secretary of State, M. J. Moriarty.
Assistant Secretaries, J. C. Davey; W. J. A. Innes; C. L. Scoble.
Principals, F. H. Eggleston; R. J. D. Hazell; W. R. Fittall; Miss P. M. Strong.
Senior Executive Officer, R. G. Martin.

Community Programmes and Equal Opportunities Department
Assistant Under-Secretary of State, A. P. Wilson.
Assistant Secretary, J. L. Goddard.
Principals, M. J. Gillespie; Mrs. C. Lehman; Mrs. P. W. Nice; Dr. G. L. Thomas.

Voluntary Services Unit
Assistant Secretary, Mrs. P. A. Lee.
Senior Principal, D. F. Scagell.
Principal, F. N. Jasper.
Senior Executive Officers, A. J. Lewis; J. R. Thew.

Criminal Department
Assistant Under-Secretary of State, W. J. Bohan.
Assistant Secretaries, Mrs. B. H. Fair; W. A. Jeffrey; G. P. Pratt; N. R. Varney; R. R. G. Watts.

Principals, M. P. Bolt; Mrs. M. E. Bowden; A. Cogbill; R. G. W. Cook; B. R. Gange; Miss L. F. Gill; Miss R. E. Henn; R. W. B. Hurley; Mrs. S. J. Jarvis; B. Johnson; Miss B. Latimer; Miss J. MacNaughton; Mrs. R. M. Mitev; S. S. Mundy; K. R. North; J. S. Nottingham; Mrs. S. Street; G. Sutton; Mrs. D. M. White; M. Youngs.

Senior Executive Officers, I. F. Rutherford; G. R. Sampher; R. A. Wright.

Chief Probation Inspector, R. S. Taylor.

Assistant Chief Probation Inspectors, R. A. Betteridge; D. F. Duchemin; Miss M. D. Samuels; C. T. Swann.

Research and Planning Unit

Head of Unit, Dr. R. V. G. Clarke.

Senior Principal Research Officer, Mrs. M. Tuck.

Senior Principal Scientific Officer, S. F. J. Butler.

Principal Research Officers, J. M. Hough; T. F. Marshall; Mrs. P. Mayhew; Miss J. W. Mott; Ms. M. J. Shaw; Dr. D. E. Smith; P. Softley; R. Tarling; G. R. Walmsley.

Principal Scientific Officers, Dr. H. Goldman; Dr. S. Korman; A. D. Maclean; J. F. Macleod; Miss. P. M. Morgan.

Establishment Department

Assistant Under Secretary of State, Miss M. A. Clayton (*Personnel*).

Assistant Secretaries, M. H. Davies; J. A. Ingham; W. J. Stephens; F. J. A. Warne.

Senior Principals, S. W. Bennett; F. R. Hayhurst; J. Smedley; P. G. Spurgeon.

Senior Librarian, D. B. Gibson.

Principals, Miss M. V. A. Allibone; R. J. Baxter; R. C. Case; Miss A. Edwards; B. J. Flaherty; D. W. French; D. H. Gannon; D. Grant; P. H. Gibson; Mrs. M. G. Hollocks; E. C. Huggett; D. G. Jones; W. R. Mann; Miss S. Marshall; K. E. R. Rogers; M. P. Scandrett; J. C. Smith; J. Wake.

Senior Executive Officers, J. Ainge; Mrs. P. A. Almond; D. G. Andrews; K. A. Aylen; W. A. Black; Mrs. W. P. Boyle; G. Brindle; G. J. Edwards; B. Elliott; J. F. Fleming; E. W. A. Fryer; Miss J. A. Grady; K. S. Griffiths; N. Hancock; R. A. Hemmings; Miss H. I. McKinnon; A. E. Mantle; Mrs. J. Morgan; D. T. Nash; H. A. O'Connor; J. L. Osborne; F. J. Parker; R. Ritchie; D. G. Ross; Miss J. Rumble; G. Ryan; A. Silver; E. F. Sprunt; W. A. Syme; G. Thomson; C. Thursby; P. F. Vallance; J. Waud; D. West; S. Wharton.

Home Office Unit at Civil Service Selection Board
Standard House, 28 Northumberland Avenue, W.C.2
[01–273 3529]

Assistant Secretary, R. J. Miles.
Principal Psychologist, R. T. Feltham.

Finance and Manpower Department

Assistant Under-Secretary of State (*Principal Finance Officer*), J. F. Halliday.

Assistant Secretaries, A. J. Butler; J. V. Dance; C. H. Taylor.

Senior Principals, J. W. Cane; Mrs. V. V. R. Harris; R. M. Hoare; J. P. Nicholson.

Principals, G. Allison; J. Bowles; M. J. Brown; J. I. Chisholm; I. M. Clark; D. R. Dewick; C. I. Dickinson; R. Hulley; D. J. McDonough; D. Mullarky; A. Norbury; G. C. Robertson; Mrs. M. R. Ryan; A. V. H. Stainer.

Senior Executive Officers, R. D. Ainslie; A. T. Ashpool; P. Barham; J. W. Bowden; I. R. Burley; Mrs. M. A. Cooper; J. A. Couch; C. Darracott; R. I. Henderson; W. E. James; A. J. Jones; P. W. Jones; R. S. H. Kettle; R. G. LeMarechal; M. R. Mullard; K. Sheehan; J. D. Smith; S. M. Thornton; A. T. Williams; D. F. Williams; D. R. Wiltshire; D. I. H. Wright.

Fire Department

Assistant Under-Secretary of State, R. M. Morris.

Assistant Secretaries, P. R. Burleigh; P. Canovan; Miss G. M. B. Owen.

Principals, W. F. Bryant; T. K. Cobley; T. P. R. Crompton; C. Farrington; Mrs. D. M. Grice; D. C. Houghton; A. D. Jackson; Miss S. R. Muir; I. Rich; T. J. Wilson.

Senior Executive Officers, D. H. Evans; D. J. Mould; N. J. Neathey; R. J. Rice; R. M. Sutcliffe.

Fire Service Inspectorate

Chief Inspector, P. H. Darby, C.B.E., Q.F.S.M.

Inspectors (*Grade I*), A. R. Brannon, O.B.E.; T. D. Jones, O.B.E.; H. J. Porter, O.B.E., Q.F.S.M.; P. G. Robinson, O.B.E.; N. F. Roundell, Q.F.S.M.; A. A. Winning, C.B.E.

Inspectors (*Grade II*), F. C. Best; C. G. Burgon; S. D. Christian; C. Green; T. Greenwood; E. R. May; S. Platt; H. V. Reed.

Senior Engineering Inspector, R. M. Simpson

Fire Service College
Moreton-in-Marsh, Gloucestershire
[Moreton-in-Marsh: 50831]

Commandant, G. Clarke, C.B.E.
Deputy Commandant, D. Holland, M.B.E..
Secretary (*Principal*), J. A. Gibbs.

General Department

Assistant Under-Secretary of State, M. E. Head.

Assistant Secretaries, S. S. Bampton; Miss P. C. Drew; N. M. Johnson; N. Nagler.

Principals, Mrs. F. Clarkson; J. C. Dilling; A. H. Hewins; R. G. Ferguson; Miss G. M. Griffiths; Mrs. E. J. Grimsey; D. J. Hardwick; A. N. Pickersgill; Miss G. M. Romney; R. B. Snow; Miss C. J. Stewart; R. J. Weatherill; Miss M. S. Wooldridge.

Senior Executive Officers, L. D. Hay; Miss J. Odiam; P. Storr; M. J. I. Hill; M. W. Jarvis; J. S. Lawson; D. C. McIntosh; Mrs. D. Sangway; E. Waters.

Chief Inspector of Drugs, H. B. Spear.

Cruelty to Animals Inspectorate

Chief Inspector, M. A. Richards.
Superintending Inspector, C. B. Hart.

Immigration and Nationality Department
Lunar House, Wellesley Road, Croydon, Surrey
[01–686 0333]

Assistant Under-Secretary of State, G. H. Phillips.

Assistant Secretaries, R. J. Fries; J. K. Moore; A. R. Rawsthorne; Mrs. J. E. Reisz; E. Soden.

Senior Principals, R. A. McDowell; D. M. McQueen.

Principals, M. Copley; J. G. Daly; J. P. Emery; Mrs. E. I. France; T. M. Harris; R. Haugh; Mrs. J. M. Kidd; J. F. C. Love; R. C. Mansfield; A. Parkinson; G. H. Sonnenberg.

Senior Executive Officers, K. S. Batten; B. Bishop; J. W. Bradley; J. A. Byrd; T. Chapman; P. R. Curwen; C. Dolphin; A. N. Gammons; S. C. Handley; Mrs. V. R. Hatcher; Mrs. D. Hewett; D. A. Hills; R. A. Homes; D. Howarth; R. B. Ingham; I. Jackson; P. Kirwen; R. Laurence; M. R. Matthews; N. F. Montgomery-Pott; R. Parsons; P. M. Pawsey; F. G. Pegg; D. A. Peters; R. W. Pitcher; A. J. Plunkett; D. J. Ridout; M. I. Saunders; P. W. Sommer; Mrs. A. Underhill; G. A. Wheeler; Mrs. A. Wickington; Mrs. N. W. Williams; D. J. Wilmott; R. D. Wilson.

Immigration Service

Chief Inspector, P. Tompkins.
Deputy Chief Inspectors, C. B. Manchip; A. A. Holton; D. G. Stephens.
Assistant Chief Inspectors, G. Boiling; K. Butterworth; J. M. de Llanos; J. M. Durose; A. L. Raven; G. H. C. Thomas; G. A. Treadwell.
Inspectors, R. J. Brown; A. C. Harris; E. T. Lawrence.

Passport Department

Clive House, Petty France, SW1H 9HD
[01–213 3000]

Head of Unit, A. Holmes, C.B.E.
Deputy Head of Unit, F. H. Keens.
Principals, Miss M. A. N. Ashton; R. Harrod; T. Lonsdale; J. F. Nicholson; Miss H. E. Wells.
Senior Executive Officers, G. S. Austin; V. Hogg; A. R. James; R. F. E. Jones; G. R. Napthine; J. Y. Waddell; Miss M. M. Williamson.

Legal Adviser's Branch

Legal Adviser, J. Nursaw, C.B.
Principal Assistant Legal Advisers, A. H. Hammond; J. Pakenham-Walsh.
Assistant Legal Advisers, D. Bentley; R. J. Clayton; Miss P. Edwards; Mrs. S. A. Evans; A. W. D. Wilson.
Senior Legal Assistants, A. B. Cole; A. M. C. Inglese; J. O'Meara; D. Seymour; R. W. Tomlinson.

Police Department

Assistant Under-Secretaries of State, J. L. Bantock; D. H. J. Hilary; R. M. Morris; G. J. Wasserman.
Assistant Secretaries, D. J. Belfall; B. O. Bubbear; B. A. Emes; Miss J. M. Goose; A. Harding; R. A. Harrington; J. A. Howard.
Senior Principals, Mrs. J. Thompson; K. H. Heal; M. H. Rumble.
Principals, C. E. Birt; Miss K. J. Collins; K. H. Cooper; A. F. C. Crook; G. E. Dunkley; N. K. Finlayson; E. A. Grant; P. R. A. Fulton; P. Harris; R. E. Hawkes; P. F. Hewett; N. F. M. Home; P. J. Honour; A. P. Jackson; Miss S. G. Kippax; Mrs. L. Pallett; N. L. Sanderson; P. A. Stanton; A. G. Thomson; A. Walmsley; M. L. Winspear; R. C. Yeates.
Senior Executive Officers, D. Brooker; K. A. Day; B. Ferguson; J. A. Gunderson; D. Massey; K. B. Mitchell; P. Newton; S. Spence; K. F. Templar.

Police National Computer Unit
Horseferry House,
Dean Ryle Street, S.W.1
[01–211 3000]

Assistant Secretary, A. G. Bailey.
Senior Principals, G. F. Atherton; W. D. Clements; G. M. Cole; D. W. Punshon.
Principals, D. Blackwood; E. L. Brannan; G. Coulthard; Mrs. A. Cowley; R. F. Cumings; D. C. Moulton; D. A. Quarmby; R. Reason; R. T. Robinson; K. M. Shewry; B. G. Stocking; R. H. Watt; T. W. Wrighton.
Senior Executive Officers, Miss M. Berry; Mrs. H. Buttery; Mrs. J. Cant; R. J. Cardy; D. W. L. Chapman; Mrs. P. Cocks; I. Desmond; D. H. Faulks; A. Fishwick; K. Gadsdon; D. S. Gregory; I. Hardy; J. A. Henderson; P. D. Hill-Jones; L. G. Hunt; D. W. Jones; M. B. Jones; P. J. Kelly; D. F. J. Lovering; J. R. C. Murray; G. I. Nelson; F. W. Parfrement; D. E. F. Perkins; Miss M. Portlock; Mrs. E. Price; P. T. Price; A. K. Ring; A. Rouse; J. A. Somerville; P. C. W. Taylor; D. W. Thompson; B. T. Williams; M. H. Williams.

Directorate of Telecommunications
Horseferry House,
Dean Ryle Street, S.W.1
[01–211 3000]

Director of Telecommunications, P. L. T. Owen, O.B.E.
Deputy Directors, G. E. Guy; R. M. Hughes; S. R. Temple; H. Woodmansey.
Principals, D. R. Birleson; D. J. Moss.
Senior Executive Officers, N. C. L. Hackney; J. S. Sarjantson; Miss M. P. Symon.
Senior Communications Officer, D. W. Hart.
Chief Wireless Engineers, I. Aitken; A. Hulme; A. N. Kent; J. E. Lebutt; G. J. Mewett; J. L. Mumford; D. S. Oldnall; M. J. Phillips; J. A. W. Portanier; D. C. J. Theobald; P. M. Tomlinson

H.M. Inspectorate of Constabulary

H.M. Chief Inspector of Constabulary, Sir Lawrence Byford, C.B.E., Q.P.M.
H.M. Inspectors, R. S. Barratt, C.B.E., Q.P.M.; J. H. Brownlow, C.B.E., Q.P.M.; P. A. Myers, O.B.E., Q.P.M.; B. Weigh, C.B.E., Q.P.M.; J. Woodcock, C.B.E., Q.P.M.
Senior Executive Officer, J. L. Gilhespy.

Scientific Research and Development Branch
Horseferry House,
Dean Ryle Street, S.W.1
[01–211 3000]

Director, A. N. Rapsey.
Deputy Directors, Dr. R. A. Hinder; Dr. B. S. Luetchford; Dr. D. M. S. Peace; Dr. G. Turnbull; Dr. P. A. Young.
Principal Scientific Officers, Dr. B. J. Blain; G. J. Church; Dr. R. W. Eagle; Dr. A. Ganson; Dr. J. A. Harwood; T. Kent; T. R. Mann; D. J. Meakin; J. A. Miles; D. D. O'Brien; C. D. Payne; Dr. F. H. Preston; J. E. Simes; Dr. J. R. Stealey; R. C. Stephen; Dr. R. J. Stevens; F. Venables; Dr. R. W. Walker; A. M. Western; Dr. I. P. Williamson.
Senior Scientific Officers, C. J. Aldridge; B. G. Barnard; P. R. Bentley; D. R. Boyle; R. J. Brett; F. C. Brown; Dr. P. L. Camwell; Dr. G. A. Carr-Hill; D. J. Dean; R. H. Doney; Dr. S. Hadjipavlou; Mrs. K. E. Howard; D. S. Keen; A. J. G. Kitson; Dr. S. R. Lewis; R. A. Livermore; K. Millard; Dr. G. E. Scott; Dr. A. Stevens; P. A. Stringer; A. J. Thomas.
Principal Professional and Technology Officer, R. Oliver.
Professional & Technology Officers I, R. J. Harry; D. Hicks.
Senior Executive Officer, J. L. Ward.

Police Staff College
Bramshill House, Basingstoke, Hampshire
[Hartley Wintney 2931]

Commandant, B. N. Pain, C.B.E., Q.P.M.
Deputy Commandant and Director of Courses, J. Radley, Q.P.M.
Dean of Academic Studies, I. A. Watt.
Principal, A. F. G. Hitchman.

Civil Defence College
The Hawkhills, Easingwold, Yorks.
[Easingwold: 21406]

Acting Principal, G, E. Harrison.
Vice-Principal, (vacant).

Home Office H.Q. U.K. Warning and Monitoring Organization
James Wolfe Road, Cowley, Oxford
[Oxford 776005]

Director, R. F. Cooke.
Deputy Director, W. P. Lawrie.

Headquarters Forensic Science Service
Horseferry House
Dean Ryle Street, S.W.1.
[01–211 3000]

Controller, Miss M. Pereira.
Assistant to Controller, Dr. T. J. Rothwell.
Principal, Mrs. J. W. Harvey.
Principal Scientific Officer, V. J. Emmerson.
Senior Executive Officer, G. F. Holden.

Prison Department
89 Eccleston Square, S.W.1
[01–828–9848]

Director-General of the Prison Service, C. J. Train.
Deputy Director-General of the Prison Service, W. A. Brister, C.B.

Prisons Board

Assistant Under Secretaries of State (Directors), vacant (*Personnel and Finance*); A. J. Langdon (*Operational Policy*); T. C. Platt (*Regimes and Services*); Dr. J. Kilgour (*Medical Services*).
Regional Directors, K. Gibson (*South-East*); D. G. Higman (*Northern*); G. Lister (*Midland*); A. W. Driscoll (*South West*).
Non-Executive Members, P. Custis; Mrs. J. Hughes.
Assistant Secretaries, M. J. Addison; P. C. Edwards; J. E. Hayzelden; P. J. C. Mawer; Q. J. Thomas; A. H. Turney; R. M. Whalley; L. P. Wright.
Assistant Controller, C. P. Honey.
Deputy Director of Prison Medical Services, Dr. P. J. Hynes.
Principal Medical Officers, Dr. D. O. Topp; Dr. D. A. F. Doherty; Dr. R. J. Wool.
Senior Principals, D. L. Smith; L. A. Scudder.
Governors I, D. Atkinson; A. M. E. de Frisching; T. J. Gadd.
Principals, Mrs. P. R. Atkins; N. Benger; M. D. Boyle; Miss A. Carden; B. G. Chaplin; J. D. Cleary; P. Cook; D. A. L. Cooke; Mrs. C. Crawford; H. M. C. Crudge; P. Done; M. Goddard; D. J. Hollis; M. J. D. Jones; B. J. Jordan; E. J. Kings; J. LeVay; B. Lockett; W. F. McCay; Ms. E. B. Moody; M. J. Murphy; Mrs. S. Murray; Ms. M. C. Pedler; T. R. Peters; P. G. V. Pike; J. Plumridge; D. E. Powell; J. A. K. de Quidt; M. J. A. Prowse; Ms. P. Ransford; P. M. Scott; G. N. Stadlen; C. P. Stevens; R. S. Weekes; Mrs. H. Wigoder.
Governors II, J. F. Bailey; A. J. Barclay; J. J. Childs; R. Clarke; Mrs. M. M. Donnelly; H. D. Jones; P. J. Kitteridge; D. G. Longley; A. K. Rawson; R. Tilt.
Prison Service Chaplaincy, Ven. P. L. Ashford.
Director of Psychological Services, P. H. Shapland.
Chief Education Officer, A. S. Baxendale.
Chief Physical Education Officer, M. Denton.
Governors III, Miss M. Carden; R. Curtis; J. W. Dring; C. F. Lambert; I. Lockwood; T. M. O'Sullivan.
Senior Executive Officers, F. J. Archer; E. H. Armstrong; M. Carr; J. J. Courtney; J. Glaze; A. Hall; Miss N. M. Holden; R. W. Knight; A. D. McFarlane; T. G. McQuaid; W. H. Millar; I. A. Newton; S. A. Oattes; K. O'Sullivan; R. K. W. Parker; J. W. Plumb; A. L. Reeves; M. J. Rickman; D. S. Roberts; C. J. Roden; J. Simpson; G. H. Thomas; Ms. J. Thorpe; R. E. Smith; Mrs. V. K. Storey; Miss K. Walsh; B. J. Wells; R. J. White; G. Williams.

Chief Architect's Branch and Directorate of Works
St. Vincent House, 30 Orange Street, W.C.2
[01–930 8499]

Chief Architect and Director of Works, H. J. M. McMaster.
Superintending Architects, M. A. Brooks; J. H. Cooper; G. E. F. Slatter; R. W. T. Haines; T. R. Jones; P. A. G. Walker.

Principal Professional and Technology Officers, D. G. Baines; H. G. S. Banks; M. J. Bridgford; G. F. Burgess; B. D. Charlson; G. W. Chrisp; C. R. Cope; H. J. Davies; C. F. Drewitt; A. W. Gillman; D. W. Harris; M. C. Hayes; G. E. Hickey; J. V. R. Hillyer; F. Home; M. J. Ireson; J. F. Keeler; R. T. Lewis; S. L. Mahraj; T. G. G. Norman; A. W. Orchard; R. J. Perham; C. A. G. Poole; R. S. Putland; J. F. Sheldon; B. A. Stickley; M. Sweeny; E. C. Webber.
Principal, D. Mannings.
Senior Executive Officer, S. J. Baggott.
Professional & Technology Officer I, D. K. Acland; M. G. Adnett; N. Ashton; B. V. Atkinson; P. J. Attwater; O. P. Astaniotis; G. G. Bailey; C. R. Ball; A. Bareham; J. R. Beetles; J. E. Bingham; P. J. Bleet; D. H. Bringloe; D. G. Bullion; G. F. Burgess; J. K. Chamberlain; M. C. Cliffe; P. Clinton; J. Creigh; R. D'Cruz; T. W. Daniels; A. L. Dick; J. A. Doohan; D. E. Dunbar; S. C. Dunkin; P. E. Dyne; G. J. Easterbrook; D. G. Ellis; P. Enticknap; A. G. Fyvie; P. J. Gates; J. Gleed; K. W. Granger; G. A. Harvey; P. D. Heath; L. W. Herbert; J. L. Howells; G. S. H. Jackson; B. H. D. James; D. Kathuria; K. E. Keenan; D. W. M. Key; B. R. Lawrence; D. R. Lees; F. S. Leeson; V. Levett; A. J. Lloyd; R. Lord; R. C. Lucy; J. M. Manley; R. R. Mansfield; J. E. T. Mason; G. A. M. Miller; P. D. Morris; G. Munday; W. Murney; D. H. Newton; C. W. Nicholls; A. H. Pearson; A. H. M. Peters; M. J. Prout; M. J. Ramsey; S. W. Richards; J. M. Richmond; P. N. Roberts; M. F. Ryland; W. Sampson; A. Shaw; N. Schneider; D. Skipper; K. T. Stannard; C. Stubbs; D. A. Toms; E. J. Warwick; J. S. Watterson; A. C. Weeks; R. H. J. Whitby; E. H. Wilks; D. T. Williams; N. L. Willson; F. A. C. Wilson; O. R. Wood; S. G. Wood; E. H. Wright.

Directorate of Industries and Farms
Tolworth Tower, Tolworth, Surbiton, Surrey
[01–399 5191]

Director, C. J. Walters.
Group Managers, M. Codd; N. Fennemore; A. M. Gold; J. H. Smith; P. D. Stevens; C. J. Welsh.
Principals, J. H. Henderson; J. F. Rogers; C. Tredger.
Senior Executive Officers, P. W. Bond; W. G. Floyd; D. P. King; P. R. Symes; M. Tall.
Principal Professional & Technology Officers, D. Beaton; G. A. Hallam; G. H. A. Playford; T. Senior; A. Williams.
Professional & Technology Officers, P. J. Anderson; J. E. Belcher; C. B. Bendy; W. F. Blacker; R. W. Cardy; L. M. Cohen; K. Cunliffe; D. E. Davies; R. Daw; D. H. Fields; W. A. Heppolette; J. Irwin; A. Keenan; F. J. King; J. B. Lamb; M. W. McGuire; K. Monk; D. J. Moore; J. D. Snowdon.
Senior Farms & Gardens Managers, R. Cunningham; D. Neville; A. Gillcrist.
Farms & Garden Managers, N. Carver; J. W. Fallows; R. A. Fletcher; H. Johnstone; D. W. Webber.

Supply and Transport Branch
Crown House, 53 Elizabeth Street,
Corby, Northants.
[Corby 2101]

Director, J. D. Lodder.
Principals, R. C. Brett; M. Fitzgerald; J. Harvey; A. S. Thompson.
Senior Executive Officers, R. M. Bowley; D. J. Brown; R. M. T. England; A. H. Sutton.
Professional and Technology Officers, Grade I, P. E. G. Stone; A. W. Stimson.

Prison Department Regional Offices

Birmingham:
Regional Director, G. Lister.
Deputy Regional Director, F. B. O'Friel.

Assistant Regional Directors, E. C. Bennett (*Administration*); W. E. Cowper-Johnson (*Young Offenders*); I. A. E. Boon (*Operations*).

Bristol:
Regional Director, L. A. W. Driscoll.
Deputy Regional Director, J. Williams.
Assistant Regional Directors, T. C. Newell (*Adult Offenders*); D. V. Horsley (*Administration*); G. W. A. Ellington (*Young Offenders*).

Manchester:
Regional Director, D. W. Higman.
Deputy Regional Director, W. R. Booth.
Assistant Regional Directors, L. Edgar (*Administration*); D. M. Brooke (*Adult Males*); M. Langdon (*Females*); G. Walker (*Young Offenders*).

Tolworth:
Regional Director, K. Gibson.
Deputy Regional Director, J. R. Sandy
Assistant Regional Directors, J. Walsh (*Administration*); J. Dugdale (*Operations*); J. H. Rumball (*Young Offenders*).

PRISONS
Governors

Acklington, Northumberland, A. Stapleton
£16,343 to £19,317
Albany, I.O.W., P. D. R. Meech £21,529
Ashwell, Leics., B. J. Frisby ..... £16,343 to £19,317
Askham Grange, Yorks., J. Hunter
£13,269 to £15,947
Bedford, E. P. Polkinghorne ..... £13,269 to £15,947
Birmingham, R. J. Kendrick £21,529
Blundeston, Suffolk, G. H. Cropper £16,343 to £19,317
Bristol, J. Williams .... £16,343 to £19,317
Brixton, S.W.2, A. J. Pearson £21,529
Camp Hill, I.O.W., S. Brumby .... £16,343 to £19,317
Canterbury, Maj. R. A. Stratford-Tuke
£16,343 to £19,317
Cardiff, G. W. Axe .... £16,343 to £19,317
Channings Wood, Devon, W. J. Keast
£13,269 to £15,947
Chelmsford, J. R. Penson .... £16,343 to £19,317
Coldingley, Surrey, D. Shaw ..... £16,343 to £19,317
Cookham Wood, J. D. Yates...... £13,269 to £15,947
Dartmoor, D. Thompson .... £16,343 to £19,317
Dorchester, P. R. Pope......... £13,269 to £15,947
Drake Hall, Stafford, R. Mitchell . £13,269 to £15,947
Durham, A. H. Papps £21,529
Exeter, D. Alderson .... £16,343 to £19,317
Featherstone, Wolverhampton, D. A. Marsden
£16,343 to £19,317
Ford, Sussex, P. L. Pye .... £16,343 to £19,317
Frankland, Durham, G. Dadds.............£21,529
Gartree, Leics., M. Brown £21,529
Gloucester, W. E. McEvoy ...... £13,269 to £15,947
Grendon and Spring Hill, Bucks., M. F. G. Selby
£21,529
Haverigg, Cumbria, P. Buxton ... £16,343 to £19,317
Highpoint, Newmarket, D. V. Hickson
£13,269 to £15,947
Holloway, N.7, Miss J. A. M. Kinsley £21,529
Hull, J. F. Perriss...........................£21,529
Kingston, Portsmouth, Miss M. R. Allen
£13,269 to £15,947
Kirkham, Lancs., J. L. Rham .... £16,343 to £19,317
Lancaster, C. B. Scott .... £13,269 to £15,947
Leeds, W. A. Martin £21,529
Leicester, R. Mole .... £16,343 to £19,317
Lewes, D. A. Brown .... £16,343 to £19,317
Leyhill, Glos., R. L. D. Skrine ... £16,343 to £19,317
Lincoln, P. L. Harrap .... £16,343 to £19,317
Liverpool, J. Richardson £21,529
Long Lartin, Worcs., M. D. Jenkins.........£21,529
Maidstone, C. J. Allen .... £16,343 to £19,317
Manchester, J. D. U. Lewis £21,529

Northeye, Sussex, D. C. Ozanne .. £13,269 to £15,947
Norwich, R. E. Withers .... £16,343 to £19,317
Nottingham, J. R. Marriott ..... £13,269 to £15,947
Oxford, J. Horsfall............... £13,269 to £15,947
Parkhurst, I.O.W., A. H. Rayfield...........£21,529
Pentonville, B. A. Marchant £21,529
Preston, K. L. Taylor .... £16,343 to £19,317
Ranby, T. Davies .... £16,343 to £19,317
Reading, B. C. Hayday .... £13,269 to £15,947
Rudgate, N. Berry .... £13,269 to £15,947
Shepton Mallet, D. L. Long ..... £13,269 to £15,947
Shrewsbury, L. M. Wiltshire..... £13,269 to £15,947
Stafford, C. Heald.........................£21,529
Standford Hill, J. M. Reid .... £16,343 to £19,317
Styal, Cheshire, J. H. M. Anderson £16,343 to £19,317
Sudbury, L. Stones .... £16,343 to £19,317
Swansea, L. Lewis .... £13,269 to £15,947
The Verne, Dorset, B. V. Smith .. £16,343 to £19,317
Wakefield, J. E. Simmons £21,529
Wakefield Service College, R. S. Duncan £21,529
Wandsworth, S.W.18, W. Guinan...........£21,529
Wayland, C. A. Brown .... £16,343 to £19,317
Winchester, M. V. Roberts ...... £16,343 to £19,317
Wormwood Scrubs, W.12, I. Dunbar £21,529
Wymott, Preston, E. S. Nash ..... £16,343 to £19,317

YOUTH CUSTODY CENTRES
Governors

Aylesbury, T. C. H. Newth .... £16,343 to £19,317
Bullwood Hall, Essex, Miss U. M. B. McCollam
£13,269 to £15,947
Castington, D. M. Twiner .... £16,343 to £19,317
Deerbolt, P. A. Whitehouse ...... £16,343 to £19,317
Dover, D. Aram .... £16,343 to £19,317
East Sutton Park, Kent, B. H. Coatsworth
£13,269 to £15,947
Erlestoke, Wilts., A. F. Mills ..... £13,269 to £15,947
Everthorpe, Humberside, R. Cooper
£16,343 to £19,317
Feltham, A. F. H. Arnold .... £16,343 to £19,317
Gaynes Hall, Cambs, K. D. Wyatt £13,269 to £15,947
Glen Parva, Leics., E. V. H. Williams £21,529
Guys Marsh, Dorset, J. Blakey ... £13,269 to £15,947
Hatfield, Yorks., R. Elvy .... £13,269 to £15,947
Hewell Grange, Worcs., T. M. Turner
£13,269 to £15,947
Hindley, Lancs, G. Shore .... £16,343 to £19,317
Hollesley Bay Colony, Suffolk, J. C. G. Williams
£16,343 to £19,317
Huntercombe and Finnamore Wood, Oxon., E. R. Campbell .... £13,269 to £15,947
Lowdham Grange, Notts., W. J. Cooper
£16,343 to £19,317
Northallerton, F. Weigh .... £13,269 to £15,947
Onley, Warwicks., J. Whitty ..... £16,343 to £19,317
Portland, Dorset, E. R. E. Skelton £16,343 to £19,317
Rochester, J. S. Shulman .... £16,343 to £19,317
Stoke Heath, Salop, A. Cruikshank
£16,343 to £19,317
Swinfen Hall, Staffs., J. Semple .. £13,269 to £15,947
Usk, Gwent, J. Capel .... £13,269 to £15,947
Wellingborough, E. Martin ...:.. £16,343 to £19,317
Wetherby, Yorks., F. E. C. Jones .. £13,269 to £15,947

REMAND CENTRES
Governors

Ashford, Middx., S. C. A. Pryor . £16,343 to £19,317
Brockhill, Worcs., J. Wilkinson .. £13,269 to £15,947
Latchmere House, Surrey, J. L. Smith
£13,269 to £15,947
Low Newton, Co. Durham, M. R. J. Gander
£13,269 to £15,947
Pucklechurch, Bristol, Miss S. F. McCormick
£13,269 to £15,947
Risley, Cheshire, N. F. Low £21,529
Thorp Arch, Wetherby, R. A. Dalton
£13,269 to £15,947

DETENTION CENTRES
Governors

Aldington, Kent, G. Gregory-Smith
£13,269 to £15,947
Blantyre House, Kent, R. Croxford £13,269 to £15,947
Buckley Hall, Lancs., R. M. Parfitt £13,269 to £15,947
Campsfield House, Oxford, K. B. Owen
£11,182 to £12,814
Eastwood Park, Glos., D. W. Chapman
£11,182 to £12,814
Foston Hall, Derby, Maj. L. J. Henwood
£11,182 to £12,814
Gringley, R. McGlasson .... £11,182 to £12,814
Haslar, Hants., B. Sutton .... £13,269 to £15,947
Kirklevington, Cleveland, A. J. Brackenborough
£11,182 to £12,814
Medomsley, D. Whitehead .... £13,269 to £15,947
New Hall, Yorks., B. E. N. Lyte ... £13,269 to £15,947
North Sea Camp, Lincs., J. W. Hanson
£13,269 to £15,947
Send, Surrey, J. R. Dovell .... £11,182 to £12,814
Werrington House, Staffs., M. K. Pascoe
£13,269 to £15,947
Whatton, Notts., Miss J. M. Fowler
£13,269 to £15,947

Inspectorate of Prisons

H.M. Chief Inspector of Prisons, Sir James Hennessy, K.B.E., C.M.G.
H.M. Deputy Chief Inspector of Prisons, G. H. Lakes, M.C.
Inspectors, D. Campbell; D. J. Blackman; H. D. Hillier; C. J. Jones; Dr. D. Macleod; J. A. Pemberton; J. Tuck; B. J. Wells; B. Wilson, B.E.M.
Principal, G. Underwood.

Public Relations Branch

Director of Information Services, B. L. Mower.
Chief Information Officer, B. J. Sutlieff.
Principal Information Officers, Ms. E. Drummond; Mrs. S. M. L. May.
Senior Information Officers, G. R. Cotterell; G. H. Moores; Miss M. J. Palau; J. Porter; B. R. Richardson; B. R. Willis.

Statistical Department

Tolworth Tower, Tolworth, Surrey
[01–399 5191]

Assistant Under-Secretary of State, Miss R. J. Maurice.
Chief Statisticians, C. G. Lewis; P. W. Ward; J. R. Williams.
Statisticians, W. R. L. Alldrift; P. H. Atkinson; G. C. Barclay; Dr. A. J. Bishop; K. D. Childs; P. F. Collier; L. Davidoff; J. Imber; K. M. Jackson; W. Lister; G. J. O. Phillpotts; G. C. Reed; S. M. Speller; R. M. Taylor; D. H. Ward; C. F. Woolf.
Senior Executive Officers, E. C. Curson; J. D. Fuller.

Women's Royal Voluntary Service

17 Old Park Lane, W1Y 4AJ
[01–499 6040]

National Chairman, Mrs. B. Shenfield.

HORSERACE TOTALISATOR BOARD

74 Upper Richmond Road, S.W.15
[01–874 6411]

Established by the Betting, Gaming and Lotteries Act, 1963, as successor in title to the Racecourse Betting Control Board established by the Racecourse Betting Act, 1928.

Its function is to operate totalisators on approved racecourses in Great Britain, and it also provides off-course cash and credit offices. Under the Horserace Totalisator and Betting Levy Board Act, 1972, it is further empowered to offer bets at starting price (or other bets at fixed odds) on any sporting event.
Chairman, Sir Woodrow Wyatt £21,509
Members, Sir Alexander Glen, K.B.E., D.S.C.; Dame Elizabeth Ackroyd, D.B.E.; F. J. Chapple; The Duke of Devonshire, P.C., M.C.; Hon. D. Montagu; P. S. Winfield; J. F. Sanderson.

HOUSING CORPORATION

149 Tottenham Court Road, W1P 0BN
[01–387 9466]

A Government agency established in 1964 which registers, supervises and funds non-profit making housing associations throughout the United Kingdom. Under the 1974 Housing Act the Corporation was given a new and central role in promoting the housing association movement and funding an expanded programme of housing schemes by associations mainly for fair rent. The Act also gave the Corporation the responsibility for the registering of the housing associations before they could be eligible for public funds and supervising and controlling their activities to ensure accountability for the public money in their care. The Corporation has now registered over 2,500 associations under the 1974 Act.

Since 1974 the Corporation has supported housing associations in the rehabilitation of older houses and in new building, much of it to help people with special needs, including the elderly, the handicapped, and the single homeless. Following the 1980 Housing Act the Corporation is encouraging and backing new initiatives by housing associations to extend the range of housing available through schemes for shared equity, leasehold for the elderly and improvement for sale. All housing associations may now sell to their tenants and tenants of non-charitable housing associations have the right to buy their homes. *Chairman,* Sir Hugh Cubitt, C.B.E.

INDEPENDENT BROADCASTING AUTHORITY

70 Brompton Road, S.W.3
[01–584 7011]

The Independent Television Authority was created by Act of Parliament in July, 1954 to provide an additional television broadcasting service to that provided by the British Broadcasting Corporation. In July, 1972, under the Sound Broadcasting Act, 1972, it was renamed the Independent Broadcasting Authority and its functions were extended to cover the provision of Independent Local Radio. The Television Act, 1964, and the Sound Broadcasting Act, 1972 were consolidated into the Independent Broadcasting Authority Act, 1973. The Broadcasting Act, 1980, provided for the setting up of the Channel Four Television Company as a subsidiary of the IBA; it started broadcasting in England, Scotland and Northern Ireland on Nov. 2, 1982. A separate Welsh Fourth Channel Authority was also established by this Act and started broadcasting on Nov. 2, 1982. The Broadcasting Act, 1981 has consolidated a number of Acts relating to the IBA. As part of its review of the ITV system, the Authority, in December 1980, offered a contract to broadcast a new national breakfast-time television service (which started in Feb. 1983) to TV-AM. In addition, changes were made to some ITV companies.

The Authority consists of a Chairman and eleven members appointed by the Home Secretary (of whom three make Scotland, Wales and Northern Ireland their respective responsibilities) and a permanent staff under the Director General. The four main functions of the Authority are to appoint the ILR and ITV programme companies; to own and operate the transmitters; to supervise the programmes provided by the contractors and the Channel Four Television Company and their scheduling; and to control the advertising. The programme companies pay the Authority a rental to enable it to carry out its duties. Fifteen ITV programme companies provide programmes in 14 regions (two companies operate in London, one at the weekends, the other during the week). By June, 1984, 43 Independent Local Radio contractors were broadcasting in 42 areas of the U.K. (in London, there are two companies, one providing a news and information service, and the second general entertainment and information). Further areas will be covered by Independent Local Radio during the 1980s. Both Independent Television and ILR are financed mainly by the sale of advertising time.

Chairman, The Lord Thomson of Monifieth, p.c., k.t.
£23,520

Deputy Chairman, Sir John Riddell, Bt. £6,115
Members, Mrs. P. Ridley; M. H. Caine; R. A. Grantham; Mrs. J. D. M. Jowitt; Mrs. J. McIvor *(Northern Ireland)*; Rev. W. J. Morris, ph.d. *(Scotland)*; G. R. Peregrine *(Wales)*; Mrs. Y. Conolly; G. Russell; Prof. A. Cullen, o.b.e., f.r.s.
£3,060

Director General, J. Whitney.
Director of Administration, Mrs. S. Littler.
Director of Television, D. Glencross.
Director of Radio, J. B. Thompson, c.b.e.
Director of Engineering, T. Robson, o.b.e.
Director of Finance, P. Rogers.
Head of Advertising Control, H. Theobalds.
Head of Information, Miss B. Hosking.
Secretary, B. Rook.
Regional and National Officers, F. W. L. G. Bath *(South-West England, Channel Islands)*; vacant *(Yorkshire)*; E. Lewis *(Wales and West of England)*; A. D. Fleck *(Northern Ireland)*; Miss S. Thane *(East of England)*; D. Lee *(North-West England)*; B. Marjoribanks *(Scotland)*; R. J. F. Lorimer *(North-East England and the Borders)*; N. J. Reedy *(East and West Midlands)*; J. B. Scott *(South and South-East England)*.

CENTRAL OFFICE OF INFORMATION
Hercules Road, SE1 7DU
[01–928 2345]

The Central Office of Information is a common service department which produces information and publicity material, and supplies publicity services, for other Government departments on a repayment basis. In the United Kingdom it conducts Government display press, television and poster advertising, produces and distributes booklets, leaflets, films, television material, exhibitions, photographs and other visual material; and distributes departmental press notices. For the overseas departments it supplies British Information posts overseas with press, radio and television material, booklets, magazines, reference services, films, exhibitions, photographs, display and reading room material; arranges tours in the United Kingdom for official visitors from overseas. Administrative responsibility for the Central Office of Information rests with H.M. Treasury Ministers, while the ministers whose departments it serves are responsible for the policy expressed in its work.

Salary List
Director General £30,375
Deputy Director General £26,236
Principal Establishment Officer . £23,159 *(maximum)*
Principal Finance Officer . . . . £23,159 *(maximum)*
Group Director . . . . £23,159 *(maximum)*

Head of Career Management Unit
£23,159 *(maximum)*
Director . . . . £20,794 *(maximum)*
Regional Director (Leeds, London, Birmingham and Manchester) . . . . £20,794 *(maximum)*
Regional Director (Newcastle, Cambridge and Bristol) . . . . £16,656 *(maximum)*
Director-General, D. D. Grant.
Private Secretary, Mrs. M. L. Evans.
Head of Career Management Unit for the Information Officer Group, A. J. Brooks.
Deputy Director-General, Miss S. Jefferies.

Establishment and Organization Division
Atlantic House, Holborn Viaduct, E.C.1.
[01–583 5744]

Principal Establishment Officer, E. Bridger.

Finance and Accounts Division
Principal Finance Officer, A. H. Robinson.

OVERSEAS PUBLICITY GROUP
Group Director, A. E. Bevens.

Overseas Press Services
Director, R. N. Hooper.

Overseas Publications & Foreign Languages
Director, S. C. Lyle-Smythe.

Overseas Visitors & Information Studies
Director, D. A. Smith.

VISUAL MEDIA AND RADIO GROUP
Group Director, E. R. I. Allan, o.b.e.

Films & Television
Director, R. J. Hall.

Radio and Photographic Services
Director, J. A. Leys.

Exhibitions
Director, D. A. Low.

HOME PUBLICITY GROUP
Group Director, (vacant).

Advertising
Director, (vacant).

Home Publications & Printing
Director, D. A. Loxley.

Research
Director, R. J. H. Jones.

CLIENT SERVICES GROUP
Group Director, P. T. Brazier.

Media Co-ordination & Customer Relations
Director, J. W. Coe.

Regional Offices
North Eastern
Wellbar House, Gallowgate,
Newcastle upon Tyne
Regional Director, J. F. Dougray.

Yorkshire and Humberside
City House, New Station Street, Leeds
Regional Director, A. S. Poole.

Eastern
Three Crowns House, 72–80 Hills Road, Cambridge
Regional Director, P. J. Woodford.

London and South Eastern
Atlantic House, Holborn Viaduct, E.C.1

Regional Director, J. K. Holroyd.

South Western
The Pithay, Bristol, 1

Regional Director, P. D. Yorke.

Midlands
Five Ways Tower, Frederick Road, Edgbaston,
Birmingham 15

Regional Director, R. F. Long.

North Western
Sunley Building, Piccadilly Plaza, Manchester

Regional Director, O. J. B. Prince-White.

BOARD OF INLAND REVENUE
Somerset House, WC2R 1LB
[01–438 6622]

The Board of Inland Revenue was constituted under the Inland Revenue Board Act, 1849, by the consolidation of the Board of Excise and the Board of Stamps and Taxes. In 1909 the administration of excise duties was transferred to the Board of Customs. The Board of Inland Revenue administers and collects direct taxes—mainly income tax, corporation tax, capital gains tax, capital transfer tax, stamp duty, development land tax and petroleum revenue tax—and advises the Chancellor of the Exchequer on policy questions involving them. The Head Office is in London and there are Inspectors of Taxes offices and Collection offices throughout the United Kingdom. The Department's Valuation Office is responsible for valuing property for tax purposes, for compensation and for compulsory purchase and (in England and Wales) for local rating purposes. In 1983/84 Inland Revenue collected over £45,800,000,000 tax.

SALARY LIST

Unified Grade 1	£45,500
2	£36,500
3	£29,500
4	£25,455
5	£23,159 (*maximum*)
6	£20,794 (*maximum*)

Departmental Variations:
Deputy Chief Valuer (England and Wales)
    £29,500 (*maximum*)
Chief Valuer (Scotland) £25,184
Assistant Chief Valuer (England and Wales) £24,628
Solicitor (Scotland) £24,030
Senior Legal Assistant (Scotland)
    £19,317 (*maximum*)
Chief Examiner (CTO) & Controller of Stamps
  (Scotland) .... £16,789 (*maximum*)

The Board

Chairman (Grade 1), Sir Lawrence Airey, K.C.B.
  Private Secretary, A. J. Walker.
Deputy Chairmen (Grade 2), J. M. Green, C.B.; A. J. G. Isaac.
Directors General (Grade 2), J. H. Gracey, C.B.; D. B. Rogers, C.B.
Commissioners : Chief Valuer (Grade 2), A. B. Fallows; *(Grade 3)*, J. D. Taylor-Thompson.

Policy Divisions

Grade 3, J. D. Taylor-Thompson; B. T. Houghton; P. L. O'Leary; L. J. H. Beighton; J. M. Crawley; R. A. Blythe.
Grade 5, P. W. Fawcett; D. G. Draper; I. R. Spence; J. P. B. Bryce; R. G. Lusk; B. A. Mace; J. D. Farmer; O. T. Morgan; D. Y. Pitts; J. B. Shepherd; R. I.

McConnachie; M. J. G. Elliott; C. W. Corlett; P. J. Driscoll; N. C. Munro; M. A. Johns; M. Prescott; M. F. Cayley; E. McGiven; C. Stewart.
Controller of Development Land Tax Office (Grade 6), R. A. Hutton.

Central Division

Grade 3, T. J. Painter.
Grade 5, P. Lewis; R. R. Martin.
Senior Economic Adviser (Grade 5), R. Weeden.
Press Officer (Grade 6), J. P. O. Lewis.

Technical Division

Directors (Grade 3), J. E. Lawrance; B. Pollard.
Assistant Directors (Grade 4), M. D. Whitear; K. Skinner; R. E. German; R. W. Parker; J. Moule; M. D. E. Newstead; E. K. Pearson; P. Tyrer, C.B.E.; E. Pattison; G. F. Hamilton; W. Northend; D. W. Muir; J. C. Campbell; P. C. H. Crozier.
Assistant Directors (Grade 5), G. H. Bush; T. A. Symons; J. Bishton; D. W. Hugo; I. N. Hunter; B. Sadler; J. F. Hall.
Principal Inspectors of Taxes (Grade 5), M. Templeman; J. Potter; M. L. Gordon; E. J. Smith; R. E. Creed; J. White; P. C. Fielder; I. R. Drummond; R. J. Ramage; G. Guest; K. H. Colmer; J. S. Marshall; D. A. Johnson; E. J. Gribbon.
Controller of Oil Taxation Office (Grade 5), R. M. Elliss.
Board's Investigating Officer (Grade 6), D. Ward.

Management Divisions

Director of Personnel (Grade 3), D. B. Vernon.
Assistant Directors (Grade 5), P. H. Dennis; C. E. Howick; F. W. Newcombe; J. T. Tudor; J. K. Ward; B. O'Connor.
Controller of Office Services (Grade 6), B. R. Spooner.
Director of Manpower and of Training (Grade 3), D. J. L. Moore.
Assistant Directors, K. W. H. Benson (*Grade 4*); J. Marshall; H. A. White; D. K. Matthews; J. W. Waters (*Grade 5*).
Principal Inspector of Taxes (Grade 5), G. J. Shaw.
Head of Operational Research Services (Grade 6), Dr. A. A. Holt.
Director of Data Processing (Grade 3), P. B. G. Jones.
Assistant Directors, S. C. T. Matheson (*Grade 4*); A. R. Brunsdon; D. Selwood (*Grade 5*).
Director of Operations (Grade 3), J. H. Roberts.
Assistant Directors, C. Cherry (*Grade 4*); J. M. Phalp; R. H. Allen; D. H. Stanton; P. J. Hodgson; J. C. Jones; J. Gant; F. Colloff (*Grade 5*).
Controller Enforcement Office (Grade 6), R. F. Bruford.

Finance Division

Principal Finance Officer (Grade 3), D. J. L. Moore.
Assistant Secretaries (Grade 5), A. G. Nield; J. A. Pinder.
Controller, Central Accounting Office (Grade 6), L. J. Lee.
Chief Internal Auditor (Grade 6), T. D. C. Meadows.

Statistics Division

Director (Grade 3), J. W. S. Walton.
Chief Statisticians (Grade 5), J. B. Dearman; W. Gonzalez; F. A. Fitzpatrick.
Management (Grade 6), E. F. Smith.

Office of the Controller of Stamps
Bush House, South-West Wing, Strand, W.C.2
and Barrington Road, Worthing, Sussex

Controller (Grade 6), D. E. Pipe.

Capital Taxes Office
Minford House, Rockley Road, W.14

Controller (Grade 4), P. H. Fletcher.
Deputy Controllers (Grade 5), G. A. Spencer; B. D. Kent.

Asst. Controllers (Grade 6), W. H. Rundle; G. Allcock; A. S. Johnson; M. Swann; R. J. Draper; A. L. Barton; G. Wilkinson; I. P. Gunn; D. J. Ferley; C. A. Oldridge; H. V. Capon.

Solicitor of Inland Revenue
Somerset House, W.C.2

Solicitor (Grade 2), R. S. Boyd.
Principal Assistant Solicitors (Grade 3), P. D. Hall; J. F. Easton; R. K. Miller.
Assistant Solicitors (Grade 5), A. L. L. Alexander; C. J. C. Baron; R. T. Brand; K. O. Butterfield; B. R. D. Clarke; B. E. Cleave; M. C. Furey; J. F. W. Hinson; E. O. Jackson; J. D. H. Johnston; N. R. Phillips; J. G. H. Bates; P. L. Ridd.

Superannuation Funds Office
Lynwood Road, Thames Ditton, Surrey

Controller (Grade 5), H. B. Thompson.
Assistant Controllers (Grade 6), J. Horrell; I. A. Young.

Inspector of Foreign Dividends Office
Lynwood Road, Thames Ditton, Surrey

Inspector of Foreign Dividends (Grade 6), D. J. Critchley.

Office of the Chief Valuer
New Court, Carey Street, W.C.2

Chief Valuer (Grade 2), A. B. Fallows.
Deputy Chief Valuers, P. G. Heard; R. R. B. Shutler.
Assistant Chief Valuers, P. J. Borett; R. D. E. Gilbard; G. Williams; R. J. Sellick; S. H. Keith; A. J. Langford.
Superintending Valuers (Grade 5), D. B. Hardy; D. I. Mabey; A. S. Murton; A. B. Prior; E. G. Rogers; A. K. L. Ryde; R. J. Schumacher; C. V. Thompson.

INLAND REVENUE (SCOTLAND)
80 Lauriston Place, Edinburgh

Controller (Grade 4), W. S. Linkie.
Group Controllers (Grade 5), F. W. Provan; H. S. MacRae; O. J. Clarke; M. J. Hodgson.

Controller (Stamps)
16 Picardy Place, Edinburgh

Controller, Mrs. M. M. Wynne.

Capital Taxes Office
16 Picardy Place, Edinburgh

Registrar (Grade 5), J. B. M. McKean.
Deputy Registrar (Grade 6), P. G. Bruce, M.B.E.
Chief Examiners, Miss M. M. M. Armstrong; F. F. King; G. Mackie; T. E. Naysmith; Mrs. J. A. Templeton; J. R. Telford; W. Young.

Solicitor's Office
80 Lauriston Place, Edinburgh

Solicitor, T. H. Scott.
Senior Legal Assistants, I. K. Laing; Miss E. M. M. McLean; D. S. Wishart.

Office of the Chief Valuer, Scotland
15 Drumsheugh Gardens, Edinburgh

Chief Valuer, J. Gilchrist, C.B.E.
Assistant Chief Valuers (Grade 5), J. Fergus; J. A. Sutherland.

INTERVENTION BOARD FOR AGRICULTURAL PRODUCE
Fountain House, 2 Queen's Walk, Reading RG1 7QW
[Reading: 583626]

The Board was formed as a Government Department on November 22, 1972, and is responsible under the Agricultural Ministers for the implementation within the United Kingdom of the guarantee functions of the Common Agricultural Policy of the European Economic Community. Policy matters are the responsibility of the Agricultural Ministers of the United Kingdom.
Chairman, D. C. G. Jessel.
Chief Executive (Under Secretary), A. K. H. Atkinson
£27,750
Secretary and Information Officer (Higher Executive Officer), D. J. Ward .... £8,000 to £10,200

Establishments Branch
Establishments Officer (Principal), J. Bird
£12,400 to £16,600
Senior Executive Officers, D. H. Potter; G. Donkin
£10,000 to £12,500

Finance and Audit Division
Finance Officer (Assistant Secretary), P. G. Horscroft
£19,200 to £23,100
Senior Principal, E. M. Abbott . £16,300 to £20,800

Finance Branch
Principals, D. D. Morris; P. J. Offer; H. Mac-Kinnon .... £12,400 to £16,600
Senior Executive Officers, C. M. Collins; R. H. Ebsworth; G. E. Lambert; A. D. Reed; J. Palethorpe
£10,000 to £12,500

Audit Branch
Chief Accountant (Principal), R. Howes
£12,400 to £16,600
Senior Executive Officers, J. O'Neill; G. Evans
£10,000 to £12,500

Internal Market Division
Assistant Secretary, D. M. L. Macgregor
£19,200 to £23,100
Senior Principal, G. R. Holloway . £16,300 to £20,800
Principals, D. F. Horler; M. E. Statham; J. P. Bradbury .... £12,400 to £16,600
Commodity Specialists, J. R. Edmunds; D. G. Griffiths
£13,300 to £17,700
Senior Executive Officers, C. D. Perrin; D. J. H. F. Lee; R. W. Hughes; D. J. Sweet £10,000 to £12,500

Import and Export Division
Assistant Secretary, R. J. Attwell £19,200 to £23,100
Principals, N. Dixon; E. R. Asprey; N. P. J. Rowe
£12,400 to £16,600
Senior Executive Officers, L. J. Frampton; A. J. Butler; Mrs. S. Banham; J. Fitzgerald; A. E. Holden; J. W. C. Williams; J. F. Springate
£10,000 to £12,500

United Kingdom Seeds Executive
Prof. J. D. Ivins *(Chairman)*; R. E. Aiken; Prof. J. P. Cooper; J. S. Denton; P. R. Hayward; D. J. Palmer; F. H. Goodwin; D. C. Todd; W. P. Watt.
Secretary, D. J. Ward *(H.E.O.)*.

H.M. LAND REGISTRY
Lincoln's Inn Fields, WC2A 3PH
[01-405 3488]

The registration of title to land was first introduced in England and Wales by the Land Registry Act, 1862. Many changes have been made to the original system by subsequent legislation and H.M. Land Registry operates today under the Land Registration Acts, 1925 to 1971. The object of registering title to land is for dealings with it to be made more simple and economical. This is achieved by maintaining a register of land owners whose title is guaranteed by the State and by providing simple forms for the transfer, mortgage and other dealings with real property. Under the Land Registration Act, 1966, the voluntary first registration of land in non-compulsory areas was severely curtailed in order to facilitate an accelerated programme for the extension of the compulsory system to cover all the built-up areas of the country as soon as possible. The intention is that registration of title shall ultimately be universal throughout England and Wales. Nevertheless, before the 1966 Act a great deal of land became registered voluntarily and it is still possible in non-compulsory areas to register building estates, upon certain conditions, and other classes of property in specified circumstances. H.M. Land Registry is administered under the Lord Chancellor by the Chief Land Registrar and the work is decentralized to a number of regional offices. The Chief Land Registrar is also responsible for the Land Charges Department and the Agricultural Credits Department.

Headquarters Office

Chief Land Registrar, E. J. Pryer £35,278
Chief Executive, C. Hotham £28,583
Senior Land Registrar, C. J. West £19,243 to £23,159
Land Registrar, Mrs. J. G. Totty . £19,243 to £23,159
Assistant Land Registrars, J. V. Timothy; M. L. Wood
                                         £14,401 to £19,317
Assistant Secretaries, J. J. Manthorpe (*Controller Registration*); R. B. Parker (*Controller of Management Services*). . . . . £19,243 to £23,159
Senior Principal, P. J. Smith . . . . . £15,605 to 20,794
Principals, E. G. Beardsall; P. J. Brenchley; J. E. Deas; I. Leach; P. Morris; P. J. Reader; V. J. C. Shorney; J. W. Wallis . . . . £12,399 to £16,656

Establishment and Accounts

Principal Establishment Officer, E. F. Martin
                                         £19,243 to £23,159
Assistant Establishment Officers, A. D. Gould; B. Gaskell . . . . £12,399 to £16,656
Principal Finance Officer, B. R. Elliott
                                         £12,399 to £16,656
Head of Office Services, R. A. Davis £12,399 to £16,656

Birkenhead District Land Registry
76 Hamilton Street, Birkenhead,
Merseyside L41 5JW
[051–647 5661]

District Land Registrar, J. L. Inskipp
                                         £19,243 to £23,159
Assistant Land Registrars, G. A. Hughes; C. Tate; I. E. Hardman; M. Taylor . . . . £14,401 to £19,317
Area Manager, M. H. Spooner . . . £12,399 to £16,656

Croydon District Land Registry
Sunley House, Bedford Park, Croydon CR9 3LE
[01–686 8833]

District Land Registrar, M. H. Baines
                                         £19,243 to £23,159
Assistant Land Registrars, A. E. Farwell; C. H. Johnson . . . . £14,401 to £19,317
Area Manager, J. O. Sheldon . . . . £15,605 to £20,794

Durham District Land Registry
Southfield House, Southfield Way,
Durham DH1 5TR
[0385–66151]

District Land Registrar, P. H. Curnow
                                         £19,243 to £23,159
Assistant Land Registrars, S. R. Coveney; Miss C. A. Lever; H. M. Taylor; R. E. P. Underwood; A. J. Pain; G. J. Wadsworth . . . . £14,401 to £19,317
Area Manager, D. F. Price . . . . £15,605 to £20,794

Gloucester District Land Registry
Twyver House, Bruton Way,
Gloucester GL1 1DQ
[0452–28666]

District Land Registrar, A. M. Phillips
                                         £19,243 to £23,159
Assistant Land Registrars, D. M. Adams; M. E. Burn; D. M. J. Moss; P. M. Ratcliffe; S. G. Taverner
                                         £14,401 to £19,317
Area Manager, G. M. Chere . . . . . £15,605 to £20,794

Harrow District Land Registry
Lyon House, Lyon Road, Harrow,
Middlesex HA1 2EU
[01–427 8811]

District Land Registrar, H. S. Early
                                         £19,243 to £23,159
Assistant Land Registrars, Miss J. E. Bagshaw; M. G. Garwood; T. H. O. Lewis; C. J. T. Brierley; J. H. Gill . . . . £14,401 to £19,317
Area Manager, D. I. Whyte . . . . . . £15,605 to £20,794

Land Charges and Agricultural Credits Department
Burrington Way, Plymouth PL6 3LP
[0752–779831]

Superintendent of Land Charges, J. C. O'Brien
                                         £12,399 to £16,656

Lytham District Land Registry
Birkenhead House, Lytham St. Annes,
Lancs. FY8 5AB
[0253–736999]

District Land Registrar, R. E. Shorrocks
                                         £19,243 to £23,159
Assistant Land Registrars, J. F. Bamber; J. G. Dickinson; J. B. Duckworth; R. H. Hargreaves; L. D. Jefferies; P. J. Timothy . . . . . £14,401 to £19,317
Area Manager, E. J. Stringer . . . . £15,605 to £20,794

Nottingham District Land Registry
Chalfont Drive, Nottingham NG8 3RN
[0602–291111]

District Land Registrar, D. L. Groom
                                         £19,243 to £23,159
Assistant Land Registrars, P. A. Brown; J. G. Cooper; K. G. Harvey; M. C. Jefferies; I. M. Jeffrey; P. D. Smith; Mrs. P. M. Reeson . . . . . £14,401 to £19,317
Area Manager, P. F. Taylor . . . . . . £15,605 to £20,794

Peterborough District Land Registry
Aragon Court, Northminster Road,
Peterborough PE1 1XN
[0733 46048]

District Land Registrar, M. Avens £19,243 to £23,159
Assistant Land Registrars, T. J. Reacher; J. T. Scott; S. T. Abdulhusein . . . . £14,401 to £19,317
Area Manager, G. N. French . . . . . £12,399 to £16,656

Plymouth District Land Registry
Plumer House, Tailyour Road,
Crownhill, Plymouth PL6 5HY
[0752–701234]

District Land Registrar, P. A. Meehan
                                         £19,243 to £23,159
Assistant Land Registrars, W. J. Perry; E. G. Thomas; M. Crocker; S. P. Kelway . . . . . £14,401 to £19,317
Area Manager, B. Hall . . . . £15,605 to £20,794

Stevenage District Land Registry
Brickdale House, Danestrete, Stevenage,
Herts. SG1 1XG
[0438–314488]

District Land Registrar, D. M. T. Mullett
                                         £19,243 to £23,159

Assistant Land Registrars, F. G. D. Emler; C. W.
Martin; O. D. Christopherson . £14,401 to £19,317
Area Manager, R. J. Fenn . . . . £15,605 to £20,794

Swansea District Land Registry
37, The Kingsway, Swansea, Glam. SA1 5LF
[0792–476677]

District Land Registrar, A. P. Roberts
£19,243 to £23,159
Assistant Land Registrars, C. D. Hinds; N. M. Jones
£14,401 to £19,317
Area Manager, B. E. G. Martin . . £12,399 to £16,656

Tunbridge Wells District Land Registry
Curtis House, Hawkenbury, Tunbridge Wells,
Kent TN2 5AQ
[0892–26141]

District Land Registrar, A. Gould £19,243 to £23,159
Assistant Land Registrars, J. S. R. Bevington; P. L.
Cook; G. R. Tooke . . . . £14,401 to £19,317
Area Manager, B. E. Kitching . . . £15,605 to £20,794

Weymouth District Land Registry
1 Cumberland Drive, Weymouth,
Dorset DT4 9TT
[03057–76161]

District Land Registrar, K. L. Charles
£19,243 to £23,159
Assistant Land Registrars, W. W. Budden; J. B.
Rhodes; M. A. Roche . . . . £14,401 to £19,317
Area Manager, R. R. C. Green . . . £12,399 to £16,656

Computer Services Division
Plumer House, Tailyour Road,
Crownhill, Plymouth PL6 5HY
[0752–701234]

Head of Computer Services Division, A. A. Restorick
£15,605 to £20,794
Principals, N. G. Worcester; R. J. Smith; R. T. Davis
£12,399 to £16,656

LAW OFFICERS' DEPARTMENT
Attorney-General's Chambers,
Royal Courts of Justice, W.C.1.

The Law Officers of the Crown for England and
Wales (the Attorney-General and the Solicitor-
General) represent the Crown in courts of justice,
advise Government departments and represent them
in court. The Attorney-General has also certain
administrative functions, including supervision of
the Director of Public Prosecutions.
Attorney General, THE RT. HON. SIR (ROBERT)
MICHAEL (OLDFIELD) HAVERS, Q.C., M.P. . . £32,224†
Parliamentary Private Secretary, N. W. Lyell, Q.C.,
M.P.
Solicitor General, SIR PATRICK (BARNABAS BURKE)
MAYHEW, Q.C., M.P. £26,364†
Parliamentary Private Secretary, M. Howard, Q.C.,
M.P.
Legal Secretary, H. Steel, C.M.G., O.B.E. £35,278
Asst. Legal Sec., M. L. Saunders £28,583
† Plus Parliamentary and Ministerial Allowances.

LIBRARIES

THE BRITISH LIBRARY
2 Sheraton Street, W1V 4BH
[01–636 1544]

The British Library was established on July 1,
1973, under the British Library Act, 1972, to provide,
on a national scale, comprehensive reference, lending, bibliographic and other services based on its vast
collections of books, manuscripts, maps, music,
periodicals and other material. It was created by
bringing together under a management board a
number of national library organizations

The Library is organized into three divisions:
Reference, Lending and Bibliographic Services, and
two departements: the National Sound Archive and
the Research and Development Department. It has a
Central Administration.

The Reference Division comprises the Departments
of Printed Books, Manuscripts, Oriental Manuscripts
and Printed Books; the India Office Library and
Records (since 1982), the Newspaper Library at
Colindale, the Library Association Library, the
Science Reference Library and, since 1983, the
Preservation Service. The Division contains about
11,330,000 volumes of printed books and periodicals,
about 83,900 volumes of Western Manuscripts and
37,800 volumes of Oriental Manuscripts, and outstanding collections of newspapers, official papers,
papyri, charters, seals, maps, music and postage
stamps. Admission to the Great Russell Street
reading rooms and those of the Department of
Oriental Manuscripts and Printed Books, the India
Office Library and Records and the Newspaper
Library is by reader's pass only. The Science
Reference Library is the principal public reference
library in the U.K. for contemporary literature of
science and technology; no reader's pass is needed.
In 1983, the Library established a Preservation
Service within the Division. It is concerned with
preservation policies and practices including management of conservation studios and binderies,
reprographic and photographic services, research,
training and the provision of consultancy services.

The Lending Division in Yorkshire operates a
rapid postal loan or photocopy service for organizations and currently receives 2,772,000 requests a year
from British and foreign libraries. Individuals should
apply through their local libraries. The stock contains 4,500,000 volumes of books and periodicals,
3,500,000 documents in microfilm and large quantities
of semi-published materials such as reports, translations and theses.

The Bibliographic Services Division creates records both for forthcoming publications, from advance
information received under the cataloguing-in-
publication scheme, and for books and other items
received by legal deposit at the Copyright Receipt
Office. The Division publishes the records in a range
of printed bibliographies, including the British
National Bibliography, and in machine-readable form
as UKMARC, available on-line through the BLAISE-
LINE information retrieval scheme, or on magnetic
tape, through various record supply services. These
records can be further processed by the BLAISE-
LOCAS service which offers centralized file building
and catalogue production facilities. In addition, the
Division offers the specialist biomedical and toxico-
logical information service, BLAISE-LINK.

The National Sound Archive (founded as the
British Institute of Recorded Sound in 1948) became
a department of the British Library in April 1983. Its
collections include nearly 500,000 discs and over
35,000 hours of recorded tape. Public access to the
collections is through a free listening service.

The Research and Development Department promotes and supports research and development related
to library and information operations in all subject
fields and is directed to the benefit of the national
library and information system as a whole.

Board Members
Chairman, Sir Frederick Dainton, F.R.S.
Deputy Chairman and Chief Executive, K. R. Cooper.
Directors General, A. Wilson; P. R. Lewis; M. B. Line.

Part-time Members, Sir Robert Clayton, C.B.E.; W. G. Graham, M.C.; Sir Denis Hamilton, D.S.O.; Prof. B. Morris; D. Owen; Miss D. Park; Prof. I. G. Stewart; Prof. P. A. Larkin.

Central Administration
2 Sheraton Street, W1V 4BH
[01–636 1544]

Secretary to the Board and Director of Central Administration, L. Bell.
Head of Press and Public Relations, Mrs. M. Treen.

Reference Division
Director General, A. Wilson.

Department of Printed Books
Gt. Russell St., London, W.C.1
[01–636 1544]

Keepers, R. J. Fulford; I. P. Gibb.

Library Association Library
7 Ridgmount St., W.C.1.
[01–636 1544]

Librarian, A. N. Macgregor.

Newspaper Library
Colindale Ave., N.W.9
[01–200 5515]

Head of Newspaper Library, S. P. Green.

Department of Manuscripts
Gt Russell St., W.C.1
[01–636 1544]

Director and Keeper, Dr. D. P. Waley.

Department of Oriental Manuscripts and Printed Books
14 Store St., W.C.1
[01–636 1544]

Keeper, B. C. Bloomfield.

India Office Library and Records
Orbit House, 197 Blackfriars Rd., S.E.1
[01–928 9531]

Director, B. C. Bloomfield.

Science Reference Library
25 Southampton Buildings, Chancery Lane, W.C.2
and
9 Kean St., W.C.2

Director, M. W. Hill.

The Preservation Service
Great Russell Street, W.C.1.
[01–636 1544]

Director, Dr. D. W. G. Clements.

Lending Division
Boston Spa, Wetherby, West Yorks.
[0937 843434]

Director General, M. B. Line.
Executive Director, K. P. Barr.

Bibliographic Services Division
2 Sheraton St., W.1
[01–636 1544]

Director General, P. R. Lewis.
Director of Automated Services, M. D. Martin.

National Sound Archive
29 Exhibition Road, S.W.7
[01–589 6603]

Director, Dr. C. Roads.

Research and Development Department
2 Sheraton St., W.1
[01–636 1544]

Director, B. J. Perry.

NATIONAL LIBRARY OF SCOTLAND
George IV Bridge, Edinburgh EH1 1EW
[031–226 4531]

Open free. Reading Room, weekdays, 9.30 a.m. to 8.30 p.m. Saturdays 9.30 to 1. Map Room, weekdays, 9.30 to 5 p.m.; Saturdays, 9.30 to 1. Exhibition, weekdays, 9.30 a.m. to 5 p.m. Saturdays, 9.30 to 1; Sundays 2 to 5 (closed on Sundays Oct. to April).

The Library, which had been founded as the Advocates' Library in 1682, became the National Library of Scotland by Act of Parliament in 1925. It continues to share the rights conferred by successive Copyright Acts since 1710. Its collections of printed books and MSS., augmented by purchase and gift, are very large and it has an unrivalled Scottish collection. The present building was opened by H.M. the Queen in 1956.

The Reading Room is for reference and research which cannot conveniently be pursued elsewhere. Admission is by ticket issued to an approved applicant.

Chairman of the Trustees, M. F. Strachan, C.B.E. F.R.S.E.
Librarian and Secretary to the Trustees, Prof. E. F. D. Roberts, PH.D., F.R.S.E. £23,159
Secretary of the Library and Deputy Librarian, B. G. Hutton . . . . £19,243 to £21,678
Curators Grade C, S. Holland; J. E. McIntyre; A. M. Marchbank, PH.D.; Elspeth D. Yeo
£11,076 to £16,656
Curator Grade D, E. A. Harpley . . . £9,470 to £12,518
Keepers of Printed Books, W. H. Brown, E.R.D.; R. Donaldson, PH.D.; I. D. McGowan; Ann Matheson, PH.D . . . . £15,652 to £19,317
Curators Grade C, M. A. Begg; A. M. Cain, PH.D.; T. A. F. Cherry; R. Duce; M. C. Graham; Alison E. Harvey Wood; B. P. Hillyard, D.PHIL.; Ruth I. Hope; Alexia F. Howe; W. A. Kelly; J. M. Morris; J. Margaret Wilkes . . . . £11,076 to £16,656
Curators Grade D, R. E. Adams; Eunice M. Souter; Christian E. G. Wright . . . . £9,470 to £12,518
Keepers of Manuscripts, P. M. Cadell; T. I. Rae, PH.D.
£15,652 to £19,317
Curators Grade C, I. G. Brown, PH.D.; I. C. Cunningham; I. F. Maciver; S. M. Simpson
£11,076 to £16,656
Director of Scottish Library Network (SCOLCAP), B. Gallivan. . . . . £15,652 to £19,317
Curator Grade C, B. Royan . . . . . . £11,076 to £16,656

THE NATIONAL LIBRARY OF WALES
Llyfrgell Genedlaethol Cymru
Aberystwyth, Dyfed SY23 3BU

Readers' room open on weekdays, 9.30 a.m. to 6 p.m. (Saturdays, 5 p.m.); closed on Sundays. Admission by Reader's Ticket.

Founded by Royal Charter, 1907, and maintained by annual grant from the Treasury. One of the six libraries entitled to most privileges under Copyright Act. Contains about 2,500,000 printed books, 30,000 manuscripts, 3,500,000 deeds and documents, and numerous maps, prints and drawings. Specializes in manuscripts and books relating to Wales and the Celtic peoples. Repository for pre-1858 Welsh probate records. Approved by the Master of the Rolls as a repository for manorial records and tithe documents, and by the Lord Chancellor for certain legal records. Bureau of the Regional Libraries Scheme for Wales.
Librarian, R. G. Gruffydd, D.PHIL.
Secretary, D. B. Lloyd.
Heads of Departments, D. Huws (*Manuscripts and Records*); P. A. L. Jones (*Printed Books*); vacant (*Pictures and Maps*).

COMMISSION FOR LOCAL ADMINISTRATION IN ENGLAND
21 Queen Anne's Gate, SW1H 9BU
[01–222 5622]

Local Commissioners are responsible for investigating complaints from members of the public in England who claim to have suffered injustice because of maladministration by a local authority, a water authority or a police authority. Certain types of action are excluded from investigation, particularly personnel matters and commercial transactions unless they relate to the purchase or sale of land. Complaints must normally be made through a member of the authority against which the complaint is made although a complaint can be put to a Local Commissioner direct if a member fails or refuses to refer it. A free booklet "Your Local Ombudsman" is available from the Commission's office.

Chairman of the Commission and Local Commissioner, D. C. M. Yardley, D.Phil. £44,033
Vice Chairman and Local Commissioner, (vacant).
Local Commissioner, F. P. Cook £35,728
Member, The Parliamentary Commissioner for Administration
Secretary, M. R. Hyde £26,691

LONDON REGIONAL TRANSPORT
55 Broadway, SW1H 0BD
[01–222 5600]

Subject to the financial objectives and principles approved by the Secretary of State for Transport, London Regional Transport has a general duty to provide or secure the provision of public transport services for Greater London. It will form companies to run the former London Transport bus and Underground services.

Chairman, Dr. K. Bright £47,500
Managing Director (Railways), Dr. T. M. Ridley
                                             £41,000
Managing Director (Buses), (vacant).
Member, I. Phillips £35,500
Part-time Members, D. Hardy (*Vice-Chairman*) (£13,000); K. Brown; Miss E. Cole; Dr. S. Glaister; S. Jenkins; K. Joyner; Mrs. H. Robinson; Miss P. Steel . . . . each £4,500

LORD ADVOCATE'S DEPARTMENT
Fielden House, 10 Great College Street,
SW1P 3SL

The Law Officers for Scotland are the Lord Advocate and the Solicitor-General for Scotland. The Lord Advocate's Department is responsible for drafting Scottish legislation, for providing legal advice to other departments on Scottish questions and for assistance to the Law Officers for Scotland in certain of their legal duties.

Lord Advocate, The Lord Cameron of Lochbroom,
P.C., Q.C. £33,320
Solicitor-General for Scotland, P. L. Fraser, Q.C., M.P.
                                             £22,991
Legal Secretary and First Parliamentary Draftsman,
N. J. Adamson, C.B., Q.C. £36,500
Senior Asst. Legal Secs. and Parlty. Draftsmen, G. M. Clark; D. J. S. Duncan; J. C. McCluskie . . . £29,500
Asst. Legal Secs. and Deputy Parlty. Draftsmen, P. J. Layden, T.D.; J. D. Harkness; C. A. M. Wilson; G. Kowalski . . . . £20,051 to £23,159
Junior Legal Sec. and Asst. Parlty. Draftsman, D. C. Macrae . . . . £14,401 to £19,317

LORD CHANCELLOR'S DEPARTMENT
See **Law Courts and Offices**

LORD GREAT CHAMBERLAIN'S OFFICE
House of Lords, S.W.1
[01–219 3100]

The Lord Great Chamberlain is a Great Officer of State, the office being hereditary since the grant of Henry I to the family of De Vere, Earls of Oxford.

Lord Great Chamberlain, The Marquess of Cholmondeley, G.C.V.O., M.C.
Secretary to the Lord Great Chamberlain, Lt.-Gen. Sir David House, G.C.B., C.B.E., M.C.
Clerk to the Lord Great Chamberlain, Miss C. A. Sansbury.

LORD PRIVY SEAL
Privy Council Office,
Whitehall, SW1A 2AT

Lord Privy Seal, and Leader of the House of Commons,
THE RT. HON. JOHN BIFFEN, M.P..
Principal Private Secretary, D. R. Morris.
Private Secretary, C. Marshall.

OFFICE OF MANPOWER ECONOMICS
22 Kingsway, WC2B 6JY
[01–405 5944]

The Office of Manpower Economics was set up in 1971. It is an independent non-statutory organization which is responsible for servicing independent review bodies which advise on the pay of various public service groups (*see* entries under "Review Bodies"), the Pharmacists Review Panel, the Police Negotiating Board and the Civil Service Arbitration Tribunal. The Office is also responsible for servicing *ad hoc* bodies of inquiry and for undertaking research into pay and associated matters as requested by Government.

Director, R. W. Williams
Assistant Secretaries, G. E. Johnson; D. A. Roberts; D. R. Bower.
Chief Statistician, H. J. M. Jones.

MANPOWER SERVICES COMMISSION
Head Office: Moorfoot, Sheffield S1 4PQ
[0742 753275]

Chairman, (vacant) £40,500
Members, F. A. Baker, C.B.E.; Miss S. I. Elkin, O.B.E.; K. Graham, O.B.E.; Dr. M. R. Green; W. H. Keys; J. A. Lawton, C.B.E.; W. Longden; H. Orr-Ewing; N. J. Payne, C.B.E.
Director, G. Holland £32,500

Employment Division

Chief Executive, B. D. Emmett £26,250
General Employment Service, M. Weston £21,654
Planning, J. S. Child £20,500
Disabled Person's Services, B. Swindell £23,159
SEPACS and Sheltered Employment, D. J. Sullivan
                                            £20,550
Special Employment Measures, J. B. Surr . . £22,302
PER Director, D. Rees £22,700
Executive Directors:
  T. O'Conor (*Wales and the South*); M. Weston (*Scotland and the North*).

Training Division

Chief Executive, R. J. Dawe, O.B.E. £28,265
Director of Occupational Training, Miss J. H. Bacon
                                            £26,250
Director of Youth Training, K. N. Atkinson . £25,000
Open Tech Unit, J. D. Tinsley £23,159
Occupational Policy, J. Wiltshire £23,159
Adult Training, J. A. Robertson £20,728
Sectors Training, P. D. Carr £23,421
YTS Programmes, Mrs. V. J. Bayliss £23,387

YTS Strategy, Evaluation and Research, M. G. Mellish.
Quality Branch, Dr. G. Tolley.
Training, Economics and Statistics Branch, Mrs. J. Marquand.
Statistics, N. H. W. Davis.
Regional and Area Operations, J. Wild £23,387

Skillcentre Training Agency

Chief Executive, R. C. Stephenson £24,077
Skill Centre Operations, S. Loveman £21,426
Product Development, J. Mannell £20,794
Promotional Services, J. Turner.
Financial and Accounting Services, T. Kent.

Personnel and Central Services Division

Director, D. B. Price.
Personnel, A. T. Wisbey.
Computer Branch, I. E. Turl.
Marketing Information Branch, N. Stone.
Psychological Services, Dr. M. C. Killcross.
Staff Training, J. Corbett.

Planning and Resources Division

Director, I. A. Johnston.
Accounts, J. S. Cousins.
Finance Policy, D. J. Howells.
Manpower and Efficiency, G. Kendall.
Central Planning, J. F. Smith.

MEDICAL RESEARCH COUNCIL
20 Park Crescent, W1N 4AL
[01–636 5422]

Chairman, The Earl Jellicoe, P.C., D.S.O., M.C.
Deputy Chairman and Secretary, Sir James Gowans, C.B.E., F.R.S.
Members, E. D. Acheson, D.M., F.R.C.P.; B. H. Bailey, O.B.E.; Belinda Banham, C.B.E.; Sir Christopher Booth, M.D., F.R.C.P.; Prof. I. D. Bouchier, M.D., F.R.C.P.; J. T. Carter; Prof. A. Cowey, D.Phil.; D. L. Crouch, M.P.; Prof. C. T. Dollery, F.R.C.P.; Prof. M. A. Epstein, M.D., D.SC., F.R.S.; Prof. R. B. Garland, PH.D., F.R.S.E.; Prof. P. J. Morris, PH.D.; Prof. J. M. Newsom-Davis, M.D., F.R.C.P.; Prof. F. W. O'Grady, T.D., M.D., M.SC., F.R.C.P.; Prof. C. G. Phillips, D.M., F.R.C.P., F.R.S.; Sir Desmond Pond, M.D., F.R.C.P.; J. A. Reid, C.B., T.D., M.D., D.SC., F.R.C.P.; Sir Michael Stoker, C.B.E., F.R.S..
Administrative Secretary, D. Noble.

Neurobiology and Mental Health Board
Chairman, Prof. J. M. Newsom-Davis, M.D., F.R.C.P.

Cell Biology and Disorders Board
Chairman, Prof. M. A. Epstein, M.D., D.SC., F.R.S.

Physiological Systems and Disorders Board
Chairman, Prof. C. T. Dollery, F.R.C.P.

Tropical Medicine Research Board
Chairman, Sir Christopher Booth, M.D., F.R.C.P.

HEADQUARTERS OFFICE
Medical Division
Head of Division, T. Vickers, PH.D.
Board Secretaries, Katherine Levy; Barbara Rashbass; J. Alwen, PH.D.; D. R. James, PH.D.

Grants and Training Awards
Head of Division, B. C. Dodd.

Administrative Division
Head of Division, D. Noble.

National Institute for Medical Research
Mill Hill, N.W.7
[01–959 3666]

Director, D. A. Rees, D.SC., F.R.S.

Clinical Research Centre
Watford Road, Harrow, Middlesex
[01–864 5311]

Director, Sir Christopher Booth, M.D., F.R.C.P.

Institute of Hearing Research
University Park, Nottingham

Director, M. Haggard, PH.D.

Research Units

Applied Psychology Unit, 15 Chaucer Road, Cambridge. *Director*, A. D. Baddeley, PH.D.
Biochemical Parasitology Unit, Molteno Institute, Downing Street, Cambridge. *Director*, B. A. Newton, PH.D.
Biostatistics Unit, University Medical School, Hills Road, Cambridge. *Director*, I. Sutherland, D.Phil.
Blood Group Unit, University College, London, Wolfson House, 4 Stephenson Way, N.W.1. *Director*, Patricia Tippett, PH.D.
Blood Pressure Unit, Western Infirmary, Glasgow. *Director*, A. F. Lever, F.R.C.P.
Brain Metabolism Unit, University Dept. of Pharmacology, 1 George Square, Edinburgh. *Director*, G. Fink, M.D.
Cell Biophysics Unit, Dept. of Biophysics, King's College, 26–29 Drury Lane, W.C.2. *Hon. Director*, Prof. B. B. Boycott, F.R.S.
Cell Mutation Unit, University of Sussex, Falmer, Brighton. *Director*, Prof. B. A. Bridges, PH.D.
Cellular Immunology Unit, Sir William Dunn School of Pathology, Oxford. *Director*, Dr. A. F. Williams.
Clinical and Population Cytogenetics Unit, Western General Hospital, Crewe Road, Edinburgh. *Director*, Prof. H. J. Evans, PH.D., F.R.S.E.
Clinical Oncology and Radiotherapeutics Unit, Medical School, Hills Road, Cambridge. *Hon. Director*, Prof. N. M. Bleehen, F.R.C.P.
Clinical Pharmacology Unit, University Department of Clinical Pharmacology, Radcliffe Infirmary, Oxford. *Hon. Director*, Prof. D. G. Grahame-Smith, PH.D., F.R.C.P.
Cognitive Development Unit, 17–19 Gordon Street, W.C.1. *Director*, J. Morton, PH.D.
Cyclotron Unit, Hammersmith Hospital, Ducane Road, W.12. *Director*, D. D. Vonberg, C.B.E.
Dental Unit, Dental School, Lower Maudlin Street, Bristol. *Hon. Director*, (vacant).
Unit on the Development and Integration of Behaviour, Subdept. of Animal Behaviour, Madingley, Cambridge. *Hon. Director*, Prof. R. A. Hinde, SC.D., F.R.S
Development Neurobiology Unit, 33 St. John's Mews, W.C.1. *Director*, R. Balàzs, M.D., D.Phil.
Dunn Nutrition Unit, Milton Road, Cambridge. *Director*, R. G. Whitehead, PH.D.
Environmental Physiology Unit, Southampton General Hospital. *Director*, Prof. D. J. P. Barker, M.D., PH.D., F.R.C.P.
Epidemiology and Medical Care Unit, Northwick Park Hospital, Harrow, Middx. *Director*, T. W. Meade.
Epidemiology Unit (South Wales), 4 Richmond Road, Cardiff. *Director*, P. C. Elwood, M.D.
Unit for Epidemiological Studies in Psychiatry, University of Psychiatry, Royal Edinburgh Hospital, Morningside Park, Edinburgh. *Director*, N. B. Kreitman, M.D.
Experimental Embryology and Toxicology Unit, M.R.C. Laboratories, Woodmansterne Road, Carshalton, Surrey. *Director*, D. G. Whittingham.

Human Biochemical Genetics Unit, Galton Laboratory University College London, Wolfson House, 4 Stephenson Way, N.W.1. *Hon. Director*, D. A. Hopkinson, M.D.

Immunochemistry Unit, University Department of Biochemistry, South Parks Road, Oxford. *Hon. Director*, Prof. R. R. Porter, Ph.D., F.R.S.

Institute of Hearing Research, The Medical School, University of Nottingham. *Director*, M. P. Haggard, Ph.D.

M.R.C. Laboratories, Carshalton, Woodmansterne Road, Carshalton, Surrey. *Admin. Officer*, B. H. Goodfellow.

M.R.C. Laboratories, The Gambia, Fajara, The Gambia, W. Africa. *Director*, B. M. Greenwood, M.D.

M.R.C. Laboratories, Jamaica, University of the West Indies, Mona, Kingston, Jamaica. *Director*, G. R. Serjeant, M.D.

Leukaemia Unit, Royal Postgraduate Medical School, Ducane Road, W.12. *Hon. Director*, Prof. D. A. G. Galton, M.D., F.R.C.P.

Mammalian Development Unit, University College London, Wolfson House, 4 Stephenson Way, N.W.1. *Director*, Anne McLaren, D.Phil., F.R.S.

Mammalian Genome Unit, Dept. of Zoology, University of Edinburgh, West Mains Road, Edinburgh. *Director*, E. M. Southern, Ph.D.

Mechanisms in Tumour Immunity Unit, University Medical School, Hills Road, Cambridge. *Director*, Prof. P. J. Lachmann, Sc.D., F.R.C.P.

Medical Sociology Unit, Institute of Medical Sociology, Westburn Road, Aberdeen. *Director*, Sally Macintyre, M.Sc., Ph.D.

Mineral Metabolism Unit, The General Infirmary, Great George Street, Leeds. *Acting Director*, M. Peacock, F.R.C.P.

Laboratory of Molecular Biology, University Postgraduate Medical School, Hills Road, Cambridge. *Director*, S. Brenner, D.Phil., F.R.S.

Molecular Haematology Unit, John Radcliffe Hospital, Headington, Oxford. *Director*, Prof. D. J. Weatherell, M.D., F.R.C.P., F.R.S.

Unit of Neural Mechanisms of Behaviour, 3 Malet Place, W.C.1. *Director*, I. Steele Russell, Ph.D.

Neurochemical Pharmacology Unit, University Dept. of Pharmacology, Hills Road, Cambridge. *Director*, (vacant).

Neuroendocrinology Unit, Newcastle General Hospital, Westgate Road, Newcastle upon Tyne. *Director*, J. A. Edwardson, Ph.D.

Neurological Prostheses Unit, Institute of Psychiatry, De Crespigny Park, Denmark Hill, S.E.5. *Hon. Director*, Prof. G. S. Brindley, M.D., F.R.C.P., F.R.S.

Neuro-Ontology Unit, Institute of Neurology, National Hospital, Queen Square, W.C.1. *Director*, J. D. Hood, Ph.D., D.Sc.

Neuropathogenesis Unit, West Mains Road, Edinburgh. *Director*, A. G. Dickinson, Ph.D.

Perceptual and Cognitive Performance Unit, Experimental Psychology Laboratory, University of Sussex, Falmer, Brighton. *Director*, Prof. W. P. Colquhoun, Ph.D.

Pneumoconiosis Unit, Llandough Hospital, Penarth, Glam. *Director*, (vacant)

Radiobiology Unit, Harwell, Didcot, Oxon. *Director*, Prof. G. E. Adams, Ph.D., D.Sc.

Reproductive Biology Unit, 37 Chalmers St., Edinburgh. *Director*, D. W. Lincoln, Ph.D., D.Sc.

Social and Applied Psychology Unit, Dept. of Psychology, University of Sheffield. *Director*, P. B. Warr, Ph.D.

Social Psychiatry Unit, Institute of Psychiatry, De Crespigny Park, Denmark Hill, S.E.5. *Director*, Prof. J. K. Wing, M.D., Ph.D.

Toxicology Unit, M.R.C. Laboratories, Woodmansterne Road, Carshalton, Surrey. *Director*, T. A. Connors, D.Sc.

Trauma Unit, Oxford Road, Manchester. *Director*, Prof. H. B. Stoner, M.D.

Unit for Laboratory Studies in Tuberculosis, Royal Postgraduate Medical School, Ducane Road, W.12. *Hon. Director*, Prof. D. A. Mitchison, F.R.C.P.

Tuberculosis and Chest Diseases Unit, Brompton Hospital, Fulham Road, S.W.3. *Director*, Prof. W. Fox, C.M.G., M.D., F.R.C.P.

Virology Unit, Institute of Virology, Church Street, Glasgow. *Hon. Director*, Prof. J. H. Subak-Sharpe, Ph.D., F.R.S.E.

THE ROYAL MINT

Llantrisant, nr. Pontyclun,
Mid-Glamorgan CF7 8YT
[0443–222111]

Master Worker and Warden, The Chancellor of the Exchequer (*ex officio*).

Deputy Master and Comptroller, Dr. D. J. Gerhard.

MONOPOLIES AND MERGERS COMMISSION

48 Carey Street, WC2A 2JT
[01–831 6111]

The Commission was established under the Monopolies and Restrictive Practices (Inquiry and Control) Act, 1948 as the Monopolies and Restrictive Practices Commission and was reconstituted on subsequent occasions. It became the Monopolies and Mergers Commission when the Fair Trading Act, 1973, came into operation on November 1, 1973. The Commission has the duty of investigating and reporting on questions referred to it in accordance with the Act with respect to (*a*) the existence or possible existence of monopolies not registrable under the Restrictive Trade Practices Act, 1976, which consolidated earlier legislation, and relating to the supply of goods or services in the United Kingdom or part of the United Kingdom or to the supply of goods for export; (*b*) the transfer of a newspaper or newspaper's assets; (*c*) the creation or possible creation of a merger qualifying for investigation within the meaning of the Act.

In monopoly references (except those "limited to the facts") and in merger references it is the duty of the Commission to report on the effect of the facts which they find on the public interest and to consider and, if they think fit, to recommend the action to be taken to remedy or prevent adverse effects. In addition the Fair Trading Act, 1973, provides for references to the Commission on the general effect on the public interest of specified monopoly or other uncompetitive practices and of restrictive labour practices.

The Competition Act, 1980, provides for the reference to the Commission of particular anti-competitive practices and of questions of efficiency, costs, service provided and possible abuse of monopolies in the public sector.

Chairman, Sir Godfray Le Quesne, Q.C. £51,120
Deputy Chairmen, (*part-time*), J. D. Eccles (£21,008); Sir Alan Neale, K.C.B., M.B.E. (£18,268); D. G. Richards (£21,008).
Members, J. G. Ackers; M. B. Bunting; K. S. Carmichael, C.B.E.; Sir Robert Clayton, C.B.E.; P. H. Dean; Prof. K. D. George; H. L. G. Gibson, O.B.E.; Prof. R. M. Goode, O.B.E.; D. G. Goyder; G. D. Gwilt; H. H. Hunt; L. Kelly; M. S. Lipworth; Prof. S. C. Littlechild; S. R. Lyons; L. A. Mills; B. C. Owens; Prof. A. R. Prest; J. S. Sadler, C.B.E.; N. L. Salmon; R. G. Smethurst; Sir Ronald Swayne, M.C.; C. A. Unwin, M.B.E.; J. J. Wallis ...... *each* £6,180
Secretary, N. E. D. Burton.

MUSEUMS

MUSEUMS AND GALLERIES COMMISSION
2 Carlton Gardens, SW1Y 5AA
[01–930 0995]

The Commission was established in 1931 as the Standing Commission on Museums and Galleries. From its inception its remit has covered the whole of Great Britain. In 1981, the Government decided to strengthen the Commission, changing its name with a revised formal mandate:— (i) to advise generally on the most effective development of museums and galleries and to advise, and take action as appropriate, on any specific matters which may be referred to them from time to time; (ii) to promote co-operation between musuems and galleries and particularly between the national and provincial institutions; (iii) to stimulate the generosity and direct the efforts of those who aspire to become public benefactors. The Commission is funded through the Office of Arts and Libraries. Its present executive functions include the control of the services of the National Security Adviser, the allocation of grants to the 7 Area Museum Councils (AMCs) in England and the monitoring of the 9 U.K. AMCs generally, and co-ordination of the funding and monitoring the work of the Museum Documentation Association. The Commission also directly administers a capital grant scheme for non-national museums and, in 1984, a significant new scheme of conservation grants. In addition, the Commission exercises an important role in advising the Government on indemnities and the acceptance of works of art in lieu of Capital Transfer Tax.

Chairman, The Lord Howard of Henderskelfe.
Members, The Marchioness of Anglesey, D.B.E.; T. Clifford; Prof. Sir John Hale, F.B.A.; T. W. I. Hodgkinson, C.B.E.; T. A. Hume, C.B.E., F.S.A.; J. Last; H. F. J. Leggatt; Admiral of the Fleet the Lord Lewin, K.G., G.C.B., M.V.O., D.S.C.; Prof. B. Morris, D.Phil.; Prof. G. D. Sims, O.B.E.; Prof. H. A. D. Miles; Prof. B. Yamey, C.B.E.
Secretary, S. Ridley.

THE BRITISH MUSEUM
Great Russell Street, W.C.1
[01–636 1555]

Antiquities Departments: Egyptian, Greek and Roman, Medieval and Later, Oriental, Prehistoric and Romano-British; Western Asiatic; also, Coins and Medals, Prints and Drawings, Ethnography. *Main entrance*, Great Russell Street, W.C.1; *North entrance*, Montague Place, W.C.1. Open weekdays (including Bank Holidays) 10 to 5 and Sundays 2.30 to 6. Closed on Good Friday, Christmas Eve, Christmas Day, Boxing Day, New Year's Day and the first Monday in May. The ethnographical collections are displayed in The Museum of Mankind at 6 Burlington Gardens, W.1. Opening times as above.

The British Musuem may be said to date from 1753, when Parliament granted funds to purchase the collections of Sir Hans Sloane and the Harleian manuscripts, and for their proper housing and maintenance. The building (Montagu House) was opened in 1759. The present buildings were erected between 1823 and the present day, and the original collection has increased to its present dimensions by gifts and purchases. The administrative expenses were estimated at £12,455,000 in 1984–85, and were met by a vote under "Museums, Galleries and the Arts", Class X of the Civil Estimates. The constitution of the British Museum was revised under the terms of the British Museum Act, 1963.

Under the provisions of the British Library Act 1972 and the British Library Act (Appointed Day) Order 1973, the Library Departments of the British Museum were transferred on July 1, 1973, from the responsibility of the Trustees of the British Museum to that of the British Library Board and became part of the British Library.

Board of Trustees

Appointed by the Sovereign: H.R.H. The Duke of Gloucester, G.C.V.O. *Appointed by the Prime Minister:* The Lord Trend, P.C., G.C.B., C.V.O., (*Chairman*); Sir Arthur Drew, K.C.B.; Graham C. Greene; Prof. E. T. Hall, D.Phil., F.S.A.; Sir Denis Hamilton, D.S.O.; Prof. H. Hinsley, O.B.E., F.B.A.; Simon Hornby; Sir Denys Lasdun, C.B.E., F.R.I.B.A.; J. L. Thorn; The Lord Windlesham, P.C., C.V.O.; The Lord Charteris of Amisfield, P.C., G.C.B., G.C.V.O., O.B.E.; Mrs. M. Moore; Prof. G. H. Treitel, D.C.L., F.B.A., Q.C.
Nominated by the Royal Society, Royal Academy, British Academy and Society of Antiquaries of London: The Lord Adrian, M.D., F.R.S. (*Royal Society*); Dame Elisabeth Frink, D.B.E., R.A. (*Royal Academy*); The Lord Blake, F.B.A. (*British Academy*); Prof. W. Watson, C.B.E., F.S.A., F.B.A. (*Society of Antiquaries*)
Appointed by the Trustees of the British Museum: David Attenborough, C.B.E.; Sir Martyn Beckett, BT., M.C., R.I.B.A.; Prof. Rosemary Cramp, F.S.A.; Prof. P. Lasko, C.B.E., F.S.A., F.B.A.; Sir Francis Sandilands, C.B.E.

Officers

Director, Sir David Wilson	£34,250
Deputy Director, Jean M. Rankine £21,825 to £23,159	
Secretary, G. B. Morris	£15,652 to £19,317
Administrative Assistant, Marjorie L. Caygill	
	£9,470 to £16,656
Deputy Keeper, Public Services, G. A. L. House	
	£15,652 to £19,317
Assistant Keeper, Design Office, Margaret Hall, O.B.E.	
	£9,470 to £16,656
Assistant Keeper, Education Office, J. F. Reeve	
	£9,470 to £16,656
Senior Information Officer, Press and Public Relations, E. Balfour.	
Senior Principal, C. W. Berry	£15,605 to £20,794
Principals, B. A. Wilson; P. E. Youngs	
	£12,399 to £16,656
Senior Executive Officers, G. E. Cooper; P. D. Jill Campbell; Barbara A. Hughes; G. S. Barber; A. W. Newton	£10,079 to £12,518
Keeper of Prints and Drawings, J. K. Rowlands	
	£19,243 to £21,678
Deputy Keeper, A. V. Griffiths	£16,652 to £19,317
Assistant Keepers, Frances A. Carey; N. J. L. Turner; Lindsay Stainton; J. A. R. Wilton	
	£9,470 to £16,656
Keeper of Coins and Medals, J. P. C. Kent	
	£19,243 to £21,678
Deputy Keepers, M. J. Price; N. M. Lowick	
	£15,652 to £19,317
Assistant Keepers, M. G. Powell-Jones; Marion M. Archibald; A. M. Burnett	£9,470 to £16,656
Keeper of Egyptian Antiquities, T. G. H. James	
	£19,243 to £21,678
Deputy Keeper, W. V. Davies	£15,652 to £19,317
Assistant Keepers, M. L. Bierbrier; A. J. Spencer	
	£9,470 to £16,656
Keeper (Acting) of Western Asiatic Antiquities, T. C. Mitchell	£19,243 to £21,678
Assistant Keepers, J. E. Curtis; C. B. F. Walker; I. L. Finkel; J. N. Tubb	£9,470 to £16,656
Keeper of Greek and Roman Antiquities, B. F. Cook	
	£19,243 to £21,678
Deputy Keeper, K. S. Painter	£15,652 to £19,317
Assistant Keepers, Susan E. C. Walker; Veronica Tatton-Brown	£9,470 to £16,656

Keeper of Medieval and Later Antiquities, N. M.
Stratford .... £19,243 to £21,678
Deputy Keepers, G. H. Tait; J. Cherry
£15,652 to £19,317
Assistant Keepers, Leslie E. Webster; D. Kidd; D.
Buckton; M. D. Collins; T. H. Wilson
£9,470 to £16,656
Keeper of Prehistoric and Romano-British Antiquities, I. H. Longworth .... £19,243 to £21,678
Deputy Keepers, G. de G. Sieveking; I. M. Stead
£15,652 to £19,317
Assistant Keepers, I. A. Kinnes; T. W. Potter
£9,470 to £16,656
Keeper of Oriental Antiquities, L. R. H. Smith
£19,243 to £21,678
Deputy Keepers, Jessica M. Rawson; J. M. Rogers
£15,652 to £19,317
Assistant Keepers, W. Zwalf; R. Whitfield; J. R. Knox
£9,470 to £16,656
Keeper of Ethnography, M. D. McLeod
£19,243 to £21,678
Deputy Keeper, B. Durrans ...... £15,652 to £19,317
Assistant Keepers, Elizabeth M. Carmichael; Shelagh
G. Weir; Dorota Starzecka; J. C. H. King; J. B.
Mack; N. F. Barley .... £9,470 to £16,656
Keeper of Scientific Research and Conservation, M.
Tite .... £19,243 to £21,678
Principal Scientific Officers, P. T. Craddock; M. J.
Hughes...................... £11,343 to £14,931
Head of Conservation, W. A. Oddy £15,652 to £19,317
Principal Scientific Officer, V. D. Daniels
£11,343 to £14,931

THE BRITISH MUSEUM (NATURAL HISTORY)
Cromwell Road, SW7 5BD
[01–589 6323]

Open free Monday to Saturday (except New Year's
Day, Good Friday, May Day, Christmas Eve, Christmas Day and Boxing Day) 10 to 6, and on Sundays
from 2.30 to 6.

The Natural History Museum originates from the
natural history departments of the British Museum,
Bloomsbury. During the 19th century the natural
history collections grew so extensively that it became
necessary to find new quarters for them and in 1881
they were moved to South Kensington. The British
Museum Act, 1963, made the Natural History Museum completely independent with its own body of
Trustees. The Zoological Museum, Tring, bequeathed
by the second Lord Rothschild, has formed part of the
Museum since 1938. Research workers are admitted
to the libraries and study collections by Student's
Ticket, applications for which should be made in
writing to the Director. There are lectures for
visitors at 3 p.m. on week-days and lectures are also
available at other times for special parties by arrangement with the Department of Public Services.

The administrative expenses were estimated at
£9,429,000 in 1983–84.

Board of Trustees

Chairman, Prof. Sir Richard Harrison, F.R.S.
Appointed by the Prime Minister: Sir Hugh Casson,
K.C.V.O., P.R.A.; The Earl of Cranbrook; Prof. Sir
Frederick Stewart, F.R.S.; The Lord Swann, F.R.S.;
The Lord Adrian, F.R.S.; Dr. W. F. Bodmer, F.R.S.;
Prof. D. Spencer-Smith.
Nominated by the Royal Society: Prof. Sir Andrew
Huxley, P.R.S.
*Appointed by the Trustees of the British Museum
(Natural History):* Prof. G. E. Fogg, C.B.E., F.R.S.;
Sir Michael Perrin, C.B.E.; Prof. H. B. Whittington,
F.R.S.; Sir James Hamilton, K.C.B., M.B.E.
Director, R. H. Hedley, D.SC. £31,625

Deputy Director, A. C. Bishop, PH.D.
£20,493 to £24,409
Secretary, R. Saunders .... £16,855 to £22,044
Assistant to the Director, R. F. Eastwood, PH.D.
£10,220 to £12,726

Department of Administrative Services

Head and Establishment Officer, R. Saunders
£16,855 to £22,044
Deputy Head and Administration Officer, B. Johnston, I.S.O. .... £13,649 to £17,906
Finance and Organization, E. G. Hartman
£13,649 to £17,906

Department of Botany

Keeper, J. F. M. Cannon .... £20,493 to £24,409
Deputy Keeper, P. W. James ..... £16,855 to £22,044
Principal Scientific Officers, A. O. Chater; A. Eddy;
A. C. Jermy; R. J. Pankhurst; J. M. Pettitt, PH.D.;
J. H. Price; N. K. B. Robson, PH.D.; C. J. Humphries,
PH.D.; D. M. John, PH.D. .... £12,593 to £16,181

Department of Central Services

Head, G. B. Corbet, PH.D. .... £16,855 to £22,044
Biometrics and Computing Services, R. F. Eastwood,
PH.D. .... £10,220 to £12,726
Publications Officer, R. S. Cross .. £13,649 to £17,906

Department of Entomology

Keeper, L. A. Mound, D.SC. .... £16,855 to £20,567
Deputy Keepers, D. R. Ragge, PH.D.; R. I. Vane-
Wright .... £16,855 to £22,044
Senior Principal Scientific Officers, R. W. Crosskey,
D.SC.; V. F. Eastop, D.SC. .... £16,855 to £20,567
Principal Scientific Officers, R. L. Blackman, PH.D.; B.
Bolton; P. M. Hammond; D. Hollis; W. J. Knight,
PH.D.; R. D. Pope; J. Quinlan; A. J. Shelley, PH.D.;
K. G. V. Smith; R. T. Thompson; W. G. Tremewan;
Miss C. M. F. von Hayek; A. Watson; P. E. S.
Whalley, D.SC.; K. S. O. Sattler, PH.D.; A. C. Pont
£12,593 to £16,181

Department of Library Services

Head, A. P. Harvey .... £16,855 to £22,044
Deputy Head, R. E. R. Banks..... £12,593 to £16,181
Principal Scientific Officer, Miss P. Gilbert
£12,593 to £16,181

Department of Mineralogy

Keeper, A. C. Bishop, PH.D........ £20,493 to £24,409
Deputy Keeper, D. R. C. Kempe, D.PHIL.
£16,855 to £22,044
Senior Principal Scientific Officer, P. Henderson,
D.PHIL........................ £16,855 to £22,044
Principal Scientific Officers, A. M. Clark, PH.D.; A. J.
Easton, PH.D.; P. G. Embrey; A. L. Graham, PH.D.;
R. Hutchison, PH.D.; R. F. Symes; A. R. Woolley,
PH.D. .... £12,593 to £16,181

Department of Palaeontology

Keeper, H. W. Ball, PH.D. .... £20,493 to £24,409
Deputy Keepers, L. R. M. Cocks, D.S.C.; M. K. Howarth,
PH.D. .... £16,855 to £22,044
Senior Principal Scientific Officers, C. Patterson,
PH.D.; C. G. Adams, PH.D. ...... £16,855 to £22,044
Principal Scientific Officers, P. J. Andrews, PH.D.; C.
H. C. Brunton, PH.D.; A. J. Charig, PH.D.; P. L.
Forey, PH.D.; A. W. Gentry, D.PHIL.; R. G. Harvey,
PH.D.; R. P. S. Jefferies, PH.D.; N. J. Morris, D.PHIL.;
C. P. Nuttall; H. G. Owen, PH.D.; J. B. Richardson,
PH.D.; B. R. Rosen, PH.D.; A. J. Sutcliffe, PH.D.; R.
A. Fortey, PH.D.; C. B. Stringer, PH.D.
£12,593 to £16,181

Sub-Department of Physical Anthropology
Principal Scientific Officer, D. Tills, PH.D.
£12,593 to £16,181

Department of Public Services

Head, R. S. Miles, D.SC. . . . . £16,855 to £22,044
Deputy Head, G. C. S. Clarke, PH.D.
£12,593 to £16,181
Operations Manager, M. B. McBratney
£13,649 to £17,906

Department of Zoology

Keeper, J. G. Sheals, PH.D. . . . . £20,493 to £24,409
Deputy Keepers, C. R. Curds, D.SC.; J. F. Peake
£16,855 to £22,044
Senior Principal Scientific Officer, P. H. Greenwood,
D.SC. . . . . £16,855 to £22,044
Principal Scientific Officers, E. N. Arnold, PH.D.; K. E.
Banister, PH.D.; I. R. Bishop; G. A. Boxshall, PH.D.;
Miss A. M. Clark; Miss P. L. Cook; P. F. S.
Cornelius, PH.D.; A. A. Fincham, PH.D.; J. D. George,
PH.D.; D. I. Gibson, PH.D.; J. E. Hill; R. W. Ingle,
PH.D.; Mrs. J. Jewell, PH.D.; R. J. Lincoln, PH.D.; D.
Rollinson, PH.D.; R. W. Sims; V. R. Southgate,
PH.D.; J. D. Taylor, PH.D.; A. C. Wheeler; P. J. P.
Whitehead, PH.D. . . . . £12,593 to £16,181

Sub-Department of Ornithology
Park Street, Tring, Herts.
[Tring: 4181]

Senior Principal Scientific Officer, D. W. Snow, D.SC.
£15,605 to £20,794
Principal Scientific Officers, I. C. J. Galbraith (*Head*)
(£11,843 to £15,431); P. J. K. Burton, PH.D.; C. J. O.
Harrison, PH.D. . . . . £11,343 to £14,931

MUSEUM OF LONDON

The Museum of London was opened in December
1976 in its new building at the corner of London Wall
and Aldersgate Street in the City. It is based on the
amalgamation of the former Guildhall Museum and
London Museum. The Museum is controlled by a
Board of Governors, appointed (6 each) by the
Government, the Corporation of London and the
Greater London Council. The exhibition illustrates
the history of London from prehistoric times to the
present day.
Chairman of Board of Governors, R. M. Robbins,
C.B.E., F.S.A.
Director, M. G. Hebditch, F.S.A.

THE SCIENCE MUSEUM
South Kensington, SW7 2DD
[01–589 3456]

Open on weekdays 10 to 6; Sundays 2.30 to 6.
Closed on Good Friday, Christmas Eve, Christmas
Day, Boxing Day, New Year's Day and May Day
Bank Holiday.
For Science Museum Library, *see* below.
The Science Museum, which is the National
Museum of Science and Industry, was instituted in
1853 under the Science and Art Department as a
part of the South Kensington Museum, and opened
in 1857; to it were added in 1883 the collections of
the Patent Museum. In 1909 the administration
of the Science Collections was separated from that of
the Art Collections, which were transferred to the
Victoria and Albert Museum. The collections in the
Science Museum illustrate the development of science
and engineering and related industries.
The administrative expenses of the Museum,
Library, the National Railway Museum and the
National Museum of Photography, Film and Tele-
vision were estimated at £8,158,000 for 1983–84.
Director and Secretary, Dame Margaret Weston,
D.B.E. £28,583
Museum Administrator, K. J. Rhodes
£16,343 to £20,794

Department of Physics

Keeper I, Dr. D. B. Thomas . . . . . . £19,243 to £21,678
Assistant Keepers, Dr. D. Vaughan; Dr. A. Q. Morton
£11,076 to £16,658

Department of Chemistry

Keeper I, Dr. R. G. W. Anderson . . £19,243 to £21,678
Assistant Keepers, Dr. J. Darius; Dr. R. F. Bud; Dr.
A. K. Newmark . . . . £11,076 to £16,658

Wellcome Museum of the History of Medicine

Keeper I, Dr. B. Bracegirdle . . . . . £19,243 to £21,678
Assistant Keeper, Dr. G. M. Skinner
£11,076 to £16,658

Department of Electrical Engineering, Communications, Earth, Space and Mathematical Sciences

Keeper I, Dr. E. J. S. Becklake . . . . £19,243 to £21,678
Assistant Keepers, Dr. B. P. Bowers; W. K. E. Geddes;
J. Robinson (£11,076 to £16,658); O. B. R. Strimpel
£9,470 to £12,518

Department of Transport

Keeper I, G. W. B. Lacey . . . . £19,243 to £21,678
Assistant Keepers, Dr. T. Wright; J. A. Bagley; A.
Hall-Patch; P. R. Mann . . . . £11,076 to £16,658

Department of Mechanical and Civil Engineering

Keeper I, J. T. van Riemsdijk . . . . £19,243 to £21,678
Assistant Keepers, R. J. Law; A. K. Corry; A. E.
Butcher . . . . £11,076 to £16,658

Department of Museum Services

Keeper I, Dr. D. A. Robinson . . . . . £19,243 to £21,678
Keeper II, M. R. Preston . . . . £15,652 to £19,317
Assistant Keepers, I. M. Ball; Dr. A. W. Wilson
£11,076 to £16,658

Library

SCIENCE MUSEUM LIBRARY, South Kensington,
S.W.7.—A national library of science, specializing in
the history of science and technology, 480,000 volumes, 21,000 periodicals and transactions of learned
societies, about 6,400 current. Bibliographies supplied.—Open on weekdays 10 to 5.30. Closed on
Sundays and Bank Holiday weekends. Photocopying
and microfilm service.
Keeper I, L. R. Day . . . . £19,243 to £21,678
Assistant Keepers, D. J. Bryden; Dr. L. D. Will
£11,076 to £16,658

National Railway Museum
Leeman Road, York
[0904–21261]

Keeper I, Dr. J. A. Coiley . . . . £19,243 to £21,678
Assistant Keeper, P. W. B. Semmens
£11,076 to £16,658

National Museum of Photography, Film and Television
Princes View, Bradford
[0274 727488]

Keeper II, C. Ford . . . . £15,652 to £19,317
Assistant Keeper, (vacant) . . . . . . £11,076 to £16,658

THE VICTORIA AND ALBERT MUSEUM
South Kensington, S.W.7
[01–589 6371]

Hours 10 to 5.50 (weekdays and Bank Holidays);
Sundays, 2.30 to 5.50. Closed every Friday, Christmas
Eve, Christmas Day, Boxing Day, New Year's Day
and May Day. The National Art Library is open on
weekdays (except Fridays) from 10 to 5.45 and the

Print Room from 10 to 4.30 (except Fridays). A museum of all branches of fine and applied art, descends direct from the Museum of Manufactures (later called Museum of Ornamental Art), opened in Marlborough House in 1852. The Museum was moved in 1857 to become part of the collective South Kensington Museum. It was renamed the Victoria and Albert Museum in 1899. The branch museum at Bethnal Green was opened in 1872 and the building is the most important surviving example of the type of glass and iron construction used by Paxton for the Great Exhibition of 1851. The Victoria and Albert Museum also administers the Wellington Museum (Apsley House), Ham House, Richmond, Osterley Park, Middlesex, and the Theatre Museum. Administrative expenses of the Museum are estimated at £9,376,000 in 1982–83.

Director and Secretary, Sir Roy Strong, PH.D., F.S.A.
£26,826

Deputy Director, M. D. Darby.

Department of Ceramics

Keeper, J. V. Mallet .... £19,243 to £21,678
Deputy Keeper, D. M. Archer.
Assistant Keepers, C. H. Truman; Dr. O. Watson.

Department of Conservation

Keeper, Dr. J. Ashley-Smith ..... £19,243 to £21,678
Conservator C, V. J. Murrell.
Conservators D, P. D. Young; J. H. Larson; Miss S. Edmonds.

Department of Education

Keeper, G. Opie .... £18,525 to £20,777
Assistant Keeper, R. D. Parkinson.

Far Eastern Department

Keeper, J. V. Earle .... £19,243 to £21,678
Assistant Keepers, A. C. Clunas; Miss R. Kerr.

Department of Furniture and Woodwork

Keeper, P. K. Thornton .... £19,243 to £21,678
Deputy Keeper, S. S. Jervis.
Assistant Keeper, J. J. S. L. Hardy

Indian Department

Keeper, R. W. Skelton .... £19,243 to £21,678
Assistant Keeper, Dr. D. Swallow.

Library

Keeper, R. Lightbown .... £19,243 to £21,678
Deputy Keepers, D. Haldane; C. Hogben.
Assistant Keeper, Dr. R. Watson.

Metalwork Department

Keeper, Mrs. S. J. Bury .... £19,243 to £21,678
Assistant Keepers, Miss A. G. Somers-Cocks; Mrs. P. Glanville; Miss M. Campbell.

Museum Services Department

Keeper, M. D. Darby .... £19,243 to £21,678
Assistant Keeper, B. M. Griggs (*Design*).

Prints, Drawings, Photographs and Paintings Department

Keeper, Dr. C. M. Kauffmann .... £19,243 to £21,678
Deputy Keepers, Miss S. B. Lambert (*Prints and Drawings*); J. D. W. Murdoch (*Paintings*)
Assistant Keepers, L. S. Lambourne (*Paintings*); M. Haworth-Booth (*Photographs*); M. Snodin (*Prints and Drawings*).

Department of Sculpture

Keeper, A. F. Radcliffe .... £19,243 to £21,678
Assistant Keepers, M. Baker; P. E. D. Williamson.

Department of Textiles and Dress

Keeper, Miss S. Levey .... £19,243 to £21,678
Deputy Keeper, Miss N. K. A. Rothstein
Assistant Keepers, Mrs. M. Ginsburg; Mrs. V. D. Mendes; Miss W. Hefford.

Secretariat

Chief Administrative Officer, J. Close
£16,343 to £20,794
Deputy Superintendent, G. D. Lawrence
£10,079 to £12,518

Theatre Museum

Keeper, A. Schouvaloff .... £19,243 to £21,678
Assistant Keeper, Dr. J. Fowler.

Bethnal Green Museum of Childhood
Cambridge Heath Road, Bethnal Green, E2 9PA
[01–980 3204]

Hours 10 to 6 on Mondays to Thursdays and Saturdays (including Bank Holidays); Sundays 2.30 to 6. Closed every Friday, May Day, Christmas Eve, Christmas Day, Boxing Day and New Year's Day. A branch of the Victoria and Albert Museum, opened in 1872. Toys, dolls, dolls' houses, model theatres, optical toys, games and children's costume. Also Spitalfields silk and wedding dresses.
Keeper, A. P. Burton .... £15,652 to £19,317

THE COMMONWEALTH INSTITUTE
Kensington High Street, W.8
[01–603 4535]

The Commonwealth Institute is a centre for information about the Commonwealth. It is funded by the British Government with contributions from other Commonwealth Governments. The Institute is controlled by a Board of Governors which includes the High Commissioners of all Commonwealth countries represented in London. The Institute has permanent exhibitions on all Commonwealth nations, an arts centre, library and education department.

Gallery opening hours: Monday to Saturday 10 a.m. to 5.30 p.m.; Sundays 2 p.m. to 5 p.m. Admission is free. Closed Good Friday, May Day, Christmas Eve, Christmas Day, Boxing Day and New Year's Day.

Director, J. F. Porter.
Deputy Director, R. R. Bourne.
Chief Education Officer, J. F. Callander
£13,649 to £17,906
Chief Exhibition Officer, A. E. Cobbold
£13,649 to £17,906
Art Director, R. Atkins .... £13,649 to £17,906
Establishment and Finance Officer, M. J. Dunleavy
£11,329 to £13,768
Librarian, M. J. Foster .... £11,329 to £13,768
Senior Education Officer, Miss M. Butcher
£11,329 to £13,768
Senior Exhibition Officer, R. Varney
£11,329 to £13,768

IMPERIAL WAR MUSEUM
Lambeth Road, SE1 6HZ
[01–735 8922]

Open daily (except Good Friday, Christmas Eve, Christmas Day, Boxing Day, New Year's Day and May Bank Holiday) 10 a.m.–5.50 p.m. (Sundays 2 p.m.–5.50 p.m.) Reference Depts. open Monday–Friday (except on public holidays), 10 a.m.–5.00 p.m.

The Museum, which was founded in 1917 and established by Act of Parliament in 1920, illustrates and records all aspects of the two world wars and other military operations involving Britain and the

Commonwealth since 1914. It was opened in its present home, formerly Bethlem Hospital or Bedlam, in 1936. Its extensive collections include aircraft, armoured fighting vehicles, artillery, uniforms, models, orders and decorations, badges and insignia, works of art, posters, photographs, films, books, documents and sound recordings. The Museum also administers H.M.S. *Belfast* in the Pool of London, Duxford Airfield near Cambridge and The Cabinet War Rooms in Westminster.

The Museum provides regular programmes of films and talks for visiting parties from schools, colleges and the armed services. Expenses for 1984–85 are estimated at £4,383,000.

Director, A. C. N. Borg, PH.D., F.S.A.
£19,243 to £23,159
Deputy Director and Head of the Research and Information Office, R. W. K. Crawford
£19,243 to £21,678
Secretary, J. J. Chadwick . . . . £15,652 to £19,317
Special Assistant to the Director, Mrs. J. C. Andrew
£11,076 to £16,656
Establishment and Finance Officer (Principal), J. F. Golding . . . . £12,399 to £16,656
Senior Keeper and Keeper of Audio-Visual Records, G. T. C. Coultass . . . . £19,243 to £21,678
Keeper of Duxford Airfield, E. O. Inman
£19,243 to £21,678
Keeper of H.M.S. Belfast, Capt. A. W. Wheeler, R.N.
£19,243 to £21,678
Keeper of the Department of Museum Services, C. Dowling, D.Phil. . . . . £15,652 to £19,317
Keeper of the Department of Documents, R. W. A. Suddaby . . . . £15,652 to £19,317
Keeper of the Department of Exhibits and Firearms, D. J. Penn . . . . £15,652 to £19,317
Keeper of the Department of Printed Books, G. M. Bayliss, PH.D. . . . . £15,652 to £19,317
Keeper of the Department of Art, Miss A. H. Weight
£11,076 to £16,656
Keeper of the Department of Film, Miss A. E. Fleming
£11,076 to £16,656
Keeper of the Department of Information Retrieval, R. B. N. Smither . . . . £11,076 to £16,656
Keeper of the Department of Photographs, Miss K. J. Carmichael . . . . £11,076 to £16,656
Keeper of the Department of Sound Records, Mrs. M. A. Brooks . . . . £11,076 to £16,656
Curator of the Cabinet War Rooms, E. J. Wenzel
£7,759 to £10,218

NATIONAL MARITIME MUSEUM
Greenwich, SE10 9NF
[01–858 4422]

Open weekdays 10 till 6 (Mon.–Fri. in winter, 10–5, Sats. 10–5.30); Sundays 2 to 5.30 (2 to 5 in winter). Closed Good Friday, Christmas Eve, Christmas Day, Boxing Day, New Year's Day and May Day.

Reading Room open on weekdays 10 to 5; tickets of admission on written application to the Director.

The National Maritime Museum was established by Act of Parliament in 1934, for the illustration of the maritime history, archæology, art and science of Great Britain. The museum is in two groups of buildings, in Greenwich Park, the Main Buildings, centred round the Queen's House (built by Inigo Jones, 1616–35) and the Old Royal Observatory, including Wren's Flamsteed House, to the south. The collections include paintings; actual craft and ship-models; ships' lines; prints and drawings; maps, atlases and charts; navigational and astronomical instruments; uniforms and relics; books and MSS. The amount for salaries and expenses, including a Grant-in-Aid, was estimated at £4,080,000 for 1983–84.

Director and Accounting Officer, Dr. N. Cossons, O.B.E.
£26,236
Deputy Director (Curator A), P. G. W. Annis
£19,243 to £21,678
Assistant Deputy Director (Conservator A), Miss G. M. Lewis . . . . £19,243 to £21,678
Secretary (Principal), Col. W. B. Mansell, M.C., R.M. (ret.) . . . . £12,399 to £16,656

Information Project Group

Curator B, Dr. R. J. B. Knight . . . £15,652 to £19,317
Curators C, Dr. J. L.Cutbill; S. M. Riley
£11,076 to £16,656
Curator D, B. K. W. Booth . . . . £9,470 to £12,518

Department of Museum Services

Curator B, C. St. J. H. Daniel . . . . £15,652 to £19,317
Curator C, L. J. Willis (*Design Services*)
£11,076 to £16,656
Curators D, P. Sugg (*Film Officer*); G. P. Stewart (*D.O.E. Liaison Officer*) . . . . £9,470 to £12,518

Department of Astronomy and Navigation

Curator A, Prof. S. R. C. Malin . . . £19,243 to £21,678
Curator B, A. N. Stimson M.V.O. (*Navigation*)
£15,652 to £19,317
Curators C, C. W. Terrell (*Hydrography*); B. Hutchinson (*Horology*) . . . . £11,076 to £16,656
Curator D, Ms. C. Stott (*Astronomy*)
£9,470 to £12,518

Department of Pictures

Curator A, R. L. Ormond . . . . £19,243 to £21,678
Curator B, Dr. D. M. B. Cordingly £15,652 to £19,317
Curator C, H. H. Preston (*Prints and Drawings*)
£11,076 to £16,656
Curator D, D. S. Stonham (*Historic Photographs*)
£9,470 to £12,518

Department of Conservation

Conservator A, Miss G. M. Lewis . £19,243 to £21,678
Chief Antiques Conservator (Conservator C), P. C. Van Geersdaele . . . . £11,076 to £16,656
Conservators C, Miss K. Leane; Mrs. C. E. Hampton
£11,076 to £16,656
Conservators D, Mrs. E. Boyd; C. J. Wheatley; Miss E. G. Hamilton-Eddy . . . . £9,470 to £12,518

Department of Printed Books and Manuscripts

Curator A, D. V. Proctor . . . . £19,243 to £21,678
Curators C, Mrs. M. Patrick (*Librarian*); A. W. H. Pearsall; Dr. M. W. B. Sanderson; Mrs. A. M. Shirley; Mrs. S. G. Vaz . . . . £11,076 to £16,656

Department of Ships

Curator A, Dr. A. P. McGowan . . . £19,243 to £21,678
Curators C, Miss R. Prentice (*Weapons and Antiquities*); F. M. Walker (*Naval Architecture & Shipbuilding*); A. J. Viner . . . . £11,076 to £16,656
Curator D, D. J. Lyon . . . . £9,470 to £12,518

Archaeological Research Centre

Curator A, Dr. J. F. McGrail . . . . . £19,243 to £21,678
Curator D, Miss S. V. E. Heal . . . . . £9,470 to £12,518

Department of Administration

Principal, Col. W. B. Mansell, M.C., R.M. (*ret.*)
£12,399 to £16,656
Senior Executive Officers, E. A. Skinner, M.B.E. (*Finance Officer*); Miss D. E. Williams (*Establishments Officer*) . . . . £10,079 to £12,518
Security Officer, J. Stacey . . . . £8,455 to £9,392

NATIONAL ARMY MUSEUM
Royal Hospital Road, SW3 4HT
[01–730 0717]

Established by Royal Charter (1960). History of five centuries of the British Army: includes the story of the Indian Army up to Independence in 1947. Open, Mon.–Sat., 10–5.30; Sun. 2–5.30. Indian Army room and the regimental collections of 5 Irish infantry regiments disbanded in 1922 at R.M.A. Sandhurst, Camberley, Surrey may be viewed by appointment only, Mon. to Fri.
Director, W. Reid, F.S.A.
Personal Assistant to the Director, Miss E. Christie.
Deputy Director and Keeper of Records, B. Mollo, T.D.
Assistant Director and Keeper of Uniform, Mrs. D. B. Willcox.

ROYAL AIR FORCE MUSEUM
Hendon, NW9 5LL
[01–205 2266]

The museum covers all aspects of the history of the Royal Air Force and its predecessors, and the history of aviation generally. The museum building is sited on ten acres of the historic former airfield at Hendon. Its aircraft hall, which occupies two hangars dating from the First World War, displays some 40 aircraft from the museum's total collection of over 100 machines. Admission is free.

Adjacent to the R.A.F. Museum is the Battle of Britain Museum, which contains a unique collection of British, German and Italian aircraft. Admission: £1·00; children and O.A.P.s 50p.

Also located on the same site is the new Bomber Command Museum which contains an impressive collection of historic bomber aircraft. Admission: £1; children and O.A.P.s 50p. Open Mons.–Sats., 10 a.m.–6 p.m. (Sundays, 2 p.m.–6 p.m.). Closed 24, 25, 26 Dec., 1 Jan., Good Fri. and May Day.
Director, J. Tanner, C.B.E., LL.T., F.S.A. £24,000
Keepers, R. F. Barker; M. Fopp; R. Lee, F.R.S.A., F.S.A. scot.; D. C. R. Elliott; P. Murton; Gp. Capt. W. S. O. Randle, C.B.E., A.F.C., D.F.M.; Wg. Cmdr. W. Wood, O.B.E. £18,000

GEOLOGICAL MUSEUM
Exhibition Road, South Kensington, SW7 2DE
[01–589 3444]

Open weekdays 10 a.m. to 6 p.m. Sundays 2.30 p.m. to 6 p.m. Closed on New Year's Day, Good Friday, May Day, Christmas Eve, Christmas Day and Boxing Day.

The Museum, forming part of the British Geological Survey, is the national museum of earth sciences. Its three public galleries have major displays of gems, basic earth science, British regional geology and the economic geology of the world. There is also the national reference library of geological literature.
Director, G. M. Brown, D.SC, F.R.S., F.R.S.E.
Curator, F. W. Dunning, O.B.E.

(For other Museums in England—*see* Index)

THE NATIONAL MUSEUM OF WALES
(Amgueddfa Genedlaethol Cymru)
Cardiff CF1 3NP
[0222 397951]

Open on weekdays, 10 a.m. to 5 p.m. Sundays 2.30 to 5 p.m. Closed on Christmas Eve, Christmas Day, Boxing Day, New Year's Day, May Day and Good Friday. Admission free.
President, W. A. Twiston-Davies.
Vice-President, Hon. J. Davies.
Director, D. A. Bassett, PH.D.

Secretary, D. W. Dykes, PH.D., F.S.A.
Keepers, (*Geology*) M. G. Bassett, PH.D.; (*Botany*) S. G. Harrison; (*Zoology*) P. M. Morgan; (*Archaeology*) G. C. Boon, F.S.A.; (*Art*) P. Cannon-Brookes, PH.D.

Welsh Folk Museum
(Amgueddfa Werin Cymru)
St. Fagans, Nr. Cardiff

The museum is situated 4 miles west of Cardiff. Open weekdays 10–5, Sundays 2.30–5. Admission 30p, children and pensioners 15p. Closed on Christmas Eve, Christmas Day, Boxing Day, New Year's Day, Good Friday and May Day.
Curator, T. M. Owen, F.S.A.
Keepers, V. H. Phillips; E. Scourfield.

Legionary Museum of Caerleon
Caerleon, Gwent.

Contains material found on the site of the Roman fortress of Isca and its suburbs. [NOTE. The Museum is closed for redevelopment until 1987.]

Turner House
Penarth, Nr. Cardiff

Open Tues.–Sat. 11 a.m.–12.45 p.m. and 2 p.m. to 5 p.m. Sundays, 2 p.m. to 5 p.m. Closed Mondays, except Bank Holidays, and on Christmas Eve, Christmas Day, Boxing Day, New Year's Day, Good Friday, and May Day. Admission free.

Oriel Eryri
Llanberis, Gwynedd

Open mid-June till mid-Sept.; weekdays 10–5; Sundays 2.30–5.

Welsh Slate Museum
Llanberis, Gwynedd

Open 9.30 a.m.–5.30 p.m. Easter to 30 April; 9.30 a.m. to 6.30 p.m. May to Sept. Admission 60p; children and pensioners 30p.

Segontium Roman Fort Museum
Beddgelert Road, Caernarfon, Gwynedd

Open weekdays at 9.30, Sundays at 2. Closes at 6 from May to September, at 5.30 in March, April and October, at 4 from November to February. Closed Christmas Eve, Christmas Day, Boxing Day, New Year's Day, Good Friday and May Day. Admission free. On the site of the fort, in the guardianship of the Welsh Office. Contains mostly material excavated there.

Museum of the Woollen Industry
Dre-fach Felindre, Dyfed

It occupies part of a working mill, the Cambrian Mills. Open 10 a.m. to 5 p.m. Monday–Saturday from April 1 to September 30. Closed May Day. Admission free.

Welsh Industrial and Maritime Museum
Bute Street, Cardiff

Open weekdays 10–5; Sundays 2.30–5. Closed Christmas Eve, Christmas Day, Boxing Day, New Year's Day, Good Friday and May Day. Admission free.
Curator, J. G. Jenkins, F.S.A.

Yr Hen Gapel
Tre'r-ddôl, nr. Aberystwyth, Dyfed

The museum portrays 19th century religious life in Wales. Open 10–5 Monday–Saturday from April–September. Closed May Day. Admission free.

ROYAL SCOTTISH MUSEUM
Chambers Street, Edinburgh EH1 1JF
[031–225 7534]

Open, Mon.–Sat., 10 a.m. to 5 p.m.; and Sun., 2 to 5 p.m.

Director, N. Tebble, D.SC., F.R.S.E. £23,159
Keeper, Department of Art and Archaeology, Miss D. Idiens . . . . £19,243 to £21,678
Keeper, Department of Geology, C. D. Waterston, D.SC., F.R.S.E. . . . . £19,243 to £21,678
Keeper, Department of Natural History, M. Shaw, D.Phil. . . . . £19,243 to £21,678
Keeper, Department of Technology, J. D. Storer
£19,243 to £21,678
Deputy Keepers, Sheila Brock, ph.D.; H. G. Macpherson, ph.D.; I. H. J. Lyster; S. Wood
£15,652 to £19,317

NATIONAL MUSEUM OF ANTIQUITIES OF SCOTLAND
Queen Street, Edinburgh
[031–557 3550]

Founded in 1781 by the Society of Antiquaries of Scotland, and transferred to the Nation in 1858. Open free. Weekdays, 10 a.m. to 5 p.m.; Sundays 2–5 p.m.

Director, Dr. A. Fenton £22,003
Deputy Keeper, Dr. D. V. Clarke.
Assistant Keepers, G. Sprott; Miss M. Bryden; Dr. D. Caldwell; H. G. Cheape.

Scottish Agricultural Museum
Royal Highland Showground, Ingliston,
Midlothian

Open weekdays 10 a.m.–4 p.m. May to September; at other times by arrangement. Admission free.

NATIONAL AUDIT OFFICE
Audit House, Victoria Embankment, EC4Y 0DS
[01–353 8901]

The National Audit Office, created by the National Audit Act 1983, replaced the Exchequer and Audit Department on January 1, 1984. The Comptroller and Auditor General, who is head of the National Audit Office, is an Officer of the House of Commons and is appointed by Letters Patent under the Great Seal on an address from the House of Commons made by the Prime Minister after agreement with the Chairman of the Committee of Public Accounts. He can be removed from Office only by the Queen on an address from both Houses of Parliament. His full title is "Comptroller General of the Receipt and Issue of Her Majesty's Exchequer and Auditor General of Public Accounts". As Comptroller General, he authorizes the issue of public funds to Government Departments and other public sector bodies. As Auditor General, his statutory duties are to certify the accounts of all Government Departments and a wide range of other public sector bodies; to examine revenue and store accounts; and to report the results of his examinations to Parliament. He also has wide statutory powers to carry out and report to Parliament on, examinations of economy, efficiency and effectiveness in the use of resources by those bodies he audits or to which he has rights of access. In addition to his statutory audits, the Comptroller and Auditor General is also the auditor by agreement of the accounts of many bodies, generally in receipt of public funds, and of certain international organizations.

Comptroller and Auditor General, Sir Gordon Downey, K.C.B. £40,500

Deputy Comptroller and Auditor General, P. Cousins, C.B. £32,500
Assistant Auditor Generals, H. D. Myland; J. A. Collens; D. A. Dewar £26,750
Director of Establishments and Accounts, P. J. Beck.
Directors of Audit, P. M. Jefford; G. W. Garside; M. R. J. Paul; J. A. Davies; I. R. W. Hargest; R. W. Locke; T. Dobson; P. O'Keefe; A. G. Brown; E. S. Young; M. J. Goodson; T. J. Lovett; G. R. L. Osborne; A. C. Pyatt; G. H. B. Spear; G. J. S. Frith; D. A. Reeve; R. N. Le Marechal; A. I. A. Oyarzabal; C. L. Press; W. D. Turner . . . . . . £19,243 to £23,159
Deputy Directors of Audit, A. W. Bird; W. E. Harle; E. J. Weeks; C. J. Day; D. C. Page; G. T. Morgan; J. E. Smith; B. D. Baker; J. A. Higgins; C. K. Beauchamp; K. E. Turner; B. Hogg; R. J. McCourt; A. R. Murray; W. L. Ewing; G. J. McKeown; L. H. Hughes; J. M. Pearce; M. C. Pfleger; R. M. Bennett; M. V. Pettet; R. E. Spurgeon; A. G. Roberts; R. A. Skeen . . . . £16,343 to £20,794

NATIONAL BUS COMPANY
172 Buckingham Palace Road, SW1W 9TN
[01–730 3453]

The National Bus Company is a statutory body under the provisions of the Transport Act, 1968. It controls 45 operating companies covering almost every part of England and Wales outside London and the municipal and Passenger Transport Executive undertakings. The N.B.C. bus and coach fleets total about 14,000 vehicles and it employs a staff of about 51,000.

Chairman, The Lord Shepherd, P.C. *(part-time)*
£26,860
Deputy Chairman and Chief Executive, R. Brook, C.B.E. £42,750
Members (part-time), R. H. Grierson; R. T. Kanter; G. Heywood, M.B.E.; I. S. Irwin, C.B.E.; Miss K. Mortimer; J. D. Orme; G. J. Parker   *(each £3,825)*

NATIONAL COAL BOARD
Hobart House, Grosvenor Place, S.W.1.
[01–235 2020]

The National Coal Board was constituted in 1946. It took over the mines on January 1, 1947.

Chairman, I. MacGregor £59,325
Deputy Chairman, J. R. Cowan, C.B.E.
£39,550 to £50,055
Members, D. Davies, C.B.E.; F. B. Harrison, C.B.E.; H. M. Spanton, O.B.E. . . . . £32,130 to £40,480
Members (part-time), Sir Melvyn Rosser; R. T. S. Macpherson, C.B.E.; P. C. Michael, C.B.E.; D. L. Donne; D. K. Newbigging, O.B.E.; C. Barker.
Secretary, D. G. Brandrick, C.B.E.

NATIONAL CONSUMER COUNCIL
18 Queen Anne's Gate, S.W.1
[01–222 9501]

Chairman, M. J. Montague, C.B.E. £11,044
Director, J. Mitchell.

NATIONAL DEBT OFFICE, *see* NATIONAL INVESTMENT AND LOANS OFFICE

NATIONAL DOCK LABOUR BOARD
22–26 Albert Embankment, SE1 7TE

The National Dock Labour Board administers the scheme for giving permanent employment to dock workers under the Dock Workers (Regulation of Employment) (Amendment) Scheme 1967. The Board was reconstituted as a body corporate on August 1, 1977 under the Dock Work Regulation Act 1976 which made further provision for regulating the

allocation and performance of the work of cargo-handling in and about the ports of Great Britain.
Chairman, R. H. Thompson.
General Manager, K. T. Percy.

NATIONAL ECONOMIC DEVELOPMENT OFFICE
Millbank Tower, Millbank, SW1P 4QX
[01–211 6998]

Council
Government Members, The Chancellor of the Exchequer (*Chairman*); the Secretaries of State for Employment, Education and Science, Energy, Environment and Trade and Industry. *Management Members,* Sir Terence Beckett, C.B.E.; Sir Donald Barron; Sir James Cleminson, M.C.; Dr. J. S. McFarlane; Dr. P. T. Main; J. J. R. Pope; R. E. Utiger, C.B.E. *Trade Union Members,* D. Basnett; R. Bickerstaffe; T. Duffy; A. M. Evans; C. Jenkins; The Right Hon. L. Murray, O.B.E. *Independent Members,* Sir George Jefferson, C.B.E.; R. Leigh-Pemberton; Sir Walter Marshall, C.B.E., F.R.S.; Mrs. R. E. Waterhouse, C.B.E.; D. Young.
Director-General, J. Cassels, C.B. £42,000
Secretary, P. V. Dixon.
Industrial Director, P. McGregor.
Economic Director, Dr. D. Morris.

NATIONAL ENTERPRISE BOARD
See British Technology Group

NATIONAL FREIGHT CONSORTIUM p.l.c.
The Merton Centre,
45 St. Peters Street, Bedford.
[0234 67444]

The National Freight Consortium p.l.c. purchased the whole of the issued share capital of the National Freight Company Limited from the Secretary of State for Transport in February 1982. 82½ per cent of the issued share capital of the Consortium is held by the employees, pensioners and their families, whilst the remaining 17½ per cent is held by a consortium of bankers.
Chairman and Chief Executive, Sir Peter Thompson.
Deputy Chairmen (non-executive), V. G. Paige, C.B.E.; F. S. Law, C.B.E.
Executive Directors, J. D. Mather; J. K. Watson (*Finance*); D. H. White; G. F. Pygall; P. A. Mayo (*Legal Services*); G. S. Abel; J. L. Copland.
Non-Executive Directors, Sir Ronald Swayne, M.C.; R. H. Watson; H. L. Batty; J. W. Robb.
Secretary, A. J. Staley, M.B.E.

NATIONAL GALLERIES
See Art Galleries

NATIONAL INVESTMENT AND LOANS OFFICE
Royex House, Aldermanbury Square, EC2V 7LR
[01–606 7321]

The National Investment and Loans Office was set up on April 1, 1980 by merging the staffs of the National Debt Office and the Public Works Loan Board. The Department provides staff and services for the National Debt Commissioners and the Public Works Loan Commissioners.
Director, P. A. Goodwin.
Establishment Officer, A. G. Ladd.

National Debt Office
Comptroller General, P. A. Goodwin.

Public Works Loan Board
Chairman, J. E. A. R. Guinness.
Deputy Chairman, W. Bowdell, C.B.E.
Other Commissioners, Miss F. M. Cook; R. W. E. Law; Miss V. J. Di Palma; G. R. Russell; W. H. P. Davison; T. E. Carter; P. Brackfield; S. G. Dunster; D. H. Adams.
Secretary, P. A. Goodwin.
Assistant Secretary, I. H. Peattie.

NATIONAL RADIOLOGICAL PROTECTION BOARD
Chilton, Didcot, Oxon. OX11 0RQ
[0235–831600]

The National Radiological Protection Board is an independent statutory body created by the Radiological Protection Act 1970. The Government's purpose was to establish a national point of authoritative reference in radiological protection.
Chairman, Sir Frederick Dainton, F.R.S.
Director, H. J. Dunster, C.B.

NATIONAL RESEARCH DEVELOPMENT CORPORATION
See British Technology Group

DEPARTMENT FOR NATIONAL SAVINGS
Charles House, 375 Kensington High Street,
W14 8SD
[01–603 2000]

The Department for National Savings was established as a Government Department when the former Post Office Savings Department became separated from the Post Office on October 1, 1969. The Department operates the National Savings Bank and maintains the records of holdings of National Savings Certificates, Income Bonds, Deposit Bonds, Save as You Earn contracts, Premium Savings Bonds, British Savings Bonds (and their forerunners Defence and National Development Bonds) and Government stock on the National Savings Stock Register.
Director of Savings, S. W. Gilbert, C.B. £36,500
Deputy Director, J. A. Patterson £29,500
Establishment Officer, R. T. Rowland
£19,243 to £23,159
Finance Officer, D. E. L. Whittall . £19,243 to £23,159
Controllers, J. Stamp; P. N. S. Hickman Robertson (*Marketing & Information*); R. S. Watts; G. R. Wilson . . . . £19,243 to £23,159
Senior Principals (Grade 6), R. L. H. Gurney, M.B.E.; W. E. H. Westlake; C. Ward; E. B. Senior; D. W. Kellaway; I. T. Standen; R. H. Lee
£15,605 to £20,794
Principals, J. G. Booth; I. B. Arkinstall; F. Bardsley; J. H. Fife; H. Johnson; B. E. Smith; N. Booth; D. H. Monaghan; J. S. Creighton; K. M. J. Harbridge; J. K. Hill; A. S. McGill; D. S. Speedie; I. Forsyth; A. R. Young; D. Newton; W. J. Herd; C. B. Taylor; J. W. Davison; T. Threlfall; A. Brown; R. H. Stansfield; W. J. Ferrier; A. G. Muir; J. Boyd; A. J. V. Cummings; W. A. Norris; F. McGourty; T. J. F. Mahon; D. K. Paterson . . . . . £12,399 to £16,656
Statistician, M. J. Barker . . . . £12,399 to £16,656
Principal Information Officers, P. G. Hutchings; D. C. Robinson . . . . £12,399 to £16,656
Principal Research Officer, T. J. Bedeman
£12,399 to £16,656

NATIONAL TRUST
36 Queen Anne's Gate, SW1H 9AS
[01–222 9251]

The National Trust was founded in 1895 by Miss Octavia Hill, Sir Robert Hunter and Canon Rawnsley, their object being to preserve as much as possible the history and beauty of their country for its people. It became an organization incorporated by Act of Parliament (1907) to ensure the preservation of lands and buildings of historic interest or natural beauty for public access and benefit. It is independent of the State and relies on the voluntary support of private individuals for working funds. As a charity, however, it is allowed certain tax exemptions.

The Trust protects more than 530,000 acres, much of it superb hill country in the Lake District, Snowdonia, the Peak District and other National Parks. The Trust also owns and opens to the public some 250 country houses, other buildings and gardens and preserves villages, nature reserves, archæological sites and many farms.

In 1965 the Trust launched a campaign to acquire as much as possible of the most beautiful stretches of coastline which were under threat from development. The Trust now protects about 450 miles of coastline.

The Trust has now over 1,000,000 members paying an annual subscription and more than 150,000 new members are joining each year. Rents, admission fees, legacies and gifts are other important sources of support and income.

The policy of the Trust is determined by the governing body, the Council. Half of its members are appointed by national institutions, such as the British Museum, the National Gallery, the Ramblers' Association and the Royal Horticultural Society; the other half are elected by Trust members at the annual general meeting. The Council appoints the Executive Committee, which in turn has established Regional Committees responsible for the management of the Trust's properties.

NATIONAL TRUST FOR SCOTLAND
5 Charlotte Square, Edinburgh 2

The National Trust for Scotland was founded in 1931, and its objects are similar to those of the National Trust. Like that organization, it is incorporated by Act of Parliament, is dependent for finance upon legacies, donations and the subscriptions of its members, is recognized as a charity for tax exemption purposes, and enjoys certain privileges under various Finance Acts regarding capital transfer tax and capital gains tax.

The Trust administers 96 major properties covering over 100,000 acres. Great houses in its care include:— The House of The Binns, West Lothian; Brodick Castle, Isle of Arran; Crathes Castle, Kincardineshire; Culzean Castle, Ayrshire; Falkland Palace, Fife; Hill of Tarvit and Kellie Castle, Fife; Drum Castle, Castle Fraser, Leith Hall, Craigievar Castle and Haddo House, Aberdeenshire; and Brodie Castle, Morayshire. In Edinburgh are two contrasting houses—the Georgian House in the New Town and Gladstone's Land in the Old Town; and in Helensburgh is Charles Rennie Mackintosh's The Hill House.

In the Trust's care are also several noteworthy gardens. Some are associated with the great houses, others are:—Inverewe, in Wester Ross; the recreated 17th century garden of Pitmedden in Aberdeenshire; Threave in Kirkcudbrightshire, where a School of Gardening is run; Branklyn Garden, Perth; Inveresk Lodge Garden, near Edinburgh, and Greenbank, Clarkston, Glasgow.

Among the mountainous country owned by the Trust is the Pass of Glen Coe and the mountain group "The Five Sisters of Kintail" and the estate of Torridon in Wester Ross, and Ben Lomond.

Islands in the Trust's care include the St. Kilda group, Fair Isle, Iona and Canna. At Bannockburn, Killiecrankie, Glenfinnan and Culloden, the Trust owns sites associated with Scottish history.

Among smaller properties are houses associated with famous Scots:— the birthplaces of Barrie in Kirriemuir, Carlyle in Ecclefechan, and Hugh Miller in Cromarty; and Burns' Bachelors' Club, Tarbolton and Souter Johnnie's House, Kirkoswald in Ayrshire.

At Culross, in other Fife coastal villages, and at Dunkeld, Perthshire, the restoration of architecturally attractive groups of houses led to the creation of the Little Houses Improvement Scheme, under which properties are bought, restored and re-sold. Since its inception over 160 houses reflecting the vernacular architecture of Scotland have been restored throughout the country. The operation was one of the four pilot projects in the U.K. selected for special allocation during European Architectural Heritage Year, 1975 and in 1976 was awarded the European Prize for the Preservation of Ancient Monuments, given by the F.V.S. Foundation of Hamburg.

NATURAL ENVIRONMENT RESEARCH COUNCIL
Polaris House, North Star Avenue, Swindon, Wilts. SN2 1EU
[0793 40101]

The Natural Environment Research Council was established by Royal Charter on June 1, 1965, under the Science and Technology Act, 1965, to encourage, plan and conduct research in the physical and biological sciences which relate to man's natural environment and its resources.

The Council carries out research and training through its own institutes and grant-aided institutes, and by grants, fellowships and post-graduate awards to universities and other institutions of higher education.
Chairman, Sir Hermann Bondi, K.C.B., F.R.S.
Secretary, J. C. Bowman, Ph.D.

RESEARCH INSTITUTES

British Geological Survey
Nicker Hill, Keyworth, Nottingham
[06077 6111]
Director, G. M. Brown, D.SC., Ph.D., F.R.S., F.R.S.E.

Institute of Oceanographic Sciences
Wormley Laboratory, Godalming, Surrey
[042879 4141]
Director, A. S. Laughton, Ph.D., F.R.S.
Bidston Observatory, Birkenhead
[051–052 8639]
Taunton Laboratory, Crossway, Taunton
[0823 86211]

Institute for Marine Environmental Research
Prospect Place, The Hoe, Plymouth
[0752 21371]
Director, B. L. Bayne, Ph.D.

Institute of Marine Biochemistry
St. Fittick's Road, Aberdeen
[0224 875695]
Acting Director, Dr. J. R. Sargent.

Sea Mammal Research Unit
c/o British Antarctic Survey,
Madingley Road, Cambridge
[0223 311354]
Director, R. M. Laws, C.B.E., Ph.D., F.R.S.

Institute of Hydrology
Maclean Building, Crowmarsh Gifford,
Wallingford, Oxon.
[0491 38800]
Director, J. S. G. McCulloch, Ph.D.

Institute of Terrestrial Ecology
Merlewood Research Station,
Grange-over-Sands, Cumbria
[04484 2264/6]
Director, J. N. R. Jeffers.
Research Stations: Cambridge; Monks Wood; Furzebrook; Edinburgh; Banchory; Bangor; Culture Centre of Algae and Protozoa, Cambridge.

Institute of Virology
Mansfield Road, Oxford
[0865–512361]
Director, Dr. D. H. L. Bishop.

Unit of Comparative Plant Ecology
Department of Botany, University of Sheffield,
Western Bank, Sheffield
[0742 78555]
Head of Unit, Prof. I. H. Rorison, D.Phil.

British Antarctic Survey
Madingley Road, Cambridge
[0223 61188]
Director, R. M. Laws, C.B.E., Ph.D., F.R.S.

GRANT-AIDED INSTITUTES

Marine Biological Association of the U.K.
The Laboratory, Citadel Hill, Plymouth
[0752 21761]
Director, Prof. E. J. Denton, C.B.E., F.R.S.

Scottish Marine Biological Association
Dunstaffnage Marine Research Laboratory
P.O. Box No. 3, Oban, Argyll
[0631 62244]
Director, Prof. R. I. Currie, C.B.E.

Freshwater Biological Association
The Ferry House, Far Sawrey,
Ambleside, Cumbria
[09662 24689]
Director, R. T. Clarke, Ph.D.

SPECIAL SERVICES

N.E.R.C. Scientific Services
Polaris House, North Star Avenue,
Swindon, Wilts.
[0793 40101]
Director, B. F. Rule.

NATURE CONSERVANCY COUNCIL
19–20 Belgrave Square, SW1X 8PY
[01–235 3241]

Establishes, maintains and manages National Nature Reserves, advises generally on nature conservation, gives advice to the Government on nature conservation policies and on how other policies may affect nature conservation, and supports, commissions and undertakes relevant research.
Chairman, W. H. N. Wilkinson.
Director General, R. C. Steele.
Chief Scientist, Dr. D. A. Ratcliffe (based at P.O. Box 6, Godwin House, George Street, Huntingdon, Cambs. PE18 6BU).
Country Headquarters:
England: Calthorpe House, Calthorpe Street, Banbury, Oxon. OX16 8EX.
[0295–57601]
Director, Dr. F. B. O'Connor.
Scotland: 12 Hope Terrace, Edinburgh EH9 2AS.
[031–447 4784]
Director, Dr. J. Morton Boyd.
Wales: Plas Penrhos, Penrhos Road, Bangor, Gwynedd LL57 2LQ.
[0248–355141]
Director, Dr. T. Pritchard.

NORTHERN IRELAND OFFICE
Whitehall, SW1A 2AZ
[01–273 3000]
Stormont House, Belfast
[0232 63255]
Stormont Castle, Belfast
[0232 63011]
Dundonald House,
Upper Newtownards Road, Belfast
[0232 650111]

The Secretary of State for Northern Ireland in the Cabinet is responsible for Government administration in Northern Ireland. The Northern Ireland Act, 1974, made, *inter alia*, temporary arrangements for the government of Northern Ireland, exercised through the Secretary of State.
Secretary of State for Northern Ireland, THE RT. HON. DOUGLAS HURD, C.B.E., M.P. £42,980
Private Secretary, G. K. Sandiford.
Assistant Private Secretaries, R. P. Cleasby*; D. A. Hill.
Parliamentary Clerk, Miss S. Marshall.
Special Adviser, E. S. C. Bickham.
Parliamentary Private Secretary, R. Needham, M.P.
Minister of State, DR. RHODES BOYSON, M.P. ... £33,590
Private Secretary, W. R. Gamble.
Parliamentary Private Secretary, G. M. Wolfson, M.P.
Parliamentary Under Secretaries of State, The Lord Lyell (£24,229); N. Scott, M.B.E., M.P.; C. Patten, M.P.
£28,120
Private Secretaries, S. L. Rickard; Ms. C. A. Marson; R. Crawford.
Permanent Under Secretary of State, R. J. Andrew, C.B. £45,500
Private Secretary, S. A. Marsh.
Second Permanent Under Secretary of State, Head of the NICS, Sir Ewart Bell, K.C.B.* £42,000
Private Secretary, K. G. Donnelly*.
Deputy Secretaries, J. B. Bourn*; A. J. E. Brennan, C.B. £36,500
Under Secretaries, G. L. Angel; I. M. Burns; P. W. Buxton*; D. Gilliland, C.B.E.*; B. D. Palmer*; A. J. Merifield*; S. G. Norris (*Principal Establishment and Finance Officer*) £29,500
Assistant Secretaries, N. C. Abbott; P. M. Coston; P. Coulson*; P. N. Bell*; W. J. Kerr O.B.E.*; J. R. Ingram*; R. S. Reeve*; S. C. Jackson*; L. J. McClelland*; C. Radcliffe*; N. R. Cowling; J. M. Lyon; S. McKillop*; D. G. McNeil*.
Chief Information Officer 'A', A. Wood.
Deputy Chief Scientific Officer, Dr. W. H. D. Morgan*.

* Located in Northern Ireland.

ORDNANCE SURVEY
Romsey Road, Maybush, Southampton SO9 4DH
[Southampton 775555]

Director-General, W. P. Smith, C.B., O.B.E.
Directors:
Surveys and Production, A. S. Macdonald . £20,794
Marketing, Planning and Development, P. McMaster £22,996
Overseas Survey, E. Furmston.
Finance, D. Mason .... £19,243 to £23,159
Heads of Functions:
Production, J. Leonard.
Topographic Surveys, P. Wesley.
Geodesy, Photogrammetry and Computations, A. Atkinson.
Marketing, A. Marles.
Research and Development, S. Sowton.
Accounting, J. Evenett.
Establishments, W. Rayer.
Overseas Survey, I. Logan.

OVERSEAS DEVELOPMENT ADMINISTRATION

Eland House, Stag Place, SW1E 5DH
[01–213 3000]
Abercrombie House, Eaglesham Road, East Kilbride,
Glasgow G75 8EA
[03552 41199]

The Overseas Development Administration deals with British development assistance to overseas countries. This includes both capital aid on concessional terms and technical assistance (mainly in the form of specialist staff abroad and training facilities in the United Kingdom), whether provided directly to developing countries or through the various multilateral aid organizations, including the United Nations and its specialized agencies.

Minister for Overseas Development, THE RT. HON. TIMOTHY RAISON, M.P.
Private Secretary, M. C. McCulloch.
Permanent Secretary, Sir William Ryrie, K.C.B.
£42,000
Private Secretary, J. G. Lingham.
Deputy Secretary, R. A. Browning £36,500
Under Secretaries, R. M. Ainscow; N. B. Hudson; J. L. F. Buist; J. M. M. Vereker; A. T. Wilson; Dr. R. M. Oliver; H. J. Arbuthnot; Dr. J. M. Healey
£29,500

Economic Service

Head of the Economic Service (Under Secretary), Dr. J. M. Healey £29,500
Senior Economic Advisers, Dr. B. E. Cracknell; J. C. H. Morris; J. T. Roberts; G. P. Sandersley; J. T. Winpenny . . . . £19,243 to £23,159
Economic Advisers, P. R. Carter; A. G. Coverdale; A. D. Davis; Dr. G. D. Gwyer; K. E. Gubbins; E. Hawthorn; P. L. Owen; J. N. Stevens; C. J. B. White; Mrs. J. M. White . . . . . £12,399 to £16,656
Chief Statistician, R. M. Allen . . . £19,243 to £23,159
Statisticians, C. J. Allison; B. N. Downie; B. W. Hammond; M. W. Kirsop; M. C. Walmsley
£12,399 to £16,656

Information Department

Principal Information Officer, J. E. Murphy
£12,399 to £16,656
Senior Information Officers, M. E. Alderton; Mrs. H. Dean; D. Harris . . . . £10,079 to £12,518

Heads of Development Divisions

Caribbean (Bridgetown), K. A. F. Woolverton; *East Africa (Nairobi)*. R. M. Graham-Harrison; *Pacific (Suva)*, R. W. Wootton; *South-East Asia (Bangkok)*, V. J. McLean; *Southern Africa (Lilongwe)*, J. V. Kerby . . . . £19,243 to £23,159
U.K. Permanent Delegation to U.N.E.S.C.O. (Paris)
Permanent Delegate, J. Gordon . . £19,243 to £23,159
Assistant Secretaries, M. G. Bawden; R. L. Baxter; G. A. Beattie; M. L. Cahill; W. T. A. Cox; R. F. R. Deare; J. A. L. Faint; K. G. W. Frost; W. Hobman; B. R. Ireton; C. R. O. Jones; W. D. Maniece; R. G. M. Manning; Dr. D. G. Osborne; M. A. Pattison; R. G. Pettitt; J. E. Rednall; D. F. Smith; D. L. Stanton; Ms. S. Unsworth . . . . £19,243 to £23,159
Senior Principals, F. Crampsey; L. E. Fitzpatrick; A. F. Watkins; J. L. West . . . . £16,343 to £20,794
Principals, J. D. Aitken; S. I. Alexander; M. D. Allen; J. A. Anning; Miss A. Archbold; G. A. Armstrong; D. W. Baker; E. T. Barnes; D. J. Batt; W. T. Birrell; H. Britton; W. A. Brownlie; P. J. Burton; D. G. Camps; R. O. Carter; J. H. S. Chard; P. H. Charters; Miss D. W. Cherry; D. J. Church; B. Cook; G. Crabtree; D. Craxton; D. R. Curran; T. J. David; M. J. Dinham; A. S. Findlay; D. S. Fish; C. T. Gerard; J. R. Gilbert; M. J. Graham; K. D. Grimshaw; Miss J. U. Hanna; N. Hoult; W.

Jardine; Mrs. S. Jay; B. T. Jordan; Mrs. B. M. Kelly; R. O. Kiernan; Mrs. J. Laurance; D. Lawless; G. G. Leader; M. C. McCulloch; J. C. Millett; B. A. Mitchell; M. H. Pennington; S. C. Pennock; P. T. Perris; B. G. Peskett; M. A. Power; S. Ray; R. S. Ridgwell; G. F. Roberts; M. K. Robson; C. R. Roth; D. S. Sands-Smith; J. M. Scoular; R. J. Smith; M. J. Sexton; I. F. Stickels; I. D. Stuart; A. J. Sutherland; C. M. Taylor; N. Thomas; B. A. Thorpe; D. Trotter; D. P. Turner; Miss M. H. Vowles; R. J. Walsgrove; C. W. Warren; S. A. Wheeler; R. S. White; D. M. Whitecross; Mrs. P. H. Wilkinson; G. A. Williams; T. D. Wright, M.V.O.
£12,399 to £16,656
Senior Executive Officers, R. Allen; R. F. Barnes; D. G. Bell; J. W. Block; K. A. Cardy; R. J. Cattermole; T. W. Church; T. F. G. Connor; Miss C. Coppard; T. Cousins; P. Dean; J. M. Gray; C. W. Hall; J. M. Harris; B. Hefferon; M. I. Holland; Miss B. Holt; Miss H. Howden; Mrs. L. T. Jenkins; Mrs. C. B. Johnson; P. D. Johnson; M. Joseph; B. F. Kavanagh; J. Kelly; J. Last; G. G. Leader; R. A. Ludford; T. B. H. McCall; J. M. McDonough; P. McVey; G. H. Malley; S. M. Milne; Mrs. R. Mustard; V. R. Pheasant; D. T. Richards; F. C. Scutt; G. Snow; P. A. Tilley; P. J. Watson; D. A. Wilcock; P. M. Wilson; I. H. Woods; A. N. Young
£10,079 to £12,518

Advisory and Specialist Staff

Principal Education Adviser, Dr. R. O. Iredale
£19,243 to £23,159
Education Advisers, M. D. Francis; P. G. Scopes; Dr. B. L. Steele . . . . £15,605 to £19,317
Principal Engineering Adviser, M. B. Grieveson
£19,243 to £23,159
Engineering Advisers, T. D. Pike; J. N. Bulman; J. R. Hyde . . . . £15,605 to £19,317
Assistant Engineering Advisers, C. I. Ellis; H. B. Jackson; J. R. Plumb; C. S. Reid £11,343 to £14,931
Energy Adviser, Dr. J. L. D. Harrison.
Architectural Adviser, J. B. Shelley
£15,605 to £19,317
Architectural & Planning Adviser, H. W. Housego-Woolgar.
£15,605 to £19,317
Manpower and Employment Adviser, Prof. J. Fyfe
£15,605 to £19,317
Chief Medical Adviser, Dr. R. M. Oliver (*see also Department of Health & Social Security*)
Principal Medical Adviser, Dr. A. M. Baker.
Medical Advisers, (one vacancy); Dr. N. A. Ward
£15,235 to £21,329
Principal Nursing and Health Services Adviser, Mrs. B. M. Bubb . . . . £22,130 to £24,714
Nursing and Health Services Adviser, (vacant)
£16,251 to £19,113
Chief Natural Resources Adviser, (vacant) . . £26,750
Deputy Chief National Resources Adviser, A. W. Peers . . . . £19,243 to £23,159
Deputy Chief Natural Resources Adviser, Dr. J. C. Davies (*Research*) . . . . £19,243 to £23,159
Agricultural Advisers, J. R. Goldsack; R. W. Smith (*Research*); P. Tuley; R. L. Waddell
£15,605 to £19,317
Assistant Agricultural Advisers, A. J. Tainsh; J. R. F. Hansell . . . . £11,343 to £14,931
Animal Health Advisers, G. G. Freeland; J. M. Scott . . . . £15,605 to £19,317
Co-operatives Adviser, D. W. Heffer
£11,343 to £14,931
Financial Institutions Adviser, (vacant)
£15,605 to £19,317
Fisheries Advisers, J. Stoneman; Dr. J. Tarbit
£15,605 to £19,317
Forestry Advisers, R. H. Kemp; W. J. Howard
£15,605 to £19,317

Overseas Police Adviser,
(vacant) } *See also Foreign and Commonwealth Office.*
Deputy Overseas Police Adviser,
R. G. W. Lamb
Senior Social Development Adviser, Dr. D. A. P.
Butcher . . . . £15,605 to £19,317
Social Development Adviser, Dr. S. J. Conlin
£11,343 to £14,931

Land Resources Development Centre
Tolworth Tower, Surbiton, Surrey
[01–399 5281]

Director, A. J. Smyth . . . . £19,243 to £23,159

Tropical Development Research Institute
56–62 Gray's Inn Road, W.C.1
[01–242 5412]
College House, Wrights Lane, W.8

Director, Dr. E. M. Thain £24,077

OFFICE OF THE PARLIAMENTARY COMMISSIONER AND HEALTH SERVICE COMMISSIONER
Church House, Great Smith Street, SW1P 3BW
[01–212 7676]

The Parliamentary Commissioner for Administration is responsible for investigating complaints referred to him by Members of the House of Commons from members of the public who claim to have sustained injustice in consequence of maladministration in connection with administrative action taken by or on behalf of Government Departments. Certain types of action by Departments are excluded from investigation. Actions taken by other public bodies (such as local authorities, the police, the Post Office and nationalised industries) are outside the Commissioner's scope.

The Health Service Commissioners for England, for Scotland and for Wales are responsible for investigating complaints against National Health Service authorities that are not dealt with by those authorities to the satisfaction of the complainant. Complaints can be referred direct by the member of the public who claims to have sustained injustice or hardship in consequence of the failure in a service provided by a relevant body, failure of that body to provide a service or in consequence of any other action by that body. Certain types of action are excluded, in particular, action taken solely in consequence of the exercise of clinical judgment. The three offices are presently held by the Parliamentary Commissioner.

Parliamentary Commissioner and Health Service Commissioner, (vacant) £45,500
Secretaries, D. G. Allen, C.M.G.; G. V. Marsh . £29,500
Directors, V. J. Dean; K. H. Green; Mrs. J. M. Fowler; M. D. Randall; J. C. Bateman; J. H. Carruthers
£20,493 to £24,409
Principals, P. J. Belsham; Miss A. Burdett; C. H. Hemmings; J. F. Hanna (*Establishment Officer*); G. M. Keil; H. Lederman; D. S. Martin; C. McCabe; J. C. McCloud; Miss J. A. McGregor; B. J. Orr; M. Padgham; R. A. Smith; A. Watson
£13,649 to £17,906

PARLIAMENTARY COUNSEL
36 Whitehall, SW1A 2AY
[01–273 3000]

First Counsel, Sir George Engle, K.C.B., Q.C. . . £42,750
Second Counsel, C. H. de Waal, C.B. £36,875
Counsel, P. Graham, C.B.; J. D. M. Rennie; J. C. Jenkins; J. S. Mason; Miss S. P. Burns; D. W. Saunders; E. G. Caldwell . . . . *up to* £34,250

PAROLE BOARD
50 Queen Anne's Gate, SW1H 9AT
[01–213 3000]

The Board was constituted under section 59 of the Criminal Justice Act, 1967.

The function of the Board is to advise the Secretary of State for the Home Department with respect to: (1) Release on licence under section 60 (i) or 61 and recall under section 62 of the Criminal Justice Act, 1967 of persons whose cases have been referred to the Board by the Secretary of State; (2) The conditions of such licences, and the variation and cancellation of such conditions; and (3) any other matter so referred which is connected with release on licence or recall of persons to whom section 60 or 61 of the Act applies.

Chairman, The Lord Windlesham, P.C., C.V.O.
Vice-Chairman, The Hon. Mr. Justice Lloyd.
Secretary, J. Glaze.

PATENT OFFICE
(and Industrial Property and Copyright Department)
Department of Trade and Industry,
25 Southampton Buildings, WC2A 1AY
[01–405 8721]
Sale Branch: Orpington, Kent

The duties of the Department consist in the administration of the Patent Acts, the Registered Designs Act and the Trade Marks Act and in dealing with questions relating to the Copyright Acts. The Department also provides information service about patent specifications. In 1983 the Office granted 28,254 patents and registered 6,878 designs and 11,925 trade marks.

Comptroller-General, I. J. G. Davis, C.B. £31,625
Assistant Comptrollers, R. Bowen; V. Tarnofsky
£27,486
Superintending Examiners, F. J. Kearley; V. S. Dodd; D. O. Westrop; D. C. L. Blake; N. G. Tarnofsky; T. W. Sage; J. P. Britton; M. F. Vivian; A. Sugden
£24,409
Principal Examiners, A. H. W. Kennard; J. G. Clark; R. E. Bridges; C. G. Harrison; R. M. Bennett; C. S. Richenberg; M. Fox; J. F. Elliott; P. E. Taylor; C. I. C. Byrne; M. G. Currell; S. A. Goodchild; J. Winter; A. J. Needs; R. M. Ruby; H. R. Bailey; J. Sharrock; P. L. Eggington; Miss C. M. Edwards; D. A. Foley; A. C. N. Woodcock; E. F. Blake; G. K. Lindsey; D. R. Barrett; P. A. Gill; N. L. Sands; B. C. Faulkner; S. J. Rutland; W. J. Lyon; K. E. Panchen; C. D. Kopkin; D. H. Rowland; E. J. Lawrence; B. J. Phillips; D. B. Johnson; C. G. M. Hoptroff; S. Southworth . . . . . £21,966 to £23,493
Assistant Registrar, Trade Marks, J. M. Myall
£20,493 to £24,493
Senior Principals, A. B. Clarke; R. V. Egan; A. Holt
£16,855 to £22,044
Senior Examiner, Information Retrieval Services, W. Preacher . . . . £14,519 to £20,567

Manchester Office
Baskerville House, Browncross Street, Salford
[061–832 9571]

Keeper, A. A. Bryant . . . . £8,166 to £10,218

PAYMASTER GENERAL
70 Whitehall, S.W.1
[01–233 7051]
Sutherland House, Russell Way, Crawley, West Sussex RH10 1UH

The Paymaster General's Office was formed by the consolidation in 1835 of various separate pay departments then existing, some of which dated back at least to the Restoration of 1660. Its function is that of paying agent for Government Departments, other than the Revenue Departments. Most of its payments are made through banks, to whose accounts the necessary transfers are made at the Bank of England. The payment of approximately one million public service pensions is an important feature of its work.

Paymaster General, JOHN SELWYN GUMMER, M.P.
Assistant Paymaster General, L. A. Andrews
£19,243 to £23,159
Senior Principals, D. R. L. Breed; A. J. McClatchey
£15,605 to £20,794
Principals, D. R. Alexander; O. J. Breeden; E. D. Hatswell; K. Sullens; G. Thomas; M. D. West
£12,399 to £16,656
Senior Executive Officers, J. V. Allard; Mrs. D. F. Ambrose; R. S. Atkins; K. F. M. Bridle; R. F. Brigden; M. L. Card; K. J. Collins; L. T. Corner; C. R. Cowley; A. D. Edwards; T. R. George; R. G. Hollands; R. S. Juett; E. McGroarty; J. A. Payne; A. G. Rodgers; C. A. Ulph; R. Wilmer
£10,079 to £12,518

POLICE COMPLAINTS BOARD
Waterloo Bridge House, Waterloo Road, SE1 8UT
[01–275 3236]

The Police Complaints Board was established under the Police Act 1976 to introduce an independent element into the procedure for dealing with complaints by members of the public against police officers in England and Wales. The Board accordingly has certain statutory functions in relation to the disciplinary aspects of such complaints.

Chairman, Prof. Sir Cyril Philips.
Deputy Chairman, Rear-Admiral J. A. Bell.
Members, G. A. D. Coghlan; Mrs. S. Flather; D. G. Haffenden; D. J. Hodges; T. Jenkins; Mrs. J. Kellock; B. B. Mitchell; Hon. Mrs. Lindy Price; Dr. R. Rathbone; Dr. J. Robinson; The Lady Staughton; Mrs. R. Wolff.
Secretary, P. E. Bolton.

POLITICAL HONOURS SCRUTINY COMMITTEE
Cabinet Office, Great George Street, SW1P 3AL
[01–233 3000]

Chairman, The Lord Shackleton, K.G., P.C., O.B.E.
Members, The Lord Carr of Hadley, P.C.; The Lord Franks, P.C., O.M., G.C.M.G., K.C.B., C.B.E., F.B.A.
Secretary, Mrs. M. Hedley-Miller, C.B.

OFFICE OF POPULATION CENSUSES AND SURVEYS
St. Catherine's House, 10, Kingsway, WC2B 6JP
[01–242 0262]

The Office of Population Censuses and Surveys was created by a merger in May 1970 of the General Register Office and the Government Social Survey Department. The Registrar General controls the local registration service in England and Wales in the exercise of its registration and marriage duties. Copies of the original registrations of births, stillbirths, marriages and deaths are kept in London. A register of adopted children is held at Titchfield. Central indexes are compiled quarterly and certified copies of entries may be obtained on payment of certain fees. Since 1841 the Registrar General has been responsible for taking the census of population. He also prepares and publishes a wide range of statistics and appropriate commentary relating to population, fertility, births, still-births, marriages, deaths and cause of death, infectious diseases, sickness and injuries. The Registrar General also maintains, at Southport, a central register of persons on doctors' lists, for the purposes of the National Health Service.

Hours of public access, Mon.–Fri., 8.30 a.m.–4.30 p.m.

Director and Registrar General, A. R. Thatcher, C.B.
£34,250
Deputy Director, F. W. Whitehead £27,750
Deputy Registrar General, J. V. Ribbins
£19,243 to £23,159
Assistant Secretaries, Miss R. D. B. Pease (*Establishment Officer*); P. H. Kenney . . . . £19,243 to £23,159
Chief Statisticians, M. R. Alderson (*Medical*); J. Craig (*Population*); Miss J. H. Thompson (*Population*) . . . . £19,243 to £23,159
Senior Statisticians (*Medical*), J. S. Ashley; A. G. McCormick; A. J. Swerdlow £22,996
Chief Social Survey Officer "A", R. Barnes
£19,243 to £23,159
Senior Principals, G. P. Barnes; R. H. Birch; J. P. Hisley; M. L. Pennington; W. Jenkins; D. L. Pearce
£16,343 to £20,794
Chief Social Survey Officers "B", Mrs. K. H. Dunnell; Mrs. M. L. Durant; R. K. Thomas; I. B. Knight
£16,343 to £20,794
Statistician (*Medical*), M. F. G. Murphy.
Statisticians, R. I. Armitage; F. L. Ashwood; R. J. Beacham; M. S. Britton; Miss A. C. Brown; L. Bulusu; Miss S. B. Claydon; T. L. F. Devis; J. M. Dixie; A. J. Fox; P. O. Goldblatt; Mrs. M. E. Lane; M. E. McDowall; J. B. Werner . £12,399 to £16,656
Principals, B. S. T. Alcock; Mrs. P. E. Astbury; N. E. Auckland; E. Barton; T. B. Bryson; J. Denton; I. M. Golds; P. Howell; A. F. Jones; J. H. Kempf; Miss E. M. McCrossan; R. McLeod; Mrs. J. S. Morris; R. M. Nicholls; Miss D. M. Pace; J. A. Rampton; T. A. Russell; K. J. Stalker; T. O. Youlten
£12,399 to £16,656
Principal Social Survey Officers, Miss J. Atkinson; Mrs. M. R. Bone; M. J. Bradley; R. J. Butcher; Mrs. J. R. Gregory; P. J. Heady; A. J. Marsh; Mrs. J. Martin; Mrs. I. Rauta; R. U. Redpath; K. K. Sillitoe; Miss J. E. Todd; P. R. Wilson
£12,399 to £16,656
Principal Information Officer, Mrs. S. F. Brown
£12,399 to £16,656
Principal Research Officer, C. J. Denham
£12,399 to £16,656
Senior Social Survey Officers, N. Bateson; Miss E. Breeze; Mrs. H. Green; T. B. Kenney; A. J. Manners; Miss V. A. Mason; P. H. White
£10,079 to £12,518
Senior Executive Officers, T. Anderson; Mrs. B. Arm; R. A. P. Bailey; D. E. Birch; Miss N. Blackshaw; B. E. Brotherton; R. J. Carpenter; A. M. Clark; J. M. Cloyne; R. W. Dunk; Miss M. C. Ellis; Miss C. E. Finch; F. B. Gentle; J. E. Good; P. C. Gregory; Miss J. A. Higgins; Mrs. C. M. Holmes; J. T. J. Hume; Mrs. P. E. John; A. C. P. L'Hours; W. O. Laurie; B. G. Little; Miss C. S. J. Lloyd; Miss M. Y. Machin; Miss M. L. F. McCall; T. McCormick; Mrs. M. Mansfield; R. W. Massingham; B. W. Meakings; R. S. Merrett; D. J. Mountjoy; J. R. O'Donnell; Mrs. V. A. Osborn; A. Parr; N. L. Perryman; S. J. Robinson-Grindey; J. A. Salvetti; C. F. Savage; A. A. Sellar; D. Stewart; Mrs. D. M. Stobart; Mrs L. M. Street; A. C. Taylor; D. Taylor; A. W. Tester; S. R. Turner; Mrs. M. J. Wagget; P. A. Wake; Miss D. M. A. E. Waldron; J. R. Watkins; I. S. G. White; R. D. Whymark; J. G. Wright . . £10,079 to £12,518

PORT OF LONDON AUTHORITY
Head Office, Leslie Ford House,
Tilbury Docks,
Tilbury, Essex RM18 7EH
[03752 3444]

Under the Port of London Authority (Constitution) Revision Order 1975, the membership of the Board consists of a minimum of nine and a maximum of 17 members. In addition to the Chairman a minimum of seven and a maximum of 10 non-executive members are appointed by the Minister of Transport.

A minimum of one executive member and a maximum of six executive members may be appointed by the Chairman and other non-executive members.

The continuing operations of the Port for the year ended Dec. 31, 1982, showed a loss of £3,300,000.
Chairman, V. G. Paige, C.B.E..
Vice-Chairman, Sir Robin Gillett, Bt., G.B.E.
Chief Executive, J. N. Black.
Director of Tilbury, J. S. McNab.
Director of Administration, J. C. Jenkinson, M.V.O.
Director of Finance, T. R. MacMaster.
Secretary, G. E. Ennals.

THE POST OFFICE
St. Martins le Grand, EC1A 1PG
[01–432 1234]

Crown services for the carriage of Government despatches were set up about 1516. The conveyance of public correspondence began in 1635 and the mail service was made a Parliamentary responsibility with the setting up of a Post Office in 1657. Telegraphs came under the Post Office control in 1870 and the Post Office Telephone Service began in 1880. The National Girobank service of the Post Office began in 1968. The Post Office ceased to be a Government Department on October 1, 1969, following the Post Office Act 1969. The office of Postmaster General was abolished and responsibility for the running of the postal, telecommunications, and giro and remittance services was transferred to the new public authority called the Post Office. The 1981 British Telecommunications Act separated the functions of the Post Office. The Post Office is now solely responsible for postal services and National Girobank. The Act reaffirmed the Post Office basic letter monopoly but added some specific exclusions. The Chairman and members of the Post Office Board are appointed by the Secretary of State but responsibility for the running of the Post Office as a whole rests with the Board in its corporate capacity.

Post Office Board
Chairman, Sir Ronald Dearing, C.B.
Deputy Chairman and Managing Director, National Girobank, S. Wainwright.
Members, R. A. Clinton (*Managing Director, Counter Services and Corporate Services*); W. Cockburn (*Royal Mail Operations*); K. M. Young, C.B.E. (*Personnel and Industrial Relations*); A. D. Garrett (*Royal Mail Marketing*); P. E. Sellers (*Finance*).
Part-time Members, C. E. Beauchamp, C.B.E.; D. O. Gladwin, C.B.E.; E. Cole; Sir Clifford Cornford, K.C.B.; P. E. Moody, C.B.E.

PRIVY COUNCIL OFFICE
Whitehall, SW1A 2AT

Lord President of the Council (and Leader of the House of Lords), THE VISCOUNT WHITELAW, C.H., M.C.
Private Secretary, Miss J. Lewis-Jones.

Clerk of the Council, G. I. de Deney £30,750
Deputy Clerk of the Council, C. E. S. Horsford, C.V.O. £24,409
Senior Clerk, R. P. Bulling £13,369

PUBLIC HEALTH LABORATORY SERVICE
Headquarters Office:
Colindale Avenue, N.W.9
[01–200 1295]

Members of the Board: C. E. G. Smith, C.B., M.D. (*Chairman*); A. D. Bostock; D. F. R. Crofton; A. E. Earnes; T. H. Flewett, M.D.; A. Haines; E. L. Harris, C.B.; J. R. Hepple; R. G. Hoare, C.B.E.; P. Higham; Prof. R. Hurley, M.D.; W. C. D. Lovett, O.B.E., M.D.; Prof. F. W. O'Grady, C.B.E., T.D., M.D.; Prof. M. H. Richmond, SC.D., F.R.S.; A. J. Rowland; M. Sackwood; C. C. Stevens, O.B.E.
Director, J. E. M. Whitehead, M.D.
Deputy Directors, Miss J. R. Davies, M.D.; P. D. Meers, M.D.
Secretary, R. B. Paget.

(With name of Director)
Central Public Health Laboratory
Colindale Avenue, N.W.9
A. A. Glynn, M.D.

Enteric Pathogens Division: B. Rowe.
Epidemiological Research Laboratory: (vacant).
Food Hygiene Laboratory: R. J. Gilbert, Ph.D.
Hospital Infection, Division: Mrs. E. M. Cooke, M.D.
Microbiological Reagents and Quality Control Division: (vacant).
National Collection of Type Cultures: L. R. Hill, D.SC.
Virus Reference Laboratory: Mrs. M. S. Pereira, M.D.

Centre for Applied Microbiology and Research
Porton Down, Salisbury

Director, P. M. Sutton.
Microbial Technology Laboratory: Prof. A. Atkinson, Ph.D.
Molecular Genetics Laboratory: P. J. Greenaway, Ph.D.
Environmental Microbiology and Safety Reference Laboratory: G. J. Harper (*acting*).
Pathogenic Microbes Research Laboratory: Prof. D. C. Ellwood, Ph.D.
Special Pathogens Reference Laboratory: E. T. W. Bowen (*acting*).
Therapeutic Products Laboratory: H. E. Wade, Ph.D.
Vaccine Research and Production Laboratory: J. Melling, Ph.D.
Bacterial Metabolism Research Laboratory, M. J. Hill, Ph.D.

Other Reference and Special Laboratories

Anaerobe Reference Unit, Public Health Laboratory, Luton: A. T. Willis, M.D.
Communicable Diseases Surveillance Centre, 61 Colindale Avenue, N.W.9: N. S. Galbraith, M.B.
Leptospira Reference Unit, Public Health Laboratory, Hereford: S. Waitkins, Ph.D.
Malaria Reference Laboratory, London School of Hygiene and Tropical Medicine, W.C.1; Prof. D. J. Bradley, D.M.; Prof. W. Peters, M.D., D.SC.
Mycobacterium Reference Unit, Public Health Laboratory, Cardiff: P. A. Jenkins, Ph.D.
Mycological Reference Laboratory, London School of Hygiene & Tropical Medicine, W.C.1: Prof. D. W. R. Mackenzie, Ph.D.

Regional Laboratories

Birmingham, J. G. P. Hutchison, M.D.; *Bristol*, A. E. Jephcott, M.D.; *Cambridge*, C. E. D. Taylor, M.D.; *Cardiff*, C. H. L. Howells, M.D.; *Leeds*, G. L. Gibson, M.D.; *Liverpool*, G. C. Turner, M.D.; *Manchester*, D. M. Jones, M.D.; *Newcastle*, A. E. Wright, T.D., M.D.; *Oxford*, J. B. Selkon, T.D.; *Portsmouth*, O. A. Okubadejo, M.D.; *Sheffield*, B. W. Barton.

Area Laboratories

Ashford, C. Dulake; *Bath*, C. J. Hall, M.D. (*acting*); *Brighton*, B. T. Thom; *Carlisle*, M. Knowles; *Carmarthen*, H. D. S. Morgan; *Chelmsford*, (vacant); *Chester*, Miss P. M. Poole, M.D.; *Coventry*, P. R. Mortimer, M.D.; *Dorchester*, Mrs. Patricia Gill; *Epsom*, D. R. Gamble; *Exeter*, R. J. C. Hart; *Gloucester*, K. A. V. Cartwright; *Guildford*, R. Y. Cartwright; *Hereford*, I. R. Ferguson; *Hull*, S. L. Mawer; *Ipswich*, P. H. Jones; *Leicester*, C. J. Mitchell; *Lincoln*, J. G. Wallace; LONDON: *Central Middlesex Hospital*, D. A. McSwiggan (*Honorary*); *Dulwich*, Miss A. H. C. Uttlay; *Tooting*, D. G. Fleck, M.D.; *Whipps Cross*, B. Chattopadhyay, M.D.; *Luton*, A. T. Willis, M.D.; *Middlesbrough*, E. McKay-Ferguson, M.D.; *Norwich*, W. Shepherd, M.D.; *Nottingham*, M. J. Lewis, M.D.; *Peterborough*, R. S. Jobanputra, M.D.; *Plymouth*, P. J. Wilkinson; *Poole*, W. L. Hooper; *Preston*, D. N. Hutchinson; *Reading*, J. V. Dadswell; *Rhyl*, F. B. Jackson; *Salisbury*, Miss S. Patrick; *Shrewsbury*, C. A. Morris, M.D.; *Southampton*, A. D. Pearson; *Stoke-on-Trent*, J. Gray; *Swansea*, W. Kwantes; *Taunton*, J. V. S. Pether; *Truro*, W. A. Telfer Brunton; *Watford*, M. T. Moulsdale; *Wolverhampton*, R. G. Thompson.

PUBLIC RECORD OFFICE
See **Record Offices**

PUBLIC TRUSTEE OFFICE
Stewart House, Kingsway, WC2B 6JX
[01–405 4300]

The Public Trustee is a Trust corporation created to undertake the business of executorship and trusteeship; he can act as executor or administrator of the estate of a deceased person, or as a trustee of a will or settlement (either by original appointment or by transfer at a later stage) alone or jointly with others in the same manner and under the same legal obligations as a private individual or commercial trust corporation, but with a guarantee that all breaches of trust will be made good out of the Consolidated Fund. He cannot accept a trust which is foreign, exclusively charitable or for the benefit of creditors, nor an insolvent estate. He can accept the trusteeship of and manage pension funds, disaster funds and the funds of private individuals or institutions. He also administers common investment funds for moneys in Court. Fees are charged for his services, the Office being self supporting but non profit making.

Public Trustee, J. A. Boland £27,750
Assistant Public Trustee, R. C. Annis
£21,301 to £24,409
Chief Administrative Officer, J. P. Hamilton
£20,493 to £24,409
Chief Investment Manager, T. H. Nicholls
£20,493 to £24,409
Finance Officer, F. A. Boocock ... £17,593 to £22,044
Chief Property Adviser, R. Myers . £14,461 to £16,961
Acceptance Officer, R. A. Cunningham
£13,649 to £17,906

PUBLIC WORKS LOAN BOARD
See **National Investment and Loans Board**

COMMISSION FOR RACIAL EQUALITY
Elliot House, 10–12 Allington Street, SW1E 5EH
[01–828 7022]

Established on June 13, 1977, under the Race Relations Act 1976, to work towards elimination of discrimination and promote equality of opportunity and good relations between different racial groups generally. (Replaces Community Relations Commission and Race Relations Board).
Chairman, P. Newsam.
Deputy Chairman, C. Robinson, O.B.E.
Members, Mrs. S. Flather; A. W. Gayton; Dr. F. Hashmi, O.B.E.; G. E. B. Tyler; L. Crawford; Mrs. L. Khan; Prof. B. Parekh; G. S. Sarang; K. Gill; Ethel M. Houston, O.B.E.; E. Gilmour Jones; W. Morris; K. R. Whitesides.

RECORD OFFICES, ETC.

THE PUBLIC RECORD OFFICE
Chancery Lane, WC2A 1LR
[01-405 0741]
Ruskin Avenue, Kew,
Richmond, Surrey TW9 4DU
[01-876 3444]

National Records since the Norman Conquest brought together from Courts of Law and Government Departments. Search rooms open from Monday to Friday to holders of readers' tickets from 9.30 to 5 (Kew and Chancery Lane). Information about the location and availability of records can be obtained either by writing or by telephone enquiry. The Museum (at Chancery Lane) is open Monday to Friday, 1 to 4 p.m., and to organized parties at other times by arrangement; it contains *Domesday Book* (2 vols.), made by order of William the Conqueror in 1085, and *Domesday Chest*; the *Gunpowder Plot* papers (1605); bull of Pope Clement VII, confirming Henry VIII as *Fidei Defensor* (1524); the Log Book of H.M.S. *Victory* at Trafalgar (1805); and many other documents of national interest.

Keeper of Public Records, G. H. Martin, D.Phil., F.S.A.
£29,000
Deputy Keeper, Dr. P. M. Barnes . £19,943 to £23,859
Records Administration Officer, M. Roper
£19,943 to £23,859
Officer-in-Charge, Chancery Lane, Dr. R. F. Hunnisett
£20,493 to £22,928
Establishment Officer, J. G. Wickham
£13,099 to £17,356
Principal Assistant Keepers, C. D. Chalmers; Mrs. J. M. Cox; Dr. N. G. Cox; N. E. Evans; Dr. A. A. H. Knightbridge; Mrs. A. N. Nicol; J. L. Walford
£16,352 to £20,567
Assistant Keepers, Miss G. L. Beech; J. D. Cantwell; Dr. T. M. Chalmers; Miss M. M. Condon; Dr. D. Crook; Dr. H. Forde; Dr. M. R. Foster; Dr. E. M. Hallam Smith; Dr. E. J. Higgs; Mrs. H. E. Jones; Dr. M. J. Jubb; Mrs. A. E. Morton; T. R. Padfield; Dr. J. B. Post; Dr. A. M. S. Prochaska; Dr. N. A. M. Rodger; Dr. D. L. Thomas
scale rising to max. of £17,906
Principal, Repository and Reprographic Services, P. F. McCaffrey................. £13,099 to £17,356
Principal Inspecting Officer, D. Ashton
£13,099 to £17,356
Inspecting Officers, D. Barlow; A. W. H. Medlicott; C. J. Edwards; J. S. Harley; J. A. Keene; C. B. Townshend; K. J. Smith ...... £10,779 to £13,218
Senior Executive Officers, T. J. Donovan; F. McCall
£10,579 to £13,218

ADVISORY COUNCIL ON PUBLIC RECORDS

Public Record Office, Chancery Lane, WC2A 1LR

[01–405 0741]

Chairman, The Master of the Rolls.

Members, The Lord Bancroft, G.C.B.; Dr. R. D'O. Butler, C.M.G.; W. Clarke, C.B.E.; P. T. Cormack, M.P.; Prof. D. N. Dilks; Prof. G. R. Elton, F.B.A.; Prof. R. C. Floud; Prof. P. D. A. Harvey; Prof. M. E. Howard, C.B.E., M.C., F.B.A.; Dr. M. Hughes, M.P.; Prof. Sir Hans Kornberg, F.R.S.; Rt. Hon. Sir Robert Megarry, F.B.A.; Dr. J. Morgan; Sir Paul Osmond, C.B.; W. R. Serjeant; R. S. Wainwright, M.P.

Assessors, D. J. Wiblin; Dr. G. H. Martin.

Secretary, M. J. Jubb.

HOUSE OF LORDS RECORD OFFICE

House of Lords, SW1A 0PW

[01–219 3074]

Since 1497, the records of Parliament have been kept within the Palace of Westminster. They are in the custody of the Clerk of the Parliaments, who in 1946 established a record department to supervise their preservation and their production to students. The Search Room of this office is open to the public throughout the year, Mondays to Fridays inclusive from 9.30 a.m. to 5.30 p.m. The records preserved number some 3,000,000 documents, and include Acts of Parliament from 1497, Journals of the House of Lords from 1510. Minutes and Committee proceedings from 1610, and Papers laid before Parliament from 1531. Amongst the records are the Petition of Right, the Death Warrant of Charles I, the Declaration of Breda and the Bill of Rights. The House of Lords Record Office also has charge of the Journals of the House of Commons (from 1547), and other surviving records of the Commons (from 1572), which include plans and annexed documents relating to Private Bill legislation from 1818. Among other documents are the records of the Lord Great Chamberlain, the political papers of certain members of the two Houses (including the papers of Lloyd George, Bonar Law and other statesmen previously preserved in the Beaverbrook Library), and documents relating to Parliament acquired on behalf of the nation. All the manuscripts and other records are preserved in the Victoria Tower of the Houses of Parliament. A permanent exhibition was established in the Royal Gallery in 1979.

Clerk of the Records, H. S. Cobb, F.S.A.

           £20,493 to £24,409

Deputy Clerk of the Records, D. J. Johnson, F.S.A.

           £16,902 to £20,567

Assistant Clerks of the Records, J. C. Morgan (*Sound Archives*); S. K. Ellison £12,326 to £17,906.

ROYAL COMMISSION ON HISTORICAL MANUSCRIPTS

Quality House, Quality Court, Chancery Lane, W.C.2

[01–242 1198]

The Commission was set up by Royal Warrant in 1869 to enquire and report on collections of papers of value for the study of history in private hands. In 1959 a new warrant enlarged these terms of reference to include all historical records, wherever situated, outside the Public Records and gave it added responsibilities, as a central co-ordinating body, to promote, assist and advise on their proper preservation and storage. The Commission has published over 200 volumes of reports. It holds a further 26,000 unpublished reports in the National Register of Archives, available for consultation in its search room. It also administers the Manorial and Tithe Documents Rules on behalf of the Master of the Rolls.

Chairman, The Lord Blake, F.B.A.

Commissioners, Prof. J. C. Beckett; Sir Robert Somerville, K.C.V.O., F.S.A.; The Lord Kenyon, C.B.E., F.S.A.; The Lord Fletcher, P.C., Ll.D., F.S.A.; ; The Duke of Northumberland, K.G., P.C., G.C.V.O., F.R.S.; J. P. W. Ehrman, F.B.A., F.S.A.; The Earl of Wemyss and March, K.T.; Prof. S. F. C. Milsom, F.B.A.; Sir John Habakkuk, F.B.A.; G. E. Aylmer, F.B.A.; P. T. Cormack, F.S.A., M.P.; H. M. Colvin, C.B.E., F.B.A., F.S.A.; Prof. G. W. S. Barrow, F.B.A.; Valerie L. Pearl, F.S.A.

Secretary, B. S. Smith, F.S.A.

SCOTTISH RECORD OFFICE

H.M. General Register House, Edinburgh EH1 3YY

[031–556 6585]

The history of the national archives of Scotland can be traced back to the 13th century. The present headquarters of the Scottish Record Office, the General Register House, was founded in 1774 and built to designs by Robert Adam, later modified by Robert Reid. Here are preserved the administrative records of pre-Union Scotland, the registers of central and local courts of law, the public registers of property rights and legal documents, and many collections of local and church records and private archives. Certain groups of records, mainly the modern records of government departments in Scotland, the Scottish railway records, and the plans collection, are preserved in the branch repository at the West Register House in Charlotte Square—the former St. George's Church which was designed by Robert Reid. The Search Rooms in both buildings open daily from 9 to 4.45 (Mondays to Fridays). A permanent exhibition at the West Register House and changing exhibitions at the General Register House are open to the public on weekdays from 10 to 4. The National Register of Archives (Scotland), which is a branch of the Scottish Record Office, is based in the West Register House.

Keeper of the Records of Scotland, J. Imrie.

DEPARTMENT OF THE REGISTERS OF SCOTLAND

Meadowbank House, 153 London Road, Edinburgh EH8 7AU

[031–661 6111]

The Registers of Scotland consist of:—

(1) General Register of Sasines and Land Register of Scotland; (2) Register of Deeds in the Books of Council and Session; (3) Register of Protests; (4) Register of English and Irish Judgments; (5) Register of Service of Heirs; (6) Register of the Great Seal; (7) Register of the Quarter Seal; (8) Register of the Prince's Seal; (9) Register of Crown Grants; (10) Register of Sheriffs' Commissions; (11) Register of the Cachet Seal; (12) Register of Inhibitions and Adjudications; (13) Register of Entails; (14) Register of Hornings.

The General Register of Sasines and the Land Register of Scotland form the chief security in Scotland of the rights of land and other heritable (or real) property.

Keeper of the Registers of Scotland, W. S. Penman

           £24,077

Deputy Keeper, W. Russell . . . . £19,243 to £23,159

Senior Assistant Keepers, T. M. Nichol; J. Robertson; P. G. Skea . . . . £16,343 to £20,794

Assistant Keepers, R. C. Brown; A. M. Falconer; R. C. Fulton; W. G. Lobban; J. MacDonald; A. G. Rennie; J. Shaw; I. M. Tainsh; A. A. Snowdon; G. C. Warrender . . . . £12,399 to £16,656

Accountant, Mrs. A. McDonald . . £10,079 to £12,518

Senior Examiners, J. Anderson; A. J. G. Balfour; J. F. Campbell; R. C. Clarke; J. Cogle; B. J. Corr; A. B. Farmer; P. P. M. Gordon; K. G. Herbertson; J.

Knox; D. Lorimer; D. Manson; J. B. Marshall; J. F. Morrison; L. J. Morrison; D. L. Nicoll; A. W. Ramage; J. Rynn; E. B. Sanderson; R. M. Stewart; Miss I. Thom .... £10,079 to £12,518

CORPORATION OF LONDON RECORDS OFFICE
Guildhall, EC2P 2EJ
[01–606 3030]

Contains the municipal archives of the City of London which are regarded as the most complete collection of ancient municipal records in existence. Includes charters of William the Conqueror, Henry II, and later Kings and Queens to 1957; ancient custumals: Liber Horn, Dunthorne, Custumarum, Ordinacionum, Memorandorum and Albus, Liber de Antiquis Legibus, and collections of Statutes; continuous series of judicial rolls and books from 1252 and Council minutes from 1275; records of the Old Bailey and Guildhall Sessions from 1603, and financial records from the 16th century, together with the records of London Bridge from the 12th century and numerous subsidiary series and miscellanea of historical interest. A Guide was published in 1951. Readers' Room open Monday to Friday, 9.30 a.m. to 4.45 p.m.
Keeper of the City Records, The Town Clerk.
Deputy Keeper, J. R. Sewell.
Assistant Keeper, Mrs. J. M. Bankes.

REVIEW BODIES

ARMED FORCES PAY

The Review Body on Armed Forces Pay was appointed in September 1971 to advise the Prime Minister on the pay and allowances of members of Naval, Military and Air Forces of the Crown and of any women's service administered by the Defence Council.
The members of the Review Body are: Sir David Orr (*Chairman*); M. Bett; Sir Richard Cave; D. P. M. Hudson; Mrs. J. Hughes; L. A. Mills; Admiral Sir Anthony Morton, G.B.E., K.C.B.; J. R. Sargent.

DOCTORS' AND DENTISTS' REMUNERATION

The Review Body on Doctors' and Dentists' Remuneration was appointed in July 1971 to advise the Prime Minister on the remuneration of doctors and dentists taking any part in the National Health Service.
The members of the Review Body are: Sir Robert Clark, D.S.C. (*Chairman*); Dr. Anne Hogg; J. L. Kirkpatrick, C.B.E.; Prof. P. G. Moore, T.D.; D. G. Richards; Prof. G. F. Thomason, C.B.E.; Sir Graham Wilkins; J. K. Warburton, C.B.E.

TOP SALARIES

The Review Body on Top Salaries was appointed in May, 1971 to advise the Prime Minister on the remuneration of the higher judiciary and other judicial appointments; senior civil servants; and senior officers of the armed forces. Until August 1980 the remit also included the Chairmen and members of the Boards of nationalized industries. The Review Body has also been asked on a number of occasions to advise on the remuneration of Members of Parliament and of Ministers and on the level of the Peers' expenses allowances.

The members of the Review Body are: The Lord Plowden, K.C.B., K.B.E. (*Chairman*); Sir Harold Atcherley; The Lord Chorley; Sir Robin Ibbs; A. Morritt, Q.C.; Sir David Orr; Sir Thomas Skyrme, K.C.V.O., C.B., C.B.E.

NURSING STAFF, MIDWIVES, HEALTH VISITORS AND PROFESSIONS ALLIED TO MEDICINE

The Review Body for nursing staff, midwives, health visitors and professions allied to medicine was set up in July 1983 to advise the Prime Minister on the remuneration of nursing staff, midwives and health visitors employed in the National Health Service; and physiotherapists, radiographers, remedial gymnasts, occupational therapists, orthoptists, chiropodists, dietitians and related grades employed in the National Health Service.
The members of the Review Body are: Sir John Greenborough, K.B.E. (*Chairman*); Miss B. Cooper, Q.C.; Mrs. S. Harold; Sir John Herbecq, K.C.B.; Dr. G. Hills; Mrs. J. Hughes; I. H. Phillipps; Prof. G. F. Thomason, C.B.E.
NOTE.—The secretariat for the above bodies is provided by the Office of Manpower Economics (*see separate entry*).

ROYAL COMMISSION FOR THE EXHIBITION OF 1851
1 Lowther Gardens, Exhibition Road, SW7 2AA
[01–589 3665]

Incorporated by Supplemental Charter as a permanent Commission after winding up the affairs of the Great Exhibition of 1851. It has for its object the promotion of scientific and artistic education by means of funds derived from its Kensington Estate, purchased with the surplus left over from the Great Exhibition.
President, H.R.H. The Duke of Edinburgh, K.G., P.C., K.T., O.M., G.B.E.
Chairman, Board of Management, Sir Richard Way, K.C.B., C.B.E.
Secretary to Commissioners, C. A. H. James.

SCIENCE AND ENGINEERING RESEARCH COUNCIL
Polaris House, North Star Avenue, Swindon, Wilts. SN2 1ET
[0793–26222]

Chairman, Prof. J. F. C. Kingman, F.R.S.
Members of the Council, Prof. J. I. G. Cadogan, F.R.S.; Prof. D. C. Colley; D. Downs, C.B.E.; G. R. Hall; Dr. M. W. Holdgate, C.B.; P. A. B. Hughes, C.B.E.; Prof. Sir Jack Lewis, F.R.S.; Prof. A. G. J. MacFarlane, F.R.S.; Prof. E. W. J. Mitchell, C.B.E.; Sir Alan Muir Wood, F.R.S.; Prof. R. O. C. Norman, F.R.S.; Prof. K. A. Pounds, C.B.E., F.R.S.; Prof. M. H. Richmond, F.R.S.; O. Roith; Sir Francis Tombs; Prof. J. J. Turner; Prof. W. L. Wilcock; Dr. W. L. Wilkinson.

SCOTTISH OFFICE
Dover House, Whitehall, SW1A 2AU
[01–233 3000]

Secretary of State for Scotland, THE RT. HON. GEORGE KENNETH HOTSON YOUNGER, T.D., M.P. . . . £40,930
Private Secretary, J. S. Graham   £19,243 to £23,159
Assistant Private Secretaries, E. S. Gowans; Ms. S. M. McCabe.
Minister of State for Agriculture and Fisheries, The Lord Gray of Contin, P.C. £26,670

Parliamentary Under Secretaries of State, J. Allan Stewart, M.P. (*Industry and Education*); J. MacKay, M.P. (*Health and Social Work*); M. Ancram, M.P. (*Home Affairs and the Environment*) £26,780
Permanent Under Secretary of State, Sir William Fraser, G.C.B. £44,033
Private Secretary, Mrs. E. Lewis.
Parliamentary Clerk, Ms. M. P. Morrow.
Liaison Staff:
  Assistant Secretaries, G. Murray; R. H. Scott
               £19,243 to £23,159
  Principals, A. C. King; G. A. D. Philip
               £12,399 to £16,656

New St. Andrew's House,
Edinburgh EH1 3SK
[031–556 8400]

MANAGEMENT GROUP SUPPORT STAFF
Principal, E. C. Davison .... £12,399 to £16,656

CENTRAL SERVICES
Deputy Secretary (*Central Services*), I. D. Penman
               £35,278

Establishment Division
Under Secretary, A. H. Bishop (*Principal Establishment Officer*) £28,583
Assistant Secretaries, Miss M. Maclean; G. R. Wilson .... £19,243 to £23,159
Senior Principals, J. N. Davison; A. B. Fairweather, T.D.; W. A. Smith .... £15,605 to £20,794
Principals, W. E. Bennett; J. Blaikie; D. J. Chalmers; D. A. Christie; W. Davidson; M. Finnigan; J. R. M. Flucker; I. C. Freeman; H. J. Graham; D. Macniven; Mrs. J. Niven; B. V. Surridge; Miss M. A. Wood .... £12,399 to £16,656
Senior Executive Officers, A. G. Aitken; J. Calderwood; J. W. A. Chalmers; T. Chalmers; B. W. Clark; J. B. Currie; E. D. Ewing; G. H. Fox; J. P. Garvie; Mrs. M. D. K. Kemp; B. J. Lincoln; H. M. MacKenzie; R. R. Morrison; H. M. Muir; Mrs. C. Peden; A. S. Robertson; J. B. Roddin; B. W. J. Sharry; A. J. Stewart; A. G. Templeman; E. Thomson; S. J. B. Walker; B. F. Warren; A. G. Young; H. Young .... £10,079 to £12,518
Librarian, H. A. Colquhoun ..... £10,079 to £12,518

Directorate of Computers and Telecommunications
Broomhouse Drive, Edinburgh
[031–443 4040]
Computer Services
Manager (*Assistant Secretary*), F. Ibbotson
               £19,243 to £23,159
Deputy Manager, C. B. Knox .... £15,605 to £20,794
Principals, A. M. Brown; J. A. Brown; I. W. Goodwin
               £12,399 to £16,656
Senior Executive Officers, I. S. Barclay; R. Barrie; L. J. D. Boyd; P. Boyd; Mrs. S. M. Crearie; R. G. Donaldson; W. M. Ferguson; I. D. Hunter; A. R. McCowan; K. A. Macdonald; A. D. Paterson; B. U. Pearson; J. H. Robertson; T. G. Whitehead
               £10,079 to £12,518

Telecommunications
St. Andrew's House, Edinburgh
(031–556 8501)
Director, A. F. Harrison .... £18,374 to £20,794

Finance Division
Finance Group
Under Secretary, R. R. Hillhouse (*Principal Finance Officer*) £28,583

Assistant Secretaries, T. M. Band; I. G. F. Gray; K. J. MacKenzie; H. Robertson, M.B.E.
               £19,243 to £23,159
Senior Principals, I. Nicholson; W. T. Tait; A. Walker .... £15,605 to £20,794
Principals, J. S. Aldridge; R. Anderson; R. A. Catto; S. W. E. Davidson; J. W. Elvidge; L. P. S. Dunbar; T. W. Forsyth; C. D. Henderson; D. A. Howe; T. Hunter; W. A. Lamberton; R. C. Lawson; D. R. Mayer; W. Moyes; I. M. Nicol; I. M. Smith; I. T. Wallace; R. K. West; R. G. B. Wilkie
               £12,399 to £16,656
Senior Executive Officers, P. E. Anderson; E. G. J. Bee; I. S. Brown; R. S. Buchan; R. G. Carter; R. J. Chisholm; W. D. Fairbairn; D. M. Ferguson; F. D. Garvie; J. L. Gordon; A. A. Harper; N. Harvey; M. W. Jarron; N. J. H. Kernohan; G. C. Kincaid; R. MacCallum; J. A. McCabe; R. McGregor; W. McLauchlan; D. A. McNiven; W. M. Martin; W. Malone; W. E. M. Maxwell; D. Muir; C. Naldrett; R. S. Pryor; Mrs. C. Ritchie; E. F. Rose; R. R. Ross; A. P. Smart; J. Symington; G. F. Talbot; M. W. Thomson; Miss K. T. Wallace; W. P. Young
               £10,079 to £12,518

Local Government Finance Group
Assistant Secretaries, N. G. Campbell; B. V. Philp
               £19,243 to £23,159
Principals, A. G. Beattie; J. A. Rennie; R. Tait; T. Winwick .... £12,399 to £16,656

Solicitor's Office
(*For the Scottish Departments and certain U.K. services including H.M. Treasury, in Scotland.*)
Solicitor, A. A. McMillan £35,278
Deputy Solicitor, R. Brodie £28,583
Divisional Solicitors, J. B. Allan; K. F. Barclay; N. W. Boe; *R. Eadie; G. Jackson; J. L. Jamieson; *A. J. Sim; J. A. Stewart; T. G. Walters
               £19,243 to £23,159
*Seconded to Scottish Law Commission

Scottish Information Office
(*For the Scottish Departments and certain U.K. services*)
Director, C. F. Corbett .... £19,243 to £23,159
Deputy Director, D. C. M. Beveridge
               £15,605 to £20,794

Statistics Directorate
Director of Statistics, D. Wishart, PH.D.
               £19,243 to £23,159

Inquiry Reporters
16 Waterloo Place, Edinburgh
[031–556 9191]
Chief Reporter, A. G. Bell £28,583
Deputy Chief Reporter, W. D. Campbell
               £19,243 to £23,159
Senior Executive Officer, Miss C. B. Forbes
               £10,079 to £12,518

DEPARTMENT OF AGRICULTURE AND FISHERIES FOR SCOTLAND
Chesser House, 500 Gorgie Road, Edinburgh
EH11 3AW
[031–443 4020]
Dover House, Whitehall, London, SW1A 2AU
[01–233 3000]
Secretary, L. P. Hamilton £35,278
Under Secretary, D. G. Mackay £28,583
Fisheries Secretary, B. Gordon £28,583
Assistant Secretaries, T. A. Cameron; A. D. F. Findlay; J. W. L. Lonie; A. I. Macdonald; L. V. McEwan; Miss J. L. Ross; A. B. Scott; D. C. Todd; I. M. Whitelaw .... £19,243 to £23,159

Principals, D. J. Baird; C. Barbour; D. I. Dalgetty; D. R. Dickson; J. H. F. Finnie; J. N. Johnston; F. J. Lawrie; A. Lindsey; B. E. McAdam; J. McGhee; C. K. McIntosh; D. Reid; W. B. Ritchie; D. A. Robertson; N. A. Stewart; D. Stott
£12,399 to £16,656

Senior Executive Officers, L. J. D. Boyd; W. M. Bremner; R. A. J. Dalziel; A. R. Donaldson; R. T. McGeorge; W. Malcolm; A. B. Patton; M. T. A. Vance; R. J. Walker; D. Watson £10,079 to £12,518
Chief Agricultural Officer (Under Secretary), C. Mackay £28,583
Deputy Chief Agricultural Officer, A. H. Boggon
£19,243 to £23,159
Assistant Chief Agricultural Officers, J. F. Hutcheson; R. Macdonald; W. A. Macgregor; G. M. B. Redpath; J. I. Woodrow .... £15,605 to £20,794
Chief Agricultural Economist, J. M. Dunn, D.Phil.
£15,605 to £20,794
Chief Fatstock Officer, A. Bain ... £12,399 to £16,656
Chief Food and Dairy Officer, M. E. M. Anderson
£13,345 to £17,748
Chief Surveyor, N. Taylor .... £15,605 to £20,794
Scientific Adviser, A. M. Raven, PH.D.
£19,243 to £23,159
Senior Principal Scientific Officers, T. W. Hegarty; D. D. Thornton .... £15,605 to £20,794

Royal Botanic Garden
Inverleith Row, Edinburgh EH3 5LR
[031–552 7171]

Regius Keeper, Prof. D. M. Henderson, F.R.S.E.
£19,243 to £23,159
Assistant Keeper, J. Cullen, PH.D. £15,605 to £20,794

Agricultural Scientific Services
East Craigs, Edinburgh EH12 8NJ
[031–339 2355]

Director, D. C. Graham, PH.D., F.R.S.E.
£19,243 to £23,159
Deputy Director, R. D. Seaton .... £15,605 to £20,794
Senior Principal Scientific Officers, J. R. Cutler; M. J. Richardson .... £15,605 to £20,794

Fisheries Research Services
Marine Laboratory, P.O. Box 101,
Victoria Road, Torry, Aberdeen AB9 8DB
[0224 876544]

Director, Prof. A. D. McIntyre, D.SC., F.R.S.E. . £24,077
Deputy Director, A. D. Hawkins, PH.D.
£19,243 to £23,159
Senior Principal Scientific Officers, R. Jones; D. N. MacLennan; A. Saville, F.R.S.E.; C. S. Wardle, PH.D. .... £15,605 to £20,794

Freshwater Fisheries Laboratory,
Faskally, Pitlochry, Perthshire PH16 5LB
[0796 2060]

Senior Principal Scientific Officers, R. G. J. Shelton, PH.D.; J. E. Thorpe, PH.D. ...... £15,605 to £20,794

Sea Fisheries Inspectorate

Chief Inspector of Sea Fisheries, J. W. S. Kinnaird
£15,605 to £20,794
Inspector of Salmon and Freshwater Fisheries, R. B. Williamson .... £11,812 to £14,931
Marine Superintendent, Captain D. R. Corse
£17,271 to £17,566

Crofters Commission
4/6 Castle Wynd, Inverness IV2 3EQ
[0463 237231]

Chairman (part-time), J. F. M. Macleod £18,500
Members (part-time), N. A. MacAskill (£12,025); A. Fraser, PH.D.; B. T. Hunter; J. MacDonald; D. Morrison; I. G. Munro £6,013

Secretary, I. A. Macpherson ..... £15,605 to £20,794
Assistant Secretaries, A. W. Gladwin, W. T. Peters
£12,399 to £16,656
Chief Technical Officer, W. Macfarlane
£13,211 to £15,711

Red Deer Commission
Knowsley, 82 Fairfield Road, Inverness IV3 5LH
[0463 231751]

Chairman, I. K. Mackenzie £9,715
Secretary, N. H. McCulloch ...... £10,079 to £12,518

SCOTTISH DEVELOPMENT DEPARTMENT
New St. Andrew's House, Edinburgh EH1 3SZ
[031–556 8400]
Dover House, Whitehall, London, SW1A 2AU
[01–233 3000]

Secretary, T. R. H. Godden, C.B. £35,278
Under Secretaries, H. H. Mills; W. W. Scott . £28,583
Assistant Secretaries, D. A. Bennet; Ms. L. Clare; M. J. P. Cunliffe; D. J. Essery; K. W. Moore; J. S. B. Martin; F. H. Orr; G. Robson; N. W. Smith; R. E. Smith .... £19,243 to £23,159
Principals, M. T. Affolter; J. R. Brown; A. M. Burnside; D. J. Christie; M. A. Duffy; R. Gordon; J. L. Helm; J. C. Henderson; A. R. Irons; J. W. H. Irvine; C. M. A. Lugton; I. J. MacKenzie; P. M. McLaren; Mrs. M. J. Martyn; A. J. Matheson; J. Meldrum; D. N. G. Reid; P. J. Robinson; D. M. Rowand; P. M. Russell; J. M. Thornton; R. Walker; J. O. Wastle; M. R. Wilson..... £12,399 to £16,656
Senior Executive Officers, S. S. Anderson; J. Black; A. Brown; N. P. Burnett; J. K. Clark; J. S. Graham; J. B. Jolly; P. Kemp; Miss E. M. Livingstone; I. F. McEwan; I. A. McLeod; A. H. Meldrum; M. J. Rogers; R. M. Russell; Miss F. A. Stenhouse
£10,079 to £12,518

Professional Staff

Chief Engineer, S. C. Agnew £28,583
Deputy Chief Engineer, E. H. Nicoll, C.B.E. ... £23,159
Assistant Chief Engineers, W. Ferguson; R. McGillivray; J. O. Thorburn ..... £15,605 to £20,794
Director of Building and Chief Architect, J. E. Gibbons, PH.D........................... £28,583
Deputy Director of Building and Deputy Chief Architect, (vacant) .... £19,243 to £23,159
Deputy Director of Building and Chief Quantity Surveyor, D. C. Russell .... £19,243 to £23,159
Assistant Director and Deputy Chief Quantity Surveyor, A. Duncan .... £15,605 to £20,794
Assistant Director and Chief Mechanical and Electrical Engineer, R. A. E. Quartermaine
£15,605 to £20,794
Assistant Directors, A. R. H. Bott; M. R. Miller; R. W. Naismith; R. I. Watson .... £15,605 to £20,794
Superintending Architects, S. G. E. Shipman; W. W. M. Beal....................... £15,605 to £20,794
Chief Planner, W. D. C. Lyddon, C.B., D.Litt. . £28,583
Deputy Chief Planner, A. Mackenzie
£19,243 to £23,159
Assistant Chief Planners, D. R. Dare; A. W. Denham; S. G. Fulton; P. D. McGovern, PH.D.
£15,605 to £20,794
Chief Research Officer, C. C. MacDonald
£19,243 to £23,159
Senior Principal Research Officers, C. P. A. Levein, PH.D.; C. L. Wood .... £15,605 to £20,794
Chief Road Engineer, J. A. M. MacKenzie ... £28,583
Deputy Chief Engineer (Roads), J. R. Lake
£19,243 to £23,159
Deputy Chief Engineer (Bridges), W. R. Varley
£19,243 to £23,159
Assistant Chief Engineers, J. Patience; G. F. Storey; G. S. Marshall................ £15,605 to £20,794

H.M. Chief Industrial Pollution Inspector, R. R. A.
Pride .... £19,243 to £23,159
Chief Estates Officer, (vacant) .... £15,605 to £20,794
Principal Inspector of Ancient Monuments for Scotland, I. MacIvor .... £15,382 to £17,518
Principal Inspector of Historic Buildings, D. M.
Walker .... £15,382 to £17,518

INDUSTRY DEPARTMENT FOR SCOTLAND
New St. Andrew's House, Edinburgh
[031–556 8400]
and
Dover House, Whitehall, S.W.1
[01–233 3000]

*Secretary and Chief Economic Adviser to the Secretary
of State for Scotland,* R. G. L. McCrone, C.B., Ph.D.
£35,278
Under Secretaries, J. F. Laing; J. F. McClellan
£28,583
Assistant Secretaries, D. Connelly; R. S. Crofts; W. J.
Fearnley; Miss E. A. Mackay; A. M. Russell
£19,243 to £23,159
Senior Economic Advisers, C. M. Baxter; W. M.
McNie .... £19,243 to £23,159
Principals, Mrs. M. H. Borowski; D. J. Crawley; A.
W. Fraser; M. A. Grant; D. M. Henderson; K. W.
McKay; W. A. McKenzie; Mrs. R. N. Menlowe; B.
Naylor; E. C. Reavley; D. R. Semple
£12,399 to £16,656
Senior Executive Officers, R. M. Aitken; A. D.
Fleming; S. W. Fox; I. A. Snedden; J. H. Turgoose
£10,079 to £12,518

Industrial Expansion
Alhambra House, 45 Waterloo Street, Glasgow
[041–248 2855]

Under Secretary, G. R. Wilson £28,583
Industrial Adviser, D. J. Bain.
Assistant Secretaries, S. F. Hampson; P. McKinlay
£19,243 to £23,159
Senior Principal, J. E. Milne, O.B.E.
£15,605 to £20,794
Principals, W. C. Alison; G. J. Heffernan; I. Gordon;
E. D. F. McGaughrin; K. MacRae
£12,399 to £16,656
Senior Executive Officers, D. S. Chalmers; C. H.
Coulthard; J. H. B. Fleming, T.D.; R. E. Magowan;
Mrs. S. M. Quinn; J. Scullion .. £10,079 to £12,518

Locate in Scotland
120 Bothwell Street, Glasgow
[041–248 2700]

Director, I. S. Robertson £26,236
Senior Principal, T. E. McGreevy £15,605 to £20,794
Principal, J. P. Laydon .... £12,399 to £16,656
Senior Executive Officer, (vacant) £10,079 to £12,518

SCOTTISH EDUCATION DEPARTMENT
New St. Andrew's House, St. James Centre,
Edinburgh
[031–556 8400]
and
Dover House, Whitehall, London, S.W.1
[01–233 3000]

Secretary, J. A. Scott, M.V.O. £35,278
Under Secretaries, Miss P. A. Cox; I. M. Wilson
£28,583
Assistant Secretaries, D. A. Campbell; J. R. Cuthbert,
Ph.D. (*Chief Statistician*); J. J. Farrell; E. Frizzell;
J. Keeley; T. J. Kelly; R. M. Laidlaw; J. Linn
£19,243 to £23,159
Senior Principal, G. E. Brewerton £15,605 to £20,794

Principals, Mrs. E. E. R. Barnwell; T. Blacklock; R.
G. H. Brown; D. G. Campbell; T. B. Haig, O.B.E.; J.
C. Halley; I. C. Henderson; F. H. Hunter; M. J.
Hunter; Miss J. M. Lawson; J. McCallum; N.
MacLeod; Miss M. M. Marshall; N. Pittman; G. T.
Reed; I. M. Watt; W. Weir..... £12,399 to £16,656
Senior Executive Officers, I. R. Anderson; Miss M. E.
Graham, M.V.O.; A. Lister; E. M. C. Mackay; D. C.
MacNab; R. E. Merrall; B. R. Morgan; A. Naismith;
W. H. Stein .... £10,079 to £12,518

H.M. Inspectors of Schools

Senior Chief Inspector, J. A. Ferguson £28,583
Deputy Senior Chief Inspectors, W. R. Ritchie; H. F.
Smith £25,182
Chief Inspectors, W. F. L. Bigwood; L. Clark; A. H.
Ferguson; T. N. Gallacher; D. S. Graham; J.
Howgego; R. S. Johnston; S. E. McClelland, Ph.D.;
D. W. Mack; J. H. Thomson.... £19,243 to £23,159
Inspectors, J. N. Alison; M. T. J. Axford; P. Banks;
W. T. Beveridge; J. Boyes; Miss C. L. Boyle; M. J.
Brown; Mrs. M. M. Browning; J. W. Burdin; D. C.
Burgess; Miss G. C. Campbell; T. N. Carr; D. G.
Carter; C. Cleall; A. W. Constable; M. Q. Cramb;
A. H. B. Davidson; G. B. Debling; G. A. Dell; R. F.
Dick; J. C. Dignan; G. H. C. Donaldson; J. T.
Donaldson; D. W. Duncan; Miss K. M. Fairweather; A. W. Finlayson; B. Fryer; A. R. Gallon;
A. B. Giovanazzi; G. P. D. Gordon; G. D. Gray,
Ph.D.; T. O. Greig; R. A. Hawke; J. Hay, Ph.D.; K.
A. Hope; L. A. Hunter; M. Jack; J. Jackson, Ph.D.;
A. W. Jeffrey; E. S. Kelly; J. Kiely; D. G.
Kirkpatrick; I. Lawson; R. E. Lygo; M. McAllan;
J. McAlpine; I. M. MacAskill; L. McCallum; D.
McCalman; H. K. McCorkindale; J. J. McDonald;
Mrs. M. A. Macfarlane; A. S. McGlynn; H. M.
MacLaren; M. Macleod; D. R. McNicoll; A. J.
Macpherson; A. Maltby; H. L. Martin; A. C. T.
Mascarenhas; G. Mathieson; W. M. Mein; Mrs. J.
M. Millar; A. Milne; S. Milne, Ph.D.; J. Mitchell;
H. Morris; Miss W. Morrison; Miss E. R. Mowat;
R. H. Nelson; W. Nicol; D. A. Osler; I. P. Pascoe; J.
Picken; Miss A. H. M. Prain; R. B. Prescott; A. M.
Rankin; T. A. Rankin; J. C. Rankine; W. M. Roach,
Ph.D.; I. D. S. Robertson; J. N. Robertson; A. L.
Robson; M. Roebuck; J. Rorrison; D. M. Russell;
A. L. Small; E. P. Spencer; H. Stalker; A. M. Steele;
Mrs. J. A. Stewart; W. P. Stewart; H. Walker; G.
Wallis; R. S. Weir; R. G. Wilson; J. G. L. Wright;
D. B. Young; R. W. J. Young, Ph.D.
£14,401 to £20,801

Social Work Services Group
43 Jeffrey Street, Edinburgh
[031–556 9233]

The Social Work Services Group, which is attached
to the Scottish Education Department, administers
the provisions of the Social Work (Scotland) Act,
1968.
Under-Secretary, D. A. Leitch £28,583
Assistant Secretaries, J. M. Francis; R. E. S. Robinson;
D. Stevenson .... £19,243 to £23,159
Senior Principal, G. W. Tucker .. £15,605 to £20,794
Principals, D. J. Baird; Miss A. E. Hamilton; D. G.
Kerr; J. C. McLean; I. F. Munro; W. F. Robertson;
D. Stewart; Mrs. G. M. Stewart £12,399 to £16,656
Senior Executive Officers, H. W. Bradford; R. Crawford; Miss L. E. Hardie; Miss E. B. Hewitt; D. K.
Meikle .... £10,079 to £12,518
Chief Social Work Adviser, D. Colvin £25,455
Deputy Chief Social Work Advisers, D. S. Roulston;
D. K. Naik .... £19,243 to £23,159
Senior Advisers, A. C. Adams; Miss D. M. Boardman;
J. Gallacher; Ms. M. L. Hunt; W. J. McCollam; F.
A. O'Leary; R. Percival; A. R. Sabine; J. I. Smith
£17,504 to £21,676

SCOTTISH HOME AND HEALTH
DEPARTMENT
St. Andrew's House,
Edinburgh
[031–556 8501]
Dover House, Whitehall, London, S.W.1
[01–233 3000]

Secretary, W. K. Reid, C.B. £35,278
Under Secretaries, W. Baird; J. E. Fraser; H. Morison;
J. Walker £28,583
Assistant Secretaries, G. P. H. Aitken, T.D.; R. J. W.
Clark; Mrs. E. C. G. Craghill; J. Hamill; G. G.
Lyall; A. M. Macpherson; G. N. Munro; G. J.
Murray; N. E. Sharp; J. W. Sinclair; E. J. Weeple
£19,243 to £23,159
Principals, D. C. Anderson; J. W. Barron; P. A.
Brady; D. H. Brown; J. T. Brown; J. A. Clare; D.
J. Davidson; Mrs. W. A. Dickson; J. G. Donnelly;
M. Ewart; P. J. Fleming; C. C. Forsyth; J. D.
Gallagher; W. M. Giles; P. G. Glynn; W. A. Howat;
D. K. C. Jeffrey; A. Johnston; J. C. Judson; J. F.
Kerr; S. M. Liddle; M. J. Lowndes; R. S. T.
MacEwen; G. A. McHugh; K. B. T. MacKenzie; C.
Moir; Mrs. N. S. Munro; R. Patton; G. A. Paul; A.
J. Rushworth; A. Simmen; A. Stephenson; P. D.
Stephenson; R. S. Stewart; E. S. Wall, O.B.E.; G. P.
Walker; A. W. Wallace .... £12,399 to £16,656
Senior Executive Officers, Miss M. R. M. Bald; J.
Ballantyne; M. Bunney; D. Burnett; D. O. Camp-
bell; Mrs. E. M. Chalmers; Mrs. F. M. Cruick-
shanks; L. C. Cunning; D. H. F. Dee; Miss W. M.
Doonan; S. M. Ellis; G. J. G. Halford; Miss W. W.
Hamilton; E. E. Hancock; N. M. Keegan; J. B.
Lyall; D. MacDonald; H. M. MacLean; I. A.
McLeod; J. K. Melville; A. J. Murray; D. J. Palmer;
G. Pearson; J. S. Ross; R. N. Shaw; M. P. Sivell; T.
Spence; I. C. Stewart; I. R. N. Stewart; Miss M. B.
M. Talbot .... £10,079 to £12,518

Medical Services

Chief Medical Officer, J. J. A. Reid, C.B., T.D. . .£32,500
Deputy Chief Medical Officers, I. S. Macdonald; G. A.
Scott £26,750
Principal Medical Officers, M. Ashley-Miller; J. H.
Grant; A. D. McIntyre; A. T. B. Moir; W. M.
Prentice; R. A. Ratcliff; B. C. S. Slater, O.B.E.
£23,431
Senior Medical Officers, A. E. Bell; J. T. Boyd; P. W.
Brooks; R. G. Covell; D. C. Drummond; J. B. P.
Ferguson; C. F. Fleming; G. I. Forbes; W. Forbes;
G. Gilray; Margaret Hennigan; L. F. Howitt; H.
McBain; R. M. Melville, O.B.E.; J. A. Morton; J. S.
Patterson; O. A. Thores; A. B. Young £22,996
Medical Officers, R. E. G. Aitken; J. M. Forrester
£15,235 to £21,329
Senior Regional Medical Officers, A. C. McBlane; D.
E. Walker £23,431
Regional Medical Officers, Elspeth C. Carrick; I. G.
Conn; J. A. Fergusson; T. E. S. Fergusson; W. M.
Gilmour; W. T. D. McKenzie; J. B. Morris; R. C.
Nimmo-Smith; J. Pearson; W. M. Reid; P. I. T.
Walker .... £15,235 to £21,329
Chief Scientist, Prof. A. P. M. Forrest.
Chief Dental Officer, N. K. Colquhoun £23,434
Deputy Chief Dental Officer, J. Gall £22,996
Regional Dental Officers, T. G. L. Bell; F. D. Murray;
G. A. Reid .... £15,235 to £21,329
Chief Nursing Officer, Miss M. G. Auld £24,990
Chief Pharmacist, G. Calder ..... £18,374 to £20,794

Miscellaneous Appointments

H.M. Chief Inspector of Constabulary, A. Morrison,
Q.P.M., C.V.O. £32,756
H.M. Chief Inspector of Prisons, D. A. P. Barry, C.B.E.

Commandant, Scottish Police College, Maj.-Gen. D. C.
Alexander, C.B. £25,419
H.M. Chief Inspector of Fire Services, R. J. Knowlton,
C.B.E., Q.F.S.M. .... £23,942 to £25,661
Commandant, Scottish Fire Service Training School,
A. Jones, O.B.E., Q.F.S.M. .... £12,891 to £13,482
Secretary, Scottish Health Service Planning Council,
(vacant).

Prisons Group
St. Margaret's House, 151 London Road,
Edinburgh 8
[031–661 6181]

Director of Scottish Prison Service, A. M. Thomson
£24,077
*Assistant Secretary, Deputy Director (Administra-
tion)*, R. C. Allan, M.V.O. .... £19,243 to £23,159
*Assistant Controller, Deputy Director (Operations and
Industries)*, D. M. MacIver £22,996
*Assistant Secretary, Deputy Director (Personnel and
Services)*, R. D. Jackson .... £19,243 to £23,159
Senior Principal, Assistant Director (Industries), T.
Collinson .... £16,343 to £20,794

Prison Governors

Aberdeen, M. J. Milne .... £13,269 to £15,947
Castle Huntly Young Offenders Institution, R. R. H.
Glen .... £13,269 to £15,947
Cornton Vale, W. Finlayson ..... £16,343 to £19,317
Dumfries Young Offenders Institution, J. Meikle-
john .... £13,269 to £15,947
Dungavel, Strathaven, Mrs. A. Curran
£13,269 to £15,947
Edinburgh, C. W. Hills £21,529
Glasgow (Barlinnie), A. Gallacher £21,529
Glasgow (Barlinnie Special Unit), J. Wyper
£13,269 to £15,947
*Glenochil Young Offenders Institution and Detention
Centre*, W. McVey £21,529
Greenock, (vacant) .... £13,269 to £15,947
Inverness, F. Sankey .... £13,269 to £15,947
Longriggend Remand Institution, A. M. Webster
£13,269 to £15,947
Low Moss, J. Dow .... £13,269 to £15,947
Noranside Young Offenders Institution, L. W. G.
Hewitson .... £13,269 to £15,947
Penninghame, R. L. Houchin .... £11,182 to £12,814
Perth, W. G. Walker .... £16,343 to £19,317
Perth (Friarton Detention Centre), R. Park
£11,182 to £12,814
Peterhead, A. J. Smith £21,529
Polmont Young Offenders Institution, G. B. Duncan
£16,343 to £19,317
Shotts, T. Binnie .... £13,269 to £15,947
Scottish Prison Service College, A. Thomson
£13,269 to £15,947

Mental Welfare Commission for Scotland
22 Melville Street, Edinburgh EH3 7NS

Chairman, P. C. Millar, O.B.E.
Commissioners, Prof. Annie T. Altschul, C.B.E.; Prof.
T. D. Campbell; R. G. Davis; Mrs. J. B. M. Ellis,
O.B.E.; Ms. A. M. Green; Mrs. A. I. Huggins; D. A.
Macdonald, O.B.E.; Mrs. H. S. Mein; Dr. A. F.
Rodger; Dr. H. S. Ross; H. F. Smith, M.B.E.; J. G.
Sutherland.
Medical Commissioners, H. C. Fowlie; W. Boyd.
Secretary, Mrs. D. Mellon.

*Counsel to the Secretary of State for Scotland under
the Private Legislation Procedure (Scotland) Act,
1936* (50 Frederick Street, Edinburgh)
Senior Counsel, G. S. Douglas, Q.C.
Junior Counsel, P. K. Vandore, Q.C.

NATIONAL HEALTH SERVICE, SCOTLAND

Health Boards

Argyll and Clyde, Gilmour House, Paisley. *Chairman,* J. D. Ryan. *Secretary,* A. K. Skirving.
Ayrshire and Arran, P.O. Box 13, Hunters Avenue, Ayr. *Chairman,* W. S. Fyfe. *Secretary,* M. S. Abbott.
Borders, Huntlyburn, Melrose, Roxburghshire. *Chairman,* J. Gibb. *Secretary,* D. A. Peters.
Dumfries and Galloway. Nithbank, Dumfries. *Chairman,* J. M. Miller. *Secretary,* R. B. K. MacGregor.
Fife, Glenrothes House, North Street, Glenrothes. *Chairman,* J. C. Balfour. *Secretary,* I. G. Dorward.
Forth Valley, 33 Spittal Street, Stirling. *Chairman,* G. J. V. Horsman, o.b.e. *Secretary,* J. M. Eckford.
Grampian, 1–5 Albyn Place, Aberdeen. *Chairman,* C. W. Ellis. *Secretary,* Dr. H. R. M. Wilson.
Greater Glasgow, 225 Bath Street, Glasgow. *Chairman,* D. F. McQuaker. *Secretary,* R. D. R. Gardner, c.b.e.
Highland, Reay House, 17 Old Edinburgh Road, Inverness. *Chairman,* J. McWilliam. *Secretary,* R. R. W. Stewart.
Lanarkshire, 14 Beckford Street, Hamilton, Lanarkshire. *Chairman,* Mrs. B. M. Gunn, o.b.e. *Secretary,* R. M. Morrison.
Lothian, 11 Drumsheugh Gardens, Edinburgh. *Chairman,* J. Dunning. *Secretary,* R. Mitchell.
Orkney, Balfour Hospital, New Scapa Road, Kirkwall, Orkney. *Chairman,* J. D. M. Robertson. *Secretary,* J. A. Muir.
Shetland, 28 Burgh Road, Lerwick. *Chairman,* R. Adair. *Secretary,* D. C. March.
Tayside, P.O. Box 75, Vernonholme, Riverside Drive, Dundee. *Chairman,* D. B. Grant. *Secretary,* G. G. Savage, o.b.e.
Western Isles, 37 South Beach Street, Stornoway, Isle of Lewis. *Chairman,* Mrs. M. A. Macmillan. *Secretary,* J. Glover.

Common Services Agency

Trinity Park House, South Trinity Road, Edinburgh
Secretary, J. R. Y. Mutch. *Treasurer,* J. W. Morrison.

GENERAL REGISTER OFFICE (Scotland)
New Register House, Edinburgh EH1 3YT
[031–556 3952]

Registrar General, Dr. C. M. Glennie £24,077
Deputy Registrar General, J. S. Wheeler
£19,243 to £23,159
Statisticians, D. Salmond; D. A. Orr
£12,399 to £16,656
Principals, G. F. Baird; I. G. Bowie; I. G. Dewar
£12,399 to £16,656
Senior Executive Officers, W. McMaster; J. M. Nicol; D. M. Robertson; J. Rose; R. I. Perrett
£10,079 to £12,518

SEA FISH INDUSTRY AUTHORITY
Sea Fisheries House, 10 Young Street,
Edinburgh EH2 4JQ
[031–225 2515]

Chairman, J. P. Rettie, t.d.
Chief Executive, J. R. Richman.
Technical Director, P. D. Chaplin.
Financial Director, A. Downie.
Marketing Director, R. M. Kennedy.
Secretary, R. A. Davie.

SOCIAL SCIENCE RESEARCH COUNCIL
See **Economic and Social Research Council**

OFFICE OF THE SOCIAL SECURITY COMMISSIONERS
6 Grosvenor Gardens, SW1W 0DH
[01–730 9236]
23 Melville Street, Edinburgh EH3 7PW
[031–225 2201]
16 Park Grove, Cardiff CF1 3BN
[0222 387898]

The Commissioners are the final Statutory Authority to decide claims under the Social Security Acts, and the Child Benefit Acts.
Chief Commissioner, L. J. Bromley, q.c.
Secretary, Mrs. P. M. Hall.

HER MAJESTY'S STATIONERY OFFICE
St. Crispins, Duke Street, Norwich NR3 1PD
[0603–22211]

Her Majesty's Stationery Office was established in 1786 and is the British Government's central organization for the supply of printing, binding, office supplies and office machinery of all kinds, for the Public Service at home and abroad; H.M.S.O. is also the Government's publisher and has bookshops for the sale of Government publications in London, Edinburgh, Manchester, Bristol, Birmingham and Belfast. H.M.S.O. obtains most of its supplies from commercial sources by competitive tender, except that about one quarter of its printing requirements is done in its own printing works.
Since April 1, 1980, H.M.S.O. has been financed by means of a trading fund established under the Government Trading Funds Act, 1973.
Controller and Chief Executive, W. J. Sharp, c.b.
£36,500
Executive Assistant, Mrs. M. E. Nisbet.
Senior Personal Secretary, Miss J. A. Moran (*London*).
Principal Establishment and Finance Officer, D. T. J. Rutherford £26,236
Director General of Printing and Publishing, K. A. Allen £26,236
Head of Internal Audit and Manpower Branch, C. G. Wood .... £12,399 to £16,656
Adviser on Typography, Matthew Carter.

Publications Division

Director, C. J. Penn .... £19,243 to £23,159
Head of Publications Distribution, S. M. Rae
£15,605 to £20,794
Deputy Directors, vacant (*Publications 1*); B. Wilson (*Publications 2*); J. Saville (*Graphic Design*); A. M. Cole (*Publications, Publications Centre*); vacant (*Publications/Management Accounting*)
£12,399 to £16,656

Supply Division

Director, D. W. Ray .... £19,243 to £23,159
Deputy Directors, F. R. Payne; C. E. Harrold; A. A. Gummett; V. G. Bell; C. N. Southgate
£12,399 to £16,656
Manager, Office Machinery Technical Services, L. Crawford .... £10,079 to £12,163

Finance and Planning Division

Director, M. D. Lynn .... £19,243 to £23,159
Deputy Directors, R. T. Wykes; A. J. Davies
£12,399 to £16,656

Personnel Services Division

Director, D. J. Balls .... £19,243 to £23,159
Deputy Directors, R. C. Barnard; R. A. Dunn
£12,399 to £16,656

Industrial Personnel Division

Director, D. J. Wintle . . . . £15,605 to £20,794
Deputy Directors, M. B. Moore; G. A. James
£12,399 to £16,656

Computer Services Division

Director, J. V. Moore . . . . £15,605 to £20,794
Deputy Directors, B. L. Cleland; M. J. M. Salt; D. C.
Kerry . . . . £12,399 to £16,656

Production Division

Director, E. B. McKendrick . . . . . . £19,243 to £23,159
Director of Parliamentary and Classified Printing,
D. G. Forbes . . . . £15,605 to £20,794
Director of Reprographics, R. S. Moore
£12,399 to £16,656
General Managers, G. H. R. Parfitt; A. Mackie; E.
Hendry . . . . £12,399 to £16,656
Head of Works Management Accounting, R. W.
Chapman . . . . £12,399 to £16,656

Technical Services

Head of Technical Services (Origination), T. J. Soutar
£12,399 to £16,656
Head of Technical Services (Printing), H. S. Todd
£12,399 to £16,656
*Head of Engineering Services, Safety Adviser &
Energy Manager*, R. Miller . . . . £13,211 to £15,711

Print Procurement Division

Director, A. A. Smith . . . . £19,243 to £23,159
Deputy Directors, J. N. Palmer; J. McDonald
£12,399 to £16,656
Deputy Director Management Accounting, P. J.
Macdonald . . . . £12,399 to £16,656

Scotland
Bankhead Avenue, Edinburgh EH11 4AB

Bookshop: 13A Castle Street, Edinburgh EH2 3AR.
Director, G. A. H. Turner . . . . £12,399 to £16,656

Northern Ireland
Chichester Street, Belfast BT1 4PS

Retail and Trade Bookshop: Chichester Street,
Belfast BT1 4JY.
Director, Miss V. J. Wilson . . . . . £10,079 to £12,518

London
Britannia House, 7 Trinity Street, SE1 1DA

Publications Centre: 51 Nine Elms Lane, SW8 5BR.
Bookshops: Retail—49 High Holborn, W.C.1.
Wholesale and Post Orders—P. O. Box 276,
SW8 5DT.

Manchester
Broadway, Chadderton, Oldham, Lancs. OL9 9QH

Bookshop: Brazennose Street, Manchester M60 8AS.

Bristol
Ashton Vale Road, Bristol BS3 2HN

Bookshop: Southey House, Wine Street, Bristol
BS1 2BQ.

Birmingham

Bookshop: 258 Broad Street, Birmingham B1 2HE.

STATUTE LAW COMMITTEE
House of Lords, SW1A 0PW

Chairman, The Lord Chancellor.
Vice-Chairman, Mr. Justice Ralph Gibson.
Members, The Attorney-General; the Lord Advocate; N. J. Adamson, C.B., Q.C.; P. K. Archer, Q.C.,
M.P.; K. A. Bradshaw, C.B.; The Lord Brightman,
P.C.; Sir Antony Buck, Q.C., M.P.; Sir Brian Cubbon,
K.C.B.; The Lord Diplock, P.C.; Sir George Engle,

K.C.B.; Sir William Fraser, K.C.B.; H. W. Gamon,
C.B.E.; Sir Michael Kerry, K.C.B.; P. Le Cheminant,
C.B.; The Lord Lowry, P.C.; The Hon. Lord Maxwell;
J. Morris, Q.C., M.P.; Sir George Moseley, K.C.B.; Sir
Derek Oulton, K.C.B.; D. Rippengal, C.B., Q.C.; J. C.
Sainty; W. J. Sharp, C.B.; T. R. F. Skemp, C.B.
Secretary, Miss F. M. MacLeod.

Statutory Publications Office
Queen Anne's Chambers,
28 Broadway, SW1H 9JS
[01–273 3000]

Editor, C. R. Crockett.

NATIONAL THEATRE BOARD
South Bank, SE1 9PX
[01–928 2033]

Chairman, The Lord Rayne.
Members, T. Banks, M.P.; R. Brew, C.B.E.; T. Burrill;
The Lord Chorley; R. Clutton; J. C. Hannam, M.P.;
H. Hinds; The Lady Melchett; Richard M. Mills;
The Lord Mishcon; Sir Derek Mitchell, K.C.B.,
C.V.O.; J. C. Mortimer, Q.C.; The Lady Plowden,
D.B.E.; Mrs. L. Sieff; J. Whitney.
Director of National Theatre, Sir Peter Hall, C.B.E.
Secretary, D. Gosling.

DEPARTMENT OF TRADE AND INDUSTRY
1 Victoria Street, SW1H 0ET
[01–215 7877]

The Department is responsible for:
(a) International trade policy, including the promotion of U.K. trade interests in the European Community, G.A.T.T., O.E.C.D., U.N.C.T.A.D. and other
international organizations.
(b) Under the direction of the British Overseas Trade
Board, the promotion of U.K. exports and assistance
to exporters.
(c) Policy in relation to industry, including the
general promotion of the interests of industry and
assistance to industry; specific interest in all manufacturing and service industries apart from those
covered by other Departments; regional policy and
regional industrial assistance (some of this applying
only to England; policy towards small firms; and
policy in relation to the public bodies British
Shipbuilders, the British Steel Corporation, the Post
Office, British Telecom and the British Technology
Group.
(d) Competition policy and consumer protection,
including relations with the Office of Fair Trading
and the Monopolies and Mergers Commission, and
the National Weights and Measures Laboratory.
(e) Policy on science and technology and research
and development matters, standards and designs,
support for innovation, and the administration of
the National Physical Laboratory, National Engineering Laboratory, Warren Spring Laboratory and
the Laboratory of the Government Chemist.
(f) The administration of company legislation and
the Companies Registration Office; the Insolvency
Service; the regulation of the insurance industry;
the regulation of radio frequencies; and the Patent
Office.
(g) The Business Statistics Office.

SALARY LIST

Secretary of State £30,304
Ministers of State £21,364
Parliamentary Under Secretaries of State . . . £16,154
Permanent Secretary (Grade 1) £42,750
Deputy Secretary (Grade 2) £34,250
The Solicitor (Grade 2) £34,250
Under Secretary (Grade 3) £27,750

Grade 4 .... £24,077
Grade 5 .... £19,243 to £23,159
Grade 6 .... £15,605 to £20,794
Principal .... £12,399 to £16,656
Controller, Export Licensing Branch
                £12,399 to 16,656
Inspector General of the Insolvency Service (Grade 3)
           £27,750
Deputy Inspectors General £24,628
Inspector of Companies £24,628

Research Establishments

Director, National Physical Laboratory £30,375
Director, National Engineering Laboratory .. £27,750
Government Chemist £27,750
Director, Warren Spring Laboratory £27,750

Secretary of State for Trade and Industry and President of the Board of Trade, THE RT. HON. NORMAN TEBBIT, M.P.
  Principal Private Secretary, M. C. McCarthy.
  Parliamentary Private Secretary, I. Mills, M.P.
Minister for Trade, THE RT. HON. PAUL CHANNON, M.P.
  Private Secretary, S. Nicklen.
  Parliamentary Private Secretary, D. Atkinson, M.P.
Minister of State for Information Technology, GEOFFREY EDWIN PATTIE, M.P.
  Private Secretary, N. M. McMillan.
Minister of State for Industry, NORMAN LAMONT, M.P.
  Private Secretary, Miss L. C. Rhind.
Parliamentary Under Secretary of State for Corporate and Consumer Affairs, Alexander Fletcher, M.P.
  Private Secretary, D. P. Griffiths.
Parliamentary Under Secretary of State for Industry, John Butcher, M.P.
  Private Secretary, Dr. D. J. Saunders.
Parliamentary Under Secretary of State for Industry, David Trippier, M.P.
  Private Secretary, P. D. Madden.
Parliamentary Under Secretary of State, The Lord Lucas of Chilworth.
Joint Permanent Secretaries, Sir Brian Hayes, K.C.B.; Sir Anthony Rawlinson, K.C.B.
  Private Secretaries, P. J. Smith; P. Smee.
Deputy Secretaries, D. M. Dell; R. H. F. Croft, C.B.; O. Roith (Chief Scientist and Engineer); R. Mountfield; B. W. Oakley, C.B.E. (Alvey Directorate); J. Caines, C.B.; C. W. Roberts; H. H. Liesner, C.B. (Chief Economic Adviser); W. C. Beckett, C.B. (The Solicitor); R. C. M. Cooper, C.B. (Principal Establishment and Finance Officer).
Parliamentary Clerk, T. A. Hardbattle.
Policy Planning Unit (G5), J. P. Spencer.

International Trade Policy Division
[01–215 7877]

Under Secretary, R. Williams.
Heads of Branch (G5), A. J. Pryor; P. Gent; W. J. Hall; J. C. Octon.

Overseas Trade Divisions
[01–215 7877]

Division 1 (Projects and Export Policy)

Under Secretary, C. B. Benjamin.
Heads of Branch (G5), Miss M. T. Neville-Rolfe; P. S. Salvidge; A. C. Hutton; J. P. S. Crawford; J. H. Chapman.

Division 2
(N. America, N.E. and S.E. Asia and Australasia)

Under Secretary, G. R. Sunderland.
Heads of Branch (G5), A. Dunning; J. M. Healey.

Division 3

Under Secretary, S. N. Burbridge

Administration and Finance
Head of Branch (G5), R. M. Rumbelow.

Export to Europe Branch
Head of Branch (G5), L. F. Standen.

Export Data Branch
Director (G5), M. J. Morrison.
(1 Victoria Street, SW1H 0ET. Tel. 01–215 7877.)

Fairs and Promotion Branch
Director (G5), P. Robinson.

Division 4 (E. Europe, China and S. Asia)
Under Secretary, P. M. S. Corley.
Heads of Branch (G5), K. W. N. George; D. J. Hall.

Division 5 (Middle East, Africa and Latin America)
Under Secretary, A. Titchener.
Heads of Branch (G5), H. R. Owen; D. R. Ford; W. B. Lello.

European Commercial and Industrial Policy Division
[01–215 7877]

Under Secretary, Miss M. J. Lackey, O.B.E.
Heads of Branch (G5), A. Berry; J. B. Ingram.

British Overseas Trade Board
1 Victoria Street, S.W.1
[01–215 7877]

Chairman, The Earl Jellicoe, P.C., D.S.O., M.C.
Vice-Chairman, H.R.H. The Duke of Kent, G.C.M.G., G.C.V.O.
Members, P. E. G. Bates; Sir Gordon Booth, K.C.M.G., C.V.O.; Sir Neville Bowman-Shaw; Gisela Burg; T. T. Candlish; T. Duffy; A. K. Edwards, M.B.E.; R. H. George, C.B.E.; J. Gill, C.B.; R. Haslam; G. W. Mackworth-Young; R. G. S. Messervy; M. R. Rendle; C. W. Roberts; C. F. Sedcole; The Lord Selsdon; Dr. N. B. Smith, C.B.; N. C. Thompson; Sir Crispin Tickell, K.C.V.O.; G. S. Tucker, C.B.E.; R. J. Withers, C.B.E.
Chief Executive, C. W. Roberts.
Secretary (G5), R. M. Rumbelow.
Chief Information Officer (G6), P. W. Probert.

Patent Office and Industrial Property and Copyright Department
25 Southampton Buildings, W.C.2
[01–405 8721]

Comptroller General of Patents, Designs and Trade Marks, I. J. G. Davis.
Assistant Comptrollers, R. Bowen; V. Tarnofsky.
Assistant Registrar of Trade Marks, J. M. Myall.

Insurance Division
Sanctuary Bldgs., 16–20 Gt. Smith Street, S.W.1
[01–215 7877]

Under Secretary, T. Muir.
Heads of Branch (G5), V. F. Lane; M. Z. Wasilewski; D. M. Hoddinott.

Financial Services and Companies Division
Sanctuary Bldgs., 16–20 Gt. Smith Street, S.W.1
[01–215 7877]

Under Secretary, B. J. G. Hilton.
Heads of Branch (G5), A. C. G. Lowry; D. Steel; R. H. S. Wells.

2–14 Bunhill Row, E.C.1
[01–606 4071]

Companies Investigation Branch, Inspector of Companies, R. B. Howard.

Companies Registration Office
Companies House, Crown Way, Maindy, Cardiff
[0222 388588]

Registrar of Companies for England and Wales (G5),
D. B. Nottage.
London Search Room, 55–71 City Road, E.C.1
[01–253 9393]

102 George Street, Edinburgh
[031–225 5774]
Registrar for Scotland, E. T. K. Lougheed.

Department of Commerce
64 Chichester Street, Belfast
[0232 34488]
Registrar for Northern Ireland, H. Lytk.

The Insolvency Service
2–14 Bunhill Row, E.C.1
[01–606 4071]

Inspector General of the Insolvency Service, A. D.
Gwyther.
Deputy Inspectors General, P. D. Pink; J. B. Clemetson; M. Clark.

Consumer Affairs Division
Millbank Tower, Millbank, S.W.1
[01–211 3000]

Under Secretary, Miss J. Blow.
Heads of Branch (G5), N. P. Brecknell; D. L. Gatland;
R. P. Hope.
Director Engineer, G. Souch.
Trading Standards Adviser, D. Jones.

Air Division
Ashdown House, 123 Victoria Street, S.W.1
[01–212 7676]

Under Secretary, P. G. Hudson.
Heads of Branch (G5), B. E. P. MacTavish; M. J.
Michell; M. M. Baker.
Grade 6, J. R. Collingbourne; A. W. R. Allcock.

Space, Post Office and Films Division
29 Bressenden Place, S.W.1
[01–213 3000]

Under Secretary, J. C. Leeming.
Heads of Branch (G5), A. C. Nicholas; M. J. C.
Butcher; A. A. George.

Research and Technology Policy Division
Ashdown House, 123 Victoria Street, SW1E 6RB
[01–212 7676]

Under Secretary, A. Williams.
Heads of Branch (G5), E. Barlow Wright; Dr. T. B.
Copestake; T. Garrett, C.B.E.

International Technology Group
Culham Laboratory, Abingdon, Oxfordshire.
[0235 21840]

Head of Group, Dr. R. Roberts.

National Physical Laboratory
Teddington, Middlesex
[01–977 3222]

Director (G3), Dr. P. Dean, C.B.

Laboratory of the Government Chemist
Cornwall House, Stamford Street, S.E.1
[01–928 7900]

Government Chemist, Dr. R. F. Coleman

National Engineering Laboratory
East Kilbride, Glasgow
[03552 20222]

Director (G3), Dr. D. A. Bell.

Warren Spring Laboratory
Gunnels Wood Road, Stevenage, Herts.
[0438 3388]

Director, P. J. Cooper.

General Policy Division
1 Victoria Street, SW1H 0ET
[01–215 7877]

Under Secretary, E. Wright.
Heads of Branch (G5), Dr. M. Howe; A. Whiting; G.
M. Field; M. J. Vile.

Quality and Education Division
Ashdown House, 123 Victoria Street, S.W.1
[01–212 7676]

Under Secretary, J. H. M. Solomon.
Heads of Branch (G5), Dr. E. B. Bates; E. E. Williams,
O.B.E.; P. Goodman.

**Inward Investment, Tourism and Service
Industries Division**
Kingsgate House, 66–74 Victoria Street, S.W.1
[01–212 7676]

Under Secretary, J. F. J. Jardine.
Heads of Branch (G5), A. R. Gordon-Cumming, C.M.G.,
C.V.O.; D. Harrison-Harvey; J. Woodrow.

Regional Policy Division
Kingsgate House, 66/74 Victoria Street, S.W.1
[01–212 7676]

Under Secretary, J. E. Cammell.
Heads of Branch (G5), E. W. Pearcey; J. G. Walmsley;
B. Winkett; D. W. F. Johnson.

Small Firms Division
Ashdown House, 123 Victoria Street, S.W.1
[01–212 7676]

Under Secretary, J. F. J. Jardine.
Heads of Branch (G5), O. H. Kemmis; P. J. Graham.

Industrial Development Unit
Kingsgate House, 66–74 Victoria Street, S.W.1
[01–212 7676]

Director (G2), D. M. Dell.
Deputy Directors, I. Boyce; H. J. Middleton; J. G.
Allen; R. Ford.
Secretariat and General Policy:
Head of Branch (G5), D. R. Coates.

Radio Regulatory Division
Waterloo Bridge House, Waterloo Road, S.E.1
[01–275 3000]

Under Secretary, G. P. Renton.
Heads of Branch (G5), A. Marshall; A. J. Niedoszynski.
Director (G5), Dr. J. Durkin.

Alvey Directorate
Millbank Tower, Millbank, S.W.1.
[01–211 3000]

Minerals and Metals Division
Ashdown House, 123 Victoria Street, S.W.1
[01–212 7676]

Under Secretary, B. Murray.
Heads of Branch (G5), N. M. K. Worman; J. F. Mogg;
M. A. R. Lunn; R. L. Long.

**Chemicals, Textiles, Paper, Timber and Other
Miscellaneous Industries Division**
Ashdown House, 123 Victoria Street, S.W.1
[01–212 7676]

Under Secretary, P. G. Bryant.
Heads of Branch (G5), M. W. Hunt; M. S. Bremner;
B. E. Armstrong; J. E. Avery

Shipbuilding Policy Division
Ashdown House, 123 Victoria Street, S.W.1
[01–212 7676]

Under Secretary, S. W. Treadgold.
Heads of Branch (G5), M. E. Farry; J. E. M. Beale; D. R. C. Durie.

Mechanical and Electrical Engineering Division
Ashdown House, 123 Victoria Street, S.W.1
[01–212 7676]

Under Secretary, F. R. Mingay.
Heads of Branch (G5), J. C. S. Priston; Mrs. P. A. Denham; R. McVickers; Dr. R. C. Dobbie.

Vehicles Division
Ashdown House, 123 Victoria Street, S.W.1
[01–212 7676]

Under Secretary, R. A. Lingard.
Heads of Branch (G5), M. J. A. Cochlin; R. J. Meadway; A. J. Mantle.

Information Technology Division
29 Bressenden Place, S.W.1
[01–213 3000]

Under Secretary, W. B. Willott.
Heads of Branch (G5), B. W. Smith; R. Foster; A. A. Duguid.

Electronics Applications Division
29 Bressenden Place, S.W.1
[01–213 3000]

Under Secretary, J. H. Major.
Heads of Branch (G5), J. G. Noyes; R. J. F. Franklin; H. J. Ivey; A. Conway.

Telecommunications Division
Ashdown House, 123 Victoria Street, S.W.1
[01–212 7676]

Under Secretary, A. J. P. Macdonald.
Heads of Branch (G5), T. Sharp; I. K. C. Ellison; J. F. R. Martin.

DEPARTMENT OF TRADE AND INDUSTRY SERVICES ORGANIZATION
Sanctuary Buildings, 16/20 Great Smith Street, S.W.1
[01–215 7877]

Deputy Secretaries, H. H. Liesner, C.B. (*Chief Economic Adviser*); W. C. Beckett, C.B. (*The Solicitor*); R. C. M. Cooper, C.B. (*Principal Establishment and Finance Officer*).

Personnel Management Division
Sanctuary Buildings
16–20 Great Smith Street, S.W.1
[01–215 7877]

Under Secretary, N. F. Ledsome.
Heads of Branch (G5), Dr. J. Morton; Mrs. S. E. Brown; Dr. R. Wood.

Management Services and Manpower Division
Sanctuary Buildings,
16–20 Great Smith Street, S.W.1
[01–215 7877]

Under Secretary, P. E. Dougherty.
Heads of Branch (G5), R. Nicholls; K. J. Doyle; R. W. Simpson; R. A. C. Hewes.
Senior Principal Scientific Officer (G6), J. P. Corneille.

Finance and Resource Management Division
Kingsgate House, 66/74 Victoria Street, S.W.1
[01–212 7676]

Under Secretary, A. C. Russell.
Heads of Branch (G5), E. H. Whitaker; H. V. B. Brown.

Accounts Branch
24–26 Newport Road, Cardiff
[0222 492611]

Director of Accounts, A. C. Elkington.

Internal Audit
Ebury Bridge House, Ebury Bridge Road, S.W.1
[01–730 9678]

Head of Internal Audit, K. Holt

Solicitor's Department
10–18 Victoria Street, S.W.1
[01–215 7877]

The Solicitor, W. C. Beckett, C.B.
Under Secretaries, R. J. Ayling; J. B. Evans; J. B. K. Rickford.
Assistant Solicitors (G5), P. H. Bovey; Mrs. N. M. P. Chappell; Mrs. T. J. Dunstan; Miss P. A. E. Granados; R. Higgins; K. A. M. Johnson; C. S. Kerse; J. R. Mallinson; R. M. Malbey; C. B. Robson; Mrs. F. A. Scarborough; J. M. Stanley; G. H. Taylor; E. A. Thompson; J. R. Wollman.

Information Division
1 Victoria Street, SW1H 0ET

Head of Information (G5), Miss C. Bowe.
Deputy Head of Information (G6), A. Williams.
Chief Press Officers, Miss J. Silver; H. Jarmany.

Economics Divisions
1 Victoria Street, S.W.1
[01–215 7877]

Chief Economic Adviser (G2), H. H. Liesner, C.B.

Division 1
Ashdown House, 123 Victoria Street, S.W.1
[01–212 7676]

Under Secretary, J. R. Shepherd.
Heads of Branch (G5), R. D. Rees; B. M. Nonehebel; J. M. Barber.

Division 2
1 Victoria Street, S.W.1
[01–215 7877]

Under Secretary, N. K. Gardner.
Heads of Branch (G5), R. Van Slooten; P. J. Goate; M. S. Bradbury.

Statistics Divisions
1 Victoria Street, S.W.1
[01–215 7877]

Division 1
Millbank Tower, Millbank, S.W.1
[01–211 3000]

Under Secretary, S. F. James.
Heads of Branch (G5), D. B. Manwaring; R. L. Butchart; J. Walker.

Division 2
1 Victoria Street, S.W.1
[01–215 7877]

Under Secretary, J. Hibbert.
Heads of Branch (G5), W. E. Boyd; P. H. Richardson; G. Jenkinson.

Business Statistics Office
Cardiff Road, Newport, Gwent
[0633 56111]

Director, R. Ash.
Heads of Branch (G5), C. C. Maskall; Dr. B. Mitchell; R. M. Norton; S. R. Curtis; D. R. Lewis.
Grade 6, W. D. Knight.

Accountancy Services Division
Millbank Tower, Millbank, S.W.1
[01–211 3000]

Under Secretary, J. A. Knox.
Directors (G5), G. T. Pearson; H. J. Charman.

REGIONAL ORGANIZATION

North Eastern Regional Office
Stanegate House, 2 Groat Market, Newcastle upon
Tyne
[0632 324722]

Regional Director (Under Secretary), W. R. Atkinson.
Regional Industrial Adviser, F. A. Green.

North Western Regional Office
Sunley Bldg., Piccadilly Plaza, Manchester
[061–236 2171]

Regional Director (G3), Dr. J. C. J. Thynne.
Regional Industrial Adviser, G. D. Yates.

Yorkshire and Humberside Regional Office
Priestley House, Park Row, Leeds
[0532 443171]

Regional Director (Under Secretary), J. W. Preston.

West Midlands Regional Office
Ladywood House, Stephenson Street, Birmingham
[021–632 4111]

Regional Director (G5), H. M. Lanyon.

East Midlands Regional Office
Severns House, 20 Middle Pavement, Nottingham
[0602 56181]

Regional Director (G5), K. J. Green.

South Western Regional Office
The Pithay, Bristol
[0272 291071]

Regional Director (G5), H. M. Dawson.

South West Industrial Development Office
Phoenix House, Notte Street, Plymouth
[0752 21891]

Deputy Director, S. C. Finn.

South Eastern Regional Office (Industry)
Charles House, 375 Kensington High Street, W.14
[01–603 2060]

Regional Director (G5), G. J. Bradshaw.

South Eastern Regional Office (Exports)
Ebury Bridge House, Ebury Bridge Road, London,
S.W.1
[01–730 9678]

Director (G6), F. E. Wildman.

DEPARTMENT OF TRANSPORT
2 Marsham Street, SW1P 3EB
[01–212 3434]

The Department of Transport has overall responsibility for land, sea and air transport. This entails general sponsorship of the transport industries, with particular responsibility for the nationalized airline, rail and bus industries; domestic and international civil aviation policy; shipping policy and the ports industry; navigational lights; pilotage; H.M. Coastguard; oversight of road transport, including vehicle registration and licensing, driver licensing and road safety; responsibility for construction and maintenance of motorways and trunk roads; and general oversight of the transport planning of local authorities, including payments of grant from central Government.

Secretary of State £30,304
Minister of State £21,364
Parliamentary Secretary £16,154
Permanent Secretary (Grade 1) £45,500
Deputy Secretary (Grade 2) £36,500
Director TRRL (Grade 3) £30,375
Chief Highway Engineer (Grade 3) £29,500
Under Secretary (Grade 3) £29,500
Director of Regional Offices (Grade 3) £29,500
Director, (Transport) (Grade 4) £25,455
Chief Inspecting Officer, Railways (Grade 4) . £25,455
Deputy Chief Highway Engineer (Grade 4) .. £25,455
Deputy Chief Scientific Officer (Grade 5)
　　　　　　　　　　　　　£19,243 to £23,159
Assistant Chief Planner (Grade 5) £19,243 to £23,159
Chairman of Traffic Commissioners (Grade 5) £23,159
Assistant Secretary (Grade 5) .... £19,243 to £23,159
Controller, Regional Office (Grade 5)
　　　　　　　　　　　　　£19,243 to £23,159
Senior Economic Adviser (Grade 5)
　　　　　　　　　　　　　£19,243 to £23,159
Chief Statistician (Grade 5) ...... £19,243 to £23,159

Secretary of State for Transport, THE RT. HON.
NICHOLAS RIDLEY, M.P.
　Private Secretary, Miss D. A. Nichols.
　Parliamentary Private Secretary, Mrs. A. Rumbold,
　　C.B.E., M.P.
Minister of State, MRS. LYNDA CHALKER, M.P.
　Private Secretary, Dr. J. H. Denning.
　Parliamentary Private Secretary, R. Squire, M.P.
Parliamentary Under Secretaries, D. Mitchell, M.P.;
　M. Spicer, M.P.
　Private Secretary, A. J. C. Poulter.
　Private Secretary, B. D. Glatt.
　Parliamentary Clerk, M. Carty.
Permanent Under Secretary of State, P. E. Lazarus,
　C.B.
　Private Secretary, Mrs. J. C. Cotton.

Information
Head of Information, G. M. Devereau.

DEPUTY SECRETARY: J. Palmer.

Railways
Under Secretaries, E. B. C. Osmotherly; R. C. D.
Walker.
Grade 5, G. D. Miles; B. D. Goodfellow; P. Wood.
Chief Inspecting Officer, Maj. C. F. Rose (*ret.*).

Bus Industry
Under Secretary, A. P. Brown.
Grade 5, P. E. Pickering; Mrs. G. M. Ashmore.

Public Transport London
Under Secretary, A. J. Goldman.
Grade 5, F. Gale; A. S. D. Whybrow.

Freight and Local Transport
Under Secretary, W. P. Jackson.
Grade 5, M. S. Albu; H. C. T. Fawcett.
Grade 6, J. Winder; R. A. O'Sullivan.

Traffic Area Offices
*Chairmen of Traffic Commissioners and Licensing
Authorities*

Eastern (Nottingham and Cambridge), K. Peter.
Metropolitan (Acton), A. S. Robertson.
North Eastern (Newcastle upon Tyne and Leeds),
Maj.-Gen. V. H. J. Carpenter, C.B., M.B.E.
North Western (Manchester), R. D. Hutchings.
Scottish (Edinburgh), H. McNamara.
South Eastern (Eastbourne), R. S. Thornton.

West Midlands (Birmingham), R. R. Jackson.
Western (Bristol), A. A. Crabtree, T.D.
South Wales (Cardiff), R. R. Jackson.

DEPUTY SECRETARY: W. M. Knighton, C.B.

Shipping Policy

Under Secretary, G. R. Sunderland.
Grade 5, J. D. Henes; M. L. Fielder.

Marine and Ports

Under Secretary, J. W. S. Dempster.
Grade 5, J. A. Battersby; I. C. Douek; J. R. Fells; Capt. J. H. Shone; D. J. Fowler; D. C. Gilbert; G. Thompson.
Chief Coastguard, Lt.-Cdr. J. T. Fetherstone-Dilke, R.N. (ret.).

Marine Pollution Control Unit

Director, Rear-Adm. M. L. Stacey, C.B.
Surveyor General, Dr. J. Cowley, C.B.E.

Road and Vehicle Safety

Under Secretary, T. W. Hall.
Grade 5, D. J. Lyness; J. B. W. Robins; E. Dunn.

Vehicle Engineering Development Unit

Chief Mechanical Engineer, D. V. Jones.

Driver and Vehicle Licensing

Director, J. A. Fowles, C.B.E.
Grade 5, G. R. Wattley; M. A. Robinson; R. Bird.

Driver Licensing, Vehicle Taxation and Insurance

Grade 5, D. S. Evans.

DEPUTY SECRETARY: J. E. Hannigan, C.B.

Highways Policy and Programme

Under Secretary, J. R. Coates.
Grade 5, D. A. R. Peel; M. R. Egerton; P. E. Butler.

Highways, Contracts, Administration and Maintenance

Under Secretary, A. A. Pelling.
Grade 5, W. Walker; P. R. Smith; J. W. Fellows; B. J. Bennett.

Highways Engineering

Chief Highway Engineer, K. Sriskandan.
Grade 4, T. A. Rochester.
Grade 5, M. F. Maggs; G. P. Mallett; R. S. Wilson; S. Chatterjee.

Traffic and Greater London Roads

Under Secretary, Mrs. J. M. Bridgeman.
Grade 5, A. M. White; N. T. Rees; W. E. Gallagher.

PRINCIPAL FINANCE OFFICER AND DEPUTY SECRETARY: D. Holmes.

Civil Aviation Policy

Under Secretary, H. J. Blanks.
Grade 5, R. E. Clarke; P. H. Twyman; A. T. Baker; R. I. Varney.

International Aviation

Under Secretary, H. M. G. Stevens.
Grade 5, A. Fortnam; E. J. Lindley.

Accidents Investigation Branch

Chief Inspector of Accidents, G. C. Wilkinson, A.F.C.
Grade 5, P. J. Bardon, D.F.C., A.F.C.

International Transport

Under Secretary, A. G. Lyall.
Grade 5, C. M. Woodman; D. R. Instone.

Finance

Under Secretary, I. Yass.
Grade 5, M. W. Jackson; P. R. Smethurst; B. J. Billington; J. D. Noulton; J. A. Rhodes.
Accountancy Adviser, G. M. Dennett.

Transport Policy Review Unit

Grade 5, D. C. Moss.

ECONOMICS AND STATISTICS (TRANSPORT)

Chief Economic Adviser, H. J. D. Cole.
Grade 5, G. A. C. Searle; M. B. Egerton; C. T. B. Smith; A. J. Nichols.

Statistics (Transport)

Under Secretary, E. J. Thompson.
Grade 5, H. M. Dale; Miss B. J. Wood; H. Collings; G. R. Emes.

Science and Research

Chief Scientific Adviser, Deputy Secretary, Dr. M. W. Holdgate, C.B.

DEPUTY SECRETARY, RESEARCH AND DEVELOPMENT: H. J. D. Cole.

Transport and Road Research Laboratory

Director, G. Margason.
Deputy Director, D. F. Cornelius.
Grade 5, N. W. Lister; Dr. L. J. Griffin; Dr. A. J. M. Hitchcock; F. V. Webster.

Science and Research Policy and Programmes

Grade 5, P. G. O'Neill.

DEPARTMENTS OF THE ENVIRONMENT AND TRANSPORT REGIONAL OFFICES

See under **Department of the Environment**

THE TREASURY
Parliament Street, SW1P 3AG
[01–233 3000]

The Office of the Lord High Treasurer has been continuously in commission for well over 200 years. The Lord High Commissioners of H.M. Treasury consist of the First Lord of the Treasury (who is also the Prime Minister), the Chancellor of the Exchequer and five Junior Lords. This Board of Commissioners is assisted at present by the Chief Secretary, a Parliamentary Secretary who is the Chief Whip, a Financial Secretary, an Economic Secretary, a Minister of State and the Permanent Secretary. The Prime Minister and First Lord is not primarily concerned in the day-to-day aspects of Treasury business. The Parliamentary Secretary and the Junior Lords are Government Whips in the House of Commons. The management of the Treasury devolves upon the Chancellor of the Exchequer and, under him, the Chief Secretary, the Financial Secretary, the Economic Secretary and Minister of State. The Chief Secretary is responsible for the control of public expenditure. The Financial Secretary discharges the traditional responsibility of the Treasury for the voting of funds by Parliament; is responsible for direct taxation and has general oversight of the Inland Revenue. The Economic Secretary is responsible for monetary policy, the financial system and taxes on industry. The Minister of State is responsible for indirect taxation, public sector pay and Civil Service manpower.

Prime Minister and First Lord of the Treasury, THE RT. HON. MARGARET HILDA THATCHER, M.P., F.R.S. £30,304
Parliamentary Private Secretary, M. Alison, M.P.
Lord Commissioners of the Treasury, The Hon. D. Thompson, M.P.; The Hon. I. Lang, M.P.; The Hon. T. Garel-Jones, M.P. £13,474

Chancellor of the Exchequer, THE RT. HON. NIGEL LAWSON, M.P. £30,304
Principal Private Secretary, D. L. C. Peretz.
Private Secretary, Miss M. O'Mara.
Parliamentary Private Secretary, M. Lennox-Boyd, M.P.
Chief Secretary to the Treasury, THE RT. HON. PETER REES, Q.C., M.P. £30,304
Private Secretary, E. J. W. Gieve.
Assistant Private Secretary, P. Peglar.
Parliamentary Secretary to the Treasury and Government Chief Whip, THE RT. HON. JOHN WAKEHAM, M.P. £25,174
Private Secretary, M. Maclean.
Financial Secretary, JOHN MOORE, M.P. £21,364
Private Secretary, A. P. Hudson.
Economic Secretary, IAN STEWART, M.P.
Private Secretary, A. M. Ellis.
Minister of State, BARNEY HAYHOE, M.P. £21,364
Private Secretary, M. E. Corcoran.
Treasurer of H.M. Household and Deputy Chief Whip, J. Cope, M.P. £21,364

(NOTE.—All salaries shown above do not include Parliamentary salary.)

Assistant Whips, Hon. A. Hamilton, M.P.; Hon. D. Hogg, M.P.; Hon. T. Sainsbury, M.P.; J. Major, M.P.; M. Neubert, M.P.
Permanent Secretary, Sir Peter Middleton, K.C.B.
Private Secretary, D. R. H. Board.
Second Permanent Secretaries, J. G. Littler, C.B. (*Overseas Finance*); A. M. Bailey, C.B. (*Public Services*) £39,500
Head of Government Economics Service and Chief Economic Adviser to the Treasury, Sir Terence Burns.
Deputy Secretaries, F. Cassell (*Public Finance*); J. B. Unwin (*Overseas Finance*); J. Anson, C.B. (*Public Services*); vacant (*General Expenditure*); E. P. Kemp (*Pay and Allowances*); N. J. Monck (*Industry*) £34,250
Deputy Chief Economic Adviser to the Treasury, I. C. R. Byatt £34,250

Public Services Sector

Industry, Agriculture and Employment Group:
Under Secretary, A. H. Lovell £27,750
Assistant Secretaries, D. Bostock; Ms. E. Conn; P. R. Gordon...................... £19,243 to £23,159
Public Enterprises:
Under Secretary, T. U. Burgner £27,750
Assistant Secretaries, S. A. Robson; G. E. Grimstone; R. H. Wilson .... £19,243 to £23,159
Social Services and Territorial:
Under Secretary, G. W. Watson £27,750
Assistant Secretaries, Ms. D. Seammen; P. M. Rayner; W. J. E. Norton .... £19,243 to £23,159
Local Government:
Under Secretary, J. E. Pestell £27,750
Assistant Secretaries, A. C. Pirie; C. C. Allan £19,243 to £23,159
Home Transport and Education:
Under Secretary, Miss J. Kelley £27,750

Assistant Secretaries, F. K. Jones; M. J. C. Faulkner £19,243 to £23,159
Expenditure Support:
Under Secretary, Miss M. P. Brown £27,750
Assistant Secretaries, M. L. Taylor; R. B. Willis £19,243 to £23,159
Chief Statistician, J. Draper ..... £19,243 to £23,159
Chief Scientific Officer, T. P. Turner £19,243 to £23,159
Senior Economic Adviser, M. J. Spackman £19,243 to £23,159

Accounts and Purchasing:
Under Secretary, C. H. A. Judd £27,750
Assistant Secretary, A. J. Perry .. £19,243 to £23,159
Senior Principal, R. J. Allwood .. £15,605 to £20,794
Central Computer and Telecommunications Agency:
Under Secretary, P. Freeman £27,750
Assistant Secretaries, W. A. Beard; C. D. Butler; W. Houldsworth; R. A. Ballard; R. M. Paynter; M. O'Connor .... £19,243 to £23,159
Directing Grade Engineer B, C. R. D. Tatham £19,243 to £23,159
General Expenditure Policy:
Under Secretary, M. C. Scholar £27,750
Assistant Secretaries, P. R. C. Gray; Miss M. E. Peirson; N. J. King .... £19,243 to £23,159
Senior Principal, E. I. Cooper .... £15,605 to £20,794
Defence Policy and Material:
Under Secretary, P. J. Kitcatt £27,750
Assistant Secretaries, I. P. Wilson; K. T. King £19,243 to £23,159
Civil Service Catering Organization:
Executive Director, D. S. B. Simpson £27,750

Overseas Finance Sector

Overseas Finance:
Finance Economic Unit:
Under Secretary, P. N. Sedgwick £27,750
Aid and Export Finance:
Under Secretary, P. Mountfield £27,750
Assistant Secretaries, J. S. Beastall, Mrs. A. F. Case £19,243 to £23,159
European Community:
Under Secretary, G. E. Fitchew £27,750
Assistant Secretaries, J. E. Mortimer; G. W. Hopkinson .... £19,243 to £23,159
External Finance:
Under Secretary, R. G. Lavelle £27,750
Assistant Secretaries, C. W. Kelly; A. R. H. Bottrill..................... £19,243 to £23,159

Chief Economic Adviser's Sector

Forecast and Analysis:
Under Secretary, H. P. Evans £27,750
Senior Economic Advisers, J. H. Shields; C. J. Mowl £19,243 to £23,159
Senior Principal, R. James ...... £15,605 to £20,794
Medium Term and Policy Analysis:
Under Secretary, J. C. Odling-Smee £27,750
Senior Economic Advisers, C. Mellis; C. J. Riley £19,243 to £23,159

Domestic Economy Command

Domestic Economy Unit:
Under Secretary, I. C. Byatt £27,750
Assistant Secretary, G. A. C. D. Houston £19,243 to £23,159
Senior Economic Advisers, J. H. Rickard; G. M. White; G. P. Smith .... £19,243 to £23,159
Fiscal Policy:
Under Secretary, G. W. Monger £27,750
Assistant Secretaries, R. I. G. Allen; H. M. Griffiths £19,243 to £23,159
Home Finance:
Under Secretary, T. P. Lankester £27,750

Assistant Secretaries, M. A. Hall; Mrs. J. R. Lomax;
D. R. Collinson, M.V.O. .... £19,243 to £23,159
Senior Principal, L. Watts .... £15,605 to £20,794

Pay and Allowances Command

Pay:
Under Secretary, J. B. Pearce £27,750
Assistant Secretaries, Miss C. E. C. Sinclair; P. G. F.
Davis; D. M. Williams......... £19,243 to £23,159
Industrial Relations:
Assistant Secretary, D. A. Truman £19,243 to £23,159
Superannuation:
Assistant Secretary, W. L. St. Clair £19,243 to £23,159

Central Area

Establishment and Organization:
Under Secretary, B. T. Gilmore............. £27,750
Assistant Secretary, B. M. Fox .... £19,243 to £23,159
Senior Economic Adviser, J. Dixon
£19,243 to £23,159
Senior Principal, P. F. Chambers; E. J. Needle; R. N.
Edwards .... £15,605 to £20,794
Principal, Mrs. P. Waugh .... £12,399 to £16,656
Central Unit:
Under Secretary, A. M. W. Battishill........ £27,750
Economic Briefing (Assistant Secretary), M. T. Folger.
Information:
Assistant Secretary, R. P. Culpin . £19,243 to £23,159
*Deputy Head of Division and Press Secretary to the
Chief Secretary*, J. J. Monaghan £15,605 to £20,794

Treasury Representatives in U.S.A.

*Economic Minister and U.K. Representative IMF/
IBRD*, N. L. Wicks, C.B.E.

Rating of Government Property Department
Jameson House, 69 Notting Hill Gate, W.11

Treasury Valuer, P. J. Dahlhoff.
Deputy Treasury Valuer, J. F. Olney.

THE TREASURY SOLICITOR
Department of H.M. Procurator-General and Treasury Solicitor
Queen Anne's Chambers, 28 Broadway, SW1H 9JS
[01–273 3000]

Procurator-General and Treasury Solicitor, J. B.
Bailey, C.B. £40,500
Deputy Treasury Solicitor, G. A. Hosker £32,500

Advisory Division

Under Secretary (Legal), (vacant) £26,750
Assistant Solicitors, R. P. Ellis; A. D. Osborne; J. E.
Collins; Miss J. L. Wheldon; R. Venables
£20,051 to £23,159
Senior Legal Assistants, J. A. Catlin; M. R. M. Davis;
Mrs. J. B. C. Douglas; A. J. Perrett
£14,401 to £19,317

Litigation Divisions

Under Secretaries, *(Legal)*, W. H. Godwin; R. D.
Munrow; D. A. Watson £26,750
Assistant Solicitors, M. J. C. Haines; J. A. Hornsby,
T.D.; N. D. Ing; A. Leithead; C. G. Leonard; M. E.
Mead; Miss V. M. Peto; A. D. Preston; R. N. Ricks;
J. H. Wilkinson .... £20,051 to £23,159
Senior Legal Assistants, A. P. M. Aylett; Mrs. D.
Babar; A. Belchambers; J. R. J. Braggins; Mrs. G.
Dagtoglou; J. N. Desai; Miss V. F. Dewhurst; H.
Grange; P. D. F. Grant; N. J. Harington; M. J.
Hemming; D. A. Hogg; I. Hood; J. D. Howes; R. A.
D. Jackson; P. C. Jenkins; J. E. Jones; Mrs. A. D.
B. McFee; B. E. McHenry; D. A. Pearson; R. J.
Phillips; A. J. Sandal; R. E. Seely; G. Stimson; M.
B. Sturdy; K. M. Treitel; A. Turek; J. Ward; P. F.
O. Whitehurst .... £14,401 to £19,317

Principals, D. Palmer; D. A. Stalker; J. M. Hawkins;
F. G. O'Connell .... £12,399 to £16,656

Queen's Proctor Division

Queen's Proctor, J. B. Bailey, C.B.
Assistant Queen's Proctor, G. F. Sills
£20,051 to £23,159

Conveyancing Division

Under Secretary (Legal), I. T. Lewis £26,750
Assistant Solicitors, D. E. T. Bevan; R. W. M. Cooper;
A. P. Millar; P. L. Noble; D. A. J. Simpson; E. W.
Wills; J. Wyer .... £20,051 to £23,159
Senior Legal Assistants, M. H. M. Anderson; M.
Benmayor; J. J. Briars; P. W. M. Cooke; R. L.
Coward; M. Drayton; Miss R. C. Farmer; T.
Forrester; D. J. C. Garnett; Miss G. Gilder; D. M.
Gleed; L. Gunatilleke; M. W. Harrison; J. B. Howe;
Mrs. M. Jordan; L. Levy; A. R. Lilleystone; Miss
P. E. Mathias; Miss J. M. Matthews; P. F. Nockles;
C. L. Oastler; G. E. Papes; R. M. Pierce; M. F.
Rawlins; S. W. Rock; M. R. Rosenfeld; A. M. Scarfe;
Miss P. E. Slatter; R. J. B. Stenhouse; T. J.
Sylvester-Jones; S. A. Tobin; Miss C. E. M.
Troddyn; M. A. Widdrington; W. F. Williams; Mrs.
J. M. Wills; H. W. C. Wilson ... £14,401 to £19,317
Principals, R. D. Harris; F. F. H. Hayter
£12,399 to £16,656

Statutory Publications Office

Assistant Solicitor, C. R. Crockett.
Senior Legal Assistants, C. E. J. Carey; J. M. Gibson.

Establishment, Finance and General Services Division

Legal Personnel Officer (Assistant Solicitor), R. M. C.
Venables .... £20,051 to £23,159
Establishment Officer, G. Roberts. £12,399 to £16,656
Chief Accountant, B. C. Shephard £12,399 to £16,656
Head of Costs Branch, A. M. Niven
£12,399 to £16,656

Bona Vacantia Division

Assistant Solicitor, J. C. Leck .... £20,051 to £23,159
Senior Legal Assistant, Miss S. L. Sargant
£14,401 to £19,317
Principal, D. B. Green .... £12,399 to £16,656

Department of Energy Branch
Thames House South, Millbank, S.W.1
[01–211 6046]

Legal Adviser (Under Secretary (Legal)), G. B.
Claydon £26,750
Assistant Solicitors, D. R. M. Long; D. F. Pascho; B.
J. Ecclestone................. £20,051 to £23,159
Senior Legal Assistants, M. A. Blythe; F. Croft; R.
Lines; D. A. E. Michaels; D. F. W. Pickup
£14,401 to £19,317

Department of Education and Science Branch
Elizabeth House, York Road, S.E.1
[01–928 9222]

Legal Adviser (Under Secretary), J. E. Coleman.
Assistant Solicitor, D. H. Ingham £20,051 to £23,159
Senior Legal Assistants, Miss M. Trefgarne; D. J.
Aries .... £14,401 to £19,317

Department of Transport Branch
2 Marsham Street, SW1P 3EB
[01–212 3434]

Under Secretary, G. H. Beetham.
Assistant Solicitors, R. G. Bellis; C. W. M. Ingram; B.
W. James; A. G. Jones; L. Oates.
Senior Legal Assistants, F. D. W. Clarke; M. L.
Davies; Mrs. P. A. Dayer; J. H. Francis; B. J.
Hammersley; A. K. Johnston; D. W. Jordan; Miss
M. Lind-Smith; J. S. Reynolds.

COUNCIL ON TRIBUNALS
St. Dunstan's House, Fetter Lane, EC4A 1BT
[01-404 4954]

The Council on Tribunals are an independent body established in 1958 by the *Tribunals and Inquiries Act* of that year, to act as an advisory body in the field of administrative tribunals and statutory inquiries. They now operate under the Tribunals and Inquiries Act, 1971. Under the Act they keep under review the constitution and working of the various tribunals which have been placed under their general supervision, and consider and report on administrative procedures relating to statutory inquiries.

The Council must be consulted both about procedural regulations for the tribunals under their supervision and about many procedural rules for statutory inquiries. They are also frequently consulted on proposals for legislation affecting tribunals and inquiries and on proposals where the need for an appeals procedure may arise.

The numerous tribunals which have been placed under the Council's supervision are concerned with a wide variety of matters ranging from agriculture and road traffic to immigration, taxation, pensions, and the allocation of school places. They include social security and National Health Service Tribunals, the Lands Tribunal, Industrial Tribunals, Mental Health Review Tribunals, Local Valuation Courts and the Civil Aviation Authority. The Council's jurisdiction is from time to time extended to additional tribunals, inquiries and hearings.

The Scottish Committee of the Council generally considers Scottish tribunals and matters relating only to Scotland.

Members of the Council are appointed by the Lord Chancellor and the Lord Advocate. The Scottish Committee is composed partly of members of the Council designated by the Lord Advocate and partly others appointed by him. The Parliamentary Commissioner for Administration is *ex officio* a member of both the Council and the Scottish Committee.

The Council submit an annual report on their work and that of the Scottish Committee to the Lord Chancellor and the Lord Advocate, which must be laid before Parliament.

Chairman, The Lord Gibson-Watt, P.C., M.C.
Members, Prof. L. N. Brown; D. C. Calcutt, Q.C.; Sir Cecil Clothier, K.C.B., Q.C.; Sir Kenneth Clucas, K.C.B.; Mrs. M. S. Courtenay; P. R. Everett, D.S.C.; I. R. Guild, W.S. (*also Chairman of Scottish Committee*); A. C. Heywood; Mrs. B. M. Hoggett; D. W. Jones-Williams, O.B.E., M.C., T.D.; Miss E. R. Littlejohn, O.B.E.; N. Robertson; The Lord Wigoder, Q.C.
Secretary, M. W. Sayers.

Scottish Committee
20 Walker Street, Edinburgh EH3 7HR
[031-225 3236]

Chairman, I. R. Guild, W.S.
Members, Sir Cecil Clothier, K.C.B., Q.C.; Mrs. E. Anderson; R. N. M. MacLean, Q.C.; G. S. Peterkin; N. Robertson; R. B. Weatherstone.
Secretary, Mrs. E. M. Chalmers.

SPECIAL COMMISSIONERS OF INCOME TAX
Turnstile House, 98 High Holborn, WC1V 6LQ
[01-438 7413]

The Special Commissioners are an independent body appointed by the Treasury to hear appeals concerning income tax, surtax, corporation tax, capital gains tax, capital transfer tax and petroleum revenue tax.

Presiding Special Commissioner, R. H. Widdows.

Special Commissioners, R. H. Widdows; A. K. Tavare; Miss E. Wix; B. M. F. O'Brien; T. H. K. Everett .... £21,350 to £23,450
Clerk to Special Commissioners, A. G. Cumbers
£12,399 to £16,656

CORPORATION OF TRINITY HOUSE
Trinity House, Tower Hill, EC3N 4DH
[01-480 6601]

Trinity House, the first General Lighthouse and Pilotage Authority in the Kingdom, was a body of importance when Henry VIII granted the institution its first charter in 1514. The Corporation is the General Lighthouse Authority for England and Wales, the Channel Islands and Gibraltar, with certain statutory jurisdiction over aids to navigation maintained by local harbour authorities. It is also responsible for dealing with wrecks dangerous to navigation, except those occurring within port limits or wrecks of H.M. ships. The Trinity House Lighthouse Service is maintained out of the General Lighthouse Fund which is provided from light dues levied on ships using the ports of the United Kingdom and Eire. The Corporation is also the principal pilotage authority in the United Kingdom and is responsible for London and 39 other districts. Certain charitable trusts are administered by the Corporation for the relief of aged or distressed mariners and their dependants. The affairs of the Corporation are managed by a Board of ten active Elder Brethren and the Secretary, assisted by administrative, engineering and marine staff. The active Elder Brethren also act as nautical assessors in marine causes in the Admiralty Division of the High Court of Justice.

Elder Brethren

Master, H.R.H. the Duke of Edinburgh, K.G. *Deputy Master*, Captain Sir Miles Buckley Wingate, K.C.V.O. *Elder Brethren*, Capt. D. A. G. Dickens; H.R.H. The Prince of Wales, K.G.; Capt. G. P. McCraith; Capt. R. J. Galpin, R.D. R.N.R.(ret.); Capt. Sir George Barnard; Capt. R. N. Mayo, C.B.E.; Capt. Sir David Tibbits, D.S.C., R.N.(ret.); Capt. J. E. Bury; Capt. D. J. Cloke; The Lord Wilson of Rievaulx, P.C., K.G., O.B.E., F.R.S.; Rt. Hon. E. R. G. Heath, M.B.E., M.P.; Capt. I. R. C. Saunders; The Visct. Runciman of Doxford, O.B.E., A.F.C.; Capt. P. F. Mason, C.B.E.; Capt. T. Woodfield, O.B.E.; Sir Eric Drake, C.B.E; The Lord Simon of Glaisdale, P.C.; Admiral of the Fleet The Lord Lewin, K.G., G.C.B., M.V.O., D.S.C.; Captain D. T. Smith, R.N.; Commander Sir Robin Gillett, Bt., G.B.E., R.D., R.N.R.(ret.); Capt. P. M. Edge, The Lord Shackleton, K.G., P.C., O.B.E.; Sir John Cuckney; Capt. D. J. Orr.

Officers

Secretary, J. R. Backhouse.
Deputy Secretary, A. W. Snook.
Engineer-in-Chief, R. J. Shergold.
Principal, Lights Department, M. J. Faulkner.
Administration Manager, J. B. Fuller.
Establishment Officer, A. J. Smith.
Surveyor of Shipping, J. K. Rankin.
Principal, Pilotage Department, H. E. Oliver.
Principal, Corporate Department, J. A. Liddle.
Public Relations Officer, P. W. Ridgway.

CLYDE PORT AUTHORITY
16 Robertson Street, Glasgow G2 8DS

Chairman, R. W. S. Easton, C.B.E.
Managing Director, J. Mather.
Secretary and Solicitor, J. B. Maxwell.

COMMISSIONERS OF NORTHERN LIGHTHOUSES
84 George Street, Edinburgh.
[031-226 7051]

The Commissioners of Northern Lighthouses are the General Lighthouse Authority for Scotland and the Isle of Man. The present Board owes its origin to an Act of Parliament passed in 1786 which authorized the erection of 4 lighthouses; 19 Commissioners were appointed to carry out the Act. At the present time the Commissioners operate under the Merchant Shipping Act, 1894 and are 19 in number.

The Commissioners control 50 Major manned Lighthouses, 41 Major unmanned Lighthouses, 100 Minor Lights and many Lighted and Unlighted Buoys. They have a fleet of 3 Motor Vessels.

Commissioners

The Lord Advocate, the Solicitor General, the Lords Provost of Glasgow and Aberdeen; the Convenor of Edinburgh District Council; the Provost of Inverness; the Chairman of Argyll & Bute District Council; the Sheriffs-Principal of North Strathclyde; Tayside, Central & Fife; Grampian, Highlands & Islands: South Strathclyde, Dumfries & Galloway; Lothians & Borders; and Glasgow & Strathkelvin; W. D. H. Gregson, C.B.E.; T. Macgill; Capt. J. A. MacLeod; Capt. A. F. Dickson, O.B.E.; Rev. Capt. A. W. G. Kissack; A. J. Struthers.

Officers

General Manager, Cdr. J. M. Mackay, M.B.E.
Engineer-in-Chief, J. H. K. Williamson.
Secretary, J. R. Welsh.

UNIVERSITY GRANTS COMMITTEE
14 Park Crescent, W1N 4DH
[01-636 7799]

The Committee was appointed by the Chancellor of the Exchequer in July, 1919, and its present terms of reference are as follows;

"To enquire into the financial needs of university education in the U.K.; to advise the Government as to the application of any grants made by Parliament towards meeting them; to collect, examine, and make available information relating to university education throughout the United Kingdom; and to assist, in consultation with the universities and other bodies concerned, the preparation and execution of such plans for the development of the universities as may from time to time be required in order to ensure that they are fully adequate to national needs."

Chairman, Sir Peter Swinnerton-Dyer, F.R.S. £39,500
Other Members, Sir Peter Baxendell; Prof. P. M. Bromley; Prof. J. Cannon; D. Clarke; Prof. K. M. Clayton, C.B.E.; Sir Robert Clayton; Dr. S. Cotson; Prof. C. T. Dollery; Prof. A. J. Forty; Prof. B. G. Gowenlock, F.R.S.E.; Prof. Mary Hesse; Prof. G. R. Higginson; Prof. C. B. Howe; R. S. Johnson; Prof. D. S. Jones, M.B.E., F.R.S.; Prof. P. G. Moore; Prof. J. G. Morris; W. D. C. Semple; Prof. J. Sizer; Mrs. T. Thomas, O.B.E..
Secretary, N. T. Hardyman, C.B. £27,750
Assist. Secretaries, E. C. Appleyard; M. B. Baker; H. W. B. Davies .... £19,243 to £23,159
Principals, Miss M. J. Darby; G. F. Hawker; G. E. Huggins; M. C. Hutchison (*Statistician*); Mrs. R. McDonagh; Miss A. Lawson; A. H. Prosser; M. H. Sharpe.

VALUE ADDED TAX TRIBUNALS

A person dissatisfied with a decision of the Commissioners of Customs and Excise relating to certain aspects of value added tax may appeal to a tribunal. VAT Tribunals are entirely independent of the Commissioners and are under the supervision of the Council on Tribunals. They are intended to determine disputes concerning VAT speedily and with a minimum of formality and to assist in the uniform application of the tax throughout the United Kingdom. VAT Tribunals are established in London, Manchester and Edinburgh. Tribunals also sit in Belfast, Birmingham, Bristol, Cardiff, Exeter, Leeds and Newcastle as necessary.

15/17 Great Marlborough Street, W1V 1AF
[01-437 8340/8330]

President, The Lord Grantchester, Q.C.
Registrar, J. M. Busby.

Tribunal Centres

London: 15/17 Great Marlborough Street, W1V 1AF [01-437 7495/8244].
Chairman, N. P. M. Elles.
Edinburgh (including Belfast and Newcastle): 44 Palmerston Place, Edinburgh [031-226 3551].
Vice-President, Scotland, R. A. Bennett, Q.C.
Manchester: Warwickgate House, Warwick Road, Old Trafford, Manchester [061-872-6471]
Chairman, P. A. Ferns, T.D.

COMMONWEALTH WAR GRAVES COMMISSION
2 Marlow Road, Maidenhead, Berkshire SL6 7DX
[Maidenhead: 34221]

The Commonwealth War Graves Commission (formerly Imperial War Graves Commission) was founded by Royal Charter in 1917. It is responsible for the commemoration of 1,695,000 members of the forces of the Commonwealth who fell in the two world wars. More than one million graves are maintained in 23,459 burial grounds throughout the world. Over three-quarters of a million men and women who have no known grave or who were cremated are commemorated by name on memorials built by the Commission.

The funds of the Commission are derived from the six Governments participating in its work—the United Kingdom, Canada, Australia, New Zealand, South Africa and India.

President, H.R.H. The Duke of Kent, G.C.M.G., G.C.V.O.
Chairman, The Secretary of State for Defence.
Vice-Chairman, Air Chief Marshal Sir John Barraclough, K.C.B., C.B.E., D.F.C., A.F.C., F.R.S.A.
Members, The Minister for Housing and Construction; The High Commissioners for Canada, the Commonwealth of Australia, New Zealand, and India; the Ambassador for the Republic of South Africa; Sir Edward Gardner, Q.C., M.P.; The Lord Wallace of Coslany; Sir Edward Goschen, Bt., D.S.O.; Admiral Sir David Williams, G.C.B.; General Sir Robert Ford, G.C.B., C.B.E.; Sir David Muirhead, K.C.M.G., C.V.O; Sir Donald Maitland, G.C.M.G., O.B.E.; The Baroness McFarlane of Llandaff.
Director-General, Sir Arthur Hockaday, K.C.B., C.M.G.
Deputy Director-General, P. R. Matthew.
Assistant Directors-General, W. J. Symons, O.B.E. (*Operations*); J. Saynor (*Administration*).
Legal Adviser and Solicitor, G. C. Reddie.
Director of External Relations, P. H. M. Swan.
Director of Works, N. B. Osborn.
Director of Horticulture, J. B. Paton.
Director of Informations Services, S. G. Campbell. M.C.
Establishment Officer, H. Westland.
Chief Finance Officer, M. S. Johnson.
Organization and Audit Officer, (vacant).
Hon. Consulting Engineer, P. A. Scott.
Hon. Botanical Adviser, Prof. E. A. Bell, Ph.D.
Hon. Artistic Adviser, Prof. Sir Peter Shepheard, C.B.E.

Imperial War Graves Endowment Fund

Trustees, Sir John Hogg, T.D.; E. M. P. Welman; Air Chief Marshal Sir John Barraclough, K.C.B., C.B.E., D.F.C., A.F.C., F.R.S.A.
Hon. Secretary to the Trustees, M. S. Johnson.

WELSH OFFICE

Gwydyr House, Whitehall, SW1A 2ER
[01–233 3000]

Cathays Park, Cardiff CF1 3NQ
[0222 825111]

Plas Crug, Aberystwyth,
Dyfed SY23 1NG
[0970 3162]

(All staff are based in Cardiff unless otherwise indicated. Staff marked * are located in London and those marked † in Aberystwyth.)
Secretary of State, THE RT. HON. (ROGER) NICHOLAS EDWARDS, M.P* £30,304
Special Adviser, C. J. Butler.*
Private Secretary, C. L. Jones.*
Assistant Private Secretaries, J. Carter*; Ms. J. H. Roberts.
Parliamentary Private Secretary, K. Best, M.P.*
Minister of State, JOHN STRADLING THOMAS, M.P.*
£21,365
Private Secretary, M. D. Chown.*
Parliamentary Under-Secretary of State, I. W. P. Roberts, M.P.* £16,154
Private Secretary, S. Morris.*
Permanent Secretary, Sir Trevor Hughes, K.C.B.
£45,500
Private Secretary, R. I. Dewey.
Deputy Secretaries, R. A. Lloyd-Jones, C.B.; I. H. Lightman, C.B. £36,500

Permanent Secretary's Division

Assistant Secretary, Mrs. M. Evans*
£19,243 to £23,159
Principal, Miss E. M. Jones ...... £12,339 to £16,656

Establishment Group

Principal Establishment Officer, J. W. Lloyd . £29,500
Assistant Secretaries, W. L. Chapman; Miss E. N. M. Davies; B. H. Evans .... £19,243 to £23,159
Senior Economic Adviser, O. T. Hooker
£19,243 to £23,159
Chief Statistician, D. Adams Jones £19,243 to £23,159
Superintending Architect, J. D. Hogg
£15,605 to £20,794
Principal Inspector of Ancient Monuments and Historic Buildings, R. Avent ...... £15,382 to £17,518
Principals, R. J. Bolus; P. Davenport; R. F. Patterson; W. A. Vinall .... £12,399 to £16,656
Economic Adviser, W. K. Griffiths £12,399 to £16,656
Principal Research Officer, I. I. Thomas
£12,399 to £16,656
Statisticians, G. J. Cockell; K. Francombe; R. Jones; E. Swires Hennessey; Mrs. B. J. M. Wilson
£12,399 to £16,656
Inspectors of Ancient Monuments and Historic Buildings, J. K. Knight; A. D. McLees; Dr. S. E. Rees
£9,136 to £15,841

Finance Group

Principal Finance Officer, M. G. Jeremiah ... £29,500
Assistant Secretaries, L. L. Ginn; R. D. Potter; L. Pritchard .... £19,243 to £23,159
Principals, M. G. Horlock; G. Morgan; D. A. Pritchard; C. E. Taylor; N. E. Thomas; B. O. Valentine
£12,399 to £16,656
Chief Internal Auditor, B. R. Davies
£12,399 to £16,656

Architects and Surveyors Division

Chief Architect, G. J. Kelly ...... £19,243 to £23,159
Principal Professional and Technology Officers, R. Broad; T. A. Campden; H. O. M. Coleman; C. Eyres; G. N. Harding; E. T. Williams.. £13,211 to £15,711

Health and Social Work Department
Group 1

Chief Medical Officer, G. Crompton £29,500
Principal Medical Officers, A. M. George; Deidre J. Hine £25,176
Senior Medical Officers, R. B. Morley-Davies; G. J. Moses; D. J. W. Anderson; D. M. Gambier; D. Ferguson-Lewis £23,159
Chief Dental Officer, D. R. Edwards £23,159
Medical Officers, R. Buntwal; Mary Cotter; D. E. Davies; P. I. Harry; Jennifer Lloyd; D. H. Richards; N. E. Thomas .... £15,235 to £21,329
Dental Officers, A. Cobb; J. D. O. Parkholm; T. A. Williams .... £15,235 to £21,329
Scientific Adviser, J. A. V. Pritchard
£15,605 to £19,317
Pharmaceutical Adviser, D. L. Thomas
£15,605 to £20,794

Group 2

Under Secretary, R. A. Pengelly £29,500
Assistant Secretaries, P. R. Gregory; L. M. Lloyd, M.B.E.; J. A. Morgan; J. C. Price £19,243 to £23,159
Chief Social Work Service Officer, Miss Z. E. Williams
£19,243 to £23,159
Principal Social Work Service Officers, D. G. Evans; B. F. Norman .... £17,504 to £21,676
Senior Principal, G. T. Evans .... £15,605 to £20,794
Principals, W. M. Cooper; G. Davies; T. G. Davies; A. S. Dredge; J. A. Grimes; N. S. Jones; S. H. Martin; B. J. Mitchell; Miss J. E. Paulett; G. P. Thomas
£12,399 to £16,656
Social Work Service Officers, G. H. Davies; J. K. Fletcher; J. F. Mooney; Miss A. Perrott; C. D. Vyvyan; A. G. Williams; R. C. Woodward
£12,399 to £17,031
Ambulance Adviser, P. J. Hunt .. £12,399 to £16,656
Principal Professional and Technology Officers, M. W. Grist; J. Jarvis; I. Smith ... £13,211 to £15,711
Catering and Domestic Services Adviser, C. H. Bearpark .... £10,079 to £12,518

Nursing Division

Chief Nursing Officer, Mrs. Y. Moores....... £24,178
Deputy Chief Nursing Officer, Mrs. G. M. Stephens
£21,273
Nursing Officers, Mrs. P. A. Bryant; Mrs. B. Melvin; M. F. Tonkin; Mrs. D. J. Vass; Miss M. D. Wells; Miss M. Yeo .... £16,251 to £19,113

Legal Division

Legal Adviser, A. J. Beale £29,500
Assistant Solicitors, D. G. Lambert; P. J. Murrin
£20,051 to £23,159
Senior Legal Assistants, J. D. H. Evans; A. K. Gillard; C. P. Jones; C. G. Longville; Mrs. A. T. Parkes; Mrs. T. C. Shellens; J. H. Turnbull; H. Warman; A. J. Watkins.................... £14,401 to £19,317

Information Division

Chief Information Officer, H. G. Roberts
£19,243 to £23,159
Principal Information Officer, E. M. Bowen
£12,399 to £16,656

Economic and Regional Policy Group

Under Secretary, J. A. Annand............. £29,500
Assistant Secretaries, H. R. Bollington; G. C. G. Craig; H. K. Trimnell .... £19,243 to £23,159

Principals, R. Abel; L. Conway; Ms. J. M. Gordon; Mrs. C. Peat; Mrs. E. A. Taylor; F. G. Watson; B. Wilcox; R. C. Williams .... £12,399 to £16,656

Industry Department

Director, O. Rees £29,500
Industrial Director, J. P. Driscoll £21,500
Assistant Secretaries, J. F. Craig; C. W. Harris
£19,243 to £23,159
Senior Principal, J. N. M. Firth .. £16,343 to £20,794
Principals, P. Bishop; C. J. Burdett; R. O. Evans; N. Firstbrook; S. R. Lindsay; D. Pugh; C. J. Tudor
£12,399 to £16,656
Principal Research Officer, W. P. Roderick
£12,399 to £16,656
Principal Professional and Technology Officer, F. J. Davies .... £13,211 to £15,711
Principal Scientific Officers, P. Bragg; G. A. Madden
£11,343 to £14,931

Housing Division

Assistant Secretary, J. I. Davies, M.B.E.
£19,243 to £23,159
Principals, A. C. Elmer; D. T. Richards; G. A. Thomas
£12,399 to £16,656

Water and Environmental Protection Division

Director 'B', L. E. Taylor .... £19,243 to £23,159
Superintending Engineers, A. S. R. Mutch; W. D. A. Waters .... £15,605 to £20,794
Senior Principal, B. S. Millwood . £15,605 to £20,794
Principals, J. A. Evans; L. A. Pavelin; A. Whitaker
£12,399 to £16,656
Principal Professional and Technology Officers, A. A. Houlden; H. Ruttley; J. E. Saunders; H. G. Taylor
£13,211 to £15,711
Principal Scientific Officers, J. C. Finnigan; R. A. Page .... £11,343 to £14,931

Education Department

Under Secretary, R. H. Jones, c.v.o. £29,500
Assistant Secretaries, L. H. Hayward; J. C. Lewis
£19,243 to £23,159
Senior Principal, D. M. Timlin ... £15,605 to £20,794
Principals, D. F. J. Beames; D. A. Bullen; R. J. Callen; J. B. Davies; H. Evans; J. W. Jones
£12,399 to £16,656

H. M. Inspectorate

Chief Inspector, I. R. Lloyd £25,176
Staff Inspectors, L. M. Evans; G. Lloyd-Jones; R. E. Jones; P. Thomas; R. Thomas; P. C. Webb; M. J. F. Wynn .... £19,243 to £23,159
H. M. Inspectors, C. Abbott; S. J. Adams; H. W. Davies; R. G. Davies; J. R. N. Evans; K. M. Evans; N. B Evans; Mrs. L. Gainsbury; A. Higgins; Mrs. R. James; R. L. James; W. R. Jenkins; A. H. Jones; G. D. Jones; O. E. Jones; J. M. Laugharane; M. J. Law; I. M. Lewis; R. A. Lowe; A. Morgan; I. G. Morgan; J. Nicholas; Miss P. A. Nicholas; T. E. Parry; T. G. Prosser; G. O. Roberts; Miss D. Selleck; Mrs. V. Scott; M. W. Stone; R. Taylor; G.

Thomas; Glyndwr Thomas; Miss L. Thomas; W. E. Thomas; P. B. Walker; G. Warren; B. Wigley
£15,605 to £20,794

Transport, Highways and Planning Group

Under Secretary, R. W. Jarman £29,500
Director of Engineering, G. Mercer £25,176
Assistant Secretaries, G. G. Elliott; A. H. H. Jones; A. W. E. Peat .... £19,243 to £23,159
Chief Planner, C. J. Curry ...... £19,243 to £23,159
Principal Housing and Planning Inspector, H. S. Crow....................... £19,823 to £21,977
Superintending Engineers, J. G. Evans; J. E. Morgan, o.b.e........................ £15,605 to £20,794
Superintending Estates Officer, G. K. Hoad
£18,374 to £20,794
Senior Housing and Planning Inspectors, T. W. Barnes; R. Pierce; E. M. Roberts; J. L. S. Whalley; D. J. Grainger; A. D. R. Saunders; G. Sloan
£14,951 to £19,730
Principals, R. W. Jenkins; A. V. Price; D. M. Rolph; R. C. Simpson; K. L. Smith; H. I. W. Sparkes; S. J. Sutherland .... £12,399 to £16,656
Principal Planning Officers, D. B. Courtier; G. Fairhurst; J. O. Pryce; B. G. Taylor
£12,399 to £16,656
Principal Research Officers, J. G. Evans; I. E. Thompson .... £12,399 to £16,656
Landscape Adviser, C. W. W. Smart
£13,211 to £15,711
Principal, Professional and Technology Officers, P. I. Adams; P. C. Dunstan; J. A. L. Harries; B. H. Hawker; R. Lober; D. G. Minas; B. J. W. Martin; S. D. Padfield; W. H. Prosser; D. P. Soane; E. G. Whitcutt .... £13,211 to £15,711

Agriculture Department

Under Secretary, R. Hall Williams £29,500
Assistant Secretaries, M. E. Bevan; G. Owen; D. J. Palmer† .... £19,243 to £23,159
Principals, D. R. Davies; P. Finnigan†; R. E. Hughes†; D. H. Jones; D. J. Pierce†; J. M. Thomas; D. I. Westlake .... £12,399 to £16,656
Divisional Executive Officers, J. C. Alexander (*Carmarthen*); D. W. Evans (*Ruthin*); R. G. Gairey (*Cardiff*); D. R. Thomas (*Caernarfon*); R. J. E. Wilcox (*Llandrindod Wells*) .. £12,399 to £16,656

LAND AUTHORITY FOR WALES
Brunel House, Cardiff CF2 1SQ
[0222 499077]

The Land Authority for Wales was established under the provisions of the Community Land Act 1975 and continued in operation by the Local Government Planning and Land Act 1980. It is responsible for acquiring and disposing of land needed for private development in Wales under the provisions of that Act.
Chairman, D. H. P. Thomas, c.b.e. (*part-time*) £17,150
Members, J. D. Allen; I. Davies; H. R. Hicks; C. Hudson; H. H. Roberts; W. R. Webb; (two vacancies) .... (*Members, part-time* £3,395)
Chief Executive, E. W. G. C. Howell.

SAVINGS

PREMIUM BONDS

These bonds are a United Kingdom Government security and were first introduced on November 1, 1956. Instead of earning interest, however, each bond offers to its holder the chance of winning a money prize in a prize draw. Bonds are issued in values ranging from £5 (the minimum purchase) to £2,000, and may be purchased in multiples of £5; each £1 buys one bond unit, which has one chance in each prize draw. Individual holdings are limited to £10,000.

Prizes are paid from a fund formed by the interest, at present 7¼ per cent *per annum*, on each bond eligible for the draw. A bond becomes eligible for the draw three clear calendar months following the month of purchase and goes into every subsequent draw whether or not it has won a prize until the end of the month in which it is repaid.

Bonds belonging to a deceased bondholder will remain eligible for all Prize Draws held in the month of death and in the following 12 calendar months, provided they have not been repaid earlier. They will then become ineligible for all further draws. These terms also apply to bonds purchased before August 1, 1960 (Series "A").

The winning numbers are selected by the electronic random number indicator equipment—usually called "ERNIE". Winning numbers are printed monthly in the *London Gazette*.

It is estimated that by the end of April 1984, bonds to the value of £3,296,131,800 had been sold. Of these £1,613,795,035 had been cashed, leaving £1,682,336,765 still invested. After the draws in July 1984, 22,821,193 prizes, totalling £1,238,619,800 had been distributed since the inception of the Premium Savings Bond Scheme.

INCOME BONDS

National Savings Income Bonds were introduced on August 2, 1982. They are particularly suitable for those who want to receive regular monthly payments of interest while preserving the full cash value of their capital. The Bonds are sold in multiples of £1,000. The minimum holding is £2,000 and the maximum £50,000.

Interest is calculated on a day-to-day basis and paid monthly. The rate may be varied from time to time, but it will be kept competitive. Interest is taxable, but is paid without deduction of tax at source. The Bonds have a guaranteed life of ten years, but may be repaid at par before maturity on giving three months' notice. No formal period of notice for repayment is required if the holder dies.

Net investment in National Savings Income Bonds was £2,141,752,000 at the end of June 1984.

SAVINGS BANKS

National Savings Bank.—On May 31, 1984, there were approximately 19,851,000 active accounts with the sum of £1,765,613,000 due to depositors in Ordinary accounts and approximately 2,755,266 active accounts with the sum of £4,806,289,000 due to depositors in Investment accounts.

Interest is earned at 6 per cent per year on each Ordinary account with a balance of £500 or more maintained throughout 1984 and at 3 per cent per year for all other Ordinary accounts. The minimum deposit is £1; maximum balance £10,000 plus current interest. On May 31, 1984 the average amount held in Ordinary accounts was £88·94.

The Investment account pays a higher rate of interest (the current rate can be ascertained at any Savings Bank Post Office). The minimum deposit is £1; maximum balance £50,000 plus current interest. On May 31, 1984 the average amount held in Investment accounts was £1,744·40.

Trustee Savings Banks.—There are 14 Trustee Savings Banks with more than 1,612 branches in the United Kingdom. On November 20, 1983, the Banks operated nearly 13,000,000 active accounts and total customer balances exceeded £8,222,800,000. *Central Board*, P.O. Box 33, 25 Milk Street, E.C.2.

DEPOSIT BONDS

National Savings Deposit Bonds were introduced on October 17, 1983. They offer a premium rate of interest on lump sum savings and are best suited for money not needed in less than a year. The minimum purchase is £250, larger purchases can be made in multiples of £50 and the maximum holding is £50,000 plus current interest.

Interest is taxable, but tax is not deducted at source. The interest rate is variable but will remain competitive. Interest is calculated on a daily basis and credited on the anniversary of purchase. Minimum amount of repayment is £50 and 3 months notice is required. Any amount repaid within a year of purchase earns interest at half the published rate. No interest is lost once a Bond has been held for a full year. Net investment in National Savings Deposit Bonds was £137,746,593 at May 31, 1984.

YEARLY PLAN

The National Savings "Yearly Plan" was introduced on July 2, 1984, following the withdrawal of Third Issue Save As You Earn. It offers a guaranteed tax-free return. Applicants agree to make 12 monthly payments, leading to the issue of a Yearly Plan Certificate which can be held for at least four years. Applications may be made by any individuals aged 7 or over; in the name of children under 7; and by not more than two trustees for a sole beneficiary.

Payments must be made on the same date every month by standing order from a bank or other acceptable account. Only one payment may be made in any one month and must be in multiples of £5. Minimum monthly contribution is £20, maximum £100.

On receipt of an application the applicant will be sent an Offer Letter telling him the interest rates he will receive on his agreement if he accepts. The Certificate will be sent at the end of the first year. It will show the total value of the payments made and the value of the Certificate if held for four years. The Certificate will earn interest compounded annually on the anniversaries of the Certificate Date. Maximum interest is earned if the Certificate is held for the full four years. At the end of each year, providing at least seven payments have been made during that year, the applicant is given the option to take up a subsequent agreement, leading to the issue of a further Certificate.

NATIONAL SAVINGS CERTIFICATES

The amount, including accrued interest, index-linked increase or bonus remaining to the credit of investors in National Savings Certificates on March 31, 1984 was approximately £14,725m. In 1983–84, approx. £1,636m was subscribed and £1,138m (excluding interest, index-linked increase or bonus) was repaid. Interest, index-linked increase, bonus or other sum payable is free of United Kingdom income tax (including investment income surcharge) and capital gains tax. The 1st–11th issues continue to attract interest.

Issue and Maximum Holding (in units)	Unit Cost £	Value after		Interest Per Unit
		Years	£ p	
12th (1966–70) . . . . (1,500)	1	12	1·81½	During 12th year, 3½p per completed 4 months.
				During 13th year, 4p per completed 4 months.
				During 14th year, 5p per completed 4 months.
		15	2·27	During 15th year, 6p per completed 4 months plus ½p bonus at end of 15th year.
		16	2·49½	During 16th year, 7½p per completed 4 months.
		17	2·70½	During 17th year, 7p per completed 4 months.†
Decimal (1970–74) . . . (1,500)	1	9	1·74½	During 9th year, 4p per completed 4 months.
		10	1·90	During 10th year, 5p per completed 4 months plus ½p bonus at end of 10th year.
		11	2·08½	During 11th year, 6p per completed 4 months plus ½p bonus at end of 11th year.
		12	2·26½	During 12th year, 6p per completed 4 months.†
Fourteenth . . . . June 17, 1974 to Dec. 11, 1976 and April 1, 1977–Jan. 27, 1979 (3,000)	1	5	1·43	During 5th year, 3p per completed 4 months.
		6	1·55	During 6th year, 4p per completed 4 months.
		7	1·70½	During 7th year, 5p per completed 4 months plus ½p bonus at end of 7th year.
		8	1·85	During 8th year, 4½p per completed 4 months plus 1p bonus at end of 8th year.†
Index-Linked Retirement Issue (June 2, 1975–Nov. 15, 1980) (120)	10			Unlike conventional issues where interest is accrued periodically the repayment value of Index-Linked Certificates, subject to their being held a year, is related to the movement of the United Kingdom General Index of Retail Prices.** N.B. Certificates of the Retirement Issue were on sale only to men aged 65 years and over and women aged 60 years and over, but may now be transferred to anyone.
Sixteenth . . . . (Dec. 13, 1976 to Mar. 31, 1977) (300)	5	6	8·51½	After 1st year, 20p is added, during 2nd year, 10p per completed 4 months, during 3rd year, 20p per completed 4 months, during 4th year, 20p per completed 4 months plus 30p bonus at year end, during 5th year, 24p per completed 4 months, during 6th year, 26½p per completed 4 months.†
Eighteenth . . . . (Jan. 29, 1979–Feb. 2, 1980) (150)	10	5	15·00	After 1 year, 50p is added, during 2nd year, 25p per completed 4 months, during 3rd year, 33p per completed 4 months, during 4th year, 42p per completed 4 months, during 5th year, 50p per completed 4 months.†
Nineteenth . . . . (Feb. 4, 1980–May 9, 1981) (500)	10	5	16·35	After 1 year 50p is added, during 2nd year 30p per completed 4 months, during 3rd year 35p per completed 4 months, during 4th year 55p per completed 4 months and during 5th year 75p per completed 4 months.*
2nd Index-Linked Issue (Nov. 17, 1980–) (1,000)	10			Like Retirement Issue, the repayment value of 2nd Index-Linked Issue Certificates, subject to their being held a year, is related to the movement of the United Kingdom General Index of Retail Prices.** N.B. Certificates of the 2nd Index-Linked Issue were made available to anyone, regardless of age, from September 7, 1981.
Twenty-First . . . . Issue (May 11, 1981–Nov. 7, 1981) (500)	10	5	15·40	After 1 year, 75p is added, during 2nd year, 28p per completed 4 months, during 3rd year, 33p per completed 4 months, during 4th year, 40p per completed 4 months and during 5th year 54p per completed 4 months.*
Twenty-Third . . . . . . (Nov. 9, 1981–March 10, 1982) (200)	25	5	41·20	After 1 year, £2·25 is added, during 2nd year, 87p per completed 4 months, during 3rd year, £1·02 per completed 4 months, during 4th year, £1·23 per completed 4 months and during 5th year £1·53 per completed 4 months.*

Issue and Maximum Holding (in units)	Unit Cost £	Value after		Interest Per Unit
		Years	£ p	
Twenty-Fourth ..... (April 19, 1982–Nov. 4, 1982) (200)	25	5	38·32	After 1 year, £1·80 is added, during 2nd year, 53p per completed 3 months, during 3rd year, 63p per completed 3 months, during 4th year, 77p per completed 3 months and during 5th year 95p per completed 3 months.*
Twenty-Fifth .... (Nov. 17, 1982–Aug. 13, 1983) (200)	25	5	35·90	After 1 year, £1·50 is added, during 2nd year, 43p per completed 3 months, during 3rd year, 51p per completed 3 months, during 4th year, 62p per completed 3 months and during 5th year 79p per completed 3 months.*
Twenty-Sixth .... (Aug. 15, 1983–Mar. 19, 1984) (200)	25	5	37·17	After 1 year, £1·53 is added, during 2nd year, 47p per completed 3 months, during 3rd year, 58p per completed 3 months, during 4th year, 72p per completed 3 months and during 5th year 89p per completed 3 months.*
Twenty-Seventh .... (April 5, 1984–Aug. 7, 1984) (200)	25	5	35·48	After 1 year, £1·32 is added, during 2nd year, 41p per completed 3 months, during 3rd year, 50p per completed 3 months, during 4th year, 62p per completed 3 months and during 5th year 76p per completed 3 months.*
Twenty-Eighth ..... (Aug. 8, 1984–) (200)	25	5	38·47	After 1 year, £1·63 is added, during 2nd year, 51p per completed 3 months, during 3rd year, 64p per completed 3 months, during 4th year, 80p per completed 3 months and during 5th year £1·01 per completed 3 months.*

* As announced by the Treasury.

† From June 1982, savings certificates of the 7th to 14th, 16th and 18th Issues will be extended on common interest terms as they reach the end of their existing extension periods. The percentage interest rate is determined by the Treasury and any change in this common interest rate will be applicable from the 1st of the month following its announcement.

Under the new system, a certificate earns interest for each complete period of three months beyond the expiry of the previous extension terms. Within each three month period interest is calculated separately for each month at the rate applicable from the beginning of that month. The interest for each month is 1/12 of the annual rate (*i.e.* it does not vary with the number of days in the month) and is capitalised annually on the anniversary of the date of purchase. The current rate of interest under the common extension terms is displayed on special posters at most post offices.

** Index-linked certificates are eligible for an annual supplement of 3 per cent for the year to November 1, 1985. There have been two previous annual supplements of 2·4 per cent for 1982–83 and 1983–84. Certificates bought after October 31, 1985, kept for a full year, earn 0·25 per cent of the purchase price for each whole calendar month up to the end of October 1985. At the 5th anniversary there is a bonus of 4 per cent of the purchase price and at the 10th anniversary there is a second bonus of 4 per cent of the full 5th anniversary value. All supplements and bonuses are fully index-linked once earned.

LAW COURTS AND OFFICES

LAW SITTINGS (1985)—*Hilary*, Jan. 11 to April 3; *Easter*, April 16 to May 24; *Trinity*, June 4 to July 31; *Michaelmas*, Oct. 1 to Dec. 21.

THE JUDICIAL COMMITTEE

The Judicial Committee of the Privy Council includes the Lord Chancellor, the Lords of Appeal in Ordinary (*see* below) and such other members of the Privy Council as shall from time to time hold or have held "high judicial office," and certain judges from the Commonwealth.

Office—Downing Street, S.W.1. (Tel. 01–233 4394).
Registrar of the Privy Council, E. R. Mills, C.B.E.
Chief Clerk, D. H. O. Owen.

THE HOUSE OF LORDS

The Supreme Judicial Authority for Great Britain and Northern Ireland is the House of Lords, which is the ultimate Court of Appeal from all the Courts in Great Britain and Northern Ireland (except criminal courts in Scotland).

The Lord High Chancellor—
The Rt. Hon. the Lord Hailsham of St. Marylebone, C.H. (*born* 1907, *apptd.* 1979), £58,500.

Lords of Appeal in Ordinary (each £51,750)

	Apptd.
Rt. Hon. Lord Diplock, *born* 1907	1968
Hon. Lord Fraser of Tullybelton, *born* 1911	1975
Rt. Hon. Lord Keith of Kinkel, *born* 1922	1977
Rt. Hon. Lord Scarman, O.B.E., *born* 1911	1977
Rt. Hon. Lord Roskill, *born* 1911	1980
Rt. Hon. Lord Bridge of Harwich, *born* 1917	1980
Rt. Hon. Lord Brandon of Oakbrook, M.C., *born* 1920	1981
Rt. Hon. Lord Brightman, *born* 1911	1982
Rt. Hon. Lord Templeman, M.B.E., *born* 1920	1982

Registrar: The Clerk of the Parliaments, J. Sainty.

SUPREME COURT OF JUDICATURE

Court of Appeal

Ex officio Judges.—The Lord High Chancellor, the Lord Chief Justice of England, the Master of the Rolls, the President of the Family Division, and the Vice-Chancellor.

The Master of the Rolls (£51,750)
The Rt. Hon. Sir John Donaldson (*born* 1920, *apptd.* 1982).

Secretary, Miss V. Seymour; *Clerk*, K. H. L. Smeeton.

Lords Justices of Appeal (each £49,000)—

	Apptd.
Rt. Hon. Sir John Frederick Eustace Stephenson, *born* 1910	1971
Rt. Hon. Sir Frederick Horace Lawton, *born* 1911	1972
Rt. Hon. Sir George Stanley Waller, O.B.E., *born* 1911	1976
Rt. Hon. Sir (James) Roualeyn Hovell-Thurlow-Cumming-Bruce, *born* 1912	1977
Rt. Hon. Sir Edward Walter Eveleigh, E.R.D., *born* 1917	1977
Rt. Hon. Sir Desmond James Conrad Ackner, *born* 1920	1980
Rt. Hon. Sir Robin Horace Walford Dunn, M.C., *born* 1918	1980
Rt. Hon. Sir Peter Raymond Oliver, *born* 1921	1980
Rt. Hon. Sir Tasker Watkins, V.C., *born* 1918	1980
Rt. Hon. Sir Patrick McCarthy O'Connor, *born* 1914	1980
Rt. Hon. Sir (William) Hugh Griffiths, M.C., *born* 1923	1980
Rt. Hon. Sir Michael Fox, *born* 1921	1981
Rt. Hon. Sir Michael Robert Emanuel Kerr, *born* 1921	1981
Rt. Hon. Sir John Douglas May, *born* 1923	1982
Rt. Hon. Sir Christopher John Slade, *born* 1927	1982
Rt. Hon. Sir Francis Brooks Purchas, *born* 1919	1982
Rt. Hon. Sir Robert Lionel Archibald Goff, *born* 1926	1982
Rt. Hon. Sir George Brian Hugh Dillon, *born* 1923	1982
Rt. Hon. Sir Stephen Brown, *born* 1929	1983
Rt. Hon. Sir Roger Jocelyn Parker, *born* 1923	1983
Rt. Hon. Sir Nicolas Christopher Henry Browne-Wilkinson, *born* 1930	1983

HIGH COURT OF JUSTICE

Chancery Division

President, The Lord High Chancellor

The Vice-Chancellor (£49,000)
The Rt. Hon. Sir Robert Edgar Megarry (*born* 1910, *apptd.* 1976)

Secretary, Mrs. P. Joseph; *Clerk*, R. W. Murrell.

Judges (each £45,500)—

	Apptd.
Hon. Sir John Norman Keates Whitford, *born* 1913	1970
Hon. Sir (Ernest) Irvine Goulding, *born* 1910	1971
Hon. Sir Raymond Henry Walton, *born* 1915	1973
Hon. Sir John Evelyn Vinelott, *born* 1923	1978
Hon. Sir Martin Charles Nourse, *born* 1932	1980
Hon. Sir Douglas William Falconer, M.B.E., *born* 1914	1981
Hon. Sir Jean-Pierre Frank Eugene Warner, *born* 1924	1981
Hon. Sir Peter Leslie Gibson, *born* 1934	1981
Hon. Sir David Herbert Mervyn Davies, M.C., T.D., *born* 1918	1982
Hon. Sir Jeremiah LeRoy Harman, *born* 1930	1982
Hon. Sir Donald James Nicholls, *born* 1933	1983
Hon. Sir Richard Rashleigh Folliott Scott, *born* 1934	1983

Queen's Bench Division

The Lord Chief Justice of England (£56,500)
The Rt. Hon. The LORD LANE, A.F.C. (*born* 1918, *apptd.* 1980)

Secretary, Mrs. J. Simpson; *Clerk*, G. Curtis.

Judges (each £45,500)—

	Apptd.
Hon. Sir Joseph Donaldson Cantley, O.B.E., *born* 1910	1965
Hon. Sir Hugh Eames Park, *born* 1910	1965
Hon. Sir Bernard Caulfield, *born* 1914	1968
Hon. Sir William Lloyd Mars-Jones, M.B.E., *born* 1915	1969
Hon. Sir Ralph Kilner Brown, O.B.E., T.D., *born* 1909	1970
Hon. Sir Peter Henry Rowley Bristow, *born* 1913	1970
Hon. Sir Hugh Harry Valentine Forbes, *born* 1917	1970
Hon. Sir David Powell Croom-Johnson, D.S.C., V.R.D., *born* 1914	1971
Hon. Sir Leslie Kenneth Edward Boreham, *born* 1918	1972
Hon. Sir (Alfred William) Michael Davies, *born* 1921	1973
Hon. Sir John Dexter Stocker, M.C., T.D., *born* 1918	1973
Hon. Sir Kenneth George Illtyd Jones, *born* 1921	1974

Hon. Sir Haydn Tudor Evans, *born* 1920 1974
Hon. Sir Peter Richard Pain, *born* 1913 1975
Hon. Sir Kenneth Graham Jupp, M.C., *born* 1917 1975
Hon. Sir Ralph Brian Gibson, *born* 1922...... 1977
Hon. Sir (Walter) Derek (Thornley) Hodgson, *born* 1917 1977
Hon. Sir James Peter Comyn, *born* 1921...... 1978
Hon. Sir (Anthony) John Leslie Lloyd, *born* 1929 1978
Hon. Sir (Frederick) Maurice Drake, D.F.C., *born* 1923 1978
Hon. Sir Brian Thomas Neill, *born* 1923 1978
Hon. Sir Michael John Mustill, *born* 1931 1978
Hon. Sir Barry Cross Sheen, *born* 1918....... 1978
Hon. Sir David Bruce McNeill, *born* 1922 1979
Hon. Sir Harry Kenneth Woolf, *born* 1933.... 1979
Hon. Sir Christopher James Saunders French, *born* 1925 1979
Hon. Sir Thomas Patrick Russell, *born* 1926 .. 1980
Hon. Sir Peter Edlin Webster, *born* 1929 1980
Hon. Sir Thomas Henry Bingham, *born* 1933 . 1980
Hon. Sir Iain Derek Laing Glidewell, *born* 1924 1980
Hon. Sir Henry Albert Skinner, *born* 1926 ... 1980
Hon. Sir Peter Murray Taylor, *born* 1930 1981
Hon. Sir Murray Stuart-Smith, *born* 1927 1981
Hon. Sir Christopher Stephen Thomas Jonathan Thayer Staughton, *born* 1933 1981
Hon. Sir Donald Henry Farquharson, *born* 1928 1981
Hon. Sir Anthony James Denys McCowan, *born* 1928 1981
Hon. Sir (Iain) Charles (Robert) McCullough, *born* 1931 1981
Hon. Sir Hamilton John Leonard, *born* 1926 .. 1981
Hon. Sir Alexander Roy Asplan Beldam, *born* 1925 1981
Hon. Sir David Cozens-Hardy Hirst, *born* 1925 1982
Hon. Sir John Stewart Hobhouse, *born* 1932 .. 1982
Hon. Sir Michael Mann, *born* 1930 1982
Hon. Sir Andrew Peter Leggatt, *born* 1930 ... 1982
Hon. Sir Michael Patrick Nolan, *born* 1928 ... 1982
Hon. Sir Oliver Bury Popplewell, *born* 1927 .. 1983
Hon. Sir William Alan Macpherson, T.D., *born* 1926...................................... 1983
Hon. Sir Philip Howard Otton, *born* 1933 1983
Hon. Sir Paul Joseph Morrow Kennedy, *born* 1935 1983
Hon. Sir Michael Hutchison, *born* 1933 1983

Court of Appeal (Criminal Division)

Judges, The Lord Chief Justice of England, The Master of the Rolls, Lord Justices of Appeal and all the Judges of the Queen's Bench Division.

Family Division

President (£49,000)

Rt. Hon. Sir John Lewis Arnold (*born* 1915, *apptd.* 1979).
Sec., Mrs. E. Coles; *Clerk,* C. Beardsmore.
Judges (each £45,500)—   Apptd.
Hon. Sir John Brinsmead Latey, M.B.E., *born* 1914 1965
Hon. Sir (Alfred) Kenneth Hollings, M.C., *born* 1918...................................... 1971
Hon. Sir (Charles) Trevor Reeve, *born* 1915 .. 1973
Hon. Dame Rose Heilbron, D.B.E., *born* 1914... 1974
Hon. Sir Brian Drex Bush, *born* 1925 1976
Hon. Sir Alfred John Balcombe, *born* 1925 ... 1977
Hon. Sir John Kember Wood, M.C., *born* 1922 . 1977
Hon. Sir Ronald Gough Waterhouse, *born* 1926...................................... 1978
Hon. Sir (John) Gervase (Kensington) Sheldon, *born* 1913 1978
Hon. Sir (Thomas) Michael Eastham, *born* 1920...................................... 1978

Hon. Dame Margaret Myfanwy Wood Booth, D.B.E., *born* 1933 1979
Hon. Sir Anthony Leslie Julian Lincoln, *born* 1920...................................... 1979
Hon. Dame (Ann) Elizabeth (Oldfield) Butler-Sloss, D.B.E. *born* 1933 1979
Hon. Sir Anthony Bruce Ewbank, *born* 1925 . 1980
Hon. Sir John Douglas Waite, *born* 1932 1982
Hon. Sir Anthony Barnard Hollis, *born* 1927 . 1982

Judge Advocate of the Fleet, W. M. Howard, Q.C.
Queen's Proctor, Sir Henry Ware, K.C.B.

LORD CHANCELLOR'S DEPARTMENT
House of Lords, SW1A 0PW
[01–219 3000]

The Lord Chancellor is responsible for promoting general reforms in the civil law, for the procedure of the civil courts and for the administration of the Supreme Court (Court of Appeal, High Court and Crown Court) and county courts in England and Wales, and for legal aid schemes. He is responsible for advising the Crown on the appointment of judges and certain other officers and is himself responsible for the appointment of Masters and Registrars of the High Court and District and County Court Registrars and magistrates. He is responsible for ensuring that letters patent and other formal documents are passed in the proper form under the Great Seal of the Realm, of which he is the custodian. The work in connection with this is carried out under his direction in the Office of the Clerk of the Crown in Chancery.

Lord Chancellor, THE RT. HON. THE LORD HAILSHAM OF ST. MARYLEBONE, C.H. £63,800
Private Secretary to the Lord Chancellor, R. C. Stoate £12,399 to £16,656
Permanent Secretary, Sir Derek Oulton, K.C.B. £45,500
Private Secretary to the Permanent Secretary, R. V. Sams .... £8,166 to £10,218

Crown Office

Deputy Clerk of the Crown in Chancery, P. D. Robinson, C.B. £36,500
Clerk of the Chamber, Miss J. L. Waine £10,079 to £12,518

Legal Administration Division
Neville House, Page Street, S.W.1
[01–211 8104]

Deputy Secretary, P. D. Robinson, C.B. £36,500
Under Secretary, R. E. K. Holmes £29,500
Assistant Solicitors, J. A. C. Watherston; R. H. H. White .... £20,051 to £23,159
Assistant Secretaries, C. W. Everett; D. E. Staff £19,243 to £23,159

Appointments Division
House of Lords, S.W.1.
[01–219 3000]

Deputy Secretary, T. S. Legg £36,500
Assistant Solicitor, M. D. Huebner £20,051 to £23,159

Secretary of Commissions
4th Flr, Thames House North, Millbank, S.W.1.
[01–211 0067]

Secretary of Commissions (Under Secretary), B. Cooke £29,500
Joint Deputy Secretaries of Commissions, R. V. Grobler; W. B. Scott.

Legislation Division
House of Lords, S.W.1.
[01–219 3000]

Under Secretary, C. R. Seaton £29,500
Assistant Solicitors, P. M. Harris; M. H. Collon £20,051 to £23,159

Establishment and Finance Division
Neville House, Page Street, S.W.1
[01–211 8623]

Principal Establishment and Finance Officer, D. J.
Wiblin £29,500
Assistant Secretaries, Miss J. E. Court; A. D. Fagin;
D. S. Mortimer; I. R. Tapster; F. C. Yeomans
£19,243 to £23,159
Senior Principal, C. F. Tye.
Principal Information Officer, G. E. Moggridge.

Ecclesiastical Patronage
10 Downing Street, S.W.1
[01–233 3000]

Secretary for Ecclesiastical Patronage, J. R. Catford.
Assistant Secretary for Ecclesiastical Patronage, Brigadier G. B. Curtis, O.B.E., M.C. .. £12,399 to £16,656

**SUPREME COURT DEPARTMENTS
AND OFFICES**
Royal Courts of Justice, WC2A 2LL

Administrator, J. M. Parkin ..... £19,243 to £23,159
Conveyancing Counsel of the Supreme Court, J.
Monckton; S. G. Maurice; M. J. Roth.

Examiners of the Court
(Empowered to take Examination of Witnesses in all
Divisions of the High Court)
M. F. Meredith-Hardy; B. Rathbone; N. W. Briggs;
R. Jacobs.

Official Referees of the Supreme Court
His Honour Judge Sir William Stabb, Q.C.; His Honour
Judge Hawser, Q.C.; His Honour Judge Newey,
Q.C.; His Honour Judge Smout, Q.C.

Official Solicitor's Department
Penderel House, 287 High Holborn, W.C.1.

Official Solicitor to the Supreme Court, H. D. S.
Venables £29,500
Dep. Do., H. J. Baker .... £20,051 to £23,159
Assistant Solicitor, W. H. McBryde
£20,051 to £23,159
Chief Clerk, A. J. Simpson ...... £12,399 to £16,656

Court Funds Office
Royal Courts of Justice, WC2A 2LL

Accountant General, Sir Derek Oulton, K.C.B.
Deputy Accountant General, P. D. Lewis, T.D.
£19,243 to £23,159
Head of Courts Fund Office, I. J. MacBean
£12,399 to £16,656

Central Office of the Supreme Court
Royal Courts of Justice, WC2A 2LL

*Senior Master of the Supreme Court (Q.B.D.), and
Queen's Remembrancer,* J. R. Bickford-Smith, T.D.
£29,750
Masters of the Supreme Court (Q.B.D.), S. J. Wald-
man; I. S. Warren; C. W. S. Lubbock; P. B.
Creightmore; K. W. Topley; D. L. Prebble; A. A.
Grant; G. H. Hodgson; R. L. Turner £25,750
Chief Clerk (Central Office), F. Simmons
£12,399 to £16,656
Chief Clerk to the Q.B. Judges in Chambers, F. W.
Simpson .... £12,399 to £16,656

Criminal Appeal Office
Royal Courts of Justice, WC2A 2LL

Registrar, D. R. Thompson, C.B., Q.C. £29,750
Assistant Registrar, J. A. D. Heal . £20,051 to £23,159
Assistant Solicitor, R. A. Venne .. £20,051 to £23,159
Chief Clerk, A. F. P. Ottway ..... £12,399 to £16,656

Courts-Martial Appeals Office
Royal Courts of Justice, WC2A 2LL

Registrar, D. R. Thompson, C.B., Q.C. £29,750
Chief Clerk, A. F. P. Ottway.

Supreme Court Taxing Office

Chief Master, F. T. Horne £29,750
Masters of the Supreme Court, M. A. Clews; F. G.
Berkeley; A. J. Wright; C. R. N. Martyn; M. N.
Devonshire, T.D.; P. T. Hurst; C. A. Prince £25,750
Chief Clerk, D. Hutchings .... £12,399 to £16,656

CHANCERY DIVISION
Chancery Chambers,
Royal Courts of Justice, WC2A 2LL

Masters of the Supreme Court, E. R. Heward, C.B.
(Chief Master), £27,750; M. B. Cholmondeley
Clarke; J. M. Dyson; J. S. Gowers; G. A. Barratt;
R.Chamberlain, T.D. £25,750
Chief Clerk, W. E. Loveday ...... £12,399 to £16,656

Companies Court
Thomas More Building,
Royal Courts of Justice, W.C.2

Judges, The Hon. Mr. Justice Vinelott; The Hon. Mr.
Justice Nourse; The Hon. Mr. Justice Mervyn
Davies; The Hon. Mr. Justice Harman.
Registrar, J. Bradburn.
Chief Clerk, J. R. Baker .... £12,399 to £16,656
Senior Official Receiver, Companies Department,
J. B. Clemetson.

Bankruptcy (High Court) Department
Thomas More Building, Royal
Courts of Justice, Strand, W.C.2

Judges, The Rt. Hon. the Vice-Chancellor; The Hon.
Mr. Justice Goulding; The Hon. Mr. Justice
Walton; The Hon. Mr. Justice Vinelott; The Hon.
Mr. Justice Nourse; The Hon. Mr. Justice Warner;
The Hon. Mr. Justice Peter Gibson; The Hon. Mr.
Justice Mervyn Davies; The Hon. Mr. Justice
Harman; The Hon. Mr. Justice Nicholls; The Hon.
Mr. Justice Scott.
Chief Registrar, J. Bradburn £29,750
Registrars, T. L. Dewhurst, M.C.; G. L. Pimm; D. G.
Scott.................................... £25,750
Principal Clerk, R. L. Jones.

Official Receivers' Department

Senior Official Receiver, J. B. Clemetson.
Official Receivers, D. A. Thorne; D. E. Dolman.
Assistant do. E. A. Ashcroft; A. G. L. Billing; D. E. I.
Peet; W. Jenner; S. E. Rhodes; J. A. Booth; M. J.
Pugh.

FAMILY DIVISION
Principal Registry
Somerset House, W.C.2

Senior Registrar, B. P. Tickle £29,750
Registrars, B. Garland; C. F. Turner; T. G. Guest; D.
H. Colgate; D. E. Morris; J. E. Artro-Morris; R. B.
Rowe; G. B. N. A. Angel; B. P. F. Kenworthy-
Browne; G. A. Terian; Mrs. K. T. Moorhouse;
D. T. A. Davies; Mrs. N. Pearce £25,750
Secretary, R. Conn .... £12,399 to £16,656
Establishment Officer, R. C. Sturtivant
£12,399 to £16,656

District Probate Registrars

Birmingham and Stoke-on-Trent, A. M. Teasdale.
Brighton and Maidstone, G. R. Garrett.
Bristol, Exeter and Bodmin, P. L. Speyer.
Ipswich, Norwich and Peterborough, E. R. Alexander.
Leeds, Lincoln and Sheffield, C. S. Fisher.
Liverpool, Lancaster and Chester, J. D. Hemingway.

Llandaff, Bangor, Carmarthen and Gloucester,
D. W. Jones.
Manchester and Nottingham, M. A. Moran.
Newcastle, Carlisle, York and Middlesbrough, A.
Bertram.
Oxford and Leicester, Miss M. L. Farmborough.
Winchester, A. K. Biggs.

Admiralty Registry and Marshal's Office
Royal Courts of Justice, WC2A 2LL

Registrar, J. D. H. Rochford £25,750
Marshal and Chief Clerk, V. E. Ricks
£12,399 to £16,656

COURT OF PROTECTION
25 Store Street, W.C.1.

Master, Mrs. A. B. MacFarlane.
Chief Clerk, P. D. Lewis, T.D.

Protection Division
Head of Protection Division, E. J. Dober.

Management Division
48–49 Chancery Lane, W.C.2.
Head of Management Division, J. R. Ellis.

OFFICE OF THE LORD CHANCELLOR'S
VISITORS
Neville House, Page Street, S.W.1

Legal Visitor, M. H. Fauvelle.
Medical Visitors, W. A. Heaton-Ward; E. Carr; F. E.
Kenyon; R. J. Kerry; P. A. Morris £22,901

RESTRICTIVE PRACTICES COURT
Thomas More Building,
Royal Courts of Justice, W.C.2

Judicial Members, The Hon. Mr. Justice Anthony
Lincoln (*Principal*); Lord Ross; Lord Justice
Gibson; The Hon. Mr. Justice McNeill; The Hon.
Mr. Justice Warner.
Lay Members, N. C. Pearson, O.B.E., T.D.; N. L.
Salmon; I. G. Stewart; B. M. Currie; C. J. Risk; L.
Robertson.
Clerk of the Court, J. Bradburn.
Chief Clerk, J. R. Baker.

LAW COMMISSION

England and Wales
Conquest House, 37–38 John Street,
Theobalds Road, WC1N 2BQ
[01–242 0861]

Set up on June 16, 1965, under the Law Commissions
Act, 1965, to make proposals to the Government for
the examination of the law and for its revision where
it is unsuited for modern requirements, obscure, or
otherwise unsatisfactory. It recommends to the Lord
Chancellor programmes for the examination of different branches of the law and suggests whether the
examination should be carried out by the Commission
itself or by some other body. The Commission is also
responsible for the preparation of Consolidation and
Statute Law (Repeals) Bills.
Chairman, The Hon. Mr. Justice Ralph Gibson.
Members, B. J. Davenport, Q.C.; Prof. J. T. Farrand;
Mrs. B. M. Hoggett; Dr. P. M. North.
Secretary, J. G. H. Gasson.

CIRCUIT JUDGES
(*each* £29,750)

Midland and Oxford Circuit
W. A. L. Allardice; F. A. Allen; F. A. Blennerhassett, Q.C.; J. F. Blythe, T.D.; F. L. Clark, Q.C.; J. M.

Coulson; W. N. Davison; A. de Piro, Q.C.; A. R. M.
Ellis; J. F. Evans, Q.C.; H. G. A. Gosling; M. K.
Harrison-Hall; T. R. Heald; J. R. Hopkin; P. G.
Hughes; R. H. Hutchinson; J. E. M. Irvine; J. G.
Jones; E. F. Jowitt, Q.C.; T. O. Kellock, Q.C.; J. T. C.
Lee; D. T. Lloyd; J. R. Macgregor; K. Matthewman,
Q.C.; P. W. Medd, O.B.E., Q.C.; K. S. W. Mellor, Q.C.; N.
Micklem; A. J. H. Morrison; P. C. Northcote; F. M.
Potter; H. C. Rigby, D.F.C.; D. E. Roberts; J. Ross,
Q.C.; C. S. Stuart-White; H. C. Tayler, Q.C.; K. J.
Taylor; R. J. Toyn; G. M. Vos; M. B. Ward; R. L.
Ward, Q.C.; G. G. A. Whitehead, D.F.C.; H. Wilson;
J. W. Wilson; B. Woods; C. H. Wootton; C. G. Young.

Northern Circuit
H. H. Andrew, Q.C.; J. R. Arthur, D.F.C.; A. W. Bell;
R. M. Bingham, T.D., Q.C.; A. J. Blackett-Ord (*Vice
Chancellor, County Palatine of Lancaster*); A. S.
Booth, Q.C.; J. Booth; Joyanne W. Bracewell, Q.C.; D.
D. Brown, Q.C.; G. P. Crowe, Q.C.; J. W. Da Cunha; J.
M. Davies, Q.C.; B. Duckworth; Ann Marian Ebs-
worth; A. A. Edmondson; J. FitzHugh, Q.C.; D. M.
Forster; D. G. F. Franks; R. J. Hardy; Mary Holt; G.
W. Humphries; W. H. W. Jalland; A. C. Jolly; J. E.
Jones; H. A. Kershaw; H. L. Lachs; K. K. F. Lawton;
R. R. Leech; C. N. Lees; J. M. Lever, Q.C.; R. Lockett;
J. H. Lord; I. H. Morris-Jones, Q.C.; F. J. Nance; M.
O' Donoghue; F. D. Paterson; R. E. I. Pickering; A.
M. Prestt, Q.C.; M. A. G. Sachs; N. W. M. Sellers,
V.R.D.; J. A. Stannard; E. S. Temple, M.B.E., Q.C.
(*Recorder of Liverpool*); I. R. Taylor, Q.C.; V. B.
Webster; W. R. Wickham; R. Wood.

North Eastern Circuit
G. Baker, Q.C.; P. Baker, Q.C.; J. M. A. Barker; H.
C. Beaumont, M.B.E.; H. G. Bennett, Q.C.; B. Bush; C.
D. Chapman, Q.C.; Myrella Cohen, Q.C.; J. A. Cotton;
C. R. Dean, Q.C.; D. S. Forrester-Paton, Q.C.; S. S. Gill;
M. Gosnay; H. G. Hall; P. H. Hallam; J. A. Henham;
D. Herrod, Q.C.; H. Hewitt; V. R. Hurwitz; J. R.
Johnson; A. C. Lauriston, Q.C.; A. C. Macdonald; G.
Milner; A. L. Myerson, Q.C.; D. A. Orde; R. A. Percy;
J. Pickles; J. H. E. Randolph; D. M. Savill, Q.C.; L. B.
Stephen; J. Stephenson; R. A. R. Stroyan, Q.C.; J. D.
Walker; M. Walker; P. H. C. Walker; O. Wrightson.

South Eastern Circuit
J. S. R. Abdela, T.D., Q.C.; F. J. Aglionby; A. K.
Allen, O.B.E.; M. J. Anwyl-Davies, Q.C.; M. V. Argyle,
M.C., Q.C.; A. P. Babington; J. A. Baker; J. B. Baker,
Q.C.; P. V. Baker; R. M. N. Band, M.C., Q.C.; R. A.
Barr; P. T. S. Batterbury, T.D.; F. E. Beezley; G. J.
Binns; M. Birks; J. C. C. Blofeld, Q.C.; P. M.
Blomefield; J. Bolland; G. N. Butler; N. M.
Butter, Q.C.; H. J. Byrt, Q.C.; C. V. Callman; Sir
Harold Cassel, Bt., T.D., Q.C.; B. R. Clapham; A. W.
Clark; D. J. Clarkson, Q.C.; J. L. Clay, T.D.; Patricia
Coles, Q.C.; C. C. Colston, Q.C.; R. K. Cooke, O.B.E.; J.
F. Coplestone-Boughey; P. J. Corcoran; Margaret D.
Cosgrave; A. G. W. Coulthard; P. H. Counsell; A. E.
Cox; P. V. Crocker; N. H. Curtis-Raleigh; W. L. M.
Davies, Q.C.; J. J. Dean; K. M. Devlin; G. L. S. Dobry,
C.B.E., Q.C.; The Lord Dunboyne; J. B. S. Edwards; Q.
T. Edwards, Q.C.; J. H. Ellison, V.R.D.; J. K. Q. Evans;
P. R. Faulks, M.C.; A. L. Figgis; I. Finestein, Q.C.; J.
A. R. Finlay, Q.C.; A. G. Friend; A. Garfitt; L. Gerber;
E. B. Gibbens, Q.C.; F. E. H. G. Gibbens; P. W.
Goldstone; M. B. Goodman; J. H. Gower, Q.C.; D. A.
Grant, D.S.O., Q.C.; P. B. Greenwood; Jean Graham
Hall; D. J. Griffiths; R. E. Hammerton; J. P. Harris,
D.S.C., Q.C.; C. L. Hawser, Q.C.; J. D. W. Hayman; J. B.
R. Hazan, Q.C.; A. H. Head; M. R. Hickman; C. R.
Hilliard; D. E. Hill-Smith, V.R.D.; F. Honig; A. C. W.
Hordern, Q.C.; J. Hunter; C. P. James; W. Kee; J. F.
Kingham; L. G. Krikler; C. G. Lea, M.C.; N. Lermon,
Q.C.; A. C. L. Lewisohn; A. Lipfriend; G. D. Lovegrove,
Q.C.; D. B. D. Lowe; Noreen M. Lowry; R. J. Lowry,

Q.C.; R. D. Lymbery, Q.C.; D. L. McDonnell, O.B.E.; K. M. McHale; I. G. McLean; J. L. E. MacManus, T.D., Q.C.; M. B. Macmullen; M. J. P. Macnair; K. A. Machin; J. R. Main, Q.C.; A. Marder, Q.C.; O. S. Martin, Q.C.; G. F. P. Mason, Q.C.; J. H. E. Mendl; Sir James Miskin, Q.C. (*Recorder of London*); E. F. Monier-Williams; S. A. Morton, T.D.; J. D. F. Moylan; J. I. Murchie; M. Myers, Q.C.; J. H. R. Newey, Q.C.; Suzanne F. Norwood; C. R. Oddie; A. Owen; D. A. Paiba; R. H. S. Palmer; M. C. Parker, Q.C.; R. B. H. Pearce, Q.C.; D. E. Peck; J. C. Perks, M.C., T.D.; F. H. L. Petre; A. L. Phelan; T. H. Pigot, Q.C.; D. W. Tudor Price (*Common Serjeant in the City of London*); J. E. Pullinger; R. D. Ranking; J. W. Rant, Q.C.; E. V. P. Reece; G. R. Rice; E. B. B. Richards; G. H. Rooke, T.D., Q.C.; Deborah M. Rowland; K. W. Rubin; J. H. A. Scarlett; J. D. Sheerin; G. J. Shindler, Q.C.; M. Singh, Q.C.; J. K. E. Slack, T.D.; S. C. Sleeman; P. M. J. Slot; M. B. Smith; D. A. L. Smout, Q.C.; A. P. Solomon; Sir William Stabb, Q.C.; R. O. C. Stable, Q.C.; D. J. Stinson; E. Stockdale; J. S. Streeter; J. H. A. Stucley, D.S.C.; J. B. Taylor, M.B.E., T.D.; D. A. Thomas, M.B.E.; A. H. Tibber; A. S. Trapnell; A. M. Troup; S. Tumim; J. T. Turner; A. O. R. Vick, Q.C.; M. T. Underhill, Q.C.; L. J. Verney, T.D.; R. W. Vick; G. M. Vos; B. J. Wakley, M.B.E.; A. F. Waley, V.R.D., Q.C.; M. E. Ward; J. R. Warde; D. B. Watling, Q.C.; V. B. Watts; D. S. West-Russell; F. J. White; D. H. Wild; J. E. Williams; Sir Thomas Williams, Q.C.; W. G. Wingate, Q.C.; G. N. Worthington; E. E. Youds.

Wales and Chester Circuit

R. D. G. David, Q.C.; T. M. Evans, Q.C.; W. N. Francis; M. Gibbon, Q.C.; B. F. Griffiths, Q.C.; D. W. Howells; T. E. I. Lewis-Bowen; J. D. Seys Llewellyn; D. T. Lloyd-Jones, V.R.D.; G. Morgan; P. T. Hopkin Morgan, Q.C.; D. Morgan Hughes; D. A. Phillips; C. N. Pitchford; D. W. Powell; H. W. J. ap Robert; H. E. P. Roberts, Q.C.; J. C. Rutter; E. P. Wallis-Jones; D. B. Williams, T.D., Q.C.; H. Williams; R. G. Woolley.

Western Circuit

G. B. Best; N. R. Blaker, Q.C.; B. R. Braithwaite; A. C. Bulger: R. C. Chope; Sir Jonathan Clarke; P. H. F. Clarke; Hazel Counsell; J. A. Cox; M. Dyer; P. Fallon, Q.C.; B. J. F. Galpin; A. C. Goodall, M.C.; I. Starforth Hill, Q.C.; G. B. Hutton; J. H. Inskip, Q.C.; M. G. King; Sir Ian Lewis; I. P. Llewellyn Jones; D. McCarraher, V.R.D.; H. E. L. McCreery, Q.C.; Sheila M. D. McKinney; G. G. Macdonald; E. B. McLellan; G. Neville; K. C. L. Smithies; R. Stock, Q.C.; H. M. J. Tucker; D. H. W. Vowden, Q.C.; K. M. Willcock, Q.C.; J. H. Wroath.

CENTRAL CRIMINAL COURT
Old Bailey, E.C.4

Courts Administrator, John Howe.
Secondary and Under-Sheriff, Col. Leonard Bindon Arrowsmith Thacker.

COURTS SERVICE

First-tier centres deal with both civil and criminal cases and are served by High Court and Circuit Judges. Second-tier centres deal with criminal cases only but are served by both High Court and Circuit Judges. Third-tier centres deal with criminal cases only and are served only by Circuit Judges.

Midland and Oxford Circuit

First-tier—Birmingham, Lincoln, Nottingham, Stafford, Warwick. Second-tier—Leicester, Northampton, Oxford, Shrewsbury, Worcester. Third-tier—Coventry, Derby, Dudley, Grimsby, Hereford, Peterborough, Stoke-on-Trent, Walsall, Wolverhampton.

Circuit Administrator, M. C. Blair, 2 Newton Street, Birmingham B4 7LU.
Courts Administrators, Birmingham Group, C. A. Green; *Nottingham Group,* P. H. Martin; *Stafford Group,* A. F. Parker.

North Eastern Circuit

First-tier—Leeds, Newcastle upon Tyne, Sheffield, Teesside. Second-tier—York. Third-tier—Beverley, Doncaster, Durham, Huddersfield, Kingston-upon-Hull, Wakefield.
Circuit Administrator, C. W. Pratley, National Westminster House, 4th Floor, 29 Bond Street, Leeds LS1 5BQ.
Courts Administrators, Leeds and Sheffield Groups, C. A. White; *Newcastle upon Tyne Group,* F. I. Lance.

Northern Circuit

First-tier—Carlisle, Liverpool, Manchester, Preston. Third-tier—Barrow-in-Furness, Bolton, Burnley, Kendal, Lancaster.
Circuit Administrator, R. Potter, Aldine House, West Riverside, New Bailey Street, Salford M3 5EU.
Courts Administrators, Manchester Group, G. F. Addicott; *Liverpool Group,* B. H. Whittaker; *Preston Group,* G. Davies.

South Eastern Circuit

First-tier—Greater London, Lewes, Norwich (The High Court in Greater London sits at the Royal Courts of Justice. The Crown Court in Greater London sits at the following locations: Acton, Central Criminal Court, Croydon, Kingston-upon-Thames, Knightsbridge, Newington Causeway, Snaresbrook, Southwark and Wood Green). Second-tier—Chelmsford, Ipswich, Maidstone, Reading, St. Albans. Third-tier—Aylesbury, Bedford, Bury St. Edmunds, Cambridge, Canterbury, Chichester, Southend.
Circuit Administrator, J. L. Heritage, New Cavendish House, 18 Maltravers Street, W.C.2.
Deputy Circuit Administrator, M. McKenzie.
Courts Administrators, Chelmsford Group, K. H. A. Henderson; *Maidstone Group,* G. R. Nicholls; *Kingston Group,* P. M. Thomas.

Wales and Chester Circuit

First-tier—Caernarvon, Cardiff, Chester, Mold, Swansea. Second-tier—Carmarthen, Newport, Welshpool. Third-tier—Dolgellau, Haverfordwest, Knutsford, Merthyr Tydfil, Warrington.
Circuit Administrator, S. W. L. James, Churchill House, Churchill Way, Cardiff.
Courts Administrators, Cardiff Group, G. Jones; *Chester Group,* A. H. Howard.

Western Circuit

First-tier—Bodmin, Bristol, Exeter, Winchester. Second-tier—Dorchester, Gloucester, Plymouth. Third-tier—Barnstaple, Bournemouth/Poole, Devizes, Newport (I.O.W.), Portsmouth, Salisbury, Southampton, Swindon, Taunton.
Circuit Administrator, I. E. Ashworth, Bridge House, Clifton, Bristol BS8 4BN.
Courts Administrators, Bristol Group, A. C. Burden; *Exeter Group,* J. F. Brindley; *Winchester Group,* J. K. W. Phipps.

RECORDERS

J. R. S. Adams; I. D. G. Alexander; J. D. Alliott, Q.C.; W. P. Andreae-Jones; B. J. Appleby, Q.C.; J. F. A. Archer, Q.C.; The Rt. Hon. P. K. Archer, Q.C., M.P.; A. J. Arlidge; R. Ashton; P. Ashworth, Q.C.; M. J. Astill; T. G. F. Atkinson; R. E. Auld, Q.C.; P. Back, Q.C.; P. G. N. Badge; M. J. D. Baker; T. S. G. Baker,

Q.C.; A. F. Balston; D. Barker, Q.C.; R. O. Barlow; C. J. A. Barnett, Q.C.; W. E. Barnett, Q.C.; A. R. Barrowclough, Q.C.; S. T. Bates, Q.C.; R. J. A. Batt; P. M. Beard; C. H. Beaumont; C. O. M. Bedingfield, T.D., Q.C.; R. E. Bell, Q.C.; P. Bennett, Q.C.; D. M. Berkson; Miss I. Bernstein; R. H. Bernstein, D.F.C., Q.C.; M. Bethel, Q.C.; J. C. Beveridge, Q.C.; I. J. Black, Q.C.; J. W. Black, Q.C.; M. S. Blackburn; C. Bloom; L. A. F. Borrett; M. R. Bowley, Q.C.; P. C. Bowsher, Q.C.; I. R. Boyd; P. N. Brandt; D. J. Brennan; G. J. B. G. Brice, Q.C.; J. N. W. Bridges-Adams; P. J. Briggs; S. E. Brodie, Q.C.; N. J. L. Brodrick; L. J. Bromley, Q.C.; H. Brooke, Q.C.; A. E. Brooks; R. Brown; S. D. Brown; J. M. Bull, Q.C.; J. P. Burke, Q.C.; J. K. Burke; B. Bush; J. W. A. Butler-Sloss; A. N. L. Butterfield; D. C. Calcutt, Q.C.; Mrs. B. A. Calvert, Q.C.; The Lord Campbell of Alloway, Q.C.; I. B. Campbell; B. E. Capstick, Q.C.; H. B. H. Carlisle, Q.C.; M. Carlisle, Q.C., M.P.; F. B. Carter, Q.C.; J. A. Chadwin, Q.C.; D. R. Chance; P. J. Charlesworth; B. W. Chedlow, Q.C.; P. N. R. Clark; D. C. Clarke, Q.C.; P. C. Clegg; R. N. B. Clegg, Q.C.; R. R. B. Cole; G. J. K. Coles, Q.C.; J. M. Collins, Q.C.; J. M. Collins; C. D. Compston; M. B. Connell, Q.C.; M. J. Cook; G. H. Coombe; M. R. Coombe; Miss B. P. Cooper, Q.C.; Rt. Hon. Sir Frederick Corfield, Q.C.; Miss D. R. Cotton, Q.C.; J. S. Coward, Q.C.; D. M. Cowley, Q.C.; B. R. E. Cox, Q.C.; P. J. Cox, D.S.C., Q.C.; J. Crabtree; P. F. Crane; P. J. Crawford, Q.C.; W. H. R. Crawford, Q.C.; C. J. Crespi, Q.C.; M. A. L. Cripps, C.B.E., D.S.O., T.D., Q.C.; F. P. Crowder, Q.C.; J. D. Crowley, Q.C.; E. J. R. Crowther, O.B.E., Q.C.; T. R. Crowther; Miss E. A. M. Curnow; R. H. Curtis, Q.C.; G. H. W. Daniel; G. W. Davey; I. T. R. Davidson, Q.C.; Sir Alun T. Davies, Q.C.; R. E. Davies, Q.C.; J. J. Deave; J. B. Deby, Q.C.; C. F. Dehn, Q.C.; W. N. Denison, Q.C.; W. E. Denny, C.B.E., Q.C.; S. C. Desch, Q.C.; J. B. S. Diehl; T. M. Dillon, Q.C.; Miss A. E. Downey; D. P. Draycott, Q.C.; G. A. Draycott; J. M. Drinkwater, Q.C.; R. D. L. Du Cann, Q.C.; W. H. Dunn, Q.C.; C. H. Durman.

D. E. H. Edwards; G. O. Edwards; D. F. Elfer; G. Elias, Q.C.; The Lord Elystan-Morgan; G. A. Ensor; A. H. M. Evans, R.D., Q.C.; D. A. Evans, Q.C.; Miss M. A. P. Evans; E. C. Evans-Lombe, Q.C.; G. N. Eyre, Q.C.; W. D. Fairclough; P. D. Fanner; B. A. Farrer, Q.C.; D. J. Farrer, Q.C.; M. H. Fauvelle; S. J. D. Fawcus; J. D. A. Fennell, O.B.E., Q.C.; T. G. Field-Fisher, T.D., Q.C.; J. J. Finney; Miss E. N. Fisher; W. R. Fitch; J. E. Fletcher; J. R. B. Fox-Andrews, Q.C.; A. N. Fricker, Q.C.; M. Gale, Q.C.; Sir Edward Gardner, Q.C., M.P.; P. N. Garland, Q.C.; L. N. H. George; R. J. H. Gibbs, Q.C.; W. J. Glover, Q.C.; Miss A. F. Goddard; H. K. Goddard, Q.C.; S. A. Goldstein; A. A. Gordon; J. P. Gorman, Q.C.; The Lord Grantchester, Q.C.; G. Gray, Q.C.; R. I. Gray, Q.C.; A. D. Green; B. S. Green, Q.C.; R. D. Grey, Q.C.; R. Grey, Q.C.; W. P. Grieve, Q.C.; I. O. Griffiths, Q.C.; L. Griffiths; M. G. Grills; Mrs. H. M. Grindrod, Q.C.; R. B. Groves; M. F. Haigh; J. Hall; D. T. Hallchurch, T.D.; P. J. Halnan; J. H. Hames, Q.C.; A. W. Hamilton, Q.C.; G. M. Hamilton, T.D., Q.C.; R. G. Hamilton; J. A. Hammond; J. Hampton; Miss R. S. A. Hare, Q.C.; B. Hargrove, O.B.E., Q.C.; R. D. Harman, Q.C.; J. N. Harper; F. D. Hart, Q.C.; C. A. Hart-Leverton, Q.C.; C. S. Harvey, M.B.E., T.D.; R. J. S. Harvey, Q.C.; T. S. A. Hawkesworth, Q.C.; G. E. Heggs; R. A. Henderson, Q.C.; R. H. Q. Henriques; D. R. M. Henry, Q.C.; J. C. Hicks, Q.C.; A. B. Hidden, Q.C.; B. J. Higgs, Q.C.; A. M. Hill, Q.C.; E. M. Hill, Q.C.; J. D. Hitchen; T. D. T. Hodson; D. Holden; D. A. Hollis, V.R.D., Q.C.; A. T. Hoolahan, Q.C.; The Lord Hooson, Q.C.; R. Houlker, Q.C.; W. M. Howard, Q.C.; M. J. Hubbard; F. M. S. Hudson; Maj.-Gen. Sir David Hughes-Morgan, Bt, C.B.E.; J. Hugill, Q.C.; J. G. Hull, Q.C.; P. J. Hunt; R. Hunt; A. E. Hutchinson, Q.C.; M. Hutchison, Q.C.; M. J. Hyman; B. A. Hytner, Q.C.; N. E. J. Inglis-Jones, Q.C.; N. F. Irvine, Q.C.; F. C. Irwin, Q.C.; D. M. Jack; P. J. E. Jackson; C. E. F. James; N.

F. B. Jarman; D. A. Jeffreys, Q.C.; J. Jeffs, Q.C.; C. W. L. Jervis; D. B. Johnson, Q.C.; M. H. Johnson; R. L. Johnson, Q.C.; G. J. Jones; E. S. Jones, Q.C.; G. R. Jones; T. G. Jones; W. H. Joss; I. Judge, Q.C.; J. W. Kay, Q.C.; D. St. J. Keane, Q.C.; D. N. Keating, Q.C.; R. W. M. Keeling, D. A. M. Kemp, Q.C.; I. A. Kennedy, Q.C.; M. D. Kennedy, Q.C.; A. M. Kenny; P. M. Kershaw, Q.C.; R. I. Kidwell, Q.C.; G. E. Kilfoil; R. C. Klevan, Q.C.

D. N. R. Latham; G. F. B. Laughland, Q.C.; T. Lawrence; L. D. Lawton, Q.C.; M. K. Lee, Q.C.; R. T. L. Lee; Sir Godfrey Le Quesne, Q.C.; S. Levine; M. E. Lewer, Q.C.; A. K. Lewis, Q.C.; E. ap G. Lewis, Q.C.; M. ap G. Lewis, Q.C.; L. J. Libbert, Q.C.; C. C. D. Lindsay; R. J. D. Livesey, Q.C.; C. G. Llewellyn-Jones; J. Lloyd-Eley, Q.C.; R. H. Lownie; F. D. Loy; E. Lyons, Q.C.; J. R. V. McAulay, Q.C.; D. D. McEvoy, Q.C.; I. S. Mackintosh; N. R. B. Macleod, Q.C.; Miss M. B. MacMurray, Q.C.; J. G. McNaught; E. A. Machin, Q.C.; B. C. Maddocks; R. G. Marshall-Andrews; R. B. Martin, Q.C.; H. R. Mayor; M. Meggerson; J. A. Meredith; A. L. Mildon, Q.C.; R. A. Miller; Mrs. B. J. L. Mills; J. B. M. Milmo, Q.C.; N. A. Miscampbell, Q.C., M.P.; H. J. Montlake; L. J. J. Morgan; W. G. O. Morgan, Q.C.; G. E. Moriarty, Q.C.; M. Morland, Q.C.; D. G. Morris; The Rt. Hon. J. Morris, Q.C., M.P.; P. C. W. Morris; J. B. Mortimer, Q.C.; T. H. Moseley; M. D. Mott; F. J. Muller, Q.C.; A. S. Myerson, Q.C.; G. K. Naylor, T.D.; C. W. F. Newman, Q.C.; J. D. Newton; A. J. D. Nicholl; C. V. Nicholls, Q.C.; C. A. A. Nicholls, Q.C.; A. T. C. Nicholson; M. C. Nicholson; A. S. T. E. Nicol; Mrs. M. F. Norrie; M. Nunan; D. P. O'Brien, Q.C.; E. M. Ogden, Q.C.; H. H. Ognall, Q.C.; B. R. Oliver; S. K. O'Malley; S. K. Overend; G. V. Owen, Q.C.; J. A. D. Owen, Q.C.; S. R. Page; Miss H. E. Paling; A. W. Palmer, Q.C.; E. O. Parry; N. S. K. Pascoe; J. G. Paulusz; Miss V. A. Pearlman; J. R. Peppitt, Q.C.; Sir Ian Percival, Q.C., M.P.; D. S. Perrett, Q.C.; N. A. Phillips, Q.C.; D. A. Pirie; M. T. Pill, Q.C.; C. J. Pitchers; Miss E. F. Platt, Q.C.; D. A. Poole, Q.C.; F. H. Potts, Q.C.; H. C. Pownall, Q.C.; M. J. Pratt, Q.C.; T. W. Preston, Q.C.; A. J. Price, Q.C.; J. A. Price, Q.C.; V. W. C. Price, Q.C.; E. J. Prosser, Q.C.; B. H. Pryor; A. G. Purnell, Q.C.

A. Rankin, Q.C.; A. D. Rawley, Q.C.; L. F. Read, Q.C.; P. Rees; H. A. Richardson; K. A. Richardson; Miss S. A. Ritchie, Q.C.; G. Rivlin, Q.C.; P. B. Roberts; J. M. G. Roberts, Q.C.; D. E. H. Robson, Q.C.; J. O. Roch, Q.C.; D. A. H. Rodwell, Q.C.; A. M. T. Rogers, Q.C.; J. W. Rogers, Q.C.; P. H. Rolf; A. M. T. Rose, M.C.; C. D. R. Rose, Q.C.; R. G. Rougier, Q.C.; J. J. Rowe, Q.C.; R. R. Russell; T. R. E. F. Ryland; A. F. B. Scrivener, Q.C.; C. Seagroatt, Q.C.; R. A. W. Sears, Q.C.; H. M. Self, Q.C.; J. A. O. Shand; M. D. Sherrard, Q.C.; L. Shield; L. S. Shields, Q.C.; J. M. Shorrock; A. Simpson; R. M. G. Simpson, Q.C.; H. S. Singer; A. T. Smith, Q.C.; C. H. Smith; D. A. Smith, Q.C.; J. R. S. Smyth; R. E. Snape; R. J. Southan; Miss J. M. Southworth, Q.C.; G. C. H. Spafford; D. H. Spencer, Q.C., M.P.; J. A. C. Spokes, Q.C.; S. A. Stamler, Q.C.; D. H. Stembridge; S. M. Stephens, Q.C.; J. S. H. Stewart, Q.C.; R. M. Stewart, Q.C.; E. D. R. Stone, Q.C.; P. J. Stretton; F. R. C. Such; D. M. Sumner; A. J. C. Sumption, D.S.C.; L. Swift, Q.C.; A. B. Taylor; E. Taylor; N. Taylor, Q.C.; R. C. Taylor; K. J. Tetley; D. M. Thomas, Q.C.; D. O. Thomas, Q.C.; J. Thomas, Q.C.; Rt. Hon. P. J. M. Thomas, Q.C., M.P.; S. B. Thomas, Q.C.; R. N. Titheridge, Q.C.; M. A. Thorpe, Q.C.; J. K. Toulmin, Q.C.; J. B. S. Townend, Q.C.; R. H. Tucker, Q.C.; S. L. Tuckey, Q.C.; M. J. Turner, Q.C.; R. L. Turner; C. J. M. Tyrer; A. R. Tyrrell, Q.C.; A. R. Vandermeer, Q.C.; D. C. Waddington, Q.C., M.P.; J. P. Wadsworth, Q.C.; D. St. J. R. Wagstaff; R. M. Wakerley, Q.C.; W. H. Waldron, Q.C.; J. J. Walker-Smith; B. Walsh, Q.C.; C. D. G. P. Waud; D. McL. Webster, Q.C.; P. A. Webster; M. Weisman; P. Weitzman, Q.C.; C. P. C. Whelon; C. H. Whitby, Q.C.; A. Whitfield, Q.C.; J. R. Whitley; D. J.

R. Wilcox; Miss N. Wilkins; G. H. G. Williams, q.c.;
G. W. Williams, q.c.; J. G. Williams, q.c.; S. W.
Williamson, q.c.; J. C. Willis; S. M. Willis; J. G.
Wilmers, q.c.; A. M. Wilson, q.c.; C. Wilson Smith;
D. R. Woolley, q.c.; N. G. Wootton; J. M. Wright,
q.c.; E. G. Wrintmore; G. N. Barr Young; K. H.
Zucker, q.c.

INNER LONDON MAGISTRATES' COURTS

Chief Metropolitan Stipendiary Magistrate and Chairman of Committee of Magistrates for Inner London Area, David Armand Hopkin
    3rd Floor, North-West Wing,
    Bush House, Aldwych, WC2B 4PJ
Principal Chief Clerk and Clerk to the Committee,
I. Fowler £26,229
Chief Clerk (Training), J. W. Greenhill £23,004

Bow Street, W.C.2

The Chief Magistrate. £33,000
Magistrates, William Edward Charles Robins; Ronald
    David Bartle; Terence Maher ..... *(each)* £28,500
Senior Chief Clerk, Mrs. J. M. Ferley £22,758
Chief Clerk, D. O'Connor ..... £20,298 to £22,266

Camberwell Green, D'Eynsford Road, S.E.5

Magistrates, Maurice Juniper Guymer, o.b.e.; Ralph
    Hamilton Lownie; George Alfred Bathurst Norman; Sir Bryan Clieve Roberts, k.c.m.g., q.c.;
    Charles Peter Morton Davidson .. *(each)* £28,500
Senior Chief Clerk, J. A. Laing £22,758
Chief Clerk, T. N. Blake .... £20,298 to £22,266

Clerkenwell, Kings Cross Road, W.C.1

Magistrates, John Denis Purcell; Mark Lemon Robert
    Romer; Christopher John Bourke .. *(each)* £28,500
Senior Chief Clerk, W. A. W. Strachan £22,758
Chief Clerk, M. Pascoe .... £20,298 to £22,266

Greenwich, Blackheath Road, S.E.10

Magistrates, Stanley Graham Clixby; Miss Pamela
    Marjorie Long; David Quentin Miller £28,500
Senior Chief Clerk, P. C. Unwin £22,758

Woolwich, Market Street, S.E.18

Magistrates (as Greenwich).
Chief Clerk, I. W. Pepper .... £20,298 to £22,266

Hampstead Magistrates' Court
Downshire Hill, N.W.3.

Chief Clerk, J. D. Heywood ...... £19,350 to £20,754

Highbury Corner, Holloway Road, N.7

Magistrates, David Barr; Michael Anthony Johnstone; David Melvyn Fingleton; Geoffrey Parkinson .... *(each)* £28,500
Senior Chief Clerk, A. L. Gooch £22,758
Chief Clerk, J. A. Patron .... £20,298 to £22,266

Horseferry Road, Horseferry Road, S.W.1

Magistrates, Eric Crowther, o.b.e.; James Hobson
    Jobling; Ronald Trevor Moss; Mrs. Norma Negus
    (each) £28,500
Senior Chief Clerk, D. M. Davies £22,758
Chief Clerk, K. A. Thompson .... £20,298 to £22,266
Chief Clerk (Licensing), L. G. Bowerman
    £20,298 to £22,266

Marlborough Street,
Great Marlborough Street, W.1

Magistrates, St. John Bernard Vyvyan Harmsworth;
    Jeremy George Connor .... *(each)* £28,500
Chief Clerk, E. L. Yabsley........ £20,298 to £22,266

Marylebone, 181 Marylebone Road, N.W.1

Magistrates, Peter Duncan Fanner; Brian John
    Canham; John Quentin Campbell .. *(each)* £28,500
Senior Chief Clerk, D. V. Wainwright....... £22,758
Chief Clerk, W. G. Johnston £22,758

Old Street, E.C.1

Magistrates, Kenneth John Heastey Nichols; Terence
    Maher .... *(each)* £28,500
Chief Clerk, S. R. Samjee .... £20,298 to £22,266

South Western, Lavender Hill, S.W.11

Magistrates, Miss Dawn Angela Freedman; John
    Jeremy Fordham; Anura Cooray .. *(each)* £28,500
Senior Chief Clerk, C. E. Hollingdale....... £22,758
Chief Clerk, G. D. Painter .... £20,298 to £22,266

Thames, Aylward Street, E.1

Magistrates, Peter Gilmour Noto Badge; Patrick
    John Halnan.................... *(each)* £28,500
Senior Chief Clerk, J. S. L. Pulford £22,758
Chief Clerk, Miss E. Thompson ... £20,298 to £22,266

Tower Bridge, Tooley Street, S.E.1

Magistrates, Roger Benedict Sanders; Christopher
    David Voelcker; Mrs. Jacqueline Roberta Comyns
    (each) £28,500
Chief Clerk, P. W. Johnson ...... £20,298 to £22,266

Wells Street, 59/65 Wells Street, W.1

Magistrates, Christopher Besley; Edward James
    Branson; Miss Audrey Mary Jennings; Geoffrey
    Lindsay James Noel .... *(each)* £28,500
Senior Chief Clerk, R. N. W. Harbord £22,758
Chief Clerk, Miss M. Noon .... £20,298 to £22,266

West London, Southcombe Street, W.14

Magistrates, David Fairbairn; Harold Cook
    (each) £28,500
Senior Chief Clerk, Miss P. M. Austin....... £22,758

Walton Street Magistrates' Court, 1A Walton Street, S.W.3

Chief Clerk, J. B. Jordan .... £20,298 to £22,266

Juvenile Courts, 185 Marylebone Road, N.W.1

Senior Chief Clerk, A. C. Austin............. £23,004
Chief Clerk, Mrs. H. Mitcham .... £20,298 to £22,266

Unattached Magistrate, David Kennett Brown
    £28,500

STIPENDIARY MAGISTRATES

Greater Manchester, William Derrick Fairclough
    (1982); Cecil Thomas Latham, o.b.e. (1976).
Humberside, Ian Robertson Boyd (1972); Peter Fingret (1982).
W. Yorks., Francis David Lindley Loy (1972).
Merseyside, Norman Geoffrey Wootton (1976).
Mid Glamorgan, David Powys Rowland (1961); Benjamin Rhys Oliver (1983).
South Glamorgan, Sir (Adrian) Lincoln Hallinan
    (1976).
South Yorkshire, Ian William Crompton (1983).
West Midlands, Frederick Henry Hatchard (1981);
    James Robert Staples Smyth (1978); William
    Michael Probert (1983).

DIRECTOR OF PUBLIC PROSECUTIONS
4/12 Queen Anne's Gate, S.W.1

Director, Sir Thomas Hetherington, k.c.b., c.b.e., t.d.,
    q.c.
Deputy Director, K. Dowling.
Principal Assistant Directors, D. G. Williams; J.
    Wood.

OFFICE OF THE JUDGE ADVOCATE GENERAL OF THE FORCES

(Lord Chancellor's Establishment; Joint Service for the Army and the Royal Air Force)
4th Floor, St. Dunstan's House, Fetter Lane,
EC4A 1BT

Judge Advocate General, J. Stuart-Smith ... £32,750
Vice Judge Advocate General, G. L. Chapman
£29,000
Assistant Judge Advocates General, C. G. Gould; G.
E. Empson; G. R. Canner; E. G. Moelwyn-Hughes;
A. P. Pitts; S. B. Spence .... £19,243 to £23,159
Deputy Judge Advocate, A. Labor £14,401 to £19,317

METROPOLITAN POLICE OFFICE
New Scotland Yard, Broadway, SW1H 0BG
[01–230 1212]

Commissioner, Sir Kenneth Newman, Q.P.M. £42,750
Deputy Commissioner, A. Laugharne, C.B.E., Q.P.M.
£35,064
Receiver, A. D. Gordon-Brown £35,278
Deputy Receiver, B. G. David £26,236

"A" Department
Administration and Operations

Assistant Commissioner, W. H. Gibson, C.B.E., Q.P.M.
£31,875
Deputy Assistant Commissioners, J. H. Cracknell,
M.V.O.; D. J. Hanson, Q.P.M.; R. Innes £25,890
Commanders, J. Hilton; J. F. Newing; C. J. Rideout
£23,199
Principal, D. R. Pidgeon .... £12,399 to £16,656
Metropolitan Special Constabulary, Chief Commandant, A. A. Hammond, O.B.E.

"B" Department
Traffic and Technical Support

Assistant Commissioner, G. D. McLean, Q.P.M.
£31,875
Deputy Assistant Commissioners, M. J. Evans; C. B.
J. Sutton £25,890
Senior Principal, W. T. Davis .... £16,343 to £20,794
Commanders, L. Adams, M.B.E., Q.P.M.; A. M. Hayward, Q.P.M.; K. E. Hunter; E. Mitchell £23,199
Principals, E. R. Bright; M. Brothers; D. H. Burr; J.
E. Geater; D. F. F. Hannaford.. £12,399 to £16,656

"C" Department
Criminal Investigation

Assistant Commissioner, J. A. Dellow, O.B.E. . £31,875
Deputy Assistant Commissioners, C. V. Hewett, O.B.E.,
Q.P.M.; D. Powis, O.B.E., Q.P.M.; B. R. C. Worth
£25,890
Commanders, D. R. E. Bicknell, Q.P.M.; F. E. Cater,
Q.P.M.; P. H. Corbett; W. H. Hucklesby; P. Phelan;
G. E. Stockwell; D. H. Williams; C. B. Wood
£23,199

Metropolitan Police Laboratory

Director, R. L. Williams £25,087
Deputy Directors, B. J. Culliford; G. J. O. Lee; M. R.
Loveland; E. F. Pearson .... £15,605 to £20,794
Senior Principal Scientific Officer, B. B. Wheals
£15,605 to £20,794
Principal Scientific Officers, B. Arnold; R. R. Berrett;
C. F. Candy; K. Chaperlin; B. E. Connett; D. R.
Cousins; R. J. Davis; D. M. Ellen; O. E. Facey; N.
F. Fuller; J. V. Jackson; Mrs. S. M. Keating; R. H.
Keeley; Mrs. F. R. Lewington; P. D. Martin; B. H.
Parkin; D. Rudram; R. A. Stedman; M. J. Whitehouse; Miss J. M. Wiles; W. D. C. Wilson
£11,343 to £14,931

"D" Department
Personnel and Training

Assistant Commissioner, G. J. Dear, Q.P.M. ... £31,875
Deputy Assistant Commissioners, H. N. Annersley;
J. H. Thornton, Q.P.M. £25,890
Commanders, J. M. M. Huins; B. H. Skitt, B.E.M.; A.
W. Young £23,199
Principals, J. Clarke; J. H. Mailing; B. A. Phillips
£12,399 to £16,656
Welfare Officer, K. F. T. Rivers, M.B.E
£10,079 to £12,518

Metropolitan Police Cadet Corps

Commander, A. W. Young £23,199
Director of Academic Studies, (vacant).

Medical and Dental Branch

Chief Medical Officer, E. C. A. Bott.
*Consulting Physician and Deputy to Chief Medical
Officer*, Dr. N. F. Jones.
Consulting Surgeon, R. W. Lloyd-Davies.
Dental Officer, W. C. Keys.

"P" Department
Public Information

Director of Information, R. B. Wells £25,890
Deputy Director of Information, H. B. Colver
£16,343 to £20,794
Head of News Branch, M. C. Johnson
£12,399 to £16,656
Head of Publicity Branch, J. H. V. Bradley
£12,399 to £16,656

"S" Department
Solicitors

Solicitor, D. M. O'Shea £35,278
Deputy Solicitor, C. N. Winston £28,583
Assistant Solicitors, H. J. Drake; P. R. Essex; W. S.
Frost; H. B. Hargrave; R. L. Kiley; R. E. Marsh; R.
G. Mays; J. R. McCann; C. S. Porteous; R. M. D.
Thorne; J. M. Tuff; D. W. Warran
£20,051 to £23,159
Senior Legal Assistants, R. E. Cuffe-Adams; D. L.
Brodie; Miss S. D. M. Burrows; R. P. Coupland;
Miss J. M. Craig; G. R. Edwards; Mrs. K. M. Ferris;
C. L. Foster; Miss S. B. Gale; R. J. A. Glass; G.
Gibb; D. Hamilton; S. M. Howard; J. R. P. Hyde;
Miss S. M. James; J. P. McCooey; A. M. McLellan;
Miss S. M. Norton; S. A. O'Doherty; P. A. Shawdon;
R. N. Short; C. E. Swann; S. T. Suchak; R. B.
Vince; Miss S. E. Woollam; H. A. Youngerwood
£14,401 to £19,317
Legal Assistants, Miss H. Argue; C. A. Baylis; Mrs.
S. M. Charlton-Brown; S. F. Cain; Mrs. I. S.
Chandler; Miss C. J. Davies; Miss C. F. Forshaw;
G. A. Green; G. J. Harding; Miss D. J. Harman; D.
C. Hewett; Miss L. D. Hyams; M. W. James; C. R.
Lake; Miss A. M. Martin; Miss C. M. Mather; Miss
W. J. Megeney; G. Morgan; Mrs. V. A. Murdie;
Miss A. S. Pugh; Mrs. B. B. P. Reynolds; Miss H.
M. C. Rushmore; M. J. N. Sage; Mrs. A. P. Sassoli;
Miss J. T. Sullivan; S. Taylor ... £7,342 to £13,523
Senior Principal Legal Executive, P. G. Stenning
£16,343 to £20,794
Principal Legal Executives, A. W. G. Astill; J. P.
Clarke; A. W. Kirkwood; J. R. Niblett; B. Tickner
£12,399 to £16,656

Area Headquarters

Deputy Assistant Commissioners, E. F. Maybanks,
Q.P.M.; R. A. Hunt; C. R. Smith; M. D. Richards
£25,890
Commanders, J. D. Atkins, Q.P.M.; S. R. A. Crawshaw;
A. W. F. Hemmingway £23,199

Complaints Investigation Bureau

Deputy Assistant Commissioner, J. M. Sewell, Q.P.M.
.... £25,890
Commander, K. J. Merton £23,199
Principal, J. S. Steele ...... £12,399 to £16,656

Force Inspectorate

Deputy Assistant Commissioner, D. W. Halsey, O.B.E.,
Q.P.M. £25,890
Commanders, B. Dovey, Q.P.M.; R. Paterson, Q.P.M.
.... £23,199
Principal, P. J. Groom .... £12,399 to £16,656

Management Services Department

Director, N. E. Hand .... £19,243 to £23,159
Deputy Director, J. E. Tubb ...... £16,343 to £20,794
Principal, R. C. Vivian .... £12,399 to £16,656
Chief Work Study Officer, J. E. Holbrow
.... £12,399 to £16,656
Principal Psychologist, J. Jones-Lloyd
.... £12,399 to £16,656
Principal Scientific Officers, J. Gaughan; Mrs. S.
Merchant; R. P. Du Parcq ..... £11,343 to £14,931

"E" Department
Establishments and Secretariat

Establishment Officer, M. Lee .... £19,243 to £23,159
Deputy Establishment Officers, J. A. Crutchlow; R. B.
Jones; M. W. Maidment....... £16,343 to £20,794
Principals, P. I. May; A. Clague; B. W. Smyth; J. R.
Hamilton .... £12,399 to £16,656

"F" Department
Finance

Director of Finance, R. V. Clark .. £19,243 to £23,159
Deputy Directors of Finance, J. L. Davies; A. M. J.
Williams; D. Wilson .... £16,343 to £20,794
Assistant Directors of Finance, D. W. Brown; T. S.
Diaper; A. Fearon; R. A. Saines; B. H. Neilson; M.
J. Pratt; C. E. D. Reeves .... £12,399 to £16,656

Supplies and Services Department

Director, N. N. I. Batten .... £16,343 to £20,794
Principals, C. E. Ford; R. W. Smith
.... £12,399 to £16,656
Statistical Advisers, H. P. Redway; J. Custance
.... £12,399 to £16,656
Principal Professional and Technology Officer, I.
Cohen...................... £13,211 to £15,711

Catering Department

Director of Catering, Col. R. R. Owens, O.B.E.
.... £16,343 to £20,794
Deputy Directors, R. J. Downing; N. Pitts; T.
Whittaker .... £14,503 to £16,656

Property Services Department

Director of Property Services, M. L. Belchamber
.... £23,159
Deputy Directors, J. A. Chipchase (*Building*); K. R.
Sewell....................... £18,374 to £20,794
Principal (Administration), D. J. Chambers
.... £12,399 to £16,656
Principal Professional and Technology Officers, C. J.
Brown; J. W. Burton; G. F. Cornelia; P. Fredericks;
J. Grunberg; N. F. Hammond; D. F. Hobart; K. R.
Hunt; I. G. Mowat; P. F. Newton; E. D. Page; M.
Randall; E. G. Ricketts .... £13,211 to £15,711

Chief Engineer's Department

Chief Engineer, Col. J. E. Owen £23,159
Deputy Chief Engineers, N. Boothman; D. Hale,
O.B.E.; J. M. Wardle; D. A. Woolgar
.... £18,374 to £20,794
Principals, H. D. Walton, Q.P.M.; P. R. Williams
.... £12,399 to £16,656

Principal Professional and Technology Officers, R. P.
J. Astington; D. C. Chapman; C. W. Cornock; G.
A. Crocker; G. R. Fuller; I. G. Giles; R. E. Ginman;
J. E. Grant; S. J. Haydock; D. J. Hopkins; D. E.
Keech; A. P. Lambert; R. Matthews; R. G. Ramsay;
G. Sudbury; E. J. Willis; P. J. Wright
.... £13,211 to £15,711

Department of Computing Services

Director of Computing Services, R. G. Gregory
.... £19,243 to £23,159
Deputy Directors of Computing Services, D. K. Dun-
kin; T. Egan .... £16,343 to £20,794
Principals, Miss B. Arnold; M. J. Bloomfield; K. G.
Daly; J. C. Day; I. J. Joyce; J. E. G. King; C. R.
Muid; H. A. Williams .... £12,399 to £16,656

*General Secretary of the Association of Chief Police
Officers of England, Wales and Northern Ireland,*
B. Morrissey, Q.P.M............ £12,399 to £16,656

CITY OF LONDON POLICE
26 Old Jewry, EC2R 8DJ

Commissioner, P. Marshall, Q.P.M. £35,064
Assistant Commissioner, O. Kelly £27,333
Commander, H. J. Moore £23,199
Chief Superintendents, A. Martin (*Administration*);
J. Moss ("*B*" *Div.*); R. Fowlie ("*C*" *Div.*); K.
Richiardi (*Traffic & Communications*); B. A. Tar-
bun (*C.I.D.*); M. Kirkwood (*C.I.D/Fraud*)
.... £20,553 to £21,750

City of London Special Constabulary

Chief Commandant, F. A. D. Ralfe.
Staff Officer, P. Redman.

INDUSTRIAL AND OTHER TRIBUNALS
The Industrial Tribunals

Central Office (England and Wales)
93 Ebury Bridge Road, S.W.1
President, D. S. West-Russell £36,000

Central Office (Scotland)
St. Andrew House, 141 West Nile Street, Glasgow
President, R. C. Hay, W.S................... £32,750

Lands Tribunal
5 Chancery Lane, W.C.2

President, Sir Douglas Frank, Q.C.
Members, J. H. Emlyn Jones, M.B.E.; V. G. Wellings,
Q.C.; W. H. Rees; C. R. Mallett; Wm. Hall, D.F.C.
Registrar, O. L. Mott.

Patents Court (Appellate Section)
Room 163, Chancery Chambers,
Royal Courts of Justice, W.C.2

Judges, The Hon. Mr. Justice Whitford; The Hon.
Mr. Justice Falconer.

Performing Right Tribunal
Room 1509, State House, 66–71 High Holborn, W.C.1

Chairman, A. M. Morison, Q.C.
Secretary, E. J. Barnett.

Transport Tribunal
Golden Cross House,
Duncannon Street, WC2N 4JF

President, Judge Inskip, Q.C.

Parliamentary and Local Government Election
Petitions Office
Room 120, Royal Courts of Justice, W.C.2

Prescribed Officer, J. R. Bickford Smith.

Pensions Appeal Tribunals
St. Dunstan's House, Fetter Lane, EC4A 1BT
President, Sir Geoffrey Briggs.

Immigration Appeal Tribunal
Thanet House, 231 Strand, W.C.2
President, D. L. Neve.
Vice-Presidents, G. W. Farmer; Prof. D. C. Jackson.

SCOTTISH LAW COURTS AND OFFICES

COURT OF SESSION (Established 1532) and HIGH COURT OF JUSTICIARY

The Lord President and Lord Justice General, The Rt. Hon. the Lord Emslie, M.B.E.

INNER HOUSE.—*First Division.*

The Lord President, The Rt. Hon. Lord Emslie,
George Carlyle Emslie, M.B.E. £58,500
Hon. Lord Cameron, Sir John Cameron, K.T., D.S.C.
Rt. Hon. Lord Stott, George Gordon Stott.
Hon. Lord Grieve, William Robertson Grieve, V.R.D.

Second Division

Lord Justice Clerk, The Rt. Hon. Lord Wheatley,
John Wheatley......................... £55,500
Hon. Lord Hunter, John Oswald Mair Hunter, V.R.D.
Hon. Lord Robertson, Ian Macdonald Robertson, T.D.
Hon. Lord Dunpark, Alastair McPherson Johnston,
T.D.

OUTER HOUSE

Hon. Lord Brand, David William Robert Brand
Hon. Lord Kincraig, Robert Smith Johnston
Hon. Lord Maxwell, Peter Maxwell (*seconded to Scottish Law Commission*)
Hon. Lord McDonald, Robert Howat McDonald, M.C.
Rt. Hon. Lord Wylie, Norman Russell Wylie, V.R.D.
Hon. Lord Stewart, Ewan George Francis Stewart,
M.C.
Hon. Lord Ross, Donald MacArthur Ross
Hon. Lord Allanbridge, William Ian Stewart

Hon. Lord Cowie, William Lorn Kerr Cowie
Hon. Lord Jauncey, Charles Eliot Jauncey
Rt. Hon. Lord Murray, Ronald King Murray
Hon. Lord Mayfield, Ian MacDonald, M.C.
Hon. Lord Davidson, Charles Kemp Davidson
Rt. Hon. Lord Mackay of Clashfern, James Peter
Hymers Mackay
(SALARIES: All judges other than the Lord President
and Lord Justice Clerk................. £51,250)

Principal Clerk of Session and Justiciary, A. M.
Campbell .... £19,243 to £23,159
Deputy Principal Clerk of Session and Extractor, H.
S. Foley .... £12,399 to £16,656
*Deputy Principal Clerk (Administration) and of
Justiciary*, W. Howard .... £12,399 to £16,656
Keeper of the Rolls, V. A. Woods .. £12,399 to £16,656
Depute Clerks of Session, Outer House, W. Gillon; M.
Weir; A. Hogg; M. Bonar; N. J. Dowie; I. Smith; J.
A. R. Cowie; T. Fyffe; T. Higgins; E. A. Cumming;
B. Watson; P. J. McGonigle; A. Brown; E. Smith;
W. McCulloch................. £10,079 to £12,518
Depute Clerks of Justiciary, J. Robertson; W. J.
Burns; P. Feeney; J. Cumming £10,079 to £12,518

Crown Office
5/7 Regent Road, Edinburgh

Crown Agent, I. Dean £34,250
Deputy Crown Agent, J. D. Lowe £25,455

Crown Estate Commissioners
10 Charlotte Square, Edinburgh

Crown Estate Receiver, D. B. Cooke.

Companies Registration Office
102 George Street, Edinburgh EH2 3DJ

Registrar, E. T. K. Lougheed.

Sheriff Court of Chancery
16, North Bank Street, Edinburgh

Sheriff of Chancery, Sir Frederick O'Brien, Q.C.

H.M. Commissary Office
16, North Bank Street, Edinburgh

Commissary Clerk, D. B. White.

SCOTTISH COURTS ADMINISTRATION
26–27 Royal Terrace, Edinburgh EH7 5AH

Director, W. A. P. Weatherston.

SCOTTISH LAND COURT
1 Grosvenor Crescent, Edinburgh

Chairman, The Hon. Lord Elliott, M.C.
Members, A. B. Campbell, O.B.E.; A. Gillespie, M.B.E.;
D. D. McDiarmid.

LANDS TRIBUNAL FOR SCOTLAND
1 Grosvenor Crescent, Edinburgh

President, The Hon. Lord Elliott, M.C.
Members, W. Hall, D.F.C. (*full-time*); W. D. C. Andrews, C.B.E., W.S.; T. Finlayson (*part-time*).

SCOTTISH LAW COMMISSION
140 Causewayside, Edinburgh

Chairman, The Hon. Lord Maxwell.
Commissioners, Dr. E. M. Clive; C. G. B. Nicholson
(*full-time*); R. D. D. Bertram, W.S.; J. Murray, Q.C.
(*part-time*).

SHERIFFS PRINCIPAL, SHERIFFS, SHERIFF CLERKS AND PROCURATORS FISCAL IN
SCOTLAND

SHERIFFDOM AND SHERIFF PRINCIPAL	SHERIFFS	SHERIFF CLERKS	PROCURATORS FISCAL
Grampian, Highland and Islands.— S. E. Bell, Q.C.	*Aberdeen, Stonehaven,* A. M. G. Russell, Q.C.; A. L. Stewart; D. J. Risk; R. J. D. Scott; A. G. Johnston.	J. Rodden .... I. P. Smith	M. T. NacNeill. J. T. O'Donnell.
	Banff and Peterhead, N. Mc-Partlin.	J. G. Barr.......... P. J. O'Hara	P. W. Johnston. I. S. McNaughtan.
	Elgin, R. A. Wilson	I. Munro	A. Wither.
	Wick and Dornoch, E. Stewart (*also Tain*).	K. A. MacColl	D. R. Hingston. J. D. McNaughton. T. F. Aitchison.
	Inverness, Lochmaddy, Portree, Stornoway, Dingwall, Tain, W. J. Fulton; D. Booker-Milburn; J. D. A. Fraser.	R. M. Sinclair ...... W. Dunn	A. Haughney. C. S. Mackenzie. W. M. S. Carnegie. H. T. Westwater.
	Kirkwall, Lerwick, A. A. Mac-Donald.	J. Rodden	A. W. Wright. D. J. McLeay.
	Fort William, D. Noble (*also Oban and Campbeltown*)	R. M. Sinclair	J. I. M. MacGillivray.
Tayside, Central and Fife.— R. R. Taylor, Q.C., PH.D.	*Arbroath, Forfar,* S. O. Kermack	A. G. Pryde .... R. G. Davis	C. D. G. Hillary. A. L. Ingram.
	Dundee, E. F. Bowen; G. L. Cox	A. A. Steele	D. R. Smith.
	Perth, J. F. Wheatley	Miss J. Telfer	M. MacPhail.
	Falkirk, A. V. Sheehan; R. E. G. Younger (*also Stirling*)	R. D. S. Mercer	G. E. Scott.
	Stirling, W. C. Henderson	K. MacKenzie	K. Valentine.
	Alloa, W. M. Reid	R. D. Sinclair	Miss M. W. Robertson.
	Cupar, J. C. McInnes (*also Perth*)	Miss A. I. Thompson	R. A. S. Brown.
	Dunfermline, J. S. Forbes; W. M. Reid (*also Alloa*)	J. M. Hay	R. T. Hamilton.
	Kirkcaldy, W. J. Christie; C. R. Macarthur, Q.C.	J. M. Clark	Mrs. I. Guild.
Lothian and Borders.— Sir Frederick O'Brien, Q.C.	*Edinburgh,* N. Macvicar, Q.C.; N. E. D. Thomson; W. T. Hook; K. W. B. Middleton (*also Haddington*); R. D. Ireland, Q.C.; J. L. M. Mitchell; Miss I. A. Poole*; G. W. S. Presslie*; P. G. B. McNeill, PH.D.; Miss H. J. Aronson; R. G. Craik, Q.C.; G. I. W. Shiach.	D. B. White	J. D. Allan.
	Peebles, N. E. D. Thomson (*also Edinburgh*).	D. B. White	F. J. M. Brown.
	Linlithgow, I. D. MacPhail; M. Stone	G. W. Waddell	H. R. Annan.
	Haddington, K. W. B. Middleton (*also Edinburgh*).	D. V. Flynn	I. D. Douglas.
	Jedburgh, Duns, J. V. Paterson.	J. R. Jenkins.......	D. W. Batchelor. J. C. Whitelaw.
	Selkirk, J. V. Paterson	G. C. McKillop	D. J. F. Howdle.
North Strathclyde.— R. A. Bennett, Q.C. (*Temporary*)	*Oban and Campbeltown,* D. Noble (*also Fort William*).	J. Shaw .... J. S. Doig	D. H. McNeill. I. Henderson. J. I. M. MacGillivray.
	Dumbarton, J. P. Murphy; D. Kelbie; F. H. Hamilton*.	J. S. Doig	J. Cardle.
	Paisley, A. K. F. Hunter; H. R. MacLean; R. S. Smith.	J. Shaw	J. B. R. Mackinnon.
	Greenock, J. Irvine Smith; Sir Stephen Young (*also Dunoon and Rothesay*).	A. P. McPherson ...	A. T. W. Wilson. W. D. Stewart. Miss C. McNaughton.
	Kilmarnock, T. M. Croan; D. B. Smith; T. F. Russell.	W. B. Davidson	J. L. McLeod.

*Floating Sheriffs.

Sheriffdom and Sheriff Principal	Sheriffs	Sheriff Clerks	Procurators Fiscal
Glasgow and Strathkelvin.— J. A. Dick, M.C., Q.C.	*Glasgow*, N. D. MacLeod; A. C. Horsfall; J. J. Maguire; A. A. Bell, Q.C.; J. S. Mowat; B. Kearney; G. H. Gordon, Q.C.; A. C. McKay; A. Lothian; J. C. M. Jardine; Mrs. D. J. B. Robertson; B. A. Lockhart; I. G. Pirie; Miss A. L. A. Smith; W. G. Stevenson, Q.C.; G. J. Evans; E. H. Galt; F. J. Keane; I. R. Hamilton, Q.C.; A. C. Henry; J. A. Farrell; C. Smith*.	C. McLay	J. M. Tudhope.
South Strathclyde, Dumfries and Galloway.— M. G. Gillies, T.D., Q.C.	*Hamilton*, J. R. Fiddes, Q.C.; L. S. Lovat; A. C. MacPherson; A. M. Bell; I. A. MacMillan, C.B.E.	B. J. Young	S. W. Lockhart.
	Lanark, R. G. McEwan, Q.C.	J. Gallagher	S. R. Houston.
	Ayr, D. M. K. Grant; N. Gow, Q.C.	E. L. McGowan	N. G. O'Brien.
	Stranraer, Kirkcudbright, N. J. G. Ramsay (*also Dumfries*).	L. McFarlane	F. Walkinshaw. R. F. Gibb.
	Dumfries, K. G. Barr; N. J. G. Ramsay.	W. Jones	J. T. MacDougall.
	Airdrie, A. R. McIlwraith; J. S. Boyle.	H. Findlay	W. G. Carmichael.

*Floating Sheriffs.

BRITISH FORCES BROADCASTING SERVICE
(A division of the Services Sound & Vision Corporation)
King's Buildings, Dean Stanley Street, S.W.1

The service came into existence during the middle of the Second World War to provide radio programmes of entertainment and information, and a link with home. No exact date can be given for the inception of the service because it began in many different places almost simultaneously during 1943.

In 1960 B.F.B.S. was reorganized: a Director was appointed and a Head Office was created in London to co-ordinate the activities of the service and to provide programme material specifically aimed at H.M. Forces, and their dependents overseas, and featuring leading personalities in all walks of life which the stations cannot produce themselves. These programmes are recorded in London and flown to B.F.B.S. stations abroad, as well as to H.M. Ships in many parts of the world, and for the benefit of personnel serving in places such as Belize and Dharan.

Over the years output has increased considerably and the stations in Germany, Cyprus and Gibraltar are now on the air round the clock. In Cyprus and Gibraltar a second channel for minority tastes is also available on medium wave. In Hong Kong and Brunei, B.F.B.S. stations provide services in Gurkhali and in English.

B.F.B.S. Television—a service combining programmes from B.B.C. and I.T.V., with some specially produced, started at Celle, near Hanover on September 18, 1975. When the full transmitter chain is completed, it will serve all the main concentrations of personnel and their families in West Germany.

The Combined Services Entertainment section of B.F.B.S. arranges stage and cabaret shows, as well as solo artistes, to tour Northern Ireland and Commands overseas.

The staff of B.F.B.S. are all civilian, professional broadcasters and engineers. A trainee scheme is in operation, details of which may be obtained from the Head Office. The Service is administered by the Army on behalf of the other two Services, and is financed from Ministry of Defence funds.

On April 1, 1983, B.F.B.S. was merged with the Services Kinema Corporation to form the Services Sound & Vision Corporation (S.S.V.C.). B.F.B.S. now forms the broadcasting division of S.S.V.C., still transmitting under its original title.

B.F.B.S. supplies two programme staff and one engineer in support of Falkland Islands Broadcasting Station.

Managing Director, S.S.V.C., J. Grist.

THE ARMED FORCES
(*See also* "Occurrences During Printing")

MINISTRY OF DEFENCE
Main Building, Whitehall, SW1A 2HB
[01–218 9000]

Secretary of State for Defence, THE RT. HON. MICHAEL HESELTINE, M.P. £38,910
Private Secretary, R. C. Mottram.
Assistant Private Secretaries, N. R. H. Evans; B. P. Neale; S. H. Lowe; Miss W. Anderton.
Parliamentary Private Secretary, N. B. Baker, M.P.
Minister of State for the Armed Forces, THE RT. HON. JOHN STANLEY, M.P. £30,410
Private Secretary, P. M. W. Francis.

Minister of State for Defence Procurement, THE RT. HON. ADAM COURTAULD BUTLER, M.P. £30,410
Private Secretary, Dr. A. S. Kemp.
Parliamentary Under Secretary of State for the Armed Forces, The Lord Trefgarne £20,390
Parliamentary Under Secretary of State for Defence Procurement, J. Lee, M.P. £25,460
Chief of Defence Staff, Field Marshal Sir Edwin Bramall, G.C.B., O.B.E., M.C., A.D.C. (*Gen.*)
Deputy Chief of The Defence Staff, Air Marshal Sir Donald Hall, K.C.B., C.B.E., A.F.C.

Assistant Chief of The Defence Staff (Programmes), Rear-Admiral J. J. R. Oswald.

Assistant Chief of The Defence Staff (Commitments), Air Vice Marshal J. M. D. Sutton, C.B.

Assistant Chief of The Defence Staff (Command, Control, Communications and Information Systems), Major-General G. R. Oehlers.

Director-General of Intelligence, Vice-Admiral Sir Roy Halliday, K.B.E., D.S.C. (retd.).

Deputy Chief of The Defence Staff (Intelligence), Air Marshal Sir Michael Armitage, K.C.B., C.B.E.

Defence Services Secretary, Major-General J. M. Palmer.

Chief of The Naval Staff and First Sea Lord, Admiral Sir John Fieldhouse, G.C.B., G.B.E., A.D.C.

Vice Chief of The Naval Staff, Vice-Admiral Sir Peter Stanford, K.C.B., M.V.O.

Commandant-General Royal Marines, Lt.-Gen. M. C. L. Wilkins, O.B.E.

Chief of The General Staff, General Sir John Stanier, G.C.B., M.B.E., A.D.C. (Gen.).

Vice Chief of The General Staff, Lt.-Gen. Sir James Glover, K.C.B., M.B.E.

Chief of The Air Staff, Air Chief Marshal Sir Keith Williamson, G.C.B., A.F.C., A.D.C.

Vice Chief of The Air Staff, Air Marshal Sir Peter Harding, K.C.B.

Chief Scientific Adviser, Prof. R. O. C. Norman £42,750

Assistant Chief Scientific Advisers, N. H. Hughes (Projects); H. G. R. Robinson, O.B.E. (Research); J. D. Culshaw (Studies); D. C. Fakley, O.B.E. (Nuclear) £27,750

Director, Defence Operational Analysis Establishment, J. D. Culshaw £27,750

Chief Scientist (Royal Navy), Dr. F. A. Johnson £27,750

Chief Scientist (Army), L. R. Gray £27,750

Chief Scientist (Royal Air Force), D. E. Humphries £27,750

Vice Chief of The Defence Staff (Personnel and Logistics), Admiral Sir Peter Herbert, K.C.B., O.B.E.

Assistant Chief of The Defence Staff (Personnel and Logistics), Major-General K. Burch, C.B.E.

Chief of Naval Personnel and Second Sea Lord, Vice-Admiral Sir Simon Cassels, K.C.B., C.B.E.

Naval Secretary, Rear-Admiral W. R. S. Thomas, O.B.E.

Matron-in-Chief, Queen Alexandra's Royal Naval Nursing Service, Miss J. Robertson, R.R.C., Q.H.N.S., Q.A.R.N.N.S.

Director, Women's Royal Naval Service, Commandant D. P. Swallow, W.R.N.S.

Chaplain of The Fleet, Ven. N. D. Jones, Q.H.C.

Chief of Fleet Support, Vice-Admiral A. S. Tippett.

Chief Executive Royal Dockyards, Rear-Admiral A. S. George, C.B. £30,375

General Managers of H.M. Dockyards, J. H. Bedbrook (Devonport); R. Bleasby (Portsmouth); Rear-Admiral J. Burgess (Rosyth).

Principal Director of Planning and Policy, D. Whitwam.

Director of Management Systems and Audit, G. Allin.

Director of Establishments and Personnel, R. J. C. Stone.

Director, Finance, A. G. Maxfield.

Military Secretary, Lt.-Gen. Sir David Mostyn, K.C.B., C.B.E.

Adjutant-General, Gen. Sir Roland Guy, K.C.B., C.B.E., D.S.O.

Quartermaster-General, Gen. Sir Richard Trant, K.C.B.

Chaplain-General, Ven. W. F. Johnston, C.B., Q.H.C.

Matron-in-Chief (Army) and Directorate of Army Nursing, Brig. V. M. Rooke, C.B.E., R.R.C., Q.H.N.S.

Director, Women's Royal Army Corps, Brig. H. G. Meechie, W.R.A.C.

Air Member for Personnel, Air Chief Marshal Sir Thomas Kennedy, K.C.B., A.F.C.

Chaplain-in-Chief, R.A.F., Ven. G. R. Renowden, Q.H.C.

Matron-in-Chief, Princess Mary's R.A.F. Nursing Service, Air Commodore I. J. Harris, C.B., R.R.C.

Director, Women's Royal Air Force, Air Cdre. Helen Renton, C.B., A.D.C., W.R.A.F.

Air Member for Supply and Organisation, Air Marshal Sir Michael Knight, K.C.B., A.F.C.

Permanent Under Secretary of State, Sir Clive Whitmore, K.C.B., C.V.O. £42,750

Second Permanent Under Secretary of State, Sir Ewen Broadbent, K.C.B., C.M.G. £39,500

Deputy Under-Secretaries of State, J. N. H. Blelloch, C.B. (Policy and Programmes); J. D. Bryars, C.B. (Finance and Budget); R. M. Hastie-Smith, C.B. (Civilian Management); C. W. France (Personnel and Logistics); A. R. M. Jaffray, C.B. (Navy); B. E. Robson (Army); D. C. Humphreys (Air) ... £34,250

Assistant Under-Secretaries of State, W. D. Reeves (Resources and Programmes); D. A. Nicholls (Defence Staff); M. Gainsborough (Naval Staff); C. T. McDonnell (General Staff); N. H. Nichols (Air Staff); J. G. Ashcroft (General Finance); J. S. Goldsmith, C.B. (Director-General of Defence Accounts); M. J. V. Bell (Director-General of Management Audit); J. L. L. Imrie (Civilian Management (Administrators)); J. Roberts (Civilian Management (Specialists)); P. Mehew (Civilian Management (C)); J. Dromgoole (Personnel and Logistics); D. A. J. West (Naval Personnel); B. H. Cousins, C.B.E. (Fleet Support); M. J. Culham (Adjutant-General); L. Salthouse (Personnel (Air)); M. J. M. Erritt (Statistics); B. M. Day (Supply and Organisation (Air)); K J. Pritchard, C.B. (Director-General Supplies and Transport (Naval)) £27,750

Commandant, Royal College of Defence Studies, Gen. Sir Michael Gow, K.C.B., O.B.E.

Procurement Executive

Chief of Defence Procurement, D. H. Perry ... £42,750 Private Secretary, Miss E. G. Cassidy.

Deputy Under-Secretary of State (Policy) (P.E.), K. C. Macdonald, C.B. £34,250

Assistant Under-Secretary of State (International and Industrial Policy) J. L. Roberts £27,750

Assistant Under-Secretary of State (Royal Ordnance Factories Bill), B. M. Norbury £27,750

Director-General Quality Assurance, P. Corner £25,000

Director-General of Defence Contracts, B. R. Haigh £27,750

Head of Defence Sales, J. Blyth.

Director-General of Marketing, T. F. W. B. Knapp.

Assistant Under-Secretary, E. Pendlebury (Sales Admin.) £27,750

Controller Research and Development Establishments, Research and Nuclear, C. C. Fielding, C.B. £36,875

Assistant Under-Secretary of State Research and Development Establishments, and Research Administration, W. F. Mumford £27,750

Deputy Controller and Adviser (Research and Technology), Dr. G. G. Pope £34,250

Deputy Controller Research and Development Establishments Resources and Personnel, J. F. Barnes, C.B. £34,250

Director-General Research (General), H. G. R. Robinson £27,750

Director-General Research A and Chief Scientist (Royal Navy), Dr. F. A. Johnson £27,750

Director, Admiralty Marine Technology Establishment, A. B. Mitchell £27,750
Director, Admiralty Surface Weapons Establishment, K. F. Slater £30,375
Director, Admiralty Underwater Weapons Establishment, I. L. Davies, C.B. £30,375
Director, Royal Signals and Radar Establishment, Dr. A. C. Baynham £30,375
Director-General Research B and Chief Scientist (Army), L. R. Gray £27,750
Director, Atomic Weapons Research Establishment, P. G. E. F. Jones £36,650
Director, Chemical Defence Establishment, Dr. A. Bebbington £27,750
Director, Military Vehicles and Engineering Establishment, J. Ellis £30,375
Director, Propellants, Explosives and Rocket Motor Establishment, Dr. B. H. Newman £27,750
Director, Royal Armament Research and Development Establishment, Dr. T. P. McLean £30,375
Director-General Research C and Chief Scientist (Royal Air Force), D. E. Humphries £27,750
Commandant, Aeroplane and Armament Experimental Establishment, Air Commodore G. C. Williams.
Director, Royal Aircraft Establishment, T. H. Kerr, C.B. £34,250
Assistant Controller (Nuclear), Dr. E. D. Dracott
        £28,075
Controller of the Navy, Vice-Admiral Sir Derek Reffell, K.C.B.
Assistant Under-Secretary of State (Material-Naval), C. H. O'D. Alexander £27,750
Principal Director of Navy and Nuclear Contracts, A. J. Figes.............................. £26,236
Deputy Controller Warships, P. W. Jarvis ... £34,250
Director-General Surface Ships, Rear Admiral M. A. Vallis.
Director-General Submarines, S. A. T. Warren
        £27,750
Chief Naval Weapons Systems Engineer, Dr. D. G. Kiely £27,750
Director-General Future Material Projects (Naval), W. G. Sanders......................... £27,750
Deputy Controller Warship Equipment, Rear-Admiral J. E. K. Croydon.
Director-General Surface Weapons, H. Perkins
        £27,750
Director-General Underwater Weapons, Commodore C. L. Wood.
Director-General Marine Engineering/Chief Marine Systems Engineer, Commodore H. L. O. Thompson.
Chief Strategic Systems Executive, Rear Admiral J. S. Grove, C.B., O.B.E.
Deputy Chief Strategic Systems Executive, Cdre. B. C. Foyston.
Master-General of the Ordnance, Lt. General Sir Richard Vincent, K.C.B., D.S.O.
Vice Master-General of the Ordnance, Major-General S. J. Beardsworth, C.B.
Assistant Under-Secretary of State (Ordnance), A. W. Stephens £27,750

Principal Director of Contracts (Ordnance), R. G. Woodman £26,236
Director-General Guided Weapons and Electronics, Dr. P. G. Smith......................... £27,750
Director-General of Fighting Vehicles and Engineer Equipment, Major-General J. H. B. Dent, C.B., O.B.E.
Director-General of Weapons (Army), Major-General R. J. Crossley, C.B.E.
Controller, Aircraft, Air Chief Marshal Sir John Rogers, K.C.B., C.B.E.
Assistant Under-Secretary of State/Air (Procurement Executive), J. M. Moss £27,750
Principal Director of Contracts/Air, B. J. Slade
        £26,236
Deputy Controller Aircraft, I. H. Johnston, C.B.
        £34,250
Director-General Engines (Procurement Executive), M. C. Neale £27,750
Director-General Aircraft 1, D. M. Spiers £27,750
Director-General Aircraft 2, Air Vice-Marshal J. A. Porter, O.B.E.
Director-General Aircraft 3, C. Redmayne ... £27,750
Deputy Controller Aircraft Weapons and Electronics, P. R. Wallis £30,375
Director-General of Air Weapons Electronic Systems, Dr. T. Buckley £27,750
Director-General of Strategic Electronic Systems, Air Vice-Marshal F. M. Holroyd £27,750
Chairman Royal Ordnance Factories, F. Clarke
        £39,500
Managing Director Royal Ordnance Factories, W. Meakin, C.B. £34,250
Managing Directors, R.O.F.s, T. Truman (*Explosives*); H. Butterworth (*Ammunition*); R. L. Goldsmith (*Weapons & Fighting Vehicles*); S. Carroll (*Small Arms*) £27,750

Meteorological Office

London Road, Bracknell, Berks.
[Bracknell: 20242]
The Meteorological Office is the State Meteorological Service. It forms part of the Ministry of Defence, the Director General being ultimately responsible to the Secretary of State for Defence.

Except for the common services provided by other government departments as part of their normal functions, the cost of the Meteorological Office is borne by Defence Votes.

Of the expenditure chargeable to Defence Votes about £32,900,000 represents expenditure associated with staff and £29,400,000 on stores, communications and miscellaneous services. About £19,700,000 is recovered from outside bodies for special services rendered, sales of meteorological equipment, etc.

Director-General, Prof. J. T. Houghton, C.B.E., D.Phil., F.R.S. £34,250
Director of Research, P. Goldsmith £26,236
Director of Services, F. H. Bushby £27,750

THE ROYAL NAVY

THE QUEEN

Admirals of the Fleet

H.R.H. The Prince Philip, Duke of Edinburgh, K.G., P.C., K.T., O.M., G.B.E., *born* June 10, 1921	Jan. 15, 1953
Sir Varyl Begg, G.C.B., D.S.O., D.S.C., *born* Oct. 1, 1908	Aug. 12, 1968
The Lord Hill-Norton, G.C.B., *born* Feb. 8, 1915	March 12, 1971
Sir Michael Pollock, G.C.B., M.V.O., D.S.C., *born* Oct. 19, 1916	March 1, 1974
Sir Edward Ashmore, G.C.B., D.S.C., *born* Dec. 11, 1919	Feb. 9, 1977
The Lord Lewin, K.G., G.C.B., M.V.O., D.S.C., *born* Nov. 19, 1920	July 6, 1979
Sir Henry Leach, G.C.B., *born* Nov. 18, 1923	Dec. 1, 1982

Admirals

Cassidi, Sir Desmond, G.C.B., A.D.C., (*C.-in-C. Naval Home Command*).

Fieldhouse, Sir John, G.C.B., G.B.E., A.D.C., (*First Sea Lord and Chief of Naval Staff*).

Staveley, Sir William, G.C.B., (*C.-in-C. Fleet, Allied C.-in-C. Channel and C.-in-C. Eastern Atlantic Area*).

Herbert, Sir Peter, K.C.B., O.B.E., (*Vice-Chief of the Defence Staff, Personnel and Logistics*).

Bryson, Sir Lindsay, K.C.B., (*Controller of the Navy*).

Vice-Admirals

Cassels, Sir Simon, K.C.B., C.B.E., (*Second Sea Lord and Chief of Naval Personnel and Admiral President Royal Naval College Greenwich*).

Hallifax, Sir David, K.B.E., (*Deputy Supreme Allied Commander Atlantic*).

Cadell, J. F., (*Chief of Staff to Commander Allied Naval Forces Southern Europe*).

Anson, Sir Edward, K.C.B., (*Chief of Staff to Commander-in-Chief Fleet*).

Brown, Sir David, K.C.B., (*Flag Officer, Plymouth, Port Admiral Devonport, Commander Central Sub Area Eastern Atlantic and Commander Plymouth Sub Area Channel*).

Stanford, Sir Peter, K.C.B., M.V.O., (*Vice Chief Naval Staff*).

Tippet, Sir Anthony, K.C.B., (*Chief of Fleet Support*).

Reffell, Sir Derek, K.C.B., (*Controller of the Navy*).

Hunt, N. J. S., M.V.O., (*Flag Officer Scotland and Northern Ireland and Port Admiral Rosyth*).

Woodward, Sir John, K.C.B.

Rear-Admirals

Haslam, Sir David, K.B.E., C.B., (*Hydrographer of the Navy*).

Greening, P. W., (*Flag Officer Royal Yachts*).

Fitch, R. G. A. (*Flag Officer Third Flotilla and Commander Anti-Submarine Group Two*).

Grove, J. S., C.B., O.B.E., (*Chief Strategic Systems Executive and Chief Naval Engineering Officer*).

Eckersly-Maslin, D. M., (*Assistant, Command, Control, Communications and Information Systems*).

Walters, J. W. T., (*Assistant Chief of the Defence Staff (Personnel and Logistics)*).

Warsop, J. C., (*Flag Officer and Port Admiral Portsmouth*).

Macey, D. E., C.B., (*Deputy Assistant, Chief of Staff (Operations) on the Staff of the Supreme Allied Commander Europe*).

Gerken, R. W. F., C.B.E., (*Director-General Naval Manpower and Training*).

Croydon, J. E. K. (*Controllerate (Warship Equipment)*).

Dalton, G. T. J. O., (*Assistant Chief Naval Staff (Policy)*).

Webster, J. M., (*Chief of Staff to C.-in-C. Fleet*).

Symons, P. J., (*Commander British Navy Staff Washington Naval Attache Washington UK National Liaison Representative to SACLANT*).

Higgins, W. A., C.B.E., (*Director-General Naval Personnel Services and Chief Naval Supply and Secretariat Officer*).

Lockyer, A. A., M.V.O., (*Chief Staff Officer (Engineering) to Commander-in-Chief Fleet*).

Marsh, G. G. W., O.B.E., (*Deputy Controller Warship Equipment*).

Oswald, J. J. R., (*Assistant Chief of the Defence Staff (Programmes)*).

Baxter, G. A., (*Senior Naval Member of the Directing Staff, Royal College of Defence Studies and Chief Naval Instructor Officer*).

Bowen, F., (*Special Project Director, S.R.A. Systems*).

Vallings, G. M. F., (*Flag Officer and Port Admiral Gibraltar and COMGIBMED*).

Vallis, M. A., (*Director-General Surface Ships and Senior Naval Representative Bath*).

Thomas, W. R. S., O.B.E., (*Naval Secretary*).

Middleton, L. E., D.S.O.

Barker, J. P., (*Chief of Staff to Commander-in-Chief Naval Home Command*).

Simpson, M. F., (*Director-General Aircraft (Navy)*).

Black, J. J., D.S.O., M.B.E., (*Assistant Chief of Naval Staff (Operational Requirements)*).

MacLean, E., (*Director-General Fleet Support Policy and Services*).

Thompson, H. L. O., (*Director-General Marine Engineering*).

Bathurst, D. B., (*Flag Officer Second Flotilla*).

Burgess, J., M.V.O., (*Managing Director, H.M. Dockyard, Rosyth*).

Heaslip, R. G., (*Deputy Asst. Chief of Staff (Operations) on the staff of the Supreme Allied Commander, Europe*).

Hogg, R. I. T., (*Flag Officer First Flotilla*).

Livesay, M. H., (*Flag Officer Sea Training*).

Snow, K. A., (*Asst. Chief of Naval Staff (Operations)*).

HER MAJESTY'S FLEET

Type/Class	No.	Operational or engaged in preparing for service or trials or training	No.	Undergoing restorative or major refit or conversion, on standby etc.
Submarines				
Polaris	3	Renown, Repulse, Revenge	1	Resolution
Fleet	10	Valiant, Warspite, Churchill, Courageous, Swiftsure, Sceptre, Spartan, Splendid, Trafalgar, Turbulent*	3	Conqueror, Superb, Sovereign
Oberon Class	8	Orpheus, Oberon, Otter, Oracle, Ocelot, Osiris, Opossum, Opportune	5	Odin, Olympus, Onslaught, Onyx, Otus
Porpoise Class	2	Sealion, Walrus		
ASW Carrier	2	Invincible, Illustrious		
ASW/Commando Carriers	1	Hermes†		
Assault Ships	1	Fearless†	1	Intrepid
Guided-Missile Destroyers				
County	3	Glamorgan, Fife, Antrim		
Type 82	1	Bristol		
Type 42	12	Birmingham, Cardiff, Newcastle, Glasgow, Exeter, Southampton, Nottingham, Liverpool, Manchester, Gloucester*, Edinburgh*, York*		

Frigates

Type 22	6	Broadsword, Battleaxe, Brilliant, Brazen, Boxer, Beaver*		
Type 21	5	Active, Ambuscade, Arrow, Alacrity, Avenger	1	Amazon
Leander Class	22	Leander, Ajax, Galatea, Naiad, Aurora, Euryalus, Arethusa, Cleopatra, Phoebe, Sirius, Argonaut, Minerva, Danae, Penelope, Andromeda, Charybdis, Achilles, Diomede, Apollo, Ariadne, Hermione, Jupiter	2	Scylla, Juno
Rothesay Class	6	Rothesay, Plymouth, Yarmouth, Lowestoft, Berwick, Falmouth		
Type 12	1	Torquay		

Offshore Patrol

Island Class	7	Alderney, Anglesey, Guernsey, Jersey, Lindisfarne, Orkney, Shetland		
Castle Class	2	Dumbarton Castle, Leeds Castle		

MCMVs

Minesweepers Ton Class	13	Alfriston, Bickington, Crichton, Cuxton, Hodgeston, Lewiston, Pollington, Shavington, Soberton, Stubbington, Upton, Walkerton, Wotton		
Fleet	4	Waveney, Carron*, Helford*, Dovey*		
Minehunters Ton Class	14	Bildeston, Bossington, Brereton, Brinton, Bronington, Gavinton, Iveston, Kedleston, Kellington, Kirkliston, Maxton, Nurton, Sheraton, Wilton	1	Hubberston
Hunt Class	8	Brecon, Brocklesby, Cattistock, Cottesmore, Dulverton, Ledbury, Middleton*, Chiddingfold*		
Hovercraft			1	BH7

Patrol Craft

Bird Class	4	Cygnet, Kingfisher, Peterel†, Sandpiper†	
Loyal Class	2	Alert, Vigiliant	
20m Class	5	Attacker, Fencer, Hunter, Chaser, Striker	
Coastal Patrol Craft	5	Beachampton, Monkton, Wasperton, Wolverton, Yarnton	
Peacock Class	3	Peacock, Plover, Starling*	
Falkland Islands Patrol Vessels	3	Protector, Guardian, Sentinel	

Support Ships

Submarine Tender	1	Wakeful
MCM Support Ship	1	Abdiel
Seabed Operations Vessel	1	Challenger*

Royal Yacht/Hospital Ship .. 1 Britannia

Training Ships

Ex Survey Vessels	2	Waterwitch, Woodlark
Fleet Tenders	4	Manly, Mentor, Messina, Millbrook

Ice Patrol Ship .... 1 Endurance

Survey Ships .... 12 Beagle, Bulldog, Echo, Egeria, Enterprise, Fawn, Fox, Hecate, Hecla, Herald, Hydra, Gleaner

Notes:

(i) This table includes ships due for completion or disposal during the course of 1984/85 and the numbers of each type are not therefore an accurate indication of the ships available at any one time. It does not include those ships solely engaged in harbour training duties.

(ii) Ships marked * were under construction on 1 April 1984 and are planned to enter service during 1984/85.

(iii) Ships marked † are engaged partially on trials or training.

(iv) Ships approved during 1983/84 for disposal: Dido, Rhyl, Londonderry, Gurkha, Tartar, Zulu, St. David, Venturer, Crofton, Droxford.

Royal Naval Auxiliary Service.—The Royal Naval Auxiliary Service (RNXS) is a uniformed civilian volunteer service, administered by the Ministry of Defence and trained by the Royal Navy to operate at ports and anchorages, for duty in emergencies and war. RNXS units are situated on the coasts of the United Kingdom and organised and run by the Area Flag Officers. The role of the RNXS is to assist with the defence of ports and anchorages by manning local headquarters and supporting the Naval Control of Shipping Organisation. The strength is 2,800.

ROYAL MARINES

The Corps of Royal Marines, about 7,700 strong, first formed in 1664, is part of the Naval Service. The Royal Marines provide Britain's sea soldiers and in particular 3 Commando Brigade Royal Marines, two thirds of which is trained and equippped for arctic warfare. Royal Marines also serve in H.M. Ships, provide landing craft crews, special boat sections and other detachments for naval and amphibious operations. They also provide the Naval Band Service.

The Royal Marines Reserve of about 1,200 volunteers consists of five main centres in London, Bristol, Liverpool, Newcastle and Glasgow.
Commandant-General, Royal Marines, M. C. L. Wilkins, O.B.E.
Major-Generals, J. C. Hardy, M.V.O. (*H.Q. ARNFORTH*); J. M. C. Garrod, O.B.E. (*Chief of Staff*); J. H. A. Thompson, C.B., O.B.E. (*Training, Reserve and Special Forces*); J. St. J. Grey (*Commando Forces*).

QUEEN ALEXANDRA'S ROYAL NAVAL NURSING SERVICE (Q.A.R.N.N.S.)

The first nursing sisters were appointed to naval hospitals in 1884 and the service gained its current title under the patronage of Queen Alexandra in 1902. Nursing ratings were introduced in 1960 and from 1982 a number of men have taken the opportunity to join Q.A.R.N.N.S. as both officers and ratings. Still largely based at the Royal Naval Hospitals, Q.A.R.N.N.S. continue their responsibility for the health and fitness of naval personnel. The strength is about 600.
Patron, H.R.H. Princess Alexandra.
Matron-in-Chief and Director of Naval Nursing Services, Miss J. Robertson, R.R.C., Q.H.N.S., Q.A.R.N.N.S.

WOMEN'S ROYAL NAVAL SERVICE (W.R.N.S.)

Originally founded in 1917, the W.R.N.S. were temporarily disbanded between World Wars I and II. The contribution of the Service is now firmly established as a professional and integral part of the Royal Navy with personnel serving in the United Kingdom and abroad in a wide range of specialist roles. Although W.R.N.S. do not serve at sea, they provide an essential nucleus of about 3,000 trained personnel ashore in order to release men to H.M. Ships.
Chief Commandant, H.R.H. Princess Anne.
Director W.R.N.S., Commandant D. P. Swallow, W.R.N.S.

THE ARMY

THE QUEEN

Field-Marshals

H.R.H. The Prince Philip, Duke of Edinburgh, K.G., P.C., K.T., O.M., G.B.E., Field-Marshal, Australian Military Forces, Col.-in-Chief, Q.R.I.H., D.E.R.R., Q.O. Hldrs., Corps of Royal Electrical and Mechanical Engineers, A.C.F., Col. G.G., *born* June 10, 1921 .... Jan. 15, 1953
The Lord Harding of Petherton, G.C.B., C.B.E., D.S.O., M.C., *born* Feb. 10, 1896 .... July 21, 1953
Sir Richard A. Hull, K.G., G.C.B., D.S.O., *born* May 7, 1907 .... Feb. 8, 1965
Sir A. James H. Cassels, G.C.B., K.B.E., D.S.O., *born* Feb. 28, 1907 .... Feb. 29, 1968
The Lord Carver, G.C.B., C.B.E., D.S.O., M.C., *born* April 24, 1915 .... July 18, 1973
Sir Roland Gibbs, G.C.B., C.B.E., D.S.O., M.C., *born* June 22, 1921................................ July 13, 1979
Sir Edwin Bramall, G.C.B., O.B.E., M.C. (*Chief of Defence Staff*), *born* Dec. 18, 1923 .... Aug. 1, 1982

Generals

Creasey, Sir Timothy, K.C.B., O.B.E., Col. Comdt. R. Anglian (*C.D.S. & Chief of Operations Sultan of Oman's Armed Forces*).

Stanier, Sir John, G.C.B., M.B.E., A.D.C. (*Gen.*), Col. Comdt. R.A.C. (*Chief of the General Staff*).

Gow, Sir Michael, G.C.B., Col. Comdt. Int. Corps (*Comdt. Royal College of Defence Studies*).

Kitson, Sir Frank, K.C.B., C.B.E., M.C., A.D.C. (*Gen.*), Col. Comdt. R.G.J., Col. Comdt. 2 R.G.J. (*C.-in-C. U.K. Land Forces*).

Bagnall, Sir Nigel, K.C.B., C.V.O., M.C., Col. Comdt. A.P.T.C. (*Commander Northern Army Group and C.-in-C. B.A.O.R.*).

Morony, Sir Thomas, K.C.B., O.B.E., A.D.C. (*Gen.*), Col. Comdt. R.A. (*U.K. MILREP N.A.T.O.*).

Lawson, Sir Richard, K.C.B., D.S.O., O.B.E. (*C.-in-C. Allied Forces Northern Europe*).

Guy, Sir Roland, K.C.B., C.B.E., D.S.O., A.D.C. (*Gen.*), Col. Comdt. 1 R.G.J., Col. Comdt. S.A.S.C. (*Adjutant General*).

Burgess, Sir Edward, K.C.B., O.B.E., Col. Comdt. R.A. (*DSACEUR*).

Trant, Sir Richard, K.C.B., Col. Comdt. R.A., Col. Comdt. R.A.O.C., Col. Comdt. R.A.E.C. (*Quartermaster General*).

Lieutenant-Generals

Reay, Sir Alan, K.B.E., Q.H.P., M.B., Ch.B., F.R.C.P. (*Director General Army Medical Services*).

Glover, Sir James, K.C.B., M.B.E., Col. Comdt. 3 R.G.J., Col. Comdt. R.M.P. (*Vice-Chief of the General Staff*).

Boswell, Sir Alexander, K.C.B., C.B.E., Col. Comdt. The Scottish Division (*G.O.C. Scotland & Governor of Edinburgh Castle*).

Richardson, Sir Robert, K.C.B., C.V.O., C.B.E., Col. R.S. (*G.O.C. Northern Ireland*).

Farndale, Sir Martin, K.C.B., Col. Comdt. R.A. and A.A.C. (*Commander I (B.R.) Corps*).

Mostyn, Sir David, K.C.B., C.B.E., Col. Comdt. The Light Division, Col. Comdt. A.L.C. (*Military Secretary*).

Howlett, Sir Geoffrey, K.B.E., M.C., Col. Comdt. P.A.R.A., Col. Comdt. A.C.C. (*G.O.C. South East District*).

Akehurst, Sir John, K.C.B. C.B.E., Dep. Col. R. Anglian (*Comd. U.K. Fd. Army & Insp. Gen. T.A.*).

Vincent, Sir Richard, K.C.B., D.S.O., Col. Comdt. R.A. and R.E.M.E. (*Master General of the Ordnance*).

Huxtable, Sir Charles, K.C.B., C.B.E., Col. Comdt. The King's Division, Col. D.W.R. (*Comd. Training Establishments*).

Major-Generals

Palmer, J. M., Col. 14/20H (*Defence Services Secretary*).

Langley, Sir Desmond, K.C.V.O., M.B.E. (*C.B.F. Cyprus & Administrator Sovereign Base Area*).

Watts, J. P. B. C., C.B.E., M.C. (*Comd. Sultan of Oman's Land Forces*).

Boorman, D., C.B., Col. 6 G.R. (*C.B.F. Hong Kong & Major General Brigade of Gurkhas*).

Gerrard-Wright, R. E. J., C.B.E., Col. Comdt. The Queen's Division (*Director Territorial Army & Cadets*).

Swindells, G. M. G. (*Director Management Support (Intelligence)*).

Chapple, J. L., C.B.E. (*Director Military Operations*).

Matthews, M., C.B. (*Engineer-in-Chief (Army)*).

Reynolds, M. F., C.B. (*Assistant Director, Plans & Policy Division, International Military Staff N.A.T.O.*).

Arthur, J. N. S., Col. Comdt. M.P.S.C., Col. Scots D.G. (*Director of Personal Services (Army)*).

Dent, J. H. B., C.B., O.B.E. (*Director General Fighting Vehicles & Equipment*).

Lane, B. M., C.B., O.B.E., Col. L.I. (*G.O.C. South West District*).

Chiswell, P. I., C.B.E. (*G.O.C. Wales*).

Kenny, B. L. G., C.B.E., Col. Comdt. R.A.V.C. (*Director Army Staff Duties*).

Reilly, J. C., D.S.O., Dep. Col. R.R.F. (*Director Battle Development*).

Thorne, Sir David, K.B.E., Dep. Col. R. Anglian (*Comd. 1 Armd. Div.*).

Woodford, D. M., C.B.E., Col. R.R.F. (*Comdt. Joint Service Defence College*).

Gray, M. S., O.B.E. (*Chief of Staff H.Q. B.A.O.R.*).

Pascoe, R. A., M.B.E. (*Chief of Staff United Kingdom Land Forces*).

Walker, A. K. F., Col. Comdt. R.T.R.

Boam, T. A., C.B.E. (*Head of British Defence Staff Washington*).

Boyne, J., M.B.E. (*Vice Adjutant General & Director of Manning*).

Carleton-Smith, M. E., C.B.E. (*Head of British Defence Staff & Defence Adviser CANBERRA*).

Davis, B. W., C.B.E. (*Vice Quartermaster General*).

Dennis, A. W., O.B.E. (*Director Military Assistant Office*).

Keightley, R. C. (*Comdt. R.M.A.S.*).

MacMillan, J. R. A., C.B.E., Col. Gordons (*G.O.C. Eastern District*).

Palmer, C. P. R., C.B.E., Col. A. & S.H. (*Comdt. Staff College*).

Watkins, G. H., O.B.E. (*Comd. The Artillery Division*).

Eyre, J. A. C. G., C.V.O., C.B.E. (*G.O.C. London District & Major General Comd. The Household Division*).

Rougier, C. J. (*Director Army Training*).

Steele, M. C. M., M.B.E. (*Chief Joint Liaison Organisation Bonn*).

Bartlett, J. L. (*Paymaster in Chief*).

Davies, P. M., O.B.E. (*G.O.C. North West District*).

Palmer, T. B., C.B. (*Director General of Electrical and Mechanical Engineering*).

Whalley, W. L. (*Director General Ordnance Services*).

Pryn, W. J., C.B., Q.H.S. (*Director of Army Surgery*).

Pearson, R. M., M.B.E., A.H.D.S. (*Director of Army Dental Services*).

Benbow, R. (*Signal Officer in Chief (Army)*).

Bowman, J. F. (*Director Army Legal Services*).

Goodman, J. D. W. (*Director Army Air Corps*).

Gordon Lennox, B. C., M.B.E. (*G.O.C. Berlin*).

New, L. A. W., C.B.E. (*Assistant Chief of the General Staff (Operational Requirements)*).

Shortis, C. T., C.B.E., Col. Comdt. P.O.W. Div. (*Director of Infantry*).

Stibbon, J. J., O.B.E. (*Comdt. R.M.C.S.*).

Waters, C. J., C.B.E. (*Comd. 4 Armd. Div.*).

Webster, B. C., C.B.E. (*Director of Army Quartering*).

Welsh, P. M., O.B.E., M.C. (*President Regular Commissions Board*).

Braggins, D. H. (*Director General of Transport & Movements*).

Miller, D. E., C.B.E., M.C., Col. King's Own Border (*Chief of Staff LIVE OAK*).

Pank, J. D. G. (*Comd. Land Forces Northern Ireland*).

Spacie, K., O.B.E.

Ryan, D. E., L.L.B. (*Director of Army Education*).

Thompson, C. N. (*Director Military Survey*).

Airy, C. J., C.B.E. (*Senior Army Member R.C.D.S.*).

Inge, P. A. (*G.O.C. North East District & Comd. 2 Inf. Div.*).

McGuinness, B. P. (*G.O.C. Western District*).

Paton, D. S., C.B.E., Q.H.P. (*Comd. Medicine B.A.O.R.*).

Moffat, W. C., O.B.E., Q.H.S. (*Comdt. R.A.M.C. Training Group & Principal Medical Officer U.K.L.F.*).

Livesey, B., Q.H.S. (*Comdt. Royal Army Medical College*).

Roberts, D. M., Q.H.P. (*Director Army Medicine*).

Burch, K., C.B.E. (*Assistant Chief Defence Staff (Personnel & Logistics)*).

Yeoman, A. (*Comd. Communications B.A.O.R.*).

Cornock, C. G., M.B.E. (*Director Royal Artillery*).

Crossley, R. J., C.B.E. (*Director General Weapons (Army)*).

Oehlers, G. R. (*Assistant Chief Defence Staff (Communication & Information Systems)*).

Billiere, P. E. de la C. de la, C.B.E., D.S.O., M.C. (*C.B.F. Falkland Islands*).

Cooper, S. C. (*Director Royal Armoured Corps*).

Ramsbotham, D. J., C.B.E. (*Comd. 3 Armd. Div.*).

CONSTITUTION OF THE BRITISH ARMY

The Regular Forces include the following Arms, Branches and Corps. Soldiers' Record Offices are shown at the end of each group; records of officers are maintained at the Ministry of Defence.

The Arms

Household Cavalry.—The Life Guards; The Blues and Royals (Royal Horse Guards and 1st Dragoons). *Records,* Horse Guards, London, S.W.1.

Royal Armoured Corps.—Cavalry Regiments: 1st The Queen's Dragoon Guards; The Royal Scots Dragoon Guards (Carabiniers and Greys); 4th/7th Royal Dragoon Guards; 5th Royal Inniskilling Dragoon Guards; The Queen's Own Hussars; The Queen's Royal Irish Hussars; 9th/12th Royal Lancers (Prince of Wales's); The Royal Hussars (Prince of Wales's Own), 13th/18th Royal Hussars (Queen Mary's Own); 14th/20th King's Hussars; 15th/19th

The King's Royal Hussars; 16th/5th The Queen's Royal Lancers; 17th/21st Lancers; Royal Tank Regiment comprising four regular regiments. *Records,* Queen's Park, Chester.

Artillery.—Royal Regiment of Artillery. *Records,* Imphal Barracks, Fulford Road, York.

Engineers.—Corps of Royal Engineers. *Records,* Ditchling Road, Brighton.

Signals.—Royal Corps of Signals. *Records,* Balmore House, Caversham, Reading.

Infantry.—The Brigades/Regiments of Infantry of the Line are grouped in Divisions as follows:—

Guard's Division—Grenadier, Coldstream, Scots, Irish and Welsh Guards. Divisional HQ: HQ Household Division, Horse Guards, S.W.1. *Depot:* Pirbright Camp, Brookwood, Surrey. *Records:* The Foot Guards Regimental Manning and Record Office, Wellington Barracks, Birdcage Walk, London, S.W.1.

Scottish Division—The Royal Scots (The Royal Regiment); The Royal Highland Fusiliers (Princess Margaret's Own Glasgow and Ayrshire Regiment); The King's Own Scottish Borderers; The Black Watch (Royal Highland Regiment); Queen's Own Highlanders (Seaforth and Camerons); The Gordon Highlanders; The Argyll and Sutherland Highlanders (Princess Louise's). *Divisional HQ*, The Castle, Edinburgh. *Depôts*, Scottish Divisional Depôts, Glencorse, Milton Bridge, Midlothian and Gordon Barracks, Bridge of Don, Aberdeen. *Records*, Imphal Barracks, Fulford, York.

Queen's Division—The Queen's Regiment, The Royal Regiment of Fusiliers, The Royal Anglian Regiment. *Divisional HQ*, Bassingbourn Barracks, Royston, Herts. *Depôt*, Bassingbourn Barracks, Royston, Herts. *Records*, Higher Barracks, Exeter, Devon.

King's Division—The King's Own Royal Border Regiment, The King's Regiment; The Prince of Wales's Own Regiment of Yorkshire; The Green Howards (Alexandra, Princess of Wales's Own Yorkshire Regiment); The Royal Irish Rangers (27th (Inniskilling) 83rd and 87th); The Queen's Lancashire Regiment; The Duke of Wellington's Regiment (West Riding). *Divisional HQ*, Imphal Barracks, York. *Depôts*, The King's Division Depôt (Yorkshire), Queen Elizabeth Barracks, Strensall, Yorks. The King's Division Depôt (Royal Irish Rangers), St. Patrick's Barracks, Ballymena, Northern Ireland. *Records*, Imphal Barracks, Fulford, York.

Prince of Wales's Division—The Devonshire and Dorset Regiment; The Cheshire Regiment; The Royal Welch Fusiliers, The Royal Regiment of Wales (24th/ 41st Foot); The Gloucestershire Regiment; The Worcestershire and Sherwood Foresters Regiment (29th/45th Foot); The Royal Hampshire Regiment; The Staffordshire Regiment (Prince of Wales's); The Duke of Edinburgh's Royal Regiment (Berkshire and Wiltshire). *Divisional HQ*, Whittington Barracks, Lichfield, Staffs. *Depôts*, Mercian Depôt, The Prince of Wales's Division, Whittington Barracks, Lichfield, Staffs; Welsh Depôt, The Prince of Wales's Division, Cwrt-y-Gollen, Crickhowell, Powys. *Records*, Imphal Barracks, Fulford, York.

Light Division—The Light Infantry; The Royal Green Jackets. *Divisional HQ*, Peninsula Barracks, Winchester, Hants. *Depôts*, The Light Division Depôt (Shrewsbury), Sir John Moore Barracks, Copthorne, Shrewsbury, Salop. The Light Division Depôt (Winchester), Peninsula Barracks, Winchester, Hants. *Records*, Higher Barracks, Exeter.

Brigade of Gurkhas—2nd King Edward VII's Own Gurkha Rifles (The Sirmoor Rifles); 6th Queen Elizabeth's Own Gurkha Rifles; 7th Duke of Edinburgh's Own Gurkha Rifles; 10th Princess Mary's Own Gurkha Rifles, The Queen's Gurkha Engineers, Queen's Gurkha Signals, Gurkha Transport Regt. *Brigade HQ*, H.M.S. *Tamar*, Hong Kong, B.F.P.O. 1. *Depôt*, Training Depôt, Brigade of Gurkhas, Malaya Lines, Sek Kong, B.F.P.O. 1. *Records*, Record Office, Brigade of Gurkhas, Hong Kong, B.F.P.O. 1.

The Parachute Regiment (Three regular battalions)—*Depôt*, Browning Barracks, Aldershot, Hants. *Records*, Higher Barracks, Exeter.

Special Air Service Regiment—*Regimental HQ*, Duke of York's Headquarters, Sloane Square, S.W.3. *Depôt*, Bradbury Lines, Hereford. *Records*, Higher Barracks, Exeter, Devon.

Army Air Corps—Regimental H.Q. and Depôt, Middle Wallop, Hants. *Records*, Higher Barracks, Exeter.

The Services

Royal Army Chaplain's Department—Regimental H.Q. and Depôt, Bagshot Park, Surrey.

Royal Corps of Transport, *Records*, Ore Place, Hastings.

Royal Army Medical Corps, Royal Army Dental Corps, Queen Alexandra's Royal Army Nursing Corps, and Women's Royal Army Corps. *Records*, Queen's Park, Chester.

Royal Army Ordnance Corps, Corps of Royal Electrical and Mechanical Engineers. *Records*, Glen Parva Barracks, Saffron Road, Wigston, Leicester.

Small Arms School Corps. *Records*, Higher Barracks, Exeter.

General Service Corps. *Records*, Imphal Barracks, Fulford Road, York.

Corps of Royal Military Police, Royal Army Pay Corps, Royal Army Veterinary Corps, Royal Pioneer Corps, Intelligence Corps, Army Catering Corps, Military Provost Staff Corps, Royal Army Educational Corps, Army Physical Training Corps, Army Legal Corps, Band of the Royal Military Academy, Sandhurst, Officers Training Corps. *Records*, Higher Barracks, Exeter, Devon.

The Territorial Army (T.A.) is designed to provide a highly trained and well equipped force which will complete the Regular Army order of battle in a time of national emergency. Its establishment is approximately 75,000 and it is planned that this will rise to 86,000 by 1990. A new element of the T.A., The Home Service Force, designed to produce a low cost guard force, is being expanded to some 5,000 posts by 1990.

The Ulster Defence Regiment (U.D.R.) was raised under authority of the *U.D.R. Act* 1969 and assists the Regular Army in Northern Ireland. H.Q., Magheralave Road, Lisburn, Co. Antrim. *Records*, Imphal Barracks, Fulford Road, York.

QUEEN ALEXANDRA'S ROYAL ARMY NURSING CORPS (Q.A.R.A.N.C.)

Founded in 1902 as Q.A.I.M.N.S., became Q.A.R.A.N.C. in 1959. Q.A.R.A.N.C. has trained nurses for the register and roll since 1950 and has four other employment categories. There was an introduction of a non-nursing officer element in 1959 for personnel work. The Q.A.R.A.N.C. provides service in military hospitals world-wide—United Kingdom (including N. Ireland), B.A.O.R., Hong Kong, Dharan, Cyprus, Falkland Islands and Belize.

Colonel-in-Chief, H.R.H. Princess Margaret.

WOMEN'S ROYAL ARMY CORPS (W.R.A.C.)

The W.R.A.C. was formed on February 1, 1949 as a Corps of the Regular Army. The Corps predecessors were Q.M.A.A.C. in World War I, and A.T.S. in World War II. The present role of the W.R.A.C. is to be organised and trained, as an integral part of the Army, to carry out those tasks for which its members are best suited and qualified, so that it will contribute to the maximum efficiency of the Army as a whole. The Corps is approximately 8,500 (Regular and T.A.) and is employed by 36 sponsors in 60 employments in 500 units world-wide in the British Army.

Commandant-in-Chief, H.M. Queen Elizabeth The Queen Mother.

Controller Commandant, H.R.H. The Duchess of Kent.

Deputy Controller Commandant, Brigadier E. J. Nolan, c.b.

Director Women's Royal Army Corps, Brigadier H. G. Meechie, m.a.

THE ROYAL AIR FORCE

THE QUEEN

Marshals of the Royal Air Force

H.R.H. the Prince Philip, Duke of Edinburgh, K.G., P.C., K.T., O.M., G.B.E. (*Air Commodore-in-Chief, Air Training Corps, Marshal of the R.A.A.F.*) *born* June 10, 1921 .... Jan. 15, 1953
Sir William F. Dickson, G.C.B., K.B.E., D.S.O., A.F.C., *born* Sept. 24, 1898 .... June 1, 1954
Sir Dermot A. Boyle, G.C.B., K.C.V.O., K.B.E., A.F.C., *born* Oct. 2, 1904 .... Jan 1, 1958
The Lord Elworthy, K.G., G.C.B., C.B.E., D.S.O., M.V.O., D.F.C., A.F.C., *born* March 23, 1911 ... April 1, 1967
Sir John Grandy, G.C.B., K.B.E., D.S.O., *born* Feb. 8, 1913 (*Governor and Constable of Windsor Castle*) .... April 1, 1971
Sir Denis Spotswood, G.C.B., C.B.E., D.S.O., D.F.C., *born* Sept. 26, 1916 .... March 31, 1974
The Lord Cameron, G.C.B., C.B.E., D.S.O., D.F.C., A.F.C., *born* July 8, 1920 .... July 31, 1977
Sir Michael Beetham, G.C.B., C.B.E., D.F.C., A.F.C., A.D.C., *born* May 17, 1923 .... Oct. 15, 1982

Air Chief Marshals

Williamson, Sir Keith, G.C.B., A.F.C., A.D.C. (*Chief of the Air Staff*).
Kennedy, Sir Thomas, K.C.B., A.F.C., A.D.C. (*Air Member for Personnel*).
Craig, Sir David, G.C.B., O.B.E. (*A.O.C.-in-C. U.K. Air Forces*).
Rogers, Sir John, K.C.B., C.B.E. (*Controller Aircraft*).
Beavis, Sir Michael, K.C.B., C.B.E., A.F.C. (*Deputy C.-in-C., Allied Forces Central Europe*).

Air Marshals

Pedder, Sir Ian, K.C.B., O.B.E., D.F.C. (*Controller, National Air Traffic Service*).
Knight, Sir Michael, K.C.B., A.F.C. (*Air Member for Supply and Organisation*).
Harding, Sir Peter, K.C.B. (*Vice-Chief of the Air Staff*).
Hine, Sir Patrick, K.C.B. (*C.-in-C., R.A.F. Germany and Cmdr. 2A. T.A.F.*).
Hall, Sir Donald, K.C.B., C.B.E., A.F.C. (*Deputy Chief of the Defence Staff*).
Armitage, Sir Michael, K.C.B., C.B.E. (*Deputy Chief of the Defence Staff* (*Intelligence*)).
Fitzpatrick, Sir John, K.B.E., C.B. (*A.O.C. No. 18 Group*).
Harcourt-Smith, Sir David, K.C.B., D.F.C. (*A.O.C.-in-C., R.A.F. Support Command*).
Gilbert, J. A., C.B., C.B.E. (*Deputy C.-in-C. Strike Command*).
Dunn, Sir Eric, K.B.E., C.B., B.E.M. (*Chief Engineer (R.A.F.)*).

Air Vice-Marshals

Sutton, J. M. D., C.B. (*Assistant Chief of the Defence Staff* (*Commitments*)).
Howe, J. F. G., C.B.E., A.F.C. (*Director-General of Security and Commandant-General R.A.F. Regiment*).
Ward, P. A. (*Deputy Chief of Staff* (*Operations*), *Allied Air Forces Central Europe*).
Skingsley, A. G., C.B. (*Assistant Chief of the Air Staff (Policy)*).
Hayr, K. W., C.B., C.B.E., A.F.C. (*Air Officer Commanding, No. 11 Group*).
Bennett, E. P., C.B. (*Commander, Sultan of Oman's Air Force*).
Parry-Evans, D., C.B.E. (*Air Officer Commanding No. 1 Group*).
Peirse, R. C. F., C.B. (*Commandant, R.A.F. College, Cranwell*).
Duxbury, J. B., C.B.E. (*Air Secretary*).
Jones, L. A., C.B., A.F.C. (*Assistant Chief of the Air Staff (Operations)*).
White, G. A., C.B., A.F.C. (*Deputy Comander, R.A.F. Germany*).
Collins, P. S., A.F.C. (*Director-General of Organisation (R.A.F.)*).
Adams, M. K., A.F.C. (*Assistant Chief of the Air Staff (Operational Requirements)*).
Ashford, R. G., C.B.E. (*Director-General of Personal Services (R.A.F.)*).
Sanderson, K. F. (*Air Officer Administration, Strike Command*).
Spottiswood, J. D., C.V.O., A.F.C. (*Director-General of Training (R.A.F.)*).
Stuart-Paul, R. I., M.B.E. (*Air Officer Training R.A.F. Support Command*).

Tetley, J. H. F., C.V.O. (*Commander, Northern Maritime Air Region and Air Officer Scotland and N. Ireland*).
Newton, B. H. (*Senior Directing Staff (Air), Royal College of Defence Studies*).
Simmons, M. G., A.F.C. (*Senior Air Staff Officer, Strike Command*).
Hann, D. N. (*Chief of Staff, No. 18 Group*).
Richardson, D. W. (*Air Officer Engineering Strike Command*).
White, T. P. (*Air Officer Maintenance, R.A.F. Support Command*).
Holroyd, F. M. (*Director-General Strategic Electronic Systems*).
Perrin, N. A. (*President Ordnance Board*).
Porter, J. B., O.B.E. (*Director-General Aircraft 2*).
Martindale, A. R., C.B. (*Director-General of Supply (R.A.F.)*).
Lees, R. L., M.B.E. (*Air Officer Administration, R.A.F. Support Command*).
Cooke, J. N. C., C.B., O.B.E., Q.H.P. (*Senior R.A.F. Consultant*).
Riseley-Pritchard, R. A., Q.H.S. (*Principal Medical Officer, R.A.F. Support Command*).
Donald, J. G., O.B.E., Q.H.S. (*Principal Medical Officer, Strike Command*).
Hills, D. G. M., O.B.E., Q.H.S. (*Director of Medical Policy and Plans*).
King, P. F., O.B.E., Q.H.S. (*Dean of Air Force Medicine*).
Jones, J. M., Q.H.D.S. (*Director of Dental Services (R.A.F.)*).
Forman, G. N. (*Director of Legal Services (R.A.F.)*).

PRINCESS MARY'S ROYAL AIR FORCE NURSING SERVICE (P.M.R.A.F.N.S.)

The Princess Mary's Royal Air Force Nursing Service is open to suitable male and female candidates who wish to train for or already hold the Enrolled Nurse Certificate (G). Registered General Nurses are eligible to apply for an initial 4 years' short service commission.

WOMEN'S ROYAL AIR FORCE (W.R.A.F.)

Formed on 1 April 1918, the Women's Royal Air Force was disbanded on 1 April 1920 and reformed on 1 February 1949 from the Women's Auxiliary Air Force, the World War II Service, which had been formed on 28 June 1939, and from the R.A.F. Companies of the Auxiliary Territorial Service.

W.R.A.F. officers and airwomen, respectively, serve in most of the R.A.F. ground branches and trades and also as Air Loadmaster aircrew. W.R.A.F. personnel are employed at R.A.F. stations and higher formations at home and abroad, and they compete, on equal terms, with their R.A.F. counterparts for appointments, promotion and places on training courses.

Commandant-in-Chief, H.M. Queen Elizabeth the Queen Mother.
Air Chief Commandant, H.R.H. Princess Alice, Duchess of Gloucester.
Director, Air Commodore H. F. Renton, C.B., A.D.C.

CONSTITUTION OF THE ROYAL AIR FORCE

The Royal Air Force consists of 3 Commands: Strike Command and Support Command in the United Kingdom, and R.A.F. Germany. Strike Command is responsible for providing the air defence of the United Kingdom and reinforcement forces for N.A.T.O.; its roles include strike/attack, air defence, control and reporting, maritime surveillance, air reconnaissance, air-to-air refuelling, offensive support, air transport, aero-medical facilities, and search and rescue. Support Command is responsible for air and ground training, communications, engineering support, logistics, hospitals and for providing a range of administrative support. R.A.F. Germany provides

tactical air support in N.A.T.O.'s Central Region; its roles include strike/attack, interdiction, counter air operations, air defence, close air support of land forces, tactical reconnaissance and helicopter support.

To carry out its tasks, the Royal Air Force is equipped with Victor, Tornado, Buccaneer, Phantom, Lightning, Harrier, Jaguar, Canberra, Hunter, Nimrod, Shackleton, VC10, Hercules, Hawk, Jet Provost, Chipmunk and Bulldog aircraft; Puma, Wessex, Sea King and Chinook helicopters; miscellaneous communications aircraft, etc.; and Bloodhound and Rapier missiles.

ROYAL OBSERVER CORPS
Bentley Priory, Stanmore, Middlesex

Established 1925, the Royal Observer Corps is a uniformed voluntary civilian organization originally set up to identify and track the movement of aircraft in war. In 1955 the Corps assumed the modern role of detecting nuclear bursts and monitoring radioac-

tive fall-out in support of the United Kingdom Warning and Monitoring Organization. The Corps is affiliated to the Royal Air Force and is administered by Strike Command.

Air Commodore-in-Chief, H.M. THE QUEEN.
Commandant, Air Commodore G. P. Black, O.B.E., A.F.C.

THE UNION JACK SERVICES CLUBS

Patron-in-Chief: Her Majesty the Queen.
Patron: Major-Gen. Sir Julian Gascoigne, K.C.M.G., K.C.V.O., C.B., D.S.O.
President: Major-Gen. Sir Robert Pigot, Bt., C.B., O.B.E., R.M.
Comptroller: Brig. J. N. Ghika, C.B.E.
Club Secretary: L. F. Moulton.

THE UNION JACK CLUB
Sandell Street, S.E.1
[Tel.: 01–928 6401]

The Union Jack Club provides residential accommodation for service and ex-service men and women

and their families. All serving men and women below commissioned rank are members. Ex-service membership is by election. Honorary membership is extended to the Forces of other nations visiting the United Kingdom, to members of the Police, Fire, Ambulance and Prison Services, to members of the Merchant Navy, Royal Observer Corps, Coast Guards, Civil Service, Royal British Legion, and Corps of Commissionaires, and those sponsored by various other organizations approved by the Governing Council.

RELATIVE RANK—SEA, LAND AND AIR

ROYAL NAVY	ARMY	ROYAL AIR FORCE
1. Admiral of the Fleet.	1. Field-Marshal.	1. Marshal of the R.A.F.
2. Admiral.	2. General.	2. Air Chief Marshal.
3. Vice-Admiral.	3. Lieutenant-General.	3. Air Marshal.
4. Rear-Admiral.	4. Major-General.	4. Air Vice-Marshal.
5. Commodore (1st & 2nd Class).	5. Brigadier.	5. Air Commodore.
6. Captain.	6. Colonel.	6. Group Captain.
7. Commander.	7. Lieutenant-Colonel.	7. Wing Commander.
8. Lieutenant-Commander.	8. Major.	8. Squadron Leader.
9. Lieutenant.	9. Captain.	9. Flight-Lieutenant.
10. Sub-Lieutenant.	10. Lieutenant.	10. Flying Officer.
11. Acting Sub-Lieutenant.	11. Second Lieutenant.	11. Pilot Officer.

SERVICE SALARIES AND PENSIONS

The following rates of pay have been introduced as part of the 1984 pay award for service personnel. The Government, although accepting the recommendations of both the Armed Forces Pay Review Body, which advises on pay levels for all ranks up to and including Brigadier, and the Top Salaries Review Body, which advises on ranks above Brigadier, decided to stage in two parts the increases in salary. The First stage took effect from 1 April 1984 with the full amount (shown below) being introduced from 1

November 1984. Salaries for the Women's Services reflect equal pay for equal work and conditions, but because the X-Factor addition for women is lower than for men (7½% compared to 10%) women's rates approximate to 97·73% of the rates for men. Since 1970 the determining factor of the Review Body's recommendations has been the relation of forces' salaries to civilian earnings by a carefully detailed process of job evaluation.

ROYAL NAVY AND ROYAL MARINES
Normal Rates

Rank (and equivalent rank, R.M.)	Daily	Annual
	£	£
Midshipman	13·44	4,906
After 1 year	16·70	6,095
Sub-Lieutenant	19·14	6,986
After 2 years	24·67	9,005
After 3 years	26·62	9,716
Lieutenant R.N.	31·04	11,330
After 1 year	31·88	11,636
After 2 years	32·72	11,943
After 3 years	33·56	12,249
After 4 years	34·40	12,556
After 5 years	35·24	12,863
After 6 years	36·08	13,169
Lieutenant R.M.	24·67	9,005
After 1 year	31·04	11,330
After 2 years	31·88	11,636
After 3 years	32·72	11,943
After 4 years	33·56	12,249
After 5 years	34·40	12,556
After 6 years	35·24	12,863
After 7 years	36·08	13,169
Lieutenant-Commander/Captain R.M.	39·13	14,282
After 1 year	40·10	14,636
After 2 years	41·07	14,991
After 3 years	42·04	15,345
After 4 years	43·01	15,699
After 5 years	43·98	16,053
After 6 years	44·95	16,407
After 7 years	45·92	16,761
After 8 years	46·89	17,115
Commander R.N./Major R.M.	53·23	19,429
After 2 years or with 19 years' service	54·63	19,940
After 4 years or with 21 years' service	56·03	20,451
After 6 years or with 23 years' service	57·43	20,942
After 8 years or with 25 years' service	58·83	21,473
Captain R.N./Lieutenant-Colonel R.M.	61·69	22,517
After 2 years	63·31	23,108
After 4 years	64·93	23,699
Captain R.N. with 6 years' seniority/Colonel R.M.	74·25	27,101
Rear-Admiral/Major-General R.M.	80·82	29,500
Vice-Admiral/Lieutenant-General R.M.	100·00	36,500
Admiral/General R.M.	124·66	45,500
Admiral of the Fleet	140·41	51,250

ARMY
Normal Rates

Rank	Daily	Annual
	£	£
Second Lieutenant	19·14	6,986
Lieutenant—On appointment	24·67	9,005
After 1 year	25·32	9,242
After 2 years	25·97	9,479
After 3 years	26·62	9,716
After 4 years	27·27	9,954
Captain—On appointment	31·04	11,330
After 1 year	31·88	11,636
After 2 years	32·72	11,943
After 3 years	33·56	12,249
After 4 years	34·40	12,556
After 5 years	35·24	12,863
After 6 years	36·08	13,169
Major—On appointment	39·13	14,282
After 1 year	40·10	14,636
After 2 years	41·07	14,991
After 3 years	42·04	15,345
After 4 years	43·01	15,699
After 5 years	43·98	16,053
After 6 years	44·95	16,407
After 7 years	45·92	16,761
After 8 years	46·89	17,115
Special List—Lieutenant-Colonel	53·01	19,349
Lieutenant-Colonel—On appointment with less than 19 years' service	53·23	19,429
After 2 years or with 19 years' service	54·63	19,940
After 4 years or with 21 years' service	56·03	20,451
After 6 years or with 23 years' service	57·43	20,962
After 8 years or with 25 years' service	58·83	21,473
Colonel—On appointment	61·69	22,517
After 2 years	63·31	23,108
After 4 years	64·93	23,699
After 6 years	66·55	24,291
After 8 years	68·17	24,882
Brigadier	74·25	27,101
Major-General	80·82	29,500
Lieutenant-General	100·00	36,500
General	124·66	45,500
Field Marshal	140·41	51,250

ROYAL AIR FORCE

Rank	Daily	Annual	Rank	Daily	Annual
	£	£		£	£
Acting Pilot Officer............	16·70	6,096	After 7 years................	45·92	16,761
After 6 months in the rank			After 8 years................	46·89	17,115
(aircrew only).............	17·09	6,238	Wing Commander—On appoint-		
Pilot Officer	19·14	6,986	ment with less than 19 years'		
Flying Officer................	24·67	9,005	commissioned service	53·23	19,429
After 1 year.................	25·32	9,242	After 2 years or 19 years' com-		
After 2 years................	25·97	9,479	missioned service	54·63	19,940
After 3 years................	26·62	9,716	After 4 years or 21 years' com-		
After 4 years................	27·27	9,954	missioned service	56·03	20,451
Flight Lieutenant	31·04	11,330	After 6 years or 23 years' com-		
After 1 year.................	31·88	11,636	missioned service	57·43	20,962
After 2 years................	32·72	11,943	After 8 years or 25 years' com-		
After 3 years................	33·56	12,249	missioned service	58·83	21,473
After 4 years................	34·40	12,556	Group Captain	61·69	22,517
After 5 years................	35·24	12,863	After 2 years................	63·31	23,108
After 6 years................	36·08	13,169	After 4 years................	64·93	23,699
Squadron Leader..............	39·13	14,282	After 6 years................	66·55	24,291
After 1 year.................	40·10	14,636	After 8 years................	68·17	24,882
After 2 years................	41·07	14,991	Air Commodore	74·25	27,101
After 3 years................	42·04	15,345	Air Vice-Marshal	80·82	29,500
After 4 years................	43·01	15,699	Air Marshal	100·00	36,500
After 5 years................	43·98	16,053	Air Chief Marshal.............	124·66	45,500
After 6 years................	44·95	16,407	Marshal of the Royal Air Force .	140·41	51,250

ROYAL NAVY AND ROYAL MARINES SPECIAL DUTIES LIST OFFICERS
Army Male Officers commissioned from the ranks, and Royal Air Force Branch Officers

Years of commissioned service	Years of Rating/Soldier/Airman Service					
	Under 12 years		12 years and under 15 years		15 years and over	
	Daily	Annual	Daily	Annual	Daily	Annual
	£	£	£	£	£	£
On commissioning.................	34·26	12,505	35·86	13,089	37·46	13,673
After 1 year.....................	35·06	12,797	36·66	13,381	38·06	13,892
After 2 years....................	35·86	13,089	37·46	13,673	38·66	14,111
After 3 years....................	36·66	13,381	38·06	13,892	39·26	14,330
After 4 years....................	37·46	13,673	38·66	14,111	39·86	14,549
After 5 years....................	38·06	13,892	39·26	14,330	40·46	14,768
After 6 years....................	38·66	14,111	39·86	14,549	41·06	14,987
After 8 years....................	39·26	14,330	40·46	14,768	41·66	15,206
After 10 years...................	39·86	14,549	41·06	14,987	41·66	15,206
After 12 years...................	40·46	14,768	41·66	15,206	41·66	15,206
After 14 years...................	41·06	14,987	41·66	15,206	41·66	15,206
After 16 years...................	41·66	15,206	41·66	15,206	41·66	15,206

ROYAL NAVY
Artificers, Medical and Communications Technicians—Daily Rates

Rating	Less than 6 years Scale A	6 years but less than 9 years Scale B	9 years or more Scale C
	£	£	£
5th Class Technician (Able)	18·56	18·86	19·31
Acting Leading Artificer..........................	19·51	19·81	20·26
Leading Artificer .... }	21·56	21·86	22·31
Acting/4th Class Technician			
4th Class Technician (Leading)	22·95	23·25	23·70
Probationary or Acting PO Artificer .... }	26·32	26·62	27·07
3rd Class Technician			
PO Artificer .... }	27·60	27·90	28·35
2nd Class Technician			
CPO Artificer....... } Scale II................	31·25	31·55	32·00
1st Class Technician . }			
CPO Artificer....... } Scale I	32·49	32·79	33·24
1st Class Technician . }			
CCPO Artificer/Technician	33·80	34·10	34·55
FCPO Artificer/Technician	35·22	35·52	35·97

ROYAL NAVY AND ROYAL MARINES—OTHER BRANCHES

New rates of pay for those committed to serve for:

Rating	Scale	Less than 6 years Scale A	6 years but less than 9 years Scale B	9 years or more Scale C
		£	£	£
Ordinary Rating/Marine 2nd Class............	II	12·87	13·17	13·62
	I	14·01	14·31	14·76
Able Rating/Marine 1st Class.................	III	15·91	16·21	16·66
	II	17·42	17·72	18·17
	I	18·56	18·86	19·31
Corporal	III	20·24	20·54	20·99
Leading Rating/Corporal	II	21·56	21·86	22·31
	I	27·95	23·25	23·70
Sergeant	III	24·94	25·24	25·69
Petty Officer/Sergeant	II	25·16	25·46	25·91
	I	25·62	25·92	26·37
Colour Sergeant	III	27·26	27·56	28·01
	II	27·82	28·12	28·57
Chief Petty Officer	II	28·23	28·53	28·98
Colour Sergeant	I	28·38	28·68	29·13
Chief Petty Officer	I	28·75	29·05	29·50
Warrant Officer Class 2	I	30·61	30·91	31·36
Fleet Chief Petty Officer/Warrant Officer Class I	I	32·56	32·86	33·31

ARMY

Daily rates of pay for those committed to serve for:

Rank	Less than 6 years Scale A			6 years but less than 9 years Scale B			9 years or more Scale C		
	Band 1	Band 2	Band 3	Band 1	Band 2	Band 3	Band 1	Band 2	Band 3
	£	£	£	£	£	£	£	£	£
Private Class IV ...	12·87	—	—	13·17	—	—	13·62	—	—
Class III ...	13·86	15·91	—	14·16	16·21	—	14·61	16·66	—
Class II	14·92	16·97	—	15·22	17·27	—	15·67	17·72	—
Class I	15·94	17·99	20·22	16·24	18·29	20·52	16·69	18·74	20·97
Lance Corporal									
Class III ...	15·94	17·99	—	16·24	18·29	—	16·69	18·74	—
Class II	17·04	19·09	—	17·34	19·39	—	17·79	19·84	—
Class I	18·22	20·27	22·50	18·52	20·57	22·80	18·97	21·02	23·25
Corporal Class II ...	19·51	21·56	—	19·81	21·86	—	20·26	22·31	—
Class I	20·90	22·95	25·18	21·20	23·25	25·48	21·65	23·70	25·93

	Band 4	Band 5	Band 6	Band 7	Band 4	Band 5	Band 6	Band 7	Band 4	Band 5	Band 6	Band 7
	£	£	£	£	£	£	£	£	£	£	£	£
Sergeant	22·91	25·16	27·60	—	23·21	25·46	27·90	—	23·66	25·91	28·35	—
Staff Sergeant ..	24·35	26·60	29·04	31·70	24·65	26·90	29·34	32·00	25·10	27·35	29·79	32·45
Warrant Officer 2	26·03	28·28	30·72	33·38	26·33	28·58	31·02	33·68	26·78	29·03	31·47	34·13
Warrant Officer 1	27·87	30·12	32·56	35·22	28·17	30·42	32·86	35·52	28·62	30·87	33·31	35·97

ROYAL AIR FORCE
Airmen (Aircrew)

New rates of pay for those committed to serve for:

Rank	Less than 6 years Scale A	6 years but less than 9 years Scale B	9 years or more Scale C
	£	£	£
Pilots, Navigators, Air Electronics Operators and Air Engineers (A)			
Sergeant (Band 6)	27·60	27·90	28·35
Flight Sergeant (Band 7)	32·52	32·82	33·27
Master Aircrew (Band 7)	35·22	35·52	35·97
Air Signallers and Air Loadmasters			
Sergeant (Band 5)	25·16	25·46	25·91
Flight Sergeant (Band 6)	29·86	30·16	30·61
Master Aircrew (Band 6)	32·56	32·86	33·31

ROYAL AIR FORCE

Airmen (Ground Trades) and P.M.R.A.F.N.S.

New rates of pay for those committed to serve for:

Rank	Less than 6 years Scale A			6 years but less than 9 years—Scale B			9 years or more Scale C		
Band	1	2	3	1	2	3	1	2	3
	£	£	£	£	£	£	£	£	£
Aircraftman	12·87	12·87	12·87	13·17	13·17	13·17	13·62	13·62	13·62
Leading Aircraftman	13·86	15·91	18·14	14·16	16·21	18·44	14·61	16·66	18·89
Senior Aircraftman	15·94	17·99	20·22	16·24	18·29	20·52	16·69	18·74	20·97
Junior Technician	18·22	20·27	22·50	18·52	20·57	22·80	18·97	21·02	23·25
Corporal	20·65	22·70	25·18	20·95	23·00	25·48	21·40	23·45	25·93
Band	4	5	6	7	4	5	6	7	4	5	6	7
	£	£	£	£	£	£	£	£	£	£	£	£
Sergeant	22·91	25·16	27·60	—	23·21	25·46	27·90	—	23·66	25·91	28·35	—
Chief Technician	24·04	26·29	28·73	31·39	24·34	26·59	29·03	31·69	24·79	27·04	29·48	32·14
Flight Sergeant	25·17	27·42	29·86	32·52	25·47	27·72	30·16	32·82	25·92	28·17	30·61	33·27
Warrant Officer	27·87	30·12	32·56	35·22	28·17	30·42	32·86	35·52	28·62	30·87	33·31	35·97

Officers of W.R.N.S.

Rank	Daily	Annual
	£	£
Probationary 3rd Officer	18·70	6,825
3rd Officer	20·50	7,482
After 2 years	24·11	8,800
After 3 years	24·74	9,030
After 4 years	25·38	9,264
After 5 years	26·01	9,494
After 6 years	26·65	9,727
2nd Officer	30·33	11,070
After 1 year	31·16	11,373
After 2 years	31·98	11,673
After 3 years	32·80	11,972
After 4 years	33·62	12,271
After 5 years	34·44	12,571
After 6 years	35·26	12,870
1st Officer	38·24	13,958
After 1 year	39·19	14,304
After 2 years	40·14	14,651
After 3 years	41·08	14,994
After 4 years	42·03	15,341
After 5 years	42·98	15,688
After 6 years	43·93	16,034
After 7 years	44·88	16,351
After 8 years	45·82	16,724
Chief Officer—On appointment	52·02	18,987
After 2 years or 19 years' service	53·39	19,487
After 4 years or 21 years' service	54·76	19,987
After 6 years or 23 years' service	56·16	20,498
After 8 years or 25 years' service	57·56	21,009
Superintendent	60·85	22,210
After 2 years	62·47	22,802
After 4 years	64·09	23,393
After 6 years	65·71	23,984
After 8 years	67·33	24,575
Director, W.R.N.S.	73·84	26,952

Officers of W.R.A.C., and Q.A.R.A.N.C.

Rank	Daily	Annual
	£	£
Officer Cadet	—	
Second-Lieutenant	18·70	6,826
Lieutenant—On appointment	24·11	8,800
After 1 year	24·74	9,030
After 2 years	25·38	9,264
After 3 years	26·01	9,494
After 4 years	26·65	9,727
Captain—On appointment	30·33	11,070
After 1 year	31·16	11,373
After 2 years	31·98	11,673
After 3 years	32·80	11,972
After 4 years	33·62	12,271
After 5 years	34·44	12,571
After 6 years	35·26	12,870
Major—On appointment	38·24	13,958
After 1 year	39·19	14,304
After 2 years	40·14	14,651
After 3 years	41·08	14,994
After 4 years	42·03	15,341
After 5 years	42·98	15,688
After 6 years	43·93	16,034
After 7 years	44·88	16,381
After 8 years	45·82	16,724
Lieutenant-Colonel—On appointment with less than 19 years' service	52·02	18,987
After 2 years or with 19 years' service	53·39	19,487
After 4 years or with 21 years' service	54·76	19,987
After 6 years or with 23 years' service	56·16	20,498
After 8 years or with 25 years' service	57·56	21,009
Colonel—On appointment	60·85	22,210
After 2 years	62·47	22,802
After 4 years	64·09	23,393
After 6 years	65·71	23,984
After 8 years	67·33	24,575
Brigadier	73·84	26,952

Officers of W.R.A.F.

Rank	Daily	Annual
	£	£
Acting Pilot Officer..............	16·32	5,957
Pilot Officer	18·70	6,826
Flying Officer	24·11	8,800
After 1 year	24·74	9,030
After 2 years	25·38	9,264
After 3 years	26·01	9,494
After 4 years	26·65	9,727
Flight Lieutenant	30·33	11,070
After 1 year..................	31·16	11,373
After 2 years	31·98	11,673
After 3 years	32·80	11,972
After 4 years	33·62	12,271
After 5 years	34·44	12,571
After 6 years	35·26	12,870
Squadron Leader	38·24	13,958
After 1 year..................	39·19	14,304
After 2 years	40·14	14,651
After 3 years	41·08	14,994
After 4 years	42·03	15,341
After 5 years	42·98	15,688
After 6 years	43·93	16,034
After 7 years	44·88	16,381
After 8 years	45·82	16,724
Wing Commander on appointment with less than 19 years' commissioned service	52·02	18,987
After 2 years or 19 years' commissioned service	53·39	19,487
After 4 years or 21 years' commissioned service	54·76	19,987
After 6 years or 23 years' commissioned service	56·16	20,498
After 8 years or 25 years' commissioned service	57·56	21,009
Group Captain	60·85	22,210
After 2 years..................	62·47	22,802
After 4 years..................	64·09	23,393
After 6 years..................	65·71	23,984
After 8 years..................	67·33	24,575
Air Commodore	73·84	26,952

W.R.N.S. Ratings and Naval Nurses

Rating	Scale	New rates of pay		
		Band 1	Band 2	Band 3
		£	£	£
Ordinary Rating	under 17½	9·51	—	—
	at 17½	12·57	—	—
Able Rating	III	13·54	15·54	17·72
	II	15·02	17·02	19·20
	I	16·12	18·12	20·30
Leading Rating	II	19·06	21·06	23·24
	I	20·42	22·42	24·60

		Band 4	Band 5	Band 6	Band 7
		£	£	£	£
Petty Officer	II	22·14	24·34	26·72	29·32
	I	22·62	24·82	27·20	29·80
Chief Petty Officer	II	23·96	26·16	28·54	31·14
	I	24·54	26·74	29·12	31·72
Fleet Chief Petty Officer	I	27·23	29·43	31·81	34·41

Note: Wrens/Naval Nurses who have served for:
(a) 6 years but less than 9 years will receive an additional £0·30 a day.
(b) 9 years or more will receive an additional £0·75 a day.

W.R.A.C. and Q.A.R.A.N.C.
New rates of pay for those who have served for:

Rank		Less than 6 years			6 years but less than 9 years			9 years or more		
	Band	1	2	3	1	2	3	1	2	3
		£	£	£	£	£	£	£	£	£
Private Class IV Age 17–17½ .		9·21	—	—	—	—	—	—	—	—
Class IV		12·57	—	—	12·87	—	—	13·32	—	—
Class III		13·54	15·54	—	13·84	15·84	—	14·29	16·29	—
Class II		14·58	16·58	—	14·88	16·88	—	15·33	17·33	—
Class I.............		15·57	17·57	19·75	15·87	17·87	20·05	16·32	18·32	20·50
Lance Corporal Class III		15·57	17·57	—	15·87	17·87	—	16·32	18·32	—
Class II		16·65	18·65	—	16·95	18·95	—	17·40	19·40	—
Class I		17·80	19·80	21·98	18·10	20·10	22·28	18·55	20·55	22·73
Corporal Class II...........		19·06	21·06	—	19·36	21·36	—	19·81	21·81	—
Class I		20·42	22·42	24·60	20·72	22·72	24·90	21·17	23·17	25·35
	Band	4	5	6	7	4	5	6	7	4	5	6	7
		£	£	£	£	£	£	£	£	£	£	£	£
Sergeant		22·38	24·58	26·96	—	22·68	24·88	27·26	—	23·13	25·33	27·71	—
Staff Sergeant		23·79	25·99	28·37	30·97	24·09	26·29	28·67	31·27	24·54	26·74	29·12	31·72
Warrant Officer Class 2		25·43	27·63	30·01	32·61	25·73	27·93	30·31	32·91	26·18	28·38	30·76	33·36
Class 1		27·23	29·43	31·81	34·41	27·53	29·73	32·11	34·71	27·98	30·18	32·56	35·16

W.R.A.F. AIRWOMEN (Ground Trades) and P.M.R.A.F.N.S.
Daily rates of pay for those who have served for:

Rank	Less than 6 years			6 years but less than 9 years			9 years or more		
	Band 1	Band 2	Band 3	Band 1	Band 2	Band 3	Band 1	Band 2	Band 3
	£	£	£	£	£	£	£	£	£
Aircraftwoman under age 17¼	9·51	—	—	—	—	—	—	—	—
Aircraftwoman at age 17¼	12·57	12·57	12·57	—	—	—	—	—	—
Leading Aircraftwoman	13·54	15·54	17·72	13·84	15·84	18·02	14·29	16·29	18·47
Senior Aircraftwoman	15·57	17·57	19·75	15·87	17·87	20·05	16·32	18·32	20·50
Junior Technician	17·80	19·80	21·98	18·10	20·10	22·28	18·55	20·55	22·73
Corporal	20·18	22·18	24·60	20·48	22·48	24·90	20·93	22·93	25·35

Rank	Band 4	Band 5	Band 6	Band 7	Band 4	Band 5	Band 6	Band 7	Band 4	Band 5	Band 6	Band 7
	£	£	£	£	£	£	£	£	£	£	£	£
Sergeant	22·38	24·58	26·96	—	22·68	24·88	27·26	—	23·13	25·33	27·71	—
Chief Technician	23·48	25·68	28·06	30·66	23·78	25·98	28·36	30·96	24·23	26·43	28·81	31·41
Flight Sergeant	24·59	26·79	29·17	31·77	24·89	27·09	29·47	32·07	25·34	27·54	29·92	32·52
Warrant Officer	27·23	29·43	31·81	34·41	27·53	29·73	32·11	34·71	27·98	30·18	32·56	35·16

Charges for Married Quarters

Type of quarter	Weekly	Annual
Standard Accommodation	£	£
Other Ranks		
A	11·06	576·70
B	15·82	824·90
C	17·99	938·05
D/WO	20·23	1,054·85
Officers		
V	25·83	1,346·85
IV	29·47	1,536·65
III	33·46	1,744·70
II	38·22	1,992·90
I	42·63	2,222·85
Sub-Standard Accommodation		
Other Ranks		
A	6·37	332·15
B	8·47	441·65
C	9·59	500·05
D/WO	10·92	569·40
Officers		
V	13·93	726·35
IV	15·75	821·25
III	17·85	930·75

Charges for Single Quarters

Rank	Weekly	Annual
Standard Accommodation	£	£
Young servicemen receiving less than the minimum adult rate (i.e. Private IV rate)	3·99	208·05
Corporal and below	5·39	281·05
Warrant Officer and Senior N.C.O.	10·22	532·90
Captain and below	14·49	755·55
Major and above	17·29	901·55
Senior Officers occupying single rooms		
Major and above	14·49	755·55
Sub-Standard Accommodation		
Young servicemen receiving less than the minimum adult rate (i.e. Private IV rate)	2·17	113·15
Corporal and below	2·87	149·65
Warrant Officer and Senior N.C.O.	5·46	284·70
Captain and below	7·91	412·45
Major and above	9·31	485·45

Female officers of Q.A.R.N.N.S.

Rank	Daily	Annual
	£	£
Nursing Officer/Lieutenant	24·11	8,800
After 1 year	24·74	9,030
After 2 years	25·38	9,264
After 3 years	26·01	9,494
After 4 years	26·65	9,727
Senior Nursing Officer/Captain	30·33	11,070
After 1 year	31·16	11,373
After 2 years	31·98	11,673
After 3 years	32·80	11,972
After 4 years	33·62	12,271
After 5 years	34·44	12,571
After 6 years	35·26	12,870
Superintending Nursing Officer/ Major	38·24	13,958
After 1 year	39·19	14,304
After 2 years	40·14	14,651
After 3 years	41·08	14,994
After 4 years	42·03	15,341
After 5 years	42·98	15,668
After 6 years	43·93	16,034
After 7 years	44·88	16,381
After 8 years	46·82	16,724
Chief Nursing Officer/Lieutenant-Colonel	52·02	18,987
After 2 years or 19 years' commissioned service	53·39	19,487
After 4 years or 21 years' commissioned service	54·76	19,987
After 6 years or 23 years' commissioned service	56·16	20,498
After 8 years or 25 years' commissioned service	57·56	21,009
Principal Nursing Officer/ Colonel	60·85	22,210
After 2 years	62·47	22,802
After 4 years	64·09	23,393
After 6 years	65·71	23,984
After 8 years	67·33	24,575
Matron-in-Chief/Brigadier	73·84	26,952

SERVICE RETIREMENT BENEFITS, ETC.

NOTE—Those who leave the Forces having served at least five years, but not long enough to qualify for the appropriate immediate pension, now qualify for a preserved pension and terminal grant both of which are payable at age 60. The tax-free resettlement grants shown below are payable on release to those who qualify for a preserved pension and who have completed 9 years service from age 21 (officers) or 12 years from age 18 (other ranks).

†RETIREMENT BENEFITS (MEN) Officers*—All Services

No. of years reckonable service over age 21	Capt. (incl. Q.M.) and below	Major (incl. Q.M.)	Lt.-Col. (Q.M.)	Lt.-Col.	Col. and Deputy Chaplain General	Brigadier	Major-General, etc.	Lieutenant-General, etc.	General, etc.
	£p.a.	£p.a.	£p.a.	£p.a.	£p.a.	£p.a.	£p.a.	£p.a.	£p.a.
16	3,753	4,474	5,087	5,683					
17	3,927	4,687	5,300	5,946					
18	4,101	4,899	5,512	6,209	7,195				
19	4,274	5,112	5,725	6,471	7,500				
20	4,448	5,324	5,937	6,734	7,804				
21	4,622	5,537	6,150	6,997	8,109				
22	4,796	5,750	6,363	7,260	8,413	9,531			
23	4,969	5,962	6,575	7,523	8,718	9,832			
24	5,143	6,175	6,788	7,786	9,022	10,133	11,029		
25	5,317	6,387	7,000	8,048	9,327	10,434	11,357		
26	5,491	6,600	7,213	8,311	9,632	10,735	11,685		
27	5,665	6,813	7,426	8,574	9,936	11,036	12,012	14,864	
28	5,838	7,025	7,638	8,837	10,241	11,337	12,340	15,270	
29	6,012	7,238	7,851	9,100	10,545	11,638	12,668	15,675	
30	6,186	7,451	8,064	9,363	10,850	11,940	12,996	16,081	20,046
31	6,360	7,663	8,276	9,625	11,154	12,241	13,324	16,486	20,552
32	6,533	7,876	8,489	9,888	11,459	12,542	13,651	16,892	21,057
33	6,707	8,088	8,701	10,151	11,763	12,843	13,979	17,297	21,563
34	6,881	8,301	8,914	10,414	12,068	13,144	14,307	17,703	22,068

* Including those male officers holding equivalent ranks in the Q.A.R.N.N.S.
† Admirals of the Fleet, Field Marshals and Marshals of the Royal Air Force receive Active List Retired Pay at the rate of £24,856 per annum.

Ratings, Soldiers and Airmen*

Number of years reckonable service	Below Corporal	Corporal	Sergeant	Staff Sergeant	Warrant Officer Class II	Warrant Officer Class I
	£p.a.	£p.a.	£p.a.	£p.a.	£p.a.	£p.a.
22	2,241	2,829	3,127	3,543	3,643	3,998
23	2,319	2,928	3,236	3,667	3,772	4,143
24	2,398	3,027	3,345	3,790	3,902	4,288
25	2,476	3,125	3,454	3,914	4,031	4,433
26	2,554	3,224	3,564	4,037	4,161	4,577
27	2,632	3,323	3,673	4,161	4,290	4,722
28	2,711	3,422	3,782	4,285	4,420	4,867
29	2,789	3,521	3,891	4,408	4,549	5,012
30	2,867	3,619	4,000	4,532	4,679	5,157
31	2,945	3,718	4,109	4,655	4,808	5,302
32	3,024	3,817	4,218	4,779	4,938	5,447
33	3,102	3,916	4,327	4,903	5,067	5,592
34	3,180	4,015	4,437	5,026	5,197	5,736
35	3,258	4,113	4,546	5,150	5,326	5,881
36	3,337	4,212	4,655	5,273	5,456	6,026
37	3,415	4,311	4,764	5,397	5,585	6,171

* Including male nurses serving in the Q.A.R.N.N.S. holding equivalent rank.

RETIREMENT BENEFITS (WOMEN)

Q.A.R.N.N.S., W.R.N.S., Q.A.R.A.N.C., W.R.A.C., P.M.R.A.F.N.S., W.R.A.F. (The annual rates for W.R.A.C. are given: these apply to equivalent ranks in all Services, including the Nursing Services).

OFFICERS (16–34 years' service).—Captain, £3,669–£6,726; Major, £4,373–£8,114; Lt.-Col., £5,555–£10,180; Colonel, £7,105–£11,917; Brigadier, £9,483–£13,078.

SERVICEWOMEN (22–37 years' service).—Below Corporal, £2,191–£3,338; Corporal, £2,765–£4,214; Sergeant, £3,057–£4,657; Staff Sergeant, £3,463–£5,276; Warrant Officer II, £3,561–£5,459; Warrant Officer I, £3,908–£6,032.

NOTES

Terminal grants are in each case three times the rate of retired pay or pension. There are special rates of retired pay for Chaplains, Flight Lieutenants (Specialist Aircrew), and certain other ranks not shown above. Deductions may be made in cases of voluntary retirement.

The normal rates of gratuity for officers with short service commissions are £1,275 (men) and £1,246 (women) for each year completed. Resettlement grants are: officers £4,390 (men) and £4,291 (women); non-commissioned ranks £2,950 (men), £2,884 (women).

THE CHURCH OF ENGLAND
Province of Canterbury

CANTERBURY £24,625

102nd Archbishop and Primate of All England,
Most Rev. and Rt. Hon. Robert Alexander
Kennedy Runcie, M.C., D.D. (Lambeth Palace,
S.E.1), *cons.* 1970, *trs.* 1980. [Signs Robert
Cantuar] 1980

Bishops Suffragan

Dover, Rt. Rev. Richard Henry McPhail Third,
M.A. (Upway, St. Martin's Hill, Canterbury)
(*cons.* 1976) 1980
Croydon, Rt. Rev. Geoffrey Stuart Snell, M.A. (52
Selhurst Road, S.E. 25) 1977
Maidstone, Rt. Rev. Robert Maynard Hardy, M.K.
(Bishop's House, Egerton, Ashford, Kent) 1980
Assistant Bishops, Rt. Rev. John Taylor Hughes,
C.B.E. (*cons.* 1956), 1977; Rt. Rev. Harold
Isherwood, M.V.O., O.B.E. (*cons.* 1974), 1979; Rt.
Rev. The Lord Coggan, P.C., D.D. (*cons.* 1956),
1980; Rt Rev. Ross Hook, M.C., D.Litt. (*cons.*
1965) 1980

Dean (£10,640)

Very Rev. Victor Alexander de Waal, M.A. 1976

Canons Residentiary (£8,590)

A. M. Allchin, M.A.,	Archd. Simpson 1981
B.Litt., D.D........1973	P. Brett, M.A........1983
J. H. R. De	
Sausmarez 1981	
Organist, Allan Wicks, M.A., F.R.C.O. 1961	

Archdeacons

Canterbury, Ven. J. A. Simpson, M.A. 1981
Croydon, Ven. F. R. Hazell, M.A. 1978
Maidstone, Ven. A. M. Percival-Smith, M.A. 1979
    Clergy, 241.
Vicar-General of Province and Diocese, Miss S.
Cameron, Q.C.
Commissary General, J. H. R. Newey, Q.C., M.A.,
LL.B. 1971
Joint Registrars of the Province, F. E. Robson, 16
Beaumont Street, Oxford; B. J. T. Hanson,
Church House, Dean's Yard, S.W.1.
Registrar of the Diocese of Canterbury, A. O. E.
Davies, 9 The Precincts, Canterbury.

LONDON £19,990

130th Bishop, Rt. Rev. and Rt. Hon. Graham
Douglas Leonard, D.D., *cons.* 1964, *trs.* 1973 and
1981 (8 Barton Street, S.W.1.) [Signs Graham
Londin:] 1981

Bishops Suffragan

Kensington, Rt. Rev. Mark Santer, M.A. (19
Campden Hill Square, W.8) 1981
Willesden, Rt. Rev. Geoffrey Hewlett Thompson,
M.A. (173 Willesden Lane, Brondesbury,
N.W.6) 1974
Edmonton, (vacant)
Stepney, Rt. Rev. James Lawton Thompson, M.A.
(23 Tredegar Square, E.3).................1978
Fulham, Rt. Rev. Brian John Masters, M.A. (13
North Audley Street, W.1) 1982

Dean of St. Paul's (£10,640)

Very Rev. Alan Brunskill Webster, M.A., B.D.,
The Deanery, 9 Amen Court, E.C.4 1977

Canons Residentiary (each £8,590)

Archd. Harvey 1978	K. G. Routledge, M.A.1982
K. J. Woollcombe,	P. Ball, M.A.........1984
M.A., S.T.D. 1981	
Organist, C. H. Dearnley, M.A., B.MUS., F.R.C.O. ..1968	
Receiver of St. Paul's, Commander C. Shears,	
O.B.E., R.N. (*ret.*)	

Archdeacons

London, Ven. F. W. Harvey, M.A. 1978
Middlesex, Ven. T. J. Raphael, B.A. 1983
Northolt, Ven. T. F. Butler, M.SC., Ph.D.........1980
Hampstead, Ven. F. Pickering, M.A. 1974
Hackney, Ven. R. E. D. Sharpley, M.A...........1981
  Beneficed Clergy, 403; *Curates, &c.,* 185
*Chancellor and Commissary of the Dean and
Chapter,* G. H. Newsom, Q.C., M.A. 1971
Registrar, D. W. Faull, 22 Greencoat Place,
S.W.1 1969

WESTMINSTER

The Collegiate Church of St. Peter—(A Royal Peculiar)
Dean, Very Rev. Edward Frederick Carpenter,
M.A., B.D., Ph.D. 1974

Canons Residentiary (£8,590)

Bishop E. G. Knapp-	S. Charles, B.comm.,
Fisher 1975	B.D. 1978
T. R. Beeson, M.A.,	A. E. Harvey, M.A. ..1982
A.K.C. 1976	
Archdeacon, Rt. Rev. E. G. Knapp-Fisher, M.A. .1975	
Chapter Clerk, Registrar and Receiver General,	
W. R. J. Pullen, C.V.O., Ll.B. 1959	
Organist, S. Preston, M.A., B.MUS. 1980	
Legal Secretary, C. L. Hodgetts, Ll.B. 1973	

WINCHESTER £14,550

94th Bishop, Rt. Rev. John Vernon Taylor, M.A.,
D.D. (Wolvesey, Winchester) [Signs John
Winton:] 1975

Bishops Suffragan

Southampton, Rt. Rev. Edward David Car-
twright, M.A. (Sparsholt Vicarage, Winchester
SO21 2NS) 1984
Basingstoke, Rt. Rev. Michael Richard John
Manktelow, M.A. (1 The Close, Winchester) ..1977

Dean (£10,640)

Very Rev. Michael Staffurth Stancliffe, M.A. ...1969

Dean of Jersey, Very Rev. Thomas Ashworth
Goss, M.A...................................1971
Dean of Guernsey, Very Rev. John William
Foster 1978

Canons Residentiary (£8,590)

A. G. Wedderspoon,	E. G. Job, M.A. 1979
M.A., B.D.........1970	P. A. Britton, M.A. ..1980
Bp. of Basingstoke ..1977	
Organist, Martin Neary, M.A., F.R.C.O...........1972	

Archdeacons

Winchester, (vacant).
Basingstoke, Ven. T. G. Nash, M.A. 1982
  Beneficed Clergy, 247; *Curates, &c.,* 61
Chancellor, (vacant).
Registrar and Legal Secretary, P. M. White, B.A. 1981

BATH AND WELLS £13,070

74th *Bishop*, Rt. Rev. John Monier Bickersteth, M.A. (*cons.* 1970). (The Palace, Wells BA5 2PD) [Signs John Bath & Wells] 1975

Bishop Suffragan

Taunton, Rt. Rev. Peter John Nott, M.A. 1977

Dean (£10,640)

Very Rev. Patrick Reynolds Mitchell, M.A., F.S.A. 1973

Canons Residentiary of Wells (each £8,590)

D. R. Vicary, M.A....1975 | C. E. Thomas.......1983
S. R. Cutt, M.A. .....1979 |
Organist, A. Crossland 1970

Archdeacons

Bath, Ven. J. E. Burgess, B.D. 1975
Taunton, Ven. L. E. Olyott, B.A. 1977
Wells, Ven. C. E. Thomas, B.A.................1983
    Beneficed Clergy, 235; *Other Clergy*, 47.
Chancellor, G. H. Newsom, Q.C. 1970
Registrar, Sec. & Chapt. Clerk, N. M. Cavender, Wells.

BIRMINGHAM £13,070

6th *Bishop*, Rt. Rev. Hugh William Montefiore, D.D. (*cons.* 1970) (Bishop's Croft, Harborne, Birmingham) [Signs Hugh Birmingham] 1978

Bishop Suffragan

Aston, Rt. Rev. Michael Humphrey Dickens Whinney, M.A. (60 Handsworth Wood Road, Birmingham) 1982

Provost

Very Rev. Basil Stanley Moss, M.A. 1972

Canons Residentiary

D. McLean, M.A.....1972 | Archd. Cooper 1982
L. M. Davies, B.A....1981 |

Archdeacons

Aston, Ven. J. L. Cooper, B.D. 1982
Birmingham, Ven. G. Hollis, M.A. 1974
    Beneficed Clergy, 159; *Curates, &c.*, 73
Organist, H. Best, B.MUS., A.R.C.O.............1978
Chancellor, His Honour Judge Aglionby, M.A. ..1970
Registrar and Legal Secretary, M. Shaw (85 Cornwall Street, Birmingham).

BRISTOL £13,070

53rd *Bishop*, Rt. Rev. Ernest John Tinsley, M.A., B.D. (Bishop's House, Clifton Hill, Bristol BS8 1BW) [Signs John Bristol] 1976

Bishop Suffragan

Malmesbury, Rt. Rev. Peter James Firth, M.A. ..1983

Dean

Very Rev. Alfred Hounsell Dammers, M.A.......1973

Canons Residentiary

D. E. R. Isitt, M.A....1977 | J. Rogan, M.A. 1983
J. M. Free, B.D. .....1982 |
Organist, M. Archer, M.A., F.R.C.O., A.R.C.M. 1983

Archdeacons

Bristol, Ven. A. J. Balmforth, M.A...............1979
Swindon, Ven. K. Clark, M.A. 1982
    Beneficed Clergy, 123; *Curates, &c.*, 30
Chancellor, D. C. Calcutt, LL.B., MUS.B..........1971
Registrar and Sec., T. R. Urquhart 1972

CHELMSFORD £13,070

6th *Bishop*, Rt. Rev. Albert John Trillo, F.K.C., B.D., M.Th. (*cons.* 1963) (Bishopscourt, Margaretting) [Signs John Chelmsford] 1971

Bishops Suffragan

Colchester, Rt. Rev. Roderic Norman Coote, D.D. (Bishop's House, 32 Inglis Road, Colchester) (*cons.* 1951) 1966
Barking, Rt. Rev. James William Roxburgh, M.A. (670 High Road, Buckhurst Hill) 1983
Bradwell, Rt. Rev. Charles Derek Bond, A.K.C. (188 New London Road, Chelmsford) 1976
Provost, Very Rev. J. H. Moses, Ph.D., B.A. 1982
Organist, G. Elliott, MUS.B., F.R.C.O. 1981

Archdeacons

Southend, Ven. J. S. Bailey, M.A. 1982
West Ham, Ven. P. S. Dawes, B.A..............1980
Colchester, Ven. E. C. F. Stroud, B.A...........1983
    Beneficed Clergy, 384; *Curates, &c.*, 99
Chancellor, Miss S. M. Cameron, M.A. 1970
Diocesan Registrar, D. W. Faull, 22 Greencoat Place, S.W.1 1963

CHICHESTER £13,070

99th *Bishop*, Rt. Rev. Eric Waldram Kemp, D.D. (The Palace, Chichester) [Signs Eric Cicestr:] 1974

Bishops Suffragan

Lewes, Rt. Rev. Peter John Ball, M.A. (Litlington Rectory, nr. Polegate) 1977
Horsham, Rt. Rev. Ivor Colin Docker, M.A. (Bishop's Lodge, Worth, nr. Crawley).......1975
Assistant Bishops, Rt. Rev. James Herbert Lloyd Morrell, (*cons.* 1959) 1978; Rt. Rev. William Warren Hunt, M.A. (*cons.* 1955) 1980; Rt. Rev. Mark Green (*cons.* 1972) 1982

Dean

Very Rev. Robert Tinsley Holtby, M.A., B.D......1977

Canons Residentiary

R. T. Greenacre, | C. C. Luxmoore,
M.A., ...1975 | M.A. 1981
Organist, A. J. Thurlow, B.A.., F.R.C.O..........1980

Archdeacons

Chichester, Ven. K. Hobbs, M.A. 1981
Horsham, Ven. W. C. L. Filby, ...1983
Lewes and Hastings, Ven. M. L. Godden, M.A....1975
    Beneficed Clergy, 320; *Curates, &c.*, 69
Chancellor, Q. T. Edwards, Q.C.................1978
Legal Secretary to the Bishop, and Diocesan Registrar, C. L. Hodgetts, LL.B.

COVENTRY £13,070

6th *Bishop*, Rt. Rev. John Gibbs, B.A., B.D. (*cons.* 1973) (The Bishop's House, 23 Davenport Road, Coventry) [Signs John Coventry] 1976

Bishop Suffragan

Warwick, Rt. Rev. Keith Appleby Arnold, M.A...1980
Provost, Very Rev. Colin Semper, M.A. 1982
Organist, P. Wright, M.A., F.R.C.O. 1984

Canons Residentiary

P. A. Berry, M.A.....1973 | S. J. L. King, M.A....1977
S. S. Smalley, M.A.,
B.D., Ph.D ....1977 |

Archdeacons

Warwick, Ven. P. S. G. Bridges 1977
Coventry, Ven. A. W. Morgan, B.A. 1983

Beneficed Clergy, 104; *Curates, &c.*, 49
Chancellor, W. M. Gage, M.A. 1980
Registrar, D. J. Dumbleton, LL.B., Coventry 1978

DERBY £13,070

4th Bishop, Rt. Rev. Cyril William Johnston Bowles, M.A. (The Bishop's House, 6 King Street, Duffield, Derby) [Signs Cyril Derby] ..1969

Bishop Suffragan

Repton, Rt. Rev. Stephen Edmund Verney, M.C., M.A. (Repton House, Lea, Matlock) 1977
Assistant Bishops, Rt. Rev. Thomas Richards Parfitt, M.A. (cons. 1952) 1961; Rt. Rev. Cecil Allan Warren, M.A. (cons 1965) 1983
Provost, Very Rev. Benjamin Hugh Lewers, M.A.1981

Canons Residentiary

J. B. Potter, B.A. 1978	M. R. Austin 1981
Archd. Dell 1981	I. Gatford..........1984

Archdeacons

Chesterfield, Ven. G. R. Phizackerley, M.A. 1978
Derby, Ven. R. S. Dell, M.A. 1973
Organist, P. Gould, F.R.C.O. 1982
Beneficed Clergy, 190; *Curates, &c.*, 23
Chancellor, J. W. M. Bullimore, LL.B. 1981
Registrar, J. R. S. Grimwood-Taylor, M.A., Derby.

ELY £13,070

66th Bishop, Rt. Rev. Peter Knight Walker, D.D. (cons. 1972, trans. 1977) (The Bishop's House, Ely) [Signs Peter Elien:] 1977

Bishop Suffragan

Huntingdon, Rt. Rev. William Gordon Roe, M.A., D.Phil. (Powchers Hall, The College, Ely) 1980

Dean (£10,640)

Very Rev. William James Patterson, M.A. 1984

Canons Residentiary (each £8,590)

D. J. Green 1980	M. S. MacDonald,
Bp. of Huntingdon..1980	M.A. 1982

Organist, A. W. Wills, MUS. DOC., F.R.C.O........1959

Archdeacons

Ely, Ven. D. Walser, M.A. 1981
Wisbech, Ven. D. Fleming 1984
Huntingdon, Ven. R. K. Sledge, M.A. 1978

Incumbents, 155; *Curates, &c.*, 10
Chancellor, Rev. Canon K. G. Routledge, M.A., LL.B.
Registrar, W. H. Godfrey 1978
Joint Registrar, P. F. B. Beesley, LL.B. 1 The Sanctuary, S.W.1.

EXETER £13,070

68th Bishop, Rt. Rev. Eric Arthur John Mercer (cons. 1965) (The Palace, Exeter) [Signs Eric Exon:] 1973

Bishops Suffragan

Crediton, Rt. Rev. Peter Coleman, M.A. (10 The Close, Exeter) 1984
Plymouth, Rt. Rev. K. A. Newing, M.A. 1982
Assistant Bishops, Rt. Rev. John Armstrong, C.B., O.B.E. (cons. 1963); Rt. Rev. Charles Robert Claxton, D.D. (cons. 1946); Rt. Rev. John Maurice Key, D.D. (cons. 1947); Rt. Rev. Ronald Cedric Osbourne Goodchild, M.A. (cons. 1964).

Dean (£10,640)

Very Rev. Richard Montague Stephens Eyre, M.A. 1981

Canons Residentiary (£8,590)

Archd. Richards ...1981	A. C. Mawson, M.A. ..1979
J. A. Thurmer, M.A. .1973	

Organist, L. Nethsingha, M.A., F.R.C.O. 1972
Chapter Clerk, J. F. Eden, M.A. 1966

Archdeacons

Barnstaple, Ven. R. G. Herniman, B.A. 1970
Totnes, Ven. R. S. Hawkins, M.A., B.Phil. 1981
Plymouth, Ven. R. G. Ellis, M.A. 1982
Exeter, Ven. J. Richards, M.A. 1981
Beneficed Clergy, 275; *Curates, &c.*, 38
Chancellor, D. C. Calcutt, Q.C., M.A., LL.B., MUS.B .1971
Registrar, J. F. G. Michelmore, T.D., M.A., 18 Cathedral Yard, Exeter 1963
Diocesan Secretary, Sqn. Ldr. W. McDonald, D.F.C., Diocesan House, Palace Gate, Exeter ..1976

GIBRALTAR IN EUROPE

Bishop, Rt. Rev. John Richard Satterthwaite (5A Gregory Place, W8 4NG).

Bishop Suffragan

In Europe, Rt. Rev. Ambrose Walter Marcus Weekes, C.B.

Auxiliary Bishops, Rt. Rev. E. M. H. Capper, O.B.E.; Rt. Rev. D. de Pina Cabral; Rt. Rev. H. Isherwood, M.V.O., O.B.E.
Bishop's Commissaries, Canon J. A. Taylor; Canon H. Wybrew; Preb. D. W. C. Mossman, O.B.E.
Dean, Cathedral Church of the Holy Trinity, Gibraltar, Very Rev. D. J. Rowlands.
Chancellor, Pro-Cathedral of St. Paul, Valletta, Malta, Ven. J. W. Evans.
Chancellor, Pro-Cathedral of the Holy Trinity, Brussels, Belgium, Ven. J. Lewis.

Archdeacons

Aegean, Ven. G. B. Evans.
N.W. Europe, Ven. J. Lewis.
N. France, Ven. P. Sertin.
Gibraltar, Ven. R. B. Ney, O.B.E.
Italy, Ven. J. W. Evans.
Riviera, Ven. J. Livingstone.
Scandinavia, Ven. B. Horlock, O.B.E.
Switzerland, Ven. A. R. Nind.
Office Commissary, Canon J. D. Beckwith.

GLOUCESTER £13,070

37th Bishop, Rt. Rev. John Yates, M.A. (cons. 1972) (Bishopscourt, Gloucester GL1 2BQ) [Signs John Gloucestr:] 1975

Bishop Suffragan

Tewkesbury, Rt. Rev. Thomas Carlyle Joseph Robert Hamish Deakin, M.A. (Green Acre, Hempsted, Gloucester) 1973

Dean (£10,640)

Very Rev. K. N. Jennings, M.A. 1982

Canons Residentiary (£8,590)

Archd. Evans 1969	A. L. Dunstan, M.A. ..1978
D. C. St. V. Welan-	R. D. M. Grey,
der, B.D. 1975	A.K.C. 1982

Organist, J. D. Sanders, M.A., MUS.B., F.R.C.O., A.R.C.M. 1967

Archdeacons

Gloucester, Ven. C. J. H. Wagstaff, B.A.
Cheltenham, Ven. T. E. Evans, M.A..............1975
    Beneficed Clergy, 184; *Curates, &c.*, 23
Chancellor & Vicar-Gen., Rev. E. Garth Moore,
    M.A. 1957
Registrar, H. A. Gibson, 34 Brunswick Road,
    Gloucester.
Legal Sec., Dr. D. M. Moir Carey, M.A., 1 The
    Sanctuary, Westminster, S.W.1.
Diocesan Sec., Brig. J. S. Cooper, O.B.E.

GUILDFORD £13,070

7th Bishop, Rt. Rev. Michael Edgar Adie, M.A. (Willow
    Grange, Woking Road, Guildford) [Signs Michael
    Guildford] 1983

Bishop Suffragan

Dorking, Rt. Rev. Kenneth Dawson Evans, M.A.
    (3 New Inn Lane, Burpham, Guildford) 1968
Assistant Bishop, Rt. Rev. Gilbert Hindley
    Baker, (cons. 1966)........................1983
Dean, Very Rev. Antony Cyprian Bridge 1968

Canons Residentiary

F. S. Telfer, M.A.....1973 | P. G. Croft, M.A. 1983
Organist, A. T. S. Millington, M.A., F.R.C.O. 1983

Archdeacons

Surrey, Ven. P. E. Barber, M.A. 1980
Dorking, Ven. P. G. Hogben 1982
    Beneficed Clergy, 147; *Curates, &c.*, 55
Chancellor, M. B. Goodman, M.A.
Legal Sec., P. F. B. Beesley, Ll.B.
Registrar of Diocese, P. F. B. Beesley, Ll.B.
Registrar of the Archdeaconries, P. F. B. Beesley, Ll.B.

HEREFORD £13,070

103rd Bishop, Rt, Rev. John Richard Gordon
    Eastaugh, B.A. (The Palace, Hereford) [Signs
    John Hereford] 1973

Bishop Suffragan

Ludlow, Rt. Rev. Stanley Mark Wood (cons.
    1971)......................................1982

Dean (£10,640)

Very Rev. Peter Haynes......................1982

Canons Residentiary (£8,590)

Archd. Woodhouse .1982 | P. Iles 1983
Organist, Roy Massey, B.Mus., F.R.C.O...........1974

Archdeacons

Hereford, Ven. A. H. Woodhouse 1982
Ludlow, Ven. I. Griggs 1984
    Beneficed Clergy, 98; *Curates, &c.*, 43
Chancellor, J. M. Henty 1977
Joint Registrars, V. T. Jordan, 5 St. Peter Street,
    Hereford; P. Beesley, 1 The Sanctuary, Westmins-
    ter, S.W.1.

LEICESTER £13,070

4th Bishop, Rt. Rev. Cecil Richard Rutt, C.B.E.,
    M.A. (cons. 1966) (Bishop's Lodge, Leicester
    LE2 3BD) [Signs Richard Leicester] 1978
Assistant Bishop, Rt. Rev. John Ernest Llewellyn
    Mort, (cons. 1952)................1972
Provost, Very Rev. Alan Christopher Warren,
    M.A. 1978

Canons Residentiary

D. W. Gundry, B.D., | Bp. Mort 1970
  M.Th. ....1963 |
Organist, Peter White, M.A., Mus.B., F.R.C.O......1968

Archdeacons

Leicester, Ven. R. D. Silk, B.A.................1980
Loughborough, Ven. H. Lockley, Ph.D. 1963
    Beneficed Clergy, 169; *Curates, &c.*, 23
Chancellor, N. H. Freeman 1979
Registrar, G. K. J. Moore, 10 Friar Lane, Leices-
    ter.

LICHFIELD £13,070

97th Bishop, Rt. Rev. Keith Norman Sutton, M.A.
    (cons. 1978) (Bishop's House, The Close, Lich-
    field WS13 7LG) [Signs Keith Lichfield] 1984

Bishops Suffragan

Shrewsbury, Rt. Rev. Leslie Lloyd Rees (68
    London Road, Shrewsbury) 1980
Stafford, Rt. Rev. John Stevens Waller, M.A.
    (Park Lodge, 3 Beech Court, Stone, Staffs.) ...1979
Wolverhampton, Rt. Rev. Barry Rogerson, B.A.
    (61 Richmond Road, Wolverhampton) 1979

Dean (£10,640)

Very Rev. John Harley Lang, M.A. 1980

Canons Residentiary (each £8,590)

Archd. Ninis.......1974 | G. M. Smallwood,
A. N. Barnard, M.A. .1977 | M.A. 1978
                | W. J. Turner, B.A. ..1983
Organist, J. Rees-Williams, M.A., F.R.C.O. 1978

Archdeacons

Lichfield, Ven. R. B. Ninis, M.A. 1974
Salop, Ven. R. M. C. Jeffery, B.D. 1980
Stoke on Trent, Ven. J. D. Delight, B.A. 1982
    Beneficed Clergy, 352; *Curates, &c.*, 76
Chancellor, Rev. Canon K. G. Routledge, M.A., LL.B.
Diocesan Registrar and Bishop's Sec., M. B. S.
    Exham.

LINCOLN £13,070

69th Bishop, Rt. Rev. Simon Wilton Phipps, M.C.,
    M.A. (cons. 1968, trans. 1974), (Bishop's House,
    Eastgate, Lincoln LN2 1QQ) [Signs Simon
    Lincoln:] 1974

Bishops Suffragan

Grimsby, Rt. Rev. David Tustin, M.A. (43 Abbey
    Park Road, Grimsby) 1979
Grantham, Rt. Rev. Dennis Gascoyne Hawker,
    M.A. (Fairacre, Barrowby High Road,
    Grantham) 1972
Assistant Bishops, Rt. Rev. Anthony Otter, M.A.
    (cons. 1949) (1965); Rt. Rev. Kenneth Healey,
    M.A. (cons. 1958) (1965); Rt. Rev. Gerald Fitz-
    maurice Colin, M.A. (cons. 1966) 1979

Dean (£10,640)

Very Rev. the Hon. Oliver William Twisleton-
    Wykeham-Fiennes, M.A.....................1968

Canons Residentiary (£8,590)

D. C. Rutter, M.A. ...1965 | B. R. Davis, M.A. 1977
Archd. Dudman, | J. S. Nurser, M.A.,
  B.A. ....1971 | Ph.D 1977
Organist, Philip Marshall, Mus.Doc., F.R.C.O. 1966

Archdeacons

Stow, Ven. D. Scott, M.A. 1975
Lincoln, Ven. R. J. Milner, M.A. 1983
Lindsey, Ven. R. W. Dudman, B.A. 1971
    Beneficed Clergy, 280; *Curates, &c.*, 50
Chancellor, His Honour Judge M. B. Goodman,
    M.A......................................1971
Registrar, D. M. Wellman, M.A., 5-6 Bank
    Street, Lincoln.

NORWICH £13,070

69th Bishop (and 110th of East Anglia), Rt. Rev. Maurice Arthur Ponsonby Wood, D.S.C., M.A. (The Bishop's House, Norwich) [Signs Maurice Norvic] 1971

Bishops Suffragan

Lynn, Rt. Rev. William Aubrey Aitken, M.A. (Broad House, Ranworth, Norwich) 1973
Thetford, Rt. Rev. Timothy Dudley-Smith, M.A. .1981

Dean (£10,640)

Very Rev. John Paul Burbridge, M.A. 1983

Canons Residentiary (£8,590)

J. F. Poulton, B.A. ...1979	C. Beswick 1984
D. H. Bishop 1980	

Organist, M. B. Nicholas, M.A., F.R.C.O. 1971

Archdeacons

Norfolk, Ven. P. Dawson, M.A..................1977
Norwich, Ven. A. M. Handley, M.A. 1981
Lynn, Ven. G. F. Grobecker, M.A. 1980
   Beneficed Clergy, 225; Curates, &c., 15
Chancellor, His Hon. J. H. Ellison, V.R.D., M.A. ..1955
Registrar and Sec., B. O. L. Prior, M.B.E., T.D.

OXFORD £13,070

40th Bishop, Rt. Rev. Patrick Campbell Rodger (cons. 1970, trs. 1978), (Diocesan Church House, North Hinksey, Oxford) [Signs Patrick Oxon] 1978

Bishops Suffragan

Buckingham, Rt. Rev. Simon Hedley Burrows, M.A. (Sheridan, Grimms Hill, Great Missenden) 1974
Dorchester, Rt. Rev. Conrad John Eustace Meyer, M.A. (151 Wroslyn Road, Freeland, Oxon.) 1979
Reading, Rt. Rev. Ronald Gregory Graham Foley, B.A. (Greenbanks, Old Bath Road, Sonning, Reading) 1982
Assistant Bishops, Rt. Rev. David Goodwin Loveday, M.A., 1971; Rt. Rev. Sydney Cyril Bulley, M.A., D.D., 1979; Rt. Rev. A. K. Cragg, M.A., D.D., 1982; Rt. Rev. Eric Wild, M.A. 1982

Dean of Christ Church (£10,640)

Very Rev. Eric William Heaton, M.A. 1979

Canons Residentiary

W. R. F. Browning, M.A., B.D. (Canon of the Cathedral Church) 1965	M. F. Wiles, D.D. 1970
	J. McManners, D.Litt. 1972
J. Macquarrie, D.Litt 1969	J. C. Fenton, M.A., B.D. 1978
	Archd. Weston 1982
	O. M. T. O'Donovan, D.Phil. 1982

Organist, F. Grier, F.R.C.O.

Archdeacons

Oxford, Ven. F. V. Weston, M.A.................1982
Berks., Ven. J. E. Brown, B.D. 1978
Bucks., Ven. J. F. E. Bone, M.A. 1978
Chancellor, P. T. S. Boydell 1958
Registrar and Legal Sec., F. E. Robson 1969

WINDSOR

(The Queen's Free Chapel of St. George within Her Castle of Windsor—A Royal Peculiar)
Dean, Rt. Rev. Michael Ashley Mann..........1976

Canons Residentiary

D. I. T. Eastman, M.C., M.A...............1977	J. D. Treadgold 1981
	J. A. White 1982
D. J. Burgess, M.A. ...1978	

Organist, C. J. Robinson, M.A., B.MUS., F.R.C.O. ...1975
Chapter Clerk, Maj.-Gen. R. L. C. Dixon, C.B., M.C. 1981

PETERBOROUGH £13,070

36th Bishop, Rt. Rev. William John Westwood, M.A. (The Palace, Peterborough) [Signs William Petriburg] 1984
Assistant Bishops, Rt. Rev. Alan Francis Bright Rogers, M.A. (cons. 1959) (1975); Rt. Rev. William Alfred Franklin, O.B.E., 1978; Rt. Rev. J. P. Burrough, M.B.E. 1981

Dean (£10,640)

Very Rev. Randolph George Wise, M.A. 1981

Canons Residentiary (each £8,590)

Archd. Fernyhough 1977	T. R. Christie, M.A. ...1980
	J. Higham, M.A. 1983

Master of the Music, C. S. Gower, M.A., F.R.C.O. ..1977

Archdeacons

Northampton, Ven. B. R. Marsh, B.A. 1964
Oakham, Ven. B. Fernyhough, B.A.............1977
   Beneficed Clergy, 259; Curates, &c, 30
Chancellor, Rev. Canon K. C. Routledge, M.A., LL.B.
Registrar, R. Hemingray, 37 Priestgate, Peterborough.

PORTSMOUTH £13,070

7th Bishop, Rt. Rev. Timothy John Bavin, M.A. (Bishopswood, Fareham, Hants.) [Signs Timothy Portsmouth] 1984
Provost, Very Rev. David Staffurth Stancliffe, M.A...1982
Organist, A. Froggatt, MUS.B., A.R.C.O.

Canons Residentiary

N. H. Crowder, M.A. .1975	R. Eckersley 1984
S. G. Platten 1982	P. J. Cotton 1984

Archdeacons

Portsmouth, Ven. R. V. Scruby, M.A. 1977
I. of Wight, Ven. F. C. Carpenter, M.A...........1977
   Beneficed Clergy, 94; Curates, &c., 54
Chancellor, His Honour Judge Aglionby, M.A. ..1978
Registrar, T. S. Blower, M.A. 1976

ROCHESTER £13,070

104th Bishop, Rt. Rev. Richard David Say, D.D. (Bishopscourt, Rochester) [Signs David Roffen:] 1961

Bishop Suffragan

Tonbridge, Rt. Rev. David Henry Bartleet, M.A. (Bishop's Lodge, St. Botolph's Road, Sevenoaks) 1982

Dean (£10,640)

Very Rev. John Robert Arnold, M.A............1978

Canons Residentiary

P. A. Welsby, M.A., Ph.D. 1966	E. R. Turner, M.A. ..1981
	Achd. Turnbull 1984
H. E. G. Stapleton, M.A. 1980	

Organist, B. Ferguson, M.A., F.R.C.O. 1977

Archdeacons

Bromley, Ven. E. R. Francis 1979
Rochester, Ven. A. M. A. Turnbull, M.A. 1984

Tonbridge, Ven. R. J. Mason 1977
  Beneficed Clergy, 200; *Curates, &c.*, 50
Chancellor, His Honour Judge M. B. Goodman,
  M.A. 1971
Registrar, O. R. Woodfield, Rochester 1955
Sec. D. W. Faull, 22 Greencoat Place, S.W.1. 1963

ST. ALBANS £13,070

8th Bishop, Rt. Rev. John Bernard Taylor, M.A.
(Abbey Gate House, St. Albans) [Signs John
St. Albans] 1980

Bishops Suffragan

Bedford, Rt. Rev. David John Farmbrough, M.A. 1981
Hertford, Rt. Rev. Kenneth Harold Pillar, M.A. . . .1982

Dean (£10,640)

Very Rev. Peter Clement Moore, M.A., D.Phil. . . .1973
Organist, S. H. Darlington, B.A., F.R.C.O. 1978

Archdeacons

St. Albans, Ven. E. M. Norfolk 1982
Bedford, Ven. C. J. Mayfield 1979
  Beneficed Clergy, 249; *Curates, &c.*, 83
Chancellor, G. H. Newsom, Q.C., M.A. 1958
Registrar and Legal Sec., D. N. Cheetham,
Holywell Lodge, 41 Holywell Hill, St. Albans . 1978

ST. EDMUNDSBURY AND IPSWICH £13,070

7th Bishop, Rt. Rev. John Waine, B.A. (Bishop's
House, Ipswich IP1 3ST), *cons.* 1975 [Signs
John St. Edm. & Ipswich] 1978

Bishop Suffragan

Dunwich, Rt. Rev. Eric Nash Devenport, B.A. 1980
Provost, Very Rev. Raymond Furnell 1981

Canons Residentiary

D. A. Payne, M.A. . . .1973 | G. J. Tarris, M.A. . . .1982

Archdeacons

Ipswich, Ven. G. D. J. Walsh, M.A. 1976
Suffolk, Ven. T. A. Gibson, M.A. 1984
Sudbury, Ven. D. J. Smith 1984
Organist, T. F. H. Oxley, M.A., B.MUS., F.R.C.O. . .1957
Beneficed Clergy, 138; *Clergy of incumbent status*, 45;
  Curates, 20
Chancellor, His Honour Judge Blofeld, Q.C., M.A. 1974
Registrar, J. D. Mitson, M.A., LL.B. 22–28 Museum
Street, Ipswich.

SALISBURY £13,070

76th Bishop, Rt. Rev. John Austin Baker, M.A.,
M. Litt. (South Canonry, The Close, Salisbury
SP1 2ER) [Signs John Sarum] 1982

Bishops Suffragan

Sherborne, Rt. Rev. John Dudley Galtrey Kirk-
ham, M.A. (Little Bailie, Sturminster Marshall,
Wimborne) 1976
Ramsbury, Rt. Rev. John Robert Geoffrey
Neale, A.K.C. (Chittoe Vicarage, Bromham,
Chippenham) 1974

Dean (£10,640)

Very Rev. Sydney Hall Evans, C.B.E., M.A., D.D. . .1977

Canons Residentiary (£8,590)

I. G. D. Dunlop, M.A., | C. Moxon, M.A. 1975
  F.S.A. . . . . .1972 | R. G. Askew, M.A. . . .1983
Organist, R. G. Seal, M.A., F.R.C.O. 1968

Archdeacons

Sherborne, Ven. E. J. G. Ward, M.V.O., M.A. 1967
Sarum, Ven. N. S. McCulloch, M.A. 1979
Wilts, Ven. B. J. Smith 1980
Dorset, Ven. G. E. Walton 1982
  Beneficed Clergy, 255; *Curates, &c.*, 38
Chancellor of the Diocese, His Hon. J. H. Ellison,
  V.R.D., M.A. 1955
Registrar and Legal Secretary, F. M. Broadbent,
M.A., 42 Castle Street, Salisbury.

SOUTHWARK £13,070

7th Bishop, Rt. Rev. Ronald Oliver Bowlby, M.A.
(Bishop's House, 38 Tooting Bec Gardens,
S.W.16) (*cons.* 1973, *trans.* 1980) [Signs Ronald
Southwark] 1980
Assistant Bishops, Rt. Rev. Edward George
Knapp-Fisher, M.A. (*cons.* 1960), 1975; Rt. Rev.
Edmund Michael Hubert Capper, O.B.E. (*cons.*
1967), 1981; Rt. Rev. Archibald Ronald Mc-
Donald Gordon (*cons.* 1975) 1984

Bishops Suffragan

Kingston on Thames, Rt. Rev. Peter Stephen
Maurice Selby, M.A. 1984
Woolwich, Rt. Rev. Albert Peter Hall, M.A.
(Homestead, Hillyfields Crescent, S.E.4) 1984
Provost, Very Rev. David Lawrence Edwards,
M.A. 1983

Canons Residentiary

P. H. Penwarden, | G. A. Parrott 1977
  M.A. . . . . .1971 | R. Garrard 1979
I.G. Smith-Cameron, | J. S. Cox, M.A. 1983
  B.A. . . . . .1972 |
Organist, H. Bramma 1976

Archdeacons

Southwark, Ven. W. D. Wood 1982
Lewisham, Ven. I. G. Davies, B.A., B.D. 1972
Kingston, Ven. B. V. Jacob, M.A. 1977
Wandsworth, Ven. P. B. Coombs, M.A. 1975
Chancellor, Rev. E. Garth Moore, M.A. 1948
Registrar, D. W. Faull, 30 Causton Street, S.W.1. 1963

TRURO £13,070

12th Bishop, Rt. Rev. Peter Mumford, M.A. (Lis
Escop, Truro) [Signs Peter Truron:] 1981

Bishop Suffragan

St. Germans, Rt. Rev. Michael, S.S.F., M.A. (Regin-
ald Lindsay Fisher) (32 Falmouth Road,
Truro) 1979
Assistant Bishop, Rt. Rev. R. F. Cartwright,
M.A. 1982

Dean

Very Rev. David John Shearlock, B.A. 1982

Canons Residentiary

M. S. F. Thornton, | P. L. Maddock, B.A. .1976
  M.A., S.T.D. . . . . . . .1975 | Archd. Wood 1981
Organist, J. Winter 1971

Archdeacons

Cornwall, Ven. A. Wood 1981
Bodmin, Ven. G. Temple 1981
  Beneficed Clergy, 164; *Curates, &c.*, 20
Chancellor, P. T. S. Boydell, Q.C. 1957
Registrar and Secretray, R. W. Money, 2
Princes Street, Truro.

WORCESTER £13,070

111th *Bishop*, Rt. Rev. Philip Harold Ernest Goodrich, M.A. (The Bishop's House, Hartlebury Castle, Kidderminster) [Signs Philip Worcester] 1982

Assistant Bishops, Rt. Rev. David Howard Nicholas Allenby, M.A. (*cons.* 1962) (1968); Rt. Rev. Oliver Stratford Tomkins, D.D. (*cons.* 1959) 1975

Bishop Suffragan

Dudley, Rt. Rev. Anthony Charles Dumper, M.A. (The Bishop's House, Brooklands, Halesowen Road, Cradley Heath) 1977

Dean (£10,640)

Very Rev. Thomas George Adames Baker, M.A. .1975

Canons Residentiary (£8,590)

J. R. Fenwick, M.A. ..1978	Archd. Bentley 1984
N. Robinson 1983	

Organist, D. Hunt, MUS.D., F.R.C.O. 1975

Archdeacons

Dudley, (vacant).
Worcester, Ven. F. Bentley 1984
  Beneficed Clergy, 120; *Curates*, &c., 50
Chancellor, P. T. S. Boydell, Q.C. 1959
Registrar, Rev. J. A. Dale, Diocesan Registry, Little Comberton Rectory, Pershore.

Province of York

YORK £21,495

95th *Archbishop and Primate of England* Most Rev. and Rt. Hon. John Stapylton Habgood, P.C., D.D., *cons.* 1973 (Bishopthorpe, York) [Signs John Ebor:] 1983

Assistant Bishops, Rt. Rev. George Eyles Irwin Cockin, B.A. (*cons.* 1959) (1969); Rt. Rev. Richard Knyvet Wimbush, M.A. (*cons.* 1963) (1977); Rt. Rev. George Edward Holderness (*cons.* 1955) 1979

Bishops Suffragan

Selby, Rt. Rev. Clifford Condor Barker, M.A. (8 Bankside Close, Upper Poppleton, York) 1983

Whitby, Rt. Rev. Gordon Bates (60 West Green, Stokesley, Middlesbrough) 1983

Hull, Rt. Rev. Donald George Snelgrove, T.D., M.A. (Hullen House, Woodfield Lane, Hessle, Hull) 1981

Dean (£10,640)

(vacant).

Canons Residentiary (£8,590)

M. E. Bowering 1981	R. Mayland 1982
R. A. Hockley, M.A. ..1976	J. Toy, M.A., Ph.D. ...1983

Organist, P. J. Moore, B.MUS., A.R.C.M., F.R.C.O.

Archdeacons

York, Ven. L. C. Stanbridge, M.A. 1972
East Riding, Ven. M. E. Vickers, M.A. 1981
Cleveland, Ven. J. E. Southgate, B.A. 1974
  Beneficed Clergy, 264; *Curates*, &c., 43
Official Principal and Auditor of the Chancery Court, J. A. D. Owen, Q.C.
Chancellor of the Diocese, T. A. C. Coningsby, M.A. 1977
Vicar-General of the Province and Official Principal of the Consistory Court, T. A. C. Coningsby, M.A.
Registrar and Secretary, G. P. Knowles, M.A., LL.B. 1968

DURHAM £17,575

92nd *Bishop*, Rt. Rev. David Edward Jenkins, M.A. (Auckland Castle, Bishop Auckland) [Signs David Dunelm] 1984

Bishop Suffragan

Jarrow, Rt. Rev. Michael Thomas Ball, M.A., C.G.A. (Melkridge House, Gilesgate, Durham) .1980

Dean (£10,640)

Very Rev. Peter Richard Baelz, M.A., B.D. 1980

Canons Residentiary (£8,590)

D. R. Jones, M.A. 1964	R. L. Coppin, M.A. 1974
Archd. Perry 1970	Archd. Hodgson ...1983
S. W. Sykes, M.A. ...1974	T. Hart, M.A. 1983

Organist, R. Lloyd, MUS.B., F.R.C.O. 1974

Archdeacons

Durham, Ven. M. C. Perry, M.A. 1970
Auckland, Ven. J. D. Hodgson, B.A. 1983
  Clergy, 306
Chancellor, Rev. E. Garth Moore, M.A. 1954
Registrar and Legal Secretary, W. K. Wills, Ll.B. .1975

BLACKBURN £13,070

6th *Bishop*, Rt. Rev. David Stewart Cross, M.A. (Bishop's House, Ribchester Road, Blackburn) [Signs Stewart Blackburn] 1982

Bishops Suffragan

Lancaster, Rt. Rev. Dennis Fountain Page, M.A. (Winmarleigh Vicarage, nr. Preston) 1975

Burnley, Rt. Rev. Richard Charles Challinor Watson, M.A. (Palace House, Burnley) 1970

Provost, Very Rev. Lawrence Jackson, A.K.C. ...1973

Canons Residentiary

G. A. Williams, M.A. ..1965	B. M. Beaumont,
J. M. Taylor 1975	M.A. 1977

Archdeacons

Lancaster, Ven. K. H. Gibbons, B.SC............1981
Blackburn, Ven. C. W. D. Carroll, M.A. 1973
Organist, D. A. Cooper, M.A., F.R.C.O. 1983
  Beneficed Clergy, 240; *Curates*, &c., 54
Chancellor, Quentin T. Edwards, Q.C. 1977
Registrar, Leslie Ranson, LL.B. 1954

BRADFORD £13,070

7th *Bishop*, Rt. Rev. Robert Kerr Williamson (Bishopscroft, Ashwell Road, Heaton, Bradford) [Signs Robert Bradford] 1984

Provost, Very Rev. Brandon Donald Jackson, Ll.B. 1977

Canons Residentiary

K. H. Cook, A.K.C. ....1977 | C. Hayward.......1983
Organist, G. Weaver, M.A., A.R.C.O. 1982

Archdeacons

Bradford, Ven. D. H. Shreeve, M.A. 1984
Craven, Ven. D. A. Rogers, M.A. 1977
  Beneficed Clergy, 123; *Curates*, &c., 23

Chancellor, D. M. Savill, Q.C. 1976
Registrar and Secretary, J. G. H. Mackrell, 18
Devonshire Street, Keighley 1977

CARLISLE £13,070

64th Bishop, Rt. Rev. Henry David Halsey, B.A.
(Rose Castle, Dalston, Carlisle CA5 7BZ), (*cons.*
1968) [Signs David Carliol] 1972

Bishop Suffragan

Penrith, Rt. Rev. George Lanyon Hacker, M.A.
(The Rectory, Gt. Salkeld, Penrith). 1979

Dean (£10,640)

Very Rev. John Howard Churchill, M.A. 1973

Canons Residentiary

R. A. Chapman, M.A. 1978 | R. J. W. Bevan 1982
Organist, R. A. Seivewright, M.A., A.R.C.O. 1960

Archdeacons

Carlisle, Ven. C. P. Stannard 1984
West Cumberland, Ven. T. R. B. Hodgson, B.D. . .1979
Westmorland and Furness, Ven. P. Vaughan,
M.A. 1983
Beneficed Clergy, 190
Chancellor, His Hon. D. J. Stinson, M.A. 1971
Registrar and Sec., I. S. Sutcliffe, M.A., LL.B.,
Carlisle 1964

CHESTER £13,070

39th Bishop, Rt. Rev. Michael Alfred Baughen,
B.D. (Bishop's House, Chester) [Signs Michael
Cestr:] 1982

Bishops Suffragan

Stockport, Rt. Rev. Frank Pilkington Sargeant,
B.A. (32 Park Gate Drive, Cheadle Hulme,
Cheshire SK8 7DS) 1983
Birkenhead, Rt. Rev. Ronald Brown, B.A. (Traf-
ford House, Queen's Park, Chester) 1974

Dean (£10,640)

Very Rev. Thomas Wood Ingram Cleasby, M.A. .1978

Canons Residentiary (£8,590)

K. M. Maltby, M.A., | W. H. Vanstone, M.A.,
B.D. . . . . .1974 | S.T.M. 1978
K. M. Whittam, M.A. 1975 | L. R. Barker, M.A. . .1984
Organist, R. A. Fisher, M.A., F.R.C.O. 1967

Archdeacons

Chester, Ven. H. L. Williams, B.A. 1975
Macclesfield, Ven. R. Simpson, M.V.O., M.A. 1978
Chancellor, H. H. Lomas, M.A. 1977
Registrar and Legal Secretary, A. K. McAllester,
Friars, 20 White Friars, Chester.

LIVERPOOL £13,070

6th Bishop, Rt. Rev. David Stuart Sheppard, M.A.
(*cons.* 1969) (Bishop's Lodge, Woolton Park,
Liverpool) [Signs David Liverpool] 1975

Bishop Suffragan

Warrington, Rt. Rev. Michael Henshall, B.A.
(Martinsfield, Elm Avenue, Great Crosby,
Liverpool) 1975
Asst. Bishops, Rt. Rev. William Scott Baker, M.A.
(*cons.* 1943), 1968; Rt. Rev. John William
Hawkins Flagg (*cons.* 1969) 1978

Dean (£10,640)

Very Rev. R. D. C. Walters, B.SC 1983

Canons Residentiary

M. M. Wolfe . . . . . . .1982 | K. J. Riley 1983
D. J. Hutton . . . . . . .1983 | N. A. Frayling 1983
Organist, Ian Tracey 1980

Archdeacons

Liverpool, Ven. G. H. G. Spiers 1979
Warrington, Ven. C. D. S. Woodhouse 1981
Beneficed Clergy, 188; *Curates, &c.*, 125
Chancellor, R. G. Hamilton, M.A.
Registrar and Cathedral Chapter Clerk, R. H.
Arden, 1 Hanover Street, Liverpool 1.

MANCHESTER £13,070

9th Bishop, Rt. Rev. Stanley Eric Francis Booth-
Clibborn, M.A. (Bishopscourt, Bury New Road,
Manchester 7) [Signs Stanley Manchester] . . .1979

Bishops Suffragan

Bolton, Rt. Rev. David George Galliford, M.A. (4
Standfield Drive, Lostock, Bolton) 1984
Hulme, Rt. Rev. Colin Scott, M.A. (1 Raynham
Avenue, Didsbury, Manchester 20) 1984
Middleton, Rt. Rev. Donald Alexander Tytler,
M.A., (The Hollies, Manchester Road,
Rochdale) 1982
Assistant Bishops, Rt. Rev. Edward Ralph Wick-
ham, B.D. (*cons.* 1959), 1982; Rt. Rev. Kenneth
Venner Ramsey, M.A., B.D. (*cons.* 1953) 1975

Dean (£10,640)

Very Rev. Robert Waddington, B.A. (The
Deanery, 44 Shrewsbury Road, Prestwich M25
8GQ) 1984

Canons Residentiary (£8,590)

G. O. Morgan, B.SC. .1971 | J. Nicholls, A.K.C. 1983
Archd. R. B. Harris .1980 | J. R. Atherton, M.A.,
| ph.D. 1984
Organist, G. Stewart.

Archdeacons

Manchester, Ven. R. B. Harris, M.A. 1980
Bolton, Ven. F. J. Hoyle, M.A. 1982
Rochdale, Ven. D. Bonser, M.A. 1982
Beneficed Clergy, 300; *Curates, &c.*, 110
Chancellor, G. C. H. Spafford, M.A., Ll.B. 1976
Registrar and Bishop's Secretary, J. Maloney, 90
Deansgate, Manchester .1972

NEWCASTLE £13,070

10th Bishop, Rt. Rev. Andrew Alexander Kenny
Graham (*cons.* 1977) (Bishop's House, 29 Moor
Road South, Gosforth, Newcastle upon Tyne)
[Signs A. Newcastle] 1981
Assistant Bishop, Rt. Rev. Kenneth Edward Gill
(*cons.* 1972) 1980
Provost, Very Rev. Christopher Garnett Howsin
Spafford, M.A. 1976

Canons Residentiary

A. Wilson, M.A. . . . . . .1964 | W. J. Thomas, M.A. .1983
D. A. Carrette, M.A. .1978
Organist, Russell A. Missin, F.R.C.O. 1967

Archdeacons

Northumberland, Ven. W. J. Thomas, M.A. 1983
Lindisfarne, Ven. D. J. Smith 1981
Beneficed Clergy, 121; *other Clergy of incumbent
status*, 36; *Curates, &c.*, 33
Chancellor, His Hon. A. J. Blackett-Ord, M.A. 1971
Registrar and Sec., R. R. V. Nicholson, 46
Grainger Street, Newcastle upon Tyne.

RIPON £13,070

11th *Bishop,* Rt. Rev. David Nigel de Lorentz Young, M.A. (Bishop Mount, Ripon.) [Signs David Ripon] 1977

Bishop Suffragan

Knaresborough, Rt. Rev. John Dennis, M.A. (16 Shaftesbury Avenue, Leeds) 1979

Dean (£10,640)

Very Rev. Christopher Russell Campling, M.A. . . 1984

Canons Residentiary (each £8,590)

| R. B. McFadden, M.A. ....1979 | D. G. Ford, A.L.C.D., L.Th. ....1980 |

Organist, Ronald Perrin, F.R.C.O. 1966

Archdeacons

Leeds, Ven. A. J. Comber, M.SC. 1982
Richmond, Ven. N. G. L. R. McDermid, M.A. 1983
    Beneficed Clergy, 132; *Curates, &c.,* 40
Chancellor, J. B. Mortimer, Q.C., M.A. 1971
Registrar and Legal Secretary, J. R. Balmforth, M.A., Phoenix House, South Parade, Leeds.

SHEFFIELD £13,070

5th *Bishop,* Rt. Rev. David Ramsay Lunn, M.A. (Bishopscroft, Snaithing Lane, Sheffield 10) [Signs David Sheffield] 1980

Bishop Suffragan

Doncaster, Rt. Rev. William Michael Dermot Persson (5 Park Lane, Sheffield 10) 1982
Provost, Very Rev. Wilfred Frank Curtis, A.K.C. 1974

Archdeacons

Sheffield, Ven. M. J. M. Paton, M.A. 1978
Doncaster, Ven. I. Harland, M.A. 1979
Organist, G. Matthews, B.MUS., F.R.C.O. 1967
    Beneficed Clergy, 163; *Curates, &c.,* 46
Chancellor, G. B. Graham, Q.C. 1971
Registrar and Legal Sec. P. T. Ward, 30 Bank Street, Sheffield.

SODOR AND MAN £13,070

78th *Bishop,* Rt. Rev. Arthur Henry Attwell, B.D., M.Th., M.A. (Bishop's House, Quarterbridge Road, Douglas, Isle of Man) [Signs Arthur Sodor and Man] 1983
Archdeacon, D. A. Willoughby, B.A.

Canons Residentiary

| B. H. Kelly, M.A. | J. D. Gelling, M.A. |
| D. Baggaley, M.A. | J. M. Payne, M.A. |

    Beneficed Clergy, 20; *Curates, &c.,* 21
Vicar-General and Registrar, P. W. S. Farrant, 24 Athol Street, Douglas.
Assistant Secretary, J. Wilson.

SOUTHWELL £13,070

7th *Bishop,* Rt. Rev. John Denis Wakeling, M.C., M.A. (Bishop's Manor, Southwell) [Signs Denis Southwell] 1970

Bishop Suffragan

Sherwood, Rt. Rev. Harold Richard Darby, B.A. (Applegarth, Halam, Southwell) 1975
Provost, Very Rev. John Murray Irvine, M.A. 1978

Canons Residentiary

| D. P. Keene, M.A. ...1981 | L. J. Morley, B.D., M.Th. ....1980 |

Organist, K. Beard, M.A., MUS.B., F.R.C.O. 1959

Archdeacons

Newark, Ven. D. Leaning 1979
Nottingham, Ven. G. C. Handford 1984
    Beneficed Clergy, 172; *Curates, &c.,* 42
Chancellor, J. Shand, M.A., LL.B. 1981
Registrar, P. H. Mellors, M.A., Ll.B. 1970

WAKEFIELD £13,070

9th *Bishop,* Rt. Rev. Colin Clement Walter James, M.A. (Bishop's Lodge, Woodthorpe Lane, Wakefield) (*cons.* 1973) [Signs Colin Wakefield] 1977

Bishop Suffragan

Pontefract, Rt. Rev. Thomas Richard Hare, M.A. (306 Barnsley Road, Wakefield) 1971
Asst. Bishops, Rt. Rev. Philip William Wheeldon, O.B.E., M.A. (*cons.* 1954) 1977; Rt. Rev. Patrick Burnet Harris, M.A. (*cons.* 1973) 1981; Rt. Rev. Ralph Emmerson, B.D. (*cons.* 1972) 1979; Rt. Rev. Anselm Genders, M.A. (*cons.* 1977) 1982
Provost, Very Rev. John Edward Allen. 1982

Archdeacons

Pontefract, Ven. K. Unwin, M.A. 1981

Halifax, Ven. J. R. Alford, M.A. 1972
Organist, J. L. Bielby, M.A., MUS.B., F.R.C.O. 1971
    Beneficed Clergy, 176; *Curates, &c.,* 27
Chancellor, G. B. Graham, Q.C., LL.B. 1959
Registrar and Sec., E. Chapman, B.A., Burton Street, Wakefield.........................1979

The General Synod of the Church of England

Church House, Dean's Yard, SW1P 3NZ—*Presidents,* The Archbishop of Canterbury; The Archbishop of York; *Sec.-Gen.,* W. D. Pattinson. THE HOUSE OF BISHOPS.—*Chairman,* The Archbishop of Canterbury; *Vice-Chairman,* The Archbishop of York. THE HOUSE OF CLERGY.—*Chairman,* The Archdeacon of Leicester; *Vice-Chairman,* Canon P. H. Boulton. THE HOUSE OF LAITY, *Chairman,* O. W. H. Clark, C.B.E.; *Vice-Chairman,* Prof. J. D. McClean.

THE CHURCH IN WALES

BANGOR £13,428

79th *Bishop,* Rt. Rev. John Cledan Mears, M.A., *b.* 1922 (Ty'r Esgob, Bangor, Gwynedd), *cons.* 1982.

LLANDAFF £13,428

100th *Bishop,* Rt. Rev. John Richard Worthington Poole Hughes, M.A., *b.* 1916 (Llys Esgob, The Cathedral Green, Llandaff, Cardiff, *cons.* 1962, *trans.* 1976 1976

MONMOUTH £13,428

6th *Bishop* and 8th *Archbishop of Wales,* Most Rev. Derrick Greenslade Childs, B.A., *b.* 1918 (Bishopstow, Stow Hill, Newport, Gwent NPT 4EA), *cons.* 1972, *elected* Archbishop of Wales, 1983.

ST. ASAPH £13,428

74th *Bishop,* Rt. Rev. Alwyn Rice Jones, M.A., *b.,* 1934 (Esgobty, St. Asaph, Clwyd LL17 0TW) ..1982

ST. DAVID'S £13,428

124th *Bishop*, Rt. Rev. George Noakes, B.A., *b.* 1924 (Llys Esgob, Abergwili, Carmarthen, Dyfed) 1982

SWANSEA AND BRECON £13,428

6th *Bishop*, Rt. Rev. Benjamin Noel Young Vaughan, M.A., *b.* 1917 (Ely Tower, Brecon, Powys) 1976

OVERSEAS

Sees	Apptd.

CANADA

Primate

The Most Rev. Edward Walter Scott 1971

Province of Canada

The Most Rev. Archbishop

Fredericton, Harold Lee Nutter, *b.* 1923 (cons.1971), *Archbishop and Metropolitan* 1980

The Rt. Rev. Bishops

Central Newfoundland, M. Genge 1975
Eastern Newfoundland and Labrador M. Mate .1980
Montreal, R. Hollis 1975
Nova Scotia, L. F. Hatfield 1980
Quebec, A. Goodings 1977
Western Newfoundland, S. S. Payne, *b.* 1932 1978

Province of Rupert's Land

The Most Rev. Archbishop

Qu'Appelle, Michael Geoffrey Peers, *b.* 1934 (cons. 1977), *Archbishop and Metropolitan* 1982

The Rt. Rev. Bishops

Arctic, J. R. Sperry, *b.* 1924 1974
Athabasca , G. F. Woolsey 1983
Brandon, J. F. S. Conlin 1975
Calgary, J. B. Curtis 1983
Edmonton, E. K. Clarke (cons. 1976) 1980
Keewatin, H. J. P. Allan, *b.* 1928 1974
Qu' Appelle (see above)
Rupert's Land, W. Jones (cons. 1970) 1983
Saskatchewan, H. V. R. Short, *b.* 1914 1970
Saskatoon, R. A. Wood 1981

Province of Ontario

The Most Rev. Archbishop

Toronto, Lewis Samuel Garnsworthy, *b.* 1922 (cons. 1968), *Archbishop and Metropolitan* ...1980

The Rt. Rev. Bishops

Algoma, F. F. Nock, *b.* 1916 1975
Huron, D. D. Jones (cons. 1982) 1984
Moosonee, C. Lawrence 1980
Niagara, J. C. Bothwell (cons. 1971) 1973
Ontario, A. A. Read (cons. 1972) 1981
Ottawa, E. K. Lackey 1981
Toronto (see above)

Province of British Columbia

The Most. Rev. Archbishop

New Westminster, Douglas Walter Hambidge, *b.* 1927 (cons. 1969), *Archbishop and Metropolitan* 1981

The Rt. Rev. Bishops

British Columbia (vacant).
Caledonia, J. E. Hannen 1981
Cariboo, J. S. P. Snowden 1974
Kootenay, R. E. F. Berry.....................1971
New Westminster (see above)
Yukon, R. C. Ferris 1981

Sees	Apptd.

AUSTRALIA

Primate of Australia

The Most Rev. John Basil Rowland Grindrod, K.B.E., Archbishop of Brisbane.

Province of New South Wales

Archbishop and Metropolitan

Sydney, D. W. B. Robinson, *b.* 1922 (cons. 1973)..1982
Asst. Bps., J. R. Reid, *b.* 1928 (1972); K. H. Short, *b.* 1927 (1975); E. D. Cameron, *b.* 1926 (1975); R. H. Goodhew, *b.* 1931 (1982).
Armidale, P. Chiswell, *b.* 1934 1976
Bathurst, H. A. J. Witt (cons. 1965) 1981
Canberra and Goulburn, O. D. Dowling (cons. 1981) 1983
Grafton (vacant).
Newcastle, A. C. Holland *b.* 1927 (cons. 1970) 1978
Riverina, B. R. Hunter, *b.* 1927 (cons. 1971) 1971

Province of Victoria

Archbishop and Metropolitan

Melbourne, The Most Rev. David John Penman, *b.* 1936 (cons. 1982)..........................1984
Bps. Coadj., J. A. Grant, *b.* 1931 (1970); D. H. W. Shand; *b.* 1921 1973

The Rt. Rev. Bishops

Ballarat, J. Hazlewood, *b.* 1924 1975
Bendigo, O. S. Heyward, *b.* 1926 1975
Gippsland, N. J. Chynoweth, *b.* 1922 (cons. 1974) 1980
Wangaratta, M. McN. Thomas, *b.* 1926 1975

Province of Queensland

Archbishop and Metropolitan

Brisbane, The Most Rev. J. B. R. Grindrod, K.B.E., *b.* 1919 1980
Bp. Administrator, R. Wicks, O.B.E., *b.* 1921 1973

The Rt. Rev. Bishops

Carpentaria, A. Hall-Matthews, *b.* 1940 1984
N. Queensland, H. J. Lewis, *b.* 1926 1971
Northern Territory, C. Wood, *b.* 1936 1983
Rockhampton, G. A. Hearn, *b.* 1935 1981

Province of Western Australia

Archbishop and Metropolitan

Perth, The Most Rev. Peter Frederick Carnley, (cons. 1981) 1981
Asst. Bps., M. B. Challen (1978); B. R. Kyme ..1982

The Rt. Rev. Bishops

Bunbury, H. J. U. Jamieson 1984
N. W. Australia, G. B. Muston 1982

Province of South Australia

Archbishop and Metropolitan

Adelaide, The Most Rev. Keith Rayner, *b.* 1929 (cons. 1969) 1975

Sees	Apptd.

The Rt. Rev. Bishops
The Murray, R. G. Porter, *b.* 1924 (*cons.* 1967)...1970
Willochra, S. B. Rosier, *b.* 1928 (*cons.* 1967) 1970

Extra-Provincial Diocese

Tasmania, P. K. Newell, *b.* 1930 (*cons.* 1982) 1982

PROVINCE OF PAPUA NEW GUINEA
Archbishop

Popondota, The Most Rev. G. S. Ambo (*cons.*
1960) 1984

The Rt. Rev. Bishops
Aipo Rongo, J. C. Ashton.....................1976
Asst. Bps., B. Kerina 1981
Dogura, R. Sanana 1976
New Guinea Is., B. S. Meredith 1967
Port Moresby, I. R. Gadebo 1983

PROVINCE OF NEW ZEALAND
Primate and Archbishop

Auckland, The Most Rev. Paul Alfred Reeves, *b.*
1932, *cons.* 1971, *trans.* 1979 1980
Asst. Bps., G. E. A. Wilson, *b.* 1926 (1980); E.
G. Buckle, *b.* 1926 (1981)

The Rt. Rev. Bishops
Aotearoa, W. Vercoe, *b.* 1928 1981
Christchurch, M. J. Goodall, *b.* 1928 1984
Dunedin, P. W. Mann, *b.* 1924..................1976
Nelson, P. E. Sutton, *b.* 1923 1965
Polynesia, J. L. Bryce, *b.* 1935 1975
Waiapu, P. G. Atkins, *b.* 1936 1983
Waikato, B. N. Davis, *b.* 1934..................1980
Wellington, E. K. Norman, K.B.E., *b.* 1916 1973
Asst. Bp., W. J. W. Rosevear, *b.* 1918 1981

PROVINCE OF MELANESIA
Archbishop

Central Melanesia, The Most Rev. Norman
Kitchener Palmer, C.M.G., M.B.E., *b.* 1928 1975

The Rt. Rev. Bishops
Malaita, W. A. Pwaisiho 1981
Temotu, A. S. Waiaru 1981
Vanuatu, H. Tevi (*cons.* 1979) 1980
Ysabel, E. Pogo...............................1981

PROVINCE OF SOUTH AFRICA
Archbishop and Metropolitan

Cape Town, The Most Rev. Philip Welsford
Richmond Russell, *b.* 1919 (*cons.* 1966) 1981
Bps. Suff., P. M. Matolengwe, *b.* 1937 (1976);
C. H. Albertyn *b.* 1928 (1983).

The Rt. Rev. Bishops
Bloemfontein, T. S. Stanage, *b.* 1932 1982
George, (vacant).
Grahamstown, K. C. Oram, *b.* 1919 1974
Johannesburg, (vacant).
Bps. Suff., M. S. Ndwandwe, *b.* 1928 (1978);
J. S. Nkoane, *b.* 1929 (1982).
Kimberley & Kuruman, G. A. Swartz, *b.* 1928 ...1983
Lebombo, D. S. Sengulane, *b.* 1946 1976
Lesotho, P. S. Mokuku, *b.* 1935 1978
Bp. Suff., D. P. Nestor, *b.* 1938................1980
Namibia, J. H. Kauluma, *b.* 1933 1981
Natal, M. Nuttall, *b.* 1934 1982
Bp. Suff., A. Mkhize, *b.* 1929 1980
Niassa, (vacant).
Port Elizabeth, B. R. Evans, *b.* 1929 1974

Sees	Apptd.

Pretoria, R. A. Kraft, *b.* 1936 1982
Bp. Suff., J. H. G. Ruston, *b.* 1929 1983
St. Helena, E. A. C. Cannan, *b.* 1920............1979
St. John's, G. W. E. C. Ashby, *b.* 1930...........1980
Bp. Suff., J. Z. Dlamini, *b.* 1935 1980
Swaziland, B. L. N. Mkhabela, *b.* 1926 1975
Zululand, L. B. Zulu, *b.* 1937 1975

PROVINCE OF THE WEST INDIES
Archbishop of West Indies

Windward Islands, The Most Rev. George Cuthbert Manning Woodroffe, K.B.E., *Archbishop
and Metropolitan*, *b.* 1918 (*cons.* 1969) 1980

The Rt. Rev. Bishops
Antigua, O. U. Lindsay, *b.* 1928 (*cons.* 1970).....1970
Barbados, D. W. Gomez, *b.* 1937 (*cons.* 1972) 1972
Belize, K. A. McMillan (*cons.* 1980) 1980
Guyana, R. O. George, *b.* 1924 (*cons.* 1976) 1980
Jamaica, N. W. de Souza (*cons.* 1973) 1979
Bps. Suff. (*Mandeville*), W. A. Murray (1976);
(*Montego Bay*), A. C. Reid (1980)
Nassau and the Bahamas, M. H. Eldon, C.M.G.
(*cons.* 1971) 1972
Trinidad, C. O. Abdulah (*cons.* 1970)...........1970
Windward Islands, (see above).

As the Province of Nigeria came into being on
Feb. 24, 1979, the rest of the Province of West Africa
continues to function as the (On-going) Province of
West Africa:

PROVINCE OF WEST AFRICA
Archbishop

Liberia, The Most Rev. George Daniel Browne,
D.D.

The Rt. Rev. Bishops
Accra, F. W. B. Thompson; *Bo*, M. Keili; *Cape
Coast*, J. Ackon; *Freetown*, P. E. S. Thompson;
Kumasi, J. B. Arthur; *Gambia and Guinea*, J.
R. Elisee; *Liberia*, (see above); *Koforidua*, R.
Okine; *Sekondi*, T. Annobil; *Sunyani/Tamale*,
J. Dadson

PROVINCE OF NIGERIA
Archbishop

Ibadan, The Most Rev. Timothy Omotayo Olu-
fosoye (*cons.* 1965) *elected Archbp. of Nigeria* .1979

The Rt. Rev. Bishops
Lagos, F. O. Segun...........................1970
The Niger, J. A. Onyemelukwe...............1975
Niger Delta, S. O. Elenwa 1981
Ondo, S. O. Aderin 1981
Kaduna, T. E. Ogbonyomi 1975
Owerri, B. C. Nwankiti.......................1968
Benin, J. W. I. Idahosa 1977
Ekiti, J. A. Adetiloye 1970
Enugu, G. N. Otubelu 1969
Aba, H. A. I. Afonya 1957
Kwara, H. Haruna 1974
Ilesa, G. I. O. Olajide 1981
Egba-Egbado, T. I. Akintayo 1977
Ijebu, E. O. I. Ogundana......................1984
Asaba, R. N. C. Nwosu 1977
Kano, B. Ayam 1980
Jos, S. C. N. Ebo 1980
Warri, J. O. Dafiewhare 1980
Akure, E. B. Gbonigi 1983
Owo, A. O. Awosan 1983
Akoko, J. L. Akeredolu 1983

Sees   Apptd.

PROVINCE OF CENTRAL AFRICA

Archbishop

Botswana, The Most Rev. W. P. K. Makhulu, *b.*
1935 (*cons.* 1979) 1980

The Rt. Rev. Bishops

Central Zambia, C. W. Hlanya, *b.* 1933 (*cons.*
1984) 1984
Lake Malawi, P. N. Nyanja, *b.* 1940 (*cons.* 1978) .1978
Lundi, J. Siyachitema, *b.* 1932 (*cons.* 1981) 1981
Lusaka, S. S. Mumba, *b.* 1939 (*cons.* 1981) 1981
Manicaland, E. Masuko (*cons.* 1981) 1981
Mashonaland, R. P. Hatendi, *b.* 1927 (*cons.* 1979) 1981
Matabeleland, R. W. S. Mercer, *b.* 1935 (*cons.*
1977) 1977
Northern Zambia, J. Mabula, *b.* 1922 (*cons.* 1971) 1971
Southern Malawi, D. D. Ainani, *b.* 1921 (*cons.*
1979) 1981

PROVINCE OF KENYA

Archbishop

Nairobi, The Most Rev. Manasses Kuria 1979

The Rt. Rev. Bishops

Maseno North, J. Mundia 1970
Maseno South, H. Okullu.....................1974
   Asst. Bp., D. J. Omolo 1981
Mombasa, P. Mwang'ombe 1964
   Bp. Coadjutor, C. Nzano, (*cons.* 1975) 1978
Mount Kenya East, D. Gitari 1975
Mount Kenya South, S. Magua 1976
Nakuru, L. Kamau 1979

PROVINCE OF TANZANIA

Archbishop

Zanzibar and Tanga, The Most Rev. J. Ramad-
hani 1984

The Rt. Rev. Bishops

Central Tanganyika, Y. Madinda, *b.* 1926 (*cons.*
1964) 1971
Dar es Salaam, C. Mlangwa 1984
Masasi, C. R. Norgate.........................1984
Morogoro, G. Chitemo 1965
Ruvuma, M. Ngahyoma 1971
South West Tanganyika, C. Mwaigoga 1983
Victoria Nyanza, J. Rusibamayila 1976
Western Tanganyika, G. E. Mpango 1983
Mount Kilimanjaro, A. Mohamed 1982

PROVINCE OF UGANDA

Archbishop

Kampala, The Most Rev. Dr. Y. Okoth (*cons.*
1972) 1984

The Rt. Rev. Bishops

Ankole, A. Betungura 1970
Bukedi, N. E. Okille 1984
   Asst. Bp., A. L. Gonahasa 1978
Bunyoro, Y. Rwakaikara 1981
Busoga, C. Bamwoze..........................1972
   Asst. Bp., T. T. T. Nabeta 1983
Karamoja, H. Davies...........................1981
Kigezi, F. Kivengere 1972
   Asst. Bp., W. Rukirande 1975
Lango, M. Otim 1976
   Asst. Bp., W. Okodi 1979
Madi and West Nile, R. Ringtho (*cons.* 1976) 1977
Mbale, A. M. Wesonga 1981
Mityana, Y. Mukasa 1977
Namirembe, D. K. Nsubuga (*cons.* 1964) 1965
   Asst. Bps., M. Kauma 1975; L. Mpalanyi-
Nkoyoyo 1980

Sees   Apptd.

North Kigezi, Y. Ruhindi.....................1981
Northern Uganda, B. Ogwal 1974
   Asst. Bp., G. Oboma 1979
Ruwenzori, E. Kamanyire 1981
Soroti, G. Ilukor 1976
West Ankole, Y. Bamunoba 1977
West Buganda, C. Senyonjo 1974

PROVINCE OF BURUNDI, RWANDA AND ZAIRE

Archbishop

Butare, The Most Rev. J. Ndandali (*cons.*
1975) 1982

The Rt. Rev. Bishops

Boga Zaire, P. Njojo 1980
Bukavu, B. Dirokpa 1982
   Asst. Bp., M. Kolini 1980
Bujumbura, S. Sindamuka 1975
Buye, S. Ndayisenga 1979
Kisangani, M. Tibafa 1980

PROVINCE OF THE INDIAN OCEAN

Archbishop

(vacant)

The Rt. Rev. Bishops

Antananarivo, R. Rabenirina 1984
Antsiranana, K. Benzies 1982
Mauritius, R. Donat 1984
Seychelles, F. C. Him 1979
Toamasina, (vacant).

ANGLICAN COUNCIL OF SOUTH AMERICA

The Rt. Rev. Bishops

Argentina and E. S. America, R. S. Cutts.......1975
Chile, C. F. Bazley (*cons.* 1969) 1977
   Asst. Bps., I. Morrison (1977); B. Skinner 1978
Northern Argentina, D. Leake (*cons.* 1969).....1980
   Asst. Bp., M. Mariño 1975
Paraguay, D. Milmine 1973
   Aux. Bp., O. Ortiz 1982
Peru and Bolivia, D. Evans 1978

UNDER THE ARCHBISHOP OF CANTERBURY

The Rt. Rev. Bishops

Bermuda, (vacant).
Pusan, W. Choi 1974
Kuching, B. Temengong.......................1968
Lusitanian Church in Portugal, F. Soares 1981
Sabah, Chhoa Heng Sze 1971
Seoul, P. Lee 1965
Singapore, M. Tay 1982
Spanish Reformed Episcopal Church, A.
   Sanchez 1982
Taejon, M. Pae 1974
West Malaysia, J. G. Savarimuthu 1973

THE EPISCOPAL CHURCH IN JERUSALEM AND THE MIDDLE EAST

President-Bishop, Rt. Rev. H. B. Dehqani-Tafti .1976
   Asst. Bp., A. K. Cragg......................1970
Jerusalem, S. Kafity 1984
Iran, H. B. Dehqani-Tafti.....................1961
Egypt, G. Abdel Malik 1984
Cyprus and the Gulf, H. Moore 1983

ARCHBISHOPS OF CANTERBURY SINCE 1414

1414 Henry Chichele	1633 William Laud	1828 William Howley
1443 John Stafford	1660 William Juxon	1848 John Bird Sumner
1452 John Kemp	1663 Gilbert Sheldon	1862 Charles Thomas Longley
1454 Thomas Bourchier	1678 William Sancroft	1868 Archibald Campbell Tait
1486 John Morton	1691 John Tillotson	1883 Edward White Benson
1501 Henry Dean	1695 Thomas Tenison	1896 Frederick Temple
1503 William Warham	1716 William Wake	1903 Randall Thomas Davidson
1533 Thomas Cranmer	1737 John Potter	1928 Cosmo Gordon Lang
1556 Reginald Pole	1747 Thomas Herring	1942 William Temple
1559 Matthew Parker	1757 Matthew Hutton	1945 Geoffrey Francis Fisher
1576 Edmund Grindal	1758 Thomas Secker	1961 Arthur Michael Ramsey
1583 John Whitgift	1768 Hon. Frederick Cornwallis	1974 Frederick Donald Coggan
1604 Richard Bancroft	1783 John Moore	1980 Robert Runcie
1611 George Abbot	1805 Charles Manners Sutton	

ARCHBISHOPS OF YORK SINCE 1606

1606 Tobias Matthew	1724 Launcelot Blackburn	1891 William Connor Magee
1628 George Montague	1743 Thomas Herring	1891 William Dalrymple Maclagan
1629 Samuel Harsnett	1747 Matthew Hutton	1909 Cosmo Gordon Lang
1632 Richard Neile	1757 John Gilbert	1929 William Temple
1641 John Williams	1761 Robert Hay Drummond	1942 Cyril Forster Garbett
1660 Accepted Frewen	1777 William Markham	1956 Arthur Michael Ramsey
1664 Richard Sterne	1808 Edward Venables Vernon	1961 Frederick Donald Coggan
1683 John Dolben	Harcourt	1975 Stuart Yarworth Blanch
1688 Thomas Lamplugh	1848 Thomas Musgrave	1983 John Stapylton Habgood
1691 John Sharp	1860 Charles Thomas Longley	
1714 William Dawes	1862 William Thomson	

ECCLESIASTICAL COURTS

Judge, John Arthur Dalziel Owen, Q.C.

[Judge of the Provincial Courts of Canterbury and York under "The Ecclesiastical Jurisdiction Measure, 1963."].

Court of Arches

Registry, 16 Beaumont Street, Oxford.
Dean, J. A. D. Owen, Q.C.

Court of Faculties

[Registry and Office for Marriage Licences (Special and Ordinary). Appointment of Notaries Public, &c., 1, The Sanctuary, Westminster, S.W.1. Office hours, 10 to 4; Saturdays, 10 to 12].
Master, J. A. D. Owen, Q.C.

Vicar General's Office

16 Beaumont Street, Oxford

Vicar General and Chancellor, Miss S. M. Cameron, Q.C.

OFFICE OF THE VICAR GENERAL OF THE PROVINCE OF YORK.
Vicar General, T. A. C. Coningsby.
Chancellor, T. A. C. Coningsby.
Registrar, G. P. Knowles.

Chancery Court of York

Auditor, J. A. D. Owen, Q.C.
Registrar, G. P. Knowles.

THE CHURCH OF SCOTLAND

Church Office, 121 George Street, Edinburgh 2

THE CHURCH OF SCOTLAND is Presbyterian in constitution, and is governed by Kirk Sessions, Presbyteries, Synods, and the General Assembly, which consists of both clerical and lay representatives from each of the Presbyteries. It is presided over by a Moderator (chosen annually by the Assembly), to whom Her Majesty the Queen has granted precedence in Scotland, during his term of office, next after the Lord Chancellor of Great Britain. The Sovereign, if not present in person, is represented by a Lord High Commissioner, who is appointed each year by the Crown. The country, for Church purposes, is divided into 12 Synods and 46 Presbyteries, and there are about 2,000 ministers and licentiates engaged in ministerial and other work. The figures at Dec. 31, 1981, were:—

Congregations, 1,780; total membership 902,714. In 21 Overseas Mission fields there are 152 European missionaries (and in addition many missionaries' wives, most of whom are doing mission work in the various fields).

LORD HIGH COMMISSIONER (1984), The Lord Maclean, P.C., K.T., G.C.V.O., K.B.E.

MODERATOR OF THE ASSEMBLY (1984), Right Rev. J. M. K. Paterson, M.A.
Principal Clerk, Rev. D. F. M. Macdonald, C.B.E., M.A., Ll.B.
Deputy Clerk, Rev. A. G. McGillivray, M.A., B.D.
Procurator, G. Penrose, Q.C.
Law Agent and Solicitor of the Church, R. A. Paterson, M.A. Ll.B.
Parliamentary Solicitor, Colin McCulloch (London).
General Treasurer, W. G. P. Colledge, C.A.

THE PRESBYTERIAN CHURCH IN IRELAND.—The largest of the Presbyterian churches in Ireland consists of 22 presbyteries, 444 ministers, 566 congregations, with 133,141 communicants, 125,592 families and 6,700 Sunday-school teachers. During the 12 months ended Dec. 31, 1983, there was contributed by congregational effort £2,518,973 plus IR£197,766 for religious, charitable, and missionary purposes. The total income for the period raised by congregations for all purposes was £13,416,007 plus IR£979,330.—
General Sec., Very Rev. A. J. Weir, M.SC., D.D., Church House, Belfast, 1.

UNITED REFORMED CHURCH

The United Reformed Church was formed by the union of the Congregational Church in England and Wales and the Presbyterian Church of England on October 5, 1972. The Re-formed Association of Churches of Christ were joined to the URC on September 26, 1981. It is divided into 12 Provinces, each with a Provincial Moderator, and 70 Districts. There are 140,000 members and 900 serving ministers of whom 100 are auxiliary and give voluntary service. It shares an international mission through the Council for World Mission and is a member of the British and World Council of Churches. Its ministers are trained at five recognized colleges.

General Sec., Rev. B. G. Thorogood, M.A., 86 Tavistock Place, WC1H 9RT

The majority of those members of the Congregational Church who did not join the United Reformed Church comprise the Congregational Federation. *Sec.*, J. B. Wilcox, The Congregational Centre, 4 Castle Gate, Nottingham.

THE EPISCOPAL CHURCH IN SCOTLAND

Sees. The Rt. Rev. Bishops.	Cons. Clgy.	Stipd.
Aberdeen and Orkney, Frederick Charles Darwent	1978..12	£8,125
Argyll and the Isles, George Kennedy Buchanan Henderson, M.A., *b.* 1921	1977..11	£9,780
Brechin, Lawrence Edward Luscombe, *b.* 1925	1975..16	£6,217
Edinburgh, Alastair Iain Macdonald Haggart, M.A., *b.* 1915. .1975..65		£7,272

Sees. The Rt. Rev. Bishops.	Cons. Clgy.	Stipd.
Glasgow and Galloway, Derek Alec Rawcliffe, O.B.E., *b.* 1919	1981..41	£8,349
Moray, Ross and Caithness, George Minshull Sessford, M.A., *b.* 1928	1970..17	£6,300
St. Andrews, Dunkeld and Dunblane, Michael Geoffrey Hare-Duke, M.A., *b.* 1925	1969..26	£6,420

Registrar of the Episcopal Synod, I. R. Guild, W.S., 16 Charlotte Square, Edinburgh EH2 4YS Churches, Mission Stations, &c., 339. Clergy, 221; Communicants, 38,420.

THE CHURCH OF IRELAND

Sees	Archbishops	Apptd.	Clgy.
*Armagh**	Most Rev. John Ward Armstrong, D.D., *b.* 1915 (*cons.* 1968)	1980	54
Dublin	Most Rev. Henry Robert McAdoo, Ph.D., D.D., *b.* 1916 (*cons.* 1962)	1977	74
	BISHOPS		
Meath & Kildare	Most Rev. Donald Arthur Richard Caird, B.D., *b.* 1925 (*cons.* 1970)	1976	25
Cashel & Ossory.	Rt. Rev. Noel Vincent Willoughby, M.A., *b.* 1926	1980	44
Clogher	Rt. Rev. Gordon McMullan, Ph.D., B.SC., *b.* 1934	1980	32
Connor	Rt. Rev. William John McCappin, B.D., *b.* 1919	1981	101
Cork, Cloyne & Ross	Rt. Rev. Samuel Greenfield Poyntz, Ph.D., B.D., *b.* 1926	1978	28
Derry & Raphoe.	Rt. Rev. James Mehaffey, B.D., Ph.D., *b.* 1931	1980	56
Down & Dromore	Rt. Rev. Robert Henry Alexander Eames, Ll.B., Ph.D., *b.* 1937 (*cons.* 1975)	1980	103
Kilmore, Elphin & Ardagh	Rt. Rev. William Gilbert Wilson, B.D., Ph.D., *b.* 1918	1981	27
Limerick & Killaloe	Rt. Rev. Walton Newcombe Francis Empey, B.D., *b.* 1934	1981	20
Tuam	Rt. Rev. John Coote Duggan, B.D., *b.* 1918	1969	11

*Primate.

ST. PATRICK'S NATIONAL CATHEDRAL, DUBLIN. *Dean and Ordinary,* Very Rev. V. G. B. Griffin, Ph.D., B.A.

Chief Officer and Secretary to the REPRESENTATIVE CHURCH BODY, H. R. Roberts, Church of Ireland House, Church Avenue, Rathmines, Dublin 6.

THE METHODIST CHURCH

The Methodist Church is governed primarily by the Conference, secondarily by the District Synods (held in the autumn and the spring), consisting of all the ministers and of selected laymen in each district, over which a chairman, who is a minister, is appointed by the Conference; and thirdly by the circuit meeting of the ministers and lay officers of each circuit. The authority of both Synods and Circuit Meetings is subordinate to the Conference, which has the supreme legislative and judicial power in Methodism.

President of the Conference (July 1984–85), Rev. G. E. Barritt, O.B.E., M.A.
Vice-President of the Conference (July 1984–85), Mrs. J. E. Lunn.
Secretary of the Conference, Rev. B. E. Beck, D.D., 1 Central Buildings, Westminster, S.W.1.
President Designate (1985–86), Rev. C. Hughes Smith, M.A.
Vice-President Designate (1985–86), L. Murray.

Statistics.—In 1984 in association with the Conference in Great Britain there were 3,457 Ministers, 13,984 Local Preachers, 458,592 Members in 7,659 churches. Statistics are published triennially.

The World Methodist Council, founded 1881, reorganized 1951, associates Methodism throughout the world in 90 countries.

The Methodist Church was founded in 1739 by the two brothers Wesley and rapidly spread throughout the British Isles and to America before 1770. The Methodist Church in Great Britain was united in 1932 by the fusion of the Wesleyan Methodist Church which was the original section, the Primitive Methodist Church, which arose through the evangelists Hugh Bourne and William Clowes in 1810, and the United Methodist Church, itself a fusion in 1907 of the Methodist New Connexion which dated from 1797, the Bible Christian Methodist Church, which dated from 1815 and the United Methodist Free Churches which originated in controversies in 1828 and 1849. The United Methodist Church of America was formed by a union of United Methodist denominations with the United Evangelical Brethren.

Methodist Church in Ireland

The Methodist Church in Ireland has 198 Ministers, 275 Lay Preachers, 21,339 Adult and 14,659 Junior Members.

President, (1984–85), Rev. P. Kingston.

Secretary, Rev. C. G. Eyre, B.A., 3 Upper Malone Road, Belfast, 9.

The United Church of Canada

85 St. Clair Ave. E., Toronto, Ontario

The United Church of Canada is the result of the union (1925) of Methodist, Presbyterian and Congregational Churches in Canada. Subsequently several other communions have become part of the Church.

Moderator, Rt. Rev. Clarke MacDonald, D.D.

Secretary, Rev. P. A. Cline.

Independent Methodists

Independent Methodists.—This body is Congregational in its organization, with an unpaid Ministry. Its first Conference was held in 1805. In 1983 there were in Great Britain 151 Ministers, 4,430 Members, 118 Churches and 4,763 Sunday scholars. *Gen. Sec.,* Rev. J. M. Day, The Old Police House, Croxton, Stafford ST21 6PE

Wesleyan Reform Union

This Union is Methodist in doctrine, Congregational in government, with, if any church desires it, a paid ministry. It is the remnant of the original Reformers expelled from Wesleyan Methodism in 1849. The adherents are mainly in the Midland and Northern counties. In 1984 there were in Great Britain 21 Ministers, 165 Lay Preachers, 3,403 Members, 134 Chapels and 2,549 Sunday School scholars.—*President,* A. Fisher, Sheffield.

General Secretary and Connexional Editor, Rev. D. A. Morris, Wesleyan Reform Church House, 123 Queen Street, Sheffield 1.

THE PRESBYTERIAN CHURCH OF WALES

The PRESBYTERIAN OR CALVINISTIC METHODIST CHURCH OF WALES is the only Church of purely Welsh origin, and embraces a very large section of the Welsh-speaking population. Its form of government is Presbyterian, and it is a constituent of the World Alliance of Reformed Churches.

In 1983 the body numbered—chapels and other buildings, 1,200; ministers in pastoral charge, 181; elders, 4,917; communicants, 75,092; Sunday scholars, 25,343.

The *Association in the East* which includes nine of the English Presbyteries was formed in 1947.

Moderator of General Assembly (1984–85), Miss M. Roberts, Amlwch.

Moderators of Associations (1984–85) *South Wales,* R. Nantlais Williams, Swansea; *North Wales,* Rev. E. Idris Davies, Menai Bridge; *East Wales,* L. Morgan, Bronllys.

General Secretary, Rev. D. H. Owen, 53 Richmond Road, Cardiff CF2 3UP

The **Baptists** have over 35,000,000 members in all countries. In Britain they are for the most part grouped in Associations of churches, and the majority of these belong to the Baptist Union, which was formed in 1812. Current statistics show that there are 2,052 churches and 168,582 members. There also exist separate Baptist Unions of Scotland (159 churches and 16,471 members); Wales (607 churches and 34,179 members); Ireland (92 churches and 7,949 members). *President of the Baptist Union of Great Britain and Ireland,* (1984–85), Rev. F. Cooke, B.D. *Secretary,* Rev. B. Green, M.A., B.D. *Office,* 4 Southampton Row, WC1B 4AB

THE JEWS

It is estimated that about 410,000 Jews are resident in the British Isles, some 280,000 being domiciled in Greater London.

The *Board of Deputies of British Jews,* established in 1760, is the representative body of British Jewry and is recognized by H.M. Government. The basis of representation is mainly synagogal, but secular organizations are also represented. It is a deliberative body and its objects are to watch over the interests of British Jewry, to protect Jews against any disability which they may suffer by reason of their creed and to take such action as may be conducive to their welfare.

President, The Hon. Greville Janner, Q.C., M.P.

Secretary General, Hayim Pinner.

Office, Woburn House, Upper Woburn Place, W.C.1.

CHIEF RABBI—The Very Rev. I. Jakobovits, KT., Ph.D.

Executive Director, M. Davis. *Office,* Adler House, Tavistock Square, W.C.1.

The *Beth Din* (Court of Judgment) is a rabbinic body consisting of *Dayanim* (Assessors) and the Chief Rabbi, who is President of the Court. The Court arbitrates when requested in cases between Jew and Jew and non-Jew and gives decisions on religious questions. The decisions are based on Jewish Law and practice and do not conflict with the law of the land. The *Beth Din* also deals with matters concerning dietary law and marriages and divorces, according to Jewish Law.

Dayanim, M. Swift; Dr. I. Lerner; C. D. Kaplin; Rabbi I. D. Berger.

Clerk to the Court, Marcus Carr, Adler House, Tavistock Square, W.C.1.

OTHER RELIGIOUS DENOMINATIONS

The General Assembly of Unitarian and Free Christian Churches has about 95 ministers, 250 chapels and other places of worship in Great Britain and Ireland. *Gen. Sec.*, Dr. R. W. Smith, Essex Hall, Essex Street, WC2R 3HY

The Salvation Army, first known as the Christian Mission, was founded by William Booth in the East End of London in 1865. In 1878 it took its present name and adopted a quasi-military method of government. Since then it has become established in over 80 countries of the world. The head of the denomination, known as the General, is elected by a High Council, consisting of all active Commissioners and Territorial Commanders who have held the rank of Colonel for at least two years. In 1983 there were in Great Britain, 1,044 Corps (Churches), 125 Social Services Centres and 1,812 Officers engaged in evangelistic and social work. The latest statistics for the world (1983) are 15,135 Corps, 4,449 Social Services Centres (including institutions and schools) and 24,808 Officers. *General*, Jarl Wahlström. *International Headquarters:*— 101 Queen Victoria Street, E.C.4.

The Religious Society of Friends (Quakers), founded in the 17th century, has no separated ministry. There are in Great Britain 444 places of worship and 18,303 members (world membership 204,457). *Central Offices (Great Britain)*, Friends House, Euston Road, N.W.1; *(Ireland)*, 6 Eustace Street, Dublin.

The First Church of Christ, Scientist, in Boston Massachusetts, U.S.A. (District Manager, Committees on Publication for Great Britain and Ireland, 108 Palace Gardens Terrace, W.8), has about 260 branch churches and societies in Great Britain and Ireland.

The Moravian Church, 5 Muswell Hill, N.10, has in the U.K. 40 congregations with 4,000 members.

The Free Church of England (otherwise called The Reformed Episcopal Church) has 33 churches in England. *Gen. Sec.*, Rt. Rev. A. Ward, 28 Sedgebrook, Swindon, Wilts.

The Seventh Day Adventists (*Hdqrs.*, Stanborough Park, Watford, Herts.), have more than 200 organized churches and companies and more than 15,500 members in the British Isles. *Executive Sec.*, E. W. Howell.

The Spiritualists in Britain have 900 churches and societies.

THE ROMAN CATHOLIC CHURCH

HIS HOLINESS POPE JOHN PAUL II (Karol Wojtyla), *born* in Wadowice, Poland, May 18, 1920; *ordained priest* November 1, 1946; appointed *Archbishop of Krakow* January 13, 1964, created *Cardinal* at a Consistory on June 26, 1967. Formally assumed Pontificate October 16, 1978.

THE SACRED COLLEGE OF CARDINALS, when complete, consisted of six Cardinal Bishops, fifty Cardinal Priests and fourteen Cardinal Deacons. This number was fixed by Pope Sixtus V in 1586. Pope John XXIII created 52 new Cardinals. Pope Paul VI created 27 new Cardinals on Feb. 22, 1965, 27 on June 26, 1967, 33 on Apr. 28 1969, 30 on March 5, 1973, 20 on May 24, 1976, 4 on June 27, 1977; Pope John Paul II created 15 new Cardinals on June 30, 1979. In July 1983 there were 120 Cardinals. The Cardinals are advisers and assistants of the Sovereign Pontiff and form the supreme council or Senate of the Church. On the death of the Pope they elect his successor. The assembly of the Cardinals at the Vatican for the election of a new Pope is known as the Conclave in which, in complete seclusion, the Cardinals elect by secret ballot; a two-thirds majority is necessary before the vote can be accepted as final. When a Cardinal receives the necessary votes the Dean of the Sacred College formally asks him if he will accept election and the name by which he wishes to be known. On his acceptance of the office the Conclave is dissolved and the First Cardinal Deacon announces the election to the assembled crowd in St. Peter's Square. On the first Sunday or Holyday following the election the new Pope assumes the pontificate at High Mass in St. Peter's Square. A new pontificate is dated from the assumption of the pontificate.

FORMS OF ADDRESS: *Cardinal*, "His Eminence Cardinal . . ." (if an Archbishop, "His Eminence the Cardinal Archbishop of . . ."); *Archbishop*, "The Most Rev. Archbishop of . . ."; *Bishop*, "The Rt. Rev. Bishop of . . ."

THE CURIA

The Curia or governing body of the Roman Catholic Church is made up of various administrative departments headed by the Secretariat of State and the Sacred Council for the Public Affairs of the Church. Below these are congregations, secretariats and tribunals assisted by commissions and offices. All are headed by Cardinals who have as their British equivalent the Ministers or Secretaries of State heading the various government departments.

The Vatican State has as with any nation its own diplomatic service although its representatives are officially acknowledged in different ways throughout the countries of the World. Where the representation is only to the local churches and not to the government of that country then the man appointed is an Apostolic Delegate as was the case in Britain until recently. However where the representative is recognized as having diplomatic status by a particular government then he is known as either a nuncio, pro nuncio or inter nuncio. Nuncios are Papal Ambassadors who are given precedence over all other ambassadors by their appointed country and are the doyens of the diplomatic corps. In countries where precedence is not recognized, as in Britain, the papal representative is known as a pro nuncio.

Apostolic Pro Nuncio to Great Britain, His Excellency Archbishop Bruno Bernard Heim, 54 Parkside, Wimbledon, SW19.

British Ambassador Extraordinary and Plenipotentiary to the Holy See, His Excellency Sir Mark Evelyn Heath, K.C.V.O., C.M.G., 00179 Roma, Villa Drusiana, Via di Porta, San Sebastiano, 13/A.

THE BISHOPS' CONFERENCES

The Roman Catholic church **in England and Wales** is governed by:

1. **The Bishops' Conference** which consists of the local ordinaries (the Diocesan Bishops) of any rite; coadjutor bishops and auxiliaries; and titular bishops with special tasks. They are headed by the President, Cardinal Basil Hume and Vice President, Archbishop Worlock, Archbishop of Liverpool.

2. **The Bishops' Standing Committee** made up of the Metropolitans (Archbishops) and department heads. It has general responsibility for continuity and policy between the Plenary Sessions of the Conference and for the preparation of the agenda and implementation of Conference decisions. This committee is serviced by the General Secretariat.

There are six departments each with an episcopal chairman which look after the life of the church within England and Wales. The departments and their heads are as follows:

(a) Department for Christian Life and Worship: Archbishop Bowen (*Southwark*).

(b) Department for Mission and Unity: Bishop Clark (*East Anglia*).

(c) Department for Christian Doctrine and Formation: Bishop Konstant (*Central London*).

(d) Department for Social Responsibility: Bishop Harris (*Middlesbrough*).

(e) Department for Christian Citizenship: Bishop McCartie (*Auxiliary in Birmingham*).

(f) Department for International Affairs: Bishop O'Brien (*Hertfordshire*).

As well as the above the Conference has agencies and consultative bodies affiliated to it and all are serviced by the General Secretariat headed by a General Secretary namely:

England & Wales: *President*, H. E. Cardinal George Basil Hume, Archbishop of Westminster, Archbishop's House, Westminster, London, SW1P 1QJ

Scotland: *President*, H. E. Cardinal Gordon Joseph Gray, Archbishop of St. Andrews and Edinburgh, Archbishop's House, 42 Grenhill Gardens, Edinburgh, EH10 4BJ

Ireland (there is one hierarchy covering both North and South): *President*, H. E. Cardinal Tomás Ó Fiaich, Archbishop of Armagh, "Ara Coeli", Armagh, Ireland.

ENGLAND AND WALES

Apostolic Delegate to Gt. Britain and Gibraltar, The Most Rev. Bruno Heim.

The Most Revd. Archbishops	Cons.	Clgy.
Westminster, H.E. Cardinal Basil Hume (1976)	1976	937
Auxil., Basil C. Butler	1966	
Auxil., Victor Guazzelli	1970	
Auxil., Philip Harvey	1977	
Auxil., David Konstant	1977	
Auxil., Gerald Mahon	1970	
Auxil., James J. O'Brien	1977	
Birmingham, Maurice Couve de Murville (1982)	1982	522
Auxil., Joseph Cleary	1965	
Auxil., Patrick L. McCartie	1977	
Cardiff, John A. Murphy (1961)	1948	186
Auxil., Daniel Mullins	1970	
Liverpool, Derek Worlock (1976)	1965	599
Auxil., Anthony Hitchen	1979	
Auxil., Kevin O'Connor	1979	
Auxil., John Rawsthorne	1982	
Southwark, Michael Bowen (1977)	1970	573
Auxil., Charles Henderson	1972	
Auxil., Howard Tripp	1980	
Auxil., John Jukes	1980	

The Rt. Revd. Bishops		
Arundel and Brighton, Cormac Murphy-O'Connor	1977	331
Brentwood, Thomas McMahon (1980)	1980	214
Clifton, Mervyn Alexander (1975)	1972	246
East Anglia, Alan Clark (1976)	1969	125
Hallam, Gerald Moverley (1980)	1968	106

	Cons.	Clgy.
Hexham and Newcastle, Hugh Lindsay (1975)	1970	340
Auxil., Owen Swindelhurst	1977	
Lancaster, Brian C. Foley	1962	265
Auxil., Thomas Pearson	1949	
Leeds, William Gordon Wheeler (1966)	1964	299
Menevia (*Wales*), John Ward (1981)	1980	141
Middlesbrough, Augustine Harris (1978)	1966	208
Auxil., Thomas O'Brien	1982	
Northampton, Francis Thomas	1982	182
Nottingham, James McGuinness (1975)	1972	250
Plymouth, Cyril Restieaux	1955	187
Portsmouth, Anthony Emery (1976)	1968	355
Salford, Thomas Holland, D.S.C. (1964)	1961	490
Auxil., Geoffrey Burke	1967	
Shrewsbury, Joseph Gray (1980)	1969	255
Auxil., John Brewer	1971	

SCOTLAND

The Most Revd. Archbishops		
St. Andrews & Edinburgh, H.E. Cardinal Gordon Gray	1951	250
Auxil., James Monaghan	1970	
Glasgow, Thomas Winning (1974)	1972	374
Auxil., Joseph Devine	1977	
Auxil., Charles Renfrew	1977	

The Rt. Revd. Bishops		
Aberdeen, Mario Conti	1977	57
Argyll & Isles, Colin MacPherson	1969	39
Dunkeld, Vincent Logan	1981	75
Galloway, Maurice Taylor	1981	82
Motherwell, Francis Thompson	1965	203
Paisley, Stephen McGill (1969)	1960	94

NORTHERN IRELAND†

Nuncio to Ireland, Most Rev. Gaetano Alibrandi (Archbishop of Bindi)

The Most Revd. Archbishop		
Armagh, H.E. Cardinal Thomas O'Fiaich	1977	278
Auxil., James Lennon	1980	

The Rt. Revd. Bishops		
Clogher, Joseph Duffy	1979	140
Derry, Edward Daly	1974	155
Down & Connor, Cahal Daly (1982)	1967	*
Dromore, Francis Brooks	1976	74
Kilmore, Francis McKiernan	1972	133

RESIDENTIAL ARCHBISHOPRICS THROUGHOUT THE WORLD

Abidjan (Ivory Coast), Bernard Yago.
Acerenza (Italy), Francis Cuccarese.
Addis Ababa (Ethiopia), Paul Tzadua.
Adelaide (Australia), James William Gleeson.
Agra (India), vacant.
Ahwaz (Iran), Hanna Zora.
Aix (France), Bernard Panafieu.
Akka, San Giovanni d'Acri, Tolemaide (Israel) [Greek Melekite Catholic Rite], Maximos Sauoum.
Albi (France), Robert Coffy.
Alep, Beroea, Halab (Syria) [Greek Melekite Catholic Rite], Néophytos Edelby.
Alger (Algeria), Cardinal Leon-Etienne Duval.
Amalfi (Italy), Ferdinand Palatucci.

---

† There is one hierarchy for the whole of Ireland. Several of the Dioceses listed above have territory partly in the Republic of Ireland and partly in Northern Ireland.

Anchorage (U.S.A.), Francis Thomas Hurley.
Ancona (Italy), Carlo Maccari.
Anking, Huai-Ning (China), vacant.
Antequera, Oaxaca (Mexico), Bartolomé Carrasco Briseno.
Antofagasta (Chile), Carlos Oviedo Cavada.
Aparecida (Brazil), Geraldo Maria de Morais Penido.
Aracajú (Brazil), Luciano José Cabral Duarte.
Arbil, Erbil (Iraq), Stephane Babeka.
Arequipa (Peru), Fernando Vargas Ruiz de Somocurcio.
Armagh (Ireland), Cardinal Tomás Ó Fiaich.
Asunción (Paraguay), Ismael Bias Roion Silvero.
Athenai (Greece), Nicola Foscolos.
Atlanta (U.S.A.), Thomas A. Donnellan.
Auch (France), Maurice Rigaud.
Avignon (France), Raymond Bouchex.
Ayacucho o Huamanga (Peru), Federico Richter Fernandez-Prada.

Baalbek, Eliopoli (Libya) [Greek Melekite Catholic Rite], Elias Zoghbi.
Baghdad (Babilonia) (Iraq), Ernest Charles Albert Nyary.
Bahia Blanca (Argentina), Jorge Mayer.
Baltimore (U.S.A.), William D. Borders.
Bamako (Mali), Luc Auguste Sangaré.
Bamberg (Federal Republic of Germany), Elmar Maria Kredel.
Bamenda (Cameroon), Paul Verdzekov.
Bangalore (India), Packiam Arokiaswamy.
Bangkok (Thailand), Michael Michai Kitbunchu.
Bangui (Central Africa), Joachim N'Dayen.
Baniyas, Cesarea di Filippo, Paneade (Libya), Athanase Ach-Chaer.
Bar, Antivari (Yugoslavia), Petar Perkolić.
Barcelona (Spain), Cardinal Narciso Jubany Arnau.
Bari (Italy), Mariano Magrassi.
Barquisimeto (Venezuela), Julio Manuel Chirivella Varela.
Barranquilla (Colombia), Germán Villa Gaviria.
Beirut (Lebanon) [Greek Melekite Catholic Rite], Habib Bacha.
Belém do Pará (Brazil), Alberto Gaudêncio Ramos.
Belo Horizonte (Brazil), João Rezende Costa.
Benvento (Italy), Carlo Minchiatti.
Beograd (Yugoslavia), Alojz Turk.
Besançon (France), Lucien Daloz.
Bhopal (India), Eugene D'Souza.
Birmingham (England), Maurice N. L. Couve de Murville.
Blantyre (Malawi), James Chiona.
Bloemfontein (S. Africa), Peter John Butelezi.
Bogotá (Colombia), Cardinal Aníbal Munoz Duque.
Bologna (Italy), Cardinal Antonio Poma.
Bombay (India), Simon Ignatius Pimenta.
Bordeaux (France), Marius Maziers.
Bosra, Bostra (Syria), vacant.
Boston (U.S.A.), Cardinal Humberto S. Medeiros.
Botucatú (Brazil), Vincent Marchetti Zioni.
Bourges (France), Paul Vignancour.
Braga (Portugal), Eurico Dias Nogueira.
Brasilia (Brazil), José Newton de Almeida Batista.
Brazzaville (Congo), Barthélémy Batantu.
Brindisi (Italy), Settimio Todisco.
Brisbane (Australia), Francis Roberts Rush.
Bucaramanga (Colombia), Hector Rueda Hernández.
Bucarest (Rumania), vacant.
Buenos Aires (Argentina), Cardinal Juan Carlos Aramburu.
Burgos (Spain), Garcia de Sierra y Méndez.

Caceres (Philippines), Teopisto Alberto y Valderrama.
Cagayan de Oro (Philippines), Patrick H. Cronin.
Cagliari (Italy), Giuseppe Bonfiglioli.
Calcutta (India), Cardinal Lawrence Trevor Picachy.

Cali (Colombia), Alberto Uribe Urdaneta.
Cambrai (France), Jacques Delaporte.
Camerino (Italy), Bruno Frattegiani.
Campinas (Brazil), Gilberto Pereira Lopes.
Campobasso-Boiano (Italy), Pietro Santoro.
Campo Grande (Brazil), Antonio Barbosa.
Canberra (Australia), Edward B. Clancy.
Canton (China), Dominic Tang Yee-Ming.
Cape Coast (Ghana), John Kodwo Amissah.
Cape Town (South Africa), Cardinal Owen McCann.
Capiz (Philippines), Antonio Frondosa.
Capua (Italy), Luigi Diligenza.
Caracas, Santiago di Venezuela (Venezuela), José Alí Lebrún Moratinos.
Cardiff (Wales), John Murphy.
Cartegena (Colombia), Rubén Isaza Restrepo.
Cascavel (Brazil), Armando Cirio.
Cashel (Ireland), Thomas Morris.
Castries (West Indies), Kelvin Edward Felix.
Catania (Italy), Domenico Picchinenna.
Catanzaro (Italy), Antonio Cantisani.
Cebu, Nome di Gesù (Philippines), Ricardo Vidal.
Chambéry (France), André Bontems.
Changanacherry (India), Anthony Padiyara.
Changsha (China), vacant.
Chicago (U.S.A.), Joseph L. Bernardin.
Chieti (Italy), Vincenzo Fagiolo.
Chihuahua (Mexico), Adalberto Almeida Merino.
Chungking (China), vacant.
Cincinnati (U.S.A.), Daniel E. Pilarczyk.
Cipro (Libya), Elie Farah.
Ciudad Bolivar (Venezuela), Crisanto Mata Cova.
Cochabamba (Bolivia), Gennaro Prata.
Colombo (Sri Lanka), Nicholas Marcus Fernando.
Conakry (Guinea), Robert Sarah.
Concepcion (Chile), Manuel Sánchez Beguiristáin.
Conza (Italy), Antonio Nuzzi.
Cordoba (Argentina), Cardinal Raúl Francisco Primatesta.
Corfu (Greece), Antonio Varthalitis.
Corrientes (Argentina), Jorge Manuel Lopez.
Cosenza (Italy), Dino Trabalzini.
Cotabato (Philippines), Philip Frances Smith.
Cotonou (Bènin), Christophe Adimou.
Cuenca (Ecuador), Alberto Luna Tobar.
Cuiaba (Brazil), Bonifacio Piccinini.
Curitiba (Brazil), Pedro Antonio Fedalto.
Cuttack-Bhubaneswar (India), Henry Sebastian D'Souza.
Cuzco (Peru), vacant.

Dakar (Sénégal), Cardinal Hyacinthe Thiandoum.
Damascus (Syria) [Greek Melekite Catholic Rite], vacant.
Dar-es-Salaam (Tanzania), Cardinal Laurean Rugambwa.
Davao (Philippines), Antonio Mabutas y Lloren.
Delhi (India), Angelo Innocent Fernandes.
Denver (U.S.A.), James Vincent Casey.
Detroit (U.S.A.), Edmund C. Szoka.
Dhaka (Bangladesh), Michael Rozario.
Diamantina (Brazil), Geraldo Majelo Reis.
Diarbekir (Turkey), Paul Karatas.
Diégo-Suarez (Madagascar), Albert Joseph Tsiahoana.
Douala (Cameroons), Simon Tonyé.
Dublin (Ireland), Dermot J. Ryan.
Dubuque (U.S.A.), James J. Byrne.
Durango (México), Antonio López Aviña.
Durban (South Africa), Denis Eugene Hurley.
Durrës (Albania), vacant.

Edmonton (Canada), Joseph N. MacNeil.
Eger (Hungary), László Kádár.
Ende (Indonesia), Donatus Djagom.
Ernakulam (India), Cardinal Joseph Parecattil.

Esztergom (Hungary), Cardinal László Lekai.
Évora (Portugal), Maurilio Jorge Quinjal de Gouveia.

Fermo (Italy), Cleto Bellucci.
Ferrara (Italy), Luigi Maverna.
Fianarantsoa (Madagascar), Gilbert Ramanantoan-
    ina.
Firenze (Florence) (Italy), vacant.
Florianópolis (Brazil), Afonso Niehues.
Foggia (Italy), Salvatore De Giorgi.
Foochow, Min-Hou (China), vacant.
Fortaleza (Brazil), Cardinal Aloisio Lorscheider.
Fort-de-France (Martinique), Maurice Marie-Sainte.
Freetown and Bo (Sierra Leone), Joseph Ganda.
Freiburg im Breisgau (West Germany), Oskar Saier.

Gaeta (Italy), Luigi Carli.
Garoua (Cameroons), Yves Plumey.
Genova (Genoa) (Italy), Cardinal Giuseppe Siri.
Gitega (Burundi), Joachim Ruhuna.
Glasgow (Scotland), Thomas Winning.
Gniezno (Poland), Józef Glemp. (See also Warszawa.)
Goa and Damão (India), Raul Nicolau Gonsalves.
Goiânia (Brazil), Fernando Gomes Dos Santos.
Gorizia and Gradisca (Italy), Antonio Vitale Bom-
    marco.
Granada (Spain), José Méndez Asensio.
Grouard-McLennan (Canada), Henri Légaré.
Guadalajara (México), Cardinal José Salazar López.
Guayaquil (Ecuador), Bernardino Echeverria Ruiz.
Guetemala (Guatemala), Cardinal Mario Casariego.

Halifax (Canada), James Martin Hayes.
Hangchow (China), vacant.
Hankow (China), vacant.
Hanoi (Vietnam), Cardinal Joseph-Marie Trinh văn-
    Căn.
Harare (Zimbabwe), Patrick Chakaipa.
Hartford (U.S.A.), John F. Whealon.
Hassaké-Nisibi (Syria), Georges Habib Hafouri.
Hermosillo (Mexico), Carlos Quintero Arce.
Hobart (Australia), Guilford Clyde Young.
Homs, Emesa (Syria) [Greek Melekite Catholic Rite],
    Denys Gaith.
Homs, Emesa (Syria) [Syrian Catholic Rite], vacant.
Honiara (Oceania), Daniel Stuyvenberg.
Huambo (Angola), Manuel Franklin da Costa.
Huancayo (Peru), Eduardo Picher Peña.
Huê (Vietnam), Philippe Nguyen-Kim-Diên.
Hyderabad (India), Saminini Arulappa.

Ibagué (Colombia), José Joaquin Flórez Hernández.
Indianapolis (U.S.A.), Edward T. O'Meara.
Istanbul, Constantinople (Turkey), Jean Tcholakian.
Izmir (Turkey), Domenico Caloyera.

Jakarta (Indonesia), Leo Soekoto.
Jalapa (Mexico), Sergio Obeso Rivero.
Juiz de Fora (Brazil), Juvenal Roriz.

Kaduna (Nigeria), Peter Yariyok Jatau.
Kaifeng (China), vacant.
Kalocsa (Hungary), József Ijjas.
Kampala (Uganda), Cardinal Emmanuel Nsubuga.
Kananga (Zaire), Bakole wa Ilunga.
Kansas City in Kansas (U.S.A.), Ignatius J. Strecker.
Karachi (Pakistan), Cardinal Joseph Cordeiro.
Kasama (Zambia), Elias Mutale.
Kaunas (Lithuania), vacant.
Keewatin—Le Pas (Canada), Paul Dumouchel.
Kerkük (Iraq), André Sana.
Khartoum (Sudan), Gabriel Zubeir Wako.
Kigali (Rwanda), Vincent Nsengiyumva.
Kingston (Canada), Francis John Spence.
Kingston in Jamaica (Jamaica), Samuel Emmanuel
    Carter.
Kinshasa (Zaire), Cardinal Joseph Malula.

Kisangani (Zaire), Fataki.
Köln (Cologne) (Germany), Cardinal Joseph Höffner.
Kraków (Poland), Cardinal Franciszek Macharsili.
Kuala Lumpur (Malaysia), Dominic Vendargon.
Kuching (Sarawak, Malaysia), Peter Chung Hoan
    Ting.
Kunming (China), vacant.
Kwang Ju (Korea), Victorinus Kong-Hi Youn.
Kweyang (China), vacant.

Lagos (Nigeria), Anthony Okogie.
Lanchow (China), vacant.
Lanciano (Italy), Enzio d'Antonio.
Laodicea di Siria (Syria) [Greek Melekite Catholic
    Rite], Michel Yatim.
La Paz (Bolivia), Jorge Manrique Hurtado.
La Plata (Argentina), Antonio José Plaza.
L'Aquila (Italy), Carlo Martini.
La Serena (Chile), Juan Francisco Fresno Larrain.
Lecce (Italy), Michele Mincuzzi.
Libreville (Gabon), André Fernand Anguilé.
Lima (Peru), H.E. Cardinal Juan Landázuri Ricketts.
Lingayen-Dagupan (Philippines), Federico G. Limon.
Lipa (Philippines), Mariano Gaviola Garcés.
Liverpool (England), Derek Worlock.
Ljubljana (Yugoslavia), Alojzij Suštar.
Lomé (Togo), Robert Casimir Dosseh-Anyron.
Londrina (Brazil), Geraldo Majela Agnelo.
Los Angeles (U.S.A.), H.E. Cardinal Timothy Man-
    ning.
Louisville (U.S.A.), Thomas C. Kelly.
Luanda (Angola), Eduardo André Muaca.
Lubango (Angola), Alexandre do Nascimento.
Lubumbashi (Zaire), Kabanga Songasonga.
Lucca (Italy), Giuliano Agresti.
Lusaka (Zambia), Emmanuel Milingo.
Lwów (Poland), vacant. (Apostolic Administrator:
    Monsignor Marian Rechowicz.)
Lyon (France), Albert Decourtray.

Maceió (Brazil), Miguel Fenelon Câmara Filho.
Madang (Papua New Guinea), Leo Arkfeld.
Madras and Mylapore (India), Rayappa Arulappa.
Madrid (Spain), H.E. Cardinal Vicente Enrique y
    Tarancón.
Madurai (India), Justin Diraviam.
Malabo (Equatorial Guinea), Rafael Nze Abuy.
Malta (Malta), Joseph Mercieca.
Managua (Nicaragua), Miguel Obando Bravo.
Manaus (Brazil), Milton Corrêa Pereira.
Mandalay (Burma), Alphonse U Than Aung.
Manfredonia (Italy), Valentino Vailati.
Manila (Philippines), H.E. Cardinal Jaime L. Sin.
Manizales (Colombia), José de Jesús Pimiento Rod-
    riguez.
Maputo (Mozambique), Alexandre José Maria dos
    Santos.
Maracaibo (Venezuela), Domingo Roa Pérez.
Mariana (Brazil), Oscar de Oliveira.
Maringá (Brazil), Jaime Luis Coelho.
Marseilles (France), H.E. Cardinal Roger Etchegaray.
Maseru (Lesotho), Alfonso Liguori Morapeli.
Matera (Italy), Michele Giordano.
Mbandaka-Bikoro (Zaire), Etsou-Nzabi-Bamung-
    wabi.
Malines-Bruxelles (Belgium), Godfried Danneels.
Medan (Indonesia), Alfred Gonti Pius Datubara.
Medellín (Colombia), Alfonso López Trujillo.
Melbourne (Australia), Thomas Francis Little.
Mendoza (Argentina), Cándido Genaro Rubiolo.
Merauke (Indonesia), Jacobus Duivenvoorde.
Meridia (Venezuela), Miguel Antonio Salas Salas.
Messina (Italy), Ignazio Cannavó.
Mexico (Mexico), H.E. Cardinal Ernesto Corripio
    Ahumada.
Miami (U.S.A.), Edward A. McCarthy.
Milano (Italy), Carlo Maria Martini.

Milwaukee (U.S.A.), Rembert G. Weakland.
Mobile (U.S.A.), Oscar H. Lipscomb.
Modena (Italy), Bruno Foresti.
Mohilev (U.S.S.R.): there is an **unnamed** Apostolic Administrator in the following Russian Dioceses: Mohilev, Moscow, Leningrad, Kharkov, Kazan, Samara and Sinibirsk.
Monaco (Monaco), Charles Brand.
Moncton (Canada), Donat Chiasson.
Monreale (Italy), Salvatore Cassisa.
Monrovia (Liberia), Michael Kpakala Francis.
Monterrey (Mexico), José de Jesús Tirado Pedraza.
Montevideo (Uruguay), Carlos Parteli.
Montréal (Canada), Paul Grégoire.
Morelia (Mexico), Estanislao Alcaraz Figueroa.
Mossul (Iraq), Georges Garmo.
Mount Hagen (Papua New Guinea), George Bernarding.
Mukden (China), vacant.
Munchen (Munich) and Freising (West Germany), Friedrich Wetter.

Nagasaki (Japan), H.E. Cardinal Joseph Asajiro Satowaki.
Nagpur (India), Leobard D'Souza.
Nairobi (Kenya), H.E. Cardinal Maurice Otunga.
Nanchang (China), vacant.
Nanking (China), vacant.
Nanning (China), vacant.
Napoli (Italy), H.E. Cardinal Corrado Ursi.
Natal (Brazil), Nivaldo Monte.
Naxos (Greece), Jean Perris.
N'Djamena (Chad), Charles Vandame.
Newark (U.S.A.), Peter L. Gerety.
New Orleans (U.S.A.), Philip M. Hannan.
New York (U.S.A.), H.E. Cardinal Terence J. Cooke.
Niterói (Brazil), José Gonçalves da Costa.
Nouméa (Oceania), Michel-Marie-Bernard Calvet.
Nueva Pamplona (Colombia), Mario Revollo Bravo.
Nueva Segovia (Philippines), José T. Sánchez.

Oklahoma City (U.S.A.), Charles A. Salatka.
Olinda & Recife (Brazil), Helder Reçsoa Câmara.
Olomouc (Czechoslovakia), vacant.
Omaha (U.S.A.), Daniel E. Sheehan.
Onitsha (Nigeria), Francis Arinze.
Oristano (Italy), Francesco Spanedda.
Osaka (Japan), Paul Hisao Yasuda.
Otranto (Italy), Vincenzo Franco.
Ottawa (Canada), Joseph Aurèle Plourde.
Ouagadougou (Haute Volta), H.E. Cardinal Paul Zoungrana.
Oviedo (Spain), Gabino Diaz Merchán.

Paderborn (West Germany), Johannes Joachim Degenhardt.
Palermo (Italy), H.E. Cardinal Salvatore Pappalardo.
Palo (Philippines), Cipriano Urgel Villahermosa.
Pamplona (Spain), José Mariá Cirardo Lachiondo.
Panamá (Panamá), Marcos Gregorio McGrath.
Papeete (French Polynesia), Michel Coppenrath.
Paraíba (Brazil), José M. Pires.
Paraná (Argentina), Adolfo Servando Tortolo.
Paris (France), Jean-Marie Lustiger.
Peking (China), vacant.
Perth (Australia), Launcelot John Goody.
Perugia (Italy), Cesare Pagani.
Pescara-Penne (Italy), Antonio Jannucci.
Petra and Filadelfia (Jordan) [Greek Melekite Catholic Rite], Saba Youakim.
Philadelphia (U.S.A.), H.E. Cardinal John Joseph Krol.
Pisa (Italy), Benvenuto Matteucci.
Pittsburgh (U.S.A.), Stephen J. Kocisko.
Piura (Perú), Oscar Rolando Cantuarias Pastor.
Pondicherry and Cuddalore (India), Venmani S. Selvanather.

Pontianak (Indonesia), Hieronymus Herculanus Bumbun.
Popayán (Colombia), Samuel Silverio Buitrago.
Port-au-Prince (Haiti), François-Wolff Ligondé.
Portland in Oregon (U.S.A.), Cornelius M. Power.
Port Moresby (New Guinea), Peter Kurongku.
Porto Alegre (Brazil), Claudio Colling.
Port of Spain (Trinidad), Gordon Anthony Pantin.
Porto Velho (Brazil), José Martins da Silva.
Potenza (Italy), Giuseppe Vairo.
Pouso Alegre (Brazil), José D'Angelo Neto.
Poznán (Poland), Jerzy Stroba.
Praha (Czechoslovakia), H.E. Cardinal František Tomášek.
Pretoria (South Africa), George Francis Daniel.
Puebla de los Angeles (Mexico), Rosendo Huesca Pacheco.
Puerto Montt (Chile), Eladio Vicuña Aránguiz.

Québec (Canada), Louis-Albert Vachon.
Quito (Ecuador), H.E. Cardinal Pablo Muñoz Vega.

Rabat (Morocco), vacant. (Apostolic Administrator: Monsignor J. Chabbert.)
Rabaul (Papua New Guinea), Albert Bundervoet.
Ranchi (India), Pius Kerketta.
Rangoon (Burma), Gabriel Thohey.
Ravenna (Italy), Ersilio Tonini.
Reggio Calabria (Italy), Aurelio Sorrentino.
Regina (Canada), Charles Halpin.
Reims (France), H.E. Cardinal Paul Gouyon.
Rennes (France), Jacques Ménager.
Ribeirão Preto (Brazil), Romeu Alberti.
Rijeka-Senj (Yugoslavia), Josip Paulišić.
Rimouski (Canada), Gilles Ouellet.
Rodi (Greece), vacant. (Apostolic Administrator: Michel Pierre Franzidis.)
Rosario (Argentina), vacant.
Rossano (Italy), Serafino Sprovieri.
Rouen (France), Joseph Duval.

Saïdā (Libya) [Greek Melekite Catholic Rite], Ignace Raad.
St. Andrews and Edinburgh (Scotland), H.E. Cardinal Joseph Gray.
St. Boniface (Canada), Antoine Hacault.
St. John's, Newfoundland (Canada), Alphonsus L. Penney.
St. Louis (Missouri), John L. May.
St. Paul and Minneapolis (U.S.A.), John Robert Roach.
Salerno (Italy), Gaetano Pollio.
Salta (Argentina), Carlos Mariano Pérez Eslava.
Salzburg (Austria), Karl Berg.
Samoa-Apia and Tokelau (Oceania), H.E. Cardinal Pio Taofinu'u.
San Antonio (U.S.A.), Patrick F. Flores.
San Cristóbal de la Habana (Cuba), Jaime Lucas Ortega y Alamino.
San Fernando (Philippines), Oscar Cruz.
San Francisco (U.S.A.), John R. Quinn.
San José de Costa Rica (Costa Rica), Román Arrieta Villalobos.
San Juan de Cuyo (Argentina), Italo Severino Di Stefano.
San Juan de Puerto Rico (Puerto Rico), H.E. Cardinal Luis Aponte Martinez.
San Salvador (El Salvador), vacant. (Apostolic Administrator: Monsignor Arturo Rivera Damas.)
Santa Cruz de la Sierra (Bolivia), Luis Rodriguez Pardo.
Santa Fe (U.S.A.), Robert F. Sanchez.
Santa Fe (Argentina), Vicente Faustino Zazpe.
Santa Severina (Italy), Giuseppe Agostino.
Santiago de Chile (Chile), H.E. Cardinal Raúl Silva Henriquez.

Santiago de Compostela (Spain), Angel Suquia Goicoechea.
Santiago de Cuba (Cuba), Pedro Meurice Estiu.
Santo Domingo (Dominican Republic), Nicolás de Jesús López Rodriguez.
São Luis do Maranhão (Brazil), João José da Motta e Albuquerque.
São Paulo (Brazil), H.E. Cardinal Paulo Evaristo Arns.
São Salvador da Bahia (Brazil), H.E. Cardinal Avelar Brandão Vilela.
São Sebastião do Rio de Janeiro (Brazil), H.E. Cardinal Eugenio de Araújo Sales.
Sassari (Italy), Salvatore Isgrò.
Seattle (U.S.A.), Raymond G. Hunthausen.
Semarang (Indonesia), vacant.
Sens (France), Eugene Ernoult.
Seoul (Korea), H.E. Cardinal Stephen Sou Hwan Kim.
Sevilla (Spain), Carlos Amigo Vallejo.
Sherbrooke (Canada), Jean Marie Fortier.
Shillong-Gauhati (India), Hubert D'Rosario.
Shkodrë (Albania), vacant. (Apostolic Administrator: Monsignor Ernesto Coba.)
Sian (China), vacant.
Siena (Italy), Ismaele Mario Castellano.
Singapore (Singapore), Gregory Yong Sooi Nghean.
Siracusa (Italy), Calogero Lauricella.
Sorrento (Italy), Antonio Zama.
Southwark (England), Michael G. Bowen.
Split-Makarska (Yugoslavia), Frane Franić.
Spoleto (Italy), Ottorino Pietro Alberti.
Sucre (Bolivia), H.E. Cardinal José Clemente Maurer.
Suiyuan (China), Francis Wang Hsueh-Ming.
Suva (Oceania), Petero Mataca.
Sydney (Australia), H.E. Cardinal James Darcy Freeman.

Tabora (Tanzania), Mark Mihayo.
Tae Gu (Korea), John B. Bong-Kil Sye.
Taipeh (Taiwan), Matthew Kia Yen-Wen.
Taiyuan (China), Dominic Luke Capozi (expelled 11th April 1946, now living in Nazareth, Israel).
Tamale (Ghana), Peter Poreiru Dery.
Tananarive (Madagascar), H.E. Cardinal Victor Razafimahatratra.
Tanger (Morocco), vacant. (Apostolic Administrator: Ramón Lourido Diaz.)
Taranto (Italy), Guglielmo Motolese.
Tarragona (Spain), José Pont y Gol.
Tegucigalpa (Honduras), Hector Enrique Santos Hernández.
Teheran (Iran), Youhannan Semaan Issayi.
Teresina (Brazil), José Freire Falcão.
Thanh-Phô Hôchiminh (Vietnam), Paul Nguyên Van Binh.
Tharé and Nonseng (Thailand), Lawrence Khai Saen-Phon-On.
Tôkyô (Japan), Peter Seiichi Shirayanagi.
Toledo (Spain), H.E. Cardinal Marcelo González Martin.
Torino (Italy), H.E. Cardinal Anastasio Alberto Ballestrero.
Toronto (Canada), H.E. Cardinal Gerald Emmett Carter.
Toulouse (France), André Collini.
Tours (France), Jean Honoré.
Trani and Barletta (Italy), Giuseppe Calata.
Trento (Italy), Alessandro Maria Gottardi.
Tripoli del Libano (Libya) [Maronite Rite]: Antoine Joubeir; [Greek Melekite Catholic Rite]: Elias Nijmé.
Trivandrum (India) [Syrian Melekite Rite]: Benedict Varghese Mar Gregorios Thangalathil.
Trnava (Czechoslovakia), vacant. (Apostolic Administrator: Monsignor Julius Gábriš.)
Trujillo (Peru), Manuel Prado Pérez-Rosas.

Tsinan (China), vacant. (Apostolic Administrator: John P'ing Ta-kuam.)
Tuam (Ireland), Joseph Cunnane.
Tuguegaro (Philippines), Teodulfo S. Domingo.
Tunja (Colombia), Augusto Trujillo Arango.
Tyr (Libya) [Greek Melekite Catholic Rite]: Georges Haddad; [Maronite Rite]: Joseph Khoury.

Uberaba (Brazil), Benedito de Ulhôa Vieira.
Udine (Italy), Alfredo Battisti.
Ujung Pendang (Indonesia), vacant.
Urmyā (Iran), vacant.
Utrecht (Netherlands), H.E. Cardinal Johannes Willebrands.

Valencia (Spain), Miguel Roca Cabanellas.
Valencia (Venezuela), Luis Eduardo Henriquez Jiménez.
Valladolid (Spain), José Delicado Baeza.
Vancouver (Canada), James Francis Carney.
Verapoly (India), Joseph Kelanthara.
Vercelli (Italy), Albino Mensa.
Vilna (Lithuania), vacant. (Apostolic Administrator: Monsignor Edward Kisiel.)
Vitória (Brazil), João Batista da Mota e Albuquerque.
Vrhbosna (Yugoslavia), Marko Jozinović.

Warszawa (Poland), Józef Glemp.
Washington (U.S.A.), James A. Hickey.
Wellington (New Zealand), Thomas Stafford Williams.
Westminster (England), H.E. Cardinal George Basil Hume.
Wien (Austria), H.E. Cardinal Franz Konig.
Winnipeg (Canada), Latin Rite: Adam Exner; Ukrainian Rite: Maxim Hermaniuk.
Wroclaw (Poland), Henryk Roman Gulbinowicz.

Yaoundé (Cameroons), Jean Zoa.
Yucatán (Mexico), Manuel Castro Ruiz.

Zadar (Yugoslavia), Marijan Oblak.
Zagreb (Yugoslavia), Franjo Kuharić.
Zahleh and Furzol (Libya) [Greek Melekite Catholic Rite]: Augustin Farah.
Zamboanga (Philippines), Francisco Raval Cruces.
Zaragoza (Spain), Eliaz Yanez Alvarez.

ARCHBISHOPS OF TITULAR SEES

Amasya, James Patrick Carroll.
Amida, Flavien Zacharie Melkie.
Cesarea in Palaestina [Greek Melekite Catholic Rite]: Hilarion Capucci.
Claudiopolis in Honoriade, Alfredo Bruniera.
Colonia in Armenia, Paul Coussa.
Corinthus, Gennaro Verolino.
Damiata [Greek Melekite Catholic Rite]: Nicholas Hajj.
Dara, Nicholas T. Elko.
Doclea, Jozef Tomko.
Edessa in Osrhoëne [Greek Melekite Catholic Rite]: Pierre Rai; [Syrian Catholic Rite]: Gregoire Ephrem Jarjour.
Emerita Augusta, Justo Mullor Garcia.
Egina, Raffaele Forni.
Ephesus, John Henry Boccella.
Gabala, Gérard de Milleville.
Gangra, Antonio Ferreira de Macedo.
Gradum, José López Ortiz.
Hadrianopolis in Haemimonto, Lino Zanini.
Heraclea in Europa, Mario Cagna.
Justiniana prima, Aurelio Sabbatani.
Kaškar, Emmanuel-Karim Delly.
Laodicea in Syria, Martin John O'Connor.
Macra, John Dooley.
Marcianopolis, Teofilo Camomot Bastida.

Maronea, Franz Jáchym.			*Salamis,* Joseph Kuo.		

Maronea, Franz Jáchym.
Mesembria, Loris Francesco Capovilla.
Myra, Basile Khoury.
Nazareth, Giuseppe Carata.
Nicaea Parva, Paolino Limongi.
Nicosia, Aurelio Signora.
Nubia, Paul Antaki.
Pelusium [Greek Melekite Catholic Rite]: Pierre Medawar.

Salamis, Joseph Kuo.
Scytopolis, Joseph Raya.
Selymbria, Emile Socquet.
Soteropolis, Ettore Cunial.
Tarsus [Maronite Rite]: Nasrallah Sfeir; [Greek Melekite Catholic Rite]: Loutfi Laham.
Tiburnia, Donato Squicciarini.
Tyrus, Bruno Wüstenberg.
Viminacium, Franco Brambilla.

POPES FROM 1800

Sovereign Pontiff	*Family Name*	*Elected*
Pius VII	Chiaramonti	1800
Leo XII	della Genga	1823
Pius VIII	Castiglioni	1829
Gregory XVI	Cappellari	1831
Pius IX	Mastai-Ferretti	1846
Leo XIII	Pecci	1878
Pius X	Sarto	1903
Benedict XV	della Chiesa	1914
Pius XI	Ratti	1922

Sovereign Pontiff	*Family Name*	*Elected*
Pius XII	Pacelli	1939
John XXIII	Roncalli	1958
Paul VI	Montini	1963
John Paul I	Luciani	1978
John Paul II	Wojtyla	1978

Adrian IV (Nicholas Breakspear, the only Englishman elected Pope) was born at Langley, near St. Albans; elected Pope, on the death of Anastasius IV, 1154; died 1159.

ORTHODOX CHURCH

Greek Orthodox Church (*Archdiocese of Thyateira and Great Britain*), Most Rev. Archbishop Methodios Fouyas, Ph.D., D.D., 5 Craven Hill, W.2.

Serbian Orthodox Church (*Patriarchate of Serbia*) Right Rev. Bishop Lavrentije, 89 Lancaster Road, W.11.

Polish Orthodox Church Abroad, Right Rev. Bishop Matthew, 53 Shakespeare Road, NW7 4BA

Russian Orthodox Church (*Patriarchate of Moscow*), Most Rev. Metropolitan Anthony of Sourozh, Russian Cathedral, Ennismore Gardens, S.W.7.

Russian Orthodox Church Outside Russia. His Grace Bishop Constantine, Dormition Cathedral, Emperor's Gate, S.W.7. Mission Administrator Igounen Seraphim, 14 St. Dunstan's Road, N.W.6.

The Ukrainians, Latvians, Byelorussians and Romanians also have congregations in this country.

LONDON CATHEDRALS, CHURCHES, ETC.

Church of England

ST. PAUL'S CATHEDRAL, City of London, EC4M 8AD (1675–1710), cost £747,660. The cross on the dome is 365 ft. above the ground level, the inner cupola 218 ft. above the floor. "Great Paul," in S.W. tower weighs 17 tons. Organ by Father Smith (enlarged by Willis and rebuilt by Mander) in case carved by Grinling Gibbons (who also carved the choir stalls). The choir and high altar were restored in 1958 after war damage and the North Transept in 1962. The American War Memorial Chapel was consecrated in November, 1958. The Chapel of the Most Excellent Order of the British Empire in the Crypt of the Cathedral was dedicated on May 20, 1960. Nave and transepts free; Fees to the following parts (on weekdays only, 10 a.m. (Sat. 11 a.m.) to 3.15 p.m. and—during Summer Time only—to 4.15 p.m.); Crypt, Treasury and historical display, 70p; whispering gallery, stone gallery, 75p (children reduced price). Service on Sundays at 8, 10.30, 11.30 and 3.15. Weekdays at 7.30, 8, 4 (winter), 5 (summer).

WESTMINSTER ABBEY, S.W.1. (built A.D. 1050–1745).—Open on weekdays 9 a.m. to 6 p.m., (8 p.m., Wednesdays). Admission to the Royal Chapels, Poets' Corner, Quire and Statesmen's Aisle £1.30 (student card holders 60p; O.A.P.s and children 30p). Last admission Monday–Friday 4 p.m., Saturday 5 p.m. Wednesdays 6 p.m.–8 p.m. free. Nave open on Sundays between services. Services: Sundays, Holy Com-munion 8 a.m., Matins 10.30, Holy Communion 11.40 (sung every second and fourth Sundays in month), Evensong 3 p.m., Congregational Service 6.30 p.m., generally preceded by an organ recital. Monday–Friday, Matins 7.30 a.m., Holy Communion 8 a.m., Holy Communion 12.30 p.m. (Wednesdays, Lunch-hour Service), Evensong 5 p.m. Saturdays, Holy Communion 8 a.m., Matins 9 a.m., Evensong 3 p.m. Chapel of Henry VII, Chapter House and Cloisters; King Edward the Confessor's shrine, A.D. 1269, tombs of kings and queens (Henry III, Edward I, Edward III, Henry V, Mary Queen of Scots, Queen Elizabeth I), and many other monuments and objects of interest, including the grave of "The Unknown Warrior" and Poets' Corner. The Coronation Chair encloses the "Stone of Scone", which was removed from Scotland by Edward I in 1296.

SOUTHWARK CATHEDRAL, south side of the Thames, near London Bridge, S.E.1.—Mainly 13th century, but the nave is largely rebuilt. Open 7.30 a.m. to 6 p.m., free. Sunday services, Eucharist 11 a.m., Even-song 3 p.m. Weekdays: Matins 12.30 p.m., Holy Communion 12.45 p.m., Evensong (sung on Tuesdays and Fridays) 5.30 p.m., Saturdays, Holy Communion, 12 noon.

The tomb of John Gower (1330–1408) is between the Bunyan and Chaucer memorial windows, in the N. aisle; Shakespeare effigy backed by view of Southwark and Globe Theatre in S. aisle; the altar screen (erected 1520) has been restored; the tomb of Bishop Andrews (died 1626) is near screen. The Early English Lady Chapel (behind the choir), restored 1930, was the scene of the Consistory Courts of the reign of Mary (Gardiner and Bonner); and is still used as a Consistory Court. John Harvard, after whom Harvard University is named, was baptized here in 1607.

TEMPLE CHURCH, The Temple, E.C.4.—The nave formed one of five remaining round churches in England, the others being at Cambridge, Northampton, Little Maplestead (Essex), and Ludlow Castle. Rebuilding of the church was completed in 1958. Sunday morning services, open to the public, 11.15 a.m., except in August and September. *Master of the Temple*, Rev. Canon J. Robinson, M.Th., B.D. *Reader*, Rev. Preb. W. D. Kennedy-Bell, M.A.

Church of Scotland
CROWN COURT CHURCH, Russell Street, Covent Garden, W.C.2.—Sundays, 11.15 (Holy Communion, first Sunday of Month) and 6.30. Mid week Service, Thursdays, 1.30. *Minister*, Rev. J. M. Scott, M.A., B.D., F.S.A.Scot.

ST. COLUMBA'S, Pont Street, SW1X 0BD. Sundays, 11 and 6.30. *Minister*, Very Rev. J. F. McLuskey, M.C., D.D.

United Reformed
CITY TEMPLE, Holborn Viaduct, E.C.1.—Sundays, 11 and 6.30 and Thursdays, 1.15. *Minister*, Rev. B. Johanson, B.A., B.D., D.D.

Independent Evangelical
WESTMINSTER CHAPEL, Buckingham Gate, SW1E 6BS—Sundays, 11 and 6.30. *Minister*, Rev. Dr. R. T. Kendall.

Methodist
WESLEY'S CHAPEL, City Road, EC1Y 1AU—Sunday service 11 a.m. *Minister*, Rev. Dr. R. C. Gibbins.

CENTRAL HALL, Westminster, SW1H 9NU—Sunday Services, 11 a.m. and 6.30 p.m. *Minister*, Rev. Dr. R. J. Tudor.

WEST LONDON MISSION, Hinde Street Methodist Church, W.1.—Sundays at 10, 11 and 6.30. *Superintendent*, Rev. J. A. Newton, M.A., Ph.D.

Baptist
BLOOMSBURY CENTRAL BAPTIST CHURCH, Junction of Shaftesbury Avenue and New Oxford Street, W.C.2.—Sundays 11 and 6.30. *Minister*, Rev. H. Howard Williams, Ph.D.

Religious Society of Friends
FRIENDS' HOUSE, Euston Road, N.W.1.

Roman Catholic
WESTMINSTER CATHEDRAL, Ashley Place, Westminster, S.W.1 (close to Victoria Station), built 1895–1903 from the designs of J. F. Bentley (the campanile is 283 feet high.—*Sundays:* Masses, 7, 8, 9, 10.30 (sung), 12 noon, 5.30 p.m. and 7 p.m.; Solemn Vespers and Benediction, 3.30. *Weekdays.* (Mon.-Fri.) Masses, 7, 8, 8.30, 9, 10.30, 12.30, 1.05 5.30 (sung). Lauds, 7.40 a.m.; Vespers, 4.15 p.m.; (Saturday) Masses, 7, 8, 8.30, 9, 10.30 (sung), 12.30, 6 p.m.; Lauds, 7.40 a.m.; Vespers, 5.30 p.m. *Holy days of obligation.* Low Masses, 7, 8, 8.30, 9, 10.30, 12.30, 1.05, 5.30 (sung), 7 p.m. Cathedral open 6.45 a.m. to 8 p.m.

THE ORATORY, Brompton, S.W.7.—*Sundays:* Masses, 7, 8, 9, 10, 11; (High Mass); 12.30, 4.30, 7; Vespers and Benediction, 3.30. *Weekdays:* Masses, 7, 7.30, 10; 12.30, 6 p.m. (no 12.30 on Sats.). Service Thurs. 8 p.m. *Holy days:* Masses 7, 8, 10, 12.15, 1.15, 4.30, and 8 p.m.; 6 p.m. (High Mass). On the eve, Vespers and Benediction, 5.30 p.m.

PATRON SAINTS

St. George, Patron Saint of England.—St. George is believed to have been born in Cappadocia, of Christian parents, in the latter part of the 3rd century and to have served with distinction as a soldier under the Emperor Doicletian, including a visit to England on a military mission. When the persecution of Christians was ordered, St. George sought a personal interview to remonstrate with the Emperor and after a profession of faith resigned his military commission. Arrest and torture followed and he was martyred at Nicomedia on April 23, 303, a day ordered to be kept in remembrance as a national festival by the Council of Oxford in 1222, although it was not until the reign of Edward III that he was made patron saint of England. His connection with a dragon seems to date from the close of the 6th century and to be due to the transfer of his remains from Nicomedia to Lydda, close to the scene of the legendary exploit of Perseus in rescuing Andromeda and slaying the sea monster, credit for which became attached to the Christian martyr.

St. David, Patron Saint of Wales.—St. David is believed to have been born near the beginning and to have died towards the end of the 6th century. St. David was an eloquent preacher, who founded the monastery at Menevia, now St. David's. He became the patron of Wales, but there is no record of any

papal Canonization before 1181. His annual festival is observed on March 1.

St. Andrew, Patron Saint of Scotland.—St. Andrew, one of the Christian Apostles and brother of Simon Peter, was born at Bethsaida on the Lake of Galilee and lived at Capernaum. He preached the Gospel in Asia Minor and in Scythia along the shores of the Black Sea and became the patron saint of Russia. It is believed that he suffered crucifixion at Patras in Achaea, on a *crux decussata* (now known as St. Andrew's Cross) and that his relics were removed from Patras to Constantinople and thence to St. Andrews, probably in the 8th century, since which time he has been the patron saint of Scotland. The festival of St. Andrew is held on November 30, a church festival indicated in the calendar by red letters.

St. Patrick, Patron Saint of Ireland.—St. Patrick was born in England about 389 and was carried off to Ireland as a slave about sixteen years later, escaping to Gaul at the age of 22. He was ordained deacon at Auxerre and having been consecrated Bishop in 432 was despatched to Wicklow to reorganize the Christian communities in Ireland. He founded the see of Armagh and introduced Latin into Ireland as the language of the Church. He died in 461 and his festival is celebrated on March 17.

EDUCATION DIRECTORY

UNIVERSITIES

The universities have power to award their own degrees. They grant 70 per cent. of all first degrees awarded in Britain and 95 per cent. of all higher degrees. They provide most of the basic and much of the applied research undertaken in Britain, and are responsible for the initial training of virtually all research workers. The universities make the chief contribution to wholly new knowledge through fundamental research.

THE UNIVERSITY OF OXFORD

FULL TERMS, 1985

Hilary, Jan. 20 to Mar. 16; *Trinity*, April 28 to June 22; *Michaelmas*, Oct. 13 to Dec. 7

Number of Undergraduates in Residence 1983–84: *Men*, 5,972; *Women*, 3,429

UNIVERSITY OFFICES, etc.   Elect.

Chancellor, Rt. Hon. the Earl of Stockton, O.M., F.R.S., *Balliol* 1960
High Steward, The Lord Wilberforce, P.C., C.M.G., O.B.E., M.A., *All Souls* 1967
Vice-Chancellor, G. J. Warnock, M.A., Principal of *Hertford* 1981
Proctors, W. H. Newton-Smith, M.A., D.Phil., *Balliol*; R. C. S. Walker, M.A., D.Phil., *Magdalen* 1984
Assessor, E. P. Wilson, M.A., *Worcester* 1984
Public Orator, G. W. Bond, M.A., *Pembroke* 1980
Bodley's Librarian, J. W. Jolliffe, M.A. 1982
Keeper of Archives, T. H. Aston, M.A., Corpus Christi 1969
Director of the Ashmolean Museum, Sir David Piper, M.A., *Worcester* 1973
Registrar of the University, A. J. Dorey, M.A., D.Phil., *Linacre* 1979
Surveyor to the University, J. Lankester, M.A., St. Catherine's 1956
Secretary of Faculties, R. Butler, M.A. University 1980
Secretary of the Chest and Chief Accountant, W. Hyde, M.A., *Linacre* 1980
Deputy Registrar (Admin.), D. W. Roberts, M.A., *Pembroke*

Oxford Colleges and Halls
(With dates of foundation)

All Souls (1438), Sir Patrick Neill, Q.C., B.C.L., M.A., *Warden* (1977).
Balliol (1263), A. J. P. Kenny, Ph.D., M.A., D.Phil., D.Litt., F.B.A., F.R.S.E., *Master* (1978).
Brasenose (1509) Prof. J. K. B. M. Nicholas, M.A., *Principal* (1978).
Christ Church (1546), Very Rev. E. W. Heaton, M.A., *Dean*, (1979).
Corpus Christi (1517), Sir Kenneth Dover, M.A., D.Litt., F.R.S.E., F.B.A., *President* (1976).
Exeter (1314), The Lord Crowther-Hunt, Ph.D., M.A., *Rector* (1982).
Green (1979), Sir John Walton, M.A., D.Sc., *Warden* (1983).
Hertford (1874), J. R. Torrance, M.A., *Principal* (acting).
Jesus (1571), Dr. P. M. North, D.C.L., M.A., *Principal* (1984).
Keble (1868), C. J. E. Ball, M.A., *Warden* (1979).
Lady Margaret Hall (1878), D. M. Stewart, M.A., *Principal* (1979).
Linacre (1962). J. B. Bamborough, M.A., *Principal* (1962).

Lincoln (1427), Rev. V. H. H. Green, D.D., *Rector* (1983).
Magdalen (1458), K. B. Griffin, M.A., D.Phil., *President* (1979).
Merton (1264), C. S. G. Phillips, M.A., D.Sc., *Warden* (acting).
New College (1379), A. H. Cooke, M.B.E., M.A., D.Phil., *Warden* (1976).
Nuffield (1937), M. G. Brock, C.B.E, M.A., *Warden* (1978).
Oriel (1326), Rt. Hon. Sir Zelman Cowen, A.K., G.C.M.G., G.C.V.O., Q.C., M.A., D.C.L., *Provost* (1982).
Pembroke (1624), P. J. Cuff, M.A., D.Phil., *Vice-gerent.*
Queen's (1340), The Lord Blake, M.A., D.Litt., F.B.A., *Provost* (1968).
St. Anne's (1952) (Originally Society of Oxford Home-Students (1879)), Dr. C. Palley, Ph.D., *Principal* (1984).
St. Antony's (1950), A. R. M. Carr, M.A., *Warden* (1968).
St. Catherine's (1962), Rt. Hon. Sir Patrick Nairne, G.C.B., M.C., M.A., *Master* (1981).
St. Cross (1965), G. H. Stafford, C.B.E., M.A., Ph.D., F.R.S., *Master* (1980).
St. Edmund Hall (c. 1278), J. C. B. Gosling, M.A., *Principal* (1983).
St. John's (1555), Sir John Kendrew, C.B.E., SC.D., Ph.D., M.A., D.SC., D.Phil., F.R.S., *President* (1981).
St. Peter's (1929), Prof. G. E. Aylmer, M.A., D.Phil., F.B.A., *Master* (1978).
Trinity (1554), The Lord Quinton, M.A., F.B.A., *President* (1978).
University (1249), The Lord Goodman, C.H., LL.M., M.A., *Master* (1976).
Wadham (1612), Sir Claus Moser, K.C.B., C.B.E., F.B.A., *Warden* (1984).
Wolfson (1966), The Hon. Sir Henry Fisher, M.A., Q.C., *President* (1975).
Worcester (1714), The Lord Briggs, M.A., F.B.A., *Provost* (1976).
Campion Hall (1896), Rev. P. Hackett, M.A., *Master* (1984).
St. Benet's Hall (1897), Rev. P. D. Holdsworth, O.S.B., M.A., S.T.L., *Master* (1980).
Mansfield (1886), D. A. Sykes, M.A., D.Phil., *Principal* (1977).
Regent's Park (1810), Rev. B. R. White, M.A., D.Phil., *Principal* (1972).
Greyfriars (1910), Very Rev. T. M. Mann, M.A., *Warden* (1981).

* denotes college for men only.

COLLEGES FOR WOMEN ONLY

St. Hilda's (1893), Mrs. G. M. Moore, M.A., *Principal* (1980).
St. Hugh's (1886), Miss M. R. Trickett, M.A., *Principal* (1973).
Somerville (1879), Miss D. M. S. D. Park, C.M.G., O.B.E., M.A., *Principal* (1980).

THE UNIVERSITY OF CAMBRIDGE

FULL TERMS, 1985

Lent, Jan. 15 to Mar. 15; *Easter*, Apr. 16 to June 7; *Michaelmas*, Oct. 8 to Dec. 9

Number of Undergraduates in Residence 1983–84: *Men*, 6,352; *Women*, 3,153

UNIVERSITY OFFICES, &C.   Elect.

Chancellor, H.R.H. The Duke of Edinburgh, K.G., K.T., O.M., G.B.E. 1977

† *Vice-Chancellor*, Sir John Butterfield, O.B.E.,
M.A., D.M., M.D., *Master of Downing College* .. 1983
High Steward, The Lord Devlin, P.C., M.A.,
F.B.A., *Chr*.................................... 1966
Deputy High Steward, The Lord Richardson of
Duntisbourne, P.C., M.B.E., T.D. 1983
Commissary, The Lord Salmon, P.C., M.A.,
Pemb...................................... 1979
Proctors, K. J. Pascoe, M.A., *St. John's*; R. B.
Rickards, SC.D., *Emm*. 1984
Orator, J. Diggle, M.A., PH.D., *Queen's*.......... 1982
Registrary, S. G. Fleet, M.A., PH.D., *Down* 1983
Deputy Registrary, R. F. Holmes, M.A.,*Darw*.... 1972
Librarian, F. W. Ratcliffe, M.A., PH.D., *Corp*. ... 1980
Treasurer, A. B. Shone, M.A., *Rob*. 1984
Secretary General of the Faculties, K. J. R.
Edwards, M.A., *St. John's* 1984
Director of the Fitzwilliam Museum, Prof.
A. M. Jaffé, M.A., *King's* 1973

Cambridge Colleges
(With dates of foundation)

Christ's (1505), Prof. Sir Hans Kornberg, SC.D., F.R.S.,
Master (1983).
Churchill (1960), Prof. Sir Hermann Bondi, K.C.B.,
M.A., F.R.S., *Master* (1982).
Clare (1326), Prof. R. C. O. Matthews, C.B.E., M.A.,
F.B.A., *Master* (1975).
Clare Hall (1966), Sir Michael Stoker, C.B.E., M.A.,
M.D., F.R.S., *President* (1980).
Corpus Christi (1352), M. W. McCrum, M.A., *Master*
(1980).
Darwin (1964), Sir Arnold Burgen, M.D., F.R.S., *Master*
(1982).
Downing (1800), Sir John Butterfield, O.B.E., M.A.,
D.M., M.D., *Master* (1978).
Emmanuel (1584), D. S. Brewer, M.A., PH.D., LITT.D.,
Master (1977).
Fitzwilliam (1966), Prof. J. C. Holt, M.A., D.PHIL., F.B.A.,
Master (1981).
Girton (1869), Dame Mary Warnock, M.A., *Mistress*
(1984).
Gonville & Caius (1348), Prof. H. W. R. Wade, M.A.,
LL.D., D.C.L., F.B.A., Q.C., *Master* (1976).
Jesus (1496), Sir Alan Cottrell, M.A., PH.D., SC.D., F.R.S.,
Master (1974).
King's (1441), B. A. O. Williams, M.A., F.B.A., *Provost*
(1979).
Pembroke (1347), Prof. Lord Adrian, M.A., M.D., F.R.S.,
Master (1981).
Peterhouse (1284), Lord Dacre of Glanton, M.A., F.B.A.,
Master (1980).
Queens' (1448), Prof. E. R. Oxburgh, M.A., F.R.S.,
President (1982).
Robinson (1977), Prof. Sir Jack Lewis, M.A., PH.D.,
D.SC., M.A., SC.D., F.R.S., *Warden* (1977).
St. Catharine's (1473), *Master* (vacant).
St. Edmund's House (1896), Rev. J. Coventry, M.A.,
Master (1976).
St. John's (1511), Prof. F. H. Hinsley, O.B.E., M.A.,
Master (1979).
Selwyn (1882), Prof. A. H. Cook, SC.D., F.R.S., *Master*
(1983).
Sidney Sussex (1596), Prof. D. H. Northcote, PH.D.,
SC.D., F.R.S., *Master* (1976).
Trinity (1546), Sir Andrew Huxley, P.R.S., *Master*
(1984).
Trinity Hall (1350), J. Lyons, M.A., PH.D., *Master*
(1984).
Wolfson (1965), Prof. D. G. T. Williams, M.A., LL.B.,
President (1980).

---

† Correspondence for the *Vice-Chancellor* and other
administrative officers should be sent to the *University Offices*, The Old Schools, Cambridge.

COLLEGE FOR MEN ONLY

Magdalene (1542), Sir Derman Christopherson, O.B.E.,
D.Phil., Ph.D., F.R.S., *Master* (1978).

COLLEGES FOR WOMEN ONLY

New Hall (1954), Mrs. V. L. Pearl, M.A., D.Phil.,
President (1981).
Newnham (1871), Miss S. J. Browne, M.A., C.B.,
Principal (1983).

APPROVED SOCIETIES

Homerton (1824) (for B.Ed. Students), Miss A. C.
Shrubsole, C.B.E., M.A., *Principal* (1971).
Hughes Hall (formerly Cambridge T.C.) (1885), (for
post-graduate students), B. M. Herbertson, M.A.,
M.D., *President* (1984).
Lucy Cavendish Collegiate Society (1965) (for women
research students and mature undergraduates),
Lady Bowden, M.A., *President* (1979).

THE UNIVERSITY OF ASTON IN BIRMINGHAM (1966)
Gosta Green, Birmingham B4 7ET

Students (1983–84), 4,100.
Chancellor, Sir Adrian Cadbury, M.A.
Vice-Chancellor Prof. F. W. Crawford, M.SC., PH.D.,
D.Eng., D.SC.
Secretary, (vacant).

UNIVERSITY OF BATH (1966)
Claverton Down, Bath BA2 7AY

Full-time Students (1983–84), 3,716.
Chancellor, Lord Kearton, O.B.E., F.R.S.
Vice-Chancellor, J. R. Quayle, M.A., B.SC., PH.D., F.R.S.
Registrar and Secretary, R. M. Mawditt.

THE UNIVERSITY OF BIRMINGHAM (1900)
Birmingham B15 2TT

Full-time Students (1984), 8,519.
Chancellor, Sir Alex Jarratt, C.B.
Vice-Chancellor and Principal, Prof. E. A. Marsland,
PH.D., F.R.C. Path.
Secretary, H. Harris, B.SC. (ECON.), LL.B.
Registrar, Mrs. A. M. Hutton, M.A.

UNIVERSITY OF BRADFORD (1966)
Bradford BD7 1DP

Students (1983–84), 4,475.
Chancellor, The Lord Wilson of Rievaulx, K.G., P.C.,
O.B.E., M.A., F.R.S.
Vice-Chancellor and Principal, Prof. J. C. West, C.B.E.,
PH.D., D.SC.
Registrar and Secretary, I. M. Sanderson, M.B.E., B.SC.

THE UNIVERSITY OF BRISTOL (1909)
Bristol BS8 1TH

Full-time Students (1983–84), 6,976.
Chancellor, Prof. Dorothy Hodgkin, O.M., M.A., PH.D,
F.R.S. (1971).
Vice-Chancellor, Prof. P. Haggett, M.A., PH.D., D.SC.
(*acting*).
Registrar and Secretary, E. C. Wright, M.A. (1978).

BRUNEL UNIVERSITY (1966)
Uxbridge, Middlesex UB8 3PH

Students (1983–84), 3,851.
Chancellor, The Earl of Halsbury, F.R.S.
Vice-Chancellor, Prof. R. E. D. Bishop, C.B.E., PH.D.,
SC.D., F.R.S.
Secretary General and Registrar, D. Neave, B.A., L.L.M..

UNIVERSITY OF BUCKINGHAM (1983)
(Founded 1976 as University College at Buckingham)
Buckingham MK18 1EG

Students (1984), 527
Independent of state finance.
Chancellor, The Lord Hailsham of St. Marylebone, P.C., C.H., F.R.S.
Vice-Chancellor, Dr. A. M. Barrett, PH.D.
Registrar, S. P. J. Ellis, M.A.
Bursar and Sec., P. Quick, M.A.

THE CITY UNIVERSITY (1966)
Northampton Square, EC1V 0HB

Students (1983–84), 3,100.
Chancellor, The Lord Mayor of London.
Vice-Chancellor, R. N. Franklin, M.A., D.Phil., D.SC.
Academic Registrar, A. H. Seville, M.A., PH.D.
Secretary, M. M. O'Hara.

THE UNIVERSITY OF DURHAM
(Founded 1832; re-organized 1908, 1937 and 1963)
Old Shire Hall, Durham DH1 3HP

Full-time Students (1984–85), 4,636.

Chancellor, Dame Margot Fonteyn de Arias.
Vice-Chancellor and Warden, Prof. F. G. T. Holliday, C.B.E., F.R.S.E.
Registrar and Secretary, I. E. Graham, M.A.

Colleges

University, E. C. Salthouse, PH.D., *Master*
Hatfield, J. P. Barber, M.A., P.H.D., *Master*.
Grey, E. Halladay, M.A., *Master*.
Van Mildert, A. T. von S. Bradshaw, M.A., *Master*.
Collingwood, J. A. Tuck, M.A., PH.D., *Master*.
St. Chad's, Rev. R. C. Trounson, M.A., *Principal*.
St. John's, Miss D. R. Etchells, M.A., *Principal*.
St. Mary's, Miss J. M. Kenworthy, M.A., *Principal*.
St. Aidan's, Miss I. Hindmarsh, M.A., *Principal*.
Trevelyan, Miss D. Lavin, M.A., *Principal*.
St. Hild and St. Bede, J. V. Armitage, PH.D., *Principal*.
St. Cuthbert's Society, Prof. J. L. Brooks, M.A., *Principal (acting)*.
The Graduate Society, G. Kohnstam, PH.D., *Principal*.
Ushaw, Very Rev. Canon P. F. J. Walton, *President*.

THE UNIVERSITY OF EAST ANGLIA (1963)
Norwich NR4 7TJ

Students (1983–84), 4,123.
Chancellor, (vacant).
Vice-Chancellor, Prof. M. W. Thompson, D.SC.
Registrar and Secretary, M. G. E. Paulson-Ellis, M.A.

THE UNIVERSITY OF ESSEX (1964)
Wivenhoe Park, Colchester CO4 3SQ

Students (1983–84), 3,157.
Chancellor, Rt. Hon. Sir Patrick Nairne G.C.B., M.C., M.A., LL.D.
Vice-Chancellor, A. E. Sloman, C.B.E., M.A., D.Phil.
Registrar and Sec., E. Newcomb, B.A.

THE UNIVERSITY OF EXETER (1955)
Northcote House, Exeter EX4 4QJ

Full-time Students (1983–84), 4,856.
Chancellor, Sir Rex Richards, D.SC., F.R.S., F.R.S.C. (1982).
Vice-Chancellor, D. Harrison, M.A., PH.D., SC.D., F.R.S.C.
Academic Registrar and Secretary, M. J. Hislop.

THE UNIVERSITY OF HULL (1954)
Cottingham Road, Hull HU6 7RX

Full-time Students (1983–84), *Men*, 2,916; *Women*, 2,681.
Chancellor, The Lord Wilberforce, P.C., C.M.G., O.B.E. (1978).
Vice-Chancellor, Sir Roy Marshall, C.B.E., M.A., PH.D. (1979).
Registrar, F. T. Mattison, M.A., LL.B.

THE UNIVERSITY OF KEELE (1962)
Keele, Staffordshire ST5 5BG

Full-time Students (1983–84), 2,682.
Chancellor, H.R.H. The Princess Margaret, Countess of Snowdon, C.I., G.C.V.O. (1962).
Vice-Chancellor, B. E. F. Fender, PH.D.
Registrar, D. Cohen, M.A., PH.D., F.R.S.C.

UNIVERSITY OF KENT AT CANTERBURY (1965)
Canterbury, Kent CT2 7NZ

Students (1983–84), 4,108.
Chancellor, The Lord Grimond, P.C., T.D.
Vice-Chancellor, D. J. E. Ingram, M.A., D.Phil., D.SC.
Registrar and Finance Officer, A. D. Linfoot, M.A.
Academic Secretary, G. D. Millyard, M.A.

THE UNIVERSITY OF LANCASTER (1964)
Bailrigg, Lancaster LA1 4YW

Full-time Students (1983–84), 4,499.
Chancellor, H.R.H. The Princess Alexandra, G.C.V.O.
Vice-Chancellor, Prof. P. A. Reynolds, M.A.
Registrar, M. D. Forster, M.A.
Secretary, G. M. Cockburn, M.A.

THE UNIVERSITY OF LEEDS (1904)
Leeds LS2 9JT

Full-time Students (1983–84), 10,411.
Chancellor, H.R.H. The Duchess of Kent, G.C.V.O. (1966).
Vice-Chancellor, Sir Edward Parkes, M.A., PH.D., SC.D.
Registrar, J. J. Walsh, M.A. (1979).
Bursar, R. Head (1976).

THE UNIVERSITY OF LEICESTER (1957)
Leicester LE1 7RH

Full-time Students (1983–84), 4,677.
Chancellor, Prof. Sir Alan Hodgkin, O.M., K.B.E., M.A., SC.D., F.R.S. (1971).
Vice-Chancellor, M. Shock, M.A.
Registrar, J. W. Walmsley (1983).

THE UNIVERSITY OF LIVERPOOL (1903)
Senate House, Liverpool L69 3BX

Students (1983–84), 7,453.
Chancellor, The Viscount Leverhulme, T.D.
Vice-Chancellor, R. F. Whelan, M.D., PH.D., D.SC.
Registrar, R. A. Hind.
Secs., D. R. Holmes (*Academic*); S. Guy (*Admin.*).

THE UNIVERSITY OF LONDON (1836)
Senate House, WC1E 7HU

Internal Students (1982–83), 40,696, External Students, 19,095.
Visitor, H.M. The Queen in Council.
Chancellor, H.R.H. The Princess Anne, G.C.V.O.
Vice-Chancellor, Prof. Randolph Quirk, C.B.E., F.B.A.
Chairman of the Court, The Lord Scarman, P.C., O.B.E. M.A.

Chairman of Convocation, Prof. J. P. Quilliam, M.B., D.SC.
Principal, W. Taylor, C.B.E., PH.D.

Principal Officers

Clerk of the Court, P. Holwell.
Clerk of the Senate, P. Taylor.
Academic Registrar, Mrs. G. Roberts.
Secretary to University Entrance and School Examinations Council, A. R. Stephenson, M.A.
Director of Central Library Services, V. T. H. Parry, M.A.

Schools of the University*

Bedford College, Inner Circle, Regent's Park, NW1 4NS, Prof. Dorothy E. C. Wedderburn, M.A., *Principal.*
Birkbeck College, Malet Street, WC1 7HX, Prof. W. G. Overend, PH.D., D.SC., *Master.*
Chelsea College, 552 King's Road S.W.10, Prof. H. Tyrrell, *Principal.*
Imperial College of Science and Technology, South Kensington, SW7 2AZ, The Lord Flowers, M.A., M.SC., D.SC., F.R.S., *Rector.*
Institute of Education, 20 Bedford Way, WC1H 0AL, Prof. D. Lawton, PH.D., *Dir*
King's College, Strand, WC2R 2LS, The Lord Cameron of Balhousie, G.C.B., C.B.E., D.S.O., D.F.C., *Principal.*
London School of Economics and Political Science, Houghton Street, WC2A 2AE, Prof. I. Patel, *Director.*
Queen Elizabeth College, Campden Hill Road, W8 7AH, R. S. Barnes, D.SC., *Principal.*
Queen Mary College, Mile End Road, E1 4NS, Sir James Menter, M.A., PH.D., SC.D., F.R.S., *Principal.*
Royal Holloway College, Egham Hill, Egham, Surrey TW20 0EX, R. F. Miller, PH.D., *Principal.*
Royal Veterinary College, Royal College Street, NW1 0TU, A. O. Betts, M.A., PH.D., *Principal and Dean.*
School of Oriental and African Studies, Malet Street, WC1E 7HP, Prof. C. D. Cowan, M.A., PH.D., *Dir.*
School of Pharmacy, 29–39 Brunswick Square, WC1N 1AX, F. Fish, PH.D., *Dean.*
University College, Gower Street, WC1E 6BT, Sir James Lighthill, F.R.S., *Provost.*
Westfield College, Kidderpore Avenue, Hampstead, NW3 7ST, Prof. J. E. Varey, PH.D., D.Litt., *Principal.*
Wye College, Wye nr. Ashford, Kent TN25 5AH, I. A. M. Lucas, C.B.E., M.SC., *Principal.*
***Heythrop College,** 11 Cavendish Square, W.1., Rev. F. X. Walker, S.J., P.H.D., *Principal.*

Senate Institutes

British Institute in Paris, 9–11 Rue de Constantine, 75007, Paris, Prof. C. L. Campos, L-ès-L., PH.D., *Dir.* London office: 15 Woburn Square, WC1H 0NS.
Courtauld Institute of Art, 20 Portman Square, W1H 0BE, Prof. P. E. Lasko, C.B.E., F.B.A., F.S.A., *Dir.*
Institute of Advanced Legal Studies, Charles Clore House, 17 Russell Square, WC1B 5DR, Prof. A. L. Diamond, LL.M., *Dir.*
Institute of Archæology, 31–34 Gordon Square, WC1H 0PY, Prof. J. D. Evans, M.A., PH.D., Litt.D., F.B.A., F.S.A., *Dir.*
Institute of Classical Studies, 31–34 Gordon Square, WC1H 0PY, Prof. E. W. Handley, M.A., F.B.A., *Dir.*
Institute of Commonwealth Studies, 27–28 Russell Square, WC1B 5DS, Prof. Shula E. Marks, PH.D., *Dir.*
Institute of Germanic Studies, 29 Russell Square, WC1B 5DP, Prof. J. P. Stern, M.A., PH.D., Litt.D., *Hon. Dir.*

* For Medical Schools, Training Colleges and Veterinary Colleges, *see under* Professional Education.
**Not in receipt of U.G.C. grants.

Institute of Historical Research, Senate House, WC1E 7HU, Prof. F. M. L. Thompson, M.A., D.Phil., F.B.A., *Dir.*
Institute of Latin American Studies, 31 Tavistock Square, WC1H 9HA, Prof. J. Lynch, M.A., PH.D., *Dir.*
Institute of United States Studies, 31 Tavistock Square, WC1H 9EZ, Prof. P. J. Parish, *Dir.*
School of Slavonic and E. European Studies, University of London, Senate House, WC1E 7HU, M. A. Branch, PH.D., *Dir.*
Warburg Institute, Woburn Square, WC1H 0AB, Prof. J. B. Trapp, M.A., F.B.A., *Dir.*

Institutions having Recognised Teachers

Goldsmiths' College, Lewisham Way, New Cross, SE14 6NW, A. Rutherford, M.A., *Warden.*
Jews' College, Finchley Synagogue, Kinloss Gardens, N3 3DU, Rabbi Dr. J. Sacks, *Principal.*
London Graduate School of Business Studies, Sussex Place, NW1 4SA, Prof. P. G. Moore, PH.D., *Principal.*
Royal Academy of Music, Marylebone Road, NW1 5HT, D. Lumsden, M.A., D.Phil., MUS.B., F.R.C.M., *Principal.*
Royal College of Music, Prince Consort Road, SW7 2BS, M. G. Matthews, F.R.C.M., *Director.*
Trinity College of Music, Mandeville Place, W1M 6AQ, M. Davies, C.B.E., B.Mus., M.A., F.R.C.M., *Principal.*

LOUGHBOROUGH UNIVERSITY OF TECHNOLOGY (1966)
Loughborough LE11 3TU

Students (1983–84), 5,313.
Chancellor, Sir Arnold Hall, M.A., F.R.S.
Vice-Chancellor, Sir Clifford Butler, PH.D., F.R.S.
Registrar, H. Brooks, B.SC. (Econ.).

THE UNIVERSITY OF MANCHESTER
Oxford Road, Manchester MI3 9PL

(Founded 1851; re-organized 1880 and 1903).

Full-time Students (1983–84), 17,073.
Chancellor, The Duke of Devonshire, P.C., M.C. (1965).
Vice-Chancellor, Prof. M. H. Richmond, PH.D., SC.D., F.R.S. (1981).
Registrar, K. E. Kitchen, M.A. (1979).

UNIVERSITY OF MANCHESTER INSTITUTE OF SCIENCE AND TECHNOLOGY (1824)
P.O. Box 88, Manchester M60 1QD

Full-time Students (1983–84), 4,271.
President, Sir William Mather, O.B.E., M.C., T.D.
Principal, Prof. H. C. A. Hankins, PH.D.
Secretary and Registrar, D. H. McWilliam, B.A.

THE UNIVERSITY OF NEWCASTLE UPON TYNE
(Founded 1852; re-organized 1908, 1937 and 1963)
Newcastle upon Tyne NE1 7RU

Students (1983–84), 7,410.
Chancellor, The Duke of Northumberland, K.G., P.C., G.C.V.O., T.D., F.R.S. (1963).
Vice-Chancellor, Prof. L. W. Martin, M.A., PH.D.
Registrar, D. E. T. Nicholson, M.A.

THE UNIVERSITY OF NOTTINGHAM (1948)
University Park, Nottingham NG7 2RD

Full-time Students (1983–84), 6,800.
Chancellor, Sir Gordon Hobday, PH.D., F.R.S.C.
Vice-Chancellor, B. C. L. Weedon, C.B.E., PH.D., D.SC., F.R.S., F.R.S.C.

Registrar, G. E. Chandler, B.A.
Bursar, J. E. Madocks, C.B.E.

THE UNIVERSITY OF READING (1926)
Whiteknights, Reading RG6 2AH

Number of Students (1983–84), 5,617.
Chancellor, The Lord Sherfield, G.C.B., G.C.M.G. (1970).
Vice-Chancellor, E. S. Page, B.SC., M.A., PH.D. (1979).
Registrar, T. Bottomley, B.A. (1982).
Bursar, R. H. C. Ascott, M.A.

UNIVERSITY OF SALFORD (1967)
Salford M5 4WT

Full-time Students (1983–84), 3,700.
Chancellor, H.R.H. The Prince Philip, Duke of Edinburgh, K.G., P.C., K.T., O.M., G.B.E., F.R.S.
Vice-Chancellor, J. M. Ashworth, PH.D., M.A., D.SC.
Registrar, S. R. Bosworth, B.A.

THE UNIVERSITY OF SHEFFIELD (1905)
Sheffield S10 2TN

Full-time Students (1983–84), 7,535.
Chancellor, Sir Frederick Dainton, PH.D., SC.D., M.A., F.R.S. (1979).
Vice-Chancellor, Prof. G. D. Sims, O.B.E., M.SC., PH.D. (1974).
Registrar and Secretary, J. S. Padley, PH.D. (1982).

THE UNIVERSITY OF SOUTHAMPTON (1952)
Highfield, Southampton SO9 5NH

Students (1983–84), 6,396.
Chancellor, The Earl Jellicoe, P.C., D.S.O., M.C.
Vice-Chancellor, Prof. J. M. Roberts, M.A., D.Phil. (1979).
Secretary and Registrar, D. A. Schofield, M.A. (1978).
Academic Registrar, Miss A. E. Clarke, B.A. (1978).

UNIVERSITY OF SURREY (1966)
Guildford, Surrey GU2 5XH

Full-time Students (1983–84), 3,227.
Chancellor, H.R.H. The Duke of Kent, G.C.M.G., G.C.V.O.
Vice-Chancellor, A. Kelly, PH.D., SC.D., F.R.S.
Academic Registrar, G. Haigh, PH.D.
Secretary, L. J. Kail.

THE UNIVERSITY OF SUSSEX (1961)
Falmer, Brighton BN1 9RH

Full-time Students (1983–84), 4,292.
Chancellor, The Lord Shawcross, P.C., G.B.E., Q.C.
Vice-Chancellor, Prof. Sir Denys Wilkinson, M.A., PH.D., SC.D., F.R.S.
Registrar and Secretary, G. Lockwood, D.Phil.

THE UNIVERSITY OF WARWICK (1965)
Coventry CV4 7AL

Students (1983–84), 5,539.
Chancellor, The Lord Scarman, P.C., O.B.E., M.A.
Vice-Chancellor, J. B. Butterworth, C.B.E., M.A.
Registrar, M. L. Shattock, M.A.

THE UNIVERSITY OF YORK (1963)
Heslington, York YO1 5DD

Full-time Students (1983–84), 3,423.
Chancellor, The Lord Swann, M.A., PH.D., F.R.S.
Vice-Chancellor, Prof. S. B. Saul, B.com., PH.D.
Registrar, Anne B. Riddell.

ROYAL COLLEGE OF ART, 1837
Kensington Gore SW7 2EU

Under Royal Charter (1967) the Royal College of Art grants the degrees of Doctor, Doctor of Philos-
ophy, Doctor of Arts, Master of Arts and Master of Design (RCA).
Students (1984), 602 (all postgraduate).
Provost, Sir Hugh Casson, K.C.V.O., P.R.A., M.A.
Registrar, B. M. Cooper, B.A..

CRANFIELD INSTITUTE OF TECHNOLOGY 1969
Cranfield, Bedford MK43 0AL

Under Royal Charter (1969) the Cranfield Institute of Technology grants degrees in applied science, engineering, technology and management.
Students (1983–84), 1,605.
Chancellor, The Lord Kings Norton, PH.D., D.I.C.
Vice-Chancellor, Sir Henry Chilver, PH.d., D.SC., M.A., F.R.S.
General Secretary, P. A. Digger.

THE OPEN UNIVERSITY (1969)
Walton Hall, Milton Keynes MK7 6AA

Students (1982), 100,850.
Tuition by correspondence linked with special radio and television programmes, summer schools and a locally-based tutorial and counselling service. Under Royal Charter the University awards degrees of B.A., B.Phil., M.Phil., PH.D., D.SC. and D.Litt. There are six faculties—arts, School of Education, mathematics, science, social sciences and technology and a wide range of continuing education courses.
Chancellor, The Lord Briggs, M.A.
Vice-Chancellor, J. H. Horlock, PH.D., SC.D., F.R.S.
Secretary, D. J. Clinch.

THE UNIVERSITY OF WALES (1893)
Cathays Park, Cardiff

Chancellor, H.R.H. The Prince of Wales, K.G., K.T., G.C.B., A.D.C. (1976).
Pro-Chancellor, The Lord Cledwyn, P.C., C.H. (1985).
Vice-Chancellor, A. F. Trotman-Dickenson, M.A., PH.D., D.SC. (1983).
Registrar, M. A. R. Kemp, PH.D.

Colleges

University College of Wales, Aberystwyth.—*Princ.,* G. Owen, D.SC. (1979).
University College of North Wales, Bangor.—*Princ.,* Prof. E. Sunderland, M.A., PH.D.
University of Wales Institute of Science and Technology, Cardiff.—*Princ.,* A. F. Trotman-Dickenson, M.A., PH.D., D.SC. (1968).
Cardiff (University College).—*Princ.,* C. W. L. Bevan, C.B.E., D.SC. (1966).
Lampeter (St. David's College).—*Princ.,* Prof. B. R. Morris, M.A., D.Phil. (1980).
Swansea (University College).—*Princ.,* Prof. B. L. Clarkson, B.SC., PH.D., (1982).
University of Wales College of Medicine, Cardiff.—*Provost,* Prof. H. L. Duthie, M.D., ch.M., F.R.C.S. (1979).

SCOTLAND

UNIVERSITY OF ABERDEEN (1495)
Regent Walk, Aberdeen AB9 1FX

Undergraduates (1983), 4,994.
Chancellor, Lord Polwarth, T.D., F.R.S.E., F.R.S.A.
Principal, Prof. G. P. McNicol, M.D., PH.D., F.R.C.P. (1981).
Secretary, W. M. Bradley.
Rector (1981–84), R. J. Perryment, M.A.

UNIVERSITY OF EDINBURGH (1583)
Old College, South Bridge, Edinburgh EH8 9YL

Students (1983–84), 9,860.

Chancellor, H.R.H. The Prince Philip, Duke of Edinburgh, K.G., K.T., O.M., G.B.E., P.C., F.R.S. (1952).
Vice-Chancellor and Principal, J. H. Burnett, M.A., D.Phil., F.R.S.E. (1979).
Secretary, A. M. Currie, O.B.E. (1978).
Rector, Rt. Hon. David Steel, M.A., M.P. (1982–85).

UNIVERSITY OF DUNDEE (1967)
Dundee DD1 4HN

Full-time Students (1983–84), 3,527.
Chancellor, The Earl of Dalhousie, K.T., G.C.V.O., G.B.E., M.C. (1977).
Principal and Vice-Chancellor, Prof. A. M. Neville, M.C., T.D., M.SC., Ph.D., D.SC., F.R.S.E. (1978).
Secretary, R. Seaton, M.A., LL.B. (1973).
Rector, R. Gordon Wilson, M.P. (1983–86).

UNIVERSITY OF GLASGOW (1451)
Gilmorehill, Glasgow G12 8QQ

Students (1983–84), 10,043.
Chancellor, Sir Alec Cairncross, K.C.M.G., F.B.A.
Vice-Chancellor, Sir Alwyn Williams, Ph.D., F.R.S., F.R.S.E. (1976).
Registrar, F. Gillanders, M.A.
Secretary to the University Court, J. McCargow, M.A.
Rector, M Kelly, Ph.D. (1984–87).

HERIOT-WATT UNIVERSITY (1966)
Chambers Street, Edinburgh EH1 1HX

Students (1983–84), 3,244.
Chancellor, The Lord Thomson of Monifieth, P.C. (1977).
Principal and *Vice-Chancellor,* T. L. Johnston, M.A., Ph.D., F.R.S.E. (1981).
Registrar, D. Sturgeon, B.L.
Secretary, D. I. Cameron, B.L. (1966).

UNIVERSITY OF ST. ANDREWS (1411)
College Gate, St. Andrews KY16 9AJ

Students (1983–84), 3,672.
Chancellor, Sir Kenneth Dover, M.A., D.Litt., F.R.S.E., F.B.A. (1981).
Principal and Vice-Chancellor, J. S. Watson, M.A., F.R.S.E. (1966).
Registrar and Secretary, M. J. B. Lowe, Ph.D. (1981).
Rector, Katharine Whitehorn (1982–85).

UNIVERSITY OF STIRLING (1967)
Stirling FK9 4LA

Full-time Students (1983–84), 2,540.
Chancellor, Sir Monty Finniston, Ph.D., F.R.S. (1978).
Principal and Vice-Chancellor, Sir Kenneth Alexander, B.SC., F.R.S.E. (1980).
Secretary, R. G. Bomont, B.SC. (Econ.) (1973).

UNIVERSITY OF STRATHCLYDE (1964)
16 Richmond Street, Glasgow G1 1XQ

Full-time Students (1983–84), 7,099.
Chancellor, The Lord Todd, O.M., M.A., D.SC., D.Phil., F.R.S., F.R.S.C. (1965).
Principal and Vice-Chancellor, G. J. Hills, Ph.D., D.SC., F.R.S.E., F.R.S.C. (1980).
Registrar, D. W. J. Morrell, M.A., LL.B. (1973).

NORTHERN IRELAND

THE QUEEN'S UNIVERSITY OF BELFAST (1908)

Full-time Students (1983–84), 6,645.
Chancellor, (vacant).
President and Vice-Chancellor, P. Froggatt, M.A., M.D., Ph.D. (1976).
Secretary, R. G. Topping, V.R.D., M.A. (1977).
Secretary to the Academic Council, A. H. Graham, M.A. (1978).

UNIVERSITY OF ULSTER (1984)
Coleraine, Co. Londonderry BT52 1SA
(Amalgamation of New University of Ulster and Ulster Polytechnic)

Full-time Students (1983–84), 7,316.
Chancellor, The Lord Grey of Naunton, G.C.M.G., G.C.V.O., O.B.E. (1980).
Vice-Chancellor, D. S. Birley, M.A.
Secretary, J. A. Hunter, M.A.

REPUBLIC OF IRELAND

UNIVERSITY OF DUBLIN TRINITY COLLEGE (1592)
Dublin 2

Full-time Students (1983–84), 6,153.
Chancellor, W. B. Stanford, M.A., Litt.D. (1983).
Provost, W. A. Watts, M.A., SC.D. (1981).
Registrar, E. Sagarra, M.A., D.Phil. (1981).
Secretary, G. H. H. Giltrap, M.A.

NATIONAL UNIVERSITY OF IRELAND, DUBLIN (1908)
49 Merrion Square, Dublin 2

Full-time Students (1983–84), 19,119.
Chancellor, Dr. T. K. Whitaker.
Vice-Chancellor, Dr. T. ó Ciardha, M.A., Ph.D.
Registrar, Dr. M. Gilheany, B.A., B.comm., M.Econ.SC.

Constituent Colleges
Presidents
Univ. Coll., Dublin, T. Murphy, M.D., D.SC.
Univ. Coll., Cork, T. ó Ciardha, M.A., Ph.D.
Univ. Coll. Galway, C.ó h Eocha, Ph.D.

THE ASSOCIATION OF COMMONWEALTH UNIVERSITIES
36 Gordon Square, WC1H 0PF

The Association holds quinquennial Congresses of the Universities of the Commonwealth and other meetings in the intervening years; publishes the *Commonwealth Universities Yearbook,* handbooks listing scholarships and fellowships, etc.; acts as a general information centre on universities in U.K. and other Commonwealth countries; provides an advisory service for the filling of university teaching staff appointments overseas; administers travelling fellowships for university administrators as well as Commonwealth Foundation and Edward Boyle bursaries for medical students; and runs the Third World Academic Exchange Programme. It also supplies the secretariat for the Commonwealth Scholarship Commission in the United Kingdom, for the Marshall Aid

Commemoration Commission and for the Kennedy Memorial Trust.
Secretary General, A. Christodoulou, C.B.E., M.A.

COUNCIL FOR NATIONAL ACADEMIC AWARDS
344–354 Gray's Inn Road, WC1X 8BP

Established in 1964 with powers to award degrees and other academic distinctions, comparable in standard with awards granted and conferred by universities to students in polytechnics and other institutions of higher education in the United Kingdom which do not have the power to award their own degrees. The Council awards degrees and honours degrees of B.A., B.Ed., B.SC., B.Eng. and M.Eng. and higher and research degrees and doctorates. On Sept. 1, 1974, the Council assumed responsibility for the work formerly undertaken by the National

Council for Diplomas in Art and Design, and in September, 1976, for the Diploma on Management Studies.
President, H.R.H. The Prince of Wales, K.G., K.T., G.C.B.
Chairman, Sir Alastair Pilkington, F.R.S.
Chief Officer, E. Kerr, B.SC., PH.D.

POLYTECHNICS

The 30 polytechnics constitute a substantial part of the higher education system in England and Wales. Overall they provide an educational environment for some 260,000 students each year, about half of them following full-time or sandwich courses. Within the public sector their total entry includes over 75% of all first-year enrolments to degree courses and others recognised as being of the same standard. In many cases, their student enrolments at this level match those of most universities. In addition the polytechnics play a major part in the national provision of other advanced courses which do not lead to a degree or degree-equivalent qualifications. The polytechnics' function is to provide virtually the full range of courses, albeit with a pronounced vocational flavour. Together engineering, science and technology currently account for little more than one-third of the enrolments. A further third is involved in administrative, business and social studies and some 13% occur in education. The remaining 22% are spread over other professional and vocational subjects (e.g. architecture, librarianship and catering); music, drama and visual arts; languages (3%) and other arts (3%). Full-time students for the year 1983–84 are shown in parentheses.

CITY OF BIRMINGHAM POLYTECHNIC, Perry Barr, Birmingham B42 2SU (4,541).—*Dir.,* R. J. W. Hammond.
BRIGHTON POLYTECHNIC, Moulsecoomb, Brighton BN2 4AT (4,065).—*Dir.,* G. R. Hall.
BRISTOL POLYTECHNIC, Coldharbour Lane, Frenchay, Bristol BS16 1QY (5,247).—*Dir.,* Dr. W. Birch.
COVENTRY (LANCHESTER) POLYTECHNIC, Priory Street, Coventry CV1 5FB (5,348).—*Dir.,* G. Holroyde.
HATFIELD POLYTECHNIC, College Lane, Hatfield, Herts. (3,460).—*Dir.,* J. Illston, PH.D., D.SC.
HUDDERSFIELD POLYTECHNIC, Queensgate, Huddersfield HD1 3DH (4,600).—*Rector,* K. J. Durrands.
KINGSTON POLYTECHNIC, Penrhyn Road, Kingston upon Thames KT1 2EE (5,182).—*Dir.,* R. C. Smith, PH.D.
LANCASHIRE POLYTECHNIC, Corporation Street, Preston PR1 2TQ (3,500).—*Dir.,* E. E. Robinson.
LEEDS POLYTECHNIC, Calverley Street, Leeds LS1 3HE (5,494).—*Dir.,* P. J. Nuttgens, C.B.E., PH.D.
LEICESTER POLYTECHNIC, P.O. Box 143, Leicester LE1 9BH (6,295).—*Dir.,* D. Bethel, C.B.E.
LIVERPOOL POLYTECHNIC, Rodney House, 70 Mount Pleasant, Liverpool L3 5UX (4,600).—*Rector,* J. C. McKenzie.
LONDON:
  CITY OF LONDON POLYTECHNIC, 117–119 Houndsditch, EC3A 7BU (3,500).—*Prov.,* J. M. Edwards, Q.C..
  MIDDLESEX POLYTECHNIC, 114 Chase Side, N.14.—*Dir.,* R. M. W. Rickett, PH.D.
  NORTH-EAST LONDON POLYTECHNIC, Romford Road, E15 4LZ (6,000).—*Dir.,* G. T. Fowler, M.A.
  POLYTECHNIC OF CENTRAL LONDON, 309 Regent Street, W1R 8AL (4,120).—*Rector.,* Prof. T. E. Burlin, D.SC., PH.D.
  POLYTECHNIC OF NORTH LONDON, Holloway Road, N.7.—*Dir.,* D. W. MacDowall, M.A., D.Phil., F.S.A.
  POLYTECHNIC OF THE SOUTH BANK, Borough Road, SE1 0AA (4,758).—*Dir.,* J. Beishon, D.Phil.
THAMES POLYTECHNIC, Wellington Street, Woolwich, SE18 6PF (3,489).—*Dir.,* N. Singer, PH.D.

MANCHESTER POLYTECHNIC, All Saints, Manchester.—*Dir.,* K. Green, M.A.
NEWCASTLE UPON TYNE POLYTECHNIC, Ellison Place, Newcastle upon Tyne.—*Dir.,* Prof. L. Barden.
NORTH STAFFORDSHIRE POLYTECHNIC, Beaconside, Stafford ST18 0AD (4,250).—*Dir.,* J. F. Dickenson, PH.D.
OXFORD POLYTECHNIC, Headington, Oxford OX3 0BP (4,150).—*Dir.,* B. L. Tonge, PH.D.
PLYMOUTH POLYTECHNIC, Drake Circus, Plymouth PL4 8AA (4,800).—*Dir.,* R. F. M. Robbins, PH.D.
PORTSMOUTH POLYTECHNIC, Museum Road, Portsmouth PO1 2QQ (6,463).—*Pres.,* H. D. Law, PH.D.
SHEFFIELD CITY POLYTECHNIC, Pond Street, Sheffield S1 1WB (8,400).—*Principal,* J. M. Stoddart.
SUNDERLAND POLYTECHNIC, Langham Tower, Ryhope Road, Sunderland SR2 7EE (4,604).—*Rector,* E. P. Hart, PH.D.
TEESSIDE POLYTECHNIC, Borough Road, Middlesbrough, Cleveland.—*Dir.,* M. D. Longfield, PH.D.
TRENT POLYTECHNIC, Burton Street, Nottingham NG1 4BU (7,292).—*Dir.,* E. A. Freeman, PH.D., D.SC.
WOLVERHAMPTON POLYTECHNIC, Wulfruna Street, Wolverhampton WV1 1LY (5,517).—*Dir.,* G. A. Seabrooke.
POLYTECHNIC OF WALES, Pontypridd, Mid Glamorgan CF37 1DL (3,828).—*Dir.,* J. D. Davies, M.SC., PH.D., D.SC.

COLLEGES

It is not possible to name here all the colleges offering courses of higher or further education. The list that follows is confined to colleges providing at least one full-time course leading to a *first degree* granted by a university or by the Council for National Academic Awards (C.N.A.A.). It does not include colleges forming part of a polytechnic or of a university.
After the name of each college the abbreviated title of the appropriate degree or degrees is given, but the very many *other* qualifications for which the colleges also provide courses are not listed.

ABERDEEN COLLEGE OF EDUCATION (*B.Ed.*), Hilton Place, Aberdeen AB9 1FA.—*Principal,* D. Adams.
AVERY HILL COLLEGE (*B.A., B.Sc., B.Ed.*), Bexley Road, London SE9 2PQ.—*Principal,* M. Lovitt.
BATH COLLEGE OF HIGHER EDUCATION (incorporating BATH ACADEMY OF ART) (*B.A., B.Sc., B.Ed.*), Newton Park, Bath BA2 9BN.—*Director,* N. P. Payne.
BEDFORD COLLEGE OF HIGHER EDUCATION (*B.A., B.Ed.*), 37 Lansdowne Road, Bedford MK40 2BZ.—*Director,* D. G. Lyne.
BISHOP GROSSETESTE COLLEGE (*B.Ed.*), Lincoln, Lincolnshire LN1 3DY.—*Principal,* L. G. Marsh.
BOLTON INSTITUTE OF HIGHER EDUCATION (*B.A., B.Sc., B.Ed.*), Deane Road, Bolton BL3 5AB.—*Principal,* Dr. R. Oxtoby.
BRADFORD AND ILKLEY COMMUNITY COLLEGE (*B.A., B.Ed.*), Great Horton Road, Bradford BD7 1AY.—*Principal,* Dr. P. J. Gallagher.
BRETTON HALL COLLEGE OF HIGHER EDUCATION (*B.A., B.Ed.*), West Bretton, Wakefield, West Yorkshire WF4 4LG.—*Principal,* Dr. J. L. Taylor.
BUCKINGHAMSHIRE COLLEGE OF HIGHER EDUCATION (*B.A., B.Sc.*), Queen Alexandra Road, High Wycombe, Bucks. HP11 2JZ.—*Director,* D. J. Everett.
BULMERSHE COLLEGE OF HIGHER EDUCATION (*B.A., B.Ed.*), Woodlands Avenue, Earley, Reading RG6 1HY.—*Principal,* H. Silver, PH.D.
CAMBERWELL SCHOOL OF ART AND CRAFTS (*B.A.*), Peckham Road, London S.E.5.—*Principal,* I. E. T. Jenkin.
CAMBORNE SCHOOL OF MINES (*B.Sc.*), Trevenson, Pool, Redruth, Cornwall TR15 3SE.—*Principal,* P. Hackett.

CAMBRIDGESHIRE COLLEGE OF ARTS AND TECHNOLOGY (*B.A., B.Sc.*), Cambridge.—*Principal*, R. L. Helmore, C.B.E.

CANTERBURY COLLEGE OF ART (*B.A.*), New Dover Road, Canterbury CT1 3AN.—*Principal*, G. G. Bellamy.

CENTRAL SCHOOL OF ART AND DESIGN (*B.A.*), Southampton Row, London WC1 4AP.—*Principal*, T. H. Pannell.

CENTRAL SCHOOL OF SPEECH AND DRAMA (*B.Ed., B.Sc.*), Embassy Theatre, Eton Avenue, London NW3 3HY.—*Principal*, G. Kitson.

CHARLOTTE MASON COLLEGE (*B.Ed.*), Ambleside, Cumbria LA22 9BB.—*Principal*, J. Thorley, M.A., PH.D.

CHELMER INSTITUTE OF HIGHER EDUCATION (*B.A., B.Sc., B.Ed.*), Victoria Road South, Chelmsford, Essex CM1 1LL.—*Director*, M. Salmon.

CHELSEA SCHOOL OF ART (*B.A.*), Manresa Road, London S.W.3.—*Principal*, J. Barnicoat.

CHESTER COLLEGE (*B.A., B.Ed.*), Cheyney Road, Chester CH1 4BJ.—*Principal*, Dr. M. V. J. Seaborne.

CHRIST CHURCH COLLEGE OF HIGHER EDUCATION (*B.A., B.Sc., B.Ed.*), North Holmes Road, Canterbury, Kent.— *Principal*, M. H. A. Berry, T.D.

COLCHESTER INSTITUTE (*B.A.*), Sheepen Road, Colchester CO3 3LL.—*Director*, J. M. Threlfall.

CREWE AND ALSAGER COLLEGE OF HIGHER EDUCATION (*B.A., B.Ed.*), Crewe Road, Crewe CW1 1DU.—*Director*, Miss B. P. R. Ward, C.B.E.

DARTINGTON COLLEGE OF ARTS (*B.A.*), Totnes, Devon TQ9 6EJ.—*Principal*, C. Roosevelt.

DE LA SALLE COLLEGE (*B.A., B.Sc., B.Ed.*), Hopwood Hall, Middleton, Manchester M24 3XH.—*Principal*, Rev. Br. Wilfrid, M.A.

DERBYSHIRE COLLEGE OF HIGHER EDUCATION (*B.Comb.Studs., B.A., B.Sc., B.Ed.*), Kedleston Road, Derby DE3 1GB.—*Director*, J. May, T.D., PH.D.

DORSET INSTITUTE OF HIGHER EDUCATION (*B.A., B.Sc.*), Wallisdown Road, Wallisdown, Poole.—*Director*, C. B. Brewington.

DUNCAN OF JORDANSTONE COLLEGE OF ART (*B.A., B.Sc., B. Arch.*), Perth Road, Dundee DD1 4HT.—*Principal*, M. Lacome.

DUNDEE COLLEGE OF EDUCATION (*B.Ed.*), Gardyne Road, Dundee DD5 1NY.—*Principal*, W. A. Illsley, PH.D.

DUNDEE COLLEGE OF TECHNOLOGY (*B.A., B.Sc.*), Bell Street, Dundee DD1 1HG.—*Principal*, H. G. Cuming, PH.D.

DUNFERMLINE COLLEGE OF PHYSICAL EDUCATION (*B.Ed., B.A.*), Cramond Road North, Edinburgh EH4 6JD.—*Principal*, Miss J. A. Carroll.

EALING COLLEGE OF HIGHER EDUCATION (*B.A.*), St. Mary's Road, Ealing, London W.5.—*Director*, N. Merritt.

EDGE HILL COLLEGE OF HIGHER EDUCATION (*B.A., B.Ed., B.Sc.*), Ormskirk, Lancs. L39 4QP.—*Director*, H. Webster.

EDINBURGH COLLEGE OF ART (*B.A., B.Sc., B.Arch.*), Lauriston Place, Edinburgh EH3 9DF.—*Principal*, J. L. Paterson.

EXETER COLLEGE OF ART AND DESIGN (*B.A.*), Earl Richards Road North, Exeter EX2 6AS.—*Principal*, D. Jeremiah, PH.D.

FALMOUTH SCHOOL OF ART (*B.A.*), Woodlane, Falmouth, Cornwall.—*Principal*, T. Cross.

GLASGOW COLLEGE OF BUILDING AND PRINTING (*B.Sc.*), 60 North Hanover Street, Glasgow G1 2BP.—*Principal*, D. McEwan.

GLASGOW COLLEGE OF TECHNOLOGY (*B.A., B.Sc.*), Cowcaddens Road, Glasgow G4 0BA.—*Director*, Dr. N. G. Meadows.

GLASGOW SCHOOL OF ART (*B.A., B.Arch.*), 167 Renfrew Street, Glasgow G3 6RQ.—*Director*, Prof. A. E. Jones.

GLOUCESTERSHIRE COLLEGE OF ARTS AND TECHNOLOGY (*B.A., B.Sc.*), Oxstalls Lane, Gloucester GL2 9HW.—*Principal*, R. D. Williams.

GWENT COLLEGE OF HIGHER EDUCATION (*B.A., B.Sc., B.Ed.*), Clarence Place, Newport, Gwent NPT 0UW.—*Principal*, M. I. Harris.

HARROW COLLEGE OF HIGHER EDUCATION (*B.A.*), Watford Road, Northwick Park, Harrow, Middlesex.—*Principal*, Dr. H. R. Harris.

HERTFORDSHIRE COLLEGE OF HIGHER EDUCATION (*B.Ed.*), Wall Hall, Aldenham, Nr. Watford.—*Principal*, D. Haslam, PH.D.

HUMBERSIDE COLLEGE OF HIGHER EDUCATION (*B.A., B.Ed., B.Sc.*), Cottingham Road, Hull HU6 7RT.—*Director*, J. Earls, PH.D.

JEWS' COLLEGE (*B.A.*), Albert Road, Hendon, N.W.4.—*Principal*, Rabbi Dr. J. Sacks.

JORDANHILL COLLEGE OF EDUCATION (*B.Ed.*), Southbrae Drive, Jordanhill, Glasgow G.13.—*Principal*, Dr. T. R. Bone.

KIDDERMINSTER COLLEGE OF FURTHER EDUCATION (*B.A.*), Hoo Road, Kidderminster, Worcs DY10 1LX. *Principal*, W. J. Cotterell.

KING ALFRED'S COLLEGE OF HIGHER EDUCATION (*B.A., B.Ed.*), Sparkford Road, Winchester SO22 4NR.—*Principal*, J. A. Cranmer.

LABAN CENTRE FOR MOVEMENT AND DANCE, GOLDSMITHS' COLLEGE (*B.A.*), New Cross, London SE14 6NW.—*Director*, Marion North, PH.D.

LA SAINTE UNION COLLEGE OF HIGHER EDUCATION (*B.A., B.Th., B.Ed.*), The Avenue, Southampton SO9 5HB.—*Principal*, H. N. Dickenson.

COLLEGE OF LIBRARIANSHIP WALES (*B.Lib.*), Llanbadarn Fawr, Aberystwyth SY23 3AS.—*Principal*, F. N. Hogg.

LIVERPOOL INSTITUTE OF HIGHER EDUCATION (*B.A., B.Ed.*), *Rector*, Dr. J. Burke, Stand Park Road, Liverpool L16 9JD; Christ's and Notre Dame College—*Principal*, Mgr. B. Doyle; S. Katharine's College—*Head of College*, Rev. E. V. Binks.

LONDON BIBLE COLLEGE (*B.A.*), Green Lane, Northwood, Middlesex HA6 2UW.—*Principal*, Dr. M. C. Griffiths.

LONDON COLLEGE OF PRINTING (*B.A.*), Elephant and Castle, London S.E.1.—*Principal*, R. Hedley Lewis.

LOUGHBOROUGH COLLEGE OF ART AND DESIGN (*B.A.*), Radmoor, Loughborough, Leics.—*Principal*, R. H. Hampson.

LUTON COLLEGE OF HIGHER EDUCATION (*B.Sc.*), Park Square, Luton.—*Director*, Dr. R. W. Steed.

MAIDSTONE COLLEGE OF ART (*B.A.*), Oakwood Park, Oakwood Road, Maidstone, Kent.—*Principal*, K. Gribble.

MORAY HOUSE COLLEGE OF EDUCATION (*B.Ed.*), Holyrood Road, Edinburgh EH8 8AQ.—*Principal*, G. Kirk.

NAPIER COLLEGE OF COMMERCE AND TECHNOLOGY (*B.A., B.Sc.*), Colinton Road, Edinburgh EH10 5DT and Sighthill Court, Edinburgh.—*Principal*, Dr. W. A. Turmeau.

NENE COLLEGE (*B.A., B.Sc., B.Ed.*), Moulton Park, Northampton NN2 7AL.—*Director*, Dr. E. Ogilvie.

NEWMAN COLLEGE (*B.Ed.*), Genners Lane, Bartley Green, Birmingham B32 3NT.—*Principal*, Joan Cuming, PH.D.

NONINGTON COLLEGE (*B.A.*), Nonington, Dover, Kent CT15 4HH.—*Principal*, S. Beaumont.

NORMAL COLLEGE (*B.A., B.Ed.*), Bangor, North Wales.—*Principal*, Dr. J. A. Davies.

NORTH CHESHIRE COLLEGE (*B.A.*), Fearnhead, Warrington WA2 0DB.—*Director*, W. E. Buckley.

NORTH E. WALES INSTITUTE OF HIGHER EDUCATION (*B.A., B.Ed.*), Cefn Road, Wrexham, Clwyd LL13 9HL.—*Principal*, Prof. G. O. Phillips, PH.D.

NORTH RIDING COLLEGE OF EDUCATION (*B.Ed.*), Filey Road, Scarborough, North Yorkshire YO11 3AZ.—*Principal*, F. W. Wright.

NORWICH SCHOOL OF ART (*B.A.*), St. George Street, Norwich, Norfolk NR3 1BB.—*Principal*, W. G. English.

OAK HILL COLLEGE (*B.A.*), Chase Side, Southgate, N14 4PS.—*Principal*, Rev. Canon D. H. Wheaton.

PAISLEY COLLEGE OF TECHNOLOGY (*B.A., B.Sc.*), High Street, Paisley PA1 2BE.—*Principal*, T. M. Howie.

QUEEN MARGARET COLLEGE (*B.A., B.Sc.*), 36 Clerwood Terrace, Edinburgh EH12 8TS.—*Principal*, Miss C. L. Morgan.

THE QUEEN'S COLLEGE, GLASGOW (*B.A., B.Sc.*), 1 Park Drive, Glasgow G3 6LP.—*Principal*, Dr. G. A. Richardson.

RAVENSBOURNE COLLEGE OF ART AND DESIGN (*B.A.*), Walden Road, Chislehurst, Kent BR7 5SN.—*Principal*, N. J. Frewing.

RIPON AND YORK ST. JOHN COLLEGE OF HIGHER EDUCATION (*B.A., B.Sc., B.Ed.*), Lord Mayor's Walk, York YO3 7EX.—*Principal*, Dr. G. P. McGregor.

ROBERT GORDON'S INSTITUTE OF TECHNOLOGY (*B.A., B.Sc.*), Schoolhill, Aberdeen AB9 1FR.—*Principal*, P. Clarke, PH.D.

ROEHAMPTON INSTITUTE OF HIGHER EDUCATION (*B.A., B.Sc., B.Ed.*), Roehampton Lane, London SW15 5PJ.—*Rector*, K. W. Keohane, C.B.E., PH.D.

ROLLE COLLEGE (*B.A., B.Ed.*), Exmouth, Devon EX8 2AT.—*Principal*, M. Preston, PH.D.

ROSE BRUFORD COLLEGE OF SPEECH AND DRAMA (*B.A.*), Lamorbey Park, Sidcup, Kent DA15 9DF.—*Principal*, J. N. Benedetti.

ROYAL ACADEMY OF MUSIC (*B.Mus.*), Marylebone Road, London NW1 5HT.—*Principal*, Dr. D. Lumsden.

ROYAL COLLEGE OF MUSIC (*B.Mus.*), Prince Consort Road, South Kensington, London SW7 2BS.—*Director*, M. G. Matthews, F.R.C.M.

ROYAL MILITARY COLLEGE OF SCIENCE (*B.Sc., B.Eng.*), Shrivenham, Swindon, Wilts. SN6 8LA.—*Dean*, Prof. F. R. Hartley, D.PHIL.

ROYAL NAVAL ENGINEERING COLLEGE (*B.Sc.*), Manadon, Plymouth PL5 3AQ.—*Dean*, Capt. A. O. Holding.

ROYAL SCOTTISH ACADEMY OF MUSIC AND DRAMA (*B.A.*), St. George's Place, Glasgow G.2.

S. MARTIN'S COLLEGE OF EDUCATION (*B.A., B.Ed.*), Bowerham, Lancaster LA1 3JD.—*Principal*, R. Clayton.

ST. ANDREW'S COLLEGE OF EDUCATION (*B.Ed.*), Bearsden, Glasgow G61 4QA.—*Principal*, Sr. Margaret Sheridan.

ST. JOSEPH'S COLLEGE OF EDUCATION (*B.Ed.*), Trench House, Stewartstown Road, Belfast.—*Principal*, Very Rev. Canon M. Dallat.

COLLEGE OF ST. MARK AND ST. JOHN (*B.A., B.Ed.*), Derriford Road, Plymouth PL6 8BH.—*Principal*, J. E. Anderson.

ST. MARTIN'S SCHOOL OF ART (*B.A.*), 107 Charing Cross Road, London WC2H 0DU.—*Principal*, I. Simpson.

ST. MARY'S COLLEGE (*B.A., B.Sc., B.Ed.*), Strawberry Hill, Twickenham, Middlesex.—*Principal*, Rev. D. A. Beirne.

ST. MARY'S COLLEGE OF EDUCATION (*B.Ed.*), 191 Falls Road, Belfast BT12 6FE.—*Principal*, Very Rev. Canon M. Dallat.

COLLEGE OF ST. PAUL AND ST. MARY (*B.A., B.Sc., B.Ed.*), The Park, Cheltenham, Glos. GL50 2RH.—*Principal*, G. D. Barnes.

SCOTTISH COLLEGE OF TEXTILES (*B.A., B.Sc.*), Netherdale, Galashiels, Selkirkshire TD1 3HF.—*Principal*, J. C. Furniss.

SOUTHAMPTON COLLEGE OF HIGHER EDUCATION (*B.A., B.Sc.*), East Park Terrace, Southampton SO9 4WW.—*Principal*, J. W. Longden.

SOUTH GLAMORGAN INSTITUTE OF HIGHER EDUCATION (*B.A., B.Sc., B.Ed.*), Western Avenue, Llandaff, Cardiff CF5 2YB.—*Principal*, Dr. E. J. Brent.

SPURGEON'S COLLEGE (*B.A.*), South Norwood Hill, London SE25 6DJ.—*Principal*, Rev. R. Brown, PH.D.

STOURBRIDGE COLLEGE OF TECHNOLOGY AND ART (*B.A.*), Hagley Road, Stourbridge, West Midlands.—*Principal*, T. H. Jenkins.

STRANMILLIS COLLEGE (*B.Ed.*), Stranmillis Road, Belfast BT9 5DY.—*Principal*, R. J. Rodgers, PH.D.

TRINITY AND ALL SAINTS' COLLEGE (*B.A., B.Sc., B.Ed.*), Brownberrie Lane, Horsforth, Leeds LS18 5HD.—*Principal*, Dr. H. M. Hallaway.

TRINITY COLLEGE (*B.A.*), Stoke Hill, Bristol.—*Principal*, Rev. G. Carey, PH.D.

TRINITY COLLEGE (*B.A., B.Ed.*), Carmarthen, Dyfed, South Wales.—*Principal*, D. C. Jones-Davies.

TRINITY COLLEGE OF MUSIC (*B.Mus.*), Mandeville Place, London W1M 6AQ.—*Principal*, M. Davies, C.B.E.

WATFORD COLLEGE (*B.Sc.*), Hempstead Road, Watford, WD1 3EZ.—*Principal*, T. J. Howard, PH.D.

WELSH COLLEGE OF MUSIC AND DRAMA (*B.A., B.Ed.*), Castle Grounds, Cathays Park, Cardiff.—*Principal*, P. Fletcher.

WEST GLAMORGAN INSTITUTE OF HIGHER EDUCATION (*B.A., B.Ed.*), Townhill Road, Cockett, Swansea SA2 0UT.—*Principal*, G. Stockdale, PH.D.

WESTHILL COLLEGE (*B.Ed.*), Hamilton Building, Weoley Park Road, Selly Oak, Birmingham B29 6LL.—*Principal*, A. G. Bamford.

WEST LONDON INSTITUTE OF HIGHER EDUCATION (*B.A., B.Sc., B.Ed.*), Lancaster House, Borough Road, Isleworth, Middlesex TW7 5DU.—*Principal*, J. E. Kane, M.ED., PH.D.

WEST MIDLANDS COLLEGE OF HIGHER EDUCATION (*B.A., B.Ed.*), Gorway, Walsall.—*Principal*, T. J. Cox.

WESTMINSTER COLLEGE (*B.A., B.Ed.*), North Hinksey, Oxford.—*Principal*, Rev. Dr. K. B. Wilson.

WEST SURREY COLLEGE OF ART AND DESIGN (*B.A.*), Falkner Road, The Hart, Farnham, Surrey GU9 7DS.—*Principal*, R. J. Morris.

WEST SUSSEX INSTITUTE OF HIGHER EDUCATION (*B.A., B.Ed.*), The Dome, Upper Bognor Road, Bognor Regis, West Sussex PO21 1HR.—*Director*, J. F. Wyatt.

WIMBLEDON SCHOOL OF ART (*B.A.*), Merton Hall Road, Wimbledon, London SW19 3QA.—*Principal*, M. Murphy.

WINCHESTER SCHOOL OF ART (*B.A.*), Park Avenue, Winchester, Hampshire SO23 8DL.—*Principal*, D. C. Sherlock, F.R.S.A..

WORCESTER COLLEGE OF HIGHER EDUCATION (*B.A., B.Ed.*), Henwick Grove, Worcester WR2 6AJ.—*Principal*, D. R. Shadbolt, D.PHIL.

GRANTS FOR STUDENTS

Post-School

Students in England and Wales who plan to take a full-time or sandwich course of further study after leaving school may be eligible for a grant from their local education authority (L.E.A.). Enquiries should be made to the authority in the area in which the student normally lives. There is a list on pages 513–515. Application forms are available from schools and L.E.A.s. Completed forms should be sent to the appropriate L.E.A. as early as possible. For courses beginning in the autumn, applications should, however, not be made earlier than the preceding January.

Types of grant. Grants are of two kinds: mandatory and discretionary. *Mandatory grants* (354,500 in 1981–82) are those which L.E.A.s *must* pay to students who are attending what are called "designated courses" and who can satisfy certain other conditions; such a grant is normally to enable the student to attend only one designated course and there is no general entitlement to an award for any particular number of years. *Discretionary grants* (44,800 full value awards in 1981–82) are those for which each L.E.A. has discretion to decide its own policy.

Designated courses include those which are *full-time or sandwich* and lead to a university or C.N.A.A. (*see* p. 509–510) degree; the diploma of higher education; the higher national diploma of the Business & Technician Education Council; and initial teacher-training courses including courses for the postgraduate certificate in education and the art teachers' certificate or diploma. Also included may be *part-time* initial teacher-training courses designated for this purpose.

Eligibility. To be eligible for a grant, students admitted to a designated course must, *inter alia:*—

(a) have been ordinarily resident in the United Kingdom, Isle of Man or the Channel Islands for the three years immediately preceding the academic year in which the course begins. (If the student was absent because he or she, spouse or parent were temporarily employed abroad, the student may still be eligible.)

(b) have not previously attended one or more courses of advanced further education of more than two years' duration. Attendance for up to one term on such a course is disregarded;

(c) apply for the grant before the end of the first term of the course.

Condition (b) above does not apply to students wishing to take a course leading to a postgraduate certificate in education or the art teachers' certificate or diploma.

Value. A means-tested maintenance grant, usually paid once a term through the university or college office, covers periods of attendance during term and the Christmas and Easter vacations but not the summer vacation. It is subject to deduction on account of the student's own income and his/her parents' or spouse's income. (66 per cent of students in 1981–82 getting full value awards had parents who were assessed as having to pay a contribution towards the maintenance element of the grant.) Tuition fees in full are usually paid direct to the university or college by the L.E.A.

Cost. Local authority expenditure on student maintenance in 1981–82 was £498·6 million.

In Scotland corresponding awards are made by the Scottish Education Department and in Northern Ireland by Education and Library Boards.

Postgraduate awards

A number of schemes of postgraduate bursaries or studentships for U.K. residents are administered by the Department of Education and Science and the five research councils (agricultural and food, economic and social science, medical, natural environment, science and engineering). 15,500 awards were made in 1981–82.

LOCAL EDUCATION AUTHORITIES

English and Welsh Counties

Avon, Avon House North, St. James Barton, Bristol.—*Director,* G. F. Crump.

Bedfordshire, County Hall, Bedford.—*Chief Education Officer,* D. P. J. Browning.

Berkshire, Shire Hall, Shinfield Park, Reading.—*Director,* P. E. Edwards.

Buckinghamshire, County Hall, Aylesbury.—*Chief Education Officer,* C. Garrett.

Cambridgeshire, Shire Hall, Castle Hill, Cambridge.—*Chief Education Officer,* G. H. Morris.

Cheshire, County Hall, Chester.—*Director,* J. R. G. Tomlinson, C.B.E.

Cleveland, Woodlands Road, Middlesbrough.—*Director,* A. H. R. Calderwood.

Clwyd, Shire Hall, Mold.—*Director,* J. H. Davies.

Cornwall, County Hall, Truro.—*Secretary for Education,* N. W. Barr.

Cumbria, 5 Portland Square, Carlisle.—*Director,* P. C. Boulter.

Derbyshire, County Offices, Matlock.—*Director,* J. G. Evans.

Devon, County Hall, Exeter.—*Chief Education Officer,* J. G. Owen, C.B.E.

Dorset, County Hall, Dorchester.—*Director,* P. L. Gedling.

Durham, County Hall, Durham.—*Director,* D. J. W. Sowell.

Dyfed, Pibwrlwyd, Carmarthen.—*Director,* W. J. Phillips.

Essex, Threadneedle House, Market Road, Chelmsford.—*County Education Officer,* J. O. Morris.

Gloucestershire, Shire Hall, Gloucester. *Chief Education Officer,* K. D. Anderson.

Gwent, County Hall, Cwmbran.—*Director,* E. H. Loudon.

Gwynedd, County Offices, Shirehall Street, Caernarfon.—*Director,* G. E. Humphreys.

Hampshire, The Castle, Winchester.—*County Education Officer,* R. D. Clark.

Hereford and Worcester, Castle Street, Worcester.—*County Education Officer,* J. W. Turnbull.

Hertfordshire, County Hall, Hertford.—*County Education Officer,* D. Fisher.

Humberside, County Hall, Beverley.—*Director,* J. Bower.

Isle of Wight, County Hall, Newport.—*County Education Officer,* R. O. Burton.

Kent, Springfield, Maidstone.—*County Education Officer,* W. H. Petty, C.B.E.

Lancashire, County Hall, Preston.—*Chief Education Officer,* A. J. Collier.

Leicestershire, County Hall, Glenfield, Leicester.—*Director,* K. H. Wood-Allum.

Lincolnshire, County Offices, Lincoln.—*Director,* F. G. Rickard.

Mid Glamorgan, County Hall, Cathays Park, Cardiff.—*Director,* K. S. Hopkins.

Norfolk, County Hall, Norwich.—*County Education Officer,* M. H. Edwards.

Northamptonshire, Northampton House, Northampton.—*County Education Officer,* M. J. Henley.

Northumberland, County Hall, Morpeth.—*Director,* C. C. Tipple.

Nottinghamshire, County Hall, West Bridgford, Nottingham.—*Director,* A. J. Fox.

Oxfordshire, Macclesfield House, New Road Oxford.—*Director,* T. R. P. Brighouse.

Powys, The Lindens, Spa Road, Llandrindod Wells.—*Director,* R. W. Bevan.

Shropshire, Shirehall, Abbey Foregate, Shrewsbury.—*County Education Officer,* N.

Somerset, County Hall, Taunton.—*Director,* B. Taylor.

South Glamorgan, County Offices, Kingsway, Cardiff.—*Director,* L. J. Cule.

Staffordshire, County Education Offices, Tipping Street, Stafford.—*Chief Education Officer,* T. W. Hadley.

Suffolk, County Hall, Ipswich.—*County Education Officer,* D. G. Graham.

SURREY, County Hall, Kingston upon Thames.— *County Education Officer*, M. C. Pinchin.

SUSSEX (East), County Hall, Lewes.—*County Education Officer*, J. A. Carter.

SUSSEX (West), County Hall, Chichester.—*Director*, G. R. Potter.

WARWICKSHIRE, 22 Northgate Street, Warwick.— *Director*, M. L. Ridger.

WEST GLAMORGAN, County Hall, Swansea.—*Director*, J. Beale.

WILTSHIRE, County Hall, Trowbridge.—*Chief Education Officer*, I. M. Slocombe.

YORKSHIRE (North), County Hall, Northallerton.— *County Education Officer*, F. F. Evans.

London

INNER LONDON EDUCATION AUTHORITY.—*Controller of Education*, W. H. Stubbs.

Education Officers

BARKING, Town Hall, Dagenham.—A. W. Bush.

BARNET, Town Hall, Friern Barnet, N.11.—J. Dawkins.

BEXLEY, Town Hall, Crayford.—*Director*, P. Geen.

BRENT, Chesterfield House, Park Lane, Wembley.— *Director*, A. Parsons.

BROMLEY, Sunnymead, Bromley Lane, Chislehurst, Kent.—G. Grainge.

CROYDON, Taberner House, Park Lane.—*Director*, D. Naismith.

EALING, Hadley House, Uxbridge Road, W.5.—R. J. Hartles.

ENFIELD, Civic Centre, Enfield.—*Director*, G. Hutchinson.

HARINGEY, 48–62 Station Road, N.22.—A. Lenney.

HARROW, Civic Centre, Station Road, Harrow.— *Director*, J. F. Mann.

HAVERING, Mercury House, Mercury Gardens, Romford, Essex.—*Director*, B. H. Laister.

HILLINGDON, Civic Centre, High Street, Uxbridge, Middx.—*Director*, J. Lyn-Jones.

HOUNSLOW, Civic Centre, Lampton Road.—*Director*, J. Cooper.

KINGSTON UPON THAMES, Guildhall.—*Director*, R. J. McCloy.

MERTON, Station House, London Road, Morden, Surrey.—*Director*, R. Davies.

NEWHAM, 29 Broadway, Stratford, E.15.—J. Pailing.

REDBRIDGE, Lynton House, 255–259 High Road, Ilford, Essex.—K. G. M. Ratcliffe.

RICHMOND UPON THAMES, Regal House, London Road, Twickenham, Middx.—*Director*, I. Waters.

SUTTON, The Grove, Carshalton, Surrey.—*Director*, C. Melville.

WALTHAM FOREST, Municipal Offices, High Road, Leyton, E.10.—I. Smith.

Metropolitan District Councils

BARNSLEY, Berneslai Close, Barnsley.—*Education Officer*, T. Brooks.

BIRMINGHAM, Margaret Street, Birmingham 3.— *Chief Education Officer*, J. M. Crawford.

BOLTON, Paderborn House, Civic Centre.—*Director*, B. Hughes.

BRADFORD, Provincial House, Bradford.—*Director*, W. R. Knight.

BURY, Athenaeum House, Market Street.—*Director*, M. Gray.

CALDERDALE.—Northgate House, Northgate, Halifax.—*Chief Education Officer*, A. Pickvance.

COVENTRY, Council House, Earl Street.—*Education Officer*, R. Aitken.

DONCASTER, Princegate.—*Director*, M. J. Pass.

DUDLEY, 2 St. James's Road, Dudley.—*Education Officer*, R. K. Westerby.

GATESHEAD, Prince Consort Road South.—*Education Officer*, W. H. Cubitt.

KIRKLEES, Oldgate House, Oldgate, Huddersfield.— *Education Officer*, (vacant).

KNOWSLEY, Huyton Hey Road, Huyton, Liverpool.— *Education Officer*, P. M. Neafsey.

LEEDS, Merrion House, Merrion Centre.—*Director*, R. S. Johnson.

LIVERPOOL, 14 Sir Thomas Street.—*Education Officer*, K. A. Antcliffe.

MANCHESTER, Cumberland House, Crown Square.— *Chief Education Officer*, G. Hainsworth.

NEWCASTLE UPON TYNE, Civic Centre.—*Director*, B. M. O'Reilly.

NORTH TYNESIDE, The Chase, North Shields.—*Education Officer*, J. F. Partington.

OLDHAM, Old Town Hall, Chadderton.—*Education Officer*, T. J. Farrington.

ROCHDALE, Municipal Offices, Smith Street, Rochdale.—*Chief Education Officer*, A. N. Naylor.

ROTHERHAM, Norfolk House, Walker Place.—*Education Officer*, K. Snowden.

ST. HELENS, Century House, Hardshaw Street.— *Education Officer*, N. D. Nelson.

SALFORD, Chapel Street.—*Education Officer*, J. A. Barnes.

SANDWELL, Highfields, High Street, West Bromwich.—*Education Officer*, G. A. Brinsdon.

SEFTON, Town Hall, Bootle.—*Education Officer*, K. Robinson.

SHEFFIELD, P.O. Box 67, Leopold Street.—*Education Officer*, G. M. A. Harrison, C.B.E.

SOLIHULL, The Council House.—*Education Officer*, C. Humphrey.

SOUTH TYNESIDE, Town Hall, Jarrow.—*Director*, K. Stringer.

STOCKPORT, Stopford House, Town Hall.—*Education Officer*, N. J. Fitton.

SUNDERLAND, Town Hall.—*Education Officer*, J. Hall.

TAMESIDE, Council Offices, Wellington Road, Ashton-under-Lyne.—*Education Officer*, D. Marbeck.

TRAFFORD, P.O. Box 19, Town Hall, Sale.—*Education Officer*, D. J. Hatfield.

WAKEFIELD, 8 Bond Street.—*Education Officer*, W. H. Wright.

WALSALL, Civic Centre, Darwall Street, Walsall.— *Director*, R. D. Nixon.

WIGAN, Gateway House, Standishgate.—*Education Officer*, R. C. Hopkinson.

WIRRALL, Municipal Offices, Cleveland Street, Birkenhead.—*Director*, M. Nichol.

WOLVERHAMPTON, Civic Centre.—*Director*, P. N. Harris.

Channel Islands, etc.

JERSEY, P.O. Box 142, Highlands, St. Saviour.— *Director*, J. S. Rodhouse.

GUERNSEY, P.O. Box 32, La Couperderie, St. Peter Port.—*Director*, M. D. Hutchings.

ISLE OF MAN, Government Offices, Bucks Road, Douglas.—*Director*, J. A. Davies.

ISLES OF SCILLY, Town Hall, St. Mary's.—*Secretary for Education*, I. Glover.

Scottish Regional and Islands Councils

BORDERS, Regional Headquarters, Newtown St. Boswells.—*Director*, J. McLean.

CENTRAL, Viewforth, Stirling.—*Director*, I. Collie.

DUMFRIES AND GALLOWAY, 30 Edinburgh Road, Dumfries.—*Director*, J. K. Purves.

FIFE, Fife House, North Street, Glenrothes.—*Director*, I. S. Flett.

GRAMPIAN, Woodhill House, Ashville Road West, Aberdeen.—*Director*, J. A. D. Michie.

HIGHLAND, Regional Buildings, Glenurquhart Road, Inverness.—*Director*, Dr. C. E. Stewart.

LOTHIAN, 40 Torphichen Street, Edinburgh.—*Director*, W. D. C. Semple.

ORKNEY, Council Offices, Kirkwall.—*Director*, A. Bain.

SHETLAND, 1 Harbour Street, Lerwick.—*Director*, R. A. Barnes.

STRATHCLYDE, Strathclyde House, 20 India Street, Glasgow.—*Director*, E. Miller.

TAYSIDE, Tayside House, Crichton Street, Dundee.—*Director*, D. G. Robertson.

WESTERN ISLES, Council Offices, Sandwick Road, Stornoway.—*Director*, N. R. Galbraith.

Northern Ireland

Education and Library Boards

BELFAST, Board Headquarters, 40 Academy Street, Belfast 1.—*Chief Officer*, T. G. J. Moag.

NORTH-EASTERN, County Hall, 182 Galgorm Road, Ballymena, Co. Antrim.—*Chief Officer*, R. A. Hamilton.

SOUTH-EASTERN, 18 Windsor Avenue, Belfast 9.—*Chief Officer*, T. Nolan.

SOUTHERN, 3 Charlemont Place, The Mall, Armagh.—*Chief Officer*, J. G. Kelly.

WESTERN, 1 Hospital Road, Omagh, Co. Tyrone.—*Chief Officer*, M. H. F. Murphy.

ADULT EDUCATION

'Adult Education' covers a broad spectrum of educational activities ranging from non-vocational courses of general interest, through the acquiring of special vocational skills needed in industry or commerce, to study for a degree at the Open University. It has been defined as "the provision of non-formal and informal education for adult people: that is, courses excluding the normal range of provision in colleges and universities for young people immediately following the statutory school leaving age, but including the full range of recurrent educational opportunities designed for people of more mature years, and related to any or all aspects of adult life".

Providers. Courses are provided by many bodies: local education authorities (regional authorities in Scotland, education and library boards in Northern Ireland), residential colleges, the Open University, the extra-mural departments of other universities (and Birkbeck College of the University of London), the BBC, ITV and local radio stations, and various voluntary bodies. The local education authorities operate through 'area' adult education centres, institutes or colleges and the adult studies departments of colleges of further education. The Open University, in partnership with the BBC, provides distance teaching leading to ordinary or honours first degrees, and also offers post-experience and higher degree courses. Nearly 40 other universities have extra-mural or adult or continuing education departments which serve their local areas or regions. The BBC has a Continuing Education Advisory Council and the Independent Broadcasting Authority an Educational Advisory Council which has an Adult Education Section. Of the voluntary bodies the biggest and best-known is the Workers' Educational Association (*see below*).

Courses. Although lengths vary, most courses are part-time. Long-term residential colleges (*see below*) provide full-time courses lasting one or two years. Adult education courses are of two main kinds – those involving face-to-face teaching with teacher and student in the same room and the distance teaching provided through TV and radio, and/or correspondence courses.

Numbers. There are no comprehensive statistics covering all aspects of adult education but it is known that enrolments in November 1983 at L.E.A. adult education and youth centres in England were about 1·6 million, an increase of 6 per cent over the previous year. About 110,000 students were enrolled at the Open University in 1983, including 66,000 undergraduates and 43,000 students on continuing education courses. In 1982–83, there were 375,564 enrolments at other U.K. universities' extra-mural departments, joint courses with the W.E.A., and in other departments; this is 4 per cent up on the previous year.

NATIONAL INSTITUTE OF ADULT CONTINUING EDUCATION (England and Wales), 19b De Montfort Street, Leicester LE1 7GE. (*Dir.*, A. K. Stock). The institute provides a means of consultation and cooperation between all the forces in adult education. It provides information and advice to organisations and individuals on all aspects of adult continuing education; it conducts enquiries into problems of adult education; organises conferences and other meetings; and issues publications. Recently, it has set up a special Unit for the Development of Adult Continuing Education with additional D.E.S. finance and also administers the local development of the D.E.S.'s Education for Adult Unemployed project. The government-funded Adult Literacy and Basic Skills Unit operates as an agency of the National Institute.

SCOTTISH INSTITUTE OF ADULT EDUCATION, 30 Rutland Square, Edinburgh EH1 2BW. (*Dir.*, Dr. Elizabeth Gerver). The institute is an advisory and consultative body which arranges conferences and training courses, undertakes research, acts as an information centre on current activities, and issues publications.

UNIVERSITIES COUNCIL FOR ADULT AND CONTINUING EDUCATION, consisting of one representative from each university, was established in 1947 for the interchange of ideas and the formulation of common policies on extra-mural education – *Hon. Secretary*, W. Forster, M.A., Dept. of Adult Education, The University, Leicester.

WORKERS EDUCATIONAL ASSOCIATION, Temple House, 9 Upper Berkeley Street, London W1H 8BY. (*Gen. Secretary*, R. Lochrie). Founded in 1903, the WEA consists of about 900 branches and nearly 1,500 affiliated educational and workers' organisations. Non-sectarian and non-party-political, it aims to stimulate and to satisfy the demands of workers for education, and to further the advancement of education generally. The WEA is organised in 21 districts. Each district in England and Wales is recognised by the Department of Education and Science as a 'responsible body' for the provision of educational facilities in respect of which it receives grants under Departmental regulations. LEAs also make grants towards administrative expenses.

RESIDENTIAL COLLEGES FOR ADULT EDUCATION

Long term:
The eight long-term colleges listed below offer one- and two-year courses for adults and are grant-aided by the Department of Education and Science. Students are eligible for grants from the colleges.

COLEG HARLECH, Harlech, Gwynedd LL46 2PU. (For men and women).—*Warden*, J. W. England.

CO-OPERATIVE COLLEGE, Stanford Hall, Loughborough, Leics. (For men and women).—*Principal*, Dr. R. Houlton.

FIRCROFT COLLEGE, 1018 Bristol Road, Selly Oak, Birmingham B29 6LH. (For men and women).—*Principal*, B. J. Wicker.

HILLCROFT COLLEGE, Surbiton, Surrey KT6 6DF. (For women).—*Principal*, Ms. P. Lambert.

NEWBATTLE ABBEY, Dalkeith, Midlothian. (For men and women).—*Principal*, A. D. Reid.

NORTHERN COLLEGE, Wentworth Castle, Stainborough, Barnsley, South Yorks. S75 3ET. (For men and women).—*Principal*, R. H. Fryer.

PLATER COLLEGE, Pullens Lane, Oxford. (For men and women).—*Principal*, D. G. Chiles.

RUSKIN COLLEGE, Oxford OX1 2HE. (For men and women).—*Principal*, J. D. Hughes.

Short term:

The short-term colleges and centres listed below offer residential courses, lasting from a day or two to two or three weeks, in a wide range of subjects. LEAs directly sponsor many of the colleges while others are sponsored by universities or voluntary organisations. A booklet listing such *Residential Short Courses* is published by the National Institute of Adult Education (see above).

ALSTON HALL COLLEGE, Longridge, Nr. Preston; ASHRIDGE MANAGEMENT COLLEGE, Berkhamsted, Herts.; AVONCROFT COLLEGE, Stoke Heath, Bromsgrove, Worcs.; BEAMISH HALL RESIDENTIAL COLLEGE FOR ADULT EDUCATION, Stanley, County Durham; BELSTEAD HOUSE, Nr. Ipswich, Suffolk; BRAZIERS ADULT COLLEGE, Ipsden, Oxford; BURTON MANOR, Burton, South Wirral, Cheshire; BURWELL HOUSE RESIDENTIAL CENTRE, Burwell, Cambridge; DEBDEN HOUSE, Debden Green, Loughton, Essex; DENMAN COLLEGE, Marcham, Nr. Abingdon, Oxon.; DEVON

CENTRE FOR FURTHER EDUCATION, Dartington College of Arts, Totnes; DILLINGTON HOUSE COLLEGE AND ARTS CENTRE, Ilminster, Somerset; DYFFRYN HOUSE, St. Nicholas, Nr. Cardiff; EARNLEY CONCOURSE, Nr. Chichester, Sussex; EASTHAMPTEAD PARK EDUCATIONAL CENTRE, Wokingham, Berkshire; GRAFHAM WATER RESIDENTIAL CENTRE, West Perry, Huntingdon; GRANTLEY HALL, Ripon, North Yorkshire; HAWKWOOD COLLEGE, Stroud, Glos.; HENLEY—THE MANAGEMENT COLLEGE, Greenlands, Henley-on-Thames, Oxon.; HIGHAM HALL, Bassenthwaite Lake, Cockermouth, Cumbria; THE HILL, Pen-y-Pound, Abergavenny, Gwent; HOLLY ROYDE COLLEGE, West Didsbury, Manchester; HORNCASTLE RESIDENTIAL COLLEGE, Horncastle, Lincs.; KINGSGATE HOUSE, Convent Road, Broadstairs, Kent; KNUSTON HALL, Irchester, Wellingborough, Northants.; LANCASHIRE COLLEGE FOR ADULT EDUCATION, Southport Road, Chorley; LOSEHILL HALL, Castleton, Derbyshire; MADINGLEY HALL, Madingley, Cambridge; MARYLAND COLLEGE, Woburn, Milton Keynes; MISSENDEN ABBEY, Great Missenden, Bucks.; THE OLD RECTORY, Fittleworth, Pulborough, Sussex; PENDLEY MANOR, Tring, Herts.; PENDRELL HALL, Codsall Wood, Wolverhampton; REWLEY HOUSE, 3–7 Wellington Square, Oxford; ROFFEY PARK MANAGEMENT COLLEGE, Horsham, Sussex; RURAL MUSIC SCHOOLS ASSOCIATION, Little Benslow Hills, Ibberson Way, Hitchin, Herts.; SPODE CONFERENCE CENTRE, Hawkesyard Priory, Rugeley, Staffs.; THEOBALDS PARK COLLEGE, Waltham Cross, Herts.; URCHFONT MANOR, Nr. Devizes, Wilts.; WANSFELL COLLEGE, Theydon Bois, Epping, Essex; WEDGWOOD MEMORIAL COLLEGE, Barlaston, Stoke-on-Trent, Staffs.; WENSUM LODGE, King Street, Norwich, Norfolk; WEST DEAN COLLEGE, West Dean, Chichester, Sussex; WESTHAM HOUSE COLLEGE, Barford, Warwick.

PROFESSIONAL EDUCATION
(excluding *postgraduate* study)

NOTE.—References to university courses in the sections following are not claimed to be comprehensive and cover only *full-time* courses leading to *first degrees*. A full list appears in the *Compendium of University Entrance Requirements* produced annually by the universities. The considerable facilities available for postgraduate study or research are not treated here.

POSTGRADUATE STUDY AND RESEARCH. All universities provide facilities for postgraduate study and research. They co-operatively issue each year the *British Universities' Guide to Graduate Study* which lists all "taught courses" (except in medicine, dentistry and veterinary science) but does not cover research. In general, universities can provide facilities for research in at least some aspects of all the subjects in which first degrees are offered.

Courses at postgraduate level leading to master's-level degrees of the Council for National Academic Awards (C.N.A.A.) are offered by polytechnics and other colleges. They are listed in the C.N.A.A.'s annual *Directory of Postgraduate and Post-Experience Courses*. It is also possible to undertake research at polytechnics leading to an M. Phil. or Ph.D. granted by the C.N.A.A.

ACCOUNTANCY

(*See also* Business, Management and Administration).

First Degrees in *Accounting* or *Accountancy* are granted by the Universities of Belfast, Birmingham, Dundee, East Anglia, Exeter, Glasgow, Hull, Kent, Liverpool, Stirling, Strathclyde, Ulster and Wales (Aberystwyth and Cardiff University Colleges and Institute of Science and Technology). At several

other universities one of these subjects can be combined with, e.g., Financial Administration, Finance or Economics.

Courses leading to first degrees in *Accounting, Accountancy* or *Accounting and Finance* granted by the Council for National Academic Awards are provided by City of Birmingham Polytechnic, Brighton Polytechnic, Bristol Polytechnic, City of London Polytechnic, Dundee College of Technology, Ealing College of Higher Education, Glasgow College of Technology, Huddersfield Polytechnic, Humberside College of Higher Education, Kingston Polytechnic, Leeds Polytechnic, Liverpool Polytechnic, Manchester Polytechnic, Middlesex Polytechnic, Napier College of Commere and Technology, Newcastle upon Tyne Polytechnic, North East London Polytechnic (*Finance with Accounting*), Polytechnic of North London, Portsmouth Polytechnic, Preston Polytechnic, Sheffield City Polytechnic (*Accounting and Financial Control*), Trent Polytechnic and Polytechnic of Wales.

Professional Bodies.—The main bodies granting membership on examination after a period of practical work are:

INSTITUTE OF CHARTERED ACCOUNTANTS IN ENGLAND AND WALES, Chartered Accountants' Hall, Moorgate Place, EC2P 2BJ.

INSTITUTE OF CHARTERED ACCOUNTANTS OF SCOTLAND, 27 Queen Street, Edinburgh EH2 1LA and 218 St. Vincent Street, Glasgow.

ASSOCIATION OF CERTIFIED ACCOUNTANTS, 29 Lincolns Inn Fields, WC2A 3EE.

CHARTERED INSTITUTE OF PUBLIC FINANCE AND ACCOUNTANCY, 3 Robert Street, WC2N 6BH.

INSTITUTE OF COST AND MANAGEMENT ACCOUNTANTS, 63 Portland Place, W1N 4AB.

ACTUARIAL SCIENCE

First Degrees in *Actuarial Science* are granted by the City University and the Universities of Kent and London (London School of Economics and Political Science); and in *Actuarial Mathematics and Statistics* by Heriot-Watt University.

Two professional organizations grant qualifications after examination:

INSTITUTE OF ACTUARIES, Staple Inn Hall, High Holborn, WC1V 7QJ.

FACULTY OF ACTUARIES IN SCOTLAND, *Hall and Library,* 23 St. Andrew Square, Edinburgh EH2 1AQ.

AERONAUTICS
and Aeronautical Engineering

First Degrees in *Aeronautical Engineering* are granted by the Universities of Bath, Belfast, Bristol, Cambridge, the City University, the Universities of Glasgow, London (Imperial College of Science and Technology; Queen Mary College (also *Avionics— Aeronautical/Electrical* and *Industrial Aerodynamics & Light Structures*), Loughborough (*Aeronautical Engineering and Design*), Manchester, Salford and (*Aeronautics and Astronautics* and *Aerospace Systems Engineering*) Southampton; and in *Air Transport Engineering* by the City University.

Courses leading to first degrees in *Aeronautical Engineering* granted by the Council for National Academic Awards are provided by Hatfield Polytechnic and Kingston Polytechnic.

CHELSEA COLLEGE OF AERONAUTICAL AND AUTOMOBILE ENGINEERING, Shoreham Airport, Sussex BN4 5FJ.

AGRICULTURE

First Degrees in *Agriculture* or *Agricultural Science(s)* are granted by the Universities of Aberdeen, Belfast, Edinburgh, Glasgow, Leeds, London (Wye College), Newcastle upon Tyne, Nottingham, Reading and Wales (University Colleges of Aberystwyth and Bangor); and in *Horticulture* by Bath, London (Wye College), Nottingham, Reading and Strathclyde.

Courses leading to first degrees in *Agriculture* granted by the Council for National Academic Awards are provided by Plymouth Polytechnic/Seale Hayne College and Wolverhampton Polytechnic/ Harper Adams Agricultural College.

Other schools of agriculture are:

ABERDEEN, North of Scotland College of Agriculture, 581 King Street, AB9 1UD.—*Principal,* Prof. G. A. Lodge, PH.D.

CIRENCESTER, Royal Agricultural College, GL7 6JR.— *Principal,* H. V. Hughes.

EDINBURGH SCHOOL OF AGRICULTURE, THE, West Mains Road, Edinburgh EH9 3JG.—*Principal,* Prof. P. N. Wilson, PH.D.

SHUTTLEWORTH AGRICULTURAL COLLEGE, Old Warden Park, Biggleswade, Bedfordshire SG18 9DX.— *Principal,* J. E. Scott.

WEST OF SCOTLAND AGRICULTURAL COLLEGE, Auchincruive, Ayr KA6 5HW.—*Principal,* Prof. J. M. M. Cunningham, C.B.E., Ph.D., F.R.S.E.

There are in addition over twenty country Agricultural Institutes giving a one-year course.

ARCHÆOLOGY

First Degrees in *Archæology* or *Archæological Sciences/Studies* are granted by the Universities of Belfast, Bradford, Durham, Edinburgh, Exeter, Glasgow, Lancaster, Leicester, Liverpool, London (Institute of Archæology, King's and University Colleges;

School of Oriental and African Studies), Newcastle upon Tyne, Nottingham, Reading, Southampton, Wales (University College of Cardiff), and York. At several other universities archæology can be combined with another subject, e.g. ancient history, classics or anthropology.

ARCHITECTURE

The Education and Professional Development Committee of THE ROYAL INSTITUTE OF BRITISH ARCHITECTS, 66 Portland Place, W1N 4AD, sets standards and guides the whole system of architectural education throughout the United Kingdom. Courses at the following Schools are recognized by the R.I.B.A. They are visited regularly by the R.I.B.A. Visiting Board to ensure that they meet the minimum standards for exemption from the R.I.B.A.'s own examinations.

UNIVERSITY SCHOOLS

(Subject to exceptions noted below, courses are full-time for five years, leading to a first degree and final diploma; number of students and name of Head of School or Department of Architecture are included.)

BATH: University School of Architecture and Building Engineering, Claverton Down (277).—Prof. E. Happold (6-yr. sandwich course in architecture in conjunction with 4-year sandwich course in building engineering).

BELFAST: Queen's University (156).—Prof. W. J. Kidd.

CAMBRIDGE: Department of Architecture (190).— Prof. C. St. J. Wilson.

CARDIFF: The Welsh School of Architecture, University of Wales Institute of Science and Technology (270).— Prof. J. Eynon.

DUNDEE: Dept. of Architecture, University of Dundee: Duncan of Jordanstone College of Art, Perth Road (203).—Prof. J. Paul.

EDINBURGH: University of Edinburgh, Dept. of Architecture (176).—E. C. Ruddock.

—Heriot-Watt University (joint course with Edinburgh College of Art), Lauriston Place (200).—Prof. J. D. Dunbar-Nasmith.

GLASGOW: Mackintosh School of Architecture, Glasgow University and Glasgow School of Art, 177 Renfrew Street (299).—Prof. A. MacMillan. University of Strathclyde, Dept. of Architecture and Building Science, 131 Rottenrow (190).—Prof. T. W. Maver.

LIVERPOOL: The Liverpool School of Architecture, Liverpool University (180).—Prof. J. N. Tarn.

LONDON: Bartlett School of Architecture and Planning, University College London (190).—Prof. J. Musgrove.

MANCHESTER: University of Manchester School of Architecture (196).—Prof. J. A. M. Bell, Prof. T. Dannatt and Prof. W. Whitfield.

NEWCASTLE UPON TYNE: University School of Architecture (180).—Prof B. Farmer.

NOTTINGHAM: University Dept. of Architecture (179).—Prof. C. Riley.

SHEFFIELD: University Dept. of Architecture (200).— Prof. K. H. Murta.

OTHER SCHOOLS

(Subject to the exceptions noted below, courses are full-time for five years, leading to a first degree and final diploma. Number of students and name of Head of School are shown.)

ABERDEEN: Scott Sutherland School of Architecture, Robert Gordon's Institute of Technology (200).— D. Kinghorn (*Acting Head*).

BIRMINGHAM: School of Architecture, City of Birmingham Polytechnic (212).—A. D. Collier.

BRIGHTON: School of Architecture and Interior Design, Brighton Polytechnic, Lewes Road, Brighton (217).—R. Macleod.

CANTERBURY: School of Architecture, Canterbury College of Art, New Dover Road, CT1 3AN (172).—M. Crux.

HUDDERSFIELD: Polytechnic School of Architecture, Queensgate.—Dr. A. Forward. (Part 1 only).

HULL: School of Architecture, Humberside College of Higher Education, Strand Close. (100).—C. Padamsee.

KINGSTON UPON THAMES: Polytechnic School of Architecture, Knights Park, KT1 2QJ (210).—D. Berry.

LEEDS: School of Architecture and Landscape, Leeds Polytechnic, Brunswick Terrace, LS2 8BU (353).—W. T. Bradshaw.

LEICESTER: Polytechnic School of Architecture, P.O. Box 143, LE1 9BH (184, part-time 70).—Prof. T. Matoff.

LIVERPOOL: Polytechnic (B.A. (Hons.) Architectural Studies).—K. E. Martin.

LONDON: Architectural Association School of Architecture, 34–36 Bedford Square, W.C.1 (400).—A. Boyarsky.

Department of Architecture, Polytechnic of the South Bank, S.W.8 (121).—H. Haenlein.

School of Architecture, Faculty of Environment. Polytechnic of Central London, 35 Marylebone Road, NW1W 5LS (260, part-time 110).—A. Cunningham.

Dept. of Environmental Design, Polytechnic of North London, Holloway, N7 8DB (450).—W. Briscoe.

School of Architecture, North East London Polytechnic, Holbrook Road, E15 3EA (172 full- and part-time).—N. Silver.

Thames Polytechnic, School of Architecture and Landscape, Oakfield Lane, Dartford, Kent DA1 2SZ (292, part-time 189).—Dr. J. Paul.

MANCHESTER: Polytechnic School of Architecture, Dept. of Architecture and Landscape, Loxford Tower, All Saints, M15 6BR (290).—M. H. Darke.

OXFORD: Dept. of Architecture, Oxford Polytechnic, Gypsy Lane (340).—R. Maguire.

PLYMOUTH: Polytechnic School of Architecture, Hoe Centre, Notte Street, PL1 2AR (211).—Prof. A. Gale.

PORTSMOUTH: Polytechnic School of Architecture, King Henry I Street, PO1 2DY (198).—Prof. G. H. Broadbent.

ART AND DESIGN

First Degrees in *Art, Fine Art* or *History of Art* are granted by the University of Aberdeen, Cambridge, East Anglia, Edinburgh, Essex, Lancaster (*Visual Arts*),Leeds, Leicester, London (Courtauld Institute of Art; Birkbeck, University and Westfield Colleges), Loughborough (*Design and Technology*), Manchester, Manchester Institute of Science and Technology (*Textile Design and Design Management*), Newcastle upon Tyne, Nottingham, Oxford, Reading, St. Andrews, Stirling, Sussex, Wales (University College, Aberystwyth—*Visual Art*; Cardiff University College—*Textiles and Design*) and Warwick. At several other universities art or history of art can be combined with another subject. The degrees in *Art* granted by the Royal College of Art are higher degrees.

Courses leading to first degrees in *Art and Design* (*Fine Art, Graphic Design, Textiles/Fashion or Three-Dimensional Design*) granted by the Council for National Academic Awards are provided by some 50 colleges/schools of art and polytechnics some of which also offer C.N.A.A. degree courses in other subjects

in the field of Art and Design, including *Furniture Design, Industrial Design and Interior Design.*

LONDON.—Royal Academy Schools of Painting and Sculpture, Burlington Gardens, W.1 (65).—*Keeper*, Peter Greenham, C.B.E., R.A.; *Secretary*, Laura Scott; *Curator*, W. Woodington; *Registrar*, L. Bray.

LONDON.—The Slade School of Fine Art, University College, W.C.1, provides undergraduate and graduate courses in Fine Art.—*Slade Professor*, Sir Lawrence Gowing, C.B.E.; *Sec.*, M. Watson.

LONDON.—Royal College of Art, *see* p. 512.

OXFORD, The Ruskin School of Drawing and Fine Art, at 74 High Street, Oxford OX1 4BG (60 undergraduates).—*Ruskin Master of Drawing*, vacant. Course in Drawing, Painting, Print-making, Sculpture and History of Art. The University awards a Bachelor of Fine Art degree.

ASTRONOMY

First Degrees in *Astronomy* are granted by the Universities of Glasgow, London (Queen Mary and University Colleges); and in *Astrophysics* by the Universities of Edinburgh, London (Queen Mary College) and Wales (University College, Cardiff). Various combinations of Astronomy, Mathematics, Physics and Astrophysics are also available.

Astronomy may be taken as part of a C.N.A.A. degree course at certain polytechnics.

BANKING

First Degrees with specialization in *Banking and Finance* are granted by the Universities of Birmingham (*Money, Banking and Finance*), Loughborough, Ulster and Wales (Institute of Science and Technology; also *Banking, Insurance and Finance* at Bangor University College), and the City University (*Banking and International Finance*).

Professional organizations granting qualifications after examination:—

THE INSTITUTE OF BANKERS, 10 Lombard Street, EC3V 9AS.

THE INSTITUTE OF BANKERS IN SCOTLAND, 20 Rutland Square, Edinburgh EH1 2DE.

BIOLOGY, CHEMISTRY, PHYSICS

First Degrees in these subjects are granted by many universities. Courses leading to first degrees, granted by the Council of National Academic Awards, are provided by many polytechnics. Professional qualifications are awarded by:—

THE INSTITUTE OF BIOLOGY, 20 Queensberry Place, SW7 2DZ.—*Gen. Sec.*, P. N. O'Donoghue.

THE INSTITUTE OF PHYSICS, 47 Belgrave Square, SW1X 8QX.

THE ROYAL SOCIETY OF CHEMISTRY, Burlington House, Piccadilly, W.1.—*President*, Prof. R. O. C. Norman, D.S.C., F.R.S.C., F.R.S., *Gen. Sec.*, Dr. R. D. Guthrie, F.R.S.C.

BREWING

First Degrees in Brewing are granted by Heriot-Watt University.

BUILDING
(*See also* Architecture, Estate Management and Surveying)

First Degrees in *Building, Building Engineering* or *Building Technology* are granted by the following Universities: Aston in Birmingham, Bath, Heriot-Watt (also *Building Economics and Quantity Surveying*), Liverpool (*Building Construction Engineering,*

Building Services Engineering), London (University College), Manchester (Manchester Institute of Science and Technology—also *Building Services Engineering* and *Construction Management*), Reading (*Building Construction & Management, Quantity Surveying* and *Building Surveying*), Salford (*Building Surveying*, also *Quantity Surveying and Construction Economics*) and Ulster (also *Building Services Engineering* and *Quantity Surveying*).

Courses leading to first degrees in *Building* granted by the Council for National Academic Awards are provided by Brighton Polytechnic, Bristol Polytechnic, Polytechnic of Central London, Coventry (Lanchester) Polytechnic, Glasgow College of Technology with Glasgow College of Building and Printing, Leeds Polytechnic, Liverpool Polytechnic, Sheffield City Polytechnic (*Construction*), the Polytechnic of the South Bank, Trent Polytechnic, and Polytechnic of Wales; in *Building Surveying* by Leicester Polytechnic, Liverpool Polytechnic, Polytechnic of the South Bank, Thames Polytechnic; and in *Building Services Engineering* by Newcastle upon Tyne Polytechnic and the Polytechnic of the South Bank (*Environmental Engineering*).

Examinations are conducted by:—

THE CHARTERED INSTITUTE OF BUILDING, Englemere, King's Ride, Ascot, Berks. SL5 8BJ.

THE INSTITUTE OF CLERKS OF WORKS OF GREAT BRITAIN, 41 The Mall, Ealing, W5 3TJ.

THE INSTITUTION OF MUNICIPAL ENGINEERS, 25 Eccleston Square, S.W.1 (Chartered Engineers', Building Control Officers' Ordinary and Higher Certificates).

BUSINESS, MANAGEMENT AND ADMINISTRATION

First Degrees in *Business Studies* are granted by the Universities of Bath (*Business Administration*), Belfast (*Business Administration*), Bradford, City, Edinburgh, Heriot-Watt (*Business Organization*), Liverpool, Loughborough (*Business Administration with a Modern Language*), Salford (*Business and Administration, Business Operation and Control*), Sheffield, Stirling, Ulster (also *European Business Studies*), Wales (University College, Aberystwyth: *Economics and Business*) (University College, Swansea: also *European Business Studies*), Wales (Institute of Science and Technology) (*Business Administration*; also *Business Economics*); in *Administration* by the Universities of Aston in Birmingham (*Managerial and Administrative Studies*), Birmingham (*Public Policy Making and Administration*), Dundee, Essex (*Policy-making and Administration*) and Salford (*Business and Administration*); in *Management Sciences/Studies* by the City University (*Systems and Management*), Loughborough University of Technology, and the Universities of Bradford, Hull, Kent at Canterbury (also *Public Administration and Management*, and *European Management Science*), Lancaster, Leeds (*Textile Management*), London (London School of Economics), Loughborough, Manchester (Institute of Science and Technology; also *Textile Economics and Management*), St. Andrews, Stirling, Wales (Cardiff University College; Swansea University College: also *American Management Studies* and *European Management Science*), and Warwick; in *Marketing* by the Universities of Lancaster and Strathclyde; and in *Commerce* by the University of Birmingham. A variety of other combinations in these fields are available at some of these universities and these subjects also form part of degree courses in other universities.

Courses leading to first degrees in *Business Studies* or *Business Administration* granted by the Council for National Academic Awards are provided by City of Birmingham Polytechnic, Brighton Polytechnic, Bristol Polytechnic, Polytechnic of Central London, City of London Polytechnic, Coventry (Lanchester) Polytechnic, Dorset Institute of Higher Education, Dundee College of Technology (also *Commerce*), Ealing College of Higher Education, Glasgow College of Technology (also *Commerce*), Hatfield Polytechnic, Huddersfield Polytechnic, Humberside College of Higher Education, Kingston Polytechnic, Leeds Polytechnic, Leicester Polytechnic, Liverpool Polytechnic, Manchester Polytechnic, Middlesex Polytechnic, Napier College of Commerce and Technology (also *Commerce*), Newcastle upon Tyne Polytechnic, North East London Polytechnic, Polytechnic of N. London, N. Staffordshire Polytechnic, Oxford Polytechnic, Paisley College of Technology (*Business Economics*), Plymouth Polytechnic, Portsmouth Polytechnic, Preston Polytechnic, Robert Gordon's Institute of Technology, Sheffield City Polytechnic, Polytechnic of the South Bank, Sunderland Polytechnic, Teesside Polytechnic, Thames Polytechnic, Trent Polytechnic, Polytechnic of Wales, and Wolverhampton Polytechnic.

Courses leading to first degrees in *European Business Studies/Administration* granted by the Council for National Academic Awards are provided by Buckinghamshire College of Higher Education, Humberside College of Higher Education, Middlesex Polytechnic and Trent Polytechnic.

The Thames Polytechnic provides courses for C.N.A.A. first degrees in *International Marketing*; Huddersfield Polytechnic courses for C.N.A.A. degrees in *Marketing (Engineering)* and *Textile Marketing*; and Humberside College of Higher Education and Newcastle upon Tyne Polytechnic courses for C.N.A.A. degrees in *Secretarial Studies*.

Leicester, Manchester, Sheffield City, Teesside and Trent Polytechnics, the Polytechnic of Wales, Glasgow College of Technology, Robert Gordon's Institute of Technology provides courses for C.N.A.A. first degrees in *Public Administration*.

Glasgow College of Technology provides courses for C.N.A.A. first degrees in *Risk Management*.

Professional bodies conducting training and/or examinations in Administration and Management include:

ROYAL INSTITUTE OF PUBLIC ADMINISTRATION, 3 Birdcage Walk, SW1H 9JH.

THE INSTITUTE OF HEALTH SERVICE ADMINISTRATORS, 75 Portland Place, W1N 4AN.

THE INSTITUTE OF PERSONNEL MANAGEMENT, IPM House, Camp Road, Wimbledon, S.W.19.

INSTITUTION OF INDUSTRIAL MANAGERS, Industrial Management House, Cardiff Road, Luton, Beds. LU1 1RQ.

INSTITUTE OF HOUSING, 12 Upper Belgrave Street, S.W.1.

INSTITUTE OF ADMINISTRATIVE MANAGEMENT, 40 Chatsworth Parade, Petts Wood, Orpington, Kent BR5 1RW.

HENLEY—THE MANAGEMENT COLLEGE, Greenlands, Henley-on-Thames, Oxon RG9 3AU.—*Princ.*, Prof. T. Kempner (1972).

LONDON BUSINESS SCHOOL, Sussex Place, Regent's Park, NW1 4SA.—*Princ.*, Prof. R. J. Ball, M.A., PH.D.

MANCHESTER BUSINESS SCHOOL, Booth Street West, Manchester.—*Dir.*, Prof. T. Lupton.

SCOTTISH BUSINESS SCHOOL, 69 St. George's Place, Glasgow G2 1EU.

INSTITUTE OF MARKETING, Moor Hall, Cookham, Maidenhead, Berks. SL6 9QH.—*Dir.-Gen.*, P. B. Blood.

Courses of advanced training in most branches of commerce, including preparation for examinations of the recognized professional organizations as well as for the National Certificates in Business Studies are available at the Polytechnics listed by cities on p. 510.

Throughout the country commercial education at a lower level is provided at *Evening Institutes*, particulars of which may be obtained from the Local Education Authority.

There are also numbers of well-established private schools awarding certificates which are widely accepted.

Institutions awarding Professional Qualifications in Commerce:—

A. GENERAL

THE ROYAL SOCIETY OF ARTS EXAMINATIONS BOARD, John Adam Street, Adelphi, WC2N 6EZ.

THE LONDON CHAMBER OF COMMERCE AND INDUSTRY, Commercial Education Scheme, Marlowe House, Station Road, Sidcup, Kent.

THE EAST MIDLAND FURTHER EDUCATIONAL COUNCIL, Robins Wood House, Robins Wood Road, Aspley, Nottingham NG8 3NH.

THE NORTHERN COUNCIL FOR FURTHER EDUCATION, 5 Grosvenor Villas, Grosvenor Road, Newcastle upon Tyne NE2 2RU.

THE WEST MIDLANDS ADVISORY COUNCIL FOR FURTHER EDUCATION (incorporating Union of Educational Institutions), Norfolk House, Smallbrook Queensway, Birmingham B5 4NB.

NORTH WESTERN REGIONAL ADVISORY COUNCIL FOR FURTHER EDUCATION (incorporating the Union of Lancashire and Cheshire Institutes), Town Hall, Walkden Road, Worsley, Manchester.

THE YORKSHIRE AND HUMBERSIDE ASSOCIATION FOR FURTHER AND HIGHER EDUCATION, Bowling Green Terrace, Leeds LS11 9SX.

WELSH JOINT EDUCATION COMMITTEE, 245 Western Avenue, Cardiff CF5 2YX.

B. SPECIALIZED

THE INSTITUTE OF CHARTERED SECRETARIES AND ADMINISTRATORS, 16 Park Crescent, W1N 4AH.

THE FACULTY OF SECRETARIES AND ADMINISTRATORS LTD., 51 Tormead Road, Guildford, Surrey GU1 2JB.

THE INSTITUTE OF EXPORT, World Trade Centre, E1 9AA.

THE INSTITUTE OF CHARTERED SHIPBROKERS, 24 St. Mary Axe, EC3A 8DE.

INSTITUTE OF MARKETING, Moor Hall, Cookham, Maidenhead, Berks. SL6 9QH.

THE CHARTERED INSTITUTE OF TRANSPORT, 80 Portland Place, W1N 4DP.

THE CAM FOUNDATION, Abford House, 15 Wilton Road, S.W.1.

INSTITUTE OF PRACTITIONERS IN ADVERTISING, 44 Belgrave Square, SW1X 8QS.

INSTITUTE OF PURCHASING AND SUPPLY, Easton House, Easton on the Hill, Stamford, Lincs. PE9 3NZ.

INSTITUTE OF PERSONNEL MANAGEMENT, IPM House, Camp Road, Wimbledon, S.W.19.

BUSINESS AND TECHNICIAN EDUCATION COUNCIL Central House, Upper Woburn Place, WC1H 0HH

The Business & Technician Education Council (BTEC) is responsible for planning, administering and reviewing a wide range of courses, below degree level, in areas such as business, finance, distribution, public sector administration, computing, engineering, construction, science, agriculture, catering and design in England, Wales and Northern Ireland.

Chairman, H. N. Raine.
Chief Executive, J. E. Sellars.

COMPUTER SCIENCE

First Degrees in *Computer/Computing Science(s)/Computing, Computational Science* are granted by Brunel (also *Applied Computer Systems*), City (also *Business Computing Systems*), Heriot-Watt and Loughborough (also *Data Processing*) Universities and by the Universities of Aberdeen, Aston in Birmingham, Belfast (also *Information Technology*), Birmingham (*Computer Science/Software Engineering*), Bradford (also *Computing & Information Systems Science*), Bristol, Cambridge, Dundee, East Anglia, Edinburgh, Essex (also *Computer & Microprocessor Systems*), Exeter, Glasgow, Hull, Keele, Kent (also *Computer Systems Engineering*), Lancaster, Leeds (also *Data Processing*), Liverpool, London (Imperial (also *Software Engineering*), King's, Queen Mary (also *Computer Systems with Microelectronics*), Royal Holloway, and University Colleges; London School of Economics and Political Science), Manchester (also *Computing & Information Systems*), Manchester Institute of Science and Technology, Newcastle upon Tyne, Reading, St. Andrews (also *Information Processing*), Salford (*Electronic Computer Systems*), Sheffield, Southampton, Stirling, Strathclyde (also *Computer Science and Microprocessor Systems*), Sussex, Ulster (also *Computing Science for Business* and *Computing Science* (*Data Processing*)), Wales (University College, Aberystwyth; University College, Cardiff: *Computer Systems*; University College, Swansea) Warwick and York (also *Computer Systems & Software Engineering*).

Courses leading to first degrees in *Computer Science/Studies* or *Computing* granted by the Council for National Academic Awards are provided by Brighton Polytechnic, Bristol Polytechnic (*Systems Analysis*), Coventry (Lanchester) Polytechnic, Glasgow College of Technology (*Computer Information Systems*), Hatfield Polytechnic, Huddersfield Polytechnic (*Computing in Business*), Kingston Polytechnic (also *Information Systems Design*), Leeds Polytechnic (*Computing and Operational Research*), Leicester Polytechnic, Napier College of Commerce and Technology (*Computing and Data Processing*), North East London Polytechnic, North Staffordshire Polytechnic (also *Information Systems*), Paisley College of Technology, Plymouth Polytechnic (*Computing and Informatics*), Portsmouth Polytechnic, Sheffield City Polytechnic (also *Systems Modelling*), Teesside Polytechnic (also *Computer Technology*), Thames Polytechnic (also *Computer and Communications Systems*), Wolverhampton Polytechnic and Polytechnic of Wales; in *Control and Computer Engineering* by Polytechnic of Central London; in *Computer and Control Systems* by Coventry (Lanchester) Polytechnic; and in *Data Processing* by Sunderland Polytechnic.

These subjects also form part of other degree courses, often as *Mathematics/Statistics and Computer Science*, at many universities and colleges.

DANCE

(*See also* Physical Education)
First degrees in *Dance in Society* are granted by the University of Surrey.

Courses leading to first degrees in *Dance* granted by the Council for National Academic Awards are provided by the Laban Centre for Movement and Dance in association with Goldsmiths' College. Dance also forms part of C.N.A.A. degree courses, often called *Performing Arts* or *Creative Arts*, at several polytechnics and colleges. For first degree courses in *Human Movement Studies* see under 'Physical Education'.

THE ROYAL ACADEMY OF DANCING (incorporated by Royal Charter), 48 Vicarage Crescent, SW11 3LT.—

Directors, Julia Farron, D. Scrimgeour, Priscilla Yates.

THE ROYAL BALLET SCHOOL, 155 Talgarth Road, W14 9DE, and White Lodge, Richmond Park.—*Director,* Merle Park, C.B.E.

IMPERIAL SOCIETY OF TEACHERS OF DANCING (1904), Euston Hall, Birkenhead Street, WC1H 8BE.—*Gen. Sec.,* P. J. Pearson.

DEFENCE

First Degrees in *Peace Studies* are granted by the universities of Bradford and Ulster.

Royal Naval Colleges

ROYAL NAVAL COLLEGE
Greenwich, SE10 9NN

Admiral President, Vice-Admiral Sir Simon Cassels, K.C.B., C.B.E.
Head of Dept. of History and International Affairs, Prof. P. Nailor.
Dean of the College and Director, Dept. of Nuclear Science and Technology, Prof. J. R. A. Lakey, PH.D.

INSTITUTE OF NAVAL MEDICINE
Alverstoke, Hants PO12 2DL

Medical Officer-in-Charge, Surgeon Captain E. P. Beck.

ROYAL NAVAL HOSPITAL
Haslar, Gosport, Hants.

Surgeon Commodore and Dean of Naval Medicine, Surgeon Cdre. J. W. Richardson O.B.E., Q.H.S., F.R.C.S.

BRITANNIA ROYAL NAVAL COLLEGE
Dartmouth, Devon TQ6 0HJ

Captain, Capt. G. M. Tullis.
Commander, Cdr. C. J. Esplin-Jones, O.B.E.
Dir. of Studies, C. H. Christie, M.A.

ROYAL NAVAL ENGINEERING COLLEGE
Manadon, Plymouth.

Officers of the Royal Navy and Commonwealth and Foreign Navies and sponsored civilian students are prepared for C.N.A.A. degrees in Naval Engineering.
Captain, Capt. R. A. Isaac.
Dean, Capt. G. C. George.
Executive Officer, Cdr. A. W. M. Stephens.
Dir. of Naval Engineering, Cdr. M. L. D. Kendrick.
Dir. of Postgraduate Studies, Cdr. D. J. Cooke.
Dir. of Undergraduate Studies, Cdr. K. S. Hart.

Military Colleges

STAFF COLLEGE, CAMBERLEY
Surrey GU15 4NP

Officers who graduate at the college have the letters *psc.* after their names in Service Lists.
Commandant, Maj.-Gen. C. P. R. Palmer, C.B.E.
Deputy Commandant, Brig. J. A. M. Evans.

ROYAL MILITARY ACADEMY
SANDHURST
Camberley, Surrey GU15 4PQ

The Royal Military Academy, Woolwich, founded in 1741, and the Royal Military College, Sandhurst, founded in 1799, were amalgamated in 1947 under the above title.

Mons Officer Cadet School, Aldershot, opened in 1942 for the training of short service officers, also became part of RMA Sandhurst in 1972.
Commandant, Maj.-Gen. R. C. Keightley.

ROYAL MILITARY COLLEGE OF SCIENCE
Shrivenham, nr. Swindon, Wilts SN6 8LA

The College was founded at Woolwich in 1864 and transferred to Shrivenham in 1946. Officer students from U.K., Commonwealth and foreign armies and some civilian students are prepared for first degrees in Applied Science and Engineering and for higher degrees in various aspects of technology of the Council for National Academic Awards.

Commandant, Maj.-Gen. J. J. Stibbon, O.B.E.
Dean, Prof. F. R. Hartley, D.Phil.
Academic Registrar, vacant.

ARMOUR SCHOOL
R.A.C. CENTRE
Bovington Camp, nr. Wareham,
Dorset BH20 6LZ

Commanding Officer and Chief Instructor, Col. A. A. Mathieson, M.C.

WELBECK COLLEGE
Worksop, Notts. S80 3LN

Headmaster, M. J. Maloney.
Bursar, Col. R. Mathews.

INSTITUTE OF ARMY EDUCATION
Court Road, Eltham, SE9 5NR

Director, Maj.-Gen. D. E. Ryan.

Royal Air Force Colleges

ROYAL AIR FORCE STAFF COLLEGE
Bracknell, Berks.

Opened at Andover on 3 April 1922, the College is now the centre for Command and Staff Training in the Royal Air Force. The principal course held each year aims to prepare selected senior officers, from the UK Armed Forces and many countries overseas, for high-grade command and staff appointments and for promotion to the highest ranks in their Services.
Air Officer Commanding and Commandant, Air Vice-Marshal A. G. Skingsley, C.B.

ROYAL AIR FORCE COLLEGE
Cranwell, Lincs NG34 8HB

Founded in 1920, the College provides initial officer training for Royal Air Force, Women's Royal Air Force and Princess Mary's Royal Air Force Nursing Service officers, and initial specialist training for officers of the Engineer and Supply Branches. Advanced specialist training is provided for officers of the General Duties, Engineer and Supply Branches. Flying training for pilots of the General Duties Branch is provided by the Flying Training School, Cranwell. The headquarters of the University Air Squadrons is at the College.
Air Officer Commanding and Commandant, Air Vice-Marshal R. C. F. Peirse.

ROYAL AIR FORCE SCHOOL OF
EDUCATION AND TRAINING SUPPORT
R.A.F. Newton, Nottingham NG13 8HL

Commanding Officer, Gp. Capt. R. C. Travis, M.B.E.

DENTISTRY

First Degrees in Dentistry are granted by the University of Belfast, Birmingham, Bristol, Dundee, Edinburgh, Glasgow, Leeds, Liverpool, London (United Medical and Dental Schools of Guy's and St.

Thomas's Hospitals, King's College School of Medicine and Dentistry, London Hospital Medical College, University College), Manchester, Newcastle upon Tyne, Sheffield, Wales (University College, Cardiff, and Welsh National School of Medicine).

To be entitled to be registered in the Dentists Register a person must hold the degree or diploma in dental surgery of a University in the United Kingdom or Republic of Ireland or the diploma of any of the Licensing Authorities (The Royal College of Surgeons of England, of Edinburgh and in Ireland, and the Royal College of Physicians and Surgeons of Glasgow).

DIETETICS
(*See also* Food and Nutrition Science)

Courses in *Dietetics* leading to first degrees granted by the University of Wales are provided by South Glamorgan Institute of Higher Education. Courses leading to first degrees in *Dietetics* granted by the Council for National Academic Awards are provided by Leeds Polytechnic, Queen Margaret College, Queen's College and Robert Gordon's Institute of Technology (*Nutrition and Dietetics*).

The professional association is The British Dietetic Association, Daimler House, Paradise Street, Birmingham. Full membership is open to dietitians holding a recognized qualification, who may also become State Registered Dietitians through the Council for Professions Supplementary to Medicine (*q.v.*).

DRAMA

First Degrees in *Drama* are granted by the Universities of Birmingham (*Drama and Theatre Arts*), Bristol, East Anglia, Exeter, Glasgow (*Dramatic Studies*—in conjunction with Royal Scottish Academy of Music and Drama), Hull, Kent (*Drama and Theatre Studies*), London (Royal Holloway College: *Drama and Theatre Studies*), Loughborough, Manchester and Wales (University Colleges of Aberystwyth and Bangor); and in *Theatre Studies* by the University of Warwick. Drama also forms part of degree courses in other universities. Courses in Drama leading to first degrees granted by the University of Lancaster are provided at the City of Liverpool College of Higher Education and by the University of Leeds at Bretton Hall College of Higher Education.

Courses leading to first degrees granted by the Council for National Academic Awards are provided by Crewe and Alsager College of Higher Education (*Drama Studies*), Dartington College of Arts (*Theatre*), King Alfred's College of Higher Education (*Drama (Theatre and TV Studies*)) and Rose Bruford College of Speech and Drama (*Theatre Arts*).

The national validating body for courses providing training in drama is the National Council for Drama Training. It currently has courses at the following: Arts Educational Schools; Birmingham School of Speech Training & Dramatic Art; Bristol Old Vic Theatre School; Central School of Speech and Drama; Drama Centre, London; Guildford School of Acting; Guildhall School of Music and Drama (see p. 529); London Academy of Music and Dramatic Art; Rose Bruford College of Speech and Drama; Royal Academy of Dramatic Art (*see below*); Royal Scottish Academy of Music and Drama; Webber Douglas Academy of Dramatic Art; Welsh College of Music and Drama.

Royal Academy of Dramatic Art (founded by Sir Herbert Beerbohm Tree, 1904), 62–64 Gower Street, W.C.1.—*Principal*, O. Neville, ph.d.; *Administrator-Registrar*, R. O'Donoghue.

British Theatre Association (formerly British Drama League), 9 Fitzroy Square, W1P 6AE.

ECONOMICS

Almost all universities grant first degrees in economics. Courses leading to first degrees in Economics granted by the Council for National Academic Awards are provided by some 20 Polytechnics and Colleges.

ENGINEERING
(*See separate subjects below*)

The Council of Engineering Institutions ceased operations in Sept. 1983 and its major functions are now carried on by The Engineering Council, Canberra House, Maltravers Street, W.C.2. The sixteen principal qualifying bodies are:—

Royal Aeronautical Society, 4 Hamilton Place, W.1.

Institution of Energy, 18 Devonshire Street, W.1.

Institution of Chemical Engineers, 165/171 Railway Terrace, Rugby, Warwickshire CV21 3HQ; London Office, 12 Gayfere Street, SW1P 3HP.

Institution of Civil Engineers, Great George Street, S.W.1.

Institution of Electrical Engineers, Savoy Place, WC2R 0BL.

Institution of Electronic and Radio Engineers, 99 Gower Street, WC1E 6AZ.

Institution of Gas Engineers, 17 Grosvenor Crescent, S.W.1.

Institute of Marine Engineers, 76 Mark Lane, EC3R 7JN.

Institution of Mechanical Engineers, 1 Birdcage Walk, SW1H 9JJ.

Institution of Metallurgists, P.O. Box 471, 1 Carlton House Terrace, S.W.1.

Institution of Mining Engineers, Danum House, 6A South Parade, Doncaster DN1 2DY.

Institution of Mining and Metallurgy, 44 Portland Place, W1N 4BR.

Institution of Municipal Engineers, 25 Eccleston Square, S.W.1.

Institution of Production Engineers, Rochester House, 66 Little Ealing Lane, W5 4XX.

Institution of Structural Engineers, 11 Upper Belgrave Street, SW1X 8BH.

Royal Institution of Naval Architects, 10 Upper Belgrave Street, S.W.1.

ENGINEERING, GENERAL AND ENGINEERING SCIENCE

First Degrees in *General Engineering* or *Engineering Science* are granted by the Universities of Aberdeen, Cambridge, Durham, Edinburgh, Exeter, Lancaster, Leicester, Liverpool, London (Queen Mary College), Loughborough, Oxford, Reading, Surrey, Ulster and Warwick. Courses leading to first degrees in *Engineering* granted by the Council for National Academic Awards are provided by polytechnics and colleges.

Aeronautical Engineering

See main heading:
Aeronautics and Aeronautical Engineering

Agricultural Engineering

First Degrees in *Agricultural Engineering* and *Agricultural Mechanisation* are granted by the University of Newcastle upon Tyne. Courses in *Agricultural Engineering* leading to degrees granted by Cranfield Institute of Technology are provided at Silsoe College.

Chemical Engineering

First Degrees are granted by the Universities of Aston in Birmingham (also *Chemical Process Engineering*), Bath, Belfast, Birmingham, Bradford, Cambridge, Edinburgh, Exeter, Heriot-Watt, Leeds, London (Imperial College of Science and Technology; University College), Loughborough, Manchester (Manchester Institute of Science and Technology), Newcastle upon Tyne, Nottingham, Salford, Sheffield (*Chemical Process Engineering*), Strathclyde, Surrey, Wales (University College, Swansea).

Courses leading to first degrees granted by the Council for National Academic Awards are provided by North East London Polytechnic, Polytechnic of the South Bank, Teesside Polytechnic and Polytechnic of Wales.

Civil, Electrical & Mechanical Engineering

First Degrees in *Civil, Electrical* (or *Electrical and Electronic*) and *Mechanical Engineering* are granted by Aberdeen, Aston in Birmingham, Bath, Belfast, Birmingham, Bradford, Bristol, Brunel (*E. & M.*), Cambridge, City, Dundee, Durham, Edinburgh, Exeter, Glasgow, Heriot-Watt, Lancaster, Leeds, Leicester, Liverpool, London (Imperial College of Science and Technology, King's College, Queen Mary College, University College), Loughborough, Manchester, *also* Manchester Institute of Science and Technology, Newcastle upon Tyne, Nottingham, Reading (*E. & M.*), Salford, Sheffield, Southampton, Strathclyde, Surrey, Sussex, Ulster (*C. & Manufacturing E.*), Wales (University Colleges at Cardiff and Swansea; Institute of Science and Technology, Cardiff; University College, Bangor *E.*), and Warwick.

Some 40 polytechnics or colleges provide courses (in one or more of civil, electrical/electronic and mechanical engineering) leading to first degrees granted by the Council for National Academic Awards.

Electronic Engineering & Electronics

First Degrees in *Electronic Engineering* or *Electronics* or *Electrical and Electronic Engineering* or *Electrical Engineering (including Electronics)* are granted by the following universities: Aberdeen, Aston, Bath, Belfast, Birmingham, Bradford, Bristol, Brunel, City, Dundee, East Anglia (*Electronic Systems Engineering*), Edinburgh, Essex, Exeter, Glasgow, Heriot-Watt, Hull, Keele, Kent at Canterbury, Lancaster, Leeds, Leicester, Liverpool, London (Imperial College of Science and Technology, King's, Queen Mary and University Colleges), Loughborough, Manchester (*also* Manchester Institute of Science and Technology), Newcastle upon Tyne, Nottingham, Reading, Salford, Sheffield, Southampton, Strathclyde, Surrey, Sussex, Ulster, Wales (University Colleges of Bangor (also *Ocean Electronics*), Cardiff and Swansea, Institute of Science and Technology), Warwick (*Engineering Electronics*), York.

Courses leading to first degrees in *Electronic Engineering* or in *Electrical and Electronic Engineering*, granted by the Council for National Academic Awards are provided by nearly 30 polytechnics or colleges.

Marine Engineering and Naval Architecture

First Degrees in *Marine Engineering* and *Naval Architecture and Shipbuilding* are granted by the University of Newcastle upon Tyne; in *Naval Architecture and Ocean Engineering* by the Universities of Glasgow and London (University College); in *Naval Architecture* by the University of Strathclyde; in *Ship Science* by the University of Southampton, in *Maritime Technology* by the University of Wales (Institute of Science and Technology) and in *Civil and Maritime Engineering* by the University of Liverpool.

Courses leading to first degrees in *Marine Engineering* granted by the Council for National Academic Awards are provided by Southampton College of Higher Education, in *Mechanical Engineering (Marine)* by Liverpool Polytechnic and in *Naval Engineering* by the Royal Naval Engineering College (open only to naval officers).

Nuclear Engineering

First Degrees are granted by the Universities of London (Queen Mary College—also *Nuclear Reactor Science and Technology*), Manchester, and Salford (*Applied Chemistry—Nuclear Technology*).

Offshore Engineering

First Degrees are granted by Heriot-Watt University.

Production Engineering

First Degrees in *Production Engineering, Manufacturing Engineering* or *Industrial Engineering* are granted by the following Universities: Aston in Birmingham, Bath, Birmingham, Bradford, Brunel, Cambridge, City, Hull (*Engineering Design and Manufacture*), Loughborough, Manchester *and* Manchester Institute of Science and Technology, Nottingham, Strathclyde, Ulster and Wales (Institute of Science and Technology).

Courses leading to first degrees in *Production Engineering* granted by the Council for National Academic Awards are provided by Coventry (Lanchester) Polytechnic, Kingston Polytechnic, Leeds Polytechnic, Trent Polytechnic; in *Industrial Engineering* by Hatfield Polytechnic, Paisley College of Technology; in *Manufacturing Engineering* by Liverpool Polytechnic; in *Manufacturing Studies* by North East London Polytechnic; in *Manufacturing Systems Engineering* by Sheffield City Polytechnic; and in *Plant Engineering* by Trent Polytechnic.

Structural Engineering

First Degrees in *Civil and Structural Engineering* are granted by the Universities of Aberdeen, Bath, Bradford, Cambridge, Heriot-Watt (*Structural Engineering*), Liverpool, London (University College: *Civil, Structural and Environmental Engineering*), Sheffield, Sussex, and Wales (University College, Cardiff).

ESTATE MANAGEMENT AND SURVEYING
(*See also* Building)

First Degrees are granted by the Universities of Aberdeen (*Land Economy*), Cambridge (*Land Economy*), Heriot-Watt (*Estate Management*), Reading (*Land Management*) and Ulster (*Estate Management*).

First Degrees in *Surveying Science* are granted by the University of Newcastle upon Tyne, in *Building Economics and Measurement* by the University of Aston in Birmingham, in *Building Economics and Quantity Surveying* by Heriot-Watt and Ulster Universities, in *Property Valuation and Management* by the City University, in *Quantity Surveying* and *Building Surveying* by the University of Reading, and in *Quantity Surveying and Construction Economics* and *Building Surveying* by the University of Salford.

Courses leading to first degrees granted by the Council for National Academic Awards are provided by the following: in *Estate Management* by the City of Birmingham Polytechnic, Kingston Polytechnic, Oxford Polytechnic, Polytechnic of the South Bank and Thames Polytechnic; in *General Practice Surveying* by Newcastle upon Tyne Polytechnic; in *Housing* by Bristol Polytechnic; in *Housing Studies* by Sheffield City Polytechnic; in *Land Administration* by North East London Polytechnic; in *Land Economics* by Paisley College of Technology; in *Land Management* by Leicester Polytechnic; in *Minerals Estate Management* by Sheffield City Polytechnic; in *Quantity Surveying* by City of Birmingham Polytechnic, Bristol Polytechnic, Polytechnic of Central London, Dundee College of Technology, Glasgow College of Technology with Glasgow College of Building and Printing, Kingston Polytechnic, Leeds Polytechnic, Liverpool Polytechnic, Newcastle upon Tyne Polytechnic, Portsmouth Polytechnic, Robert Gordon's Institute of Technology, Polytechnic of the South Bank, Thames Polytechnic, Trent Polytechnic and Polytechnic of Wales; in *Surveying and Mapping Sciences* by North East London Polytechnic; in *Urban Estate Management* by Polytechnic of Central London, Liverpool Polytechnic and the Polytechnic of Wales; in *Urban Estate Surveying* by Trent Polytechnic; in *Urban Land Administration* by Portsmouth Polytechnic; in *Urban Land Economics* by Sheffield City Polytechnic; and in *Valuation and Estate Management* by Bristol Polytechnic.

Qualifying professional bodies include:

THE INCORPORATED SOCIETY OF VALUERS AND AUCTIONEERS, 3 Cadogan Gate, SW1X 0AS.

RATING AND VALUATION ASSOCIATION, 115 Ebury Street, SW1W 9QT.

THE INCORPORATED ASSOCIATION OF ARCHITECTS AND SURVEYORS, Jubilee House, Billing Brook Road, Weston Favell, Northampton.

THE ROYAL INSTITUTION OF CHARTERED SURVEYORS (incorporating The Institute of Quantity Surveyors), 12 Great George Street, Parliament Square, SW1P 3AD.

THE FACULTY OF ARCHITECTS AND SURVEYORS, with which is incorporated the Institute of Registered Architects, 15 St. Mary Street, Chippenham, Wilts.

FISHERY SCIENCE

First Degrees in *Wildlife and Fisheries Management* are granted by the University of Edinburgh.

Courses leading to first degrees in *Fishery Science/Studies* granted by the Council for National Academic Awards are provided by Humberside College of Higher Education, Plymouth Polytechnic.

FOOD AND NUTRITION SCIENCE
(*See also* Dietetics, Home Economics and Hotelkeeping)

First Degrees in *Food Science* are granted by the Universities of Belfast, Leeds, London (King's College), Loughborough (*Food Processing Engineering*), Nottingham, Reading (also *Food Science, Food Economics & Marketing* and *Food Technology*), Strathclyde and Surrey (*Nutrition & Food Science*); and in *Nutrition* by the Universities of London (King's College), Nottingham and Surrey.

Courses leading to first degrees in *Food Science* granted by the Council for National Academic Awards are provided by the Polytechnic of the South Bank; in *Catering* by Oxford Polytechnic; in *Catering Administration* by Dorset Institute of Higher Education; in *Catering and Applied Nutrition* by Huddersfield Polytechnic; in *Catering Systems* by Sheffield City Polytechnic; in *Food and Accommodation*

Studies by Leeds Polytechnic; in *Food Marketing Sciences* by Sheffield City Polytechnic; in *Industrial Food Technology* by Humberside College of Higher Education; in *Nutrition and Dietetics* by Robert Gordon's Institute of Technology.

Scientific and professional bodies include: NUTRITION SOCIETY, Chandos House, 2 Queen Anne Street, W1M 9LE; FOOD SCIENCE & TECHNOLOGY INSTITUTE, 20 Queensberry Place, SW7 2DR.

FORESTRY AND TIMBER STUDIES

First Degrees in Forestry are granted by the Universities of Aberdeen, Edinburgh, and (also *Wood Science*) Wales (University College, Bangor).

Courses leading to first degrees in *Timber Technology* granted by the Council for National Academic Awards are provided by Buckinghamshire College of Higher Education.

Professional Organizations

THE COMMONWEALTH FORESTRY ASSOCIATION, c/o CFI, South Parks Road, Oxford OX1 3RB.

THE ROYAL FORESTRY SOCIETY OF ENGLAND, WALES AND NORTHERN IRELAND, 102 High Street, Tring, Herts. HP23 4HU.

THE ROYAL SCOTTISH FORESTRY SOCIETY, 1 Rothesay Terrace, Edinburgh.

THE INSTITUTE OF CHARTERED FORESTERS, 22 Walker Street, Edinburgh EH3 7HR.

FUEL AND ENERGY STUDIES
(*See also* Nuclear Engineering)

First Degrees in *Fuel and Combustion Science* and in *Fuel and Energy Engineering* are granted by the University of Leeds; in *Petroleum Engineering* by London (Imperial College of Science and Technology); in *Mining and Petroleum Engineering* by the University of Strathclyde; in *Natural Gas Engineering* by the University of Salford; in *Energy Studies* by the Universities of Ulster and Wales (University College, Swansea); in *Fuel Technology* by the University of Sheffield; in *Fuel and Energy and Management Studies* by the University of Leeds; and in *Thermal Power Engineering* by the University of Bath. These subjects may also form part of other degree courses.

Courses leading to first degrees in *Energy Engineering* granted by the Council for National Academic Awards are provided by Napier College of Commerce and Technology, and in *Power Engineering* by Derbyshire College of Higher Education.

Courses leading to certificates and qualification by professional bodies are available at many Technical Colleges.

The principal professional bodies are:—

THE INSTITUTION OF GAS ENGINEERS, 17 Grosvenor Crescent, S.W.1.

THE INSTITUTE OF ENERGY, 18 Devonshire Street, W.1.

THE INSTITUTE OF PETROLEUM, 61 New Cavendish Street, W.1.

GEOLOGY

First Degrees in *Geology* or *Geological Sciences* or *Applied Geology* are granted by the Universities of Aberdeen, Aston in Birmingham, Belfast, Birmingham, Bristol, Cambridge, Dundee, Durham, East Anglia (*Environmental Sciences*), Edinburgh, Exeter, Glasgow, Hull, Keele, Lancaster (*Geophysical Sciences*), Leeds, Leicester, Liverpool, London (Bedford College, Birkbeck College, Goldsmith's College, Imperial College of Science and Technology, Queen

Mary College, University College), Manchester, Newcastle upon Tyne, Nottingham, Oxford, Reading, St. Andrews, Sheffield, Southampton, Strathclyde, Wales (University Colleges at Aberystwyth, Cardiff and Swansea).

Courses leading to first degrees in *Geology* granted by the Council for National Academic Awards are provided by City of London Polytechnic, Derbyshire College of Higher Education (*Earth and Life Studies*), Kingston Polytechnic and Portsmouth Polytechnic; in *Geology and Environment* by Oxford Polytechnic; and in *Engineering Geology and Geotechnics* by Portsmouth Polytechnic.

HOME ECONOMICS AND CATERING
(See also Dietetics, Food, Hotelkeeping and Institutional Management).

First Degrees are granted by the Universities of Ulster (*Home Economics* and *Catering Administration*), Wales (Cardiff University College: *Home Economics*), Strathclyde (*Hotel and Catering Management*) and Surrey (*Hotel and Catering Management*). Courses leading to first degrees in *Home Economics* granted by the University of Bath are provided at Bath College of Higher Education and by the University of Manchester at Manchester Polytechnic.

Courses leading to first degrees granted by the Council for National Academic Awards are provided by Bradford and Ilkley Community College (*Home and Community Studies*), Dorset Institute of Higher Education (*Catering Administration*), Huddersfield Polytechnic (*Catering and Applied Nutrition; Hotel and Catering Administration*); Leeds Polytechnic (*Home Economics* and *Food and Accommodation Studies*); Liverpool Polytechnic (*Home Economics*), Manchester Polytechnic (*Hotel and Catering Studies*); Middlesex Polytechnic (*Catering Studies*); Napier College of Commerce and Technology (*Catering and Accommodation Studies*); Newcastle upon Tyne Polytechnic (*Home Economics*) Oxford Polytechnic (*Catering*); Portsmouth Polytechnic/Highbury College of Technology (*Hotel and Catering Management*); Queen Margaret College (*Home Economics*); Queen's College (*Home Economics*); Robert Gordon's Institute of Technology (*Home Economics; Hotel, Catering and Institutional Management*); and Sheffield Polytechnic (*Catering Systems*).

HOTELKEEPING
(See also Home Economics)

First Degrees are granted by the Universities of Strathclyde (*Hotel and Catering Management*), Surrey (*Hotel Management* and *Hotel and Catering Management*) and Ulster (*Hotel and Tourism Management*).

Courses leading to first degrees in *Hotel and Catering Administration/Studies/Management* granted by the Council for National Academic Awards are provided by Huddersfield, Manchester and Middlesex Polytechnics and by Portsmouth Polytechnic/Highbury College of Technology; and in *Hotel, Catering and Institutional Management* by Robert Gordon's Institute of Technology.

INDUSTRIAL RELATIONS

First Degrees in Industrial Relations are granted by the Universities of Birmingham, Kent at Canterbury, London (London School of Economics and Political Science), and Wales (Cardiff University College). Industrial relations also forms part of degree courses at other universities.

INSTITUTIONAL MANAGEMENT

First Degrees in Institutional Management are granted by the University of Wales (Cardiff University College).

Courses leading to first degrees in *Institutional Management* granted by the Council for National Academic Awards are provided by the Polytechnic of North London; and in *Hotel, Catering and Institutional Management* by Robert Gordon's Institute of Technology.

Qualifying professional body in the three subjects above is:

HOTEL, CATERING AND INSTITUTIONAL MANAGEMENT ASSOCIATION, 191 Trinity Road, S.W.17.

INSURANCE

First Degrees in *Banking, Insurance and Finance* are granted by the University of Wales (University College, Bangor).

Courses leading to first degrees in *Risk Management* granted by the Council for National Academic Awards are provided by the Glasgow College of Technology.

Organizations conducting examinations and awarding diplomas:—

THE CHARTERED INSURANCE INSTITUTE, 20 Aldermanbury, EC2V 7HY.

THE ASSOCIATION OF AVERAGE ADJUSTERS, Irongate House, Dukes Place, EC3A 7LP.

THE CHARTERED INSTITUTE OF LOSS ADJUSTERS, Manfield House, 376 Strand, W.C.2.

JOURNALISM

Courses for trainee newspaper journalists are available at 11 centres. One-year full-time courses are available for selected students. Particulars of all these courses are available from the Director of the National Council for Training of Journalists, Carlton House, Hemnall Street, Epping, Essex.

Short courses for experienced journalists are also arranged by the National Council. For periodical journalists courses are offered at a London college through N.C.T.J. enrolment including a one-year full-time course.

LANGUAGES

First Degrees in a very wide range of Languages (including Oriental and African languages) are granted by universities. Degrees in *Linguistics* are awarded by the Universities of East Anglia, Essex (also *Language Studies; Psycholinguistics; Linguistics and Language Pathology*), Hull, Lancaster, Leeds (*Linguistics and Phonetics*), London (School of Oriental and African Studies and University College), Newcastle upon Tyne, Reading (also *Linguistics and Language Pathology*), Sussex and Wales (University College, Bangor); in *Language and Linguistics* (*African, Asian and European Languages*) by the University of York; and in *Languages* (*Interpreting and Translating*) by Heriot-Watt University. These subjects also form part of degree courses at many other universities.

Courses leading to first degrees in various *Languages* granted by the Council for National Academic Awards are provided by some 16 Polytechnics and Colleges.

LAW

First Degrees in Law are granted by the Universities of Aberdeen, Belfast, Birmingham, Bristol, Brunel, Cambridge, Dundee, Durham, East Anglia, Edinburgh, Essex, Exeter, Glasgow, Hull, Kent at

Canterbury (also *Industrial Relations* (*Law*)), Lancaster, Leeds, Leicester, Liverpool, London (King's College; London School of Economics and Political Science; Queen Mary College; School of Oriental and African Studies; University College), Manchester, Newcastle upon Tyne, Nottingham, Oxford, Reading, Sheffield, Southampton, Stirling (*Business Law*), Strathclyde (also *Business Law*), Sussex, Wales (University Colleges at Aberystwyth and Cardiff, Institute of Science and Technology) and Warwick.

Courses leading to first degrees in Law granted by the Council for National Academic Awards are provided by City of Birmingham Polytechnic, Bristol Polytechnic, Polytechnic of Central London, Chelmer Institute of Higher Education, City of London Polytechnic (also *Business Law*), Coventry (Lanchester) Polytechnic (*Business Law*), Ealing College of Higher Education, Huddersfield Polytechnic (*Business Law*), Kingston Polytechnic, Leeds Polytechnic, Leicester Polytechnic, Liverpool Polytechnic, Manchester Polytechnic, Middlesex Polytechnic, Newcastle upon Tyne Polytechnic, North East London Polytechnic, Polytechnic of North London, North Staffordshire Polytechnic, Preston Polytechnic, Polytechnic of the South Bank, Trent Polytechnic and Wolverhampton Polytechnic; and Polytechnic of Wales.

Qualifications for Barrister are obtainable only at one of the Inns of Court or Faculty of Advocates; for Solicitor, from the Law Society or its equivalent in Scotland or Ireland.

THE INNS OF COURT
THE SENATE OF THE INNS OF COURT AND THE BAR
11 South Square, Gray's Inn, WC1R 5EL

The governing body of the Barristers' branch of the legal profession, established in 1974 assuming the functions of the former Senate of the Four Inns of Court and the former General Council of the Bar.
President, The Rt. Hon. Lord Justice Browne-Wilkinson.
Chairman, D. Calcutt, Q.C.
Treasurer, A. Park, Q.C.
Secretary, Sir Arthur Power, K.C.B., M.B.E.

THE INNER TEMPLE, E.C.4

Treasurer (1984), The Lord Rawlinson of Ewell, P.C., Q.C.
Sub-Treasurer, Rear. Adm. T. B. Homan, C.B.
Deputy Sub-Treasurer, Miss J. Morris.
Master of the Library, The Hon. Mr. Justice Hobhouse.

THE MIDDLE TEMPLE, E.C.4

Treasurer (1984), The Lord Justice Ackner, P.C.
Under-Treasurer, Rear Adm. J. R. Hill.
Deputy Under-Treasurer, P. F. Gee.

LINCOLN'S INN, W.C.2

Treasurer (1984), Master Ian Warren.
Master of the Library, Mr. Justice Warner.
Under-Treasurer, Capt. P. M. Carver.
Deputy do., E. M. T. Segar.

GRAY'S INN, W.C.1

Treasurer (1984), His Honour Judge Gibbens, Q.C.
Master of Library, L. Caplan, Q.C.
Under-Treasurer, Rear Adm. C. M. Bevan, C.B.
Deputy do., P. A. A. Simmonds.

COUNCIL OF LEGAL EDUCATION
Gray's Inn Place, WC1R 5DX

Established by the four Inns of Court to superintend the Education and Examination of Students for the Bar of England and Wales.

Chairman, The Hon. Mr. Justice Bingham.
Vice-Chairman and Chairman, Board of Studies, The Hon. Mr. Justice Hobhouse.
Vice-Chairman and Chairman of the Finance Committee, His Hon. Judge E. F. Monier-Williams.
Inns of Court School of Law, Dean of Faculty, C. A. Morrison, Q.C.
Sub-Dean, E. Tenenbaum.

FACULTY OF ADVOCATES
Advocates' Library, Edinburgh EH1 1RF

Application for admission as an Advocate of the Scottish Bar is made by Petition to the Court of Session. The candidate is remitted for examination to the Faculty of Advocates. Enquiries should be addressed to The Clerk of Faculty.
Dean of Faculty, W. D. Prosser, Q.C.
Vice-Dean, J. A. Cameron, Q.C.
Treasurer, A. C. M. Johnston, Q.C.
Clerk of Faculty, N. M. P. Morrison.
Keeper of the Library, J. T. Cameron, Q.C.
Law Agent, P. C. Millar.

NORTHERN IRELAND
Admission to the Bar of Northern Ireland is controlled by the Honorable Society of the Inn of Court of Northern Ireland (established Jan. 11, 1926), Royal Courts of Justice, Belfast BT1 3JF.
Treasurer (1984), His Honour Judge Pringle, Q.C.
Under-Treasurer and Librarian, J. A. L. McLean, Q.C.

THE LAW SOCIETY
113 Chancery Lane, WC2A 1LP

The Society controls the education and examination of articled clerks, and the admission of solicitors in England and Wales. It also regulates professional standards and conduct. Number of members, over 40,000.
President of the Society (1984–85), A. H. Hoole.
Vice-President (1984–85), C. A. B. Leslie.
Secretary-General, J. L. Bowron.
Secretaries, D. Edwards (*Deputy Sec. Gen., and Legal Aid*); G. C. E. Snowling (*Education and Training*); J. M. D. Hoyle (*Professional Purposes*); G. Lee (*Professional and Public Relations* and *Professional Development*); A. J. Merrett (*Finance and Administration*); M. T. Sennett (*Contentious Business*); M. C. Leaf (*Non-Contentious Business*); H. Adamson (*Law Reform and International Relations*); Mrs. A. N. Brice (*Council Business*).

THE COLLEGE OF LAW, Braboeuf Manor, St. Catherine's, Guildford, Surrey GU3 1HA (and at 33–35 Lancaster Gate, W2 3LU, 2 Breams Buildings, Chancery Lane, EC4A 1DP, and Christleton Hall, Chester CH3 7AB), provides courses for The Law Society examinations.

LAW SOCIETY OF SCOTLAND
Law Society's Hall, 26 Drumsheugh Gardens, Edinburgh EH3 7YR

The Society comprises all practising solicitors in Scotland. It controls the examination of legal trainees and the admission of solicitors in Scotland and acts as registrar of solicitors under the Solicitors (Scotland) Act, 1980.

The Law Society of Scotland administers the Legal Aid and Advice Scheme set up under the Legal Aid and Advice (Scotland) Acts, 1967 and 1972.
President of the Society (1984–85), G. R. G. Graham.
Secretary, K. W. Pritchard.
Secretary (*Legal Education*), Mrs. C. Slater.

LIBRARIANSHIP AND INFORMATION SCIENCE

First Degrees are granted by the University of Belfast (*Library and Information Studies*), Loughborough University of Technology (*Library Studies*), and the University of Wales (Aberystwyth) (*Librarianship*) (jointly with the College of Librarianship, Wales), and by the University of Strathclyde (*Librarianship* with another subject).

Courses leading to first degrees in *Librarianship* or *Library Studies* granted by the Council for National Academic Awards are provided by City of Birmingham Polytechnic, Brighton Polytechnic, Ealing College of Higher Education, Leeds Polytechnic, Liverpool Polytechnic, Manchester Polytechnic, Newcastle upon Tyne Polytechnic, Polytechnic of North London (*Librarianship and Information Studies*) and Robert Gordon's Institute of Technology; and in *Information Science* by Leeds Polytechnic.

The Library Association, 7 Ridgmount Street, WC1E 7AE, maintains the professional register of Chartered Librarians (Fellows and Associates).

MATERIALS STUDIES (including Metallurgy)

First Degrees in *Metallurgy* and/or *Metallurgical Engineering* are granted by the following universities: Birmingham (*Metallurgy and Materials*), Brunel, Cambridge (*Metallurgy and Materials Science*), Leeds, Liverpool, London (Imperial College of Science and Technology: *Metallurgy and Materials*), Manchester and Manchester Institute of Science and Technology, Newcastle upon Tyne, Nottingham (*Metallurgy and Materials Science*), Oxford (*Metallurgy and Science of Materials*), Salford (*Engineering Metallurgy*), Sheffield, Strathclyde, Surrey, Wales (University Colleges at Cardiff (also *Metallurgy and Materials Science*) and Swansea). First Degrees in *Materials Science, Materials Technology, or Materials Science and Technology* are granted by the following universities: Bath, Birmingham (also *Metallurgy and Materials*), Brunel, Cambridge (*Metallurgy and Materials Science*), Leeds, Liverpool, London (Imperial College of Science and Technology: *Metallurgy and Materials*, Queen Mary College), Loughborough (*Materials Engineering*), Manchester and Manchester Institute of Science and Technology, Newcastle upon Tyne, Nottingham (*Metallurgy and Materials Science*), Oxford (*Metallurgy and Science of Materials*), Sheffield, Strathclyde (*Science of Engineering Materials*), Surrey and Wales (University College, Swansea, and (*Metallurgy and Materials Science*) Cardiff). First Degrees in *Polymer Technology/Polymer Science* are granted by London (Queen Mary College) and Sheffield. First Degrees in *Ceramics Science and Engineering/Technology* are granted by the Universities of Leeds and Sheffield.

Courses leading to first degrees in *Metallurgy* or *Metallurgy and Materials* or *Materials Science/Technology* granted by the Council for National Academic Awards are provided by the City of London Polytechnic, Coventry (Lanchester) Polytechnic, Sheffield City Polytechnic (*Metallurgy and Microstructural Engineering*), Sunderland Polytechnic, Thames Polytechnic. Courses leading to first degrees in *Polymer Science and Technology* granted by the Council for National Academic Awards are provided by Manchester Polytechnic and the Polytechnic of North London; and in *Mineral Processing Technology* by Camborne School of Mines.

THE INSTITUTION OF METALLURGISTS, P.O. Box 471, 1 Carlton House Terrace, S.W.1, is a qualifying body.

MATHEMATICS

First Degrees in *Mathematics* and/or *Applied Mathematics* are granted by all universities.

Courses leading to first degrees in *Mathematics* granted by the Council for National Academic Awards are provided by a dozen Polytechnics and Colleges.

MEDICINE

First Degrees in *Medicine and Surgery* are granted by the Universities of Aberdeen, Belfast, Birmingham, Bristol, Cambridge, Dundee, Edinburgh, Glasgow, Leeds, Leicester, Liverpool, London (medical schools/colleges:— Charing Cross and Westminster M.S., King's College S.M.D., London H.M.C., Middlesex H.M.S., Royal Free H.M.S., St. Bart's. H.M.C., St. George's H.M.S., St. Mary's H.M.S., United M.D.S. (Guy's and St. Thomas's), University College), Manchester, Newcastle upon Tyne, Nottingham, Oxford, Sheffield, Southampton, Wales (University College, Cardiff, and Welsh National School of Medicine).

MEDICAL SCHOOLS OF THE UNIVERSITY OF LONDON

CHARING CROSS AND WESTMINSTER MEDICAL SCHOOL, The Reynolds Building, St. Dunstan's Road, W6 8RP; Horseferry Road, Westminster, SW1P 2AR.— *Dean*, Prof. T. W. Glenister, C.B.E., T.D., D.S.C.; *Secretary*, G. K. Buckley.

THE LONDON HOSPITAL MEDICAL COLLEGE, Turner Street, E1 2AD.—*Dean*, Prof. M. A. Floyer, M.A., M.D., F.R.C.P.; *Secretary*, D. L. Edwards.

THE MIDDLESEX HOSPITAL MEDICAL SCHOOL, Mortimer Street, W1P 7PN.—*Dean*, W. W. Slack, M.A., F.R.C.S.; *Secretary*, Dr. D. Sanders.

ROYAL FREE HOSPITAL SCHOOL OF MEDICINE, Rowland Hill Street, NW3 2PF.—*Dean*, B. B. MacGillivray, F.R.C.P.; *Secretary*, G. W. Fenn, M.A.

ST. BARTHOLOMEW'S HOSPITAL MEDICAL COLLEGE, West Smithfield, EC1A 7BE.—*Dean*, Dr. I. Kelsey Fry, D.M., F.R.C.P.; *Secretary*, D. J. Brown, M.B.E., M.A.

ST. GEORGE'S HOSPITAL MEDICAL SCHOOL, Cranmer Terrace, Tooting, SW17 0RE.—*Dean*, R. J. West, M.D., F.R.C.P., D.Ch.; *Secretary*, R. B. Hill, M.A., M.SC.

ST. MARY'S HOSPITAL MEDICAL SCHOOL, Norfolk Place, Paddington, W2 1PG.—*Dean*, Prof. P. Richards, M.A., Ph.D., M.D., F.R.C.P.; *Secretary*, K. Lockyer.

UNITED MEDICAL AND DENTAL SCHOOLS OF GUY'S AND ST. THOMAS'S HOSPITALS, Guy's Campus: London Bridge, SE1 9RT; Leicester Square Campus: 32 Leicester Square, W.C.2; St. Thomas's Campus: Lambeth Palace Road, SE1 7EH.—*Deans*, B. Creamer, M.D., F.R.C.P., Prof. T. J. H. Clark, M.D., F.R.C.P.; *Dean of Dental Studies*, Prof. W. J. Tulley, PH.D.; *Secretary*, D. G. Bompas, C.M.G., M.A.

POSTGRADUATE MEDICAL SCHOOLS OF THE UNIVERSITY OF LONDON

LONDON SCHOOL OF HYGIENE AND TROPICAL MEDICINE, Keppel Street, WC1E 7HT. C. E. Gordon Smith, C.B., M.D., F.R.C.P., *Dean*.

ROYAL POSTGRADUATE MEDICAL SCHOOL, Du Cane Road, W.12. Dr. D. N. S. Kerr, F.R.C.P., *Dean*.

BRITISH POSTGRADUATE MEDICAL FEDERATION (University of London), 33 Millman Street, WC1N 3EJ. D. Innes Williams M.D., M.Chir., F.R.C.S., *Director*. Comprises:—

INSTITUTE OF BASIC MEDICAL SCIENCES, 35–45 Lincoln's Inn Fields, WC2A 3PN. Prof. G. P. Lewis, *Academic Dean*.

INSTITUTE OF CANCER RESEARCH, Fulham Road, S.W.3. Prof. A. M. Neville, PH.D., M.D., *Dean.*

CARDIOTHORACIC INSTITUTE, Fulham Road, SW3 6HP. Prof. Margaret Turner-Warwick, *Dean.*

INSTITUTE OF CHILD HEALTH, 30 Guilford Street, W.C.1. Prof. O. H. Wolff, M.D., F.R.C.P., *Dean.*

INSTITUTE OF DENTAL SURGERY, Eastman Dental Hospital, Gray's Inn Road, WC1X 8LD. Prof. G. B. Winter, D.ch., F.D.S.R.C.S., *Dean.*

INSTITUTE OF DERMATOLOGY, St. John's Hospital for Diseases of the Skin, Lisle Street, W.C.2. Prof. E. Wilson Jones, F.R.C.P., F.R.C.Path, *Dean.*

INSTITUTE OF LARYNGOLOGY AND OTOLOGY, Royal National Throat, Nose and Ear Hospital, 330–336 Gray's Inn Road, WC1X 8EE. P. McKelvie, F.R.C.S., *Dean.*

INSTITUTE OF NEUROLOGY, National Hospital, Queen Square, WC1N 3BG. Prof. J. Marshall, D.SC., M.D., F.R.C.P., *Dean.*

INSTITUTE OF OBSTETRICS AND GYNÆCOLOGY, Queen Charlotte's Maternity Hospital, Goldhawk Road, W6 0XG. Prof. Sir John Dewhurst, F.R.S.E., F.R.C.O.G., *Dean.*

INSTITUTE OF OPHTHALMOLOGY, Judd Street, WC1H 9QS. B. S. Jay, M.D., F.R.C.S., *Dean.*

INSTITUTE OF ORTHOPÆDICS, Royal National Orthopædic Hospital, Brockley Hill, Stanmore, Middx. HA7 4LP. E. L. Trickey, F.R.C.S., *Dean.*

INSTITUTE OF PSYCHIATRY, De Crespigny Park, Denmark Hill, SE5 8AF. Dr. R. M. Murray, M.D., M.R.C.Psych., *Dean.*

INSTITUTE OF UROLOGY, 172 Shaftsbury Avenue, WC2H 8JE. J. P. Pryor, F.R.C.S., *Dean.*

Licensing Corporations granting Diplomas

THE ROYAL COLLEGE OF PHYSICIANS OF LONDON AND THE ROYAL COLLEGE OF SURGEONS OF ENGLAND, Examining Board in England, Lincoln's Inn Fields, WC2A 3PN.

THE SOCIETY OF APOTHECARIES, Black Friars Lane, EC4V 6EJ.

ROYAL COLLEGE OF OBSTETRICIANS AND GYNÆCOLOGISTS, 27 Sussex Place, Regent's Park, N.W.1.

THE ROYAL COLLEGE OF PHYSICIANS OF EDINBURGH, 9 Queen Street, Edinburgh EH2 1JQ.

THE ROYAL COLLEGE OF SURGEONS OF EDINBURGH, Nicolson Street, Edinburgh EH8 9DW.

THE ROYAL COLLEGE OF PHYSICIANS AND SURGEONS OF GLASGOW, 234–242 St. Vincent Street, Glasgow G2 5RJ.

THE SCOTTISH TRIPLE QUALIFICATION BOARD, Nicolson Street, Edinburgh EH8 9DW and 242 St. Vincent Street, Glasgow.

Professions Supplementary to Medicine

The standard of professional education in chiropody, dietetics, medical laboratory sciences, occupational therapy, orthoptics, physiotherapy, radiography and remedial gymnastics is the responsibility of eight professional boards, which also publish an annual register of qualified practitioners. The work of the Boards is co-ordinated and supervised by The Council for Professions Supplementary to Medicine (Park House, 184 Kennington Park Road, SE11 4BU).

CHIROPODY

Professional qualifications are granted by the Society of Chiropodists, 53 Welbeck Street, W1M 7HE, to students who have passed the qualifying examination after attending a course of full-time training for three years at one of the nine recognized schools in England and Wales, two in Scotland and one in Northern Ireland. Qualifications granted by the Society are approved by the Chiropodists Board for the purpose of State Registration, which is a condition of employment within the National Health Service.

DIETETICS
(*See* main heading, p. 522)

MEDICAL LABORATORY SCIENCE

First Degrees in *Medical Laboratory Science* are granted by the University of Ulster.

Courses leading to first degrees in Medical Laboratory Science granted by the Council for National Academic Awards are provided by Portsmouth Polytechnic.

Qualifications from higher or further education establishments and training in medical laboratories are required for progress to the professional examinations and qualifications of the Institute of Medical Laboratory Sciences, 12 Queen Anne Street, W1M 0AU.

OCCUPATIONAL HYGIENE

Courses leading to first degrees in *Occupational Hygiene* granted by the Council for National Academic Awards are provided by the Polytechnic of the South Bank.

OCCUPATIONAL THERAPY

Professional qualifications are awarded after examination by the College of Occupational Therapists, 20 Rede Place, Bayswater, W.2, which recognizes 16 training schools in England, Wales, Scotland, N. Ireland and Eire.

ORTHOPTICS

Orthoptists undertake the diagnosis and treatment of all types of squint and other anomalies of binocular vision, working in close collaboration with ophthalmologists. The training and maintenance of professional standards are the responsibility of the Orthoptists Board of the Council for the Professions Supplementary to Medicine. The examining and qualifying body is the British Orthoptic Council. Training consists of a three-year course at one of 10 approved Orthoptic Schools in England and Wales and 1 in Scotland.

The Professional Association is the British Orthoptic Society, Norvic House, Hilton Street, Manchester. The registered office of the Council is at Manchester University Department of Ophthalmology, Lister House, Nelson Street, Manchester M13 9PL.

(*See also* under Ophthalmic Optics.)

PHYSIOTHERAPY

First Degrees are granted by the University of Ulster.

Courses leading to first degrees in *Physiotherapy* granted by the Council for National Academic Awards are provided by North East London Polytechnic and the Queen's College.

Full-time three- or four-year degree or diploma courses available at 32 recognised Schools in the U.K. Examinations leading to Membership of the Chartered Society of Physiotherapy and to State Registration. Information from The Chartered Society of Physiotherapy, 14 Bedford Row, London W.C.1.

RADIOGRAPHY AND RADIOTHERAPY

Examinations leading to qualification are conducted by The College of Radiographers, 14 Upper Wimpole Street, W.1.

There are recognized training centres in radiography and radiotherapy at many cities and towns in England and Wales, Scotland and Northern Ireland.

In London courses are available at the London Teaching Hospitals listed on p. 527; and at Hammersmith, St. Thomas' and Royal Northern Hospitals, at Bromley and Greenwich.

METEOROLOGY

First Degrees in *Meteorology* are granted by the University of Reading. The subject is also included in degree courses at some other universities.

MINING AND MINING ENGINEERING

First Degrees in *Mining* or *Mining Engineering* are granted by the following universities: Birmingham (*Minerals Engineering*), Leeds (also *Mineral Engineering*), London (Imperial College of Science and Technology (also *Mineral Technology*)), Newcastle upon Tyne, Nottingham, Strathclyde (*Mining and Petroleum Engineering*), Wales (University College, Cardiff: also *Mineral Processing*).

Courses leading to first degrees granted by the Council for National Academic Awards are provided by Camborne School of Mines (*Mining* and *Mineral Processing Technology*) and North Staffordshire Polytechnic (*Mining Engineering*).

Miscellaneous Authorities

THE INSTITUTION OF MINING ENGINEERS, Danum House, 6A South Parade, Doncaster DN1 2DY.

THE ENGINEERING COUNCIL, Canberra House, Maltravers Street, W.C.2.

MUSIC

First Degrees in *Music* are granted by the Universities of Aberdeen, Bath (course at Bath College of Higher Education), Belfast, Birmingham, Bristol, Cambridge, City, Durham, East Anglia, Edinburgh, Exeter, Glasgow (also *Music Education* and *Music Performance* in conjunction with Royal Scottish Academy of Music and Drama), Hull, Lancaster, Leeds (also at Bretton Hall College), Leicester (*Musicianship*), Liverpool, London (King's College, Royal Holloway College; *also* Goldsmiths' College, Royal Academy of Music, Royal College of Music, and Trinity College of Music), Manchester, Newcastle upon Tyne, Nottingham, Oxford, Reading, Sheffield, Southampton, Stirling, Surrey, Sussex, Ulster, Wales (University Colleges at Aberystwyth, Bangor and Cardiff; also at Welsh College of Music and Drama), and York.

Courses leading to first degrees in Music granted by the Council for National Academic Awards are provided by City of Birmingham Polytechnic, Colchester Institute, Dartington College of Arts, Huddersfield Polytechnic and Kingston Polytechnic (*Music Education*).

ASSOCIATED BOARD OF THE ROYAL SCHOOLS OF MUSIC
14 Bedford Square, WC1B 3JG

Conducts the local examinations in music and speech for the four Royal Schools of Music—the Royal Academy of Music and the Royal College of Music in London, the Royal Northern College of Music, Manchester and the Royal Scottish Academy of Music and Drama, Glasgow.
Chief Exec. and Dir. of Examinations, R. Smith.

ROYAL ACADEMY OF MUSIC (1822)
Marylebone Road, N.W.1

Full training facilities are provided for students seeking a professional career in all branches of music.

Courses lead to Professional Certificate, G.R.S.M. (Hons) or B.Mus. (London) after three years' full time study. Dip.R.A.M. (Performers) may be obtained after four years. The L.R.A.M. Diploma is open to both internal and external candidates.
Principal, D. Lumsden, M.A., D.PHIL., MUS.B.
Administrator, J. Bliss.
Warden, P. James, PH.D., B.MUS.

ROYAL COLLEGE OF MUSIC (1883)
Prince Consort Road, South Kensington, S.W.7

M.MUS., B.MUS., G.R.S.M., DIP.R.C.M. and A.R.C.M. awarded by examination.
No. of Students, 600.
Director, M. G. Matthews, F.R.C.M., A.R.C.O.
Vice-Director, I. Horsbrugh.
Registrar, J. Thorogood.
Bursar, A. P. Millar.

GUILDHALL SCHOOL OF MUSIC AND DRAMA (1880)
Silk Street, Barbican, EC2Y 8DT

Full-time and part-time courses in Music, Speech, Drama and Stage Management. Awards Diplomas of Graduate (G.G.S.M.), Associate (A.G.S.M.) and Licentiate (L.G.S.M.). The Diploma of Graduate (G.G.S.M.) carries graduate honours status.
Principal, J. Hosier, C.B.E., F.R.C.M.
Director of Drama, T. Church.
Director of Music, L. East.
Director of Administration, G. Derbyshire.

TRINITY COLLEGE OF MUSIC (1872)
11–13 Mandeville Place, W1M 6AQ

Complete training in music for teachers and performers. Courses lead to the university degree of B.MUS., the Graduate Diploma which carries Graduate Honours status, the Teacher's Diploma in Music and the Performer's Diploma in Music.
Principal, M. Davies, C.B.E., F.R.C.M.
Vice-Principal, C. Cork.
Dir. of Examinations, D. Gulliver.

LONDON COLLEGE OF MUSIC
47 Great Marlborough Street, W1V 2AS

Comprehensive full-time musical training for performers and teachers. Graduate Course recognised by the Dept. of Education and Science and Burnham Committee.
Director, J. McCabe, MUS.B., F.R.C.M.
Secretary, K. R. Beard.

ROYAL COLLEGE OF ORGANISTS (1864)
Kensington Gore, SW7 2QS

For the promotion of the highest standard in organ playing and choir-training. Awards Diplomas of Associateship (A.R.C.O.) and Fellowship (F.R.C.O.); and Choir-Training (CHM).
Clerk, K. B. Lyndon.

BIRMINGHAM SCHOOL OF MUSIC
Paradise Circus, Birmingham B3 3HG
Head, L. Carus.

THE JOHN CURWEN SOCIETY
108 Battersea High Street, SW11 3HP

International examining body maintaining the Curwen Institute (1975).

ROYAL SCHOOL OF CHURCH MUSIC
Addington Palace, Croydon CR9 5AD
Founded (1927) for the advancement of good
music in the Church.

Director, L. Dakers, C.B.E., D.MUS., F.R.C.O., F.R.A.M.
Secretary, V. E. Waterhouse.

ROYAL NORTHERN COLLEGE OF MUSIC
124 Oxford Road, Manchester M13 9RD

Principal, J. Manduell, C.B.E., F.R.A.M., F.R.N.C.M.,
F.R.C.M., F.R.S.A.M.D.

ROYAL MILITARY SCHOOL OF MUSIC
Kneller Hall, Twickenham TW2 7DU (42)

Commandant, Col. D. J. St. J. Loftus, O.B.E.
Director of Music and Chief Instructor, Lt.-Col. D. R.
Beat, M.V.O.

ROYAL MARINES SCHOOL OF MUSIC
Deal, Kent CT14 7EH

Commandant, Lt.-Col. E. D. Watson, R.M.
Principal Director of Music, Lt.-Col. G. A. C. Hoskins,
M.V.O., A.R.A.M., R.M. (Nine Bands in Commission in
1983).

ROYAL SCOTTISH ACADEMY OF MUSIC AND
DRAMA
St. George's Place, Glasgow G2 1BS (725)

Curriculum provides for all branches of study
necessary for entry into the professions of music and
drama. Special Degree Courses for those who wish to
teach music and drama in schools.
Principal, P. Ledger, MUS.B., L.R.A.M.

NAUTICAL STUDIES
(*See also* Fishery Science)

The University of Wales grants first degrees in
Maritime Technology, Maritime Commerce and *Mar-
itime Geography* (courses at Institute of Science and
Technology).

Courses leading to first degrees in *Nautical Studies*
granted by the Council for National Academic
Awards are provided by Liverpool Polytechnic (*Maritime Studies*), Plymouth Polytechnic and Sunderland Polytechnic.

Merchant Navy Training Schools
For Officers

MERCHANT NAVY COLLEGE, Greenhithe, Kent DA9
9NY.—*Principal*, G. Emmons, M.SC., PH.D.
THE COLLEGE OF NAUTICAL STUDIES, Warsash,
Southampton. *Director*, Capt. C. N. Phelan.

For Seamen

INDEFATIGABLE AND NAUTICAL SEA TRAINING SCHOOL
FOR BOYS (Independent; in receipt of government
grant (Residential)), Plas Llanfair, Llanfairpwll,
Anglesey (150); *Captain Headmaster*, Capt. R. T.
Youngman; *Sec.*, L. R. Ridyard, Room 22, Oriel
Chambers, 14 Water Street, Liverpool, 2.
NATIONAL SEA TRAINING COLLEGE, Denton, Graves-
end, Kent. *Princ.*, Capt. P. H. Adlam.

NURSING

Courses in which academic study at a University
may be combined with nursing training/practical
nursing in hospitals are provided by the following universities: Brunel (*Mental Nursing*), City,
Edinburgh, Glasgow, Hull, Liverpool, London (Gold-

smiths', King's and Queen Mary Colleges),
Manchester, Southampton, Surrey, Ulster and Wales
(Welsh National School of Medicine).

Courses leading to first degrees in *Nursing* granted
by the Council for National Academic Awards are
provided by Bristol Polytechnic, Dundee College of
Technology, Glasgow College of Technology, Leeds
Polytechnic, Queen Margaret College, Sheffield City
Polytechnic and Polytechnic of the South Bank.

Three-year courses for State Registration in general, sick children's mental and mental deficiency
nursing. Two-year course for State enrolment.
Training schools in many parts of Great Britain.

THE ROYAL COLLEGE OF NURSING
OF THE UNITED KINGDOM
20 Cavendish Square, W1M 0AB

The Royal College of Nursing, within its Institute
of Advanced Nursing Education, provides education
at post-basic level in hospital, occupational health
and community health fields. Advanced courses are
held in preparation for senior posts in administration
and teaching; and other short and special courses.
Director of Education, Miss M. D. Green.

NATIONAL BOARDS FOR NURSING,
MIDWIFERY AND HEALTH VISITING
FOR ENGLAND
170 Tottenham Court Road, W1P 0HA
Chief Exec., Dr. E. Bendall.

FOR SCOTLAND
22 Queen Street, Edinburgh EH2 1JX
Chief Exec., Miss M. W. Thomson.

FOR WALES
Pearl Assurance House, Greyfriars Road,
Cardiff CF1 3AG
Chief Exec., W. Preece.

FOR NORTHERN IRELAND
79 Chichester Street, Belfast BT1 4JE
Chief Exec., Mrs. M. P. Scott.

OPHTHALMIC OPTICS

First Degrees in *Ophthalmic Optics* are granted by
the following Universities: Aston in Birmingham,
Bradford, City, Manchester (Manchester Institute of
Science and Technology), and Wales (Institute of
Science and Technology). Courses leading to first
degrees in *Ophthalmic Optics* granted by the Council
for National Academic Awards are provided by the
Glasgow College of Technology.

Examining bodies granting qualifications as an
ophthalmic or dispensing optician:—
THE BRITISH COLLEGE OF OPHTHALMIC OPTICIANS
(OPTOMETRISTS), 10 Knaresborough Place, SW5
0TG.
THE ASSOCIATION OF DISPENSING OPTICIANS, 22 Not-
tingham Place, W1M 4AT (training institution;
qualification as dispensing optician).
FACULTY OF DISPENSING OPTICIANS, Apothecaries'
Hall, Blackfriars Lane, EC4V 6EL.

OSTEOPATHY

LONDON COLLEGE OF OSTEOPATHIC MEDICINE (Incorporating London College of Osteopathy), 8–10
Boston Place, N.W.1.

PHARMACY

First Degrees in *Pharmacy* are granted by the
Universities of Aston in Birmingham, Bath, Belfast,
Bradford, Heriot-Watt, London (King's College and
the School of Pharmacy), Manchester, Nottingham,

Strathclyde, Wales (Institute of Science and Technology).

Courses leading to first degrees in Pharmacy granted by the Council for National Academic Awards are provided by Brighton Polytechnic, Leicester Polytechnic, Liverpool Polytechnic, Portsmouth Polytechnic, Robert Gordon's Institute of Technology, and Sunderland Polytechnic.

Further information may be obtained from The Registrar, The Pharmaceutical Society of Great Britain, 1 Lambeth High Street, SE1 7JN.

PHOTOGRAPHY, FILM AND TV STUDIES

First Degrees in *Film and Media Studies* are granted by the University of Stirling. At some other universities *Film* may be studied as part of a first degree course.

Courses leading to first degrees granted by the Council for National Academic Awards are provided by Derbyshire College of Higher Education (*Photographic Studies*), Harrow College of Higher Education (*Applied Photography, Film and TV*), London College of Printing (*Photography, Film and TV*), Polytechnic of Central London (*Film and Photographic Arts* and *Photographic Sciences*), Trent Polytechnic (*Photography*), West Surrey College of Art and Design (*Photography, Film and Video, Animation*).

BRITISH INSTITUTE OF PROFESSIONAL PHOTOGRAPHY, Amwell End, Ware, Herts. SG12 9HN.—*Secretary*, P. A. Large.

PRINTING

First Degrees in *Typography and Graphic Communication* are awarded by the University of Reading.

Courses leading to first degrees in *Printing and Packaging Technology* granted by the Council for National Academic Awards are provided by Watford College of Technology.

Courses in technical and general, design and administrative aspects of printing are available at technical colleges throughout the United Kingdom. Details can be obtained from the Institute of Printing and the British Printing Industries Federation (*see below*).

In addition to the examining and organizing bodies listed below, examinations are held by various independent regional examining boards in further education.

INSTITUTE OF PRINTING (1961), 8 Lonsdale Gardens, Tunbridge Wells, Kent TN1 1NU.

JOINT COMMITTEE (AND SCOTTISH JOINT COMMITTEE) FOR NATIONAL CERTIFICATES IN PRINTING.

BRITISH PRINTING INDUSTRIES FEDERATION, 11 Bedford Row, WC1R 4DX.

RECREATION, SPORT, AND HUMAN MOVEMENT STUDIES

(*See also* Dance)

First Degrees are granted by the University of Birmingham (*Physical Education*), by Loughborough University of Technology (*Physical Education and Sports Science*; also *Physical Education, Sports Science and Recreation Management*) and Ulster (*Sports Studies*).

Courses in *Sports Science/Studies* leading to first degrees granted by the Council for National Academic Awards are provided by Bedford College of Higher Education, Brighton Polytechnic, Crewe and Alsagar College of Higher Education, Liverpool Polytechnic, Newcastle upon Tyne Polytechnic with Sunderland Polytechnic, North Staffordshire Polytechnic (*Sport and Recreation Studies*), Sheffield City

Polytechnic, Trent Polytechnic (*Sport—Administration and Science*) and West Sussex Institute of Higher Education; and in *Recreation* by Dunfermline College of Physical Education, College of St. Mark and St. John (*Recreation and Community*), and West Midlands College of Higher Education (*Leisure and Recreational Studies*).

First degrees in *Human Movement Studies* or *Movement Studies* are granted by the University of Kent at Canterbury (courses at Nonington College), the University of Wales (courses at South Glamorgan Institute of Higher Education) and the Council for National Academic Awards (courses at Leeds Polytechnic: also *Leisure Studies*).

Physical Education and *Sports Science/Studies* also form part of a degree course at many other colleges/polytechnics.

ROBOTICS

(*See also* Computer Science)

First Degrees in *Electronic Control and Robot Engineering* are granted by the University of Hull.

SOCIAL WORK

First Degrees in *Social Studies* or in *Social Sciences* are granted by most universities. Courses leading to first degrees in *Social Science* or *Social Sciences/ Applied Social Science or Sociology* granted by the Council for National Academic Awards are provided by some 30 polytechnics and colleges.

Courses leading to first degrees in *Health and Community Studies* granted by the University of Liverpool are provided by Chester College; and courses leading to first degrees in *Public Service Studies* granted by the University of Manchester are provided by Manchester Polytechnic. Courses leading to first degrees in *Community Studies* granted by the Council for National Academic Awards are provided by Bradford and Ilkley Community College.

CENTRAL COUNCIL FOR EDUCATION AND TRAINING IN SOCIAL WORK, Derbyshire House, St. Chad's Street, London WC1H 8AD.—*Dir.*, Miss P. H. F. Young, C.B.E. The Council is an independent body financed by the Government. It has statutory authority throughout the U.K. to promote education and training for social work and for certain other kinds of work in the personal social services. It recognizes or approves courses, schemes or programmes. The C.C.E.T.S.W.'s award, the Certificate of Qualification in Social Work, is the professional qualification for social workers and courses that lead to it are available at universities, polytechnics, colleges and institutes.

BRITISH ASSOCIATION OF SOCIAL WORKERS, 16 Kent Street, Birmingham B5 6RD.

THE INSTITUTE OF HOUSING, 12 Upper Belgrave Street, S.W.1.—*Dir.*, P. J. McGurk.

SPEECH SCIENCE

(*See also* Languages)

First Degrees in *Speech* are awarded by the University of Newcastle upon Tyne, in *Speech Science* by the University of Sheffield, in *Speech Sciences* by the University of London (University College), in *Speech Pathology and Therapy* by the University of Manchester (and at Manchester Polytechnic), in *Speech Pathology and Therapeutics* (with courses at Jordanhill College of Education) by the University of Glasgow; and in *Speech Therapy* by the University of Ulster and (with courses at South Glamorgan Institute of Higher Education) by the University of Wales.

Courses leading to first degrees in *Speech Therapy* granted by the Council for National Academic

Awards are provided by Central School of Speech and Drama, City of Birmingham Polytechnic (*Speech and Language Pathology and Therapeutics*), Leeds Polytechnic, Leicester Polytechnic (*Speech Pathology and Therapy*) and Queen Margaret College (*Speech Pathology and Therapy*).

The Directory of qualified Speech Therapists is published by the College of Speech Therapists, Harold Poster House, 6 Lechmere Road, NW2 5BU. Courses leading to B.Sc.(Hons.) degree in Speech Therapy and Licentiateship of The College of Speech Therapists are available at:

THE CENTRAL SCHOOL OF SPEECH AND DRAMA (Department of Speech Therapy), Embassy Theatre, Swiss Cottage, NW3 3HY.

CITY OF BIRMINGHAM POLYTECHNIC SCHOOL OF SPEECH THERAPY, Perry Bar, Birmingham.

LEEDS POLYTECHNIC, School of Health and Applied Sciences, Speech Therapy Section, Calverley Street, Leeds LS1 3HE.

QUEEN MARGARET COLLEGE, Department of Speech Therapy, Clerwood Terrace, Edinburgh EH12 8TS.

CARDIFF SCHOOL OF SPEECH THERAPY, South Glamorgan Institute of Higher Education, Western Avenue, Cardiff.

LEICESTER POLYTECHNIC, School of Speech Pathology, Scraptoft, Leicester.

NATIONAL HOSPITALS COLLEGE OF SPEECH-SCIENCES, 59 Portland Place, W.1.

SURVEYING

(*See* Estate Management and Surveying)

TEACHING

There are now three main ways to gain the qualification needed to become a teacher:

(a) The first is to follow a three- or four-year course leading to a B.Ed. degree. B.Ed. courses are provided by nearly 80 colleges of education/institutes of higher education/polytechnics. The degrees are awarded either by universities or by the Council for National Academic Awards (C.N.A.A.).

(b) The second, for those who are already graduates with a degree other than a B.Ed., is to follow a one-year course leading to a postgraduate certificate in education.

(c) The third is to take a course at one of the few institutions, mainly universities, that offer concurrent courses (normally four years) leading to a degree (other than B.Ed.) *and* a teaching qualification.

TECHNICAL EDUCATION

First Degrees in one or more technologies are awarded by almost all universities; and many polytechnics and colleges of technology provide courses leading to first degrees granted by the Council for National Academic Awards. Details are given under individual subject headings.

(*See also:* Aeronautics; Building; Computer Science; Engineering; Fuel Technology; Mining; Optics; Patent Agency; Printing and Textiles.)

CITY AND GUILDS OF LONDON INSTITUTE
76 Portland Place, W1N 4AA

An independent educational organisation founded in 1878 and incorporated by Royal Charter. The Institute offers examinations on its published regulations and syllabuses, and awards certificates of prevocational and vocational training in a wide range of technical subjects. Its syllabuses are taught in secondary schools, colleges of further education, and other educational and training establishments in the United Kingdom and overseas. The Institute provides the administrative services for the National

Examinations Board for Supervisory Studies, and, with the Business and Technician Education Council, has established the Joint Board for Pre-Vocational Education.

President, H.R.H. the Duke of Edinburgh, K.G., K.T.
Chairman, H. M. Neal.
Director-General, H. Knutton, C.B.
Secretary, B. B. Phillips.
Dean of the City and Guilds College, Prof. H. Sawistowski.

TECHNICIAN EDUCATION COUNCIL
(*See* "Business and Technician Education Council" on page 520).

Regional Advisory Councils

Set up in 1947 (i) to bring education and industry together to find out the needs of young workers and advise on the provision required, and (ii) to secure reasonable economy of provision. They also have certain responsibilities in connection with the procedure for the approval by the Department of Education and Science of advanced courses, and issue handbooks, etc., giving, for the guidance of students and teachers, information about the facilities available within a region or district for various types of training (*e.g.* electrical engineering, textiles, building and chemistry). There are ten Regional Advisory Councils in England and Wales:—

1 (LONDON AND SOUTH EASTERN).—Regional Advisory Council for Technological Education, Tavistock House South, Tavistock Square, WC1H 9LR.
2 (SOUTHERN).—Regional Council for Further Education, 26 Bath Road, Reading RG1 6NT.
3 (SOUTH WEST).—Regional Council for Further Education, Wessex Lodge, 11–13 Billetfield, Taunton TA1 3NN.
4 (WEST MIDLANDS).—Advisory Council for Further Education, Norfolk House, Smallbrook Queensway, Birmingham B5 4NB.
5 (EAST MIDLANDS).—East Midlands Further Education Council, Robins Wood House, Robins Wood Road, Aspley, Nottingham NG8 3NH.
6 (EAST ANGLIAN).—Regional Advisory Council for Further Education, Shirehall, Bury St. Edmunds, Suffolk.
7 (YORKSHIRE AND HUMBERSIDE).—Association for Further and Higher Education, Bowling Green Terrace, Green Terrace, Leeds LS11 9SX.
8 (NORTH-WESTERN).—North Western Regional Advisory Council for Further Education (incorporating the Union of Lancashire and Cheshire Institutes), Town Hall, Walkden Road, Worsley, Manchester.
9 (NORTHERN).—Northern Council for Further Education, 5 Grosvenor Villas, Grosvenor Road, Newcastle upon Tyne NE2 2RU.
10 (WALES).—Welsh Joint Education Committee, 245 Western Avenue, Cardiff CF5 2YX.

Industry Training Boards

AGRICULTURAL, Bourne House, 32–34 Beckenham Road, Beckenham, Kent BR3 4PB.—*Dir.*, R. C. Swan.
CLOTHING AND ALLIED PRODUCTS, Tower House, Merrion Way, Leeds LS2 8NY.—*Director*, J. W. Dearden.
CONSTRUCTION, Radnor House, London Road, Norbury, SW16 4EL.—*Sec.*, G. R. Gardner.
ENGINEERING, 54 Clarendon Road, Watford, Herts. WD1 1LB.—*Sec.*, E. P. Jones.
HOTEL AND CATERING INDUSTRY TRAINING BOARD, Ramsey House, Central Square, Wembley, Middx. HA9 7AP.—*Sec.*, B. Smart.
LOCAL GOVERNMENT TRAINING BOARD, 4th Floor, Arndale Centre, Luton, Beds. LU1 2TS.—*Dir.*, M. Clarke.

MAN-MADE FIBRES INDUSTRY TRAINING ADVISORY BOARD, Langwood House, 63–81 High Street, Rickmansworth, Herts. WD3 1EQ.—*Gen. Manager*, D. W. Ashby.

OFFSHORE PETROLEUM, Forties Road, Montrose, Angus DD10 9ET.—*Sec.*, P. J. Bing, O.B.E.

PLASTICS PROCESSING, Brent House, 950 Great West Road, Brentford, Middx. TW8 9ES.—*Gen. Manager.*, D. Titterton.

ROAD TRANSPORT, Capitol House, Empire Way, Wembley, Middx.—*Dir. Gen.*, T. E. Tindall.

Industrial Training Foundation
91 Waterloo Road, S.W.1.

The Industrial Training Foundation provides a consultancy service to British and overseas governments, industry and commerce, on technical education and training. It is a non profit-making institution registered under the Charities Act and charges fees only to cover its costs. Its objectives are to promote the development of vocational and industrial education and training in its broadest sense.

ITF has acted for, or in association with, all relevant Government departments, and international and institutional bodies. It was formed in 1964 with British Government support and the experience gained in Britain was later put to use in developing training services for overseas countries.

ITF advises Governments and industry on the necessary steps for the institution, development and implementation of training programmes ranging from courses to cover a specific problem to fully integrated comprehensive projects.

TEXTILES

First Degrees in *Textiles* are awarded by the Universities of Leeds and Manchester (Manchester Institute of Science and Technology). Courses leading to first degrees in *Textile Marketing* granted by the Council for National Academic Awards are provided by Huddersfield Polytechnic; in *Textile Technology* by Leicester Polytechnic; in *Textile and Knitwear Technology* by Leicester Polytechnic; in *Textiles with Clothing Studies* by Scottish College of Textiles; in *Clothing Studies* by Manchester Polytechnic; in *Food, Textiles and Consumer Studies* by Polytechnic of the South Bank; and in various aspects of *Textiles/Fashion* by some 30 Polytechnics and Colleges.

THE TEXTILE INSTITUTE, 10 Blackfriars Street, Manchester M3 5DR.—*Gen. Sec.*, R. G. Denyer.

THEOLOGY

First Degrees in *Theology* or *Divinity* are granted by the Universities of Aberdeen, Belfast, Birmingham, Bristol (*Theology and Religious Studies*), Cambridge (*Theological and Religious Studies*), Durham, Edinburgh, Exeter, Glasgow, Hull, Kent at Canterbury, Leeds (*Theology and Religious Studies*), Liverpool (at Liverpool Institute of Higher Education), London (Heythrop and King's Colleges), Manchester, Nottingham, Oxford, St. Andrews, Southampton (at La Sainte Union College of Higher Education), and Wales (Aberystwyth, Bangor, Cardiff, and, also *Theology and Religious Studies*, St. David's University Colleges); in *Biblical Studies* by the Universities of London (King's College), Manchester, Newcastle upon Tyne, Sheffield and Wales (Bangor University College); and in *Religious Studies* by the Universities of Aberdeen, Bristol (*Theology and Religious Studies*), Cambridge (*Theological and Religious Studies*), Edinburgh, Lancaster, Leeds (*Theology and Religious Studies*), London (King's College), Newcastle upon Tyne, Stirling, and Wales (University College, Cardiff

and, *Theology and Religious Studies*, St. David's University College).

Courses leading to first degrees in *Theology* or *Theological Studies* granted by the Council for National Academic Awards are provided by Avery Hill College, London Bible College, Spurgeon's College, Trinity College, Bristol and Westminster College, Oxford; in *Theological and Pastoral Studies* by Oak Hill College; and in *Jewish Studies* by Jews' College.

Theological Colleges
Church of England and Church in Wales

BANGOR (University Anglican Chaplaincy) (Church Hostel) (28).—*Warden*, Rev. Canon B. C. Morgan.

BIRMINGHAM (Queen's Coll., Somerset Road, Edgbaston, B15 2QH) (70).—*Princ.*, Rev. G. S. Wakefield (Ecumenical College).

BRISTOL (Trinity College, BS9 1JP) (120).—*Princ.*, Rev. G. Carey, PH.D.

CAMBRIDGE (Ridley Hall, CB3 9HG) (56).—*Princ.*, Rev. H. F. de Waal.

CAMBRIDGE (Westcott House, Jesus Lane, CB5 8BP) (50).—*Princ.*, Rev. Dr. R. W. N. Hoare.

CHICHESTER (Westgate, PO19 3ES) (54).—*Princ.*, Rev. Canon J. W. Hind.

CUDDESDON (Ripon College, Oxon OX9 9EX) (70).—*Princ.*, Rev. Canon D. P. Wilcox.

DURHAM.—*See* University of Durham—St. Chad's; St. John's.

LAMPETER (St. David's College)—*See* University of Wales.

LINCOLN (Theological College, LN1 3BP) (70).—*Warden*, Rev. Canon F. H. A. Richmond.

LLANDAFF (St. Michael's, Cardiff CF5 2YJ) (35).—*Warden*, Rev. Canon J. G. Hughes, PH.D.

LONDON (King's College, W.C.2.).—*See* University of London.

MIRFIELD (College of the Resurrection, WF14 0BW) (43).—*Princ.*, Rev. D. Lloyd.

NOTTINGHAM (St. John's College, Bramcote, NG9 3DS) (132).—*Princ.*, Rev. Canon C. O. Buchanan.

OAK HILL (Southgate, N14 4PS) (80).—*Princ.*, Rev. Canon D. H. Wheaton.

OXFORD (St. Stephen's House, OX4 1JX) (58).—*Princ.*, Rev. D. Thomas.

OXFORD (Wycliffe Hall) (80).—*Princ.*, Rev. G. N. Shaw.

SALISBURY AND WELLS (19 The Close, Salisbury SP1 2EE) (150).—*Princ.*, Rev. Canon R. J. A. Askew.

Church of Scotland

ABERDEEN (Christ's Coll., AB1 1YD) (118).—*Master*, Rev. H. R. Sefton, PH.D.

EDINBURGH (New Coll., Faculty of Divinity, Univ. of Edinburgh, EH1 2LX) (280).—*Princ.*, Rev. Prof. A. C. Cheyne.

GLASGOW (Trinity Coll.) (106).—*Princ.*, Rev. Prof. R. Davidson, B.D.

ST. ANDREWS (College of St. Mary, University of St. Andrews) (170).—*Princ.*, Very Rev. W. McKane.

Scottish Episcopal Church

EDINBURGH (Rosebery Crescent, EH12 5JT) (28).—*Princ.*, Rev. Canon J. M. Armson.

Presbyterian

BELFAST (Union Theological Coll.) (40).—*Princ.*, Rev. Prof. E. A. Russell.

Presbyterian Church of Wales

ABERYSTWYTH (United Theological Coll.) (35).—*Princ.*, Rev. Prof. E. ap Nefydd Roberts.

Methodist

BELFAST (Edgehill Theological Coll.) (40).—*Princ.,* Rev. Dr. Dennis Cooke.

BRISTOL (Wesley Coll., Westbury-on-Trym) (55).—*Princ.,* Rev. Dr. W. D. Stacey.

CAMBRIDGE (Wesley House) (25).—*Princ.,* Rev. Dr. I. H. Jones.

Congregational and United Reformed

ABERYSTWYTH (Memorial College) (14).—*Princ.,* Rev. Dr. D. E. Davies.

BANGOR (Bala-Bangor Independent Coll., LL57 2EH) (16).—*Princ.,* R. T. Jones, D.Phil., D.D.

CAMBRIDGE (Westminster Coll., Madingley Road, CB3 0AB) (30).—*Princ.,* Rev. M. H. Cressey.

EDINBURGH (Scottish Congregational College, 9 Rosebery Crescent, EH12 5JT) (25).—*Princ.,* Rev. H. Smith.

MANCHESTER (Northern College, College Road, M16 8BP) (35).—*Princ.,* Rev. Dr. R. J. McKelvey.

OXFORD (Mansfield College) (140).—*Princ.,* D. A. Sykes, D.Phil.

Roman Catholic
(Colleges for the Diocesan Clergy)

ALLEN HALL, 28 Beaufort Street, Chelsea, S.W.3 (50).—*Rector,* Rt. Rev, Mgr. J. Coghlan.

GLASGOW (St. Peter's Coll., 33 Briar Road, Glasgow) (37).—*Rector,* Very Rev. M. Ward, PH.L.

OSCOTT COLL., Sutton Coldfield, West Midlands B73 5AA (93).—*Rector,* Rev. Father M. J. Kirkham.

OSTERLEY, Middlesex (Campion House, 112 Thornbury Road, TW7 4NN) (60).—*Superior,* Rev. D. Blackledge, S.J.

UPHOLLAND, Skelmersdale, Lancs. WN8 0PZ (now St. Joseph's College School and the Upholland Northern Institute for Adult Christian Education) (114).—*Pres.,* Rt. Rev. Bishop J. Rawsthorne.

USHAW (Durham DH7 9RH) (180).—*Pres.,* V. Rev. P. Walton.

WONERSH, Guildford GU5 0QX (St. John's) (70).—*Rector,* Rev. Mgr. H. C. Budd.

Baptist

BANGOR (North Wales Baptist Coll., LL57 2EH) (4).—*Princ.,* to be appointed.

BRISTOL (Baptist Coll., Woodland Road, BS8 1UN) (40).—*Pres.,* Rev. Dr. W. M. S. West.

CARDIFF (S. Wales Baptist Coll.) (16).—*Princ.,* D. G. Davies.

GLASGOW (The Scottish Baptist College, 12 Aytoun Road, G41 5RT) (17).—*Princ.,* Rev. G. W. Martin, PH.D.

LONDON (Spurgeon's Coll., South Norwood Hill, SE25 6DJ) (70).—*Princ.,* Rev. R. Brown, PH.D.

MANCHESTER (Northern Baptist College, Brighton Grove, Rusholme, M14 5JP) (affiliated to Manchester Univ.) (100).—*Princ.,* Rev. M. H. Taylor.

OXFORD (Regent's Park College, OX1 2LB) (87).—*Princ.,* Rev. B. R. White, D.Phil.

Unitarian

MANCHESTER (Unitarian College, Victoria Park, M14 5QL) (4).—*Princ.,* Rev. A. J. Long.

Interdenominational—Unitarian

OXFORD (Manchester Coll.) (65).—*Princ.,* Rev. B. Findlow.

Jewish

JEWS' COLLEGE, Albert Road, Hendon, N.W.4 (49).—*Princ.,* Rabbi Dr. J. Sacks.

LEO BAECK COLLEGE, The Manor House, 80 East End Road, N3 2SY (95).—*Princ.* Prof. J. B. Segal.

TOWN AND COUNTRY PLANNING

First Degrees are granted by Heriot-Watt University (*Town Planning*), and by the Universities of Dundee (*Town and Regional Planning* in association with Duncan of Johnstone College of Art), Glasgow (*Planning*), London (University College: *Environmental Studies* and *Planning*), Manchester (*Town and Country Planning*), Newcastle upon Tyne (*Town and Country Planning, Landscape Design*), Nottingham (*Architecture and Environmental Design*), Sheffield (*Urban Studies*), Stirling (*Urban Studies and Social Policy*), and Wales (Institute of Science and Technology: *Town Planning Studies*).

Courses leading to first degrees in *Town Planning* granted by the Council for National Academic Awards are provided by City of Birmingham Polytechnic, Leeds Polytechnic and Polytechnic of the South Bank; in *Town and Country Planning* by Bristol Polytechnic, Glasgow School of Art, Gloucestershire College of Arts and Technology and Trent Polytechnic; in *Planning Studies* by Oxford Polytechnic; in *Environmental Planning* by Chelmer Institute of Higher Education; in *Strategic Environmental Planning Studies* by Liverpool Polytechnic; in *Urban Planning Studies* by the Polytechnic of Central London; and in *Urban and Regional Planning* by Coventry (Lanchester) Polytechnic.

The ROYAL TOWN PLANNING INSTITUTE, 26 Portland Place, W.1, conducts examinations in town planning.

TRANSPORT

First Degrees are granted by the Universities of Aston (*Transport Operation and Planning*), Loughborough (*Transport Management and Planning*), Wales (*Institute of Science and Technology: International Transport*) and Ulster (*Transport Technology*). Courses leading to first degrees granted by the Council for National Academic Awards are provided by Huddersfield Polytechnic (*Transport and Distribution*) and Napier College of Commerce and Technology (*Transportation Engineering*).

THE CHARTERED INSTITUTE OF TRANSPORT, 80 Portland Place, London W.1, conducts qualifying examinations in transport management leading to chartered professional status.

VETERINARY STUDIES

First Degrees in *Veterinary Science/Medicine and Surgery* are granted by the Universities of Bristol, Cambridge, Edinburgh, Glasgow, Liverpool and London (Royal Veterinary College).

HEADMASTERS' CONFERENCE SCHOOLS

THE HEADMASTERS' CONFERENCE.—*Chairman* (1984), D. A. Emms (Dulwich); *Principal Sec.*, T. P. Snape, Chancery House, 107 St Paul's Road, N.1.; *Deputy Sec.*, F. G. R. Fisher. The annual meetings are, as a rule, held at the end of September.

In considering applications for election to membership the Committee will have regard to the scheme or other instrument under which the school is administered (taking particularly into consideration the degree of independence enjoyed by the Headmaster and the Governing Body); the number of pupils over thirteen years of age in the school; the number of pupils in proportion to the size of the school who are in the sixth form, *i.e.* engaged on studies at the Advanced Level of the General Certificate of Education.

Name of School	F'ded.	No. of Boys	Annual Fees D = Day Boys	Headmaster *(With date of Appointment)*
England and Wales				
Abingdon, Oxfordshire	1256	700	£3,648 .... D£1,824	M. St. J. Parker (1975)
Aldenham, Elstree, Herts.	1597	350†	£4,560 .... D£3,180	M. Higginbottom (1983)
Alleyn's School, Dulwich, S.E.22	1619	850†	D£2,070	D. A. Fenner (1976)
Allhallows, Rousdon, Dorset	1515	273†	£4,608 .... D£2,148	P. S. Larkman (1983)
Ampleforth College *(R.C.)*, York	1802	700	£4,350	Rev. D. L. Milroy, O.S.B. (1980)
Ardingly Coll., Haywards Heath, Sussex*	1858	455†	£4,755 .... D£3,615	J. W. Flecker (1980)
Arnold School, Blackpool	1896	737†	£3,036 .... D£1,521	R. D. W. Rhodes (1979)
Ashville College, Harrogate	1877	400†	£3,576 .... D£1,875	D. E. Norfolk (1977)
Bancroft's, Woodford Green, Essex	1727	675†	D£2,100	I. M. Richardson (1965)
Barnard Castle, Co. Durham	1883	500†	£2,970 .... D£1,560	F. S. McNamara (1980)
Bedales, Petersfield, Hants.	1893	350†	£4,950 .... D£1,100	E. A. M. MacAlpine (1981)
Bedford School	1552	890	£4,020 .... D£2,286	C. I. M. Jones (1975)
Bedford Modern School	1566	904	£3,066 .... D£1,626	P. J. Squire (1977)
Berkhamsted, Herts.	1541	451	£4,005 .... D£2,142	C. J. Driver (1983)
Birkenhead, Merseyside	1860	690	D£1,605	J. A. Gwilliam (1963)
Bishop's Stortford College, Herts.	1868	348†	£4,140 .... D£2,925	S. G. G. Benson (1984)
Bloxham School, Banbury, Oxon.*	1860	350†	£4,755 .... D£3,186	M. W. Vallance (1982)
Blundell's, Tiverton	1604	450†	£4,950 .... D£3,015	A. J. D. Rees (1980)
Bolton	1524	998	D£1,509	A. W. Wright (1983)
Bootham, York	1823	240†	£4,194 .... D£2,496	J. H. Gray (1972)
Bradfield College, Berks.	1850	490†	£4,980 .... D£3,486	A. O. H. Quick (1971)
Bradford Grammar, Yorks.	1662	1000†	D£1,410	D. A. G. Smith (1974)
Brentwood School, Essex	1557	855†	£3,660 .... D£2,052	J. A. E. Evans (1981)
Brighton College, Sussex	1845	450†	£4,095 .... D£2,655	W. S. Blackshaw (1971)
Bristol Cathedral School	1542	410†	D£1,650	C. S. Martin (1979)
Bristol Grammar School	1532	1000†	D£1,650	J. R. Avery (1975)
Bromsgrove, Worcs.	1553	400†	£4,152 .... D£2,721	Rev. J. N. F. Earle (1971)
Bryanston School, Blandford	1928	600†	£4,800 .... D£3,200	T. D. Wheare (1983)
Bury Grammar, Lancs.	1634	650	D£1,248	J. Robson (1969)
Canford, Wimborne, Dorset	1923	520†	£4,800 .... D£3,360	M. Marriott (1976)
Caterham, Surrey	1811	440	£3,870 .... D£2,124	S. R. Smith (1974)
Charterhouse, Godalming	1611	690†	£5,400 .... D£4,455	P. J. Attenborough (1982)
Cheadle Hulme	1855	860†	£3,810 .... D£1,770	D. C. Firth (1977)
Cheltenham College	1841	545†	£4,950 .... D£3,240	R. M. Morgan (1978)
Chigwell, Essex	1629	300†	£3,999 .... D£2,505	B. J. Wilson (1971)
Christ College, Brecon	1541	295	£3,297 .... D£2,472	S. W. Hockey (1982)
Christ's Hospital, Horsham	1553	720	Various	D. Baker (1979)
Churcher's College, Petersfield, Hants.	1722	450†	£3,786 .... D£1,830	D. I. Brooks (1973)
City of London, E.C.4	1442	780	D£2,412	J. M. Hammond (1984)
Clifton College, Bristol	1862	470	£5,130 .... D£3,525	S. M. Andrews (1975)
Colfe's School, Lee, S.E.12	1652	650†	D£1,830	V. S. Anthony (1976)
Colston's, Bristol	1710	300†	£3,780 .... D£2,385	G. W. Searle (1975)
Coventry School (Bablake and King Henry VIII, *amal.* 1977)	—	1669†	D£1,386	R. Cooke (*Director*) (1977)
Cranleigh, Surrey	1863	570†	£5,730 .... D£3,990	A. Hart (1984)
Culford School, Bury St. Edmunds	1881	460†	£3,837 .... D£2,304	D. Robson (1971)
Dame Allan's Sch., Newcastle on Tyne	1705	450	D£1,605	F. Wilkinson (1970)
Dauntsey's, Devizes	1543	463†	£4,206 .... D£2,376	G. E. King-Reynolds (1969)
Dean Close, Cheltenham	1884	420†	£5,025 .... D£3,225	C. J. Bacon (1979)
Denstone College, Uttoxeter, Staffs.*	1873	440†	£4,520 .... D£3,330	T. G. Beynon (1978)
Douai *(R.C.)*, Woolhampton	1903	330	£4,798 .... D£2,592	Rev. P. W. Sollom, O.S.B. (1975)
Dover College, Kent	1871	370†	£4,875 .... D£3,195	J. K. Ind (1981)
Downside *(R.C.)*, Stratton-on-the-Fosse, Somerset	1607	500	£4,326 .... D£2,898	Rev. P. Jebb (1980)
Dulwich College, S.E.21	1619	1350	£4,770 .... D£2,370	D. A. Emms (*Master*) (1975)
Durham	1414	340	£4,500 .... D£3,000	M. A. Lang (1982)
Eastbourne College, Sussex	1867	540†	£4,642 .... D£3,416	C. J. Saunders (1981)

† Pupils.   * A Woodard Corporation School.

Name of School	F'ded.	No. of Boys	Annual Fees D = Day Boys		Headmaster *(With date of Appointment)*
Ellesmere College, Shropshire*	1884	385†	£4,645	D£3,180	F. E. Maidment (1981)
Eltham College, S.E.9	1842	514	£4,149	D£1,869	C. D. Waller, ph.d. (1983)
Emanuel School, S.W.11.	1594	620		D£2,160	P. F. Thomson (1984)
Epsom College, Surrey	1855	630†	£4,725	D£3,255	J. B. Cook, ph.d. (1982)
Eton College, Windsor	1440	1250	£4,725		W. E. K. Anderson (1980)
Exeter, Devon	1633	600	£3,234	D£1,734	G. T. Goodall (1979)
Felsted, Dunmow, Essex	1564	450†	£4,863	D£3,894	E. J. H. Gould (1983)
Forest School, Snaresbrook, E.17	1834	625†	£3,471	D£2,385	J. C. Gough *(Warden)* (1983)
Framlingham College, Suffolk	1864	500†	£3,975	D£2,559	L. I. Rimmer (1971)
Giggleswick, Settle, Yorks.	1512	295†	£4,770	D£3,180	I. D. Watson (1978)
Gresham's, Holt, Norfolk	1555	415†	£4,575	D£2,985	Dr. T. P. Woods (1981)
Haberdashers' Aske's, Elstree, Herts.	1690	1100		D£2,226	B. H. McGowan (1973)
Haileybury, Herts.	1862	620†	£4,908	D£2,943	D. M. Summerscale *(Master)* (1976)
Hampton, Middlesex	1557	840		D£1,800	H. G. Alexander (1970)
Harrow, Middlesex	1571	740	£5,400		I. D. S. Beer (1981)
Hereford, Cathedral School	1384	566†	£3,348	D£1,863	B. B. Sutton (1975)
Highgate, N.6	1565	625	£4,386	D£2,496	R. C. Giles (1974)
Hulme Grammar School, Oldham	1611	680		D£1,344	D. R. Ward (1980)
Hurstpierpoint College, Sussex*	1849	410	£4,620	D£3,600	R. N. P. Griffiths (1964)
Hymers College, Hull	1889	630†		D£1,248	B. G. Bass (1983)
Ipswich, Suffolk	1390	592†	£3,663	D£2,115	Dr. J. M. Blatchly, f.s.a. (1972)
The John Lyon School, Harrow	1876	470		D£1,815	D. Dixon (1983)
Kelly College, Tavistock	1877	315†	£4,989	D£3,327	D. W. Ball, m.b.e. (1972)
Kent College, Canterbury	1885	579†	£3,753	D£2,034	R. J. Wicks (1980)
Kimbolton, Cambs.	1600	500†	£4,029	D£1,977	D. W. Donaldson (1973)
King Edward VI School, Southampton	1553	858		D£1,815	C. Dobson (1971)
King Edward VII School, Lytham	1908	545		D£1,368	D. Heap (1982)
King Edward's, Bath, Avon	1552	600†		D£1,497	J. P. Wroughton (1982)
King Edward's, Birmingham	1552	700		D£1,854	M. J. W. Rogers *(Master)* (1982)
King Edward's, Witley, Surrey	1553	520†	£3,900	D£2,460	R. D. H. Roberts (1980)
King's College, Taunton*	1880	510†	£4,230	D£3,015	J. M. Batten (1969)
King's College Sch., Wimbledon, S.W.19	1829	630	£4,050	D£2,250	R. M. Reeve (1980)
King's School, Bruton	1519	300†	£4,635	D£3,255	G. H. G. Doggart (1972)
King's School, Canterbury	600	700†	£5,220	D£3,510	Rev. Canon P. Pilkington (1975)
King's School, Chester	1541	440		D£1,770	A. R. D. Wickson (1981)
King's School, Ely	970	430†	£4,476	D£2,856	H. Ward (1970)
King's School, Macclesfield	1502	1050		D£1,725	A. H. Cooper (1966)
King's School, Rochester	604	440†	£3,795	D£2,175	R. A. Ford (1975)
King's School, Worcester	1541	630†	£3,543	D£1,980	Dr. J. M. Moore (1983)
Kingston Grammar, Surrey	1561	570†		D£2,040	S. J. Miller (1977)
Kingswood School, Bath	1748	460†	£4,530	D£2,844	L. J. Campbell (1970)
Lancing College, Sussex*	1848	513†	£4,980	D£3,375	J. S. Woodhouse (1981)
Latymer Upper, Hammersmith, W.6	1624	950		D£2,100	M. L. R. Isaac (1971)
Leeds Gr. School, Leeds 6	1552	1204†		D£1,580	A. C. F. Verity (1976)
Leighton Park Sch., Reading	1890	300†	£4,356	D£3,051	J. Hunter (1981)
The Leys School, Cambridge	1875	430†	£4,605	D£3,405	B. T. Bellis (1975)
Liverpool College, Liverpool 18	1840	540†	£3,210	D£1,710	R. V. Haygarth (1979)
Llandovery College	1848	250†	£3,600	D£2,400	R. Brinley Jones, ph.d. (1976)
Lord Wandsworth Coll., Long Sutton, Hants.	1912	400	£4,104	D£3,204	G. A. G. Dodd (1982)
Loughborough Grammar	1495	800	£3,918	D£1,806	D. N. Ireland (1984)
Magdalen College School, Oxford	1480	500	£3,693	D£1,794	W. B. Cook *(Master)* (1972)
Malvern College, Worcester	1865	600	£5,100	D£3,660	R. de C. Chapman (1983)
Manchester Grammar School	1515	1440		D£1,770	D. Maland *(High Master)* (1978)
Marlborough College, Wilts.	1843	900†	£4,725		R. W. Ellis, c.b.e. *(Master)* (1972)
Merchant Taylors', Crosby	1620	640		D£1,629	D. R. Johnston-Jones (1979)
Merchant Taylors', Northwood	1561	700	£3,900	D£2,670	D. J. Skipper (1982)
Mill Hill, N.W.7	1807	550†	£4,560	D£3,030	A. C. Graham (1979)
Monkton Combe, Bath	1868	340†	£4,599	D£3,411	R. A. C. Meredith (1978)
Monmouth	1614	525	£3,546	D£1,920	R. D. Lane (1982)
Mount St. Mary's College, Spinkhill, Derbyshire *(R.C.)*	1842	260†	£3,816	D£2,529	Rev. J. F. Grumitt, s.j. (1976)
Newcastle-under-Lyme School	1874	1200†		D£1,500	J. W. Donaldson *(Principal)* (1974)
Norwich School	1250	600	£3,921	D£1,734	C. D. Brown (1984)
Nottingham High School	1513	800		D£1,560	D. T. Witcombe, ph.d. (1970)
Oakham, Rutland, Leics.	1584	948†	£4,656	D£2,469	O. R. S. Bull (1977)
The Oratory *(R.C.)*, Woodcote, Reading	1859	350	£4,335	D£3,024	A. Snow (1972)

† Pupils.   * A Woodard Corporation School.

Name of School	F'ded.	No. of Boys	Annual Fees D = Day Boys	Headmaster (With date of Appointment)
Oundle, Peterborough, Northants......	1556	750	£5,235............	D. B. McMurray (1984)
Pangbourne College, Berks.	1917	365	£4,275.... D£3,030	P. D. C. Points (1969)
Perse Sch., Cambridge	1615	455	£3,585.... D£1,680	A. E. Melville (1969)
Plymouth College	1877	650†	£3,465.... D£1,770	A. M. Joyce (1983)
Pocklington School, York.	1514	634†	£3,462.... D£1,680	A. D. Pickering (1981)
Portsmouth Gr. Sch.....................	1732	700†	.... D£1,560	A. C. V. Evans (1983)
Prior Park Coll. (R.C.), Bath	1830	275†	£4,132.... D£2,340	P. F. J. Tobin (1981)
Queen Elizabeth's Gr., Blackburn	1567	1066†	.... D£1,461	P. F. Johnston (1978)
Queen Elizabeth Gr. Sch., Wakefield ...	1591	713	£2,841.... D£1,716	J. G. Parker (1975)
Queen Elizabeth's Hospital, Bristol.....	1590	442	£3,084.... D£1,662	R. N. Pittman (1978)
Queen's College, Taunton, Som.........	1843	430†	£4,755.... D£2,715	A. P. Hodgson (1979)
Radley Coll., Abingdon	1847	589	£4,920............	D. R. W. Silk (*Warden*) (1968)
Ratcliffe Coll. (R.C.), Leicester	1844	300†	£3,800.... D£2,530	Rev. W. F. Fearon (1982)
Reed's, Cobham, Surrey	1813	285†	£4,005.... D£2,955	D. E. Prince (1983)
Reigate Grammar	1675	880†	.... D£1,899	J. G. Hamlin (1982)
Rendcomb Coll., Cirencester, Glos.	1920	260†	£4,035............	R. M. A. Medill (1971)
Repton School, Derby	1557	555†	£4,560.... D£3,360	D. J. Jewell (1979)
Rossall, Fleetwood, Lancs...............	1844	500†	£4,998.... D£3,498	J. Sharp, D.Phil. (1973)
Royal Grammar School, Guildford	1552	700	.... D£1,950	J. Daniel (1977)
Royal Grammar Sch., Newcastle-upon-Tyne	1545	950	.... D£1,560	A. S. Cox (1972)
Rugby, Warwickshire	1567	760†	£5,175.... D£3,675	O. R. S. Bull (1985)
Rydal, Colwyn Bay, Clwyd	1885	330†	£3,810.... D£2,700	P. F. Watkinson (1968)
Ryde School, Isle of Wight.............	1921	386†	£3,270.... D£1,635	P. D. V. Wilkes (1984)
St. Albans, Herts.	1570	670	.... D£1,872	S. C. Wilkinson (1984)
St. Anselm's Coll., Birkenhead.	1933	700	.... D£1,287	Rev. Br. M. G. Miller (1981)
St. Bees, Cumbria	1583	380†	£4,560.... D£3,060	M. T. Thyne (1980)
St. Benedict's, Ealing, W.5 (R.C.).......	1902	580†	.... D£1,815	Dom. A. Gee (1978)
St. Dunstan's, Catford, S.E.6...........	1888	670	.... D£1,890	B. D. Dance (1973)
St. Edmund's, Canterbury.............	1749	280†	£4,029.... D£2,913	J. V. Tyson (1978)
St. Edmund's Coll. (R.C.), Ware, Herts. .	1568	250†	£4,143.... D£2,478	D. J. J. McEwen (1984)
St. Edward' Coll., Liverpool	—	670	.... D£1,500	B. D. Sassi (1984)
St. Edward's, Oxford..................	1863	542†	£4,800.... D£3,600	J. C. Phillips (*Warden*) (1978)
St. George's Coll., Weybridge (R.C.)	1869	750†	£3,600.... D£2,445	Rev. P. C. Hunting (1977)
St. John's, Leatherhead	1851	440	£3,900.... D£2,700	E. J. Hartwell (1970)
St. Lawrence Coll., Ramsgate	1879	320†	£4,710.... D£3,120	J. H. Binfield (1983)
St. Mary's College, Gt. Crosby	1919	625†	.... D£1,350	Rev. Br. N. D. O'Halloran (1972)
St. Paul's, Lonsdale Rd., Barnes, S.W.13	1509	750	£4,287.... D£2,661	J. W. Hele (*High Master*) (1973)
St. Peter's, York	627	435†	£4,350.... D£2,450	D. G. Cummin (1984)
Sedbergh, Cumbria	1525	470	£4,875.... D£3,414	R. G. Baxter (1982)
Sevenoaks School, Kent...............	1418	800†	£4,743.... D£2,853	R. P. Barker (1981)
Sherborne, Dorset	1550	660	£5,070.... D£3,750	R. D. Macnaghten (1974)
Shrewsbury School....................	1552	658	£4,740.... D£3,255	S. J. B. Langdale (1981)
Silcoates, Wakefield	1820	364†	£3,450.... D£1,998	J. C. Baggaley (1979)
Solihull, Warwicks	1560	920†	£3,252.... D£1,833	A. Lee (1983)
Stamford, Lincs.	1532	780	£3,240.... D£1,620	G. J. Timm (1978)
Stockport Grammar Sch., Cheshire.....	1487	920†	.... D£1,665	H. R. Wright (1979)
Stonyhurst Coll. (R.C.), nr. Whalley, Lancs..............................	1794	480	£4,470............	Rev. M. Bossy, S.J. (1972)
Stowe, Bucks.........................	1923	618†	£5,280.... D£3,750	C. G. Turner (1979)
Sutton Valence, Kent..................	1576	350†	£4,530.... D£2,925	M. R. Haywood (1980)
Taunton, Somerset	1847	644†	£4,701.... D£3,042	N. S. Roberts (1970)
Tettenhall College, Staffs.	1863	300†	£3,765.... D£2,319	W. J. Dale (1968)
Tonbridge, Kent	1553	625	£5,055.... D£3,504	C. H. D. Everett (1975)
Trent Coll., Long Eaton, Derbyshire....	1868	575†	£4,440.... D£2,472	A. J. Maltby (1968)
Trinity School, Croydon	1596	730	.... D£1,953	R. J. Wilson (1972)
Truro, Cornwall	1879	850†	£2,994.... D£1,764	D. W. Burrell (1959)
University Coll. School, Frognal, N.W.3	1830	520	.... D£2,340	G. D. Slaughter (1983)
Uppingham, Leics.....................	1584	650†	£4,980............	N. R. Bomford (1982)
Warwick	914	806	£3,468.... D£1,587	J. A. Strover (1977)
Wellingborough, Northants	1595	393†	£3,858.... D£2,358	G. Garrett (1973)
Wellington Coll., Crowthorne, Berks. ..	1856	800†	£4,590.... D£3,330	D. H. Newsome, Ph.D. (1980)
Wellington Sch., Somerset	1841	760†	£3,390.... D£1,800	J. Kendall-Carpenter (1973)
Wells Cathedral School, Somerset	1180	490†	£3,483.... D£1,956	A. K. Quilter (1964)
Westminster, Dean's Yard, S.W.1	1560	572†	£4,620.... D£2,805	J. M. Rae, Ph.D. (1970)
Whitgift, Croydon....................	1596	850	.... D£2,079	D. A. Raeburn (1970)
William Hulme's G. S..................	1887	765	.... D£1,761	P. A. Filleul (1974)
Winchester College	1382	630	£5,310.... D£3,984	J. L. Thorn (1968)
Wolverhampton Grammar School	1512	580†	.... D£1,890	P. H. Hutton (1978)

† Pupils.

Name of School	F'ded.	No. of Boys	Annual Fees D = Day Boys	Headmaster (With date of Appointment)
Woodbridge School, Suffolk	1662	500†	£3,645 .... D£2,058	A. F. Vyvyan-Robinson (1976)
Woodhouse Grove School, Bradford	1812	510†	£3,450 .... D£1,995	D. A. Miller (1972)
Worcester Coll. for the Blind	1866	79	£8,010 .... D£5,340	Rev. B. R. Manthorp (1980)
Worksop Coll., Notts.*	1895	350†	£4,485 .... D£3,075	R. J. Roberts (1975)
Worth School, Crawley, Sussex (R.C.) ..	1959	323	£4,380	Rev. R. S. Ortiger (1983)
Wrekin Coll., Wellington, Shropshire ..	1880	305†	£4,725 .... D£3,285	J. H. Arkell (1983)
Wycliffe Coll., Stonehouse, Glos.	1882	350†	£4,752 .... D£3,036	R. C. Poulton (1980)

Scotland

Daniel Stewart's and Melville Coll., Edinburgh (amalgamated, 1973)	1832	770	£3,375 .... D£1,680	R. M. Morgan (1977)
Dollar Academy, Perthshire	1818	889†	£3,156 .... D£1,338	L. Harrison (Rector) (1984)
Dundee High School, Tayside	1239	1135†	.... D£1,440	R. Nimmo (Rector) (1977)
The Edinburgh Academy	1824	660†	£4,125 .... D£2,055	L. E. Ellis (Rector) (1977)
Fettes College, Edinburgh	6870	460†	£4,500 .... D£3,060	A. J. C. Cochrane (1979)
George Heriot's, Edinburgh	1659	1250†	.... D£1,515	K. P. Pearson (1983)
George Watson's Coll., Edinburgh	1741	1200†	£3,375 .... D£1,680	Sir Roger Young (1958)
Glasgow Academy	1845	580	.... D£1,515	C. W. Turner (Rector) (1983)
Glenalmond College, Perthshire	1841	400	£4,725	J. N. W. Musson (Warden) (1972)
Gordonstoun, Elgin, Morayshire	1934	460†	£4,980 .... D£3,192	M. B. Mavor (1979)
Hutcheson's Gr. School, Glasgow	1641	1100†	.... D£962	P.Brian (Rector) (1984)
Kelvinside Academy, Glasgow	1878	500	.... D£1,545	J. H. Duff (Rector) (1980)
Loretto Sch., Musselburgh, Midlothian .	1827	298†	£4,500 .... D£2,700	Rev. N. W. Drummond (1984)
Merchiston Castle, Edinburgh	1833	325	£4,440 .... D£2,880	D. M. Spawforth (1981)
Morrison's Academy, Perthshire	1860	650†	£3,180 .... D£1,254	H. A. Ashmall (Rector) (1979)
Robert Gordon's Coll., Aberdeen	1729	850	£2,774 .... D£1,199	G. A. Allan (1978)
Strathallan, Forgandenny, Perthshire..	1913	370†	£4,470	C. D. Pighills (1975)

Northern Ireland

Bangor Gr. School, Co. Down	1856	890	.... D£615	T. W. Patton (1979)
Belfast Methodist College	1868	1640†	£2,500 ...... D£850	J. Kincade, ph.d. (1974)
Belfast Royal Academy	1785	1247†	.... D£759	W. M. Sillery (1980)
Campbell Coll., Belfast	1894	470	£3,684 .... D£1,599	B. W. J. G. Wilson (1977)
Coleraine Academical Institution	1856	1200	£3,870 .... D£2,070	R. S. Forsythe (1984)
Portora Royal School, Enniskillen	1618	450	£2,793 ...... D£903	R. L. Bennett (1983)
Royal Belfast Academical Instn.	1810	955	.... D£933	T. J. Garrett (1978)

Channel Islands, Isle of Man, etc.

Elizabeth Coll., Guernsey	1563	534	£2,310 ...... D£780	R. A. Wheadon (1972)
Victoria Coll., Jersey	1852	600†	£3,801 ...... D£759	M. H. Devenport (1967)
King William's Coll., Isle of Man	1668	300†	£4,290 .... D£2,850	P. K. Bregazzi, ph.d. (1979)

OVERSEAS

Africa

Diocesan Coll., Rondebosch, S. Africa...	1849	600	R5,400 ... DR3,000	J. S. B. Peake (1983)
Falcon College, Esigodini, Zimbabwe ...	1954	400	$22,880	D. E. Turner (1962)
Peterhouse, Maranderer, Zimbabwe	1955	434	$Z2,850 .... D$Z450	Rev. Dr. A. J. Megahey (Rector) (1984)
St George's Coll., Harare, Zimbabwe	1896	780	$Z2,520 .... D$Z960	J. C. Berry (Rector) (1984)

Australia

A.C.T.:

Canberra G.S.	1929	844	$5,973 .... D$2,607	P. J. McKeown (1959)

N.S.W.:

Armidale Sch., Armidale	1894	582	$6,417 .... D$2,898	G. C. S. Andrews (1982)
Barker Coll., Hornsby	1890	1120†	$5,730 .... D$2,640	T. J. McCaskill (1963)
Church of England G.S. N. Sydney	1889	950	$6,720 .... D$3,300	R. A. I. Grant (1983)
Cranbrook Sch., Sydney	1918	780	$7,110 .... D$3,630	M. Bishop, o.b.e. (1963)
The King's School, Parramatta	1831	920	$7,320 .... D$4,140	J. A. Wickham (acting)
Knox G.S., Wahroonga	1924	1200	$6,400 .... D$3,100	Dr. I. Paterson (1969)
Newington Coll., Stanmore...........	1863	1050	$7,380 .... D$3,630	A. J. Rae (1972)
St. Patrick's College, Goulburn	1874	600	$2,568 .... D$444	Br. F. D. Marzorini (President) (1956)
The Scots College, Sydney	1893	979	$7,515 .... D$3,975	G. A. W. Renney (1980)
Sydney Grammar School	1857	1160	.... D$3,720	A. M. Mackerras (1969)

Queensland:

Church of England G.S. Brisbane	1912	1267	$4,785 .... D$2,145	W. Hayward (1974)
Southport School......................	1901	782	$5,100 .... D$2,400	J. H. Day (1972)

† Pupils.　　　* A Woodard Corporation School.

Name of School	F'ded.	No. of Boys	Annual Fees D=Day Boys	Headmaster (With date of Appointment)
South Australia:				
Prince Alfred Coll., Adelaide	1869	740	$6,600 .... D$3,165	G. B. Bean (1970)
St. Peter's Coll., Adelaide	1847	732	$6,735 .... D$3,085	Dr. A. J. Shinkfield (1978)
Scotch Coll., Adelaide.................	1919	......	....	W. M. Miles (1975)
Tasmania:				
Hutchins School, Hobart	1846	600	$4,800 .... D$2,400	Dr. D. B. Clarke (1971)
Victoria:				
Ballarat and Clarendon Coll., Ballarat ..	1864	750†	$6,660 .... D$3,210	R. M. Horner (1967)
Brighton Grammar School, Brighton ...	1882	1051	.... D$4,104	R. L. Rofe (1967)
Carey Baptist School, Kew	1923	1130†	.... D$3,150	G. L. Cramer (1965)
Caulfield Grammar Sch., East Kilda	1881	1290†	$6,870 .... D$3,420	Rev. A. S. Holmes (1977)
Church of England G.S., Melbourne	1856	782	$6,750 .... D$3,450	N. A. H. Creese (1970)
Eltham College.......................	1974	636†	.... D$2,970	Dr. B. J. Webber (1984)
Geelong Coll., Geelong, Corio	1861	1323†	$8,175 .... D$3,840	S. P. Gebhardt (1976)
Haileybury Coll., Keysborough	1892	......	....	A. M. H. Aikman (1974)
Peninsular Church of England, Mt. Eliza...............................	1961	779	$6,624 .... D$3,924	H. A. Macdonald (1971)
Scotch Coll., Hawthorn, Melbourne	1851	1300	$7,080 .... D$3,700	Dr. F. G. Donaldson (1983)
Wesley Coll., Melbourne	1866	1450†	.... D$3,660	D. H. Prest (1972)
West Australia:				
Christ Church Grammar School, Claremont...........................	1910	748	$6,090 .... D$2,955	A. J. de V. Hill (1982)
Guildford Grammar Sch...............	1896	750	$4,805 .... D$2,820	J. M. Moody (1979)
Hale School, Wembley Downs..........	1858	650	$5,925 .... D$2,835	Dr. K. G. Tregonning, M.B.E. (1967)
Scotch Coll., Swanbourne	1897	729	$5,910 .... D$2,835	W. R. Dickinson (1972)
Canada				
Appleby Coll., Ontario	1911	246	$10,950 . D$7,250	A. S. Troubetzkoy (1981)
Ashbury Coll., Ottawa	1891	290†	$10,950 . D$5,850	A. M. Macoun (1981)
Brentwood Coll., School, Vancouver ...	1961	......	....	W. T. Ross (1976)
Hillfield Strathallan Coll.,Ont..........	1901	878†	.... D$5,200	M. B. Wansbrough (1969)
Pickering Coll., Ont..................	1842	155	$10,750 . D$6,000	S. H. Clark (1972)
St. Andrew's Coll., Ont.	1899	435	$10,950 ... D$6,250	R. P. Bedard (1981)
Shawnigan Lake School, B.C...........	1916	......	....	D. J. Farrant (1978)
Toronto French School, Ont.	1962	340†	$10,800 ... D$5,700	W. H. Giles (1962)
Trinity Coll. Sch., Port Hope, Ont.	1865	345	$11,300 ... D$6,500	R. C. N. Wright (1983)
Upper Canada Coll., Toronto	1829	590	$10,750 ... D$5,850	R. H. Sadleir (1975)
Europe				
Aiglon Coll., Switzerland	1949	......	....	P. Parsons (1976)
British School of Brussels	1970	1050†	.... D*Fb*277,000	J. Jackson, PH.D. (1983)
British School in the Netherlands......	......	550†	*Dfl*11,250	B. D. Davidson (1979)
Campion School, Athens	1970	528†	*Drachmae*787,500 D *Drachmae*300,000	A. F. Eggleston, O.B.E. (1983)
The English School, Cyprus	1900	770†	£C1,816 .... £C976	D. H. Humphreys, O.B.E. (1968)
St. Columba's Coll., Dublin	1843	280†	*IR*£3,795 D*IR*£1,980	D. S. Gibbs, O.B.E. (*Warden*) (1974)
St. George's English School, Rome	1958	470†	.......D*L*8,000,000	H. J. Deelman (1980)
Far East				
Island School, Hong Kong	1967	1150†	.... D$16,700	C. H. R. Niven (1983)
India				
Lawrence School, Lovedale, ...	1858	450†	*Rs.*6,500	L. A. Vyas (1972)
Lawrence School, Sanawar............	1847	542†	*Rs.*6,000	S. R. Das (1974)
St. Paul's School, Darjeeling...........	1823	......	....	H. Dang (*Rector*) (1977)
Yadavindra Public School, Patiala	1947	500†	*Rs.*6,300 . D*Rs.*2,300	H. N. Kashyap (1969)
New Zealand				
Christchurch Boys' High Sch., Canterbury	1881	1110	$2,145 .... D$25	I. D. Leggat (1976)
Christ's Coll., Christchurch, Canterbury	1850	620	$4,200 .... D$2,100	A. M. Brough (1970)
The Collegiate School, Wanganui	1854	524	$5,655 .... D$2,850	I. D. McKinnon (1980)
King's Coll., Auckland	1896	712†	$5,025 .... D$2,880	I. P. Campbell (1973)
Rathkeale Coll., Masterton	1963	485†	$5,190 .... D$2,151	J. S. Taylor (1979)
St. Andrew's Coll., Christchurch.......	1916	620	$5,000 .... D$2,400	A. J. Rentoul, PH.D. (1982)

† Pupils.

Name of School	F'ded.	No. of Boys	Annual Fees D=Day Boys	Headmaster (With date of Appointment)
Timaru Boys' High Sch., Canterbury ..	1880	722	$1,950 .... D*Nil*	I. W. Sawers (1981)
Waitaki Boys' High School	1883	713	$2,385 .... D$69	K. A. Laws (1976)
South America				
Markham Coll., Lima, Peru............	1946	470	... D*Soles*3,400,000	R. C. Pinchbeck, O.B.E. (1966)
St. George's Coll., Argentina	1898	195†	$5,000 .... D$3,250	C. T. Gill Leech (1980)
West Indies				
Harrison Coll., Barbados	1729	......	....	A. G. Williams (1965)
Munro Coll., Jamaica	1856	......	....	R. B. D. Roper (1954)

SOCIETY OF HEADMASTERS OF INDEPENDENT SCHOOLS
Secretary, A. E. R. Dodds, Green Garth, Horsell Rise, Woking, Surrey.

Name of School	F'ded.	No. of Boys	Annual Fees D=Day Boys	Headmaster (With date of Appointment)
Abbotsholme, Uttoxeter, Staffs.	1889	256†	£4,788 .... D£3,192	D. J. Farrant (1984)
Ackworth, Pontefract	1779	420†	£3,726 .... D£2,160	G. R. McKee (1971)
Austin Friars, Carlisle (*R.C.*)	1951	290	£3,075 .... D£1,674	Rev. T. Lyons, O.S.A. (1981)
Bearwood Coll., Wokingham, Berks.....	1827	340	£4,500 .... D£2,700	The Hon. Martin Penney (1980)
Bedstone College, Shropshire	1948	200†	£3,885 .... D£2,250	G. S. Wilson (1971)
Belmont Abbey, Hereford (*R.C.*)	1926	273	£3,450 .... D£1,875	Rev. S. McGurk (1983)
Bembridge, Isle of Wight	1919	230†	£2,970 .... D£2,040	R. L. Whitby, M.V.O. (1974)
Bentham Grammar, N. Yorks..........	1726	300†	£3,060 .... D£1,575	R. S. Repper (1983)
Bethany School, Goudhurst, Kent	1866	290	£3,786 .... D£2,526	C. A. H. Lanzer (1970)
Carmel Coll., Wallingford, Oxon.......	1948	248†	£5,674 .... D£3,135	P. D. Skelker (1984)
Chetham's School of Music, Manchester	1653	267†	£6,980 .... D£5,405	J. Vallins, O.B.E. (1974)
City of London Freeman's Sch., Ashtead Park, Surrey	1854	345†	£3,528 .... D£2,241	M. J. Kemp (1964)
Clayesmore, Iwerne Minster, Blandford	1896	320†	£4,350 .... D£3,110	M. P. Hawkins (1979)
Cokethorpe School, Nr. Witney, Oxon. .	1957	140†	£4,650 .... D£3,210	D. F. Goldsmith (1979)
Cotton College, Oakamoor, Staffs. (*R.C.*)	1763	180†	£3,075 .... D£1,920	R. J. Hutchings (1983)
Cranbrook, Kent	1518	730†	£2,181 .... D*Nil*	M. C. Pavey (1981)
Fort Augustus School, Inverness-shire (*R.C.*)	1878	110	£3,624 .... D£2,174	Rev. G. F. Davidson, O.S.B. (1972)
Frensham Heights, Farnham, Surrey ...	1925	240†	£5,070 .... D£3,045	A. L. Pattinson (1973)
Fulneck Boys' School, W. Yorkshire....	1753	300	£3,200 .... D£1,655	I. D. Cleland (1980)
Grenville College, Bideford, Devon*....	1954	351	£3,981 .... D£2,028	D. C. Powell-Price, T.D., Ph.D. (1975)
Keil School, Dumbarton	1915	130†	£3,624 .... D£2,103	C. H. Tongue (1984)
Kingham Hill School, Oxon.	1886	250	£3,360 .... D£2,240	D. Shepherd (1981)
King's School, Gloucester	1541	356†	£3,627 .... D£2,154	Rev. A. C. Charters (1983)
Kirkham Grammar, nr. Preston, Lancs..	1549	510†	£2,751 .... D£1,431	M. J. Summerlee (1972)
Milton Abbey Sch., nr. Blandford, Dorset	1954	280	£4,590	S. R. D. Hall (1979)
Oswestry, Shropshire.................	1407	330†	£3,432 .... D£2,100	F. E. Gerstenberg (1974)
Pierrepont School, Farnham, Surrey ...	1947	260†	£4,320 .... D£2,634	J. Payne (1983)
Purcell School (Music), Harrow, Middx.	1962	160†	£4,890 .... D£2,490	K. J. Bain (1983)
Rannoch School, Perthshire	1959	235†	£3,840 .... D£2,280	M. Barratt (1982)
Reading Blue Coat School, Berks.	1646	470	£3,540 .... D£2,034	A. C. E. Sanders (1974)
Rishworth School, Ripponden, W. Yorks.	1724	430†	£3,465 .... D£1,890	Rev. J. Williams (1961)
Royal Russell School, Croydon, Surrey .	1853	410†	£3,825 .... D£2,391	R. D. Balaam (1981)
Royal Wolverhampton Sch., Staffs......	1850	350†	£3,648 .... D£2,136	R. Hawkins (1977)
Ruthin School, Clwyd	1574	180	£3,960 .... D£2,586	A. S. Hill (1967)
St. David's Coll., Llandudno	1965	230	£3,750 .... D£2,400	J. A. Mayor (1965)
Scarborough College, Yorks...........	1898	450†	£3,810 .... D£2,025	R. W. Wilkinson (1974)
Seaford College, Petworth, Sussex	1884	430	£3,555	Rev. C. E. Johnson (1944)
Shebbear College, Beaworthy, Devon ...	1841	305	£3,429 .... D£1,734	R. J. Buley (1983)
Shiplake College, Henley, Oxon.	1959	320	£4,305 .... D£2,700	P. H. Lapping (1979)
Sidcot School, Winscombe, Somerset ...	1808	270†	£4,110 .... D£2,160	T. C. Leimdorfer (1977)
Stanbridge Earls School, Romsey	1952	170†	£5,070 .... D£3,380	H. Moxon (1984)
West Buckland Sch., Barnstaple, Devon.	1858	367†	£3,510 .... D£1,890	M. Downward (1979)

† Pupils. * A Woodard Corporation School.

NOTE.—The Headmasters of Bedales School, Colston's School, Churcher's College, Lord Wandsworth College, Pangbourne College, Rendcomb College, Ryde School, St. Edmund's College, St. George's College, Weybridge, Silcoates School, Tettenhall College, Wells Cathedral School and Woodbridge School are also Members of the Society. Details of these schools are included in the list of Headmasters' Conference Schools.

GIRLS' SCHOOLS ASSOCIATION MEMBERS

THE GIRLS' SCHOOLS ASSOCIATION, 29 Gordon Square, W.C.1.—*Sec.*, Miss S. M. Chapman.

Name of School	F'ded.	No. of Girls	Annual Fees D = Day Girls	Headmistress (a) Headmaster (With date of Appointment)
The Abbey School, Reading	1887	700	.... D£1,560	S. M. Hardcastle (1960)
Abbot's Hill, Hemel Hempstead	1912	140	£3,900 .... D£2,700	Mrs. J. Kingsley (1979)
Adcote School, Shrewsbury	1907	133	£3,672 .... D£2,274	Mrs. S. B. Cecchet (1979)
The Alice Ottley School, Worcester	1883	550	£3,540 .... D£1,785	E. D. Millest (1964)
All Hallows School, Ditchingham, Bungay, Suffolk	1864	180	£3,030 .... D£1,839	D. M. Handford (1983)
Ancaster House, Bexhill-on-Sea	1906	170	£3,750 .... D£2,280	Mrs. S. J. Grattidge (1978)
The Atherley School, Southampton (CSC)	1925	470	.... D£1,530	A. Ward (1973)
Badminton School, Bristol	1858	250	£4,140 .... D£2,100	(a) C. J. T. Gould (1981)
*Bath High School	1875	530	.... D£1,440	D. J. Chapman (1969)
Battle Abbey School, E. Sussex	1912	120	£3,525 .... D£2,025	(a) D. J. A. Teall (1982)
Bedford High School	1882	870	£3,417 .... D£1,701	Mrs. M. E. A. Kaye (1976)
Bedgebury School, Goudhurst, Kent	1860	360	£4,269 .... D£2,529	(a) J. H. Delany (1978)
*Belvedere School, Liverpool	1880	491	.... D£1,440	S. Downs (1972)
Benenden School, Cranbrook, Kent	1923	385	£4,610	J. R. Allen (1976)
Beresford House, Eastbourne	1902	200	£3,585 .... D£1,875	A. M. Barnett (1964)
Berkhamsted School for Girls	1888	434	£3,246 .... D£1,632	V. E. M. Shepherd (1980)
*Birkenhead High	1901	923	.... D£1,440	F. Kellett (1971)
*Blackheath High	1880	528	.... D£1,521	Mrs. H. E. W. Williams (1978)
Bolton School, Lancs	1877	700	....	Mrs. M. A. Spurr (1979)
Bradford Grammar School for Girls	1875	600	.... D£1,395	R. M. Gleave (1976)
*Brighton and Hove High, Brighton	1876	728	£3,024 .... D£1,440	Mrs. J. B. E. Wells (1978)
*Bromley High School	1883	592	.... D£1,521	J. A. Plowman (1984)
Bruton School for Girls, Somerset	1900	578	£3,030 .... D£1,680	J. M. Thomson (1980)
Burgess Hill, Sussex	1906	278	£3,561 .... D£2,025	Mrs. B. H. Webb (1979)
Bury Grammar School	1884	740	.... D£1,248	J. E. Batty (1979)
Casterton School, Kirkby Lonsdale, Cumbria	1823	300	£3,528 .... D£2,130	(a) G. Vinestock (1984)
*Central Newcastle High School	1895	766	.... D£1,440	Mrs. A. M. Chapman (1985)
Channing School, Highgate, N.6	1885	280	.... D£2,160	Mrs. I. R. Raphael (1984)
Charters Towers, Bexhill-on-Sea	1929	160	£3,615 .... D£1,845	D. L. Howe (1970)
Cheltenham Ladies' College	1853	824	£4,188 .... D£2,631	J. Sadler (1979) (*Principal*)
Christ's Hospital, Hertford	1552	230	*Various*	B. J. Morrison (1982)
City of London, Barbican, E.C.2	1894	552	.... D£1,875	L. E. Mackie (1972)
Clarendon School, Bedford	1898	224	£4,200 .... D£2,280	J. L. Howell (1978)
Clifton High School for Girls, Bristol	1877	627	£3,045 .... D£1,455	P. M. Stringer (1965)
Cobham Hall, Gravesend, Kent	1962	300	£4,785 .... D£3,195	(a) C. J. Dixon (1981)
Colston's Girls' School, Bristol	1891	630	.... D£1,392	A. C. Parkin (1981)
Combe Bank, Sevenoaks, Kent	1863	242	£3,538 .... D£1,675	Mrs. A. J. K. Austin (1982)
Commonweal Lodge, Purley, Surrey	1916	131	.... D£1,860	J. M. Brown (1982)
The Convent of the Assumption, Richmond, Yorks.	1852	200	£3,615 .... D£1,965	Sr. M. Connor (1978)
Cranborne Chase, Tisbury, Wilts.	1946	116	£4,350 .... D£1,800	Mrs. M. Simmons (1983)
Cranford House, Wallingford	1931	123	.... D£1,695	T. A. Spencer (1980)
Croft House, Shillingstone, Dorset	1941	184	£3,975 .... D£2,655	Mrs. B. M. Warley (1971)
Croham Hurst, S. Croydon, Surrey	1899	315	.... D£1,590	D. J. Seward (1970)
*Croydon High School	1874	1025	.... D£1,521	A. M. Mark (1980)
Dame Alice Harpur School, Bedford	1882	750	.... D£1,407	S. M. Morse (1970)
Dame Allan's Girls', Newcastle-on-Tyne	1705	440	.... D£1,605	J. Graham (1970)
Derby High School	1892	320	.... D£1,882	(a) G. H. Goddard (1983)
Dodderhill School, Droitwich	1973	125	.... D£1,725	(a) I. U. Andersson (1984)
Downe House, Cold Ash, Newbury	1907	380	£4,125 .... D£2,595	S. E. Farr (1978)
Durham High School	1884	260	.... D£1,404	B. E. Stephenson (1978)
Edgbaston Church of England Coll.	1886	330	.... D£1,395	(a) I. J. Walkley (1979)
Edgbaston High School	1876	540	.... D£1,389	V. R. Belton (1967)
Edgehill Coll., Bideford, Devon	1884	350	£3,297 .... D£1,647	D. W. Ballantyne (1980)
Ellerslie, Great Malvern	1922	260	£4,335 .... D£2,985	P. M. Binyon (1974)
Elmslie School, Blackpool	1918	420	.... D£1,335	E. M. Smithies (1978)
Eothen, Caterham ,Surrey (CSC)	1892	205	.... D£1,725	D. C. Raine (1973)
Farlington, Horsham, W. Sussex	1896	245	£3,570 .... D£2,160	Mrs. O. M. Peto (1977)
Farnborough Hill Convent, Hants.	1889	497	.... D£1,674	Sr. S. Cousins (1983)
Farringtons, Chislehurst	1911	300	£3,570 .... D£2,010	Mrs. F. V. Hatton (1972)
Felixstowe College, Suffolk	1929	350	£4,185 .... D£2,550	E. D. Guinness (1979)
Fernhill Manor, New Milton, Hants.	1890	145	£3,150 .... D£2,205	D. M. Brooke (1984)
Francis Holland, Clarence Gate, N.W.1.	1878	350	.... D£1,860	A. E. Holt (1974)
Francis Holland, Graham Terr., S.W.1.	1881	320	.... D£1,950	Mrs. J. A. Anderson (1982)
Godolphin, Salisbury	1726	264	£4,170 .... D£2,490	E. A. S. Hannay (1980)

Name of School	F'ded.	No. of Girls	Annual Fees D = Day Girls	Headmistress (a) Headmaster (With date of Appointment)
Godolphin and Latymer Sch., W.6	1905	700	.... D£1,920	B. F. Dean (1974)
Greenacre, Banstead, Surrey	1933	265	£3,510 .... D£1,875	M. E. Haggerty (1977)
The Grove, Hindhead, Surrey	1891	140	£3,834 .... D£2,322	(a) C. Brooks (1984)
Guildford High School (CSC)	1887	397	.... D£1,800	J. E. Dutton (1977)
Haberdashers' Aske's, Elstree	1873	......		Mrs. S. Wiltshire (1974)
Haberdashers' Monmouth School for Girls	1892	480	£2,829 .... D£1,518	Mrs. P. M. Phillips (1981)
Harrogate College	1893	440	£3,810 .... D£2,535	Mrs. J. C. Lawrance (1974)
Headington School, Oxford	1915	530	£3,570 .... D£1,830	E. M. Tucker (1982)
Heathfield School, Ascot	1899	170	£4,725	Mrs. S. E. Watkins (1982)
Hethersett Old Hall, Norwich	1928	150	£3,165 .... D£1,695	Mrs. V. M. Redington (1983)
Holy Child School, Edgbaston	1933	263	£2,535 .... D£1,395	Sr. W. Gradon (1983)
Howell's School, Denbigh	1859	320	£4,350 .... D£2,745	(a) Dr. J. T. Armstrong (1983)
*Howell's School, Llandaff	1860	521	£3,285 .... D£1,521	J. P. Turner (1978)
Hull High School (CSC)	1890	340	£2,205 .... D£1,575	C. M. B. Radcliffe (1976)
Hulme Grammar School, Oldham	1895	430	.... D£1,344	M. A. Winfield (1975)
Hunmanby Hall, nr. Filey	1928	317	£3,654 .... D£2,379	J. E. Jefferson (1979)
Huyton College, Liverpool	1894	309	£3,726 .... D£1,752	W. E. Edwards (1984)
*Ipswich High School	1878	606	.... D£1,440	P. M. Hayworth (1971)
James Allen's Girls', Dulwich, S.E.22	1741	600	.... D£1,650	Mrs. B. Davies (1984)
School of Jesus and Mary, Ipswich	1860	160	.... D£1,365	Mrs. E. A. McKay (1982)
Kent College, Tunbridge Wells	1886	340	£3,582 .... D£2,220	(a) Rev. J. C. A. Barrett (1983)
King Edward VI H.S., Birmingham	1883	515	.... D£1,677	E. W. Evans (1977)
King's High School, Warwick	1879	530	.... D£1,479	M. Leahy (1970)
Kingsley School, Leamington	1884	325	£2,805 .... D£1,500	E. C. Fairhurst (1977)
La Sagesse Convent High, Newcastle-upon-Tyne	1906	350	.... D£1,557	Sr. Pauline (1967)
La Sagesse Convent, Romsey	1896	150	£2,385 .... D£1,065	Sr. Thomas (1977)
Lady Eleanor Holles, Hampton, Middx.	1711	580	.... D£1,755	E. M. Candy (1981)
Lavant House, Chichester	1952	120	£3,480 .... D£2,040	D. M. Ellis (1982)
Lawnside, Great Malvern	1818	140	£4,095	D. M.M. Stewart (1971)
Leeds Girls' High	1876	586	.... D£1,470	P. A. Randall (1977)
Loughborough High School	1850	527	£2,928 .... D£1,608	J. E. L. Harvatt (1978)
Luckley-Oakfield School, Wokingham	1895	266	£2,745 .... D£1,695	(a) R. C. Blake (1984)
Malvern Girls' College	1893	520	£4,320 .... D£2,880	Mrs. E. Stamers-Smith (1984)
Manchester High School for Girls	1874	733	.... D£1,593	M. M. Moon (1983)
Maynard School, Exeter	1877	425	.... D£1,545	F. Murdin (1980)
Merchant Taylors' School, Crosby	1888	500	.... D£1,629	Mrs. M. E. Davies (1963)
Micklefield School, Seaford, Sussex	1910	220	£3,840 .... D£1,995	Mrs. M. M. Payton (1969)
Moira House, Eastbourne	1875	250	£4,020 .... D£2,685	(a) A. R. Underwood (1975)
More House School, Pont Street, S.W.1	1953	240	.... D£2,475	Mrs. P. M. Mathias (1974)
Moreton Hall, Oswestry	1913	310	£4,410 .... D£2,940	(a) E. J. Cussell (1976)
Mount School, York	1831	290	£3,870	D. J. Ellis (1977)
New Hall, Chelmsford	1642	515	£4,455 .... D£2,688	Sr. M. Francis (1963)
Newcastle-upon-Tyne Church H.S.	1885	370	.... D£1,530	P. E. Davies (1974)
North Foreland Lodge, Sherfield-on-Loddon, Hants.	1909	160	£4,275	D. L. Matthews (1983)
North London Collegiate School, Edgware	1850	700	.... D£1,680	M. M. N. McLauchlan (1965)
Northampton High School	1878	500	.... D£1,515	S. Lightburne (1964)
Northwood College, Middx.	1878	310	£2,649 .... D£1,467	M. D. Hillyer-Cole (1966)
*Norwich High School	1875	712	.... D£1,440	R. H. M. Standeven (1976)
*Nottingham High School for Girls	1875	960	.... D£1,440	Mrs. C. Bowering (1984)
*Notting Hill and Ealing High	1873	725	.... D£1,521	Mrs. C. J. Fitz (1983)
Oakdene, Beaconsfield	1911	400	£2,985 .... D£1,935	C. S. Artley, Ph.D. (1983)
Old Palace School, Croydon	1887	620	.... D£1,284	K. L. Hilton (1974)
*Oxford High School	1875	604	.... D£1,440	Mrs. J. Townsend (1981)
Park School, Yeovil	1851	140	£3,834 .... D£1,701	(a) D. M. Upton
Parsons Mead, Ashstead, Surrey	1897	400	£3,951 .... D£2,181	M. M. Dees (1979)
Penrhos Coll., Colwyn Bay	1880	300	£4,020 .... D£2,580	(a) N. C. Peacock (1974)
Perse School for Girls, Cambridge	1881	550	.... D£1,713	M. R. Bateman (1980)
Pipers Corner School, High Wycombe	1950	230	£3,435 .... D£1,920	(a) J. H. P. Maas (1974)
Polam Hall, Darlington	1848	330	£3,780 .... D£1,875	J. E. Ridley (acting) (1984)
Portland House, Leicester	1906	249	.... D£1,575	Mrs. D. Buchan (1982)
*Portsmouth High School	1882	602	.... D£1,440	Mrs. J. M. Dawtrey (1984)
Princess Helena Coll., Hitchin, Herts.	1820	181	£4,170 .... D£2,775	(a) D. Clarke, Ph.D. (1971)
Prior's Field, Godalming	1902	200	....	Mrs. M. W. Dawson
*Putney High School, S.W.15	1893	727	.... D£1,521	Mrs. N. Silver (1979)
Queen Anne's, Caversham	1698	365	£3,900 .... D£2,400	A. M. Scott (1977)
†Queen Ethelburga's, Harrogate	1912	200	£3,885 .... D£2,460	Mrs. M. C. James (1984)

Name of School	F'ded.	No. of Girls	Annual Fees D = Day Girls	Headmistress (a) Headmaster (With date of Appointment)
†Queen Margaret's, Escrick Park, York	1901	215	£3,895 .... D£2,430	(a) C. S. McGarrigle (1983)
Queen Mary, Lytham	1930	620	.... D£1,368	M. C. Ritchie (1981)
Queen's College, Harley Street, W.1 ...	1848	390	£3,000 .... D£1,800	Mrs. P. J. Fleming (1983)
Queen's Gate School, Queen's Gate, S.W.7	1891	200	£4,200 .... D£2,325	Mrs. C. M. Newnham (1971)
Queen's School, Chester	1878	420	.... D£1,410	M. Farra (1973)
Queenswood, Hatfield, Herts.	1894	350	£4,350	Mrs. A. M. B. Butler (1981)
Redland High School, Bristol	1882	450	.... D£1,446	W. M. Hume (1969)
The Red Maids', Bristol	1634	465	£2,700 .... D£1,400	E. Castle (1982)
Rickmansworth Masonic School	1788	500	£3,950 .... D£2,370	(a) D. L. Curtis (1980)
Roedean School, Brighton	1885	435	£4,266	Mrs. A. R. Longley (1984)
Rosemead, Littlehampton	1919	222	£3,375 .... D£1,830	Mrs. S. Dickerson (1981)
Royal Naval School, Haslemere, Surrey	1840	300	£3,996 .... D£2,664	D. M. Otter (1970)
Royal School for Daughters of Officers of the Army, Bath	1864	400	....	Mrs. S. Greig (1982)
Runton Hill, Runton, Cromer	1911	180	£3,675 .... D£2,460	Mrs. M. Sheelin Cuthbert (1976)
Rye St. Anthony, Oxford	1930	300	£3,150 .... D£1,635	P. M. Sumpter (1976)
Sacred Heart, Tunbridge Wells	1915	240	£3,531 .... D£2,196	(a) J. A. Fallon, ph.d. (1977)
St. Albans High School	1889	660	.... D£1,500	E. M. Diggory (1983)
St. Andrew's, Bedford	1896	195	.... D£1,245	K. M. Smith (1981)
St. Anne's, Windermere	1863	310	£3,600 .... D£2,250	(a) M. B. McC. Brown (1984)
St. Audries, West Quantoxhead, nr. Taunton	1906	194	£3,603 .... D£2,013	(a) A. J. Tough (1975)
St. Brandon's, Clevedon, Avon	1831	400	£3,750 .... D£1,950	(a) J. S. Davey (1978)
St. Catherine's, Bramley, Guildford ...	1885	400	£3,795 .... D£2,325	(a) J. R. Palmer (1982)
†School of St. Clare, Penzance	1889	180	£3,642 .... D£2,070	M. M. Coney (1969)
St. David's, Ashford, Middx.	1716	300	....	J. M. Gardner (1973)
St. Dunstan's Abbey, Plymouth	1850	228	£2,685 .... D£1,500	H. L. Abley (1970)
St. Elphin's Church of England School, Matlock	1844	280	£3,717 .... D£2,058	(a) A. P. C. Pollard (1979)
St. Felix, Southwold, Suffolk	1897	365	£4,086 .... D£2,877	Mrs. A. Mustoe (1978)
S. Gabriel's, Newbury	1929	133	.... D£1,842	Mrs. P. Gott (1980)
St. George's, Ascot	1923	200	£4,425 .... D£2,670	Mrs. J. M. Goodland (1983)
S. Helen & S. Katharine, Abingdon	1903	508	£2,797 .... D£1,455	Y. Paterson (1973)
S. Helen's, Northwood, Middx.	1899	550	£3,405 .... D£1,815	J. D. Leader (1966)
S. Hilary's, Alderley Edge	1880	245	.... D£1,575	(a) N. H. Norman (1976)
St. Hilary's, Sevenoaks	1942	212	.... D£1,389	Mrs. P. Miles (1977)
St. James's and the Abbey, West Malvern (amalgamated 1979)	—	200	£4,200 .... D£2,802	J. M. Nixon (1978)
St. Joseph's Convent, Reading	1909	......	....	Mrs. J. Effendowicz
St. Leonards-Mayfield School, East Sussex (amalgamated 1954)	—	520	£3,060 .... D£2,040	Sr. J. Sinclair (1980)
St. Margaret's, Bushey, Herts	1749	331	£3,627 .... D£2,229	Mrs. E. M. Perryer (1983)
†St. Margaret's, Exeter	1902	420	£2,436 .... D£1,455	Mrs. J. M. Gidding (1984)
Saint Martin's, Solihull	1941	230	.... D£1,725	(a) D. J. Cobb (1984)
St. Mary's Convent, Ascot	1885	300	£4,200 .... D£2,520	Sr. M. Orchard (1982)
St. Mary's Convent, Cambridge	1898	500	£2,500 .... D£1,500	Sr. M. C. Kenworthy-Browne (1977)
St. Mary's Convent, Shaftesbury	1945	300	£3,500 .... D£1,850	Sr. L. Le Marchand (1976)
St. Mary's Hall, Brighton	1836	391	£3,525 .... D£2,145	M. F. C. Harvey (1981)
St. Mary's, Calne, Wilts.	1873	314	£4,380 .... D£2,580	Mrs. J. D. Walters (1982)
St. Mary's, Colchester	1908	300	.... D£1,455	Mrs. G. M. G. Mouser (1981)
St. Mary's, Gerrards Cross	1872	263	.... D£1,755	J. Smith (1984)
St. Mary's, Wantage, Oxon.	1873	300	.... D£4,050	Mrs. P. H. Johns (1980)
St. Michael's, Limpsfield, Oxted	1850	191	£3,525 .... D£2,055	(a) B. F. Long, ph.d. (1983)
†St. Michael's, Petworth, Sussex	1844	......	....	Mrs. M. Steeves (1981)
St. Paul's Girls', Brook Green, W.6	1904	590	.... D£2,502	Mrs. H. Brigstocke (High Mistress) (1974)
St. Stephen's Coll., Broadstairs	1867	132	£4,080 .... D£2,520	B. Seymour (1974)
St. Swithun's, Winchester	1884	410	£4,254 .... D£2,700	N. O. Davies (1973)
*Sheffield High School	1878	620	.... D£1,440	D. M. Skilbeck (1983)
Sherborne School, Dorset	1899	455	£4,155 .... D£2,775	E. M. Coulter (1975)
*Shrewsbury High School	1885	551	.... D£1,440	E. M. Gill (1982)
Sir William Perkins's, Chertsey	1725	440	.... D£1,530	Mrs. A. F. Darlow (1982)
*South Hampstead High School	1876	646	.... D£1,521	Mrs. D. A. Burgess (1975)
Stamford High School, Lincs.	1877	700	£3,228 .... D£1,614	G. K. Bland (1978)
Stonar, Atworth, Melksham, Wilts.	1921	270	£3,825 .... D£1,650	F. D. Denmark (1962)
Stover School, Newton Abbot	1932	190	£3,594 .... D£1,965	Mrs. W. Lumel (1984)
Stratford House School, Bromley	1912	245	.... D£1,710	Mrs. A. Williamson (1974)
*Streatham Hill and Clapham High	1887	438	.... D£1,521	G. M. Ellis (1979)

Name of School	F'ded.	No. of Girls	Annual Fees D = Day Girls	Headmistress (a) Headmaster (With date of Appointment)
Sunderland High School (CSC)	1884	220	.... D£1,515	Mrs. M. Thrush (1980)
Surbiton High School (CSC)	1884	400	.... D£1,665	Mrs. R. A. Thynne (1979)
*Sutton High School, Surrey	1884	818	.... D£1,521	A. E. Cavendish (1980)
*Sydenham High School, S.E.26	1887	643	.... D£1,521	M. I. J. Hamilton (1966)
Talbot Heath, Bournemouth	1886	485	£3,162 .... D£1,650	C. E. Austin-Smith (1976)
Teesside High, Cleveland	1970	409	.... D£1,470	J. Sawyer (1982)
Tormead School, Guildford	1905	345	£3,390 .... D£1,665	Mrs. J. V. Crouch-Smith (1977)
Truro High School	1880	420	£3,216 .... D£1,623	Mrs. J. F. Marshall (1984)
Upper Chine, Shanklin, I.O.W.........	1799	300	£2,925 .... D£2,055	B. A. Philpott (1981)
Ursuline Convent, Westgate-on-Sea ...	1904	350	£3,450 ... D£1,827	Sr. M. Murphy
Ursuline High School, Ilford	1903	420	.... D£1,470	P. Dixon (1984)
Wadhurst College, Sussex	1930	230	£3,711 .... D£2,325	D. Swatman (1972)
Wakefield High School	1878	710	.... D£1,551	Y. J. Hand (1974)
Walthamstow Hall, Sevenoaks, Kent ..	1838	451	£3,285 .... D£1,785	Mrs. J. S. Lang (1984)
Wentworth Milton Mt., Bournemouth	1871	315	£3,000 .... D£1,935	M. Vokins (1982)
Westfield, Newcastle-upon-Tyne	1960	230	.... D£1,536	Mrs. M. Hill (1979)
West Heath, Sevenoaks, Kent	1867	140	£4,125 .... D£2,970	R. M. Rudge (1965)
Westholme, Blackburn	1923	600	.... D£1,260	J. Bond, ph.d. (1968)
Westonbirt, Tetbury, Glos.	1928	250	£4,440 ... D£2,985	(a) H. A. Nickols (1981)
*Wimbledon High School	1880	641	.... D£1,521	Mrs. R. A. Smith (1982)
Withington School, Manchester	1890	460	.... D£1,512	M. Hulme (1961)
Woldingham School, Surrey	1842	400	£3,855 ... D£2,370	Sr. M. Hinde (1974)
Wroxhall Abbey School, Warwick.....	1872	155	£4,146 .... D£2,499	Mrs. I. D. M. Iles (1980)
Wycombe Abbey, Bucks.	1896	470	£4,680	P. M. Lancaster (1974)
York College (CSC)	1908	210	.... D£1,710	Mrs. J. L. Clare (1982)
Scotland				
Laurel Bank, Glasgow	1903	400	.... D£1,425	L. G. Egginton (1984)
Mary Erskine School, Edinburgh	1694	540	£3,375 .... D£1,680	(a) R. M. Morgan (1978)
Park School, Glasgow	1880	408	.... D£1,665	J. Rutherford (1974)
St. Denis and Cranley, Edinburgh	1855	203	£3,450 ... D£1,650	....
St. George's, Edinburgh	1888	580	£3,510 .... D£1,710	Mrs. J. L. Clanchy (1976)
St. Leonards, St. Andrews, Fife	1877	400	£4,455 ... D£2,250	M. Hamilton (1970)
St. Margaret's, Aberdeen.............	1846	225	£2,847 .... D£1,197	M. D. Bosomworth (1970)
St. Margaret's, Edinburgh	1890	700	£3,210 .... D£1,560	Mrs. M. J. Cameron (1984)
Channel Islands				
The Ladies' College, Guernsey	1872	350	.... D £708	J. Honey (1976)

* Girls' Public Day School Trust, 26 Queen Anne's Gate, S.W.1

† Woodard Corporation School.

CSC Church Schools Company, 1a Doughty Street, W.C.1

G.B.A. and G.B.G.S.A.

The Governing Bodies Association (G.B.A.) and the Governing Bodies of Girls' Schools Association (G.B.G.S.A.) together comprise 531 independent secondary schools all of which are educational charities. Both Associations are constituent members of the Independent Schools Joint Council. The Headmasters or Headmistresses of almost all these schools are members of either the Headmasters Conference (H.M.C.), the Girls Schools Association (G.S.A.) or the Society of Headmasters of Independent Schools (S.H.M.I.S.). The total number of pupils in G.B.A. and G.B.G.S.A. schools is approximately 274,000. *Sec.,* Lt. Col. C. J. M. Hamilton, o.b.e., The Flat, The Lambdens, Beenham, Reading, Berks.

EVENTS OF THE YEAR (*SEPT. 1, 1983–AUG. 31, 1984*)

THE ROYAL HOUSE

(1983) **Sept. 7.** Princess Margaret visited Skye. **16.** Princess Anne opened the National Exhibition of Children's Art in London. Princess Margaret left Heathrow Airport to represent the Queen at the independence celebrations of St. Christopher and Nevis. **18.** Prince Andrew visited R.A.F. Finningley and started the King's Cup Air Race, presenting the awards afterwards. **19.** Princess Anne visited Glasgow. **25.** The Queen Mother was present at a service in Dunblane Cathedral to mark the 750th anniversary of the commencement of the building. **27.** Princess Anne visited Hampshire.

Oct. 3. Princess Anne attended the gala night of the Horse of the Year Show at Wembley Arena. **5.** Princess Anne visited Bristol Grammar School on the 450th anniversary of the granting of its charter. The Prince of Wales attended a banquet to celebrate the British Film Institute's 50th anniversary at Guildhall. **9.** The Duke of Edinburgh left Heathrow Airport for Hong Kong (and subsequently visited Thailand and Malaysia) to undertake engagements as President of the World Wildlife Fund International. **12.** The Queen Mother visited Aberdeen University. Princess Margaret visited the Intelligence Centre at Ashford. **19.** The Queen gave a lunch at Buckingham Palace for the President of Mozambique and later attended the annual national service for seafarers at St. Paul's Cathedral. **20.** The President of the French Republic (Mr. Mitterrand) visited the Queen at Buckingham Palace. **21.** The Queen opened the new Burrell Gallery in Glasgow. **25.** The Queen and the Duke of Edinburgh gave a lunch at Buckingham Palace for the King and Queen of Tonga. **27.** The Queen opened an exhibition at the Commonwealth Institute to mark the silver jubilee of Voluntary Service Overseas. The Queen Mother was present at a service of thanksgiving in St. Paul's Cathedral to mark the centenary of the Boys' Brigade. **30.** The Prince of Wales began a three-day visit to the Isles of Scilly.

Nov. 2. The Queen unveiled a statue of Admiral of the Fleet Earl Mountbatten of Burma on Foreign Office Green. **3.** Princess Anne visited Northampton. **7.** The Queen was present at a Royal Variety Performance at the Theatre Royal, Drury Lane. **8.** The Queen Mother was present at a special performance of the musical *Blondel* at the Old Vic to mark the re-opening of the Theatre. **9.** The Queen left Heathrow Airport for State visits to Kenya, Bangladesh and India; she was subsequently joined by the Duke of Edinburgh. The Prince of Wales accompanied

by the Princess of Wales attended the dedication of the Falkland Islands Campaign Memorial at the Guards Chapel, London. Princess Margaret visited Nottinghamshire. **10.** The Queen Mother planted a cross in the Royal British Legion Field of Remembrance at St. Margaret's Church, Westminster. **12.** The Queen Mother was present at the Royal British Legion Festival of Remembrance at the Royal Albert Hall and other members of the royal family attending included the Prince and Princess of Wales, Prince Andrew and Princess Anne. **13.** The Prince of Wales, on behalf of the Queen, and Prince Andrew laid wreaths at the Cenotaph on Remembrance Day; other members of the royal family present included the Queen Mother, the Princess of Wales and Princess Anne. **17.** The Queen Mother visited Hertfordshire. **28.** Princess Anne, President, Save the Children Fund, visited Scotland.

Dec. 5. The Prince of Wales accompanied by the Princess of Wales attended a concert at Kensington Palace given by Mstislav Rostropovich and the English Chamber Orchestra in aid of the centenary appeal of the Royal College of Music. **6.** The Queen Mother visited the Royal Smithfield Show at Earls Court. **7.** The Prince of Wales visited Tyne and Wear. The Duke of Kent attended the 100th Association football match between Oxford and Cambridge universities at Wembley. **8.** The Queen opened the new London South Western District Office of the Post Office at Nine Elms. **14.** The Queen opened Newham General Hospital in London. The President of Lebanon visited the Queen at Buckingham Palace. Princess Margaret visited Cardiff. **15.** The Queen visited the Board of Customs and Excise in London and toured the tercentenary exhibition. The Duke of Edinburgh visited Cumbria. **19.** The Prince and Princess of Wales went to Westminster Hospital and St. Thomas' Hospital to visit victims of the Harrods I.R.A. bomb. **20.** The Prince and Princess of Wales visited Greater Manchester. **25.** The Queen made her traditional broadcast to the Commonwealth. **31.** The New Year's Honours List was published and included four life peers in a total of 668 people honoured.

(1984) **Jan. 23.** Princess Anne, President of British Olympic Association, left Gatwick Airport for visit to U.S.A. **24.** The Queen visited R.A.F. Marham.

Feb. 1. The Prince and Princess of Wales visited the "Genius of Venice" exhibition at the Royal Academy of Arts. Princess Margaret undertook engagements in Greater Manchester. **6.** The Duke of Edinburgh presided at a dinner at St. John's College,

Cambridge, to celebrate 400 years of printing and publishing by the University Press. 7. The Prince of Wales visited the National Hospital, Queen Square, London. 10. The Prince of Wales arrived at Liverpool and subsequently spent the day at sea on *H.M.S. Walkerton.* 11. Princess Anne left R.A.F. Lyneham for Yugoslavia to visit the Winter Olympics at Sarajevo; subsequently she visited Morocco, The Gambia, and Upper Volta as President of the Save the Children Fund. The Princess of Wales flew to Norway to attend a performance of the London City Ballet in Oslo. 13. The Prince and Princess of Wales announced they were expecting their second child late in September. 14. The Prince of Wales visited the Police Staff College, Bramshill, Hampshire; on the following day he visited Jaguar Cars, Allesley, Coventry. 16. The President of Zimbabwe visited the Queen at Buckingham Palace. 21. The Prince of Wales left Heathrow Airport for Brunei to represent the Queen at the first national independence celebrations. The Princess of Wales visited the Royal Marsden Hospital, Sutton, Surrey. 22. The Queen with the Duke of Edinburgh was present at a lunch at the Bank of England to mark the 250th anniversary of the Bank's occupation of its present site. The Princess of Wales visited the national Headquarters of the British Red Cross Society in London. 23. The President of Italy visited the Queen and the Duke of Edinburgh at Buckingham Palace and later they visited the "Genius of Venice" exhibition at the Royal Academy of Arts. The Queen Mother was present at a concert in Westminster Abbey to mark the 50th anniversary of the death of Sir Edward Elgar. 24. The Duke of Edinburgh carried out engagements in Yorkshire.

Mar. 2. The Duke of Edinburgh visited Nottingham. 4. Princess Anne attended the children's royal variety performance in aid of the N.S.P.C.C. at Her Majesty's Theatre, Haymarket. 6. The Crown Prince and Crown Princess of Japan, with Prince Naruhito, visited the Queen and Duke of Edinburgh at Buckingham Palace. 7. The Queen gave a reception at Buckingham Palace to mark 125th anniversary of the Corps of Commissionaires. The Duke of Edinburgh visited Headquarters, U.K. Land Forces, Wilton, Wilts. 8. Princess Anne visited the British School of Osteopathy in London. 9. The Prince of Wales visited the Fire Service College, Moreton-in-Marsh, Gloucestershire. 12. The Queen and the Duke of Edinburgh attended the Commonwealth Day Observance service in Westminster Abbey. 13. The Duke of Edinburgh visited London Dockyards and later Bexley. 14. The President of the Gambia visited the Queen at Buckingham Palace. 15. The Prince and Princess of Wales visited Sheffield. 16. The Queen and the Duke of

Edinburgh visited Clwyd. The Queen Mother visited the British Military Hospital in Munster, West Germany. 18. The Prince of Wales left Heathrow Airport to visit Tanzania, Zambia, Zimbabwe, and Botswana. 19. The Queen with the Duke of Edinburgh was present at the Royal Film Performance of "The Dresser" in London. Princess Anne opened the Portland Hospital for Women and Children in London. 21. The Queen attended a service in London at St. Columba's Church of Scotland to mark its centenary. 22. Princess Margaret was present at a thanksgiving service and dedication at Chelmsford Cathedral on the completion of restoration work. 23. The Princess of Wales opened the new spinal injuries unit at Royal National Orthopaedic Hospital, Stanmore, Middlesex. 25. The Queen and the Duke of Edinburgh left Heathrow Airport for Cyprus and flew next day to Amman for a five-day State visit to Jordan. The Queen Mother was present at the Milk Cup Final at Wembley Stadium. 28. The Queen Mother unveiled a memorial to Sir Noel Coward in Westminster Abbey. 29. The Princess of Wales visited the Metropolitan Police training establishment at Hendon.

April 1. Prince Andrew left R.A.F. Brize Norton to visit St. Helena on the occasion of 150th anniversary of the Island becoming a Crown Colony, and Ascension Island. 2. The President of Israel visited the Queen and Duke of Edinburgh at Windsor Castle. 3. Princess Anne visited the Borders region of Scotland. The Duke and Duchess of Kent arrived in Belfast for a 24-hour visit to Northern Ireland. 5. Princess Margaret visited Canvey Island. 6. The Queen Mother opened the new paddock complex at Kempton Park racecourse. 9. The Queen, with the Duke of Edinburgh, opened the Joint European Torus at Culham, Oxfordshire, and accompanied by President Mitterrand of France, viewed a presentation on the JET project. 10. The Amir of Bahrain arrived in Windsor on a State visit. 12. The Princess of Wales visited British Airways and the British Airports Authority, Heathrow Airport. 15. Prince Andrew left Heathrow Airport for Los Angeles to attend functions arranged by the British Olympic Association and the Gordonstoun Golden Jubilee Committee. 18. Princess Anne carried out engagements in Coventry and Birmingham. 19. The Queen and the Duke of Edinburgh attended the Maundy Service in Southwell Minster at which the Queen distributed the Royal Maundy. 26. The Prince of Wales gave a reception at Kensington Palace for the 50th anniversary year of the British Council. 27. Princess Margaret visited Cambridge University.

May 1. The Duke of Edinburgh attended a dinner at Guildhall to mark 250th anniversary of *Lloyd's List.* 2. The Queen, accompanied by the Duke of Edinburgh, opened the International Garden Festival in Liverpool. **8.** The Queen, accompanied by the Duke of Edinburgh, opened the Thames Barrier. **9.** The Prince of Wales opened a power station at Llanberis, Gwynedd. **11.** Princess Margaret visited Edinburgh. **15.** Princess Anne opened the Wilde Theatre in Bracknell. **16.** The Queen and the Duke of Edinburgh visited Cambridge and Cambridge University. **17.** The Queen opened the new extension of St. Joseph's Hospice at Hackney in London. The Prince of Wales visited York. **19.** The Duke of Edinburgh, President of the World Wildlife Fund International, left London airport for the U.S.A. to attend meetings of the Fund in Washington D.C. Princess Anne visited Hereford. Princess Margaret visited Shropshire. **20.** The Duke of Kent and the Duchess of Kent were present at the F.A. Cup Final at Wembley. **21.** The Queen and other members of the royal family visited the Chelsea Flower Show. **22.** The Queen left Heathrow Airport for West Germany to visit The Royal Regiment of Artillery and The Royal Green Jackets in B.A.O.R. **23.** The Prince of Wales visited Wormwood Scrubs prison in London. Princess Margaret opened the exhibition of court dress and the restored rooms at Kensington Palace. **24.** Princess Margaret visited Birmingham. **29.** The Duke of Edinburgh visited Tideswell and Chapel-en-le-Frith, Derbyshire. The Queen Mother embarked in *Britannia* at Portsmouth for a visit to the Channel Islands. **30.** The Queen, accompanied by the Duke of Edinburgh, opened the new terminal at Birmingham international airport. The Prince and Princess of Wales visited Cheshire.

June 3. The Queen Mother was present at a service in Portsmouth Cathedral to mark 40th anniversary of D-Day and also opened the D-Day Museum. **4.** Princess Margaret visited Derbyshire. **5.** President Reagan and Mrs. Reagan visited the Queen and the Duke of Edinburgh at Buckingham Palace; later the Queen and the Duke of Edinburgh arrived at Havant Station and then sailed in *Britannia* for Normandy. **6.** The Queen and the Duke of Edinburgh attended the 40th anniversary commemoration of the D-Day landings in Normandy. The Queen Mother was present at Epsom Races. Princess Margaret left for two-day visit to Northern Ireland. **9.** The Queen and the Duke of Edinburgh gave a dinner party at Buckingham Palace for leaders of countries attending the London economic summit. **12.** Princess Anne visited Clwyd. **13.** The Duke of Edinburgh attended a garden party given by the Cambridge University Press in celebration of 400 years of printing and publishing, and later attended a dinner at Peterhouse marking the seventh centenary of the College's foundation. **14.** The Queen visited the headquarters of the British Council in London to mark their golden jubilee. Princess Anne and Capt. Mark Phillips attended the Royal International Horse Show at the National Exhibition Centre, Birmingham. **16.** The Queen was present at her Birthday Parade on Horse Guards Parade, being accompanied by the Duke of Edinburgh, the Prince of Wales, and the Duke of Kent. The Queen's Birthday Honours List was published. **18.** The Queen visited the Royal Highlands Show at Ingliston to mark its bicentenary. **19.** The Queen and the Duke of Edinburgh were present at Ascot Races (they also attended on June 20, 21, and 22). Princess Anne visited Bath. **20.** The Duke and Duchess of Kent left Heathrow Airport for Washington D.C. to attend the 350th anniversary celebrations of the founding of the State of Maryland. **24.** Prince Andrew attended the British helicopter championships at Castle Ashby, Northants. **25.** The President of Sri Lanka visited the Queen at Buckingham Palace. **26.** The President of Costa Rica visited the Queen at Buckingham Palace. The Duke of Edinburgh attended Meridian Day festivities in Greenwich Park. **29.** The Prince of Wales was present at the memorial service for Sir John Betjeman held in Westminster Abbey.

July 2. The Queen and the Duke of Edinburgh visited Napier College, Edinburgh, and opened the new library extension. **3.** The Queen visited an exhibition to mark the centenary of the Royal Scottish Geographical Society in Edinburgh. The Duke of Edinburgh visited the summer exhibition of the Royal Scottish Academy in Edinburgh. The Queen Mother was present at a service in Westminster Abbey to mark the 50th anniversary of the death of Marie Curie. **5.** The Queen and the Duke of Edinburgh visited Berwickshire. Princess Anne visited Glenrothes. **7.** Princess Anne left Gatwick Airport for the U.S.A. to visit Los Angeles, Atlanta, Raleigh and Manteo. Princess Margaret undertook engagements in Hampshire. **9.** The Prince of Wales opened the *Mary Rose* exhibition in Portsmouth. **11.** Princess Margaret was present at the British Museum for the inauguration of the exhibition of treasures from the Treasury of St. Mark's Cathedral in Venice. **12.** The Queen Mother was present at the "topping out" ceremony of Lloyd's new building in London. **13.** Princess Anne attended the 400th anniversary celebrations of the first English settlement in the New World in Manteo, North Carolina; she returned to London on July 14. **17.** Princess Margaret visited Liverpool. **22.** The Prince of Wales opened the world wheelchair games (Paralympics) at Stoke Mandeville, Bucks. **23.** Princess Margaret visited Glasgow. **25.** The Duke of Edinburgh, President of the Federation Equestre Internationale, left Heathrow Airport for the U.S.A. to attend the Olympic

Games. **27.** Princess Anne, President of the British Olympic Association, left Gatwick Airport for the U.S.A. to attend the Olympic Games. **31.** The Queen attended a performance of "Arabella" at Glyndebourne to mark the Festival's golden jubilee.

Aug. 4. The Queen from *Britannia* watched the Tall Ships' Parade of Sail as they left the Mersey. The Prince of Wales left R.A.F. Brize Norton to visit Papua New Guinea. **8.** The Queen, accompanied by Princess Margaret, opened the new Kylesku Bridge, Sutherland; on Aug. 10 Her Majesty opened the new Queen Elizabeth Bridge over the River Dee. **30.** Princess Margaret undertook engagements in Argyll and Bute.

BRITISH POLITICS

(1983) Sept. 8. Mr. Fowler, Social Services Secretary, issued an instruction to health authorities to let private contractors tender for cleaning, catering and laundry services in hospitals. **11.** The Social Democratic Party at their conference in Salford ruled out a merger with the Liberals before the next General Election by an overwhelming majority and rejected an amendment calling for joint selection of all Alliance candidates. **14.** Mr. John Selwyn Gummer was appointed as chairman of the Conservative Party in succession to Mr. Cecil Parkinson. **15.** The Cabinet agreed to try to limit pay rises in the public sector in 1984–85 to three per cent. **17.** Mr. Steel, the Liberal leader, announced he intended to lead his party into the next General Election after his 2½ month break from politics. **20.** The Liberal Assembly opened in Harrogate; on the following day the Assembly endorsed the reunification of Ireland as a long-term aim with the withdrawal of British troops from Ulster. **25.** Mrs. Thatcher arrived in Ottawa at the start of a six-day visit to Canada and the U.S.A. for talks with Mr. Trudeau and President Reagan. **26.** Sir Percy Cradock, Britain's Ambassador to China, was given the role of special supervisor of the Hong Kong negotiations and foreign affairs adviser to Mrs. Thatcher. **28.** The National Executive of the Labour Party approved a statement of revised aims and decided to recommend to the party conference that Polaris should be kept as a bargaining counter in arms negotiations. **29.** A Soviet trade official, who had been accused of spying, was ordered to leave Britain within seven days. The Employment Secretary (Mr. Tebbit) held his first meeting with the T.U.C. since the unions decided to lift their boycott on talks with the Government. **30.** The Social Services Secretary (Mr. Fowler) announced that cuts in N.H.S. manpower had been agreed with all 14 regional health authorities and that 4,837 jobs were to go by Mar. 31 to save about £40 million a year.

Oct. 2. Mr. Neil Kinnock was elected Labour's new leader when the party's electoral college voted him the winner on the first ballot of a four-cornered contest at the annual conference at Brighton; voting was: Kinnock 71·272 per cent, R. Hattersley 19·288, E. Heffer 6·303, P. Shore 3·137; the deputy leadership was won by Mr. Roy Hattersley who had a first ballot win over three other candidates. **3.** The Labour Party conference voted by a 3–1 majority to reject appeals against expulsion from five leading members of the Trotskyist Militant Tendency; on the following day the conference elected a national executive with no single group dominant; Mr. Foot, outgoing leader, made his farewell address; on Oct. 5 conference voted overwhelmingly in favour of unilateral nuclear disarmament. **5.** The Environment Secretary (Mr. Jenkin) said he was taking measures to improve the management system of the Property Services Agency as it was disclosed that 61 employees had been dismissed for various forms of corruption. Mr. Cecil Parkinson, Trade and Industry Secretary, in a statement admitted a relationship with Miss Sara Keays, his former secretary, who was expecting his child in Jan. **7.** The Government's White Paper on local government reorganization, with a commitment to abolish the Greater London Council and the six Metropolitan County Councils on April 1, 1986, was published. **11.** The Conservative Party conference opened in Blackpool; the Home Secretary (Mr. Brittan) announced a package of tougher prison sentences including minimum 20-year terms for some murderers; on the following day, conference was told that the deposit at Parliamentary elections was to be increased possibly to £1,000 and people on holiday on the day of an election were to be given the right to vote by post or proxy; on Oct. 13 conference decisively rejected a motion to ban further coloured immigration, encourage repatriation and abolish the race relations laws. **14.** Mr. Cecil Parkinson resigned as Trade and Industry Secretary after Miss Sara Keays issued a statement to "put the record straight" about their affair; on Oct. 16 the Prime Minister appointed Mr. Norman Tebbit as Trade and Industry Secretary in succession to Mr. Parkinson; Mr. Tebbit was replaced as Employment Secretary by Mr. Tom King whose position as Transport Secretary was assigned to Mr. Nicholas Ridley, Financial Secretary to the Treasury. **18.** A Government statement announced that the Navy was to have a new class of frigate and that tenders were to be invited for construction of the first of 12 Type 23 frigates at a total cost of about £1·2 billion. Mrs. Thatcher completed Government changes with five appointments in non-Cabinet posts. **19.** Mr. Ian Gow, Minister of Housing, announced the Government was to cut house improvement grants next year from 90 per cent of the cost to 75 per cent. **20.** The

THE NEW PRINCE

The Prince and Princess of Wales leaving hospital with Prince Harry the day after his birth.

THE ROYAL VISIT TO JORDAN

The Queen paid a five-day State visit to Jordan in March amid tight security.

THE QUEEN IN WEST GERMANY

The Queen visiting B.A.O.R. units in May.

THE 40TH ANNIVERSARY OF D-DAY

The Queen with other Heads of State during the anniversary commemorations in Normandy.

THE HARRODS BOMBING

The wreckage left by the I.R.A. car bomb at Harrods in December 1983.

THE LIBYAN EMBASSY SIEGE

An intermediary leading Libyans from the building at the end of the police siege.

THE ABBEYSTEAD DISASTER

The aftermath of the explosion at the underground water treatment plant in Lancashire in which a number of local visitors were killed.

THE MINERS' STRIKE

Massed police confronting pickets at Orgreave Colliery in South Yorkshire.

THE YORK MINSTER FIRE

The Archbishop of Canterbury surveys the devastated south transept.

THE PEAT BOG MAN

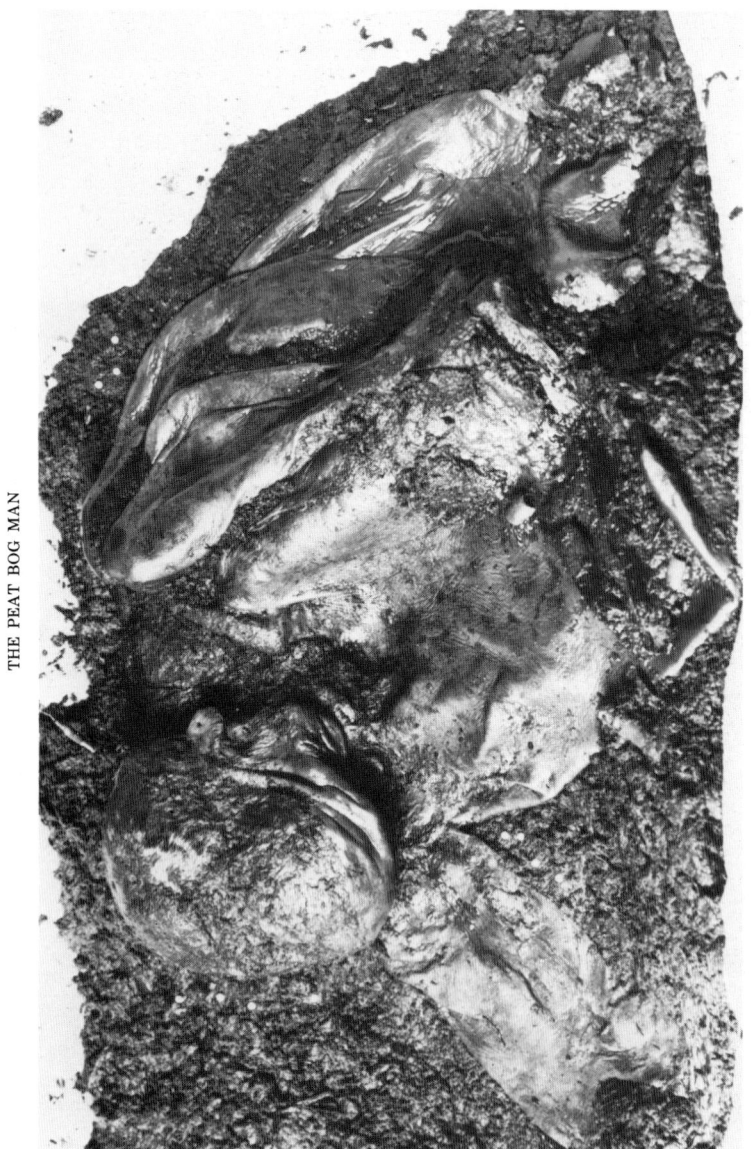

The 2,500 years-old remains of a man discovered in a peat bog at Lindow Moss in Cheshire.

FREE-FLYING IN SPACE

U.S. astronaut Bruce McCandless making the first untethered human flight in space.

OBITUARIES

Sir John Betjeman (*top left*), J. B. Priestley (*top right*), Marshal of the R.A.F. Sir Arthur ("Bomber") Harris (*bottom left*) and Dame Flora Robson.

OBITUARIES

James Mason (*top left*), Richard Burton (*top right*), Eric Morecambe (*bottom left*) and Tommy Cooper.

TRIUMPHANT FAREWELL

Jayne Torvill and Christopher Dean, Olympic gold medallists, and world ice dance champions for the fourth consecutive year.

CRICKETING FEATS

Richard Hadlee (*left*), the first man since 1967 to score 1,000 runs and take 100 wickets in a season. Gordon Greenidge, Man of the Series, in which the West Indies beat England in all five Tests.

THE LOS ANGELES OLYMPICS

Mary Decker, the U.S. favourite, crashes out of the 3,000 metres following a controversial collision with Britain's Zola Budd. The U.S. athlete Carl Lewis, who equalled Jesse Owens' record of four gold medals in track and field events.

Chancellor of the Exchequer (Mr. Lawson) said strict control over public spending would continue for years and that the Government's long-term aim was zero inflation. The Environment Secretary (Mr. Jenkin) announced the Government was to impose penalties on local councils to curb their spending with rate support grants only £90 million higher next year than this at £11,870 million. The Anglo-French summit opened at Downing Street between Mrs. Thatcher and President Mitterrand. **21.** The Government announced it had agreed to write off outstanding loans of £22·5 million to Mozambique. **24.** It was disclosed Britain had given political asylum to Mr. Oleg Bitov, a Soviet defector. **25.** The Prime Minister and the Foreign Secretary (Sir Geoffrey Howe) both made statements in the Commons on the U.S.–Caribbean invasion of Grenada and an emergency debate was held on Oct. 26 when Labour's attack on the Government's handling of the crisis was rejected on a procedural motion to adjourn by 336 to 211 votes. **26.** The Government published its new Trade Union Bill requiring unions to hold secret ballots before authorizing or declaring official any strike or disruptive action which interfered with or broke employment contracts. **27.** The Prime Minister told the Commons she did not regard the special relationship between Britain and the U.S.A. as having been damaged by President Reagan's decision to order the invasion of Grenada against her advice. The Government's revised Police and Criminal Evidence Bill was reintroduced in Parliament. In the Commons, a Labour motion calling on the Government to reverse its policy of cutting the N.H.S. was defeated by 338 to 205 votes, and the Government motion endorsing its efforts to ensure the best value for money spent on patient care was carried by 331 to 204 votes. **31.** Mr. Heseltine, Defence Secretary, said in the Commons the Government would deploy cruise missiles without insisting on a "dual key" arrangement with the U.S.A. and that the "damaging" disagreement over Grenada should not reduce Britain's trust of the U.S.A. over defence.

Nov. 2. The Commons voted by 164 to 159 to give Mr. Austin Mitchell, Labour M.P. for Great Grimsby, leave to introduce a private member's Bill to allow Commons' debates and committee hearings to be televised. **7.** Mrs. Thatcher and Dr. Fitzgerald, the Irish Prime Minister, had talks at Chequers. The Commons gave a second reading to the new Police and Criminal Evidence Bill by 339 votes to 188. **8.** A second reading was given in the Commons to the Trade Union Bill by 362 to 189 votes. **11.** Mr. Eric Varley, Labour M.P. for Chesterfield, announced he was to resign his seat. The Commons gave an unopposed second reading to a private member's Bill which would introduce a system of certifica-

tion for video cassettes and would ban video "nasties". Mrs. Thatcher lunched with Mr. Trudeau, Canadian Prime Minister, at Downing Street before he returned home after his visit to six West European capitals. **14.** Mr. Heseltine, Defence Secretary, announced in the Commons the arrival of the first cruise missiles to Greenham Common airbase; on Nov. 15, 300 demonstrators were arrested as they blocked the entrance to the Commons in a protest against the arrival of the missiles. **17.** The Chancellor of the Exchequer (Mr. Lawson) made his autumn economic statement to the Commons. **23.** Mr. Fowler, Social Services Secretary, announced in the Commons he was setting up a ministerial inquiry into State, occupational, and private pension schemes and that he would be chairman. **24.** Mr. Jenkin, Environment Secretary, announced new figures for the Housing Investment Programme which showed a reduction of 20 per cent in the Government contribution to amounts which councils in England and Wales could spend on housing next year. **28.** The Social Services Secretary announced legislation would be introduced to allow opticians to advertise their services and to enable non-opticians to sell spectacles, as recommended by the Office of Fair Trading.

Dec. 2. Lord Whitelaw, the Prime Minister's deputy, took over the role of co-ordinating Government information from Mr. Biffen, leader of the Commons. **7.** The Prime Minister rejected calls for British troops to be withdrawn from Lebanon. **8.** On a free vote, the House of Lords passed by 74 to 24 a motion instructing their Sound Broadcasting Committee to report on how to implement the decision made in 1966 in favour of the public televising of some of the Lords' proceedings. **13.** A Home Office report was published showing that expenses of £6,100,000 were spent by 2,578 candidates contesting 650 seats in the General Election in June. Mr. Tebbit, Trade and Industry Secretary, published a White Paper on regional industrial development. **14.** Mr. Jenkin, Environment Secretary, announced the total Government grant for local authorities next year would be £11,872 million or £90 million more than in the current year, the rate of grant being cut by nearly one per cent to 51·9 per cent of total spending. Mr. Brittan, Home Secretary, announced measures to curb drug traffickers and doctors who over-prescribed dangerous drugs with the promise of more Government finance for the treatment of addicts. **15.** The Bill to turn British Telecom into a private company completed all its stages in the Commons. **19.** The Home Secretary told the Commons that an extra 700 police as well as special vehicle patrols were being deployed in London to deter further I.R.A. bomb attacks. **20.** It was announced that a 22-year-old administrative trainee in the Department of

Employment, who was not named and was not to be charged under the Official Secrets Act, was dismissed for leaking a sensitive memorandum to the magazine *Time Out.* The Government Bill to limit the rates of high-spending councils was published. 22. The Cabinet decided to defer proscribing Sinn Fein.

(1984) Jan. 9. Mr. Fowler, Social Services Secretary, announced extra money totalling £83 million for the N.H.S. to add an average of one per cent. to health authorities' budgets. 16. The Chancellor of the Exchequer (Mr. Lawson) stated that the Queen and other members of the Royal Family had been given a four per cent. increase in the Civil List. 17. The Government's Rates Bill, aimed at curbing high-spending local authorities, was given a second reading in the Commons by 346 to 247 votes; 13 Tories, including the former Prime Minister, Mr. Edward Heath, voted against the Government and some 20 other Tories abstained. 19. Three Tories voted against the Government and a few others abstained in the Commons on a Labour motion critical of proposed cuts in housing benefits which was lost by 330 to 198 votes. 22. Stokeley Carmichael, a former leader of the Black Panther revolutionary group in America, was barred from entering Britain when he arrived at Heathrow Airport. 23. The Government's proposals for reduced rate support grants were approved in the Commons by 332 to 203 votes; four Tories voted against the Government and about a dozen others abstained. 25. The Foreign Secretary (Sir Geoffrey Howe) announced to M.P.s that the Government had decided to ban workers at its top secret communications headquarters in Cheltenham from belonging to trade unions "in the interests of national security", the ban being accompanied by an offer of £1,000 to each employee as recompense for giving up trade union rights; later the six main Civil Service unions said they would fight the decision. The Commons gave a third reading by 184 to 84 votes to the Prevention of Terrorism (Temporary Provisions) Bill which re-enacted existing legislation with changes recommended by Lord Jellicoe following his review of the powers. 26. After making a statement on the publication of the report of inquiry into the mass escape from the Maze Prison, Belfast, in Sept. 1983, Mr. Prior, Northern Ireland Secretary, rejected demands in the Commons for his own resignation and for that of Mr. Nicholas Scott, the Under-Secretary with responsibility for Ulster prisons. The Home Secretary announced that 16 cases, including six of murder, in which evidence against the accused had been given by Dr. Alan Clift, the discredited forensic scientist, were to be referred for review by the Court of Appeal. 28. It was revealed that Mr. Oleg Bitov, a leading Russian editor and writer

who escaped to the West four months ago, had been given asylum in Britain. 31. Changes in electoral law allowing holidaymakers and Britons abroad to vote and increasing the deposit paid by candidates were proposed by the Government in a White Paper.

Feb. 1. Mr. Tebbit, Trade and Industry Secretary, announced that a pilot plant was to be built in Britain by Nissan, the Japanese motor-vehicle manufacturer, before decisions were made to expand output to 100,000 cars a year. In the Commons, an Opposition motion calling on the Government to help in the formation of a new corporate plan for the shipbuilding industry was defeated by 285 to 198 votes. 2. The Government announced the sites for Britain's first six freeports: Belfast, Birmingham, Cardiff, Liverpool, Prestwick, and Southampton. 6. Mr. Fowler, Social Services Secretary, said the proposed cuts in housing benefits were to be reduced by £45 million after all-party protests. 9. The Government had a majority of 141 after a debate in the Commons on last year's I.R.A. escape from the Maze Prison. 10. Mr. Harold Macmillan, former Conservative Prime Minister, received an earldom on his 90th birthday. 15. The report on the Select Committee on Employment's investigation into the Government's decision to ban trade union membership at G.C.H.Q. in Cheltenham was published and recommended the ban should be withdrawn and the unions' offer of a legally-binding no-disruption agreement be accepted (on the following day, Mrs. Thatcher disagreed with the Select Committee's recommendations during exchanges in the Commons). The D.H.S.S. announced a cut of £33 million in social security spending to pay for concessions in the housing benefit scheme. The Government announced the proposed £10,000 maximum fine for the most serious offences under the private member's Bill to outlaw video nasties was to be doubled to £20,000. 16. The Government's expenditure plans until the end of 1987 were published as a White Paper. A record total of 17 candidates were in the field for the Chesterfield by-election when nominations closed. 17. It was announced that the Government hoped to introduce legislation in the next session of Parliament to allow suitably qualified non-solicitors as well as banks and building societies to compete with solicitors for house conveyancing work. 20. Mr. Brittan, Home Secretary, introduced an order in the Commons which doubled maximum fines which could be imposed by magistrates in England and Wales. 23. At a meeting with union leaders at Downing Street Mrs. Thatcher refused to compromise on the Government's plan to ban union membership at G.C.H.Q. in Cheltenham. 27. After a heated Commons debate on the Cheltenham G.C.H.Q. issue, the Government had a majority in a division forced by Alliance M.P.s, but with Labour abstaining, of 176; about a dozen Tories abstained; on Feb. 28, Mr. Kinnock, Labour leader, dismissed two of his Front-bench spokesmen for voting against the Government after the Labour leadership had decided not to vote; they were among seven Labour M.P.s voting against the Government on a technical motion on which the debate took place; the Speaker rebuked M.P.s who had disrupted the Commons on Feb. 23 following concern from senior M.P.s on both sides that the Commons was being brought into disrepute by rowdy behaviour. **29.** Mr. David Nellist, Labour M.P. for Coventry, S.E., was ordered out of the Commons after he refused to withdraw a remark that a Conservative M.P. was "well paid" to support the South African Government.

Mar. 1. Mr. Wedgwood Benn won the Chesterfield by-election for Labour with a majority of 6,264 over the Lib./S.D.P. Alliance candidate, with the Conservatives third. **8.** The Social Services Secretary (Mr. Fowler) announced N.H.S. prescription charges would be increased by 20p an item from April. **13.** The Chancellor of the Exchequer (Mr. Nigel Lawson) presented his first Budget in the Commons. **14.** The Home Secretary told the Commons that five Libyans detained in connection with recent bomb explosions were being deported. **16.** The Video Recordings Bill was given an unopposed third reading in the Commons. **21.** An Opposition motion attacking the Government over energy price rises was defeated in the Commons by 289 to 202 votes. **22.** The Foreign Secretary (Sir Geoffrey Howe) announced the complete withdrawal of the British contingent which served in Lebanon in the Multinational Force. **24.** A statement from 10 Downing Street after an emergency meeting of ministers at Chequers said the Queen's visit to Jordan should go ahead; this followed fears for the Queen's safety after a bomb explosion in Amman. **26.** Mrs. Thatcher was cleared by the Commons Select Committee on Members' Interests over her son Mark's involvement in a £300 million deal to build a university in Oman. The Defence Secretary (Mr. Heseltine) told the Commons that the Territorial Army was to be expanded to 86,000 by 1990. **28.** The Foreign Secretary told M.P.s that Britain would not pay the E.E.C. the £100 million advance it wanted to save the Community from running out of money following the failure of the E.E.C. foreign ministers to reach agreement on a solution to the dispute over Britain's budget payments. The Industry Minister (Mr. Lamont) announced Government approval for the takeover by a consortium of the Scott Lithgow shipyard on Clydeside at a cost of £88 million to the taxpayer. In the Commons, the Government had a majority of 125 on the third reading of the Rates Bill. **29.** The report

of the Security Commission investigation into the case of an Intelligence Corps N.C.O. jailed last year for offering secrets to the Russians was published and Mrs. Thatcher told the Commons she had ordered a tightening of security throughout government departments, the intelligence agencies, and the armed forces.

April 2. Mr. Fowler, Social Services Secretary, announced a review of social security benefits. Forty Tory M.P.s voted against the Government on report stage of the Trade Union Bill and supported an amendment calling for an end to the arrangement under which union members could "contract out" of paying the political levy. **4.** D.H.S.S. announced an investigation was to be carried out into the way services were provided by family doctors. **9.** The London Regional Transport Bill was given a third reading in the Commons by 254 to 168 votes. **10.** After a three-hour emergency debate initiated by Labour on the civil liberty aspects of the miners' strike, during which Labour M.P.s were critical of some police tactics, the Government had a majority of 157 on a formal motion to adjourn. In a Commons written reply, the Government rejected the Greek Government's request for the return of the Elgin Marbles. **11.** Mr. Edward Heath and three ex-Cabinet ministers—Mr. Francis Pym, Mr. Geoffrey Ripon, and Sir Ian Gilmour—led a Commons revolt by a minority of Tory M.P.s against the Government on the Bill paving the way for the abolition of the G.L.C. and six Metropolitan authorities; the second reading of the Bill was carried by 301 to 208 votes, 19 Tories joining Labour in opposing the measure with about 20 others abstaining. **12.** The Government announced that it had decided to buy U.S. missiles for the Navy instead of the British Sea Eagle. **25.** Mr. Brittan, Home Secretary, told the Commons that in the light of the Libyan Embassy crisis the Government was to review the Vienna Convention on diplomatic relations. In the Commons, a Labour motion attacking Government transport policy was defeated by 247 to 168 votes. **26.** Mrs. Thatcher, in a Commons written reply, promised a full investigation of MI5 by the Security Commission following the conviction of Michael Bettaney, an MI5 officer, for attempting to spy for the Russians. The Trade Union Bill received a third reading in the Commons by 231 to 149 votes.

May 2. Mr. Tam Dalyell, Labour M.P. for Linlithgow, was ordered from the Commons and suspended for five days for refusing to withdraw a claim that the Prime Minister had lied over the sinking of the Argentine cruiser *General Belgrano*. **3.** In three by-elections, the Conservatives held Surrey South-West and Stafford, but with considerably reduced majorities, and Labour retained

Cynon Valley. In local government elections, the Tories suffered a series of setbacks and lost control of a number of councils including Birmingham. **12.** Dr. Keith Hampson, Conservative M.P. for Leeds North-West, resigned as Parliamentary Private Secretary to the Defence Secretary, following his arrest in a Soho homosexual striptease club. **14.** The Defence White Paper was published. **16.** The Police and Criminal Evidence Bill was given a third reading in the Commons by 286 to 190 votes. **22.** The Foreign Office disclosed it had expelled Mr. Arkadi Gouk, described during the Bettaney spy trial as the KGB controller in London, following Russia's demand on May 21 for the withdrawal of Mr. John Burnett, security officer at the British Embassy in Moscow. **23.** The Commons held its longest post-war sitting (32 hours 13 minutes) during discussion of the Government Bill to pave the way for the abolition of the G.L.C. and six metropolitan councils; business overspilled from the all-night session on May 22 and the Government defeated a closure motion to obtain the third reading a day earlier than scheduled. The Social Services Secretary (Mr. Fowler) announced proposals for legislation to give employees who changed jobs the right to take their pension entitlements with them. **30.** It was announced that salary increases of up to 18 per cent. for State industry chairmen had been approved by Mr. Ridley, Transport Secretary.

June 2. Mr. P. W. Botha, the South African Prime Minister, had talks at Chequers with Mrs. Thatcher before flying on to Zurich. **4.** President Reagan arrived in London as the first of the six leaders of the visiting heads of state attending the London Economic Summit. **7.** Police arrested over 120 people when fighting broke out in Parliament Square, Westminster, as miners staged a mass lobby of the Commons while M.P.s began a debate on the strike; an Opposition motion condemning the Government's mishandling of the dispute was defeated by 272 to 179 votes. Britain demanded the withdrawal of a Czech Embassy clerk within 14 days in the third expulsion of Czech officials from London in a month. The Prime Minister announced the country's nurses were to be paid in full the 7·5 per cent. pay increase recommended by a review body, but that doctors, dentists, the armed forces and top people in public service were to be kept to an immediate increase of three per cent. with further rises of 3·5 to 4·6 per cent. in November. **11.** In the Lords, the Government secured a second reading for its bill to cancel next year's elections to the G.L.C. and six Metropolitan authorities when a Liberal amendment supported by Labour and S.D.P. peers as well as some Tories was defeated by 237 to 217 votes. **14.** Elections took place for Britain's 81 seats in the European Parliament; results announced on

June 17 and 18 gave Labour 15 gains from Tories who held 45 of their previous 60 seats; Labour seats totalled 32; the Scottish National Party retained its one seat and in Northern Ireland the Rev. Ian Paisley was re-elected together with Mr. John Taylor (Official Unionist) and Mr. John Hume (S.D.L.P.); the Liberal/S.D.P. Alliance failed to win a solitary constituency although polling almost 20 per cent. of the votes. In the Portsmouth South by-election, the Liberal/S.D.P. Alliance won a sensational victory by capturing the seat held by the Conservatives for over 60 years and overturning a Tory majority of 12,335 at the General Election. **18.** Mr. Fowler, Social Services Secretary, announced that the cost of pensions, child benefit, unemployment pay and other social security benefits was to be increased by £1,600 million, raising the total cost to £39,000 million a year. **19.** The Government was defeated in the Lords on its Trade Union Bill when peers voted by a majority of 20 that trade union executives should be elected by postal ballot. **28.** The Lords voted by a big majority to stop the proposed suspension of elections for the G.L.C. and the Metropolitan Councils until royal assent was given to a Bill which the Government planned to introduce in the next session; they carried by 191 votes to 143, a majority of 48 against the Government, a new clause to the Local Government (Interim Provisions) Bill which prevented the Secretary of the Environment from setting up interim councils composed of nominated councillors from the boroughs to take over county functions next May. **29.** In a Green Paper, the Government outlined proposals for day and weekend imprisonment as an alternative for some full-time custodial sentences.

July 1. The Foreign Secretary (Sir Geoffrey Howe) arrived in Moscow for two days of talks with President Chernenko and Mr. Gromyko, Soviet Foreign Minister. **5.** The Cabinet approved changes to the Bill to cancel next year's G.L.C. and metropolitan council elections following the defeat in the Lords; the lives of the existing councils would be extended for 11 months until April, 1986, instead of temporary councils being installed for that period; the Government won the backing of the Lords for its new measures on July 16. An Opposition motion attacking the Government over the National Health Service was defeated in the Commons by 297 to 174 votes. It was announced that new excursion documents would be issued for trips to France lasting up to 60 hours and valid for one month after the abandonment of the old system of no-passport excursions. **10.** Eighteen Tory M.P.s abstained in the Commons on a vote approving the recent agreement on the financing of the E.E.C. budget but the Government won the two divisions with majorities of 165 and 161. **12.** The Foreign Secretary told the Commons that two Nigerian diplomats must leave Britain within seven days because of the Dikko kidnap affair and that in view of the Nigerian refusal to permit police questioning of the High Commission staff in London it would be inappropriate for the High Commissioner to return from Lagos, where it was announced that two British envoys must leave the country within a week; on July 13, Nigeria requested Britain to recall its High Commissioner in Lagos; Britain agreed on July 15. **12.** Mr. Jenkin, Environment Secretary, in a Commons written reply, said the Government was withholding £452 million in grants this year from councils planning to overspend its targets. **13.** It was announced in the Commons that laws were to be introduced to deprive drug traffickers and other major criminals of the proceeds of their crimes and that an extra £1 million was being made available for local services to help drug misusers. **16.** Social Services Secretary (Mr. Fowler) announced proposed legislation to give people the right to be responsible for their own pension arrangements. **18.** A reorganisation of the Defence Ministry was announced. The Foreign Office announced that Britain and Argentina held direct talks in Berne for the first time since the Falklands Conflict; the talks broke down on the following day. The Home Secretary announced a review of extradition treaties and new initiatives to combat international terrorism and abuses of diplomatic status. **24.** Mr. Jenkin, Environment Secretary, named the 18 "worst over-spenders" among local authorities, which were to have their rates limited next year under the new rate-capping legislation which would lead to a total saving of £400 million; Mr. Jenkin also said that his specific consent would be needed for any cash help from the G.L.C. to other councils. Thirty-five Tory M.P.s voted against the Government in the Commons on a motion seeking stronger action in the Trade Union Bill for postal ballots for the election of officials, but the Government defeated the proposal by 467 to 52 votes. **25.** Mr. Tebbit, Trade and Industry Secretary, told M.P.s of the decision to sell British Shipbuilders' seven warship yards to private ownership. The Chancellor of the Exchequer announced that the income tax system was to be computerised with the loss of 6,000 jobs. Mr. Kinnock, Labour's leader, won by 15 to 12 votes support from his Party's National Executive for his plan to give constituency parties the option of holding ballots instead of leaving decisions on whether or not to re-select M.P.s to management committees. **31.** Mr. Martin Flannery, Labour M.P. for Sheffield Hillsborough, was suspended from the Commons for five sitting days after being "named" by the Speaker when he refused to withdraw a claim that "tame Tory judges" were being used by the Government against striking miners.

Aug. 7. Television broadcasts of House of Lords debates were expected to begin early next year following the recommendations by the Lords Select Committee on Sound Broadcasting published in a report. **23.** Mr. Clarke, Health Minister, announced an extra 6,800 jobs were to be created in the N.H.S. to provide better services for patients. **29.** The Prime Minister decided to postpone a two-week tour of South East Asia because against the background of the present industrial situation it would not be right for her to be so far from Britain for this period.

IRELAND

(1983) Sept. 7. The Republic of Ireland rejected abortion by a two to one majority in a national referendum, but only 54 per cent of the electorate voted. **9.** The Irish Republic expelled two Soviet diplomats accused of spying, the first such action ever taken by a Dublin Government. **26.** Mr. Patrick Gilmour, held prisoner for 11 months by Provisional I.R.A. in a vain attempt to force his "supergrass" son, Ian Gilmour, from giving evidence against 60 terrorist suspects, was freed.

Oct. 5. An inquiry was ordered into the use of dummy soldiers for guard duty in Northern Ireland after claims that dummies were manning observation posts when 38 I.R.A. terrorists broke out of the Maze Prison. **10.** An agreement was reached to provide natural gas from the Irish Republic to Northern Ireland. **13.** Northern Ireland Office released figures showing the Army, police, and other services spent £500 million of public money to combat crime and terrorism in Ulster last year. **18.** The Irish Government published its Criminal Justice Bill under which terrorists who used guns in the Republic were liable to get life sentences. **21.** Eleven terrorist suspects were freed in Belfast because a "supergrass" who had named them changed his mind; on Oct. 24 another seven walked free from a Belfast court after another informer refused to give evidence against them. **28.** Sir George Terry, who investigated the R.U.C.'s handling of the Kincora Boys' Home inquiry, stated that he had found no evidence of a police cover-up.

Nov. 3. The New Ireland Forum published figures in Dublin showing that terrorism in Ulster between 1969 and 1982 cost the British taxpayer £9 billion and Eire £2 billion. **21.** The Official Unionist party voted to boycott the Northern Ireland Assembly following the murders of three men at a Protestant chapel in Co. Armagh.

Dec. 2. Two Eire policemen were held up and divested of their uniforms by a man believed to be Dominic McGlinchey, the Irish

National Liberation Army terrorist, at a cottage near Cork. **7.** Mr. Edgar Graham, aged 29, a prominent Unionist politician, was murdered by Provisional I.R.A. in Belfast when on his way to the law faculty at Queen's University to give a tutorial. **23.** Mrs. Thatcher made a one-day visit to Ulster.

(1984) Jan. 8. The Prime Minister (Dr. Fitzgerald) announced a greater proportion of the police in the Irish Republic was to be armed. **24.** The Northern Ireland Secretary (Mr. Prior) announced that Londonderry City Council could in future refer to itself as "Derry," but the change applied only to the council and not to the City itself. **26.** The report of the inquiry by the Chief Inspector of Prisons into the security arrangements at the Maze Prison, following the mass escape of I.R.A. prisoners in Sept. 1983, was published; Mr. Ernest Whittington, the governor of the prison, resigned as soon as the report was published.

Feb. 20. The Irish Republic banned the public representatives of Sinn Fein from having access to ministers or state departments.

Mar. 6. It was stated in the Commons that economic support for Ulster last year was £1,149 million and the cost of the Army's role was £143 million.

April 3. The Duke and Duchess of Kent arrived at Hillsborough, near Belfast, to start a 24-hour visit to the Province. **5.** Britain apologised for "apparent" undercover activity in the Irish Republic by the R.U.C. in 1982. **10.** A review of the Operation of the Northern Ireland (Emergency Provisions) Act, 1978, was published.

May 2. The three main political parties in the Irish Republic and the S.D.L.P. of Northern Ireland launched the report of the New Ireland Forum. **17.** The Government gave approval for a private enterprise scheme (near Crumlin) for the first big coal mining operation in Northern Ireland. **23.** The Official Ulster Unionists decided to end their six-month-old boycott of the Northern Ireland Assembly.

June 1. President Reagan arrived at Shannon for a three-day visit to the Irish Republic. **6.** Princess Margaret began a two-day visit to Northern Ireland.

July 31. The Republic of Ireland's Supreme Court ruled that I.R.A. suspect Seamus Shannon should be extradited to Northern Ireland to face charges of murdering Sir Norman Strong, a former Speaker of the Ulster Parliament, and his son.

Aug. 12. A man was killed and 20 people injured in Belfast when police charged into a crowd of pro-I.R.A. demonstrators in an attempt to arrest Martin Galvin, publicity director of Noraid, the I.R.A.'s American fund-raising organisation. **21.** The Northern Ireland Assembly, in a special sitting called following increased violence and tension, passed a motion deploring the failure of the Secretary of State (Mr. Prior) to consistently uphold Government policy and condemned the gross imbalance of reporting of recent events in Ulster.

ACCIDENTS AND DISASTERS

(1983) Sept. 12. Over sixty South African miners, most of them black, were killed in an explosion at a colliery in Natal. **22.** Thirty passengers were taken to hospital after the overnight Inverness–Glasgow train jumped the rails at Aldour, south of Pitlochry. **23.** A Gulfair Boeing 737 airliner crashed near Abu Dhabi airport after it caught fire in mid-air, all 111 passengers and crew being killed.

Oct. 1. U.S. intelligence sources reported that three Russian cosmonauts narrowly escaped death when their rocket blew up as it was being launched from central Asia on Sept. 27. **25.** Five people were killed and 18 others injured in a gas explosion at the Royal Darroch Hotel, Aberdeen. **26.** Five Asian women died after being trapped by a fire which destroyed a clothing workshop in East London. **30.** A remote area of eastern Turkey was devastated by an earthquake with great loss of life and thousands injured and made homeless.

Nov. 5. Five men—three of them Britons—died and one was injured when a diving bell and a decompression chamber separated on board a Norwegian drilling rig in the North Sea. **6.** Six members of an Asian family—three women and three children—were killed when equipment in an illicit shoe-making business in the basement of their home in Gravesend exploded. **8.** Belgium suffered its most severe earthquake since 1938 when a woman was killed and several people were badly injured in the eastern part of the country. **9.** It was reported that at least 1,500,000 people were made homeless by storms and floods along the coast of Vietnam between late Sept. and early Nov. **27.** A Colombian jumbo jet crashed into a field and burst into flames minutes before it was due to land at Madrid Airport, killing 181 of the 192 people aboard. **28.** A Nigeria Airways Fokker F-28 crashed while landing at Enugu, 62 of the 66 passengers and three of the five crew being killed.

Dec. 7. Ninety-two people lost their lives when a Spanish airline pilot lost his way taxiing a DC9 jet at Madrid's fog-covered international airport and collided with another jet. **8.** Ten people were killed when an executive jet aircraft crashed into the sea off Stornoway. **9.** Helicopters rescued 108 passengers and 20 crew members of the Sealink ferry *Antrim Princess* after fire crippled her two engines during gales off the east coast of Ulster; earlier helicopters lifted 24 sailors to safety from a fishery protection vessel, which was drifting in heavy seas towards the coast of Co. Down after her engines failed. **17.** Eighty-three people died when fire swept through a crowded Madrid discothèque. **18.** Thirty-four Italian sailors were killed when their lorry crashed on the motorway linking Genoa and Turin. **30.** The death toll in America's "big freeze" reached over 430 as fresh low temperature records were set and damage to fruit and vegetable crops in Florida, Texas, and Louisiana was put at £275 million.

(1984) Jan. 6. It was announced that the final death toll in December's earthquake in Guinea was 275. **14.** Thirty-six persons died in hotel fire in Pusan, South Korea. **24.** Seventeen seamen were drowned after abandoning the sinking freighter, *Radiant Med*, in gales off Guernsey; nine of the crew aboard a raft were rescued by lifeboat.

Feb. 25. At least 69 Brazilians were killed when petrol leaked from a pipeline and exploded in a slum area close to the coastal refinery of Cubatao.

Mar. 15. A death toll of 35 was confirmed when divers ended their search for bodies in a U.S. oil-drilling ship, which sank off Vietnam last October. **19.** It was reported that an earthquake in Soviet Central Asia had caused serious damage to the city of Bukhara. **24.** A U.S. helicopter carrying 18 American and 11 South Korean Marines crashed into a mountain near Pohang killing everyone on board. **29.** A freak storm in the Carolinas which moved on to major cities of the north-east of the U.S.A. caused 67 people to lose their lives.

April 1. Four Britons were killed in an avalanche near Zermatt, Switzerland. **10.** Eight people died in a fire at the hospital on the Falkland Islands.

May 5. Eight British holidaymakers and a Spanish courier were killed in coach crash on Majorca. **23.** Nine people were killed and over 30 injured by an explosion at the underground water treatment plant at Abbeystead, Lancs., as a group of local visitors from the village of St. Michael's on Wyre were being shown around the installation; on June 4 the death toll rose to 15.

June 3. Nineteen people, including a baby, were missing in heavy seas north of Bermuda

after the British barque, *Marques*, sank when participating in a tall ships sailing race; nine crew members were rescued. **13.** The Navy frigate, *Jupiter*, collided with London Bridge while turning in the Thames. **21.** Three oil rig workers died when fire swept through a production platform 200 miles north-east of the Shetlands. **22.** It was reported that a big explosion at a Soviet naval arsenal in Northern Russia had destroyed surface-to-air missiles and killed an unknown number of Russians. **24.** An overnight Aberdeen-to-London express train hurtled off the rails on a bend near Morpeth Station in Northumberland, injuring 38 passengers.

July 8. About 40 people were injured when a coach crashed through a brick wall at Lynton, Devon. **9.** Lightning was blamed for causing a fire which destroyed the south transept at York Minster and caused damage estimated at over £1 million. **14.** Thirty-six people were killed in a train crash on the Yugoslav frontier near Trieste. **30.** Thirteen people were killed when a crowded commuter train crashed near Falkirk in Central Scotland.

Aug. 19. Eleven people were killed and three injured when a twin-engined Vickers Varsity plane carrying a party of aircraft enthusiasts crashed and exploded near Uttoxeter, Staffs. **20.** A London Transport driver was killed when his Central Line train crashed into the rear of a stationary train outside Leyton station; 30 passengers were injured. **22.** It was stated in New Delhi that floods and landslides had killed over 400 people in India in the past few months. **25.** A French cargo ship, the *Mont Louis*, sank after being in collision with the German ferry, *Olau Britannia*, 12 miles off the Belgian coast; on Aug. 26 it was disclosed that the *Mont Louis* was carrying a shipment of nuclear material. **27.** Fifty-five people were rescued from a pleasure boat after it struck rocks near the Needles lighthouse, Isle of Wight.

CRIMES, TRIALS, ETC.

(1983) Sept. 6. Seventy-five neighbourhood watch schemes were launched in London to encourage residents to improve local crime prevention and protect their properties. **7.** An incendiary letter bomb was delivered to each of the offices of Mr. Tebbit, Employment Secretary, and Mr. Younger, Scottish Secretary. **9.** Derek Devine, aged 25, a seaman, who started a fire which killed another crew-member and destroyed a Royal Navy Fleet Auxiliary ship four years ago, was jailed for life at the Central Criminal Court after being convicted of arson and manslaughter. **12.** Two privately-owned Picasso paintings valued at nearly $1,000,000 were stolen from the Art Museum of South Texas. **15.** Mr. Anthony

Hamilton, a consultant gynaecologist of Luton accused of attempting to murder a baby who survived an abortion operation, had the test case prosecution against him dismissed by Luton magistrates. **25.** Thirty-eight Republican terrorist prisoners armed with guns and knives fought their way out of the Maze Prison, near Belfast; a prison officer was stabbed to death, another was shot in the head, and five more received knife wounds; by nightfall 11 prisoners had been recaptured; Ulster Secretary, Mr. Prior, ordered an immediate rigorous inquiry at the highest level into all aspects of the escape; on Sept. 26 Sir James Hennessy, Chief Inspector of Prisons, arrived in Belfast to lead an inquiry; on Sept. 27 two more escaped prisoners were caught in Co. Down. **27.** Pte Michael McAleavey, of the Irish Army, was jailed for life at a court martial at The Curragh camp for killing three comrades in the Irish peace-keeping force in the Lebanon in 1982, after a row. **30.** Reported crime rose by 10 per cent in 1982 in England and Wales, the Home Office stated.

Oct. 9. Four of South Korea's Cabinet ministers on an official visit and at least 15 other people were killed by a bomb in the Burmese capital Rangoon. **11.** David Martin, aged 36, of London, was jailed for 25 years at the Central Criminal Court; he was convicted of causing grievous bodily harm to a policeman he had shot and also possessing firearms with intent to resist arrest when confronted by armed officers six weeks later; he was also convicted of theft during a bank robbery and found guilty of burglary. **17.** Det. Con. Peter Finch, of Croxley Green, one of two detectives accused of trying to kill Stephen Waldorf, when he was mistaken for criminal David Martin, was acquitted of attempted murder at the Central Criminal Court on the direction of the judge; on Oct. 19 Det. Con. Finch and Det. Con. John Jardine, of Pinner, were acquitted of wounding charges and Jardine was also acquitted of attempted murder. **24.** A wealthy solicitor, Mr. Basil Laitner, his wife and their son, were stabbed to death by an intruder at their home at Dore, near Sheffield, only hours after the wedding of their eldest daughter; another daughter was held at knifepoint for several hours.

Nov. 4. Dennis Nilsen, aged 37, of Cranley Gardens, Muswell Hill, London, was jailed for life at the Central Criminal Court after being found guilty of six murders and two attempted murders; he was stated to have confessed to a total of 15 or 16 killings; the judge recommended he serve at least 25 years. **8.** Ronald Waldron, of Anfield, who was alleged to have claimed while in custody he had worked for the Special Branch and British secret service and to have committed 19 political killings, was jailed for life at Liverpool Crown Court for murdering his five-year-old nephew. **9.**

Mr. Alfred Heineken, aged 60, head of Holland's Heineken brewery, was kidnapped in Amsterdam; on Nov. 30 he was freed after a police raid on an empty factory near the city. **20.** Three men were shot dead and seven people wounded when two masked gunmen burst into the Mountain Lodge Pentecostal Gospel Hall in the village of Keady, Co. Armagh, and opened fire with machine guns on the congregation of 70 men, women and children; a group calling itself the "Republican Action Force" claimed responsibility. **21.** The Home Secretary (Mr. Brittan) announced the largest new prison building programme this century costing nearly £250 million; four prisons were to be built in addition to 10 announced earlier. **24.** Terrorists dressed as police kidnapped Mr. Don Tidey, executive director of an Irish supermarket chain, near Dublin; on Dec. 16 Mr. Tidey was rescued unharmed during a gun battle near Ballinamore, Co. Leitrim, in which an Irish Republican soldier and a policeman were killed by Provisional I.R.A. terrorists; another policeman and soldier were injured but four terrorists were later caught. **26.** Gold bars, stated to be worth £26 million, were stolen in Britain's biggest robbery by a six-man gang in a raid on the Brinks-Mat security warehouse near Heathrow Airport. **29.** A Circuit Court judge, Keith Bruce Campbell, and a second-hand car dealer, Alan Foreman, of Wimbledon, were each fined £2,000 at Ramsgate after admitting smuggling whisky and cigarettes into Britain from Guernsey aboard the judge's motor cruiser; on Dec. 5 Judge Campbell became the first English judge this century to be removed from office for misbehaviour.

Dec. 2. Bruce Lee, the Humberside arsonist, was cleared in the Court of Appeal of causing the deaths of 11 elderly men in a fire at an old people's home; Lee was still detained, however, in a mental hospital for other fires which killed another 15 people. **6.** Lord Lane, Lord Chief Justice, stated in the Appeal Court that a handful of hair which a dying girl plucked from the head of her killer seven years ago pointed inescapably to the fact that Jane Bigwood, a 20 year-old art student, could not have been murdered by Mervyn John Russell who squatted in the block of Deptford flats where she lived; Russell, who had been in jail since 1977, was freed. **8.** Following a rampage in the city of Luxembourg after the European soccer championship game between Luxembourg and England on Nov. 16, nine English soccer supporters were jailed for up to four months. **9.** Explosives believed planted by terrorists outside the guardroom of 17th Training Regt, Royal Artillery, Woolwich, blew a hole in a wall and injured four soldiers and a woman passer-by. **12.** Two brothers, Khalig Raja, and Ahmed Raja, of Glasgow, who sold glue sniffing kits to children, were each jailed for three years in Glasgow High Court. **13.** A 10lb terrorist bomb discovered in a holdall at the entrance to a block of flats in Kensington High Street, London, was destroyed in a controlled explosion. **16.** George Panae, member of a South London kidnap gang, who kept their victims Emmanuel Xuereb and his wife tied up for four days in an attempt to obtain £2 million ransom from the family, was sent to jail for 18 years at the Central Criminal Court; the other two gang members were jailed for 10 and eight years. **17.** Five people, including a police sergeant and a police woman, were killed and 91 injured when an I.R.A. terrorist bomb exploded outside a rear entrance to Harrods in Hans Crescent, Knightsbridge; on Dec. 24 a police inspector became the sixth victim when he died from his injuries. **31.** Terrorist bombings in Marseilles station and on a high-speed train travelling from Marseilles to Paris caused four deaths with over 40 injured.

(1984) Jan. 12. Charles McCormick, aged 45, a former member of the Royal Ulster Constabulary's special branch, who had served three years and five months in custody after being convicted on the evidence of a "supergrass", was freed at a Belfast Court after successfully appealing against a 20-year sentence for armed robbery and other violent crimes, which was quashed. **20.** Four armed masked raiders broke into the viewing room at Christie's in St. James's, London, and stole jewellery valued at about £1,500,000. **27.** The parents of a boy aged 14 who sent a letter bomb to Mrs. Thatcher at Downing Street were ordered at the Central Criminal Court to pay £200 towards the costs of the case; the judge held them "partly responsible" for their son's actions; the boy was freed on a three-year supervision order. Samuel Murphy, aged 33, an Ulster Defence Association terrorist, of Belfast, was given three life sentences at Belfast Crown Court for his responsibility for three murders and also received a total of 439 years in concurrent jail terms for other terrorist crimes. **30.** Dr. Roger Thomas, Labour M.P. for Carmarthen, was fined £75 at Gowerton magistrates' court, Swansea, for importuning for immoral purposes at a men's public lavatory. **31.** Kathleen Calhaem, of Cheddar, Somerset, a 57-year-old spinster who arranged the contract killing of her rival in love, Mrs. Shirley Rendell, was jailed for life at Winchester Crown Court.

Feb. 3. An Indian diplomat, Mr. Ravindara Mhatre, was kidnapped in Birmingham; his body was found in Leicestershire two days later; a Kashmiri political group claimed responsibility. **6.** A committee of inquiry for the syndicate of owners of the kidnapped racehorse *Shergar* reported it was convinced the horse was taken by the I.R.A. and almost certainly killed shortly afterwards. **17.** An-

thony Black, a security guard, was jailed for six years at the Central Criminal Court for his part in a multi-million pound bullion robbery near Heathrow in Nov. 1983, after he agreed to inform on the rest of the gang. **22.** Six of a gang's middlemen were jailed at the Central Criminal Court for between 14 and five years for their parts in the £3 million burglary at Lloyds Bank, Holborn Circus, in July, 1982. **24.** Norman Smith, aged 18, of Castleton, was found guilty at Nottingham Crown Court of murdering Susan Renhard, an art student, in the Derbyshire Peak District; Smith was ordered to be detained during Her Majesty's pleasure.

Mar. 6. In Belfast, three I.R.A. terrorists shot dead a deputy governor at the Maze Prison as his wife and three-year-old daughter watched him leave for work. Two Hell's Angels, Michael Bardell and Stephen Parkinson, were jailed for life at Northampton Crown Court for the murder by stabbing of David Cox, aged 21, while his fiancée watched before she was tied to a tree and strangled to death with her own scarf. **11.** Police opened fire to rescue a couple and their son and his school-friend who had been taken hostage from their home in Sussex by two gunmen attempting to escape a manhunt; the gunmen had earlier shot a policeman near Arundel Castle and kidnapped two others in their patrol car. **12.** Police held and questioned a number of Libyans about a weekend wave of bomb attacks in London and Manchester in which 27 people were injured. **14.** Gerry Adams, leader of Sinn Fein, was shot and wounded in Belfast in an assassination attempt by Loyalist terrorists. **15.** Thieves escaped with silverware worth an estimated £5 million from Woburn Abbey, Beds.; it was later recovered. **17.** Dominic McGlinchey, the I.N.L.A. terrorist, was captured after a gun battle with police near Shannon Airport in the Irish Republic. **23.** Sarah Tisdall, aged 23, the Foreign Office clerk who passed secret Government documents about the arrival in Britain of cruise missiles to the *Guardian* newspaper, was jailed for six months at the Central Criminal Court.

April 3. It was disclosed that porcelain pieces valued at an estimated £1 million had been stolen in a robbery at a Mayfair gallery. **13.** Seven young Servicemen stationed in Cyprus were flown into Britain and appeared at Bow Street Magistrates' Court charged under the Official Secrets Act. **16.** Michael Bettaney, the Secret Service officer who had plotted to give the Russians information which could have resulted in the deaths of British agents, was jailed for 23 years at the Central Criminal Court after being convicted by a jury of all 10 spying charges. **17.** Armed police surrounded the Libyan Embassy (known as the "People's Bureau" in St.

James's Square, London after a shooting incident in which a woman police constable, Yvonne Fletcher, aged 25, died after machine-gun fire from the Embassy also wounded 12 anti-Gaddafi Libyan demonstrators who were protesting peacefully; the Home Secretary (Mr. Brittan) condemned the shooting as the "most disgraceful and barbaric outrage in London for some time"; meanwhile hundreds of Libyan revolutionary guards besieged the British Embassy in Tripoli chanting anti-British slogans and the Ambassador (Mr. Oliver Miles) and his staff were prevented from leaving; on April 18 three Britons including Mr. Douglas Ledingham, British Caledonian Airways manager in Tripoli, were being held prisoner by Libyan authorities as armed police in London continued their siege of the Embassy; the 25 Britons, including 11 women and two children, trapped in the British Embassy in Tripoli were allowed to go to their homes; Mr. Richard Luce, Minister of State, Foreign Office, met an intermediary for the "People's Bureau," and insisted all persons in the building should leave and allow it to be searched for arms and explosives; Libya denied shots had been fired from the "Bureau". On April 22 Britain broke off diplomatic relations with Libya and told the Libyan students and diplomats under siege at the "Bureau" to leave the country within seven days; the 8,000 Britons in Libya were warned by the Foreign Office to consider their safety and welfare as a result of the break in diplomatic relations; on April 23 a member of the Libyan Students' Revolutionary Committee which took over the Embassy in Feb. was expelled from Britain; on April 24, Col. Gaddafi sent a three-man delegation to London to supervise the evacuation of the Embassy; simultaneously, the secretary of the "student" group which seized the Embassy was deported; on April 26 families of British diplomats in Libya flew home and a plane carrying 140 Libyans including women and children left London for Tripoli; 18 diplomatic bags from St. James's Square were not searched; on April 27, 30 Libyans, including the killer of W.P.C. Fletcher, flew home to Tripoli after the Embassy siege ended; before leaving, the Libyan diplomats and "students" were questioned by police and other officials; earlier a plane carrying the British Ambassador and nine of his diplomatic staff left Tripoli for home; the last of the four-man revolutionary committee at the "Bureau," was deported from Britain; on April 30, Army and police explosives experts made a room-by-room search of the "Bureau" and in Tripoli Libyan police entered the British Embassy to carry out a search in retaliation; on May 1, the Home Secretary announced tighter restrictions on Libyans wishing to enter Britain; arms found in the Embassy included pistols, body armour, and two magazines from sub-machine guns; Mrs. Thatcher told M.P.s she had instructed the Cabinet Office that the siege events be thoroughly reviewed in an internal inquiry; on May 2, police found 3,600 rounds of ammunition and an automatic pistol in a further search of the Embassy and more sets of body armour. **20.** Twenty-two people were injured when a bomb exploded in Terminal Two at London Airport. **24.** More than 100 people were arrested in connection with police inquiries into the printing and distribution of forged £50 notes and 10 people were detained overseas. **27.** The Supreme Court in Providence, Rhode Island, overturned the conviction of Claus Von Bulow and ordered a new trial on charges that he twice attempted to murder his wife.

May 2. At Belfast Crown Court James Doherty was given 10 life sentences and Charles Crumley nine when a 10-man I.R.A. gang was jailed for 62 crimes between Oct. 1981 and Nov. 1982 in Londonderry. **16.** Dennis Skinner, the British banker and double agent who fell 12 floors to his death from his Moscow flat, was "unlawfully killed", an inquest jury at Croydon decided. **18.** Two off-duty soldiers were killed and 11 other people were injured when the I.R.A. set off a car bomb at a fishing festival in Enniskillen, Co. Fernmanagh. **22.** A terrorist trial ended after two sittings when the judge at Belfast Crown Court discharged himself because of a dispute about the credibility of the evidence of a "supergrass" and ordered a new trial for 36 men and women, all from Londonderry. **25.** John Goodwin, of Bishop's Stortford, was freed from a seven-year jail sentence when the Appeal Court quashed his conviction of jury nobbling at the Central Criminal Court.

June 20. The all-party Commons Foreign Affairs Select Committee published figures from a Foreign Office report showing that 546 serious crimes, including rape, incest and blackmail, were said to have been committed by foreign diplomats in London over the past 10 years. **22.** Dr. Brian Richards, of Sandwich, Kent, was found guilty by a jury in Santa Monica, California, on two counts of soliciting the murder of Peter Stephan, his partner in a Harley Street clinic. **29.** Michael Telling, a second cousin of Lord Vestey, was cleared of murdering his wife, but jailed for life for manslaughter at Exeter Crown Court.

July 5. Nigeria's former Transport Minister, Mr. Umaru Dikko, was found drugged and in a crate at Stansted airport a few hours after he had been kidnapped outside his London home; in the same crate aboard a Nigerian Airways freight plane was an Israeli mercenary who had drugs and a syringe; another Israeli mercenary and a Nigerian who were in a second crate were among 17 people detained by police; eight of these were later freed; in Lagos, the Nigerians detained a British Caledonian jumbo jet; on July 7 the Nigerian Airways freight plane took off from Stansted and the British Caledonian plane returned safely to Gatwick; on July 9 Mr. Dikko was released from hospital; on July 10, a Nigerian and three Israeli nationals were charged with kidnapping Mr. Dikko and administering stupefying drugs with intent to kidnap and were subsequently remanded in custody. **6.** Dr. Mark Patterson, a blood specialist, was jailed for three years at the Central Criminal Court after being convicted of a four-year swindle in which blood given by civilians and soldiers for N.H.S. transfusions was systematically stolen and sold to a Danish laboratory for a total of £158,000; two other men in the plot were also jailed. **10.** Two brothers, Patrick Smyth, aged 25, of Westgate, Kent, and Anthony Smyth, aged 27, of Ramsgate, were jailed at the Central Criminal Court over a letter bomb campaign against selected targets including the Prince of Wales and the Prime Minister; Patrick Smyth was jailed for 10 years and his brother was sentenced to three years. **11.** At Swansea Crown Court jail terms of up to 10 years were given to eight members of a drug smuggling ring convicted of charges including plotting to land nearly £6 million worth of cannabis on a secluded Welsh beach. **19.** James Huberty, aged 41, shot dead 21 people, including children, in a restaurant in the border town of San Ysidro, California before a police marksman shot him dead; another 19 victims were wounded, one of whom died the next day. **20.** The Court of Appeal freed Geoffrey Mycock, aged 37, who had spent 15 years in jail after being convicted of murder mainly on evidence given by the discredited Home Office forensic scientist, Dr. Alan Clift. **25.** Five bronze sculptures by the late Dame Barbara Hepworth with an art value of at least £100,000, were reported stolen from a park near Wakefield. **27.** Paul Davies, aged 21, a R.A.F. telegraphist, accused of passing N.A.T.O. secrets to a so-called "Mata Hari" while serving at a secret signals base in Cyprus, was cleared of all charges at the Central Criminal Court. **30.** Michael Haines, of Maidenhead, Berks., sentenced to life imprisonment on a charge of murdering his wife, was cleared by the Court of Appeal in London which quashed his conviction and set aside his sentence of which he had served 14 months.

Aug. 6. Two American Mafia operators, both from Chicago, were jailed for 15 years each at the Central Criminal Court for armed robbery at a Knightsbridge jewellers in 1980. **9.** Peter Fell, aged 23, of Aldershot, who stabbed two women to death on a public footpath in May 1982, because one of them looked like his mother, whom he hated, was sentenced to life imprisonment at Winchester Crown Court. **16.** John De Lorean was

acquitted in Los Angeles of plotting to distribute cocaine worth £18 million in an attempt to save the Belfast factory which produced his sports car. **20.** A Libyan on bail on terrorist bombing charges, was found murdered in a Marylebone flat in London.

ECCLESIASTICAL

(1983) Sept. 13. The Pope ended his four-day visit to Austria.

Nov. 10. The Church of England General Synod provisionally approved procedures to allow some divorcees to re-marry in the Church after a vote in all three houses. **18.** The new Archbishop of York (Dr. John Habgood) was enthroned in York Minster.

Dec. 1. The Archbishop of Canterbury (Dr. Runcie) arrived in Peking for the first official visit to China by the head of the Anglican Church, his stay lasting 15 days. **11.** The Pope preached in the Lutheran Church of Rome.

(1984) Jan. 21. Church of England clergy in York and Chelmsford voted decisively against proposals for re-marrying divorced people in church, bringing the total votes cast in the 20 dioceses where a ballot had been taken to 761 for and 2,757 against. **25.** The Italian Government presented a draft revision of its 55-year-old concordat with the Vatican which would end Roman Catholicism's status as the State religion. **31.** The Church of England House of Bishops meeting in private in Westminster unanimously decided to recommend that the General Synod should drop the plan to allow divorcees to re-marry in the Church of England, but supported a proposal which could allow divorcees to re-marry in church after consulting local clergymen.

Feb. 19. Ninety-nine Roman Catholic martyrs of the French Revolution were proclaimed "blessed" by the Pope.

Mar. 1. The Church of England General Synod accepted proposals by the bishops for a simplified procedure under which divorcees could apply for marriage in church.

May 6. The Pope canonized 103 martyrs in Seoul; on May 7 the Pope flew to Papua New Guinea for a three-day visit. **21.** The General Assembly of the Church of Scotland decided Mr. James Nelson, who served 10 years in jail after being sentenced to life imprisonment for murdering his mother, could become a minister of religion. **30.** The National Association of Head Teachers conference at Brighton overwhelmingly carried a resolution which favoured changing the law so that schools did not have to hold daily assemblies and daily acts of worship. **31.** A report by a Church of England group appointed by the Archbishop

of Canterbury recommended marriages between step-parents and step-children over 21
should be allowed.

June 25. The Dalai Lama of Tibet arrived
in London on a fortnight's visit at the
invitation of the Dean of Westminster.

July 4. The Archbishop of York rejected a
petition signed by more than 12,000 people
asking him to postpone the consecration of
Prof. David Jenkins as Bishop of Durham; on
July 6 the consecration service in York
Minster was twice interrupted by protestors.
10. The Church of England General Synod
gave provisional approval to the bishops'
proposed new procedure to allow the marriage
in church of divorced persons in suitable
cases. **19.** A requiem mass was held at
Portsmouth Cathedral for the sailors and
soldiers who lost their lives off Spithead when
the Tudor warship, *Mary Rose*, sank.

EDUCATION

(1983) Oct. 23. The Catholic Education
Council instructed all diocesan schools' commissioners in England and Wales to phase out
corporal punishment in R.C. schools.

(1984) Jan. 5. The Labour-controlled Derbyshire education committee voted to accept
a plan to allow sixth-form pupils aged 18 and
over who had been appointed to the governing
bodies of all 81 comprehensive schools in the
county to take an active part in the appointment of heads, teachers, and non-teaching
staff; the plan was subject to Ministerial
approval. **6.** Sir Keith Joseph, Education
Secretary, outlined wide changes in the
examination system for 16-year-olds and a
campaign to improve standards of education
and conduct.

April 5. Sir Keith Joseph, Education Secretary, told the Commons that the successor
body to the Inner London Education Authority would be directly elected when the G.L.C.
had been abolished.

May 23. A Green Paper was published
containing reforms to raise standards and the
effectiveness of schools and give parents
increased representation on governing bodies.

June 20. Sir Keith Joseph announced in
the Commons that O-level and C.S.E. examinations were to be replaced by a single system
of 16-plus examinations to be called the
General Certificate of Secondary Education
with courses starting in England and Wales
in the autumn of 1986.

Aug. 13. It was reported that the handover
of the Bedford College site in Regent's Park,
London, to a consortium of American colleges
had been completed.

ENVIRONMENT AND LOCAL AFFAIRS

(1983) Sept. 16. Two more satellite television channels were to be authorized by the
Government and would come under the
supervision of the I.B.A., the Home Secretary
announced. **29.** Lady Donaldson was elected
the first woman Lord Mayor of London.

Oct. 17. Details were announced of a
Thames-side development plan costing £250
million covering a site extending about half a
mile from London Bridge to Tower Bridge on
the southern bank of the river. **25.** Mr.
Patrick Jenkin, Environment Secretary, told
the Commons that a disused mine in Cleveland and a site in Bedfordshire were possible
locations for the dumping of radioactive waste
but that public inquiries would be held into
the proposals.

Nov. 3. The Environment Secretary announced the north block of Somerset House
in the Strand would be leased to the Courtauld
Institute and its gallery. **20.** A stretch of
beach near Sellafield, Cumbria, closed over
the weekend after radio-active material was
washed ashore, was re-opened and British
Nuclear Fuels—who operate the Windscale
nuclear plant—said there was no danger; on
Dec. 1 the Environment Department said
Government scientists were monitoring a 50-
mile stretch of coastline around the Sellafield
plant and had started an investigation into
the source of the contamination; on Dec. 5
the Government announced it would stop the
dumping of low-level radio-active waste at
sea while it carried out a joint safety inquiry
with the T.U.C.

(1984) Feb. 7. Mr. Ridley, Transport Secretary, ordered a two-year feasibility study for
a second Severn Bridge. **8.** The Post Office
announced a cut in the number of post offices
and a £100 million automation programme.
14. Two Government reports of inquiries into
last year's leak of radio-active waste from
British Nuclear Fuels, Sellafield, were published. **22.** The tenth report of the Royal
Commission on Environmental Pollution was
published.

Mar. 6. A report was published stating that
defects in up to a million purpose-built homes,
nearly all flats, of the 1960s and early 1970s
meant councils faced a bill approaching £5,000
million. **13.** The Government announced
additional funds for the National Heritage

Fund so that Calke Abbey, the early 18th century Derbyshire mansion, could be preserved intact for the nation. **30.** The Government published the Local Government (Interim Provisions) Bill to prepare the way for abolition of the Greater London Council and six metropolitan counties by cancelling the elections due to be held in May, 1985.

May 2. The Queen opened the Liverpool International Garden Festival. **8.** The Queen opened the Thames Barrier at Woolwich. **29.** It was announced that the Duke of Edinburgh was to chair an inquiry into housing.

June 1. The Post Office announced that letter charges were to rise from 16p to 17p for first-class and from 12½p to 13p for second-class on Sept. 3. **12.** Mr. Anthony Peter Bull became the first person to be accepted by the City of London Court of Aldermen after having been previously vetoed since the present system was introduced in 1710. **20.** London Transport announced that smoking was to be banned on all tube trains from July 9.

July 2. It was announced that the Central Electricity Generating Board had awarded a contract to a consortium to convert Battersea power station into a £40 million entertainment centre, with a funfair and other leisure facilities. **4.** It was announced that the Government was to abolish national dog licences and allow local authorities to introduce schemes of their own. **7.** It was stated that water restrictions and hosepipe bans had been imposed on more than nine million people as much of England and Wales experienced the driest weather since the drought of 1976. **9.** Liverpool district Labour Party voted to accept the Government deal for a legal budget giving a 17 per cent rate rise; the budget was approved by the City Council on July 11. **19.** The biggest earthquake to be experienced in the British Isles in 100 years shook much of the country. **23.** Radioactivity from Sellafield nuclear power station was largely cleared of causing cancer in local children by the Government-appointed inquiry chaired by Sir Douglas Black in its report which was published. **27.** The Government announced preparations for water rationing with rota cuts to homes and the setting up of street standpipes in Devon and Cornwall as the water shortage worsened; 21 million people, over 40 per cent of the population, were now affected by the drought and banned from using hosepipes.

Aug. 2. Mr. Ken Livingstone, G.L.C. leader, his deputy, and two other members of the Labour group resigned their seats on the G.L.C. to force and fight by-elections. **10.** The statue of Eros was removed from its pedestal in Piccadilly Circus for renovation.

FINANCE

(1983) Sept. 22. The International Monetary Fund suspended all new negotiations for large-scale loans for the first time. **27.** The Hong Kong Government enacted emergency legislation to take over the colony's privately-owned Hang Lung Bank.

Oct. 3. U.K. clearing banks cut lending rates by ½ per cent to nine per cent. **6.** It was announced that Centre Radio, Leicester's independent station, had gone into liquidation. **11.** Israel devalued the shekel by 23 per cent. **13.** Reed International confirmed it was to float off its Mirror Group Newspapers subsidiary early in 1984. **21.** Building societies voted to end their 40-year-old interest rate cartel.

Nov. 9. Brazil's National Congress voted to accept the terms of an economic austerity package the I.M.F. insisted on before it provided billions of dollars in loans.

(1984) Jan. 12. The New Cross Building Society was closed down on instructions from the Treasury and the Chief Registrar of Friendly Societies. **15.** Israel announced a record inflation rate for 1983 of 190 per cent.

Feb. 1. The Chancellor of the Exchequer stated that the halfpenny coin was to be phased out by the end of the year. **23.** The Inland Revenue told the building societies that profits on Government issued gilt-edged stocks would now be taxed when realized.

Mar. 1. The Government announced it would invest £250 million in British Aerospace to enable it to participate in the latest European Airbus A320 project. **6.** Talbot, the French-controlled car firm, announced it was to invest £20 million to ensure the future of its Coventry plant. **16.** Building societies cut their mortgage rate by one per cent from 11¼ to 10¼. **19.** Government announced £120 million microchip investment aid.

April 18. British Rail reported its best financial results for six years with an £8 million profit for 1983 compared with a £175 million loss during 1982. **26.** Western bankers agreed to re-schedule £1·3 billion of Poland's commercial debts covering four years' outstanding loans.

May 1. British Airways made a profit of £214 million for the year to Mar. 31. **15.** Israel's consumer price index rose by 20·6 per cent. in April. **29.** Britain had a trade deficit of £838 million in April, the worst on record, partly because the miners' strike had increased imports of fuel oil.

June 13. The National Bus Company made a record profit of nearly £7 million last year.

July 3. The Government approved changes in building society activities to allow them to provide banking services, but their interest rate-fixing "cartel" was to be broken by ending its exemption from the Restrictive Trade Practices Act. **6.** The banks raised their base lending rates by ¾ per cent to 10 per cent because of the slide in the pound; on July 11 there was a further increase by two points to 12 per cent. **12.** Reed International, owners of Mirror Group Newspapers, accepted the offer of £113 million by Mr. Robert Maxwell's Pergamon Press organisation for the *Daily Mirror* and five other newspapers. **13.** The Building Societies Association recommended a 2½ per cent rise in the mortgage interest rate from 10¼ per cent to 12½ per cent, the second largest rise on record. **18.** British Rail's Sealink subsidiary was sold for £66 million to Sea Containers, a Bermuda-based American company. **19.** British Telecom produced profits of £990 million for the year ending in March, compared with £1,031 million for the previous year. An investment of £10 million of public money in British film development and production over the next five years was announced by the Government. **24.** British Gas announced record profits of £668 million. **26.** Mr. Ian MacGregor, Chairman of the National Coal Board, announced losses of £875 million in the last financial year, double the deficit of the previous year, and Mr. Walker, Energy Secretary, said the industry was insolvent and able to carry on only because the taxpayer had provided £1.3 billion last year in aid.

Aug. 2. The Central Electricity Generating Board announced increased profits of £901 million. **8.** A cut in base lending rates from 12 to 11½ per cent was announced by the banks; on Aug. 17, the rates were again cut to 10½ per cent. **9.** Mr. Tiny Rowland and his trading group, Lonrho, were cleared by a Government-appointed inspector of allegations of improper dealings to try to acquire more influence over the Harrods stores group House of Fraser.

LABOUR AND TRADE UNIONS

(1983) Sept. 1. The T.U.C. General Council voted 20 to 17 to support discussions with Mr. Tebbit, Employment Secretary, on his proposed union reform legislation. **2.** Unemployment dropped for the first time in almost four years during August, the total of 3,009,907 being a fall of 10,688. **5.** The annual conference of the T.U.C. opened in Blackpool; on Sept. 6 Congress voted to talk to the Government about further trade union reform proposals; on Sept. 7 the conference endorsed a motion demanding selective import controls and reaffirmed support for free collective bargaining; on Sept. 8 Congress delegates passed a resolution calling for immediate cancellation

of the Cruise and Trident missile programmes, and another expressing total opposition to the Government's policy of privatisation. **16.** The five-week dispute which stopped production at the oil platform construction yard at Nigg in the north of Scotland ended when strikers voted to accept a peace formula. **19.** Cunard announced it had decided that the annual refit of the *QE2* should be done in West Germany because British Shipbuilders could not do the work in time or at the right price. **22.** It was disclosed that up to 1,000 jobs were to be lost by the sale by Dunlop of its European tyre-making interests to a Japanese company. **29.** Unemployment in Sept. rose by 157,532 to 3,167,439, or 13·3 per cent, mainly due to school-leavers joining the register. **30.** The National Coal Board offered miners rises amounting to 5·2 per cent in reply to a union claim for increases of between 17 and 23 per cent on basic rates.

Oct. 4. The Vauxhall pay strike collapsed when two-thirds of the workers voted to accept a revised 7·75 per cent 12-month deal. **21.** A pay rise of 7·8 per cent was awarded to firemen and fire control staff. Miners' union delegates at a special conference in London voted unanimously to impose an overtime ban in all coalfields from Oct. 31 in protest at pit closures and the N.C.B.'s pay offer.

Nov. 2. Agreement was reached between British Shipbuilders and unions on improved productivity deals in return for union commitments to change working practices. **3.** Unemployment in Oct. dropped by 73,441 to 3,093,998. **9.** It was announced that the Civil and Public Services' Association had rejected by a 2–1 majority a move to affiliate to the Labour Party. **11.** Land-Rover announced it was to close nine plants and reduce its workforce by 1,560. British Printing and Communications Corporation announced it was immediately closing its *Radio Times* plant at Park Royal, West London, because of a dispute in which 400 workers were losing their jobs. British Steel Corporation reached agreement with the Iron and Steel Trades Federation to negotiate for local pay deals after refusing to approve a national award. Members of the Association of Broadcasting Staff and the National Association of Television, Theatrical and Kine Employees voted by a large majority to form jointly the Entertainment Trades Alliance. **15.** The dispute which blacked out sport and other live events on B.B.C. Television ended after a peace formula was accepted over demands by outside broadcast staff about allowances when working away from base. **22.** The national executive of the N.G.A. voted unanimously to defy the High Court by not paying a £50,000 fine for contempt of court; on Nov. 23 the T.U.C. announced moral support for the N.G.A. but gave no undertaking to reimburse sequestrated funds. **25.** Print-workers' strike stopped publication of the national newspapers on Nov. 26 and the Sunday newspapers on Nov. 27 when N.G.A. members walked out after a court decision ordering all the N.G.A.'s assets to be sequestrated up to £175,000. **29.** Violence erupted when pickets besieged the Warrington plant of the Messenger Group of newspapers and scores of arrests were made, but work on Fleet Street newspapers returned to normal. The Post Office Engineering Union ordered 1,100 telephone engineers to end their disruptive action in protest against plans to privatise British Telecom.

Dec. 1. The majority of Ford's 24 plants accepted the company's 7·5 per cent pay offer and the threat of an all-out strike by the workforce from Jan. was removed; 13 plants voted for the offer, 10 plants against, with one plant a "split vote". **8.** The executive of the Post Office Engineering Union decided to order back to work another 1,500 strikers and to end their disruptive campaign against the privatisation of British Telecom while continuing to oppose the Telecommunications Bill with a publicity drive and parliamentary lobbying. **10.** The N.G.A. called a national 24-hour strike of all its members for Dec. 14 after a High Court judge in Manchester imposed contempt of court fines totalling £525,000 on the union for illegal picketing at the Messenger Group plant at Warrington; on Dec. 12 the High Court in London ordered the N.G.A. to call off its threatened strike after considering an application by certain national and regional newspapers for an injunction restraining the union from further inducing breaches of contract of employment; on Dec. 13, T.U.C. Employment Policy and Organization Committee voted 9–7 to support the strike, the vote being repudiated by Mr. Len Murray, the General Secretary; the action was suspended by N.G.A. national council because of the confusion following the vote; on Dec. 14 the T.U.C. General Council declined by 29 to 21 votes to endorse the committee decision to support the 24-hour strike. **12.** Increases of 5·2 per cent in the national minimum wage for engineering workers were agreed. **19.** Britoil cancelled an order for an £88 million oil rig at the Scott Lithgow shipbuilding yard on the Clyde because work was two years behind timetable.

(1984) Jan. 5. After three consecutive days of talks, the shipbuilding unions reached agreement with British Shipbuilders and called off the national shipbuilding strike which was due to start on Jan. 6. **6.** It was officially confirmed that 700 jobs were to be cut at the Navy's main dockyard at Devonport over the next four years. **11.** It was announced that British Rail's engineering division was to cut 3,500 more jobs by the end of the year with redundancies at Swindon, Shildon, Doncaster, York, Derby, Glasgow, and Wolverton. **12.** The N.U.M. executive meeting in Sheffield voted unanimously to continue the overtime ban over the N.C.B.'s pay offer. **16.** Ford announced that the company's foundry at Dagenham would close in April next year with the loss of 2,000 jobs. **18.** The National Graphical Association decided to purge its contempt of the High Court over its closed shop dispute at the Messenger Newspaper Group and seek the return of sequestrated assets. **24.** Mr. Peter Heathfield was elected as general secretary of the National Union of Miners. **25.** British Shipbuilders announced that three more yards must close and over 1,800 workers lose their jobs by the end of March and union leaders agreed to end demarcation rules and fall into line with working practices of other West European shipyards. **29.** Ford workers at Dagenham voted to suspend a threatened strike in protest at the company's decision to close the foundry.

Feb. 2. Sogat '82 clerical workers at the *Times* and *Sunday Times* whose 20-day dispute stopped publication of the papers since Jan. 26 voted to accept a return-to-work formula. **3.** British American Tobacco announced it was withdrawing from direct sales and distribution in Britain with the loss of over 1,800 jobs. **14.** British Petroleum cancelled a £60 million rig contract at Scott Lithgow. **27.** The T.U.C.'s "inner cabinet" proposed a series of further measures including a "freeze" on relations with the Government in retaliation for the ban on unions at G.C.H.Q. Cheltenham. **28.** Strikes and protest rallies by unions took place throughout the country over the ban on union membership at G.C.H.Q. Cheltenham and no national newspapers were printed in London. It was revealed that about 90 per cent. of the 7,000 staff at Cheltenham G.C.H.Q. and out-stations had accepted the Government's offer of £1,000 to renounce their trade union rights. **29.** The T.U.C. decided to call a 24-hour general strike if any civil servant at G.C.H.Q. Cheltenham was dismissed.

Mar. 6. The N.C.B. announced plans to cut up to 20,000 more jobs in the next financial year. **8.** The national executive of the N.U.M. meeting in Sheffield decided to give official support to an indefinite strike by 70,000 men in Yorkshire and Scotland from midnight. **12.** It was reported that about 100,000 miners had joined the strike throughout the coalfields amid mass picketing and violent scenes in places. **14.** Miners from Yorkshire defied a High Court injunction granted earlier which banned them picketing in other coalfields and returned to Nottinghamshire in an effort to close down pits where miners wished to continue working normally. **15.** After three days of picketing violence Nottinghamshire's miners began a 24-hour stoppage while a strike ballot was held. **16.** Miners in the Midlands, Lancashire, South Derbyshire, Cumberland, North Wales, and Durham mechanics voted against striking over pit closures and on Mar. 17 Nottinghamshire voted by 3 to 1 against striking; the only area vote in favour of the strike was in Northumberland; on Mar. 22 Lancashire miners' leaders reversed a 2 to 1 ballot vote by the men against a strike and called them out from Mar. 26. **28.** Miners' pickets besieged power stations in several areas of the country and the National Union of Seamen said it had stopped coasters carrying coal to power stations in the southeast; other pickets continued their attempts to block roads. **29.** Leaders of six unions—N.U.R., A.S.L.E.F., T.G.W.U., N.U.S., Transport Salaried Staffs' Association, and the Iron & Steel Trades Confederation—agreed on a complete ban on coal movements in support of the miners' strike and asked all their union members not to cross N.U.M. picket lines. **30.** Nissan, the Japanese motor vehicle manufacturer, confirmed the company was to locate its car plant at Washington New Town, near Sunderland.

April 2. The N.U.R. instructed its members to black movement of coal and coke and not to cross miners' picket lines; on April 3, the National Union of Seamen blacked all movement of coal in British ships. **5.** Delegates representing miners in Nottinghamshire voted overwhelmingly to reject a recommendation of their area executive not to cross picket lines. A walk-out by some 2,000 London staff in protest at the dismissal of 595 scenery workers caused management to take BBC-1 off the air; on April 11 the BBC and Entertainment Trades Alliance agreed terms for settling the scenery workers' strike. **12.** The N.U.M.'s executive voted 21 to 3 to call a special delegate conference; Mr. Scargill, the President, ruled out of order a proposal by the Leicestershire area to hold an immediate ballot on national strike action. **30.** Gas industry manual workers accepted a 4·6 per cent. across-the-board pay offer after a ballot.

May 1. Mr. Len Murray, T.U.C. General Secretary, announced he was to retire in the autumn. **11.** The siege by N.U.M. pickets of the Ravenscraig steel plant ended when mining, steel and rail unions agreed on a deal allowing two trains a day to deliver coal; four transport unions promised extra support for striking miners in an effort to stop the flow of coal and other fuels into and around Britain. The National Union of Teachers decided to stage a series of three-day strikes starting on May 22 in an attempt to force employers to improve their 4·5 per cent. pay offer, or go to arbitration. The N.U.R. and A.S.L.E.F. gave notice of a ban on overtime and rest-day

working over a pay dispute, but action was called off on May 24 after improved pay offer. **22.** Miners crossing picket lines in north Derbyshire had their union membership "suspended indefinitely". British Leyland announced plans to close the lorry and engine plant at Bathgate, Scotland. **23.** Talks at N.C.B. headquarters to prepare the way for negotiations to resolve the miners' strike collapsed after an hour. **29.** Seamen began a 48-hour ferry strike at midnight in a N.U.S. protest at Government plans to denationalize the British Rail part of the Sealink fleet. **31.** Leaders of the N.C.B. and the N.U.M. met for talks at a secret location in the Yorkshire area; colliery winders at Barnsley decided to return to work on June 4.

June 7. At a meeting of six unions in London—N.U.M., N.U.R., A.S.L.E.F., N.U.S., transport workers, and steelworkers—it was announced they had unanimously agreed to blockade the movement of oil and other fuels into power stations and of all coke and coal into steelworks. **8.** The N.C.B. chairman, Mr. Ian MacGregor, and the miners' leader, Mr. Arthur Scargill, had talks in Edinburgh. **13.** Talks between the N.C.B. and N.U.M. leaders at a Rotherham hotel broke down. Coal, rail, and steel unions in South Wales vetoed national instructions to halt coke and coal deliveries to the Llanwern steelworks. **22.** Teachers at local authority schools in England and Wales suspended all disruptive action when their 11-week-old pay dispute was referred to arbitration. **26.** Three Fleet Street newspapers—*Financial Times, The Sun,* and *The Daily Mirror*—failed to publish after their editors refused to print a statement from the five print unions in support of striking miners; other newspapers were printed later than usual or in truncated form after managements agreed to carry the statement in various forms.

July 2. Representatives of 14 unions in the steel industry decided after a meeting in London that the call by the miners to reduce work to "safety" level without any production was "not practicable". **5.** Talks aimed at resolving the miners' strike were adjourned in London; the talks broke up in stalemate on July 9. **9.** The T.G.W.U. ordered a national dock strike from midnight in protest at British Steel's alleged use of non-dockers at Immingham to unload ore "blacked" because of the miners' strike; however, the union claimed the main issue was the continued existence of the national dock scheme to protect jobs of registered dockers. **11.** The miners' union defied a High Court order when at a special conference in Sheffield, delegates approved a new disciplinary code which provided for sanctions against any action which might be detrimental to the union.

The National Union of Railwaymen instructed its 4,000 members in the docks not to cross transport union picket lines and the General, Municipal, Boilermakers and Allied Trades Union called out its 1,500 members in the docks. The National Union of Seamen decided not to allow commercial vehicles to use British Sealink ferries from midnight on July 13 in their campaign to stop denationalisation of the British Rail shipping subsidiary. **18.** More talks to try and end the coal strike broke down after 13 hours. **19.** Dockers at Dover yielded to threats from stranded lorry drivers and called off the strike which has been stopping freight movements; the blockade by British lorry drivers at French Channel ports was also lifted and freight sailings resumed. **20.** The national dock strike effectively ended with employers and union negotiators agreeing a peace formula. The N.U.S. abandoned its attempts to prevent the denationalisation of Sealink and decided to have talks with Sea Containers, the buyers of the subsidiary. **21.** Delegates representing striking dockers voted to accept the peace agreement and returned to work at midnight. **24.** Miners' pickets closed the Humber Bridge for three hours. **25.** An improved pay offer of 4.5 per cent for N.H.S. ancillary workers was accepted by the General, Municipal and Boilermakers' Union.

Aug. 10. The Ministry of Defence announced that cuts in the labour force at Devonport naval dockyard were to be brought forward and 400 jobs were to go by March. **15.** A £6 billion plan for training Britain's workforce of the future, jointly produced by the Labour Party and the T.U.C., was published. **21.** A 4.5 per cent pay offer to N.H.S. clerks and administrators was accepted by a delegate meeting of N.A.L.G.O. **22.** British Steel decided to bring in a "blacked" bulk carrier, *Ostia*, to its depot at Hunterston on the Clyde and unload its cargo of coal for the Ravenscraig steelworks; on Aug. 23 the 18 members of the T.G.W.U. at Hunterston walked out in protest at the unloading and on Aug. 24 delegates at a conference called by the Union voted for a national strike; nearly all Scotland's 2,500 dockers had walked out during the morning shift; on Aug. 26 dockers at Immingham and Grimsby decided at a mass meeting to work normally in defiance of the strike call; on Aug. 27 dockers at Belfast and Larne, Co. Antrim, voted not to join the strike; on Aug. 28 dockers at over a dozen ports also decided not to participate; on Aug. 30 there was confusion about the result of the vote at a mass meeting of dockers at Tilbury; dockers at Immingham and Grimsby voted almost unanimously to return to work after a brief walk-out; on Aug. 31 men at Felixstowe and Dover voted overwhelmingly not to strike. **23.** Leaders of 14 unions called on the N.C.B. to resume talks with the miners' union

immediately in a move to end the coal strike on the basis of efforts to mediate by Mr. Stanley Orme, Labour's Shadow Energy Secretary. **30.** N.U.M leaders and T.U.C. leaders held discussions in Brighton to try to resolve their differences over the pit strike preparatory to the T.U.C. conference; on Aug. 31, T.U.C. General Council voted 38 to 5 to extend the coal strike into other industries, including power stations and steelworks, but the decision was condemned by the steel and electricity unions.

LEGAL

(1983) Sept. 26. The Employment Appeal Tribunal ruled that the white-collar union A.S.T.M.S. had acted illegally when it contributed £43,000 towards the cost of the Labour Party's Southwark Headquarters; the judge rejected an appeal by the union against a finding by the Government Certification Officer that it was a political payment.

Oct. 31. In the Court of Appeal, two judges ruled that parents could not in law be convicted of kidnapping their own children.

Nov. 8. A White Paper was published giving the Government's response to the recommendations of the Royal Commission on Legal Services, which reported in 1979, and stated a major review of civil court procedure was to be started to see how the conduct and trial of cases could be speeded up and made more economical. **9.** The Appeal Court in London decided unanimously to grant an injunction restraining the Post Office Engineering Union from continuing disruption of Mercury private enterprise tele-communications company, which had been blacked for eight months; on Nov. 10 there was an overwhelming vote by delegates at the Union's annual conference at Blackpool to obey the injunction. **17.** National Graphical Association, the print union, was fined £50,000 for contempt of court after defying two High Court orders during its dispute with Messenger Group newspapers in Warrington. **23.** The Federation of London Wholesale Newspaper Distributors obtained a High Court injunction restraining the London Central branch of SOGAT '82, a print union, from continuing to black supplies of magazines in the London area. **25.** An order for sequestration of the entire assets of the N.G.A. was made in the High Court in Manchester because of the Union's failure to pay a £50,000 fine in the Messenger Group newspapers' dispute; the judge also imposed a fine of £100,000 for mass picketing outside the Group's premises at Warrington which he said was a clear breach of an earlier court order; later an application by the N.G.A. for a stay of the High Court order pending an appeal was refused by the

Court of Appeal, after the Union declined to give certain undertakings. **29.** The National Union of Journalists lost its appeal against a High Court order outlawing a strike at David Dimbleby's Richmond-based newspaper group in south-west London; the N.U.J. ordered the strike after the group had transferred production to a non-union printers in Nottingham; on Dec. 1 the N.U.J. told the Court of Appeal it would not obey the court order whereupon the Master of the Rolls said the injunction would now take effect; on Dec. 6 the Appeal Court ruled the Union was not engaged in a legitimate trade dispute and dismissed its appeal against the strike ban. **30.** The Court of Appeal reimposed a total freeze on the assets of the N.G.A. and in the High Court seven national newspaper publishers were granted injunctions restraining the N.G.A. from inducing sympathetic industrial action.

Dec. 1. Greenpeace, the environment protection group, was fined £50,000 in the High Court, London, for breaking a court order not to interfere with the discharge of nuclear waste into the Irish Sea from the Sellafield re-processing plant in Cumbria. **2.** In the High Court, London, the judge granted an interim order to B.B.C. Publications and the British Printing and Communications Corporation and Waterlow and Sons to halt an official strike by SOGAT '82 members which had stopped work on the Christmas edition of *Radio Times*; on Dec. 6, SOGAT '82 decided to obey the High Court injunction. **6.** A claim for £30,000 damages by Jim Brown, former captain of Dunfermline Athletic, over a tackle which ended his football career, was settled out of court in Edinburgh but the terms were not disclosed. **9.** The High Court in Manchester imposed additional contempt of court fines totalling £525,000 on the N.G.A. over illegal picketing in the dispute at Messenger Group newspapers. **16.** The Appeal Court in London ruled that protection of national security required that the *Guardian* should hand over a secret Government memorandum so that the "mole" who had leaked it anonymously to the newspaper might be identified; the Court dismissed an appeal by the *Guardian* against an order requiring it to hand over the document immediately.

(1984) Jan. 13. British Nuclear Fuels was granted a permanent injunction in the High Court, London, banning the Greenpeace environmental group from interfering with its nuclear waste pipeline at Sellafield, but the Court upheld the right to protest in the vicinity of the pipeline and to monitor radioactive levels in the sea and on the beach. **26.** In the High Court, London, a judge granted the B.B.C. an injunction requiring the print union, Sogat '82, to withdraw any instructions to its members likely to interfere with the printing, delivery or distribution of

the *Radio Times*. **27.** A High Court judge in Manchester decided that the assets of the National Graphical Association, seized under a High Court order, were to be returned to the union; after an apology by Mr. Joe Wade, the union's general secretary, the judge said the union had purged its contempt but he refused to reduce fines totalling £525,000 it had yet to pay following action at the Messenger Newspaper Group plant at Warrington, Cheshire.

Feb. 1. A High Court judge ruled that computers were so much a part of everyday life that tax officials or any other employee could not object to using them in their work; he dismissed an application by eight tax officers in the West Midlands for a declaration that the change in work required to operate the new central PAYE computer went beyond their existing contracts of employment and could not be imposed on them without their consent. Sogat '82 was fined £10,000 for contempt of a High Court order to lift "blacking" of London editions of the *Radio Times*.

Mar. 1. Mr. Eddy Shah, owner of the Messenger Newspaper Group, was awarded £73,653 against the N.G.A. in respect of damage and the cost of security measures against mass picketing at his Warrington plant in Nov. 1983, at a High Court appeal hearing in Chester. **20.** Two Kent miners failed in the High Court, London, to obtain an injunction barring police from trying to prevent them leaving the county to join mining pickets in other areas. **29.** In the House of Lords, five law lords unanimously ruled that a woman who was reasonably suspected of having committed an arrestable offence had not been falsely imprisoned; they upheld a Court of Appeal decision that a county court judge had been wrong in ruling the woman suspect had been falsely imprisoned for six hours at a Hampshire police station.

April 12. The 15th Report of the Criminal Law Revision Committee on sexual offences was published. **13.** The High Court ruled that Mr. Arthur Scargill, President of the N.U.M., and his four fellow union officials were in breach of their fiduciary duty as trustees of the miners' pension fund by refusing to allow new investments abroad or in industries competing with coal. **19.** A judge fined the Society of Graphical and Allied Trades '82 and the N.G.A. £75,000 each at a hearing in London for contempt of court orders to end the sit-in of the London headquarters of British Printing and Communications Corporation.

May 21. Lord Beaumont, the Liberal peer, lost his claim in the High Court against the

National Trust decision to allow the Defence Ministry to lease land at the foot of the Chiltern Hills for the construction of an underground bunker for a N.A.T.O. strike command headquarters in a future war; the judge ruled the Trust had the power and right to grant leases to the Ministry. **25.** A High Court judge granted an interim injunction to 631 Nottinghamshire miners banning the N.U.M. from giving them an instruction or direction to strike or not to cross picket lines within the Nottinghamshsire coalfield although if a national ballot or other lawful strike call were made the orders would cease to operate.

June 21. Solicitors were allowed for the first time to advertise their services and their charges after a decision by the Law Society's governing council. **26.** A judge ruled in Manchester High Court that the N.U.M. could not call an official strike without an official ballot of members when he heard a case between non-striking men at Agecroft Colliery, Salford, and the Lancashire N.U.M., the judge making it clear his decision only affected the union's Lancashire area.

July 4. A House of Lords committee granted permission to Mr. Alan Monk, from Ashford, Kent, and his former mother-in-law to promote a private Parliamentary Bill to enable them to overcome the ban on the marriage of in-laws. **6.** A High Court judge in London ordered a stay in the implementation of two resolutions passed by the South Yorkshire police committee earlier in the week to withhold funds from its chief constable for policing pickets in the miners' dispute. Seven young people who suffered brain damage after whooping cough vaccinations as babies were given permission by a High Court judge in London to sue the D.H.S.S. **10.** At a special hearing in the High Court in London, the Vice-Chancellor, Sir Robert Megarry, ruled that the miners' conference opening on July 11 in Sheffield should not discuss or vote on a proposed rule change aimed at disciplining miners who had refused to strike until Nottingham pitmen had been given the chance to tell their delegates how to vote; on Aug. 18 Sir Robert granted a declaration sought by 17 Nottinghamshire miners against the N.U.M. and its national officials and declared void and invalid N.U.M. plans to discipline working miners approved at the union conference in defiance of the court order. **16.** A High Court judge ruled that the Government's ban on unions at G.C.H.Q. in Cheltenham was "invalid and of no effect"; on Aug. 6, the Appeal Court declared that the ban was legal and overturned the High Court decision. **19.** In a unanimous ruling, five law lords allowed an appeal by the liquidator of Laker Airways against injunctions granted by the Court of Appeal last year to stop him

suing British Airways and British Caledonian in America over an alleged fares-fixing conspiracy to put Laker out of business. **23.** A High Court judge in London ordered a scientologist father to hand over his 10-year-old son and eight-year-old daughter to their mother and ordered the Church of Scientology, which he described as "corrupt, sinister and dangerous", to stop intimidating and harassing the mother. **27.** At an emergency hearing in the High Court in London, a judge banned the G.L.C. from incurring expense or liability on at least £2 million-worth of contracts which its finance and general purposes committee wished to proceed with by July 31, after which contracts of £100,000 or more and building contracts worth over £250,000 would need the consent of the Environment Secretary. **30.** The South Wales area of the N.U.M. was fined £50,000 in the High Court in London for contempt over its members' continued picketing outside the Port Talbot steelworks. In the High Court in Manchester, Mr. Eddy Shah's Messenger Newspapers Group was awarded £125,051 against the National Graphical Association for its unlawful picketing, intimidation and conspiracy during last year's closed shop dispute with the company.

Aug. 16. A report of the Criminal Law Revision Committee recommended laws to deal with kerb crawlers which would punish male clients with fines of up to £400 as well as the prostitutes they solicited. **22.** Three Staffordshire miners won their High Court application for reinstatement as branch union officers at Lea Hall colliery, Rugeley, in the Midlands, when the judge granted them orders preventing the N.U.M. treating the Midlands area strike as having been officially sanctioned.

SPORT

(1983) Sept. 4. Steve Ovett of England regained his 1,500 metres world record in Reiti, Italy. **13.** Steve O'Shaughnessey, aged 22, scored a century in 35 minutes for Lancashire against Leicestershire at Old Trafford to equal the world record time set by Percy Fender 63 years ago. **26.** Australia captured the America's Cup yachting trophy from the U.S.A. for the first time in 132 years when the challenger *Australia II*, snatched victory from the defender, *Liberty*, in the deciding best-of-seven race series.

Oct. 3. Geoffrey Boycott, the England batsman, was dismissed by Yorkshire County Cricket Club. **5.** In Nevada, Richard Noble of Britain broke the world land speed record in his jet car, *Thrust 2*, at an average speed of 633·468 m.p.h. on the required two runs.

Nov. 19. England defeated New Zealand 15 to 9 in the rugby international at Twicken-

ham, their first win there over the All Blacks
since 1936.

(1984) Jan. 20. Bob Willis passed Fred
Trueman's England Test wicket record when
he took his 308th wicket during the New
Zealand versus England match in Wellington.
21. Members of Yorkshire County Cricket
Club voted decisively to reverse the decision
to dismiss Geoffrey Boycott at a special
meeting at Harrogate; on Jan. 23 all members
of the Club's committee resigned.

Feb. 8. The Winter Olympics opened in
Sarajevo, Yugoslavia. **29.** John Francombe
became only the second National Hunt jockey
to ride 1,000 winners.

March 8. Charlton Athletic Football Club
was allowed to remain in business after being
given a financial base approved by a High
Court judge and the Official Receiver. **17.** The
University Boat Race was postponed for 24
hours, less than an hour before it was timed
to begin, after the Cambridge boat was
smashed in a collision with a barge during a
practise start; on the next day Oxford won in
a record time. Scotland won the Rugby Union
grand slam for the first time since 1925 when
they beat France at Murrayfield. **24.** Jayne
Torvill and Christopher Dean of Britain won
the world ice dance title at the championships
in Ottawa for the fourth successive year. **30.**
The Rugby Football Union voted decisively
to send an England team to tour South Africa.

April 2. Derby County, the Second Division
football club, was saved from extinction after
paying in full its tax debts. **6.** Zola Budd, a
South African athlete, was granted British
citizenship. **12.** The Test and County Cricket
Board executive committee cleared England's
cricketers who had been accused of drug-
taking and bad behaviour on their New
Zealand tour. **13.** Ian Botham, the England
Test cricketer, was fined £1,000 and severely
reprimanded by the Test and County Cricket
Board for his comments about Pakistan in a
radio interview. **23.** Anne Ferris became the
first woman jockey to win the Irish Grand
National.

May 8. It was officially announced in
Moscow that Russia would not take part in
the Los Angeles Olympic Games. **12.** Liverpool
won the First Division Championship for the
third year in succession. **13.** Charles Spedding, of Durham, won the London marathon.
24. Rumania announced it would not be
joining the Eastern bloc boycott of the
Olympic Games. **26.** Scotland and England
drew 1-1 at Hampden Park in the last British
Championship match.

June 19. Rory McCarthy, of Hampstead,
set a new world hang-gliding record after

being released from a hot-air balloon at
34,500 ft. and landing safely in a field near
Diss, Norfolk.

July 3. The British Medical Association at
its annual meeting in Manchester agreed to
promote a campaign to achieve a total ban on
all forms of boxing because of "alarming
evidence" of brain damage to boxers. **22.** The
Prince of Wales opened the seventh world
wheelchair games (Paralympics) at Stoke
Mandeville, Bucks. **29.** President Reagan
opened the 23rd Olympic Games in Los
Angeles; the Games closed on Aug. 12.

Aug. 14. England suffered the first 5-0 home
defeat in their history when at the Oval the
West Indies won the final Test. **16.** A report
by a Government working party aimed at
dealing with soccer hooliganism was published.

TRANSPORT

(1983) Sept. 21. British Airways lost its
High Court action to prevent British Midland
Airways from setting up in competition on
the Heathrow–Belfast route. **22.** A world
speed record for scheduled passenger trains
was set by French Railways with the 264
miles from Paris to Lyons covered in two
hours at an average of 132 m.p.h. **27.** A £7,000
million road programme to meet the country's
needs beyond the end of the century was set
out by Mr. King, Transport Secretary, in a
White Paper.

Oct. 11. British Caledonian placed a £150
million order for the A320 European Airbus
jet liner. **24.** It was announced that British
Railways would receive £200 million less in
Government subsidy over the next three
years than they had asked for in their
corporate plan.

Dec. 12. Mr. Ridley, Transport Secretary,
told M.P.s that British Airways was to become
a public limited company on April 1, 1984 and
that the Government would like to privatise
it as soon as possible, preferably in early 1985.

(1984) Jan. 2. British Rail disclosed plans
to reduce passenger services by up to 30 per
cent in some areas in May.

Feb. 8. It was announced that heavy lorries
and coaches would be allowed to travel faster
on dual carriageways under proposed speed
limit changes.

April 5. Virgin Atlantic Airways, the new
British airline, was granted conditional permission for a licence to operate a daily
economy service between London and New
York with an introductory one-way fare of
£99. **11.** It was announced that the Man-

chester Ship Canal was to close for most of its length because of heavy losses due to falling traffic.

May 26. The 40-mile Danube–Black Sea Canal was opened.

June 29. The new London Regional Transport Board took over control of London Transport from the G.L.C.

July 12. A widespread reorganisation of bus and taxi services throughout the country was proposed in a White Paper. **16.** A report by the Civil Aviation Authority on its review of implications of privatising British Airways for competition and the development of the British airline industry was published.

Aug. 15. The Government provisionally approved plans to build a short take-off and landing airport in London's dockland. **30.** The Government's decision to approve British Rail's programme costing £306 million for the electrification of the East coast line to Edinburgh was announced in the Commons.

COMMONWEALTH

(1983) Sept. 9. Air Vice-Marshal Hugh Slatter and Air Cdre Philip Pile, after more than a year in jail and detention in Zimbabwe, were freed on the orders of the Home Affairs Minister who the previous week detained them and four other officers in prison after they were acquitted of treason; on Sept. 14 Zimbabwe freed a third Air Force officer, Wing-Cdr Peter Briscoe, who was also detained after being acquitted of treason. **13.** Zimbabwe announced a commission of inquiry into alleged atrocities by security forces against civilians in Matabeleland. **18.** The U.K. Associated State of St. Kitts and Nevis in the Caribbean became fully independent at midnight.

Oct. 7. Mrs. Gandhi dismissed the State government in the Punjab and introduced direct rule from New Delhi after Sikhs killed eight Hindus in two incidents. **19.** In Grenada, Mr. Maurice Bishop, the Prime Minister, and three other ministers were shot dead by troops in a state of disorder which had existed since Oct. 13, and a military council seized control on Oct. 20; on Oct. 21, it was reported that a U.S. Naval task force was heading for southern Caribbean as U.S. Administration became concerned for the 1,100 American citizens on Grenada; on Oct. 25 U.S. troops and forces from six Caribbean nations invaded Grenada and captured the island's two airports and Cuban personnel; a force of 1,900 U.S. Marines and Army Rangers supported by 11 warships led the dawn invasion accompanied by 300 troops and police from the Caribbean nations; Mrs. Thatcher, in a tele-

phone call, tried to dissuade President Reagan from ordering the invasion, but he told her it would go ahead; the Prime Minister immediately called senior Ministers to talks at Downing Street; the Prime Minister and the Foreign Secretary both made statements in the House of Commons; on Oct. 26 resistance by the Cubans collapsed in all but one stronghold after the Americans were reinforced by 800 paratroops and attacked the Cubans' main base with helicopter gunships; it was stated that 600 Cubans had been taken prisoner; Grenada's Governor-General, Sir Paul Scoon, was freed with his family and taken off the island; on Oct. 27 the Pentagon announced the last major pocket of resistance—at Richmond Hill Prison—had fallen to U.S. troops; on Oct. 28 Sir Paul Scoon ordered the closing of all Grenadian high commissions and embassies and said he hoped to hold free elections within six months; U.S.A. used its veto to block a resolution in the U.N. Security Council which would have deplored the invasion of Grenada; on Oct. 29 U.S. Marines captured Grenadian deputy prime minister Bernard Coard believed to be the *coup* leader; on Oct. 30, Sir Paul Scoon directed government offices, shops and schools to re-open on Oct. 31 and appealed for reconciliation; on Oct. 31, the Pentagon admitted that U.S. forces bombed and shelled a mental hospital which formed part of a military complex during their initial assault; up to 47 patients were reported killed but the White House said the toll was "substantially less"; on Nov. 3 President Reagan declared that U.S. objectives had been achieved in Grenada and that troops would begin to withdraw over the next few days; on Nov. 9 the Governor-General announced the formation of a nine-member Advisory Council to run the island's government until general elections could be held; on Nov. 10 the number of U.S. troops wounded in the invasion was officially increased from 97 to 113 with 31 non-combat injuries; the number of U.S. dead remained at 18.

Nov. 1. It was reported that Bishop Abel Muzorewa, leader of a Zimbabwe minority opposition party, was being detained in Harare under the country's emergency laws. **16.** Lt. Nigel Lewis-Walker, a white air force officer, detained in 1982 after the sabotage attack at Thornhill airbase, was released from detention in Zimbabwe on condition he left the country. **23.** The member states of the Commonwealth opened their biennial summit in New Delhi; it ended on Nov. 29. **30.** Bangladesh ordered the expulsion of 18 Russian diplomats.

Dec. 8. The Australian Government refused dry-dock facilities to the carrier *Invincible* in Sydney following refusal of the British High Commission in Canberra to deny or confirm the ship was carrying nuclear weapons. **22.** The Zimbabwe Government released three remaining detained white air force officers and ordered them and their families to leave the country within a week. **31.** At midnight, Brunei gained full independence from Britain. In Nigeria, the government of President Shagari was ousted in a bloodless military *coup*, led by Maj.-Gen. Muhammad Buhari.

(1984) Jan. 13. The Government of Mauritius closed down Libya's Embassy in Port Louis. **25.** Mr. Pierre Trudeau, Canadian Prime Minister, began three-nation (Czechoslovakia, East Germany, and Rumania) Soviet bloc visit. **29.** A massacre of about 30 people was reported from near the Ugandan capital of Kampala.

Feb. 9. Sultan Mahmood Iskandar of Johore was elected Malaysia's king. **14.** Eleven people were killed in clashes between Sikhs, Hindus, and police in India's Punjab state; on Feb. 21 nine people were shot dead in further Hindu-Sikh violence; it was stated on Feb. 24 that more than 50 people had died in 11 days of disturbances in Punjab and Haryana States. **23.** Brunei celebrated its independence. **29.** Mr. Pierre Trudeau announced he was stepping down after more than 15 years as Canada's Prime Minister.

Mar. 7. Nigerian police put the number of those killed in the religious riots in northeastern town of Yola at 535. **8.** It was announced that India was to build a 2,000-mile security fence along its border with Bangladesh in Assam to try to curb the flow of illegal immigrants. **30.** Publication in Australia of the contents of a top-secret document outlining the country's defence strategy caused a major Government crisis although a censure motion was defeated on party lines in the House of Representatives.

April 2. Security forces in the Punjab and Haryana were alerted and a strict curfew imposed after a series of terrorist attacks and mob violence resulting in killings in the Sikh holy city of Amritsar, and in Batala; on April 3, 10 people were shot dead by police and two policemen were killed when rioting continued in Amritsar. **3.** India's first spaceman was put into orbit with two Russian cosmonauts in a spacecraft launched from Soviet Central Asia. **6.** The Cocos Islands voted to be integrated with Australia. **11.** Australian Government replaced "God Save the Queen" with "Advance Australia Fair" as its national anthem, but it was announced that "God Save the Queen" would be kept as the royal anthem for when the Queen was present. **12.** It transpired that a detailed report alleging that Zimbabwean troops had conducted a campaign of starvation, beatings, torture, rape,

and murder in south Matabeleland since February when a strict curfew was imposed had been presented in Harare by the R.C. Church. **16.** About 150 people were arrested in Punjab State as three others were murdered, two within the Golden Temple complex in Amritsar. **20.** Sir Geoffrey Howe, Foreign Secretary, said in Hong Kong that negotiations with China over the territory's future were based on handing over the colony's sovereignty in 1997. **26.** The Sultan of Johore took the oath as the King of Malaysia.

May 15. The Chinese Prime Minister said in Peking that China had no intention of altering the way of life in Hong Kong and "due regard" would be given to Britain's economic interests. **25.** Mrs. Gandhi placed the state of Sikkim under direct rule by the President in New Delhi. **26.** The death-toll in the week-long Hindu-Moslem communal riots in Bombay rose to more than 230.

June 2. Mrs. Gandhi announced that the Army was to be responsible for security in the Punjab; on June 6 Indian troops seized the Sikhs' holiest shrine, the Golden Temple in Amritsar after a day-long battle in which at least 325 people died; soldiers were reported to have stormed 38 other Sikh shrines in the Punjab; on June 7 violence flared in many areas of India. **16.** Mr. John Turner was chosen leader of the Liberal Party and successor to Mr. Pierre Trudeau as Prime Minister of Canada at a convention in Ottawa.

July 2. The Australian Government decided to appoint a judge and two scientists to conduct an inquiry into British nuclear tests in the country in the 1950s. **11.** According to a document issued by the Indian Government, 495 civilians were killed in the battle for the Golden Temple. **14.** New Zealand's Labour Party, led by Mr. David Lange, decisively defeated the National Party of the Prime Minister, Sir Robert Muldoon; on July 24, two women Cabinet Ministers were appointed for the first time in New Zealand's new Government.

Aug. 1. The Foreign Secretary (Sir Geoffrey Howe) announced in Hong Kong the framework of the pact with China to relinquish sovereignty over the colony in exchange for a pledge to maintain its lifestyle 50 years beyond 1997. **2.** The six-month-old dusk-to-dawn curfew in southern Matabeleland province was lifted by the Zimbabwe Government. **8.** Uganda suspended a military aid programme from America because of reports in the U.S.A. that the Ugandan army was carrying out mass killings of civilians in a reign of terror; on Aug. 9 the U.S.A. called on President Obote to stop the slaughter of innocent civilians by troops engaged in operations against anti-government rebels; on

Aug. 19, the Ugandan Government stated the death toll in massacres and other atrocities committed by both sides in the bush war was around 15,000 in the period since President Obote took office in 1980. **9.** Clashes between Government forces and Tamil separatists continued in Sri Lanka and the Government claimed about 70 separatists had been killed.

MIDDLE EAST

(1983) Sept. 1. President Reagan ordered an amphibious force with 1,600 Marines to sail to Lebanon to support U.S. troops in Beirut and directed the carrier *Eisenhower* to stay in position off the Lebanese coast. **3.** Israel began the withdrawal of its troops from areas north of the Awali River. **6.** Druze forces captured the Christian-held town of Bhamdoun and two U.S. Marines were killed in shelling near Beirut. **8.** A U.S. frigate, standing off Beirut, opened fire at a battery in the mountains which had shelled close to U.S. Marine positions. **9.** Britain sent six R.A.F. Buccaneer long-range strike aircraft to Cyprus to provide air support for British troops in the Lebanon international peace-keeping force. **10.** A massacre of Christian villagers in a Chouf mountain village was reported in Beirut. **11.** Buccaneer aircraft of the R.A.F. drew small-arms fire when they twice flew low over Beirut. **15.** Mr. Begin submitted his formal resignation as Prime Minister of Israel. **17, 19 and 20.** U.S. warships fired at targets in Lebanon. **22.** French Super-Etendard fighters attacked anti-government artillery positions in the hills behind Beirut after six soldiers in France's peace-keeping contingent were wounded. **25.** Syrian special forces surrounded a force of 1,000 P.L.O. guerrillas loyal to Yasser Arafat and ordered them to hand over their arms in a remote valley in the Hermel region. **26.** The Lebanese Prime Minister submitted the resignation of his Cabinet to clear the way for the formation of a government of national reconciliation.

Oct. 10. Israel's Parliament gave a vote of confidence to the new Government of Mr. Yitzhak Shamir, the Prime Minister-designate, by a majority of seven votes. **16.** A U.S. Marine was killed and three others wounded in seven hours of sniping and grenade attacks against the American peace-keeping troops manning a position near Beirut international airport. **19.** The Israeli Government survived a vote of no confidence in the Knesset by seven votes. **23.** Nearly 300 American and French troops of the Lebanese peace-keeping force were killed at dawn in separate "suicide" bomb attacks on their bases in Beirut; terrorists drove trucks loaded with explosives into the buildings; on Oct. 24 President Reagan declared the U.S. forces would remain in Lebanon; President Mitter-

rand visited the scene where French troops were killed.

Nov. 3. Yasser Arafat and his loyal P.L.O. supporters were fighting for survival as rival Palestinians backed by Syrians and Libyans attacked the P.L.O.'s last major stronghold near Tripoli in northern Lebanon; more than 60 people were killed. **4.** In a suicide mission, Arab guerrillas crashed a lorry filled with explosives through barriers at the Israeli military command post at Tyre in Lebanon and killed 29 Israeli soldiers and 10 Arab prisoners; within hours the Israeli air force bombed and strafed three towns in the hills east of Beirut. **6.** Yasser Arafat gave the order to evacuate Nahr Al Bared, a P.L.O camp, which was cut off by Palestinian rebels. **15.** Turkish Cypriots declared their sector of Cyprus independent and the Turkish Government announced its recognition. **16.** Palestinian rebels claimed to have captured the Beddawi refugee camp, last stronghold of Yasser Arafat, whose main forces were reported to be retreating to Tripoli. **18.** The Defence Ministry in London announced the amphibious assault ship, *Fearless*, was being sent to the Lebanon to support British troops ashore. **23.** Yasser Arafat, trapped in Tripoli by Palestinian rebels, agreed in principle to a peace agreement involving him abandoning the city. **24.** Israel freed 4,800 Palestinian prisoners in exchange for six captured Israeli soldiers from the civil war in Tripoli. **29.** President Reagan announced new measures of strategic co-operation between the U.S.A. and Israel.

Dec. 4. Eight U.S. Marines were killed when the American base in Beirut was shelled by Druze rebels and guns of the U.S. 6th Fleet were called in to help reply to the attack; earlier two U.S. Navy jets were shot down over Lebanon in the first U.S. air strike against Syrian positions. **5.** A car bomb exploded outside a high-rise block of flats in south Beirut killing 14 people and wounding over 80. **6.** A terrorist bomb exploded in a bus as it waited at traffic lights in Jerusalem and killed four people and injured 43. **13.** Israeli and American ships shelled Lebanon in separate and unco-ordinated attacks on Palestinian and Syrian bases. **14.** U.S. battleship, *New Jersey*, opened fire and blasted Syrian anti-aircraft batteries 15 miles inland after U.S. reconnaissance jets came under ground attack for second day running over Lebanon. **20.** Yasser Arafat and 4,000 of his guerrillas evacuated Tripoli in Greek merchant vessels escorted by French warships for Algeria, Tunisia, and North Yemen. **21.** At least 11 people, including a French soldier of the multi-national peace-keeping force, were reported to have been killed in two bomb explosions in Beirut.

(1984) Jan. 2. P.L.O. chairman, Yasser Arafat, rejected President Reagan's Middle East peace plan. **3.** Syria released a U.S. airman who had been shot down over Lebanon following a visit to Damascus by the Rev. Jesse Jackson, the black American civil rights leader. **9.** Talks between Lebanon, Syria and Saudi Arabia aimed at resolving the security situation in Lebanon collapsed in Beirut. **15.** U.S. warships off the Lebanese coast bombarded Druze militia positions after U.S. Marines came under heavy fire. **24.** Chancellor Kohl of West Germany arrived in Israel for a five-day visit. **25.** The Israeli Government survived three no-confidence votes in the Knesset over their economic policies.

Feb. 5. In Lebanon, President Gemayel's Cabinet resigned; on Feb. 6 it was reported Beirut had erupted into open civil war; on Feb. 7 Moslem militiamen over-ran and seized control of Beirut's western sector aided by mass desertion of pro-Moslem Lebanese Army soldiers; President Reagan ordered the phased withdrawal of the 1,600 U.S. Marines from Beirut to be based on ships offshore; on Feb. 8 British troops moved out at dawn from their positions in suburbs of Beirut and were flown by helicopters to a Royal Fleet Auxiliary support ship standing by offshore; on Feb. 10 more than 500 civilians were evacuated from Beirut by the Royal Navy as fighting continued in the city. **19.** The U.S.A. refused to succumb to Soviet-Syrian pressure to remove its fleet from Lebanon waters as the price of introducing a U.N. peacekeeping force in Beirut; heavy fighting continued at Souk al Gharb, still held by the Lebanese Army, and Israeli warplanes attacked Syrian-held positions in the mountains; the Italian contingent of the peace force departed on Feb. 20; on Feb. 26 the last of the U.S. Marines left Beirut. **29.** President Gemayel of Lebanon visited Damascus for talks with President Assad of Syria.

Mar. 1. Jordan and the P.L.O. ended four days of talks in Amman. **5.** Lebanon cancelled the troop withdrawal agreement it reached with Israel 10 months ago to prepare the way for national reconciliation talks between Lebanese factions. **20.** The Lebanese peace conference in Lausanne, Switzerland ended. **22.** The Israeli Parliament voted to dissolve and hold an early general election. **25.** The French peace-keeping force in Beirut began withdrawing from the city and the total evacuation was completed within a week.

April 13. Lebanon entered its 10th year of civil war with artillery, machine-gun and mortar fire being exchanged in Beirut. **20.** Syria's state news agency reported that President Gemayel of Lebanon and President Assad had agreed principles to reunite the Lebanese at their talks in Damascus.

May 27. Egypt's general election was won by the ruling National Democratic Party.

June 12. The Lebanese Parliament gave a vote of confidence to its 10-man Cabinet to enable it to rule by decree. **23.** The Lebanese Cabinet agreed on a comprehensive package deal designed to set the nation on the way to peace. **28.** Syria and Israel exchanged prisoners taken during the 1982 war in Lebanon.

July 23. Israeli general election took place and resulted in stalemate.

Aug. 14. British and French naval minehunters entered the Suez Canal to help clear the Red Sea of mines which had damaged 17 ships in five weeks.

U.S.A.

(1983) Sept. 8. President Reagan ordered a review of the U.S.' military presence in Lebanon following the deaths of four marines in Beirut. **26.** The President, in an address to U.N. General Assembly, offered three new concessions in nuclear arms negotiations. **28.** The U.S. Congress voted to accept a compromise which allowed President Reagan to keep U.S. Marines in Lebanon for another 18 months.

Oct. 3. President Reagan cancelled his planned visits to the Philippines, Indonesia and Thailand in Nov. which were scheduled as part of a Far East tour. **4.** The President announced that America was to propose at the Strategic Arms Reduction Talks (START) in Geneva a "build-down" approach of scrapping an agreed number of long-range missile warheads for every new one deployed. **9.** Mr. James Watt, Secretary of the Interior, resigned; on Oct. 13 President Reagan nominated Mr. William Clark, his national security adviser, to succeed Mr. Watt; on Oct. 17 Mr. Robert McFarlane, Middle East envoy, was appointed national security adviser. **19.** The Senate voted in favour of making the third Monday in January a national holiday in memory of Martin Luther King, the assassinated black civil rights leader. **22.** A man with a revolver evaded security men and crashed his pick-up truck through the gates of a Georgia golf course where President Reagan was playing; the gunman took hostages before surrendering.

Nov. 1. The President lifted some of the economic sanctions imposed on Poland after martial law was declared in 1981. **7.** Production of the MX intercontinental missile was approved finally when the Senate rejected an amendment which would have cut $2·1 billion from the defence budget. **13.** It was disclosed that the U.S.A. was sending 1,000 army engineers to Costa Rica for "civil action". **14.** In a move to break the deadlock at the START talks in Geneva, the U.S.A. suggested a global limit of 420 medium-range warheads for each side. **18.** Record military spending of $249·8 billion was approved by the House of Representatives. **28.** The space shuttle *Columbia*, carrying six astronauts, the largest crew to date and including a West German, the first non-American to travel in a U.S. spacecraft, took off from Cape Canaveral; it returned on Dec. 8.

Dec. 8. The President announced the lifting of the U.S. embargo on arms sales to Argentina. **27.** U.S. Steel Corporation announced it would close all or part of several steel plants with the loss of over 4,500 jobs. **28.** A Pentagon inquiry into the Beirut suicide bomb disaster, which killed 241 U.S. Servicemen in Oct., blamed the whole military chain of command for lack of security and questioned the continuing presence of U.S. troops in Lebanon. **29.** It was announced that President Reagan had decided to withdraw the U.S.A. from Unesco.

(1984) Jan. 10. China's Premier, Zhao Ziyang, started his visit to the U.S.A.; on Jan. 12 America signed two agreements with China on economic and technological co-operation. **11.** The Kissinger Commission's report on Central America was published. **16.** President Reagan pledged his commitment to East-West dialogue. **25.** The President, in his State of the Union address, called for improved relations with the Soviet Union and said in 1984 he would "seize the opportunities for peace." **29.** President Reagan announced he was to seek re-election for a second term of office. **30.** U.S. Administration broke a seven-year embargo on military sales to Guatemala by authorizing the delivery of $2 million worth of helicopter spare parts to the Guatemalan army.

Feb. 1. The President submitted to Congress a budget for a 14·5 per cent rise in military spending. **3.** The space shuttle *Challenger* was launched on an eight-day mission from Cape Canaveral; on Feb. 7, astronaut Bruce McCandless floated from the space craft to make the first human space free-flight. **15.** Mr. Kinnock, the Labour Party leader, ended a week-long visit to the U.S.A. which included a meeting with President Reagan at the White House. **22.** The Senate voted in support of a Bill to allow the federal government to execute terrorists, spies, and people who attempted to assassinate presidents. **29.** Senator Gary Hart won an unexpected victory in the New Hampshire primary for the Democratic presidential candidature by defeating Mr. Walter Mondale, the favourite.

Mar. 16. Senator John Glenn, the former astronaut, withdrew from the campaign for the Democratic presidential nomination. The White House announced new security measures to protect the President after an "emotionally-disturbed" man armed with a sawn-off shotgun had been shot in the arm while loitering nearby.

April 5. A child-killer and a double murderer were electrocuted in separate executions in Florida and Louisiana. **6.** Five astronauts on board the space shuttle *Challenger* lifted off from Cape Canaveral, Florida; on April 10, after three days of trouble, they captured a damaged satellite and carried out repairs; the shuttle touched down at Edwards Air Force Base, California on April 13. **11.** The Senate voted 84 to 12 against U.S. support for mining of Nicaraguan waters on a "non-binding resolution"; on April 13 the House of Representatives passed by 281 to 111 a non-binding "sense of the Congress" resolution calling for an end to the mining of Nicaraguan ports. **24.** President Reagan called on the Chinese Government as well as other Asian states to align with America in economic and other policies to combat "expansionist aggression" in the Pacific.

May 7. Seven American chemical companies agreed to pay $180 million in settlement of a law suit brought on behalf of 15,000 Vietnam war veterans who claimed use of the herbicide Agent Orange had wrecked their health. **10.** A Federal Judge ruled in Salt Lake City that the U.S. Government caused deaths and illnesses with its Nevada atom-bomb tests 30 years ago and awarded $2,600,000 to nine people. **17.** The House of Representatives voted against resuming production of nerve gas weapons, the figures being 247 to 179 to reject the President's request for money. **24.** Congress voted overwhelmingly in favour of banning American combat troops being sent to El Salvador or Nicaragua except to rescue embassy staff or other U.S. citizens, but approved a £45 million military aid package to El Salvador by 267 to 154 votes in the House of Representatives. **29.** U.S.A. delivered anti-aircraft missiles and a tanker plane to help protect Saudi Arabian oil installations and shipping from attack.

June 11. The Pentagon announced that for the first time a non-nuclear U.S. weapon had destroyed an intercontinental ballistic missile in an outer space test. **15.** The first sale of U.S. weapons to China since the Communists took power in 1949 was agreed in principle during three days of talks in Washington between the U.S. Defence Secretary and his Chinese counterpart. **21.** The Senate gave final approval to a $291 billion Defence Authorisation Bill. **27.** President Reagan disclosed he had proposed establishing bilateral contacts with the Russians in a number of areas, including high-level military discussions.

July 12. Mr. Walter Mondale, the Democratic presidential candidate, named Mrs. Geraldine Ferraro, New York Congresswoman, as his vice-presidential running mate. **14.** Merrell Dow Pharmaceuticals agreed to pay £92 million to settle claims that its drug, Debendox, caused birth defects in hundreds of children. **16.** The Democratic national convention opened in San Francisco.

Aug. 10. The Pentagon dispatched five warships to central America for two weeks to "underscore American support for friendly countries in the region". **16.** The American National Bank in McLean, Texas, was declared insolvent and closed, the 50th bank failure this year in the U.S.A. **20.** The Republican national convention opened in Dallas. **30.** The new shuttle, *Discovery*, lifted off from Cape Canaveral with a six-member crew.

COMMON MARKET

(1983) Oct. 12. The European Parliament agreed to pay back to Britain a £180 million rebate on its 1982 contributions to the E.E.C. by a majority of only seven against a blocking amendment. The E.E.C. Commission President, M. Gaston Thorn, announced stop-gap measures to halt the run on E.E.C. funds by farmers and said, "the till is closed". **20.** The E.E.C. Commission in Brussels announced a package of measures aimed to keep the Community out of debt for the remainder of the year. **27.** The European Parliament voted by 262 to 56 votes to freeze Britain's promised E.E.C. rebate for this year until permanent reform of the financing system was agreed.

Nov. 5. Common Market governments agreed on a substantial programme of investment in computer research to help European companies compete with their American and Japanese rivals. **8.** The Common Market Commission produced a new formula in Brussels which purported to reveal that Britain's net unadjusted contribution to the E.E.C. budget in 1982 was just half of the generally accepted figure; Mr. Christopher Tugendhat, the British Commissioner in charge of budget policy, voted against the Commission findings which, he said, amounted to "cooking the books". **13.** The E.E.C. in Brussels set minimum prices from Dec. 1 for basic steel products to end a price-cutting war between European steel companies.

Dec. 6. The Common Market summit held in Athens, which was to have decided on fundamental reforms of the Community's financial system, ended in complete failure and the 10 member countries could not even agree on a final communiqué. **15.** The European Parliament in Strasbourg voted by 268 to 73 to withhold payment of £457 million due to Britain as a rebate on its 1983 Common Market budget contribution, placing the refund into a suspense account pending agreement by E.E.C. member governments on comprehensive reform of the Market's financial system; later Mrs. Thatcher told the U.K. Parliament that Britain would withhold payments if the refund was not handed over. **20.** The European Parliament in Brussels formally approved a £15 billion budget for the Common Market next year; ministers of the member countries had opposed the budget as exceeding the Parliament's authority in a number of areas. **23.** E.E.C. officials said the Common Market was to end economic sanctions it had imposed on Russia over Poland in 1982 at the end of the current year.

(1984) Jan. 9. An emergency programme to reform the Common Market's agricultural policy by Mar. 31 was launched by E.E.C. agriculture ministers in Brussels. **11.** Common Market grants to Britain worth £149 million were announced by the Commission in Brussels to assist over 600 development projects throughout the country. **13.** The Common Market introduced higher tariffs and curbs on American exports to Europe worth £78 million a year. **30.** The E.E.C. Commission confirmed it had begun two actions against the British Government in the European Court of Justice claiming the entire subsidy scheme operated by the English and Welsh Milk Marketing Boards in the past three or four years was illegal.

Feb. 14. The European Parliament in Strasbourg approved a draft treaty under which the right of Common Market countries to veto E.E.C. policies judged to be against their national interest would be removed.

Mar. 13. E.E.C. farm ministers agreed to curb the Community's soaring milk production. **19.** At an E.E.C. summit in Brussels, Mrs. Thatcher rejected a French compromise scheme for ending Britain's E.E.C. budget problems; on Mar. 20, the Summit meeting collapsed amid disagreement over the U.K.'s contribution when Heads of Government failed to close a gap of £138 million between differing proposals on a rebate to Britain next year; France and Italy blocked payment of a £450 million rebate to the U.K. owed since last year; on Mar. 27 E.E.C. Foreign Ministers met in Brussels but also failed to resolve Britain's budget payments dispute with no country prepared to make extra concessions. **31.** Common Market farm ministers meeting in Brussels decided to curb the E.E.C. milk surpluses with West Germany, Britain, and Holland cutting production by up to seven per cent and France by two per cent, but Ireland was allowed an increase of 4·65 per cent.

April 18. The E.E.C. Commission said in Brussels it would formally appeal to Governments for a loan of some £1·4 billion to meet its commitments for 1984.

May 23. The E.E.C. Commission proposed a budget for 1985 of £17·2 billion. **24.** President Mitterrand of France proposed to the European Parliament a new European Union and an end to the practice of majority voting under which individual members could veto E.E.C. policies.

June 17. Elections took place for the European Parliament in all member countries except Britain, which polled on June 14. **25.** The E.E.C. summit meeting began in Fontainebleau near Paris and Mrs. Thatcher rejected new proposals from France and the E.E.C. Commission which set a time limit on future rebates to Britain; on June 26 Mrs. Thatcher secured a new budget deal for Britain and in return promised a 40 per cent. increase in the tax revenue the Government would hand over to Brussels to help run the Community; the settlement also ended the long-standing dispute over the £450 million owed to Britain by the Community as its 1983 budget rebate.

July 4. The Common Market Commission fined British Leyland £208,000 for charging traders £100 when they re-imported Metro cars from the Continent. **10.** Capt. Kent Kirk, the Danish fisherman and former Euro-M.P., won his claim that British fishery protection rules under which he was fined £30,000 for unlawful fishing violated Common market law; judges of the European Court of Justice ruled that the U.K. had no right to introduce a temporary order banning Danish fishing vessels from fishing in Britain's 12 mile territorial limit before a community fisheries policy was agreed in late Jan. 1983. **19.** Britain was the only country to refuse to raise the limit of contributions to the E.E.C. Budget at a meeting in Brussels. **27.** The European Parliament voted to block once again Britain's £457 million rebate from the 1983 Budget.

AFRICA

(*see also* Commonwealth)

(1983) Sept. 2. A Libyan-led dawn attack was made on the desert cross-roads of Oum Chalouba in Chad. **8.** It was confirmed that Unita guerrillas had captured the Angolan town of Calulo after a week-long battle with Cuban and Russian-backed government forces. **29.** A commission of inquiry into malpractices in South African prisons was ordered after six warders, four whites and two blacks, had been jailed for what the judge called "an orgy of assault" on prisoners.

Oct. 4. President Mitterrand of France and 40 African leaders reached concensus at Vittel, in the Vosges Mountains, that there would be no partition of Chad in their appeal for national reconciliation, the African leaders reaffirming support for President Habre of Chad. **6.** It was stated that forces loyal to President Seyni Kountche of Niger foiled an attempted *coup* on Oct. 5 when a group of armed men tried to take advantage of the President's absence in France to seize power. **17.** South African commandos destroyed an office used by the African National Congress in a central residential area of Maputo, the Mozambique capital.

Nov. 2. Polling took place in a referendum on a new constitution for South Africa when the country's whites voted on whether to allow limited political rights to the Indian and Coloured population; over 65 per cent of voters approved the plan. **10.** The Unita guerrilla movement in Angola claimed to have shot down the Boeing 737 which crashed on Nov. 8 shortly after take-off from Lubango airport, killing all 150 people on board; the official Angolan news agency said the airliner crashed after developing a technical fault.

Dec. 20. President Machel of Mozambique confirmed that the Governments of South Africa and Mozambique were meeting in Swaziland to work out a policy of peaceful co-existence. **23.** South Africa admitted its troops were in action in southern Angola but that they were involved only in a "limited" campaign against guerrillas of the South West Africa People's Organization.

(1984) Jan. 6. President Bourguiba of Tunisia announced that a 100 per cent price increase for bread which had led to widespread riots, would be cancelled. **22.** More than 100 people were feared to have died in northern Morocco in weekend rioting. **31.** South Africa began to disengage its forces from Southern Angola.

Feb. 15. South African police resumed the removal of 250 black families from the Magopa area of the Western Transvaal to the black homeland of Bophuthatswana. **20.** Mozambique agreed to sign a formal peace agreement with South Africa outlawing guerrilla attacks across the border after talks in Maputo between the two countries. **24.** Unita rebels captured 77 foreigners, including 16 Britons, during a raid on the State-owned diamond mines in north-east Angola.

Mar. 16. Sudan blamed Libya for an air attack near Khartoum which killed three people.

April 3. The armed forces seized power in Guinea 10 days after the death of President Sekou Toure. **7.** The President of Cameroon announced that calm had been restored and loyal troops had won a "complete victory" over rebels of the Republican Guard. **28.** President Numeiry of Sudan imposed an indefinite state of emergency and the introduction of martial law.

May 2. South Africa and Mozambique signed an agreement for the supply of power from the Cabora Bassa hydro-electric scheme on the Zambesi River. **13.** Unita guerillas in Angola released 16 British hostages after 11 weeks of captivity. **14.** The African National Congress was blamed by South Africa's Police Minister for the firing of at least eight rockets at a Durban oil refinery. **15.** Morocco announced it had sealed off the Algerian frontier by completing a new line of fortifications designed to prevent incursions by guerrillas into the Western Sahara. **28.** The South African Prime Minister, Mr. P. W. Botha, left Cape Town on an eight-nation European tour.

June 17. President Machel of Mozambique dismissed three ministers.

July 13. The last session of South Africa's all-white Parliament and of the country's Westminster-style system, ended in Cape Town.

Aug. 1. South Africa broke off diplomatic relations with New Zealand. **13.** A treaty binding Morocco to Libya was signed by Col. Gaddafi and King Hassan. **29.** The South African Government confirmed it would go ahead with constitutional changes despite low turnouts and violence during the elections for the Indian and Coloured Houses of the new Legislature. **21.** Col. Gaddafi freed two of the six Britons detained in Libya since the London embassy siege in April.

OTHER COUNTRIES

(1983) Sept. 1. U.S.A. accused the Russians of deliberately shooting down a *South Korean* jumbo jet carrying 269 people which had apparently strayed into Russian airspace north of Japan on Aug. 31; on Sept. 6 the Russian Government admitted in a statement that a Soviet fighter pilot carried out orders from ground control "to stop the flight" of the airliner after it "tried to evade pursuit"; on Sept. 8, President Reagan ordered the closure of Aeroflot offices in the U.S.A. and prohibited American carriers from having any dealings with the Soviet airline; on Sept.

12 Russia vetoed a resolution in the U.N. Security Council deploring the destruction of the airliner; on Sept. 30 the International Federation of Air Line Pilots' Association recommended the 60-day ban on flights (imposed on Sept. 6) to and from Moscow should be lifted on Oct. 3. **8.** Gen. Zia ul-Haq, *Pakistan's* military ruler, began a four-day tour of Sind Province where 40 people had died in over three weeks of anti-Government riots with at least 2,000 arrests. **9.** *Chile* extended for a further six months the country's "state of public disturbance" after a night of anti-Government protest during which four people were reported killed. **12.** It was stated that a vice-consul at the U.S. consulate in Leningrad had been ordered to leave *Russia* for allegedly spying and that his wife was involved; the Americans disclosed that they had expelled two Soviet diplomats in August for alleged spying. **22.** President Marcos of the **Philippines** threatened to re-impose martial law unless anti-Government riots in Manila stopped.

Oct. 5. Lech Walesa, leader of Solidarity, the banned *Polish* trade union, became the 1983 winner of the Nobel Peace Prize. The *U.S.A.* and *Russia* resumed the Strategic Arms Limitation Talks (START) in Geneva. **7.** *France* and *Spain* signed a military co-operation agreement. **10.** *Spain* confirmed that its secret service agents had foiled a plot by Argentine saboteurs to cross into Gibraltar to attack British military installations during the Falklands Conflict. **17.** It was reported that in the past seven days of fighting in *El Salvador*, 276 soldiers and civilians had been killed. **21.** *Iran* claimed its forces had penetrated 10 miles into *Iraqi* territory along a 100-mile front on the second day of its new offensive, but Iraq said the assault had been completely foiled. **28.** The *French* Minister for Tourism announced that from Dec. 20 the financial restrictions imposed on taking currency abroad would be lifted. **30.** *Argentina* went to the polls to choose a civilian government for the first time in a decade; the Radical Party led by Senor Raul Alfonsin won an absolute majority.

Nov. 5. *Turkey* staged its first parliamentary elections since the military *coup*; the Motherland Party won more than half the seats in the National Assembly. **9.** Emperor Hirohito welcomed President Reagan at the start of his visit to *Japan*; on Nov. 13, the President concluded his Far East tour with a visit to the demilitarized zone in *Korea*. **21.** Thousands of anti-missile demonstrators tried to invade the Bundestag in Bonn as the *West German* Parliament debated deployment of new U.S. missiles; on Nov. 22, after a two-day debate, the Parliament approved by 286 to 226 votes the deployment of the missiles.

23. Two *Russian* cosmonauts returned to earth after nearly five months in the *Salyut*-7 space station. Pershing-2 missile parts began arriving in *West Germany*. *Russian* negotiators walked out of the medium-range missile talks in Geneva. **24.** President Andropov said *Russia* intended to implement retaliatory measures in response to the deployment of American cruise and Pershing-2 missiles in Europe.

Dec. 6. *Turkey's* ruling generals stepped down from office and handed over to the elected administration. **8.** N.A.T.O. foreign ministers unanimously agreed to appoint Lord Carrington, former British Foreign Secretary, to succeed Dr. Joseph Luns as Secretary General. **10.** *Argentina* ended eight years of military rule when Senor Raul Alfonsin was sworn in as President. **13.** The Office of the U.N. High Commissioner for Refugees said in Geneva a total of about 330,000 refugees from *Central American* countries had fled to other countries in the region. **14.** President Alfonsin of *Argentina* announced that the generals who had ruled the country were to be put on trial on murder and torture charges. **27.** Most of Sweden, Finland, and Denmark were blacked out after an unexplained explosion at a transformer station in central *Sweden*, which stopped all electricity within Sweden and exports to Denmark and Finland.

(1984) Jan. 2. *France* announced it was to withdraw more than a quarter of its troops from the multi-national peace-keeping force in Beirut. *Portugal* abolished its departure tax for tourists. **6.** Britain and the U.S.A. abstained in the U.N. Security Council on a resolution which condemned South Africa for its latest military operation in Angola. **11.** Production restarted at the *French* Talbot car factory at Poissy after talks between management, employers, and the Government following serious clashes between striking and non-striking workers. **12.** *French* farmers, who ambushed two British lorries and seized their cargoes of lamb, obeyed an order of President Mitterrand and freed the two drivers whom they had held captive. **17.** A conference of 35 nations on disarmament and security in Europe opened in *Stockholm*. **24.** President Andropov of the *U.S.S.R.* declared himself ready for a genuine dialogue with the U.S.A. but rejected "talks for the sake of talks". **25.** The *Japanese* Cabinet approved an austerity Budget. **30.** The New *China* News agency announced that an experimental satellite had been launched.

Feb. 1. Gen. Gunther Kiessling, dismissed as a security risk in Jan. after allegations of homosexuality, was rehabilitated and reinstated as *West Germany's* top commander in N.A.T.O., but because of his health would take early retirement at the end of March.

Norway declared nine Russian diplomats and trade delegates unacceptable. **2.** Mrs. Thatcher arrived in Budapest for talks with *Hungarian* leaders. **7.** Western diplomatic despatches stated that Soviet forces had killed hundreds of *Afghan* civilians, mainly women and children, in the town of Istalef. **8.** A Russian *Soyuz* capsule lifted three cosmonauts into space, making with the five Americans in the shuttle *Challenger*, a total of eight men in orbit—a new space record. **9.** It was stated that *Pakistan* could now make atomic bombs. **12.** *Iranian* troops claimed to have advanced 15 miles inside north-east *Iraq*. **13.** Mr. Konstantin Chernenko, aged 72, was named as the new general-secretary of the *Soviet* Communist Party in succession to Mr. Andropov, who died on Feb. 9; Mr. Andropov's funeral took place on Feb. 14 in Moscow and was attended by world leaders, including Mrs. Thatcher, who later had a meeting with Mr. Chernenko; Mr. George Bush, U.S. Vice-President, handed Mr. Chernenko a letter from President Reagan during their meeting. **17.** *French* riot police and troops with helicopters and bulldozers moved in on Government orders to clear roads which had been paralysed by lorry drivers protesting at delays caused by go-slow strikes by French and Italian customs officers at both ends of the Mont Blanc tunnel; on Feb. 21, blockades by the lorry drivers spread to Paris; on Feb. 22 nearly all main roads were blocked by heavy lorries and thousands of lorries were stranded along the Alpine routes; on Feb. 24 the blockade ended after the two transport unions appealed to their members to unblock the roads and a second round of negotiations between the Government and the hauliers' unions was reaffirmed. **22.** The *West German* Cabinet approved £400 million worth of State aid for the new four-nation European A-320 airbus project. **23.** Brig. Lami Dozo, former Commander of the *Argentine* Air Force and member of the military junta which ordered the invasion of the Falklands, was under arrest at an air base near Buenos Aires following the arrests of ex-President Galtieri and Jorge Anaya, former Navy Commander, after the trio had testified at a court martial. **27.** *Iraq* announced its aircraft had attacked oil tankers berthed at the *Iranian* oil terminal at Kharg Island in the Gulf.

Mar. 1. *Iran* announced it had launched a new attack against *Iraqi* positions north of Basra; on Mar. 4, Iran accused Britain of supplying Iraq with chemical weapons and claimed 1,000 of its soldiers had been wounded by gas-shells fired by Iraqi artillery; the British Foreign Office denied the allegations; on Mar. 5, U.S.A. stated that it had confirmed that Iraq was using chemical weapons. **5.** It was reported that Russian forces in *Afghanistan* had launched a major offensive against the Panjshir Valley, the stronghold of the resistance. **7.** A British merchant ship, *Charming*, had been badly damaged by an *Iraqi* missile in the Gulf War zone, the Foreign Office stated. A *French* Navy patrol boat fired tear gas grenades at two Spanish trawlers fishing illegally in European Community waters, injuring nine trawlermen. **12.** *Iraq* claimed to have repulsed an *Iranian* offensive across the border north-east of Basra. **14.** It was stated *East Germany* was building a concrete barricade parallel to the Berlin Wall. **27.** A U.N. report stated there was concrete evidence that chemical weapons in the form of aerial bombs had been used in the *Gulf War*. **28.** Mr. Kenneth Whitty, first secretary at the British Embassy in *Athens*, was shot dead while driving home for lunch.

April 4. The *French* Cabinet decided that unemployed immigrant workers who wished to return home would be given substantial financial assistance. **11.** Mr. Konstantin Chernenko was declared President of the *Soviet Union*. **15.** Sir Geoffrey Howe, Foreign Secretary, arrived in *Peking* for talks on Hong Kong. **17.** The Prime Minister (Mrs. Thatcher) began visit to *Portugal*. **18.** A draft treaty for a complete and verifiable ban on chemical weapons throughout the world was presented to the disarmament conference in *Geneva* by Mr. George Bush, the U.S. Vice-President; on April 26 Russia rejected the plan. **24.** *Afghanistan* régime claimed the strategic Panjshir Valley had been captured after Russia launched a major offensive to defeat the Afghan rebels. **26.** President Reagan arrived in Peking for visit to *China*.

May 6. The *French* Government announced it was ending no-passport excursions by Britons to France after nearly 30 years on July 8. **8.** Reports stated that an attempt on the life of Col. Gaddafi in Tripoli had been defeated by forces loyal to the *Libyan* leader. **14.** Four tankers were ablaze or damaged in the Gulf, two of them having been hit by missiles near Kharg Island, the *Iranian* oil port. **16.** A *Saudi Arabian* supertanker in its own territorial waters was struck by a missile from an aircraft reported to be Iranian. **19.** A Panamanian cargo vessel sank after being hit by a missile at the head of the Gulf when bound for an *Iranian* port. **20.** In a referendum, *Swiss* voters decisively rejected a move to open up the country's traditional banking secrecy. *Russia* stated that it had increased the number of its nuclear-armed submarines off the coast of the U.S.A. as a retaliatory measure following the deployment of Cruise and Pershing missiles in Europe. **22.** Western diplomats reported that heavy fighting between Russian troops and rebels was continuing around *Afghanistan*'s Panjshir Valley. **25.** *Iraq* claimed eight vessels were destroyed and set alight in an attack on an inshore Iranian shipping convoy

in the Gulf. **29.** President Mitterrand of *France* and Chancellor Kohl of *West Germany* ended their two-day summit talks near Paris. **31.** N.A.T.O. foreign ministers ended a two-day review of East–West relations in *Washington* with a renewal of their commitment to a "constructive dialogue" with Russia.

June 1. The *Dutch* Government decided to take all its quota of 48 Cruise missiles but not until 1988 and subject to conditions. **4.** Two British diplomats were expelled from *Prague* in retaliation for the expulsion of two Czechoslovak diplomats from London. Mr. P. W. Botha, South African Prime Minister, arrived in *Bonn* for talks with Chancellor Kohl. **5.** *Saudi Arabian* jet fighters shot down two Iranian jet fighters over the Gulf and the U.S.A. ordered a second aircraft carrier to the region. **6.** The Queen and President Reagan paid homage to the men who died on the *Normandy* beaches on D-Day during a day-long 40th anniversary programme of commemoration and remembrance on the French coast; the ceremonies were also attended by President Mitterrand of France, King Badouin of Belgium, King Olaf of Norway, Queen Beatrix of the Netherlands, and Mr. Pierre Trudeau, Prime Minister of Canada. **10.** A *Kuwaiti* tanker was attacked by Iranian jets off Qatar. **11.** President Chernenko proposed that *Russia* and *America* begin without delay formal negotiations for an agreement to ban further testing of anti-satellite weapons and dismantle existing anti-satellite systems. The Pope received Mr. P. W. Botha, Prime Minister of South Africa, in audience in *Rome*. **20.** President Mitterrand of France arrived in *Moscow* for talks with President Chernenko. **24.** *Iraq* claimed that its planes had hit "four large naval targets" at Kharg Island, the Iranian oil terminal. **25.** Lord Carrington, former British Foreign Secretary, took over as secretary-general of N.A.T.O. **26.** Count Otto Lambsdorff, *West German* Economics Minister, facing trial on corruption charges, resigned. **27.** *West German* engineering workers and employers reached agreement to settle a seven-week dispute on working hours. It was reported that a supertanker had been hit by an *Iraqi* missile while sailing from Iran's Kharg Island oil terminal. **29.** *Russia* announced it was ready to begin talks in the autumn with the *U.S.A.* aimed at controlling anti-satellite space weapons.

July 1. An *Iraqi* Military communique claimed that Iraqi air and sea attacks had destroyed a convoy of seven ships and shot down an Iranian fighter plane. **3.** *West German* car assembly lines re-started work after being halted for over a month in a strike which laid off more than 450,000 employees. **7.** *Russia* named a new ambassador to *Egypt* as full diplomatic relations were restored after a three-year rift. **17.** *France's* Industry Minister, M. Laurent Fabius, was appointed Prime Minister after the Government headed by M. Mauroy resigned; on July 19 the Communist Party declined an invitation to hold office in the new Cabinet. **21.** The *Polish* Parliament approved an amnesty for thousands of prisoners including dissidents and jailed members of the banned Solidarity movement. **25.** The *West German* Cabinet approved a new £250 million credit for East Germany in return for the easing of restrictions in a number of areas. *Soviet* cosmonaut, Svetlana Savitskaya, became the first woman to walk in space. **31.** Western diplomats said in Islamabad that heavy Russian bombing of *Afghanistan's* western city of Herat the previous week had caused "hundreds of casualties".

Aug. 25. *Paris* celebrated the 40th anniversary of its liberation from German forces. **26.** Crown Prince Hans Adam took over executive power in *Liechtenstein* from his father, Prince Franz Josef II. **28.** According to Western diplomatic dispatches reaching Islamabad, 37 civilians had been killed or wounded when Soviet bombers attacked an *Afghan* tourist centre near Kabul.

THE FALKLANDS

(1983) Oct. 13. Harland and Wolff shipyard, Belfast, won the £4 million contract for a floating harbour for use in the Falklands. **15.** Mr. John Stanley, Armed Forces Minister, flew into Port Stanley on a fact-finding tour. **24.** The White Paper, "The Future Defence of the Falkland Islands", was published. **25.** The Queen's approval was published for the awarding of battle honours for the Falklands campaign. **28.** A livestock ship arrived in the Falklands with replacements for many of the animals lost in the conflict.

Nov. 9. The Prince of Wales, accompanied by the Princess of Wales, laid a wreath as Colonel of the Welsh Guards in the Guards Chapel, Westminster, during the dedication of a memorial plaque to 42 Guardsmen who died in the Falklands; later the Duke of Kent as Colonel of the Scots Guards laid a wreath in honour of eight members of the Regiment killed in the campaign. **11.** A large granite cross given by the people of Wales was dedicated at Fitzroy Farm, East Falkland, near where many Welsh Guards were killed.

Dec. 2. A report prepared by Argentina's Army Chief of Staff, as an analysis of the Falklands Conflict, was published in Buenos Aires; the Argentine Army admitted it was never adequately organized, equipped or trained to confront British forces. **22.** The Falkland Islands surrender documents went on public display at the Imperial War Museum, London.

(1984) Jan. 4. Mrs. Thatcher indicated she was ready to lift the total exclusion zone around the Falklands the moment the newly-elected government in Argentina made clear that hostilities over the Islands were ended. **22.** Mr. Heseltine, Defence Secretary, ended his three-day tour of the Falklands.

April 26. The new £20 million Falkland Islands port was opened.

July 18. In Berne, Switzerland, Argentina held direct discussions for the first time since the Falklands conflict; the talks, however, collapsed on the following day. **30.** The Queen approved the award to the Parachute Regiment of battle honours for three engagements in which it fought during the Falklands conflict at Goose Green, Mount Longdon, and Wireless Ridge; battle honours were also won by the Scots Guards for their part in the Tumbledown Mountain action; six regiments won "theatre" honours for their overall part in the campaign.

MISCELLANEOUS

(1983) Sept. 14. Mrs. Thatcher inaugurated Britain's Magnus oilfield in the North Sea.

Oct. 3. The Ministry of Defence commissioned an investigation into whether 12,000 Servicemen who took part in the British nuclear weapons tests in the South Pacific and Australia between 1952 and 1967 had suffered from a higher than normal rate of cancer.

Nov. 9. Britain's first freeport was officially launched on the Isle of Man. **14.** Fees for passports and visas were increased. **18.** The report by the Policy Studies Institute on a three-year independent study into the Metropolitan Police was published. Girl sextuplets were born to Mrs. Janet Walton in Liverpool.

Dec. 6. A world record auction price for a work of art was set in London when £7,400,000 was paid for a 12th century manuscript called the Gospels of Henry the Lion. **13.** The Department of Health banned the drug, Flosint, taken by people with arthritis, after reports looking into the deaths of seven patients.

(1984) Jan. 3. The first French long-life milk allowed into Britain was released by the health authorities at Newhaven. **16.** Britain's first satellite television channel was launched in Swindon using the cable network. **22.** It was announced that Britain's first test tube triplets had been born in London.

Feb. 24. The "Revolutionary Students' Force" in Britain announced it had taken over the Libyan People's Bureau in London.

Mar. 7. Stephen Waldorf, who was shot by police who mistook him for a wanted man, was paid £120,000 compensation by the Metropolitan Police, in an out-of-court settlement. **15.** Defence Secretary (Mr. Heseltine) introduced three Service officers and a civilian from whom Britain would choose its first two astronauts.

April 4. The main women's peace camp at Greenham Common was cleared by bailiffs supported by police.

May 2. Britain's first test tube quadruplets were born in London.

June 22. Princess Margaret made her début as a radio actress, playing herself in an episode of *The Archers*, the BBC serial. **26.** A report into the circumstances in which a veterinary surgeon was allowed to take part in an operation on a hospital patient was ordered

by Mr. Fowler, Health and Social Services Secretary.

July 5. A Turner painting called "Seascape: Folkestone" was sold for an auction record of £6.7 million at Sotheby's. **16.** A private test tube baby centre at Cambridge, announced that several women had become pregnant after deep-frozen embryos were thawed and implanted in their wombs. **17.** A nuclear fuel flask survived a 100 m.p.h. impact when a train was crashed into it in a demonstration staged by the C.E.G.B. **18.** The report of the Committee of inquiry chaired by Dame Mary Warnock into human fertilisation and embryology was published. **25.** It was announced that the Home Service Force was to be expanded to nearly 5,000 men. **28.** Ten-day-old Hollie Roffey was given the heart of another baby at the National Heart Hospital in London; she was the world's youngest heart transplant patient, but died on Aug. 17 after developing respiratory problems.

Aug. 6. Britain's first freeport opened at Southampton. **14.** Surgeons carried out a pioneering operation at the London Hospital on a 21 year old deaf woman patient; five platinum electrodes were implanted into her inner ear. **29.** The National Consumer Council published a major social security report.

OBITUARY, SEPT. 16, 1983–SEPT. 15, 1984

Adeane, Michael, P.C., G.C.B., G.C.V.O., Baron, former Private Secretary to the Queen, aged 73—*April* 30.

Andropov, Yuri, Soviet leader, aged 69—*Feb.* 9.

Aron, Raymond, French philosopher, aged 78—*Oct.* 17, 1983.

Astor of Hever, Gavin Astor, Baron, former owner of *The Times*, aged 66—*June* 28.

Baillie, Dame Isobel, D.B.E., oratorio singer, aged 88—*Sept.* 24, 1983.

Barker, *Gen.* Sir Evelyn, K.C.B., K.B.E., D.S.O., M.C., distinguished military career, aged 89—*Nov.* 23, 1983.

Basie, Count, jazz pianist and bandleader, aged 79—*April* 26.

Beaufort, Duke of, K.G., G.C.V.O., P.C., former Master of the Queen's Horse, aged 83—*Feb.* 5.

Berryman, Gwen, M.B.E., actress, aged 77—*Dec.* 20, 1983.

Betjeman, Sir John, C.B.E., Poet Laureate, aged 77—*May* 19.

Blackwell, Sir Basil, the doyen of booksellers, aged 94—*April* 9.

Booth, Webster, the singer, aged 82—*June* 21.

Bosanquet, Reginald, television newsreader, aged 51—*May* 27.

Brandt, Bill, photographer, aged 79—*Dec.* 20, 1983.

Brooke of Cumnor, P.C., C.H., Baron, former Conservative Home Secretary, aged 80—*March* 29.

Bull, Peter, actor and author, aged 72—*May* 21.

Burton, Richard, C.B.E., stage and film star, aged 58—*Aug.* 5.

Byers, Charles Frank, P.C., O.B.E., Baron, Liberal leader in the Lords, aged 68—*Feb.* 6.

Capote, Truman, author, aged 59—*Aug.* 25.

Carson, Violet, O.B.E., actress, pianist and singer, aged 85—*Dec.* 26, 1983.

Coogan, Jackie, famous child film star, aged 69—*March* 1.

Cooper, Tommy, comedian, aged 62—*April* 15.

Clark, *General* Mark, famous U.S. wartime commander, aged 87—*April* 17.

Culver, Roland, O.B.E., actor, aged 83—*March* 1.

Cutforth, René, journalist and broadcaster, aged 75—*April* 1.

Docker, Lady Norah, society figure, aged 77—*Dec.* 11, 1983.

Dods, Marcus, conductor, aged 66—*April* 30.

Dolin, Sir Anton, dancer and choreographer, aged 79—*Nov.* 25, 1983.

Dors, Diana, actress, aged 52—*May* 4.

Empson, Sir William, distinguished poet and critic, aged 77—*April* 15.

Evans, Ioan, Labour M.P. for Cynon Valley, aged 56—*Feb.* 10.

Follows, Sir Denis, C.B.E., sports administrator, aged 75—*Sept.* 17, 1983.

Foreman, Carl, film producer and screenwriter, aged 69—*June* 26.

Fraser, *Rt. Hon.* Sir Hugh, M.B.E., former Conservative Minister, aged 66—*March* 6.

Gaynor, Janet, film actress, aged 77—*Sept.* 14.

Gibberd, Sir Frederick, C.B.E., R.A., architect-planner, aged 76—*Jan.* 9.

Gobbi, Tito, opera singer, aged 68—*March* 5.

Goudge, Elizabeth, author, aged 83—*April* 1.

Hale, Binnie, musical comedy actress, aged 84—*Jan.* 10.

Harris, *Marshal of the Royal Air Force* Sir Arthur, G.C.B., O.B.E., A.F.C., Chief of Bomber Command 1942–45, aged 91—*April* 5.

Headley, George, former West Indian Test cricketer, aged 74—*Nov.* 30, 1983.

Hellman, Lillian, playwright, aged 77—*June* 30.
Hibberd, Stuart, M.B.E., radio announcer, aged 90—*Nov.*, 1983.
Holst, Imogen, C.B.E., musician, aged 76—*March* 9.
Holyoake, *Rt. Hon.* Sir Keith, K.G., G.C.M.G., C.H., former Prime Minister of New Zealand, aged 79—*Dec.*, 1983.
Hooker, Sir Stanley, C.B.E., aero engine designer, aged 76—*May* 24.
John, *Admiral of the Fleet* Sir Caspar, G.C.B., distinguished naval career, aged 81—*July* 11.
Keating, Tom, art faker, aged 67—*Feb.* 12.
Kennedy, Jimmy, O.B.E., songwriter, aged 81—*April* 6.
Lee of Newton, Frederick, P.C., Baron, former Labour Cabinet Minister, aged 77—*Feb.* 4.
Le Mesurier, John, actor, aged 71—*Nov.* 15, 1983.
Leopold III, former King of the Belgians, aged 81—*Sept.* 25, 1983.
Llewellyn, Richard, author, aged 77—*Nov.* 30, 1983.
Lord, Cyril, former textile magnate, aged 72—*May* 29.
Losey, Joseph, film director, aged 75—*June* 22.
Macmillan of Ovenden, Maurice, Visct., P.C., former Conservative Minister, aged 63—*March* 10.
Mason, James, actor, aged 75—*July* 27.
Melville, Alan, revue writer and author, aged 73—*Dec.* 24, 1983.
Merman, Ethel, musical stage star, aged 75—*Feb.* 15.
Miró, Joan, artist, aged 90—*Dec.* 25, 1983.
Moorehead, Alan, C.B.E., journalist and author, aged 73—*Sept.* 29, 1983.

Morecambe, Eric, O.B.E., comedian, aged 58—*May* 28.
O'Brien, Pat, film actor, aged 83—*Oct.* 15, 1983.
O'Flaherty, Liam, novelist, aged 88—*Sept.* 7.
Pilkington, Harry, Baron, businessman and public figure, aged 78—*Dec.* 22, 1983.
Pink, Ralph, C.B.E., Conservative M.P. for Portsmouth South, aged 71—*May* 6.
Powell, Margaret, authoress and broadcaster, aged 76—*April* 25.
Powell, William, film actor, aged 91—*March* 5.
Priestley, John Boynton, O.M., author and playwright, aged 89—*Aug.* 14.
Rees, Dai, C.B.E., golfer, aged 70—*Nov.* 16, 1983.
Renault, Mary, novelist, aged 78—*Dec.* 13, 1983.
Richardson, Sir Ralph, actor, aged 80—*Oct.* 10, 1983.
Ridley, Arnold, O.B.E., dramatist and actor, aged 88—*March* 12.
Robbins, Lionel, C.H., Baron, educationalist, aged 85—*May* 15.
Robinson, *Rt. Rev.* John, former Bishop of Woolwich, aged 64—*Dec.* 5, 1983.
Robson, Dame Flora, D.B.E., actress, aged 82—*July* 7.
Shaw, Irwin, American writer, aged 71—*May* 16.
Sholokhov, Mikhail, Soviet author, aged 78—*Feb.* 20.
Skeaping, Mary, M.B.E., ballet director and producer, aged 81—*Feb.* 9.
Vaizey, John Ernest, Baron, economist and educationalist, aged 54—*July* 19.
Voce, Bill, famous cricketer, aged 74—*June* 6.
Weissmuller, Johnny, film star and champion swimmer, aged 79—*Jan.*

CENTENARIES

One Hundred Years Ago (1885).—A selection follows of "Remarkable Occurrences" (as "Events of the Year" was then called) as printed in the 1886 and 1887 editions of *Whitaker's Almanack* covering the year 1885:

JANUARY, 1885.

1. Time reckoning at Greenwich Observatory changed, the day commencing from midnight, in accordance with universal time, instead of noon.
12. General Stewart's force reach Gakdul.
17. Battle of Abu Klea; victory with heavy losses of the British forces under General Stewart.
19. British victory near Metamneh; General Stewart wounded.
24. Attempts to blow up the House of Commons, Westminster Hall, and the Tower of London with dynamite; several persons badly injured.
26. Fall of Khartoum; General Gordon killed.
28. Col. Sir C. Wilson reaches Khartoum, and finds it in the hands of the enemy.
29. Bank rate reduced to 4 per cent.

FEBRUARY.

5. News reaches England of the fate of Khartoum on the 26th January; intense excitement in London.
8. The Italian flag hoisted with that of Egypt at Massowah.
10. A victory gained near Dulka Island by forces under General Earle, who was killed.
12. Langson, in Cochin China, captured by French troops.
13. Opening of the Mersey Tunnel.
14. Gubat evacuated by Major-General Buller.
20. The Grenadier Guards embark at Gravesend for the Soudan.
21. Dedication of the Washington Monument at Washington, U.S.A.: the tallest structure known, being 555 feet high.
23. John Lee, convicted of the murder of Miss Keyse, respited after a third unsuccessful attempt to hang him.
—. Sir C. Warren proclaims military law in Bechuanaland, and takes over the administration into his own hands.

MARCH.

3. The New South Wales Contingent leave Sydney for the Soudan: the first occasion of Australian troops sharing in the defence of the Empire.
15. Telephonic tickets at half a franc issued in Paris.
19. Bank rate reduced to 3½ per cent.
22. Severe fighting near Suakim; British losses 700 men.
25. Reconnoitring at Suakim by means of a balloon; the first ascent made on active service in the English army.
26. Message from the Queen read in the House of Commons to the effect that the Reserve Forces and Militia Reserves are to be called out.
28. Langson, in Cochin China, evacuated by General Négrier, who was seriously wounded.
30. Attack by the Russians, under General Komaroff, on the Afghan positions between the Murghab and the Kushk.
31. Arrival of the Ameer at Rawal Pindi.

APRIL.

6. Peace concluded between France and China.
7. The Prince and Princess of Wales and Prince Edward of Wales leave London for Ireland.
23. Explosion at the Admiralty in the room of Mr. E. W. Swainson, Assistant Under-Secretary, who was badly injured.
24. Opening conflict at Fish Creek, Canada, with the half-breed and Indian rebels under Louis Riel.
27. The Prince and Princess of Wales leave Ireland after a visit of nearly three weeks' duration.

MAY.

2. Destruction by fire of the Japanese Village erected at Albert Gate, Knightsbridge.

4. Opening of the International Inventions Exhibition at South Kensington by the Prince and Princess of Wales.

5. A treaty concluded between the United States Government and the Columbian Government at Bogotá, providing a joint protectorate over the Isthmus of Panama.

7. Bank rate reduced to 3 per cent.

9. General Middleton, with 1,000 men, leaves Gabriel's Crossing. A gunboat fired on near Batoche, and a short engagement takes place; the rebels routed.

14. Bank rate reduced from 3 per cent. to 2½ per cent.

15. Capture, near Batoche, of Louis Riel, the instigator of the Canadian Rebellion.

18. The "Revised Bible" published.

—. Burton and Cunningham, convicted of treason-felony in connection with the late dynamite outrages in London, sentenced to penal servitude for life.

23. Daring robbery of diamonds in Hatton Garden from the firm of Alexander Brothers, and attempt to shoot Mr. James Alexander.

28. Bank rate reduced from 2½ to 2 per cent.

31. Lying-in-state of Victor Hugo under the Arc de Triomphe.

JUNE.

1. First meet of the season of the Four-in-Hand Club.

—. Funeral of Victor Hugo at the Panthéon, Paris.

3. Lord Hastings's Melton won the Derby.

5. Opening of the Albert Palace at Battersea.

7. Demonstration in Hyde Park to protest against an increase in the beer and spirit duties.

9. Treaty of peace between France and China signed at Tientsin.

12. Lord Salisbury has an audience with the Queen at Balmoral, and accepts office.

18. Disastrous explosion in the Clifton Hall Colliery at Pendlebury.

20. The Spanish Ministry tender their resignation in consequence of the king's determination to visit the cholera-stricken districts.

24. The seals of office transferred from Mr. Gladstone's Cabinet to that of the Marquis of Salisbury.

29. The death of the Mahdi, Mohammed Achmed, is reported to have taken place.

JULY.

1. Postal arrangements accelerated from this date in all parts of the United Kingdom.

9. Buildings of the new University of Wales, at Aberystwith, in great part destroyed by fire.

18. Strike of between 15,000 and 20,000 cotton spinners at Oldham against a reduction of 10 per cent. in wages.

23. Princess Beatrice married at Whippingham Church to Prince Henry of Battenberg.

26. The Rev. Coker Adams, rector of Soham Toney, Norfolk, publicly excommunicated an octogenarian parishioner.

AUGUST.

4. A religious service in memory of the late General Grant held in Westminster Abbey.

6. Meeting of the Emperors of Germany and Austria at Gastein.

12. Thanks to the officers and men engaged in the Soudan are moved in both Houses.

20. The occupation of the Caroline Islands by Germany caused much excitement in Spain.

25. Meeting of the Emperors of Russia and Austria at Kremsier.

31. Announcement made that of 223,546 persons attacked by cholera in Spain, 82,619 had died from the epidemic.

SEPTEMBER.

5. Five hundred thousand sovereigns, weighing five tons, received in Dublin from London, to meet a run upon the Bank of Ireland.

—. Completion of the Severn Tunnel, and passage of the first train with directors.

10–11. Arrival in London of the Guards from the Soudan.

14. After four abortive attempts the first International Yacht Match takes place off New York, the American yacht Puritan beating the Genesta.

15. "Jumbo", the elephant formerly in the Zoological Gardens, received such injuries in a railway collision at St. Thomas, Ontario, that he died in a few minutes.

18. Revolution in Eastern Roumelia. The Governor-General placed under arrest, and allegiance sworn to Prince Alexander of Bulgaria.

24. Eighteen persons crushed to death and about forty injured in Stockholm on the occasion of Madame Nilsson singing from a balcony of the Grand Hotel.

29. The death-rate in London announced as only 13·8 per thousand.

OCTOBER.

1. The system of sixpenny telegrams first came into operation.

4. First meeting of the Ambassadors at Constantinople on the Eastern Crisis.

21. Prince Albrecht of Prussia elected Regent of the Duchy by the Brunswick Diet.

22. Marriage of Prince Waldemar of Denmark and Princess Marie Amélie d'Orléans at the Château d'Eu.

24. James Malcolm sentenced to seven years' penal servitude for a bigamous marriage under the name of Captain Macdonald.

28. The *Great Eastern* steamship sold by auction to Mr. Frederick de Mattos for £26,200.

NOVEMBER.

1. The first detachment of the Burmese Expedition started from Calcutta for Rangoon.

12. Bank rate raised to 3 per cent.

14. Opening of the Indian Village at the Albert Palace.

16. Hostilities against the Burmese commenced under Lieut.-General Prendergast.

25. The Queen presented medals to non-commissioned officers for gallantry in the Soudan.

27. Mr. Gladstone returned for Midlothian.

30. King of Burmah surrenders unconditionally.

DECEMBER.

10. Mr. Charles Pulman, Clerk of the Works at British Museum, fined for feeding the pigeons with seeds steeped in spirits of wine. No legal offence having been committed, fine was made nominal.

12. Grand funeral service at Madrid for late King Alfonso; thirty-four Bishops were present at the altar.

14. In consequence of the new regulations respecting care of dogs, 7,000 dogs had been taken into custody up to this date.

15. The Crown recovered in the Court of Queen's Bench £1,986 penalties for smuggling against a Leeds tobacconist. The tobacco was brought to Hull in coffins and hollow balks of timber.

17. Bank rate raised for 3 to 4 per cent.

18. Last day of polling in the General Election.

21. Funeral of King Ferdinand of Portugal at Lisbon.

22. Suicide from Clifton Suspension Bridge, making the 19th since the opening of the bridge.

30. Queen Christina of Spain took the oath before Congress to be faithful to the heir to the crown during "his or her" minority.

THE CENTENARIES OF 1985

Died 1885

Jan. 26 — General Charles G. Gordon, soldier and governor of Egypt and the Sudan.

May 22 — Victor Hugo, French writer.

July 23 — General Ulysses S. Grant, American Civil War general, and President.

Oct. 1 — 7th Earl of Shaftsbury, social reformer.

Born 1885

Jan. 31 — Anna Pavlova, Russian ballerina.

Sept. 11 — David Herbert Lawrence, writer.

Oct. 30 — Ezra L. Pound, American writer.

Born 1785

Aug. 15 — Thomas De Quincey, essayist and critic.

Oct. 18 — Thomas Love Peacock, novelist.

Died 1685

Feb. 6 — Charles II.

July 15 — Duke of Monmouth, pretender to the English throne.

Born 1685

Feb. 23 — George Frederick Handel, German composer.

Mar. 12 — Bishop George Berkeley, philosopher and writer.

Mar. 21 — Johann Sebastian Bach, German composer.

June 30 — John Gay, poet.

Oct. 26 — Domenico Scarlatti, Italian composer.

Died 1585

Nov. 23 — Thomas Tallis, composer.

Born 1585

Sept. 9 — Cardinal Richelieu, French statesman.

Died 1485

Aug. 22 — Richard III, at Bosworth Field.

THE CENTENARIES OF 1986

Died 1886

Jan. 16 — Amilcare Ponchielli, Italian composer.

May 15 — Emily Dickinson, American poet.

May 23 — Leopold von Ranke, German historian.

July 31 — Franz Liszt, Hungarian pianist and composer.

Nov. 8 — Fred Archer, champion jockey.

Nov. 18 — Chester A. Arthur, U.S. President 1881–85.

Born 1886

July 23 — Sir Arthur Whitten Brown, aviator and companion of Alcock on first transatlantic flight.

Oct 16 — David Ben-Gurion, first Prime Minister of Israel.

Died 1786

Aug. 17 — Frederick the Great, King of Prussia 1740–86.

Born 1786

Feb. 24 — Wilhelm Grimm, German philologist and folklorist.

Aug. 17 — Davy Crockett, American frontiersman and Congressman.

Nov. 18 — Carl von Weber, German composer.

Died 1686

Nov. 11 — Louis, Prince of Condé, French soldier.

Born 1686

May 14 — Gabriel D. Fahrenheit, German physicist and inventor of the mercury thermometer.

Died 1586

Oct. 17 — Sir Philip Sidney, Elizabethan poet and soldier.

Events 1886

Jan. 29 — Patenting of first successful petrol-driven car, built by Karl Benz.

March 10 — First Cruft's Dog Show in London.

Sept. 4 — Surrender of Geronimo, leader of the last great American Indian rebellion.

Oct. 28 — Statue of Liberty unveiled.

Events 1586

July 28 — First potatoes arrive in Britain (at Plymouth) from Colombia.

Sept. 22 — Battle of Zutphen.

THE CINQUE PORTS

As their name implies the Cinque Ports were originally five in number, Hastings, New Romney, Hythe, Dover and Sandwich. They were in existence before the Norman Conquest and were the Anglo-Saxon successors to the Roman system of coast defence organized from the Wash to Spithead to resist Saxon onslaughts. William the Conqueror reconstituted them and granted peculiar jurisdiction, most of which was abolished in 1855. Only jurisdiction in Admiralty still survives.

At some time after the Conquest the "antient towns" of Winchelsea and Rye were added with equal privileges. The other members of the Confederation, known as Limbs, are:—Lydd, Faversham, Folkestone, Deal, Tenterden, Margate and Ramsgate.

The Barons of the Cinque Ports have the ancient privilege of attending the Coronation Ceremony and are allotted special places in Westminster Abbey.

Lord Warden, H.M. Queen Elizabeth the Queen Mother.

Judge, Court of Admiralty, Gerald Darling, R.D., Q.C.

Registrar, I. G. Gill, P.O. Box 9, Margate, Kent.

Lord Wardens since 1904

Marquess Curzon 1904
The Prince of Wales 1905
Earl Brassey 1908
Earl Beauchamp 1913
Marquess of Reading 1934
Marquess of Willingdon.......................1936
Sir Winston Churchill 1941
Sir Robert Menzies 1965
H.M. Queen Elizabeth the Queen Mother 1978

HOME FINANCE
Central government financial transactions
£ million

| | Consolidated Fund | | | National Loans Fund | | | | Central government borrowing requirement |
| | | | | | Other transactions | | Other funds and accounts | |
	Revenue	Expenditure	Consolidated fund deficit	Receipts	Payments	Deficit		
1981	71,890	−82,352	−10,462	10,733	−11,668	−11,397	999	−10,398
1982	84,896	−89,237	−4,341	11,023	−14,008	−7,326	−529	−7,855
1983	86,610	−96,257	−9,647	11,511	−16,201	−14,337	−100	−14,437
Financial years								
1981−82	76,754	−84,803	−8,049	11,224	−11,969	−8,794	1,180	−7,614
1982−83	83,270	−90,470	−7,200	10,824	−15,288	−11,664	−1,069	−12,733
1983−84	88,364	−97,450	−9,086	11,833	−15,245	−12,498	288	−12,210
1983 1st quarter	25,787	−25,832	−45	3,288	−5,023	−1,780	−489	−2,269
2nd quarter	18,448	−22,676	−4,228	2,293	−3,929	−5,864	410	5,454
3rd quarter	20,333	−23,544	−3,211	3,342	−3,862	−3,731	229	−3,502
4th quarter	22,042	−24,205	−2,163	2,588	−3,387	−2,962	−250	−3,212
1984 1st quarter	27,541	−27,025	516	3,610	−4,067	59	17	−42
1983 March	9,379	−11,304	−1,925	2,802	−2,157	−1,280	−1,675	−2,955
April	6,166	−7,528	−1,362	528	−886	−1,720	463	−1,257
May	6,491	−7,866	−1,375	1,359	−1,617	−1,633	−43	−1,676
June	5,791	−7,282	−1,491	406	−1,426	−2,511	−10	−2,521
July	7,236	−8,430	−1,194	1,537	−1,849	−1,506	494	−1,012
August	6,297	−7,130	−833	783	−605	−655	−599	−1,254
September	6,800	−7,984	−1,184	1,022	−1,408	−1,570	334	−1,236
October	8,249	−7,691	558	603	−614	547	−482	65
November	7,041	−9,003	−1,962	1,488	−2,122	−2,596	477	−2,119
December	6,752	−7,511	−759	497	−651	−913	−245	−1,158
1984 January	11,803	−8,000	3,803	273	−2,336	1,740	483	2,223
February	7,451	−7,471	−20	349	−720	−391	47	−438
March	8,287	−11,554	−3,267	2,988	−1,011	−1,290	−537	−1,827
April	6,321	−8,128	−1,807	702	−696	−1,801	−59	−1,860

Public sector borrowing requirement
£ million

	Total		Contributions by			Financed by				
						Non-bank private sector		Monetary sector	Overseas sector	
									External finance	
	Unadjusted	Seasonally adjusted†	Central government*	Local authorities	Public corporations	Notes and coin	Other	Borrowing in sterling from banks	Foreign currency borrowing from banks	Direct external finance
1981	10,587		10,398	993	−804	585	8,702	252	−790	1,947
1982	4,953		7,855	−2,108	−794	465	5,817	−2,272	−52	1,491
1983	11,541		14,437	−2,424	−472	698	11,428	−2,066	135	1,453
Financial years										
1981−82	8,629		7,614	971	44	492	7,044	114	−863	2,007
1982−83	8,856		12,733	−2,629	−1,248	1,419	9,072	−3,332	−64	2,055
1983−84	9,652		12,210	−2,181	−377					
1982 1st quarter	−2,110	143	−2,609	508	−9	−412	−726	−864	12	−152
2nd quarter	2,748	1,531	3,199	−151	−300	124	2,173	−24	−4	585
3rd quarter	1,708	1,676	2,551	−745	−98	270	1,906	−477	11	−55
4th quarter	2,607	1,219	4,714	−1,720	−387	483	2,464	−907	−71	1,113
1983 1st quarter	1,793	4,430	2,269	−13	−463	542	2,529	−1,924	—	412
2nd quarter	3,149	1,665	5,454	−1,467	−838	−346	3,349	−88	−20	885
3rd quarter	3,691	2,971	3,502	89	100	244	2,775	−124	−50	408
4th quarter	2,908	2,546	3,212	−1,033	729	258	2,775	70	205	−252
1984 1st quarter	−96	2,470	42	230	−368					

†Financial year constrained.   *An increase in debt is shown positive.

BALANCE OF PAYMENTS OF THE UNITED KINGDOM (£ million)

	1977	1978	1979	1980	1981	1982
Current account						
Visible trade						
Exports (fob)	31,728	35,063	40,687	47,415	50,977	55,546
Imports (fob)	34,012	36,605	44,136	46,182	47,969	53,427
Visible balance	−2,284	−1,542	−3,449	+1,233	+3,008	+2,119
Invisibles						
Credits	16,847	19,130	23,804	25,943	29,760	31,724
Debits	14,509	16,430	21,008	23,941	26,221	28,415
Invisible balance	+2,338	+2,700	+2,796	+2,002	+3,539	+3,309
of which:						
Services balance	*+3,338*	*+3,816*	*+4,071*	*+4,267*	*+4,249*	*+3,844*
Interest, profits and dividends balance	*+116*	*+661*	*+990*	*−186*	*+1,257*	*+1,577*
Transfers balance	*−1,116*	*−1,777*	*−2,265*	*−2,079*	*−1,967*	*−2,112*
CURRENT BALANCE	+54	+1,158	−653	+3,235	+6,547	+5,428
Capital transfers	−	−	−	−	−	−
Investment and other capital transactions						
Overseas investment in United Kingdom						
Direct	+1,326	+1,261	+1,793	+2,573	+902	+1,154
Investment by oil companies	+1,131	+666	+1,215	+1,714	+1,882	+1,770
Portfolio	+1,853	−85	+1,253	+853	+508	+415
of which: British government stocks	*+979*	*−3*	*+929*	*+571*	*+201*	*+495*
Miscellaneous investment	+89	+35	+75	+100	+70	+120
Total overseas investment in United Kingdom	+4,399	+1,877	+4,336	+5,240	+3,362	+3,459
United Kingdom private investment overseas						
Direct	−1,885	−2,710	−2,777	−3,430	−5,103	−2,638
Investment by oil companies and miscellaneous investment	−461	−821	−2,858	−1,566	−1,418	−1,960
Portfolio	+12	−1,073	−909	−3,150	−4,150	−6,170
Total	−2,334	−4,604	−6,544	−8,146	−10,671	−10,768
Official long-term capital	−303	−336	−401	−91	−336	−337
Import credit	+280	+292	+64	−254	+122	−224
Export credit	−635	−922	−856	−902	−969	−1,165
Foreign currency borrowing or lending abroad	+364	−433	+1,623	+2,054	+1,462	+4,173
Exchange reserves in sterling:						
British government stocks	+6	−113	+247	+945	+267	−32
Banking and money market liabilities, etc.	−16	—	+509	+317	−118	+440
Other external banking and money market liabilities in sterling	+1,481	+293	+2,580	+2,558	+2,607	+4,164
External sterling lending by United Kingdom banks	+58	−504	+205	−2,500	−2,954	−3,243
Other external borrowing or lending						
United Kingdom public sector	+750	+22	−7	−173	−18	−105
United Kingdom private sector	+63	+84	+467	−692	−449	+537
Other transactions	+53	+81	−66	−243	+101	+250
Total investment and other capital transactions	+4,166	−4,263	+2,157	−1,887	−7,594	−2,851
Allocation of SDRs	—	—	+195	+180	+158	—
Official financing						
Net transactions with overseas monetary authorities	+1,113	−1,016	−596	−140	−145	−163
Foreign currency borrowing (net)	+1,114	−187	−250	−941	−1,587	+26
Official reserves (drawings on +/additions to −)	−9,588	+2,329	−1,059	−291	+2,419	+1,421
Total official financing	−7,361	+1,126	−1,905	−1,372	+687	+1,284
Balancing item	+3,141	+1,979	+206	−156	+202	−3,861

PERSONAL INCOME AND EXPENDITURE (£ million)

	1977	1978	1979	1980	1981	1982
Income before tax						
Income from employment:						
Wages and salaries	73,235	83,821	97,839	115,828	123,600	131,774
Pay in cash and kind of HM Forces	1,506	1,645	2,020	2,436	2,708	2,904
Total	74,741	85,466	99,859	118,264	126,308	134,678
Employers' contributions:						
National insurance, etc.	5,702	6,084	6,947	8,330	8,931	9,476
Other	5,766	6,887	7,959	9,315	11,071	10,979
Total income from employment	86,209	98,437	114,765	135,909	146,310	155,133
Income from self-employment:						
After deducting stock appreciation	10,945	12,515	14,492	16,286	17,639	19,738
Stock appreciation	566	454	810	832	659	330
Total	11,511	12,969	15,302	17,118	18,298	20,068
Rent, dividends and net interest:						
Receipts by life assurance and superannuation schemes	4,012	4,766	6,406	7,790	8,795	9,873
Imputed rent of owner-occupied dwellings	4,669	5,371	6,537	7,827	8,826	9,681
Other receipts, net	2,861	3,344	5,096	6,228	5,564	6,669
Total	11,542	13,481	18,039	21,845	23,185	26,223
Current transfers to charities from companies	43	44	45	46	47	48
National insurance benefits and other current grants from general government	15,092	17,871	20,957	25,484	31,173	36,169
Imputed charge for capital consumption of private non-profit making bodies	179	199	226	269	296	302
Total personal income	124,576	143,001	169,334	200,671	219,309	237,943
Deductions from income						
UK taxes on income	18,149	19,501	21,668	25,851	29,147	32,304
National insurance, etc. contributions	9,508	10,107	11,531	13,944	15,911	18,659
Transfers abroad (net)	—	74	207	256	278	268
Personal disposable income	96,919	113,319	135,928	160,620	173,973	187,302
Expenditure						
Consumers' expenditure	86,712	99,596	118,383	136,890	152,239	167,128
Balance saving	10,207	13,723	17,545	23,730	21,734	20,174
Total	96,919	113,319	135,928	160,620	173,973	187,302
Memorandum items						
Saving ratio (per cent)	*10.5*	*12.1*	*12.9*	*14.8*	*12.5*	*10.8*
Real personal disposable income:						
At 1980 prices	139,318	149,602	158,295	160,620	156,630	155,627
1980 = 100	86.7	93.1	98.6	100.0	97.5	96.9

CONSUMERS' EXPENDITURE

£ million

	Total consumers' expenditure	Durable goods				Other goods								Services	
		Total	Cars, motor cycles and other vehicles	Furniture and floor coverings	Other durable goods	Food (household expenditure)	Beer	Other alcoholic drink	Tobacco	Clothing other than footwear	Footwear	Energy products	Other goods	Rent, rates and water charges	Other services
At current prices															
1978	99,596	9,762	4,489	2,556	2,717	17,927	4,182	3,280	3,885	6,393	1,343	7,210	10,482	11,334	23,798
1979	118,503	12,677	6,180	3,194	3,303	20,364	4,839	4,009	4,233	7,454	1,613	8,819	12,420	13,364	28,711
1980	137,324	13,019	6,120	3,357	3,542	22,873	5,655	4,486	4,822	7,983	1,750	10,957	14,220	16,040	35,519
1981	153,099	13,820	6,436	3,555	3,829	24,170	6,378	4,992	5,515	8,328	1,798	13,367	15,294	19,406	40,031
1982	168,390	15,511	7,136	3,972	4,403	25,564	7,039	5,314	5,882	8,820	1,944	14,954	16,507	22,558	44,297
1983	184,456	18,801	9,234	4,555	5,012	27,072	7,861	5,891	6,199	9,874	2,155	16,212	17,853	23,955	48,583
Unadjusted															
1981 1st quarter	35,604	3,626	1,796	909	921	5,753	1,342	937	1,193	1,767	379	3,466	3,445	4,456	9,240
2nd quarter	36,889	3,291	1,662	820	809	5,901	1,578	1,058	1,405	1,885	432	2,983	3,599	4,805	9,952
3rd quarter	39,199	3,749	1,999	846	904	6,159	1,759	1,173	1,455	1,949	451	2,920	3,711	4,968	10,905
4th quarter	41,407	3,154	979	980	1,195	6,357	1,699	1,824	1,462	2,727	536	3,998	4,539	5,177	9,934
1982 1st quarter	39,261	3,815	1,881	940	994	6,102	1,489	990	1,396	1,830	402	3,992	3,681	5,332	10,232
2nd quarter	40,485	3,463	1,694	887	882	6,511	1,753	1,117	1,460	1,983	463	3,322	3,874	5,634	10,905
3rd quarter	43,061	4,311	2,274	967	1,070	6,319	1,948	1,216	1,496	2,080	490	3,254	4,015	5,748	12,184
4th quarter	45,583	3,922	1,287	1,178	1,457	6,632	1,849	1,991	1,530	2,927	589	4,386	4,937	5,844	10,976
1983 1st quarter	43,445	4,843	2,577	1,094	1,172	6,341	1,629	1,090	1,486	1,990	424	4,523	3,981	5,869	11,269
2nd quarter	44,349	4,258	2,152	1,063	1,043	6,669	1,896	1,244	1,550	2,247	530	3,779	4,216	5,961	11,999
3rd quarter	47,380	5,273	3,024	1,082	1,167	6,832	2,273	1,360	1,568	2,349	550	3,421	4,329	6,031	13,394
4th quarter	49,282	4,427	1,481	1,316	1,630	7,230	2,063	2,197	1,595	3,288	651	4,489	5,327	6,094	11,921
1984 1st quarter	46,516	5,050	2,635	1,190	1,225	6,761	1,795	1,183	1,577	2,131	452	4,880	4,211	6,171	12,305
Revalued at 1980 prices															
1978	131,485	12,109	5,736	3,253	3,120	22,501	5,840	4,276	4,982	7,484	1,729	10,759	14,424	15,512	31,869
1979	138,004	13,930	6,763	3,616	3,551	22,893	5,897	4,660	4,960	8,040	1,838	11,114	14,824	15,787	34,061
1980	137,324	13,019	6,120	3,357	3,542	22,873	5,655	4,486	4,822	7,983	1,750	10,957	14,220	16,040	35,519
1981	137,559	13,415	6,296	3,394	3,725	22,676	5,345	4,450	4,470	8,258	1,781	10,992	14,182	16,263	35,727
1982	139,390	14,483	6,580	3,678	4,225	22,570	5,285	4,355	4,128	8,645	1,936	11,038	14,323	16,531	36,096
1983	144,812	16,875	7,959	4,088	4,828	22,772	5,443	4,565	4,080	9,476	2,126	11,129	14,569	16,781	36,996
Unadjusted															
1981 1st quarter	33,543	3,584	1,803	879	902	5,559	1,203	887	1,129	1,768	373	3,118	3,268	4,045	8,609
2nd quarter	33,340	3,215	1,644	784	787	5,576	1,320	950	1,126	1,884	426	2,484	3,366	4,060	8,933
3rd quarter	34,687	3,605	1,917	807	881	5,736	1,455	1,034	1,127	1,934	449	2,291	3,415	4,073	9,568
4th quarter	35,989	3,011	932	924	1,155	5,805	1,367	1,579	1,088	2,672	533	3,099	4,133	4,085	8,617
1982 1st quarter	33,396	3,578	1,735	884	959	5,427	1,160	845	1,027	1,810	403	3,120	3,277	4,107	8,642
2nd quarter	33,516	3,233	1,567	820	846	5,685	1,323	919	1,027	1,952	462	2,488	3,388	4,127	8,912
3rd quarter	35,389	4,001	2,074	896	1,031	5,620	1,451	981	1,034	2,041	488	2,377	3,464	4,139	9,793
4th quarter	37,089	3,671	1,204	1,078	1,389	5,838	1,351	1,610	1,040	2,842	583	3,053	4,194	4,158	8,749
1983 1st quarter	34,643	4,427	2,298	998	1,131	5,445	1,160	868	1,001	1,932	419	3,116	3,324	4,173	8,778
2nd quarter	34,894	3,818	1,866	952	1,000	5,670	1,318	965	1,018	2,177	520	2,615	3,451	4,188	9,154
3rd quarter	36,977	4,642	2,548	972	1,122	5,703	1,569	1,042	1,026	2,255	544	2,374	3,502	4,206	10,114
4th quarter	38,298	3,988	1,247	1,166	1,575	5,954	1,396	1,690	1,035	3,112	643	3,024	4,292	4,214	8,950
1984 1st quarter	35,357	4,411	2,184	1,036	1,191	5,465	1,198	896	1,003	2,088	446	3,237	3,351	4,229	9,033
Seasonally adjusted															
1981 1st quarter	34,458	3,309	1,515	870	924	5,697	1,374	1,132	1,185	2,055	437	2,735	3,544	4,045	8,945
2nd quarter	34,383	3,428	1,656	850	922	5,629	1,322	1,106	1,105	2,046	438	2,747	3,544	4,060	8,958
3rd quarter	34,297	3,352	1,589	839	924	5,676	1,336	1,112	1,103	2,052	447	2,705	3,546	4,073	8,895
4th quarter	34,421	3,326	1,536	835	955	5,674	1,313	1,100	1,077	2,105	459	2,805	3,548	4,085	8,929
1982 1st quarter	34,263	3,273	1,419	872	982	5,568	1,323	1,079	1,075	2,110	473	2,748	3,555	4,107	8,952
2nd quarter	34,605	3,437	1,543	892	1,002	5,733	1,334	1,075	1,011	2,126	475	2,751	3,567	4,127	8,969
3rd quarter	34,949	3,698	1,674	935	1,089	5,570	1,328	1,062	1,011	2,173	487	2,775	3,603	4,139	9,103
4th quarter	35,573	4,075	1,944	979	1,152	5,699	1,300	1,139	1,031	2,236	501	2,764	3,598	4,158	9,072
1983 1st quarter	35,505	4,052	1,912	983	1,157	5,595	1,323	1,110	1,048	2,253	492	2,759	3,610	4,173	9,090
2nd quarter	36,095	4,079	1,861	1,035	1,183	5,716	1,338	1,140	1,004	2,374	536	2,876	3,630	4,188	9,214
3rd quarter	36,527	4,308	2,109	1,013	1,186	5,652	1,437	1,133	1,003	2,404	544	2,766	3,645	4,206	9,429
4th quarter	36,685	4,436	2,077	1,057	1,302	5,809	1,345	1,182	1,025	2,445	554	2,728	3,684	4,214	9,263
1984 1st quarter	36,224	4,063	1,833	1,019	1,211	5,615	1,363	1,138	1,050	2,426	521	2,870	3,632	4,229	9,317

UNEMPLOYMENT (Thousands)

	United Kingdom		Great Britain				Northern Ireland			
	Total	Percent-age rate	Total	Percent-age rate	Males	Females	Total	Percent-age rate	Males	Females
1979	1,295·7	5·3	1,233·9	5·2	887·2	346·7	61·8	10·7	43·0	18·9
1980 Monthly	1,664·9	6·8	1,590·5	6·7	1,129·1	461·3	74·5	12·8	51·5	22·9
1981 averages	2,520·4	10·4	2,422·4	10·2	1,773·3	649·1	98·0	16·8	70·0	27·9
1982	2,916·9	12·1	2,808·5	11·9	2,055·9	752·6	108·3	18·7	77·3	31·0
1983	3,104·7	12·9	2,987·6	12·7	2,133·5	854·0	117·1	20·2	85·1	32·0
1980 October 9	1,916·4	7·9	1,831·6	7·7	1,294·0	537·5	84·8	14·6	58·7	26·1
November 13	2,016·0	8·3	1,929·4	8·1	1,328·8	546·6	86·5	14·9	60·2	26·4
December 11	2,099·9	8·6	2,011·3	8·5	1,459·8	551·5	88·6	15·2	62·3	26·3
1981 January 15	2,271·1	9·4	2,177·5	9·2	1,583·4	594·2	93·5	16·1	66·4	27·2
February 12	2,312·4	9·5	2,218·1	9·4	1,621·6	596·2	94·3	16·2	67·3	27·0
March 12	2,333·5	9·6	2,239·1	9·5	1,646·7	592·5	94·3	16·2	67·7	26·6
April 9	2,372·7	9·8	2,279·2	9·6	1,681·6	597·7	93·5	16·1	67·5	26·0
May 14	2,407·4	9·9	2,311·5	9·8	1,710·3	601·2	95·9	16·5	69·0	26·9
June 11	2,395·2	9·9	2,299·3	9·7	1,706·1	593·2	95·9	16·5	69·1	26·8
July 9	2,511·8	10·4	2,413·9	10·2	1,775·1	638·7	97·9	16·8	70·0	27·9
August 13	2,586·3	10·7	2,488·3	10·5	1,819·8	668·6	98·0	16·8	70·4	27·5
September 10	2,748·6	11·3	2,643·2	11·2	1,908·8	734·5	105·4	18·1	74·7	30·8
October 8	2,771·6	11·4	2,667·7	11·3	1,932·0	735·7	103·9	17·9	73·4	30·5
November 12	2,769·5	11·4	2,667·7	11·3	1,941·7	726·0	101·8	17·5	72·5	29·4
December 10	2,764·1	11·4	2,663·0	11·2	1,952·9	710·0	101·2	17·4	72·3	28·9
1982 January 14	2,896·3	12·0	2,790·5	11·8	2,047·2	743·3	105·8	18·3	75·5	30·2
February 11	2,870·2	11·9	2,765·5	11·7	2,031·6	734·0	104·7	18·1	74·9	29·8
March 11	2,820·8	11·7	2,717·6	11·5	1,999·4	718·1	103·2	17·8	74·1	29·2
April 15	2,818·5	11·7	2,714·3	11·5	2,000·3	714·0	104·2	18·0	74·7	29·5
May 13	2,800·5	11·6	2,694·3	11·4	1,988·1	707·2	105·1	18·2	75·3	29·8
June 10	2,769·6	11·5	2,663·8	11·3	1,967·1	696·7	105·8	18·3	75·8	30·0
July 8	2,852·5	11·8	2,744·4	11·6	2,011·6	732·8	108·2	18·7	76·7	31·4
August 12	2,898·8	12·0	2,789·7	11·8	2,036·6	753·1	109·0	18·8	77·2	31·9
September 9	3,066·2	12·7	2,950·3	12·5	2,127·3	823·0	115·8	20·0	81·3	34·5
October 14	3,049·0	12·6	2,935·3	12·4	2,127·4	807·9	113·7	19·7	80·1	33·7
November 11	3,063·0	12·7	2,950·8	12·5	2,147·6	803·2	112·2	19·4	80·8	31·4
December 9	3,097·0	12·8	2,984·7	12·6	2,186·4	798·3	112·3	19·4	81·6	30·7
1983 January 13	3,225·2	13·4	3,109·0	13·2	2,270·6	838·4	116·2	20·1	84·2	32·0
February 10	3,199·4	13·3	3,084·7	13·1	2,252·7	832·0	114·7	19·8	83·9	30·8
March 10	3,172·4	13·2	3,058·7	13·0	2,236·0	822·7	113·7	19·6	83·4	30·2
April 14	3,169·9	13·2	3,053·5	13·0	2,221·1	832·5	116·4	20·1	85·3	31·1
May 12	3,049·4	12·7	2,934·4	12·5	2,115·0	819·4	115·0	19·9	84·4	30·6
June 9	2,983·9	12·4	2,870·5	12·2	2,061·8	808·7	113·4	19·6	82·9	30·5
July 14	3,020·6	12·6	2,903·5	12·4	2,059·4	844·1	117·1	20·2	84·6	32·6
August 11	3,009·9	12·5	2,892·9	12·3	2,040·6	852·4	117·0	20·2	84·5	32·5
September 8	3,167·4	13·2	3,043·7	13·0	2,116·3	927·4	123·7	21·4	88·3	35·4
October 13	3,094·0	12·9	2,974·2	12·7	2,075·9	898·3	119·8	20·7	86·5	33·4
November 10	3,084·4	12·8	2,964·7	12·6	2,072·4	892·2	119·7	20·7	86·6	33·2
December 8	3,079·4	12·8	2,960·9	12·6	2,080·7	880·3	118·4	20·5	86·2	32·2
1984 January 12	3,199·7	13·3	3,077·4	13·1	2,156·6	920·9	122·2	21·1	88·8	33·5
February 9	3,186·4	13·2	3,063·8	13·0	2,147·4	916·5	122·5	21·2	89·5	33·0
March 8	3,142·8	13·1	3,021·9	12·9	2,116·6	905·3	120·9	20·9	88·4	32·4
April 5	3,107·7	12·9	2,987·6	12·7	2,092·5	895·2	120·1	20·7	87·6	32·5
May 10	3,084·5	12·8	2,963·9	12·6	2,073·4	890·5	120·6	20·8	87·7	32·8

Employees in employment: all industries

At June Industries analysed according to the Standard Industrial Classification 1980 Thousands

	1975	1976	1977	1978	1979	1980	1981	1982	1983
Total employees in employment..	22,710	22,543	22,619	22,777	23,158	22,972	21,871	21,418	21,081
Males	13,536	13,392	13,363	13,389	13,479	13,306	12,547	12,160	11,855
Females	9,174	9,152	9,256	9,388	9,679	9,666	9,324	9,258	9,226
of which: Total production and construction industries	9,507	9,254	9,260	9,215	9,234	8,918	8,069	7,634	7,267
Agriculture, forestry and fishing....	397	393	388	382	368	361	352	354	349
Coal, oil and natural gas extraction and processing	356	350	353	358	356	357	344	329	313
Electricity, gas, other energy and water supply	370	370	365	358	366	370	365	354	342
Manufacturing industries..........	7,524	7,281	7,328	7,290	7,258	6,940	6,221	5,898	5,609
Construction	1,256	1,252	1,215	1,208	1,253	1,252	1,138	1,053	1,003
Wholesale distribution and repairs ..	1,047	1,039	1,058	1,087	1,128	1,163	1,127	1,112	1,097
Retail distribution	2,085	2,061	2,087	2,101	2,174	2,175	2,090	2,031	2,018
Hotels and catering..............	840	864	877	898	950	979	950	965	935
Transport	1,051	1,025	1,030	1,048	1,051	1,047	985	935	896
Postal services and communications	448	431	419	415	422	437	438	434	427
Banking, finance, insurance	1,489	1,494	1,518	1,571	1,663	1,714	1,740	1,748	1,755
Public administration	1,991	1,990	1,989	1,999	2,001	1,972	1,905	1,869	1,883
Education	1,568	1,618	1,602	1,608	1,647	1,630	1,604	1,591	1,590
Medical and other health services, veterinary services..............	1,144	1,174	1,184	1,207	1,229	1,254	1,289	1,313	1,315
Other services	1,138	1,193	1,204	1,245	1,291	1,323	1,325	1,323	1,297

Distribution of working population

Thousands

			Unadjusted						Seasonally adjusted	
	Working population	Unemployed excluding students	Employed labour force	Employees in employment			Self-employed persons (with or without employees)	HM Forces	Working population	Employees in employment
				Total	Males	Females				
At June										
1975	25,878	838	25,040	22,710	13,536	9,174	1,994	336	25,922	22,711
1976	26,093	1,265	24,828	22,543	13,392	9,152	1,949	336	26,131	22,524
1977	26,209	1,359	24,850	22,619	13,363	9,256	1,904	327	26,241	22,606
1978	26,342	1,343	24,999	22,777	13,389	9,388	1,904	318	26,372	22,762
1979	26,610	1,235	25,375	23,158	13,479	9,679	1,903	314	26,646	23,139
1980	26,819	1,513	25,306	22,972	13,306	9,666	2,011	323	26,869	22,950
1981										
Mar.	26,716	2,334	24,382	21,957	12,656	9,301	2,091	334	26,840	22,095
June	26,718	2,395	24,323	21,871	12,547	9,324	2,118	334	26,781	21,845
Sept.	27,026	2,749	24,277	21,799	12,496	9,303	2,143	335	26,881	21,718
Dec.	26,872	2,764	24,108	21,608	12,312	9,296	2,168	332	26,831	21,572
1982										
Mar.	26,724	2,821	23,903	21,382	12,186	9,197	2,193	328	26,842	21,519
June	26,730	2,770	23,960	21,418	12,160	9,258	2,218	324	26,803	21,390
Sept.	26,942	3,066	23,876	21,310	12,119	9,191	2,243	323	26,790	21,224
Dec.	26,842	3,097	23,745	21,156	11,967	9,189	2,268	321	26,803	21,126
1983										
Mar.	26,703	3,172	23,531	20,917	11,837	9,079	2,293	321	26,816	21,052
June	26,705	2,984	23,721	21,081	11,855	9,226	2,318	322	26,786	21,054
Sept.	27,003	3,167	23,836	21,168	11,910	9,258	2,343	325	26,845	21,081
Dec.	26,960	3,079	23,881	21,188	11,845	9,344	2,368	325	26,922	21,162

FUEL AND POWER

ELECTRICITY SUPPLY

England and Wales

In the year ended March 31, 1984, the electricity industry sold 199,690 million units to all customers, a reduction of 3·4 per cent over 1982–83. Average price per unit to customers was 4·435p compared with 4·478p in 1982–83. At the end of the year there were 21,047,102 customers, 1·05 per cent more than at March 31, 1983.

75,911 million units were supplied to industry (an increase of 3·2 per cent), 71,890 million to domestic users (2·7 per cent more) and 42,431 million to commercial users (5·8 per cent more), 14,789 million units were sold on off-peak tariffs, an increase of 7·7 per cent over 1982–83.

On March 31, 1984, the Central Electricity Generating Board had 90 power stations (1983, 100) with a maximum output capacity of 51,028 *MW*, a decrease of 0·8 per cent in capacity over 1983. In 1983–84, 932 *MW* of new plant was commissioned. C.E.G.B. power stations supplied 212,728 million kWh in 1983–84, 0·9 per cent more than in 1982–83. Maximum simultaneous demand met during the year was 42,243 *MW* (1982–83, 42,067).

Transmission lines (double and single circuit) in service at the end of the year totalled 7·679 route km., and distribution lines 602,903 circuit km.

The industry employed 137,210 persons at March 31, 1984, 4,175 less than in 1982–83.

Electricity Industry Finance 1982–84

	£ million	
	1982–83	1983–84
Turnover		
Sales of Electricity	8,650·8	8,856·7
Contracting and Appliance Marketing	469·1	535·7
Other	150·1	169·6
TOTAL	9,270·0	9,562·0
Expenditure		
Generation and Purchases	5,879·0	5,979·2
Main Transmission and Distribution	1,167·8	1,236·3
Consumer Service	166·9	171·5
Administration, Collection of Accounts etc.	424·4	460·8
Contracting and Appliance Marketing	459·7	513·9
Other	287·2	295·2
TOTAL	8,385·0	8,656·9
Operating Profit before working capital deducted: Electricity Supply	875·6	883·3
Contracting and appliance marketing	9·4	21·8
	885·0	905·1
Less monetary working capital	17·5	4·1
Total operating profit	867·5	901·0
Interest	535·9	444·5
Profit	331·6	456·5

COAL PRODUCTION†

Year (*March*)	NCB Mines	Open Cast	Other	Total
1982	108·6	14·3	1·4	124·3
1983	104·7	14·7	1·5	120·9
1984	90·0	13·8	1·5	105·3

† million tonnes.

Income	£ million	
	1983†	1984†
From Sales (Net)		
Coal	4,412	4,153
Coke	164	137
Gas, Benzole, Tar, etc.	34	37
Processed Fuel	101	112
Miscellaneous Products, Services and Rents	237	221
	4,948	4,660
Other Receipts	345	367
NET INCOME	5,293	5,027
Expenditure		
Wages, Salaries, Pensions, etc.	2,646	2,457
Past Employee Costs	340	445
Contract work	345	328
Materials, Repairs, Power	1,280	1,250
Depreciation and other expenses	810	957
TOTAL EXPENDITURE	5,421	5,437
PROFIT (LOSS)	(128)	(410)
Less Interest Payable, etc.	357	465
Surplus (Deficit) for year	(485)	(875)
Government deficit grant	374	875
SURPLUS (DEFICIT) CARRIED TO RESERVES	(111)	—

† April to March.

GAS SUPPLY

	1982–83	1983–84
	(Million Therms)	
GAS SOLD AND USED		
Domestic	8,616	9,128
Industrial	5,605	5,753
Commercial	2,242	2,400
Total gas sold	16,463	17,281
Used for own purposes	117	133
TOTAL GAS SOLD AND USED	16,580	17,414

British Gas Corporation Finance

	1982–83	1983–84
	£ million	
TURNOVER		
Gas and oil	5,520·2	5,964·0
Installation and contracting	211·7	229·3
Appliance Trading	226·1	229·1
TOTAL TURNOVER	5,958·0	6,422·4
OPERATING COSTS		
Cost of sales	3,035·7	3,430·2
Distribution costs	1,701·4	1,733·1
Administrative expenses	557·8	591·2
CURRENT COST PROFIT ON ORDINARY ACTIVITIES	663·1	667·9
Net interest receivable	88·5	99·4
Taxation	(254·4)	(350·4)
Extraordinary charge	(295·0)	(3·2)
Interest payable on capital liabilities	(13·8)	(12·7)
CURRENT COST PROFIT RETAINED	188·4	401·0

AGRICULTURE

Agricultural land: area and harvest

	Area at the June Census (thousand hectares)				Estimated quantity harvested (thousand tonnes)			
	1980	1981	1982	1983	1980	1981	1982	1983†
Cereals								
Wheat	1,441	1,491	1,663	1,695	8,470	8,710	10,320	10,880
Barley	2,330	2,327	2,222	2,143	10,320	10,230	10,960	10,080
Oats	148	144	129	108	600	620	575	465
Mixed corn for threshing	13	11	10	8	59	44	39	35
Rye for threshing	6	6	6	7	25	25	25	25
Potatoes								
Early crop	27	24	25	24	455	375	430	
Main crop	179	167	167	171	6,650	5,840	6,445	
Fodder crops								
Beans for stockfeeding	48	45	40	34	149	123	122	105
Turnips and swedes	84	79	71	66	5,065	4,795	4,575	3,655
Fodder beet and mangolds	6	5	5	5	370	320	370	295
Maize for threshing or stockfeeding	22	18	16	15	785	635	635	550
Kale, cabbage, savoys, kohl rabi and rape for stockfeeding	54	49	43	40	2,115	2,195	1,985	1,660
Peas harvested dry for stockfeeding				29				85
Other crops for stockfeeding	29	26	31	25				
Horticultural crops								
Orchards and small fruit	66	62	61	58				
Vegetables grown in the open:								
Brussels sprouts	14	13	13	11	222	203	216	
Cabbage (all kinds), cauliflower and broccoli	26	26	27	25	893	897	829	
Carrots	16	17	14	13	521	711	576	
Parsnips			3	2	52	54	52	
Turnips and swedes	4	3	3		129	110	82	
Beetroot	2	2	2	2	107	99	102	
Onions	8	8	9	8	253	258	259	
Leeks					34	37	39	
Beans (broad, runner and french)	13	11	12	11	102	83	105	
Peas, green for market	59	55	56	47	18	25	24	
Peas, green for processing					205	256	242	
Peas, for harvesting dry	34	28	27	18	111	87	88	
Celery	1	1	1	1	54	50	50	
Lettuce	4	4	4	4	132	131	146	
Rhubarb					41	39	37	
Other vegetables	10	10	9	10				
Flowers, nursery stock, bulbs grown in open:								
Hardy nursery stock	7	7	7	7				
Bulb flowers and bulbs	4	5	5	4				
Other flowers	1	1	1	1				
Area under glass	2	2	2	2				
Other crops								
Sugar beet	213	210	204	199	7,380	7,395	10,005	
Rape grown for oilseed	92	125	174	222	300	325	581	563
Hops	6	6	6	6	10	9	10	
Other crops not for stockfeeding	7	7	6	7				
Bare fallow	59	76	55	97				
Total tillage	5,031	5,071	5,127	5,124				
Lucerne								
All grasses under five years old	1,965	1,911	1,859	1,846				
Total arable	6,996	6,982	6,986	6,970				
All grasses five years old and over	5,140	5,103	5,097	5,107				
Total crops and grass	12,136	12,085	12,083	12,078				
Rough grazing								
Sole rights	5,119	5,021	4,984	4,927				
Common (estimated)	1,214	1,214	1,214	1,212				
Woodland on agricultural holdings	271	277	285	292				
All other land on agricultural holdings	214	211	217	227				
Total agricultural area	18,953	18,808	18,783	18,735				
Total area of the United Kingdom	24,088	24,089	24,088	24,088				

† Provisional.

AGRICULTURE

Cattle, Sheep, Pigs and Poultry on Agricultural Holdings (Thousands)

Cattle and Calves	Total cattle and calves	Cows and heifers in milk		Cows in calf but not in milk		Heifers in calf with first calf		Bulls for service	All other cattle and calves		
		Dairy	Beef	Dairy	Beef	Dairy	Beef		2 years old and over	1 year old and under 2	Under 1 year old
1978 June	13,670	2,958	1,345	316	243	678	180	92	1,029	3,251	3,578
December	13,538	2,707	735	685	867	459	200	89	1,101	3,127	3,569
1979 June	13,589	2,975	1,303	317	240	684	180	90	1,033	3,123	3,644
December	13,363	2,662	739	690	797	442	169	86	1,044	3,114	3,621
1980 June	13,426	2,938	1,241	290	238	677	161	86	1,005	3,153	3,636
December	13,062	2,608	701	669	750	449	171	82	972	3,086	3,575
1981 June	13,138	2,907	1,191	284	228	700	162	84	963	3,041	3,676
December	12,959	2,615	678	678	732	441	178	82	948	3,034	3,573
1982 June	13,244	2,984	1,161	266	227	688	163	84	937	3,057	3,676
December	13,173	2,684	673	673	708	437	177	82	970	3,095	3,574
1983 June	13,290	3,058	1,132	274	225	688	159	83	904	3,059	3,707
December†	13,131	2,729	704	687	645	414	167	80	932	3,124	3,649

Sheep and Lambs	Total sheep and lambs	Sheep 1 year old and over				Lambs under 1 year old
		Ewes for breeding	Two tooth ewes (shearlings)	Rams for service	Others	
1978 June	29,772	11,475	2,724	333	957	14,282
December	21,715	13,472		367	803	7,073
1979 June	29,946	11,709	2,870	342	974	14,051
December	21,609	13,640		375	889	6,705
1980 June	31,446	12,178	2,745	353	927	15,243
December	21,604	14,038		378	714	6,473
1981 June	32,097	12,528	2,743	358	841	15,628
December	22,200	14,430		386	709	3,683
1982 June	33,067	12,909	2,871	366	877	16,044
December	22,944	14,926		397	838	6,783
1983 June	34,069	13,310	2,933	383	831	16,612
December†	23,246	15,139		412	811	6,883

Pigs	Total pigs	Sows and gilts for breeding				Boars for service	Barren sows for fattening	All other pigs				
		Sows in pig	Gilts in pig	Other sows kept for breeding	50 kg gilts (110 lb) and over expected to be used for breeding			110 kg (240 lb) and over	80 kg (175 lb) and under 110 kg (240 lb)	50 kg (110 lb) and under 80 kg (175 lb)	20 kg (45 lb) and under 50 kg (110 lb)	Under 20 kg (45 lb)
1978 June	7,728	512	118	215	90	42	12	105	671	1,777	2,221	1,965
December	7,986	536	109	223	91	43	13	128	681	1,838	2,263	2,060
1979 June	7,864	528	109	215	82	43	14	112	695	1,770	2,258	2,040
December	7,813	521	91	208	91	42	13	107	661	1,766	2,288	2,026
1980 June	7,815	517	109	204	84	42	12	102	657	1,772	2,240	2,074
December	7,770	514	101	203	89	42	14	109	634	1,773	2,244	2,047
1981 June	7,828	522	112	203	87	43	11	90	638	1,776	2,227	2,119
December	7,910	532	108	197	90	43	12	93	627	1,837	2,281	2,090
1982 June	8,023	543	122	200	89	45	12	117	630	1,824	2,281	2,163
December	8,210	558	114	204	92	46	15	105	661	1,892	2,308	2,216
1983 June	8,174	542	110	204	82	45	15	100	605	1,868	2,362	2,241
December†	7,769	510	96	184	75	42	16	85	608	1,824	2,243	2,085

Poultry	Total poultry	Fowls for producing eggs for eating			Fowls for breeding (including cocks and cockerels)	Broilers and other table fowls	Total fowls	Other poultry		
		Birds that have been in the laying flock for:		Growing pullets (from day old to point of lay)				Ducks	Geese	Turkeys
		less than 12 months	12 months or more							
1978 June	137,973	39,024	11,961	17,343	6,447	56,340	131,116	1,343	139	5,376
December	129,863	39,382	11,125	14,447	6,258	50,754	121,966	1,237	117	6,543
1979 June	135,345	35,890	12,230	15,504	6,657	57,153	127,433	1,552		6,359
December	124,542	33,502	13,140	13,642	6,651	49,045	115,979	1,269	109	7,186
1980 June	135,105	34,415	11,596	14,457	6,676	59,917	127,063	1,390	133	6,519
December	119,297	32,296	12,074	11,959	5,642	47,975	109,947	1,226	123	9,001
1981 June	132,286	31,737	12,736	14,219	6,117	57,830	122,639	1,333	148	8,167
December	123,596	31,368	11,760	12,663	6,039	53,032	114,862	1,316	120	7,298
1982 June	135,363	32,711	12,081	14,766	6,457	60,075	126,091	1,443	157	7,672
December	113,866	32,408	11,726	12,726	5,586	49,788	112,234	1,402	122	
1983 June	128,260	29,971	11,546	12,079	6,012	58,887	118,496	1,410	138	8,198
December†	101,973	24,002	10,235	10,358	3,948	41,529	90,073	1,450	115	10,335

† Provisional

ROADS

On April 1, 1983, the total mileage of public roads in Great Britain, excluding green lanes, was 214,359 of which 162,981 were in England, 31,257 in Scotland and 20,121 in Wales.

motorway were open to traffic in Great Britain (England 1,435, Scotland 147 and Wales 74), 76 miles were under construction, all of them in England.

Highway Authorities

The powers and responsibilities of highway authorities in England and Wales are set out in the Highways Acts 1980. They are concerned mainly with the construction, improvement and maintenance of highways. The Secretary of State for Transport and the Secretary of State for Wales are the highway authorities for the trunk roads in England and in Wales respectively. (Trunk roads constitute the national system of routes for through traffic and include most motorways.)

Under the Local Government Act 1972, since April 1, 1974, the county councils are the highway authorities for all highways in England (outside Greater London) and Wales, other than trunk roads. However, the district councils have a right to maintain unclassified urban roads, footpaths and bridleways and may under agency arrangements carry out other highway functions on behalf of the county councils. In Greater London the most important non-trunk roads are metropolitan roads, for which the Greater London Council is highway authority. The Common Council of the City of London and the London borough councils are highway authorities for all other non-trunk roads in their areas.

For Scotland there is separate legislation under which the Secretary of State for Scotland is the highway authority for trunk roads. The highway authorities for non-trunk public roads are the Regional and Islands Councils. There are general powers available in the Local Government (Scotland) Act 1973, which would enable them if they wished to delegate functions to the District Councils.

On April 1, 1975, a new system of grant-aiding local authority expenditure on transport came into effect. From that date transport expenditure by the G.L.C., and all county councils in England and Wales became eligible for an annual block grant. The grant, known as Transport Supplementary Grant, represents about 21 per cent of expenditure accepted for T.S.G.-grant aid; the balance being assisted through the rate support grant along with other rate borne expenditure. For the financial year 1984–85 local authorities in England received a total of £400,000,000 in transport supplementary grants.

Motorways

The network in England and Wales is based on five main routes—London–Yorkshire (M1), London–South Wales (M4), Birmingham–Bristol–Exeter (M5), Birmingham–Carlisle (M6) and Lancashire–Yorkshire (M62). Other important motorways in use or under construction include: Medway Towns (M2); London–Basingstoke (M3); London–Cambridge (M11); Rotherham–Goole (M18); London–Folkestone (M20); London orbital route (M25); London–Oxford (M40); North Cheshire (M56); and South Humberside (M180). Motorways in use in Scotland include: Edinburgh–Glasgow–Greenock (M8); Edinburgh–Stirling (M9); Maryville–Mollisburn (M73); Millbank–Maryville (M74); Stirling–Haggs (M80); Friarton Bridge, Perth (M85); Inverkeithing–Perth (M90) and (M80)–Kincardine Bridge (M876).

On April 1, 1983, 1,683 miles of trunk and principal

Motor Vehicles

The number of vehicles in Great Britain with current licences in 1983 totalled 20,216,000; private and light goods vehicles 17,158,000; motor cycles, scooters and mopeds 1,290,000; public transport vehicles 113,000; heavy goods vehicles 1,565,000; agricultural tractors 376,000. There were 628,000 vehicles exempt from licensing.

Driving Tests

The number of driving tests conducted in Great Britain in the year 1983 was 1,892,300, of which 51·3 per cent resulted in failure.

Expenditure

Expenditure on roads in England during 1982–83 was £2,031m compared with £1,799m in 1981–82. The expenditure during 1982–83 may be broken down as follows: New Construction and Improvement £978m (Trunk roads £533m; Principal and other roads, £445m); Maintenance (including road safety), £1,053m (Trunk roads, £206m, Principal and other roads, £847m); Cleansing, Gritting and Snow-Clearing, and other expenditure. Road Lighting costs of £139m are included. In addition the cost of vehicle parking was £80m (gross).

Expenditure on new construction and in improvement of trunk roads and motorways in England during 1982–83 was £533m. In Scotland and Wales, the figures were £95·2m and £109·9m respectively. Expenditure on new construction and improvement of principal and other roads in 1982–83 was £445m in England, £104·9m in Scotland and £64·6m in Wales.

Road Casualties

In 1983 in Great Britain there were 59 vehicles for every kilometre of road or one vehicle for every 17 metres. Fifteen road users were killed and 826 injured on an average day. Of those killed 37% were car users, 35% pedestrians, 18% users of two-wheeled motor vehicles; 10% of all those killed were children.

Year	Killed	Injured	Year	Killed	Injured
1964	7,820	377,679	1974	6,833	318,035
1965	7,952	389,985	1975	6,366	318,584
1966	7,985	384,472	1976	6,570	333,103
1967	7,319	362,659	1977	6,614	341,447
1968	6,810	342,398	1978	6,831	342,964
1969	7,365	345,529	1979	6,362	328,000
1970	7,499	355,869	1980	6,010	323,000
1971	7,699	344,328	1981	5,846	318,994
1972	7,763	351,964	1982	5,934	328,362
1973	7,406	346,374	1983	5,445	303,139

Deaths more than 30 days after the accident are excluded.

BRITISH RAILWAYS IN 1983

The British Railways Board was set up, along with our other separate nationalized transport undertakings, by the terms of the Transport Act, 1962. This Act dissolved the British Transport Commission and shared its assets between the new bodies which assumed their responsibilities on January 1, 1963. Under the Act the finances of the railways were reconstructed and previous restrictions were modified to give them greater commercial freedom than they had enjoyed in the past.

The Transport Act of 1968 reduced the railways' commencing debt and enabled the Secretary of State for the Environment to make grants for the maintenance of unremunerative passenger services.

The Railways Act of 1974 further reduced the Board's capital debt but increased its borrowing powers. It also introduced a new system of financial support in accordance with E.E.C. regulations; the Secretary of State is authorized to impose general obligations on the Board in respect of passenger services and is empowered to compensate the Board for meeting these obligations. The Secretary of State's power to make grants for unremunerative passenger services was withdrawn.

For the purposes of management and operation the railways are divided into Regions. They cover the following areas:

1. London Midland Region—bounded by a line joining Carlisle, Oldham, Nottingham, Bedford, London, Banbury, Kidderminster, Aberystwyth.
2. Western Region—west of a line joining Yeovil, Westbury, Reading, London and the southern border of the L.M. Region.
3. Southern Region—south of a line joining Dorchester, Salisbury, London and the Thames.
4. Eastern Region—east of a line joining London, Peterborough, Sheffield, Bradford and Carlisle.
5. Scottish Region—north of a line joining Carlisle and Berwick.

Staff.—On Dec. 31, 1983, British Rail employed a total staff of 155,423 compared with 161,407 on Dec. 31, 1982.

Financial Results, 1983.—The Profit and Loss Account for 1983 showed a surplus of £7·8m compared with a deficit of £173·6m for 1982, while the railway working surplus (before taking interest charges or revenue from other activities into account) was £64m, compared with a loss of £96·7m for the previous year.

	£ million 1983	
Railways		
Gross receipts:		
Passenger (including Grants)..	2,082·9	
Freight (inc. parcels and mails)	632·8	
Miscellaneous	22·8	
TOTAL....................		2,738·5
Working expenses:		
Train services	1,120·3	
Terminal	277·4	

Miscellaneous traffic expenses .	52·5	
Track and signalling..........	692·5	
General expenses..............	469·9	
Provision for replacement of assets	93·0	
TOTAL....................		2,705·6
Railway net surplus		20·9
Net income from Operational Property (Letting), Advertising and Catering....		41·3
OPERATING PROFIT		62·2

OPERATING STATISTICS

At the end of 1983, British Rail had 25,664 miles of standard gauge lines and sidings in use, representing 10,541 miles of route of which 2,330 miles were electrified. Standard rail on main line has a weight of 110 lbs. per yard. British Rail had 2,850 locomotives (diesel and diesel electric, 2,603 and electric, 247); 2,703 diesel multiple-unit vehicles, 7,306 electric multiple-unit vehicles and 4,059 locomotive-hauled passenger carriages with a capacity of 971,097 seats or berths in 1983. Loaded train miles run in passenger service totalled 202·2m. 695·2m passenger journeys were made during the year, including 308·8m made by holders of season tickets. The average distance of each passenger journey on ordinary fare was 35·7 miles; and on season ticket, 15·7 miles. Passenger stations in use in 1983 numbered 2,363 and freight stations 253.

Freight.—There were 54,510 freight-vehicles and 2,156 other vehicles in the non-passenger-carrying stock. 87·9m tonnes of coal and coke were carried in 1983, 16·1m tonnes of iron and steel and 33·9m tonnes of other traffic. Loaded train miles run in freight service totalled 28·2m.

Casualties in Train Accidents
(includes British Railways, London Transport and other railways).

	1981	1982
Fatal accidents....	7	5
Passengers killed ..	4	0
Passengers seriously injured ...	12	3
Railwaymen killed	1	8
Railwaymen seriously injured ...	3	12
Other persons killed	2	3
Other persons seriously injured ...	6	3
Passengers carried per passenger killed	300,000,000	—
Passenger miles run per passenger killed	5,400,000,000	—

Railway Accidents in which 20 Persons and over were Killed in the United Kingdom since 1948

Year	Date	Name of Accident	Railway	Number Killed	Cause
1948	Apl. 17	Winsford	L.M. Region	24	Collision.
1952	Oct. 8	Harrow	L.M. Region	112	Collision.
1957	Dec. 4	Lewisham	S. Region	90	Collision in fog.
1967	Nov. 5	Hither Green	S. Region	49	Track failure.
1975	Feb. 28	Moorgate	L.T.E.	43	Terminal overrun.

AERODROMES AND AIRPORTS

Aerodromes in Great Britain, Northern Ireland, the Isle of Man and the Channel Islands which are either State owned, operated by the Civil Aviation Authority or licensed for use by civil aircraft. A number of unlicensed airfields not included in this list are also available for private use by permission of the owner or controlling authority. Aerodromes designated as Customs airports are printed in bold type. Customs facilities are available at certain other aerodromes by special arrangement.

S = Owned and operated by the State.
CAA = Operated by the Civil Aviation Authority.
BAA = Operated by the British Airports Authority.
M = Owned or operated by Municipal Authority.

J = Military airfield available for civil use by prior permission.
H = Licensed helicopter station.

ENGLAND AND WALES

Aberporth, Dyfed. S
Abingdon, Oxon. J
Andrewsfield, Essex.
Barrow (Walney Island), Cumbria.
Bembridge, I.O.W.
Benson, Oxon. J
Biggin Hill, Kent.
Binbrook, Lincolnshire. J
Birmingham, W. Midlands. M
Blackbushe, Hants.
Blackpool, Lancs. M
Bodmin, Cornwall.
Bourn, Cambridge.
Bournemouth, (Hurn), Dorset. M
Bridlington, Humberside.
Bristol, Avon. M
Caernarfon, Gwynedd.
Cambridge.
Cardiff, S. Glamorgan. M
Carlisle, Cumbria. M
Chichester (Goodwood), Sussex.
Chivenor, Devon. J
Church Fenton, N. Yorks. J
Clacton, Essex.
Coltishall, Norfolk. J
Compton Abbas, Dorset.
Coventry, W. Midlands. M
Cranfield, Beds.
Cranwell, Lincs. J
Culdrose, Cornwall. J
Denham, Bucks.
Dishforth, N. Yorks. J
Doncaster, S. Yorks.
Dunkeswell, Devon.
Duxford, Cambs. M
East Midlands, Derby. M
Elstree, Herts.
Elvington, Yorks. J
Exeter, Devon.
Fairoaks, Surrey.
Farnborough, Hants. S
Fenland, Lincs.
Finningley, S. Yorks. J
Gloucester/Cheltenham (Staverton), Glos. M
Great Yarmouth (North Denes), Norfolk.
Halfpenny Green, Staffs.
Hamble, Hants.
Hatfield, Herts.
Haverfordwest, Dyfed. M
Hawarden, Clwyd.
Hucknall, Notts.
Humberside. M
Ipswich, Suffolk.
Isle of Wight (Sandown).
Kemble, Glos. J
Land's End (St. Just), Cornwall.
Lashenden, Headcorn, Kent.
Leavesden, Herts.
Leeds and Bradford, Yorks. M
Leeming, N. Yorks. J

Lee-on-Solent, Hants. J
Leicester, Leics.
Linton-on-Ouse, Yorks. J
Liverpool, Merseyside. M
London (Gatwick). BAA
London (Heathrow). BAA
London (Stansted). BAA
London (Westland Heliport). H
Luton, Beds. M
Lydd, Kent.
Lyneham, Wilts. J
Manchester International. M
Manchester (Barton).
Manston, Kent. J
Nether Thorpe, S. Yorks.
Newcastle, Tyne and Wear. M
Newton, Notts. J
Northampton (Sywell), Northants.
Northolt, Mddx. J
Norwich, Norfolk. M
Nottingham, Notts.
Odiham, Hants. J
Oxford (Kidlington), Oxfordshire.
Pansanger, Herts.
Penzance, Cornwall. H
Peterborough (Conington).
Peterborough (Sibson), Cambs.
Plymouth (Roborough), Devon.
Portland Naval, Dorset. JH
Redhill, Surrey.
Rochester, Kent.
St. Mawgan, Cornwall. J
Sandtoft, Humberside.
Scilly Isles (St. Mary's).
Seething, Norfolk.
Shawbury, Shropshire. J
Sherburn-in-Elmet, N. Yorks.
Shipham, Norfolk.
Shobdon, Herefordshire.
Shoreham, W. Sussex. M
Silverstone, Northants.
Skegness (Ingoldmells), Lincs.
Sleap, Shropshire.
Southampton, Hants.
Southend, Essex. M
Stapleford, Essex.
Sturgate, Lincs.
Swansea, W. Glam. M
Teesside, Cleveland. M
Thruxton, Hants.
Topcliffe, N. Yorks. J
Tresco, Isles of Scilly. H
Valley, Gwynedd. J
Waddington, Lincs. J
Warton, Lancs.
Wattisham, Suffolk. J
Wellesbourne Mountford, Warwick.
Weston, Avon. H
White Waltham, Berks.
Wickenby, Lincs.
Wittering, Cambs. J
Woodford, Gtr. Manchester.

Woodvale, Merseyside. J
Wycombe Air Park (Booker), Bucks.
Yeovil, Somerset.
Yeovilton, Somerset. J

SCOTLAND

Aberdeen (Dyce). BAA
Barra, Hebrides.
Benbecula, Hebrides. CAA
Dounreay (Thurso). S
Dundee, Angus. M
Eday. M
Edinburgh. BAA
Fair Isle.
Fetlar, Shetlands.
Fife/Glenrothes.
Flotta, Orkneys.
Fort William. H
Glasgow. BAA
Hoy, Orkneys. M
Inverness (Dalcross). CAA
Islay (Port Ellen). CAA
Isle of Skye. M
Kinloss. J
Kirkwall. CAA
Lerwick (Tingwall). M
Leuchars. J
Lochgilphead, Argyll. H
Lossiemouth. J
Machrihanish, Kintyre, J
North Ronaldsay, Orkneys. M
Oban, Argyll. H
Papa Westray, Orkneys. M
Perth (Scone).
Prestwick, BAA
Rothesay, Bute. H
Sanday, Orkneys. M
Scatsta.
Stornoway, Hebrides. CAA
Stronsay, Orkneys. M
Sumburgh, Shetlands. CAA
Tiree. CAA
Unst, Shetland. M
West Freugh, Wigtown. S
Westray, Orkneys. M
Whalsay, Shetlands.
Wick. CAA

NORTHERN IRELAND

Belfast (Aldergrove). S
Belfast (Harbour).
Enniskillen (St. Angelo). M
Londonderry (Eglinton). M
Newtownards.

ISLE OF MAN

Ronaldsway.

CHANNEL ISLANDS

Alderney. S
Guernsey. S
Jersey. S

MERCHANT SHIPPING

PRINCIPAL MERCHANT FLEETS OF THE WORLD. Source: *Lloyd's Register of Shipping*

Flag	1968 No.	1968 Tons Gross	1973 No.	1973 Tons Gross	1978 No.	1978 Tons Gross	1983 No.	1983 Tons Gross
Liberia	1,613	25,719,642	2,289	49,904,744	2,523	80,191,329	2,062	67,564,201
Japan	6,877	19,586,902	9,469	36,785,094	9,321	39,182,079	10,593	40,751,915
Greece	1,634	7,415,984	2,536	19,295,143	3,666	33,056,093	3,169	37,477,642
Panama	798	5,096,956	1,692	9,568,951	3,640	20,748,679	5,316	34,655,508
U.S.S.R.	4,206	12,061,833	7,123	17,386,900	7,991	22,261,927	7,753	24,549,350
*U.S.A.	3,232	19,668,421	4,063	14,912,432	4,746	16,187,636	6,437	19,358,496
Norway	2,881	19,667,441	2,758	23,621,096	2,646	26,128,428	2,340	19,299,966
United Kingdom	4,020	21,990,980	3,628	30,159,543	3,359	30,896,606	2,570	19,131,457
†China, People's Republic of	456	548,060			157	6,528,463	1,085	11,153,805
France	1,490	6,023,643	1,736	8,880,205	1,694	11,491,473	1,609	10,015,211
Spain	1,495	5,796,360	1,376	8,298,773	1,317	12,197,354	1,173	9,868,075
Singapore	2,046	2,820,784	2,420	4,833,048	2,753	8,056,080	2,589	7,504,690
Germany, Fed. Republic of	2,732	6,527,946	2,234	7,914,679	954	7,489,205	855	7,009,106
Korea (South)	232	473,991	387	2,004,269	1,969	9,736,667	1,769	6,896,961
India	383	1,945,037	617	1,103,925	1,148	2,975,389	1,733	6,386,002
Brazil	398	1,294,190	469	2,886,585	591	5,759,224	677	6,226,646
Saudi Arabia	39	49,625	43	58,530	565	3,701,731	698	5,807,906
Denmark	1,140	3,294,040	1,362	4,106,525	154	1,246,112	435	5,296,798
Netherlands	1,721	5,267,681	1,989	5,091,443	1,397	5,853,408	1,112	5,115,097
Hong Kong	135	1,766,213	98	342,529	1,258	5,183,492	1,927	4,939,380
Poland	446	1,341,665	631	2,072,531	150	871,850	294	4,383,526
Cyprus	109	652,588	589	2,935,775	796	3,490,587	812	3,686,127
Sweden	1,074	4,865,365	831	5,669,340	793	2,599,529	593	3,450,211
Canada	1,296	2,402,983	1,235	947,210	696	6,508,255	674	3,432,683
Philippines	278	854,256	404	676,879	1,289	2,954,499	1,300	3,384,677
Kuwait	42	149,123	162	1,667,183	577	1,264,995	884	2,961,472
Yugoslavia	337	1,266,592	382	756,807	251	2,240,030	235	2,548,112
Turkey	298	648,171	353	1,453,552	468	2,305,630	479	2,546,638
Argentina	315	1,196,817	396	1,574,497	460	1,358,779	687	2,524,374
Romania	56	324,999	96	1,545,936	432	2,000,879	532	2,469,686
Finland	399	1,122,996	390	1,161,609	239	1,428,041	379	2,380,764
Belgium	218	927,900	236	1,160,205	388	2,258,623	339	2,358,127
Australia	314	818,247	373	668,964	426	1,684,692	322	2,273,503
Indonesia	479	711,500	573	192,386	1,093	1,531,739	578	2,022,481
Iran	37	74,448	93	228,274	208	1,272,387	270	1,949,699
Iraq	35	36,547	46	453,024	115	1,194,675	161	1,734,642
Mexico	114	403,573	248	226,350	336	1,305,907	619	1,561,417
Malaysia	85	40,465	117		182	727,201	376	1,475,104
German Dem. Rep.	361	806,074	432	1,219,037	452	1,539,994	416	1,475,048
Algeria	6	15,644	56	162,832	121	1,152,086	143	1,420,834
Portugal	348	771,643	438	1,271,815	342	1,239,963	357	1,368,652
Bulgaria	112	548,102	169	756,749	189	1,082,477	197	1,357,681

* Including ships of the United States Reserve Fleet. † Including 2,225,377 tons gross for Taiwan.

TONNAGE CLASSED WITH LLOYD'S REGISTER.

At 30th June, 1983, 25·52 per cent (107,824,213 tons) of the tonnage owned in the world was classed by Lloyd's Register.

MERCHANT SHIPPING

STEAMSHIPS AND MOTORSHIPS COMPLETED IN THE WORLD DURING 1983
Source: *Lloyd's Register of Shipping*

Country of Build	Steamships No.	Steamships Tons Gross	Motorships No.	Motorships Tons Gross	Total No.	Total Tons Gross	For Registration in	Total S. & M. No.	Total S. & M. Tons Gross
Japan	5	359,710	750	6,310,607	755	6,670,317	Japan	439	2,302,952
U.S.A.	3	112,460	156	268,439	159	380,899	Liberia	62	1,639,003
France			37	307,609	37	307,609	U.S.A.	133	432,459
United Kingdom			60	496,835	60	496,835	U.S.S.R.	249	921,863
Brazil			28	258,741	28	258,741	United Kingdom	59	404,772
Spain			106	500,706	106	500,706	Norway	71	680,662
Korea (South)			88	1,538,592	88	1,538,592	Brazil	36	165,230
Poland			39	345,830	39	345,830	Greece	39	853,109
Sweden			24	328,187	24	328,187	Spain	50	132,849
Germany, Federal Republic of			130	798,461	130	798,461	Germany, Federal Republic of	115	551,030
U.S.S.R.			144	352,796	144	352,796	France	22	255,950
German Democratic Republic			55	336,929	55	336,929	Sweden	13	55,492
Norway			61	182,036	61	182,036	Netherlands	97	505,550
Finland			38	259,621	38	259,621	China, People's Republic of }	28	427,669
Netherlands			126	231,758	126	231,758	Taiwan, Province of }		
Denmark			48	443,861	48	443,861	Korea (South)	29	301,837
Italy	2	100,288	39	155,600	41	255,888	Kuwait	11	307,944
Yugoslavia			15	304,476	15	304,476	Panama	186	1,915,200
†China, People's Republic of			30	184,858 }	48	529,592	Singapore	69	293,054
Taiwan, Province of			18	344,734 }			Denmark	34	296,163
Canada			12	70,057	12	70,057	Australia	32	254,007
Portugal	2	293,318	12	19,993	14	312,311	Portugal	10	176,759
Bulgaria			12	125,666	12	125,666	Bulgaria	3	28,101
Belgium			16	299,809	16	299,809	Belgium	17	301,772
†Romania			14	207,111	14	207,111	Poland	9	64,360
Singapore			70	47,985	70	47,985	Italy	27	61,826
Argentina			11	55,271	11	55,271	Nigeria	13	1,779
India			11	61,398	11	61,398	Rumania	12	201,449
Greece			8	38,024	8	38,024	India	28	226,494
Egypt			3	19,038	3	19,038	Malaysia	18	82,482
Turkey			30	56,766	30	56,766			
Irish Republic			2	40,036	2	40,036			
Other Countries			71	72,347	71	72,347	Other Countries	365	2,069,326
WORLD TOTAL	12	864,776	2,264	15,046,367	2,276	15,911,143		2,276	15,911,143

Tonnage completed to Lloyd's Register Class.—Of the world tonnage completed during 1983, 32·3 per cent (5,138,163 gross tonnage) was to Lloyd's Register Class.
† Information incomplete.

DEFENCE MANPOWER STRENGTHS

At 1 April   Thousands

U.K. Service Personnel	1977	1978	1979	1980	1981	1982	1983
All services: total	330·5	320·7	315·0	320·6	333·8	327·6	320·6
Male	316·0	306·1	299·7	304·4	316·8	311·9	305·2
Female	14·5	14·6	15·3	16·2	16·9	15·7	15·4
Royal Navy: total	68·5	67·8	65·1	64·4	66·4	65·1	64·0
Male	64·6	63·8	61·2	60·5	62·3	61·1	60·1
Female	4·0	4·0	3·8	3·8	4·1	4·0	3·9
Royal Marines: total	7·7	7·5	7·4	7·6	7·9	7·9	7·8
Male	7·7	7·5	7·4	7·6	7·9	7·9	7·8
Army: total	167·3	160·8	156·2	159·0	166·0	163·2	159·1
Male	161·6	155·1	150·4	152·8	159·4	157·2	152·9
Female	5·8	5·7	5·8	6·3	6·6	6·0	6·1
Royal Air Force: total	86·9	84·6	86·3	89·6	93·5	91·5	89·8
Male	82·2	79·7	80·7	83·5	87·2	85·7	84·5
Female	4·8	4·9	5·6	6·1	6·3	5·8	5·4
Personnel Locally Entered overseas: total	8·5	8·4	8·4	8·2	9·7	10·1	10·1
Regular Reserves: total	174·9	179·5	188·5	192·6	196·5	196·4	193·4
Royal Navy	27·9	26·3	28·4	27·0	26·8	24·7	23·9
Royal Marines	2·4	2·4	2·4	2·2	2·2	2·2	2·2
Army	111·2	118·5	127·0	133·1	137·5	140·2	138·3
Army General Reserve	–	–	–	–	–	–	–
Royal Air Force	33·4	32·3	30·8	30·3	30·1	29·3	28·9
Volunteer Reserves and Auxilliary Forces: total	75·2	75·3	73·5	77·0	83·9	86·3	87·0
Royal Navy	5·4	5·4	5·4	5·0	5·4	5·4	5·4
Royal Marines	0·9	1·0	0·9	0·8	0·9	1·1	1·1
Territorial Army	60·9	60·6	59·4	63·3	69·5	72·1	72·8
Ulster Defence Regiment	7·6	7·9	7·6	7·4	7·5	7·1	7·1
Royal Air Force	0·3	0·4	0·3	٭ 0·5	0·6	0·6	0·6
Cadet Forces: total	141·6	142·2	140·0	141·5	144·1	144·6	142·0
Royal Navy	25·1	25·0	23·9	22·7	24·5	24·6	22·4
Army	72·7	73·4	72·6	74·6	75·1	74·1	74·5
Royal Air Force	43·7	43·8	43·5	44·1	44·4	45·9	45·1

Recruitment of U.K. Service personnel to each Service

Number

	1975/76	1976/77	1977/78	1978/79	1979/80	1980/81	1981/82	1982/83
All Services: total	46,906	40,244	38,237	43,366	50,652	50,488	22,607	21,647
Male	41,686	36,390	34,188	38,774	46,206	46,693	21,188	19,342
Female	5,220	3,854	4,049	4,592	4,446	3,795	1,419	2,305
Royal Navy: total	8,910	8,195	7,167	6,791	8,526	9,088	3,805	3,584
Male	7,732	7,238	6,269	5,978	7,701	8,130	3,353	3,078
Female	1,178	957	898	813	825	958	452	506
Royal Marines: total	1,154	929	903	1,282	1,676	1,674	699	447
Male	1,154	929	903	1,282	1,676	1,674	699	447
Army: total	29,591	24,088	22,550	25,254	29,189	28,871	14,204	13,071
Male	27,238	22,344	20,868	23,528	27,164	27,241	13,603	11,679
Female	2,353	1,744	1,682	1,726	2,025	1,630	601	1,392
Royal Air Force: total	7,251	7,032	7,617	10,039	11,261	10,855	3,899	4,545
Male	5,562	5,879	6,148	7,986	9,665	9,648	3,533	4,138
Female	1,689	1,153	1,469	2,053	1,596	1,207	366	407

HOUSING

Permanent dwellings completed

	United Kingdom				England and Wales			
	Total	For local housing authorities	For private owners	Other	Total	For local housing authorities	For private owners	Other
1961	303,161	116,118	180,727	6,316	268,832	92,880	170,366	5,586
1962	313,643	128,577	178,211	6,855	278,667	105,302	167,016	6,349
1963	307,714	123,903	177,787	6,024	270,655	97,015	168,242	5,398
1964	383,192	154,754	221,264	7,174	336,505	119,468	210,432	6,605
1965	391,234	164,957	217,162	9,115	347,181	133,024	206,246	7,911
1966	396,009	176,871	208,647	10,491	349,480	142,430	197,502	9,548
1967	415,455	199,749	204,208	11,498	362,898	159,347	192,940	10,611
1968	425,835	187,984	226,068	11,783	371,726	148,049	213,273	10,404
1969	378,324	180,958	185,916	11,450	324,165	139,850	173,377	10,938
1970	362,226	176,926	174,342	10,958	307,266	134,874	162,084	10,308
1971	364,475	154,894	196,313	13,268	309,776	117,215	179,998	12,563
1972	330,936	120,131	200,755	9,750	287,294	93,635	184,622	9,037
1973	304,637	102,604	191,080	10,953	264,047	79,289	174,413	10,345
1974	279,582	121,017	145,177	13,388	241,173	99,423	129,626	12,124
1975	321,936	150,526	154,528	16,882	278,694	122,857	140,381	15,456
1976	324,769	151,824	155,229	17,716	278,660	124,152	138,477	16,031
1977	314,093	143,250	143,905	26,938	276,011	121,246	128,688	26,077
1978	288,603	112,340	152,166	24,097	254,001	96,752	134,578	22,671
1979	251,695	88,481	143,949	19,265	220,722	77,192	125,306	18,224
1980	240,221	88,222	130,516	21,483	213,204	78,261	114,761	20,182
1981	204,021	68,144	116,354	19,523	177,354	58,219	101,803	17,332
1982	176,766	39,827	123,959	12,980	154,123	33,298	109,577	11,248

	Scotland				Northern Ireland			
	Total	For local housing authorities	For private owners	Other	Total	For local housing authorities	For private owners	Other
1961	27,230	19,541	7,147	542	7,099	3,697	3,214	188
1962	26,761	18,788	7,784	189	8,125	4,487	3,411	317
1963	28,217	21,164	6,622	431	8,842	5,724	2,923	195
1964	37,171	29,156	7,662	353	9,516	6,130	3,170	216
1965	35,116	26,584	7,553	979	8,937	5,349	3,363	225
1966	36,029	27,515	7,870	644	10,500	6,926	3,275	299
1967	41,458	33,222	7,498	738	11,099	7,180	3,770	149
1968	41,989	32,011	8,720	1,258	12,120	7,924	4,075	121
1969	42,628	33,932	8,326	370	11,531	7,176	4,213	142
1970	43,126	34,360	8,220	546	11,834	7,692	4,038	104
1971	40,783	28,577	11,614	592	13,916	9,102	4,701	113
1972	31,992	19,593	11,835	564	11,650	7,203	4,298	149
1973	30,033	17,349	12,215	469	10,557	5,966	4,452	139
1974	28,336	16,182	11,239	915	10,073	5,412	4,312	349
1975	34,323	22,784	10,371	1,168	8,919	4,885	3,776	258
1976	36,527	21,154	13,704	1,669	9,582	6,518	3,048	16
1977	27,320	14,328	12,132	860	10,762	7,676	3,085	1
1978	25,759	9,907	14,443	1,409	8,843	5,681	3,145	17
1979	23,672	7,853	15,069	750	7,301	3,436	3,574	291
1980	20,537	7,448	12,187	902	6,480	2,513	3,568	399
1981	19,910	7,066	10,994	1,850	6,757	2,859	3,557	341
1982	16,569	3,715	11,710	1,144	6,074	2,814	2,672	588

BIRTHS AND MARRIAGES (Thousands)

	Live births					Marriages				
	United Kingdom	England and Wales		Scotland	Northern Ireland	United Kingdom	England and Wales		Scotland	Northern Ireland
		Total	Wales				Total	Wales		
1978	687·0	596·4	33·3	64·3	26·2	416·4	368·3	20·6	37·8	10·3
1979	734·6	638·0	36·2	68·4	28·2	416·9	368·9	20·2	37·9	10·2
1980	753·7	656·2	37·4	68·9	28·6	418·4	370·0	21·1	38·5	9·9
1981	730·8	634·5	35·8	69·1	27·3	397·8	352·0	19·8	36·2	9·6
1982	719·2	625·9	35·7	66·2	27·0	387·0	342·2	19·0	34·9	9·9
†1983	721·4	629·1	35·5	65·1	27·3				35·0	
1981 1st quarter	180·5	156·2	8·9	17·5	6·7	71·6	63·7	3·6	6·3	1·6
2nd quarter	184·9	160·8	9·2	17·1	7·0	111·0	98·4	5·4	9·9	2·6
3rd quarter	188·5	164·3	9·2	17·2	7·0	135·7	119·8	6·9	12·1	3·8
4th quarter	176·9	153·1	8·5	17·2	6·6	79·6	70·1	3·9	7·8	1·6
1982 1st quarter	176·7	153·4	8·6	16·6	6·7	62·2	54·9	3·1	5·8	1·5
2nd quarter	180·2	157·0	9·0	16·3	6·9	108·8	96·5	5·3	9·6	2·7
3rd quarter	185·9	162·1	9·3	16·7	7·0	138·0	121·9	6·7	12·1	4·1
4th quarter	176·5	153·4	8·8	16·7	6·4	78·0	68·9	3·9	7·5	1·7
1983 1st quarter	175·3	152·4	8·7	16·1	6·8	61·9	54·7	4·0	5·6	1·6
2nd quarter	184·6	161·3	9·0	16·3	7·0		96·7	5·2	9·5	
3rd quarter	187·4	163·4	9·1	16·9	7·1				12·3	
4th quarter	174·1	151·9	8·6	15·8	6·3				7·6	
1984 1st quarter†		154·0			6·9					

† Estimated.

DEATHS REGISTERED* (Thousands)

	Total					Infants under one year				
	United Kingdom	England and Wales		Scotland	Northern Ireland	United Kingdom	England and Wales		Scotland	Northern Ireland
		Total	Wales				Total	Wales		
1978	667·2	585·9	36·0	65·1	16·1	9·13	7·88	0·44	0·83	0·42
1979	675·6	593·0	36·1	65·7	16·8	9·47	8·18	0·45	0·89	0·41
1980	661·5	581·4	35·1	63·3	16·8	9·11	7·90	0·43	0·83	0·38
1981	658·0	577·9	35·0	63·8	16·2	8·16	7·02	0·45	0·78	0·36
†1982	662·8	581·9	35·2	65·0	15·9	7·90	6·78	0·38	0·75	0·37
†1983	659·0	579·6	35·2	63·5		7·36	6·38	0·38	0·65	
1981 1st quarter	182·4	160·6	9·8	17·3	4·6	2·30	1·96	0·15	0·24	0·09
2nd quarter	156·8	137·6	8·4	15·2	3·9	1·96	1·70	0·10	0·17	0·09
3rd quarter	146·7	128·8	7·8	14·3	3·5	1·78	1·55	0·09	0·16	0·07
4th quarter	172·1	150·9	9·0	17·0	4·2	2·12	1·82	0·12	0·20	0·09
1982 1st quarter†	190·5	166·5	9·9	19·4	4·7	2·24	1·95	0·09	0·18	0·11
2nd quarter†	160·1	141·1	8·6	15·2	3·9	1·83	1·55	0·08	0·19	0·09
3rd quarter†	144·5	126·9	7·9	14·2	3·4	1·73	1·47	0·09	0·19	0·07
4th quarter†	167·6	147·4	8·8	16·3	3·9	2·08	1·80	0·11	0·20	0·08
1983 1st quarter†	190·5	167·6	10·5	18·1	4·8	2·10	1·86	0·11	0·17	0·08
2nd quarter†	157·5	138·3	8·4	15·3	3·9	1·80	1·54	0·08	0·15	0·10
3rd quarter†	147·8	130·0	8·0	14·2	3·5	1·65	1·41	0·10	0·16	0·08
4th quarter†	163·3	143·6	8·3	15·8	3·8	1·81	1·57	0·09	0·17	0·07
1984 1st quarter†		158	9		4·4		1·8	0·08		0·08

* Excluding stillbirths. † Provisional.

Deaths Analysed by Cause (United Kingdom)

	1978	1979	1980	1981*	1982†
Total deaths	667,177	675,577	661,519	657,974	(646,883)
Deaths from natural causes	641,542	649,920	637,030	634,251	(624,191)
Infective and parasitic diseases	2,826	2,620	2,598	2,460	(2,399)
Cholera	—	—	—	—	(—)
Typhoid fever	1	2	1	3	(3)
Shigellosis and amoebiasis	6	9	5	9	(4)
Enteritis and other diarrhoeal diseases	353	204	156	163	(146)
Tuberculosis of respiratory system	602	573	557	518	(504)
Other tuberculosis, including late effects	456	516	502	390	(361)
Diphtheria	—	—	—	—	(1)
Whooping cough	17	8	6	6	(16)
Streptococcal sore throat and scarlet fever	4	8	4	4	(3)
Meningococcal infection	110	105	81	92	(80)
Acute poliomyelitis	—	—	—	—	(—)
Smallpox	—	—	—	—	(—)
Measles	21	19	34	19	(15)
Typhus and other rickettisioses	2	1	—	—	(—)
Malaria	9	7	8	2	(11)
Syphilis and its sequelae	101	84	66	62	(48)
Neoplasms	144,845	146,752	147,497	148,837	(146,695)
Malignant neoplasm of stomach	12,979	12,754	12,286	12,006	(11,268)
Malignant neoplasm of trachea, bronchus and lung	39,017	39,547	39,795	39,530	(38,948)
Malignant neoplasm of breast	13,499	13,623	13,755	14,075	(13,728)
Malignant neoplasm of uterus	4,170	4,045	3,966	3,948	(3,843)
Leukaemia	3,793	3,695	3,750	3,719	(3,764)
Benign neoplasms and neoplasms of unspecified nature	1,348	1,265	1,189	1,391	(1,662)
Endocrine, nutritional, metabolic diseases and immunity disorders	7,683	7,458	7,392	7,204	(6,781)
Diabetes mellitus	5,610	5,543	5,477	5,381	(5,125)
Nutritional deficiencies	233	117	129	157	(110)
Diseases of blood and blood-forming organs	1,722	1,984	1,911	1,803	(1,750)
Anaemias	1,416	1,427	1,320	1,270	(1,137)
Mental disorders	2,986	3,815	3,928	4,039	(4,397)
Diseases of nervous system and sense organs	6,996	7,854	7,367	7,916	(8,286)
Meningitis	324	338	324	303	(311)
Diseases of the circulatory system	340,372	342,144	332,088	328,127	(317,525)
Acute rheumatic fever	37	8	9	8	(7)
Chronic rheumatic heart disease	6,254	3,902	3,656	3,504	(3,240)
Hypertensive disease	7,677	7,240	6,258	6,018	(5,658)
Ischaemic heart disease	184,819	179,017	177,114	178,558	(173,238)
Diseases of pulmonary circulation and other forms of heart disease	27,582	41,106	38,802	36,664	(35,166)
Cerebrovascular disease	84,971	86,319	82,800	80,952	(78,024)
Diseases of the respiratory system	93,651	94,828	92,448	92,164	(95,639)
Influenza	1,626	925	658	704	(951)
Pneumonia	57,020	59,303	58,860	58,996	(60,724)
Bronchitis, emphysema	25,371	23,912	21,228	19,229	(18,687)
Asthma	1,325	1,672	1,687	1,791	(1,773)
Diseases of the digestive system	16,343	18,663	18,699	19,053	(18,572)
Ulcer of stomach and duodenum	4,650	4,888	5,019	5,060	(5,099)
Appendicitis	232	244	208	188	(168)
Intestinal obstruction and hernia	2,483	2,384	2,262	2,193	(2,115)
Chronic liver disease and cirrhosis	2,364	2,676	2,696	2,727	(2,544)
Diseases of the genito-urinary system	9,120	8,981	8,819	9,127	(9,065)
Nephritis, nephrotic syndrome and nephrosis	3,796	5,006	5,079	5,478	(5,522)
Hyperplasia of prostate	952	914	821	807	(730)
Complications of pregnancy, child birth and puerperium	72	82	82	71	(48)
Abortion	6	11	15	11	(6)
Diseases of the skin and subcutaneous tissue	468	486	531	573	(544)
Diseases of musculo-skeletal system & connective tissue	3,387	3,360	3,369	3,424	(3,469)
Congenital anomalies	4,056	4,049	3,907	4,470	(3,330)
Causes of perinatal mortality	3,670	3,988	3,647	3,129	(2,788)
Birth trauma, hypoxia, birth asphyxia and respiratory	2,260	2,243	2,002	1,705	(1,509)
Symptoms and other ill-defined	3,345	2,856	2,751	2,854	(2,903)
Deaths by violence	25,635	25,657	24,489	23,726	(22,692)
All accidents	18,495	18,289	17,115	2,856‡	(15,542)
Motor vehicle accidents	7,901	7,078	6,863	953‡	(6,051)
Suicide and other self-inflicted injuries	4,531	4,765	4,917	5,025	(4,840)
All other external causes	2,609	2,603	2,457	476‡	(2,301)

* Provisional   † Provisional figures for Great Britain only   ‡ Scotland and N. Ireland only

THE UNITED KINGDOM

Area.—The land area of the United Kingdom* (England, Wales, Scotland and N. Ireland) is 93,051 sq. miles. The area of inland water in the United Kingdom is 1,196 sq. miles. Total 94,247 sq. miles.

Sq. miles	England	Wales	Scotland	N. Ireland
Land	50,081	7,969	29,795	5,206
Inland Water	281	50	619	246
Total	50,362	8,019	30,414	5,452

* Excludes the Isle of Man (227 sq. miles) and the Channel Islands (75 sq. miles)

POPULATION: CENSUS RESULTS, 1801–1981   Thousands

	United Kingdom			England and Wales			Scotland			Northern Ireland†		
	Total	Male	Female	Total	Male	Female	Total	Male	Female	Total	Male	Female
1801	11,944	5,692	6,252	8,893	4,255	4,638	1,608	739	869	1,443	698	745
1811	13,368	6,368	7,000	10,165	4,874	5,291	1,806	826	980	1,397	668	729
1821	15,472	7,498	7,974	12,000	5,850	6,150	2,092	983	1,109	1,380	665	715
1831	17,835	8,647	9,188	13,897	6,771	7,126	2,364	1,114	1,250	1,574	762	812
1841	20,183	9,819	10,364	15,914	7,778	8,137	2,620	1,242	1,378	1,649	800	849
1851	22,259	10,855	11,404	17,928	8,781	9,146	2,889	1,376	1,513	1,443	698	745
1861	24,525	11,894	12,631	20,066	9,776	10,290	3,062	1,450	1,612	1,396	668	728
1871	27,431	13,309	14,122	22,712	11,059	11,653	3,360	1,603	1,757	1,359	647	712
1881	31,015	15,060	15,955	25,974	12,640	13,335	3,736	1,799	1,936	1,305	621	684
1891	34,264	16,593	17,671	29,003	14,060	14,942	4,026	1,943	2,083	1,236	590	646
1901	38,237	18,492	19,745	32,528	15,729	16,799	4,472	2,174	2,298	1,237	590	647
1911	42,082	20,357	21,725	36,070	17,446	18,625	4,761	2,309	2,452	1,251	603	648
1921	44,027	21,033	22,994	37,887	18,075	19,811	4,882	2,348	2,535	*1,258*	*610*	*648*
1931	46,038	22,060	23,978	39,952	19,133	20,819	4,843	2,326	2,517	*1,243*	*601*	*642*
1951	50,225	24,118	26,107	43,758	21,016	22,742	5,096	2,434	2,662	1,371	668	703
1961	52,709	25,481	27,228	46,105	22,304	23,801	5,179	2,483	2,697	1,425	694	731
1971	55,515	26,952	28,562	48,750	23,683	25,067	5,229	2,515	2,714	1,536	755	781
1981	55,776	27,064	28,701	49,154	23,873	25,281	5,130	2,466	2,664	1,491	725	756

NOTES.—1. Before 1801 there existed no official return of the population of either England or Scotland. Estimates of the population of England at various periods, calculated from the number of baptisms, burials and marriages, are: in 1570, 4,160,221; 1600, 4,811,718; 1630, 5,600,517; 1670, 5,773,646; 1700, 6,045,008; 1750, 6,517,035. Because of the War there was no Census in 1941.

2. The last official Census of Population in respect of England and Wales, Scotland, Northern Ireland, the Isle of Man and Guernsey, was taken on the night of April 5, 1981.

3. † All figures refer to the area which is now Northern Ireland. Figures for N. Ireland in 1921 and 1931 are estimates based on the Censuses held in 1926 and 1937.

ISLANDS.—*The figures given above do not include islands of the British seas.* Populations of these islands at census years since 1900 were:—

	Isle of Man			Jersey			Guernsey		
	Total	Male	Female	Total	Male	Female	Total	Male	Female
1901	54,752	25,496	29,256	52,576	23,940	28,636	43,042	21,140	21,902
1911	52,016	23,937	28,079	51,898	24,014	27,884	45,001	22,215	22,786
1921	60,284	27,329	32,955	49,701	22,438	27,263	40,529	19,303	21,226
1931	49,308	22,443	26,865	50,462	23,424	27,038	42,743	20,675	22,068
1951	55,123	25,749	29,464	57,296	27,282	30,014	45,747	22,094	23,380
1961	48,151	22,060	26,091	57,200	27,200	30,000	47,178	22,890	24,288
1971	56,289	26,461	29,828	72,532	35,423	37,109	52,708	25,382	27,326
1981	64,679	30,901	33,778	77,000	37,000	40,000	56,000	27,000	29,000

INCREASE OF THE PEOPLE, ETC.

In Great Britain 6·3 per cent of the usually resident population was born outside the United Kingdom, and in England and Wales this figure was 6·6 per cent. Some 4·5 per cent of the population of England and Wales lived in households whose head was born in the New Commonwealth or Pakistan. Britain's total population is expected, on 1979 estimates, to be 56·4 million in 1986, 58·4 million in 2001 and 59·6 million in 2016. Annual births have fallen since the mid-1960s and the average size of family in 1982 was 1·75, below the level of 2·1 required for replacement of the population. The number of live births in 1982

was 692,000 (11,000 less than in 1981), of which over 13 per cent were illegitimate.

Although the total population has remained relatively stable in the last decade there have been changes in the age and sex structure. The proportion of people under 16 is about 22 per cent; 16–64 years, 63 per cent; 65 and over, 15 per cent. Some 18 per cent were over normal retirement age (60 for women, 65 for men). There are about 6 per cent more male than female births every year, but the higher mortality of men at all ages, means that at about 50 years of age the number of women begins to exceed the number of men.

LOCAL GOVERNMENT IN ENGLAND AND WALES

The Local Government Act, 1972 provided for the reorganisation of local government in England (outside Greater London whose local government was reorganised in 1965) and Wales. On April 1, 1974 the former county, county borough, and county district councils were abolished. Two tiers of new local authorities, county and district councils, covering metropolitan and non-metropolitan counties and districts, replaced them.

Structures and Areas in England

Six *metropolitan counties* cover the main conurbations outside Greater London: Tyne and Wear, West Midlands, Merseyside, Greater Manchester, West Yorkshire and South Yorkshire. They range in population from 1,142,515 (Tyne and Wear) to 2,654,000 (West Midlands). Each metropolitan county extends to the edge of the general continuously built-up area of the conurbation.

The six metropolitan counties are divided into 36 *metropolitan districts*. These range in population from 159,867 (South Tyneside) to 1,011,000 (Birmingham). Most of them have a population of over 200,000 and most include a former county borough. They form compact areas.

There are 39 *non-metropolitan counties* ranging in population from 120,400 (Isle of Wight) and 301,400 (Northumberland) to 1,498,600 (Essex).

Each of the non-metropolitan counties is divided into *non-metropolitan districts*, of which there are 296. These districts have populations broadly between 60,000 and 100,000. About one third of the non-metropolitan districts, however, have populations above this range because of the need to avoid dividing large towns. Some districts, mainly in sparsely populated areas, have populations below 60,000 though less than 10 have populations below 40,000.

Permanent Local Government Boundary Commissions for England and Wales have been set up to keep the areas and electoral arrangements of the new local authorities under review.

Constitution and Elections

The county and district councils consist of directly elected councillors. The broad range of sizes of councils are: county councils 60–100 members; metropolitan district councils 50–80 members; non-metropolitan district councils 30–60 members. The councillors elect annually one of their number as chairman.

The general pattern in England is that councillors serve 4 years and there are no elections of district and parish councillors in county elections year. All new authorities were elected *en bloc* in 1973 (as "shadow" authorities until they took on their functions on April 1, 1974). All county councils were elected together in 1977 and every four years thereafter (i.e. 1979, 1981, 1985, etc.). In metropolitan districts one-third of the councillors for each ward are elected each year except in the year of county elections. Non-metropolitan districts can choose whether to have elections by thirds or whole council elections. In the former case, one-third of the council, as nearly as may be, is elected in each year of metropolitan district elections. If they choose whole council elections these are held in the mid-year of the county cycle (i.e. 1979, 1983, etc.). Local elections are normally held on the first Thursday in May.

Elections to local authorities in *Greater London* have been brought into line with the rest of England so that the normal term of office for councillors on the G.L.C. and the London Borough Councils is now four years instead of three. Greater London Council elections have taken place in the same year as county council elections since 1977.

Internal Organisation and Local Government Services in England

The council are the final decision making body within any authority. They are free to a great extent to make their own internal organisational arrangements. Normally questions of major policy are settled by the full council, while the administration of the various services is the responsibility of committees of members. Day to day decisions are delegated to the council's officers, who act within the policies laid down by the members.

Many councils have set up corporate management teams of the Chief Executive and chief officers. Such teams consider the operations of their authority as a whole, rather than dealing with each service separately, as was often the case in the past.

Local authorities are empowered or required by various Acts of Parliament to carry out functions in their areas. The legislation concerned comprises public general Acts and "local" Acts which local authorities have promoted as private bills. Functions are divided everywhere between two tiers of authorities, though their allocation within the metropolitan areas is somewhat different from outside, the metropolitan district councils exercising more functions than the non-metropolitan district councils.

Responsibility for the main local government functions is allocated as follows (though responsible authorities may involve other authorities in the provision of certain of their services through agency arrangements):

County councils: Strategic planning (e.g. structure plans; major projects); traffic, transport and highways; police; fire service; consumer protection (other than hygiene); refuse disposal; smallholdings.

Non-metropolitan county and metropolitan district councils: Education; social services; libraries.

District Councils: Local planning; housing; highways (maintenance of certain urban roads and off-street car parks); building regulations; environmental health; refuse collection; cemeteries and crematoria.

Concurrent (county and district councils): Recreation (e.g. parks, playing fields, swimming pools); museums; encouragement of the arts.

The sewerage and sewage disposal functions of local authorities have been transferred to 9 new water authorities in England and the Welsh Water Authority. Water authorities, however, are expected to make agreements whereby the new district councils discharge sewerage functions on an agency basis. Apart from these functions, the water authorities are responsible for water supply and conservation; river pollution control and river management; fisheries; land drainage; and use of water space for recreation and amenity purposes.

The personal health functions of local authorities were transferred in 1977 to area health authorities, whose areas were the same as non-metropolitan and Welsh counties and metropolitan districts. From April 1982 this two-tier structure was replaced by about 199 District Health Authorities. They work in close collaboration with local education, social services and environment health authorities.

London.—The Greater London Area embraces the old counties of London and Middlesex (except Potters Bar, Staines and Sunbury-on-Thames) and parts of the neighbouring counties of Essex, Herts., Kent and Surrey and the whole of the county boroughs of Croydon, East Ham and West Ham.

The Greater London Council is responsible for traffic, major roads and overall planning. All other matters are the concern of the 32 London borough councils; the City of London, besides retaining its previous functions, has the powers of a London borough.

Parishes

The rural parishes in England were not, in general, affected by local government reorganisation except that the powers of parish councils were extended and a few of them were divided by the boundaries of new counties and districts. 300 former small borough and urban district councils became parish councils with the same powers as other parish councils.

Parishes with 200 or more electors must generally have parish councils, and about three-quarters of the parishes have councils. A parish council comprises at least 5 members, the number being fixed by the district council. All parishes have parish meetings, comprising the electors of the parish.

Parish council functions include: allotments; arts and crafts; community halls, recreational facilities (e.g. open spaces, swimming pools), cemeteries and crematoria; and many minor functions. They must also be given an opportunity to comment on planning applications. They may, like county and district councils, spend up to a 2p rate for the general benefit of the parish. They precept on the district councils for their rate funds. In general, parish councils are elected every four years, in the year in which the local district councillor is elected.

Civic dignities

District councils may petition for a royal charter granting borough status to the district. In boroughs the chairman of the council is the mayor. The status "city" and the right to call the mayor "Lord Mayor" may also be granted by letters patent. Parish councils may call themselves "town councils", in which case their chairman is the "town mayor".

Charter trustees are established for those former boroughs which are too large to have parish councils and are situated in districts without city or borough status. The charter trustees are the district councillors representing the former borough and they elect a mayor, continue civic tradition, and look after the charters, insignia and civic plate of the former borough.

Local Government Elections

Generally speaking, all British subjects or citizens of the Republic of Ireland of 18 years or over, resident on the qualifying date in the area for which the election is being held are entitled to vote at local government elections. A register of electors is prepared and published annually by local electoral registration officers.

A returning officer has the overall responsibility for an election. Voting takes place at polling stations, arranged by the local authority and under the supervision of a presiding officer specially appointed for the purpose. Candidates, who are subject to various statutory qualifications and disqualifications designed to secure that they are suitable persons to hold office, must be nominated by electors for the electoral area concerned.

Local Commissioners for England and Wales

There exist Local Commissioners for England and Wales whose duty it is to investigate complaints of maladministration in many aspects of local government.

Wales

Since 1974 Wales, including the former Monmouthshire, has been divided into eight counties; Gwynedd; Clwyd; Powys; Dyfed; West, Mid and South Glamorgan; and Gwent. They range in population from 112,000 (Powys) to 541,800 (Mid-Glamorgan). There are 37 districts in Wales, many of those in the less populated parts reflecting the areas of former Welsh counties. Their populations range from 21,600 (Radnor) to 279,800 (Cardiff).

The arrangements for Welsh counties and districts are generally similar to those for English non-metropolitan counties and districts. There are some differences in functions: Welsh district councils have refuse disposal as well as refuse collection functions and they may provide on-street as well as off-street car parks with the consent of the county council. A few districts have also been designated as library authorities.

In Wales parishes have been replaced by communities. Unlike England, where many areas are not in any parish, communities have been established for the whole of Wales; approximately 1,000 communities in all. Community meetings may be convened as and when desired. Community councils exist in about 750 communities and further councils may be established at the request of a community meeting. Community councils have broadly the same range of powers as English parish councils. Community councillors are elected *en bloc* on the same basis as parish councillors in England, i.e. at the same time as a district council election and for a term of four years.

Local Government Finance

Local government is financed from various sources.

(1) *Rates.*—Levied by district councils and in London by the City Corporation and the London boroughs. Sums required by the Greater London Council, by county councils and parish or community councils are included in the rates levied by London boroughs and district councils. Rates are levied by a poundage tax on the rateable value of property in the area of the rating authority. Under the General Rate Act, 1967, rating authorities are required to charge a lower rate in the pound on dwellings than on property generally in their area. A differential of 18½p for both England and Wales has been prescribed since 1982–83. Rental values are annual rental values, on certain statutory assumptions, determined as at the date of the current valuation lists. The current valuation lists, prepared by valuation officers of the Board of Inland Revenue, came into force on April 1, 1973. New property is added to the list and significant changes to existing property necessitate amendments to the rateable value. The lists remain in force until the next general revaluation. Certain types of property are exempt from rates, e.g. agricultural land and buildings, and places of public religious worship. Some charities and other non-profit-making organizations can receive full or partial exemption. Under the General Rate Act, 1967, as amended by the Local Government Act, 1974 and the Local Government and Land Act 1980, local authorities can resolve to rate specified classes of empty property by an amount up to 100 per cent of the full rates, subject to a maximum of 50 per cent on non-domestic properties from 1 April 1981. From April 1, 1984 local authorities' powers to levy rates on empty industrial properties have been suspended. The Social Security and Housing Benefits Act 1982 (administered by the D.H.S.S.) makes provision for rate rebates for domestic ratepayers, eligibility depending on income, rates payable and number of people in the household. The Rating (Disabled Persons) Act 1978 provides rate relief in respect of certain facilities needed by disabled persons.

(2) *Government Grants.*—In addition to specific Government grants in aid of revenue expenditure on particular services, from April 1, 1981 grants known as rate support grants are payable to local authorities under the provisions of Part VI of the Local Government, Planning and Land Act, 1980. These grants, which replace the block grants previously paid under the Local Government Act, 1974, consist of two elements: block grant and domestic rate relief grant. The block grant, which is a single grant payment, replaces the needs and resources element under the previous system, and is payable to non-metropolitan counties and districts, metropolitan districts, London boroughs, the City of London, and the Isles of Scilly. The block grant is intended to enable all authorities to provide comparable standards of service at the same poundage cost to local ratepayers. The domestic rate relief grant, like the previous domestic element, is payable to all rating authorities to reimburse them for the cost of giving the domestic rate relief prescribed for the year.

In order to arrive at the total amount of the rate support grants to local authorities in England for any year (the new grant system provides for Wales to be administered separately), the aggregate of Exchequer grants to local authorities in respect of their relevant expenditure for the year is determined in advance (housing subsidies and specific grants towards expenditure on rate rebates and mandatory awards to students and trainee teachers are outside this aggregate amount) and from this is deducted the estimated amount of specific grants for the year in aid of revenue expenditure and the supplementary grants for transport purposes and in connection with national parks; the resulting balance is the amount of rate support grant. The Local Government Finance Act 1982 gives the Secretary of State power to abate the block grant of local authorities which exceed expenditure guidance which he has issued.

Forecasts of local authority relevant expenditure for 1984–85 in England adopted by the Government for rate support grant purposes were as follows. The amounts given are at 1984–85 cash prices.

Service	£M
Education	9,532
School Meals and Milk	263
Libraries, Museums and Art Galleries	327
Personal Social Sevices and Port Health	2,159
Police	2,358
Fire	513
Other Home Office Services	333
Local Transport	1,555
Local Environmental Services	2,307
Land Drainage and Flood Protection	86·5
Consumer Protection	52
Employment	70·5
Non-Housing Revenue Account Housing	91
Housing Benefits	82
Allocated Current Expenditure	£19,729
Unallocated Current Expenditure	660
Total Current Expenditure	£20,389
Revenue Contributions to Capital Outlay	513
Loan Charges (including leasing)	2,030
Rate Fund Contributions to Housing Revenue Account	246
Interest Receipts	−295
Total Relevant Expenditure	£22,883

The aggregate amount of Exchequer grants for 1984–85 was determined at £11,872 million. Of this, the specific revenue grants and the Transport and National Parks Supplementary grants were estimated at £2,459 million, giving a total for rate support grants of £9,323 million, of which £8,631 million was in respect of the block grant and £692 million the domestic rate relief grant.

Rates and Rateable Values.—The total rateable value for England on April 1, 1984 was £7,444 million and an estimate of the amount to be raised in rates, gross of rebates, in 1984–85 is £12,265 million.

Average Rates.— The estimated average rates levied in England in 1984–85 were: Inner London Boroughs, *domestic* rate 187·04p, *non-domestic* rate 181·91p; Outer London, 154·92p and 176·18p; Metropolitan Districts, 182·13p and 204·93p. The average rates levied in England were estimated at 154·90p (domestic) and 180·15p (non-domestic). In Wales the estimated average rates levied were, *domestic* rate 124·03p, *non-domestic* rate 180·40p.

SCOTLAND

Since 1975 Scotland has been divided into 9 regions, and 3 islands areas covering respectively Orkney, Shetland and the Western Isles. Within the regions there is a second independent tier of 53 districts. Regional and district councils have separate responsibility for specific functions. Islands councils are most-purpose authorities and are each responsible in their areas for the functions (except police, fire and valuation) which are carried out by regions and districts.

Regional Functions.—The regional authorities are responsible for strategic planning, for the provision of infrastructure such as roads, water and sewerage, for flood prevention, coast protection, and for certain public transport services. They also carry out among others the education, social work and consumer protection functions and have responsibility for police, fire, civil defence and electoral registration.

District Functions.—The district authorities deal with more local matters such as local planning; development control; building control; housing; leisure and recreation; tourism; libraries; environmental health including cleansing, refuse collection and disposal, food hygiene, inspection of shops, offices and factories, clean air, markets and slaughterhouses, burial and cremation; licensing, including liquor, cinemas and theatres, betting, gaming and dogs, taxis, charitable collections.

Community Councils.—Provision is also made in the Act for setting up community councils under schemes prepared by each district and islands authority. Such councils are not local authorities but have a statutory base. They have no statutory functions but are expected to take such action in the community as appears to their members to be desirable and practicable.

Local Government Electors.—In April 1984 there were 3,957,276 electors in Scotland. Elections are next due to take place in 1986 for region and island councils and in 1988 for district councils.

Rates and Rateable Values.—In 1980–81, the latest year for which final figures were available, a total of £975,679,000 was received from the general rates of local government in Scotland and £47,355,000 from domestic water rates. The rateable value on which rates were leviable was £1,280,598,000 on the general rates and £462,029,000 on the domestic water rates. The average general rate levied was 81p and the domestic water rate levied was 6·6p.

Provisional figures for 1983–84 show total receipts from general rates of £1,459,944,541 and £56,332,037 from domestic water rates. The rateable value leviable for 1983–84 was £1,184,569,515 (general) and

£600,520,909 (domestic water rate). The average rate per £ levied for 1983–84 was 123·4p (general) and 9·4p (domestic water rate).

NORTHERN IRELAND

For the purpose of local government Northern Ireland has a system of 26 single-tier district councils. There are 526 members of the councils, elected for periods of four years at a time on the principle of proportional representation.

The district councils all have the same three main roles. These are:

(a) an executive role in which the councils are responsible for a wide range of local services including the provision of recreational, social, community, and cultural facilities; environmental health; consumer protection; the enforcement of building regulations; the promotion of tourist development schemes; gas supply; street cleansing; refuse collection and disposal; litter prevention; and miscellaneous licensing and registration provisions, including dog control;

(b) a representative role in which they nominate representatives to sit as members of the various statutory bodies responsible for the administration of regional services such as education and libraries, health and personal social services, drainage, fire and electricity; and

(c) a consultative role in which they act as the media through which the views of local people are expressed on the operation in their area of other regional services notably planning, roads, and conservation (including water supply and sewerage services) provided by those departments of central government which have an obligation, either statutorily or otherwise, to consult the district councils about proposals affecting their areas.

WATER AUTHORITIES

The Water Act 1973, which provided for the reorganization of the water services in England and Wales, resulted in the creation of ten autonomous multipurpose water authorities (nine regional authorities in England and the Welsh Water Authority), and of the National Water Council and the Water Space Amenity Commission. Under the Water Act 1983 these latter two bodies were wound up and the Water Authorities Association was set up by the regional water authorities. The Association enables the water authorities to discuss amongst themselves and with the Government and other bodies matters of common concern, co-ordinates any necessary joint action by the water authorities, and provides press and public relations services.

The water authorities are responsible for water supply; water conservation, sewerage and sewage disposal, prevention of river pollution, fisheries, land drainage and the recreational use of their waters. Between them the authorities employ about 57,000 people, have an annual revenue expenditure of some £1,872 million and an investment budget of about £717 million a year.

THE WATER AUTHORITIES ASSOCIATION, 1 Queen Anne's Gate, S.W.1.—*Sec.*, A. Semple.

Regional Water Authorities

THAMES WATER AUTHORITY, New River Head, Rosebery Avenue, London, E.C.1.—*Managing Director*, K. West.

SOUTHERN WATER AUTHORITY, Guildborne House, Worthing, Sussex.—*Chief Executive*, B. R. Thorpe.

SEVERN TRENT WATER AUTHORITY, Abelson House, 2297 Coventry Road, Sheldon, Birmingham.—*Chief Executive*, D. A. D. Reeve.

WESSEX WATER AUTHORITY, Wessex House, Passage Street, Bristol.—*Chief Executive*, K. F. Roberts, C.B.E.

ANGLIAN WATER AUTHORITY, Ambury House, Huntingdon.—*Chief Executive*, P. H. Bray.

SOUTH WEST WATER AUTHORITY, 3–5 Barnfield Road, Exeter.—*Chief Executive*, A. G. C. Williams.

NORTHUMBRIAN WATER AUTHORITY, Northumbria House, Regent Centre, Gosforth, Newcastle-upon-Tyne.—*Chief Executive*, W. F. Ridley.

NORTH WEST WATER AUTHORITY, Dawson House, Great Sankey, Warrington.—*Chief Executive*, J. B. Oldfield.

YORKSHIRE WATER AUTHORITY, West Riding House, 67 Albion Street, Leeds.

WELSH WATER AUTHORITY, Cambrian Way, Brecon, Powys.—*Chief Executive*, B. Doyle.

Party Representation

Abbreviations: *A.* = Liberal/S.D.P. Alliance; *C.* = Conservative; *Com.* = Communist; *D.Lab.* = Democratic Labour; *Ind.* = Independent; *Lab.* = Labour; *L.* = Liberal; *M.K.* = Mebyon Kernow; *N.P.* = Non-Political/ Non-Party; *P.C.* = Plaid Cymru; *R.A.* = Ratepayers'/Residents' Associations; *S.D.P.* = Social Democratic Party; *S.N.P.* = Scottish National Party.

ENGLAND

Non-Metropolitan Counties (as at end May 1984)

Avon .... *Lab.* 39, *C.* 32, *L.* 3, *A.* 1, *Ind.* 1.
Bedford ..... *C.* 38, *Lab.* 33, *L.* 9, *Ind.* 1, (2 Vac.).
Berkshire .. *C.* 43, *Lab.* 27, *A.* 16, *Ind.* 1.
Bucks. ...... *C.* 47, *Lab.* 14, *Ind.* 5, *L.* 2, *A.* 1, *R.A.* 1.
Cambridge.. *C.* 34, *Lab.* 19, *L.* 12, *Ind.* 2, *Ind. C.* 1.
Cheshire .... *Lab.* 34, *C.* 30, *L.* 6, *Ind.* 1.
Cleveland ... *Lab.* 61, *C.* 26, *Ind.* 1, (1 Vac.).
Cornwall .... *Ind.* 44, *C.* 14, *L.* 14, *Lab.* 4, *S.D.P.* 1, *Ecology* 1, (1 Vac.).
Cumbria..... *Lab.* 41, *C.* 33, *Ind.* 4, *L.* 3, *Ind. Lab.* 1, (1 Vac.).
Derbyshire .. *Lab.* 58, *C.* 23, *A.* 1, *Ind. Lab.* 1, *L.* 1.
Devon ...... *C.* 65, *Lab.* 16, *L.* 11, *Ind.* 6.
Dorset ...... *C.* 55, *L.* 15, *Lab.* 11, *Ind.* 10.
Durham ..... *Lab.* 52, *C.* 7, *L.* 6, *Ind.* 4, *S.D.P.* 3.
Essex .... *C.* 49, *Lab.* 30, *L.* 14, *RA.* 2, (3 Vac.).
Gloucester .. *C.* 26, *Lab.* 17, *L.* 10, *Ind.* 7, *R.A.* 1.
Hampshire . *C.* 64, *Lab.* 26, *L.* 8, *Ind.* 2, *S.D.P.* 2.
Hereford and Worcester . *C.* 51, *Lab.* 19, *L.* 15, *Ind.* 7.
Herts........ *C.* 44, *Lab.* 27, *A.* 5, *R.A.* 1.
Humberside . *Lab.* 42, *C.* 33.
Kent........ *C.* 65, *Lab.* 22, *L.* 10, *Ind.* 1, *S.D.P.* 1.
Lancashire .. *Lab.* 53, *C.* 35, *A.* 7, *R.A.* 2, *Ind.C.* 1, (1 Vac.).

Leicester .... *C.* 44, *Lab.* 43, *L.* 5, (1 Vac.).
Lincolnshire . *C.* 39, *Lab.* 13, *L.* 10, *Ind.* 8, *S.D.P.* 2, *Ind. C.* 1, *R.A.* 1, (2 Vac.).
Norfolk ..... *C.* 52, *Lab.* 26, *L.* 4, *N.P.* 1.
Northants. .. *C.* 31, *Lab.* 31, *L.* 4, *Ind.* 2.
Northumb. .. *Lab.* 33, *C.* 15, *L.* 14, *Ind. C.* 2, *Ind.* 1, *S.D.P.* 1.
Notts........ *Lab.* 55, *C.* 32, *R.A.* 1.
Oxfordshire . *C.* 36, *Lab.* 19, *A.* 11, *Ind.* 3.
Shropshire .. *C.* 25, *Lab.* 22, *L.* 10, *N.P.* 7, *R.A.* 1, *S.D.P.* 1.
Somerset .... *C.* 34, *Lab.* 9, *L.* 8, *Ind.* 6.
Staffordshire *Lab.* 48, *C.* 26, *Ind.* 4, *L.* 4
Suffolk ...... *C.* 49, *Lab.* 31, *Ind.* 2.
Surrey ...... *C.* 62, *Lab.* 7, *L.* 4, *Ind.* 3.
Sussex, East . *C.* 53, *L.* 15, *Lab.* 13, *S.D.P.* 2, *Ind.* 1.
Sussex, West . *C.* 59, *L.* 13, *Lab.* 7, *Ind.* 1.
Warwicks.... *C.* 30, *Lab.* 26, *L.* 2, *Ind.* 1, *R.A.* 1, *S.D.P.* 1, (1 Vac.).
Wight, I.o. .. *L.* 26, *C.* 11, *N.P.* 4, *Ind.* 2.
Wiltshire .... *C.* 41, *Lab.* 19, *L.* 11, *Ind.* 1, *R.A.* 1, (1 Vac.).
Yorks., N. ... *C.* 48, *Lab.* 17, *L.* 14, *Ind.* 12, (2 Vac.).

Metropolitan Counties (as at end May 1984)

Greater Manchester . *Lab.* 77, *C.* 18, *L.* 10, *S.D.P.* 1.
Merseyside .... *Lab.* 54, *C.* 27, *L.* 17, (1 Vac.).
South Yorkshire .... *Lab.* 82, *C.* 13, *A.* 2, *L.* 2, *R.A.* 1.

Tyne and Wear ..... *Lab.* 72, *C.* 23, *L.* 7, *Ind.* 1, *R.A.* 1.
West Midlands ...... *Lab.* 74, *C.* 25, *L.* 5.
West Yorkshire ..... *Lab.* 62, *C.* 14, *L.* 11, (1 Vac.).

Metropolitan District Councils (as at end May 1984)

GREATER MANCHESTER

Bolton .... *Lab.* 36, *C.* 20, *L.* 4.
Bury .... *C.* 26, *Lab.* 22.
Manchester........ *Lab.* 79, *C.* 14, *L.* 6.
Oldham............ *Lab.* 40, *C.* 16, *L.* 4.
Rochdale .... *Lab.* 28, *C.* 17, *L.* 13, *A.* 2.
Salford .... *Lab.* 53, *C.* 6, *A.* 1.
Stockport .... *C.* 28, *Lab.* 17, *L.* 15, *Ind.* 3.
Tameside .... *Lab.* 45, *C.* 9, *L.* 3.
Trafford .... *C.* 36, *Lab.* 19, *L.* 7, (1 Vac.).
Wigan .... *Lab.* 60, *L.* 8, *C.* 4.

MERSEYSIDE

Knowsley .... *Lab.* 55, *C.* 9, *L.* 2.
Liverpool.......... *Lab.* 57, *L.* 28, *C.* 13, (1 Vac.).
St. Helens .... *Lab.* 39, *C.* 12, *L.* 2, *S.D.P.* 1.
Sefton............. *C.* 36, *Lab.* 21, *A.* 10, *Ind.* 1, (1 Vac.).
Wirral .... *C.* 34, *Lab.* 24, *A.* 8.

SOUTH YORKSHIRE

Barnsley .... *Lab.* 59, *C.* 3, *A.* 1, *Ind.* 1, *R.A.* 1, (1 Vac.).
Doncaster .... *Lab.* 50, *C.* 11, *L.* 1, (1 Vac.).
Rotherham .... *Lab.* 60, *C.* 4, *S.D.P.* 2.
Sheffield........... *Lab.* 61, *C.* 17, *L.* 9.

TYNE AND WEAR

Gateshead .... *Lab.* 57, *C.* 7, *L.* 1, *R.A.* 1.
Newcastle upon Tyne .... *Lab.* 45, *C.* 22, *L.* 10, *S.D.P.* 1.
North Tyneside ..... *Lab.* 33, *C.* 20, *A.* 3, *L.* 2, *Ind. Lab.* 1, (1 Vac.).
South Tyneside ..... *Lab.* 47, *C.* 3, *L.* 1, *Others* 9.
Sunderland .... *Lab.* 53, *C.* 13, *A.* 7, *Ind. Lab.* 2.

WEST MIDLANDS

Birmingham .... *Lab.* 61, *C.* 52, *L.* 3, *S.D.P.* 1.
Coventry .... *Lab.* 34, *C.* 20.
Dudley .... *Lab.* 36, *C.* 35, *S.D.P.* 1.
Sandwell .... *Lab.* 53, *C.* 13, *L.* 6.
Solihull .... *C.* 33, *Lab.* 13, *Ind.* 2, *R.A.* 2, *L.* 1.
Walsall .... *Lab.* 25, *C.* 19, *L.* 9, *Ind.* 7.
Wolverhampton..... *Lab.* 35, *C.* 23, *A.* 2.

WEST YORKSHIRE

Bradford .... *Con.* 44, *Lab.* 40, *L.* 5, *S.D.P.* 1.
Calderdale.......... *Lab.* 22, *C.* 16, *L.* 15, *Ind. Lab.*1.
Kirklees............ *Lab.* 37, *C.* 18, *L.* 14, *S.D.P.* 3.
Leeds .... *Lab.* 53, *C.* 33, *L.* 10, *A.* 2, *Ind.* 1.
Wakefield .... *Lab.* 54, *A.* 4, *C.* 4, *Ind.* 1.

Non-Metropolitan District Councils (as at end May 1984)

(* one-third of councillors of Councils so denoted retire each year, except in those years when County Council elections are held)

*Adur .... C. 19, L. 18, R.A. 2.
Allerdale .... Lab. 26, Ind. 19, C. 10.
Alnwick .... N.P. 9, L. 8, C. 6, Ind. 3, Ind. Lab. 2, Lab. 1.
*Amber Valley .. Lab. 22, C. 10, A. 7, Ind. 3, N.P. 1.
Arun .... C. 51, A. 4, Lab. 1.
Ashfield .... Lab. 28, L. 3, C. 1, S.D.P. 1.
Ashford .... C. 26, A. 8, Ind. 7, Lab. 6, Ind. L. 1, R.A. 1.
Aylesbury Vale .. C. 34, Ind. 14, A. 6, Lab. 4.
Babergh .... C. 19, Ind. 7, Lab. 3, A. 2, Others 11.
*Barrow-in-
Furness .... Lab. 25, C. 12, Ind. 1.
*Basildon .... Lab. 24, C. 15, L. 3.
*Basingstoke &
Deane .... C. 29, Lab. 19, Ind. 7, L. 2, S.D.P. 2.
*Bassetlaw ..... Lab. 26, C. 17, Ind. 2, Ind. C. 1, Others 4.
*Bath .... C. 31, Lab. 11, A. 6.
Berwick upon .. C. 8, L. 7, Ind. 4, Lab. 3, Others 5, (1
Tweed .... Vac.).
Beverley .... C. 37, L. 10, Lab. 5, Ind. 1.
Blaby .... C. 20, A. 4, Ind. 4, R.A. 1, Others 10.
*Blackburn ..... Lab. 30, C. 23, L. 3, R.A. 3, Ind. Lab. 1.
Blackpool .... C. 32, Lab. 9, L. 3.
Blyth Valley .... Lab. 32, A. 11, C. 3, L. 1.
Bolsover .... Lab. 35, Ind. 2.
Boothferry ...... C. 20, Ind. 8, Lab. 6, S.D.P. 1.
Boston .... C. 17, Ind. 9, Lab. 4, L. 4.
Bournemouth ... C. 39, Ind. 5, Lab. 5, A. 4, Ind. C. 3, L. 1.
Bracknell .... C. 40.
Braintree .... C. 27, Lab. 16, Ind. 11, L. 4, R.A. 2.
Breckland ...... C. 25, N.P. 15, Lab. 8, Ind. 4, A. 1.
*Brentwood .... C. 28, L. 9, Lab. 2.
Bridgnorth ..... Ind. 19, C. 9, L. 3, Lab. 2.
Brighton .... C. 23, Lab. 21, L. 3, S.D.P. 1.
*Bristol .... Lab. 33, C. 29, L. 6.
*Broadland ..... C. 39, Ind. 6, A. 4.
Bromsgrove .... C. 29, Lab. 8, R.A. 3, L. 1.
*Broxbourne .... C. 33, Lab. 5, A. 4.
Broxtowe .... C. 38, Lab. 10, Ind. 1.
*Burnley .... Lab. 39, C. 12, A. 2, L. 1.
*Cambridge ..... Lab. 21, C. 11, A. 10.
*Cannock Chase . Lab. 19, L. 17, C. 5, Ind. 1.
Canterbury ..... C. 37, Lab. 7, A. 3, Ind. 2.
Caradon .... Ind. 31, C. 5, A. 2, R.A. 2, Lab. 1.
Carlisle .... Lab. 26, C. 22, L. 2, Ind. 1.
Carrick .... C. 22, Ind. 11, L. 11, (1 Vac.).
Castle Morpeth .. N.P. 10, C. 7, A. 6, L. 4, Ind. 3, Lab. 2, R.A. 2.
Castle Point .... C. 37, Lab. 2.
Charnwood ..... C. 38, Lab. 13, Ind. C. 1.
Chelmsford ..... A. 31, C. 26, Ind. 3.
*Cheltenham ... L. 14, C. 12, R.A. 4, Lab. 2, Ind. 1.
*Cherwell ...... C. 35, Lab. 12, A. 4, Ind. 1.
*Chester .... C. 33, Lab. 16, L. 10, Ind. 1.
Chesterfield .... Lab. 37, C. 9, A. 1.
Chester-le-Street Lab. 23, Ind. 5, L. 4, C. 1.
Chichester ...... C. 27, A. 13, Ind. 4, N.P. 4, R.A. 2.
Chiltern .... C. 43, A. 2, Lab. 2, Ind. 1, L. 1, R.A. 1.
*Chorley .... C. 23, Lab. 22, Ind. 1, S.D.P. 1.
Christchurch .... C. 15, Ind. 7, Lab. 3.
Cleethorpes .... C. 17, Lab. 8, L. 8, Ind. 7, Ind. Lab. 1.
*Colchester ..... C. 35, Lab. 11, A. 10, R.A. 3, Ind. 1.
*Congleton ..... C. 27, L. 13, Lab. 5.
Copeland .... Lab. 29, C. 16, Ind. 4, A. 1, R.A. 1.
Corby .... Lab. 24, C. 3.
Cotswold .... N.P. 23, C. 10, Ind. 6, A. 2, L. 2, Ind. C. 1, Lab. 1.
*Craven .... C. 19, L. 8, Ind. 4, Lab. 2, S.D.P. 1.

*Crawley .... Lab. 18, C. 14.
*Crewe and
Nantwich ..... C. 27, Lab. 25, L. 3, S.D.P. 2.
Dacorum .... C. 37, Lab. 17, S.D.P. 2, Ind. 1, L. 1.
Darlington ...... Lab. 27, C. 20, Ind. 3, A. 2.
Dartford .... C. 26, Lab. 15, R.A. 3, Ind. Lab. 1.
*Daventry ...... C. 20, Lab. 8, Ind. 5, A. 2.
*Derby .... Lab. 24, C. 18, L. 2.
Derwentside .... Lab. 36, Ind. 12, C. 4, A. 3.
Dover .... C. 39, Lab. 17.
Durham .... Lab. 27, Ind. 8, L. 5, A. 4, C. 2, Ind. Lab. 1, Others 2.
Easington ...... Lab. 34, L. 7, Ind. 6, A. 2, Ind. Lab. 2.
*Eastbourne .... C. 14, A. 9, L. 6, Lab. 1.
East Cambs. .... Ind. C. 4, C. 3, Ind. 3, A. 2, Ind. L. 2, L. 1, Lab. 1, Others 21.
*East Devon .... C. 43, A. 13, Ind. 3, Lab. 1.
East Hampshire . C. 27, A. 7, Ind. 6, (2 Vac.).
East Herts...... C. 32, Ind. 7, R.A. 6, A. 2, Lab. 2, Ind. C. 1.
*Eastleigh ...... C. 20, A. 14, Lab. 10.
East Lindsey .... N.P. 38, C. 7, Ind. 5, A. 4, L. 3, Lab. 3.
East Northants. . C. 30, Lab. 6.
East Staffs....... C. 21, Lab. 21, Ind. C. 2, L. 2.
East Yorkshire .. C. 30, Ind. 7, Lab. 2, L. 1, Others 3.
Eden .... N.P. 37.
*Ellesmere Port &
Neston .... Lab. 27, C. 12, Ind. Lab. 1, (1 Vac.).
*Elmbridge ..... C. 31, R.A. 19, A. 5, Lab. 5.
*Epping Forest .. C. 36, Lab. 12, R.A. 6, Ind. 2, S.D.P. 2, Ind. C. 1.
Epsom & Ewell .. R.A. 33, A. 3, Lab. 3.
Erewash .... C. 27, Lab. 19, Ind. 2, N.P. 2, Ind. Lab. 1.
Exeter .... C. 16, Lab. 14, A. 5, Ind. 1.
*Fareham .... C. 26, A. 11, R.A. 3, Ind. 1, Lab. 1.
Fenland .... C. 20, Lab. 8, Ind. 6, L. 5, A. 1.
Forest Heath .... C. 13, N.P. 6, Ind. 4, Lab. 2.
Forest of Dean .. Lab. 21, Ind. 20, A. 4, C. 4.
Fylde .... C. 23, R.A. 11, N.P. 9, Ind. C. 2, A. 1, Ind. 1, L. 1, Lab. 1.
Gedling .... C. 39, Lab. 8, A. 4, Ind. 3, Ind. C. 1.
*Gillingham ..... C. 24, L. 9, Lab. 7, Ind. L. 2.
Glanford .... C. 25, Ind. 12, Lab. 2, A. 1, SDP. 1.
*Gloucester ..... C. 16, Lab. 11, L. 6.
*Gosport........ C. 24, L. 3, Lab. 3.
Gravesham ..... C. 23, Lab. 20, S.D.P. 1.
*Great Grimsby . Lab. 19, C. 18, A. 7, Ind. 1.
Great Yarmouth . C. 26, Lab. 18, L. 4.
Guildford .... C. 31, Lab. 6, A. 5, L. 2, Ind. 1.
*Halton .... Lab. 34, C. 8, S.D.P. 2, Ind. 1, L. 1, N.P. 1
Hambleton ...... NP. 19, C. 14, Ind. 10, Lab. 3, A. 1.
Harborough ..... C. 17, N.P. 11, Ind. 6, Lab. 2, A. 1.
*Harlow .... Lab. 33, L. 5, C. 4.
Harrogate ...... C. 36, Ind. 9, L. 7, Lab. 2, A. 1, Others 5.
*Hart .... C. 12, L. 11, Ind. 7, S.D.P. 2, Ind. C. 1, Others 1, (1 Vac.).
*Hartlepool ..... Lab. 33, C. 11, Ind. 2, L. 1.
*Hastings .... C. 13, L. 10, Lab. 8, Ind. 1.
*Havant .... C. 24, Lab. 9, A. 5, Ind. 2, R.A. 1, (1 Vac.).
*Hereford ...... L. 14, C. 7, Lab. 4, Ind. 2.
*Hertsmere ..... C. 23, Lab. 12, A. 4.
High Peak ...... C. 19, Lab. 14, Ind. 6, L. 3, R.A. 1, (1 Vac.).
Hinckley and
Bosworth ..... C. 27, Lab. 4, L. 3.
Holderness...... Ind. 28, C. 3.
Horsham .... C. 36, Ind. 3, A. 2, R.A. 1.
Hove .... C. 24, Lab. 3, L. 2, Ind. 1.

*Huntingdon ...*C*. 36, *Lab.* 7, *Ind.* 5, *S.D.P.* 2, *A.* 1,
    Ind. C. 1, *Ind. L.* 1.
Hyndburn ......*C.* 24, *Lab.* 20, *A.* 2, *L.* 1.
*Ipswich ....*Lab.* 30, *C.* 17, (1 Vac.)
Kennet ....*NP.* 19, *C.* 9, *Ind.* 7, *A.* 4, (1 Vac.).
Kerrier ....*Ind.* 19, *C.* 17, *Lab.* 4, *A.* 3, *M.K.* 1.
Kettering ......*C.* 23, *Lab.* 12, *Ind.* 5, *L.* 2, *S.D.P.* 1,
    Others 2.
King's Lynn & *C.* 41, *Lab.* 14, *Ind. C.* 2, *Ind.* 1,
  W. Norfolk .... *S.D.P.* 1, (1 Vac.).
*Kingston upon
  Hull ....*Lab.* 49, *C.* 10, *A.* 1.
Kingswood ......*C.* 25, *Lab.* 18, *Ind.* 2, *L.* 2.
Lancaster.......*C.* 37, *Lab.* 15, *A.* 6, *RA.* 1, (1 Vac.)
Langbaurgh.....*Lab.* 30, *C.* 29, (1 Vac.).
*Leicester ......*Lab.* 42, *C.* 14.
*Leominster ....*Ind.* 24, *A.* 6, *C.* 3, *Ind. C.* 1, *L.* 1,
    Lab. 1.
Lewes ....*C.* 38, *Ind.* 6, *L.* 4.
Lichfield ....*C.* 38, *Lab.* 15, *Ind.* 2, *Ind. C.* 1.
*Lincoln ....*Lab.* 25, *C.* 8.
Luton ....*C.* 25, *Lab.* 17, *L.* 6.
*Macclesfield ....*C.* 39, *Lab.* 5, *L.* 4, *Ind.* 3, *R.A.* 3,
    S.D.P. 3, *Others* 3.
*Maidstone ....*C.* 23, *A.* 20, *Lab.* 8, *Ind.* 3, (1 Vac.)
Maldon ....*C.* 15, *A.* 9, *Ind.* 4, *Ind. C.* 1, *Lab.* 1.
Malvern Hills ..*C.* 17, *Ind.* 12, *N.P.* 11, *A.* 7, *Lab.* 2,
    Ind. C. 1, *L.* 1.
Mansfield ......*Lab.* 39, *C.* 5, *S.D.P.* 2.
Medina ....*L.* 20, *C.* 10, *Ind.* 5, *A.* 1.
Melton ....*C.* 16, *Ind.* 5, *Ind. C.* 2, *L.* 2, *R.A.* 1.
Mendip ....*C.* 22, *Ind.* 7, *NP.* 7, *Lab.* 4, *A.* 2, *L.*
    1.
Mid Beds. ......*C.* 26, *N.P.* 17, *Lab.* 7, *Ind.* 2, *A.* 1.
Mid Devon ......*Ind.* 30, *A.* 8, *L.* 2.
Middlesbrough ..*Lab.* 35, *C.* 16, *A.* 1, *Ind.* 1.
Mid Suffolk ....*C.* 17, *N.P.* 10, *Lab.* 6, *Ind.* 5, *A.* 1,
    Ind. C. 1.
*Mid Sussex ....*C.* 39, *A.* 10, *Ind.* 4, *Ind. C.* 1.
*Milton Keynes .*Lab.* 18, *C.* 17, *A.* 9, *Ind.* 1, *Ind. C.*
    1.
*Mole Valley ....*C.* 17, *Ind.* 15, *L.* 7, *Ind. C.* 1, *Lab.* 1.
Newark ....*C.* 25, *Lab.* 25, *Ind.* 3, *A.* 2, *Ind. Lab.*
    1.
Newbury ....*C.* 35, *L.* 10.
*Newcastle under
  Lyme ....*Lab.* 37, *C.* 10, *L.* 6, *Ind.* 2, *S.D.P.* 1.
New Forest ....*C.* 40, *Ind.* 7, *A.* 4, *R.A.* 3, *Lab.* 1,
    Others 3.
Northampton ...*C.* 21, *Lab.* 18, *L.* 4.
Northavon ......*C.* 35, *A.* 10, *Lab.* 10, *Ind.* 2.
*North Beds. .....*C.* 30, *Lab.* 11, *L.* 9, *Ind.* 1, *S.D.P.* 1,
    (1 Vac.).
North Cornwall .*L.* 5, *C.* 1, *Others* 32.
North Devon ....*Ind.* 12, *N.P.* 12, *L.* 9, *C.* 6, *Lab.* 1,
    Others 4.
North Dorset ...*N.P.* 25, *L.* 6, *C.* 2.
N.-E. Derbys....*Lab.* 31, *C.* 17, *Ind.* 4, *Ind. Lab.* 1.
*North Herts. ...*C.* 31, *Lab.* 12, *R.A.* 3, *A.* 2, *Ind.* 2.
North Kesteven .*Ind.* 21, *C.* 14, *L.* 2, *Lab.* 2.
North Norfolk ..*N.P.* 24, *C.* 13, *Ind.* 7, *Lab.* 2.
North Shropshire*N.P.* 33, *C.* 5, *Ind.* 1, *Ind. C.* 1.
N. Warwicks. ...*Lab.* 20, *C.* 12, *Ind.* 1, *Ind. L.* 1.
N.-W. Leics.....*Lab.* 19, *C.* 12, *Ind.* 5, *A.* 4.
North Wiltshire .*C.* 35, *L.* 10, *Ind.* 4, *Lab.* 3.
*Norwich ......*Lab.* 39, *C.* 7, *L.* 2.
Nottingham......*Lab.* 28, *C.* 27.
*Nuneaton &
  Bedworth .....*Lab.* 32, *C.* 11, *A.* 2.
*Oadby &
  Wigston ......*C.* 23, *L.* 3.
Oswestry ....*L.* 4, *C.* 3, *Ind.* 3, *Lab.* 3, *S.D.P.* 1,
    Others 15.
*Oxford ....*Lab.* 27, *C.* 15, *A.* 3.
*Pendle.........*Lab.* 19, *L.* 16, *C.* 14, *Ind.* 1, *SDP.* 1.
*Penwith .......*N.P.* 24, *C.* 6, *Lab.* 2, *L.* 1, *M.K.* 1.

*Peterborough ..*Lab.* 22, *C.* 18, *L.* 8.
Plymouth ....*C.* 32, *Lab.* 24, *Ind. C.* 3, *S.D.P.* 1.
Poole ....*C.* 27, *L.* 8, *A.* 1.
Portsmouth .....*C.* 25, *Lab.* 11, *Ind.* 2, *S.D.P.* 1.
*Preston ....*Lab.* 31, *C.* 21, *L.* 5.
*Purbeck ....*C.* 7, *N.P.* 6, *R.A.* 3, *A.* 2, *Ind.* 2, *L.*
    2.
Reading ....*C.* 23, *Lab.* 17, *L.* 5.
*Redditch ......*Lab.* 19, *C.* 9, *Ind.* 1.
*Reigate &
  Banstead .....*C.* 38, *Lab.* 10, *A.* 1.
Restormel ......*N.P.* 20, *A.* 8, *Ind.* 8, *C.* 6, *Lab.* 1, (1
    Vac.).
Ribble Valley ....*C.* 32, *Ind.* 3, *Lab.* 2, *A.* 1.
Richmondshire . .*N.P.* 34.
Rochester upon
  Medway ......*C.* 27, *Lab.* 22, *Ind.* 1.
*Rochford ......*C.* 29, *L.* 8, *Lab.* 2, *Ind.* 1.
*Rossendale.....*C.* 19, *Lab.* 15, *Ind.* 1, *L.* 1.
Rother ....*C.* 23, *Ind.* 8, *A.* 5, *R.A.* 4, *Lab.* 3,
    Ind. C. 1, (1 Vac.).
*Rugby ....*C.* 23, *Lab.* 16, *R.A.* 6, *Ind.* 2, *L.* 1.
*Runnymede ....*C.* 30, *Lab.* 6, *R.A.* 4, *Ind. C.* 1, *L.* 1.
Rushcliffe.......*C.* 51, *Lab.* 2, *A.* 1.
*Rushmoor ....*C.* 31, *Ind. C.* 9, *A.* 5.
Rutland .........*N.P.* 11, *C.* 4, *L.* 4, *Ind.* 1.
Ryedale ........*N.P.* 15, *C.* 7, *Ind.* 7, *L.* 6, *A.* 4, *Ind.*
    C. 1, *Lab.* 1, (1 Vac.).
St. Albans ......*C.* 25, *A.* 23, *Lab.* 7, *Ind.* 2.
St. Edmondsbury *C.* 30, *Lab.* 9, *A.* 3, *Ind.* 2.
Salisbury ....*C.* 25, *Ind.* 13, *L.* 10, *R.A.* 5, *Lab.* 4,
    S.D.P. 1.
Scarborough ....*C.* 20, *Ind.* 16, *Lab.* 8, *A.* 5.
*Scunthorpe ....*Lab.* 29, *C.* 6, *A.* 5.
Sedgefield.......*Lab.* 41, *S.D.P.* 3, *C.* 2, *Ind.* 1, *L.* 1,
    Others 1.
Sedgemoor ......*C.* 25, *Lab.* 11, *Ind.* 6, *A.* 3, *L.* 3, (1
    Vac.).
Selby ....*C.* 29, *Ind.* 11, *Lab.* 7, *Ind. Lab.* 3.
Sevenoaks ......*C.* 37, *Ind.* 11, *L.* 3, *Lab.* 1, *SDP.* 1.
Shepway ....*C.* 32, *L.* 17, *Ind.* 5, *Lab.* 2.
*Shrewsbury &
  Atcham ......*C.* 22, *Lab.* 16, *A.* 7, *Ind.* 3.
*Slough ....*Lab.* 20, *C.* 15, *L.* 3, (1 Vac.).
*Southampton ..*Lab.* 23, *C.* 20, *A.* 2.
*South Beds. .....*C.* 41, *Lab.* 9, *Ind.* 1, *Ind. C.* 1, *L.* 1.
South Bucks. ....*C.* 29, *R.A.* 5, *Ind.* 4, *A.* 1, *N.P.* 1, (1
    Vac.).
*South Cambs. ...*Ind.* 35, *A.* 9, *C.* 8, *Lab.* 3.
South Derbys. ...*Lab.* 18, *Ind.* 8, *C.* 5, *L.* 2, *A.* 1.
*Southend-on-
  Sea ....*C.* 25, *A.* 11, *Lab.* 3.
South Hams .....*C.* 26, *N.P.* 10, *A.* 3, *Ind.* 3, *Ind. C.*
    1, *L.* 1.
*Sth. Hereford ..*N.P.* 21, *Ind.* 6, *C.* 5, *L.* 1, *S.D.P.* 1,
    (1 Vac.).
South Holland...*C.* 11, *Ind.* 9, *A.* 2, *Others* 15, (1
    Vac.).
South Kesteven .*C.* 28, *N.P.* 11, *Lab.* 10, *L.* 7, (1 Vac.).
*South Lakeland *C.* 24, *Ind.* 9, *A.* 5, *L.* 3, *Lab.* 3,
    Others 8.
South Norfolk ...*C.* 34, *Ind.* 7, *L.* 3, *S.D.P.* 2, *Lab.* 1.
S. Northants.....*C.* 28, *Ind.* 3, *Lab.* 3, *Others* 6.
S. Oxfordshire ..*C.* 35, *Lab.* 7, *Ind.* 6, *A.* 5, *Ind. C.* 2,
    (1 Vac.).
South Ribble ....*C.* 38, *Lab.* 11, *L.* 5.
S. Shropshire ...*NP.* 25, *Ind.* 5, *A.* 4, *C.* 4, *Lab.* 1,
    RA. 1.
South Staffs. .....*C.* 33, *Ind.* 7, *Lab.* 4, *L.* 3, *Others* 3.
South Wight ....*C.* 13, *Ind.* 6, *L.* 4, *R.A.* 1.
Spelthorne ......*C.* 36, *Lab.* 4.
Stafford ....*C.* 35, *Lab.* 19, *A.* 6.
Staffordshire
  Moorlands ....*Ind. C.* 34, *Lab.* 14, *Ind.* 7, *S.D.P.* 1.
*Stevenage .....*Lab.* 26, *L.* 6, *S.D.P.* 5, *C.* 2.
Stockton-on-Tees *Lab.* 28, *C.* 26, *A.* 1.
*Stoke-on-Trent .*Lab.* 57, *C.* 3.

*Stratford-on-
Avon. ....C. 37, Ind. 10, L. 5, Lab. 2, (1 Vac.).
*Stroud ....C. 28, Ind. 9, SDP. 9, Lab. 8, (2 Vac).
Suffolk Coastal . . C. 44, Ind. 5, N.P. 4, Lab. 2.
Surrey Heath . . . C. 36.
*Swale ....C. 27, Lab. 12, A. 8, Ind. 1, Ind. C. 1.
*Tamworth .....C. 17, Lab. 10.
*Tandridge .....C. 35, A. 3, Lab. 3, Ind. 1.
Taunton Deane . . C. 32, Lab. 10, Ind. 6, S.D.P. 1.
Teesdale ....Ind. 28, Lab. 3.
Teignbridge.....C. 21, N.P. 21, Ind. 8, A. 4, Lab. 3, (1 Vac.).
Tendring ....C. 31, Lab. 8, R.A. 8, L. 7, Ind. 4, A. 1, (1 Vac.).
Test Valley ......C. 31, N.P. 6, A. 4, Ind. 2, Lab. 1.
Tewkesbury ....C. 13, Ind. 8, N.P. 4, A. 1, L. 1, Others 18
*Thamesdown . . . Lab. 31, C. 15, A. 2, Ind. 1.
Thanet ....C. 29, Ind. 14, Lab, 7, A. 2, Ind. C. 1, Ind. Lab. 1.
*Three Rivers . . C. 24, L. 13, Lab.9, A. 1.
*Thurrock ......Lab. 27, C. 10, Ind. Lab. 2.
*Tonbridge & Malling.......C. 35, A. 11, Lab. 5, Ind. 1.
*Torbay ....C. 29, A. 3, R.A. 2, Ind. 1, L. 1.
Torridge........Ind. 29, A. 3, C. 3, Lab. 1.
*Tunbridge Wells C. 40, A. 5, Ind. 2, Lab. 1.
Tynedale ....Ind. 16, C. 12, L. 12, Lab. 7.
Uttlesford ......C. 27, A. 6, Ind. 3, Others 6.
Vale of White Horse ....C. 40, A 8, Ind. 2, Lab. 1.
Vale Royal .....C. 28, Lab. 23, Ind. 5, L. 1, R.A. 1, S.D.P. 1, (1 Vac.).
Wansbeck ....Lab. 36, L. 9, Ind. 1.
Wansdyke ......C. 33, Lab. 11, Ind. 3.
Warrington......Lab. 36, C. 22, A. 2.
Warwick ....C. 31, Lab. 7, A. 4, R.A. 3.
*Watford ....Lab. 23, C. 13.
Waveney ....C. 26, Lab. 19, L. 2, Ind. 1.

Waverley ....C. 46, A. 4, Ind. 4, Lab. 2, Ind. C. 1.
Wealden ....C. 48, R.A. 6, A. 2, Ind. 2.
Wear Valley ....Lab. 26, Ind. 4, C. 3, L. 2, Others 4, (1 Vac.).
Wellingborough . C. 18, Lab. 12, Ind. 3, L. 1.
*Welwyn Hatfield ......Lab. 24, C. 19.
West Derbyshire C. 26, A. 4, N.P. 4, Lab. 2, Ind. 1, Ind. C. 1, L. 1.
*West Devon ....NP. 14, C. 9, Ind. 5, A. 1, (1 Vac.).
*West Dorset....N.P. 24, C. 17, L. 5, Ind. 4, Ind. C. 3, A. 1, Lab. 1.
*W. Lancashire .C. 32, Lab. 19, A. 2, Ind. 2.
*West Lindsey ..A. 15, Ind. 12, C. 7, Lab. 3.
*W. Oxon. ......C. 23, Ind. 13, A. 8, Lab. 4, Ind. C. 1.
West Somerset ..C. 4, N.P. 4, Ind. 3, R.A. 2, A. 1, Others 18.
West Wilts. ......C. 33, Lab. 4, A. 2, Ind. 2, L. 2.
*Weymouth and Portland ......C. 17, Lab. 12, R.A. 3, Ind. 2, L. 1.
Wimborne ......C. 26, Ind. 3, A. 2, L. 2, RA. 2, SDP. 1.
*Winchester ....C. 37, A. 7, Ind. 5, Lab. 5.
Windsor and Maidenhead ..C. 48, L. 6, R.A. 4.
*Woking........C. 20, A. 8, Lab. 7.
*Wokingham....C. 46, L. 7, Lab. 1.
*Woodspring....C. 47, Ind. 5, Lab. 4, A. 3.
*Worcester .....C. 18, Lab. 18.
Worthing ....C. 24, A. 7, L. 5.
Wrekin.........Lab. 33, C. 7, Ind. 6.
Wychavon ......C. 18, Ind. 8, L. 5, Lab. 3, A. 1, Others 14.
Wycombe ....C. 50, Lab. 6, R.A. 3, L. 1.
Wyre ....C. 46, Lab. 8, L. 2.
*Wyre Forest ...C. 19, L. 14, Lab. 7, Ind. 2.
Yeovil ....L. 26, C. 21, Ind. 11, Lab. 1, SDP. 1.
*York ....Lab. 19, C. 18, L. 8.

Greater London Boroughs (as at end July 1984)

Barking and Dagenham........Lab. 37, Ind. 5, C. 3, L. 3.
Barnet ....C. 47, Lab. 13.
Bexley ....C. 41, Lab. 14, L. 7.
Brent ....Lab. 32, C. 31, L. 3.
Bromley............C. 51, Lab. 5, S.D.P. 4.
Camden ....Lab. 33, C. 26.
Croydon............C. 62, Lab. 5, Ind. 3.
Ealing ....C. 35, Lab. 29, L. 3, Ind. C. 1, Ind. Lab. 1, (1 Vac.).
Enfield ....C. 47, Lab. 19.
Greenwich ....Lab. 43, C. 16, L. 2, S.D.P. 1.
Hackney ....Lab. 50, L. 7, C. 3.
Hammersmith .....Lab. 25, C. 23, L. 2.
Haringey ....Lab. 35, C. 24.
Harrow ....C. 41, L. 13, Lab. 6, Ind. 3.
Havering...........C. 37, Lab. 12, R.A.Ind. 9, A. 5.
Hillingdon.........C. 57, Lab. 10, A. 2.
Hounslow ....Lab. 33, C. 27.

Islington ....Lab. 49, S.D.P. 3.
Kensington and Chelsea ....C. 39, Lab. 15.
Kingston-on-Thames C. 38, L. 9, Lab. 3.
Lambeth ....Lab. 34, C. 27, S.D.P. 3.
Lewisham ....Lab. 41, C. 26.
Merton.............C. 43, Lab. 13, Ind. 1.
Newham ....Lab. 55, S.D.P. 3, L. 2.
Redbridge ....C. 50, Lab. 12, L. 1.
Richmond-on-Thames ....C. 25, L. 25, S.D.P. 2.
Southwark ....Lab. 51, C. 8, Ind. Lab. 2, L. 2, (1 Vac.).
Sutton ....C. 42, Lab. 7, L. 6, (1 Vac.).
Tower Hamlets.....Lab. 30, L. 19, Ind. 1.
Waltham Forest.....C. 25, Lab. 25, L. 7.
Wandsworth........C. 33, Lab. 26, L. 1.
Westminster........C. 43, Lab. 16, Ind. 1.

WALES
County Councils (as at end May 1984)

Clwyd.......Lab. 28, Ind. 21, C. 13, L. 3, S.D.P. 1.
Dyfed ....Ind. 39, Lab. 29, L. 5, P.C. 5, R.A. 1, (1 Vac.).
Gwent ....Lab. 65, C. 12, L. 1.
Gwynedd ....N.P. 45, P.C. 8, L. 5, Lab. 5, C. 2, A. 1.
Mid Glam. . . . Lab. 64, P.C. 7, Ind. 4, C. 3, L. 2, R.A. 2, Com. 1, Others 2.

Powys.......N.P. 39, Ind. 6, Lab. 4, L. 2, C. 1, S.D.P. 1.
S. Glam. .....Lab. 41, C. 35, L. 2, A. 1, P.C. 1.
W. Glam. ....Lab. 56, C. 10, Ind. 1, Ind. Lab. 1, N.P. 1, R.A. 1.

District Councils (as at end May 1984)

Aberconwy ..... N.P. 20, C. 11, A. 8, Lab. 2.
Afan .... Lab. 25, R.A. 6.
Alyn & Deeside.. Lab. 23, C. 13, A. 4, Ind. 4, R.A. 1.
Arfon .... Ind. 15, Lab. 12, P.C. 11, L. 2.
Blaenau Gwent.. Lab. 39, Ind. 3, P.C. 2, R.A. 2, C. 1,
    Ind. 1, Ind. Lab. 1, L. 1.
Brecknock ...... Ind. 32, Lab. 16, L. 1, P.C. 1, (1
    Vac.).
Cardiff .... C. 34, Lab. 26, A. 4, Ind. 1.
Carmarthen..... Ind. 28, Lab. 6, L. 2.
Ceredigion...... Ind. 28, L. 7, A. 3, Lab. 2, P.C. 2,
    S.D.P. 1.
Colwyn .... N.P. 13, L. 12, C. 6, Ind. C. 1, Lab.
    1, R.A. 1.
Cynon Valley ... Lab. 28, P.C. 6, Com. 1, Ind. 1,
    Others 2.
Delyn .... Lab. 18, Ind. 14, L. 3, C. 2, P.C. 2,
    N.P. 1.
Dinefwr .... Lab. 14, Ind. 10, P.C. 4, Ind. Lab. 2,
    N.P. 2.
Dwyfor .... P.C. 3, Others 26.
Glyndwr .... Ind. 31, Lab. 2.
Islwyn .... Lab. 24, P.C. 8, Ind. 2, S.D.P. 1.
Llanelli .... Lab. 30, L. 2, Ind. 1.
Lliw Valley ..... Lab. 25, Ind. 2, Ind. Lab. 2, C. 1,
    P.C. 1, Other 1.

Meirionnydd .... P.C. 5, Lab. 3, Ind. 1, Others 30.
Merthyr Tydfil .. Lab. 30, R.A. 2, Ind. Lab. 1.
Monmouth ...... C. 26, Lab. 7, Ind. 4, A. 2.
Montgomery .... Ind. 5, P.C. 2, C. 1, L. 1, Lab. 1,
    Others 39.
Neath .... Lab. 28, Ind. 2, PC. 2, A. 1, (1 Vac.).
Newport .... Lab. 35, C. 11, A. 1.
Ogwr .... Lab. 28, C. 19, Ind. 6, P.C. 2, L. 1,
    R.A. 1.
Preseli.......... Ind. 43, Lab. 1.
Radnor .... Ind. 32, (1 Vac.).
Rhondda........ Lab. 26, R.A. 4, P.C. 2, Ind. 1.
Rhuddlan .... N.P. 11, Ind. 10, C. 4, Lab. 4, A. 2,
    R.A. 1.
Rhymney Valley. Lab. 35, P.C. 8, Ind. 2, R.A. 2, A. 1.
S. Pembroke. ....N.P. 11, Lab. 4, Ind. 1, Others 13.
Swansea .... Lab. 31, C. 16, Ind. 2, A. 1, R.A. 1.
Taff-Ely .... Lab. 30, Ind. 6, P.C. 5, L. 3, R.A. 2,
    C. 1, (1 Vac.).
Torfaen......... Lab. 32, Ind. 8, Com. 1, C. 1, RA. 1.
Vale of
    Glamorgan.... C. 32, Lab. 10, Ind. 2, P.C. 2.
Wrexham Maelor Lab. 23, C. 6, Ind. 4, L. 3, P.C. 1,
    Others 8.
Ynys Môn ...... Ind. 41, Lab. 2, (2 Vac.).

SCOTLAND
Scottish Regional Councils (as at end May 1984)

Borders ..... Ind. 13, C. 8, A. 2.
Central ...... Lab. 22, S.N.P. 5, C. 4, Ind. 2, A. 1.
Dumfries &   N.P. 12, Ind. 10, C. 4, Lab. 4, S.N.P. 3,
    Galloway ..   A. 2.
Fife .... Lab. 27, C. 9, A. 5, Ind. 2, Com. 1, SNP.
    1.
Grampian ... C. 26, Lab. 15, A. 6, S.N.P. 4, Ind. 2, (1
    Vac.).
Highland .... Ind. 16, Lab. 5, C. 2, L. 2, S.N.P. 2,
    Others 24, (1 Vac.).

Lothian ..... Lab. 22, C. 21, A. 3, Ind. 1, S.N.P. 1, (1
    Vac.).
Orkney ..... N.P. 24.
Shetland .... Ind. 22, Lab. 3.
Strathclyde .. Lab. 79, C. 15, A. 4, S.N.P. 3, Ind. 2.
Tayside ..... C. 27, Lab. 13, S.N.P. 4, Ind. 2.
Western Isles N.P. 30.

Scottish District Councils (as at end May 1984)

Aberdeen .... Lab. 28, A. 14, C. 8.
Angus .... S.N.P. 11, C. 8, Ind. 2.
Annandale
    & Eskdale ..... Ind. 9, A. 4, N.P. 3.
Argyll & Bute ... Ind. 12, C. 3, S.N.P. 1, Others 10.
Badenoch and
    Strathspey .... Ind. 6, N.P. 4, S.N.P. 1.
Banff & Buchan .Ind. 6, N.P. 6, S.N.P. 5, C. 1.
Bearsden and
    Milngavie .... C. 6, A. 2, Ind. 1, Lab. 1.
Berwickshire ... C. 8, Ind. 3, S.D.P. 1.
Caithness .... Ind. 15, L. 1.
Clackmannan ... Lab. 9, S.N.P. 2, C. 1.
Clydebank ...... Lab. 11, C. 1.
Clydedale ...... Lab. 16, Ind. 4, S.N.P. 3, Ind. Lab. 1,
    Others 2.
Cumbernauld
    & Kilsyth ..... Lab. 8, S.N.P. 4.
Cumnock &
    Doon Valley ... Lab. 10.
Cunn'ghame .... Lab. 23, C. 5, N.P. 2.
Dumbarton ..... Lab. 11, C. 2, A. 1, Ind. 1, N.P. 1.
Dundee .... Lab. 25, C. 15, A. 2, S.N.P. 2.
Dunfermline .... Lab. 24, A. 6, C. 2, Com. 1, SNP. 1.
East Kilbride .... Lab. 14, C. 2.
East Lothian .... Lab. 11, C. 6.
Eastwood .... C. 10, R.A.2.
Edinburgh ..... Lab. 34, C. 22, A.4, SNP. 2.
Ettrick and
    Lauderdale ... Ind. 13, Lab. 2, C. 1
Falkirk .... Lab. 24, SNP. 7, C. 2, Ind. 2, (1 Vac).
Glasgow .... Lab. 59, C. 5, A. 2.
Gordon .... Ind. 7, C. 3, L. 2.

Hamilton .... Lab. 17, A. 2, C. 1.
Inverclyde ...... Lab. 11, A. 9.
Inverness .... Ind. 18, Lab. 8, L. 2.
Kilmarnock and
    Loudoun...... Lab. 14, C. 3, S.N.P. 1.
Kincardine and
    Deeside .... Ind. 7, C. 3, L. 1, S.N.P. 1.
Kirkcaldy ...... Lab. 30, A. 3, C. 3, Ind. 2, R.A. 1, (1
    Vac.).
Kyle & Carrick .. Lab. 12, C. 11, Others 2.
Lochaber .... Ind. 8, Lab, 5, Ind. Lab. 2.
Midlothian ..... Lab. 14, A. 1.
Monklands ..... Lab. 18, C. 2.
Moray .... N.P. 10, Ind. 5, S.N.P. 2, Lab. 1.
Motherwell ..... Lab. 24, C. 2, SNP. 2, Com. 1, NP. 1.
Nairn .... Ind. 9, Lab. 1.
Nithsdale .... Ind. 10, S.N.P. 7, Lab. 6, C. 3, Ind.
    Lab. 1, N.P. 1.
N.-E. Fife .... A. 10, C. 6, Ind. 2.
Perth & Kinross .C. 14, Lab. 6, A. 4, Ind. 4, SNP. 1.
Renfrew .... Lab. 35, C. 5, S.N.P. 3, A. 2.
Ross &
    Cromarty ..... N.P. 15, Ind. 4, Lab. 2, C. 1.
Roxburgh .... Ind. 6, C. 5, A. 4, Others 1.
Skye & Lochalsh .Ind. 10, A. 1.
Stewartry ...... N.P. 9, Ind. 3.
Stirling......... Lab. 11, C. 8, Ind. 1.
Strathkelvin .... Lab. 11, C. 4.
Sutherland ..... N.P. 14.
Tweeddale ..... . Ind. 10.
West Lothian ... Lab. 19, Ind. 3, S.N.P. 2.
Wigtown .... N.P. 13, S.N.P. 1.

POLICE AUTHORITIES IN THE UNITED KINGDOM

POLICE FORCE	HEADQUARTERS	CHIEF CONSTABLE	CHAIRMAN OF POLICE AUTHORITY/COMMITTEE
England			
Avon and Somerset	Bristol	R. Broome, O.B.E., Q.P.M.	T. E. Turvey
Bedfordshire	Bedford	A. K. Sloan, Q.P.M.	F. S. Lester
Cambridgeshire	Huntingdon	I. Kane, Q.P.M.	Mrs. M. J. Shaw, O.B.E.
Cheshire	Chester	D. J. Graham, Q.P.M.	J. H. Collins, O.B.E.
Cleveland	Middlesbrough	C. Payne, Q.P.M.	E. A. Dickinson, M.B.E.
Cumbria	Penrith	B. D. K. Price, Q.P.M.	J. H. Duffield
Derbyshire	Ripley	A. Parrish	H. Lowe
Devon and Cornwall	Exeter	D. Elliott, Q.P.M.	A. L. Goodrich, O.B.E.
Dorset	Dorchester	B. H. Weight, Q.P.M.	Maj. Gen. H. M. G. Bond
Durham	Durham	E. G. Boothby, Q.P.M.	J. McCallum
Essex	Chelmsford	R. S. Bunyard, Q.P.M.	G. C. Waterer, M.B.E.
Gloucestershire	Cheltenham	L. A. G. Soper, Q.P.M.	A. N. C. Ussher
Hampshire (*incl. I. of W.*)	Winchester	J. Duke, Q.P.M.	Capt. M. P. R. Boyle
Hertfordshire	Welwyn Garden City	T. A. Morris	Maj. A. J. Hughes, M.C., T.D.
Humberside	Kingston upon Hull	D. Hall, C.B.E., Q.P.M.	C. Brady
Kent	Maidstone	F. L. Jordan, Q.P.M.	J. A. Spence
Lancashire	Preston	R. B. Johnson, Q.P.M.	J. Entwhistle
Leicestershire	Leicester	A. Goodson, O.B.E., Q.P.M.	The Duke of Rutland, C.B.E.
Lincolnshire	Lincoln	S. W. Crump	C. R. H. Bennett
Greater Manchester	Manchester 16	C. J. Anderton, C.B.E., Q.P.M.	Mrs. G. Cox
Merseyside	Liverpool 69	K. G. Oxford, C.B.E., Q.P.M.	Mrs. M. B. Simey
Norfolk	Norwich	G. Charlton, Q.P.M.	Capt. J. Peel
Northamptonshire	Northampton	M. Buck, O.B.E., Q.P.M.	C. E. Grimmer, B.E.M.
Northumbria	Newcastle upon Tyne	S. E. Bailey, C.B.E., Q.P.M.	J. Hornsby
Nottinghamshire	Nottingham	C. McLachlan, Q.P.M.	F. Taylor
Staffordshire	Stafford	C. H. Kelly, Q.P.M.	H. Brown
Suffolk	Ipswich	S. L. Whiteley, C.B.E., Q.P.M.	Lt. Col. J. M. H. R. Tomkin, M.C.
Surrey	Guildford	B. Hayes	A. J. Blowers
Sussex	Lewes	R. Birch, Q.P.M.	J. Chatfield, C.B.E.
Thames Valley	Oxford	P. M. Imbert, Q.P.M.	R. J. Clibbon
Warwickshire	Warwick	P. Joslin, Q.P.M.	Maj. S. W. T. Birch, T.D.
West Mercia	Worcester	R. W. Cozens, Q.P.M.	J. W. C. Bowers
West Midlands	Birmingham 4	Sir Philip Knights, C.B.E., Q.P.M.	E. Shore
Wiltshire	Devizes	D. Smith, O.B.E., Q.P.M.	Lt. Col. D. B. W. Jarvis, D.F.C.
Yorkshire, North	Northallerton	K. Henshaw, Q.P.M.	C. Thorpe
Yorkshire, South	Sheffield	P. Wright, O.B.E.	G. H. Moores
Yorkshire, West	Wakefield	C. Sampson, Q.P.M.	R. Darrington
Wales			
Dyfed-Powys	Carmarthen	R. B. Thomas, O.B.E., Q.P.M.	W. V. Morris
Gwent	Cwmbran	J. C. Over, Q.P.M.	E. V. Ovens
North Wales	Colwyn Bay	D. Owen, Q.P.M.	W. R. Webb
South Wales	Bridgend	D. A. East, Q.P.M.	P. Squire, C.B.E.
Scotland			
Central Scotland	Stirling	I. T. Oliver, Q.P.M.	W. Douglas
Dumfries and Galloway	Dumfries	J. M. Boyd, Q.P.M.	Rev. R. Hamill
Fife	Kirkcaldy	W. Moodie	W. G. Anderson
Grampian	Aberdeen	A. Lynn, Q.P.M.	J. A. S. McPherson, C.B.E.
Lothian and Borders	Edinburgh 4	W. G. M. Sutherland, Q.P.M.	B. A. Meek, O.B.E.
Northern	Inverness	D. B. Henderson, Q.P.M.	J. S. Munro
Strathclyde	Glasgow 2	Sir Patrick Hamill, Q.P.M.	J. Irvine
Tayside	Dundee	J. Bowman, Q.P.M.	W. Johnston, M.B.E.
Northern Ireland			
Royal Ulster Constabulary	Belfast 5	Sir John Hermon, O.B.E.	Sir Myles Humphreys
Islands			
Isle of Man	Douglas	F. Weedon, Q.P.M.	E. M. Ward, B.E.M.
States of Jersey	St. Helier	†D. Parkinson	J. W. Ellis
Guernsey	St. Peter Port	†A. D. G. Wallen, M.B.E.	M. W. Torode

† Chief Officer
LONDON.—City of London Police and Metropolitan Police Area (*see* pages 460–1).

The Kingdom of England

Position and Extent.—The Kingdom of England lies between 55° 46′ and 49° 57′ 30″ N. latitude (from the mouth of the Tweed to the Lizard), and between 1° 46′ E. and 5° 43′ W. (from Lowestoft to Land's End). England is bounded on the north by the Cheviot Hills; on the south by the English Channel, on the east by the Straits of Dover (Pas de Calais) and the North Sea; and on the West by the Atlantic Ocean, Wales and the Irish Sea.

It has a total area of 50,362 sq. miles (land 50,081; inland water 281). The population (1981 Census) was 46,362,836 (males 22,520,723; females 23,842,113). The average density of the population in 1981 was 915 per square mile.

Relief.—There is a marked division between the upland and lowland areas of England. In the extreme north the Cheviot Hills (highest point, *The Cheviot*, 2,674 ft.) form a natural boundary with the Kingdom of Scotland. Running south from the Cheviots, though divided from them by the Tyne Gap, is the Pennine range (highest point, *Cross Fell*, 2,930 ft.), the main orological feature of the country. The Pennines culminate in the Peak District of Derbyshire (*Kinder Scout*, 2,088 ft.). West of the Pennines are the Cumbrian Mountains, which include *Scafell Pike* (3,210 ft.), the highest peak in England, and to the east are the Yorkshire Moors, their highest point being *Urra Moor* (1,490 ft.).

In the west, the foothills of the Welsh mountains extend into the bordering English counties of Shropshire (the *Wrekin*, 1,334 ft.; *Long Mynd*, 1,694 ft.) and Hereford and Worcester (the Malvern Hills—*Worcestershire Beacon*, 1,394 ft.). Extensive areas of high land and moorland are also to be found in the southwestern peninsular formed by Somerset, Devon and Cornwall: principally Exmoor (*Dunkery Beacon*, 1,704 ft.), Dartmoor (*High Willhays*, 2,038 ft.) and Bodmin Moor (*Brown Willy*, 1,377 ft.). Ranges of low, undulating hills run across the south of the country, including the Cotswolds in the Midlands and southwest, the Chilterns to the north of Greater London, and the North (Kent) and South (Sussex) Downs of the south-east coastal areas.

The lowlands of England lie in the Vale of York, East Anglia and the area around the Wash, the lowest lying being the Cambridgeshire Fens in the valleys of the Great Ouse and the River Nene, which are below sea-level in places; since the 17th century extensive drainage has brought much of the Fens under cultivation. The North Sea coast between the Thames and the Humber, low-lying and formed of sand and shingle for the most part, is subject to erosion and defences against further incursion have been built along many stretches.

Hydrography.—The *Severn* is the longest river in Great Britain, rising in the north-eastern slopes of Plinlimmon (Wales) and entering England in Shropshire with a total length of 220 miles from its source to its outflow into the Bristol Channel, where it receives on the east the Bristol Avon, and on the west the Wye, its other tributaries being the Vrynwy, Tern, Stour, Teme and Upper (or Warwickshire) Avon. The Severn is tidal below Gloucester, and a high bore or tidal wave sometimes reverses the flow as high as Tewkesbury (13½ miles above Gloucester). The scenery of the greater part of the river is very picturesque and beautiful, and the Severn is a noted salmon river, some of its tributaries being famous for trout. Navigation is assisted by the Gloucester and Berkeley Ship Canal (16¼ miles), which admits vessels of 350 tons to Gloucester. The *Severn Tunnel*, begun

in 1873 and completed in 1886 (at a cost of £2,000,000) after many difficulties from flooding, is 4 miles 628 yards in length (of which 2¼ miles are under the river). The Severn road bridge between Haysgate, Gwent, and Almondsbury, Glos., with a centre span of 3,240 ft. was opened in 1966.

The longest river wholly in England is the *Thames*, with a total length of 215 miles from its source in the Cotswold hills to the Nore, and is navigable by ocean-going ships to London Bridge. The Thames is tidal to Teddington (69 miles from its mouth) and forms county boundaries almost throughout its course; on its banks are situated London, Windsor Castle, the home of the Sovereign, Eton College, the first of the public schools, and Oxford, the oldest university in the kingdom.

Of the remaining English rivers those flowing into the North Sea are the Tyne, Wear, Tees, Ouse and Trent from the Pennine Range, the Great Ouse (160 miles) from Northamptonshire, and the Orwell and Stour from the hills of East Anglia. Flowing into the English Channel are the Sussex Ouse from the Weald, the Itchen from the Hampshire Hills, and the Axe, Teign, Dart, Tamar and Exe from the Devonian Hills; and flowing into the Irish Sea are the Mersey, Ribble and Eden from the western slopes of the Pennines and the Derwent from the Cumbrian Mountains. The *English Lakes*, noteworthy for their picturesque scenery and poetic associations, lie in Cumbria, the largest being Windermere (10 miles long), Ullswater and Derwentwater.

Islands.—The *Isle of Wight* is separated from Hampshire by the Solent; total area 147 sq. miles, population about 120,400. The climate is mild and healthy, making the island a popular holiday resort. Capital, Newport, at the head of the estuary of the Medina, Cowes (at the mouth) being the chief port; other centres are Ryde, Sandown, Shanklin, Ventnor, Freshwater, Yarmouth, Totland Bay, Seaview and Bembridge.

Lundy (= Island) 11 miles N.W. off Hartland Point, Devon, is about 2 miles long and about ½ mile broad (average), with a total area of about 1,116 acres, and a population of about 20; it became the property of the National Trust in 1969 and is now principally a bird sanctuary.

(*See also* The Isles of Scilly, p. 692.)

Climate.—England has a generally mild and temperate climate. Because of the prevailing south-westerly winds, the weather day to day is variable, being affected mainly by depressions moving eastwards across the Atlantic Ocean. This maritime influence means that the west of the country tends to experience wetter but also milder weather than the east. Rainfall also increases with altitude, the mountainous areas of the north and west having more rain than the lowlands of the south and east. Rain is fairly well-distributed throughout the year in all areas but, on average, the driest months are March to June, and the wettest September to January.

The mean annual temperature reduced to sea-level varies from 11°C in the south-west to 9°C near Berwick-on-Tweed. In winter, temperatures tend to be higher in the south and west than in the east, while the warmest in summer are the south and inland areas. Latitude for latitude the mean annual temperature is lower in the east; the decrease of mean temperature with height is about 0·6°C per 100 metres.

EARLY INHABITANTS

Prehistoric Man.—Archaeological evidence suggests that England has been inhabited since at least the Palaeolithic period, though the extent of the various Palaeolithic cultures was dependent upon the degree of glaciation. The succeeding Neolithic and Bronze Age cultures have left abundant remains throughout the country, the best-known of these being the henges and stone circles of Stonehenge (10 miles north of Salisbury, Wilts.) and Avebury (Wilts.), both of which are believed to have been of religious significance. In the latter part of the Bronze Age the *Goidels*, a people of Celtic race, and in the Iron Age other Celtic races of *Brythons* and *Belgae*, invaded the country and brought with them Celtic civilization and dialects, place names in England bearing witness to the spread of the invasion over the whole kingdom.

The Roman Conquest.—The Roman conquest of Gaul (57–50 B.C.) brought Britain into close contact with Roman civilization, but although Julius Cæsar raided the south of Britain in 55 B.C., and 54 B.C., conquest was not undertaken until nearly 100 years later. In A.D. 42 the Emperor Claudius dispatched Aulus Plautius, with a well-equipped force of 40,000, and himself followed with reinforcements in the same year. Success was delayed by the resistance of *Caratacus* (Caractacus), the British leader from A.D. 48–51, who was finally captured and sent to Rome, and by a great revolt in A.D. 61 led by *Boudicca* (Boadicea), Queen of the Iceni; but the south of Britain was secured by A.D. 70, and Wales and the area north to the Tyne by about A.D. 80.

In A.D. 122, the Emperor Hadrian visited Britain and built a continuous rampart, since known as *Hadrian's Wall*, from Wallsend to Bowness (Tyne to Solway). The work was entrusted by the Emperor Hadrian to Aulus Platorius Nepos, legate of Britain from 122 to 126, and it formed the northern frontier of the Roman Empire in the west for three and a half centuries.

The Romans administered Britain as a Province under a Governor, with a well-defined system of local government, each Roman municipality ruling itself and surrounding territory, while London was the centre of the road system and the seat of the financial officials of the Province of Britain. Colchester, Lincoln, York, Gloucester and St. Albans stand on the sites of five Roman municipalities, and Wroxeter, Caerleon, Chester, Lincoln and York were at various times the sites of legionary fortresses. Well-preserved Roman towns have been uncovered at (or near) *Silchester* (Calleva Atrebatum), 10 miles south of Reading, *Wroxeter* (Viroconium), near Shrewsbury, and *St. Albans* (Verulamium) in Hertfordshire.

Four main groups of roads radiated from London, and a fifth (the Fosse) ran obliquely from Lincoln through Leicester, Cirencester and Bath to Exeter. Of the four groups radiating from London one ran S.E. to Canterbury and the coast of Kent, a second to Silchester and thence to parts of Western Britain and South Wales, a third (later known as *Watling Street*) ran through Verulamium to Chester, with various branches, and the fourth reached Colchester, Lincoln, York and the eastern counties.

In the 4th century Britain was subject to raids along the east coast by Saxon pirates, which led to the establishment of a system of coast defence from the Wash to Southampton Water, with forts at Brancaster, Burgh Castle (Yarmouth), Walton (Felixstowe), Bradwell, Reculver, Richborough, Dover, Lympne, Pevensey and Porchester (Portsmouth). The Irish (Scoti) and Picts in the north were also becoming more aggressive; from about A.D. 350 incursions became more frequent and more formidable. As the Roman Empire came under attack increasingly towards the end of the 4th century many troops were removed from Britain for service in other parts of the Empire. The island was cut off from Rome by the Teutonic conquest of Gaul early in the 5th century, and with the withdrawal of the last Roman garrison in A.D. 442, the Romano-British were left to themselves.

According to legend, the British King *Vortigern* called in the Saxons to defend him against the Picts, the Saxon chieftains being *Hengist* and *Horsa*, who landed at Ebbsfleet, Kent, and established themselves in the Isle of Thanet; but the events during the 150 years between the final break with Rome and the re-establishment of Christianity are unclear. However, it would appear that in the course of this period the raids turned into large-scale settlement by invaders traditionally known as Angles (England north of the Wash and East Anglia), Saxons (Essex and southern England) and Jutes (Kent and the Weald), which pushed the Romano-British into the mountainous areas of the north and west, Celtic culture outside Wales and Cornwall surviving only in topographical names. Various kingdoms were established at this time which attempted to claim overlordship of the whole country, hegemony finally being achieved by *Wessex* (capital, Winchester) in the 9th century. This century also saw the beginning of raids by the Vikings (Danes), which were resisted by *Alfred the Great* (871–899), the greatest of the Wessex kings, who fixed a limit to the advance of Danish settlement by the Treaty of Wedmore (878), giving them the area north and east of Watling Street, on condition they adopt Christianity.

In the 10th century the Kings of Wessex recovered the whole of England from the Danes, but subsequent rulers were unable to resist a second wave of invaders. England paid tribute (*Danegeld*) for many years, and was invaded in 1013 by the Danes and ruled by Danish Kings from 1016 until 1042, when Edward the Confessor was recalled from exile in Normandy. In 1066 Harold Godwineson (brother-in-law of Edward and son of Earl Godwin of Wessex) was chosen King of England, but after defeating (at Stamford Bridge, Yorkshire, Sept. 25) an invading army under Harald Hadraada, King of Norway (aided by Harold Godwineson's younger brother, the outlawed Earl Tostig of Northumbria), he was himself defeated at the *Battle of Hastings* on Oct. 14, 1066, and the Norman Conquest secured the throne of England for Duke William of Normandy, a cousin of Edward the Confessor.

Christianity reached the Roman province of Britain from Gaul in the 3rd century (or possibly earlier), *Alban*, traditionally Britain's first martyr, being put to death as a Christian during the persecution of Diocletian (June 22, 303), at his native town Verulamium; and the Bishops of Londinium, Eboracum (York), and Lindum (Lincoln) attended the Council of Arles in 314. However, the Anglo-Saxon invasions submerged the Christian religion in England until the 6th century when conversion was undertaken in the north from 563 by Celtic missionaries from Ireland led by St. Columba, and in the south by a mission sent from Rome in 597 which was led by St. Augustine, who became the first archbishop of Canterbury. England appears to have been converted again by the end of the 7th century and followed, after the Council of Whitby in 663, the practices of the Roman Church, which brought the country into the mainstream of European thought and culture.

AREA AND POPULATION OF ENGLISH COUNTIES

County	Administrative Headquarters	Area (*hectares*)	Population	Actual Rateable Value per head§	Maximum Rates Levied
				£	p.
Avon	Avon House, The Hay-market, Bristol	134,614	934,000	132·61	179·00
Bedfordshire......	*Bedford	123,460	514,500	166·48	150·10
Berkshire	†Reading	125,890	715,400	178·56	142·80
Buckinghamshire .	*Aylesbury	188,284	599,400	168·06	139·50
Cambridgeshire ...	†Cambridge	340,892	611,095	141·84	142·00
Cheshire	*Chester	232,846	948,300	146·06	169·00
Cleveland	Municipal Buildings, Middlesbrough	58,308	563,900	140·39	190·00
Cornwall	*Truro	354,792‡	433,700	109·17	138·70
Cumbria..........	The Courts, Carlisle	681,012	482,500	101·68	157·00
Derbyshire	County Offices, Matlock	263,094	912,500	117·26	176·50
Devon............	*Exeter	671,088	970,200	118·60	141·25
Dorset	*Dorchester	265,375	614,200	141·12	142·00
Durham	*Durham	243,592	606,150	97·42	154·00
Essex	*Chelmsford	367,192	1,498,600	159·10	141·00
Gloucestershire ...	†Gloucester	264,266	508,400	130·34	141·48
Hampshire	The Castle, Winchester	377,698	1,497,000	143·30	138·50
Hereford and Worcester	*Worcester	392,650	643,000	136·28	141·00
Hertfordshire.....	*Hertford	163,415	970,400	178·73	148·10
Humberside	*Beverley, N. Humberside	351,212	857,500	115·87	163·00
Kent.............	*Maidstone	373,060	1,494,200	127·92	137·49
Lancashire	*Preston	306,346	1,388,300	104·73	144·50
Leicestershire	*Leicester	255,293	865,800	134·13	139·00
Lincolnshire......	County Offices, Lincoln	591,485	556,900	114·04	137·00
Greater London ...	*S.E.1.	157,946	6,745,891	297·26	34·70
Greater Manchester.....	*Piccadilly Gardens, Manchester	128,674	2,595,700	128·89	48·00
Merseyside	Metropolitan House, Old Hall Street, Liverpool	65,202	1,489,200	131·49	65·00
Norfolk	*Norwich	536,776	713,400	130·68	135·00
Northamptonshire	*Northampton	236,737	542,930	137·71	145·00
Northumberland ..	*Morpeth	503,165	301,400	111·26	166·00
Nottinghamshire..	*Nottingham	216,365	991,400	127·66	171·50
Oxfordshire	*Oxford	260,782	554,600	150·81	140·00
Shropshire	†Shrewsbury	349,014	386,600	117·06	134·00
Somerset	*Taunton	345,094	437,400	119·00	143·00
Staffordshire	County Buildings, Stafford	271,615	1,020,500	124·54	154·00
Suffolk	*Ipswich	379,663	618,800	129·75	144·00
Surrey	*Kingston-upon-Thames	167,924	1,023,300	172·03	145·40
Sussex, East	Pelham House, St. Andrew's Lane, Lewes	179,512	677,600	149·63	140·60
Sussex, West......	*Chichester	198,935	681,600	149·21	131·00
Tyne and Wear ...	Sandyford House, Archbold Terrace, Newcastle	54,006	1,142,515	113·37	54·50
Warwickshire	†Warwick	198,053	480,500	143·67	143·30
West Midlands	*Lancaster Circus, Birmingham	89,943	2,654,000	156·76	43·60
Wight, Isle of	*Newport, I.O.W.	38,066	120,400	115·19	146·00
Wiltshire.........	*Trowbridge	348,070	532,800	116·03	136·00
Yorkshire, North .	*Northallerton	830,865	683,000	113·47	139·00
Yorkshire, South..	*Barnsley	156,049	1,311,600	106·82	83·30
Yorkshire, West...	*Wakefield	203,912	2,065,000	105·62	47·00

* County Hall. † Shire Hall. ‡ Excluding Isles of Scilly. § Actual Rateable Value per head at April 1, 1983.

ENGLISH COUNTIES AND SHIRES

LORD LIEUTENANTS AND HIGH SHERIFFS

County or Shire	Lord Lieutenant	*High Sheriff, 1984–85
Avon	Sir John Wills, Bt., T.D.	C. W. Thomas, C.B.E.
Bedfordshire	Lt. Col. H. C. Hanbury, M.V.O., M.C.	S. C. Y. Farmbrough
Berkshire	Col. The Hon. G. W. N. Palmer, O.B.E., T.D.	D. J. Simonds
Buckinghamshire	Cdr. The Hon. J. Tapling Fremantle	Maj. G. A. G. Selby-Lowndes
Cambridgeshire	Sir Peter Proby, Bt.	Brig. A. N. Breitmeyer
Cheshire	The Rt. Hon. The Viscount Leverhulme, T.D.	R. C. Roundell
Cleveland	The Rt. Hon. The Lord Gisborough	R. N. Spark
Cornwall	The Rt. Hon. The Viscount Falmouth	R. D. Lyle
Cumbria	Sir Charles Graham, Bt.	E. P. Ecroyd
Derbyshire	Col. P. Hilton, M.C.	Maj. C. L. Stephenson, T.D.
Devon	Lt. Col. The Rt. Hon. The Earl of Morley	A. M. Sutton-Scott-Tucker
Dorset	The Rt. Hon. The Lord Digby	M. Roper
Durham	The Rt. Hon. The Lord Barnard, T.D.	J. W. Snowdon
Essex	Adm. Sir Andrew Lewis, K.C.B.	P. B. Lake, T.D.
Gloucestershire	Col. M. St. J. V. Gibbs, C.B., D.S.O., T.D.	J. A. B. Baillie-Hamilton
Hampshire	Lt. Col. Sir James Scott, Bt.	Maj. H. L. St. V. Rose
Hereford and Worcester	Capt. T. R. Dunne	Lt. Col. P. C. Britten (Rtd)
Hertfordshire	Maj.-Gen. Sir George Burns, K.C.V.O., C.B., D.S.O., O.B.E., M.C.	R. M. Abel Smith
Humberside	R. A. Bethell	J. G. Gordon, T.D.
Kent	R. Leigh-Pemberton	R. J. Corben
Lancashire	S. Towneley	Surgeon Lt.-Cdr. P. J. J. Wren, V.R.D., R.N.R
Leicestershire	Col. R. A. St. G. Martin, O.B.E.	A. W. Fenwick
Lincolnshire	H. N. Nevile	Lt. A. J. Massingberd-Mundy, R.N. (Rtd)
Greater London	The Baroness Phillips	Sir Arthur Taylor
Greater Manchester	Sir William Downward	B. Hodgkiss
Merseyside	Wing Cmdr. K. M. Stoddart, A.E.	Lt. Col. C. H. Elston, T.D.
Norfolk	T. Colman	Capt. J. S. Peel, M.C.
Northamptonshire	J. L. Lowther, C.B.E.	W. D. Morton
Northumberland	The Rt. Hon. The Viscount Ridley, T.D.	L. G. Allgood
Nottinghamshire	Sir Gordon Hobday	Col. J. M. A. Gunn, O.B.E., T.D.
Oxfordshire	Sir Ashley Ponsonby, Bt., M.C.	Miss I. J. Hutchinson
Shropshire	J. R. S. Dugdale	C. R. Thompson
Somerset	Lt. Col. G. W. F. Luttrell, M.C.	C. E. B. Clive-Ponsonby-Fane
Staffordshire	Sir Arthur Bryan	J. H. Leigh
Suffolk	Sir Joshua Rowley, Bt.	N. Longe
Surrey	The Rt. Hon. The Lord Hamilton of Dalzell, K.C.V.O., M.C.	Sir Richard Meyjes
Sussex, East	The Most Hon. The Marquess of Abergavenny, K.G., O.B.E.	Capt. S. R. Le H. Lombard-Hobson, C.V.O., O.B.E., R.N.
Sussex, West	Lavinia, Duchess of Norfolk, C.B.E.	Maj. Gen. J. C. Cowley, C.B.
Tyne and Wear	Sir Ralph Carr-Ellison, T.D.	D. C. Souter, V.R.D.
Warwickshire	C. M. T. Smith-Ryland	H. L. Gray-Cheape
West Midlands	The Rt. Hon. The Earl of Aylesford	D. M. P. Lea
Wight, Isle of	Sir John Nicholson, Bt., K.B.E.	Mrs. D. M. C. Grey
Wiltshire	Col. H. Brassey, O.B.E., M.C.	Maj. Gen. J. H. S. Bowring, C.B., O.B.E., M.C.
Yorkshire, North	The Most Hon. The Marquess of Normanby, C.B.E.	A. T. Preston
Yorkshire, South	G. F. Young, C.B.E.	R. N. Horne
Yorkshire, West	Sir William Bulmer	S. A. Barr

* High Sheriffs are nominated by the Queen on November 12 and come into office after Hilary Term.

ENGLISH COUNTIES AND SHIRES

CHIEF EXECUTIVES, TREASURERS AND CHAIRMEN OF COUNTY COUNCILS

County or Shire	Chief Executive	County Treasurer	Chairman of C.C.
Avon	N. J. L. Pearce	D. G. Morgan	T. E. Turvey
Bedfordshire........	J. W. Elven	V. F. Phillips	A. C. Chapman
Berkshire	R. W. Gash	M. C. Beasley	I. E. Morgan
Buckinghamshire ...	M. White	E. Deung	R. Parker-Jervis
Cambridgeshire	J. K. Barratt	J. E. Barton	R. S. James
Cheshire	R. G. Wendt	J. E. H. Whiteoak	B. S. Jeuda
Cleveland	A. J. Hodgkinson†	B. Stevenson	Mrs. I. M. Cole
Cornwall	G. K. Burgess	C. E. J. Cainey	F. J. Williams
Cumbria............	T. J. R. Whitfield	J. R. Ford	E. A. Martlew
Derbyshire	E. Cobb*	E. Cobb	J. J. Carty
Devon..............	D. D. Macklin	B. J. Weston	G. E. H. Creber, C.B.E.
Dorset	K. A. Abel, C.B.E.	D. M. Gasson	Air Cmmdre. K. J. McIntyre, C.B., C.B.E.
Durham	P. Dawson	K. W. Smith	J. McCallum
Essex	R. W. Adcock	E. A. Twelvetree	R. M. Williams
Gloucestershire	J. V. Miller	T. N. Hobson	H. W. G. Elwes
Hampshire	L. K. Robinson, C.B.E.	J. E. Scotford	L. S. White, M.B.E., T.D.
Hereford and Worcester	G. A. Price	J. Rocke	Mrs. M. J. T. Hadley, O.B.E.
Hertfordshire	M. J. Le Fleming	K. S. Cliff	F. J. Cogan
Humberside	K. J. Bridge	J. A. Parkes	G. V. Chapman, B.E.M.
Kent	W. U. Jackson	W. B. Taylor	Wing Cdr. R. H. C. Powling
Lancashire	B. Hill	W. O. Jolliffe	Mrs. L. J. Ellman
Leicestershire	S. Jones	R. Hale	Dr. P. Hill
Lincolnshire........	R. J. D. Procter	D. G. Barrett	F. L. Marshall
Greater London	Sir James Swaffield, C.B.E., R.D.	M. F. Stonefrost, C.B.E.	H. Hinds
Greater Manchester.......	G. A. Harrison	J. M. Marriott	H. Davies
Merseyside	R. F. O'Brien	D. F. Smith	B. Shaw
Norfolk	B. J. Capon	G. M. Ellis	Mrs. F. M. Roualle
Northamptonshire ..	A. J. Greenwell	J. Smith	Mrs. J. Green
Northumberland	W. H. Foakes	R. Wolstenholme	Mrs. E. W. Mitchell, O.B.E.
Nottinghamshire....	A. Sandford	G. S. Luff	W. J. Morris
Oxfordshire	A. T. Brown, C.B.E.	J. T. Vokins	Mrs. O. F. Gibbs
Shropshire	W. N. P. Jones	M. N. Davis	R. A. H. Lloyd, T.D.
Somerset	J. E. Whittaker	B. M. Tanner	W. R. Meadows
Staffordshire	B. A. Price	B. Smith	F. A. Cholerton, C.B.E.
Suffolk	C. W. Smith	C. Stephenson	Miss M. M. P. MacRae
Surrey	F. A. Stone	D. J. Thomas	J. Macfarlane
Sussex, East	R. M. Beechey	M. R. Hancock	R. E. Brown, O.B.E.
Sussex, West........	J. R. Hooley	B. E. Fieldhouse	C. S. Buckle
Tyne and Wear	J. J. Gardner	P. J. Smith	A. Potts
Warwickshire	J. W. Hayes	J. P. Hunt	Dr. J. W. Bland
West Midlands	J. D. Hender	K. E. Rose	V. E. Turton
Wight, Isle of	J. S. Horsnell	D. A. Tuck	P. G. Harris
Wiltshire...........	I. A. Browning	A. F. Gould	Capt. P. S. Beale, R.N.
Yorkshire, North ...	H. J. Evans	K. R. Housome	Lt. Col. M. J. B. Burnett, D.S.O.
Yorkshire, South....	J. C. Harris	D. B. Chynoweth	T. P. Concannon
Yorkshire, West.....	W. Miles	G. S. Pollard	St. J. Binns, M.B.E.

† Secretary.   * Director.

MUNICIPAL DIRECTORY OF ENGLAND

A list of METROPOLITAN BOROUGH AND CITY COUNCILS. Those accorded CITY status are in SMALL CAPITALS.

Metropolitan Boroughs	Population	Rateable Value 1984 £	Chief Executive	Mayor †Lord Mayor *Chairman 1984–85
GREATER MANCHESTER				
Bolton	260,500	28,668,542	K. P. Bounds	Mrs. B. A. Hurst
Bury	176,500	19,800,000	J. A. McDonald	Mrs. C. Ormrod
MANCHESTER	457,500	77,759,298	J. Hetherington	†H. Tucker
Oldham	220,600	23,425,157	C. Smith	J. K. Leyden
Rochdale	206,400	21,603,861	J. Towey	J. N. Angus
SALFORD	245,000	32,379,879	R. C. Rees	Mrs. J. Bryans
Stockport	289,400	39,323,496	A. L. Wilson	G. E. Lowe
Tameside	216,800	21,671,652	G. Mayall	J. G. Brierley
Trafford	218,700	39,515,757	R. M. C. Shields	Mrs. M. Hinchcliffe
Wigan	309,083	31,866,000	A. E. Hart	P. Hull
MERSEYSIDE				
Knowsley	171,100	21,805,989	R. Penn	G. S. Taylor
LIVERPOOL	497,300	°70,973,297	A. J. Stocks, C.B.E.	*H. Dalton
St. Helens	189,600	23,258,822	B. S. Lace	T. Chisnall
Sefton......................	299,800	36,984,954	J. P. McElroy	Mrs. J. Jessop
Wirral	338,500	42,831,101	C. D. Darley	M. J. Moore
SOUTH YORKSHIRE				
Barnsley	225,860	19,790,321	A. Bleasby	D. Baines
Doncaster	289,800	30,005,324	C. B. Jeynes	Mrs. N. Wilson
Rotherham	252,000	23,560,570	D. I. Shackleton	G. S. Etchells
SHEFFIELD	546,700	67,529,692	I. L. Podmore	†G. R. Munn
TYNE AND WEAR				
Gateshead	212,900	21,883,000	L. Elton	Mrs. M. Robson
NEWCASTLE UPON TYNE	283,000	42,779,801	C. T. Davies	†N. Stockdale
North Tyneside	197,000	21,385,442	E. B. Lincoln	S. Ingles
South Tyneside	159,867	15,794,612	F. Thompson	Mrs. C. Cox
Sunderland	298,000	28,336,291	G. P. Key	G. Elliott
WEST MIDLANDS				
BIRMINGHAM	1,011,000	165,215,000	T. Caulcott	†R. J. Hales
COVENTRY	314,000	44,542,846	R. Tarr	†W. Brandish
Dudley	301,100	44,725,779	J. F. Mulvehill	Mrs. L. Hingley
Sandwell	307,300	50,031,204	G. A. Hadley	J. G. Smith
Solihull	199,000	30,349,549	J. Scampion	Mrs. M. Harris
Walsall	265,300	39,567,512	A. V. Astling	J. M. Gavin
Wolverhampton...............	255,400	42,745,591	K. Williams	S. A. Ledsam
WEST YORKSHIRE				
BRADFORD	454,198	45,182,172	G. C. Moore	†Mrs. O. Messer
Calderdale..................	192,000	16,996,495	M. Ellison	J. Bradley, O.B.E.
Kirklees	377,100	33,013,640	(vacant)	S. Dawson
LEEDS	716,100	90,400,000	J. Rawnsley‡	†D. E. Gabb, O.B.E.
WAKEFIELD	312,100	33,670,063	J. G. Stanbury	Mrs. J. Beech

° 1983 figure. Rate for 1984 not yet set by the City Council.
‡ Chief Officer.

DISTRICT COUNCILS

A list of non-Metropolitan District Councils in England. Those accorded CITY status are in SMALL CAPITALS, those with Borough status are distinguished by having § prefixed.

District	Population	Rateable value 1984 £	Chief Executive (*Clerk)	Chairman 1984–85 (a) Mayor (b) Lord Mayor
Adur, West Sussex	58,300	8,502,000	Maj.-Gen. R. J. Buckland, C.B., M.B.E.	A. J. A. Merrick
Allerdale, Cumbria	94,244	9,111,637	A. C. Crane	W. P. Ralph
Alnwick, Northumberland	28,800	3,121,101	A. G. A. Groome	W. J. Mitchell
Amber Valley, Derbyshire......	109,100	12,084,140	J. Ragsdale	R. Jowett
Arun, West Sussex	120,200	16,936,429	J. V. Midgley	Mrs. G. M. Tullett
Ashfield, Nottinghamshire	106,000	10,560,307	S. Beedham	R. S. Chamberlain
§Ashford, Kent................	84,710	11,821,099	E. H. W. Mexter	(a) G. Fortescue

District	Population	Rateable value 1984 £	Chief Executive (* Clerk)	Chairman 1984–85 (a) Mayor (b) Lord Mayor
Aylesbury Vale, Bucks.	138,000	20,326,875	J. L. Guest	W. J. Hanson
Babergh, Suffolk	75,400	9,473,000	D. C. Bishop	A. C. Goodwin, M.B.E.
§Barrow in Furness, Cumbria ..	73,800	6,518,954	D. G. B. Lyon	(a) H. K. Gahan
Basildon, Essex	154,800	25,700,000	R. C. Mitchinson	D. G. Marks
§Basingstoke and Deane, Hants.	134,000	20,781,533	D. W. Pilkington	(a) R. B. Gaiger
Bassetlaw, Notts.	103,300	16,820,114	R. D. Blair	Mrs. M. McCarthy
BATH, Avon	84,200	11,275,832	D. C. Beeton	(a) A. J. Rhymes
§Berwick-upon-Tweed, Northumberland	26,400	3,181,981	J. Healy	(a) A. Easton
§Beverley, Humberside	107,400	12,244,858	W. J. H. Thomas	(a) Mrs. M. Weeks
Blaby, Leics.	77,100	9,344,615	J. E. Meakin	Mrs. J. A. Dixon
§Blackburn, Lancs.	142,800	13,826,000	C. H. Singleton, O.B.E.	(a) C. West
§Blackpool, Lancs.	147,000	18,820,583	I. B. Prosser	(a) C. Lowe
§Blyth Valley, Northumberland	78,000	7,294,792	P. W. Ferry	(a) R. A. Lee
§Bolsover, Derbys.	70,358	6,240,325	C. A. Tucker	Mrs. M. Braddon
§Boothferry, Humberside	61,600	5,761,887	J. W. Barber	W. Bray
§Boston, Lincs.	53,002	6,476,329	R. E. Coley	(a) T. W. North
§Bournemouth, Dorset	144,300	24,321,000	K. Lomas	(a) M. H. Filer
Bracknell, Berks.	85,900	14,948,777	A. J. Targett	T. G. Ainscough
Braintree, Essex	113,800	15,632,919	C. Daybell	J. W. Amies
Breckland, Norfolk	98,200	11,616,000	J. B. Heath	L. P. R. Brown
Brentwood, Essex	72,800	13,269,772	C. P. Sivell	D. E. Ramsey
Bridgnorth, Shropshire	50,200	5,992,197	G. C. Nutley	Mrs. R. E. J. Yeomans
§Brighton, East Sussex	150,500	25,321,926	R. G. Morgan	(a) J. C. Blackman
BRISTOL, Avon	399,600	60,115,000	P. M. McCarthy	(b) C. Draper
Broadland, Norfolk	98,900	10,507,510	B. R. Grayling	E. W. Trafford
Bromsgrove, Hereford and Worcs.	88,200	11,810,053	R. P. Bradshaw	A. G. Williams
§Broxbourne, Herts.	80,000	12,753,818	C. Campbell	L. W. Goodman
§Broxtowe, Notts.	102,400	11,912,785	A. E. Hodder	(a) J. Sutton
§Burnley, Lancs.	92,200	8,597,006	B. Whittle	(a) K. Butterworth
CAMBRIDGE	101,000	21,554,275	G. G. Datson	(a) E. G. Cowell
Cannock Chase, Staffs.	85,800	11,111,603	B. E. Rastall	J. O'Leary
CANTERBURY, Kent	123,000	14,975,000	C. C. Gay	(a) C. Windsor
Caradon, Cornwall	69,300	6,848,686	L. J. Gawley	L. C. Chapman, D.S.C.
CARLISLE, Cumbria	100,900	11,104,582	R. Wilson	(a) I. Stockdale
Carrick, Cornwall	76,500	9,334,217	Lt. Cdr. A. R. Grint	Mrs. S. Perkin
§Castle Morpeth, Northumberland	51,700	6,404,290	M. Cole	(a) G. M. Green
Castle Point, Essex	85,900	11,678,308	A. R. Neighbour	N. J. Firman
§Charnwood, Leics.	140,700	19,739,950	D. L. Harris	(a) R. Burton
§Chelmsford, Essex	139,200	23,865,188	R. M. C. Hartley	(a) Mrs. C. Johnson
§Cheltenham, Glos.	85,800	14,772,106	B. N. Wynn	(a) G. Bingham
Cherwell, Oxon.	110,212	16,977,117	A. M. Brace	R. F. Moffatt
CHESTER, Cheshire	116,657	18,478,800	D. F. Burton	(a) C. M. Eimerl
§Chesterfield, Derbys.	96,600	12,051,021	D. R. Harrison	(a) M. G. Caulfield
Chester-le-Street, Durham	52,300	4,613,965	A. Golightly	Mrs. M. N. Potter
Chichester, West Sussex	97,612	14,046,859	P. G. Lomas	N. Best, M.C.
Chiltern, Bucks.	91,837	16,159,663	D. G. Sainsbury	E. J. E. Powell
§Chorley, Lancs.	91,500	8,791,977	A. B. Webster	(a) G. Simons
§Christchurch, Dorset	40,300	6,544,778	C. H. Dewsnap	(a) E. N. S. Spreadbury
§Cleethorpes, Humberside	68,700	8,782,028	R. W. Bull	(a) R. C. Portess
§Colchester, Essex	140,000	19,352,439	J. Cobley	(a) J. I. Fulford
§Congleton, Cheshire	82,000	10,620,276	A. Molyneux	(a) R. Tomlinson
§Copeland, Cumbria	72,900	7,439,826	P. N. Denson	(a) O. J. Coyles
Corby, Northants.	52,100	8,087,619	D. Hall	J. J. Sims
Cotswold, Glos.	69,000	9,268,167	D. Waring	H. N. E. Groves
Craven, North Yorks	47,653	4,998,825	*A. Howell	T. Cardus
§Crawley, West Sussex	82,000	18,046,690	M. Sander	(a) P. Milton
§Crewe and Nantwich, Cheshire	100,500	12,747,531	H. Bamford	(a) Mrs. A. B. Blacklay
Dacorum, Herts.	131,300	23,229,941	R. H. Davis	C. M. Barling
§Darlington, Durham	97,219	13,196,196	H. R. C. Owen	(a) P. S. Bewlay
§Dartford, Kent	77,315	11,889,323	R. J. Duck	(a) R. F. Maxted
Daventry, Northants.	57,334	9,236,989	R. J. Symons	A. K. Rickett
§DERBY	214,900	30,776,937	F. R. Tagg	(a) R. Longdon
Derwentside, Durham	87,500	7,537,629	T. M. Hodgson	B. Charlton
Dover, Kent	102,800	11,568,229	J. P. Moir	P. E. Buss
DURHAM	89,100	9,182,890	R. J. B. Morris	(a) E. Shuker

District	Population	Rateable value 1984 £	Chief Executive (*Clerk)	Chairman 1984–85 (a) Mayor (b) Lord Mayor
Easington, Durham............	102,402	7,587,647	D. C. Kelly	G. W. Laidler
§Eastbourne, East Sussex	79,000	14,080,567	C. A. Bloor	L. Mason
East Cambridgeshire	54,300	5,772,791	T. T. G. Hardy	Mrs. M. R. Cook
East Devon	108,400	13,314,720	C. A. Moseley	Capt. C. G. E. Cottrell
East Hampshire	91,600	12,016,171	H. S. Fry	S. A. Postle
East Hertfordshire	111,200	17,114,857	D. J. Anstey	N. G. Murphy
§Eastleigh, Hants.	95,500	14,347,254	D. A. Tranah	(a) Mrs. M. Kyrle
East Lindsey, Lincs.	107,525	12,717,098	A. W. Silcox-Crowe	H. M. Dale
East Northamptonshire	62,400	6,865,500	D. N. Adnitt	C. Wood
East Staffordshire	95,800	12,887,103	F. W. Saunders	S. Deeming
§East Yorkshire, Humberside ...	77,200	7,270,612	J. H. Gibson	(a) P. G. Martin
Eden, Cumbria	43,400	4,490,017	J. D. Brown	E. Bain
§Ellesmere Port and Neston, Cheshire	82,200	16,759,754	S. Ewbank	N. L. Angel
§Elmbridge, Surrey	111,700	22,705,772	D. W. L. Jenkins	(a) P. L. Jackson
§Epping Forest, Essex	116,204	19,443,937	A. V. Hackman	M. M. Aldworth
§Epsom and Ewell, Surrey	68,000	11,591,675	D. R. Grimes	(a) Ms. N. Fryer
§Erewash, Derbys.	103,500	11,742,714	J. M. Parker	A. C. Colclough
EXETER, Devon	101,800	14,739,576	B. Frowd	(a) J. E. Pollitt, B.E.M.
§Fareham, Hants.	90,875	12,656,822	O. D. Ellis	(a) Dr. H. G. Jerrard
Fenland, Cambs.	68,200	7,958,316	E. S. Thompson	P. M. Skoulding
Forest Heath, Suffolk	56,100	6,461,689	J. F. Gale	Lady Petre
Forest of Dean, Glos.	72,500	6,951,519	K. W. Harris	A. C. Cooper
§Fylde, Lancs.	68,400	8,945,022	B. J. Smith	(a) Ms. C. M. Hodgson
§Gedling, Notts.	104,000	11,371,763	W. Brown	(a) E. Frost
§Gillingham, Kent..............	95,000	10,532,277	G. C. Jones	(a) G. L. Smith
§Glanford, Humberside	67,300	8,656,545	D. D. H. Cameron	(a) W. T. Smart
GLOUCESTER	94,400	12,978,961	H. R. T. Shackleton	(a) T. B. Wathen
§Gosport, Hants.	77,100	9,647,000	W. D. Hooper	Mrs. I. G. McBryde
§Gravesham, Kent	95,600	12,543,691	R. D. Dewar	(a) J. T. Taylor
§Great Grimsby, Humberside ...	92,200	11,655,626	R. V. Hughes	A. M. Webster
§Great Yarmouth, Norfolk	82,100	11,785,853	K. G. Ward	(a) H. D. McGee
§Guildford, Surrey	124,000	22,868,753	B. E. Twyford	(a) Mrs. J. Golding
§Halton, Cheshire	122,900	17,613,866	R. Turton	(a) K. J. Ebbrell
Hambleton, North Yorks.	75,350	8,287,139	C. Spencer	Col. M. C. W. P. Consett
Harborough, Leics.	61,900	7,963,809	F. T. Berry	Mrs. J. M. White
Harlow, Essex	78,700	14,108,801	H. Platt	J. M. Hobbs
§Harrogate, North Yorks.	141,300	16,765,022	J. V. Lovell	(a) R. A. McCarrol
Hart, Hants.	80,000	10,270,663	H. V. Hill	Maj. P. A. Duckworth
§Hartlepool, Cleveland	93,400	10,302,265	N. D. Abram	(a) M. Lennon
§Hastings, East Sussex	77,800	9,817,837	R. A. Carrier	(a) R. A. C. Saunders
§Havant, Hants.	116,080	15,469,066	D. E. Ridley	(a) K. M. Moss
HEREFORD	48,300	6,890,000	C. E. S. Willis	(a) G. R. G. Beynon
§Hertsmere, Hertfordshire	88,400	16,517,303	S. J. Evans	Mrs. D. M. Nelson
§High Peak, Derbys.	82,100	9,086,613	G. D. Jones	(a) Mrs. D. M. Livesley
§Hinckley and Bosworth, Leics..	89,300	11,733,898	F. Shaw†	(a) G. E. J. Chapman
§Holderness, Humberside	47,100	4,760,000	D. B. Law	(a) K. B. Graville
Horsham, West Sussex	100,745	14,337,193	D. M. Balmford	Mrs. E. M. Mauchel
§Hove, East Sussex	88,600	15,304,225	R. Hinton	(a) I. Moy-Loader
Huntingdon, Cambs............	127,000	15,790,173	L. Bly	C. W. Bridge
§Hyndburn, Lancs.	78,210	6,800,582	N. D. Macgregor	(a) J. Grime
§Ipswich, Suffolk	120,447	19,136,295	J. R. Savage	(a) P. K. Gardiner
Kennet, Wilts.	66,300	6,729,093	S. L. A. Jaques	J. M. Read
Kerrier, Cornwall	84,900	8,481,143	S. G. Stevens	S. J. Jeffery
§Kettering, Northants.	71,700	8,336,745	R. M. Eagland	(a) J. B. Poole
§King's Lynn and W. Norfolk ...	119,335	16,448,981	J. McGhee	(a) B. Seaman
KINGSTON UPON HULL, Humberside	271,100	29,029,957	A. B. Wood	(b) Mrs. F. Brady
Kingswood, Avon	85,900	8,461,800	A. Smith	I. H. Smith
LANCASTER, Lancs.	125,300	13,937,473	W. Pearson	(a) W. Mashiter
§Langbaurgh, Cleveland	150,600	23,645,000	K. Abigail*	(a) S. M. Kay
LEICESTER	282,300	42,255,433	D. Mellor	(b) M. J. Cufflin, O.B.E.
Leominster, Hereford and Worcs.	37,400	3,704,992	G. A. Robson	P. Jones
§Lewes, East Sussex	81,400	12,263,913	C. W. Mann	A. R. Peters
LICHFIELD, Staffs.	89,500	12,289,000	J. T. Thompson	R. H. Blewitt
LINCOLN	76,600	10,549,138	C. J. Thomas	(a) F. Wright
§Luton, Beds.	165,000	31,891,021	A. Collins	(a) Mrs. M. McCarroll
§Macclesfield, Cheshire	149,800	22,668,328	B. W. Longden	(a) J. H. Carter

† Director of Administration.

District	Population	Rateable value 1984 £	Chief Executive (*Clerk)	Chairman 1984–85 (a) Mayor (b) Lord Mayor
§Maidstone, Kent	130,800	17,296,411	A. F. Hargraves	(a) M. D. Nightingale
Maldon, Essex	48,500	7,424,041	E. Robinson	D. J. Fisher
Malvern Hills, Hereford and Worcs.	85,100	10,198,399	L. J. Martin	Mrs. J. M. Dereham
Mansfield, Notts.	99,600	10,230,142	C. Evans	M. Sims
§Medina, Isle of Wight	68,700	8,151,890	K. L. Heath	(a) R. W. Ford
§Melton, Leics.	43,700	5,547,190	P. J. G. Herrick*	(a) A. E. Lovett
Mendip, Somerset	90,400	10,139,418	G. Jeffo	E. G. Wright
Mid Bedfordshire	106,000	14,057,659	P. A. Freeman	A. Sherwood-King
Mid Devon (Tiverton)	58,700	5,524,240	R. C. Greensmith	Mrs. D. C. Bruton
§Middlesbrough, Cleveland	149,100	17,798,164	J. R. Foster	(a) M. H. Kiril
Mid Suffolk	69,342	8,348,721	H. McFarlane	H. F. Griffiths, O.B.E.
Mid Sussex, West Sussex	114,235	16,919,863	B. J. Grimshaw	E. L. Cox
§Milton Keynes, Bucks.	143,700	24,171,462	M. J. Murray	(a) F. E. Atter
Mole Valley, Surrey	77,300	12,600,727	A. A. Huggins	Lt. Cdr. H. C. Syms
Newark, Notts.	104,300	11,423,261	J. R. Spencer	B. J. B. Fisher
Newbury, Berks.	125,200	18,877,603°	B. J. Thetford	R. Roberts
§Newcastle under Lyme, Staffs.	120,000	13,572,183	A. G. Owen	(a) T. Naylor
§New Forest, Hants.	147,400	23,728,165	P. A. Bassett	J. E. Coles
§Northampton	162,200	28,141,323	A. C. Parkhouse	(a) S. T. James
Northavon, Avon	120,100	16,511,132	F. Maude	A. G. Higgs
§North Bedfordshire	132,400	21,063,662	J. F. Hayward	(a) V. Storrow
North Cornwall	65,300	7,290,497	I. Whiting	G. Facks-Martin
North Devon	78,500	8,236,628	M. J. Clare	G. E. Andrews
North Dorset	49,000	5,257,843	A. J. Bridgeman	Mrs. M. E. Cossins
North East Derbyshire	97,600	9,195,225	R. S. Billington	G. W. Marshall
North Hertfordshire	108,400	19,206,000	J. S. Philp	K. F. Emsall
North Kesteven, Lincs.	79,511	8,050,627	Dr. G. J. Coady	L. Young
North Norfolk	83,800	10,625,549	T. V. Nolan	Mrs. V. H. Bensley
North Shropshire	51,500	4,984,798	K. Flood	Mrs. P. M. Collins
§North Warwickshire	60,000	8,492,000	D. Monks	(a) P. R. Collins
North West Leicestershire	79,100	10,312,393	J. E. White	Maj. S. Southworth, M.M.
North Wiltshire	105,400	10,524,398	H. Miles	M. E. Flintoff
NORWICH, Norfolk	126,100	23,234,286	A. R. H. Glover	(b) S. B. Petersen
NOTTINGHAM	277,800	42,601,216	M. H. F. Hammond	(b) Mrs. I. F. Matthews
§Nuneaton and Bedworth, Warks.	114,500	13,894,500	I. J. Clarke	(a) S. Williams
§Oadby and Wigston, Leics.	53,100	7,005,619	J. B. Burton	(a) Mrs. E. Ridley
§Oswestry, Shropshire	30,078	3,095,531	D. A. Towers	(a) J. R. Bowyer
OXFORD	115,900	21,243,536	E. J. Patrick	(b) F. A. Garside
§Pendle, Lancs.	86,300	6,378,988	C. A. Simmonds	(a) Mrs. M. H. Heaton
Penwith, Cornwall	55,662	6,047,208	J. C. Moore, M.B.E.	J. J. Daniel
PETERBOROUGH, Cambs.	138,365	21,323,847	P. B. Sidebottom	R. Palmer
PLYMOUTH, Devon	253,600	30,238,003	A. F. Watson	(b) P. Whitfield
§Poole, Dorset	122,669	20,384,945	I. K. D. Andrews	J. Breckell
PORTSMOUTH, Hants.	184,300	27,671,000	R. Trist	(b) J. S. Marshall, O.B.E.
§Preston, Lancs.	126,500	15,636,974	H. Kirby	(a) Mrs. N. Taylor
Purbeck, Dorset	40,600	5,517,000	A. J. James	D. B. Humphry
§Reading, Berks.	136,300	28,173,744	W. H. Tee	(a) R. W. Jewitt
§Redditch, Hereford and Worcs.	70,500	11,091,897	J. D. Weth	(a) R. D. Watton
§Reigate and Banstead, Surrey	116,600	19,219,118	C. T. Pollard	(a) A. K. Gulati
§Restormel, Cornwall	79,100	10,152,925	D. Brown	(a) J. Parnall
§Ribble Valley, Lancs.	52,600	5,294,649	M. Jackson	(a) R. B. Thornton
Richmondshire, North Yorks.	44,400	4,412,958	M. F. Tooze	A. F. P. Abraham
ROCHESTER UPON MEDWAY, Kent	144,700	22,970,226	R. E. Painter	(a) T. G. Mason
Rochford, Essex	74,400	10,504,241	A. G. Cooke	Mrs. J. Jones
§Rossendale, Lancs.	64,900	5,136,000	J. S. Hartley‡	(a) Mrs. E. Graham
Rother, East Sussex	77,200	11,275,626	D. F. Powell	Mrs. E. E. Armstrong
§Rugby, Warwicks.	87,100	12,619,974	J. S. R. Lawton	(a) W. M. Clarke
Runnymede, Surrey	72,600	12,257,573	E. W. Andrews	(a) S. L. E. Brunger
§Rushcliffe, Notts.	93,000	12,900,397	J. Saxton	(a) G. E. Green
§Rushmoor, Hants.	79,400	12,240,662	D. Hartley	J. H. Marsh
Rutland, Leics.	33,400	3,911,957	A. S. Jowett	R. A. Pedder
Ryedale, North Yorks.	86,600	8,071,752	D. Cudworth	E. J. Pile
ST. ALBANS, Herts.	125,600	22,933,772	R. H. Braddon	(a) F. Perham
§St. Edmundsbury, Suffolk	87,820	12,125,555	G. R. N. Toft	(a) M. L. Lacey
Salisbury, Wilts.	102,800	13,050,909	F. W. Colquhoun	D. A. Alford
§Scarborough, North Yorks.	102,100	11,337,721	R. Bradley	(a) M. F. Pitts

° 1983 figure. Rate for 1984 not yet set by the Borough Council.   ‡ Borough Director.

District	Population	Rateable value 1984 £	Chief Executive (*Clerk)	Chairman 1984–85 (a) Mayor (b) Lord Mayor
§Scunthorpe, Humberside	66,000	11,970,091	K. Lescure	(a) Mrs. B. A. Kirk
Sedgefield, Durham	92,300	9,347,637	A. J. Roberts	T. Ward
Sedgemoor, Somerset	90,000	10,798,405	(vacant)	Mrs. H. M. Ellis-Jones
Selby, North Yorks.	80,400	13,260,156	D. J. Jenkins	M. Johnson
Sevenoaks, Kent	109,871	13,712,905	P. Hodgson	L. C. E. Robus
Shepway, Kent	86,500	12,174,912	R. H. Summers	J. F. Setterfield
§Shrewsbury and Atcham, Shropshire	88,500	12,293,840	D. M. Clark	(a) F. Jones
§Slough, Berks.	97,400	24,117,803	C. F. Lakin	(a) Mrs. L. E. Simmons
SOUTHAMPTON, Hants.	208,400	31,883,873	E. A. Urquhart	(a) Mrs. I. F. Candy, C.B.E.
South Bedfordshire	109,000	20,281,750	T. D. Rix	A. E. Whinnett
South Bucks.	62,000	13,774,532	S. R. Jobson	P. N. Janes
South Cambridgeshire	111,600	16,443,607	B. J. Hancock	K. C. Collett
South Derbyshire	68,500	9,818,801	I. F. Baylis	J. E. J. Parkinson
§Southend-on-Sea, Essex	157,700	27,365,968	F. G. Laws	Mrs. J. A. Carlile
South Hams, Devon	68,371	7,912,785	S. W. Bradley	G. South
South Herefordshire	47,587	5,060,420	D. T. Cole	Mrs. E. M. Saunders
South Holland, Lincs.	61,734	6,798,505	J. T. Brindley	D. Dewsberry
South Kesteven, Lincs.	99,500	11,946,039	K. R. Cann	J. H. Foster
South Lakeland, Cumbria	95,900	10,890,458	A. F. Winstanley	H. E. Newman
South Norfolk	97,100	10,564,654	A. G. T. Kellett	A. W. Cook
South Northamptonshire	65,196	7,715,839	C. M. Major	G. V. Smith
South Oxfordshire	131,900	18,415,771	J. B. Chirnside	Mrs. P. Clarke
§South Ribble, Lancs.	97,900	10,054,801	R. N. L. Hamm*	(a) G. Thorpe
South Shropshire	34,200	3,387,633	G. Kellet, M.B.E.	T. J. Marston
South Staffordshire	98,400	12,479,082	G. J. Hayward	Mrs. P. M. Yates
§South Wight, I.O.W.	50,200	5,995,564	C. M. Simpson	(a) A. Philpott
§Spelthorne, Surrey	92,032	21,453,045	G. F. Hilbert	(a) N. L. Renfree
§Stafford	117,300	16,384,338	R. E. Humphreys	(a) H. Lowry
Staffordshire Moorlands	95,800	9,726,380	A. W. Law	D. Machin
§Stevenage, Herts.	75,000	13,900,000	S. W. Catchpole	(a) K. R. Hopkins
§Stockton-on-Tees, Cleveland	173,800	28,270,297	F. F. Theobalds*	(a) J. Munsey
STOKE-ON-TRENT, Staffs.	252,300	32,387,170	S. W. Titchener	(b) J. T. Dimmock
Stratford-on-Avon, Warwicks.	101,200	15,937,650	T. J. W. Foy	Rr. Adm. R. C. P. Wainwright
Stroud, Glos.	102,400	11,927,405	D. F. Collins	R. P. Nicholas
Suffolk Coastal	99,500	14,351,255	D. L. Blay	C. W. Webb
§Surrey Heath	77,700	13,206,193	M. Orlik	(a) J. Hall
§Swale, Kent	110,000	12,680,273	H. White, C.B.E., D.F.C., A.F.C.	(a) W. Boggia
§Tamworth, Staffs.	68,000	7,990,775	P. E. Thorpe	(a) A. J. Whitefoot
Tandridge, Surrey	77,900	10,133,946	D. Brunton	(a) J. F. Farrell
§Taunton Deane, Somerset	88,300	10,770,000	P. F. Berman	(a) L. J. Lane
Teesdale, Durham	24,400	2,262,708	A. E. Pooley	A. Makepeace
Teignbridge, Devon	96,200	11,260,000	P. B. Young	P. C. Riggs
Tendring, Essex	116,600	15,826,689	D. Mitchell-Gears	Miss A. P. R. Overton
§Test Valley, Hants.	93,900	13,620,386	G. Blythe	(a) M. J. C. Bigwood
§Tewkesbury, Glos.	80,815	11,473,577	R. A. Wheeler	(a) Mrs. P. A. Roberts
§Thamesdown, Wilts.	154,909	21,697,073	D. M. Kent	(a) H. E. Garrett
Thanet, Kent	121,400	15,131,607	I. G. Gill	B. R. White, B.E.M.
Three Rivers, Herts.	79,300	12,996,193	G. A. Deans	R. Clements
§Thurrock, Essex	125,300	28,371,133	G. V. Semain	(a) S. P. Davis
Tonbridge and Malling, Kent	98,600	13,407,679	T. J. Shellard	Miss J. R. Browne
§Torbay, Devon	113,100	16,905,900	D. P. Hudson	(a) Mrs. M. E. Thairlwall
Torridge, Devon	48,700	4,039,049	L. S. Mogridge	R. G. Braine
§Tunbridge Wells, Kent	98,600	12,231,983	W. E. Battersby	(a) Maj. J. T. G. Liles
Tynedale, Northumberland	54,500	6,094,954	A. Baty	J. N. Davison
Uttlesford, Essex	63,850	9,141,388	J. F. Vernon	P. M. MacPhail
Vale of White Horse, Oxon.	104,900	18,073,000	J. C. Neville Wood	V. G. Day
Vale Royal, Cheshire	111,800	15,228,381	W. R. T. Woods	F. T. Dolphin
Wansbeck, Northumberland	62,112	7,865,761	J. D. McHardy	F. L. McKenzie
Wansdyke, Avon	77,500	8,660,071	†H. St. J. Smith	J. F. Neville-Dove
§Warrington, Cheshire	178,000	25,989,076	W. H. Lawton, T.D.	(a) Mrs. V. I. Edwards
Warwick	115,600	19,358,685	M. J. Ward	M. F. Coker
§Watford, Herts.	75,200	16,678,181	R. B. McMillan	(a) Mrs. M. I. Hughes
Waveney, Suffolk	101,000	11,750,589	M. Berridge	J. R. Aldous
Waverley, Surrey	112,700	17,245,206	G. W. Nuttal	Mrs. A. E. Hoath
Wealden, East Sussex	121,800	14,401,416	K. Wilson	E. W. Ellison, O.B.E.
Wear Valley, Durham	64,100	5,949,203	M. R. Sutcliff	A. Brooksbank

† Secretary.

District	Population	Rateable value 1984 £	Chief Executive (* Clerk)	Chairman 1984–85 (a) Mayor (b) Lord Mayor
§Wellingborough, Northants....	64,500	8,581,669	W. B. Veal	(a) R. Fairhurst
Welwyn Hatfield, Herts.	92,665	19,127,276	L. Asquith	U. G. Bennett
West Derbyshire	67,600	7,117,786	R. Bubb	Mrs. M. E. Gillan
§West Devon..................	42,998	4,041,454	J. S. Ligo	(a) J. R. Philpott
West Dorset	81,200	9,230,998	M. B. Taylor	H. W. Haward
West Lancashire	107,600	12,882,353	J. C. Cowdall	W. M. Cox
West Lindsey, Lincs.	76,100	8,094,743	A. W. Hancock	B. Stallman
West Oxfordshire	81,029	10,550,000	M. G. Knapman	G. C. Kellow
West Somerset	29,300	5,971,625	H. Close	D. Merson
West Wiltshire................	100,500	11,533,000	G. A. F. Garland	G. C. Allden
§Weymouth and Portland, Dorset	58,300	6,468,891	R. E. F. Norman	(a) E. Webb
Wimborne, Dorset.............	70,466	10,296,810	W. G. Press	D. A. Goodwin
WINCHESTER, Hants.	92,500	13,418,377	D. H. Cowan	(a) J. F. C. H. Broadway
§Windsor and Maidenhead, Berks.......................	134,300	25,978,143	G. B. Blacker	(a) F. A. Robinson
§Woking, Surrey	83,500	15,323,499	P. Russell	(a) J. A. Jewson
Wokingham, Berks.	124,400	18,583,030	N. E. Butler	Col. J. R. Cole
Woodspring, Avon	167,638	19,731,896	R. H. Moon	Mrs. A. Birks
WORCESTER	75,900	12,926,083	P. Stanton	(a) J. H. Carpenter
§Worthing, West Sussex	93,400	14,595,688	T. L. Elliott	(a) A. R. Clare
Wrekin, Shropshire	128,000	16,261,454	R. E. Paine	Mrs. E. Harrison
Wychavon, Hereford and Worcs.	96,300	13,929,585°	P. G. Rust, M.B.E.	Mrs. J. M. Jones
Wycombe, Bucks................	157,600	29,205,957	W. C. Roberts	S. A. Goulborn
§Wyre, Lancs...................	99,400	11,207,798	A. K. B. Boatswain	(a) T. E. Croft
Wyre Forest, Hereford and Worcs.	92,000	13,293,035	A. S. Dick	Mrs. V. Pargeter
Yeovil, Somerset	134,700	15,366,337	D. J. Ashford	S. C. Harding
YORK, North Yorks.	99,910	11,593,537	D. A. Ansbro	(b) Rt. Hon. K. Cooper

° 1983 figure

THE PRINCIPAL ENGLISH CITIES

BIRMINGHAM

BIRMINGHAM (West Midlands), Britain's second city and the largest metropolitan district in the country, is the chief centre of the hardware trade and motor components industry. It is estimated that over 1,500 distinct trades are carried on in the city. The generally accepted derivation of "Birmingham" is the *ham* or dwelling-place of the *ing* or the family of *Beorma* presumed to have been a Saxon. Between the 11th and 16th centuries the de Berminghams were Lords of the Manor. Recent development includes the National Exhibition Centre (opened in 1976), the Aston Science Park for high technology industries, and the setting up of a partnership between the City Council, Lloyd's Bank and Aston University to provide risk-capital for such industries. Birmingham is also a regional centre for the media.

The principal buildings are the Town Hall, built in 1832–1834; the Council House (1878); Victoria Law Courts (1891); the University (1909); the 13th century Church of St. Martin (rebuilt 1873); the Cathedral (formerly St. Philip's Church); the Roman Catholic Cathedral of St. Chad (Pugin) and the Methodist Central Hall.

Under local government reorganization in 1974, Birmingham was merged with Sutton Coldfield, to become a Metropolitan District in the West Midlands Metropolitan County.

BRADFORD

BRADFORD (West Yorkshire), 192 miles N.N.W. of London, is the administrative centre of the Metropolitan District of Bradford. The District covers an area of 91,444 acres and lies on the southern edge of the Yorkshire Dales National Park, including within its boundaries the village of Haworth, home of the Brontë sisters, and Ilkley Moor.

Originally a Saxon township, Bradford received a market charter in 1251 but developed only slowly until the industrialisation of the textile industry brought rapid growth during the 19th century. The prosperity of that period is reflected in much of the city's architecture, particularly the public buildings—City Hall (1873), Wool Exchange (1867), St George's Hall (Concert Hall, 1853), Cartwright Hall (Art Gallery, 1904) and Technical College (1882). Other chief buildings are the Cathedral (15th century) and Bolling Hall (14th century).

Textiles still play an important part in the city's economy but industry is now more broadly based, including engineering and micro-electronics. The city has a strong banking, insurance and building society sector, and a growing tourism industry.

BRISTOL

BRISTOL (Avon) is the largest non-metropolitan district in population in the country, and lies 119 miles W. of London. The present municipal area is 10,954 hectares.

Bristol's port systems at Avonmouth, Royal Portbury and Portishead are the largest municipally owned docks in the country, handling imports of fresh and processed foods, sugar, molasses, tobacco, chemicals, petroleum products, metals and forest products. Goods exported through the port include vehicles, metals and all types of manufactured goods. The Royal Portbury Dock is capable of handling six 70,000 d.w.t. vessels at any one time.

The chief buildings include the 12th century Cathedral (with later additions), with Norman Chapter House and gateway, the 14th century Church of St. Mary Redcliffe, Wesley's Chapel, Broadmead, the Merchant Venturers' Almshouses, the Council House (1956), Guildhall, Exchange (erected from the designs of John Wood in 1743), Cabot Tower, the University and Clifton College, Red Lodge (Tudor), Georgian House and Blaise Folly and Mansion. The Roman Catholic Cathedral at Clifton was opened in 1973.

The *Clifton Suspension Bridge*, with a span of 702 feet over the Avon, was projected by Brunel in 1836 but was not completed until 1864. Brunel's SS *Great Britain*, the first ocean going propeller driven ship, is now being restored in the City Docks from where she was launched in 1843.

Bristol was a Royal Borough before the Norman Conquest. The earliest form of the name is *Bricgstow*. In 1373 it received from Edward III a charter granting it county status.

CAMBRIDGE

CAMBRIDGE, a settlement far older than its ancient University, lies on the Cam or Granta, 51 miles north of London and 65 miles south-west of Norwich. It has an area of 10,060 acres.

The city is a county town and regional headquarters. Its industries include electronics, flour milling, cement making and the manufacture of scientific instruments. Among its open spaces are Jesus Green, Sheep's Green, Coe Fen, Parker's Piece, Christ's Pieces, the University Botanic Garden, and the Backs, or lawns and gardens through which the Cam winds behind the principal line of college buildings. East of the Cam, King's Parade, upon which stand Great St. Mary's Church, Gibbs' Senate House and King's College Chapel with Wilkins' screen, joins Trumpington Street to form one of the most beautiful throughfares in Europe.

University and College buildings provide the outstanding features of Cambridge architecture but several churches (especially St. Benet's, the oldest building in the City, and St. Sepulchre's the Round Church) also are notable. The modern Guildhall (1939) stands on a site of which at least part has held municipal buildings since 1224.

CANTERBURY

CANTERBURY, the Metropolitan City of the Anglican Communion, has a history going back to prehistoric times. It was the Roman Durovernum and the Saxon Cant-wara-byrig (stronghold of the men of Kent). Here in 597 St. Augustine began the conversion of the English to Christianity, when Ethelbert, King of Kent, was baptized.

Of the Benedictine St. Augustine's Abbey, burial place of the Jutish Kings of Kent (whose capital Canterbury was) only extensive ruins remain. St. Martin's Church, on the eastern outskirts of the City, is stated by Bede to have been the place of worship of Queen Bertha, the Christian wife of King Ethelbert, before the advent of St. Augustine.

In 1170 the rivalry of Church and State culminated in the murder in Canterbury Cathedral, by Henry II's knights, of Archbishop Thomas Becket, whose shrine became a great centre of pilgrimage as described by Chaucer in his *Canterbury Tales*. After the Reformation pilgrimages ceased, but the prosperity of the City was strengthened by an influx of Huguenot refugees, who introduced weaving. The Elizabethan poet and playwright Christopher Marlowe was born and reared in Canterbury, and there are literary associations also with Defoe, Dickens, Joseph Conrad and Somerset Maugham.

The Cathedral, with architecture ranging from the eleventh to the fifteenth centuries, is world famous. Modern pilgrims are attracted particularly to the Martyrdom, The Black Prince's Tomb, the Warriors' Chapel and the many examples of mediæval stained glass.

The medieval City Walls are built on Roman foundations and the fourteenth century West Gate is one of the finest buildings of its kind in the country.

The University of Kent at Canterbury admitted its first students in 1965.

The city's district has an area of 120 square miles, including the towns of Whitstable and Herne Bay. Before the institution of the Mayoralty in 1448 it was governed by bailiffs and earlier still by prefects or provosts.

CARLISLE

CARLISLE is situated at the confluence of the River Eden and River Caldew, 309 miles north west of London and a few miles from the Scottish border. It has an area of 254,955 acres, and was granted a charter in 1158.

The city stands at the western end of Hadrian's Wall and dates from the original Roman settlement of *Luguvalium*. Granted to Scotland in the 10th century, Carlisle is not included in the Doomsday Book. William Rufus reclaimed the area in 1092 and the Castle and city walls were built to guard Carlisle and the western border; the Citadel is a Tudor addition to protect the south of the city. Until the Union of the Crowns in 1603, Carlisle changed hands several times and was frequently besieged. During the Civil War the city remained Royalist; in 1745 it supported the Young Pretender.

The Cathedral, originally a 12th century Augustinian priory, was enlarged in the 13th and 14th centuries after the diocese was created in 1133. To the south are the restored remains of the medieval priory and nearby the 18th century church of St. Cuthbert, the third to stand on a site dating from the 7th century.

Carlisle is the major commercial and agricultural centre for the area, and industries include the manufacture of metal goods, biscuits and textiles. However, the largest employer is the services sector, notably in retailing and transport. The city has an important communications position at the centre of a network of major roads, as an important stage on the main west coast rail services and with its own airport at Crosby.

CHESTER

CHESTER is situated on the River Dee, 189 miles north west of London. The city administers an area of 173 square miles and was granted Borough and City status in 1974.

Chester's recorded history dates from the 1st century when the Romans founded the fortress of *Deva*. The city's name is derived from the Latin *castra* (a camp or encampment). During the Middle Ages, Chester was the principal port of north west England but declined with the silting of the Dee estuary and competition from Liverpool. The city was also an important military centre, notably during Edward I's Welsh campaigns and the Elizabethan Irish campaigns. During Civil War, Chester supported the King and was besieged from 1643-6. Chester's first charter was granted c 1175 and the city was incorporated in 1506. The office of Sheriff is the earliest created in the country (c 1120's), and the Mayor also enjoys the title "Admiral of the Dee".

The city's architectural features include the city walls (an almost complete two mile circuit), the unique Rows (covered galleries above the street level shops), the Victorian Gothic Town Hall (1869), the Castle (rebuilt 1788 and 1822) and numerous half-timbered buildings. The Cathedral was a Benedictine abbey until the Dissolution. Remaining monastic buildings include the chapter house, refectory and cloisters and there is a modern free-standing bell tower. The Norman church of St. John the Baptist was a Cathedral church in the early Middle Ages.

Chester's principal industry is tourism, and the city is also a shopping centre for North Wales and the North West. Other industries include light engineering and manufacture of car components.

COVENTRY

COVENTRY (West Midlands) is a city 92 miles N.W. of London, and an important industrial centre, producing cars, machine tools, agricultural machinery and telecommunications equipment.

The city owes its beginning to Leofric, Earl of Mercia and his wife Godiva who, in 1043, founded a Benedictine monastery. The guildhall of St. Mary dates from the 14th century, three of the city's churches date from the 14th and 15th centuries and 16th century almshouses may still be seen. Coventry's first cathedral was destroyed at the Reformation, its second in the 1940 blitz (its walls and spire remain) and the new cathedral designed by Sir Basil Spence, consecrated in 1962, now draws innumerable visitors.

Post-war public buildings include the Art Gallery and Museum, Lanchester Polytechnic, the Civic Theatre, Museum of British Road Transport, new swimming baths and sports centre.

DERBY

DERBY stands on the banks of the River Derwent, 127 miles N.N.W. of London, and covers an area of 30 square miles. The name Derby dates back to 880 when the Danes settled in the locality and changed the original Saxon name of "Northworthy" to "Deoraby".

Derby has a wide range of industries, supported by excellent communications. It is an engineering centre with products including aero engines, lawn mowers, and sugar refining machinery. Other industries include textiles, chemicals, plastics and porcelain. The city is an established railway centre and in recent years British Rail has added a training centre and technical centre with research laboratories to its engineering complex in which has been developed the Advanced Passenger Train.

Buildings of interest include St Peter's Church, (14th century), the Cathedral (1525), St Mary's Roman Catholic Church (1839), the Industrial Museum, formerly the Old Silk Mill (1721), and the Old Abbey Building dating from the 14th century. Two recent developments are the Assembly Rooms in the Market Place and the Eagle Centre, a shopping precinct covering twelve acres, including a market and the new Derby Playhouse.

The first charter granting a Mayor and Aldermen was that of Charles I in 1637. Previous charters date back to 1154. It was granted City status in 1977.

DURHAM

The city of DURHAM is a district in the county of Durham and covers an area of 73 square miles. The city is the major tourist attraction in the county because of its prominent Norman Cathedral and Castle set high on a wooded peninsula overlooking the River Wear. The Cathedral was founded as a shrine for the body of St. Cuthbert in 995. The present building dates from 1093 and among its many treasures is the tomb of the Venerable Bede (673-735). Durham's Prince Bishops had unique powers up to 1836, being lay rulers as well as religious leaders. As a palatinate Durham could have its own army, nobility, coinage and courts. The Castle was the main seat of the Prince Bishops for nearly 800 years; it is now used as a Hall of Residence by the University.

The University, founded on the initiative of Bishop William Van Mildert, is England's third oldest. Its students live in 14 colleges spread across the city.

Among other buildings of interest is the Guildhall in the Market Place which dates originally from the 14th century. Much work has been carried out to conserve this area, forming part of the city's major contribution to the Council of Europe's Urban Renaissance Campaign. Annual events include Durham's Regatta in June (claimed to be the oldest rowing event in Britain) and the Miners' Gala in July.

In the past 20 years the economy of Durham has undergone a significant change with the replacement of mining as the dominant feature by "white collar" employment. The majority of this employment is in local government service industries and the University.

EXETER

EXETER lies on the River Exe 170 miles south west of London and 10 miles from the sea. It covers an area of 11,037 acres and was granted a Royal Charter by Henry II.

The Romans founded *Isca Dumnoniorum* in the 1st century A.D., and in the 3rd century a stone wall (most of which remains) was built, providing protection against Saxon, and then Danish invasions. After the Conquest, the city led resistance to William in the west, until reduced by siege. The Normans built the motte and bailey castle of Rougemont, the gatehouse and one tower of which remain, although the rest was pulled down in 1784. The first bridge across the Exe was built in the 13th century. The city's role as a port declined due to the silting of the river, but was somewhat restored by the construction in the 1560's of the first ship canal in England. Exeter was the Royalist headquarters in the West during the Civil War.

The diocese of Exeter was established by Edward the Confessor in 1050, although a church existed on the Cathedral site in the early 10th century. A new cathedral was built in the 12th century but the present building was begun *c* 1275 in the Gothic style, although incorporating the Norman towers, and completed about a century later with the West Front. The Guildhall dates from the 12th century and there are many other medieval buildings in the city, as well as architecture in the Georgian and Regency styles (Custom House, The Quay). Damage suffered by bombing in 1942 led to the redevelopment of the city centre.

Exeter's prosperity from medieval times was based on trade in wool and woollen cloth (commemorated by Tuckers Hall), which remained at its height until the late 18th century when export trade was hit by the French Wars. Subsequently Exeter has developed as an administrative and commercial centre, notably in the distributive trades and light manufacturing industries.

KINGSTON UPON HULL

HULL (officially "Kingston upon Hull") lies in the mostly rural County of Humberside, at the junction of the River Hull with the Humber, 22 miles from the North Sea and 205 miles N. of London. The municipal area is 17,535 acres.

Hull is one of the great seaports of the United Kingdom. It has docks covering a water area of 172 acres, equipped to handle cargoes by unit-load techniques, and is a departure point for car ferry services to the continent. There is a great variety of industry and service industries, as well as increasing tourism and conference business.

The city, restored after very heavy air raid damage during World War II, has good office and administrative buildings, its municipal centre being the Guildhall, its educational centre the University of Hull and its religious centre the Parish Church of the Holy Trinity. The old Town area is being renovated, and this also includes a Town Docks Scheme to develop defunct docks as a marina. Just west of the city is the Humber Bridge, the world's longest single span suspension bridge, which was officially opened by H.M. the Queen in July 1981.

Kingston upon Hull was so named by Edward I. City status was accorded in 1897 and the office of Mayor raised to the dignity of Lord Mayor in 1914.

LEEDS

LEEDS (West Yorkshire), a Metropolitan District from April 1, 1974, is a junction for road, rail, canal and air services and an important commercial centre, situated in the lower Aire Valley, 195 miles by road N.N.W. of London. The municipal area is 138,441 acres.

Leeds has a wide variety of manufacturing industries, notably cloth and ready-made clothing, engineering of all kinds, leather and chemical products, food and drink, furniture and plastics.

The principal buildings are the Civic Hall (1933), the Town Hall (1858), the Municipal Buildings and Art Gallery (1884) with the Henry Moore Gallery (1982), the Corn Exchange (1863) and the University. The Parish Church (St. Peter's) was rebuilt in 1841; the 17th century St. John's Church has a fine interior with a famous English renaissance screen; the last remaining 18th century church is Holy Trinity, Boar Lane (1727). Kirkstall Abbey (about 3 miles from the centre of the city), founded by Henry de Lacy in 1152, is one of the most complete examples of Cistercian houses now remaining. Temple Newsam, birthplace of Lord Darnley, was acquired by the Council in 1922. The present house was largely re-built by Sir Arthur Ingram in about 1620. Adel Church, about 5 miles from the centre of the city, is a fine Norman structure.

Leeds was first incorporated by Charles I in 1626. The earliest forms of the name are *Loidis* or *Ledes*, the origins of which are obscure.

LEICESTER

LEICESTER is situated geographically in the centre of England, 100 miles north of London. The City dates back to pre-Roman times and was one of the five Danish *Burhs*. In 1589 Queen Elizabeth I granted a Charter to the City and the ancient title was confirmed by Letters Patent in 1919. Under local government reorganization Leicester's area remained unchanged at 18,141 acres, and it retains its designation as a City.

The principal industries of the city are hosiery, and knitwear, footwear manufacturing and engineering. The growth of Leicester as a hosiery centre increased rapidly from the introduction there of the first stocking frame in 1670 and to-day it has some of the largest hosiery factories in the world, with much of the output being exported.

The principal buildings in the city are the Town Hall; the New Walk Centre; the University; Leicester Polytechnic and De Montfort Hall, one of the finest concert halls in the provinces seating over 2,750 persons. The ancient Churches of St. Martin (now Leicester Cathedral), St. Nicholas, St. Margaret, All Saints, St. Mary de Castro, and buildings such as the Guildhall, the 14th century Newarke Gate, the Castle and the Jewry Wall Roman site still exist. The

Haymarket Theatre, an integral part of a large new shopping and car-parking complex, was opened in 1973.

LINCOLN

Situated 143 miles north of London and 40 miles inland on the River Witham, LINCOLN derives its name from a contraction of *Lindum Colonia*, the settlement founded in A.D. 48 by the Romans to command the crossing of Ermine Street and Fosse Way. Sections of the 3rd century Roman city wall can be seen, including an extant gateway (Newport Arch), and excavations have discovered traces of a sewerage system unique in Britain. The Romans also drained the surrounding fenland and created a canal system, laying the foundations of Lincoln's agricultural prosperity, and also of the city's importance in the medieval wool trade as a port and Staple town. As one of the Five Boroughs of the Danelaw, Lincoln was an important trading centre in the 9th and 10th centuries and medieval prosperity from the wool trade lasted until the 14th century, enabling local merchants to build parish churches (of which three survive), and attracting in the 12th century a Jewish community (Jew's House and Court, Aaron's House). However, the removal of the Staple to Boston in 1369 heralded a decline from which the city only recovered fully in the 19th century when improved fen drainage made Lincoln agriculturally important, and improved canal and rail links led to industrial development, mainly in the manufacture of machinery, components and engineering products.

The Castle was built shortly after the Conquest and is unusual in having two mounds; on one motte stands a Keep (Lucy's Tower) added in the 12th century. The Cathedral was begun c1073 when the first Norman bishop moved the see of Lindsey to Lincoln, but was mostly destroyed by fire and earthquake in the 12th century. Rebuilding was begun by St. Hugh and completed over a century later. The Wren library contains manuscripts including one of the four surviving originals of the Magna Carta. Other notable architectural features of the city are the 12th century High Bridge, the oldest in Britain still to carry buildings, and the Guildhall situated above the 15–16th century Stonebow gateway.

LIVERPOOL

LIVERPOOL (Merseyside) on the right bank of the river Mersey, 3 miles from the Irish Sea and 194 miles N.W. of London, is one of the greatest trading centres of the world and the principal port in the United Kingdom for the Atlantic trade. The municipal area of 27,819 acres includes 2,840 acres in the bed of the river Mersey.

Quays on both sides of the river are about 38 miles long, and the Gladstone Dock can accommodate the largest vessels afloat. Gross tonnage of ships entering and leaving the port annually exceeds 15,375,000 tonnes. The main imports are petroleum, grain, ores, non-ferrous metals, sugar, wood, oil, fruit and cotton. The Seaforth Container Terminal was opened in 1972, covering 500 acres and costing £50m.

Liverpool was created a borough in 1207 and a city in 1880. From the early eighteenth century it expanded rapidly with the growth of the port. Surviving buildings from this date include the Bluecoat Chambers (1718, formerly the Bluecoat School), the Town Hall (1754, rebuilt to the original design, 1795), and buildings in Rodney Street, Canning Street and the suburbs. Notable from the nineteenth and twentieth centuries are the Anglican Cathedral, built from the designs of Sir Giles Gilbert Scott (the foundation stone was laid in 1904, and the building was only completed in 1980): the Catholic Metropolitan Cathedral (designed by Sir Frederick Gibberd, consecrated 1967) and St. George's Hall, (1838–1854), regarded as one of the finest modern examples of classical architecture. In 1852 an Act was obtained for establishing a public library, museum and art gallery; as a result Liverpool had one of the first public libraries in the country. The Brown, Picton & Hornby libraries now form the largest city central libraries in Europe. The Victoria Building of Liverpool University, The Royal Liver, Cunard and Mersey Docks & Harbour Company buildings at the Pier Head, the Municipal Buildings and the Philharmonic Hall are other examples of the City's fine buildings.

Constructed between 1925 and 1934 the first Mersey Tunnel was named "Queensway". When the volume of traffic increased far beyond earlier expectations, the second Mersey Tunnel—"Kingsway"—was opened on 24 June 1971, and a similar tunnel adjacent to it was opened on 14th February 1974.

Strenuous efforts were made after 1945 to improve employment prospects. The City Council developed large industrial estates at Kirby, Speke and Aintree and is now tackling the problem of the "inner city". In 1984 a 250 acre area of Liverpool's southern waterfront was cleared and landscaped to accommodate Britain's first International Garden Festival.

In 1969 the Merseyside Passenger Transport Executive was formed to improve and co-ordinate local transport throughout Merseyside, and, in partnership with British Rail, developed the Merseyside Loop/Link system, opened in 1977 to link Southport, Ormskirk and Garston with the City Centre stations and lines to the Wirral.

MANCHESTER

MANCHESTER (the *Mancunium* of the Romans, who occupied it in A.D. 78) is 189 miles N.W. of London and covers about 43 square miles.

Manchester is a commercial and industrial centre with a population engaged in engineering, chemical, clothing, food processing and textile industries. Banking and insurance are among the prime commercial activities. The city is connected with the sea by the Manchester Ship Canal, opened in 1894, 35½ miles long, and accommodating ships up to 15,000 tons. Manchester Airport handles more than 5 million passengers yearly.

The principal buildings are the Town Hall, erected in 1877 from the designs of Alfred Waterhouse, R.A., together with a large extension of 1938; the Royal Exchange (1869, enlarged 1921) the Central Library (1934); Heaton Hall; the 17th century Chetham Library; the Rylands Library (1899), which includes the Althorp collection; the University precinct; the 15th-century Cathedral (formerly the parish church) and the Free Trade Hall. Manchester is the home of the Hallé Orchestra, the Royal Northern College of Music, the Royal Exchange Theatre and seven public art galleries.

The town received its first charter of incorporation in 1838 and was created a city in 1853. The title of city was retained under local government reorganization.

NEWCASTLE UPON TYNE

NEWCASTLE UPON TYNE (Tyne and Wear) a Metropolitan District on the north bank of the River Tyne, is 8 miles from the North Sea, 272 miles N. of London and has an area of 27,640 acres. A Cathedral and University City, it is the administrative, commercial and cultural centre for north-east England and the principal port. It is an important manufacturing centre with a wide variety of industries.

The principal buildings include the Castle Keep (12th century), Black Gate (13th century), Blackfriars (13th century), West Walls (13th century), St. Nicholas's Cathedral (15th century, fine lantern tower), St. Andrew's Church (12th–14th century), St. John's (14th–15th century), All Saints (1786 by Stephenson), St. Mary's Roman Catholic Cathedral (1844), Trinity House (17th century), Sandhill (16th century houses), Guildhall (Georgian), Grey Street (1834–39), Central Station (1846–50), Laing Art Gallery (1904), University of Newcastle Physics Building (1962), Civic Centre (1963), Central Library (1969) and Eldon Square Development (1976). Open spaces include the Town Moor (927 acres) and Jesmond Dene. Eight bridges span the Tyne at Newcastle.

The City derives its name from the "new castle" (1080) erected as a defence against the Scots. In 1400 it was made a County, and in 1882 a City.

NORWICH

NORWICH (Norfolk) is an ancient City 110 miles N.E. of London. It grew from an early Anglo-Saxon settlement near the confluence of the Rivers Yare and Wensum, and now serves as provincial capital for the predominantly agricultural region of East Anglia. The name is thought to relate to the most northerly of a group of Anglo-Saxon villages or "wics". The present City has an area of 9,655 acres. The City's first known Charter was granted in 1158 by Henry II.

Norwich serves its surrounding area as a market town and commercial centre, banking and insurance being prominent among the City's businesses. From the 14th century until the Industrial Revolution, Norwich was the regional centre of the woollen industry, but now the biggest single industry is the manufacturing of shoes and other principal trades are engineering, printing, and the production of chemicals, clothing, confectionery and other foodstuffs. Norwich is accessible to seagoing vessels by means of the River Yare, entered at Great Yarmouth, 20 miles to the east.

Among many historic buildings are the Cathedral (completed in the twelfth century and surmounted by a fifteenth century spire 315 feet in height), the Keep of the Norman Castle (now a museum and art gallery), the fifteenth century flint-walled Guildhall, some thirty medieval parish churches, St. Andrew's and Blackfriars' Halls, the Tudor houses preserved in Elm Hill and the Georgian Assembly House. The University of East Anglia has been established in Norwich on a spacious site at Earlham on the City's western boundary and received its first students in 1963.

NOTTINGHAM

NOTTINGHAM (Nottinghamshire) stands on the River Trent, 124 miles N.N.W. of London in one of the most valuable coalfields of the country connected by canal with the Atlantic and the North Sea. The municipal area is 18,364 acres.

The principal industries are hosiery, lace, bleaching, dyeing and spinning, tanning, engineering and cycle works, brewing, the manufacture of tobacco, chemicals, furniture, typewriters and mechanical products.

The chief buildings are the 17th century Nottingham Castle (restored in 1878, and now the City Museum and Gallery of Art), Wollaton Hall (1580–88) owned by the City Council and now a Natural History Museum, St. Mary's, St. Peter's, and St. Nicholas's Churches, the Roman Catholic Cathedral (Pugin, 1942–4), the Council House (1929), the Guildhall and Court House (1888), Shire Hall, Albert Hall, the University, Trent Polytechnic, Newstead Abbey, home of Lord Byron, the Theatre Royal (1865), the Playhouse (1963) and the Royal Concert Hall (1982).

Snotingaham or *Notingeham*, "the village or home of the sons of Snot" (the Wise), is the Anglo-Saxon name for the Celtic *Tuigogobauc*, "Cave Homes". The City possesses a Charter of Henry II, and was created a City in 1897. Under local government reorganization, the style of city was reaccorded from April, 1974.

OXFORD

OXFORD is a University City, an important industrial centre, and a market town, with an area of 8,785 acres. Industry played a minor part in Oxford until the motor industry was established in 1912.

It is for its architecture that Oxford is of most interest to the visitor, its oldest specimens being the reputed Saxon tower of St. Michael's church, the remains of the Norman castle and city walls and the Norman church at Iffley. It is chiefly famous however, for its Gothic buildings, such as the Divinity Schools, the Old Library at Merton College, William of Wykeham's New College, Magdalen College and Christ Church and many other college buildings. Later centuries are represented by the Laudian quadrangle at St. John's College, the Renaissance Sheldonian Theatre by Wren, Trinity College Chapel, and All Saints Church; Hawksmoor's mock-Gothic at All Souls College, and the eighteenth century Queens' College. In addition to individual buildings, High Street and Radcliffe Square, just off it, both form architectural compositions of great beauty. Most of the Colleges have gardens, those of Magdalen, New College, St. John's (designed by "Capability" Brown) and Worcester being the largest.

PLYMOUTH

PLYMOUTH is situated on the borders of Devon and Cornwall at the confluence of the Rivers Tamar and Plym, 210 miles from London, with an area of 19,572 acres. The city has a long maritime history; it was the home port of Sir Francis Drake and the starting point for his circumnavigation of the world, as well as the last port of call for the Mayflower when the Pilgrim Fathers sailed for the New World in 1620. The Barbican harbour area has many Elizabethan buildings, and on Plymouth Hoe stands the first lighthouse to be built on the Eddystone Rocks, some miles offshore.

Following extensive war damage, the city centre comprising a large shopping centre, municipal offices, law courts and public buildings, has been re-built. The main employment is provided by H.M.Dockyard, though many new industrial firms have become established in the post-war period and the city is a growing tourism centre. In conjunction with the Cornwall County Council, the Tamar Bridge was constructed linking the City by road with Cornwall.

PORTSMOUTH

PORTSMOUTH occupies Portsea Island, Hampshire, with boundaries extending to the mainland. It has an area of 15½ sq. miles and is 70 miles from London.

Portsmouth is a centre of industry and commerce, including many high technology and manufacturing industries. It is the U.K. headquarters of a major computer company and two insurance companies. H.M. Naval Base still has a substantial work force, although this has decreased in recent years. The commercial port and Continental Ferry Port is owned and run by the City Council, and carries passengers and vehicles to France and the Channel Islands.

A major port since the 16th century, Portsmouth is also a thriving seaside resort catering for thousands of visitors and day-trippers annually. Among many historic attractions are Lord Nelson's flagship, H.M.S. *Victory*; the Tudor warship *Mary Rose*; Charles Dickens' birthplace at 393 Old Commercial Road; the Royal Naval and Royal Marine museums; Southsea Castle (built by Henry VIII), the Round Tower and Point Battery, which for hundreds of years have guarded the entrance to Portsmouth Harbour; and Fort Widney on Portsdown Hill.

ST. ALBANS

Twenty-five miles north west of London and situated on the River Ver, ST. ALBANS' origins stem from the major Roman town of *Verulamium*. Named after the first Christian martyr in Britain, who was executed here, St. Albans has developed around the Norman Abbey and Cathedral Church (consecrated 1115), the second longest in Britain, built partly of materials from the old Roman city. The museums house Iron Age and Roman artifacts and the Roman Theatre, unique in Britain, has a stage as opposed to an amphitheatre. Archæological excavations in the city centre continue also to reveal evidence of pre-Roman, Saxon and medieval occupation.

The town's significance grew to the extent that it was a signatory and venue for the drafting of the Magna Carta. It was also the scene of major riots during the Peasants' Revolt; the French King John was imprisoned there after the Battle of Poitiers, and heavy fighting took place during the Wars of the Roses; but it is as a Roman town that it is best recognized.

Previously controlled by the Abbot, the town achieved a Royal Charter in 1553 and City status in 1877. The street market, first established in 1553, is still an important feature of the city, as are many hotels and inns which survive from the days when St. Albans was an important coach stop. Tourist attractions include historic churches and houses, and a 15th century clock tower.

The advent of the railway saw the gradual expansion of the city, and the area now contains a wide range of firms, with special emphasis on microtechnology and electronics, particularly in the medical field. In addition, it is the home of the Royal National Rose Society, and of Rothamsted Park, the agricultural research centre.

In 1974 the City and District of St. Albans was formed, taking in the town of Harpenden and many villages, and it now covers an area of 63 square miles.

SHEFFIELD

SHEFFIELD (South Yorkshire), the centre of the special steel and cutlery trades, is situated 159 miles N.N.W. of London, at the junction of the Sheaf, Porter, Rivelin and Loxley with the River Don.

Sheffield has an area of 91,000 acres (nearly 150 square miles), including 4,619 acres of publicly owned parks and woodland. Though its cutlery, silverware and plate have long been famous, Sheffield has other and now more important industries—special and alloy steels, engineering and tool-making. Research in glass, metallurgy, radiotherapy and other fields is carried on.

The parish church of St. Peter and St. Paul, founded in the twelfth century, became the Cathedral Church of the Diocese of Sheffield in 1914. The Roman Catholic Cathedral Church of St. Marie (founded 1847) was created Cathedral for the new diocese of Hallam in 1980. Parts of the present building date from about 1435. The principal buildings are the Town Hall (1897, 1923 and 1977), the Cutlers' Hall (1832), the University (1905 and recent extensions, including 19-storey Arts Tower), City Hall (1932), Graves Art Gallery (1934), Castle Market Building

(1959), the retail market (1973), Mappin Art Gallery and the Crucible Theatre.

Sheffield was created a city in 1893 and on April 1, 1974 became a Metropolitan District Council incorporating Stocksbridge and most of the Wortley Rural area, and retained city status.

Master Cutler (1983–84) 360th *Master of the Company of Cutlers in Hallamshire,* W. J. D. Carr.

SOUTHAMPTON

SOUTHAMPTON is Britain's premier passenger and a fast-growing container port. The first Charter was granted by Henry II and Southampton was created a county of itself in 1447. In February, 1964, Her Majesty the Queen granted city status by Royal Charter. The city has an area of 12,071 acres excluding tidal waters.

There have been Roman and Saxon settlements on the site of the city, which has been an important port since the time of the Conquest due to its natural deep-water harbour. The oldest church is St. Michael's (1070) which has a black tournai marble font and an unusually tall tower, a landmark for navigators of Southampton Water. Other buildings and monuments within the city walls are the Tudor Merchants Hall, the Weigh-house, West Gate, King John's House, Long House, Holy Rood Church, St. Julien's Church and the Mayflower Memorial. From 1982 a naval destroyer, H.M.S. Cavalier went on show as a floating museum in the Eastern Docks. Public open spaces total over 1,000 acres in extent and comprise 9 per cent. of the city's area. The Common covers an area of 328 acres in the central district of the city and is mostly natural parkland.

STOKE-ON-TRENT

STOKE-ON-TRENT (Staffordshire), familiarly known as The Potteries, stands on the River Trent 157 miles N. of London. The present municipal area is 22,916 acres (36 square miles) and the city is the main centre of employment for the population of North Staffordshire. It is the largest clayware producer in the world (china, earthenware, sanitary goods, refractories, bricks and tiles) and has a considerable coal mining output drawn from one of the richest coalfields in Western Europe. The city has steelworks, foundries, chemical works, engineering plants, rubber works, paper mills, and a very wide range of manufactures.

Extensive reconstruction has been carried on in recent years. A unique feature of the city is that it has six "centres" and more shops and public halls than other areas of comparable size. The City was formed by the federation in 1910 of the separate municipal authorities of Tunstall, Burslem, Hanley, Stoke-upon-Trent, Fenton, and Longton, all of which are now combined in the present City of Stoke-on-Trent.

WINCHESTER

WINCHESTER, the ancient capital of England, is situated on the River Itchen 65 miles S.W. of London and 12 miles north of Southampton. Since local government reorganization in 1974, the style of City has been accorded to the whole of the new district of Winchester, which embraces an area of 162,921 acres of Mid-Hampshire.

Winchester is rich in architecture of all types but the cathedral takes first place. The longest Gothic cathedral in the world, it was built in 1079–1093 and exhibits examples of Norman, Early English and Perpendicular styles. Winchester College, founded in 1382, is one of the most famous public schools, the original building (of 1393) remaining unaltered. St. Cross Hospital, another great medieval foundation, lies 1 mile south of the city. Founded in 1136 by Bishop Henry de Blois, the Almshouses were re-established in 1445 by Cardinal Henry Beaufort. The Chapel and dwellings are of great architectural interest, and visitors may still receive the "Wayfarer's Dole" of bread and ale.

Recent excavations have done much to clarify the origins and development of Winchester. Excavations in the Cathedral Close have uncovered the entire site of the Anglo-Saxon cathedral (known as the Old Minster) and parts of the New Minster, built by Alfred's son Edward the Elder, and the burial place of the Alfredian dynasty. The original burial place of St. Swithun, before his remains were translated to a site in the present cathedral, was also uncovered.

Excavations in other parts of the City have thrown much light on Norman Winchester, notably on the site of the Royal Castle, adjacent to which the new Law Courts have been built, and in the grounds of the Bishop's Palace at Wolvesey, where the great house built by Bishops Walkelin and Henry of Blois in the early 12th century has been uncovered.

YORK

The City of YORK is a District in the County of North Yorkshire, and is an archiepiscopal seat. The City has an area of 7,295 acres.

The recorded history of York dates from A.D. 71, when the Roman Ninth Legion established a base under Petilius Cerealis which later became the fortress of Eboracum. In Anglo-Saxon times the city was the royal and ecclesiastical centre of Northumbria, and was captured by a Viking army in A.D. 866, after which it became the capital of the Viking kingdom of Jorvik. By the 14th century the city had become a great mercantile centre, chiefly owing to its control of the wool trade, and was used as the chief base against the Scots. Under the Tudors its fortunes declined, though Henry VIII made it the headquarters of the Council of the North. Recent excavations on many sites, including Coppergate, has greatly expanded knowledge of Roman, Viking and medieval urban life.

With its development as a railway centre in the 19th century the commercial life of York expanded and it is now a flourishing modern city. The principal industries are the manufacture of chocolate, railway coaches, scientific instruments, glass containers and sugar. The City is also an important tourist centre.

It is rich in examples of architecture of all periods. The earliest church (built, 627) was succeeded by several others until, in the 12th to the 15th centuries, the present Minster was built in a succession of styles. The finest features are the West front with its two towers, the spacious transepts and the stained glass. Other examples within the city are the medieval city walls and gateways, churches and guildhalls. Domestic architecture includes the Georgian mansions of The Mount, Micklegate and Bootham. Its museums are world-famous and include the Castle Museum, one of the best-known folk museums in Great Britain, and the National Railway Museum.

THE NATIONAL PARKS

The ten National Parks described below in their order of designation have been established in England and Wales. These areas are not public property and visitors are not free to wander over private land within the Park boundaries. They have been marked out for special care aimed at two prime purposes: to conserve and enhance their natural beauty, and to promote their enjoyment by the public.

Peak District National Park (542 sq. miles).— Mainly in Derbyshire but extending into Staffordshire, Cheshire, South Yorkshire, West Yorkshire and Greater Manchester. In the south and east are limestone uplands, and finely wooded dales, while northwards, moorlands, edged by gritstone crags, attract hill walkers and climbers. There are information centres at Bakewell, Edale (open all year) and Castleton (Easter–October and possibly winter weekends), and information points in Goyt Valley and at Hartington (summer weekends and Bank Holidays). An information caravan tours the Park and there is a residential study centre at Nosehill Hall.

Lake District National Park (866 sq. miles).—In Cumbria. Spectacular mountain scenery with wooded lower slopes enhanced by lakes and tarns. The area includes England's highest mountains (Scafell Pike, Helvellyn and Skiddaw) and largest lakes. Walking and rock-climbing are the principal recreations, but there are fishing, swimming, sailing, boating and winter sports as well. There are information centres at Keswick, Kendal, Ambleside, Waterhead, Hawkshead, Seatoller and Bowness. Information vans are sited at Coniston, Glenridding and Pooley Bridge. At Brockhole on the shore of Windermere, is a National Park centre and there is a residential study centre near Keswick.

Snowdonia National Park (838 sq. miles).—In Gwynedd in North Wales. A mountainous region of lakes, forest, wooded valleys, reservoirs and power stations and traversed by high passes, offering some of the finest rock-climbing and mountain walking for both beginner and expert. There are information centres at Aberdyfi, Bala, Betws y Coed, Blaenau Ffestiniog, Conwy, Harlech, Dolgellau, Llanberis, Llanrwst and Plas Tan y Bwlch, at which there is also a residential study centre.

Dartmoor National Park (365 sq. miles).—In Devon, the highest area of high moorland in southern England, famous for its granite "tors" often weathered into strange shapes. Fine hanging oak woods adorn the river valleys which lead up into the Moor. The Park is rich in prehistoric relics and offers fine walking and riding. Information vans are sited at Newbridge, Tavistock, Bovey Tracey, Steps Bridge, Princeton and Postbridge.

Pembrokeshire Coast National Park (225 sq. miles).—A spectacular section of Britain's coastline, where rock cliffs alternate with bays and sandy coves. In the north is Mynydd Preseli, abounding in prehistoric relics. The Park includes the fine Milford Haven waterway reaches, Tenby, the cathedral of St. David's, and Carew and other Norman castles. There are information centres at Tenby, St. David's, Pembroke, Newport, Kilgetty, Haverfordwest and Broad Haven.

North York Moors National Park (553 sq. miles).—In North Yorkshire and Cleveland, the Park stretches from the Hambleton Hills in the west to the coastline above Scarborough. On the coast sheltered bays and sandy beaches alternate with headlands harbouring villages such as Staithes and Robin Hood's Bay. The heart of the Park offers tracts of open moorland, intersected by wooded valleys. Mount Grace Priory and the abbeys of Rievaulx and Byland are within the Park. There are information centres at Danby Lodge, Pickering, Sutton Bank, Ravenscar, Helmsley and Hutton-le-Hole, and a day study centre at Danby Lodge.

Yorkshire Dales National Park (680 sq. miles).— An area of upland moors, cut by deep valleys, mostly in North Yorkshire but extending into Cumbria. The Park includes some of the finest limestone scenery in Britain: Kilnsey Crag in Wharfedale, Gordale Scar, and Malham Cove in Malhamdale. In the Park also are Swaledale and Wensleydale, the three peaks of Ingleborough, Whernside and Pen-y-Ghent, and many relics of the past such as the Roman fort at Bainbridge and Bolton Abbey in Wharfedale. There are information centres at Clapham, Grassington, Hawes, Aysgarth Falls, Malham and Sedbergh, and a national park cave and fell centre at Whernside Manor.

Exmoor National Park (265 sq. miles).—Mainly in Somerset but extending into Devon, this is a moorland plateau with finely wooded combes encompassing the well-known coastline between Minehead and Combe Martin Bay in the north and the Brendon Hills in the east. There are information centres at Lynmouth, County Gate and Dulverton. An information van is sited at Combe Martin.

Northumberland National Park (398 sq. miles).—A region of hills and moorland, stretching from Hadrian's Roman Wall in the south to the Cheviot Hills on the Scottish Border. The area is rich in historic interest. There are information centres at Byrness, Ingram, Once Brewed, Rothbury, Housesteads, Hexham and Harbottle Hills. An information caravan is sited at Cawfields.

Brecon Beacons National Park (519 sq. miles).— The most recent National Park, established in 1957, is centred on "The Beacons" with its three peaks: Pen y Fan, Corn Du and Cribyn rising to nearly 3,000 feet. But it includes the Black Mountains to the east and the Black Mountain to the west, thus taking in parts of Gwent and Dyfed as well as southern Powys and a small area of Mid-Glamorgan. The Upper Usk Valley, Llangorse Lake, Brecon Cathedral, Carreg Cennen Castle and Llanthony Priory are all within the Park. There are information centres at Brecon, Craig-y-nos Country Park, Abergavenny, Llandovery, a study centre at Danywenallt and a day visitor centre near Libanus. Brecon.

AREAS OF OUTSTANDING NATURAL BEAUTY

These are designated solely for landscape conservation purposes. They are listed below, in alphabetical order, having been designated between December, 1956 and October, 1983.

Anglesey (83 sq. miles).—Except for breaks around the urban areas and in the vicinity of Wylfa, the designated area extends along the entire coastline. The varied scenery is famed for its beauty, as also are

the Menai Straits, separating the island from the mainland.

Arnside and Silverdale (29 sq. miles).—Lying along the upper half of Morecambe Bay, the area embraces the Kent estuary where it adjoins the Lake District National Park and includes extensive tidal flats in the Bay. The varied coastal landscape contains several limestone hills, woodland and bog areas locally known as "mosses". Known for its wildfowl breeding grounds, the whole area is of considerable ecological value.

Cannock Chase (26 sq. miles).—This is an area of high heathland in Staffordshire, relieved by varied scenery in which parklands adjoin farms, woodlands and pleasant villages. Deer continue to roam over the Chase.

Chichester Harbour (29 sq. miles).—Well known for its small boating and sailing facilities, the area extends from Hayling Island in the west to Apuldram in the east and contains the whole of Thorney Island.

Chilterns (309 sq. miles).—The well-known chalk downlands from Goring in South Oxfordshire north-eastwards through Buckinghamshire, Hertfordshire and Bedfordshire to Dunstable and Luton, including the outlying group of hills beyond Luton. Contains several National Trust properties and Whipsnade Zoo.

Cornwall (360 sq. miles).—Comprising a number of separate areas including Bodmin Moor and some of the finest and best-known coastal scenery in Britain. Most of the Land's End peninsula; the coast between St. Michael's Mount and St. Austell with Falmouth omitted; and the Fowey Estuary are all included: in north Cornwall most of the coast to Bedruthan Steps, north of Newquay, and between Perranporth and Godrevy Towans. In 1983 10 sq. miles of the Camel Estuary were added to the designated area.

Cotswolds (582 sq. miles).—Contains the great limestone escarpment overlooking the Vales of Gloucester and Evesham. The remainder is high undulating country and narrow wooded valleys traversed by shallow rapid streams. Noted for its beautiful villages.

Cranborne Chase and West Wiltshire Downs (370 sq. miles).—This area, covering parts of Wiltshire, Dorset, Hampshire and Somerset, contains extensive tracts of chalkland, with steep-sided combes and scarps, and the wooded remnants of the ancient Chase. To the west the area is bounded by wooded greens and hills and the Vale of Wardour.

Dedham Vale (28 sq. miles).—This is the flat land of water meadows with hedges and woodland, bordering Essex and Suffolk, where John Constable (1776–1837) painted during much of his life. Flatford Mill, Willy Lott's Cottage and the church of Stoke-by-Nayland still stand.

East Devon (103 sq. miles).—The area comprises the fine stretch of coastline between Orcombe Rocks, near Exmouth, and the Dorset area near Lyme Regis, with Sidmouth, Beer and Seaton omitted, Inland Gittisham Hill, East Hill and Woodbury and Aylebeare Commons are all included.

North Devon (66 sq. miles).—Comprising three sections of fine coastline—the whole of the Hartland peninsula; from Bideford Bar to the western limits of Ilfracombe, and from east of Ilfracombe to the boundary of the Exmoor National Park. Clovelly, Braunton Burrows, Woolacombe and Combe Martin are all included.

South Devon (128 sq. miles).—It includes the magnificent coast between Bolt Head and Bolt Tail, a National Trust property; Salcombe, Slapton Sands and Dartmouth, and the four estuaries and valleys of the Yealm, Erme, Avon and Dart.

Dorset (400 sq. miles).—Takes in the whole of the coastline between Lyme Regis and Poole, with the Isle of Portland and Weymouth omitted, and stretches inland to include the Purbeck Hills and the downs, heaths and wooded valleys of the Hardy country.

Forest of Bowland (310 sq. miles).—A fine tract of high open moorland running westward from near Settle and Bolton by Bowland in the Pennines, to Caton and Scorton in Central Lancashire. A small outlying area east of the River Ribble includes Pendle Hill and Pendleton Moor.

Gower (73 sq. miles).—In the county of West Glamorgan, South Wales, the area is known for its beautiful coastline, its rocky limestone cliffs, sandy bays and coves and for its wooded ravines stretching inland.

East Hampshire (151 sq. miles).—This mainly chalkland area stretches from the outskirts of Winchester to the Hampshire/Sussex border at a distance of about 10 miles inland from the south coast.

South Hampshire Coast (30 sq. miles).—14 miles of coastline on the northern shores of the Solent, between Hurst Castle and Calshot Castle, south-east of Fawley, with the central part of the area extending inland up the Beaulieu River for about six miles, including a beautiful part of the New Forest. Along much of the coast woods of oak and Scots pine stretch down to the water's edge, while at the western end are some attractive salt marshes.

High Weald (560 sq. miles).—Based on the central sandstone hills of the Weald of South-East England, the area covers parts of East and West Sussex, Kent and Surrey. It is predominantly wooded, with copses of deciduous woodland as well as larger heathland areas like Ashdown Forest, the remnants of the old Wealden forests. Orchards and cultivated land are also characteristic, as are landscaped parks, historic buildings and villages, and hammer ponds, the relics of the ancient iron industry.

Kent Downs (326 sq. miles).—Running from the Surrey border near Westerham (its boundary adjoining that of the Surrey Hills area), about 60 miles to the coast near Dover and Folkestone, with a coastal outlier at South Foreland and a narrow strip of the old sea cliff escarpment west of Hythe overlooking Romney Marsh. Pleasant pastoral scenery, picturesque villages, ancient churches and castles, with the Downs rising to 600 feet.

Lincolnshire Wolds (216 sq. miles).—The area extends in a south-east direction from Laceby and Caistor in the north to the region of Spilsby, about ten miles west of Skegness. Its charm is derived from the undulating terrain, sparse settlement pattern and the excellent views from the chalk escarpments. The wolds are extensively farmed and contain numerous small, attractive villages.

Lleyn (60 sq. miles).—An isolated peninsula in Gwynedd, North Wales, of unique character, still largely unspoilt by the hand of man.

Malvern Hills (40 sq. miles).—The area embodies the whole range of the Malvern Hills in the county of Hereford and Worcester, just touching Gloucestershire. Such well-known features as the Worcestershire Beacon, North Hill, the Herefordshire Beacon, and Midsummer Hill, a National Trust property, are within the area.

Mendip Hills (78 sq. miles).—Comprising over half of the Mendip Hills, the area stretches, west to east, from Bleadon Hill to the A.39 road north of Wells. Blagdon Lake and Chew Magna Lake are within the boundary which, in the south, takes in Cheddar Gorge. The plateau, rising to over 1,000 ft., commands fine views over the Bristol Channel and surrounding countryside. Noted for its caves, including Wookey Hole, the area is of great scientific and historic interest.

Norfolk Coast (174 sq. miles).—With coastal scenery ranging from salt marsh and mudflats, sand-dunes and shingle ridges to sea cliffs, this area includes six miles of the south-east coast of the Wash, an almost continuous coastal strip three to five miles in depth from Hunstanton to Bacton, with a further small strip between Sea Palling and Winterton-on-Sea. The area, which is rich in wild-life, also includes part of the Sandringham Estate.

Northumberland Coast (50 sq. miles).—Low cliffs and rocky headlands with active fishing villages comprise this area which stretches from just south of Berwick to Amble. It includes Holy Island, with the oldest monastic ruins in the country; the Farne Islands, and the great castles of Bamburgh, Dunstan-burgh and Warkworth.

Quantock Hills (38 sq. miles).—The main feature of this area in Somerset is the range of red sandstone hills rising to a height of 1,260 feet at Will's Neck above Crow Combe.

Isles of Scilly (6 sq. miles).—There are about 140 islands and skerries in the Scillies group of which only five are inhabited. Geologically, the formation is similar to Land's End and other granite areas in Cornwall. The coastline is dramatically rocky, inter-spersed with sheltered sandy beaches and areas of dune of bleached decomposed granite, glistening with mica and shells. There are coastal paths round the larger islands, and a number of sites of special scientific interest, identified by the Nature Conservancy Council.

Shropshire Hills (300 sq. miles).—This area includes the fine landscape around Church Stretton, with Caer Caradoc, the Long Mynd, the Stiperstones, and the long ridge of Wenlock Edge from which it extends north-east to the Wrekin and the Ercall.

Solway Coast (41 sq. miles).—A stretch of beautiful coastline in Cumbria from above Maryport to the estuaries of the Rivers Eden and Esk (with Silloth omitted) backed by the Solway Plain and noted for its historic and scientific interests.

Suffolk Coast and Heaths (151 sq. miles).—Takes in 38 miles of coastline and parts of the Stour and Orwell estuaries, while the Deben, Alde and Blyth

flow through it. With heath, woodland, marsh and beaches, the scenery is attractively varied and the area important to ornithologists.

Surrey Hills (160 sq. miles).—The Hog's Back and the ridge of the North Downs from Guildford to Titsey in the east are within this area, as are Leith Hill, Hindhead Common, the Devil's Punch Bowl; the well-known villages of Abinger, Shere, Hamble-don and Chiddingfold; Box Hill and Frensham Ponds.

Sussex Downs (379 sq. miles).—The area includes the chalk escarpment of the South Downs from Beachy Head to the West Sussex/Hampshire border, with such well-known features as Firle Beacon and Chanctonbury Ring, and stretches down to the coast between Eastbourne and Seaford. In the west the boundary adjoins the East Hampshire and Surrey Hills areas.

North Wessex Downs (671 sq. miles).—An upland area in Hampshire, Wiltshire, Oxfordshire and Berk-shire, bounded by the Marlborough and Lambourn Downs in the west and the Chiltern Hills in the east. To the south of the downs the area is intersected by the Kennet Valley, the Vale of Pewsey and Enbourne Vale, with Savernake Forest in the midst. The southern section comprises the North Hampshire Downs where they descend to the Test Valley which, together with Salisbury Plain, form the southern limit of what is so far the largest area designated.

Isle of Wight (73 sq. miles).—A number of separate areas comprising unspoiled stretches of coastline, the Yar Valley, the high downland behind Ventnor and the fine chalk downland ridge east of Newport to Culver Cliff and Foreland.

Wye Valley (125 sq. miles).—This area lies within the counties of Gwent, Gloucestershire and Hereford and Worcester. The lower Wye Valley landscape is characterised by its steeply-wooded slopes, cliffs and gorges where the river has cut through limestone outcrops. Further north the valley is broader and the river meanders through pleasant pastureland. Tintern Abbey and the well-known viewpoint from Symonds Yat are within this beautiful area. The flora include many rare species.

HISTORIC MONUMENTS

England

A select list of monuments under the control, since its creation in April 1984, of the Historic Buildings and Monuments Commission for England.

Charges for admission represent the figures obtaining in 1984.

Reduced admission prices for retirement pension-ers and children under 16. 10 per cent. discount for parties of 11 or more. Annual membership passes are available at £8 for adults and £4 for pensioners and children upon application to the Commission, 25 Savile Row, London W1X 2BT.

Standard hours of opening (marked *) are as follows:

	Weekdays	Sundays
Mar. 15–Oct. 15	9.30 a.m.–6.30 p.m.	2.00–6.30 p.m.
Oct. 16–Mar. 14	9.30 a.m.–4.00 p.m.	2.00–4.00 p.m.

Monuments not marked * open April–Sept. only.

Those marked † open on Sundays at 9.30 a.m. from April–Sept. inclusive.

All monuments are closed on Christmas Eve, Christmas Day, Boxing Day and New Year's Day. Some smaller sites may close for the lunch-hour, which is normally 1–2 p.m.

BEESTON CASTLE, Cheshire. 60p*. Thirteenth-century inner ward with gatehouse and towers, and considerable remains of large outer ward.

BERKHAMSTED CASTLE, Hertfordshire*. Extensive remains of a large 11th-century motte-and-bailey castle with later stone wall.

BOLSOVER CASTLE, Derbyshire. 50p†*. established in Norman times, it is now notable for its exception-ally interesting 17th-century buildings.

BOSCOBEL HOUSE, Salop. 50p*†. Timber-framed early 17-century hunting lodge with later alterations. Charles II's "Royal Oak" is nearby.

BRINKBURN PRIORY, Northumberland. 40p†*. An Augustinian priory; the church (c. 1200, repaired in 1858) and parts of the claustral buildings survive.

BROUGHAM CASTLE, Cumbria. 50p†*. Extensive remains of the keep (c. 1170), and of other buildings of periods up to the 17th century.

BYLAND ABBEY, North Yorkshire. 40p*. Consider-able remains of church and conventual buildings date from the abbey's foundation in 1177 by the Cistercians.

CARISBROOKE CASTLE, Isle of Wight. Summer £1.20, Winter 60p†*. Extensive motte-and-bailey castle with shell keep.

CARLISLE CASTLE, Cumbria. Summer 90p, Winter 50p†*. The Castle was begun by William Rufus. The keep houses the Regimental Museum of the Border Regiment.

CASTLE ACRE PRIORY, Norfolk. 40p†*. Extensive remains include the church with its elaborate west front, and the prior's lodgings.

CASTLE RISING, Norfolk. 50p†*. A fine 12th-century keep stands in a massive earthwork with its gatehouse and bridge.

CHESTERS ROMAN FORT, Northumberland. Summer 80p, Winter 40p†*.

CHYSAUSTER ANCIENT VILLAGE, Cornwall, 40p†*. Iron-Age village of courtyard houses.

CLEEVE ABBEY, Somerset. 60p†* Much of the claustral buildings survive including timber-roofed frater, but only foundations of the church.

CORBRIDGE ROMAN STATION, Northumberland. 50p*. Excavations have revealed the central area of the Roman town and military base of Corstopitum.

DEAL CASTLE, Kent. 50p†*. The largest and most complete of the castles erected by Henry VIII for coastal defence.

DOVER CASTLE, Kent. Keep—Summer £1, Winter 60p†*; Underground Works 50p*; Grounds—free. One of the largest and most important English castles.

DUNSTANBURGH CASTLE, Northumberland. 40p†*. The castle, standing on a cliff above the sea, has a 14th-century gatehouse-keep.

FARLEIGH CASTLE, Somerset. 40p†*. Late 14th-century castle of two courts. The chapel contains fine relics of Sir Thomas Hungerford.

FARNHAM CASTLE, Surrey. 30p. Keep, April–Sept. Built by the Bishops of Winchester, the motte of the castle is enclosed by a large 12th-century shell keep.

FINCHALE PRIORY, Durham. 30p†. Benedictine house on banks of River Wear with considerable 13th-century remains.

FOUNTAINS ABBEY, North Yorkshire. Summer 90p, Winter 50p†*. Finest monastic ruin in W. Europe.

FRAMLINGHAM CASTLE, Suffolk. 40p†*. Impressive castle with high curtain-walls of late 12th-century enclosing a poor-house of 1639.

FURNESS ABBEY, Cumbria. 50p*. Founded in 1127 by Stephen, afterwards King of England; extensive remains of church and conventual buildings.

GOODRICH CASTLE, Hereford and Worcester. 50p†*. Extensive remains of beautiful 14th-century castle incorporating interesting 12th-century keep.

GRIMES GRAVES, Norfolk. 50p†*. Extensive group of flint mines dating from the Stone Age. Several shafts can be inspected.

HAILES ABBEY, Gloucestershire. 50p†*. Ruins of a Cistercian monastery founded in 1246. Museum contains some fine architectural fragments.

HELMSLEY CASTLE, North Yorkshire. 40p†*. Twelfth-century keep and curtain wall with 16th-century domestic buildings against west wall.

HOUSESTEADS ROMAN FORT, Northumberland. Summer 80p, Winter 40p†*. Excavation has exposed this infantry fort on Hadrian's Wall with its extra-mural civilian settlement.

KENILWORTH CASTLE, Warwickshire. 50p*. One of the finest and most extensive castles in England, showing many styles of building from 1155 to 1649.

LANERCOST PRIORY, Cumbria. 40p. The nave of the priory church is still used and there are remains of other claustral buildings.

LINDISFARNE PRIORY, Northumberland. 40p†*. An Anglican monastery destroyed by the Danes, it was re-established by the Benedictine abbey of Durham.

LULLINGSTONE ROMAN VILLA, Kent. Summer 90p, Winter 50p†*. A large villa occupied through much

of the Roman period; fine mosaics and a unique Christian chapel.

MIDDLEHAM CASTLE, North Yorkshire. 50p*. The fine keep of 1170 stands in the centre of 13th-century inner ward.

MOUNT GRACE PRIORY, North Yorkshire. 50p*. Carthusian monastery, with remains of monks' separate houses.

NETLEY ABBEY, Hampshire. 40p*. Extensive remains of 13th-century church, claustral buildings and abbot's house, incorporating much fine detail.

OLD SARUM, Wiltshire. 40p†*. Large 11th-century earthworks enclosing the excavated remains of the castle and the cathedral.

ORFORD CASTLE, Suffolk. 40p*†. Circular keep of c. 1170 and remains of coastal defence castle built by Henry II.

PENDENNIS CASTLE, Cornwall. 50p†*. Well-preserved castle erected by Henry VIII for coast defence and enlarged by Elizabeth I.

PEVENSEY CASTLE, East Sussex. 40p†*. Extensive remains of a Roman fort of the Saxon Shore enclosing an 11th-century castle.

PEVERIL CASTLE, Derbyshire. 50p*†. In a picturesque and nearly impregnable position, this 12th-century castle is defended on two sides by precipitous rocks.

PORTCHESTER CASTLE, Hampshire. 50p†*. A Roman fort of the Saxon Shore enclosing a fine Norman keep and priory church.

RECULVER CASTLE and ROMAN FORT, Kent. 30p. Remains of Saxon church with 12th-century towers standing in a Roman fort.

RICHBOROUGH CASTLE. Kent. 50p†*. The landing-site of the Claudian invasion, it became a supply-base and a Saxon Shore fort.

RICHMOND CASTLE, North Yorkshire. 60p†*. This very fine 12th-century keep, with 11th-century curtain-wall and gatehouse, commands Swaledale.

RIEVAULX ABBEY, North Yorkshire. Summer 80p, Winter 40p†*. Extensive remains include an early Cistercian nave (1140) and fine 13th-century choir and claustral buildings.

ROCHESTER CASTLE, Kent. 50p*†. Eleventh-century wall, partly overlying the Roman city wall, encloses splendid square keep of c. 1130.

ST. AUGUSTINE'S ABBEY, Canterbury, Kent. 40p†*. Founded by St. Augustine in 598; 7th- and 11th-century churches underlie the mediaeval abbey.

ST. MAWES CASTLE, Cornwall. 40p†*. Coast defence castle built by Henry VIII consisting of central tower and three bastions.

SCARBOROUGH CASTLE, North Yorkshire. 50p†*. Remains of 12th-century keep and curtain-walls dominating the town.

STONEHENGE, Wiltshire. 60p†*. Sundays from 9.30 a.m. all year. World-famous prehistoric monument consisting of central stone circles surrounded by bank and ditch.

TILBURY FORT, Essex. 50p*. Built to guard the Thames against the Dutch, the fort is a fine example of 17th-century fortification.

TINTAGEL CASTLE, Cornwall. 60p†*. Twelfth-century castle on cliff-top site and remains of a Celtic monastery.

TYNEMOUTH PRIORY and CASTLE, Tyne and Wear. 50p†*. Anglian monastery destroyed by the Danes and re-established in 1090, with 14th-century defensive system.

WALMER CASTLE, Kent. Summer 90p, Winter 50p†*. Closed Mon. (unless Bank Holiday) and when Lord Warden is in residence. One of Henry VIII's coast defence castles, it is the residence of the Lord Warden of the Cinque Ports.

WARKWORTH CASTLE, Northumberland. 50p†. Magnificent early 15th-century keep built by the Percys, with other remains from earlier periods.

WHITBY ABBEY, North Yorkshire. 40p†*. A Saxon foundation destroyed by the Danes with considerable remains of fine 13th-century church.

WROXETER ROMAN CITY, Shropshire 40p†*. The public baths and part of the forum remain of the Roman town of Viroconium.

Wales

A select list of monuments under the control of the Welsh Office. Charges for admission represent the figures obtaining in 1984. Concessionary rates are available for children, etc. Hours of opening are as shown for English monuments.

BEAUMARIS CASTLE, Anglesey, Gwynedd. 80p†. The finest example of the concentrically planned castle in Britain, it is still almost intact.

CAERLEON ROMAN AMPHITHEATRE, Gwent. 50p†. late 1st-century oval arena surrounded by bank for spectators with entrance passages.

CAERNARFON CASTLE, Gwynedd. Summer £1.65, Winter £1.00†. The most important of the Edwardian castles, built together with the town wall between 1283 and 1330.

CAERPHILLY CASTLE, Glamorgan. 80p†. Concentrically planned castle (c. 1270) notable for its great scale and use of water defences.

CASTELL COCH, S. Glamorgan. £1.00. Rebuilt 1875–90 on medieval foundations.

CHEPSTOW CASTLE, Gwent. 80p†. Fine rectangular keep in the middle of extensive fortifications.

CONWY CASTLE, Gwynedd. 80p†. Built by Edward I to guard the Conway ferry, it is a magnificent example of mediaeval architecture.

CRICCIETH CASTLE, Gwynedd. 60p†. A native Welsh castle of the early 13th century, much altered by Edward I.

DENBIGH CASTLE, Clwyd. 60p†. The remains of the castle, which dates from 1282–1322, include unusual triangular gatehouse.

HARLECH CASTLE, Gwynedd. 80p†. Well preserved Edwardian castle with a concentric plan sited on rocky outcrop above the former shore-line.

RAGLAN CASTLE, Gwent. 70p†. Extensive and imposing remains of 15th-century castle with moated hexagonal keep.

ST. DAVID'S, BISHOP'S PALACE, Dyfed. 60p†. Extensive remains of principal residence of Bishop of St. David's dating from 1280–1350.

TINTERN ABBEY, Gwent. 50p†. Very extensive remains of the fine 13th-century church and conventual buildings of this Cistercian monastery.

Scotland

A select list of monuments under the control of the Scottish Development Department.

Charges for admission represent the figures obtaining in 1984. Concessionary rates are available for children, etc.

Standard hours of opening (marked S.) are as follows:

	Weekdays	Sundays
April–Sept.	9.30–7.00 p.m.	2.00–7.00 p.m.
Oct.–March	9.30–4.00 p.m.	2.00–4.00 p.m.

Monuments open at any reasonable time are indicated by A.

ABERLEMNO, Tayside. Four Pictish stones. A. Closed in Winter. Admission free.

ANTONINE WALL, Central and Strathclyde Regions. A. Admission free.

ARNOL BLACKHOUSE, Western Isles. S. 40p. Traditional Hebridean dwelling.

BONAWE, Strathclyde. A. Closed in Winter. 50p. Mid-18th century iron-furnace.

BROUGH OF BIRSAY, Orkney. A. 40p. Remains of the Norse period.

BROWN AND WHITE CATERTHUNS, Tayside. A. Admission free. Iron Age hill forts.

CAERLAVEROCK CASTLE, Dumfries and Galloway. S. 40p.

CAIRNPAPPLE HILL, Lothian. S. 35p. A prehistoric ritual complex and Bronze Age cairn.

CALLANISH, Western Isles. A. Admission free. Standing Stones.

CAMSTER CAIRNS, Highland. A. Admission free.

CLAVA CAIRNS, Highland. A. Admission free.

DRYBURGH ABBEY, Borders. S. 60p.

EARLS AND BISHOPS PALACES, Kirkwall, Orkney. S. 50p.

EDINBURGH CASTLE, including Scottish National War Memorial, Scottish United Services Museum and Historic Apartments. Admission to War Memorial, free; to all other areas, Nov.–March £1.30, April–Oct. £1.70. There is no reduction for parties. Members of H.M. Forces in uniform free. Open Oct.–March, weekdays 9.30–5.05, Sun. 12.30–4.20; April–Sept. weekdays 9.30–5.50, Sun. 11.00–5.50.

Alterations may also be made to opening hours during the Tattoo, State and Military events.

EDZELL CASTLE, Tayside. S. 40p.

ELGIN CATHEDRAL, Grampian. S. 50p.

FORT GEORGE, Highland. S. 40p.

GLASGOW CATHEDRAL, Strathclyde. S. Admission free.

GLENELG BROCHS, Highland. A. Admission free.

HERMITAGE CASTLE, Borders. S. 30p.

HUNTLY CASTLE, Grampian. S. 40p.

JARLSHOF, Shetland. S. 50p. Remains of villages from Bronze Age to Viking times.

JEDBURGH ABBEY, Borders. S. 50p.

KELSO ABBEY, Borders. S. Admission free.

LINLITHGOW PALACE, Lothian. S. 60p.

LOANHEAD STONE CIRCLE, Grampian. A. Admission free.

MAES HOWE, Orkney. S. 60p. Prehistoric tomb.

MEIGLE MUSEUM, Tayside. S. 35p. Pictish stones.

MELROSE ABBEY, Borders. S. 70p.

MOUSA BROCH, Shetland. A. Admission free.

NETHER LARGIE CAIRNS, Strathclyde. A. Admission free.

NEW ABBEY CORN MILL, Dumfries and Galloway. S. 40p.

RING OF BROGAR, Orkney. A. Admission free.

RUTHWELL CROSS, Dumfries and Galloway. A. Admission free.

ST. ANDREWS' CASTLE AND CATHEDRAL, Fife. S. 50p. Cathedral, admission free.

SKARA BRAE, Orkney. S. 80p. Prehistoric village.

SMAILHOLM TOWER, Borders. S. Closed in Winter. 50p.

STIRLING CASTLE, Central. Oct.–March, weekdays 9.30–5, Sun. 12.30–4.20; April–Sept., weekdays 9.30–6, Sun. 11–6. £1.20.

TANTALLON CASTLE, Lothian. S. 60p.

THREAVE CASTLE, Dumfries and Galloway. S. Admission free. Ferry charge 50p.

HOUSES OPEN TO THE PUBLIC

Times of summer opening and admission fees shown are those which obtained in 1984, and are subject to modification. Space permits only a selection of some of the more noteworthy houses in the U.K. which are open to the public. A fuller description of some houses in or near London will be found on pages 665–675. (*Property of the National Trust.)

ALNWICK CASTLE, Northumberland. Seat of the Duke of Northumberland.—May 6–Sept. 28, Daily (except Sat.) 1–5. Admission, £1.30.

A LA RONDE, Exmouth.—April–Oct., Mon.–Sat., 10–6; Sun., 2–7. Admission, £1.20p.

ALTHORP, Northampton.—All year (Sun., Tues., Wed., Thurs., Sat.) 2.30–5.30. Aug., (incl. Mon. and Fri.) 2.30–6, Bank Holidays, 11.30–6. Admission, £2.50, Weds., £3.50 (Connoisseurs' Day).

*ANGLESEY ABBEY, Cambs.—April 21–Oct. 14, Wed., Thurs., Fri., Sat., Sun. and Bank Holiday Mons. 2–6. Mar. 31–April 15, weekends only. Admission, £1.80.

ARUNDEL CASTLE, W. Sussex. Seat of the Duke of Norfolk.—April 1–Oct. 26, 1–5; June–Aug. and Bank Hols., 12–5. Closed Sats.

*AVEBURY MANOR, Marlborough.—April–Oct., Mon. to Sat., 11.30–6.30; Sun. 1.30–6.30. Nov.–March, Sat. and Sun., 1.30–5.

BADMINTON, Avon.—One Wednesday only in June, July, Aug. and Sept., 2.30–5.30. Admission, £1.

BANTRY HOUSE, Co. Cork.—All year, Daily, 9–6. Admission, £2.

*BASILDON PARK, Berks.—April–Oct., 2–6 (Wed. to Sat.); Suns. and Bank Holiday Mons., 12–6. Admission, £1.50.

BEAULIEU, Hants.—Easter–Sept., Daily, 10–6. Oct.–Easter, Daily 10–5 (see also page 653).

*BELTON HOUSE, Grantham.—April–Oct., Weds.–Suns. and Bank Hol. Mons., 1–5.30. Admission, £2.

BELVOIR CASTLE, nr. Grantham. Seat of the Duke of Rutland.—March 27–Sept. 30, Tues., Wed., Thurs., Sat and Good Friday, 12–6; Bank Holidays, 11–7; Suns., 12–7. Oct., Suns., 2–6. Admission, £1.80.

BERKELEY CASTLE, Glos.—May–Aug., Daily, except Mon. (but including Bank Holidays), 11–5; Sun. 2–5; April and Sept., 2–5; Bank Holidays, 11–5; Oct., Suns., 2–4.30. Admission, £1.70.

BLAIR CASTLE, Perths. Seat of the Duke of Atholl.—April, Suns. and Mons. April 19–Oct. 14., Daily, 10–5 (Suns. 2–5). Admission, £1.80.

BLENHEIM PALACE, Oxon. Seat of the Duke of Marlborough.—March 12–Oct. 31, Daily, 11–6.

BOUGHTON HOUSE, Northants. Seat of the Duke of Buccleuch & Queensberry.—April weekends; 2 weekends in May; July 28—Sept. 16, Daily (except Fri.); Sept. 19–Oct. 31, Wed., to Sun., 2–6. Admission, £2.

BOWHILL, Selkirk.—May–Sept., Mon., Wed., Thurs., Sat. and Sun. (July and Aug., Daily except Fri.) 12.30–5; Suns., 2–6. Admission, £1.50.

BROADLANDS, Hants.—April–Sept., Daily (closed Mon., except Aug., Sept. and Bank Holidays), 10–6. Admission, £2.25.

BROUGHTON CASTLE, Oxon.—mid May–mid Sept., Weds. and Suns. (also Thurs. in July and Aug.) and Bank Holidays, 2–5. Admission, £1.50.

*BUCKLAND ABBEY, Devon. Including Drake relics.—Good Fri.–Sept. (also Bank Holidays) 11–6; Suns. 2–6. Oct.–Easter, Wed. and weekends, 2–5. Admission, £1.20.

BURGHLEY HOUSE, Stamford.—April–7 Oct. (closed Sept. 8), Daily 11–5; Good Fri. and Suns., 2–5.

CARDIFF CASTLE.—May–Sept., Daily, 10–6; Nov.–Feb., Daily, 10–4; Mar., April, Oct., Daily, 10–5.

CARLTON TOWERS, N. Yorks.—May, June and Sept., Suns. only; July and Aug., Sun., Mon. and Wed., 1–5. Admission charged.

CASTLE ASHBY, Northants.—August. Daily (except day of Horse Trials), 2–6. Open all year to parties by prior arrangement.

*CASTLE COOLE, Enniskillen.—Closed for restoration work. Parklands remain open.

*CASTLE DROGO, Devonshire.—April–Oct., Daily, 11–6. Admission, £2.

CASTLE HOWARD, E. Yorks.—March 25–Oct., Daily, 11.30–5.

CAWDOR CASTLE, Inverness.—May–Sept., Daily, 10–5.30. Admission, £1.60.

*CHARTWELL, Kent. Home of Sir Winston Churchill.—March–Nov., Sat., Sun. and Bank Holidays, 11–6; Tues.–Thurs., 2–6 (July and Aug., Wed. and Thurs., 11–6). Admission, £2.20.

CHATSWORTH, Derbyshire. Seat of the Duke of Devonshire.—March 25–Oct. 28, Daily, 11.30–4.30.

CHICHELEY HALL, Newport Pagnell.—April 20–Sept. 30, Suns. and Bank Holidays, also Weds. in Aug., 2.30–6. Admission, £1.50.

*CLIVEDEN, Maidenhead.—Gardens, Daily, 11–6 (closed Jan. and Feb.); House, April.–Oct., Sats. and Suns., 2–6, (closed Bank Holidays and Good Friday). Admission, £2.

*COMPTON CASTLE, nr. Paignton.—April–Oct., Mons., Weds. and Thurs., 10–12.15, 2–5. Admission, £1.10.

*CROFT CASTLE, Herefordshire.—May–Sept., Weds.–Suns., 2–6 (also Bank Holidays). Apr. and Oct., weekends and Easter Bank Hol. Mon., 2–5. Admission £1.30.

DARWIN AND DOWN HOUSE, Downe, Orpington, Kent.—March–Jan., 1–6; not Mons. (except Bank Hols.), Fris. or Dec. 24–26. Admission, £1; O.A.P.s, 50p; children, 20p.

DRUMLANRIG CASTLE, Dumfries.—Easter and April 28–9; May and June, Daily (except Fri.), 12.30–5 (Sun. 2–6); July and Aug., Daily (except Fri.), 11–5; Suns., 2–6. Admission, £1.50.

GLAMIS CASTLE, Angus.—May–Sept., Daily (except Sats.), also Easter, 1–5. Admission, £1.50.

*HARDWICK HALL, Derbyshire.—Apr.–Oct., Daily (not Mons. (except Bank Hols.) Tues. and Fris.), 1–5.30. Admission, £2.

HAREWOOD HOUSE, Leeds.—April–Oct., Daily, from 11 a.m.

HATFIELD HOUSE, Herts.—March 25–Oct. 7, Daily (except Mons.), 12–5; Suns., 2–5.30; Bank Holidays, 11–5. Admission, £2.35.

HEVER CASTLE, Kent.—April–Sept., Daily (except Thurs.), 12–6.

HOLKER HALL, Cumbria.—Easter Sun.–Oct. 28, Daily (except Sats.), 10.30–5.15.

HOLKHAM HALL, Wells.—June–Sept., Sun., Mon., Thurs., 1.30–5; also Weds. in July and Aug. (and Spring and Summer Bank Hol. Mons.,) 11.30–5. Admission £1.

HOPETOUN HOUSE, nr. Edinburgh.—Easter and April 28–Sept. 17, Daily, 11–5.30. Admission charge.

HOUGHTON HALL, Norfolk.—Easter Sun.–Sept. 30; Thurs. and Bank Holidays, 12–5.30; Suns., 1.30–5.30. Admission, £1.50.

*HUGHENDEN MANOR, High Wycombe. Disraeli's home—April–Oct., Weds.–Sats., 2–6; Suns. and Bank Hol. Mons., 12–6. Mar. weekends, 2–6 or dusk. Admission, £1.50.

INVERARAY CASTLE, Argyll. Seat of the Duke of Argyll.—April 7–Oct. 14, Daily (except Fri.), 10–1, 2–6 (July and Aug., Daily, 10–6); Suns., 1–6. Admission, £1.80.

KELMSCOTT MANOR, nr. Lechlade.—April–Sept., 1st Wed. in each month, 11–1, 2–5. Admission, £2.

KNEBWORTH HOUSE, Herts.—April–May, Suns. and Bank Hols.; June 1–Sept. 15, Daily (except Mons.); Sept. 16–30, Suns. only; also Bank Hol. Mons. 11.30–4.30.

*KNOLE, Kent.—April–Nov., Weds. to Sats., 11–5 (also Bank Holidays); Suns., 1–5. Admission, £2.

LEEDS CASTLE, Kent.—April–Oct., Daily (except non Bank Hol. Mons. in April, May and Oct.), 12–5. Nov.–March, weekends only, 12–4.

*LITTLE MORETON HALL, Cheshire.—April–Sept., Daily (except Tues.), Mar. and Oct., weekends, 2–6. Admission, £1.40.

LONGLEAT HOUSE, Warminster.—All year, Daily, 10–6 (Oct.–Easter, 10–4).

LUTON HOO, Beds.—March 31–mid Oct., Daily (except Tues. and Fris.), also Good Friday, 11–6; Suns., 2–6. Admission, £1.60.

MELBOURNE HALL, Derbyshire.—June 1–Oct. 1, Suns., 2–6. Admission, £2.

MICHELHAM PRIORY, E. Sussex.—April 20–Oct. 21, Daily, 11–5.30. Admission, £1.30.

*MONTACUTE HOUSE, Yeovil.—April–Nov. 4, Daily (except Tues.), 12.30–6. Admission, £2.

*MOUNT STEWART, Co. Down.—April–Sept., Daily (except Fris.), 2–6. Also Good Friday. Admission, £1.30.

OSBORNE HOUSE, I.O.W. State and Private Apartments. —April 2–Oct. 13, 11–5, (July and Aug., 10–5); not Suns. Admission, £2.

*PENRHYN CASTLE, Bangor.—April 20–Nov. 4, Daily (except Tues.), 2–5 (June–Sept., Bank Holidays 11–5). Admission, £1.80.

PENSHURST PLACE, Kent.—April–Oct. 7, Daily (except Mons.), 1–5.30. Admission, £2.35.

*PETWORTH HOUSE, W. Sussex.—April–Oct., Daily (except Mons., Tues. and Fris.), also Bank Holiday Mons., 2–6. Admission, £1.80.

PORTMEIRION, Gwynedd.—April–Oct., Daily, 9.30–5.30. Admission, £1.45.

POWDERHAM CASTLE, Exeter.—For opening times contact the Administrator, (0626) 890 243.

*POWIS CASTLE, Powys.—April 21–Sept., Weds. to Suns. (also Tues. in July and Aug.). 1–6. Bank Hol. Mons., 11.30–6. Admission, £1.80.

RABY CASTLE, Durham.—April 25–June 27 and Sept., Weds. and Suns.; July–Aug., Daily (except Sats.), 2–5. Also Bank Hols. Admission, £1.20.

RAGLEY HALL, Warwicks.—April–Sept., Daily (except Mons. and Fris.), also Bank Hols., 1.30–5.30. Admission, £2.

ROCKINGHAM CASTLE, Corby.—Easter Sun.–Sept., Suns., Thurs., Tues. in Aug and Bank Hols. (Mon. and Tues.), 2–6. Admission, £1.50.

*RUFFORD OLD HALL, Lancashire—April–Oct., Daily (except Fri., but incl. Good Fri.), 2–6. Admission, £1.30.

RUSSBOROUGH, Co. Wicklow.—Easter–Oct., Suns., Bank Hols.; also Weds. (June–Aug.), Sats. (July–Aug.), 2.30–6.30. Admission, £1.50.

SANDRINGHAM, Norfolk.—April 22–Sept. 27 (except Fris. and Sats., and closed July 16–Aug. 4), 11–4.45 (Suns., 12–4.45). Admission, £1.50.

SCONE PALACE, Perth.—Good Friday–mid Oct., Daily, 10–5.30; Suns., 2–5.30 (July and Aug., 11–5.30). Admission, £1.80.

SHEFFIELD PARK, East Sussex.—May, June, Sept. and Oct., Weds., Thurs., Suns. and Bank Holidays, 2–5. Also Easter Sun. and Mon. Admission, £1.25.

SHERBORNE CASTLE, Dorset.—Easter Sat.–Sept., Thurs., Sat., Sun. and Bank Hol. Mons., 2–6.

*SHUGBOROUGH, Staffs.—mid March–Oct., Tues. to Fris. and Bank Hol. Mons., 10.30–5.30; Sats. and Suns., 2–5.30. Admission, £1.40.

*SISSINGHURST, Kent.—April–Oct. 14, Tues.–Fri., 1–6.30; Sats., Suns. and Good Friday, 10–6.30. Closed Bank Holidays. Admission, £2.20 (Suns. £2.60).

SKIPTON CASTLE, N. Yorks.—Mons.–Sats., 10–6; Suns, 2–6. Admission, 80p.

*SMALLHYTHE PLACE, Tenterden. Dame Ellen Terry's home.—Mar. weekends, April–Oct., Daily (except Tues. and Fris.) 2–6. Admission, £1.

*SNOWSHILL MANOR, Broadway.—April and Oct., Sats., Suns. and Easter Mon., 11–1, 2–5; May–Sept., Weds. to Suns. (incl. Bank Holidays), 11–1, 2–6. Admission, £1.90.

STANFORD HALL, Leics.—Easter Sun.–Sept., Thurs., Sats. and Suns. (also Bank Hol. Mons. and following Tues.), 2.30–6. Admission, £1.50.

STONOR PARK, Oxon.—April–Sept., Weds., Thurs. and Suns. (also Sats. in Aug.), 2–5.30. Bank Hol. Mons., 11–5.30. Admission £1.50.

STONELEIGH ABBEY, Warwicks.—April 22–June 28, July 8–Aug. 24 and Sept., Suns., Mons. and Thurs. (also Weds. in July and Aug.), 1–5.30. Admission, £2.20.

*STOURHEAD, Wilts.—May–Sept., Daily (except Fris.); Apr. and Oct.–Nov. 4, Daily (except Tues., Thurs., Fri.), 2–6. Admission, £1.60. Gardens, Daily, 8–7. Admission, £1.20.

STRATFIELD SAYE HOUSE, Reading.—April 21–Sept., Daily (except Fris.), 11.30–5.30.

*SUDBURY HALL, Derbys.—April–Oct., Daily (except Mons. and Tues.), also Bank Hols. 1–5.30. Admission, £1.80.

SUDELEY CASTLE, Glos.—April–Oct., Daily, 12–5.30. Admission, £2.80.

SULGRAVE MANOR, Northants. Home of the Washington family.—Feb.–Dec., Daily (except Weds.), 10.30–1, 2–5.30 (closes 4 p.m. in winter). Admission, 80p.

*TRERICE, Cornwall.—April–Oct., Daily, 11–6. Admission, £1.80.

*THE VYNE, Basingstoke.—April–Oct. 14, Daily (except Mons. and Fris.), 2–6; Bank Hol. Mons., 11–6. Admission, £1.50.

TYN-Y-RHOS HALL, Shropshire—May–Sept., Weds., Thurs., Sats., Suns. and Bank Hol. Mons., 2.30–6. Admission, 80p.

*WADDESDON MANOR, Bucks.—March 28–Oct. 28, Weds. (except after Bank Hol.) to Suns., 2–6. Also Bank Hols., 11–6. Admission, £1.80.

WARWICK CASTLE.—March–Oct., Daily, 10–5.30; Nov.–Feb., Daily, 10–4.30.

WILTON HOUSE, Wilts.—April 10–Oct. 14, Tues. to Sats. and Bank Hol. Mons., 11–6; Suns., 1–6. Admission, £2.

*WIMPOLE HALL, Cambs.—March 31–Nov. 4, Daily (except Fris.) and Bank Hol. Mons., 2–6. Admission, £1.80.

WINSLOW HALL, Bucks.—July to Sept. 15, Daily (except Mons.) also Bank Hols., 2.30–5.30. Sept. 15–30, weekends only. Admission, £1.

WOBURN ABBEY, Beds. Seat of the Duke of Bedford.—March 26–Oct. 26, 11–5.45, Suns., 11–6.15. Oct. 27–March 25, weekends only, 11–4.45.

MUSEUMS AND ART GALLERIES OUTSIDE LONDON

(*For National Art Galleries and Museums outside London see pages 375–6, 418 and 421–22.*)

Avebury.—*Great Barn Folk Life Museum.* April–Oct., open weekdays, 10–6; Sundays, 10.30–6: most weekends Nov.–Mar. Admission charge.

Barnard Castle, Co. Durham.—*The Bowes Museum.* Important collections of British and European fine art, from medieval period to 19th century Fine porcelain and glass, tapestries and furniture. Music and costume galleries. English period rooms from Elizabeth I to Victoria; French decorative arts of 18th and 19th centuries; local antiquities. Temporary Exhibitions. Open weekdays, May–Sept., 10–5.30; March, April and October, 10–5; Nov.–Feb., 10–4. Sundays, 2–5 (Summer); 2–4 (Winter). Admission £1·00; children and O.A.P.s, 25p. *Curator,* Elizabeth Conran.

Bath.—*Roman Baths Museum.* Roman Baths complex including newly excavated Temple precinct. Admission (including Pump Room), £1·40; children 80p. *Museum of Costume,* Assembly Rooms. Fashion from 16th century to current year. (Winter) weekdays 9–5; Sundays 11–5. (Summer) weekdays 9–6; Sundays 10–6. Admission £1.10; children 60p. *American Museum in Britain,* Claverton Manor. American decorative arts from late-17th to mid-19th centuries. Open 30 Mar.–3 Nov., daily (except Mons.), 2–5; Bank Holiday Mons. and preceding Suns., 11–5. During winter only on application. Admission charge. *Victoria Art Gallery,* Bridge Street. Open Mon.–Fri. 10–6; Sat. 10–5. Closed Suns. and Bank Holidays. Admission free.

Beaulieu.—*National Motor Museum.* Displays of vehicles dating from 1895 to present day. Open daily 10–6 (winter, 10–5). Admission charge.

Belfast.—*Ulster Museum,* Botanic Gardens. Collections of Irish antiquities, natural and local history, fine and applied arts. Open Mon.–Fri. 10–5, Sat. 1–5, Sun. 2–5. *Ulster Folk Museum,* Holywood. Indoor and outdoor exhibits of all aspects of Ulster folklife. Open Oct.–April, weekdays 11–5, Sun. 2–5 (May–Sept. open to 7 p.m.). Admission 50p, children and O.A.P.s, 20p. *Transport Museum,* Holywood and Witham Street. History of land, sea and air transport in Ireland and road, rail and sea vehicles. Holywood site—open as for Folk Museum. Witham Street site open weekdays 10–6. Admission 20p, children and O.A.P.s 10p. Special arrangements apply at both museums over Christmas and Easter.

Birmingham.—*City Museum and Art Gallery.* British and European masters from 14th to 20th centuries (particularly of the Pre-Raphaelite movement), sculpture, European gold, silver and jewellery, pottery and porcelain, furniture, textiles and costume, archaeology, local and natural history. Open, free, Weekdays, 10–5; Sundays, 2–5. Closed Christmas Day, Boxing Day, New Year's Day and Good Friday.

Museum of Science and Industry, Newhall Street. The history of science from the Industrial Revolution to the present; many working machines under steam, gas, etc. Open, free, Weekdays, 10–5; Saturdays, 10–5, Sundays, 2–5. Other Birmingham museums are: *Aston Hall, Blakesley Hall, Birmingham Nature Centre, Sarehole Mill,* and *Weoley Castle.*

Bradford.—*Cartwright Hall,* Lister Park. Contains European and British fine art from the 16th century onwards. *Bolling Hall,* off Wakefield Road, a furnished house dating from the 15th century. *Industrial Museum,* Moorside Mills, illustrates the local wool and worsted industries and transport. *Cliffe Castle,* Keighley. Natural and local history. *Manor House,* Ilkley, is an Elizabethan Manor House with exposed wall of Roman Fort. All show changing temporary exhibitions. Open 10–5 (April–Sept., 10–6,

except Industrial museum). Closed Good Friday, Christmas Day, Boxing Day and Mons. (except Bank Holidays). Admission free.

Brighton.—*The Royal Pavilion, Palace of George IV.* Chinoiserie interiors, much of the original furniture returned on loan from H.M. the Queen. Open daily 10–5 (10–6.30, June to September). Closed Christmas Day and Boxing Day. Admission £1·85 (reduced rates for children, O.A.P.s, parties, etc.).

Art Gallery and Museum, Church Street (adjacent Royal Pavilion). Old master paintings; Willett pottery and porcelain collection, 20th-century art and furniture, ethnography, archæology, costume gallery. Open, free, 10–5.45 Tuesdays to Saturdays; Sundays 2–5. Closed Christmas Day, Boxing Day, Good Friday and Mondays.

Preston Manor, Preston Park. (Thomas-Stanford: Macquoid bequests of English period furniture, furnishings, china and silver.) Closed Christmas Day, Boxing Day, Good Friday and Mondays and Tuesdays. Open weekdays 10–5, Sundays, 2–5. Admission 80p (reduced rates for children, O.A.P.s, parties). Gardens open, free.

The Grange, Art Gallery, Rottingdean. Sussex Room, Kipling Room and collections of National Toy Museum. Open, free, 10–5 weekdays; Sundays, 2–5. Closed Christmas Day, Boxing Day and Wednesdays.

The Booth Museum of Natural History, Dyke Road. Open, free, weekdays, 10–5, Sundays, 2–5. Closed Christmas Day, Boxing Day, Good Friday and Thursdays.

Bristol.—*City Museum and Art Gallery.* Collections of Egyptology, British archæology, natural and local history. Collection of Old Masters, 19th cent. and modern paintings, Chinese ceramics, glass, English silver, glass, porcelain and delftware, English and foreign embroideries. Open weekdays, 10–5. *Bristol Industrial Museum,* Prince's Wharf. Collections of manufacturing equipment and transport, including unique steam carriage and Bristol-built aero-engines. Open daily (except Thurs. and Fri.) 10–1, 2–5. *St. Nicholas Church Museum.* Church plate and vestments, local medieval antiquities, Hogarth altarpiece. Brass-rubbing centre. Open Mon.–Sat. 10–5. Also *Red Lodge, Blaise Castle House Museum, Kingsweston Roman Villa* and *Georgian House.*

National Life-boat Museum, Princes Wharf, Wapping Road. Displays of life-boats, models and equipment dating from 1904. Open Easter Mon. to early Oct., daily 10.30–4.30. Closed Fri. Admission 30p, children 20p, O.A.P.s 15p.

Cambridge.—*Fitzwilliam Museum.* The Fine Art collections of the University, and one of the most important museums outside London. The chief collections, largely due to private benefaction, comprise Egyptian, Greek and Roman antiquities, coins and medals, medieval manuscripts, paintings and drawings, prints, pottery and porcelain, textiles, arms and armour, medieval and renaissance objects of art, and a library. Open free, Tues.–Sat., Lower Galleries 10–2, Upper Galleries 2–5; Sun. 2.15–5. Closed Dec. 24 to Jan. 1 and Good Friday. Closed Mons. incl. May Day Bank Holiday but not Easter and Bank Holiday Mons.

Canterbury.—*Royal Museum and Art Gallery, and Buffs Regimental Museum.* Collections include archaeology, porcelain, prints and pictures. Open free weekdays, 10–5. *Roman Pavement Museum.* Roman material from post-war excavations of Canterbury. *Westgate Tower Museum.* Arms and armour and display of city walls and gates. (Roman and Westgate Museums open 10–1, 2–5; Oct.–March, 2–4 only.) Admission 25p, children, 10p.

Carisbrooke.—*Castle Museum.* History of Isle of Wight, and personal relics of Charles I, who was imprisoned in Castle from 1647 to 1648. Open, 15 March–15 Oct. 9.30–6.30 daily; 16 Oct.–14 March 9.30–4 (Sundays 2–4). Admission to Castle and Museum, £1.40 (in winter, 70p).

Carlisle.—*Tullie House Museum and Art Gallery,* Castle Street. Collections of archæology, natural and social history, fine and decorative arts in Jacobean house. Open weekdays 9–7 (Oct.—March, 9–5); Spring and Summer Bank Holidays, and Suns. June–Aug., 2.30–5. *Guildhall,* Greenmarket. Civic and Guild history and artefacts. Contact Tullie House Museum for opening information.

Chester.—*Grosvenor Museum,* Grosvenor Street. Collection of Roman antiquities from legionary fortress; natural history, art and folk-life. Open weekdays 10.30–5, Sun., 2–5. *King Charles Tower* on City Walls. Civil War displays. Open daily (summer), weekends (winter), times vary. Admission charge.

Colchester.—*Colchester and Essex Museum, The Castle* contains local archæological antiquities, especially those from Roman Colchester. The *Holly Trees Mansion* (1718) covers social life of the 18th and 19th centuries. *Natural History Museum,* All Saints Church. Natural history of Essex. *Museum of Social History,* Holy Trinity Church. Domestic life and crafts. Open, weekdays, 10–5, Sat, 10–4 (branches closed 1–2 p.m.). Castle only, Sundays 2.30–5 (April–Sept.); admission 55p; Children 20p, O.A.P.s free. Branches free all year.

Coventry.—*Herbert Art Gallery and Museum,* Jordan Well. Archæology, natural and local history, fine and decorative arts. Open weekdays 10–6, Sun., 2–5. Closed Good Friday and Christmas period. *Museum of British Road Transport,* Cook Street. Easter–Sept., 10–4 (Mon.–Fri.), 10–5.30 (weekends); Oct.–March, Fri., Sat. and Sun. only. Admission 30p; children and O.A.P.s 20p. *Lunt Roman Fort,* Baginton. June–Oct., 12–6 (closed Mons. and Thurs.).

Crich, Nr. Matlock, Derbyshire—*National Tramway Museum.* Open air working museum with collection of trams from Britain and abroad. Open, Sats., Suns. and Bank Holidays 10.30–5.30 (Easter–Oct.); also daily (except Fri.) 10.00–4.30 (May–Sept.)

Derby.—*Museum and Art Gallery,* Strand. Archaeology, military, social history, natural history. Collections of paintings by Joseph Wright of Derby; Derby porcelain, costume, model theatres. Open Tues.–Sat. 10–5. *Industrial Museum,* Silk Mill, Full Street, Rolls Royce collection of aero engines etc. Tues.–Fri. 10–5. (Saturdays 10–4.45). Closed on all Bank Holidays.

Dorchester.—*Dorset County Museum.* Geology, archæology, local and natural history and rural crafts of Dorset. Collection of Thomas Hardy's manuscripts, books, notebooks, drawings, etc. Open weekdays 10–5, closed Christmas Day, Boxing Day and Good Friday. Admission 50p, children 25p.

Durham.—*Light Infantry Museum and Arts Centre.* County Regiment's 200 year history displayed; arts and crafts exhibitions. Open weekdays (except Mons.) 10–5, Sun. and Bank Holiday Mons., 2–5. Closed Christmas Day and Boxing Day. Admission 30p, children and O.A.P.s 10p. *Oriental Museum,* The University. Collections ranging from Ancient Egypt to China and Japan. Open weekdays 9.30–1, 2.15–5. Weekends, closed Nov.–Feb.; Mar.–Oct. Sats. 9.30–12, 2.15–5, Suns. 2.15–5. *Cathedral Treasury.* Relics of St. Cuthbert, church plate, medieval seals, manuscripts and vestments. Open weekdays 10–4.30, Sun., 2–4.30. Admission 45p, children 10p.

Edinburgh.—*City Art Centre,* 2 Market Street. Late 19th and 20th century art, mostly Scottish, and temporary exhibitions. Open weekdays 10–5 (June–Sept., 10–6). Admission free. *Canongate Tolbooth,* 163 Canongate. Courthouse and prison for 300 years; collection of highland dress. Open weekdays 10–5 (June–Sept., 10–6). Admission free. *Huntly House,* 142 Canongate. Local history, collections of Edinburgh silver, glass and Scottish pottery. Open weekdays 10–5 (June–Sept., 10–6). Admission free. Also: *Lady Stair's House,* Lawnmarket. Mon.–Sat., 10–5 (June–Sept., 10–6). *Lauriston Castle,* Cramond Road South, April–Oct., Daily (except Fri.), 11–1, 2–5; Nov.–March, weekends only.

Exeter.—*Royal Albert Memorial Museum and Art Gallery,* Queen Street. English art, ceramics and glass, Exeter silver, costume, natural and social history. Open Tues.–Sat. 10–5.15. *Maritime Museum,* The Quay. Collection of working boats. Open daily 10–5 (Jun.–Sept., 10–6). Admission charge. *Underground Passages,* Princesshay. Medieval aqueducts. Tues.–Sat., 2–4.40.

Fort William.—*West Highland Museum,* Cameron Square. Historical, natural history and folk exhibits, including those of the '45 Rising. Monday to Saturday, 9.30–1, 2–5; July and Aug., 9.30–9.

Glasgow.—*Art Gallery and Museum,* Kelvingrove. Old Masters, 19th century French paintings; archæology and natural history, special collection of armour. *Museum of Transport,* 25 Albert Drive. Road and rail vehicles, ship models. *People's Palace,* Glasgow Green. History of city from 1175 to present. *The Burrell Collection,* Pollok Park. Textiles, furniture, ceramics, stained glass, silver and other art objects, paintings, especially 19th century French. All open weekdays 10–5, Sun. 2–5. Admission free.

Guildford.—*Guildford Museum,* Castle Arch. Local museum for archæology and history of Surrey including collections of the Surrey Archæological Society. Open every day except Sunday, 11–5. Closed on Good Friday and Christmas.

Hull.—*Ferens Art Gallery.* Collection of European art, especially Dutch 17th century; British portraits of 18th–20th centuries; Humberside marine paintings; contemporary art and changing exhibitions. *Wilberforce House.* Jacobean merchant's house, birthplace of Wilberforce; collection of slavery relics, period furniture, costume and ceramics. *Transport and Archæology Museum.* Veteran cars, trams, coaches and velocipedes; archæological finds from Humberside, including Roman mosaics. *Town Docks Museum.* Whaling, fishing, trawling, ships and shipping. All open Mon.–Sat., 10–5; Sun., 2.30–4.30. *Posterngate Gallery.* Exhibitions and one-man shows. Tues.–Sat.

Huntingdon.—*Cromwell Museum.* Remaining portion of the 12th-century Hospital of St. John housing portraits of Cromwell, his family and Parliamentary notables (by Walker, Lely etc.); as well as reproductions and engravings covering the whole Puritan field. Unique collection of Cromwelliana—objects, documents, armour, coins and medals. Open, free, Sun. 2–4; Tues. to Fri., 11–1, 2–5, Sat., 11–1, 2–4. Closed Mon. and Bank Holidays other than Good Friday.

Ipswich.—*Ipswich Museum.* Collections of Suffolk geology, archæology and natural history and ethnology. Temporary exhibitions. *Christchurch* (Branch Museum) Tudor house contains furniture, Suffolk portraits, English porcelain, pottery and glass. *Wolsey Art Gallery,* attached, houses Borough collections of paintings (local artists, Gainsborough, Constable, Munnings, etc.). Modern prints, sculpture. *Both:* Open, weekdays 10–5, Sundays (Christchurch only) 2.30–4.30. (Christchurch closing at dusk in winter.) Closed on some Bank Holidays.

Leeds.—*City Art Gallery.* English watercolours. British and European painting, modern sculpture, incl. Henry Moore gallery. Open weekdays, 10–6, Suns., 2–5. Print Room and Art library contains study collection of drawings and prints. Wed., 10–9, Sat., 10–4, other weekdays 10–5.30, closed Sun.

Temple Newsam House. Tudor/Jacobean house, furnished in style of 17th and 18th cents., with silver, European porcelain and pottery, pictures, etc. Open daily (except Mons.), 10.30–6.15 or dusk; Weds. (May–Sept.), 10.30–8.30. Open all Bank Holidays (except Christmas). Admission 50p; children (with adults 20p), O.A.P.s 20p. *Lotherton Hall,* Gascoigne art and silver collection, oriental gallery, costume collection, 19th century furniture, ceramics, park and gardens. open daily (except Mons.), 10.30–6.15 or dusk; Thurs. (May–Sept.), 10.30–8.30. Open all Bank Holidays (except Christmas). Admission to Hall, 50p; children (with adults 20p), O.A.P.s 20p. *Abbey House Museum,* folk museum including three full-sized streets. Open Oct.–Mar., weekdays 10–5, Sun. 2–5, (to 6, April–Sept.). *Industrial Museum.* Open April–Sept., Tues.–Sat. 10–5, Sun. 2–5 (to 4, Oct.–March). Open Bank Holidays.

Leicester.—*Leicestershire Museum and Art Gallery,* New Walk (1849). Natural history, geology, Egyptology, 18th–20th century English paintings, ceramics, silver. *Newarke Houses,* The Newarke. Social history of Leicestershire from 1500 A.D.; musical instruments; local clocks. *Jewry Wall Museum,* St. Nicholas Circle. Archaeology (prehistoric–1500). Roman Jewry Wall and Baths, mosaics *in situ.* *Belgrave Hall,* Church Road. A Queen Anne house with furniture and garden of note. Coaches and agricultural collection. *Museum of the Royal Leicestershire Regiment,* The Magazine, Oxford Street. *Museum of Technology,* Corporation Road. Knitting industry and Power galleries. Horse-drawn and motor vehicles, beam engines. *Wygston's House Museum of Costume,* Applegate. Costume from 1789–1924. All museums open weekdays (except Fri.) 10–5.30; Sun., 2–5.30. Closed Christmas Day, Boxing Day and Good Friday.

Lewes.—*Museum of Sussex Archæology,* Barbican House, near Castle. Prehistoric, Roman, Saxon and mediæval collections relating to Sussex; local pictures and prints. Open weekdays, 10–5, Sundays (April–Oct.), 11–5. Admission, 75p; Children, 40p. *Anne of Cleves House,* Southover. Local history and folk museum. Open weekdays (mid. Feb.–mid. Nov.), 10–5. Suns. (April–Oct.), 2–5. Admission, 70p; Children 35p.

Lincoln.—*Usher Gallery.* Watches, miniatures, porcelain, silver, etc., Peter de Wint collection of oils and watercolours, Lincolnshire topographical drawings, *personalia* associated with Tennyson family. Coins and medals. Open weekdays, 10–5.30; Sun., 2.30–5. *City and County Museum,* The Greyfriars. Geology, natural history and archæology of Lincolnshire. Special collection of armour. Open weekdays, 10–5.30; Sun., 2.30–5. *Museum of Lincolnshire Life.* Collections illustrate life and work in Lincolnshire since 17th century. Open weekdays 10–5.30; Sun., 2.30–6. Closed December and January.

Liverpool.—*Walker Art Gallery.* European painting from 14th century–present day, particularly strong in early Italian and Northern, Pre-Raphaelite and Academic 19th century paintings. Open, weekdays, 10–5; Suns., 2–5. Closed on Good Friday, Christmas Eve, Christmas Day, Boxing Day and New Year's Day. *Sudley Art Gallery* (Emma Holt Bequest), Mossley Hill Road. 18th and 19th-century paintings, mainly English, including Gainsborough, Millais and Turner. Open as for Walker Art Gallery.

Merseyside County Museums, William Brown Street. Established on the Mayer and Derby collec-

tions, now supplemented by the Mayer-Fejervary Gothic ivories, the Bryan Fausett group of Anglo-Saxon antiquities, the Liverpool University Herbarium and the Lord Derby and Tristram ornithological collections. Displays include vivarium and aquarium, land transport, local and natural history, archæology, ethnology, timekeeping and space gallery; also a Planetarium. Open weekdays, 10–5; Sun., 2–5. Closed New Year's Day, Good Friday, Christmas Eve, Christmas Day and Boxing Day. Admission free (except to Planetarium). *Merseyside Maritime Museum,* Pier Head. The Old Pilotage building houses display on history of R. Mersey, and pleasure and workboats of the area. Quays and restored docks show cargo-handling and dock machinery, and boats displayed afloat. Open Easter–Autumn, daily 10.30–5.30. Admission charge. *Prescot Museum of Clock and Watch Making,* 34 Church Street, Prescot. Craft tools, workshops and industrial development. Open Tues.–Sat. and Bank Hol. Mon. 10–5; Sun. 2–5. Closed Mon., Christmas Eve, Christmas Day, Boxing Day, New Year's Day and Good Friday. Admission free.

Speke Hall. Half-timbered Tudor house administered by the County Museums for the National Trust. Open weekdays 10–5, Sun. 2–5 (2–5 Oct.–March). Admission charge. *Croxteth Hall and County Park.* A working estate within the boundary of a major city. Hall, farm etc. open daily, Easter to Sept., 11–5. Admission charge. Park open all year; free.

Manchester.—*City Art Gallery,* Mosley Street. Old Masters, Turner, Impressionists; sculpture, porcelain, silver. *Gallery of Modern Art,* Princess Street. British and European decorative and fine art since 1900. *Both* Mon.–Sat., 10–6. Admission free. *Whitworth Art Gallery,* Oxford Road. Watercolours, drawings, prints, textiles and wallpapers collections, and 20th century British art. Mon.–Sat., 10–5 (Thurs. 10–9); closed Suns. *North Western Museum of Science and Industry,* Grosvenor Street. Development of industry in region. *National Paper Museum,* history of papermaking. *Both* open Mon.–Sat. 10–5. Admission free. *Gallery of English Costume,* Platt Hall, Rusholme. Exhibits from 17th century to present. Also *Heaton Hall,* Prestwich, *Wythenshawe Hall,* Northenden and *Fletcher Moss Museum,* Didsbury. Opening times vary.

Newcastle-upon-Tyne.—*Laing Art Gallery,* Higham Place. Fine art from 17th century, pottery, glass, silver and metalwork. Open weekdays 10–5.30 (Sat. 4.30), Sun. 2.30–5.30. *Keep Museum,* St. Nicholas Street. History of site. Oct.–March, Mon. 2–4, Tues.–Sat. 10–4 (April–Sept. open to 5 p.m.). Closed Christmas Day, Boxing Day, New Year's Day and Good Friday.

Newmarket.—*National Horse racing Museum.* Five galleries of displays relating to the development of horseracing and to the horses and people connected with the sport. Open 9 March–15 Dec., Tues.–Sat. 10–5, Sun. 2–5. Closed Mon. except June–Aug. and Bank Holidays. Admission £1, children, O.A.P.s 50p.

Norwich.—*Castle Museum.* Exhibits of art (Colman collection of the Norwich School), local archæology, social and natural history, pottery and glass. Open, weekdays, 10–5; Sun. 2–5. Headquarters of the Norfolk Museums Service, comprising 15 museums. *Strangers' Hall,* Charing Cross. Late medieval mansion furnished as a museum of urban domestic life, 16th–19th centuries. Open, weekdays, 10–5. *Bridewell Museum of Local Industries,* Bridewell Alley. Transport, crafts and industries of Norfolk and North Suffolk. Open, weekdays, 10–5. *St. Peter Hungate Church Museum,* Princes Street. 15th century church used for display of church art and antiquities. Open, weekdays, 10–5.

Nottingham.—*Castle Museum and Art Gallery.* English and Netherlands paintings and drawings

17th–20th centuries; special collections of Bonington and Paul Sandby. Ceramics, silver, glass, medieval Nottingham alabaster carvings, local historical and archaeological displays, classical, oriental and ethnographical antiquities; the regimental collection of the Sherwood Foresters. Open, Summer, 10–5.45; Winter, 10–4.45. Closed Christmas Day. Admission free, small charge on Sundays and Bank Holidays.

Industrial Museum, Wollaton Park. Industrial, lacemaking machinery, steam engines, transport. Open, April–Sept., Mon.–Sat. 10–6; Sunday, 2–6; Oct.–April, Thurs. and Sat., 10–4.30; Sunday, 1.30–4.30. Closed Christmas Day. Admission free, small charge on Sun. and Bank Holidays.

Canal Museum, Canal Street. Open Easter–Oct., Wed.–Sat., 10–5.45, (Sun. 1–5.45); Oct.–Easter, Wed.–Sat., 1–5.00; Sun. 1–5. Admission free.

Natural History Museum, Wollaton Hall. Open, Summer 10–7 (Sun. 2–5); Winter, 10 till dusk (Sun. 1.30–4.30). Closed Christmas Day. Admission free except Sun. and Bank Holidays.

Newstead Abbey, 11½ miles N. of Nottingham. Collections associated with poet Byron. Abbey open Good Friday to end of September, every day, 2–6, admission charge.

Castlegate Museum of Costumes and Textiles. Open daily 10–5. Closed Christmas Day. Admission free.

Brewhouse Yard Museum, Castle Boulevard. Everyday life from the 17th century to present. Open daily 10–12, 1–5, admission free. Closed Christmas Day.

Oakham, *Rutland County Museum*, Catmose Street.—Archæology, local history, craft tools and agricultural implements. Open Tues.–Sat., 10–1, 2–5; Sun. (April–Oct.) 2–5, and Bank Holiday Mons.

Oxford, *Ashmolean Museum*.—Department of Western Art, Department of Antiquities, Heberden Coin Room, Department of Eastern Art. Open Tues.–Sat., 10–4, Sundays, 2–4.

Plymouth.—*City Museum and Art Gallery*, Drake Circus. Fine art, including Cottonian collection and Reynolds' portraits, Plymouth porcelain, archaeology, local and natural history. Mon.–Fri., 10–6; Sat., 10–5. Admission free.

Portsmouth.—*City Museum and Art Gallery*, Museum Road. Decorative and fine arts, local and social history. Daily 10.30–5.30. Admission charge. Also 6 branch museums including fortifications, military history, archæology, natural science, technology and D-Day Museum. *Royal Naval Museum*, H.M. Naval Base. Nelson collection, ship and naval artifacts, the Victorian Navy, W.W.2 at Sea and The South Atlantic campaign displays. Weekdays 10.30–5; Sundays 1–5. Admission charge.

Port Sunlight Village, Merseyside. *Lady Lever Art Gallery*. Paintings and watercolour drawings (mainly British School), antique, renaissance and British sculpture, English furniture, mainly 18th cent., Chinese pottery and porcelain, and important collection of old Wedgwood. Open weekdays 10–5, Sundays 2–5.

St. Albans.—*City Museum*, Hatfield Road. Natural history, geology, craft and trade tools. Open weekdays 10–5. Admission free. *Verulamium Museum*, St. Michael's. Roman and Belgic material including mosaics, one *in situ* in Hypercaust annexe. Open weekdays 10–4, Sun. 2–4 (to 5.30 p.m. in summer). Admission, 60p; children, students and O.A.P.s, 35p.

Sheffield.—*City Museum*, Weston Park. Includes the Bateman Collection of antiquities from the Bronze Age barrows of the Peak District, cutlery and old Sheffield plate collections. Open, weekdays, Sept.–May, 10–5; June–Aug. 10–8; Sun. 11–5 (Closed Christmas Eve, Christmas Day and Boxing Day).

Mappin Art Gallery, Weston Park. Paintings and sculpture of 18th–20th centuries (mainly British School) and contemporary works. Open weekdays 10–5 (Jun.–Aug. open to 8 p.m.), Sun. 2–5. *Abbeydale Industrial Hamlet*, Abbeydale Road South. A late 18th–early 19th century scythe and steel works with associated housing. Open, weekdays 10–5, Sun. 11–5. *Kelham Island Industrial Museum*. Open Wed.–Sat., 10–5; Sun. and Bank Holiday Mon., 11–5. *Shepherd Wheel*, Whiteley Wood. Water-powered cutlery grinding establishment. Open 10–12.30, 1.30–5 (opens at 11 on Sun.). Closed Mon. and Tues. *Bishops' House, Meersbrook Park*; museum of local history in timber-framed domestic building. Open, Wed.–Sat., 10–5; Sun. 11–5.

Stratford-upon-Avon.—*Shakespeare's Birthplace*, contains period furniture, rare books, MSS and objects of Shakespearean interest. Garden contains new Shakespeare Centre. *Anne Hathaway's Cottage*, Shottery, early home of Shakespeare's wife. *Mary Arden's House*, Wilmcote, Tudor farmhouse home of Shakespeare's mother. *Hall's Croft*, half-timbered home of Shakespeare's daughter and her family. *Grammar School* attended by Shakespeare. *Royal Shakespeare Theatre* burnt down 1926, rebuilt 1932 with 1,500 seats.

Styal.—*Quarry Bank Mill*, Cheshire. History of the cotton industry, weaving demonstrations. Closed Mon. except June–Aug. Oct.–March, daily, 11–4. April–Sept., daily, 11–5. Admission £1·80; children £1·20.

Winchester.—*City Museum*. Weekdays 10–5; Sundays 2–5 (closed Mons. in winter). *Cathedral Library*. MSS and other exhibits from 10th century onwards. Weekdays 10.30–12.30, 2.30–4.30. Admission charge. *Cathedral Treasury*. Exhibition of church silver and other pieces. Weekdays 11–5; Sundays 2.30–4.30. Admission charge.

Worcester.—*City Museum and Art Gallery*. Natural history of Worcestershire and temporary art exhibitions; also museum of the Worcestershire Regiment and the Worcester Yeomanry Cavalry. Open weekdays 9.30–6, Sat. 9.30–5. Closed Thurs. *The Commandery*, Sidbury. 15th century building housing local history and Civil War display. Weekdays (not Mon.) 10.30–5; Sun. 2.30–5. *Tudor House Museum*, Friar Street. Local domestic and social history. Mon.–Sat., 10.30–5 (closed Thurs.). *Dyson Perrins Museum of Worcester Porcelain*, Severn Street. Mon. to Fri. 10–1, 2–5, Sat. (April–Sep.).

York.—*Castle Museum*. Folk museum of Yorkshire life of the past four centuries. Open weekdays, 9.30–5, Suns., 10–5 (closes 6.30 p.m., April–Sept.). Admission, £1.50; children and O.A.P.s 75p (special party rates Nov.–March).

Jorvik Viking Centre, Coppergate. Reconstruction of Viking York and display of artifacts. Open daily (incl. Suns.) 9–5.30 (7 p.m. Easter–Oct.). Admission £2, children £1.

Yorkshire Museum and Gardens, Museum Street. Archæology, decorative arts, geology, natural history. Open weekdays, 10–5; Sun., 1–5. Admission, £1; children, O.A.P.s, etc., 50p. Gardens, Roman, Anglian and medieval ruins. Open weekdays, 8–dusk; Sun. 10–dusk. *The York Story*, Castlegate. Open weekdays 10–5; Sun. 1–5. Admission, 75p; children 40p.

Art Gallery, Exhibition Square. European paintings, 14th–20th century; watercolours and prints of Yorkshire; modern English stoneware pottery. Open weekdays, 10–5; Sun., 2.30–5. Admission free.

Treasurer's House (National Trust). Chapter House Street. Open, April–Oct., 10.30–6. Admission charge.

LONDON BOROUGHS

City or Borough (*Inner London Borough)	Municipal Offices	Population	Rateable Value April 1, 1984	Town Clerk (*Chief Executive)	Mayor or Lord Mayor
			£		
CITY OF WESTMINSTER*	City Hall, Victoria St., S.W.1.	163,892	331,572,063	R. G. Brooke	J. Bull
Barking	‡Dagenham, Essex.	151,200	26,988,602	D. C. J. Farr	C. J. Fairbrass
Barnet	†The Burroughs, Hendon, N.W.4.	296,500	61,209,331	E. M. Bennett	L. Sussman
Bexley	‡Bexleyheath, Kent.	217,900	31,079,172	*T. Musgrave	D. C. Bale
Brent	†Forty Lane, Wembley.	254,000	52,066,302	*M. G. Bichard	C. Shaw
Bromley........	†Bromley, Kent.	299,500	50,755,654	*N. T. Palk	C. G. Priest
Camden*	†Euston Road, N.W.1.	172,014	117,010,089	F. Nickson	Ms. B. Hughes
Croydon........	†Taberner House, Park Lane, Croydon.	318,700	69,263,178	F. S. H. Birch	Mrs. M. Horden
Ealing	†Ealing, W.5.	282,000	56,753,704	B. T. Collins	Mrs. M. E. Heywood
Enfield	‡Enfield.	257,200	49,413,228	W. D. Day	J. W. E. Jackson
Greenwich*	†Wellington St., Woolwich, S.E.18.	209,873	33,026,000	*A. Glover	P. Graham
Hackney*	Mare St., E.8.	183,300	37,596,562	D. Wood	K. Hanson
Hammersmith and Fulham* .	†King St., W.6.	148,447	35,941,754	*A. J. Allen	P. Ward
Haringey.......	Wood Green, N.22.	204,600	36,447,113	*R. C. Limb	Ms. V. Fenwick
Harrow	‡Station Rd., Harrow.	198,800	34,785,382	*D. Adams	A. C. Cocksedge
Havering.......	†Romford, Essex.	241,200	38,367,988	*R. W. J. Tridgell	W. B. S. Todd
Hillingdon......	‡Uxbridge.	229,280	58,893,738	*P. A. Johnson	F. E. Walsh
Hounslow	‡Lampton Rd., Hounslow	200,900	49,381,878	*P. McQuail	J. Kenna
Islington*	†Upper St., N.1.	162,900	54,933,815	*E. W. Dear	Ms. R. Dale
Kensington and Chelsea (Royal Borough)*	†Hornton St., W.8.	136,800	72,526,917	R. S. Webber	A. J. A. D. Fitzgerald
Kingston upon Thames (Royal Borough).....	Guildhall, Kingston upon Thames.	133,700	28,777,714	G. N. Hollis (Co-ordinator)	D. V. Weston
Lambeth*	Brixton Hill, S.W.2.	246,000	59,227,823	A. J. George	Mrs. P. Williams
Lewisham*	†Catford, S.E.6.	233,600	35,008,186	J. W. Harwood	J. L. H. Eyte
Merton........	†Broadway, Wimbledon, S.W.19	167,960	31,396,113	*W. McKee	A. Nicholson
Newham	†East Ham Road, E.6.	212,300	36,371,138	*J. J. Warren	C. Flemwell
Redbridge	High Road, Ilford	227,000	36,735,465	*G. U. Price	J. J. M. Smith
Richmond upon Thames	§Twickenham, Middx.	161,600	32,433,940	M. J. Honey	D. V. Wainwright
Southwark*	†Peckham Rd., S.E.5.	215,400	59,826,018	A. G. Corless	J. Greening
Sutton	‡St. Nicholas Way, Sutton, Surrey.	170,100	29,237,000	*A. Taylor	Mrs. J. Bowley
Tower Hamlets*.	†Patriot Square, E.2.	144,500	46,763,828	*J. Wolkind, C.B.E.	R. W. Ashkettle
Waltham Forest .	†Walthamstow, E.17.	214,000	31,700,544	*L. G. Knox	D. B. Arnold
Wandsworth*...	†Wandsworth, S.W.18.	258,500	43,386,000	*A. J. Newman	P. D. Donaghue

†Town Hall.　　‡Civic Offices.　　§Municipal Offices.

GREATER LONDON COUNCIL

The Greater London Council and 32 London Borough Councils were constituted under the London Government Act, 1963. They replaced, on April 1, 1965, the London County Council, the Middlesex County Council, the County Borough Councils of Croydon, East Ham and West Ham, 28 metropolitan borough, 39 non-county borough and 15 urban district councils. The boundaries and constitution of the Corporation of the City of London were not affected.

Under the Act, Greater London became for the first time a clearly defined local government area including, in addition to the former counties of London and the greater part of Middlesex, parts of Metropolitan Essex, Kent, Surrey and Hertfordshire.

The Greater London Council at present consists of 92 councillors. Councillors are elected for single-member electoral divisions which are coterminous with the parliamentary constituencies. Councillors hold office for four years. The Chairman, Vice-Chairman and Deputy Chairman are elected annually by the councillors. The political head of the administration is the Leader of the Council, elected by the majority party. The Council meets at three weekly intervals at 2.30 p.m. on Tuesdays except in holiday periods. Most committees and sub-committees meet at three- or six-weekly intervals.

GREATER LONDON COUNCIL

Chairman, I. Harrington.
Vice-Chairman, H. Kay.
Deputy-Chairman, V. Langton.
Leader of the Council, K. Livingstone*.
Leader of the Opposition, A. Greengross.
Arbour, A. F. (*C.*).......... *Surbiton*
Avery, Dr. D. J. (*C.*) .... *The City of London and Westminster South*
Bailey, Dr. G. N. A. (*C.*) .... *Brentford and Isleworth*
Banks, A. L., M.P. (*Lab. & Co-op*)................... *Tooting*
Bays, A. W. (*C.*) .... *Upminster*
Beale, N. (*C.*)............... *Finchley*
Bell, W. A. O. J. (*C.*) .... *Chelsea*
Black, P. B. (*C.*) .... *Hendon South*
Boateng, P. (*Lab.*) .... *Walthamstow*
Bolton, S. C. (*C.*) .... *Wimbledon*
Bramall, Sir Ashley (*Lab.*).. *Tower Hamlets*
Branagan, J. (*Lab.*) .... *Stepney and Poplar*
Brew, R. M., C.B.E. (*C.*) ..... *Chingford*
Brook-Partridge, B. (*C.*).... *Romford*
Bundred, S. (*Lab.*) .... *Islington North*
Carr, J. A. (*Lab.*) .... *Hackney Central*
Cassidy, B. M. D. (*C.*) ...... *Hendon North*
Clack, Mrs. J. E. (*C.*) ...... *Harrow Central*
Copland, Mrs. S. (*C.*) ...... *Carshalton*
Cutler, Sir Horace, O.B.E.
(*C.*) .... *Harrow West*
Daniel, G. J. (*Lab.*) .... *Ealing North*
Davies, B. H. (*Lab.*) .... *Vauxhall*
Davies, N. (*Lab.*) .... *Woolwich West*
Dawe, P. J. (*Lab.*) .... *Leyton*
Dimson, G. F. C.B.E. (*Lab.*) .. *Battersea North*
Dobson, J. C. (*C.*) .... *Acton*
Edwards, A. F. G. (*Lab.*).... *Newham North West*
Fletcher, Ms. J. (*Lab.*) ..... *Tottenham*
Gardner of Parkes, Baroness
(*C.*) .... *Southgate*
Garside, M. E. (*Lab.*)....... *Woolwich East*
Gent, R. C. (*C.*)............ *Sidcup*
Gill, P. S. (*C.*) .... *Croydon South*
Gouge, E. S. (*Lab.*)........ *Ilford South*
Greengross, A. D. (*C.*) ...... *Hampstead*
Gumbel, Mrs. M. (*C.*)....... *Sutton and Cheam*
Hammond, L. (*Lab.*) .... *Dulwich*
Handy, E. (*Lab.*)........... *Erith and Crayford*
Hardy, A. (*C.*) .... *Brent North*
Harrington, I. (*Lab.*) .... *Brent South*
Harris, A. P. (*Lab.*) .... *Putney*
Hart, Dr. A. B. (*Lab.*) ...... *Hornsey*
*Herbert, A. L. (*Lab.*) .... *Lewisham West*
Hinds, H. W. (*Lab. & Co-op*) *Peckham*
Howard, N. (*Lab.*) .... *Brent East*

Hughes, R. G. (*C.*) .... *Croydon Central*
Jenkinson, T. A. (*Lab.*) .... *Newham South*
Judge, A. R. (*Lab.*) .... *Mitcham and Morden*
Kay, H. (*Lab.*)............. *Dagenham*
Langton, V. R. M. (*C.*) .... *Bexleyheath*
Lemkin, J. A. (*C.*) .... *Uxbridge*
*Little, K. W. (*Lab.*) .... *Edmonton*
*Livingstone, K. R. (*Lab.*)... *Paddington*
McBrearty, A. (*Lab.*) ..... *Enfield North*
*McDonnell, J. (*Lab.*)....... *Hayes and Harlington*
Mackay, A. C. (*Lab.*)...... *Deptford*
Major, J. R. (*C.*) .... *Chipping Barnet*
Mitchell, R., O.B.E. (*C.*) .... *Wanstead and Woodford*
Moore, P. D. (*Lab.*) .... *Lambeth Central*
Morgan, Ms. J. M. (*Lab.*) ...*Hackney South and Shoreditch*
Morrell, Ms. F. M. (*Lab.*) ...*Islington South and Finsbury*
Mote, H. T. (*C.*)............ *Harrow East*
Nicholson, G. E. (*Lab.*) .....*Bermondsey*
Pitt, P. S. (*Lab.*) .... *Feltham and Heston*
Randall, S. J. C. (*C.*) ...... *Beckenham*
Ripley, S. W. L. (*C.*) .... *Kingston upon Thames*
Roe, Mrs. M. A., M.P. (*C.*) .. *Ilford North*
Rolfe, A. J. (*C.*) .... *Croydon North East*
Ross, G. (*Lab. & Co-op*)..... *Hackney North and Stoke Newington*
Rossi, C. A. (*Lab.*) .... *Holborn and St. Pancras South*
Rossi, P. N. (*S.D.P.*) .... *Lewisham*
Sandford, H. H., O.B.E. (*C.*) .. *St. Marylebone*
Sieve, Mrs. Y. (*Lab.*) ...... *Southall*
Slade, A. C. (*Lib.*) .... *Richmond*
Smith, Prof. N. J. D. (*C.*).... *Norwood*
Sofer, Ms. A. (*S.D.P.*) ...... *St. Pancras North*
Stead, B. J. (*Lab.*) .... *Fulham*
Stewart, S. J. (*C.*).......... *Croydon North-West*
Tatham, Mrs. J. (*C.*) .... *Orpington*
Taylor, C. J. H. (*C.*) .... *Ruislip-Northwood*
Tremlett, G., O.B.E. (*C.*)..... *Twickenham*
Turney, S. J. (*Lab.*) .... *Islington Central*
Vigars, R. L. (*C.*) .... *Kensington*
Ward, J. B. (*Lab.*) .... *Barking*
Ward, M. (*Lab.*) .... *Wood Green*
Wetzel, D. C. (*Lab.*) .... *Hammersmith North*
Weyer, F. W. (*C.*) .... *Streatham*
Wheeler, M. J. (*C.*)........ *Ravensbourne*
Williams, A. R. (*Lab.*) ..... *Hornchurch*
Wilson, J. (*Lab.*) .... *Newham North East*
Wise, Ms. V. (*Lab.*) .... *Battersea South*
Wood, D. F. M. (*Lab.*) ..... *Greenwich*
Wykes, Mrs. J. K. (*C.*)...... *Chislehurst*

* Resigned Aug. 1984 to fight by-elections on Sept. 20. Livingstone replaced as Leader of the Council by J. Wilson.

Director-General and Clerk to the Council, M. F. Stonehurst, C.B.E.

G.L.C. SERVICES

The services provided by the G.L.C. include planning, roads, traffic management and control, fire services, refuse disposal, housing, parks and licensing. For certain services it shares responsibility with the London Borough Councils and the City Corporation.

Education.—The local education authority for an area corresponding with the area of the twelve inner London boroughs and the City of London is the Inner London Education Authority, a special committee of the G.L.C. consisting of the members of the Council elected for the inner London boroughs together with a representative of each inner London Borough Council and of the Common Council. The Council charges to the rating authorities in the Inner London Education Area the expenditure of the I.L.E.A., the amount being determined by the Authority. This unique arrangement preserves the continuity of the service which has developed since 1870 as a unity without regard to local boundary divisions.

The total number of pupils on the rolls of the Authority's nursery, primary and secondary schools (including special schools for handicapped children) is 310,643. There are 1,113 schools, staffed by the equivalent of 21,077 full-time teachers. Vocational instruction, cultural studies and recreational activities for persons over compulsory school age are arranged at the various establishments for further education. The Authority maintains 26 colleges and makes grants to 5 polytechnics and 3 other institutions. Part-time classes are offered at 24 adult education and literary institutes, and 76 youth centres, including 2 drama centres. The 20 outer London Borough Councils are the education authorities for their Boroughs.

Housing.—The Council shares with the London Borough Councils responsibility for housing in London. In line with the development of its strategic housing role the Council has now transferred most of its housing management functions to the Borough Councils. For the future, the Council intends to concentrate on analysing London's overall housing needs, presenting a co-ordinated view of action required, with a much reduced range of executive activities, although it will continue to carry out new building programmes and improvement work on older properties. This work is set out in the Council's London Housing Appraisal and its annual Housing Investment Programme submission to the Department of the Environment.

Planning and Transportation.—Planning responsibilities in London are shared between the G.L.C. and the London Borough Councils. The G.L.C. is the planning authority for London as a whole and its strategic policies are set out in the G.L.D.P.—the structure plan for Greater London. Within the framework of the G.L.D.P., London Borough Councils may prepare their own local plans which together with the G.L.D.P. then form the basis for controlling development.

Town planning control of development proposals is mainly the concern of the London Boroughs (or the London Docklands Development Corporation), but the G.L.C. has some responsibilities in this field. As planner and developer the Council is involved in many major schemes. The Council and its District Surveyors are responsible for making and administering building control regulations in the inner London boroughs, and the Council is also responsible for planning controls respecting buildings of historical or architectural interest, or in conservation areas.

The Council is responsible for the construction, improvement and maintenance of principal roads. As the traffic authority for all roads in Greater London it prepares or approves traffic management schemes and devises special projects for assisting cyclists and pedestrians, installs and controls traffic signals, bus only lanes, waiting and loading restrictions and speed limits and makes the orders which enforce them. It maintains the Thames tunnels, all but four of the Thames bridges (London, Tower, Blackfriars and Southwark, which are maintained by the Corporation of London), and maintains and operates the Woolwich free ferry.

The G.L.C.'s responsibility, through the London Transport Executive, for transport services in London was transferred in June 1984 to the London Regional Transport board, which is responsible to the Secretary of State for Transport.

Expanding towns.—The Council continues to have agreements with a number of towns for the provision of homes and jobs out of London, but negotiations are now well advanced for their termination where this can be done by agreement.

Parks and Open Spaces.—The Council maintains some 5,500 acres of parks and open spaces. The London Borough Councils and the City Corporation between them provide a further 28,500 acres. Up to 800 open-air entertainments are arranged in G.L.C. parks each summer and almost all games and sports are provided for. At Crystal Palace, in addition to the Council's 106 acre park is the Crystal Palace National Sports Centre, owned by the Council and managed by the Sports Council.

Other features of the G.L.C.'s administration include its responsibility for the Royal Festival Hall, Queen Elizabeth Hall and Purcell Room, and the Hayward Gallery, which is leased by the G.L.C. to the Arts Council; the maintenance of The Iveagh Bequest, Kenwood, many other buildings of historic interest and two museums, and the maintenance and operation of Thames piers. The Greater London Record Office and Library house official records and other manuscripts, books, maps, drawings and photographs relating to London and are open to the public for reference purposes. The Research and Intelligence unit is concerned with information and research on any matters concerning Greater London. The results of its work will be available to government departments, local authorities and the public.

Solid waste disposal.—The Council is responsible for the disposal of refuse throughout Greater London—some 3,250,000 tonnes currently being handled each year. It operates a number of transfer stations and one incinerator. Refuse is used for infilling at thirty-four land reclamation sites. The Boroughs continue to be responsible for refuse collection. Over 12,000 old vehicles and more than 300,000 tonnes of bulky household refuse (the latter deposited direct by members of the public but included in the total of 3,250,000 tonnes) are also dealt with as a means of improving the environment under the Refuse Disposal (Amenity) Act, 1978. The Council provide separate containers for glass, metal, textiles, etc. to facilitate re-cycling. The G.L.C. is also responsible, under the Control of Pollution Act, 1974, for the issue of waste disposal licences and for monitoring the movement of hazardous waste through the London area.

Land Drainage and Flood Prevention.—The G.L.C. and the Borough Councils exercise land drainage functions on certain watercourses within a 400 sq. mile area in and adjoining Greater London known as the London Excluded Area. The G.L.C. undertakes flood prevention works and maintains unobstructed flows in main metropolitan watercourses including the Ravensbourne, Beverley Brook, Wandle, Crane and Brent rivers. The Council also has flood prevention functions along some 120 miles of riverbank of the Thames and its tidal tributaries. A moveable barrier across the Thames at Silvertown was completed in 1982 and, with associated bank raising schemes, will provide flood protection against surge tides.

Licensing.—The Council is the licensing authority in Greater London for certain places of entertainment, greyhound race tracks and petroleum installations.

Fire Services.—The Council is the fire authority for its whole area.

The London Fire Brigade set up on April 1, 1965, under the London Government Act, 1963, consists of the Brigades of the former counties of London and Middlesex (excluding the districts of Staines, Sunbury and Potters Bar), the former county boroughs of East Ham, West Ham and Croydon and of parts of Essex, Herts., Kent and Surrey. *Headquarters*, 8 Albert Embankment, S.E.1.

The Brigade has 114 land stations. Wholetime authorized establishment, 7,067. There are 640 firefighting appliances and support vehicles and a new fire-boat was recently commissioned.

Chief Officer, R. A. Bullers, Q.F.S.M.

Deputy Chief Officer, S. D. Clarkson.

Finance.—The Greater London Council's budget for 1984–85 (including London Transport Executive) amounts to £3,570 million of which £3,063 million is revenue expenditure (including £1,066 million for the Inner London Education Authority) and £507 million capital expenditure (£20 million for the Inner London Education Authority).

Revenue expenditure during the year will be met by precept on the London Borough Councils (£1,631 million); income from loan repayments, rents, reimbursements for fees and salaries, etc. (£651 million); London Transport fares etc. (£488 million); and by Exchequer grants for certain works and services (£293 million). The Inner London Education Authority determines the amount the Council must precept on the rating authorities in Inner London for education purposes.

Capital expenditure on housing and education is financed by external borrowing; capital expenditure on all other services is financed internally through a capital fund.

THE CORPORATION OF LONDON

The City of London is the historic centre at the heart of London known as "the square mile" around which the vast metropolis has grown over the centuries. The City's residential population is 5,300 (1981 Census). The civic government is carried on by the Corporation of London through the Court of Common Council, a body consisting of the Lord Mayor, 24 other Aldermen and 136 Common Councilmen. The legal title of the Corporation is "the Mayor and Commonalty and Citizens of the City of London."

The City is the financial and business centre of London and includes the head offices of the principal banks, insurance companies and mercantile houses, in addition to buildings ranging from the historic interest of the Roman Wall and the 15th century Guildhall, to the massive splendour of St. Paul's Cathedral and the architectural beauty of Wren's spires.

The City of London was described by Tacitus in A.D. 62 as "a busy emporium for trade and traders". Under the Romans it became an important administration centre and hub of the road system. Little is known of London in Saxon times when it formed part of the kingdom of the East Saxons. In 886 Alfred recovered London from the Danes and reconstituted it a burgh under his son-in-law. In 1066 the citizens submitted to William the Conqueror who in 1067 granted them a charter, which is still preserved, establishing them in the rights and privileges they had hitherto enjoyed. The mayoralty was established on the recognition of the corporate unity of the citizens by Prince John in 1191, the first Mayor being Henry Fitz Ailwyn who filled the office for 21 years and was succeeded by Fitz Alan (1212–15). A new charter was granted by King John in 1215, directing the Mayor to be chosen annually, which has ever since been done, though in early times the same individual often held the office more than once. A familiar instance is that of "Whittington, thrice Lord Mayor of London" (in reality four times, A.D. 1397, 1398, 1406, 1419); and many modern cases have occurred. The earliest instance of the phrase "Lord Mayor" in English is in 1414. It is used more generally in the latter part of the 15th century and becomes invariable from 1535 onwards. At Michaelmas the Liverymen in Common Hall choose two Aldermen who have served the office of Sheriff for presentation to the Court of Aldermen, and one is chosen to be Lord Mayor for the ensuing mayoral year. The Lord Mayor is presented to the Lord Chief Justice at the Royal Courts of Justice on the second Saturday in November to make the final declaration of office, having been sworn in at Guildhall on the preceding day. The procession to the Royal Courts of Justice is popularly known as the *Lord Mayor's Show*.

Aldermen are mentioned in the 11th century and their office is of Saxon origin. They were elected annually between 1377 and 1394, when a charter of Richard II directed them to be chosen for life. The *Common Council*, elected annually on December 17, was, at an early date, substituted for a popular assembly called the *Folkmote*. At first only two representatives were sent from each ward, but the number has since been greatly increased.

Sheriffs were Saxon officers: their predecessors were the *wic-reeves* and *portreeves* of London and Middlesex. At first they were officers of the Crown, and were named by the Barons of the Exchequer; but Henry I (in 1132) gave the citizens permission to choose their own Sheriffs, and the annual election of Sheriffs became fully operative under King John's charter of 1199. The citizens lost this privilege, as far as the election of Sheriff of Middlesex is concerned, by the Local Government Act, 1888; but the Liverymen continue, as heretofore, to choose two Sheriffs of the City of London, who are appointed on Midsummer Day, and take office at Michaelmas.

Officers.—The Recorder was first appointed in 1298. The office of Chamberlain is an ancient one, the first contemporary record of which is 1276. The Town Clerk (or Common Clerk) is mentioned in 1274 and the Common Serjeant in 1291.

Activities.—The work is assigned to a number of committees which present reports to the Court of Common Council. These Committees are:—City Lands and Bridge House Estates, Policy and Resources, Coal, Corn and Rates Finance, Planning and Communications, Central Markets, Billingsgate and Leadenhall Markets, Spitalfields Market, Police, Port and City of London Health and Social Services, Library (Library, Records, Art Gallery and Museum), Boards of Governors of Schools, Music (Guildhall School of Music and Drama), Establishment, Housing, Gresham (City side), Epping Forest and Open Spaces, West Ham Park, Privileges, Barbican Development, Barbican Residential and Barbican Centre (Barbican Arts and Conference Centre).

The Honourable the *Irish Society*, which manages the Corporation's Estates in Ulster, consists of a

Governor and 5 other Aldermen, the Recorder, and 19 Common Councilmen, of whom one is elected Deputy Governor.

The *City's Estate*, in the possession of which the Corporation of London differs from other municipalities, is managed by the City Lands and Bridge House Estates Committee, the Chairmanship of which carries with it the title of "Chief Commoner."

The Right Honourable the Lord Mayor 1983–1984*

Dame Mary Donaldson, G.B.E., *born* 1921; Alderman of *Coleman Street*, 1975; *Sheriff of London*, 1981; *Lord Mayor*, 1983.

Secretary, Rear-Admiral A. J. Cooke, C.B.

Recorder, Sir James Miskin, Q.C., 1975; *Chamberlain*, Bernard Peter Harty, 1983; *Town Clerk*, Geoffrey William Rowley, 1982; *Common Serjeant*, David William Tudor Price, 1982.

The Aldermen

Aldermen	Ward	Born	C.C.	Ald.	Shff.	Lord Mayor
Sir Edward de Coucey Howard, Bt., G.B.E.	*Cornhill*	1915	1951	1963	1966	1971
Cdr. Sir Robin Danvers Penrose Gillett, Bt., G.B.E., R.D., R.N.R.	*Bassishaw*	1925	1965	1969	1973	1976
Sir Peter Drury Haggerston Gadsden, G.B.E.	*Farringdon Wt.*	1929	1969	1971	1970	1979
Col. Sir Ronald Laurence Gardner-Thorpe, G.B.E., T.D.	*Bishopsgate*	1917	....	1972	1978	1980
Sir Christopher Leaver, G.B.E.	*Dowgate*	1937	1973	1974	1979	1981
Dame Mary Donaldson, G.B.E.	*Coleman St.*	1921	1966	1975	1981	1983
	All the above have passed the Civic Chair					
Alan Towers Traill	*Langbourn*	....	1970	1975	1982	....
William Allan Davis	*Cripplegate*	1921	1971	1976	1982	....
Richard Christopher Larkins Charvet, R.D.	*Aldgate*	1936	1970	1976	1983	....
David Kenneth Rowe-Ham	*Bridge*	1935	....	1976	1984	....
Col. Greville Douglas Spratt, T.D.	*Castle Baynard*	1927	....	1978	1984	....
Christopher Collett	*Broad Street*	1931	1973	1979	....	....
Hugh Charles Philip Bidwell	*Billingsgate*	1934	....	1979	....	....
Alexander Michael Graham	*Queenhithe*	1938	1978	1979	....	....
Brian Garton Jenkins	*Cordwainer*	1935	....	1980	....	....
Francis McWilliams	*Aldersgate*	1926	1978	1980	....	....
Paul Henry Newall, T.D.	*Walbrook*	1934	1980	1981	....	....
Christopher Rupert Walford	*Farringdon Wn.*	1935	....	1982	....	....
Roderic Neil Young	*Bread Street*	1933	1980	1982	....	....
Roger William Cork	*Tower*	1947	1978	1983	....	....
Brian Edward Toye	*Lime Street*	1938	....	1983	....	....
Richard Everard Nichols	*Candlewick*	1938	1983	1984	....	....
Peter Anthony Bull	*Cheap*	1937	1968	1984	....	....

NB. At the time of going to press, the Wards of *Portsoken* and *Vintry* were vacant.

* The Lord Mayor for 1984–85 was elected on Michaelmas Day (*See* "Occurrences During Printing").

The Sheriffs 1984–1985

David Kenneth Rowe-Ham (*see above*) and Greville Douglas Spratt, T.D. (*see above*), *elected* June 25; *assumed office* September 28, 1984.

THE COMMON COUNCIL OF LONDON

Allday, P. F. (1972) .... *Bishopsgate*
Angell, O. D. (1964) .... *Bishopsgate*
Ballard, K. A., M.C. (1969) .... *Castle Baynard*
Balls, *Deputy* H. D. (1970) .... *Cripplegate*
Barker, J. A. (1981) .... *Cripplegate Wt.*
Beale, M. J. (1949) .... *Lime Street*
Begg, M. Henderson (1977) .... *Coleman Street*
Bigley, Miss A. F. (1982) .... *Cripplegate Wn.*
Bird, J. L. (1977) .... *Bridge*
Birkett, *Lt. Col.*, D., M.C. (1983) ..... *Aldersgate*
Block, S. A. A. (1983) .... *Cheap*
Bramwell, F. M. (1983) .... *Langbourn*
Brighton, A. G. (1966) .... *Portsoken*
Brooks, W. I. B. (1979) .... *Cripplegate Wn.*
Brown, B. J., C.B.E. (1973) .... *Aldersgate*
Brown, D. C. G. (1976) .... *Aldgate*
Brown, D. T. (1971) .... *Walbrook*
Cassidy, M. J. (1980) .... *Aldersgate*
Catt, B. F. (1982) .... *Farringdon Wn.*
Challis, G. H. (1978) .... *Langbourn*

Champness, *Deputy* P. H. (1966) ..... *Walbrook*
Chalstrey, L. J. (1981) .... *Farringdon Wt.*
Chandler, E. G., C.B.E. (1982) .... *Cornhill*
Clements, *Deputy* G. E. I. (1960) ...... *Farringdon Wt.*
Cohen, J. M. (1980) .... *Queenhithe*
Cohen, *Deputy* S. E., C.B.E. (1951) ... *Farringdon Wt.*
Cole, *Lt.-Col.*, Sir Colin, K.C.V.O., T.D. (1964) .... *Castle Baynard*
Colover, D. (1975) .... *Bishopsgate*
Cope, Dr. J. (1963) .... *Farringdon Wt.*
Coulson, A. G. (1961) .... *Broad St.*
Coven, *Deputy* Mrs. E. O. (1972) ..... *Dowgate*
Daltrey, D. H. J. (1973) .... *Billingsgate*
Deith, R. C. (1944) .... *Farringdon Wn.*
Delderfield, D. W. (1982) .... *Aldersgate*
Denny, A. M. (1971) .... *Billingsgate*
De Silva, (1980) .... *Farringdon Wt.*
Dewhurst, *Deputy* W. (1971) .... *Cripplegate*
Donnelly, T. A., M.B.E. (1982) .... *Bread Street*
Duckworth, *Deputy* H. (1960) .... *Lime St.*

Durand, Mrs. B. J. (1975)	*Farringdon Wt.*	Mizen, *Deputy* D. H. (1979)	*Broad Street*
Durnin, J. C. (1976)	*Cordwainer*	Morgan, *Deputy* B. L., C.B.E. (1963)	*Bishopsgate*
Edwards, R. D. K. (1978)	*Bassishaw*	Murkin, *Deputy* C. H., O.B.E. (1969)	*Vintry*
Eskenzi, A. N. (1971)	*Farringdon Wn.*	Nash, Mrs. J. C. (1983)	*Aldersgate*
Evans, Mrs. J. (1975)	*Farringdon Wt.*	Neary, J. E. (1982)	*Aldgate*
Eve, R. A. (1980)	*Cheap*	Newby, J. (1982)	*Lime Street*
Ewin, *Deputy* Sir David Floyd-,		Oliver, J. M. Y. (1980)	*Bishopsgate*
M.V.O., O.B.E. (1963)	*Castle Baynard*	Olson, A. H. F. (1972)	*Dowgate*
Farrow, M. W. W. (1983)	*Cripplegate*	Oram, *Deputy* M. H., T.D. (1963)	*Cordwainer*
Farthing, R. B. C. (1981)	*Aldgate*	Owen, Mrs. J. (1975)	*Langbourn*
Fell, J. A. (1982)	*Queenhithe*	Owen-Ward, J. R. (1983)	*Bridge*
Fisher, *Deputy* D. G. (1958)	*Cornhill*	Packard, Brig. J. J. (1973)	*Cripplegate*
Fitzgerald, R. C. A. (1981)	*Bread Street*	Peacock, R. W., C.B.E. (1956)	*Vintry*
Fordham, W. E. (1966)	*Aldgate*	Pearson, T. A. S. (1979)	*Queenhithe*
Frankenberg, *Deputy* J. (1964)	*Portsoken*	Pembroke, *Deputy* Mrs. A. M. F.	
Frappell, C. E. (1973)	*Bread St.*	(1978)	*Cheap*
Fraser, W. B. (1981)	*Vintry*	Ponsonby of Shulbrede, The Lady	
Galloway, A. D. (1981)	*Broad Street*	(1981)	*Farringdon Wt.*
Gass, *Deputy* G. J. (1967)	*Coleman St.*	Prince, *Deputy* L. B., C.B.E. (1950)	*Bishopsgate*
Gold, R. (1965)	*Castle Baynard*	Pulman, G. A. (1983)	*Tower*
Gordon, Miss C. F. (1978)	*Cripplegate Wn.*	Ratner, R. A., T.D. (1981)	*Broad Street*
Gugan, K., PH.D. (1974)	*Dowgate*	Reed, E. J. (1978)	*Tower*
Harding, N. H. (1970)	*Farringdon Wn.*	Reed, *Deputy* J. L., M.B.E. (1967)	*Farringdon Wn.*
Harris, R. P. (1980)	*Cripplegate.*	Rigby, P. P. (1972)	*Farringdon Wn.*
Harris, W. H. Wylie (1957)	*Farringdon Wn.*	Rodgers, S. C. (1969)	*Farringdon Wt.*
Hart, *Deputy* M. G. (1970)	*Bridge*	Rogers, Miss E. H. L. (1982)	*Cornhill*
Hatfield, A. F. R. (1968)	*Bishopsgate*	Roney, *Deputy* E. P. T. (1974)	*Bishopsgate*
Henderson, *Deputy* J. S. (1975)	*Langbourn*	Rowlandson, Sir Graham, M.B.E.	
Holland, *Deputy* J. (1972)	*Aldgate*	(1961)	*Coleman Street*
Horlock, *Deputy* H. W. S. (1969)	*Farringdon Wn.*	Samuel, Mrs. I. (1972)	*Portsoken*
Howard, D. H. S. (1973)	*Cornhill*	Saunders, *Deputy* R. (1975)	*Candlewick*
Humphrays, Mrs. R. (1976)	*Cripplegate*	Savory, M. B. (1980)	*Broad Street*
Ide, W. R. (1972)	*Castle Baynard*	Shalit, D. M. (1973)	*Farringdon Wn.*
Jackson, L. St. J. T. (1978)	*Bassishaw*	Sharp, *Deputy* Mrs. I. M. (1974)	*Queenhithe*
James, A. J. (1973)	*Cordwainer*	Sheppard, S., O.B.E. (1957)	*Billingsgate*
James, J. F. (1977)	*Farringdon Wt.*	Shindler, *Deputy* A. B. (1966)	*Billingsgate*
Jenks, M. A. B. (1972)	*Coleman Street*	Silk, D. (1979)	*Cripplegate*
Keith, J. M., C.B.E., T.D. (1962)	*Candlewick*	Smith, P. A. Revell- (1959)	*Vintry*
Langmead, A. D. G., T.D. (1982)	*Tower*	Spurrier, H. J. (1974)	*Dowgate*
Laurie, P. D. Northall- (1975)	*Walbrook*	Stevenson, J. L. (1970)	*Coleman Street*
Lawson, G. C. H. (1972)	*Portsoken*	Stitcher, G. M., C.B.E. (1966)	*Farringdon Wt.*
Lawrence, D. W. O. (1979)	*Bridge*	Sunderland, O., T.D. (1968)	*Billingsgate*
Levene, P. K. (1983)	*Candlewick*	Turner, *Deputy* R. L. (1973)	*Tower*
Liss, *Deputy* H. (1965)	*Aldersgate*	Welch, Sir John, Bt. (1975)	*Walbrook*
Luke, A. L. (1968)	*Bishopsgate*	Wilmot, R. T. D. (1973)	*Cordwainer*
McAuley, *Deputy*, C. (1957)	*Bread St.*	Wilson, *Deputy* A. B. (1960)	*Aldersgate*
McNeil, I. D. (1977)	*Lime Street*	Wilson, E. S. (1979)	*Aldersgate*
Malins, J. H. (1981)	*Farringdon Wt.*	Wixley, *Deputy* G. R. A., C.B.E., T.D.	
Mills, A. P. (1969)	*Bassishaw*	(1964)	*Bassishaw*
Mitchell, C. R. (1972)	*Castle Baynard*	Woodward, C. D. (1972)	*Cripplegate*

Deputies.—In the preceding list each Common Councilman so described serves as *Deputy* to the Alderman of his Ward.

FREEMEN'S GUILDS

London.—Guild of Freemen of the City of London, 4 Dowgate Hill, EC4M 7DE. *Clerk,* D. Reid.

Berwick upon Tweed.—Freemen's Guild of Berwick upon Tweed. *Sec.,* J. R. Reay, 9 Church Street.

Chester.—Freemen and Guilds of the City of Chester. The Guildhall, Chester.

Coventry.—City of Coventry Freemen's Guild. *Hon. Clerk.,* H. J. McCranor, 89 Brinklow Road, Binley, Coventry, CV3 2JB.

Grimsby.—Enrolled Freemen of Grimsby. *Clerk,* W. J. Savage, St. Mary's Chambers, Grimsby.

Lincoln.—Lincoln Freemen's Committee. *Clerk,* A. J. Gadd, 45 Skellingthorpe Road, Lincoln.

Newcastle upon Tyne.—Gild of Freemen of the City of Newcastle upon Tyne. *Hon. Sec.,* G. T. Henzell, 8 Leyburn Drive, High Heaton, Newcastle-upon-Tyne, NE7 7AP.

Oxford.—Oxford Freemen's Committee. *Sec.,* C. R. Butterfield, 126 High Street, Oxford.

Shrewsbury.—Association of Shrewsbury Freemen. *Hon. Sec.* D. Morris, 7 Canonbury, Kingsland, Shrewsbury.

York.—Gild of Freemen of the City of York. *Hon. Clerk,* Mrs. J. Steel, 9 Spalding Avenue, Clifton, York.

THE CITY GUILDS (LIVERY COMPANIES)

The Livery Companies of the City of London derive their name from the assumption of a distinctive dress or livery by their members in the 14th century.

The order of precedence (according to 2nd Report of Municipal Corporations' Commissioners, 1837), omitting extinct companies, is given in parentheses after the name of each Company.

About 20,400 Liverymen of the Guilds are entitled to vote at elections in *Common Hall.*

MERCERS (*1*). *Hall*, Ironmonger Lane, EC2V 8HE. *Livery*, 220.—*Clerk*, G. M. M. Wakeford; *Master*, J. P. G. Wathen.

GROCERS (*2*). *Hall*, Princes Street, EC2R 8AQ. *Livery*, 334.—*Clerk*, C. P. G. Chavasse; *Master*, H. C. P. Bidwell.

DRAPERS (*3*). *Hall*, Throgmorton Street, EC2N 2DQ. *Livery*, 230.—*Clerk*, R. C. G. Strick; *Master*, Capt. P. A. Bence-Trower, R.N.

FISHMONGERS (*4*). *Hall*, London Bridge, EC4R 9EL. *Livery*, 319.—*Clerk*, E. S. Earl; *Prime Warden*, The Viscount Leverhulme, T.D.

GOLDSMITHS (*5*). *Hall*, Foster Lane, EC2V 6BN. *Livery*, 270.—*Clerk*, C. P. de B. Jenkins, M.B.E., M.C.; *Prime Warden*, A. G. Grimwade.

SKINNERS (*6 and 7*). *Hall*, 8 Dowgate Hill, EC4R 2SP. *Livery*, 320.—*Clerk*, M. H. Glover; *Master*, Prof. J. R. Batchelor.

MERCHANT TAYLORS (*6 and 7*). *Hall*, 30 Threadneedle Street, EC2R 8AY. *Livery* 340.—*Clerk*, A. T. Langdon-Down; *Master*, P. A. S. Blomfield.

HABERDASHERS (*8*). *Hall*, Staining Lane, EC2V 7DD. *Livery*, 320.—*Clerk*, Capt. M. E. Barrow, D.S.O., R.N.; *Master*, G. L. Bourne.

SALTERS (*9*). *Hall*, Fore Street, EC2Y 5DE. *Livery*, 150.—*Clerk*, J. M. Montgomery; *Master*, Maj. C. A. Park.

IRONMONGERS (*10*). *Hall*, Barbican, EC2Y 8AA. *Livery*, 101.—*Clerk*, R. B. Brayne, M.B.E.; *Master*, J. R. C. Twallin.

VINTNERS (*11*). *Hall*, Upper Thames Street, EC4V 3BE. *Livery*, 319.—*Clerk*, Cdr. R. D. Ross, O.B.E., R.N.; *Master*, J. A. Metcalfe.

CLOTHWORKERS (*12*). *Hall*, Dunster Court, Mincing Lane, EC3R 7AH. *Livery*, 185.—*Clerk*, C. M. Mowll; *Master*, Lt. Cdr. P. Angell, D.S.C.

The above are the Twelve "Great" London Companies in order of Civic precedence.

ACCOUNTANTS (*86*). *Livery*, 307.—*Clerk*, O. Sunderland, T.D., Shelley House, 3 Noble Street, EC2V 7DQ; *Master*, M. R. Harris.

ACTUARIES (*91*). *Livery*, 112.—*Clerk*, A. K. Tudor, 8 Madgeways Close, Great Amwell, Herts., SG12 9RW; *Master*, L. G. Hall.

AIR PILOTS AND AIR NAVIGATORS, GUILD OF (*81*). *Grand Master*, H.R.H. the Prince Philip, Duke of Edinburgh, K.G.; *Clerk*, W. T. F. Rossiter, 30 Eccleston Square, S.W.1; *Master*, Capt. C. Klimcke.

APOTHECARIES, SOCIETY OF (*58*). *Hall*, Black Friars Lane, EC4V 6EJ. *Livery*, 1,150.—*Clerk*, Maj. J. C. O'Leary; *Master*, Prof. N. Ashton.

ARBITRATORS (*93*). *Livery*, 155.—*Clerk*, B. W. Vigrass, O.B.E., V.R.D., 75 Cannon Street, EC4N 5BH; *Master*, N. A. Royce.

ARMOURERS AND BRASIERS (*22*). *Hall*, 81 Coleman Street, EC2R 5BJ. *Livery*, 120.—*Clerk*, Lt. Col. R. R. F. Cowe; *Master*, P. W. Trumper.

BAKERS (*19*). *Hall*, Harp Lane, Lower Thames Street, E.C.3. *Livery*, 360.—*Clerk*, P. F. Wilson, D.F.C.; *Master*, D. Goble.

BARBERS (*17*). *Hall*, Monkwell Square, E.C.2. *Livery*, 178.—*Clerk*, B. W. Hall, *Master*, P. Lambert.

BASKETMAKERS (*52*). *Livery*, 500.—*Clerk*, B. Stroulger, 87–95 Tooley Street, SE1 2RA; *Prime Warden*,

Sir William Woolf Harris, O.B.E.

BLACKSMITHS (*40*). *Livery*, 250.—*Clerk*, J. Green, 41 Tabernacle Street, E.C.2; *Prime Warden*, A. W. Pennington.

BOWYERS (*38*). *Livery*, 86.—*Clerk*, J. G. McCagney, 7 Chandos Street, W1M 9DE; *Master*, B. MacDermot.

BREWERS (*14*). *Hall*, Aldermanbury Square, EC2V 7HR. *Livery*, 110.—*Clerk*, Rr. Adm. M. La Touche Wemyss, C.B; *Master*, Dr. B. C. Kilkenny.

BRODERERS (*48*). *Livery*, 96.—*Clerk*, S. G. B. Underwood, 11A Bridge Road, East Molesey, KT8 9EY; *Master*, R. H. Mann.

BUILDERS MERCHANTS (*88*). *Livery*, 200.—*Clerk*, A. G. P. Lincoln, M.C., T.D. 128 Queen Victoria Street, E.C.4; *Master*, M. H. Vinden.

BUTCHERS (*24*). *Hall*, 87 Bartholomew Close, EC1A 7EB. *Livery*, 650.—*Clerk*, Cmdr. P. B. Cowan, R.N.; *Master*, J. W. Brewster, O.B.E.

CARMEN (*77*). *Livery*, 430.—*Clerk*, Lt. Col. G. T. Pearce, M.B.E., St. Olave's Rectory, 8 Hart Street, EC3R 7NB; *Master*, C. F. W. Birch.

CARPENTERS (*26*). *Hall*, Throgmorton Avenue, EC2N 2JJ. *Livery*, 150.—*Clerk*, Capt. K. G. Hamon, R.N.; *Master*, Maj. R. P. G. Dill.

CITY OF LONDON SOLICITORS (*79*). *Livery*, 417.—*Clerk*, A. Ellery, 13–14 Charterhouse Square, EC1M 6AX; *Master*, D. F. Gray.

CLOCKMAKERS (*61*). *Livery*, 275.—*Clerk*, Air Cdre. B. G. Frow, D.S.O, D.F.C., 2 Greycoat Place, SW1P 1SD; *Master*, B. G. L. Jackman.

COACHMAKERS (*72*). *Livery*, 376.—*Clerk*, J. A. Nicholson, 9 Lincoln's Inn Fields, W.C.2; *Master*, T. J. Connolly.

COOKS (*35*). *Livery*, 75.—*Clerk*, H. J. Lavington, T.D. 49 Queen Victoria Street, E.C.4; *Master*, H. H. Tickler.

COOPERS (*36*). *Hall*, 13 Devonshire Square, EC2M 4TH. *Livery*, 255.—*Clerk*, J. A. Newton; *Master*, A. Grant, O.B.E., M.C., T.D.

CORDWAINERS (*27*).—*Clerk*, Capt. C. T. Codrington, 30 Fleet Street, E.C.4; *Master*, D. T. B. Blanford.

CURRIERS (*29*). *Livery*, 80.—*Clerk*, I. R. McNeil, 43 Church Road, Hove, BN3 2BT; *Master*, N. F. Martin.

CUTLERS (*18*). *Hall*, 4 Warwick Lane, EC4M 7BR. *Livery*, 100.—*Clerk*, K. S. G. Hinde; *Master*, I. S. Ball.

DISTILLERS (*69*). *Livery*, 225.—*Clerk*, B. Dehn, 1 Vintners Place, E.C.4; *Master*, D. Lamdin.

DYERS (*13*). *Hall*, 10 Dowgate Hill, EC4R 2ST. *Livery*, 130.—*Clerk*, A. J. Boyall, O.B.E., D.S.C.; *Prime Warden*, C. H. Christie.

FAN MAKERS (*76*). *Livery*, 209.—*Clerk*, R. Southcombe, Ludgate House, 107–111 Fleet Street, E.C.4; *Master*, D. A. Collins, T.D.

FARMERS (*80*). *Livery*, 295.—*Clerk*, I. G. Williamson. 7/8 King's Bench Walk, Temple, EC4Y 7DT; *Master*, C. T. Muddiman.

FARRIERS (*55*). *Livery*, 375.—*Clerk*, H. W. H. Ellis, 37 The Uplands, Loughton, Essex, IG10 1NQ; *Master*, H.R.H. The Princess Anne, Mrs. Mark Phillips, G.C.V.O.

FELTMAKERS (*63*). *Livery*, 292.—*Clerk*, E. J. P. Elliott, 53 Davies Street, Berkeley Square, W1Y 2BL; *Master*, A. G. I. Wontner.

FLETCHERS (*39*). *Livery*, 110.—*Clerk*, F. N. Steiner, 23 College Hill, E.C.4; *Master*, H. L. Waterman.

FOUNDERS (*33*). *Hall*, 13 St. Swithin's Lane, EC4N 8AL. *Livery*, 160.—*Clerk*, H. Wilson Wiley; *Master*, N. C. Crighton.

FRAMEWORK KNITTERS (*64*). *Livery*, 225.—*Clerk*, H. C. Weale, 51 Dulwich Wood Avenue, SE19 1HG; *Master*, R. Noskwith.

FRUITERERS (*45*). *Livery*, 270.—*Clerk*, J. C. Airey, 1 Serjeants' Inn, EC4Y 1JD; *Master*, H. M. Arthur.

FURNITURE MAKERS (83). *Livery*, 233.—*Clerk*, G. Benbow, T.D., c/o G. Benbow & Co., Grove Mills, Cranbrook Road, Hawkhurst, Kent, TN18 4AS; *Master*, M. Leigh, PH.D.

GARDENERS (66). *Livery*, 250.—*Clerk*, F. N. Steiner, 23 College Hill, E.C.4; *Master*, Rear-Adm. M. J. Ross.

GIRDLERS (23). *Hall*, Basinghall Avenue, E.C.2. *Livery*, 80.—*Clerk*, P. H. White; *Master*, D. N. Seaton.

GLASS-SELLERS (71). *Livery*, 180.—*Hon. Clerk*, P. J. Willoughby, 25 New Street Square, EC4A 3LN; *Master*, P. C. Northam.

GLAZIERS (53). *Livery*, 290.—*Clerk*, R. B. Hodgetts, Glaziers Hall, 9 Montague Close, London Bridge, S.E.1; *Master*, Col. M. H. Seys-Phillips.

GLOVERS (62). *Livery*, 285.—*Clerk*, Capt. D. G. F. Palmer, O.B.E., Glovers, Tismans Common, Rudgwick, W. Sussex, RH12 3DU; *Master*, H. S. Kirsch.

GOLD AND SILVER WYREDRAWERS (74). *Livery*, 350.— *Clerk*, D. Reid, 40a Ludgate Hill, EC4M 7DE; *Master*, B. E. Toye.

GUNMAKERS (73). *Livery*, 200.—*Clerk*, F. B. Brandt, 12 Devonshire Square, E.C.2; *Master*, Hon. R. Blackett Beaumont.

HORNERS (54). *Livery*, 450.—*Clerk*, Dr. E. M. Hunt, 11 Hobart Place, SW1W 0HL; *Master*, E. R. Nicholson.

INNHOLDERS (32). *Hall*, College Street, Dowgate Hill, E.C.4. *Livery*, 107.—*Clerk*, J.R. Edwardes Jones; *Master*, H. J. Lavington, T.D.

INSURERS (92). *Livery*, 271.—*Clerk*, V. D. Webb, The Hall, 20 Aldermanbury, E.C.2; *Master*, J. A. S. Neave, C.B.E.

JOINERS (41). *Livery*, 117.—*Clerk*, D. A. Tate, Parkville House, Bridge Street, Pinner, HA5 3JD; *Master*, R. M. Rayner.

LAUNDERERS (89). *Livery*, 180.—*Clerk*, W. E. Kingsland, 34 Broadhurst, Ashtead, Surrey, KT21 1QD; *Master*, J. Pennell.

LEATHERSELLERS (15). *Hall*, 15 St. Helens Place, EC3A 6DQ. *Livery*, 150.—*Clerk*, Capt. C. N. MacEacharn, C.B.E., R.N.; *Master*, A. G. Williams.

LORINERS (57). *Livery*, 352.—*Clerk*, J. R. Williams, 2/5 Benjamin Street, EC1M 5QL; *Master*, A. J. Gunton.

MARKETORS (90). *Livery*, 175.—*Clerk*, B. F. Catt, 29 Queen Street, EC4R 1BH; *Master*, The Lord Mais of Walbrook, G.B.E., E.R.D., T.D.

MASONS (30). *Livery*, 108.—*Clerk*, H. J. Maddocks, 9 New Square, WC2A 3QN; *Master*, C. J. Jeffries, M.B.E.

MASTER MARINERS, HONOURABLE COMPANY OF (78). H.Q.S. *Wellington*, Temple Stairs, WC2R 2PN. *Livery*, 300.—*Clerk*, D. H. W. Field; *Admiral*, H.R.H. the Duke of Edinburgh, K.G.; *Master*, Capt. O. Elsom.

MUSICIANS (50). *Livery*, 250.—*Clerk*, W. R. I. Crewdson, 4 St. Paul's Churchyard, E.C.4; *Master*, H. F. Winckler.

NEEDLEMAKERS (65). *Livery*, 230.—*Clerk*, M. G. Cook, 4 Staple Inn, WC1V 7QW; *Master*, N. C. Green, D.S.O., D.F.C.

PAINTER STAINERS (28). *Hall*, 9 Little Trinity Lane, EC4V 2AD. *Livery*, 405.—*Clerk*, A. G. P. Lincoln, M.C., T.D.; *Master*, S. F. Everson.

PATTENMAKERS (70). *Livery*, 250.—*Clerk*, A. J. Hucker, 6 Raymond Bldgs., Gray's Inn, W.C.1; *Master*, C. A. Prendergast, C.B.E.

PAVIORS (56). *Livery*, 250.—*Clerk*, R. F. Coe, Cutlers' Hall, Warwick Lane, EC4M 7BR; *Master*, H. Olson.

PEWTERERS (16). *Hall*, Oat Lane, EC2V 7DE. *Livery*, 110.—*Clerk*, Maj. J. M. Halford, R.M.; *Master*, Lt. Col. P. B. Wakelin, M.C.

PLAISTERERS (46). *Hall*, 1 London Wall, EC2Y 5JU. *Livery*, 199.—*Clerk*, H. Mott; *Master*, R. A. Hills.

PLAYING CARD MAKERS (75). *Livery*, 142.—*Clerk*, M. J. Smyth, 1 Serjeants' Inn, Fleet Street, E.C.4; *Master*, His Hon. Judge Argyle, M.C., Q.C.

PLUMBERS (31). *Livery*, 260.—*Clerk*, Col. E. M. P. Hardy, Ironmongers Hall, Barbican, E.C.2.; *Master*, P. L. Steer.

POULTERS (34). *Livery*, 160.—*Clerk*, I. G. Williamson, 7-8 King's Bench Walk, Temple, EC4Y 7DT; *Master*, C. W. H. Longley.

SADDLERS (25). *Hall*, Gutter Lane, Cheapside, EC2V 6BR. *Livery*, 65.—*Clerk*, Gp. Capt. K. M. Oliver, R.A.F. (*retd.*); *Master*, C. C. Taylor.

SCIENTIFIC INSTRUMENT MAKERS (84). *Livery*, 214.— *Clerk*, Maj. Gen. E. Younson, O.B.E., 9 Montague Close, SE1 9DD; *Master*, J. B. S. Savage, T.D.

SCRIVENERS (44).—*Clerk*, H. J. W. Harman, Chancery House, 53/64 Chancery Lane, W.C.2; *Master*, R. A. D. Urquart.

SECRETARIES AND ADMINISTRATORS (87). *Livery*, 206.—*Hon. Clerk*, G. H. Challis, The Irish Chamber, Guildhall Yard, EC2V 5AE; *Master*, Miss S. I. M. Tutt.

SHIPWRIGHTS (59). *Livery*, 500.—*Clerk*, C. H. Baylis, C.B., Ironmongers' Hall, Barbican, E.C.2; *Permanent Master*, H.R.H. the Duke of Edinburgh, K.G., K.T.; *Prime Warden*, Sir Charles Alexander.

SPECTACLEMAKERS (60). *Livery*, 303.—*Clerk*, C. J. Eldridge, Apothecaries' Hall, EC4V 6EL; *Master*, M. Rawling.

STATIONERS AND NEWSPAPER MAKERS (47). *Hall*, Stationers' Hall, Ave Maria Lane, Ludgate Hill, EC4M 7DD. *Livery*, 450.—*Clerk*, Capt. P. Hames, R.N.; *Master*, L. W. M. Viney.

SURVEYORS (85). *Livery*, 283.—*Clerk*, B. C. Briant, C.V.O., M.B.E., 12 Great George Street, Parliament Square, SW1P 3AD; *Master*, P. W. Grafton, C.B.E.

TALLOWCHANDLERS (21). *Hall*, 4 Dowgate Hill, EC4R 2SH. *Livery*, 175.—*Clerk*, Col. M. ff. Woodhead, O.B.E.; *Master*, N. M. Wells.

TIN PLATE WORKERS (67). *Livery*, 205.—*Clerk*, A. Hill, 71 Lincolns Inn Fields, WC2A 3JF; *Master*, Rear Adm. Sir Anthony Miers, V.C.

TOBACCO PIPE MAKERS AND TOBACCO BLENDERS (82). *Livery*, 189.—*Clerk*, I. J. Kimmins, Bouverie House, 154 Fleet Street, EC4A 2HX; *Master*, H. E. P. Spearing, T.D.

TURNERS (51). *Livery*, 163.—*Clerk*, N. M. A. Evelegh, 1 Serjeants' Inn, EC4Y 1JD; *Master*, J. E. Borrett.

TYLERS AND BRICKLAYERS (37). *Livery*, 123.—*Clerk*, J. C. Peck, 6 Bedford Row, WC1R 4DQ; *Master*, C. N. Stokes.

UPHOLDERS (46). *Livery*, 203.—*Clerk*, W. R. Wallis, Imperial Buildings, 56 Kingsway, WC2B 6DX; *Master*, J. H. Ayerst.

WAX CHANDLERS (20). *Hall*, Gresham Street, EC2V 7AD. *Livery*, 100.—*Clerk*, T. Wood; *Master*, J. E. P. Titman, C.V.O.

WEAVERS (42). *Livery*, 125.—*Clerk*, J. G. Ouvry, 1 The Sanctuary, SW1P 3JT; *Upper Bailiff*, The Rt. Hon. The Lord Brain.

WHEELWRIGHTS (68). *Livery*, 265.—*Clerk*, M. R. Francis, Greenup, Milton Avenue, Gerrards Cross, Bucks., SL9 8QW; *Master*, H. F. J. Fenton.

WOOLMEN (43). *Livery*, 145.—*Clerk*, R. J. R. Cousins, 192-198 Vauxhall Bridge Rd., S.W.1; *Master*, R. E. Auld, Q.C.

PARISH CLERKS (*No livery*) (*Brethren*, 100).—*Clerk*, R. H. Adams, T.D., F.S.A., 14 Dale Close, Oxford, OX1 1TU; *Master*, T. D. Wilkin.

WATERMEN AND LIGHTERMEN (*No livery*).—*Hall*, 18 St. Mary-at-Hill, EC3R 8EE.—*Clerk*, B. G. Wilson; *Master*, A. C. Clark-Kennedy.

ENVIRONMENTAL CLEANERS.—*Hall*, Mark Lane, E.C.3.—*Clerk*, E. W. Hill, T.D.; *Master*, R. L. Turner.

NOTE.—In certain companies the election of Master or Prime Warden for the year does not take place till the autumn. In such cases the Master or Prime Warden for 1983-84 is given.

LONDON AND ITS ENVIRONS

(For National Art Galleries and Museums in London see pages 374–5 and 416–21; for London Cathedrals, Churches, etc. see pages 502–3.)

Adelphi, Strand, W.C.2.—Adelphi Terrace and district commemorate the four Adam brothers, James, John, Robert and William, who laid out the district (formerly Durham House) at the close of the 18th century, though few 18th century buildings now remain. Four of the streets were formerly called after the brothers but are now Adam Street, John Adam Street, Robert Street and Durham House Street. In the neighbourhood of the Adelphi was York House, built by the Duke of Buckingham in 1625 (the Water Gate of which still stands in Embankment Gardens), the commemorative streets being *Charles* Street, *Villiers* Street, *Duke* Street, *Buckingham* Street.

Alexandra Palace and Park, Muswell Hill, N.10.—Set in a park of 200 acres, the second Palace was completed in 1875 at a cost of £400,000. Although it suffered severe damage from a fire in July 1980 plans for restoration include the provision of facilities for exhibitions, concerts, sport and leisure activities. Meanwhile, events continue in the ALEXANDER PAVILION adjacent to the Palace. Trusteeship of the Palace devolved onto the G.L.C. in 1965, who passed it to Haringey Council on Jan. 1, 1980.

Baltic Exchange, St. Mary Axe, E.C.3.—The world market for the chartering of cargo ships. The present Exchange was built in 1903 and the new wing opened by H.M. The Queen on Nov. 21, 1956.

Bank of England, Threadneedle Street, E.C.2. (Not open to the public)—The Bank of England, founded in 1694, has always been closely connected with the Government. The present building, completed in 1940 to the designs of Sir Herbert Baker, incorporates features reminiscent of the earlier architects, Sampson (1734), Sir Robert Taylor (1765) and Sir John Soane (1788).

Banqueting House, Whitehall, S.W.1.—The only important building left of the great Palace of Whitehall. The previous banqueting house was burnt down in 1619, and replaced by the present structure designed by Inigo Jones. In 1635 it was enriched with Rubens' ceiling paintings. Charles I was executed on a scaffold set up just in front of the present entrance. Open, Tues.–Sat., 10–5; Sun., 2–5. Closed Mons. Admission (1984), 50p; children and O.A.P.s 25p.

Barbican Arts Centre, E.C.2.—The final phase of the Barbican complex in the City of London was opened on 3 March 1982 by H.M. The Queen. The Arts Centre, the largest of its kind in Western Europe, houses the 1,166 seat Barbican Theatre, now the London base of the Royal Shakespeare Company along with a smaller 200 seat studio theatre, and the 2,026 seat Barbican Hall for concerts by the London Symphony Orchestra. There are also three cinemas, an art gallery, a sculpture court and a large lending library, in addition to facilities for exhibitions and conferences, and to bars and restaurants.

Bridges.—The bridges over the Thames (from East to West) are the *Tower Bridge* (built by the Corporation of London and opened in 1894), with its bascules, operated now by new electrically-run machinery. The walkway was opened to the public in 1982 and a museum in 1983. *London Bridge* (opened after rebuilding in 1831 by Rennie; the new London Bridge was completed in 1973 and opened by H.M. The Queen on March 16, 1973); *Southwark Bridge* (opened in 1819, also by Rennie; rebuilt by the Corporation of London, 1922); *Blackfriars Bridge* (opened in 1769, rebuilt, 1869, and widened by the Corporation of London in 1909); *Waterloo Bridge* (Rennie), opened in 1817, commanding a fine view of

western London, rebuilt by L.C.C. and reopened 1944; *Hungerford Bridge,* 1863 (railway bridge with a footbridge); *Westminster Bridge* (built in 1750 and then presenting a view that inspired Wordsworth's sonnet; rebuilt and re-opened in 1862; width, 84 ft.) with Thomas Thornycroft's *Boadicea* at the north-eastern end; this bridge leads from Westminster Abbey and the Houses of Parliament to the County Hall and St. Thomas's Hospital; *Lambeth Bridge* (built 1862, rebuilt 1932) leading from Lambeth Palace to Millbank; *Vauxhall Bridge* (built in 1811–16, rebuilt in 1906), leading to Kennington Oval; *Chelsea Bridge,* leading from Chelsea Hospital to Battersea Park (reconstructed and widened; 1937) and *Albert Bridge* (1873); *Battersea Bridge* (opened in 1890); *Wandsworth Bridge* opened in 1873; rebuilt and re-opened in 1940); *Putney Bridge* (built 1729, rebuilt 1884, widened in 1933), where the Oxford and Cambridge Boat Race is started for Mortlake; *Hammersmith Bridge* (rebuilt 1887); *Barnes Bridge* (for pedestrians only, 1933); *Chiswick Bridge* (opened in 1933); *King Edward VII Bridge, Kew* (rebuilt in 1902, opened 1903), leading to the Royal Botanic Gardens, Kew; *Twickenham Lock Bridge; Twickenham Bridge* (opened 1933); *Richmond Bridge* (opened in 1777); *Kingston Bridge* (built 1828 and widened 1914) and *Hampton Court Bridge* (rebuilt, 1933).

Buckingham Palace, St. James's Park, S.W.1. (Not open to the public.)—Purchased by King George III in 1762 from the heir of the Duke of Buckingham, the Palace has been the London home of the Sovereign since Queen Victoria's accession in 1837. It was altered by Nash for King George IV, and refronted in stone (part of the Queen Victoria Memorial) by Sir Aston Webb in 1913.

The Queen's Gallery, containing a changing selection of the finest pictures and works of art from all parts of the royal collection, was opened to the public on July 25, 1962. Open: Tues.–Sat., and Bank Holidays 11–5 p.m.; Sundays. 2–5 p.m. Admission charges are payable, entering from Buckingham Palace Road.

The Royal Mews is open to visitors on Weds. and Thurs. throughout the year (except in Ascot Week), 2–4 p.m. Admission charges, the net proceeds of which are devoted to charities, are payable at the entrance.

Canada House, Trafalgar Square, S.W.1.—Designed by Sir Robert Smirke and built in 1824–7, it underwent major alterations to incorporate the former Royal College of Physicians building, also by Smirke, between 1964–67. Certain interior features of the original building, now housing the Canadian High Commission, are preserved including the spacious, richly furnished room now occupied by the High Commissioner.

Canonbury Tower, Canonbury, N.1.—The largest remaining part of a 16th-century house originally built by the Priors of St. Bartholomew, and since 1952 used as the headquarters of a non-professional theatre company. Contains the "Spencer" and "Compton" oak-panelled rooms. Other relics of Canonbury House can be seen nearby.

Carlyle's House, 24 Cheyne Row, Chelsea, S.W.3. The home of Thomas Carlyle for 47 years until his death in 1881, and containing many of his effects. Now the property of the National Trust. Open daily, except Mons., Tues. and Sun. 11–5, from April 1–Oct. 31. Admission £1; children 50p, O.A.P.s 70p.

Catholic Central Library, St. Francis Friary, 47 Francis Street, S.W.1.—Founded as a private library in 1914, it was taken over in 1959 by the Franciscan Friars of the Atonement. It is an up-to-date lending and research library of over 55,000 volumes, 150 periodicals, for the general reader, student and ecumenist. Books are sent by post when required. Hours of opening: Mon.-Fri. 10–5; Sat. 10–1.30.

Cemeteries.—In *Kensal Green Cemetery*, North Kensington, W.10 (70 acres), are tombs of W. M. Thackeray, Anthony Trollope, Sydney Smith, Shirley Brooks, Wilkie Collins, Tom Hood, W. Mulready, George Cruikshank, John Leech, Leigh Hunt, Brunel ("Great Eastern"), Ross (Arctic), Charles Kemble and Charles Mathews (actors). In *Highgate Cemetery*, N.6, are the tombs of George Eliot, Herbert Spencer, Michael Faraday, Karl Marx and G. J. Holyoake. In *Abney Park Cemetery*, Stoke Newington, N.16 are the tomb of General Booth, founder of the Salvation Army, and memorials to many Nonconformist Divines. In the *South Metropolitan Cemetery*, Norwood, S.E.27, are the tombs of C. H. Spurgeon, Lord Alverstone, Douglas Jerrold, John Belcher, R.A., Theodore Watts-Dunton, Dr. Moffat (missionary), Sir H. Bessemer, Sir H. Maxim, Sir J. Barnby, Sir A. Manns, Mrs. Beeton, Sir Henry Tate and J. Whitaker, F.S.A. (*Whitaker's Almanack*). In the churchyard of the former *Marylebone Chapel* are buried Allan Ramsay (poet), Hoyle (whist), Ferguson (astronomer), Charles Wesley (hymn writer) and his son Samuel Wesley (musician). The chapel itself was demolished in 1949. **Crematoria.**—*Ilford* (City of London); *Norwood*; *Hendon*; *Streatham Park*; *Finchley* (St. Marylebone) and *Golder's Green* (12 acres), near Hampstead Heath, with "Garden of Rest" and memorials to famous men and women.

Cenotaph, Whitehall, S.W.1.—(Literally "empty tomb"). Monument erected "To the Glorious Dead", as a memorial to all ranks of the Sea, Land and Air Forces who gave their lives in the service of the Empire during the First World War. Designed by Sir Edwin Lutyens. Erected as a temporary memorial in 1919 and replaced by a permanent structure in 1920. Unveiled by King George V on Armistice Day, 1920. An additional inscription was added after the 1939–45 War, to commemorate those who gave their lives in that conflict.

Charterhouse. Sutton's Hospital, Charterhouse Square, E.C.1. (*Master*, E. E. Harrison, M.A., F.S.A.; *Registrar and Clerk to the Governors*, J. C. Moss), a Carthusian monastery from 1371–1537, when it came into the possession of Sir Edward (later first Lord) North, who sold it in 1565 to the fourth Duke of Norfolk, who renamed it Howard House. After his execution in 1572, following the Ridolfi Plot, hatched at Charterhouse, it was eventually granted by Queen Elizabeth, in 1587, to Norfolk's second son, Thomas Howard, Earl of Suffolk, who in 1608 sold it to Thomas Sutton, who endowed it as a Hospital for aged men "of gentle birth" and a School for Boys (removed to Godalming in 1872). The buildings are partly 14th but mainly 15th and 16th century. The Duke's private palace was destroyed by enemy action in the second World War, but the Hall, Chapel and Great Chamber are intact or restored and now accommodate some 30 Brothers. Roger Williams, founder and governor of Rhode Island, was a scholar on the Foundation. Among other famous pupils were John Wesley, Lord Baden-Powell, the poets and writers Crashaw, Lovelace, Beddoes and Thackeray, who described the School as "Greyfriars" in "The Newcombes" and more recently Lord Beveridge, Lord Isenay and Lord Weeks. Visitors are shown round on Wednesdays at 2.45 p.m. from April to July inclusive (charge £1).

Chelsea Physic Garden, 66 Royal Hospital Road, S.W.3.—A garden of general botanical research, established in latter part of 17th century by the Society of Apothecaries, occupies site presented in 1772 by Sir Hans Sloane. Administered by the Chelsea Physic Garden Ltd. Open to the public on a regular basis during summer months. All enquiries to the Curator at above address.

Chelsea, Royal Hospital (founded by Charles II, in 1682, and built by Wren; opened in 1692), Royal Hospital Road, Chelsea, S.W.3, for old and disabled soldiers. Great Hall, Chapel and Museum open daily 10 to 12 and 2 to 4 (Museum closed on Sunday afternoons from October to March). The extensive grounds include the former Ranelagh Gardens, and are the venue for the Chelsea Flower Show held each May by the Royal Horticultural Society. *Governor*, General Sir Robert Ford, G.C.B., C.B.E.; *Lieut-Governor and Secretary*, Major-Gen. A. L. Watson, C.B.

City Business Library (Corporation of London), 55 Basinghall Street, E.C.2. Open Mon.-Fri. 9.30-5.00.

College of Arms or Heralds' College, Queen Victoria Street, E.C.4—Her Majesty's Officers of Arms (Kings, Heralds and Pursuivants of Arms) were first incorporated by Richard III, and granted Derby House on the site of the present College building by Philip and Mary. The building now in use dates from 1671–88. The powers vested by the Crown in the Earl Marshal (The Duke of Norfolk) with regard to State ceremonial are largely exercised through the College, which is also the official repository of English pedigrees and all Arms granted to subjects of the Queen (except in Scotland). Enquiry may be made to the Officer on duty in the Public Office, Mon.-Fri. between 10 a.m. and 4 p.m.

Commonwealth Institute, Kensington High Street, W.8.—A permanent exhibition opened on Nov. 6, 1962, by Her Majesty the Queen, replacing the former Imperial Institute opened in 1893 in S. Kensington. An interesting feature of the building is its paraboloid copper-sheathed roof. The Institute contains, in 60,000 square feet arranged in 3 galleries, a visual representation of the history, geography and ways of life of the Commonwealth countries and dependencies; on the ground floor, exhibits of Australia, New Zealand, Bangladesh, Canada, India, Sri Lanka, the Pacific and Atlantic islands and Antarctica; on the middle gallery, the African countries, Mauritius and Seychelles; and on the upper gallery, the Caribbean countries, Bermuda, Cyprus, Gibraltar and Malta, Brunei, Hong Kong, Malaysia, Singapore, Belize, Guyana, Papua New Guinea, Isle of Man and the Channel Islands. Art Galleries; Cinema; Theatre; Library services; Restaurant, Bookshop.
Open, weekdays, 10–5.30; Sundays, 2.00–5.00. Admission free. Closed Christmas Eve, Christmas Day, Boxing Day, New Year's Day, Good Friday and May Day.

County Hall, Westminster Bridge, S.E.1.—The Headquarters of the Greater London Council (*see* pp. 658–60) built on the Pedlar's Acre, Bishop's acre, Four Acres and Float Mead, Lambeth, from the designs of Ralph Knott, with a river façade of 750 ft. The main building was completed in 1933. The building of the North and South blocks on a site to the East of the main building started in the early 1930s. They were occupied in 1939 but not finally completed until 1963. The Council, when in session, meets in public in the council chamber every third Tuesday afternoons at 2.30 p.m.

Courtauld Institute Galleries, University of London, Woburn Square, WC1.—The galleries of the University of London contain the Lee collection and the Gambier–Parry collections (14th century to 18th century old masters); the important Courtauld collection of Impressionist and Post-Impressionist paintings; the Roger Fry collection and the Witt and Spooner collections (old master drawings and English water-colours). A major new bequest, the Princes Gate collection of old master paintings and drawings, was opened to the public in July 1981. Open weekdays, 10–5; Sundays, 2–5. Admission £1; children, OAPs, and students (except London University students), 50p.

Custom House, Lower Thames Street, E.C.3.— Built 1813–17, with a wide quay on Thames. The *Long Room* is about 190 ft. long.

Dickens House, 48, Doughty Street, W.C.1.—In this house Charles Dickens lived from 1837 to 1839, and here he completed *Pickwick Papers.* It is the headquarters of the Dickens Fellowship and contains many relics of the novelist. It is open to the public daily, 10 to 5 (Sundays and Bank Holidays excepted); admission £1; students 75p; children, 50p; families, £2.

Downing Street.—Number 10, Downing Street, S.W.1, is the official town residence of the Prime Minister, No. 11 of the Chancellor of the Exchequer and No. 12 is the office of the Government Whips. The street was named after Sir George Downing, Bt. soldier and diplomatist, who was M.P. for Morpeth from 1660 to 1684.

Chequers, a Tudor mansion in the Chilterns, about 3 miles from Princes Risborough, was presented together with a maintenance endowment by Lord and Lady Lee of Fareham in 1917 to serve, from Jan. 1, 1921, as a country residence for the Prime Minister of the day, the Chequers estate of 700 acres being added to the gift by Lord Lee in 1921. The mansion contains a famous collection of Cromwellian portraits and relics.

Dr. Johnson's House, Gough Square, Fleet Street, E.C.4.—A tall late 17th-century house in which Samuel (and his wife) lived between 1748 and 1759. His *Dictionary* was compiled here. The house is furnished with 18th century pieces and there is an excellent collection of Johnsoniana. Open daily (except Sundays and Bank Holidays) from 11 to 5.30 (Winter 5). Admission £1; students and O.A.P.s, 50p.

Dulwich, S.E.21.—Contains *Dulwich College* (founded by Edward Alleyn in 1619), the *Horniman Museum* (q.v.) and the *Dulwich Picture Gallery,* built by Sir John Soane to house the collection bequeathed by the artist Sir Francis Bourgeois. The gallery was damaged in the Second World War but rebuilt with the aid of a grant from the Pilgrim Trust and reopened in 1953. *Dulwich Village* retains many of the rural characteristics of the pre-suburban period.

Eltham, S.E.9.—Contains remains of 13th–15th century *Eltham Palace,* the birthplace of John of Eltham (1316), son of Edward II. The hall, built by Edward IV, has a hammer-beam roof of chestnut. In the churchyard of St. John the Baptist is the tomb of *Thomas Doggett,* the comedian and founder of the Thames Watermen's championship (Doggett's Coat and Badge).

Ely Place, Holborn Circus, E.C.1.—Previously the site of the London house of the Bishop of Ely, Ely Place is a private street (built in 1773) whose affairs are administered by Commissioners under a special Act of Parliament. The 14th-century chapel, now St. Etheldreda's (R.C.) Church, is open daily until dusk.

Eton College.—The most famous of English public schools, founded by Henry VI in 1440. Buildings date from 1442.

Fulham Palace, Bishop's Avenue, Fulham, S.W.6.—The courtyard is 16th century, remainder 18th and 19th century. Former residence of the Bishop of London. Grounds of about 9 acres.

Geffrye Museum, Kingsland Road, E.2.—Open on Tuesdays to Saturdays 10 to 5, Sundays 2 to 5. Closed on Christmas Day and on Mondays except Bank Holidays. Admission free.

The Museum is housed in a building erected originally as almshouses in 1713. It was eventually purchased by the London County Council and opened as a museum in 1914. The Exhibits are shown in a series of period rooms dating from 1600 to 1939, each containing furniture and domestic equipment of middle-class English home. An 18th century woodworker's shop, an openhearth kitchen and the original chapel are also shown, together with a selection of costume. Temporary exhibitions are held in the Exhibition Hall. There is a reference library of books on furniture, social history and art. Special arrangements for children visiting the Museum in school parties (which must be booked in advance) and in their leisure time. *Director,* J. Daniels.

George Inn, Southwark.—Near London Bridge Station. Given to National Trust in 1937. Last galleried inn in London, built in 1677. Open during licensed hours.

Greenwich, S.E.10.—*Greenwich Hospital* (since 1873, the Royal Naval College) was built by Charles II, largely from designs by John Webb, and by Queen Anne and William III, from designs by Wren, on the site of an ancient royal palace, and of the more recent *Palace of Placentia,* an enlarged edition of the palace, constructed by Humphrey, Duke of Gloucester (1391–1447), son of Henry IV. Henry VIII, Queen Mary I and Queen Elizabeth I were born in the Royal Palace (which reverted to the Crown in 1447) and King Edward VI died there. In the principal quadrangle is a marble statue of George II, by Rysbraeck. (For *National Maritime Museum,* see Index.) *Painted Hall* and *Chapel* open daily except Thursdays from 2.30 p.m. to 5 p.m. Visitors are also admitted to Sunday Service in the Chapel at 11 a.m., summer and winter, except during College vacations. *Greenwich Park* (196¼ acres) was enclosed by Humphrey, Duke of Gloucester, and laid out by Charles II, from the designs of Le Nôtre. *The Queen's House,* begun in 1616, was designed for Anne of Denmark by Inigo Jones (Closed for repairs from Oct. 1984). On a hill in Greenwich Park is the former Royal Observatory (founded 1675). Part of its buildings at Greenwich have been taken over by the Maritime Museum and named *Flamsteed House,* after John Flamsteed (1646–1719), first Astronomer Royal. Astronomical and navigational equipment is exhibited, and the time ball and zero meridian of longitude can also be seen. The Parish church of Greenwich (*St. Alfege*) was rebuilt by Hawksmoor (Wren's pupil) in 1728, and restored after severe damage during the Second World War. General Wolfe (Heights of Abraham) and Tallis ("the father of Church Music") are buried in the church. Henry VIII was christened in the former church. *Charlton House:* built in the early 17th century (1607–1612) for Adam Newton, tutor to Prince Henry, brother to Charles I. The house is largely in the Jacobean style of architecture. *Cutty Sark,* the last of the famous tea clippers, which has been preserved as a memorial to ships and men of a past era. The ship is fully restored and re-rigged, with a museum of sail on board. Open to visitors: weekdays, 11 to 5 (Summer, 6 p.m.); Sundays and Boxing Day, 2.30 to 5. The yacht *Gipsy Moth IV* in which Sir Francis Chichester sailed single-handed round the world, 1966–67, is preserved alongside the *Cutty Sark.*

Guildhall, Gresham Street, City, E.C.2.—Scene of civic government for the City for more than a thousand years. Built *c.* 1440; façade built 1788–9;

damaged in the Great Fire, 1666, and by incendiary bombs, 1940. The main hall and crypt (the most extensive medieval crypt in London) have been restored. Events in Guildhall include the annual election of Lord Mayor, election of Sheriffs, receptions in honour of Sovereigns and Heads of State, and the meetings of the Court of Common Council (*see* "Corporation of London"). Open free; weekdays, 10–5; Sundays (May to Sept.) 10–5. *Keeper of the Guildhall*, J. H. Lucioni.

The Library and Museum of the Clockmakers' Company are housed in new premises, and are open to the public, Mon. to Fri., 10–5. Admission free (entrance in Aldermanbury). The Library contains Plans of London, 1570; Deed of Sale with Shakespeare's signature; first, second and fourth folios of Shakespeare's plays etc. *see also* City Business Library).

Ham House, Richmond.—A notable example of 17th-century domestic architecture, long the home of the Tollemache family (Earls of Dysart). The contents, described as "probably the finest and most varied collection of Charles II's reign to survive", were purchased for the Victoria and Albert Museum which now administers the house. Ham House may be seen on Tues.–Sun. inclusive and on Bank Holidays, 2–6 p.m., April–Sept., 12–4 p.m., Oct.–March. Closed Mon. (except Bank Holidays), Christmas Eve, Christmas Day, Boxing Day, Good Friday, New Year's Day and May Day. Admission £1·50; children, students and O.A.P.s, 75p.

Hampton Court.—Sixteenth-century Palace built by Cardinal Wolsey, with additions by Sir Christopher Wren for William and Mary, 15 miles from London. Fine view of river. Beautiful gardens with maze and prolific grape vine (planted in 1769). State Apartments and collection of pictures. Tennis Court, built by King Henry VIII in 1530. The Palace is *closed* on Christmas Eve, Christmas Day, Boxing Day, New Year's Day and Good Friday. April–September: State Apartments: (1984) £2; (Oct.–March £1). Children under sixteen and O.A.P.s £1 (Oct.–March 60p). Royal Mews 20p. Mantegna Gallery 10p. Maze 25p. Tennis Court, *closed* Oct.–March. Maze *closed* Nov.–Feb. Open April–Sept. 9.30–6 (Sundays 11–6) (Maze 10.00–6.00; 11–6). Nov.–March, 9.30–5 (Sundays 2–5) (Maze 10–5, 11–5).

Harrow.—Public school founded by John Lyon in 1571. The "Fourth Form Room" dates from 1608.

Honourable Artillery Company's Headquarters, City Road, E.C.1.—The H.A.C. (*Chief Exec.* Capt. G. C. Lloyd, C.B.E., R.N.) received its charter of incorporation from Henry VIII in 1537, and has occupied its present ground since 1641. The Armoury House dates from 1735. The present castellated barracks date from 1860. Four of its members who emigrated in the 17th century, founded in 1638 the Ancient and Honorable Artillery Company of Massachusetts. The H.A.C. is the senior regiment of the Territorial Army Volunteer Reserves, and maintains a Headquarters with an Officer Training Wing, and four squadrons.

Horniman Museum and Library, London Road, Forest Hill, S.E.23. Open daily (except Christmas Eve and Christmas Day), 10.30 to 6, Sundays 2 to 6. Only the Lecture Hall is open on Boxing Day afternoon. Admission free. The Museum was presented in 1901 to the London County Council by the founder, Mr. F. J. Horniman, M.P. It is now administered by the I.L.E.A. on behalf of the G.L.C. The Museum has three main departments, ethnography, musical instruments and natural history. In the ethnography department the large collections include exhibits illustrating man's progress in the arts and crafts from

prehistoric times. The natural history department includes an aquarium. Reference library (except Mondays). Schools Service. Free concerts and lectures (autumn and spring). Special exhibitions. *Director,* D. M. Boston, O.B.E.

Horse Guards, Whitehall, S.W.1.—Archway and offices built about 1753. The mounting of the guard (Life Guards, or the Blues and Royals) at 11 a.m. (10 a.m. on Sundays) and the dismounted inspection at 4 p.m. are picturesque ceremonies. Only those on the Lord Chamberlain's list may drive through the gates and archway into *Horse Guard's Parade* (230,000 sq. ft.), where the Colour is "trooped" on the Queen's Official Birthday.

The Houses of Parliament, Westminster, S.W.1.—An ordinance issued in the reign of Richard II stated that "Parliament shall be holden or kepid wheresoever it pleaseth the King" and at the present day the Sovereign summons Parliament to meet and prescribes the time and place of meeting. The royal palace of Westminster, originally built by Edward the Confessor (Westminster Hall (*q.v.*) being added by William Rufus), was the normal place of Parliament from about 1340. St. Stephen's Chapel (first mentioned in the reign of John) was used from about 1550 for the meetings of the House of Commons, which had previously been held in the Chapter House or Refectory of Westminster Abbey. The House of Lords met in an apartment of the royal palace.

The fire of 1834 destroyed the whole palace, except Westminster Hall, and the present Houses of Parliament were erected on the site from the designs of Sir Charles Barry and Augustus Welby Pugin between 1840 and 1867, at a cost of £2,198,000. The Chamber of the House of Commons was destroyed by enemy action in 1941 and the foundation stone of a new building, from the designs of Sir Giles Gilbert Scott, was laid by the Speaker on May 26, 1948. The new Chamber was used for the first time on Oct. 26, 1950.

The Victoria Tower of the House of Lords is about 330 ft. high, and when Parliament is sitting the Union Flag flies by day from its flagstaff. *The Clock Tower* of the House of Commons is about 320 ft. high and contains "Big Ben", the hour bell said to be named after Sir Benjamin Hall, First Commissioner of Works when the original bell was cast in 1856. This bell, which weighed 16 tons 11 cwt., was found to be cracked in 1857. The present bell (13¼ tons) is a recasting of the original and was first brought into use in July, 1859. The dials of the clock are 23 ft. in diameter, the hands being 9 ft. and 14 ft. long (including balance piece). A light is displayed from the Clock Tower at night when Parliament is sitting.

The Houses of Parliament are not open to the general public. All arrangements for visits must be made direct with a Member of Parliament.

Admission to the Strangers' Gallery of the House of Lords as arranged by a Peer or by queue *via* the St. Stephen's Entrance. Admission to the Strangers' Gallery of the House of Commons, by Members' order (Members' orders should be sought well in advance), or by queue *via* St. Stephen's Entrance. Queues are sometimes shorter after 6 p.m., Mon.–Thurs. Overseas visitors may obtain cards of introduction from their Embassy or High Commission.

Inns of Court.—The *Inner* and *Middle Temple*, S. of Fleet Street, E.C.4, and N. of Victoria Embankment, to which the gardens extend, have occupied (since early 14th century) the site of the buildings of the Order of Knights Templars. *Inner Temple Hall* (rebuilt in 1955 after bomb damage) is open to the public Mon.–Fri. 10.30–11.30, 3–4 on application to Treasurer's Office during law sittings. *Temple Church,* restored in 1958 after severe damage by bombing, is open on weekdays 9.30–4.30 p.m. and the public are admitted to Sunday services. *Middle Temple Hall* (1562–70) is open to the public when not in use, Monday–Friday, 10–12 and 3–4.30 p.m.; Saturday when staff are available. Closed, Public Holidays. In Middle Temple Gardens (not open to the public) Shakespeare (Henry VI, Part I) places the incident which led to the "Wars of the Roses" (1455–85). *Lincoln's Inn*, from Chancery Lane to Lincoln's Inn Fields, W.C.2, occupies the site of the palace of a former Bishop of Chichester and of a Black Friars monastery. The records show the Society as being in existence in 1422. The Hall and Library Buildings are of 1845, although the Library is first mentioned in 1474, and the old Hall early 16th century, the Chapel was rebuilt *c.* 1619–23. Halls open to public by appointment, Chapel and Gardens, Mon.–Fri. 12–2.30. Chapel services, Sun. 11.30 a.m. during Law Terms. *Lincoln's Inn Fields* (7 Acres); the Square, laid out by Inigo Jones, contains many fine old houses with handsome interiors. *Gray's Inn,* Holborn/Gray's Inn Road, W.C.1. Early 14th century. Hall (1556–60); Chapel (largely rebuilt in 1698). Services 11.15 a.m. (during Law Dining Terms only.) Holy Communion 1st Sunday in every month except Aug.–Sept. Public welcome. Library (41,000 vols., mss. and printed books) may be viewed by appointment. Gardens open to the public from 12 noon to 2.30 p.m. (May–Sept.). The Inn, although badly damaged during the last war, has been completely restored to its former beauty with gracious red brick buildings overlooking grass covered squares and gardens. Strong Elizabethan associations. No other "Inns" are active, but what remains of *Staple Inn* is worth visiting as a relic of Elizabethan London; though heavy damage was done by a flying-bomb, it retains a picturesque gabled front on Holborn (opposite Gray's Inn Road). *Clement's Inn* (near St. Clement Danes' Church), *Clifford's Inn,* Fleet Street, and *Thavies Inn,* Holborn Circus, are all rebuilt. *Serjeant's Inn,* Fleet Street (damaged by bombing) and another (demolished 1910) of the same name in Chancery Lane, were composed of Serjeants-at Law, the last of whom died in 1922.

Jewish Museum, Woburn House, Upper Woburn Place, W.C.1.—Opened in 1932, the Museum contains a comprehensive collection of objects and antiquities, illustrating Jewish life, history and religion. Open Tues.–Thurs. (and Fri. in summer) 10–4, Sun. (and Fri. in winter) 10–12.45. Closed Mon., Sat., Public and Jewish holidays. Group visits by arrangement with Secretary.

Keats House, Keats Grove, Hampstead, N.W.3.— In two houses here, now made into one, John Keats lived at various times between 1818 and 1820. Restored 1974–75. Open weekdays, 10–1 a.m., 2–6 p.m.; Sundays and Bank Holidays, 2 p.m.–5 p.m. Closed—Christmas Day, Boxing Day, New Year's Day, Good Friday, Easter Eve and May Day. The Keats Memorial Library contains over 7,000 volumes.

Kensington Palace, W.8.—The original house was bought by William III in 1689 and enlarged by Christoper Wren. The birthplace of Queen Victoria in 1819. The state apartments are open to the public and contain pictures and furniture from the royal collections. A suite of rooms devoted to the memory of Queen Victoria is also shown. Admission: £1; children, O.A.P.s 50p.
The *Court Dress Collection* is also open, and includes three restored rooms, the Red Salon, the Teck Drawing Room and the room where Queen Victoria is said to have been born. Admission: £1·50; children, O.A.P.s, 75p. *Both open,* weekdays 9–5; Suns. 1–5. *Joint Tickets:* £2; children, O.A.P.s, £1.

Kew, Surrey.—A favourite home of the early Hanoverian monarchs. Kew House, the residence of Frederick, Prince of Wales, and later of his son,

George III, was pulled down in 1803, but the earlier Dutch House, now known as Kew Palace, survives. It was built in 1631 and acquired by George III as an annexe to Kew House in 1781. The famous Kew Gardens (*see* p. 674) were originally laid out as a private garden for Kew House for George III's mother in 1759 and were much enlarged in the nineteenth century, notably by the inclusion of the grounds of the former Richmond Lodge.

Kneller Hall, Twickenham.—Royal Military School of Music. A band of up to 120 instrumentalists gives concerts in the grounds on Wednesdays throughout the summer, commencing at 8 p.m. Admission 50p (Grand concerts, £1). Season tickets available.

Lambeth Palace, S.E.1.—The official residence of the Archbishop of Canterbury, on south bank of Thames; the oldest part is 13th century, the house itself is early 19th century. For leave to visit the historical portions, applications should be made by letter to the Archbishop's Chaplain.

Livery Companies' Halls.—The Principal Companies (*see* pp. 663–4) have magnificent halls but admission to view them has generally to be arranged beforehand. Among the finest or more interesting may be mentioned the following: Goldsmiths' Hall, Foster Lane. The present hall was completed in 1835, and contains some magnificent rooms. Exhibitions of plate have been shown here periodically in recent years. Fishmongers' Hall, London Bridge (built 1831–3), now admirably restored after severe bomb damage, also contains fine rooms. Apothecaries' Hall, Black Friars Lane, was rebuilt in 1670, after the Great Fire, and has library, hall and kitchen which are good examples of this period, together with a pleasant courtyard. Vintners' Hall, Upper Thames Street, was also rebuilt after the Great Fire, and its hall has very fine late 17th century panelling. The Watermen and Lightermen's Company is not, strictly speaking, a Livery Company, but its hall, in St. Mary at Hill, is a good example of a smaller 18th century building, with pilastered façade. It was completed in 1780. Stationers' Hall, in Stationers' Hall Court, behind Ludgate Hill, another post-fire Hall, standing in its own court, has a particularly finely carved screen; its façade dates from 1800. Barbers' Hall, Monkwell Street, with a Hall attributed to Inigo Jones, was completely destroyed by bombing, but has now been rebuilt. The new hall was built some 30 ft. from the old site to enable one of the bastions and part of the wall of the Roman fort to remain exposed to view.

Lloyd's, Lime Street, E.C.3.—Housed in the Royal Exchange for 150 years and in Leadenhall Street from 1928–1957. The present building was opened by H.M. Queen Elizabeth the Queen Mother on Nov. 14, 1957. The underwriting space has an area of 44.250 sq. ft. and houses the Lutine Bell.

London Planetarium, Marylebone Road, N.W.1.—Open daily (except Dec. 25), presentations from 11–4.30. Admission charge.

London Transport Museum, Covent Garden, W.C.2.—Housed in the former Flower Market, the Museum contains a collection of buses, trams, trolley-buses, trains, working displays and London Transport paraphernalia. There is a research library and lecture theatre. Open every day, 10 a.m. to 6.00 p.m. (except Dec. 25 and 26). Admission: £2; children and O.A.P.s, £1.

Lord's Cricket Ground, St. John's Wood Road, N.W.8.—The headquarters (since 1814) of the Marylebone Cricket Club (founded 1787), the premier cricket club in England, the scene of some of the principal matches of the season and Middlesex

County headquarters. Real tennis court and squash courts in building behind members' pavilion.

The Cricket Memorial Gallery, a museum of cricket, open to the public on match days (except Sundays) until 5 p.m. Adults, 50p; children and O.A.P.s, 25p. In winter and on non-match days admission is by prior arrangement with the Curator.

Madame Tussaud's Exhibition, Marylebone Road, N.W.1.—Open daily (except Dec. 25), 10–5.30; July–Aug., 10–6. Admission charge.

Marble Hill House, Twickenham.—Example of the English Palladian style, built 1724–9 for Henrietta Howard, Countess of Suffolk, mistress of George II. Reopened 1966, after restoration work on the elevations of the house, entrance hall, main staircase and first floor rooms. The Great Room and mahogany staircase are noteworthy. Open daily (except Fri.) 10 a.m.–5 p.m. (closes 4, Nov.–Jan.). Admission free. Now houses fine collection of early 18th century paintings and furniture.

Mansion House, City, E.C.4.—(Built 1739–53, reconstructed 1930–31.) The official residence of the Lord Mayor; the Egyptian Hall and Ballroom are the chief attractions. Admission by order from the Lord Mayor's Secretary.

Markets.—The London markets (administered by the Corporation of the City of London) provide foodstuffs for 8,500,000 to 9,000,000 people. *Central Meat, Fish, Fruit, Vegetable, and Poultry Markets,* Smithfield (present buildings, 1866) the largest meat market in the world and site of St. Bartholomew's Fair from 9th to 19th century; *Leadenhall Market* (Meat and Poultry built 1881, part recently demolished); *Billingsgate* (Fish), Thames Street (built 1875, part recently demolished) a market site for over 1,000 years (moved to the Isle of Dogs in Jan. 1982); *Spitalfields,* E.1. (Vegetables, Fruit, etc.), enlarged 1928, and opened by the late Queen Mary; *London Fruit Exchange,* Brushfield Street (built by Corporation of London 1928–29) faces Spitalfields Market. Other markets are—*Covent Garden* (now moved to Nine Elms) established under a charter of Charles II, in 1661, and *Borough Market,* S.E.1, for vegetables, fruit, flowers, etc.

Marlborough House, Pall Mall, S.W.1.—Built by Wren for the first Duke of Marlborough and completed in 1711, the house finally reverted to the Crown in 1835. Prince Leopold lived there until 1831, and Queen Adelaide from 1837 until her death in 1849. In 1863 it became the London house of the Prince of Wales and was the London home of Queen Mary until her death in 1953. The Queen's Chapel, Marlborough Gate, begun in 1623 from the designs of Inigo Jones for the Infanta Maria of Spain, and completed for Queen Henrietta Maria, is open to the public for services on Sundays at 8.30 a.m. and 11.15 a.m. between Easter Day and end July (*see also* St. James's Palace for winter services in The Chapel Royal). In 1959 Marlborough House was given by the Queen as a centre for Commonwealth Government conferences and it was opened as such in March, 1962.

London Monument (commonly called "The Monument"), Monument Street, E.C.3.—Built from designs of Wren, 1671–77, to commemorate the *Great Fire of London,* which broke out in Pudding Lane, Sept. 2, 1666. The fluted Doric column is 120 ft. high (the moulded cylinder above the balcony supporting a flaming vase of gilt bronze is 42 ft. in addition), and is based on a square plinth 40 ft. high, with fine carvings on W. face (making a total height of 202 ft.). Splendid views of London from gallery at top of column (311 steps). Admission (until 20 minutes before closing time), Monday to Saturday, 9 a.m. to 6

p.m. (Oct.-March to 4 p.m.). Sundays—May to Sept. 2–6 p.m. Entrance fee. Closed Christmas Day, Boxing Day and Good Friday.

Monuments.—*Albert Memorial,* South Kensington; *Royal Air Force,* Victoria Embankment, *Beaconsfield,* Parliament Square; *Beatty, Jellicoe* and *Cunningham,* Trafalgar Square; *Belgian Gratitude* (Reginald Blomfield), Victoria Embankment; *Boadicea* (or "Boudicca"), Queen of the Iceni, E. Anglia (Thomas Thornycroft), Westminster Bridge; *Brunel* (Marochetti), Victoria Embankment; *Burghers of Calais* (Rodin), Victoria Tower Gardens, Westminster; *Burns,* Embankment Gardens; *Carlyle* (Boehm), Cheyne Walk, Chelsea; *Cavalry,* Hyde Park; *Cavell,* St. Martin's Place (Frampton); *Cenotaph* (Lutyens), Whitehall; *Charles I,* Trafalgar Square; *Charles II,* inside the Royal Exchange; *Churchill,* Parliament Square; *Cleopatra's Needle* (68½ ft. high *c.* 1,500 B.C. erected on the Thames Embankment in 1877–8)—the Sphinxes are Victorian; *Clive,* Whitehall; *Captain Cook* (Brock), The Mall; *Crimean,* Broad Sanctuary; *Oliver Cromwell* (Thornycroft), outside Westminster Hall; *Duke of Cambridge,* Whitehall; *Duke of York* (124 ft.), Carlton House Terrace; *Edward VII* (Mackennal), Waterloo Place; *Elizabeth I* (1586, oldest outdoor statue in London) (from Ludgate), Fleet Street; *Eros* (Shaftesbury Memorial) (Gilbert), Piccadilly Circus; *Marechal Foch,* Grosvenor Gardens; *Charles James Fox,* Bloomsbury Square; *George III,* Cockspur Street; *George IV* (Chantrey), riding without stirrups, Trafalgar Square; *George V,* Old Palace Yard; *George VI,* Carlton Gardens; *Gladstone,* facing Australia House, Strand; *Guards'* (Crimea), Waterloo Place; (Great War), Horse Guards' Parade; *Haig* (Hardiman), Whitehall; *Irving* (Brock), N. side of National Portrait Gallery; *James II,* Trafalgar Square; *Samuel Johnson,* opposite St. Clement Danes; *Kitchener,* Horse Guards' Parade; *Abraham Lincoln,* Parliament Square; *Milton,* St. Giles, Cripplegate; *Monument, The* (see above); *Mountbatten,* Foreign Office Green; *Nelson* (170 ft. 1½ in.), Trafalgar Square, with Lanseer's lions (cast from guns recovered from the wreck of the *Royal George*); *Florence Nightingale,* Waterloo Place; *Palmerston,* Parliament Square; *Peel,* Parliament Square; *Pitt,* Hanover Square (Chantrey); *Portal,* Embankment Gardens; *Prince Consort,* Holborn Circus; *Raleigh,* Whitehall; *Richard Coeur de Lion* (Marochetti), Old Palace Yard; *Roberts,* Horse Guards' Parade; *Franklin D. Roosevelt,* Grosvenor Square (Reid Dick); *Royal Artillery* (South Africa), The Mall; (Great War), Hyde Park Corner; *Captain Scott,* Waterloo Place (Lady Scott); *Shackleton,* Kensington Gore; *Shakespeare,* Leicester Square; *Smuts* (Epstein), Parliament Square; *Sullivan,* Victoria Embankment; *Trenchard,* Victoria Embankment; *Victoria Memorial,* in front of Buckingham Palace; *George Washington* (Houdon copy), Trafalgar Square; *Wellington,* Hyde Park Corner; *Wellington* (Chantrey) riding without stirrups, Royal Exchange; *John Wesley,* City Road; *William III,* St. James's Square; *Wolseley,* Horse Guards' Parade.

Osterley Park, Isleworth.—House and park of 140 acres given to the National Trust by the Earl of Jersey in 1949. The Elizabethan house, built in 1577 for Sir Thomas Gresham, was largely remodelled by Robert Adam, and the staterooms are among the best examples of Adam decoration. Open daily, except Mondays, (April–Sept.) 2–6 p.m.; (Oct–Mar.) 12 noon– 4 p.m. Closed Monday (except Bank Holidays), Christmas Eve, Christmas Day, Boxing Day, New Year's Day, Good Friday and May Day. Admission £1·50, children 75p.

Percival David Foundation of Chinese Art, 53 Gordon Square, W.C.1.—Set up in 1951 to promote the study and teaching of the art and culture of China and the surrounding regions, and provide facilities necessary to that end. The Foundation contains the collection of Chinese ceramics formed by Sir Percival David and his important library of books on Chinese art. To these was added a gift from the Hon. Mountstuart Elphinstone of part of his collection of Chinese monochrome porcelains. The galleries were opened to the public in 1952. The Foundation is administered on behalf of the University of London by the School of Oriental and African Studies. *Hours of opening:* Galleries, Mon. 2 to 5 p.m.; Tues. to Fri. 10.30 a.m. to 5 p.m.; Sat. 10.30 a.m. to 1 p.m.; Closed Sats. in August and Bank Holidays. Library available to ticket holders only; applications in writing to the Curator, Miss R. Scott.

Port of London.—The Port of London comprises the tidal portion of the River Thames from Teddington to the seaward limit (Tongue light vessel), a distance of 95 miles and one operational dock system and land for redevelopment, covering an area of 3,718 acres, of which 512 acres are water. The governing body is the Port of London Authority, whose Head Office is at Leslie Ford House, Tilbury Docks, Tilbury, Essex. Particulars of the docks are as follows:—*India & Millwall Docks,* E.14—remaining area vested in Docklands Development Corporation. *Royal Albert & King George V Docks,* E.16.—Area 512 acres. *Tilbury Docks, Essex.*—Area 1,037 acres, incuding 155 acres water. These docks are 26 miles below London Bridge and are used principally by vessels plying on the Australian, North American, Indian, other Eastern routes, West Africa and the Continent. Tilbury Passenger Landing Stage provides accommodation for liners at all states of the tide and adjoins Tilbury Riverside Station. A development and extension scheme at Tilbury added nearly 2 miles of deepwater quays, in addition to a £7 million Grain Terminal. With the recently completed Northfleet Hope Development, Tilbury is capable of handling forest products, containers and roll-on/roll-off traffic.

The St. Katherine Docks were sold to the G.L.C. in 1969 and the London Docks were closed on May 31, 1969 and sold to Tower Hamlets Council in 1976. Surrey Commercial Docks were closed in 1970 and were sold to the G.L.C. and Southwark Council in 1976 and 1977.

Prince Henry's Room, 17 Fleet Street, E.C.4.— Early 17th century timber-framed house containing fine room on first floor with panelling and moulded plaster ceiling. Includes an exhibition on Samuel Pepys and the London in which he lived. Open Mon. to Fri. 1.45 p.m. to 5 p.m.; Sat to 4.30 p.m. Admission free. Closed Christmas Day, Good Friday and Bank Holidays. Available for morning or evening lettings on application to The Town Clerk, Guildhall, E.C.2.

Richmond, Surrey. Contains the red brick gateway of *Richmond Palace* (Henry VII, 1485–1509) and buildings of the Jacobean, Queen Anne, and early Georgian periods, including *White Lodge* in Richmond Park, the former home of Queen Mary's mother (the Duke of Windsor was born there, June 23, 1894), and now the home of the Royal Ballet School. The *Star and Garter* Home for Disabled Soldiers, Sailors, and Airmen (the Women's Memorial of the Great War) was opened by Queen Mary in 1924. *Richmond Park* (2,469 acres) contains herds of fallow and red deer.

Roman London.—Although visible remains from this period are few, excavations carried out in the City on sites due for redevelopment often reveal Roman features. Sections of the City Wall are the most striking remains to be seen of Roman *Londinium,* although even these are largely medieval due to the Roman wall being rebuilt during the medieval

period. Sections may be seen near the White Tower in the Tower of London; at Tower Hill; at Coopers' Row; at All Hallows, London Wall, its vestry being built on the remains of a semi-circular Roman bastion; at St. Alphage, London Wall, showing a striking succession of building repairs from Roman until the late medieval period, and at St. Giles Cripplegate. Excavations in the Cripplegate area have revealed that a Roman fort was built there in about A.D.100–120. It was later incorporated into the city wall when this was built about A.D.200.

The administrative centre of the Roman city was the great forum and basilica, more than 165 metres square, sections of which have been encountered during excavations in the area of Leadenhall, Gracechurch Street and Lombard Street. Excavations during the past few years have revealed Roman activity along the river. Traces of a massive riverside wall, built in the late Roman period, have been found and a succession of Roman timber quays have been excavated along Lower and Upper Thames Street helping to prove that Roman London was a thriving commercial centre.

Other major buildings found are the Provincial Governor's Palace in Cannon Street; remains of a bath-building, preserved in Lower Thames Street; and the Temple of Mithras in Walbrook. The fine sculptures from this temple are displayed in the Museum of London, where many other relics from the Roman City may be seen. There is also an Ordnance Survey map of Roman London.

Royal Albert Hall, Kensington Gore, S.W.7.— The elliptical hall, one of the largest in the world, was completed in 1871, and since 1941 has been the venue each summer for the Promenade Concerts founded in 1895 by Sir Henry Wood. Also used for public meetings, concerts, sports and other entertainments. *Gen. Manager,* D. C. McNicol.

Royal Exchange, E.C.3. (founded by Sir Thomas Gresham, 1566, opened as "The Bourse" and proclaimed "The Royal Exchange" by Queen Elizabeth I, 1571, rebuilt 1667–69 and 1842–44). The building is occupied by the Guardian Royal Exchange Assurance Group and by the London International Financial Futures Exchange, and is administered by the Gresham Committee (*Clerk,* Mercers' Hall, Ironmonger Lane, E.C.2.).

Royal Geographical Society, Kensington Gore, S.W.7.—Map room open to public, *free.*

Royal Opera House, Covent Garden, W.C.2.— Home of the Royal Ballet (1931) and Royal Opera (1946) companies, the Opera House is the third theatre to be built on the site, opening May 15, 1858: the first was opened Dec. 7, 1732. The season of the resident companies runs mid Sept.–Aug. *General Director,* Sir John Tooley.

Runnimede.—A meadow of about 100 acres, on S. bank of Thames (part of the Crown Lands), between Windsor and Staines. From June 15–23, 1215, the hostile Barons encamped on this meadow during negotiations with King John, who rode over each day from Windsor. The 48 "Articles of the Barons" were accepted by the King on June 15, and were subsequently embodied in a charter, since known as *Magna Carta,* of which several copies were sealed on June 19. About half a mile N.E. of the meadow is *Magna Carta Island* (claimed as the actual site of the sealing), presented to the National Trust in 1930.

A memorial at *Cooper's Hill,* near Runnimede, to members of the Commonwealth air forces who lost their lives in the Second World War while serving from bases in the United Kingdom and north-western Europe and have no known grave, was unveiled by the Queen on October 17, 1953. Her Majesty on May 14, 1965, unveiled a memorial to the late President of the United States, John F. Kennedy, on ground nearby.

St. James's Palace, in Pall Mall, S.W.1.—(Not open to the public.) Built by Henry VIII; the Gatehouse and Presence Chamber remain, later alterations by Wren and Kent. The Chapel Royal is open to the public for services on Sundays at 8.30 a.m. and 11.15 a.m. between beginning October and Good Friday (*see also* Marlborough House for summer services in The Queen's Chapel). Representatives of Foreign Powers are still accredited "to the Court of St. James's". Clarence House (1825) in the palace precinct is the home of H.M. the Queen Mother.

St. John's Gate, Clerkenwell, E.C.1.—Now the Chancery of the Order of St. John of Jerusalem, and formerly the entrance of the Priory of that Order, of which the gate house (early 16th century) and crypt of Church (12th century) alone survive. They may be inspected on application to the Curator.

Sir John Soane's Museum, 13 Lincoln's Inn Fields, W.C.2. The house and galleries, built 1812–24, are the work of the founder, Sir John Soane (1753–1837) and contain his collections, arranged as he left them, in pursuance of an Act procured by him in 1833. Exhibits include the Sarcophagus of Seti 1 (*c.* 1290 B.C.), classical vases and marbles, Hogarth's *Rake's Progress* and *Election* series, paintings by Canaletto, Reynolds, Turner, Lawrence, etc., and sculpture by Chantrey, Flaxman, etc. Soane's library of 8,000 vols, and collection of 20,000 architectural drawings are available for study. Open Tues.–Sat. inclusive, 10 a.m. to 5 p.m. Closed Bank Holidays. *Curator,* Sir John Summerson, C.B.E., F.B.A. *Inspectress,* Miss D. Stroud, M.B.E., F.S.A.

Somerset House, Strand, W.C.2, and Victoria Embankment, W.C.2.—The beautiful river façade (600 ft. long) was built in 1776–86 from the designs of Sir W. Chambers; the eastern extension, which houses part of King's College, was built by Smirke in 1829. Somerset House was the property of Lord Protector Somerset, at whose attainder in 1552 the palace passed to the Crown, and it was a royal residence until 1692.

South Bank, S.E.1.—The arts complex on the south bank of the River Thames includes the South Bank Concert Halls, owned and managed by the G.L.C. and consisting of the 2,900-seat *Royal Festival Hall* (opened in 1951 for the Festival of Britain), a major venue for concert and ballet seasons, with the adjacent 1,100-seat *Queen Elizabeth Hall* and 370-seat *Purcell Room,* accommodating smaller-scale performances.
The *National Film Theatre* (opened 1958), administered by the British Film Institute, has two auditoria showing films, television and video of outstanding historical, artistic or technical merit. The London Film Festival is held here every November.
The *National Theatre* opened in 1976 and stages classical, modern, new and neglected plays in its three auditoria; the 1,160-seat Olivier theatre (apron stage), the 890-seat Lyttleton theatre (proscenium stage) and the experimental Cottesloe theatre, which holds up to 400.

Stock Exchange, E.C.2.—The market floor of the new Stock Exchange building in London opened for trading in June, 1973. A tower, 331 feet high, and the new Market replace the complex of buildings started in 1801 on the same site. The new building is the headquarters of The Stock Exchange, following the amalgamation of all the Stock Exchanges in Great Britain and Ireland on March 25, 1973.

The Stock Exchange provides a market for the purchase and sale of over 7,000 securities officially listed, and valued at nearly £832,099,100,000 and also securities listed on other Stock Exchanges throughout the World. At present the members of The Stock Exchange, who consist of brokers (agents for clients) and Jobbers (dealers in specific securities) number about 4,200. The Visitors Gallery is open between 9.45 a.m. and 3.15 p.m. Monday to Friday. Admission free and without ticket; film show. Advance bookings are advisable; last complete programme begins at 2.30 p.m.

Syon House, Brentford.—The summer home of the Duke of Northumberland. The House is built on the remains of the Nunnery of Syon, founded by the order of Henry V in 1415. At the Dissolution of the Monasteries the estate reverted to the Crown. In 1594 it was granted to the 9th Earl of Northumberland, who altered and improved the property. In the eight years, 1762–1770, the interior was transformed and furnished by Robert Adam. Open Easter to Sept. 29 (Sun. to Thurs.), 12–5·00 p.m.

Thames Embankments.—The Victoria Embankment, on the N. side (from Westminster to Blackfriars), was constructed by Sir J. W. Bazalgette for the Metropolitan Board of Works, 1864–70 (the seats, of which the supports of some are a kneeling camel, laden with spicery, and of others a winged sphinx, were presented by the Grocers' Company, and by Rt. Hon. W. H. Smith, M.P., in 1874); the Albert Embankment, on the S. side (from Westminster Bridge to Vauxhall), 1866–69; the Chelsea Embankment, 1871–74. The total cost exceeded £2,000,000. Sir J. W. Bazalgette (1819–91) also inaugurated the London main drainage system, 1858–65. A medallion has been placed on a pier of the Victoria Embankment to commemorate the engineer of the Thames waterside improvements ("Flumini vincula posuit"). The headquarters of the G.L.C. include an embankment on the Surrey side.

Thames Flood Barrier.—Officially opened in May 1984, though first used in Feb. 1983, the Barrier consists of ten rising sector gates which span 570 yards from bank to bank of the Thames at Woolwich Reach. When not in use the gates lie horizontally, allowing shipping to navigate the river normally; when the Barrier is closed, the gates turn through 90 degrees to stand vertically more than 50 feet above the river bed. The Barrier took eight years to complete and can be raised within about 30 minutes.

Thames Tunnels.—The *Rotherhithe Tunnel,* constructed by the L.C.C. and opened in 1908, connects Commercial Road, E.14, with Lower Road, Rotherhithe; the total length is 1 mile 332 yards, of which 474 yards are under the river. The cost of the tunnel and its approaches was £1,506,914. The first *Blackwall Tunnel* (pedestrians and vehicles) was constructed by the L.C.C. and opened in 1897, connecting East India Dock Road, Poplar, with Blackwall Lane, East Greenwich. The cost of the tunnel with its approaches was about £1,323,663. A second tunnel (for southbound vehicles only) was opened in August, 1967, at a cost of about £9,750,000 and the old tunnel was improved at a cost of about £1,350,000 and made one-way northbound. Both tunnels are for vehicles only. The relative lengths of the tunnels measured from East India Dock Road to the Gate House on the south side are 6,215 ft. (old tunnel) and 6,152 feet. *Greenwich Tunnel* (pedestrians only), constructed by the L.C.C. and opened in 1902, connects the Isle of Dogs, Poplar, with Greenwich. The length of the subway is 406 yards, and the cost was about £180,000. The *Woolwich Tunnel* (pedestrians only), constructed by the L.C.C. and opened in 1912, connects North and South Woolwich below the passenger and vehicular ferry from North Woolwich Station, E.16, to High Street, Woolwich, S.E.18. The length of the subway is 552 yards, and its cost was about £86,000. The *Thames Tunnel* (1,300 feet) was opened in 1843 to connect Wapping (N.) with Rotherhithe (S.). In 1866 it was closed to the public, and purchased by the East London Railway Company. The *Tower Subway* for pedestrians was opened in 1870, and has long been closed.

Tower Hill, E.C.1 and E.C.3, was formerly the place of execution for condemned prisoners from the Tower, the site of the scaffold being marked in the gardens of Trinity Square.

Tower of London, E.C.3.—Admission to a general view of the Tower, the White Tower (Armouries), the History, Oriental, Ordnance and 18–19th Century Galleries, and the Wall Walk Phases I and II. Admission (1983): Oct.–Mar., £2 (children £1); April–Sept. £3 (children £1·50); to the Jewel House, 80p, children 40p. (The Jewel House is usually closed for cleaning in Feb. Precise dates available from the Receiver of Fees Office at the Tower.) On Sundays throughout the year (except August) the public is admitted to Holy Communion, 9.15 a.m. and Morning Service, 11 a.m. Open on weekdays, Mar. 1 to Oct. 31, 9.30–5; Nov. 1 to Feb. 28, 9.30–4; Sundays, 2 p.m. to 5 p.m., Mar. 1–Oct. 31 only; Tower closed Christmas Eve, Christmas Day, Boxing Day, Good Friday and New Year's Day. *Constable*, Gen. Sir Peter Hunt, G.C.B., D.S.O., O.B.E.; *Lieutenant*, Lieut. Gen. Sir Hugh Cunnigham, K.B.E.; *Resident Governor and Keeper of the Jewel House*, Maj.-Gen. A. P. W. MacLellan, M.B.E.; *Master of the Armouries*, A. V. B. Norman; *Chaplain at the Chapel Royal of St. Peter ad Vincula*, Rev. J. F. M. Llewellyn.

The White Tower is the oldest and central building in Her Majesty's Royal Palace and Fortress of the Tower of London. It was built at the order of William I and constructed by Gundulph, Bishop of Rochester, in the years 1078–98. The Inner Wall, with thirteen towers, was constructed by Henry III in the 12th century. The Moat was extended and completed by Richard I and the Wharf first mentioned in 1228. The Outer Wall was completed in the reign of Edward I and now incorporates 6 towers and 2 bastions. The last Monarch to reside in the Tower of London was James I. The Crown Jewels came to the Tower in the reign of Henry III. All coinage used in Great Britain was minted in the Outer Ward of the Tower of London until 1810 when the Royal Mint was formed. The Tower of London has had a military garrison since 1078. The Chapel Royal of St. John the Evangelist, within the White Tower (1080–1088) is the oldest Norman church in London. The chapel of St. Peter ad Vincula was built in the early 16th century.

Waltham Abbey (or **Waltham Holy Cross**), Essex.—The Abbey ruins, Harold's Bridge (14th century), the Nave of the former cruciform Abbey Church and the traditional burial place of King Harold II (1066), and a Lady Chapel of Edward II, with crypt below. New evidence of the position and style of several buildings, which once stood on the site of the Augustinian monastery, were revealed by the prolonged drought in the summer of 1933 and by subsequent excavations. At Waltham Cross, 1 mile from the Abbey, is one of the crosses (partly restored) erected by Edward I to mark a resting place of the corpse of Queen Eleanor on its way to Westminster Abbey. (Ten crosses were erected, but only those at Geddington, Northampton and Waltham remain; "Charing" Cross originally stood near the spot now occupied by the statue of Charles I at Whitehall.)

Wellington Museum, Apsley House, 149 Piccadilly, at Hyde Park Corner, W.1.—Admission 60p, children 30p. Open weekdays, 10 to 6; Sundays, 2.30 to 6. Closed Mondays and Fridays, Christmas Eve, Christmas Day, Boxing Day and New Year's Day. Apsley House was designed by Robert Adam for Lord Bathurst and built 1771–8. It was bought in 1817 by the Duke of Wellington, who in 1828–29 employed Benjamin Wyatt to enlarge it, face it with Bath stone and add the Corinthian portico. The museum contains many fine paintings, services of porcelain and silver plate and personal relics of the 1st Duke of Wellington (1769–1852) and was given to the Nation by the 7th Duke. It was first opened to the public in 1952, under the administration of the Victoria and Albert Museum.

Westminster Hall, S.W.1.—The only part of the old Palace of Westminster to survive the fire of 1834, Westminster Hall is adjacent to and incorporated in the Houses of Parliament. Westminster Hall was built by William Rufus from 1097–99 and altered by Richard II, 1394–1401. It is about 240 ft. long, 69 ft. wide and 90 ft. high; the hammer beam roof of carved oak dates from 1396–98. The Hall was the scene of the trial of Charles I. Westminster Hall is included on the route followed by those who have arranged a visit to the Houses of Parliament (*q.v.*) with their M.P.

Whitechapel Art Gallery, High Street, E.1.—Opened in 1901; administered by a charitable trust. There is no permanent collection; temporary exhibitions, mainly of modern art, are presented, and community and educational projects are run. Open Tues.–Suns. 11–5.50 p.m. (7.05 p.m. Tues. and Thurs.), closed Mons. The Gallery is closed for improvements and extension and will re-open in June 1985.

Windsor Castle (begun by William the Conqueror, A.D. 1066–87).—22 miles from London, by Western and Southern Regions. The Castle Precincts are open daily, free of charge, from 10 a.m. to 4.15 p.m. late October to late March; 5.15 p.m. late March and April and September to late October; and 7.15 p.m. May to August. When the Queen is not in official residence, the *State Apartments* of Windsor Castle are open to the public on every weekday and on Sunday afternoons during the summer months. When the State Apartments are open, the charges for admission are for Adults, £1·20 and for Children and O.A.P.s 60p. By the Queen's command, the net proceeds go to charities. The hours of admission to the State Apartments are: Jan. to late Mar., late Oct. to Dec., 10.30–3; May to late Oct., 10.30–5; Sundays, May to late Oct. 1.30–5; Closed, mid-March, April and mid-June. *Queen Mary's Doll's House, the Exhibition of Dolls, the Exhibition of Drawings by Holbein, Leonardo da Vinci and other artists and the Royal Mews Exhibition* can be seen on the same days and hours as the State Apartments; admission, adults 50p, children and O.A.P.s 20p. When the State Apartments are closed, Queen Mary's Doll's House, the Exhibition of Drawings and the Royal Mews Exhibition remain open to the public. The *Albert Memorial Chapel* is open throughout the year from 10–1; 2–3.45; closed on Sundays; Admission free. A fee is charged to visit *St. George's Chapel*. The *Curfew Tower* may be seen under the guidance of the Keeper to whom application must be made at the entrance.

The *Royal Mausoleum*, Frogmore Gardens, Home Park, is open annually on two days in early May in conjunction with the opening of Frogmore Gardens in aid of the National Garden Scheme, 10 a.m.–7 p.m. Also open on the Wednesday nearest to May 24 (Queen Victoria's birthday) from 11 a.m. to 4 p.m. Admission free.

Zoological Gardens, Regent's Park, N.W.1.—(Opened in 1828). Open daily (except Dec. 25) March–Oct. 9–6 or dusk (7 p.m. Suns. and Bank Hols.), opens 10 a.m. in winter. Admission, £2·95, children under 16, £1·45, under 5 free. Special rates for parties and O.A.P.s. Aquarium and Children's Zoo free.

[London Tourist Board.—26 Grosvenor Gardens, S.W.1. (*Tel.*, 01–730 3450.)]

PARKS, SPACES AND GARDENS

The principal Parks and Open Spaces in the Metropolitan area are maintained as under:—

By the Crown

BUSHY PARK (1,099 acres).—Adjoining Hampton Court, contains avenue of horse-chestnuts enclosed in a four-fold avenue of limes planted by William III. "Chestnut Sunday" (when the trees are in full bloom with their "candles") is usually about May 1 to 15.

GREEN PARK (49 acres), W.1.—Between Piccadilly and St. James's Park with *Constitution Hill*, leading to Hyde Park Corner.

GREENWICH PARK (196½ acres), S.E.10.

HAMPTON COURT GARDENS (54 acres).

HAMPTON COURT GREEN (17 acres).

HAMPTON COURT PARK (622 acres).

HYDE PARK (341 acres).—From Park Lane, W.1, to Kensington Gardens, W.2 containing the Serpentine. Fine gateway at Hyde Park ,Corner, with Apsley House, the Achilles Statue, Rotten Row and the Ladies' Mile. To the north-east is the *Marble Arch*, originally erected by George IV at the entrance to Buckingham Palace and re-erected in present position in 1851.

KENSINGTON GARDENS (275 acres), W.2.—From western boundary of Hyde Park to Kensington Palace, containing the Albert Memorial.

KEW, ROYAL BOTANIC GARDENS (300 acres).—Open daily, except Christmas Day and New Year's Day, from 10 a.m. The closing hour varies from 4 p.m. in mid-winter to 7 p.m. on week-days, and 8 p.m. at week-ends and Bank Holidays, in mid-summer. Admission, 15p. Museums open 10 a.m.; Glasshouses, 11 a.m. to 4.50 p.m. (weekdays); to 5.50 p.m. (Sundays). No dogs except guide-dogs for the blind.

REGENT'S PARK and PRIMROSE HILL (464 acres), N.W.1.—From Marylebone Road to Primrose Hill surrounded by the Outer Circle and divided by the *Broad Walk* leading to the Zoological Gardens.

RICHMOND PARK (2,469 acres).

ST. JAMES'S PARK (93 acres), S.W.1.—From Whitehall to Buckingham Palace. Ornamental lake of 12 acres. The original suspension bridge built in 1857 was replaced in 1957. The *Mall* leads from the Admiralty Arch to the Queen Victoria Memorial and Buckingham Palace. *Birdcage Walk* from Storey's Gate, past Wellington Barracks, to Buckingham Palace.

By the Corporation of London

BURNHAM BEECHES and FLEET WOOD, Bucks. (510 acres).—Purchased by the Corporation for the benefit of the public in 1879, Fleet Wood (65 acres) being presented in 1921.

COULSDON COMMON, Surrey (127 acres).

EPPING FOREST (6,000 acres).—Purchased by the

Corporation for £250,000 and thrown open to the public in 1882. The present forest is 12 miles long by 1 to 2 miles wide, about one-tenth of its original area.

FARTHINGDOWN, Surrey (121 acres).

HIGHGATE WOOD (70 acres).

KENLEY COMMON, Surrey (85 acres).

QUEEN'S PARK, Kilburn (30 acres).

RIDDLESDOWN, Surrey (90 acres).

SPRING PARK, West Wickham (51 acres).

WEST HAM PARK (77 acres).

WEST WICKHAM COMMON, Kent (25 acres).

With smaller open spaces within the City of London, including FINSBURY CIRCUS GARDENS.

By the Greater London Council

ABBEY WOOD PARK (19 acres), S.E.2.

ARCHBISHOP'S PARK (10 acres), S.E.1.

AVERY HILL (87 acres), S.E.9, with winter garden and nursery.

BATTERSEA PARK (200 acres), S.W.11, with zoo and lake.

BLACKHEATH (272 acres), S.E.10.—*Morden College*, founded in 1695 as a home for "decayed Turkey merchants", is near the S.E. corner. The building was designed by Wren and its Chapel doors have carvings attributed to Grinling Gibbons. Concerts and poetry recitals are held at *Rangers House*, an early 18th century mansion, which houses the Suffolk collection of English portraits from the Elizabethan to the Georgian period.

BOSTALL HEATH AND WOODS (159 acres), S.E.2.

BURGESS PARK (85 acres), S.E.5.

CASTLEWOOD, see JACKWOOD.

CRYSTAL PALACE PARK (106 acres), S.E.19, with zoo, and open air concerts in summer.

CUTTY SARK GARDENS (4 acres), S.E.10.

DULWICH PARK (72 acres), S.E.21.

ELTHAM PARK (including Shepherdsleas Wood, 109 acres), S.E.9.

FINSBURY PARK (115 acres), N.4.

GEFFRYE'S GARDEN (2 acres), E.2.

GOLDERS HILL (36 acres), N.W.3, adjoining West Heath, Hampstead.

HACKNEY MARSH (336 acres), E.9. 106 football pitches.

HAINAULT FOREST (958 acres), Hainault, Essex.

HAMPSTEAD HEATH and Extension (283 acres), N.W.3.

HAVERING COUNTRY PARK (168 acres).

HERNE HILL STADIUM (9 acres), S.E.24. Cycle racing track.

HOLLAND PARK (55 acres), W.8. Open air theatre and concerts; floodlit gardens; King George VI Memorial Youth Hostel; Restaurant.

HORNIMAN GARDENS (26 acres), S.E.23. Adjoining Horniman Museum.

HOUNSLOW HEATH (204 acres), Staines Road, Hounslow.

JACKWOOD (266 acres), S.E.18. Includes Castlewood, Oxleas Wood and Meadow, Eltham Common.

KENWOOD (200 acres), N.W.3, the northern part of Hampstead Heath. Part purchased in 1922 by public subscription. Open air symphony concerts each summer. The Iveagh Bequest, in an 18th-century mansion (open to the public), includes valuable art treasures. Recitals and poetry readings in the Orangery.

LESNES ABBEY WOODS (215 acres), Erith, S.E.2.— Ruins of an Augustinian abbey.

MARBLE HILL (66 acres).—Twickenham, Middlesex.—A beautiful park, running down to the riverside, on the left bank of the Thames; includes a mansion (open to the public). Open air theatre.

MILE END PARK, E.3. (56 acres). Includes the East London Stadium.

PARLIAMENT HILL (271 acres), N.W.3.—Part of Hampstead Heath. Lido and swimming bath. Important cross-country events are held here.

SOUTH BANK (10 acres, including Jubilee Gardens), Belvedere Road, S.E.1.

THAMESMEAD (176 acres), S.E.2. Sailing.

TOWER HAMLETS CEMETERY (28 acres), E.3. Conversion to public open spaces.

TRENT PARK (413 acres), Cockfosters, Enfield. Country park with nature trail, riding school, golf course, picnic sites, fishing, etc.

VICTORIA PARK (218 acres), E.9.

WARREN HOUSE ESTATE (now known as Stanmore Country Park) (78 acres), Stanmore, Middlesex.

WORMWOOD SCRUBS (191 acres), Hammersmith, W.12. West London Stadium.

LATIN NAMES OF ENGLISH TOWNS AND CITIES

Bath	*Aquae Sulis*	Lincoln	*Lindum*
Canterbury	*Durovernum*	London	*Londinium*
Carlisle	*Luguvalium*	Manchester	*Mancunium*
Chelmsford	*Caesaromagus*	Newcastle	*Pons Aelius*
Chester	*Deva*	Pevensey	*Anderida*
Cirencester	*Corinium*	Rochester	*Durobrivae*
Colchester	*Camulodunum*	St. Albans	*Verulamium*
Doncaster	*Danum*	Salisbury	*Sorbiodunum*
Dorchester	*Durinum, Durnovaria*	(Old Sarum)	
Dover	*Dubris*	Silchester	*Calleva Atrebatum*
Exeter	*Isca Dumnoniorum*	Winchester	*Venta Belgarum*
Gloucester	*Glevum*	Worcester	*Wigornia*
Lancaster	*Lunecastrum*	Wroxeter	*Viroconium*
Leicester	*Ratae Coritanorum*	Yarmouth	*Magna Gernemutha*
		York	*Eboracum*

The Principality of Wales

Position and extent.—Wales (Cymru) occupies the extreme west of the central southern portion of the island of Great Britain, with a total area of 8,019 sq. miles; it is bounded on the N. by the Irish Sea, on the S. by the Bristol Channel, on the E. by the English counties of Cheshire, Shropshire, Hereford and Worcester, and Gloucester, and on the W. by St. George's Channel. Across the Menai Straits is the Welsh island of *Anglesey* or Ynys Môn (276 sq. miles), communication with which is facilitated by the Menai Suspension Bridge (1,000 ft. long), built by Telford in 1826 and by the tubular railway bridge (1,100 ft. long) built by Stephenson in 1850. Holyhead harbour, on Holy Isle (N.W. of Anglesey), provides accommodation for ferry services to Dublin (70 miles).

Population.—The population at the Census of 1981 was 2,791,851 (males 1,352,639; females 1,439,212). The average density of population in 1981 was 343 per square mile.

Relief.—Wales is a country of extensive tracts of high plateau and shorter stretches of mountain ranges deeply dissected by river valleys. Lower-lying ground is largely confined to the coastal belt and the lower parts of the valleys. The highest mountains are those of Snowdonia in the north-west (*Snowdon*, 3,559 ft.), Berwyn (*Aran Fawddwy*, 2,971 ft.), Cader Idris (*Pen y Gadair*, 2,928 ft.), Dyfed (*Plynlimon*, 2,467 ft.), and the Black Mountain, Brecon Beacons and Black Forest ranges in the south-east (*Carmarthen Van*, 2,630 ft., *Pen y Fan*, 2,906 ft., *Waun Fâch*, 2,660 ft.).

Hydrography.—The principal river of those rising in Wales is the *Severn* (*see* England), which flows from the slopes of Plynlimon to the English border. The *Wye* (130 miles) also rises in the slopes of Plynlimon. The *Usk* (56 miles) flows into the Bristol Channel, through Gwent. The *Dee* (70 miles) rises in Bala Lake and flows through the Vale of Llangollen, where an aqueduct (built by Telford in 1805) carries the Pontcysyllte branch of the Shropshire Union Canal across the valley. The estuary of the Dee is the navigable portion, 14 miles in length and about 5 miles in breadth, and the tide rushes in with dangerous speed over the "Sands of Dee". The *Towy* (68 miles), *Teifi* (50 miles), *Taff* (40 miles), *Dovey* (30 miles), *Taf* (25 miles), and *Conway* (24 miles), the last named broad and navigable, are wholly Welsh rivers.

The largest natural lake in Wales is Bala (Llyn Tegid) in Gwynedd, 4 miles long and about 1 mile wide; *Lake Vyrnwy* is an artificial reservoir, about the size of Bala, and forms the water supply of Liverpool, and Birmingham is supplied from a chain of reservoirs in the Elan and Clærwen valleys.

The Welsh Language.—According to the 1981 Census results, the percentage of persons of three years and over able to speak Welsh were:

Clwyd	18·7	Powys	20·2
Dyfed	46·3	S. Glamorgan	5·8
Gwent	2·5	W. Glamorgan	16·4
Gwynedd	61·2		
Mid Glamorgan	8·4	**Wales**	18·9

The 1981 figure represents a slight decline from 20·8 per cent in 1971 (1961, 26 per cent; 1951, 28·9 per cent).

Flag.—A red dragon on a green and white field (per fess argent and vert a dragon passant gules). The flag was augmented in 1953 by a royal badge on a shield encircled with a riband bearing the words *Ddraig Goch Ddyry Cychwyn* and imperially crowned. Only the unaugmented flag is flown on Government offices in Wales and, where appropriate, in London. Both flags continue to be used elsewhere.

EARLY HISTORY

Celts and Romans.—The earliest inhabitants of whom there is any record appear to have been subdued or exterminated by the *Goidels* (a people of Celtic race) in the Bronze Age, and a further invasion of Celtic *Brythons* and *Belgae* followed in the ensuing Iron Age. The *Roman* conquest of South Britain and Wales was for some time successfully opposed by *Caratacus* (Caractacus or Caradog), Chieftain of the Catuvellauni and son of *Cunobelinus* (Cymbeline) King of the Trinobantes. In A.D. 78 the conquest of Wales was completed under Julius Frontinus, and communications were opened up by the construction of military roads from Chester to Caerleon-on-Usk and Caerwent, and from Chester to Conway (and thence to Camarthen and Neath). *Christianity* was introduced (during the Roman occupation) in the 4th century.

The Anglo-Saxon Attacks.—The Anglo-Saxon invaders of South Britain drove the Celtic Goidels and Brythons into the mountain fastness of Wales, and into Strathclyde (Cumberland and S.W. Scotland) and Cornwall, giving them the name of *Waelisc*, or Welsh (= Foreign). The West Saxons' victory of Deorham (577) isolated Wales from Cornwall and the battle of Chester (613) cut off communication with Strathclyde. In the 8th century the boundaries of the Welsh were further restricted by the annexations of Offa, King of Mercia, and counter-attacks were largely prevented by the construction of an artificial boundary from the Dee to the Wye (Offa's Dike). In the 9th century Rhodri Mawr united the country against further incursions of the Saxons by land and against the raids of Norse and Danish pirates by sea, but at his death his three provinces of *Gwynedd* (N.), *Powys* (Mid.) and *Deheubarth* (S.) were divided among his three sons—Anarawd, Mervyn and Cadell—the son of the last named being Hywel Dda, who codified the laws of the country, while Llewelyn ap Seisyll (husband of the heiress of Gwynedd) again united the provinces and reigned as Prince from 1018 to 1023.

The Norman Conquest.—After the Norman conquest of England, William I created Palatine counties along the Welsh frontier, and Robert FitzHamon, the Norman Earl of Gloucester, raided South Wales and erected fortresses from the Wye to Milford Haven. Henry I introduced Flemish settlers into South Wales, but after his death the Welsh rose under the leadership of Griffith ap Rhys and routed the Norman-Flemish forces at the fords of the Teifi (Cardigan) in 1136. From the early years of the 13th century the house of Gwynedd, in the north, gained an ascendancy over the whole of Wales, and Llywelyn ap Iorwerth was in constant strife with England for recognition as an independent sovereign. Llywelyn ap Gruffydd (grandson of Llywelyn ap Iorwerth), the last native prince, was killed in 1282 during hostilities between the Welsh and English, allowing Edward I of England to establish his authority over the country. On Feb. 7, 1301, Edward of Caernarvon, son of Edward I, was created *Prince of Wales*, a title which has subsequently been borne by the eldest son of the sovereign. Strong Welsh national feeling continued, expressed in the early 15th century in the rising led by Owain Glyndŵr, but the situation was altered by the accession to the English throne in 1485 of Henry VI of the Welsh House of Tudor. Wales was politically assimilated to England under the Act of Union of 1535, which extended English laws to the

Principality and gave it parliamentary representation for the first time.

Eisteddfod.—The Welsh are a distinct nationality, with a language and literature of their own, and the national bardic festival (Eisteddfod), instituted by Prince Rhys ap Griffith in 1176, is annually maintained. These *Eisteddfodau* (sessions) form part of the *Gorsedd* (assembly), which is believed to date from the time of Prydian, a ruling prince in an age many centuries before the Christian era.

AREA AND POPULATION OF THE WELSH COUNTIES

County	Administrative Headquarters	Area (hectares)	Population	Actual Rateable Value per head
				£
Clwyd	Shire Hall, Mold	242,650	394,500	100·67
Dyfed	*Carmarthen	576,577	336,100	95·45
Gwent	*Cwmbran	137,599	439,100	105·23
Gwynedd	County Offices, Caernarfon	386,708	323,400	102·50
Mid Glamorgan	*Cathays Park, Cardiff	101,867	541,800	73·64
Powys	*Llandrindod Wells	507,741	112,000	87·32
South Glamorgan	County Headquarters, Newport Road, Cardiff	41,629	391,600	132·43
West Glamorgan	*The Guildhall, Swansea	81,657	365,700	104·61

* County Hall.

COUNTY OFFICIALS AND CHAIRMEN OF COUNTY COUNCILS

County	Chief Executive	County Treasurer	Chairmen of C.C.
Clwyd	M. H. Phillips	R. C. Greening	J. C. Epsley
Dyfed	D. H. Davies	B. H. R. Evans	T. G. Parry
Gwent	M. J. Perry	R. Emmott	V. L. H. Etheridge
Gwynedd	I. B. Rees	J. L. Williams	E. E. Davies
Mid Glamorgan ...	D. H. Thomas*	R. K. Lacey	T. I. W. A. Davies
Powys	M. J. Greenwood	M. J. Greenwood	J. H. Lloyd
South Glamorgan .	W. P. Davey	R. G. Tettenborn	A. A. Huish, CBE
West Glamorgan ..	M. E. J. Rush	S. G. Dunster	T. L. Thomas

* County Clerk.

PRINCIPAL WELSH CITIES

CARDIFF

CARDIFF (South Glamorgan), at the mouth of the rivers Taff, Rhymney and Ely, is the capital City of Wales and one of Britain's major administrative, commercial and office centres. It has many industries, including steel works, car component manufacturing, cigars and a flourishing port with a substantial and varied trade. There are many fine buildings in the civic centre started early this century which includes the City Hall, the National Museum of Wales, University Buildings, Law Courts, Welsh Office, County Hall, Police Headquarters and the Temple of Peace and Health. Also in the city are Llandaff Cathedral, the Welsh National Folk Museum at St. Fagans, Cardiff Castle, the New Theatre, the Sherman Theatre and the Cardiff College of Music and Drama. New buildings include St. David's Hall, a 2,000-seat concert and conference hall.

SWANSEA

SWANSEA (in Welsh, Abertawe) is a City and a seaport of West Glamorgan with its own municipal airport. The beautiful Gower Peninsula was brought within the City boundary under local government reform on April 1, 1974. The trade of the port includes coal, patent fuel, ores, and the import and export of oil. The municipal area is 60,511 acres.

The principal buildings are the Norman Castle (rebuilt in 1330), the Royal Institution of South Wales, founded in 1835 (containing Museum and Library), the University College at Singleton and the Guildhall, containing the Brangwyn panels. New buildings include the Industrial and Maritime Museum and the new Maritime Quarter and Marina. Swansea was chartered by the Earl of Warwick, *circa* 1158–1184, and further charters were granted by King John, Henry III., Edward II., Edward III. and James II., 2 from Cromwell and 1 Lord Marcher.

LORD LIEUTENANTS AND HIGH SHERIFFS OF WELSH COUNTIES

County	Lord Lieutenant	High Sheriff (1984–85)
Clwyd	Col. J. Ellis Evans, C.B.E., T.D.	D. H. Griffith
Dyfed	D. C. Mansel Lewis	J. D. D. Williams
Gwent	R. Hanbury-Tenison	T. R. Baxter-Wright
Gwynedd	The Most Hon. The Marquess of Anglesey	Wing-Cdr. R. W. Turner, D.F.C., A.F.C., R.A.F. (*Rtd.*)
Mid Glamorgan	Sir Cennydd Traherne, K.G., T.D.	E. Rea
Powys	Col. J. L. Corbett-Winder, O.B.E., M.C.	D. S. Baird-Murray
South Glamorgan	} (*See* Mid Glamorgan)	C. H. Rapport, M.B.E.
West Glamorgan		B. B. Hickey, T.D.

MUNICIPAL DIRECTORY OF WALES

District Councils

Those accorded CITY Status are shown in SMALL CAPITALS; those with
Borough Status are distinguished by having § prefixed.

District	Popula- tion	Rateable Value 1984 £	Chief Executive	Chairman 1984–85 (a) Mayor (b) Lord Mayor
§Aberconwy, Gwynedd	51,300	5,524,452	J. P. Hughes	(a) G. G. Williams
§Afan, West Glamorgan	55,000	8,478,484	C. A. Millward	(a) W. J. Harris
Alyn and Deeside, Clwyd	72,800	8,230,684	W. E. Rogers	V. G. Kindlin
§Arfon, Gwynedd	54,659	5,421,858	D. L. Jones	(a) G. Buckley-Jones
§Blaenau Gwent, Gwent	79,200	5,885,715	R. Leadbeter	(a) E. L. Williams
§Brecknock, Powys	40,800	3,469,358	E. F. Jones	(a) J. A. T. Elston
CARDIFF, South Glamorgan	279,800	39,202,011	H. T. Crippin	(b) A. W. Buttle
Carmarthen, Dyfed	51,733	4,072,764	V. M. Williams	V. L. James
Ceredigion, Dyfed	61,600	5,117,434	D. Morgan	J. R. Davies
§Colwyn, Clwyd	49,800	5,406,375	O. Morris	(a) T. H. Roberts
§Cynon Valley, Mid Glamorgan	67,200	4,520,739	G. W. Hosgood	(a) E. D. Jenkins
§Delyn, Clwyd	65,700	6,030,000	J. R. Packer	(a) S. Roberts
§Dinefwr, Dyfed	36,413	2,326,871	E. W. Harries	(a) A. H. Phillips
Dwyfor, Gwynedd	25,900	2,584,000	E. Davies	H. Evans
Glyndwr, Clwyd	40,000	3,508,572	D. Bowen	W. Owen
§Islwyn, Gwent	64,769	4,557,994	B. Bird	(a) R. H. Cooke
§Llanelli, Dyfed	75,200	6,440,644	A. B. Thomas	(a) F. Owens
§Lliw Valley, West Glamorgan	60,000	4,644,471	J. C. Howells	(a) I. I. Williams
Meirionnydd, Gwynedd	31,300	4,094,752	G. W. Hughes	I. Thomas
§Merthyr Tydfil, Mid Glamorgan	61,000	4,660,810	S. Jones	(a) J. Bromley
Monmouth, Gwent	74,300	7,513,483	G. Cummings	T. R. Spencer
Montgomery, Powys	47,700	4,251,733	I. W. Williams	R. J. Bainbridge
§Neath, West Glamorgan	66,200	6,288,406	I. H. K. Thorne	(a) R. Bennett
§Newport, Gwent	130,200	19,571,533	G. N. Cook	(a) C. Summers
§Ogwr, Mid Glamorgan	130,100	10,581,692	J. G. Cole	(a) F. G. Embling
Preseli, Dyfed	67,682	7,427,348	I. W. R. David	J. D. E. Codd
Radnor, Powys	21,600	2,200,000	K. M. Francis	D. O. Evans
§Rhondda, Mid Glamorgan	81,268	3,942,321	G. Evans	(a) Mrs. K. Rees
§Rhuddlan, Clwyd	52,800	6,054,943	F. J. K. Davies	(a) N. H. Taylor
Rhymney Valley, Mid Glamorgan	107,100	7,471,664	P. A. Bennett	R. Parry
South Pembrokeshire, Dyfed	38,300	7,220,088	D. R. Jones	J. E. Feetham
SWANSEA, West Glamorgan	188,100	18,668,453	A. N. F. Rees	(b) M. Murphy
§Taff-Ely, Mid Glamorgan	92,301	9,261,257	D. Gethin	(a) E. P. Lewis
§Torfaen, Gwent	90,700	9,105,357	M. B. Mehta	(a) C. Little
§Vale of Glamorgan, South Glamorgan	109,100	13,724,350	J. R. Gau	(a) Mrs. R. E. E. Parsons
§Wrexham Maelor, Clwyd	113,900	11,442,298	S. F. Tongue	(a) J. W. Coleman
§Ynys Môn (Isle of Anglesey), Gwynedd	68,500	7,552,307	E. L. Gibson	(a) Mrs. A. Lloyd Jones

THE KINGDOM OF SCOTLAND

Position and Extent.—The Kingdom of Scotland occupies the northern portion of the main island of Great Britain and includes the Inner and Outer Hebrides, and the Orkney, Shetland, and many other islands. The Kingdom lies between 60° 51′ 30″ and 54° 38′ N. latitude and between 1° 45′ 32″ and 6° 14′ W. longitude, its southern neighbour being the Kingdom of England, with the Atlantic Ocean on the N. and W., and the North Sea on the E. The greatest length of the mainland (Cape Wrath to the Mull of Galloway) is 274 miles, and the greatest breadth (Buchan Ness to Applecross) is 154 miles. The customary measurement of the Island of Great Britain is from the site of John o' Groats house, near Duncansby Head, Caithness (at the N.E. extremity of the island) to Land's End, Cornwall (at the S.W. extremity), a total distance of 603 miles in a straight line and (approximately) 900 by road.

The total area of the Kingdom is 30,414 square miles (land 29,795; inland water 619). The population (1981 Census) was 5,130,735 (males 2,466,437; females 2,664,298). The average density of the population in 1981 was 168 persons per square mile.

Relief.—There are three natural orographic divisions of Scotland. The Southern Uplands have their highest points in Merrick (2,766 feet), Rhinns of Kells (2,669 feet), and Cairnsmuir of Carsphairn (2,614 feet), in the west; and the Tweedsmuir Hills in the east (*Hartfell* 2,651 ft., *Dollar Law* 2,682 ft., *Broad Law* 2,756 ft.). The Central Lowlands, formed by the valleys of the Clyde, Forth and Tay, divide the Southern Uplands from the heather-clad Northern Highlands, which extend almost from the extreme north of the mainland to the central lowlands, and are divided into a northern and southern system by the *Great Glen*. The Grampian Mountains, which entirely cover the southern Highland area, include in the west *Ben Nevis* (4,406 ft.), the highest point in the British Isles, and in the east the Cairngorm Mountains (*Cairn Gorm* 4,084 ft., *Braeriach* 4,248 ft., *Ben Macdui* 4,296 ft.). The north-western Highland area contains in the mountains of Wester and Eastern Ross *Carn Eige* (3,880 ft.) and *Sgurr na Lapaich* (3,775 ft.).

Created, like the Central Lowlands, by a major geological fault, the *Great Glen* (60 miles long) runs between Inverness and Fort William, and contains Loch Ness, Loch Oich and Loch Lochy. These are linked to each other and to the north-east and south-west coasts of Scotland by the Caledonian Canal, providing a navigable passage between the Moray Firth and the Inner Hebrides.

Hydrography.—The western coast of Scotland is fragmented by peninsulas and islands, and indented by fjords (sea-lochs), the longest of which is *Loch Fyne* (42 miles long) in Argyllshire. Although the east coast tends to be less fractured and lower, there are several great drowned inlets (firths), e.g. Firth of Forth, Firth of Tay, Moray Firth, as well as the Firth of Clyde in the west.

The lochs are the principal hydrographic feature of the Kingdom, both on the mainland and in many of the islands. The largest in the Kingdom and in Great Britain is *Loch Lomond* (27 square miles in area), in the Grampian valleys; the longest and deepest is *Loch Ness* (24 miles long and 800 feet deep), in the Great Glen; and Lochs Shin (20 miles) and Maree in the northern Highlands.

The longest river in Scotland is the *Tay* (117 miles), noted for its salmon. It flows into the North Sea, with Dundee on the estuary, which is spanned by the *Tay Bridge* (10,289 ft.) opened in 1887 and the *Tay Road Bridge* (7,365 ft.) opened in 1966. Other noted salmon rivers are the *Dee* (90 miles) which flows into

the North Sea at Aberdeen, and the *Spey* (110 miles), the swiftest flowing river in the British Isles, which flows into Moray Firth. The *Tweed*, which gave its name to the woollen cloth produced along its banks, marks in the lower stretches of its 96-mile course the border between Scotland and England.

The most important river commercially is the *Clyde* (106 miles), formed by the junction of the Daer and Portrail water, which flows through the city and port of Glasgow to the Firth of Clyde. During its course it passes over the picturesque *Falls of Clyde*, Bonnington Linn (30 ft.), Corra Linn (84 ft.), Dundaff Linn (10 ft.) and Stonebyres Linn (80 ft.), above and below Lanark. The *Forth* (66 miles), upon which stands Edinburgh, the capital, is spanned by the *Forth (Railway) Bridge* (1890), which is 5,330 feet long, and the *Forth (Road) Bridge* (1964), which has a total length of 6,156 ft. (over water) and a single span of 3,000 ft.

The highest waterfall in Scotland, and the British Isles, is *Eas a'Chùal Aluinn* with a total height of 658 ft., which falls from Glas Bheinn in Sutherland. The *Falls of Glomach*, on a head-stream of the Elchaig in Wester Ross, have a drop of 370 ft.

Gaelic Language.—According to the 1981 Census, 82,620 people, mainly in the Highlands and western coastal regions, were able to speak, read or write the Scottish form of Gaelic.

THE SCOTTISH ISLANDS

The Hebrides did not become part of the Kingdom of Scotland until 1266, when they were ceded to Alexander III by Magnus of Norway. Orkney and Shetland fell to the Scottish Crown as a pledge for the unpaid dowry of Margaret of Denmark, wife of James III, in 1468, the Danish suzerainty being formally relinquished in 1590.

Orkney.—The Orkney Islands (total area 375½ square miles) lie about six miles north of the mainland, separated from it by the Pentland Firth. Of the 90 islands and islets (holms and skerries) in the group, about one-third are inhabited. The total population at the 1981 Census was 19,040; the 1981 populations of the islands shown here include those of smaller islands forming part of the same civil parish.

Mainland	14,299	Shapinsay	345
Eday	154	South Ronaldsay	1,188
Hoy and Graemsay	80	Stronsay	462
Papa Westray	94	Walls and Flotta	761
Rousay and Egilsay	264	Westray	741
Sanday and North Ronaldsay	652		

The islands are rich in Pictish and Scandinavian remains, the most notable being the Stone Age village of Skara Brae, the burial chamber of Maeshowe, the many brochs (Pictish towers) and St. Magnus Cathedral. Scapa Flow, between the Mainland and Hoy, was the war station of the British Grand Fleet from 1914–19 and the scene of the scuttling of the surrendered German High Seas Fleet (June 21, 1919).

Most of the islands are low-lying and fertile, and farming (principally beef cattle) is the main industry. Flotta, to the south of Scapa Flow, is now the site of the oil terminal for the Piper, Claymore and Tartan fields in the North Sea.

Capital.—Kirkwall (population 6,881) on Mainland.

Shetland.—The Shetland Islands (total area, 551 square miles; population (1981 Census) 27,271) lie about 50 miles north of the Orkneys, with Fair Isle about half way between the two groups. Out Stack, off Muckle Flugga, one mile north of Unst, is the most northern part of the British Isles (60° 51′ 30″ N. lat.). There are over 100 islands, of which 16 are inhabited.

Mainland	22,184	Muckle Roe	101
Bressay	335	Out Skerries	79
East and West Burra,		Papa Stour	29
and Trondra	930	Unst	1,206
Fair Isle	69	Whalsay	1,026
Fetlar	102	Yell	1,168
Foula	39		

Shetland's many archaeological sites include Jarlshof, Mousa and Clickhimin, and its long connection with Scandinavia has resulted in a strong Norse influence on its place names and dialect. Industries include fishing, knitwear and farming. In addition to the fishing fleet there are fish processing factories, while the traditional handknitting of Fair Isle and Unst is supplemented now with machine knitted garments,. Farming is mainly crofting, with sheep being raised on the moorland and hills of the islands. Latterly the islands have become an important centre of the North Sea oil industry, with pipelines from the Brent and Ninian fields running to the terminal at Sullom Voe, the largest of its kind in Europe. Lerwick is the main centre for supply services for offshore oil exploration and development.

Capital.—Lerwick (population 7,901) on Mainland.

The Hebrides.—Until the closing years of the 13th century "The Hebrides" included other Scottish islands in the Firth of Clyde, the peninsula of Kintyre (Argyllshire), the Isle of Man, and the (Irish) Isle of Rathlin. The origin of the name is stated to be the Greek *Eboudai*, latinized as *Hebudes* by Pliny, and corrupted to its present form. The Norwegian name *Sudreyjar* (Southern Islands) was latinized as *Sodorenses*, a name that survives in the Anglican bishopric of "Sodor and Man."

There are over 500 islands and islets, of which about 100 are inhabited, though mountainous terrain and extensive peat bogs mean that only a fraction of the total area is under cultivation. Stone, Bronze and Iron Age settlement has left many remains, including those at Callanish on Lewis, and Norse colonization has influenced language, customs and place-names. Occupations include farming (mostly crofting and stock-raising), fishing and the manufacture of tweeds and other woollens. Tourism is also an important factor in the economy.

The **Inner Hebrides** lie off the west coast of Scotland and relatively close to the mainland. The largest and best-known is *Skye* (area 643 sq. miles; pop. 8,139; chief town, Portree), which contains the Cuillin Hills (*Sgurr Alasdair* 3,257 feet), the Red Hills (*Beinn na Caillich* 2,403 feet) as well as *Bla Bheinn* (3,046 feet) and *The Storr* (2,358 feet). Skye is also famous as the refuge of Prince Charles Edward (The Young Pretender) in 1746. Other islands in the Highland Region include *Raasay* (pop. 182) *Rum, Eigg* and *Muck*. Islands in the Strathclyde Region include *Arran* (pop. 4,726) containing *Goat Fell* (2,868 feet); *Coll and Tiree* (pop. 933); *Colonsay and Oronsay* (pop. 137); *Islay* (area 235 sq. miles; pop. 3,997); *Jura* (area 160 sq. miles; pop. 239) with a range of hills culminating in the Paps of Jura (*Beinn-an-Oir*, 2,576 feet, and *Beinn Chaolais*, 2,477 feet); *Mull* (area 367 sq. miles; pop. 2,605; chief town Tobermory) containing *Ben More* (3,171 feet).

The **Outer Hebrides**, separated from the mainland by the Minch, now form the Western Isles Islands Council area (area 1,119 sq. miles; pop. (1981 Census) 31,842). The main islands are *Lewis with Harris* (area 770 sq. miles, pop. 23,390), whose chief town, Stornoway (pop. 13,409), is the administrative headquarters of the Islands Council; *North Uist* (pop. 1,454); *South Uist* (pop. 2,223); *Benbecula* (pop. 1,988) and *Barra*

(pop. 1,232). Other inhabited islands include *Bernera* (292), *Berneray* (134), *Eriskay* (219), *Grimsay* (206), *Scalpay* (461) and *Vatersay* (108).

EARLY HISTORY

Prehistoric Man.—The *Picts*, believed to be of non-Aryan origin, seem to have inhabited the whole of North Britain and to have spread over the north of Ireland. Remains are most frequent in Caithness and Sutherland and the Orkney Islands. Celtic *Goidels, Brythons* and *Belgae* arrived from Belgic Gaul during the latter part of the Bronze Age and in the early Iron Age, and except in the extreme north of the mainland and in the islands, the civilization and speech of the people were definitely Celtic at the time of the Roman invasion of Britain.

The Roman Invasion.—In A.D. 80 Julius Agricola extended the Roman conquests in Britain by advancing into Caledonia, but after a victory at *Mons Graupius* he was recalled. About 60 years later the Roman frontier was carried to the isthmus between the Forth and Clyde and marked by the *Wall of Pius*, but before the close of the second century the northern limit of Roman Britain had receded to *Hadrian's Wall*.

The Scots.—*Christianity* was introduced into Southern Caledonia about 380 by missionaries from Romanized Britain, who penetrated to the northern districts and islands. After the withdrawal (or absorption) of the Roman garrison of Britain there were many years of tribal warfare between the Picts and Scots (the Gaelic tribe then dominant in Ireland), the Brythonic Waelisc (Welsh) of Strathclyde (Southwest Scotland and Cumberland), and the Anglo-Saxons of the Lothians. The Waelisc were isolated from their kinsmen in Wales by the victory of the West Saxons at Chester (613), and towards the close of the 9th century the Scots under *Kenneth Macalpine* became the dominant power in Caledonia. In the reign of Malcolm I (943–954) Strathclyde was brought into subjection, the English lowland kingdom (Lothian) being conquered by Malcolm II (1005–1034). From the late 11th century until the middle of the 16th there were constant wars between Scotland and England, the outstanding figures in the struggle being *William Wallace*, who defeated the English at Stirling Bridge (1297) and *Robert Bruce*, who won the victory of Bannockburn (1314). James IV and many of his nobles fell at the disastrous battle of *Flodden* (1513).

In 1603 James VI of Scotland succeeded Queen Elizabeth I on the throne of England (his mother, Mary Queen of Scots, was the great-granddaughter of Henry VII), his successors reigning as Sovereigns of Great Britain. After the abdication (by flight) in 1689 of James VII and II, the crown devolved upon William III (grandson of Charles I) and Mary (daughter of James VII and II) and then upon Anne (second daughter of James VII and II). Anne's children died young, and the throne devolved upon George I (great-grandson of James VI and I). In 1689 Graham of Claverhouse "roused the Highlands" on behalf of James VII and II, but died after a military success at Killiecrankie. In 1715, armed risings led to the indecisive battle of Sheriffmuir, but the Jacobite movement died down until 1745, when Prince Charles Edward defeated the Royalist troops at Prestonpans and advanced to Derby in England (1746). From Derby, the adherents of "James VIII and III" (the title claimed for his father by Prince Charles Edward) fell back on the defensive, and the movement was finally crushed by the Royalist troops under the Duke of Cumberland at *Culloden* (April 16, 1746).

AREA AND POPULATION OF SCOTTISH REGIONS

Region	Administrative Headquarters	Area (acres)	Population	Rateable value £
Borders	Newtown St. Boswells	1,154,366	100,953	19,041,472
Central	Stirling	1,015†	272,662	74,800,105
Dumfries and Galloway	Dumfries	1,574,074	146,156	28,424,100
Fife	Glenrothes, Fife	322,960	342,826	86,473,076
Grampian	Aberdeen	2,150,731	494,491	132,534,620
Highland	Inverness	10,091†	196,079	45,566,472
Lothian	Edinburgh	433,600	744,802	215,580,126
Orkney	Kirkwall	217,600	19,239	13,735,255
Shetland	Lerwick	551†	23,454	32,894,539
Strathclyde	Glasgow	5,348†	2,338,077	577,541,930
Tayside	Dundee	2,897†	394,895	94,417,599
Western Isles	Stornoway, Lewis	1,119†	31,519	4,950,084

† Sq. miles

CHIEF EXECUTIVES, DIRECTORS OF FINANCE AND CHAIRMEN OF REGIONAL AND ISLANDS COUNCILS

Region	Chief Executive	Director of Finance	Convener
Borders	K. J. Clark	P. Jeary	T. Hunter
Central	E. Geddes	J. Broadfoot	J. Anderson, C.B.E.
Dumfries and Galloway	L. T. Carnegie, C.B.E.	J. C. Stewart	J. V. M. Jameson
Fife	J. M. Dunlop, C.B.E.	D. Mitchell	R. Gough
Grampian	J. D. Macnaughton	T. E. Carter	J. Sorrie
Highland	R. H. Stevenson	J. W. Bremner	I. S. Campbell, O.B.E.
Lothian	R. G. E. Peggie	B. Grosset	B. A. Meek, O.B.E.
Orkney	H. A. G. Lapsley	R. H. Gilbert	E. R. Eunson
Shetland	M. Gerrard	M. Green	A. I. Tulloch
Strathclyde	R. Calderwood	K. R. Paterson	J. Burns
Tayside	J. A. Wallace	I. B. McIver	W. K. Fitzgerald, C.B.E.
Western Isles	R. MacIver	D. G. Macleod	A. Matheson

PRECEDENCE IN SCOTLAND

The Sovereign.

The Prince Philip, Duke of Edinburgh.

The Lord High Commissioner to the General Assembly (while that Assembly *is sitting*).

The Duke of Rothesay (eldest son of the Sovereign). H.R.H. Prince Andrew. H.R.H. Prince Edward.

Nephews of the Sovereign.

Lords Lieutenant of Counties, Lord Provosts of Counties of Cities, and Sheriffs Principal (successively—within their own localities and during holding of office).

Lord Chancellor of Great Britain.

Moderator of the General Assembly of the Church of Scotland.

The Prime Minister.

Keepers of the Great Seal and of the Privy Seal (successively—if Peers).

Hereditary Lord High Constable of Scotland. Hereditary Master of the Household.

Dukes (successively) of England, Scotland, Great Britain and United Kingdom (including Ireland since date of Union).

Eldest sons of Dukes of the Blood Royal.

Marquesses, in same order as Dukes.

Dukes' eldest sons.

Earls, in order as Dukes.

Younger sons of Dukes of Blood Royal.

Marquesses' eldest sons.

Dukes' younger sons.

Keepers of the Great Seal and of the Privy Seal (successively—if not Peers).

Lord Justice General.

Lord Clerk Register.

Lord Advocate.

Lord Justice Clerk.

Viscounts, in order as Dukes.

Earls' eldest sons.

Marquesses' younger sons.

Lord-Barons, in order as Dukes.

Viscounts' eldest sons.

Earls' younger sons.

Lord-Barons' eldest sons.

Knights of the Garter.

Privy Councillors not included in above ranks.

Senators of Coll. of Justice (Lords of Session).

Viscounts' younger sons.

Lord-Barons' younger sons.

Sons of Life Peers.

Baronets.

Knights of the Thistle.

Knights of other Orders as in England.

Solicitor-General for Scotland.

Lord Lyon King of Arms.

Sheriffs Principal (except as shown in column 1).

Knights Bachelor.

Sheriffs Substitute.

Companions of Orders as in England.

Commanders of Royal Victorian and British Empire Orders.

Eldest sons of younger sons of Peers.

Companions of Distinguished Service Order.

Members (Class 4) Royal Victorian Order.

Officers of British Empire Order.

Knights' eldest sons successively (from Garter to Bachelor).

Members of Class 5 of Royal Victorian Order.

Members of British Empire Order.

Baronets' younger sons.

Knights' younger sons.

Queen's Counsel.

Barons-feudal.

Esquires.

Gentlemen.

SCOTTISH DISTRICT COUNCILS

District	Administrative Headquarters	Population	Rateable Value £	Chief Executive	Chairman (a) Convener (b) Provost (c) Lord Provost
Aberdeen City (5)	Aberdeen	214,100	69,840,000	J. M. Wilson	(c) H. E. Rae
Angus (9)	Forfar	93,163	18,314,424	W. S. McCulloch	(b) A. Welsh
Annandale and Eskdale (3)	Annan	35,701	6,318,500	J. A. Whitecross	(a) R. G. Greenhow
Argyll and Bute (8) ...	Lochgilphead	63,684	14,894,990	M. A. J. Gossip	D. C. Currie
Badenoch and Strathspey (6)......	Kingussie	10,003	2,500,000	H. G. McCulloch	A. J. McCook
Banff and Buchan (5) .	Banff	83,086	23,254,129	R. W. Jackson†	(a) N. Cowie
Bearsden and Milngavie (8)	Bearsden	39,697	9,392,528	A. R. Rae	(b) R. W. Robinson
Berwickshire (1)	Duns	18,370	3,255,000	R. A. Christie	Capt. J. Evans
Caithness (6).........	Wick	27,239	4,202,000	A. Beattie	(a) J. M. Young
Clackmannan (2)	Alloa	48,116	11,444,700	A. E. O'Neill	(a) J. Millar
*Clydebank (8)	Clydebank	51,500	10,410,975	J. M. Brown	(b) H. Duffy
Clydesdale (8)	Lanark	57,361	10,944,320	P. W. Daniels	(a) Miss M. T. Hodgson
Cumbernauld and Kilsyth (8)	Cumbernauld	62,794	°14,257,000	J. Hutton	(b) J. Pollock
Cumnock and Doon Valley (8)	Cumnock	44,500	6,668,681	D. T. Hemmings	(a) D. Shankland
Cunninghame (8).....	Irvine	137,683	30,799,500	J. M. Miller	(a) Mrs. T. Beattie
Dumbarton (8)	Dumbarton	78,780	20,656,958	L. MacKinnon	(b) R. McNamara
Dundee City (9)	Dundee	180,748	49,414,307	J. F. Hoey	(c) T. Mitchell
Dunfermline (4)	Dunfermline	127,484	32,232,793	G. Brown	(b) R. Mill
East Kilbride (8)......	East Kilbride	82,524	20,783,375	W. G. McNay, O.B.E.	(b) G. McKillop
East Lothian (7)	Haddington	80,838	19,287,203	D. B. Miller	T. Wilson
Eastwood (8)	Giffnock	54,371	11,156,600	M. D. Henry	(b) Mrs. J. M. Edmondson
Edinburgh City (7) ...	Edinburgh	440,902	149,086,584	M. M. Duncan	(c) Rt. Hon. J. H. McKay
Ettrick/Lauderdale (1)	Galashiels	33,291	6,428,366	J. D. Bell	(b) A. L. Tulley
Falkirk (2)	Falkirk	143,921	42,376,000	J. P. H. Paton	(b) J. Docherty
Glasgow City (8)	Glasgow	747,486	205,998,000	S. F. Hamilton	(c) Rt. Hon. R. Gray
Gordon (5)	Inverurie	67,684	11,226,693	A. C. Kennedy	(a) J. B. Presly, M.B.E.
Hamilton (8)	Hamilton	107,222	21,248,614	F. T. Malcolm	(b) S. Casserly
Inverclyde (8)	Greenock	100,229	24,259,890	I. C. Wilson	(b) Sir Simpson Stevenson
Inverness (6)	Inverness	57,526	16,172,000	B. Wilson	(b) A. G. Sellar
Kilmarnock and Loudoun (8)	Kilmarnock	81,459	17,520,813	R. W. Jenner Miss E. M. G. Cockburn	(b) T. Ferguson
Kincardine and Deeside (5).........	Stonehaven	44,314	8,387,031		D. J. Mackenzie
Kirkcaldy (4)	Kirkcaldy	149,500	37,523,000	J. M. Smith†	(a) R. King
Kyle and Carrick (8) ..	Ayr	112,934	28,300,931	I. R. D. Smillie	(b) G. Macdonald
Lochaber (6)	Fort William	19,561	4,633,000	D. A. B. Blair	C. Neilson
Midlothian (7)	Dalkeith	82,362	15,853,000	D. W. Duguid	(a) W. Steele
Monklands (8)	Coatbridge	109,984	21,435,570	J. S. Ness	(b) E. Cairns
Moray (5)............	Elgin	84,880	19,517,695	J. P. C. Bell	E. Aldridge
Motherwell (8)	Motherwell	149,914	35,090,000	J. Bonomy	(b) J. McGhee
Nairn (6)	Nairn	10,039	1,850,000	F. T. Milne†	(b) Lt. Col. H. McLean, M.B.E.
Nithsdale (3)	Dumfries	57,076	12,046,128	(vacant)	(b) K. Cameron
North-East Fife (4) ...	Cupar	65,851	15,365,000	Brig. D. Anderson, C.B.E.	D. A. Barrie
Perth and Kinross (9) .	Perth	119,749	26,827,000	J. E. D. Cormie	(b) J. M. Mathieson
Renfrew (8)	Paisley	206,971	51,450,107	W. McIntosh	(b) W. McCready
Ross and Cromarty (6)	Dingwall	47,351	12,326,608	A. Cuthbertson	(a) G. D. Finlayson
Roxburgh (1).........	Hawick	35,210	6,290,712	J. F. A. Richardson	J. R. Irvine
Skye and Lochalsh (6).	Portree	10,963	1,696,373	D. H. Noble	J. F. Munro
Stewartry (3)	Kirkcudbright	23,033	4,436,853	W. L. Dick-Smith	(a) J. Nelson, T.D.
Stirling (2)	Stirling	80,800	20,455,723	J. Cairns	(a) J. Wyles
Strathkelvin (8)	Kirkintilloch	88,534	16,600,000	C. Mallow	(b) R. M. Coyle
Sutherland (6)	Golspie	13,000	1,712,220	D. W. Martin	Mrs. L. Mackenzie
Tweeddale (1)	Peebles	14,373	3,155,821	G. Gardiner	J. P. Campbell
West Lothian (7)	Bathgate	140,700	31,501,118	D. Morrison	(a) D. McCauley
Wigtown (3)	Stranraer	30,150	5,268,526	A. Geddes	(a) D. R. Robinson

° 1983 figure.　　† Director of Administration.

REGIONS.—(1) Borders; (2) Central; (3) Dumfries and Galloway; (4) Fife; (5) Grampian; (6) Highland; (7) Lothian; (8) Strathclyde; (9) Tayside.

LORD LIEUTENANTS IN SCOTLAND

Region	Title	Name
Borders	Berwickshire	Lt. Col. W. B. Swan, C.B.E., T.D.
	Roxburgh, Ettrick and Lauderdale	The Duke of Buccleuch and Queensbery, K.T., V.R.D
	Tweeddale	Lt. Col. A. M. Sprot of Haystoun, M.C.
Central	Clackmannan	The Earl of Mar and Kellie
	Stirling and Falkirk	Lt. Col. J. Stirling of Garden
Dumfries & Galloway	Dumfries	Lt. Col. A. J. Jardine Paterson, O.B.E.
	The Stewartry of Kirkcudbright	The Lord Sinclair, M.V.O.
	Wigtown	Maj. H. J. Brewis
Fife	Fife	Sir John Edward Gilmour, Bt., D.S.O., T.D.
Grampian	Aberdeenshire	Sir Maitland Mackie, C.B.E.
	Banffshire	Col. T. R. Gordon-Duff of Drummuir, M.C.
	Kincardineshire	The Viscount of Arbuthnott, D.S.C.
	Morayshire	Capt. I. M. Tennant
Highland	Caithness	The Viscount Thurso
	Inverness	Col. Sir Donald Hamish Cameron of Lochiel, K.T., C.V.O., T.D.
	Nairn	The Earl of Leven and Melville
	Ross and Cromarty	Vice-Adm. Sir John Hayes, K.C.B., O.B.E.
	Sutherland	Col. A. MacD. Gilmour, O.B.E., M.C.
Lothian	East Lothian	The Earl of Wemyss and March, K.T.
	Midlothian	Sir John Dutton Clerk of Penicuik, Bt., C.B.E., V.R.D.
	West Lothian	The Marquess of Linlithgow, M.C.
Strathclyde	Argyll and Bute	The Lord Maclean, K.T., P.C., G.C.V.O., K.B.E.
	Ayr and Arran	Col. B. M. Knox, M.C., T.D.
	Dunbartonshire	Brig. A. S. Pearson, C.B., D.S.O., O.B.E, M.C., T.D.
	Lanarkshire	Col. The Lord Clydesmuir, K.T., C.B., M.B.E., T.D.
	Renfrewshire	Maj. J. D. M. Crichton Maitland
Tayside	Angus	The Earl of Dalhousie, K.T., G.C.V.O., G.B.E., M.C.
	Perth and Kinross	Maj. D. H. Butter, M.C.
Orkney	Orkney	Col. R. A. A. S. Macrae, M.B.E.
Shetland	Shetland	M. M. Shearer
Western Isles	Western Isles	The Earl Granville, M.C.

NOTE.—The Lord Provosts of the four city districts of Aberdeen, Dundee, Edinburgh and Glasgow are Lord Lieutenants for those districts *ex officio.*

PRINCIPAL SCOTTISH CITIES

EDINBURGH

EDINBURGH, the Capital of Scotland, has a municipal area of 100·6 sq. miles. The city is built on a group of hills and contains in Princes Street one of the most beautiful thoroughfares in the world. The principal buildings are the Castle, which includes St. Margaret's Chapel, the oldest building in Edinburgh, and near it, the Scottish National War Memorial; the Palace of Holyroodhouse; Parliament House, the present seat of the judicature; two universities (Edinburgh and Heriot-Watt); St. Giles' Cathedral (restored 1879–83); St. Mary's (Scottish Episcopal) Cathedral (Sir Gilbert Scott); the General Register House (Robert Adam): the National and the Signet Libraries; the National Gallery; the Royal Scottish Academy; and the National Portrait Gallery. The city is governed by the City of Edinburgh District Council which includes the area of South Queensferry, Kirkliston, Currie, Ratho and Balerno.

GLASGOW

GLASGOW, a Royal Burgh, City, largest District in the Strathclyde Region, and the principal commercial and industrial centre in Scotland, has a municipal area of 49,743 acres. The city occupies the north and south banks of the Clyde, one of the chief commercial estuaries in the world. The principal industries include engineering, aero and marine engines, chemicals, printing, etc. The city has also developed recently as a tourism and conference centre. The chief buildings are the 13th century Gothic Cathedral, the University (Sir Gilbert Scott), the City Chambers, Pollok House, the Transport Museum, Kelvingrove Art Galleries, the Burrell Collection museum and the Mitchell Library. The city is home of the Scottish National Orchestra, Scottish Opera, Scottish Ballet, etc.

ABERDEEN

ABERDEEN, 126 miles N.E. of Edinburgh, received its charter as a Royal Burgh from William the Lion in 1179. Scotland's third largest city, it covers an area of 73·25 square miles. Aberdeen is the principal commercial and administrative centre in the N. of Scotland, the second largest Scottish fishing port and the main European centre for offshore oil exploration. It is also an ancient university town and distinguished research centre. Other industries include engineering, shipbuilding, food processing, textiles, paper manufacturing and chemicals. Places of interest: King's College, St. Machar's Cathedral, Brig o' Balgownie, the Kirk of St. Nicholas, Mercat Cross, Marischal College, Provost Skene's House, Art Gallery, James Dun's House (children's museum) and Provost Ross's House (maritime museum).

DUNDEE

DUNDEE, a Royal Burgh, City, is the administrative centre of Tayside Region. Situated on the north bank of the Tay estuary, it extends over 96 square miles. The city's first class port and dock installations are important to the offshore oil industry and the airport also provides servicing facilities. Principal industries include textiles, watches and clocks, computers and other electronic industries, printing, tyre manufacture, food processing, carpets, heavy electrical engineering, shipbuilding and marine engineering and clothing manufacture. Six sites, totalling 210 acres, have Enterprise Zone status. These include the Technology Park, airport and port, as well as city centre commercial sites and general industrial sites. The University of Dundee was established in 1967. The unique City Churches—three churches under one roof, together with the 15th century St. Mary's Tower—are the most prominent architectural feature.

CHIEFS OF CLANS AND NAMES IN SCOTLAND

THE ROYAL HOUSE: H.M. The Queen

AGNEW: Sir Crispin Hamlyn Agnew of Lochnaw, Bt., 6 Palmerston Road, Edinburgh.

ARBUTHNOTT: Viscount of Arbuthnott, D.S.C., Arbuthnott House, Laurencekirk, Kincardineshire.

BARCLAY: Peter C. Barclay of that Ilk, Gatemans, Stratford St. Mary, Colchester, Essex.

BORTHWICK: Maj. J. H. S. Borthwick of Borthwick, T.D., Crookston, Midlothian.

BOYD: Lord Kilmarnock, Casa de Mondragon, Ronda (Malaga), Spain.

BOYLE: Rr. Adm. The Rt. Hon. The Earl of Glasgow, C.B., D.S.C., Kelburn, Fairlie, Ayrshire.

BRODIE: Ninian Brodie of Brodie, Brodie Castle, Forres.

BRUCE: Earl of Elgin and Kincardine, Broomhall, Dunfermline, Fife.

BUCHAN: David S. Buchan of Auchmacoy, Auchmacoy, Ellon, Aberdeenshire.

BURNETT: J. C. A. Burnett of Leys, Crathes Castle, Kincardineshire.

CAMERON: Col. Sir Donald Hamish Cameron of Lochiel, K.T., C.V.O., T.D., Achnacarry, Spean Bridge, Inverness.

CAMPBELL: Duke of Argyll, Inveraray, Argyll.

CARMICHAEL: Richard John Carmichael of Carmichael, Carmichael, Thankerton, Biggar, Lanarkshire.

CARNEGIE: Earl of Southesk, K.C.V.O., Kinnaird Castle, Brechin.

CATHCART: Maj. Gen. The Rt. Hon. The Earl Cathcart, C.B., D.S.O., M.C., 2 Pembroke Gardens, W.8.

CHARTERIS: Earl of Wemyss and March, K.T., Gosford House, Longniddry, East Lothian.

CHISHOLM: Alastair Chisholm of Chisholm (*The Chisholm*), Silver Willows, Bury St. Edmunds.

CLAN CHATTAN: M. K. Mackintosh of Clan Chattan, Maxwell Park, Gwelo, Zimbabwe.

COCHRANE: Earl of Dundonald, Lochnell Castle, Ledaig, Argyllshire.

COLQUHOUN: Sir Ivar Colquhoun of Luss, Bt., Rossdhu, Luss, Dunbartonshire.

CRANSTOUN: Lt. Col. Alastair Cranstoun of that Ilk, M.C., Corehouse, Lanarkshire.

CRIGHTON: Charles Crighton of that Ilk, Monzie, Perth.

DARROCH: Captain Duncan Darroch of Gourock. The Red House, Branksome Park Rd., Camberley.

DRUMMOND: Earl of Perth, P.C., Stobhall, Perth.

DUNBAR: Sir Jean Ivor Dunbar of Mochrum, Bt., 45/55 39th Street, Long Island City, New York.

DUNDAS: David D. Dundas of Dundas, 8 Derna Road, Kenwyn 7700, South Africa.

ELIOTT: Sir Arthur Eliott of Stobs, Bt., Redheugh, Newcastleton, Roxburghshire.

ERSKINE: Earl of Mar and Kellie, Claremont House, Alloa.

FARQUHARSON: Capt. A. A. C. Farquharson of Invercauld, M.C., Invercauld, Braemar.

FERGUSSON: Sir Charles Fergusson of Kilkerran, Bt., Kilkerran, Maybole, Ayrshire.

FORBES: Lord Forbes, K.B.E., Balforbes, Alford, Aberdeenshire.

FORSYTH: Alistair Forsyth of that Ilk, Ethie Castle, by Arbroath, Angus.

FRASER: Lady Saltoun, Cairnbulg Castle, Fraserburgh, Aberdeenshire.

FRASER (OF LOVAT)*: Lord Lovat, D.S.O., M.C., T.D., Balblair House, Beauly, Inverness-shire.

GAYRE: Lt. Col. Robert Gayre of Gayre and Nigg, 1–3 Gloucester Lane, Edinburgh.

GORDON: Marquess of Huntly, Aboyne Castle, Aberdeenshire.

GRAHAM: Duke of Montrose, Auchmar, Drymen, Stirlingshire.

GRANT: Lord Strathspey, 111 Elms Ride, West Wittering, Sussex.

HAIG: Earl Haig, O.B.E., Bemersyde, Melrose, Roxburgh.

HANNAY: Ramsey W. R. Hannay of Kirkdale and of that Ilk, Cardoness House, Gatehouse-of-Fleet, Kirkcudbright.

HAY: Earl of Erroll, Wolverton Farm, Wolverton, Basingstoke, Hants.

HUNTER: Neil A. Hunter of Hunterston, Tour d'Escas, Carretera d'Escas, La Massana, Andorra.

IRVINE OF DRUM: C. F. Irvine of Drum, 29 Forest Road, Hoylake, Wirral, Merseyside.

JARDINE: Col. Sir William Jardine of Applegirth, Bt., O.B.E., T.D., Denbie, Lockerbie, Dumfriesshire.

JOHNSTONE: Patrick Johnstone of Annandale and of that Ilk, Raehills, Dumfriesshire.

KEITH: The Earl of Kintore, Glenton House, Rickarton, Stonehaven, Aberdeenshire.

KENNEDY: Marquess of Ailsa, O.B.E., Cassillis House, Maybole, Ayrshire.

KERR: Marquess of Lothian, Monteviot, Ancrum, Roxburgh.

KINCAID: A. C. Kincaid of Kincaid, Murarashi, Kenya.

LAMONT: Peter N. Lamont of that Ilk, St. Patrick's College, Manley, N.S.W. 2095, Australia.

LENNOX: Dennis P. H. Lennox of that Ilk, Pools Farm, Dowton on the Rock, Ludlow, Shropshire.

LESLIE: Earl of Rothes, Tanglewood, West Tytherley, Salisbury, Wilts.

LINDSAY: Earl of Crawford and Balcarres, P.C., Balcarres, Colinsburgh, Fife.

LOCKHART: Angus Hew Lockhart of the Lee, Newholme, Dunsyre, Lanark.

McBAIN: J. H. McBain of McBain, 7025, North Finger Rock Place, Tucson, Arizona, U.S.A.

MALCOLM (MACCALLUM): Robin N. L. Malcolm of Poltalloch, Duntrune Castle, Lochgilphead, Argyll.

MACDONALD: Lord Macdonald (*The Macdonald of Macdonald*), Ostaig House, Skye.

MACDONALD OF CLANRANALD*: Ranald A. Macdonald of Clanranald, 55 Compton Road, N.1.

MACDONALD OF SLEAT (CLAN HUSTEAIN)*: Sir Ian Bosville-Macdonald of Sleat, Bt., Thorpe Hall, Rudston, Driffield, Yorks.

MACDONELL OF GLENGARRY*: Air Cdre. Aeneas R. MacDonell of Glengarry, C.B., D.F.C., Elonbank, Castle Street, Fortrose, Ross-shire.

MACDOUGALL: Madame Coline MacDougall of MacDougall, Dunollie, Argyll.

MACGREGOR: Sir Gregor MacGregor of MacGregor, Bt., Bannatyne, Newtyle, Angus.

MACKAY: Lord Reay, 11 Wilton Crescent, S.W.1.

MACKENZIE: Earl of Cromartie, M.C., T.D., Castle Leod, Strathpeffer, Ross-shire.

MACKINNON: The Mackinnon of Mackinnon, Field End, Nailsbourne, nr. Taunton, Somerset.

MACKINTOSH: The Mackintosh of Mackintosh, O.B.E., Moy Hall, Inverness.

MACLACHLAN: Madame Marjorie MacLachlan of MacLachlan, Castle Lachlan, Argyll.

MACLAREN: Donald MacLaren of MacLaren and Achleskine, British Military Government, Berlin (B.F.P.O. 45).

MACLEAN: Lord Maclean, P.C., K.T., G.C.V.O., K.B.E., Duart Castle, Mull.

MACLENNAN: Ronald G. MacLennan of MacLennan, Clachan, Lochbroom, Ullapool, Ross-shire.

MACLEOD: J. MacLeod of MacLeod, Dunvegan Castle, Skye.

MACMILLAN: Gen. Sir Gordon MacMillan of Mac-Millan, K.C.B., K.C.V.O., C.B.E., D.S.O., M.C., Finlay-stone, Langbank, Renfrewshire.

MACNAB: J. C. Macnab of Macnab (*The Macnab*), Finlanrig, Killin, Perthshire.

MACNAGHTEN: Sir Patrick Macnaghten of Macnaghten and Dundarave, Bt., Dundarave, Bushmills, Co. Antrim.

MACNEIL OF BARRA: Ian R. Macneil of Barra (*The Macneil of Barra*), Kismull Castle, Barra.

MACPHERSON: Sir William Macpherson of Cluny, T.D., Q.C., Newtown Castle, Blairgowrie, Perth-shire.

MACTHOMAS: Andrew P. C. MacThomas of Finegand, c/o The Clan MacThomas Society, 29 Bennan Gardens, Broughty Ferry, Dundee.

MAITLAND: Earl of Lauderdale, The Tower, Castle Gogar, Costorphine, Edinburgh.

MAR: Countess of Mar, 10 Cranberry Drive, Stour-port-on-Severn, Worcs.

MARJORIBANKS: William Marjoribanks of that Ilk, Kirklands of Forglen, Turriff, Aberdeenshire.

MATHESON: Sir Torquhil Matheson of Matheson, Bt., Sanderwick Court, Frome, Somerset.

MENZIES: David R. Menzies of Menzies, 20 Nardina Crescent, Dalkeith, Western Australia.

MOFFAT: Francis Moffat of that Ilk, Redacres, Moffat, Dumfriesshire.

MONCREIFFE: Sir Iain Moncreiffe of that Ilk, Bt., C.V.O., Easter Moncreiffe, Bridge of Earn, Per-thshire.

MONTGOMERIE: Earl of Eglinton and Winton, The Dutch House, West Green, Hartley Wintney, Hants.

MORRISON: Dr. Iain M. Morrison of Ruchdi, Todhurst Farm, Lake Lane, Barnham, Sussex.

MUNRO: Patrick G. Munro of Foulis, T.D., Foulis Castle, Ross.

MURRAY: Duke of Atholl, Blair Castle, Blair Atholl, Perthshire.

NICOLSON (OF SCORRYBREAC)*: Ian Nicolson of Scor-rybreac, P.O. Box 420, Ballina, N.S.W. 2478.

OGILVY: Earl of Airlie, Cortachy Castle, Kirriemuir, Angus.

RAMSAY: Earl of Dalhousie, K.T., G.C.V.O., G.B.E., M.C., Brechin Castle, Angus.

RATTRAY: James S. Rattray of Rattray, Craighall, Rattray, Perthshire.

ROBERTSON: Alexander Gilbert Haldane Robertson of Struan (*Struan-Robertson*), The Breach Farm, Goudhurst Road, Cranbrook, Kent.

ROLLO: Rt. Hon. Lord Rollo, Pitcairns, Dunning, Perthshire.

ROSE: Miss Elizabeth Rose of Kilravock, Kilravock Castle, Croy, Inverness-shire.

ROSS: David C. Ross of that Ilk, Shandwick, Glen-rothes, Fife.

RUTHVEN: Earl of Gowrie, Castlemartin, Kilcullen, Co. Kildare, Eire.

SCOTT: Duke of Buccleuch and Queensberry, K.T., V.R.D., Bowhill, Selkirk.

SCRYMGEOUR: The Earl of Dundee, Birkhill, Cupar, Fife.

SEMPILL: Lady Sempill, Druminnor Castle, Rhynie, Aberdeenshire.

SHAW: John Shaw of Tordarroch, Newhall, Balblair, By Conon Bridge, Ross-shire.

SINCLAIR: Earl of Caithness, Rangers Lodge, Charl-bury, Oxon.

STIRLING: Sir Charles Norman Stirling of Cader, K.C.M.G., K.C.V.O., 17 Park Row, Farnham, Surrey.

SUTHERLAND: Countess of Sutherland, House of Tongue, Borea, Sutherland.

SWINTON: W. F. H. Swinton of that Ilk, 23301 8th Avenue S.S., Calgary, Alberta, Canada.

URQUHART: Kenneth T. Urquhart of that Ilk, 4713 Orleans Blvd., Jefferson, Louisiana, U.S.A.

WALLACE: Lt.-Col. M. R. Wallace of that Ilk, Hilton of Gask, Auchterarder, Perthshire.

WEDDERBURN OF THAT ILK: The Master of Dundee, Birkhill, Cupar, Fife.

WEMYSS: David Wemyss of that Ilk, Wemyss Castle, Fife.

Only chiefs of *whole* Names or Clans are included (except certain special instances (marked *), who though not chiefs of a "whole name", were, or are, for some reason, (*e.g.* the Macdonald forfeiture), independent. Under decision (*Campbell-Gray*, 1950) that a bearer of a "double or triple-barrelled" surname cannot be held chief of a part of such, several others cannot be included in the list at present.

NEW TOWNS IN GREAT BRITAIN

Commission for the New Towns. Glen House, Stag Place, S.W.1.—The Commission was established on October 1, 1961, under the New Towns Act, 1959, to take over new towns in England and Wales from development corporations whose purposes have been achieved or substantially achieved. The assets and liabilities of Crawley and Hemel Hempstead Development Corporations were transferred to the Commission in 1962 and those of the Hatfield and Welwyn Garden City Development Corporations in 1966. In April, 1978, the Commission transferred to the local authorities under the New Towns (Amendment) Act 1976 the housing and related assets of its four towns. The Commission assumed responsibility for the residual industrial and commercial assets in Corby, Harlow and Stevenage in 1980 and in Bracknell in 1982 and will do so later in such other new towns as the Government may decide. All local offices, except at Corby, have now been closed.

Chairman, Sir Neil Shields, M.C.
Deputy Chairman, A. Jones.
Members, R. B. Caws; J. N. C. James; M. A. Hastilow; W. J. Mackenzie, O.B.E.; The Lord Sefton of Garston; P. M. Vine, C.B.E.; Sir Gordon Roberts, C.B.E.
Chief Executive, D. M. Woodhall.

BRACKNELL, Berks.—Area, 3,303 acres. Population, 48,800.
CORBY, Northants.—*Manager,* M. V. P. Hart. *Offices,* 9 Queen's Square, Corby, Northants. Area, 4,423 acres. Population, 47,200.
CRAWLEY, Sussex.—Area 6,047 acres. Population, 72,200.
HARLOW, Essex.—Area, 6,395 acres. Population, 79,300.
HATFIELD, Herts.—Area, 2,340 acres. Population, 25,200.
HEMEL HEMPSTEAD, Herts.—Area, 5,910 acres. Population, 76,300.
STEVENAGE, Herts.—Area, 6,256 acres. Population, 74,400.
WELWYN GARDEN CITY, Herts.—Area, 4,317 acres. Population, 40,500.

DEVELOPMENT CORPORATIONS
England and Wales

AYCLIFFE, Co. Durham.—Formed 1947. *Chairman,* Sir Michael Straker, C.B.E. *General Manager,* G. Philipson, D.F.C. *Offices,* Acorn House, Newton Aycliffe, nr. Darlington, Co. Durham. Area, 3,150 acres. Population, 25,500. Estimated eventual population, 32,000.
BASILDON, Essex.—Formed 1949. *Chairman,* Dame Elizabeth Coker, D.B.E. *General Manager,* D. Galloway. *Offices,* Gifford House, Basildon, Essex. Area, 7,818 acres. Population, 101,833. Estimated eventual population, 130,000.
CENTRAL LANCASHIRE NEW TOWN, Lancs.—Formed 1970. *Chairman,* Sir Frank Pearson. *General Manager,* R. W. Phelps. *Offices,* Cuerden Hall, Bamber Bridge, Preston, Lancs. Area, 35,255 acres. Population, 250,000. Estimated eventual population, 260,000.
CWMBRAN, Gwent.—Formed 1949. *Chairman,* Lt. Col. G. D. Inkin, O.B.E. *Managing Director,* W. Howlett. *Offices,* Gwent House, Town Centre, Cwmbran, Gwent. Area, 3,500 acres. Population, 45,600. Estimated eventual population, 50,000.
MILTON KEYNES, Bucks.—Formed 1967. *Chairman,* Sir Henry Chilver. *General Manager,* F. C. Henshaw. *Offices,* Saxon Court, 502 Avebury Boulevard, Milton Keynes. Area, 22,000 acres. Population, 115,000. Estimated eventual population, 200,000.
NORTHAMPTON.—Formed 1968. *Chairman,* A. R. Davis, C.B.E. *General Manager,* L. Austin-Crowe.

Offices, Cliftonville House, Bedford Road, Northampton. Area, 20,000 acres. Population, 163,000. Estimated eventual population, 180,000.
PETERBOROUGH.—Formed 1967. *Chairman,* J. Rowe, C.B.E. *General Manager,* J. R. Beckett. *Offices,* Touthill Close, City Road, Peterborough. Area, 15,940 acres. Population, 125,450. Estimated eventual population, 150,000.
PETERLEE, Co. Durham.—Formed 1948. *Chairman,* Sir Michael Straker, C.B.E. *Managing Director,* G. Philipson, D.F.C. *Offices,* Lee House, Town Centre, Peterlee. Co. Durham. Area, 2,977 acres. Population, 23,400. Estimated eventual population, 30,000.
REDDITCH, Worcs.—Formed 1964. *Chairman,* Prof. D. Hinton. *Managing Director,* N. More. *Offices,* Holmwood, Plymouth Road, Redditch, Worcs. Area, 7,180 acres. Population, 71,000. Estimated eventual population, 85,000. (Redditch Development Corporation was wound up in April 1984 and will be dissolved in June 1985).
SKELMERSDALE, Lancs.—Formed 1962. *Chairman,* W. A. D. Windham. *Managing Director,* E. Bradbury. *Offices,* Pennylands, Skelmersdale, Lancs. Area, 4,124 acres. Population, 42,000. Estimated eventual population, 60,500. (It is intended to wind up Skelmersdale Development Corporation in April 1985.)
TELFORD, Shropshire.—Formed 1963. *Chairman,* The Lord Northfield. *General Manager,* J. Boyce. *Offices,* Priorslee Hall, Telford, Shropshire. Area, 19,300 acres. Population, 108,000. Estimated eventual population, 150,000
WARRINGTON AND RUNCORN, Cheshire.—Amalgamated 1981 (Warrington formed 1968; Runcorn formed 1964). *Chairman,* D. Forster. *General Manager,* D. J. Binns. *Offices,* New Town House, Buttermarket St., Warrington, Cheshire. Area, Warrington 18,612 acres; Runcorn 7,234 acres. Population, Warrington 140,000; Runcorn 66,000. Estimated eventual population, Warrington 170,000; Runcorn 90,000.
WASHINGTON, Tyne and Wear.—Formed 1964. *Chairman,* Prof. W. G. McClelland. *Managing Director,* R. G. Tilmouth. *Offices,* Usworth Hall, Washington. Area, 5,610 acres. Population, 55,500. Estimated eventual population, 80,000.

DEVELOPMENT BOARD FOR RURAL WALES.—Formed 1977. *Chairman,* F. L. Morgan, M.B.E.. *Offices,* Ladywell House, Newtown, Powys.

Scotland

CUMBERNAULD, Strathclyde.—Formed 1956. *Chairman,* F. M. Cook, O.B.E. *Chief Executive,* Brig. C. H. Cowan, C.B.E.. *Headquarters,* Cumbernauld House, Cumbernauld. Area, 7,788 acres. Population, 49,500. Estimated eventual population, 70,000.
EAST KILBRIDE, Strathclyde.—Formed 1947. *Chairman,* J. A. Denholm. *Managing Director,* G. B. Young, C.B.E. *Offices,* Atholl House, East Kilbride. Area, 10,250 acres. Population, 70,500. Estimated eventual population, 82,500.
GLENROTHES, Fife.—Formed 1948. *Chairman,* Sir George Sharp, O.B.E. *Chief Executive,* W. M. Cracknell. *Offices,* Balbirnie House, Glenrothes, Fife. Area, 5,765 acres. Population, 37,500. Estimated eventual population, 55,000.
IRVINE, Ayrshire.—Formed, 1966. *Chairman,* Sir Charles O'Halloran. *Managing Director,* Brig. R. A. S. Rickets. *Offices,* Perceton House, Irvine, Ayrshire. Area, 12,440 acres. Population, 56,600. Estimated eventual population, 95,000.
LIVINGSTON, West Lothian.—Formed, 1962. *Chairman,* R. S. Watt. *Chief Executive,* J. Wilson. *Offices,* Sidlaw House, Almondvale, Livingston. Area, 6,868 acres. Population, 39,300. Estimated eventual population, 70,000.

Northern Ireland

(For geographical and historical notes on Ireland, see Index)

The usually resident population of Northern Ireland, as revised, at the 1981 Census was 1,556,039 (males, 761,882; females, 794,157) compared with a total population of 1,536,065 at the Census of 1971. (N.B. This revised figure takes account of the population effect of non-enumerated households, estimated at 74,000 persons.) In 1981 the number of persons in the various religious denominations (expressed as percentages of the total usually resident population) were: Roman Catholic, 28·0; Presbyterian, 22·9; Church of Ireland, 19·0; Methodist, 4·0; others 7·6; not stated, 18·5. Northern Ireland has a total area of 5,516 sq. miles (land, 5,267 sq. miles; inland water and tideways, 249 sq. miles) with a density of population of 282 persons per sq. mile in 1981.

Constitution and Government. A separate parliament and executive Government was established for Northern Ireland in 1921 by the Government of Ireland Act. The Northern Ireland Constitution Act, 1973, abolished the post of Governor and Parliament of Northern Ireland and provided for the transfer of certain legislative functions to a Northern Ireland Assembly and Executive. Devolved Government came into operation with effect from January 1, 1974 but when the Executive collapsed the Northern Ireland Assembly was prorogued on May 29, 1974. The Northern Ireland Constitution Act, 1974, which became law in July 1974, made provision for temporary arrangements for the government of Northern Ireland by the Secretary of State for Northern Ireland and also provided for the holding of elections and a Constitutional Convention. Direct Rule continues in being under the terms of the Northern Ireland Act 1974.

In April 1982, the Government published a White Paper entitled "Northern Ireland : A Framework for Devolution", in which it signified its intention to hold elections for a Northern Ireland Assembly, which would initially perform a consultative and deliberative role, but in due course would also be able to assume administrative and legislative responsibility for transferred functions if a sufficient level of agreement on how these powers should be exercised could be reached by the parties represented in it. The Government subsequently presented to Parliament a Northern Ireland Bill aimed at giving effect to these proposals, and elections to a 78 member Ulster Assembly were held on October 20th, 1982. The first meeting of the Assembly took place on November 11, 1982, although Nationalist members have not taken their seats. In November 1983 Ulster Unionist Party members withdrew but have since returned and the Assembly and its Departmental Committees (one for each N.I. Department) continue to function.

The Assembly, pending agreement on the devolution of powers, has consultative and scrutinising functions; by May 1984 it had produced 66 reports, considered 18 proposals for draft Orders in Council, and in addition some 380 pieces of subordinate legislation had been referred to it. In May 1984 the Assembly set up a Committee on devolution to consider and report on how the Assembly might be strengthened and progress made towards legislative and selective devolution.

Members of the Northern Ireland Assembly

Abbreviations: All. = Alliance Party; D.U.P. = Democratic Unionist Party; Ind.U. = Independent Unionist; O.U.P. = Official Unionist Party; S.D.L.P. = Social Democratic and Labour Party; S.F. = Sinn Fein; U.P.U.P = Ulster Popular Unionist Party.

G. Adams (S.F.) *Belfast West*; W. A. F. Agnew (O.U.P.) *South Antrim*; J. A. Allen (O.U.P.) *Londonderry*; J. H. Allister (D.U.P.) *North Antrim*; Rev. W. J. Beattie (D.U.P.) *South Antrim*; J. R. Beggs (O.U.P.) *North Antrim*; W. B. Bell (O.U.P.) *South Antrim*; W. G. Bleakes (O.U.P.) *North Down*; W. Brown (O.U.P.) *South Down*; D. J. M. Burchill (O.U.P.) *Belfast East*; D. N. Calvert (D.U.P.) *Armagh*; G. L. Campbell (D.U.P.) *Londonderry*; O. G. Carron (S.F.) *Fermanagh, South Tyrone*; J. Carson (O.U.P.) *Belfast North*; S. A. Close (All.) *South Antrim*; D. S. Cook (All.) *Belfast South*; C. J. Cousley (D.U.P.) *North Antrim*; J. A. Currie (S.D.L.P.) *Fermanagh, South Tyrone*; J. W. Cushnahan (All.) *North Down*; I. Davis (D.U.P.) *South Antrim*; W. A. B. Douglas (O.U.P.) *Londonderry*; Col. Rt. Hon. Lord Dunleath (All.) *North Down*; Mrs. D. Dunlop (O.U.P.) *Belfast East*; S. N. Farren (S.D.L.P.) *North Antrim*; F. Feely (S.D.L.P.) *South Down*; R. Ferguson (O.U.P.) *Fermanagh, South Tyrone*; C. J. Forsythe (O.U.P.) *South Antrim*; Rev. T. J. I. Foster (D.U.P.) *Fermanagh, South Tyrone*; J. A. Gaston (O.U.P.) *North Antrim*; H. J. S. Gibson (D.U.P.) *North Down*; W. Glendinning (All.) *Belfast West*; G. Graham (D.U.P.) *South Down*; P. D. Haughey (S.D.L.P.) *Mid-Ulster*; Dr. J. G. Hendron (S.D.L.P.) *Belfast West*; J. Hume (S.D.L.P.) *Londonderry*; A. J. Kane (D.U.P.) *Mid-Ulster*; J. A. Kilfedder (U.P.U.P.) *North Down*; T. J. Kirkpatrick (O.U.P.) *Belfast South*; H. A. Logue (S.D.L.P.) *Londonderry*; J. McAllister (S.F.) *Armagh*; R. L. McCartney (O.U.P.) *North Down*; W. J. McClure (D.U.P.) *Londonderry*; R. S. McCrea (D.U.P.) *Belfast South*; Rev. R. T. W. McCrea (D.U.P.) *Mid-Ulster*; R. R. McCullough (O.U.P.) *South Down*; J. H. McCusker (O.U.P.) *Armagh*; J. McDonald (S.D.L.P.) *South Antrim*; K. W. Maginnis (O.U.P.) *Fermanagh, South Tyrone*; E. K. McGrady (S.D.L.P.) *South Down*; J. M. McGuinness (S.F.) *Londonderry*; P. Maguire (All.) *Belfast North*; J. McKee (D.U.P.) *North Antrim*; A. J. Morrow (All.) *Belfast East*; Mrs. M. K. McSorley (S.D.L.P.) *Mid-Ulster*; G. H. Mawhinney (All.) *South Antrim*; F. Millar (Ind.U.) *Belfast North*; F. Millar (O.U.P.) *Belfast South*; J. H. Molyneaux (O.U.P.) *South Antrim*; D. G. Morrison (S.F.) *Mid-Ulster*; O. J. Napier (All.) *Belfast East*; J. L. Neeson (All.) *North Antrim*; H. News (S.D.L.P.) *Armagh*; J. F. Nicholson (O.U.P.) *Armagh*; P. O'Donoghue (S.D.L.P.) *South Down*; P. J. O'Hare (S.D.L.P.) *Belfast North*; Rev. Dr. I. R. K. Paisley (D.U.P.) *North Antrim*; T. Passmore (O.U.P.) *Belfast West*; J. W. Pentland (D.U.P.) *North Down*; P. D. Robinson (D.U.P.) *Belfast East*; G. Seawright (D.U.P.) *Belfast North*; Mrs. M. Simpson (O.U.P.) *Armagh*; J. A. Speers (O.U.P.) *Armagh*; Rev. W. M. Smyth (O.U.P.) *Belfast South*; Rt. Hon. J. D. Taylor (O.U.P.) *North Down*; R. Thompson (D.U.P.) *South Antrim*; W. J. Thompson (O.U.P.) *Mid-Ulster*; D. Vitty (D.U.P.) *Belfast East*; J. H. Wells (D.U.P.) *South Down*.

Seats: O.U.P. 27; D.U.P. 21; S.D.L.P. 13; All. 10; S.F. 5; Ind.U. 1; U.P.U.P. 1.

THE PRIVY COUNCIL

Sir John Andrews, K.B.E. (1957); R. J. Bailie (1971); D. W. Bleakley (1971); R. H. Bradford (1969); Capt. Viscount Brookeborough (1971); W. Craig (1963); Sir Lancelot Curran (1957); J. Dobson (1969); W. K. Fitzsimmons (1965); Lt. Col. the Lord Glentoran (1953); *Lord Justice* Jones (1965); Mr. Justice Kelly (1969); H. V. Kirk (1962); Capt. W. J. Long (1966); Lord Lowry (*Lord Chief Justice*) (1971); R. W. B. McConnell (1964); W. B. McIvor (1971); W. J. Morgan (1961); The Lord Moyola (1966); Sir Ivan Neill (1950); The Lord O'Neill of the Maine (1956); Sir Robert Porter, Q.C. (1969); Lord Rathcavan (1969); R. Simpson (1969); J. D. Taylor (1970); H. W. West (1960).

GOVERNMENT OFFICES

Department of Finance and Personnel

Permanent Secretary, Dr. W. G. H. Quigley.
Under Secretaries, P. Carvill; J. S. Crozier; J. B. C. Lyttle; W. J. Hodges; J. L. Semple; R. B. Spence.
Assistant Secretaries, D. W. Alexander; J. M. Dowdall.
Asst. Secs., Resources Group, Dr. J. J. M. Harbison; Dr. D. G. Slattery; P. J. Small (*Financial Planning*); R. G. Smartt.
Asst. Secs., Efficiency Services, Dr. D. J. Allott; W. G. Purdy.
Asst. Secs., Personnel Group, R. J. Anderson; J. B. Forsythe; J. Maguire.
Asst. Sec., Central Secretariat, T. Pearson.
Senior Principals, J. E. Henderson; R. J. Reid.
Solicitor, W. E. M. Reid.
Commissioner of Valuation, D. W. M. Deyermond.
First Legislative Draftsman, T. R. Erskine.

Department of Education

Permanent Secretary, J. H. Parkes.
Under Secretaries, A. J. Green; E. G. Martin.
Senior Chief Inspector, I. H. N. Wallace.
Asst. Secretaries, A. M. Dodds; N. R. Jennings; R. T. Holmes; K. H. Clark; R. D. Hill; P. S. Holmes; J. S. Smith; T. Johnston.
Chief Inspectors, N. Morrison; J. B. S. O'Kelly.

Department of Environment

Permanent Secretary, D. Barry.
Under Secretaries, J. M. Beckett (*Personnel, Information Systems Unit, Solicitors Branch, Central Management, Local Government, Conservation, Historic Monuments and Buildings, Environmental Protection*); D. J. Clement (*Works Service, Public Records Office, Ordnance Survey, Land Registry, Registry of Deeds, Finance, Rates*); J. B. McAllister (*Housing*); F. McCann (*Planning, Comprehensive Development, Lands Service, Development Officer Services*); J. A. G. Whitlaw (*Roads, Water, Transport*).
Director, Town and Country Planning Service, J. B. Davidson.
Director, Water Service, E. O'Hara.
Director, Roads Service, T. A. Warnock.
Director, Works Services, J. Brennan.
Assistant Secretaries, W. Black; W. N. Campbell; H. E. Carson; J. Cowan; W. E. C. Ford; N. Hamilton; J. J. McClenahan; R. H. MacKenzie; A. Miller; F. R. Rodgers; E. A. Simpson; J. Kirk; J. McCormick; J. M. Irvine; D. C. White; J. F. Russell.
Chief Local Government Auditor, S. J. Bailie.
Chief Engineer (Roads Service), Dr. W. M. C. Stevenson.
Chief Planning Officer, (vacant).
Chief Engineer (Water Service), S. T. Bratty.
Chief Quantity Surveyor, T. O'Hara.
Chief Survey Officer, M. J. D. Brand.
Chief Civil Engineer, C. E. Ronaldson.
Chief Architect, V. L. Corbett.
Chief M. & E. Engineer, E. Clarke.
Chief Structural Engineer, K. Turkington.

Department of Health & Social Services

Permanent Secretary, Dr. M. N. Hayes.
Under Secretaries, F. A. Elliott; G. Buchanan; R. F. Mills; R. S. Sterling; Miss Z. Davies.
Assistant Secretaries, A. N. Burns; C. McN. Davie; J. G. Hunter; R. J. Minnis; E. H. Elliott; J. Scott; R. Wilson; J. A. Wylie; R. McMurray; A. S. Treacy; D. H. McNally; Miss J. Mills; P. Simpson; Dr. R. W. McQuiston.
Chief Medical Officer, Dr. R. J. Weir.
Deputy Chief Medical Officers, Dr. D. J. Sloan; Dr. W. D. Thornton.
Chief Social Work Adviser, P. J. Armstrong.

Department of Economic Development

Permanent Secretary, K. P. Bloomfield, C.B.*
Under Secretaries, W. N. Drummond; G. F. Loughran; E. Mayne.
Asst. Secretaries, W. T. McCrory; R. J. O'Hara; Miss M. L. Johnston; J. D. M. Thompson; J. J. Monaghan; D. C. Gowdy; D. J. Alexander; Miss J. Dixon; I. W. McMurtry; D. J. Watkins.
Director of Industrial Science Division, J. T. McCullins.
Director of Industrial Accountancy Services, D. Gibson.
Economic Adviser, Prof. W. Black.

Industrial Development Board

Chief Executive, H. S. Tate.
Deputy Chief Executives, A. S. Hopkins; D. Fell.
Directors of Industrial Development, A. I. Devitt; R. A. Burden; F. O. Higgins; W. G. Wilson; P. T. Bill; J. H. Caldwell; P. S. McDowell; F. Hewitt.

Department of Agriculture

Permanent Secretary, Dr. W. H. Jack.
Under Secretaries, J. C. Chalmers; J. Murray.
Chief Scientific Officer, Dr. W. O. Brown.
Chief Agriculture Officer, T. A. Larmour.
Chief Veterinary Officer, E. W. Sullivan.
Chief Forest Officer, J. C. Phillips.
Assistant Secretaries, W. H. Parker; D. M. Carnson; R. E. Aiken; S. R. Armstrong; N. E. Morrison; I. C. Henderson; K. E. Brady.

Head of Northern Ireland Civil Service and Central Secretariat

Head of Northern Ireland Civil Service, K. P. Bloomfield, C.B. (*from Dec. 1, 1984).
Under Secretary, P. Carvill.
Assistant Secretary, T. Pearson.
Director of Information, D. Gilliland, C.B.E.

Exchequer and Audit Department

Comptroller and Auditor-General, L. V. D. Calvert.
Secretary, J. F. Younger.
Directors of Audit, D. A. Kerr; K. G. McCormick; B. H. Poulter; J. G. W. McComish.

Northern Ireland Trade Centre
11 Berkeley Street, W.1.

Principal, R. Bennett.

THE JUDICATURE

Supreme Court of Judicature, The Royal Courts of Justice, Belfast.

The Rt. Hon. The Lord Lowry, *Lord Chief Justice of Northern Ireland.*
The Rt. Hon. Lord Justice (Sir Maurice White) Gibson; The Rt. Hon. Lord Justice (Turlough) O'Donnell; The Rt. Hon. Lord Justice (Sir John William Basil) Kelly; The Hon. Mr. Justice (John Clarke) MacDermott; The Hon. Mr. Justice (Donald Bruce) Murray; The Hon. Mr. Justice (James Brian Edward) Hutton; The Hon. Mr. Justice (John Patrick Basil) Higgins; The Hon. Mr. Justice (Robert Douglas) Carswell.

Lord Chief Justice's Office

Principal Secretary to the Lord Chief Justice and Clerk of the Crown for Northern Ireland, J. A. L. McLean, Q.C.
Legal Secretary to the Lord Chief Justice, R. T. Millar.

Central Office

Master, D. S. Stephens, Q.C.

Office of Care and Protection

Master, R. L. G. Davison.

Chancery Office
Master, V. G. Bridges.

Bankruptcy and Companies Office
Master, J. M. Hunter, C.B.E.

Probate and Matrimonial Office
Master, D. W. G. Heatly.

High Court
Master, V. A. Care, Q.C.

Taxing Office
Master, A. E. Anderson, C.B.E.

Court Funds Office
Accountant, R. A. Guiler.

Recorders
Belfast, J. K. Pringle, Q.C.
Londonderry, J. J. Curran, Q.C.

County Court Judges

Judge Babington, D.S.C., Q.C.; Judge Chambers, Q.C.; Judge Donaldson, Q.C.; Judge Gibson, Q.C.; Judge McKee, Q.C.; Rt. Hon. Judge Sir Robert Porter, Q.C.; Judge Rowland, Q.C.; Judge Russell, Q.C.; Judge Watt, Q.C.

Crown Solicitor, H. A. Nelson.
Director of Public Prosecutions, Sir Barry Shaw, C.B., Q.C.

FLAG.—The national flag is that of the United Kingdom.

BELFAST

BELFAST, a City, the seat of Government of Northern Ireland, situated at the mouth of the River Lagan at its entrance to Belfast Lough, has a municipal area of 16,017 acres, exclusive of tidal water (2,034) and a population (mid-1983) of 322,600. The city received its first charter of incorporation in 1613 and has since grown, owing to its easy access by sea to Scottish coal and iron, to be a great industrial centre. The chief industries are ship-building and the manufacture of aircraft, aerostructure, heavy and light engineering, textiles, ropes and tobacco. Belfast is an important seaport with extensive docks.

The principal buildings are of a relatively recent date and include the Parliament Buildings at Stormont, the City Hall, the Law Courts, the Public Library and the Museum and Art Gallery. The Queen's University (previously Queen's College) was chartered in 1908.

Belfast was created a city in 1888 and the title of Lord Mayor was conferred in 1892.

LONDONDERRY

LONDONDERRY, a City situated on the River Foyle, has a population (mid-1983) of 96,100 and was reputedly founded in 546 by St. Columba. Londonderry (formerly *Derry*) has important associations with the City of London. The Irish Society, under its royal charter of 1613, fortified the city and was for long closely associated with its administration.

Famous for the great siege of 1688–89, when for 105 days the town held out against the forces of James II until relieved by sea, Londonderry was an important naval base throughout the Second World War. Interesting buildings are the Protestant Cathedral of St. Columb's (1633) and the Guildhall reconstructed in 1912 and containing a number of beautiful stained glass windows, many of which were presented by the livery companies of London. The famous Walls are still intact and form a circuit of almost a mile around the old city. The traditional activity in Londonderry is shirtmaking. Other industries include mechanical engineering, automobile components including rubber tyres, cord and synthetic fibre. New industries include the manufacture of bicycles. A large part of Ulster's agricultural export trade passes through the port.

FINANCE

Taxation in Northern Ireland is largely imposed and collected by the United Kingdom Government. After deducting the cost of collections and of Northern Ireland's contributions to the European Economic Community the balance, known as the Attributed Share of Taxation, is paid over to the Northern Ireland Consolidated Fund. Northern Ireland's revenue is insufficient to meet its expenditure and is supplemented by a grant in aid.

	1983–84*	1984–85**
	£	£
Public income.....	2,878,209,314	3,021,719,000
Public expenditure	2,878,079,116	3,021,619,000
	* Outturn	** Estimate

EXTERNAL TRADE*

Tonnes (000)

	1981	1982	1983
Total imports ...	10,154	10,748	10,179
Total exports ...	3,284	3,256	2,524

* Including cross-Channel trade with Great Britain.

PRODUCTION

Industries.—The total value of the industrial production (manufacturing, gas, electricity and water) in Northern Ireland by firms employing 20 or more persons in 1981 was approximately £3,652 million and the number of persons employed about 116,000. The products of the engineering, shipbuilding and aircraft industries which employed 35,000 persons, were valued at £591 million. The textile industries, employing about 13,000 persons, produced products valued at approximately £227 million. The food and drink industry, employing about 20,000 persons, produced goods valued at £1,529 million. The value of clothing manufactured in 1981 was about £131 million.

Minerals.—1,530 persons were employed in mining and quarrying operations in Northern Ireland in 1982 and the minerals raised were valued at £20,727,887.

COMMUNICATIONS

Seaports.—The total number of ships using the principal ports in 1983 was 9,906. Regular ferry and container services operate to ports on the Western coast of Great Britain and the Continent of Europe from Belfast, Larne and Warrenpoint.

Road and Rail Transport.—The Northern Ireland Transport Holding Company is responsible for the supervision of the subsidiary companies, Ulsterbus and Citybus (which operate the public road passenger services), Northern Ireland Railways, and Northern Ireland Airports, which is responsible for running the main airport at Aldergrove, near Belfast. A few privately operated bus services are provided in rural areas under licence. Road freight services are also provided by a large number of hauliers operating competitively under licence.

Air Transport.—Passenger and freight services operate between Belfast International Airport and airports throughout Great Britain. Scheduled air services are available from Belfast (Harbour) Airport to five destinations in Great Britain. In 1983 some 1,400,000 passengers and 22,251 tonnes of freight, including mail, were carried, making it the seventh busiest airport in the United Kingdom. The third stage of a major development programme costing £25 million was completed in 1983; it has doubled the size of the terminal and improved other operational facilities to cater for a continuing growth of traffic.

There are three other licensed aerodromes in Northern Ireland and, apart from some scheduled services in the summer, these are used principally by flying clubs, by private owners and by expanding air taxi businesses flying to destinations in Ireland, Great Britain and continental Europe.

COUNTIES OF NORTHERN IRELAND

Counties and County Boroughs	Area* sq. miles	Lord Lieutenant	High Sheriff, 1984
(1) Antrim	1,093	Capt. R. A. F. Dobbs	J. P. Cooke
Belfast County Borough	25	Lt. Col. the Lord Glentoran, P.C., K.B.E.	Mrs. P. Whittley
(2) Armagh..............	484	Capt. F. M. A. Torrens-Spence, D.S.O., D.S.C., A.F.C., R.N. (retd).	W. H. Jordan
(3) Down	945	Col. W. N. Brann, O.B.E., E.R.D.	J. E. C. Lewis-Crosby, O.B.E.
(4) Fermanagh............	647	Viola, Duchess of Westminster	R. R. A. Eadie
(5) Londonderry†	798	Col. M. W. McCorkell, O.B.E.,	G. A. McIlrath
Londonderry City	3·4	T.D.	Dr. J. Hart
		T. F. Cooke	
(6) Tyrone	1,211	Lt.-Col. J. H. Hamilton Stubber	J. T. Ward

* Excluding inland waters and tideways.   † Excluding the City of Londonderry.

MUNICIPAL DIRECTORY OF NORTHERN IRELAND

District and *Borough Councils	Population	Net Annual Value	Council Clerk	Mayor (†) or Chairman 1984
		£		
*Antrim, (1)	45,500	5,690,078	S. J. Magee	†J. H. Allen
*Ards, (3)...............	59,700	6,515,273	D. J. Fallows	†O. W. Johnston
Armagh, (2)...........	49,900	4,102,105	N. C. H. Megaw	S. Foster
*Ballymena, (1)	55,400	6,862,840	J. S. McIlroy	†A. Spence
*Ballymoney, (1)	24,400	2,075,831	W. J. Williamson	†Mrs. M. G. Holmes
Banbridge, (3)..........	30,600	2,876,918	R. J. Weatherall	S. J. Cowan
Belfast, (1 & 3)	322,600	47,833,894	C. Ward	Rt. Hon. A. Ferguson (*Lord Mayor*)
*Carrickfergus, (1)	28,400	3,875,879	R. Boyd	†C. Johnston
*Castlereagh, (3)	59,800	6,710,697	A. D. Nichol	†E. S. Harper
*Coleraine, (5)	47,400	6,382,060	W. E. Andrews	†W. H. King
Cookstown, (6)	29,300	2,424,328	W. A. Bownes	V. M. McGahie
*Craigavon, (2)	73,400	8,906,945	E. A. McKinley	†G. A. Hatch
Derry, (5)..............	96,100	9,715,051	C. M. Geary	†J. Tierney
Down, (3)..............	54,000	4,864,362	S. Byrne	C. W. Maxwell
Dungannon, (6)	45,700	3,622,951	R. Paisley	W. R. Brown
Fermanagh, (4).........	51,600	4,109,097	G. Burns	C. McClaughry
*Larne, (1).............	29,300	3,485,854	G. McKinley	J. McKee
Limavady, (5)	28,000	2,304,216	(vacant)	S. Gault
*Lisburn, (1 & 3)	87,900	10,566,207	H. A. Duff	†M. McKinney
Magherafelt, (5)	34,200	2,685,672	R. S. McMaster	P. Sweeney
Moyle, (1)	14,500	1,221,051	J. O'Kane	M. McSparren
Newry and Mourne, (3) .	83,400	6,440,728	P. J. O'Hagan	J. F. McEvoy
*Newtownabbey, (1)	71,900	9,773,760	E. Craig	†R. L. Caul
*North Down, (3)........	66,800	7,893,145	J. McKimm	†Mrs. H. E. Bradford
Omagh, (6).............	46,900	3,304,962	D. R. D. Mitchell	B. McGrath
Strabane, (6)	37,000	2,436,684	J. N. McMorran	J. P. Gallagher
Northern Ireland	1,572,700	176,680,588		

Note.—Rates in Northern Ireland are collected by the Department of the Environment (N.I.) and consist of two rates, a regional rate made by the Department of Finance and Personnel and a district rate made by individual District Councils.

THE ISLE OF MAN (MONA)

An island in the Irish Sea, in lat. 54° 3′–54° 25′ N. and long. 4° 18′–4° 47′ W., nearly equidistant from England, Scotland, and Ireland. Although the early inhabitants were of Celtic origin, the Isle of Man was part of the Norwegian Kingdom of the Hebrides until 1266, when this was ceded to Scotland. Subsequently granted to the Stanleys (Earls of Derby) in the 15th century, it was brought under the direct administration of the Crown in 1765. The island forms the bishopric of Sodor and Man.

The total land area is 141,263 acres (221 sq. miles), of which 78,853 acres are under cultivation. The report on the 1981 Census showed a resident population of 64,679 (males, 30,901; females, 33,778). In 1982 births numbered 724 and deaths 981. 284 persons were returned at the Census of 1971 as able to speak the Manx language, compared with 4,657 in 1901, 355 in 1951 and 165 in 1961.

CAPITAL, ΨDouglas. Population (1981), 19,944; ΨCastletown (3,141) is the ancient capital; the other towns are ΨPeel (3,688), and ΨRamsey (5,818).

FLAG.—Three legs in white and gold armed conjoined on a red ground.

GOVERNMENT

The Isle of Man is a self-governing Crown dependency, the Lieutenant-Governor being the Queen's personal representative in the Island. The legislature, called the Tynwald, has two branches—the Legislative Council and the House of Keys. The Council consists of the Bishop of Sodor and Man, the Attorney-General and 8 members chosen by the House of Keys, one of whom is appointed President of the Council. The House of Keys, one of the most ancient legislative assemblies in the world, consists of 24 members, elected by the adult male and female population. Bills after having passed both Houses are signed by the members, and then sent for the Royal Assent. After receiving the Royal Assent, a Bill does not become law unless promulgated within the ensuing twelve months, and on the first "Tynwald Day" (July 5) following it is announced in the English and Manx languages on the Tynwald Hill. On the promulgation taking place a certificate thereof is signed by the Lieutenant-Governor, the President of the Legislative Council and the Speaker of the House of Keys.

ECONOMY

Most of the income generated in the Island is earned in the services sector with financial and business services being considerably larger than the traditional industry of tourism. Manufacturing industry is also a major generator of income whilst the Island's other traditional industries of agriculture and fishing now play a minor role in the economy.

Under the terms of the Island's special relationship with the European Community the Island has free access to E.E.C. markets.

The establishment of a "Freeport" in the Island is seen as a potential area for growth.

The Island's unemployment rate is approximately 8 per cent and price inflation is around 6 per cent per annum.

FINANCE

The Island's Budget for 1984–85 provided for net revenue and capital expenditure of £97,300,000. The principal sources of Government revenue are taxes on income and expenditure. Income tax is payable at a flat rate of 20 per cent. of both personal and company income after the deduction of various allowances. By agreement with the United Kingdom Government, the Island keeps most of its rates of indirect taxation (Value Added Tax and duties) the same as those in the United Kingdom, but this agreement may be terminated by either party. The Island has a reciprocal arrangement with the United Kingdom regarding social security benefits and pensions and the basic rates of contribution are the same in the Isle of Man and United Kingdom. Taxes are also charged on property (rates), but these are comparatively low.

Apart from the social security system, the major Government expenditure items are education and health services. The Island makes a voluntary annual contribution to the United Kingdom for defence and other external services.

Although the Island has a special relationship with the European Community it neither contributes money to nor receives funds from the E.E.C. Budget.

Lieutenant-Governor, His Excellency Rear-Adm. Sir Nigel Cecil, K.B.E., C.B.
A.D.C. to the Lieutenant-Governor, M. M. Wood.
President of the Legislative Council, J. C. Nivison, C.B.E.
Speaker, House of Keys, Sir Charles Kerruish, K.B.E.
Clerk of Tynwald and Secretary to the House of Keys, R. B. M. Quayle.
Attorney-General, T. W. Cain.
Government Secretary, P. J. Hulme.
Government Treasurer, W. Dawson.

THE CHANNEL ISLANDS

Situated off the north-west coast of France (at distances of from ten to thirty miles), are the only portions of the *Dukedom of Normandy* now belonging to the Crown, to which they have been attached ever since the Conquest. They consist of Jersey (28,717 acres), Guernsey (15,654 acres), and the dependencies of Guernsey—Alderney (1,962 acres), Brechou (74), Great Sark (1,035) Little Sark (239), Herm (320), Jethou (44) and Lihou (38)—a total of 48,083 acres, or 75 square miles. In 1981 the population of Jersey was 76,050; and of Guernsey, 54,380; Alderney, 2,000 and Sark, 604.

GOVERNMENT

The islands are Crown dependencies with their own legislative assemblies (the States in Jersey, Guernsey and Alderney, and the Court of Chief Pleas in Sark), and systems of local administration and of law, and their own courts. Acts passed by the States require the sanction of The Queen-in-Council. The British Government is responsible for defence and international relations.

In both Bailiwicks the Lieutenant-Governor and Commander-in-Chief, who is appointed by the Crown, is the personal representative of the Queen and the channel of communication between the Crown (via the Privy Council) and the insular government. The Bailiffs of Jersey and Guernsey, also appointed by the Crown, are President of the States and of the Royal Courts of their respective islands. The government of each Bailiwick is conducted by committees appointed by the States. Justice is administered by the Royal Courts of Jersey and Guernsey, each consisting of the Bailiff and 12 elected Jurats.

Each Bailiwick constitutes a deanery within the diocese of Winchester (*see* page 483).

ECONOMY

A mild climate and good soil have led to the development of intensive systems of agriculture and horticulture, which form a significant part of the economy of the Channel Islands. Equally important are invisible earnings, principally from the tourist trade and from banking and finance, the low rate of income tax (20p. in the £ in Jersey and Guernsey; no tax of any kind in Sark) and the absence of super-tax and death duties making the Channel Islands a popular tax-haven. Principal exports are agricultural produce and flowers; imports are chiefly machinery, manufactured goods, food, fuel and chemicals. Trade with the U.K. is regarded as internal trade.

British currency is legal tender in the Channel Islands but each Bailiwick issues its own coins, and some notes, of the same values as those of the U.K. They also issue their own postage stamps; U.K. stamps are not valid.

LANGUAGE

The official languages are English and French, but French is gradually being supplanted by English, which is the language in daily use. In country districts of Jersey and Guernsey and throughout Sark a Norman-French *patois* is also in use, though to a declining extent.

CHIEF TOWNS, Ψ St. Helier on the south coast of Jersey; Ψ St. Peter Port, on the east coast of Guernsey, and St. Anne's on Alderney.

JERSEY

Lieutenant-Governor and Commander-in-Chief of Jersey, His Excellency Admiral Sir William Pillar, G.B.E., K.C.B. (from 1985) £18,938
Secretary and A.D.C., Comdr. D. M. L. Braybrooke, M.V.O., R.N.
Bailiff of Jersey, Sir Frank Ereaut.
Deputy Bailiff, P. L. Crill, C.B.E.
Attorney-General and Receiver-General, V. A. Tomes.
Solicitor-General, P. M. Bailhache.
Greffier of the States, E. J. M. Potter.
States Treasurer, L. May.

Year to Dec. 31:	1982	1983
Revenue	£130,074,676	£143,680,497
Revenue Expenditure	112,535,570	115,902,191
Capital Expenditure ..		14,825,425
Public Debt	349,543	− 71,254

FLAG.—A white field charged with a red saltire, and coat of arms.

GUERNSEY AND DEPENDENCIES

Lieutenant-Governor and Commander-in-Chief of the Bailiwick of Guernsey and its Dependencies, His Excellency Air Chief Marshal Sir Peter Le Cheminant, G.B.E., K.C.B., D.F.C.(1980).

Secretary and A.D.C., Capt. D. P. L. Hodgetts.
Bailiff of Guernsey, Sir Charles Frossard.
Deputy Bailiff, G. M. Dorey.
H. M. Procureur, de Vic G. Carey.
H. M. Comptroller, A. C. K. Day.
Receiver-General, R. H. Collenette.
States Supervisor, F. N. Le Cheminant.

	1981	1982
Revenue	£54,512,965	£60,464,344
Expenditure	44,318,956	51,537,384
Net Funded Debt ..	955,893	826,354
Note and Coin Issue	24,550,582	27,085,783

FLAG.—White, bearing a red cross of St. George.

Alderney

President of the States, J. Kay-Mouat.
Clerk of the States, W. R. Jones.
Clerk of the Court, P. Beer.

Sark

Le Seigneur of Sark, J. M. Beaumont.
The Seneschal, H. Carré, M.B.E.
The Greffier, J. P. Hamon.
Brechou and Lihou are uninhabited; Herm and Jethou are leased to private tenants.

THE ISLES OF SCILLY

There are about 140 islands and skerries in the Scillies group (total area, 6 square miles) situated 28 miles south-west of Land's End, of which only five are inhabited; Bryher, St. Agnes, St. Martin's, St. Mary's and Tresco. The population is 1,850. The entire group has been designated an Area of Outstanding Natural Beauty, and given National Nature Reserve status by the Nature Conservancy Council because of its unique flora and fauna. Tourism is the basis of the economy of the Isles. The island group is a recognised rural development area.

The islands are administered by the Council of the Isles of Scilly, a 25-member non-political body, which combines the powers and duties of a County Council and a District Council under the Local Government Act 1972 and the Isles of Scilly Orders 1978. Legisla-

tion is specifically applied to the Isles of Scilly by Special Order. The Council is responsible for education, fire services, highways, planning and social services, and Cornwall County Council provides other services on an agency basis: the police service is administered by the Devon and Cornwall Police Authority. The Isles are part of the St. Ives electoral division.

Administrative Headquarters, Town Hall, St. Mary's.
Chairman of the Council, W. C. M. Mumford.
Clerk and Chief Executive, I. Glover.
Chief Financial Officer, L. W. Michell.
Chief Technical Officer, B. M. Lowen.

THE COMMONWEALTH

The Commonwealth is a free association of the 49 sovereign independent states listed below together with their associated states and dependencies.

ANTIGUA AND BARBUDA	MALDIVES
AUSTRALIA	MAURITIUS
BAHAMAS	NAURU
BANGLADESH	NEW ZEALAND
BARBADOS	NIGERIA
BELIZE	PAPUA NEW GUINEA
BOTSWANA	SAINT KITTS-NEVIS
BRUNEI	SAINT LUCIA
CANADA	SAINT VINCENT AND THE
CYPRUS	GRENADINES
DOMINICA	SEYCHELLES
FIJI	SIERRA LEONE
GAMBIA (THE)	SINGAPORE
GHANA	SOLOMON ISLANDS
GREAT BRITAIN	SRI LANKA
GRENADA	SWAZILAND
GUYANA	TANZANIA
INDIA	TONGA
JAMAICA	TRINIDAD AND TOBAGO
KENYA	TUVALU
KIRIBATI	UGANDA
LESOTHO	VANUATU
MALAWI	WESTERN SAMOA
MALAYSIA	ZAMBIA
MALTA	ZIMBABWE

Area and Population.—The total area of the independent Commonwealth is estimated at 10,684,847 square miles. Details of the areas and populations of the Member States and dependencies appear in the following pages. The total population of the Commonwealth is estimated to be about one quarter of the world total.

History and Government.—The status and relationship of member nations was first defined by the Inter-Imperial Relations Committee of the 1926 Imperial Conference, under the chairmanship of Lord Balfour, in what came to be known as the "Balfour Declaration": "They are autonomous communities . . . equal in status, in no way subordinate one to another in any aspect of their domestic or external affairs, though united by a common allegiance to the Crown and freely associated as members of the British Commonwealth of Nations." This formula was given legal substance by the Statute of Westminster 1931.

The concept of a group of countries owing allegiance to a single Crown changed in 1949 when India decided to become a republic, and her continued membership of the Commonwealth was agreed by the other members on the basis of her "acceptance of the King as the symbol of the free association of its independent member nations and as such the Head of the Commonwealth". All member nations continue to acknowledge The Queen as Head of the Commonwealth.

Most members of the Commonwealth are parliamentary democracies.

Queen Elizabeth II is Head of State of 18 member countries of the Commonwealth: Antigua and Barbuda, Australia, the Bahamas, Barbados, Belize, Britain, Canada, Fiji, Grenada, Jamaica, Mauritius, New Zealand, Papua New Guinea, St. Kitts-Nevis, Saint Lucia, Saint Vincent and the Grenadines, Solomon Islands and Tuvalu. In each of these countries (except Britain) The Queen is personally represented by a Governor-General, who holds in all' essential respects the same position in relation to the administration of public affairs in the realm as is held by Her Majesty in Britain (with the exception of certain constitutional functions which are performed by The Queen personally). The Governor-General is

appointed by The Queen on the advice of the Government of the country concerned.

Twenty-five member countries are republics: Bangladesh, Botswana, Cyprus, Dominica, The Gambia, Ghana, Guyana, India, Kenya, Kiribati, Malawi, The Maldives, Malta, Nauru, Nigeria, Seychelles, Sierra Leone, Singapore, Sri Lanka, Tanzania, Trinidad & Tobago, Uganda, Vanuatu, Zambia and Zimbabwe. In Malaysia, the Head of State is elected from among the nine hereditary Malay rulers and holds office for five years. Brunei, Lesotho, Tonga, and Swaziland have their own monarchs. Western Samoa has a Head of State whose functions are analogous to those of a constitutional monarch.

Membership of the Commonwealth is subject only to the approval of existing members. Four countries, The Maldives, Nauru, St. Vincent and Tuvalu, are special members, with the right to participate in all functional Commonwealth meetings and activities, but not to attend Meetings of Commonwealth Heads of Government.

Consultation.—Commonwealth Heads of Government meet every two years to discuss international developments and to consider cooperation among members. These meetings, the successors to the prewar Imperial Conferences, have grown in importance as they are the only regular forum of leaders from both developed and developing countries, constituting a broad sample of the world community. Decisions are reached by consensus, and the views of the meeting are set out in a communiqué.

In addition, there are annual meetings of Finance Ministers, and frequent meetings of Ministers and officials in the fields of trade, education, health, law, science, agriculture, labour and employment, and youth affairs.

Defence.—The Commonwealth is not a military alliance and members make their own defence arrangements in the light of their particular requirements. Some are parties to multi-lateral treaties, for example A.N.Z.U.S. and N.A.T.O. Various members of the Commonwealth cooperate with each other in combined exercises, joint research organizations and exchanges of personnel and training facilities.

Law.—English common law forms the basis of the legal system in many Commonwealth countries, although in most cases it has been radically adapted by statute to suit the individual needs and aspirations of a country, and there are countries where other systems have been adopted—for example, the law of Quebec Province and of Mauritius is founded on that of France, and Roman Dutch law forms the basis in Sri Lanka and Lesotho. Of the non-realms in the Commonwealth, Dominica, The Gambia, Kiribati, Malaysia, Singapore, and Trinidad and Tobago retain the right of appeal to the Judicial Committee of the Privy Council in the United Kingdom, which also hears appeals from a number of realms (Antigua and Barbuda, the Australian States, the Bahamas, Barbados, Belize, Fiji, Jamaica, Mauritius, New Zealand, St. Kitts-Nevis, St. Lucia, St. Vincent and the Grenadines, Tuvalu) and the dependent territories.

Citizenship and Nationality.—Each member of the Commonwealth defines the citizenship and nationality of its own people and determines the status of other Commonwealth nationals within its own boundaries. Members of the Commonwealth differentiate, in greater or lesser degree, as regards the grant of privileges, between citizens of the Commonwealth and aliens. The Republic of Ireland, which in

1949 ceased to be a member of the Commonwealth, is not regarded by the other Commonwealth nations as a foreign country nor her citizens as foreigners.

Finance and Development.—Complete financial autonomy is enjoyed by all members of the Commonwealth. In some countries, customs tariffs are lower for merchandise of Commonwealth origin than for imports from foreign countries. Developing countries, including those in the Commonwealth, obtain preference for exports of industrial goods and some agricultural exports from the developed countries under the Generalised Scheme of Preferences (G.S.P.). Many smaller Commonwealth countries are also party to the Lomé Convention which accords preferential access to the European Economic Community. Many former Commonwealth preferences have been replaced by these arrangements.

British aid for the development needs of the Commonwealth countries and dependent territories are dealt with under the provisions of the Overseas Aid Act 1966, administered by the Overseas Development Administration. This Act succeeds the former Colonial Development and Welfare Acts. Those countries which are party to the Lomé Convention also receive aid under that Convention from the European Community.

Commonwealth Secretariat.—This was established by decision of Commonwealth Heads of Government in 1965, and is the main agency for multilateral communication between Commonwealth Governments on issues relating to the Commonwealth as a whole. It promotes consultation and disseminates information on matters of common concern, organizes meetings and conferences, coordinates Commonwealth activities and provides technical assistance for economic and social development through the Commonwealth Fund for Technical Cooperation. (*See also* p. 381.)

Dependent Territories and Associated States. —Britain, Australia and New Zealand have a number of dependent territories. New Zealand also has two associated states: Cook Islands (since 1965) and Niue (since 1974).

Member States of the Commonwealth
(with dates of independence)

1867* Canada
1901* Australia
1907* New Zealand
1947 India (Republic, 1950)
1948 Sri Lanka (Republic, 1972)
1957 Ghana (Republic, 1960)
     Federation of Malaya (Federation of Malaysia since 1963—indigenous monarchy)
1960 Cyprus (Republic on independence; joined Commonwealth 1961)
     Nigeria (Republic, 1963)
1961 Sierra Leone (Republic, 1971)
     Tanganyika (Republic, 1962; united 1964 with Zanzibar as TANZANIA)

1962 Western Samoa (Republic on independence; joined Commonwealth 1970)
     Jamaica
     Trinidad and Tobago (Republic, 1976)
     Uganda (Republic, 1967)
1963 Kenya (Republic, 1964)
     Singapore (as State in Federation of Malaysia; seceded as Republic, 1965)
1964 Malawi (Republic, 1966)
     Malta (Republic, 1974)
     Zambia (Republic on independence)
1965 The Gambia (Republic, 1970)
     Maldives (Republic, 1968; joined Commonwealth as a Special Member 1982)
1966 Guyana (Republic, 1970)
     Botswana (Republic on independence)
     Lesotho (indigenous monarchy)
     Barbados
1968 Mauritius
     Nauru (Republic on independence—Special Member)
     Swaziland (indigenous monarchy)
1970 Tonga (indigenous monarchy)
     Fiji
1971 Bangladesh (Republic on independence; joined Commonwealth 1972)
1973 Bahamas
1974 Grenada
1975 Papua New Guinea
1976 Seychelles (Republic on independence)
1978 Solomon Islands
     Tuvalu (Special Member)
     Dominica (Republic on independence)
1979 Saint Lucia
     Kiribati (Republic on independence)
     Saint Vincent and the Grenadines (Special Member)
1980 Zimbabwe (Republic on independence)
     Vanuatu (Republic on independence)
1981 Belize
     Antigua and Barbuda
1983 Saint Kitts-Nevis
1984 Brunei (indigenous monarchy)

* These are the effective dates of independence, given legal effect by the Statute of Westminster, 1931.

(The above member states are realms unless otherwise stated.)

Associated States

The Cook Islands and Niue are self-governing states in association with New Zealand, which likewise remains responsible for their external affairs and defence.

Countries which have left the Commonwealth

1949 Republic of Ireland
1961 South Africa
1972 Pakistan

AREA AND POPULATION

Provinces or Territories and Capitals (with official contractions)	Area (English Sq. Miles). Land and Water	Population Census, 1976	Population Census, 1981
Alberta, *Alta.* (Edmonton)...................	255,285	1,838,037	2,237,724
British Columbia, *B.C.* (Victoria)	366,255	2,466,608	2,744,467
Manitoba, *Man.* (Winnipeg)	251,000	1,021,506	1,026,241
New Brunswick, *N.B.* (Fredericton)...........	28,354	677,250	696,403
Newfoundland and Labrador, *Nfld.* (St. John's) .	156,185	574,600	567,681
Nova Scotia, *N.S.* (Halifax)	21,425	828,571	847,442
Ontario, *Ont.* (Toronto)	412,582	8,264,465	8,625,107
Prince Edward Island, *P.E.I.* (Charlottetown) ..	2,184	118,229	122,506
Quebec, *Que.* (Quebec)	594,860	6,234,445	6,438,403
Saskatchewan, *Sask.* (Regina)	251,700	921,323	968,313
Yukon Territory, *Y.T.* (Whitehorse)	207,076	21,836	23,153
Northwest Territories, *N.W.T.* (Yellowknife) ..	1,304,903	42,609	45,741
Total...............	3,851,809	22,992,604	24,343,181

Land Area, 3,560,238 square miles; Water Area, 291,571 square miles.
Of the total immigration of 121,147 in 1982, 9,360 were from the United States, 16,445 from the United Kingdom and Ireland, and 8,674 from the West Indies.

Increase of the People

Census Year	Population Males	Population Females	Population Total	Decennial Increase	Immigrants during Census Year
1901..........	2,751,708	2,619,607	5,371,315	538,076	55,747
1911..........	3,821,995	3,384,648	7,206,643	1,835,328	331,288
1921..........	4,529,643	4,258,306	8,787,949	1,581,306	91,728
1931..........	5,374,541	5,002,245	10,376,786	1,588,837	27,530
1941..........	5,900,536	5,606,119	11,506,655	1,129,869	9,329
1951..........	7,088,873	6,920,556	14,009,429	2,502,774	194,391
1961..........	9,218,893	9,019,354	18,238,247	4,228,818	71,689
1966..........	10,054,344	9,960,536	20,014,880	3,934,087	194,743
1971..........	10,795,370	10,772,940	21,568,310	3,330,063	121,900
1976..........	11,449,520	11,543,080	22,992,605	2,977,725	149,429
1981..........	12,068,290	12,274,890	24,343,180	1,350,575	128,421

Mother Tongues of the Population

In the 1981 Census a distinction was made for the first time between the many aboriginal languages used in Canada, and a greater number of languages were identified as separate mother tongues than in the 1976 Census. N.B. Processing procedures in 1981 were not strictly comparable to those used in 1976.

	1976	1981		1976	1981
English	14,122,770	14,918,445	Indo-Pakistani Languages	58,415	116,990
French	5,887,205	6,249,095	Punjabi	..	53,680
European Languages			Japanese	15,525	20,130
Croatian, Serbian, etc.	77,575	87,870	Korean	..	17,100
Czech and Slovak	34,955	42,825	Philippino and Tagalog	..	44,865
Finnish	28,470	33,380	Semitic Languages	37,100	58,900
German	476,715	522,855	Arabic	..	50,115
Greek	91,530	122,960	African Languages	..	3,270
Italian	484,050	528,775	North American Languages		
Magyar (Hungarian)	69,300	83,720	Native Indian Languages	117,105	127,450
Netherlandic Languages	122,555	156,640	Algonkian Langs.	..	102,905
Dutch and Frisian	114,760	146,830	Cree	..	67,495
Polish	99,845	127,960	Ojibway	..	19,770
Portuguese	126,535	165,510	Athapaskan Langs	..	11,665
Russian	23,485	31,490	Inuktituk	15,900	18,840
Scandinavian Languages	59,410	67,725	Indian, not otherwise specified	..	20,285
Spanish	44,135	70,160	Not Stated	445,020	..
Ukrainian	282,060	292,265			
Yiddish	23,435	32,760	Total	22,992,605	24,343,180
Asian Languages			Indian population (1961) 208,286; (1971), 295,215; (1981), 367,810.		
Armenian	10,335	17,140			
Chinese	132,560	224,030	Eskimo population (1961), 11,835; (1971), 17,550; (1981), 25,390.		
Indo-Chinese Languages	..	41,615			
Vietnamese	..	30,105			

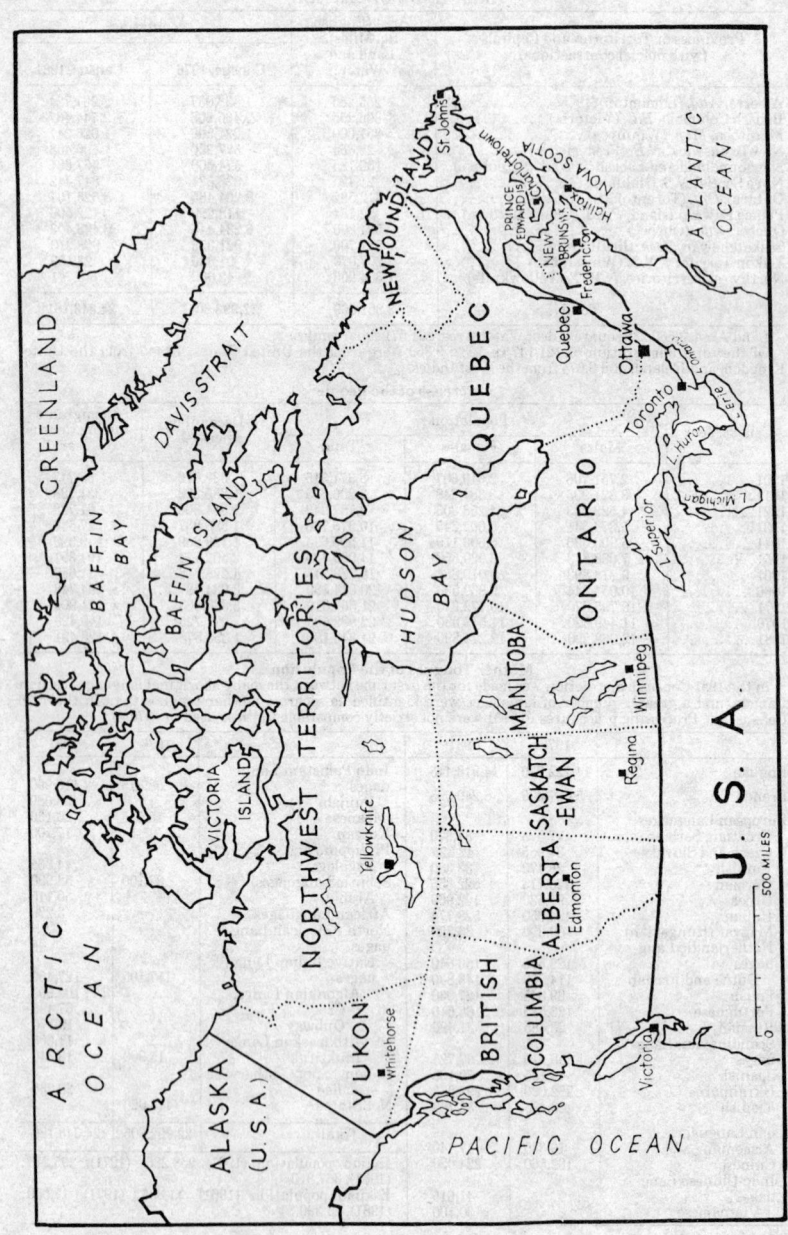

PHYSIOGRAPHY

Canada was originally discovered by Cabot in 1497, but its history dates only from 1534, when the French took possession of the country. The first permanent settlement at Port Royal (now Annapolis), Nova Scotia, was founded in 1605, and Quebec was founded in 1608. In 1759 Quebec was captured by the British forces under General Wolfe, and in 1763 the whole territory of Canada became a possession of Great Britain by the Treaty of Paris of that year. Nova Scotia was ceded in 1713 by the Treaty of Utrecht, the Provinces of New Brunswick and Prince Edward Island being subsequently formed out of it. British Columbia was formed into a Crown colony in 1858, having previously been a part of the Hudson Bay Territory, and was united to Vancouver Island in 1866.

Canada occupies the whole of the northern part of the North American Continent (with the exception of Alaska), from 49° North latitude to the North Pole, and from the Pacific to the Atlantic Ocean. In Eastern Canada, the southernmost point is Middle Island in Lake Erie, at 41° 41'.

Relief.—The relief of Canada is dominated by the mountain ranges running north and south on the west side of the Continent, by the pre-Cambrian shield on the east, with, in between, the northern extension of the North American Plain. From the physiographic point of view Canada has six main divisions. These are: (1) Appalachian-Acadian Region, (2) the Canadian Shield, (3) the St. Lawrence-Great Lakes Lowland, (4) the Interior Plains, (5) the Cordilleran Region and (6) the Arctic Archipelago. The first region occupies all that part of Canada lying southeast of the St. Lawrence. In general, the relief is an alternation of highlands and lowlands and is hilly rather than mountainous. The lowlands area seldom rises over 600 feet above sea level. The great Canadian Shield comprises more than half the area. The interior as a whole is an undulating, low plateau (general level 1,000 to 1,500 feet), with the more rugged relief lying along the border between Northern Quebec and Labrador. Throughout the whole area water or muskeg-filled depressions separate irregular hills and ridges, 150 to 200 feet in elevation. Newfoundland, an outlying portion of the shield, consists of glaciated, low rolling terrain broken here and there by mountains.

The flat relief of the St. Lawrence-Great Lakes lowland varies from 500 feet in the east to 1,700 feet south of Georgian Bay. The whole area in the western part slopes gently to the Great Lakes. The most striking relief is provided by the eastward facing scarp of the Niagara escarpment (elevation 250 to 300 feet). The interior plains, comprising the Pacific Provinces, slope eastward and northward a few feet per mile. The descent from west to east is made from 5,000 feet to less than 1,000 feet in three distinct levels, with each new level being marked by an eastward facing *conteau* or scarp. Horizontal strata and peneplanation make for slight relief of the level to rolling type. Five fairly well-developed topographic divisions mark out the Cordilleran region of western Canada. These are : (1) coastal ranges, largely above 5,000 feet with deep fiords and glaciated valleys, (2) the interior plateau, around 3,500 feet and comparatively level, (3) the Selkirk ranges, largely above 5,000 feet, (4) the Rocky Mountains with their chain of 10,000 to 12,000 feet peaks, and (5) the Peace River or Tramontane region with its rolling diversified country.

The Arctic Archipelago, with its plateau-like character has an elevation between 500 and 1,000 feet, though in Baffin Land and Ellesmere Island the mountain ranges rise to 8,500 and 9,500 feet. Two tremendous waterway systems, the St. Lawrence and

the Mackenzie, providing thousands of miles of water highway, occupy a broad area of lowland with their dominant axis following the edge of the shield.

Climate.—The climate of the eastern and central portions presents greater extremes than in corresponding latitudes in Europe, but in the southwestern portion of the Prairie Region and the southern portions of the Pacific slope the climate is milder. Spring, summer, and autumn are of about seven to eight months' duration, and the winter four to five months.

GOVERNMENT

The Constitution of Canada had its source in the British North America Act of 1867 which formed a Dominion, under the name of Canada, of the four provinces: Ontario, Quebec, New Brunswick and Nova Scotia; to this Federation the other Provinces have subsequently been admitted. Under this Act Canada came into being on July 1, 1867 (Dominion Day), and under the Statute of Westminster, which received the royal assent on Dec. 11, 1931, Canada and the Provinces were exempted (in common with other self-governing Dominions of the Commonwealth of Nations) from the operation of the Colonial Laws Validity Act, the Statute of Westminster having removed all limitations with regard to the legislative autonomy of the Dominions, except that the British North America Act could be amended in important respects only by Acts of the British Parliament.

Provinces admitted since 1867 are: Manitoba (1870), British Columbia (1871), Prince Edward Island (1873), Alberta and Saskatchewan (1905) and Newfoundland (1949).

Agreement was reached in Nov. 1981 between the Federal and Provincial Governments (except Quebec) to patriate the Constitution so that it was amendable only in Canada. The inclusion in the Constitution of a Charter of Rights was also agreed. At the request of the Canadian Parliament, legislation was passed at Westminster and the Constitution formally patriated on 17th April 1982.

The Executive power is vested in a Governor-General appointed by the Sovereign on the advice of the Canadian Ministry, and aided by a Privy Council.

FLAG.—Red maple leaf with 11 points on white square, flanked by vertical red bars one half the width of the square.

Governor General's Household

Governor-General and Commander-in Chief, Her Excellency, The Rt. Hon. Jeanne Sauvé, C.C., C.M.M., C.D.
Secretary to the Governor-General, E. U. Butler, C.V.O.
Deputy Secretary, J. Noiseux.
Comptroller of Household, D. C. McKinnon, C.V.O., C.D.
Director of the Chancellery, R. de C. Nantel, M.V.O., C.D.
Administrative Secretary, E. Joly de Lotbinière.
Cultural Attaché, J.-N. Tremblay.
Travel Officer and Assistant Secretary to the Governor-General, Maj. C. A. Sangster, C.D.
Press Secretary, Mlle. M. Bender.
Aides-de-Camp, Lt. (N) B. Simchison; Capt. P. Richard; Capt. A. Levesque.
Attaché, Mlle. L. Benoit.

The Cabinet

Mr. Pierre Trudeau stood down as Prime Minister at the end of June 1984 and was replaced by Mr. John Turner, who appointed a Cabinet on June 30, and subsequently called a General Election for Sept. 4, 1984.

Prime Minister, John N. Turner.
Government Leader in the Senate, Hon. Allan J. MacEachen.
Deputy P.M.; External Affairs, Hon. Jean Chrétien.
President of the Treasury Board, Hon. Herbert E. Gray.
President of Privy Council; Regional Economic Development; Labour, Hon. André Ouellet.
Finance, Hon. Marc Lalonde.
Employment and Immigration, Hon. John Roberts.
National Health and Welfare, Hon. Monique Bégin.
National Defence, Hon. Jean-Jacques Blais.
International Trade, Hon. Francis Fox.
Energy, Mines and Resources, Hon. Gerald Regan.
Solicitor-General, Hon. Robert Kaplan.
Minister of State (Transport), Hon. William Rompkey.
Public Works; Supply and Services, Hon. Charles Lapointe.
Regional Industrial Expansion; Science and Technology; Communications, Hon. Edward Lumley.
Justice; Attorney-General, Hon. Donald Johnston.
Transport; Wheat Board, Hon. Lloyd Axworthy.
Consumer and Corporate Affairs; Social Development; Women, Hon. Judy Erola.
Environment, Hon. Charles Caccia.
Secretary of State, Hon. Serge Joyal.
Veterans Affairs, Hon. W. Bennett Campbell.
Minister of State (Multi-culturalism), Hon. David M. Collenette.
Minister of State (Small Businesses and Tourism), Hon. David P. Smith.
Revenue, Hon. Roy MacLaren.
Fisheries, Hon. Herb Breau.
Minister of State (Regional Development), Hon. Remi Bujold.
Minister of State (Youth; Fitness and Amateur Sport), Hon. Jean Lapierre.
Agriculture, Hon. Ralph Ferguson.
Indian and Northern Affairs, Hon. Douglas Frith.

The Prime Minister receives remuneration of $124,600; other ministers, each $105,600. In every case—including the Prime Minister's—a sessional allowance of $67,100 *per annum* is paid to members of the House of Commons. In addition, members of the House of Commons receive an expense allowance. Certain Members of Parliament for large northern constituencies have larger expense allowances.

CANADIAN HIGH COMMISSION
Macdonald House, 1 Grosvenor Square, W.1.
[01–629–9492]

High Commissioner, His Excellency Donald C. Jamieson (1983).
Deputy High Commissioner, P. Lapointe.
Ministers, C. M. Forsyth-Smith (*Commercial*); M. Phillips (*Public Affairs*).
Minister-Counsellors, D. Stockwell (*Administration*); G. H. Stewart (*Immigration*).

BRITISH HIGH COMMISSION
80 Elgin Street, Ottawa

High Commissioner, His Excellency Sir Derek Day, K.C.M.G.
Deputy High Commissioner and Head of Chancery, R. H. Baker.
Counsellor, J. Brasnett (*Economic and Commercial*).
Defence and Air Adviser, Air Cdre. D. Whittaker, M.B.E.
Naval Adviser, Capt. J. Laybourne.
Military Adviser, Col. W. M. R. Addison.
1st Secretaries, R. H. T. Bates (*Administration*); R. M. Publicover (*Economic*); J. C. Beck, O.B.E.; M. Rafferty; M. H. Connor (*Chancery*).
Cultural Affairs and British Council Representative, C. M. Chadwick, O.B.E.

THE LEGISLATURE

Parliament consists of a Senate and a House of Commons. The *Senate* consists of 104 members, nominated by the Governor-General (age limit 75). They are distributed between the various provinces thus: 24 each for *Ontario* and *Quebec,* 10 each for *Nova Scotia* and *New Brunswick,* 6 each for *Newfoundland, British Columbia, Manitoba, Alberta,* and *Saskatchewan* and 4 for *Prince Edward Island,* 1 for *North West Territories* and 1 for *Yukon*; each Senator must be at least thirty years old, a resident in the province for which he is appointed, a natural-born or naturalized subject of the Queen, and the owner of a property qualification amounting to $4,000. The Speaker of the Senate is chosen by the Government of the day.

The *House of Commons* has 282 members and is elected every five years at longest. Representation by provinces is at present as follows: Newfoundland 7, Prince Edward Island 4, Nova Scotia 11, New Brunswick 10, Quebec 75, Ontario 95, Manitoba 14, Saskatchewan 14, Alberta 21, British Columbia 28, Yukon 1, Northwest Territories 2.

THE SENATE

The state of the parties in the Senate in mid-1984 was *Liberal* 74, *Conservative* 23, *Independent* 4, *Independent Liberal* 1 (2 vacant).
Speaker of the Senate, Hon. Maurice Riel, Q.C. $82,900
Clerk of the Senate & Clerk of the Parliaments, C. A. Lussier.

THE HOUSE OF COMMONS

The state of parties in the House of Commons in mid-1984 was *Liberal* 145, *Conservative* 100, *N.D.P.* 31, *Independent* 1 (5 vacant).
Speaker of the House of Commons, Hon. Lloyd Francis $105,600
Deputy Speaker, Eymard G. Corbin $87,300
Clerk of the House of Commons, Dr. C. B. Koester.

THE JUDICATURE

The Judicature is administered by judges following the Civil Law in Quebec Province and Common Law in other Provinces. Each Province has its Court of Appeal. All Superior, County and District Court Judges are appointed by the Governor-General, the others by the Lieutenant-Governors of the Provinces.

The highest federal court is the Supreme Court of Canada, composed of a Chief Justice and eight puisne judges, which exercises general appellate jurisdiction throughout Canada in civil and criminal cases, and which usually holds three sessions each year. There is one other federally constituted Court, the Federal Court of Canada, which has jurisdiction on appeals from its Trial Division, from Federal Tribunals and reviews of decisions and references by Federal Boards and Commissions. The Trial Division has jurisdiction in claims by or against the Crown, its officers or servants or Federal bodies. It also deals with inter-Provincial and Federal-Provincial disputes.

SUPREME COURT OF CANADA

Chief Justice of Canada, Rt. Hon. Brian Dickson, P.C. $111,900
Puisne Judges, Hon. R. A. Ritchie; Hon. J. Beetz; Hon. W. Z. Estey; Hon. W. R. McIntyre; Hon. J. Chouinard; Hon. A. Lamer; Hon. Bertha Wilson; Hon. G. Le Dain
                                        each $103,000

FEDERAL COURT OF CANADA

Chief Justice, Hon. A. L. Thurlow	$96,700
Associate Chief Justice, Hon. J. A. Jerome.	$96,700

Appeal Division Judges, Hon. W. F. Ryan; Hon. L. Pratte; Hon. D. V. Heald; Hon. J. J. Urie; Hon. J. K. Hugessen; Hon. P. M. Mahoney, P.C.; Hon. L. Marceau; Hon. M. MacGuigan, P.C.; Hon. A. J. Stone each $91,100

Trial Division Judges, Hon. Allison Walsh; Hon. J. E. Dubé; Hon. F. U. Collier; Hon. G. A. Addy; Hon. P. Rouleau; Hon. J. C. McNair; Hon. F. C. Muldoon; Hon. Barbara J. Reed; Hon. B. L. Strayer; Hon. Y. Pinard; Hon. L. M. Joyal; Hon. P. Denault; Hon. B. Cullen .... each $91,100

VITAL STATISTICS

BIRTHS, DEATHS AND MARRIAGES, 1982

Province	Births	Deaths	Marriages
Alberta	45,036	12,968	22,312
British Columbia .	42,747	20,707	23,831
Manitoba........	16,123	8,490	8,264
New Brunswick ..	10,489	5,197	4,923
Newfoundland ...	9,173	3,385	3,764
Nova Scotia	12,325	6,941	6,486
Ontario	124,856	63,696	71,595
P.E.I.	1,924	980	855
Quebec	90,800	43,497	38,354
Saskatchewan ...	17,722	8,202	7,491
Yukon	525	118	225
N. W. Territories	1,362	232	260
	373,082	174,413	188,360

Canada's birth rate per 1,000 population (1982) 15·1; Death Rate 7·1; Marriage Rate 7·6. Divorces 70,436.

FINANCE

Gross general revenue and expenditure was:—

	1982–83 $ millions	1983–84 $ millions
Total Revenue	74,056	77,269
Total Expenditure.........	93,774	104,221

DEBT

	1982–83 $ millions	1983–84 $ millions
Gross Public Debt	159,500	185,000
Net Public Debt	119,500	145,000

Banking.—There were 72 chartered banks on March 31, 1984, with assets of $378,014 m. Deposits were $330,247 m. of which $103,224 m. were personal savings.

NATIONAL DEFENCE

The Minister of National Defence has the control and management of the Canadian Armed Forces and all matters relating to National Defence establishments and works for the defence of Canada.

The Canadian Forces are organized on a functional basis to reflect the major commitments assigned by the government and are formed into National Defence Headquarters and five major Commands reporting to the Chief of the Defence Staff. The roles of the five Commands are: *Mobile Command*—Provision of ground forces for the protection of Canadian territory, combat forces in Canada for support of overseas commitments, and forces for support of United Nations or other peace-keeping operations. *Maritime Command*—Provision of sea forces on the Atlantic and Pacific coasts for the defence of Canada, anti-submarine defence in support of NATO. Support to Canadian Military operations and the conduct of search and rescue operations within the Atlantic and Pacific search and rescue areas. Maritime Command also has operational control of Maritime aircraft. *Air Command*—Provision of operationally ready air forces to national, continental and international commitments. *Canadian Forces Communication Command*—Manages, operates and maintains strategic communications for the Canadian Forces. *Canadian Forces Europe*—Canadian Forces allocated to support NATO in Europe consisting of land and air elements.

National Defence expenditures for the fiscal year 1983–84—$7,595 million. Canadian Armed Forces strength at Dec. 1983, 86,381.

EDUCATION AND LANGUAGE

Education is under the control of the Provincial Governments, the cost of the publicly controlled schools being met by local taxation, aided by provincial grants. In 1982–83 there were 15,627 publicly controlled elementary and secondary schools with 4,996,388 pupils. Of these, 1,121 were private schools with 225,830 pupils; 354 Indian schools with 37,678 pupils and 22 special schools for the blind and deaf with 3,074 pupils.

In 1983–84 there were 66 degree-granting universities with a full-time enrolment of 439,920, as well as 296,100 students in 196 other post-secondary, non-university institutions.

Canada has two official languages, English and French. At the 1981 census 61·3 per cent. of the total population gave English as their mother language and 25·7 per cent. French.

CANADIAN PRODUCTION

Agriculture.—About 7 per cent. of the total land area of Canada is classified as farm land and approximately half of this is under cultivation, the remainder being woodland or suitable only for grazing purposes. More than three-quarters of the land now cultivated is found in the prairie region of Western Canada. Farm cash receipts from the sale of farm products in 1983 were $18,664,907. Livestock, poultry and eggs contributed $9,032,648,000; field crops $9,109,951,000.

Grain crop production ('000 tonnes)

	1982	1983
Wheat	27,620·2	26,914·1
Oats	3,775·9	2,773·1
Barley	14,073·6	10,616·0
Rye	888·4	830·5
Flaxseed	747·0	465·0
Rapeseed	2,114·0	2,681·0
	49,219·1	44,279·7

Livestock.—In Jan. 1984 the livestock included 11,335,100 cattle, 548,300 sheep, 10,380,200 hogs and 24,170,000 chickens (layers).

Fur Production.—Canada in 1982–83 produced pelts valued at $91,130,048. Wild life pelts made up 51% of the total, with a value of $46,839,019.

Fisheries.—The marketed value of catches in 1983 was $2,109,950,000.

Forestry.—About 48 per cent. of the total land areas is in forests. The value of forest products in 1983 was: newsprint $4,057,487,000; paper (other than newsprint) $1,799,404,000; lumber $3,103,734,000; wood pulp $3,383,915,000.

Minerals.—('000 tonnes)

	1982	1983
Copper	612·5	625·0
Nickel	88·6	121·8
Lead	272·2	258·9
Molybdenum	14·0	10·5
Zinc	965·6	970·8
Iron Ore	33,198·0	32,382·0
Asbestos	834·0	829·0
Gypsum	5,987·0	7,481·0
Cement	8,426·0	7,828·0
Lime	2,197·0	2,126·0
Salt	7,940·0	8,590·0
Potash	5,309·0	6,203·0

Production of gold was 70,746,000 grams in 1983 (64,735,000 in 1982) and of silver was 1,106,000 kg. (1,314,000 kg. in 1982). Uranium production in 1983 was 7,035,000 kilograms (7,643,000 kg. in 1982).

TRADE

Merchandise imports into Canada in 1983 were valued at $75,586,566,000 and merchandise exports (including re-exports) at $90,882,662,000. Value of trade with Canada's largest trading partners in 1983 was as follows:

Country	Imports ($'000)	Domestic Exports ($'000)
United States	54,106,207	64,527,697
Japan	4,409,441	4,728,174
United Kingdom	1,809,806	2,448,796
West Germany	1,576,555	1,155,674
Venezuela	1,004,451	231,779
USSR	33,252	1,761,789
France	840,977	626,034
Italy	798,389	549,357
Netherlands	349,382	958,139
Australia	357,487	437,996
Belgium/ Luxemburg	296,024	700,126
South Korea	791,405	556,088
China	245,767	1,607,242
Brazil	499,958	596,246
Taiwan	925,451	342,180
Hong Kong	820,316	221,176
Sweden	415,843	146,727
Switzerland	408,161	197,805
Mexico	1,079,233	375,260
Iran	526,750	206,177

COMMUNICATIONS

Railways.—The total track of railways in operation on Dec. 31, 1982, was 98,927 km.

	1982
Capital	$12,516,114,417
Operating Revenues	6,301,314
Operating Expenses	6,185,181

In 1982 revenue freight was 219,417,717,282 tonne-kilometres.

Shipping.—The registered shipping on Dec. 31, 1982 including inland vessels, was 34,832 vessels with gross tonnage 5,193,490. The volume of international shipping handled at Canadian ports in 1982 was

125,281,616 metric tonnes loaded and 48,729,336 metric tonnes unloaded.

Canals.—The bulk of canal shipping in Canada is handled through the two sections of the St. Lawrence Seaway. In 1982, transits on the Montreal-Lake Ontario section numbered 4,376 for a total of 42,815,314 cargo tonnes; transits in the Welland Canal section numbered 5,184 for a total of 49,024,104 cargo tonnes. Principal commodities carried were iron ore, wheat, corn, barley, soybeans, fuel oil, manufactured iron and steel, coal and coke.

Civil Aviation.—The number of passengers carried in 1981 (all carriers) was 30,565,578. 668,771,378 ton-miles of freight were carried in 1980.

Motor Vehicles.—Total motor vehicle registrations numbered 14,310,717 in 1982.

Post.—There were 8,095 postal facilities operating in Canada on March 31, 1983. Total postal revenue in the fiscal year 1982–83 was $2,200 m. (estimated); total expenditure $2,600 m. (estimated).

FEDERAL CAPITAL

OTTAWA, the Federal Capital, 111 miles west of Montreal and 247 miles north-east of Toronto, is a city on the south bank of the Ottawa river. The city was chosen as the Capital of the Province of Canada in 1857 and was later selected as the site of the Dominion capital. Ottawa contains the Parliamentary Buildings, the Public Archives, Royal Mint, National Museum, National Art Gallery and the Dominion Observatory.

A National Arts Centre opened on June 2, 1969, near the Parliament buildings. Facilities provided on 6¼ acres of terraced land include an opera house with seating for 2,300, a theatre (800 seats), an experimental studio (300 seats) and a hall (100 seats).

Manufacturing is also carried on, high technology (communications, defence), printing and publishing being of greatest importance. Ottawa is connected with Lake Ontario by the Rideau Canal. The City population was 303,114 at the Census of 1981; Metropolitan Ottawa 710,000 (1981 census).

YUKON TERRITORY

The Yukon Act, 1970, as amended, provides for the administration of the Territory by a Commissioner acting under instructions from time to time given by the Governor in Council or the Minister of Indian Affairs and Northern Development. Legislative powers, analogous to those of a provincial government, are exercised by a Legislative Assembly of 16 members elected from electoral districts in the Territory. The Executive Council of the Assembly consists of the government leader as chairman and four elected members. The area of the Territory is 207,076 square miles with a population (1981 Census) of 23,153. Mining is the chief industry, though trapping remains important and there is considerable timber production. Mining production, including copper, silver, lead, zinc and gold, was valued at $59,362,000 in 1983.

Seat of Government, Whitehorse. Pop. (1981) 14,814.
Commissioner, D. L. D. Bell.

NORTHWEST TERRITORIES

The Northwest Territories Act, 1979, as amended, provides for a Legislative Assembly of 24 elected members, of which the Executive Committee under the chairmanship of the Commissioner is the senior decision-making body of the government in the province.

The Northwest Territories are subdivided into the districts of Mackenzie, Keewatin and Franklin.

The area of the Northwest Territories is 1,304,903 square miles with a population (1981 Census) of 45,741. The chief industry is mining, with a total value of $516,671,000 in 1983. Zinc and lead contributed 62 per cent. of the total; gold and silver 37 per cent., and since 1982 there have been major developments in natural gas and petroleum extraction on- and off-shore.

Seat of Government, Yellowknife. Pop. (1981) 9,483.
Commissioner, John Parker.

PROVINCES OF CANADA

ALBERTA

Area and Population.—The Province of Alberta has an area of 255,285 square miles, including about 6,485 square miles of water, with a population (Jan. 1984 estimate) of 2,361,000.

Government.—The Government is vested in a Lieutenant-Governor and Legislative Assembly composed of 79 members, elected for five years, representing 79 electoral districts in the Province. At a provincial election held in Nov. 1982, the Progressive Conservative party took 75 seats, the New Democratic Party 2 seats, and Independents 2 seats.

Lieut.-Governor, His Honour Frank Lynch-Staunton.

EXECUTIVE

Premier, and President of Council, Hon.
Peter Lougheed........................ $99,613
Speaker of the Legislative Assembly, Hon. G.
Amerongen 72,617
Deputy Speaker, F. P. Appleby 48,326
Leader of the Opposition,W. G. Notley 75,386
Deputy Minister of the Executive Council, G.
de Rappard.
Clerk of the Legislative Assembly, B. J. D.
Stefaniuk.

London Office, Alberta House, 1, Mount Street, W.1.

THE JUDICATURE

Court of Appeal of Alberta, Hon. William McGillivray (*C.J.*)
Judges, Hons. N. D. McDermid; S. S. Lieberman; D. C. Prowse, A. F. Moir; W. J. Haddad; J. H. Laycraft; J. W. McClung; A. M. Harradence; R. P. Kerans; R. H. Belzil; W. A. Stevenson.
Court of Queen's Bench of Alberta, Hon. W. R. Sinclair (*C.J.*); Hon. W. K. Moore (*Associate C.J.*).

ECONOMY

The Gross Domestic Product at factor cost in 1982 was ($ millions):—

Agriculture and forestry 1,789
Mining 8,294
Manufacturing 3,125
Construction 3,648
Transportation 3,489
Utilities 1,326
Trade..................................... 4,140
Finance................................... 10,390
Services 7,113
Public Administration 2,643
Total G.D.P. at factor cost 45,957

Mineral Production 1983
(preliminary estimates)

	$ m.
Crude Oil............................	12,282·9
Natural Gas	6,227·6
Natural Gas By-Products	2,523·4
Coal	462·4
Sulphur (elemental)	413·4
Sand & Gravel	116·0
Cement	138·6
Other	53·9
Total................................	22,218·2

Manufacturing.—The value of manufacturing shipments (1983 preliminary) was $12,762,530,000. Number of industrial establishments 2,452, total employees 86,356 (1981). The leading industries are slaughtering and meat processing, petroleum refining, chemicals and chemical products, non-metallic mineral products, primary metal and metal fabricating products.

GOVERNMENT FINANCE
Budgetary Estimates $'000

	1983–84	1984–85
Revenue	8,840,000	9,386,000
Expenditure	9,685,452	9,644,337
Deficit	845,452	258,337

NOTE: The Budgetary revenue figure does not include funds allocated to the Alberta Heritage Savings Trust Fund.

CAPITAL.—Edmonton—city population (1983) 560,085, metropolitan area, 682,000. Other centres are Calgary (620,692), Grande Prairie (24,076), Lethbridge (58,086), Medicine Hat (41,493) and Red Deer (50,257).

BRITISH COLUMBIA

Area and Population.—British Columbia has a total area estimated at 366,255 square miles, with a population of 2,823,900 (1983).

Government.—The Government consists of a Lieutenant-Governor and an Executive Council together with a Legislative Assembly of 57 members.

Lieut.-Governor, Hon. Robert Gordon Rogers.

EXECUTIVE COUNCIL

Premier and President of the Council, Hon.
William Richards Bennett $41,357
Human Resources, Hon. Grace Mary McCarthy.
Attorney-General, Hon. Brian R. D. Smith, Q.C.
Minister of Finance, Hon. Hugh Austin Curtis.
Minister of Agriculture and Food, Hon. Harvey W. Schroeder.
Education, Hon. John H. Heinrich.
Provincial Secretary and Minister of Government Services, Hon. James R. Chabot.
Lands, Parks and Housing and Environment, Hon. Anthony J. Brummeto.
Labour, Hon. Robert H. McClelland.
Health, Hon. James Arthur Nielsen.
Transportation and Highways, Hon. Alexander Vaughan Fraser.
Municipal Affairs, Hon. William S. Ritchie.
Consumer and Corporate Affairs, Hon. James J. Hewitt.
Forests, Hon. Thomas Manville Waterland.
Energy, Mines and Petroleum Resources, Hon. C. Stephen Rogers.
Industry and Small Business Development, Hon. Donald McGray Phillips.
Universities, Sciences and Communications, Hon. Patrick Lucey McGeer.

Intergovernmental Relations, Hon. Garde
Basil Gardom.
Tourism, Hon. Claude H. Richmond.
(Members of the Executive Council, other
than the Premier, receive a salary of
$31,283).
Speaker, Legislative Assembly, Hon. K. Walter Davidson $24,918

Agent-General in London, A. Hart, Q.C., British
Columbia House, 1 Regent Street, S.W.1.

THE JUDICATURE

Court of Appeal—Chief Justice of British Colombia,
Hon. N. T. Nemetz.
Justices of Appeal, Hons. J. D. Taggart; P. D. Seaton;
A. B. B. Carrothers; E. E. Hinkson; W. A. Craig; J.
S. Aikins; J. D. Lambert; J. A. Macdonald; R. P.
Anderson; H. E. Hutcheon; A. B. Macfarlane; W.
A. Esson.
Supreme Court—Chief Justice, Hon. A. McEachern.
Puisne Judges, Hons. J. G. Gould; H. C. McKay; K.
E. Meredith; A. A. Mackoff; S. M. Toy; J. C. Bouck;
L. G. McKenzie; G. L. Murray; H. P. Legg; W. J.
Trainor; P. M. Proudfoot; H. A. Callaghan; A. G.
MacKinnon; M. R. Taylor; C. C. Locke; W. A.
Esson; W. J. Wallace; P. D. Dohm; R. M. P. Paris;
D. B. Hinds; A. A. W. Macdonell; J. E. Spencer; B.
M. McLachlin; W. S. Davies; C. R. Lander; B. D.
McDonald; K. M. Lysyk; L. S. G. Finch; J. Wood;
R. J. Gibbs.

FINANCE (1984–85)

Estimated Revenue................. $7,719,000,000
Estimated Expenditure 8,390,000,000
Direct Debt (31/3/83)............... 1,572,000,000

ECONOMY

Production and Industry.—Manufacturing activity is based largely on the processing of the output of
the logging, mineral, fishing and agriculture industries. The principal manufacturing centres are
Vancouver, New Westminster, Victoria, North Vancouver, Kelowna and Prince George. Forestry and
forest-based industries form the most important
economic activity, accounting for approximately 40
per cent of total production. British Columbia is the
leading province of Canada in the quantity and value
of its timber and sawmill products. Mining, the
second most important non-service economic activity, is based on copper, zinc, lead, iron concentrates,
molybdenum, coal, natural gas, crude petroleum,
asbestos and silver. Molybdenum production is
approximately 90 per cent of the Canadian total.
The production levels for important industries
were estimated for 1983 as follows:—

Lumber .... 30,777,000 cu. metres.
Paper .... 2,158,000 tonnes
Pulp .... 5,572,000 tonnes
Coal .... 11,800,000 tonnes
Gas .... 7,016 million cu. metres

Mineral production for 1983 was valued at $2,859·6
million.
The most important agricultural products are
livestock, eggs and poultry, fruits and dairy products.
Salmon accounts for approximately 50 per cent of the
value of fisheries. Other species include halibut,
herring, sole, cod, flounder, perch, tuna and shellfish.
In recent years the sale of herring roe to Japan has
become an important source of fishery revenue. In
1983 farm cash receipts were valued at $898·8 million.
The economy is dependent upon markets outside
the province for the disposal of most of the products

of her industry. An estimated 55–60 per cent of
production is exported to foreign markets. Manufacturing shipments in 1983 were valued at $16,867
million.
Transport.—The province has deep water harbours
which are well serviced by railways and modern
highways. Vancouver is the base for regular scheduled air routes to other parts of Canada, the United
States, Europe, Mexico, South America, Hawaii, Fiji,
Australia, Japan, Hong Kong and the Middle East.
CAPITAL, ΨVICTORIA, Metropolitan population
(1982) 236,400. ΨVANCOUVER metropolitan population (1982) 1,283,000, is the western terminus of the
Canadian Pacific Railway and the Canadian National
Railways (the C.N.R. also has a terminus at Prince
Rupert) and the southern terminus of the British
Columbia Railway, and possesses one of the finest
natural harbours in the world, servicing a variety of
vessels, including large bulk cargo carriers. Other
principal cities are Prince George, Kamloops, Kelowna and Nanaimo.

MANITOBA

Area and Population.—Manitoba, originally the
Red River settlement, is the central province of
Canada. The Province has a considerable area of
prairie land but is also a land of wide diversity
combining 400 miles of sea-coast, large lakes and
rivers covering an area of 30,225 square miles and
pre-cambrian rock which covers about three-fifths of
the Province. The total area is 250,946 square miles
with a population (1984 estimate) of 1,051,500.
Government.—The Government is administered by
a Lieutenant-Governor, assisted by an Executive
Council of Ministers, who are members of the
Legislative Assembly of 57 members. Each member of
the Legislative Assembly receives an annual sessional
indemnity totalling $31,824 for the year ending
March 31, 1984.
The New Democratic Party formed the government
of Manitoba in November 1981. The standing in the
House at May 1, 1984 was: New Democratic Party 32,
Progressive Conservative 23, Independent 2.
Lieut.-Governor, Her Honour Pearl McGonigal (1981).

EXECUTIVE

Premier, Federal-Provincial Relations, Hon. Howard
R. Pawley, Q.C.
Health, Recreation and Sport, Hon. Laurent L.
Desjardins.
Business Development and Tourism, Hon. Samuel
Uskiw.
Employment Services and Economic Security, Hon.
Leonard S. Evans.
Agriculture, Hon. Billie Uruski.
Government Services, Hon. A. R. Adam.
*Co-operative Development, Chairman of Treasury
Board,* Hon. Jay M. Cowan.
Energy and Mines, Hon. Wilson D. P. Parasiuk.
Finance and Crown Investments, Hon. Victor Schroeder.
Education, Hon. Maureen L. Hemphill.
*Culture, Heritage and Recreation; Industry, Trade
and Technology,* Hon. Eugene M. Kostyra.
Attorney-General, Consumer and Corporate Affairs,
Hon. Roland Penner.
Community Services, Hon. Muriel A. Smith.
Natural Resources, Hon. Alvin H. Mackling.
Labour and Urban Affairs, Hon. Mary E. Dolin.
Northern Affairs, Hon. J. T. Storie.
Housing, Hon. John Bucklaschuk.
Highways and Transportation, Hon. John G. Plohman.
Municipal Affairs, Government House Leader, Hon.
Andre Anstett.

Environment and Workplace Safety and Health, Hon. Gérard Lécuyer.

THE JUDICATURE

Court of Appeal:—
  Chief Justice of Manitoba, Hon. A. M. Monnin.............................. $96,700
  Puisne Judges, Hons. R. J. Matas; G. C. Hall; J. F. O'Sullivan; C. R. Huband; A. R. Philp............................ 89,100
Queen's Bench, Chief Justice, Q.B.D. Hon. A. S. Dewar.............................. 96,700
  Associate Chief Justice (Family Division), Hon. A. C. Hamilton.................. $96,700

ECONOMY

Finance.—The revenue of the provincial government, 1984–85, is estimated at $3,458 million and the expenditure $2,969 million.

Agriculture.—The total land area in Manitoba is 135,342,565 acres, of which 18,819,359 acres are in occupied farms. The gross value of agriculture production in 1983 was estimated at $1,905 million.

Manufactures.—Manufacturing enterprises employed about 59,000 persons on average in 1983. The chief manufacturing centres are Winnipeg, Brandon, Selkirk and Portage la Prairie. The largest manufacturing industry is the food and beverage industry, followed by the machinery and metal fabricating industries.

CAPITAL.—Winnipeg, population 584,842. Other cities are Brandon (36,242), Thompson (14,288), Portage la Prairie (13,086) and Flin Flon (7,894).

NEW BRUNSWICK

Area and Population.—New Brunswick is situated between 45°–48° N. lat. and 63° 47′–69° W. long. and comprises an area of 28,354 square miles with a population (Jan. 1984 estimate) of 710,500. It was first colonized by British subjects in 1761, and in 1783 by inhabitants of New England, who had been dispossessed of their property in consequence of their loyalty to the British Crown.

Government.—Government is administered by a Lieutenant-Governor, an Executive Council, and a Legislative Assembly of 58 members elected by the people. At the General Election of October 12, 1982, 39 Progressive Conservative, 18 Liberal and 1 New Democratic Party members were returned.

Lieutenant-Governor, His Honour Dr. George F. G. Stanley.

EXECUTIVE

Premier, Hon. Richard B. Hatfield.
Justice, Hon. Ferdinand Dubé, Q.C.
Transportation, Hon. W. G. Bishop.
Agriculture and Rural Development, Hon. Malcolm MacLeod.
Commerce and Development, Hon. Paul Dawson.
Health, Hon. Charles Gallagher.
Education, Hon. Clarence Cormier.
Continuing Education, Hon. Mabel Deware.
Natural Resources, Hon. Gerald Merrithew.
Labour and Human Resources, Hon. Joseph Mombourquette.
Finance, Hon. John Baxter.
Municipal Affairs, Hon. Yvon Poitras.
Fisheries, Hon. Jean Gauvin.
Tourism, Hon. Omer Leger.
Chairman, Treasury Board, Hon. Harold Fanjoy.

Social Services, Hon. Nancy Clark Tweed.
Youth, Hon. Leslie Hull.
Supply and Services, Hon. Edwin Allen.
Environment, Hon. William Harmer.
Historical and Cultural Resources, Hon Jean-Pierre Ouellet.
Chairman, Social Program Reform, Hon. Brenda Robertson.
Chairman, Public Service Delivery Reform, Hon. Jean-Maurice Simard.
Ministers, each $55,354 (salary and allowance).
Speaker of the House, Hon. James Tucker.... $41,515

THE JUDICATURE

Court of Appeal

Chief Justice, Hon. S. G. Stratton.
Judges of Appeal, Hons. H. E. Ryan; La Forest; J. C. Angers; W. Hoyt.

Queen's Bench Division

Chief Justice, Hon. G. A. Richard.

ECONOMY

Finance.—The estimated revenue for the year ending March 31, 1983, was $1,945,154,091 and ordinary expenditure, $2,147,955,484.

Manufactures.—New Brunswick's largest manufacturing group, in terms of shipments, is the food and beverage industry followed by the paper and allied wood industries. Together these industries accounted in 1982 for over 50 per cent. of the total value of manufacturing shipments of $3,323,696,723. Saint John has a major ice-free port and is the principal manufacturing centre of the province.

Agriculture.—Total land area 27,633 sq. miles; farms numbered 4,063 and averaged 266 acres each in 1981. Dairy products and potatoes are the leading agricultural products. Both industries together accounted for 46·4 per cent of total farm cash receipts in 1983. Farm cash receipts in 1983 totalled $187,887,000.

Fisheries.—The chief commercial fish are lobsters, herring, tuna, crab and cod. Total direct employment exceeds 12,000, of whom 6,579 are fishermen. Landings reached 106,548 metric tons valued at $78,260,000 in 1983.

Minerals.—Extensive zinc, lead and copper deposits are now being mined in the north-eastern part of the Province with New Brunswick being the second largest producer of zinc in Canada. A lead smelter, fertilizer plant and port facilities have been constructed at Belledune. Canada's only primary antimony producer is located at Lake George. There is exploration and development near Sussex and Salt Springs, where potash and salt deposits have been found. Coal is mined at Grand Lake and exploration for other deposits is being undertaken. Total mineral production was valued at $513,673,000 in 1983.

Principal Cities.—CAPITAL ΨFredericton: population (1981), 64,439. ΨSaint John (114,048); Moncton (98,354); Bathurst (24,267); Edmundston (21,901); Campbellton (15,508).

NEWFOUNDLAND AND LABRADOR

Area and Population.—The Island of Newfoundland is situated between 46° 37′–51° 37′ N. latitude and 52° 44′–59° 30′ W. longitude, on the north-east side of the Gulf of St. Lawrence, and is separated from the North American Continent by the Straits of Belle Isle on the N.W. and by Cabot Strait on the S.W. The island is about 317 miles long and 316 miles broad and is triangular in shape, with Cape Bauld (N.), Cape Race (S.E.) and Cape Ray (S.W.) at the angles. It comprises an area of 43,359 sq. miles with a population (1981 Census) (inclusive of Labrador) of 567,681.

Labrador forms the most easterly part of the North American continent, and extends from Point St. Charles, at the northeast entrance to the Straits of Belle Isle, on the south, to Cape Chidley, at the eastern entrance to Hudson's Straits on the north. It has an area estimated at 112,826 sq. miles, with a population (1981 census) of 31,318.

Government.—On March 31, 1949 Newfoundland became the 10th Province of the Dominion of Canada. The Government is administered by a Lieutenant-Governor, aided by an Executive Council and a Legislative Assembly of 52 members. A General Election was held on April 6, 1982. The standings in the current House of Assembly are: 44 Progressive Conservatives and 8 Liberals.

Lieutenant-Governor, Hon. W. Anthony Paddon, C.M., M.D. (July 10, 1981).

EXECUTIVE

Premier and Intergovernmental Affairs, Hon. A. Brian Peckford.
President of the Council, and Minister responsible for Labrador Hydro and the Petroleum Directorate, Hon. William Marshall, Q.C.
Finance, and President of Treasury Board, Hon. Dr. John Collins.
Justice and Attorney General, Hon. G. Ottenheimer.
Education, Hon. Lynn Verge.
Fisheries, Hon. James Morgan.
Transportation, Mines and Energy, Hon. Ronald Dawe.
Environment, Hon. Hal D. Andrews.
Development, Hon. Neil Windsor.
Rural, Agricultural and Northern Development, Hon. Joseph Goudie.
Health, Hon. Wallace House.
Forest Resources and Land, Hon. Charles Power.
Municipal Affairs, Hon. Hazel Newhook.
Labour and Manpower, Hon. Jerome Dinn.
Culture, Recreation and Youth, Hon. Leonard A. Simms.
Social Services, Hon. Thomas V. Hickey.
Public Works and Services, Hon. Haig Young.
Communications, Hon. Norman Doyle.

Speaker of the House of Assembly, J. Russell.
Clerk of the Executive Council, D. Vardy.

ECONOMY

Finance.—The estimated gross capital and current account revenues for 1984–85 were $2,009,243,000 and the gross current and capital account expenditures $2,215,571,000.

Production and Industry.—The main primary industries are fishing, forestry and mining. In 1982 shipments of fish products were valued at $504·5 million. In 1983 newsprint shipments from the three pulp and paper mills were valued at $260·7 million. In 1983 the mining operations plus the structural materials producers had combined shipments estimated at $690·4 million of which $601·1 million was from the 3 iron ore mines in Labrador. Manufacturing shipments with the exclusion of fish and paper products totalled approximately $500 million in 1983. The hydro-electric plant on the Churchill river is the largest underground plant in the world, with a capacity of 5,225,000 kw.

Transport.—The province is connected to mainland Canada by a ferry service from North Sydney, Nova Scotia to Port aux Basques and Argentia. The main line of the railway extends from St. John's on the east coast to Port aux Basques on the west coast. Transport between various points on the island is by

highway but the south coast and Labrador still rely on the coastal boat service.

CAPITAL, St. John's (population 1981 Census, Greater St. John's 154,820) is North America's oldest city, and thus of historical interest and is the seat of the provincial legislature, the site of most provincial and federal government offices and the principal port for the island of Newfoundland. Newfoundland's second city of Corner Brook (population 1981 Census, 24,339) is situated on the west coast, its principal industry being its pulp and paper mill.

Labrador

Labrador, the most northerly area of the Province of Newfoundland, forms the most easterly part of the North American continent, and extends from Blanc Sablon, at the north-east entrance to the Straits of Belle Isle, on the south, to Cape Chidley, at the eastern entrance to Hudson's Straits on the north. Labrador is noted for its cod fisheries and also possesses valuable salmon, herring, trout and seal fisheries. Newfoundland (Labrador) produces more iron ore than any other province in Canada.

NOVA SCOTIA

Area and Population.—Nova Scotia is a peninsula between 43° 25′–47° N. lat. and 59° 40′–66° 25′ W. long., and is connected with New Brunswick by a low fertile isthmus about 17·5 miles wide. It comprises an area of 21,425 square miles including 1,023 square miles of lakes and rivers and 6,479 miles of shoreline. No place is more than 35 miles from the Atlantic Ocean. Population (1984) 866,100.

Government.—The Government consists of a Lieutenant-Governor and a 52-member elected Legislative Assembly, from which the Executive Council (Cabinet) is selected. The Lieutenant-Governor represents the Queen and is appointed by the Governor-in-Council.

Lieutenant-Governor, Hon. Alan R. Abraham $41,600

EXECUTIVE COUNCIL

Premier, Hon. John M. Buchanan, Q.C. $39,100
Without Portfolio, Hon. G. Henley.
Health, Hon. G. Sheehy.
Attorney General, Hon. R. Giffen, Q.C.
Mines and Energy, Hon. J. Matheson, Q.C.
Agriculture and Marketing, Hon. R. S. Bacon.
Lands and Forests, Hon. K. Streatch.
Tourism, Hon. R. F. Hudson, Q.C.
Municipal Affairs, Hon. T. J. McInnes.
Transportation, Hon. J. MacIsaac.
Management Board, Hon. R. S. Russell.
Education, Hon. T. Donahoe, Q.C.
Fisheries, Hon. J. Leefe.
Finance, Hon. G. Kerr.
Social Services, Hon. E. Morris.
Government Services, Hon. J. Lawrence.
Environment, Hon. G. Moody.
Consumer Affairs, Hon. L. Stirling.
Culture, Recreation and Fitness, Hon. W. J. MacLean.
Housing, Hon. M. Laffin.
Resource Development Board, Hon. M. Pickings.
Labour and Manpower, Hon. D. Nantes.

Cabinet Ministers receive $30,300 a year, *plus* member's sessional indemnity $19,400 and expense allowance $9,700.
Agent-General in London, Donald M. Smith, 14 Pall Mall, S.W.1.

THE JUDICATURE

Supreme Court—Appeal Division
Chief Justice, Hon. I. M. MacKeigan $111,900
Judges, Hons. T. H. Coffin; A. G. Cooper;
A. L. Macdonald; G. L. S. Hart; L. L. Pace;
M. C. Jones; V. A. Morrison 103,000

Trial Division

Chief Justice, Hon. Constance R. Glube 111,900
Judges, Hons. A. M. MacIntosh; W. J. Grant;
    J. D. Hallett; K. P. Richard; C. Denne
    Burchell; L. Clarke; R. M. Rogers; H.
    Nathanson; M. Nunn 103,000

ECONOMY

Finance.—The revenue for the fiscal year ending
March 31, 1983, was $2,119,065,000 and expenditure
was $2,387,755,000. The net direct debt was
$1,875,332,000.

Manufacturing.—Manufacturing constitutes the
most important goods producing sector of the economy. Shipments were worth $3,962 million in 1983
with a total added value estimated to be more than
$1,340 million. Manufacturing plants provide em-
ployment for 41,000 or 13 per cent of the labour force.
Capital expenditure in the manufacturing sector has
decreased from $238 million in 1983 to $155 million in
1984.

Utilities.—Electric power in Nova Scotia is supplied
by the Nova Scotia Power Corporation, a Crown
corporation. The Corporation's generating stations,
which are predominantly coal fired have a nameplate
capacity of 2,198,827 kilowatts. The Corporation's
generating system is made up of seven thermal plants,
three gas turbines and 31 hydro stations scattered
throughout the province.

The number of telephones in Nova Scotia was
550,044 in December, 1983, or approximately 65 per
100 population.

Petroleum Activity.—During 1983–84 exploration
activity on the Shelf and Slope regions of Nova Scotia
reached record levels with eight rigs currently
working offshore. By mid-1984 a total of 90 wells had
been completed off-shore since drilling began in 1967,
with the current drilling being done by six major
operations; and gas is now expected from the Ventura
field by 1989.

An onshore drilling programme began during 1983–
84 in which two wells were completed and four
additional wells were spudded.

Mining.—The total value of mineral production
in 1983 was estimated at $290,678,584, Dollar value of
production was:—

Coal $167,377,000
Sand, gravel and crushed rock 46,125,107
Gypsum and anhydrite 37,831,468
Salt 31,692,290
Limestone 3,845,586
Barite 1,088,650

Agriculture.—Farm cash receipts were $239,254,000
in 1983. About 3 per cent of the total area, or 439,803
acres, is classified as farm land. Dairy and poultry
products form the largest sectors.

Fishing.—The value of fish landed in 1983 was
$276,451,000. Products have been diversified and
enlarged into a variety of processed foods that are
increasing in number. Primary fishing and fish
processing employed 19,843 persons in 1983 (12,543
fishermen and 7,300 plant workers).

Forest Products.—The gross value of primary and
secondary forestry was $400,000,000 in 1983. Forest
lands total 10,800,000 acres or 84 per cent of the land
area. About 75 per cent of forest land is privately
owned. Forest based industries employ about 8,000.

Tourism.—Between June 1 and October 31, 1983,
about 1,113,184 visitors spent about $183,826,400 in
the province.

CAPITAL ΨHalifax, including the neighbouring city
of Dartmouth, has a population of 176,871. In addition
to a container-handling terminal in South Halifax a
new terminal at the north end of Halifax Harbour
was opened in 1981. A 90-acre autoport has been built

at Port Halifax to handle both the export and import
of motor vehicles. A shipyard, with dry-dock, can
build and repair the largest ocean-going liners. The
harbour, ice-free the year round, is the main Atlantic
winter port of Canada. Other cities and towns
include ΨSydney (29,444), ΨGlace Bay (21,466), Amherst (9,684) and New Glasgow (10,464).

Cape Breton Island

This has been part of Nova Scotia since 1819. It is
the centre of the steel manufacturing and coal mining
industries, and is also noted for its large lakes and
beautiful coastal scenery, making it a tourist attraction in Canada.

ONTARIO

Area and Population.—The Province of Ontario
contains a total area of 412,582 sq. miles, with a
population (1981) of 8,625,107.

Government.—The Government is vested in a
Lieutenant-Governor and a Legislative Assembly of
125 members elected for five years. After the last
election, in 1981, there were 70 Progressive Conservatives, 33 Liberals, 21 New Democrats.

Lieutenant-Governor, Hon. John Black Aird, Q.C.
    (1980).

EXECUTIVE COUNCIL

Premier and President of the Council, Hon. William
    G. Davis, Q.C.
Deputy Premier and Minister for Women's Issues,
    Hon. R. Welch.
Citizenship and Culture, Hon. Susan Fish.
Chairman of Management Board of Cabinet, Hon.
    G. R. McCague.
Education, Colleges and Universities, Hon. Bette M.
    Stephenson, M.D.
Health, Hon. Keith Norton, Q.C.
Community and Social Services, Hon. F. Drea.
Agriculture and Food, Hon. D. R. Timbrell.
Environment, Hon. Andrew Brandt.
Labour, Hon. R. G. Elgie, M.D.
Transport and Communications, Hon. J. W. Snow.
Consumer and Commercial Relations, Hon. R. G.
    Elgie, M.D.
Treasurer and Minister of Economics, Hon. L. Grass-
    man, Q.C.
Revenue, Hon. B. Gregory.
Resources Development, Hon. Norman Sterling, Q.C.
Natural Resources, Hon. A. W. Pope.
Municipal Affairs and Housing, Hon. C. Bennett.
Social Development, Hon. Gordon Dean.
Attorney-General, Hon. R. R. McMurtry, Q.C.
Northern Affairs, Hon. L. E. Bernier.
Correctional Services, Hon. N. Leluk.
Government Services, Hon. George Ashe.
Intergovernmental Affairs, Hon. T. L. Wells.
Industry and Trade, Hon. Frank Miller.
Tourism and Recreation, Hon. Reuben Baetz.
Without Portfolio, Hon. R. Eaton.
Solicitor-General, Hon. G. W. Taylor, Q.C.
Energy, Hon. Philip Andrewes.
Justice, Hon. Gordon Walker, Q.C.

Secretary of the Cabinet, Dr. E. E. Stewart.
Speaker, Legislative Assembly, Hon. J. M. Turner.

JUDICATURE

Chief Justice of Ontario, Hon. W. G. C. Howland.
Chief Justice of the High Court, Hon. G. T. Evans.

Agent-General in London, W. R. DeGeer, 13 Charles
    II Street, S.W.1.

ECONOMY

Agriculture.—Ontario has the highest total of
agricultural production in Canada with a gross value

of $5,029,900,000 and a total net farm income of $843,100,000 in 1982.

Forestry.—Productive forested lands cover 377,000 sq. km. or 35·3 per cent of the land area of the Province. Paper and allied industries are by far the most important sector of Ontario's forest industry: production in 1981 was worth $1,915,400,000 and accounted for 27·1 per cent by value and 25·5 per cent by quantity of Canada's production.

Minerals.—Ontario's natural resources include 15 basic minerals, such as copper, iron ore, zinc, silver, gold and platinum. The province has half the world's supply of nickel and the largest amount of uranium in the Western World. Total value of the mineral production in 1983 was estimated at $3,532,700,000.

Energy.—Total electrical energy generated in Ontario in 1983 was 117,971 million kWh (31 per cent hydro, 32·4 per cent nuclear and 30·4 per cent other conventional fossil fuels).

Manufacture.—Ontario is the chief manufacturing province in Canada, producing 50 per cent of all manufactured goods. It represents over 43 per cent of total Canadian exports of fully manufactured products. During 1982 Ontario's exports totalled $36,842 million, an increase in value of $2,800 million over 1981. A $3,791 million growth in the value of end products—the sector which contains the bulk of Ontario's manufactured exports—was also achieved.

CAPITAL.—ΨToronto (metropolitan population, 2,137,395) has a wide range of manufacturing and service industries and is a centre of education, business and finance. Other major urban areas are: Ottawa, the national capital (295,163); ΨHamilton (306,434), with iron and steel industry, metal fabrication, machinery, electrical and chemical industries; London (254,280), a business and manufacturing centre; ΨWindsor (192,083); Kitchener (139,734) and Sudbury (91,829).

PRINCE EDWARD ISLAND

Area and Population.—Prince Edward Island lies in the southern part of the Gulf of St. Lawrence, between 46°–47° N. lat. and 62°–64° 30′ W. long. It is about 140 miles in length, and from 4 to 40 miles in breadth; its area is 2,184 square miles and its population (1983) 123,700.

Government.—The Government is vested in a Lieutenant-Governor and an Executive Council, and Legislative Assembly of 32 members elected for a term of 5 years, 16 as Councillors and 16 as Assemblymen. Party representation at Sept. 27, 1982, was: *Conservative* 21; *Liberal* 11.

Lieutenant-Governor, His Honour J. A. Doiron (1980) $38,500
(and expense allowance)

EXECUTIVE

Premier and President of the Executive Council, Hon. J. M. Lee, P.C.
Industry, Hon. P. G. Binns.
Finance and Tourism, Hon. L. G. MacPhail.
Health and Social Services, Hon. A. P. Fogarty.
Justice, Attorney-General and Community and Cultural Affairs, Hon. G. R. McMahon, Q.C.
Agriculture, Hon. P. G. Chappell.
Education, Hon. L. Bagnall.
Transportation and Public Works, Hon. G. Lank.
Fisheries and Labour, Hon. R. B. Pratt.
Energy and Forestry, Hon. F. L. Driscoll.
Premier $37,400 *(plus expenses).* Ministers $26,400 *(plus expenses)*
Speaker of the Legislative Assembly Hon. Marion Reid $8,450
(plus M.L.A. salary and expenses)

Members of the Legislative Assembly receive a salary of $14,600 *plus* $6,900 expense allowance; Ministers receive their salary and allowance as members in addition to their Ministerial salary.

SUPREME COURT

Chief Justice, Hon. J. P. Nicholson $89,000
Associate Justices, Hon. F. A. Large; Hon. G. Mitchell; Hon. C. R. McQuaid; Hon. K. R. MacDonald; Hon. A. B. Campbell; Hon. G. J. Mullally .... each $84,000

Finance.—The ordinary revenue in 1983–84 was $373,925,914 and the expenditure was $389,956,897.

Education.—A university and a college of applied arts and technology were established in 1969, estimated enrolment for 1983–84 being (University of Prince Edward Island), 2,386; college of applied arts and technology (Holland College) 823 full and part-time students.

CAPITAL, ΨCharlottetown (pop. July 1981 census, 15,282), on the shore of Hillsborough Bay, which forms a good harbour.

QUEBEC

Area and Population.—The Province of Quebec contains an area estimated at 594,860 square miles (1,540,668 sq. km.) with a population (June, 1982), of 6,470,300.

Government.—The Government of the Province is vested in a Lieutenant-Governor, a Council of ministers and a National Assembly of 122 members elected for five years. At June 24, 1984, there were 71 *Parti Quebecois,* 48 Liberals, 2 Independents and 1 vacant seat.

Lieut.-Governor, The Hon. Gilles Lamontagne.

EXECUTIVE

Premier, René Lévesque.
Justice and Intergovernmental Affairs, Pierre Marc Johnson.
Finance, Jacques Parizeau.
Education, Yves Bérubé.
Citizens' Affairs, Denis Lazure.
Overseas Trade and International Relations, Bernard Landry.
Regional Development and Management, François Gendron.
Leisure, Hunting and Fishing, Guy Chevrette.
Environment, Adrien Ouellette.
Government Leader in Parliament and Minister for Communications, Jean-François Bertrand.
Women's Affairs, Mme. Denise Leblanc-Bantey.
Treasury, Robert Dean.
Agriculture, Fisheries and Food, Jean Garon.
Energy and Resources, Yves Duhaime.
Social Affairs, Camille Laurin.
Transport, Jacques Léonard.
Manpower and Incomes, Mme. Pauline Marois.
Industry, Commerce and Tourism, Roderigue Biron.
Public Works and Municipal Affairs, Alain Marcoux.
Ethnic Culture and Immigration, Gérald Godin.
Administrative Reform, Michel Clair.
Cultural Affairs, Clément Richard.
Labour, Raynald Fréchette.
Housing and Consumer Affairs, Guy Tardif.
Science and Technology, Gilbert Paquette.

Agent-General in London, Gilles Loiselle, 12 Upper Grosvenor Street, W.1.

JUDICATURE

Court of Appeal, Chief Justice of Quebec, Hon. Marcel Crête.
Superior Court, Chief Justice of Quebec (Montreal), Hon. Alan B. Gold.

ECONOMY

Finance.—The revenue for the year 1982–83 was $19,210,266,000; expenditure amounted to 22,259,296,000. The net debt (March 31, 1983) was $14,225,644,000.

Production and Industry.—The principal manufacturing centres are Montreal, Montreal East, Quebec, Trois-Rivières, Sherbrooke, Shawinigan Drummondville and Lachine. Forest lands cover 684,480 sq. km., of which 490,693 sq. km. are productive. Forest products in 1982 included: wood pulp, 6,282,713 metric tons; paper and paperboard, 5,490,888 metric tons.

Total estimated value of shipments in the manufacturing industries in 1983 was $52,704,661,000. Value of 1983 shipments in the chief industries:—

Food and beverages.................	$9,230,877,000
Paper and allied industries..........	5,387,018,000
Primary metal industries	3,731,093,000
Textiles	2,407,719,000
Clothing	2,559,340,000

Agriculture and Fisheries.—In 1983 total farm receipts were: Crops, $412,872,000; Livestock and livestock products, $2,200,933; Other farm receipts, $230,566,000. 68,784,270 metric tons of fish to the value of $54,705,846 were landed in 1983.

Mineral Production.—Minerals to the value of $2,015,715,315 were mined during 1982, compared with $2,385,090,364 in 1981. Distribution of the 1982 total was: copper, $165,413,220; zinc, $71,896,718; asbestos, $298,145,512.

CAPITAL, ΨQuebec (population (Census 1981), 166,474) historic city visited annually by thousands of tourists, and one of the great seaport towns of Canada; and ΨMontreal (municipal population, 980,354) with suburbs, 2,828,349 (Metropolitan Montreal), the commercial metropolis. Other important cities are Laval (268,335); Verdun (61,287) and Sherbrooke (74,075), Montreal-Nord (94,914) and La Salle (76,299).

SASKATCHEWAN

Area and Population.—The Province of Saskatchewan lies between Manitoba on the east and Alberta on the west and has an area of 251,700 square miles (of which the land area is 220,182 sq. miles), with a population (estimated, 1983) of 992,700. Saskatchewan extends along the Canada–U.S.A. boundary for 393 miles and northwards for 761 miles. Its northern width is 276 miles.

Government.—The Government is vested in the Lieutenant-Governor, with a Legislative Assembly of 64 members. There is an Executive Council of 25 members. The Legislative Assembly is elected for 5 years and the state of the parties in May 1984 was: Progressive Conservative 55; New Democratic Party 8; Liberal 1.

Lieut.-Governor, His Honour F. W. Johnson (1983)	$38,900

EXECUTIVE COUNCIL

Premier and President of the Council, Hon. G. Devine	$63,880

Deputy Premier, Minister of Economic Development and Provincial Secretary, Hon. E. Berntson.
Attorney-General, Minister for Justice, Hon. G. Lane.
Consumer and Commercial Affairs, Hon. Joan Duncan.
Co-operation and Co-operative Development, Hon. J. Sandberg.
Energy and Mines, Hon. P. Schoenhals.
Education, Hon. Patricia Smith.
Environment, Hon. N. Hardy.
Finance, Hon. R. Andrew.
Health, Hon. G. Taylor.
Highways and Transportation, Hon. J. Garner.
Revenue and Financial Services, Hon. P. Rousseau.
Labour, Hon. L. McLaren.
Science and Technology, Hon. G. Currie.
North Saskatchewan, Supply and Services, Hon. G. McLeod.
Parks and Renewable Resources, Hon. R. Pickering.
Rural Development, Hon. L. Domotor.
Social Services, Hon. G. Dirks.
Agriculture, Hon. L. Hepworth.
Urban Affairs, Hon. T. Embury.
Advanced Education and Manpower, Hon. C. Maxwell.
Culture and Recreation, R. Folk.
Tourism and Small Business, Hon J. Klein.
Minister without Portfolio, Hon. S. Dutchak, Hon. G. Muirhead.
Ministers, each $54,942.

Agent-General in London.—R. A. Larter, 21 Pall Mall, S.W.1.

Finance.—Combined* revenue for year ending March 1984 is $3,011,719,800 and combined* expenditure $3,278,925,320 (*Consolidated Fund and Heritage combined).

CAPITAL.—Regina. Population (estimated 1983), 165,952. Other cities: Saskatoon (159,581), Moose Jaw (34,677); Prince Albert (32,522) and Yorkton (15,862).

The Commonwealth of Australia

AREA AND POPULATION

States and Capitals	Area (English Sq. Miles)	Estimated Resident Population		
		June 30, 1976 (a)	June 30, 1981 (a)	Dec. 31, 1983 (preliminary)
States				
New South Wales (Sydney).............	309,433	4,959,600	5,234,900	5,378,300
Queensland (Brisbane).................	667,000	2,092,400	2,345,200	2,488,000
South Australia (Adelaide).............	380,070	1,274,100	1,318,800	1,347,000
Tasmania (Hobart)	26,383	412,300	427,200	434,700
Victoria (Melbourne)	87,884	3,810,400	3,946,900	4,053,400
Western Australia (Perth)	975,920	1,178,300	1,300,100	1,373,700
Territories				
Australian Capital Territory (Canberra).	939	207,700	227,600	240,100
Northern Territory (Darwin)..........	520,280	98,200	122,600	136,800
Total........................	2,967,909	14,033,100	14,923,300	15,451,900

Population of Aboriginal or Torres Strait Islander Origin
(from Census of 1981)

	Aboriginal	Torres Strait Islanders	Total
States			
New South Wales	33,414	1,953	35,367
Queensland	33,966	10,732	44,698
South Australia	9,476	349	9,825
Tasmania	2,334	354	2,688
Victoria	5,283	774	6,057
Western Australia	30,749	602	31,351
Territories			
Australian Capital Territory	763	60	823
Northern Territory	28,680	408	29,088
Total	144,665	15,232	159,897

Inter-Censal Increases, 1961–1981

Year of Census	Population at Census			Inter-Censal Increase	Net Immigration during Period	
	Males	Females	Total			
1961	5,333,185	5,215,082	10,548,267	(b) 1,521,656	1954–1961 ..	584,754
1966	5,841,588	5,757,910	11,599,498	1,051,231	1961–1966 ..	395,485
1971 (a)	6,567,936	6,499,329	13,067,265	(c) 1,156,140	1966–1971 ..	521,139
1976 (a)	7,032,034	7,001,049	14,033,083	965,818	1971–1976 ..	281,074
1981 (a)	7,448,267	7,474,993	14,923,260	890,177	1976–1981 ..	370,865

(a) Based on Census counts, place of usual residence, adjusted for under-enumeration, and including an estimate of Australian residents temporarily overseas on Census night.
(b) Excludes full-blood Aboriginals.
(c) Based on 1971 Census figure as enumerated.

Increase of Population

Year	Births	Deaths	Net Overseas Migration (a)	Net Increase (b)	Marriages
1978	224,181	108,425	47,397	149,297	102,958
1979	223,129	106,568	68,611	171,651	104,396
1980	225,527	108,695	100,940	204,889	109,240
1981	235,842	109,003	121,785	242,083	113,905
1982	239,895	114,771	102,228	227,352	117,275
1983*	242,722	109,839	42,210	175,093	n/a

* Preliminary.
(a) Net permanent and long-term overseas migration gain with an adjustment for the net effect of category jumping.
(b) Prior to June 30, 1981, differences between the net increase shown and the sum of natural increase and net overseas migration were due to the distribution of intercensal discrepancy.

PHYSICAL FEATURES

Australia, including Tasmania, comprises a land area of 7,682,300 square kilometres lying between latitudes 10°41′S (Cape York) and 43°39′S (South East Cape, Tasmania) and longitudes 113°09′E (Steep Point) and 153°39′E (Cape Byron). The latitudinal distance between Cape York and South East Cape is about 3,680 kilometres and the longitudinal distance between Steep Point and Cape Byron is about 4,000 kilometres. (The latitudinal distance between Cape York and the most southerly point on the mainland South Point, Wilson's Promontory, is about 3,180 kilometres.)

Australia has three major landforms: the western plateau, the interior lowlands and the eastern uplands. The western half of the continent consists mainly of a great plateau. The interior lowland includes the Channel country of southwest Queensland (drainage to Lake Eyre) and the Murray-Darling river system to the south. The eastern uplands consist of a broad belt of varied width extending from north Queensland to Tasmania and composed largely of tablelands, ranges and ridges with only limited mountain areas above 1,000 metres.

Australia's large area and latitudinal range have resulted in climatic conditions ranging from the alpine to the tropical. Two thirds of the continent is arid or semi-arid although good rainfalls (over 800 mm annually) occur in the northern monsoonal belt under the influence of the Australian Asian Monsoon and along the eastern and southern highland regions under the influence of the great atmospheric depressions of the Southern Ocean. The effectiveness of the rainfall is greatly reduced by marked alternations of wet and dry seasons, unreliability from year to year, high temperatures and high potential evaporation.

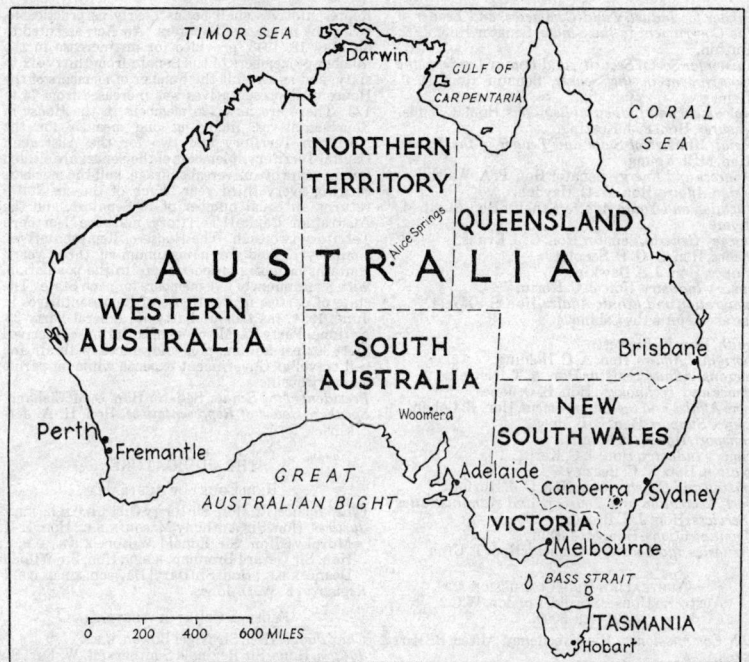

Fifty per cent of the area of Australia has a medium rainfall of less than 300 mm per year and 80 per cent has less than 600 mm. Extreme minimum temperatures are not as low as those recorded in other continents because of the absence of extensive mountain masses and because of the expanse of ocean to the south. However, extreme maxima are comparatively high, reaching 50 C. over the inland, mainly due to the great east–west extent of the continent in the vicinity of the Tropic of Capricorn.

Only one third of the Australian land mass drains directly to the ocean, mainly on the coastal side of the Main Divide and inland with the Murray–Darling system. With the exception of the Murray–Darling system, most rivers draining to the ocean are comparatively short and account for the majority of the country's average annual discharge.

GOVERNMENT

The Commonwealth of Australia was constituted by an Act of the Imperial Parliament dated July 9, 1900, and was inaugurated Jan. 1, 1901. The Government is that of a Federal Commonwealth within the British Commonwealth of Nations, the executive power being vested in the Sovereign (through the Governor-General), assisted by a Federal Ministry of twenty-seven Ministers of State. Under the Constitution the Federal Government has acquired and may acquire certain defined powers as surrendered by the States, residuary legislative power remaining with the States. Trade and customs passed under Federal control immediately on the establishment of

the Commonwealth; posts, telegraphs and telephones, naval and military defence, lighthouses and quarantine on proclaimed dates. The Federal Government also controls such matters as social services, patents and copyrights, naturalization, navigation, &c. The right of a State to legislate on these and other matters is not abrogated except in connection with matters exclusively under Federal control, but where a State law is inconsistent with a law of the Commonwealth the latter prevails to the extent of the inconsistency.

FLAG.—The British Blue Ensign, consisting of a blue flag, with the Union Jack occupying the upper quarter next the staff, differenced by a large white star (representing the six States of Australia and the Territories of the Commonwealth) in the centre of the lower quarter next the staff and pointing direct to the centre of the St. George's Cross in the Union Jack and five white stars, representing the Southern Cross, in the fly.

AUSTRALIA DAY.—January 26.

Governor-General and Staff

Governor-General, His Excellency The Rt. Hon. Sir Ninian Stephen, A.K., G.C.M.G., G.C.V.O., K.B.E., *born* June 15, 1923; *assumed office* July 29, 1982.
Official Secretary, D. I. Smith, C.V.O.
Deputy Official Secretary, K. L. Brown.

Ministry

Prime Minister, Hon. R. J. L. Hawke.
Deputy Prime Minister; Minister for Trade; Vice-President of the Executive Council, Hon. L. F. Bowen.

Minister for Industry and Commerce, and Leader of the Government in the Senate, Senator Hon. J. N. Button.

Minister for Social Security, and Deputy Leader of the Government in the Senate, Senator Hon. D. J. Grimes.

Employment and Industrial Relations, Hon. R. Willis.

Treasurer, Hon. P. J. Keating.

Special Minister of State and Leader of the House, Hon. M. J. Young.

Resources and Energy, Senator Hon. P. A. Walsh.

Foreign Affairs, Hon. W. G. Hayden.

Education and Youth Affairs, Senator Hon. Susan M. Ryan.

Attorney-General, Senator Hon. G. J. Evans.

Defence, Hon. G. G. D. Scholes.

Finance, Hon. J. S. Dawkins.

Primary Industry, Hon. J. C. Kerin.

Immigration and Ethnic Affairs, Hon. S. J. West.

(The above form the Cabinet.)

Health, Hon. N. Blewett.

Aboriginal Affairs, Hon. A. C. Holding.

Veterans' Affairs, Senator Hon. A. T. Gietzelt.

Science and Technology, Hon. B. O. Jones.

Home Affairs and the Environment, Hon. B. Cohen.

Defence Support, Hon. B. L. Howe.

Transport, Hon. P. F. Morris.

Primary Industry, Hon. J. C. Kerin.

Aviation, Hon. K. C. Beazley.

Housing and Construction, Hon. C. J. Hurford.

Sport, Recreation and Tourism, and Administrative Services, Hon. J. J. Brown.

Communications, Hon. M. J. Duffy.

Territories and Local Government, Hon. T. Uren.

AUSTRALIAN HIGH COMMISSION

Australia House, Strand, London, W.C.2.

[01–438–8000]

High Commissioner, His Excellency Alfred R. Parsons.

Deputy High Commissioner, R. H. Robertson.

Official Secretary, G. E. C. Gibson.

Ministers, J. A. Benson; G. H. Watkins (*Commercial*); J. H. Cosgrave (*Treasury*); A. J. McFarlane.

Head of Defence Staff, Rear Adm. K. Vonthethoff, A.O., R.A.N.

BRITISH HIGH COMMISSION

Commonwealth Avenue, Canberra

High Commissioner, His Excellency Sir John Leahy, K.C.M.G. (1984).

Defence and Military Adviser and Head of British Defence Liaison Staff, Maj. Gen. M. E. Carleton-Smith, C.B.E.

First Secretaries, R. D. C. Scarlett; D. E. Kipping (*Administration*); D. R. Upton; P. S. Collecott (*Economic, Commercial, Agriculture*); A. N. George; Dr. R. M. Allen (*Defence Research*); R. C. Russell (*Passports*); J. E. Bent.

Naval Adviser, Capt. B. W. Turner, R.N.

Air Adviser, Group Capt. H. Marshall, O.B.E., D.F.C.

Consuls-General, H. J. O. R. Tunnell (*Brisbane*); M. A. Cafferty (*Melbourne*); H. J. Sharland (*Perth*); M. S. Berthoud (*Sydney*).

Honorary Consul-General, H. C. Schmidt (*Adelaide*).

Cultural Adviser and British Council Representative, P. J. Prescott, 203 New South Head Road (P.O. Box 88), Edgecliff, Sydney.

THE LEGISLATURE

Parliament consists of the Queen, a Senate and a House of Representatives. The Constitution provides that the number of members of the House of Representatives shall be, as nearly as practicable, twice the number of Senators. An Act, assented to on May 18, 1948, provided for an increase in the number of members of the Senate from thirty-six to sixty, and as a result the number of members of the House of Representatives was increased from 74 to 123. There are now 125 members in the House of Representatives, including one member for the Northern Territory and two for the Australian Capital Territory. Members of the Senate are elected for six years by universal suffrage, half the members retiring every third year. Each of the six States returns an equal number of 10 Senators, and the Australian Capital Territory and the Northern Territory two each. The House of Representatives, similarly elected for a maximum of three years, contains members proportionate to the population, with a minimum of five members for each State. The state of parties in the House of Representatives in June, 1984 was Labour Party 75, Liberal Party 33, National Party 17. Members of both Houses received $A41,802 per annum, plus allowances, with air and rail travel at Government expense while on parliamentary business.

President of the Senate, Senator Hon. D. McClelland.

Speaker, House of Representatives, Hon. H. A. Jenkins.

THE JUDICATURE

HIGH COURT OF AUSTRALIA

Chief Justice, Rt. Hon. Sir Harry Gibbs, G.C.M.G., K.B.E.

Justices, Hon. Sir Anthony Mason, K.B.E.; Hon. L. K. Murphy; Hon. Sir Ronald Wilson, K.B.E., C.M.G.; Hon. Sir Gerard Brennan, K.B.E.; Hon. Sir William Deane, K.B.E.; Hon. Sir Daryl Dawson, K.B.E., C.B.

Registrar, F. W. D. Jones.

FEDERAL COURT OF AUSTRALIA

Chief Judge, Hon. Sir Nigel Bowen, K.B.E.

Judges, Hons. Sir Reginald Smithers; R. W. Fox; Sir Richard Blackburn, O.B.E.; C. A. Sweeney, O.B.E.; Sir William Forster; Sir Albert Woodward, O.B.E.; R. J. A. Franki; J. H. Muirhead; P. G. Evatt, D.S.C.; R. J. B. St. John; R. M. Northrop; J. A. Keely; J. L. Toohey; D. G. P. McGregor; F. R. Fisher; J. F. Gallop; J. D. Davies; J. S. Lockhart; I. F. Sheppard; J. J. A. Kelly; T. R. Morling; G. E. Fitzgerald; K. J. Jenkinson; A. R. Neaves; M. D. Kirby, C.M.G.; B. A. Beaumont; M. R. Wilcox; J. E. J. Spender; P. R. A. Gray.

Registrar, J. T. Howard, E.D.

SUPREME COURT OF THE AUSTRALIAN CAPITAL TERRITORY

Judges, Hons. Sir Richard Blackburn, O.B.E. (*Chief Justice*); J. J. A. Kelly; J. F. Gallop (*Resident Judges*); Sir Reginald Smithers; Sir Albert Woodward, O.B.E.; R. J. A. Franki; P. G. Evatt, D.S.C.; R. J. B. St. John; R. M. Northrop; J. D. Davies; J. S. Lockhart; D. G. P. McGregor; I. F. Sheppard; T. R. Morling; G. E. Fitzgerald; K. J. Jenkinson; B. A. Beaumont (*Additional Judges*).

Registrar, B. J. Proctor.

SUPREME COURT OF THE NORTHERN TERRITORY

Chief Justice, Hon. Sir William Forster.

Judges, Hons. J. H. Muirhead; J. A. Nader; Sir William Kearney (*Resident Judges*); J. L. Toohey; J. F. Gallop.

Master, N. Patel.

DEFENCE

A single Department of Defence was created on November 30, 1973, following the abolition of the Departments of the Navy, Army and Air, though the separate identities of the three services have been retained. The defence research and development elements of the former Department of Supply, along with other research groups on the three services, were incorporated in 1978 into the Defence, Science and Technology Organization. The Chief of Defence Force Staff is responsible for command of the Defence Force through the three Service Chiefs of Staff and is also the principal military adviser to the Minister.

The Secretary to the Department of Defence is responsible to the Minister for Defence for advice on policy, resources and organization.

Total defence expenditure amounted to $A3,646 million in 1980–81.

Royal Australian Navy

The Royal Australian Navy consists of an Anti-Submarine Warfare and strike aircraft carrier, 4 destroyers, 7 destroyer escorts, 6 submarines, 3 mines counter-measure vessels, 15 patrol boats, 2 survey ships, 2 fleet support ships, 6 heavy landing craft, 2 oceanographic ships, one training ship, 2 guided missile frigates, one heavy lift ship and one oiler. The Fleet Air Arm is equipped with Skyhawk, Tracker, Macchi, Jindivik and HS748 fixed-wing aircraft, and with Sea King, Wessex, Iroquois and Bell 206 helicopters.

The strength of the Royal Australian Navy on June 30, 1981 was 17,298.

Army

The three Australian Army commands are: Field Force Command (H.Q. Sydney), responsible for the operation of the Army's fighting formations; Logistic Command (H.Q. Melbourne) responsible for the broad military functions of transport, supply and repair; Training Command (H.Q. Sydney) responsible for the operation of all Army schools and training establishments.

On June 30, 1981 the Australian Army comprised a volunteer Regular Army component of 32,898 and a volunteer Army Reserve component (formerly known as the Citizen Military Force) of 32,737.

Air Force

The Royal Australian Air Force consists of 16 operational units, operating F111 strike aircraft, Mirage fighters, Hercules and Caribou transports, Orion maritime reconnaissance aircraft, Iroquois and Chinook helicopters, Macchi, HS748, Winjeel and CT4A trainers, HS748, Mystere and BAC1–11 special transports, and Canberra photo reconnaissance aircraft. In addition the R.A.A.F. has six maintenance squadrons, two control and reporting units, three aircraft depots, three stores depots, one ammunition depot, and many training and support establishments. Two squadrons of Mirage fighters, backed by a maintenance squadron and supporting personnel, are based at Butterworth in Malaysia. The total strength of the R.A.A.F. at June 30, 1981, was 22,322.

COMMONWEALTH FINANCE

Revenue and expenditure of the consolidated revenue fund balanced at $A44,476 million in 1982–83, compared with $A40,593 million in 1981–82. Total loan fund expenditure was $A7,356 million in 1982–83 (1981–82, $A5,487 million).

DEBT

The total of the Commonwealth Debt on June 30, 1983, was $A22,858,500,000. Adding the indebtedness of the States, viz. $A16,269,400,000, the "face" or "book" value of Commonwealth government securities on issue amounted (June 30, 1983) to $A39,127,900,000.

The Debt per head of population at June 30, 1983, was $A2,543·85.

BANKING

The weekly average of liabilities and assets (excluding shareholders' funds, interbranch accounts and contingencies) of the 6 major trading banks operating in Australia (March) were:

	1983	1984
	\$ millions	
Liabilities	44,020	48,794
Assets.........................	45,426	51,517
Total Deposits in Savings Banks	28,692	33,899

STATE AND LOCAL GOVERNMENT FINANCE

State	1981–82		
	Outlay	Receipts	Financing items
	\$Amillion	\$Amillion	\$Amillion
N.S.W.	9,699·8	8,054·1	1,645·7
Victoria	8,192·7	6,465·3	1,727·4
Queensland....	4,914·6	4,059·0	855·6
S. Australia....	2,519·3	2,197·8	321·5
W. Australia...	2,741·2	2,387·5	353·7
Tasmania......	1,071·1	892·4	178·7
N.T.	731·8	568·5	145·3
Total Six States and N.T......	29,852·5	24,624·7	5,227·8

GENERAL GOVERNMENT PERSONAL BENEFIT PAYMENTS

	1981–82	1982–83
	\$A,000	\$A,000
Hospital, Medical and Pharmaceutical Benefits......	1,948	2,302
Age and Invalid Pensions ..	5,484	5,936
Family Allowances	1,045	1,376
War and Service Pensions..	1,322	1,710
Unemployment Benefits ...	1,224	2,249
Other	2,391	2,798
Total.................	13,414	16,371

PRODUCTION AND INDUSTRY

In 1982–83, 63·0 per cent of the Australian land area consisted of agricultural establishments, with the remainder being urban areas, State forests, mining leases and unoccupied land. Crop-growing areas constituted up to 4·0 per cent of the total agricultural establishments, emphasizing the relative importance of the livestock industries in Australia (sheep in the warm, temperate, semi-arid lands and beef cattle in the tropics).

The wide range of climatic and soil conditions over the agricultural regions of Australia has resulted in a diversity of crops being grown throughout the country. Generally, cereal crops (excluding rice and sorghum) are grown in all States over wide areas, while other crops are confined to specific locations in a few States. However, scanty or erratic rainfall, limited potential for irrigation and unsuitable soils or topography have restricted intensive agriculture.

The estimated gross values of agricultural commodities ($A,000):—

	1981–82	1982–83
Crops	6,311,900	5,002,600
Livestock slaughterings ...	3,295,600	3,489,600
Livestock products	3,100,600	3,210,200

AGRICULTURAL PRODUCTION

The principal products (tonnes) were:—

	1981–82	1982–83
Cotton	324,920	285,558
Sunflower	115,123	104,021
Wheat	16,359,766	8,875,571
Oats	1,617,082	848,166
Barley	3,450,124	1,938,763
Maize	212,397	139,126
Grain Sorghum	1,316,706	958,010
Sugar-cane*	25,093,841	24,817,109
Wool (greasy basis)	717,368	701,700
Butter	74,240	n/a
Cheese	152,593	n/a
Bacon and Hams (on bone)	18,410	n/a

* Cut for crushing.

Wool production was valued (preliminary figure) at \$A1,765,800,000. Total meat production (beef, veal, mutton, lamb, pig meat) was 2,313,000 tonnes carcase weight.

Livestock (in thousands)

	1979	1980	1981	1982	1983
Sheep ..	134,222	135,985	134,407	137,976	133,237
Cattle..	27,112	26,203	25,168	24,553	22,478
Pigs....	2,301	2,518	2,430	2,373	2,490

Mines and Minerals.—Significant mineral resources comprise bauxite, coal, copper, crude petroleum, gems, gold, ilmenite, iron ore, lead, limestone, manganese, nickel, rutile, salt, silver, tin, tungsten, uranium, zinc and zircon. Recently, geological exploration has significantly increased the mineral resources of the nation.

Australia now has fourteen oilfields in production: Alton, Bennett, Conloi, Kincora, Moonie and Trinidad in Queensland; Barracouta, Cobia, Halibut, Kingfish, Mackerel and Tuna in Victoria in the offshore Gippsland Basin and from Dongara and Barrow Island in Western Australia.

Stabilised crude oil production from the Australian fields in the year 1980 amounted to 23·24 million cubic metres or some 69% of the country's total requirement. Commercial production of natural gas in 1980 amounted to 26,980,000 cubic metres per day.

In 1982–83, value added by the mining industry was estimated at \$A8,147 million. Mine production of black coal was 107, 768,000 tonnes, crude oil (incl. condensate) was 22,069 megalitres and natural gas 11,654 gigalitres. Refinery production of principal metals was:—

Aluminium	403,917 tonnes
Copper	172,456 „
Lead	212,176 „
Zinc	288,250 „
Gold	25,784 k.g.

Manufactures.—In 1982–83 there were in Australia 27,705 industrial establishments, employing 1,053,202 persons; wages paid amounted to \$A17,409m; purchases, transfers in and selected expenses \$A51,256m; value added by manufacture \$A31,074m; and turnover \$A82,326m.

Trade Unions.—On December 31, 1983, there were 319 separate trade unions in Australia with a total membership of 2,985,200.

TRADE

Total external trade (including Bullion and Specie.)

Years	Imports	Exports
1977–78....	11,166,553,000	12,269,530,000
1978–79....	13,751,845,000	14,242,747,000
1979–80....	16,217,505,000	18,870,079,000
1980–81....	18,964,266,000	19,169,243,000
1981–82.....	23,012,990,000	19,581,480,000

MAIN TRADING PARTNERS

Country	Imports from 1982–83 (\$A,000)	Exports to
Japan	4,506,447	5,964,716
China	278,296	643,792
Hong Kong	485,308	349,691
New Zealand	694,293	1,155,472
Papua New Guinea	69,042	508,321
Indonesia	561,376	384,893
Malaysia	214,502	480,010
India.................	142,288	211,512
Pakistan	23,521	55,353
Sri Lanka	11,305	22,208
Saudi Arabia	976,780	351,882
Iran	39,687	231,945
South Africa...........	84,944	144,533
U.S.A.	4,766,435	2,240,286
Canada	434,663	285,892
U.K.	1,466,957	1,178,684
Other E.E.C. countries .	2,719,798	1,875,441
Non E.E.C. European countries (incl. U.S.S.R.)	531,658	865,769

IMPORTS FROM ALL COUNTRIES, 1982–83

	\$A'000
Live animals	27,509
Meat and meat preparations	14,731
Dairy products and eggs	58,690
Fish	216,369
Cereals.............................	38,269
Fruit and Vegetables	170,122
Sugar	14,560
Coffee, tea, cocoa, spices, etc.	218,147
Feeding-stuff for animals	39,018
Miscellaneous preparations chiefly for food	38,183
Beverages	100,471
Tobacco	83,336
Hides and skins	2,452
Oil-seeds, etc.	15,316
Crude rubber	47,201
Wood, timber and cork	164,163
Pulp and waste paper	81,554
Textile fibres.......................	76,410
Crude fertilizers and minerals	194,099
Metalliferous ores and metal scrap	16,509
Crude animal and vegetable materials ...	47,716
Coal and coke	5,275
Petroleum and products................	3,092,463
Petroleum gases	678
Oils and fats	81,508
Chemical elements and compounds	700,702
Mineral tar, etc......................	17,574
Dyeing, tanning and colouring materials	78,008
Medicinal and pharmaceutical products .	193,356
Essential oils and perfume materials.....	106,108
Fertilizers, manufactured	89,557
Explosives	9,299
Plastic materials, etc.	364,228
Chemical materials and products........	234,782
Leather	45,537
Rubber manufactures	244,916
Wood and cork manufactures...........	93,370
Paper, paperboard and manufactures	484,069
Textile yarn and fabrics	1,011,440
Non-metallic mineral manufactures	368,533
Iron and steel	550,026
Non-ferrous metals	93,370
Manufactures of metal	554,262
Machinery	5,681,231
Transport equipment	2,340,857
Sanitary, plumbing, heating and lighting fixtures and fittings	40,751

Furniture	112,374
Travel goods, etc.	88,998
Clothing and clothing accessories	389,821
Footwear	144,704
Scientific instruments	437,988
Photographic apparatus, equipment, etc..	373,677
Miscellaneous manufactured articles	1,145,472
Merchandise trade, not elsewhere shown	390,132
Non-merchandise trade	590,434

MAJOR EXPORTS 1982–83

	$A'000
Meat and meat preparations	1,677,927
Dairy products and eggs	328,368
Fish and fish preparations	357,344
Cereal grains and cereal preparations	1,855,712
Fruit and vegetables	239,779
Sugar, sugar preparations and honey	581,107
Hides, skins and fur skins, undressed	232,489
Textile fibres and their waste	1,926,338
Metalliferous ores and scrap	3,753,393
Coal, coke and briquettes	3,079,742
Petroleum and petroleum products	1,152,921
Animal oils and fats	78,543
Chemical elements and compounds	45,217
Chemical materials and products, n.e.s.	85,792
Non-metallic mineral manufactures, n.e.s	110,151
Iron and steel	483,516
Non-ferrous metals	1,251,419
Manufactures of metal, n.e.s.	178,161
Machinery	770,558
Transport equipment	362,309
Miscellaneous manufactured articles, n.e.s.	167,197
Merchandise trade, not elsewhere classified, etc.	645,713

FOOD EXPORTS TO U.K. 1982–83

	$A'000
Meat and meat preparations	
Beef	18,847
Sheep, lamb and goats	4,623
Edible offal	9,903
Dairy products	6,604
Fruit and nuts, fresh or dried	7,996
Sugar, sugar preparations and honey	5,536

COMMUNICATIONS

Railways.—Gross earnings 1981–82:

	$A,000
New South Wales	663,216
Victoria	360,049
Queensland	520,265
South Australia	37,714
Western Australia	211,385
Tasmania	
Trans-Australian	
Central Australia	195,267
Northern Territory	
Capital Territory	
Total	1,887,896

Shipping.—Total arrivals and departures (one arrival and one departure per voyage, irrespective of the number of ports visited) of vessels engaged in overseas trade at the various Australian ports in 1982–83 were: arrivals 5,519 (233,978,422 deadweight tonnes); departures 5,686 (230,010,573 deadweight tonnes).

The total number of vessel calls made in 1982–83 were: arrivals 9,998 (315,465,880 dead-weight tonnes); departures 9,914 (316,847,814 dead-weight tonnes).

The total overseas shipping (excluding local shipping) which called at the ports of capital cities during 1982–83 was:

	Arrivals		Departures	
	Calls	Dead Wt. Tonnes	Calls	Dead Wt. Tonnes
Adelaide .	461	7,613,955	454	7,556,090
Brisbane .	909	16,513,235	884	16,036,966
Darwin ..	80	991,434	85	1,062,089
Fremantle	1,038	25,154,568	1,046	25,412,789
Hobart ...	172	3,116,876	158	2,907,867
Melbourne	1,259	22,759,539	1,188	21,686,696
Sydney ...	1,187	23,798,233	1,200	24,432,091

Posts and Telegraphs.—In the year ended June 30, 1983, there were 4,843 post offices dealing with 2,506,565,000 letters, 398,421,000 packets and newspapers, 6,948,000 registered articles and 32,054,000 parcels. 4,050,740 internal telegrams and 1,300,000 international telegrams were despatched. At June 30, 1983, there were 5,353 telephone exchanges with 5,591,667 services and 8,266,662 instruments.

Broadcasting and Television.—On June 30, 1983, the Australian Broadcasting Corporation operated 136 stations, including 6 short-wave stations in Australia. Privately owned commercial broadcasting stations totalled 137. On June 30, 1983, 272 television stations were in operation.

Motor Vehicles.—At June 30, 1983, there were 8,574,200 motor vehicles registered in Australia. These comprised 6,462,700 cars and station wagons, 401,900 motor cycles, and 1,709,500 commercial vehicles.

Civil Aviation.—At June 30, 1983, there were 443 licensed public aerodromes in the various States and Territories. Aircraft on the Australian Register at June 30, 1983, numbered 6,773.

FEDERAL CAPITAL

CANBERRA is the capital of Australia. It is situated in the Australian Capital Territory which has an area of 939 sq. miles (2,395 sq. km.) and was acquired from New South Wales in 1911. Canberra, which is the seat of the federal government, had a population at June 30, 1982, of 230,800. Apart from Parliament House, the city also contains other National institutions, such as the Australian War Memorial, National Library, Royal Australian Mint and the Australian National University. Most Government departments have their headquarters in Canberra. An artificial lake is a central feature of this planned city, based on Walter Burley Griffin's design.

THE NORTHERN TERRITORY

The Northern Territory has a total area of 1,346,200 square km. and lies between 129°–138° east longitude and 11°–26° south latitude. The estimated population in the Northern Territory at the 1981 Census was 126,300, of which about a quarter are Aboriginals.

The administration was taken over by the Commonwealth on January 1, 1911, from the government of the State of South Australia.

The Northern Territory (Self-Government) Act 1978 established the Northern Territory as a body politic as from 1 July 1978, with Ministers having control over and responsibility for Territory finances and the administration of the functions of government as specified by the Federal Government by regulations made pursuant to the Act. Proposed laws passed by the Legislative Assembly in relation to a transferred function require the assent of the Administrator. Proposed laws in all other cases may be assented to by the Administrator or reserved by the

Administrator for the Governor-General's pleasure. The Governor-General may disallow any laws assented to by the Administrator within six months of the Administrator's assent.

The Northern Territory has federal representation electing one member to the House of Representatives and two members to the Senate.

Administrator, His Hon. Commodore E. E. Johnston, O.B.E.

THE MINISTRY

Chief Minister, Minister for Industrial Development and Tourism, Hon. P. A. E. Everingham.
Deputy Chief Minister and Minister for Health, Youth, Sport, Recreation and Ethnic Affairs, Hon. N. Dondas.
Treasurer, Minister of Lands, Hon. M. B. Perron.
Mines and Energy, and Primary Production, Hon. I. L. Tuxworth.
Leader of the House, Attorney-General, Minister for Transport and Works, Hon. J. M. Robertson.
Education, Hon. T. Harris.
Housing and Conservation, Hon. C. N. Padgham-Purich.
Community Development, Hon. D. W. Manzie.

Various Aboriginal Land Trusts hold title to land previously called Reserves, totalling about one-fifth of the Northern Territory.

The Aboriginal Land Rights (N.T.) Act of 1976 provides for the investigation and determination of Aboriginal traditional claims to vacant Crown land or land already owned by or on behalf of Aboriginals. Successful land claims to date have increased Aboriginal ownership to 27% of the Northern Territory whilst a further 18% is the subject of claims.

A number of major Aboriginal communities previously administered by Church Mission Societies and the Federal Government are now controlled by the Aboriginal people themselves, through local Aboriginal Councils. A recent phenomenon is the voluntary movement of some Aboriginals to their traditional homeland areas where they feel that their culture will be better preserved.

ECONOMY

Northern Territory's primary production is concentrated in two industries—extensive beef cattle production and fishing. However, following the introduction of a number of government measures designed to expand and diversify primary production, the Territory's agricultural and horticultural industries are also beginning to contribute an increasing amount to Territory rural output.

The beef cattle industry continues to be the major user of pastoral lands with a herd of 1·5 million head or approximately 7 per cent of Australia's national herd. Income from cattle and beef production in 1982–83 was:—

Live cattle—sold interstate $A55,000,000
          —exported overseas 4,500,000
N.T. export abattoirs 56,000,000
N.T. domestic abattoirs 6,000,000

The buffalo population, estimated at 190,000 head is confined to the Darwin and Gulf districts. In 1982–83, the estimated gross value of production was $A5 million, derived from live exports, slaughtering for home and overseas markets and meat processing.

Egg production was 1,537,000 in 1981–82; the estimated gross value of production was in excess of $2·5 million.

The area planted to grain and seed crops expanded from just over 2,000 hectares in 1981–82 to approximately 4,000 hectares in the 1982–83 season, and the Territory is approaching self-sufficiency in maize and sorghum. Grain production in 1982–83 was 6,150

tonnes. Promising results are also being obtained with the development of fruit and vegetable crops. The climatic conditions that prevail during the Top End's dry season permit a range of out-of-season crops to be produced at a time when supplies in southern Australia are limited.

Horticultural production

	Yield (tonnes)	Area (hectares)	Estimated Wholesale Value ($A)
1981–82	2,850	190	1,140,000
1982–83	4,600	230	2,300,000

The annual gross value of production of the Northern Territory's fishing industry has averaged about $20 million over the last few years. The industry is based on barramundi and prawn production, with attempts now being made to establish shark fishing locally. To preserve the basic resource and ensure long term profitability, further expansion will depend primarily on the success of developing new, predominantly low-unit value fisheries.

Mining has played a major part in the development of the Northern Territory and is now its major industry with production in 1982 as follows:—

		Value ($A)
Uranium concentrate...	4,488*	325,000,000
Manganese ore	1,700,000*	n/a
Copper	7,150*	3,600,000
Gold	2,700,000g	32,000,000
Silver	527,000g	95,000

*Tonnes

The total value of production in 1982 was $A625 million.

Tourism is of importance to the Territory's economy. It is a major growth industry and generates over $220 million annually.

COMMUNICATIONS

The Northern Territory has three main ports—Darwin, managed by the Northern Territory Port Authority; and the private mining ports of Gove, operated by Nabalco Pty. Ltd., and Groote Eylandt, operated by Groote Eylandt Mining Co. Pty. Ltd.

The new standard gauge rail link between Southern Australia and Alice Springs was officially opened in October, 1980. The link between Alice Springs and Darwin is provided by a fully co-ordinated rail-road service.

The main population centres are linked by the Stuart Highway, which connects Alice Springs to Darwin via Tennant Creek and Katherine. The Barkly Highway (444 km.) east from Tennant Creek, and the Victoria Highway (468 km.) west from Katherine, connect to the National Highway networks of Queensland and Western Australia. Of special interest to the Northern Territory is the operation of "road trains". These are basically massive trucks hauling two or three trailers, having a net capacity of about 100 tonnes and measuring up to 45 metres in length.

The two national domestic carriers, Trans-Australia Airlines (T.A.A.) and Ansett Airlines of Australia, both operate daily services to and from all Australian capital cities and main Northern Territory centres. In addition to the two national domestic carriers, intra-Territory services are provided by Airlines of Northern Australia (A.N.A.), plus a number of smaller commuter operators. There are also a number of charter and general aviation operators providing feeder type services. Qantas currently operates one international flight out of Darwin each week and Garuda provides two services weekly to Bali and Jakarta. Royal Brunei provide a weekly service linking Darwin and Bandar Seri Beyawan, with connections to Hong Kong, etc.

AUSTRALIAN EXTERNAL TERRITORIES

ASHMORE AND CARTIER ISLANDS

Ashmore Islands (known as Middle, East and West Islands) and Cartier Island are situated in the Indian Ocean some 850 km. and 790 km. west of Darwin respectively. The Islands lie at the outer edge of the continental shelf. They are small and low and are composed of coral and sand. Vegetation consists mainly of grass. Turtles are plentiful at certain times of the year and beche-de-mer is abundant. The Islands are uninhabited.

Great Britain took formal possession of the Ashmores in 1878 and Cartier was annexed in 1909. By Imperial Order in Council of July 23, 1931, the Islands were placed under the authority of the Commonwealth of Australia, and were accepted in 1933 under the name of the Territory of Ashmore and Cartier Islands. The Territory was annexed to and deemed to form part of the Northern Territory of Australia with relevant laws of the Northern Territory applying to the Territory of Ashmore and Cartier Islands. From July 1, 1978, responsibility for the administration of Ashmore and Cartier Islands became a direct responsibility of the Commonwealth of Australia.

In accordance with an agreement between the governments of Indonesia and Australia, Indonesian fishermen who have traditionally plied the area may fish within the Territory and land to collect water at certain locations.

THE AUSTRALIAN ANTARCTIC TERRITORY

The *Australian Antarctic Territory* was established by an Order in Council, dated February 7, 1933, which placed under the government of the Commonwealth of Australia all the islands and territories, other than Adélie Land, which are situated south of the latitude 60° S. and lying between 160° E. longitude and 45° E. longitude. The Order came into force on August 24, 1936, after the passage of the Australian Antarctic Territory Acceptance Act, 1933. The boundaries of Terre Adélie were definitely fixed by a French Decree of April 1, 1938, as the islands and territories south of 60° S. latitude lying between 136° E. longitude and 142° E. longitude. The Australian Antarctic Territory Act, 1954 declared that the laws in force in the Australian Capital Territory are, so far as they are applicable, in force in the Australian Antarctic Territory.

On February 13, 1954, the Australian National Antarctic Research Expeditions (ANARE) opened a station in Mac-Robertson Land at latitude 67° 36′ S. and longitude 62° 53′ E. The station was named Mawson in honour of Sir Douglas Mawson and was the first permanent Australian station to be set up on the Antarctic continent. Scientific research conducted at Mawson includes upper atmosphere physics, cosmic ray physics, meteorology, earth sciences, biology and medical science. Mawson is also a centre for coastal and inland exploration.

A second Australian scientific research station was opened on the coast of Princess Elizabeth Land on January 13, 1957, at latitude 68° 35′ S. and longitude 77° 58′ E., and was named in honour of Captain John King Davis. Scientific programmes carried out at Davis include meteorology, biology, upper atmosphere physics, with field investigations in biology.

In February, 1959, the Australian Government accepted from the U.S. Government custody of Wilkes Station on the Budd Coast, Wilkes Land at about 66° 15′ S. and longitude 110° 31′ E. The station was closed in February 1969, and activities were transferred to Casey station. Casey station was named in honour of Lord Casey, a former Governor-General of Australia. The station, at 66° 17′ S., 110° 32′ E., is of advanced design and scientific programmes carried out there include geophysics, meteorology with field programmes in glaciology, geology, etc.

Since 1948 ANARE has also operated a station on Macquarie Island, a dependency of Tasmania, situated at 54° 30′ S. and 158° 57′ E., about 900 miles north of the Antarctic Continent.

For other Commonwealth dependencies in the Antarctic *see* New Zealand; British Antarctic Territory.

CHRISTMAS ISLAND

Until the end of 1957 a part of the then Colony of Singapore, Christmas Island was administered as a separate colony until October 1, 1958, when it became Australian territory. It is situated in the Indian Ocean about 224 miles S. of Java Head. Area 52 sq. miles. Population (estimated, June 30, 1982) is 3,018, consisting of employees of the Phosphate Mining Company and the Administration, and their families. There is no indigenous population.

The island is densely wooded and contains extensive deposits of phosphates, the recovery of which is the major economic activity. An Australian Government company, the Phosphate Mining Company of Christmas Island, carries out the mining activities. New Zealand has the right to purchase up to half of the Island's phosphate rock output. The island is administered by the Australian Government through the Department of Territories and Local Government in Canberra.

Administrator, T. F. Paterson.

COCOS (KEELING) ISLANDS

The Cocos (Keeling) Islands were declared a British possession in 1857. In 1878 they were placed under the control of the Governor of Ceylon and were later annexed to the Straits Settlements and incorporated with the colony of Singapore. On Nov. 23, 1955, their administration was transferred to Australia. On April 6, 1984, the Cocos community, in an Act of Self-Determination observed by a U.N. mission, chose to integrate with Australia.

The Islands are two separate atolls (North Keeling Island and, 24 km. to the south, the main atoll) comprising some 27 small coral islands with a total area of about 5½ square miles, situated in the Indian Ocean in latitude 12° 5′ South and longitude 96° 53′ East. The main islands of the southern atoll are West Island (the largest, about 6 miles from north to south) on which are the administrative centre, the aerodrome, and the Australian-based employees of government departments; Home Island, where the Cocos Malay community lives; Direction Island, Horsburgh and South Island.

The main economic activity is the production of copra: total exports 1982–83 were 165 metric tons. The climate is equable and pleasant, being usually under the influence of the south-east trade winds for about three-quarters of the year. A weekly air charter service operates between Perth, the Cocos (Keeling) Islands and Christmas Island. Population (June 30, 1983), 559. The islands are administered by the Australian Government through the Department of Territories and Local Government in Canberra, although all proposed Ordinances, Regulations and By-laws for the Islands must be submitted to the Islands Council (est. 1979) for its consideration.

Administrator, Dr. K. Chan.

CORAL SEA ISLANDS TERRITORY

The territory lies between the Great Barrier Reef and longitude 157° 10′ E., and between latitudes 12° and 24° S. It comprises scattered reefs and islands, often little more than sandbanks, spread over a sea area of 1,035,995 sq. km. The islands are formed, mainly of coral and sand; some have a cover of grassy or scrub-type vegetations. Large populations of sea birds nest and breed in the area.

The Australian Government bases its claim to the islands on numerous acts of sovereignty since early this century and enacted the Coral Sea Islands Act 1969 which declares the islands a Territory of the Commonwealth of Australia.

HEARD ISLAND AND McDONALD ISLANDS

The islands, about 4,100 km. south-west of Fremantle, comprise all the islands and rocks lying between 52° 30′ and 53° 30′ S. latitude and 72° and 74° 30′ E. longitude. Sovereignty over the islands was transferred by the U.K. to the Commonwealth of Australia in 1947. The Heard Island and McDonald Islands Act 1953 provides for the government of the islands as one Territory and under this Act the law operating there is that of the Australian Capital Territory. The Islands are administered by the Department of Science and Technology.

NORFOLK ISLAND

The island is situated in latitude 29° 02′ S. and longitude 167° 57′ E., being about 1,042 miles from Sydney and 400 miles north of New Zealand. It is about five miles in length by three in breadth, with an area of 8,528 acres and circumference of 20 miles. The climate is mild, with a mean temperature of 20° C. The descendants of the mutineers of the *Bounty* were brought here from Pitcairn Island in 1856. The island is a popular tourist resort, and a large proportion of the population depends on tourism and its ancillaries for employment. Resident population at the 1981 Census was 1,849.

Seat of Government and Administration Offices, Kingston. A Legislative Assembly was elected in 1979, enabling the island to run its affairs to the greatest practical extent, and it is intended that the island will achieve full internal self-government as a Territory under the authority of the Commonwealth. The island is currently administered by the Australian Government through the Department of Territories and Local Government in Canberra.

Regular air services operate from Australia and New Zealand.

Administrator, Air Vice-Marshal R. E. Trebilco, A.O., D.F.C.

STATES OF THE COMMONWEALTH OF AUSTRALIA

NEW SOUTH WALES

The State of New South Wales is situated entirely between the 28th and 38th parallels of S. lat. and 141st and 154th meridians of E. long., and comprises an area of 309,433 square miles (exclusive of 939 sq. miles of Australian Capital Territory which lies within its borders).

POPULATION.—Estimated resident population (June 30, 1983): Males, 2,671,200; Females, 2,689,200. Total, 5,360,400.

Births, Deaths and Marriages

Year	Births	Deaths	Marriages
1980	79,455	40,282	38,965
1981	81,530	39,959	40,679
1982	83,489	42,352	41,955
1983	82,739	40,324	39,995

Vital Statistics.—Annual rate per 1,000 of estimated resident population in 1983:—Births, 15·4; Deaths, 7·5; Marriages, 7·5. Deaths under 1 year per 1,000 live births, 9·7.

Religions

The members of the Church of England in New South Wales, according to the Census of 1981, numbered, 1,569,374. Roman Catholic (including "Catholic") 1,424,499, Presbyterian 252,725, Uniting 179,271, Orthodox 171,427, Methodist 148,992, Baptist 64,663, Lutheran 31,696, other Christian 239,895, Hebrew 25,176 and Muslim 38,527. The religion of 934,305 persons was either not stated in the census schedules or was stated as "none".

PHYSIOGRAPHY

Natural features divide the State into four strips of territory extending from north to south, viz., the Coastal Divisions; the Tablelands, which form the Great Dividing Range between the coastal districts and the plains; the Western Slopes of the Dividing Range; and the Western Plains. The highest points are Mounts Kosciusko, 7,314 feet, and Townsend,

7,251 feet. The western portion of the State is watered by the rivers of the Murray-Darling system and immense reservoirs have been constructed for irrigation purposes, as well as many artesian bores. The Darling, 1,712 miles, and the Murrumbidgee, 981 miles, are both tributaries of the Murray, part of which forms the boundary between the States of New South Wales and Victoria.

Climate.—New South Wales is situated entirely in the Temperate Zone. The climate is generally mild and mostly free from extremes of heat and cold. At Sydney the average mean shade temperature is 18° C. The mean (shade) temperature ranges for the various divisions of the State are as follows: coastal, 15° C in the south to 20°C in the north; northern and central tableland, 12° C to 16° C; southern tableland, 7° C to 14° C; and for the rest of the State (western slope, central plains, Riverina and western), 15° C in the south to 20° C in the north.

GOVERNMENT

New South Wales was first colonized as a British possession in 1788, and after progressive settlement a partly elective legislature was established in 1843. In 1855 Responsible Government was granted, the present Constitution being founded on the Constitution Act of 1902. New South Wales federated with the other States of Australia in 1901. The executive authority of the State is vested in a Governor (appointed by the Crown), assisted by a Council of Ministers.

GOVERNOR

Governor of New South Wales, His Excellency Air Marshal Sir James Rowland, K.B.E., D.F.C., A.F.C., *assumed office* Jan. 20, 1981.
Lieutenant-Governor, Hon. Sir Laurence Whistler Street, K.C.M.G.

THE MINISTRY
(at June 4, 1984)

Premier and Minister for Arts, Hon. N. K. Wran, Q.C.
Deputy Premier, Minister for Health, Hon. R. J. Mulock.

Youth and Community Services, and Housing, Hon.
F. J. Walker, Q.C.
Public Works and Ports; Roads, Hon. L. J. Brereton.
Attorney-General, Hon. D. P. Landa.
Industrial Relations, Hon. P. D. Hills.
Agriculture and Fisheries, Hon. J. R. Hallam.
Police and Emergency Services, Hon. P. T. Anderson.
Treasurer, Hon. K. G. Booth.
Planning and Environment, Hon. T. W. Sheahan.
Transport and Vice-President of the Council, Hon.
B. J. Unsworth.
Education, Hon. R. M. Cavalier.
Mineral Resources and Energy, Hon. P. F. Cox.
Local Government, Hon. K. J. Stewart.
*Industry and Decentralisation; Small Business and
Technology,* Hon. E. L. Bedford.
Consumer Affairs; Aboriginal Affairs, Hon. G. Pa-
ciullo.
Natural Resources, Hon. J. A. Crosio.
Employment; Finance, Hon. R. J. Debus.
Corrective Services, Hon. J. E. Akister.
Sport and Recreation; Tourism, Hon. M. A. Cleary.

The annual salaries of Ministers are: Premier,
$A78,090; Deputy Premier, $A70,304; Leader of the
Government members in the Legislative Council,
$A71,095; (Deputy $A67,719); other Ministers
$A66,380 each. Ministers also receive expense allow-
ances and electoral allowances, and a special expense
allowance is paid to Ministers who represent or
reside in outlying electorates.

AGENT-GENERAL IN LONDON,
N.S.W. House, 66 Strand, W.C.2

Agent-General, R. F. W. Watson, C.M.G.

THE LEGISLATURE

The *Legislative Council* consists of 45 members,
elected by popular vote and the *Legislative Assembly*
consists of 99 members elected for a maximum period
of 3 years. Party representation in the Council at
May 1, 1984 was: Labour 24, Liberal 11, National 7,
Australian Democrat 1, and Independent 2. The
annual salaries of members of the Legislative Council
and Legislative Assembly who are not Ministers are
$A29,450 and $A38,000 respectively. Members also
receive expense and electoral allowances, and a
special expense allowance is paid to members who
reside in, or represent, outlying electorates. Party
representation in the Assembly at May 1, 1984 was:
Labour 58, Liberal 22, National 15 and Independent
4.

President of the Legislative Council, Hon. J. R.
Johnson.
Speaker, Legislative Assembly, Hon. L. B. Kelly.

THE JUDICATURE

The judicial system includes a Supreme Court
(with Chief Justice, President of the Court of Appeal,
six Judges of Appeal, three Chief Judges, five Masters
and 26 Judges), Industrial Commission (President
and nine Deputy Presidents), District Court (Chief
Judge and 35 Judges), Land and Environment Court,
Workers' Compensation Commission and Police Tribunal.

Chief Justice, Supreme Court, Hon. Sir Laurence
Street (+ allce. $A5,134) $A95,394
President, Court of Appeal, Hon. Mr. Justice Moffit
(+ allce. $A4,140) $A89,930
Chief Justice, District Court, Hon. Judge Staunton
(+ allce. $A4,140) $A87,445

GOVERNMENT FINANCES

Consolidated Fund, for year ended June 30th,
vas:—

	1982	1983
	$A'000	$A'000
Receipts	5,915,854	6,531,024
Expenditure	5,975,670	6,571,146
Public Debt	5,108,066	5,327,886

Banking, etc.—There were (March 1984) 8 trading
banks with deposits of $A16,659 million. Savings
bank deposits amounted to $A9,426 million, repre-
senting $A1,757 per head of the population.

EDUCATION

Education.—Education is compulsory between the
ages of 6 and 15 years. It is non-sectarian and free at
all government schools. The enrolment in July 1983
in 2,237 government schools was 778,410. In addition
to the government schools there were, in 1983, 831
non-government schools, with an enrolment of
251,506 students. The six universities had an enrolment of 64,521 students in 1983. Colleges of Advanced
Education which provide courses at tertiary level,
but with a more vocational emphasis than universities, had 45,619 students enrolled in 1983. Students
enrolled in technical and further education colleges
in 1983 numbered 347,031. State Government expenditure on education was $A2,007,300,000 in the year
1982–83.

PRODUCTION AND INDUSTRY

Local value of production in 1982–83 was:—

Agricultural commodities	$A2,668,603,889
Crops	879,476,074
Livestock products	889,153,400
Slaughterings.	889,974,415
Mining and Quarrying	1,851,505,000
Manufacturing	11,347,000,000

Crops.—The production of wheat in 1982–83 was
1,499,406 tonnes of grain and 29,340 tonnes of hay.
Other important crops in 1982–83 were (tonnes):
Barley 189,398; Oats 134,899; Rice 525,488; Cotton
205,501; Oilseed 47,546; Potatoes 108,799; Sugar-cane
crushed 1,702,342; 913,381 kilograms of dried leaf
tobacco and 68,645,900 kilograms of bananas were
obtained; almost every kind of fruit and vegetable is
grown.
Livestock and Livestock Products.—A large area is
suitable for sheep-raising, the principal breed of sheep
being the merino, which was introduced in 1797. On
March 31, 1983, there were 5,018,022 cattle, 48,094,638
sheep and lambs, and 794,346 pigs. In 1982–83,
218,071,088 kg. (stated as in the grease) of wool were
produced, 1,956,000 kg. of butter, 11,667,000 kg. of
cheese, and 22,457,000 kg. of bacon and ham.
Mining Industry.—The principal minerals are coal,
lead, zinc, tin, rutile, copper and zircon. The total
value of minerals won in 1982–83 was $A2,520,134,000,
of which the value of output of the coal mining
industry was $A1,922,720,000 and of the silver-lead-
zinc industry, $A273,345,000 and the construction
materials industry, including stone, gravel and sand,
was $A212,514,000. The average number of persons
employed in the mining industry during 1982–83 was
28,607. In 1982–83, 66,297,478 tonnes of coal were
produced.
Manufacturing Industry.—At June 30, 1983, there
were 10,508 manufacturing establishments (employing four of more persons). The average number of
persons employed during 1982–83 was 386,334. Large
iron and steel works with subsidiary factories are in
operation at Newcastle and Port Kembla in proximity
to the coalfields. Products of the regions include iron
and steel, pipes, boilers, steel wire and wire netting,
copper wire, copper and brass cables and tin-plate.
The production (1982–83) of pig-iron was 4,084,000
tonnes, and of raw steel 4,533,000 tonnes.

OVERSEAS TRADE

Year ended June 30	Overseas Imports $A(f.o.b.)	Overseas Exports $A(f.o.b.)
1980	6,704,649,000	4,103,985,000
1981	7,951,738,168	4,103,507,000
1982	9,235,665,000	4,194,662,855
1983	8,610,737,630	4,956,144,989

The chief exports in 1982–83 were coal and coke, meat, wool, petroleum products and wheat. Chief imports were machinery, office and transport equipment, petroleum and petroleum products, telecommunications and recording equipment, and printed matter.

TRANSPORT AND COMMUNICATIONS

Shipping.—2,498 vessels entered the major ports of N.S.W. from overseas during the year ended June 30, 1983, the gross tonnage being 45,933,823. The shipping entries at Sydney were 1,701 vessels of 25,591,431 gross tonnage.

Roads and Bridges.—Expenditures by the State Government and the local authorities on road systems and regulation in 1981–82 was $A788,800,000. Sydney Harbour Bridge carries eight lanes of roadway and two lines of railway. At mean high water there is a headway of 52·6 m.

Motor Vehicles.—At June 30, 1983, there were 2,821,100 registered motor vehicles (cars, 1,788,800).

Railways.—The railways of New South Wales are controlled by the State, which also operates bus and ferry services in the Sydney and Newcastle metropolitan areas. At June 30, 1983, the route kilometres of the State railways open for traffic was 9,883, revenue in the year 1982–83 being $A1,295,112,000.

Aviation.—Sydney is the principal overseas terminal in Australia. Traffic movements at Sydney airport in 1982 were: passengers 8,101,465; freight 158,876 tonnes; aircraft, 99,101.

Postal and Telecommunication Services.—The postal and telecommunication services are administered by the Australian Government. At June 30, 1983, there were 1,537 post offices in New South Wales. Transmit time between Sydney and London is approximately 2½ days for airborne mail and between 4 and 6 weeks for seaborne mail. Telephone and telex services in operation numbered 2,098,615 and 14,252 respectively.

Radio and Television.—At June 30, 1983, there were 22 National Broadcasting Stations in New South Wales and 41 commercial stations operating under licence. There were also 23 licensed non-profit radio stations providing special interest services not catered for by the national and commercial services. At June 30, 1983, there were 28 television stations (14 national, 14 commercial) in operation.

TOWNS

ΨSYDNEY, the chief city and State capital and the largest city in Australia, stands on the shores of Port Jackson, Sydney Harbour extends inland for 21 km.: the total area of water is about 55 sq. km.

The estimated resident population at June 30, 1983 of the Sydney Statistical Division was 3,332,550. The Newcastle and Wollongong Statistical Districts contain populations of 414,250 and 234,800 respectively.

The populations of principal municipalities located outside the boundaries of these statistical areas are: Albury 38,600, Bathurst 24,250, Broken Hill 27,400, Dubbo 29,800, Goulburn 22,400, Greater Lithgow 21,000, Greater Taree 33,900, Hastings 38,200, Lismore 36,200, Orange 31,950, Queanbeyan 20,450, Shoalhaven 54,000, Tamworth 33,100, Wagga Wagga 49,350.

LORD HOWE ISLAND

Lord Howe Island, which is part of New South Wales, is situated 702 kilometres north-east of Sydney. Lat. 31° 33′ 4″ S., Long. 159° 4′ 26″ E. Area 17 sq. km. Pop. June 30, 1983, 300. The island is of volcanic origin with Mount Gower reaching an altitude of 866 m. The affairs of the Island are administered by the Lord Howe Island Board.

QUEENSLAND

This State, situated in lat. 10° 40′–29° S. and long. 138°–153° 30′ E., comprises the whole north-eastern portion of the Australian continent.

Queensland possesses an area of 1,727,000 square km. (*i.e.*, equal to more than 5½ times the area of the British Isles).

POPULATION.—At June 30, 1983, the estimated resident population numbered 2,471,600 persons.

Births, Deaths and Marriages

Year	Births	Deaths	Marriages
1981	38,834	17,175	18,305
1982	40,540	18,419	18,928
1983	42,000	17,200	18,645

Vital Statistics:—Annual rate per 1,000 of mean population in 1982–83; Births, 17·0; Deaths, 7·0; Marriages 7·5. Deaths under 1 year, 10·0 per 1,000 live births.

Religions

At the Census of 1981, there were 601,537 Anglican, 554,912 Roman Catholics (including Catholics undefined), 146,898 Uniting Church, 132,525 Presbyterians, 86,750 Methodists, 50,401 Lutherans, 34,323 Baptists, and 166,611 other Christians.

PHYSIOGRAPHY

The Great Dividing Range on the eastern coast of the continent produces a similar formation to that of New South Wales, the eastern side having a narrow slope to the coast and the western a long and gradual slope to the central plains, where the Selwyn and Kirby Ranges divide the land into a northern and southern watershed. The Brisbane, Burnett, Fitzroy and Burdekin rise in the eastern ranges and flow into the Pacific, the Flinders, Mitchell, and Leichhardt into the Gulf of Carpentaria, and the Barcoo and Warrego rise in the central ranges and flow southwards.

GOVERNMENT

Queensland was constituted a separate colony with responsible government in 1859, having previously formed part of New South Wales. The executive authority is vested in a Governor (appointed by the Crown), aided by an Executive Council of 18 members.

GOVERNOR

Governor of Queensland, His Excellency Commodore Sir James Maxwell Ramsay, K.C.M.G., K.C.V.O., C.B.E., D.S.C. $A50,000

EXECUTIVE COUNCIL.
(H.E. the Governor presides.)

Premier and Treasurer, Hon. Sir Johannes Bjelke-Petersen, K.C.M.G. $A82,627
Deputy Premier and Minister assisting the Treasurer, Hon. W. A. M. Gunn $A70,934
Mines and Energy, Hon. I. J. Gibbs.
Industry, Small Business and Technology, Hon. M. J. Ahern.

Transport, Hon. D. F. Lane.
Lands and Forestry, and Police, Hon. W. H. Glasson.
Health, Hon. B. D. Austin.
Education, Hon. L. W. Powell.
Water Resources and Maritime Services, Hon. J. P. Goleby.
Primary Industry, Hon. N. J. Turner.
Employment and Industrial Affairs, Hon. V. P. Lester.
Environment, Valuation and Administrative Services, Hon. M. J. Tenni.
Justice and Attorney General, Hon. N. J. Harper.
Welfare Services and Ethnic Affairs, Hon. G. H. Muntz.
Tourism, National Parks, Sport and the Arts, Hon. P. R. McKechnie.
Northern Development and Aboriginal and Island Affairs, Hon. R. C. Katten.
Ministers, each $A65,145.

AGENT-GENERAL IN LONDON

Agent-General for Queensland, J. Hayward Andrews, 392–393 Strand, W.C.2.

THE LEGISLATURE

Parliament consists of a *Legislative Assembly* of 82 members, elected by all persons aged 18 years and over. Members of the Assembly receive $A39,833 per annum plus an electorate allowance. The Assembly, as elected on October 22, 1983, was composed of: National Party, 41; Liberal Party, 8; Australian Labour Party, 32.

Speaker, Hon. J. H. Warner............ $A54,526
Chairman of Committees, E. C. Row...... $A44,618

THE JUDICATURE

There is a Supreme Court, with a Chief Justice, a Senior Puisne Judge and 16 Puisne Judges; District Courts, with 22 Judges; an Industrial Court, with a Supreme Court Judge as President; a Land Court and a Medical Assessment Tribunal, each presided over by a Judge of the Supreme Court; a Local Government Court, presided over by a District Court Judge; the Industrial Conciliation and Arbitration Commission consisting of 5 members; Inferior Courts at all the principal towns, presided over by Stipendiary Magistrates; a Small Claims Tribunal; and a Licensing Court.

Chief Justice, Supreme Court, Hon. Sir Walter Campbell $A93,675
Senior Puisne Judge, Hon. D. G. Andrews 82,800

EDUCATION

Education is compulsory between the ages of 6 and 15 years and is provided free in Government schools. At July 1983 the State administered 1,047 primary, 78 primary/secondary, and 148 secondary schools with 250,955 primary students, 122,622 secondary students, and 21,525 teachers. Special education, which is included in the above figures, was provided to 5,348 children by 746 teachers at 62 special schools and 55 primary schools with special classes. Non-government enrolments at July 1983 were 58,264 primary students and 49,727 secondary students taught by 5,654 teachers at 225 primary, 60 primary/secondary and 78 secondary schools.

Post-secondary education involves technical and further education (TAFE), advanced education, and university education. During 1982, 335 full-time and 508 part-time students were enrolled in tertiary courses at TAFE colleges and 5,968 full-time and 98,613 part-time students (including apprenticeship students) were enrolled in non-tertiary courses at these colleges and rural training schools. At 30 April 1982, there were 10,713 full-time and 12,440 part-time students enrolled in approved advanced education courses at colleges of advanced education and 149 full-time and 1,014 part-time students were enrolled

in other courses. The three universities had enrolments of 12,464 full-time students and 10,064 part-time students at April 30, 1982.

PRODUCTION AND INDUSTRY

Agriculture and Livestock.—The gross value of agricultural commodity production in 1982–83 was $A2,366,802,000 (including crops $A1,267,886,000, livestock disposals $A784,575,000, livestock products $A314,341,000.

The most important crop in 1982–83 was sugarcane, producing 3,325,000 tonnes of raw sugar. Wheat yielded 1,754,384 tonnes, maize 87,393 tonnes, sorghum 757,704 tonnes and barley 268,471 tonnes. The livestock on March 31, 1983 included 9,349,455 cattle, 368,729 being dairy cattle, 12,225,003 sheep and 551,469 pigs.

Forestry.—Total Australian grown timber processed in 1982–83 amounted to 1,085,385 cubic metres (gross volume measure).

Minerals.—There are rich deposits of both metallic and non-metallic minerals. Coal is mined extensively in Central Queensland and on a lesser scale in North Queensland and Ipswich districts.

Output in 1982–83

	$A
Bauxite	100,554,201
Coal	1,446,733,300
Copper concentrate.................	164,354,091
Crude oil and natural gas	43,597,792
Gold (various forms)	12,759,922
Lead concentrate	191,066,794
Mineral sands......................	27,914,566
Nickel ore	12,476,150
Scheelite and wolfram concentrate...	227,660
Tin concentrate	24,204,439
Uranium concentrate...............	31,603,183
Zinc concentrate	47,441,654

Manufacturing.—In 1981–82 there were 3,556 establishments with four or more workers, employing 122,717 persons, and producing goods and services worth $A10,590 million. The value added was $A3,448 million. Much of the production was the processing of primary products, *e.g.* foodstuffs, timber and minerals. Included in other factory production were the products from engineering, transport equipment, basic and fabricated metal, chemical and fertilizer works, cement, paper and textile mills and oil refineries.

FINANCE

Government finance ($A'000) was:—

	1982	1983
Revenue	3,276,756	3,690,187
Expenditure	3,276,926	3,690,956
Gross Debt	2,112,070	2,197,901

Banking.—Advances made by Trading Banks (including the Commonwealth Trading Bank of Australia) at June 30, 1983, totalled $A4,096,347,000. The deposits at the same date amounted to $A5,886,578,000. Depositors' balances in Queensland savings banks at June 30, 1983, $A4,136,077,000, averaged $A1,696 for each inhabitant. There were 3,394,000 operative accounts.

OVERSEAS TRADE

Year	Imports	Exports
1980–81	$A1,882,815,000	$A4,501,290,000
1981–82	2,179,752,000	4,414,452,000
1982–83	1,994,608,000	4,470,870,000

The chief overseas exports are coal, non-ferrous metals, meat, sugar, wool, and cereal grains.

COMMUNICATIONS

Road and Rail.—The State is served by 9,979 kilometres of railways, practically all of 1,067 milli-metres gauge. During 1982–83, 34,749,000 passengers and 43,706,000 tonnes of goods and livestock were carried. At June 30, 1983, there were 141,120 kilometres of formed roads in the State, and 1,496,100 motor vehicles were on the register.

Aviation.—Regular services operate between Brisbane, the main Queensland coastal and inland towns and the southern capitals. Brisbane, Townsville and Cairns are also ports of call on several international services.

Radio and Television.—On June 30, 1983, 27 national and 29 commercial sound broadcasting and 32 national and 11 commercial television stations were operating in Queensland. There were five public broadcasting stations.

TOWNS

CAPITAL, ΨBRISBANE, is situated on the Brisbane River, which is navigable by large vessels to the city, over 23 kilometres from Moreton Bay. The estimated resident population of the Brisbane Statistical Division at June 30, 1983 was 1,138,370. This area includes the cities of Brisbane (740,130), Ipswich (73,950), Logan (99,930) and Redcliffe (45,290).

Other cities and towns with population over 10,000 at June 30, 1983, are: ΨTownsville, 82,450; Gold Coast, 113,690; Toowoomba, 74,450; ΨRockhampton, 54,700; ΨCairns, 38,110; ΨBundaberg, 32,670; Mount Isa, 25,350; ΨMaryborough, 22,400; ΨMackay, 22,750; ΨGladstone, 25,310; ΨHervey Bay, 15,700; Gympie, 11,380.

Transmission of mails from London to Brisbane, by air, 3 days; by sea 5 to 6 weeks.

SOUTH AUSTRALIA

The State of South Australia is situated between 26° and 38° S. lat. and 129° and 141° E. long., the total area being 380,070 sq. miles.

POPULATION.—At June 30, 1983, the resident population was estimated to be 1,340,400.

Births, Deaths and Marriages

Year	Births	Deaths	Marriages
1980	18,499	9,582	10,064
1981	19,310	9,706	10,252
1982	19,294	10,457	10,935
1983	19,865	9,882	10,550

Religions

Religion is free and receives no State aid. At the Census, 1981, the persons belonging to the principal religious denominations were as follows: Church of England, 260,919; Methodists, 85,935; Congregationalists, 2,834; Baptists, 22,287; Lutherans, 63,860; Roman Catholics, 255,332; Presbyterians, 21,725; Churches of Christ, 18,657; Greek Orthodox, 36,423; Uniting Church, 108,857; and Pentecostal, 11,232.

PHYSIOGRAPHY

The most important physical features of South Australia are broad plains, divided longitudinally by four great secondary features, which form barriers to east-west movement, and which have thus largely determined the direction of roads and railways, the sites of towns and villages and the manner of distribution of the population. These four barriers

are Spencer Gulf, Gulf St. Vincent, the Mt. Lofty-Flinders Ranges and the River Murray. The long, deeply-indented coast-line, which provides a few major, and a multitude of lesser harbours, trends generally south-eastward. Pleasant weather conditions and good rainfall are experienced in most coastal areas.

The north-western portion of the State is mostly desert, while north of latitude 32° S. the country is unpromising by comparison with the fertile land which surrounds the hill country of the east. The Murray, which flows for some 400 miles through the south-eastern corner, is the only river of importance.

The lack of rivers and fresh-water lakes in the settled areas has necessitated the building of a number of reservoirs, which have been supplemented since 1941 by the construction of pipelines from the River Murray.

Climate.—The mean annual temperature at Adelaide is 17·1°C, the winter temperature (June-August) averaging 11·9°C, and the summer (Nov.-Mar.) 22·3°C. During the summer months the maximum temperature at times exceeds 40°C, but is associated with a relatively low humidity. The average annual rainfall at Adelaide, derived from over 140 years' record is 21 inches. This total is rather higher than the approximate average annual rainfall over the whole of the agricultural areas.

GOVERNMENT

South Australia was proclaimed a British Province in 1836, and in 1851 a partially elective legislature was established. The present Constitution rests upon a Law of Oct. 24, 1856, the executive authority being vested in a Governor appointed by the Crown, aided by a Council of 13 Ministers.

GOVERNOR

Governor of South Australia, His Excellency Lt. Gen. Sir Donald B. Dunstan, K.B.E., C.B. (1982) $A30,000
Lieut.-Governor, Hon. Sir Condor Laucke, K.C.M.G. (1982).

THE MINISTRY

Premier, Treasurer, Minister of State Development, and for the Arts, Hon. J. C. Bannon.
Deputy Premier; Chief Secretary; Minister of Labour and of Emergency Services, Hon. J. D. Wright.
Attorney-General; Minister of Consumer Affairs, Corporate Affairs, and Ethnic Affairs, Hon. C. J. Sumner.
Environment and Planning, of Lands and Repatriation, Hon. D. J. Hopgood.
Transport and Marine, Hon. R. K. Abbott.
Health, Hon. J. R. Cornwall.
Education and Technology, Hon. L. M. F. Arnold.
Tourism and Local Government, Hon. G. F. Keneally.
Mines and Energy, Hon. R. G. Payne.
Community Welfare and Aboriginal Affairs, Hon. G. J. Crafter.
Water Resources, and Recreation and Sport, Hon. J. W. Slater.
Housing and Construction; Public Works, Hon. T. H. Hemmings.
Agriculture, Fisheries and Forests; Correctional Services, Hon. F. T. Blevins.

AGENT-GENERAL IN LONDON

Agent-General for South Australia, J. L. Rundle, South Australia House, 50 Strand, W.C.2.

THE LEGISLATURE

Parliament consists of a *Legislative Council* of 22 members elected for 6 years, one-half retiring every 3 years; and a *House of Assembly* of 47 members, elected for a maximum duration of 3 years. Election is by ballot, with universal adult suffrage for both the Legislative Council and the House of Assembly for all British subjects, male and female. The number of electors in 1983 was 880,455.

The representation in the House of Assembly is 22 Liberals, 23 Labour, 1 National Party and 1 Independent.

President of the Legislative Council, Hon.
A. M. Whyte $A60,655
Speaker of the House of Assembly, Hon. T.
M. McRae $A60,655

THE JUDICATURE

Law and Justice.—The Supreme Court is presided over by the Chief Justice and thirteen Puisne Judges.

EDUCATION

Education at the primary and secondary level is available at Government schools controlled by the Education Department and at non-government schools, most of which are denominational. In 1983 there were 714 Government schools with 205,517 students, and 173 independent schools with 48,270 students. The Department of Further Education administers the South Australian College of External Studies, apprentice training and contributing education in 8 metropolitan and 4 country community colleges and 5 metropolitan and 11 country colleges of further education.

The two universities had, in 1983, a total enrolment of 8,842 full-time students. There is also a College of Advanced Education.

FINANCE

Revenue and expenditure of the Consolidated Revenue Account and debt of Southern Australia (year ended June 30) was:—

	1982	1983
Revenue	$A1,705,499,000	1,923,808,000
Expenditure	1,766,772,000	2,032,765,000
Debt	1,962,590,000	2,035,762,000

Banking.—There are 7 trading banks in Adelaide, including the Commonwealth Trading Bank and the State Bank of South Australia, having total average deposits of $A1,933,067,000 in June 1983. The eight savings banks had deposits of $A2,978,561,000 at June 30, 1983.

PRODUCTION AND INDUSTRY

The gross value of primary production in 1982–83 was:—

Crops $A497,099,000
Livestock products 348,230,000
Slaughterings..................... 338,486,000
Fisheries 61,234,000

Agriculture.—Wheat harvest 1982–83, 692,364 tonnes; barley, 667,518 tonnes. Oranges, lemons, apples, apricots, peaches, and all stone fruits and olives are successfully grown, and a quantity of this fruit is dried. In 1982–83, 200,283,000 litres of wine and 3,743 tonnes of sultanas, currants and raisins were produced. Considerable quantities of fruits (fresh and dried), wine and brandy, are annually sent to overseas countries, and to other Australian States. Some areas of the State, particularly near Adelaide, are also very suitable for growing all kinds of root crops and vegetables.

Livestock (March 31, 1984).—There were 16,738,900 sheep, 873,100 cattle, 414,600 pigs. Wool production (1982–83), 96,081,000 kg.

Minerals.—Iron, pyrite, gypsum, salt, coal, limestone, clay, &c., are found. The total mineral output was valued at $A404,899,000 in 1982–83, including iron ore valued at $A12,000,000.

OVERSEAS TRADE

Year	Imports	Exports
	$A	$A
1980–81	1,072,425,000	1,400,028,000
1981–82	1,337,301,000	1,275,938,000
1982–83	1,244,243,000	1,227,125,000

The principal exports are live sheep and lambs, wool, wheat, barley, meat, lead and lead alloys.

TRANSPORT AND COMMUNICATIONS

There were (June, 1983) 152 kilometres of railway operated by State Transport Authority, 976 kilometres of tram and bus routes and 102,400 kilometres of roads, including roads and tracks outside local government areas. There are a number of excellent harbours, of which Port Adelaide is the most important. The number of vessels (exceeding 200 net tons) entering South Australia from overseas during 1982–83 was 753 with 2,392,231 import tonnes and leaving with 3,000,249 export tonnes. There are 597 post offices in the State.

Civil Aviation.—There are 32 Government and licensed airports; the largest of these, Adelaide airport, recorded 1,635,663 passenger movements during 1982–83.

Motor Vehicles.—The registration on 30 June, 1983, totalled 763,667.

Radio and Television (Jan. 1983)—Broadcasting stations 24; Television stations 30 (including translator and satellite fed stations).

TOWNS

ΨADELAIDE, the chief city and capital, estimated resident population on June 30, 1983, 969,160, inclusive of suburbs. Other centres (with 1983 populations) are: ΨWhyalla (31,200); ΨMt. Gambier (21,340); ΨPort Pirie (14,760); ΨPort Augusta (16,100); and ΨPort Lincoln (12,940).

Transit.—Transmission of mails from London to Adelaide, approximately 35 days by sea and 5 days by air.

TASMANIA

Tasmania is an island state of Australia situated in the Southern ocean off the south-eastern extremity of the mainland. It is separated from the Australian mainland by Bass Strait and incorporates King Island and the Furneaux group of islands which are in the Strait. It lies between 40° 38′–43° 39′ S. lat. and 144° 36′–148° 23′ E. long., and contains an area of 26,383 square miles.

POPULATION.—The estimated resident population at Sept. 30, 1983 was 433,300.

Births, Deaths and Marriages

Year	Births	Deaths	Marriages
1978	6,788	3,311	3,148
1979	6,757	3,167	3,254
1980	6,735	3,392	3,433
1981	7,188	3,320	3,515
1982	7,002	3,432	3,576
1983	7,028	3,311	3,644

Vital Statistics.—The birth rate in 1983 was 16·3, death rate 7·6, marriage rate 8·4 per 1,000. Infant mortality (1983) 10·5 per 1,000 births.

Religions

In 1981 there were 151,207 members of the Anglican Church of Australia, 78,143 Roman Catholics, 17,668

United Church of Australia, 19,906 Methodists, 11,575 Presbyterians, 1,790 Congregationalists and 7,965 Baptists.

PHYSIOGRAPHY

The surface of the country is generally hilly and timbered, with mountains from 1,500 to 5,300 ft. in height, and expanses of level, open plains. There are numerous rivers, the South Esk, Gordon, Derwent and Huon being the largest. The climate is fine and salubrious, and well suited to European constitutions; the hot winds of Australia do not often reach the island. At Hobart the mean maximum temperature ranges from about 12°C in winter to 21°C in summer, the mean minimum from 5°C to 11°C. The western side of the island is very wet, the eastern side being much drier.

GOVERNMENT

The island was first settled by a British party from New South Wales in 1803, becoming a separate colony in 1825. In 1851 a partly elective legislature was inaugurated, and in 1856 responsible government was established. In 1901 Tasmania became a State of the Australian Commonwealth. The State executive authority is vested in a Governor (appointed by the Crown), but is exercised by Cabinet Ministers responsible to the Legislature, of which they are members.

GOVERNOR

Governor of Tasmania, His Excellency Sir James Plimsoll, A.C., C.B.E.; *assumed office* Oct. 1982.

THE MINISTRY

Premier, Treasurer and Minister for State Development, Energy and Forests, Hon. R. T. Gray.
Deputy Premier, Leader of the House, Attorney-General and Minister for Industrial Relations, Tourism, Racing and Gaming, Hon. G. A. Pearsall.
Environment, Licensing, Construction and Administrative Services, Hon. G. B. Davies.
Small Businesses, Housing, Consumer Affairs, and Inland Fisheries, Hon. N. M. Robson.
Local Government, Main Roads, Primary Industry, and Water Resources, Hon. I. M. Braid.
Health, Ethnic Affairs, Community Welfare and the Elderly, Hon. T. J. Cleary.
Education, Lands and National Parks, Hon. R. J. Beswick.
Transport, Mines, and Police and Emergency Services, Hon. F. R. Groom.

THE LEGISLATURE

Parliament consists of two Houses, a *Legislative Council* of 19 members, elected for six years (3 retiring annually, in rotation, except in every sixth year, when four retire) and a *House of Assembly* of 35 members, elected by proportional representation for four years in five 7-member constituencies, the electors for both Houses being all Tasmanians of 18 years and over who have resided continuously in the State for at least 6 months. Elections for the Assembly are held every four years.

The election of May 1982 resulted in the election of the Liberal Government. The state of parties in June 1983 was: Liberals 19, Labour 14, Independent 2.
President of the Legislative Council, Hon. A. J. Broadby.
Speaker of the House of Assembly, Hon. M. H. Bushby.

THE JUDICATURE

The Supreme Court of Tasmania, with civil, criminal ecclesiastical, admiralty and matrimonial jurisdiction, was established by Royal Charter on October 13, 1823.

Local Courts established under the Local Courts Acts, 1896, are held before Commissioners who are legal practitoners with a jurisdiction up to $A1,500 in the case of liquidation claims ($A1,000, unliquidated claims). Courts of General Sessions, constituted by a chairman who is a Justice of the Peace and at least one other Justice, are established in the municipalities for the recovery of debts and demands not exceeding $A100. Courts of Petty Sessions are established under the Justices Act, 1959, constituted by Police Magistrates sitting alone, or any two or more justices. A single justice may hear and determine certain matters.
Chief Justice, Supreme Court, Hon. Sir Guy Green.

EDUCATION

Government schools are of three main types: primary, secondary and matriculation schools. On July 1, 1983, there were 68,387 scholars enrolled in 257 Government schools. There were also 70 independent schools with an enrolment of 15,940. The University of Tasmania at Hobart, established 1890, had 3,101 full-time students and 2,128 part-time (including external) students in 1983. A College of Advanced Education offering degree and diploma courses was established in 1972. Enrolments in 1982 were 929 full-time students and 1,251 part-time students.

FINANCE

Revenue and expenditure of the Consolidated Revenue Fund and debt of Tasmania at current rates of exchange (June 30) was:—

	1981–82	1982–83
Revenue	$A683,231,327	$A764,989,770
Expenditure	717,628,276	772,753,011
Debt	1,071,605,763	1,114,396,841

Banking.—The weekly average of depositors' balances at trading banks in April 1984 was $A629,179,000; the savings bank balances at the end of April 1984, were $A1,071,117,000.

PRODUCTION AND INDUSTRY

Gross value of agricultural production in 1982–83 was $A339m. The estimated value added for agricultural enterprises in 1980–81 was $A107·3m. Total value added in manufacturing in 1981–82 was $A713·4m.; value added in mining was $A170m. in 1981–82.

Agriculture and Livestock.—The principal crops are apples, potatoes, green peas, oil poppies, hops, barley, beans and onions.
The livestock included (March 31, 1983) 562,000 cattle, 4,451,000 sheep and 51,000 pigs. The wool production (1982–83) was 19,804 tonnes.
Electrical Energy.—Tasmania, the smallest Australian state, ranks fourth as a producer of electrical energy—most of it derived from water power, with a total installed generator capacity of 1,862,144 kW. By reason of its low-cost electrical energy, Tasmania has large plants producing ferro-manganese and newsprint. A large aluminium plant is situated at Bell Bay and Tasmania is the source of the bulk of Australian requirements of zinc and fine papers. The Hydro-Electric Commission has completed a network of 27 stations including a dual machine oil fired station at Bell Bay. Work is continuing on three hydro-electric developments in the remote western region of the State, which will increase the installed generator capacity to 2·17 million kW.
Forestry.—The quantity of timber (excluding firewood) of various species cut in 1982–83 was 3,853,100 cubic metres, including 3,182,000 cubic metres for woodchip and wood-pulp.

Minerals.—The chief ores mined are those containing copper, tin, iron, silver, zinc and lead.

Manufactures.—The chief manufactures for export are: refined metals, pelletized iron ore, preserved fruit and vegetables, butter, cheese, textiles, paper, confectionery, wood chips and sawn timber. In 1982–83, 528 manufacturing establishments employed 24,088 persons, including working proprietors. Salaries and wages paid totalled $A387·7m.

OVERSEAS TRADE

Year	Imports	Exports
	$A'000	$A'000
1980–81	172,456	658,013
1981–82	166,032	647,617
1982–83	179,814	773,044

The principal overseas exports are ores and concentrates, refined metals, woodchips, greasy wool, meat, abalone, fresh fruit, cheese and hides and skins.

COMMUNICATIONS

Road and Rail.—Tasmania is served by a 1,067 mm gauge Federal Government railway system of 864 route kms. An additional 134 route kms of the same gauge is privately operated. Regular passenger services no longer operate. At June 30, 1983 there were 22,211 kilometres of road normally open to traffic. Of this total 8,441 kilometres were sealed. Motor vehicles on the register at Dec. 31, 1983 were: cars and station wagons, 193,300; commercial vehicles, 53,400 and motor cycles, 6,100.

Aviation.—Regular services operate between Tasmania and the other Australian States. During 1982 more than 982,000 passengers were carried on these services. The main cities and town in the State are served by regular internal services.

TOWNS

CAPITAL, ΨHOBART, founded 1804. Population (June 30, 1981), 128,603.

Other towns (with population at June 30, 1981) are ΨLaunceston (64,555), ΨDevonport (21,424), Burnie-Somerset (20,368), Ulverstone (9,413), New Norfolk (6,243) and Kingston-Blackmans Bay (8,556).

VICTORIA

The State of Victoria comprises the south-east corner of Australia, at the part where its mainland territory projects farthest into the southern latitudes; it lies between 34°–39° S. latitude and 141°–150° E. longitude. Its extreme length from east to west is about 493 miles, its greatest breadth is about 290 miles, and its extent of coast-line is about 1,043 geographical miles, including the length around Port Phillip Bay, Western Port and Corner Inlet, the entire area being 87,876 square miles.

Population.—The estimated resident population at June 30, 1983 was 4,034,600.

Births, Deaths and Marriages

Year	Births	Deaths	Marriages
1980	58,206	29,374	27,724
1981	59,513	29,034	28,648
1982	59,983	30,611	28,851

Vital Statistics.—Preliminary annual rate per 1,000 of estimated resident population in 1982: Births, 15·02; Deaths, 7·67; Marriages, 7·23. Deaths under 1 year per 1,000 live births, 10·69.

Religions

At the Census in 1981, members of the Catholic Church numbered 1,064,514, Church of England 777,551, Uniting (union of Presbyterian, Congregationalist and Methodist) 213,257, Presbyterian 175,291, Orthodox 171,131, Methodist 90,444 and Baptist 40,790. The number of persons who did not state their religion was 451,550.

PHYSIOGRAPHY

The *Australian Alps* and the *Great Dividing Range* pass through the centre of the State, and divide it into a northern and southern watershed, the latter sloping down to the ocean and containing, especially in the south-east, well-wooded valleys. The length of the Murray River, which forms part of the northern boundary of Victoria, is about 1,196 miles along the Victorian bank. Melbourne, the capital city, stands upon the Yarra-Yarra, which rises in the southern slopes of the Dividing Range.

Climate.—The climate of Victoria is characterized by warm to hot summers and rather cold winters. The highest temperature ever recorded in the State is 50·8°C, the lowest being −12·8°C. Normally, rain falls at most places throughout the year, with a maximum in winter or spring. In Melbourne, the mean annual temperature is 14·8°C.

GOVERNMENT

Victoria was originally known as the Port Phillip District of New South Wales and was created a separate colony in 1851, with a partially elective legislature. In 1855 Responsible Government was conferred. The executive authority is vested in a Governor, appointed by the Crown, aided by an Executive Council of Ministers.

Governor of the State of Victoria, His Excellency Rear Adm. Sir Brian Stewart Murray, K.C.M.G., A.O., *assumed office* March 1, 1982.

Lieutenant-Governor, Hon. Sir John McIntosh Young, K.C.M.G. (1974).

THE MINISTRY

Premier, Hon. J. Cain.

Deputy Premier, and Minister of Education, Hon. R. C. Fordham.

Attorney-General, Hon. J. H. Kennan.

Planning and Environment; Public Works, Hon. E. Walker.

Housing and Industry, Commerce and Technology, Hon. I. R. Cathie.

Transport and Industrial Affairs, Hon. S. M. Crabb.

Consumer Affairs, and Ethnic Affairs, Hon. P. C. Spyker.

Treasurer, Hon. R. A. Jolly.

Agriculture, Hon. D. E. Kent.

Conservation, Forests and Lands, Hon. R. A. Mackenzie.

Arts, and Police and Emergency Services, Hon. C. R. T. Mathews.

Health, Hon. T. W. Roper.

Employment and Training, Hon. J. L. Simmonds.

Minerals, and Energy and Water Supply, Hon. D. R. White.

Local Government, Hon. F. N. Wilkes.

Labour and Industry; Property and Services, Hon. J. L. Simpson.

Community Welfare Services, Hon. P. T. Toner.

Youth, Sport and Recreation, Hon. N. B. Trezise.

AGENT-GENERAL IN LONDON

Agent-General for Victoria, Hon. I. M. Haig, Victoria House, Melbourne Place, Strand, WC2B 4LG.

THE LEGISLATURE

Parliament consists of a *Legislative Council* of 44 members, elected for the 22 Provinces for 6 years, one-half retiring every 3 years; and a *Legislative*

Assembly of 81 members, elected for a maximum duration of 3 years. Voting is compulsory. The electors on the rolls at March 12, 1982 numbered 2,453,642.

President of the Legislative Council, Hon.
F. S. Grimwade $A72,279
Speaker of the Legislative Assembly, Hon.
C. T. Edmunds 72,279

THE JUDICATURE

There is a Supreme Court with a Chief Justice and 21 Puisne Judges, a County Court and Magistrates' Courts.

Chief Justice, Supreme Court, Hon. Sir
John Young, K.C.M.G. $A89,698
Chief Judge, County Court, Hon. G. R. D.
Waldron $A79,112
Solicitor-General, H. C. Berkeley, Q.C. $A79,737

EDUCATION

Primary education is compulsory, secular and free between the ages of 6 and 15. At July 1, 1983, there were 1,634 Government Primary Schools attended by 327,681 pupils, 19 Primary–Secondary Schools with 3,678 pupils, and 288 Secondary Schools (excluding Secondary Technical Schools) with an enrolment of 173,022. There were also 108 Government Secondary Technical Schools with 70,112 pupils and 75 Special Schools with 5,408 pupils. In addition there are technical and further education institutions and Colleges of Advanced Education.

At July 1, 1983, 234,171 pupils attended 659 non-Government schools, 492 of which were Roman Catholic.

There are four State-aided Universities.

FINANCE

Revenue and expenditure from the Consolidated Fund, and the debt of Victoria were:—

	1981–82	1982–83
Revenue	$A5,478,776	$A7,209,261
Expenditure	5,478,776	7,209,261
Debt	3,932,415	4,045,328

Banking, etc.—State Savings Bank deposits at June 30, 1983, amounted to $A5,383,653,000; in addition, deposits in the Commonwealth Savings Bank (in the State of Victoria) amounted to $A2,290,942,000, and in other savings banks $A3,632,884,000.

PRODUCTION AND INDUSTRY

The gross value of primary production (excluding mining and quarrying) in 1982–83 was $A2,580,566,804, crops $A736,347,042, livestock $A1,844,219,762. The local value of production of primary industries, excluding mining, was $A2,291,115,957. Wool, wheat, flour, butter, livestock, fruits, milk and cream, meats, poultry and eggs are staple products.

Livestock.—There were on rural holdings in March, 1983, 22,748,412 sheep, 3,408,274 cattle, and 386,901 pigs. The quantity of wool produced in 1982–83 was valued at $A324,132,830.

Minerals.—Minerals raised include oil and natural gas, brown coal, limestone, clays and stone for construction material. Production of brown coal in 1983 amounted to 34,988,498 tonnes.

Crude Oil and Natural Gas.—In 1965 natural gas was first discovered in commercial quantities in the offshore waters of the Gippsland Basin in eastern Victoria and in 1966–67, three more valuable oilfields were located in the same general area. These fields are still the largest yet found in Australia. Following the development of the four fields, commercial gas and crude oil came on stream in October, 1969. Production from the Gippsland fields during the

calendar year 1983 was: stabilized crude oil, 21,834,881 cubic metres; treated natural gas, 5,646,298,600 cubic metres; commercial propane, 1,590,379 cubic metres, and commercial ethane, 172,070,548 cubic metres.

Secondary Industry.—In 1981–82 there were 12,625 manufacturing establishments in which 284,465 males and 115,829 females were employed. Value added in the course of manufacture by all manufacturing establishments with four or more persons employed was $A10,578 million.

OVERSEAS TRADE

The export trade (excluding inter-state trade) consists largely of agricultural and mining products, machinery and transport equipment. The principal overseas imports of the State are apparel and textiles, electrical and other machines and machinery, motor vehicles and tractors, metals and metal manufactures, iron and steel, chemicals, petroleum and petroleum products, artificial resins and plastic materials.

Year	Imports	Exports
	$A	$A
1980–81	5,929,278,000	3,989,429,000
1981–82	7,167,614,000	4,177,187,000
1982–83	6,989,885,000	4,323,907,000

TRANSPORT

Victoria State Railways—At June 30, 1982, there were 5,812 kms of railway open for traffic. The revenue and expenditure for the year ended June 30, 1982, were $A260,197,702 and $A496,858,103 respectively. Total distance travelled was 31,135,564 kms and passenger journeys numbered 76,313,000. Goods and livestock carried amounted to 11,622,571 tonnes.

Shipping.—During the year ended June 30, 1982, 2,347 overseas vessels with dead-weight tonnage of 49,404,527 arrived at Victorian ports and 2,260 overseas vessels with dead-weight tonnage of 47,066,387 departed.

Motor Vehicle Registration.—The number of vehicles on the register at June 30, 1983, was: cars and stationwagons, 1,796,500; utilities and panel vans, 187,100; trucks and omnibuses, 194,400, and motor cycles, 79,600.

TOWNS

ΨMELBOURNE, the capital city, had a resident population at June 30, 1982, estimated at 2,836,8000. Other urban centres are ΨGeelong, 142,890; Ballarat, 73,630; Bendigo, 60,980; Moe-Yallourn, 17,660; Shepparton-Mooroopna, 36,760; ΨWarrnambool, 22,390; Morwell, 17,230; Traralgon, 19,010, Wodonga, 20,630.

WESTERN AUSTRALIA

Includes all that portion of the continent west of 129° E. long., the most westerly point being in 113° 9′ E. long. and from 13° 44′ to 35° 8′ S. lat. Its extreme length is 1,480 miles, and 1,000 miles from east to west; total area 975,920 sq. miles.

POPULATION.—At June 1983, the estimated resident population was 1,363,239.

Births, Deaths and Marriages

Year	Births	Deaths	Marriages
1978	20,611	7,794	10,404
1979	20,469	8,020	9,239
1980	20,607	8,166	9,594
1981	21,877	7,993	10,111
1982	22,236	8,187	10,455

Religions

Census of 1981—Church of England 375,848, Roman Catholics 316,337, Methodists 51,225, Uniting Church 32,592, and Presbyterians 32,033.

PHYSIOGRAPHY

Large areas of the State, for some hundreds of miles inland, are hilly and even mountainous, although the altitude, so far as ascertained, rises nowhere above that of Mount Meharry (4,097 ft.) in the north-west division or that of Bluff Knoll (3,640 ft.) in the Stirling Range in the south-west. The coastal regions are undulating, with an interior slope to the unsettled central portion of Australia. The Darling and Hamersley ranges of the west have a seaward slope to the Indian Ocean, into which flow many streams, notably the Preston, Collie, Murray, Swan, Murchison, Gascoyne, Ashburton, Fortescue and De Grey. In the north the Fitzroy flows from the King Leopold ranges into the Indian Ocean, and the Drysdale and Ord into the Timor Sea. The greater portion of the State may be described as an immense tableland, with an average elevation of 1,000 to 1,500 ft. above sea-level, the surface of which varies from stretches of clay soils to the sand dunes of the far interior. The climate is one of the most temperate in the world. Of the total area two-thirds is suitable for pastoral purposes.

GOVERNMENT

Western Australia was first settled by the British in 1829, and in 1870 it was granted a partially elective legislature. In 1890 Responsible Government was granted, and the Administration vested in a Governor, a Legislative Council, and a Legislative Assembly. The present consititution rests upon the Constitution Act, 1889, the Constitution Acts Amendment Act, 1899, and amending Acts. The Executive is vested in a Governor appointed by the Crown and aided by a Council of responsible Ministers.

The Legislative Assembly (elected February, 1983) is composed of Australian Labour Party 32, Liberal Party 20, National Country Party 3, National Party 2.

Governor of Western Australia, His Excellency Prof. Gordon Reid.

Lieut.-Governor and Administrator, Hon. Sir Francis Burt, K.C.M.G.

THE MINISTRY

Premier, Treasurer, Minister Co-ordinating Economic and Social Development, Minister for Forests, for Tourism, and for Women's Interests, Hon. B. T. Burke, M.L.A. $A78,151
Deputy Premier, Minister for Industrial Development and Technology, and Defence Liaison, Hon. M. J. Bryce, M.L.A. $A71,611
Minister for Industrial Relations and Administrative Services, and Leader of the Government in the Legislative Council, Hon. D. K. Dans, M.L.C.
$A69,958
Attorney-General, Minister for Budget Management and Prisons, Hon. J. M. Berinson, M.L.C.
Water Resources, Parliamentary and Electoral Reform, and Leader of the House, Hon. A. R. Tonkin, M.L.A.
Police and Emergency Services, and Local Government, Hon. J. P. Carr, M.L.A.
Environment, Multi-cultural and Ethnic Affairs, and the Arts, Hon. R. Davies, M.L.A.
Agriculture, Fisheries, and Wildlife, Hon. H. D. Evans, M.L.A.
Education, Hon. R. J. Pearce, M.L.A.
Health, Hon. B. J. Hodge, M.L.A.

Works, and Lands and Surveys, Hon. K. F. McIver, M.L.A.
Minerals and Energy, and Minister assisting the Minister co-ordinating Economic and Social Development, Hon. D. C. Parker, M.L.A.
Transport, Regional Development and the North West, Hon. J. F. Grill, M.L.A.
Housing, Youth and Community Services, and Sport and Recreation, Hon. K. J. Wilson, M.L.A.
Planning, Employment and Training, and Consumer Affairs, Hon. P. M. Dowding, M.L.C.
Ministers, each $A64,490 to $A79,376, according to location of electorate.

AGENT-GENERAL IN LONDON

Offices, Western Australia House 115 Strand, London, W.C.2.

Agent-General, R. Douglas.

THE LEGISLATURE

Parliament consists of a *Legislative Council* and a *Legislative Assembly,* elected by adult suffrage subject to qualifications of residence and registration. The qualifying age for electors for both the Legislative Council and Legislative Assembly is 18 years. There are 34 members in the Legislative Council, two from each Province, for a period of 6 years, one member from each Province retiring triennially. The Legislative Assembly is composed of 57 members, who are elected for a term of 3 years.

President of the Legislative Council, Hon.
C. E. Griffiths $A60,567
Speaker of the Legislative Assembly, Hon.
J. J. Harman 61,400

THE JUDICATURE

Chief Justice, Hon. Sir Francis Burt, K.C.M.G. (*+allce.* $A3,960)............ $A87,133
Senior Puisne Judge, Hon. A. R. A. Wallace (*+allce.* $A3,465) 80,162
Puisne Judges, Hons. P. F. Brinsden; C. H. Smith; G. A. Kennedy; H. W. Olney; W. P. Pidgeon; B. W. Rowland (*+allce.* $A3,300)........................ *each* 77,957

EDUCATION

In 1982 there were 712 government schools and 213 non-government schools (excluding kindergartens) with 208,428 and 51,538 pupils respectively. The total amount expended on education (by State authorities) during the year ended June 30, 1981, was $A627,362,000, including grants totalling $A63,543,000 to the University of Western Australia (9,835 enrolments in 1981), and to Murdoch University (2,785 enrolments in 1981). These amounts included Commonwealth monies.

PRODUCTION AND INDUSTRY

The gross value of agricultural production in 1981–82 was: crops $A1,067,289,000; livestock slaughterings, etc., $A349,487,000; livestock products $A454,153,000; fishing and gross value of fisheries was $A99,254,000.

Crops and Livestock.—The production of wheat for grain in 1981–82 was 4,803,439 tonnes. On March 31, 1982, the livestock included 1,942,361 cattle, 30,268,181 sheep, and 262,977 pigs. Wool production in 1981–82 was 151,304 tonnes in the grease.

Manufacturing Industries.—There were 3,693 manufacturing establishments operating in the State at June 30, 1981. The total number of persons employed (including working proprietors) by these establishments at the end of June, 1981 was 71,359.

Forestry.—The forests contain some of the finest hardwoods in the world. The total quantity of sawn timber produced during 1981–82 was 333,594 cubic metres.

Minerals.—The State has large deposits of a wide range of minerals, many of which are being mined or are under development for production. The ex-mine value of all minerals produced during 1981–82 was $A2,067,762,000.

Communications.—On June 30, 1982, there were 5,609 kms. of State government railway open for general and passenger traffic; and 728 kms. (Kalgoorlie-W.A. border) of the Trans-Australian railway. In the year ended June 30, 1981, 1,871 vessels entered Western Australian ports direct from, and 1,887 were cleared direct to overseas. The number of registered motor vehicles at June 30, 1982, was 789,076 (555,588 motor cars and station wagons, 197,424 light and heavy commercials, and 36,064 motor cycles and motor scooters).

FINANCE

	1981–82	1982–83
	$A	$A
Revenue	2,061,893,781	2,324,874,369
Expenditure	2,061,893,781	2,339,070,164
Public Debt (June 30)	1,485,788,284	1,547,497,840

OVERSEAS TRADE

Year	Imports	Exports
	$A	$A
1979–80	1,449,682,816	3,854,046,635
1980–81	1,663,189,694	3,791,113,894
1981–82	2,535,112,015	3,907,613,384

Overseas exports in 1981–82 included:

	$A
Iron ore and concentrates	1,195,485,520
Wheat	594,991,862
Wool	394,366,899
Live sheep and lambs	94,825,458
Petroleum and petroleum products	89,442,596
Beef and veal	72,642,109
Gold bullion	72,059,924
Rock lobster tails	65,643,223
Barley	48,744,499
Ilmenite, leucoxene and rutile	47,291,846
Salt	43,217,906
Mutton and lamb	37,057,418
Zirconium	23,961,055

TOWNS

CAPITAL.—ΨPERTH. Estimated resident population (estimate for June 30, 1982) of Perth Statistical Division, including the port of Fremantle, 948,850.

Perth stands on the right bank of the Swan River estuary, 12 miles from Fremantle.

New Zealand

AREA AND POPULATION

Islands	Area (English) Sq. Miles)	Population	
		Census Mar. 24, 1981†	Estimated Mar. 31, 1983
(a) Exclusive of Island Territory:			
North Island	44,281	2,322,989	2,379,500
South Island	58,093	852,748	850,500
Stewart Island	670	600*	540*
Chatham Islands	372	751*	770*
Minor Islands:			
Inhabited—			
Kermadec Islands	13	5*	5*
Campbell Island	44	10*	10*
Uninhabited—			
Three Kings	3	..	..
Snares	1	..	..
Solander	¼	..	..
Antipodes	24	..	..
Bounty	½	..	..
Auckland	234	..	..
Total exclusive of Island Territory	103,736	3,175,737	3,230,000
(b) Island Territory:			
Tokelau Islands	..	1,572‖	1,595§
(c) Niue island¶‡	..	3,226§	3,002**
Cook Islands¶††	..	18,000‡	17,400**
Ross Dependency	175,000	..	..

* Included in North Island and South Island totals.
† Excluding members of the Armed Forces overseas—979 in 1981.
¶ The Cook Islands have had complete internal self-government since Aug. 4, 1965, as has Niue since Oct. 19, 1974, but Cook Islanders and Niueans remain New Zealand citizens.
‖ Nov. 2, 1981.   § Oct. 1, 1983.   ‡ Dec. 31, 1980.   ** March 31, 1983.   †† Sept. 30, 1980.
Maori Population included in the totals for New Zealand proper—1976 Census, 257,770; 1981 Census, 279,252; 1983 estimate, 286,500.

Vital Statistics

Year	Births	Deaths	Natural Increase	Deaths of Infants under one year	Infant Mortality per 1,000 live births	Marriages
1979	52,279	25,340	26,939	653	12·49	22,326
1980	50,542	26,676	23,866	650	12·86	22,981
1981	50,794	25,150	25,644	592	11·65	23,660
1982	49,938	25,532	24,406	587	11·75	25,537
1983	50,474	25,991	24,483	633	12·54	24,678

Inter-Censal Increases

Year	Results of Census			Numerical Increase	Net Inflow or Outflow from Total Migration
	Males	Females	Total		
1966	1,343,743	1,333,176	2,676,919	261,935	+12,950
1971	1,430,856	1,431,775	2,862,631	185,712	+8,481
1976	1,562,042	1,567,341	3,129,383	266,752	+6,567
1981	1,578,927	1,596,810	3,175,737	46,354	−15,328

Excluding 1,936 members of the Armed Forces overseas at the time of the 1966 census, 1,482 at the 1971 census, 1,333 at the 1976 census and 979 at the 1981 census.

Races and Religions

Races	1976	1981	Religions	1976	1981
				Per cent	Per cent
Europeans..............	2,672,919	2,696,568	Church of England	29·2	25·7
Maoris	269,954	279,084	Presbyterians............	18·1	16·7
Chinese	14,236	18,480	Roman Catholics	15·3	14·3
Polynesians (other than			Methodists	5·5	4·7
N.Z. Maoris)	60,971	88,827	Baptists	1·6	1·6
Other races	85,185	60,348			

PHYSIOGRAPHY

New Zealand consists of a number of islands of varying size in the South Pacific Ocean, and has also administrative responsibility for a large tract in the Antarctic Ocean. The two larger and most important islands, the North and South Islands of New Zealand, are separated by only a relatively narrow strait. The remaining islands are very much smaller and, in general, are widely dispersed over a considerable expanse of ocean. The boundaries, inclusive of the most outlying islands and dependencies, range from 33° to 53° South latitude, and from 162° East longitude to 173° West longitude.

Geographical Features.—The two principal islands have a total length of 1,040 miles, and a combined area of 102,344 square miles. A large proportion of the surface is mountainous in character. The principal range is that of the Southern Alps, extending over the entire length of the South Island and having its culminating point in Mount Cook (12,349 ft.). The North Island mountains include several volcanoes, two of which are active, others being dormant or extinct. Mt. Ruapehu (9,175 ft.) and Mt. Ngauruhoe (7,515 ft.) are the most important. Of the numerous glaciers in the South Island, the Tasman (18 miles long by 1¼ wide), the Franz Josef and the Fox are the best known. The North Island is noted for its hot springs and geysers. For the most part the rivers are too short and rapid for use in navigation. The more important include the Waikato (270 miles in length); Wanganui (180), and Clutha (210). Lakes (Taupo, 234 sq. miles in area; Wakatipu, 113; and Te Anau, 133) are abundant, many of them of great beauty.

Climate.—New Zealand has a moist-temperate marine climate, but with abundant sunshine. A very important feature is the small annual range of temperature which permits of some growth of vegetation, including pasture, all the year round. Very little snow falls on the low levels even in the South Island. The mean temperature ranges from 15° C. in the North to about 9° C. in the South. Rainfall over the more settled areas in the North Island ranges from 35 to 70 inches and in the South Island from 25 to 45 inches. The total range is from approximately 13 to over 250 inches. The number of rainy days is generally in the neighbourhood of 160 to 180 in the North Island and between 110 and 140 in the South, except in the southern portion of the west coast. The amount of sunshine is generally over 2,000 hours per annum and ranges between 1,600 to 2,500 hours.

GOVERNMENT

The discoverers and first colonists of New Zealand were Polynesian people, ancestors of the Maoris of today. Whether there was a single colonization, several, or many, is not known. By the 13th or 14th century early exploration was over and there were well established Maori settlements.

The first European to discover New Zealand was a Dutch navigator, Abel Tasman, who sighted the coast on December 13, 1642 but did not land. It was the British explorer James Cook who circumnavigated New Zealand and landed in 1769. Traders, whalers and sealers made up the majority of Europeans in New Zealand during the 18th century and until the late 1830s, when the proportion of permanent European settlers became significant.

Largely as a result of increased British emigration, the country was annexed by the British Government in 1840. The British Governor, William Hobson, RN, proclaimed sovereignty over the North Island by virtue of the Treaty of Waitangi, signed by him and many Maori chiefs, and over the South Island and Stewart Island by right of discovery.

On May 3, 1841, New Zealand was, by letters patent, created a separate colony distinct from New South Wales. Organized colonization on a large scale commenced in 1840 with the New Zealand company's settlement at Wellington. On Sept. 26, 1907, the designation was changed to *The Dominion of New Zealand.* The Constitution rests upon the Imperial Act of 1852, and on the New Zealand Constitution (Amendment) Act of Dec. 10, 1947. The Statute of Westminster was formally adopted by New Zealand in 1947. The executive authority is entrusted to a Governor-General appointed by the Crown and aided by an Executive Council, within a Legislature consisting of one chamber, the House of Representatives.

FLAG: Blue ground, with Union Jack in top left quarter, four five-pointed red stars with white borders on the fly. On June 20, 1968, a naval ensign bearing the Southern Cross was adopted, replacing the British white ensign.

Governor-General and Staff

Governor-General and Commander-in-Chief of New Zealand, His Excellency Hon. Sir David Stuart Beattie, G.C.M.G. (1981).
Official Secretary, J. Brown.

THE EXECUTIVE COUNCIL

His Excellency the GOVERNOR-GENERAL

Prime Minister; Minister of Foreign Affairs, and in charge of Security Intelligence Service, Hon. David Lange.
Deputy P.M.; Leader of the House; Minister of Justice; Attorney-General, Hon. Geoffrey Palmer.
Overseas Trade and Marketing; Tourism, Recreation, Publicity and Sport, Hon. Michael Moore.
Finance; Inland Revenue, Hon. Roger Douglas.
Transport; Pacific Island Affairs, Hon. Richard Prebble.
Maori Affairs; Lands and Forests; Valuation, Hon. Coro Wetere.

Trade and Industry, Hon. David Caygill.
Education; Environment, Hon. Russell Marshall.
Minister of State; Minister of Defence, Hon. Frank O'Flynn.
Health; Local Government, Hon. Michael Bassett.
Police; Social Welfare; Women's Rights, Hon. Ann Hercus.
Energy; Science and Technology; Audit Department; Statistics, Hon. B. Tizard.
Agriculture and Fisheries; Rural Bank and Finance Corporation, Hon. Colin Moyle.
Labour; State Services, Hon. S. Rodger.
Broadcasting; Postmaster-General, Hon. Jonathan Hunt.
Works and Development, Hon. Fraser Colman.
Regional Development; Employment; Immigration, Hon. Kerry Burke.
Customs; Consumer Affairs, Hon. Margaret Shields.
Internal Affairs; Civil Defence; Arts, Hon. Peter Tapsell.
Housing, Hon. P. Goff.

The Prime Minister receives $79,717 per annum with an allowance of $14,000 for expenses of his office and the Ministerial residence. The salary of each Minister holding a portfolio is $55,115 with expense allowance of $5,750 and that of each Minister without portfolio $44,572, with $4,500 expense allowance.

NEW ZEALAND HIGH COMMISSION
New Zealand House, Haymarket, SW1Y 4TQ

High Commissioner, His Excellency William Young (1982).
Deputy High Commissioner, B. M. Brown.
Minister (Commercial), D. J. Walker.
Head, Defence Liaison Staff, Air Cdre. P. Neville, R.N.Z.A.F.

BRITISH HIGH COMMISSION
Reserve Bank of New Zealand Building,
2 The Terrace (P.O. Box 1812), Wellington, 1

High Commissioner, His Excellency Terence Daniel O'Leary, C.M.G., apptd, 1984.
Deputy High Commissioner, Head of Chancery and Counsellor (Political and Economic), J. H. Fawcett.
Defence Adviser, Capt. R. D. Ferguson, R.N.
1st Secretaries, R. Crawshaw (*Agriculture and Food*); S. Prince (*Commercial*); P. Cooper (*Chancery, Information*).
2nd Secretary, H. C. R. Price (*Consular and Administration*).
Attaché, M. R. Rogers (*Consular*).

British Council Representative, D. R. Howell.

THE LEGISLATURE

Parliament consists of a House of Representatives consisting of 92 members elected for 3 years. There are four Maori electorates. Women have been entitled to vote since 1893, and to be elected Members of the House of Representatives since the passing of the Women's Parliamentary Rights Act, 1919. Following the General Election of July 14, 1984, the state of the parties in Parliament was Labour 56, National Party 37 and Social Credit 2.

Members of the House receive $NZ32,271 *per annum,* with an allowance of $NZ2,500 *per annum* for expenses, plus an electorate allowance. The Leader of the Opposition receives $NZ55,115 *per annum* and $NZ5,750 *per annum* for expenses, plus house and travelling allowances.

Speaker of the House of Representatives,
  Hon. J. R. Harrison (*plus expense allowance and residential quarters in Parliament House*) $NZ51,161

THE JUDICATURE

The judicial system comprises a High Court and a Court of Appeal; also District Courts having both civil and criminal jurisdiction.

Chief Justice, Rt. Hon. Sir Ronald Davison, G.B.E., C.M.G. $NZ81,891
Court of Appeal, Rt. Hon. Sir Arthur Owen Woodhouse, K.B.E., D.S.C. (*President*) 78,377
Judges, Rt. Hon. Sir Robin Cooke; Rt. Hon. I. L. Richardson; Rt. Hon. D. W. McMullin; Hon. E. J. Somers 75,741
High Court Puisne Judges, Hons. L. F. Moller; G. M. Roper; J. P. Quilliam; N. F. Chilwell; M. E. Casey; J. A. Ongley; J. F. Jeffries; R. I. Barker; M. H. Vautier; J. B. Sinclair; G. E. Bisson; A. D. Holland; T. M. Thorp; L. M. Greig; J. P. Cook, O.B.E., E.D.; E. M. Prichard; R. C. Savage; M. Hardie-Boys; J. H. Wallace; J. T. Eichelbaum; P. G. Hillyer; R. G. Gallen ....
High Court Administrative Divn., Rt. Hon. Sir Ronald Davison (*Chief Justice*); Hons. D. W. McMullin; C. M. Roper; N. F. Chilwell; M. E. Casey; J. F. Jeffries; G. E. Bisson.
Judge, Court of Arbitration, Judge A. P. Blair ....

POLICE

On March 31, 1983 the strength of the New Zealand Police Force was 5,014 of all ranks, equivalent to 1 for every 644 of the population. Total police expenditure for the year 1982–83 was $NZ181,223,000.

DEFENCE

A unified Ministry of Defence which retained the three single services was set up in 1964. The Minister of Defence is responsible for national defence, and, with the other members of the Defence Council, commands and administers the three services:

The *Royal New Zealand Navy* consists of 2,857 officers and ratings as at March 31, 1983, as well as the Volunteer Reserve in four divisions. The strength is four frigates, one survey ship and one research vessel, as well as patrol and inshore survey craft.

The *New Zealand Army* consists of the Regular Force, the Territorial Force and the Army Reserve. The strength of the Regular Force at March 31, 1983 was 5,590, and of the Territorial Force and Army Reserve, 7,926. The Army is structured to provide a Regular Force battalion group which is available for rapid deployment on military operations or civil assistance tasks, as well as a framework of integrated Regular Force/Territorial Force Units as a basis for expansion when required. One infantry battalion is based in Singapore.

The *Royal New Zealand Air Force* had a Regular Force strength of 4,409 at March 31, 1983, with 1,377 Territorial and Reserve Forces. Operational units include fighter ground attack, maritime, medium and short-range transport, and helicopter squadrons, and flying training units. A helicopter support unit is based in Singapore, and there is a helicopter detachment serving with the Multinational Force and Observers in the Sinai.

FINANCE

Into the Consolidated Account (New Zealand's main public account) are paid the proceeds of income tax, sales tax, customs and excise duties and other taxes, also interest, profits from trading undertakings, and departmental receipts (departmental expenditure is included gross). Revenue from taxation is also paid into the National Roads Fund principally from a tax on motor spirits and registration and licence fees for motor vehicles.

Year ended March 31	Revenue	Expenditure
	$NZ	$NZ
1979	6,517,986,000	6,512,800,000
1980	7,530,560,000	7,529,100,000
1981	8,994,215,000	8,992,465,000
1982	11,137,401,000	11,124,976,000
1983	13,012,815,000	12,992,323,000*

*Includes:	$NZ,000
Education	1,652,373
Social Welfare	3,700,258
Health	1,767,751
Development of Industry	1,641,598
Defence	652,131
Debt services	1,636,428
Law and order	318,552

Revenue from taxation in 1982–83 amounted to $NZ10,097,466,000 of which $NZ9,864,509,000 represented receipts into the Consolidated Account, and $NZ232,957,000 receipts into the National Roads Fund.

DEBT

The gross *Public Debt* amounted on March 31, 1983, to $NZ18,732,776,000 of which $NZ4,470,601,000 was domiciled in Europe, $NZ1,862,023,000 in U.S.A. and $NZ1,355,986,000 in Japan; $NZ13,122,000 represented World Bank loans.

BANKING

There are four trading banks, two of which are predominantly New Zealand banks. At Dec. 28, 1983, assets of all trading banks in respect of New Zealand business amounted to $NZ9,185,900,000, liabilities, $NZ8,349,900,000; and the value of notes in circulation amounted, in the December quarter of 1983, to $NZ604,400,000 (The Reserve Bank of New Zealand notes are the legal tender). New Zealand's official overseas reserves at Dec. 1983, amounted to $NZ1,240,100,000. Trading banks' advances in 1983 averaged $NZ5,887,700,000 weekly, and deposits with the trading banks averaged $NZ7,857,000,000.

Post-office, trustee and private savings banks had, at March 31, 1983, over 7,722,000 accounts having $NZ5,578,400,000 to their credit.

EDUCATION

Schools are free and attendance is compulsory between the ages of 6 and 15. There are opportunities for apt pupils to proceed to university. At July 1982 there were 458,968 pupils attending public primary schools, and 27,199 pupils attending registered private primary schools. The secondary education of boys and girls in the cities and large towns is carried on in 273 state secondary schools, and 45 private secondary schools. The total number of pupils receiving full-time secondary education in July 1982 was 223,501 and in addition there were 137,574 students attending technical classes including 29,837 receiving part-time tuition from the Technical Correspondence School. Almost all the students attending technical classes are part-time. There are six universities; the Lincoln university college of agriculture is associated with the University of Canterbury. The university system is co-ordinated by the

University Grants Committee. The Universities had a total of 54,149 students in 1982.

The total expenditure on education out of public funds in 1982–83 is estimated at $NZ12,466,000,000.

PRODUCTION AND INDUSTRY
Gross Agricultural Production (Gross Output)

	Year ended March		
	1980	1981	1982*
	$NZ(million)		
Sheep and lambs	477	560	605
Wool	823	811	803
Cattle	630	545	564
Pigs	64	65	80
Dairy products	691	850	1,022
Crops and seeds	168	221	279
Fruit and nuts	124	154	183
Vegetables	153	183	227
Poultry and eggs	97	110	124
Agricultural services	223	261	295
Other horticulture	79	104	125
Other products n.e.c.	33	50	58
Physical change of live- stock	200	100	93
Sales of live animals	592	536	557
Gross Output	4,354	4,549	5,013

*Provisional

Agricultural and Pastoral Production

	1982	1983
*Wheat, metric tons	292,100	. .
*Wool, metric tons	363,000	371,000
†Butter, metric tons	247,100	254,040
†Cheese, metric tons	110,910	114,390
‡Stock Slaughtered—		
Lambs, No.	32,115,000	35,995,000
Sheep, No.	9,021,000	9,234,000
Cattle, No.	2,172,000	2,156,000
Calves, No.	1,069,000	962,000
Pigs, No.	716,000	720,000

* Year ended June 30.
† Year ended May 31.
‡ Year ended Sept. 30. Provisional.

Forestry.—The output of sawn timber for 1983 was 2,045,000 cubic metres, of which 1,899,000 cubic metres represented exotic varieties, mainly radiata pine.

Livestock.—Livestock on farms at June 30, 1983, included 3,134,000 dairy cattle (of which 2,098,000 were dairy cows in milk during season), 4,497,000 beef cattle (of which 1,448,000 were beef breeding cows), and 408,000 pigs. Sheep numbered 70,263,000.

Minerals.—Non-metallic minerals such as coal, clay, limestone and dolomite are both economically and industrially more important than metallic ones. Coal output in 1982 was 2,244,384 tonnes. Of the metals, the most important is ironsand, which is mined for export. In 1982, 2,386,000 tonnes of concentrate were exported. Natural gas deposits in Taranaki are being used for electricity generation and as a premium fuel, piped to an increasing number of North Island centres. Gas and oil exploration continue, and expenditure on exploration for other minerals reached $NZ8,609,000 in 1982.

TRADE

	1981–82	1982–83
Imports (v.f.d.) . .	$NZ7,044,800,000	$NZ6,928,200,000
Exports (f.o.b.) . .	6,733,800,000	7,694,300,000

Trade with U.K.

	1982	1983
Imports from U.K. .	$NZ636,100,000	$NZ637,800,000
Exports to U.K. . . .	962,500,000	990,100,000

New Zealand produce exported to the U.K. in the 12 months ending June, 1983, included butter, valued at $NZ295,700,000; beef ($NZ6,900,000); wool ($NZ115,400,000); lamb ($NZ368,800,000).

COMMUNICATIONS

Railways.—The national railway system is owned and operated by the New Zealand Railways Corporation. In March, 1983, there were 4,332 kilometres of Government railway in operation. The number of passengers carried on Government lines in 1982–83 was 13,697,799. Goods railed amounted to 11,090,000 tonnes. Railway total revenue and expenditure were $NZ661,500,000 and $NZ637,300,000 in 1982–83.

Motor Vehicles.—In the year ended June 30, 1983 there were 2,386,052 licensed motor vehicles. These included 1,431,739 cars and 154,602 motor and power cycles. This gives a ratio of 2·2 persons to each passenger car.

Shipping.—During 1983 the vessels entered from overseas ports numbered 3,085 (net tonnage 13,067,000) and those cleared for overseas 3,073 (net tonnage 13,011,000).

Post Office Statistics.—During 1982–83 internal postal services handled 660,475,000 items, including 564,530,000 letters. Overseas mails included 1,736,180 kg. of airmail received and 994,224 kg. despatched. Telephones connected at March 31, 1983 totalled 1,192,809.

Civil Aviation.—In 1982 domestic scheduled services flew 26,362,000 kilometres and carried 2,248,000 passengers. Freight carried amounted to 38,600 tonnes. In 1982 international services to and from New Zealand carried 1,664,000 passengers, 70,484 tonnes of freight and 3,099 tonnes of mail.

CAPITAL.—ΨWellington, in the North Island (estimated population March 31, 1983, Wellington statistical division, 342,500).

Other large centres; ΨAuckland, 863,900; ΨChristchurch, 322,200; ΨDunedin, 112,000; Palmerston North, 93,700; Hamilton, 164,600; ΨNapier-Hastings, 114,400.

NATIONAL DAY (Waitangi Day).—Feb. 6.

THE TERRITORIES OF NEW ZEALAND

In addition to North, South, Stewart and Chatham Islands:—

The Three Kings (discovered by Tasman on the Feast of the Epiphany), in 34° 9′ S. lat. and 172° 8′ 8″ E. long. (uninhabited). *Auckland Islands*, about 290 miles south of Bluff Harbour, in 50° 32′ S. lat. and 166° 13′ E. long. *Antipodes Group*, 40° 41′ 15″ S. lat. and 178° 43′ E. long. *Bounty Islands*, 47° 4′ 43″ S. lat., 170° 0′ 30″ E. long. *Snares Islands and Solander*. All these islands are uninhabited.

The Kermadec Group (population normally 9 or 10) between 29° 10′ to 31° 30′ S. lat., and 177° 45′ to 179° W. long., includes Raoul or Sunday, Macaulay, Curtis Islands, L'Esperance, and some islets. All the inhabitants are government employees at a meteorological station. *Campbell Island* (used as a weather station).

TOKELAU (OR UNION ISLANDS)

A group of atolls (Fakaofo, Nukunono and Atafu) (estimated population 1,595 at Oct. 1, 1983), proclaimed part of New Zealand as from Jan. 1, 1948.

THE ROSS DEPENDENCY

The *Ross Dependency*, placed under the jurisdiction of New Zealand by Order in Council dated July

30, 1923, and defined as all the islands and territories between 160° E. and 150° W. longitude which are situated south of the 60° S. parallel. The Ross Dependency includes Edward VII Land and portions of Victoria Land. For some years there have been permanent bases in the area, staffed by survey and scientific personnel.

ASSOCIATED STATES

COOK ISLANDS

Included in the boundaries of New Zealand since June, 1901, the group consists of the islands of Rarotonga, Aitutaki, Mangaia, Atiu, Mauke, Mitiaro, Manuae, Takutea, Palmerston, Penrhyn or Tongareva, Manihiki, Rakahanga, Suwarrow, Pukapuka or Danger and Nassau. The total population of the group was estimated at 17,400 (March 1983). The chief exports of the Cook Islands are fruit juice, clothing, copra, bananas, citrus fruit and pulp, and pearl shell. The trade is chiefly with New Zealand, Australia, Japan, the U.K. and the U.S.A. The New Zealand Government continues to give financial aid to the Cook Islands.

The High Commissioner of the Cook Islands is employed in a dual role, since he represents both the Queen and the New Zealand Government. Since Aug. 4, 1965, the Islands have enjoyed complete internal self-government, executive power being in the hands of a Cabinet consisting of the Premier and five other ministers. The new Constitution Act was passed by the New Zealand Parliament in November 1964, but did not come into force until it had been endorsed by the 22-member Legislative Assembly of the Cook Islands, elected in April 1965.

The New Zealand citizenship of the Cook Islanders is embodied in the Constitution, and assurances have been given that the changed status of the Islands will in no way affect the consideration of subsidies or the right of free entry into New Zealand for exports from the group.

NIUE

Geographically part of Cook Islands, but administered separately. Had a population (1983) of 3,002.

A New Zealand Representative is stationed at Niue, which since October 1974 has been self-governing in free association with New Zealand, which is responsible for external affairs and defence, and continues to give financial aid. Executive power is in the hands of a Premier and a Cabinet of 3 drawn from the Assembly of 20 members.

Antigua and Barbuda

Antigua and Barbuda comprises the islands of Antigua (108 square miles; population, 78,000), Barbuda (62 square miles; population, 1,500) 25 miles north of Antigua, and Redonda (¼ square mile; uninhabited) 25 miles south-west of Antigua. Antigua is part of the Leeward Islands in the Eastern Caribbean and lies 17° 3′ N. and 61° 48′ W. It is distinguished from the rest of the Leeward group by its absence of high hills and forest, and a drier climate than most of the W. Indies. Barbuda, formerly a possession of the Codrington family, is very flat with a large lagoon and well wooded in the north east. Antigua was first settled by the English in 1632, and was granted to Lord Willoughby by Charles II.

CAPITAL.—ΨSt. John's. Population, 22,000. The town of Barbuda is Codrington.

FLAG.—Inverted triangle (centred on a red field) divided horizontally into three bands of black over blue over white; rising sun device in gold on black band.

GOVERNMENT

Antigua became internally self-governing in 1967 and fully independent on Nov. 1, 1981, as a constitutional monarchy with H.M. The Queen as Head of State, represented by the Governor-General. There is a Senate of 17 members and a House of Representatives.

Governor-General, Sir Wilfred Ebenezer Jacobs, K.C.V.O., O.B.E., Q.C.
Prime Minister and Minister of Finance, Rt. Hon. Vere C. Bird, Sr.
Deputy P.M. and Minister for Foreign Affairs, Economic Development, Tourism and Energy, Hon. Lester Bird.

HIGH COMMISSION FOR THE
EASTERN CARIBBEAN STATES
10 Kensington Court, W8 5DL.

High Commissioner for Eastern Caribbean States, His Excellency Dr. Claudius C. Thomas, C.M.G.

BRITISH HIGH COMMISSION
38 St. Mary's Street (P.O. 483), St. John's

High Commissioner, (resides at Bridgetown, Barbados).

Resident Representative, J M. Crane (*Second Secretary*).

ECONOMY

Tourism is the main feature of the economy, with several hotels (and a number under construction) to take advantage of the many white sand beaches which made Antigua one of the first Caribbean islands to attract tourists.

For many years sugar was the dominant crop but is now produced primarily for local consumption. Areas of agricultural development include livestock, sea island cotton, corn (for cornmeal production) and improved vegetable and fruit production. An oil refinery on the island was reopened in 1982.

FINANCE

	1981	1982
Revenue	EC$77,244,549	EC$99,193,039
Expenditure (recurrent)	85,859,391	106,371,017

Trade with U.K.

	1982	1983
Imports from U.K.	£12,606,000	£10,465,000
Exports to U.K.	6,245,000	1,718,000

The Bahamas
(The Commonwealth of the Bahamas)

The Bahama Islands are an archipelago lying in the Atlantic Ocean between 20° 55'–25° 22' N. Lat; 72° 35'–79° 35' W. Long. They extend from the coast of Florida on the north-west almost to Haiti on the south-east. The group consists of 700 islands, of which 30 are inhabited and 2,400 cays comprising an area of more than 5,382 square miles. The population, at the census of 1980 was 237,090. The principal islands include: Abaco, Acklins, Andros, Berry Islands, Bimini, Cat Cay, Cat Island, Crooked Island, Eleuthera, Exumas, Grand Bahama, Harbour Island, Inagua, Long Cay, Long Island, Mayaguana, New Providence (on which is located the capital, Nassau), Ragged Island, Rum Cay, San Salvador and Spanish Wells. San Salvador was the first landfall in the New World of Christopher Columbus on October 12, 1492.

The Bahamas were settled by British subjects when the islands were deserted. The ownership of the Bahamas was taken over in 1782 by the Spanish, but the Treaty of Versailles in 1783 restored them to the British.

CAPITAL.—ΨNassau. Population (1980 census), 135,437. Nassau is distant from Liverpool 4,000 miles.

GOVERNMENT

The Bahamas gained independence on July 10, 1973. There are a Senate of 16 members and an elected House of Assembly of 43 members.

Governor-General, His Excellency Sir Gerald Cash, G.C.M.G., K.C.V.O., O.B.E.
Prime Minister, Rt. Hon. Sir Lynden Pindling, K.C.M.G.
Deputy Prime Minister and Minister of Finance, Hon. A. D. Hanna.
Transport, Hon. P. M. Bethel.
Economic Affairs, Hon. A. T. Maycock.
Education, Hon. D. E. Rolle.
Agriculture and Fisheries and Local Government, Hon. G. A. Smith.
Works and Utilities, Hon. A. L. Roker.
Foreign Affairs and Attorney General, Hon. P. L. Adderley.
Labour and Home Affairs, Hon. C. T. Maynard.
Health, Hon. L. N. Coakley.
Youth, Sports and Community Affairs, Hon. K. W. Nottage.
Tourism, Hon. P. G. Christie.
Housing and National Insurance, Hon. H. A. Ingraham.

Chief Justice, Hon. P. T. Georges.
Puisne Judges, Sir Denis Malone; Hon. K. C. Henry.

BAHAMAS HIGH COMMISSION
39 Pall Mall, SW1Y 5JG
[01–930 6967]

High Commissioner, His Excellency R. F. A. Roberts.

BRITISH HIGH COMMISSION
Bitco Building, East St.
P.O. Box N7516, Nassau.

High Commissioner, His Excellency Peter William Heap (1980).
Deputy High Commissioner, M. Holmes, M.B.E. (*Head of Chancery*).

ECONOMY

Tourism is the economic mainstay of the Bahamas, employing about two-thirds of the labour force. It provides about two-thirds of Government revenue and about half the country's foreign exchange earnings. The second main industry is international banking and trust business, the Bahamas' absence of any direct taxation and internal stability enabling the country to become one of the world's leading financial centres.

Agricultural production is mainly of fresh vegetables, fruit, meat and dairy products for the domestic market, and crawfish, mostly for export. There are large reserves of aragonite, and reserves of limestone and salt, all of which are being commercially exploited. Freeport is the country's leading industrial centre, with a cement and pharmaceutical plant, an oil refinery, and port and bunkering facilities. There is also a rum distillery on New Providence.

EDUCATION

Education is compulsory between the ages of 5 and 14. More than 62,000 students are enrolled in Ministry of Education and Independent schools in New Providence and the Family Islands.

COMMUNICATIONS

The main ports are Nassau (New Providence), Freeport (Grand Bahamas), Matthew Town (Inagua). International air services are operated from Nassau and Freeport, and there are also airports at West End (Grand Bahama) and Rock Sound (Eleuthera). About 50 smaller airports and landing strips facilitate services between the islands, the services being provided by Bahamasair, the national carrier. There are roads on the larger islands, and roads are under construction on the smaller islands. There are no railways. Wireless and telephone services are in operation to all parts of the world. There are 132 radio-telephone channels among the islands.

FINANCE AND TRADE

	1982	1983
Public revenue	B$305,109,400	B$339,860,000
Expenditure	304,130,584	310,610,000

Trade with U.K.

	1982	1983
Imports from U.K.	£26,364,000	£17,815,000
Exports to U.K.	18,273,000	24,013,000

The imports are chiefly foodstuffs, manufactured articles, building material, vehicles and machinery. The chief exports are petroleum and petroleum products, hormones, salt, rum, crawfish and aragonite.

Bangladesh
(The People's Republic of Bangladesh)

AREA, POPULATION, CLIMATE, ETC.—The People's Republic of Bangladesh consists of the territory which was formerly East Pakistan (the old province of East Bengal and the Sylhet district of Assam), covering an area of 55,126 sq. miles in the region of the Gangetic delta, and has a population, according to the 1981 census, of 89,940,000.

The country is crossed by a network of navigable rivers, including the eastern arms of the Ganges, the Jamuna (Brahmaputra) and the Meghna, flowing into the Bay of Bengal. The climate is tropical and monsoon; hot and extremely humid during the summer, and mild and dry during the short winter. The rainfall is heavy, varying from 50 inches to 135 inches in different districts and the bulk of it falls during monsoon season from June to September. The mean temperature during the winter (November to February) is about 20°C. (68°F.) and during the hot season 30°C. (86°F.).

Prior to becoming East Pakistan, the territory had been part of British India. It acceded to Pakistan in October, 1947, which became a Republic on March 23, 1956.

By a proclamation of March 26, 1971, Bangladesh purported to secede from the central government, and a government-in-exile was set up in April in Calcutta. The short war between India and Pakistan, in both the East and the West, and India's overwhelming defeat of the Pakistani Army in the East, brought about a *de facto* secession of the East wing. The Indo-Pakistan war was concluded on December 16, 1971, and Mr. Zulfiqar Ali Bhutto became President of Pakistan on December 20. Sheikh Mujib was sworn in as Prime Minister of Bangladesh on January 12, 1972. Recognition of the new state was accorded swiftly by many countries. Bangladesh was admitted to the Commonwealth on April 18, and to the United Nations in 1974. Pakistan and Bangladesh accorded one another mutual recognition in Feb. 1974 and established diplomatic relations in Jan. 1976.

CAPITAL.—Dhaka. Population 3,458,602, according to the results of the 1974 census.

GOVERNMENT

From 1975 a non-political administration ran the country under martial law, initially under President Mr. Justice A. M. Sayem, then from April 1977 under Major General Ziaur Rahman. A Presidential election was held on June 3, 1978, and President Zia was elected by a considerable majority. Parliamentary elections were held in February 1979 and martial law was lifted in April 1979. The 1974 Proclamation of Emergency, which suspended certain sections of the constitution concerned with fundamental rights, was revoked in November 1979. Zia was assassinated in May 1981 in an unsuccessful coup, but the military, led by Lt.-Gen. Ershad, took over in March 1982 and martial law was again imposed. Parliamentary elections are scheduled for Dec. 8, 1984.

President and Chief Martial Law Administrator, Lt.-Gen. H. M. Ershad (*also holds Finance and Foreign Affairs portfolios*).

Deputy Chief Martial Law Administrators, Rr. Adm. M. A. Khan (*Minister of Agriculture*); Air Vice Marshal Sultan Mahmud (*Minister of Industries*).

Prime Minister, Minister of Law and Justice, Ataur Rahman Khan.

Energy and Mineral Resources, S. M. Shafiul Azam.

Food, Air Vice Marshal (ret'd) A. G. Mahmood.

Irrigation, Water Development and Flood Control, A. R. Shams-ud Doha.

Jute and Textiles, Air Vice Marshal (ret'd) K. M. Aminul Islam.

Religious Affairs and Endowments, Khandakar Abu Bakr.

Home Affairs, Maj. Gen. Abdul Mannan Siddique.

Health and Population Control, Maj. Gen. M. Shamsul Haque.

Local Government, Rural Development and Cooperatives, Mahbubur Rahman.

Communications, A. Z. M. Obaidullah Khan.

Social Welfare and Women's Affairs, Dr. Shafia Khatun.

Planning, Dr. Abdul Majeed Khan.

Establishment, Maj. Gen. Mahabbat Jan Chowdhury.

Works, Maj. Gen. Abdul Munim.

Education, Shamsul Huda Chowdhury.

Commerce, Dr. M. A. Martin.

Information, Md Shamsul Huq.

Land Administration and Land Reforms, M. A. Haque.

Ports, Shipping, Reazuddin Ahmed.

Labour and Manpower, Shah Moazzem Hossain.

BANGLADESH HIGH COMMISSION
28 Queen's Gate, S.W.7
[01-584 0081]

High Commissioner, His Excellency Fakhruddin Ahmed.

Deputy High Commissioner, Mohiuddin Ahmed.

BRITISH HIGH COMMISSION
Abu Bakr House, P.O. Box 6079, Gulshan
Dhaka-12

High Commissioner, His Excellency Terence George Streeton, C.M.G. (1983).

Deputy High Commissioner, A. Burgess.

British Council Representative, Dr. R. E. Wright, O.B.E., 5 Fuller Road, (P.O. Box 161), Ramna, Dhaka 2.

EDUCATION

Primary education is free but not universal. Most primary schools are under government management. The majority of secondary schools and colleges are privately managed, but many receive government grants. There are six Universities. In 1980 literacy was estimated at 22 per cent of the whole of Bangladesh and 26 per cent of the male population.

TRANSPORT AND COMMUNICATIONS

Principal seaports are ΨChittagong, and ΨChalna. The Bangladesh Shipping Corporation has been set up by the Government to operate the Bangladesh merchant fleet. The principal airports are Dhaka-Zia and Chittagong. The international airline, Bangladesh Biman, serves Europe, the Middle East, South and South-East Asia, and an internal network.

There are about 6,880 miles of roads in Bangladesh; 4,724 miles are metalled. There are 2,798 miles of railway track.

Radio Bangladesh is the main national broadcasting service. A television service was introduced in 1965 and colour transmissions began in 1981.

PRODUCTION

Bangladesh is a principal producer of raw jute. Other agricultural products are rice, tea, oil seeds, pulses, and sugar cane. The chief industries are jute, cotton, tea, leather, pharmaceuticals, fertilizer, sugar, fishing (prawns), and natural gas.

Trade with U.K.

	1982	1983
Imports from U.K.	£58,179,000	£51,000,000
Exports to U.K.	25,558,000	25,200,000

AID

Bangladesh is a major recipient of bilateral and multilateral development aid. Aid disbursement in 1982 totalled U.S. $1,236 million, of which food aid was U.S. $231 million, commodity aid U.S. $421 million and project aid U.S. $584 million.

Barbados

Barbados, the most easterly of the Carribean islands, is situated in latitude 13° 14′ N. and longitude 59° 37′ W. The island has a total area of 166 square miles, the land rising in a series of tablelands marked by terraces to the highest point, Mt. Hillaby (1,104 ft.). It is nearly 21 miles long by 14 miles broad. Some 46 acres are covered by forest. The climate is equable with annual average temperature 26·5°C. (79·8°F.) and rainfall varying from a yearly average of 75 inches in the high central district to 50 inches in some of the low-lying coastal areas.

POPULATION.—The population of Barbados (census 1980) was 248,983. There are eleven administrative areas (parishes); St. Michael; Christ Church; St. Andrews; St. George; St. James; St. John; St. Joseph; St. Lucy; St. Peter; St. Philip, and St. Thomas.

CAPITAL.—ΨBridgetown (population, estimated April, 1980, 17,552) in the parish of St. Michael. There are three other towns, Oistins in Christ Church, Holetown in St. James and Speightstown in St. Peter.

FLAG.—Three vertical stripes, dark blue, gold and dark blue, with trident devises on gold stripe.

NATIONAL DAY.—Nov. 30 (Independence Day).

GOVERNMENT

The first inhabitants of Barbados were Arawak Indians but the island was uninhabited when first settled by the British in 1627. It was a Crown Colony from 1652 until it became an independent state within the Commonwealth on November 30, 1966. The Legislature consists of the Governor-General, a Senate and a House of Assembly. The Senate comprises 21 Senators appointed by the Governor-General, of whom 12 are appointed on the advice of the Prime Minister, 2 on the advice of the Leader of the Opposition and 7 by the Governor-General at his discretion to represent religious, economic or social interests in the Island or such other interests as the Governor-General considers ought to be represented. The House of Assembly comprises 27 members elected every five years by adult suffrage. In 1963 the voting age was reduced to 18. The last General Election took place on June 18, 1981 and, as a result, seats in the House of Assembly were distributed as follows: Barbados Labour Party 17; Democratic Labour Party 10. A General Election is due before the end of 1984.

Governor-General, Sir Hugh Springer, K.C.M.G., C.B.E., *apptd* 1984.

CABINET

Prime Minister, Minister of Finance and Planning, Rt. Hon. J. M. G. Adams, Q.C.
Deputy Prime Minister and Minister of Trade, Industry and Tourism, Hon. B. St. John, Q.C.
Culture and Information and Leader of the Senate, Senator Hon. N. A. Barrow.
Attorney-General and Minister of Foreign Affairs, Hon. L. R. Tull.
Education, Hon. Miss B. A. Miller.
Health, Dr. Hon. D. G. Blackman.
Agriculture, Food and Consumer Affairs, Hon. Dr. R. L. Cheltenham.
Labour and Social Security, Hon. D. O. Bradshaw.
Parliamentary Affairs and Leader of the House, Hon. L. S. Craig.
Transport and Works, Hon. V. Johnson.
Housing and Lands, Hon. L. Braithwaite.
Minister of State, Finance and Planning, Sen. C. A. Griffith.
President of the Senate, Senator Hon. Sir Arnott Cato, K.C.M.G.
Speaker, House of Assembly, Hon. W. C. B. Hinds.

BARBADOS HIGH COMMISSION
6 Upper Belgrave Street, SW1X 8A2
[01–235 8686]

High Commissioner, His Excellency Dr. The Hon. H. McDonald Forde.

BRITISH HIGH COMMISSION
147–9 Roebuck Street (P.O. Box 676C)
Bridgetown

High Commissioner, His Excellency Giles Lionel Bullard, C.M.G. (1983).

JUDICATURE

There is a Supreme Court of Judicature consisting of a High Court and a Court of Appeal. In certain cases a further appeal lies to the Judicial Committee of H.M. Privy Council. The Chief Justice and Puisne Judges are appointed by the Governor-General on the recommendation of the Prime Minister and after consultation with the Leader of the Opposition.
Chief Justice, Rt. Hon. Sir William Douglas, K.C.M.G.

EDUCATION

Primary and secondary education is free in Government schools. There are 120 primary schools, 21 Government Secondary schools and 17 approved Government secondary schools.

COMMUNICATIONS

Barbados has some 965 miles of roads, of which about 917 miles are asphalted. The Grantley Adams International airport is situated at Seawell, 12 miles from Bridgetown, and frequent scheduled services connect Barbados with the major world air routes. Bridgetown, the only port of entry, has a deep-water harbour with berths for 8 ships, but oil is pumped ashore at Spring Gardens and at an Esso installation on the West Coast. Barbados has a colour television service, three radio broadcasting services, and a wired broadcasting service.

FINANCE

	1982–83
Current revenue	BDS$495,712,000
Current expenditure	477,164,000
Capital expenditure	112,669,000

ECONOMY

The economy of the island is based on tourism, sugar and light manufacturing. In 1982 over 300,000 tourists visited Barbados. Chief exports are sugar, molasses, rum and electrical components.

	1981	1982
	BDS$	BDS$
Total imports	1,150,941,117	1,107,490,000
Total exports	391,039,019	517,505,000

Trade with U.K.

	1982
Imports from U.K.	BDS$99,500,000
Exports to U.K.	47,000,000

Belize

Belize lies on the east coast of Central America, bounded on the north and north-west by Mexico, and on the west and south by Guatemala. The total area (including offshore islands) is about 8,867 sq. miles, with a length and breadth of 174 miles and 68 miles respectively. The climate is sub-tropical, with a mean annual temperature of 79°F, but is tempered by sea breezes. There are two dry seasons, the main one from March to May and the other (the Maugre Season) from August to September. The country is occasionally affected by hurricanes.

The coastal areas are mostly flat and swampy but the country rises gradually towards the interior. The northern and western districts are hilly, and in the south the Maya Mountains and the Cockscombs form the backbone of the country, reaching a height of 3,800 feet at Victoria Peak. There are 17 principal rivers, of which the Belize River is the most important, but few are navigable for any distance.

The population is 148,300 (1981 estimate), of which the main racial groups are Creoles, Mestizos (Maya-Spanish) and Caribs, plus a number of East Indian and Spanish descent. The races are now heavily inter-mixed. The majority of the population is Christian, about 60 per cent Catholic and most of the remainder Protestant.

The early history of Belize is little known, although the numerous ruins in the area indicate that it was heavily populated by the Maya Indians. The first British settlement was established in 1638 but was subject to repeated attacks by the Spanish, who claimed sovereignty over the area, until the decline of Spanish power in the Americas in the 19th century. In 1862 the area was recognised by Britain as a Colony and called British Honduras. On June 1, 1973 the colony was officially renamed Belize, and was granted independence on September 21, 1981. The long-standing territorial dispute with Guatemala, which had delayed independence earlier, remains unresolved despite efforts to reach a settlement.

CAPITAL.—Belmopan (estimated population, Dec. 31, 1975, 4,000). The largest city and the former capital is ΨBelize City (population, estimated, 1978 50,000), which was badly damaged by a hurricane in October 1961. Other towns are ΨCorozal (6,000), San Ignacio (6,000), Dangriga (9,000), Orange Walk (7,000), Punta Gorda (2,700).

GOVERNMENT

The Queen is Head of State, represented in Belize by a Governor-General, who is a citizen of the country, appointed in consultation with the Prime Minister of Belize. There is a National Assembly, comprising a House of Representatives (18 members elected for 5 years) and a Senate (8 members appointed by the Governor-General). Executive power is vested in the Cabinet, which is responsible to the National Assembly.

Governor-General, Her Excellency Dr. Minita Elvira Gordon, G.C.M.G.
Prime Minister, Rt. Hon. George Price.

EDUCATION

Education is compulsory from 6 to 14 years of age. In 1980 free primary education was provided by 21 state schools and 180 grant-aided schools (usually run by the churches), with a total enrolment of 35,000. Secondary education was provided by 5 state and 17 grant-aided schools with an enrolment of over 6,000. There are 5 post-secondary institutions, but no universities although the Government offers scholarships for students to go abroad. There is an extra-mural faculty of the University of the West Indies, with a resident tutor.

ECONOMY

About 42 per cent of the population is engaged in agriculture. Corn (maize), rice, red kidney beans, root crops and fruit are the main food crops, although main agricultural exports are sugar, bananas and citrus products. The country is more or less self-sufficient in fresh beef, pork and poultry, but processed meat and dairy products are imported. About 25 per cent of timber production (mostly mahogany) is exported, and there is a large U.S. market for lobster, conch and scale fish. Tourism is also a valuable source of income.

FINANCE

	1981–82	1982–83
Revenue	BZ $82,700,000	$86,000,000
Expenditure	81,100,000	75,900,000
Surplus	15,600,000	10,100,000

The Belize dollar (BZ $) is tied to the U.S. dollar: BZ $2 = U.S. $1.

TRADE

	1982
Total imports	BZ $262,900,000
Total exports	187,500,000

Trade with U.K.

	1982	1983
Imports from U.K.	£10,450,000	£11,565,000
Exports to U.K.	13,320,000	8,726,000

COMMUNICATIONS

There is a Government-operated radio service but no official television service in the country. An automatic telephone service covers the whole country; internal services are handled by the Belize Telecommunication Authority and external services by Cable and Wireless Ltd. through the earth satellite system (opened 1978).

The principal airport is at Belize City and various airlines operate international flights to U.S. and other Central American states. The main port is also Belize City, where construction of deep water quays was recently completed. There are 1,865 miles of road, including four main highways, but there is no railway system.

BELIZE HIGH COMMISSION
c/o West Indies Committee,
48 Albermarle Street, W.1.
(01–486 8381)
High Commissioner, His Excellency Rudolph I. Castillo, M.B.E.

BRITISH HIGH COMMISSION
P.O. Box 91, Belmopan.
High Commissioner, His Excellency John M. Crosby, M.V.O.
Deputy High Commissioner, S. S. Calder.

Botswana
(The Republic of Botswana)

Botswana (formerly the British Protectorate of Bechuanaland) lies between latitudes 18° and 26° S. and longitudes 20° and 28° W. and is bounded by the Cape and Transvaal Provinces of South Africa on the south and east, by Zimbabwe, the Zambesi and Chobe (Linyanti) Rivers on the north and north-east and by South West Africa on the west. Botswana extends some 500 miles by 550 miles, with a total area of 220,000 square miles. The climate of the country is generally sub-tropical, but varies considerably with latitude and altitude. A plateau at a height of about 4,000 feet divides Botswana into two main topographical regions. To the east of the plateau streams flow into the Marico, Notwani and Limpopo Rivers; to the west lies a flat region comprising the Kgalagadi Desert, the Okavango Swamps and the Northern State Lands area. The Kgalagadi Desert is a level tract closely covered with thorn bush and grass, extending 300 miles to the west and bounded by the Makgadikgadi salt pans and the Boteti River in the north. Its rainfall varies from 20 inches in the east to 9 inches in the south-west. The Okavango Swamps, 6,500 square miles in area, lie in the remote north-western corner of Botswana, and, apart from the Limpopo and Chobe Rivers, are the only source of permanent surface water in the country. North of the Boteti River and the Makgadikgadi depression the Kgalagadi Desert gives way to forest and dense bush of the Northern State Lands. Large areas of the country support only herds of game. Elephant numbers have been estimated at 15–30,000.

POPULATION.—Botswana has an estimated population (1981) of about 937,000. The eight principal Botswana tribes are Bakgatla, Bakwena, Bangwaketse, Bamalete, Bamangwato, Barolong, Batawana and Batlokwa. The principal languages in use in Botswana are Setswana and English.

CAPITAL.—Gaborone, estimated population 60,000. Other business centres are Francistown (31,000), Lobatse (19,000), and Selebi-Phikwe (30,000).

FLAG.—Horizontal bands of blue, white, blue, with a black stripe on the white band.

GOVERNMENT

On September 30, 1966, Bechuanaland became a Republic within the Commonwealth under the name Botswana. The President of Botswana is Head of State and appoints as Vice-President a member of the National Assembly who is his principal assistant and leader of Government business in the National Assembly. The Assembly consists of the President, 32 members elected on a basis of universal adult suffrage, 4 specially elected members, the Attorney-General (non-voting) and the Speaker. There is also a House of Chiefs.

President, His Excellency Dr. Q. K. J. Masire.

CABINET

Vice President, Minister of Finance and Development Planning, Hon. P. S. Mmusi.
External Affairs, Hon. A. M. Mogwe, M.B.E.
Public Service and Information, Hon. D. K. Kwela-gobe.
Assistant Minister, Finance and Development Planning, Hon. O. I. Chilume.
Health, Hon. L. Makgekgenene.
Agriculture, Hon. W. Meswele.
Local Government and Lands, Hon. E. M. K. Kgabo.
Works and Communications, Hon. C. Blackbeard.
Commerce and Industry, Hon. M. P. K. Nwako.
Education, Hon. K. P. Morake.
Mineral Resources and Water Affairs, Hon. Dr. G. K. T. Chiepe, M.B.E.
Home Affairs, Hon. Mrs. K. L. Disele.
Assistant Minister, Local Government and Lands, Hon. J. L. T. Mothibamele.
Assistant Minister, Agriculture, Hon. G. U. S. Matlha-baphiri.

A General Election was to be held on Sept. 8, 1984.

BOTSWANA HIGH COMMISSION
162 Buckingham Palace Road, S.W.1
(01–730 5216)

High Commissioner, His Excellency S. A. Mpuchane.

BRITISH HIGH COMMISSION
Private Bag 0023, Gaborone

High Commissioner, His Excellency Wilfred Jones, C.M.G. (1981)
British Council Representative, D. Munro.

AGRICULTURE

Botswana is a predominantly pastoral country, with a national herd of over 3 million cattle and over 2 million smallstock. Eighty per cent of agricultural income is derived from cattle. The country is embarking on a Tribal Grazing Land Programme which will encourage the adoption of modern ranching techniques. Measures are being taken to combat soil erosion and to increase livestock and crop production.

MINERAL PRODUCTION

Mineral extraction and processing has recently become a major source of income for the country, following the opening of large mines for diamonds and copper-nickel. Large deposits of coal have been discovered, and are being mined on a small scale; further development, including coal exports, is anticipated. Much of the country has yet to be fully prospected. Manufacturing industry is expected to grow slowly in the future, as communications improve.

EDUCATION

In 1984 there were 512 primary schools with an enrolment of 208,433 and 56 secondary schools with 27,275 enrolments. There were also three teacher training establishments with an enrolment of 1,070 (two more open in 1985), one Polytechnic with 567 students and the University of Botswana with 1,200 undergraduates.

COMMUNICATIONS

The railway from Cape Town to Zimbabwe passes through eastern Botswana. The main roads in the country are the north–south road, which closely follows the railway, and the road running east–west that links Francistown and Maun. A new road from Nata to Kazungula provides a direct link to Zambia from Botswana. Air services are provided on a scheduled basis between the main towns, linking with services from South Africa, Zambia and Zimbabwe.

FINANCE

	1981–82	1982–83*
Actual Revenue (Recurrent and development)	*P*322,620,000	*P*365,780,000
Actual Expenditure	341,360,000	435,460,000

* estimate.

Currency: In August 1976 Botswana introduced its own currency, the *pula*, to replace the South African *rand* formerly in use. It is linked to a basket of currencies. *P*1 = \$US0·846 (June, 1984).

TRADE

Principal exports are diamonds, copper-nickel matte, and beef and beef products.

	1981	1982
Imports	*UA* 695,059	*UA* 744,042
Exports	347,837	494,243

(*U.A.* = Units of Account, the common currency unit for the Southern African Common Customs Area, which is based on the South African *Rand*.)

Trade with U.K.

	1983
Imports from U.K.	£3,250,000
Exports to U.K.	21,713,000

Brunei
(Negara Brunei Darussalem)

Brunei is situated on the north-west coast of the island of Borneo, total area about 2,226 sq. miles, population (1982), approximately 200,000 of whom 68 per cent are of Malay or other indigenous race and 25 per cent Chinese. The country has a humid tropical climate.

CAPITAL.—Bandar Seri Begawan (population, 58,000).

FLAG.—Yellow, with diagonal bands of white over narrow black band (from top by staff), with red device on diagonal bands.

GOVERNMENT

In 1959, the Sultan of Brunei promulgated the first written Constitution, which provides for a Privy Council, a Council of Ministers and a Legislative Council. On January 1, 1984 Brunei resumed full independence. A ministerial system of government was established at independence, the seven Ministers being appointed by the Sultan and responsible to him. The Sultan presides over the Privy Council and the Council of Ministers.

Sultan, H.H. Sir Muda Hassanal Bolkiah Mu'izzadin Waddaulah, G.C.M.G., *acceded* 1967, *crowned* Aug. 1, 1968.

BRUNEI HIGH COMMISSION
49 Cromwell Road, S.W.7

High Commissioner, Pengiran Haji Idriss.

BRITISH HIGH COMMISSION
Hong Kong and Shanghai Bank
Building (3rd floor), Bandar
Seri Begawan.

High Commissioner, His Excellency Robert Francis Cornish, M.V.O. (1983).

FINANCE

	1984 (forecast)
Revenue	*B*\$6,500 million
Expenditure*	2,600 million

*Including development expenditure.

Currency.—The unit of currency is the *Brunei dollar* of 100 *cents*, which is fully interchangeable with the currency of Singapore.

Cyprus

AREA, CLIMATE AND POPULATION.—Cyprus with an area of 3,572 square miles, is the third largest island in the Mediterranean Sea, exceeded in size by Sicily and Sardinia. Its greatest length is 140 miles and greatest breadth 60 miles, situated at latitude 35°N. and longitude 33° 30'E. It is about 40 miles distant from the nearest point of Asia Minor, 60 miles from Syria and 240 miles from Port Said. The main topographical features of Cyprus are: (*a*) A narrow limestone range of mountains extending in an unbroken chain for nearly 100 miles along the north coast, at an average height of 2,000 feet; (*b*) A broad central plain, running for some 60 miles from west to east; (*c*) An extensive igneous massif rising to over 6,000 feet in the west of the island; and (*d*) Narrow coastal plains between the mountains and the sea. The rivers are little more than mountain torrents. There is no permanent stream of any volume.

Cyprus has a somewhat intense Mediterranean climate with a hot dry summer and a variable warm winter, while the intermediate seasons are short and transitional. The winter is generally sunny with frequent cold spells between the beginning of December and end of February. The rainy season lasts from October to April with average total rainfall of about 20 inches. July and August are the warmest months.

In 1978 the estimated population was 618,300. There are two major communities, Greek Cypriots (78 per cent) and Turkish Cypriots (18·2 per cent); and minorities of Armenians, Maronites and others. The population growth in 1978 was 0·7 per cent. The birth rate in 1978 was estimated to be 19·3 and the death rate 8·4 per thousand.

CAPITAL.—Nicosia, near the centre of the island, with a population of 233,500 (1974 estimate); the other principal towns are ΨLimassol, ΨFamagusta, ΨLarnaca, Paphos and Kyrenia. Nicosia is distant from London 2,028 miles by air.

FLAG.—Gold map of Cyprus on a white ground, surmounting crossed olive branches (green).

GOVERNMENT

Cyprus passed under British administration from 1878. Cyprus was formally annexed to Great Britain on Nov. 5, 1914, on the outbreak of war with Turkey. From 1925 to 1960 it was a Crown Colony administered by a Governor, assisted by an Executive Council and also for a time by a partly-elected Legislative Council. Following the launching in April 1955 of an armed campaign by EOKA in support of ENOSIS (union with Greece), a state of emergency was declared in November, 1955, which lasted for four years. Following a meeting at Zürich between the Prime Ministers of Greece and Turkey, a conference was held in London and an agreement was signed on February 19, 1959, between the United Kingdom, Greece, Turkey and the Greek and Turkish Cypriots which provided that Cyprus would be an independent Republic.

CONSTITUTION

Under the Cyprus Act, 1960, the island became an independent sovereign republic on August 16, 1960. The constitution provided for a Greek Cypriot President and a Turkish Cypriot Vice-President elected for a five-year term by the Greek and Turkish communities respectively. The House of Representatives, elected for five years by universal suffrage of each community separately, was to consist of 35 Greek and 15 Turkish members. The 1960 Constitution proved unworkable in practice and led to intercommunal troubles. The mandate of the U.N. Peace Keeping Force in Cyprus (UNFICYP) was last renewed on June 15, 1984.

On July 15, 1974, mainland Greek officers of the Greek Cypriot National Guard launched a *coup d'état* against President Makarios and installed a former E.O.K.A. member, Nikos Sampson, in his place. Turkey reserved to itself the right to maintain constitutional order and the independence and territorial integrity of the island, invaded Northern Cyprus and occupied over a third of the island. In 1975 a "Turkish Federated State of Cyprus" under Mr. Rauf Denktash was declared in this area, and in November 1983 a "Declaration of Statehood" was issued which purported to establish the "Turkish Republic of Northern Cyprus". The declaration has been condemned by the U.N. Security Council and only Turkey has recognized the new "state".

Since 1974 attempts to reach a settlement have focused on the procedure of intercommunal talks under the auspices of the U.N. These have been in suspense since May 1983, but the U.N. Secretary General has continued to explore ways of bringing the two sides together.

A general election was held for the Greek House of Representatives on May 24, 1981, resulting in the parties gaining the following number of seats: AKEL (Communist) 12; Democratic Rally 12; Democratic Party (Centre) 8; EDEK (Socialist) 3. (In a 1982 by-election, one Democratic Rally M.P. was replaced by one from the Democratic Party.)

President, Spyros Kyprianou, *elected* Feb. 28, 1978, *re-elected*, Feb. 13, 1983.

COUNCIL OF MINISTERS

Foreign Affairs, George Iacovou.
Interior & Defence, Christodoulos Veniamin.
Finance, Simos Vasiliou.
Commerce & Industry, Georgios Andreou.
Education, Stellos Katsellis.
Communications & Works, Christos Mavrellis.
Agriculture & Natural Resources, Demetrios Christodoulou.
Labour & Social Insurance, Pavlos Papageorgiou.
Health, Christos Pelekanos.
Justice, Phivos Clerides.

Minister to the President, Dinos Michaelides.
Deputy Minister of Interior, Elias Eliades.

CYPRUS HIGH COMMISSION
93 Park Street, W1Y 4ET
[01-499 2810]

High Commissioner, His Excellency Tasos Panayides.

BRITISH HIGH COMMISSION
Alexander Pallis Street (P.O. Box 1978)
Nicosia

High Commissioner, His Excellency William John Antony Wilberforce, C.M.G. (1981).
British Council Representative, J. Mulholland, O.B.E., P.O. Box 1995, 3 Museum Street, Nicosia.

ECONOMY

Following a period of rapid growth in the years 1975–79 the economy has settled to a more modest and sustainable growth rate averaging about 3·5 per cent over the past two years. Continued growth at about 4 per cent is the aim of the 1982–86 development plan which will also promote Cyprus as a centre for Middle East trade.

Agriculture still occupies a prime position in the Cyprus economy but little further growth is expected. Main products are citrus fruits, grapes and vine products, potatoes and other vegetables. Manufacturing, construction, distribution and other service industries are other major employers. Tourism is the main growth industry with 621,000 long-stay tourists producing C£170 million in foreign exchange earnings in 1983. Plans to establish an "industrial free zone" to attract new foreign investment for exportable commodities are in hand. Some 2,700 foreign firms and individuals have registered as "offshore companies" in Cyprus which supports Cyprus' claim to be a centre for Middle East trade.

Britain is still the country's most important trading partner, taking some 16·5 per cent of its exports in 1983 and supplying 13·5 per cent of its imports. Cyprus is seeking to diversify its export markets and now sells almost half its exports to the Middle East. The trading account continues in deficit and is offset by invisible earnings, mainly from tourism, foreign aid and development loans, capital inflows and income derived from the Sovereign Base Areas and United Nations personnel.

FINANCE

	1982
Total Revenue	C£245 million
Ordinary Expenditure	C£302 million

TRADE

	1982	1983
Imports	C£577·6 m	C£641·9 m
Exports (including re-exports)	263·8 m	260·5 m

Trade with U.K.

	1982	1983
Imports from U.K.	£111,882,000	£127,800,000
Exports to U.K.	89,908,000	87,400,000

BRITISH SOVEREIGN AREAS

The United Kingdom retained full sovereignty and jurisdiction over two areas of 99 square miles in all—Akrotiri–Episkopi–Paramali and Dhekelia–Pergamos–Ayios Nicolaos–Xylophagou—and use of roads and other facilities. The British Administrator of these areas is appointed by the Queen and is responsible to the Secretary of State for Defence.

Administrator of the British Sovereign Areas, Maj.-Gen. Sir Desmond Langley, K.C.V.O., M.B.E.

Dominica
(The Commonwealth of Dominica)

Dominica, the loftiest of the Lesser Antilles, lies in the Windward Group, between 15° 20′ and 15° 45′ N. lat. and 61° 13′ and 61° 30′ W. long., 95 miles S. of Antigua. It is about 29 miles long and 15 broad comprising an area of 290 sq. miles. The island is of volcanic origin and very mountainous and picturesque, abounding in streams fairly well stocked with fish, and the soil is very fertile. The temperature varies, according to the altitude, from 55° to 85°F. The climate is healthy, and during the winter months is very pleasant. Population (1981 census, 74,069).

CAPITAL.—ΨRoseau, on the south-west coast, population, 8,346. The other principal town is Portsmouth, population, 2,220.

GOVERNMENT

The island was discovered by Columbus in 1493, when it was a stronghold of the Caribs, who remained virtually the sole inhabitants until the French established settlements in the 18th century. It was captured by the British in 1759 but passed back and forth between France and Britain until 1805, after which British possession was not challenged. From 1871–1939 Dominica was part of the Leeward Islands Colony, then from 1940 the island was a unit of the Windward Islands group. Internal self-government from 1967 was followed on Nov. 3, 1978 by independence as a republic with the name The Commonwealth of Dominica. Executive authority is vested in the President, who is elected by the House of Assembly for not more than two terms of five years. Parliament consists of the President and the House of Assembly (representatives elected by universal adult suffrage) and nine Senators, who may be appointed by the President or elected. Parliament has a life of five years.

President, His Excellency Aurelius Marie, M.B.E.
Prime Minister and Minister for Finance, Foreign Affairs, Trade, Industry and Tourism, Hon. Mary Eugenia Charles.

DOMINICA HIGH COMMISSION
1, Collingham Gardens, S.W.1.
(01–370 5194/5)

High Commissioner, His Excellency Arden Shillingford, M.B.E.

BRITISH HIGH COMMISSION
High Commissioner, (resides at Bridgetown, Barbados).

FINANCE

	1983–84*
Recurrent Revenue	*$70,456,830
Recurrent Expenditure	70,170,010
Capital Revenue	76,326,690
Capital Expenditure	82,831,120

* Estimated

ECONOMY

Agriculture is the principal occupation, with tropical and citrus fruits the main crops. Products for export are bananas, lime juice, lime oil, bay oil, copra and rum. Forestry and fisheries are being encouraged. The only commercially exploitable mineral is pumice, used chiefly for building purposes. Manufacturing consists largely of the processing of agricultural products.

TRADE

	1982
Imports	$128,250,000
Exports	66,150,000

Trade with U.K.

	1982
Imports from U.K.	£7,423,000
Exports to U.K.	11,376,000

Fiji

Fiji is made up of about 332 islands and over 500 islets (including numerous atolls and reefs) in the South Pacific Ocean, about 1,100 miles north of New Zealand. About 100 islands are permanently inhabited. The gross area of the group, which extends 300 miles from east to west, and 300 north to south, between 15° 45′—21° 10′ S. lat. and 176° E.—178° W. long. is 7,072 square miles. The International Date Line has been diverted to the east of the island group. The largest islands are Viti Levu and Vanua Levu. The main groups of islands are Lomaiviti, Lau and Yasawas. Most of the larger islands are mountainous with sharp peaks and crags, but also have conspicuous areas of flat land and many of the rivers have built extensive deltas. The climate is tropical, without extremes of heat and temperatures rarely exceed 32°C. and seldom fall below 15°C.

The population (mid-1983) was 671,712, of which about 44 per cent are indigenous Fijians and about 50 per cent Indians.

CAPITAL.—ΨSuva, in the island of Viti Levu. Population (mid-1983) 71,000.

GOVERNMENT

Fiji was a British colony from 1874 until October 10, 1970, when it became an independent state and a member of the Commonwealth. Under the Constitution there is a Governor-General appointed by the Queen. The House of Representatives has 52 members—22 Fijians, 22 Indians and 8 General Elector representatives. For the Fijians and Indians, 12 are elected by voters registered on the Communal Roll and 10 by voters on the National Roll. Three General Elector representatives are elected by voters on the Communal Roll and five by voters on the National Roll. General members are in the main representatives of the European, part-European and Chinese communities.

There is a Senate of 22 members, 8 nominated by the Great Council of Chiefs, 7 by the Prime Minister,

6 by the Leader of the Opposition and one by the Council of Rotuma, an island dependency 400 miles from Suva, discovered in 1879 and annexed in 1881.

Governor-General, His Excellency Ratu Sir Penaia Ganilau, G.C.M.G., K.C.V.O., K.B.E., D.S.O., E.D.

CABINET

Prime Minister, Minister for Fijian Affairs, and Information, Rt. Hon. Ratu Sir Kamisese Mara, G.C.M.G., K.B.E.
Deputy P.M. and Minister for Economic Planning and Development, Hon. Ratu David Toganivalu.
Cabinet Secretary, Hon. Dr. Isireli Lasaqa.
Employment and Industrial Relations, Hon. Mohammed Ramzan, M.B.E.
Communications, Transport and Works, Hon. Semesa Sikivou.
Home Affairs, Hon. Militoni Leweniqila.
Lands, Energy and Mineral Resources, Hon. Jone Naisara.
Attorney-General, Minister for Justice, Hon. Qoriniasi Bale.
Primary Industries, Hon. Charles Walker.
Finance, Hon. Mosese Qionibaravi.
Housing and Urban Affairs, Hon. Edward Beddoes.
Foreign Affairs, Tourism and Civil Aviation, Hon. Jonati Mavoa, C.M.G.
Health and Social Welfare, Hon. Dr. Apenisa Kurisaqila.
Education, Hon. Dr. Ahmed Ali.

Speaker, House of Representatives, Hon. Tomasi Vakatora.
President of the Senate, Hon. Senator W. M. Barrett.

FIJI HIGH COMMISSION
34 Hyde Park Gate, SW7 5BN
[01-584 3661/2]

High Commissioner, His Excellency Ratu Josua B. Toganivalu, C.B.E.

BRITISH HIGH COMMISSION
Civic Centre, Stinson Parade,
P.O. Box 1355, Suva

High Commissioner, His Excellency Roger Arnold Rowlandson Barltrop, C.V.O. (1982).

JUDICIARY

The Constitution guarantees the independence of the judiciary. Judges are appointed by the Governor-General.

Chief Justice of Fiji, Hon. Sir Timoci Tuivaga.

FINANCE

	1981	1982
Public Income	$259,450,000	$276,843,000
Public Expenditure	239,582,000	276,692,000

Currency.—Currency is the *Fiji dollar.*

ECONOMY

The economy is primarily agrarian, with about 600,000 acres under cultivation. The principal cash crop is sugar cane, which is the main export, followed by coconuts, ginger and copra. A variety of other fruit, vegetables and root crops are also grown, and self-sufficiency in rice is a major aim. Forestry, fishing and beef production are being encouraged in order to diversify the economy. The processing of agricultural, marine and timber products are the main industries, along with gold mining.

Tourism is also a major factor in the economy, second only to sugar as a money-earner. There were 203,600 visitors in 1982.

TRADE

	1981	1982
Total Imports	$540,071,695	$475,591,000
Total Exports (including Re-exports)	268,968,183	267,557,000

Trade with U.K.

	1982	1983
Imports from U.K.	£9,088,000	£12,184,000
Exports to U.K.	39,826,000	46,943,000

The chief imports are foodstuffs, machinery, mineral fuels, chemicals, beverages, tobacco and manufactured articles. Chief exports are sugar, coconut oil, gold, lumber, molasses, ginger and canned fish.

COMMUNICATIONS

Fiji is one of the main aerial crossroads in the Pacific. Air Pacific Ltd. is based at Nausori Airport near Suva and operates scheduled domestic services within the Fiji Islands and from Suva provides services to New Zealand, Australia, Tonga, Western Samoa, Vanuatu, the Solomon Islands, Kiribati, Tuvalu, New Caledonia and American Samoa. Fiji Air Services Ltd. operates charter flights within the Fiji group of islands and South Pacific and provides scheduled services within the Fiji group.

Fiji has three ports of entry, at Suva, Lautoka and Levuka.

The Gambia

The Gambia takes its name from the Gambia River, which it straddles for over 200 miles inland from the west coast of Africa. It is a narrow strip, surrounded by the Republic of Senegal, except at the coast, lying between 13° 10′–13° 45′ N. and 13° 90′–16° 50′ W. The area is 4,004 sq. miles of which one fifth is the river. Ocean-going vessels can go up-river for 150 miles and river craft up to 300 miles from the mouth. The Gambia River basin was part of the region dominated in the 10th–16th centuries by the strong Songhai and Mali kingdoms centred on the upper Niger. The population comprises mainly Wolof, Mandinka and Fula peoples who originally migrated there from the north and east. Population (1983 Census) is approximately 700,000.

The first recorded Europeans to reach the Gambia River were the Portuguese in 1447. In 1588 Queen Elizabeth I gave the first charter to English merchants to trade along the river. Merchants from France, Courland (now part of Latvia) and the Netherlands also established trading posts there. The English presence was strongly challenged by the French, who were dominant further north up the coast, but in 1783 the Treaty of Versailles acknowledged English rights. In 1816, after the Napoleonic Wars, and in order to enforce abolition of the slave trade, the British stationed a garrison on a low sandy island called Banjul at the river mouth. Renamed Bathurst, this became the capital of a small British-administered colony, initially under the Governor of Sierra Leone. Negotiations with France continued sporadically until 1889 when it was agreed that the British rights along the upper river should extend 10 km on either bank. British administration was extended from the Colony to this Protectorate. The Gambia became independent within the Commonwealth on February 18, 1965, and a Republic on April 24, 1970.

The Gambia's relationship with Senegal has always been an important factor in political and economic policy. Moves towards a closer association were accelerated after an abortive coup in The Gambia in July 1981 was put down with the help of Senegalese troops. In February 1982 the Senegambia Confederation was formally instituted based on certain joint institutions and integration of policies, but each country remains sovereign and independent.

Except during the rainy season from June to October, when it sometimes becomes uncomfortably humid, Banjul's climate is very pleasant. Rainfall is 32–40 inches a year.

CAPITAL.—ΨBanjul. Population (1983 Census) of island of Banjul was 44,536; and of adjacent Kombo St. Mary district 102,858. Total population of Banjul/Kombo St. Mary, 147,394.

FLAG.—Horizontal stripes of red, blue and green, separated by narrow white stripes.

GOVERNMENT

The constitution is democratic and Parliamentary, with an executive President elected for five years. The House of Representatives has 35 elected members, 5 elected Chiefs Representatives and up to 8 nominated members plus the Attorney-General (ex-officio). The Vice President and other Ministers are appointed by the President. Parliament must be dissolved after five years. The last general elections were held in May 1982. The present state of the parties for elected members is PPP (People's Progressive Party) 29; NCP (National Convention Party) 3; Independents 3.

PRESIDENT AND CABINET

President, His Excellency Alhaji Sir Dawda Kairaba Jawara, G.C.M.G.
Vice-President, Hon. Bakary B. Darbo.
External Affairs, Hon. L. K. Jabang.
Finance and Trade, Hon. S. S. Sisay.
Attorney-General, Hon. F. M'Bai.
Health, Labour and Social Welfare, Hon. M. C. Jallow.
Agriculture, Hon. S. Sabally.
Information and Tourism, Hon. L. J. Sonko.
Economic Planning and Industrial Development, Hon. Dr. M. S. K. Manneh.
Water Resources and the Environment, Hon. O. A. Jallow.
Works and Communications, Hon. L. B. M'Boge.
Education, Youth, Sports and Culture, Hon. A. A. N'Jie.
Local Government and Lands, Hon. A. Janneh.
Interior, Hon. A. W. Badji.

Chief Justice, Hon. E. O. Ayoola.
Speaker, Alhaji Hon. M. B. N'Jie.

GAMBIA HIGH COMMISSION
57 Kensington Court, W8 5DG
[01-937 6316/7/8]

High Commissioner, His Excellency Samuel J. O. Sarr.

BRITISH HIGH COMMISSION
48 Atlantic Road, Fajara (P.O. Box 507), Banjul

High Commissioner, His Excellency David Le Breton, C.B.E. (1981).

COMMUNICATIONS

There is an international airport at Yundum, 17 miles from Banjul, with scheduled services flying to other West African states and to the U.K. Banjul is the main port. Internal communication is by road and river. There is no railway system. There are two broadcasting stations and a U.H.F. telephone service linking Banjul with the principal towns in the provinces. There is no television service.

EDUCATION

There are 23 secondary high schools and technical colleges with a total enrolment of 12,500 students. Two High Schools provide 'A' level education.

Gambia College provides post-secondary courses in education, agriculture, public health and nursing. There are seven vocational training institutions with a total enrolment of 800. Higher education and advanced training courses are taken outside The Gambia, currently by over 200 students.

PRODUCTION

Eighty-five per cent of the population depend for their livelihood on agriculture (40 per cent of Gross Domestic Product). The chief product, groundnuts, is also the most important export item, forming over 90 per cent of all domestic exports. Other crops are rice, millet, sorghum, maize and cotton. Fishing and livestock industries are being developed. Thirty per cent of the country's basic food requirements are imported. There are no significant deposits of minerals. Manufactures are limited to groundnut processing, minor metal fabrications, paints, furniture, soap and bottling. Tourism is developing quickly, with 54,000 visitors in 1983–84. The entrepôt trade through The Gambia, re-exporting imported goods to neighbouring countries, is an important element in the national economy.

FINANCE 1983–84*

	Recurrent *D*'000	Development ment *D*'000
Revenue	157,362	..
Expenditure	151,827	119,400

*Approved estimates

Over 80 per cent of capital expenditure comes from external aid grants and loans. The Five Year Development Plan 1981–86 envisages an annual GDP growth rate of 5·1 per cent or 2·5 per cent per capita (at 1980–81 prices).

The Government financial year begins on July 1.

Currency.—Decimal currency was introduced in the Gambia on July 1, 1971. The unit is the *dalasi* of 100 *butut.*

TRADE

	1982	1983
Total imports	*D*221,216,000	*D*262,107,000
Total exports	98,512,000	114,700,000

Trade with U.K.

	1982	1983
Imports from U.K.	£10,087,000	£10,565,000
Exports to U.K.	2,031,000	3,800,000

Ghana

Ghana (formerly known as the Gold Coast) is situated on the Gulf of Guinea, between 3° 07′ W. long. and 1° 14′ E. long. (about 334 miles), and extends 441 miles north from Cape Three Points (4° 45′ N.) to 11° 11′ N. It is bounded on the north by Upper Volta, on the west by the Ivory Coast, on the east by Togo, and on the south by the Atlantic Ocean. Although a tropical country, Ghana is cooler than many countries within similar latitudes.

AREA AND POPULATION.—Ghana has a total area of 92,100 sq. miles. The population at the Census of 1970 was 8,545,561; estimates put the current figure at around 14 million. Almost all Ghanaians are Sudanese Negroes, although Hamitic strains are common in Northern Ghana. The official language is English. The principal indigenous language group is Akan, of which Twi and Fanti are the most commonly used. Ga, Ewe and languages of the Mole–Dagbani group are common in certain regions.

CAPITAL.—ΨACCRA. Population of the Greater Accra Region (including Tema) was (1970 Census, provisional total) 851,614. Other towns are Kumasi, Tamale, Sekondi-Takoradi, Cape Coast, Sunyani, Ho, Koforidua, Tarkwa and Winneba. Accra is 3,920 miles by sea from Liverpool, transit 12 to 30 days.

FLAG.—Equal horizontal bands of red over yellow over green; five-point black star on gold stripe.

INDEPENDENCE DAY.—March 6.

GOVERNMENT

There is no recorded history of the Gold Coast region before the coming of Europeans in the fifteenth century. The constituent parts of the State came under British administration at various times, the original Gold Coast Colony (the coastal and Southern areas) being first constituted in 1874; Ashanti in 1901; and the Northern Territories Protectorate in 1901. The territory of Trans-Volta-Togoland, part of the former German colony of Togo, was mandated to Britain by the League of Nations after the First World War, and remained under British administration as a United Nations Trusteeship after the Second World War. After a plebiscite in May, 1956, under the auspices of the United Nations, the territory was integrated with the Gold Coast Colony.

The former Gold Coast Colony and associated territories became the independent state of Ghana and a member of the British Commonwealth on March 6, 1957 and adopted a Republican constitution on July 1, 1960. A *coup* in June 1979 led to the formation of an Armed Forces Revolutionary Council chaired by Flt.-Lt. Jerry Rawlings. Civilian rule was restored in Sept. 1979 but overthrown on Dec. 31, 1981, when another *coup* brought back into power Flt.-Lt. Rawlings.

PROVISIONAL NATIONAL DEFENCE COUNCIL
Chairman, Flt.-Lt. J. J. Rawlings.
Members, W/O. J. A. Buadi; E. Tawiah; Mrs. A. Enin; Naa Polkuu Konku Chiiri.
Secretary to P.N.D.C., Dr. E. Hansen.
Secretary, P.N.D.C. Coordinating Secretariat, P. V. Obeng.

GHANA HIGH COMMISSION
13 Belgrave Square, SW1H 8PR
[01-235 4142/5]

High Commissioner, His Excellency Kenneth Kweku Sinaman Dadzie (1982).

BRITISH HIGH COMMISSION
P.O. Box 296, High Street, Accra

High Commissioner, His Excellency Kevin Francis Xavier Burns, C.M.G. (1983).

British Council Representative, D. Clare, Liberia Road (P.O. Box 771), Accra, and an Office in *Kumasi*.

PRODUCTION, ETC.

Agriculture.—Agriculture forms the basis of Ghana's economy, employing 70 per cent. of the working population. Crops of the *Forest Zone* include cocoa, which is the largest single source of revenue, rice and a variety of other foodstuff crops grown on mixed-crop farms. Fruits such as avocado pears, oranges and pineapples are grown. Cassava is the most important crop of the *Coastal Savannas Zone*, of the lower Volta area. Production of pulses such as groundnuts is widespread. Near the Togo border oil palms, yams, maize, cassava, fruit and vegetables are produced. Livestock is raised in the uncultivated areas. The *Northern Savanna Zone* is Ghana's principal cattle rearing area and other livestock production there is important for home consumption. Corn and millet crops are produced in the far north and maize, yams, rice and groundnut crops in more southerly parts of the Zone.

Attempts are being made to diversify agricultural production, with cash crops being extensively cultivated for export and to provide raw materials for local industry.

Fisheries.—Fishing is important in coastal areas and in the Volta itself. However production cannot meet demand and there are considerable imports of fish products. About 80 per cent of home supply is obtained from sea fisheries, but production from the Volta Lake and other inland fisheries is increasing rapidly thanks to greatly increased fish population.

Mineral Production.—The area within a 60 mile radius of Dunkwa produces 90 per cent of Ghana's mineral exports. Manganese production from Nsuta ranks among the world's highest and gold, industrial diamonds and bauxite are also produced. Some 30,000 persons are employed by the mining companies.

Manufactures.—Examples of the small-scale traditional industries are tailoring, goldsmithing and carpentry. Priority has been given in recent years to the establishment of a number of "Pioneer Industries" including timber products, vehicle and refrigerator assembly, cigarettes, boatbuilding, food processing, cotton textiles, clothing, footwear, printing and other light industries. A modern industrial complex is growing in the Accra-Tema area.

Volta River Project.—The Volta River is formed at the confluence of the Black and White Voltas, both of which rise in the neighbouring republic of Upper Volta. With its tributaries the Volta drains an area of 150,000 sq. miles of which 61,000 sq. miles lie in Ghana. From 1966 the Volta Dam at Akosombo has generated hydro-electric power for the processing of bauxite and fed a power transmission network for the Accra-Kumasi-Takoradi area. Electricity is now also sent to Togo and Dahomey. The lake raised by the Volta Dam has a maximum area of 3,275 sq. miles, a length of 250 miles and a shore line of 4,500 miles. A water transport service from Akosombo to various points on the lake has been instituted.

COMMUNICATIONS

Accra Airport is an international airport and Ghana Airways Corporation is the national airline. There are also internal airports at Takoradi, Kumasi and Tamale.

There are 20,000 miles of motorable roads, of which 2,335 miles are bituminised. There are 600 miles of railway, linking Accra and the principal ports of Takoradi and Tema with their hinterlands, and with each other.

Takoradi Harbour consists of seven quay berths—five are used for the handling of general cargo, one is leased specially for manganese exports and one is used for shallow draft colliers. Tema Harbour has 10 berths for larger ocean going vessels and the largest dry dock on the West African coast. An oil berth has also been built to serve the Ghaip refinery which has been constructed at Tema.

Trade with U.K.

	1982	1983
Imports from U.K.	£66,709,000	£82,234,000
Exports to U.K.	78,438,000	58,192,000

Principal exports are cocoa, timber and gold. Principal imports are raw materials, manufacturing equipment, petroleum and food.

The currency of Ghana is the *cedi* (¢) (of 100 *pesawas*).

Grenada

Grenada is situated between the parallels of 12° 13'–11° 58' N. lat. and 61° 20'–61° 35' W. long., and is about 80 miles north of Trinidad, 68 miles S.S.W. of St. Vincent, and about 120 miles S.W. of Barbados. The island is about 21 miles in length and 12 miles in breadth, with an area of 120 square miles. Also included in the territory of Grenada are some of the Grenadines islets, the largest of which is Carriacou, 13 square miles in area. The population was estimated at Dec. 1982 as 110,410. The country is mountainous and very picturesque, and the climate is healthy.

CHIEF TOWN.—ΨSt. George's (population 7,500) lies on the southwest coast, and possesses a good harbour.

GOVERNMENT

Grenada was discovered by Columbus in 1498, and named Conception. It was originally colonized by the French, and was ceded to Great Britain by the Treaty of Versailles in 1783. It became an Associated State in 1967 and an independent nation on Feb. 7, 1974.

The government of Sir Eric Gairy was overthrown on March 13, 1979 by the New Jewel Movement and a People's Revolutionary Government was set up, headed by Mr. Maurice Bishop, one of the leaders of the revolution. Disagreements within the P.R.G. led, in Oct. 1983, to violence and the death of Mr. Bishop, whose government was replaced by a Revolutionary Military Council. These events prompted the intervention of Caribbean and U.S. forces. The Governor-General installed an advisory council in Nov. 1983 to act as an interim government until elections for a parliament and a new government are held, probably in late 1984.

Governor-General, Sir Paul Scoon, G.C.M.G., O.B.E. apptd. 1978.

ADVISORY COMMITTEE

Chairman (responsible for Foreign Affairs, Security, Information, Electoral Matters, Immigration, Tourism), Nicholas Braithwaite.

Deputy Chairman, and Finance, Trade and Planning, Allan Kirton.

Agriculture, Natural Resources and Industrial Development, Arnold Cruickshank.

Construction, Environment, Science and Technology, James De Vere Pitt.

Education, Labour and Civil Aviation, Patrick Emmanuel.

Health and Telecommunications, Ray Smith.

Social Affairs and Women's Affairs, Joan Purcell.

Members without Portfolio, Christopher Williams; Randolph Mark.

GRENADA HIGH COMMISSION
1 Collingham Gardens, SW5 0HW
[01–373 7808/9 and 7800]

High Commissioner, His Excellency Oswald M. Gibbs, C.M.G.

BRITISH HIGH COMMISSION
14 Church Street, St. George's.

High Commissioner, (resides at Bridgetown, Barbados).

Resident Representative, J. P. Kelly (*Second Secretary*).

ECONOMY

The economy is principally agrarian, with cocoa, nutmegs and bananas the major crops. Fruit and vegetables are grown and livestock raised for domestic consumption. The fishing industry is being developed. Manufacturing is mostly confined to processing agricultural products.

Total value of imports in 1982 was EC$152 million. Principal domestic exports for 1982 were cocoa (EC$12·5m), nutmeg (EC$8·2m), mace (EC$2·5m) and bananas (EC$8·9m).

Guyana

Guyana, the former colony of British Guiana, which includes the Counties of Demerara, Essequibo and Berbice, is situated on the north-east coast of South America, bordering on Venezuela, Brazil and Suriname. It has a total area of 83,000 square miles with a seaboard of about 270 miles. The population at May 1980, was estimated at 793,000, but subsequent years have seen heavy emigration. There are three distinct areas. (1) A narrow alluvial coastal belt 10 to 40 miles deep, the eastern part of which is intensively cultivated and contains some 90 per cent of the population. Much of this is below the level of the sea and is drained and irrigated by an intricate system of canals constructed by the Dutch. (2) A mountainous area of dense rain forest behind the coastland, still partly unexplored, which reaches its highest point at *Mount Roraima* (9,000 ft.) on the junction of the Guyana–Brazil–Venezuela borders. (3) The open savannah country of the Rupununi in the south-west where cattle ranching is practised and oil deposits have been discovered.

The entire country is intersected by numerous large rivers, though these are of limited navigational use because of rapids and waterfalls, the most notable of which are the *Kaieteur Fall* on the Potaro River with a sheer drop of 741 ft., the *Horse Shoe Falls* on the Essequibo and the *Marina Fall* on the Ipobe River.

Climate.—The two dry seasons normally last from the middle of February to the end of April, and from the middle of August to the end of November. The climate on the coast is pleasant and healthy for the greater part of the year. In the Aug.–Oct. period it is hot. The mean temperature is 80·3°, the usual extremes being 70° and

90°. In the interior the mean temperature is higher—82·6°, its extremes ranging from 66° to 103°. The yearly rainfall is subject to marked variation, its mean on the coast lands averaging about 90 inches with an average of 58 inches on the savannahs.

CAPITAL.—ΨGeorgetown. Estimated population, including environs, 185,000. Other towns are: Linden (population 29,000); ΨNew Amsterdam (population 23,000); Corriverton (population 17,000).

FLAG.—Red triangle with black border, pointing from hoist to fly, on a yellow triangle with white border, all on a green field.

GOVERNMENT

Guyana became independent on May 26, 1966, with a Governor-General appointed by the Queen. It became a Cooperative Republic on Feb. 23, 1970, and Mr. Arthur Chung was elected first President on March 17, 1970, for a term of six years. The electoral system is a Proportional Representation or "single list" system, each voter casting his vote for a party list of candidates. The voting age is 18. Under the Independence Constitution the Prime Minister and Cabinet were responsible to a National Assembly of 53 members elected by secret ballot every 5 years. The last election under this Constitution was in 1973 and the term of that Assembly was later extended to October 1980.

On April 10, 1978, the Constitution Amendment Bill was passed in the National Assembly. The Bill sought to amend Article 73 of the existing Constitution so as to remove the requirement for the holding of a Referendum and to enable provisions of that kind to be amended by a Bill which has been supported by the vote of not less than two-thirds of all the elected members of the National Assembly. After the Constitution had been so amended it would be competent for the Assembly to repeal the existing Constitution and to replace it by another without the necessity for a Referendum. A Referendum permitting the Assembly so to act was held on July 10, 1978. The new Constitution was passed into law in February 1980 and promulgated in October 1980. It provides for an Executive President, a National Assembly of 65 members, and also for a National Congress of Local Democratic Organs responsible for local government. The Supreme Congress of the People consists of all members of these two assemblies.

Executive President.—L. F. S. Burnham, *elected*, December 15, 1980.

CABINET

Executive President and Minister of Defence and National Security, L. F. S. Burnham.
Prime Minister and First Vice-President (Production), D. Hoyte.
Vice-President and Attorney General, Dr. M. Shahabudeen.
Vice-President (Social Infrastructure), Hamilton Green.
Vice-President (Party and State Matters), B. Ramsaroop.

SENIOR MINISTERS

Home Affairs, J. R. Thomas.
Mobilisation, R. H. O. Corbin.
Energy and Mines, Haroon Rashid.
Foreign Affairs, R. E. Jackson.
Education and Social Development, R. Chandisingh.
Economic Planning and Finance, C. Greenidge.

GUYANA HIGH COMMISSION
3 Palace Court, Bayswater Road, W2 4LP
[01-229 7684/8]

High Commissioner, His Excellency Cedric Joseph.

BRITISH HIGH COMMISSION
44 Main Street (P.O. Box 10849),
Georgetown

High Commissioner, His Excellency William Kenneth Slatcher, C.M.G., C.V.O (1982).

JUDICATURE

The Supreme Court of Judicature consists of a Court of Appeal and a High Court. There are also Courts of Summary Jurisdiction. The Court of Appeal consists of the Chancellor as President, the Chief Justice and such number of Justices of Appeal as may be prescribed by Parliament.

The High Court consists of the Chief Justice, as President, and nine Puisne Judges. It is a court with unlimited jurisdiction in civil matters and exercises exclusive jurisdiction in probate, divorce and admiralty, and certain other matters.

Chancellor, K. S. Massiah.
Chief Justice, K. M. George.

PRODUCTION, ETC.

The economy is based almost entirely on the main export items of sugar, rice, bauxite and alumina. Diamonds and gold are also mined, timber and rum are produced and there is some cattle ranching. The fishing industry is being expanded. Industry is fairly small-scale.

COMMUNICATIONS

Georgetown and New Amsterdam are the principal ports, though bauxite ships also sail to Linden, on the R. Demerara, and Everton, on the R. Berbice. There are no public railways and the few roads are confined mainly to the coastal areas. Air transport is the easiest form of communication between the coast and the interior. There are two state-owned radio broadcasting stations; there is no television service.

EDUCATION

In September 1976 Government assumed total control of the education system and made education free from nursery to university level. At Aug. 1981 there were 374 nursery schools with 27,955 pupils, 425 primary schools with 130,832 pupils. There were 75,325 students in secondary schools. Government trains teachers for primary and secondary schools at its own institutions.

Approximately 1,800 students were enrolled at the University of Guyana in degree programmes and certificate and diploma courses.

There are five technical and vocational institutions, and 36 Home Economics and Industrial Arts Centres in various parts of the country; many primary and secondary schools have departments attached to them. There are also a number of technical and vocational institutions not under the aegis of the Ministry of Education.

Trade with U.K.

	1982	1983
Imports from U.K.	£13,145,000	£13,685,000
Exports to U.K.	50,495,000	42,810,000

India

AREA AND POPULATION.—The Republic of India has an area of 1,261,816 square miles, composed of three well-defined regions: the mountain range of the Himalayas; the Indo-Gangetic plain; and the Southern Peninsula. The main mountain ranges are the Himalayas in the north (over 29,000 feet) and the Western and Eastern Ghats (over 8,000 feet). Major rivers include the Ganges, Indus, Krishna, Godavari and Mahanadi.

There are four seasons: the cold season (Dec.–March); the hot season (April–May); the rainy season (June–Sept.); and the season of the retreating S.W. monsoon (Oct.–Nov.). Temperatures vary over the whole country, between averages of about 50° F and 92° F, reaching over 100° F in some parts during the hot season. There are similar variations in rainfall, from only a few inches a year falling in the western Thar Desert to about 300 inches in parts of Assam.

India is the second most populous country in the world. The population at the 1981 census was 683,880,051, of which slightly more than 20 per cent was urban. The majority of the population are Hindu (453 million = 82 per cent), the rest being Muslim (61 million = 11 per cent), Christian (14 million = 2·5 per cent), Sikh (10 million = 1·8 per cent), Buddhist (4 million = 0·7 per cent) and Jain (2·5 million = 0·5 per cent). The official languages are Hindi in the Devanagari script and English, though 14 regional languages also are recognized for adoption as official State languages.

HISTORY.—The Indus civilization was fully developed by c. 2,500 B.C. but collapsed c. 1,750 B.C., subsequently being replaced by an Aryan civilization spread from the west. The first Arabic invasions of the north west began in the seventh century and Moslem, Hindu and Buddhist states developed until the establishment of the Mogul dynasty in 1526. The British East India Company established settlements throughout the 17th century; clashes with the French and native princes led to the British government taking control of the Company in 1784. The separate dominions of India and Pakistan became independent within the Commonwealth in 1947 and India became a Republic in 1950.

FLAG.—The National Flag is a horizontal tricolour with bands of deep saffron, white and dark green in equal proportions. On the centre of the white band appears an Asoka wheel in navy blue.

CAPITAL.—Delhi (population in 1981 was 6,196,414).

NATIONAL DAY.—January 26 (Republic Day).

President of the Republic of India, Giani Zail Singh, *elected* July 12, 1982.
Vice-President, M. Hidayatullah.

CABINET

Prime Minister, Mrs. Indira Gandhi.
Finance, Pranab Mukherjee.
External Affairs, (vacant).
Defence, S. B. Chavan.
Home, P. V. Narasimha Rao.
Planning and Immigration, P. C. Sethi.
Railways, A. B. A. Ghani Khan Chaudhury.
Energy and Petroleum, P. Shiv Shankar.
Chemicals and Fertilizers, Vasant Sathe.
Industry, Vijay Bhaskara Reddy.
Law, Justice and Company Affairs, Jagannath Kaushal.
Labour and Rehabilitation, Transport and Shipping, Veerendra Patil.
Health and Family Welfare, B. Shankaranand.
Agriculture, Rao Birendra Singh.
Commerce, V. P. Singh.
Parliamentary Affairs and Sports, Works and Housing, Buta Singh.

INDIAN HIGH COMMISSION
India House, Aldwych, WC2B 4NA
[01–836 8484]

High Commissioner, Dr. V. A. Seyid Muhammad.
Deputy High Commissioner, P. Johari.

BRITISH HIGH COMMISSION
Chanakyapuri, New Delhi, 21, 1100–21.

High Commissioner, His Excellency Sir Robert Wade-Gery, K.C.M.G., K.C.V.O. (1982).
British Council Representative in India, J. M. Ure, O.B.E., AIFACS Building, Rafi Marg, New Delhi 110 001. Offices also at *Bombay, Madras* and *Calcutta.* There are British Council libraries at these four centres and British libraries at *Ahmedabad, Bangalore, Bhopal, Hyderabad, Lucknow, Patna, Pune, Ranchi* and *Trivandrum.*

CONSTITUTION

The Constitution of India came into force in 1950. Executive power is vested in the President, who is elected for a five year term by an electoral college consisting of the elected members of the Union and State Legislatures. He appoints the Prime Minister and, on the latter's advice, the Ministers, and can dismiss them. The Council of Ministers is collectively responsible to the *Lok Sabha* (Lower House). The Vice President is *ex-officio* chairman of the *Rajya Sabha* (Upper House).

Legislative power rests with the President, the *Rajya Sabha* (which has up to 250 members) and the *Lok Sabha* (which has up to 542 members). Twelve members of the *Rajya Sabha* are nominated by the President, the rest are indirectly elected representatives of the State and Union Territories. They hold office for six years. The 525 members of the *Lok Sabha* representing the States are directly elected by universal adult franchise, and 17 representatives of the Union Territories are chosen, for a maximum term of six years. Subject to the provisons of the Constitution, the Union Parliament can make laws for the whole of India and the State legislatures for their respective units.

The Supreme Court consists of the Chief Justice and not more than 13 other judges, appointed by the President. It is the highest court in respect of all constitutional matters and the final Court of Appeal.

STATES AND TERRITORIES OF THE UNION

Each State is governed by a Governor appointed by the President who holds office for five years, and a Council of Ministers. All States have a Legislative Assembly, and some have also a Legislative Council, elected directly by adult suffrage for a maximum period of five years. The judges of the High Court of a State are appointed by the President.

The Union Territories are administered, except where otherwise provided by Parliament, by the President acting through an Administrator or other authority appointed by him.

The 22 States (State capitals in brackets) are: Andhra Pradesh (Hyderabad), Assam (Dispur), Bihar (Patna), Gujarat (Gandhinagar), Haryana (Chandigarh), Himachal Pradesh (Simla), Jammu and Kashmir (an area disputed between India, China and Pakistan; capital, Srinagar in summer, Jammu in winter), Karnataka (Bangalore), Kerala (Trivandrum), Madhya Pradesh (Bhopal), Maharashtra (Bombay City), Manipur (Imphal), Meghalaya (Shillong), Nagaland (Kohima), Orissa (Bhubaneswar), Punjab (Chandigarh), Rajasthan (Jaipur), Sikkim

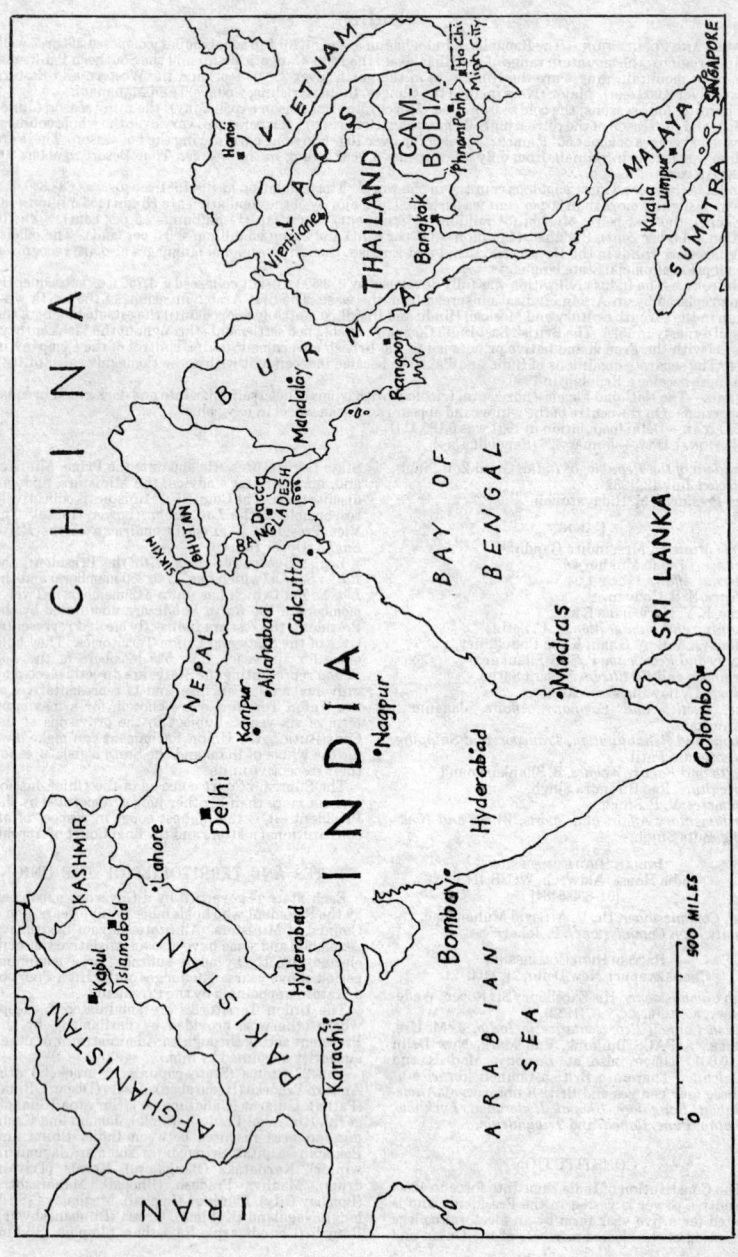

(Gangtok), Tamil Nadu (Madras), Tripura (Agartala), Uttar Pradesh (Lucknow), West Bengal (Calcutta).

The nine Union Territories are: Andaman and Nicobar Islands; Arunachal Pradesh; Chandigarh; Dadra and Nagar Haveli; Delhi; Goa, Daman and Diu; Lakshadweep (formerly the Laccadive, Minicoy and Amindivi Islands); Mizoram; and Pondicherry.

DEFENCE

The supreme command of the armed forces is vested in the President. Administrative and operational control resides in the Army, Navy and Air Headquarters under the supervision of the Ministry of Defence.

The *Army* has five Commands, Southern, Eastern, Northern, Western and Central.

The *Indian Navy* consists of an aircraft-carrier, two cruisers, a number of frigate squadrons, including some of the latest type of anti-submarine and anti-aircraft frigates, a squadron of anti-submarine patrol vessels, a minesweeping squadron, conventional type submarines, a submarine depot ship and fast boats carrying surface-to-surface guided missiles. A Naval aviation wing and a hydrographic office have also been set up. India has started building her own naval craft.

The *Indian Air Force* is organized in five major formations, the Western, Eastern and Central Air Commands, and the Training and Maintenance Commands and an independent Operational Group. Aircraft in use include SU-7, Hunter, Gnat, Mig 21 and HF24; Canberra bomber, helicopter and training planes.

PRODUCTION
Agriculture

Agriculture is the chief industry, supporting about 70 per cent of the population, and in 1981 providing nearly 40 per cent of the Gross Domestic Product. The area under cultivation has been increased by irrigation schemes, but most holdings are less than five acres. Production has grown by three per cent each year since 1951, remaining slightly ahead of the two per cent increase necessary to keep pace with the rising population. Food grains occupy three-quarters of the total cropped area and production of these amounted to 127 million tonnes in 1982–83. The main crops are rice, cereals (principally wheat), pulses, sugar cane, jute, cotton and tea. Other products include oil seeds, spices, groundnuts, tobacco, rubber and coffee. Livestock is raised, principally for dairy purposes or for the hides: cattle (181 million), goats (71 million), sheep (41 million) and pigs (9·9 million).

Industry

India's major industries are based on the exploitation and processing of her mineral resources, principally coal, oil and iron. The coal industry, nationalized in 1973, reached an output in 1981–82 of 130·8 million tonnes. Production of crude oil, from the main fields in Assam and offshore in the Gulf of Cambay (the Bombay High field) was about 16·2 million tonnes in 1981–82. Steel production is mainly in the hands of the public sector, with five public and one private sector integrated steel plants producing 10·4 million tonnes of ingot steel in 1981–82: the engineering industry, heavy and light, is also primarily in the hands of the public sector. The manufacture of chemicals, fertilizers, petrochemicals, automobiles and commercial vehicles has been expanded.

Other principal manufactures are those derived from agricultural products, textiles, jute goods, sugar, leather, which along with tea, fish and iron ore and concentrates, are India's major exports.

FINANCE

The budget estimates for 1983–84, placed expenditure (on revenue account) at *Rs.*224,190 million. Revenue (excluding States' shares) was estimated at *Rs.*200,100 million.

Trade with U.K.

	1982	1983
Imports from U.K.	£805,321,000	£804,779,000
Exports to U.K.	379,169,000	366,928,000

COMMUNICATIONS

Civil Aviation.—Four international airports—Palam (Delhi), Santa Cruz (Bombay), Dum Dum (Calcutta), Meenambakkam (Madras)—are managed by the International Airports Authority. The other 84 aerodromes are controlled and operated by the Civil Aviation Department of the Government. The national airlines are Indian Airlines (internal) and Air India (international).

Railways.—The railways are grouped into nine administrative zones, Southern, Central, Western, Northern, North-Eastern, North-East Frontier, Eastern, South-Eastern and South-Central.

Gross Traffic Receipts (1983–84), crores of rupees, 5,146. Working expenses, 4,521. Net railway revenues, 671.

Ψ *Ports.*—The chief seaports are Bombay (Mumbai), Calcutta, Madras, Mormugao, Cochin, Visakhapatnam, Kandla, Paradip, Mangalore and Tuticorin. There are 167 intermediate and minor ports with varying capacity.

Shipping.—On Dec. 31, 1981, 403 ships totalling 58·89 lakh gross tons were on the Indian Register.

Jamaica

Jamaica is situated in the Caribbean Sea south of the eastern extremity of Cuba and lies between latitudes 17° 43′ and 18° 32′ North, and longitude 76° 11′ and 78° 21′ West. The island was discovered by Columbus on May 4, 1494, and occupied by the Spanish from 1509 until 1655 when a British expedition, sent out by Oliver Cromwell, under Admiral Penn and General Venables, attacked the island, which capitulated after a token resistance. In 1670 it was formally ceded to England by the Treaty of Madrid. Jamaica became an independent state within the British Commonwealth on August 6, 1962.

AREA AND POPULATION.—Jamaica is 4,243·6 square miles in area and is divided into three counties (Surrey, Middlesex and Cornwall) and 14 parishes. The surface of the island is extremely mountainous, the highest peak being 7,402 ft. above sea level. The greatest length from east to west (Morant Point to Negril Point) is 146 miles and the extreme breadth 51 miles. At Dec. 31, 1982 Jamaica's population was estimated to be 2,265,400. Jamaica for climatic and other reasons is a popular tourist resort, attracting visitors mainly from the U.S.A. The total number of visitor arrivals in 1982 was 670,202. Tourist expenditure in 1982 was estimated at US$284,300,000.

PHYSICAL FEATURES.—The topography consists mainly of coastal plains, divided by the Blue Mountain Range in the east, and the hills and limestone plateaux which occupy the central and western areas of the interior. The central chain of high peaks of the Blue Mountains is over 6,000 feet above sea level, and the Blue Mountain Peak, the highest of these, reaches an elevation of 7,402 feet. The rivers flow down from the central mountainous area. Most of the rivers are narrow and fast flowing, and some have rapids. In general those flowing south are longer and are fed by more tributaries than those flowing north. None is navigable except the Black River, and that only for small craft.

CAPITAL.—The seat of government is Kingston, the largest town and seaport (estimated population of the Corporate area of Kingston and St. Andrew in 1979, 662,501). Other towns are Montego Bay, Spanish Town, Mandeville and May Pen.

FLAG.—Gold diagonal cross forming triangles of green at top and bottom, triangles of black at hoist and in fly.

NATIONAL DAY.—First Monday in August (Independence Day).

GOVERNMENT

The Legislature consists of a Senate of 21 nominated members and a House of Representatives consisting of 60 members elected by universal adult suffrage. The Senate has no power to delay money bills for longer than one month or other bills for longer than seven months against the wishes of the House of Representatives. The Constitution provides for a Leader of the Opposition.

At the General Election of Dec. 15, 1983, the Jamaica Labour Party won all 60 seats after the People's National Party decided not to contest the election.

Governor-General, His Excellency Sir Florizel Glasspole, G.C.M.G., G.C.V.O.

CABINET

Prime Minister, Minister of Finance and Planning, and of Information and Culture, Rt. Hon. E. Seaga, P.C., M.P.
Deputy Prime Minister, Minister of Foreign Affairs and Foreign Trade, Rt. Hon. H. Shearer.
Construction, Hon. B. Golding.
Agriculture, Hon. Dr. P. Broderick.
National Security and Justice, and Attorney General, Hon. W. Spaulding.
Local Government, Hon. N. B. Lewis.
Labour and the Public Service, Hon. J. A. G. Smith.
Public Utilities and Transport, Hon. P. Charles.
Education, Hon. Dr. Mavis Gilmour.
Industry and Commerce, Hon. D. Vaz.
Public Service and Social Security, Hon. E. M. Anderson.
Youth and Community Development, Hon. E. C. Barlett.
Tourism, Hon. A. Abrahams.*
Health, Hon. Dr. K. Baugh.
Environment, Science and Technology, Hon. Dr. R. A. Irvine.*
*Resigned Aug. 1984.

JAMAICAN HIGH COMMISSION
50 St. James's Street, SW1A 1JS
[01–499 8600]

High Commissioner, His Excellency H. S. Walker.

BRITISH HIGH COMMISSION
P.O. Box 575, Trafalgar Road, Kingston 10.

High Commissioner, His Excellency Harold Martin Smith Reid, C.M.G. (1984).

JUDICATURE

Chief Justice and Keeper of Records, Hon. K. G. Smith.
Judges of the Court of Appeal, Hon. L. H. U. Robinson (*President*); Hons. H. D. Carberry; K. C. Henry; E. Zacca; J. S. Kerr; I. D. Rowe.

COMMUNICATIONS

There are several excellent harbours, Kingston being the principal port. The island has 2,944 miles of main roads and over 7,000 miles of subsidiary roads. There are about 204 miles of railway open. Telegraph stations and post offices are established in every town and in very many villages.

There are two international airports capable of handling the largest civil jet aircraft, the Norman Manley International Airport on the south coast serving Kingston, and Sangster Airport on the north coast serving the major tourist areas. In addition there are licensed aerodromes at Port Antonio, Ocho Rios, Mandeville and Negril. There are 16 privately owned, seven public and two military airstrips.

Air Jamaica, the national airline, operates international services; Trans-Jamaica Airlines operates scheduled internal services.

PRODUCTION

Agriculture.—Most of the staple products of tropical climates are grown; sugar, bananas, pimento, coffee and citrus fruit. Some of the sugar is used to produce rum and molasses. Chief products exported in 1982 were sugar (J$85 million), bananas (J$13 million), citrus fruit and citrus products (J$12 million).

Industry.—Jamaica is the fourth largest producer of bauxite in the world; output for 1982 was 8,300,000 tonnes of which 1,700,000 tonnes were processed into alumina before being exported. The bauxite deposits are worked, and processed into alumina, by one Canadian and four U.S. companies in partnership with the Government. In 1982 exports of bauxite and alumina were valued at J$862 million. Cement is manufactured locally, the output being 208,000 long tons in 1982. The ESSO Oil Refinery processed 6,103,230 barrels of crude oil during 1982.

The Jamaica Industrial Development Corporation is responsible for implementing the Government's industrial development programme. This Corporation administers incentive legislation which was enacted to stimulate the establishment of industries locally. In addition to undertaking promotional activities both locally and abroad, the Corporation maintains offices in the U.S. and the U.K. In the last decade, manufacturing has grown from the processing of a few agricultural products into the production of a whole range of commodities dependent on both local and foreign raw materials.

FINANCE

	1983–84*
Revenue	J$3,226,824,846
Expenditure	3,254,716,213

*Estimates
Public Debt (March 1983) J$5,825,433,020

TRADE		Trade with U.K.	
1981	1982	1982	1983
Total imports .... J$2,098,708,715	J$2,460,308,780	Imports from U.K...... £56,025,000	£116,188,000
Total exports 1,679,023,456	1,328,107,986	Exports to U.K. 92,760,000	94,036,000

Kenya

Kenya is bisected by the equator and extends approximately from latitude 4° N. to latitude 4° S. and from longitude 34° E. to 41° E. From the coast of the Indian Ocean in the east, the borders of Kenya are with Somalia in the east and Ethiopia and Sudan in the north and north-west. To the west lie Uganda and Lake Victoria. On the south is Tanzania. The total area is 224,960 square miles (including 5,171 square miles of water). The country is divided into 7 Provinces (Nyanza, Rift Valley, Central Coast, Western, Eastern and North-Eastern). The population is estimated to be about 17 million, and increasing by 3·8 per cent annually. The main tribal groups are the Kikuyu, Luhya, Luo, Kamba, Kalenjin and Masai. The official languages are Swahili, which is generally understood throughout Kenya, and English: numerous indigenous languages are also spoken.

CAPITAL.—Nairobi, population about 1,000,000.

Nairobi: transit from London about 25 days by sea; by air, 10 hrs.

FLAG.—Three equal horizontal bands of black over red over green; red and white spears and shield device in centre.

NATIONAL DAY.—December 12.

GOVERNMENT

Kenya became an independent state and a member of the British Commonwealth on December 12, 1963, after six months of internal self-government. The national assembly consists of a single House of Representatives. Kenya became a Republic on Dec. 12, 1964. In 1982 the Government introduced amendments to the constitution and election law, making the country a one-party (K.A.N.U.) state.

President, Daniel T. arap Moi, *took office,* Oct. 14, 1978.
Vice-President and Minister of Home Affairs, Hon. Mwai Kibaki.
Finance and Planning, Hon. Prof. George Saitoti.
Water Development, Hon. Jeremiah Nyageh.
Cooperative Development, Hon. Dr. A. Mukasa Mango.
Agriculture and Livestock Development, Hon. Odongo Omamo.
Local Government, Hon. Moses Mudavadi.
Information and Broadcasting, Hon. Robert Matano.
Foreign Affairs, Hon. Elijah W. Mwangale.
Lands and Settlement, Hon. Paul J. Ngei.
Energy and Regional Development, Hon. Kiprono N. K. Biwott.
Works, Housing and Physical Planning, Hon. Arthur K. Magugu.
Commerce and Industry, Hon. Andrew J. O. Manga.
Culture and Social Services, Hon. Kenneth Matiba.
Tourism and Wildlife, Hon. Maina Wanjigi.
Transport and Communications, Hon. Henry K. Kosgey.
Environment and Natural Resources, Hon. Eliud Mwamunga.
Labour, Hon. Dr. Robert J. Ouko.
Health, Hon. Gilbert K. M'mbijjewe.
Ministers of State, Hon. Justus ole Tipis; Hon. Peter Nyakiamo; Hon. Hussein M. Mohammed.
Attorney-General, Hon. Matthew G. Muli.

KENYA HIGH COMMISSION IN LONDON
45 Portland Place, W1N 4AS
[01–636 2371]

High Commissioner, His Excellency Benjamin K. Kipkulei (1984).

BRITISH HIGH COMMISSION
Bruce House, Standard Street, P.O. Box 30465
Nairobi

High Commissioner, His Excellency Sir Leonard Allinson, K.C.V.O., C.M.G. (1982).

British Council Representative, D. Aspinell, O.B.E., (P.O. Box 40751) ICEA Building, Kenyatta Avenue, Nairobi. There are offices at *Kisumu* and *Mombasa.*

PRODUCTION

Agriculture provides about 52 per cent of total export earnings (excluding processed oil products). The great variation in altitude and ecology provide conditions under which a wide range of crops can be grown. These include wheat, barley, pyrethrum, coffee, tea, sisal, coconuts, cashew nuts, cotton, maize and a wide variety of tropical and temperate fruits and vegetables. The total area of well-farmed land on which concentrated mixed farming can be practised is small and the remainder is arid or semi-arid country but population pressure and the need to increase agricultural production for export has led to attempts to develop such areas.

Prospecting and mining are carried on in some parts of the country, the principal minerals produced being soda ash, salt and limestone.

Hydro-electric power has been developed, particularly on the Upper Tana River. Kenya is now almost self-sufficient in electric power generation but the connection with Owen Falls in Uganda is still in being.

There has been considerable industrial development over the last 15 years and Kenya has a wide variety of industries processing agricultural produce and manufacturing an increasing range of products from local and imported raw materials. New industries have recently come into being such as steel, textile mills, dehydrated vegetable processing and motor tyre manufacture as well as many smaller schemes which have added to the country's already considerable consumer goods. There is an oil refinery in Mombasa supplying both Kenya and Uganda, and a fuel pipeline now connects Mombasa and Nairobi. Industrial areas have been developed in all the principal towns and light industrial estates are being developed for African entrepreneurs. The Kenya Government is actively encouraging investment in the industrial sector and has a Foreign Investments Protection Act to protect such investments.

COMMUNICATIONS

The Kenya Railways Corporation has 1,300 miles of railway open to traffic. There are also 31,000 miles of road, of which 2,700 are bitumen surfaced.

The principal port is Mombasa, operated by the Kenya Ports Authority.

International air services operate from airports at Nairobi and Mombasa.

TRADE

Principal exports are coffee and tea, which account for 33 per cent of total export earnings. Also exported are fruit, vegetables, and crude animal and vegetable material. Petroleum products account for about 37 per cent of imports; other imports are manufactured goods, particularly machinery, transport equipment, metals, pharmaceuticals and chemicals.

Trade with U.K.

	1982	1983
Imports from U.K.	£153,858,000	£111,249,000
Exports to U.K.	104,312,000	128,464,000

Kiribati

Kiribati, the former Gilbert Islands, became an independent Republic in 1979. Kiribati comprises 33 islands—the Gilberts Group (17) including Banaba, formerly Ocean Island, the Phoenix Islands (8) and the Line Islands (8)—situated in the South West Central Pacific around the point at which the International Date Line cuts the Equator. The total land area of 264 square miles is spread over some 2 million square miles of ocean. Few of the atolls are more than half a mile in width or more than 12 feet high. The vegetation consists mainly of coconut palms, breadfruit trees and pandanus. The population (1982 estimate) is about 60,000. Tarawa is the capital with an est. population of 20,000. The Phoenix and Line Islands now have no indigenous populations. Christianity is widespread, 44 per cent of the population being Protestant and 50 per cent Roman Catholic.

GOVERNMENT

The President is Head of State as well as Head of Government and is elected nationally. There is an elected House of Assembly (36 members); executive authority is vested in the Cabinet.

President and Minister of Foreign Affairs, Hon. Ieremia Tabai, G.C.M.G..
Vice-President and Minister of Home Affairs and Decentralization, Hon. T. Teannaki.
Finance, Hon. Boanereke Boanereke.
The Line and Phoenix Groups, Hon. Uera Rabaua.
Trade, Industry and Labour, Hon. Teewe Arobati.
Health and Family Planning, Hon. Binata Tetaeka.
Natural Resource Development, Hon. Babera Kirata, O.B.E.
Education, Hon. Baitika Toum.
Communications, Hon. Taomati Iuta.
Works and Energy, Hon. Tiwau Awira.
Chief Justice, Hon. J. R. Jones, C.B.E.
Attorney-General, Hon. Michael N. Takabwebwe.

ECONOMY

Most people still practise a semi-subsistence economy, the main staples of their diet being coconuts and fish, supplemented by some imported staples.

The unit of currency is the Australian dollar. Estimated recurrent revenue for 1983 is $A13,973,448, of which $A2,750,000 is provided by the United Kingdom as budgetary assistance under the Independence Financial Settlement. This assistance is necessary following the expiry of the phosphate industry, which previously accounted for approximately 50 per cent. of recurrent revenue. The principal imports are foodstuffs, consumer goods and building materials. The principal exports are copra, most of which is produced by small landowners and which earned $A1,454,000 in 1982; phosphate, valued at $A17,952,995; and fish, income from which was $A641,000 in 1982. Estimated value of total exports in 1982 was $A2,400,000.

COMMUNICATIONS

Air communication exists between most of the islands, and is operated by Air Tungaru, a statutory corporation. Air Tungaru operates a fortnightly service between Tarawa and Tuvalu, and Air Nauru flies weekly between Tarawa and Nauru. Inter-island shipping is operated by a statutory corporation, the Shipping Corporation of Kiribati.

SOCIAL WELFARE

The Government maintains a teacher training college and a secondary school. Four junior secondary schools are maintained by missions. Throughout the Republic there are about a hundred primary schools. The total enrolment of children of school age is about 14,000. The Marine Training School at Tarawa trains seamen for service with overseas shipping lines. There is a general hospital at Tarawa. The other inhabited islands have dispensaries.

BRITISH HIGH COMMISSION
P.O. Box 61, Bairiki Tarawa
High Commissioner, His Excellency Charles Thompson (1983).

Lesotho

Lesotho is a landlocked mountainous state entirely surrounded by the Republic of South Africa. Of the total area of 11,716 sq. miles a belt between 20 and 40 miles in width lying across the western and southern boundaries and comprising about one-third of the total is classed as Lowlands, being between 5,000 and 6,000 ft. above sea level. The remaining two-thirds are classed as Foothills and Highlands, rising to 11,425 ft. The land is held in trust for the nation by the state. The population was estimated at 1,204,000 in 1981.

CAPITAL.—Maseru, population, 240,081.

FLAG.—Blue with conical white Basotho hat in centre, red and green vertical stripes (next staff).

GOVERNMENT

Lesotho became a constitutional monarchy within the Commonwealth on October 4, 1966. The independence constitution was suspended in January 1970, when the country was governed by a Council of Ministers, until the establishment of a nominated National Assembly in April 1974.

The country is divided into ten administrative districts. In each district there is a District Coordinator who co-ordinates all Government activity in the area, working in co-operation with hereditary chiefs.

Head of State, His Majesty King Moshoeshoe II.

COUNCIL OF MINISTERS

Prime Minister and Minister of Defence and Internal Security, Rt. Hon. Dr. Leabua Jonathan.
Interior, Hon. N. S. 'Maseribane.
Foreign Affairs, Hon. E. R. Sekhonyana.
Finance, Hon. K. T. J. Rakhetla.
Water, Energy and Mining, Hon. P. M. Majara.
Commerce and Industry, Hon. M. Molapo.
Works, Hon. L. Joanathan.
Transport and Communications, Hon. Dr. K. T. Maphathe.
Health and Social Welfare, Hon. P. L. Lehleonya.
Education, Sport, Culture and Youth, Hon. B. A. Tlelase.
Rural Development, Hon. V. M. Makhele.
Agriculture, Hon. P. N. Peete.
Law and Justice, Hon. N. Nkuatsana.
Information and Broadcasting, Hon. D. Sixishe.
Ministers of State, Hon. P. J. Khasoane, Hon. I. J. Mokone.

JUDICIARY

The Lesotho Courts of Law consist of: the Court of Appeal, the High Court, Magistrates' Courts, Judicial Commissioners' Court, Central and local Courts. Magistrates' and higher courts administer the laws of Lesotho which are framed on the basis of the Roman–Dutch law. They also adjudicate appeals from the Judicial Commissioner's and Subordinate Courts.

Chief Justice, Hon. T. S. Cotran, C.B.E.

LESOTHO HIGH COMMISSION
10 Collingham Road, SW5 0NR
[01–373 8581]

High Commissioner, His Excellency O. T. Sefako (1983).

BRITISH HIGH COMMISSION
P.O. Box 521, Maseru

High Commissioner, His Excellency Peter Edward Rosling, M.V.O. (1984).
British Council Representative, B. P. Chenery, Hobson's Square, P.O. Box 429, Maseru.

EDUCATION

Most schools are mission-controlled, the Government providing grants for salaries and buildings. There are over 1,000 primary and over 100 secondary schools; few areas lack a school and there is a high literacy rate of about 70 per cent. Increasing emphasis is being laid on agricultural and vocational education. The National University of Lesotho at Roma was established in 1975.

COMMUNICATIONS

A tarred road of 110 miles links Maseru to several of the main lowland towns, and this is being extended in the south of the country. The mountainous areas are linked by a 1,300 miles of gravelled and earth roads and tracks. Roads link border towns in South Africa with the main towns in Lesotho. Maseru is connected by rail with the main Bloemfontein–Natal line of the South African Railways. Scheduled international air services are operated daily between Maseru and Johannesburg and other scheduled international flights are to Gaborone, Manzini and Maputo. There are 30 airstrips. Internal scheduled services are operated by the Lesotho Airways Corporation.

The telephone network is fully automated in all urban centres. Radio telephone communication is used extensively in the remote rural areas.

PRODUCTION

The economy of Lesotho is based on agriculture and animal husbandry, and the adverse balance of trade (mainly consumer goods) is offset by the earnings of the large numbers of the population who work in South Africa. Apart from some diamonds, Lesotho has few natural resources and little industrial development. The Lesotho National Development Corporation was set up to promote the development of industry, mining, trade and tourism. Using Lesotho's potential as a source of water is presently under consideration, and the commercial development of diamonds is intended. Drilling is being carried out for oil. Tourism is being developed and is rapidly playing a major role in the economic progress of the country: a National Park has been established at Sehlabathebe in the Maluti mountains. A number of light manufacturing and processing industries have recently been established.

FINANCE AND TRADE

The main sources of revenue are customs and excise duty. Estimates of expenditure and revenue (1982) are recurrent revenue M127,000,000; recurrent expenditure M107,900,000; capital revenue M77,000,000; capital expenditure M104,000,000.

On Jan. 19, 1980 the *Maloti* was introduced as Lesotho's currency, on the basis of parity with the S. Africa *rand*.

Trade with U.K.

	1982	1983
Imports from U.K......	£1,260,000	£2,080,000
Exports to U.K.	682,000	216,000

Malawi

MALAWI, formerly the Nyasaland Protectorate, comprises Lake Malawi (formerly Lake Nyasa) and its western shore, with the high table-land separating it from the basin of the Luangwa River, the watershed forming the western frontier with Zambia; south of the lake, Malawi reaches almost to the Zambesi and is surrounded by Mozambique, the frontier lying on the west on the watershed of the Zambesi and Shire Rivers, and to the east on the Ruo, a tributary of the Shire, and Lakes Chiuta and Chirwa. This boundary reaches the eastern shore of Lake Malawi and extends up to the mid-point of the lake for about half its length where it returns to the eastern and northern shores to form a frontier with Tanzania.

Malawi has a total area of 45,747 sq. miles. The population of Malawi according to the Census held in September 1977 is 5,547,460.

CAPITAL.—Lilongwe (population, 102,924). The city of Blantyre in the Southern Region, incorporating Blantyre and Limbe (population, 222,153), is the major commercial and industrial centre. Other main centres are: Mzuzu, Thyolo, Mulanje, Mangochi, Salima, Dedza and Zomba, the former capital.

FLAG.—Horizontal stripes of black, red and green, with rising sun in the centre of the black stripe.

GOVERNMENT

Malawi became a republic on July 6, 1966, having assumed internal self-government on February 1, 1963, and achieved independence on July 6, 1964, and is a member of the Commonwealth. There is a Cabinet consisting of the life President and other Ministers. The Parliament consists of 101 members, each elected by universal suffrage. Under the 1981 Amendment to the Constitution, the life President has the power to nominate as many Members of Parliament as he wishes. Being a one-party State (the Malawi Congress Party), all elected members are required to be members of the Party. The Parliament, which usually meets twice a year, is presided over by a Speaker.

President, Minister of External Affairs, Works and Supplies, Agriculture and Justice, Dr. H. Kamuzu Banda, *elected* 1966, *sworn in as* President for Life, July 6, 1971.

CABINET

Minister Without Portfolio, Hon. Robson W. Chirwa.
Minister at Large, Hon. Sidney B. Somanje.
Finance, Hon. Edward C. I. Bwanali.
Labour, Hon. Wadson B. Deleza.
Local Government, Hon. B. L. R. Kapichira Banda.
Transport and Communications, Hon. S. Chimwemwe Hara.
Education and Culture, Hon. Louis Chimango.
Youth, Hon. Stanford Demba.
Forestry and Natural Resources, Hon. P. C. Mtenje.
Health, Hon. Dalton S. Katopola.
Trade, Industry and Tourism, Hon. E. C. Katola Phiri.
Community Services, Hon. G. A. Kandawire.

JUDICIARY

Chief Justice, J. J. Skinner.
Puisne Judge, N. S. Jere.

MALAWI HIGH COMMISSION
33 Grosvenor Street, W1X 0DE
[01-491 4172/7]

High Commissioner, His Excellency C. M. Mkona (1981).

BRITISH HIGH COMMISSION
Lingadzi House (P.O. Box 30042),
Lilongwe 3

High Commissioner, His Excellency Arthur Henry Brind, C.M.G. (1983).
Deputy High Commissioner, M. E. J. Gore.
British Council Representative, C. G. Housden, (P.O. Box 30222), Lilongwe. There is also a library at Blantyre.

EDUCATION

Primary education is the responsibility of local authorities in both urban and rural areas, although policy, curricula and inspection are the responsibility of the Ministry of Education and Culture. The Ministry is also responsible for secondary schools, technical education and primary teacher training. Religious bodies, with Government assistance, still play an important part in these fields. In 1981–82 there were 882,903 pupils enrolled in primary schools and 16,338 pupils in secondary schools. There were 13,120 primary school teachers and 932 secondary teachers. The University of Malawi was opened in 1965 and in 1980–81 there were 1,723 students in its three constituent colleges.

COMMUNICATIONS

A single-track railway runs from Mchinji on the Zambian border, through Lilongwe and Salima on Lake Malawi (itself served by two passenger and a number of cargo boats) through Blantyre to the southern frontier into Mozambique, crossing the Zambesi River by a bridge 12,050 feet long, and connecting with the Mozambique port of Beira, which handles the bulk of the country's imports and exports. In 1970 a 70-mile line was opened from Liwonde to Nayuchi, linking the Malawi rail system with the Mozambique network to the port of Nacala. There are about 11,000 miles of maintained roads in Malawi of which about 2,000 are bituminized.

FINANCE
(excluding Development Account)

	1981–82	1982–83
Revenue	K187m	K218m
Expenditure	207m	252m*

*less appropriations in aid.

The unit of currency is the *kwacha* (K1·80 = £1 sterling approx.).

TRADE

	1981	1982
Imports	K322m	K322m
Exports	246m	270m

Trade with U.K.

	1982	1983
Imports from U.K.	£20,893,000	£18,893,000
Exports to U.K.	42,478,000	42,060,000

Agriculture is the country's mainstay. In 1982 principal exports were tobacco (K146m), tea (K45m), sugar (K23m), groundnuts (K5m) and coffee (K2m). Other cash crops include coffee and tung oil. Main imports are fuels and fertilizer, transport and agricultural machinery and equipment.

Malaysia

Malaysia, comprising the 11 states of Peninsula Malaya plus Sabah and Sarawak, forms a crescent well over 1,000 miles long between latitudes 1° and 7° N. and longitudes 100° and 119° E. It occupies two distinct regions—the Malay Peninsula which extends from the Isthmus of Kra to the Singapore Strait and the North-West Coastal area of the Island of Borneo. Each is separated from the other by 400 miles of the South China Sea. The total area of Malaysia, including the Federal Territory of Kuala Lumpur (94 sq. miles), is estimated to be

130,000 sq. miles, containing a population of 13,435,588 (1980 census). The principal racial groups are the Malays, the Chinese and those of Indian and Sri Lankan origin, as well as the indigenous races of Sarawak and Sabah. Bahasa Malaysia (Malay) is the sole official language, but English, various dialects of Chinese, and Tamil are also widely spoken. There are a few indigenous languages widely spoken in Sabah and Sarawak.

RELIGION.—Islam is the official religion of Malaysia, each Ruler being the head of religion in his State, though the Heads of State of Sabah and Sarawak are not heads of the Muslim religion in their States. The Yang di-Pertuan Agung is the head of religion in Malacca and Penang. The Constitution guarantees religious freedom.

Climate.—The year is commonly divided into the Southwest and Northwest monsoon seasons. Rainfall averages about 100 inches throughout the year, though the annual fall varies from place to place. The average daily temperature throughout Malaysia varies from 70° F. to 90° F., though in higher areas temperatures are lower and vary widely.

CAPITAL.—Kuala Lumpur was proclaimed Federal Territory on February 1, 1974. Its population is (1980) 997,100.

NATIONAL DAY.—August 31 (*Hari Kebangsaan*).

FLAG.—Equal horizontal stripes of red (7) and white (7); 14 point yellow star and crescent in blue canton.

STATES OF THE FEDERATION

The 13 States of the Federation of Malaysia (State capitals in brackets) and their populations at the 1980 Census are:

Johore (Johore Bahru)	1,638,200
Kedah (Alor Setar)	1,116,100
Kelantan (Kota Baru)	893,800
ΨMelaka (Melaka)	464,800
Negri Sembilan (Seremban)	573,600
Pahang (Kuantan)	798,800
ΨPenang (Georgetown)	954,600
Perak (Ipoh)	1,805,200
Perlis (Kangar)	148,300
ΨSabah (Kota Kinabalu)	1,011,000
ΨSarawak (Kuching)	1,307,600
Selangor (Shah Alam)	1,515,500
Trengganu (Kuala Trengganu)	540,600
ΨSeaport	

GOVERNMENT

The Federation of Malaya became an independent country within the Commonwealth on August 31, 1957, as a result of an agreement between H.M. the Queen and the Rulers of the Malay States, whereby Her Majesty relinquished all powers and jurisdiction over the Malay States and over the Settlements of Penang and Malacca which then became States of the Federation. On Sept. 16, 1963, the Federation was enlarged by the accession of the states of Singapore, Sabah (*formerly* British North Borneo) and Sarawak, and the name of MALAYSIA was adopted from that date. On Aug. 9, 1965, Singapore seceded from the Federation.

The Constitution was designed to ensure the existence of a strong Federal Government and also a measure of autonomy for the State Governments. It provides for a constitutional Supreme Head of the Federation (His Majesty the *Yang di-Pertuan Agung*) to be elected for a term of five years by the Rulers from among their number, and for a Deputy Supreme Head (His Royal Highness the *Timbalan Yang di-Pertuan Agung*) to be similarly elected. The Malay Rulers are either chosen or succeed to their position in accordance with the custom of the particular state. In other states of Malaysia choice of the Head of State is in the discretion of the *Yang di-Pertuan Agung* after consultation with the Chief Minister of the State. Save in certain instances provided in the Constitution, the Supreme Head acts in accordance with the advice of a Cabinet appointed by him from among the members of Parliament on the advice of the Prime Minister. The Supreme Head appoints as Prime Minister the person who in his judgment is likely to command the confidence of the majority of the members of the House of Representatives. He also has the powers to promulgate emergency ordinances.

Supreme Head of State, His Majesty Sultan Mahmood Iskandar Al-Haj ibni Al-Marhun Sultan Ismail (Sultan of Johore), *assumed office for a term of 5 years*, April 1984.

Deputy Supreme Head of State, His Royal Highness Raja Tun Azlan Shah (Sultan of Perak).

MINISTRY

Prime Minister and Minister of Defence, Datuk Seri Dr. Mahathir bin Mohamed.

Deputy Prime Minister and Minister of Home Affairs, Dato Musa bin Hitam.

Justice, Datuk James Ongkili.

Minister without Portfolio, Datuk Khalil Yaacob.

Transport, Tan Sri Chong Hon Nyan.

Science, Technology and Environment, Datuk Stephen Yong.

Foreign Affairs, Tunku Ahmad Rithaudeen.

Welfare Services, Datuk Abu Hassan Omar.

Trade and Industry, Tunku Razaleigh Hamzah.

Finance, Daim Zaimuddin.

Health, Datuk Chin Hon Ngiam.

Land and Regional Development, Datuk Adib Adam.

Information, Datuk Rais Yatim.

Labour and Manpower, Datuk Mak Hon Kam.

Primary Industries, Dato Paul Leong Khee Seong.

Agriculture, Annuar Ibrahim.

Energy, Telecommunications and Posts, Datuk Leo Moggie Anak Irok.

Housing and Local Government, Dato Dr. Neo Yee Pan.

Works and Utilities, Dato S. Samy Vellu.

Culture, Youth and Sport, Datuk Sulaiman Daud.

Public Enterprises, Datin Paduka Rafidah Aziz.

Education, Dr. Sulaiman bin Haji Daud.

Federal Territory, Dato Shahrir bin Abdul Samad.

National and Rural Development, Datuk Sanusi bin Junid.

NOTE.—The words "Tunku/Tengku", "Tun", "Tan Sri", and "Datuk" are titles. The word "Tunku/Tengku" is equivalent to "Prince". "Tun" denotes membership of a high Order of Malaysian Chivalry and "Tan Sri" and "Datuk" ("Datuk Seri" in Perak and "Datu" in Sabah) are each the equivalent of a knighthood. The wife of a "Tun" is styled "Toh Puan", that of a "Tan Sri" is styled "Puan Sri" and of a "Datuk" "Datin". The honorific "Tuan" or "Encik" is equivalent to "Mr." and the honorific "Puan" is equivalent to "Mrs.". The words "Al-Haj" or "Haji" indicate that the person so named has made the pilgrimage to Mecca.

MALAYSIAN HIGH COMMISSION
45 Belgrave Square, SW1X 8QT
[01–235 8033]

High Commissioner, His Excellency M. H. Kassim (1983).

BRITISH HIGH COMMISSION
Wisma Damansara, Jalan Semantan
(P.O. Box 11030), Kuala Lumpur 23–03

High Commissioner, David Howe Gillmore, C.M.G.
(1983).

British Council Representative, E. T. J. Phillips, Jalan
Bukit Aman, Kuala Lumpur 10–01; offices at *Kota
Kinabalu* (Sabah) and *Kuching* (Sarawak), and a
library in Penang.

LEGISLATURE

The Federal Parliament consists of two houses, the
Senate and the House of Representatives. The Senate
(*Dewan Negara*) consists of 58 members, under a
President (*Yang di-Pertua Dewan Negara*), 26 elected
by the Legislative Assemblies of the States (2 from
each) and 32 appointed by the *Yang di-Pertuan Agung*
from persons who have achieved distinction in major
fields of activity or are representative of racial
minorities, including the Aborigines (*Orang Asli*).
The House of Representatives (*Dewan Rakyat*),
consists of 154 members (Peninsular Malaysia, 114;
Sarawak, 24; and Sabah, 16). Members are elected on
the principle of universal adult suffrage with a
common electoral roll. The House of Representatives
is presided over by a Speaker who is either a member
of the House or is qualified to be elected as a member.

The Constitution provides that each State shall
have its own Constitution not inconsistent with the
Federal Constitution, with the Ruler or Governor
acting on the advice of an Executive Council
appointed on the advice of the *Menteri Besar* or Chief
Minister and a single chamber Legislative Assembly.
Three *ex officio* members sit in the Executive Council
besides these elected members. They are the State
Secretary, the State Legal Adviser and the State
Financial Officer. The State Constitutions provide
for the Ruler or Governor to appoint as *Menteri
Besar* or Chief Minister, to preside over the Executive
Council, a member of the Legislative Assembly who
in his judgement is likely to command the confidence
of the majority of the members of the Assembly. The
Legislative Assemblies are fully elected on the same
basis as the Federal Parliament.

Legislative powers are divided into a Federal List,
a State List and a Concurrent List, with residual
powers vested in the State Legislatures. The Federal
List comprises broadly, external affairs, defence, civil
and criminal law and justice, the machinery of
government, finance, commerce and industry, communications and transport, power, education, medicine and labour and social security. The State List
includes land, agriculture and forestry, local government and services and the machinery of state
government. In the Concurrent List are, *inter alia*,
social welfare, wild-life, animal husbandry, town and
country planning, public health and drainage and
irrigation.

JUDICATURE

The Judicial System consists of a Federal Court
and two High Courts, one in Peninsular Malaysia
and one for Sabah and Sarawak (sitting alternately
in Kota Kinabalu and Kuching). The High Court in
Peninsular Malaysia known as the High Court in
Malaya has its principal registry in Kuala Lumpur
while the High Court in Sabah/Sarawak known as
the High Court in Borneo has its principal registry
in Kuching.

The Federal Court comprises a President, the two
Chief Justices of the High Courts and other judges.
It possesses appellate, original and advisory jurisdic-
tion.

Each of the High Courts consists of a Chief Justice
and not less than 4 other judges. The Federal
Constitution allows for a maximum of twelve such
judges for Malaya and eight for Borneo. In Peninsular Malaysia the Subordinate Courts consist of the
Sessions Courts and the Magistrates' Courts. In
Sabah/Sarawak the Magistrates' Courts constitute
the Subordinate Courts.

DEFENCE

The Malaysian Armed Forces consist of the Army,
Navy and Air Force, together with volunteer forces
for each arm. The defence of the country is largely
borne by the army in its role of providing defence
against external threat and counter-insurgency operations and also to assist the police in the performance of public order duties. The *Royal Malaysian
Navy (RMN)* has the responsibility of defending the
3,000 miles of the country's coastline and maintaining
constant patrol of 500 miles of the high seas that
separate Sabah and Sarawak from the mainland. The
Royal Malaysian Air Force (RMAF) is capable of
providing close strategic and tactical support to the
army and police in the defence and internal security
of the country.

FINANCE

	M$million	
	1981	1982*
Revenue	15,806	16,434
Expenditure	27,044	26,619
*Latest estimate		

PRODUCTION AND TRADE

The agricultural sector continues to be the mainstay of the Malaysian economy. However, diversification of crops and rapid growth in the
manufacturing sector has made Malaysia less vulnerable to fluctuations in the price of its primary crop,
natural rubber.

Malaysia is the largest exporter of natural rubber,
tin, palm oil and tropical hardwoods. Other major
export commodities are manufactured and processed
products, petroleum, oil, and other minerals, palm
kernel oil, tea and pepper.

Exports of the four major primary commodities:
rubber, tin, palm oil and tropical hardwoods accounted for 45·2 per cent of the total exports in 1981.
Export of petroleum, crude and partly refined oil
accounted for 25.5 per cent of total exports. The
expansion of the manufacturing sector led to a rise
in exports of manufactured goods from 21.6 per cent
in 1980 to 23.2 per cent in 1981. Estimated figures for
1982 indicate that exports of the four major primary
commodities account for 41 per cent of total exports,
petroleum, crude and partly-refined oil for 27 per
cent, and manufactured goods for 25 per cent.

Another commodity which is produced throughout
Malaysia is rice, the staple food. To achieve self-
sufficiency, various measures aimed at increasing
output and productivity are being introduced. They
include wider use of improved seeds and fertilizers,
expansion of double-cropping through the provisions
of large scale irrigation schemes and research programmes to improve rice yields. The rapid increase
in oil production means that Malaysia is a net
exporter, and as her own oil is almost sulphur free,
she obtains a considerably higher price than she has
to pay for her imports.

Imports consist mainly of machinery and transport
equipment, manufactured goods, foods, mineral fuels,

chemicals and inedible crude materials for her growing population and to accelerate the pace of her economic growth and development.

Malaysia's main trading partners are the other member states of A.S.E.A.N., Japan, Singapore, U.S.A., E.E.C. countries, the U.K. and Australia.

	M$million	
	1981	1982
Imports	26,674·7	28,893·0
Exports	27,099·7	26,440·0
Balance of trade (visibles)	425·0	−2,453·0
*Estimated		

The Maldives

Area, etc.—The Maldives are a chain of coral atolls, some 400 miles to the south-west of Sri Lanka, stretching from just south of the equator for about 600 miles to the north. There are about 20 coral atolls comprising over 1,200 islands, 202 of which are inhabited. No point in the entire chain of islands is more than 8 feet above sea-level. The population of the islands (1982) is 160,200. The people are Sunni Moslems and the Maldivian language is akin to Elu or old Sinhalese.

CAPITAL.—Malé (population, 1982, 37,000). There is an international airport at Malé.

FLAG.—Green field bearing a white crescent, with wide red border.

GOVERNMENT

Until 1952 the islands were a Sultanate under the protection of the British Crown. Internal self-government was achieved in 1948 and full independence in 1965. In 1982 the Republic of the Maldives became a special member of the Commonwealth.

The Maldives form a Republic which is elective. There is a Parliament (the *Citizens' Majlis*) with representatives elected from all the atolls. The life of the Majlis is 5 years. The Government consists of a Cabinet, which is responsible to the Majlis.

President, His Excellency Maumoon Abdul Gayoom, *elected* 1978, *re-elected* Sept. 30, 1983 (also *Minister of Defence and National Security*).

CABINET

Justice, Hon. Abdulla Hameed (*acting*).
Home Affairs and Social Services, Hon. Umar Zahir.
Education, Hon. Mohamed Zahir Hussain.
Health, Hon. Abdulla Jameel.

Fisheries, Hon. Abdul Sataar Moosa Didi.
Agriculture, (vacant).
Transport and Shipping, Hon. Ahmed Mujathaba.
External Affairs, Hon. Fathulla Jameel.
Atolls Administration, Hon. Abdulla Hameed.
Trade and Industries, Hon. Ilyas Ibrahim.

BRITISH HIGH COMMISSION

High Commissioner, (*resident* at Colombo).

PRODUCTION

The vegetation of the islands is coconut palms with some scrub. Hardly any cultivation of crops is possible and nearly all food to supplement the basic fish diet has to be imported. The principal industry is fishing and considerable quantities of fish are exported to Japan. Dried fish is exported to Sri Lanka, where it is a delicacy. The tourist industry is expanding very rapidly. Maldives Shipping Ltd. has a fleet of some 30 merchant ships.

Malta

Malta lies in the Mediterranean Sea, 58 miles from Sicily and about 180 miles from the African coast, about 17 miles in length and 9 in breadth, and having an area of 94·9 square miles. Malta includes also the adjoining island of *Gozo* (area 25·9 sq. miles); *Comino* and minor islets. The estimated population at March 1981 was 341,000. Malta's climate, although not tropical, is hot in summer.

Malta was in turn held by the Phœnicians, Greeks, Carthaginians, Romans and Arabs. In 1090 it was conquered by Count Roger of Normandy. In 1530 it was handed over to the Knights of St. John, who made of it a stronghold of Christianity. In 1565 it sustained the famous siege, when the last great effort of the Turks was successfully withstood by Grandmaster La Valette. The Knights expended large sums in fortifying the island and carrying out many magnificent works, until they were expelled by Napoleon in 1798. The Maltese rose against the French garrison soon afterwards, and the island was subsequently blockaded by the British fleet. The Maltese people freely requested the protection of the British Crown in 1802 on condition that their rights and privileges would be preserved and respected. The islands were finally annexed to the British Crown by the Treaty of Paris in 1814.

Malta was again closely besieged in the last war. From June, 1940, to the end of the war, 432 members of the garrison and 1,540 civilians were killed by enemy aircraft, and about 35,000 houses were destroyed or damaged.

CAPITAL.—ΨValletta. Population (estimated 1981), 14,096. Valletta Grand Harbour is one of the finest in the world; it is very deep, and large vessels can anchor alongside the shore. It is an important port of call and ship repairing centre for vessels, being half-way between Gibraltar and Port Said.

FLAG.—Two equal vertical stripes, white at the hoists and red at the fly. A representation of the George Cross is carried edged in red in the top corner of the white stripe.

NATIONAL DAY—March 31.

President, Her Excellency Miss Agatha Barbara, *elected* 16 Feb. 1982.

GOVERNMENT

On Sept. 21, 1964, under the Malta Independence Order, 1964, Malta became an independent state within the Commonwealth; on December 13, 1974, Malta became a republic within the Commonwealth. In the 1981 general election the Malta Labour Party was returned to office. State of the parties; Malta Labour Party, 34 seats; Nationalist Party, 31 seats. The Nationalist Party received 51 per cent of the votes cast but failed to obtain a majority of seats and boycotted Parliament after the election, but eventually took their seats in March 1983.

Maltese and English are the official languages of administration and Maltese is ordinarily the official language in all the courts of law and the language of general use in the islands.

CABINET

Prime Minister and Minister of the Interior, Hon. Dom Mintoff.
Senior Deputy P.M. and Minister of Education, Hon. Karmenu Mifsud Bonnici.
Senior Deputy P.M. and Minister of Justice and Parliamentary Affairs, Hon. Joseph Cassar.
Deputy P.M. and Minister of Finance and Customs, Hon. Wistin Abela.
Works and Housing, Hon. Lorry Sant.
Labour and Social Services, Hon. F. Micallef.
Foreign Affairs, Hon. A. Sceberras Trigona.
Economic Planning and Trade, Hon. Lino Spiteri.
Industry, Hon. Karmenu Vella.
Tourism, Hon. Joseph Grima.
Parastatal and People's Investments, Hon. Philip Muscat.
Health, Hon. Vincent Moran.
Fisheries and Agriculture, Hon. J. Debono Grech.

MALTESE HIGH COMMISSION
16 Kensington Square, W.8
[01–938 1712]
High Commissioner, (vacant).

BRITISH HIGH COMMISSION
7 St. Anne Street, Floriana, Malta
High Commissioner, His Excellency Charles L. Booth, C.M.G., M.V.O.

EDUCATION

In June 1983 there were 83 Government Primary Schools with 24,403 pupils and 38 Secondary Schools and new Lyceums, with a total of 15,397 pupils.

The Government also runs 4 Technical Institutes and 18 Trade Schools (with an enrolment of 5,271 students). Schools of Art, Music, Secretarial Studies, Catering, Nursing and Dramatic Art sponsored by the Government. Evening courses in a number of academic, commercial, technical and practical subjects are run by both the Government and private institutions. Tertiary education is available at the University of Malta, which has 1,010 students.

A number of private schools offer more or less the same facilities that exist in Government schools. Private schools are fee-paying with the exception of one college for boys.

In religion, the Maltese are Roman Catholics. The Maltese language is of Semitic origin and held by some to be derived from the Carthaginian and Phoenician tongues.

AGRICULTURE

Agriculture plays a significant role in the economy. There are 4,332 full time farmers and about 11,026 part time farmers. The yearly crop production is about 99,727 tonnes consisting mainly of tomatoes, potatoes, onions, cabbages and cauliflowers, and some 2,922 tonnes of fruit. Grape is the largest fruit crop. Flowers and cuttings are produced for export markets.

INDUSTRY

The island's leading industry is the state-owned Malta Drydocks, employing about 5,000 people. The main port of Grand Harbour handled traffic (excluding mineral oils) of 1,696,584 tonnes in 1982.

At the end of 1983 manufacturing firms employed some 29,440 people. The wide range of produce includes food processing, textiles and clothing, plastics and chemical products, electronic equipment and components. The gross output of the manufacturing industry in 1983 was £M223·5 million, of which £M141·6 million were export sales.

Tourism has assumed primary importance, with over 490,000 tourists visiting the island in 1983, and there are plans to develop Marsamxett Harbour as a yachting centre. Gross income from this industry stood at £M65 million.

FINANCE AND TRADE

	1983	1984
Revenue	£M226,100,000	£M228,100,000
Expenditure	222,624,000	227,213,000

The Central Bank of Malta has the sole right of issuing legal tender currency notes and coins. The Maltese pound is divided into 100 *cents* and 1,000 *mils*. The Malta £ was revalued in June 1981.

TRADE

The principal imports for home consumption are foodstuffs—mainly wheat, meat and bullocks, milk and fruit—fodder, beverages and tobacco, fuels, chemicals, textiles and machinery (industrial, agricultural and transport). The chief domestic exports are vegetables, flowers and cuttings, processed food and other manufactures.

	1983
Imports	£M316,600,000
Exports	156,700,000

Trade with U.K.

	1982	1983
Imports from U.K.	£71,823,000	£71,895,000
Exports from U.K.	42,792,000	40,852,000

Mauritius

Mauritius is an island group lying in the Indian Ocean, 550 miles east of Madagascar, between 57° 17′–57° 46′ E. long. and lat. 19° 58′–20° 33′ S., and comprising with its dependencies an area of 805 square miles. The estimated resident population in 1982 was: Mauritius, 949,686; Rodrigues, 33,649; Lesser Dependencies about 350, made up of Asiatic races (Hindus 52·6 per cent, Muslims 16·5 per cent), and persons of European (mainly French extraction), mixed and African descent (28·3 per cent).

Mauritius was discovered in 1511 by the Portuguese; the Dutch visited it in 1598, and named it Mauritius, after Prince Maurice of Nassau. From 1638 to 1710 it was held as a small Dutch colony and in 1715 the French took possession but did not settle it until 1721. Mauritius was taken by a British Force in 1810. A British garrison remained on the island until its withdrawal in June 1960. The French language and French law have been preserved under British rule. English is the official language but French may be used in the Legislative Assembly and lower law courts. However, Creole is the mostly commonly used language.

CLIMATE.—Mauritius enjoys a sub-tropical maritime climate, with a wide range of rainfall and temperature resulting from the mountainous nature of the island. Humidity is rather high throughout the year and rainfall is sufficient to maintain a green cover of vegetation, except for a brief period in the driest districts.

CAPITAL.—ΨPort Louis, population (1982), 147,599; other centres are Beau Bassin-Rose Hill (87,117); Curepipe (57,191); Vacoas-Phoenix (55,494) and Quatre Bornes (56,291) (all figures provisional).

FLAG.—Red, blue, yellow and green horizontal stripes.

GOVERNMENT

A Crown Colony for 158 years, Mauritius became an independent state within the Commonwealth on March 12, 1968. The Constitution defined by Order in Council in 1964 was slightly altered in 1966 on the recommendation of the Banwell Commission, the effect being to increase the membership of the Legislative Assembly to 70, 62 elected by block voting in multi-member constituencies (including 2 members for Rodrigues) and 8 specially-elected members. Of the latter, 4 seats go to the "best loser" of whichever communities in the island are under-represented in the Assembly after the General Election and the four remaining seats are allocated on the basis of both party and community. The Constitution provides for the appointment of a Governor-General who acts on the advice of the Council of Ministers, collectively responsible to the Legislative Assembly.

In the August 1983 General Election, the Mouvement Socialiste Mauricien, allied with the Labour Party and the Parti Mauricien Social Democrate, defeated the Mouvement Mauricien Militant and formed the Government, with a majority of 43 seats.

Governor-General, Dr. The Rt. Hon. Sir Seewosagur Ramgoolan, G.C.M.G.

COUNCIL OF MINISTERS

Premier and Minister of Defence, Internal Security, External Communications, Information and Reform Institutions, Hon. Aneerood Jugnauth.
Deputy Prime Minister and Minister of Justice, Hon. Sir Gaetan Duval.
Women's Rights and Family Affairs, Hon. Mrs. Sheilabia Bappoo.
Works, Dr. The Hon. Rohit Niemo Beedassy.
Commerce, Shipping, Prices and Consumer Protection, Hon. Abdool Kader Ahmed Bhayat.
Economic Planning and Development, Hon. Sir Satcam Boolell.
Employment and Social Security and National Solidarity, Dr. The Hon. Diwakur Bundhun.
Industry and Cooperatives, Hon. Ramsamy Chedumbarum Pillay.
Agriculture, Fisheries and Natural Resources, Hon. Nunkeswarsingh Deerpalsingh.
Labour and Industrial Relations, Hon. Joseph Herve Duval.
Rodrigues and The Outer Islands, Hon. France Felicite.
External Affairs, Tourism and Emigration, Hon. Anil Kumarsingh Gayan.
Health, Dr. The Hon Beergoonath Ghurburren.
Youth and Sports, Hon. Michael James Kevin Glover.
Housing, Lands and the Environment, Hon Dwarkanath Gungah.
Finance, Hon. Seetanah Lutchmeenaraidoo.
Local Government, Hon. Louis Sylvio Michel.
Education and the Arts and Cultural Affairs and Leisure, Hon. Armoorgum Parsuraman.
Energy and Internal Communications, Hon. Mahyendrah Utchanah.

MAURITIUS HIGH COMMISSION
32–33 Elvaston Place, S.W.7
[01–581 0294]

High Commissioner, His Excellency Gian Nath (1983).

BRITISH HIGH COMMISSION
P.O. Box 586, Cerne House, Chaussée Street, Port Louis

High Commissioner, His Excellency James Nicholas Allan, C.B.E. (1981).

EDUCATION

Primary education is free and in 1983 was provided for over 128,091 children at 267 primary schools. Although education is not compulsory it is estimated that about 90 per cent of children of primary age attend school. At post-primary level there are a total of 81,946 students attending 8 government senior secondary schools, 6 government junior secondary schools, 3 junior technical schools and 127 private secondary schools: fees and teachers' salaries in the private secondary schools are paid by government. 194 students attend the Industrial Trade Training Centre. The College of Education trains primary school teachers. The Institute of Education is responsible for training secondary school teachers and for curriculum development. The University of Mauritius consists of Schools of Agriculture, of Administration and of Industrial Technology, and had 430 students in 1983. Estimated expenditure on education in 1982–83 was: recurrent *Rs.*510,185,000; capital *Rs.*38,730,087.

COMMUNICATIONS

Port Louis, on the N.W. coast, handles the bulk of the island's external trade. A bulk sugar terminal capable of handling the total crop began operating in 1980. The international airport is located at Plaisance in the southeast of the island about 5 miles from Mahébourg. There are 8 daily newspapers and 2 weeklies, mostly in French, and 2 Chinese daily papers and one weekly paper. The Mauritius Broadcasting Corporation has a monopoly of radio broadcasting in the country: television was introduced in 1965. There is a satellite communications ground station near Port Louis.

PRODUCTION

Sugar is the main industry of the island, employing over 50,000 people. About 55 per cent of the total crop is produced on a plantation scale, while smaller owners (cultivating less than 10 acres) cultivate about 24 per cent of the land under cane. Tea and tobacco are also grown commercially but on a smaller scale than sugar.

	1982	1983
	tonnes	
Sugar	687,940	604,741
Tea (manufactured)	5,287	6,142
Tobacco (leaves).............	624	785

The bulk of the island's requirements in manufactured products still has to be imported, though there is a diverse and growing local manufacturing sector. The most important industry is the processing of sugar. In 1983 production of molasses, mainly for export, was 162,143 tonnes. Other products include alcohol, rum, denatured spirits, perfumed spirits and vinegar.

FINANCE

The main sources of Government revenue are private and company income tax, customs and excise duties, mainly on imports, but also on sugar exports.

	1981–82	1982–83
Public revenue	Rs.3,503 m	Rs.3,771 m
Public expenditure	4,166 m	4,719 m
National Debt	—	97 m
	Currency—Rs. = Rupee.	

TRADE

Most foodstuffs and raw materials have to be imported from abroad. Apart from local consumption (about 36,500 metric tons per annum), the sugar produced is exported, mainly to Britain, U.S.A. and Canada.

	1982	1983
Total imports	Rs.5,048 m	Rs.5,156 m
Total exports	3,989 m	4,311 m

Trade with U.K.

	1982	1983
Imports from U.K.	Rs.446 m	Rs. 449 m
Exports to U.K.	2,123 m	2,182 m

RODRIGUES AND DEPENDENCIES OF MAURITIUS

Rodrigues, formerly a dependency but now part of Mauritius, is about 350 miles east of Mauritius. Area, 40 square miles. Population (1982) 33,649. Cattle, salt fish, sheep, goats, pigs and onions are the principal exports. The island is administered by a Resident Commissioner.

Resident Commissioner, Maxime Labour.

The islands of Agalega and St. Brandon are dependencies of Mauritius. Other small islands, formerly Mauritian dependencies, including Six Islands, Peros Banhos, Salomon, Diego Garcia and Trois Frères, have since 1965 constituted the British Indian Ocean Territory.

Republic of Nauru

The Republic of Nauru is an island of 8·2 sq. miles in size, situated in 166° 55′ E. longitude and 0° 32′ S. of the Equator. It has a population (Census Jan. 1977) of 7,254 (Nauruans 4,174; other Pacific Islanders 1,890; Chinese 626; Caucasians 564). About 43 per cent of Nauruans are adherents of the Nauruan Protestant Church and there is a Roman Catholic Mission on the island.

FLAG.—Twelve-point star (representing the 12 original Nauruan tribes) below a gold bar (representing the Equator), all on a blue ground.

GOVERNMENT

From 1888 until the First World War Nauru was administered by Germany, in 1920 becoming a British mandated territory under the League of Nations administered by Australia. A Trusteeship superceding the Mandate was approved in 1947 by the U.N. and Nauru continued to be administered by Australia until it became an Independent State on February 1, 1968. It was announced in November, 1968, that a limited form of membership of the Commonwealth had been devised for Nauru at the request of its Government. Parliament has eighteen members including the Cabinet and Speaker. Voting is compulsory for all Nauruans over 20 years of age, except in certain specified instances. Elections are held every three years. The Cabinet is chosen by the President and comprises not fewer than five nor more than six members including the President.

President and Minister for External Affairs, Internal Affairs, Island Development and Industry, Civil Aviation Authority and the Public Service, His Excellency Hammer DeRoburt, G.C.M.G., O.B.E.

CABINET

Minister for Finance, Hon. K. Aroi.
Health and Education, Hon. L. Stephen.
Works and Community Services, Hon. R. B. B. Detudamo.
Justice, Hon. B. Dowiyogo.

JUDICIARY

A Supreme Court of Nauru is presided over by the Chief Justice. The District Court, which is subordinate to the Supreme Court, is presided over by a Resident Magistrate. Both the Supreme Court and the District Court are Courts of Record. The Supreme Court exercises both original and appellate jurisdiction.

EDUCATION AND WELFARE

Nauru has a hospital service and other medical and dental services. There is also a maternity and child welfare service. Education is available in 9 primary and 2 secondary schools on the island with a total enrolment of about 1,600 pupils receiving primary education and 500 secondary education.

PRODUCTION, ETC.

The only fertile areas are the narrow coastal belt and local requirements of fruit and vegetables are mostly met by imports. The economy is heavily dependent on the extraction of phosphate, of which the island has one of the world's richest deposits. About two million tonnes of phosphate are mined each year, providing employment for over 1,000 people. The industry has been run since 1970 by the Nauru Phosphate Corporation. Considerable investments have been made abroad with the royalties on phosphate exports to provide for a time when production declines.

The Nauru Pacific Line owns six ships: the Government-owned Air Nauru operates scheduled air services throughout the Pacific and to Australia, New Zealand, Japan, Singapore and the Philippines.

Trade with U.K.

	1982	1983
Imports from U.K.	£1,843,000	£1,715,000
Exports to U.K.	32,000	1,421,000

BRITISH HIGH COMMISSION (*see* Suva, Fiji).

Nigeria

AREA AND POPULATION.—The Republic of Nigeria is situated on the west coast of Africa. It is bounded on the south by the Gulf of Guinea, on the west by the Republic of Benin, on the north by Niger and on the east by Cameroon. It has an area of 356,669 sq. miles with a population (1963 Census) of 55,654,000. U.N. estimates of the present population suggest a figure of 85 million. The population is almost entirely African. The main ethnic groups are Hausa/Fulani, Yoruba and Ibo, and the principal languages are English, Hausa, Yoruba and Ibo. Over half the population are Muslim, these being concentrated in the north and west. In the southern areas in particular there are many Christians.

A belt of mangrove swamp forest 10–60 miles in width lies along the entire coastline. North of this there is a zone 50–100 miles wide of tropical rain forest and oil-palms. North of this the country rises and the vegetation changes to open woodland and savannah. In the extreme north the country is semi-desert. There are few mountains, but in Northern Nigeria the central plateau rises to an average level of 4,000 feet. The Niger, Benue, and Cross are the main rivers.

The climate varies with the types of country described above, but Nigeria lies entirely within the tropics and temperatures are high. Temperatures of over 100° in the north are common while coast temperatures are seldom over 90°. The humidity at the coast, however, is much higher than in the north. The rainy season is from about April to October; rainfall varies from under 25 inches a year in the extreme north to 172 inches on the coast line. During the dry season the *harmattan* wind blows from the desert; it is cool and laden with fine particles of dust.

CAPITAL.—ΨLAGOS, estimated population, 3,000,000. Other important towns are Ibadan, Kaduna, Kano, Benin City, Enugu and ΨPort Harcourt. Work on a new capital under construction at Abuja was suspended when the military took power.

FLAG.—Three equal vertical bands, green, white and green.

NATIONAL DAY.—October 1 (Republic Day).

GOVERNMENT

The Federation of Nigeria attained independence as a member of the Commonwealth on Oct. 1, 1960 and became a republic in 1963. On Jan. 15, 1966 the military took power, suspended the Constitution and dissolved the legislature. In 1979 civil rule was restored under a new constitution similar to that of the United States after elections at National and State level. After similar elections in 1983 the new administration was removed by the military on Dec. 31, political activity was banned and parts of the Constitution suspended. The military government comprises a Supreme Military Council, Federal and State Executive Councils, Military governors and a National Council of State to coordinate Federal and State affairs. Originally regional in structure the Federation was divided into 12 states in 1967 and into the present 19 states in 1976.

Head of State, Commander-in-Chief of the Armed Forces, Chairman of the Supreme Military Council, Maj. Gen. Muhammadu Buhari.

SUPREME MILITARY COUNCIL

Brig. T. Idiagbon (*Chief of Staff, Supreme Headquarters*); Maj. Gen. D. Y. Bali; Maj. Gen. I. Babangida (*Chief of Army Staff*); Cdre. A. Aikhomu (*Chief of Naval Staff*); Air Vice Marshal I. Alfa (*Chief of Air Staff*); Maj. Gen. M. Vatsa; Brig. M. Magoro; Brig. S. Abacha; Brig. O. Oni; Brig. M. G. Nasko; Brig. Y. Y. Kure; Col. S. Ibrahim; J. E. Inyang (*Inspector-General of Police*); C. Ofodile; M. L. Rafindadi (*Dir.-Gen. of National Security Organisation*); Brig. P. U. Omu; Capt. O. E. Ukiwe; Air Cdre. L. D. Koinyan.

FEDERAL EXECUTIVE COUNCIL

Without Portfolio, Maj. Gen. D. Y. Bali.
Internal, Brig. M. Magoro.
Federal Capital Territory, Maj. Gen. M. Vatsa.
Communications, Lt. Col. A. Abdullahi.
Employment, Labour and Productivity, Brig. S. A. Omojokun.
Information, Social Development, Youth, Sports and Culture, Gp. Capt. S. E. Omeruah.
Health, Cdre. P. S. Koshoni.
Attorney-General & Minister of Justice, C. Ofodile.
Education, Science and Technology, A. I. Y. Abdullahi.

Transport and Aviation, A. A. Ibrahim.
Agriculture and Water Resources, and Rural Development, Dr. B. Shaib.
Commerce and Industries, Dr. M. Tukur.
Mines, Power and Steel, A. R. Lukman.
External Affairs, Dr. I. A. Gambari.
Finance, Dr. Ona O. Soleye.
National Planning, Chief M. S. Adigun.
Petroleum and Energy, Prof. T. David-West.
Works and Housing, Dr. E. N. Nsan.

NIGERIAN HIGH COMMISSION
Nigeria House, 9 Northumberland Avenue,
WC2N 5BX
[01–839 1244]

High Commissioner, His Excellency Maj. Gen. H. A. Hananiya.

BRITISH HIGH COMMISSION
Eleke Crescent, Victoria Island, Lagos

High Commissioner, His Excellency William Erskine Hamilton Whyte (1983).

British Council Representative, E. H. Semmens, O.B.E., Plot 1650, Olosa Street, Opposite Eko Hotel, Victoria Island (P.O. Box 3702), Lagos. Branch offices at Kano, Kaduna and Enugu.

EDUCATION

A programme was introduced in September 1976 intended to achieve universal primary education. Numbers of pupils in 1982–83 are: 15·4 million in primary schools, 3·5 million in secondary schools, 53,766 in polytechnics and 88,636 in universities. There are 13 universities.

COMMUNICATIONS

The Nigerian railway system, which is controlled by the Nigerian Railway Corporation, is the most extensive in West Africa. There are 2,178 route miles of lines. The principal international airlines operating from Lagos, Kano and Port Harcourt bring Nigeria within about six hours of the Western European capitals. There are also services to other parts of Africa and to the United States. A network of internal air services connects the main centres. The principal seaports are served by a number of shipping lines, including the Nigerian National Line.

A nationwide television and radio network is being developed, with each State eventually having its own television and radio station. There is a network of meteorological reporting stations.

PRODUCTION AND INDUSTRY

Nigeria was a predominantly agricultural country until the early 1970s with agriculture contributing over 60 per cent of export revenue and 45 per cent of Gross National Product. Tin and calumbite mining on the Jos plateau, textiles and coal mining were also important. The major exports were ground nuts, palm products, tin, cocoa, rubber and timber. Recently oil has provided over 90 per cent of exports revenue and agricultural exports have greatly declined. Nigeria now imports wheat, rice and other food. Though agriculture still employs half the labour force it contributes only 20 per cent of G.N.P., exceeded by trading and oil. The construction sector is twice as large as the manufacturing sector and industries dependent on imported raw materials such as vehicle assembly have faltered recently. Three oil refineries are in operation at Port Harcourt, Warri and Kaduna. A steel plant has been opened near Warri and a larger one is being completed at Ajaokuta. Other projects include natural gas liquifaction, petro-chemicals, fertilizers and several power stations plus the Abuja Federal Capital. Several large irrigation schemes have been completed and more are planned.

TRADE

Oil revenues have been falling since 1981 and are now restricted by an OPEC production quota and lower prices to half their peak level. In March 1982 imports curbs and payments restrictions were introduced but exchange reserves have fallen and debts have increased while shortages of both consumer and production goods and inflation have became worse. New currency notes were introduced in May 1984. The exchange rate for the *Naira* was N1 = US$1.31 in June 1984.

	1982
Total imports (including invisibles)	US$22,381,000 m
Total exports	17,055,000 m

The unit of currency is the *Naira*.

Trade with U.K.

	1982	1983
Imports from U.K.	£1,225,164,000	£798,276,000
Exports to U.K.	356,802,000	387,975,000

Papua New Guinea

Papua New Guinea extends from the equator to Cape Baganowa in the Louisiade Archipelago at 11° S. latitude and from the border with Irian Jaya to 160° E. longitude. The total area of Papua New Guinea is 178,260 square miles, of which approximately 152,420 form the mainland, on the island of New Guinea. The country has many island groups, principally the Bismarck Archipelago, a portion of the Solomon Islands, the Trobriands, the D'Entrecasteaux Islands and the Louisade Archipelago.

The main islands of the Bismark Archipelago are New Britain, New Ireland and Manus. Bougainville is the largest of the Solomon Islands within Papua New Guinea.

Papua New Guinea lies within the tropics and has a typically monsoonal climate. Temperature and humidity are uniformly high throughout the year. The average rainfall is about 80 inches per year but there are wide variations—from 47 inches at Port Moresby to over 200 inches in mountainous western areas.

POPULATION.—The estimated population of Papua New Guinea in 1983 was 3,160,000. The inhabitants of the country comprise a great diversity of physical types and a large number of linguistic groups. The population increases by approximately 2·7 per cent annually.

CAPITAL.—Port Moresby. Estimated population 138,500. Other major towns are Lae, Rabaul, Madang, Wewak, Goroka and Mount Hagen.

FLAG.—A rectangle divided diagonally from the top of the hoist to the bottom of the fly, the upper segment scarlet and containing a soaring yellow bird of paradise. The lower segment is black charged with five white five-pointed stars representing the Southern Cross.

GOVERNMENT

New Guinea was sighted by Portuguese and Spanish navigators in the early sixteenth century. In 1884, a British Protectorate was proclaimed over the southern coast of New Guinea (Papua) and the adjacent islands. British New Guinea, as the Protectorate was called, was annexed outright in 1888. In 1906 the Territory of British New Guinea was placed under the authority of the Commonwealth of Australia. Also in 1884 Germany had formally taken possession of certain northern areas, which later came to be known as the Trust Territory of New Guinea. In 1914 the German areas were occupied by Australian troops and remained under military administration until 1921, when the League of Nations conferred on Australia a mandate for their government.

New Guinea was administered under the Mandate and Papua under the Papua Act until the invasion by the Japanese in 1942 when the civil administration was suspended. Following the surrender of the Japanese in 1945, civil administration was progessively restored.

The first House of Assembly for the whole country met in 1964 and included an elected majority and ten nominated official members. After 1970 there was a gradual assumption of powers by the Papua New Guinea Government, culminating in formal self-government in December 1973. Final reserve powers held by Australia over defence and foreign relations were relinquished to Papua New Guinea in March 1975, and Papua New Guinea achieved full independence on September 16, 1975.

Elections are held every five years. The House of Assembly comprises 109 elected Members, 20 from Regional electorates, the remainder from Open electorates. There are 19 provinces, which have their own provincial governments with certain legislative and administrative powers.

Governor-General, Sir Kingsford Dibela, G.C.M.G.

NATIONAL EXECUTIVE COUNCIL
(CABINET)

Prime Minister, Michael Somare, C.H.
Deputy P.M. and Minister for National Planning and Development, Paias Wingti.
Defence, Boyamo Sali.
Provincial Affairs, John Nilkare.
Industrial Development, K. Stack.
Foreign Affairs and Trade, R. Namaliu, C.M.G.
Culture and Tourism, M. Javopa.
Environment, H. Mai.
Finance, P. Bouraga.
Health, M. Tovadek.
Lands, B. Koroworo.
Transport, M. Bendum.
Works and Supply, P. Kakaraya.
Public Services, T. Siaguru.
Broadcasting and Information, Epel Tito.
Justice, T. Bais.
Posts and Telecommunications, R. Evara.
Physical Planning, K. Swokim.
Police, J. Gihena.
Education, Sir Barry Holloway, K.B.E.
Correction Institutions and Liquor Licensing, P. Kange.
Forests, L. Waka.
Labour and Employment, C. Anggua.
Minerals and Energy, F. Pusal.
Religion, Youth, Women and Recreation, T. Awasa.
Administrative Services, Sir Pita Lus.
Primary Industry, D. Young.
Civil Aviation, T. Pais.

PAPUA NEW GUINEA HIGH COMMISSION
3rd Floor, 14 Waterloo Place, SW1R 4AR
[01–930 0922]

High Commissioner, His Excellency Ilinome F. Tarua, O.B.E.

BRITISH HIGH COMMISSION
P.O. Box 739, Port Moresby

High Commissioner, His Excellency Arthur John Collins, O.B.E. (1982).

COMMUNICATIONS

Road communications are very limited, the most important road being that linking Lae with the populous Highlands.

Air Niugini (the national airline) and Qantas operate regular air services between Port Moresby and Australia, and under a tripartite agreement Air Niugini/Cathay Pacific/Air New Zealand operate between Hong Kong and Auckland *via* Port Moresby. Air Niugini also operates services to Manila (Philippines), Honiara (Solomon Islands), Jayapura (Indonesia), Honolulu and Singapore. Internal air services are operated by Air Niugini, Douglas Airways, and Talair.

Several shipping companies operate cargo services between Papua New Guinea and Australia, Europe, the Far East and U.S.A. There are very limited cargo and passenger services between Papua New Guinea main ports, outports, plantations and missions.

Papua New Guinea is linked *via* the Seacom international cable to Australia, Guam, Hong Kong, Kota Kinabalu, the Far East and U.S.A. There is also a link to Australia *via* the A/PNG cable. Telex services are also available.

ECONOMY

Until the 1970s the Papua New Guinea economy was based almost entirely on agriculture. At the beginning of the 20th century copra plantations formed the basis of the cash economy. Further crops which have been introduced over the years are cocoa, tea, coffee, palm oil, rubber, groundnuts, spices and timber. A variety of commercial agricultural developments now co-exist with the traditional informal rural economy. Government expenditure is still reliant on Australian budgetary support, to the extent of just under 30 per cent in 1983.

In 1972, Bougainville Copper Pty Ltd (BCL) began mining in the North Solomons Province, producing copper, silver and gold. B.C.L.'s contribution to the economy increased rapidly and in recent years it has provided some 50 per cent of Papua New Guinea's total exports by value. There are extensive mineral deposits throughout Papua New Guinea, including nickel, chromite, bauxite and possibly commercial deposits of oil and gas. The most important new development is the exploitation of large copper and gold deposits on the Ok Tedi, in the Western Province. This project, due to start production in 1984, should provide substantial export earnings for Papua New Guinea well into the 21st century.

In 1982–83 the Papua New Guinea economy was affected by the world recession but new commercial sugar development enabled the country to phase out sugar imports, and significant progress was made in palm oil production. New developments to promote export crops and increase employment, typically involving foreign investment, are planned for the future.

Secondary industry, originally orientated towards processing primary products, now also partly services the local market. Successful operations include brewing, bottling and packaging, paint, plywood, and metal manufacturing and the construction industries.

Although the formal economy is still dominated by non-Papua New Guineans, the participation of Papua New Guineans is increasing.

Trade with U.K.

	1982	1983
Imports from U.K.	£15,911,000	£18,236,000
Exports to U.K.	28,031,000	28,142,000

CURRENCY

The unit of currency is the *Kina.*

St. Kitts-Nevis

The State of St. Kitts-Nevis is located at the northern end of the Eastern Caribbean. It comprises the islands of St. Kitts (65 sq. miles, population about 35,000) and Nevis (36 sq. miles, 9,300).

St. Kitts, lat. 17° 18′ N. and long. 62° 48′ W. was the first island in the British West Indies to be colonised (1623). Its economy has been based on sugar for over three centuries. Tourism and light industry is being developed. The central area of the island is forest-clad and mountainous, rising to the 3,792 ft. Mount Misery.

CAPITAL—ΨBasseterre, is a port of registry and now has deep water harbour facilities. Golden Rock airport can take most large jet aircraft.

Nevis, lat. 17° 10′ N. and long. 62° 35′ W. is separated from the southern tip of St. Kitts by a strait two miles wide. The sea ferry route from Basseterre, St. Kitts to Charlestown, Nevis is 11 miles. Newcastle airstrip can take small aircraft, e.g. Islanders: and night landing facilities are available. The economy of Nevis centres on small peasant farmers. A sea-island cotton is being developed for export to Japan. The island is dominated by the central Nevis Peak, 3,232 ft.

CHIEF TOWN—ΨCharlestown (pop. 1,200), is a port of entry.

FLAG—Three diagonal bands, green, black and red; each colour separated by a stripe of yellow. Two white stars on the black band.

GOVERNMENT

The Territory of St. Kitts-Nevis became a State in Association with Britain on Feb. 27, 1967. The State of St. Kitts-Nevis became an independent nation on Sept. 19, 1983, with a new constitution under which Great Britain relinquished its responsibility for defence and external affairs. Under the new Constitution, H.M. The Queen is Head of State, represented in the islands by the Governor-General. There is a central Cabinet Government with a Ministerial system, the Head of which is the Prime Minister of St. Kitts-Nevis, and a National Assembly located on St. Kitts. On Nevis there is a Nevis Island Administration, the Head being styled Premier of Nevis, and a Nevis Island Assembly.

Governor-General, His Excellency Sir Clement Athelston Arrindell, G.C.M.G. (1981).

CABINET

Prime Minister and Minister of Finance, Home Affairs and Foreign Affairs,, Hon. Dr. K. A. Simmonds.
Deputy P.M. and Minister of Labour and Tourism, Hon. M. O. Powell.
Natural Resources and Environment, Hon. S. Daniel.
Education, Health and Community Affairs, Hon. S. E. Morris.
Communications, Works and Public Utilities, Hon. I. A. W. Stevens.
Agriculture, Lands, Housing and Development, Hon. H. C. Heyliger.
Women's Affairs, Hon. Constance Mitcham.
Trade and Industry, Hon. F. Jones.
In Ministry of Finance, Hon. R. Caines.
Without Portfolio, Hon. U. S. Swanston.
Attorney-General, Hon. S. W. T. Seaton.
Cabinet Secretary, C. Farier.

St. Lucia

St. Lucia, the second largest and the most picturesque of the Windward group, situated in 13° 54′ N. lat. and 60° 50′ W. long., at a distance of about 90 miles W.N.W. of Barbados, 21 miles N. of St. Vincent, and 24 miles S. of Martinique, is 27 miles in length, with an extreme breadth of 14 miles. It comprises an area of 238 square miles with an estimated population (1982) of 124,000. It possesses perhaps the most interesting history of all the smaller islands. Fights raged hotly around it, and it constantly changed hands between the English and the French. It is mountainous, its highest point being Mt. Gimie (3,145 feet) and for the most part it is covered with forest and tropical vegetation.

CAPITAL.—ΨCastries (estimated population 1982, 50,282) is recognized as being one of the finest ports in the West Indies on account of its reputation as a safe anchorage in the hurricane season.

FLAG.—Blue, bearing in centre a device of yellow over black over white triangles having a common base.

GOVERNMENT

St. Lucia became independent within the Commonwealth on Feb. 22, 1979. The Head of State is H.M. The Queen, represented in the island by a St. Lucian Governor-General, and there is a bicameral legislature. The Senate has 11 members, 6 appointed by the ruling party, 3 by the Opposition and 2 by the Governor-General. The House of Assembly, which has a life of five years, has 17 elected Members and a Speaker, who may be elected from outside the House.

Governor-General, His Excellency Sir Allen Lewis, G.C.M.G., Q.C.
Prime Minister, Minister of Finance, Development and Foreign Affairs, Rt. Hon. J. G. M. Compton.
Deputy P.M. and Minister of Trade, Industry and Tourism, Hon. G. Mallet.

ST. LUCIA HIGH COMMISSION
10 Kensington Court, W.8.
[01–937 9522]

High Commissioner, His Excellency Dr. Claudius C. Thomas, C.M.G.

BRITISH HIGH COMMISSION (*see* Barbados).

ECONOMY

The economy is mainly agrarian, with manufacturing based on the processing of agricultural products. Principal crops are bananas, coconuts, cocoa, mangoes, avocado pears, breadfruit, spices, root crops such as cassava and yams, and citrus fruit. Attempts are being made to diversify the economy, in particular through greater industrialization.

The principal exports are bananas, coconut products (copra, edible oils, soap), cardboard boxes, beer and textile manufactures. The chief imports are flour, meat, machinery, building materials, motor vehicles, cotton piece goods, petroleum and fertilisers.

St. Vincent and the Grenadines

The territory of the State of St. Vincent includes certain of the Grenadines, a chain of small islands stretching 40 miles across the Caribbean Sea between Grenada and St. Vincent, some of the larger of which are Bequia, Canouan, Mayreau, Mustique, Union Island, Petit St. Vincent and Prune Island. The whole territory extends 150 square miles (96,000 acres).

The main island, St. Vincent, is situated between 13° 6′ and 14° 35′ N. latitude and 61° 6′ and 61° 20′ W. longitude, approximately 21 miles south west of St. Lucia and 100 miles west of Barbados. The island is 18 miles long and 11 miles wide at its extremities comprising an area of 133 square miles and a population (1982 estimate) of 127,883 of whom about 118,660 inhabit the main island. St. Vincent was discovered by Christopher Columbus in 1498. It was granted by Charles I to the Earl of Carlisle in 1627 and after subsequent grants and a series of occupations alternately by the French and English, it was finally restored to Britain in 1783.

CAPITAL and principal port is ΨKingstown, population approximately 33,694.

GOVERNMENT

St. Vincent and the Grenadines achieved full independence within the Commonwealth on Oct. 27, 1979.

St. Vincent has a constitution under which there is a Governor-General who is Her Majesty's Representative. Except where otherwise provided, the Governor-General is required to act in accordance with the advice of the Prime Minister.

The House of Assembly consists of 13 elected members and 6 Senators appointed by the Governor-General. It is presided over by a Speaker elected by the House from within or without it.

Governor-General, His Excellency Sir Sydney Douglas Gun-Munro, G.C.M.G., M.B.E.

Prime Minister, Minister of Finance and Foreign Affairs, Hon. James Mitchell.

ST. VINCENT AND THE GRENADINES
HIGH COMMISSION
10 Kensington Court, W.8
[01-937 9522]

High Commissioner, His Excellency Dr. Claudius C. Thomas, C.M.G.

BRITISH HIGH COMMISSION (*see* Barbados).

ECONOMY

This is based mainly on agriculture but the tourist and manufacturing industries have been expanding. The main products are bananas, arrowroot, coconuts, sugar, cocoa, spices and various kinds of food crops. The main imports are foodstuffs (meat, rice, beverages), textiles, lumber, cement and other building materials, fertilizers, motor vehicles and fuel.

EDUCATION

Primary and secondary education in Government schools is free but not compulsory. In 1982 there were 24,569 enrolments in state primary schools and 5,123 enrolments in state secondary schools.

Seychelles

The Republic of Seychelles, in the Indian Ocean, consists of 115 islands with a total land area of 171·4 square miles, spread over 400,000 square miles of ocean. There is a relatively compact granitic group, 32 islands in all, with high hills and mountains (highest point about 2,990 ft.), of which Mahé is the largest and most populated (90 per cent of the population live on Mahé): and the outlying coralline group, for the most part, only a little above sea-level. Although only 4° S. of the Equator, the climate is pleasant though tropical. The population was estimated (mid-1983) to be 64,410. The average natural growth rate (1981) was 0·9 per cent.

CAPITAL.—ΨVictoria (population, 1982, 24,733), on the N.E. side of Mahé.

GOVERNMENT

Proclaimed as French territory in 1756, the Mahé group began to be settled as a dependency of Mauritius from 1770, was captured by a British ship in 1794, changed hands several times between 1803 and 1814, when it was finally assigned to Great Britain. By Letters Patent of September, 1903, these islands, together with the coralline group, were formed into a separate Colony. On June 29, 1976, the Islands became an independent republic within the Commonwealth. A *coup d'état* took place on June 5, 1977.

A new constitution making Seychelles a one-party state came into force in June 1979. The executive power lies with the President, who is elected by universal suffrage for a five year term. Legislative power lies with the President and the People's Assembly (which has 23 elected members and two nominated by the President), an independent judiciary commission and an integrity commission.

President, France Albert René, *assumed office* June 5, 1977; *elected* June 26, 1979; *re-elected* June 18, 1984.

SEYCHELLES HIGH COMMISSION
50 Conduit Street, W1A 4PE
[01-439 0405]

High Commissioner, Her Excellency Mrs. Danielle de St. Jorre.
Counsellor, R. F. Delpech.

TRADE

	1982	1983
Imports	Rs.641,322	Rs.594,082
Exports	20,279	25,250
Re-exports	79,787	111,997

The principal imports are foodstuffs, beverages, tobacco, mineral fuels, manufactured items, building materials, machinery and transport equipment. The chief exports are copra, fish (fresh and frozen), cinnamon bark and guano. Re-exports cover a large proportion of exports from Seychelles and include such items as petroleum products, fuel and services for both aviation and shipping needs.

BRITISH HIGH COMMISSION
Victoria House, P.O. Box 161,
Victoria, Mahé.

High Commissioner, His Excellency Colin G. Mays.

Sierra Leone

AREA AND POPULATION, ETC.—Sierra Leone, with a total land area of 27,925 square miles, is on the west coast of Africa, between Guinea and Liberia. There was a population at the Census of 1974 of 3,123,000; a U.N. estimate put the population in 1980 at 3,470,000. The origins of the country date back to the late 18th century when a project was begun to settle destitute Africans from England on Freetown peninsula. In 1808 the settlement was declared a Crown Colony and became the main base in West Africa for enforcing the 1807 Act outlawing the slave trade. The Colony was also used as a settlement for Africans from North America and the West Indies, and great numbers of Africans rescued from slave ships, also settled there. Their descendants, known as Creoles, still live on Freetown peninsula. The southern half of Sierra Leone is inhabited by peoples whose languages fall into the Mende group; the northern half by the Temne, and smaller groups such as the Limba, Loko, Koranko and Susu.

CAPITAL.—Freetown (population at 1974 census, 274,000).
FLAG.—Three horizontal stripes of leaf green, white and cobalt blue.
NATIONAL DAY.—April 19 (Republic Day).

GOVERNMENT

Sierra Leone became a fully independent state within the Commonwealth on April 27, 1961. On April 19, 1971 a Republican Constitution was adopted and Dr. Siaka Stevens became the first Executive President. In June 1978 Sierra Leone became a one-Party State, following approval by Parliament and a Referendum. Opposition Members of Parliament declared for the ruling A.P.C., rather than lose their seats.

The first General Election under the one party system was held on May 1, 1982. The Parliament now comprises 85 elected members and 12 Paramount Chiefs, plus seven nominated members, two of whom are the Army Commander and the Commissioner of Police.

President, His Excellency Dr. Siaka P. Stevens, G.C.M.G.
First Vice-President, Hon. S. I. Koroma.
Second Vice-President, Hon. F. M. Minah.

SIERRA LEONE HIGH COMMISSION
33 Portland Place, W1N 5AG
[01–636 6483/5]

High Commissioner, His Excellency Victor E. Sumner (1980).

BRITISH HIGH COMMISSION
Standard Bank of Sierra Leone Building
Lightfoot Boston Street, Freetown

High Commissioner, His Excellency Richard Dennis Clift, C.M.G.
British Council Representative, B. T. Chadwick, P.O. Box 124, Tower Hill, Freetown.

COMMUNICATIONS

Since the phasing out of the railway system in 1974 the road network has been developed considerably and there are now 5,000 miles of roads in the country, over 2,000 miles being surfaced. A bridge has been constructed over the Mano River linking Sierra Leone and Liberia.

The Freetown international airport is situated at Lungi, across the Sierra Leone River from Freetown. The main port is Freetown, which has one of the largest natural harbours in the world, and where there is a deep water quay providing about six berths for medium sized ships. There are smaller ports at Pepel and Bonthe.

Radio and television are operated by the Department of Broadcasting of the Sierra Leone Government. There are two shortwave transmitting and receiving stations in Freetown. A 250 KW radio transmitter has been installed which covers the whole country. Broadcasts are made in several of the more important indigenous languages in addition to English. There is also a weekly broadcast in French.

EDUCATION

In 1982 there were 1,279 primary schools in Sierra Leone and 160 secondary schools. Technical education is provided in the two Government Technical Institutes, situated in Freetown and Kenema, in two Trade Centres and in the technical training establishments of the mining companies. Teacher training is carried out at the university, six colleges in the Provinces and in the Milton Margai Training College near Freetown. The University of Sierra Leone (1967), consists of Fourah Bay College (1827) and Njala University College (1964).

PRODUCTION AND TRADE

On the Freetown Peninsula, farming is largely confined to the production of cassava and garden crops, such as maize and vegetables, for local consumption. In the hinterland, the principal agricultural product is rice, which is the staple food of the country, and cash crops such as cocoa, coffee, palm kernels, and ginger.

The economy depends largely on mineral exports mainly diamonds, bauxite and rutile. Iron ore production recommenced in 1982. Diamonds provide about 60 per cent of export earnings. Total exports in 1983–84 were estimated at Le102·1 million.

Trade with U.K.

	1982	1983
Imports from U.K.	£19,110,000	£13,735,000
Exports to U.K.	14,438,000	17,710,000

FINANCE

In 1964, Sierra Leone adopted decimal currency. The basic unit is the *Leone*.
The revenue for 1984-85 is estimated at Le317·1 million and total expenditure at Le507·1 million resulting in a projected deficit of Le190 million).

Singapore

The Republic of Singapore consists of the island of Singapore and 54 smaller islands, covering a total area of 230 square miles. Singapore Island is 26 miles long and 14 miles in breadth and is situated just north of the Equator off the southern extremity of the Malay Peninsula, from which it is separated by the Straits of Johore.

A causeway, carrying a road and railway, crosses the three-quarters of a mile to the mainland. The highest point of the island is 581 feet above sea level.

CLIMATE.—The climate is hot and humid and there are no clearly defined seasons. Rainfall averages 96 inches a year and temperature ranges from 24°–32° C (76°–89° F).

POPULATION.—At the 1980 census this was 2,362,700. (Chinese, 1,819,600; Malays, 359,700; Indians, 162,800; others (Europeans, Eurasians, etc.), 48,700). At the end of 1983 the population was estimated at 2,502,400 (Chinese, 1,917,100; Malay, 368,500; Indians, 160,600; others, 55,800). At least 8 Chinese dialects are used and Malay, Mandarin, Tamil and English are the official languages.

FLAG.—Horizontal bands of red over white; crescent with five five-point stars on red band near staff.

NATIONAL DAY.—August 9.

GOVERNMENT

Singapore, where Sir Stamford Raffles had first established a trading post under the East India Company in 1819, was incorporated with Penang and Malacca to form the Straits Settlements in 1826. The Straits Settlements became a Crown Colony in 1867. Singapore fell into Japanese hands in 1942 and civil government was not restored until 1946, when it became a separate colony. Internal self-government and the title "State of Singapore" were introduced in 1959. Singapore became a state of Malaysia when the Federation was enlarged in September, 1963, but left Malaysia and became an independent sovereign state within the Commonwealth on August 9, 1965. Singapore adopted a Republican constitution from that date, the Yang di-Pertuan Negara being restyled President. There is a Cabinet collectively responsible to a fully-elected Parliament of 75 members.

HEAD OF STATE

President, C. V. Devan Nair, *elected* Oct. 23, 1981.

CABINET

Prime Minister, Lee Kuan Yew, G.C.M.G., C.H.
First Deputy Prime Minister (Education), Dr. Goh Keng Swee.
Second Deputy Prime Minister (Foreign Affairs), M. S. Rajaratnam.
Defence, Goh Chok Tong.
Foreign Affairs and Culture, S. Dhanabalan.
Home Affairs, Chua Sian Chin.
National Development, Teh Cheang Wan.
Social Affairs, Dr. Ahmed Mattar.
Environment, Ong Pang Boon.
Health, Howe Yoon Chong.
Law, E. W. Barker.
Finance, Trade and Industry, Tony Tan Keng Yam.
Minister Without Portfolio, Ong Teng Cheong.
Communications, Dr. Yeo Ning Hong.
Labour, Prof. Shanmugam Jayakumar.

Speaker of Parliament, Dr. Yeoh Ghim Seng.

SINGAPORE HIGH COMMISSION
2 Wilton Crescent, SW1X 8RW
[01–235 8315]

High Commissioner, His Excellency Dr. Ho Guan Lim.

BRITISH HIGH COMMISSION
Tanglin Circus, Singapore 1024

High Commissioner, His Excellency Sir Peter Moon, K.C.V.O., C.M.G. (1982).
British Council Representative, Dr. J. L. Munby, Rubber House, Collyer Quay, Singapore 1.

COMMUNICATIONS

Singapore is one of the largest seaports in the world, with deep water wharves and ship repairing facilities. Ships also anchor in the roads, unloading into lighters. In 1983, 63,885,170 freight tons of cargo were handled. The Airport is at Changi, in the east of the island. There are 25·75 km. of metric gauge railway connected to the Malaysian rail system by the causeway across the Straits of Johore, and 2,529 kilometres of roads. There are both wireless and wired broadcasting services carrying commercial advertising. Television was introduced in 1963 and a colour service on two channels in 1974. Radio Singapore and Television Singapore amalgamated to form the Singapore Broadcasting Authority Corporation in February 1980.

PRODUCTION, ETC.

Historically Singapore's economy was largely based on the sale and distribution of raw materials from surrounding countries and on entrepot trade in finished products. In the last decade, however, new manufacturing industries have been introduced, including ship building and repairing, iron and steel, textiles, footwear, wood products, micro-electronics, scientific instruments, detergents, confectionery, pharmaceuticals, petroleum products, sanitary-ware, building materials, domestic electrical appliances, plastic articles, transport equipment, etc. Singapore has also become a financial centre with over 100 banks established in the Republic, and an oil-refining centre.

Projects now being undertaken include the construction of a Mass Rapid Transit Rail system; further reclamation of marshy land at Jurong Town; extension of other industrial estates; the building of more low-cost housing units by the Housing & Development Board; a new drainage system throughout the island; the development of additional water-supply catchments and expansion of the airport.

FINANCE

	1984–85
Estimated revenue	S$9,969,349,000
Estimated expenditure	16,560,640,970

TRADE

	1982	1983
Total imports	S$60,244·6m	S$59,504·2m
Total exports	44,472·8m	46,154·9m

Trade with U.K.

	1982	1983
Imports from U.K.	£406,172,000	£469,155,000
Exports to U.K.	245,453,000	404,122,000

Solomon Islands

Forming a scattered archipelago of mountainous islands and low-lying coral atolls, Solomon Islands stretches about 900 miles in a south-easterly direction from Bougainville, in Papua New Guinea, to the Santa Cruz islands. The archipelago covers an area of about 249,000 square nautical miles while the land area is approximately 11,500 square miles. Solomon Islands lies between the east longitudes 155° 30′ and 170° 30′ and between south latitudes 5° 10′ and 12° 45′. The six biggest islands are: Choiseul, New Georgia, Santa Isabel, Guadalcanal, Malaita and Makira. They are characterised by precipitous, thickly-forested mountain ranges intersected by deep, narrow valleys, and vary between 90 to 120 miles in length and between 20 to 30 miles in width.

Distribution of population at the Census of 1976 was: Melanesian 183,665; Polynesian 7,821; Micronesian 2,783; European 1,359; Chinese 452; Others 773. Total 196,823. A mid-1982 estimate put the total population at 244,000.

CAPITAL, Honiara (population (1979), 18,346).

Governor-General, Sir Baddeley Devesi, G.C.M.G, G.C.V.O. (1978).
Prime Minister, Hon. Solomon Mamaloni.
Deputy Prime Minister and Minister for Home Affairs, Guadalcanal, Hon. Kamilio Teke.

FINANCE AND TRADE

Revenue (1983), SI$59,400,000.
The main imports are foodstuffs, consumer goods, machinery and transport materials. Principal exports are timber, fish, copra, and palm oil. Other exports include cocoa and marine shells.

JUDICIARY

The High Court of Solomon Islands, constituted by the Solomon Islands Independence Order, consists of a Chief Justice and not fewer than two nor more than three Puisne Judges. The Court of Appeal Act was enacted on May 8, 1978.

COMMUNICATIONS

An internal air service, Solair, serves 22 airstrips throughout the country, four of which are designated international airports. Air Pacific makes two air connections weekly to Brisbane via Honiara, one of which is a combined service with Solair. Air Nauru makes two flights a week, and Air Niugini also provides flights between Honiara/Port Moresby twice a week. Solair has also extended its services to Bougainville three times a week and to Santo in the New Hebrides once a week.

There are about 52 miles of secondary and minor roads in the urban areas of Honiara, Auki and Gizo. About 18 miles of road in and around Honiara and one mile in Auki and Gizo are bitumen sealed, the remainder being coral or gravel surfaced. In the rural areas there are some 800 miles of road, including those in private plantations, forestry areas and roads built and maintained by councils. All main islands have transreceivers to maintain communications with Honiara and there is a telephone link between Honiara and Auki, Gizo and Tulagi.

Soltel, a company jointly owned by Cable and Wireless Limited and Solomon Islands Government operates the international telephone circuits from a ground station in Honiara via the Intelsat Pacific Ocean communication satellite.

BRITISH HIGH COMMISSION
Soltel House, Mendana Avenue, Honiara.
High Commissioner, His Excellency George N. Stansfield, O.B.E. (1982).

Sri Lanka
(The Democratic Socialist Republic of Sri Lanka)

AREA AND POPULATION.—Sri Lanka (formerly Ceylon) is an island in the Indian Ocean, off the southern tip of the peninsula of India and separated from it by a narrow strip of shallow water, the Palk Strait. Situated between 5° 55′–9° 50′ N. latitude and 79° 42′–81° 52′ E. longitude, it has an area of 25,332 square miles, including 33 square miles of inland water. Its greatest length is from north to south, 270 miles; and its greatest width 140 miles, no point in Sri Lanka being more than 80 miles from the sea.

The population at the 1981 census was 14,800,001.

RACES AND RELIGIONS.—At the 1981 Census the total population was found to be 14·8 million. Of these 74 per cent were Sinhalese, 12·6 per cent Sri Lankan Tamils, 5·6 per cent Indian Tamils, 7·1 per cent Sri Lankan Moor and 0·7 per cent Burghers, Malays and others. The religion of the great majority of inhabitants is Buddhism, introduced from India, according to ancient Sinhalese chronicles, in 247 B.C. Next to Buddhism (69·3 per cent), Hinduism has a large following (15·5 per cent); 7·6 per cent of the population are Muslims and 7·5 per cent Christians. The national languages are Sinhalese, Tamil and English.

PHYSIOGRAPHY.—From a central massif of mountains the land slopes down to the sea on all sides in a series of three peneplains. These lie at approximately 6,000 feet, 1,600 feet and 100 feet. The lowest is broadest towards the north and continues for a distance out to sea as a continental shelf; a coral reef, for the most part submerged, lies close to the coast. The highest peaks are Pidurutalagala (8,281 ft.), Kirigalpota (7,857 ft.), Totapola Kanda (7,741 ft.), Adam's Peak (7,360 ft), a place of pilgrimage for Buddhists, Hindus and Moslems, and Great Western (7,269 ft.). The Peninsula of Jaffna and the island of Mannar are featureless level stretches.

The Mahaweli-Ganga, 208 miles long, is the largest river of Sri Lanka, rising on the western side of the central hilly ridge, and flowing north east into Trincomalee Bay. None of the rivers is navigable by ocean-going vessels. Dunhinda (Badulla), Diyaluma (Koslanda), Elgin (Hatton Plateau) and Perawella are among the outstanding waterfalls. Forests, jungle and scrub cover the greater part of the island, often being intermingled. The forests, of varying species, extend from fairly near the coast right into the hill country. In areas over 2,000 feet above sea level grasslands (*patanas* or *talawas*) are found.

CLIMATE.—The climate of Sri Lanka is warm throughout the year, with a high relative humidity. Temperatures average 80° F. during the year in the lowlands, falling off in the hills to 60° F. at elevations over 6,000 ft. Day humidity is over 70 per cent and night humidity over 85 per cent. Temperature ranges vary little between wet and dry seasons. In the hills the climate is more temperate. Traces of ground frost appear occasionally at night and thunderstorms occasionally give hail, but snow is completely absent. Rainfall is generally heavy, with marked regional variations; the heaviest falls (200–250 inches) are recorded on the south-west slopes of the central hills. The two main monsoon seasons are mid-May to September (south-west) and November to March (north-east).

CAPITAL.—ΨColombo, population (1981, 585,776). Other principal towns are ΨJaffna (118,215), Kandy (101,281), ΨGalle (77,183), ΨNegombo (51,376) and ΨTrincomalee (44,913).

FLAG.—On a dark red field, within a golden border, a golden lion passant holding a sword in its right paw, and a representation of a *bo*-leaf, issuing from each corner; and to its right, two vertical stripes of saffron and green also placed within a golden border, to represent the minorities of the country.

INDEPENDENCE DAY.—Feb. 4.

GOVERNMENT

Early in the sixteenth century the Portuguese landed in Ceylon and founded settlements, eventually conquering much of the country. Portuguese rule in Ceylon lasted 150 years during which the Roman Catholic religion was established among the Sinhalese inhabitants and to some extent Portuguese modes of living adopted. In 1658, following a twenty-year period of decline, Portuguese rule gave place to that of the Dutch East India Company which was to exploit Ceylon with varying fortunes until 1796.

The Maritime Provinces of Ceylon were ceded by the Dutch to the British on February 16, 1798, becoming a British Crown Colony in 1802 under the terms of the Treaty of Amiens. With the annexation of the Kingdom of Kandy in 1815, all Ceylon came under British rule.

On February 4, 1948, Ceylon became a self-governing state and a member of the British Commonwealth of Nations under the *Ceylon Independence Act* 1947. A republican Constitution was adopted on May 22, 1972, providing for a unicameral legislature, the National State Assembly, which has a six year term, and the country was renamed the Republic of Sri Lanka (meaning 'Resplendent Island'). On Sept. 5, 1978 a new Constitution introduced the title the Democratic Socialist Republic of Sri Lanka and a system of proportional representation.

A referendum in Dec. 1982 extended the life of the 1977 Parliament by six years from Aug. 1983.

President, Minister of Defence, Plan Implementation, Energy and Power, Higher Education, Janata Estates Development and State Plantations, His Excellency Junius Jayewardene, *acceded,* Feb. 4, 1978, *elected* Oct. 20, 1982.

Prime Minister, Minister of Local Government, Housing, Construction and Highways, and Leader of the House of Parliament, Hon. R. Premadasa.

SRI LANKA HIGH COMMISSION
13 Hyde Park Gardens, W2 2LX
[01–262 1841]

High Commissioner, His Excellency Chandra Monerawela.

BRITISH HIGH COMMISSION
Galle Road, Kollupitiya (P.O. Box 1433),
Colombo 3

High Commissioner, His Excellency Sir John Nicholas, K.C.V.O., C.M.G. (1979).

British Council Representative, R. A. K. Baker, 47 Alfred House Gardens, Colombo 3. Office also in *Kandy.*

THE LEGISLATURE

According to the Constitution, the legislative power of the people is to be exercised by Parliament, the executive power being exercised by the President.

THE JUDICATURE

The Judicial System provides for a Supreme Court, a Court of Appeal, a High Court and other Courts of First Instance.

PRODUCTION

Agriculture.—The staple products of the island are tea, rubber, copra, spices and gems. There is increasing emphasis on local production of food, especially rice, and plans for the large-scale production of sugar cane, cotton and citrus fruits.

Industry.—Factories are established for the manufacture or processing of ceramic ware, vegetable oils and by-products, paper, tobacco, tanning and leather goods, plywood, cement, chemicals, sugar, flour, salt, textiles, ilmenite, tiles, tyres, fertilizers, clothing, jewellery and hardware and there is a petroleum refinery.

Trade with U.K.

	1982	1983
Imports from U.K.	£60,211,000	£70,136,000
Exports to U.K.	42,000,000	39,784,000

COMMUNICATIONS

There are over 15,660 miles of motorable roads in Sri Lanka and a government-run railway system with 984 miles of lines.

On May 6, 1976, Sri Lanka inaugurated a satellite earth station at Padukka, in south-west Sri Lanka. Constructed with assistance from the Asian Development Bank, the earth satellite station provides instant telecommunication links *via* satellite with any part of the globe.

The principal airports are at Katunayake, 19 miles north of Colombo, and Ratmalana, nine miles south of the capital. Air Lanka operates on 76 flights weekly to the Gulf States, the Maldives, Western Europe and throughout the Far East.

Swaziland
(Kingdom of Swaziland)

Surrounded by South Africa on its northern, western and southern borders and by Mozambique to the east, this small land-locked country is geographically and climatically divided into three principal areas. The broken mountainous Highveld along the western border with an average altitude of 4,000 feet has been densely afforested mainly with conifers and eucalyptus; the Middleveld, averaging about 2,000 feet, is a mixed farming area including cotton and pineapples; and the Lowveld in the east which was mainly scrubland until the introduction of large sugar cane plantations west of the Lubombo mountain range and the Mozambique border. Four rivers, the Komati, Usutu, Mbuluzi and Ngwavuma, flow from west to east, cutting their way through the Lubombo mountains to the Indian Ocean. The exploitation of these rivers is particularly important to the agricultural development of the Middle and Lowveld, where irrigation schemes have promoted the introduction of sugar cane and have effectively altered the landscape of the Bushveld (Lowveld). The total area of Swaziland is 6,782 sq. miles and the population is estimated at some 600,000.

CAPITAL.—Mbabane (population, estimated 30,000), the headquarters of the Government, is situated at an average altitude of 3,800 ft. Other main townships are: Manzini (population, estimated, 30,000), Big Bend, Mhlambanyati, Mhlume, Nhlangano, Pigg's Peak and Simunye.

FLAG.—Five horizontal bands, crimson, bearing shield and spears device, bordered by narrow yellow bands; blue bands at top and foot.

GOVERNMENT

The Kingdom of Swaziland came into being on April 25, 1967, under a new internal self-government constitution and became an independent kingdom, headed by H.M. Sobhuza II, in membership of the Commonwealth on September 6, 1968. On April 12, 1973, the King, in response to a motion passed by both Houses of Parliament, repealed the Parliamentary Constitution of 1968 and assumed supreme legislative, executive and judicial power, to be exercised in collaboration with a Council constituted by his Cabinet Ministers. A new electoral law was introduced in 1978, under which each of the 40 traditional Tinkhundla elect two members to the electoral college who elect 40 members to the House of Assembly. The King nominates 10 members to the House of Assembly, making 50 in all, who then elect 10 members (not of their own number) to the Senate. To these are added 10 senators nominated by the King, bringing the full membership of the Senate to 20. Under the Establishment of the Parliament of Swaziland Order, 1978, the Head of State, advised by the Supreme Council of State (the Liqoqo), continues to reserve a large measure of executive, legislative and judicial authority.

Head of State, Queen Regent Ntombi Tfwala, mother of the designated heir to the throne, Crown Prince Makhosetive, who may not accede to the throne until he comes of age.
Prime Minister, Rt. Hon. Prince Bhekimpi Dlamini, M.P.

SWAZILAND HIGH COMMISSION
58 Pont Street, SW1X 0AE
[01–581 4976/8]

High Commissioner, His Excellency G. M. Mamba (1978).

BRITISH HIGH COMMISSION
Mbabane

High Commissioner, His Excellency Martin Reith (1983).

EDUCATION

In 1982, there were 125,303 pupils enrolled at 470 primary schools and 26,576 at 86 secondary schools.

COMMUNICATIONS

Swaziland's railway is about 150 miles long and runs from Ngwenya in the west to the Mozambique border near Goba in the east, and thence to the Mozambique port of Maputo. A southern link from Phuzumoya in central Swaziland joins up with the South African railway network to Richards Bay. A rail link from Mpaka in central Swaziland to the north-west border is under construction and will provide a link to Komatipoort when completed.

Most passenger and goods traffic is carried by privately-owned motor transport services. There are daily scheduled air services by Royal Swazi National Airways to Johannesburg and scheduled routes to Durban, Harare, Lusaka, Nairobi and Dar-es-Salaam. International telecommunications and television services are provided through a satellite earth station opened in 1983. There is also a national telephone network through a series of microwave links.

FINANCE

Government revenue for 1984–85 is estimated at E208,780,000, of which E130,410,000 (or 62·4 per cent) is anticipated revenue from the South African Common Customs Union with South Africa, Botswana and Lesotho. Total Government-financed recurrent and capital expenditure in 1984–85 is estimated at E210,840,000.

CURRENCY

Swaziland is a member of the Rand Monetary Union and its unit of currency *Emalangeni* (singular *Lilangeni*) has a par value with the South African Rand.

Trade with U.K.

	1982	1983
Imports from U.K.	£7,654,000	£3,536,000
Exports to U.K.	£40,049,000	£23,966,000

Tanzania
(United Republic of Tanzania)

Tanganyika, the mainland part of the United Republic of Tanzania (Tanganyika and Zanzibar), occupies the east-central portion of the African continent, between 1°–11° 45′ S. lat. and 29° 20′–40° 38′ E. long. It is bounded on the N. by Kenya and Uganda; on the S.W. by Lake Malawi, Malawi and Zambia; on the S. by Mozambique; on the W. it is bounded by Rwanda, Burundi and Zaire; on the E. the boundary is the Indian Ocean. Tanganyika has a coastline of about 500 miles and an area of 362,820 sq. miles (including 20,650 sq. miles of water). The greater part of the country is occupied by the Central African plateau from which rise, among others, Mt. Kilimanjaro, the highest point on the continent of Africa (19,340 ft.) and Mt. Meru (14,974 ft.). The Serengeti National Park, which covers an area of 6,000 sq. miles in the Arusha, Mwanza and Mara Regions, is famous for its variety and number of species of game.

The African population consists mostly of tribes of mixed Bantu race. The total population of Tanzania at the Census held in August, 1978 was 17,551,925; Africans form a very large majority, while the Europeans, the Asians, and other non-Africans form a small minority. Annual average population growth is 3·3 per cent. The population of Zanzibar at the 1978 census was 475,655. Swahili is the national and official language. English is the second official language, both for educational and government purposes.

Zanzibar.—Formerly ruled by the Sultan of Zanzibar, and a British Protectorate until Dec. 10, 1963. Zanzibar consists of the islands of Zanzibar, Pemba and Latham. It has a total area of approximately 1,000 sq. miles. The islands produce a large part of the world's supply of cloves and clove oil, and coconuts, coconut oil and copra are also produced.

Zanzibar became internally self-governing on June 24, 1963, and fully independent on Dec. 10, 1963. The revolutionary Afro-Shirazi party seized power on Jan. 12, 1964, and the Sultan was forced to leave the country. Later Zanzibar united with Tanganyika (*see* below).

CAPITAL.—ΨDar es Salaam (population about 757,346 (mid-1978)). Other towns (1978 population) are ΨTanga (103,409); Mwanza (110,611); Arusha (55,281); Moshi (52,223); Morogoro (61,890); Dodoma (45,703); Tabora (67,392) and Mtwara (48,510). In Zanzibar, the chief town and seaport of that name (population, 110,669) provides facilities for shipping and trade. The principal international airports are Dar es Salaam and Kilimanjaro. Other airports include Zanzibar, Arusha, Mwanza and Tanga.

FLAG.—Green (above) and blue; divided by diagonal black stripe bordered by gold, running from bottom (next staff) to top (in fly).

NATIONAL DAY.—April 26 (Union Day).

GOVERNMENT

Following a constitutional conference held in Dar es Salaam in March, 1961, Tanganyika became an independent state and a member of the British Commonwealth on December 9, 1961.

Tanganyika became a Republic, within the Commonwealth, on December 9, 1962, with an executive President, elected by universal suffrage, who is both the Head of State and Head of the Government. Tanzania is a one-party state. General and Presidential elections have been held every five years since 1965. The President is elected by a national referendum on a simple majority. Two candidates stand in each parliamentary constituency, selected by the ruling party in primary elections. In 1977 the Tanganyika African National Union (TANU) and the Afro-Shirazi party of Zanzibar merged to form the C.C.M. Party.

On April 25, 1964, following a Parliamentary ratification of an agreement signed by the President of the Republic of Tanganyika and the President of the People's Republic of Zanzibar and Pemba, Tanganyika united with Zanzibar to form a new sovereign state. The present Constitution of April 1977 provides that the President should come from one part of the Union and the Vice-President from the other. Zanzibar retains some internal autonomy and has its own Constitution (adopted in 1980) and government for non-Union matters. Zanzibar Ministers and MPs take part in the Union government, which is also responsible for mainland affairs. 111 members of the National Assembly are elected, 10 nominated, 20 *ex officio*, 40 indirectly elected and 64 from Zanzibar (from the Zanzibar Revolutionary Council as chosen by the Zanzibar House of Representatives) and the Vice-President—a total of 246 members. In addition there is a speaker. The C.C.M. (Revolutionary Party) is the supreme organ of the state in policy matters. The National Assembly is the legislature and subordinate to the Party, which is the only one permitted. Currently, further changes to the Constitution are under consideration.

President of the United Republic, Hon. Mwalimu Julius K. Nyerere, *b.* 1922; *elected* Nov. 1962; *took office* Dec. 9, 1962; *re-elected* Sept., 1965, Nov., 1970, Oct., 1975 and Oct. 1980.

Vice-President of the United Republic and President of Zanzibar, Hon. Ali Hassan Mwinyi.

CABINET

Prime Minister, Hon. Salim Ahmed Salim.
Foreign Affairs, Hon. Benjamin Mkapa.
Agriculture and Livestock Development, Hon. John Machunda.
Finance, Hon. Cleopa Msuya.
Industry and Trade, Hon. Basil Mramba.
Defence and National Service, Hon. Brig. M. Kimario.

Communications and Works, Hon. John Malecela.
National Education, Hon. Jackson Makweta.
Lands, National Resources and Tourism, Hon. Paul Bomani.
Home Affairs, Hon. Salmin Amour.
Health, Hon. Dr. A. D. Chiduo.
Information, Hon. D. Mwakawago.
Water, Energy and Minerals, Hon. Al-Noor Kassum.
Justice and Attorney-General, Hon. Joseph Warioba.
Labour and Manpower Development, Hon. Daudi Mwakawago.
Planning and Economic Affairs, Hon. Prof. Kighoma Malima.

TANZANIA HIGH COMMISSION
43 Hertford Street, W1Y 7TF
[01–499 8951]

High Commissioner, His Excellency Anthony B. Nyakyi (1982).

BRITISH HIGH COMMISSION
Hifadhi House, Samora Avenue (P.O. Box 9200), Dar es Salaam.

High Commissioner, His Excellency John A. Sankey, C.M.G. (1982).
British Council Representative, J. Mayatt, Samora Avenue, (P.O. Box 9100), Dar es Salaam.

EDUCATION

Education, almost entirely under state control, is characterised by official insistence that education must serve the aims of overall Government policy and planning. All Tanzanian Secondary Schools are expected to include practical subjects in the basic course. All who receive secondary (or equivalent) education are called up for a period of National Service. The school system is administered in Swahili and the intention is for the national language to become the medium at all levels. For higher education most Tanzanian students go to the University of Dar es Salaam, other East African universities, or to Universities and Colleges outside East Africa, mainly in Britain.

PRODUCTION AND TRADE

The economy is based mainly on the production and export of primary produce and the growing of foodstuffs for local consumption. The chief export crops are coffee, cotton, sisal, cloves, tea, tobacco and cashew nuts. The most important minerals are diamonds. Hides and skins are another valuable export. Industry is at present largely concerned with the processing of raw material for either export or local consumption. There is also a healthy growth of secondary manufacturing industries, including factories for the manufacture of leather and rubber footwear, knitwear, razor blades, cigarettes and textiles, and a wheat flour mill.

Trade with U.K.

	1982	1983
Imports from U.K.	£71,985,000	£62,100,000
Exports to U.K.	19,521,000	46,500,000

Tonga
(Kingdom of Tonga)

Tonga, or the Friendly Islands, comprises a group of islands situated in the Southern Pacific some 450 miles to the E.S.E. of Fiji, with an area of 288 sq. miles, and population (end 1981 estimate) of 98,000. The largest island, Tongatapu, was discovered by Tasman in 1643. Most of the islands are of coral formation, but some are volcanic (Tofua, Kao and Niuafoou or "Tin Can" Island). The limits of the group are between 15° and 23° 30′ S., and 173° and 177° W.

CAPITAL.—Nuku'alofa (21,000).
FLAG.—Truncated red cross on rectangular white ground (next staff) on a red field.

GOVERNMENT

The Kingdom of Tonga is an independent constitutional monarchy within the Commonwealth. Prior to June 4, 1970 it had been a British-protected state for 70 years. The constitution provides for a Government consisting of the Sovereign, a privy council and cabinet, a legislative assembly and a judiciary. The legislative assembly has 28 members, with a Speaker, and includes the Ministers of the Crown, the two Governors of Island groups, and the representatives of the Nobles and of the people (nine of each), who are elected triennially.

Head of State, H.M. King Taufa'ahau Tupou IV, G.C.M.G., G.C.V.O., K.B.E., *acceded* Dec. 16, 1965.
Heir, H.R.H. Crown Prince Tupouto'a.

Prime Minister and Minister of Agriculture, H.R.H. Prince Fatafehi Tu'ipelehake, K.B.E.
Deputy Prime Minister, Minister of Lands, Survey and Natural Resources, Hon. Baron Tuita, C.B.E.
Governor of Vava'u, Hon. Dr. Ma'afu Tupou.
Governor of Ha'apai, Hon. Fakafanua.

FINANCE AND TRADE 1982-83

Revenue	T$16,093,571
Expenditure	*16,005,299
National Debt (1982)	21,632,671
*estimate	

Soil generally is fertile, the principal exports are copra, other coconut products, tropical root crops and bananas.

TRADE

Total imports	T$41,700,000
Total exports	6,500,000

Trade with U.K.

	1982	1983
Imports from U.K.	£764,000	£648,000
Exports to U.K.	38,000	25,000

The unit of currency is the *Pa'anga* (T$), which is close to parity with the Australian dollar.

TONGA HIGH COMMISSION
New Zealand House, Haymarket, SW1Y 4TE
[01–839 3287/8]

High Commissioner, His Excellency Sonatane Tu'a Taumoepeau-Tupou (1983).

BRITISH HIGH COMMISSION
P.O. Box 56, Nuku'alofa

High Commissioner, His Excellency Gerald F. Rance, M.B.E.

Trinidad and Tobago
(The Republic of Trinidad and Tobago)

AREA, ETC.—*Trinidad,* the most southerly of the West Indian Islands, lies close to the north coast of S. America, the nearest point being Venezuela, 7 miles distant. The island is situated between 10° 3′–10° 50′ N. lat. and 60° 55′–61° 56′ W. long., and is about 50 miles in length by 37 miles in width, with an area of 1,864 sq. miles. The island was discovered by Columbus in 1498, was colonized in 1532 by the Spaniards, capitulated to the British under Abercromby in 1797, and was ceded to Britain under the Treaty of Amiens (March 25, 1802). Two mountain systems, the Northern and Southern Ranges, stretch across almost its entire width and a third, the Central Range, lies diagonally across its middle portion; otherwise the island is mostly flat. The highest peaks are in the Northern Range (Aripo 3,085 ft., El Tucuche 3,072 ft.). The climate is tropical with temperatures averaging 82° F. (27·8° C) by day and 74° F. (23·3° C) by night, and a rainfall averaging 82·7 inches a year. There is a well-marked dry season from January to May and wet season from June to December. The nights are invariably cool. The main tourist season is from December to April.
The population (1980) was estimated at 1,016,300 for Trinidad only, and at 1,055,800 for both Trinidad and Tobago.
Tobago lies between 11° 9′ and 11° 21′ N. lat. and between 60° 30′ and 60° 50′ W. long., 19 miles north-east of Trinidad, and 120 miles S.W. of Barbados. It was ceded to the British Crown in 1814 and amalgamated with Trinidad in 1888. The island is 26 miles long, and 7½ wide, and has an area of 116 sq. miles. The population was

39,530 at the 1980 Census. It is one of the healthiest of the West Indies and a popular tourist resort. The main town is ΨScarborough.

Other Islands.—Corozal Point and Icacos Point, the N.W. and S.W. extremities of Trinidad, enclose the Gulf of Paria. West of Corozal Point lie several islands, of which Chacachacare, Huevos, Monos and Gaspar Grande are the most important.

CAPITAL.—Port-of-Spain (population approximately 55,800 in 1980) is the administrative centre of the islands. About 33 miles south of the capital is San Fernando (population approximately 33,490 in 1980), a town of growing importance which is emerging as the industrial centre of Trinidad, and which is in close proximity to a number of large industrial plants.

FLAG.—Black diagonal stripe bordered with white stripes, running from top by staff, all on a red field.

NATIONAL DAYS.—August 31 (Independence Day); September 24th (Republic Day).

GOVERNMENT

The Territory of Trinidad and Tobago became an independent state and a member of the British Commonwealth on August 31, 1962, under the Trinidad and Tobago Independence Act, 1962, and a republic in 1976. The President is elected for 5 years by all members of the Senate and the House of Representatives. The House of Representatives has 36 members elected by universal adult suffrage and the Senate has 31, of whom 16 are appointed on the advice of the Prime Minister, 6 on the advice of the Leader of the Opposition and 9 on the advice of the President. Legislation was passed in Sept. 1980 which afforded Tobago a degree of self-administration.

President, His Excellency Sir Ellis Emmanuel Innocent Clarke, G.C.M.G.

CABINET

Prime Minister and Minister of Finance and Planning, Hon. G. Chambers.

Agriculture, Lands and Food Production, Hon. K. Mohammed.

National Security, Senator Hon. J. S. Donaldson.

Labour, Co-operatives and Social Security, Hon. E. Mahabir.

Health and Environment, Senator Hon. Dr. N. Connell.

Attorney-General and Legal Affairs, Senator Hon. S. R. Martineau.

Education, Hon. O. R. Padmore.

Works, Maintenance and Drainage, Hon. H. Francis.

Public Utilities and National Transportation, Senator Hon. J. Eckstein.

Housing and Resettlement, Senator Hon. W. Mottley.

Energy and Natural Resources, Hon. P. Manning.

Local Government and Community Development, Hon. Dr. C. Joseph.

Industry, Commerce and Consumer Affairs, Hon. D. Cartey.

External Affairs, Senator Hon. Dr. B. Ince.

State Enterprises, Hon. R. J. Williams.

Sport, Culture and Youth Affairs, Hon. Marilyn Gordon.

Information, Senator Hon. Muriel Green.

President of the Senate, Dr. the Hon. W. Ali.
Speaker of the House of Representatives, Hon. M. Ramacharan.

TRINIDAD AND TOBAGO HIGH COMMISSION
42 Belgrave Square, SW1X 8NT
[01–245 9351]

High Commissioner, His Excellency F. O. Abdulah (1983).
Deputy High Commissioner, H. H. Broomes.
Counsellor, Dr. V. Lasse.

BRITISH HIGH COMMISSION
Furness House, 90 Independence Square
(P.O. Box 778) Port of Spain

High Commissioner, His Excellency David Neil Lane, C.M.G. (1980).

EDUCATION

The education system is based on the British model and covers primary and secondary schools and university. The system provides for free education at all state-owned and government-assisted denominational schools and certain faculties at the University of the West Indies. In addition there are various private teaching establishments. Selection to secondary schools is by common entrance examination at 11 years. There are three technical institutes, two teachers' training colleges, and one of the three branches of the University of the West Indies is located in Trinidad, at the St. Augustine campus.

COMMUNICATIONS

There are some 6,435·4 km. of all-weather roads in Trinidad and Tobago. The only general cargo port is Port-of-Spain but there are specialized port facilities elsewhere for landing crude oil, loading refinery products and sugar, and for storing and transmitting bauxite and cement. Regular shipping services call here and many inter-island craft use the port. Another, rapidly growing, port is at Port Lisas where new industries powered by local natural gas are located.

International scheduled airlines, including the national airline, Trinidad and Tobago Airways (BWIA) Corporation, use Piarco International Airport outside Port-of-Spain. The airline also flies between Piarco and Crown Point Airport in Tobago.

Four commercial broadcasting stations and one commercial television station operate in Trinidad and Tobago. There is an internal telephone system and external telephone and telegraph connections.

PRODUCTION

Oil, which is extracted both offshore and onshore, is the main source of the islands' revenue. Production of domestic crude in 1982 was approximately 10·2 million cu. metres, a decline by some 7 per cent from the previous year. The decline in crude petroleum production continued in 1983. The two major oil refineries have a combined capacity of 71,595 cu. metres per day, and refine in the main imported crude, which is subsequently re-exported. With large reserves of natural gas there is emphasis on the development of manufacturing industries, which are energy intensive. An integrated steel plant and an anhydrous ammonia plant have been constructed; a methanol plant started production in 1984; and an aluminium smelter and an LNG plant are planned.

Fertilisers, tyres, clothing, soap, furniture and foodstuffs are manufactured locally while motor vehicles, radios, TV sets, and electro-domestic equipment are assembled from parts, mainly from Japan.

FINANCE

	1981	1982*
Revenue	TT$7,007·8m	TT$7,887·8m
Expenditure	7,392·4m	9,311·7m
Gross public debt	1,961·3m	2,098·0m

*estimate

	1982
Imports	TT$8,813,·1m
Exports	7,372·4m

The petroleum sector accounted for 88·3 per cent of total exports; other main export commodities were chemicals and machinery. The petroleum sector accounted for 22·2 per cent of total imports.

	1982	1983
Imports from U.K.	£158,436,000	£148,811,000
Exports to U.K........	65,154,000	52,748,000

Tuvalu

Tuvalu, formerly the Ellice islands, formed part of the Gilbert and Ellice Islands Colony until October 1, 1975. Separation from the Gilbert Islands took place on January 1, 1976.

Tuvalu comprises nine coral atolls situated in the South West Pacific around the point at which the International Date Line cuts the Equator. The total land area is only about 10 square miles. Few of the atolls are more than 12 feet above sea level or more than half a mile in width. The vegetation consists mainly of coconut palms. The resident population according to the 1979 Census was 7,349, but it is estimated that about 1,500 Tuvaluans work overseas, mostly in Nauru, or as seamen. The entire population is Christian and is predominantly Protestant. The principal languages are Tuvaluan and English.

CAPITAL.—Funafuti. Estimated population 2,120. The capital has a grass strip airfield from which a service operates regularly to Fiji and Kiribati, and is also the only port.

FLAG.—Blue ground with Union Jack in top left quarter and nine five-pointed gold stars in the fly.

GOVERNMENT

On October 1, 1978, Tuvalu became fully independent as a sovereign state within the Commonwealth. The Constitution provides for a Prime Minister and four other Ministers who must be members of the 12-member elected Parliament. The Prime Minister presides at meetings of the Cabinet, which consists of the five Ministers, and is attended by the Attorney General. Local Government services are provided by elected Island Councils.

Governor-General, His Excellency Sir Fiatau Penitala Teo, G.C.M.G., G.C.V.O., M.B.E., I.S.O.

CABINET

Prime Minister, Rt. Hon. Dr. Tomasi Puapua.
Deputy Prime Minister and Minister for Finance, Hon. Henry Naisali, C.M.G., C.B.E.
Commerce and Natural Resources, Hon. Lale Seluka.
Works and Communications, Hon. Metia Tealofi.
Social Services, Hon. Falaile Pilitai.

Attorney-General, Hon. Beith Atkinson

ECONOMY

Most people still practise a subsistence economy, the main staples of their diet being coconuts and fish. The main imports (valued at A$2,890,937 in 1982) are foodstuffs, consumer goods and building materials. The only export is copra (180,000 kilos valued at A$26,671 in 1982), but philatelic sales provide a major source of revenue. The unit of currency is the Australian dollar.

EDUCATION AND WELFARE

There are eight primary schools in Tuvalu and a church secondary school run jointly with the Government. The total of enrolled children of school age in 1980 was 1,573. A Maritime Training School started in 1979.

There is a 31-bed hospital at Funafuti. All islands are served by a dispensary and a primary school.

Uganda
(Republic of Uganda)

Situated in Eastern Africa, Uganda is flanked by Zaire, the Sudan, Kenya and on the south by Tanzania and Rwanda. Large parts of Lakes Victoria, Edward and Albert (Mobutu) are within its boundaries, as are Lakes Kyoga, Kwania, George and Bisina (formerly Salisbury) and the course of the River Nile from its outlet from Lake Victoria to the Sudan frontier post at Nimule. Despite its tropical location, Uganda's climate is tempered by its situation some 3,000 ft. above sea level, and well over that altitude in the highlands of the Western and Eastern Regions. In South Uganda, temperatures seldom rise above 85° F. (29° C.) or fall below 60° F. (15° C.). The rainfall averages about 50 inches a year which means that the country is covered in a lush green cloak for most of the year. Uganda has three National Parks with a wide variety of wildlife and flora, and a fourth (Lake Mburo) has been designated.

AREA AND POPULATION.—Uganda has an area of 91,000 sq. miles (water and swamp 16,400 sq. miles) and population (estimated, 1980) of 12,600,000. The official language of Uganda is English. The main local vernaculars are of Bantu, Luo and Hamitic origins. Ki-Swahili is generally understood in trading centres.

CAPITAL.—Kampala (population of Greater Kampala, 400,000).

FLAG.—Six horizontal stripes of black, yellow and red (repeated) with a crested crane emblem on a white orb in the centre.

NATIONAL DAY.—October 9 (Independence Day).

GOVERNMENT

Uganda became an independent state and a member of the Commonwealth on October 9, 1962, after some 70 years of British rule. A Republic was instituted on September 8, 1967, under an executive President, assisted by a Cabinet of Ministers.

Early in 1971, while the President was abroad, the Uganda Army, with the co-operation of the police forces, assumed control of the country. All political activity in Uganda was suspended and Maj.-Gen. Idi Amin, the Army Commander, proclaimed himself Head of State, later suspending those sections of the constitution dealing with executive and legislative powers, and subsequently ruling by decree. In 1979, following on risings and military intervention by Tanzania, President Amin was overthrown. Dr Yusof Lule became President in April, but in June was succeeded by Mr. Godfrey Binaisa. Mr. Binaisa was in turn replaced by the Military Commission of the Uganda National Liberation Front, which governed the country until elections were held in December 1980.

President and Minister for Foreign Affairs and Finance, Dr. A. Milton Obote, *elected* Dec. 1980.
Vice-President and Minister of Defence, Paulo Muwanga.
Prime Minister, Otema Allimadi.

UGANDA HIGH COMMISSION
Uganda House, 58–59 Trafalgar Square, WC2N 5DX
[01–839 5783]

High Commissioner, His Excellency Shafiq Arain.

BRITISH HIGH COMMISSION
10/12 Obote Avenue, P.O. Box 7070, Kampala

High Commissioner, His Excellency Colin McLean, C.M.G. M.B.E. (1983).
British Council Representative, K. F. Burd.

EDUCATION

Education is a joint undertaking by the Govern-ment, local authorities and, to some extent, voluntary agencies. In 1981 Uganda had 4,276 primary schools with an enrolment of 1,421,615 children. Secondary schools numbered 199 with 78,727 students enrolled; and 4,979 students in various technical training institutions.

The National University is Makerere University, Kampala, founded as a trade school in 1921 and becoming an independent University in 1970.

COMMUNICATIONS

There is an international airport at Entebbe, with direct flights to destinations in Africa, Asia and Europe. There are 8 other state airports and airfields in Uganda. Having no sea coast, Uganda is heavily dependent upon rail and road links to Mombasa for her trade. There are 2,226 kilometres of bituminized and 25,310 kilometres of gravel roads. The state of the roads at present is very poor. A railway network joins the capital to the western, eastern and northern centres. National Corporations have been estab-lished to provide rail and air services.

TRADE, ETC.

The principal export earner is coffee but attempts are being made to increase production of cotton and tea for export. Hydro-electricity is produced from the Owen Falls power station which has a capacity of 150 MW and about 30 MW is exported to Kenya. The principal food crops are plantains, bananas, cassava, sweet potatoes, potatoes and sorghum.

Trade with U.K.

	1982	1983
Imports from U.K.	£31,272,000	£21,092,000
Exports to U.K.	23,107,000	29,645,000

Vanuatu
(Republic of Vanuatu)

The former Condominium of the New Hebrides became an independent republic and a member of the Commonwealth under the name of Vanuatu on July 30, 1980. The *Vanuatu* Group, in the South Pacific Ocean, is situated between 13° and 21° S. and 166° and 170° E. It includes 13 large and some 70 small islands, of coral and volcanic origin, including the Banks and Torres Islands in the North, and has a total land area of about 6,050 square miles. The principal islands are Vanua Lava and Gaua (Banks), Espiritu Santo, Maewo, Pentecost, Aoba, Malekula, Ambrym, Epi, Efate, Erromango, Tanna and Aneityum. Most islands are mountainous and there are active volcanoes on several. The climate is oceanic tropical, moderated by the south-east trade winds which blow between May and October. At other times winds are variable and cyclones may occur. Temperatures range between 62° F. and 83° F, with annual rainfall averaging 90 in. in the south and 155 in. in the north.

The 1979 Census showed a population of 112,596. The national language is Bislama (Pidgin), but English and French are also official languages.

Seat of Administration—ΨVila, Efate, population (1979), 14,801.

President, His Excellency Ati George Sokomanu, M.B.E., *elected* 1980, *re-elected* 1984.

COUNCIL OF MINISTERS

Prime Minister, Hon. Father Walter Lini, C.B.E.
Deputy P.M. and Minister for Home Affairs, Hon. S. J. Regenvanu.
Finance, Commerce, Industry and Tourism, Hon. K. Kalsakau.
Lands, Energy and Water Supply, Hon. D. Kalpokas.
Foreign Affairs and External Trade, Hon. S. Molisa.
Education, Youth and Sports, Hon. O. Tahi.

Transport, Communications and Public Works, Hon. A. Sande.
Health, Hon. W. Korisa.
Agriculture, Fisheries and Forestry, Hon. J. Hopa.

Chief Justice, Hon. Mr. Justice F. G. Cooke.
Attorney-General, S. Hakwa.

BRITISH HIGH COMMISSION
Melitco House, Rue Pasteur, Vila.

High Commissioner, His Excellency Richard B. Dorman, C.B.E. (1982)

ECONOMY

Most of the population is employed on plantations or in subsistence agriculture. Subsistence crops include yams, toro, manioc, sweet potato and breadfruit; principal cash crops are copra, cocoa and coffee. Large numbers of cattle are kept on the plantations and an export trade in meat is being developed. On the island of Santo a plant freezes tuna and bonito for export.

Principal exports are copra, meat (frozen, tinned and chilled), fish and cocoa.

Tourism is an increasingly important revenue earner, and the absence of direct taxation has led to some growth in the finance and associated industries.

The unit of currency is the *Vatu*.

Western Samoa

Western Samoa consists of the islands of Savai'i (662 sq. miles) and of Upolu, which, with seven other islands, has an area of 435 sq. miles. All islands are mountainous. Upolu, the most fertile, contains the harbours of Ψ Apia and ΨSaluafata and Savai'i the harbour of ΨAsau. The islanders are Christians of different denominations. The population at the 1981 census was 158,130, the largest numbers being on Upolu (114,980) and Savai'i (43,150). The main languages spoken are Samoan and English.

CAPITAL.—ΨApia, on Upolu (population 33,100). Robert Louis Stevenson died and was buried at Apia in 1894.

FLAG.—Five white stars (depicting the Southern Cross) on a quarter royal blue at top next staff, and three quarters red.

GOVERNMENT

Formerly administered by New Zealand (latterly with internal self-government), Western Samoa became, on January 1, 1962, the first fully-independent Polynesian State.The State was treated as a member country of the Commonwealth until its formal admission on August 28, 1970.

The 1962 Constitution provides for a Head of State to be elected by the Legislative Assembly for a five year term. However, it was decided that initially two of the four Paramount chiefs should jointly hold the office of Head of State for life. When one of the chiefs died in April 1963, Malietoa Tanumafili II became the holder of the office of Head of State for life. The Head of State's functions are analogous to those of a constitutional monarch. Executive government is carried out by a Cabinet of Ministers.

Head of State, H. H. Malietoa Tanumafili II, G.C.M.G., C.B.E. (April 15, 1963).

Prime Minister, Minister of Internal Affairs, Foreign Affairs, Legislative, Police and Prisons, Attorney-General and Immigration, Hon. Tofilau Eti.

ECONOMY

Agriculture is the basis of Western Samoa's economy, the principal cash crops (and exports) being coconuts (copra), cocoa and bananas. Other agricultural exports include coffee, timber, tropical fruits and seeds. Efforts are being made to develop fishing on a commercial scale. Manufacturing is very small in scope and concerned largely with processing agricultural products, but is being encouraged by the Government. Tourism is increasing rapidly.

The unit of currency is the *tala* (WS $).

Trade with U.K.

	1982	1983
Imports from U.K.	£285,000	£468,000
Exports to U.K.	107,000	156,000

BRITISH HIGH COMMISSION (*see* New Zealand)

Zambia
(Republic of Zambia)

The Republic of Zambia lies on the plateau of Central Africa between the longitudes 22° E. and 33° 33′ E. and between the latitudes 8° 15′ S. and 18° S. It has an area of 290,587 square miles within boundaries 3,515 miles in length and a population (mid-year estimate, 1982) of 6,050,000, including about 50,000 non-Africans.

With the exception of the valleys of the Zambesi, the Luapula, the Kafue and the Luangwa Rivers, and the Luano valley, elevations vary from 3,000 to 5,000 feet above sea level, but in the north-eastern districts the plateau rises to occasional altitudes of over 6,000 feet. In many localities the evenness of the plateau is broken by hills, sometimes occurring as chains which develop into areas of broken country.

Although Zambia lies within the tropics, and fairly centrally in the great land mass of the African continent its elevation relieves it from the extremely high temperatures and humidity usually associated with tropical countries. The lower reaches of the Zambesi, Luangwa and Kaufe rivers in deeper valleys do experience high humidity and extremes of heat.

CAPITAL.—Lusaka, situated in the Central Province. Population (estimated, 1980), 641,000. Other centres are Livingstone, Kabwe, Chipata, Mazabuka, Mbala, Kasama, Solwezi, Mongu, Mansa, Ndola, Luanshya, Mufulira, Chingola, Chililabombwe, Kalulushi and Kitwe, the last six towns being the main centres on the Copperbelt.

FLAG.—Green with three small vertical stripes, red, black and orange (next fly); eagle device on green above stripes.

GOVERNMENT

At the dissolution of the Federation of Rhodesia and Nyasaland, on December 31, 1963, Northern Rhodesia (as Zambia was then known) achieved internal self-government under a new constitution. Zambia became an independent republic within the Commonwealth on October 24, 1964—75 years after coming under British rule and nine months after achieving internal self-government.

In July 1973, a new Constitution was introduced, making the United National Independence Party (U.N.I.P.) the only party.

President, Dr. Kenneth David Kaunda, *assumed office* Oct. 24, 1964; *re-elected*, Dec. 1973, Dec. 1978 and Oct. 1983.

CABINET

Prime Minister, Nalumino Mundia.
Defence, Clement Mwananshiku.
Foreign Affairs, Prof. Lameck Goma.
Finance, Luke Mwananshiku.
Legal Affairs (Attorney-General), Gibson Chigaga.
Higher Education, Rajah Kunda.
General Education and Culture, Kebby Musokotwane.
Health, Mark Tambatamba, M.P.
Commerce and Industry, I. Subulwa
Home Affairs, Frederick Chomba.
Mines, Basil Kabwe.
Agriculture and Water Development, Gen. Kingsley Chinkuli.
Power, Transport and Communications, Fitzpatrick Chuula.
Works and Supply, Haswell Mwale.
Labour and Social Services, Frederick Hapunda.
Tourism, Roger Sakuhuka.
Information and Broadcasting Services, Cosmos Chibanda.
Youth and Sports, Ben Kakoma.
Lands and Natural Resources, Fabiano Chelah.
National Guidance, Arnold Simuchimba.
Co-operatives, Justin Mukando.
National Commission for Development Planning, Dr. Henry Meebelo.

ZAMBIA HIGH COMMISSION
2 Palace Gate, W8 5LS
[01–589 6655]

High Commissioner, His Excellency Peter D. Zuze.

BRITISH HIGH COMMISSION
Independence Avenue (P.O. Box 50050), Lusaka

High Commissioner, His Excellency William Kelvin Kennedy White, C.M.G. (1984).
British Council Representative, R. B. Timms, Heroes Place, (P.O. Box 34571), Lusaka.

JUDICATURE

There is a Chief Justice appointed by the President, all other judges being appointed on the recommendation of the Judicial Service Commission consisting of the Chief Justice, the chairman of the Public Service Commission, a senior Justice of Appeal and one Presidential nominee.

PRODUCTION

Principal products are maize, sugar, groundnuts, cotton, livestock, vegetables and tobacco.

Mineral production was valued at K861,300 in 1982. The production of copper in 1983–84 totalled 550,000 tonnes.

FINANCE AND TRADE

The unit of currency is the *Kwacha*.

Gross Domestic Product (current prices) was K3,563·7m in 1982 and K4,205·6m in 1983. G.D.P. per capita (current prices) was K589 in 1982 and K674 in 1983.

	1982	1983 (provisional)
Imports	K909m	K870m
Exports	960·4m	1,060m

Trade with U.K.

	1983
Imports from U.K.	K55,501,000
Exports to U.K.	50,242,000

Zimbabwe
(Republic of Zimbabwe)

Zimbabwe, the former Southern Rhodesia (named after Cecil Rhodes) comprising eight provinces (Manicaland, Masvingo, Matabeleland North, Matabeleland South, Midlands, Mashonaland West, Central and East), lies south of the Zambesi river. The political neighbours are Zambia and Mozambique on the N.: South Africa and Botswana on the S. and W., and Mozambique on the E. It has a total area of 150,820 square miles and a population (estimated 1982) of 7,539,000 (Africans over 7 million; Europeans, Asians and coloured, approximately 250,000). The population is increasing at around 3·5 per cent. annually.

CAPITAL.—Harare (Salisbury) situated on the Mashonaland plateau, altitude 4,850 ft., estimated population (August 1982) 656,000. Bulawayo—the largest town in Matabeleland, altitude 4,450 ft., estimated population (August 1982) 413,800. Other centres are Mutare, Gweru, Kadoma, Kwe Kwe, Masvingo and Hwange.

Harare is 5,600 miles from London (air route), transit 12 hours; by sea via Cape Town, 17 days (approx.).

FLAG.—Seven horizontal stripes (green, gold, red, black, red, gold, green) with white triangle at the hoist containing the Zimbabwe bird superimposed on red five-point star.

GOVERNMENT

Southern Rhodesia was granted responsible government in 1923. An illegal declaration of independence on November 11, 1965 was finally terminated on December 12, 1979. Following elections in February 1980 the country obtained independence on April 18, 1980 as the Republic of Zimbabwe, a member of the British Commonwealth. The Parliament consists of a House of Assembly of 100 members and a Senate of 40 Senators and has a maximum life of five years. The President is elected by the Members of Parliament and holds office for a period of six years.

Legislation has reformed the system of local government and established district councils for rural areas.

President, Rev. The Hon. Canaan Banana, *elected* April, 11 1980.

MINISTRY

Prime Minister and Minister of Defence, Hon. Robert G. Mugabe.

Deputy Prime Minister, S. V. Muzenda.
Labour, Manpower Planning and Social Welfare, F. Shava.
Home Affairs, Simbi Mubako.
Youth, Sport and Culture, Simba Makoni.
Information, Posts & Telecommunications, N. Shamuyarira.
Mines, C. Ndlovu.
Community Development and Women's Affairs, Mrs. T. R. Nhongo.
Finance, Economic Planning and Development, B. Chidzero.
Lands, Resettlement and Rural Development, M. Mahachi.
Trade and Commerce, R. Hove.
Agriculture, Sen. D. Norman.
Education and Culture, D. Mutumbuka.
Natural Resources & Tourism, Mrs. V. Chitepo.
Foreign Affairs, W. Mangwende.
Transport, H. Ushewokunze.
Local Government and Town Planning, E. Chikowore.
National Supplies, Sen. E. Nkala.
Construction and National Housing, S. Mumbengegwi.
Justice, Legal and Parliamentary Affairs, E. Zvobgo.
Health, S. Sekeramayi.
Without Portfolio, Sen. F. Masango; D. Ngwenya.

ZIMBABWE HIGH COMMISSION
Zimbabwe House, Strand, WC2R 0SA
[01-836 7755]

High Commissioner, His Excellency Dr. M. Murerwa.

BRITISH HIGH COMMISSION
Stanley House, Stanley Avenue,
(PO Box 4490), Harare

High Commissioner, His Excellency Martin Kenneth Ewans, C.M.G.
British Council Representative, C. W. Perchard, O.B.E,
23 Stanley Avenue, (P.O. Box 664), Harare.

EDUCATION

Since independence, a policy of free primary education has resulted in rapidly expanding enrolment. In 1984, an estimated 2,897,890 children were enrolled in Government and Government aid schools. Although about 80 per cent of schools are private, many receive grants and all teaching staff are paid by the Government.

ECONOMY

Agriculture is the chief source of income for more than 75 per cent of the population, and the source of more than one third of the country's earnings. Major crops are maize, wheat, cotton, tobacco and sugar, with diversification occurring significantly in livestock; Zimbabwe's beef herds and daily herds have been badly affected by three years of drought.

Although mining accounts for only 5 per cent of the Gross National Product and employs only 6 per cent of the labour force, it plays an important role in the economy as almost 90 per cent of output is exported, accounting for 42 per cent of all exports in 1982. Direct mineral exports, including gold, in 1982 were valued at about Z$345 million. The most important minerals are gold and silver (accounting for nearly 40 per cent of total output in 1982), asbestos, nickel, copper, coal, chrome ore, tin, iron ore and cobalt.

Manufacturing industries contributed more than 25 per cent of the Gross National Product in 1982, employing about 16 per cent of the labour force. Principal products in the light industry sector are foodstuffs, drink and tobacco, textiles, clothing and footwear, wood and furniture, and paper, printing and publishing. Heavy industry includes chemical and petroleum products, non-metallic mineral products, metal and metal products, and transport equipment. Growth in this sector, however, continues to be inhibited by the current shortage of foreign exchange for raw materials.

FINANCE AND TRADE

	1981–82	1982-83
Revenue	$1,361,867,000	$1,789,000
Expenditure	1,570,372,000	2,012,000

Trade with U.K.

	1982	1983
Imports from U.K.	£95,019,000	£64,746,000
Exports to U.K.	£62,584,000	£68,449,000

Dependent Territories, etc.

ANGUILLA

Anguilla is a flat coralline island, about 16 miles in length, 3¼ miles in breadth at its widest point and its area is about 35 sq. miles. It lies approximately 18° N. latitude and 63° W longitude, to the north of the Leeward Islands group.

The island is covered with low scrub and fringed with some of the finest white coral-sand beaches in the Caribbean. The climate is pleasant and healthy with temperatures in the range of 75-85°F. throughout the year. The population is about 7,000.

CAPITAL.—The Valley (population 50).

GOVERNMENT

Anguilla has been a British colony since 1650. For most of its history it has been linked administratively with St. Kitts, but three months after the Associated State of Saint Christopher (St. Kitts)-Nevis-Anguilla came into being in 1967 the Anguillans repudiated government from St. Kitts. A Commissioner was installed in 1969 and in 1976 Anguilla was given a new status and separate constitution. Final separation from St. Kitts-Nevis was effected on Dec. 19, 1980 and Anguilla reverted to a British Dependency. A new Constitution was introduced in 1982, providing for a Governor, an Executive Council comprising the Governor, four elected Ministers and two *ex-officio* members (Attorney General and Permanent Secretary, Finance), and an 11-member legislative House of Assembly presided over by a Speaker.

Governor, His Excellency Alastair Turner Baillie (1983).

EXECUTIVE COUNCIL
President, The Governor.
Chief Minister and Minister of Labour, Communications and Agriculture, Hon. Emile Gumbs.
Works, Public Utilities and Health, Hon. Eric Reid.

Education, Tourism and Development, Hon. Mrs. Albena Lake-Hodge.
Finance and Lands, Hon. Hubert Hughes.
Attorney-General, A. Hoole.
Permanent Secretary (Finance), F. Connor.

ECONOMY

Low rainfall limits agricultural output and export earnings are mainly from sales of lobsters and salt. Tourism is being developed. The unit of currency is the East Caribbean dollar (*EC$*)

FINANCE 1983

Government revenue	*EC*$11,061,000
Government expenditure	11,776,000
Grant-in-aid	715,000

ASCENSION
See ST. HELENA

BERMUDA

The Bermudas, or Somers Islands, are a cluster of about 100 small islands (about 20 only of which are inhabited) situated in the west of the Atlantic Ocean, in 32° 18′ N. lat. and 64° 46′ W. long., the nearest point of the mainland being Cape Hatteras in North Carolina, about 570 miles distant. The colony derives its name from Juan Bermudez, a Spaniard, who sighted it before 1515, but no settlement was made until 1609, when Sir George Somers, who was shipwrecked here on his way to Virginia, colonized the islands.

The total area is approximately 20·59 sq. miles which includes 2·3 sq. miles leased to the U.S.A. The civil population was 57,237 at the 1980 Census.
CAPITAL.—Hamilton (population, 1980, 1,617).

GOVERNMENT

Internal self-government was introduced on June 8, 1968. There are a Senate of 11 Members and an elected House of Assembly of 40 Members. The Governor retains responsibility for external affairs, defence, internal security and the police, although administrative matters for the Police Service have been delegated to the Minister of Home Affairs.

Governor and Commander-in-Chief, His Excellency The Viscount Dunrossil, C.M.G. (1983).
Deputy Governor, M. Herdman.

CABINET

Premier, Hon. J. W. Swan.
Deputy Premier and Minister of Finance, Dr. Hon. C. James.
Tourism, Hon. C. V. Woolridge.
Education, Dr. Hon. G. Thomas.
Works, Housing, Agriculture and Fisheries, Hon. Q. L. Edness.
Industry and Technology, Dr. Hon. J. D. Stubbs.
Health and Social Services, Sen. Hon. C. T. M. Collis.
Transport, Hon. S. D. W. McPhee.
Planning and the Environment, Hon. T. E. Davis.
Home Affairs, Hon. Sir John Sharpe.
Community and Cultural Affairs, Sen. Hon. G. Simons.
Youth, Sport and Recreation, Hon. J. I. Pearman.

President of the Legislative Council, Hon. H. Richardson, C.B.E.
Speaker of the House of Assembly, Hon. F. J. Barritt.

Chief Justice, Hon. Sir James R. Astwood, C.B.E.
Puisne Judges, Hon. G. Collett, C.B.E., Q.C.; Hon. J. Melville.

ECONOMY

Locally manufactured concentrates and pharmaceuticals are now the colony's leading exports. Little food is produced except vegetables and fish, other foodstuffs being imported.

The Islands' economic structure is based on tourism, which continues to be the major industry and source of revenue. In 1983 a total of 567,640 visitors arrived in Bermuda. Cruise ships dock at Hamilton and St. George.

Free elementary education was introduced in May, 1949. Free secondary education was introduced in 1965 for those children in the aided and maintained schools who were below the upper limit of the statutory school age of 16 (from 1969 onwards).

There are 5 radio and 2 television stations, one daily and 2 weekly newspapers and overseas telephone and telegraph services are maintained.

FINANCE

	1983–84	1984–85
Public revenue	$165,498,190	$186,553,800
Public expenditure	165,466,440	169,299,755
Public debt (March 31) .	(Nil)	(Nil)

Currency.—The unit of currency is the Bermudan dollar (*Bd* $).

Trade with U.K.

	1982	1983
Imports from U.K.	£18,222,000	£24,924,000
Exports to U.K.	5,128,000	4,019,000

THE BRITISH ANTARCTIC TERRITORY

The British Antarctic Territory was designated in 1962 and consists of the areas south of 60°S. latitude which were previously included in the Falkland Islands Dependencies. The territory lies between longitudes 20° and 80°W., south of latitude 60°S. and includes the South Orkney Islands, the South Shetland Islands, the mountainous Antarctic Peninsula (highest point *Mount Jackson,* 13,620ft, in Palmer Land) and all adjacent islands, and the land mass extending to the South Pole. The territory has no indigenous inhabitants and the British population consists of the scientists and technicians who man the British Antarctic Survey stations. The number averages about 60 to 70 in winter, but increases considerably in the summer months with the arrival of field workers; Argentina, Brazil, Chile, Poland, U.S.A., U.S.S.R. and West Germany also have scientific stations in the territory.

The first two British Antarctic Survey stations were established in the South Shetland Islands in 1944, and by 1956 the number of stations had risen to twelve. Due to the completion of field work in some areas and increased mobility, the number has now been reduced to five. These are Signy (Signy Island, S. Orkney Islands), Faraday (Argentine Islands, Graham Coast), Rothera (Adelaide Island), Halley (Caird Coast) and, in summer only, Fossil Bluff (George VI Sound). Fifteen other stations have been established but are at present unoccupied.

The territory is administered by a High Commissioner, resident in the Falkland Islands.

High Commissioner, Sir Rex Hunt, C.M.G. (1980).
(*see index also for* The Antarctic)

778 BRI *Dependent Territories, etc.* CAY [1985

THE BRITISH INDIAN OCEAN TERRITORY

The British Indian Ocean Territory was established by an Order in Council in 1965 and included islands formerly administered by Mauritius and the Seychelles. After the independence of both, the territory was redefined in 1976 as comprising only the islands of the Chagos Archipelago.

The Chagos Archipelago consists of six main groups of islands situated on the Great Chagos Bank and covering some 21,000 square miles. The largest and most southerly of the Chagos Islands is *Diego Garcia*, a sand cay with a land area of about 17 square miles approximately 1,100 miles east of Mahe, used as a joint naval support base by Britain and U.S.A.

The other main island groups of the archipelago, *Peros Banhos* (29 islands with a total land area of 4 square miles) and *Salomon* (11 islands with a total land area of 2 square miles) are uninhabited. The islands have a typical tropical maritime climate, with average temperatures between 77°F and 84°F in Diego Garcia, and rainfall in the whole archipelago of 90–100 inches a year.

Commissioner, W. N. Wenban-Smith.
Administrator, D. H. Doble.

THE BRITISH VIRGIN ISLANDS

The Virgin Islands are a group of islands at the eastern extremity of the Greater Antilles, divided between Great Britain and the U.S.A. Those of the group which are British number 36, of which 11 are uninhabited, and have a total area of about 59 square miles. The principal are Tortola, the largest (situate in 18° 27′ N. lat. and 64° 40′ W. long., area, 21 sq. miles), Virgin Gorda (8¼ sq. miles), Anegada (15 sq. miles) and Jost Van Dyke (3½ sq. miles). The 1980 Census of Population showed a total population of 12,034 (Tortola (9,322); Virgin Gorda (1,443); Anegada (169); Jost Van Dyke (136); and other islands (82). Apart from Anegada, which is a flat coral island, the British Virgin Islands are hilly, being an extension of the Puerto Rico and the U.S. Virgin Islands archipelago. The highest point is Sage Mountain on Tortola which rises to a height of 1,780 feet. Tourism is the main industry, but there is some cattle raising and fishing. Other products are vegetables, fruit, charcoal and rum.

The islands lie within the Trade Winds belt and possess a pleasant and healthy sub-tropical climate. The average temperature varies from 71°–82° F. in winter and 78°–88° F. in summer. The summer heat is tempered by sea breezes and the temperature usually falls by about 10° at night. Average rainfall is 53 inches. Hurricanes are very rare—the last occurrence being in 1928.

CAPITAL.—ΨRoad Town, on the south-east of Tortola. Population, 2,479.

GOVERNMENT

Under the 1977 Constitution, the Governor, appointed by the Crown, remains responsible for defence and internal security, external affairs and the civil service but in other matters acts in accordance with the advice of the Executive Council. The Executive Council consists of the Governor as Chairman, one *ex officio* member (the Attorney-General), the Chief Minister and three other ministers. The Legislative Council consists of a Speaker chosen from outside the Council, one *ex officio* member (the Attorney-General), and nine elected members returned from nine one-member electoral districts.

Governor, His Excellency David R. Barwick, C.B.E., Q.C.
Deputy Governor, E. Georges.
Financial Secretary, K. Bain, O.B.E.

THE EXECUTIVE COUNCIL

Chairman, The Governor.
Chief Minister and Minister of Finance, Hon. C. B. Romney.
Deputy Chief Minister and Minister for Health, Education and Welfare, Hon. W. Wheatley, M.B.E.
Communications and Works, Hon. E. W. Brewley.
Natural Resources and Labour, Hon. C. Maduro.
Attorney-General, Hon. L. S. Hunte.

Puisne Judge (resident), Hon. Miss M. Joseph.

FINANCE

	1981	1982 (estimated)
Revenue	$U.S. 14,462,599	$U.S. 14,750,000
Expenditure	14,211,871	13,035,615

ECONOMY

Tourism is the main industry but other industries include a rum distillery, three stone-crushing plants and factories manufacturing concrete blocks and paint. The major export items are fresh fish, gravel, sand, fruits and vegetables: exports are largely confined to the U.S. Virgin Islands. Chief imports are building materials, machinery, cars and beverages.

COMMUNICATIONS

The principal airport is on Beef Island, linked by bridge to Tortola, and an extended runway of 3,600 feet enables larger aircraft to call. There is a second airfield on Virgin Gorda and a third on Anegada. There are direct shipping services to the United Kingdom and the United States and fast passenger services connect the main islands by ferry.

THE CAYMAN ISLANDS

The Cayman Islands, between 79° 44′ and 81° 26′ W. and 19° 15′ and 19° 46′ N., consist of three islands, Grand Cayman, Cayman Brac, and Little Cayman, with a total area of 100 square miles. Population (1983), 18,750.

CAPITAL.—ΨGeorge Town, in Grand Cayman, population (1981) 8,200.

GOVERNMENT

The constitution provides for a Governor, Legislative Assembly and an Executive Council. The Legislative Assembly consists of the Governor, three official members and 12 elected members. The Governor presides over the Executive Council, which consists of three official members appointed by the Governor, and four elected members, chosen by the elected members of the Assembly from among their own number. The normal life of the Assembly is four years.

Governor, His Excellency George Peter Lloyd, C.V.O., C.M.G.

EXECUTIVE COUNCIL

President, The Governor.
Chief Secretary, Hon. D. H. Foster, C.V.O., C.B.E.
Financial Secretary, Hon. T. C. Jefferson.
Attorney-General, Hon. M. J. Bradley.
Member for Health, Education and Social Services, Hon. T. M. Bodden.

Member for Communications and Works, Hon. G. H. Bodden.
Member for Tourism, Aviation and Trade, Hon. J. M. Bodden.
Member for Agriculture, Lands and Natural Resources, Hon. J. McLean.

FINANCE

	1982	1983
Revenue	CI\$47,920,000	CI\$49,692,616
Expenditure	45,967,000	39,355,604
Public Debt	8,500,000	9,090,000

TRADE

	1981	1982 (estimated)
Total imports	CI\$109,000,000	CI\$110,000,000
Total exports	3,000,000	2,000,000

FALKLAND ISLANDS

The Falkland Islands, the only considerable group in the South Atlantic, lie about 300 miles east of the Straits of Magellan, between 52° 15'–53° S. lat. and 57° 40'–62° W. long. They consist of East Falkland (area 2,610 sq. miles), West Falkland (2,090 sq. miles) and upwards of 100 small islands in the aggregate. Mount Usborne (E. Falkland), the loftiest peak, rises 2,312 feet above the level of the sea.

The climate is cool. At Stanley the mean monthly temperature varies between 49° F. in January and 35·5° F. in July. The air temperature has never been known to exceed 77° F. or to fall below 12° F.; it is notably windy. The islands are chiefly moorland.

The Falklands were sighted first by Davis in 1592, and by Hawkins in 1594: the first known landing was by Strong in 1690. A settlement was made by France in 1764; this was subsequently sold to Spain, but the latter country recognized Great Britain's title to a part at least of the group in 1771. The settlement was destroyed by the Americans in 1831. In 1833 occupation was resumed by the British for the protection of the seal-fisheries, and the islands were permanently colonized as the most southerly organized colony of the British Empire. Argentina has long claimed sovereignty over the Islands (known to them as las Islas Malvinas), and in pursuance of this claim invaded the Islands on April 2, 1982 and also occupied South Georgia. A Task Force despatched from Great Britain recaptured South Georgia on April 25, and after landing at San Carlos Bay on May 21, recaptured the Islands from the Argentines, who surrendered on June 14, 1982. A large British naval and military presence remains in the area.

The population of 1,813 (at Census of Dec. 5, 1980) is almost totally British, and is principally engaged in sheep-farming to which practically all the land in the colony is devoted, 663,367 sheep being carried in 1979–80. Wool, hides and skins are exported. Main imports are foodstuffs, manufactured goods, timber and machinery.

CHIEF TOWN.—ΨStanley, population 1,050 (1980). The size of the British garrison is about 4,000. Stanley is distant from England about 8,103 miles.

GOVERNMENT

The Civil Commissioner is advised by an Executive Council, over which he presides, composed of the Chief Executive, the Financial Secretary, two nominated members, and two elected members, elected by and from the elected members of the Legislative Council. The Legislative Council is composed of two *ex officio* members, namely, the Chief Executive and the Financial Secretary, and six representatives elected by the people, with the Civil Commissioner as President.

Civil Commissioner, Sir Rex Hunt, C.M.G.
Military Commissioner and Commander, British Forces, Falkland Islands, Maj. Gen. P. E. de la C. de la Billiere, C.B.E., D.S.O., M.C..
Chief Executive, D. G. P. Taylor.

FINANCE AND TRADE

	1982–83	1983–84†
Public Revenue	£3,538,708	£3,295,590
Expenditure	3,456,164	3,531,475
	†Estimated.	

Falkland Islands and Dependencies Trade with U.K.

	1982	1983
Imports from U.K.	£4,150,000	£7,269,000
Exports to U.K.	2,568,000	4,022,000

Dependencies

SOUTH GEORGIA, An island 800 miles east-south-east of the Falkland group, with an area of 1,450 sq. miles. The population comprises the staff of the British Antarctic Survey Station at King Edward Point, which is at present manned by service personnel, and of the laboratory on Bird Island, in the north-west of S. Georgia.

THE SOUTH SANDWICH ISLANDS lie some 470 miles S.E. of South Georgia. The group is a chain of uninhabited, actively volcanic islands about 150 miles long, with a wholly Antarctic climate.
(*See* Index for other entries).

GIBRALTAR

Gibraltar is a rocky promontory, 2¾ miles in length, three-quarters of a mile in breadth and 1,396 feet high at its greatest elevation, near the southern extremity of Spain, with which it is connected by a low isthmus. It is about 14 miles distant from the opposite coast of Africa. In a total area of 2¼ sq. miles, the population at the census of Nov. 1981 was 28,719.

Gibraltar is a naval base of strategic importance to Great Britain. It was captured in 1704, during the war of the Spanish Succession, by a combined Dutch and English force, under Sir George Rooke, and was ceded to Great Britain by the Treaty of Utrecht, 1713. Several attempts have been made to retake it, the most celebrated being the great siege in 1779–83, when General Eliott, afterwards Lord Heathfield, held it for 3 years and 7 months against a combined French and Spanish force. The town stands at the foot of the promontory on the W. side.

GOVERNMENT

The Constitution of Gibraltar, approved in 1969, made formal provision for certain domestic matters to devolve on Ministers appointed from among elected members of the House of Assembly then set up to replace the former Legislative Council. The House of Assembly consists of an independent Speaker, 15 elected members and the Attorney-General and Financial and Development Secretary.

Governor and Commander-in-Chief, His Excellency Admiral Sir David Williams, G.C.B.
Flag Officer, Gibraltar, and Admiral Supr., H.M. Naval Base, Gibraltar, Rear Admiral G. Vallings.
Deputy Governor, J. K. E. Broadley £23,601

Financial and Development Secretary, B. Traynor
£22,201
Attorney-General, E. Thistlethwaite £22,201
Chief Justice, Sir Dermot Davis, O.B.E. £22,415
Chief Minister, Sir Joshua Hassan, C.B.E., M.V.O., Q.C.
Speaker, A. J. Vasquez, C.B.E.

ECONOMY

Gibraltar enjoys the advantages of an extensive shipping trade and is a popular shopping centre. The chief sources of revenue are the port dues, the rent of the Crown estate in the town, and duties on consumer items. The free port tradition of Gibraltar is still reflected in the low rates of import duty. The gradual change from a fortress city to an attractive holiday centre has led to a flourishing tourist trade.

A total of 2,226 merchant ships (21,545,985 gross registered tons aggregate) entered the port during 1983. Of these 1,254 were deep-sea ships (20,963,577 gross registered tons aggregate). In addition 5,573 yachts (106,523 gross registered tons) called at the port. There are 26·75 miles of roads.

Education is compulsory and free between the ages of 4 and 15 and scholarships are available for higher education in Britain. The total enrolment in Government schools was 5,483 in Dec. 1983. Government expenditure on education in 1983 was £4,365,900.

FINANCE AND TRADE

	1981/82	1982/83
Revenue	£44,552,019	£47,900,000
Expenditure	42,124,294	47,400,000

	1982	1983
Total imports	£68,392,879	£61,700,000
Total exports	23,847,825	24,500,000

Trade with U.K.

	1982	1983
Imports from U.K.	£29,712,000	£26,495,000
Exports to U.K.	4,229,000	4,266,000

Distance from London 1,209 miles; transit. 3¼ days. G.B. Airways and British Airways operate regular direct air services to the U.K. Transit times average 3 hours.

HONG KONG

Hong Kong, consisting of a number of islands and of a portion of the mainland (Kowloon and the New Territories), on the south-eastern coast of China, is situated at the eastern side of the mouth of the Pearl River, between 22° 9′ and 22° 37′ N. lat. and 113° 52′–114° 30′ E. long. The total area of the territory is 404 sq. miles (including recent reclamation) with a population which at the end of 1983 was 5,344,400.

The island of *Hong Kong* is about 11 miles long and from 2 to 5 miles broad, with a total area of 29 square miles; at the eastern entrance to the harbour it is separated from the mainland by a narrow strait. The island was first occupied by Great Britain in January, 1841, and formally ceded by the Treaty of Nanking in 1842; *Kowloon* was subsequently acquired by the Peking Convention of 1860; and the *New Territories*, consisting of a peninsula in the southern part of the Guangdong province, together with adjacent islands, by a 99-year lease signed June 9, 1898. Hong Kong Island is now linked to the Kowloon peninsula by a mile-long underwater road tunnel and an underground railway system which began operation on Oct. 1, 1979.

The island is broken in shape and mountainous, the highest point being Victoria Peak, which is 1,805 feet high. The New Territories contain several peaks

higher than this, the highest being Tai Mo Shan, 3,140 ft.

Climate.—Although Hong Kong lies within the tropics it enjoys unusually varied weather for a tropical area. The mean monthly temperature ranges from 15° C. in February to 29° C. in July, though summer temperatures can exceed 33° C and winter temperatures drop below 10° C. The average annual rainfall is 2,246 mm., of which nearly 80 per cent falls between May and September. Tropical cyclones passing at various distances from Hong Kong occur between July and September, causing high winds and heavy rain.

CAPITAL.—Victoria, situated on the island of Hong Kong, is about 81 miles S.E. of Canton and 40 miles E. of the Portuguese province of Macau at the other side of the Pearl River. It lies along the northern shore of the island and faces the mainland; the harbour (23 sq. miles water area) lies between the city and the mainland.

GOVERNMENT

Hong Kong is administered as a Crown Colony with a Governor, aided by an Executive Council, consisting of 4 *ex-officio* and 13 appointed members, and a Legislative Council, which consists of 27 official and 27 unofficial members. There is also an Urban Council, financially autonomous, which provides services relating to public health and sanitation, culture and recreation. In 1982, District Boards with elected members were set up for public consultation and participation.

Governor, His Excellency Sir Edward Youde, G.C.M.G., M.B.E., *appointed* 1982.
Commander, British Forces, Maj.-Gen. D. Boorman, C.B.
Chief Justice, Hon. Sir Denys Roberts, K.B.E.
Chief Secretary, Hon. Sir Philip Haddon-Cave, K.B.E., C.M.G.
Attorney-General, Hon. M. Thomas, Q.C.
Secretary for Home Affairs, Hon. D. C. Bray, C.M.G., C.V.O.
Financial Secretary, Hon. Sir John Bremridge, K.B.E..
Secretary for the Civil Service, Hon. M. Rowlands, C.B.E.
Secretary for Economic Services, Hon. P. Jacobs, O.B.E.
Secretary for City and New Territories Administration, Hon. D. Akers-Jones, C.M.G.
Secretary for Housing, Hon. D. Liao, C.B.E.
Secretary for Security, Hon. D. G. Jeaffreson, C.B.E.
Secretary for Health and Welfare, Hon. H. Ching, C.B.E.
Secretary for Education and Manpower, Hon. J. N. Henderson, O.B.E.
Secretary for Transport, Hon. A. J. Scott, C.B.E..
British Council Representative, O. R. Siddle, O.B.E. Easey Commercial Building, 225 Hennessy Road, Hong Kong.

LONDON OFFICE
Hong Kong Government Office
6 Grafton Street, W1X 3LB
[01-499 9821]

Commissioner in London, Sir Jack Cater, K.B.E.

COMMUNICATIONS

Hong Kong, one of the world's finest natural harbours, possesses excellent wharves. The Kwai Chung container terminal is the third busiest in the world. It has six berths which can accommodate six "third-generation" container ships simultaneously. An ocean terminal pier with an overall length of 1,250 ft. can accommodate large liners and cargo vessels. Tankers up to 920 ft. in length and 51 ft.

draught can be berthed. Buoy moorings in the harbour are available to vessels of up to 37 ft. draught. Excellent dockyard facilities are available and include five floating drydocks, the largest of which has a lifting capacity of over 100,000 tonnes. In 1983 some 11,400 ocean-going vessels called at Hong Kong and loaded and discharged more than 37,000,000 tonnes of cargo.

Hong Kong International Airport, Kai Tak, situated on the north shore of Kowloon Bay, is an important link on the main air routes of the Far East. It is regularly used by over 30 international airlines, providing some 1,000 frequent scheduled passenger and cargo services each week between Hong Kong and the United Kingdom, the People's Republic of China, North and South America, Europe, East and South Africa, the Middle East, Australasia, the South Pacific region, and Asian countries. In addition, some 7 airlines operate about 16 non-scheduled services a week.

British Airways operate 13 passenger services per week from and to London, Africa and Japan. Cathay Pacific Airways, the Hong Kong based airline, operate 392 passenger and cargo services from Hong Kong weekly to points in the Far East, Australia and the Middle East and, since 1980, the U.K. British Caledonian Airways also flies the London–Hong Kong route.

During 1983, 54,281 aircraft on international flights arrived and departed, carrying 8,800,000 passengers and 368,000 metric tonnes of freight.

EDUCATION

In 1983 there were 2,592 schools with 1,376,443 pupils. In 1980 free education for all children up to the age of 15 was made compulsory. Post-secondary education is provided by five technical institutes (enrolment, 40,028), four teacher training colleges, three post-secondary colleges, two universities and two polytechnics. The University of Hong Kong has six faculties and three schools, with an undergraduate enrolment of 5,610. The Chinese University of Hong Kong comprises three foundation colleges and has four faculties with 4,719 undergraduates. The Hong Kong Polytechnic has an enrolment of 25,600 full-time and part-time students.

FINANCE

	1982–83 HK$	1983–84 HK$
Public revenue	31,097,600,000	32,269,700,000
Public expenditure	34,597,800,000	35,474,900,000

TRADE

Hong Kong is an industrial territory with an economy based on exports rather than the domestic market. Domestic industry, producing mainly light manufactures, has grown rapidly in recent years and now provides the bulk of goods for the export trade; but the secondary role as an *entrepôt*, has also been sustained. In 1983 the value of the re-export trade was 35 per cent of total exports.

Hong Kong produces a wide range of articles, although the economy is very dependent upon textiles (40 per cent of export earnings and 41 per cent of industrial jobs) and the electronics industry (second largest export earner).

Diversification of manufacture continues to be a major feature of recent industrial development, as are industrial partnerships with overseas companies in a wide and varied field of manufactures. Modern manufacturing processes have also been introduced to local industry. The marked improvement in both

quality and output of items for which precision engineering is required, has continued.

Attempts are being made to promote the high technology and financial services sectors in the interests of broadening the base of the economy.

The adverse balance on visible trade is offset by a favourable balance on invisible account-remittances from overseas Chinese, investments, exchange, shipping and insurance profits, and the spending of tourists, etc. In 1983 Hong Kong's principal customers for its domestic products, in order of value of trade, were U.S.A., the United Kingdom, the Federal Republic of Germany, China, Japan, Canada, Australia, Singapore, the Netherlands and Switzerland. China was its principal supplier, followed by Japan, U.S.A., Taiwan, Singapore, the United Kingdom and South Korea.

	1982 H.K.$	1983 H.K.$
Total Exports	127,385m	160,699m
Total Imports	142,893m	175,442m

Trade with U.K.

	1982	1983
Imports from U.K....	£732,489,000	£726,711,000
Exports to U.K.	872,545,000	1,178,343,000

MONTSERRAT

Situated in 16° 45′ N. lat. and 61° 15′ W. long., 27 miles S.W. of Antigua, the island is about 11 miles long and 7 wide, with an area of 39 square miles and a population (1980), 12,073. Discovered by Columbus in 1493, it was settled by Irishmen in 1632, conquered and held by the French for some time, and finally assigned to Great Britain in 1783. It contains two active volcanoes and several hot springs. About two-thirds of the island is mountainous, the rest capable of cultivation.

CHIEF TOWN.—ΨPlymouth (1,623).

GOVERNMENT

A Ministerial system was introduced in Montserrat in 1960. The Executive Council is presided over by the Governor and is composed of 4 elected members (the Chief and 3 other Ministers) and two *ex-officio* members (the Attorney-General and the Financial Secretary). The 4 Ministers are appointed from the members of the political party holding the majority in the Legislative Council. The Legislative Council consists of the Speaker, two *ex officio* members (the Attorney General and the Financial Secretary), two nominated unofficial members and 7 elected members.

Governor, His Excellency D. K. H. Dale, C.B.E.

EXECUTIVE COUNCIL

President, The Governor.
Attorney-General, Hon. O. Adams.
Financial Secretary, Hon. J. E. Ryan.
Chief Minister and Minister of Finance, Hon. J. A. Osborne.
Education, Health and Welfare, Hon. Mrs. M. M. Dyer.
Agriculture, Trade, Lands and Housing, Hon. J. B. Chalmers.
Communications and Works, Hon. N. Tuitt.

Speaker of the Legislative Council, Hon. H. A. Fergus, O.B.E.

ECONOMY

The chief exports are flour bags, sea island cotton, tomatoes, hot peppers and other fruits and vegetables. Real estate development and tourism have done much to aid the island's economy. Revenue (1983) EC$23,172,700; Expenditure EC$22,378,140.

PITCAIRN ISLANDS

Pitcairn, a small volcanic island of less than two square miles in area, is the chief of a group of Islands situated about midway between New Zealand and Panama in the South Pacific Ocean at longitude 130° 06′ W. and latitude 25° 04′ S.

The island rises in cliffs to a height of 1,100 feet and access from the sea is possible only at Bounty Bay, a small rocky cove, and then only by whaleboats. Mean monthly temperatures vary between 66° F. in August and 75° F. in February and the average annual rainfall is 80 inches. Moderate easterly and north-easterly winds predominate but short easterly and south-easterly gales occasionally occur from April to September. With an equable climate, the island is very fertile and produces both tropical and sub-tropical trees and crops.

The small community, numbering 61 (1984), are descendants of the Bounty mutineers and their Tahitian companions who did not wish to remain on Norfolk Island when the entire community was transferred there in 1856, and returned to Pitcairn three years later.

Pitcairn became a British Settlement under the British Settlement Act, 1887, and was administered by the Governor of Fiji from 1952 until 1970, when the administration was transferred to the British High Commission in New Zealand and the British High Commissioner was appointed Governor. The local Government Ordinance of 1964 provides for a Council of ten members of whom four are elected.

Governor of Pitcairn, Ducie, Henderson and Oeno Islands, His Excellency T. O'Leary, C.M.G. (*British High Commissioner to New Zealand*).
Island Magistrate and Chairman of Island Council, I. Christian.
Education Officer and Government Adviser, L. Salt.

The Islanders live by subsistence farming and fishing, and their limited monetary needs are satisfied by the manufacture of wood carvings and other handicrafts which are sold to passing ships and to a few overseas customers. Other than small fees charged for gun and driving licences there are no taxes and Government revenue is derived almost solely from the sale of postage stamps. Communication with the outside world is maintained by cargo vessels travelling between New Zealand and Panama which call at irregular intervals; and by means of a telegraphic link with New Zealand.

The New Zealand Education Department provides assistance in recruiting a teacher for the sole-charge school. Education is compulsory between the ages of five and fifteen. Secondary education in New Zealand is encouraged by the Administration which provides scholarships and bursaries for the purpose. Medical care is provided by a registered nurse. Since 1887 the islanders have all been adherents of the Seventh Day Adventist Church.

The other three islands of the group (Henderson lying 105 miles E.N.E. of Pitcairn, Oeno lying 75 miles N.W. and Ducie lying 293 miles E.) are all uninhabited. Henderson Island is occasionally visited by the Pitcairn Islanders to obtain supplies of "miro" wood which is used for their carvings. Oeno is visited for excursions of about a week's duration every two years or so.

ST. HELENA

Probably the best known of all the solitary islands in the world, St. Helena is situated in the South Atlantic Ocean, 955 miles S. of the Equator, 760 S.E. of Ascension, 1,140 from the nearest point of the African Continent, 1,800 from the coast of S. America,

1,694 from Cape Town and 4,477 from Southampton (transit 5 days and 16 days respectively), in 15° 55′ S. lat. and 5° 42′ W. longitude. It is 10½ miles long, 6½ broad, and encloses an area of 47 square miles, with a population of 5,499 (end 1982).

St. Helena is of volcanic origin, and consists of numerous rugged mountains, the highest rising to 2,700 feet, interspersed with picturesque ravines. Although within the tropics, the south-east "trades" keep the temperature mild and equable. St. Helena was discovered by the Portuguese navigator, Juan da Nova Castella, in 1502 (probably on St. Helena's Day) and remained unknown to other European nations until 1588. It was used as a port of call for vessels of all nations trading to the East until it was annexed by the Dutch in 1633. It was never occupied by them, however, and the English East India Company seized it in 1659. In 1834 it was ceded to the Crown. During the period 1815 to 1821 the island was lent to the British Government as a place of exile for the Emperor Napoleon Bonaparte who died in St. Helena on May 5, 1821. It was formerly an important station on the route to India, but its prosperity decreased after the construction of the Suez Canal. Since the collapse of the New Zealand flax (*phormuim tenax*) industry in 1965, there have been no significant exports, but a second five year development plan, launched in 1979, seeks primarily to increase the island's productivity in its limited land and sea resources. ѱSt. James's Bay, on the north-west of the Island, possesses a good anchorage. There is no airport or airstrip.

CAPITAL.—ѱJamestown. Population (1978), 1,516.

GOVERNMENT

The government of St. Helena is administered by a Governor, with the aid of a Legislative Council, consisting of the Governor, two *ex-officio* members (Government Secretary and Treasurer) and twelve elected members. Six committees of the Legislative Council are reponsible for general oversight of the activities of Government Departments and have in addition a wide range of statutory and administrative functions. The Governor is also assisted by an Executive Council of the two *ex-officio* members and the Chairmen of the Council committees.

Governor, His Excellency Francis E. Baker (1984).
Government Secretary, P. Dale, O.B.E.
Treasurer and Development Secretary, R. J. Saltwell.
Senior Medical Officer, Dr. D. W. Young.
Agricultural and Forestry Officer, M. D. Holland.
Education Officer, B. A. George.

FINANCE AND TRADE

	1980–81	1981–82
Public revenue	£4,488,257	£5,656,518
Expenditure	4,551,657	5,681,934
Total imports	2,117,126	2,485,819

Imports from U.K. were valued at £986,758 in 1980–81, and at £1,245,322 in 1981–82.

ASCENSION

The small island of Ascension lies in the South Atlantic (7° 56′ S., 14° 22′ W.) some 700 miles north-west of the island of St. Helena. It is a rocky peak of purely volcanic origin, the highest point (Green Mountain) some 2,817 ft. is covered with lush vegetation, which with each rainy season is slowly creeping down to the lower areas. B.B.C. (Ascension Island Services) operate a farm of some 10 acres on the mountain, permitting the production of vegetables and livestock. The island is famous for turtles, which land on the beaches from January to May to lay their eggs. It is also a breeding area for the sooty tern, or wideawake, large numbers of which settle on the south-western coastal section every eighth month to hatch their eggs. Other wild life on the island includes feral donkeys and cats, rabbits and francolin partridge. All wild life except rabbits and cats is protected by law. The ocean surrounding the island abounds with shark, barracuda, tuna, bonito and many other fish.

Ascension is said to have been discovered by Juan da Nova Castella, on Ascension Day, 1501, and two years later was visited by Alphonse d'Albuquerque, who gave the island its present name. It was uninhabited until the arrival of Napoleon in St. Helena in 1815 when a small British naval garrison was stationed on the island. It remained under the supervision of the Board of Admiralty until 1922, when it was made a dependency of St. Helena by Royal Letters Patent.

The British Foreign Secretary appoints the Administrator. There is a small Police Force and Post Office. The British organizations provide and operate various common services for the island (school, hospital, public works etc).

Ascension Island is a main relay point of the coaxial submarine cable system laid between South Africa, Portugal and the United Kingdom, which is operated by the South Atlantic Cable Company. Cable & Wireless Ltd operates the international telephone and cable services, maintains an internal telephone service, and also operates an Earth Station on behalf of N.A.S.A. The B.B.C. opened its Atlantic relay station broadcasting to Africa and South America in 1967.

The resident population in March 1984 totalled 1,438, of whom 969 were from St. Helena, 285 from the U.K., 173 from the U.S.A. and 11 from the Republic of South Africa. The residents consist of the employees and families of the British organizations, of the contractors for the U.S. Air Force and N.A.S.A. (Pan American Airways, Radio Corporation of America and Bendix Field Engineering Corporation) and of the St. Helena Government.

British forces returned to the island in April 1982 in support of operations in the Falkland Islands. At present there are about 450 R.A.F. personnel on the island who are supporting the air bridge to the Falklands.

Administrator, M. T. Blick.

TRISTAN DA CUNHA

Tristan da Cunha is the chief of a group of islands of volcanic origin lying in lat. 37° 6' S. and long. 12° 2' W., discovered in 1506 by a Portuguese admiral (Tristão da Cunha), after whom they are named. They have a total area of 45 square miles. The main island, with a peak rising to 6,760 ft., is about 1,500 miles W. of the Cape of Good Hope, 3,600 miles N.E. of Cape Horn, and about 1,320 miles S.S.W. of St. Helena. It was the resort of British and American sealers from the middle of the 18th century, and in 1760 a British naval officer visited the group and gave his name to Nightingale Island. On August 14, 1816, the group was annexed to the British Crown and a garrison was placed on Tristan da Cunha, but this force was withdrawn in 1817, William Glass, a corporal of artillery (*died* 1853), remaining at his own request, with his wife and two children. This party, with five others, formed a settlement. In 1827 five coloured women from St. Helena, and afterwards others from Cape Colony, joined the party.

The islands form a dependency of St. Helena, being administered by the Foreign and Commonwealth Office through a resident Administrator, with headquarters at the settlement of Edinburgh. Under a new constitution introduced in 1969, he is advised by an elected Island Council of 8 members of whom one must be a woman, and three appointed members, with universal suffrage at 18. The population numbered 298 persons in 1984, plus 5 expatriate Government officers and their families, and a resident chaplain.

In October, 1961, a volcano, believed to have been extinct for thousands of years, erupted and lava was thrown up in some cases to a height of 75 feet. In view of the danger of further volcanic activity, the inhabitants were evacuated and reached the United Kingdom on Nov. 23, 1961, where they remained for nearly two years. An advance party returned to Tristan da Cunha in the spring of 1963, and the main body of the islanders has now returned to the island.

A boat harbour was completed in 1967. The first freezing factory was re-established in 1966. There are no taxes on Tristan, income being derived from royalties paid by the fishing company and from the sale of stamps. The new Camogli Hospital was opened early in 1971 and a new school was opened in 1975.

Administrator, C. F. Redston.

INACCESSIBLE ISLAND is a lofty mass of rock with sides 2 miles in length; the island is the resort of penguins and sea-fowl. Cultivation was started in 1937, but has been abandoned.

THE NIGHTINGALE ISLANDS are three in number, of which the largest is 1 mile long and ¾ mile wide, and rises in two peaks, 960 and 1,105 ft. above sea-level respectively. The smaller islands, Stoltenhoff and Middle Isle, are little more than huge rocks. Seals, innumerable penguins, and vast numbers of sea-fowl visit these islands.

GOUGH ISLAND (or Diego Alvarez), in 40° 20' S. and 9° 44' W., lies about 250 miles S.S.E. of Tristan da Cunha. The island is about 8 miles long and 4 miles broad, with a total area of 40 square miles, and has been a British possession since 1816. The island is the resort of penguins and sea-elephants and has valuable guano deposits. There is no permanent population, but there is a meteorological station maintained on the island by the South African Government and manned by South Africans.

TURKS AND CAICOS ISLANDS

The Turks and Caicos Islands are situated between 21° and 22° N. latitude and 71° and 72° W. longitude, about 100 miles north of the Dominican Republic and 50 miles south-east of the Bahamas of which they are geographically an extension. There are over 30 islands of which eight are inhabited covering an estimated area of 193 square miles. The principal is Grand Turk. The present population is 7,436 (Grand Turk 3,146).

The Islands lie in the Trade Wind but with an excellent climate. The average temperature varies from 75°–80°F. in the winter and 85°F.–90°F. in the summer and humidity is generally low. Average rainfall is 21 inches per annum. Hurricanes are rare, the last occurring in 1960.

A new Constitution was introduced in 1976, providing for an Executive Council and Legislative Council, and for the appointment of a Chief Minister and three other Ministers from elected members of the Legislative.

Governor, His Excellency C. J. Turner, O.B.E.
Chief Minister, Hon. N. B. Saunders.

The principal airports are on the islands of Grand Turk, South Caicos and Providenciales. There are direct shipping services to the U.S.A. (Miami). There is an air service between Miami and Grand Turk via the Dominican Republic. An internal air service provides a twice daily service between the principal islands. A comprehensive telephone and telex service is provided by Cable and Wireless (W.I.) Ltd.

The most important industry is fishing but tourism is of increasing importance with about 13,342 visitors in 1982.

FINANCE

	1981–82	1982–83
Revenue	U.S.$7,948,797	U.S.$9,343,667
Expenditure	7,505,878	8,848,758

Budgetary Aid (1982–83), $2,100,152.

Trade with U.K.

	1982
Imports	£405,000
Exports	5,000

VIRGIN ISLANDS,
see BRITISH

DISTANCES FROM LONDON BY AIR

A list of the distances in statute miles from London to various places abroad. They have been supplied by IAL, Southall, Middx.

To	Miles	To	Miles	To	Miles
Ajaccio	790	Dublin	279	New York (J. F. Kennedy)	3,440
Algiers	1,035	Düsseldorf	310	Nice	645
Alicante	911	Entebbe	4,033	Oporto	806
Amsterdam	230	Faro	1,063	Oslo (Fornebu)	723
Ankara	1,770	Frankfurt	406	Palermo	1,128
Athens	1,500	Geneva	468	Palma/Majorca	836
Auckland	11,404	Gibraltar	1,084	Paris	215; (Orly 227)
Baghdad	2,551	Gothenburg (Landvetter)	664	Perth/Australia	9,008
Bahrain	3,163	Hamburg	463	Prague	649
Bangkok	5,928	Helsinki (Vantaa)	1,147	Rangoon	5,581
Barbados	4,193	Hong Kong	5,990	Reykjavik	1,167
Barcelona	712	Honolulu	7,220	Rhodes	1,743
Basle	447	Istanbul	1,560	Rome (Fiumicino)	895
Beirut	2,161	Johannesburg	5,634	Salzburg	652
Bergen	648	Karachi	3,935	Shannon	369
Berlin (Templehof)	592	Khartoum	3,071	Singapore (Changi)	6,756
Bermuda	3,428	Kingston/Jamaica	4,668	Sofia	1,266
Bombay	4,478	Kuala Lumpur	6,557	Stockholm (Arlanda)	908
Bordeaux	458	Kuwait	2,903	Sydney (Australia)	10,568
Brisbane	10,273	Larnaca/Cyprus	2,036	Tangier	1,120
Brussels	217	Leningrad	1,314	Teheran	2,741
Budapest	923	Lisbon	972	Tel Aviv	2,229
Cagliari	959	Madrid	773	Tokyo (Narita)	5,956
Cairo	2,194	Malaga	1,041	Toronto	3,545
Calcutta	4,958	Malta	1,305	Trinidad (Port of Spain)	4,405
Chicago (O'Hare)	3,941	Marseilles	614	Tripoli	1,468
Cologne	331	Mauritius	6,075	Turin (Caselle)	570
Colombo	5,411	Milan	609	Valencia	826
Copenhagen	608	Montego Bay	4,687	Venice (Tessera)	715
Corfu	1,273	Montreal (Mirabel)	3,241	Vienna (Schwechat)	790
Dar-es-Salaam	4,662	Moscow (Sheremetievo)	1,557	Warsaw	912
Darwin	8,613	Munich	588	Zagreb	848
Delhi	4,180	Nairobi	4,247	Zürich	490
Detroit	3,754	Naples	1,011		
Doha	3,253	Nassau	4,332		

UNIVERSITIES OF THE COMMONWEALTH
(outside the United Kingdom)

With date of foundation, number of full-time students and name of Executive Head
(*Vice-Chancellor, President* or *Principal*)

Australia

ADELAIDE (1874). (Full-time students, 6,300).—*Vice-Chancellor*, Prof. D. R. Stranks, A.O., Ph.D.

AUSTRALIAN NATIONAL (1946), Canberra. (3,931).—*Vice-Chancellor*, Prof. P. H. Karmel, A.C., C.B.E., Ph.D., LL.D, D.Litt., D. Univ.

DEAKIN (1974), Geelong. (1,597).—*Vice-Chancellor*, Prof. F. R. Jevons, Ph.D., D.Sc.

FLINDERS, SOUTH AUSTRALIA (1966), Adelaide. (2,541).—*Vice-Chancellor*, Prof. K. J. Hancock, Ph.D.

GRIFFITH (1971), Brisbane. (1,709).—*Vice-Chancellor*, Prof. L. R. Webb, Ph.D.

JAMES COOK, NORTH QUEENSLAND (1970), Townsville. (1,915).—*Vice-Chancellor*, Prof. K. J. C. Back, A.O., Ph.D., D.Sc.

LA TROBE (1964), Melbourne. (5,455).—*Vice-Chancellor*, Prof. J. F. Scott.

MACQUARIE (1964), Sydney. (4,464).—*Vice-Chancellor*, Prof. E. C. Webb, Ph.D., D.Sc.

MELBOURNE (1853). (11,407).—*Vice-Chancellor*, Prof. D. E. Caro, O.B.E., Ph.D., LL.D.

MONASH (1958), Melbourne. (9,659).—*Vice-Chancellor*, Prof. R. L. Martin, Ph.D., Sc.D.

MURDOCH (1973), Perth. (1,344).—*Vice-Chancellor*, Prof. P. J. Boyce, Ph.D.

NEWCASTLE (1965). (2,580).—*Vice-Chancellor*, Prof. D. W. George, A.O., Ph.D.

NEW ENGLAND (1954), Armidale. (2,358).—*Vice-Chancellor*, vacant.

NEW SOUTH WALES (1949), Sydney. (12,499).—*Vice-Chancellor*, Prof. L. M. Birt, C.B.E., Ph.D., D.Phil., D.Litt.

QUEENSLAND (1909), Brisbane. (9,881).—*Vice-Chancellor*, Prof. B. G. Wilson, Ph.D.

SYDNEY (1850). (14,127).—*Vice-Chancellor*, Prof. J. M. Ward.

TASMANIA (1890), Hobart. (3,101).—*Vice-Chancellor*, Prof. A. Lazenby, Ph.D.

WESTERN AUSTRALIA (1911), Perth. (6,658).—*Vice-Chancellor*, Prof. R. Street, Ph.D., D.Sc.

WOLLONGONG (1975). (2,468).—*Vice-Chancellor*, K. McKinnon, D.Ed.

Bangladesh

BANGLADESH AGRICULTURAL (1961), Mymensingh. (Full-time students, 3,784).—*Vice-Chancellor*, Prof. A. K. M. Aminul Haque, Ph.D.

BANGLADESH U. OF ENGINEERING AND TECHNOLOGY (1961), Dacca. (3,015).—*Vice-Chancellor*, Prof. A. M. Patwari, Ph.D.

CHITTAGONG (1966). (32,657).—*Vice-Chancellor*, Prof. M. A. Aziz Khan, Ph.D.

DHAKA (1921). (65,672).—*Vice-Chancellor*, Prof. M. S. Huq, Ph.D.

JAHANGIRNAGAR (1970), Dacca. (1,674).—*Vice-Chancellor*, Prof. A. F. M. Kamuluddin, Ph.D.

RAJSHAHI (1953). (51,473).—*Vice-Chancellor*, Prof. M. A. Raqib, Ph.D.

Botswana

BOTSWANA (1976), Gabarone. (Full-time students, 1,195).—*Vice-Chancellor*, Prof. T. Tlou, Ph.D.

Canada

ACADIA (1838), Wolfville. (Full-time students, 3,256).—*President*, J. R. C. Perkin, D.Phil.

ALBERTA (1906), Edmonton. (22,908).—*President*, M. Horowitz, Ed.D., LL.D.

ATHABASCA (1970), Athabasca.—*President*, S. Griew, Ph.D.

BISHOP'S (1843), Lennoxville. (945).—*Principal*, C. I. H. Nicholl, Ph.D.

BRANDON (1967). (1,387).—*Interim President*, Dr. E. J. Tyler.

BRITISH COLUMBIA (1908), Vancouver. (21,803).—*President*, K. G. Pedersen, Ph.D.

BROCK (1964), St. Catharines. (3,437).—*President and Vice-Chancellor*, A. J. Earp, LL.D.

CALGARY (1966). (14,557).—*President*, N. E. Wagner, Ph.D.

U. COLL. OF CAPE BRETON (1982), Sydney (1,845).—*President*, W. M. Reid, Ph.D.

CARLETON (1942), Ottawa. (10,348).—*President*, W. E. Beckel, Ph.D.

CONCORDIA (1929), Montreal. (12,285).—*Principal*, P. J. Kenniff, Ph.D.

DALHOUSIE (1818), Halifax. (7,813).—*President*, W. A. MacKay, Q.C., LL.D.

UNIV. OF KING'S COLL. (1789), Halifax. (501).—*President*, J. F. Godfrey, D.Phil.

DOMINICAN COLL. OF PHILOSOPHY AND THEOLOGY (1967), Ottawa. (116).—*President*, Rev. Father G.-D. Mailhiot.

GUELPH (1964). (11,070).—*Vice-Chancellor*, B. C. Matthews, Ph.D., D.U.

LAKEHEAD (1965), Thunder Bay. (3,561).—*Interim Vice-Chancellor*, R. G. Rosehart, Ph.D.

LAURENTIAN, SUDBURY (1960). (3,100).—*President*, J. S. Daniel, DèsSc.

LAVAL (1852), Quebec. (19,500).—*Rector*, J.-G. Paquet, D.SC.

LETHBRIDGE (1967). (2,442).—*President*, J. H. Woods, Ph.D.

McGILL (1821), Montreal. (17,140).—*Principal*, D. L. Johnston, LL.D.

McMASTER (1887), Hamilton. (11,518).—*President*, A. A. Lee, Ph.D.

MANITOBA (1877), Winnipeg. (22,681).—*President*, A. Naimark, M.D.

ST. JOHN'S COLL. (1866), Winnipeg.—*Warden*, Rev. M. R. McLean, D.Phil.

ST. PAUL'S COLL. (1926), Winnipeg.—*Rector*, D. J. Lawless, Ph.D.

MEMORIAL, NEWFOUNDLAND (1949), St. John's. (7,904).—*Vice-Chancellor*, L. Harris, Ph.D.

MONCTON (1963), Moncton, Edmundston and Shippagan. (3,662).—*Rector*, G. Finn, O.C., LL.D.

MONTREAL (1876). (20,348).—*Rector*, P. Lacoste, D.U.

MOUNT ALLISON (1858), Sackville. (1,636).—*President*, G. R. MacLean, Ph.D.

MOUNT ST. VINCENT (1925), Halifax. (1,787).—*President*, E. Margaret Fulton, Ph.D., D.Ed.

NEW BRUNSWICK (1785), Fredericton and St. John. (7,540).—*President*, J. Downey, Ph.D.

ST. THOMAS (1934), Fredericton.—*President*, Fr. G. W. Martin.

NOVA SCOTIA AGRICULTURAL COLL. (1905), Truro. (471).—*Principal*, H. F. MacRae, Ph.D.

NOVA SCOTIA COLL. OF ART AND DESIGN (1887), Halifax. (490).—*President*, G. N. Kennedy.

OTTAWA (1848). (12,079).—*Rector*, A. D'Iorio, Ph.D

ST. PAUL (1848), Ottawa (422).—*President*, Rev. Father H. Gouldreault, D.Th.

PRINCE EDWARD ISLAND (1969), Charlottetown (1,676).—*President*, P. P. M. Meincke, Ph.D.

QUEBEC (1968), Chicoutimi, Hull, Montreal, Rimouski, Trois-Rivières, and other centres (23,748).—*President*, G. Boulet.

QUEEN'S, KINGSTON (1841). (11,368).—*Principal*, D. C. Smith, Ph.D.

REGINA (1974). (5,291).—*President*, L. I. Barber, O.C., Ph.D.
    CAMPION COLL. (1918), Regina.—*President*, Rev. J. B. Gavin, Ph.D.
    LUTHER COLL. (1926), Regina.—*President*, M. A. Anderson, LL.D.
ROYAL MILITARY COLL. OF CANADA (1876), Kingston. (828).—*Principal*, B. J. Plant, Ph.D.
ROYAL ROADS MILITARY COLLEGE (1942), Victoria. (262). *Principal*, J. S. Mothersill, Ph.D.
RYERSON POLYTECHNICAL INSTITUTE (1963), Toronto. (8,801).—*President*, B. Segal, Ph.D.
STE.-ANNE (1892), Church Point, N.S. (143).—*President*, R. Runte, Ph.D.
ST. FRANCIS XAVIER (1853), Antigonish. (2,494).—*President*, Rev. G. A. MacKinnon, Ph.D.
ST. MARY'S (1841), Halifax. (3,131).—*President*, K. L. Ozmon, Ph.D.
SASKATCHEWAN (1907), Saskatoon (12,562).—*President*, L. F. Kristjanson, Ph.D., LL.D.
    ST. THOMAS MORE COLL. (1936), Saskatoon.—*Principal*, Rev. J. T. Hanrahan.
SHERBROOKE (1954). (7,670).—*Rector*, C. Hamel.
SIMON FRASER (1963), Burnaby. (7,779).—*President*, W. G. Saywell, Ph.D.
TECHNICAL U. OF NOVA SCOTIA (1909), Halifax. (1,093).—*President*, J. C. Callaghan.
TORONTO (1827). (35,672).—*President*, G. E. Connell, Ph.D
    UNIV. OF ST. MICHAEL'S COLL. (1852), Toronto. (2,778).—*President*, Rev. J. K. McConica, D.Phil.
    UNIV. OF TRINITY COLL. (1851), Toronto. (1,078).—*Vice-Chancellor*, F. K. Hare, O.C., Ph.D., LL.D., D.SC.
    VICTORIA (1836), Toronto. (2,400).—*President*, G. S. French, C.D., Ph.D.
    ONTARIO INSTITUTE FOR STUDIES IN EDUCATION (1965), Toronto. (614).—*Director*, B. J. Shapiro, Ed.D.
TRENT (1963), Peterborough. (2,819).—*President*, D. F. Theall, Ph.D.
TRINITY WESTERN COLL. (1962), Langley.—*President*, R. N. Snider, Ph.D.
VICTORIA (1963), British Columbia. (7,200).—*President*, H. E. Petch, Ph.D., D.SC, LL.D.
WATERLOO (1959). (15,912).— *Vice-Chancellor*, D. T. Wright, Ph.D., D.Eng., LL.D., D.SC.
    ST. JEROME'S COLL., Waterloo.—*President*, Rev. N. L. Choate.
WESTERN ONTARIO (1878), London. (20,056).—*Acting President*, A. K. Adlington.
    BRESCIA COLL. (1919), London.—*Principal*, Sister Dolores Kuntz, Ph.D.
    HURON COLL. (1863), London.—*Principal*, J. A. Trentman, Ph.D.
    KING'S COLL. (1912), London.—*Principal*, J. D. Morgan, Ph.D.
WILFRED LAURIER (1973), Waterloo. (4,468).—*President*, J. A. Weir, Ph.D.
WINDSOR (1857). (8,396).— *Vice-Chancellor*, R. W. Ianni, Ph.D.
WINNIPEG (1967). (3,273).—*President*, R. H. Farquhar, Ph.D.
YORK (1959), Toronto. (16,294).—*President*, H. W. Arthurs.

Ghana

CAPE COAST (1962). (Full-time students 1,592).— *Vice-Chancellor*, Prof. K. B. Dickson, Ph.D.
GHANA (1961), Legon. (3,139).—*Acting Vice-Chancellor*, K. E. Senanu, Ph.D.
UNIV. OF SCIENCE AND TECHNOLOGY (1961), Kumasi. (2,979).— *Vice-Chancellor*, F. O. Kwami, Dr.Ing.

Guyana

GUYANA (1963), Georgetown. (Full-time students, 1,091).—*Actg. Vice-Chancellor*, G. L. Walcott, Ph.D.

Hong Kong

CHINESE UNIV. OF HONG KONG (1963). (Full-time students, 5,111).—*Vice-Chancellor*, Prof. Ma Lin, HON.C.B.E., Ph.D.
HONG KONG (1911). (5,586).—*Vice-Chancellor*, R. L. Huang, C.B.E., D.Phil., D.SC.

India

AGRA (1927). (Full-time students, 36,767).—*Vice-Chancellor*, A. P. Mathur, Ph.D.
AGRICULTURAL SCIENCES (1964), Bangalore. (3,395).— *Vice-Chancellor*, N. G. Perur, Ph.D.
ALIGARH MUSLIM (1920). (10,438).— *Vice-Chancellor*, Prof. S. Hamid.
ALLAHABAD (1887). (29,773).—*Vice-Chancellor*, Dr. R. P. Misra.
ALL-INDIA INSTITUTE OF MEDICAL SCIENCES (1956), New Delhi. (980).—*Director*, H. D. Tandon, M.D.
AMRAVATI (1983). (11,679).—*Vice-Chancellor*, K. G. Deshmukh, Ph.D.
ANDHRA (1926), Waltair. (69,042).—*Vice-Chancellor*, Prof. K. Ramakyishna Rao.
ANDHRA PRADESH OPEN (1982), Hyderabad. (6,406).— *Vice-Chancellor*, Prof. G. Ram Reddy, Ph.D.
ANNA (1978), Madras. (3,593).—*Vice-Chancellor*, V. C. Kulandaiswamy, Ph.D., D.Litt.
ANNAMALAI (1928), Annamalainagar. (5,553).—*Vice-Chancellor*, Prof. S. V. Chittibabu.
ASSAM AGRICULTURAL (1969), Jorhat. (891).—*Acting Vice-Chancellor*, Dr. P. C. Borah.
AVADH (1975), Faizabad. (35,505).—*Vice-Chancellor*, A. P. Mehrotra, D.Phil.
AWADHESH PRATAP SINGH VISHWAVIDYALAYA (1968), Rewa. (54,770).—*Vice-Chancellor*, H. L. Nigam, D.Phil., Ph.D.
BANARAS HINDU (1915). (17,271).—*Vice-Chancellor*, I. Narain, Ph.D.
BANASTHALI VIDYAPITH (1983). (867).—*Director*, Miss Sushila Vyas.
BANGALORE (1964). (72,217).—*Vice-Chancellor*, Dr. D. Shankar Narayan.
BARODA (1949). (22,418).—*Vice-Chancellor*, Prof. B. C. Parekh, Ph.D.
BERHAMPUR (1967). (21,878).—*Vice-Chancellor*, Prof. B. K. Mohanty.
BHAGALPUR (1960). (57,290).—*Vice-Chancellor*, M. Q. Towheed, Ph.D.
BHARATHIAR (1982), Coimbatore. (9,812).—*Vice-Chancellor*, R. Subbayyan, Ph.D.
BHARATHIDASAN (1982), Tiruchirapalli. (30,000).— *Vice-Chancellor*, Prof. P. S. Mani Sundaram.
BHAVNAGAR (1978). (4,523).—*Vice-Chancellor*, Prof. I. J. Dhruv.
BHOPAL VISHWAVIDYALAYA (1970). (25,887).—*Vice-Chancellor*, R. C. Shukla, Ph.D.
BIDHAN CHANDRA KRISHI VISWA VIDYALAYA (1974), Kalyani. (1,260).—*Vice-Chancellor*, J. C. Sengupta.
BIHAR (1952), Muzaffarpur. (80,803).—*Vice-Chancellor*, L. K. Mishra.
BIRLA INSTITUTE OF TECHNOLOGY AND SCIENCE (1964), Pilani. (2,210).—*Director*, C. R. Mitra, Eng.SC.D.
BOMBAY (1857). (133,930).—*Vice-Chancellor*, M. S. Gore, Ph.D.
BUNDELKHAND (1975), Jhansi. (32,532).—*Vice-Chancellor*, Prof. H. L. Sharma, Ph.D, D.Litt.
BURDWAN (1960). (64,003).—*Vice-Chancellor*, S. P. Banerjee, Ph.D.
CALCUTTA (1857). (130,390).—*Vice-Chancellor*, Prof. S. Bhattacharya.
CALICUT (1968). (106,367).—*Vice-Chancellor*, K. Srinivasan.
CENTRAL INSTITUTE OF ENGLISH AND FOREIGN LANGUAGES (1958), Hyderabad. (281).—*Director*, R. Mohan, Ph.D.

CHANDRA SHEKHAR AZAD U. OF AGRICULTURE AND TECHNOLOGY (1975), Kanpur. (967).—*Vice-Chancellor*, Dr. M. B. L. Bharadwaj.

COCHIN (1971), Tripunithura. (836).—*Vice-Chancellor*, K. Gopalan, DR.ING.

DAKSHINA BHARAT HINDI PRACHAR SABHA (1918), Hyderabad. (143).—*Hon. Vice-Chancellor*, P. V. Narasimha Rao.

DAYALBAGH EDUCATIONAL INST. (1981), Agra. (1,153).—*Director*, Mrs G. P. Sherry, PH.D.

DELHI (1922). (71,481).—*Vice-Chancellor*, Gurbaksh Singh, PH.D.

DEVI AHILYA VISHWAVIDYALAYA (1964), Indore. (24,101).— *Vice-Chancellor*, K. K. Dave.

DIBRUGARH (1965). (65,025).— *Vice-Chancellor*, S. D. Gogoi, PH.D.

DOCTOR HARISINGH GOUR VISHWAVIDYALAYA (1964), Sagar. (6,177).—*Vice-Chancellor*, M. B. Malhotra.

GANDHIGRAM RURAL INSTITUTE (1956), Madurai. (576).—*Vice-Chancellor*, M. Aram, PH.D.

GARHWAL (1973), Srinagar. (26,969).—*Vice-Chancellor*, D. S. Rawat, PH.D.

GAUHATI (1948). (108,871).—*Vice-Chancellor*, Prof. J. M. Choudhury, PH.D.

GORAKHPUR (1956). (6,144).—*Vice-Chancellor*, Prof. B. M. Shukla.

GOVIND BALLABH PANT U. OF AGRICULTURE AND TECHNOLOGY (1960), Pantnagar. (2,347).—*Vice-Chancellor*, K. Narain, PH.D.

GUJARAT (1949), Ahmedabad. (93,950).—*Vice-Chancellor*, Prof. K. S. Shastri.

GUJARAT AGRICULTURAL (1969), Ahmedabad. (1,685).—*Vice-Chancellor*, R. B. Shukla.

GUJARAT AYURVED (1966), Jamnagar. (1,881).—*Vice-Chancellor*, V. J. Thacker.

GUJARAT VIDYAPITH (1920), Ahmedabad. (90).—*Vice-Chancellor*, Prof. R. Parikh.

GULBARGA (1980).—*Vice-Chancellor*, Dr. M. Nagraj.

GURU GHASIDAS (1983), Bilaspur.—*Vice-Chancellor*, S. C. Behar.

GURUKULA KANGRI VISHWAVIDYALAYA (1900), Saharahpur. (517).—*Vice-Chancellor*, Dr. G. B. K. Hooja.

GURU NANAK DEV (1969), Amritsar. (58,830).—*Vice-Chancellor*, J. S. Grewal, PH.D., D.LITT.

HARYANA AGRICULTURAL (1970), Hissar. (2,416).—*Vice-Chancellor*, L. D. Kataria.

HIMACHAL PRADESH (1970), Simla. (17,335).—*Vice-Chancellor*, L. P. Sinha.

HYDERABAD (1974). (690).—*Vice-Chancellor*, Prof. B. S. Ramakrisha, PH.D.

INDIAN AGRICULTURAL RESEARCH INSTITUTE (1905), New Delhi. (468).—*Director*, H. K. Jain, PH.D.

INDIAN INSTITUTE OF SCIENCE (1909), Bangalore. (1,176).—*Director*, Prof. C. N. R. Rao, PH.D, D.SC.

INDIAN INST. OF TECHNOLOGY, BOMBAY (1958). (2,667).—*Director*, A. K. De, PH.D.

INDIAN INST. OF TECHNOLOGY, DELHI (1961). (2,966).—*Director*, Prof. N. M. Swani, PH.D.

INDIAN INST. OF TECHNOLOGY, KANPUR (1960). (1,893).—*Director*, Prof. S. Sampath.

INDIAN INST. OF TECHNOLOGY, KHARAGPUR (1951). (2,544).—*Director*, Prof. G. S. Sanyal.

INDIAN INST. OF TECHNOLOGY, MADRAS (1959). (2,219).—*Director*, Prof. L. S. Srinath.

INDIAN SCHOOL OF MINES (1926), Dhanbad. (668).—*Director*, Prof. G. S. Marwaha.

INDIAN STATISTICAL INST. (1932), Calcutta. (366).—*Director*, A. Maitra, PH.D

INDIAN VETERINARY RESEARCH INST., Izatnagar.—*Director*, Dr. B. S. Rajya.

INDIRA KALA SANGIT VISHAVIDYALAYA (1956), Khairagarh. (121).—*Vice-Chancellor*, B. Mukherjee.

JADAVPUR (1955), Calcutta. (4,533).—*Vice-Chancellor*, M. M. Chakrabarty, PH.D.

JAMMU (1969). (11,232).—*Vice-Chancellor*, M. R. Puri.

JAWAHARLAL NEHRU KRISHI VISHWA VIDYALAYA (1964), Jabalpur. (2,872).—*Vice-Chancellor*, Prof. S. V. Arya.

JAWAHARLAL NEHRU TECHNOLOGICAL (1972), Hyderabad. (2,904).—*Vice-Chancellor*, G. Lakshminarayana, PH.D.

JAWAHARLAL NEHRU U. (1969), New Delhi. (2,372).—*Vice-Chancellor*, Prof. P. N. Srivastava, D.PHIL.

JIWAJI (1964), Gwalior. (32,095).—*Vice-Chancellor*, K. K. Tiwari, PH.D.

JODHPUR (1962). (8,594).—*Vice-Chancellor*, S. N. Mehrotra, D.PHIL.

KAKATIYA (1976), Warangal. (11,360).—*Vice-Chancellor*, Prof. T. Vasudev, PH.D.

KALYANI (1960). (2,189).—*Vice-Chancellor*, S. Mookerjee, PH.D.

KAMESHWARA SINGH DARBHANGA SANSKRIT VISHWAVIDYALAYA (1961), Darbhanga.—*Vice-Chancellor*, J. Mishra, PH.D.

KANPUR (1965). (126,132).—*Vice-Chancellor*, Dr. D. D. Tewari.

KARNATAK (1949), Dharwar. (50,997).—*Vice-Chancellor*, Dr. S. G. Desai.

KASHI VIYAPITH (1921), Varanasi. (4,617).—*Vice-Chancellor*, D. N. Chaturdevi, PH.D.

KASHMIR (1969), Srinagar. (11,997).—*Vice-Chancellor*, Prof. S. M. Alam, PH.D.

KERALA (1937), Trivandrum. (200,751).—*Actg. Vice-Chancellor*, K. Gopalan.

KERALA AGRICULTURAL (1971), Trichur. (1,545).—*Vice-Chancellor*, T. M. Menon.

KONKAN KRISHI VIDYAPEETH (1972), Ratnagiri. (986).—*Vice-Chancellor*, P. V. Salvi, PH.D.

KUMAUN (1973), Nainital.—*Vice-Chancellor*, S. N. Srivastava, PH.D.

KURUKSHETRA (1956). (4,662).—*Vice-Chancellor*, K. K. Sharma.

L. N. MITHILA (1972), Darbhanga. (110,355).—*Vice-Chancellor*, C. D. Singh, PH.D.

LUCKNOW (1921).—*Vice-Chancellor*, R. P. Agarwal, PH.D.

MADRAS (1857). (75,000).—*Vice-Chancellor*, M. Santappa, PH.D.

MADURAI-KAMARAJ (1966). (117,681).—*Vice-Chancellor*, Prof. J. Ramachandran.

MAGADH (1962), Gaya. (113,161).—*Vice-Chancellor*, F. Ahmad.

MAHARSHI DAYANAND (1976), Rohtak. (53,293).—*Vice-Chancellor*, H. Lal.

MAHATMA PHULE AGRICULTURAL (1967), Ahmednagar. (1,776).—*Vice-Chancellor*, D. K. Salunkhe, PH.D.

MANGALORE (1980).—*Vice-Chancellor*, Prof. B. Sheik Ali.

MANIPUR (1980), Imphal. (10,485).—*Vice-Chancellor*, Prof. K. J. Mahale, PH.D.

MARATHWADA (1958), Aurangabad. (36,320).—*Vice-Chancellor*, M. P. Kanade.

MARATHWADA AGRICULTURAL (1972), Parbhani. (1,408).—*Vice-Chancellor*, Dr. N. G. P. Rao.

MEERUT (1966). (57,765).—*Vice-Chancellor*, Prof. R. L. Singh, PH.D.

MOHAN LAL SUKHADIA (1962), Udaipur. (15,466).—*Vice-Chancellor*, P. N. Bhandari.

MYSORE (1916). (53,577).—*Vice-Chancellor*, Prof. K. S. Hegde.

NAGARJUNA (1976), Nagarjunanagar. (23,210).—*Vice-Chancellor*, Dr. K. R. R. Mohan Rao.

NAGPUR (1923). (44,750).—*Vice-Chancellor*, G. B. Kadam.

NARENDRA DEV. U. OF AGRICULTURE AND TECHNOLOGY (1974), Faizabad. (231).—*Acting Vice-Chancellor*, Dr. K. Singh.

NORTH BENGAL (1962), Darjeeling. (19,410).—*Vice-Chancellor*, Prof. D. B. Dutta.

NORTH-EASTERN HILL (1973), Shillong. (21,143).—*Vice-Chancellor*, B. D. Sharma, PH.D.

OSMANIA (1918), Hyderabad. (58,303).—*Vice-Chancellor*, S. H. Ali.

PANJAB (1947), Chandigarh. (74,975).—*Vice-Chancellor*, Prof. R. C. Paul, PH.D., SC.D.

PATNA (1917). (17,375).—*Vice-Chancellor*, G. P. Sinha, PH.D.

POONA (1948). (87,629).—*Vice-Chancellor*, Prof. R. G. Takwale, PH.D

PUNJAB AGRICULTURAL (1962), Ludhiana. (2,928).—*Vice-Chancellor*, S. Singh, PH.D.

PUNJABI (1961), Patiala. (35,656).—*Vice-Chancellor*, S. S. Johl, PH.D.

PUNJABRAO KRISHI VIDYAPEETH (1969), Akola. (2,839).—*Vice-Chancellor*, K. R. Thakare, PH.D.

RABINDRA BHARATI (1962), Calcutta. (3,601).—*Vice-Chancellor*, Prof. R. Das.

RAJASTHAN (1947), Jaipur. (120,252).—*Vice-Chancellor*, Prof. T. K. N. Unithan, PH.D., D.Litt.

RANCHI (1960). (52,946).—*Vice-Chancellor*, Dr. B. Prasad.

RANI DURGAVATI VISHWAVIDYALAYA (1957), Jabalpur. (18,180).—*Vice-Chancellor*, K. Chaudhuri.

RAVISHANKAR (1963), Raipur. (39,662).—*Vice-Chancellor*, B. K. Shrivastava, PH.D.

ROHILKHAND (1975), Bareilly. (32,042).—*Vice-Chancellor*, Prof. J. N. Rai.

ROORKEE (1949). (2,558).—*Vice-Chancellor*, B. Singh, PH.D.

SAMBALPUR (1967). (49,197).—*Vice-Chancellor*, S. Sahu, PH.D.

SAMPURNANAND SANSKRIT VISHWAVIDYALAYA (1958), Varanasi. (43,143).—*Vice-Chancellor*, Dr. D. S. Misra.

SARDAR PATEL (1955), Vallabh Vidyanagar. (10,343).—*Vice-Chancellor*, K. N. Shah.

SAURASHTRA (1966), Rajkot. (34,871).—*Vice-Chancellor*, Dr. H. G. Desai.

SCHOOL OF PLANNING AND ARCHITECTURE (1955), New Delhi. (244).—*Director*, Prof. B. D. Souza.

SHIVAJI (1962), Kolhapur. (42,699).—*Vice-Chancellor*, K. Bhagishayana.

SHREEMATI N. D. THACKERSEY WOMEN'S (1951), Bombay. (16,010).—*Vice-Chancellor*, Mrs. Jyoti H. Trivedi, M.D.

SOUTH GUJARAT (1966), Surat. (26,141).—*Vice-Chancellor*, Prof. U. V. Baxi.

SREE CHITRA TIRUNAL INST. FOR MEDICAL SCIENCES AND TECHNOLOGY (1981), Trivandrum. (24).—*Director*, Dr. M. S. Valiathan.

SRI KRISHNADEVARAYA (1981), Anantapur. (1,220).—*Vice-Chancellor*, M. Abel, PH.D.

SRI PADMAVATI MAHILA VISWA VIDYALAYAM, Tirupati.—*Vice-Chancellor*, Mrs. Varaja Iyengar.

SRI SATHYA SAI INSTITUTE OF HIGHER LEARNING (1981), Anantapur. (749).—*Vice-Chancellor*, Prof. V. K. Gokak.

SRI VENKATESWARA (1954), Tirupati. (35,056).—*Vice-Chancellor*, Prof. G. N. Reddy.

TAMIL (1981), Thanjavur. (37).—*Vice-Chancellor*, V. I. Subramoniam, PH.D.

TAMIL NADU AGRICULTURAL (1971), Coimbatore, (2,717).—*Vice-Chancellor*, A. Venkataraman.

TATA INSTITUTE OF SOCIAL SCIENCES (1936), Bombay. (241).—*Director*, Miss A. S. Desai, PH.D.

UTKAL (1943), Bhubaneswar. (87,170).—*Vice-Chancellor*, M. K. Rout, PH.D, D.SC.

VIDYA SAGAR, Midnapore.—*Vice-Chancellor*, Prof. B. C. Mukherjee.

VIKRAM (1957), Ujjain. (31,427).—*Vice-Chancellor*, K. K. Kemkar, PH.D.

VISVA-BHARATI (1951), Santiniketan. (3,270).—*Vice-Chancellor*, Prof. A. Datta.

Kenya

NAIROBI (1970). (Full-time students, 5,456).—*Vice-Chancellor*, Prof. J. M. Mungai, PH.D.

KENYATTA UNIV. COLL. (1972), Nairobi. (2,201).—*Principal*, Prof. J. K. Maitha, PH.D.

Lesotho

NATIONAL U. OF LESOTHO (1975), Roma. (Full-time students, 1,143).—*Vice-Chancellor*, B. A. Tlelase.

Malawi

MALAWI (1964), Zomba and other centres. (Full-time students, 1,849).—*Vice-Chancellor*, D. Kimble, O.B.E., PH.D.

Malaysia

UNIV. OF AGRICULTURE, MALAYSIA (1971), Serdang. (Full-time students, 6,039).—*Vice-Chancellor*, Prof. Nayan bin Ariffin, PH.D.

MALAYA (1962), Kuala Lumpur. (9,216).—*Vice-Chancellor*, Royal Prof. Ungku A. Aziz, D.ECON., D.Litt.H., ED.D.

NATIONAL UNIV. OF MALAYSIA (1970), Kuala Lumpur. (6,445).—*Vice-Chancellor*, Prof. Dato Abdul Hamid Abdul Rahman.

NORTHERN MALAYSIA (1984), Alor Star. (350).—*Vice-Chancellor*, Tan Sri Dato Prof. Awang Had Salleh, PH.D.

SCIENCE U., MALAYSIA (1969). (3,893).—*Vice-Chancellor*, Yang Berbahagia Datuk Musa bin Mohamad.

U. OF TECHNOLOGY (1972), Kuala Lumpur. (5,416).—*Vice-Chancellor*, Y. B. Tan Sri Dato Hj. Ainuddin bin Abdul Wahid.

Malta

MALTA (1980), Msida. (Full-time students, 1,234).—*Rector*, Prof. G. P. Xuereb, D.Phil., M.D.

Mauritius

NATIONAL U., MAURITIUS (1965), Réduit. (Full-time students, 117).—*Vice-Chancellor*, Prof. J. Manrakhan.

New Zealand

AUCKLAND (1882). (Full-time students, 8,790).—*Vice-Chancellor*, C. J. Maiden, D.Phil.

CANTERBURY (1873), Christchurch. (5,269).—*Vice-Chancellor*, Prof. A. D. Brownlie.
  LINCOLN COLL. (1878). (1,623).—*Principal*, Emeritus Prof. B. J. Ross.

MASSEY (1964), Palmerston North. (4,855).—*Vice-Chancellor*, T. N. M. Waters, PH.D., D.SC.

OTAGO (1869), Dunedin. (5,438).—*Vice-Chancellor*, R. O. H. Irvine, M.D.

VICTORIA, WELLINGTON (1897). (4,767).—*Vice-Chancellor*, W. I. Axford, PH.D.

WAIKATO (1964), Hamilton. (2,282).—*Vice-Chancellor*, vacant.

Nigeria

AHMADU BELLO (1962), Zaria. (Full-time students, 18,770).—*Vice-Chancellor*, Prof. A. Abdullahi, PH.D.

ANAMBRA STATE U. OF TECHNOLOGY (1980), Enugu and Awka. (983).—*President*, Prof. C. A. Onwumechili, PH.D., D.SC.

BAYERO (1975), Kano. (3,592).—*Vice-Chancellor*, Prof. I. H. Umar, PH.D.

BENIN (1970). (8,092).—*Vice-Chancellor*, Prof. D. A. Baikie, ED.D.

CALABAR (1975). (4,873).—*Vice-Chancellor*, Prof. A. N. Mohammed, PH.D.

FEDERAL U. OF TECHNOLOGY, AKURE (1980). (299).—*Vice-Chancellor*, Prof. T. I. Francis.

FEDERAL U. OF TECHNOLOGY, MINNA.—*Vice-Chancellor*, Prof. J. O. Ndagi.

FEDERAL U. OF TECHNOLOGY, OWERRI (1980). (366).—*Vice-Chancellor*, Prof. U. D. Gomwalk, PH.D.

IBADAN (1948). (11,140).—*Acting Vice-Chancellor*, Prof. L. A. Banjo.

IFE (1961), Ile-Ife. (10,227).—*Vice-Chancellor*, Prof. W. Abimbola, Ph.D.

ILORIN (1975). (4,623).—*Vice-Chancellor*, S. A. Toye, Ph.D.

IMO STATE (1981), Etiti and other centres. (1,225).—*Vice-Chancellor*, Prof. M. J. C. Echeruo, Ph.D.

Jos (1975). (4,556).—*Vice-Chancellor*, Prof. E. U. Emovon, Ph.D.

LAGOS (1962). (15,104).—*Vice-Chancellor*, Prof. A. O. Adesola.

MAIDUGURI (1975). (5,426).—*Vice-Chancellor*, Prof. J. M. Aminu, Ph.D.

NIGERIA (1960), Nsukka and Enugu. (12,620).—*Vice-Chancellor*, Prof. F. N. Ndili, Ph.D.

OBAFEMI AWOLOWO (1982), Ado-Ekiti. (136).—*Vice-Chancellor*, Prof. I. O. Oladapo, Ph.D

PORT HARCOURT (1975). (2,546).—*Vice-Chancellor*, Prof. S. J. S. Cookey, Ph.D.

RIVERS STATE U. OF SCIENCE AND TECHNOLOGY (1980), Port Hartcourt and other centres. (3,509).—*Vice-Chancellor*, Prof. T. T. Isoun, D.V.M., Ph.D.

SOKOTO (1975). (1,347).—*Vice-Chancellor*, Prof. M. Adamu, Ph.D.

Papua New Guinea

PAPUA NEW GUINEA (1965), Port Moresby. (Full-time students, 1,458).—*Vice-Chancellor*, E. T. Brash, D.Phil.

PAPUA NEW GUINEA UNIV. OF TECHNOLOGY (1973), Lae. (874).—*Vice-Chancellor*, M. Moramoro.

Sierra Leone

SIERRA LEONE (1966), with colleges at Freetown and Njala. (Full-time students, 2,379).—*Vice-Chancellor*, A. T. Porter, Ph.D., L.H.D., LL.D.

Singapore

NATIONAL U. OF SINGAPORE (1980). (Full-time students, 12,955).—*Vice-Chancellor*, Lim Pin M.D.

  NANYANG TECHNOLOGICAL INST. (1981), Singapore. (582).—*President*, Cham Tao Soon, Ph.D.

South Pacific

SOUTH PACIFIC (1967), Suva and Alafua. (Full-time students, 1,639).—*Vice-Chancellor*, G. K. Caston.

Sri Lanka

BUDDHIST AND PALI (1982), Colombo. (Full-time students, 68).—*Vice-Chancellor*, Ven. K. Anuruddha Thera, Ph.D.

COLOMBO (1979). (3,110).—*Vice-Chancellor*, Prof. S. Wijesundera, D.Phil.

JAFFNA (1979). (2,479).—*Vice-Chancellor*, Prof. S. Vithiananthan, Ph.D.

KELANIYA (1979). (2,535).—*Vice-Chancellor*, Prof. M. P. Perera, Ph.D.

MORATUWA (1979), Katubedda. (941).—*Vice-Chancellor*, Prof. M. W. J. G. Mendis.

OPEN U. OF SRI LANKA (1980), Nugegoda, (13,018 part-time).—*Vice-Chancellor*, Prof. P. D. Gunatilake, Ph.D.

PERADENIYA (1979). (6,192).—*Vice-Chancellor*, Prof. B. L. Panditharatne, Ph.D.

  BATTICALOA U. COLL. (1981). (207).—*Director*, Prof. S. Rajaratnam.

RUHUNA (1979), Matara. (901).—*Vice-Chancellor*, Prof. G. P. Samarawickrama, Ph.D.

SRI JAYEWARDENEPURA (1979), Gangodawila. (3,217).—*Vice-Chancellor*, K. Kodithuwakku.

Swaziland

SWAZILAND (1976), Kwaluseni. (Full-time students, 1,067).—*Vice-Chancellor*, Prof. S. M. Guma, D.Litt. & Phil.

Tanzania

DAR ES SALAAM (1970). (Full-time students, 3,360).—*Vice-Chancellor*, N. A. Kuhanga.

SOKOINE U. OF AGRICULTURE (1984), Morogoro.—*Vice-Chancellor*, Prof. G. R. V. Mmari, Ph.D.

Uganda

MAKERERE (1970), Kampala. (Full-time students, 5,042).—*Vice-Chancellor*, Prof. A. Wandira.

West Indies

UNIV. OF THE WEST INDIES (1962), Jamaica, with campuses in Trinidad and Barbados. (Full-time students, 7,165).—*Vice Chancellor*, A. Z. Preston, LL.D.

Zambia

ZAMBIA (1965), Lusaka and Ndola. (Full-time students, 3,628).—*Vice-Chancellor*, J. M. Mwanza, Ph.D.

Zimbabwe

ZIMBABWE (1955), Salisbury. (Full-time students, 3,215).—*Principal*, Prof. W. J. Kamba, LL.D.

FOREIGN COUNTRIES

The following Articles have been revised under the direction of the various Governments or of the British Representatives at Foreign Capitals and by the Foreign and Commonwealth Office in London, to whom the Editor desires to express his warmest thanks. The Editor is also greatly indebted to the Embassies and Consulates-General in London for various corrections and additions.

AFGHANISTAN

(Afghānistān)

President, Babrak Karmal.

COUNCIL OF MINISTERS

Chairman of the Council, Sultan Ali Kishtmand.
President of State Planning Committee, Savivar Mangal.
Deputy Chairmen (without portfolio), Maj. Gen. Mohammad Rafi; Abdul Majid Sarbuland; Prof. Guldad.
Foreign Affairs, Shah M. Dost.
Interior, Maj. Gen. Sayed M. Gulabzoi.
Defence, Col. Gen. Abdul Qadar.
Communications, Lt. Col. M. Aslam Watanjar.
Finance, Muhammad Kabir.
Tribes and Nationalities, Suleiman Laeq.
Transport, Lt. Col. Sher Jan Mazdooryar
Power, Dr. Raz M. Pakteen.
Mines and Industries, M. Ismail Danesh.
Public Works, Nazar Mohammad.
Agriculture and Land Reform, Abdul Ghaffar Lakanwal.
Commerce, Mohammad Khan Jalalar.
Public Health, Dr. M. Nabi Kamyar.
Justice, Mohan Bashir Baghliani.
Education, Abdul Samad Qayumi.
Higher Education, Burhanuddin Ghiasi.
Irrigation, Ahmad Shah Sorkhabi.
Without Portfolio, Dr. Faqir M. Yaqubi.

AFGHAN EMBASSY IN LONDON
31 Prince's Gate, SW7 1QQ.
[01–589 8891/2]

Chargé d'Affaires, Mohammad Homayon Mokammil.

Afghanistan lies to the N. and W. of Pakistan. Its ancient name was Aryana, by which title it is referred to by Strabo, the Greek geographer who lived in the 1st century B.C. The estimated area is 250,000 sq. miles, and the population (Government estimate, 1979) 15,500,000, although it is estimated that two to three million have become refugees in Pakistan and Iran since the Soviet invasion. The population is very mixed. The most numerous race is the Pathan which predominates in the South and West, the main divisions being the Durranis, from whom the Royal Family came, and the Ghilzais. Then come the Tadjiks, an Iranian people mainly cultivators and small traders. There are also Uzbeks and Turkomen in the North, Hazaras in the centre, Baluchis in the South-West and the Nuristanis who live near the Chitral border. All are Sunni Moslems, except the Hazaras and Kizilbashes, who belong to the Shia sect.

Afghanistan is bounded on the W. by Iran (boundary fixed 1857 and 1904), on the S. by Baluchistan (now Pakistan) (boundary fixed 1896–7), on the N. by the U.S.S.R. (boundary fixed 1886–7 and 1893–5), and on the E. by the N.W. Frontier Province (now Pakistan) (boundary fixed 1895) and China. The northern boundary runs from Zulfikar on the Iran frontier to Kushk, the Russian railway terminus,

and thence N.E. to the Oxus (or Amu Darya, "Mother of Rivers") which forms the boundary from Khamiab to Lake Victoria, whence the line to the Chinese frontier was fixed by the Pamir agreement of 1895. The Russo-Afghan frontier was demarcated by the Tashkent Boundary Commission in 1948. An Afghan-Chinese border treaty was signed in 1963 and the border demarcation in 1964. The Pakistan-Afghan frontier was settled by the Durand agreement of 1893.

By treaty of Nov. 22, 1921 (renewed in 1930), Great Britain and Afghanistan agreed to respect one another's internal and external independence; to recognize boundaries then existent, subject to a slight re-adjustment near the Khyber; and to establish Legations and consular offices. As successor state to the British Government, Pakistan has agreed that her relations with Afghanistan shall be based on the 1921 treaty.

Mountains, chief among which are the Hindu Kush, cover three-quarters of the country, the elevation being generally over 4,000 feet. There are three great river basins, the Oxus, Helmand, and Kabul. The climate is dry, with extreme temperatures.

Afghanistan is divided into 26 provinces each under a local Party Secretary.

Government.—The Constitutional Monarchy, introduced by the 1964 Constitution, was overthrown by a *coup d'etat* on July 17, 1973. The country was ruled by Presidential decree until February 1977 when a constitution was approved by a Loya Jirgah (Grand Assembly). Mohammad Daoud was elected President of the Republic for a term of six years.

On April 27, 1978, President Daoud was overthrown by the Armed Forces and power handed to the People's Democratic Party of Afghanistan (PDPA). Noor Mohammad Taraki was appointed Secretary-General of the PDPA, President of the Revolutionary Council and Prime Minister. He was ousted and succeeded by Hafizullah Amin in September 1979. In December 1979 Soviet troops invaded Afghanistan and Babrak Karmal was installed in place of Amin, becoming Secretary-General of the PDPA, President of the Revolutionary Council and Head of State.

Judiciary.—Hitherto Afghanistan has been ruled on the basis of Shariat or Islamic law. However, the Constitution introduced in 1965 provided for the creation of a legal code, and for a new structure of courts, consisting of a lower court in each *wuluswal* (sub province), and a court of appeal in each province, with a Supreme Court in Kabul. The complete separation of executive and judiciary in this constitution was abolished by Presidential Decree in July, 1973. In late 1976 and early 1977 new Penal and Civil Codes were published.

Defence.—The Army, which numbered about 80,000 before the Soviet invasion, has been greatly depleted by desertions. Men between the ages of 18 and 40 are liable to three years' military service. A military academy and military colleges are located in Kabul; some regular officers are trained in the U.S.S.R. A small Air Force is maintained. All military and air force equipment is now of Russian pattern.

Production.—Agriculture and sheep raising are the principal industries. There are generally two crops a year, one of wheat (the staple food), barley, or lentils, the other of rice, millet, maize, and *dal.* Sugar beet and cotton are grown. Afghanistan is rich in fruits. Sheep, including the Karakuli, and transport animals are bred. Silk, woollen and hair cloths and carpets are manufactured. Salt, silver, copper, coal, iron, lead, rubies, lapis lazuli, gold, chrome and talc are found.

The following main roads are open to motor traffic.

(a) Internal: Kabul–Kandahar (310 miles); Kanda-har–Herat (350 miles); Herat–Maimana to Mazar-i-Sharif (500 miles); Mazar-i-Sharif–Kabul (380 miles). Also Kabul–Khanabad–Faizabad (450 miles); Kabul–Gardez (80 miles); Kabul–Bamian (140 miles). The road from Kabul to the North was shortened by the completion in 1964 of the Salang pass. (b) Roads to the frontiers: Kabul–Khyber (175 miles); Kandahar–Chaman (70 miles) and roads from Herat to the Russian and Iranian borders. Five of the major roads in Afghanistan were surfaced by U.S. and Soviet Aid. The Kabul–Khyber, Kandahar–Spin Baldak and Kabul–Kunduz–Qizil Qala roads are also surfaced. A network of minor roads fit for motor traffic in fine weather links up all important towns and districts.

Motor transport has taken the place of pack transport as the chief means of conveyance. The chief trade routes to Pakistan and India are the Khyber Pass route, from Kabul to Peshawar (190 miles), and the road from Kandahar to Chaman (70 miles). In 1982 the Afghan and Soviet shores of the River Oxus were linked by a road and rail bridge which joins the Afghan port of Hairatan and the Soviet port of Termez. A network of internal air services operates between the main towns.

Language and Literature.—The principal languages of the country are Dari (a form of Persian) and Pushtu, although a number of minority languages are also spoken in various provinces. All schoolchildren learn both Persian and Pushtu. Education is free and nominally compulsory, elementary schools having been established in most centres; there are secondary schools in large urban areas and two universities, one in Kabul (established 1932) and one in Jalalabad (established early 1970's).

The annual revenue consists largely of payments in kind. There are taxes on land, sales of animals, a grazing tax, customs duties, stamps, fines, receipts from State lands, monopolies, and factories and mining royalties; in addition certain businesses and individuals have become eligible for income-tax.

Trade with U.K.

	1982	1983
Imports from U.K.	£9,344,000	£10,310,000
Exports to U.K.	20,855,000	19,837,000

Exports are mainly Persian lambskins (Karakul), dried fruits, nuts, cotton, raw wool, carpets, spice and natural gas, while the imports are chiefly oil, cotton yarn and piece goods, tea, sugar, machinery and transport equipment.

CAPITAL, Kabul (about 1,500,000). The chief commercial centres are Kabul and Kandahar (185,000). Other provincial capitals are Herat (145,000), Mazar-i-Sharif (105,000), Jalalabad (55,000).

FLAG.—Black, red and green horizontal stripes with a device in top left-hand corner.

BRITISH EMBASSY
Karte Parwan, Kabul

Chargé d'Affaires a.i., J. D. Garner, M.V.O.

Kabul is distant 5,000 miles from London.

ALBANIA

Chairman of the Praesidium of the People's Assembly (i.e. *Head of State*), Ramiz Alia, *assumed office*, Nov. 22, 1982.
Chairman, Council of Ministers, Adil Çarçani.

Labour (= *Communist*) Party

Politbureau of the Central Committee, R. Alia; M. Asllani; A. Carcani; H. Celiku; Enver Hoxha; H.

Isai; R. Marko; P. Miska; M. Myftiu; L. Cuko; S. Stefani (*full members*); L. Gegprifti; Q. Mihali; B. Bekteshi; F. Çami; P. Murra (*candidate members*).
Secretariat of the Central Committee, Enver Hoxha (*First Secretary*); R. Alia; V. Cerava; L. Cuko; H. Isai; S. Stefani.

Situated on the Adriatic Sea, Albania is bounded on the north and east by Yugoslavia and on the south by Greece. The area of the Republic is estimated at 10,700 sq. miles, with a population (1981) of 2,752,300.

Albania was under Turkish suzerainty from 1468 until 1912, when independence was declared. After a period of unrest, a republic was declared in 1925, and in 1928 a monarchy. The King went into exile in 1939 when the country was occupied by the Italians: Albania was liberated in Nov. 1944. Elections in Dec. 1945 resulted in a Communist-controlled Assembly; the King was deposed *in absentia* and a republic declared in Jan. 1946. United Kingdom diplomatic relations with Albania ceased in 1939 and have so far not been restored.

Much of the country is mountainous and nearly a half is covered by forest. There are fertile areas along the Adriatic coast and the Koritza Basin and there have been land reclamation and irrigation programmes. The main crops are wheat, maize, sugar-beet, potatoes and fruit.

All industry is nationalised. The principal industries are agricultural product processing, textiles, oil products and cement. Output is small at present but the chemical and engineering industries are being built up and the country's considerable mineral resources are being increasingly exploited.

Exports include crude oil, minerals (bitumen, chrome, nickel, copper), tobacco, fruit and vegetables.

Trade with U.K.

	1983
Imports from U.K.	£2,983,000
Exports to U.K.	240,000

CAPITAL, Tirana (pop. 200,000).
FLAG.—Black-two-headed eagle surmounted by yellow outline star, all on a red field.

ALGERIA

President of State, Secretary-General of the Party, Bendjedid Chadli, *elected*, Feb. 1979, *re-elected*, Jan. 1984.

Ministers

Prime Minister, Abdelhamid Brahimi.
Secretary-General of the Government, Mohamed Tayebi.
Foreign Affairs, Ahmed Taleb Ibrahimi.
Interior, Mohamed Yala.
Finance, Boualem Benhamouda.
Trade, Abdelaziz Khellef.
Heavy Industry, Salim Saadi.
Light Industry, Zitouni Messaoudi.
Hydraulics, Environment and Forestry, Mohamed Rouighi.
Energy and Petrochemicals, Belkacem Nabi.
Information, Bachir Rouis.
Primary Education, Mohamed Cherif Kherroubi.
Higher Education, Rafik Abdelhak Brerhi.
Vocational Training, Mohamed Nabi.
Transport, Salah Goudjil.
Labour, Mouloud Oumeziane.
Agriculture and Fisheries, Abdellah Khalef dit Kasdi Merbah.
Justice, Boualem Baki.
Culture and Tourism, Abdelmadjid Meziane.
Youth and Sports, Kamal Bouchama.
Planning and Organization of National Territory, Ali Oubouzar.

Public Health, Djamel Eddine Houhou.
Posts and Telecommunications, Boualem Bessaih.
Public Works, Ahmed Benfreha.
Housing and Construction, Abderrahmane Belayat.
Religious Affairs, Abderrahman Chibane.
Social Affairs, Mme. Z'hor Ounissi.
Ex-Combatants, Dejlloul Bakhti Nemiche.

ALGERIAN EMBASSY IN LONDON
54 Holland Park, W11 3RS
[01–221 7800]

Ambassador Extraordinary and Plenipotentiary, (vacant).

Algeria lies between 8° 45′ W. to 12° E. longitude 27° 6′ N. to a southern limit about 19° N. Area, 855,200 sq. miles (estimated). The population in 1983 was estimated at 20,200,000.

Government.—Algiers surrendered to a French force on July 5, 1830, and Algeria was annexed to France in Feb. 1842. From 1881 the three northern departments of Algiers, Oran and Constantine formed an integral part of France. Between 1955 and 1960 these were reorganized to form 13 departments. The Southern Territories of the Sahara, formerly a separate colony, became an integral part of Algeria on the attainment of independence. In June 1974 there was a further administrative reorganisation resulting in 31 departments. An armed rebellion led by the Moslem *Front de Liberation Nationale (F.L.N.)* against French rule broke out on Nov. 1, 1954. French control of Algeria came to an end when President de Gaulle declared Algeria independent on July 3, 1962; by October, 1963, all agricultural land held by foreigners had been expropriated and by 1965 more than 80 per cent. of the French population had left Algeria.

Ben Bella was elected President of the Republic in Sept., 1963, but was deposed and a Council of the Revolution presided over by Col. Boumediène assumed power on June 19,1965.

A new constitution was established by referendum on Nov. 19, 1976, and on Dec. 10, 1976 President Boumediène was elected for a six-year term of office. Elections for a national popular assembly were held in Feb. 1977. Following President Boumediène's death in December 1978, M. Bendjedid Chadli was elected President in February 1979.

Development in Algeria is regulated by a series of national development plans. The 1970–73 Plan placed particular emphasis on industrial development. The 1974–77 Plan provided for expenditure on infrastructure development and social services. The 1980–84 Plan concentrates on housing, water supply and agriculture.

Trade with U.K.

	1982	1983
Imports from U.K.	£199,234,000	£233,426,000
Exports to U.K.	176,304,000	157,645,000

Algeria's main exports are crude oil and liquefied natural gas. Principal imports from the United Kingdom are capital plant and equipment for industrial use.

Algeria's main industry is the hydrocarbons industry. Oil and natural gas are pumped from the Sahara to terminals on the coast before being exported; the gas is first liquefied at liquefaction plants at Skikda and Arzew.

Other major industries being developed include a steel industry, motor vehicles, building materials, paper making, chemical products and metal manufactures. All major industrial enterprises are now under State control.

Algeria has a rapidly expanding network of roads and railways. Considerable sums are also being spent

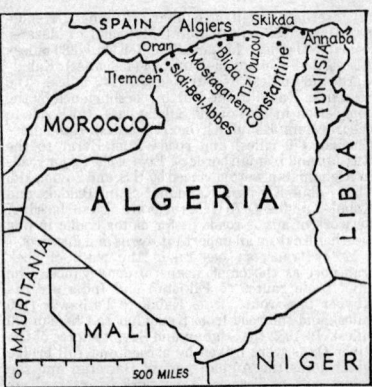

on the development of the State airline, the national shipping company and telecommunications.

CAPITAL.—ΨAlgiers, population 3,250,000 (approx). It is one of the principal ports of the Mediterranean as well as an important industrial centre. Other towns include ΨOran; Constantine; ΨAnnaba; Blida; Setif; Sidi-Bel-Abbès; Tlemcen; Mostaganem; Ψ Skikda; ΨBejaia and Tizi Ouzou.

FLAG.—Red crescent and star on vertically divided green and white background.

NATIONAL DAY.—November 1.

BRITISH EMBASSY
Résidence Cassiopée, 7 Chemin de Glycines,
Algiers.

Ambassador Extraordinary and Plenipotentiary, His Excellency Alan Gordon Munro, C.M.G.
Counsellor, Head of Chancery and Consul General, M. Gowlland.
Cultural Attaché, British Council Representative, J. M. S. Whittell, O.B.E., 6 Avenue Souidani Boudjemaa, Algiers. There is a British Council library in *Algiers*.

ANDORRA

A small, neutral principality (formed by a treaty in 1278), situated on the southern slopes of the Pyrenees between Spain and France, with an approximate area of 190 square miles and population of about 41,600, less than one-fifth of whom are native Andorrans. It is surrounded by mountains of 6,500 to 10,000 feet. Andorra is divided into seven Parishes, each of which has four Councillors elected by vote to the Valleys of Andorra Council of Twenty-eight. The Council appoints the head of the executive government, who designates the members of his government. Constitutionally, the sovereignty of Andorra is vested in two "Co-Princes", the President of the French Republic and the Spanish Bishop of Urgel. These two "co-princes" can veto certain decisions of the Council of the Valleys but cannot impose their own decisions without the consent of the Council. They are represented by Permanent Delegates of whom one is the French Prefect of the Pyrenees Orientales Department at Perpignan and the other is the Spanish Vicar-General of the Diocese of Urgel. They are in turn represented in Andorra la Vella by two resident "Viguiers" known as the Viguier Français and the Viguier Episcopal, who have a joint responsibility for law and order and overall administration policy, together with judicial powers as members of the Supreme Court.

The language of the country is Catalan, but French and Spanish (Castilian) are also spoken. Spanish *pesetas* and French *francs* are the accepted currency and the Budget is expressed in *pesetas*. The estimated national revenue (1981) was US$327 million, with a per capita income of $8,643. The climate is naturally cold for six months, but mild in spring and summer. Potatoes are produced in the highlands and tobacco in the valleys. The mountain slopes have been developed for skiing, and it is estimated that 10,000,000 tourists visit the Valleys during the year. The economy is largely based on tourism, commerce, tobacco, construction and forestry; a third of the country is classified as forest in which pine, fir, oak, birch and box-tree predominate.

A good road into the Valleys from Spain is open all year round, and that from France is closed only occasionally in winter. An airport at Seo d'Urgell just outside Andorra provides daily air connections with Barcelona. There are two radio stations in Andorra, one privately-owned and one operated by a French Government corporation. Both pay dues to the Council of the Valleys.

CAPITAL: Andorra la Vella (population 16,000).

FLAG.—Three vertical bands, blue, yellow, red; Andorran coat of arms frequently imposed on central (yellow) band but not essential.

H.M. Consul-General, Miss P. M. Hutchinson, C.M.G., C.B.E. (*Resident at Barcelona*).

ANGOLA

President, Jose Eduardo Dos Santos.

Angola, which has an area of 488,000 square miles, lies on the western coast of Africa; its population in 1983 was estimated at 7,100,000 although in the wake of fighting between the rival liberation movements the white population, formerly of several hundred thousand, has been greatly reduced, by a mass exodus.

After a Portuguese presence of at least four centuries, and an anti-colonial war since 1961, Angola became independent on Nov. 11, 1975 in the midst of civil war. Soviet-Cuban military assistance to the Popular Movement for the Liberation of Angola (M.P.L.A.) enabled it to defeat its rivals early in 1976. However, the M.P.L.A. government remains under pressure from the U.N.I.T.A. guerrilla movement which now controls up to one-third of the country and operates freely in another third.

The M.P.L.A., a Marxist-Leninist party, is the sole legal party. The Constitution provides for an executive President, who appoints a Council of Ministers to assist him, and a 203-member National People's Assembly.

Angola has valuable oil and diamond deposits and exports of these two commodities account for 70–80 per cent of total exports.

Principal agricultural crops are cassava, maize, bananas, coffee, palm oil and kernals, cotton and sisal. Coffee, sisal, maize and palm oil are exported: exports also include mahogany and other hardwoods from the tropical rain forests in the north of the country. Economic activity fell after independence although progress has been made in the provision of electricity supplies, health services and primary education.

Trade with U.K.

	1982	1983
Imports from U.K.	£25,781,000	£22,847,000
Exports to U.K.	7,368,000	45,732,000

CAPITAL.—ΨLuanda (Est. over 1 million in 1984).

FLAG.—Red and black with a yellow star, machete and cog-wheel.

BRITISH EMBASSY

Rua Diogo Cao 4 (Caixa Postal 1244), Luanda.

Ambassador Extraordinary and Plentipotentiary, His Excellency Marrack Irvine Goulding, C.M.G. (1983).

ARABIA

The area known as Arabia is a peninsula in the south-west of the Asiatic continent, forming the connecting link between Asia and Africa, and lies between 30° 30'—60° E, long. and 12° 45'—34° 50' N. lat. The north-western limit is generally taken from 'Aqaba at the head of the Gulf of 'Aqaba, to a point in the Syrian Desert about 150 miles north-east, and thence northwards to a point about 50 miles due east of Damascus. The remaining land boundaries are in the form of a horse-shoe, encompassing the Syrian Desert, and descending in a south-easterly direction to the head of the Persian Gulf, and thus excluding the whole of Mesopotamia and the Euphrates Valley. The other boundaries of Arabia are the Red Sea and Gulf of Aden, the Arabian Sea and the Persian Gulf and Gulf of Oman. Generally speaking, the peninsula consists of a plateau sloping from south-west to north-east towards the Euphrates Valley, except that the broad south-eastern promontory, which encloses the Persian Gulf, contains a coastal range in Oman.

Language and Literature.—Arabic is spoken not only in this region, but in many other countries, either as the principal or auxiliary tongue, notably in Egypt and the Sudan, Libya, Morocco, Algeria, Iraq, Jordan, Syria, Lebanon; and to some extent also in Nigeria, Madagascar and Zanzibar. Owing to Moorish incursions it was formerly spoken in Spain, the Balearic Islands and Sicily. There are anthologies of pre- and post-Islamic poetry and a considerable prose literature, including popular romances and story cycles (such as "The Thousand and One Nights"), historical and biographical studies, and, resulting from the westernizing movement, there is a general revival of learning among Arabic speaking peoples. Many daily newspapers are published in Arabic and there is a native Arabic drama.

See also—BAHRAIN; KUWAIT; OMAN; QATAR; SAUDI ARABIA; THE YEMEN REPUBLICS: UNITED ARAB EMIRATES.

ARGENTINE REPUBLIC
(República Argentina)

President, Dr. Rául Alfonsín, *took office* Dec. 10, 1983.

CABINET

Interior, Dr. Víctor Martínez.
Foreign Affairs, Sr. Dante Caputo.
Labour, Sr. Juan Manuel Casella.
Economy, Sr. Bernardo Grinspun.
Education and Justice, Dr. Carlos Alconada Aramburú.
Defence, Dr. Raúl Barras.
Health and Social Welfare, Dr. Aldo Neri.
Public Works, Sr. Roque Carranza.

The Embassy closed after the Argentine invasion of the Falkland Islands. Argentine interests in Great Britain are currently handled by the Brazilian Embassy.

Argentina is a wedge-shaped country, occupying the greater portion of the southern part of the South American Continent, and extending from Bolivia to Cape Horn, a total distance of nearly 2,300 miles; its greatest breadth is about 930 miles. It is bounded on the north by Bolivia, on the north-east by Paraguay, Brazil and Uruguay, on the south-east and south by the Atlantic, and on the west by Chile, from which Republic it is separated by the Cordillera de los Andes. On the west the mountainous Cordilleras, with their plateaux, extend from the northern to the southern boundaries: on the east are the great plains. Those in the north are thickly wooded and are known as *El Gran Chaco*, and further south lie the treeless pampas extending from Cordoba in the north to the Rio Negro; and south of the Río Negro are the vast plains of Patagonia. Argentine thus contains a succession of level plains, broken only in Córdoba by the San Luis and Córdoba ranges, in the north-western states by the eastern spurs of the Andes, and in the southern portion of the Province of Buenos Aires by the Tandil Hills (about 1,000 ft.) and the Sierra De La Ventana, near Bahia Blanca (about 3,000 ft.). The Paraná River, formed by the junction of the Upper Paraná with the Paraguay River, flows through the north-eastern states into the Atlantic, and is navigable throughout its course in Argentina; the Pilcomayo, Bermejo, and Salado del Norte are also navigable for some distance from their confluence with the Paraná. In the Province of Buenos Aires the Salado del Sud flows south-east for some 300 miles into Samborombon Bay (Atlantic). In the south Colorado and Río Negro rise in the extreme west and flow across the pampas into the Atlantic, many similar streams in Patagonia (notably the Chubut

and Santa Cruz) traversing the country from the Andes to the Atlantic. The climate ranges from sub-tropical to cold temperate.

The Republic consists of 22 provinces, one territory (Tierra del Fuego) and one federal district (Buenos Aires), comprising in all an area of 1,079,965 square miles, with a population (Census of 1980) of 27,862,771, an increase of 19·3 per cent. since 1970.

Government.—The estuary of La Plata was discovered in 1515 by Juan Díaz de Solís, but it was not until 1534 that Pedro de Mendoza founded Buenos Aires. This city was abandoned and later founded once more by Don Juan de Garay in 1580. In 1810 (May 25) Spanish rule was defied, and in 1816 (July 9), after a long campaign of liberation conducted by General José de San Martín, the independence of Argentina was declared by the Congress of Tucumán.

The first decades after independence were dominated by the dictatorship of Juan Manuel de Rosas. Following his overthrow in 1852, constitutional rule was restored and Buenos Aires was finally established as the seat of the federal government. Compulsory male suffrage was introduced in 1912, but in 1930 the government of Hipólito Irigoyen was overthrown in a military *coup*. In 1945 Juan Domingo Perón became President until overthrown in 1955. There followed eighteen years of political and economic instability, and eventually in 1973, Perón was recalled from exile. Elected President he died within a year and was succeeded by his widow, Vice President María Estela Martínez de Perón. However, warring factions in the Perónist movement and increasing terrorist activity eventually led to a bloodless *coup* when the armed forces on March 24, 1976. A Junta, consisting of the three commanders of the Armed Forces, was established and one of their number, Lt.-General Videla, was also sworn in as President on March 29, 1976 and was later nominated to serve until March 1981. His successor, former Army Chief of Staff, Lt.-Gen. Viola, was ousted in December 1981 and replaced by Gen. Galtieri. Following the Falkland Islands defeat Gen. Galtieri resigned and the Army appointed Gen. Bignone as President. The Navy and Air Force withdrew from the Junta but this was reconstituted shortly afterwards. Elections for a civilian government to replace the military one were held on October 30, 1983 and the Radical Party's candidate, Raúl Alfonsín, was elected President.

Agriculture.—Of a total land area of approximately 700,000,000 acres, farms occupy about 425,000,000. About 60 per cent. of the farmland is in pasture, 10 per cent. in annual crops, 5 per cent. in permanent crops and the remaining 25 per cent. in forest and wasteland. A large proportion of the land is still held in large estates devoted to cattle raising but the number of small farms is increasing. The principal crops are wheat, maize, oats, barley, rye, linseed, sunflower seed, alfalfa, sugar, fruit and cotton. Argentina is pre-eminent in the production of beef, mutton and wool, being self-sufficient in basic foodstuffs and conducting a large export trade in many others. Pastoral and agricultural products provide about 85 per cent. of Argentina's exports and they originate mainly from the pampas or rich central plain which embraces the provinces of Buenos Aires, Santa Fé, Entre Rios, Córdoba and La Pampa.

Mineral Production.—Oil is found in various parts of the Republic and is obtained to a considerable extent at Comodoro Rivadavia (Chubut), Mendoza, Plaza Huincul (Neuquen), Tartagal (Salta) and in other districts. There are a natural gas pipeline between Comodoro Rivadavia and Buenos Aires, an oil pipeline from Campo Duran (Salta) to a refinery in San Lorenzo (Santa Fé), a natural gas pipeline from the same source to the outskirts of Buenos Aires and a natural gas pipeline between Neuquén and Bahía Blanca. The production of oil is of first importance to Argentina's industries and, to some extent, to her economic and financial development. Total petroleum output for 1980 was 28,400,000 cubic metres.

Coal, lead, zinc, tungsten, iron ore, sulphur, mica and salt are the other chief minerals being exploited. There are small worked deposits of beryllium, manganese, bismuth, uranium, antimony, copper, kaolin, arsenate, gold, silver and tin. Coal production in 1980 was 4,156,000 tons; this is produced at the Rio Turbio mine in the province of Santa Cruz. The output of other materials is not large but greater attention is now being paid to the development of these natural resources, especially copper for which the Government and private companies are carrying out exploration.

Industries.—Meat-packing is one of the principal industries; flour-milling, sugar-refining, and the wine industry are also important. In recent years great strides have been made by the textile, plastic and machine tool industries and engineering, especially in the production of motor vehicles and steel manufactures.

Communications.—There are 25,386 miles of railways of which 14,000 miles are broad gauge (5′ 6″), 2,000 miles standard (4′ 8½″), 8,720 miles of narrow 1 metre, 537 miles of 0·75 metre and 129 miles of 0·60 metre. They are all State property. Plans are in hand for complete re-organization of the railways in order to improve their operating efficiency and reduce a very large financial deficit. The combined national and provincial road network totals approximately 137,000 miles of which 23,180 miles are surfaced. There are air services between Argentina and all the neighbouring republics, Europe, Asia, Canada, the U.S.A. and South Africa. Total tonnage entering Argentine ports in 1979 was 13,879,391.

There are 16 short-wave broadcasting stations, 150 medium wave (of which 65 are official). In addition there are 65 television stations, of which 4 are in Buenos Aires. About 3·8 million television receivers are in use.

Defence.—The Army consists of four corps organized into 12 brigades, including mountain, jungle, airborne and armoured troops. It numbers about 5,000 officers, 15,000 N.C.O.s and 65–70,000 conscripts who serve 1 year.

The Navy consists of 1 aircraft carrier, 9 destroyers, 4 frigates/corvettes, 3 submarines, 4 minesweepers, 1 minehunter and ancillary craft. Strength is about 3,000 officers and 30,000 ratings, including 11,000 conscripts.

The Air Force consists of 9 brigades and a training force, with a strength of 1,600 officers, 15,000 other ranks and 20,000 civilians.

Education—Primary and Secondary. The government is formulating a new education policy. At the moment, education is compulsory for the 7 grades of primary school (6 to 13). Secondary schools (14 to 17+) are available in and around Buenos Aires and in most of the important towns in the interior of the country. Most secondary schools are administered by the Central Ministry of Education in Buenos Aires, while primary schools are administered by the Central Ministry or by Provincial Ministries of Education. Private schools, of which there are many, are also loosely controlled by the Central Ministry. *Teacher-Training* now takes place at post school level, courses lasting from 2 to 5 years. *Universities*—Many new universities have been created over the last two years. The total is now over 50 with 24 national (including the Federal Technological University), 25 private and a small number of provincial universities.

Language and Literature.—Spanish is the language of the Republic and the literature of Spain is accepted as an inheritance by the people. There is little indigenous literature before the break from Spain,

but all branches have flourished since the latter half of the nineteenth century. About 450 daily newspapers are published in Argentina, including 7 major ones in the city of Buenos Aires. The English language newspaper is the *Buenos Aires Herald* (daily). There are several other foreign language newspapers.

Trade with U.K.

	1982	1983
Imports from U.K.	£37,349,000	£4,500,000
Exports to U.K.	58,728,000	200,00

CAPITAL.—ΨBuenos Aires, Pop. (Dec. 1980), Metropolitan area 2,908,000; with suburbs, 9,677,200. Other large towns are: ΨRosario de Santa Fé (798,292), Córdoba (798,663), ΨLa Plata (408,300), ΨMar del Plata (317,444), San Miguel de Tucuman (326,000), Santa Fé (312,427) and Mendoza (118,568).

FLAG.—Horizontal bands of blue, white, blue; gold sun in centre of white band.

NATIONAL DAY.—July 9.

BRITISH EMBASSY

The British Embassy was closed after the Argentine invasion of the Falkland Islands. British interests are currently handled by a section at the Swiss Embassy, Dr. Luis Agote 2412, Buenos Aires.

AUSTRIA

President of the Republic of Austria, Dr. Rudolf Kirchschläger, *born* 1915; *elected* June 23, 1974, re-elected May 18, 1980.

CABINET

Chancellor, Dr. Fred Sinowatz.
Vice-Chancellor and Minister of Commerce and Industry, Dr. Norbert Steger.*
Interior, Karl Blecha.
Justice, Dr. Harald Ofner.*
Finance, Dr. Franz Vranitzky.
Transport, Ferdinand Lacin.
Foreign Affairs, Dr. Leopold Gratz.
Agriculture and Forestry, Dip. Ing. Günter Haiden.
Defence, Dr. Friedhelm Frischenschlager.*
Construction and Technology, Karl Sekanina.
Science and Research, Dr. Heinz Fischer.
Health and Environment, Dr. Kurt Steyrer.
Social Services, Alfred Dallinger.
Education and Arts, Dr. Helmut Zilk.
Family Affairs, Gertrude Frölich-Sandner.
* Members of the Freedom Party (Liberals). Other Ministers belong to the Socialist Party.

AUSTRIAN EMBASSY IN LONDON
18 Belgrave Mews West, SW1X 8HU
[01–235 3731]

Ambassador Extraordinary and Plenipotentiary, His Excellency Dr. Reginald Thomas (1982).
Defence Attaché, Col. G. S. M. Trofaier.
Minister-Counsellor, Dr. H. Wessely.

Austria is a country of Central Europe bounded on the north by Czechoslovakia, on the south by Italy and Yugoslavia, on the east by Hungary, on the north-west by Germany and on the west by Switzerland. Its area is 32,376 square miles and its population (1983 estimate), 7,551,300.

Government.—The Republic of Austria comprises nine provinces (Vienna, Lower Austria, Upper Austria, Salzburg, Tyrol, Vorarlberg, Carinthia, Styria and Burgenland) and was established in 1918 on the break-up of the Austro-Hungarian Empire. In March 13, 1938, as a result of the *Anschluss,* Austria (*Oesterreich*) was incorporated into the German

Reich under the name *Ostmark.* After the liberation of Vienna in 1945, the Austrian Republic was reconstituted within the frontiers of 1937 and a freely-elected Government took office on December 20, 1945. The country was divided at this time into four zones occupied respectively by the U.K., U.S.A., U.S.S.R. and France, while Vienna was jointly occupied by the four Powers. On May 15, 1955, the Austrian State Treaty was signed in Vienna by the Foreign Ministers of the four Powers and of Austria. This Treaty recognized the re-establishment of Austria as a sovereign, independent and democratic state, having the same frontiers as on January 1, 1938.

There is a National Assembly of 183 Deputies. In the elections of April 1983, the Socialists formed a coalition with the Freedom Party.

The state of the parties in the Nationalrat (Lower House) in April 1983, was:

Socialist Party (Social Democrat)	90
People's Party (Conservative)	81
Freedom Party (Liberal)	12

In the Bundesrat (Upper House) in March 1983 the People's Party held 32 seats and the Socialist Party, 31.

Religion and Education.—The predominant religion is Roman Catholic. Elementary education is free and compulsory between the ages of 6 and 15 and there are good facilities for secondary, technical and professional education. There are 12 state-maintained Universities and six colleges of art.

Language and Literature.—The language of Austria is German, but the rights of the Slovene- and Croat-speaking minorities in Carinthia, Styria and Burgenland are protected. The press is free.

Communications.—Internal communications in Austria are partly restricted because of the mountainous nature of the country, and road and rail routes must, of necessity, follow the river valleys. The railways in Austria are state-owned and in 1982 had 5,759 km. of track, much of which has been electrified. There were, in 1982, 37,132 km. of roads, including a network of *autobahn* between major cities which also links up with the West German and Italian networks. Of the 1,733 km. of waterways, 595 km. are navigable and there is considerable trade through the Danube ports by both local and foreign shipping. There are six commercial airports.

Tourism.—In 1983, 14,481,500 tourists visited Austria. Foreign exchange receipts from tourism were 91,030 million Schillings—a major contribution to the balance of payments.

PRODUCTION AND INDUSTRY

The origin of Gross Domestic Product in 1983 was as follows (in per cent.):

Agriculture and forestry	5·0
Mining and material goods production	29·4
Energy and water supply	3·2
Construction	6·9
Commerce, hotels, restaurants	16·9
Transport and communications	6·1
Asset management	12·0
Other services and producers	17·1
Import duties and other items	3·4

The value of G.D.P. in 1983 (at current prices) was AS1,207,700 million: G.D.P. per capita (at current prices) was AS159,920.

Agriculture.—The arable land produces wheat, rye, barley, oats, maize, potatoes, sugar beet, turnips, and miscellaneous crops. Many varieties of fruit trees flourish and the vineyards produce excellent wine. The pastures support horses, cattle and pigs. Timber forms a valuable source of Austria's indigenous wealth, about 44·2 per cent. of the total land area consisting of forest areas. Coniferous species predominate (81 per cent. of afforested area).

Energy.—Energy production in 1983 was:—

Crude oil		
—production	1,269,000	tonnes
—imports	5,339,000	,,
(from U.S.S.R.	1,392,600	,,)
(from Saudi Arabia	1,248,600	,,)
Natural gas		
—production	1,213m.	cu. metres
—imports	2,495m.	cu. metres
(from U.S.S.R.	2,451m.	cu. metres)
Electric power		
—output	42,609m.	kWh.
—imports	4,398m.	kWh.
—exports	7,893m.	kWh.

A 700 mw nuclear power station had already been constructed when in November 1978 the Austrian people decided by a very small margin in a national referendum not to allow the introduction of nuclear power stations in Austria.

Mining.—Production in 1982 was (tonnes):—

Lignite	3,297,488
Iron/manganese ore	3,330,000
Raw magnesite	1,031,404
Lead/zinc ore	841,027
Crystal salt	433,557
Graphite	24,451

In addition 2,159,931 cu. metres of brine was produced.

Industry.—Heavy industry production in 1982 included pig iron 3,114,985 tonnes, raw steel 4,258,156 tonnes and rolled steel 3,380,743 tonnes. In addition, petroleum, non-ferrous metals and chemicals are processed in quantity and construction materials, industrial machinery, vehicles, paper and textiles are produced.

FINANCE

	1982	1983*
	Schillings, million	
Federal Budget:		
Expenditure	372,775	407,786
Revenue	300,955	316,667
Gross Budget Deficit	—	91,119
* estimated.		

Federal Budget expenditure (preliminary figures) 1983 (AS million):—

Agriculture, forestry	11,150
Defence	15,750
Education and tuition	35,520
International security, justice	13,210
Public services	7,010
Roads	16,640
Science and research	12,320
Social welfare	103,020
Transportation	80,700
Expenditure on debts	51,906
Other purposes	60,560

TRADE

Main exports are processed goods (iron and steel, textiles, paper and cardboard products), machinery and transport equipment, other finished goods (including clothing) and foodstuffs. Main imports are machinery and transport equipment, processed goods, chemical products, foodstuffs, fuel and energy.

	1982	1983
	Schillings, million	
Imports	332,550	348,339
Exports	226,860	277,120

Over 80 per cent. of all trade is with other European countries, E.E.C. countries accounting for 61·1 per cent., Eastern Europe for 11·1 per cent. and E.F.T.A. members for 7·7 per cent.

Trade with U.K.

	1982	1983
Imports from U.K.	£251,032,000	£273,702,000
Exports to U.K.	404,318,000	438,446,000

Currency.—The unit of currency is the *Schilling* (AS) of 100 *Groschen.* For rate of exchange *see* p. 81.

CAPITAL, Vienna, on the Danube, population 1,531,346. Other towns are Graz (243,166), Linz (199,910), Innsbruck (117,287), Salzburg (139,426), and Klagenfurt (87,321).

FLAG.—Horizontal stripes of red, white, red, with eagle crest on white stripe.

NATIONAL DAY.—October 26.

BRITISH EMBASSY
Reisnerstrasse 40, 1030 Vienna

Ambassador Extraordinary and Plenipotentiary, His Excellency Michael O'Donel Bjarne Alexander (1981).
Counsellor, A. H. Morgan.
1st Secretaries, A. L. Free-Gore (*Head of Chancery*); J. R. Bruce-Lockhart; J. A. Towner; D. J. Harding (*Commercial*); A. E. Clarke (*H.M. Consul*); F. Holroyd (*Administration*).
Defence Attaché, Lt.-Col. M. Legg.
There is a British Consular Office at *Vienna,* and Honorary Consulates at *Innsbruck, Graz and Salzburg.*
British Council Representative, R. Adlam, O.B.E., Schenkenstrasse 4, A-1010 Vienna.

BAHRAIN

Amir, H.H. Shaikh Isa bin Sulman Al Khalifa, G.C.M.G., *born* 1932; *acceded* Dec. 16, 1961.
Crown Prince and C.-in-C., Bahrain Defence Force, H.E. Shaikh Hamad bin Isa Al Khalifa, K.C.M.G.

CABINET

Prime Minister, H.E. Shaikh Khalifa bin Sulman Al-Khalifa.
Minister of Defence, The Crown Prince.
Foreign Affairs, Shaikh Mohammed bin Mubarak Al-Khalifa.
Justice and Islamic Affairs, Shaikh Abdullah bin Khalid Al-Khalifa.
Development and Industry, and Cabinet Affairs, Yusuf Ahmad Shirawi.
Education, Dr. Ali Fakhroo.
Health, Jawad Salim Al-Arayyed.
Legal Affairs, Dr. Hussain Al-Baharna.
Transportation, Ibrahim Mohammed Humaidan.
Interior, Shaikh Mohammed bin Khalifa Al-Khalifa.
Information, Tariq Abdulrahman Al Moayyed.
Labour and Social Affairs, Shaikh Khalifa bin Sulman bin Mohammed Al-Khalifa.
Works, Power and Water, Majid Jawad Al-Jishi.
Housing, Shaikh Khalid bin Abdullah Al-Khalifa.
Finance and National Economy, Ibrahim Abdulkarim Mohammed.
Commerce and Agriculture, Habib Ahmed Kassim.

BAHRAIN EMBASSY IN LONDON
98 Gloucester Road, SW7 4AU
[01–370 5132]

Ambassador Extraordinary and Plenipotentiary, His Excellency Sheik Abdul-Rahman Faris Al-Khalifa.

Area and population.—Bahrain consists of a group of low-lying islands situated about half-way down the Gulf, some 20 miles off the east coast of Arabia. The largest of these, Bahrain island itself, is about 30 miles long and 10 miles wide at its broadest. The capital, Manama, is situated on the north shore of this island. The next largest, Muharraq, with the town and Bahrain International Airport, is connected to Manama by a causeway 1¼ miles long.

The population (1981 Census) is 350,798, of whom 112,378 are foreign. About 65 per cent. of the Bahrainis are Sunni Moslems, the remaining 35 per cent. being Shias; the ruling family and many of the most prominent merchants are Sunnis.

Climate.—The climate is humid all the year round, with rainfall of about 3 in., concentrated in the mild winter months, December to March; in summer, May to October, temperatures can exceed 110°F.

Government.—Bahrain has been a fully independent state since 1971. Government takes the form of a constitutional monarchy, in which traditional consultative procedures continue to play an important role.

Economy.—The largest source of revenue is oil. The Bahrain field, discovered in 1932, is now wholly owned by the Bahrain National Oil Co. Production now stands at about 41,800 bpd. The Sitra refinery derives about 70 per cent. of its crude oil by submarine pipeline from Saudi Arabia. Bahrain also has a half share with Saudi Arabia in the profits of the offshore Abu Sa'afa field. A reservoir of unassociated gas has recently been developed on Bahrain island.

Heavy industry is currently limited to the Aluminium Bahrain smelter, with an annual capacity of 170,000 tonnes of ingots, billets and slabs; it used alumina from Australia and the local natural gas. The Bahrain Government owns 59·9 per cent. of the shares. A dry dock built for a consortium of the OPEC countries and capable of taking tankers of up to 500,000 dwt was opened in 1977. A large petrochemical plant to produce ammonia and methanol is part of Bahrain's industrial development.

The pearling industry, once the basis of the economy, has virtually ceased to exist. There is however a variety of light industries.

The state has developed as a financial centre. Apart from commercial banks, led by the National Bank of Bahrain, the Chartered Bank, the British Bank of the Middle East and the Bank of Bahrain and Kuwait, many international banks have been licensed as "offshore banking units"; there are also money brokers and merchant banks.

The currency is the Bahraini Dinar (BD) divided into 1,000 fils.

Trade with U.K.

	1982	1983
Imports from U.K.	£152,272,000	£150,264,000
Exports to U.K.	35,459,000	37,488,000

Communications.—The port of Mina Sulman has sixteen alongside berths for ships up to 36′ draft.

Bahrain International airport is the main air traffic centre of the Gulf; it is the headquarters of Gulf Air, and a stopping point on routes between Europe and Australia and the Far East, including British Airways and Cathay Pacific.

A world-wide telephone and telex service, by satellite, is operated by Bahrain Telecommunications Company.

FLAG.—Red, with vertical serrated white bar next to staff.

CAPITAL.—Manama; population (1981 Census), 121,986.

BRITISH EMBASSY
21 Government Avenue,
Manama 306, P.O. Box 114

Ambassador Extraordinary and Plenipotentiary, His Excellency Francis S. E. Trew, C.M.G. (1984).

1st Secretaries, P. R. Holmes (Commercial);
W. H. Stevens.
2nd Secretaries, R. P. Smith (Consul); R. J. Cork
(Commercial).
British Council Representative, D. R. Thomas, 21
Government Avenue (P.O. Box 452), Manama 306.

BELGIUM
(Royaume de Belgique)

King of the Belgians, H.M. King Baudouin, K.G., born
Sept. 7, 1930; succeeded July 17, 1951, on the
abdication of his father, King Leopold III, after
having acted as Head of the State since August 11,
1950; married Dec. 15, 1960, Doña Fabiola de Mora
y Aragòn.
Heir Presumptive, H.R.H. Prince Albert, born June 6,
1934, brother of the King; married July 2, 1959,
Donna Paola Ruffo di Calabria, and has issue Prince
Philippe Léopold Louis Marie, b. April
15, 1960; Princess Astrid Josephine-Charlotte
Fabrizia Elisabeth Paola Marie, b. June 5, 1962;
Prince Laurent, b. Oct. 20, 1963.

Prime Minister, Dr. Wilfred Martens (CVP).
Deputy Prime Minister and Minister of Finance and
Foreign Trade, W. de Clerq (PVV).
Deputy Prime Minister and Minister for Justice and
Constitutional Reform, Jean Gol (PRL).
Deputy Prime Minister and Minister for the Interior
and for the Civil Service, Charles-Ferdinand Noth-
omb (PSC).
Public Works and the Middle Classes, Louis Oliver
(PRL).
Foreign Affairs, Léo Tindemans (CVP).
National Defence, Freddy Vreven (PVV).
Flemish Education, Daniel Coens (CVP).
French Language Education, André Bertouille
(PRL).
Economic Affairs, Mark Eyskens (CVP).
Labour and Employment, Michel Hansenne (PSC).
Communications, Posts and Telecommunications,
Herman de Croo (PVV).
Budget, Scientific Policy and Planning, Philippe
Maystadt (PSC).
Brussels Regional Affairs, Paul Hatry (PRL).
Social Affairs and Institutional Reform, Jean-Luc
Dehaene (CVP).

CVP—Social Christian Party (Flemish wing);
PSC—Social Christian Party (Francophone wing);
PVV—Liberals (Flemish); PRL—Liberals (Franco-
phone).

BELGIAN EMBASSY IN LONDON
103 Eaton Square, SW1W 9AB
[01–235 5422]

Ambassador Extraordinary and Plenipotentiary, His
Excellency Jean-Paul van Bellinghen.
Minister Plenipotentiary, M. N. Cockx.
Minister Counsellor, M. B. Lauwaert (Economic).
Military, Naval and Air Attaché, Capt. N. H. Stradiot.

A Kingdom of Western Europe, with a total area of
11,781 square miles and a population, (1981) of
9,863,374 (Greater Brussels, 1,000,221; Flanders,
5,634,152; Wallonia, 3,229,001, of whom 64,713 are
German-speaking). The majority of Belgians are
Roman Catholics. The Kingdom of Belgium is
bounded on the N. by the Kingdom of the Netherlands,
on the S. by France, on the E. by Germany and
Luxemburg, and on the W. by the North Sea.
Belgium has a frontier of 898 miles, and a seaboard
of 41 miles. The Meuse and its tributary, the Sambre,
divide it into two distinct regions, that in the west
being generally level and fertile, while the table-land

of the Ardennes, in the east, has for the most part a
poor soil. The "polders" near the coast, which are
protected by dykes against floods, cover an area of
193 sq. miles. The highest hill, Signal de Botranges,
rises to a height of 2,276 feet, but the mean elevation
of the whole country does not exceed 526 feet. The
principal rivers are the Scheldt and the Meuse.
Brussels has a mean temperature of 49° F. (summer
65°, winter 37°).
Government.—The kingdom formed part of the
"Low Countries" (Netherlands) from 1815 until Oct.
14, 1830, when a National Congress proclaimed its
independence, and on June 4, 1831, Prince Leopold of
Coburg was chosen hereditary king. The separation
from the Netherlands and the neutrality and inviol-
ability of Belgium were guaranteed by a Conference
of the European Powers, and by the Treaty of London
(April 19, 1839), the famous "Scrap of Paper," signed
by Austria, France, Great Britain, Prussia, The
Netherlands, and Russia. On Aug. 4, 1914, the
Germans invaded Belgium, in violation of the terms
of the treaty. The Kingdom was again invaded by
Germany on May 10, 1940. The whole Kingdom
eventually fell and was occupied by Nazi troops until
liberated by the Allies in September 1944.
According to the Constitution of 1831 the form of
government is a constitutional representative and
hereditary monarchy with a bicameral legislature,
consisting of the King, the Senate and the Chamber
of Representatives. The parliamentary term is four
years.
The last general election was held on November 8,
1981. The results were as follows (seats):
Chamber of Deputies: CVP, 43; PSC, 18; PVV, 28;
PRL, 24; SP (Socialist), 26; PS (Socialist), 35; VU
(Flemish Nationalist), 20; FDF (Brussels Franco-
phones)/RW (Walloon Regionalists), 8; UDRT (Anti-
tax), 3; Ecologists, 4; PCB/KPB (Communist), 2;
VLAAMS, 1.
Senate: CVP, 22; PSC, 8; PVV, 14; PRL, 11; PS, 18;
SP, 13; VU, 10; FDF/RW, 4; UDRT, 1; Ecologists, 4;
PCB/KPB, 1. Besides these directly elected represen-
tatives the Senate also includes 50 members who are
elected by the Provincial Councils and 25 who are co-
opted in the proportions of the directly elected seats.
H.R.H. Prince Albert is a "sénateur de droit".
Regional Governments.—The 1980 regionalization
law made provision for the establishment of three
Regional Parliaments (Assemblies) with executive
councils which were set up in November 1981 and

became effective in January 1982. The executives are autonomous from the central government, and their members are elected by the members of the Assemblies to whom they are responsible. They prepare Bills within the limits of their regional/community competences, and once these Bills have been passed by the regional assembly and published in the *Moniteur Belge*, they have the force of law.

The Flemish Regional Assembly (182 members) and Executive (a President and 8 Regional Ministers) covers the provinces of Antwerp, East and West Flanders, Limbourg and the Flemish *arrondissements* (Hall, Vilvoorde, Leuven) in the province of Brabant, and is also responsible for the Flemish population of Brussels. The Walloon Regional Assembly (106 members) and Executive (a President and 5 Regional Ministers) covers the provinces of Hainault, Liege, Luxembourg and Naumur, and the *arrondissement* of Nivelles in the province of Brabant. The French Community Assembly (137 members) and Executive (a President and 2 Community Ministers) has no fixed territory but is responsible for the francophone population of Brussels and, in concert with the Walloon Regional Assembly, deals with certain Walloon regional affairs.

Although the regionalization laws defined the City of Brussels as a region, there is no autonomous regional parliament for the City and its affairs are handled by a Brussels Executive within the national government. The German community (about 60,000) also has no autonomous regional assembly; German community affairs are handled by the German Cultural Council based in Eupen.

Language and Literature.—Belgium is divided between those who speak Dutch (the Flemings) and those who speak French (the Walloons). Dutch is spoken in the provinces of West Flanders, East Flanders, Antwerp, Limburg, and the northern half of Brabant, and French in the provinces of Hainault, Namur, Luxemburg, Liège and the southern half of Brabant. Dutch is recognized as the official language in the northern areas and French in the southern (Walloon) area and there are guarantees for the respective linguistic minorities. Brussels is officially bi-lingual. There is a small German-speaking area (Eupen and Malmedy) along the German border, east of Liège.

The literature of France and the Netherlands is supplemented by an indigenous Belgian literary activity, in both French and Dutch. Maurice Maeterlinck (1862–1949) was awarded the Nobel Prize for Literature in 1911. Emile Verhaeren (1855–1916) was a poet of international standing. Of contemporary Belgian writers, perhaps the most celebrated is Georges Simenon (*born* at Liège in 1903). There are 39 daily newspapers in Belgium (23 in French, 15 in Dutch and 1 in German).

Education.—The nursery schools provide free education for the 2½ to 6 age group. There are over 8,000 primary schools (6 to 12 years) of which approximately 5,000 are administered by the State, province or commune and the remainder are free institutions (predominantly Roman Catholic). There are more than 1,100 secondary schools offering a general academic education slightly over half of which are free institutions (predominantly Roman Catholic but subsidized by the State) and the remainder official institutions. The official school leaving age is 14.

Production.—Belgium is essentially a manufacturing country. With no natural resources except coal, annual production of which was 6,136,000 tonnes in 1981, industry is based largely on the processing for re-export of imported raw materials. Gross National Product per capita in 1979 was B.Fr.297,400. Principal industries are coal, steel and metal products (Mons, Charleroi, Liège, Namur, Hainault, Brabant and Limburg), textiles (Ghent, Bruges, Courtrai, Verviers, etc.), glass, nitrogen, heavy chemicals, sugar, breweries, etc.

FINANCE

Budget	1981	1982
	B. Fr. (millions)	
Revenue	1,158,800	1,151,000
Expenditure	1,609,000	1,458,800

The unit of currency is the Belgian *franc.* (*See also* p. 81). External trade figures relate to Luxemburg as well as Belgium since the two countries formed an Economic Union in 1921.

TRADE

	1981	1982
	B. Fr. (millions)	
Total Imports	2,296,600	2,424,000
Total Exports	2,059,900	2,307,000

Trade with U.K.

	1982	1983
Imports from U.K.	£2,298,118,000	£2,572,673,000
Exports to U.K.	2,861,809,000	3,133,905,000

Communications.—In 1983, there were 3,920 kilometres of normal gauge railways operated by the Belgian National Railways, of which 1,763 kilometres were electrified. The Belgian National Light Railways (SNCV) also operated 27,671 kilometres of regular bus routes. In 1982 there were 2,722,107 telephone subscribers in Belgium.

Ship canals include *Ghent-Terneuzen* (18 miles, of which half is in Belgium and half in the Netherlands) which permits the passage to Ghent of ships up to 60,000 tons; the Canal of *Willebroek Rupel-Brussels* (20 miles, by which ships drawing 18 ft reach Brussels from the sea; opened in 1922); and *Bruges* (from Zeebrugge on the North Sea to Bruges, 6¼ miles). The *Albert Canal* (79 miles), links Liège with Antwerp; it was completed in 1939 and accommodates barges up to 1,350 tons. The modernization of the port of Antwerp is well advanced. Inland waterway approaches to Antwerp are also to be improved. The river Meuse from the Dutch to the French frontiers, the river Sambre between Namur and Monceau, the river Scheldt from Antwerp-Ghent and the Brussels-Charleroi Canal are being widened or deepened to take barges up to 1,350 tons. Most of the maritime trade of Belgium is carried in foreign shipping.

In 1981 there were 13,093 km. of trunk roads of which about 1,315 km. are motorways.

The Belgian National Airline *Sabena* operates regular services between Brussels and London, and many continental centres, as well as overseas services to Northern and Central America, Africa, Middle East, Far East, etc. Many foreign airlines call at Brussels.

Cities and Towns.—The Capital, BRUSSELS, has a population (1981) of 1,000,221 (with suburbs). Other towns are ΨAntwerp, the chief port (923,547); Ψ Ghent (486,081), which has large cotton and flax spinning mills, and is the second port of importance after Antwerp; Liège (609,066), the centre of the iron industry, and Charleroi (441,017), an important coal-mining and metallurgical centre; ΨBruges (252,430); ΨOstend (270,888); Malines (291,459). Brussels is 224 miles from London; transit, by rail and sea, 8 hrs.; by air, 50 mins.

NATIONAL FLAG.—Three vertical bands, black, yellow, red.

NATIONAL DAY.—July 21 (Accession of King Leopold I, 1831).

BRITISH EMBASSY.
Britannia House, 28 rue Joseph II,
1040 Brussels.

Ambassador Extraordinary and Plenipotentiary, His
Excellency Sir Edward Jackson, K.C.M.G.
Counsellors, A. L. S. Coltman (*Head of Chancery*); M.
B. Collins, M.B.E. (*Commercial*).
Defence and Military Attaché, Col. K. J. Marchant.
Air and Naval Attaché, Wing Cdr. A. L. Terrett,
R.A.F.
There are British Consular Offices at *Brussels,
Antwerp, Ghent* and *Liège.*

*British Council Representative to Belgium and Lux-
emburg,* J. P. Harniman, O.B.E., Avenue Galilée-
Galileilaan 5 (Boîte 10), 1030, Brussels (Council
Library at *Brussels*).
BRITISH CHAMBER OF COMMERCE FOR BELGIUM AND
LUXEMBURG (INC.), 30 Rue Joseph II, 1040 Brussels.

BENIN
(People's Republic of Benin)

*President of the Military Revolutionary Government
and Head of State,* Gen. Ahmed Mathieu Kerekou;
assumed office, Oct. 26, 1972, re-elected, Aug. 1984.

A republic situated in West Africa, between 2° and
3° W. and 6° and 12° N., Benin (formerly known as
Dahomey) has a short coast line of 78 miles on the
Gulf of Guinea but extends northwards inland for
437 miles. It is flanked on the west by Togo, on the
north by Upper Volta and Niger and on the east by
Nigeria. It has an area of about 47,000 square miles
and a population of 3,338,240 at the 1979 Census.
Although poor in resources, Benin is one of the most
thickly populated areas in West Africa, with a high
level of education. It is divided into four main regions
running horizontally: a narrow sandy coastal strip,
a succession of inter-communicating lagoons, a clay
belt and a sandy plateau in the north.

The first treaty with France was signed by one of
the kings of Abomey in 1851 but the country was not
placed under French administration until 1892.
Benin became an independent republic within the
French Community on Dec. 4, 1958; full independence
outside the Community was proclaimed on August 1,
1960. In October, 1963, a popular revolution led to
the fall of the government of the first President of
Benin, Hubert Maga. The Army held power until
Sourou-Migan Apithy was elected President and
Justin Ahomadegbé Chief of Government in January,
1964, after a new constitution had been agreed. This
government was overthrown in November, 1965,
following a long-standing disagreement between
Maga and Apithy. It was replaced by President
Tahirou Congacou, who was in turn dismissed in
December of the same year by the Army. Christophe
Soglo then assumed control and dismissed the Assem-
bly. Soglo was in his turn overthrown by an Army
coup d'état on December 17, 1967. Seven months later
Dr. Zinsou was installed, with the support of the
Army, as President, an appointment which was
confirmed by a national referendum on July 28, 1968.

Dr. Zinsou was overthrown by a military coup on
December 10, 1969 and for five months the country
was ruled by a military "Directoire". Following
abortive elections in March, 1970, a Presidential
Council was set up in May, 1970 consisting of MM.
Maga, Ahomadégbé and Apithy, with M. Maga as
President of the Council and Head of State. He was
succeeded in May, 1972 by M. Ahomadégbé, who in
turn would have been succeeded in May 1974 by M.
Apithy, but for the *coup d'état* of October 26, 1972
which brought the Military Revolutionary Govern-

ment, headed by Lt.-Col. Kerekou, to power. General
elections were held in Nov. 1979, and a new Constitution and National Assembly were established.

Benin is a member of the *Conseil de l'Entente,* the
Organisation Commune Africaine et Malgache
(OCAM), the Organization of African Unity (O.A.U.)
and the Economic Community of West African States
(ECOWAS). The official language is French.
Finance.—The currency of Benin is the *Franc
CFA* of 100 *centimes.*
Trade.—The principal exports are palm products
(80 per cent.) followed by ground nuts, shea-nuts,
cotton and coffee. Small deposits of gold, iron and
chrome have been found; oil production is scheduled
to begin in 1983.

Trade with U.K.

	1982	1983
Imports from U.K.	£14,941,000	£10,577,000
Exports to U.K.	1,227,000	2,887,000

CAPITAL.—Porto Novo (104,000). Political capital
and principal commercial town and port, ΨCotonou
(178,000).
FLAG.—Green, with five pointed red star in the top
left corner.
NATIONAL DAY.—November 30.
British Embassy (see Lagos, Nigeria).

BHUTAN

King of Bhutan, H.M. Jigme Singye Wangchuck,
born Nov. 11, 1955; succeeded his father, July, 1972;
crowned, June 2, 1974.

COUNCIL OF MINISTERS
H.M. Representative in the Ministry of Finance,
H.R.H. Ashi S. C. Wangchuk.
H.M. Representative in the Ministry of Development,
H.R.H. Ashi D. W. Wangchuk.
Trade, Industry and Forests, H.R.H. Namgyel
Wangchuk.
Home Affairs and Speaker of the National Assembly,
Lyonpo Tamji Jagar.
Foreign Affairs, Lyonpo Dawa Tshering.
Communications and Tourism, Lyonpo Sangye
Penjor.
Deputy Minister of Defence, Col. Lam Dorji.

Bhutan is a small Himalayan Kingdom situated
between Tibet (to the north) and India (to the west,
south and east). The total area is about 18,000 sq.
miles, with a mountainous northern region which is
infertile and sparsely populated, a central zone of
upland valleys where most of the population and
cultivated land is found, and in the south the densely
forested foothills of the Himalayas, which are mainly
inhabited by Nepalese settlers and indigenous tribes-
people.

The population of Bhutan is estimated (mid-1981)
at 1,300,000, about three-quarters of whom are
Buddhists. The remainder (mostly the Nepali Bhu-
tanese) are Hindu. The official language, for administrative and religious purposes, is Dzongkha, a
variant of Tibetan, which functions as a *lingua franca*
amongst a variety of languages and dialects. It is
government policy to make the study of Dzongkha
compulsory in schools, although English is the
medium of instruction and has become widely used
within the administration.

In 1949, a treaty was concluded with the Government of India under which the Kingdom of Bhutan
agreed to be guided by the Government of India in
regard to its external relations, but it still retains
independence, issues its own passports, has its own
diplomatic representatives and is a member of the
U.N.

It also receives from the Government of India an annual payment of *Rs.*500,000 as compensation for portions of its territory annexed by the British Government in India in 1864. India provides 50 per cent of the budget for Bhutan's 5-year plan (1982–7).

Government.—Bhutan has a 150-member National Assembly which meets twice a year. The 8-member Royal Advisory Council, nominated by the King and the National Assembly, acts as a consultative body when the National Assembly is not in session. The King is also assisted by a Council of Ministers.

Economy.—The economy is based on agriculture and animal husbandry, which engage over 90 per cent of the workforce in what is largely a self-sufficient rural society. The principal food crops are rice, wheat, maize and barley. Vegetables and fruit are also produced. Bhutan is the world's largest producer of cardamom, which forms its principal export to countries other than India. Mineral resources include dolomite and small amounts of coal, which are exported to India. Industry is little developed, the principal industrial units being a cement plant, a distillery and a food processing plant. Tourism and postage stamps are increasingly important sources of foreign exchange. Over 90 per cent of foreign trade is with India. Principal exports are agricultural products, timber, cement and coal; main imports are textiles, cereals and consumer goods. With Indian assistance a network of roads has been constructed and Bhutan's airline, Druk Air, has become operational, flying between the capital and Calcutta.

CURRENCY.—*Ngultrum* (parity with Indian rupee).
CAPITAL.—Thimphu.
FLAG.—Orange and crimson divided diagonally, with dragon device in centre.

BOLIVIA
(República de Bolivia)

President of the Republic, Dr. Hernan Siles Zuazo, *took office,* October 10, 1982.

BOLIVIAN EMBASSY IN LONDON
106 Eaton Square, SW1W 9AD
[01–235 2257/4248]

Minister Counsellor, C. Quintanilla.
1st Secretary, Srta. Marta Bosacoma Bonel.
There is a Bolivian Consular Office in *Liverpool.*

The land-locked Republic of Bolivia extends between lat. 10° and 23° S. and long. 57° 30′ and 69° 45′ W. It has an area estimated at 415,000 square miles with a population of 6,000,000. (*For* MAP, *see* Index.) The Republic derives its name from its liberator, Simon Bolivar (1783–1830).

The chief topographical feature is the great central plateau (65,000 square miles) over 500 miles in length, at an average altitude of 12,500 feet above sea level, between the two great chains of the Andes, which traverse the country from south to north, and contain, in Illampu, Illimani, and Sajama, three of the highest peaks of the western hemisphere. The total length of the navigable streams is about 12,000 miles, the principal rivers being the Itenez, Beni, Mamore and Madre de Dios.

Language and Literature.—The official language of the country is Spanish, but many of the Indian inhabitants (about two-thirds of the population) speak Quechua or Aymará, the two linguistic groups being more or less equal in numbers.

The Roman Catholic religion was disestablished in 1961 but relations between it and the State are good. Elementary education is compulsory and free and there are secondary schools in urban centres. Provision is also made for higher education; in addition to St. Francisco Xavier's University at Sucre, founded in 1624, there are six other universities, the largest being the University of San Andres at La Paz. Bolivian literature has not yet produced authors of world-wide renown. There are nine principal daily newspapers in Bolivia.

Production.—Mining, natural gas, petroleum and agriculture are the principal industries. The ancient silver mines of Potosí are now worked chiefly for tin, but gold, partly dug and partly washed, is obtained on the Eastern Cordillera of the Andes; the tin output is one of the largest in the world, and together with other minerals (copper, antimony, lead, zinc, asbestos, wolfram, bismuth salt and sulphur), provides over half of Bolivia's exports.

In 1982 Bolivia produced 1·4 million cubic metres of oil, sufficient for internal consumption. Gas (currently providing about a quarter of Bolivia's export income) is piped to Argentina and there are plans to build a pipeline to Sao Paulo, Brazil, by 1985. Bolivia's agricultural produce consists chiefly of rice, barley, oats, wheat, sugar-cane, maize, cotton, indigo, rubber, cacao, potatoes, cinchona bark, medicinal herbs, brazil nuts etc. Total exports (c.i.f.) in 1982 were U.S. $898 million.

Transport and Communications.—There are 2,200 miles of railways in operation including the lines from Corumbá to Santa Cruz (312 miles). There are about 10,950 miles of telegraphs, and microwave telephone communications between La Paz, Santa Cruz, Cochabamba, Oruro and Sucre; there are plans to include other cities in the network soon. Most other towns of any size have radio/telephone communication with the main cities. There is direct railway communication to the sea at Antofagasta (32 hours), Arica (10 hours), and Mollendo (2 days), and also to Buenos Aires (3½ days); branch lines run from Oruro to Cochabamba, and from Río Mulato to Potosí, and from Potosí to Sucre, the legal capital. The Antofagasta (Chile) and Bolivia Railroad was formerly an all-British concern, but the Bolivian sector has now been nationalized. Communication with Peru is effected by rail to Guaqui and thence by steamer across Lake Titicaca to the railhead at Puno.

Commercial aviation in Bolivia is conducted by Eastern Airlines (American), Lufthansa, Aeroperu, Aerolineas Argentinas, Cruzeiro do Sul (Brazil), and Lloyd Aereo Boliviano (Bolivian), providing international connections with U.S.A., West coast South American countries, Canal Zone, Europe, Brazil and Argentina; local flights provided by Lloyd Aereo Boliviano and Transporte Aereo Militar link La Paz, Oruro, Cochabamba, Santa Cruz, Tarija, Sucre, Trinidad and other towns.

Bolivia is without a sea-coast, having been deprived of the ports of Tocopilla, Cobija, Mejillones and Antofagasta by the "Pacific War" of 1879–1884.

FINANCE

The economy has deteriorated since 1977, with disappointing petroleum reserves and a large external debt. The position worsened in 1981 when world tin prices remained low. The peso was devalued to 2,000 to 1 U.S. dollar in April 1984. The inflation rate in 1984 was about 560 per cent.

Trade with U.K.

	1982	1983
Imports from U.K.	£4,943,000	£4,711,000
Exports to U.K.	20,899,000	14,834,000

Mineral exports represent about 83 per cent of these totals. A large part of Bolivia's minerals were shipped to U.K. for smelting and re-export, but Bolivia is now developing her own smelters and will in future be exporting metals. The chief imports are wheat and flour, iron and steel products, machinery, vehicles and textiles.

Seat of Government.—La Paz.' Population (census 1976) 654,700. Other large centres are Cochabamba (194,000), Oruro (124,000), Santa Cruz (237,000), Potosí (77,000), Sucre, the legal capital and seat of the judiciary (63,000) and Tarija (38,500).

FLAG.—Three horizontal bands; red, yellow, green.
NATIONAL DAY.—August 6 (Independence Day).

BRITISH EMBASSY
Avenida Arce 2732–2754,
(Casilla 694) La Paz.

Ambassador Extraordinary and Plenipotentiary, His Excellency Stanley Frederick St. Clare Duncan, C.M.G. (1981).
1st Secretary, P. Sullivan (*Commercial and Head of Chancery*).

BRITISH CONSULAR OFFICES

There is a British Consular Office at *La Paz*.

BRAZIL
(The Federative Republic of Brazil)

President, General João Baptista de Figueiredo; *elected*, October 15, 1978; *inaugurated*, March 15, 1979.
Vice-President, Aureliano Chaves.

BRAZILIAN EMBASSY IN LONDON
32 Green Street, W1Y 3FD
[01–499 0877]

Ambassador Extraordinary and Plenipotentiary, His Excellency Mario Gibson-Barboza (1982).
Minister-Counsellor, José Olympio Rache de Almeida.
Minister, Thereza Maria Machado Quintella (*Consular*).
Air Attaché, Gp. Capt. S. L. Millon.
Naval Attaché, Capt. D. A. Luiz.
Military Attaché, Col. J. de Oliveira Brazida.
Consular Section, 6 Deanery Street, W1Y 5LH (01–499 7441).
Commercial Section, 15 Berkeley Street, W1X 5AE (01–499 0877).

There are also a Brazilian Consulate-General at *Liverpool* and honorary consular offices at *Cardiff* and *Glasgow*.

POSITION AND EXTENT

Brazil, the most extensive State of South America, discovered in 1500 by Pedro Alvares Cabral, Portuguese navigator, is bounded on the north by the Atlantic Ocean, the Guianas, Colombia and Venezuela; on the west by Peru, Bolivia, Paraguay, and Argentina; on the south by Uruguay; and on the east by the Atlantic Ocean. Brazil extends between lat. 5° 16′ N. and 33° 45′ S. and long. 34° 45′ and 73° 59′22″ W., being 2,685 miles from north to south, and 2,690 from west to east, with a coast-line on the Atlantic of 4,604 miles. The Republic comprises an area of 3,289,440 square miles, with a population (1980 census) of 119,098,922.

The northern States of Amazonas and Pará are mainly wide, low-lying, forest-clad plains. The central states of Mato Grosso are principally plateau land and the eastern and southern States are traversed by successive mountain ranges interspersed with fertile valleys. The principal ranges are *Serra do Mar* in São Paulo; the *Serra Geral* (Caparao 9,393 feet) between Minas Gerais and Espirito Santo, the *Serra da Mantiqueira* (Itatiaia, 9,163 feet) and the *Serra do Espinhaco* (Itacolumi, 5,748 feet), in the south-east of Minas Gerais; the *Serra do Paraná*, between Goiás and Minas Gerais, the *Serra dos Aimorés*, which divide Espírito Santo from Minas Gerais; and the *Serra do Gurgueia, Branca* and *Araripe*, which envelop Piaui.

Brazil is unequalled for its rivers. The River *Amazon* has tributaries which are themselves great rivers, and flows from the Peruvian Andes to the Atlantic, with a total length of some 4,000 miles. Its principal northern tributaries are the *Rio Branco, Rio Negro*, and *Japurá*; its southern tributaries are the *Juruá, Purus, Madeira* and *Tapajós*, while the *Xingú* meets it within 200 miles of its outflow into the Atlantic. The *Tocantins* and *Araguaia* flow northwards from the Plateau of Mato Grosso and the mountains of Goiás to the Gulf of Pará. The *Parnaiba* flows from the encircling mountains of Piaui into the Atlantic. The *São Francisco* rises in the South of Minas Gerais and traverses Bahia on its way to the eastern coast, between Alagoas and Sergipe. The *Paraguai*, rising in the south-west of Mato Grosso, flows through Paraguay to its confluence with the *Paraná*, which rises in the mountains of that name and divides Brazil from Paraguay. On the *Iguaçú or Iguassú*, which unites with the Upper Paraná at the Brazil-Argentine-Paraguay boundary, are the majestic *Falls of the Iguaçú* (200 ft.), and on the *São Francisco* are the no less famous falls of *Paulo Afonso* (260 ft.).

Government.—Brazil was colonized by Portugal in the early part of the sixteenth century, and in 1822 became an independent empire under Dom Pedro, son of the refugee King Joao VI. of Portugal. On Nov. 15, 1889, Dom Pedro II., second of the line, was dethroned and a republic was proclaimed.

The Federative Republic of Brazil is made up of the Federal District, 23 States and 3 Territories (the most under-developed frontier regions). The constitution of January 1967 draws on the same conceptual basis as that of the United States, and envisages an equal distribution of power between the Executive, the Legislature and the Judiciary. The President, who heads the Executive of the Federal Government, is elected for a 6-year term by an electoral college consisting of the Congress and representatives of the State Legislative Assemblies. The next Presidential elections will be in January 1985.

The Congress consists of a Senate (3 Senators per State elected for an 8-year term) and a Chamber of Deputies which is re-elected every 4 years. (The number of Deputies per State depends upon the State's population). Each State has a Governor, and a Legislative Assembly with a 4-year term.

Production.—There are large and valuable mineral deposits including among others, iron ore (hematite), manganese, bauxite, beryllium, chrome, nickel, tungsten, cassiterite, lead, gold, monazite (containing rare earths and thorium) and zirconium. Diamonds and precious and semi-precious stones are also found. The mineral wealth is being exploited to an increasing extent. The iron ore deposits of Minas Gerais and the untapped ones of the Amazon region are particularly rich and plans for mining them are advanced. Production is increasing all the time.

Electric power production in 1983 was 161,970 Gwh. In the same year, the total output of pig-iron was 12,945,000 tonnes. Production of oil was 123,700,000 barrels. Of these 72,000,000 barrels were produced from offshore fields.

Agriculture production in 1982 was:

Black Beans	2,907,213	tonnes
Cassava	24,039,008	,,
Castor Beans	192,428	,,
Cocoa	318,400	,,
Cotton	1,935,091	,,
Maize	21,865,439	,,
Oranges	57,971,264	,,
Peanuts	317,383	,,
Potatoes	2,147,918	,,
Rice	9,718,074	,,
Sisal	249,236	,,
Soya	12,834,624	,,
Tobacco	421,532	,,
Jute	14,222	,,
Wheat	1,819,504	,,

Defence.—The peace-time strength of the Army is 182,750 of which 15,280 are officers and warrant officers and 35,500 are N.C.O.s and 132,000 conscripts. The Navy consists of 1 aircraft carrier, 7 submarines, 10 destroyers, 6 frigates, 9 patrol vessels, 5 river patrol ships, 1 river monitor, 1 river transport, 6 coastal mine sweepers, 7 survey ships, and 29 other vessels. The strength of the Navy is 49,000. The Air Force, with a strength of 43,000, has 696 aircraft, of which 192 are fast-jet.

Education.—Primary education is compulsory and is the responsibility of State governments and municipalities. At this level approximately 10 per cent. attend private schools. Secondary education is largely the responsibility of the State and Municipal Governments, although a small number of very old foundations (the Pedro II Schools) remain under direct federal control. Over 50 per cent. of all pupils at this level attend Private Schools. Higher education is available in Federal State, Municipal and private universities and faculties.

Language and Literature.—Portuguese is the language of the country, but Italian, Spanish, German, Japanese and Arabic are spoken by immigrant minorities, and newspapers of considerable circulation are produced in those languages. English and French are currently spoken by educated Brazilians.

Until the second quarter of the nineteenth century Brazilian literature was dominated by Portugal. French influence is traceable for the next half century, since when a national school has come into existence and there are many modern authors of high standing. Public libraries have been established in urban centres and there is a flourishing national press with widely circulated daily and weekly newspapers.

Communications.—In 1982 there were 1,394,165 km. of highways. The route-length of railways in 1980 was 35,100 km. Seventy-eight aviation companies (25 foreign) provide air-mail and passenger services. There are 21,944 miles of navigable inland waterways. During 1982, 9,574 vessels entered Rio de Janeiro and Santos, the two leading ports.

FINANCE

	1983 *Cruzeiros*
Revenue	11,335,500 million
Expenditure	11,321,209 million

In 1983 (up to September) Brazil's foreign debt stood at U.S.$77,005·6 million. Reserves in 1982 were $3,994·4 million.

TRADE 1983

Total imports	U.S.$15,408 million
Total exports	U.S.$21,899 million

Trade with U.K.

	1982	1983
Imports from U.K.	£158,837,000	£157,758,000
Exports to U.K.	443,956,000	560,277,000

Principal imports are fuel and lubricants, machinery, chemicals, wheat, metals and metal manufactures. Principal exports are coffee, iron ore, soya and its products, steel and orange juice. In 1983 the Brazilian automobile industry produced 836,314 vehicles. Of these, 168,674 vehicles (worth U.S. $1,327,000,000) were exported.

CAPITAL.—Brasilia (inaugurated on April 21, 1960). Population (Census 1980), 1,176,748. Other important centres are São Paulo (8,490,763); the former capital ΨRio de Janeiro (5,094,396); ΨBelo Horizonte (1,774,712); ΨRecife (1,204,794); ΨSalvador (1,017,591); ΨPorto Alegre (1,125,091); ΨFortaleza (1,308,859); and Belem (934,330).

FLAG.—Green, with yellow lozenge in centre; blue sphere with white band and stars in centre of lozenge. NATIONAL DAY.—September 7 (Independence Day).

BRITISH EMBASSY

Setor de Embaixadus Sul, Quadra 801, Conjunto K, 70.408 Brasilia, D.F.

Ambassador Extraordinary and Plenipotentiary, His Excellency John Burns Ure, C.M.G., M.V.O. (1984). There are British Consulates-General at Rio de Janeiro and São Paulo.

BRITISH COUNCIL.—*Representative*, E. J. Rayner, P.O. Box 14-2336, 70,740 Brasilia D.F. Regional Directors in *Rio de Janeiro*, *Recife* and *São Paulo*. BRITISH AND COMMONWEALTH CHAMBER OF COMMERCE IN SÃO PAULO, Rua Barão de Itapetininga 275, Caixa Postal 1621, São Paulo. (Correspondents at *Santos* and *Porto Alegre*.)

Rio de Janeiro, 5,750 miles distant from London: transit, 15 days.

BULGARIA
(Bulgariya)
COUNCIL OF STATE

Chairman of the Council of State, Todor Zhivkov, *elected*, July 7, 1971; *re-elected*, June 1981 (*Head of State*).
First Deputy Chairman, Petur Tanchev.
Deputy Chairmen, Peko Takov; Georgi Dzhagarov; Mitko Grigorov; Yaroslav Radev.

Secretary, Nikola Manolov.
Chairman of the Committee for State and People's Control, (vacant).

COUNCIL OF MINISTERS

Chairman and Prime Minister, Grisha Filipov.
First Deputy Prime Minister, Chudomir Alexsandrov.
Deputy Prime Ministers, Andrei Lukanov; Grigor Stoichkov; Georgi Yordanov; Stanish Bonev (*Chairman, State Planning Committee*); Georgi Karamanev; Todor Bozhinov (*Minister of Energy and Raw Material Resources*).
Finance, Belcho Belchev.
Interior, Col. Gen. Dimiter Stoyanov.
Defence, Gen. Dobri Dzhurov.
Foreign Affairs, Peter Mladenov.
Education, Prof. Alexander Fol.
Chemical Industry, Georgi Pankov.
Machine Building, Ognyan Doynov.
Construction and Territorial Settlement Organisation, Grigor Stoichkov.
Production and Trade in Consumer Goods, Georgi Karamanev.
Foreign Trade, Khristo I. Khristov.
Forests and Forest Industry, Yanko Markov.
Communications, Pando Vanchev.
Health, Prof. Radoy Popivanov.
Justice, Svetla Daskalova.
Ambassador to the U.S.S.R., Dimiter Zhulev.
Chairmen of the Committees, Nikola Todoriev (*Science and Technical Progress*); Stanish Bonev (*State Planning*); Alexander Petkov (*National Agro-Industrial Union*); Georgi Yordanov (*Culture*); Toncho Chakurov (*without Portfolio*).
Chairman of the Bulgarian National Bank, Vesselin Nikiforov.

THE COMMUNIST PARTY

The Politbureau of the Central Committee, G. Filipov; P. Kubadinski; S. Todorov; T. Zhivkov; D. Dzhurov; O. Doynov; P. Mladenov; T. Bozhinov; M. Balev; C. Aleksandrov; Y. Yotov (*full members*); A. Lukanov; G. Yordanov; P. Dyulgerov; G. Atanasov; G. Stoichkov; S. Bonev; D. Stoyanov (*candidate members*).
The Secretariat of the Central Committee, Todor Zhivkov (*Secretary-General*); O. Doynov; G. Atanasov; D. Stanishev; S. Mikhailov; M. Balev; V. Tsanov; K. Zarev; E. Khristov.

BULGARIAN EMBASSY AND CONSULATE IN LONDON 186–188 Queen's Gate Gardens, SW7 5HL [01–584 9400/9433]

Ambassador Extraordinary and Plenipotentiary, His Excellency Kiril Shterev (1980).

The Republic of Bulgaria is bounded on the north by Rumania, on the west by Yugoslavia, on the east by the Black Sea, and on the south by Greece and Turkey. The total area is approximately 43,000 square miles, with a population in December, 1982 of 8,929,000. The largest religion of the Bulgarians is the Bulgarian Orthodox Church. The Gregorian (Western) Calendar is in use.

A Principality of Bulgaria was created by the *Treaty of Berlin* (July 13, 1878) and in 1885 Eastern Roumelia was added to the newly-created principality. In 1908 the country was declared to be an independent kingdom. In 1912–13 a successful war of the *Balkan League* against Turkey increased the size of the kingdom, but in August, 1913, a short campaign against the remaining members of the League reduced the acquired area, and led to the surrender of Southern Dobrudja to Rumania. On Oct. 12, 1915,

Bulgaria entered the War on the side of the Central Powers by declaring war on Serbia. She thus became involved in the defeats of 1918, and on Sept. 29, 1918, made an unconditional surrender to the Allied Powers. On Nov. 29, 1919, she signed the *Treaty of Neuilly*, which ceded to the Allies her Thracian territories (later handed over to Greece) and some territory on the western frontier to Yugoslavia.

Nazi troops entered the country on March 3, 1941, and occupied Black Sea ports, but Bulgaria was not at war with the Soviet Union. On August 26, 1944, the government declared Bulgaria to be "neutral in the Russo-German war" and delegates to Cairo sought terms of peace from Great Britain and the United States. The Soviet Union refused to recognize the so-called "neutrality" and called upon Bulgaria to declare war against Germany, and no satisfactory reply being received on Sept. 5, 1944, the U.S.S.R. declared war on Bulgaria. Bulgaria then asked for an armistice and on Sept. 7 declared war on Germany, hostilities with U.S.S.R. ending on Sept. 10. The armistice with the Allies was signed in Moscow, Oct. 28. On Sept. 9 a *coup d'état* gave power to the Fatherland Front, a coalition of Communists, Agrarians, Social Democrats and officers and intellectuals. In August, 1945, the main body of Agrarians and Social Democrats left the Government. The Peace Treaty with Bulgaria was signed on Feb. 22, 1947, and came into force on Sept. 15, 1947. It recognized the return of Southern Dobrudja to Bulgaria.

On Sept. 8, 1946, a referendum was held, at which, according to the published results, an overwhelming majority declared for the abolition of the Monarchy and the setting up of a Republic. On Oct. 27, a general election to a Grand National Assembly (with power to make a constitution) was held; the Opposition won 101 seats out of 465.

On May 16, 1971 a referendum was held, at which a new Constitution was adopted. According to the Constitution the legislature is a single chamber National Assembly or *Subranie* elected by adult suffrage for a maximum term of 5 years and consisting of 400 deputies representing constituencies of equal size. The 1971 Constitution also established the Council of State, being the supreme permanent body of the National Assembly with both legislative and executive functions. The opposition Agrarian Party was suppressed in 1947, but its remnant was later revived as the Agrarian Union which now constitutionally shares power with the Communist Party.

Production.—Until 1939 Bulgaria was a predominantly agricultural country, but has since pursued an elaborate programme of industrialization. About 90 per cent of the country's agriculture has been turned over to co-operatives, and a smaller proportion mechanized. The principal crops are wheat, maize, beet, tomatoes, tobacco, oleaginous seeds, fruit, vegetables and cotton. The livestock includes cattle, sheep, goats, pigs, horses, asses, mules and water buffaloes.

There is now a substantial engineering industry producing *inter alia* machine tools, electric trucks of all kinds, agricultural machinery, cranes, electric motors and electronic components, which accounts for about two-thirds of Bulgaria's exports; and considerable production of ferrous and non-ferrous metals. In 1982 production of electricity was 40,438 million kilowatt-hours, of steel 2,586,000 tons and of coal 32,182,000 tons (of which about one-quarter was soft coal).

There are mineral deposits of varying importance. Bulgaria's heavy industry includes the Kremikovtsi Steel Plant near Sofia and the Lenin steel mill at Pernik, the chemical complex at Devnia, the petrochemical plant at Bourgas with an annual capacity of 6 million tons of processed oil and various other chemical and metallurgical works situated around the country. The Soviet-designed nuclear power station at Kozlodui will have four reactors, each with a capability of producing 800 million kilowatt/hours; in 1983 four were in operation.

Defence.—Under the Peace Treaty signed between Bulgaria and the Allies, the Bulgarian Army is limited to 55,000 men, but it is believed at present to be at least 152,000 strong.

Education.—Free basic education is compulsory for children from 7 to 15 years inclusive. The Bulgarian educational system was reorganized on Soviet lines in September, 1950, and in 1982 there were 5,733 kindergartens, and a total of 4,238 educational establishments for primary and secondary education including vocational, technical and other specialized schools for secondary age pupils. The total number of pupils attending these establishments was 1,498,316. There are three Universities (at Sofia, Plovdiv and Veliko Turnovo) and 21 higher educational establishments whose pupils total 83,633.

Language and Literature.—Bulgarian is a Southern Slavonic tongue, closely allied to Serbo-Croat and Russian (*see* U.S.S.R.) with local admixtures of modern Greek, Albanian and Turkish words. There is a modern literature chiefly educational and popular. The alphabet is Cyrillic. In 1983 there were 8 daily newspapers in Sofia.

Finance.—Planned budget revenue for 1984 is 17,754,200,000 *leva*, expenditure 17,739,200,000 *leva*. Currency in Bulgaria is the *lev*.

TRADE

The principal imports are industrial and agricultural machinery, industrial raw materials, machine tools, chemicals, dyestuffs, pharmaceuticals, rubber, paper. The principal exports are non-ferrous metals, electric trucks and motors, pumps, ships, accumulators and machine tools, cereals, tobacco, fruit, vegetables, oil seeds, oils, fats, textiles, eggs, chemicals and oils including attar of roses. In 1983, 77·1 per cent of Bulgaria's foreign trade was within the C.M.E.A., including 57 per cent with the Soviet Union.

Trade with U.K.

	1982	1983
Imports from U.K.	£46,104,000	£44,630,000
Exports to U.K.	21,009,000	12,340,000

CAPITAL.—Sofia, Pop. (1982), 1,082,315, at the foot of the Vitosha Range, the capital and commercial centre is on the main railway line to Istanbul, 338 miles from the Black Sea port of ΨVarna (295,038) and 125 miles from Lom (28,500), on the Danube;

ΨBourgas (178,239) is also a Black Sea Port, those on the Danube being ΨRousse (178,920), ΨVidin (60,877). Other important trading and industrial centres are Plovdiv (367,195), Pleven (135,899), Stara Zagora (141,722), Pernik (94,854), Sliven (100,637), Yambol (86,216), Khaskovo (87,639) and Tolbukhin (98,857).

FLAG.—3 horizontal bands, white, green, red; national emblem on white stripe near hoist.

NATIONAL DAY.—Sept. 9 (Day of Freedom).

BRITISH EMBASSY
Boulevard Marshal Tolbukhin, 65–67, Sofia.

Ambassador Extraordinary and Plenipotentiary, His Excellency John Michael Owen Snodgrass, C.M.G. (1983).

1st Secretaries, E. A. Burner (*Consul and Head of Chancery*); J. Daly (*Commercial*).

2nd Secretary, S. M. Williams (*Chancery and Cultural*).

Defence, Naval, Military and Air Attaché, Lt.-Col. G. A. Attard Manche.

3rd Secretaries, M. Snell (*Administration*); Miss B. Lawson (*Consular*).

BURMA
(The Socialist Republic of the Union of Burma)
Government of the Union

President, Gen. U San Yu, *elected* Nov. 9, 1981.

COUNCIL OF MINISTERS

Prime Minister, U Maung Maung Kha.
Deputy Prime Minister and Planning and Finance, Thura U Tun Tin.
Deputy Prime Minister and Defence, General Thura Kyaw Htin.
Home and Religious Affairs, Maj.-Gen. Min Gaung.
Agriculture and Forests, U Ye Gaung.
Industry I, Tint Swe.
Education, U Kyaw Nyein.
Industry II, Maung Cho.
Trade, Khin Maung Gyi.
Co-operatives, Livestock and Fisheries, Sein Tun.
Labour and Social Welfare, U Ohn Kyaw.
Foreign Affairs, U Chit Hlaing.
Culture and Information, U Aung Kyaw Myint.
Construction, Hla Tun.
Transport and Communications, Thura Saw Pru.
Health, U Tun Way.
Mines, Brigadier-General Than Tin.

BURMESE EMBASSY AND CONSULATE
19A Charles St., Berkeley Square, W1X 8ER
[01–499 8841]

Ambassador Extraordinary and Plenipotentiary, His Excellency U Myo Aung (1981).

Area and Population.—Burma forms the western portion of the Indo-Chinese district of the continent of Asia, lying between 9° 58′ and 28° N. latitude and 92° 11′ and 101° 9′ E. longitude, with an extreme length of approximately 1,200 miles and an extreme width of 575 miles. It has a sea coast on the Bay of Bengal to the south and west and a frontier with Bangladesh along the Naaf River, defined in 1964 by a Memorandum of Agreements, and India to the north-west defined in 1967. In the north and east the frontier with China was determined by a treaty with the People's Republic in October, 1960, and has since been demarcated; there is a short frontier with Laos in the east, while the long finger of Tenasserim

stretches southward along the west coast of the Malay Peninsula, forming a frontier with Thailand to the east. (*For* MAP, *see* Index). The total area of the Union is about 262,000 square miles, with a population of 35,313,905 (1983 Census)—about 135 persons to the square mile.

Physical Features.—Burma falls into four natural divisions. Arakan (with the Chin Hills region) the Irrawaddy basin, the old Province of Tenasserim, including the Salween basin and extending southwards to the Burma-Siam peninsula, and the elevated plateau on the east made up of the Shan State. Mountains enclose Burma on three sides, the highest point being Hka-kabo Razi (19,296 ft.) in the northern Kachin hills. Mt. Popa, 4,981 ft., in the Myingyan district is an extinct volcano and a well-known landmark in Central Burma. The principal river systems are the Kaladan-Lemro in Arakan, the Irrawaddy-Chindwin and the Sittang in Central Burma, and the Salween which flows through the Shan Plateau.

Races, Language and Religions.—The indigenous inhabitants who entered Burma from the north and east are of similar racial types and speak languages of the Tibeto-Burman, Mon-Khmer and Thai groups. The three important non-indigenous elements are Indians, Chinese and those from the former East Pakistan. Numbers of resident foreigners have shown a sharp decline in recent years. Burmese is the official language, but minority languages include Shan, Karen, Chin, Kayah and the various Kachin dialects. English is still spoken in educated circles in Rangoon and elsewhere. Buddhism is the religion of 85 per cent of the people, with 5 per cent Animists, 4 per cent Moslems, 4 per cent Hindus and rather less than 3 per cent Christians.

Government.—Burma became an independent republic outside the British Commonwealth on January 4, 1948, and remained a parliamentary democracy for 14 years.

On March 2, 1962 the army took power, and suspended the parliamentary Constitution. A Revolutionary Council of senior officers under General Ne Win took measures to create a Socialist State.

In January 1974 a new Constitution was adopted after a national referendum. The highest authority is the People's Assembly (476 representatives) which meets twice a year. When the Assembly is not in session the Council of State (29 members) is vested with wide powers. The senior executive body is the Council of Ministers. The Chairman of the Council of State is also President of the Socialist Republic of the Union of Burma.

Political Divisions.—Burma is comprised of fourteen States and Divisions. Amongst the former are the Kachin State (34,000 sq. miles), Kayah State (4,500 sq. miles); Karen (formerly Kawthoolei) State (12,000 sq. miles), Chin State (14,000 sq. miles), Mon State, Arakan State and the Shan State (60,000 sq. miles).

Education.—The literacy rate is high compared with other Asian countries, there is no caste system and women engage freely in social intercourse and play an important part in agriculture and retail trade.

Most Burmese children attend primary school, and about four million are currently enrolled; in middle and high schools, 11 million. There are two universities, at Rangoon and Mandalay, and in 1982–83 the numbers graduating were 6,610. A number of autonomous institutes of university standard award their own degrees: three Institutes of Medicine (two at Rangoon, one at Mandalay), one each of Economics, Technology, Education and Dental Medicine at Rangoon, and Animal Husbandry and Veterinary Science and Agriculture at Yezin and Pyinmana. Under the two universities are affiliated Degree

Colleges at Moulmein, Magwe, Bassein and the Workers' College, Rangoon. There are also 14 two-year colleges affiliated to Rangoon or Mandalay University, spread throughout the country. After completion of the two-year courses at these colleges students can join the third-year classes of the universities.

Teachers' Training Institutes at Rangoon, Moulmein and Mandalay train teachers for middle and primary schools, and 13 Teachers' Training Schools for primary only. Seven Government Technical Institutes offer post-secondary technical training courses. Fourteen Technical High Schools train semi-skilled tradesmen. Six Agricultural Institutes offer training courses in agriculture and veterinary science; nine Agricultural High Schools train semi-skilled agriculturists. There are 34 Vocational Schools for weaving, handicrafts and so on. Britain grants aid to Burma under the Colombo Plan.

Finance.—The chief sources of revenue are profits on state trading, income-tax, customs duties, commercial taxes and excise duties; the chief heads of expenditure are general administration, defence, education, police and development. The budget estimates for 1984–85 were: Revenue, *K*36,625,070,000; Expenditure, *K*40,884,733,000. The monetary unit is the *Kyat* of 100 *Pyas*. (For rate of exchange, *see* p. 81.)

Production, Industry and Commerce.—Three-quarters of the population depend on agriculture; the chief products are rice, oilseeds (sesamum and groundnut), maize, millet, cotton, beans, wheat, grain, tea, sugarcane, Virginia and Burmese tobacco, jute and rubber. Rice has traditionally been the mainstay of Burma's economy and the quantity of rice and by-products available for export was 722,000 tons in 1982–83. The principal export after rice is teak, of which 136,200 cubic tons was exported in 1982–83.

Burma is rich in minerals, including petroleum, lead, silver, tungsten, zinc, tin, wolfram and gem-stones. Of these, petroleum products are the most important. Oil is now being produced from oilfields in Myanaung, Prome and Shwepyitha and at Chauk, Yenangyaung, Mann, and Letpando. Production of crude oil in 1982–83 totalled 9,789,000 U.S. barrels. There is a refinery at the main oilfield, Chauk, another at Syriam near Rangoon and a third is being built at Mann. There has been a slight decline in Burma's oil production in recent years and the country is no longer self-sufficient. Onshore exploration continues. In 1982–83 there was also some offshore oil exploration on a small scale. Oil extraction and the production and distribution of petroleum are monopolies of the Myanma Oil Corporation and the Petrochemical Industries Corporation respectively. Major reserves of natural gas have been discovered in the Martaban Gulf, which Burma is hoping to develop.

All industrial activity of any size is in the public sector. Under development plans, projects completed or under construction with overseas financial and technical assistance include the production of cement, bricks and tiles, sheet glass, steel sections, jute bags and twine, cotton yarns, cotton and cotton mixture cloth, pharmaceuticals, sugar, paper, plywood, urea fertilizers, soda ash, tractors and tyres; also a hydro-electric scheme and various irrigation works. Japan continues to be the major individual donor of soft loans and grant aid in the industrial and agricultural sectors. West Germany has also been an important contributor of soft loans.

Loans amounting to US $125 million have been extended by the World Bank. As a member of the Colombo Plan since 1952 Burma continues to receive technical assistance from a number of countries and international agencies.

Trade with U.K.

	1982	1983
Imports from U.K.	£44,242,000	£21,927,000
Exports to U.K.	5,342,000	4,726,000

Communications.—The Irrawaddy and its chief tributary, the Chindwin, form important waterways, the main stream being navigable beyond Bhamo (900 miles from its mouth) and carrying much traffic.

The chief seaports are Rangoon, Moulmein, Akyab and Bassein. Transit from London to Rangoon: by sea, 35 days; by air (via Bangkok), 16 hours.

The Burma Railways network covers 2,764 route miles, extending to Myitkyina, on the Upper Irrawaddy. There are now 219 diesel locomotives in service, as well as 141 steam. There were 2,452 miles of Union highways and 11,767 miles of other main roads in 1982–83. The airport at Mingaladon, about 13 miles north of Rangoon, only handles limited international air traffic.

CAPITAL.—The chief city of Lower Burma, and the seat of the government of the Union is Rangoon, on the left bank of the Rangoon river, about 21 miles from the sea. The city contains the Shwe Dagon pagoda, much venerated by Burmese Buddhists. Population (1983): Rangoon District, 3,973,872; city population, 2,458,712.

Mandalay is the chief city of Upper Burma, population (1983): Mandalay district, 4,580,923; city, 532,985; Moulmein of 219,991 and Bassein of 144,092. Pagan, on the Irrawaddy, S.W. of Mandalay, contains many sacred buildings.

FLAG.—The Union flag is red, with a canton of dark blue, inside which are a cogwheel and two rice ears surrounded by 14 white stars.

NATIONAL DAY.—January 4.

BRITISH EMBASSY
80 Strand Road (Box No. 638), Rangoon

Ambassador Extraordinary and Plenipotentiary, His Excellency Nicholas Maxted Fenn, C.M.G. (1982).
1st Secretaries, D. L. Smallman (*Head of Chancery and Consul*); D. Rees (*Commercial*).
2nd Secretary, S. D. Butt (*Vice Consul*).
Cultural Attaché and British Council Representative, R. P. Hale.

BURUNDI
(Republic of Burundi)

President, Col. Jean-Baptiste Bagaza, *assumed office* Nov. 1, 1976, *elected* Dec. 1979, *re-elected*, Sept. 1984.

Formerly a Belgian trusteeship under the United Nations, Burundi was proclaimed an independent State on July 1, 1962. Situated on the east side of Lake Tanganyika, the State has an area of 10,747 sq. miles and a population (estimated, 1984) of 4,480,000. The majority of the population are of the Bahutu ethnic group, but power rests in the hands of the minority Batutsi ethnic group.

Burundi became independent as a constitutional monarchy but this was overthrown on November 28, 1966 and the country became a republic. On Nov. 1, 1976, the government of President Micombero was overthrown and a Supreme Revolutionary Council led by Col. Jean-Baptiste Bagaza took power. In 1980 the S.R.C. was replaced by a political bureau and central committee as part of a process of political normalization, which continued with elections to the National Assembly, a 65-member legislature. The most recent elections were in November 1982.

The chief crop is coffee, representing about 80 per cent of Burundi's export earnings. Cotton is the second most important crop. Minerals, tea, hides and skins exports are also important. Joint economic arrangements of Burundi with Rwanda ended in 1964 and each country now has its own national bank, coffee organization, etc.

Trade with U.K.

	1982	1983
Imports from U.K.	£8,737,000	£3,200,000
Exports to U.K.	1,522,000	3,500,000

The currency is the Burundi *Franc.*

CAPITAL.—Bujumbura *(formerly* Usumbura), with about 150,000 inhabitants. Kitega (18,000 inhabitants) is the only other sizeable town. Official languages are Kirundi, a Bantu language, and French. Kiswahili is also used.

FLAG.—White diagonal cross on green and red quarters, with a circular white panel in the centre.

NATIONAL DAY.—July 1.

British Ambassador (see Kinshasa, Zaire).

CAMBODIA
(Democratic Kampuchea)

President, Prince Norodom Sihanouk.
Vice-President responsible for Foreign Affairs, Khieu Samphan.
Prime Minister, Son Sann.

Area and Population.—Situated between Thailand and the south of Vietnam and extending from the border with Laos on the north to the Gulf of Thailand, Cambodia covers an area of some 70,000 square miles. It has a population (1981) of approximately 6 million. (*For* MAP, *see* Index.)

Fifty per cent. of the total land area is forest or jungle, abounding in wild life of all kinds, including big game. The climate is tropical monsoon with a rainy season from May to October.

History.—Once a powerful kingdom, which, as the Khmer Empire, flourished between the tenth and fourteenth centuries, Cambodia became a French protectorate in 1863 and was granted independence within the French Union as an Associate State in 1949. Full independence was proclaimed on November 9, 1953, and the process was completed when, in January, 1955, the Kingdom of Cambodia became financially and economically independent not only of France but also of Laos and Vietnam. For the next fifteen years the political life of the country was dominated by Prince Norodom Sihanouk, first as King, then as Head of Government after he had abdicated in favour of his father and finally (following his father's death in 1960) as Head of State.

On March 18, 1970, during his absence from the country, Prince Sihanouk was deposed as Head of State by a vote of the National Assembly. A Republic was declared on October 9, 1970, and the name of the country changed to the Khmer Republic.

In April 1970 widespread fighting developed between communist Vietnamese and Khmer forces which gradually developed into a general civil war with republican forces controlling the major centres of population and large areas of the country falling under the control of the Khmer Rouge supported by North Vietnamese. With large-scale assistance from the United States the armed forces of the Republic were increased from 35,000 in 1970 to 250,000 in 1973.

In March 1973 a State of National Emergency was declared, various clauses of the constitution were suspended and a coalition "government of exception" was formed.

In April 1975 Phnom-Penh fell to the Khmer Rouge. Prince Sihanouk returned to Cambodia on September 9, as nominal Head of State. However, a new Constitution was promulgated in Jan. 1976 and elections to a People's Representative Assembly were held in March. Prince Sihanouk resigned as Head of

State in April, and when the Assembly met on April 11 Khieu Samphan was elected President of the State Presidium. A Government led by Pol Pot, the leader of the Communist party, was appointed.

On Dec. 25, 1978 Vietnamese troops invaded Cambodia in support of an uprising by the Cambodian National United Front. The Cambodian capital, Phnom-Penh, fell on Jan. 7, 1979. The following day the Cambodian National United Front for National Salvation established a People's Revolutionary Council, recognized by Vietnam, U.S.S.R. and by other, chiefly Soviet-aligned, countries. The regime, which remains almost totally dependent on the Vietnamese, is opposed to the Khmer Rouge forces and non-communist nationalist groups which in June 1982 formed the Coalition Government of Democratic Kampuchea. The C.G.D.K. replaces the purely Khmer Rouge government; and it occupies Cambodia's seat at the U.N.

Economy.—Cambodia has an economy based on agriculture, fishing and forestry, the bulk of its people being rice-growing farmers living in the basins of the Mekong and Tonlé Sap rivers. In addition to rice, which is the staple crop, the major products are rubber, livestock, maize, timber, pepper, palm sugar, fresh and dried fish, kapok, beans, soya and tobacco. Rice and rubber used to be the main exports though production was brought to a standstill by the hostilities. Following the Khmer Rouge victory, the populations of Phnom-Penh and other towns were forcibly evacuated to the country to work on the land, and re-establish the plantations producing such crops as cotton, rubber and bananas. Following the Vietnamese invasion of 1978 the towns were repopulated and commerce revived; currency was reintroduced. Factories, in particular textile mills, iron smelting works and cement works were put back in production.

Trade with U.K.

	1983
Imports from U.K.	£826,000
Exports to U.K.	184,000

Communications.—The country had over 5,000 kilometres of roads, of which nearly half are hard-surfaced and passable in the rainy season. There are two railways. One runs from Phnom-Penh to the Thai border; the other from Phnom-Penh to Kampot and on to Kompong Som. Operations and repairs are hindered by the continuing fighting. Phnom-Penh is on a river capable of receiving ships of up to 2,500 tons all the year round. The deep water port at Kompong Som on the Gulf of Thailand can receive ships up to 10,000 tons. The port is linked to Phnom-Penh by a modern highway.

Religion and Education.—The state religion was Buddhism of the "Little Vehicle". The new constitution guaranteed religious freedom, but in practice Buddhism was suppressed by the Khmer Rouge. There has been some revival recently. There were also small Muslim and Christian communities, but many members of them died or fled the country during Khmer Rouge rule. The national language is Khmer. In the years preceding the civil war considerable efforts were devoted to the development of education and new schools, colleges and technical institutes had been established. Until April 1975 there was a Buddhist University in Phnom-Penh, and several residential teachers' training colleges were in operation. However, most of the country's educated elite died under the Khmer Rouge regime, which closed all institutions of higher education.

CAPITAL.—Phnom-Penh.

FLAG.—Red, with a yellow three-towered temple in the middle.

CAMEROON REPUBLIC
(Republic of Cameroon)

President, Head of State, Government and Commander in Chief of the Armed Forces, Paul Biya, *acceded* Nov. 6, 1982 on resignation of Pres. Ahidjo, *elected* Jan. 14, 1984, *sworn in* Jan. 21, 1984.

MINISTRY

Youth and Sports, Mbombo Njoya.
Foreign Affairs, William Eteki Mboumoua.
Territorial Administration, Jean-Marcel Mengueme.
Finance, Etienne Ntsama.
Public Service, René Ze Nguele.
Higher Education and Scientific Research, Bol Alima Gibering.
Animal Husbandry, Fisheries and Animal Industries, Hamadjoda Adjoudji.
Social Affairs, Mrs. Rose Zang Nguele.
Posts and Telecommunications, Félix Tonye Mbog.
Town Planning and Housing, Babale Abdoulaye.
Transport, Benjamin Itoe.
Information and Culture, François Sengat Kuo.
Equipment, Thomas Dakayi Kamga.
Agriculture, Sadou Hayatou.
Computer Services and Public Contracts, Daniel Kamgueu.
Mines and Power, Michael Tabong Kima.
National Education, Robert Mbella Mbappe.
Women's Affairs, Mrs. Yaou Boubakari.
Commerce and Industry, Edouard Nomo Ongolo.
Labour and Social Insurance, Dr. Joseph Fofe.
Public Health, Prof. Victor Anomah Ngu.
Ministers of State, Gilbert Anze Tsoungi (*Armed Forces*); André Ngongang Ouandji (*Justice*); Youssoufa Daouda (*Planning and Territorial Development*).
Ministers Delegate, Dr. Joseph Zambo (*Relations with Assemblies*); Mahamat Paba Sale (*Foreign Affairs*); Joseph C. Awunti (*General State Inspectorate and Administrative Reforms*).
Ministers at the Presidency of the Republic with special functions, Dr. Joseph Zambo; Georges Ngango; Joseph C. Doumba.

CAMEROON EMBASSY
84 Holland Park, W11 3SB
[01-727 0771]

Ambassador Extraordinary and Plenipotentiary, His Excellency E. H. M. Haman Dicko (1982).

The Republic of Cameroon lies on the Gulf of Guinea between Nigeria to the west, Chad and the Central African Republic to the east and Congo and Gabon and Equatorial Guinea to the south. It has an area of 475,400 sq. km. and a population of 8,320,000 (1980 estimate).

The whole territory was administered by Germany from 1884 to 1916. From 1916 to 1959, the former East Cameroon was administered by France as a League of Nations (later U.N.) trusteeship. On Jan. 1, 1960 it became independent as the Republic of Cameroon. The Republic was joined on October 1, 1961, by the former British administered trust territory of the Southern Cameroons, after a plebiscite held under United Nations auspices. Cameroon became a Federal Republic with separate East and West Cameroon state governments. Subsequently, after plebiscite held in May, 1972, Cameroon became a United Republic.

Cameroon is the only country in Africa where French and English are both official languages enjoying equal status, and the government's declared long-term objective is to achieve complete "bilingualism" and "biculturalism".

The main economic emphasis is on agricultural development, both through encouraging small-scale peasant agriculture, and through the development of large-scale agro-industrial complexes, with the aim of making the country agriculturally self-sufficient and a major food exporter.

Principal products are cocoa, coffee, bananas, cotton, timber, ground-nuts, aluminium, rubber and palm products. There is an aluminium smelting plant at Edéa with an annual capacity of 50,000 tons. Oil is now also one of Cameroon's principal products with an estimated production of 6·4m. tonnes during 1983.

TRADE

	1981
Total imports	FCFA364,000 m.
Total exports	290,000 m.

Trade with U.K.

	1982	1983
Imports from U.K.	£22,462,000	£25,445,000
Exports to U.K.	9,108,000	52,481,000

CAPITAL.—Yaoundé (337,000). Ψ Douala (458,000) is the commercial centre.

FLAG.—Vertical stripes of green, red and yellow with single five-pointed yellow star in centre of red stripe.

BRITISH EMBASSY
Avenue Winston Churchill, B.P. 547
Yaoundé

Ambassador Extraordinary and Plenipotentiary, His Excellency James Glaze (1984).
1st Secretaries, Miss K. Oliver (*Head of Chancery and Consul*); R. Godfrey (*Aid*).
2nd Secretary, D. M. Gray (*Commercial/Information*).
British Council Representative, C. H. Mogford, Les Galéries, Rue J. F. Kennedy, (B.P. 818), Yaoundé.

CAPE VERDE ISLANDS
(Republic of Cape Verde)

President, Aristides Pereira *born* 1924, *assumed office,* July 5, 1975.
Prime Minister, Pedro Pires.

The Cape Verde Islands, off the west coast of Africa, consist of two groups of islands, *Windward* (Santo Antão, São Vicente, Santa Luzia, São Nicolau Boa Vista and Sal) and *Leeward* (Maio, São Tiago, Fogo and Brava) with a total area of 1,516 sq. miles. The population at the 1980 Census was 296,093, the majority of whom are Roman Catholic.

The Islands, colonized in c. 1460, achieved independence from Portugal on July 5, 1975, under the nationalist party of Guinea Bissau and Cape Verde. A federation of the islands with Guinea Bissau was planned (till 1879 Guinea-Bissau and the Islands were a single administrative unit) but this was dropped following the 1980 coup in Guinea Bissau.

The Republic is a one-party (the P.A.I.C.V.) state with a President elected by the National Assembly. He has a mandate of 5 years, as do Assembly deputies, who are elected by universal adult suffrage.

The islands have had little rain since 1969, and agriculture is mostly confined to irrigated inland valleys, the chief products being bananas and coffee (for export), maize, sugarcane and nuts. Fish and shellfish are important exports. Salt is obtained on Sal, Boa Vista and Maio; volcanic rock is also mined for export. The main ports are Praia and Mindelo, and there is an international airport on Sal.

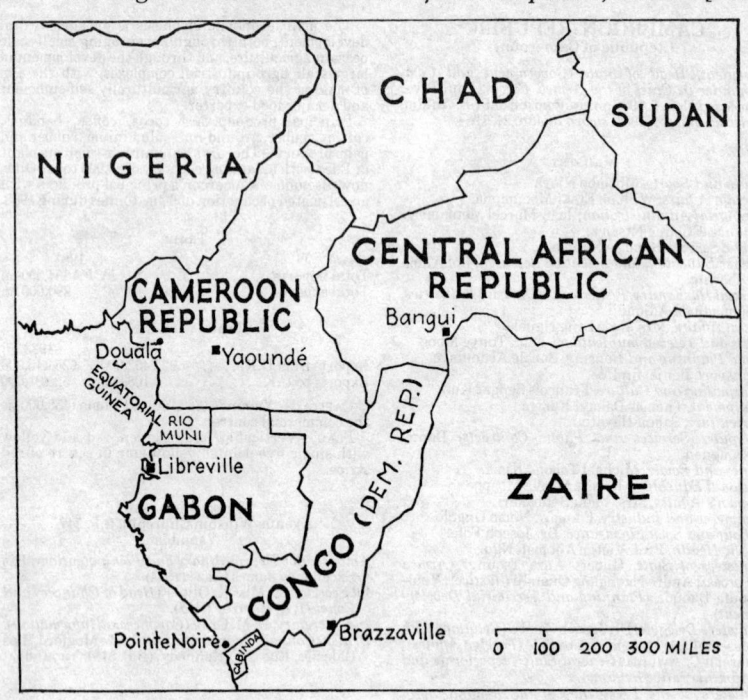

Trade with U.K.

	1982	1983
Imports from U.K.	£2,068,000	£1,246,00
Exports to U.K.	49,000	122,000

CAPITAL, ΨPraia (1970, 6,000).
British Ambassador (resident at Dakar, Senegal.)

CENTRAL AFRICAN REPUBLIC

Head of State, Gen. Andre Kolingba, *assumed power* Sept. 1, 1981.

Formerly the French colony of Ubanghi Shari, the Republic lies just north of the Equator between the Cameroon Republic, the Republic of Chad, the southern part of Sudan and Zaire. The Republic has an area of about 234,000 sq. miles and a population (1981 estimate) of 2,379,000. On December 1, 1958, Ubanghi Shari elected to remain within the French Community and adopted the title of the Central African Republic. It became fully independent on August 17, 1960. The first President of the Central African Republic, M. David Dacko, held office from 1960 until Jan. 1, 1966, when he was replaced by the then Col. Bokassa after a *coup d'état.* On Dec. 4, 1976, President Bokassa proclaimed himself Emperor and a new constitution (Parliamentary Monarchy) was introduced, the country being known as the Central African Empire. On Sept. 20, 1979, Emperor Bokassa was deposed by M. David Dacko in a bloodless *coup* and the country reverted to a Republic. President Dacko surrendered power on 1st September 1981 to army commander Gen. Andre Kolingba in a bloodless *coup.*

Economy.—A programme of economic reconstruction is under way, concentrating on agricultural production and private investment. Cotton, diamonds, coffee and timber are the major exports;

Trade with U.K.

	1982	1983
Imports from U.K.	£579,000	£536,000
Exports to U.K.	878,000	902,000

CAPITAL.—Bangui, near the border with Zaire (350,000).

FLAG.—Four horizontal stripes, blue, white, green, yellow, crossed by central vertical red stripe with a yellow five-pointed star in top left-hand corner.

CHAD REPUBLIC

Situated in north-central Africa, the Chad Republic extends from 23° N. latitude to 7° N. latitude and is flanked by the Republics of Niger and Cameroon on the west, by Libya in the north, by the Sudan on the east and by the Central African Republic on the south. (*For* MAP, *see* Index.) It has an area of 488,000 sq. miles and a population now estimated at 4,000,000. Chad became a member state of the French Community on Nov. 28, 1958, and was proclaimed fully independent on August 11, 1960. On April 14, 1962, a new Constitution was adopted involving a presidential-type regime. This was suspended on

April 13, 1975 when President Tombalbaye was killed in a military coup. The country was run by a Supreme Military Council, under General Felix Malloum until his overthrow in February 1979. A Transitional Government of National Unity, headed by Goukouni Oueddei, was replaced in June 1982 by one headed by Hissein Habre. Forces commanded by Oueddei, and supported by Libyan troops, occupy the north of Chad.

About 90 per cent of the workforce is occupied in agriculture, fishing and forestry. There is an oilfield in Kanem and salt is mined around Lake Chad, but the most important activities are cotton growing (mostly in the south) and animal husbandry (in central areas). Raw cotton and meat are the main exports.

Trade with U.K.

	1982	1983
Imports from U.K	£1,082,000	£2,244,000
Exports to U.K.	3,000	8,000

CAPITAL.—Ndjaména (formerly known as Fort Lamy) south of Lake Chad (150,000).

FLAG.—Vertical stripes, blue, yellow and red.

British Ambassador (Non-Resident), His Excellency Michael Daly.

CHILE

(República de Chile)

Head of State, General Augusto Pinochet (Ugarte), *born*, November 25, 1915, Army Commander-in-Chief and President of the Republic.

Junta Members, Admiral José Toribio Merino (Castro), C.-in-C. Navy; General Fernando Matthei (Aubel), C.-in-C. Air Force; General César Mendoza (Durán), Director-General of Carabineros; General César Raul Benavides Escobar (Army).

CABINET

Foreign Affairs, Jaime del Valle Alliende.
Interior, Sergio O. Jarpa Reyes.
Defence, Vice Adm. Patricio Carvajal.
Education, Horacio Aranguiz.
Mines, Samuel Lira.
Finance, Luis Escobar Cerda.
Justice, Hugo Rosende.
Public Works, Brig.-Gen. Bruno Siebert.
Transport, Gen. Enrique Escobar.
Agriculture, Jorge Prado Aranguiz.
National Patrimony, Gen. René Peri Fagerstrom.
Labour and Social Security, Hugo Galvez.
Health, Winston Chinchon.
Housing, Miguel Angel Poduje.
Economic Affairs, Modesto Collados.
Planning, Hernan Bucci.
Energy, Gen. Hernan Brady.
Secretary General of the Government, Alfonso Marquez de la Plata.

CHILEAN EMBASSY AND CONSULATE IN LONDON
12 Devonshire Street, W1N 2DS
[01–580 6392/4]

Ambassador Extraordinary and Plenipotentiary, His Excellency Prof. Francisco Orrego.
Military Attaché, Brig. Gen. Daniel Gaston Frez.
Air Attaché, Brig. Gen. Vargas del Campo.
Naval Attaché, Rear Adm. Jorge Sepulveda.
Press Attaché, Srta Olga Kliwadenko.
Minister Counsellor, Sr. Ricardo Lira.
Consul General, Sr. Juan Martabit.

A State of South America, of Spanish origin, lying between the Andes and the shores of the South Pacific, extending coastwise from just north of Arica to Cape Horn south, between lat. 17° 15′ and 55° 59′ S. and long. 66° 30′ and 75° 48′ W. Extreme length of the country is about 2,800 miles, with an average breadth, north of 41°, of 100 miles. The great chain of the Andes runs along its eastern limit, with a general elevation of 5,000 to 15,000 feet above the level of the sea; but numerous summits attain a greater height. The chain, however, lowers considerably towards its southern extremity. The Andes form a boundary with Argentina, and at the head of the pass where the international road from Chile to Argentina crosses the frontier, has been erected a statue of *Christ the Redeemer*, 26 feet high, made of bronze from old cannon, to commemorate the peaceful settlement of a boundary dispute in 1902. There are no rivers of great size, and none of them is of much service as a navigable highway. In the north the country is arid. (*For* MAP, *see* p. 794.)

Among the island possessions of Chile are the *Juan Fernandez group* (3 islands) about 360 miles distant from Valparaiso, where a wireless station has been erected. One of these islands is the reputed scene of Alexander Selkirk's (Robinson Crusoe) shipwreck. *Easter Island* (27° 8′ S. and 109° 28′ W.), about 2,000 miles distant in the South Pacific Ocean, contains stone platforms and hundreds of stone figures, the origin of which has not yet been determined. The area of the island is about 45 sq. miles.

Chile is divided into 12 regions and the Metropolitan Area and the total area of the Republic is estimated at 290,000 square miles, with a population (estimated, 1979) of 11,000,000. Two of these regions, Arica and Antofagasta, were annexed from Peru and Bolivia respectively after the War of the Pacific (1879–84). The province of Tacna was also annexed but under a treaty signed in 1929 was returned to Peru which at the same time received payment of £1,200,000 for Arica. The Chilean population has four main sources: (*a*) Spanish settlers and their descendants; (*b*) indigenous Araucanian Indians, Fuegians, and Changos; (*c*) mixed Spanish Indians; and (*d*) European immigrants. Only the few remaining indigenous Indians and some originally Bolivian Indians in the north are racially separate. Following extensive intermarriage there is no effective distinction among the remainder.

Government.—Chile was discovered by Spanish adventurers in the 16th century and remained under Spanish rule until 1810, when a revolutionary war, culminating in the *Battle of Maipu* (April 5, 1818), achieved the independence of the nation.

At a general election held on Sept. 4, 1970, the Marxist candidate Dr. Allende was elected President by a narrow margin. A new Cabinet took office on Oct. 30, 1970.

After severe industrial unrest and widespread violent incidents, the Government of Dr. Salvador Allende was overthrown on September 11, 1973, by a coup planned, and carried out within a few hours, by leaders of the Armed Forces and National Police. President Allende was said to have committed suicide.

After a national plebiscite, the Constitution of 1925 was replaced early in 1981 and Gen. Pinochet was sworn in as President, to serve until 1989. Economically, the regime is pursuing a free-market economy and the level of inflation has been reduced, from 1,000 per cent in 1973 to about 23 per cent in 1983.

Production.—Wheat, maize, barley, oats, beans, peas, rice, lentils, wines, tobacco, hemp, chilipepper, potatoes, sugar beet, onions, grapes, peaches and melons are grown extensively and livestock accounts for nearly 40 per cent of agricultural production. The vine and all European fruit trees flourish in the central zone and fruit and wines are important export items. Sheep farming predominates in the extreme south (Province of Magallanes). There are large timber tracts in the central and southern zones of Chile, some types of which are exported, along with wood derivatives such as cellulose, to Europe and the Argentine and other markets.

The mineral wealth is considerable, the country being particularly rich in copper-ore, iron-ore and nitrate. Uranium is also said to have been discovered in small quantities. Copper production in 1983 totalled 1,257,200 metric tons, and represented 48 per cent of total exports earnings, the remainder of which are derived mainly from other minerals, wool, fruit, fish and forestry derivatives. The rainless north is the scene of the only commercial production of nitrate of soda (Chile saltpetre) from natural resources in the world. Production in 1983 of both potassium and sodium nitrate was 622,513 metric tons. Chile also produces iodine, manganese ore, coal, mercury, molybdenum, zinc, lead and a small quantity of gold. In 1983 1,077,831 metric tons of coal were produced. The country has also large deposits of high grade sulphur, but mostly around high extinct volcanoes in the Andes Cordillera, difficult of access. Oil was struck in Magallanes (Tierra del Fuego) in December, 1945. Production in 1983 was 2,283,782 cu. metres of crude oil and 4,802,800,000 cu. metres of natural gas—all in the Magallanes area from on_ and off-shore wells. This total production, which covers approximately 50 per cent of total oil requirement, plus imported crude oil is refined at Concon and San Vicente in the central part of the country. There is a steel plant at Huachipato, near Concepción. Current production is about 593,200 metric tons of steel ingots per year.

Some consumer goods are manufactured locally—copper, steel and oil derivatives, pulp and paper, cement and other building materials, tobacco, cutlery, food products and beverages, sugar refining, textiles, clothing and footwear, plastic products, household equipment, motor-vehicles, tyres and other rubber products, chemicals, pharmaceutical products, soaps, detergents and cosmetics.

Communications.—Chilean ships have a virtual monopoly in the coastwide trade, though, with the improvement of the roads, an increasing share of internal transportation is moving by road and rail. The Chilean mercantile marine numbers about 60 vessels (of over 100 tons gross) with a total deadweight tonnage of 825,076 (1982). Recently introduced changes to navigation laws now facilitate the operation of regular shipping services on a flag-of-convenience basis. A cargo reserve of 50 per cent to Chilean vessels is only applicable when there are flag protection policies in other countries at whose ports such vessels call. Chilean and foreign shipping companies serving the Pacific coast and northern Europe route are now operating container, bulk and general cargo services under two pooling arrangements which compete with each other.

There are 6,575 miles of railway track. A metre-gauge line (the *Longitudinál*) runs from La Calera, just north of Santiago, to Iquique. The wide gauge railway (1·676 metres) runs from Valparaiso through La Calera, 60 miles inland, and after passing through Santiago ends at Puerto Montt.

With the completion of a section of 435 miles from Corumba, Brazil, to Santa Cruz, Bolivia, the Trans-Continental Line will link the Chilean Pacific port of Arica with Rio de Janeiro on the Atlantic. Another line from Antofagasta to Salta (Argentine) was opened in 1948. Further south, the Trans-Andine Railway connects Valparaiso on the Pacific with Buenos Aires, crossing the Andes at 11,500 ft. However services have now been suspended due to financial difficulties.

Chile is served by about 20 international airlines.

The domestic traffic is carried by the State-owned Linea Aerea Nacional and the privately-owned LADECO, which also operate internationally, and smaller regional carriers. Chile has an extensive system of airports.

Chile's road system is about 65,000 kilometres in length, but only an estimated 7,000 kilometres are first-class paved highways. At the end of 1983 there were some 850,000 cars, 19,500 buses and taxis, 195,000 goods vehicles and 17,000 tractors in circulation.

Defence.—Military service is compulsory, but not all those who are liable are required. Recruitment for the Navy is voluntary. The Navy consists of 3 cruisers, 12 destroyers, frigates and escorts, some patrol vessels and FPBs and 3 submarines. There is a support force of transports, tankers, 1 submarine depôt ship and ancillary small craft. The strength of the Navy is 1,000 officers and 14,000 men, plus a Marine Force of 60 officers and 2,000 men. The Army's total strength is 50,000, which includes 3,000 officers and 25,000 conscripts (2 years). In addition there is a police force of "Carabineros" of 30,000 officers and men. The Air Force has 800 officers and 8,700 other ranks, with a strength of 200 aircraft.

Education.—Elementary education is free, and has been compulsory since 1920. There are 8 Universities (3 in Santiago, 2 in Valparaiso, 1 in Antofagasta, 1 in Concepción and 1 in Valdivia). The religion is Roman Catholic.

Language and Literature.—Spanish is the language of the country, with admixtures of local words of Indian origin. Recent efforts have reduced illiteracy and have thus afforded access to the literature of Spain, to supplement the vigorous national output. The Nobel Prize for Literature was awarded in 1945 to Señorita Gabriela Mistral, for Chilean verse and prose, and in 1971 to the poet Pablo Neruda. There are over 100 newspapers and a large number of periodicals, including some devoted to professional, scientific and social subjects.

Finance.—Total revenue for 1982 is estimated at U.S. $3,309,700,000, expenditure U.S. $3,603,300,000, a deficit of 8·1 per cent. Foreign debt at December 31, 1981 was provisionally quoted at U.S. $17,000 million.

EXTERNAL TRADE
($U.S. ,000)

	1982	1983
Total imports	3,831,000	2,969,000
Total exports	3,821,500	3,836,000

Trade with U.K.

	1982	1983
Imports from U.K.	£56,897,000	£43,520,000
Exports to U.K.	111,206,000	107,644,000

The principal exports are metallic and non-metallic minerals (refined copper, ingots and bars, iron ore, etc.), wood derivatives, some metal products, fish products, vegetables, fruit and wool. The principal imports are wheat, sugar and other food products, industrial raw materials, machinery, equipment and spares, oil fuels, lubricants and transportation equipment.

CAPITAL, Santiago, 4,000,000 (Greater Santiago), Other large towns are:—ΨValparaiso (500,000), Concepción (170,000), Temuco (110,000), ΨAntofagasta (110,000), Chillán (79,461), ΨTalcahuano (75,643), Talca (75,354); ΨValdivia (70,000), ΨIquique (50,000), ΨPunta Arenas (50,000). Punta Arenas on the Straits of Magellan, is the southernmost city in the world.

FLAG.—2 horizontal bands, white, red; in top sixth a white star on blue square, next staff.

NATIONAL DAY.—September 18 (National Anniversary).

BRITISH EMBASSY

Avenida La Concepción 177, Santiago 9
(Casilla 72D)

Ambassador Extraordinary and Plenipotentiary,
John K. Hickman, C.M.G.

1st Secretary, C. J. Edgerton (*Commercial*).

Defence Attaché, Capt. M. S. Ashley, R.N.

Cultural Attaché, D. J. Harvey.

Head of Chancery, E. J. Hughes.

2nd Secretaries, P. Armstrong (*Commercial*); J.
Cummins, M.B.E. (*Consul*).

BRITISH CONSULAR OFFICES

There are British Consular Offices at *Santiago,
Arica, Valparaiso* and *Punta Arenas.*

BRITISH COUNCIL

Representative, D. J. Harvey, Eliodoro Yañez 832,
Santiago (Casilla 154-D). The Council supplies
books to the libraries of the *Instituto Chileno-
Britanico* in *Santiago, Viña del Mar/Valparaiso*
and *Concepción.*

Valparaiso is distant from London 9,000 miles via
Panama, and 11,000 via the Strait; transit 28 to 45
days; by air, 22 hrs.

CHINA
(Zhonghua Renmin Gongheguo—
The People's Republic of China.)

President of the People's Republic of China, Li
Xiannian.

Vice President, Ulanhu.

*Chairman of the Standing Committee of the Sixth
National People's Congress,* Peng Zhen.

Chairman of the Central Military Commission, Deng
Xiaoping.

Premier, Zhao Ziyang.

Vice-Premiers, Wan Li; Yao Yilin; Li Peng; Tian
Jiyun.

Auditor General, Yu Mingtao.

Secretary-General, Tian Jiyun.

State Councillors, Chen Muhua; Fang Yi; Gu Mu; Ji
Pengfei; Kang Shien; Song Ping; Wang Bingqian;
Wu Xueqian; Zhang Aiping; Zhang Jingfu.

MINISTERS

Agriculture, Animal Husbandry and Fisheries, He
Kang.

Aviation Industry, Mo Wenxiang.

Chemical Industry, Qin Zhongda.

Civil Affairs, Cui Naifu.

Coal Industry, Gao Yangwen.

Commerce, Lui Yi.

Communications, Li Qing.

Culture, Zhu Muzhi.

Economic Relations and Foreign Trade, Chen Muhua.

Education, He Dongchang.

Electronics Industry, Jiang Zemin.

Finance, Wang Bingqian.

Foreign Affairs, Wu Xueqian.

Forestry, Yang Zhong.

Geology and Minerals, Sun Daguang.

Justice, Zou Yu.

Labour and Personnel, Zhao Shouyi.

Light Industry, Yang Bo.

Machine Building Industry, Zhou Jiannan.

Metallurgical Industry, Li Dongye.

National Defence, Zhang Aiping.

Nuclear Industry, Jiang Xinxiong.

Ordnance Industry, Yu Yi.

Petroleum Industry, Tang Ke.

Posts and Telecommunications, Wen Minsheng.

Public Health, Cui Yueli.

Public Security, Liu Fuzhi.

Radio and Television, Wu Lengxi.

Railways, Chen Puru.

Space Industry, Zhang Jun.

State Security, Ling Yun.

Textile Industry, Wu Wenying.

*Urban and Rural Construction and Environmental
Protection,* Li Ximing.

Water Conservancy and Power, Qian Zhengying.

MINISTERS IN CHARGE OF STATE COMMISSIONS

Economic, Zhang Jingfu.

Family Planning, Wang Wei.

Nationalities Affairs, Yang Jingren.

Physical Culture and Sports, Li Menghua.

Planning, Song Ping.

Restructuring the Economic System, Zhao Ziyang.

Scientific and Technological, Fang Yi.

President of the People's Bank of China, Lu Peijian.

THE CHINESE COMMUNIST PARTY

General Secretary, Hu Yaobang.

The Politburo Standing Committee, Hu Yaobang; Ye
Jianying; Deng Xiaoping; Zhao Ziyang; Li Xiannian; Chen Yun.

The Politburo of the Central Committee, Wan Li; Xi
Zhongxun; Wang Zhen; Wei Guoqing; Ulanhu;
Fang Yi; Deng Xiaoping; Deng Yingchao; Ye
Jianying; Li Xiannian; Li Desheng; Yang Shang-
kun; Yang Dezhi; Yu Qiuli; Song Renqiong; Zhang
Tingfa; Chen Yun; Zhao Ziyang; Hu Qiaomu; Hu
Yaobang; Nie Rongzhen; Ni Zhifu; Xu Xiangqian;
Peng Zhen (*full members*); Yao Yilin; Qin Jiwei;
Chen Muhua (*alternate members*).

The Secretariat of the Central Committee, Wan Li; Xi
Zhongxun; Deng Liqun; Yu Qiuli; Gu Mu; Chen
Pixian; Hu Qili; Hu Yaobang; Yao Yilin (*full
members*); Qiao Shi; Hao Jianxiu (*alternate members*).

The Advisory Commission, Deng Xiaoping (*Chairman*); Bo Yibo; Xu Shiyou; Li Weihan (*Vice
Chairmen*).

The Discipline Inspection Commission, First Secretary, Chen Yun; Second Secretary, Huang Kech-
eng; Standing Secretary, Wang Heshou.

Membership, 40,000,000.

EMBASSY IN LONDON

31 Portland Place, W1N 3AG
[01-636 5726]

Ambassador Extraordinary and Plenipotentiary,
Chen Zhaoyuan.

AREA AND POPULATION.—The area of China is
about 3,700,000 square miles. A nationwide census
(the third) was held in July 1982, which recorded a
total population of 1,008,175,288. China is anxious to
control the growth of the population and has
introduced stringent policies intended to result in a
population of 1·2 billion by the year 2,000. About 6
per cent of the population belong to around 60 ethnic
minorities. Among the largest are the Zhuang of
Guangxi, the Uygurs of Xinjiang, the Tibetans and
the Mongols.

THE PROVINCES OF CHINA

1982 census results were:

Anhui	49,665,724
Fujian	25,931,106
Gansu	19,569,261
Guangdong	59,299,220
Guangxi Zhuang Autonomous Region	36,420,960
Guizhou	28,552,997
Hebei	53,005,875
Heilongjiang	32,665,546
Henan	74,422,739
Hubei	47,804,150
Hunan	54,008,851

Jiangsu	60,521,114
Jiangxi	33,184,827
Liaoning	35,721,693
Nei Monggol Autonomous Region	19,274,279
Ningxia Hui Autonomous Region	3,895,578
Peking	9,230,687
Qinghai	3,895,706
Shaanxi	28,904,423
Shandong	74,419,054
Shanghai	11,859,748
Shanxi	25,291,389
Sichuan	99,713,310
(Taiwan	18,270,749)
Tianjin	7,764,141
Tibet Autonomous Region	1,892,392
Xinjiang Uygur Autonomous Region	13,081,681
Yunnan	32,553,817
Zhejiang	38,884,603
Armed Forces	4,238,210

Xinjiang is the largest region or province in area (about one sixth of the whole area of China) and Sichuan the most populous.

Government.—On October 10, 1911, the party of reform forced the Imperial dynasty to a "voluntary" abdication, and a Republic was proclaimed at Wuchang.

On September 30, 1949, the Chinese People's Political Consultative Conference (C.P.P.C.C) met in Peking and appointed the National People's Government Council under the Chairmanship of Mao Tse-tung. On October 1, Mao proclaimed the inauguration of the Chinese People's Republic. The Soviet Union broke off relations with the Nationalists and established relations with the new *régime* on October 2. The *régime* was recognized by all the Communist *bloc* countries in quick succession, and soon after by the Asian countries of the Commonwealth, the United Kingdom and by a number of other countries. Others, led by the United States, continued to recognize the Chiang Kai-shek *régime* on Taiwan as the rightful Government of China. China's ideological quarrel with the Soviet Union flared up into open conflict across the Ussuri River in 1969. In early 1979 China made an incursion into Vietnam. China has concentrated on wooing developing countries, the West and Japan. In 1971 the People's Republic won acceptance into the United Nations on the expulsion of Taiwan. Since then many more countries have accorded recognition, including, among the most recent, the United States and Japan. To date, 129 countries have established diplomatic relations with China.

The C.P.P.C.C. continued to be the supreme legislative body of the new state until September 20, 1954, when a new constitution was adopted. It was then replaced as the highest organ of state power by the National People's Congress which exercised legislative power, and the National People's Government Council was replaced by the State Council. This body was the supreme administrative body, responsible for the day-to-day running of the country.

A new Constitution was adopted in December 1982, under which the National People's Congress is the highest organ of state power. It is elected for a term of five years and is supposed to hold one session a year. It is empowered to amend the Constitution, make laws, select the President and Vice-President and other leading officials of the state, approve the national economic plan, the state budget and the final state accounts, and to decide on questions of war and peace. The post of President of the People's Republic was abolished at the insistence of Mao Tse-tung but has now been restored. Li Xiannian was elected President at the First Session of the Sixth National People's Congress in June 1983. The State Council is the highest organ of the state administration. It is

composed of the Premier, the Vice Premiers, the State Councillors, heads of Ministries and Commissions, the Auditor General and the Secretary General. Command over the armed forces is vested in the newly established Central Military Commission, of which Deng Xiaoping is the Chairman.

The system of elections to local People's Congresses and to the National People's Congress is maintained. Deputies to congresses at the primary level are "directly elected" by the voters "through a secret ballot after democratic consultation". This is now being extended to county level. These Congresses elect the Deputies to the Congress at the next higher level. Deputies to the National People's Congress are elected by the People's Congresses of the provinces, autonomous regions and municipalities directly under the Central Government, and by the armed forces.

Local government is conducted through People's Governments at provincial, municipal and county levels. Autonomous regions, prefectures and counties exist for national minorities and are described as self-governing. The system prevailing is that found elsewhere, i.e. People's Congresses and People's Governments. Peking, Shanghai and Tientsin continue to come directly under the central government.

In 1966 Mao Tse-tung launched the Cultural Revolution to ward off what he saw as revisionism within the Communist Party. The Party apparatus was virtually swept away, and with it many of China's top leaders, including the senior Party Vice-Chairman and Chairman of the People's Republic Liu Shao-Chi. Mao's second prospective heir Lin Biao was disgraced in 1971, and at the 10th Congress in 1973 Premier Chou En-lai was placed second to Mao at the head of the newly-reconstructed Communist Party. Both men died in 1976 to be succeeded as Party Chairman and Premier by Hua Guofeng. The so-called "Gang of Four", headed by Mao's widow, Chiang Ching, were promptly arrested for allegedly attempting to seize power. This led to pressure for the recall of Vice-Premier Deng Xiaoping, dismissed shortly after Chou's death for betraying Maoist orthodoxy. At the 11th Congress in 1977 Deng was elected Vice-Chairman under Chairman Hua. He has since become the dominant force within the Party by eliminating leftist influence, rehabilitating fallen leaders and adjusting Maoist policies to meet the needs of a developing economy. Hua was replaced as Premier by Zhao Ziyang in 1980, and resigned from the Party Chairmanship in 1981, being replaced by Hu Yaobang. Deng's policies were reaffirmed at the 12th Congress in 1982. The Congress also elected a new Party leadership dominated by Deng and his supporters. The post of Chairman of the Party was abolished. Hu Yaobang, as General Secretary, remained the Party leader.

Armed Forces.—All three military arms in China are parts of the People's Liberation Army (P.L.A.) The size of this body has not been formally given, but it is estimated that China has approximately 3·5 million men under arms, with a further 12 million (or perhaps many more) reserves who take part in militia activities. Until 1955 the P.L.A. did not have a rank structure, but one was introduced in that year similar to that of the Russian Army. In the same year compulsory military service was introduced for all men between the ages of 18 and 40. This service was on a selective basis. The present length of service for those conscripted is three years in the Army, four years in the Air Force and five years in the Navy. With effect from June 1, 1965, the rank structure was abolished, together with all marks of distinction of branch of service. Both are expected to be reinstated.

China exploded her first experimental nuclear device on October 16, 1964 and made further tests in 1965 and in May, October and December, 1966. Her first hydrogen bomb was tested in June, 1967. Further

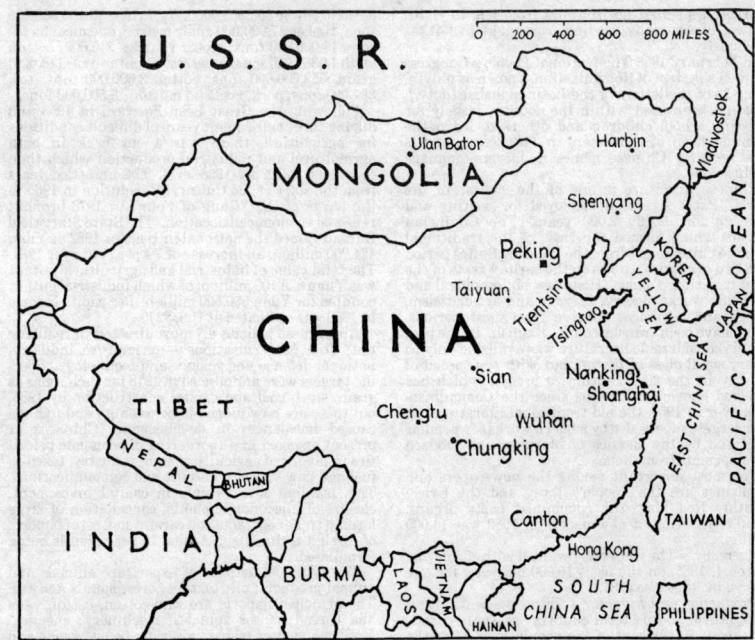

tests of nuclear devices and hydrogen bombs have since been announced, the latest being in November 1976. China embarked on a programme of earth-satellite launchings in April 1970, the latest being made in January 1978. A long-range I.C.B.M. was tested in May 1980.

Religion.—The indigenous religions of China are Confucianism (which includes ancestor worship), Taoism (originally a philosophy rather than a religion) and, since its introduction in the first century of the Christian era, Buddhism. There are also Chinese Moslems (officially estimated at about 12 million) and Christians (unofficially estimated at about 50 million). Religious freedoms, severely curtailed during the Cultural Revolution, are reviving slightly under more liberal policies.

Education.—Although primary education was compulsory under the Nationalists, mass education did not become a fact until after the Communists had taken over. All major educational establishments closed down at the start of the Great Proletarian Cultural Revolution in 1966. Primary and middle schools began to re-open in 1968 and universities in 1970. The Cultural Revolution caused considerable disruption to the educational system and since 1976 attempts have been made to raise academic standards. Primary education now lasts five years, and has a claimed enrolment of 139,720,000 pupils. Secondary education lasts five years (three years in Junior Middle School and two years in Senior Middle School). There were 46,844,000 Middle School pupils in 1982. The proportion of illiterates and semi-illiterates in 1982 was 23·5 per cent, but efforts are being made to expand secondary education, particularly in the rural areas. Particular attention is being paid to higher education where there are over 600 universities, colleges and institutes with an enrolment of 1,159,000 students.

Language and Literature.—The Chinese language has many dialects, notably Cantonese, Hakka, Amoy, Foochow, Changsha, Nanchang, Wu (Shanghai) and the northern dialect. The Common Speech or *Putonghua* (often referred to as "Mandarin") which is being taught throughout the country is based on the northern dialect. The Communists, when they came into power, continued the Kuomintang policy of promoting it as the national language and made much more intensive efforts to propagate it throughout the country. Since the most important aspect of this policy is the use of the spoken language in writing, the old literary style of writing has fallen into disuse.

Chinese writing is ideographic and not phonetic. While the number of sounds in *Putonghua* is limited, the use of four tones expands the variety of meanings that a sound may have. These meanings are distinguished visually by different characters. Whereas originally the language was monosyllabic and confusion was avoided by the use of different characters, thus producing texts which were visually clear but ambiguous to the ear, with the increasing use of the spoken language for writing people are increasingly making use of polysyllabic compounds both in speech and writing in order to avoid confusion. In 1956, after some 4 years of study, the Government decided to introduce 230 simplified characters with a view to making reading and writing easier. The list was enlarged; there are now over 2,000 simplified characters in use. In January, 1956, all Chinese newspapers and most books began to appear with the characters printed horizontally from left to right, instead of vertically reading from right to left, as previously.

In February 1958 The National People's Congress adopted a system of Romanization, known as pinyin, using 25 of the letters of the Latin alphabet (not v). This has been used within the country largely for assisting school children and others to learn the pronunciation of characters in *Putonghua*, and is now used for Chinese names in foreign-language publications.

Chinese literature is one of the richest in the world. Paper has been employed for writing and printing for nearly 2,000 years. The Confucian classics which formed the basis of the traditional Chinese culture date from the Warring States period (4th–3rd centuries B.C.) as do the earliest texts of the rival tradition, Taoism. Histories, philosophical and scientific works, poetry, literary and art criticism, novels and romances survive from most periods. Many have been translated into English. In the past all this considerable literature was available only to a very small class of *literati*, but with the spread of literacy in the 20th century, a process which has received enormous impetus since the Communists took over in 1950, the old traditional literature has been largely superseded by modern works of a popular kind and by the classics of Marxism and modern developments from them.

The most important among the newspapers and magazines are the People's Daily and the twice-monthly Red Flag, the communist party organs. Total circulation of newspapers in 1982 was 14,000 million.

Currency.—The *yuan* was revalued with effect from March 1, 1955, on the basis 10,000 old *yuan* for one new *yuan*. (*See also* p. 81.)

Production and Industry.—China is essentially an agricultural and pastoral country: peasants constitute about 80 per cent of the population. After the establishment of the Chinese People's Government at which time land for the most part was privately owned, there occurred several stages of land reform culminating in the formation of the people's communes in 1958. With the exception of the State farms, the communes embrace the whole rural population. In all there are 50,000 communes and each is subdivided into production brigades and teams.

The communes lost their administrative functions under the new Constitution and remain as purely economic enterprises. New agricultural policies, designed to give greater incentives to the rural population, have meant that the responsibility for agricultural production has been devolved down to individual households, whereas previously work was generally assigned on a collective basis.

Wheat, barley, maize, millet and other cereals, with peas and beans, are grown in the northern provinces, and rice and sugar in the south. Rice is the staple food of the inhabitants. Cotton (mostly in valleys of the Yangtze and Yellow Rivers), tea (in the west and south), with hemp, jute and flax, are the most important crops.

Livestock is raised in large numbers. Silkworm culture is one of the oldest industries. Cottons, woollens and silks are manufactured in large quantities. The mineral wealth of the country is very great. Coal of excellent quality is produced. Iron ore, tin, antimony, wolfram, bismuth and molybdenum are also abundant. Oil is produced in several northern provinces, particularly in Heilongjiang and Shandong, and off-shore deposits are to be tapped in co-operation with Western and Japanese companies.

The Chinese State Statistical Bureau issues production figures annually. The following are of note for 1983:

Steel 40,000,000 tons; pig iron 37,400,000 tons;

electric power 350,000,000 kWs; crude oil 105,900,000 tons; timber 47,000,000 cubic metres; chemical fertilizers 14,000,000 tons; motor vehicles 240,000; cotton cloth 14,864,000 square metres; machine tools 118,000; grain, 353,000,000 tons; cotton 3,600,000 tons; tea, 397,000 tons; pork, beef and mutton 13,500,000 tons.

Following the Great Leap Forward in 1958 and during three subsequent years of difficult conditions for agriculture, there was a cut back in both agricultural and industrial production which then recovered to its pre-1958 level. The unsettled years from the start of the Cultural Revolution in 1966 to the purge of the "Gang of Four" in 1976 brought renewed economic dislocation. The State Statistical Bureau valued the national income for 1982 at Yuan 424,700 million, an increase of 7·4 per cent over 1981. The total value of industrial and agricultural output was Yuan 829,100 million, of which industrial output counted for Yuan 550,600 million. Per capita income in 1980 was estimated at U.S. $270.

All Chinese policies are now directed to realising the "Four Modernisations"—agriculture, industry, national defence and science and technology. Specific targets were announced in 1978 for such items as grain, steel, coal and capital construction by 1985, but these are now judged to be too high and to have caused imbalances in development. China is at present engaged in a reordering of economic priorities in favour of agriculture, light industry, textiles, fuel and power, and transport and communications. This involves severe cuts in capital investment, closure of uneconomic plants, cancellation of large foreign trade contracts and careful control of imports of foreign technology. A new 10-year plan is being formulated.

The principal articles of export are animals and animal products; oil; textiles; ores, metals and tea. The principal imports are raw cotton, cotton yarn and thread; motor vehicles; machinery; chemical fertilizer plants; wheat; aircraft; books, paper and paper-making materials; chemicals; metals and ores; and dyes.

Trade with U.K.

	1982	1983
Imports from U.K.	£103,051,000	£159,722,000
Exports to U.K.	193,231,000	231,417,000

Communications.—Of the total area of China over half consists of tableland and mountainous areas where communications and travel are generally difficult. By 1949, the communications system, as a result of years of neglect and civil war, was more or less completely paralysed. In any case such roads and railways as did exist were largely confined to the eastern plains. After the Communists achieved complete control they devoted much attention to restoring and improving the communication system. The country now has more than 50,000 kilometres of railway trunk and branch lines (as compared to 21,000 kilometres in 1949) and some 890,000 kilometres of highway (as compared with 70,000 kilometres in 1949). In addition, internal civil aviation has been developed, with routes now totalling more than 340,000 kilometres. As a result the communications network now covers most of the country. In the past where roads did not exist the principal means of communications east to west was provided by the rivers, the most important of which are the Yangtze (Changjiang) (3,400 miles long), the Yellow River (Huanghe) (2,600 miles long) and the West River (Xihe) (1,650 miles). These, together with the network of canals connecting them are still much used, but their overall importance is less than it was. Coastal port facilities are being improved and the merchant fleet expanded. In the past 10 years great progress has been made in developing postal services and telecommunications. It is now claimed that 95 p.c. of all rural communes are on the telephone and that postal routes reach practically every production brigade headquarters.

CAPITAL.—Peking, population (Chinese official figure, 1982), 9,230,687. The population of ΨShanghai (Chinese official figure, 1982) is given as 11,859,748; Nanking (estimate, 1974) 2,400,000; Tianjin (Chinese official figure, 1980) 7,390,000; Shenyang (Chinese official figure 1975) 4,400,000; Wuhan (Chinese official figure, 1976) 3,500,000; Chongqing (Chinese official figure, 1979) 6,200,000; ΨGuangzhou (Canton) (estimate, 1973) 5,000,000; Harbin (estimate, 1974) 2,100,000; Luda (Lushun and Dalien) (estimate, 1973) 4,200,000.

FLAG.—Red, with large gold five-point star and four small gold stars in crescent, all in upper quarter next staff.

NATIONAL DAY.—October 1 (Founding of People's Republic).

BRITISH EMBASSY
11 Guang Hua Lu,
Jian Guo Men Wai, Peking.

Ambassador, His Excellency Sir Richard Evans, K.C.M.G. (1984)
Counsellors, P. Thomson (*Head of Chancery*); G. E. Clerk, O.B.E. (*Commercial*); A. D. Johnson (*Cultural, and British Council Representative*).
Defence Attaché, Col. B. Aldridge.
1st Secretaries, O. M. O'Brien; N. N. Inkster; A. Maley, O.B.E.; F. J. Savage; W. D. W. Dennis; W. G. Ehrman.
2nd Secretaries, G. Voysey (*Commercial*); P. S. Johnson; Miss V. P. Hart (*Cultural*); R. Peirce; A. E. C. Cowan; Miss R. C. Manning; J. Ashton; G. Andrews, M.B.E.; J. V. Everard.

TIBET

Tibet is a plateau seldom lower than 10,000 feet, forms the northern frontier of India (boundary imperfectly demarcated), from Kashmir to Burma, but is separated therefrom by the Himalayas. The area is estimated at 463,000 square miles with a population of 1,892,392 in 1982.

From 1911 to 1950, Tibet was virtually an independent country but its status was never officially so recognised. In October 1950, Chinese Communist forces invaded Eastern Tibet. The Dalai Lama later left Lhasa and set up his Government at Yadong, near the Sikkim frontier. On May 23, 1951, an agreement was reached whereby the Chinese army was allowed entry into Tibet. A Communist military and administrative headquarters was set up. In 1954 the Government of India recognized that Tibet was an integral part of China, in return for the right to maintain trade and consular representation there.

A series of revolts against Chinese rule over several years culminated on March 17, 1959, in a rising in Lhasa. Heavy fighting continued for several days before the rebellion was suppressed by Chinese troops and military rule imposed. The Dalai Lama fled to India where he and his followers were granted political asylum. On March 28, 1959, the Chinese Premier issued an order dissolving the Tibetan Government. In its place the 16-member Preparatory Committee for the Tibetan Autonomous Region, originally set up in 1955 with the Dalai Lama as Chairman, was to administer Tibet under the State Council. The Preparatory Committee was to have the Panchen Lama as Acting Chairman and also to include 4 Chinese Officials. Elections were held to choose local People's Congresses in Tibet, thus indicating that the government organization there no longer differed significantly from that of any ordinary province in China.

In December, 1964, the Dalai Lama was declared to be a traitor, and both he and the Panchen Lama were dismissed. The position of Acting Chairman of the Preparatory Committee was assumed by Ngapoi Ngawang Jigmi, who had long been the most prominent secular figure in Tibet. This move marked the end of the period of co-operation by the Chinese Government with the traditional religious authorities, and the eclipse of the latter. The Preparatory Committee completed its work with the setting up of Tibet as an Autonomous Region of China on Sept. 9, 1965. The Panchen Lama is now rehabilitated as an official of the C.P.P.C.C., and the Chinese have invited the Dalai Lama to return from exile.

TAIWAN
(Formosa)

President, Chiang Ching-kuo, *elected,* March, 1978, re-elected, March 21, 1984.
Vice-President, Lee Teng-hui, *elected,* March 22, 1984.
Premier, Yu Kuo-hwa (May 20, 1984).

An island of some 13,800 sq. miles in the China Sea, Taiwan lies 90 miles east of the Chinese mainland in latitude 21° 45′N.—25° 38′N. The population (18,203,000 in March, 1982), is almost entirely Chinese in origin and includes about 2,000,000 mainlanders who came to the island with Chiang Kai-shek in 1947–49. The territories administered by the Chinese Nationalists include the Pescadores Islands (50 sq. miles), some 35 miles west of Taiwan, as well as Quemoy (68 sq. miles) and Matsu (11 sq. miles) which are only a few miles from the mainland. Settled for centuries by the Chinese, the island was administered by Japan from 1895 to 1945. General Chiang Kai-shek withdrew to Taiwan in 1949, towards the end of the war against the Communist *régime,* accompanied by 500,000 Nationalist troops, after which the territory continued under his presidency until his death on April 5, 1975. A mutual defence treaty between the United States and Taiwan Governments was signed in 1954 but this has been terminated as the United States recognized the People's Republic of China on January 1, 1979.

The eastern part of the main island is mountainous and forest covered. Mt. Morrison (Yu Shan) (13,035 ft.) and Mt. Sylvia (Tz'ukaoshan) (12,972 ft.) are the highest peaks. The western plains are watered by many rivers and the soil is very fertile, producing sugar, rice, sweet potatoes, tea, bananas, pineapples and tobacco. Coal, sulphur, iron, petroleum, copper and gold are mined. There are important fisheries. The principal seaports ΨKeelung and ΨKaohsiung are situated in the northern and southern sections of the island.

Trade with U.K.

	1982	1983
Imports from U.K.	£125,183,000	£128,467,000
Exports to U.K.	335,537,000	458,307,000

CAPITAL.—Taipei (population 1979, 2,196,237). Other towns are ΨKaohsiung (1,172,777); Tainan (572,590); Taichung (585,205); and ΨKeelung (345,392).

FLAG.—Red, with blue quarter at top next staff, bearing a twelve-point white sun.

COLOMBIA
(República de Colombia)

President, Dr. Belisario Betancur Cuartas, *assumed office*, August 7, 1982.

CABINET

Interior, Jaime Castro Castro.
Foreign Affairs, Augusto Ramirez Ocampo.
Justice, Enrique Parejo González.
Finance and Public, Roberto Junguito Bonett.
Defence, Gen. Gustavo Matamoros D'Acosta.
Agriculture, Gustavo Castro Guerrero.
Economic Development, Iván Duque Escobar.
Mines and Energy, Alvaro Leyva Durán.
Education, Doris Eder De Zambrano.
Labour, Oscar Salazar Chávez.
Health, Amaury Garcia Burgos.
Communications, Nohemí Sanin Posada.
Public Works, Hernán Beltz Peralta

COLOMBIAN EMBASSY IN LONDON
3 Hans Crescent, SW1X 0LR
[01–589 9177]

Ambassador Extraordinary and Plenipotentiary, His Excellency Dr. Augusto Espinosa (1982).
Minister Counsellor, Dr. Teresa Ivars.
There are *Consulates-General* in *London* and *Liverpool*.

The Republic of Colombia lies in the extreme north-west of South America, having a coastline on both the Atlantic and Pacific Oceans. It is situated between 4° 13′ S. to 12° 30′ N. lat. and 68° to 79° W. long., with an approximate area of 440,000 square miles, and a population (estimated 1981) of 28,100,000.

The Colombian coast was visited in 1502 by Christopher Columbus, and in 1536 a Spanish expedition under Jiménez de Quesada penetrated to the interior and established on the site of the present capital a government which continued under Spanish rule until the revolt of the Spanish–American colonies in 1811–1824. In 1819 Simón Bolívar (1783–1831) established the Republic of Colombia, consisting of the territories now known as Colombia, Panama, Venezuela and Ecuador. In 1829–1830 Venezuela and Ecuador withdrew from the association of provinces, and in 1831 the remaining territories were formed into the Republic of New Granada. In 1858 the name was changed to the Granadine Confederation and in 1861 to the United States of Colombia. In 1866 the present title was adopted. In 1903 Panama seceded from Colombia, and became a separate Republic.

There are three great ranges of the Andes, known as the Western, Central, and Eastern Cordilleras; the second contains the highest peaks, but the latter is the most important, as it consists of a series of vast tablelands. This temperate region is the most densely peopled portion of the Republic. The highest mountain in Colombia is Cristobal Colon (18,946 feet) in the Sierra Nevada de Santa Marta on the Caribbean coast.

The principal rivers are the Magdalena, Guaviare, Cauca, Atrato, Caquetá, Putumayo and Patia. The Patia flows through the famous *Minima Gorge* of the Western Cordilleras, and one of its tributaries (the Carchi, or Upper Guiatara) is spanned by the Rumichaca Arch, or *Inca's Bridge*, of natural stone. On the Rio Bogotá is the great *Fall of Tequendama*, 482 ft. in height.

Government.—During the early nineteen-fifties Colombia suffered a period of virtual civil war between the supporters of the traditional political parties, the Conservatives and the Liberals. The dictatorship of Gen. Rojas Pinilla (1953–57) put an end to the worst of the violence and following his dismissal in 1957, a military junta took over, preparing the way for a return to democratic government. Congressional elections were held on March 16, 1958, which yielded a Liberal majority. This led, the same year, to the institution of the National Front system, to run for a period of 16 years. The Presidency alternated every four years between the Liberals and Conservatives while parity of appointment was maintained between the two parties in Congress, the Government and all Government Departments.

The first election not subject to the National Front system for the Presidency and Congress was in 1974; parity in administrative appointments between the traditional parties continued, however, until 1978. Thereafter, the constitution lays down that Government portfolios and Administrative appointments shall be divided among the two majority parties in Congress in an "adequate and equitable" manner.

Defence.—The Army peace effective strength is 57,000; war effective, approx. 400,000. The Navy has four new corvettes, four destroyers, three frigates, two submarines, and other small craft. The Air Force, with 6,000 personnel, has old jet trainers and two squadrons equipped with Mirage fighters.

Production.—Colombia is rich in minerals, and produces gold (mined chiefly in Antioquia), silver, copper, lead, mercury, manganese, emeralds (mined chiefly at Muzo and Chivor), and platinum (one of the largest deposits in the world). There are also large salt deposits at Zipaquirá, the mining of which is a government-controlled monopoly. Production of oil in 1981 was 146,000 barrels per day, and exploration for new reserves is being encouraged.

Because of the range of climate, a wide variety of crops can be grown. The principal agriculture products are coffee (which accounts for over half of total exports), potatoes, rice, bananas, maize, cotton, soybean, barley, wheat and cacao. Cattle are raised in large numbers, and meat and cured skins and hides are important exports.

Industry.—Manufactures (mainly for home consumption, but with an increasing export trade) consist of textiles, leather goods, chemicals, asbestos goods, cement, pharmaceutical products, rubber goods, including motor tyres, furniture, footwear, confectionery, cigarettes, beer, glass containers and steel. Stimulus to the economy has been provided by large loans from the World Bank and IADB for project development, particularly in the power sector (in which hydroelectric projects have predominated) and for telecommunications.

Communications.—The "Atlantic Railway" links the departmental lines running down to the river, and completes the connection between Bogotá and Santa Marta. The Pacific Railway connects Bogotá with the port of Buenaventura. There are about 2,200 miles of rail in use at present. The total road network (1978) consists of 53,200 km. of roads of all types, of which 21,800 km. are classified as main trunk and transversal roads. There are daily passenger and cargo air services between Bogotá and all the principal towns. There are daily services to the U.S.A., frequent services to other countries in South America, and to Europe. The national telephone and telegraph system consists primarily of wireless links between the more important centres. Large appropriations have been made for modernization of the country's telecommunication system. There are radio stations in the main cities, and a television station in Bogotá with relays to most parts of the country.

Language and Literature.—Spanish is the language of the country and education has been free since 1870. Great efforts have been made in reducing illiteracy and it is estimated that about 70 per cent of those over 10 years of age can read and write. In addition to the National University with headquarters at Bogotá there are 26 other universities. There is a flourishing press in urban areas and a national literature supplements the rich inheritance from the time of Spanish rule.

Roman Catholicism is the established religion.

TRADE

	1981 $U.S.	1982 $U.S.
Total imports (c.i.f.)	3,863m.	6,094·7m.
Total exports (f.o.b.)	2,926m.	3,347·8m.

Trade with U.K.

	1982	1983
Imports from U.K.	£50,328,000	£51,023,000
Exports to U.K.	34,502,000	56,458,000

CAPITAL, Bogotá, population (estimated, 1978) 5,000,000. Bogotá is an inland city in the Eastern Cordilleras, at an elevation of 8,600 to 9,000 ft. above sea level. Other centres are Medellin (2,000,000); Cali (1,256,000); Barranquilla (828,000); Ψ Cartagena (420,000); Bucaramanga (390,000); Cucuta (360,000); Manizales (250,000).

FLAG.—Broad yellow band in upper half, surmounting equal bands of blue and red.

NATIONAL DAY.—July 20 (National Independence Day).

BRITISH EMBASSY
Calle 38, No. 13–35, Bogotá

Ambassador Extraordinary and Plenipotentiary, His Excellency John A. Robson, C.M.G. (1982).

There are British Consular Offices at *Bogotá, Barranquilla* and *Cali*.

British Council Representative, Dr. B. J. Lavercombe, Calle 87, No. 12–79, Bogotá 1.

THE COMOROS
(Federal and Islamic Republic of the Comoros)

President, Ahmed Abdallah, *took office* May 1978.
Prime Minister, Ali Mroudjae.

The Comoro archipelago includes the islands of Great Comoro, Anjouan, Mayotte and Moheli and certain islets in the Indian Ocean with an area of 800 sq. miles and a population (estimated 1979) of 385,000, most of whom are Muslim. The islanders voted for independence from France in December 1974 and three islands became independent on July 6, 1975. (The island of Mayotte was against independence and has remained under French administration.) On October 1, 1978 the three islands voted in a referendum to adopt a new Constitution which provides for a President, directly elected for a six year term. The Council of Government, consisting of a Prime Minister and up to nine other Ministers, is appointed by the President. There is a 39-member Federal Assembly elected for 5 years. Each island is administered by a Governor, assisted by up to four Commissioners whom he appoints, and has an elected Legislative Council.

The most important products now are vanilla, copra, cloves and essential oils, which are the principal exports; cacao, sisal and coffee are also cultivated. Great Comoro is well forested and produces some timber.

CAPITAL.—Moroni, on Great Comoro.

CONGO
(People's Republic of the Congo)

President, Col. Denis Sassou-Nguesso, *appointed* 1979, *re-elected*, July 1984 (also holds *Defence and Security Portfolio*).
Vice-President, Maj. Louis Sylvain Goma.
Prime Minister, Ange Edouard Poungui.

The Republic lies on the Equator between Gabon on the west and Zaire on the east, the River Congo and its tributary the Ubanghi forming most of the eastern boundary of the state. The Congo has a short Atlantic coastline. Area of the Republic of Congo is 129,960 sq. miles, with a population of approximately 2,100,000. Formerly the French colony of Middle Congo, it became a member state of the French Community on November 28, 1958, and was proclaimed fully independent on August 17, 1960.

In 1968, conduct of affairs was assumed by a National Council of Army officers. The Parti Congolais du Travail (*PCT*) was created by the Congress of December 29–31, 1969 and the People's Republic of the Congo was established. Under the present Constitution, approved by referendum in 1979, executive power is vested in the President, who is elected by the Congress of the P.C.T. (the only legal party). The Council of Ministers is appointed and led by the President.

Congo has its own oil deposits, though production is low, and also produces lead, zinc and gold. The principal agricultural products are cassava, sugar cane and yams. Imports are mainly of machinery.

Trade with U.K.

	1982	1983
Imports from U.K.	£9,766,000	£9,560,000
Exports to U.K.	2,393,000	4,335,000

Currency.—The currency is the CFA Franc.
CAPITAL.—Brazzaville (156,000); Ψ Pointe Noire (76,000).

FLAG.—Red, with hammer and sickle in wreath of leaves in top corner.

BRITISH EMBASSY
British Ambassador (Resident at *Kinshasa, Zaire*.)

COSTA RICA
(República de Costa Rica)

President, Luis Alberto Monge Alvarez, *took office*, May 8, 1982.

MINISTERS
For the Presidency, F. Berrocal Soto.
Foreign Affairs and Religion, C. J. Gutiérrez Gutiérrez.
Government, Dr. A. Carro Zuñiga.
Security, A. D. Solano Calderón.
Finance, P. Morera Batres.
Agriculture and Livestock, F. Morales Hernandez.
Economy and Trade, Odalier Villalobos.
Public Works and Transport, R. Araya Monge.
Education, E. Rodriquez Vega.
Health, Dr. J. Jaramillo Antillón.
Labour and Social Welfare, G. Sandoval Aguilar.
Culture, Youth and Sport, H. González Guitierréz.
Justice, H. A. Muñoz.
Industry, Energy and Mines, C. Chavez Ziamora.
Planning, J. M. Villasusa.
Exports and Investments, J. M. Dengo Obregón.

There were reports of a Cabinet reshuffle in August 1984 but no details were available at the time of going to press.

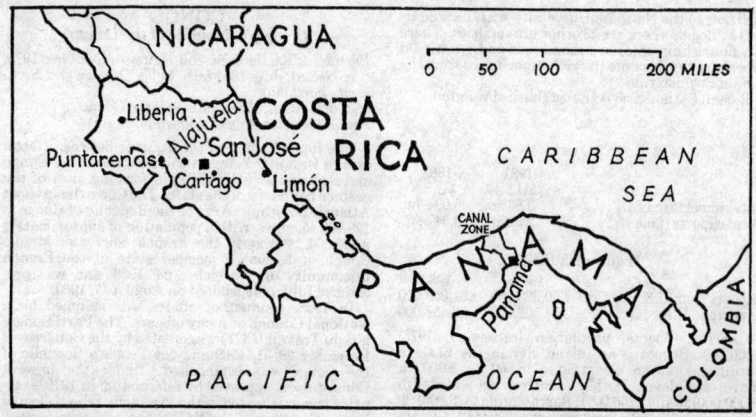

COSTA RICAN EMBASSY
93 Star Street, W2
[01–723 1772/9630]

Ambassador Extraordinary and Plenipotentiary, His Excellency Jorge Borbon Zeller (1982).

The Republic of Costa Rica in Central America extends across the isthmus between 8° 17′ and 11° 10′ N. lat. and from 82° 30′ to 85° 45′ W. long., contains an area of 19,653 sq. miles, and a population (1981 estimate) of 2,276,676. The population is basically of European stock, in which Costa Rica differs from most Latin American countries. The Republic lies between Nicaragua and Panama and between the Caribbean Sea and the Pacific Ocean. The coastal lowlands by the Caribbean Sea and Pacific have a tropical climate but the interior plateau, with a mean elevation of 4,000 feet, enjoys a temperate climate.

For nearly three centuries (1530–1821) Costa Rica formed part of the Spanish-American dominions, the seat of government being at Cartago. In 1821 the country obtained its independence, although from 1824 to 1839 it was one of the United States of Central America.

On Dec. 1, 1948, the Army was abolished, the President declaring it unnecessary, as the country loved peace.

Economy.—Agriculture is the chief industry and the principal products are coffee, bananas, sugar and cattle (for meat), all of which are important exports. Other crops are cocoa, rice, maize, potatoes and hemp. Industrial activity is principally in the manufacturing sector and manufactured goods are the largest category of exports. The main goods are foodstuffs, textiles and clothing, plastic goods, pharmaceuticals, fertilizers and electrical equipment.

Communications.—The chief ports are Limón, on the Atlantic coast, through which passes most of the coffee exported, and Puntarenas and Golfito on the Pacific coast. A new Pacific port, Caldera, currently under construction with Japanese aid, is likely to divert traffic from Puntarenas within a few years. In 1981, 1,013 ships entered Costa Rican ports handling imports and exports of approximately 2,393,374 tons of goods. The railway system is nationalised. About 500 miles of railroad are open. LACSA is the national airline, operating flights throughout Central and South America, the Caribbean and U.S.A., besides internal flights to local airports by SANSA.

Language, etc.—Spanish is the language of the country. Education is compulsory and free. The literacy rate is the highest in Latin America.

FINANCE

	1980
Revenue	8,029m. *colones*
Expenditure	8,029m. *colones*

Currency is the *colon* of 100 *centimos*.

TRADE

	1980
	$U.S., millions
Total imports	1,529
Total exports	1,018

Trade with U.K.

	1982	1983
Imports from U.K.	£5,455,000	£11,041,000
Exports to U.K.	15,068,000	22,299,000

The chief exports were manufactured goods and other products, coffee, bananas, cocoa and sugar. The chief imports were machinery, including transport equipment, manufactures, chemicals, fuel and mineral oils and foodstuffs.

CAPITAL.—San José pop. 808,919; Alajuela (377,062); Cartago (237,267); Heredia (154,943); Ψ Puntarenas (259,081); Ψ Limón (137,329); Guanacaste (209,024). (Populations shown are of provinces, cantons and districts).

FLAG.—Five horizontal bands, blue, white, red, white, blue (the red band twice the width of the others with emblem near staff).

NATIONAL DAY.—September 15.

BRITISH EMBASSY
Apartado 815, Edificio Centro Colon 1007, San José.

Ambassador Extraordinary and Plenipotentiary and Consul-General, His Excellency Peter Wayne Summerscale (1982).

San José is 5,687 miles from London; sea transit direct 18 days; via New York, 20 days; Air Mails (via New York) 4 to 8 days from London. Ocean Mail, 8 to 16 weeks.

CUBA
(Republica de Cuba)

President of Council of State and Head of Government,
Dr. Fidel Castro Ruz, *appointed* Nov. 2, 1976.

COUNCIL OF STATE

President, Dr. Fidel Castro Ruz.
First Vice-President, Raúl Castro Ruz.
Vice-Presidents, Juan Almeida Bosque; Ramiro Valdés Menéndez; Guillermo García Frías; Dr. Carlos Rafael Rodríguez; Blas Roca Calderío.
Secretary, José M. Miyar Barruecos.

COUNCIL OF MINISTERS

President, Dr. Fidel Castro Ruz.
First Vice-President, Raúl Castro Ruz.
Vice-Presidents, Dr. Carlos Rafael Rodríguez; Ramiro Valdés Menéndez; Guillermo García Frías; Sr. Pedro Miret Prieto; Sr. Diocles Torralba González; Sr. José Ramón Fernández Alvarez; Sr. Humberto Pérez González; José A. López Moreno; Osmany Cienfuegos Gorriarán; Sr. Antonio Esquivel Yedra.
Secretary, Sr. Osmany Cienfuegos Gorriarán.
Presidents of State Committees: Sr. Humberto Pérez González (*Central Planning Board*); Sr. Héctor Rodríguez Llompart (*Economic Collaboration*); Sr. Francisco Garcia Valls (*Finance*); Sr. Joaquin Benavides Rodríguez (*Labour and Social Security*); Sr. Arturo Guzmán Pascual (*Prices*); Sr. Ramón Darias Rodés (*Standardization*); Sr. Fidel Vascó González (*Statistics*); Sra. Irma Sánchez Valdés (*Technical Material Supplies*); Sr. Raúl León Torras (*National Bank of Cuba*); Dr. Wilfredo Torres Yribar (*Academy of Science*).
Ministers, Sr. Adolfo Díaz Suarez (*Agriculture*); Sr. Pedro Guelmes González (*Communications*); Sr. Marcos Portal León (*Basic Industries*); Sr. José A. López Moreno (*Construction Materials Industry*); Dr. Armando Hart Dávalos (*Culture*); Sr. José R. Fernandez Alvarez (*Education*); Sr. Ricardo Cabrisas Ruiz (*Foreign Trade*); Sr. Jorge A. Fernandez Cuervo Vinent (*Fishing Industry*); Sr. Alejandro Roca Iglesias (*Food Industry*); Sr. Isidoro Malmierca Peoli (*Foreign Affairs*); Sr. Fernando Vecino Alegret (*Higher Education*); Ramiro Valdés Menéndez (*Interior*); Col. Manuel Vila Sosa (*Internal Trade*); Dr. Juan Escalona Reguera (*Justice*); Sr. Manuel Millares Rodriguez (*Light Industry*); Dr. Sergio del Valle Jiménez (*Public Health*); Gen. Raúl Castro Ruz (*Revolutionary Armed Forces*); Sr. Diocles Torralba González (*Sugar Industry*); Ing. Marcos Lage Coello (*Sidero-Mechanic Industry*); Sr. Guillermo Garcia Frias (*Transport*); Sr. José A. Naranjo Morales, Sr. Levi Farah Balmaseda, Sr. Antonio Rodríguez Maurell (*without Portfolio*).

CUBAN EMBASSY IN LONDON
167 High Holborn, W.C.1
[01–240 2488]

Ambassador Extraordinary and Plenipotentiary, His Excellency Hermes Herrera (1981).

Cuba, the largest island in the Caribbean, lies between 74° and 85° W. long., and 19° and 23° N. lat., with a total area of 44,178 sq. miles. The country has now been divided into 14 provinces. The estimated total population in 1983 was 9,939,800.

The island of Cuba was visited by Christopher Columbus during his first voyage, on October 27, 1492, and was then believed to be part of the Western mainland of India. Early in the 16th century the island was conquered by the Spaniards, to be used later as a base of operations for the conquest of Mexico and Central America, and for almost four

centuries Cuba remained under a Spanish Captain-General. [The island was under British rule for one year, 1762–1763, when it was returned to Spain in exchange for Florida.] Separatist agitation culminated in the closing years of the 19th century in a fierce and blood-thirsty war. In 1898 the government of the United States intervened and despatched the battleship *Maine* to Havana harbour, where in February of that year the vessel was sunk by an explosion, the cause of which remains an unsolved mystery. On April 20, 1898, the U.S. Government demanded the evacuation of Cuba by the Spanish forces, and a short Spanish–American war led to the abandonment of the island, which was occupied by U.S. troops. From Jan. 1, 1899, to May 20, 1902, Cuba was under U.S. military rule, and reforms of the widest and most far-reaching character were instituted. On May 20, 1902, an autonomous government was inaugurated with an elected President, and a legislature of two houses. The island was, however, again the prey of revolution from Aug. to Sept., 1906, when the U.S. Government resumed control. On Jan. 28, 1909, a republican government was again inaugurated.

A revolution led by Dr. Fidel Castro overthrew the Government of General Batista on January 1, 1959. A provisional government was set up and elections were promised within four years. In 1961 Dr. Castro proclaimed the revolution to be Socialist and himself to be a Marxist-Leninist.

In October, 1965, the Communist Party of Cuba was formed to succeed the United Party of the Socialist Revolution. It is the only authorized political party. The First Congress of the Communist Party of Cuba was held in December 1975. The new Socialist Constitution came into force on February 24, 1976 and indirect elections to the National Assembly of People's Power were subsequently held as part of an institutionalisation of the State apparatus.

The Government has carried out programmes of land and urban reform and of nationalization of the means of production and distribution. By June, 1963, 90 per cent of industrial production, all foreign trade and about 50 per cent of small commercial companies were in state hands. In March, 1968, virtually all remaining private commercial enterprises were nationalised. About 80 per cent of the cultivated land is in state farms or State-controlled co-operatives. Private smallholders, who own the remainder, have to sell all their production to the state.

Although efforts are being made to diversify the economy, sugar is still its mainstay and Cuba's principal source of foreign exchange. It still accounts for some 80 per cent in value of total Cuban exports. The largest sugar harvest ever was produced in 1969/70, when total production reached about 8,500,000 tons. This was achieved at considerable cost to the rest of the economy, however, and subsequent harvests were much lower. In 1982–83 the harvest was 7,200,000 tons. Cuba's other main exports are nickel, seafood, citrus fruits, tobacco and rum.

Despite increased trade with Western Europe and Japan, the Communist countries, particularly the Soviet Union, form Cuba's main trading partners, covering about 86 per cent of imports and exports. In addition, the U.S.S.R. offers substantial aid through a system of subsidies which has recently been estimated to amount to $3,500 million.

There are 14,000 kms. of railway track, of which 5,000 kms. are in public service. In 1980 there were 10,000 kms. of road, 4,700 of which were unpaved. At present scheduled international air services run to North, Central and South American countries and Europe.

Language and Literature.—Spanish is the language of the island. English, formerly widely understood, is now spoken less. Education is compulsory and free. The University of Havana was founded in 1728, but until its enlargement under American auspices in the first quarter of the twentieth century no great progress was made in secondary or higher education. There are universities at Santiago de Cuba and Santa Clara. Public libraries have been established. The press and broadcasting and television are under the control of the Government.

	1982	1983
	Pesos, million	
Imports	5,537	6,224
Exports	4,939	5,531

Trade with U.K.

	1982	1983
Imports from U.K.	£64,835,484	£45,736,602
Exports to U.K.	17,688,405	14,010,254

CAPITAL.—ΨHavana (pop., est. 1981), 1,924,886; other towns are ΨSantiago (403,604), Santa Clara (189,092), Camagüey (261,831), Holgüin (239,641), and ΨCienfuegos (114,650).

FLAG.—Five horizontal bands, blue and white (blue at top and bottom) with red triangle, close to staff, charged with 5-point star.

NATIONAL DAY.—January 1 (Day of Liberation).

BRITISH EMBASSY

Edificio Bolívar, Cárcel 101–103
e Morro y Prado, Apartado 1069, Havana.

Ambassador Extraordinary and Plenipotentiary, His Excellency P. Robin Fearn, C.M.G. (1984).

Counsellor, Mrs. M. Bryan (*Head of Chancery*).

1st Secretary, J. A. Graham (*Commercial and H.M. Consul*).

CZECHOSLOVAKIA

(Československá Socialistická Republika)

President, Gustáv Husák, *born* Jan. 10, 1913; *elected* May 29, 1975, *re-elected*, May 22, 1980.

Federal Government

Prime Minister, Lubomír Štrougal.
Deputy Prime Ministers, Peter Colotka; Josef Korčák; Karol Laco; Matej Lúčan; Rudolf Rohlíček; Svatopluk Potač; Ladislav Gerle; Jaromír Obzina.

Ministers

Agriculture and Food, Miroslav Toman.
Finance, Leopold Ler.
Foreign Affairs, Bohuslav Chňoupek.
Foreign Trade, Bohumil Urban.
Fuel and Power, Vlastimil Ehrenberger.
Interior, Vratislav Vajnar.
Labour and Social Affairs, Miroslav Boďa.
Metallurgy and Heavy Engineering, Eduard Saul.
National Defence, Gen. Martin Dzúr.
Communications, Vlastimil Chalupa.
Transport, Vladimir Blažek.
People's Control, František Ondřich.
Prices, Michal Sabolčík.
General Engineering, Pavol Bahyl.
Electrical Engineering, Milan Kubat.
Chairman of State Planning Commission, Svatopluk Potac.
Prime Minister of the Czech Socialist Republic, Josef Korčák.
Prime Minister of the Slovak Socialist Republic, Dr. Peter Colotka.

CZECHOSLOVAK COMMUNIST PARTY

Presidium of the Central Committee, V. Bilak; P. Colotka; K. Hoffman; G. Husák; A. Indra; A. Kapek; J. Korčák; J. Lenárt; L. Štrougal; M. Jakeš; J. Kempný (*full members*); M. Hruškovič; J. Fojtík; J. Harman (*candidate members*).
Secretariat of the Central Committee, Gustáv Husák (*General Secretary*); M. Jakeš; M. Beňo; J. Haman; V. Bilak; J. Fojtik; J. Havlín; J. Poledník; F. Pitra (*secretaries*); M. Kabrhelová (*member*).

CZECHOSLOVAK EMBASSY

25 Kensington Palace Gardens, W8 4QY
[01–229 1255]

Ambassador Extraordinary and Plenipotentiary, His Excellency Dr. Miroslav Houštecký.
Commercial Counsellor, Václav Jarolim.
Military and Air Attaché, Col. Miroslav Merhaut.
Commercial Attaché, Jan Bittner.
Assistant Military and Air Attaché, B. Kramář.
Press Secretary, Josef Konečný.

Area and Population.—Czechoslovakia, formerly part of the Austro-Hungarian Monarchy, declared its independence on Oct. 28, 1918 (Czechoslovak Independence Day), the territory affected having an area of 53,700 square miles, reduced, by the cession of Ruthenia to U.S.S.R. in 1945, to 49,400 square miles. The population of Czechoslovakia was 15,280,148 in 1980.

Government.—The Communist Party came to power in Czechoslovakia in February, 1948, and Communist control of the country is now unqualified. On July 11, 1960, a new constitution was proclaimed, replacing that of 1948. Its purpose was to express the fact that Czechoslovakia is now deemed to have completed the construction of Socialism and to be on the road to true Communism. The official title of the State was accordingly changed to "The Czechoslovak Socialist Republic".

In January, 1968, pressures for reform of the system were realized with the removal of the First Secretary of the Communist Party, Novotný, and his replacement by Alexander Dubček. They were translated into a Party Action Programme adopted in April. Shortly afterwards the country's supreme legislative body, the National Assembly, began work on new legislation, which envisaged the democratisation of the country's political life, greater guarantees of fundamental liberties and the establishment of a federal system.

The speed of events and their implications for the internal development of the other communist regimes in Eastern Europe and the Soviet Union, as well as

for the system of alliances among these countries, alarmed the Soviet Union. On the night of August 20, Czechoslovakia was invaded by Soviet, Polish, East German, Hungarian and Bulgarian troops, the capital and all major towns being occupied.

The Russians were unable to depose the Czechoslovak leadership, but forced them to sign on August 26 an Agreement modifying their policies and, on October 18, a treaty legalising the presence of Soviet troops on Czechoslovak territory.

On April 17, 1969, Gustáv Husák took over the leadership of the Communist Party, and the reforms of 1968 were abandoned with exception of the Federal system of government, which had been set up in October 1968. Czechoslovakia now consists of the Czech Socialist Republic and the Slovak Socialist Republic, each of which has its own government responsible to its legislative body—the National Council. Areas such as the Constitution, Defence, Foreign Affairs, State Material Reserves and Currency are the responsibility of the Federal Administration. The Federal Government is responsible to the Federal Assembly, which is composed of two Chambers, the Chamber of the People, whose deputies are elected throughout the Federation, and the Chamber of the Nations, consisting of an equal number of Czech and Slovak Deputies. The federal system was not extended to the organization of the Communist Party.

The Economic System.—Under the present political system industry is state-owned, and nearly all agricultural land is cultivated by state or co-operative farms. Economic planning is centralised, and state economic plans have the force of law. Early in 1980 an experiment in limited devolution of responsibility, having been considered reasonably successful, was expanded into a "Set of Measures for the Reform of Planned Management" which affects most of the economy. Its main purpose is to introduce some devolution of production and profits control in order to encourage higher productivity and a better quality output.

Czechoslovakia is not rich in minerals, although significant quantities of coal, brown coal and lignite are mined. Principal agricultural products are sugarbeet, potatoes and cereal crops; the timber industry is also very important. The country has long been highly industrialised, and machinery, industrial consumer goods and raw materials are major exports. The 7th Five Year Plan (1981–85) aims to raise

national income by 2·8 per cent, industrial production by 2·7 per cent and agricultural production by 2·6 per cent.

Language and Literature.—Czech and Slovak are the official languages, each having its own literature. The Reformation gave a wide-spread impulse to Czech literature, the writings of Jan Hus (martyred in 1415 as a religious and social reformer) familiarizing the people with Wyclif's teaching. This impulse endured to the close of the 17th century when Jan Amos Komensky or Comenius (1592–1670) was expelled from the country. Under Austrian rule and with the persistent pursuit of Germanization, there was a period of stagnation until the national revival in the first half of the 19th century. Authors of international reputation between the Wars include K. M. Capek-Chod (1860–1927), Viktor Dyk (1877–1931), Jaroslav Hašek (1883–1923), Karel Capek (1890–1938), Vladimír Vančura (1891–1942), and Ivan Olbracht (1882–1952). Liberty of the press ceased with the loss of independence and the Nazi occupation in 1939. It was temporarily restored on the liberation of the country. After the Communist take-over of February, 1948, however, freedom of the press was curtailed. All papers and periodicals were forced to follow the Party line and a number of publications were banned. Prominent post-war writers include František Hrubín (b. 1910), Bohumil Hrabal (b. 1914), Václav Havel (b. 1936), Ladislav Mňáčko (b. 1919), Ladislav Novomesky (b. 1904), Arnošt Lustig (b. 1926), Jiří Mucha (b. 1915), and others. Poetic writing ranges from traditional lyric (Jaroslavl Seifert) to "concrete" and typographic modernism (Jiří Kolář, Josef Hiršal). In the present political conditions few of these writers are published in Czechoslovakia.

Education.—Education is compulsory and free for all children from the ages of 6 to 16. The number of pupils in basic nine-year schools is 1,875,479 (1979–80). There are 142,725 students in the secondary grammar schools and the number given for technical schools of all kinds is 331,840. There are five universities in Czechoslovakia of which the most famous is Charles University in Prague (founded 1348), the others being situated at Bratislava, Brno, Olomouc and Košice. In addition there are a considerable number of other institutions of university standing, technical colleges, agricultural colleges, etc. In 1979–80, there were 183,632 students in centres of higher education of which 44,963 were part-time.

Finance.—The Czechoslovak currency is the Czechoslovak *Koruna* (*Kčs* = Czechoslovak crown) of 100 *heller*.

Trade with U.K.

	1982	1983
Imports from U.K.	£70,105,000	£69,456,000
Exports to U.K.	82,007,000	101,302,000

CAPITAL.—Prague (Praha), on the Vltava (Moldau), the former capital of Bohemia with a population (1979) of 1,191,125. Other towns are Brno (Brünn), capital of Moravia (372,793), Bratislava (Pressburg), capital of Slovakia (374,860), Ostrava (325,473), Košice (200,943) and Plzen (Pilsen) (169,466).

FLAG.—Two equal horizontal stripes, white (above) and red; a blue triangle next to staff.

NATIONAL DAY.—May 9.

BRITISH EMBASSY
Thunovská 14, 11800 Prague 1.

Ambassador Extraordinary and Plenipotentiary, His Excellency John Rowland Rich, C.M.G.
Counsellor, A. B. P. Smart (*Head of Chancery*).
Defence and Military Attaché, Col. R. G. Lee.
Air Attaché, Wing-Cdr. M. Sparkes.
1st Secretaries, R. A. Kealy (*Commercial*); A. J. Stafford (*Consul*); R. E. Makepeace (*Press*).
2nd Secretaries (*AO*), M. Page; D. Herbert (*Commercial*).
3rd Secretary, Miss J. Wills (*Vice-Consul*).
Cultural Attaché, J. F. Green.

DENMARK
(Kongeriget Danmark)

Queen, Margrethe II, eldest daughter of King Frederik IX, *born* April 16, 1940, *succeeded* Jan. 14, 1972, *married* June 10, 1967, Count Henri de Monpezat (Prince Henrik of Denmark) and *has issue* Crown Prince Frederik *born* May 26, 1968; and Prince Joachim, *born* June 7, 1969.

CABINET

Prime Minister, Poul Schlüter.
Finance Minister, Palle Simonsen.
Foreign Affairs, Uffe Ellemann-Jensen.
Environment and Nordic Affairs, Christian Christensen.
Ecclesiastical Affairs, Mette Madsen.
Greenland, Tom Høyem.
Culture, Mimi Stilling Jacobsen.
Social Affairs, Elisebeth Kock-Petersen.
Interior, Britta Schall-Holberg.
Justice, Erik Ninn-Hansen.
Agriculture, Niels Anker Kofoed.
Fisheries, Henning Grove.
Education, Bertel Haarder.
Economic Affairs, Anders Andersen.
Taxation, Dr. Isi Foighel.
Defence, Hans Engell.
Labour, Grethe Fenger-Møller.
Industry, Ib Stetter.
Housing, Niels Bollmann.
Public Works, Arne Melchior.
Energy, Knud Enggaard.

ROYAL DANISH EMBASSY IN LONDON
55 Sloane Street, SW1X 9SR
[01–235 1255]

Ambassador Extraordinary and Plenipotentiary, His Excellency Tyge Dahlgaard (1981).
Minister Plenipotentiary, K. A. Eliasen.
Minister Counsellors, I. J. Kelland (*Economic and Consular*); H. J. Rossen (*Commercial*); J. Anker Nielson (*Press and Culture*).

Counsellor, Per Poulsen-Hansen.
Defence Attaché, Brig. Gen. B. P. Faaberg.

Area and Population.—A Kingdom of Northern Europe, consisting of the islands of Zeeland, Funen, Lolland, etc., the peninsula of Jutland, and the outlying island of Bornholm in the Baltic, the Faroes and Greenland. Denmark is situated between 54° 34′–57° 45′ N. lat., 8° 5′–15° E. 12′ long., with an area of 17,000 square miles, and a population estimated (1982) of 5,116,464. In 1982 there were 52,668 live births, and 55,426 deaths.

Government.—Under the Constitution of the Kingdom of Denmark Act of June 5, 1953, the legislature consists of one chamber, the *Folketing*, of not more than 179 members, including 2 for the Faröes and 2 for Greenland. The voting age is 18.

The Social Democrat Government of Mr. Jørgensen, formed in January 1982, resigned from office in early September 1982 after failing to obtain approval of Budget proposals and a four-party non-Socialist coalition government was formed, which continued unchanged after an election on January 10, 1984.

In 1973 Denmark joined the European Economic Community. Denmark is also a member of NATO, and the Nordic Council.

Education is free and compulsory, the schools being maintained by taxation. Special schools are numerous, commercial, technical and agricultural predominating. There are Universities at Copenhagen (founded in 1479), Aarhus (1933), Odense (1966), Roskilde (1972) and Aalborg (1974). A further University at Esbjerg is planned.

Language and Literature.—The Danish language is akin to Swedish and Norwegian. Danish literature, ancient and modern, embraces all forms of expression, familiar names being Hans Christian Andersen (1805–1875), Sören Kierkegaard (1813–1855) and Georg Brandes (1842–1927), with Henrik Pontoppidan (1857–1943) and Karl Gjellerup (1857–1919), who shared the Nobel Prize for Literature in 1917, and Johannes V. Jensen (1873–1950), who received the same award in 1944. Among recent authors of note are Klaus Rifbjerg (*b.* 1931) and Leif Panduro (1923–1977). Some 48 newspapers are published in Denmark; 10 daily papers are published in Copenhagen.

Production and Industry.—Of the labour force, 7·8
per cent is engaged in agriculture, fishing, forestry,
etc.; 26·4 per cent. in manufacturing, building and
construction; 11·4 per cent. in commerce and 54·4 per
cent. in administration, the liberal professions, etc.
The chief agricultural products are pigs, cattle, dairy
products, poultry and eggs, seeds, cereals and sugar
beet; manufactures are mostly based on imported raw
material but there are also considerable imports of
finished goods.

Communications.—Mercantile marine (ships above
100 gross tonnage) at end of 1982, totalled 834 ships,
with a gross tonnage of 4,686,000. In 1982 there was
2,461 km. of railway. In 1981 the capacity of the
telecommunications network in circuit km. was
30,193,000.

PUBLIC SECTOR FINANCE

	1984
Revenue (*Budget estimate*)	Kr. 268,600m.
Expenditure (*Budget estimate*)	299,000m.

Denmark's balance of payments on current account
showed a deficit for 1982 of Kr.20,160 million (1981,
Kr. 12,500 million).

MERCHANDISE TRADE

	1982	1983
	Kr. million	
Total Imports	137,025	145,530
Total Exports	130,640	147,545

Trade with U.K.

	1982	1983
Imports from U.K....	£1,096,642,000	£1,159,184,000
Exports to U.K.	1,335,640,000	1,512,620,000

The principal imports are petroleum and its products, machinery, raw materials, vehicles and textile
products. The chief exports are agricultural and
dairy products and machinery.

CAPITAL.—ΨCopenhagen, pop. (1982), 575,217;
Greater Copenhagen, 1,196,314. Other centres are:
ΨAarhus, 248,294; ΨOdense 170,522; ΨAalborg,
154,514; ΨEsbjerg, 80,287; ΨRanders, 61,848; Helsin-
gør 56,262; ΨKolding, 56,381; ΨHorsens, 54,724;
Roskilde, 48,692; ΨVejle, 49,637; ΨFredericia, 46,096.
FLAG.—Red, with white cross.
NATIONAL DAY.—June 5 (Constitution Day).
Copenhagen, distant from London 728 miles;
transit 26 hours by rail and sea.

BRITISH EMBASSY

36–40 Kastelsvej, DK-2100 Copenhagen.

Ambassador Extraordinary and Plenipotentiary, His
Excellency James Mellon, C.M.G. (1983).
Counsellors, R. N. Dales (*Head of Chancery*); D. P.
Small, M.B.E. (*Commercial*); H. O. Spankie.
Defence Attaché, Cmdr. J. J. M. Curtis, R.N.
1st Secretaries, S. Sadowsky (*Agriculture and Fisher-
ies*); D. G. Lambert, M.B.E.; A. T. J. Lovelock
(*Administration and H.M. Consul*); C. Dyer (*Com-
mercial*); G. S. Cowling (*Economic*); R. S. Foster
(*Labour*) (*Resident in Stockholm*).
2nd Secretary, P. J. Mathers (*Chancery and Informa-
tion*).
Chaplain, Rev. K. Povey.
There are Consulates at *Aabenraa, Aalborg, Aar-
hus, Esbjerg, Fredericia, Odense* and at *Tórshavn*
(Faröe Islands).

British Council Representative and Cultural Attaché,
Dr. W. N. Brown, O.B.E., Møntergade 1, Copenhagen.

Outlying Parts of the Kingdom

THE FARÖES, or Sheep Islands (540 sq. m.; pop.
(1976) 41,211), capital, Tórshavn, are governed by a
Lagting of 26 members, a *Landsstyre* of 4 members

which deals with special Faröes affairs, and send 2
representatives to the *Folketing* at Copenhagen. On
Sept. 14, 1946, the *Lagting*, with the consent of the
Danish Government, for its own guidance held a
plebiscite on the Faröes. About one-third of the
electors did not, however, take part in the voting: of
the rest a little more than half the votes cast were in
favour of separation from Denmark and the establishment of a republic. At subsequent general election
for the *Lagting* a great majority voted in favour of
remaining part of the Kingdom of Denmark with a
certain measure of home rule and in 1948 the Faröes
received this. The Faröes are not part of the E.E.C.

GREENLAND (ice-free portion about 132,000 sq. m.,
total area about 840,000 sq. m., population (1976)
49,666) is divided into 3 provinces (West, North and
East). Greenland (capital, Nuuk (Godthåb)) has a
Landsraad of 17 members and sends 2 representatives
to the *Folketing* at Copenhagen. Greenland attained
a status of internal autonomy on May 1, 1979. The
trade of Greenland is mainly under the management
of the Royal Greenland Trade Department. Following a plebiscite Greenland has negotiated its withdrawal from the E.E.C., but without discontinuing
relations with Denmark, and will cease to be a
member in early 1985. Mineral and oil prospecting
revealed deposits of lead, zinc, iron ore, oil, gas and
uranium. Commercial exploitation of these resources
has already begun. The United States of America has
acquired certain rights to maintain air bases in
Greenland.

DJIBOUTI
(Republic of Djibouti)

President, Hassan Gouled Aptidon.
Formerly known as French Somaliland and then
the French Territory of the Afars and the Issas, the
country became independent on June 26, 1977. It is
situated on the north-east coast of Africa (i.e. the
Horn of Africa) and has an estimated population of
over 300,000. The climate is harsh and much of the
country is semi-arid desert. The French continue to
maintain army, navy and air force bases. Djibouti
has an excellent port, international airport and a
railway line runs to Addis Ababa. *Capital*, Ψ Djibouti
(est. pop. 150,000).

DOMINICAN REPUBLIC
(República Dominicana)

President, Salvador Jorge Blanco, *took office*, 16 Aug.
1982.

CABINET

Secretary for the Presidency, Hatuey de Camps.
Administrative Secretary for the Presidency, Rafael
Flores Estrella.
Technical Secretary of the Presidency, Orlando Haza
del Castillo.
Armed Forces, Lt. Gen. Ramiro Matos Gonzalez.
Foreign Relations, Dr. José Augusto Vega Imbert.
Interior and Police, Gen. (ret.) Oscar Padilla Medrano.
Education and Fine Arts, Ivelisse Prats de Perez.
Agriculture, Domingo Marte de la Cruz.
Public Works and Communications, Pedro Delgado
Malagón.
Public Health and Social Welfare, Dr. Amiro Pérez
Mera.
Sports and Physical Education, Dr. Luis Schecker.
Labour, Pedro Franco Badía.
Industry and Commerce, José Antonio Najri.
Finance, José Santos Taveras.

EMBASSY OF DOMINICAN REPUBLIC
4 Braemar Mansions, Cornwall Gardens, SW7 4AG
[01–937 1921]

Ambassador Extraordinary and Plenipotentiary, His
Excellency Alfredo A. Ricart (1975).

The Consulate is at Flat 2, 108 Lexham Gardens,
W.8. There are also Consular Offices at *Liverpool,
Birmingham, Manchester, Grimsby, Southampton,
Cardiff, Glasgow* and *Plymouth.*

The Dominican Republic, formerly the Spanish
portion of the island of Hispaniola, is the oldest
settlement of European origin in America. The
western part of the island forms the Republic of Haiti.
(*For* Map, *see* p. 848.)

The island lies between Cuba on the west and
Puerto Rico on the east and the Republic covers an
area of about 19,322 square miles, with a population
(1981 Census) of 5,647,977. The climate is tropical in
the low lands and semi-tropical to temperate in the
higher altitudes.

Government.—Santo Domingo was discovered by
Christopher Columbus in December, 1492, and remained a Spanish Colony until 1821. In 1822 it was
subjugated by the neighbouring Haitians who remained in control until 1844 when the Dominican
Republic was proclaimed. The country was occupied
by American marines from 1916 until the adoption of
a new Constitution in 1924. From 1930 until May 30,
1961 (when he was assassinated) Generalissimo Rafael
Trujillo ruled the country.

Professor Juan Bosch, elected President in December 1962, held office until September, 1963, when he
was deposed by a military junta. A revolt in favour
of ex-President Bosch in April, 1965, developed into
civil war lasting until September the same year when
a provisional President was elected. On June 1, 1966,
Dr. Joaquin Balaguer was elected President and the
following November a new Constitution was introduced.

On May 16, 1982 Dr. Salvador Jorge Blanco was
elected President and in separate, but concurrent,
voting his P.R.D. party won an overall majority in
both the Senate and the Chamber of Deputies.

Constitution.—The constitution now in force was
introduced in Nov. 1966. Executive power is vested
in the President, who is elected by direct vote and
serves for four years. The President forms his cabinet
without reference to the Congress.

Legislative power is exercised by the Congress,
which has a term of four years concurrent with the
Presidency. The Upper Chamber is the Senate of 27
senators, one for each province and one for Santo
Domingo. The lower is the Chamber of Deputies
which has 120 members, one for each 50,000 inhabitants in each province, with the provision that no
province has less than two members. Judicial power
is exercised by the Supreme Court of Justice.

Communications.—According to local classification there are 2,932 miles of first class and 1,392 miles
of second class and inter-communal roads in the
Republic. There is a direct road from Santo Domingo
to Port-au-Prince, the capital of Haiti, but that part
of it in the border area has fallen into disuse. The
frontier has been closed since Sept., 1967, except for
that section crossed by the main road linking the two
capitals. A telephone system connects practically all
the principal towns of the republic and there is a
telegraph service with all parts of the world. There
are more than 90 commercial broadcasting stations
and six television stations.

Spanish is the language of the Republic.

The Republic is served by two national and six
foreign airlines, and an international airport 18 miles
to the east of the capital is in operation. Another has
been built near Puerto Plata on the north coast.

Economy.—Sugar, coffee, cocoa, and tobacco are

the most important crops. Other products are peanuts, maize, rice, bananas, molasses, salt, cement,
ferro-nickel, gold, silver, cattle, sisal products, honey
and chocolate. There is a growing number of light
industries producing beer, tinned foodstuffs, glass
products, textiles, soap, cigarettes, construction materials, plastic articles, shoes, papers, paint, rum,
matches, peanut oil and other products.

FINANCE

	1983	1984 (est.)
Budget		
Revenue	*RD*$1,017,191,620	*RD*$1,345,751,270

TRADE

	1982	1983
Imports	*RD*$1,255,817,161	*RD*$1,279,019,958
Exports	791,364,784	811,054,942

Trade with U.K.

	1982	1983
Imports from U.K.	£10,161,000	£11,594,000
Exports to U.K.	5,752,000	6,662,000

The chief imports are machinery, food stuffs, iron
and steel, cotton textiles and yarns, mineral oils
(including petrol), cars and other motor vehicles,
chemical and pharmaceutical products, electrical
equipment and accessories, construction material,
paper and paper products, and rubber and rubber
products; the chief exports are sugar, coffee, cocoa,
tobacco, chocolate, molasses, bauxite, ferro-nickel
and gold.

Tobacco and tobacco manufactures are the principal exports to the U.K.

CAPITAL.—Ψ Santo Domingo, population of the
Capital District (1981 census), 1,550,739. Other
centres, with populations (1981 census); Santiago de
los Caballeros (550,372); La Vega (385,043); San
Francisco De Macoris (235,544); San Juan (239,957);
San Cristóbal (446,132).

FLAG.—Red and blue, with white cross bearing an
emblem at centre.

NATIONAL DAY.—February 27 (Independence Day,
1844).

BRITISH EMBASSY
Avenida Independencia 506, Santo Domingo

Ambassador Extraordinary and Plenipotentiary, His
Excellency Roy George Marlow (1983).
2nd Secretary, I. M. T. Dinsdale.

ECUADOR
(Republica del Ecuador)

President, Oswaldo Hurtado Larrea, *assumed power*
in May 1981.
President-elect, Léon Febres Cordero, *elected* May 6,
1984; *due to take office,* Aug. 10, 1984.

CABINET
(at July 1984)

Interior, Vladimar Alvarez Grau.
Foreign Affairs, Dr. Luis Valencia Rodriguez.
Education, Dr. Claudio Malo Gonzales.
Defence, Gen. Jorge Erciniegas Salazar.
Finance, Pedro Pinto Rubianes.
Agriculture and Livestock, Fausto Jordán.
Natural Resources, Gustavo Galindo.
Industry, Commerce and Integration, Jose Bermeo
Castillo.
Education and Sport, Ernesto Alban.
Public Information, Ramiro Rivera.
Sec. Gen. of the Administration, Andrés Crespo.

EMBASSY AND CONSULATE
Flat 3B, 3 Hans Crescent, SW1X 0LS
[01–584 1367]

Ambassador Extraordinary and Plenipotentiary, His Excellency Dr. Galo Leoro.

Area and Population.—Ecuador is an equatorial State of South America, the mainland extending from lat. 1° 38′ N. to 4° 50′ S., and between 75° 20′ and 81° W. long., comprising an area reduced by boundary settlements with Peru (Jan. 29, 1942) to about 226,000 sq. miles. (*For* MAP, *see* Index.)

The Republic of Ecuador is divided into 20 provinces. It has a population (census, 1981) of approximately 8 million, mostly descendants of the Spaniards, aboriginal Indians, and Mestizoes. The territory of the Republic extends across the Western Andes, the highest peak of which is Aconcagua, in the Chilean sector (22,976 ft.), the highest peaks in Ecuador being Chimborazo (20,408 ft.), Ilinza (17,405 ft.), Carihuairazo (16,515 ft.), Cotocachi (16,301 ft.), and Pichincha (16,000 ft.) in the Western Cordillera; and Cotopaxi (19,612 ft.), Antisana (18,864 ft.), Cayambe (19,160 ft.), Altar (17,730 ft.), Sangay (17,464 ft.), Tungurahua (16,690 ft.), and Sincholagua (16,365 ft.) in the Eastern Cordillera. Ecuador is watered by the Upper Amazon, and by the rivers Guayas, Mira, Santiago, Chone, and Esmeraldas on the Pacific coast. There are extensive forests, and the cinchona bark tree is common.

The *Galápagos* (Giant Tortoise) *Islands* forming the province of the Archipelago de Colón, were annexed by Ecuador in 1832. The archipelago lies in the Pacific, about 500 miles from Saint Elena peninsula, the most westerly point of the mainland. There are 12 large and several hundred smaller islands with a total area of about 3,000 sq. miles and an estimated population (1981) of 5,000. The capital is San Cristobal, on Chatham Island. Although the archipelago lies on the equator, the temperature of the surrounding water is well below equatorial average owing to the *Antarctic Humboldt Current.* The province consists for the most part of National Park Territory, where unique marine birds, iguanas, and the giant tortoises are conserved. There is some local subsistence farming; the main industry, apart from tourism, is tuna and lobster fishing.

Government.—The former *Kingdom of Quito* was conquered by the Incas of Peru in the latter part of the 15th century. Early in the 16th century Pizarro's conquests led to the inclusion of the present territory of Ecuador in the Spanish Vice-royalty of Peru. The independence of the country was achieved in a revolutionary war which culminated in the battle of Mount Pichincha (May 24, 1822).

After seven years of military rule, Ecuador returned to democracy in 1979. The present constitution, introduced in 1978, provides for an elected President and Vice-President who serve for a five year term. (Neither may stand for re-election.) There is a Chamber of Representatives with 71 members elected every five years, 12 of whom are elected on a national basis and the rest by the provinces. The Chamber meets for two months every year (Aug.– Oct.) but can be convoked at any time for extraordinary sessions. Four Legislative Commissions meet through the year.

Voting is compulsory for all literate and (since 1980) voluntary for all illiterate citizens over the age of 18. Thirteen political groupings are recognized.

Agriculture and Industry.—Agriculture is the most important sector of the economy, supporting nearly 50 per cent of the population (particularly the poorest) and contributing 14·5 per cent of the Gross Domestic Product and 19·5 per cent of exports. The main products for export are fish (mainly shrimps, tuna and sardines), which had become the largest agricultural export by early 1982; bananas, which provide a third of agricultural exports; cocoa and coffee. Other important crops are sugar, corn, soya, rice, cotton, African palm (for oil), vegetables, fruit and timber, the temperate crops being produced mostly in the highlands.

The economy was transformed by the discovery in 1972 of major oil fields in the Oriente area, and oil accounted for two thirds of 1981 export earnings. The economy grew rapidly in the 1970s but is now faced with reduced growth, due mainly to the fall in the price of oil. The oil deposits in the Oriente are estimated at between 10–15,000 million barrels, and further exploration and development is taking place. The oil is evacuated by a trans-Andean pipeline to the port of Balao (near Esmeraldes).

Communications.—There are 23,256 km. of permanent roads and 5,044 km. of roads which are only open during the dry season. There are about 750 miles of railway, including the railway from Quito to Guayaquil. Ten commercial airlines operate international flights, linking Ecuador with major foreign cities and there are internal services between all important towns.

Defence.—The standing Army has a strength of about 38,000. There is an Air Force of some 120 aircraft of various kinds and 4,800 personnel. The small Navy is 4,500 strong.

Language and Literature.—Spanish is the principal language of the country but Quechua is also a recognized language and is spoken by the majority of the Indian population. As a result of an intensive national education programme more than 75 per cent of the population are now literate. 3 daily newspapers are published at Quito and 4 at Guayaquil. Elementary education is free and compulsory. There are 9 Universities, at Quito (2), Guayaquil (3), Cuenca, Machala, Loja and Portoviejo, Polytechnic Schools at Quito and Guayaquil and 8 technical colleges in other provincial capitals.

Finance.—The estimated government budget at Jan. 1982 was 64,770 million *sucres* (53,600 million *sucres* in 1981). The balance of payments deficit stands at U.S.$3·2 billion, and foreign exchange reserves at U.S.$500 million.

TRADE

Import licences are required for all merchandise and these are issued by the Central Bank of Ecuador.

	1982
Imports	U.S.$1,988,300,000
Exports	2,140,000,000

Trade with U.K.

	1982	1983
Imports from U.K.	£60,792,000	£35,008,000
Exports to U.K.	9,288,000	11,022,000

Manufactured goods and machinery are the main imports.

CAPITAL.—Quito. Population (1981 estimate), 800,000; Ψ Guayaquil (1,000,000) is the chief port; Cuenca (110,000).

FLAG.—Three horizontal bands, yellow, blue and red (the yellow band twice the width of the others); emblem in centre.

NATIONAL DAY.—August 10 (*Dia de la Independencia*).

BRITISH EMBASSY
Calle Gonzalez Suarez, 111 (Casilla 314),
Quito.

Ambassador Extraordinary and Plenipotentiary, His Excellency Adrian Clarence Buxton, C.M.G. (1981).

There is a British Consular Office at Guayaquil.

British Council Representative, J. T. Wright, Av. Amazonas 1615 y Orellana (Casilla 8829), Quito.

EGYPT
(Arab Republic of Egypt)

President, Muhammad Hosni Mubarak, *elected,* Oct. 14, 1981.

CABINET

Prime Minister, Kamal Hassan Ali.
Deputy P.M., Defence and Military Production, F.M. Mohammed Abdel-Halim Abu Ghazala.
Deputy P.M., Higher Education and Scientific Research, Dr. Mustapha Kamal Helmi.
Foreign Affairs, Esmat Abdel Meguid.
Agriculture and Food Security, Dr. Yousif Wali.
Cabinet Affairs, and Minister of State for Administrative Development, Atef Muhammad Ebeid.
Construction, and Minister of State for Land Reclamation, Hasaballah Muhammad el Kafraui.
Culture, Mohamed Abdul Hamid Radwan.
Electricity and Energy, Mohamed Maher Abaza.
Economy and Foreign Trade, Dr. Mustapha Kamal el Said.
Emigration Affairs, Albert Barsoum Salama.
Finance, Dr. Mahmoud Salah Hamed.
Health, Dr. Mohammed Sabri Zaki.
Housing and Infrastructures, Hassan Abdel Fattah Sedki.
Industry, Muhammad Mahmud Farag Abdel Wahab.
Information, Mohammad Safwat el-Sherif.
Interior, Gen. Ahmed Rochdi.
Irrigation, Issam Radi Abdel Hamid.
Investment Affairs and International Co-operation, Dr. Wagih Shindi.
Justice, Ahmed Mamdouh Atai.
Local Administration, Hassan Soleiman Abu Bacha.
Manpower and Vocational Training, Saad Mohammad Ahmed.
National Education, Abdel Salam Abdel Kader Abdel Ghaffar.
Oil and Mining Resources, Abdel Hadi Kandil.
People's Assembly and Shoura Council Affairs, Tewfik Abdu Ismail.
Planning, Dr. Kamal Ahmed El-Ganzouri.
Social Insurance, and Minister of State for Social Affairs, Dr. Amal Osman.
Supply and Internal Trade, Mohamed Nagi-Shatla.
Tourism and Civil Aviation, Tawfeik Abdou Ismail.
Transportation, Communications and Shipping, Soliman Metwalli Soliman.
Wakfs, El Sheik Ibrahim el Desouki.

EGYPTIAN EMBASSY
26 South Street, W1Y 8EL
[01–499 2401]

Ambassador Extraordinary and Plenipotentiary, His Excellency Hassan Abou Seeda (1980).

AREA AND POPULATION.—The total area of Egypt is estimated at 1,002,000 square kilometres (386,900 square miles), only three per cent of which is cultivated land, with a population now officially estimated (1983) at 47,000,000.

There are three distinct elements in the native population. The largest, or "Egyptian" element, is a Hamito-Semite race, known in the rural districts as *Fellahin* (*fellâh*—ploughman, or tiller of the soil). A second element is the *Bedouin,* or nomadic Arabs of the Libyan and Arabian deserts, of whom about one-seventh are real nomads, and the remainder semi-sedentary tent-dwellers on the outskirts of the cultivated end of the Nile Valley and the Fayûm. The third element is the *Nubian* of the Nile Valley between Aswân and Wadi-Halfa of mixed Arab and Negro blood. Over 90 per cent of the population are Moslems of the Sunnî denomination, and most of the rest Coptic Christians.

The territory of Egypt comprises (1) *Egypt Proper,*

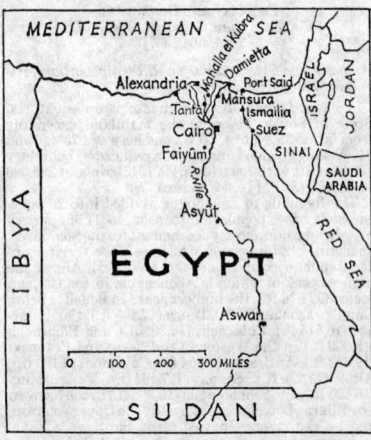

forming the N.E. corner of the African continent, divisible into (a) the valley and delta of the Nile, (b) the Western Desert, and (c) the Arabian or Eastern, Desert; (2) *The Peninsula of Sinai,* forming part of the continent of Asia; and (3) a number of *Islands* in the Gulf of Suez and Red Sea, of which the principal are Jubal, Shadwan, Gafatin and Zeberged (or St. John's Island). This territory lies between 22° and 32° N. lat. and 24° and 37° E. long. The northern boundary is the Mediterranean, and in the south Egypt is conterminous with the Sudan. The western boundary runs from a point on the coast 10 kilometres N.W. of Sollûm to the latitude of Siwa and thence due S. along the 25th meridian. The E. boundary follows a line drawn from Rafa on the Mediterranean (34° 15′ E. long.) to the head of the Gulf of 'Aqaba.

Physical Features.—The country is mainly flat but there are mountainous areas in the south-west, along the Red Sea coast and in the south of the Sinai peninsular, rising in some places to peaks of over 6,000 ft. The highest mountain in Egypt is Mt. Catherina (8,668 ft). Most of the land is desert but the Nile valley and delta are covered by silt 20–30 feet deep, and areas of desert are increasingly being reclaimed by irrigation and fertilization.

The *Nile* has a total length of 4,160 miles. In the 960 miles of its course through Egypt it receives not a single tributary stream. The river formerly had a regular yearly rise and fall of about 13 feet at Cairo, but since the completion of the Aswan High Dam in 1965, there has been no flood downstream of the dam and the water level remains almost constant throughout the year. The area of fertile land, a 5–15 mile wide strip in the Nile valley and some 6,000 square miles of the Nile delta, has been increased by the opening of the Aswan Dam. This has allowed the reclamation of about 1,300,000 acres, and a further 700,000 acres have been converted from basin to perennial irrigation. Westward from the Nile Valley stretches the *Western desert,* containing some depressions, whose springs irrigate small areas known as *Oases,* of which the principal, from S.E. to N.W., are known as Kharga, Dakhla, Farafra, Baharia and Siwa.

In the Eastern Desert between the Nile and the mountains along the Red Sea coast, are plateaux of sandstones and limestones, dissected by *wadis* (dry water-courses), often of great length and depth, with some wild vegetation and occasional wells and springs.

History.—The unification of the Kingdoms of Lower and Upper Egypt under the Pharaohs in c. 3,100 B.C. marked the establishment of the Egyptian state, with Memphis as its capital. Egypt was ruled for nearly 2,800 years by a succession of Pharaonic dynasties (31 in all), which built the pyramids at Gizeh. The oldest of these is that of Zoser, built c. 2,700 B.C., and the highest the Great Pyramid of Cheops, at 451 feet; nearby is the Sphinx, 189 feet long. A period of Hellenic rule began in 332 B.C., after the conquest of Egypt by Alexander the Great, followed by a period of rule by Rome (30 B.C. to A.D. 324) and then by the Byzantine Empire. In A.D. 640 Egypt was subjugated by Arab Muslim invaders, becoming a province of the Eastern Caliphate. In 1517 the country was incorporated in the Ottoman Empire under which it remained until early in the 19th century.

A British Protectorate over Egypt declared on Dec. 18, 1914, lasted until Feb. 28, 1922, when Sultan Ahmed Fuad was proclaimed King of Egypt. In July, 1952, following a military *coup d'état*, King Farouk abdicated in favour of his infant son, who became King Ahmed Fuad II. In June, 1953, however, Gen. Neguib's military council deposed the young king, and Egypt became a Republic.

In 1956, as a result of Egypt's trade agreements with Communist countries, Britain and U.S.A. withdrew offers of financial aid and in retaliation Pres. Nasser seized the assets of the Suez Canal Company. An Egyptian invasion of the Canal Zone, while repulsing an Israeli attack, provoked military action by Britain and France in support of their Suez Canal Company interests. A ceasefire and Anglo-French withdrawal were negotiated by the U.N.

The Israeli invasion of 1956 overran the Sinai peninsular but six months later Israel withdrew and a U.N. peace-keeping force was established in the area. However, mounting tension culminated in a second invasion of Sinai (the Six Day War of June 1967) and occupation of the peninsular by Israel. Egypt's attempt to recapture the territory (the Yom Kippur War of October 1973) was unsuccessful but Sinai was returned to Egypt in April 1982, under the treaty of 1979 which resulted from the Camp David talks between Pres. Sadat and Mr. Begin and formally terminated a 31-year old state of war between the two countries. Pres. Hosni Mubarak came to power on Oct. 6, 1981 after the assassination of Pres. Sadat by Moslem fundamentalists.

Government.—The Constitution of 1971 provides for an executive President who appoints Ministers to the Cabinet. The President determines policy which the Cabinet implements and Ministers are responsible to him. The Legislature consists of the People's Assembly (448 members); the Shura Council, or Consultative Assembly (210 members) has an advisory role. The Constitution guarantees also the independence of the Judiciary. Religious courts were abolished in 1956 and their functions transferred to the national court system. Freedom of the press is guaranteed under the Constitution.

Agriculture.—Despite increasing industrialisation, agriculture remains the most important economic activity, employing over 45 per cent of the labour force and producing nearly half of the country's exports. Agricultural output has been increased as a result of land reclamation programmes and the introduction of more efficient methods, e.g. the change from basin to perennial irrigation which yields 2–3 crops per year instead of one, the pivotal sprinkling irrigation system which uses water more efficiently, and the increasing mechanisation and use of fertilizers. Egypt is still a net importer of foodstuffs,

especially grain, and a food security programme has been set up with the aim of achieving self-sufficiency through the use of more advanced technology. Estimates suggest that an additional 3 million acres of land could be reclaimed by the end of the century.

The main cash crop is cotton, of which Egypt is one of the world's main producers. Production in 1981 was 498,000 tons. Other important summer crops are (1981 figures) maize 3,308,000 tons, rice 2,238,000 tons, millet 653,000 tons and sugar cane 8,616,000 tons. Important winter crops are wheat 1,938,000 tons, beans 208,000 tons and onions 654,000 tons. Citrus fruit and other fruits and vegetables are also grown.

Energy.—With its considerable reserves of petroleum and natural gas in Sinai, the Nile Delta and the Western Desert, and the hydro-electric power produced by the Aswan and High Dams, Egypt is self-sufficient in energy. Electricity has been provided to almost all of the country and there are plans to extend the natural gas network to all major cities.

Industry.—The production of petroleum provides Egypt with its major export and supports a growing refining industry. Steel production is another important heavy industry. The major manufacturing industries are in food processing, motor cars and electrical goods, chemical products and yarns and textiles.

Currency.—The monetary unit of Egypt is the Egyptian *pound* (L.E.) of 100 *piastres*.

TRADE

	1981 (millions)
Imports	L.E.6,187
Exports	2,263

Main Commodities Imported

	1981 (millions)
Wheat and Flour	L.E.782
Wood	264
Trucks	222

Main Commodities Exported

	1981 (millions)
Crude Petroleum	L.E.1,231
Cotton	320
Cotton Yarn	109
Oranges	33
Rice	30
Cotton Textiles	24

Trade with U.K.

	1982	1983
Imports from U.K.	£338,645,000	£370,489,000
Exports to U.K.	412,802,000	79,826,000

Communications.—The road and rail networks link the Nile Valley and Delta with the main development areas to east and west of the river.

The Suez Canal was re-opened in 1975 and a two-stage development project begun to widen and deepen the canal to allow the passage of larger shipping and to permit two-way traffic. Port Said and Suez have been reconstructed and the port of Alexandria is being improved.

CAPITAL.—Cairo (population, estimated in 1983 at 11,000,000), stands on the E. bank of the Nile, about 14 miles from the head of the Delta. Its oldest part is the fortress of Babylon in old Cairo, with its Roman bastions and Coptic churches. The earliest Arab building is the Mosque of 'Amr, dating from A.D. 643, and the most conspicuous is the Citadel, built by Saladin towards the end of the 12th century and containing in its walls the Mosque of Mohamed Ali built in the 19th century.

ΨALEXANDRIA (estimated population in 1983 of 4,000,000), founded 332 B.C. by Alexander the Great, was for over 1,000 years the capital of Egypt and a centre of Hellenic culture which vied with Athens herself. Its great *pharos* (lighthouse), 480 feet high, with a lantern burning resinous wood, was one of the "Seven Wonders of the World". Other towns are: Ismailia (400,000); ΨPort Said (285,000); Mansura (120,000); Asyût (300,000); Faiyûm (180,000); Tanta (150,000); Mahalla el Kubra (130,000); ΨSuez; Ψ Damietta (100,000).

Cairo is 2,520 miles from London: transit *via* Ancona or Venice, 5 days; *via* Marseilles, 6 days.

FLAG.—Horizontal bands of red, white and black, with an eagle in the centre of the white band.

NATIONAL DAY.—July 23 (Anniversary of Revolution in 1952).

BRITISH EMBASSY
Ahmed Ragheb Street, Garden City, Cairo

Ambassador Extraordinary and Plenipotentiary, His Excellency Sir Michael Weir, K.C.M.G.
British Council Representative, B. Vale, O.B.E., 192 Sharia el Nil, Agouza, Cairo. There is also a library in Alexandria.

EQUATORIAL GUINEA

President, Col. Teodoro Obiang Nguema Mbasogo, *took office*, Aug. 1979.

Formerly the territory of "Spanish Guinea", Equatorial Guinea consists of the Island of Bioco (formerly Macias Nguema), an island in the Bight of Biafra about 20 miles from the west coast of Africa, Pagalu Island (formerly Annobon) in the Gulf of Guinea, the Corisco Islands (Corisco, Elobey Grande and Elobey Chico) and Rio Muni, a mainland area between Cameroon and Gabon. It has a total area of about 28,000 sq. km. and a population (1980 estimate) of 150,000.

Government.—Formerly colonies of Spain, the territories now forming the Republic of Equatorial Guinea were constituted as two provinces of Metropolitan Spain, in 1960, became autonomous in 1964 and fully independent in 1968. Serious disorders in Rio Muni early in 1969 caused many of the Spanish community to leave. Following Nigerian allegations of continuing mistreatment, most of the Nigerian labour force, on whom cocoa production largely depended, were repatriated in late 1975 and early 1976.

In Aug. 1979, President Macias was deposed by a revolutionary military council headed by his nephew Col. T. Obiang Nguema. The first parliamentary elections since 1968 were held on Aug. 28, 1983, under a new constitution approved by a referendum in Aug. 1982. Forty-one representatives were elected to the National Assembly for a five-year term.

Economy.—The chief products are cocoa, coffee and wood (which is exported almost entirely from Rio Muni). Production has declined and except for cocoa, there is little commercial agriculture and the economy is now heavily dependent on outside aid, principally from Spain.

CAPITAL.—ΨMalabo (formerly known as Santa Isabel) on the island of Bioco (population 25,000). ΨBata is the principal town and port of Rio Muni.

FLAG.—Three horizontal bands, green over white over red; blue triangle next staff; coat of arms in centre of white band.

British Ambassador, (resides at Yaoundé).

ETHIOPIA

Head of State, Chairman of the Derg and of the Council of Ministers, Lt.-Col. Mengistu Haile Mariam.
Secretary General of the Derg and Deputy Chairman of the Council of Ministers, Capt. Fikre-Selassie Wogderes.

EMBASSY IN LONDON
17 Prince's Gate, SW17 1PZ
[01–589 7212]

Ambassador Extraordinary and Plenipotentiary, His Excellency Ato Ayalew Wolde Giorgis.

Position and Extent.—Ethiopia is in North-Eastern Africa, bounded on the north-west by the Sudan; on the south by Kenya; on the east by Djibouti and the Republic of Somalia; and on the north-east by the Red Sea. The area is estimated at 400,000 square miles, with a population (1981) of 31,000,000. (Other unofficial estimates put the population at 38,000,000.) About one-third are of the dominant race of Semitic origin (Amharas and Tigreans) and the remainder mainly Gallas (about 40 per cent of the population), Somalis and Afar.

Eritrea.—Eritrea was administered by Great Britain from the end of the Second World War until September 15, 1952, when it was federated with Ethiopia. It was incorporated as a province of Ethiopia in 1962. An armed campaign for independence started in 1962 and has intensified since the early 1970's.

Ethiopia has a large central plateau (average height, 6,000–7,000 ft.) which rises to nearly 15,000 ft. at Ras Dashan in the north. The plateau drops to the Nile basin in the west and the Red Sea in the east. To the north (Eritrea) and east (Ogaden) the land is mostly desert. The chief river is the Blue Nile, issuing from Lake Tana; the Atbara and many other tributaries of the Nile also rise in the Ethiopian highlands.

Those of Semitic origin (Amharas and Tigreans), and many of the Gallas, are Christians of the Ethiopian Orthodox Church, which was formerly led by the head of the Coptic Church, the Patriarch at Alexandria. Since 1959, however, the Ethiopian Church has been autocephalous and the new Patriarch, Abuna Tekle Haimanot, was enthroned in 1976. The Afar people, who inhabit lowland Eritrea, Wollo, Harargne and Bale provinces, and the Somalis, in the south-east, are Moslem.

History.—The basic Hamitic culture was heavily influenced by Semitic immigration from Arabia in the centuries about the time of Christ. Christianity was introduced in the 4th century. The empire expanded sporadically, attaining a zenith in the 6th century under the Axum rulers, but subsequently checked by Islamic expansion from the east. Modern Ethiopia dates from 1855 when Theodore succeeded in establishing supremacy over the various tribes. The last Emperor was Haile Selassie who reigned from 1930, though in exile from 1936–1941 during the Italian occupation. After considerable military and civil unrest the armed forces assumed power in Sept. 1972 and deposed the Emperor. Pending the promulgation of a new Constitution the country is ruled by a Provisional Military Administration Council (the *Derg*).

In July 1977, Somalia, claiming the Ogaden region of Ethiopia in support of Western Somalia Liberation Front guerrillas, invaded the region. Ethiopia, with Soviet arms, and the aid of Cuban troops, was able to defeat the Somalis. The Somali regular army withdrew in March 1978, but guerilla activity continues.

Production and Industry.—The principal pursuits are agriculture and cattle breeding. All agricultural land was nationalised in 1975 and tenants given rights of possession to the land they tilled. The most important crop is coffee which provided about 60 per cent of total exports (by value) in 1981. The principal food grain is teff, followed by barley, wheat, maize and durra. Sugar cane is grown, and pulses and oilseeds are produced for local consumption and export. Livestock is mainly cattle, sheep and goats, with smaller numbers of horses, donkeys, mules and camels, and hides, skins and butter are important for both home and export markets. Industry is small, mostly manufacturing, the main products being textiles, foodstuffs, tyres, beer and cement.

Ethiopia has few significant mineral deposits, apart from salt, which is produced mainly in Eritrea. Traces of gas and oil have not been exploited, though there is an oil refinery at Assab.

Communications.—With the aid of loans from the IBRD and the International Development Agency, a network of roads has been built linking the major cities with each other, and with the Sudanese and Kenyan borders and the Red Sea coast. There is a railway link from Addis Ababa to Djibouti, though this is vulnerable to guerilla activity. The narrow gauge line in Eritrea has been closed by conflict. The Ethiopian Air Lines maintain regular services from Addis Ababa to many provincial towns. External services are operated throughout Africa and to Europe and the Middle and Far East.

Defence.—Under the Ministry of Defence the armed forces comprise the Army, the Air Force and the Navy. The Army consists of 300,000 soldiers divided into 24 divisions. Nearly 200,000 of these soldiers are militia. By the end of 1984 another 100,000 will be added to serve as additional manpower and replace those lost in combat.

The Air Force comprises a transport squadron, a bomber squadron, three fighter squadrons, a training squadron, a jet conversion squadron, and an elementary training unit. There are 120 fighter planes, mostly of Russian manufacture, and a few F.5.s. The Air Force Headquarters is situated at Debre Zeit.

The Navy has a headquarters in Addis Ababa with a main base at Massawa and a smaller one at Assab. National Military Service was established on May 4, 1983.

Education.—Elementary education is provided without religious discrimination by Government schools in the main centres of population; there are also Mission schools and cadet-schools for the Army, Air Force, and Police. Government secondary schools are found mainly in Addis Ababa, but also in most of the provincial capitals. The National University (founded 1961) co-ordinates the institutions of higher education (University College, Engineering, Building and Theological Colleges in Addis Ababa, Agricultural College at Alemaya, near Harar, and Public Health Centre in Gondar, etc.). It is intended to develop the provincial colleges to university level and status. Amharic is the official language of instruction, with English as the first foreign language and main language of instruction from secondary level upwards. Arabic is taught in Koran Schools; and Ge'ez (the ancient Ethiopic) in Christian Church Schools, which abound. Adult education is met to some extent by institutes which provide evening classes in Addis Ababa.

FINANCE

	1983–84
Revenue	£1,000,981,100
Expenditure	1,195,170,700

The Ethiopian unit of currency is the *birr* of 100 cents.

Trade.—The chief imports by value are machinery and transport equipment, manufactured goods and chemicals (from U.K.); the principal exports by value being coffee, oilseeds, hides and skins, and pulses.

TRADE

	1981	1982
Total Imports	£449,678,000	£573,497,000
Total Exports	236,611,000	246,443,000

Trade with U.K.

	1982	1983
Imports from U.K.	£27,584,000	£34,092,000
Exports to U.K.	10,833,000	12,071,000

CAPITAL.— Addis Ababa (population, estimated 1,300,000), also capital of the province of Shoa; Asmara (population 250,000) is the capital of the Province of Eritrea. Dire Dawa is the most important commercial centre after Addis Ababa and Asmara, Ψ Massawa and ΨAssab (recently enlarged) are the two main ports. There are ancient architectural remains at Aksum, Gondar, Lalibela and elsewhere.

ETHIOPIAN FLAG.—Three horizontal bands; green, yellow, red.

NATIONAL DAY.—September 12 (People's Revolution Day).

BRITISH EMBASSY
Fikre Mariam Abatechan Street (P.O. Box 858), Addis Ababa

Ambassador Extraordinary and Plenipotentiary, His Excellency Brian L. Barder (1982).

There is a British Consular Office at *Addis Ababa.*

British Council Representative, L. J. Hobbs, Artistic Building, Adwa Avenue (P.O. Box 1043), Addis Ababa. There is also a library in Asmara.

FINLAND
(Suomi)

President, Dr. Mauno Koivisto, *born,* 1923, *elected,* Jan 26, 1982.

CABINET

Prime Minister, Kalevi Sorsa (*SDP*).
Foreign Affairs, Paavo Väkyrynen (*CP*).
Foreign Trade, Jermu Laine (*SDP*).
Justice, Christoffer Taxell (*SPPF*).
Interior, Matti Luttinen (*SDP*).
Environment, Matti Ahde (*SDP*).
Defence, Veikko Pihlajamäki (*CP*).

Finance, Ahti Pekkala (*CP*).
Finance II, Pekka Vennamo (*FRP*).
Education, Kaarina Suonio (*SDP*).
Education II, Gustav Björkstrand (*SPPF*).
Agriculture and Forestry, Toivo Yläjärvi (*CP*).
Transport and Communications, Matti Puhakka (*SDP*).
Trade and Industry, Seppo Lindblom (*SDP*).
Social Affairs and Health, Eeva Kuuskoski-Vikatmaa (*CP*).
Social Affairs and Health II, Vappu Taipale (*SDP*).
Labour, Urpo Leppänen (*FRP*).
(*CP*=Centre Party, *SDP*=Social Democratic Party, *SPPF*=Swedish People's Party of Finland, *FRP*=Finnish Rural Party).

FINNISH EMBASSY AND CONSULATE
38 Chesham Place, SW1X 8HW
[01–235 9531]

Ambassador Extraordinary and Plenipotentiary, His Excellency Ilkka Pastinen (1983).
Minister Counsellor, Veijo Sampovaara.
Counsellor, Jukka Seppinen.
Press Counsellor, Tom Söderman.
Defence Attaché, Lt.-Col. Ilkka Ranta.

Area and Population.—A country situated on the Gulfs of Finland and Bothnia, with a total area of 130,165 square miles, of which 70 per cent. is forest, 10 per cent. cultivated, 9 per cent. lakes and 11 per cent. waste and other land; population (December, 1982), 4,844,000. In 1981 the birth rate was 13·2, death rate 9·3 per 1,000. The infant mortality rate was 7·6 per 1,000 live births (1980). 90·3 per cent. of the people are Lutheran, 1·1 per cent. Greek Orthodox and 8·4 per cent. others.

The Aland Archipelago (Ahvenanmaa), a group of small islands at the entrance to the Gulf of Bothnia, covers about 572 square miles, with a population (December, 1980) of 21,682 (95·2 per cent. Swedish-speaking). The islands have a semi-autonomous status.

Government.—Under the Constitution there is a single Chamber (*Eduskunta*) composed of 200 members, elected by universal suffrage. The legislative power is vested in the Chamber and the President. The highest executive power is held by the President who is elected for a period of 6 years.

The present government came into office on May 6, 1983. The four parties in the coalition are the Social Democratic Party, the Centre Party, the Swedish People's Party of Finland, and the Finnish Rural Party.

Defence.—By the terms of the Peace Treaty (Feb. 10, 1947) with U.K. and U.S.S.R., the Army is limited to a force not exceeding 34,400. The Navy is limited to a total of 10,000 tons displacement with personnel not exceeding 4,500. The Air Force, including naval air arm, is limited to 60 machines with a personnel not exceeding 3,000. Bombers or aircraft with bomb-carrying facilities are expressly forbidden. The Defence Forces contain a cadre of regular officers and N.C.O.'s, but their bulk is provided by conscripts who serve for 8–11 months. Total strength of trained and equipped reserves is over 700,000, 16,500 of which have served in the U.N. peacekeeping force.

Education.—Primary education (co-educational comprehensive school) is compulsory for children from 7 to 16 years, and free of charge. In the autumn of 1981, there were 551,906 in comprehensive schools (332,887 at basic stage and 219,019 at upper stage), 103,369 in senior secondary schools and 135,000 in vocational institutions of senior level. There are 22 universities or other schools of academic level, University of Helsinki (1981), 23,900 students. Combined enrolment at universities and other schools of academic level was (1981) 84,716.

Language and Literature.—There are two official languages in Finland. 93·5 per cent of the population speak Finnish as their first language, 6·3 Swedish (1979). The remaining 0·2 per cent. speak other languages (mainly Lapps who number about 2,500 and live in the Far North). Both Finnish and Swedish are used for administration and education; newspapers, books, plays and films appear in both languages. There is a vigorous modern literature. F. E. Sillanpää, who died in 1964, was awarded the Nobel prize for Literature. Best known among the living authors are Väinö Linna, Veijo Meri and Paavo Haavikko. There are 62 daily newspapers in Finland which appear on 4 or more days per week (55 Finnish language, and 7 Swedish).

Production and Industry.—Finland is a highly industrialised country producing a wide range of capital and consumer goods. Timber and the products of the forest-based industries remain the backbone of the economy, accounting for 40 per cent. of her export earnings, but the importance of the metal-working, shipbuilding and engineering industries has been growing. This sector in 1981 accounted for 31 per cent. of Finland's exports. The textile industry is well developed and Finland's glass, ceramics and furniture industries enjoy international reputations. Other important industries are rubber, plastics, chemicals and pharmaceuticals, footwear, foodstuffs and electronic equipment.

Communications.—There are 6,976 kilometres of railroad, a fully automatic telephone system and a well-developed telegraph system. There is a railway connection with Sweden and U.S.S.R., passenger boat connection with Sweden, West Germany, Poland and U.S.S.R. Vessels on the London to Leningrad route call at Helsinki. There are also passenger/cargo services between Britain and Helsinki, Kotka and other Finnish ports. External civil air services are maintained by most European airlines. The merchant fleet at the end of March 1982 totalled 486 vessels (2,441,784 tons gross); 150 passenger vessels (257,677 tons gross), 46 tankers (1,283,583), 192 dry cargo vessels (915,299) and 98 other vessels (15,225).

FINANCE

	1982	1983
	Finnmarks	Finnmarks
Revenue (*Budget*) ...	64,916,000,000	63,157,000,000
Expenditure (*Budget*)	66,861,000,000	72,106,000,000

Currency.—The unit of currency is the *markka* of 10 penniä.

TRADE

	1981	1982
	Finnmarks	Finnmarks
Total Imports	61,263,000,000	64,722,000,000
Total Exports	60,314,000,000	62,997,000,000

Trade with U.K.

	1982	1983
Imports from U.K....	£513,558,000	£539,721,000
Exports to U.K.	849,933,000	966,017,000

The principal imports are raw materials, machinery and manufactured goods. The exports are principally the output of the paper and other forest industries, engineering, metal industry (*e.g.* paper-working machinery and ships) and chemicals.

CAPITAL.—ΨHelsinki (Helsingfors). Population (Jan. 1981), 482,800; other towns are Tampere (Tammerfors), 166,300; ΨTurku (Åbo), 163,700; Espoo, 137,500; Vantaa, 132,100; Lahti, 94,700; ΨOulu (Uleåborg), 93,800; ΨPori (Björneborg), 79,400; Kuopio, 74,600; Jyväskylä, 64,200.

NATIONAL DAY.—December 6 (Day of Independence).

FLAG.—White with blue cross.

BRITISH EMBASSY
Uudenmaankatu 16–20
00120 Helsinki 12

Ambassador Extraordinary and Plenipotentiary, His Excellency Alan Brooke Turner, C.M.G. (1983).
Counsellor (Commercial), B. T. Holmes.
1st *Secretaries,* P. G. Harborne; Miss M. Ramsay; T. I. Priest; A. Ward (*Commercial*).
Defence, Naval, Military and Air Attaché, Lt.-Col. W. J. Collings, M.B.E., R.A.
2nd *Secretaries,* R. C. Woodward (*Commercial*); Miss E. A. Rose (*Consul*).
There are British Consular offices at *Helsinki, Tampere, Turku, Pori, Kotka, Oulu, Vaasa* and *Kuopio.*
British Council Representative, A. R. Payne, Eteläesplanadi 22A, 00130 Helsinki 13.

FRANCE
(La République Française)

President of the French Republic, Francois Mitterrand, *elected* May 10, 1981.

CABINET

Prime Minister, Laurent Fabius.
Foreign Affairs, M. Claude Cheysson.
Interior and Decentralisation, Pierre Joxe.
Justice, M. Robert Badinter.
Economy, Finance and the Budget, Pierre Bérégovey.
Commerce and Tourism, M. Michel Crepeau.
Defence, M. Charles Hernu.
Education, Jean-Pierre Chevènement.
Social Affairs, Mme. Georgina Dufoix.
Agriculture, M. Michel Rocard.
Industrial Redeployment and External Trade, Mme. Edith Cresson.
Town Planning, Housing and Transport, Paul Quilès.
Planning and Regional Development, Gaston Defferre.

European Affairs and Government Spokesman, Roland Dumas.
Labour, Employment and Vocational Training, Michel Delebarre.
Environment, Mme. Huguette Bouchardeau.
Research and Technology, Hubert Curien.

FRENCH EMBASSY IN LONDON
58 Knightsbridge, SW1X 7JT
[01–235 8080].

Ambassador Extraordinary and Plenipotentiary, His Excellency Monsieur Emmanuel de Margerie (1981).

Area and Population.—The largest state in Central Europe, extending from 42° 20' to 51° 5' N. lat., and from 7° 85' E. to 4° 45' W. long. Its area is estimated at 213,000 sq. miles (544,000 sq. km.), divided into 95 departments, including the island of Corsica, in the Mediterranean, off the west coast of Italy. The population of France in 1982 was 54,334,871.

POPULATION OF THE DEPARTMENTS (1982)

Alsace		
Bas-Rhin	915,676	
Haut-Rhin....	650,372	
Aquitaine		
Dordogne.....	377,356	
Gironde	1,127,546	
Landes	297,424	
Lot-et-Garonne ...	298,522	
Pyrénées-Atlantiques.	555,696	
Auvergne		
Allier	369,580	
Cantal	162,838	
Haute-Loire ..	205,895	
Puy-de Dôme .	594,365	
Basse-Normandie		
Calvados	589,559	
Manche	465,948	
Orne	295,472	
Bourgogne		
Côte-d'Or	473,548	
Nièvre	239,635	
Saône-et-Loire.....	571,852	
Yonne	311,019	
Bretagne		
Côtes-du-Nord	538,869	
Finistère	828,364	
Ille-et-Vilaine .	749,764	
Morbihan	590,889	
Centre		
Cher	320,174	
Eure-et-Loir ..	362,813	
Indre	243,191	
Indre-et-Loire	506,097	
Loir-et-Cher ..	296,220	
Loiret........	535,669	
Champagne-Ardenne		
Ardennes.....	302,338	
Aube.........	289,300	
Marne	543,627	
Haute-Marne .	210,670	
Corse		
Corse-du-Sud .	108,604	
Haute Corse .	131,574	
Franche-Comté		
Doubs	477,163	

Haute-Saône..	231,962	
Jura	242,925	
Territoire-de-Belfort ...	131,999	
Haute-Normandie		
Eure	462,323	
Seine-Maritime ..	1,193,039	
Île-de-France		
Essonne	988,000	
Hauts-de-Seine	1,387,039	
Seine-et-Marne	887,112	
Seine-St.-Denis	1,324,301	
Val-de-Marne	1,193,655	
Val-d'Oise	920,598	
Ville de Paris	2,176,243	
Yvelines	1,196,111	
Languedoc-Roussillon		
Aude.........	280,686	
Gard.........	530,478	
Hérault	706,499	
Lozère	74,294	
Pyrénées-Orientales ..	334,557	
Limousin		
Corrèze	241,448	
Creuse	139,968	
Haute-Vienne .	355,737	
Lorraine		
Meurthe-et-Moselle..	716,846	
Meuse........	200,101	
Moselle......	1,007,189	
Vosges	395,769	
Midi-Pyrénées		
Ariège	135,725	
Aveyron ..:..	278,654	
Gers	174,154	
Haute Garonne ...	824,501	
Haute Pyrénées ...	227,922	
Lot	154,533	
Tarn	339,345	
Tarn-et-Garonne ...	190,485	

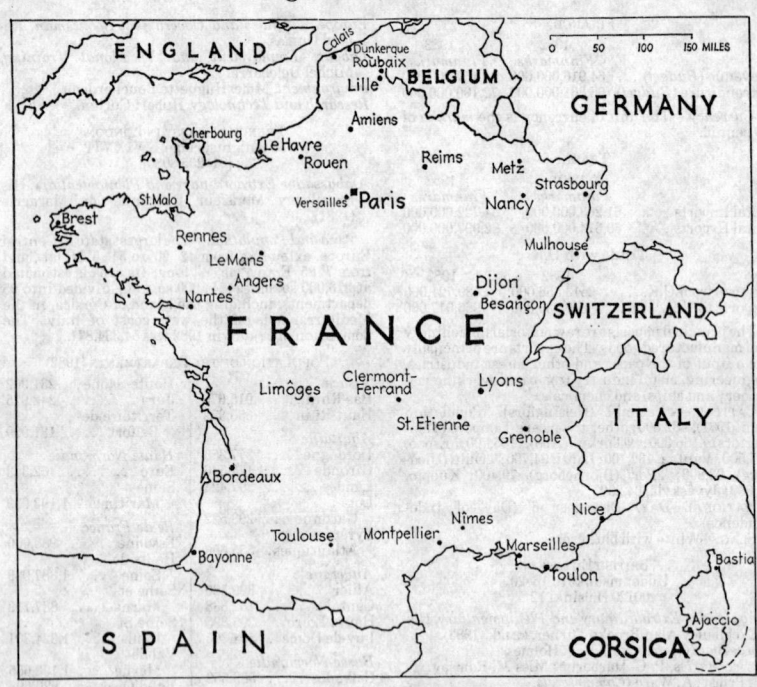

Nord-Pas-de Calais	
Nord	2,520,526
Pas-de-Calais	1,412,413

Pays de la Loire	
Loire-	
Atlantique .	995,498
Maine-et-	
Loire.......	675,321
Mayenne ...	271,784
Sarthe	504,768
Vendée.......	483,027

Picardie	
Aisne	533,970
Oise	661,781
Somme	544,570

Poitou-Charentes	
Charente	340,770
Charente-	
Maritime ...	513,220
Deux-Sèvres ..	342,812
Vienne	371,428

Provence-Alpes-	
Côte d'Azur	
Alpes-de-Haute-	
Provence ...	119,068
Alpes-	
Maritimes ..	881,198
Bouches-du-	
Rhône.....	1,724,199
Haute-Alpes ..	105,070
Var	708,331
Vaucluse	427,343

Rhône-Alpes	
Ain	418,516
Ardèche	267,970
Drôme	389,781
Haute-Savoie .	494,505
Isère	936,771
Loire.........	739,521
Rhône.......	1,445,208
Savoie	323,675

Archæology, etc.—There are dolmens and menhirs in Brittany, prehistoric remains and cave drawings in Dordogne and Ariège, and throughout France various megalithic monuments erected by primitive tribes, predecessors of Iberian invaders from Spain (now represented by the Basques), Ligurians from northern Italy and Celts or Gauls from the valley of the Danube. Julius Cæsar found Gaul "divided into three parts" and described three political groups—Aquitanians south of the Garonne, Celts between the Garonne and the Seine and Marne, and Belgae from the Seine to the Rhine. Roman remains are plentiful throughout France in the form of aqueducts, arenas, triumphal arches, &c., and the celebrated Norman and Gothic Cathedrals, including Notre Dame in Paris, and those of Chartres, Reims, Amiens (where Peter the Hermit preached the First Crusade for the recovery of the Holy Sepulchre), Bourges, Beauvais, Rouen, etc., have survived invasions and bombardments, with only partial damage, and many of the renaissance and the XVIIth and XVIIIth century châteaux survived the French Revolution.

Language and Literature.—French is the universal language of France and of a large proportion of the people of Belgium, Luxembourg, Switzerland, North and West Africa, and the Province of Quebec, Canada, to whom the literature of France is a treasured heritage. The work of the *French Academy*, founded by Richelieu in 1635, has established *le bon usage*, equivalent to "The Queen's English" in Great Britain. French authors have been awarded the Nobel Prize for Literature on 11 occasions—R.F.A. Sully-Prudhomme (1901), F. Mistral (1904), Romain Rolland (1915), Anatole France (1921), Henri Bergson (1927), Roger M. du Gard (1937), André Gide (1947), François Mauriac (1952), Albert Camus (1957), St. John Perse (Alexis Léger) (1960) and Jean Paul Sartre (1964).

GOVERNMENT

Parliament consists of the National Assembly and the Senate. Bills may be presented in either House, except money bills, which must originate in the National Assembly. The normal session of Parliament is confined to 5½ months each year and it may also meet in extraordinary session for 12 days at the request of the Prime Minister or a majority of the Assembly. Voting rights are personal and can only be delegated in special circumstances.

The *Prime Minister* is appointed by the President, as is the Cabinet on the Prime Minister's recommendation. They are responsible to Parliament. But the executive is constitutionally separate from the legislature and Ministers may not sit in Parliament. The Prime Minister is assumed to have the Assembly's confidence unless the Opposition moves a censure motion signed by not less than one-tenth of the deputies; such motion must be approved by an absolute majority; if defeated, its sponsors must not introduce another no-confidence motion in the same session.

A *Constitutional Council* is responsible for supervising all elections and referenda and must be consulted on all constitutional matters and before the President of the Republic assumes emergency powers. At the request of the Government, the *Economic and Social Council* gives advice on bills, ordinances or decrees referred to it. Any economic or social plan or bill must be submitted to it.

DEFENCE

The personnel of the Defence Forces in September 1981 totalled 265,000. National nuclear forces include medium-range ballistic missiles, submarine-launched ballistic missiles and *Mirage* IV medium bombers. The Army has a variety of new French-made equipment in service, including medium tanks, field and anti-aircraft SP guns, trucks and radio equipment. Defence Budget for 1983, 142,000 million francs.

EDUCATION

The educational system is highly developed and centralized. It is administered by the Ministry of National Education, comprising (a) the *Direction des Enseignements Supérieurs; Direction de la Pédagogie, des Enseignements Scholaires et de l'Orientation; Direction des Personnels d'Enseignement Général Technique et Professionnel; Direction des Services Administratifs et Sociaux; Direction de l'Equipement Scolaire, Universitaire et Sportif; Direction des Bibliothèques et de la Lecture Publique; Direction de la Coopération*; (b) the Superior Council of National Education (consultative); and (c) the Inspectorate. *Local Administration* comprises 25 Territorial Academies, with inspecting staff for all grades, and Departmental Councils presided over by the *Préfet*, and charged especially with *primary* education.

Primary and secondary education are compulsory, free and secular, the school age being from 6 to 16. Schools are for boys, for girls, or mixed. (i) *Primary* education is given in *écoles maternelles* (nursery schools), *écoles primaires élémentaires* (primary schools), and *collèges d'enseignement général* (4-year secondary modern course); (ii) *Secondary* education in *collèges d'enseignement technique, collèges d'enseignement secondaire* and *lycées* (7-year course leading to one of the five *baccalauréats*). (iii) *Special schools* are numerous. (iv) There are numerous *Grandes Ecoles* in France which award diplomas in many subjects not taught at university, especially applied science and engineering. Most of them are State institutions but have a competitive system of entry, unlike the universities. (v) The reform of the French university structure continues, and there are now universities in twenty-four towns in France. In the major provincial towns the existing university has been reorganized to form two, or three universities, and in Paris and the immediate surrounding district there are, since autumn 1970, thirteen universities.

In 1982–83 enrolment in primary schools was 4,390,092; in secondary schools 5,135,371, and in post-secondary education 1,096,601 (of which university students accounted for 925,370).

COMMUNICATIONS

Roads.—The length of roads in use at the end of 1981 was; motorways, 5,288 km., national roads 28,131 km., departmental roads 347,000 km., local roads 421,000 km., giving a total of 801,420 km.

Railways.—The system of railroads in France is very extensive. The length of lines open for traffic at the end of 1982 was 34,599 km., of which 10,660 km. were electrified.

Shipping.—The French mercantile marine consisted in Jan. 1982, of 393 ships of over 100 tons gross, of which 28 were passenger vessels (169,878 tons gross), 100 tankers (7,088,720 tons gross) and 265 cargo vessels (3,060,031 tons gross). The principal rivers of France are the Seine, Loire, Garonne, and Rhône, the navigable waterways in general use in 1981 were 8,568 km.

ECONOMY

Budget.—Government expenditure by function, as provided for in the 1984 general Budget, was:

	F million
Agriculture	1,887
Commerce and the Working Class	71
Culture	2,719
Economy, Finance and Budget	10,828
Education	5,611
Environment	581
Foreign Affairs	1,630
Industry and Research	25,897
Interior	4,256
Justice	525
Leisure, Youth and Sports	442
Overseas Departments and Territories	579
Social Services, Labour, Health and Employment	1,785
Tourism	81
Town Planning and Housing	23,214
Transport	10,121
Other expenditure	5,349
Total general Budget	95,576

Currency.—The unit of currency is the *franc* of 100 *centimes.* At April 1982 French gold and currency reserves stood at F282,343 million.

PRODUCTION

Gross domestic product in 1982 was F3,549,700 million, and G.D.P. per capita F65,470.

Agriculture.—Approximately 318,000 sq. km. of land is used for agricultural purposes (172 sq. km. ploughland and 129 sq. km. pasture) and 143 sq. km. is forested. Total production of cereals in 1982 was 48,044,600 tonnes, including wheat 24,975,900 tonnes, barley 10,044,400 tonnes and maize 9,762,300 tonnes. Production of sugar-beet was 31,573,400 tonnes, of potatoes 6,793,100 tonnes, oilseeds 1,823,900 tonnes, vegetables 2,727,300 tonnes and peaches, pears and apples 2,655,100 tonnes. Value of production in 1981 was crops F89,200 million and livestock F109,700 million.

The vine is extensively cultivated, regions famous for their wines including Bordeaux, Burgundy and Champagne. Production of wine in 1982 was 79,659,000 hectolitres. Cognac, liqueurs and cider are also important products.

Energy.—France produces its own oil, the greater part coming from fields in the Landes area, but is a net importer of crude oil, for processing by its important oil-refining industry. Natural gas is produced in the foothills of the Pyrenees. Electricity production was 262,800 million KWh in 1981, of which 27 per cent was hydro-electric and 36 per cent nuclear power.

Industry.—France's heavy industries include oil-refining and the production of iron and steel, and aluminium. In 1981 production of pig-iron was 17,300,000 tonnes, steel 21,300,000 tonnes and aluminium 591,000 tonnes. Other important industries produce chemicals and plastics, cement, tyres and textiles, and processed food. Engineering products include motor vehicles, and television and radio sets.

TRADE

The principal imports are raw materials for the heavy and manufacturing industries (*e.g.* oil, minerals, chemicals), machinery and precision instruments, agricultural products and vehicles. Raw materials, semi-manufactured and manufactured goods are also France's principal exports. Other member countries of the E.E.C. are France's main trading partners.

TOTAL TRADE

	1981	1982*
	Francs	*Francs*
Imports	635,186,000,000	868,292,000,000
Exports	575,796,000,000	772,636,000,000
* provisional.		

Trade with U.K.

	1982	1983
	£'000	£'000
Imports from U.K.	4,486,458	5,651,521
Exports to U.K.	4,269,103	5,043,118

CAPITAL OF FRANCE. Paris, on the Seine. Population (estimated, 1982), 2,188,918 (town); 10,073,059 (incl. suburbs).

The following towns have a population of over 200,000 inhabitants:—ΨMarseilles (878,689); Lyons (418,476); Toulouse (354,289); ΨNice (338,486); Strasbourg (252,264); Nantes (247,227); Bordeaux (211,197); Saint-Etienne (206,688); ΨLe Havre (201,067); Montpellier (200,390); Rennes (200,390).

The chief towns of Corsica are ΨAjaccio (55,279) and ΨBastia (45,081).

Paris is distant from London 267 miles; transit by air, 1 *hr.*

FLAG.—The "tricolour", three vertical bands, blue, white, red (blue next to flagstaff).

NATIONAL DAY.—July 14.

BRITISH EMBASSY
35 rue du Faubourg St. Honoré, 75383 Paris

Ambassador Extraordinary and Plenipotentiary, His Excellency Sir John Fretwell (1982).

Minister, P. C. Petrie, C.M.G.

Defence and Military Attaché, Brig. A. C. Vivian, C.B.E.

Chancellor and Head of Chancery, A. C. D. S. MacRae.

Counsellor and Consul-General, T. W. Sharp.

BRITISH CONSULAR OFFICES

There are British Consulates-General in Metropolitan France at *Paris, Bordeaux, Lille, Lyons, Marseilles.*

BRITISH CHAMBER OF COMMERCE
26 avenue Victor Hugo, 75016 Paris

President, J. Tuby.

Vice-Presidents, J. Wicker; N. Maxwell Lawford.

BRITISH COUNCIL

Representative in Paris, B. E. Swingler, C.B.E., 9 rue de Constantine, 75007 Paris.

There are British Council libraries at *Paris, Bordeaux, Lille, Lyons* and *Marseilles.*

OVERSEAS DEPARTMENTS

Legislation passed in Dec. 1982 by the French Parliament granted greater powers of self-government to four of the five overseas departments—French Guiana, Guadeloupe, Martinique and Réunion. These former colonies had enjoyed departmental status since 1947 and the status of regions of France since 1974. Elections to their new directly-elected Assemblies were held in each department in Feb. 1983 and the Assemblies will operate in parallel with the existing, indirectly constituted Regional Councils.

French Guiana.—Situated on the north-eastern coast of South America, French Guiana is flanked by Surinam on the west and by Brazil on the south and east. Area, 35,135 sq. miles. Population (1982), 73,022. Capital, ΨCayenne (38,135). Under the administration of French Guiana is a group of islands (St. Joseph, Ile Royal and Ile du Diable), known as Iles du Salut. On Devil's Isle, Captain Dreyfus was imprisoned from 1894 to 1899.

Guadeloupe.—A number of islands in the Leeward Islands group of the West Indies, consisting of the two main islands of Guadeloupe (or Basse-Terre) and Grande-Terre, with the adjacent islands of Marie-Galante, La Désirade and Iles des Saintes, and the islands of St. Martin and St. Barthélemy over 150 miles to the north-west. Area, 657 sq. miles. Population (1982), 328,400. Capital ΨBasse Terre (15,778) in Guadeloupe. Other towns are ΨPointe à Pitre (23,889) on Grande-Terre and ΨGrand Bourg (6,611) in Marie Galante.

Martinique.—An island situated in the Windward Islands group of the West Indies, between Dominica in the north and St. Lucia in the south. Area, 427 sq. miles. Population (1982), 328,566. Capital ΨFort de France (100,576). Other towns are ΨTrinité (11,214) and ΨMarin (6,104).

Mayotte.—Area, 144 sq. miles. Population (1980 estimate), 50,400. Capital, Dzaoudzi (4,147). Part of the Comoros Islands group, Mayotte remained a French dependency when the other 3 islands became independent as the Comoros Republic in 1975. Since 1976 the island has been a *collectivité particulière,* an intermediate status between Overseas Department and Overseas Territory.

Réunion.—Réunion, which became a French possession in 1638, lies in the Indian Ocean, about 569 miles east of Madagascar and 110 miles S.W. of Mauritius. Area, 969 sq. miles. Population (1982), 515,814. Capital, St. Denis (109,072).

Also lying in the Indian Ocean adjacent to Madagascar are the smaller, uninhabited islands of Bassas da India, Europa, Iles Glorieuses, Juan de Nova and Tromelin, which are administered from Réunion.

St. Pierre and Miquelon.—Area, 93 sq. miles. Population (1982), 6,041. Two small groups of Islands off the coast of Newfoundland. Became an Overseas Department in 1976 but this status is under review.

OVERSEAS TERRITORIES

French Polynesia.—Five archipelagos in the south Pacific, comprising the Society Islands (Windward Islands group includes Tahiti, Moorea, Makatea, Mehetia, Tetiaoro, Tubai Manu, etc: Leeward Islands group includes Huahine, Raiatea, Tahaa, Bora-Bora, Maupiti, etc.), the Tuamotu Islands (Rangiroa, Hao, Tureia, etc.), the Gambier Islands (Mangareva, etc.), the Tubuai Islands (Rimatara, Rurutu, Tubuai, Raivavae, Rapa, etc.) and the Marquesas Islands (Nuku-Hiva, Hiva-Oa, Fatu-Hiva, Tahuata, Ua Huka, etc.). Area, 1,522 sq. miles. Population (1983 estimate) 148,000. Capital, ΨPapeete (15,220) in Tahiti. Economy based on tourism and exports of copra, coffee, vanilla, citrus fruits and cultured pearls.

New Caledonia.—A large island in the Western Pacific, 700 miles E. of Queensland. Dependencies are the Isles of Pines, the Loyalty Islands (Mahé, Lifou, Urea, etc.), the Bélep Archipelago, the Chesterfield Islands, the Huon Islands and Walpole. New Caledonia was discovered in 1774 and annexed by France in 1854; from 1871 to 1896 it was a convict settlement. Area, 7,374 sq. miles. Population (estimate, 1979), 139,600. Capital ΨNoumea (12,000). It is one of the world's largest producers of nickel.

Southern and Antarctic Territories.—Created in 1955 from the former Réunion dependencies, the territory comprises the islands of New Amsterdam (25 sq. miles) and St. Paul (2·7 sq. miles), the Kerguelen Islands (2,700 sq. miles) and Crozet Islands (116 sq. miles) archipelagos and Adélie Land (116,800 sq. miles) in the Antarctic continent. The only population are members of staff of the scientific stations.

Wallis and Futuna Islands.—Two groups of islands (the Wallis Archipelago and the Îles du Hooru) in the central Pacific, N.E. of Fiji. Area, 106 sq. miles. Population (1982) 11,943. Capital, Mata-Utu on Urea, the main island of the Wallis group.

THE FRENCH COMMUNITY

The Constitution of the fifth French Republic promulgated on Oct. 6, 1958, envisaged the establishment of a French Community of States closely linked with common institutions. A number of the former French States in Africa have seceded from the Community but for all practical purposes continue to enjoy the same close links with France as those that remain formally members of the French Community. The Community Institutions in fact never operated as envisaged. Nevertheless, with the exception of Guinea, which opted out of the Community in the 1958 referendum, all the former French African colonies are closely linked to France by a series of financial, technical and economic agreements.

FRANCOPHONE COUNTRIES

In the following countries French is either the official or national language or the language of instruction; where there is another national language the name of it is shown after the name of the country:—Algeria (*Arabic*); Belgium (*Flemish*); Benin; Burundi (*Kirundi*); Cambodia (*Khmer*); Cameroon (*English*); parts of Canada (in Quebec, parts of Ontario and New Brunswick) (*English*); Central African Republic (*Sangho*); Chad; Congo; France; Gabon; Guinea; Haiti (*Creole*); Ivory Coast; Laos (*Laotian*); Lebanon (*Arabic*); Luxembourg (*German and Letzeburgesch*); Madagascar (*Malagasy*); Mali; Morocco (*Arabic*); Mauritania (*Arabic*); Niger; Rwanda (*Kinyarwanda*); Senegal; Switzerland (1,000,000 French speaking); Togo; Tunisia (*Arabic*); Upper Volta; Vietnam (*Vietnamese*); Zaire. French is also spoken in the Overseas Departments (*see* above).

GABON
(Gabonese Republic)

(*For* MAP, *see* Index).
President, El Hadj Omar Bongo, *assumed office*, December, 1967, *re-elected*, Feb. 1973 and Dec. 1979.

EMBASSY IN LONDON
48 Kensington Court, W.8
[01–937 5285/9]

Ambassador Extraordinary and Plenipotentiary, His Excellency Monsieur Léon N'Dong.

Gabon lies on the Atlantic coast of Africa at the Equator and is flanked on the north by Equatorial Guinea and Cameroon and on the east and south by

the People's Republic of Congo. It has an area of 101,400 sq. miles (267,667 sq. km.) and a population (estimated 1982) of 1,200,000. Gabon elected on Nov. 28, 1958, to remain an autonomous republic within the French Community and was proclaimed fully independent on August 17, 1960.

The Constitution provides for an Executive President directly elected for a seven-year term, who appoints the Council of Ministers. There is a unicameral National Assembly comprising 84 members directly elected for a five-year term and nine members nominated by the President. The sole legal party is the *Parti democratique gabonais*.

Over the past decade Gabon has known one of the fastest economic growth rates in Africa, based almost entirely on oil, production of which was 7,800,000 tonnes in 1982, making Gabon the fourth largest oil producer in Africa. Other wealth includes timber (especially okoumé wood), manganese, uranium and iron.

The GDP increased by 50 per cent. between 1978 and 1982. The 1983 budget was for £847 million. Gabon became an associate member of OPEC in 1973 and a full member in 1975.

Trade with U.K.

	1982	1983
Imports from U.K.	£14,179,000	£18,798,000
Exports to U.K.	27,634,000	66,135,000

CAPITAL.—ΨLibreville (251,000).
FLAG.—Horizontal bands, green, yellow and blue.
NATIONAL DAY.—August 17.

BRITISH EMBASSY
B.P. 476, Libreville

Ambassador Extraordinary and Plenipotentiary, His Excellency Alan H. Grey (1982).
First Secretary, M. J. Horne.

GERMANY
* Deutsches Reich (German Realm)

The term "deutsch" (German) probably began to be used in the 8th century and initially described the language spoken in the eastern part of the Frankish realm which reached its apogee in Charlemagne's reign, subsequently being divided into an eastern and western realm whose political and linguistic borders coincided. Then the term was transferred from the language to its speakers, and ultimately to the region they lived in. The first German realm was the Holy Roman Empire, established in A.D. 962 when Otto I of Saxony was crowned Emperor. The Empire endured until 1806, but from as early as the 12th century the achievement of a national state was prevented by territorial fragmentation into small principalities and dukedoms, the gradually increasing autonomy of their rulers weakening the central power.

The Holy Roman Empire was replaced by a loose association of the individual sovereign states known as the German Confederation, which survived until 1866 when it was dissolved and replaced by the Prussian-dominated North German Federation. Prussia, directed by its Prime Minister (later Chancellor) Otto von Bismarck, had translated its earlier economic predominance amongst the German states into political hegemony by the annexation of the duchies of Schleswig and Holstein from Denmark in 1864 and a decisive defeat of Austria in 1866 (the Seven Weeks War) which ended Austrian influence

---

* Nazi historians referred to the National Socialist régime as *Drittes Reich*.

over German politics. After the Franco-Prussian War of 1870–71 resulted in the defeat of France and the cession to Prussia of Alsace and Lorraine, the south German principalities united with the northern federation to form a second German Empire, the King of Prussia being proclaimed Emperor at Versailles on Jan. 18, 1871.

Germany's defeat in the 1914–18 War led to the abdication of the Emperor and the princes, and the country became a Republic. The 1919 Treaty of Versailles returned Alsace and Lorraine to France, large areas in the east of the country were lost to the newly created state of Poland, and all German colonies placed under the administration of other countries. The world economic crisis of 1929 led to the collapse of the Weimar Republic and the subsequent rise to power of the National Socialist movement of Adolf Hitler, who became Chancellor in 1933.

THE WAR OF 1939–1945.—After concluding a Treaty of Non-Aggression with Soviet Russia (Aug. 24, 1939), Germany invaded Poland (Sept. 1, 1939), thus precipitating war with France and Great Britain, which had (March 31) given a pledge to support Poland against aggression.

Hitler committed suicide on April 30, 1945. On May 8, 1945, the unconditional surrender of all German forces was accepted by representatives of the Western Allied and Soviet Supreme Commanders.

THE POST WAR PERIOD.—After the surrender the Allied Powers exercised supreme authority in Germany on lines laid down in the Potsdam agreement (August 1945) between the U.K., U.S.A. and U.S.S.R. Power was exercised by the Commanders-in-Chief, each in his own zone of occupation and jointly in matters affecting Germany as a whole through a Control Council. Berlin was governed jointly by the four occupying powers. The agreement also provided for the total disarmament and demilitarisation of Germany, the destruction of the National Socialist Party, the decentralisation of the economy and the construction of a democratic constitution. No central German government was permitted but central German administration was established in the fields of finance, industry, foreign trade, transport and communications as support organs for the Control Council. The Potsdam agreement was to have been confirmed or revised by a peace treaty but no treaty has been drawn up. Some provisions of the Potsdam agreement were carried out but differences in interpretation among the Allies made it impossible to implement in full and the system of quadripartite control broke down when the Russians withdrew from the Control Council in March 1948.

FEDERAL REPUBLIC OF GERMANY

President, Dr. Richard von Weizsäcker, *elected* May 22, 1984, *sworn in*, July 1, 1984, *for five years*.

CABINET

Federal Chancellor, Dr. Helmut Kohl (*CDU*).
Foreign Minister and Vice-Chancellor, Hans Dietrich Genscher (*FDP*).
Interior, Dr. Friedrich Zimmerman (*CSU*).
Justice, Hans Engelhard (*FDP*).
Finance, Dr. Gerhard Stoltenberg (*CDU*).
Economics, Martin Bangemann (*FDP*).
Food, Agriculture and Forestry, Ignaz Kiechle (*CSU*).
Intra-German Relations, Heinrich Windelen (*CDU*).
Labour and Social Affairs, Dr. Norbert Blüm (*CDU*).
Defence, Dr. Manfred Wörner (*CDU*).
Youth, Family Affairs and Health, Dr. Heiner Geissler (*CDU*).
Transport, Dr. Werner Dollinger (*CSU*).

Posts and Telecommunications, Dr. Christian Schwarz-Schilling (*CDU*).
Regional Planning, Building and Urban Development, Dr. Oscar Schneider (*CSU*).
Research and Technology, Dr. Heinz Riesenhuber (*CDU*).
Education and Science, Frau. Dr. Dorothee Wilms (*CDU*).
Economic Co-operation, Dr. Jürgen Warnke (*CSU*).
CDU = Christian Democratic Union; *CSU* = Christian Social Union; FDP = Free Democratic Party.

EMBASSY IN LONDON
23 Belgrave Square, SW1X 8PZ
[01–235 5033]

Ambassador Extraordinary and Plenipotentiary, His Excellency Baron Rüdiger von Wechmar (1984).
Minister Plenipotentiary, Jürgen von Alten.
Minister-Counsellor, Dr. Eike Bracklo.
1st *Counsellors*, Oskar Rudolph (*Head of Economic Dept.*); Dr. Reinhard Holubek (*Cultural*); Dr. Ulrich Däunert (*Scientific Affairs*); Dr. H. Meyer zu Drewer (*Agriculture*); Herr P. J. George (*Defence Research*).

NOTE.—Except where otherwise indicated statistical data on the Federal Republic of Germany include Berlin (West).

Area and Population.—The area of the Federal Republic is approximately 96,015 sq. miles (248,687 sq. km.). Total population of the Federal Republic in Nov. 1983 was 61,333,000. Distribution of the population among the *Länder* in 1982 was:

Baden-Wurttemberg	9,281,100
Bavaria	10,961,300
Berlin (West)	1,879,100
Bremen	689,000
Hamburg	1,630,400
Hesse	5,606,300
Lower Saxony	7,261,600
North Rhine Westphalia	17,010,400
Rhineland Palatinate	3,639,000
Saarland	1,060,400
Schleswig-Holstein	2,619,400

The population of the principal cities and towns in the Federal Republic at end June 1981, was:

Berlin (West)	1,879,100	Dortmund	603,000
ψHamburg ...	1,630,400	Düsseldorf....	585,900
Munich	1,288,200	Stuttgart.....	575,200
Cologne	967,700	Duisburg	551,700
Essen	641,500	ψBremen	551,000
Frankfurt an Main......	622,500	Hannover	527,500
		Nuremberg ...	481,000

Vital Statistics.—There were 9·7 live births per 1,000 inhabitants in the Federal Republic in 1983, compared with 19·5 per 1,000 for the same area in 1938.

Government.—The Federal Republic grew out of the fusion of the three western zones. The economic union of the U.K. and U.S. zones was later joined by the French zone and in 1948–49 Parliamentary Council, elected by the Diets of the three zones, drafted a provisional democratic federal constitution for Germany. This Basic Law came into force in the three western zones on May 23, 1949. When the Federal Government took office the Allied Military Governors were replaced by High Commissioners. In 1952 a contractual agreement was signed between the Federal Republic and the western Allies, whereby the Republic, in return for certain promises regarding a defence contribution, a foreign debt settlement, and the continuation of allied policies concerning decartelization, democratization, restitution, etc.,

regained virtual sovereignty in May, 1955, after ratification by all the parties concerned. The High Commissioners then became Ambassadors.

The Basic Law provides for a President, elected for a five-year term, a Lower House (*Bundestag*), with a four-year term of office, elected by direct universal suffrage, and an Upper House (*Bundesrat*) composed of 45 delegates of the *Länder*, without a fixed term of office.

The results of the elections held for the lower House (*Bundestag*) on March 6, 1983, were as follows:

Party	Numbers
Social Democrats	193
Christian Democratic Union	191
Christian Social Union	53
Free Democrats	34
Grüne (Green)	27

with an additional 22 representatives of Berlin elected by the Berlin Chamber of Deputies (CDU 11; SPD 9; FDP 1; Alternative Liste 1).

The Prime Ministers of the *Länder* governments in June, 1982, were:

Ministers-President

Baden-Württemberg.—Lothar Späth.
Bavaria.—Franz Josef Strauss.

Berlin.—Eberhard Diepgen (*Governing Mayor*).
Bremen.—Hans Koschnick (*Mayor*).
Hamburg.—Dr. Klaus v. Dohnanyi (*Mayor*).
Hessen.—Holger Börner.
Lower Saxony.—Dr. Ernst Albrecht.
North Rhine-Westphalia.—Johannes Rau.
Rhineland-Palatinate.—Dr. Bernhard Vogel.
Saarland.—Werner Zeyer.
Schleswig-Holstein.—Uwe Barschel.

Law and Justice.—Judicial authority is exercised by the Federal Constitutional Court, the Supreme Federal Court, and the courts of the *Länder*. Judges are independent and subject only to the law. The death sentence has been abolished.

Economy

Despite the difficulties arising from the division of Germany, which cut off from the Federal Republic the main food producing areas of Eastern Germany and some of the principal centres of light industry, Germany has regained her position as the main industrial power on the Continent, and is the most economically powerful member of the European Common Market. The Gross National Product at current prices in 1983 was estimated at *DM*.1,671,200 million, an increase of 4·5 per cent over 1982.

Agriculture.—In 1982 total area of farmland was 12,136,700 hectares, of which 7,243,900 hectares were arable land. Forest areas cover 7,328,000 hectares.

Crop yields in 1982 were (tonnes):

Rye	1,639,400
Wheat	8,631,600
Maslin	63,300
Barley	9,459,700
Oats	3,113,000
Potatoes	7,049,100
Sugar beet	22,732,000
Colza and rape	534,700
Fruit	4,217,198

Milk production was 25,464,900 tonnes. Total yield of fisheries was 276,349 tonnes, valued at *DM*.359,730,000.

Industrial Production.—The F.D.R. has a predominantly industrial economy. Principal industries are coal mining, iron and steel production, machine construction, the electrical industry, the manufacture of steel and metal products, chemicals and textiles, and the processing of foodstuffs. The index of industrial net production adjusted for irregularities of the calendar (1980 = 100) is as follows:

	1982	1983
Mining	95·3	90·6
Manufacturing industry	95·4	96·3
(i) Basic materials	91·0	93·9
(ii) Capital goods	99·1	98·8
(iii) Consumer goods	90·3	91·6
(iv) Foodstuffs	98·8	99·4
Power (electricity and gas)	98·0	101·1
Construction	88·5	86·5
Total industry	94·9	95·5

Productivity of labour in industry (excluding electricity, gas and construction) per man-hour: (1976 = 100) 1980, 115·4; 1981, 119·5; 1982, 122·8.

Annual production figures for 1983 were:

	Tonnes
Hard coal	82,202,000
Brown coal	124,281,000
Crude petroleum	4,116,000
Pig iron	25,659,000
Raw steel	35,345,000
Rolled steel	26,067,000
Fuel oils	36,991,000
Petrol, special and testing benzines	19,380,000
Chemical fibres	906,000
Cement	30,366,000

	Number
Passenger cars	3,568,000
Televisions	4,706,000
A.D.P. equipment	DM9,180m.

Labour.—Labour figures, in annual averages, were:

	1982	1983
Employment	25,632,000	25,187,000
Unemployed	1,833,000	2,258,000
Foreign Workers	1,787,000	n/a

Employment in the industrial sector was:

	1982	1983
Coal mining	209,400	203,900
Iron and steel production	257,100	238,300
Mechanical engineering	1,844,400	1,786,000
Chemicals	558,700	548,800
Textiles and clothing	470,000	435,400

FINANCE

Receipts.—As from January 1, 1979, the distribution of taxes in the Fed. Rep. of Germany between Federation, Länder, communities and local authorities has been regulated by the Basic Law (Constitution) as follows:—
(1) Of the yields of wage tax and assessed income tax, Federation and Länder receive 42·5 per cent each, and the communities 15 per cent. The yields of capital yield tax and corporation tax are distributed to Federation and Länder with 50 per cent each.
(2) The turnover taxes were made joint taxes in 1976 of which the Federation obtains 67·5 per cent and the Länder 32·5 per cent, before deduction of the E.C. share.
(3) Of the trade tax which had been fully allocated to the communities, the Federation and the Länder receive equal shares (about 15 per cent of the trade tax receipts).
(4) The yields of capital transactions taxes, insurance and bill taxes accrue to the Federation.

Excise duties, other than the beer tax, accrue to the Federal Government, all other taxes (with the exception of local taxes, *i.e.* particularly taxes on land and buildings) to the *Länder*.

Expenditure.—Figures of budgetary expenditure are:

	1983	1984
	DM million	
Total expenditure	253,200	257,100
Agriculture	5,900	6,100
Defence	46,700	47,800
Social Welfare	76,100	75,900
Transport	24,800	24,600

Currency.—The currency of the Federal Republic is the *Deutsche Mark* of 100 *Pfennig*. (*See also* p. 81.)

TRADE

	1982	1983
	DM million	
Total imports	376,463·9	390,357·3
Total exports	427,740·9	432,338·5

Of imports, 12·9 per cent were foodstuffs and 13·4 per cent industrial raw materials in 1983. Main trading partners in 1983 were (figures shown as percentage of total trade):

	Imports	Exports
E.E.C.	49·1	48·1
E.F.T.A.	13·2	15·6
U.S.A./Canada	8·4	7·2

Trade with U.K.

	1982	1983
Imports from U.K	£5,414,733,000	£6,063,989,000
Exports to U.K.	7,414,073,000	9,667,444,000

The U.K. is currently the largest supplier to the F.D.R. of petroleum and petroleum products (1983: £1,459,094,000).

Communications.—In December, 1982 the state-owned railways of the Federal Republic (*Deutsche Bundesbahn*) measured 28,369 kilometres of which 11,190 kilometres were electrified, and the privately owned railways 3,145 kilometres, a total of 31,514 kilometres. Railway rolling stock included, in 1982, 6,161 locomotives and 335,603 goods waggons; in 1982 the railways handled 320,900,000 tonnes of goods. Classified roads measured 172,490 kilometres at end 1981, of which motorways were 7,784 kilometres. On Jan. 1, 1984 there were registered 24,688,843 cars, 1,344,832 commercial vehicles (incl. buses) and 1,621,555 tractors. Ocean-going shipping under the German flag in Dec., 1982, amounted to 6,809,000 tons gross. Inland waterways handled 225,200,000 tonnes of goods in 1982. Civil aircraft in service at the same date totalled 227 aircraft.

Social Welfare.—There is compulsory insurance against sickness, accident, old age and unemployment. Children's allowances are payable in respect of the second and subsequent children. Pension schemes for widows and orphans of public servants are in operation. Public assistance is given to persons unable to earn their living, or with insufficient income to maintain a decent standard of living.

Language and Literature.—Modern (or New High) German has developed from the time of the Reformation to the present day, with differences of dialect in Austria and Alsace and in the German-speaking cantons of Switzerland. The literary language is usually regarded as having become fixed by Luther and Zwingli at the Reformation, since which time many great names occur in all branches, notably philosophy, from Leibnitz (1646–1716) to Kant (1724–1804), Fichte (1762–1814), Schelling (1775–1854) and Hegel (1770–1831); the drama from Goethe (1749–1832) and Schiller (1759–1805) to Gerhart Hauptmann (1862–1946); and in poetry, Heine (1797–1856). German authors have received the Nobel Prize for Literature on seven occasions—Theodor Mommsen (1902), R. Eucken (1908), P. Heyse (1909), Gerhart Hauptmann (1912), Thomas Mann (1929), N. Sachs (1966) and Heinrich Böll (1972). In 1978 there were 371 daily papers.

Education.—School attendance is compulsory for all children and juveniles between the ages of 6 and 18 and comprises 9 years full-time compulsory education at primary and main schools (*Grund und Hauptschulen*) and 3 years of compulsory vocational education on a part-time basis. In autumn, 1981, there were in the Federal Republic 18,541 primary and main schools (*Grund- und Hauptschulen*) with 4,775,189 pupils. Secondary modern schools (*Realschulen*) numbered 2,633 with 1,323,467 pupils. There were 2,742 other general secondary schools (*Gymnasien* including *Gesamtschulen*) with 2,331,992 pupils.

There were also 2,827 special schools (*Sonderschulen*) for retarded, physically and mentally handicapped and socially maladjusted children in the Federal Republic with 336,980 pupils.

The secondary school leaving examination (*Abitur*) entitles the holder to a place of study at a university or another institution of higher education.

Juveniles below the age of 18 who are not attending a general secondary or a full-time vocational school are obliged to take a three-year course (part-time) at a vocational school. In November, 1981, there were 2,627 full and part-time vocational schools (*Berufsschulen*) and 488 vocational extension schools (*Berufsaufbauschulen*) with 1,956,434 pupils, 2,843 full-time vocational schools (*Berufsfachschulen*) with 370,707 pupils, 1,014 schools for secondary technical studies (*Fachoberschulen/Fachgymnasien*) with 150,415 students.

Public expenditure by *Types of Schools* was in 1979 as follows:

	DM.mn
Elementary and primary schools	15,336
Special schools	2,829
Secondary modern schools	3,434
Grammar schools	7,916
Comprehensive schools	2,571
Part-time vocational schools }	5,335
Full-time vocational schools }	

Results for the winter term 1982–83 show a total of 1,203,121 students at institutions of higher education, of whom 832,363 were attending universities. The largest universities were in Munich, Berlin, Hamburg, Bonn and Cologne.

Religion.—In 1970 there were 29,696,571 Protestants in the Republic, 27,060,826 Roman Catholics, 31,684 Jews and 3,861,518 others.

CAPITAL, Bonn, in North Rhine Westphalia, 15 miles distant from Cologne. Population 292,200 (end June 1982).

FLAG.—Horizontal bars of black, red and gold.

BRITISH EMBASSY
Friedrich-Ebert Allee 77, 5300 Bonn

Ambassador Extraordinary and Plenipotentiary, His Excellency Sir Julian Bullard, K.C.M.G. (1984).

Ministers, C. L. G. Mallaby, C.M.G.; Miss C. E. Pestell, C.M.G.

Counsellors, A. J. Hunter (*Head of Chancery*); B. Smith, O.B.E. (*Commercial*); A. F. Hatfull (*Labour*); W. A. Perry (*Defence Supply*); Dr. G. W. Chantry (*Scientific*); A. J. Beamish (*Economic*); J. D. Perris (*Administration*); P. J. Fowler; G. Garrett.

1st Secretaries, R. E. Escritt; T. Macan; P. J. Torry; A. J. Alderson; M. C. Wood; D. B. Merry; J. W. Forbes-Meyler; N. J. Macsween; R. Gwilliams; M. A. Arthur; Dr. S. R. A. Brown; J. C. Suich; D. E. Lyscom; Mrs. A. M. Leslie; P. W. Sprunt; D. J. Skinner.

Defence and Military Attaché, Brig. D. Quayle.
Asst. Military Attaché, Lt.-Col W. G. C. Kenney.
Naval Attaché, Captain R. M. Venables, R.N.
Asst. Naval Attaché, Lt.-Cdr. N. L. Williams.
Air Attaché, Air Cdre. M. J. Rayson, M.V.O.
Head of Visa Section (Düsseldorf), Miss P. B. Harrison.
Chaplain, Rev. A. M. Cole.
There are British Consulates-General at *Berlin, Hamburg, Düsseldorf, Frankfurt* and *Munich*.

BRITISH CHAMBER OF COMMERCE
Heumarkt 14, 5000 Cologne 1.

Director, J. Parr.

BRITISH COUNCIL

Representative, R. Arbuthnott, Hahnenstrasse 6, 5000 Cologne 1. Offices at *Berlin, Hamburg* and *Munich* and British Council libraries at all four centres.

BERLIN

G.O.C. British Sector, Maj.-General B. C. Gordon Lennox, M.B.E.
Minister and Deputy Commandant, D. J. Wyatt, C.B.E.
Counsellor, T. C. Wood (*Political Adviser and Head of Chancery*).

GERMAN DEMOCRATIC REPUBLIC

Area and Population.—The German Democratic Republic comprises the five former German *Länder* of Brandenburg, Mecklenburg, Saxony, Saxony-Anhalt and Thuringia (an area of 41,768 sq. miles). The seat of Government is East Berlin (156 sq. miles). The population of the Republic, including East Berlin (end of 1980) is 16,740,000. In 1952 the former *Länder* were replaced by fourteen *Bezirke* (regions): Potsdam, Cottbus and Frankfurt (*formerly* Brandenburg); Rostock, Schwerin and Neubrandenburg (*formerly* Mecklenburg); Karl-Marx-Stadt, Dresden and Leipzig (*formerly* Saxony); Halle and Magdeburg (*formerly* Saxony-Anhalt); Erfurt, Gera and Suhl (*formerly* Thuringia).

Government.—The present Constitution, which defines the GDR as a Socialist state, came into force on April 9, 1968 after endorsement by a referendum. It replaced the first Constitution of October 7, 1949. The supreme organ of State power is the *Volkskammer*, which has power to elect and dismiss the Council of State, the Council of Ministers, the Chairman of the National Defence Council, the Supreme Court and the Procurator-General. The Council of State retains the presidential powers which it has exercised since the abolition of the office of President on September 12, 1960, together with responsibility for the organization of defence with the help of the National Defence Council. The Council of Ministers is responsible to the *Volkskammer* for the conduct of State policy. The present *Volkskammer* is that elected in June 1981.

As with other communist countries, effective power lies with the ruling Marxist-Leninist Party, in this case the Socialist Unity Party of Germany (SED). The other parties and mass organizations are members of the SED-controlled National Front.

COUNCIL OF STATE

Chairman, Erich Honecker.
Deputy Chairmen, Dr. Manfred Gerlach; Ernst Mecklenburg; Gerald Götting; Prof. Heinrich Homann; Horst Sindermann; Willi Stoph; Egon Krenz; Gunther Mittag.
Members, K. Anclam; W. Felfe; Prof. K. Hager; Frau B. Hanke; F. Kind; Prof. L. Kolditz; Frau M. Müller; A. Pisnik; B. Quandt; W. Seifert; Dr. K. Sorgenicht; P. Strauss; Frau I. Thiele; H. Tisch; Prof. J. Töpfer; P. Verner; Frau R. Walther.

COUNCIL OF MINISTERS

Chairman, Willi Stoph.
Chairmen, Werner Krolikowski; Alfred Neumann *(First Deputy Chairmen);* M. Flegel; H-J. Heusinger; G. Kleiber; W. Rauchfuss; Dr. H. Reichelt; G. Schürer; R. Schulze; Dr. G. Weiss; Dr. H. Weiz.
Total membership of the Council is 45, including also 29 Ministers and 4 Secretaries of State.

SOCIALIST UNITY PARTY OF GERMANY

Politbureau of the Central Committee, H. Axen; H. Dohlus; W. Felfe; Prof. H. Häber; Prof. K. Hager; J. Herrmann; Gen. H. Hoffmann; E. Honecker; W. Jarowinsky; G. Kleiber; E. Krenz; W. Krolikowski; E. Mielke; G. Mittag; E. Mückenberger; K. Naumann; A. Neumann; G. Schabowski; H. Sindermann; W. Stoph; H. Tisch *(full members);* Frau I. Lange; Frau M. Müller; G. Schürer; W. Walde *(candidate members).*
Secretariat of the Central Committee, E. Honecker *(General Secretary);* H. Axen; H. Dohlus; W. Felfe; Prof. H. Häber; Prof. K. Hager; J. Herrmann; W. Jarowinsky; E. Krenz; I. Lange; G. Mittag; K. Naumann *(secretaries).*

EMBASSY OF THE G.D.R.
34 Belgrave Square, S.W.1
[01–235 9941]

Ambassador Extraordinary and Plenipotentiary, His Excellency Dr. Gerhard Lindner (1984).
Counsellor, Dr. G. Liebig.
1st Secretaries, E. Schwager; H. Zabel; G. Menzel; Dr. A. Andres.

ECONOMY

The G.D.R. economy, including the control of industry and foreign trade, is centrally planned and administered. The State Planning Commission, which is subordinate to the Council of Ministers, is responsible for drawing up the 5- and 1-Year Plans. The 5-Year Plans determine the future development and structure of the economy; the 1-Year Plans have to achieve these aims. The implementation of these plans is the responsibility of the State Production Enterprises under the supervision of the economic and industrial Ministries. The economy is very closely integrated with those of other member countries of C.M.E.A. and particularly with the U.S.S.R.

The Budget for 1982 was: revenue, *M*182,832 million; expenditure, *M*182,071 million. The unit of currency is the *Mark of the G.D.R.* (M) of 100 *pfennig.*
Agriculture.—Land is cultivated mostly on state or collective farms, though some is cultivated independently. Crop yields in 1982 were: potatoes 8,883,000 tonnes; sugar-beet 7,193,000 tonnes; barley 4,055,000 tonnes; wheat 2,739,000 tonnes; rye 2,119,000 tonnes and oats 848,000 tonnes.
Industry.—Almost all industry is nationally or co-operatively owned; the percentage of privately owned enterprises was about 2 in 1978. G.D.R. is the leading world producer of lignite, production in 1982 was 276,000,000 tonnes, and the iron and steel industry is also important. Other highly developed industries include basic chemicals and petro-chemicals, machine tools and industrial plant, ship-building and transport equipment, electronic and engineering equipment, precision tools and optical instruments.

Trade with U.K.

	1982	1983
Imports from U.K.	£63,665,000	£60,997,000
Exports to U.K.	133,921,000	167,625,000

Principal cities and towns (population, 1980): East Berlin (1,166,641); Leipzig (1,412,037); Dresden (District) (1,801,869); Karl-Marx-Stadt (Chemnitz) (1,913,492); Magdeburg (1,260,892); Halle/Saale (1,819,034); Rostock (890,613); Erfurt (1,237,117); Zwickau (120,605); Potsdam (1,118,519).
FLAG.—Horizontal bands of black, red, gold; hammer, compasses and corn device at centre.

BRITISH EMBASSY
(108 Berlin, Unter den Linden 32/34)

Ambassador Extraordinary and Plenipotentiary, His Excellency Timothy John Everard, C.M.G. (1984).
Counsellor, D. F. Ballentyne.
1st Secretaries, Miss A. Lewis *(Head of Chancery);* F. T. Cameron; J. E. Brook *(Commercial).*
2nd Secretaries, D. A. Muat *(Administration and Consul);* D. L. Mather.
3rd Secretary, C. P. Burrows.
Cultural Attaché, G. E. B. Coe *(British Council Representative).*

GREECE
(Hellas)

President of the Hellenic Republic, Konstantinos Karamanlis, *born* 1907 *(assumed office* May 15, 1980).

CABINET

Prime Minister and Minister of Defence, Andreas Papandreou.
Prime Minister's Office, Apostolos Lazaris.
Foreign Affairs, Ioannis Haralambopoulos.
Finance and National Economy, Gerasimos Arsenis.
Interior, Agamemnon Koutsoyorgas.
Public Works, Apostolos Tsochatzopoulos.
Justice, George-Alexander Mangakis.
Education and Religion, Apostolos Kaklamanis.
Agriculture, Constantine Simitis.
Culture and Sciences, Melina Mercouri.
Environment, Antonios Tritsis.
Energy and Natural Resources, Evanghelos Kouloumbis.
Research and Technology, George Lianis.
Commerce, Vassilios Kedikoglow.
Labour, Evanghelos Yannopoulos.
Health and Welfare, George Vennimatas.
Social Insurance, Eleftherios Veryvakis.

Communications, Nikolaos Akritidis.
Public Order, Ionnis Skoularikis.
Merchant Navy, George Katsifaras.
Northern Greece, Vasilios Intzes.
Without Portfolio, Paraskevas Avgerinos; Anastasios Peponis.

GREEK EMBASSY IN LONDON
1a Holland Park, W11 3TP
[01–727 8040]

Ambassador Extraordinary and Plenipotentiary, His Excellency Nikos Kyriazides (1982).
Armed Forces Attaché, Capt. A. Logiakis.
Counsellors, Chr. Tsalikis; A. Anninos (*Consular Affairs*); T. Karavias (*Commercial*); C. Kondoyiannis (*Agricultural*); V. S. Zafiropoulos (*Political*); T. Chytiris (*Press*).
Tourist Adviser, C. Analytis.

There are Honorary Consulates at *Birmingham, Bradford, Bristol, Falmouth, Hull, Immingham, Leeds, Manchester, Newcastle, Portsmouth, Southampton, Cardiff, Edinburgh* and *Glasgow*, and at *Belfast*.

A maritime State in the south-east of Europe, bounded on the N. by Albania, Yugoslavia and Bulgaria, on the S. and W. by the Ionian and Mediterranean seas, and on the E. by Turkey, with an estimated area of 51,182 sq. miles. A census held throughout the country on April 5, 1981, recorded a population of 9,740,417.

The area of the mainland is 41,328 sq. miles, and of the islands 9,854 sq. miles. The main divisions are: *Macedonia* (which includes Mt. Athos and the island of *Thasos*), *Thrace* (including the island of *Samothrace*), *Epirus, Thessaly, Continental Greece* (which includes the island of *Euboea* and the *Sporades* or "scattered islands" of which the largest is *Skyros*), the *Peloponnese* (or *Morea*), the *Dodecanese* or *Southern Sporades* (12 islands occupied by Italy in 1911 during the Italo-Turkish War and ceded to Greece by Italy in 1947) consisting of Rhodes, Astypalaia, Karpathos, Kassos, Nisyros, Kalymnos, Leros, Patmos, Kos, Symi, Khalki and Tilos, the *Cyclades* (a circular group numbering about 200, with a total area of 923 sq. miles; the chief islands are Syros, Andros, Tinos, Naxos, Paros, Santorini, Milos and Serifos), the *Ionian Islands* (Corfu, Paxos, Levkas, Ithaca, Cephalonia, Zante and Cerigo), the *Aegean Islands* (Chios, Lesbos, Limnos and Samos). In *Crete* there was for over 1,500 years (3000 to 1400 B.C.) a flourishing civilization which spread its influence far and wide throughout the Aegean, and the ruins of the palace of Minos at Knossos afford evidence of astonishing comfort and luxury. Greek civilization emerged about 1300 B.C. and the poems of Homer, the blind poet of Chios, which were probably current about 800 B.C., record the 10-year struggle between the Achaeans of Greece and the Phrygians of Troy (1194–1184 B.C.).

Government.—A military *coup* on April 21, 1967, suspended parliamentary government and, following an unsuccessful royal counter *coup* on December 13, 1967, King Constantine went into voluntary exile in Rome. On June 1, 1973 the monarchy was abolished and a republic established under the Presidency of Mr. George Papadopoulos.

The overthrow of Archbishop Makarios, President of Cyprus, on July 15, 1974, by a military coup led by Greek Officers of the Cypriot National Guard caused an international crisis, in the wake of which the heads of the Greek armed forces decided, on July 23, to relinquish power. Mr. Konstantinos Karamanlis, Prime Minister between 1955 and 1963, returned from his self-imposed exile in Paris to form a provisional Government.

The first elections for ten years were held on November 17, 1974. Mr. Karamanlis' New Democracy Party polled 54·3 per cent of the vote and gained 220 out of the 300 seats in Parliament (this was later reduced in by-elections to 215 seats).

The constitutional position of the King, who was still in exile, remained unsettled until December 8, when by a referendum, the Greek people rejected "crowned democracy" by 69·2 per cent to 30·8 per cent and Greece became a republic. A new constitution came into force on June 11, 1975.

In Parliament Elections held on November 20, 1977, the New Democracy Party gained a reduced majority with 172 seats (later increased to 177 by the addition of members of smaller parties) and Mr. Karamanlis formed a new Government. Mr. Andreas Papandreou's Pan Hellenic Socialist Movement became the official opposition with 93 seats.

Mr. Karamanlis was elected President of the Republic by Parliament on May 15, 1980. A new government was formed on May 10 by Mr. George Rallis after his election as leader of the New Democracy party in succession to Mr. Karamanlis. The Socialist Movement under Andreas Papandreou came into office following the General Election of Oct. 1981.

Defence.—The Services are organised on the Chiefs of Staff system, the Chief of the Armed Forces Staff being a rotational appointment between the three services. The strength of the Army is 130,000 backed up by some 50,000 in the National Guard. The Navy consists of 19,500 men and is equipped with a balanced fleet of destroyers, submarines, fast patrol boats and amphibious warfare vessels, mostly of U.S., French, Dutch and German origin. The Air Force consists of 25,000 men and is equipped with a modern inventory of aircraft disposed in 12 combat squadrons supported by the necessary transport, training, helicopter and reconnaissance squadrons. National service is 2 years on average.

Communications.—The 2,650 kilometres of Greek railways are State-owned with the exception of the Athens–Piraeus Electric Railway. The railway from Athens to the Peloponnese, serving Patras and southern Greece, is metre gauge, but the other lines, except one or two minor ones, are standard gauge. Greek roads total somewhat over 35,500 kilometres, of which about 25 per cent are classified as national highways and just under 30,000 km. are classified as provincial roads.

On Dec. 31, 1983, the Greek Mercantile fleet

numbered 3,422 ships with a total tonnage of
37,377,371 tons gross. On the same day Greek-owned
ships registered under foreign flags numbered 1,194
with a total tonnage of 18,431,381 tons gross. (N.B.
These figures exclude Greek-owned vessels under 100
tons gross). Athens has direct airline links with
Australasia, North America, most countries in
Europe, Africa and the Middle East.

Religion.—Over 97 per cent of the people are
adherents of the Greek Orthodox Church, which is
the State religion, all others being tolerated and free
from interference. The Church of Greece recognizes
the spiritual primacy of the Œcumenical Patriarch
of Constantinople, but is otherwise a self-governing
body administered by the Holy Synod under the
Presidency of the Archbishop of Athens and All
Greece. It has no jurisdiction over the Church of
Crete, which has a degree of autonomy under the
Œcumenical Patriarch, nor over the Monastic Community of Mount Athos and the Church in the
Dodecanese, both of which come directly under the
Œcumenical Patriarch.

Education is free and compulsory from the age of 6
to 15 and is maintained by State grants. There are
six Universities, Athens, Salonika, Patras, Thrace,
Joannina and Crete. There are several other institutes of higher learning, mostly in Athens.

Language and Literature.—The *spoken* language
of modern Greece is descended by a process of natural
development from the "Common Greek" of Alexander's empire. *Katharevousa*, a conservative literary dialect evolved by Adamantios Corais (Diamant
Coray), who lived and died in Paris (1748–1833) and
used for official and technical matters, is to be phased
out over the next few years. Novels and poetry are
mostly composed in *dimotiki*, a progressive literary
dialect which owes much to John Psycharis (1854–
1929). The poets Solomos, Palamas, Cavafis, Sikeli-
anos, Seferis and Elytis have won a European
reputation.

Production.—Though there has in recent years
been a substantial measure of industrialization,
agriculture still employs about a quarter of the
working population. The most important agricultural
products are tobacco, wheat, cotton, sugar and rice.
The most important of the fruit trees are the olive,
peach, vine, orange, lemon, fig, almond and currant-
vine, and now exports of Greek fresh fruit and
vegetables have established themselves as an important contributor to the economy and have considerable growth potential. Currants, grown mainly
around Patras, remain one of Greece's main exports,
the United Kingdom being the principal purchaser.

The principal minerals mined in Greece are nickel,
bauxite, iron ore, iron pyrites, manganese magnesite,
chrome, lead, zinc and emery, and prospecting for
petroleum is being carried on. Oil refineries are in
operation near Athens and at Salonika, where there
is also a petro-chemical plant. The chief industries
are textiles (cotton, woollen and synthetics), chemicals, cement, glass, metallurgy, shipbuilding, domestic electrical equipment and footwear. In recent
years new factories have been opened for the
production of aluminium, nickel, iron and steel
products, tyres, chemicals fertilizers and sugar (from
locally-grown beet). Food processing and ancillary
industries have also grown up throughout the
country. The development of the country's electric
power resources, irrigation and land reclamation
schemes and the exploitation of Greece's lignite
resources for fuel and industrial purposes are also
being carried out. Tourism has developed rapidly,
but is now slowing down. Greece signed the Accession Treaty with the E.E.C. on May 28, 1979 and
became a full member on January 1, 1981.

Currency.—The Greek *drachma* has a floating
exchange rate.

TRADE

	1983
Total imports	*Drs*801,153,000,000
Total exports	392,652,100,000

Trade with U.K.

	1982	1983
Imports from U.K....	£255,281,000	£280,204,000
Exports to U.K.	151,688,000	164,917,000

CAPITAL.—Athens. Population (including
ΨPiraeus and suburbs), 3,027,331 (1981 Census).
Other large towns are ΨSalonika (706,180); ΨPatras
(154,596), ΨVolos (107,407); Larissa (102,426);
and ΨKavalla (56,705); in Crete—ΨHeraklion or
Candia (102,398), ΨCanea (47,451), and ΨRethymnon
(18,190); in the Ionian Islands—ΨCorfu (36,901);
in the Dodecanese—ΨRhodes (41,425); in the Cyclades— ΨSyros Hermoupolis (13,877); in Lesbos—Ψ
Mytilene (24,991); in Chios—ΨChios (24,070).

FLAG.—Blue and white stripes with a white cross
on a blue field in the canton.

NATIONAL DAY.—March 25 (Independence Day).

BRITISH EMBASSY
1 Ploutarchou Street, 106 75 Athens.

Ambassador Extraordinary and Plenipotentiary, His
Excellency Sir Peregrine Rhodes, K.C.M.G. (1982).
Counsellors, C. Hulse, O.B.E. (*Political and Consul-
General*); J. Thomas (*Economic and Commercial*).
Defence and Military Attaché, Brigadier J. H. Mil-
burn, O.B.E.
Naval and Air Attaché, Capt. R. N. Blair, R.N.
Embassy Chaplain, Rev. S. J. B. Peake.
Hon. Attaché, H. W. Catling, O.B.E., D.PHIL. (*Director,
British School of Archæology*).

BRITISH CONSULAR OFFICES
There are British Consular Offices at *Athens,
Corfu, Samos, Rhodes, Salonika, Heraklion* (Crete),
Kavalla and *Patras.*

BRITISH COUNCIL
17 Plateia Philikis Etairias (P.O. Box 3488),
102 10 Athens.

Representative, P. B. Naylor.
There is also an office at *Salonika* and British
Council libraries at both centres.

GUATEMALA
(República de Guatemala)

Head of State, Gen. Oscar Humberto Mejía Victores,
assumed office, Aug. 9, 1983.

Guatemala, the most northerly of the Republican
States of Central America, is situated in N. lat. from
13° 45' to 17° 49', and in W. long. from 88° 12' 49" to
92°13' 43", and has an area of 42,042 square miles, and
an estimated population of 7,500,000 (*for* MAP, *see* p.
848).

The Republic is divided into 22 departments, and is
traversed from W. to E. by an elevated mountain
chain, containing several volcanic summits rising to
13,000 feet above the sea; earthquakes are frequent,
and the capital (which is at an altitude of 4,800 ft.)
was destroyed by an upheaval in Dec. 1917. An
earthquake in Feb. 1976 killed about 25,000 people,
and caused considerable damage to property and the
infrastructure. The country is well watered by
numerous rivers; the climate is hot and malarial near
the coast, temperate in the higher regions. The
rainfall in the capital is 57 in. per annum. The chief
seaports are San José de Guatemala and Champerico
on the Pacific and Santo Tomás de Castilla and
Puerto Barrios on the Atlantic side.

The constitutionally elected president, Gen. Miguel Ydigoras Fuentes, was overthrown on March 31, 1963, by the Army, which handed executive and legislative powers to the Minister of Defence, Col. Enrique Peralta Azurdia. Important changes were included in a new constitution promulgated on Sept. 15, 1965, and elections for a new Congress and for President and Vice-President took place on March 6, 1966. The constitution was suspended "for as long as the situation demands" following a military coup in March 1982. An amnesty for guerrillas was unsuccessful and the Army is now fully occupied dealing with the proliferating subversive groups throughout the country. A Constituent Assembly was elected on July 1, 1984 whose 88 deputies will draw up a new constitution. A return to civilian rule is envisaged a year later when a presidential election should take place.

Language and Literature.—Spanish is the language of the country, and since the establishment of the University in the capital, education has received a marked impulse and the high figure of illiteracy is being reduced. The National library contains about 80,000 volumes in the Spanish tongue.

Finance.—Actual revenue and expenditure in 1978 were *Quetzales* 665,000,000 and *Quetzales* 665,300,000 respectively, compared with *Quetzales* 593,000,000 and *Quetzales* 522,600,000 in 1977.

TRADE

	1981
Imports (c.i.f.)	U.S.$1,540 m.
Exports (f.o.b.)	1,299 m.

Trade with U.K.

	1982	1983
Imports from U.K.	£8,127,000	£7,440,000
Exports to U.K.	13,476,000	9,764,000

The principal export is coffee, other articles being manufactured goods, sugar, bananas, cotton, beef and essential oils. The chief imports are petroleum, vehicles, machinery and foodstuffs.

CAPITAL.—Guatemala. Population: 1,500,000. Quezaltenango (second city of the Republic), has a pop. of 65,733. Other towns are ΨPuerto Barrios (38,956), Mazatenango (38,319), and Antigua (26,631).

FLAG.—Three vertical bands, blue, white, blue; coat of arms on white stripe.

(Guatemala and the U.K. have no formal diplomatic relations.)

GUINEA
(Republic of Guinea)

President, Col. Lansana Conté (since April 3, 1984).
Prime Minister, Col. Diara Traoré.

Formerly part of French West Africa, Guinea has a coastline on the Atlantic Ocean between Guinea-Bissau and Sierra Leone and in the interior is adjacent to Senegal, Mali, Ivory Coast, Liberia and Sierra Leone (*see* above). Area, 96,865 sq. miles. The population (1980 estimate) is 6,412,000, mostly the Fullah, Malinké and Soussou tribes.

Government.—Guinea was separated from Senegal in 1891 and administered by France as a separate colony until 1958. In a referendum held in Sept. 1958, Guinea rejected the new French Constitution. French administrative and financial assistance was terminated; and Guinea left the French Community. On October 2, 1958, Guinea became an independent republic governed by a Constituent Assembly. M. Sékou Touré, Prime Minister in the Territorial Assembly, assumed office as head of the new Government.

A provisional constitution, adopted on Nov. 12, 1958, declared Guinea "a democratic, secular and social republic", powers of government being exercised by a president assisted by the Cabinet. The President, eligible for a term of 7 years and for re-election, is head of state and of the armed forces. M. Sékou Touré was elected President of the Republic by an overwhelming vote in an election (in which he was the sole candidate) in January, 1961. Pres. Sékou Touré died in March 1984: a few days later there was a military *coup.* Guinea is now ruled by a military government, which is directed by a Military Committee for National Recovery. The country's foreign policy is one of non-alignment.

Guinea withdrew from the Franc Zone on March 1, 1960, and established her own currency, the *Guinea franc* (now the *Syli.*). Guinea is in receipt of economic aid and technical assistance from a number of countries, including the United States, Canada, the F.D.R., Yugoslavia, the Soviet Union and China.

Production, etc.—The principal products of Guinea are bauxite, alumina, iron-ore, palm kernels, millet, rice, coffee, bananas, pineapples and rubber. At Sangaredi in the mountains in the hinterland of Guinea (Fouta Djalon, 4,970 feet), where the rivers Senegal, Gambia and Niger have their sources, large deposits of bauxite (the raw material of aluminium) are mined. Deposits of iron ore, gold, diamonds and uranium have also been discovered. Principal imports are cotton goods, manufactured goods, tobacco, petroleum products, sugar, rice, flour and salt; exports, bauxite, alumina, iron-ore, diamonds, coffee, hides, bananas, palm kernels and pineapples.

Trade with U.K.

	1982	1983
Imports from U.K.	£6,840,000	£7,190,000
Exports to U.K.	1,956,000	668,000

CAPITAL.—ΨConakry (655,000). Other towns are Kankan, which is connected with Conakry by a railway, Kindia, N'Zérékoré, Mamou, Siguiri and Labé.

FLAG.—Three vertical stripes of red, yellow and green.

NATIONAL DAY.—October 2 (Anniversary of Proclamation of Independence).

BRITISH EMBASSY

British Ambassador (resident at Dakar, Senegal).

GUINEA-BISSAU

President of the Council of State (Head of State), Gen. João Bernado Vieira.
Prime Minister, Victor Saude Maria.

Guinea-Bissau, formerly Portuguese Guinea, lies in Western Africa, between Senegal and Guinea; it has an area of 14,000 sq. miles and had a population in 1979 of 760,000. The main ethnic groups are the Balante, Malinké, Fulani, Mandjako and Pepel.

Guinea-Bissau achieved independence on Sept. 10, 1974. Sr. Luis Cabral was ousted in a *coup* led by Maj. (now Gen.) Vieira in November, 1980. Following the *coup* the Assembly was suspended, and a Revolutionary Council was established as the prime political institution, overseeing the work of the Council of Ministers. Under a new constitution adopted in April 1984 the Revolutionary Council became the Council of State, and a parliament was set up.

Currency.—The *escudo* was replaced by the *peso* in March 1976.

Economy.—The country produces rice, coconuts, ground-nuts and palm oil products. Cattle are raised, and there are bauxite deposits in the south.

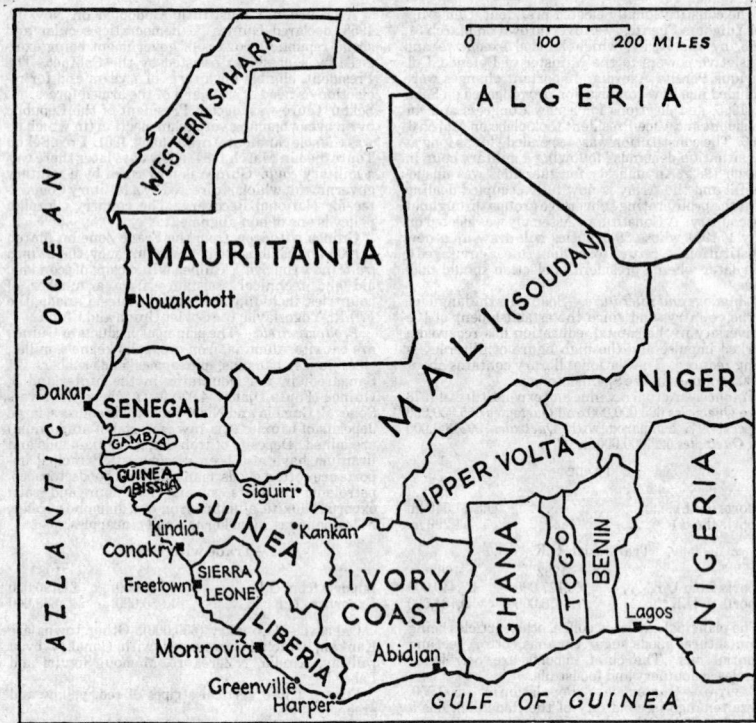

	1982	1983
Imports from U.K.	£431,000	£477,000
Exports to U.K.	—	94,000

The Capital and Chief Port is ΨBissau.

BRITISH EMBASSY

British Ambassador, (resident at Dakar, Senegal).

HAITI
(République d'Haïti)

President, Jean Claude Duvalier, *born* 1951, *installed as President for Life,* April 21, 1971.

CABINET

Interior and Defence, Roger Lafontant.
Agriculture, Natural Resources and Rural Development, Luckner Saint-Dic.
Labour and Social Affairs, Théodore Achille.
Public Health and Population, Remy Joseph Volvick.
Public Works, Transport and Communications, Alix Cineas.
National Education, Franck Saint-Victor.
Economy, Finance and Industry, Frantz Merceron.
Justice, Bertholand Edouard.
Foreign Affairs, Jean Robert Estimé.
Commerce, Odonel Fenestor.

Youth and Sports, Henri Rémy.
Planning, Yves Blanchard.
Mining and Energy, Jean E. Pierre.
Ministry for the Presidency, Information and Public Relations, Jean-Marie Chanoine.

EMBASSY AND CONSULATE
33 Abbot's House,
St. Mary Abbot's Terrace, W14 8NU.

Chargé d'Affaires, Theo Duval.

The Republic of Haiti occupies the western third of the island of Hispaniola, which, next to Cuba, is the largest island in the West Indies.

The area of the Republic, including off-shore islands, is 10,700 sq. miles (of which about three-quarters is mountainous), with a population of 6,000,000, 85 per cent of whom live in rural areas. The people are mainly negroes but there are numbers of mulattoes and others with some admixture of European blood.

Climate.—The climate is tropical with comparatively little difference in the temperatures between the summer (March–Oct.) and the winter (Nov.–Feb.). The temperature at Port-au-Prince rarely exceeds 95° F., but the humidity is high, especially in the autumn.

Language.—French is the language of the government and the press, but it is only spoken by the educated minority. The usual language of the people is Creole.

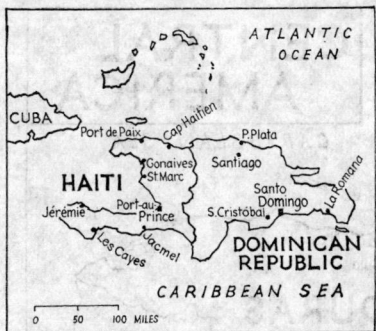

Haiti was a French colony under the name of Saint-Domingue from 1697. The slave population, estimated at 500,000, revolted in 1791 under the leadership of Toussaint L'Ouverture, who was born a slave and made himself Governor-General of the colony. He capitulated to the French in 1802 and died in captivity in 1803. Resistance was continued by Jean Jacques Dessalines, also a former negro slave, who, on January 1, 1804, declared the former French colony to be an independent state. It was at this time that the name Haiti, an aboriginal word meaning mountainous, was adopted. Dessalines became Emperor of Haiti, but was assassinated in 1806. In 1915, following a period of political upheaval, the country was occupied by a force of U.S. marines. The occupation came to an end in 1934, and U.S. control of the revenue of Haiti officially ended on October 1, 1947.

Dr. Duvalier was installed as President in 1957 and was re-elected as President for life on June 15, 1964. He died on April 21, 1971. He was succeeded as President for life on the same day by his son, Jean Claude Duvalier, whom he had nominated as his successor under Article 102 of the Constitution of 1964 as amended on January 14, 1971.

Production.—Improvident methods of peasant agriculture succeeded the colonial plantation system and resulted in the gradual impoverishment of natural resources through exhaustion of the soil, deforestation and erosion. In recent years measures for agricultural rehabilitation have been taken with the aim of a gradual restoration of productivity. The main project is a scheme for the irrigation of more than 70,000 acres of the Artibonite valley. It is estimated that eighty per cent of the people do not get enough to eat and the situation remains acute.

Coffee accounts for about one third of total exports and is still a mainstay of the country's economy though exports now rarely exceed 300,000 bags (of 60 kg.). Sugar is the second most important crop, and sisal is grown for export as or for cordage. New varieties of rice and cotton are being tried in the hope of boosting production. Rum and other spirits are distilled, and essential oils extracted. Exports of bauxite began in 1957, but known reserves are now almost exhausted.

Industry.—Industry is still on a small scale but the last few years have seen a steady and considerable expansion of light industry (the so-called transformation industries) taking advantage of cheap local labour (minimum wage, Oct. 1982, $U.S. 2·64 per day) to assemble or manufacture labour-intensive goods for the U.S. market (baseballs, brassieres, electronic equipment, etc.). Exports of manufactures now rank second after coffee at about 40 per cent of total

exports. The tourist industry is again expanding and many French Canadians are now attracted to Haiti for winter holidays. The country is one of the most beautiful in the Caribbean.

Communications.—The main roads are asphalted but secondary roads are bad. Internal air services are maintained between the capital and the principal provincial towns. International air-services connect Port-au-Prince with the U.S.A. and other Caribbean and South American cities. The principal towns and villages are connected by telephone and/or telegraph. The telephone company is now state owned (51 per cent.) and the service both in Port-au-Prince and Inter-urban has been greatly improved. External telegraph, telephone and postal services are normal. There are several commercial radio stations and a television station at Port-au-Prince.

Regular passenger liner services to New York have ceased, but cruise ships call regularly, one Norwegian line operating a weekly cruise service to Miami. Freight sailings are frequent for the U.S.A., Canada, Europe, Latin America (except Cuba) and the main Caribbean ports.

Education.—Education is free but estimates of illiteracy are as high as 75 per cent. There are four French daily newspapers. The total circulation is very small.

Finance.—New arrangements are being negotiated with the International Monetary Fund following missions to Haiti in Sept. 1981 and April 1982.

	1979 $U.S.
Revenue	94,709,000
Expenditure	94,709,000

Currency.—The unit of currency is the *gourde*, which has a fixed value of 5 *gourdes* = U.S.$1. U.S. currency is also legal tender.

Trade.—Value of imports 1979 $U.S. 224,800,000; exports 1979 $U.S. 128,000,000.

Trade with U.K.

	1982	1983
Imports from U.K....	£3,704,000	£4,171,000
Exports to U.K.	2,615,000	1,646,000

The principal exports are listed above; the principal imports are foodstuffs, textiles, machinery, mineral oils, vehicles and raw materials for industry.

CAPITAL.—Ψ Port-au-Prince. Population (census, 1971), 506,525. Other centres are: Ψ Cap Haitien (54,691); Ψ Gonaives (36,736); Ψ Les Cayes (27,222); Jérémie (25,117); Ψ St. Marc (20,504); Ψ Jacmel (16,449); Ψ Port de Paix (21,733).

FLAG.—Two vertical bands, black (next staff) and red; arms in centre on a white background.

NATIONAL DAY.—January 1.

British Ambassador, (resident at Kingston, Jamaica).

HONDURAS
(Republica de Honduras)

President of the Republic, Dr. Roberto Suazo Cordova, *assumed office,* 27 Jan. 1982.

CABINET

Interior and Justice, Abogado Oscar Mejía Arellano.
Foreign Affairs, Edgardo Paz Barniça.
Defence, Col. Amilcar Castillo Suazo.
Education, (vacant).
Finance, Manuel Fontecha.
Economy, Miguel Orellana Maldonado.
Communications, Public Works and Transport, Carlos Handal.

Health, Dr. Rubén García Martínez.
Labour and Social Security, Amado H. Nuñez.
Natural Resources, Miguel Angel Bonilla.
Culture and Tourism, Prof. Victor Cáceres Lara.
Economic Planning, Edgardo Sevilla Idiáquez.
Director of National Agrarian Institute, Ubodoro Arriaga Iraheto.
Minister for the Presidency, Ubudore Arriaga.

HONDURAS EMBASSY IN LONDON
47 Manchester Street, W1M 5PB
[01–486 3380]

Ambassador Extraordinary and Plenipotentiary, His Excellency Sr. Max Velásquez-Diaz (1984).

Honduras, one of the five Republican States of Central America, lies between lat. 13° and 16° 30′ N. and long. 83° and 89° 41′ W. with a seaboard of about 375 miles on the Caribbean Sea and an outlet, consisting of a small strip of coast 63 miles in length on the Pacific. Its frontiers are contiguous with those of Guatemala, Nicaragua and El Salvador.

The Republic contains a total area of approximately 43,278 sq. miles (112,088 km.) and is very mountainous, being traversed by the Cordilleras, with peaks rising to 1500 and 2400 metres above sea level. Most of the soil is poor and acid, except for a few acres along the North coast and in the interior. Rainfall is seasonal, May to October being wet and November to April dry. The climate varies with the altitude, being tropical throughout the year in the coastal belts and temperate and mainly healthy in the uplands. Three-

quarters of the territory is covered by pine forests which contribute to much of the country's wealth in natural resources. The population (1982 estimate) of 3,600,000 is of mixed Spanish and Indian blood. There is a foreign negro (West Indian) element in Northern Honduras.

Originally discovered and settled by the Spaniards at the beginning of the sixteenth century Honduras formed part of the Spanish American Dominions for nearly three centuries until 1821 when independence was proclaimed. Under military government from 1972–81, the present Liberal government was elected in Nov. 1981 and took office in Jan. 1982.

The Republic is divided into 18 departments, the newest of which, Gracias a Dios, formed in Feb. 1957, is now the home of thousands of Miskito Indian refugees from Nicaragua.

Agriculture is mainly confined to the large and fertile valleys on the wide Caribbean plain, and the extensive valleys found in the Comayagua and Olancho regions of the interior. Reaching inland from the Caribbean towards the eastern border with Nicaragua a vast tropical forest area called the Mosquitia constitues an untapped reserve of precious timber. Lead, zinc and silver are mined and exported.

The chief exports are coffee, bananas and timber, the most important woods being pine, mahogany and cedar. Cattle raising and the exporting of frozen meat is an important industry, and exports of shrimps and lobsters are increasing. Other products are tobacco, beans, maize, rice, cotton, palm oil, sugar cane, cement and tropical fruits. There are large tracts of uncultivated land.

There are about 1,004 km. of railway in operation, chiefly to serve the banana plantations and the Caribbean ports. There are 15,006 km. of roads, of which 1,809 are paved, excluding some 250 kms of new major highways recently inaugurated. Improvements are being made and new roads built. There are 33 smaller airstrips and three international airports, Tegucigalpa, San Pedro Sula and La Ceiba.

The language of the country is Spanish. Primary and secondary education is free, primary education being compulsory, and the Government have launched a campaign to eradicate illiteracy.

ΨThe chief ports are Puerto Cortes, Tela and La Ceiba on the North Coast, through which passes the bulk of the trade with the United States and Europe, and Amapala, situated on Tiger Island in the Gulf of Fonseca, on the Pacific side. A new deep-water port, Henecan, has been opened at San Lorenzo, on the mainland, in the Gulf of Fonseca.

The unit of currency is the *Lempira* (also known as *peso*) of 100 *centavos*.

TRADE

	1982	1983
Imports .... *Lempiras*	1,436 m.	1,511·7 m.
Exports .... „	1,308 m.	1,360·6 m.

Trade with U.K.

	1982	1983
Imports from U.K....	£4,659,000	£9,539,000
Exports to U.K.	4,693,000	7,082,000

CAPITAL.—Tegucigalpa. Pop. 533,600 (1982 est.); other towns are San Pedro Sula (397,900), ΨLa Ceiba (68,900), ΨPuerto Cortes (62,300), Choluteca (89,000) and ΨTela (61,200).

FLAG.—Three horizontal bands, blue, white, blue (with five blue stars on white band).

NATIONAL DAY.—September 15.

BRITISH EMBASSY
Apartado Postal 290, Tegucigalpa.

Ambassador Extraordinary and Plenipotentiary, His Excellency Colum John Sharkey, C.M.G., M.B.E. (1981).

Tegucigalpa is 5,930 miles from London; transit, *via* New York, 14 days; *via* Panama 20 days. By air *via* Miami 1 day.

HUNGARY
(Magyarország)

President of the Presidential Council of the Republic, Pál Losonczi, elected April, 1967.

COUNCIL OF MINISTERS

Prime Minister, György Lázár.
Deputy Prime Ministers, János Borbándi; József Marjai; Lajos Faluvégi; Istvan Sarlos.
Foreign Affairs, Peter Varkonyi.
Interior, Dr. István Horváth.
Defence, Lajos Czinege.
Finance, Dr. István Hetényi.
Justice, Imre Markója.
Industry, Lajos Méhes.
Foreign Trade, Péter Veress.
Internal Trade, Zoltán Juhar.
Agriculture and Food, Jenő Váncsa.
Health, Dr. Emil Schultheisz.
Culture and Education, Béla Köpeczi.
Building and Town Planning, Dr. Kálmán Ábrahám.
Transport and Postal Affairs, Árpád Pullai.

President, National Planning Office, Dr. Lajos Faluvégi.
President, Technical Development Committee, Gyula Szeker.

THE COMMUNIST PARTY

Politbureau of the Central Committee, G. Aczél; V. Benke; F. Havasi; M. Korom; L. Méhes; S. Gáspar; J. Kádár; G. Lázár; P. Losonczi; L. Maróthy; K. Németh; M. Ovári; I. Sárlos.
Secretariat of the Central Committee, János Kádár (*1st Secretary*); G. Aczel; F. Havasi; M. Korom; K. Németh; M. Ovári; M. Szúrös.

HUNGARIAN EMBASSY AND CONSULATE
35 Eaton Place, S.W.1.
[01–235 4048, 7191; *Consulate:* 01–235 2664]

Ambassador Extraordinary and Plenipotentiary, His Excellency Dr. Rezso Banyasz (1981).
Counsellors, Dr. L. Demus; I. Bene (*Commercial*).
Military and Air Attaché, Col. F. Esztergomi.
1st Secretaries, L. Szabados (*Scientific*); Dr. P. Kallós (*Consular*); G. Braun (*Cultural*); B. Blahó (*Consular*); K. Nagy (*Commercial*).
2nd Secretary, L. Fodor (*Press*).

Area and Population.—The area of Hungary may be stated as approximately 36,000 sq. miles with a population (1980) of 10,710,000.

Government.—Hungary was reconstituted a kingdom in 1920 after having been declared a republic on Nov. 17, 1918. She joined the Anti-Comintern Pact on Feb. 24, 1939, and entered the 1939–45 War on the side of Germany in 1941. On Jan. 20, 1945, a Hungarian provisional government of liberation, which had been set up during the preceding December, signed an armistice under the terms of which the frontiers of Hungary were withdrawn to the limits existing in 1937.

After the liberation, a coalition of the Smallholder, National Peasant, Social Democrat and Communist parties carried out major land reform and mines, heavy industry, banks and schools were nationalized. By 1949 the Communists had succeeded in gaining a monopoly of power. A campaign was opened to collectivize agriculture and by 1952 practically the entire economy had been "socialized". The Party formulates policy and the function of the Government is mainly executive.

In mid–1953 Mr. Imre Nagy became Prime Minister, introducing a more moderate policy based largely on the development of agriculture rather than heavy industry. However, in April 1955 he was removed from his position as Prime Minister and subsequently expelled from the Party.

The period from July 1956 to the outbreak of the national revolution on Oct. 23 was marked by growing ferment in intellectual circles and increased discord within the Party. The immediate signal for the revolt was a series of students' demonstrations, first in Szeged on Oct. 22 and in Budapest a day later. The chief demands put forward by students and other demonstrators were for the return of Mr. Nagy as Prime Minister, for the withdrawal of Soviet troops from the country and for free elections. Fighting broke out on the night of Oct. 23 between demonstrators, who had been joined by large numbers of factory workers, and the State Security Police (A.V.H.). Soviet forces intervened in strength early the next morning. By Oct. 30 Soviet troops had withdrawn from Budapest and on Nov. 3 Mr. Nagy formed an all-party coalition government. This government was overthrown and the revolution suppressed as the result of a renewed attack by Soviet forces on Budapest in the early hours of Nov. 4. Simultaneously the formation of a new Hungarian Revolutionary Worker Peasant Government under the leadership of Mr. Kádár was announced.

Economy.—Since 1968 the Hungarian economy has been run according to a system which allows more decentralized decision-making than in some other Eastern European countries. More difficult economic circumstances have led to more central control in vital areas such as the allocation of fuels and raw materials. Industrialization has made considerable progress in the last decade and now produces 68 per cent of national income. Industry is mainly based on imported raw materials but Hungary has her own coal (mostly brown), bauxite, considerable deposits of natural gas (some not yet under full exploitation), some iron ore and oil. Output figures in 1980 (1,000 tons), coal, 25,700; bauxite, 2,950; steel 3,763; crude oil, 2,031; cement, 4,660. Natural gas production totalled 6,127 million cubic metres.

Agriculture still occupies an important place in the Hungarian economy. Production in 1983 was some 3 per cent down on the (record) yields of 1982, mainly due to a prolonged drought. Ten and a half per cent. of the entire land area is owned by State farms and a futher 63·8 per cent is within co-operative farms. Production of the most important crops in 1980 was up on previous years; figures (1,000 tons), wheat, 6,048; rye 138; barley 926; maize 6,575; rice 25; oats 104; sugar beet 3,873; green maize and silage maize 6,253; lucerne 2,222.

In 1983, national income grew by only 0·5 per cent. Consumption and, particularly, investment continued to be squeezed by the adjustment measures necessitated by Hungary's hard currency debts. Retail prices rose by just under 8 per cent, whilst real incomes stagnated.

Religion and Education.—About two-thirds of the population are Roman Catholics, and the remainder mostly Calvinist. There are five types of schools under the Ministry of Education—kindergartens 3–6, general schools 6–14 (compulsory), vocational schools (15–18), secondary schools (15–18), universities and adult training schools (over 18). In the academic year 1978–79 there were 106,000 students at higher education institutions, 198,000 at secondary schools, and 1,107,000 at general schools.

Language and Literature.—Magyar, or Hungarian, is one of the Finno-Ugrian languages. Hungarian literature began to flourish in the second half of the sixteenth century. Among the greatest writers of the nineteenth and twentieth centuries are Mihály Vörösmarty (1800–1855), Sándor Petőfi (1823–1849), János Arany (1817–1882), Imre Madach (1823–1864), Kálmán Mikszáth (1847–1910), Endre Ady (1877–

1918), Attila József (1905–1937), Mihály Babits (1883–1941) and Dezső Kosztolányi (1885–1936).

Finance.—The budget estimates for the year 1983 were: Revenue, *Forints* 523,500 million; Expenditure, *Forints* 533,700 million. The unit of currency is the *forint* of 100 *fillér*.

TRADE

1983

	Non-convertible trade (*roubles*)	Convertible trade U.S.$
Imports	6,687,800	4,454 m.
Exports	6,158,400	4,988 m.

(1 *rouble* = 26 forints: 1 U.S.$ = 42·9 forints)

Trade with U.K.

	1982	1983
Imports from U.K.	£77,446,000	£91,845,000
Exports to U.K.	44,051,000	53,834,000

CAPITAL.—Budapest, on the Danube; population (1979), 2,093,000. Other large towns are: Miskolc (212,000); Debrecen (200,000); Szeged (178,000) and Pecs (171,000).

FLAG.—Red, white, green (horizontally).

NATIONAL DAY.—April 4 (Anniversary of Liberation, 1945).

BRITISH EMBASSY
Harmincad Utca 6, Budapest V

Ambassador Extraordinary and Plenipotentiary, His Excellency Peter William Unwin, C.M.G. (1983).
Counsellor, J. A. Fortescue (*Head of Chancery*).
Defence and Air Attaché, Wg.-Cdr. C. Campbell.
Military Attaché, Lt.-Col. A. Cowie.
Cultural Attaché and British Council Representative, W. K. Dobson.
1st Secretaries, G. Hart (*Commercial*); N. Cameron (*Information*); J. B. Greenlee (*Administration and Consul*).
2nd Secretaries, G. Reid; W. Dickson (*Commercial*).
Attachés, R. C. Mansfield; J. A. Parker; D. I. Campbell.
Vice-Consul, M. Carbine.

Budapest is distant 1,126 miles from London, transit by rail 30 hours; by air 2 hrs. 20 mins.

ICELAND
(Island)

President, Vigdís Finnbogadóttir, *born* 1930, *elected* June 29, 1980, *re-elected,* July 1984.

CABINET

Prime Minister, Steingrímur Hermannsson (*Pr.*).
Foreign Affairs, Geir Hallgrímsson (*I.*).
Finance, Albert Gudmundsson (*I.*).
Industries and Energy, Sverrir Hermannsson (*I.*).
Fisheries, Halldór Asgrímsson (*Pr.*).
Agriculture, Justice and Ecclesiastical, Jón Helgason (*Pr.*).
Education and Culture, Ragnhildur Helgadóttir (*I.*).
Commerce, Matthías A. Mathiesen (*I.*).
Health, Social Security and Communications, Matthías Bjarnason (*I.*).
Social Affairs (Housing, Local Government and Labour), Alexander Stefánsson (*I.*).
(*I.*—Independence Party; *Pr.*—Progressive Party.)

EMBASSY IN LONDON
1 Eaton Terrace, SW1W 8EY
[01–730 5131]

Ambassador Extraordinary and Plenipotentiary, His Excellency Einar Benediktsson (1982).
Counsellors, S. Björnsson; S. Gunnlaugsson (*Commercial*).

ICELAND

Iceland is a large volcanic island in the North Atlantic Ocean, extending from 63° 23' to 66° 33' N. lat., and from 13° 22' to 24° 35' W. long., with an estimated area of 40,500 square miles, or about one-sixth greater than that of Ireland. The population was 237,894 on Dec. 1, 1983.

Iceland was uninhabited before the ninth century, when settlers came from Norway. For several centuries a form of republican government prevailed, with an annual assembly of leading men called the *Althing*, but in 1241 Iceland became subject to Norway, and later to Denmark. During the colonial period, Iceland maintained its cultural integrity but a deterioration in the climate, together with frequent volcanic eruptions and outbreaks of disease led to a serious fall in the standard of living and to a decline in the population to little more than 40,000. In the nineteenth century a struggle for independence began which led first to home rule for Iceland under the Danish Crown (1918), and later to complete independence under a republican form of rule in 1944.

Government.—The parliamentary (*Althing*) elections in April 1983 gave the Independence Party 23 seats, Progressives 14, People's Alliance 10 and Social Democrats 6, Union of Social Democrats 4 and Feminists 3. In May 1983 Steingrímur Hermansson, chairman of the Progressive Party, formed a coalition government with the Independence Party, the other parties forming the opposition.

Language and Literature.—The ancient Norraena (or Northern tongue) presents close affinities to Anglo-Saxon and as spoken and written in Iceland to-day differs little from that introduced into the island in the ninth century. There is a rich literature with two distinct periods of development, from the middle of the eleventh to the end of the thirteenth century and from the beginning of the nineteenth century to the present time.

Production.—Iceland has considerable resources of hydro-electric and geothermal energy. It is estimated that exploited water power (3,900 Gigawatt hours/a) represents only about 9 per cent of that economically exploitable, whereas only 5 per cent of the estimated 80,000 Gigawatt hours/a of available geothermal power has so far been harnessed. Energy-intensive heavy industry includes an aluminium smelter, a nitrogen fertilizer factory, a diatomite plant and a ferro-silicone plant.

The principal exports are frozen fish fillets, salt fish, stock fish, fresh fish on ice, frozen scampi, fishmeal and oil, skins and aluminium; the imports consist of almost all the necessities of life, the chief items being petroleum products, transport equipment, textiles, foodstuffs animal feeds, timber, and alumina.

At January 1, 1984, the mercantile marine consisted of 542 vessels of under 100 gross tons and 398 ships of 100 gross tons and over; a total of 940 vessels (192,312 gross tons), of which 836 (111,772 gross tons) are decked fishing vessels. There are regular shipping services between Reykjavik and Felixstowe, Ipswich, Humber and Mersey ports, and the Continent.

A regular air service is maintained between Glasgow and London and Reykjavik. There are also air services from the island to Scandinavia, U.S.A., Germany, France and Luxemburg.

Road communications are adequate in summer but greatly restricted by snow in winter. Only roads in town centres and a few key highways are metalled the rest being of gravel, sand and lava dust. The climate and terrain make first-class surfaces for highways out of the question. Total number of private vehicles licensed was about 106,500 in early 1983.

FINANCE

	1982	1983
	Krónur (millions)	
Revenue	9,562	15,100
Expenditure	9,324	16,598

TRADE

	1982	1983
	Krónur (millions)	
Exports	8,479	18,623
Imports	11,647	20,596

Trade with U.K.

	1982	1983
Imports from U.K....	£46,700,000	£47,800,000
Exports to U.K.	51,500,000	53,200,000

CAPITAL: Ψ Reykjavík. Population (Dec. 1, 1983), 87,106.

Other centres in approximate order of importance are Akureyri, Kópavogur, Hafnarfjördur, Keflavík, Westmann Islands, Akranes, Isafjördur and Siglufjördur.

FLAG.—Blue, with white-bordered red cross.
NATIONAL DAY.—June 17.

BRITISH EMBASSY
Laufásvegur 49, Reykjavik

Ambassador Extraordinary and Plenipotentiary and Consul-General, His Excellency Richard Thomas (1983).

1st Secretary and Consul, P. Fluck.
Vice Consul and Attaché (Commercial), J. N. L. Burgess.

BRITISH CONSULAR OFFICES

There are Consular Offices at *Reykjavík* and *Akureyri*.

INDONESIA
(Republic of Indonesia)

President, General Soeharto, *born* June 9, 1921. *Acting President*, March 12, 1967; *confirmed as President*, Mar. 28, 1968, *re-elected for a term of 5 years*, March, 1973, March 1978 and March 1983.
Vice-President, Umar Wirahadi Kusumah, *elected* March 1983.

INDONESIAN EMBASSY AND CONSULATE
38 Grosvenor Square, W1X 9AD
[01–499 7661]

Ambassador Extraordinary and Plenipotentiary, His
Excellency Sjahabuddin Arifin (1981).
Minister, Mr. Pratjojo (*Deputy Chief of Mission*).
Minister-Counsellor, S. Siregar (*Political*).
Counsellor, I. Abidin (*Information*).
Defence Attaché, Col. P. Damanik.
Communications Attaché, R. Robbani.
Commercial Attaché, A. Darus.

Situated between latitudes 6° North and 11° South
and between longitudes 95° and 141° East, Indonesia
comprises the islands of *Java* and *Madura,* the island
of *Sumatra,* the *Riouw-Lingga Archipelago* (which
with Karimon, Anambas, Natuna Islands, Tambelan,
and part of Sumatra, forms the province of Riau), the
islands of *Bangka* and *Billiton,* part of the island of
Borneo (Kalimantan), *Sulawesi* (*formerly* Celebes)
Island, the *Molucca Islands* (Ternate, Tidore, Hal-
mahera, Buru, Seram, Banda, Timor-Laut, Larat,
Bachiam, Obi, Kei, Aru, Babar, Leti and Wetar), the
island of *Bali* and the islands of *Lombok, Sumbawa,
Sumba, Flores, Timor* and others comprising the
provinces of East and West *Nusa Tenggara* and the
western half of the island of New Guinea (*Irian Jaya*),
with a total area of 735,000 sq. miles, and a population
of about 157,000,000.

From the early part of the 17th century much of
the Indonesian Archipelago was under Netherlands
rule. Following the World War 1939–45, during
which the Archipelago was occupied by the Japanese,
a strong nationalistic movement manifested itself
and after sporadic fighting the formal transfer of
sovereignty by the Netherlands of all the former
Dutch East Indies except W. New Guinea took place
on December 27, 1949.

Dr. Sukarno was elected President of Indonesia
and held office until his deposition in 1967. He died
on June 21, 1970.

Following the establishment of Malaysia (including
Sabah and Sarawak) in 1963, President Sukarno
pursued a policy of "confrontation" against it,
involving border incursions in both West and East
Malaysia. Commonwealth forces assisted Malaysian
resistance. Western New Guinea became part of

Indonesia in 1963 under the name West Irian (now
Irian Jaya), this interpretation being confirmed in
an "Act of Free Choice" in July, 1969, of which the
United Nations took note in November 1969. Following a unilateral declaration of independence by the
Fretilin, Indonesia took over the former Portuguese
colony of East Timor, which in July 1976 was declared
the 27th province of Indonesia.

On Sept. 30, 1965, an attempted *coup d'état* assisted
by the Palace Guard resulted in the murder of six
generals. The Indonesian Communist Party was
charged with plotting to destroy the power of the
Army and to set up a Peking-oriented régime,
nominally under President Sukarno. The coup was
swiftly crushed and a widespread massacre of Communists and their supporters followed. Sukarno
remained in office but his Foreign Minister, Dr.
Subandrio, among others, was arrested and later
sentenced to death. The sentence has not been
carried out.

Following a three-week period of unrest and violent
student demonstrations the Minister of the Army,
General Soeharto, took over effective political power
in March, 1966, and announced the banning in
Indonesia of the Communist Party. The new régime
concluded an agreement ending the "confrontation"
with Malaysia on Aug. 11, 1966, and Indonesia
resumed membership of the United Nations Organization which it had left in 1965. General Soeharto
was made Acting President with full powers, on
March 11, 1967.

Using his powers as Acting President, General
Soeharto revised the membership of the two Houses
of Parliament, and on March 28, 1968, the MPRS
(Provisional People's Consultative Congress), the
highest constitutional body, appointed him full
President for a period of five years. The 1971 elections
resulted in the Government faction Golkar (functional groups) achieving a large majority, which they
have retained in all elections since.

In accordance with another instruction General
Soeharto on June 6 replaced the Ampera Cabinet
with the Development Cabinet, *i.e.* one which was
intended to reflect the emphasis to be placed hence-
forward on the development of the country, economic
affairs, efficiency and expertise in general, and to
reduce the direct influence of the military in the
Government.

In the general election of May 1982, Golkar obtained 246 seats, the Moslem Party 94, and the Democratic Party of Indonesia 24. The Fourth Development Cabinet was appointed in March 1983.

Finance.—The drop in oil prices led in March 1983 to the rupiah being devalued by 27 per cent, and a rescheduling of major projects was undertaken. More recently an increase in foreign reserves has meant that several of these projects could be re-instated.

Currency.—The unit of currency is the *rupiah* of 100 *sen.*

Production.—Nearly 70 per cent. of the population of Indonesia is engaged in agriculture and related production. Copra, kapok, nutmeg, pepper and cloves are produced, mainly by smallholders; palm oil, sugar, fibres and cinchona are produced by large estates. Rubber, tea, coffee and tobacco are also produced by both in large quantities. Timber is now the second largest foreign exchange earner after oil. Rice is a traditional staple food for the people of Indonesia and the islands of Java, Sulawesi and Sumatra are important producers. Production has risen rapidly in recent years to over 22 million tons and the country is now nearly self sufficient.

Oil and LNG are the most important assets, the export of which in 1981–82 earned about U.S. $18,800 million (about 80 per cent. of Indonesia's exports). Whilst a large improvement in rice production and an enlarged development budget pushed Indonesia's growth rate to 9·9 per cent. in 1980, it fell to 7·6 per cent. in 1981, and more recent developments have underscored the vulnerability of the economy to depressed international markets and weak oil prices.

Indonesia is rich in minerals. Tin is the second largest foreign exchange earner after oil and gas, and Indonesia is now the world's second biggest tin producer; petroleum, coal, nickel and bauxite are the other principal products; there are also considerable deposits of gold, silver, manganese phosphates and sulphur. Aid to Indonesia is channelled through the Inter-Governmental Group on Indonesia (IGGI), which pledged U.S. $2,459,000 in 1984–5.

Indonesia has ended its third five-year development programme. The Fourth Development Programme started in 1984 and its main objectives are the elimination of poverty, agriculture and urban problems, and the continued growth of installed power generation.

Trade with U.K.

	1982	1983
Direct Imports from U.K.	£212,066,000	£193,642,000
Exports to U.K.	91,700,000	169,454,000

Principal exports to the United Kingdom are rubber, timber, non-ferrous metals, tea, coffee, spices, and crude oil for refinement. Imports from the United Kingdom are mainly of machinery, transport equipment and electrical equipment.

Transport.—In Java a main line connects Jakarta with Surabaya in the East of Java and there are several branches. In Sumatra the important towns of Medan, Padang and Palembang are the centres of short railway systems.

Sea communications in the archipelago are maintained by the State-run shipping companies Djakarta-Lloyd (ocean-going) and Pelni (coastal and interisland) and other small concerns. Transport by small craft on the rivers of the larger islands plays an important part in trade. Air services in Indonesia are operated by Garuda Indonesian Airways and other local airlines, and Jakarta is served by various international services. There are approximately 50,000 miles of roads.

CAPITAL.—ΨJakarta, formerly Batavia (population 6,503,449). Other important centres are: (Java)

ΨSurabaya (7,027,913), ΨSemarang (1,026,671), Bandung (1,462,637), ΨCirebon (223,776), ΨSurakarta (469,888), Jogjakarta city (398,727); (Sumatra) Palembang (787,187), ΨPadang (480,922), Medan (1,378,955), Jambi (230,373); Pekanbaru (186,262); (Sulawesi) Menado (217,159), ΨUjung Pandang (*formerly Makassar*) (709,038); (Kalimantan) Banjarmasin (381,286), ΨPontianak (304,778), Samarinda (264,718), ΨBalikpapan (280,675); (Moluccas) Ambon (208,898); (Bali) Denpasar, Singaraja (for whole island 2,174,105); (Nusa Tenggara) Kupang (329,371); (Irian Jaya) Jayapura (107,164).

NATIONAL DAY.—August 17 (Anniversary of Proclamation of Independence).

FLAG.—Equal bands of red over white.

BRITISH EMBASSY
Jalan M. H. Thamrin 75, Jakarta

Ambassador Extraordinary and Plenipotentiary, His Excellency Alan Ewen Donald, C.M.G. (1984).

BRITISH CONSULAR OFFICES

There are British Consular Offices at *Jakarta, Medan* and *Surabaya.*

BRITISH COUNCIL

Representative, Dr. J. C. Blackwell, S Widjojo Centre, 57 Jalan Jendral Sudirman, Jakarta. There are also libraries at *Bandung* and *Medan.*

IRAN
(The Islamic Republic of Iran)

Leader of the Islamic Revolution, Ayatollah Ruholla Khomeini, *born* 1902; *assumed power,* Feb., 1979.
President, Hojatoleslam Seyed Ali Khamene'i, *elected* Oct. 2, 1981.
Prime Minister, Mir Hossein Moussavi.
Foreign Affairs, Dr. Ali Akbar Velayati.
Education, Mohammad Moyed.
Commerce, Hassan Abedi Jaafari.
Health, Dr. Ali Reza Marandi.
Justice, Hassan Ebrahim Habibi.
Defence, Col. Muhammad Reza Rahimi.
Oil, Mohammed Gharazi.
Energy, Dr. Hassan Ghaffuri-Fard.
Agriculture, Dr. Abbas Ali Zali.
Economics and Finance, Dr. Hussein Namazi.
Interior, Nateq Nouri.
Labour, Abol Hassan Sarhadi-Zadeh.
Housing, Serajeddin Kazeruni.
Mining and Metals, Hossein Nili Ahmadabadi.
Industry, Muhammad Ali Zaker.
Heavy Industry, Behzad Nabavi.
Islamic Guidance, Seyed Mohammed Khatami.
Culture and Higher Education, Muhammad Reza.
Intelligence, Mohammad Mohammadi Reyshahri.
Roads and Transport, Mohammad Hadi-Nejad Husseinian.
Construction Crusade, Bijan Namdar Zanganeh.
Islamic Revolutionary Guard, Moshen Rafiqdust.

IRANIAN EMBASSY IN LONDON
27 Princes Gate, SW7 1PX

Area and Population.—Iran has an area of 628,000 sq. miles, with a population of 39,190,000 (1982 estimate). It is mostly an arid table-land, encircled, except in the east, by mountains, the highest in the north rising to 18,934 ft. The central and eastern portion is a vast salt desert.

The Iranians are mostly Shi'ah Moslems but among them are a few hundred thousand Zoroastrians, Bahais, several million Sunni Moslems and Armenian and Assyrian Christians. Emigration has much reduced the once substantial Jewish community.

Government.—Iran was ruled from the end of the 18th century by Shahs of the Qajar Dynasty, with despotic power, subject only to the influence of interpreters of the sacred law. A nationalist movement became active in Dec., 1905, and in Aug., 1906, the Shah, Muzaffer-ud-Din, admitting the need for reforms, granted a Constitution. After the war of 1914–18, the subsequent troubles and the signature of the Soviet-Iranian Treaty of 1921, a vigorous Prime Minister, Reza Khan re-established general order. On Oct. 31, 1925, the last representative of the Qajar Dynasty, Sultan Ahmed Shah was deposed in his absence by the National Assembly, which handed over the government to the Prime Minister, Reza Khan, who was elected Shah on Dec. 13, 1925, by the Constituent Assembly, and took the title Reza Shah Pahlavi. On September 16, 1941, Reza Shah abdicated in favour of the Crown Prince, who ascended the throne under the title of Mohammed Reza Shah Pahlavi.

Following widespread and persistent opposition to his regime, the Shah departed from Iran in January, 1979. Ayatollah Khomeini, the main spiritual leader of the Shi'ah Moslems, returned to Iran from exile on February 1. Following a national referendum, Iran was declared an Islamic Republic by Ayatollah Khomeini on April 1, 1979. A new constitution, providing for a President, Prime Minister and Consultative Assembly, and also for overall leadership by Khomeini, was approved by referendum in December 1979. In January 1980 Dr. Bani-Sadr was elected President; elections to the Consultative Assembly were held in March and April. After disagreement between Dr. Bani-Sadr and the fundamentalist clergy, he was forced to resign in June 1981. From exile in Paris he became the leader of the moderates discontented with the fundamentalist policies of the government and religious leaders. Opposition to these policies led to assassination and bombings; the government's subsequent severe measures suppressed violent opposition. In Dec. 1982 an Assembly of Experts was elected to decide the eventual succession to Ayatollah Khomeini. Elections to the Consultative Assembly (Majles) were held in April and May 1984 at the end of its first four-year term.

Iran has been at war with Iraq since the Iraqi invasion of Iran in Sept. 1980. Following their defeat at Khorramshahr Iraqi forces withdrew from most Iranian territory in June 1982. The Iranians launched a major offensive against Basra in July 1982 and several subsequent minor offensives in which they have gained small areas of territory. After Iraq declared a Maritime Exclusion Zone in August 1982, shipping entering the Iranian port of Bandar Khomeini at the head of the Gulf came under Iraqi attack; since the summer of 1984 both sides have carried out attacks on neutral shipping further south in the Gulf.

Defence.—The Army has a strength of about 150,000 men, in 4 armoured divisions, 4 infantry divisions and one airborne division. The Air Force has a strength of about 35,000, with some 70 combat aircraft. The Navy has a strength of about 20,000 and consists of 3 destroyers, 4 frigates, 4 corvettes, 5 minesweepers, and patrol boats, support ships, landing craft and hovercraft. The Islamic Revolutionary Guards Corps numbers about 500,000 men, of whom approximately half are at the front. Both the regular armed forces and the police forces are in a phase of reconstruction, although the army has been expanded since the outbreak of fighting with Iraq.

Education.—Since 1943 primary education has been compulsory and free, but there is large scale absenteeism, particularly outside the towns. The establishment in 1963 of the Literacy Corps (a body of National Servicemen seconded to the Ministry of Education to work as Primary School teachers in rural districts) brought schooling to hitherto deprived villages. There are in Iran 22 universities (8 in Tehran, 14 in the provinces). They were closed in July 1981 for "Islamization" but are now gradually reopening. The educational system has not yet been fully reformed following the revolution.

Language and Literature.—Persian, or Farsi, the language of Iran, and of some other areas formerly under Persian rule, is an Indo-European tongue with many Arabic elements added; the alphabet is mainly Arabic, with writing from right to left. Among the great names in Persian literature are those of Abu'l Kásim Mansúr, of Firdausi (A.D. 939–1020), Omar Khayyám, the astronomer-poet (died A.D. 1122), Muslihu'd-Din, known as Sa'di (born A.D. 1184) and Shems-ed-Din Muhammad, or Hafiz (died A.D. 1389).

Finance.—The budget for the Iranian year beginning March 22, 1983, was revenue *Rials.* 2,930 billion; expenditure *Rials.* 3,606 billion. The unit of currency is the *Rial* of 100 *Dinars* (for rate of exchange, *see* p. 82).

Agriculture.—While petroleum is the principal product and by far the greatest export, Iran is otherwise largely an agricultural and pastoral country. After the 1979 revolution the Provisional Government announced its intention of giving greater emphasis to the development of agriculture with a view to reducing Iran's dependence on food imports. Although half of Iran's area of 165 million hectares is either mountain or desert, more than half the country's population live in rural areas, depending on the 10 million hectares under crop, sheep, goats and cattle for their livelihood. Wheat is the principal crop, using about 6 million hectares. Other important crops are barley, rice, cotton, sugar beet, fruit, nuts and vegetables. Wool is also a major product. There are extensive forests in the north and west, the conservation of which is an urgent problem.

Industry.—Under the Shah, great emphasis was given to the development of industry. Apart from oil, the principal industrial products are carpets, textiles, sugar, cement and other construction materials, ginned cotton, vegetable oil and other food products, leather and shoes, metal manufactures, pharmaceuticals, automobiles, fertilizers and plastics. Industrial output was severely curtailed by the 1979 revolution, as a result of which many industrialists left the country. In July 1979 the Provisional Government nationalized a wide range of major industrial concerns, having nationalized the banks and the insurance companies the previous month. More recently, plans to nationalize foreign trade have been dropped and more encouragement is being given to private sector companies.

Energy.—The oilfields, which lie in South Western Iran, were worked under a concession by the Anglo-Iranian Oil Company until nationalization in 1951. In 1957 the former functions of A.I.O.C. were taken over by a consortium of eight oil companies (one British, one French, one Dutch, and five U.S.), which until the 1979 revolution remained responsible for the production, refining and sale of oil through two operating companies, while "non-basic" operations were undertaken by the National Iranian Oil Company. In July 1979 N.I.O.C. assumed full control of the oil industry. In addition to that extracted from the wells in the former consortium area, oil is also produced from a number of off-shore oilfields which were developed by several oil companies formed jointly by N.I.O.C. with western oil companies. Oil production by June 1979 had reached an average of 3·5 million b.p.d., all but 700,000 b.p.d. for export. Production fell to its lowest point in 1981, but thereafter rose again to its present level of approximately 2·4 million b.p.d., of which some 1·7 million b.p.d. is exported. Iran is a member of O.P.E.C.

Communications.—The principal roads are from Tehran via Tabriz to the Turkish border at Bazargan, with a branch road to the Soviet frontier at Julfa; from Tehran via Qom, Isfahan, and Shiraz to Bushire; from Tehran to Mashad; three roads through the Alborz mountains to the Caspian coast and the Soviet borders east and west of the Caspian Sea; and from Isfahan via Yazd and Kerman to Zahedan. Mashad is connected by road with Herat (Afghanistan), and Zahedan with Quetta (Pakistan). The Trans-Iranian Railway from Bandar Turcoman (formerly Bandar Shah), on the Caspian Sea, via Tehran to Bandar Khomeini (formerly Bandar Shahpur), on the Persian Gulf, was inaugurated in 1938; this line has a total length of 872 miles and took eleven years to build. Other lines link Tehran with Tabriz and with Mashad. There are also railways from Tabriz to Julfa and from Zahedan to Quetta, and branch lines from Ahwaz to Khorramshahr and from Khorramshahr to Tanuma (Iraq). An extension from Qom to Yazd via Kashan is now in operation, as is one from Bandar Turcoman to Gorgan. An extension from Yazd to Kerman is partially complete. The Iranian rail system is linked to the Turkish system via Van. There is an international airport at Tehran (Mehrabad), and airports at all the major provincial centres. The national airline, Iranair, is government-owned and operates international and domestic routes.

TRADE

	1981 U.S.$	1982 U.S.$
Imports	10,330,000,000	11,231,000
Exports	262,000,000	16,379,000

These figures are calculated at the commercial rate of exchange and exclude oil exports.

Trade with U.K.

	1982	1983
Imports from U.K. ...	£333,700,000	£629,980,000
Exports to U.K.	225,900,000	100,545,000

Imports to Iran declined dramatically at the beginning of 1979 as a result of the economic disruption caused by the revolution. Iran's aggressive oil sales policy during 1982 enabled foreign exchange reserves to recover from the 1981 low level and made possible increased exports.

Imports into Iran consist mainly of industrial and agricultural machinery, motor vehicles and motor vehicle components for assembly, iron and steel (including manufactures), electrical machinery and goods, meat, various other foods, and certain textile fabrics and yarns. The principal exports, apart from oil, are cotton, carpets, dried fruit, nuts, hides and skins, mineral ores, wool, gums, caviare, cumin seed and spices. West Germany and Japan are Iran's leading suppliers. Japan is also the main customer for Iran's oil exports.

CAPITAL: Tehran, population 6,200,000. Other large towns are Tabriz (600,000), Isfahan (560,000) Meshed (350,000), Shiraz (250,000), Resht (150,000), Kerman (100,000), Hamadan (130,000), Yazd (70,000), Kermanshah (152,000), Ψ Abadan (300,000), Ahwaz (175,000).

FLAG.—Equal horizontal bands of green, white and red; with an emblem of the Islamic Republic.

BRITISH EMBASSY
Tehran

Minister, M. K. O. Simpson-Orlebar, C.M.G.
First Secretary, C. J. S. Rundle, O.B.E.
(The Embassy was closed on September 9, 1980, and representatives are based temporarily at the Swedish Embassy.)

IRAQ

REVOLUTIONARY COMMAND COUNCIL

Chairman, President of the Republic, and *Supreme Commander of the Armed Forces,* Saddam Hussain, assumed office July 16, 1979.
Members, Izzat Ibrahim (*RCC Vice-Chairman*); Taha Muhiddin Ma'aruf (*Vice-President of the Republic*); Taha Yasin Ramadhan (*First Deputy Prime Minister*); Na'im Haddad (*Chairman of the National Assembly*); Tariq 'Aziz (*Deputy Prime Minister and Foreign Minister*); General Adnan Khairallah (*Deputy Prime Minister and Minister of Defence*); Sa'doun Shakir (*Interior*); Hassan Ali (*Trade*); Khalid Abdul Mun'im Rasheed (*acting Secretary-General*).
In addition to those members of the R.C.C. holding departmental portfolios listed above, there are 19 other Ministers and 4 Ministers of State.

EMBASSY OF THE REPUBLIC OF IRAQ
21 Queen's Gate, SW7 5JG
[01–584 7141/6]

Ambassador Extraordinary and Plenipotentiary, Dr. Wahbi A. Al Qaraguli.

Area, etc.—Traversed by the Rivers Euphrates and Tigris, Iraq extends from Turkey on N. and N.E. to the Gulf on the S. and S.E. and from Iran on E. to Syria and Arabian Desert on W., the approximate position being between 37½° to 48½° E. long., and from 37½° to 30° N. lat. (*see* MAP, p. 854). The area of Iraq is officially estimated at 172,000 sq. miles of which 37 per cent. is desert land. About 35 to 40 per cent. of the remainder is potentially cultivable either by rainfall or by irrigation.

Population.—At the Census of October 1977 Iraq had a total population of 12,171,480. The population was estimated recently at 13·5–14 million.

The *Euphrates* (which has a total length of 1,700 miles from its source to its outflow in the Persian Gulf) is formed by two arms, of which the Murad Su (415 miles) rises in the slopes of the Ala Dagh, a mountain of Eastern Erzurum, and flows westwards to a junction with the Kara Su, or Frat Su (275 miles); the other arm rises in the north-west of Erzurum in the Dumlu Dagh. The *Tigris* has a total length of 1,150 miles from its source to its junction with the Euphrates at Qurna, 70 miles from the Gulf, and rises in two arms south of the Taurus mountains, in Kurdistan, uniting at Til, where the boundaries of the districts of Diarbekir, Van and Bitlis conjoin.

Antiquities.—In 1944 excavations at Tell Hassuna, near Shura (on the Tigris in North Iraq) unearthed abundant traces of culture dating back to 5000 B.C. Excavations in 1948 at Tel Abu Shahrain, 14 miles south of "Ur of the Chaldees," confirm Eridu's claim to be the most ancient city of the Sumerian world. Hillah, the ancient city on the left bank of the Shatt el Hillah, a branch of the Euphrates, about 70 miles south of Baghdad, is near the site of Babylon and of the "house of the lofty-head" or "gate of the god" (Tower of Babel). Mosul Governorate covers a great part of the ancient kingdom of *Assyria*, the ruins of Ninevah, the Assyrian capital, being visible on the banks of the Tigris, opposite Mosul. Qurna, at the junction of the Tigris and Euphrates, is the traditional site of the *Garden of Eden.*

Government.—Under the Treaty of Lausanne (1923), Turkey renounced sovereignty over Mesopotamia. A provisional Arab Government was set up in Nov., 1920, and in Aug., 1921, the Emir Faisal was elected King of Iraq. The country was a monarchy until July, 1958, when King Faisal II was assassinated. From 1958 Iraq has been under Presidential rule. The ruling Party is the Arab Ba'ath Socialist Party, which came to power on July 17, 1968.

Iraq has been engaged in hostilities with Iran since September 1980, originally over control of the Shatt-al-Arab waterway. In July 1982 Iranian forces moved across the border into Iraq, and since that time a series of inconclusive battles have been fought along the borders. Iraq declared a Maritime Exclusion Zone in Aug. 1982 and thereafter regularly attacked shipping entering the Iranian port of Bandar Khomeini at the head of the Gulf. The war extended further down the Gulf in the summer of 1984, with both sides attacking neutral shipping, including tankers.

Language.—The language is mainly Arabic (*see* Arabia) and English is widely used in commerce, science and the arts.

Communications and Trade.—New roads are being rapidly built, and communications between Baghdad and the provincial capitals are being improved and secured. Facilities at the port of Basrah have been improved but the port has not been used since the outbreak of hostilities with Iran in Sept. 1980. Continuous dredging of the Shatt-al-Arab has provided a navigable channel of 22½ feet at low water (as compared with 9 feet before dredging was begun), but dredging operations have also been suspended by hostilities and the channel has seriously silted. The port of Um Qasr near the Kuwaiti border has been developed for freight and sulphur handling and a container terminal is ready for operation but not in use due to the port's proximity to the war zone. Road routes from Turkey and the Mediterranean are well used, and carry through traffic to Kuwait and the south. The border between Syria and Iraq was closed in late 1977, reopened in November, 1978 and closed again in April 1982.

There is an international airport at Baghdad. Iraqi Airways and British Airways provide flights between Baghdad and London, and other international airlines operate to Europe. Iraqi Republican Railways provide regular passenger and goods services on a standard gauge line between Basra, Baghdad and Mosul, which links up through Syria and Turkey with the Mediterranean and the Bosphorus, though no through traffic has used the line since the Syrian government cut the rail link in April 1982. There is also a metre gauge line connecting Baghdad with Khanaqin, Kirkuk and Arbil.

Agriculture and Industry.—Iraq is capable of supporting a considerably greater population if irrigation is developed and extended. The Government's concern with agricultural development is shown in the large financial allocations made to the sector. Apart from the valuable revenues to be derived from oil, agricultural development makes a valuable contribution to the wealth of the country and two harvests can usually be gathered in the year. Production fluctuates from year to year according to rainfall. Salinity and soil erosion, caused by a high water table, inadequate irrigation and drainage and traditional farming methods, are the major problems now being tackled by development planners.

Increasing industrialization is taking place, mainly in the public sector. Priority is being given to petrochemicals, food industries, construction industries and engineering. Existing industries include cement, building materials, flour milling, cigarettes, soap, steel fabrications, furniture, tanning, textiles, footwear, food and drink, as well as the development of mineral resources. In 1975 there were 1,349 industrial establishments employing 134,594 persons. Iraq's major industry is oil production. It was nationalized on June 1, 1972 and accounts for approximately 98 per cent. of the total government revenue and 45 per cent. of the Gross National Product. Production was some 3·5 million barrels per day in 1979 but in 1982 the effects of war damage on the Basra terminals and the closure of the trans-Syria pipeline have reduced production to an estimated 900,000 barrels per day. Total revenues of crude oil have not been published since 1972, but they are believed to have been worth some $20,000 million in 1979, but to have dropped in 1982 to $6–8,000 million.

FINANCE

	1980*	1981*
Total revenue...	*ID*14,412,503,000	*ID*19,434,856,809
Total expenditure	14,103,423,000	19,250,261,450

* Estimates.

TRADE

(Excluding oil)

	1982
Total Imports	$17,758,000
Total Exports	142,000,000

Trade with U.K.

	1982	1983
Imports from U.K.	£874,800,000	£399,900,000
Exports to U.K.	79,800,000	30,600,000

The principal imports are iron and steel, cement and other building materials, mechanical and electrical machinery, motor vehicles, textiles and clothing, essential foodstuffs, grain, tinned foods and raw industrial materials. The chief exports are crude petroleum, dates, raw wool, raw hides and skins and raw cotton.

CAPITAL.—Baghdad. Population of the governorate (Census 1977) 3,205,645. Other towns of importance are Ψ Basrah, Mosul and Kirkuk.

FLAG.—Horizontal stripes of red, white and black, with three green stars on the white stripe.

BRITISH EMBASSY
Sharia Salah Ud-Din,
Karkh, Baghdad

Ambassador Extraordinary and Plenipotentiary, His Excellency Sir John Campbell Moberly, K.B.E., C.M.G. (1982).

Counsellor, I. R. Callan (*Consul General*).

1st Secretaries, B. V. Sims (*Consul*); D. A. Wright, O.B.E. (*Commercial*).

Defence Attaché, Col. R. G. Eccles.

Air Attaché, Wg.-Cdr. J. F. H. Marriott.

There are no British Consular Offices outside Baghdad.

British Council Representative, G. E. P. Ness, Waziriya, 301, Street 3, (P.O. Box 298), Baghdad.

IRELAND

Position and Extent.—Ireland lies in the Atlantic Ocean, to the West of Great Britain, and is separated from Scotland by the North Channel and from Wales by the Irish Sea and St. George's Channel. The land area of the island is 32,408 sq. miles and its geographical position between 51° 26′ and 55° 21′ N. latitude and from 5° 25′ to 10° 30′ W. longitude. The greatest length of the island, from N.E. to S.W. (Torr Head to Mizen Head), is 302 miles, and the greatest breadth, from E. to W. (Dundrum Bay to Annagh Head), is 174 miles. On the N. Coast of *Achill Island* (Co. Mayo) are the highest cliffs in the British Isles, 2,000 feet sheer above the sea. Ireland is occupied for the greater part of its area by the *Central Plain*, with an elevation 50 to 350 ft. above mean sea level, with isolated mountain ranges near the coastline. The principal mountains, with their highest points, are the *Sperrin Mountains* (Sawel 2,240 ft.) of County Tyrone; the *Mountains of Mourne* (Slieve Donard 2,796 ft.) of County Down, and the *Wicklow Mountains* (Lugnaquilla 3,039 ft.); the *Derryveagh Mountains* (Errigal 2,466 ft.) of County Donegal; the *Connemara Mountains* (Twelve Pins 2,695 ft.) of County Galway; *Macgillicuddy's Reeks* (Carrantuohill 3,414 ft., the highest point in Ireland); and the *Galtee Mountains* (3,018 ft.) of County Tipperary, and the *Knockmealdown* (2,609 ft.) and *Comeragh Mountains* (2,470 ft.) of County Waterford. The principal river of Ireland (and the longest in the British Isles) is the *Shannon* (240 miles), rising in County Cavan and draining the central plain; the Shannon flows through a chain of loughs to the city of Limerick, and thence to an estuary on the western Atlantic seaboard. The *Slaney* flows into Wexford Harbour, the *Liffey* to Dublin Bay, the *Boyne* to Drogheda, the *Lee* to Cork Harbour, the *Blackwater* to Youghal Harbour, and the *Suir, Barrow* and *Nore,* to Waterford Harbour. As in Scotland, the principal hydrographic feature is the *Loughs,* of which Lough Neagh (150 sq. miles) in the north-east is the largest in Ireland and the British Isles, others being the Shannon Chain of *Allen, Boderg, Forbes, Ree* and *Derg,* and the Erne Chain of *Gowna, Oughter, Lower Erne,* and *Erne; Melvin, Gill, Gara* and *Conn* in the north-west; and *Corrib* and *Mask* (joined by a hidden channel) in the west. In County Kerry, to the east of Macgillicuddy's Reeks, are the famous *lakes of Killarney.*

Primitive Man.—Although little is known concerning the earliest inhabitants of Ireland, there are many traces of neolithic man throughout the island; a grave containing a polished stone axehead assigned to 2,500 B.C. was found at Linkardstown, Co. Carlow, in 1944, and the use of bronze implements appears to have become known about the middle of the 17th century B.C. In the later Bronze Age a Celtic race of *Goidels* appears to have invaded the island, and in the early Iron Age *Brythons* from South Britain are believed to have effected settlements in the south-east, while *Picts* from North Britain established similar settlements in the north. Towards the close of the Roman occupation of Britain, the dominant tribe in the island was that of the *Scoti,* who afterwards established themselves in Scotland.

History.—According to Irish legends, the island of Ierne was settled by a Milesian race, who came from Scythia by way of Spain, and established the *Kingdom* of *Tara,* about 500 B.C. The supremacy of the *Ardri* (high king) of Tara was acknowledged by eight lesser kingdoms (Munster, Connaught, Ailech, Oriel, Ulidia, Meath, Leinster and Ossory) ruled by descendants of the eight sons of Miled. The basalt columns on the coast of Antrim, eight miles from Portrush, known as the *Giant's Causeway,* are connected with the legendary history of Ireland as the remnants of a bridge built in the time of Finn M'Coul (Fingal) to connect Antrim with Scotland (Staffa).

Hibernia was visited by Roman merchants but never by Roman legions, and little is known of the history of the country until the invasions of *Northmen* (Norwegians and Danes) towards the close of the 8th century A.D. The Norwegians were distinguished as Findgaill (White Strangers) and the Danes as Dubgaill (Black Strangers), names which survive in "Fingall," "MacDougall" and "MacDowell," while the name of the island itself is held to be derived from the Scandinavian *Ira-land* (land of the Irish), the names of the Provinces being survivals of Norse dialect forms (Ulaids-tir, Laiginstir, Mumans-tir and Kunnak-tir). The outstanding events in the encounters with the Northmen are the *Battle of Tara* (980), at which the Hy Neill king Maelsechlainn II defeated the Scandinavians of Dublin and the Hebrides under the king Amlaib Cuarán; and the *Battle of Clontarf* (1014) by which the Scandinavian power was completely broken. After Clontarf the supreme power was disputed by the O'Briens of Munster, the O'Neills of Ulster, and the O'Connors of Connaught, with varying fortunes. In 1152 Dermod MacMurrough (Diarmit MacMurchada), the deposed king of Leinster, sought assistance in his struggle with Rauidhri O'Connor (the high king of Ireland), and visited Henry II, the Norman king of England. Henry authorized him to obtain armed support in England for the recovery of his kingdom, and Dermod enlisted the services of Richard de Clare, the Norman Earl of Pembroke, afterwards known as *Strongbow,* who landed at Waterford (Aug. 23, 1170) with 200 knights and 1,000 other troops for the reconquest of Leinster, where he eventually settled, after marriage with Dermod's daughter. In 1172 (Oct. 18) Henry II himself landed in Ireland. He received homage from the Irish kings and established his capital at Dublin. The invaders subsequently conquered most of the island and a feudal government was created. In the 14th and 15th centuries, the Irish recovered most of their lands, while many Anglo-Irish lords became virtually independent, royal authority being confined to the "Pale," a small district round Dublin. Though, under Henry VII, Sir Edward Poynings, as Lord Deputy, had passed at the *Parliament of Drogheda* (1494) the act later known as *Poynings' Law,* subordinating the Irish Legislature to the Crown, the Earls of Kildare retained effective power until, in 1534, Henry VIII began the reconquest of Ireland. Parliament in 1541 recognized him as King of Ireland and by 1603 English authority was supreme.

Christianity.—Christianity did not become general until the advent of St. Patrick. *St. Patrick* was born in Britain about 389, and was taken to Ireland as a slave about sixteen years later escaping to Gaul at the age of 22. In 432 he was consecrated Bishop of Auxerre and landed in Wicklow to establish and organize the Christian religion throughout the island.

REPUBLIC OF IRELAND

Uachtarán-na-hÉireann (President), Patrick J. Hillery, *born* 1923, *assumed office,* Dec. 3, 1976, *sworn in for 2nd term,* Dec. 3, 1983.

MEMBERS OF THE GOVERNMENT

Taoiseach, Garret Fitzgerald.
Tánaiste and Minister for Energy, Dick Spring.
Finance, Alan Dukes.
Foreign Affairs, Peter Barry.
Defence, Patrick Cooney.
Industry, Trade, Commerce and Tourism, John Bruton.
Justice, Michael Noonan.
Environment, Liam Kavanagh.
Public Service, John Boland.
Education, Gemma Hussey.
Agriculture, Austin Deasy.
Gaeltacht, and Fisheries and Forestry, Paddy O'Toole.
Health and Social Welfare, Barry Desmond.
Communications, Jim Mitchell.
Labour, Ruairi Quinn.

The present Government was formed by a coalition of the Fine Gael and Labour parties following a general election on Nov. 24, 1982.

EMBASSY IN LONDON
17 Grosvenor Place, SW1X 7HR
[01-235 2171]

Ambassador Extraordinary and Plenipotentiary, His Excellency Noel Dorr (1983).

Area and Population.—The Republic has a land area of 26,600 sq. miles, divided into the four Provinces of LEINSTER (Carlow, Dublin, Kildare, Kilkenny, Laoighis, Longford, Louth, Meath, Offaly, Westmeath, Wexford and Wicklow); MUNSTER (Clare, Cork, Kerry, Limerick, Tipperary and Waterford); CONNACHT (Galway, Leitrim, Mayo, Roscommon and Sligo); and part of ULSTER (Cavan, Donegal and Monaghan).

Total population of the Republic at the Census held on April 5, 1981, was 3,443,405 (males 1,729,354; females 1,714,051), a density of 50 persons per sq. kilometre. Provisional figures showed 66,815 births, 19,181 marriages and 32,744 deaths in the year 1983.

GOVERNMENT

The Constitution.—The constitution approved by a plebiscite on July 1, 1937, came into operation on December 29, 1937.

The Constitution declares that Ireland is a sovereign independent democratic State and affirms the right of the Irish Nation to choose its own form of Government, to determine its relations with other nations, and to develop its life, political, economic and cultural, in accordance with its own genius and traditions. The national territory is declared to be the whole island of Ireland, its islands and the territorial seas. Pending the reintegration of the national territory, and without prejudice to the right of the Parliament and the Government established by the Constitution to exercise jurisdiction over the whole of the national territory, the laws enacted by that Parliament shall have the like area and extent of application as those of the Irish Free State, which did not include the six counties of Northern Ireland. The national flag is the tricolour of green, white and orange. The Irish language, being the national language, is the first official language. The English language is recognized as a second official language.

The President.—The President (*Uachtarán na hÉireann*) is elected by direct vote of the people for a period of seven years. A former or retiring President is eligible for a second term. The President summons and dissolves Dáil Éireann on the advice of the *Taoiseach* (Head of the Government). He signs and promulgates laws. The supreme command of the Defence forces is vested in him, its exercise being regulated by law. He has the power of pardon. The President, in the exercise and performance of certain of his constitutional powers and functions, is aided and advised by a Council of State.

The Legislature.—The National Parliament (*Oireachtas*) consists of the President and two Houses: a House of Representatives (*Dáil Éireann*) and a Senate (*Seanad Éireann*).

Dáil Éireann is composed of 166 members elected by adult suffrage on a basis of proportional representation by means of the single transferable vote. All citizens, and such other persons in the state as may be determined by law, who have reached the age of 18 years and are not disqualified by law have the right to vote. Each Dáil may continue for a period not exceeding five years from the date of election.

Seanad Éireann is composed of 60 members, of whom 11 are nominated by the Taoiseach and 49 are elected; six by institutions of higher education, and 43 from panels of candidates, established on a vocational basis.

Members of Dáil Éireann are paid an allowance of £16,946 per annum (and members of Seanad Éireann £9,424). They are allowed such travelling facilities between Dublin and their constituencies as may be provided for in regulations made by the Minister for the Public Service and are, subject to certain restrictions, granted free telephone and postal facilities from Leinster House and allowances for overnight stays in Dublin.

The Executive.—The executive authority is exercised by the Government subject to the Constitution. The Government is responsible to Dáil Éireann, meets and acts as a collective authority, and is collectively responsible for the Departments of State administered by the Ministers.

The Taoiseach is appointed by the President on the nomination of Dáil Éireann. The other members of the government are appointed by the President on the nomination of the Taoiseach with the previous approval of Dáil Éireann. The Taoiseach appoints a member of the Government to be the *Tánaiste* who acts for all purposes in the place of the Taoiseach in the event of the death, permanent incapacitation, or temporary absence of the Taoiseach. The Taoiseach, the Tánaiste and the Minister for Finance must be members of Dáil Éireann. The other members of the Goverment must be members of Dáil Éireann or Seanad Éireann, but not more than two may be members of Seanad Éireann.

The result of the general election on Nov. 24, 1982 was as follows: *Fianna Fáil,* 75; *Fine Gael,* 70; *Labour,* 16; *Independent,* 3; *Workers' Party,* 2. Total membership including the *Ceann Comhairle* (Chairman), 166.

JUDICIAL SYSTEM

The Judicial system comprises Courts of First Instance and a Court of Final Appeal called the Supreme Court (*Cúirt Uachtarach*). The Courts of First Instance include a High Court (*Ard-Chúirt*) invested with full original jurisdiction in and power to determine all matters and questions, whether of law or fact, civil or criminal, and also Courts of local and limited jurisdiction, with a right of appeal as determined by law. The High Court alone has original jurisdiction to entertain the question of the validity of any law having regard to the provisions of the Constitution. The Supreme Court has appellate jurisdiction from all decisions of the High Court, with such exceptions and subject to such regulations as may be prescribed by law. No law may, however, be enacted excepting from the appellate jurisdiction of the Supreme Court the question of the validity of any law, having regard to the provisions of the Constitution.

Chief Justice, Hon. Thomas F. O'Higgins . IR£45,797
President of the High Court, Hon. Thomas
A. Finlay .... IR£39,724
Judges, Supreme Court, Hon. Brian
Walsh; Hon. Seamus Henchy; Hon.
Francis Griffin; Hon. Anthony Heder-
man; Hon. Niall J. McCarthy .... IR£37,447
Judges, High Court, Hon. Donal Barring-
ton; Hon. John M. Gannon; Hon. Liam
Hamilton; Hon. James McMahon; Hon.
Herbert R. McWilliam; Hon. Rory
O'Hanlon; Hon. Declan Costello; Hon.
James A. D'Arcy; Hon. Ronan Keane;
Hon. Ms. Mella Carroll; Hon. Henry D.
Barron; Hon. Francis D. Murphy; Hon.
Thomas J. Neylon (*ex officio*) .... IR£33,652
Attorney-General, Peter D. Sutherland.

RELIGION
(Census of 1978) (Provisional)

Catholic............................	3,203,574
Church of Ireland	95,339
Presbyterians........................	14,252
Methodists	5,813
Others	124,427
Total.....................	3,443,405

DEFENCE

Under the direction of the President, and subject
to the provisions of the Defence Act, 1954, the
military command of the Defence Forces is exercisable
by the Government through the Minister for Defence.
To aid and counsel the Minister for Defence on all
matters in relation to the Department of Defence on
which he may consult it, there is a Council of Defence
consisting of the Minister of State at the Department
of Defence, the Chief of Staff, the Adjutant-General
and the Quartermaster-General. Establishments provide at present for a Permanent Defence Force of
approximately 17,958 all ranks, including the Air
Corps and the Naval Service. Recruitment is on a
voluntary basis. Minimum term of enlistment is
three years in the Permanent Defence Force followed
by six years in the Reserve Defence Force. The
Defence Vote for the year ending Dec. 31, 1984,
provides for approximately 22,214 all ranks of the
Reserve Defence Force. Recruitment is also on a
voluntary basis; minimum term of enlistment is three
years. The Defence Estimate for the year ending Dec.
31, 1984 provides for an expenditure of
IR£230,000,000.

FINANCE

	1984 (*Estimated*)
Revenue	IR£5,970·7 m.
Expenditure	7,060·0 m.

The estimated revenue for 1984 includes:

	IR£m
Customs Duties	88·0
Excise Duties	1,261·0
Estate etc. Duties	1·0
Residential Property Tax	3·0
Capital Taxes	22·5
Stamp Duties	109·7
Income Tax............................	1,952·2
Income Levy	74·0
Corporation Tax	246·0
Value-Added Tax.......................	1,380·9
Agricultural Levies (E.E.C.)	18·0
Motor Vehicle Duties	108·5
Youth Employment Levy.................	79·0
Total (including other non-tax items) ...	5,970·7

The principal items of current expenditure for 1984
are:

	IR£m.
Debt Service	1,710
Agriculture	292
Defence	264
Garda (Police)	221
Prisons, Legal etc.......................	67
Education	851
Social Welfare	1,332
Health	908
Housing................................	178
Social Service Subsidies..................	334
Roads, Transport and Sanitation	70
Industry and Labour	185
Fisheries, Forestry and Tourism	531
Total...................................	7,060

The Gross Debt at end 1983 was IR£15,754,000 and
capital assets were IR£3,253,000.

EDUCATION

Primary education is directed by the State, with
the exception of approximately 76 private primary
schools with an enrolment of about 14,147 in 1982–83.
There were 3,391 State-aided primary schools with
an enrolment of 560,397 in 1982-83.
In 1982-83 there were 516 recognized secondary
schools with 206,413 pupils under private management (mainly religious orders), and 245 vocational
schools with 71,246 pupils. All these schools and
colleges are controlled by 38 statutory local Vocational Education Committees. There were 15 State
comprehensive schools in 1982–83 with a total
enrolment of 7,668 students, and 41 community
schools with an enrolment of 23,544 students. There
were also other miscellaneous second-level schools
and the total full-time enrolment at second-level for
1982–83 was 316,878.
Third-level education is catered for by five University Colleges, two National Institutes for Higher
Education, and also by third-level courses offered by
the Technical Colleges and Regional Technical Colleges and other miscellaneous third-level institutions. There were 47,674 full-time third-level
students in 1982–83, of whom 24,533 were attending
university courses.
The estimated State expenditure on education in
the period Jan. 1, 1984 to Dec. 31, 1984, excluding
administration and inspection, is Primary
IR£350,847,000; Post-Primary IR£405,449,000. The
vote for Universities and third-level Colleges
amounted to IR£98,660,000, while, in addition, grants
of IR£9,253,000 were provided in respect of the
Faculties of General Agriculture; Veterinary Medicine and Dairy Science.

MINERALS AND FISHERIES

Minerals.—340 persons were employed in the coal
mines in 1983 and 75,000 tons of coal won.
Sea Fisheries.—8,506 persons were employed in the
fisheries in 1982. Total value of all fish landed in 1982
was IR£43,809,000.

COMMUNICATIONS

Railways.—In the year ended Dec. 31, 1982, there
were 1,235 miles of railway all of standard (5 ft. 3 in.)
gauge; 12,813,000 passengers and 3,680,000 tons of
merchandise were conveyed; the receipts were
IR£49,943,000 and expenditure IR£121,607,000.
These figures are in respect of railway working by
Coras Iompair Eireann, the national transport undertaking which is now the only concern operating
a rail service in the State.

Road Motor Services.—In 1982 road motor vehicles carried 232,918,477 passengers, the gross receipts being IR£87,247,959.

Shipping.—In 1982 the number of ships with cargo and in ballast in the foreign trade which arrived at Irish ports was 11,705 (17,829,869 net registered tons); of these 2,534 (5,042,648 net registered tons) were of Irish nationality.

CIVIL AVIATION

Shannon Airport, 15 miles W. of Limerick, is on the main transatlantic air route. In 1983 the airport handled 991,770 passengers.

Dublin Airport, 6 miles N. of Dublin, serves the cross-channel and European services operated by the Irish national airline *Aer Lingus* and other airlines. In 1983 the airport handled 2,562,308 passengers.

Cork Airport, 5 miles S. of Cork serves the cross Channel and European services operated by *Aer Lingus* and other airlines. In 1983 the airport handled 324,546 passengers.

Trade with U.K.

	1982 £ Sterling	1983 £ Sterling
Imports from U.K....	2,890,497,000	3,055,275,000
Exports to U.K.	2,000,033,000	2,290,067,000

OVERSEAS TRADE

Year	Imports	Exports	Trade Balance
	IR£	IR£	IR£
1981..	6,578,406,480	4,777,570,799	1,800,835,681
1982..	6,816,154,975	5,691,441,609	1,124,713,366
1983..	7,355,394,884	6,935,861,156	419,533,728

PRINCIPAL ARTICLES

Principal imports in 1983 were:

	IR£
Live animals	96,610,914
Food, drink and tobacco	821,286,365
Petrol and petroleum products	864,385,657
Chemicals	838,557,214
Machinery	1,714,784,847
Transport equipment	405,027,931
Metal and manufactures	444,291,213
Textiles and clothing	628,156,148
Paper, paperboard and manufactures	214,591,148
Professional, scientific etc. goods	160,791,270

Principal exports in 1983 were:

	IR£
Live animals	234,376,428
Meat and meat preparations	554,816,512
Other food, drink and tobacco	1,136,579,482
Machinery and transport equipment	1,814,131,254
Clothing, headgear and footwear ...	169,240,181
Textiles	333,103,845
Metal ores and scrap	87,688,988
Metal and manufactures	204,971,251
Non-metallic mineral manufactures .	112,974,606
Chemicals	963,616,035
Professional, scientific etc., goods ...	307,803,273

CAPITAL.—Dublin (*Baile Atha Cliath*) is a City and County Borough on the River Liffey at the head of Dublin Bay. In April, 1981, its population (1981 Census) was 525,882.

Other cities and towns, with their populations at the Census of 1981 are ΨCork (136,344); ΨLimerick (60,736); ΨDun Laoghaire (54,496); ΨWaterford (38,473); ΨGalway (37,835); ΨDundalk (25,663).

FLAG.—Equal vertical stripes of green, white and orange.

NATIONAL DAY.—March 17 (St. Patrick's Day).

BRITISH EMBASSY
33 Merrion Road, Dublin 4

Ambassador Extraordinary and Plenipotentiary, His Excellency Alan C. Goodison, C.M.G., C.V.O. (1983).
Counsellor and Head of Chancery, R. F. Stimson.
First Secretaries, Miss D. M. Mills; J. J. Beale (*Agriculture*); D. L. S. Coombe (*Commercial*); V. J. W. Auster (*Economic*); J. C. Radcliffe; J. D. F. Holt.

ISRAEL
(Yisrael)

President of Israel, Chaim Herzog, *born* 1918, *elected* Mar. 22, 1983, *inaugurated,* May 5, 1983.

CABINET

Prime Minister, Minister of the Interior and Religious Affairs, Shimon Peres (*Lab.*).
Deputy P.M. and Foreign Minister, Yitzhak Shamir (*L.H.*).
Vice-Premier, and Education and Culture, Yitzhak Navon (*Lab.*).
Vice-Premier, and Construction and Housing, David Levy (*L.H.*).
Agriculture, Ayreh Neahamkin (*Lab.*).
Commerce and Industry, Ariel Sharon (*L.H.*).
Communications, Prof. Amnon Rubinstein (*Shinui*).
Defence, Yitzhak Rabin (*Lab.*).
Economy and Planning, Gad Y'Acobi (*Lab.*).
Energy and Infrastructure, Moshe Shahal (*Lab.*).
Finance, Yitzhak Moda'i (*L.L.*).
Health, Mordechai Gur (*Lab.*).
Immigration and Absorption, Yaakov Tsur (*Lab.*).
Justice, Moshe Nissim (*L.L.*).
Labour and Social Affairs, Moshe Katzav (*L.H.*).
Police, Haim Bar-Lev.
Science and Development, Gideon Patt (*L.L.*).
Tourism, Avrahim Sharir (*L.L.*).
Transportation, Haim Corfu (*L.H.*).
In Prime Minister's Office, Ezer Weizman (*Yahad*).
Without Portfolio, Moshe Arens (*L.H.*); Yosef Shapira (*Morasha*); Dr. Yosef Bourg (*National Religious Party*); Yigael Hurwitz (*Ometz*); Rabbi Yitzhak Peretz (*Shas*).

Lab.=Labour Party; *L.H.*=Likud Party—Herut faction; *L.L.*=Likud Party—Liberal faction.

EMBASSY IN LONDON
2 Palace Green, Kensington, W8 4QB
[01–937 8050]

Ambassador Extraordinary and Plenipotentiary, His Excellency Yehuda Avner.

Area and Population.—Israel lies on the western edge of the continent of Asia at the eastern extremity of the Mediterranean Sea, between lat. 29° 30′–33° 15′ N. and longitude 34° 15′–35° 40′ E. Its political neighbours are Lebanon on the North, Syria on the North and East, Jordon on the East and the Egyptian province of Sinai on the South-West.

The area is estimated at 7,992 square miles out of the 10,429 square miles which comprised the pre-1948 mandated territory of Palestine (the remainder being occupied by Israel since the Six Day War in June, 1967, and the Golan Heights). The population was estimated in 1980 at 3,921,700. Jewish immigration has made rapid progress since the establishment of the State in 1948. In 1912 there were only 83,790 Jews in Palestine out of a total population of 752,048. During the upheavals of 1948–49 a large number of Arabs left the country as refugees and settled in neighbouring countries. Since 1948 the population of Israel has more than quadrupled.

Hebrew and Arabic are the official languages of Israel. Arabs are entitled to transact all official

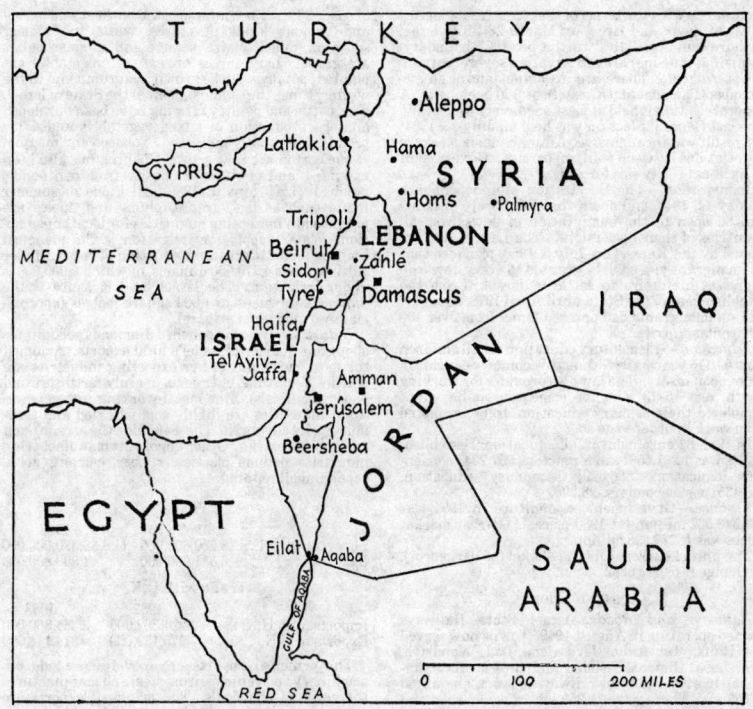

business with Government Departments in Arabic, and provision is made in the *Knesset* for the simultaneous translation of all speeches into Arabic.

Physical Features.—Israel comprises four main regions: (*a*) the hill country of Galilee and Judea and Samaria, rising in places to heights of nearly 4,000 feet; (*b*) the coastal plain from the Gaza strip to North of Acre, including the plain of Esdraelon running from Haifa Bay to the south-east, and cutting in two the hill region; (*c*) the Negev, a semi-desert triangular-shaped region, extending from a base south of Beersheba, to an apex at the head of the Gulf of 'Aqaba; and (*d*) parts of the Jordan valley, including the Hula Region, Tiberias and the south-western extremity of the Dead Sea. The principal river is the Jordan, which rises from three main sources in Israel, the Lebanon and Syria, and flows through the Hula valley and the canals which have replaced Lake Hula, drained in 1958. Between Hulata and Tiberias (Sea of Galilee) the river falls 926 ft. in 11 miles and becomes a turbulent stream. Lake Tiberias is 696 ft. below sea-level and liable to sudden storms. Between it and the Dead Sea the Jordan falls 591 ft. The other principal rivers are the Yarkon and Kishon. The largest lake is the *Dead Sea* (shared between Israel and Jordan); area 393 sq. miles, 1,286 feet below sea-level, 51·5 miles long, with a maximum width of 11 miles and a maximum depth of 1,309 ft.; it receives the waters of the Jordan and of six other streams, and has no outlet, the surplus being carried

off by evaporation. The water contains an extraordinarily high concentration of mineral substances. The highest mountain peak is Mount Meron, 3,962 feet above sea-level, near Safad, Upper Galilee.

Climate.—The climate is variable, similar to that of Lower Egypt, but modified by altitude and distance from the sea. The summer is hot but tempered in most parts by daily winds from the Mediterranean. The winter is the rainy season lasting from November to April, the period of maximum rainfall being January and February.

Antiquities.—The following are among the principal historic sites in Israel: Jerusalem: the Church of the Holy Sepulchre: the Al Aqsa Mosque and Dome of the Rock, standing on the remains of the Temple Mount of Herod the Great, of which the Western (wailing) Wall is a fragment; the Church of the Dormition and the Cœnaculum on Mount Zion; Ein Karem: Church of the Visitation, Church of St. John the Baptist. Galilee: The Sea; Church and Mount of the Beatitudes, ruins of Capernaum and other sites connected with the life of Christ. Mount Tabor: Church of the Transfiguration. Nazareth: Church of the Annunciation and other Christian shrines associated with the childhood of Christ. There are also numerous sites dating from biblical and mediæval days, such as Ascalon, Cæsarea, Atlit, Massada, Megiddo and Hazor. Other antiquities in the West Bank of Jordan and the Golan Heights at present occupied by Israel can now be visited from Israel. In accordance with the terms of the peace treaty signed between Egypt and Israel on March 26, 1979, Israel withdrew in April 1982 to the pre-1967 boundary, returning the Sinai area to Egyptian sovereignty.

Government.—There are a Cabinet and a single-chamber Parliament (*Knesset*) of 120 members. A general election is held at least once every four years. The last General Election was held on July 23, 1984; the result was inconclusive. After about six weeks of negotiations between political parties a Government of National Unity was formed.

Immigration.—The Declaration of Independence of May 14, 1948, laid down that "the State of Israel will be open to the immigration of Jews from all countries of their dispersion." The Law of Return, passed by the *Knesset* on July 5, 1950, provides that an immigrant visa shall be granted to every Jew who expresses his desire to settle in Israel. From the establishment of the State until April 1978, about 1·7 million immigrants had entered Israel from over 100 different countries.

Education.—Elementary education for all children from 5 to 15 years is free, though secondary education is not compulsory. The law also provides for working youth, age 15–18 who for some reason have not completed their primary education, to be exempted from work in order to do so.

In 1981–82 enrolment in all educational establishments was 1,261,556: kindergartens 267,234; elementary education, 586,829; secondary education, 278,435; post-secondary, 28,298.

Finance.—Government expenditure in 1981 was IS1,540,032 million (at 1980 prices). GNP at market prices was IS237,098 million.

The unit of currency, is the Shekel (of 100 agorot). Exchange rate, *see* p. 82.

COMMUNICATIONS

Railways and Roads.—Israel State Railways started operating in August 1949. Towns now served are Haifa, Tel Aviv, Jerusalem, Lod, Nahariya, Beersheba, Dimona, Ashdod and intermediate stations. In 1981 the total railway network amounted to 827 km. There were 11,950 km. of paved road and 592,916 licensed vehicles.

Shipping.—Israel's merchant marine had reached a total of 4,346,000 tons deadweight by December, 1980.

The chief ports are Haifa, a modern harbour, with a depth of 30 ft. alonside the main quay; the harbour on the Red Sea at Eilat, inaugurated in September 1965, has a capacity of 10,000 tons a day; Acre has an anchorage for small vessels; the deep-water port at Ashdod, 20 miles south of Tel Aviv, which started operations at the end of 1965, handled 5,742,000 tons of cargo in 1981. In the same year Israel's three main ports handled 12,029,000 tons of cargo.

Civil Aviation.—In 1980, 2,849,000 passengers passed through Ben Gurion airport, of which 585,051 arrived by charter flight.

PRODUCTION AND INDUSTRY

Agriculture.—The country is generally fertile and climatic conditions vary so widely that a large variety of crops can be grown, ranging from temperate crops, such as wheat and cherries, to subtropical crops such as sorghum, millet and mangoes. The famous "Jaffa" orange is produced in large quantities mostly in the coastal plain for export: high-profit export crops such as strawberries and cut flowers are increasingly important. The citrus yield during the 1980–81 season was 1,421,100 tons. Specialized glasshouse crops for export, such as flowers, tomatoes and strawberries, are becoming increasingly popular and exports of flowers in 1980 earned IS323,500,000. Olives are cultivated, mainly for the production of oil used for edible purposes and for the manufacture

of soap. The main winter crops are wheat and barley and various kinds of pulses, while in summer sorghum, millet, maize, sesame and summer pulses are grown. Large areas of seasonal vegetables are planted; potatoes can be grown in autumn and in the winter. Since the establishment of the State of Israel, beef, cattle and poultry farming have been developed and the production of mixed vegetables and dairy produce has greatly increased. Tobacco and medium staple cotton are now grown. Fishing has also been extended, and production (mostly from fish ponds) reached 24,200 tons in 1980. All kinds of summer fruits such as figs, grapes, plums and apples are produced in increasing quantities for local consumption. Water supply for irrigation is the principal limiting factor to greater production. The area under cultivation is 4,270,000 dunams, of which 2,030,000 is under irrigation. The Israel land measure is the *dunam*, equivalent to 1,000 square metres (approximately a quarter of an acre).

Industry.—In value polished diamonds account for about one quarter of Israel's total exports. Amongst the most important of her exporting industries are textiles, foodstuffs, chemicals (mainly fertilisers and pharmaceuticals). Her metal-working and science-based industries are highly sophisticated and technologically advanced. These include the aircraft and military industries. Other important manufacturing industries include plastics, rubber, cement, glass, paper and oil refining.

TRADE

	1982	1983
Imports	U.S.\$8,280,600,000	U.S.\$8,370,000,000
Exports	6,331,600,000	4,893,800,000

Trade with U.K.

	1982	1983
Imports from U.K....	£224,362,000	£354,860,000
Exports to U.K.	275,139,000	314,148,000

The principal imports are foodstuffs, crude oil, machinery and vehicles, iron, steel and manufactures thereof, and chemicals. The principal exports are citrus fruits and by-products, polished diamonds, plywood, cement, tyres, minerals, finished and semi-finished textiles.

CAPITAL.—Most of the Government departments are in Jerusalem (population, 1980, 448,200). A resolution proclaiming Jerusalem as the capital of Israel was adopted by the Israel parliament on Jan. 23, 1950. It is not, however, recognized as the capital by the United Nations. Other principal towns are ΨTel Aviv and district (1,005,000); ΨHaifa and district (566,400) and Beersheba and district (275,800).

FLAG.—White, with two horizontal blue stripes. the Shield of David in the centre.

NATIONAL DAY (1982)—April 28.

JERUSALEM

Until 1967 Jerusalem was divided between Israel and Jordan, two of the 36 recognized Christian Holy Places (in the New City) being under Jewish administration, the remainder under Arab administration in the Old City. At the conclusion of hostilities between Israel and the surrounding Arab countries in 1967 the entire city was under Israeli control.

BRITISH EMBASSY
192 Hayarkon Street, Tel Aviv.

Ambassador Extraordinary and Plenipotentiary, His Excellency C. W. Squire, C.M.G., M.V.O. (1984).

Counsellor, W. K. Prendergast (*Head of Chancery, Consul-General and Counsellor, Commercial*).

Defence, Naval and Air Attaché, Col. P. Mitchell, M.B.E.

British Council Representative, I. Watts, 140 Hayarkon Street, (P.O. Box 3302), Tel Aviv. There is a library in *Tel Aviv* and in *Jerusalem.*

ITALY
(Repubblica Italiana)

President of the Italian Republic, Alessandro Pertini, *born* 1896. *Elected* July 8, 1978.

COUNCIL OF MINISTERS

Prime Minister, Bettino Craxi (*S*).
Deputy P.M., Arnaldo Forlani (*CD*).
Regions, Carlo Vizzini.
Public Administration, Remo Gaspari (*CD*).
Relations with Parliament, Oscar Mammi (*Rep*).
Civil Defence, Giuseppe Zamberletti (*CD*).
E.E.C. Policy, Francesco Forte (*S*).
Scientific Research, Luigi Granelli (*CD*).
Southern Development, Salverino de Vito (*CD*).
Foreign Affairs, Giulio Andreotti (*CD*).
Interior, Oscar Scalfaro (*CD*).
Justice, Fermo Mino Martinazzoli (*CD*).
Budget, Pier-Luigi Romita (*SD*).
Finance, Bruno Visentini (*Rep*).
Treasury, Giovanni Goria (*CD*).
Defence, Giovanni Spadolini (*Rep*).
Education, Franca Falcucci (*CD*).

Public Works, Franco Nicolazzi (*SD*).
Agriculture, Filippo Maria Pandolfi (*CD*).
Transport, Claudio Signorile (*S*).
Posts, Antonio Gava (*CD*).
Industry, Renato Altissimo (*Lib*).
Labour, Gianni de Michelis (*S*).
Foreign Trade, Nicola Capria (*S*).
Merchant Navy, Gianuario Carta (*CD*).
State Participation, Clelio Darida (*CD*).
Health, Costante Degan (*CD*).
Tourism, Lelio Lagorio (*S*).
Cultural Heritage, Antonino Gullotti (*CD*).
Ecology, Alfredo Biondi (*Lib*).

S = Socialist; *CD* = Christian Democrat; *SD* = Social Democrat; *Rep* = Republican; *Lib* = Liberal.

ITALIAN EMBASSY IN LONDON
14 Three Kings Yard, Davies Street, W1Y 2EH
[01–629 8200]

Ambassador Extraordinary and Plenipotentiary, His Excellency Signor Andrea Cagiati (1980).
Minister-Counsellor, Sig. Umberto Vattani.
First Counsellors, Sig. Uberto Pestalozza; Sig. Ferdinando Zezza; Sig. Mario Quagliotti.
Counsellors, Sig. Gianfranco Varvesi; Sig. Leonardo Sampoli; Sig. Adolfo Treggiari.
First Secretary, Sig. Mario Polverini.
Air and Defence Attaché, Brig. Gen. Roberto Boemio.
Naval Attaché, Capt. Antonio Flamigni.

Military Attachés, Col. Salvatore Sabatino; Col. Rolando Mosca Moschini.
Cultural Attaché, Prof. Alessandro Vaciago.
Commodities Attaché, Dr. Igino Baccarini.
Financial Attaché, Sig. Corradino de Novellis.
Italian Consulate General, 38 Eaton Place, S.W.1. (01–235 9371).
Consul General, Sig. T. Fuxa.

Italy is a Republic in the South of Europe, consisting of a peninsula, the large island of Sicily and Sardinia, the island of Elba and about 70 other small islands. Italy is bounded on the N. by Switzerland and Austria, on the S. by the Mediterranean, on the E. by the Adriatic and Yugoslavia, and on the W. by France and the Ligurian and Tyrrhenian Seas. The total area is about 324,000 sq, kilometres (131,000 sq. miles).

The peninsula is for the most part mountainous, but between the Apennines, which form its spine, and the East coastline are two large fertile plains; of Emilia/Romagna in the north and of Apulia in the south. The Alps form the northern limit of Italy, dividing it from France, Switzerland, Austria and Yugoslavia. *Mont Blanc* (15,782 feet), the highest peak, is in the French Pennine Alps, but partly within the Italian borders are Monte Rosa (15,217 feet), Matterhorn (14,780 feet) and several peaks from 12,000 to 14,000 feet.

The chief rivers are the Po (405 miles), which flows through Piedmont, Lombardy and the Veneto, and the Adige (Trentino and Veneto) in the north, the Arno (Florentine Plain) and the Tiber (flowing through Rome to Ostia). The *Rubicon*, a small stream flowing into the Adriatic near Rimini formed the boundary between Italy and Cisalpine Gaul: "crossing the Rubicon" (as Cæsar did in 49 B.C., thus "invading" Italy in arms) is used to indicate definite committal to some course of action.

Population.—In Oct. 1983, Italy's population was 56,830,000. The annual rate of population increase between 1978 and 1983 was 0·3 per cent.

Government.—Italian unity was accomplished under the House of Savoy, after an heroic struggle from 1848 to 1870, in which the great patriots Mazzini (1805–72), Garibaldi (1807–82) and Cavour (1810–61) were the principal figures. It was completed when Lombardy was ceded by Austria in 1859 and Venice in 1866, and through the evacuation of Rome by the French in 1870. In 1871 the King of Italy entered Rome, and that city was declared to be the capital.

Benito Mussolini, known as *Il Duce* (The Leader) was born July 29, 1883, and was continuously in office as Prime Minister from Oct. 30, 1922, until July 25, 1943, when the Fascist *régime* was abolished. He was captured by Italian partisans while attempting to escape across the Swiss frontier and was put to death on April 28, 1945.

In fulfilment of a promise given in April, 1944, that he would retire when the Allies entered Rome a decree was signed on June 5, 1944, by the late King Victor Emmanuel III under which Prince Umberto, the King's son, became "Lieutenant-General of the Realm." The King remained head of the House of Savoy and retained the title King of Italy until his abdication on May 9, 1946, when he was succeeded by the Crown Prince.

A general election was held on June 2, 1946, together with a referendum on the question of Republic or Monarchy. The Referendum resulted in 12,717,923 votes for a Republic and 10,719,284 for a Monarchy. The Royal Family left the country on June 13, and on June 28, 1946, a Provisional President was elected.

Constitution.—The constitution of the Republic of Italy, approved by the Constituent Assembly on December 22, 1947, provides for the election of the President by an electoral college which consists of the two Houses of Parliament (the Chamber of Deputies and the Senate) sitting in joint session together with three delegates from each region (one in the case of the Valle d'Aosta). The President, who must be over 50 years of age, holds office for 7 years. He has numerous carefully defined powers, the main one of which is the right to dissolve one or both Houses of Parliament, after consultation with the Speakers.

Defence.—The period of conscription is 12 months for the Army and Air Force and 18 months for the Navy. The *Army* consists of 255,000 men with 550,000 reservists. It has three corps, each of one armed and three mechanical divisions, two independent mechanized brigades, four independent motorized brigades, five alpine brigades, one airborne brigade, two amphibious battalions and one missile brigade. There is also a para-military force, the *Carabinieri*, about 84,500 strong. The *Navy* consists of 1 helicopter carrier, 2 cruisers, 25 escorts including four G.W. destroyers, 9 submarines, 32 minesweepers and also coastal craft and fleet auxiliaries. Approximate strength: 42,000 men, with 160,000 reservists. The *Air Force* consists of 69,000 men, with 28,000 reservists and some 310 combat aircraft.

REGIONS OF ITALY

Rome and Central Italy.—Rome was founded, according to legend, by Romulus in the year now known as 753 B.C. It was the focal point of Latin civilization and dominion under the Republic and afterwards under the Roman Empire, and became the capital of Italy when the Kingdom was established in 1871. The capital is concerned mainly with tourism and government, but owing partly to the fact that the power of the Central Government is increasingly felt by industry, and that the headquarters of the giant State and parastatal companies are located there, Rome's importance as a business centre, although far from rivalling that of Milan, is steadily increasing.

Lombardy and Milan.—In the small area around Milan are to be found some 22 per cent of Italy's commercial and banking services and some 30 per cent of her industry. Here too, a market for consumer goods greatly exceeds that of any other comparable area in Italy. Lombardy's population of some 8·9 million is growing fast, both naturally and by immigration, and enjoys a *per capita* income some 40 per cent above the national average. The whole range of Italian industry is there. Most important are the steel, machine tool and motor car factories.

Turin and Piedmont.—Turin between 1861 and 1865 was Italy's first capital as the home of the Piedmontese Royal Family. Now with a population of over 1,000,000 it is famous as the headquarters of Europe's largest manufacturer of motor cars, produces 75 per cent. of Italy's motor vehicles and over 80 per cent. of its roller bearings. Turin is also Italy's second largest steel producing city. Piedmont is the centre of the Italian textile industry based mainly on Biella.

Genoa and the Ligurian Riviera.—Genoa is Europe's fourth largest port and handles one-third of Italy's foreign trade. About 80 per cent. of the goods handled are imports. Anglo-Genoese trade goes back to the 13th century and 20 per cent. of Genoa's imports still come from Britain. Genoa is Italy's third most important industrial city.

Venice and the North-East.—Venice is primarily a tourist attraction of unique beauty. It was founded in the middle of the 5th century by refugees from the mainland fleeing from Barbarian attacks. At the beginning of the 16th century it was one of the strongest and richest states of Europe, dominating Eastern Mediterranean trade. It lost its independence in 1797 when Napoleon handed it over to Austria. Industry is now developing in the Venice area, particularly on the autostrada linking Venice with her historical and now developing rivals, Verona, Vicenza, Padua and in the areas around Pordenone. Padua is known for mechanical equipment, Verona for paper and stationery, Treviso for consumer goods, and Valdagno for its woollen industry. An important electrical appliance industry is based near Treviso and at Pordenone. Near Trieste, which has a population of 277,135, is the modern Monfalcone shipyard. A Free Territory of Trieste was established in the Italian Peace Treaty of 1947 and was composed of Zone A, which included the city of Trieste and was administered by the Allied Military Government, and Zone B which was administered by Yugoslavia. In 1954 Zone A was handed over to the Italian authorities and Zone B to Yugoslavia. A treaty was signed in 1975 between Italy and Yugoslavia under which each country abandoned its residual claims to the other's zone. The Treaty was ratified in April 1977.

Tuscany, Emilia and Romagna.—Before the last war this area was the agricultural centre of Italy and there was little industry. Now there are large industrial centres at Bologna, Florence, Modena, Pistoia and Ravenna. Most of the new firms are small or medium-sized. In Prato there are about 1,000 textile firms. The footwear industry is based on Florence, reproduction furniture at Cascina and Poggibonsi, ceramics at Sassuolo, and glass and pottery at Empoli and Montelupo. Bologna is an important centre for the food industry. Florence, the capital of Tuscany was one of the greatest and most creative cities in Europe from the 11th to the 16th centuries. Under the Medici family in the 15th century flourished many of the greatest names in Italian art, including Filippo Lippi, Botticelli, Donatello and Brunelleschi. In the 16th century the tide turned to Rome where great Florentine artists like Michelangelo and Leonardo da Vinci flourished.

Naples and the Toe of Italy.—Naples, formerly the capital and administrative centre of the Kingdom of Naples and Sicily, remains the dominant city in the area, but it is beset with great problems of unemployment and the need for modernization. Around it, however, helped by Government incentives, industry is slowly developing, northwards to Caserta, southwards to Salerno and eastwards to Benevento.

Puglia.—Bari has always been a commercial centre. Fairly rapid industrial development is now taking place in the areas of Taranto, Bari, Brindisi and Foggia. At Taranto there are a highly-mechanized steel-works and a modern oil refinery. The Bari industrial zone has factories producing electronic and pneumatic valves, specialized vehicle bodies and tyres, etc. The main industry of Brindisi is a petrochemical plant. At Foggia there is a textile factory.

Sicily.—The island has a population of 5 million. The main source of income is agriculture, particularly citrus fruits, almonds and tomatoes, but this faces severe competition. Oil and oil products have recently supplanted citrus fruits as Sicily's main exports. The island is the scene of intense activity in the fields of oil, natural gas and petrochemicals. Small and medium sized industries, benefiting from the Government's incentives, are developing. Of the island's 279 factories, some 90 are in the Catania area and 60 around Palermo, the capital of the island. Tourism is bringing an increasing amount of revenue to Sicily.

Sardinia.—Sardinia is another autonomous region, with its capital at Cagliari. Six main industrial development areas have been officially designated; they are at Cagliari, Porto Vesme, Oristano, Sassari, Olbia and Arbatax. Lead and zinc mining are important. At Porto Vesme, a large smelting plant

has been constructed. In the same area, a company is investing some £60 million in an aluminium plant. There is a flourishing tourist industry.

The Economy

Italian gross domestic product in 1983 was $335,100 million. The economy developed fast in the fifties and early sixties with an average real annual increase in the gross national output of about 7 per cent. But its recovery after a setback caused by labour unrest in the last quarter of 1969, was slower than was expected. After a partial recovery came the energy crisis of 1973/74. In 1975 the balance of payments deficit was reversed and inflation halved but this was accompanied by stagnation and increasing unemployment. The rate of inflation for 1982–83 was 14·6 per cent.

Currency.—The unit of currency is the *lira*. (*see* also p. 81).

Industry.—The general index of industrial production (1980 = 100) stood at −4·9 in 1982–83. The State-owned sector of Italian industry is important, dominated by the holding companies IRI (mechanical, steel, airlines), ENI (petro-chemicals) and ENEL (electricity).

Mineral Production.—Italy is generally poor in mineral resources but since the war deposits of natural methane gas and small deposits of oil have been discovered and rapidly exploited. Production of lignite has also increased. Other minerals produced in significant quantities include iron ores and pyrites, mercury (over one-quarter of the world production), lead, zinc and aluminium. Marble is a traditional product of the Massa Carrara district. Tobacco is still a Government monopoly.

Agriculture.—Agriculture accounted for 5·8 per cent. of gross domestic product in 1982. The agricultural labour force was 22,750,000.

Tourist Traffic.—In 1980 an estimated 20 million foreign tourists visited Italy, and in 1979 foreigners spent an estimated L7,000 bn ($8·28 m). The net balance on tourism was about L5,500 bn.

Communications.—The main railway system is State-run by the *Ferrovia dello Stato*. A network of motorways (*autostrade*) covers the country, built and operated mainly by the IRI State-holding company and ANAS the State highway authority. The autostrada network covered 5,176 kms. in 1974. *Alitalia*, the principal international and domestic airline, is also State-controlled by the IRI group. Other smaller companies, including ATI (an *Alitalia* subsidiary) and Air Mediterranea operate on domestic routes. The Italian mercantile marine total of 8,378,000 tons in December, 1972, compared with 3,500,000 tons before the War.

Foreign Trade

The balance of trade in 1982 showed a deficit of 16,966 billion lire (£7·8 billion), 669 billion lire below the 1981 total.

The main markets for Italian exports in 1982 were the E.E.C. countries, which accounted for almost half of the total, and the U.S.A. Imports came principally from West Germany, France, U.S.A., Saudi Arabia and the Netherlands. The E.E.C. provided about 42 per cent. of imports.

Trade with U.K.

	1982	1983
Imports from U.K. ..	£2,022,771,000	£2,292,788,000
Exports to U.K. ...	2,745,094,000	3,188,219,000

Language and Literature.—Italian is a Romance language derived from Latin. It is spoken in its purest form at Siena (Tuscany), but there are numerous dialects, showing variously French, German, Spanish and Arabic influences. Sard, the dialect of Sardinia, is accorded by some authorities the status of a distinct Romance language. Italian literature (in addition to Latin literature, which is the common inheritance of the civilized world) is one of the richest in Europe, particularly in its golden age (Dante, 1265–1321; Petrarch, 1304–1374; and Boccaccio, 1313–1375) and in the renaissance during the fifteenth and sixteenth centuries (Ariosto, 1474–1533; Machiavelli, 1469–1527; Tasso, 1544–1595). Modern Italian literature has many noted names in prose and verse, notably Manzoni (1785–1873), Carducci (1835–1907) and Gabriele d'Annunzio (1864–1938). The Nobel Prize for Literature has been awarded to Italian authors on four occasions—G. Carducci (1906), Signora G. Deledda (1926), Luigi Pirandello (1934) and Salvatore Quasimodo (1959). In 1971, there were 85 daily newspapers published in Italy, of which 22 were published in Rome and 10 in Milan.

Education.—Education is free and compulsory between the ages of 6 and 14; this comprises five years at primary school and three in the "middle school", of which there are about 8,000. Pupils who obtain the middle school certificate may seek admission to any "senior secondary school", which is roughly equivalent to a U.K. grammar school but may be a lyceum with a classical or scientific or artistic bias, or may be an institute or school for teacher training, or may be an institute directed at technology (of which there are eight different types) or trade or industry (including vocational schools). Courses at the lyceums and technical institutes usually last for five years and success in the final examination qualifies for admission to university. There are 35 State and 14 private universities, some of ancient foundation; those at Bologna, Modena, Parma and Padua were started in the 12th century. University education is not free, but entrants with higher qualifications are charged reduced fees according to a sliding scale. In general, schools, lyceums and universities are financed by local taxation and central government grants.

CAPITAL.—Rome. Population of the commune (1981) 2,830,569.

1981 estimates of the population of the communes of the principal cities and towns are Milan, 1,634,638; Ψ Naples, 1,210,503; Turin, 1,103,520; Ψ Genoa, 760,300; Bologna, 455,853; Florence, 453,293; Ψ Palermo, 699,691; Ψ Bari, 370,781; Ψ Catania, 378,521. 1976 estimates of other towns: Ψ Venice, 362,494; Ψ Trieste, 267,857; Verona, 271,381; Padua, 242,186; Ψ Taranto, 243,750; Brescia, 215,156; Modena, 178,530; Ψ Parma, 177,894; Ψ Reggio Calabria, 177,883; Leghorn, 177,687; Ψ Salerno, 161,645; Ferrara, 155,172; Prato, 154,362; Foggia, 153,334. *Sicily,* Ψ Messina, 265,318; in *Sardinia,* Ψ Cagliari, 225,812.

ISLANDS.—*Pantelleria Island* (part of Trapani Province) in the Sicilian Narrows, has an area of 31 sq. miles and a population of 9,601. The *Pelagian Islands* (Lampedusa, Linosa and Lampione) are part of the Province of Agrigento and have an area of 8 sq. miles, pop. 4,811. The Tuscan Archipelago (including Elba), area 293 sq. km., pop. 31,861; Pontine Archipelago (including Ponza, area 10 sq. km., pop. 2,515); Flegrean Islands (including Ischia, area 60 sq. km., pop. 51,883); Capri; Eolian Islands (including Lipari, area 116 sq. km., pop. 18,636); Tremiti Islands (area 3 sq. km., pop. 426).

FLAG.—Vertical stripes of green, white and red.
NATIONAL DAY.—June 2.

BRITISH EMBASSY
Via XX Settembre 80a, 00187 Rome

Ambassador Extraordinary and Plenipotentiary, His Excellency The Lord Bridges, K.C.M.G. (1983).
Minister, G. E. Fitzherbert.

Minister, P. S. McLean, O.B.E. (*FAO*).
Defence and Military Attaché, Brig. A. Mornement.
Naval Attaché, Capt. E. H. M. Orme, R.N.
Air Attaché, Group-Capt. I. Madelin, R.A.F.
Counsellors, T. L. Richardson (*Head of Chancery*); L. C. R. Seeley.
1st *Secretaries,* C. A. Capella (*Labour*); J. Easton (*Administration*); M. J. Richardson (*Economic*); Mrs. E. T. Gregory (*Consul*); P. J. Morrice, J. H. Culver (*Commercial*); D. B. A. Evans (*Agriculture*); F. A. Doherty; (*Information*); S. M. J. Lamport.
Chaplain, Rev. Canon D. Palmer.

BRITISH CONSULAR OFFICES

There are British Consular Offices at *Milan, Rome, Naples, Genoa, Florence, Venice, Trieste* and *Cagliari* and a trade representative at *Turin.*

British Council Representative, D. J. Sharp, Palazzo del Drago, Via delle Quattro Fontane 20, 00184, Rome.

There are *British Council Offices* at Milan and Naples, each with a library.

IVORY COAST
(République de Côte d'Ivoire)

President, Félix Houphouët-Boigny, *elected* for five years in 1960; *re-elected* 1965, 1970, 1975 and 1980.

IVORY COAST EMBASSY IN LONDON
2 Upper Belgrave Street, SW1X 8BJ
[01–235 6991]

Ambassador Extraordinary and Plenipotentiary His Excellency Seydou Diarra (1983).
1st *Counsellor,* N' Goran Kouame.

The Ivory Coast is situated on the Gulf of Guinea between 5° and 10° N. and 3° and 8° W. and is flanked on the West by Guinea and Liberia, on the North by Mali and Upper Volta and on the East by Ghana. It has an area of about 127,000 square miles—tropical rain forest in the southern half and savannah in the northern—and a population of 7,000,000 (1979 estimate) divided into a large number of ethnic and tribal groups.

Although official French contact was made in the first half of the 19th century, the Ivory Coast became a Colony only in 1893 and was finally pacified in 1912. It decided on December 5, 1958 to remain an autonomous republic within the French Community; full independence outside the Community was proclaimed on August 7, 1960. Special agreements with France, covering financial and cultural matters, technical assistance, defence, etc., were signed in Paris on April 24, 1961. The Ivory Coast was a founder member of the *Conseil de l'Entente,* established on May 29, 1959, as a loose union embracing also, without abrogation of sovereignty, Dahomey, Niger and Upper Volta. Togo also adhered in June, 1966. The official language is French.

The Ivory Coast has a presidential system of government modelled on that of the United States and the French Fifth Republic. The single Chamber National Assembly of 147 members was elected in 1980. The defence of the Constitution which was promulgated on Nov. 3, 1960, is vested in a Supreme Court.

Finance.—The unit of currency of the Ivory Coast is the *Franc CFA* . In 1984, the Ivory Coast Budget allocated £731 m. for current expenditure and £350 m. for investment and equipment.

Trade.—The principal exports are coffee, cocoa, timber, palm oil, pineapples, bananas, and cotton all of which are exported to the U.K. Diamonds are exported. There are a few deposits of minerals including manganese and iron. Trade in 1982 was valued at: Imports, *Francs CFA* 718·5bn; Exports, *Francs CFA* 747·4 bn.

CAPITAL, ψAbidjan (population, 1,700,000) which is also the main port. In March 1983 the National Assembly ratified a decision to transfer the political and administrative capital from Abidjan to Yamoussoukro, but the date of the transfer is not yet known. FLAG.—3 vertical stripes, orange, white and green. NATIONAL DAY.—December 7.

BRITISH EMBASSY
Immeuble Les Harmonies, 01 B.P. 2581, Abidjan 01.

Ambassador Extraordinary and Plenipotentiary, His Excellency John Michael Willson (1983).

JAPAN
(Nihon Koku—Land of the Rising Sun)

Emperor of Japan, His Majesty Hirohito, *born* April 29, 1901; *succeeded* Dec. 25, 1926; *married* (1924) Princess Nagako (*born* March 6, 1903), daughter of the late Prince Kuniyoshi Kuni, and has issue two sons and four daughters.
Heir-Apparent, His Imperial Highness Prince Akihito, *Crown Prince*, *born* Dec. 23, 1933; *married* April 10, 1959, Miss Michiko Shoda and has issue Prince Naruhito Hironomiya, *born* Feb. 23, 1960, Prince Fumihito, *born* Nov. 30, 1965 and Princess Sayako, *born* April 18, 1969.

THE CABINET

Prime Minister, Yasuhiro Nakasone.
Justice, Eisaku Sumi.
Foreign Affairs, Shintaro Abe.
Finance, Noboru Takeshita.
Education, Yoshiro Mori.
Health and Welfare, Kozo Watanabe.
Agriculture, Forestry and Fisheries, Shinjiro Yamamura.
International Trade and Industry, Hikosaburo Okonogi.
Transport, Kichizo Hosoda.

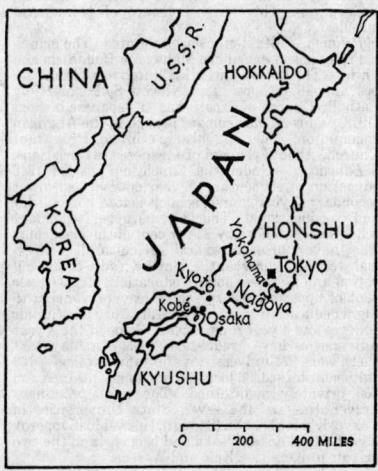

Posts and Telecommunications, Keiwa Okuda.
Labour, Misoji Sakamato.
Construction, Kiyoshi Mizuno.
Home Affairs, Seiichi Tagawa.
Administration and Coordination, Masaharu Gotoda.
Hokkaido Development Agency and National Land Agency, Sakonshiro Inamura.
Defence, Yuko Kurihara.
Economic Planning, Toshio Komoto.
Science and Technology Agency and Atomic Energy Commission, Michiyaka Isurugi.
Environment, Minoru Ueda.
Okinawa Development Agency, Ichiro Nakanishi.
Chief Cabinet Secretary, Takao Fujinami.

JAPANESE EMBASSY AND CONSULATE
43–46 Grosvenor Street, W1X 0BA
Information Centre: 9 Grosvenor Square, W1X 9LB
[01–493 6030]

Ambassador Extraordinary and Plenipotentiary, His Excellency Tsuyoshi Hirahara (1982).
Minister Plenipotentiary, Eiji Seki.
Ministers, Mitsukazu Ishikawa (*Financial*); Shunichi Uchimura (*Commercial*).
Counsellors, Katsuhisa Uchida; Shojiro Imanishi; Masao Kawase; Michio Maita; Atsushi Tokinoya; Atsushi Nagano.
Defence Attaché, Capt. Kiyomichi Terashita.

Area and Population.—Japan consists of 4 large and many small islands situated in the North Pacific Ocean between longitude 128° 6′ East and 145° 49′ East and between latitude 26° 59′ and 45° 31′ N., with a total area of 142,812 square miles and a population (1982) of 118,390,000.

Japan Proper consists of *Honshū* (or Mainland), 230,448 sq. km. (88,839 sq. m.), *Shikoku*, 18,757 sq. km. (7,231 sq. m.), *Kyūshū*, 42,079 sq. km. (16,170 sq. m.), *Hokkaido*, 78,508 sq. km. (30,265 sq. m.). Formosa and the Kwangtung Province, which had been throughout the years of Japanese expansion and aggression leased or annexed, reverted to Chinese sovereignty after the War of 1939–45.

After the unconditional surrender to the Allied Nations (Aug. 14, 1945), Japan was occupied by Allied forces under General MacArthur (Sept. 15, 1945). A Japanese peace treaty conference opened at San Francisco on Sept. 4, 1951, and on Sept. 8, 48 nations signed the treaty, which became effective on April 28, 1952. Japan then resumed her status as an independent power.

Vital Statistics.—The birth rate in 1980 was 13·6 per 1,000 (1947, 34 per 1,000; 1967, 19·7 per 1,000). It has been stated that a considerable part in reducing the birth rate to its present level was played by drastic methods, induced abortion and sterilization, the legal grounds for which had been extended by the Eugenics Law, 1948, to include economic and social hardships. The improving standard of living has also played an important part in keeping the birthrate down.

The death rate in 1980 was 6·2 per 1,000, compared with 17 per 1,000 in pre-war years.

Physiography.—The coastline exceeds 17,000 miles and is deeply indented, so that few places are far from the sea. The interior is very mountainous, and crossing the mainland from the Sea of Japan to the Pacific is a group of volcanoes, mainly extinct or dormant. Mount Fuji, the loftiest and most sacred mountain of Japan, about 60 miles from Tokyo, is 12,370 ft. high and has been dormant since 1707, but there are other volcanoes which are active, including Mount Aso in Kyūshū. There are frequent earthquakes, mainly along the Pacific coast near the Bay of Tokyo. Japan proper extends from sub-tropical in the south to cool temperate in the north. Heavy snowfalls are frequent on the western slopes of

Hokkaidō and Honshū, but the Pacific coasts are warmed by the Japan current. There is a plentiful rainfall and the rivers are short and swift-flowing offering abundant opportunities for the supply of hydro-electric power.

Government.—According to Japanese tradition, Jimmu, the First Emperor of Japan, ascended the throne on Feb. 11, 660 B.C. Under the constitution of Feb. 11, 1889, the monarchy was hereditary in the male heirs of the Imperial house. A new constitution approved by the Supreme Allied Commander was published on March 6, 1946, superseding the "*Meiji Constitution*" of 1889, and containing many radical changes based on the constitutional practices of the United Kingdom, U.S.A. and France.

The new constitution came into force on May 3, 1947. Legislative authority rests with *The Diet*, which is bicameral, consisting of a *House of Representatives* and a *House of Councillors*, both Houses being composed of elected members. Executive authority is vested in the Cabinet which is responsible to the Legislature.

The Conservatives have governed Japan almost without interruption since World War II. Since 1955, when it was formed, the Liberal Democratic Party has maintained an absolute majority in the House of Representatives, though it lost a number of seats in the December 1983 election and subsequently formed a coalition government with the 8 members of the New Liberal Club. The present strength of the parties in the House of Representatives is: Liberal Democratic Party, 246 (including New Liberal Club, 8); Japan Socialist Party, 112; Komeito, 59; Democratic Socialist Party, 39; Japan Communist Party, 27; Shaminren, 3; Independents, 5; vacant, 2.

The House of Councillors whose powers are subordinate to the House of Representatives, re-elects half of its members every three years. In July, 1984, the strength of the Parties was: Liberal Democratic Party, 136; Japan Socialist Party, 43; Komeito, 27; Japan Communist Party, 14; Democratic Socialist Party, 13; Sangiin no kai, 8; Shinsei Club, 4; Independents, 4; vacant, 3.

Agriculture and Livestock.—Owing to the mountainous nature of the country not more than one-sixth of its area is available for cultivation. The forest land includes Cryptomeria japonica, Pinus massoniana, Zeikowaskeaki, and Paulownia imperialis, in addition to camphor trees, mulberry, vegetable wax tree and a lacquer tree which furnishes the celebrated lacquer of Japan. The soil is only moderately fertile, but intensive cultivation secures good crops. The tobacco plant, tea shrub, potato, rice, wheat and other cereals are all cultivated: rice is the staple food of the people, about 10,270,000 metric tons being produced in 1982. Fruit is abundant, including the mandarin, persimmon, loquat and peach; European fruits such as apples, strawberries, pears, grapes and figs are also produced.

Minerals.—The country has mineral resources, including gold and silver, and copper, lead, zinc, iron chromite, white arsenic, coal, sulphur, petroleum, salt and uranium, but iron ore, coal and crude oil are among the principal post-war imports to supply deficiencies at home.

Industry.—Japan is the most highly industrialized nation in the Far East, with the whole range of modern light and heavy industries, including automobiles, electronics, metals, machinery, chemicals, textiles (cotton, silk, wool and synthetics), cement, pottery, glass, rubber, lumber, paper, oil refining and shipbuilding. The labour force of Japan in 1982 (average) was 58,070,000, of which 1,430,000 were unemployed. Of the total labour force, some 51,630,000 were engaged in non-agricultural industries, 5,010,000 in agriculture, forestry and fisheries.

Communications.—There were 26,587 kilometres of Government and private railroad (steam and electric) in March, 1982. The merchant fleet (ocean-going ships over 3,000 tons gross) consisted of 1,079 vessels totalling 34,220,000 tons gross in March, 1982.

Armed Forces.—After the unconditional surrender of August, 1945, the Imperial Army and Navy were disarmed and disbanded.

Although the Constitution of Japan prohibits the maintenance of armed forces, internal security forces came into being in 1950, and 1952. In July, 1954, the National Safety Agency was renamed the Defence Agency, the Forces under it the Ground Self Defence Force and the Maritime Self Defence Force respectively, and a new arm, the Air Self Defence Force was created. At the same time the mission of the forces was extended to include the defence of Japan against direct and indirect aggression.

A Treaty of Mutual Co-operation and Security between Japan and the U.S.A. was signed in January, 1960, replacing an earlier Security Treaty signed in 1951 at the same time as the Peace Treaty. By this Treaty each country recognized that an armed attack against either in the territories under the administration of Japan would be dangerous to its own safety and declared that it would act to counter the danger.

The defence budget allocated for the fiscal year 1984–85 amounted to Yen 2,935 billion, equivalent to 0·99 per cent of Japan's Gross National Product, or 4·7 per cent of the total budget. The authorized uniformed strength was: Ground Self-Defence Force (GSDF) 180,000 (Reserve 41,600); Maritime Self-Defence Force (MSDF) 43,897 (Reserve 600); Air Self-Defence Force (ASDF) 46,204. Actual strengths of all three services are slightly below their authorised figure.

In 1981 the GSDF was organized into five regional Armies, totalling thirteen Divisions, one of which had recently been reorganized as an Armoured Division. Major equipment includes tanks, APC's, towed and SP guns and rocket launchers, Hawk AA missiles, and 385 aircraft. Equipment is now largely manufactured in Japan.

The MSDF has 164 warships and auxiliaries including four DDH, four TARTAR-equipped GMDs, 42 destroyers, 14 submarines and 99 others, 205 fixed-wing aircraft and 97 helicoptors.

The ASDF has 800 aircraft including 380 trainers; 41 transports and 56 support aircraft including helicoptors). There are 6 groups of Nike SAM missiles.

Religion.—All religions are tolerated. The principal religions of Japan are Mahayana Buddhism and Shinto. The Roman Catholic Church has 2 archbishops and 16 bishops. The Nippon Seikokai (Holy Catholic Church of Japan) has 11 Japanese bishops (1978) and is an autonomous branch of the Anglican communion. There is also a United Protestant Church. About 1 per cent of Japanese are Christians.

Education.—Under the Education Law of 1948 education at elementary (6 year course) and lower secondary (3 year course) schools is free, compulsory and co-educational. The (3 year) upper secondary schools are attended by 93 per cent of the age group. They have courses in general, agricultural, commercial, technical, mercantile marine, radio-communication and home-economics education, etc. 37·4 per cent of upper secondary school leavers went on to higher education in 1981. There are 2 or 3 year junior colleges and 4 year universities. Some of the 4 year universities have graduate schools. In May 1981 there were 974 universities and junior colleges, 128 state maintained, 86 local authority maintained and 760 privately maintained. The most prominent universities are the seven State Universities of Tokyo, Kyoto, Tohoku (Sendai), Hokkaido (Sapporo), Kyushu (Fukuoka), Osaka and Nagoya, and the two private universities, Keio and Waseda.

Language and Literature.—Japanese is said to be one of the Uro-Altaic group of languages and remained a spoken tongue until the fifth–seventh centuries A.D., when Chinese characters came into use. Japanese who have received school education (99·8 per cent of the population) can read and write the Chinese characters in current use (about 1,800 characters) and also the syllabary characters called Kana. English is the best known foreign language. It is taught in all middle and high schools and universities. By 1981, the number of public libraries was 1,399 with 69,102,557 volumes. In addition there are 920 university libraries with 113,171,629 volumes. There are 125 daily newspapers in Japan. Japan's total newspaper circulation was estimated at 47,256,150 copies and 1·30 per household at the end of 1981.

FINANCE

The Budget for the financial year 1983–84, ending on March 31, was initially estimated at *Yen* 50,600,000 million for revenue and expenditure on the general account, virtually unchanged from the previous year.

For rate of exchange *see also* p. 81.

PRODUCTION AND TRADE

Being deficient in natural resources, Japan has had to develop a complex foreign trade. Principal imports in 1983 consisted of mineral oils (46·6 per cent), raw materials (14·4 per cent) e.g. metal ores and scrap, 5·2 per cent, timber, 3·1 per cent; raw cotton, 0·9 per cent; and soya beans (1·1 per cent), foodstuffs (11·8 per cent) (e.g. wheat and sugar), machinery (8·2 per cent), chemicals (5·7 per cent) and textiles (2·4 per cent).

Principal exports consist of steel (8·7 per cent), ships (4·1 per cent), automobiles (17·8 per cent), electric machinery and appliances (15·6 per cent), non-electric machinery (15·7 per cent), chemicals (4·8 per cent) and textile goods (4·5 per cent).

FOREIGN TRADE

	1982	1983
	($1,000)	($1,000)
Total imports	131,931,214	126,393,051
Total exports	138,831,166	146,902,471

Trade with U.K.

	1982	1983
	(£1,000)	(£1,000)
Imports from U.K.	1,874,196	1,940,048
Exports to U.K.	4,813,019	4,982,507

CAPITAL.—TOKYO. Population, 11,806,729. The other chief cities had the following populations: ΨOsaka (2,629,135); ΨNagoya (2,103,460); ΨYokohama (2,925,877); Kyoto, the ancient capital (1,486,873); ΨKobé (1,401,928); Kita-Kyushu (1,060,470); ΨSapporo (1,515,582); ΨKawasaki (1,076,673); ΨFukuoka (1,144,802).

FLAG.—White, charged with sun (red).

Yokohama, by sea *via* Suez Canal, 11,072 miles (30 days); *via* Panama, 12,544 miles (27 days); Tokyo, by air (British Airways polar route), 8,382 miles distant from London: transit, 17 hrs.

BRITISH EMBASSY

No. 1 Ichiban-cho, Chiyoda-ku, Tokyo 102

Ambassador Extraordinary and Plenipotentiary, His Excellency Sir Sydney Giffard, K.C.M.G. (1984).

Minister, B. Hitch, C.V.O.

Counsellors, D. J. Wright (*Economic*); J. W. Hodge (*Commercial*); M. R. Lewis (*Financial*); J. A. Barnett, C.B.E., (*Cultural*); A. P. F. Bache (*Head of Chancery*); Dr. C. C. Bradley (*Science and Technology*).

1st Secretaries, P. W. Denison-Edson, M.V.O. (*Economic*); K. C. James; W. J. A. Buckley (*Administration*); P. S. Dimond (*Commercial*); Dr. W. J. Gillan (*Science and Technology*); D. W. F. Warren-Knott, O.B.E. (*Consul*); A. F. Pinnell (*Information*); N. K. Darrock; Dr. G. Thom; P. A. Heald, M.B.E.

Defence and Military Attaché, Col. M. R. Grove.

Naval Attaché, Capt. R. H. S. Thompson, R.N.

Air Attaché, Gp. Capt. D. I. Oakden, R.A.F.

There is a British Consulate-General at *Osaka* and an Honorary Consulate at *Kita Kyushu.*

British Council Representative, J. A. Barnett, C.B.E., 1 Jimbo-cho, 2-chome, Kanda, Chiyoda-Ku, Tokyo 101. There is also an office and library in Kyoto.

JORDAN
(The Hashemite Kingdom of The Jordan)

King of the Jordan, Hussein, G.C.V.O., *born* November 14, 1935, *succeeded* on the deposition of his father, King Talal, Aug. 11, 1952, *assumed constitutional powers,* May 2, 1953, on coming of age.

Crown Prince, Prince Hassan, third son of King Talal of Jordan, *born* 1948, *appointed Crown Prince,* April 1, 1965.

CABINET

Prime Minister and Minister for Defence, Ahmad Ubeidat.

Deputy Prime Minister and Minister of the Interior, Suleiman Arar.

Labour, Dr. Taysir Abdul Jaber.

Information, Mrs. Laila Sharaf.

Education, Hikmat Saket.

Finance, Dr. Hanna Odeh.

Public Works, Rayef Nijm.

Agriculture, Mohammad Bashir.

Minister of Awqaf and Islamic Affairs, Abed Khalaf Daoudieh.

Justice (and Minister of State for Prime Ministry Affairs), Ahmad Abdul Karim Tarawneh.

Health, Dr. Kamel Ajlouni.

Communications, Dr. Mohammad Zaben.

Culture and Youth, and Antiquities, Dr. Abdullah Oweidat.

Industry and Trade, and Tourism, Dr. Jawad Anani.

Supply, Ibrahim Ayyoub.

Municipal, Rural and Environmental Affairs, Hamdullah Nabulsi.

Social Development, Abdul Salam Kana'an.

Foreign Affairs, Taher Masri.

Affairs of the Occupied Land, Shakwat Mahmoud.

Transport, Taher Hikmat.

JORDANIAN EMBASSY
6 Upper Phillimore Gardens, W8 7HB
[01-937 3685]

Ambassador Extraordinary and Plenipotentiary, His Excellency Hani Tabbara.

Counsellor, Nayef al-Kadi.

Defence Attaché, Brig. Musa Mohammad Adwan.

Service Office: 16 Upper Phillimore Gardens, W.8. (01–937–9611).

Area and Population.—The Kingdom, which covers 37,700 sq. miles, is bounded on the north by Syria, on the west by Israel, on the south by Saudi Arabia and on the east by Iraq. Since the hostilities of June, 1967, that part of the country lying to the west of the Jordan River has been under Israeli occupation. The majority of the population are Sunni Moslems and Islam is the religion of the State, freedom of belief is, however, guaranteed by the Constitution. Total population on the East Bank of the Jordan is estimated to be 2,400,000. (*For* MAP, *see* p. 861).

History.—After the defeat of Turkey in the First World War the Amirate of Transjordan was established in the area east of the River Jordan as a state under British mandate. The mandate was terminated after the Second World War and the Amirate, still ruled by its founder, the Amir Abdullah, became the Hashemite Kingdom of Jordan. Following the 1948 war between Israel and the Arab States, that part of Palestine remaining in Arab hands (but excluding Gaza) was incorporated into the Hashemite Kingdom. King Abdullah was assassinated in 1951; his son Talal ruled briefly but abdicated in favour of the present King, Hussein, in 1952. All of Jordan west of the River has been under Israeli occupation since 1967. As a result of the wars of 1948 and 1967 there are about 950,000 refugees and displaced persons living in East Jordan, about 200,000 of whom live in refugee and displaced persons camps established by the U.N. Relief and Works Agency (UNRWA). In addition there are some 300,000 entirely self-supporting Palestinian members of the East Jordanian community.

Government.—The present constitution of the Kingdom came into force in 1952. It provides for a senate of 30 members (all appointed by the King) and an elected House of Representatives of 60 persons. Half of the constituencies of the latter are on the West Bank and since the Israeli occupation of this area in 1967 it has not been possible to hold elections there. For a time membership of the House continued on the basis of pre-1967 membership but was eventually suspended in 1974. The Lower House was recalled in January 1984. By-elections were held in March 1984 to fill East Bank seats which had become vacant as a result of the death of deputies elected in 1967, and the House appointed new West Bank members to bring itself up to full strength. The King himself appoints the members of the Council of Ministers. Crown Prince Hassan normally acts as Regent when King Hussein is away from Jordan. Following the Arab summit meeting at Rabat in October 1974, and the U.N. General Assembly in November, at which the Palestinian Liberation Organization achieved recognition as the sole legitimate representative of the Palestinian people, King Hussein took measures to amend the 1952 constitution to take account of the resultant change in the status of the West Bank in relation to the administration of Jordan east of the river.

Production and Industry.—West Jordan is fertile, though many areas have suffered from soil erosion. In East Jordan the main agricultural areas are the east part of the Jordan Valley, the hills overlooking the Valley and the flatter country to the south of Amman and around Madaba and Irbid. The rest of the country is desert and semi-desert. The principal crops are wheat, barley, vegetables, olives and fruit (mainly grapes and citrus fruits). Agricultural production in the Jordan Valley has increased considerably in recent years due to the extension of the East Ghor Canal and the King Talal Dam. The only important industrial products are raw phosphates (production 1983: 4,700,000 tons)and potash, most of which is exported. There are schemes under construction for the production of potash and phosphate fertilizers. Tourism has recovered fast since the Israeli occupation of the West Bank in 1967. International-class hotels have been built to cater for the tourists visiting the archæological sites of East Jordan and the resort of Aqaba, and for businessmen visiting Jordan or stopping en route to Baghdad. The Trans-Arabian oil pipeline (Tapline) runs through North Jordan on its way from the eastern province of Saudi Arabia to the Lebanese coast of Sidon. A branch pipeline feeds a refinery at Zerqa (production 1982: 2,500,000 tons) which meets most of Jordan's requirements for refined petroleum products.

Communications.—The trunk road system is good. Amman is linked to Damascus, Baghdad and Jedda by tarred roads which are of considerable importance in the overland trade of the Middle East. The former Hejaz Railway enters Jordan east of Ramtha and runs through Zerqa and Amman to Ma'an with a spur to the top of the Ras al-Naqb escarpment. The formerly abandoned section from Ma'an to Medina in Saudi Arabia is being studied and redesigned by consultants. A total of 1,744 vessels called at Aqaba in 1981 and 9,334,748 tons of cargo were handled. Much of Jordan's trade moves overland to and from the ports in Syria and Lebanon. The Royal Jordanian Airline (ALIA) operates from Amman Airport to other cities in the Middle East and Gulf area, to most major European cities, to New York, and to Bangkok in the Far East. There is also a service to the airport at Aqaba.

FINANCE

	1982	1983
	JD (Thousands)	
Expenditure	765,000	775,000
Domestic Revenue........	338,000	424,000
Foreign Grants	215,000	183,000
Foreign Loans	64,240	101,000
Surplus/Deficit............	−26,000	−33,700

Trade with U.K.

Britain has been a leading source of supply of imported goods to Jordan for some time.

	1982	1983
Imports from U.K.	£295,000,000	£262,503,000
Exports to U.K.	17,400,000	28,688,000

CAPITAL.—Amman. Population, 750,000 (1980).

FLAG.—Black, white and green horizontal stripes, surcharged with white seven-point star on red triangle.

NATIONAL DAY.—May 25 (Independence Day).

BRITISH EMBASSY
Third Circle, Jebel Amman (P.O. Box 87),
Amman

Ambassador Extraordinary and Plenipotentiary, His Excellency Arthur John Coles (1984).
Counsellors, P. A. Rafferty, C.V.O., M.B.E. (*Consul-General*); D. R. Spedding, C.V.O., O.B.E.
Defence Attaché, Col. T. W. Hackworth, O.B.E.
Air Attaché, Wing-Cdr. N. M. J. Fraser.
1st Secretaries, A. R. Brown, M.V.O. (*Commercial*); A. J. Coulson, M.V.O. (*Information*).
2nd Secretaries, M. Hicks (*Administration*); L. B. Evans (*Development*); Miss J. James (*Consul*).

BRITISH COUNCIL
Representative, D. A. M. Latta, Amman Centre, Rainbow Street, (P.O. Box 634), Jebel Amman, Amman.

KOREA

Korea is situated between 124° 11″ and 130° 57′ E. long., and between 33° 7′ and 43° 1″ N. lat. It has an area of 85,256 sq. miles with an estimated population of about 57,000,000, of whom about 39,000,000 live south of the present dividing line. The southern and western coasts are fringed with innumerable islands, of which the largest, forming a province of its own, is Cheju.

History.—The last native dynasty (Yi) ruled from 1392 until 1910, in which year Japan formally annexed Korea. The country remained an integral part of the Japanese Empire until the defeat of Japan in 1945, when it was occupied by troops of the U.S.A. and the U.S.S.R., the 38th parallel being fixed as the boundary

between the two zones of occupation. The U.S. Government endeavoured to reach agreement with the Soviet Government for the creation of a Korean Government for the whole country and the withdrawal of all Russian and American troops. These efforts met with no success, and in September, 1947, the U.S. Government laid the whole question of the future of Korea before the General Assembly of the United Nations. The Assembly in November, 1947, resolved that elections should be held in Korea for a National Assembly under the supervision of a temporary Commission formed for that purpose by the United Nations and that the National Assembly when elected should set up a Government. The Soviet Government refused to allow the Commission to visit the Russian Occupied Zone and in consequence it was only able to discharge its function in that part of Korea which lies to the south of the 38th parallel.

A general election was held on May 10, 1948, and the first National Assembly met in Seoul on May 31. The Assembly passed a constitution on July 12, and on July 20 elected Dr. Syngman Rhee as the first President of the Republic of Korea, an office which he held until 1960. On August 15, 1948, the Republic was formerly inaugurated and American Military Government came to an end.

Meanwhile in the Russian-occupied zone north of the 38th parallel the Democratic People's Republic had been set up with its capital at Pyongyang; a Supreme People's Soviet was elected in September 1948, and a Soviet-style Constitution adopted.

The Korean War.—The country remained effectively divided into two along the line of 38th parallel until the aggression of June 25, 1950, when the North Korean forces invaded South Korea. An emergency meeting of the U.N. Security Council adopted a Resolution calling for an immediate cease fire and the withdrawal of North Korean forces. This was ignored and the communist advance continued. In response to Security Council recommendations that United Nations members should furnish assistance to repel the attack, 16 nations including the U.S.A. and the U.K. came to the aid of the Republic of Korea. However the communist advance could not be contained until eventually a front was established around Pusan. Later, following a successful U.S. marine landing at Inchon, the communist forces were driven beyond the 38th parallel. At this point the Chinese "volunteers" joined the campaign and although the U.N. forces were initially driven back beyond Seoul they regrouped and threw the communist forces back to approximately the old dividing line. The fighting was ended by an Armistice Agreement signed by the U.N. Commander-in-Chief and the Commander of the North Korean army and the Chinese People's "volunteers" on July 27, 1953. By this Agreement (which was not signed by the representatives of the Republic of Korea) the line of division between North and South Korea remained in the neighbourhood of the 38th parallel. The Geneva Conference discussed Korea in 1954, but failed to agree on measures for re-unifying the country.

Republic of Korea

President, Chun Doo Hwan (August, 1980).
Prime Minister, Chin Lee Chong (1983).

KOREAN EMBASSY
4 Palace Gate, W8 5NF
[01–581 0247]

Ambassador Extraordinary and Plenipotentiary, His Excellency Dr. Young Hoon Kang (1981).
Minister, Dong-Jin Choi.
Counsellors, Sung-Wuk Huh; Soon Tae Kwon; Pil Joo Sung.
Press and Cultural Attaché, Yun Kil Yang.

The Republic of Korea has been officially recognized by the Governments of the United States, France, Great Britain, and most other countries except the U.S.S.R. and its satellites.

President Syngman Rhee was overthrown by a popular rising in 1960. After a year of unstable government a new regime was set up on May 16, 1961 by an army officers' *coup* led by Major General Park Chung Hee. On March 22, 1962 he took over as acting President. He was elected President in December 1963 and again in 1967, 1971, 1972 and 1978.

President Park was assassinated by the head of the Korean Central Intelligence Agency, Kim Jae Kyu, on October 26, 1979. The country was placed under partial martial law. The then Prime Minister Choi Kyu Hah was elected President that December but resigned in August 1980 to be succeeded by Gen. Chun Doo Hwan. The constitution was revised and new elections held. President Chun was re-elected and his Democratic Justice Party gained a majority in the National Assembly after elections in March 1981.

Constitution.—The Constitution was revised in 1980. The President, who is Head of State, Chief of the Executive and Commander-in-Chief of the Armed Forces, is indirectly elected for a single term of seven years by an electoral college of over 5,000 members, who are directly elected. He appoints the Prime Minister with the consent of the National Assembly, and members of the State Council on the recommendation of the Prime Minister. The President is also empowered to take wide-ranging measures in an emergency, including the declaration of martial law, but must obtain the agreement of the National Assembly.

The National Assembly is directly elected for a four-year term, one third by proportional representation, two thirds from constituencies. The Assembly's powers include legislation, decision on the Budget, and approval of the Prime Minister and members of the State Council.

Armed Forces.—The Republic of Korea has an army of about 520,000, a small navy mostly for coastal patrol and protection duties, an air force with over

500 combat aircraft and a marine corps which is incorporated in the navy. About six per cent of the nation's G.N.P. is currently spent on defence.

Language and Literature.—Despite the great cultural influence of the Chinese, Koreans have developed and preserved their own cultural heritage. The Korean language is of the Ural-Altaic Group. Its script, Hangul, was invented in the 15th century; prior to this Chinese characters alone were used. Also invented around this time was the first metal movable printing type. The first works translated into Hangul were Buddhist, Confucian and other classics and it was only in the late 19th century that the European influence first began to be felt.

Education and Religion.—Primary education is compulsory for six years from the age of seven. Secondary and Higher education is extensive. The national illiteracy rate is among the lowest in Asia. There is freedom of religion. Buddhism has the most followers (13 million) followed by Protestantism (5 million) and Confucianism (4¾ million). Catholics numbered just over one million in 1977.

Agriculture and Fisheries.—The soil is fertile but the arable land is limited by the mountainous nature of the country. Staple agricultural products are rice, barley and other cereals, beans, tobacco and hemp. Fruit growing and sericulture are also practised. Ginseng, a medicinal root much used by both the Chinese and Koreans, forms a useful source of revenue. The Korean fishing industry is a major contributor to both food supply and exports.

Finance.—The budget for 1984 totals U.S.\$15·3 billion of which U.S.\$4·5 billion is for defence.

Trade and Industry.—Since the beginning of 1962 a series of successful five-year plans has resulted in real economic growth averaging around 10 per cent a year. In 1982 the annual per capita G.N.P. was U.S.\$1,700. Total imports in 1982 were U.S.\$23,473 million and exports U.S.\$20,879 million.

Until the 1960's the Republic of Korea's economy was mainly agricultural. But in 1980, 28·6 per cent of exports were textile goods, 13 per cent electrical goods and 11 per cent iron and steel. Important exports include cars, electrical and electronic equipment, footwear, ships, railway rolling stock and iron and steel products.

TRADE

	1982
Imports	U.S.\$23,473 m.
Exports	20,879 m.

Currency.—The unit of currency is the *won* of 100 *jeon.*

Trade with U.K.

	1982	1983
Imports from U.K.	£167,752,000	£168,942,000
Exports to U.K.	321,691,000	440,354,000

Minerals.—The Republic of Korea is deficient in mineral resources, except for deposits of coal on the East Coast and tungsten. There are some prospects of discovering oil in the sea between Korea and Japan.

Communications and Transport.—Modern highways mean that the whole country is now within one day's drive of Seoul. In 1980 there were 15,599 km. of paved road. Seoul has a subway system and there are national railway and airline systems. Korean Air Lines operates regular flights to Europe, the United States, the Middle East and South East Asia. Pusan and Inchon are the major ports with Pusan serving the industrial areas of the southeast. Inchon, 28 miles from Seoul, serves the capital, but development and operation at Inchon are hampered by a tidal variation of 9–10 metres.

CAPITAL.—Seoul, population (1980), 8,367,000. Other main centres are Ψ Pusan (pop. 3,160,000), Taegu (pop. 1,607,000) and Ψ Inchon (pop. 1,084,000).

FLAG.—White, with red over blue device in centre, three black parallel bars, some broken, in each quarter.

NATIONAL DAY.—August 15 (Independence Day).

BRITISH EMBASSY
No. 4, Chung-Dong, Chung-Ku, Seoul

Ambassador Extraordinary and Plenipotentiary, His Excellency John Nicholas Teague Spreckley, C.M.G. (1983).

Counsellor, P. H. D. Wetton (*Commercial*).

Defence and Military Attaché, Brig. B. S. Burditt.

1st Secretaries, Dr. J. E. Hoare (*Head of Chancery and Consul*); S. J. Hiscock (*Commercial/Information*).

Cultural Attaché and British Council Representative, S. S. Newton.

There is an Honorary British Consul at Pusan.

North Korea

Political Committee of the Central Committee, Kim Il-sung; O Chin-u; Kim Chong-il (*full members and members of the presidium*); Pak Song-chol; Yim Chun-chu; So Chol; Kim Yong-nam; Chon Mun-sop; Kim Hwan; Yon Hyong-muk; O Kuk-yol; Kang Song-san; Paek Hak-nim; Choe Yong-nim; So Yun-sok; Ho Tam; Yi Chong-ok (*full members*). Choe Kwang; Cho Se-ung; Kong Chin-tae; Chong Chun-ki; Chong Kyong-hui; Yi Kun-mo; Hyon Mu-kwang; Kim Kang-hwan; Kye Ung-tae; Kang Hui-won; Chon Pyong-ho; Kim Tu-nam; An Sung-hak; Hong Song-yong; Kim Pok-sik; Kim Chung-nin (*alternate members*).

Secretariat of the Central Committee, Kim Il-sung (*General Secretary*); Kim Chong-il; Yon Hyong-muk; Hwang Chang-yop; Hyon Mu-Kwang; Ho Chong-suk; So Kwan-hui; Chae Hui-chong; An Sung-hak; Ho Tam; Kim Yong-sun.

The population (1982) of North Korea is around 18,000,000. The capital is Pyongyang with approximately 1,500,000 inhabitants. North Korea is rich in minerals and a 7-year plan for 1978–84 gives priority to the fuel and mining industries. The armed forces are believed to number about 750,000 men.

FLAG.—Broad red horizontal band bordered by white lines bearing a five-point red star on a white disc in centre; blue horizontal bands at top and bottom.

Trade with U.K.

	1983
Imports from U.K.	£2,527,000
Exports to U.K.	362,000

KUWAIT
(The State of Kuwait)

Amir, H. H. Shaikh Jaber Al Ahmad Al Sabah, *born* 1928; acceded Jan. 1, 1978.

Crown Prince and Prime Minister, H. H. Shaikh Sa'ad Al Abdallah Al Sabah.

Deputy Prime Minister, Minister for Foreign Affairs and of Information, H. E. Shaikh Sabah al Ahmad al Jabir al Sabah.

Defence, H. E. Shaikh Salim al Sabah al Salim al Sabah.

Interior, H. E. Shaikh Nawwaf al Ahmed al Sabah.

Oil, H. E. Shaikh Ali Khalifa Al Athbi al Sabah.

KUWAIT EMBASSY IN LONDON
45–46 Queen's Gate, S.W.7.
[01–589 4533]

Ambassador Extraordinary and Plenipotentiary, His Excellency Ghazi M. A. Al-Rayes (1980).

Area and Population.—Kuwait extends along the shore of the Persian Gulf from Iraq to Saudi Arabia, with an area of 17,818 sq. km. (6,877 sq. miles). Kuwait has a dry, desert climate with a summer season extending from April to September. The mean temperature varies between 84° and 113° F. in summer, and 46° and 64° F. in winter. Humidity rarely exceeds 60 per cent except in July and August. The population is 1,786,616 (mid-1984), of which about 48 per cent are Kuwaiti citizens, the remainder being large numbers of other Arab peoples, Persians, Indians and Pakistanis. The total European and American population is about 12,500. The gross population growth rate is 6·4 per cent, a growth rate of 3·5 per cent for Kuwaiti citizens.

The official language is Arabic, and English is widely spoken as a second language. Islam is the official religion, though religious freedom is constitutionally guaranteed.

Government.—Although Kuwait had been independent for some years, the "exclusive agreement" of 1899 between the Shaikh of Kuwait and the British Government was formally abrogated by an exchange of letters dated June 19, 1961. This exchange was immediately followed by Iraqi claims to sovereignty over Kuwait, but on Oct. 4, 1963, Iraq recognized Kuwait's independence although the Kuwait-Iraqi border has not yet been determined formally. Under the Constitution legislative power is vested in the Amir and the 50-member National Assembly, and executive power in the Amir and the Cabinet. The fifth National Assembly was elected for a four year term in February, 1981 after a four year period of rule by Amiri decree following the suspension of the constitution in 1976.

Education, etc.—As a result of the very considerable oil revenues, the Kuwait Government embarked on a large scale development scheme and plans for social services. Education and medical treatment are free. New hospitals and schools continue to be built. Kuwait University was opened in 1966, and in 1984 had 13,021 students. In 1983 there were over 433,000 pupils at government and private schools.

Public Utilities.—Kuwait has a domestic water supply from water distillation plants which operate on natural gas from the oil fields. These plants can produce over 118,000,000 gallons of fresh water daily. Total water storage capacity, in reservoirs and water towers, amounts to over 1,201 million gallons. In 1961 a natural source of fresh water was discovered at Raudhatain in the north of the State. This has been developed to produce up to 3,000,000 gallons per day for at least 20 years and a pipeline has been built to carry the water to Kuwait town.

Electricity is produced by four power stations in Kuwait (Shuwaikh, Shuaiba North, Shuaiba South, Doha East, Doha West). Production in 1983 was 12,499 million Kwh.

Communications.—Ships of British, Dutch, Kuwaiti and other lines make regular calls at Kuwait. Several international and Middle Eastern airlines operate regular air services, and other companies make non-scheduled flights to Kuwait under charter. There is a network of dual-carriageway roads and more are under construction. Telecommunications, and postal services are conducted by the Kuwait Government, which has built an earth satellite station.

Finance.— Revenue for the financial year 1983–84 was budgeted at KD3,038 million. Oil revenues constitute 91·8 per cent. of total revenue. Estimated

total expenditure for the same year was KD3,376·3 million. The financial year begins on July 1. There are a large number of investment banks in some of which the Government holds equity. The banking system is controlled by the Central Bank of Kuwait.

Production.—The G.N.P. of Kuwait in 1982 was estimated at KD7,684 million, giving an average per capita income of about KD4,747.

Despite the desert terrain, 8·4 per cent of land is under cultivation, fruit and vegetables being the main crops. Shrimp fishing is becoming important.

The Government of Kuwait began to participate in the ownership of the British- and American-owned Kuwait Oil Company in 1974 and an agreement was signed in November 1975 which brought 100 per cent government ownership. After a reorganisation of the national oil industry in 1980, all the business was taken over by the Kuwait Petroleum Corporation, the national co-ordinating body for the whole industry of which the Minister of Oil is the Chairman. The Corporation is broken down into various companies responsible for crude oil products, refinery and gas plants, exploration and production, tanker operations, etc. The capital of K.P.C. was increased in 1982 to KD2,500 million to finance refinery modernisation and further overseas acquisitions.

The centre of Kuwait oil production is at Burgan, south of Kuwait City. Oil is also lifted in the Kuwait/Saudi Arabia Partitioned Zone (Wafra) area of the State. Oil is exported through a specially constructed port at Mina al Ahmadi. Production of crude oil in 1983 was approximately 1,052 million barrels per day. About 3,000 people are employed, including Kuwaitis, British, Americans, Indians, Pakistanis and citizens of other Arab countries.

Trade.—Oil exports constitute about 80 per cent. of Kuwait's total exports. Non-oil exports include chemical fertilizers, ammonia and other chemicals, metal pipes, shrimps and building materials; re-exports accounted for 73 per cent. of non-oil exports in 1982. Major trading partners are Asian countries, followed by E.E.C. countries and Arab states.

	1982*
Imports	KD2,098·0m
Exports	3,261·7m

* estimated

Trade with U.K.

	1982	1983
Imports from U.K.	£333,247,000	£333,273,000
Exports to U.K.	104,793,000	67,281,000

CAPITAL.— Ψ Kuwait (population, excluding suburbs, 400,000).

FLAG.—Three horizontal stripes of green, white and red, with black trapezoid next to staff.

NATIONAL DAY.—February 25.

BRITISH EMBASSY
P.O. Box Safat 2,
Arabian Gulf Street, Kuwait

Ambassador Extraordinary and Plenipotentiary, His Excellency Michael Ramsey Melhuish, C.M.G., (1982)

Counsellor, A. S. M. Marshall, O.B.E.

1st Secretaries, R. Bland; C. J. Hurran (*Information*); G. H. Boyce (*Financial and Economic, and Head of Chancery*); H. J. W. Coates (*Consul*); P. Newall (*Commercial*).

British Council Office Representative, T. C. White, M.B.E., P.O. Box 345, Safat, Kuwait. There is a library in *Kuwait*.

LAOS
(People's Democratic Republic of Laos)

President, Souphanouvong, *assumed office,* Dec. 2, 1975.
Prime Minister, Kaysone Phomvihane.

EMBASSY IN LONDON
5 Palace Green, W8 4QA

Ambassador Extraordinary and Plenipotentiary (vacant).
Chargé d' Affaires, Ouan Phommachack.

Position and Extent.—The People's Democratic Republic of Laos is in the northerly part of Indo-China, lying between China and Vietnam, on the north and east, and Burma and Thailand on the west. Laos has a common boundary with Cambodia to the south. The area of the country is approximately 90,000 sq. miles, with a population (estimated, 1976) of about 3,000,000.

History.—The Kingdom of Lane Xang, the Land of a Million Elephants, was founded in the 14th century, but broke up at the beginning of the 15th century into the separate kingdoms of Luang Prabang and Vientiane and the Principality of Champassac, which together came under French protection in 1893. In 1945 the Japanese executed a *coup de force* and suppressed the French administration. Under a Constitution of 1947 Laos became a constitutional monarchy under King Sisvang Vong of the House of Luang Prabang, and an independent sovereign state in 1949.

The next twenty-five years in Laos were marked by power struggles and civil war. International conferences were held in Geneva in 1954 and 1961–2 to produce a settlement based on neutrality and independence. But the resulting Coalition Governments were short-lived. Personalities involved include the present adviser to the Government, Prince Souvanna Phouma, who in 1957 formed a Government of National Union, including *Pathet Lao* (Communist) ministers, and held office as Prime Minister with intervals from 1962 to 1975; Prince Boun Oum of Champassac who formed a rightist Government in December 1960, fled Laos in 1975 and was consequently condemned to death, and Prince Souphanouvong (now President of the Republic), who took part in a later coalition with Souvanna Phouma and Boun Oum in 1962–63.

Recent Events.—After 1967 North Vietnamese forces steadily increased their military activities in Laos. Although there were regular seasonal fluctuations in the fighting, which resulted in many areas of the country changing hands several times, Government forces gradually lost ground. By February 21, 1973, when a ceasefire agreement was signed in Vientiane between the *Pathet Lao* and the Government in Vientiane, Communist forces had occupied or dominated most of the strategic areas of Laos, including the Plain of Jars in the north, and the Bolovens Plateau in the south.

After the fall of Saigon in April 1975, internal resistance to the Pathet Lao crumbled; Communist troops occupied the whole country and, though still paying lip-service to the 1973 Agreement and maintaining a façade of coalition, the *Pathet Lao* took over the government and began to implement an authoritarian régime with policies of austerity and economic self-sufficiency. On December 2, 1975, following the abdication of the King, Laos was declared a People's Democratic Republic and the *Pathet Lao* assumed full charge of the country.

Economy.—There is no significant industrial base in Laos, an estimated 85% of the work force being engaged in agriculture, largely concerned with rice cultivation. Rice production in 1982 amounted to 1·2 million tonnes, thus rendering the country theoreti-

cally self-sufficient in this staple food. In 1983, however, the authorities stated that due to late rains there was an overall shortfall of about 100,000 tons.

The main exports are electricity, timber and coffee. Total exports in 1982 were valued at $39·8 m. Imports during 1982 amounted to $124·2 m. Clearing agreements have been signed with certain socialist countries and the trade gap is largely financed by foreign aid, of which some 60% is provided by socialist countries.

Laos' economic performance so far has been poor and shows no signs of early recovery, the free market rate for the dollar is much higher than the official rate and prices of consumer items continue to increase.

Currency.—In January 1980 a "new" *Kip* replaced the former currency. In July 1983 the non-commercial rate of exchange was rectified by the State Bank.

CAPITAL.—Vientiane, population (estimated 1978) 90,000.

FLAG.—Blue background with a central white circle, framed by 2 horizontal red stripes.

NATIONAL DAY.—December 2.

BRITISH EMBASSY
P.O. Box 224
Vientiane

Ambassador Extraordinary and Plenipotentiary, and Consul-General, His Excellency William B. J. Dobbs.
3rd Secretary and Vice-Consul, R. A. Coleman.

LEBANON

President of the Republic of Lebanon, Amin Gemayel, *elected,* Sept. 21, 1982.
Prime Minister, Rashid Karami.

LEBANESE EMBASSY IN LONDON
21 Kensington Palace Gardens, W8 4QM
[01–229 7265/8485]

Ambassador Extraordinary and Plenipotentiary, His Excellency Gen. Ahmed El-Hajj (1983).
1st Secretary, Sleiman Chafic Rassi.
Counsellor, Hussein Moussawi.
Consular Section, 15 Palace Gardens Mews, W.8 (01–727 6696)

Area and Population.—Lebanon forms a strip about 120 miles in length and varying in width from 30 to 35 miles, along the Mediterranean littoral, and extending from the Israel frontier on the south to the Nahr al Kebir (15 miles north of Tripoli) on the north; its eastern boundary runs down the Anti-Lebanon range and then down the Great Central depression, the *Beqaa,* from which flow the rivers Orontes and Litani. It is divided into 5 districts, North Lebanon, Mount Lebanon, Beirut, South Lebanon and Beqaa. The seaward slopes of the mountains have a Mediterranean climate and vegetation. The inland range of Anti-Lebanon has the characteristics of steppe country. There is a mixed Arabic-speaking population of Christians, Moslems and Druses. The total area of Lebanon is about 4,300 sq. miles, population (1974), 2,780,000. (*For* MAP, *See* p. 861.)

Government.—Lebanon became an independent State on Sept. 1, 1920, administered under French Mandate until Nov. 26, 1941. Powers were transferred to the Lebanese Government from Jan. 1, 1944, and French troops were withdrawn in 1946.

In April 1975, serious fighting broke out in Beirut between members of the predominantly Christian Phalangist Party and Palestinian guerrillas based in Lebanon. The fighting continued and increased throughout 1975 and 1976. In the autumn of 1976 the Arab Deterrent Forces composed mainly of Syrian troops, imposed an effective ceasefire and brought nineteen months of civil war to an end throughout Lebanon. Major bouts of fighting took place in October 1978 and April/May 1981, interspersed with regular clashes on a smaller scale. There was renewed fighting in the summer of 1982 when Israeli forces invaded the country, penetrating as far as Beirut. Following negotiations, Palestine Liberation Organisation guerrillas left Beirut for various Arab countries. Frequent minor clashes in the following twelve months escalated into serious fighting in Aug.–Sept. 1983. The south of the country is currently occupied by Israeli troops and the north-east by Syrian and Palestinian forces.

After reconciliation talks in Lausanne, Switzerland, in March 1984, moves were made towards the disengagement of rival militias in Beirut. In April 1984, Mr. Rashid Karami formed a 10-man Cabinet which included the leaders of the principal factions.

Production.—Fruits are the most important products and include citrus fruit, apples, grapes, bananas and olives. There is a considerable amount of light industry, mostly for the production of consumer goods, but most factories have been operating below capacity since 1975. The most important industries are foods and drinks, textiles, chemicals, furniture, plastics, leather, clothing and footwear, refrigerators, cast and forged metal products, and building materials. Much of this is exported to neighbouring Arab countries. There is little remaining of the famous cedars of Lebanon.

Railways.—A narrow-gauge railway runs from Beirut to Damascus, connecting at Rayak with a branch of the standard-gauge line which runs from Tripoli through Homs, Hama and Aleppo to the Turkish frontier, from Nusaybin to the Iraq frontier at Tel Kotchek. A standard-gauge railway also runs up the coast from Nakowia to Tripoli. The railways are not functioning as a result of the 1975–6 civil war.

Archæology, etc.—Lebanon has some important historical remains, notably Baalbek (Heliopolis) which contains the ruins of first to third century Roman temples and Jubail (Biblos), one of the oldest continuously inhabited towns in the world, and ancient Tyre.

Language and Literature.—Arabic is the principal language (*see* Arabia), and French is also an official language and widely used. The use of English is also wide-spread.

Education.—There are five universities in Beirut, the American and the French (R.C.) Universities established in the last century, and the Lebanese National University, the Beirut University College and the Arab University which are recent foundations in the early stages of development. There are several institutions for vocational training, some of which have been rendered inoperative by the civil war, and there is a good provision throughout the country of primary and secondary schools, among which are a great number of private schools.

Finance.—Revenue and Expenditure, 1980 (Estimated) £L5,211,200,000, including a deficit of £L1,500m. The monetary unit is the Lebanese £(L). (*See also* p. 82.)

Principal Imports.—Gold and precious metals, machinery and electrical equipment, textiles and yarns, vegetable products, iron and steel goods, motor vehicles, mineral products, chemicals and chemical products, pharmaceuticals, prepared foods, beverages, tobacco products, live animals and animal products.

Principal Exports.—Gold and precious metals, fruits and vegetables, textiles, building materials, furniture, plastic goods, foodstuffs, tobacco and wine.

Trade with U.K.

	1982	1983
Imports from U.K.	£67,640,000	£81,435,000
Exports to U.K.	24,237,000	11,521,000

There is also a considerable and very important transit trade through Beirut, including gold, crude oil and a wide range of machinery and consumer goods. Lebanon is the terminal for two oil pipe lines, one formerly belonging to the Iraq Petroleum Company, debouching at Tripoli, the other belonging to the Trans Arabian Pipeline Company, at Sidon. The latter supplies most of Lebanon's requirements as the former has not functioned for some years.

CAPITAL.— ΨBeirut (population, 702,000). Other towns are ΨTripoli (175,000), Zahlé (46,800), ΨSidon (24,740), ΨTyre (14,000).

FLAG.—Horizontal bands of red, white and red with a green cedar of Lebanon in the centre of the white band.

NATIONAL DAY.—November 22.

BRITISH EMBASSY
Avenue de Paris, Ras Beirut, Beirut

Ambassador Extraordinary and Plenipotentiary, His Excellency Henry David Alastair Capel Miers, C.M.G.

British Council Representative, N. O. Hudson, O.B.E., Beit Fawzi Azar, Sharia Sidani, Ras Beirut.

LIBERIA
(Republic of Liberia)

Head of State, Commander-in-Chief Samuel K. Doe.

Rural Development, Maj. Yudu S. Gray.
Agriculture, Joseph Boakai.
Commerce, Industry and Transportation, Mrs. McLeod Turkett-Darpoh.
Education, Maj. G. S. Boley.
Finance, G. Alvin Jones.
Foreign Affairs, Dr. Ernest Eastman.
Health and Social Affairs, Mrs. M. S. Belleh.
Information, Cultural Affairs and Tourism, Dr. Peter Naigow.
Justice, J. K. Z. B. Scott.
Labour, Manpower and Development, Maj. J. G. Rancy.
Lands, Mines and Energy, Dr. F. Kromah.
Internal Affairs, Col. E. K. Sackor.
National Defence, Maj. Gen. Gray D. Allison.
Planning and Economic Affairs, Maj. Emmanuel O. Gardiner.
Postal Affairs, Gblorzuo S. Toweh.
Public Works, Maj. James Burphy.
State for Presidential Affairs, Dr. Bernard Blamo.
Dir.-Gen. of the Cabinet, Dr. W. Sankawulo.

LIBERIAN EMBASSY IN LONDON
21 Prince's Gate, SW7 1QB
[01–589 9405]

Ambassador Extraordinary and Plenipotentiary, His Excellency Dr. Harry F. Moniba (1981).

An independent republic of Western Africa, occupying that part of the coast between Sierra Leone and the Ivory Coast, which is between the rivers Mano in the N.W. and Cavalla in the S.E., a distance of about 350 miles, with an area of about 43,000 square miles, and extending to the interior to latitude 8° 50', a distance of 150 miles from the seaboard. It was founded by the American Colonization Society in 1822, and has been recognized since 1847 as an independent State. The population at the Census of 1974 was 1,481,524.

William V. S. Tubman, President of Liberia since 1944, died on July 23, 1971, and was succeeded by Dr. Tolbert. The Constitution was suspended following a military *coup* on April 12, 1980 led by M/Sgt. Samuel K. Doe, who then became Head of State. Executive power is now vested in the Head of State assisted by an appointed Cabinet of 18 which is supervised by the People's Redemption Council. A new Constitution was endorsed by a referendum on July 3, 1984 and on July 22 the People's Redemptive Council was dissolved and replaced by an interim National Assembly, comprising the Council and 35 civilian members, which will oversee the country's return to civilian rule. Presidential and legislative elections are scheduled for Oct. 1985, after which an elected civilian government will replace military rule.

The Army of Liberia consists of one division of 2 brigades of militia, three regular infantry battalions, one engineer battalion and a small coastguard.

The artificial harbour and free port of Monrovia was opened on July 26, 1948. There are 9 ports of entry, including 3 river ports. International and African airlines call at Robertsfield, 35 miles from Monrovia. Spriggs Payne airfield, on the outskirts of Monrovia, is used by Air Liberia for internal flights.

Liberia is receiving assistance from a number of countries, including the United Kingdom, and from the E.E.C. and various international agencies. This aid is mainly directed towards the implementation of Liberia's National Socio-Economic Development Plan.

FINANCE

	1981–82	1982–83
Revenue	$223,000,000	$237,300,000
Expenditure	303,000,000	317,800,000

$ = U.S. Dollar

TRADE

	1981	1982
Imports	$477,420,000	428,400,000
Exports	531,420,000	477,400,000

Trade with U.K.

	1982	1983
Imports from U.K.	£14,069,000	£13,877,000
Exports to U.K.	8,213,000	7,181,000

The principal exports are iron ore, crude rubber, timber, uncut diamonds, palm kernels, cocoa and coffee. The chief imports are manufactured goods of all kinds, transport and iron-ore mining equipment and foodstuffs.

The language of the Republic is English. American weights and measures are used.

CAPITAL, Ψ Monrovia. Est. Pop. 300,000. Other ports are Ψ Buchanan, Ψ Greenville (Sinoe) and Ψ Harper (Cape Palmas).

FLAG.—Alternate horizontal stripes (5 white, 6 red), with 5-pointed white star on blue field in upper corner next to flagstaff.

NATIONAL DAY.—July 26.

BRITISH EMBASSY
Mamba Point (P.O. Box 120), Monrovia

Ambassador Extraordinary and Plenipotentiary and Consul-General, His Excellency Dougal Gordon Reid, C.M.G..
2nd Secretary and Consul, R. G. Jones.
Pro-Consul, G. D. Hart.

LIBYA

Leader of the Revolution, Col. Muammar Qadhafi.
Secretary of the General People's Committee, Muhammad az-Zarruq Rajab.

LIBYAN DIPLOMATIC MISSION IN LONDON
Following the break of diplomatic relations with Libya in April 1984, the Royal Embassy of Saudi Arabia has handled Libyan interests in Britain.

Libya, on the Mediterranean coast of Africa, is bounded on the East by Egypt and the Sudan, on the South by the Republics of Chad and Niger, and on the West by Algeria and Tunisia. It consists of the three former provinces of Tripolitania, Cyrenaica and the Fezzan, with a combined area of approximately 810,000 square miles (1,760,000 sq. kms) and a population (1981 estimate) of 3,100,000. The people of Libya are principally Arab with some Berbers in the West and aboriginal tribes in the Fezzan. Islam is the official religion of Libya, but other religions are tolerated. The official language is Arabic.

Vast sand and rock deserts, almost completely barren, occupy the greater part of Libya. The Southern part of the country lies within the Sahara Desert. There are no rivers, and, as rainfall is precarious, a good harvest is infrequent. The ancient ruins in Cyrenaica, at Cyrene, Ptolemais (Tolmeta) and Apollonia, are outstanding, as are those at Leptis Magna near Homs, 70 miles from Tripoli and at Sabratha, 40 miles west of Tripoli. An Italian expedition has found in the S.W. of the Fezzan a series of rock-paintings more than 5,000 years old.

Production and Industry.—Agriculture is confined mainly to the coastal areas of Tripolitania and Cyrenaica, where barley, wheat, olives, almonds, citrus fruits and dates are produced, and to the areas of the oases, many of which are well supplied with springs supporting small fertile areas. Among the important oases are Jaghbub, Ghadames, Jofra, Sebha, Murzuq, Brach, Ghat, Jalo and the Kufra group in the South-East. In the main industry is oil and gas production. There are pipelines from Zelten to the terminal at Mersa Brega, from Dahra to Ras-es-Sider, from Amal to Ras Lanuf and from the Intisar field to Zuetina. In 1983 average production of crude oil was 1·1 million barrels per day. A major petrochemical complex is under construction at Ras Lanuf and the refinery and ethylene plant are expected to begin operations in 1984. The construction of an iron and steel plant at Misurata is well under way. However, economic constraints have slowed some

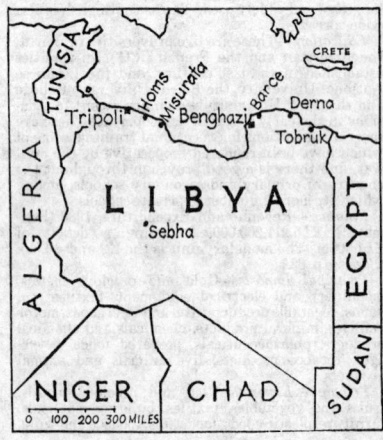

projects, particularly since Libya decided in 1983 to go ahead with a major irrigation scheme, the "Great Man-Made River".

Exports from Libya are dominated by crude oil, but some wool, cattle, sheep and horses, olive oil, and hides and skins are also exported. Principal imports are foodstuffs, including sugar, tea and coffee and most constructional materials and consumer goods. In recent years the private sector has been virtually eliminated and Libya is now a state trading country with imports controlled by state monopolies.

Communications in Libya are good in the coastal area where a motor road (of international standards) runs from the Tunisian frontier through Tripoli to Benghazi, Tobruk and the Egyptian border, serving the needs of the main population centres. In 1979 there were over 10,000 km. of paved road. There are good roads from Tripoli to Ghadames and to Sebha. There are airports at Tripoli and Benghazi (Benina), Tobruk, Mersa Bregha, Sebha, Ghadames and Kufra regularly used by commercial airlines, and military airfields near Tobruk, near Tripoli and at Al Watiya, south of Zuara.

Government.—Libya was occupied by Italy in 1911–12 in the course of the Italo-Turkish War, and under the Treaty of Ouchy (Oct. 1912) the sovereignty of the province was transferred by Turkey to Italy. In 1939 the four Provinces of Libya (Tripoli, Misurata, Benghazi and Derna) were incorporated in the national territory of Italy as *Libia Italiana.* After the Second World War Tripolitania and Cyrenaica were placed provisionally under British and the Fezzan under French administration, and in conformity with a resolution of the General Assembly on Nov. 21, 1949, Libya became on Dec. 24, 1951, the first independent state to be created by the United Nations. The monarchy was overthrown by a revolution on Sept. 1, 1969, and the country was declared a republic. It was ruled by the Revolutionary Command Council (RCC) under the leadership of Colonel Muammar Qadhafi.

In March 1977 a new form of direct democracy, the "Jamahiriya" (state of the masses) was promulgated and the official name of the country was changed to Socialist People's Libyan Arab Jamahiriya. At local level authority is now vested in 186 Basic and 25 Municipal People's Congresses which appoint Popular Committees to execute policy. Officials of these Congresses and Committees form at national level the General People's Congress, a body of some 1,000 delegates which normally meets for about a week twice a year. This is the highest policy-making body in the country. The General People's Congress appoints its own General Secretariat and the General People's Committee, whose members head the 19 government departments which execute policy at national level. The Secretary of the General People's Committee has functions similar to those of a Prime Minister.

Following the latest reorganization of March 1979 Colonel Qadhafi retains his position as leader of the Revolution. But neither he nor his former RCC colleagues any longer have any formal posts in the new administration.

Currency.—The unit of currency is the Libyan *dinar* of 1,000 *dirham. (See also* p. 81.)

Technical assistance is being provided by the United Nations to foster Libya's economic and educational development.

Trade with U.K.

	1982	1983
Imports from U.K.	£261,400,000	£274,169,000
Exports to U.K.	343,400,000	224,050,000

CAPITAL.—Tripoli.

The principal towns are: ΨTripoli, pop. 1981, about 1,000,000; ΨBenghazi (500,000); ΨMisurata (194,047).

FLAG.—Libya uses a plain emerald green flag.

NATIONAL DAY.—Sept. 1.

BRITISH EMBASSY

Diplomatic relations between the U.K. and Libya were broken in April 1984. British interests are currently handled by a section at the Italian Embassy, 1 Sharia Oran, Tripoli.

LIECHTENSTEIN
(Fürstentum Liechtenstein)

Prince, Franz Josef II., *b.* Aug. 16, 1906; *suc.* July 26, 1938; *married* March 7, 1943, Countess Gina von Wilczek.

Heir, Crown Prince Hans Adam, *b.* Feb. 14, 1945; *married* July 30, 1967, Countess Marie Kinsky.

From Aug. 26, 1984 Prince Adam takes over official duties and executive authority; Prince Franz Josef remains titular Head of State.

MINISTRY

Prime Minister, Hans Brunhart (*Foreign Affairs; Interior; Education; Finance; Culture; Construction*).

Deputy Prime Minister, Hilmar Ospelt (*Justice; Economy; Communications; Youth and Sport*).

Government Counsellors, Dr. Walter Oehry (*Agriculture and Forestry*); Dr. Egmond Frommelt (*Social Services*); Anton Gerner (*Health*).

Liechtenstein is represented in diplomatic and consular matters in the United Kingdom by the Swiss Embassy, *q.v.*

At the General Election on Feb. 7, 1982, the Patriotic Union Party won 8 seats and Progressive Citizens Party 7.

A Principality on the Upper Rhine, between Vorarlberg (Austria) and Switzerland, with an area of 62 square miles and a population in 1983 of 26,512. The main industries are metal goods, cotton spinning and weaving, measuring instruments, coating of lenses, manufacture of vacuum apparatus, electronic microscopes, ceramics, artificial teeth, sausage casings, textiles, various apparatus, foodstuffs, leatherware and woodwork. The chief products are cotton yarn, cotton material, screws, bolts and bolt-shooting apparatus, needles, knitting machinery, ceramics, artificial teeth, precision measuring instruments, vacuum pumps, coated lenses, shoes, leather gloves, bed down, conveyor belts, boilers, preserves, damask cloth, socks and stockings, and furniture.

FINANCE

	1982	1983
Revenue	*F*244,005,179	*F*260,377,610
Expenditure	237,290,038	252,146,084
	(*F* = Swiss *francs*)	

The language of the Principality is German.

CAPITAL, Vaduz. Pop. (1983), 4,896.

FLAG.—Equal horizontal bands of blue over red; gold crown on blue band near staff.

British Consul General, George Neil Smith (*office* at Dufourstrasse 56, 8008 Zürich).

LUXEMBURG
(Grand-Duché de Luxembourg)

Grand Duke, H.R.H. Jean, *born* Jan. 5, 1921, *married*, April 9, 1953, Princess Joséphine-Charlotte of Belgium, and has issue, 3 sons and 2 daughters; *succeeded* (on the abdication of his mother) Nov., 1964.

Heir Apparent, Prince Henri, born April 16, 1955, married February 14, 1981, Maria Teresa Mestre, and has issue, Prince Guillaume, born 11 Nov. 1981, and Prince Felix, born 1984.

CABINET

Christian Socialists:

Minister of State, President of the Government, Minister of Finance, National Development, Posts, Telecommunications and Information Technology, M. Jacques Santer.

Interior, the Family, Housing, Social Solidarity, M. Jean Spautz.

Education and Tourism, M. Fernand Boden.

Labour and Minister-Delegate for Finance, M. Jean-Claude Juncker.

Defence, Agriculture, Sport and the Civil Service, M. Marc Fischbach.

Agriculture and Viticulture, M. Rene Steichen.

Social Democrats:

Vice-President of the Government, Minister of the Economy, Foreign Affairs, Foreign Trade and Co-operation, Middle Classes and Treasury, M. Jacques Poos.

Public Health and Social Security, M. Benny Berg.

Justice, Cultural Affairs and the Environment, M. Robert Krieps.

Energy, Transport and Public Works, M. Marcel Schlechter.

State Secretary for Foreign Affairs, Foreign Trade and Co-operation and the Middle Classes, M. Robert Goebbels.

State Secretary for the Economy, M. Johnny Lahure.

EMBASSY AND CONSULATE
27 Wilton Crescent, SW1X 8SD
[01–235 6961]

Ambassador Extraordinary and Plenipotentiary, His Excellency Roger Hastert, C.M.G. (1978).

A Grand Duchy in Western Europe, bounded by Germany, Belgium, and France. Established as an independent State under the sovereignty of the King of the Netherlands as Grand Duke by the Congress of Vienna in 1815, it formed part of the Germanic Confederation, 1815–66, and was included in the German "Zollverein". In 1867 the Treaty of London declared it a neutral territory. On the death of the King of the Netherlands in 1890 it passed to the Duke of Nassau. The territory was invaded and overrun by the Germans at the beginning of the war in 1914, but was liberated in 1918. By the Treaty of Versailles, 1919, Germany renounced her former agreements with Luxemburg in respect of the customs union, etc., and in 1921 an economic union was made with Belgium (B.L.E.U.). The Grand Duchy was again invaded and occupied by Germany on May 10, 1940. The constitution of the Grand Duchy was modified on April 28, 1948, and the stipulation of permanent neutrality was then abandoned. Luxemburg is now a fully effective member of the Western association of powers and a signatory of the Brussels and North Atlantic Treaties. She is also a member of the European Communities.

Besides B.L.E.U., Luxemburg is also a member of the Belgium–Netherlands–Luxemburg Customs Union (Benelux, 1960). The Court of the European Communities has its seat in Luxemburg, as does the Secretariat of the European Parliament, the European Investment Bank, the European Audit Court and the European Monetary Co-operation fund.

The area is 999 square miles; the population (Jan. 1983) 365,500, nearly all Roman Catholics. There is a Chamber of 64 Deputies, elected by universal suffrage for 5 years. Legislation is submitted to the Council of State. The Grand Duchy was rich in iron-ore and possesses an important iron and steel industry with

an annual productive capacity over 5,200,000 tons. Government revenue for 1982 was estimated at L.F. 5,300 million, expenditure L.F. 5,300 million. The Luxemburg franc has at present the same value as the Belgian franc and the latter is legal tender in the Grand Duchy. There are 170 miles of railway.

Trade with U.K.

	1982	1983
Imports from U.K.	£21,000,000	£34,525,000
Exports to U.K.	49,586,000	64,238,000

The capital, Luxemburg, pop. (1983), 78,900, is a dismantled fortress. The country is well wooded, with many deer and wild boar. The language is Letzeburgesch but French is the official language; most speak German and many English.

FLAG.—Three horizontal bands, red, white and blue. NATIONAL DAY.—June 23.

BRITISH EMBASSY
28 Boulevard Royal, L-2449, Luxemburg

Ambassador Extraordinary and Plenipotentiary, His Excellency The Hon. Humphrey Maud (1982).

MADAGASCAR
(The Democratic Republic of Madagascar)

President, Didier Ratsiraka, took office 1975, re-elected Nov. 7, 1982 for a seven-year term.

Madagascar lies 240 miles off the east coast of Africa and is the fourth largest island in the world. It has an area of 228,000 sq. miles and a population of about 9,000,000. It became a French protectorate in 1895, and a French colony in 1896 when the former queen was exiled. Republican status was adopted on October 14, 1958, and independence was proclaimed on June 26, 1960.

Government.—The post-independence civilian government was replaced by a military government in Jan. 1975 and the following month martial law was declared. A Supreme Council of the Revolution of 18 members under Capitaine de Frégate (now Admiral) Didier Ratsiraka was established on June 15, 1975.

Both houses of the Malagasy Parliament, and the activities of political parties were suspended, but are now active again under the 1975 constitution.

In December 1975 a new constitution was approved in a referendum, which vested executive power in the President. He appoints a Council of Ministers to assist him, with the guidance of the Revolutionary Supreme Council. There is a 137-member National People's Assembly elected for a 5-year term by universal suffrage,

Revised agreements with France, signed on June 4, 1973, provided for the withdrawal of the French forces stationed in the country after independence. The French naval base at Diégo Suarez was turned into a civilian ship repair yard. Madagascar also withdrew from the Franc Zone and announced a claim to the Islands of Juan de Nova, Glorieuses, Isle de l'Europe, Bassa da India and Tromelin which had remained integral parts of the French Republic after independence.

The people are of mixed Polynesian, Arab and Negro origin. The languages spoken are Malagasy and French. There are sizeable French, Chinese and Indian communities.

The island's economy is still largely based on agriculture, which accounts for three-quarters of its exports. Development plans have placed emphasis on increasing agricultural and livestock production, the improvement of communications, the exploitation of mineral deposits and the creation of small industries.

TRADE

	1983
Imports	$U.S.522,000,000
Exports	432,000,000

The unit of currency is the Malagasy *franc* (FMG).

Trade with U.K.

	1982	1983
Imports from U.K........	£3,548,000	£4,907,000
Exports to U.K.	3,355,000	3,731,000

CAPITAL.—Antananarivo (population about 700,000). Other main towns are the chief port Toamasina (55,000); Mahajanga (50,000); Fianarantsoa (47,000); Antsiranana (41,000).

FLAG.—Equal horizontal bands of red (above) and green, with vertical white band by staff.

NATIONAL DAY.—June 26 (Independence Day).

BRITISH EMBASSY
(BP 167, Antananarivo)

Ambassador Extraordinary and Plenipotentiary, His Excellency David Malcolm McBain, M.V.O. (1984).
2nd Secretary, R. H. Hyde, M.B.E.
Vice-Consul (Commercial), J. A. Marcelin.

MALI
(Republic of Mali)

Head of State, President of the Government and Minister of National Defence, Gen. Moussa Traore, *born* 1937, *assumed office* Nov. 20, 1968.

The Republic of Mali, an inland state in north-west Africa has an area of 465,000 square miles and a population (1981 estimate) of 7,160,000.

Formerly the French colony of Soudan, the territory elected on Nov. 24, 1958, to remain as an autonomous republic within the French Community. It associated with Senegal in the Federation of Mali which was granted full independence on June 20, 1960. The Federation was effectively dissolved on August 22 by the secession of Senegal. The title of the Republic of Mali was adopted on Sept. 22, 1960. The Republic rejoined the CFA franc zone on June 1, 1984 when measures were taken to convert the *Franc Malien* at the rate of 2*FM* : 1 *Franc CFA*.

Government.—The *régime* of Modibo Keita was overthrown on Nov. 19, 1968, and the President arrested by a group of Army officers, who formed a National Liberation Committee and appointed a

Prime Minister. Moussa Traore assumed the functions of Head of State. A new civil constitution to come into being in 1979 was approved in a national referendum on June 21, 1974. The new government formed on May 4, 1978 contained a majority of civilians. On June 19, 1979, elections were held for an 82-member National Assembly. Presidential elections held on the same day confirmed Traore as President.

Mali's principal exports are groundnuts (raw and processed), cotton fibres, meat and dried fish. The principal rivers are the Niger and the Senegal.

Trade with UK.

	1982	1983
Imports from UK.	£4,400,000	£15,856,000
Exports to U.K.	3,400,000	3,833,000

G.N.P. per capita in 1980 was estimated at U.S.$190.

CAPITAL.—Bamako (600,000). Other towns are Gao, Kayes, Mopti, Sikasso, Segou and Timbuktu (all regional capitals).

FLAG.—Vertical stripes of green (by staff), yellow and red. NATIONAL DAY.—September 22.

BRITISH EMBASSY
British Ambassador (resident at Dakar, Senegal).

MAURITANIA
(Islamic Republic of Mauritania)

Head of State, Lt. Col. Mohamed Khouna Ould Haidalla.

Mauritania lies on the north-west coast of Africa immediately to the north of Senegal. It is bounded on the east by the Republic of Mali. To the north it is bounded by Morocco and the Western Sahara. Mauritania and Morocco took possession of that territory in February 1976 when Spain formally relinquished all right to it and in April 1976 agreed on a new frontier dividing the territory between them. In August 1979, Mauritania relinquished all claim to the southern sector of the Western Sahara after a three-year war against the Polisario front guerrilla army. Area 419,000 sq. miles. The population was estimated at 1,634,000 in 1980. (For MAP, *see* above.) The Republic of Mauritania elected on November 28, 1958, to remain within the French Community as an autonomous republic. It became fully independent on Nov. 28, 1960. In 1972 Mauritania broke with the franc zone and established its own unit of currency, the *Ouguiya*, equal in value to 5 *francs CFA*.

Mauritania's main source of potential wealth lies in rich deposits of iron ore around Zouérate, in the north of the country. Exports began in 1963, via a railway laid for the purpose from the mine to the port of Nouadhibou. The deposits are being exploited under the aegis of the *Société Nationale Industrielle Minière* following the nationalization in 1974 of the internationally based company MIFERMA. There are copper deposits at Akjoujt which are being exploited by SOMIMA, a company nationalized on Feb. 25, 1975; the mine was closed in 1978, but reopened in 1981.

	1982	1983
Imports from U.K........	£1,900,000	£1,719,000
Exports to U.K.	5,500,000	6,044,000

G.N.P. per capita in 1980 was estimated at U.S.$320.

FLAG.—Yellow star and crescent on green ground.
NATIONAL DAY.—November 28.
CAPITAL.—Nouakchott (500,000).
British Ambassador, (Resident at *Dakar, Senegal*).

MEXICO
(Estados Unidos Mexicanos)

President (1982–88), Lic. Miguel de la Madrid Hurtado, *elected*, 4 July 1982, *took office*, 1 Dec. 1982.

THE CABINET

Interior, Sr. Manuel Bartlett Diaz.
Foreign Affairs, Sr. Bernardo Sepúlveda Amor.
Finance and Public Credit, Sr. Jesús Silva Herzog Flores.
Defence, Gen. Juan José Arévalo Gardoqui.
Navy, Adm. Miguel Angel Gómez Ortega.
Budget and Planning, Sr. Carlos Salinas de Gortari.
Energy, Mines and Parastatal Industries, Sr. Francisco Labastida Ochoa.
Trade and Industrial Development, Sr. Héctor Hernández Cervantes.
Agriculture and Water Resources, Sr. Eduardo Pesqueira Olea.
Communications and Transport, Sr. Rodolfo Félix Valdez.
Education, Sr. Jesús Reyes Heroles.
Urban Development and Ecology, Sr. Marcelo Javelly Girard.
Health, Dr. Guillermo Soberón Acevedo.
Labour and Social Security, Sr. Arsenio Farell Cubillas.
Agrarian Reform, Sr. Luis Martínez Villacaña.
Tourism, Sr. Antonio Enríquez Savignac.
Fisheries, Sr. Pedro Ojeda Paullada.
Attorney-General, Sr. Sergio García Ramírez.
Attorney-General of Federal District, Sra. Victoria Adato de Ibarra.
Comptroller-General, Sr. Francisco Rojas.

MEXICAN EMBASSY IN LONDON
8 Halkin St., SW1X 7DW
[01–235 6393]

Ambassador Extraordinary and Plenipotentiary, His Excellency Francisco Cuevas-Cancino.

Area and Population.—Mexico occupies the southern part of the continent of North America, with an extensive seaboard to both the Atlantic and Pacific Oceans, extending from 14° 33′ to 32° 43′ N. lat. and 86° 46′ to 117° 08′ W. long., and comprising one of the most varied zones in the world. It contains 31 states and the federal district of Mexico, making in all 32 political divisions, covering an area of 761,604 square miles. At the 1980 Mexican General Census, the total population was 67,383,000, but a present day estimate is 76·8 million.

The two great ranges of North America, the Sierra Nevada and Rocky Mountains, are prolonged from the north to a convergence towards the narrowing

Isthmus of Tehuantepec, their course being parallel with the west and east coasts. The surface of the interior consists of an elevated plateau between the two ranges, with steep slopes both to the Pacific and Atlantic (Gulf of Mexico). In the west is the Peninsula of Lower California, with a mountainous surface, separated from the mainland by the Gulf of California. The Sierra Nevada, known in Mexico as the *Sierra Madre*, terminates in a transverse series of volcanic peaks, from Colima on the west to Citlaltepetl ("El Pico de Orizaba") on the east. The low-lying lands of the coasts form the *Tierra Caliente*, or tropical regions (below 3,000 ft.), the higher levels form the *Tierra Templada*, or temperate region (from 3,000 to 6,000 ft.), and the summit of the plateau with its peaks is known as *Tierra Fria*, or cold region (above 6,000 ft.). The only considerable rivers are the *Rio Grande del Norte* which forms part of the northern boundary, and is navigable for about 70 miles from its mouth in the Gulf of Mexico, and the *Rio Grande de Santiago*, the *Rio Balsas* and *Rio Papaloapan*. The remaining streams are governed by the formation of the land, and run in mountain torrents between deep-cut cañons or "barrancas". The largest fresh-water lakes are *Chapala* (70 miles long and 20 miles wide), and *Pátzcuaro*. In the north-west are saline lakes amid bare and dry regions. The climate varies according to the altitude, the rainy season lasting from June to October.

History and Archæology.—The present Mexico and Guatemala were once the centre of a remarkable indigenous civilization, which had unknown beginnings in the centuries before Christ, flowered in the periods from A.D. 500 to 1100 and A.D. 1300 to 1500 and collapsed before the little army of Spanish adventurers under Hernán Cortés in the years following 1519. Pre-Columbian Mexico was divided between different but connected Indian cultures, each of which has left distinctive archæological remains: the best-known of these are Chichén Itzá, Uxmal, Bonampak and Palenque, in Yucatán and Chiapas (Maya); Teotihuacon, renowned for the Pyramid of the Sun (216 feet high) in the Valley of Mexico (Teotihuacáno); Monte Albán and Mitla, near Oaxaca (Zapotec); El Tajín in the State of Veracruz (Totonac); and Tula in the State of Hidalgo (Toltec). The last and most famous Indian culture of all, the Aztec, based on Tenochtitlán suffered more than the others from the Spaniards and only very few Aztec monuments remain.

A few years after the Conquest, the Spaniards built Mexico City on the ruins of Tenochtitlán, and appointed a Viceroy to rule their new dominions, which they called New Spain. The country was largely converted to Christianity, and a distinctive colonial civilization, representing a marriage of Indian and Spanish traditions, developed and flourished, notably in architecture and sculpture. In 1810 a revolt began against Spanish rule. This was finally successful in 1821, when a precarious independence was proclaimed. Friction with the United States in Texas led to the war of 1845–48, at the end of which Mexico was forced to cede the northern provinces of Texas, California and New Mexico. In 1862 Mexican insolvency led to invasion by French forces which installed Archduke Maximilian of Austria as Emperor. The empire collapsed with the execution of the Emperor in 1867 and the austere reformer, Juárez, restored the republic. Juárez's death was followed by the dictatorship of Porfirio Diaz, which saw an enormous increase of foreign, particularly British and United States, investment in the country. In 1910 began the Mexican Revolution which reformed the social structure and the land system, curbed the power of foreign companies and ushered in the independent industrial Mexico of today.

Government.—Under the Constitution of Feb. 5, 1917 (as subsequently amended), Congress consists of a Senate of 64 members, elected for six years, and of a Chamber of Deputies, at present numbering 400, elected for three years. Presidents, who wield full executive powers, are elected for six years; they cannot be re-elected.

There are eight political parties registered in Mexico, of which by far the largest and most influential is the *Partido Revolucionario Institucional* (P.R.I.) which has for many years constituted the governing party. The Mexican Communists allied with several like-minded smaller parties to form the Mexican United Socialist Party (P.S.U.M.) in 1982.

Communications.—Veracruz, Tampico and Coatzacoalcos are the chief ports of the Atlantic, and Guaymas, Mazatlán, Puerto Lázaro Cárdenas, Acapulco, Salina Cruz and Puerto Madero on the Pacific. Work is proceeding on the reorganization, rehabilitation and re-equipment of the whole system; help in this has been forthcoming from the World Bank, the Export-Import Bank and private sources in the United States. The railways were completely nationalized in 1970.

Mexico City may be reached by at least three excellent highways (with 14 entry points) from the United States, and work is complete on roads southward from Mexico City to Yucatán as well as on two principal highways to the Guatemalan border (with three entry points).

International telegraph services to the United States frontier are provided by the government-owned Mexican Telegraph Company and then through the United States to Canada and Europe.

Teléfonos de México, a state-controlled company, controls about 98 per cent of all telephone services. In 1976 there were 9,708,000 kilometres of long distance lines. Satélite Latinoamericano, S.A. (SATELAT) is a joint government/private sector venture disseminating television programmes to Latin America through Intelstat IV satellite facilities leased by the Mexican Government.

There is a good national and international network of air services. There are 1,113 airports and landing fields in Mexico, of which eighteen are equipped to handle long-distance flights. There are 166 airline companies, including two of the major national airlines—*Mexicana de Aviación* and *Aeroméxico*. Passenger traffic is growing by about 18 per cent yearly, while cargo increases by some 14 per cent a year.

Production.—The principal agricultural crops are maize, beans, rice, wheat, sugar cane, coffee, cotton, tomatoes, chili, tobacco, chick-peas, groundnuts, sesame, alfalfa, vanilla, cocoa and many kinds of fruit, both tropical and temperate. The maguey, or Mexican cactus, yields several fermented drinks, mezcal and tequila (distilled) and pulque (undistilled). Another species of the same plant supplies sisal-hemp (henequen). The forests abound in mahogany, rosewood, ebony and chicle trees.

The principal industries (apart from agriculture) are mining and petroleum, but during recent years there has been very considerable expansion of both light and heavy industries. The mining industry has shown a growth of 20 per cent in two years. The steel industry has expanded steadily and produced 5,500,000 tons of steel in 1977. The mineral wealth is great, and principal minerals are gold, silver, copper, lead, zinc, quicksilver, iron and sulphur. Substantial reserves of uranium have been found. In the non-metals sector, Mexico continues to produce 25 per cent of the world's supply of fluorspar with a yearly output of 1·1 million metric tons.

The total proven petroleum reserves were 72 billion barrels in 1983. Crude oil production is currently about 2,600,000 barrels. Daily production of natural gas is approximately 3 billion cubic feet. Oil reserves have increased substantially due to very important

new discoveries in the Gulf of Campeche. A new refinery at Tula, State of Hidalgo is the nation's largest; and new refineries in Monterrey, State of Nuevo Leon, and Salina Cruz, State of Oaxaca, are under construction.

Textile production is led by the artificial fibres sector, which is growing by about 9 per cent each year. The natural fibre textile industry has not registered dynamic growth in the past two years and continues to lose its share of the market to the synthetics, but is being re-structured to make it more efficient and competitive.

Defence.—Supreme command is vested in the President, exercised through the Ministries of Defence (for Army and Air Force) and Marine.

Army.—The country is divided into 35 zones in which the regular army (120,000) and part-time conscripts (250,000) are trained. The Army in 1984 had three HQ Brigades, three Artillery Regiments, 25 Cavalry Regiments, Transport, Engineering and Signals Regiments, and 67 Infantry Battalions. Military education is provided for officers at the National Military School, the National War College and the National Defence College, as well as in other specialised schools. To combat illiteracy in the Army, literacy programmes have been established in regular and conscript groups.

Navy.—The Navy has a strength of about 23,000 officers and men including the Naval Air Force and Marines. It is equipped with four destroyers, six frigates, six OPVs, 19 corvettes, 17 minesweepers, 31 coastal craft patrol, 12 inshore and river patrol boats, 13 transports and tugs, and one sail training ship. Many vessels are non-operational. There are six naval zones on the Atlantic coast and 11 on the Pacific coast which provide off-shore patrol of the EEZ. The Marine Infantry has 10 battalions (4,300 officers and men). The Naval Air Force consists of four squadrons and 49 aircraft.

Air Force.—The Air Force has an approximate strength of 5,500 officers and men and 298 aircraft, including tactical/training aircraft, reconnaissance aircraft/helicopters and transport aircraft. There is a Parachute Brigade consisting of three Parachute battalions (approx. 2,000 men).

Language and Literature.—Spanish is the official language of Mexico and is spoken by about 95 per cent of the population. In addition to Spanish, there are five basic groups of Indian languages spoken in Mexico. The 1970 Census showed that of the 3,111,415 inhabitants speaking an Indian language, 25·7 per cent spoke Náhuatl; 14·6 per cent Maya; 9·1 per cent Zapotec; 7·1 per cent Otomí; 7·5 per cent Mixtec and 36 per cent one or other of the 59 dialects derived from these basic languages. The Press of Mexico is in a flourishing condition with many daily newspapers in the capital and in other urban centres. The first printing press and the first regularly issued newspaper in the New World were established by the Spaniards in Mexico City.

Education.—Education is divided into primary, secondary, preparatory and university. Primary education is free, secular and nominally compulsory.

Trade with U.K.

	1982	1983
Imports from U.K.	£162,946,000	£95,673,513
Exports to U.K.	106,067,000	160,977,775

Imports consist largely of machinery and implements for industry, mining and agriculture, and raw materials for industry. Principal exports are oil, silver, gold, molybdenum, honey, sugar, tropical fruits and nuts, polyesters and yarns, mechanical engine parts and office equipment.

CAPITAL.—Mexico City, metropolitan area 16,000,000 (est. pop.). Other cities (est. pop. 1980) are:

Guadalajara (4,371,998); Monterrey (2,513,044); León (3,006,110); Puebla (3,347,685); Mexicali (1,177,886); Chihuahua (2,005,477); San Luis Potosí (1,673,893); and Mérida (1,063,733).

FLAG.—Three vertical bands in green, white, red, with the Mexican emblem (an eagle on a cactus devouring a snake) in the centre.

NATIONAL DAY.—September 16 (Proclamation of Independence).

BRITISH EMBASSY
Calle Río Lerma 71, Colonia Cuauhtémoc,
06500 Mexico City, D.F.

Ambassador Extraordinary and Plenipotentiary, His Excellency Cynlais Morgan James, C.M.G. (1983).

There are British Consular Offices at *Mexico City, Acapulco, Mérida, Monterrey, Tampico, Veracruz* and *Cuidad Juarez.*

British Council Representative.—Dr. J. B. C. Brown, O.B.E., Maestro Antonio Caso 127, Col. San Rafael (P.O. Box 30-588), Mexico 4, D.F.

BRITISH CHAMBER OF COMMERCE, Calle Tiber 103, 6th Floor, 06500 Mexico, D.F.—*Manager,* T. King.

Transit from London to Mexico City:—By air, 13 hours; By sea, U.K.–New York, 5 to 10 days; New York–Mexico City, by rail, 3 days; by air, 4 hours. There is a direct freight service from Liverpool to ports on both the Mexican Gulf and the Pacific Coast.

MONACO
(Principauté de Monaco)

Sovereign Prince, H.S.H. Rainier III-Louis-Henri-Maxence Bertrand, *born* May 31, 1923, *succeeded his grandfather* (H.S.H. Prince Louis II), May 9, 1949; *married* April 19, 1956, Miss Grace Patricia Kelly (died Sept. 14, 1982) and *has issue* Prince Albert Alexandre Louis Pierre, *born* March 14, 1958, Princess Caroline Louise Marguerite, *born* January 23, 1957; and Princess Stephanie Marie Elisabeth, *born* Feb. 1, 1965.

President of the Crown Council, M. Pierre Blanchy.
President of the National Council, Me. Jean-Charles Rey.

Minister of State, André Saint-Mleux, *appointed* 1972.

CONSULATE-GENERAL IN LONDON
4 Audley Square, W.1
[01–629 0734]

Consul-General, I. S. Ivanovic.
Consul, A. J. Hucker, 5–6 Raymond Buildings, Gray's Inn, W.C.1 [01–242 8404].

A small Principality on the Mediterranean, with land frontiers joining France at every point, and consisting of the old town of Monaco, La Condamine, and Monte Carlo, where is the famous casino. The Principality comprises a narrow strip of country about 2 miles long (area approx. 467 acres), with approximately 28,000 inhabitants (1983) and a yearly average of over 1,000,000 visitors.

The principality, ruled by the Grimaldi family since the late 13th century, was abolished during the French Revolution and re-established in 1815 under the protection of the Kingdom of Sardinia. In 1861 Monaco came under French protection. The 1962 Constitution, which can be modified only with the approval of the National Council, maintains the traditional hereditary monarchy and guarantees freedom of association, trade union freedom and the right to strike. Legislative power is held jointly by the Prince and a uni-cameral, 18 member National Council elected by universal suffrage. Executive power is exercised by the Prince and a four-member Council of Government, headed by a Minister of State. The judicial code is based on that of France.

The whole available ground is built over, so that there is no cultivation, though there are some notable public and private gardens. Monaco has a small harbour (30 ft. alongside quay) and the import duties are the same as in France.

CAPITAL.—Monaco-ville (1,443).

FLAG.—Two equal horizontal stripes, red over white.

H.M. Consul-General, D. A. S. Gladstone (*Resident at Marseilles*).

MONGOLIA
(Mongolian People's Republic—
Bugd Nairamdakh Mongol Ard Uls)

President: Yu Tsedenbal.
Prime Minister: J. Batmunkh.

Mongolian People's Revolutionary
(= *Communist*) **Party**

Politbureau of the Central Committee, Yu Tsedenbal; J. Batmunkh; D. Molomjamts; N. Jagvaral; D. Maidar; T. Ragchaa; B. Altangerel; D. Gombojav (*full members*); S. Luvsangombo (*candidate member*).
Secretariat of the Central Committee, J. Batmunkh (*1st*); D. Molomjamts; N. Jagvaral; D. Gombojav; P. Damdin; G. Adya; M. Dash; Ts. Namsrai.

MONGOLIAN EMBASSY
7 Kensington Court, W8 5DL
[01–937 0150]

Chargé d'Affaires, Gonsurengiin Dugree.

Area and Population.—The Mongolian People's Republic (Mongolia) is a large and sparsely populated country to the north of China. Its area is over 600,000 square miles. Its population (Jan. 1984) is about 1,820,400. However, this total constitutes only part of the Mongolians of Asia, a number of whom are to be found in China and in the neighbouring regions of the Soviet Union (especially the Mongolian Buryat Autonomous Region). This country, which is almost nowhere below 1,000 metres above sea level, forms part of the Central Asiatic Plateau and rises towards the west in the high mountains of the Mongolian Altai and Khanggai Ranges. The Khentai Mountain Range, situated to the north-east of the capital Ulan Bator, is less high. The Gobi region covers much of the southern half of the country. It contains some sand deserts, but between these less hospitable areas there is semi-desert which provides pasture for great numbers of sheep, goats, camels and horses (the latter is still the characteristic means of transport for the rural population) and some cattle. In the steppe areas to the north pasturage is better and livestock more abundant. Even further north, in the better watered provinces, grain, fodder and vegetable crops are increasingly grown. There are several long rivers and many lakes, but good water is scarce since much of the lake water is salty. The climate is hard, with a short mild summer giving way to a long winter when temperatures can drop as low as minus 50° Centigrade.

History.—Mongolia, under Genghis Khan the conqueror of China and much of Asia, was for many years a buffer state between Tsarist Russia and China, although it was under general Chinese suzerainty. The outbreak of the Chinese Revolution in 1911 led to a declaration of autonomy under Chinese suzerainty which was confirmed by the Sino-Russian Treaty of Kiakhta (1915), but cancelled by a unilateral Chinese declaration in 1919. Later the country became a battleground of the Russian Civil

War, and Soviet and Mongolian troops occupied Ulan Bator in 1921: this was followed by another declaration of independence. However, in 1924 the Soviet Union in a Treaty with China again recognized the latter's sovereignty over Mongolia; but this was never properly exercised because of China's pre-occupation with internal affairs, and later by the anti-Japanese war. The Mongolian People's Republic was formally established in 1924. Under the Yalta Agreement, Chiang Kai-shek agreed to a plebiscite, held in 1945, in which the Mongolians declared their desire for independence and this was formally recognized by Nationalist China. The country entered the United Nations in 1961. The heroes of Mongolian history during the earlier part of the century were Sukhebator, who died in 1923, and the Communist Choibalsan (died 1952), who did much to turn the country into the Communist state it is today, and carried out a systematic destruction of the power of the Lamas and the old princely houses which had previously been the dominant force in both the economy and the government.

Production, etc.—The total of Mongolia's livestock was 24 million in 1980. Traditionally the Mongolian is a herdsman, tending his flock of sheep, goats and horses, cows and camels and leading a totally nomadic life. With the coming of the Communist régime (under the Mongolian People's Revolutionary Party) and especially since 1952, great efforts have been made to settle the population, but a large proportion still live nomadically or semi-nomadically in the traditional *ger* (circular tent). The pastoral population was collectivized at the end of the 1950s into huge *negdels* (co-operatives) and State farms which have hastened the process of settlement, but within these the herdsmen and their families still move with their *gers* from pasture to pasture as the seasons change. The country, and three city districts (Ulan Bator, Darkhan and Erdenet), is today divided into 18 *aimaks* (provinces) and beneath these into 258 *somons* (districts), and these form the basis of the State organization of the country, parallel with which runs the apparatus of the Revolutionary Party.

Membership of the Communist bloc has brought Mongolia considerable quantities of aid from other Socialist countries, especially the Soviet Union and China, both of which supplied many thousands of workers to help with various construction projects. Mongolia's support of the Soviet Union in the Sino-Soviet dispute resulted in the cessation of Chinese aid and a halt in the supply of Chinese workers. Mongolia is now relying on eastern European, especially Czech, Polish and East German aid to supplement the massive assistance from the Soviet Union. Soviet and Bloc aid is hastening the process of industrialization; for although the economy remains predominantly based on the herds of animals, and the principal exports of the country are still animal by-products (especially wool, hides and furs) and cattle, factories serving the needs of the country have been started up and the coal and electricity industries are being developed to provide an industrial base. A joint Mongolian/Soviet enterprise for copper and molybdenum mining was opened in 1978, at Erdenet in northern Mongolia. It is now in full production and processes 16 million tonnes of ore annually. A major geological survey is being carried out by the CMEA countries, in order to prepare for the extraction of the considerable mineral deposit known to exist in Mongolia. Coal production in 1980 was 4·5 million tons and is expected to rise to 6·8 million tons by 1985.

Ulan Bator, which contains almost a quarter of the country's population, is the main seat of industry. The second largest industrial centre is at Darkhan, north of the capital, near the Soviet frontier. Its industries include lime, cement and building materials, a flour mill and a power station. Choibalsan, in the east, is also being developed industrially. Agriculture, formerly little practised, is now being extended. Average cereal production for 1976–80 was 347,000 tons, but by 1983 had risen to 800,000 tonnes. Communication is still difficult in the country as there are very few tarmac roads. The trans-Mongolian railway, following the line of the old north-south trade route, was opened in 1955 and links Mongolia with both China and Russia. Mongolia's fundamental difficulty is its very small population and labour force.

Foreign trade is dominated by the Soviet Union, with the eastern European countries taking most of what is left. Trade with western countries and Japan is developing slowly.

CAPITAL.—Ulan Bator. (Pop. 435,000.)

FLAG.—Vertical tri-colour red, blue, red and in the hoist the traditional Soyombo symbol in gold.

NATIONAL DAY.—July 11 (Anniversary of the Mongolian People's Republic).

BRITISH EMBASSY
30 Enkh Taivny Gudamzh (P.O. Box 703)
Ulan Bator 13

Ambassador Extraordinary and Plenipotentiary, His Excellency Allan Geoffrey Roy Butler (1984).
2nd Secretary, G. N. Haycock, M.V.O.
Attachés, D. S. Scott; W. Hampson.

MOROCCO
(Kingdom of Morocco)

King, H.M. King Hassan II (Moulay Hassan Ben Mohammed), *born* July 9, 1929; *acceded* February 26, 1961, *on the death of his father,* King Mohammad V. *Heir,* Crown Prince Sidi Mohamed, *b.* August 21, 1963.

CABINET

Prime Minister, Mohamed Karim Lamrani.
Ministers of State, Abderrahim Bouabid; Hadj M'Hamid Bahnini; Ahmed Osman; Moulay Ahmed Alaoui; Me Maâti Bouabid; Me M'hamed Boucetta; Mahjoubi Aherdane; Mohamed Arsalan El Jadidi.
Justice, Moulay Mustapha Belarbi Alaoui.
Interior, Driss Basri.
Foreign Affairs, Abdelwahed Belkziz.

Religious Endowments and Islamic Affairs, Abdelke-
bir Alaoui M'Daghri.
Plan, Training of Cadres and Professional Training,
M'Hamed Douiri.
National Education, Dr. Azzedine Laraki.
Finance, Abdellatif Jouahri.
Labour and National Development, Moulay Zine
Zahidi.
Co-operation, Abdelwahed Radi.
Commerce, Industry and Tourism, Azzedine Gues-
sous.
Traditional Industry and Social Affairs, Abbes el
Fassi.
Information, Abdellatif Filali.
Transport, Mansouri Benali.
Energy and Mines, Moussa Saadi.
Public Health, Dr. Rahal Rahhali.
Youth and Sport, Abdellatif Semlali.
Maritime Fisheries and Merchant Shipping, Bensa-
lem Smili.
Secretary General of the Government, Abbès el Kaissi.
Cultural Affairs, Said Belbachir.
Housing and the Environment, M'Feddel Lahlou.
Equipment, Mohamed Kabbaj.
Posts and Telecommunications, Mohamed Laensar.
Agriculture, Othman Demnati.
Relations with Parliament, Me Ahmed Belhaj.
Prime Minister's Office, Taieb Bencheikh (Economic
Affairs); Abdelkrim Ghallab.
There are also four Secretaries and one Under
Secretary of State.

A General Election was called for Sept. 14, 1984.

EMBASSY OF THE KINGDOM OF MOROCCO AND
CONSULATE
49 Queen's Gate Gardens, SW7 5NE
[01–581 5001]

Ambassador Extraordinary and Plenipotentiary, His
Excellency Mohamed-Mehdi Benabdeljalil (1982).
Military, Naval and Air Attaché, Col. Mustapha
Jabrane.

Area and Population.—Morocco is situated in the
north-western corner of the African continent between latitude 27° 40'–36° N. and longitude 1°–13° W.
with an area estimated at approximately 180,000 sq.
miles, and a population (1982) of 20,419,555. It is
traversed in the north by the Rif Mountains and in a
general S.W. to N.E. direction, by the Middle Atlas,
the High Atlas, the Anti-Atlas and the Sarrho ranges.
The northern flanks of the Middle and High Atlas
Mountains are well wooded but their southern slopes,
exposed to the dry desert winds, are generally arid
and desolate, as are the whole of the Anti-Atlas and
Sarrho ranges. The north-westerly point of Morocco
is the peninsula of Tangier which is separated from
the continent of Europe by the narrow strait of
Gibraltar. The Jebel Mousa dominates the promontory and, with the rocky eminence of Gibraltar, was
known to the ancients as the Pillars of Hercules, the
western gateway of the Mediterranean.
Western Sahara.—Formerly the Spanish Sahara,
the territory was split between Morocco and Mauritania in 1976 after Spain withdrew in Dec. 1975. In
1979 Mauritania renounced its claim to its share of
the territory, which was added by Morocco to its
area. Morocco's annexation is being opposed by
Polisario guerrillas, who want the territory to become
an independent state.
Climate.—The climate of Morocco is generally good
and healthy, especially on the Atlantic coast, (where
a high degree of humidity is, however, prevalent) the
country being partially sheltered by the Atlas mountains from the hot winds of the Sahara. The rainy
season may last from November to April. The plains
of the interior are intensely hot in summer. Average

summer and winter temperatures for Rabat are 81°
F. and 45° F.; for Marrakesh 101° F. and 40° F.
respectively.
Government.—Morocco became an independent
sovereign state in 1956, following joint declarations
made with France on March 2, 1956, and with Spain
on April 7, 1956. The Sultan of Morocco, Sidi
Mohammad ben Youssef, adopted the title of King
Mohammad V.
Following serious disturbances in Casablanca in
March, 1965, attempts were made by King Hassan, in
consultation with all political parties, to form a
government of national union. These efforts were
unsuccessful and on June 7, 1965, the King proclaimed
a "state of exception" and suspended Parliament.
Assuming himself the office of Prime Minister, he
announced the formation of a new government and
indicated that constitutional changes were to follow.
A revised Constitution was approved by a national
referendum on July 24, 1970 and brought into effect
soon after. It was superseded by another constitution,
also approved by a national referendum, on March 1,
1972. This provides that not only political parties,
but trade unions, chambers of commerce and professional bodies will participate in the organization of
the State and representation of the people; specifies
that the King is the supreme representative of the
people; makes changes in the composition of the
Regency Council and the Sovereign's rights and
establishes a unicameral legislature. The Chamber
has 267 members, 182 elected by direct universal
suffrage and 85 members elected by electoral colleges
representing local government, industry, agriculture
and working class groups. Following disturbances in
several parts of the country in Jan. 1984, a Government of National Unity was formed with Mohamed
Karim Lamrani as Prime Minister and the heads of
all five major political parties as Ministers of State.
Defence.—The Moroccan army, formed in 1956, is
about 120,000 strong. A Moroccan air force was
formed in 1959 and a navy in 1960. The armed forces
possess quantities of French, Soviet and American
equipment, including aircraft.
Production and Trade.—Morocco's main sources
of wealth are agricultural and mineral. The present
Five Year Plan (1981–85) for economic development
places particular emphasis on social improvement.
Other priority sectors are industrial development,
agriculture and tourism. The world recession and
high energy prices, coupled with a fall in the price of
phosphates and poor harvests due to low rainfall pose
problems for the economy.
Agriculture employs more than 40 per cent. of the
working population and accounts for about 36 per
cent. of Morocco's exports. The main agricultural
products are cereals, citrus fruits, olives, grapes,
tomatoes and vegetables. Dates and figs are also
grown and exported. Cork and wood-pulp are the
most important commercial forest products. Esparto
grass is also produced. There is a fishing industry
and substantial quantities of canned fish, mainly
sardines, are exported. In 1980 3,160,500 sheep,
823,300 goats and 686,000 cattle were slaughtered in
controlled abattoirs. Horses, camels, donkeys and
pigs are also raised.
Morocco's mineral exports are phosphates, fluorite,
barite, manganese, iron ore, lead, zinc, cobalt, copper
and antimony. Production of phosphates totalled
18,562,000 tonnes in 1981, of which 15,635,500 tonnes
were exported. Production of crude oil in 1981
amounted to 17,500 tonnes. There are oil refineries
at Mohammedia and Sidi Kacem handling about 4
million tonnes of crude oil per year.
Morocco's main import requirements are petroleum products, motor vehicles, building materials,
agricultural and other machinery, chemical products,
sugar, green tea and other foodstuffs.

The trade of Morocco is chiefly with France, the U.S.A., W. Germany, Italy, the United Kingdom and Spain.

	1983
Imports	DH25,591 million
Exports	14,724 million

Trade with U.K.

	1982	1983
Imports from U.K.	£95,000,000	£99,727,000
Exports to U.K.	60,000,000	75,602,000

There is a British Chamber of Commerce at 291 Blvd Mohamed V, Casablanca.

Currency.—The unit of currency is the *dirham.* Exchange rate (*see* p. 82).

The 1984 General Budget (as amended, April 26, 1984) amounted to *DH*44,000 million.

Communications.—The railway runs south from Tangier to Sidi Kacem. From this junction, one line runs eastwards through Fez and Oujda to Algeria, and another continues southwards, through Rabat and Casablanca, to Marrakesh. A line running due south from Oujda skirts the Morocco-Algeria frontier and reaches Colomb-Bechar in Algeria, the beginning of the Mediterranean–Niger project. Moroccan railroads cover 1,250 miles and traction is electric or diesel. An extensive network of well-surfaced roads covers all the main towns in the kingdom.

Tangier is distant from London about 1,200 miles or a matter of 2 hours by air, 4 days by sea. Royal-Air-Maroc operates a service between Casablanca and London. There are air services between Tangier, Agadir (seasonal), Marrakesh and London, and also between Tangier and Gibraltar connecting with London. Royal Air Inter operates internal services. There are also regular services by many airlines with many parts of the world.

Language.—Arabic is the official language. Berber is the vernacular mainly in the mountain regions. French and Spanish are also spoken mainly in the towns. The foreign population is estimated at 61,935 (1982). The national daily press consists of 5 Arabic and 5 French newspapers.

Education.—There are government primary, secondary and technical schools. At Fez there is a theological university of great repute in the Moslem world. There is a secular university at Rabat. Schools for special denominations, Jewish and Catholic, are permitted and may receive government grants.

CAPITAL.—ΨRabat (population 518,616). Regional capitals, with municipal population figures as at 1982, are: ΨCasablanca (2,139,204); Marrakesh (439,728); Fez (448,823); Oujda (260,082); Meknes (319,783); Agadir (110,479). The towns of Fez, Marrakesh and Meknes were capitals at various times in Morocco's history.

FLAG.—Red, with green pentagram (the Seal of Solomon).

NATIONAL DAY.—March 3 (Anniversary of the Throne).

BRITISH EMBASSY
17 Boulevard de la Tour Hassan (B.P. 45), Rabat

Ambassador Extraordinary and Plenipotentiary, His Excellency John Cambridge, C.M.G., C.V.O. (1982).

1st Secretary, D. Broad (*Head of Chancery/Commercial, and Consul*).

Defence Attaché, Lt.-Col. T. C. Morris, M.V.O.

Vice Consul (*Tangier*), W. A. T. Pulleyblank, M.B.E.

There is a British Consular/Commercial Office at *Casablanca.*

British Council Representative, J. W. Edmundson, (P.O. Box 427), 22 Avenue Moulay Youssef, Rabat.

MOZAMBIQUE
(Moçambique)

President, Samora Moïses Machel, *took office,* 1975, *re-elected* April 1983.

Area and Population.—The People's Republic of Mozambique lies on the east coast of Africa, and is bounded by Swaziland in the south, South Africa in the south and west, Zimbabwe in the west, Zambia and Malawi in the north-west and Tanzania in the north. It has an area of 297,657 square miles, with a population estimated at 12,000,000 (1982).

Government.—Mozambique, discovered by Vasco de Gama in 1498, and colonized by Portugal, achieved complete independence from Portugal on June 25, 1975. The date had been agreed in September 1974 by Portugal and *Frelimo (Frente de Libertação de Moçambique),* the Marxist liberation movement.

Constitution.—The country is governed by a Council of Ministers and by the Permanent Political Committee of the *Frelimo* Party; membership of these two bodies virtually overlaps. No other political parties are permitted. The principal legislative body, the People's Assembly, consists of 216 members nominated by *Frelimo.*

The basis of the economy is subsistence agriculture, but there is an industrial sector based mainly in Beira and Maputo. After giving priority to the development of collective farms and state enterprises in all sectors, the government is now encouraging the private sector and foreign investment, particularly in agriculture and consumer goods production. Main exports are sugar, cashew nuts, copra, cotton, tea and sisal. Mozambique has a range of aid and cooperation agreements with a number of countries in Eastern Europe and in the West. A treaty of non-aggression and good neighbourliness with South Africa was signed on March 16, 1984 (the Nkomati Accord).

Trade with U.K.

	1982	1983
Imports from U.K.	£14,473,000	£28,618,000
Exports to U.K.	10,611,000	9,176,000

CAPITAL.—Ψ Maputo (pop. 850,000). Other main ports are Beira and Nacala.

BRITISH EMBASSY
C.P. 55, Av. V. I. Lenine, 310, Maputo.

Ambassador Extraordinary and Plenipotentiary, His Excellency E. V. Vines, C.M.G., O.B.E.

1st Secretary, John W. Guy (*Head of Chancery and Consul*).

2nd Secretaries, A. Featherstone; R. H. House.

NEPAL

Sovereign, H.M. King Birendra Bir Bikram Shah Dev, *born* 1945; *succeeded* January 31, 1972; *crowned* Feb. 24, 1975; *married,* Feb. 1970, H.M. Queen Aishwara Rajya Laxmi Devi Shah. *Heir,* H.H. Crown Prince Dipendra Bir Bikram Shah Dev, *born,* June 27, 1971.

COUNCIL OF MINISTERS

Prime Minister and Minister for Palace Affairs and Defence, Lokendra Bahadur Chand.

Home Affairs, Padma Sunder Lawati.

Panchayat and Local Development, Forests and Soil Conservation, Jog Mehar Shrestha.

Water Resources and Supply, Pashupati Shumsher Rana.

Commerce, Industry and Health, Narayan Dutta Bhatta.

Agriculture and Land Reform, Hem Bahadur Malla.

Foreign Affairs, Padma Bahadur Khatri.

Public Works and Transport, Damber Narayan Yadau.

Finance and Communications, Prakesh Chandra Lohani.

ROYAL NEPALESE EMBASSY IN LONDON
12A, Kensington Palace Gardens, W8 4QU
[01–229 1594/6231]

Ambassador Extraordinary and Plenipotentiary, His Excellency Ishwari Raj Pandey (1983).

1st Secretary, Prabal S. J. B. Rana, C.V.O.

Military Attaché, Lt.-Col. C. B. Gurung.

Attaché, Baikuntha Prasad Aryal.

Area and Population.—Nepal lies between India and the Tibet Autonomous Region of China on the slopes of the Himalayas, and includes Mount Everest (29,028 feet). It has a total area of 54,362 square miles and a population estimated at about 16 million. The country comprises three distinct horizontal formations. In the south, joining the Indian plains, is the Terai, a fair proportion of which was covered with jungle. It has recently been more widely cultivated but wild life is preserved in parts. The region represents 10 per cent of the total land area and nearly 40 per cent of the population live there. The central belt of the country is hilly, but with many fertile valleys, leading up to the snowline at about 14,000 feet. The hills account for 60 per cent of the area of the country and about 50 per cent of the population. The remainder of the country consists of high mountains which are sparsely inhabited. The country is drained by three great river systems rising within and beyond the Himalayan mountain ranges and eventually flowing into the Ganges in India.

The inhabitants are of mixed stock, with Mongolian characteristics prevailing in the North and Indian in the south. The official religion is Hinduism but there is also a strong Buddhist adherence. Gautama Buddha was born in Nepal.

History and Government.—The country was originally divided into numerous hill clans and petty principalities, but Nepal emerged as a nation in the middle of the 18th Century when its component parts were unified by the warrior Raja of Gorkha, Prithvi Narayan Shah, who founded the present Nepalese dynasty. In 1846 power was seized by Jung Bahadur Rana after a massacre of nobles, and he was the first of a line of hereditary Rana Prime Ministers who ruled Nepal for 104 years. During this time the role of the Monarchs was mainly ceremonial.

During the 1914–18 and 1939–45 World Wars the Nepalese Government rendered unstinted and unconditional assistance to the British Government.

In 1950/51 a revolutionary movement achieved its aim of breaking the hereditary power of the Ranas and restoring the Monarchy to its former position. After 10 years, during which various parties and individuals tried their hand at government, the late King Mahendra proscribed all political parties and assumed direct powers on December 16, 1960, with the object of leading a united country to democracy. In 1962 he introduced a new Constitution embodying a tiered, partyless system of panchayat (council) democracy under which there were elected councils at village level which in turn elect members to district council and thence to zonal councils; a referendum in May 1980 decided in favour of retaining the panchayat system, with some reforms; namely, election to the Rastriaya Panchayat (National Parliament) by universal adult franchise (over 21 years old); selection of the Prime Minister by the Rastriaya Panchayat and responsibility of his government to that body. The King retains certain reserve powers. In a general election in May 1981, 112 members were elected from the 75 districts of Nepal. The King appoints 28 other members, making a total of 140.

Economy.—Nepal exports jute, rice and other grains, hides, oil seeds, ghi, cattle, timber, etc., and imports cotton goods and yarns, sugar, salt, spices, petrol, metals, etc. Foreign aid supports 60 per cent of the development budget of the Kingdom and tourism is the single largest commercial earner of foreign exchange (U.S.$35 million in 1982–83). Revenue for the fiscal year 1983–84 is estimated at N Rps. 4,306m; foreign aid N Rps. 4,000m; and internal borrowing N Rps. 1,216m.

Trade with U.K.

	1982	1983
Imports from U.K.	£4,650,000	£5,011,000
Exports to U.K.	3,844,000	6,155,000

A State Bank was inaugurated on April 26, 1956, to issue bank notes, regulate the Nepalese currency, fix foreign exchange rates and help in the preparation of a national budget. There are three commercial banks with branches throughout Nepal.

Communications.—Kathmandu is connected with India by a road, the mountain section of which was built by India under the Colombo Plan, and to Tibet by a road to Kodari on the border which was built by the Chinese and opened on May 26, 1967. The Indian-aided Sunauli-Pokhara road (128 miles) was inaugurated in April 1972, and a road between Pokhara and Kathmandu, constructed by the Chinese, was opened in 1973. A link road between Mugling and Naryanghat, completed by the Chinese in 1981, has further improved communications between Kathmandu and the Terai. The East–West Highway (Mahendra Raj Marg) to run the length of the country, is almost complete. Work is in progress from Butwal westwards. Sections of the highway have been built, with aid from India, Great Britain, U.S.S.R., America and the Asian Development Bank. British assistance has included the building of an external communications satellite, improving telex and telephone services, and the completion in 1984 of the mountainous Dharan–Dhankuta highway.

There are daily flights from Kathmandu to New Delhi, and frequent flights to Calcutta and Patna. There are also daily flights to Bangkok, a twice weekly direct flight to Dacca, flights from Kathmandu to Rangoon, Colombo, Hong Kong and Karachi.

CAPITAL.—Kathmandu, population (1981) 235,000. Other towns of importance are Biratnagar (94,000), Lalitpur (81,000) and Bhaktapur (50,500) and Pokhara (48,500).

FLAG.—Double pennant of crimson with blue border on peaks; white moon with rays in centre of top peak; white quarter sun, recumbent in centre of bottom peak.

NATIONAL DAY.—February 18.

BRITISH EMBASSY
(Lainchaur Kathmandu, P.O. Box 106)

Ambassador Extraordinary and Plenipotentiary, His Excellency Anthony G. Hurrell, C.M.G. (1983).

First Secretary, P. H. Roberts, O.B.E. (Head of Chancery and Consul).

Defence and Military Attaché, Lt.-Col. M. G. Allen.

Vice-Consul, G. E. Perkins.

British Council Representative, A. J. Pattison, (P.O. Box 640), Kanti Path, Kathmandu.

NETHERLANDS (or HOLLAND)
(Koninkrijk der Nederlanden)

Queen of the Netherlands, Her Majesty Beatrix Wilhelmina Armgard, G.C.V.O., born Jan. 31, 1938; married March 10, 1966, H.R.H. Prince Claus George Willem Otto Frederik Geert of the Netherlands, Jonkheer van Amsberg; and has issue, Prince Willem

Alexander, *b.* April 27, 1967; Prince Johan Friso, *b.* Sept, 25, 1968; Prince Constantijn Christof, *b.* Oct. 11, 1969; *succeeded,* April 30, 1980, upon the abdication of her mother Queen Juliana.

CABINET

Prime Minister and Minister of General Affairs, Ruud Lubbers *(C.D.A.).*
Deputy P.M. and Minister for Economic Affairs, Gijs van Aardenne *(V.V.D.).*
Social Affairs and Employment, and Antilles Affairs, Dr. Jan de Konig *(C.D.A.).*
Defence, Jacob de Ruiter *(C.D.A.).*
Finance, Dr. Herman Ruding *(C.D.A.).*
Transport and Waterways, Mrs. Nellie Smit-Kroes *(V.V.D.).*
Education and Science, Dr. Wim Deetman (C.D.A.).
Welfare, Public Health and Culture, Elco Brinkman *(C.D.A.).*
Development Co-operation, Mrs. Eegje Schoo *(V.V.D.).*
Agriculture and Fisheries, Gerrit Braks *(C.D.A.).*
Housing, Planning and Environment, Pieter Winsemius *(V.V.D.).*
Justice, Frits Korthals Altes, *(V.V.D.).*
Home Affairs, Koos Rietkerk, *(V.V.D.).*
Foreign Affairs, Hans van den Broek *(C.D.A.).*
(C.D.A. = Christian Democrats; *V.V.D.* = Liberals.)

ROYAL NETHERLANDS EMBASSY IN LONDON
38 Hyde Park Gate, SW7 5DP
[01-584 5040]

Ambassador Extraordinary and Plenipotentiary, His Excellency Jonkheer J. L. R. Huydecoper (1982).
Minister Plenipotentiary, L. W. Veenendal.
Minister Plenipotentiary, J. W. Semijns de Vries van Doesburgh.
Counsellors, A. J. van der Stadt; D. Vries; A. D. H. Simonsz; J. P. Kleiweg de Zwaan; J. T. de Jonge.
1st Secretaries, Jonkheer M. D. Reuchlin; R. G. Brinks; C. W. Andrae; W. H. Ronke.
Defence, Naval and Air Attaché, Capt. W. H. van Riet.
Military Attaché, Col. J. Smit.

Area and Population.—The Kingdom of the Netherlands is a maritime country of Western Europe, situated on the North Sea, in lat. 50° 46´–53° 34´ N. and long. 3° 22´–7° 14´ E., consisting of 11 provinces plus Eastern and Southern Flevoland (reclaimed parts of the Ysselmeer) and containing a total area of 13,500 sq. miles (34,830 sq. km). The population in Jan. 1984 was estimated at 14,394,589. The live birth rate in Jan., 1983 was 11·8 per 1,000 of the population, and the death-rate was 8·2.
The land is generally flat and low, intersected by numerous canals and connecting rivers—in fact, a network of water courses. The principal rivers are the Rhine, Maas, Yssel and Scheldt.
Government.—In 1815 the Netherlands became a constitutional Kingdom under King William I, a Prince of Orange-Nassau, a descendant of the house which has taken a leading part in the destiny of the nation since the 16th century. The States-General comprise the *Eerste Kamer* (First Chamber) of 75 members, elected for 4 years by the Provincial Council; and the *Tweede Kamer* (Second Chamber) of 150 members, elected for 4 years by men and women voters of 18 years and upwards. Members of the *Tweede Kamer* are paid.
Production.—The chief agricultural products are potatoes, wheat, rye, barley, corn, sugar beet, cattle, pigs, milk and milk products, cheese, butter, poultry, eggs, beans, peas, flax seed, vegetables, fruit, flower bulbs, plants and cut flowers and there is an important fishing industry. Among the principal industries are engineering, both mechanical and electrical, elec-

tronics, nuclear energy, petro-chemicals and plastics, shipbuilding, steel, textiles of all types, leather goods, electrical appliances, metal ware, furniture, paper, cigars, sugar, liqueurs, beer, clothing, rubber products, etc.
In 1981 the production of crude oil was 1,348 million Kgs and refined oil products 36,838 million Kgs; steel 5,472 million Kgs, and gas 84,617 million cubic metres.
Defence.—As a result of a defence review in 1984 the armed forces will be re-equipped in the coming years. The armed forces are almost entirely committed to NATO. All ground and air units are assigned to the NATO Central Region, and naval forces to the Atlantic and Channel commands. Total armed forces number 108,000, which includes 50,000 conscripts and 1,450 women. In addition there are over 180,000 reservists. There is compulsory military service of 14–17 months.
Language and Literature.—Dutch is a West-Germanic language of Saxon origin, closely akin to Old English and Low German. It is spoken in the Netherlands and the northern part of Belgium. It is also used in the Netherlands Antilles. Afrikaans, one of the two South African languages, has Dutch as its origin, but differs from it in grammar and pronunciation. There are six national papers, four of which are morning papers, and there are many regional daily papers.
Education.—Illiteracy is practically non-existent. Primary and secondary education is given in both denominational and State schools, the denominational schools being eligible for State assistance on equal terms with the State schools. Attendance at primary school is compulsory. Secondary schools are numerous, well equipped and well attended. The principal Universities are at Leiden, Utrecht, Groningen, Amsterdam (2), Nijmegen (R.C.) and Rotterdam, and there are technical Universities at Delft (polytechnic); Eindhoven (polytechnic), Enschede (polytechnic) Wageningen (agriculture).
Communications.—The total extent of navigable rivers including canals, was 3,536 km. at Jan. 1, 1982, and of metalled roads 92,525 km. In 1982 the total length of the railway system amounted to 2,956 km.,

of which 1,799 km. were electrified. The mercantile marine in January 1981 consisted of 550 ships of total 3,417,000 gross registered tons. The total length of air routes covered by K.L.M. (Royal Dutch Airlines) in 1982 was 367,000 km.

FINANCE

	1983
Budget Revenue	*D.fl.* 124,400 m.
Budget Expenditure	154,700 m.

TRADE

The Dutch are traditionally a trading nation. *Entrepôt* trade, banking and shipping are of particular importance in their economy. The geographical position of the Netherlands, at the mouths of the Rhine, Meuse and Scheldt, brings a large volume of transit trade to and from the interior of Europe to Dutch ports.

Principal trading partners are the Federal Republic of Germany and Belgium/Luxemburg. U.K. supplied 8·7 per cent of Netherlands imports in 1983 and took 9 per cent of Netherlands exports.

In common with other members of the European Economic Community, the Netherlands on July 1, 1968 removed remaining duties on imports from EEC countries and brought down duties on imports from other countries into line with the Common External Tariff of the EEC.

Excluding the building industry, the index of industrial production in the Netherlands (1975 = 100) was 115 in 1983 and the index of industrial production per worker (1975 = 100) was 143·3 for the first three quarters of 1983.

Imports	*D.fl.* 175,264 m.
Exports	186,695 m.

Trade with U.K.

	1982	1983
Imports from U.K.	£4,653,416,000	£5,440,701,000
Exports to U.K.	£4,474,663,000	5,097,763,000

SEAT OF GOVERNMENT, The Hague (Den Haag or, in full, 's-Gravenhage). Pop. 449,364.

CAPITAL.—Ψ Amsterdam, 687,397. Other principal cities; Ψ Rotterdam, 558,832; Utrecht, 230,347; Eindhoven, 192,715; Haarlem, 152,529; Groningen, 166,942; Tilburg, 153,893.

FLAG.—Three horizontal bands of red, white and blue.

BRITISH EMBASSY
(Lange Voorhout, 10, The Hague, 2514 ED)

Ambassador Extraordinary and Plenipotentiary, His Excellency John William Denys Margetson, C.M.G. (1984).

British Council Representative, W. E. Moss, O.B.E., Keizersgracht 343, Amsterdam (Library).

OVERSEAS TERRITORY

The *Netherlands Antilles* comprise certain islands in the West Indies (Curaçao, Bonaire, Aruba, part of St. Martin, St. Eustatius, and Saba). The area of the Netherlands Antilles is 394·1 sq. miles with a population of 253,234. Under the Realm Statute which took effect on December 29, 1954, the Netherlands Antilles received autonomy in domestic affairs as parts of the Netherlands Realm under the Crown.

Although there are some manufacturing industries, the economy is based almost entirely upon the refining of oil. The soil is too poor to permit large-scale agriculture and most products for consumption, and industrial raw materials must be imported.

Governor
Netherlands Antilles, Dr. R. A. Römer (1983).

Trade with U.K.

Netherlands Antilles	1982	1983
Imports from U.K.	£59,359,000	£84,489,000
Exports to U.K.	76,421,000	97,486,000

The capital of Curaçao is Ψ Willemstad (pop. over 100,000), of Aruba, Ψ Oranjestad; of Bonaire, Ψ Kralendijk; of St. Martin, Philipsburg; of Statius (St. Eustatius), Oranjestad; and of Saba, Bottom.

NICARAGUA

Nicaragua is the largest State of Central America, with a long seaboard on both the Atlantic and Pacific Oceans, situated between 10° 45'–15° N. lat. and 83° 40'–87° 38' W. long., containing an area of 57,145 English square miles (*see index for* MAP). It has a population of 2,700,000 (1980), of whom about three-quarters are of mixed blood. Another 15 per cent are white, mostly of pure Spanish descent and the remaining 10 per cent are Indians or negroes. The latter group includes the Mosquitos, who live on the Atlantic coast and were formerly under British protection.

NICARAGUAN EMBASSY IN LONDON
8 Gloucester Road, SW7 4PP
[01–584 4365]

Ambassador Extraordinary and Plenipotentiary, His Excellency Señor Francisco José d'Escoto (1981).

Government.—The eastern coast of Nicaragua was touched by Columbus in 1502, and in 1518 was overrun by Spanish forces under Davila, and formed part of the Spanish Captaincy-General of Guatemala until 1821, when its independence was secured. In 1927, Augusto Cesar Sandino began a guerilla war against the occupation of Nicaragua by U.S. Marines, which continued until they were expelled in 1933. Sandino was assassinated by Anastasio Somoza, Director of the National Guard, and in 1936 Somoza assumed the Presidency. He was succeeded in power by his sons Luis and Anastasio Somoza, until 1979 when the family and the National Guard were overthrown by guerrillas of the Sandinista National Liberation Front. A Junta of National Reconstruction subsequently took power.

It was announced in March, 1981, that the ruling Junta had been reduced in membership from five to three—Sr. Rafael Cordova Rivas, Sr. Sergio Ramirez Mercado and Sr. Daniel Ortega Saavedra. Elections for President, Vice-President and a Constituent Assembly are scheduled for Nov. 4, 1984.

Agriculture and Industry.—The country is mainly agricultural. The major crops are cotton, coffee, sugar cane, tobacco, sesame and bananas. Beans, rice, maize and ipecacuanha are also important. Livestock and timber production, already considerable, are expanding. Nicaragua possesses deposits of gold and silver.

Communications.—There are 252 miles of railway, all on the Pacific side and approximately 5,500 miles of telegraph. There are 51 radio stations and two television stations in Managua. An automatic telephone system has been installed in the capital and extended to all major cities. A ground station for satellite communication was inaugurated in 1973. Transport except on the Pacific slope, is still attended with difficulty but many new roads have either been opened or are under construction. The Inter-American Highway runs from the Honduras frontier in the north to the Costa Rican border in the south; the interoceanic highway runs from the Corinto on the Pacific coast viá Managua to Rama, where there is a natural waterway to Bluefields on the Atlantic. The country's main airport is at Managua. The chief port is Corinto on the Pacific.

Language and Literature.—The official language of the country is Spanish and the majority profess Catholicism, although the English language and the Moravian Church are widespread on the Atlantic coast. There are 3 daily newspapers published at Managua, apart from the official Gazette (*La Gaceta*). A national literacy campaign in 1980 has reduced illiteracy to 12 per cent. There are universities at León and Managua.

Trade with U.K.

	1982	1983
Imports from U.K.	£4,940,000	£2,367,000
Exports to U.K.	3,282,000	1,180,000

Considerable quantities of foodstuffs are imported as well as cotton goods, jute, iron and steel, machinery and petroleum products. The chief exports are cotton, coffee, beef, gold, sugar, cottonseed, bananas and soluble coffee.

CAPITAL.—Managua, population 615,000. The centre was almost totally destroyed in the earthquake of December 1972. León, 158,577; Granada, 72,640; Masaya, 78,308; Chinandega, 144,291.

British Ambassador, (resident at San José, Costa Rica).

NIGER
(République du Niger)

President, Col. Seyni Kountché, *assumed power*, April 15, 1974.

Situated in West Central Africa, between 12° and 24° N. and 0° and 16° E., Niger has common boundaries with Algeria and Libya in the north, Chad, Nigeria, Benin, Mali and Upper Volta.

It has an area of about 459,000 square miles with a population (U.N. estimate, 1980) of 5,310,000. Apart from a small region along the Niger Valley in the south-west near the capital the country is entirely savannah or desert. The main races in Niger are the Haussas in the east, the Djermas in the south-west and the nomadic Touaregs in the north. The official language is French.

The first French expedition arrived in 1891 and the country was fully occupied by 1914. It decided on December 18, 1958, to remain an autonomous republic within the French Community; full independence outside the Community was proclaimed on August 3, 1960. Special agreements with France, covering

financial and cultural matters, technical assistance, defence, etc., were signed in Paris on April 24, 1961. These are now being revised.

The constitution of Niger, adopted on November 8, 1960, provided for a presidential system of government, modelled on that of the United States and the French Fifth Republic, and a single Chamber National Assembly. In April 1974 Lt.-Col. Seyni Kountché seized power, suspended the Constitution, dissolved the National Assembly, and suppressed all political organizations. He then set up a Supreme Military Council with himself as President.

Finance,—The currency of Niger is the *Franc CFA*. In 1982–83 the budget balanced at *CFA francs* 81,268 million.

Trade.—The cultivation of ground-nuts and the production of livestock are the main industries and provide the two main exports. Exports in 1978 were Livestock, *Francs CFA* 11,600,000,000; Ground-nuts, *Francs CFA* 300,000,000. A company formed by the Government, the French Atomic Energy Authority and private interests is exploiting uranium deposits at Arlit. Exports of uranium in 1981 were worth *Francs CFA* 98,004,000,000.

Trade with U.K.

	1982	1983
Imports from U.K.	£17,346,000	£9,660,000
Exports to U.K.	574,000	6,854,000

CAPITAL.—Niamey (100,000).

FLAG.—Three horizontal stripes, orange, white and green with an orange disc in the middle of the white stripe.

NATIONAL DAY.—December 18.

British Ambassador, (*resident at* Abidjan, Ivory Coast).

NORWAY
(Norge)

King, Olav V, K.G., K.T., G.C.B., G.C.V.O., b. July 2, 1903; *succeeded*, Sept. 21, 1957, on death of his father King Haakon VII; *married* March 21, 1929, Princess Märthe of Sweden (*born* March 29, 1901; *died* April 5, 1954); having issue, Harald (*see below*) and two daughters.

Heir-Apparent, H.R.H. Prince Harald, G.C.V.O., b. Feb. 21, 1937; m. Aug. 29, 1968, Sonja Haraldsen, and has issue Princess Märthe Louise, b.Sept. 22, 1971; and Prince Haakon Magnus, b. July 20, 1973.

CABINET

Prime Minister, Kåre Willoch.
Foreign Affairs, Svenn Stray.
Finance, Rolf Presthus.
Oil and Energy, Kåre Kristiansen.
Defence, Anders C. Sjaastad.
Justice, Mona Røkke.
Industry, Jan P. Syse.
Consumer Affairs and Government Administration, Astrid Gjertsen.
Fisheries, Thor Listau.
Local Government and Labour, Arne Rettedal.
Transport and Communications, Johann J. Jakobsen.
Environment, Rakel Surlien.
Church and Education, Kjell Magne Bondevik.
Higher Education and Culture, Lars Roar Langslet.
Agriculture, Finn T. Isaksen.
Social Affairs, Leif Arne Heløe.
Commerce, Asbjørn Haugstvedt.
Development Aid, Reidun Brusletten.
(This three-party coalition of the Conservative, Centre and Christian parties was formed in June 1983).

ROYAL NORWEGIAN EMBASSY IN LONDON
Offices: 25 Belgrave Square, SW1X 8QD
[01–235 7151]

Ambassador Extraordinary and Plenipotentiary, His Excellency Rolf Busch (1982).

Minister-Counsellor, Kai Lie.

Counsellors, Jan Flatla (*Press and Cultural*); S. Remøy (*Fisheries*); B. Syvertsen (*Economic*); Jan Enger (*Commercial*).

1st Secretaries, Eva Bugge (*Political*); Tore Karlsvik (*Consul*).

2nd Secretaries, Harald Neple (*Economic*); Oystein Steiro (*Press, Information and Cultural*).

Area and Population.—Norway ("The Northern Way"), a kingdom in the northern and western portion of the Scandinavian peninsula, was founded in 872. It is 1,752 km. in length, its greatest width about 430 km. The length of the coastline is 2,650 km., and the frontier between Norway and the neighbouring countries is 2,531 km. (Sweden 1,619 km., Finland 716 km. and U.S.S.R. 196 km.). It is divided into 19 counties (*fylker*) and comprises an area of 386,308 sq. km. of which Svalbard is 62,049 and Jan Mayen 372 sq. km., with a population (estimated, Jan. 1983) of 4,106,651. In 1979 there were for every 1,000 inhabitants: 12·7 live births; 10·2 deaths; 8·7 deaths during first year of age (per 1,000 live births); 5·7 marriages.

The Norwegian coastline is extensive, deeply indented with numerous fiords, and fringed with an immense number of rocky islands. The surface is mountainous, consisting of elevated and barren tablelands, separated by deep and narrow valleys. At the North Cape the sun does not appear to set from the second week in May to the last week in July, causing the phenomenon known as the *Midnight Sun*; conversely, there is no apparent sunrise from about Nov. 18 to Jan. 23. During the long winter nights are seen the multiple coloured *Northern Lights* or *Aurora Borealis*, which have a maximum intensity in a line crossing North America from Alaska to Labrador and Northern Europe to the Arctic coast and Siberia.

Government.—From 1397 to 1814 Norway was united with Denmark, and from Nov. 4, 1814, with Sweden, under a personal union which was dissolved on June 7, 1905, when Norway regained complete independence. Under the constitution of May 17, 1814, the *Storting* (Parliament) itself elects one-quarter of its members to constitute the *Lagting* (Upper Chamber), the other three-quarters forming the *Odelsting* (Lower Chamber). Legislative questions alone are dealt with by both parts in separate sittings.

On April 8–9, 1940, Germany invaded Norway, and it was not until June 7, 1945, that the late King Haakon was able to return from Great Britain to Oslo.

Production.—The cultivated area is about 8,636 sq. km. (2·3 per cent of total surface area); forests cover nearly 25 per cent; the rest consists of highland pastures or uninhabitable mountains.

The *Gulf Stream* pours from 140 to 170 million cubic feet of warm water per second into the sea around Norway and causes the temperature to be higher than the average for the latitude. It brings shoals of herring and cod into the fishing grounds and causes a warm current of air over the west coast, making it possible to cultivate potatoes and barley in latitudes which in other countries are perpetually frozen.

The chief industries are manufactures, agriculture and forestry, fisheries, mining, production of metals and ferro-alloys and shipping. Also in recent years industries providing both manufactured products and services for the development of North Sea oil and gas resources have assumed growing importance. In 1983, the total workforce was 1,957,000 of which

356,000 persons were employed in Norwegian industry. Manufactures are aided by great resources of hydro-electric power. Actual production in 1983 amounted to 106,200 million kwh. In normal years the quantity of fish caught by Norwegian fishing vessels is greater than that of any other European country except U.S.S.R. In 1983 the total catch amounted to 2,928,600 metric tonnes.

Defence.—Norway is a member of the North Atlantic Treaty Organization, and the Headquarters of Allied Forces, Northern Europe, is situated near Oslo. The period of compulsory national service is 15 months (without refresher training) in the Navy and Air Force, and 12 months (with refresher training) in the Army. In March 1978 Norway committed an infantry battalion with additional support to the U.N. Interim Force in the Lebanon.

Education from 7 to 16 is free and compulsory in the "basic schools" maintained by the municipalities with State grants-in-aid. The majority of the pupils receive post-compulsory schooling at "upper secondary" schools, colleges of education (19) regional colleges akin to polytechnics (12), universities (4) and other university-level specialist institutions.

Language and Literature.—Old Norse literature is among the most ancient and richest in Europe. Norwegian in both its present forms is closely related to other Scandinavian languages. Independence from Denmark (1814) and resurgent nationalism led to the development of "new Norwegian" based on dialects, which now has equal official standing with "bokmål", in which Danish influence is more obvious. This was formed in the time of the Reformation, and Ludvig Holberg (1684–1754) is regarded as the father of Norwegian literature, though the modern period begins with the patriotic and romantic writings of Henrik Wergeland (1808–1845). Some of the famous names are Henrik Ibsen (1828–1906), the dramatist, Bjørnstjerne Bjørnson (1832–1910), dramatist, novelist and Nobel Prizewinner in 1903, and the novelists Jonas Lie (1833–1908), Alexander Kielland (1849–1906), Knut Hamsun (1859–1952) and Sigrid Undset

(1882–1949), the latter two both Nobel Prizewinners, and the latter a champion of Norwegian womanhood. In 1983 there were 65 newspapers appearing six times weekly, 95 two to five times weekly and 3 once a week. Total circulation was in the region of 2,430,469. There are no Sunday newspapers.

Communications.—The total length of railways open at the end of 1983 was 4,242 km., excluding private lines. The extension of the main line from Fauske to Bodö, 60 miles north of the Arctic Circle, was completed in 1962. There are 84,032 km. of public roads in Norway (including urban streets). At the end of 1983, 2,337,705 road motor vehicles were registered.

Civil Aviation.—Scheduled internal air services are operated by Scandinavian Airlines System (SAS) on behalf of Det Norske Luftfartselskap (DNL), by Braathens South American and Far East Airtransport (SAFE), and by Wideröes Flyveselskap A.S.

Mercantile Marine.—The Mercantile Marine, 1983, consisted of 1,620 vessels of 18,125,000 gross tons (vessels above 100 gross tons, excluding fishing boats, floating whaling factories, tugs, salvage vessels, icebreakers and similar types of vessel). The fleet ranks seventh among the merchant navies of the world.

FINANCE, 1983

Sector:—

Government—	Revenue	K171,174 m
	Expenditure	153,325 m
Public—	Revenue	K215,861 m
	Expenditure	187,959 m

TRADE

	1982	1983
	million *Kroner*	
Total imports	142,257	152,581
Total exports	163,908	185,187

Trade with U.K.

	1982	1983
Imports from U.K. . . .	£924,651,000	£828,612,000
Exports to U.K.	2,023,441,000	2,820,760,000

The chief imports are raw materials, motor vehicles, chemicals, motor spirit, fuel and other oils; coal, ships and machinery; together with manufactures of silk, cotton and wool. The exports consist chiefly of crude oil and gas, manufactured goods, fish and products of fish (as canned fish, whale oils), pulp, paper, iron ore and pyrites, nitrate of lime, stone, calcium carbide, aluminium, ferro-alloys, zinc, nickel, cyanamide, etc.

CAPITAL.—Ψ Oslo (incl. Aker). Pop. (Jan. 1983), 448,747. Other towns are Ψ Trondheim, 134,652; Ψ Bergen, 207,232; Ψ Stavanger, 92,012; Ψ Kristiansand, 61,834; Ψ Drammen, 50,605; Ψ Tromsø, 47,322; Ψ Aalesund, 34,909; Ψ Haugesund, 27,043; Moss, 24,967.

FLAG.—Red, with white-bordered blue cross.

NATIONAL DAY.—May 17 (Constitution Day).

AIR TRANSIT FROM U.K.—London–Bergen or Oslo, 1 *hr.* 50 *mins.* London–Stavanger, 1 *hr.* 40 *mins.*

BRITISH EMBASSY
Thomas Heftyesgate, 8 Oslo 2.

Ambassador Extraordinary and Plenipotentiary, His Excellency William Bentley, C.M.G.

Counsellors, A. C. Hunt, *(Economic);* D. B. C. Logan *(Head of Chancery).*

BRITISH CONSULAR OFFICES

There is a British Consular Office at *Oslo* and Honorary Consulates at *Bergen, Tromsø, Alesund, Kristiansund N., Narvik, Stavanger, Trondheim, Kristiansand S.* and *Haugesund.*

BRITISH COUNCIL

Representative, P. A. Thompson, Fridtjof Nansens Plass 5, Oslo 1.

SVALBARD
(Spitsbergen and Bear Island)

By Treaty (Feb. 9, 1920) the sovereignty of Norway over the Spitsbergen ("Pointed Mountain") Archipelago was recognized by the Great Powers and other interested nations, and on Aug. 14, 1925, Norway assumed sovereignty. In September, 1941, Allied forces (British, Canadian and Norwegian) landed on the main island. After destruction of the accumulated stocks of coal and dismantling of mining machinery and the wireless installation, the Norwegian inhabitants (about 600) were evacuated to a British port and the Russians (about 1,500) to the U.S.S.R. After the war the Norwegian mining plants were rebuilt. 288,000 metric tons of coal were extracted from Norwegian mines in Svalbard in 1980.

The Svalbard Archipelago lies between 74°–81° N. lat. and between 10°–35° E. long., with an estimated area of 24,295 square miles. The archipelago consists of a main island, known as Spitsbergen (15,200 sq. miles); North East Land, closely adjoining and separated by Hinlopen Strait; the Wiche Islands, separated from the mainland by Olga Strait; Barents and Edge Islands, separated from the mainland by Stor Fjord (or Wybe Jansz Water); Prince Charles Foreland, to the W.; Hope Island, to the S.E.; Bear Island (68 square miles) 127 miles to the S.; with many similar islands in the neighbourhood of the main group. In addition to those engaged in coal-mining, the archipelago is also visited by hunters for seal, foxes and polar bears.

South Cape is 355 miles from the Norwegian Coast. Ice Fjord is 520 miles from Tromsø, 650 miles from Murmansk, and 1,300 miles from Aberdeen. Transit from Tromsø to Green Harbour 2 to 3 days; from Aberdeen 5 to 6 days.

JAN MAYEN, an island in the Arctic Ocean (70° 49'–71° 9' N. lat. and 7° 53'–9° 5' W. long.) was joined to Norway by law of Feb. 27, 1930.

Norwegian Antarctic

BOUVET ISLAND (54° 26' S. lat. and 3° 24' E. long.) was declared a dependency of Norway by law of Feb. 27, 1930.

PETER THE FIRST ISLAND (68° 48' S. lat. and 90° 35' W. long.), was declared a dependency of Norway by resolution of Government, May 1, 1931.

PRINCESS RAGNHILD LAND (from 70° 30' to 68° 40' S. lat. and 24° 15' to 33° 30' E. long.) has been claimed as Norwegian since Feb. 17, 1931.

QUEEN MAUD LAND.—On Jan. 14, 1939, the Norwegian Government declared the area between 20° W. and 45° E., adjacent to Australian Antarctica, to be Norwegian territory.

OMAN
(The Sultanate of Oman)

Sultan, Qaboos Bin-Said, *succeeded* on deposition of Sultan Said bin Taimur, July 23, 1970.
(The Sultan acts as his own Prime Minister, Minister of Foreign Affairs, Defence and Finance.)

Deputy Prime Minister for Security and Defence, Faher bin-Taimur al-Said.

Deputy Prime Minister for Legal Affairs, Fahd bin-Mahmoud al-Said.

Deputy Prime Minister for Finance and Economy, Qais Abdul Mun'Im al-Zawawi.

Special Adviser to the Sultan, governor of Muscat, Thuwaini Bin Shihab al-Said.

Minister of State for Foreign Affairs, Yousef al-Alawi Abdullah.

Special adviser to the Sultan on religious and historical affairs, Mohammad Bin-Ahmad.

Interior, Badr Bin-Saud Bin-Hareb al-Busaidi.

Justice, Hilal Bin-Hamad al-Sammar al-Said.

Post, Telegraphs and Telephones, Ahmed Suwaidam al-Baluchi.

Civil Aviation, Roads and Ports, Salem bin Nasr Albusaidi.

Commerce and Industry, Salem Abdullah al-Ghazzali.

Petroleum and Mineral Resources, Said Ahmad Said al-Shanfari.

Agriculture and Fisheries, Abdel-Hafaz Salem Rajab.

Health, Dr. Mubarak al-Khaduri.

Education, Yahya Mahfouz al-Manthari.

Social Affairs and Labour, Sheikh Mustahil Bin Ahmed al-Ma'ashani.

Land Affairs and Municipalities, Ahmad Abdullah al-Ghazzali.

Information and Youth Affairs, Abdul Al Azil al-Rowas.

National Heritage, Faisal Bin-Ali Said.

Diwan Affairs, Hamad Bin-Hamud al-Busaid.

Governor of Dhofar and Minister of State, Sayyid Hilal bin Saud bin Harub al-Busaidi.

Minister of State and Special Envoy for the Sultan, Shabib bin-Taimour al Said.

Secretary to the Council of Ministers, Salem al-Ghazali.

President of the State Consultative Council, Khalfan bin Nasir al-Wahaibi.

OMAN EMBASSY IN LONDON
44a/b Montpellier Square, SW7 1JJ
[01–584 6782/3/4]

Ambassador, His Excellency Ahmed bin Mohammed bin Nasser Al-Lamki.

The independent Sultanate of Oman lies at the eastern corner of the Arabian Peninsula. Its seaboard is nearly 1,000 miles long and extends from near Tibat on the west coast of the Musandam Peninsula round to Ras Darbat Ali, with the exception of the stretch between Dibba and Kalba on the east coast which belongs to Sharjah and Fujairah of the United Arab Emirates. Ras Darbat Ali marks the boundary between the Sultanate and the People's Democratic Republic of Yemen. The Sultanate extends inland to the borders of the Rub al Khali, or "Empty Quarter" as the South Eastern Arabian Desert is called.

Physically and historically modern Oman can be split into four main parts, the North and the South, divided by a large tract of desert. *Northern Oman* has three main sections. The *Batinah,* the coastal plain, varies in width from 30 miles in the neighbourhood of Suwaiq to almost nothing at Muscat where the mountains descend abruptly to the sea. The plain is fertile, with date gardens extending over its full length of 150 miles. The dates, which ripen in early July, well before the Basra product, are famous for their flavour. The *Hajjar,* a mountain spine running from North East to South West, reaching nearly 10,000 feet in height on Jebal Akhdar. For the most part the mountains are barren, but numerous valleys penetrate the central massif of Jabal Akhdar and in these there is considerable cultivation irrigated by wells or a system of underground canals called *falajs* which tap the water table. The two plateaus leading from the western slopes of the mountains, the *Dhahirah* or back, in the north and the *Sharqia* in the south east also have centres of settlements and cultivation. They fall from an average height of 1,000 feet into the sands of the Empty Quarter. Camels raised in this area are prized throughout Arabia. The North is separated from the South by nearly 400 miles of inhospitable country crossed by one trunk

road, the only land link. *Dhofar,* the Southern Province, is the only part of the Arabian Peninsula to be touched by the South West Monsoon. Temperatures are more moderate than in the North and sugar cane and coconuts are grown on the coastal plain, while cattle are bred on the mountains.

Government.—A Consultative Council for the State was established by Sultanic decree on October 18, 1981. The Council is a nominated body consisting of 55 members (36 representing the public and 19 representing the government). The Council's jurisdiction is confined to economic affairs and social development.

Muscat is the original capital of Oman, but the capital's commercial centre has grown around Mutrah, 3 miles away, where the main port is located, and Ruwi. Government offices and private residents are moving out to Qurm and Khuwair in increasing numbers. The other main towns on the northern coast are Sur, Khaburah and Sohar, all of which are ports but without sheltered anchorage. In the interior Nizwa and Rostaq, both former capitals, are the centres of population. The main town of Dhofar is Salalah, and Raysut and Murbat are the ports.

The area of Oman has been estimated at 120,000 sq. miles and the population at 850,000 (1982). The inhabitants of the North are for the most part Arab but along the coast there is a strong infusion of negro blood, while in the Capital Area which stretches from Muscat to Seeb there are large communities of Hindus, Khojas and Baluch, in addition to Zanzibaris of Omani origin. In Dhofar there is also an infusion of negro blood around Salalah, but in the mountains the inhabitants are either of pure Arab descent or belong to tribes of pre-Arab origin, the Qarra and Mahra, who speak their own dialects of semitic origin.

Since 1972 ships have been using Port Qaboos at Matrah, where eight deep water berths have been constructed as part of the new harbour facilities (£20m.).

The telegraph office, an automatic telephone service in Muscat and Matrah and an international telephone service are operated by the General Telecommunications Service. There are now good tarmac roads linking most main population centres of the country with the coast and with the towns of the United Arab Emirates. By the end of 1981 2,835 km. of asphalt surfaced road had been completed. Major projects including a by-pass and fly-overs to ease traffic congestion in the capital should be completed by the end of 1985.

Finance.—The main unit is the *Rial Omani* of 1,000 baiza.

Commerce and Trade.—Trade is mainly with the United Kingdom, Japan, the Netherlands, U.S., West Germany, France and India. Total imports for the year 1983 were *OR*860,900,000. Chief imports were machinery, cars, building materials, refined petroleum and food and telecommunications equipment.

Trade with U.K.

	1982	1983
Imports from U.K.	£265,283,000	£448,900,000
Exports to U.K.	46,425,000	91,400,000

Production.—Petroleum Development (Oman) Ltd. (owned 60 per cent by Oman Government and 34 per cent by Shell) began exporting oil on Aug. 1, 1967. Wintershall A.-G., Sun Oil and Elf-Erap have offshore concessions and Eif-Aquitane Sumitomo has a new inland oil concession producing about 12,000 b.p.d. Other concessions are held by B.P. Teikoko, Japex and Amoco. The current level of oil production is about 400,000 barrels per day; this will rise to 450,000 by the end of the decade.

Development.—For many years the Sultanate was

a poor country with a total annual income of less than £1,000,000. The advent of oil revenues since 1967 and the change of régime in 1970 improved prospects and have enabled the initiation of a wide-ranging development programme, especially concerned with health, education and communications. New hospitals have been completed in the main provincial centres and there are now 14 hospitals with 2,041 beds. 455 schools, with 143,000 pupils, were in operation in 1983. At Salalah, the main coastal town of the southern province of Dhofar, a new civil airport has been built. A metalled road joins Salalah to Taqa and the port of Rayzut and several housing schemes have been completed. A gas turbine power station and desalination plant are situated near Muscat and a flour mill is now in operation. Cement factories have been built near Muscat and Rayzut.

CAPITAL.—Ψ Muscat, population (estimated), 30,000.

FLAG.—Red, green and white with crossed daggers in red sector.

BRITISH EMBASSY
P.O. Box 300, Muscat

Ambassador Extraordinary and Plenipotentiary, His Excellency Duncan Slater, C.M.G. (1982).
First Secretary, R. J. Dalton (*Head of Chancery and Consul*).
Defence Attaché, Col. B. M. Lees, M.V.O., O.B.E.
Naval and Air Attaché, Wg. Cdr. M. E. Williamson, O.B.E., R.A.F.
1st Secretaries, M. Cozens; H. Marcelin.
British Council Representative, E. K. Jones, P.O. Box 7090, Mutrah, Oman.

PAKISTAN

President, Gen. Mohammad Zia-ul-Haq.
(Gen. Zia is responsible for Political Affairs, Population, Science and Technology, States and Frontier Regions, Cabinet Division, Establishment Division and is Chairman, Planning Commission).

CABINET
Defence, Ali Ahmad Talpur.
Labour and Manpower, and Pakistanis Overseas, Ghulam Dastegir Khan.
Foreign Affairs, Sahabzada Yaqub Khan.
Finance and Economics, Ghulam Ishaq Khan.
Interior, Mahmud A. Haroon.
Education, Dr. Mohammed Afzal.
Local Government and Rural Development, Mir Zafarullah Khan Jamali.
Information, Raja Zafarul Haq.
Health and Social Welfare, Dr. Basharat Jazbi (*acting*).
Communications, Moinuddin Baluch.
Culture, Sports and Tourism, Arbab Niaz Mohammed.
Industries, Ellahi Bux Soomro.
Kashmir Affairs and Northern Affairs, Lt. Gen. Jamal Said Mian.
Religious and Minority Affairs, Raja Zafarul Haq (*acting*).
Food, Agriculture and Cooperatives, Vice-Adm. M. Fazil Janjua.
Water and Power, Raja Sikander Zaman.
Petroleum and Natural Resources, (vacant).
Production, Lt. Gen. Saeed Qadir.
Railways, Sahibzada Abdul Ghafoor Khan Hoti.
Law and Parliamentary Affairs, S. Sharifuddin Pirzada (*Attorney-General*).

PAKISTAN EMBASSY
35 Lowndes Square, SW1X 9JN
[01–235 2044]

Ambassador Extraordinary and Plenipotentiary, His Excellency Ali Arshad (1981).

Ministers, Mansoor Alam; Qutubuddin Aziz (*Information*).
Defence Attaché, Brig. Mohammad Ayaz.
1st Secretaries, Imtiazul Hassan; Miss Shireen Safdar.

Area and Population.—The Islamic Republic of Pakistan consists of country situated to the north-west of the Indian sub-continent, bordered by Iran, Afghanistan, the disputed territory of Kashmir and India. It covers a total area of 310,403 sq. miles. The Government of Pakistan census in 1981 showed a population figure of 83,780,000. Of these, about 95 per cent are Moslems, about 1 per cent Hindus, 3·5 per cent Christians, and 0·5 per cent Buddhists.

Running through Pakistan are five great rivers, the Indus, Jhelum, Chenab, Ravi and Sutlej. The upper reaches of these rivers are in Kashmir, and their sources in the Himalayas.

Government.—Until April 17, 1972, when the Republic of Bangladesh seceded and was formally created to replace East Pakistan, Pakistan consisted of two geographical units, West and East Pakistan, which were separated by about 1,100 miles of Indian territory. Pakistan was constituted as a Dominion under the Indian Independence Act, 1947, which received Royal Assent on July 18, 1947.

In terms of the Act the Dominion of Pakistan consisted of former territories of British India. The States of Bahawalpur and Khairpur (in Punjab and Sind), with a Muslim population of almost 80 per cent and with Muslim rulers, acceded to Pakistan in October, 1947. Boundaries of the Provinces of East Bengal and of Punjab (West Punjab) were defined by a Boundary Commission. The following States also acceded to Pakistan : the Baluchistan States of Kalat, Mekran, Las Bela and Kharan, and the North-West Frontier States of Amb, Chitral, Dir and Swat. (All these States have since been merged in the relevant Provinces of what is now Pakistan). The States of Junagadh and Manavadar which had acceded to Pakistan were occupied by India on November 8, 1947.

Pakistan became a Republic on March 23, 1956, when a Parliamentary Constitution came into force. On October 7, 1958, however, this Constitution was abrogated and Pakistan came under martial law.

The first general elections ever held in Pakistan on a basis of "one man, one vote", were held in Dec. 1970 and Jan. 1971. The Awami League in East Pakistan, led by Shiekh Mujibur Rahman, and the Pakistan People's Party in West Pakistan, led by Zulfikar Ali Bhutto, won large majorities. Following the elections there was total disagreement between the two main parties on the question of a new Constitution for Pakistan, Sheikh Mujib insisting on complete autonomy for East Pakistan. The proposed opening of the National Assembly at Dacca on March 25, 1971, was postponed and civil war broke out.

The unofficially styled "Bangladesh" seceded from the Government of Pakistan by unilateral declaration on March 26, 1971. Fighting in East Pakistan intensified towards the end of the year and on December 3 it spread to West Pakistan and Indian forces were engaged. On December 16 the Pakistan forces on the eastern front surrendered, and the following day Pakistan accepted a cease-fire in the West. "The Democratic Government of Bangladesh" was formally proclaimed on April 17, 1972.

The United Kingdom had recognized Bangladesh on February 4; but already, on January 30, 1972, President Bhutto announced that Pakistan had left the Commonwealth as a protest against the decision by Britain, Australia and New Zealand to recognize Bangladesh.

The general elections called in March 1977 resulted in a sweeping victory for Mr Bhutto's Pakistan People's Party but the Opposition Pakistan National

Alliance alleged that the elections had been rigged. Following weeks of negotiation between the representatives of the Government and the PNA, the Armed Forces assumed power on July 5, 1977 and imposed martial law throughout the country. The military government scheduled new general elections for October 1977, but these were postponed.

From January 1978, Gen Zia-ul-Haq was assisted by a 19-member Advisory Council, which was replaced in July 1978 by a 22 member Cabinet including members of the political parties. Gen. Zia declared himself President on Sept. 16, 1978, and a federal cabinet was formed in March, 1981. In January 1982 a Federal Council (Majlis-i-Shoora) was inaugurated; a nominated advisory body, it is intended to reflect popular views until there is a return to democracy.

Education.—Formal education in Pakistan is organized into five stages. These are five years of primary education (5–9 years), three years of middle or lower secondary (general or vocational), two years of upper secondary, two years of higher secondary (intermediate) and two to five years of higher education in colleges and universities. Education is free to upper secondary level.

Provincial Governments are responsible for the total financial support of the government institutions and for grants to non-government institutions. But policy making is authorized by the national Government, which makes annual grants. The main objects of the Education Policy 1972–80 were to promote ideological solidarity and eradicate illiteracy. Since 1980 the Policy has remained much the same. It is anticipated that primary education will become universal for boys by mid-1985 and for girls by mid-1988.

At primary level enrolment has increased from 5·5 million in 1977–78 to 6·5 million in 1981–82, and the number of schools from 54,000 to 58,400. There are at present some 164,000 primary school teachers. At the middle level enrolment has increased from 1·3 million in 1977–78 to 1·5 million in 1982–83, and the number of schools from 5,000 to 6,100. At the upper secondary level it was hoped to increase enrolment from 513,000 in 1977–78 to 722,000 in 1982–83. At university level, enrolment between 1977 and 1982 rose from 41,000 to 57,000 and at college level from 324,000 to 366,000.

Production.—Pakistan's economy is chiefly based on agriculture. The principal crops are cotton, rice, wheat, sugar cane, maize and tobacco. There are large deposits of rock salt. Pakistan has one of the longest irrigation systems in the world. The total area irrigated is 33 million acres. There are substantial natural gas mains near the Baluchistan Sind border. Distribution now extends to most urban areas.

Other products: Pakistan also produces hides and skins, leather, wool, fertilizers, paints and varnishes, soda ash, paper, cement, fish, carpets, sports goods, surgical appliances and engineering goods, including switchgear, transformers, cables and wires.

Trade.—Pakistan imported manufactured goods and raw materials to the value of $6,655 million in 1982–83 and exported mainly agricultural products valued at $3,474 million. Principal imports are listed as: petroleum products, machinery, fertilizers, transport equipment, edible oils, chemicals and ferrous metals. Principal exports are raw cotton, cotton yarn and cloth, carpets, rice, petroleum products, synthetic textiles, leather, and fish.

Trade with U.K.

	1982	1983
Imports from U.K.	£199,200,000	£191,647,000
Exports to U.K.	81,500,000	80,277,000

Finance.—The unit of currency is the *Rupee* of 100 *Paisa* (1 *crore = 10 million Rupees*). For rate of exchange, see p. 81.

The 1984–85 Budget anticipated gross Revenue receipts of *Rs.*59,185 million and expenditure (excluding development expenditure) of some *Rs.*70,736 million.

Communications.—The main seaport is Karachi. The main airport at Karachi occupies an important position on international trunk routes and is equipped with modern facilities and equipment. Pakistan International Airlines (P.I.A.) operates air services between the principal cities within the country as well as abroad.

Post and telegraph facilities are available to every country in the world.

CAPITAL.—Islamabad, pop. 250,000. ΨKarachi (pop. 5,500,000) is the largest city and seaport; Lahore has a population of 2,950,000.

FLAG.—The National Flag of Pakistan is dark green, with white vertical stripes at the mast, the green portion bearing a white crescent in the centre and a five-pointed heraldic star.

NATIONAL DAYS.—March 23 (Pakistan Day), August 14 (Independence Day).

BRITISH EMBASSY
Diplomatic Enclave, Ramna 5,
P.O. Box 1122, Islamabad.

Ambassador Extraordinary and Plenipotentiary, His Excellency Richard A. Fyjis-Walker, C.M.G., C.V.O. (1984).

There is a British Consulate-General at *Karachi.*

British Council Representative, R. F. Budd, P.O. Box 1135, Islamabad. There are regional offices at Karachi and Lahore, and a library in Peshawar.

PROVINCES OF THE ISLAMIC REPUBLIC OF PAKISTAN

The Establishment of West Pakistan Act, 1955, came into force on October 3, 1955, and incorporated: (1) the former Governors' Provinces of the Punjab, North-West Frontier and Sind; (2) the former Chief Commissioners' Provinces of Baluchistan and Karachi; (3) the States of Bahawalpur and Khairpur and the Baluchistan States Union; (4) the Tribal Areas of Baluchistan, the Punjab and the North-West Frontier and the States of Amb, Chitral, Dir and Swat, into the Province of *West Pakistan* with effect from October 14, 1955. The Province was reorganized with effect from July 1, 1970, into the four separate Provinces of Punjab (including Bahawalpur), Sind (including Karachi), North West Frontier Province and Baluchistan together with Islamabad Capital Territory and the Tribal Areas.

PANAMA
(República de Panama)

President of the Republic, Dr. Jorge Illueca, *took office,* Feb. 13, 1984.
Vice-President, Dr. Carlos Ozores Typaldos.

MINISTERS OF STATE

Government and Justice, Sr. Rodolfo Chiari.
Foreign Affairs, Sr. Oyden Ortega.
Treasury and Finance, Dr. Ricaurte Vasquez.
Agricultural Development, Sr. Ramón Sieiro.
Public Works, Sr. Nestor Tomas.
Commerce and Industry, Sr. Carlos Julio Quijano.
Labour and Social Welfare, Sr. Arturo Melo.
Health, Dr. Alberto Clavo.
Housing, Sra. Zia Elena Lee.
Planning and Economic Policy, Dr. Hector Alexander.
Education, Sra. Susana Richa de Torrijos.
Presidency, Sr. Gustavo Gonzalez.

Presidential elections were held in May 1984 and the new President, Dr. Nicolas Ardito Barletta is due to take office on Oct. 11, 1984. Elections are to be held also to a new legislative assembly, which will have 69 members, but no date has been set for these.

PANAMANIAN EMBASSY IN LONDON
Eagle House, 109–110 Jermyn Street, S.W.1
[01–930 1591]

Ambassador Extraordinary and Plenipotentiary, His Excellency Lic. Guillermo Vega.
Minister-Counsellor, Prof. Dionisio Johnson.

CONSULATE
24 Tudor Street, E.C.4
[01–353 4792/3].

There are also Consular Offices of the Republic at *Glasgow* and *Liverpool*.

Panama lies on the isthmus of that name which connects N. and S. America (*see* MAP, p. 820). The area of the Republic is 31,890 sq. m., the population (1980 est.) 1,940,000. After a revolt (Nov. 3, 1903) it declared its independence from Colombia and established a separate Government.

After 1968 control of Panama was increasingly taken over by Gen. Omar Torrijos, Commander of the National Guard, following a military *coup*. On October 11, 1972, at an assembly of representatives from the 505 electoral districts, the President and Vice-President were installed for a six-year term, and General Torrijos was designated as "Leader of the Revolution" with wide overriding powers. In October 1978 he withdrew from government, and Dr. Aristides Royo was elected President by the Assembly of Representatives.

The Panama Canal Zone.—With effect from Oct. 1, 1979 the Canal Zone (647 sq. miles) was disestablished, with all areas of land and water within the Zone reverting to Panama. By the 1977 treaty with the U.S.A., the U.S.A. is allowed the use of operating bases for the Panama Canal, together with several military bases, but the Republic of Panama is sovereign in all such areas. Control of the Canal will revert to Panama in the year 2000.

The soil is moderately fertile, but nearly one-half of the land is uncultivated. The chief crops are bananas, sugar, coconuts, cacao, coffee and cereals. The shrimping industry plays an important rôle in the Panamanian economy. A railway 47 miles in length joins the Atlantic and Pacific oceans.

Education is compulsory and free from 7 to 15 years.

Language and Literature.—The official language is Spanish. There are five Spanish language and one English language newspaper published daily in the capital.

Currency.—The monetary unit is the *Balboa* (= $1 U.S.); no Panamanian paper currency is issued, and U.S. dollar bills of all values are in circulation in the Republic.

TRADE

	1980 (provisional)
Imports	U.S.$1,396 million
Exports	406 million

Trade with U.K.

	1982	1983
Imports from U.K.	£83,250,000	£42,276,000
Exports to U.K.	9,521,000	5,341,000

† Including Colon Free Zone.

The imports are mostly manufactured goods, machinery, lubricants, chemicals and foodstuffs; exports are bananas, petroleum products, shrimps, sugar, meat and fishmeal.

CAPITAL, ΨPanama City. Population (1970 Census), 418,000.

FLAG.—Four quarters; white with blue star (top, next staff), red (in fly), blue (below, next staff) and white with red star.

NATIONAL DAY.—November 3.

Dependencies of Panama.—Taboga Island (area 4 sq. miles) is a popular tourist resort of some 12 miles from the Pacific entrance to the Panama Canal. Tourist facilities are also being developed in the Las Perlas Archipelago in the Gulf of Panama. There is a penal settlement at Guardia on the island of Coiba (area 19 sq. miles) in the Gulf of Chiriqui.

BRITISH EMBASSY
(120 Via España, Panama)

Ambassador Extraordinary and Plenipotentiary, His Excellency Terence Harry Steggle (1983).
1st Secretary and Consul, D. V. Thornley.

There is a British consular office at *Panama City*.

Panama, 4,650 miles; transit from Liverpool, 15 to 19 days; from Southampton 15 days; *via* N.Y., 14 days.

PARAGUAY
(República del Paraguay)

President, General Alfredo Stroessner, *inaugurated* Aug. 15, 1954, *re-elected* 1958, 1963, 1968, 1973, 1978 and 1983.
Foreign Affairs, Dr. Carlos Augustus Saldívar.
Finance, General César Barrientos (*ret.*).
Interior, Dr. Sabino A. Montanero.
Defence, General Gaspar Germán Martínez.
Justice and Labour, Dr. José Eugenio Jacquet.
Education and Worship, Dr. Raúl Peña.
Public Works and Communications, General de División Juan A. Cáceres.
Agriculture and Livestock, Ing. Hernando Bertoni.
Industry and Commerce, Dr. Delfin Ugarte Centurión.
Public Health and Social Welfare, Dr. Adán Godoy Jiménez.
Without Portfolio, (vacant).
President of Central Bank, Dr. César Romero Acosta.

PARAGUAYAN EMBASSY AND CONSULATE IN LONDON
Braemer Lodge, Cornwall Gardens, SW7 4AQ
[01-937 1253; *Consulate*: 01-937 6629]

Ambassador Extraordinary and Plenipotentiary, His Excellency Antonio Zuccolillo.
Counsellor and Consul General, Rubén Alvarenga-Cabañas.
Consular Official, Mrs. Teresa M. de Castillo.

There is a Paraguayan Consulate in *Liverpool*.

Area and Population.—Paraguay is an inland subtropical State of South America, situated between Argentina, Bolivia and Brazil.

The area is computed at 157,000 square miles, with a population (1982 Census) of 3,026,165.

Eastern Paraguay consists of a series of plains, intersected by abrupt ranges of hills, none of which exceeds 2,300 feet above sea level. The Paraguay and Alto Paraná rivers are normally navigable for vessels of 6 to 7 feet draught. Some of the tributary streams are also navigable. The Pilcomayo river is navigable for small craft for 180 miles from Asunción. Paraguay is a country of grassy plains and dense forest, the soil being marshy in many parts and liable to floods; while the hills are covered for the most part with immense forests. The streams flowing into the Alto Paraná descend precipitously into that river. In the angle formed by the Paraná-Paraguay confluence are extensive marshes, one of which, known as "Neem-bucú," or "endless," is drained by *Lake Ypoa*, a large lagoon, south-east of the capital. The *Chaco*, lying between the rivers Paraguay and Pilcomayo and bounded on the north by Bolivia, formed the subject of a long-standing dispute with that country and led to war between Paraguay and Bolivia from 1932 to 1935. The Chaco is a flat plain, rising uniformly towards its western boundary to a height of 1,140 feet; it suffers much from floods and still more from drought, but the building of dams and reservoirs has converted part of it into good pasture for cattle raising.

Government.—In 1535 Paraguay was settled as a Spanish possession. In 1811 it declared its independence of Spain.

The 1967 constitution provides for a two-chamber parliament consisting of a 30-member Senate and a 60-member Chamber of Deputies. Two-thirds of the seats in each chamber are allocated to the majority party and the remaining one-third shared among the minority parties in proportion to the votes cast. Voting is compulsory for all citizens over 18.

The President is elected for 5 years and may be re-elected for a further term. He appoints the Cabinet, which exercises all the functions of government. During parliamentary recess it can govern by decree through the Council of State, the members of which are representative of the Government, the armed forces and various other bodies.

Production.—About three-quarters of the population are engaged in agriculture and cattle raising. Cotton, soya beans, tobacco, edible and essential oils and timber are the main exports. The forests contain many varieties of timber which find a good market abroad. Paraguay's hydroelectric power station at Acaray produces 180,000 kW. of which a surplus is exported to Argentina and Brazil.

Brazil and Paraguay are carrying out a project to develop the potential of the River Paraná—annual output is planned at 10·7 million kWh. Similarly, Paraguay and Argentina are to develop the hydro-electric complex at the Yacyreta rapids. This has a potential annual output of 3·5 million kWh. Work on the Itaipú hydroelectric scheme began early in 1976 and production started in April 1984; work on the Yacyretá scheme began in 1978.

Communications.—A railway, 985 miles in length, connects Asunción with Buenos Aires. The journey takes 55 hours. Train ferries enable the run to be accomplished without break of bulk. River steamers also connect Buenos Aires and Asunción (3 to 5 days). This service is liable to cancellation without warning when the river is low or in flood. There are direct shipping services to Asunción from England, Western Europe and the U.S.A. Eight airlines operate services from Asunción.

There are 1,176 km. of asphalted roads in Paraguay, connecting Asunción with São Paulo (26 hrs.) *via* the Bridge of Friendship and Foz de Yguazú and with Buenos Aires (24 hrs.) *via* Puerto Pilcomayo, and about 4,050 miles of earth roads in fairly good condition, but liable to be closed or to become impassable in wet weather. A 1000 km. road, of which 300 km. are paved, links Asunción with the Bolivian border. There are services to Buenos Aires, São Paulo and Paranagua, a port on the Brazilian coast.

Defence.—There is a permanent military force of about 25,000 all ranks, most of whom are conscripts doing their military service; and about 6,500 armed police (again mostly conscripts). Three gunboats and a number of small armed launches patrol inland waters.

Language and Literature.—Spanish is the official language of the country but outside the larger towns *Guarani*, the language of the largest single unit of original Indian inhabitants, is widely spoken. Three morning, one afternoon and three bi-weekly news-papers are published in Asunción. There are 48 AM, 15 FM and three TV stations in the country.

Education.—In 1980 there were 3,050 primary schools. They had 15,800 teachers and 503,000 students. The National University in Asunción had in 1980 a teaching staff of 1,184 and 12,000 students. The Catholic University had 7,000 students and about 620 teachers.

BUDGET 1984
(in million guaranies)

Central Government	*Decentralized Bodies*
Expenditure .... 89·5	216·6

Currency.—The unit is the *guarani* of 100 *céntimos.* (*See also* p. 82.)

Trade.—The imports are chiefly articles of food and drink, consumer goods, textiles, vehicles and machinery. Main exports: Soja, cotton, tobacco, meat, timber, seeds, maize, fruit and vegetable oils.

Trade with U.K.

	1982	1983
Imports from U.K.	£16,915,000	£15,263,000
Exports to U.K.	2,790,000	3,129,000

CAPITAL, ΨAsunción, about 1,000 miles up the River Paraguay from Buenos Aires. Pop. (census, 1982), 720,000; other centres being ΨEncarnación, 47,333; Concepción, 52,826; and Villarica 38,052.

FLAG.—Three horizontal bands, red, white, blue with the National seal on the obverse white band and the Treasury seal on the reverse white band.

NATIONAL DAY.—May 14.

BRITISH EMBASSY
Calle President Franco 706,
(PO Box 404)

Ambassador Extraordinary and Plenipotentiary and Consul-General, His Excellency Bernard Coleman (1984).

1st Secretary and Consul, P. T. Rouse, M.B.E.

Asunción is approximately 4,000 miles distant from London by air. Transit by sea 25 days. By air approximately 21 hours flying time *via* Rio de Janeiro.

PERU
(República del Peru)

President, Fernando Belaúnde, *assumed office,* July 28, 1980.

PERUVIAN EMBASSY AND CONSULATE
52 Sloane Street, SW1X 9SP
[01–235 1917/2545]

Ambassador Extraordinary and Plenipotentiary His Excellency Dr. Andres A. Aramburú-Menchaca.
Minister, J. Eduardo Ponce-Vivanco.
Naval and Military Attaché, Vice-Adm. Javier Llerena.
Air Attaché, Maj. Gen. Alfredo Lima.

Area and Population.—Peru is a maritime Republic of South America, situated between 0° 00′ 48″ and 18° 21′ 00″ S. latitude and between 68° 39′ 27″ and 81° 20′ 13″ W. longitude. The area of the Republic including 4,440 square kilometres of the Peruvian section of Lake Titicaca and 32 square kilometres of the coastal islands, is about 531,000 square miles with a total population (census, 1972) of 14,121,564.

Physical Features.—The country is traversed throughout its length by the Andes, running parallel to the Pacific coast, the highest points in the Peruvian sector being *Huascaran* (22,211 feet), *Huandoy* (20,855 feet), *Ausangate* (20,235 feet), *Misti* volcano (18,364 feet), *Hualcan* (20,000 feet), *Chachani* (19,037 feet), *Antajasha* (18,020 feet), Pichupichu (17,724 feet), and *Mount Meiggs* (17,583 feet).

There are three main regions, the *Costa*, west of the Andes, the *Sierra* or mountain ranges of the Andes, which include the *Punas* or mountainous wastes below the region of perpetual snow and the *Montaña*, or *Selva*, which is the vast area of jungle stretching from the eastern foothills of the Andes to the eastern frontiers of Peru. The coastal area, lying upon and near the Pacific, is not tropical, though close to the Equator, being cooled by the Humboldt Current; its chief products are cotton, sugar, and petroleum. It contains the capital, Lima, and most of the white population.

In the mountains, where most of the Indians live, are to be found minerals in great richness and variety, and cattle, sheep, llamas and alpacas are bred there. In the mountain valleys maize, potatoes and wheat are grown. Upon the eastern slopes of the Andes are to be found very large tracts suitable for cultivation and stock raising. The main products of the jungle are timber, barbasco, leche caspi and petroleum.

Government.—Peru was conquered in the early 16th century by Francisco Pizarro (born 1478, died 1541). He subjugated the Incas (the ruling caste of the Quechua Indians), who had started their rise to power some 500 years earlier, and for nearly three centuries Peru remained under Spanish rule. A revolutionary war of 1821–1824 established its independence, declared on July 28, 1821. The constitution rests upon the fundamental law of Oct. 18, 1856, and is that of a democratic Republic. A new constitution was drawn up and approved in July 1979, which replaced the early one of 1933.

Production.—The chief crops are cotton, potatoes, and other vegetables, sugar, fruit, maize, rice, wheat, barley, grapes and coffee. Mineral exports include lead, zinc, copper, iron ore and silver. Peru is normally the world's largest exporter of fishmeal. The value of fishmeal exports dropped for some years but is now recovering.

Communications.—In recent years the coastal and sierra zones have been opened up by means of roads and air routes and there is air communication, as well as communication by protracted land routes, with the tropical eastern zones, which lie east of the Andes towards the borders of Brazil, and consist

mainly of unexplored or little known country inhabited by Indians in a savage state. The completion in 1944 of the trunk road of the *Andean Highway* from the Pacific port of Callao, *via* Lima, Oroya, Cerro de Pasco (14,700 ft.), Huanuco, Tingo Maria, to Pucallpa, the river port on the Ucayali, forms a link between the Pacific, the Amazon and the Atlantic. The trunk road runs through the *Boqueron del Padre Abad*, a pass rediscovered in 1937, in the backbone of the Blue Cordillera. The Peruvian section of the Pan American highway is complete and is asphalted throughout.

The first railway was opened in 1850 and the 2,400 miles of track are now administered by the Government. There is also steam navigation on the Ucayali (*see* Andean Highway above) and Huallaga, and in the south on Lake Titicaca. Air services are maintained throughout Peru, and many international services call at Lima.

Defence.—The Army is recruited by voluntary enlistment, supplemented by conscription (2 years), and numbers about 45,000 of all ranks. Armoured units are equipped with American, Russian and French vehicles. Engineer units are employed on the construction of roadways in Peru using American equipment. *Navy.*—The Navy consists of 3 cruisers; 4 destroyers; 2 frigates; 2 corvettes; 6 U.S. submarines and 2 German submarines; 4 LST's; 5 river gunboats; 4 fleet oilers; 4 fleet auxiliaries; 2 river transports; 14 patrol boats; 2 patrol launches; 1 floating dock and 2 tugs. The main Naval base is in Callao and supports all ships of the Fleet. There are training establishments in Callao and La Punta. The Naval Air Arm consists of U.S. and French helicopters; U.S. anti-submarine aircraft and DC3's. *Air Force.*—The Air Force is equipped with British Hunter and Canberra aircraft; American training, fighter and transport aircraft plus helicopters; French Mirage aircraft and Alouette helicopters. There are military airfields at Talara, Piura, Chiclayo, Lima, Pisco, Joya, Iquitos and Arequipa plus a seaplane base at Iquitos. There are also a Civil Guard and a Republican Guard whose members number respectively 30,000 and 5,000.

Education.—Education is compulsory and free for both sexes between the ages of 6 and 15. In 1972 a new Law of Education radically changed the structure of the system.

Language and Literature.—Spanish, the language of the original Spanish stock from which the governing and professional classes are mainly recruited, was formerly the only official language of the country. However, in May 1975, the Quechua language was declared by Decree Law as the second official tongue. Quechua and Aymará are widely spoken by more than half the population of the country. Before the arrival of Pizarro, the Incas had attained a high state of culture, some traces of which survived three centuries of Spanish rule. Modern Peruvian literature includes a national drama in the Spanish tongue and many Peruvian writers have attained international fame. The national library founded at Lima in 1821 was pillaged by Chileans in the Pacific War of 1879–1883, but many of the scattered manuscripts and books have since been recovered. The greater part of the historical section of the library was destroyed by fire in 1943.

Finance.—The unit of currency is the *Sol* of 100 *centavos*. For rate of exchange, *see* p. 82.

Trade.—Import trade of Peru in 1980 totalled U.S.$3,134 million and exports U.S.$3,904 million. In 1980, Peru had an overall balance of payments surplus of about U.S.$800 million.

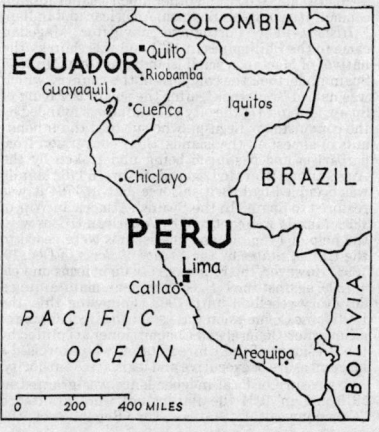

Trade with U.K.

	1982	1983
Imports from U.K.	£39,370,000	£32,947,000
Exports to U.K.	92,120,000	118,414,000

The principal imports are machinery, foodstuffs, metal and manufactured metal goods, chemicals and pharmaceutical products. The chief exports are minerals and metals, fishmeal, sugar, cotton and coffee.

CAPITAL.—Metropolitan Lima (including ΨCallao), population 3,595,000. Arequipa (561,338) Ψ Iquitos (540,560), ΨChiclayo (533,266).

FLAG.—Three vertical bands, red, white, red; coat of arms on white band. NATIONAL DAY.—July 28 (Anniversary of Independence).

BRITISH EMBASSY

Edificio El Pacifico-Washington (Piso 12), Plaza Washington, Avenida Arequipa, Lima.

Ambassador Extraordinary and Plenipotentiary, His Excellency John William Richmond Shakespeare, M.V.O. (1983).

1st Secretaries, J. W. Thorp (*Head of Chancery and Consul*); M. L. Creek, M.V.O. (*Commercial*).

Defence, Naval, Military and Air Attaché, Capt. D. H. Ross, R.N.

There are British Consular Offices at *Lima* and *Callao.*

British Council Representative, T. F. Hibbett, Apartado 11114, Edif. Pacifico-Washington, Ave Arequipa, Lima.

Lima, 7,020 miles; transit, *via.* New York and Colon, 21–27 days; *via* Liverpool and Colon, 17–30 days. Direct British Caledonian service Lima–London.

THE PHILIPPINES
(Repúblika ng Pilipinas)

President, Ferdinand Marcos, *b.* 1917, *elected* Nov. 10, 1965, *assumed office* Dec. 30, 1965, *re-elected*, June 16, 1981.

MINISTERS

Prime Minister and Minister of Finance, Cesar E. A. Virato.
Deputy P.M. and Minister of Local Government, José Rano.
Foreign Affairs, Arturo Tolentino.
Justice and Solicitor General, Estelito Mendoza.
Agriculture, Salvador Escudero.
Public Works and Highways, Jesus Hipolito.
Education, Culture and Sports, Jaime Laya.
Labour and Employment, Blas F. Ople.
Defence, Juan Ponce Enrile.
Health, Jesus Azurin.
Industry and Trade, Roberto Ongpin.
Agrarian Reform, Conrado Estrella.
Tourism, Jose D. Aspiras.
Natural Resources, Rodolfo del Rosario.
Energy, Geronimo Velasco.
Human Settlements, Imelda R. Marcos.
Transportation and Communications, Jose P. Dans.
Social Services, Sylvia Montes.
Cultural Communities, Simeon Datumanong.

PHILIPPINE EMBASSY

9a Palace Green, W8 4QE
[01–937 1609]

Ambassador Extraordinary and Plenipotentiary, His Excellency José V. Cruz.
Minister-Counsellor and Consul General, Alfredo Almendrala.
Armed Forces Attaché, Col. Reynaldo Wycoco.
Commercial Counsellor, Peregrino Sales.

Area and Population.—The Philippines are situated between 21° 20′–4° 30′ N. Lat. and 116° 55′–126° 36′ E. long., and are distant about 500 miles from the south-east coast of the continent of Asia.

The total land area of the country is 114,834 square miles, of which total 106,914 square miles are contained in the eleven largest islands, the 7,079 other islands having a combined area of 7,929 square miles. The principal islands are:—

Name	sq. miles	Name	sq. miles
Luzon	40,422	Mindoro	3,759
Mindanao	36,538	Leyte	2,786
Samar	5,050	Cebu	1,703
Negros	4,906	Bohol	1,492
Palawan	4,550	Masbate	1,262
Panay	4,446		

Other groups in the Republic are the Sulu islands (Capital, Jolo), Babuyanes and Batanes; the Catanduanes; and Culion Islands.

The population of the Philippines was estimated at the 1980 Census as 48,098,460.

The inhabitants, known as Filipinos, are basically all of Malay stock, with a considerable admixture of Spanish and Chinese blood in many localities, and about 90 per cent of them are Christians, predominantly Roman Catholics. Most of the remainder are Moslems, in the south, and animists and pagans, mainly in the north. There is a Chinese minority estimated at 500,000, and other much smaller foreign communities, notably Spanish, American and Indian.

History.—The Portuguese navigator Magellan came to the Philippines in 1521 and was slain by the natives of Mactan, a small island near Cebu. In 1565 Spain undertook the conquest of the country which was named "Filipinas", after the son of the King of Spain, and in 1571 the city of Manila was founded by the conquistador Legaspi, who subdued the inhabitants of almost all the islands, their conversion from barbarism and paganism being undertaken by the Augustinian friars in Legaspi's train. In 1762 Manila was occupied by a British force, but in 1764 it was restored to Spain. In the Spanish–American War of 1898, Manila was captured by American troops with the help of Filipinos and the Islands were ceded to the United States by the *Treaty of Paris* of Dec. 10, 1898. However, the Filipinos rose up in arms on Feb. 4, 1899, against the U.S. Government, maintaining a desultory rebellion until 1902. Following this, the Philippine Commission was established, consisting of a Governor-General and Commissioner appointed by the President of the United States, who exercised a large measure of executive and legislative authority.

A measure of local independence was granted in 1916 and in 1934 the Philippines were granted a "Commonwealth" Status. The Republic of the

Philippines came into existence on July 4, 1946 with a presidential form of government based on the American system. Martial law was imposed on September 21, 1972. This was lifted, except in two southern provinces, on January 17, 1981. On January 17, 1973, a revised constitution, providing for a parliamentary form of government with a unicameral legislative, was proclaimed after its ratification in a national referendum. Elections were held on April 7, 1978 for 165 seats in the new Interim National Assembly, which is intended to prepare the way for a permanent body. This met for the first time on June 12, 1978 when the President was sworn in as Prime Minister. Constitutional amendments were approved in April 1981 providing for a French-style system of parliamentary government with a strong executive Presidency. President Marcos subsequently fought and won a Presidential election. Parliamentary elections took place in May 1984.

Language and Literature.—The official languages are Pilipino and English. Pilipino, the national language, is based on Tagalog, one of the Malay-Polynesian languages which according to the 1970 census is spoken by 55·2 per cent of the population. English, which is the language of government and of instruction in secondary and university education, is spoken by at least 44 per cent of the population. Spanish, which ceased to be an official language in 1973, is now spoken by only 3·6 per cent. 83 per cent of the population are literate. Secondary and higher education is extensive and there are 37 private universities recognized by the Government, including the Dominican University of Santo Thomas (founded in 1611), the first in the Far East and 25 years older than Harvard; there are also 213 State-supported colleges and universities, including the University of the Philippines, founded 1908. Students at private and state colleges and universities in 1980-81 numbered 1,276,016.

Roads and Railways.—Communications suffered serious damage during the War of 1941-45 owing to the lack of proper maintenance during the Japanese occupation and destruction by bombardment. The highway system covered 153,528 kilometres in 1981 and there was a total of 1,006,130 registered road vehicles. The railways operate approximately 740 miles of track. The Philippine National Railway, on Luzon Island, has been converted to diesel traction.

Shipping.—There are 94 ports of entry in the Philippines and 12,049 vessels of various types (including 172 ocean-going vehicles), totalling 2,319,500 tons, are engaged in inter-island traffic.

Civil Aviation.—The Civil Aeronautics Administration (C.A.A.) operates and maintains 86 national airports. Philippine Air Lines have regular flights throughout the Far East and operate trans-Pacific flights to San Francisco, in addition to inter-island services. Air Manilla (Inc.) also operate charter international and local air services.

TRADE

	1980	1981
Total imports	$7,726,912,426	$7,945,680,000
Total exports	5,787,787,554	5,722,160,000

Trade with U.K.

	1982	1983
Imports from U.K.	£97,908,000	£102,949,000
Exports to U.K.	127,061,000	160,701,000

The Philippines is a predominantly agricultural country, the chief products being rice, coconuts, maize, sugar-cane, abaca (manila hemp), fruits, tobacco and lumber. There is, however, an increasing number of manufacturing industries and it is the policy of the Government to diversify its economy.

Principal exports are sugar, coconut oil, copper concentrate, logs and lumber and copra.

CAPITAL.—ΨManila, in the island of Luzon: population (1980): City area, 1,630,485; Manila with suburbs (incl. Quezon City, Pasay City, Caloocan City, Makati, Parañaque, San Juan Mandaluyong and Navota), 5,925,884. The next largest cities are ΨCebu (418,517), ΨDavao (515,520), ΨIloilo (247,956), ΨZamboanga (240,066), and Bacolod (196,492).

FLAG.—Equal horizontal bands of blue (above) and red; gold sun with three stars on a white triangle next staff.

NATIONAL DAY.—June 12 (Independence Day).

BRITISH EMBASSY
(P.O. Box 1970 MCC), Manila

Ambassador Extraordinary and Plenipotentiary, His Excellency Michael Morgan, C.M.G. (1981).
Counsellor, A. S. Payne, O.B.E.
Defence Attaché, Cdr. F. M. Flynn, R.N.
1st Secretary, N. A. Thorne (*Head of Chancery*).
2nd Secretaries, A. A. Britt (*Consul*); K. Taylor (*Commercial*).
Cultural Attaché, J. A. A. H. Moore (*British Council Representative*.

POLAND
(Polska Rzeczpospolita Ludowa)

COUNCIL OF MINISTERS

Prime Minister, Minister of Mining and Energy, and First Secretary of the Central Committee of the Communist Party, Gen. Wojciech Jaruzelski.
Deputy Prime Minister and Chairman, Planning Commission, Manfred Gorywoda.
Deputy Prime Ministers, Janusz Obodowski; Zenon Komender; Edward Kowalczyk; Zbigniew Messner; Roman Malinowski; Mieczyslaw Rakowski; Zbigniew Szalajda.
Chairman, Supreme Chamber of Control, Tadeusz Hupalowski.
Member of Presidium and Plenipotentiary for Economic Reform, Wladyslaw Baka.
Interior, Lt.-Gen. Czeslaw Kiszczak.
Foreign Affairs, Stefan Olszowski.
Defence, Gen. Florian Siwicki.
Finance, Stanislaw Nieczanz.
Foreign Trade, Tadeusz Nestorowicz.
Administration, Wlodzimierz Oliewa.
Justice, Lech Domeradzki.
Higher Education, Science and Technology, Prof. Benon Miskiewicz.
Health and Social Welfare, Tadeusz Szelachowski.
Labour, Stanislaw Gebala.
Culture, Kazimierz Zygulski.
Building and Building Materials Industry, Stanislaw Kukurywa.
Metallurgical and Engineering Industries, Janusz Maciejewicz.
Agriculture and Food, Stanislaw Zieba.
Forestry, Waldemar Kozlowski.
Internal Trade, Mrs. Anna Kedzierska.
Transport, Jan Kaminski.
Raw Materials, Jerzy Wozniak.
Education, Boleslaw Faron.
Chemical and Light Industries, Edward Grzywa.
Communications, Wladyslaw Majewski.
Religious Affairs, Adam Lopatka.
Price Affairs, Zdislaw Krasinski.
Maritime Economy, Jerzy Korzonek.
Environmental Protection and Water Economy, Stefan Jarzebski.
Without Portfolio, Wladyslaw Jablonski; Andrzej Ornat.

POLAND

POLISH EMBASSY IN LONDON
47 Portland Place, W1N 3AG
[01–580 4324]

Ambassador Extraordinary and Plenipotentiary, His Excellency Stefan Staniszewski.

Area and Population.—In 1939 the area of the Polish Republic was 150,572 square miles with a population of about 35,000,000, of whom 30 per cent. were national minorities (including over 3,000,000 Jews). Frontier changes took place at the end of the war as foreshadowed at the Tehran Conference in 1943. About 69,000 square miles of territory in the east were ceded to the Soviet Union. In exchange Poland received in the west 39,000 square miles of Eastern Germany. The southern boundary was not affected except for minor adjustments to that part formerly dividing Poland from Ruthenia (Czechoslovakia). The western boundary is formed by the Rivers Oder and Neisse. Poland now has a maritime frontier stretching from west of Kaliningrad (formerly Königsberg) to west of Szczecin (formerly Stettin). As a result of the change of frontier and of very great war-time losses, at the census of December 3, 1950, the population had fallen to 24,977,000 in an area of 121,000 square miles. In the 1982 Census it was 36,400,000. Roman Catholicism is the religion of 95 per cent. of the inhabitants.

Government.—The Republic of Poland (reconstituted within the limits of the old Polish Commonwealth) was proclaimed at Warsaw in November, 1918, and its independence guaranteed by the signatories of the Treaty of Versailles. The Polish Commonwealth had ceased to exist in 1795 after three successive partitions in 1772, 1793 and 1795, in which Prussia, Russia and Austria shared. During the Napoleonic wars, the small Grand Duchy of Warsaw was created but was dissolved by the final act of the Congress of Vienna. The so-called "Congress Kingdom" was then established on the Polish territory which had fallen to Russia's share, the Tsar assuming the title of King of Poland, and the small Republic of Cracow came into existence under the joint control of Prussia, Russia and Austria. In 1831, after an insurrection, the Congress Kingdom was dissolved and annexed by Russia and in 1848 the Austrians absorbed the Cracow Republic, Poland as an independent state ceasing to exist until the end of the War of 1914–18, when she became independent once again, after 150 years of foreign rule.

In March 1939, Great Britain entered into a treaty with Poland (France had done so in 1921) guaranteeing Polish territory against aggression, and on Hitler's invasion France and Britain implemented their guarantee. On September 17, 1939, Russian forces invaded eastern Poland and on September 21, 1939, Poland was declared by Germany and Russia to have ceased to exist. A line of demarcation was established between the areas occupied by German and Russian forces. At the end of the war a Coalition Government was formed in which the Polish Workers' Party played a large part. In December, 1948, the Polish Workers' Party and the Polish Socialist Party fused in the new Polish United Workers' Party. This is a Communist Party which closely controls every branch of State activity. A new Constitution modelled on the Soviet Constitution of 1936 was adopted on July 22, 1952, and was modified in February 1976. It changed the title of the country to the Polish People's Republic (*Polska Rzeczpospolita Ludowa*). It made no provision for a President of the Republic, whose functions were to be jointly exercised by a Council of State. Private ownership of land and freedom of religion were recognized. Church and State were to be separate.

Despite the guarantee of religious freedom in the Constitution, a campaign of encroachment in 1953 culminated in the arrest of the Primate of the Roman Catholic Church, and dissatisfaction with the *régime* and conditions of life led to riots in Poznań in June, 1956. In Jan., 1957, elections to the *Sejm* were held and in Feb., 1957, a reconstructed Government took office. Elections to the *Sejm* have been held in 1961, 1965, 1972, 1976 and 1980. The expression of severe popular discontent in December 1970 led to the ousting of Gomulka, and substantial Government and Party changes followed. In June 1976 the government introduced steep price rises for foodstuffs but after strikes and riots in a number of Polish cities these proposals were dropped. In July 1980 steep rises in food prices but static wages led to widespread strikes. The strikes continued throughout August, causing a major government reshuffle and obliging the government to agree to allow independent trade unions, the right to strike, the easing of censorship and other political and economic demands. The independent trade union movement, Solidarity, led by Lech Walesa, became a powerful force but many of its leaders, including Walesa, were detained and union activity suspended when martial law was declared on Dec. 13, 1981. Initially there was some passive resistance to martial law, which was suspended on Dec. 31, 1982.

Education.—Elementary education (ages 7–15) is compulsory and free. Secondary education is optional and free. There are universities at Kraków, Warsaw, Poznan, Lódź, Wroclaw, Lublin and Toruń and a considerable number of other towns.

Language and Literature.—Polish is a western Slavonic tongue (*see* U.S.S.R.), the Latin alphabet being used. Polish literature developed rapidly after the foundation of the University of Cracow (a printing press was established there in 1474 and there Copernicus died in 1543). A national school of poetry and drama survived the dismemberment and the former era of romanticism, whose chief Polish exponent was Adam Mickiewicz, was followed by realistic and historical fiction, including the works of Henryk Sienkiewicz (1846–1916), Nobel Prize-winner for Literature in 1905, Boleslaw Prus (1847–1912), and Stanislaw Reymont (1868–1925), Nobel Prize-winner in 1924.

Production and Industry.—On January 3, 1946, a decree was issued to provide for the nationalization of mines, petroleum resources, water, gas and electricity services, banks, textile factories and large retail stores. At present over 99 per cent of Polish industry is stated to be "socialized", but 68 per cent of agricultural land is privately farmed.

Trade with U.K.

	1982	1983
Imports from U.K.	£133,324,000	£151,721,000
Exports to U.K.	151,723,000	177,067,000

CAPITAL.—Warsaw, on the Vistula, pop. (1979) 1,572,000. Other large towns are Lódz (832,000); Kraków (705,000); Wroclaw (608,000); Poznan (544,000); Gdansk (448,000); Szczecin (388,000); Katowice (353,000); Lublin (298,000).

FLAG.—Equal horizontal stripes of white (above) and red. NATIONAL DAY.—July 22.

BRITISH EMBASSY
No. 1 Aleja Róz, Warsaw

Ambassador Extraordinary and Plenipotentiary, His Excellency John Albert Leigh Morgan, C.M.G. (1983).
Counsellor, A. E. Furness (*Head of Chancery*).
Defence and Air Attaché, Gp.-Capt. A. A. Ramus.
Naval and Military Attaché, Lt.-Col. H. V. Bates.
British Council Representative, J. J. Barnett, O.B.E., Al. Jerozolimskie 59, 00–697 Warsaw.

PORTUGAL
(República Portuguesa)

President of the Republic, General António Ramalho Eanes, *elected*, June 27, 1976, *re-elected*, 1980.

Prime Minister, Dr. Mário Soares.*
Vice P.M. and Minister for Defence, Prof. Carlos A. da Mota Pinto.†
State and Parliamentary Affairs, Dr. António Almeida Santos.*
Finance, Dr. Ernâni Lopes.
Internal Administration, Eduardo Pereira.*
Foreign Affairs, Dr. Jaime Gama.*
Maritime Affairs, Carlos Melancia.*
Health, António Maldonado Gonelha.*
Justice, Dr. Rui Machete.†
Culture, Dr. António Coimbra Martins.*
Social Infrastructure, Arq. João Rosado Correia.*
Industry, Prof. José Veiga Simão.*
Labour and Social Affairs, Dr. Amândio Anes de Azevedo.†
Education and Universities, Prof. José Augusto Seabra.†
Quality of Life and Environment, Dr. Francisco Sousa Tavares.
Trade and Tourism, Alvaro Barreto.†
Agriculture, Manuel Soares Costa.†

* *P.S.P.*, † *P.S.D.* Dr. Lopes is an Independent.

EMBASSY IN LONDON
11 Belgrave Square, SW1X 8PP
[01–235 5331]

Ambassador Extraordinary and Plenipotentiary, His Excellency João Hall Themido (1984).
Minister-Counsellor, Sr. José Maria de A. S. de Lemos Macedo.
Counsellor, Sr. Paulo G. Castilho.

Area and Population.—Continental Portugal occupies the western part of the Iberian Peninsula, covering an area of 34,000 square miles. It lies between 36° 58′–42° 12″ N. lat. and 6° 11′ 48″–9° 29′ 45″ W. long., being 362 miles in length from N. to S., and averaging about 117 in breadth from E. to W. The population (including the Azores and Madeira) was estimated at 9,862,700 in 1979.

New statutes granting greater autonomy to the Atlantic islands of the Azores were promulgated in 1980. Provisional statutes for Madeira were published in 1976. The territory of Macao remains under Portuguese administration.

Government.—From the eleventh century until 1910 the government of Portugal was a monarchy, and for many centuries included the Vice-Royalty of Brazil, which declared its independence in 1822. In 1910 an armed rising in Lisbon drove King Manuel II and the Royal family into exile, and the National Assembly of Aug. 21, 1911, sanctioned a Republican form of government. A period of great political instability ensued until eventually the military stepped in. The Constitution of 1933 gave formal expression to the corporative "Estado Novo" (New State) which was personified by Dr. Salazar, Prime Minister from 1932–68. Dr. Caetano succeeded Salazar as Prime Minister in 1968 but his failure to liberalize the régime or to provide any alternative to continuing the wars in the African colonies resulted in his government's overthrow by a military coup on April 25, 1974. The next two years were characterized by great political turmoil with no fewer than 6 provisional governments between April 1974 and July 1976 but with the failure of an attempted coup by the extreme left in November 1975 the situation began to become more stable.

Constitutional reforms introduced in Aug. 1982 have reduced the President's scope for day-to-day intervention in government but the decision to dissolve the Assembly is still largely the President's. The revisions also abolished the Council of the Revolution, ending the military's capacity for political interference, and created two new organs of state, the Constitutional Tribunal and the Council of State, to advise the President.

In the April 1983 General Election, the Portuguese Socialist Party (*P.S.P.*) won 101 seats, the Social Democratic Party (*P.S.D.*) 75 seats, the Communist Party (*P.C.P.*) 44 seats and the Democratic Social Centre Party (*C.D.S.*) 30 seats. The government is a coalition of the *P.S.P.* and *P.S.D.*

Defence.—All physically fit males are liable for military service with the exception of those who lost a near relative in the fighting during the colonial wars. But conscription is becoming increasingly selective as the armed forces were greatly reduced following the end of the colonial wars, and reorganized and re-equipped for a conventional national defence role. The present strength of the Army is about 39,000. One brigade is earmarked for N.A.T.O. service. The Navy consists of about 13,000 officers and men, including 2,600 marines, manning about 60 craft of various types, many of which are obsolete. The present serving strength of the Air Force is about 12,000, (including paratroops) and about 80 aircraft of various types.

Education is free and compulsory for six years from the age of 7. Secondary education is mainly conducted in State lyceums, commercial and industrial schools, but there are also private schools. There are also military, naval, technical and other special schools. There are old established Universities at Coimbra (founded in 1290), Oporto and Lisbon. New Universities have been established at Lisbon, Braga, Aveiro and in the Azores; a University at Faro is expected to open in 1986/87.

Language and Literature.—Portuguese is a Romance language with admixtures of Arabic and other idioms. It is the language of Portugal and Brazil, and is the *lingua franca* of Angola, Mozambique and Guinea-Bissau.

Portuguese language and literature reached the culminating point of their development in the *Lusiadas* (dealing with the voyage of Vasco da Gama) and other works of Camoens (Camões), born in 1524, died in 1580. Until the second quarter of the nineteenth century Portuguese literature dominated that of Brazil. Modern literature, both prose and verse, is flourishing.

Newspapers and Broadcasting.—There are now 9 main daily newspapers in Lisbon and 4 in Oporto, and 3 main weekly newspapers. Most have been losing money and the Government has announced plans for a radical reorganization of the newspaper industry. There are 2 TV channels (broadcasting in colour) and 5 radio stations (4 state controlled) broadcasting nationwide.

Civil aviation is controlled by the Administração Nacional Aeronaútica. There is an international airport at Portela, about 5 miles from Lisbon, and the airport of Pedras Rubras near Oporto is also used for some international services. There are direct flights between London and Faro in the Algarve.

Agriculture.—The chief agricultural products are cork, maize, wheat, rye, rice, oats, barley, potatoes, beans, onions, olives, oranges, lemons, figs, almonds, tomatoes, timber, port wine and table wines. There are extensive forests of pine, cork, eucalyptus and chestnut covering about 20 per cent of the total area of the country.

Industry.—The country is so far only moderately industrialized, but is fairly rapidly extending its industries. The principal manufactures, some of which are still protected by high tariffs, are textiles, clothing and footwear, machinery (including electric machinery and transport equipment), foodstuffs (tomato concentrates and canned fish), chemicals, fertilizers, wood, cork, furniture, cement, glassware and pottery. There is a modern steelworks, and two modern and very large shipbuilding and repair yards at Lisbon and Setúbal working mainly for foreign ship-owners. There are several hydro-electric power stations and a new thermal power station. *Minerals.*—The principal mineral products are pyrites, wolfram, tin, iron ores, copper and sodium and calcium minerals.

Finance.—Portugal is a member of the European Monetary Agreement, the World Bank, the International Monetary Fund and the International Finance Corporation. The country has substantial, but declining, gold and foreign exchange reserves.

Currency.—*Escudos* (of 100 *Centavos*). *Conto* consists of 1,000 *Escudos*.

Trade.—Portugal is a member of GATT and OECD; the country resigned its membership of EFTA in May 1984. Portugal has signed a Trade Agreement with the EEC and is expected to join the Community with effect from January 1, 1986.

The principal imports are cereals, meat, raw and semi-manufactured iron and steel, industrial machinery, chemicals, crude oil, motor vehicles and raw materials for textiles.

The principal exports are textiles, footwear, timber, cork, electrical and other machinery, and chemicals.

	1983
Total imports	E885,704 m.
Total exports	504,713 m.

Trade with U.K.

	1982	1983
Imports from U.K.	£430,684,000	£396,988,000
Exports to U.K.	379,949,000	475,902,000

The British share of the Portuguese market was 8 per cent in 1981 and the U.K. was the largest market for Portuguese exports.

CAPITAL, ΨLisbon. Population (estimated, 1974) 1,707,500. ΨOporto 1,389,800; ΨSetubal 526,000.

Lisbon distance 1,110 miles; transit 50 hours; by air, 2¼ hours.

FLAG.—Vertical band of green (next staff) and square of red, bearing arms of the Republic, framed.
NATIONAL DAY.—June 10.

BRITISH EMBASSY
35–37 Rua de S. Domingos à Lapa,
1296 Lisbon

Ambassador Extraordinary and Plenipotentiary, His Excellency Hugh Campbell Byatt, C.M.G.
There are British Consulates in *Oporto, Portimão, Funchal* (Madeira) and *Ponta Delgada* (Azores).
British Council Representative, A. J. Herbert, The British Institute, Rua de Luis Fernandes 3,1294 Lisbon. There is also an office in Porto.

MADEIRA AND THE AZORES

Madeira and The Azores are two administratively autonomous regions of Portugal, having locally elected Assemblies and Governments.

Madeira is a group of islands in the Atlantic Ocean about 520 miles south-west of Lisbon, and consist of Madeira Porto Santo and 3 uninhabited islands (Desertas). The total area is 314 square miles with a population of 265,600 (1978). ΨFunchal in Madeira, the largest island (270 square miles), is the capital, with a population of 54,068; Machico (10,905).

The Azores are a group of 9 islands (Flores, Corvo, Terceira, São Jorge, Pico, Faial, Graciosa, São Miguel and Santa Maria) in the Atlantic Ocean, with a total area of 922 square miles and a population of 254,200 (1981). ΨPonta Delgada, the capital of the group has a population of 21,347. Other ports are ΨAngra, in Terceira, (16,476) and ΨHorta (2,509).

PORTUGUESE OVERSEAS PROVINCES

ΨMACAU, in China, on an island in the Canton River, has an area of 5 square miles and a population (1970) of 248,316.

The former Portuguese overseas territories of Guinea-Bissau, Mozambique and Angola achieved independence in 1974, 1975 and 1976 respectively, and in 1976 Portuguese Timor was incorporated into Indonesia.

QATAR

Amir of Qatar, H.H. Sheikh Khalifa Bin Hamad Al-Thani, G.C.M.G.; *assumed power* February 22, 1972 (*also Prime Minister*).

COUNCIL OF MINISTERS

Heir Apparent, Minister of Defence and Commander-in Chief, H.H. Sheikh Hamad Bin Khalifa Al-Thani, K.C.M.G.
Minister of Education, H.E. Shaikh Mohammad Bin Hamad Al-Thani.
Foreign, H.E. Shaikh Suhaim bin Hamad Al-Thani.
Finance and Petroleum Affairs, H.E. Shaikh Abdul Aziz Bin Khalifa Al-Thani.
Municipal Affairs, (vacant).
Economy and Commerce, H.E. Shaikh Naser Bin Khaled Al-Thani.
Justice (vacant).
Electricity and Water, H.E. Shaikh Jasem Bin Moh'd Al-Thani.
Interior, H.E. Shaikh Khalid Bin Hamad Al-Thani.
Industry and Agriculture, H.E. Shaikh Faisal Bin Thani Al-Thani.
Health, H.E. Sayed Khalid Bin Mohammed Al-Mana.
Public Works, H.E. Sayed Khaled Bin Abdullah Al-Attiyah.

Labour and Social Welfare Affairs, H.E. Sayed Ali Bin Ahmed Al-Ansari.
Communications and Transport, H.E. Sayed Abdullah Bin Naser Al-Suwaidi.
Information, H.E. Sayed Issa Ghanim Al-Kawari.
Minister of State for Foreign Affairs, H.E. Shaikh Ahmed bin Saif Al-Thani.

EMBASSY IN LONDON
27 Chesham Place, SW1X 8HG
[01–235 0851]

Ambassador Extraordinary and Plenipotentiary, His Excellency Sherida Sa'ad Jubran Al-Ka'abi.
Minister Plenipotentiary, Abdulrahman A. Al-Wohaibi.

The state of Qatar covers the peninsula of Qatar from approximately the Northern shore of Khor al Odaid to the Eastern shore of Khor al Salwa. The area is about 4,000 sq. miles, with a population estimated in 1982 at about 250,000. The great majority of the population is concentrated in the urban district of the capital Doha. Only a small minority still pursue the traditional life of the semi-nomadic tribesmen and fisherfolk.

Until 1971, Qatar was one of the nine independent Emirates in the Arabian Gulf in special treaty relations with the Government of the United Kingdom. In that year, with the withdrawal of H.M. Forces from the area, these special treaty relations were terminated. On April 2, 1970 a Provisional Constitution for Qatar was proclaimed, providing for the establishment of a Council of Ministers and for the formation of a Consultative Council to assist the Council of Ministers in running the affairs of the State. The first Cabinet was formed of 10 members on May 29, 1970. Qatar is a member of the Arab league as well as of the United Nations.

Production.—Although Qatar is a desert country, there are gardens and smallholdings near Doha and to the North and encouragement is being given to the development of agriculture.

Current industries include a steel mill, a fertiliser plant, a cement factory, a petrochemical complex and two natural gas liquids plants. A new 50,000 b.p.d. oil refinery was commissioned in 1984 to increase domestic refinery capacity to 60,000 b.p.d. With the exception of the cement works, which is at Umm Bab, all these industries are at Umm Said, about 30 miles south of Doha. An offshore gas field (North Field), one of the largest in the world, has yet to be tapped. Qatar is also expanding its infrastructure including electrical generation and water distillation, roads, houses, and Government buildings, although reduced demand for crude oil in international markets has led to a downturn in the economy and a slower rate of development than hitherto.

The Qatar General Petroleum Corporation is the state-owned company controlling Qatar's interests in oil, gas and petrochemicals. Since its merger in 1980 with the Qatar Petroleum Producing Authority, the corporation has been responsible for Qatar's oil production through its two operational divisions; Onshore and Offshore. The production level for Qatar agreed in O.P.E.C. is currently 300,000 b.p.d. Explorations continue for further oil and also in connection with the large reserves of natural gas in the North Field.

Communications.—Doha is an expanding town with an airport built to international standards. Regular air services connect Qatar with Bahrain and the United Arab Emirates, Kuwait, Muscat, Saudi Arabia, Jordan, Syria, Lebanon, Egypt, the Indian sub-continent and Europe. The Qatar Broadcasting Service transmits on medium, shortwave, and V.H.F. Regular television transmissions in colour began in 1974 and a second channel opened in 1982.

Trade with U.K.

	1982	1983
Imports from U.K....	£245,200,000	£216,385,000
Exports to U.K.	34,100,000	10,956,000

CAPITAL.—Doha. Population (estimated) 200,000. Other towns include Khor, Dukhan, Wakra and Umm Said.

FLAG.—White and maroon, white portion nearer the mast; vertical indented line comprising 17 angles divides the colours.

BRITISH EMBASSY
P.O. Box 3, Doha

Ambassador Extraordinary and Plenipotentiary, His Excellency Julian Fortay Walker, C.M.G., M.B.E. (1984).
1st Secretary, I. S. Lockhart (*Commercial*).
2nd Secretaries, J. W. Bradley (*Consul and Administration*); P. J. Millett.
Attaché, S. H. Innes (*Commercial*).
Vice Consul, D. J. B. Torrance.
British Council Representative, W. S. Beniston, Ras Abu Aboud Road (P.O. Box 2992), Doha.

ROMANIA
(Republica Socialistă Românîa)

President of the Republic, Nicolae Ceauşescu, re-elected, March 28, 1980.
State Council, N. Ceausescu (*President*); Gheorghe Rădulescu; Stefan Voitec; Maria Ciocan; Petru Enache; M. Manescu (*Vice-Presidents*).

COUNCIL OF MINISTERS

Prime Minister, Constantin Dascalescu.
1st Deputy Prime Ministers, Elena Ceauşescu; Ion Dinca; Gheorghe Oprea.
Deputy Prime Ministers, Ioan Avram; Marin Enache; Alexandrina Gainuse; Gheorghe Petrescu; Ludovic Fazekas; Ion Nicolae; Ion Totu.
Secretary, Lucian Dragut.
Agriculture and Food Industry, Gheorghe David.
Chemical Industry, Gheorghe Dinu.
Education and Instruction, Ion Teoreanu.
Electric Power, Nicolae Busui.
Finance, Petre Gigea.
Foreign Affairs, Stefan Andrei.
Foreign Construction Dept., Ion Stanescu.
Foreign Trade, Vasile Pungan.
Forestry Administration, Ion Cioara.
Geology, Ioan Folea.
Health, Eugen Proca.
Industrial Construction, Ion Petre.
Interior, George Homostean.
Internal Trade, Ana Muresan.
Justice, Gheorghe Chivulescu.
Labour, Maxim Berghianu.
Light Industry, Ion Patan.
Machine-Building Industry, Petre Preoteasa.
Machine Tool, Electrical Engineering, and Electronics Industries, Alexandru Necula.
Metallurgy, Niculai Agachi.
Mines, Ion Lazarescu.
National Defence, Constantin Olteanu.
Oil, Gheorghe Vlad.
Technical Material Supply, Richard Winter.
Tourism and Sports, Nicolae Gavrilescu.
Transportation and Telecommunications, Vasile Bulucea.
Wood Industry and Building Materials, Ioan Florea.
Youth, Nicu Ceausescu.
Chairmen of Central Bodies, Teodor Coman (*Committee of People's Councils' Affairs*); Aneta Spornic (*State Committee for Prices*); Cornel Mihulecea

(*State Committee for Nuclear Power*); Stefan Birlea (*State Planning Committee*); Nicolae Constantin (*Central Council of General Confederation of Trade Unions*); Ion Bucur (*1st Vice-Chairman, Council of Economic and Social Organisations*); Suzana Gadea (*Council of Socialist Culture and Education*); Elena Ceausescu (*National Council of Science and Technology*); Ion Ursu (*1st Vice-Chairman, National Council of Science and Technology*); Ion Badea (*National Council for Water Resources*); Ana Muresan (*National Council of Women*); Vasile Marin (*National Union of Agricultural Production Co-operatives*).

Minister Secretaries of State, M. Capisizu (*Agriculture and Food Industry*); T. Postelnicu; Aurel Duma; Mihai Florescu; A. Rosie; I. Ceausescu; F. Nagy; E. Dobrescu; I. Albuletu; I. Bucur; I. Stanescu.

THE COMMUNIST PARTY

Political Executive Committee, N. Ceausescu; I. Banc; E. Bobu; V. Cazacu; E. Ceausescu; L. Ciobanu; I. Coman; N. Constantin; C. Dascalescu; I. Dinca; L. Fazekąs; A. Gainuşe; P. Lupu; M. Mănescu; P. Niculescu; C. Olteanu; G. Oprea; G. Pana; I. Pătan; D. Popescu; G. Rădulescu; I. Verdet; S. Voitec (*full members*); S. Andrei; S. Birlea; M. Dobrescu; M. Enache; P. Enache; S. Gadea; M. Gere; N. Giosan; C. Leonard; S. Mocuta; A. Muresan; E. Nae; C. Pacoste; I. Radu; I. Stoian; I. Szasz; I. Totu; I. Ursu; R. Winter (*candidate members*).

Secretariat of the Central Committee, N. Ceausescu (*Secretary General*); I. Banc; I. Coman; P. Enache; E. Bobu; G. Stoica; L. Ciobanu; S. Curticeanu; C. Radu; I. Radu; I. Stoian; I. Verdet.

ROMANIAN EMBASSY IN LONDON
4 Palace Green, W8 4QD
[01–937 9666]

Ambassador Extraordinary and Plenipotentiary, His Excellency Vasile Gliga (1980).

Area and Population.—Romania is a republic of South-Eastern Europe, formerly the classical *Dacia* and *Scythia Pontica*, having its origin in the union of the Danubian principalities of *Wallachia* and *Moldavia* under the *Treaty of Paris* (April, 1856). The area of Romania is 237,500 sq. km. and the population in July, 1982 was 22,480,000.

Government.—The principalities remained separate entities under Turkish suzerainty until 1859, when Prince Alexandru Ion Cuza was elected Prince of both, still under the suzerainty of Turkey. Prince Cuza abdicated in 1866 and was succeeded by Prince

Charles of Hohenzollern-Sigmaringen, in whose successors the crown was vested. By the *Treaty of Berlin* (July 13, 1878) the Principality was recognized as an independent State, and part of the *Dobrudja* (which had been occupied by the Romanians) was incorporated. On March 27, 1881, it was recognized as a Kingdom.

The outcome of the War of 1914–18 added Bessarabia, the Bukovina, Transylvania, The Banat and Crisana-Maramures, these additions of territory being confirmed in the Treaty of St. Germain, 1919, and the Treaty of Petit Trianon, 1920.

On June 27, 1940, in compliance with an ultimatum from U.S.S.R., Bessarabia and Northern Bukovina were ceded to the Soviet Government, the area affected being about 20,000 sq. miles, with a population of about 4,000,000.

In August, 1940, Romania ceded to Bulgaria the portion of Southern Dobrudja (about 3,000 sq miles) taken from Bulgaria in 1913. Romania became "The Romanian People's Republic" in December, 1947, on the abdication of King Michael.

A new Constitution, modelled on the Soviet Constitution of 1936, was adopted unanimously on September 24, 1952, by the Grand National Assembly. The Assembly was later dissolved and elections were held for a new Grand National Assembly on November 30, 1952; in each constituency there was only one candidate for election, representing the People's Democratic Front. Further elections on similar lines were held in February, 1957, in March, 1961, and in March, 1965. A new Constitution was approved by the Grand National Assembly in 1965 when the name of the state was changed to The Socialist Republic of Romania. The Constitution states (Art. 3) that the leading political force of the whole society is the Romanian Communist Party. The Constitution was modified in March, 1974.

Agriculture.—The soil of Wallachia and Moldavia is among the richest in Europe, producing wheat, maize, millet, oats, barley, rye, beans, peas and other vegetables. Grape vines and fruits are abundant. The fertile plain of Transylvania yields large crops of maize, wheat, rye, oats, flax and hemp. Agriculture and sheep and cattle raising are the principal industries of Romania, but the climate of this part of South-Eastern Europe is of the Continental character, and the intense winter cold and summer heat, and fierce summer drought sometimes defeat these principal industries. The forests of the mountainous regions are extensive, and the timber industry is important.

Socialization of agriculture was completed when plans for collectivization were fulfilled in the spring of 1962, some three years ahead of the planned date.

Natural Resources and Industry.—Before the war petroleum and agriculture were the backbone of the Romanian economy. Though the production of both industries has increased, they no longer hold the same dominant position. There are plentiful supplies of natural gas, together with various mineral deposits including coal, iron ore, bauxite, lead, zinc, copper and uranium in quantities which allow a substantial part of the requirements of industry to be met from local resources. Since 1948 industrialization has proceeded rapidly and heavy investments have been made in electrical power, the chemical, metallurgical and engineering industries and growing attention is being paid to light industry. The economy is centrally organized on the basis of Five-Year Plans which cover all branches of national activity including investment and production.

1979 production figures were: crude oil, 12,323,000 tons; coal 32,764,000 tons; electric power, 64,933,000 kwh; methane gas, 27,189,000 cu. metres; steel, 12,909,000 tons; wheat and rye, 4,716,300 tons; maize, 12,424,500 tons; sugar-beet, 6,109,100 tons.

Language and Literature.—Romanian is a Romance language with many archaic forms and with admixtures of Slavonic, Turkish, Magyar and French words. The folk-songs and folklore, composed by the people themselves, and transmitted orally through many centuries (and collected in the 19th century), form one of the most interesting of such collections. The publication of all books and reviews is controlled and authorized by the Council for Socialist Culture and Education, which has the status of a Ministry. The leading religion is that of the Romanian Orthodox Church; the Roman Catholics and some Protestant denominations are of importance numerically. The Jewish community has declined through emigration.

Education is free and nominally compulsory, with 4,680,917 in attendance in 1979–80, including 192,546 in higher education. There are Universities at Bucharest, Iasi, Cluj, Timisoara, Craiova and Brasov. A "Marxist-Leninist" University was opened in Bucharest in 1951. There are polytechnics at Bucharest, Timisoara, Cluj, Brasov, Galati and Iasi, two commercial academies at Bucharest and Brasov, and agricultural colleges at Bucharest, Iasi, Cluj, Craiova and Timisoara.

Communications.—In 1979 there were 11,113 km. of railway open for traffic. The mercantile marine had a gross tonnage of 13,220,000 tons in 1979. The principal ports are Constanta (on the Black Sea), Sulina (on the Danube Estuary), Galati, the most important, Braila, Giurgiu and Turnu Severin. Romania is a member of the Danube Commission whose seat is at Budapest.

FINANCE

	1979
	Lei
Revenue	339,309·3m
Expenditure	337,626·8m

The Romanian *Lei* (of 100 *Bani*) had been revalued three times since the war. With a 141·45 per cent. premium on all "capitalist" currencies for non-commercial transactions, the effective exchange rate in July, 1981 was *Lei* 20·96 = £1. (*See also* p. 82.)

TRADE

	1982
Imports	U.S.$7,476 million
Exports	8,493 million

No detailed statistics for foreign trade have been published since 1974. Imports are chiefly semi-manufactured goods, raw materials, machinery and metals; export consists principally of maize, wheat, barley, oats, petroleum, timber, cattle, machines and industrial equipment. Trade with U.K., although relatively small, has been growing steadily over the past few years. External trade with Communist countries dropped from 80 per cent. in 1960 to 45 per cent. in 1978.

Trade with U.K.

	1982	1983
Imports from U.K.	£115,244,000	£82,160,000
Exports to U.K.	51,515,000	58,865,000

CAPITAL, Bucharest, on the Dimbovita, population 1,960,097. Other large towns are: Constanţa (279,308); Iasi (262,493); Timişoara (281,320); Cluj-Napoca (274,095); Braşov (299,172); Ploieşti (207,009); Craiova (220,893); ΨGalaţi (252,884); ΨBrăila (208,983); Arad (172,669); Oradea (178,407); Sibiu (156,854); Piteşti (133,179); Tirgú Mures (129,284).

FLAG.—Three vertical bands, blue, yellow, red, with the emblem of the Republic in the centre band.

NATIONAL DAY.—August 23 (Liberation Day, 1944).

BRITISH EMBASSY
24 Strada Jules Michelet, Bucharest

Ambassador Extraordinary and Plenipotentiary, His Excellency Philip McKearney (1983).
Counsellor, Miss M. MacGlashan (*Head of Chancery*).
Defence, Naval and Military Attaché, Lt.-Col. S. P. Walters.
Cultural Attaché and British Council Representative, K. McGuinness.

RWANDA
(Republic of Rwanda)

President, Maj. Gen. Juvénal Habyarimana, *assumed office*, July 5, 1973, *elected*, Dec. 24, 1978, *re-elected*, Dec. 19, 1983.

Rwanda became an independent republic on July 1, 1962. Formerly part of the Belgian-administered trusteeship of Ruanda-Urundi, it has an area of 10,169 sq. miles and a population (1981 estimate) of 5,100,000, mainly of the Bahutu tribe, with Batutsi and Batwa minorities.

At a referendum held in September, 1961, under supervision of the United Nations, a large majority voted against the retention of the monarchy which was accordingly abolished on Oct. 2, 1961. Elections for a new Legislative Assembly were also held in September, 1961, and the Assembly elected M. Kayibanda as Head of State and Head of the Government. He was deposed in 1973, and replaced by a military government under Maj.-Gen. Juvénal Habyarimana.

Coffee (the chief crop), tea and sugar are grown. Tin, hides, bark of quinine and extract of pyrethrum flowers are also exported.

A University was opened at Butare in 1963.

The currency is the *Rwanda franc*. In 1979 total imports were valued at *Rw.Fr.*10,594,100,000; total exports, *Rw.Fr.*15,750,000,000.

Trade with U.K.

	1982	1983
Imports from U.K.	£510,000	£2,326,000
Exports to U.K.	2,079,000	2,919,000

CAPITAL.—Kigali (7,000).
FLAG.—Three vertical bands, red, yellow and green with letter R on yellow band.
NATIONAL DAY.—July 5.

British Ambassador (resident at *Kinshasa*, Zaire).

EL SALVADOR
(República de El Salvador)

President, José Napoleon Duarte, *elected* March 25, 1984, *assumed office*, June 1, 1984.

CABINET

Vice-President and Interior Minister, Rodolfo Castillo Claramount.
Minister of the Presidency, Julio A. Rey Prendes.
Foreign Affairs, Dr. Jorge E. Tenorio.
Planning and Co-ordination of Economic and Social Development, Dr. Fidel Chávez Mena.
Justice, Dr. Manuel F. Cardona Herrera.
Finance, Ricardo J. López.
Trade, Manuel Morales Ehrlich.
Economy, Dr. Ricardo Gonzalez Comacho.
Education, Prof. Alberto Buendía Flores.
Defence and Public Security, Gen. Carlos E. Vides Casanova.
Labour and Social Security, Dr. Julio A. Samayoa.
Agriculture, Carlos A. Duarte Funes.
Public Works, Ramón Ernesto Rodríguez.

SALVADOREAN EMBASSY AND CONSULATE
9 Welbeck House, 62 Welbeck Street, W.1
[01-486 8182/3]

Ambassador Extraordinary and Plenipotentiary, His
Excellency Dr. Alfonso Moisés-Beatriz.

Area and Population.—The Republic of El Salvador
extends along the Pacific coast of Central America
for 160 miles with a general breadth of about 50 miles,
and contains an area of 8,200 square miles with a
population (1981 estimate) of 4,939,400. It is divided
into 14 Departments.

The surface of the country is very mountainous,
many of the peaks being extinct volcanoes. The
highest peaks are the Santa Ana volcano (7,700 ft.)
and the San Vicente volcano (7,200 ft.). Much of the
interior has an average altitude of 2,000 feet. The
lowlands along the coast are generally hot, but
towards the interior the altitude tempers the severity
of the heat. There is a wet season from May to
October, and a dry season from November to April.
Earthquakes have been frequent in the history of El
Salvador, the most recent being that of May 3, 1965,
when considerable damage was done to San Salvador.

The principle river is the Rio Lempa. There is a
large volcanic lake (Ilopango) a few miles to the east
of the capital, while farther away and to the west lies
the smaller but very picturesque lake of Coatepeque,
which appears to have been formed in a vast crater
flanked by the Santa Ana volcano.

Government.—El Salvador was conquered in 1526
by Pedro de Alvarado, and formed part of the Spanish
vice-royalty of Guatemala until 1821.

After two years of government by a Junta headed
by José Napoleon Duarte, elections for a Constituent
Assembly were held in March 1982. The Assembly
has completed its principal task of adopting a new
Constitution. Presidential elections, although boycotted by the guerrilla movement, were held in March
1984 and in the run-off between the two largest
parties, Sr. Duarte, the Christian Democrat leader,
won with a 54 per cent. majority over the ARENA
candidate, Roberto d'Aubuisson. Assembly elections
are due to take place in March 1985.

Despite the new government, guerrilla warfare
continues.

Agriculture.—The principal cash crops are coffee,
which is grown principally on the slopes of the
volcanoes, cotton, which is cultivated on the coastal
plains, and sugarcane. (However, cotton and sugar
production have decreased as a result of the civil
war.) Also cultivated are maize, sesame, indigo, rice,
balsam, etc. In the lower altitudes towards the east,
sisal is produced and used in the manufacture of
coffee and cereal bags. Land reforms, announced in
March 1980, are being undertaken. The Salvadorean
Coffee Company, sugar exports and the banking
system are nationalised.

Industry.—Existing factories make textiles,
constructional steel, furniture, cement and household items. El Salvador is a member of the
Central American Common Market. The first trade
zone was inaugurated in November 1974 and the
National Assembly approved a new Export Development Law.

Education.—The illiteracy rate is about 31·5 per
cent (1979). Primary education is nominally compulsory, but the number of schools and teachers available
is too small to enable education to be given to all
children of school age. In recent Budgets, however, a
high percentage of the national revenue has been
devoted to education and great efforts are being made
to eliminate the existing shortage of schools and
teachers.

Language and Literature.—The language of the
country is Spanish. Indigenous literature has not
yet produced work of international repute. There

are 4 daily newspapers published at the capital, and 4
in the provinces.

Communications.—The former El Salvador Railways and the Salvadorean Section of International
Railways of Central America have been merged
under the Executive Autonomous Port Commission
(CEPA) which also administers the previously
foreign-owned port of Cutuco, at La Union and the
principal port of Acajutla. The new railroad organization is styled FENADESAL. There is continuous
railway communication between San Salvador and
Guatemala City and Puerto Barrios on the Caribbean
coast. The roads are paved and in good condition but
bridges are frequently dynamited. There are good
motor roads between Port Acajutla and the capital
(60 miles), and between the capital and Guatemala
City. The Pan-American Highway from the Guatemalan frontier follows this route and continues to
the Honduran frontier. The El Salvador international airport can receive jet aircraft and many
international airlines fly to San Salvador.

There are post and telegraph offices throughout
the country. There are 40 broadcasting stations and
six television stations.

BUDGET

	1981	1982
	Colones '000	
Revenue	1,068,316	1,091,532
Expenditure	1,581,292	1,649,423

TRADE

	1981	1982
	Colones '000	
Imports	2,461,458	2,207,161
Exports	1,991,940	1,760,038

Trade with U.K.

	1982	1983
Imports from U.K.	£5,244,000	£7,653,000
Exports to U.K.	2,017,000	425,000

There is strict foreign exchange control (*see also* p.
82).

Coffee to the value of ₡1,014,183 was exported in
1982. Exports of cotton were valued at ₡117,638.
Other exports are sugar (₡39,712), shrimps, sisal (in
the form of bags used for exporting coffee, sugar, etc.),
balsam, meat, towels, hides and skins. The chief
imports are chemicals, fertilizers, pharmaceutical
goods, petroleum, manufactured goods, industrial
and electronic machinery and equipment.

CAPITAL.—San Salvador. Population, (est. 1980)
425,119. Other towns are Santa Ana (204,570), San
Miguel (157,838), Ψ La Union (Cutuco), Ψ La Libertad
and Ψ Acajutia.

FLAG.—Three horizontal bands light blue, white,
light blue; coat of arms on white band. NATIONAL
DAY.—September 15.

BRITISH EMBASSY
P.O. Box 242, San Salvador

British Ambassador, (resident at Tegucigalpa, Honduras).

Chargé d'Affaires a.i., David Ridgeway (*First Secretary*).

San Salvador is 5,700 miles from London.

SAN MARINO
(Repubblica di San Marino)

Regents, Two "Capitani Reggenti".

CONSULATE GENERAL IN LONDON
86 Park Lane, W1A 3AA
Consul-General, The Lord Forte.

A small Republic in the hills near Rimini, on the Adriatic, founded, it is stated, by a pious stonecutter of Dalmatia in the 4th century. The Republic always resisted the Papal claims, and those of neighbouring dukedoms, during the 15th–18th centuries, and its integrity and sovereignty is recognized and respected by Italy. The Republic is governed by a State Congress of 10 members, under the Presidency of two Heads of State. The Great and General Council, a legislative body of 60 members, is elected by a universal suffrage for a term of 5 years. A Council of Twelve forms in certain cases a Supreme Court of Justice. The area is approximately 23 square miles, the population (March 31, 1983) is 22,053. The city of San Marino, on the slope of Monte Titano, has three towers, a fine church and Government palace, a theatre and museums. The principal products are wine, cereals, and cattle, and the main industries are tourism, ceramics, lime, concrete, cotton yarns, colour and paints. A Treaty of Extradition between the Governments of Great Britain and the Republic of San Marino has been in force since 1899.

FLAG.—Two horizontal bands, white, blue (with coat of arms of the Republic in centre).

BRITISH CONSULATE-GENERAL
Consul-General, R. A. Eilbeck (resides at Florence).

SÃO TOMÉ AND PRÍNCIPE

President, Dr. Manuel Pinto da Costa.

The islands of São Tomé and Príncipe are situated in the gulf of Guinea, off the west coast of Africa. They have an area of 372 square miles, and a population (1980 est.) of 113,000.

Following Portugal's decision to grant independence, a transitional government was installed on Dec. 21, 1974, and the islands became an independant democratic republic on July 12, 1975.

Cacao is the main product.

Trade with U.K.

	1982	1983
Imports from U.K.	£1,510,000	£597,000
Exports to U.K.	494,000	218,000

CAPITAL.—ΨSão Tomé (3,187).

British Ambassador (resident in *Luanda,* Angola).

SAUDI ARABIA
(Al Mamlaka al Arabiya as-Sa'udiyya)

King of Saudi Arabia, H.M. King Fahd bin Abdul Aziz, *born,* 1921, *ascended the throne* June 1, 1982.
Crown Prince, H.R.H. Amir Abdullah bin Abdul Aziz.

COUNCIL OF MINISTERS

Prime Minister, H.M. King Fahd bin Abdul Aziz.
First Deputy Prime Minister and Commander of the National Guard, H.R.H. Amir Abdullah bin Abdul Aziz.
Second Deputy Prime Minister and Defence, H.R.H. Amir Sultan bin Abdul Aziz.
Public Works and Housing, H.R.H. Amir Mitab bin Abdul Aziz.
Interior, H.R.H. Amir Naif bin Abdul Aziz.

Foreign Affairs, H.R.H. Amir Saud al-Faisal bin Abdul Aziz.
Finance and National Economy, Shaikh Muhammad Al Ali Aba al-Khail.
Agriculture and Water and Health (acting), Dr. Abdul Rahman bin Abdul Aziz bin Hasssan Al al-Shaikh.
Municipal and Rural Affairs, and Pilgrimages and Trusts (acting), Shaikh Ibrahim Abdullah al-Angari.
Higher Education, Shaikh Hassan Abdullah Al al-Shaikh.
Commerce, Dr Sulaiman al-Salaim.
Communications, Dr. Husain Mansouri.
Petroleum and Mineral Resources, Shaikh Ahmad Zaki Yamani.
Justice, Ibrahim bin Mohammed Al al-Shaikh.
Labour and Social Affairs, Shaikh Mohamed Ali al-Faiz.
Information, Shaikh Ali Hassan al-Sha'er.
Education, Dr. Abdul Aziz Khuwaiter.
Planning, Shaikh Hisham Mohiyiddin Nazer.
Posts, Telegraphs and Telephones, Dr. Alawi Darwish Kayyal.
Industry and Electricity, Dr. Abdul Aziz al-Zamil.
Ministers of State, Shaikh Muhammad Ibrahim Mas'oud; Dr. Muhammad al-Amran; Dr. Muhammad Abdul Latif al-Melhem; Shaikh Nasir ash-Shitri.

ROYAL SAUDI ARABIAN EMBASSY
30 Belgrave Square, SW1X 8QB
[01–235 0831]

Ambassador Extraordinary and Plenipotentiary, His Excellency Sheikh Nasser Almanqour (1980).
Minister Plenipotentiary, Naji S. Mufti.

The Kingdom of Saudi Arabia, so named since Sept. 20, 1932, is a personal union of two countries, the Sultan of Nejd becoming also King of the Hijaz.

By the Treaty of Jedda (May 20, 1927) Great Britain recognized Abdulaziz Ibn Saud as an independent ruler, King of the Hijaz and of Nejd and its Dependencies.

The total area of the Kingdom is about 927,000 sq. miles, with a population (1976 est.) of 9,160,000. Islam is the established and only permitted religion.

In the 18th century Nejd was an independent state governed from Diriya (now in ruins, 25 km. from Riyadh) and the stronghold of the Wahhabis, a puritanical Islamic sect. It subsequently fell under the Turkish yoke, but in 1913 Abdulaziz Ibn Saud threw off Turkish rule and captured the Turkish province of al Hasa. In 1920 he captured the Asir, and in 1921, by force of arms, he added to his dominions the Jebel Shammar territory of the Rashid family. In 1925 he completed the conquest of the Hejaz. The discovery of oil in 1938, the exploitation of this resource after World War II, and the increases in oil prices, and consequently in state revenues, since 1973 have enabled the Kingdom to make rapid strides towards Western standards of development. In the interim the nomadic lifestyle of the Bedouin has disappeared: in 1979 only about 5 per cent of the population was still truly nomadic.

Nejd ("Plateau"), now the Central Province, extends over Central Arabia including the Nafud and Dahna deserts. The population is estimated at about 2 million (1976) concentrated on the national capital Riyadh (approx. 1 million) and the main provincial towns of al Kharj, Unaiza, Buraidah and Hail. Apart from a concentration of light industry in Riyadh the area is agricultural: about 110,000 hectares are farmed as dry lands, with some irrigation.

Al Hasa is now incorporated into the Eastern Province, which extends from the Iraq/Kuwait borders in the north to Rub al Khali desert in the

south and from the Gulf to Dahna desert in the west.
The population is about 1 million, concentrated on
the seaboard towns of Damman, Al Khobar and Qatif,
and in Hofuf. Oil was found in commercial quantities
in Dhahran, near Dammam, in 1938. Total production
of crude oil averaged 8·3 million barrels/day in 1978,
peaked at 9·9 m.b.d. in 1980, and fell to under 5 m.b.d.
in 1983. About 97 per cent of the total is extracted by
the Arabian–American Oil Company. Aramco's 66-
year lease will terminate in 1999 but the company
was nationalized in 1980. Aramco operates a deep-
water oil terminal at Ras Tanura. The modern
commercial port at Dammam has 37 piers with an
annual capacity of 9·1 million tons: it is linked by a
railway line via Hofuf to Riyadh, where a dry port
opened in 1981. There is a concentration of manufacturing industries around Dammam. Al Hasa is
traditionally a dry farming area, and at Haradh a
major irrigation scheme will cover 16,000 hectares.
Jubail, one of the industrial poles is approx. 75 km.
north of Dammam.

The Hijaz ("the Boundary"—between Nejd and
Tihama), known as the Western Province, extends
from Asir in the south to Northern Province and
from the Red Sea to the boundaries of the Central
Province (300–350 km. inland). The population, estimated at 2·3 million, is concentrated in Jedda (1
million) and the holy towns of Mecca and Medina.
The former, about 60 km. east of Jedda, is the
birthplace of the Prophet Muhammad, and contains
the Great Mosque, within which is the Kaaba or
sacred shrine of the Muslim religion. This is the
focus of the annual Hajj ("Pilgrimage") performed by
almost 2 million in 1983. The latter, Medina al
Munawwarah ("The City of Light") some 300 km.
north of Mecca, is celebrated as the first city to
embrace Islam and as the Prophet Muhammad's
burial place (he died there on Rabia 12, 11 AH,
corresponding to June 7, 632 AD). Medina was the
terminus of the now abandoned Hejaz railway from
Damascus. The traditional wealth of the Hejaz was
founded on the pilgrimage traffic to Mecca and
Medina, and on the role of Jedda as an entrepôt for
commercial traffic on the Red Sea. The modern
commercial port at Jedda had 43 piers with an annual
capacity of 17 million tons in 1981. The city is a
centre of light industry. Dryland farming is practised
in the region. Yanbu, the second industrial pole (*see*
below) is on the coast some 350 km. north of Jedda.

Northern Province incorporates the areas north
and west of the Nafud desert, from the Red Sea
eastward along the borders of Jordan and Iraq. The
population of a little over half a million is centred on
the provincial capitals of Tabuk and al Jouf. There
is little industrial development in the region: dryland
and irrigated farming covers some 3,000 hectares.

Asir ("Inaccessible") named for its mountainous
terrain, and the coastal plain of the Tihama constitute
the Southern Province, which extends from the
border with Yemen north for some 500 km. to the
port of al Lith, and inland approx. 200 km. to include
Bishah and Najran. The population of about 1·85
million is engaged largely in agriculture, this being
the only region to enjoy substantial rainfall. Water
supplies are, however, being supplemented by dams
and irrigation. The region is served by the ports of
Qunfudah and Jizan, and is the home of the first
National Park.

Finance and Trade.—Oil has replaced customs
duties and foreign exchange accruing from the
pilgrimage traffic as the main source of receipts in
the balance of payments. In the fiscal year 1981–82
(ended April, 1982) the Government revenue was
SR368,000 million, of which 89 per cent accrued from
oil royalties, and 11 per cent from other sources
including income tax on companies and individuals.
The 1983–84 budget provided for revenue of SR214

billion, and expenditure of SR260 billion, of which 43
per cent was allocated to development projects. There
is no public debt. There are no restrictions on foreign
exchange transactions. The currency is strong,
backed by gold and foreign exchange reserves, and
maintained on a close parity to the U.S. dollar.

With the exceptions of alcohol, pork meat and
firearms there are no restrictions on imports. Imports
in 1982 were valued at SR139,335 million (up 16 per
cent on 1981), the leading suppliers being the U.S.A.
21 per cent, Japan 19 per cent, West Germany 11 per
cent, the U.K. 6·5 per cent, Italy 6 per cent and France
5 per cent. Exports in the same year were SR271,090
million (down 33 per cent on 1981), the chief customers
being Japan 24 per cent, France 9 per cent, U.S.A. 8
per cent and Singapore 5 per cent.

Trade with U.K.

	1982	1983
Imports from U.K.	£1,361,665,000	£1,478,587,354
Exports to U.K.	1,447,775,000	897,701,728

Industry.—The Government actively encourages
the establishment of manufacturing industries in the
country. The policy includes the provision of industrial estates and loans covering 50 per cent of capital
investment. By late 1982, 2,688 licences had been
granted for industrial plants. Of these 34·3 per cent
were related to the construction industry, the other
sector leaders being food and drink processing (15·4
per cent), chemicals and plastics (15·7 per cent), and
light engineering (8·5 per cent). The Government
has also established two industrial poles at Jubail
and Yanbu, financed by the state agency Saudi Basic
Industries Corp., to be the focus of heavy industrial
development. Linked by gas and oil pipelines, both
are to have petrochemical complexes producing,
initially, ethylene and methanol, for which agreements have been signed with American and Japanese
companies; two of the seven plants are now on-
stream. In addition an integrated steel complex and
a urea fertilizer factory are in production in Jubail
with West German and Taiwanese partners. Complete new cities are being built at each pole: Jubail
will eventually house 300,000 and Yanbu 150,000.
The state agency Petromin operates three refineries
and two plants which supply domestic requirements;
1982 production amounted to 310·8 million barrels.
Three joint-venture export refineries are to come on-
stream in 1984–86 in Yanbu, Jubail and Rabigh, with
a total capacity of 825,000 b.p.d.

Communications.—The railway from the port of
Dammam to the oilfields at Abqaiq and through Hofuf

to Riyadh was opened in 1951. An extension to Jedda via Medina and the reopening of the Hejaz railway are planned. A direct line Damman-Riyadh is under construction. Metalled roads connect all the cities and main towns: the network consisted of 26,000 km. in 1983. The Government-owned Saudi Arabian Airlines (Saudia) operate scheduled services to 19 domestic airports. There are international class airports at Dhahran, Jedda and Riyadh; new international airports have opened at the latter two, and work has begun on a new Dharan airport. Saudia have an extensive overseas operation including 15 flights to London per week. A large number of international airlines operate into the country. Telecommunications are being rapidly expanded. By mid-1983 16,000 telex and 807,300 telephone lines were installed; telephone and telex exchanges will be able to handle 2·25 million lines by 1990. International direct dialling is available. By 1979 there were 11 ground satellite stations for inter-city communications and two for international lines. The Government is a major participant in the Arab Satellite Communications Organisation.

Education.—With the exception of a few schools for expatriate children, all schools are Government supervised and segregated for boys and girls. In 1983 there were a total of 1·4 million schoolchildren in 6,792 primary and 2,818 intermediate and secondary schools. There are Universities in Jedda, Mecca, Riyadh (branches in Abha, to become independent, and Qassim) and Dammam (branch at Hofuf). There is a University of Petroleum and Minerals at Dhahran, and there are Islamic Universities in Medina and Riyadh. In addition there is great emphasis on vocational training. The General Organisation for Technical Education and Vocational Training runs vocational training centres providing combined literacy and artisan skill training (there were 21 centres in 1983) and more advanced technical education in industrial, commercial and agricultural institutes (20 in 1983). Education in government-owned institutes is free at all levels.

CAPITAL.—Riyadh, population about 1 million.

FLAG.—Green oblong, white Arabic device in centre: "There is no God but God, Muhammad is the Prophet of God," and a white scimitar beneath the lettering.

BRITISH EMBASSY
P.O. Box 393, Jedda.

Ambassador Extraordinary and Plenipotentiary, His Excellency Sir Patrick Wright, K.C.M.G. (1984).
Minister, I. S. Winchester, C.M.G.
Counsellors, G. L. St. L. Rollestan; R. J. S. Muir; J. Q. Greenstock (*Commercial*).
1st Secretaries, R. J. Newell (*Commercial*); M. Gathercole (*Administration*); D. H. G. Rose (*Consul-General*); S. Bonde (*Commercial*); A. M. Layden (*Chancery*).
Defence Attaché, Col. J. R. A. Daniel.
Military Attaché, Lt.-Col. G. Latham.
Naval and Air Attaché, Wing-Cdr. C. M. Quaife, M.B.E.

British Council Representative, M. R. W. Dexter, O.B.E., Mura'aba, P.O. Box 2701, Riyadh 11461. There is also an office in Jeddah.

SENEGAL
(République du Sénégal)

President and Head of Government, Abdou Diouf, *installed,* Jan. 1, 1981, *elected for 5-year term,* Feb. 27, 1983.

11 Phillimore Gardens, W8 7QG
[01–937 0925/6, 3139]

Ambassador Extraordinary and Plenipotentiary, His Excellency Ousmane Camara.

Senegal lies on the west coast of Africa between Mauritania in the north, Mali in the east, and Guinea-Bissau and Guinea in the south. The Gambia lies entirely within Senegal, except for its sea-coast. (*For* MAP, *see* index.) It has an area of 77,814 sq. miles and a population (1980 estimate) of 5,661,000.

Formerly a French colony, Senegal elected on Nov. 25, 1958, to remain within the French Community as an autonomous republic. In March, 1963 (after an attempted *coup d'état* by the then Prime Minister in the previous December) a new constitution was approved giving executive powers to the President, on the lines of the present French constitution. The process of political liberalisation continued; in 1983 fourteen political parties were officially recognised, and eight of these contested the General Election in Feb. 1983. The P.S. took 111 seats, the P.D.S. 8, and the R.N.D. 1.

In Feb. 1982, after an attempted coup in The Gambia in July 1981 had been put down with the aid of Senegalese troops, the Senegambia Confederation was established, based on certain joint institutions and the integration of defence, security and some other matters. Each country remains sovereign and independent. The President of Senegal is President of the Confederation and the President of The Gambia is Confederal Vice-President.

Senegal's principal exports are groundnuts (raw and processed) and phosphates. G.N.P. per capita in 1980 was about U.S.$450.

Trade with U.K.

	1982	1983
Imports from U.K.	£22,349,000	£13,212,000
Exports to U.K.	14,196,000	22,333,000

CAPITAL.—Ψ Dakar (1,000,000).

FLAG.—Three vertical bands, green, yellow and red; a green star on the yellow band.

NATIONAL DAY.—April 4.

BRITISH EMBASSY
B.P. 6025, Dakar.

Ambassador Extraordinary and Plenipotentiary, His Excellency Peter Laurence O'Keeffe, C.M.G., C.V.O. (1982).
1st Secretaries, N. M. McCarthy, O.B.E. (*Head of Chancery*); G. S. Hand.
2nd Secretary, M. N. Napier (*Consul*).
3rd Secretary, S. Buckley (*Administration/Vice-Consul*).
Cultural Attaché (*British Council Representative*), J. M. Tod.

SOMALIA
(Somali Democratic Republic)

President and Sec. Gen. of Council, Maj.-Gen. Mohamed Siad Barre, *assumed office* Oct. 21, 1969.
Supreme Revolutionary Council, Maj.-Gen. H. K. Afrah (*Presidential Assistant for State Affairs*); Lt.-Gen. M. A. Samatar (*Min. Defence*); Brig.-Gen. A. S. Abdallah (*Min. Planning*); Maj.-Gen. A. M. Fadil (*Min. Industry*); Col A. M. Farah (*Min. Mineral Resources*); Col. M. R. God (*Min. Presidential Affairs*); Col. M. O. Jess (*Min. Information*); Col. A. H. Musse (*Min. Public Works*); Col. A. W. Issaq (*Min. Labour and Social Affairs*); Brig.-Gen. M. A. Shire (*Head, Finance Bureau*); Col. A. M. Abukar (*Head, Party Cadre Training Bureau*),; Brig.-Gen.

M. S. Osman (*Head, Legal Affairs*); Jaalle Mohamed Ali Warsame (*Head, Research Bureau*); Col. A. H. Moh'd (*Head, Organisation and Mobilisation Bureau*); Col. F. W. Dule; Col. M. G. Yusuf.

SOMALI EMBASSY
60 Portland Place, W1N 3DG
[01–580 7148]

Ambassador Extraordinary and Plenipotentiary, His Excellency Mohamed Jama Elmi (1980).

The Somali Democratic Republic occupies part of the north-east horn of Africa, with a coast-line on the Indian Ocean extending from the boundary with Kenya (2° South latitude) to Cape Guardafui (12° N.); and on the Gulf of Aden to the boundary with Djibouti. Somalia is bounded on the west by Djibouti, Ethiopia and Kenya and covers an area of approximately 246,000 sq. miles. The population, of which a large proportion is nomadic, is estimated (Jan. 1983) at 5,000,000.

Livestock raising is the main occupation in Somalia and there is a modest export trade in livestock on the hoof, skins and hides. Italy imports the bulk of the banana crop, the second biggest export.

Government.—The Somali Democratic Republic, consisting of the former British Somaliland Protectorate and the former Italian trust territory of Somalia, was established on July 1, 1960. British rule in Somaliland lasted from 1887 until 1960 except for a short period in 1940/41 when the Protectorate was occupied by Italian forces. Somalia, formerly an Italian colony, was occupied by British forces in 1941. In 1950 it was placed under Italian administration by a resolution of the U.N.; this trusteeship lasted until independence. Following the assassination of President Shermake on October 15, 1969, the armed forces, assisted by the police, took over the Government without resistance and a Revolutionary Council under Siad Barre assumed control of the country. A new constitution was introduced following a referendum in 1979. This provides for an elected People's Assembly of 171 seats. The Assembly met for the first time in January 1980. A state of emergency was declared in October, 1980 but lifted in March 1982. There is an outstanding territorial dispute with Ethiopia and incursions by Ethiopian-backed Somali rebels occurred in disputed areas in July 1982.

Trade with U.K.

	1982	1983
Imports from U.K.	£12,095,000	£18,987,000
Exports to U.K.	883,000	681,000

CAPITAL.—ΨMogadishu (Mogadiscio), population (estimated 1982), 600,000. Other towns are Hargeisa (150,000), Kisimayu (30,000), ΨBerbera (60,000) and Burao (15,000).

FLAG.—Five-pointed white star on blue ground.
NATIONAL DAY.—July 1.

BRITISH EMBASSY
(PO Box No. 1036) Mogadishu

Ambassador Extraordinary and Plenipotentiary, His Excellency William Hugh Fullerton (1983).
1st Secretary and Consul, P. H. Gay (*Head of Chancery*).

SOUTH AFRICA
(Republiek van Suid-Afrika)

State President, Pieter Willem Botha, *sworn in*, Sept. 14, 1984.

CABINET

Defence, Gen. Magnus Malan.
Manpower, P. T. du Plessis.

Co-operation and Development and (Black) Education, Dr. V. Viljoen.
Agricultural Economics and Water Affairs, J. J. G. Wentzel.
Industries and Commerce, Dr. David J. de Villiers.
Finance, B. J. du Plessis.
Transport, H. Schoeman.
Home Affairs and National Education, F. W. De. Klerk.
Justice, H. J. Coetzee.
Environment and Tourism, J. Wiley.
Communications and Public Works, Dr. L. A. P. Munnik.
Foreign Affairs, R. F. Botha.
Mineral and Energy Affairs, D. W. Steyn.
Law and Order, L. le Grange.
Health and Welfare and Chairman, Ministers Council for White Own Affairs, Dr. C. V. van der Merwe.
Constitutional Development and Planning, J. C. Heunis.
Chairman, Ministers Council for Coloured Own Affairs, A. Hendrickse.
Chairman, Ministers Council for Indian Own Affairs, A. Rajbansi.

EMBASSY AND CONSULATE
South Africa House, Trafalgar Square, WC2N 5DP
[01–930 4488]

Ambassador Extraordinary and Plenipotentiary, His Excellency Dr. Denis John Worrall.
Minister, L. H. Evans.
Armed Forces Attaché, Col. M. J. van Niekerk.
Minister (Commercial), E. A. Erasmus.
Director of Information, J. J. Venter.

There is a consulate-general at Golden Cross House, 8 Duncannon Street, W.C.2. [01–839 2211]

Area and Population.—The Republic, comprising the Provinces of the Cape of Good Hope, Natal, the Transvaal and the Orange Free State, occupies the southernmost part of the African continent from the courses of the Limpopo, Molopo and Orange Rivers (34° 50′ 22″ South latitude) to the Cape of Good Hope, with the exception of Lesotho, Botswana and Swaziland, and part of Mozambique. It has a total area of 472,494 sq. miles (1,223,712 sq. km.) and a total population (U.N. estimate, 1980) of 29,290,000 (of which approx. 18 per cent are Whites).

The southernmost province contains many parallel ranges, which rise in steps towards the interior. The south-western peninsula contains the famous *Table Mountain* (3,582 feet), while the *Great Swartberg* and *Langeberg* run in parallel lines from west to east of the Cape Province. Between these two ranges and the *Roggeveld* and *Nuweveld* ranges to the north is

the Great Karoo Plateau, which is bounded on the east by the *Sneeuberg*, containing the highest summit in the province (Kompasberg, 7,800 feet). In the east are ranges which join the *Drakensberg* (11,000 feet) between Natal and the Orange Free State.

The Orange Free State presents a succession of undulating grassy plains, with good pasture-land, at a general elevation of some 3,800 feet, with occasional hills or kopjes. The Transvaal is also mainly an elevated plateau with parallel ridges in the *Magaliesberg* and *Waterberg* ranges of no great height. The veld or plains of this northernmost province is divisible into the High Veld of the south, the Bushveld of the centre, and the Low Veld of the north and east, the first and second forming the grazing and agricultural region of the Transvaal and the last a fertile sub-tropical area. The eastern province of Natal has pastoral lowlands and rich agriculture land between the slopes of the Drakensberg and the coast, the interior rising in terraces as in the southern provinces. The *Orange*, with its tributary the *Vaal*, is the principal river of the south, rising in the Drakensberg and flowing into the Atlantic between the Territory of South West Africa and the Cape Province. The *Limpopo*, or Crocodile River, in the north, rises in the Transvaal and flows into the Indian Ocean through Mozambique. Most of the remaining rivers are furious torrents after rain, with partially dry beds at other seasons.

Government.—The self-governing colonies of the Cape of Good Hope, Natal, the Transvaal and the Orange River Colony became united on May 31, 1910, under the South Africa Act, 1909, in a legislative union under the name of the Union of South Africa, the four colonies becoming Provinces of the Union. The Union of South Africa continued as a member of the British Commonwealth until 1961. After a referendum held among white voters on October 5, 1960, the Union of South Africa became a republic on May 31, 1961, and withdrew from the Commonwealth.

A new Constitution came into effect on Sept. 30, 1984, which provided for an executive President and a three-chamber Parliament; the House of Assembly (178 members) representing Whites, the House of Representatives (85 members) representing Coloureds, and the House of Delegates (45 members) representing Indians. The black population has no representation. There is joint parliamentary responsibility for "general" affairs (foreign policy, defence, finance, law and order, justice, transport, manpower, commerce and industry, agriculture), and each chamber has separate responsibility for the "own" affairs of the population group it represents (housing, social welfare, health, education, local government and some aspects of agriculture). Disputes between the chambers may be referred by the President to the President's Council (60 members—20 White, 10 Coloured, 5 Indian elected by their respective chambers, 15 nominated by the President, 10 nominated by Opposition parties).

The President is chosen by an 88-member electoral college (in the proportion 4 White : 2 Coloured : 1 Indian) of the majority parties of the three chambers. The President appoints the Cabinet, which he chairs, from all three communities, and also appoints each community's ministerial council for "own" affairs.

Elections to the House of Representatives and House of Delegates took place in Aug. 1984. The turnout for the Coloured assembly election was estimated at 29·6 per cent of registered voters (18 per cent of those eligible) and for the Indian assembly election at 20·3 per cent of registered voters (16·6 per cent of those eligible).

The Black Homelands.—The homelands are areas set aside for occupation by Blacks. Six areas— Gazankulu, Lebowa, KwaNdbele, KaNgwane, Qwaqwa and KwaZulu—are designated self-govern-

ing "national states". A further four areas—Bophuthatswana, Ciskei, Transkei and Venda—are regarded as independent republics by the South African government but they are not recognised as such by the United Nations.

Education.—The Provinces have been relieved of all vocational education (technical and industrial), and the Department of National Education under the Minister is concerned with universities, technical colleges, schools of industries, reformatories and State technical, housecraft and commercial high schools, State-aided vocational schools and State and State-aided special schools for the physically handicapped.

Communications.—The State-owned and controlled South African Transport Services operates the national railway system, the principal harbours, most long-distance passenger and freight road transport services, the South African Airways airline and a network of pipelines for petroleum products.

There are international airports at Johannesburg (Jan Smuts), Durban (Louis Botha) and Cape Town (D. F. Malan), with another under construction at La Mercy, Natal. South African Airways operates international services to Europe, North and South America, Australia, the Far East and the Middle East, as well as to neighbouring countries, and it is the principal operator of domestic flights.

The largest sea-port is Durban, Natal. Other major ports are Cape Town, Port Elizabeth, East London, Saldanha Bay and Mossel Bay in Cape Province and Richards Bay, Natal.

Production.—Mining is of the greatest importance to the South African economy, contributing 14·3 per cent to G.D.P. in 1982 (of which gold mining accounted for 10 per cent). Principal minerals produced are: gold, coal, iron ore, diamonds, copper, manganese, lime and limestone and asbestos.

Agriculture, forestry and fishing accounts for 6·2 per cent of G.D.P. Over 50 per cent of land is pasture so livestock farming is widespread with meat and wool important products. Principal crops are: maize, sugar-cane, fruits and vegetables, wheat, sorghum, sunflower seed and groundnuts. Cotton is widely grown because of its suitability to the climate, and viticulture is also widespread.

Industries, concentrated most heavily around Johannesburg, Pretoria and the major ports, process foodstuffs, metals and non-metallic mineral products, and also produce beverages and tobacco, motor vehicles, chemicals and chemical products, machinery, textiles and clothing, and paper and paper products.

Trade.—Principal exports are: gold, base metals and metal products, diamonds, food (especially fruit), chemicals, machinery and transport equipment, and wool. Principal imports are: machinery, chemicals, motor vehicles, metals and metal products, food, inedible raw materials and textiles. Preliminary trade figures for 1982 were:

Imports	R18,377·9 million
Exports	19,129·4 million

Trade with U.K.

	1982	1983
Imports from U.K.	£1,192,891,000	£1,109,039,000
Exports to U.K.	745,803,000	764,909,000

Currency.—The unit of currency is the *Rand* of 100 cents. For exchange rate, *see* p. 81.

Finance.—Estimated revenue for 1983–84 was R19,094 million, and estimated expenditure was R21,176 million.

Capital.—The administrative seat of the Government is PRETORIA, Transvaal; population (1980 estimate), 528,407; the seat of the Legislature is ᴪCAPE TOWN, population (1970) 1,107,764. Other large towns

(1980 figures) are Johannesburg, Transvaal (1,536,457); ΨDurban, Natal, the largest seaport (505,963); ΨPort Elizabeth, Cape (492,140); Germiston, Transvaal (155,435); BLOEMFONTEIN, capital of Orange Free State (230,688); Springs, Transvaal (153,974); Benoni Transvaal (206,810); ΨEast London, Cape (160,582); Welkom, O.F.S. (176,608); and PIETERMARITZBURG, capital of Natal (178,972).

FLAG.—Three horizontal stripes of equal width; from top to bottom, orange, white, blue; in the centre of the white stripe, the old Orange Free State flag hanging vertical, towards the pole the Union Jack horizontal, away from the pole the old Transvaal Vierkleur, all spread full.

NATIONAL DAY.—May 31.

BRITISH EMBASSY
6 Hill Street, Pretoria
91 Parliament Street, Cape Town (Jan.-June)

Ambassador Extraordinary and Plenipotentiary, His Excellency Patrick Hamilton Moberley, C.M.G. (1984).
Minister, D. Tonkin.
Defence Attaché, Gp. Capt. D. W. Hanson, O.B.E.
Counsellors, G. R. Archer (*Head of Chancery*); J. H. Owen, O.B.E.
1st Secretaries, T. D. Curran; D. W. Fall; G. W. W. Charlton (*Administration*), J. Hedley; J. W. Cox.
Cultural Attaché and British Council Representative, R. T. L. Watkins, 170 Pine Street, Arcadia, Pretoria.

There are British Consular Offices at *Cape Town, Johannesburg* and *Durban*; and Honorary Consuls at *Port Elizabeth* and *East London.*

NAMIBIA

Namibia (South West Africa) stretches from the southern border of Angola (lat. 17° 23′ S.) to part of the northern (Orange River) and north-western borders of the Cape Province of the Republic of South Africa; and from the Atlantic Ocean in the west to Botswana in the east.

The territory has an area of 318,261 sq. miles, including the area of Walvis Bay (434 sq. miles) which is claimed by South Africa. The population was estimated at 1,039,400 in 1982 and the main population groups are: Ovambo (516,600), Whites (75,000), Damara (76,800), Kavango (98,000), Herero (77,600), Nama (49,700), Coloured (43,500), Caprivians (39,500), Bushmen (29,500), Rehoboth Baster (25,800), Tswana (6,800).

Government.—A German protectorate from 1880 to 1915, South West Africa was administered until the end of 1920 by the Union of South Africa. In terms of the Treaty of Versailles the Territory was declared a "C" Mandate and entrusted to South Africa with full powers of administration and legislation over the Territory. After the dissolution of the League of Nations and in the absence of a trusteeship agreement, South Africa informed the United Nations that she would continue to administer South West Africa in the spirit of the Mandate. Since the establishment of the United Nations, South West Africa has been the subject of dispute.

Certain administrative powers held in South West Africa were in February, 1969, transferred to the South African Government, and from 1968 onwards tribal authorities were set up for the different groups.

On June 21, 1971, the International Court of Justice at The Hague delivered an advisory opinion as requested by the U.N. Security Council on the legal consequences for States of the continued presence of South Africa in "Namibia" (South West Africa). The Court decided by 13 votes to 2, that (*inter alia*) "the continued presence of South Africa being illegal, South Africa is under obligation to withdraw its administration from Namibia immediately and thus put an end to its occupation of the Territory". The South African Government rejected this opinion, but accepted the principle that the territory should attain independence. In September 1975 constitutional talks (known as the Turnhalle Conference) were begun in Windhoek between delegates from the 11 ethnic groups of the territory in order to determine the future of South West Africa. But their representative nature was contested by, *inter alia,* SWAPO, a liberation movement with substantial international support and when, in April 1977, it became clear that independence based on the Turnhalle would not solve the problem, the Five Western members of the U.N. Security Council at that time drew up a plan, later incorporated into Security Council Resolution 435, for a peaceful settlement. The plan involves free and fair elections under U.N. supervision leading to independence. The plan has been accepted by all the parties to the Namibia question and attempts to implement the plan are continuing.

Meanwhile, the South African Government appointed an Administrator-General in 1977 to establish a central administration there for those functions previously administered from Pretoria. In December 1978, the South Africans organized an election for a constituent assembly which SWAPO and most of the internal political parties boycotted. The resultant assembly was transformed into a National Assembly with legislative powers in May 1979, and a Council of Ministers was established in 1980. Both the Council and the Assembly were abolished in Jan. 1983 and the Administrator-General again rules the territory directly.

Production.—Mining, agriculture and fisheries are important. Animal husbandry accounts for 99 per cent of the total gross output of commercial agriculture. The average rainfall over 70 per cent of the Territory is below 400 mm. per annum.

Trade with U.K.

	1982	1983
Imports from U.K.	£3,973,000	£3,425,000
Exports to U.K.	45,413,000	62,437,000

CAPITAL.—Windhoek (population, 1970 census, 61,260). The only port of any size is ΨWalvis Bay.

SPAIN
(España)

Head of the Spanish State, King Juan Carlos I de Borbón y Borbón, *born* Jan. 5, 1938, *acceded to the throne,* Nov. 22, 1975, *married* May 14, 1962, Princess Sophie of Greece *and has issue,* Infante Felipe Juan Pablo Alfonso Todos Los Santos (Prince of Asturias) *born* Jan. 30, 1968; Infanta Elena Maria Isabel Dominica, *born* Dec. 20, 1963; and Infanta Christina Frederica Victoria, *born* June 13, 1965.

CABINET

Prime Minister (President of the Government), Felipe González Márquez.
Deputy P.M. (Vice-President), Alfonso Guerra González.
Foreign Affairs, Fernando Morán López.
Territorial Administration, Tomás de la Quadra Salcedo.
Defence, Narcis Serra Serra.
Minister of the Presidency, Javier Moscoso del Prado y Muñoz.

Education and Science, José María Maravall Herrero.
Labour and Social Security, José Joaquín Almunia Amann.
Health and Consumption, Ernesto Lluch Martín.
Economy and Finance, Miguel Boyer Salvador.
Public Works and Urbanisation, Julián Campo Sainz de Rozas.
Agriculture, Fisheries and Food, Carlos Romero Herrera.
Industry and Energy, Carlos Solchaga Catalán.
Justice, Fernando Ledesma Bartret.
Culture, Javier Solana Madariaga.
Interior, José Barrionuevo Peña.
Transport, Tourism and Communications, Enrique Barón Crespo.

SPANISH EMBASSY IN LONDON
24 Belgrave Square, SW1X 8QA
[01-235 5555]

Ambassador Extraordinary and Plenipotentiary, His Excellency José Joaquin Puig de la Bellacasa (1983).
Minister-Counsellor, Sr. D. Luis de la Torre.

Area and Population.—Situated in the south-west of Europe, between 36°–43° 45′ N. lat. and 4° 25′ E.–9° 20′ W. long., Spain is bounded on the south and east by the Mediterranean, on the west by the Atlantic and Portugal, and on the north by the Bay of Biscay and France, from which it is separated by the Pyrenees. Continental Spain occupies about eleven-thirteenths of the Iberian peninsula, the remaining portion forming the Republic of Portugal. Its coast-line extends 1,317 miles—712 formed by the Mediterranean and 605 by the Atlantic—and it comprises a total area of 196,700 square miles, with a population (1981) of 37,682,355.

Physical Features.—The interior of the Iberian Peninsula consists of an elevated tableland surrounded and traversed by mountain ranges—the Pyrenees, the Cantabrian Mountains, the Sierra Guadarrama, Sierra Morena, Sierra Nevada, Montes de Toledo, &c. The principal rivers are the Douro, the Tagus, the Guadiana, the Guadalquivir, the Ebro and the Minho.

Government.—Spain was a monarchy until April 1931, when King Alfonso XIII left the country and a Republic was proclaimed and a Provisional Government, drawn from the various Republican and Socialist parties, was formed. On July 18, 1936, a counter-revolution broke out in many military garrisons in Spanish Morocco and spread rapidly throughout Spain. The principal leader was General Francisco Franco Bahamonde, formerly Governor of the Canary Islands. The struggle, in its later phases, threatened to embroil some of the European Powers, those of Nazi-Fascist tendency lending aid to General Franco (leader of the Military-Fascist fusion, or *Falange*) while those of Communist views supported the Azaña (*Popular Front*) government. In October, 1938, many of the supporting troops were withdrawn, and on March 29, 1939, the Civil War was declared to have ended, the Popular Front Governments in Madrid and Barcelona surrendering to the *Nationalists* (as General Franco's followers were then named). On June 5, 1939, the Grand Council of the *Falange Española Tradicionalista y de las Juntas Ofensivas Nacional-Sindicalistas*, met at Burgos to legislate for the reorganization of the country under the Presidency of General Franco, who had assumed the title of *Caudillo* (*Leader*) *of the Empire and Chief of the State*. In the Civil War of 1936–39 over 1,000,000 lives were lost.

In July 1942, the *Cortes de España* was restored as a uni-cameral Parliament of 564 members. This was replaced under the Constitution drawn up in 1977–78 by a bi-cameral *Cortes* comprising a 350-member Congress of Deputies elected for 4 years by universal adult suffrage, and a Senate consisting of directly elected representatives of the provinces, islands, autonomous regions and Ceuta and Melilla.

On July 22, 1969, General Franco nominated Prince Juan Carlos (Alfonso) of Bourbon (grandson of the late King Alfonso XIII) to succeed him as head of state at his death or retirement. The nomination was approved in the *Cortes* by a large majority. Following the death of General Franco, on November 20, 1975, Juan Carlos acceded to the throne on Nov. 22, 1975.

At the General Election on Oct. 28, 1982, the P.S.O.E. under Sr. Felipe Gonzalez won 202 seats, the A.P. 106, the U.C.D. 13, and the P.C.E. 4 seats. In the Regional and the Municipal elections of May 1983 the P.S.O.E. won the majority of the votes. In elections held in the Basque country in February and in Cataluña in April 1984 local nationalist parties (P.N.V. and C.i.U.) retained their majorities and formed autonomous governments.

Regions.—Since the promulgation of the 1978 Constitution, 17 autonomous regions have been established, with their own parliaments and governments. These are Andalucia, Aragon, Asturias, Balaerics, the Basque country, Canaries, Castilla-La Mancha, Castilla-Leon, Cantabria, Cataluña, Extremadura, Galicia, Madrid, Murcia, Navarre, La Rioja and Valencia.

Defence.—Army: There are in Spain 1 armoured, 1 mechanized, 1 motorized, and 2 mountain divisions; 1 armoured cavalry brigade, 2 artillery brigades, 1 air-transportable brigade, 1 parachute brigade, 10 infantry brigades, 1 mountain brigade and 2 artillery brigades (including surface to air missile battalions). The *Guardia Civil* also forms part of the Army though it operates as a gendarmerie in the rural areas under the control of the Ministry of the Interior.

The active Spanish *Navy* consists of 1 aircraft carrier, 11 destroyers, 15 frigates and corvettes, 12 minesweepers, 6 major amphibious vessels, 7 submarines, 12 fast patrol craft, 6 hydrographic vessels, 1 tanker, and many smaller patrol craft and auxiliaries. The Navy also has 50 helicopters and 11 Harrier aircraft.

The *Air Force* is divided geographically into 3 Regions covering Spain plus an Air Zone for the Canaries. There are also separate functional Air Defence, Tactical and Transport Commands. The Air Force consists of 4 attack squadrons, 6 air defence squadrons, 1 maritime squadron, 9 transport squadrons, 3 search and rescue squadrons, 9 training squadrons and 1 firefighting squadron.

Spain became a member of N.A.T.O. in May 1982. The present government has frozen progress towards military integration pending a referendum on N.A.T.O. membership. It has also initiated reorganization of the military structure.

Education.—Free education for all children aged 6 to 14 is provided. 30 per cent of primary schools and 80 per cent of secondary schools are still run privately, although state spending on education multiplied fourfold between 1960 and 1970. The situation of the private schools is likely to undergo significant changes after a new Education Law of 1984 comes into force.

There are 29 state universities, the oldest of which, Salamanca, was founded in 1230. Other ancient foundations are Valencia (1245), Oviedo (1317), Valladolid (1346), Barcelona (1450), Zaragoza (1474), Santiago (1501), Seville (1502), Granada (1526), and Madrid (1590). Private universities are Deusto in Bilbao, and Navarra in Pamplona. Student numbers in the universities have risen to over 668,000.

Language and Literature.—Castilian is the language of more than three-quarters of the population of Spain and is the form of Spanish spoken in Mexico, Central and (except in Brazil) Southern America. Basque, reported to have been the original language of Iberia, is spoken in the rural districts of Vizcaya, Guipuzcoa and Alava. Catalan is spoken in Provençal Spain, and Galician, spoken in the northwestern provinces, is akin to Portuguese; the governments of these regions actively encourage use of their local languages.

The literature of Spain is one of the oldest and richest in the world, the *Poem of the Cid*, the earliest and best of the heroic songs of Spain, having been written about A.D. 1140. The outstanding writings of its golden age are those of Miguel de Cervantes Saavedra (1547–1616), Lope Felix de Vega Carpio (1562–1635) and Pedro Calderón de la Barca (1600–1681). The Nobel Prize for Literature has four times been awarded to Spanish authors—J. Echegaray (1904), J. Benavente (1922), Juan Ramón Jimenez (1956) and Vicente Aleixandre (1977).

Currency.—The peseta = 100 *céntimos. (See also* p. 81).

Production and Industry.—The country is generally fertile, and well adapted to agriculture and the cultivation of heat-loving fruits—olives, oranges, lemons, almonds, pomegranates, bananas, apricots, tomatoes, peppers, cucumbers and grapes. The agricultural products include wheat, barley, oats, rice, hemp and flax. The orange crop is exported mainly to Germany, France and the United Kingdom. The vine is cultivated widely; in the south-west, Jerez, the well-known sherry and tent wines are produced. The fishing industry is important.

Spain's mineral resources of coal, iron, wolfram, copper, zinc, lead and iron ores are variously exploited. Many of the richer and more easily worked deposits have been exhausted, but the authorities are actively engaged in stimulating the exploitation of hitherto unworked or lower grade deposits. Output of coal in 1983 was 21 million tonnes; output of iron ore (1981) was 3,816,049 tonnes and of steel (1983) 12,700,000 tonnes.

The principal goods produced are cars, steel, ships, manufactured goods, textiles, chemical products, footwear and other leather goods, ceramics, sewing machines and bicycles. In 1983 tourism contributed (net) an estimated 861,400 m. *pesetas* to the balance of payments.

TRADE

	1983
	million pesetas
Imports	4,176,470·4
Exports	2,838,601·1

The balance of payments on current account showed an estimated deficit of 332,600 m. *pesetas* in 1983 and reserves stood at $11,228 million at the end of the year.

Trade with U.K.
(inc. Canary Islands)

	1982	1983
Imports from U.K.	£958,603,000	£1,235,232,000
Exports to U.K.	1,001,509,000	1,190,334,000

The principal imports are cotton, tobacco, cellulose, timber, coffee and cocoa, fertilizers, dyes, machinery, motor vehicles and agricultural tractors, wool and petroleum products. The principal exports include iron ore, cork, salt, vegetables, citrus fruits, wines, olive oil, potash, mercury, pyrites, tinned fruit and fish, bananas and tomatoes.

CAPITAL, Madrid. Population (1981) 3,158,818. Other large cities are ΨBarcelona (1,752,627), Valencia (744,748), ΨSeville (645,817), Zaragoza (571,855), ΨMálaga (502,232), Bilbao (433,115); Murcia (284,585).

FLAG.—Three horizontal bands, red, yellow and red, with coat of arms on yellow band.

NATIONAL DAY.—October 12.

AIR TRANSIT FROM U.K.—London–Barcelona (713 miles), 2 *hrs. 25 mins.*; Madrid (775 miles), 2 *hrs.* 5 *mins.*; Valencia, 2 *hrs.* 10 *mins.*

BRITISH EMBASSY
(Calle Fernando el Santo, 16, Madrid 4)

Ambassador Extraordinary and Plenipotentiary, His Excellency Lord Nicholas Gordon Lennox, C.M.G., M.V.O. (1984).

Minister, R. B. R. Hervey, C.M.G.

Counsellor, J. Flynn.

Defence and Military Attaché, Brig. J. D. F. Alexander.

Head of Chancery, L. G. Faulkner.

1st Secretary, D. N. Reddaway, M.B.E.

British Council Representative, S. R. Smith, Almagro 5, Madrid 4. There is also an office and a library in Barcelona and Valencia, and an office and English language resource centre in Granada.

The BALEARIC ISLES form an archipelago off the east coast of Spain. There are four large islands (Majorca, Minorca, Ibiza and Formentera), and seven smaller (Aire, Aucanada, Botafoch, Cabrera, Dragonera, Pinto and El Rey). The islands were occupied by the Romans after the destruction of Carthage and provided contingents of the celebrated Balearic slingers. The total area is 1,935 square miles, with a population of 558,287. The archipelago forms a province of Spain, the capital being ΨPalma in Majorca, pop. 234,098; ΨMahon (Minorca), pop. 16,547.

The CANARY ISLANDS are an archipelago in the Atlantic, off the African coast, consisting of 7 islands and 6 uninhabited islets. The total area is 2,807 square miles, with a population of 1,170,224. The Canary Islands form two Provinces of Spain.—*Las Palmas* (Gran Canaria, Lanzarote (38,500), Fuerteventura (19,500) and the islets of Alegranza, Roque del Este, Roque del Oeste, Graciosa, Montaña Clara and Lobos), with seat of administration at ΨLas Palmas (pop. 287,038) in Gran Canaria, where major oil companies have installations for re-fueling shipping; and *Santa Cruz de Tenerife* (Tenerife, La Palma (76,000), Gomera (31,829), and Hierro (10,000)), with seat of administration at ΨSanta Cruz in Tenerife, pop. 151,361.

ISLA DE FAISANES is an uninhabited Franco-Spanish condominium, at the mouth of the Bidassoa in La Higuera bay.

ΨCEUTA is a fortified post on the Moroccan coast, opposite Gibraltar. The total area is 5 square miles, with a population (1970) of 67,187.

ΨMELILLA is a town on a rocky promontory of the Rif coast, connected with the mainland by a narrow isthmus. Melilla has been in Spanish possession since 1492. Population (1970) 64,942. Ceuta and Melilla are parts of Metropolitan Spain.

OVERSEAS TERRITORIES

Spanish settlements on the Moroccan seaboard are:—

Peñon de Alhucemas, the bay of that name includes six islands: population 366.

Peñon de la Gomera (or *Peñon de Velez*) is a fortified rocky islet about 40 miles west of Alhucemas Bay; population 450.

The Chaffarinas (or Zaffarines) are a group of three islands near the Algerian frontier, about 2 miles north of Cape del Agua; population 610.

The former provinces of Spanish Guinea, Fernando Póo and Rio Muni achieved independence on October 12, 1968, under the title of Equatorial Guinea.

The protectorate of Spanish Morocco was incorporated in Morocco on the latter's independence in 1956. Ifni, the former enclave in Morocco, was incorporated by treaty, on June 30, 1969, and the Spanish Sahara came under joint Moroccan and Mauritanian control in November 1975.

SUDAN
(Democratic Republic of the Sudan)

President and Prime Minister, Gaafar Mohamed El Nimeri, *assumed office* May 25, 1969 *elected President*, Oct. 1971, *re-elected*, 1977 and 1983.
First Vice-President and Head, State Security, Maj.-Gen. Omer Mohammed El Tayyeb.
Vice-President, Joseph Lagu.

SUDANESE EMBASSY IN LONDON
3 Cleveland Row, SW1A 1DD
[01-839 8080]

Ambassador Extraordinary and Plenipotentiary, His Excellency Abdullahi El Hassan.

Area and Population.—The Sudan extends from the southern boundary of Egypt, 22° N. lat., to the northern boundary of Uganda, 3° 36′ N. lat., and reaches from the Republic of Chad about 21° 49′ E. (at 12° 45′ N.) to the north-west boundary of Ethiopia in 38° 35′ E. (at 18° N.). The greatest length from north to south is approximately 1,300 miles, and east to west 950 miles.

The northern boundary is the 22nd parallel of North latitude; on the east lie the Red Sea and Ethiopia; on the South lie Kenya, Uganda and Zaire; and on the west the Central African Republic, Chad, and Libya.

The *White Nile* enters from Uganda at the Sudan frontier post of Nimule in Equatoria Province, as the *Bahr el Jebel*, and leaves the Sudan at Wadi Halfa. The *Blue Nile* flows from Lake Tana on the Ethiopian Plateau. Its course in the Sudan is nearly 500 miles long, before it joins the White Nile at Khartoum. The next confluence of importance is at Atbara where the main Nile is joined by the River Atbara. The total length of the Nile, now accepted as the longest river in the world, is estimated to be 4,160 miles from its source to the Mediterranean Sea. Between Khartoum and Wadi Halfa lie five of the six *Cataracts*.

The estimated area is about 967,500 sq. miles with a population of 19,500,000, partly Arabs, partly Negros, and partly of mixed Arab-Negro blood, with a small foreign element, including some 8,000 Europeans. The Arabs are mostly Moslems. The Nilotics of the Bahr el Ghazal and Upper Nile Valleys are generally animists, but some have been converted to Christianity and others are Moslems.

Government.—The Anglo-Egyptian Condominium over the Sudan which had been established in 1899 ended when the Sudan House of Representatives, on Dec. 19, 1955, voted unanimously a declaration that the Sudan was a fully independent sovereign state. A Republic was proclaimed on Jan. 1, 1956, and was recognized by Great Britain and Egypt, a Supreme Commission being sworn in to take over sovereignty. The Sudan was under military rule from Nov., 1958, until 1964 when a new civilian Cabinet was appointed. Government of the country was taken over on May 25, 1969, by a ten-man revolutionary council headed by Col. Gaafar Mohamed El Nimeri. Maj.-Gen. Nimeri became President in an uncontested election in October 1971. In February 1972 an agreement was signed at Addis Ababa which brought to an end nearly 17 years of insurrection and civil war in the six southern provinces, and which recognized southern regional autonomy within a unified Sudanese State.

Education.—School education is free for most children, but not compulsory, beginning with Primary School (of which there are 4,000) which continues for 6 years. The final examination at Primary School is highly competitive and selects children for General Secondary Schools (of which there are 700) which continues for 3 years. The Higher Secondary Stage comprises 80 academic Higher Secondary schools (3 years); 15 vocational schools—Technical (4 years); Agricultural and Commercial (3 years) and 15 Primary Teacher Training Colleges (4 years). The medium of instruction is Arabic. English is taught as the principal foreign language in all schools.

Teacher Training is carried out in 15 Primary Teacher Training Colleges, two General Secondary Teacher Training Institutes and one Higher Teacher Training Institute.

Khartoum University has 10 faculties. There is a branch of Cairo University in Khartoum, an Islamic University at Omdurman and a University at Juba. Selection for higher education is normally based on the Sudan School Certificate.

In addition to the four universities there are various technical post-secondary institutes as well as professional and vocational training establishments.

Production.—The principal grain crops are *dura* (great millet) and wheat, the staple food of the people in the Sudan. Sesame and ground-nuts are other important food crops, which also yield an exportable surplus and a promising start has been made with castor seed. The principal export crop is cotton. Main production is of long-staple (mainly Egyptian type) cotton of which the Sudan is a major producer, but increasing quantities of short and medium staple (American) type cotton are being grown. Production in 1981–82 totalled 800,000 bales. Much of the high quality, long-staple cotton is provided by the Sudan Geriza Scheme (a Government-controlled project irrigated from the Sennar Dam on the Blue Nile) and its extension, the Managil Scheme. The Sudan also produces the bulk of the world's supply of gum arabic. Sugar is an increasingly important crop. The Sudan has almost become self-sufficient in sugar and aims to produce an exportable surplus by 1986. Livestock is the mainstay of the nomadic Arab tribes of the desert and the negro tribes of the swamp and wooded grassland country in the South.

A new dam at Khashm el Girba began to store water in May, 1964, and will eventually provide irrigation to about 500,000 acres, most of which has been used to resettle the population of the Wadi Halfa area which has been flooded by the reservoir of the Egyptian High Dam. Another dam at Roseires on the Blue Nile provides increased irrigation on a further 3,000,000 acres as well as providing hydro-electric power.

Communications.—The railway system (3 ft. 6 in. gauge) has a route length of about 3,200 miles, linking Khartoum with Wadi Halfa, Karima, Port Sudan, Wad Medani, Sennar, El Damazin, Kosti, El Obeid and Nyala. A line branches out southwards to Wau from the Sennar/Nyala western line. Regular rail and Nile steamer services connect Khartoum with Juba in Equatoria Province which in turn is connected by a bus service with Nimule on the Uganda border. ΨPort Sudan is a well-equipped modern seaport. Sudan Airways fly regular services from Khartoum to many parts of the Sudan and to Egypt, Greece, Italy, the Lebanon, the United Kingdom, the Gulf States, Kenya, Uganda, W. Germany, Iraq, Saudi Arabia and Bahrain.

FINANCE

	1981–82	1982–83*
Revenue	£S 1,042 m	£S 1,342·6 m
Expenditure	1,715 m	1,910·1 m

*Proposed budget.
£S = Sudanese Pound of 100 *Piastres.*

TRADE

	1979–80 (estimated)
Total Imports	U.S.$1,370,000,000
Exports	580,000,000

Trade with U.K.

	1982	1983
Imports from U.K.	£136,636,000	£133,432,000
Exports to U.K.	9,929,000	18,693,000

The principal exports are cotton and cotton seed, ground-nuts and gum arabic. The chief imports are cotton piece goods, base metals, vehicles and transport equipment, machinery, petroleum products, sugar, tea, coffee, chemicals and pharmaceuticals.

CAPITAL, Khartoum (est. pop. 194,000). The town contains many mosques, a Catholic cathedral and an Anglican cathedral, and the University with extensive government buildings. Khartoum North and Omdurman have estimated populations of 58,000 and 167,000 respectively.

FLAG.—Three horizontal stripes of red, white and black with a green triangle next to the hoist.

NATIONAL DAY.—January 1 (Independence Day).

BRITISH EMBASSY
Khartoum

Ambassador Extraordinary and Plenipotentiary, His Excellency Sir Alexander Stirling, K.B.E., C.M.G. (1984).
Counsellor, B. S. T. Eastwood (*Head of Chancery*).
Defence and Military Attaché, Col. H. Diamond.
British Council Representative, R. A. Jarvis, O.B.E., 31 Zubeir Pasha Street, P.O. Box 1253, Khartoum. There are British Council libraries at *Khartoum, El Obeid,* and *Omdurman.*

SURINAM

Head of the National Military Council, Lt. Col. Desi Bouterse.
Prime Minister and Minister of Foreign Affairs, Wim Udenhout.

Surinam is situated on the north coast of South America and is bounded by French Guiana in the east, Brazil in the south and Guyana in the west. It has an area of 63,250 square miles, with a population (1980 estimate) of 390,000.

Formerly known as Dutch Guiana, Surinam remained part of the Netherlands West Indies until November 25, 1975, when it achieved complete independence. Surinam had received autonomy in domestic affairs under the Realm Statute which took effect on December 29, 1954. The civilian government was ousted by the military in Feb. 1982, who appointed the predominantly civilian Cabinet.

Surinam has large timber resources. Rice and sugar cane are the main crops. Bauxite is mined, and is the principal export.

TRADE

	1979 Surinam Guilders
Imports	647,500,000
Exports	777,000,000

Trade with U.K.

	1982	1983
Imports from U.K.	£10,586,000	£8,914,000
Exports to U.K.	7,593,000	11,584,000

CAPITAL.—ΨParamaribo (population, 1971, 110,000).

British Ambassador (resides at *Georgetown,* Guyana). There is a *British Consulate* at Paramaribo.
Honorary Consul, J. J. Healy.

SWEDEN
(Sverige)

King of Sweden, Carl XVI Gustaf, *born* April 30, 1946, *succeded* September 15, 1973, *married* June 19, 1976 Fraulein Silvia Renate Sommerlath *and has issue,* Crown Princess Victoria Ingrid Alice Désirée, *born* July 14, 1977; Prince Carl Philip Edmund Bertil, Duke of Värmland, *born* May 13, 1979; Princess Madeleine Thérèse Amelie Josephine, Duchess of Hälsingland and Gästrikland, *born* June 10, 1982.

COUNCIL OF MINISTERS

Prime Minister, Olof Palme.
Deputy P.M., Ingvar Carlsson.
Justice, Sten Wickbom.
Foreign Affairs, Lennart Bodström.
Agriculture, Svante Lundkvist.
Finance, Kjell-Olof Feldt.
Public Health and Medical Services, Gertrud Sigurdsen.

Housing, Hans Gustafsson.
Labour, Anna-Greta Leijon.
Education, Lena Hjelm-Wallén.
Industry, Thage Peterson.
Health and Social Affairs, Sten Andersson.
Communications, Curt Boström.
Culture, Bengt Göransson.
Equality and Immigration, Anita Gradin.
Energy, Birgitta Dahl.
State Industries, Roine Carlsson.
Public Sector, Bo Holmberg.
Foreign Trade, Mats Hellström.
Defence, Anders Thunborg.

SWEDISH EMBASSY IN LONDON
Montagu Place, W1H 2AL
[01-724 2101]

Ambassador Extraordinary and Plenipotentiary, His
Excellency Leif Leifland (1982).
Minister Plenipotentiary, H. Granqvist.
Counsellors, A. A. E. Alsterdal (*Press*); P. G. Larsson
(*Consular*); K. Wahlbäck; P. Lindström.
Defence and Naval Attaché, Capt. R. Klintebö.
Air and Military Attaché, Group Capt. J. Westberg.
Trade Commissioner, S. Widenfelt (73 Welbeck Street,
W.1.).

Area and Population.—Sweden occupies the eastern area of the Scandinavian peninsula in N.W.
Europe and comprises 24 local government districts,
"*Län*", with an area of 173,436 sq. miles, and
population Dec. 31, 1982 of 8,327,484. In 1982 there
were 92,748 births (11·1 per 1,000 inhabitants); 90,671
deaths (10·9 per 1,000 inhabitants) and infant mortality rate was 4·5 per 1,000 births.

Government.—Under the Act of Succession of June
6, 1809 (with amendments) the throne is hereditary
in the House of Bernadotte. (A 1979 amendment
vested the succession in the monarch's eldest child,
irrespective of sex.) Jean-Baptiste Jules Bernadotte,
Prince of Ponte Corvo, a Marshal of France, was
invited to accept the title of Crown Prince, with
succession to the throne. He landed at Hälsingborg
on Oct. 20, 1810, and succeeded Charles XIII in 1818.
There is a unicameral Diet (*Riksdag*) of 349 members
elected for 3 years. The Council of Ministers (*Stats-
råd*) is responsible to the *Riksdag.*

Production and Industry.—Since the end of the
First World War Sweden has become one of the
leading industrial nations of Europe. The country's
industrial prosperity is based on an abundance of
natural resources in the form of forests, mineral
deposits and water power. The forests are extensive,
covering about half the total land surface, and sustain
flourishing timber, pulp and paper milling industries.
The mineral resources include iron ore, lead, zinc,
sulphur, granite, marble and extensive deposits of
low grade uranium ore. Sweden has long had
important industries based on mining, principally
iron and steel, aluminium and copper but today it is
the general engineering industry that provides the
basis of Sweden's exports. Motor car manufacturing
and shipbuilding remain important sectors but
growth areas are largely in the specialised machinery
and systems and chemical industries. The relative
importance of agriculture has declined and in 1983
only 5·4 per cent of the population was engaged in
farming. Apart from water power Sweden has no
significant indigenous resources of conventional
hydrocarbon fuels and relies to a high degree upon
imported oil. Much of Sweden's electricity is generated by nuclear power but as a result of a referendum
in 1980 the nuclear programme is to be discontinued
by 2010. Small supplies of natural gas will be imported
from Denmark into southern Sweden from 1985.

Communications.—The total length of Swedish
railroads is about 11,750 km. In 1982 there were 828
telephones and 389 television sets for every 1,000 of

the population. The number of passenger cars in use
on December 31, 1983 was 3,676,100.

The Mercantile Marine amounted on December 31,
1983 to 3,258,000 gross tonnage. The Board of Civil
Aviation under the control of the Ministry of
Communications handles civil aviation matters.
Regular domestic air traffic is maintained by the
Scandinavian Airlines System and by A. B. Linjeflyg.
Regular European and inter-continental air traffic is
maintained by the Scandinavian Airlines System.

Defence.—Based on the policy of non-alignment in
peace leading to neutrality in war Sweden maintains
a Total Defence intended to make any attack on her
costly. Total Defence includes peacetime organizations for civil, economic and psychological defence as
well as compulsory national service for all acceptable
males. Some 50,000 National Servicemen are called
up for 7–15 months training each year and all are
recalled every fourth year for refresher training. On
mobilization the Army strength totals 4 armoured
brigades, 1 mechanised brigade and 23 infantry and
winter warfare brigades. The Navy has 12 submarines, 36 fast attack craft, a number of minor craft
and auxiliaries and 5 coast artillery units. The Air
Force has modern supersonic aircraft of Swedish
manufacture forming a standing force of 216 air
defence, 85 attack and 55 reconnaissance with support
aircraft and a modern air defence radar system.
Facilities exist for rapid dispersal from main bases in
war.

Religion.—The State religion is Lutheran Protestant, to which over 95 per cent of the people officially
adhere.

Language and Literature.—Swedish belongs, with
Danish and Norwegian, to the North Germanic
language group. Swedish literature dates back to
King Magnus Eriksson, who codified the old Swedish
provincial laws in 1350. With his translation of the
Bible, Olaus Petri (1493–1552) formed the basis for
the modern Swedish language. Literature flourished

during the reign of Gustavus III, who founded the Swedish Academy in 1786. Swedish literature is studded with names such as Almquist (1795–1866), Strindberg (1849–1912) and Lagerlöf (1858–1940), Nobel Prize Winner in 1909. Contemporary authors include Lagerquist (1891–1974), Nobel Laureate in 1951, Martinson (1904–1978) and Johnson (1900–1976), Nobel Laureates jointly in 1974. The Swedish scientist Alfred Nobel (1833–1896) founded the Nobel Prizes for Literature, Science and Peace.

Education.—Well developed and recently reorganized to provide (i) 9 years' compulsory schooling from the age of 7 to 16 in the comprehensive elementary schools; (ii) further education of 2, 3 or 4 years in the upper secondary schools, which offer a number of courses preparing for entry to the universities, other centres of higher education, the professions, etc.; (iii) a unified higher education system administered in 6 regional areas containing one of the previously founded universities—Uppsala (founded 1477); Lund (1668); Stockholm (1878); Gothenburg (1887); Umeå (1963) and Linköping (1967). At present there are 33 institutions of higher education including three technical universities in Stockholm, Gothenburg and Luleå, and the Karolinska Institute in Stockholm, which specializes in medicine and dentistry. Tuition within the State system, which is maintained by the State and by local taxation, is free.

FINANCE

	1982/83	1983/84
	Kronor million	*Kronor* million
Revenue	180,700	208,100
Expenditure	256,400	298,000

The currency is the Swedish *Krona* of 100 *Ore.* (*See also* p. 81.)

TRADE

	1981	1982
	Kronor million	*Kronor* million
Imports	146,069	173,525
Exports	144,523	167,975

Trade with U.K.

	1982	1983
Imports from U.K.	£1,935,264,000	£2,397,464,000
Exports to U.K.	1,673,165,000	2,051,931,000

Sweden's main imports from Britain are machinery and parts, road vehicles and components, crude oil and petroleum products, clothing and textiles and steel. Britain's main imports from Sweden are paper and board, road vehicles, machinery, wood, steel and pulp. There is also a substantial exchange of direct investment between the two countries.

CAPITAL.—ΨStockholm. Population (1980): City 647,115; Greater Stockholm, 1,535,539; ΨGothenburg (Göteborg) (428,171); ΨMalmö (231,532); Uppsala (147,770)

FLAG.—Yellow cross on a blue ground.
NATIONAL DAY.—June 6 (Day of the Swedish Flag).

BRITISH EMBASSY
Skarpögatan 6–8, 115 27 Stockholm

Ambassador Extraordinary and Plenipotentiary, His Excellency Sir Donald Murray, K.C.V.O., C.M.G. (1980).
British Council Representative, J. R. Day.

BRITISH CONSULAR OFFICES
There are British Consular Offices at *Göteborg* and *Stockholm.*
British-Swedish Chamber of Commerce in Sweden: Nybrokajen 7, 11140 Stockholm.

SWITZERLAND
(Schweizerische Eidgenossenschaft—Confédération Suisse—Confederazione Svizzera.)

CABINET

President of the Swiss Confederation (1984) *and Head of Transport, Energy and Communications,* Leon Schlumpf.
Vice-President (1984) *and Head of Public Economy,* Kurt Furgler.
Military, Jean-Pascal Delamuraz.
Justice and Police, Rudolf Friedrich.
Foreign Affairs, Pierre Aubert.
Interior, Alphons Egli.
Finance, Otto Stich.

SWISS EMBASSY IN LONDON
16–18 Montagu Place, W1H 2BQ
[01–723 0701]

Ambassador Extraordinary and Plenipotentiary, His Excellency F. C. Pictet.
Counsellor, H. Buchmann (*Commodities and Agriculture*).
First Secretaries, Dr. J. Kellenberger (*Economic and Labour*); H. Kunz (*Cultural*); J. Doswald (*Press*); B. Marfurt (*Finance*).
Defence Attaché, Brig. Gen. H. Mändli.
Consul and Head of Administration, C. Duboulet.

There is a Swiss Consulate-General in *Manchester.*

Area and Population.—The Helvetia of the Romans, a Federal Republic of Central Europe, situated between 45° 50′–47° 48′ N. lat. and 5° 58′–10° 3′ E. long. It is composed of 23 Cantons, 3 subdivided, making 26 in all, and comprises a total area of 15,950 square miles with a population (estimated December, 1982) of 6,365,960. In 1982 there were 74,916 live births, 59,204 deaths and 37,003 marriages. Of the total population in 1980, 44·3 per cent of the population was Protestant, 47·6 per cent Roman Catholic and 0·3 per cent Jewish.

Physical Features.—Switzerland is the most mountainous country in all Europe. The Alps, covered with perennial snow and from 5,000 to 15,217 feet in height, occupy its southern and eastern frontiers, and the chief part of its interior; and the Jura mountains rise in the north-west. The Alps occupy 61 per cent, and the Jura mountains 12 per cent, of the country. The *Alps* are a crescent-shaped mountain system situated in France, Italy, Switzerland, Bavaria and Austria, covering an area of 80,000

square miles from the Mediterranean to the Danube (600 miles). The highest peak, Mont Blanc, Pennine Alps (15,782 feet) is partly in France and Italy; Monte Rosa (15,217 feet) and Matterhorn (14,780 feet) are partly in Switzerland and partly in Italy. The highest wholly Swiss peaks are Dufourspitze (15,203 ft.), Finsteraarhorn (14,026), Aletschhorn (13,711), Jungfrau (13,671), Mönch (13,456), Eiger (13,040), Schreckhorn (13,385), and Wetterhorn (12,150) in the Bernese Alps, and Dom (14,918), Weisshorn (14,803) and Breithorn (13,685).

The Swiss lakes are famous for their beauty and include Lakes Maggiore, Zürich, Lucerne, Neuchâtel, Geneva, Constance, Thun, Zug, Lugano, Brienz and the Walensee. There are also many artificial lakes.

Production and Industry.—Agriculture is followed chiefly in the valleys, where wheat, oats, maize, barley, flax, hemp, and tobacco are produced, and nearly all English fruits and vegetables as well as grapes are grown. Dairying and stock-raising are the principal industries, about 3,000,000 acres being under grass for hay and 2,000,000 acres pasturage. The forests cover about one-quarter of the whole surface. The chief manufacturing industries comprise engineering and electrical engineering, metalworking, chemicals and pharmaceuticals, textiles, watchmaking, woodworking, foodstuffs and footwear. Banking, insurance and tourism are major industries.

Government.—The legislative power is vested in a Parliament, consisting of two Chambers, a National Council (*Nationalrat*) of 200 members, and a Council of States (*Ständerat*) of 46 members; both Chambers united are called the Federal Assembly, and the members of the National Council are elected for four years, an election taking place in October. The executive power is in the hands of a Federal Council (*Bundesrat*) of seven members, elected for four years by the Federal Assembly and presided over by the President of the Confederation. Each year the Federal Assembly elects from the Federal Council the President and the Vice-President. Not more than one of the same canton may be elected member of the Federal Council; on the other hand, there is a tradition that Italian and French-speaking areas should between them be represented on the Federal Council by at least two members.

Defence.—All Swiss males must undertake military service in the Army. *Elite* (ages 20 to 32) initial training, 118 days. Subsequently 8 training periods of 21 days; then *Landwehr* (33–42) and *Landsturm* (43 to 50). Flying personnel of the Air Force, which is part of the Army (ages 20–36): initial training 1 year, totalling 200 hours of flying. 6 weeks with squadron each year and completion of about 70 hours of flying. After 36 revert to ground duties with Air Force. Swiss Army equipment includes some British items, such as Centurion tanks, Bloodhound missiles, Vampire and Hunter aircraft and the Medium Girder Bridge. The Rapier guided missile system is being delivered.

Communications.—There are 4,993 km of railway tracks (Swiss Federal Railways, 2,941 km; Swiss privately owned railways, 2,070 km). At the end of 1981 the number of telephone subscribers amounted to 3,010,372 and the network was fully automatic throughout the country. At the same time there were 2,337,257 licensed radio receivers and 2,057,062 television receivers.

At the end of 1981 the total length of motorways was 1,258 km. The number of motor vehicles licensed in 1982 was 2,998,001.

A merchant marine, established in 1940, consisted at the end of 1982 of 33 vessels with a total gross tonnage of 319,831 tonnes. In addition 470 vessels with a total tonnage of 629,067 were engaged in Rhine shipping. In 1982, goods handled at Basle Rhine ports

amounted to 9,423,093 tonnes. In 1982 152 lake vessels transported 9,243,000 passengers and 2,757 tonnes of freight. Swiss airlines have a network covering 303,797 km and in 1982 carried 7,232,242 passengers. Swissair, the State airline, which owned 55 aircraft in 1983, flies to and from the Swiss airports at Zürich, Geneva and Basle.

Education.—Control by cantonal and communal authorities. No central organization. Illiteracy practically unknown. (i) *Primary:* Free and compulsory. School age varies, generally 7 to 14. (ii) *Secondary:* Age 12–15 for boys and girls. Schools numerous and well-attended, and there are many private institutions. (iii) *Special schools* make a feature of commercial and technical instruction. (iv) *Universities:* Basle (founded 1460), Berne (1834), Fribourg (1889), Geneva (1873), Lausanne (1890), Zürich (1832), and Neuchâtel (1909), and the technical Universities of Lausanne and Zürich and commercial University of St. Gall.

Language and Literature.—There are three official languages: French, German and Italian. In addition Romansch is recognized as a national, but not an official language. German is the dominating language in 19 of the 26 cantons; French in Fribourg, Jura, Geneva, Neuchâtel, Valais and Vaud; Italian in Ticino, and Romansch in parts of the Grisons.

Many modern authors, alike in the German school and in the Suisse Romande, have achieved international fame. Karl Spitteler (1845–1924) and Hermann Hesse (1877–1962) were awarded the Nobel Prize for Literature, the former in 1919, the latter in 1946.

FINANCE

	Budget 1983 Swiss Francs
Revenue	18,700,000,000
Expenditure	19,700,000,000

TRADE

	1983 Sw. Frs.
Total Imports	61,064,200,000
Total Exports	53,723,500,000

Trade with U.K.
(including Liechtenstein)

	1982	1983
Imports from U.K.	£1,196,203,000	£1,385,894,000
Exports to U.K.	1,669,922,000	2,154,085,000

The principal imports are machinery, electrical and electronic equipment, textiles, motor vehicles, non-ferrous metals, chemical elements, clothing, food, medicinal and pharmaceutical products. The principal exports are machinery, chemical elements, non-ferrous metals, watches, electrical and electronic equipment, textiles, dyeing, tanning and colouring equipment. Switzerland is a member of E.F.T.A.

CAPITAL.—Berne. Population (1982) 145,700. Other large towns are Zürich (367,900), Basle (181,800), Geneva (161,000), Lausanne (128,000), Winterthur (86,758), St. Gallen (75,300), Lucerne (63,278), Bienne (54,100).

FLAG.—Red, with white cross.

NATIONAL DAY.—August 1.

AIR TRANSIT FROM U.K.—London-Basle (446 miles), 1 *hr.* 30 *mins.*; Geneva (468 miles), 1 *hr.* 30 *mins.*; Zürich (491 miles), 1 *hr.* 35 *mins*; Berne, 1 *hr.* 40 *mins.*

RAIL TRANSIT FROM U.K.——London-Berne, 16 *hrs.*

BRITISH EMBASSY
Thunstrasse 50, 3000 Berne 15

Ambassador Extraordinary and Plenipotentiary, His Excellency John E. Powell-Jones (1982).

Counsellor, R. B. Crowson.

1st Secretary, G. C. Duncan.

2nd Secretary, B. England.

Defence, Naval and Military Attaché, Lt.-Col. R. G. W. Brown.

Air Attaché, Wing. Cdr. R. I. Campbell.

Attaché, P. C. Albrecht (*Commercial*).

BRITISH CONSULAR OFFICES

There is a Consular Section at H.M. Embassy, Berne; *Consulates-General* at *Zürich* and *Geneva* and Consular offices at *Lugano* and *Montreux*. The Directorate of British Export Promotion in Switzerland is in the Consulate-General Office in *Zürich*.

BRITISH-SWISS CHAMBER OF COMMERCE FOR SWITZERLAND, Dufourstrasse 51, 8008 *Zürich*.

SWISS-BRITISH SOCIETIES:
Berne.—*President*, Dr. H. Beriger.
Zürich.—*President*, Dr. R. J. Schneebeli.
Basle.—*President*, G. Simons.

SYRIA
(Syrian Arab Republic)

President, Lt.-Gen. Hafez el Assad, *b*. 1930, *assumed office* March 14, 1971, *for a term of 7 years, and re-elected for a further 7 years*, Feb. 1978.

Vice-Presidents, Abdul Halim Khaddam, Rifaat Al Assad, Zuhair Mashariqa.

Prime Minister, Abdul-Raouf Al-Kasam.

Deputy Prime Minister and Minister for Defence, Gen. Mustafa Tlass.

Deputy Prime Minister for Public Services, Brig. Walid Hamdoun.

Deputy Prime Minister for Economic Affairs, Abdul Qadir Qaddoura.

SYRIAN EMBASSY IN LONDON
8 Belgrave Square, SW1X 8PH
[01-245 9012]

Ambassador Extraordinary and Plenipotentiary, His Excellency Dr. Loutouf Allah Haydar.

Area and Population.—Syria is in the Levant, covering a portion of the former Ottoman Empire, with an estimated area of 70,800 sq. miles and a population (1981 estimate) of 10,400,000, most of whom are Arabic-speaking and Muslim. (*For Map, see* index.) The Orontes flows northwards from the Lebanon range across the northern boundary to Antakya (Antioch, Turkey). The Euphrates crosses the northern boundary near Jerablus and flows through north-eastern Syria to the boundary of Iraq.

Archæology, etc.—The region is rich in historical remains. Damascus (*Dimishq ash-Sham*) is said to be the oldest continuously inhabited city in the world (although Aleppo disputes this claim), having an existence as a city for over 4,000 years. It is situated on the river Abana (now known as Barada), in an oasis at the eastern foot of the Anti-Lebanon, and at the edge of the wide sandy desert which stretches to the Euphrates. The city contains the Omayed Mosque, the Tomb of Saladin, and the "Street Called Straight" (Acts ix. 11), while to the North-East is the Roman outpost of Dmeir and further east is Palmyra. On the Mediterranean coast at Amrit are ruins of the Phœnician town of Marath, where the *well* has been found and is being excavated and also ruins of Crusaders' fortresses at Markab, Sahyoun, and Krak des Chevaliers. At Tartous (also on the coast) the cathedral of Our Lady of Syria, built by the Knights Templars in the 12th and 13th centuries has been restored as a museum. One of the oldest alphabets in the world has been discovered at Ugarit (Ras Shamra), a Phoenician village near the port of Latakia.

Hittite cities dating from 2,000 to 1,500 B.C., have recently been explored on the west bank of the Euphrates at Jerablus and Kadesh.

Government.—Syria, which had been under French mandate since the 1914–18 war, became an independent Republic during the 1939–45 war. The first independently elected Parliament met on August 17, 1943, but foreign troops were in part occupation until April, 1946. Syria remained an independent Republic until February, 1958, when it became part of the United Arab Republic. It seceded from the United Arab Republic on Sept. 28, 1961.

A new Constitution was promulgated in March 1973; this declared that Syria is a "democratic, popular socialist State", and that the Ba'ath Party, which has been the ruling party since 1963, is "the leading party in the State and society". Elections to the 195-seat Peoples' Council in August 1977 resulted in a large majority for the Ba'ath Party.

Production and Industry.—Agriculture is the principal source of production; wheat and barley are the main cereal crops, but the cotton crop is the highest in value. Tobacco is grown in the maritime plain in Sahel, the Sahyoun and the Djebleh district of Lattakia; skins and hides, leather goods, wool and silk, textiles, cement, vegetable oil, glass, soap, sugar, plastics and copper and brass utensils are locally produced. Large new areas are coming under irrigation and cultivation in the north-east of the country as a result of the Thawra dam. There are an increasing number of light assembly plants as Syria's industrialisation programme develops. Mineral wealth is modest but oil has been found at Karachuk and other parts in the north-eastern corner of the country and exploitation and further excavations are continuing. Syria produces about 8·2 million tons of oil per year at present. A pipeline has been built to the Mediterranean port of Banias, *viâ* Homs. Two oil refineries are in production at Homs and Banias. Revenue is derived from the pipeline from the oilfields of Saudi Arabia to Sidon in Lebanon (Tapline). Another pipeline from the Iraq oilfields was closed in April 1982. Syria also has deposits of phosphate and rock salt, and produces asphalt.

Language and Literature.—Arabic is the principal language, but Kurdish, Turkish and Armenian are spoken among significant minorities and a few villages still speak Aramaic, the language spoken by Christ and the Apostles. There are 3 daily newspapers and several periodicals in Arabic published in Damascus, and also a daily newspaper in English. English has taken over from French as the main foreign language, especially among the young.

Education.—Education in Syria is under State control and, although a few of the schools are privately owned, they all follow a common system and syllabus. Elementary education is free at State Schools, and is compulsory from the age of seven. Secondary education is not compulsory and is free only at the State Schools. Because of the shortage of places, entry to these State Schools is competitive. Damascus University, founded in 1924, has faculties of law, medicine, engineering, science, arts, commerce, agriculture, divinity, fine arts, and a Higher Teachers' Training College. The number of students has risen from a few hundred in 1943 to over 60,000. There are also about 20,000 students at Aleppo University (founded 1961), over 3,000 at Tishrin University, Latakia (founded 1975) and 2,000 at Ba'ath University, Homs. Approximately 10 per cent of all students receive scholarships, and at the present time Palestinian refugees are admitted free. The rest pay fees.

Communications.—Although railway lines run from Damascus to both Beirut and Amman, train services go only as far as the border towns. A new standard-gauge track has been opened connecting Homs with Damascus but is not yet open to passengers. A standard gauge track links Homs, Hamah, Aleppo and on along the Turkish border through

Qamishliye to the Iraq frontier. Branch lines connect the ports of Tartous and Latakia to the system and another line runs from Aleppo down Euphrates valley to Deir ez Zor and thence North to Qamishliye, with a branch going to the Euphrates Dam. All the principal towns in the country are connected by roads which vary from modern dual carriageways to narrow country lanes. An internal air service operates between all major towns. The main International Airport is at Damascus and there are also flights to Eastern Europe, Turkey and Armenia from Aleppo.

Currency.—The monetary unit is the Syrian paper pound (£Syr.). Exchange rate, *see* p. 82.

Trade.—The principal imports are foodstuffs (fruit, vegetables, cereals, meat and dairy products, tea, coffee and sugar), mineral and petroleum products, yarn and textiles, iron and steel manufactures, machinery, chemicals, pharmaceuticals, fertilizers and timber.

Principal Exports.—Raw cotton, oil, cereals, fruit, phosphates, livestock and dairy products, other foodstuffs, textiles and raw wool.

Trade with U.K.

	1982	1983
Imports from U.K.	£89,535,000	£72,320,000
Exports to U.K.	25,644,000	18,859,000

CHIEF TOWNS.—Damascus (population (estimated) 2,250,000) is the capital of Syria. Other important towns are Aleppo, Homs and Hama, and the principal port is Latakia.

FLAG.—Red over white over black horizontal bands, with two green stars on central white band.

NATIONAL DAY.—April 17.

BRITISH EMBASSY
Quartier Malki, 11 rue Mohammad Kurd Ali,
Imm. Kotob, Damascus.

Ambassador Extraordinary and Plenipotentiary, His Excellency William Rodger Tomkys (1984).
British Council Representative, Dr. J. M. Compton, British Cultural Centre, 60 Atta al Ayoubi Street, Damascus.

THAILAND
(Siam)

King, His Majesty Bhumibol Adulyadej, *born* 1927; *succeeded his brother,* June 9, 1946; *married* Princess Sirikit Kityakara, April 28, 1950; *crowned* May 5, 1950; *and has issue,* Princess Ubol Ratana, *born,* April 6, 1951; Crown Prince Vajiralongkorn, *born,* July 28, 1952; Princess Sirindhorn, *born,* April 2, 1955; Princess Chulabhorn *born,* July 4, 1957.

CABINET

Prime Minister and Minister for Defence , Gen. Prem Tinsulanonda.
Deputy Prime Ministers, Gen. Prachuab Suntrangkoon; Boontheng Thongsawasdi; Bhichai Rattakul; Adm. Sonthi Boonyachai.
Ministers attached to the Prime Minister's Office, Kamol Thongthammachart; Police Lt. Charn Manootham; Meechai Ruchupan; Flt. Lt. Sulee Mahasanthana; Sawasdi Kamprakorb; Chaisiri Ruangkanchanases; Banyat Bantadtan.
Foreign Affairs, Air Chief Marshal Siddhi Savetsila.
Communications, Samak Sundaravej.
Commerce, Kosol Krairiksh.
Interior, Gen. Sitthi Jirarote.
Justice, Phipop Asitirat.
Science, Technology and Energy, Damrong Lathaphipat.

Education, Chuan Leekpai.
Public Health, Marut Bunnag.
Industry, Ob Vasuratna.
Agriculture, Narong Wongwan.
Finance, Dr. Sommai Hoontrakul.
University Affairs, Preeda Pathanathabutr.

ROYAL THAI EMBASSY IN LONDON
30 Queen's Gate, SW7 5JB
[01–589 0173]

Ambassador Extraordinary and Plenipotentiary, His Excellency Phan Wannamethee (until Sept. 1984).

Area and Population.—The Kingdom of Thailand, formerly known as Siam, has an area of 198,247 sq. miles with a population (estimated 1983) of 49,459,000. For position, *see* MAP, p. 957. It has a common boundary with Malaysia in the south, is bounded on the west by Burma and on the north-east and east by Laos and Cambodia, which were formerly part of the French colony of Indo-China. Although there is no common boundary between Thailand and China, the Chinese province of Yunnan is separated from the Thai northern border only by a narrow stretch of Burmese and Laotian territory.

The capital, Bangkok, is situated in the south of the central plain area. To the north-east there is a plateau area and to the north-west mountains. The south of Thailand consists of a narrow mountainous peninsula. The principal rivers are the Chao Phraya with its tributary the Meping and the Mekong and its tributaries, which water the eastern plateau.

Government.—Thailand became a Constitutional Monarchy in 1932. The Constitution promulgated in December 1978 provides for a National Assembly consisting of a Senate appointed by the King and a House of Representatives elected by universal adult suffrage.

Language, Religion and Education.—Thai is basically a monosyllabic, tonal language, a branch of the Indo-Chinese linguistic family, but its vocabulary especially has been strongly influenced by Sanskrit and Pali. It is written in an alphabetic script derived from ancient Indian scripts. The principal religion is Buddhism. In 1983 94·5 per cent of the population were Buddhists, 4·5 per cent Moslems, 0·6 per cent Christians and 0·4 per cent other religions. Primary education is compulsory and free and secondary education in Government Schools is free. In 1983 there were 35,846 schools and training colleges, with a total of 10,058,295 pupils and 539,680 teachers. There are 14 state universities and institutes of technology attended by a total of 780,784 students. In 1971 an open university (Ramkhamhaeng) was established in Bangkok with some 57,200 students, and a second, Sukhothai Thammathuriat, opened in 1980 and has 109,842 students.

Production and Industry.—The agricultural sector provides just under half the national income and employs about 70 per cent of the working population. Rice remains the most important crop, accounting for 63 per cent of the area planted. After rice the main crops are cassava, maize, and rubber. Also of some importance are sugar cane, kenaf, groundnuts, tobacco, and coconuts. There is a substantial forest extraction industry, the most valuable product of which is teak.

Mineral resources are mainly tin, antimony, tungsten, gypsum and fluorite. The most important of these, tin, is seeing something of a decline, mainly because of the exhaustion of reserves. The importance of lignite as a source of energy increased with higher oil prices. Natural gas, piped from the Gulf of Thailand, is expected to supply much of the country's energy requirements by the late 1980's.

Before the war, industry was mainly confined to the basic processing industries—sawmilling, rice-milling, etc. After the war, the Government set up a number of factories run by the Civil Service or the Armed Forces. The Government still has a sizeable stake in industry—notably the tobacco monopoly and factories for the manufacture of cement, glass, paper, jute, textiles, sugar and beer and spirits.

The Government in 1962 instituted a policy of encouraging the private sector to invest in industry, by means of tax reliefs and other incentives. The private sector industries are almost entirely of a secondary nature; soap products, gunny bags, textiles, car assembly, pharmaceutical preparations and packaging, dry batteries, etc. Over the last decade the size of the manufacturing sector has grown rapidly and now provides 18 per cent of national income.

Communications.—Rivers and canals provide the traditional mode of transport for much of the country. Navigable waterways have a length of about 1,100 km. in the dry season and 1,600 km. in the wet season. About 3,825 km. of State-owned railways were open to traffic in 1983. The track is metre gauge. Main lines run from Bangkok to Aranya Prathet, on the Cambodian border (160 miles E.); *via* Korat to Ubon (about 352 miles E.) and to Nongkhai (415 miles N.E.) the ferry terminal on the River Mekong opposite Vientiane, capital of Laos; to Chiangmai (411 miles N.); and to Hat Yai (600 miles S.), whence lines go down the eastern and western sides of the Malay Peninsula, *via* Sungei Golok and Penang respectively, to Singapore.

Thailand has some 25,000 km. of highways and provincial roads.

Bangkok has an international airport of importance, and services connect it direct with cities in Europe, America, and Australia, as well as countries in Asia. The airports at Chaing Mai and Hat Yai also receive international flights. Thai Airways International (THAI), was formed in 1960 in association with SAS to operate international routes. Domestic routes are operated by Thai Airways Corporation. There are some 22,000 km. of telegraph lines and improvements are being made to an already extensive micro-wave communications system. The harbour at Bangkok can take vessels up to 27′ draught and is sometimes congested. New deep-water facilities are being provided at Sattahip on the east side of the Gulf of Thailand, where the existing naval port is to be converted for commercial use.

TRADE

	1982	1983
	millions of *Baht*	
Total imports	219,025	222,888·6
Total exports	153,000	146,238·9

Trade with U.K.

	1982	1983
Imports from U.K.	£104,825,000	£131,833,000
Exports to U.K.	76,529,000	87,823,000

The exchange rate for the *Baht* was officially fixed at *Baht* 23·0 = $1 U.S. (*See also* p. 82.)

Thailand's main exports are rice, sugar, maize, tapioca products, rubber and tin. Other exports include ready-made garments, textiles, frozen shrimps, timber and articles of wood, mung beans and tobacco leaves. Main imports are petroleum and petroleum products, machinery, transport equipment, iron and steel, electrical machinery, chemicals and cotton.

CAPITAL.—ΨBangkok (population 5,733,000 (1983)); in the delta of Chao Phraya. Other centres are Chiangmai, Nakorn Sawan, Korat and Haadyai, but no other town approaches Bangkok in size or importance.

FLAG.—Five horizontal bands, red, white, dark blue, white, red (the blue band twice the width of the others).

NATIONAL DAY.—December 5 (King's Birthday).

BRITISH EMBASSY
Wireless Road, Bangkok

Ambassador Extraordinary and Plenipotentiary, His Excellency Hubert Anthony Justin Staples, C.M.G. (1981).

British Council Representative, Miss A. Lambert, O.B.E., 428 Rama 1 Road, Siam Square, Bangkok 10500.

TOGO
(Republic of Togo)

President and Minister of Defence, Gen. Gnassingbé Eyadéma, *born* 1937, *assumed office*, April 14, 1967; *re-elected for seven-year term*, Dec. 30, 1979.

Minister for Foreign Affairs and Co-operation, Dr. Anani Kuma Akakpo-Ahianyo.

EMBASSY IN LONDON
20 Wellington Court,
116 Knightsbridge, S.W.1
[01-584 7377]

Chargé d'Affaires, Fusuanu Kossi Metsoko.

The Republic is situated in West Africa between 0°–2° W. and 6°–11° N., with a coastline only 35 miles long on the Gulf of Guinea, and extends northward inland for 350 miles. It is flanked on the west by Ghana, on the north by Upper Volta and in the east by Benin (*see* MAP, p. 943). It has an area of 21,000 sq. miles and a population (estimate, 1979) of 2,470,000, including people of several African races. The official language is French.

The first President of Togo, Sylvanus Olympio, assassinated on January 13, 1963, was succeeded by Nicolas Grunitzky, who was himself overthrown by an army *coup d'état* on January 13, 1967. On April 14, 1967, the Commander-in-Chief of the Togolese army, Lt. Colonel (later promoted General) Eyadéma named himself President.

Finance.—The currency of Togo is the *Franc* C.F.A.

Production and Trade.—Although the economy of Togo remains largely agricultural, exports of phosphates have superseded agricultural products as the main source of export earnings. Other exports include palm kernels, copra and manioc. The production of phosphates entirely for export was taken over completely by the government in February 1974.

Trade with U.K.

	1982	1983
Imports from U.K.	£21,881,000	£12,212,000
Exports to U.K.	1,827,000	2,161,000

CAPITAL.—ΨLomé, population (1979), 247,000.
FLAG.—Five alternating green and yellow horizontal stripes; a quarter in red at top next staff bearing a white star.
NATIONAL DAY.—April 27 (Independence Day).

BRITISH EMBASSY
British Ambassador, (resides at *Accra, Ghana*).

TUNISIA
(Tunisian Republic)

President, Habib Bourguiba, *elected* July 25, 1957; *re-elected* 1959, 1964, 1969 and 1974. Proclaimed President for life March 1975.

Prime Minister and Minister of the Interior, Mohamed Mzali.
Special Advisor to the President, Habib Bourguiba jnr.
Justice, Mohamed Chaker.
Foreign Affairs, Beji Caid Essebsi.
National Defence, Slaheddine Baly.
Planning, Ismail Khelil.
Finance, Salah M'Barka.
National Economy, Rachid Sfar.

TUNISIAN EMBASSY IN LONDON
29 Princes Gate, SW7 1QG
[01–584 8117]

Ambassador, His Excellency Sadek Bouzayen.

Area and Population.—Tunisia lies between Algeria and Libya and extends southwards to the Sahara Desert, with a total area of 63,380 sq. miles and an estimated population in 1981 of 6,520,000.

Government.—A French Protectorate from 1881 to 1956, Tunisia became an independent sovereign State with the signing on March 20, 1956, of an agreement whereby France recognized Tunisia's independence and right to conduct her own foreign policy and to form a Tunisian Army.

Following a first general election held on March 25, 1956, a Constituent Assembly met for the first time on April 8. On July 25, 1957, the Constituent Assembly deposed the Bey, abolished the monarchy and elected M. Bourguiba first President of the Republic. On June 1, 1959, the Constitution was promulgated and on December 7, 1959, the National Assembly held its first session. In March 1975 the National Assembly proclaimed M. Bourguiba as President for life.

The country is divided into 22 regions (*gouvernorats*) each administered by a Governor.

Production, Trade, etc.—The valleys of the northern region support large flocks and herds, and contain rich agricultural areas, in which wheat, barley, and oats are grown. The vine and olive are extensively cultivated.

The chief exports are crude oil, phosphates, olive oil, finished textiles, and wine. The chief imports are machinery and equipment, foodstuffs, petroleum products, and textiles. Some oil has been discovered and production reached an annual rate of 5·6 million tons in 1983. Gas has also been discovered off the east coast but exploitation is not viable at present. Tourists numbered 1,438,872 in 1983.

	1983
Total Imports	*TD*2,109,700,000
Total Exports	1,263,900,000

France remains the main trading partner, supplying 26 per cent of the country's imports and purchasing 19 per cent of Tunisia's exports.

Trade with U.K.

	1982	1983
Imports from U.K.	£38,632,000	£44,659,000
Exports to U.K.	12,628,000	18,126,000

Currency.—The unit of currency is the *dinar* of 1,000 *millimes.*

Tunisia became an associate member of E.E.C. early in 1969, and signed a new agreement with the E.E.C. in 1976. In 1977 the introduction of import quota measures by the E.E.C. on some textile goods resulted in a reduction of growth in this important sector of the Tunisian market. The quotas for some textile products was renegotiated and increased in 1982.

CAPITAL.—Ψ Tunis, connected by canal with La Goulette on the coast, has a population (1981) of 1,133,000. The ruins of ancient Carthage lie a few miles from the city. Other towns of importance

are: Ψ Sfax (554,000); Ψ Sousse (255,000); Ψ Bizerta (376,000); Kairouan; Gabes; Menzel Bourguiba.
FLAG.—Red crescent and star in a white orb, all on a red ground.
NATIONAL DAY.—June 1.

BRITISH EMBASSY
Place de la Victoire, Tunis

Ambassador Extraordinary and Plenipotentiary and Consul-General, His Excellency William James Adams, C.M.G. (1984).
1st Secretary, D. L. Hardinge (*Head of Chancery and Consul*).
Commercial Attaché, J. F. Larner.
British Council Representative, W. D. Brown. There is a British Council Library in *Tunis.*

TURKEY

President, Gen. Kenan Evren, *assumed power,* Sept. 12, 1980; *elected for 7-year term,* Nov. 1982.

GOVERNMENT

Prime Minister, Turgut Özal.
Deputy Prime Minister, Kaya Erdem.
Ministers of State, Kazim Oksay; Mesut Yilmaz; Sudi Neşe Turel; Ahmet K. Alptemoçin; Ismail Ozdağlar; Abdullah Tenekeci.
Justice, M. Necat Eldem.
National Defence, Zeki Yavuztürk.
Interior, Ali Tanriyar.
Foreign Affairs, Vahit Halefoğlu.*
Finance and Customs, Vural Arikan.
National Education, Youth and Sport, M. Vehbi Dinçerler.
Public Works and Construction, I. Safa Giray.
Health and Social Welfare, Mehmet Aydin.
Communications, Veysel Atasoy.
Agriculture, Forestry and Rural Affairs, Hüsnü Doğan.*
Labour and Social Security, Mustafa Kalemli.
Industry and Commerce, Cahit Aral.
Energy and Natural Resources, Cemel Büyükbaş.
Culture and Tourism, Mukerrem Taşçioğlu.
Presidential Council, Pres. Kenan Evren; Gen. Nurettin Ersin; Gen. Tahsin Sahinkaya; Adm. Nejat Tumer; Gen. Sedat Celasun.
(* not an M.P.)

TURKISH EMBASSY IN LONDON
Chancery: 43 Belgrave Square, SW1X 8PA
[01–235 5252]

Ambassador Extraordinary and Plenipotentiary, His Excellency Rahmi Gümrükcüoglu (1981).

Area and Population.—People of Turkic stock are to be found scattered throughout a wide belt extending from China through the Soviet Union, Afghanistan and Iran to the present day Turkish State, and into Bulgaria.

Turkey itself extends from Edirne (Adrianople) to Transcaucasia and Iran, and from the Black Sea to the Mediterranean, Syria and Iraq. Total population at the Census of October, 1980 was 45,217,556.

Turkey in Europe consists of Eastern Thrace, including the cities of Istanbul and Edirne, and is separated from Asia by the Bosphorus at Istanbul and by the *Dardanelles*—about 40 miles in length with a width varying from 1 to 4 miles—the political neighbours being Greece and Bulgaria on the west. Population (est. 1980), 4,500,000.

Turkey in Asia comprises the whole of Asia Minor or *Anatolia* ("Land of the Rising Sun" or Orient), and extends from the Aegean Sea to the western boundaries of Georgia, Soviet Armenia and Iran, and from the Black Sea to the Mediterranean and the

northern boundaries of Syria and Iraq. Population (est. 1980), 40,500,000.

Government.—On October 29, 1923, the National Assembly declared Turkey a Republic and elected Gazi Mustafa Kemal (later known as Kemal Ataturk) President. In 1945 a multi-party system was introduced but in 1960 the government was overthrown by the Turkish Armed Forces which ruled through the Committee of National Union, a body of military officers. The committee ruled from January to November, 1961, in conjunction with a civilian House of Representatives, the two bodies together forming the Constituent Assembly. Mounting problems with the economy and terrorism led the military to assume legislative powers in Sept. 1980, a civilian technocratic government being appointed later that month.

A new Constitution, extending the powers of the President, was approved by a referendum on Nov. 7, 1982. It provided for the separation of powers between the legislature, executive and judiciary, and the holding of free elections to the unicameral Grand National Assembly, which has 400 members elected every five years. Following the General Election on Nov. 6, 1983 the military leadership handed over power to a newly elected civilian government.

Party representation in the Assembly after the General Election was: Motherland Party, 211 seats; Populist Party, 117; Nationalist Democracy Party, 67; Independents 4. (One seat was not filled at the election).

Turkey is divided for administrative purposes into 67 *il* with subdivisions into *kaza* and *nahiye*. Each *il* has a governor (*vali*) and elective council.

Religion and Education.—98·99 per cent of the population are Moslems. The main religious minorities, which are concentrated in Istanbul and on the Syrian frontier, are: Greek Orthodox, 10,000; Armenians, 42,000; Syriani Christians, 42,000; Others, 6,000. (Total Christians, 100,000); Jewish, 44,000. On April 10, 1928, the Grand National Assembly passed a law in virtue of which Islam ceased to be the State religion of the Republic. Education is free, secular and compulsory at primary level. There are elementary, secondary and vocational schools.

There are 27 universities in Turkey, including four in Istanbul, four in Ankara, two in Izmir, and one each in Erzurum and Trabzon.

The expenditure allocated to education in the 4th Five Year Plan (1979–83) was *TL*76,000,000,000,

compared with *TL*14,000,000,000 in the 3rd Five Year Plan (1973–77), but past experience has shown that targets in this field are not always met.

Language and Literature.—Until 1926, Turkish was written in Arabic script, but in that year the Roman alphabet was substituted for use in official correspondence and in 1928 for universal use, with Arabic numerals as used throughout Europe. Mainly as a consequence of this change the number of Turks who can read and write has risen steadily, from about 10 per cent in 1927 to nearly 70 per cent by 1982. Ancient Turkish literature aped the Arabic manner, but the revolution of 1908 was followed by a popular reaction against the writings of the past (which appealed only to a small class) and led to the introduction of a native literature free from foreign influences and adapted to the understanding of the people. The vehicle first employed was the newspaper, printed in the neo-Latin alphabet, with supplements for prose and dramatic fiction, poetry and literary criticism. The leading Turkish newspapers are centred in Istanbul and Ankara, although most provincial towns have their own daily papers. There are foreign language papers in French, Greek, Armenian and English and numerous magazines and weeklies on various subjects, but few trade commercial publications.

Agricultural Production.—In 1981 agricultural production accounted for some 21 per cent of the gross domestic product at constant factor prices, while exports of agricultural commodities represented some 47 per cent of the total exports. About 60 per cent of the working population are in the rural sector, but agriculture is still primitive in many areas and agricultural productivity is low. Estimated production figures for the principal crops in 1981 were ('000 tons):

Wheat	17,000	Tobacco	200
Barley	5,900	Sugar Beet	11,000
Maize	1,100	Potatoes	3,000
Rye	500	Grapes	3,600
Oilseeds	1,507	Citrus Fruits	1,200
Pulses	825	Figs	200
Cotton	500	Hazelnuts	350

With the important exception of wheat, which is mostly grown on the arid Central Anatolian Plateau, most of the crops are grown on the fertile littoral. Tobacco, sultana and fig cultivation is centred around

Izmir, where substantial quantities of cotton are also grown. The main cotton area is in the Cukurova Plain around Adana. 1980 livestock figures are as follows ('000): horses, 794; mules, 305; donkeys, 1,345; camels, 12; cattle (including buffalo), 16,925; sheep and goats, 64,015; angora goats, 3,658; hogs, 13; poultry, 61,449. The forests which lie between the littoral plain and the Anatolian Plateau, contain beech, pine, oak, elm, chestnut, lime, plane, alder, box, poplar and maple. During recent years the Government has attempted, so far not altogether successfully, to combat the depredations of peasant and goat which threaten to destroy the existing forests within the next 25 years.

Industry.—After agriculture, Turkey's second most important industry is based on her considerable mineral wealth which is, however, as yet comparatively unexploited. Coal production in 1981 amounted to 7,223,000 tons, and 17,400,000 tons of lignite. The main export minerals are chromite and boron. Production of iron ore in 1981 was 2,856,000 tons; chrome ore, 507,000 tons; copper, 45,000 tons and boron minerals, 1,333,000 tons. The research and exploitation of the principal mineral deposits are mainly in the hands of the Mineral Research and Exploration Institute of Turkey and the State-owned Etibank respectively. The latter controls directly, on behalf of the Government, all the copper, sulphur and pyrite output of Turkey, as well as much of the colemenite and chrome production. The government has plans to return some of the mines to the private sector and to open the mining field to foreign investment. Since state-sponsored industrialization began in 1935, industry has played an increasing part in the Turkish economy. Here, also, as in the case of minerals, much of the industry of the country is controlled by the Government.

Industrial production figures for 1981 ('000 tons): cement, 15,008; sugar, 1,270; pig iron, 1,830; steel ingots, 1,830; paper, 368; petroleum products, 12,606; crude oil, 2,100; artificial fertilizer, 6,609; electric energy (billion of kilowatt hours), 25; cotton fabrics (thousand metres), 228.

The progress made in the manufacture of sugar, cotton, woollen and silk textiles, and cement, has been such that the bulk of the country's requirements can now be produced locally, while other industries contributing substantially to local needs include vehicle assembly, paper, glass and glassware, iron and steel, leather and leather goods, sulphur refining, canning and rubber goods, soaps and cosmetics, pharmaceutical products, prepared foodstuffs and a host of minor industries. Legislation was passed in 1954 to encourage the investment of foreign capital in Turkey and to promote the exploitation of Turkey's petroleum resources by foreign countries.

In common with other developing countries, Turkey's economy was adversely affected by the steep rises in oil prices from 1973 onwards. This led to a succession of economic crises and high inflation culminating in Jan. 1980 in the introduction of an economic stability programme. Exports have since risen dramatically, inflation has largely been brought under control, and modest growth has resumed although the internal economy is still depressed with high unemployment.

Since the Second World War the United States Government has given Turkey financial aid totalling over 5 billion dollars, half of which has been for military and half for economic purposes. The other main official sources of foreign aid have been the O.E.C.D. (who have pledged over $3 billion since 1979); the I.B.R.D, and the I.M.F. which has made medium term loans for balance of payment support ($1·6 billion over three years in 1980). The United Kingdom has pledged over £100,000,000 of aid to Turkey since 1963.

The fourth of Turkey's Five Year Development Plans, for the years 1979–83, began in January 1979. The basic economic objective of the fourth plan was to achieve an average growth rate of 8·0 per cent in the gross national product. This had not been achieved and the plan has been dropped. Preliminary work has been started on the Fifth Plan.

COMMUNICATIONS

Railways.—The complete network became the property of the State Railways Administration in 1948. The total length of lines in operation is 8,193 kilometres.

Roads.—At the end of 1980 there were 31,976 km. of national roads (24,972 of which were macadamized). The total state and provincial road system is some 60,761 km. in length. The estimated number of vehicles in 1980 was 1,135,000, of which there were 711,000 motor cars, 66,000 minibuses, 170,000 lorries and 157,000 light-weight trucks.

Posts.—In June 1979 the number of telephone subscribers in Turkey was approximately 1,800,000.

Shipping.—In August 1980 there were 343 merchants ships over 300 gross tons, 79 passenger ships and 73 tankers, giving a total draft weight of 1,545,062 tons.

Civil Aviation.—The State airlines (T.H.Y.) operate all internal services and have services to Europe and the Middle East. Most of the leading European airlines, including British Airways, operate services to Istanbul and some also to Ankara.

FINANCE

(In 1982 the financial year is being aligned with the calendar year: these figures are for Mar. 1–Dec. 31)

	1982
	TL'000,000
Estimated Expenditure	1,755,200
Estimated Revenue	1,680,000

Currency.—The Turkish *Lira* (*TL*) is divided into 100 *Kurus*. For rate of exchange *see also* p. 82.

TRADE

	1980	1981
Total imports	$7,909,000,000	$8,911,000,000
Total exports	2,910,000,000	4,703,000,000

The 1981 foreign trade deficit figure was U.S., $4,208,000,000; for 1980 it was U.S.$4,999,000,000.

All imports are subject to licence and the issue of licences is limited to goods considered necessary for the country's economy. Lists of permitted imports are published annually at the beginning of January. The main imports are machinery, crude oil and petroleum products, iron and steel, vehicles, medicines and dyes, chemicals, fertilizers and electrical appliances. The principal exports are cotton, tobacco, fruits, nuts, minerals, livestock, textiles, glass and cement.

Trade with U.K.

	1982	1983
Imports from U.K.	£218,116,000	£244,024,000
Exports to U.K.	207,763,000	184,976,000

CAPITAL, Ankara (Angora), an inland town of Asia Minor, about 275 miles E.S.E. of Istanbul, with a population (1980) of 3,196,460. Ankara (or Ancyra) was the capital of the Roman Province of *Galatia Prima*, and a marble temple (now in ruins), dedicated to Augustus, contains the *Monumentum* (*Marmor*) *Ancyranum*, inscribed with a record of the reign of Augustus Cæsar. A new city was laid out on modern lines, with parks, statues and avenues. ΨIstanbul (4,870,747), the former capital, was the Roman city of Byzantium. It was selected by Constantine the Great as the capital of the Roman Empire about A.D. 328 and renamed Constantinople. Istanbul contains the celebrated church of St. Sophia, which, after becoming a mosque, was made a museum in 1934; it also contains Topkapi, former Palace of the Ottoman Sultans, which is also a museum. Other cities are ΨIzmir (1,968,614); Adana (1,467,346); Bursa (1,161,553); Gaziantep (387,093); and Eskişehir (543,733).

FLAG.—Red, with white crescent and star.
NATIONAL DAY.—October 29 (Republic Day).

BRITISH EMBASSY
(Ankara)

Ambassador Extraordinary and Plenipotentiary, His Excellency Robert Mark Russell, C.M.G.,(1982).
Counsellor, J. R. L. G. Varcoe.
1st Secretaries, K. R. Tebbitt (*Head of Chancery*); R. M. Kelly; R. M. D. Barrett (*Consul*); R. D. Wilkinson (*Economic and Commercial*); Ms. C. M. Street (*Cultural Affairs*); M. R. Willson (*Cultural and Science Affairs*); M. F. J. Ryder (*Administration*).
2nd Secretaries, T. J. Craddock; Miss M. S. Jack; R. Difelice.
Defence and Military Attaché, Brig. C. W. G. Bullocke, M.B.E.
Naval and Air Attaché, Wing Cdr. A. J. Raley, M.B.E.

BRITISH CONSULAR OFFICES

There is a British Consulate-General at *Istanbul*, a Vice-Consulate at *Izmir* and an Hon. British Consulate at *Iskenderun*.

BRITISH COUNCIL.—50–52 Güniz Sokak, Kavaklidere, Ankara. *Representative*, Dr. F. H. Taylor.—There is also a centre and library at *Istanbul* and a library at *Ankara*.
BRITISH CHAMBER OF COMMERCE OF TURKEY INC., Mesrutiyet Caddessi No. 34, Tepebasi Beyoğlu, Istanbul (Postal Address, P.O. Box 190 Karaköy, Istanbul). *Chairman*, A. Serdengeçti.

UNITED ARAB EMIRATES

President, Shaikh Zaid bin Sultan al Nahayyan (*Abu Dhabi*).
Vice-President and Prime Minister, Shaikh Rashid bin Said al Maktum.
Deputy Prime Ministers, Shaikh Maktum bin Rashid al Maktum; Shaikh Hamdan bin Muhammad al Nahayyan.
Interior, Shaikh Mubarak bin Muhammad al Nahayyan.
Finance and Industry, Shaikh Hamdan bin Rashid al Maktum.
Defence, Shaikh Muhammad bin Rashid al Maktum.
Minister of State for Foreign Affairs, Sayyid Rashid Abdullah al Nu'aimi.
Petroleum and Mineral Resources, Dr. Mana Said al Otaiba.
Economy and Commerce, Sayyid Saif al Jarwan.
Information and Culture, Shaikh Ahmad bin Hamid bin Butti.
Communications, Sayyid Muhammad Said al Mulla.
Public Works and Housing, Sayyid Muhammad Khalifa al Kindi.
Education, Sayyid Faraj Fadel al Mazroni.
Planning, (vacant).
Justice, Sayyid Abdullah Humaid al Mazroni.
Islamic Affairs and Awqaf, Shaikh Mohammad bin Hassan al Khazraji.
Agriculture and Fisheries, Sayyid Said al Ragabani.
Water and Electricity, Sayyid Humaid Nasser al Owais.
Labour and Social Affairs, Sayyid Khalfan al Romni.
Health, Sayyid Hamad Abdul Rahman al Madfa.

EMBASSY IN LONDON
30 Prince's Gate, SW7 1PT
[01–581 1281]

Ambassador Extraordinary and Plenipotentiary, His Excellency Sayed Mohammed Mahdi Al-Tajir.

Area and Population.—The approximate area of the U.A.E. is 33,000 square miles and the population in 1984 was estimated at about 1·3 million.

The United Arab Emirates (formerly the Trucial States) is composed of seven Emirates (Abu Dhabi, Ajman, Dubai, Fujeirah, Ras al Khaimah, Sharjah and Umm al Qaiwain) which came together as an independent state on December 2, 1971, when they ended their individual special treaty relationships with the British Government (Ras al Khaimah joined the other six on February 10, 1972).

The British Government, by virtue of a treaty made in 1892, had been responsible for the external affairs of the states through the British Political Resident in the Persian Gulf and the British Political Agents in each state, but on independence the Union Government assumed full responsibility for all internal and external affairs apart from some internal matters that remained the prerogative of the individual Emirates. Six of the Emirates lie on the shore of the Gulf between the Musandam peninsula in the East and the Qatar peninsula in the West while the seventh, Fujeirah, lies on the gulf of Oman.

Security in the area is maintained by the U.A.E. Armed Forces. The Ministry of Defence is located in Dubai with a General Headquarters in Abu Dhabi. Most of the separate police forces have also been merged.

Revenue is chiefly derived from oil, re-exports and customs dues on imports. A substantial amount is spent on overseas aid, where commitments in 1980 totalled £154·8 million, doubling those of 1979.

Trade with U.K.

	1983	1983
Imports from U.K.	£559,000,000	£567,765,000
Exports to U.K.	267,000,000	309,806,000

Abu Dhabi

Abu Dhabi is the largest Emirate of the U.A.E. in area, stretching from Khor al Odaid in the west to the borders with Dubai in the Jebel Ali area. It includes six villages in the Buraimi oasis, the other three being part of the Sultanate of Oman, and a number of settlements in the Liwa Oasis system. Following negotiations with Saudi Arabia, some adjustment of the border has now been made in the Khor al Odaid region, but the agreement has not yet been ratified. The population of the Emirate is now about 520,000

The Abu Dhabi Government controls oil, gas and petrochemical operations in the Emirate through the Abu Dhabi National Oil Company (ADNOC) which has majority shareholdings in the several oil operating and gas treatment companies. ADNOC also has majority shareholdings in oil industry related companies covering drilling, refining, distribution, chemical manufacture and investment. Offshore production began in 1962, the most important fields being Umm Shaif and Lower Zakum, near Das Island, site of a large associated gas liquefaction plant. The Upper Zakum field came on stream in late 1982, and four other offshore fields are being developed, one near Abu Dhabi city and three near Delma. Production of oil onshore began in 1963 from the Murban field. A large onshore associated gas liquefaction project based at Ruwais started production in 1981. Other large natural gas finds in recent years will consolidate Abu Dhabi's position as a holder of some of the largest reserves of natural gas in the world.

Abu Dhabi's crude oil production in 1983 was 255 million barrels.

With its oil wealth the Emirate has seen a decade of growth (which is currently slowing down), not only at Abu Dhabi, now a modern city of about 400,000 people, but also at Al Ain in the Buraimi Oasis and at the new petro-chemical city at Ruwais. A new international airport opened in 1982 at Abu Dhabi and another is under construction at Al Ain. There are airfields at Das Island and Jebel Dhanna. The port and harbour on Abu Dhabi island are now almost completed and there are port facilities at Ruwais.

Dubai

Dubai is the second largest Emirate both in size and in population, which is now about 350,000. The town of Dubai is the main port for the import of goods into the U.A.E. and has a wide re-export trade to the other Gulf States. Dubai's prosperity was established by this trade long before the discovery of oil. Oil was discovered in 1966 and production began in September 1969. The main operator of Dubai's offshore oilfields is Dubai Petroleum Company, a subsidiary of CONOCO. In 1982 an ARCO-Britoil joint venture discovered an extensive gas and condensate field onshore.

Oil income has been used to finance Dubai's infrastructure and major construction projects include an international airport, a dry dock complex and an international trade and exhibition centre. There is also a 66 berth port at Jebel Ali, forming the heart of an industrial complex which includes an aluminium smelter with an associated de-salination plant and a gas processing plant. The port and its immediate area is a free trade zone which is expected to attract more industry.

Sharjah

Sharjah, with a present population of approx. 120,000, has declined from its position 50 years ago as principal town in the area. It became the third oil producing Emirate in the summer of 1974, following the discovery of oil offshore. The field declined over the years and by 1982 was yielding less than 6,000 b.p.d. However, new oil and gas discoveries were made in 1982 in the northern emirates and production now stands at about 50,000 b.p.d. Sharjah is well connected by metalled roads to all the other Northern Emirates. It experienced a construction boom in the mid-1970's including an ambitious layout of roads and flyovers within the town. A new container port has been constructed on the Gulf of Oman at Khor Fakkan. The new international airport was officially opened in 1979.

Ras al Khaimah

Ras al Khaimah has a population of 80,000 of whom more than half live in the town. An ancient sea-port, near which archaeological remains have been found, Ras al Khaimah is developing as the most agricultural of the Emirates, producing vegetables, dates, fruit and tobacco. In 1982 Ras al Khaimah announced the discovery of oil and gas offshore and this field is currently being developed. An industrial area has been developed to the north of the Emirate, which includes 2 cement works. Ras al-Khaimah has an international airport and has also expanded its port.

Fujeirah

Fujeirah, with a population of 40,000, is the poorest and most remote of the seven Emirates lying on the Gulf of Oman coast, and only connected by a metal road to the rest of the country since the end of 1975. Largely agricultural, its population is spread between the slopes of the inland Hajar mountain range and the town of Fujeirah itself, together with a number of smaller settlements on the comparatively fertile plain on the coast. Although exploration work continues, there have been no hydrocarbon discoveries in the Emirate. However, there are some chrome and other mineral deposits. Fujeirah has a new general cargo port.

Ajman and Umm al Qaiwain

Ajman and Umm al Qaiwain are the smallest Emirates, having populations of approx. 36,000 and 30,000 respectively. Both lie on the Arabian Gulf coast although Ajman has two inland enclaves at Manama and Masfut. Exploration work continues in both Emirates for oil and gas but so far only Umm Al Qaiwain has experienced any success, with the offshore discovery of natural gas, but the field has yet to be commercially developed. The discovery of onshore gas in nearby Sharjah has increased hopes of similar discoveries in both Ajman and Umm Al Qaiwain.

BRITISH EMBASSY
P.O. Box 248, Abu Dhabi

Ambassador Extraordinary and Plenipotentiary, His Excellency Harold Berners Walker, C.M.G. (1981).
British Council Representative, W. H. Jefferson, P.O. Box 248, Abu Dhabi.

(Dubai)
Counsellor and Consul General, P. R. M. Hinchcliffe, C.V.O.
British Council Representative, J. D. Ewart, P.O. Box 65, Dubai.

UNITED STATES OF AMERICA

PHYSIOGRAPHY

The conterminous States of the Republic occupy nearly all that portion of the North American Continent between the Atlantic and Pacific Oceans, in latitude 25° 07'–49° 23' North and longitude 66° 57'–124° 44' West, its northern boundary being Canada and the southern boundary Mexico. The separate State of Alaska reaches a latitude of 71° 23' N,, at Point Barrow (2,502 miles from the U.S. geographic centre).

The general coastline of the 50 States has a length of about 2,069 miles on the Atlantic, 7,623 miles on the Pacific, 1,060 miles on the Arctic, and 1,631 miles on the Gulf of Mexico.

The principal river is the mighty Mississippi-Missouri-Red, traversing the whole country from north to south, and having a course of 3,710 miles to its mouth in the Gulf of Mexico, with many large affluents, the chief of which are the Yellowstone, Platte, Arkansas, and Ohio, Rivers. The rivers flowing into the Atlantic and Pacific Oceans are comparatively small; among the former may be noticed the Hudson, Delaware, Susquehanna, Potomac, James, Roanoke and Savannah; of the latter, the Columbia-Snake, Sacramento, and Colorado. The Nueces, Brazos, Trinity, Pearl, Mobile-Tombigbee-Alabama, Apalachicola-Chattahoochee, Suwannee and Colorado of Texas fall into the Gulf of Mexico, also the Rio Grande, a long river partly forming the boundary with Mexico. The areas of the water-basins have been estimated as follows:—Rivers flowing to the Pacific, 647,300 square miles; to the Atlantic, 488,877; and to the Gulf of Mexico, 1,683,325 square miles, of which 1,234,600 are drained by the Mississippi-Missouri-Red. The chain of the Rocky Mountains separates the western portion of the country from the remainder, communications being carried on over certain elevated passes, several of which are now traversed by railroads and major highways; west of these, bordering the Pacific coast, the Cascade Mountains and Sierra Nevada form the outer edge of a high tableland, consisting in part of stony and sandy desert and partly of grazing land and forested mountains, and including the Great Salt Lake, which extends to the Rocky Mountains. In the Eastern States (which form the more settled and most thickly inhabited portion of the country) large forests of valuable timber, as beech, birch, maple, oak, pine, spruce, elm, ash, walnut; and in the south, live oak, water-oak, magnolia, palmetto, pine, tulip-tree, cypress, etc., still exist, the remnants of the forests which formerly extended over all the Atlantic slope, but into which great inroads have been made by the advance of civilization. The mineral kingdom produces ore of iron, copper, lead, zinc, and aluminium, the non-metallic minerals include large quantities of coal, petroleum, stone, phosphate rock, and salt. The highest point is Mount McKinley (Alaska), 20,320 ft. above sea level and the lowest point of dry land is in Death Valley (Inyo, California), 282 ft. below sea-level.

AREA AND POPULATION

	Area, 1980 (sq. miles)		Population	
	Total	Land	Census 1970	Census 1980
The United States (a)	3,618,770	3,539,289	203,302,031*	226,545,805
Puerto Rico	3,515	3,459	2,712,033	3,196,520
Outlying areas under U.S. jurisdiction	1,176	1,176	314,657*	368,856
Territories	459	459	179,519**	235,927
Guam	209	209	84,996	105,979
Virgin Islands of U.S.	132	132	62,468	96,569
American Samoa	77	77	27,159	32,297
Midway Islands	2	2	2,220	453
Wake Island	3	3	1,647	302
Canton Island and Enderbury Island	27	27	—	—
Johnston Atoll (b)	0·5	0·5	1,007	327
Other (c)	9	9	—	—
Pacific Islands Trust Territory (excluding N. Mariana Is.)	533	533	81,300	116,149
N. Mariana Islands	184	184	9,640	16,780
Population abroad (d)			1,737,836†	995,546
Armed Forces			1,057,776	515,408
Total	3,543,924	3,623,461	208,066,557	231,106,727

(a) The 50 States and the Federal *District of Columbia* (see pp. 927–8).
(b) Formerly listed as Johnston and Sand Island. Sand Island uninhabited at time of enumeration.
(c) Navassa, Baker, Howland and Jarvis Islands, Kingman Reef, and Palmyra Atoll.
(d) Excludes U.S. citizens temporarily abroad on private business.
* Includes population of Swan Islands (22) and Panama Canal Zone (44,198). Jurisdiction over the Swan Islands was transferrred to Honduras in 1972. Due to the 1978 Treaty, the Census is no longer conducted in the Canal Zone.
** Includes population of Swan Islands (22).
† Includes U.S. citizens abroad for long periods who were not connected with the U.S. government (236,336) and crews of U.S. merchant vessels (15,910).

Resident Population by Race 1980
(in thousands)

White 188,372	Filipino .... 774·7	Vietnamese .... 261·7	Puerto Rican . 2,014
Black 26,495	Japanese 701	Spanish origin** 14,609	Other Spanish 3,051
American Indian* ...... 1,420·4	Asian Indian .....361·5	Cuban.......... 803	All other races .. 6,999·2
Chinese 806	Korean........... 354·6	Mexican...... 8,740	Total.... 226,546

*Includes Eskimo and Aleut.
** Persons of Spanish origin may be of any race.

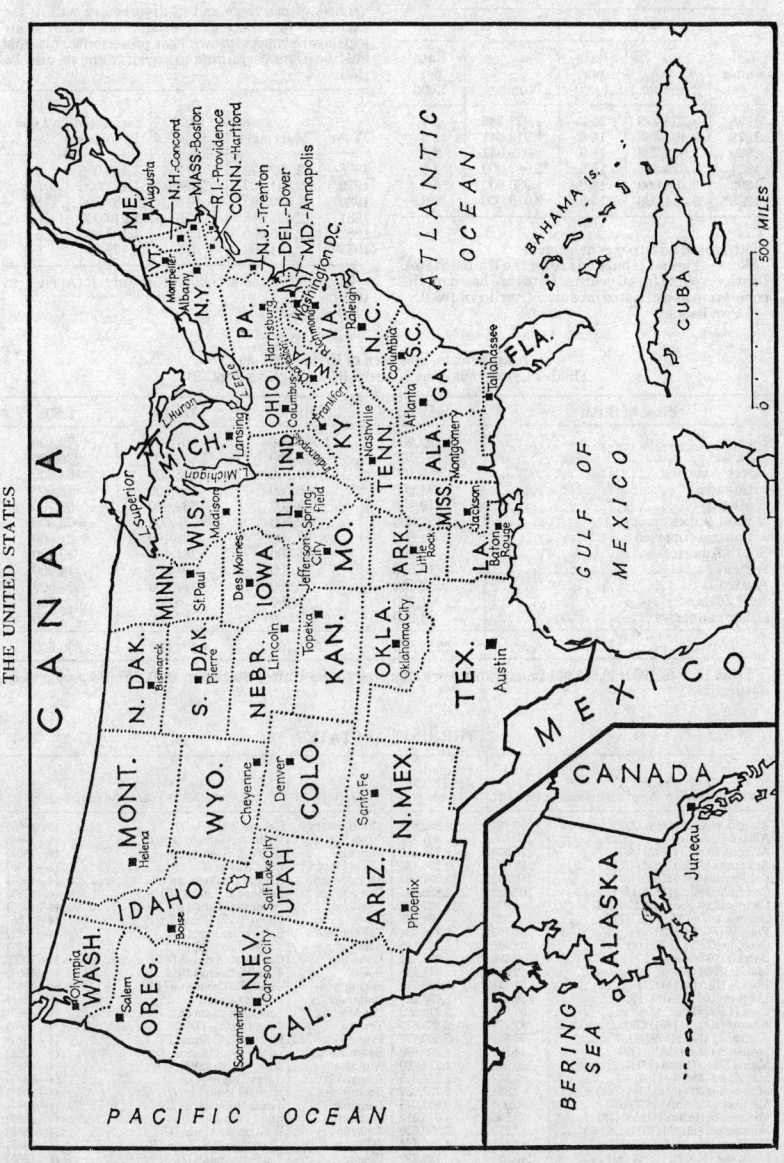

THE UNITED STATES

REGISTERED BIRTHS AND DEATHS

Cal-endar Year	Live Births Number	Live Births Rate per 1,000	Deaths Number	Deaths Rate per 1,000
1978	3,333,279	15·0	1,927,788	8·7
1979	3,494,398	15·6	1,913,841	8·5
1980	3,612,258	15·9	1,989,841	8·8
1981	3,629,238	15·8	*1,987,000	*8·7
1982	3,704,000	16·0	1,986,000	8·6
1983*	3,614,000	15·5	2,010,000	8·6

Births based on 50 per cent. sample.
Note.—Figures tabulated are for the United States. Deaths exclude foetal deaths. Rates are based on the population as estimated on July 1 (April 1 in 1980).
* Provisional.

MARRIAGE AND DIVORCE

Laws of marriage and of divorce are within the exclusive jurisdiction of each State. Each State legislature enacts its own laws prescribing rules and qualifications pertaining to marriage and its dissolution.

Year	Marriages	Per 1,000 Pop.§	Estimated Divorces	Per 1,000 Pop.§
1978	2,282,272	10·3	1,130,000	5·1
1979	2,331,337	10·4	1,181,000	5·3
1980	2,390,252	10·6	1,189,000	5·2
1981	2,422,145	10·6	1,213,000	5·3
1982*	2,495,000	10·8	1,180,000	5·1
1983*	2,444,000	10·5	1,179,000	5·0

§ Population as estimated on July 1 (April 1 in 1980).
* Provisional.

Immigrants, by Place of Birth, 1951–80
(1951–76, year ends June 30: from 1977, year ends Sept. 30)

Place of Birth	1951–60	1961–70	1971–80	1980
Europe	1,492,200	1,238,600	801,300	72,100
Asia	157,100	445,300	1,633,800	236,100
North America	769,100	1,351,100	1,645,000	164,800
Canada	274,900	286,700	114,800	13,600
Mexico	319,300	443,300	637,200	56,700
West Indies	122,800	519,500	759,800	73,300
Central America	44,600	97,700	132,400	21,000
South America	72,200	228,300	284,400	39,700
Africa	16,600	39,300	91,500	14,000
Australia	3,700	9,900	14,300	500
New Zealand	1,300	3,700	5,300	700
Other countries	3,300	5,500	17,700	1,700
TOTAL	2,515,500	3,321,700	4,493,300	530,600

From 1820 to 1980, 49,655,951 immigrants were admitted to the United States: in 1980, 157,938 people were naturalized.

THE UNITED STATES

State (with date and *order* of admission)	Land Area Sq. M.*	Population, April 1, 1980 (census)	Capital	Governor (term of office in years, and expiry year)
Alabama (Ala.) (1819) *(22)*	50,767	3,893,888	Montgomery	George Wallace *(D)* (4—1987)
Alaska (1959) *(49)*	570,833	401,851	Juneau	William Sheffield *(D)* (4—1986)
Arizona (Ariz.) (1912) *(48)*	113,508	2,718,215	Phoenix	Bruce E. Babbit *(D)* (4—1987)
Arkansas (Ark.) (1836) *(25)*	52,078	2,286,435	Little Rock	Bill Clinton *(D)* (2—1985)
California (Cal.) (1850) *(31)*	156,299	23,667,902	Sacramento	George Deukmejian *(R)* (4—1987)
Colorado (Colo.) (1876) *(38)*	103,595	2,889,964	Denver	Richard D. Lamm *(D)* (4—1987)
Connecticut (Conn.)§(1788) *(5)*	4,872	3,107,576	Hartford	William O'Neill *(D)* (4—1987)
Delaware (Del.) § (1787) *(1)*	1,932	594,338	Dover	Pierre S. du Pont IV *(R)* (4—1985)
Florida (Fla.) (1845) *(27)*	54,153	9,746,324	Tallahassee	Robert Graham *(D)* (4—1987)
Georgia (Ga.) § (1788) *(4)*	58,056	5,463,105	Atlanta	Joe F. Harris *(D)* (4—1987)
Hawaii (1959) *(50)*	6,425	964,691	Honolulu	George R. Ariyoshi *(D)* (4—1986)
Idaho (1890) *(43)*	82,412	943,935	Boise	John V. Evans *(D)* (4—1987)
Illinois (Ill.) (1818) *(21)*	55,645	11,426,518	Springfield	James R. Thompson *(R)* (4—1987)
Indiana (Ind.) (1816) *(19)*	35,932	5,490,224	Indianapolis	Robert Orr *(R)* (4—1985)
Iowa (1846) *(29)*	55,965	2,913,808	Des Moines	Terry Branstad *(R)* (4—1987)
Kansas (Kan.) (1861) *(34)*	81,778	2,363,679	Topeka	John Carlin *(D)* (4—1987)
Kentucky (Ky.) (1792) *(15)*	39,669	3,660,777	Frankfort	Martha L. Collins *(D)* (4—1987)
Louisiana (La.) (1812) *(18)*	44,521	4,205,990	Baton Rouge	Edwin W. Edwards *(D)* (4—1988)
Maine (Me.) (1820) *(23)*	30,995	1,124,660	Augusta	Joseph E. Brennan *(D)* (4—1987)
Maryland (Md.)§ (1788) *(7)*	9,837	4,216,975	Annapolis	Harry Hughes *(D)* (4—1987)
Massachusetts (Mass.)§ (1788) *(6)*	7,824	5,737,037	Boston	Michael Dukakis *(D)* (4—1987)
Michigan (Mich.) (1837) *(26)*	56,954	9,262,078	Lansing	James Blanchard *(D)* (4—1987)
Minnesota (Minn.) (1858) *(32)*	79,548	4,075,970	St. Paul	Rudy Perpich *(D)* (4—1987)
Mississippi (Miss.) (1817) *(20)*	47,233	2,250,638	Jackson	William A. Allain *(D)* (4—1988)
Missouri (Mo.) (1821) *(24)*	68,945	4,916,686	Jefferson City	Christopher S. Bond *(R)* (4—1985)
Montana (Mont.) (1889) *(41)*	145,388	786,690	Helena	Ted Schwinden *(D)*. (4—1985)
Nebraska (Nebr.) (1867) *(37)*	76,644	1,569,825	Lincoln	Bob Kerrey *(D)*. (4—1987)
Nevada (Nev.) (1864) *(36)*	109,894	800,493	Carson City	Richard Bryan *(D)* (4—1987)

State (with date and *order* of admission)	Land Area Sq. M.*	Population, April 1, 1980 (census)	Capital	Governor (term of office in years, and expiry year)
New Hampshire (N.H.)§ (1788) *(9)* . . .	8,993	920,610	Concord	John Sununu (R) . . . . (2—1985)
New Jersey (N.J.)§ (1787) *(3)*	7,468	7,364,823	Trenton	Thomas H. Kean (R) . . . . (4—1986)
New Mexico (N. Mex.) (1912) *(47)* . . .	121,335	1,302,894	Santa Fé	Toney Anaya (D) . . . . (4—1987)
New York (N.Y.)§ (1788) *(11)*	47,377	17,558,072	Albany	Mario Cuomo (D) . . . . (4—1987)
North Carolina (N.C.)§ (1789) *(12)* . .	48,843	5,881,766	Raleigh	James B. Hunt Jr. (D) . . . . (4—1985)
North Dakota (N. Dak.) (1889) *(39)* . .	69,300	652,717	Bismarck	Allen Olson (R) . . . . (4—1985)
Ohio (1803) *(17)*	41,004	10,797,630	Columbus	Richard Celeste (D) . . . . (4—1987)
Oklahoma (Okla.) (1907) *(46)*	68,655	3,025,290	Oklahoma City	George Nigh (D) . . . . (4—1987)
Oregon (Oreg.) (1859) *(33)*	96,184	2,633,105	Salem	Victor Atiyeh (R) . . . . (4—1987)
Pennsylvania (Pa.)§ (1787) *(2)*	44,888	11,863,895	Harrisburg . . .	Richard Thornburgh (R) . . . . (4—1987)
Rhode Island (R.I.)§ (1790) *(13)*	1,055	947,154	Providence . . .	J. Joseph Garrahy (D) . . . . (2—1985)
South Carolina (S.C.)§ (1788) *(8)* . . .	30,203	3,121,820	Columbia	Richard Riley (D) . . . . (4—1987)
South Dakota (S. Dak.) (1889) *(40)* . .	75,952	690,768	Pierre	William Janklow (R) . . . . (4—1987)
Tennessee (Tenn.) (1796) *(16)*	41,155	4,591,120	Nashville	Lamar Alexander (R) . . . . (4—1987)
Texas (Tex.) (1845) *(28)*	262,017	14,229,191	Austin	Mark White (D) . . . . (4—1987)
Utah (1896) *(45)*	82,073	1,461,037	Salt Lake City .	Scott M. Matheson (D) . . . . (4—1985)
Vermont (Vt.) (1791) *(14)*	9,273	511,456	Montpelier . . .	Richard A. Snelling (R) . . . . (2—1985)
Virginia (Va.)§ (1788) *(10)*	39,704	5,346,818	Richmond	Charles S. Robb (D) . . . . (4—1986)
Washington (Wash.) (1889) *(42)*	66,511	4,132,156	Olympia	John Spellman (R) . . . . (4—1985)
West Virginia (W. Va.) (1863) *(35)* . .	24,119	1,949,644	Charleston . . .	John D. Rockefeller IV (D) . . . . (4—1985)
Wisconsin (Wis.) (1848) *(30)*	54,426	4,705,767	Madison	Anthony Earl (D) . . . . (4—1987)
Wyoming (Wyo.) (1890) *(44)*	96,989	469,557	Cheyenne	Ed Herschler (D) . . . . (4—1987)
Dist. of Columbia (D.C.) (1791)	63	638,333	. .	†
OUTLYING TERRITORIES AND POSSESSIONS				
Puerto Rico (1899)	3,421	3,196,520	San Juan	Carlos Romero Barceló . . . . (4—1985)
Guam (1899)	209	105,979	Agaña	Ricardo J. Bordallo (D) . . . . (4—1987)
Samoa (1900)	77	32,297	Fagatogo	Peter T. Coleman (R) . . . . (1985)
Virgin Islands (1917)	132	96,569	Charlotte Amalie	Juan Luis (I) . . . . (4—1987)

D.—Democratic Party.   R.—Republican Party.   I.—Independent.   § The 13 Original States.
† The capital territory is governed by Congress through a Commissioner and City Council (*see* p. 931–2).

Largest Cities 1982.

Ψ New York, NY	7,086,096	San Jose, California 659,181
Ψ Los Angeles, California	3,022,247	Memphis, Tennessee 645,760
Ψ Chicago, Illinois	2,997,155	Washington, D.C. 633,425
Ψ Houston, Texas	1,725,617	Ψ Milwaukee, Wisconsin 631,509
Ψ Philadelphia, Pennsylvania	1,665,382	Columbus, Ohio 570,588
Ψ Detroit, Michigan	1,138,717	Ψ New Orleans, Louisiana 564,561
Dallas, Texas	943,848	Ψ Boston, Massachusetts 560,847
Ψ San Diego, California	915,956	Ψ Cleveland, Ohio 558,869
Phoenix, Arizona	824,230	Jacksonville, Florida 556,370
San Antonio, Texas	819,021	Denver, Colorado 505,563
Ψ Baltimore, Maryland	774,113	Ψ Seattle, Washington 490,077
Indianapolis, Indiana	707,655	Nashville-Davidson, Tennessee 455,252
Ψ San Francisco, California	691,637	Ψ Seaport

THE PRESIDENTS OF THE UNITED STATES OF AMERICA

Name (*with Native State*)	Party	Born	Inaug.	Died	Age
1. GEORGE WASHINGTON, *Va*	Fed.	1732, Feb. 22	1789	1799, Dec. 14	67
2. John Adams, *Mass.*	,,	1735, Oct. 30	1797	1826, July 4	90
3. Thomas Jefferson, *Va.*	Rep.	1743, April 13	1801	1826, July 4	83
4. James Madison, *Va.*	,,	1751, Mar. 16	1809	1836, June 28	85
5. James Monroe, *Va.*	,,	1758, April 28	1817	1831, July 4	73
6. John Quincy Adams, *Mass.*	,,	1767, July 11	1825	1848, Feb 23	80
7. Andrew Jackson, *S.C.*	Dem.	1767, Mar. 15	1829	1845, June 8	78
8. Martin Van Buren, *N.Y.*	,,	1782, Dec. 5	1837	1862, July 24	79
9. William Henry Harrison†, *Va.*	Whig.	1773, Feb. 9	1841	1841, April 4	68
10. John Tyler (*a*), *Va.*	,,	1790, Mar. 29	1841	1862, Jan. 17	71
11. James Knox Polk, *N.C.*	Dem.	1795, Nov. 2	1845	1849, June 15	53
12. Zachary Taylor† *Va.*	Whig.	1784, Nov. 24	1849	1850, July 9	65
13. Millard Fillmore (*a*), *N.Y.*	,,	1800, Jan. 7	1850	1874, Mar. 8	74
14. Franklin Pierce, *N.H.*	Dem.	1804, Nov. 23	1853	1869, Oct. 8	64
15. James Buchanan, *Pa.*	,,	1791, April 23	1857	1868, June 1	77
16. Abraham Lincoln†§, *Ky.*	Rep.	1809, Feb. 12	1861	1865, April 15	56
17. Andrew Johnson (*a*), *N.C.*	,,	1808, Dec. 29	1865	1875, July 31	66
18. Ulysses Simpson Grant, *Ohio*	,,	1822, April 27	1869	1885, July 23	63
19. Rutherford Birchard Hayes, *Ohio*	,,	1822, Oct. 4	1877	1893, Jan. 17	70
20. James Abram Garfield†§, *Ohio*	,,	1831, Nov. 19	1881	1881, Sept. 19	49
21. Chester Alan Arthur (*a*), *Vt.*	,,	1830, Oct. 5	1881	1886, Nov. 18	56

Name (*with Native State*)	Party	Born	Inaug.	Died	Age
22. Grover Cleveland, *N.J.*	Dem.	1837, Mar. 18	1885	1908, June 24	71
23. Benjamin Harrison, *Ohio*	Rep.	1833, Aug. 20	1889	1901, Mar. 13	67
Grover Cleveland, *N.J.*	Dem.	1837, Mar. 18	1893	1908, June 24	71
24. William McKinley†§, *Ohio*	Rep.	1843, Jan. 29	1897	1901, Sept. 14	58
25. Theodore Roosevelt (*a*), *N.Y.*	„	1858, Oct. 27	1901	1919, Jan. 6	60
26. William Howard Taft, *Ohio*	„	1857, Sept. 15	1909	1930, Mar. 8	72
27. Woodrow Wilson, *Va.*	Dem.	1856, Dec. 28	1913	1924, Feb. 3	67
28. Warren Gamaliel Harding†, *Ohio*	Rep.	1865, Nov. 2	1921	1923, Aug. 2	57
29. Calvin Coolidge (*a*), *Vt.*	„	1872, July 4	1923	1933, Jan. 5	60
30. Herbert Clark Hoover, *Iowa.*	„	1874, Aug. 10	1929	1964, Oct. 20	90
31. Franklin Delano Roosevelt†‡, *N.Y.*	Dem.	1882, Jan. 30	1933	1945, April 12	63
32. Harry S. Truman (*a*), *Missouri*	„	1884, May 8	1945	1972, Dec. 26	88
33. Dwight David Eisenhower, *Texas*	Rep.	1890, Oct. 14	1953	1969, Mar. 28	78
34. John Fitzgerald Kennedy, *Mass.*†§	Dem.	1917, May 29	1961	1963, Nov. 22	46
35. Lyndon Baines Johnson (*a*), *Texas*	„	1908, Aug. 27	1963	1973, Jan. 22	64
36. Richard Milhous Nixon, *California*	Rep.	1913, Jan. 9	1969	..	..
37. Gerald Rudolph Ford (*a*), *Nebraska*	„	1913, July 14	1974	..	..
38. James Earl Carter, *Georgia*	Dem.	1924, Oct. 1	1977	..	..
39. Ronald Wilson Reagan, *Illinois*	Rep.	1911, Feb. 6	1981	..	..

† Died in office.   § Assassinated.   (*a*) Elected as Vice-President.
‡ Re-elected Nov. 5, 1940, the first case of a third term; re-elected for a fourth term Nov. 7, 1944.

GOVERNMENT

The United States of America is a Federal Republic consisting of 50 States and 1 Federal District (of which 13 are Original States, 7 were admitted without previous organization as Territories, and 30 were admitted after such organization), and of organized Territories. Hawaii formally entered the Union as the 50th State on Aug. 21, 1959, from which date the flag of the United States has 13 stripes and 50 stars in 9 horizontal rows of six and five alternatively. July 4 (Independence Day) is observed as the National Day.

THE CONSTITUTION.—By the Constitution of Sept. 17, 1787 (to which ten amendments were added on Dec. 15, 1791 and eleventh to twenty-sixth, Jan. 8, 1798, Sept. 25, 1804, Dec. 18, 1865, July 28, 1868, March 30, 1870, Feb. 25, 1913, May 31, 1913, Jan. 16, 1920, Aug. 26, 1920, Feb. 6, 1933, Dec. 5, 1933, Feb. 26, 1951, March 29, 1961, Jan. 23, 1964, Feb. 10, 1967 and June 30, 1971), the government of the United States is entrusted to three separate authorities—the Executive, the Legislative, and the Judicial.

THE EXECUTIVE

THE *Executive* power is vested in a President, who is elected every four years, and is eligible for re-election for one additional term. The mode of electing the President is as follows:—Each state appoints, in such manner as the Legislature thereof directs (they are now elected by popular vote on the *first Tuesday after the first Monday in November* of the year preceding the year in which the Presidential term expires), a number of electors, equal to the whole number of Senators and Representatives to which the State may be entitled in the Congress; but no Senator or Representative, or anyone holding office under Government, shall be appointed an elector. The electors for each State meet in their respective States on the *first Monday after the second Wednesday in December* following, and there vote for a President by ballot. The ballots are then sent to Washington, and opened on the *sixth day of January* by the President of Senate in presence of Congress, and the candidate who has received a majority of the whole number of electoral votes cast is declared President for the ensuing term. If no one has a majority, then from the highest on the list (not exceeding three) the House of Representatives elects a President the votes being taken by States, the representation from each State having one vote. There is also a Vice-President, who, on the death of the President, becomes President for the remainder of the term. Under the XXth Amendment to the Constitution the terms of the President and Vice-President end at noon on the 20th day of January of the years in which such terms would have ended if the Amendment had not been ratified, and the terms of their successors then begin. In case of the removal or death of both President and Vice-President, a statute provides for the succession.

The President must be at least 35 years of age and a native citizen of the United States. He receives a taxable salary of $200,000 with a taxable expense allowance of $50,000 and a non-taxable travelling allowance not exceeding $100,000. Under the XXIInd Amendment to the Constitution, the tenure of the Presidency is limited to two terms. Executive duties:—(1) He is Commander-in-Chief of the Army and of the Navy (and of the Militias when they are in Federal service), and he commissions all officers therein. (2) With the consent of the Senate, he appoints the Cabinet officers and all the chief (and many minor) officials. (3) He exercises a general supervision over the whole Federal Administration and sees that the Federal Laws are duly carried out. Should disorder arise in any state which the authorities thereof are unable to suppress, the aid of the President is invoked. (4) He conducts the Foreign policy of the Republic, and has power, "by and with the Advice and Consent of the Senate, to make Treaties, provided two thirds of the senators present concur." The Declaration of War rests with Congress. (5) He makes recommendation of a general nature to Congress, and when laws are passed by Congress he may return them to Congress with a veto. But if a measure so vetoed is again passed by both Houses of Congress by two-thirds majority in each House, it becomes law, notwithstanding the objection of the President.

President of the United States, RONALD WILSON REAGAN, *born* Feb. 6, 1911, *sworn in* January 20, 1981. Republican.
Vice-President, George Herbert Walker Bush, *born* June 12, 1924, *sworn in* Jan. 20, 1981.

THE CABINET

Secretary of State, George Shultz.
Secretary of the Treasury, Donald T. Regan.
Secretary of Defence, Caspar W. Weinberger.
Attorney-General, William F. Smith.
Secretary of the Interior, William P. Clark.
Secretary of Agriculture, John R. Block.
Secretary of Commerce, Malcolm Baldrige.
Secretary of Labour, Raymond J. Donovan.
Secretary of Health and Human Services, Mrs. Margaret M. Heckler.
Secretary of Housing and Urban Development, Samuel R. Pierce, Jr.
Secretary of Transportation, Mrs. Elizabeth Dole.
Secretary of Energy, Donald P. Hodel.
Secretary of Education, Terrel H. Bell.

UNITED STATES EMBASSY
Grosvenor Square W.1
[01-499 9000]

Ambassador Extraordinary and Plenipotentiary, His Excellency Charles H. Price II (1983).
Minister, Hon. Raymond G. H. Seitz.
Minister for Economic and Commercial Affairs, Michael Calingaert.
Counsellors, Robert W. Maule (*Consular Affairs*); Lawrence D. Russell (*Administrative Affairs*); Gerald M. Marks (*Commercial Affairs*); Robert A. Stella (*Scientific Affairs*); Robert J. Korengold (*Public Affairs*); Turner L. Oyloe (*Agricultural Affairs*); Timothy E. Deal (*Economic Affairs*); Ernest Nagy; Richard L. McCormack (*Political Affairs*); Alan D. Wolfe (*Programme Coordinator*).
Defence Attaché, Naval Attaché and Naval Attaché for Air, Col. Alan B. Renshaw.
Army Attaché, Col. George M. Houser.
Air Attaché, Col. Kenneth W. Cordier.

CAPITAL OF THE UNITED STATES

In 1790 Congress ratified the cession of 100 sq. miles by the States of Maryland and Virginia as a site for a Federal City to be the national capital of the United States. In 1791 it was decided to name the capital *Washington* and in 1793 the foundation-stone of the Capitol building was laid. In 1800 the seat of Government was removed to Washington, which was chartered as a city in 1802. In 1846 the Virginia portion was retroceded and the present area of the *District of Columbia* (with which the City of Washington is considered co-extensive) is 63 square miles, with a population of 638,333.

The District of Columbia was formerly governed by a Commissioner and assistant and a 9-member City Council, all appointed by the President. From Nov. 5, 1974, this body has been replaced by an elected mayor and City Council.

The *City of Washington* is situated on the west central edge of Maryland, opposite the State of Virginia, on the left bank of the Potomac at its confluence with the Anacostia.

THE CONGRESS

The Legislative power is vested in two Houses, the Senate and the House of Representatives, the President having a *veto* power, which may be overcome by a two-thirds vote of each House. The Senate is composed of two Senators from each State, elected by the people thereof for the term of six years, and each Senator has one vote; and Representatives are chosen in each State, by popular vote, for two years. The average number of persons represented by each Congressman is 1 for 500,000. The *Senate* consists of 100 members. The salary of a Senator is $72,600 per annum. The *House of Representatives* consists of 435 Representatives, a resident commissioner from Puerto Rico and a delegate from American Samoa, the District of Columbia, Guam and the Virgin Islands. The salary of a Representative is $72,600 per annum. By the XIXth Amendment, sex is no disqualification for the franchise. On Nov. 1, 1980, there were 160,491,000 persons of voting age, excluding members of the armed forces overseas.

THE NINETY-EIGHTH CONGRESS

President of the Senate, George Bush (*Vice President of the United States*).
Speaker of the House of Representatives, Thomas P. O'Neill, Jr., *Massachusetts*.
Secretary of the Senate, William F. Hildenbrand, *Pennsylvania*.
Clerk of the House of Representatives, Benjamin J. Guthrie, *Virginia*.
Members of the 98th Congress were elected on Nov. 2, 1982.

The 98th Congress is constituted as follows:
Senate.—Democrats 45; Republicans, 55; Total, 100.
House of Representatives.—Democrats, 268; Republicans, 166, and 1 vacancy. Total, 435.

THE JUDICATURE

The *Federal Judiciary* consists of three sets of Federal Courts: (1) The *Supreme Court* at Washington, D.C., consisting of a Chief Justice and eight Associate Justices, with original jurisdiction in cases affecting Ambassadors, etc., or where a State is a party to the suit, and with appellate jurisdiction from inferior Federal Courts and from the judgments of the highest Courts of the States. (2) The *United States Courts of Appeals*, dealing with appeals from District Courts and from certain federal administrative agencies, and consisting of all the Circuit Judges within the circuit. (3) The 94 *United States District Courts* served by 516 District Court Judges.

THE SUPREME COURT
(U.S. Supreme Court Building, Washington, D.C.)

Chief Justice, Warren E. Burger *Va., born* Sept. 17, 1907, *appointed* June 23, 1969.

ASSOCIATE JUSTICES

Name	Born	Apptd
William J. Brennan, Jr., *N.J.*	1906	1956
Byron R. White, *Colo.*	1917	1962
Thurgood Marshall, *N.Y.*	1908	1967
Harry Blackmun, *Minn.*	1908	1970
Lewis F. Powell, Jr., *Va.*	1907	1971
William R. Rehnquist, *Ariz.*	1924	1971
John Paul Stevens, *Ill.*	1920	1975
Sandra Day O'Connor, *Ariz.*	1930	1981

Clerk of the Supreme Court, Alexander L. Stevas.

CRIMINAL STATISTICS, U.S.

Crime	No. of offences 1982	1983
Murder and Non-negligent Manslaughter	21,012	19,308
Rape	78,898	78,918
Robbery	546,204	500,221
Aggravated Assault	655,383	639,532
Burglary	3,437,206	3,120,842
Larceny—Theft	7,136,361	6,707,020
Thefts of Motor Vehicles ...	1,058,610	1,004,372
Total................	12,933,674	12,070,213

DEFENCE

Department of Defence

Secretary of Defence (in the Cabinet), Caspar W. Weinberger.
Secretary of the Army, John O. Marsh.
Secretary of the Navy, John Lehman.
Secretary of the Air Force, Verne Orr.
Chairman, Joint Chief of Staff, Gen. John W. Vessey, Jr.

The Department of Defence includes the Secretary of Defence as its head, the Deputy Secretary of Defence, the Defence staff offices, the Joint Chiefs of Staff and the Joint Staff, the three military departments and the military services within those departments, the unified and specified commands, and other Department of Defence agencies as the Secretary of Defence establishes to meet specific requirements. The Defence staff offices and the joint Chiefs of Staff, although separately organized, function in full coordination and cooperation. They include the offices of the Director of Defence Research and Engineering, the Assistant Secretaries of Defence, the General Counsel of the Department of Defence and such other staff offices as the Secretary of Defence may establish. The Joint Chiefs of Staff, as a group, are directly responsible to the Secretary of Defence for the functions assigned to them. Each member of the Joint Chiefs of Staff, other than the Chairman, is responsible for keeping the Secretary of his military department fully informed on matters considered or acted upon by the Joint Chiefs of Staff.

Each military department is separately organized under its own Secretary and functions under the direction, authority and control of the Secretary of Defence.

The Department of Defence maintains and employs armed forces: (1) to support and defend the Constitution of the United States against all enemies, foreign and domestic; (2) to insure, by timely and effective military action, the security of the United States, its possessions, and areas vital to its interests; (3) to uphold and advance the national policies and interest of the United States; and (4) to safeguard the internal security of the United States. All functions in the Department of Defence and its component agencies are performed under the direction, authority and control of the Secretary of Defence.

Commanders of unified and specified commands are responsible to the President and the Secretary of Defence for the accomplishment of military missions assigned to them.

Unified Defence Commands

COMMANDERS-IN-CHIEF

U.S. European Command, Brussels.—Gen. Bernard W. Rogers *(U.S. Army)* (concurrently *N.A.T.O. Supreme Allied Commander).*
U.S. Southern Command, Quarry Heights, Panama Canal Zone.—Lt.-Gen. Paul F. Gorman *(U.S. Army).*
Atlantic, Norfolk, Virginia.—Adm. Wesley L. Mc-

Donald *(U.S. Navy)* (concurrently *N.A.T.O. Supreme Allied Commander, Atlantic).*
Pacific, Hawaii.—Adm. William J. Crowe *(U.S. Navy).*
H.Q., Aerospace Defence Command, Gen. R. T. Herres.
*Strategic Air Command, Omaha.—Gen. Bennie L. Davis *(U.S.A.F.).*
* Military Air Lift Command, Gen. Thomas M. Ryan, Jr. *(U.S.A.F.).*
U.S. Readiness Command, Gen. Wallace H. Nutting *(U.S. Army).*
* U.S. Central Command, Lt.-Gen. Robert C. Kingston *(U.S. Army).*
*Military Sea Lift Command, Vice-Adm. William H. Rowden *(U.S. Navy).*
* A Specified Command.

Army.—The Army of U.S. had a strength on March 31, 1984, of 781,765. Stationed in Germany were four divisions.
Chief of the Staff of the Army, Gen. John A. Wickham, Jr.
Navy.—The strength of the Navy (including Marine Corps) on Sept. 30, 1983 was 557,600 active duty personnel.

The U.S. Navy had in service in 1983, 512 active fleet ships (Strategic Forces, 39; Battle Forces, 421; Support Forces, 43; Mobilization Forces, 9).
Chief of Naval Operations, Adm. James D. Watkins.
Marine Corps.—Established 1775. Strength on Sept. 30, 1983 was 194,100 active duty personnel.
Commandant, Gen. Paul X. Kelley.
Air.—The United States Air Force was established as a separate organization on September 18, 1947. On Sept. 30, 1983, there were 592,046 officers and airmen on active duty, with 251,186 civilian employees. Air Force Reserve and Air National Guard numbered 210,918.

The Air Force has up to 30 per cent of the strategic bomber fleet maintaining constant alert as well as 1,034 inter-continental ballistic missiles in hardened silos. In addition, the Air Force maintains the capability to carry out limited war and special warfare operations. In March, 1961, the Air Force was assigned primary responsibility for the Department of Defence space development programmes and projects. On June 6, 1984, the United States had a total of 1,415 spacecraft in earth or deep space orbits. These included military, other government agency and commercial equipment.
Chief of Staff of the U.S. Air Force, Gen. Charles A. Gabriel.

FINANCE

SOCIAL WELFARE EXPENDITURE

Total expenditure by programme was:

	$ million 1980	1981	1982
Social insurance	229,754	267,363	300,741
Education	121,050	128,146	133,874
Public aid	71,799	82,424	80,786
Health and medical ...	27,657	30,122	32,892
Veterans' programmes	21,466	23,441	24,708
Other social welfare ..	13,599	12,248	11,596
Housing	7,210	6,734	7,954
TOTAL.......	492,534	550,476	592,551

Expenditure per capita was ($):

	1980	1981	1982
Social insurance	995	1,145	1,277
Education	526	551	570
Public aid	312	355	344
Health and medical ...	120	130	140
Veterans' programmes	92	100	104
Other social welfare ..	59	53	49
TOTAL...........	2,137	2,362	2,519

THE UNITED STATES BUDGET
(fiscal year; in millions of dollars)

Receipts by Source	1983 (actual)	1984 (estimated)
Individual income taxes	288,900	293,300
Corporation income taxes	37,000	66,600
Social insurance taxes and contributions	209,000	239,500
Excise taxes	35,300	38,200
Estate and gift taxes	6,100	5,900
Customs duties	8,700	9,100
Miscellaneous	15,600	17,500
Total	600,600	670,100
Outlays by Function		
National defence	210,500	237,500
International affairs	9,000	13,500
General science, space, and technology	7,700	8,300
Energy	4,000	3,500
Natural resources and environment	12,700	12,300
Agriculture	22,200	10,700
Commerce and housing credit	4,400	3,800
Transportation	21,400	26,100
Community and regional development	6,900	7,600
Education, training, employment, and social services	26,600	28,700
Health	28,700	30,700
Social security and medicare	223,300	240,200
Income security	106,200	96,000
Veterans' benefits and services	24,800	25,800
Adminnstration of justice	5,100	6,000
General government	4,800	5,700
General purpose fiscal assistance	6,500	6,700
Interest	89,800	108,200
Undistributed offsetting receipts	−18,600	−17,500
Total	796,000	853,800

PUBLIC DEBT

On Sept. 30, 1982, the total gross *Federal Debt* of the United States stood at $1,147,000 million, an increase of 14·2 per cent on the 1981 figure of $1,003,900 million.

COST OF LIVING IN U.S.A.

The Consumer Price Index (for city wage-earner and clerical workers—single persons and families—in 50 cities representative of all cities in the United States) showed an annual average during the calendar year 1983 of 215·6 (1972 = 100), a rise of 3 per cent over the 1982 figure.

GROSS NATIONAL PRODUCT

Gross National Product by industry in 1982 was ($ million):—

All industries, total	3,073,000
Agriculture, forestry, fisheries	84,300
Mining	116,100
Construction	122,400
Manufacturing	630,900
Transportation	106,000
Communications	85,600
Electric, gas, sanitary services	88,200
Trade	490,200
Finance, insurance, real estate	507,100
Services	431,100
Government enterprises	363,400
Statistical discrepancy	500
Rest of the world	47,300

G.N.P., national and personal income in 1982 were ($ million):—

Gross national product	3,073,000
Net national product	2,713,800
National income	2,450,400
Compensation of employees	1,865,700
Proprietors' income	109,000
Rental income of persons	49,900
Corporate profits	164,800
Net interest	261,100
Personal income	2,578,600
Personal tax and non-tax payments	402,100
Disposable personal income	2,176,500
Personal outlays	2,051,100
Personal saving	125,400

Personal consumption expenditure in 1982 was $1,991,900 million, of which durable goods accounted for $244,500 million, non-durable goods $761,000 million and services $986,400 million. Gross private domestic investment in 1982 was $415,000 million.

UNITED STATES STOCK OF CURRENCY AND COIN

U.S. stock of currency and coin at Sept. 30, 1983 was:—

	$ million
Gold*	11,128·1
Dollars†	2,024·7
Subsidiary Coin	9,938·7
Minor Coin	3,007·6

Silver Certificates§	203·5
U.S. Notes	322·5
Federal Reserve Notes	173,093·2
TOTAL‡	199,789·1

*Held by U.S. Treasury only.

† Figures consist of $481·8 m in standard silver and the balance in cupro-nickel clad dollars.

‡ Totals include value of early issue notes in process of withdrawal, not separately shown. Value, September 1983, $70·8 m.

§ In process of withdrawal. Not redeemable in silver.

AGRICULTURE AND LIVESTOCK

The total number of farms in 1983 (preliminary figure) was 2,370,000, with a total area of land in farms of 1,035 million acres, and an average acreage per farm of 437 acres. The total number of people employed on farms in 1983 was 3,773,000, of whom, 2,250,000 were family members and 1,524,000 hired workers.

Principal crops are corn for grain, soybeans, wheat hay, cotton, tobacco, grain sorghums, rice, potatoes, oats and sugar-beets.

Livestock on farms on Jan. 1, 1983 (*Dec. 1, 1982) (preliminary figures) was:—

	Head
All cattle	115,201,000
Milk cows	11,066,000
Sheep and lambs	11,904,000
Hogs and pigs*	53,230,000
Chickens*	379,000,000
Turkeys*	3,429,000

Gross income from farming in 1982 was $162,200 million, of which cash receipts from marketing were $144,525 million and Government payments $3,500 million. Cash income from all crops in 1982 was $74,326 million and from livestock and livestock products $70,199 million.

NONFUEL MINERALS

The value of nonfuel raw mineral production in the United States in 1983 totalled an estimated $21,200 million compared with $19,700 million in 1982.

Trading Figures

	1981	1982
Imports	$28,800 m	$24,400 m
Exports	$17,600 m	$12,800 m

Production Figures
(*'000 metric tons*)

	1982	1983
Aluminium*	3,609	3,696
Iron Ore†	35,433	37,561
Phosphate rock	37,414	42,573
Zinc	300	275
Refined Copper	1,695	1,613
Lead	1,083	1,018

* measured in short tons
† measured in long tons

ENERGY

Energy Summary

(*Quadrillion (10¹⁵) Btu*)

	1981	1982	1983
Production	64·376	63·851	61·055
Consumption	73·940	70·822	70·515
Imports	13·974	12·110	11·884
Exports	4·331	4·637	3·725

Breakdown of Production and Consumption
(*Quadrillion (10¹⁵) Btu*)

	1982	1983
Production		
Crude Oil	18·309	18·324
Coal	18·603	17·286
Natural Gas (dry)	18·255	16·361
Natural Gas Plant Liquids	2·191	2·202
Hydroelectric	3·271	3·511
Nuclear	3·115	3·235
Other*	0·108	0·135
Total	63·851	61·055
Consumption		
Petroleum	30·232	29·983
Natural Gas (dry)	18·507	17·445
Coal	15·291	15·877
Hydroelectric	3·592	3·857
Nuclear	3·115	3·235
Other*	0·108	0·135
Total	70·822	70·515

* Includes geothermal power and electricity produced from wood and waste.

During 1983 oil and gas drilling rigs in operation averaged 2,232 and the number of well completions totalled 76,329. Seismic exploration work in progress involved a total of 473 crews, 47 in offshore areas and 426 on shore. Domestic crude oil production in 1983 averaged 8,656,000 barrels per day and total petroleum imports averaged 4,988,000 barrels per day, of which 1,832,000 barrels per day came from members of O.P.E.C. Production of dry natural gas in 1983 was 15,915 billion cubic feet (Bcf) and imports were 944 Bcf, supplying 15,416 Bcf required for domestic consumption. Stocks of gas available for withdrawal were estimated at 1,900 Bcf. Production of coal in 1983 was 784,865,000 short tons and imports were 1,271,000 short tons. Domestic consumption required 736,672,000 short tons, and 77,772,000 short tons were exported. In 1983 U.S. nuclear power generators produced 293,677 million net kilowatt-hours of electricity, accounting for 12·6 per cent of domestic electricity generation. Operable reactors at end Dec. 1983 totalled 80, with a maximum dependable capacity of 62·809 million net kilowatts.

LABOUR

Organized Labour.—On December 5, 1955, the American Federation of Labour (AFL), founded in 1881, and the Congress of Industrial Organizations (CIO), formally established in 1938, merged into an organization called the American Federation of Labour and Congress of Industrial Organizations. The combined membership in 1980 was 16,773,000. There are also 7,113,000 members of labour organizations not affiliated to the AFL–CIO. Of the 23,885,000 members of national and international unions with headquarters in U.S.A., 1,534,000 were employed in Canada.

Approximately 23 per cent. of the employed wage and salary workers in the United States are members of labour organizations.

Work Stoppages.—There were 81 stoppages involving 1,000 or more workers in 1983. They resulted in 17,461,000 man-days of idleness, representing 0·8 per cent. of estimated working time of all non-agricultural workers.

Employment and Unemployment.—The civilian labour force (working population) was 113,803,000 in May 1984. This includes self-employed wage and salary-earners, and unpaid family workers, employed and unemployed. Unemployment was estimated at 8,514,000 in May 1984 (7·5 per cent.) (it was 10·1 per cent. in May 1983).

Wages.—In March 1983, gross average weekly earnings in industry ranged from $648·40 per week in malt beverage industry (43·9 hours and $14·77 average hourly earnings) to $112·75 in eating and drinking places (26·1 hours and $4·32 average hourly earnings). The average for all manufacturing was $369·96 compared with $347·71 in March 1983.

On Jan. 1, 1978, the minimum wage set by federal law became $2·65 an hour for most non-agricultural employees subject to the Fair Labour Standards Act. The rate rose to $2·90 an hour on Jan. 1, 1979, $3·10 on Jan. 1, 1980 and $3·35 on Jan. 1, 1981. The law requires at least time and a half of an employee's regular rate of pay for all hours over 40 a week for most covered workers.

The Fair Labour Standards Act covers all employees of certain enterprises having workers engaged in interstate commerce, producing goods for interstate commerce, or handling, selling, or otherwise working on goods or materials that have been moved in or produced for such commerce by any person.

There are certain exemptions from these requirements in specific occupations and industries.

In addition to cash wages, most workers receive some type of "fringe" benefits—the most common forms being paid vacations, and public holidays, various types of retirement plans, insurance and health benefits financed by the employer or by employer and employees jointly.

EXTERNAL TRADE OF THE UNITED STATES

	1982	1983
	\$ million	
General Imports:		
c.i.f. value	254,884·5	269,878·2
customs value	243,951·9	258,047·8
Exports and re-exports:		
f.a.s. value†	212,193·1	200,485·8
Trade balance:		
f.a.s. exports: c.i.f. imports	− 42,691·4	− 69,392·4
f.a.s. exports: customs imports	− 31,758·8	− 57,562·0

†Excluding military aid.

EXPORTS BY PRINCIPAL COMMODITIES OF DOMESTIC ORIGIN, 1983

Commodity	Value
	\$ (million)
Food and Live Animals	24,166·0
Grain and cereal preparations	15,152·3
Beverages and Tobacco	2,813·0
Crude materials (inedible) except fuel .	18,596·0
Raw cotton	1,817·1
Metal ores, concentrates, scrap	2,275·8
Mineral fuels, lubricants, etc.	9,499·9
Coal (bituminous)	4,007·7
Petroleum and products............	4,557·4
Oils and Fats (animal and vegetable) ..	1,459·0
Chemicals and products	19,750·9
Machinery and Transport Equipment .	82,577·8
Electronic computers, parts, etc.	5,750·3
Electrical machinery, appliances, etc.	11,935·7
Motor vehicles and parts	14,462·8
Other Manufactured Goods	30,097·8
Unclassified Commodities	7,009·0

U.S. IMPORTS BY PRINCIPAL COMMODITIES, 1983

Commodity	Value
	\$ (million)
Food and Live Animals	14,452·7
Fish and fish preparations..........	3,594·2
Vegetables and fruit	2,919·9
Coffee–crude......................	2,590·4
Beverages and Tobacco	3,407·6
Crude materials (inedible), except fuels	9,590·1
Mineral fuels, lubricants, etc.	57,952·2
Crude petroleum	36,809·1
Petroleum products	15,516·1
Oils and Fats (animal and vegetable) ..	495·0
Chemicals and products	10,779·4
Machinery and Transport Equipment .	86,131·1
Telecommunications, sound recording apparatus	11,278·1
Electrical machinery, parts.........	12,498·5
Motor vehicles	28,735·6
Other Manufactured Goods	66,538·9
Unclassified Commodities	7,741·8

U.S. FOREIGN TRADE BY ECONOMIC CLASS 1983

Class	Imports	Exports*
	\$ million	
Crude Materials...	48,293	15,817
Crude Foodstuffs ..	7,664	8,969
Manufactured Foods	10,549	11,936
Semi-manufactures	39,797	37,059
Finished Manufactures...	151,745	122,188
Total.........	258,048	195,969

*Excluding the total military grant-aid of $195,918 million.

U.S. FOREIGN TRADE BY PRINCIPAL AREAS AND COUNTRIES, 1983

Area/Country	Exports and Re-exports to	General Imports from
	\$ million	
Africa..................	8,767·7	14,424·6
Asia	63,813·4	91,463·5
Japan	21,894·3	41,183·2
Saudi Arabia	7,903·3	3,627·4
Taiwan	4,666·8	11,204·2
Korea, Rep. of	5,924·9	7,147·8
Hong Kong	2,563·5	6,393·7
Oceania	4,826·5	3,043·5
Australia	3,954·3	2,222·4
Europe	58,871·0	55,243·0
Germany, West	8,736·7	12,695·3
U.K.	10,621·2	12,469·6
Other E.E.C.	24,952·9	18,727·3
Other O.E.C.D.	10,949·9	9,576·0
Communist bloc	2,890·7	1,358·6
N. & Central America....	53,450·1	77,880·5
Canada	38,244·1	52,129·7
Mexico	9,081·6	16,776·1
S. America	10,520·0	15,991·9

COMMUNICATIONS

RAILWAYS

Data on Class I line-haul railroads (*dollars in thousands*)

	1981	1982
Operating Revenues		
Freight	28,766,575	25,482,144
Passenger	534,227	571,047
Total.......	30,733,921	27,352,867
Total operating expenses	28,475,945	26,389,034
Net working capital	1,683,160	1,366,377
Average number of employees	436,397	378,906

ROADS

In 1982 there were 3·87 million miles of public roads and streets in the United States, of which 3·23 million miles were in rural areas and 641,000 miles were in urban areas. Surfaced roads and streets account for 3·40 million miles, or 87·9 per cent, of the total; 467,000 miles, or 12·1 per cent, were unimproved or graded and drained. State controlled roads total 928,056 miles, locally controlled roads total 2,676,162 miles, and federally controlled roads (in national forests and parks) total 262,078 miles.

An estimated total of $41,281 million was spent in 1982 for roads and streets in the United States. Of this total $23,916 million was spent for State highways, $6,895 million was spent for county and local rural roads, $9,250 million was spent for city streets and $1,220 million was spent on roads in Federal areas. Capital outlay accounts for 47·2 per cent of the total expenditure; 31·0 per cent was spent for maintenance, and 8·0 per cent for administration; 9·5 per cent for highway police and safety; and 4·3 per cent for interest on highway bonds.

Motor Vehicles and Taxation.—The number of motor vehicles registered in 1982 in the United States was 159,509,825, an increase of 0·7 per cent over the 1981 total of 158,456,511. In 1982 the State governments received $17,095,524,000 in State Highway-User Tax Receipts, including road and crossing tolls, and $8,325,658,000 in Federal Highway-User Tax Receipts.

Accidents.—In 1982 there were 43,846 deaths caused by motor vehicle accidents. The death rate per 100,000,000 vehicle-miles of travel was 2·75 in 1982 compared with 3·18 in 1981.

SHIPPING

The ocean-going Merchant Marine of the U.S. on June 1, 1984, consisted of 767 vessels of 1,000 gross tons and over, of which 520 were privately owned and 247 were government-owned ships. Of the 520 privately owned vessels, 409 were active including 5 combination passenger and cargo ships, 52 freighters, 19 bulk carriers, 195 tankers, 18 tug-barge units, 8 liquefied natural gas carriers and 112 intermodal ships. There were 220 ships in the National Defense Reserve Fleet of inactive government-owned vessels, of which 9 were to be sold for scrap.

AIR TRANSPORT

United States domestic and international scheduled airlines in 1983 carried 317,716,000 passengers over 281,393,000 revenue passenger miles. The freight flown by the scheduled airlines during 1983 totalled 6,030,259,000 ton miles and express 60,725,000 ton miles. In addition, the airlines flew 1,476,905,000 ton miles of mail, an increase of 5·5 per cent over 1982.

Total operating revenues of all U.S. scheduled airlines were $38,303,518,000 in 1983, an increase of 5·4 per cent from 1982.

Total operating expenses rose to a record high total of $37,913,351,000 in 1983, or a 2·2 per cent increase over 1982. Scheduled operations showed a net operating profit of $390,168,000 in 1983, compared to a net operating loss of $750,489,000 in 1982.

Three principal classes of commercial air carriers have been established in the United States based on size. They are: Majors, with annual operating revenues of over $1,000 million; Nationals, with annual operating revenues of $75–1,000 million; and Regionals, with annual operating revenues of up to $75,999,000.

U.S. SCHEDULED AIRLINE INDUSTRY STATISTICS, 1983 (Thousands)

	Majors	Nationals	Regionals	System
Revenue Passenger Carried	243,951	57,132	16,633	317,716
Revenue Passengers Miles	241,531	30,058	9,804	281,393
Air Mail Ton Miles	1,292,612	175,174	9,119	1,476,905
Express Ton Miles	59,057	1,647	51	60,725
Freight Ton Miles	3,736,308	2,140,168	153,783	6,030,259
Revenue Ton Miles	29,241,081	5,332,751	1,143,342	35,707,174
Revenue Plane Miles	2,242,247	414,439	142,071	2,798,757

EDUCATION
State School Systems

All the 50 States and the District of Columbia have compulsory school attendance laws. In general, children are obliged to attend school from 7 to 16 years of age. Officers of local administrative units, usually known as truant or attendance officers, are charged with enforcing the compulsory attendance laws.

In the autumn of 1982, 44,200,000 children were enrolled in regular elementary and secondary day schools in the United States, of whom 5·1 million or 11·5 per cent attended private schools.

The following percentages of the school-age population were estimated to be enrolled in school in the autumn of 1982; of 5- and 6-year-olds, 94 per cent; of 7- to 13-year-olds, 99 per cent; of 14- to 17-year-olds, 94 per cent; and of 18- to 24-year-olds, 30 per cent.

Data for the 1982–83 school year for public elementary and secondary regular day schools were as follows: enrolment of 39,643,476; 2,118,963 classroom teachers with an average salary of $20,715.

During the 1982–83 school year, the average daily attendance in regular public elementary and secondary day schools was 36,722,567. In the 1981–82 academic year 2,711,195 students graduated from regular public high schools, 290,000 graduated from private high school. In addition 25,000 graduated from evening schools and adult education programmes, and 490,000 received high school equivalency certificates.

Revenue for public elementary and secondary school purposes comes from the Federal, State, and local governments, sales of bonds, real property and equipment, loans and proceeds from insurance adjustments. Estimated revenue receipts from Government sources during 1982–83 amounted to $120,432,748,000; 6·8 per cent from the Federal Government, 48·4 per cent from State governments, and 44·8 per cent from local governments. Estimated current expenditure in the 1982–83 school year was $108,106,190,000, including $6,527,934,000 for sites, buildings, furniture and equipment expenditures, and $2,406,230,000 for interest on school debt.

Institutions of Higher Education

In the autumn of 1983, total enrolment in universities, colleges, professional schools, and two-year schools numbered 12,377,000.

Degrees conferred during the academic year 1981–82 were:—

Degree	
Bachelor's	952,998
Male	473,364
Female	479,634
First-Profession	72,032
Male	52,223
Female	19,809
Master's	295,546
Male	145,532
Female	150,014
Doctorates	32,707
Male	22,224
Female	10,483

The major fields for bachelor's degrees were business and management (215,817), education (101,063) and social sciences (99,898). First-profession degrees in law (35,991) and medicine (15,814) predominated. Master's degrees were heavily concentrated in education (93,104) and business and management (61,428). The most popular fields of study for doctorates were education (7,676) and social sciences (3,065).

During the 1983–84 academic year, the 3,284 colleges and universities employed about 551,000 (full-time equivalent) instructional faculty. Current-fund expenditures for colleges and universities during the 1981–82 academic year were $70,339,448,000.

Particulars of some of the Universities (with opening autumn enrolment figures, 1982) are: *Harvard* (21,252 students, including 8,274 women), founded at Cambridge, Mass. on Oct. 28, 1636, and named after John Harvard of Emmanuel College, Cambridge, England, who bequeathed to it his library and a sum of money in 1638; *Yale* (10,280 students, including 4,283 women), founded at New Haven, Connecticut, in 1701; *Bowdoin*, Brunswick, Me. (founded 1794; 1,373 students); *Brown*, Providence, R.I. (founded 1764; 6,914 students, including 3,241 women); *Columbia*, New York, N.Y. (founded 1754; 23,883 students, including 11,868 women); *Cornell* (founded at Ithaca, N.Y., 1865; 19,313 students, including 8,230 women); *Dartmouth*, Hanover, N.H. (founded 1769, 4,377 students, including 1,521 women); *Georgetown*, Washington, D.C. (founded 1789; 12,229 students, including 5,359 women); *North Carolina*, Chapel Hill, N.C. (founded in 1789; 21,612 students, including 11,756 women); *Pennsylvania*, Philadelphia, Pa. (founded 1740; 22,246 students, including 9,653 women); *Princeton*, N.J. (founded 1746; 6,088 students and 2,185 women); and *William and Mary*, Williamsburg, Va. (founded 1693; 6,520 students, including 3,345 women).

WEIGHTS AND MEASURES

The weights and measures in common use in the United States are of British origin, and date back to the American Revolution when practically all the standards were intended to be equivalent to those used in England at that period. Divergencies in these weights and measures were, however, quite common, due no doubt to the fact that the system of weights and measures in England was not itself well established, and hence the copies brought to the United States were often adjusted to different standards. Because of these discrepancies, the system of weights and measures in the United States (U.S. Customary System) is not identical with the British system.

The U.S. ton (short) = 2,000 pounds (British Imperial ton = 2,240 pounds, or 1 U.S. long ton). The U.S. gallon = 231 cubic inches (277·42 cubic inches in U.K.) or 128 fluid ounces (160 fluid ounces in U.K.). In the British system the units of dry measure are the same as those of liquid measure. In the United States these two are not the same, the gallon and its subdivisions being used in the measurement of liquids, while the bushel, with its subdivisions, is used in the measurement of certain dry commodities. The U.S. gallon is divided into 4 liquid quarts and the U.S. bushel into 32 dry quarts.

In 1971, a study recommended a concerted, co-ordinated, but voluntary national effort to make the SI the predominant form of measurement in the United States. In December 1975, legislation was passed which established the United States Metric Board to coordinate voluntary conversion to the metric system.

The International System of Units—officially abbreviated SI—is a modernized version of the metric system. It was established by international agreement to provide a logical and interconnected framework for all measurements in science, industry and commerce.

TERRITORIES, ETC. OF THE UNITED STATES

The territories and the principal islands and island groups under the sovereignty of the United States of America comprise the Commonwealth of Puerto Rico, the Commonwealth of the Northern Mariana Islands, and the following territories: Guam; American Samoa; U.S. Virgin Islands; Jarvis Island, Palmyra Island and Kingman Reef; Johnston Atoll; Midway Islands; Wake Islands.

Jarvis Island, Palmyra Island and Kingman Reef are uninhabited islands in the Line Island group. Johnston Atoll (formerly Johnston and Sand Islands) comprises two small islands, less than 1 sq. mile in area, to the south-west of Hawaii which are administered by the U.S. Air Force. The two Midway Islands (area, 2 sq. miles; population (1970), 2,200), at the western end of the Hawaiin chain, are administered by the U.S. Navy. The Wake Islands have an area of about 3 sq. miles and a population (1979) of 300. They lie about 2,300 miles west of Hawaii and are administered by the U.S. Air Force.

Under the terms of a Treaty of Friendship between the United States and Kiribati, signed in 1979 and subsequently ratified by the U.S. Senate, the United States renounced its claim to Canton and Enderbury Islands.

There are certain small guano islands, rocks, or keys which, in pursuance of action taken under the Act of Congress, August 18, 1856, subsequently embodied in Sections 5570–5578 of the Revised Statutes are considered as appertaining to the United States. Responsibility for territorial affairs generally is centred in the Office of the Assistant Secretary, Territorial and International Affairs, Dept. of the Interior, Washington, D.C. Puerto Rico was removed from the Department of the Interior's administrative jurisdiction with the acquisition of Commonwealth status in 1952.

The Trust Territory of the Pacific Islands is under the jurisdiction of the United States pursuant to a trusteeship agreement between the U.S. Government and the Security Council of the United Nations. It consists of the Mariana (except Guam), Caroline and Marshall Islands: the Northern Mariana Islands voted in 1975 to become a Commonwealth of the U.S. but this status will not come fully into effect until the trusteeship agreement is terminated.

As a result of the Panama Canal Treaty of 1977 the Canal Zone was placed under Panamanian jurisdiction. The Panama Canal Commission, an arm of the U.S. Government, will continue to operate the canal until the year 2000.

THE COMMONWEALTH OF PUERTO RICO

Puerto Rico (Rich Port) is an island of the Greater Antilles group in the West Indies, and lies between 17° 50′–18° 30′ N. lat. and 65° 30′–67° 15′ W. long., with a total area of 3,459 square miles and a population (1980) of 3,196,520. The majority of the inhabitants are of Spanish descent and Spanish and English are the official languages. The island is about 111 miles from west to east, and 36 miles from north to south. The capital is 1,600 miles distant from New York, and 1,000 miles from Miami.

Puerto Rico was discovered in 1493 by Christopher Columbus and explored by Ponce de León in 1508. It continued a Spanish possession until Oct. 18, 1898, when the United States took formal possession as a result of the Spanish-American War. It was ceded by Spain to the United States by the Treaty ratified on April 11, 1899.

The Constitution approved by the Congress and the President of the United States, which came into force on July 25, 1952, establishes the Commonwealth of Puerto Rico with full powers of local government. Legislative functions are vested in the Legislative Assembly, which consists of 2 elected houses; the Senate of 27 members (2 from each of 8 senatorial districts and 11 at large) and the House of Representatives of 51 members (1 from each of 40 representative districts and 11 at large). Membership of each house may be increased slightly to accommodate minority representatives. The term of the Legislative Assembly is 4 years. The selection of the Secretary of State must be approved also by the House of Representatives.

The Governor is popularly elected for a term of 4 years. A Supreme Court of 7 members is appointed by the Governor, with the advice and consent of the Senate. The Governor appoints all Judges. Residents of Puerto Rico are U.S. citizens. Puerto Rico is represented in Congress by a Resident Commissioner, elected for a term of 4 years, who has a seat in the House of Representatives, but not a vote, although he has a right to vote on those committees of which he is a member.

Preliminary 1982 figures for the Commonwealth Government's budget were Receipts, $4,690 million (of which $1,165 million were transfers from the Federal Government) and Expenditures, $3,909 million (including payments of $130 million to the Federal Government). Manufacturing added $5,262 million to net Commonwealth income in 1982 (preliminary figures), trade $1,732 million, finance, insurance

and real estate $1,521 million and agriculture $358 million. Principal crops are sugar cane, coffee, vegetables, fruits and tobacco. Most valuable areas of manufacturing are chemicals and allied products, metal products and machinery. Public and private schools are established throughout—enrolment in 1981 was 910,300. Enrolment in the public and private universities for 1981 was 131,900.

CAPITAL.—ΨSan Juan, population of the municipality, 518,700; Other major towns are: ΨPonce (188,500); Bayamón (205,800); ΨMayagüez (99,800); and ΨArecibo (83,300).

Governor, Carlos Romero Barceló.
Secretary of State, Carlos S. Quirós.
Resident Commissioner, Baltasar Corrada del Rio.
Chief Justice, José Trias Monge.

TRADE

	1981	1982
Total Imports	$9,329 m.	$8,167 m.
Total Exports	7,047 m.	8,888 m.

Trade with U.K.

	1983
Imports from U.K.	£35,936,000
Exports to U.K.	58,804,000

GUAM

Guam, the largest of the Ladrone or Mariana Islands in the North Pacific Ocean, lies in 13° 26′ N. lat. and 144° 39′ E. long., at a distance of about 1,506 miles east of Manila. The area of the island is estimated at 209 square miles, with a population (1980) of 105,979.

The Guamanians are of Chamorro stock mingled with Filipino and Spanish blood. The Chamorro language belongs to the Malayo-Polynesian family, but has had considerable admixture of Spanish. English is the language used throughout the island, although Chamorro is also used in Guamanian homes.

Guam was occupied by Japanese in Dec. 1941 but was recaptured and occupied throughout by U.S. forces before the end of August, 1944. Under the Organic Act of Guam of August 1, 1950 (Public Law 630 of the 81st Congress), Guam has statutory powers of self-government, and Guamanians are United States citizens. A 21-member unicameral legislature is elected biennially. The Governor and Lieutenant Governor are popularly elected. A non-voting Delegate is elected to serve in the U.S. House of Representatives. There is also a District Court of Guam, with original jurisdiction in cases under federal law.

CAPITAL, Agaña. Port of entry, ΨApra.

Governor, Ricardo J. Bordallo, *elected* Nov. 1982.
Lt. Governor, Edward D. Reyes, *elected* Nov. 1982.

AMERICAN SAMOA

American Samoa consists of the island of Tutuila, Aunu'u, Ofu, Olosega, Ta'u, Rose and Swains Islands, with a total area of 76·5 square miles and a population of 32,297 in 1980.

Tutuila, the largest of the group, has an area of 52 square miles and contains a magnificient harbour at ΨPago Pago. The remaining islands have an area of about 24 square miles. Tuna and copra are the chief exports.

American Samoans are U.S. nationals, but some have acquired citizenship through service in the United States armed forces or other naturalization procedure.

The 1960 Constitution grants American Samoa a measure of self-government, with certain powers reserved to the U.S. Secretary of the Interior. There is a bicameral legislature with popularly elected Representatives and Governors, and a popularly-elected Governor. A non-voting Delegate is elected to serve in the U.S. House of Representatives.

The constitution of American Samoa designates the village of Fagatogo as the seat of government.

Governor, Peter Tali Coleman.
Lt.-Governor, Tufele Li'e.

VIRGIN ISLANDS

Purchased by the United States from Denmark for the sum of $25 million, and proclaimed, January 25, 1917. The total area of the islands is 132 sq. miles, with a population (1980) of 96,569. There are three main islands, *St. Thomas* (28 sq. miles), *St. Croix* (84 sq. miles), *St. John* (20 sq. miles) and about 50 small islets or cays, mostly uninhabited.

The government of the Virgin Islands is organized under the provisions of the Revised Organic Act of the Virgin Islands, enacted by the Congress of the United States on July 22, 1954. Legislative power is vested in the Legislature of the Virgin Islands, a unicameral body composed of 15 senators popularly elected for two-year terms. Virgin Islanders are citizens of the United States. From the elections of November, 1970, the Governor has been popularly elected. A non-voting Delegate is elected to serve in the U.S. House of Representatives. The Virgin Islands are now a favourite tourist area in the Caribbean. The climate of the islands is delightful at all times, and particularly so during the winter months.

CAPITAL, ΨCharlotte Amalie on St. Thomas.

Governor, Juan F. Luis.
Lt.-Governor, Julio Bradley.

TRUST TERRITORY OF THE PACIFIC ISLANDS

The Trust Territory of the Pacific Islands consists of the Mariana (excluding Guam), Caroline and Marshall Islands which extend from latitude 1° to 20° N. and from longitude 130° to 172° E. They cover an ocean area of 3,000,000 square miles but have a total land area of only 687 square miles. There are 96 separate islands and island groups in the Trust Territory. The population in 1980 was 116,662 (excluding the Northern Mariana Islands). The inhabitants of the Trust Territory are broadly classed as Micronesians. The native cultures vary considerably among island groups and even more among islands and atolls in the same geographic area. Nine different languages are spoken in the territory. Copra is the principal export.

The Trust Territory is administered by the United States pursuant to a Trusteeship Agreement with the Security Council of the United Nations of July 18, 1947, administration being under the general jurisdiction of the Secretary of the Interior.

The Trust Territory has been divided into three separate and distinct governments (*see* below for Northern Mariana Islands). In May, 1979, duly constituted governments were inaugurated in the Marshall Islands and the Federated States of Micronesia (comprising Yap, Truk, Ponape and Kosrae), and in January, 1981 a constitutional government was established in Palau. A future political relationship between these governments and the United States, known as Free Association, is currently being negotiated. This relationship, detailed in the Compact of Free Association, must be approved by the people of the Trust Territory, the U.S. Congress and

the United Nations. The Trusteeship Agreement will be terminated upon the Compact's approval.

CAPITAL.—Saipan, Mariana Islands.

High Commissioner, Janet J. McCoy.
President of Palau, Harno I. Remeliik.
President of the Federated States of Micronesia, Tosiwo Nakayama.
President of the Marshall Islands, Amata Kabua.

NORTHERN MARIANA ISLANDS

The land area of the Northern Mariana Islands is 184 sq. miles with a population (1980) of 16,780.

A law enacted by Congress on March 24, 1976 provides a Covenant to establish a Commonwealth of the Northern Mariana Islands. The provisions of the Covenant will become fully effective upon termination of the Trusteeship Agreement. In the transition period, however, many aspects of the U.S. Constitution and many Federal laws have been extended to the Northern Mariana Islands. There is popularly elected bicameral legislature and popularly elected Governor.

Governor, Pedro P. Tenorio.
Lt.-Governor, Pedro A. Tenario.

THE PANAMA CANAL

With effect from October 1, 1979 the Canal Zone was disestablished, with all areas of land and water within the former Canal Zone reverting to Panama. By treaty, the United States is allowed the use of operating areas for the Panama Canal, together with several military bases, although the Republic of Panama is sovereign in all such areas.

OCEAN GOING COMMERCIAL TRAFFIC

Fiscal Year	No. of Transits	Canal, Net Tons	Cargo Tons
1979	12,935	167,470,601	154,110,866
1980	13,507	182,063,175	167,214,955
1981	13,884	188,656,491	171,221,762
1982	14,009	202,884,207	185,452,332
1983	11,707	169,503,918	145,590,759

The canal is fifty statute miles long (44·08 nautical miles), and the channel is from 500 to 1,000 feet wide at the bottom. It contains 12 locks in twin flights; 3 steps at Gatun on the Atlantic side, 1 step at Pedro Miguel and 2 at Miraflores on the Pacific side. Each lock chamber is 1,000 feet long and 110 feet wide. Transit from sea to sea takes on average 8 to 10 hours. The least width is in Gaillard Cut, and the greatest in Gatun Lake.

BRITISH EMBASSY
3100 Massachusetts Avenue, N.W.
Washington, D.C. 20008

Ambassador Extraordinary and Plenipotentiary, His Excellency Sir (John) Oliver Wright, G.C.M.G., G.C.V.O., D.S.C. (1982).
Ministers, D. M. D. Thomas; N. L. Wicks, C.B.E. (*Economic*); Dr. J. E. Green (*Defence Equipment*); R. Q. Braithwaite (*Commercial*).
Head of British Defence Staff and Defence Attaché, Maj. Gen. T. A. Boam.
Naval Attaché, Rear Adm. N. R. D. King.
Military Attaché, Brig. S. R. Stopford.
Air Attaché, Air Cdre. L. Swart.
Counsellors and Attachés, J. O. Kerr (*Head of Chancery*); D. V. Morris (*Admin. and H.M. Consul-General*); H. G. Walsh (*Economic*); T. G. Harris

(*Commercial*); R. G. M. Manning (*Overseas Development*); M. A. Goodfellow (*Hong Kong Commercial Affairs*); R. P. Maynard (*Civil Aviation and Shipping*); P. A. Escritt (*Civil Aviation Air Traffic Systems*); Dr. A. R. Cox (*Science and Technology*); B. Hampton (*Energy*); Dr. J. Gaunt (*Atomic Energy*); R. J. Harding (*Defence Supply*); J. France (*Technical Works Group*); R. J. Priestley (*Defence Supply*); V. G. Munns (*Labour*); Dr. J. Russell (*Defence Equipment*); H. G. Williams (*Defence Equipment*); Dr. D. F. Downing (*Defence Equipment*); H. G. T. P. Rissone (*Defence Equipment*); R. A. Burns (*Information*); A. F. Green; N. C. C. Girardot; A. W. Parsons; A. W. Saunders; M. E. Pellow; A. C. M. De Vere.

1st Secretaries, P. R. Jenkins (*Private Secretary to H.M. Ambassador*); Mrs. V. E. M. Hartles, M.B.E. (*Administration*); J. J. M. Exeter (*Economic*); N. F. Date, O.B.E., T. N. Young; R. Shaw (*Commercial*); Miss S. E. Brown (*Agricultural and Commercial*); Mrs. E. Mok (*Hong Kong Commercial Affairs*); R. A. Allan (*Civil Aviation and Shipping*); Dr. M. G. Norton (*Science*); Dr. R. S. Baxter (*Technology*); P. J. Bacon (*Energy*); C. V. Anson, M.V.O. (*Information*); C. G. Patterson (*Accountant*); N. D. Duckett; M. E. Flint; A. F. Goulty; S. Band; A. Robinson; S. J. Gomersall; R. O. L. Fraser Darling; C. M. R. Woodley; N. E. Sheinwald; D. E. Tarling.

Cultural Attaché and British Council Representative, H. R. Crooke, O.B.E.

Assistant Cultural Attaché, J. H. Thompson.

There are British Consulates in Atlanta, Chicago, Houston, Los Angeles, New York and San Francisco.

UPPER VOLTA
(République de Haute Volta)

Head of State, Minister of the Interior and of Security, Capt. Thomas Sankara, assumed office, Aug. 1983.

Upper Volta is an inland savannah state in West Africa, situated between 9° and 15°N. and 2°E. and 5°W. with an area of about 100,000 square miles and a population estimated in 1979 at 6,600,000. It has common boundaries with Mali on the west, Niger and Benin on the east and Togo, Ghana and the Ivory Coast on the south. The largest tribe is the Mossi whose king, the Moro Naba, still wields a certain moral influence.

Upper Volta was annexed by France in 1896 and between 1932 and 1947 was administered as part of the Colony of the Ivory Coast. It decided on December 11, 1958, to remain an autonomous republic within the French Community; full independence outside the Community was proclaimed on August 5, 1960. The official language is French.

The 1960 constitution provided for a presidential form of government with a single chamber National Assembly, but in January, 1966, the Army assumed power. A new constitution allowing for a partial return to civilian rule but with the Army still in effective control was adopted in 1970, but in 1974 this was suspended. Full legislative and presidential elections were held again in 1978. In a military *coup* in Nov. 1980, Col. Zerbo assumed power. He was overthrown in Nov. 1982 by Maj. Ouedraogo, who was himself overthrown in Aug. 1983 by radical Army officers led by Capt. Sankara.

In Aug. 1984, Upper Volta changed its name to Burkina Faso (Popular and Democratic Republic of Burkina).

Finance and Trade.—The currency of the Republic is the *Franc CFA* (*Francs CFA* 50 = 1 *French Franc*). The 1983 Budget totalled *Francs CFA* 57,940 million.

The principal industry is the rearing of cattle and sheep and the chief exports are livestock, groundnuts, shea-nuts and cotton. Small deposits of gold, manganese, copper, bauxite and graphite have been found.

Trade with U.K.

	1982	1983
Imports from U.K.	£2,166,000	£3,048,000
Exports to U.K.	1,289,000	1,514,000

CAPITAL.—Ouagadougou (200,000). Other principal towns; Bobo-Dioulasso (90,000) and Kouddougou (35,000).

NATIONAL DAY.—December 11.

BRITISH REPRESENTATION

British Ambassador (*resident in Abidjan*, Ivory Coast).

URUGUAY
(República Oriental del Uruguay)

President, General Gregorio Alvarez (1981).

CABINET

Minister of Interior, Gen. Julio C. Rapela.
Foreign Affairs, Dr. Carlos Alberto Maeso.
Economy and Finance, Ing. Alejandro Végh Villegas.
Transport and Public Works, Ing. Francisco Tourreilles.
Public Health, Cr. Luis A. Givogre.
Labour and Social Security, Col. Dr. Néstor J. Bolentini.
Agriculture and Fisheries, Sr. Carlos Mattos Moglia.
Education and Culture, Dr. Juan Bautista Schroeder Otero.
National Defence, Dr. Justo Alonso Leguisamo.
Industry and Energy, Esc. Filiberto Ginzo Gil.
Justice, Dr. Enrique V. Frigerio.
Secretariat of Planning, Co-ordination and Information, Gen. Pedro Aranco.

URUGUAYAN EMBASSY AND CONSULATE
48 Lennox Gardens, SW1X 0DL
[01–589 8835]

Ambassador Extraordinary and Plenipotentiary, His Excellency Dr. Luis M. de Posadas.
Minister, Dr. José Luis Bruno.
1st Secretary, Dr. Alberto Fajardo.
Financial Attaché, Sr. Miguel Pereira.

Area and Population.—The smallest Republic in South America, on the east coast of the Rio de la Plata situated in lat. 30°–35° S. and long. 53° 15′–57° 42′ W., with an area of 72,172 square miles, and an estimated population of 2,886,187, almost entirely white and predominantly of Spanish and Italian descent. Many Uruguayans are Roman Catholics. There is complete freedom of religion and no church is established by the State.

Physical Features.—The country consists mainly (and particularly in the south and west) of undulating grassy plains. The principal chains of hills are the Cuchilla del Haedo, which cross the Brazilian boundary and extend southwards to the Cuchilla Grande of the south and east. In no case do the peaks exceed 2,000 feet.

The principal river is the *Rio Negro* (with its tributary the Yi) flowing from north-east to south-west into the *Rio Uruguay*. The boundary river *Uruguay* is navigable from its estuary to Salto, about 200 miles north, and the Negro is also navigable for a considerable distance. Smaller rivers are the Cuareim, Yaguaron, Santa Lucia, Queguay and the Cebollati. On the south-east coast are several lagoons, and the north-east boundary crosses (the Brazilian) Lake Merin.

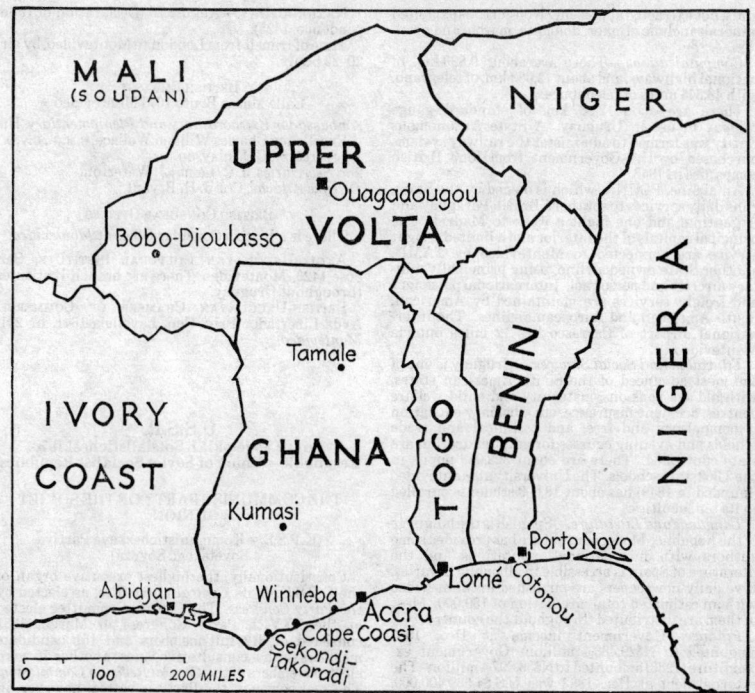

The climate is reasonably healthy. The summer is warm, but the heat is often tempered by the breezes of the Atlantic. The winter is, on the whole, mild, but cold spells, characterized by winds from the South Polar regions, are experienced in June, July and August. Rainfall is regular throughout the year, but there are occasional droughts. Floods also occur.

Government.—Uruguay—or the *Banda Oriental*, as this territory lying on the eastern bank of the Uruguay River was then called—resisted all attempted invasions of the Portuguese and Spaniards until the beginning of the 17th century, and 100 years later the Portuguese settlements were captured by the Spaniards. From 1726 to 1814 the country formed part of Spanish South America and underwent many vicissitudes during the Wars of Independence. In 1814 the armies of the Argentine Confederation captured the capital and annexed the province, and it was afterwards annexed by Portugal and became a province of Brazil. In 1825, the country threw off the Brazilian yoke. This action led to war between Argentina and Brazil which was settled by the mediation of the United Kingdom, Uruguay being declared an independent state in 1828. In 1830 a Republic was inaugurated.

According to the Constitution the President appoints a council of 11 ministers and the Vice-President presides over Congress. The legislature consists of a Chamber of 99 deputies and a Senate of 30 members (plus the Vice-President), elected for five years by a system of proportional representation.

Voting is obligatory and extends to all citizens of good repute and certain long standing residents who are not citizens, from the age of 18. However, since February, 1973 the country has been governed by presidential rule with military support. At the time of going to press, civil elections were planned for November 25, 1984.

The Republic is divided into 19 Departments each with a chief of police and a Departmental Council. The most important cities of the interior are Salto and Paysandu, both situated on the River Uruguay, which forms the main line of division from Argentina.

Production and Industry.—Wheat, barley, maize, linseed, sunflower seed and rice are cultivated. The wealth of the country is obtained from its pasturage, which supports large herds of cattle and sheep, the wool of which is of excellent quality. There are just under 11 million cattle and just under 21¼ million sheep. In addition to meat packing, other foodstuffs, (citrus, wine, beer), fishing and textile industries are of importance.

The development of local industry continues and during and since the Second World War, in addition to the greatly augmented textile industry, marked expansion in local production is notable in respect of tyres, sheet-glass, three-ply wood, cement, leather-curing, beet-sugar, plastics, household consumer goods, edible oils and the refining of petroleum and petroleum products.

Mineral Deposits.—There are some ferrous minerals, not extracted at present. Non-ferrous exploited minerals include clinker, dolomite, marble and granite.

Communications.—There are about 9,899 km. of national highways, and about 12,083 km. of telegraph, with 48,375 miles of telephones.

There are about 2,987 km. of standard gauge railway in use in Uruguay. A State Autonomous Entity was formed to administer the railway systems purchased by the Government from four British companies in 1948.

An airline, PLUNA, which is owned by the State, runs daily services to southern Brazil, Paraguay and Argentina, and one flight a week to Madrid. The principal capitals of the interior and a limited freight service are connected to Montevideo by TAMU, another State owned airline, using principally military aircraft and personnel. International passenger and freight services are maintained by American, South American and European airlines. The international airport of Carrasco lies 12 miles outside Montevideo.

Education and Social Services.—Uruguay is one of the most advanced of the South American states, with old-age pensions, maternity and child welfare centres, accident insurance, etc. Primary education is compulsory and free, and technical and trade schools and evening courses for adult education are state controlled. There are about 322,053 pupils in the 2,362 state schools. The University at Montevideo (founded in 1849) has about 18,000 students enrolled in its ten faculties.

Language and Literature.—Spanish is the language of the Republic. Modern literature has provided some authors with international reputations and the literature of Spain is accessible in all public libraries. Five daily newspapers are published in Montevideo with an estimated total circulation of 150,000. Most of them are distributed throughout the country.

Finance.—Government income at Dec. 1983 amounted to N$29,486·4 million. Government expenditure (1983) amounted to N$36,897·4 million. The external debt at Dec. 1983 was U.S.$4,589,400,000. Central Bank reserves (Dec. 1983) were US$258,400,000 million.

Currency.—The monetary unit is the *peso* (N$). For sterling exchange see p. 82.

TRADE

	1982	1983
Total exports	U.S.$975,800,000	U.S.$1,044,500,000
Total imports	1,057,900,000	705,600,000

The major exports are meat and by-products, wool and by-products, hides and bristle and agricultural products. The principal imports are raw materials, construction materials, oils and lubricants, automotive vehicles, kits and machinery.

Trade with U.K.

	1982	1983
Imports from U.K....	£13,926,000	£10,763,000
Exports to U.K.	23,107,000	33,361,000

The principal export items to the U.K. are wool and beef, the main imports are chemicals, kits, machinery, raw materials and metals.

CAPITAL.—Ψ Montevideo. Population (1981) 345,858. Other centres (with 1967 estimates) are Ψ Salto (60,000), Ψ Paysandu (60,000), Ψ Mercedes (34,000), Minas (34,000), Melo (30,000), and Rivera (40,000).

FLAG.—Four blue and five white horizontal stripes surcharged with sun on a white ground in the top corner, next flagstaff.

NATIONAL DAY.—August 25 (Declaration of Independence, 1825).

Time of transit from London to Montevideo, by air, 20–22 hours.

BRITISH EMBASSY
Calle Marco Bruto 1073 Montevideo

Ambassador Extraordinary and Plenipotentiary, His Excellency Charles William Wallace, C.M.G., C.V.O.
1st Secretary, G. Finlayson.
2nd Secretaries, J. C. Lamb; J. Waterton.
Defence Attaché, Col. J. H. Bryant.

BRITISH CONSULAR OFFICES
There is a British Consular Office at *Montevideo*.

ANGLO-URUGUAYAN CULTURAL INSTITUTE, San José 1426, Montevideo. There are branch Institutes throughout Uruguay.

BRITISH-URUGUAYAN CHAMBER OF COMMERCE, Avda Libertador Brig. Gen. Lavalleja 1641, OF 201, *Montevideo*.

U.S.S.R.
Soyuz Sovetskikh Sotsialisticheskikh Respublik = Union of Soviet Socialist Republics

THE COMMUNIST PARTY OF THE SOVIET UNION

(K.P.S.S. = Kommunisticheskaya Partiya Sovetskogo Soyuza)

Constitutionally, the highest executive organ of the C.P.S.U. is its *Central Committee*, as elected by the *Party Congress*. The Central Committee elected at the XXVIth Party Congress in March, 1981 consisted of 319 full members and 151 candidate members with a consultative voice; another 75 were elected members of the *Central Revision Commission*. The real power in the Party is vested, however, in the *Politbureau*, the *Secretariat* and the permanent Departments of the Central Committee.

Politbureau, G. A. Aliev; K. U. Chernenko; M. S. Gorbachev; V. V. Grishin; A. A. Gromyko; D. A. Kunayev; G. V. Romanov; V. V. Shcherbitsky; M. S. Solomentsev; N. A. Tikhonov; D. F. Ustinov; V. I. Vorotnikov (*full members*); V. M. Chebrikov; P. N. Demichev; V. I. Dolgikh; V. V. Kuznetsov; B. N. Ponomarev; Sh. R. Rashidov; E. A. Shevardnadze (*candidate members*).

Secretariat, Konstantin Ustinovich Chernenko (*General Secretary*) (*since* Feb. 13, 1984); V. I. Dolgikh; M. S. Gorbachev; I. V. Kapitonov; E. K. Ligachev; B. N. Ponomarev; G. V. Romanov; K. V. Rusakov; N. I. Ryzhkov; M. V. Zimyanin.

Committee of Party Control, M. S. Solomentsev (*Chairman*).

Komsomol (*Young Communist League*). V. M. Mishin (*1st Secretary*).

GOVERNMENT OF THE U.S.S.R.

The Presidium of the Supreme Soviet of the U.S.S.R.

Chairman (= *President of the U.S.S.R.*), K. U. Chernenko (*since* April 11, 1984).

Secretary, T. N. Menteshashvili.

The Supreme Soviet (= Parliament) consists of two chambers.

Chairman (= *Speaker*) *of the Council of the Union*, L. N. Tolkunov.

Chairman (= *Speaker*) *of the Council of Nationalities*, A. E. Voss.

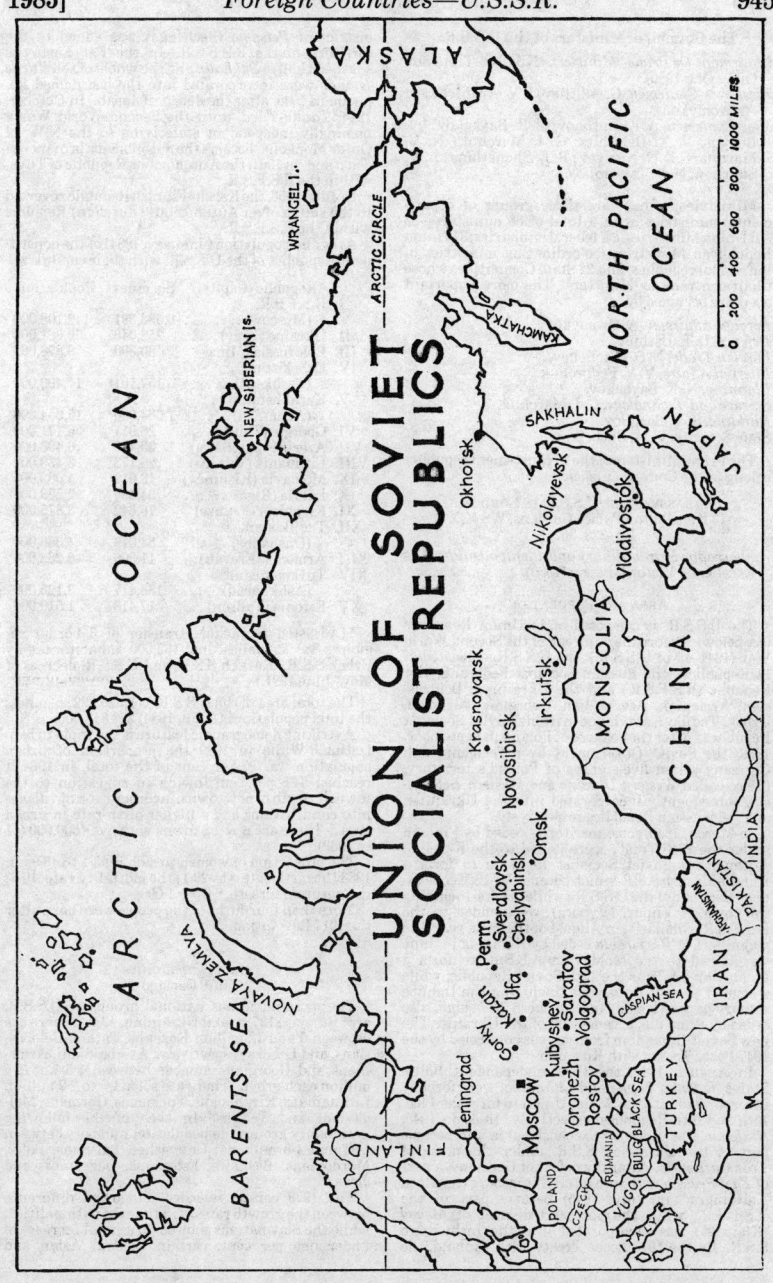

The Council of Ministers of the U.S.S.R.

Chairman (= Prime Minister), Nikolai Tikhonov (*since* Oct. 1980).

First Vice-Chairmen, G. A. Aliev; I. V. Arkhipov; A. A. Gromyko.

Vice-Chairmen, A. K. Antonov; N. K. Baybakov; I. I. Bodyul; V. E. Dymshits; G. I. Marchuk; N. V. Martynov; Z. N. Nuriyev; B. E. Shcherbina; L. V. Smirnov; N. V. Talyzin.

Ministries.—There are three groups of departmental ministries, with a total of 85 ministers—33 All Union Ministries, *i.e.* federal ministries, 31 Union Republican Ministries (co-ordinating ministries of individual republics) and 22 State Committees whose Chairmen rank as Ministers. The more important posts are occupied by:

Foreign Affairs, A. A. Gromyko.
Defence, D. F. Ustinov.
Foreign Trade, N. S. Patolichev.
Internal Affairs, V. V. Fedorchuk.
Planning, N. K. Baybakov.
Science and Technology, G. I. Marchuk.
Building, S. V. Bashilov.
State Security, V. M. Chebrikov.

The Prime Ministers of the 15 constituent republics belong to the Council *ex officio.*

EMBASSY OF THE U.S.S.R. IN LONDON
13 Kensington Palace Gardens, W8 4QX
[01–229 3628]

Ambassador Extraordinary and Plenipotentiary, His Excellency Victor I. Popov (1980).

AREA AND POPULATION

The U.S.S.R. is composed of 15 Union Republics (*see* below). Before the outbreak of the Second World War (1941–45 in U.S.S.R.), the U.S.S.R. consisted of 11 Republics—the Russian Socialist Federal Soviet Republic (R.S.F.S.R.) and the Ukrainian, Belorussian, Armenian, Azerbaidjan, Georgian, Turkmen, Uzbek, Tadjik, Kazakh and Kirghiz Soviet Socialist Republics. After the collapse of Poland in September, 1939, the Soviet Government by agreement with Germany seized five-eighths of Poland's territory, the so-called *Western Ukraine* and *Western Belorussia,* subsequently incorporated into the Ukrainian and Belorussian Republics respectively.

In March, 1940, some territories ceded by Finland under the 1940 Treaty were joined to the Karelian Autonomous Soviet Socialist Republic to form a Karelo-Finnish S.S.R. which became the 12th constituent Republic of the U.S.S.R., while others, including the town of Viipuri (Vyborg), were added to the R.S.F.S.R. Similarly, in August of the same year, the major part of *Bessarabia* ceded by Rumania in June was joined to the Moldavian A.S.S.R. to form a Moldavian S.S.R. as the 13th Soviet Republic, while a smaller part of Bessarabia, including the Danube estuary port of Izmail, and *Northern Bukovina,* also ceded by Rumania, became part of the Ukraine. The new Soviet-Rumanian frontier was confirmed by the 1947 Peace Treaty with Rumania.

In August, 1940, the three independent Baltic States, *Estonia, Latvia* and *Lithuania,* were forcibly incorporated into the Soviet Union to form the 14th, 15th and 16th Republics respectively. In June, 1945, *Ruthenia* was ceded by Czechoslovakia and became part of the Ukrainian S.S.R. under the name of *Transcarpathia.* After the defeat of Germany, a part of *East Prussia* with its capital Königsberg (renamed Kaliningrad in July, 1946) became part of the R.S.F.S.R., while the port and district of *Memel* (Klaipeda) was incorporated into the Lithuanian S.S.R. By the 1947 Peace Treaty with Finland, the

district of *Petsamo* (Pechenga) was added to the territory of the R.S.F.S.R. In the Far East, the southern half of *Sakhalin* and the whole of the *Kurile Islands* were incorporated into the last-named Republic in 1945, after the defeat of Japan. In October, 1944, *Tannu-Tuva,* until the Second World War a nominally independent state lying to the N.W. of Outer Mongolia, became the autonomous province of *Tuva* and, in 1961, the Autonomous Republic of Tuva, within the R.S.F.S.R.

In July, 1956, the Karelo-Finnish Republic reverted to the status of an Autonomous (*Karelian*) Republic within the R.S.F.S.R.

Area and population (January, 1984) of the constituent Republics of the U.S.S.R. with their capitals:—

Republic (Capital)	Sq. miles	Population
I. R.S.F.S.R.		
(Moscow)	6,593,391	142,108,000
II. Ukraine (Kiev)	252,046	50,681,000
III. Belorussia (Minsk) .	80,300	9,878,000
IV. Uzbekistan		
(Tashkent)	157,181*	17,496,000
V. Kazakhstan		
(Alma-Ata)	1,064,980*	15,654,000
VI. Georgia (Tbilisi) ...	26,911	5,171,000
VII. Azerbaidjan (Baku).	33,436	6,498,000
VIII. Lithuania (Vilnius)	26,173	3,439,000
IX. Moldavia (Kishinev)	13,912	4,083,000
X. Latvia (Riga)	24,695	2,589,000
XI. Kirghizia (Frunze) .	76,642	3,875,000
XII. Tadjikistan		
(Dushanbe)	54,019	4,366,000
XIII. Armenia (Erevan) ..	11,306	3,263,000
XIV. Turkmenistan		
(Ashkhabad)	188,417	3,123,000
XV. Estonia (Tallinn) ...	17,413	1,519,000

* (Adjusted to include transfer of 3 border regions—888 sq. miles and 162,000 inhabitants—by Uzbek S.S.R., Kazakh S.S.R. and U.S.S.R. decrees of May–June 1971.)

The total area of the U.S.S.R. is 8,620,822 sq. miles; the total population: (1 Jan. 1984) 273,843,000.

A striking demographic feature is the rapid urbanization. While in 1939 the proportion of urban population was 32 per cent of the total, in 1984 it reached 64·8 per cent, owing to migration to the towns, growth of new towns, incorporation of villages into conurbations and a higher birth-rate in urban areas. There are now 53 towns with over 500,000 (11 in 1939).

The proportion of women to men is 53·1 to 46·9. In 1983 the birth-rate was 20·1; the mortality rate, 10·3; the natural increase, 8·9 per 1,000.

More than four-fifths of the people were born after the 1917 Revolution.

Main Nationalities
(1979 Census)

The most numerous national groups of U.S.S.R. are: Russian, 137 m. and Ukrainian, 42 m. There are between 6 and 12 million Kazakhs, Tatars, Belorussians, and Uzbeks respectively. Azerbaidjani, Armenians and Georgians number between 3·5 and 5·5 million each group. There are some 1·9 to 2·9 million Lithuanians, Kirghizians, Turkmens, Germans, Moldavians and Tadjiks. In each of the following nationality groups the population numbers between 1·02 and 1·8 millions: Chuvashes, Latvians, Poles, Mordovians, Bashkirs, Estonians, Dagestanis and Jews.

The 1979 census revealed a marked difference between the growth rates of individual nationalities: while the Slav nations showed an annual increase of under one per cent, certain Central Asian and

Caucasian (mostly Moslem) nations recorded an annual net growth of 2·5 to 3·5 per cent.

THE CONSTITUTION

On October 7, 1977 a new Constitution was adopted to replace the 1936 ("Stalin") Constitution.

The Constitution is divided into a preamble and 9 Sections. The preamble describes the Soviet Union as a "developed Socialist society", which is said to be a logical stage on the road to communism. The highest aim of the Soviet state is said to be the building of a classless communist society.

Section I covers the *bases of the social-political and economic system*. The Soviet state is said to be one of the whole people (Article 1) and built on the principle of "democratic centralism", described as the electivity of all organs of state power from bottom to top, their accountability to the people, the mandatory fulfilment of decisions of higher organs by lower organs, the combination of unitary leadership with local initiative and the responsibility of each state organ and official for the work he is doing (Article 3). The Communist Party of the Soviet Union is brought from the obscurity of Article 126 of the 1936 Constitution into the prominence of Article 6 of the new text, where it is described as "the leading and guiding force of Soviet society, the nucleus of its political system and of all state and public organisations". It is said to "determine the general perspective of the development of society, the line of internal and external policies of the U.S.S.R."

The *economic system* is based on "socialist ownership of the means of production", which comprises either state ownership or ownership by collective farms and other cooperative organizations or trade unions and other public organizations (Article 9). The economy of the U.S.S.R. is said to comprise "a unitary economic complex, embracing all the elements of social production, distribution and exchange on the territory of the U.S.S.R." It is managed on the basis of state plans (Article 15).

This section also contains new chapters on *social development and culture, foreign policy*, and the *defence of the socialist Fatherland*. The foreign policy of the U.S.S.R. is said to be "directed to ensuring favourable international conditions for the building of communism in the U.S.S.R." (Article 28).

Section II is devoted to the *state and the individual*. This includes a long chapter on the *basic rights, freedoms and duties of citizens of the U.S.S.R.*, all of which are subject to the proviso that "exercise by citizens of rights and freedoms must not injure the interests of society and state, and the rights of other citizens" (Article 39). The rights listed include the right to work, leisure, health protection, maintenance in old age, housing, education, access to the achievements of culture, freedom of scientific, technical and artistic creative work "in accordance with the aims of communist construction", the right to take part in the administration of state and public affairs, to submit proposals and complaints to state public organs (Articles 40–49), as well as to freedom of speech, the press and association "in accordance with the interests of the working people and with the aim of strengthening the socialist system" (Article 50).

Freedom to profess or not profess any religion and to conduct atheistic (but not religious) propaganda, and the separation of the Church from the State and the school from the Church are provided for by Article 52. Section II also includes a list of obligations which is more comprehensive than that of the 1936 Constitution and includes the obligation to work conscientiously, to safeguard socialist property, to contribute to the strengthening of the might and prestige of the state, to do military service, to respect the national dignity of other citizens, to contribute to the maintenance of public order, to prepare their children for "socially useful labour", to protect nature and to further the consolidation of world peace (Articles 59–68).

Section III on the *national-state structure of the U.S.S.R.* describes it as a "unitary federal multinational state, formed as a result of the free self-determination of nations and the voluntary union of equal Soviet Socialist Republics (Article 69). "Each Union Republic shall retain the right freely to secede from the U.S.S.R." (Article 71).

Section IV on the *Soviets of people's deputies and the procedure for electing them* provides for the Supreme Soviet of the U.S.S.R. and the Supreme Soviets of Union and Republics to be elected for a term of 5 years and for local Soviets to be elected for 2½ years (Article 89). The minimum voting age and minimum age for deputies in all Soviets had been lowered to 18 (Article 95).

Under Section V, *the higher organs of State power and administration of the U.S.S.R.*, the *Supreme Soviet of the U.S.S.R.* is the highest organ of State power (Article 106). It consists of two chambers, a Council of the Union and Council of Nationalities, which are to be equal in rights and consist of the same number of deputies (Articles 107 and 108). Sessions of the Supreme Soviet are convoked twice a year (Article 110); between sessions the Supreme Soviet is represented by its Presidium, which consists of a Chairman (President), a First Deputy Chairman, 15 Deputy Chairmen, one from each Union Republic, a Secretary and 21 Members (Articles 117 and 118).

The highest executive organ of the State is the Council of Ministers of the U.S.S.R. (Article 127), consisting of the Chairman, his Deputies, U.S.S.R. Ministers and Chairmen of State Committees, Chairmen of the Councils of Ministers of Union Republics *ex officio* and others (Article 128). The Council of Ministers is accountable to the Supreme Soviet (Article 129). A smaller body, the Presidium of the Council of Ministers, comprising the Chairman and his Deputies, acts as the permanent organ of the Council of Ministers (Article 131).

Section VI covers the *bases of the structure of organs of state power and administration in Union Republics*. Section VII deals with *justice, arbitration and supervision by the Procuracy*. Section VIII deals with the *arms, flag, anthem and capital* of the U.S.S.R. Section IX is on the *procedure for bringing the Constitution into effect and amending it*.

Chronological System.—On February 14, 1918, the Soviet Government adopted the Gregorian (Western) Calendar. In 1981 Summer Time was introduced between April 1 and October 1, but there are some geographical anomalies in its application. The country is divided into 11 time zones (Moscow time is 3 hours ahead of G.M.T.).

LANGUAGE, LITERATURE AND ARTS

Language and Literature.—Russian is a branch of the Slavonic family of languages which is divided into the following groups: *Eastern*, including Russian, Ukrainian and White Russian; *Western*, including Polish, Czech, Slovak and Sorbish (or Lusatian Wendish); and *Southern*, including Serbo-Croat, Slovene, Macedonian and Bulgarian. The Western group and part of the Southern group are written in the Latin alphabet, the others in the Cyrillic, said to have been instituted by SS. Cyril and Methodius in the ninth century, and largely based on the Greek alphabet. Before the Westernization of Russia under Peter the Great (1682–1725), Russian literature consisted mainly of folk ballads (*byliny*), epic songs, chronicles and works of moral theology. The eighteenth and particularly the nineteenth centuries saw a brilliant development of Russian poetry and fiction. Romantic poetry reached its zenith with Alexander Pushkin (1799–1837) and Mikhail Lermontov (1814–1841). The 20th century produced great poets like Alexander Blok (1880–1921), the Nobel Prize laureate of 1958 Boris Pasternak (1890–1960), Vladimir Mayakovsky (1893–1930) and Anna Akhmatova (1888–1966). Realistic fiction is associated with the names of Nikolai Gogol (1809–1852), Ivan Turgenev (1818–1883), Fedor Dostoyevsky (1821–1881) and Leo Tolstoy (1828–1910), and later with Anton Chekhov (1860–1904), Maxim Gorky (1868–1936), Ivan Bunin (1870–1953) and Alexander Solzhenitsyn (b. 1918).

Great names in music include Glinka (1804–1857), Borodin (1833–87), Mussorgsky (1839–1881), Rimsky-Korsakov (1844–1908), Rubinstein (1829–1894), Tchaikovsky (1840–1893), Rakhmaninov (1873–1943), Skriabin (1872–1915), Prokofiev (1891–1953), Stravinsky (1882–1971) and Shostakovich (1906–1975). Performers include Igor Oistrakh, M. Rostropovich, S. Richter and the famous conductor G. Rozhdestvensky.

FINANCE

A new "heavy" Rouble was introduced on January 1, 1961. Prices and wages were changed accordingly at the rate of 10 old Roubles = 1 new Rouble. The official exchange rate bears little relation to the actual purchasing power of the currency. Banknotes in circulation are those valuing R. 1, 3, 5, 10, 25, 50 and 100. There are also coins valuing Kopecks 1, 2, 3, 5, 10, 15, 20, 50 and R. 1.

DEFENCE

Defence expenditure in the U.S.S.R. for 1984 is put officially at 17·05 billion roubles (or 4·7 per cent of total budget). It is believed, however, that this does not represent the total spent on defence in the U.S.S.R. Much of this is concealed in estimates for other ministries. The general trend is a continuing emphasis on nuclear weapons while improving the levels and capabilities of conventional arms.

The basic military service is two years in the Army and Air Force and two to three years in the Navy and Border Guards.

The total size of the Soviet regular forces is now estimated to be about 5,050,000, excluding some 400,000 Border Guard, internal security, railway and construction troops (mainly uniformed civilians), but including some 1,500,000 command and general support troops not otherwise listed.

Operational ICBMs, i.e. Inter-Continental Ballistic Missiles, now total about 1,400. SLBMs number 1,019. The number of MRBMs and IRBMs deployed is some 606. The operational personnel of the Strategic Rocket Forces totals about 325,000 (not including Air Defence Troops—500,000).

The Air Forces comprise about 11,600 operational aircraft (including about 8,640 combat aircraft). The total strength of the Air Forces, excluding the Naval Air Force (68,000) and the bomber forces of the Aviation Armies (100,000), is about 475,000 men. The total personnel of the separate Air Defence Command, now merged with the Air Defence Troops of the Ground Forces, is estimated at 630,000 men.

The total size of the Soviet Army is estimated at 1,800,000 men. It is thought to be organized in 191 divisions, distributed as follows: 30 divisions in Central and Eastern Europe, 65 in European U.S.S.R., 28 in Southern Theatre (includes 4 in Afghanistan), 52 in Far Eastern Theatre, and 16 in the Central Strategic Reserve.

The total strength of the Soviet Navy and Naval Air Force is 460,000 men. In total tonnage, it is the second largest navy in the world, and its main strength lies in the submarine fleet. There are now 276 cruise missile and attack submarines, 119 nuclear-powered and 157 diesel-powered submarines, with a further 95 attack submarines in reserve.

The Soviet Navy now has 290 major surface combat vessels, including four aircraft carriers, 37 cruisers and 73 destroyers and more than 180 frigates. The landbased Naval Air Force comprises about 755 combat aircraft, 390 of which are bombers, and some 300 helicopters.

The para-military forces number some 560,000, including 300,000 border troops and 260,000 internal security troops. There are also DOSAAF members (claimed active membership, 80 million) who participate in such activities as athletics, flight training, shooting, parachuting and pre-military training.

Minister of Defence, D. F. Ustinov (with rank of Marshal of the Soviet Union).
Chief of General Staff, Marshal S. Akhromeyev.
Chief, Political Administration, Soviet Army and Navy, Army Gen. A. A. Yepishev.

On May 14, 1955, a Treaty of Friendship, Mutual Assistance and Co-operation was signed in Warsaw between the Soviet Union and its European associates (Bulgaria, East Germany, Hungary, Poland, Rumania, and Czechoslovakia) (and Albania which left the Pact in Sept. 1968) to serve as a counterpoise to NATO. A united military command was set up in Moscow, *C.-in-C.,* Marshal V. G. Kulikov; *Chief of Staff,* Army General A. I. Gribkov. Under present arrangements, the Treaty (Warsaw Pact) is due to expire in June 1985.

INDUSTRY AND AGRICULTURE

One of the most remarkable aspects of the Soviet economy has been the transformation of an essentially agricultural country into the second-strongest industrial power in the world. The 1983 output amounted to 153 million tonnes of steel, 107 million tonnes of rolled metal, 716 million tonnes of coal, 616 million tonnes of crude oil, 128 million tonnes of cement, 1,416,000 million kW/h of electricity and 1,315,000 cars.

Agricultural development has been slower, mainly owing to lack of incentives among peasants organized in *kolkhozy* (collective farms). Repeated droughts, such as in 1980-81, were a contributing factor to a permanent shortage of grain; the 1982 harvest is estimated at 170–180 million tonnes, and the 1983 harvest was officially stated to have exceeded 190 million tonnes. Stock breeding has also suffered from the general mismanagement of farming, and from shortages of fodder in recent years. The livestock at Jan. 1, 1983 included 43,800,000 cows, 78,500,000 pigs and 151,500,000 sheep and goats. Besides *kolkhozy* (collective farms) and *sovkhozy* (state farms) a significant contribution to agricultural production is made by the private plots cultivated by individual peasants. The cultivation of these plots is encouraged by the Soviet authorities. The level of productivity remains very low. *Forests* cover nearly 40 per cent of the whole area of the Union and form a considerable source of wealth.

Trade with U.K.

	1982	1983
Imports from U.K.	£355,678,000	£445,008,000
Exports to U.K.	645,135,000	728,491,000

COMMUNICATIONS

European Russia is relatively well served by railways, Leningrad and Moscow being the two main focal points of rail routes. The centre and south have a good system of north-south and east-west lines, but the eastern part (the Volga lands), traversed as it is by trunk lines between Europe and Asia which enter Siberia *via* Sverdlovsk, Chelyabinsk, Magnitogorsk and Ufa, lacks north-south routes. In Asia, there are still large areas of the U.S.S.R., notably in the Far North and Siberia, with few or no railways. Railways built since 1928 include the Turkestan-Siberian line (*Turksib*) which has made possible a large-scale industrial exploitation of Kazakhstan, a number of lines within the system of the *Trans-Siberian Railway* (Magnitogorsk-Kartaly-Troitsk, Sverdlovsk-Kurgan, Novosibirsk-Proyektnaya, etc.), which are of great importance for the industrial development in the east, the Petropavlovsk-Karaganda-Balkhash line which has made possible the development of the Karaganda coal basin and of the Balkhash copper mines, and the Moscow-Donbass trunk line. In the northern part of European Russia, the North Pechora Railway has been completed, while in the Far East a second Trans-Siberian line (the Baikal-Amur Railway) is under construction; it will follow a more northerly alignment than the existing Trans-Siberian and will terminate in the Pacific port of Sovetskaya Gavan.

Sea Ports and Inland Waterways.—The most important ports (Odessa, Nikolayev, Batumi, Taganrog, Rostov, Kerch, Sevastopol and Novorossiisk) lie around the Black Sea and the Sea of Azov. The northern ports (Leningrad, Murmansk and Archangel) are, with the exception of Murmansk, icebound during winter. Several new ports have been built along the Arctic Sea route (between Murmansk and Vladivostok) and are now in regular use every summer. The great Far Eastern port of Vladivostok, the Pacific naval base of the U.S.S.R., is kept open by icebreakers all the year round. Inland waterways, both natural and artificial, are of great importance in the country, although all of them are icebound in winter (from 2½ months in the south to 6 months in the north). The great rivers of European Russia flow outwards from the centre, linking all parts of the plain with the chief ports, an immense system of navigable waterways which carried about 606,000,000 tons of freight in 1983. They are supplemented by a system of canals which provide a through traffic between the White, Baltic, Black and Caspian Seas. The most notable of them, built largely by forced labour, are the *White Sea-Baltic Canal*, and the *Moscow-Volga Canal*. The 63-miles long *Volga-Don Canal* linking the Baltic and the White Seas in the North to the Caspian, the Black Sea and the Sea of Azov in the South, was completed in May 1952.

FLAG OF THE U.S.S.R.—Red, with five-pointed star above hammer and sickle.

NATIONAL DAY OF THE U.S.S.R.—November 7 (Commemorating the October Bolshevist Revolution of 1917).

BRITISH EMBASSY
(Naberezhnaya Morisa Toreza 14, Moscow)

Ambassador Extraordinary and Plenipotentiary, His Excellency Sir Iain Sutherland, K.C.M.G. (1982).
Minister, D. J. E. Ratford, C.M.G., C.V.O.
1st Secretary, M. F. Sullivan, M.B.E. (*Cultural Attaché*).
Counsellors, D. Beattie (*Commercial*); C. J. R. Meyer (*Head of Chancery*); G. D. G. Murrell.
Defence and Air Attaché, Air Cdre. B. L. Robinson, R.A.F.
Military Attaché, Brig. B. K. Warner.
Naval Attaché, Capt. J. A. Marshall, R.N.
H.M. Consul, W. F. Somerset.

There are no British Consulates in the U.S.S.R. apart from the Consular Section attached to the Embassy.

I.—R.S.F.S.R.

(The Russian Soviet Federal Socialist Republic)

Chairman of the Presidium of the Supreme Soviet, M. A. Yasnov.

Chairman of the Council of Ministers, V. I. Vorotnikov.

The R.S.F.S.R. has no central Communist Party organization of its own.

The R.S.F.S.R., the largest and the most important of the Republics, occupies the major half of the European part of the U.S.S.R. and the major northern portion of its Asiatic part and makes up 77 per cent of the total territory of the U.S.S.R. with 53 per cent of the total population. It consists of 16 Autonomous Republics (the Bashkir, Buryat, Checheno-Ingush, Chuvash, Daghestan, Kabardin-Balkar, Kalmyk, Karelian, Komi, Mari, Mordovian, North-Osetian, Tatar, Tuva, Udmurt and Yakut, A.S.S.R.s); 6 regions (Altai, Khabarovsk, Krasnodar, Krasnoyarsk, Maritime and Stavropol) containing in their turn 5 autonomous provinces; 49 provinces (Amur, Archangel, Astrakhan, Belgorod, Bryansk, Chelyabinsk, Chita, Gorky, Irkutsk, Ivanovo, Kalinin, Kaliningrad, Kaluga, Kamchatka, Kemerovo, Kirov, Kostroma, Kuibyshev, Kurgan, Kursk, Leningrad, Lipetsk, Magadan, Moscow, Murmansk, Novgorod, Novosibirsk, Omsk, Orel, Orenburg, Penza, Perm, Pskov, Rostov, Ryazan, Sakhalin, Saratov, Smolensk, Sverdlovsk, Tambov, Tomsk, Tula, Tyumen, Ulyanovsk, Vladimir, Volgograd, Vologda, Voronezh and Yaroslavl).

Physical Features.—The R.S.F.S.R. may be conveniently divided into three areas, a low-lying flat Western part stretching eastwards up to the Yenisei and divided in two by the Ural ridge; an eastern part, between the Yenisei and the Pacific, consisting of a number of tablelands and ridges, and a southern mountainous part. Climatically, the R.S.F.S.R. extends over all zones, except the tropics, and may be divided into the following belts (from north to south): Arctic, Tundra, Forest, Mixed Forest-Steppe, Steppe, Sub-Tropics.

The Republic has a very long coast-line, including the longest Arctic coast-line in the world (about 17,000 miles). The most important rivers in the European part of the R.S.F.S.R. are the Volga with its tributaries Kama and Oka, the Northern Dvina and the Pechora, the short but wide Neva, the Don and the Kuban, and in the Asiatic part, the Ob with the Irtysh, the Yenisei, the Lena and the Amur, and, further north, Khatanga, Olenek, Yana, Indigirka, Kolyma and Anadyr. Lakes are abundant, particularly in the north-west. The huge Baikal Lake in Eastern Siberia is the deepest lake in the world. There are also two large artificial water reservoirs within the Greater Volga canal system, the Moscow and Rybinsk "Seas".

Minerals.—The Republic occupies one of the first places in the world for mineral wealth. Coal is mined in the Kuznetsk area, in the Urals, south of Moscow, in the Donets basin (its Eastern part lies in the R.S.F.S.R.) and in the Pechora area in the North. Oil is produced in the Northern Caucasus, in the area between the Volga and the Ural (the so-called "Second Baku") and in Western Siberia. Western Siberia also has large deposits of natural gas. Coal and gas deposits in Siberia and the Far East (especially Yakutia) are currently being developed, now that some deposits in the western parts of the U.S.S.R. are approaching exhaustion. The Ural mountains contain a unique assortment of minerals—high-quality iron ore, manganese, copper, aluminium, gold, platinum, precious stones, salt, asbestos, pyrites, coal, oil, etc. Iron ore is mined, in addition to the Urals, near Kursk, Tula, Lipetsk, in several areas in Siberia and in the Kola Peninsula. Non-ferrous metals are found in the Altai, in Eastern Siberia, in the Northern Caucasus, in the Kuznetsk-Basin, in the Far East and in the Far North. Nine-tenths of all U.S.S.R. forests are located in the R.S.F.S.R.

Production and Industry.—The vastness of the

territory of the Republic and the great variety in climatic conditions cause great differences in the structure of agriculture from north to south and from west to east. In the Far North reindeer breeding, hunting and fishing are predominant. Further south, timber industry is combined with grain growing. Vine, tobacco and other Southern crops are grown on the Black Sea shore of the Caucasus. In the southern half of the forest zone and in the adjacent forest-steppe zone, the acreage under grain crops is far larger and the structure of agriculture more complex. An extensive programme of land improvement mainly involving this zone, announced early in 1974, aims to double its total agricultural output by 1990. In the eastern part of this zone, between the Volga and the Urals, cericulture is predominant (particularly summer wheat), with cattle breeding next. Beyond the Urals, we find another important grain-growing and stock-breeding area in the southern part of the Western-Siberian plain. The southern steppe zone is the main wheat granary of the U.S.S.R., containing also large acreages under barley, maize and sunflower. In the extreme South (Krasnodar region, Stavropol region) cotton is now cultivated. Vine, tobacco and other Southern crops are grown on the Black Sea shore of the Caucasus.

Industrially, the R.S.F.S.R. occupies the first place among the Soviet Republics. Major changes in the location of industry have occurred since the revolution and again since the war with new industrial areas being developed in the Urals, the Kuznetsk basin, and more recently in Siberia and the Far East. However, Moscow and Leningrad are still the two largest industrial centres in the country. Most of the oil produced in the U.S.S.R. now comes from the R.S.F.S.R., half annual output comes from Tyumen Oblast in Western Siberia. All industries are represented in the R.S.F.S.R., including iron and steel and engineering. Industrial centres include Magnitogorsk, Chelyabinsk, Novokuznetsk, Tula, Komsomolsk, Perm, Ufa, Irkutsk, Kuibyshev, Krasnoyarsk, Nizhny-Tagil, Novosibirsk, Ormsk, Volgograd, Gorky, Saratov, Grozny, Rostov and Taganrog.

CAPITAL.—Moscow. Population 8,546,000 (Jan. 1, 1984). Moscow, founded about A.D. 1147 by Yuri Dolgoruki, became first the centre of the rising Moscow principality and, later, in the 15th century, the capital of the whole of Russia (Muscovy). In 1325, it became the seat of the Metropolitan of Russia. In 1703 Peter the Great transferred the capital to the newly built St. Petersburg, but on March 14, 1918, Moscow was again designated as the capital. ΨLeningrad (before the First World War "St. Petersburg" and from 1914–1924 "Petrograd") has a population of 4,832,000 (Jan. 1, 1984).

Other towns with populations exceeding 500,000 are:—

Gorky (Nizhny-Novgorod)	1,392,000
Novosibirsk (Novonikolayevsk)	1,386,000
Sverdlovsk (Yekaterinburg)	1,288,000
Kuibyshev (Samara)	1,251,000
Omsk	1,094,000
Chelyabinsk	1,086,000
Perm (Molotov)	1,049,000
Ufa	1,048,000
Kazan	1,039,000
Ψ Rostov-on-Don	983,000
Volgograd (Stalingrad; Tsaritsyn)	969,000
Saratov	894,000
Krasnoyarsk	860,000
Voronezh	841,000
Yaroslavl	623,000
Krasnodar	603,000
Izhevsk	603,000
Ψ Vladivostok	591,000
Irkutsk	590,000

Novokuznetsk	572,000
Togliatti	576,000
Khabarovsk	569,000
Barnaul	567,000
Tula	529,000
Myanovsk	524,000
Penza	522,000
Orenburg	513,000

Ψ Seaport.

About 83 per cent of the population are Russians.

II.—UKRAINE

First Secretary of the Party Central Committee, V. V. Shcherbitsky.
Chairman of the Presidium of the Supreme Soviet, A. F. Vatchenko.
Chairman of the Council of Ministers, A. P. Lyashko.

This Republic, second largest in population, lying in the south-western part of the European half of the U.S.S.R., was formed in December, 1917. It consists of 25 provinces—Cherkassy, Chernigov, Chernovtsy, Crimea, Dnepropetrovsk, Donetsk, Ivano-Frankovsk, Kharkov, Kherson, Khmelnitsky, Kiev, Kirovograd, Lvov, Nikolayev, Odessa, Poltava, Rovno, Sumy, Ternopol, Transcarpathia, Vinnitsa, Volhynia, Voroshilovgrad, Zaporozhye and Zhitomir.

Physical Features.—The larger part of the Ukraine forms a plain with small elevations. The Carpathian mountains lie in the south-western part of the Republic. The climate is moderate, with relatively mild winters (particularly in the south-west) and hot summers. The main rivers are the Dnieper with its tributaries, the Southern Bug and the Northern Donets (a tributary of the Don).

Production and Industry.—The main centre of Soviet coal mining and iron and steel industry is situated in the southern part of the Ukraine. Engineering and chemical industry have been greatly developed under the Soviet régime. In 1980, the Ukraine provided 36 per cent of the total Soviet steel, 51 per cent of iron ore and 27 per cent of coal. The central forest-steppe region (mainly on the right bank of the Dnieper) is the greatest sugar-producing area in the U.S.S.R. The Ukraine also leads in grain-growing and stock-raising.

There are large deposits of coal and salt in the Donets Basin, of iron ore in Krivoy Rog and near Kerch in the Crimea, of manganese in Nikopol, and of quicksilver in Nikitovka.

CAPITAL (since 1934), Kiev, one of the oldest cities in the U.S.S.R., founded in the 6th–7th century A.D., was the capital of the Russian State from 865 to 1240. Population (Jan. 1, 1983, 2,355,000. Other towns with population over 500,000 are:—

Kharkov	1,536,000
Dnepropetrovsk (Yekaterinoslav)	1,114,000
Ψ Odessa	1,113,000
Donetsk (Stalino; Yuzovka, *i.e.* Hughesovka)	1,064,000
Zaporozhye (Aleksandrovskaya)	844,000
Lvov (Lviv; Lwow; Lemberg)	728,000
Krivoy Rog	680,000
Zhdanov	520,000

III.—BELORUSSIA
(White Russia)

First Secretary of the Party Central Committee, N. N. Slyunkov.
Chairman of the Presidium of the Supreme Soviet, I. E. Polyakov.
Chairman of the Council of Ministers, V. I. Brovikov.

The Belorussian S.S.R., lying in the western part of the European area of the U.S.S.R., was formed early in 1919. It now consists of six provinces (Brest, Gomel, Grodno, Minsk, Mogilev and Vitebsk). It is largely a plain with many lakes, swamps and marshy land. Before the revolution of 1917 the area was one of the most backward parts of European Russia. Since then, agriculture has been greatly developed, thanks to draining of swamps. Most of the Republic's industry is also of recent growth. Woodworking is of great importance, but engineering has also been greatly extended with several major plants built in Gomel and Minsk.

The main rivers are the upper reaches of the Dnieper, of the Niemen and of the Western Dvina.

CAPITAL, Minsk. Population 1,442,000 (Jan. 1, 1984).

Belorussians make up four-fifths of the population, with Russians and Poles coming next.

IV.—UZBEKISTAN

First Secretary of the Party Central Committee, I. B. Usmankhodzhaev.
Chairman of the Presidium of the Supreme Soviet, A. V. Salimov.
Chairman of the Council of Ministers, N. D. Khudayberdyev.

The Uzbek S.S.R. was formed in 1924 and consists of the Kara-Kalpak A.S.S.R. and of 12 provinces (Andizhan, Bokhara, Dzhizak, Ferghana, Kashkadarya, Khorezm, Namangan, Navoi, Samarkand, Surkhan-darya, Syr-darya and Tashkent). It lies between the high Tienshan Mountains and the Pamir highlands in the east and south-east and sandy lowlands in the west and north-west. The major part of the territory is a plain with huge waterless deserts and several large oases, which form the main centres of population and economic life. The largest is the Ferghana valley, watered by the Syr-Darya. Other oases include Tashkent, Samarkand, Bokhara and Khorezm. The climate is continental and dry. Minerals include gold, natural gas, oil, copper, lead, zinc and coal.

The Uzbeks, a Turkic people, make up 68·7 per cent of the population, the Russians (10·8 per cent), Tatars (4·2 per cent) and Kazakhs (4 per cent) come next.

There are major agricultural and textile machinery plants and several chemical combines. Uzbekistan is the main cotton-growing area of the U.S.S.R. producing more than 60 per cent of all Soviet cotton. Irrigation has always been of decisive importance in this area, and the Soviet Government has done much in this field, including the construction of the Great Ferghana Canal (230 miles).

CAPITAL, Tashkent. Population 1,985,000 (Jan. 1, 1984). Samarkand contains the Gur-Emir (Tamerlane's Mausoleum), completed A.D. 1400 by Ulugbek, Tamerlane's astronomer-grandson, and a 15th-century observatory. Heavy damage was done to Tashkent by the series of earthquakes in April and May, 1966.

V.—KAZAKHSTAN

First Secretary of the Party Central Committee, D. A. Kunayev.
Chairman of the Presidium of the Supreme Soviet, B. A. Ashimov.
Chairman of the Council of Ministers, N. A. Nazarbaev.

The Kazakh S.S.R., the second-largest Union-Republic, stretching from the lower reaches of the Volga and the Caspian in the west to the Altai and Tienshan in the east, and bordering on China, was formed in 1920 as an autonomous republic (under the name of the Kirghiz A.S.S.R.) within the R.S.F.S.R., and was constituted a Union Republic in 1936. It consists of the 19 Provinces: Aktyubinsk, Alma-Ata, Chimkent, Dzhambul, Dzhezkazgan, East-Kazakhstan, Guryev, Karaganda, Kokchetav, Kustanay, Kzyl-Orda, Mangyshlak, North-Kazakhstan, Pavlodar, Semipalatinsk, Taldy-Kurgan, Tselinograd, Turgay and Uralsk.

Kazakhstan is a country of arid steppes and semideserts, flat in the west, hilly in the east and mountainous in the south-east (Southern Altai and Tienshan). The climate is continental and very dry. The main rivers are the (Upper) Irtysh, the Ural, the Syr-Darya and the Ili. Kazakhstan is very rich in minerals: copper in Kounrad and Dzhezkazgan, lead and zinc in the Altai and Karatau mountains, iron ore in Radryg and Lisakovsk, coal in Ekibastuz and Karaganda and oil and natural gas in the Mangyshlak peninsula. Major centres of metal industry exist now in the Altai Mountains, in Chimkent, north of the Balkhash Lake and in Central Kazakhstan. Stockraising is highly developed, particularly in the central and south-western parts of the Republic. Grain is grown in the north and north-east and cotton in the south and south-east. In 1954 an ambitious programme of development of "virgin" lands in the steppes was launched by the Government to increase grain production.

The Kazakhs (a Turkic people) are in a minority in the Republic named after them; they constitute only 36 per cent of its population, Russian settlers make up 41 per cent and Ukrainians 6 per cent.

CAPITAL, Alma-Ata (formerly Verny). Population 1,046,000 (Jan. 1, 1984). Karaganda, a major mining centre, has a population of 600,000 (Jan. 1, 1983).

VI.—GEORGIA

First Secretary of the Party Central Committee, E. A. Shevardnadze.
Chairman of the Presidium of the Supreme Soviet, P. G. Gilashvili.
Chairman of the Council of Ministers, D. L. Kartvelishvili.

The Georgian, S.S.R., occupying the north-western part of Transcaucasia, lies on the shore of the Black Sea and borders in the south-east on Turkey. It was formed in 1921; in 1922 it joined the Transcaucasian Federation which, in its turn, adhered to the U.S.S.R. in the same year. After the liquidation of the Transcaucasian S.F.S.R. in 1936 Georgia became a Union Republic. It contains two Autonomous Republics (Abkhazia and Adjaria) and the South-Osetian Autonomous Province. Georgia is a country of mountains, with the Greater Caucasus in the north and the Lesser Caucasus in the south. A relatively low-lying land between these two ridges is divided into two parts by the Surz Ridge: Western Georgia with a mild and damp climate and Eastern Georgia with a more continental and dry climate. The Black Sea shore and the Rioni lowland are subtropical in their climatic character. The most important mineral deposits are manganese (Chiatura), coal (Tkibuli and Tkvarcheli) and oil (Kakhetia). Georgia is a leading producer of manganese in the U.S.S.R. There are also many oil refineries. Viniculture, tea and tobacco-growing are the three main agricultural industries. The Black Sea harbours many famous holiday resorts. Georgians make up 68·8 per cent of the population, the remainder being largely composed of Armenians, Russians, Azerbaidjanis and Osetians.

CAPITAL, Tbilisi (Tiflis), population 1,140,000 (Jan. 1, 1984).

VII.—AZERBAIDJAN

First Secretary of the Party Central Committee, K. M. Bagirov.
Chairman of the Presidium of the Supreme Soviet, K. A. Khalilov.
Chairman of the Council of Ministers, G. N. Seidov.

The Azerbaidjan S.S.R. occupies the eastern part of Transcaucasia, on the shore of the Caspian Sea, and borders on Iran. It was formed in 1920. Between 1922 and 1936 it formed part of the Transcaucasian Federation. In 1936 it became a Union Republic. It contains the Nakhichevan Autonomous Republic and the Nagorno-Karabakh Autonomous Province.

The north-eastern part of the Republic is taken up by the south-eastern end of the main Caucasus ridge, its south-western part by the smaller Caucasus hills, and its south-eastern corner by the spurs of the Talysh Ridge. Its central part is a depression irrigated by the Kura and by the lower reaches of its tributary Araks. Sheltered by the mountains from the humid west winds blowing from the Black Sea, Azerbaidjan has a continental climate. The land requires artificial irrigation. Industry is dominated by oil and natural gas extraction and related chemical and engineering industries centred on Baku and Sumgait. A large power station on the Araks was completed in 1969, in conjunction with Iran. Azerbaidjan is also important as a cotton growing area. The Azerbaidjani (Turkic) make up more than three-quarters of the population of the Republic, Armenians, about 8 per cent, and Russians, 8 per cent.

CAPITAL, Ψ Baku. Population 1,661,000 (Jan. 1, 1984).

VIII.—LITHUANIA

First Secretary of the Party Central Committee, P. P. Grishkyavichus.
Chairman of the Presidium of the Supreme Soviet, A. S. Barkauskas.
Chairman of the Council of Ministers, R.-B. I. Songaila.

Lithuania, formerly a Province of the Russian Empire, was declared an independent Republic at Vilna in 1918 and was incorporated into the U.S.S.R. in August, 1940. It was occupied by German forces from June, 1941, until the autumn of 1944. The Republic forms a plain with a large number of lakes and swamps. The forests occupy 19 per cent of the whole area. The main river is the Niemen with its tributaries.

The chief industries are agriculture and forestry, the chief products being rye, oats, wheat, barley, flax, sugar-beet and potatoes. Before its incorporation into the Soviet Union, Lithuania exported a large quantity of meat and dairy produce.

The Lithuanians make up four-fifths of the population, Russians and Poles, 7–9 per cent each.

CAPITAL, Vilnius (Vilna, restored to Lithuania by U.S.S.R. after the collapse and partition of Poland in 1939, and recaptured by Soviet forces in 1944). Population 535,000 (Jan. 1, 1984).

IX.—MOLDAVIA

First Secretary of the Party Central Committee, S. K. Grossu.
Chairman of the Presidium of the Supreme Soviet, I. P. Kalin.
Chairman of the Council of Ministers, I. G. Ustiyan.

Moldavia, occupying the south-western corner of the U.S.S.R., borders in the west on Rumania with the Pruth forming the frontier. In 1918, Rumania seized the Russian Province of Bessarabia. In 1924 a Moldavian Autonomous Republic was formed within the Ukraine, and in 1940 the U.S.S.R. forced Rumania to give back Bessarabia, the major part of which was merged with the Moldavian A.S.S.R. to form a Moldavian Union Republic. Moldavia was occupied by the Germans and Rumanians from 1941 to 1944.

The northern part of the Republic consists of flat steppe lands, now all under plough. Some forests skirt the Dniester. Further south, around Kishinev, there are woody hills and further south again, low-lying steppe lands. The climate is moderate. The main river is the Dniester, navigable along the whole course.

The main industry is agriculture (viniculture, fruit-growing and market-gardening). Industry is insignificant in both parts of Moldavia, but the Republic has the densest population in the U.S.S.R. Moldavians make up 64 per cent of the population, with Ukrainians, and Russians next.

CAPITAL, Kishinev (Chisinau). Population, 605,000 (Jan. 1, 1984).

X.—LATVIA

First Secretary of the Party Central Committee, B. K. Pugo.
Chairman of the Presidium of the Supreme Soviet, P. Ya. Strautmanis.
Chairman of the Council of Ministers, Yu. Ya. Ruben.

The Latvian S.S.R., lying on the shores of the Baltic and of the Gulf of Riga, was formerly a Baltic Province of the Russian Empire. It was proclaimed an independent state in 1918 and was forcibly incorporated into the U.S.S.R. in August 1940. Between 1941 and 1944 the Republic was occupied by the German forces.

The surface of the country is generally flat, interspersed by occasional chains of hills. The climate is moderately continental. The main rivers are the lower reaches of the Western Dvina and its tributaries. Forests occupy 20 per cent of the total territory.

The Latvians make up 53·7 per cent of the Republic's population, Russians 32·8 per cent.

Latvian industry was always highly developed, with shipbuilding, engineering, chemical industry, textile industry, wood-working and dairying being the chief occupations. Both Riga and Liepaja (Libava, Libau) are important sea-ports.

CAPITAL, Ψ Riga. Population, 875,000 (Jan. 1, 1984).

XI.—KIRGHIZIA

First Secretary of the Party Central Committee, T. U. Usubaliyev.
Chairman of the Presidium of the Supreme Soviet, T. Kh. Koshoev.
Chairman of the Council of Ministers, A. D. Duisheev.

The Kirghiz S.S.R. occupies the north-eastern part of Soviet Central Asia and borders in the south-east on China. In 1924, a Kara-Kirghiz Autonomous Province was formed within the R.S.F.S.R. In 1926 it became a Kirghiz Autonomous Republic, and in 1936 a Union Republic. It contains three provinces, Issyk-Kul, Naryn and Osh. The Kirghiz Republic is a mountainous country, the major part being covered by the ridge of the Central Tienshan, while mountains of the Pamir-Altai system occupy its southern part. There are a number of spacious mountain valleys, the Alai, Susamyr, the Issyk-Kul lake and others. The majority of the population is concentrated in plains, lying at the foot of mountains—Chu, Talass, part of the Ferghana Valley where agriculture prospers. Crops include sugar beet and cotton, and sheep are important in the mountains. Industry is being developed and some mining is done. The Kirghiz constitute 47·9 per cent of the population, the

Russians 25·9 per cent. The Uzbeks (in Eastern Ferghana) amount to 12·1 per cent.

CAPITAL, Frunze (formerly Pishpek). Population, 590,000 (Jan. 1, 1984).

XII.—TADJIKSTAN

First Secretary of the Party Central Committee, R. N. Nabiev.

Chairman of the Presidium of the Supreme Soviet, G. Pallaev.

Chairman of the Council of Ministers, K. M. Makhkamov.

The Tadjik S.S.R. lies in the extreme south-east of Soviet Central Asia and borders in the south on Afghanistan and in the east on China. It was originally formed in 1924 as an Autonomous Republic within the Uzbek S.S.R. and became a Union Republic in 1929. It includes the Gorno-Badakhshan Autonomous Province and the Kulyab and Leninabad Provinces.

The country is mountainous: in the east lie the Pamir highlands with the highest point in the U.S.S.R., Pik Kommunizma (24,500 feet), in the centre the high ridges of the Pamir-Altai system. Plains are formed by wide stretches of the Syr-Darya valley in the north and of the Amu-Darya in the south.

Like the other Central-Asiatic Republics, Tadjikistan is a cotton-growing country. Its climatic conditions favour the cultivation of Egyptian cotton. Irrigation is of great importance. 58·8 per cent of the population are Tadjiks (linguistically and culturally akin to the Persians), 23 per cent Uzbeks, the rest Russians and others.

CAPITAL, Dushanbe (formerly Stalinabad; Dyushambe). Population, 539,000 (Jan. 1, 1984).

XIII.—ARMENIA

First Secretary of the Party Central Committee, K. S. Demirchyan.

Chairman of the Presidium of the Supreme Soviet, B. E. Sarkisov.

Chairman of the Council of Ministers, F. T. Sarkisyan.

The Armenian S.S.R. occupies the south-western part of Transcaucasia: it was formed in 1920. In 1922 it joined the Transcaucasian Federation, and on its liquidation in 1936 became a Union Republic. In the south it borders on Turkey. It is a mountainous country consisting of several vast table lands surrounded by ridges. The population and the economic life are concentrated in the low-lying part of Armenia, the Aras valley and the Erevan hollow; the climate is continental, dry and cold, but the Araks valley has a long, hot and dry summer. Irrigation is essential for agriculture. In Turkey, at the junction of the former Turkish, Persian and Russian boundaries, is *Mount Ararat* (17,160 ft.), the traditional resting place of "Noah's Ark." Industrial and fruit crops are grown in the low-lying districts, grain in the hills. Armenia is traditionally noted for her wine. There are large copper ore and molybdenum deposits and other minerals. The Armenian Church centred in Etchmiadzin is the oldest established Christian Church, Christianity having been recognized as the State religion in A.D. 300.

Nearly 90 per cent of the population is Armenian.

CAPITAL, Erevan. Population, 1,114,000 (Jan. 1, 1984).

XIV.—TURKMENISTAN

First Secretary of the Party Committee, M. N. Gapurov.

Chairman of the Presidium of the Supreme Soviet, B. Yazkuliev.

Chairman of the Council of Ministers, Ch. S. Karryev.

Turkmenia occupies the extreme south of Soviet Central Asia, between the Caspian and the Amu-Darya, and borders in the south on Iran and Afghanistan. It was formed in 1924 and contains five Provinces: Ashkhabad, Chardjou, Krasnovodsk, Mary and Tashauz. The country is a low-lying plain, fringed by hills in the south. Ninety per cent of the plain is taken up by the arid Kara-Kum desert. Of all Central-Asiatic Republics, Turkmenia is the lowest and driest. The cultivation of cotton, stock-raising and mineral extraction are the principal industries. The republic produces about 16 per cent of the Soviet Union's natural gas, as well as astrakhan furs and carpets. Most of the land under plough is artificially irrigated. The oil and silk industries are of old standing. There are also some fisheries in the Caspian.

Turkmens, nomadic in the past, make up 68·4 per cent of the population, Russians 12·6 per cent, and Uzbeks 8·5 per cent.

CAPITAL, Ashkhabad (formerly Askhabad, Poltoratsk). Population, 347,000 (Jan. 1, 1984).

XV.—ESTONIA

First Secretary of the Party Central Committee, K. G. Vaino.

Chairman of the Presidium of the Supreme Soviet, A. F. Ryuitel.

Chairman of the Council of Ministers, B. E. Saul.

Estonia, formerly a Baltic province of the Russian Empire, was proclaimed an independent Republic in 1918. In 1940, it was forcibly incorporated into the U.S.S.R. It lies on the shores of the Baltic and of the Finnish Gulf in the north and of the Gulf of Riga in the south-west. Some 800 islands, among them Dagö and Ösel, form part of Estonian territory. Between 1941 and 1944, Estonia was occupied by the German forces.

The country forms a low-lying plain with many lakes, among them the Chud (or Pskov) Lake, on the border with the R.S.F.S.R. Forests take up about one-fifth of the territory. Agriculture and dairy-farming are the chief industries, rye, oats, barley, flax and potatoes being the chief crops, and butter, bacon and eggs the chief products of dairy farming. There are important manufactures, including textiles, engineering, shipbuilding, woodworking, etc.

The population consists of Estonians (64·7 per cent) and Russians (27·9 per cent).

CAPITAL, Ψ Tallinn (formerly Reval). Population, 458,000 (Jan. 1, 1984).

THE VATICAN CITY STATE
(Stato della Città del Vaticano)

Sovereign Pontiff,
His Holiness Pope John Paul II (Karol Wojtyla), *born* at Wadowice (Krakow, Poland), May 18, 1920, *elected* Pope (in succession to Pope John Paul I), Oct. 16, 1978.

Secretary of State, Cardinal Agostino Casaroli, *appointed* April, 1979.

APOSTOLIC NUNCIATURE IN LONDON
54 Parkside, SW19 5NF

Apostolic Pro Nuncio, His Excellency Archbishop Bruno Heim (1982).

Counsellor, Mons. Luigi Ventura.

The office of the ecclesiastical head of the Roman Catholic Church (Holy See) is vested in the Pope, the Sovereign Pontiff. For many centuries the Sovereign Pontiff exercised temporal power, and in 1859 the Papal States had an area of 17,218 square miles, with a population of 3,124,688. During the reign of Pius IX (1846–1878), the Papal States of Romagna, Umbria and the Marches were incorporated in the Kingdom of Sardinia and with the remaining States (Rome, Comacchio, Viterbo, Civita Vecchia, Velletri and Frosinone) became part of unified Italy in 1870. The territory of the Papacy was confined to the palaces of the Vatican and the Lateran and the Villa of Castel Gandolfo and the temporal power of the Pope was in suspense until the treaty of Feb. 11, 1929, which recognized the full and independent sovereignty of the Holy See in the City of the Vatican. Accompanying the treaty were conventions regulating the condition of religion and the Catholic Church in Italy and agreeing to pay 750,000,000 *lire* in cash and the income at 5 per cent on 1,000,000,000 *lire* State bonds as a final settlement of the claims of the Holy See against Italy for the loss of temporal power. The population of the Vatican City in 1978 was 731.

FLAG.—Square flag; equal vertical bands of yellow (next staff), and white; crossed keys and triple crown device on white band.

BRITISH EMBASSY TO THE HOLY SEE
(91 Via Condotti, 00187 Rome)

Ambassador Extraordinary and Plenipotentiary, His Excellency Sir Mark Evelyn Heath, K.C.V.O., C.M.G.
1st Secretary, R. J. Griffiths.

VENEZUELA
(La Republica de Venezuela)

President, Dr. Jaime Lusinchi, *elected* Dec. 4, 1983, *assumed office* Feb. 2, 1984.

CABINET

Interior, Dr. Octovio Lepage.
Foreign Affairs, Dr. Isidro Morales Paúl.
Finance, Dr. Manuel Azpúrua Arreaza.
Defence, Gen. Humberto Alcalde Alvarez.
Development, Dr. Héctor Hurtado.
Environment and Natural Resources, Dr. Orlando Castejón.
Urban Development, Dr. Rafael Martín Guédez.
Education, Dra. Ruth Lerner de Almea.
Health and Social Assistance, Dr. Luis Manzanilla.
Agriculture and Livestock, Dr. Felipe Gómez Alvarez.
Labour, Dr. Simón Antoni Paván.
Transport and Communications, Dr. Juan Pedro del Moral.
Justice, Sr. José Manzo González.
Mines and Energy, Dr. Arturo Hernández Grisanti.
Information and Tourism, Dr. Armando Durán.
Youth, Dra. Milena Sardi de Selle.
Secretary to the Presidency, Dr. Simón Alberto Consalvi.
Minister of State for Planning, Dr. Luis Matos Azócar.
Minister of State for Culture, Dr. Ignacio Iribarren Borges.
Minister of State for Science and Technology, Dr. Luis M. Carbonell.
President, Investment Fund, Dr. Carlos Rafael Silva.
Governor of the Federal District, Dr. Carmelo Lauría.

VENEZUELAN EMBASSY IN LONDON
1 Cromwell Road, S.W.7
[01–584 4206]

Ambassador Extraordinary and Plenipotentiary, His Excellency Dr. Jose Luis Salcedo-Bastardo.
Minister Counsellor, Sr. Hector Tarchetti.
1st Secretary, Srta. Milena Santana.

There is also a Consulate-General at *Liverpool.*

Area and Population.—A South American Republic, situated approximately between 0° 45′ S. lat. and 12° 12′ N. lat. and 59° 45′–73° 09′ W. long. It consists of one Federal District, 20 states and 2 territories. Venezuela has a total area of 353,894 sq. miles and a population (1981 Census) of 14,516,735.

Venezuela lies on the north of the South American continent, and is bounded on the north by the Caribbean Sea, west by the Republic of Colombia, east by Guyana, and south by Brazil. Included in the area of the Republic are 72 islands off the coast, with a total area of about 14,650 square miles, the largest being *Margarita,* which is politically associated with Tortuga, Cubagua and Coche to form the State of *Nueva Esparta.* Margarita has an area of about 400 square miles. In 1942 Great Britain ceded to Venezuela the small island of *Patos* (170 acres) about 3 miles from the mainland.

Physical Features.—The Eastern Andes from the south-west cross the border and reach to the Caribbean Coast, where they are prolonged by the Maritime Andes of Venezuela to the Gulf of Paria on the northeast. The main range is known as the Sierra Nevada de Merida, and contains the highest peaks in the country in Pico Bolivar (16,411 feet) and Picacho de la Sierra (15,420 feet), the maritime ranges containing the Silla de Caracas (8,531 feet). Near the Brazilian border the Sierras Parima and Pacaraima, and on the eastern border the Sierras de Rincote and de Usupamo, enclose the republic with parallel northward spurs, between which are valleys of the Orinoco tributaries. The Sierra Parima contains Yaparana (7,175 feet) and Duida (8,120 feet), and Pacaraima contains Maraguaca (8,228 feet) and Roraima (9,000 feet), the latter being on the Venezuela-Guyana boundary. The slopes of the mountains and foothills are covered with dense forests, but the basin of the Orinoco is mainly *llanos,* or level stretches of open prairie, with occasional woods.

The principal river of Venezuela is the *Orinoco,* with innumerable affluents, the main river exceeding 1,600 miles in length from its rise in the southern highlands of the republic to its outflow in the deltaic region of the north-east.

The Orinoco is navigable for large steamers from its mouth for 700 miles, and by smaller vessels as far as the Maipures Cataract, some 200 miles farther upstream. Dredging operations have opened the Orinoco to ocean-going ships, of up to 40 ft. draft, as far as Puerto Ordaz (about 150 miles up-stream), which with the adjacent town of San Felix is now officially

known as Ciudad Guayana. Among the many tributaries of the main stream are the Ventuari, Caura and Caroni from the south, and the Apure (with its tributary the Portuguesa), Arauca, Meta, and Guaviare from the west, the Meta and Guaviare being principally Colombian rivers. The upper waters of the Orinoco are united with those of the Rio Negro (a Brazilian tributary of the Amazon) by a natural river or canal, known as the *Casiquiare.* The coastal regions of Venezuela are much indented and contain many lagoons and lakes, of which *Maracaibo,* with an area of 8,296 square miles, is the largest lake in South America. Other lakes are Zulia (290 square miles), south-west of Maracaibo, and Valencia (216 square miles) about 1,400 ft. above sea-level in the Maritime Andes. The *llanos* also contain lakes and swamps caused by the river floods, but they are dry in summer seasons.

The climate is tropical and, except where modified by altitude or tempered by sea breezes, is unhealthy, particularly in the coastal regions and in the neighbourhood of lowland streams and lagoons. The hot, wet season lasts from April to October, the dry, cooler season from November to March.

Language and Literature.—Spanish is the language of the country. Some Venezuelan literature is of international repute. There are 61 daily newspapers in Venezuela, of which ten are published in Caracas, and about 60 to 70 weekly news magazines. There are also a large number of fortnightly, monthly and quarterly publications.

Education is free and primary education compulsory from the age of 7 years. There are ten universities in Venezuela, five in Caracas and the others in Maracaibo, Mérida, Valencia, Cumaná and Barquisimeto.

Production and Industry.—The produce of Venezuelan forest and fields includes the following: (*a*) tropical forest region: orchids, wild rubber, timber, mangrove bark, balata gum and tonka beans. (*b*) agricultural areas: cocoa beans, coffee, cotton, rice, maize, sugar, sesame, groundnuts, potatoes, tomatoes, other vegetables, sisal and tobacco. There is an extensive beef and dairy farming industry. Despite substantial improvements in agriculture, Venezuela is heavily reliant upon food imports, which constitute about 60 per cent of total consumption.

The principal industry is that of *petroleum,* which in 1981 contributed 95 per cent of Venezuela's foreign exchange income. Daily production in the oilfields (which were nationalized on January 1, 1976) has steadily declined since 1973 in line with Venezuela's conservation policies, reaching 2·1 million barrels a day (average) in 1981 (1973—3·366 mbd). Before the war of 1939–45 over 80 per cent of the crude oil was exported to Netherlands Antilles refineries. In 1942 small refineries were established in Venezuela, capable of handling about 200,000 barrels daily. The large Shell (now Maravén) plant at Punta Cardon went into production in 1949, and the Creole refinery at Amuay a year later. Other refineries are being operated at Caripitó, San Lorenzo, Puerto La Cruz, Tucupeido, El Chaure and El Palito. Development of the Orinoco heavy oil belt is now moving ahead with the inauguration of the Lagovén continuous steam injection pilot plant at El Jobo in southern Monagas. It has been estimated conservatively that there might exist recoverable resources of 70,000 million barrels in the Orinoco region, but the initial aim of the Lagovén project is the production of 125,000 and 500,000 bpd of up-graded crude by 1988 and 2000 respectively. A high proportion of the production is exported to the U.S.A. in the form of fuel oil. The Venezuelan Government has unified income tax on firms involved in mining and petroleum at 60 per cent, and reformed the basis on which tax is calculated.

Aluminium is now the second highest source of foreign exchange after petroleum. The Venezuelan state now holds the majority stake in both the principal producing companies, Venalum and Alcasa, and is moving towards a consolidation of the aluminium industry, with both companies sharing their resources and adopting general policies of marketing and procurement of supplies. Output in 1980 was 222,100 tons, with 151,250 tons exported.

Rich iron ore deposits in Eastern Venezuela have been developed. Secondary processes for pelletizing and briqueting ore for export have been installed. The government-owned steel mill at Matanzas in the Guayana uses local iron ore and obtains its electric power from hydro-electric installations on the Caroni River. It produces seamless steel tubes, billets, wire and profiles. The production of more steel products is planned over the next few years. A new mill at Ciudad Guayana for the production of centrifugally-cast iron pipe came into operation at the end of 1970, with an annual capacity of 30,000 tons. It is planned to increase steel production to 15,000,000 tons a year by 1985.

Other industries include petrochemicals, gold, diamonds and asbestos; textiles and clothing; plastics; manufacture of paper, cement, glass and plate glass; beer and other alcoholic beverages; tyres, cigarettes, soap, animal feeding concentrates, non-alcoholic drinks, simple steel products, shoes, tins, jewellery, rope, metal and wooden furniture, sacks, paint and motor-vehicle assembly; preparation of pharmaceutical goods, lard, powdered milk, vegetable oil, flour, biscuits and other foods; fishing and fish-canning; pearl fishing, sanitary ware, electric home appliances, pumps, aluminium and aluminium products, toys, agricultural machinery, bicycles, electronic components, cosmetics and many others.

Communications.—There are about 36,563 km. of all-weather roads. The State has now acquired all but a very few of the railway lines, whose total length is only some 372 kilometres. Road and river communications have made railways of negligible importance in Venezuela except for carrying iron ore in the south-east. However, the government is restoring the Puerto Cabello-Barquisimeto line and expanding it to Turén in the agricultural heartland of Venezuela. A new line connecting Caracas with La Guaira and the Litoral is planned, and in 1983 the Caracas Metro came into operation. British, U.S. and European airlines provide Venezuela with a wide range of services. There are three Venezuelan airlines (two of them state-owned) which between them have a comprehensive network of internal lines and also connect Caracas with the United States, Central America, South America, the Caribbean and Europe. Foreign vessels are not permitted to engage in the coast trade. The telegraph, radio-telegraph and radio-telephone services are state-owned. There are two government-controlled, 150 commercial and one cultural, FM, broadcasting stations. There are four television stations in Venezuela, all in Caracas. Two are government controlled.

Trade with U.K.

	1982	1983
Imports from U.K.	£148,666,000	£87,937,000
Exports to U.K.	141,892,000	183,731,000

CAPITAL.—Caracas (3,000 ft.). Population, 1979, 3,507,800. Other principal towns are ΨMaracaibo (650,000), Barquisimeto (330,000), Valencia (360,000), Maracay (250,000), San Cristobal (150,000), Cumaná (120,000) and Ciudad Guayana (150,000).

FLAG.—Three horizontal bands, yellow, blue, red (with seven white stars on blue band and coat of arms next staff on yellow band).

NATIONAL DAY.—July 5.

BRITISH EMBASSY
Apartado 1246, Caracas 1010-A.

Ambassador Extraordinary and Plenipotentiary, His
Excellency Hugh Michael Carless, C.M.G. (1982).
Counsellor, W. Quantrill (*Head of Chancery*).
Defence Attaché, Capt. D. L. Phillips, R.N.

BRITISH CONSULAR OFFICES
There are British Consular Offices at *Caracas,
Maracaibo, Puerto La Cruz* and *Valencia.*

British Council Representative, J. W. Daniel, Aparto
1246, Caracas 1010.

VIETNAM
(Socialist Republic of Vietnam)

President, Truong Chinh.
Prime Minister, Pham Van Dong.
Deputy Premiers, Pham Hung; Vo Nguyen Giap; Do
Muoi, To Huu, Vu Dinh Lieu, Tran Phuong, Dong
Si Nguyen, Tran Quynh, Vo Van Kiet (*Chairman
of State Planning Commission*).

EMBASSY IN LONDON
12–14 Victoria Road, W8 5RD
[01–937 1912–8564]

Ambassador Extraordinary and Plenipotentiary, His
Excellency Dang Nghiem Bai.
3rd Secretary, Le Van Bang.
Attaches, Duong Danh Dinh (*Commercial*); Pham
Binh Man; Pham Binh Minh; Bui Minh Dung;
Nguyen Thi Nguyet Nga; Nguyen The Dang.

Vietnam, with an area of 129,000 square miles, and
an estimated population (1984) of 60,000,000, is
bordered on the north by China and the west by Laos
and Cambodia (*see map, p. 957*).

Government.—Following the end of the war in
Vietnam in 1975, and the establishment of a Provi-
sional Revolutionary Government to administer
South Vietnam, a National Assembly representing
the whole of Vietnam was elected on April 25, 1976.
The Assembly met in Hanoi on June 24, and on July
2 approved the reunification of North and South
Vietnam under the name of the Socialist Republic of
Vietnam. The national flag, anthem and capital of
North Vietnam were unanimously adopted for the
Socialist Republic, and Saigon was renamed Ho Chi
Minh City.

A new constitution was adopted in December 1980.
The elected National Assembly elects a Council of
Ministers and a Council of State which combines the
functions of President and Standing Committee of
the National Assembly.

Economy.—During the last five years, Vietnam's
economy has faced considerable problems. These
include harvest failures as a result of climatic
disasters, reductions in foreign aid, border hostilities
and the continued allocation of resources to military
expenditure. Efforts to integrate the economies of
the North and South have not been all that successful.
Real GDP grew on average by only 2 per cent per
annum during the period of the second Five-Year
Plan 1976-80, even declining in both 1979 and 1980.

A modest recovery was noted in 1981. Food
production reached 15 m tons. Production of light
industrial goods rose by 7 per cent over 1980 but
other sectors stagnated. In 1983 real GDP is estimated
to have risen by about 6 per cent, compared with
about 8 per cent in 1982. In the same year exports
were estimated at U.S.$538 m and imports at
U.S.$1,240 m, leaving a substantial trade gap. The
1981–85 Five Year Plan was finalised in late 1982 and
provided for more modest targets.

Trade with U.K.

	1982	1983
Imports from U.K.	£876,000	£951,000
Exports to U.K.	133,000	603,000

CAPITAL.—Hanoi (population (1984), City, 925,000;
Province, 2,800,000).
FLAG.—Red, with yellow five-point star in centre.
NATIONAL DAY.—September 2.

BRITISH EMBASSY
16 Pho Ly Thuong Kiet, Hanoi

Ambassador Extraordinary and Plenipotentiary, His
Excellency Michael Edmund Pike, C.M.G. (1982).
Head of Chancery and H.M. Consul, P. J. B. Roberts.

THE WEST INDIES

The West Indies are a number of islands and islets,
some of them mere rocks, situated between 10° to 27°
North and 59° 30′ to 85° West. The whole archipelago
extends in a curve from the Florida Channel (North
America) to within 7 miles of the coast of Venezuela
(South America), and is divided into three main
groups: I. GREATER ANTILLES, which contain the
largest islands, *Cuba* (44,000 sq. miles) and *Hispaniola*
(Haiti and the Dominican Republic) (30,000 sq. miles),
Jamaica and *Puerto Rico*; II. BAHAMAS; III. LESSER
ANTILLES. The total area of the archipelago is nearly
100,000 square miles. The West Indian Islands which
lie nearest the East have been called the *Windward
Islands*; the others the *Leeward Islands*, on account
of the winds which in this area generally blow from
the east.

YEMEN (North)
(Yemen Arab Republic)

President and Commander of the Armed Forces, Col.
Ali Abdullah Saleh, *elected* July 19, 1978, *re-elected*
May 23, 1983.
Prime Minister, Abdul Aziz al Ghani.
Deputy Prime Minister and Internal Affairs, Lt.-Col.
Mujahid Abu Shuwarib.

YEMEN EMBASSY
41 South Street, W1Y 5PD
[01–629 9905]

Ambassador Extraordinary and Plenipotentiary, His
Excellency Ahmed Daifellah Alazeib (1981).

Yemen, the *Arabia Felix* of the ancients, occupies
the S.W. corner of Arabia between the kingdom of
Saudi Arabia and the People's Democratic Republic
of Yemen, with an estimated area of 75,000 square
miles and a population of about 8,556,974 including
about 1,396,123 emigrant workers in the Arabian
peninsula and elsewhere, including the U.K. The
highlands and central plateau of Yemen, and the
highest portions of the maritime range, form the most
fertile part of Arabia, with an abundant but irregular
rainfall.

The ruins of Marib, the ancient Sabæan capital,
and its dam are in the Yemen.

Government.—A General Popular Conference was
established in Aug. 1982, consisting of 700 elected
members and 300 appointed members. It agreed a
new National Charter and elected a Permanent
Council of 75 members (50 elected, 25 appointed), with
a General Council and four sub-committees (economic; political; administrative and public works;
cultural and reform).

INDO-
CHINA

The General Popular Conference meets every two years and is re-elected every four. The Permanent Council meets regularly for two months, followed by a two-month break. The General Council and sub-committees meet regularly.

Trade.—The main exports are cotton, coffee, hides and skins.

Trade with U.K.

	1982	1983
Imports from U.K.	£52,593,000	£56,313,000
Exports to U.K.	1,340,000	1,857,000

CAPITAL.—Sana'a (pop. 277,817). Other main cities are Taiz (119,572) and Hodeida (126,386).

FLAG.—Horizontal bands of red, white and black, with 5-point green star in centre of white band.

BRITISH EMBASSY
P.O. Box 1287, Sana'a

Ambassador Extraordinary and Plenipotentiary, His Excellency David Everard Tatham (1984).
1st Secretaries, J. Dando (*Head of Chancery and Aid*); S. Robinson (*Commercial*); D. J. Baker (*Chancery*).
British Council Representative, P. J. Chenery, Beit Al-Mottahar, Harat Handhal (P.O. Box 2157), Sana'a.

YEMEN (South)
(People's Democratic Republic of Yemen)

President, Ali Nasser Mohammed, *assumed power* April 1980.

EMBASSY
57 Cromwell Road, SW7 2ED
[01–584 6607/9]

Ambassador Extraordinary and Plenipotentiary, His
Exellency Saleh Abdulla Muthana (1983).

Area and Population.—The Democratic Republic
of Yemen lies at the southern end of the Arabian
peninsula, having a frontier with the Yemen Arab
Republic, Saudi Arabia and the Sultanate of Oman,
and a coastline extending 700 miles from the Red Sea
eastwards along the Gulf of Aden. The area is largely
composed of mountains and desert. Rainfall is
generally scarce and unpredictable. The population
outside Aden is concentrated in the fertile districts.
In the more extensive desert and near-desert areas
nomadic communities depend on their livestock for a
livelihood.

Included in the State are the offshore islands of
Perim (in the Bab al-Mandeb Straits) and Socotra,
formerly part of the sultanate of Qishn and Socotra,
now merged in the People's Republic. Sovereignty
over the island of Kamaran (area 70 sq. miles) in the
Red Sea is under dispute following its occupation by
forces of the Yemen Arab Republic during border
conflicts in October, 1972. The area of the People's
Democratic Republic is 112,000 sq. miles, with a
population of 1,800,000 (Est. 1977). The population of
Aden alone (75 sq. miles) is about 270,000. The
principal districts of Aden township are: Crater,
Khormaksar, Tawahi, and Ma'alla. Neighbouring
communities are Sheikh Othman, Medinat al-Shaab,
and Little Aden, which is the site of the Aden
Refinery Company refinery. The other major coastal
town is Mukalla.

Government.—The People's Republic of South
Yemen was set up on Nov. 30, 1967 when the British
government ceded power to the National Liberation
front, thus bringing to an end 129 years of British
rule in Aden and some years of protectorate status in
the hinterland. Its name was changed to People's
Democratic Republic of Yemen on Nov. 30, 1970.
Territory of the Republic is that of the former
Federation of South Arabia and the Aden Protecto-
rates, consisting of the State of Aden and some 17
sultanates and emirates. It is now divided into six
Governorates. Under a constitution promulgated on
Nov. 30, 1970, a Supreme People's Council of 101
members was appointed in May, 1971. Elections to a
new council (112 strong) took place from 16–18
December 1978. At its first plenary session, on Dec.
27, the SPC appointed an 11-member Presidium to
replace the five-man Presidential Council. Abdel
Fattah Ismail was appointed Chairman of the Presidium, and thus head of state. Ismail resigned in April
1980 and was succeeded both as Chairman of the
Presidium and as Secretary-General of the ruling
Yemani Socialist Party by the Prime Minister Ali
Nasser Mohammed.

The Government receives substantial development
from the World Bank, Kuwait and Abu Dhabi (Arab
Development Funds). Other aid is provided by China,
the E.E.C., U.S.S.R. (including military aid) and other
Socialist Bloc countries.

Kuria Muria Islands.—The Kuria Muria Islands,
which had been administered by Great Britain from
Aden although 200 miles distant from Yemen territory, were retroceded to the Sultanate of Oman on
Nov. 30, 1967.

Production.—Agriculture is the main occupation
of the inhabitants of the 112,000 square miles of the
Republic, outside Aden town. This is largely of a
subsistence nature, sorghum, sesame and millets
being the chief crops, with wheat and barley widely
grown at the higher elevations. Disastrous floods in
1983 caused major damage to the principal agricultural areas.

Under the Five Year Development Plan 1974–79
much importance was attached to the development
of agricultural and fisheries projects. Under the
second Five Year Plan (1981–85) emphasis has shifted
to industrial development, which has been allocated
29 per cent of the total investment budget (YD508m);
agricultural development has been allocated 12 per
cent. Light industries are being established which
will replace imports and use locally produced raw
materials.

Trade with U.K.

	1982	1983
Imports from U.K.	£35·6m	£36,673,000
Exports to U.K.	26·7m	10,627,000

Following the closure of the Suez Canal in 1967 the
once prosperous trading economy of Aden fell into a
steady decline, which has not been reversed by the
re-opening of the Canal. In the main harbour, cargo
handling for larger vessels is by lighter, but wharves
at Maalla can accommodate alongside vessels up to
300 feet in length and 18 feet in draught. The Aden
Refinery Company has a refining capacity of 8 m.
tons per annum but for a number of years throughput
has not exceeded a rate equivalent to 5 m. tons
annually. Yemen is not an oil producing country but
significant traces of hydrocarbons were found during
exploration activities offshore in 1982.

Finance and Currency.—During 1977 revenue was
estimated at about £51,000,000 and expenditure
£68,000,000. Currency is the South Yemen *dinar*
(YD).

Communications.—There are no railways in the
Republic. Yemen has 760 miles of good roads and
construction of a further 300 miles is in hand. A
system of undeveloped but motorable roads links the
towns and villages outside Aden. There is an
international airport at Aden (Khormaksar) into
which a limited number of international airlines
operate.

CAPITAL.—Aden (population, 270,000).

FLAG.—A tricolour, red, white and black horizontal bands, with a triangle of light blue at the hoist
pointing towards the fly and charged with a five
pointed red star.

NATIONAL DAYS.—Independence Day, Nov. 30;
Revolution Day, Oct. 14.

BRITISH EMBASSY
Khormaksar, Aden.

Ambassador Extraordinary and Plenipotentiary, His
Excellency Peter Keegan Williams (1982).

YUGOSLAVIA
(Socijalistička Federativna Republika
Jugoslavije)

President of the Presidency, Veselin Djuranović
(*elected May 1984 for one year*).
Vice-President of the Presidency, Radovan Vlajković
(*elected May 1984 for one year*).
President of the SFRY Assembly, Dušan Alimpić.
President of the Federal Executive Council, Milka
Planinc.
*President of the Socialist Alliance of the Working
People*, Marijan Rožič.
Vice-President of the SFRY Assembly, Nuša Keršo-
van.
Vice-Presidents of the Federal Executive Council,
Borislav Srebrić; Mijat Šuković; Janez Zemljaric.
Secretary General of the SFRJ Assembly, Milan
Jonovski.
Federal Secretaries:—
Foreign Affairs, Raif Dizdarević.
National Defence, Branko Mamula.

Internal Affairs, Dobroslav Ćulafić.
Finance, Vlado Klemenčić.
Foreign Trade, Dr. Milenko Bojanić.
Trade and General Economic Affairs, Siniša Korica.
Justice and Organization of Federal Administration, Borislav Krajina.
Information, Mitko Čalovski.
Federal Committee Presidents:—
Energy and Industry, Rade Pavlović.
Agriculture, Milorad Stanojević.
Transport and Communications, Mustafa Pljakić.
Labour, Health and Social Security, Djordje Jakovljević.
Questions concerning War Veterans and Disabled Veterans, Jovko Jovkovski.
Legislature, Janko Česnik.

LEAGUE OF COMMUNISTS OF YUGOSLAVIA

Presidency of the Central Committee
President of the Presidency, Ali Šukrija (*elected for one year in June 1984*).
Secretary, Dimce Belovski (*elected for two years in June 1984*).
Members, M. Andrić; J. Bilić; D. Dragosavać; S. Dolaševic; K. Hadzivasilev; G. Jovičic; B. Krunic; M. Kučan; A. Marinc; D. Marković; P. Matić; V. Milatović; M. Pancevski; H. Pozderać; M. Radović; M. Ribičić; I. Stambolić; N. Stojanovic; M. Spiljak; D. Vidić; V. Žarković.

YUGOSLAV EMBASSY IN LONDON
5–7 Lexham Gardens W8 5JJ
[01–370 6105]

Ambassador Extraordinary and Plenipotentiary, His Excellency Dragi Stamenković (1981).
Minister Counsellors, Milutin Stajanovic; Predrag Mitic *(Economic)*.
Counsellors, Marjan Mikolic *(Press and Culture)*; Ivan Plese *(Consular)*.
Defence Attaché, Capt. Uros Trbojevic.
1st Secretaries, Neven Madey; Zdravko Dejanovic.
2nd Secretaries, Mladen Mandic; Andrej Zlebnik.
Consulate, 7 Lexham Gardens, W8 5JJ

Area and Population.—Yugoslavia is a Federation comprising the Socialist Republics of Serbia, Croatia, Slovenia, Montenegro, Bosnia and Herzegovina, and Macedonia. Serbia includes the Socialist Autonomous Provinces of Vojvodina and Kosovo. The area of Yugoslavia is estimated at 255,804 square kilometres (98,725 square miles). The population in April 1981 was 22,420,000, including 8,140,000 Serbs, 4,430,000 Croats, 1,750,000 Slovenes, 1,730,000 Albanians, 1,341,000 Macedonians and 1.220,000 "Yugoslavs", as well as a variety of other minorities.

Government.—On Nov. 29, 1945, the Constituent Assembly of Yugoslavia at a joint session of the Skupština and the House of Nationalities, proclaimed Yugoslavia a Republic.

The official name of the country, "The Socialist Federal Republic of Yugoslavia", was adopted by the 1963 Constitution.

Several amendments to the Constitution were made in 1971. The most important formed a new ruling body called the Presidency, which has 8 members, one from each Republic and Autonomous Province. Since the death of President Tito in May 1980, its members take it in turns according to a fixed order of succession to become President of the Presidency of the Republic for a period of 12 months each. A new Constitution was proclaimed in 1974 followed by the reconstitution of the Federal Assembly into two chambers consisting of the Federal Chamber (220 delegates) and the Republican/Provincial Chamber (88 delegates). A new Federal Executive Council (i.e. government) was also formed. The

current Council was elected in May 1982 with a 4 year mandate. The first election of the S.F.R.Y. Presidency since Pres. Tito's death took place in May 1984; each new member has a five-year mandate.

There is only one political party in Yugoslavia, the "League of Communists of Yugoslavia" (within which each Republic and Province has its own separate L.C.Y. organization) but there is a formal separation of State and Party; no-one may hold a post in the Federal or Republican/Provincial governments and a paid L.C.Y. post simultaneously. Political and economic decisions on many issues are devolved from Federal to Republican/Provincial level. Yugoslavia has a "self-management" form of industrial organization under which the workforce have the constitutional right to own and control their own enterprises.

Defence.—The Army, Navy and Air Force on a peace footing consist of 250,000 officers and men.

Religion and Education.—The three main faiths are the Orthodox, Catholic and Islamic, and freedom for all faiths is constitutionally guaranteed. Religion is separated from the State and no religious instruction is allowed in state schools, although it is permitted in churches.

Education.—Eight years' elementary education is compulsory and all education is free. There are 18 universities.

Language and Literature.—The language mainly used throughout Yugoslavia and in the Federal Government is Serbo-Croat but Slovenian and Macedonian (also South-Slav tongues) and Albanian, Bulgarian, Rumanian, Italian, Slovak, Ruthenian, Hungarian and Turkish are also spoken in certain areas. There is, however, no official language since all are constitutionally equal, except in the Armed Forces where Serbo Croat is obligatory. In Serbia, Macedonia and Montenegro the Cyrillic script is used and in the rest of the country the Latin. There are 4 Serbian daily newspapers in Belgrade, 2 Slovene dailies in Ljubljana, 2 Croat dailies in Zagreb, and many other dailies published in other towns. There are also many local newspapers and radio programmes in the different "minority" languages.

Production and Industry.—The share of industry in Gross Domestic Product (average annual rate in real terms of 6·5 per cent in 1981) is now 40 per cent, while agriculture is 14 per cent. In industry the high level of investment of recent years is being cut back and present efforts are directed towards development of high priority areas such as mining, energy resources and transport and communications. Agricultural policy is directed towards substantially increased production, to make the the country self-sufficient and to provide significant exports of foodstuffs. Some 80 per cent of land is still privately owned.

The main crops are wheat, maize, sugar beet, sunflower and soya. Yields in 1983 were (tons): wheat, 5·5 m; maize, 10·7 m; sugar beet, 5·6 m. According to Yugoslav official estimates, the livestock population in 1983 was approximately as follows: cattle, 5,351,000; sheep, 7,452,000; pigs, 8,370,000; poultry, 69,680,000.

Minerals are an important source of wealth particularly in the central and south eastern regions. Production in 1983 included the following (tons):—

Coal	57,900,000
Coke	3,440,000
Iron ore	5,090,000
Pig iron	2,870,000
Steel	4,165,000
Crude oil	4,130,000

Smaller quantities of copper, zinc and mercury are produced.

Communications.—In 1982 there were 9,389 kms of standard and narrow gauge railway and approximately 115,200 kms of classified roads. In 1982 there were 2,542,000 telephones in use in the country. The principal Ψports on the long Adriatic seaboard of Yugoslavia are Rijeka, Bakar, Šibenik, Split, Zadar, Kardeljeva (formerly Ploče), Dubrovnik, Bar, Kotor (Cattaro) and Koper. The Danube forms a great commercial highway and the tributary rivers Sava and Tisa provide other shipping routes.

FINANCE

	1982 million *Dinars*	1983 million *Dinars*
Revenue	1,068,000	1,140,000
Expenditure	1,068,000	1,140,000

The rate of exchange is variable. On June 6, 1980 the *dinar* was devalued against all convertible currencies and there have been several devaluations since then. (*See also* p. 82.)

Trade with U.K.

	1982	1983
Imports from U.K.	£158,881,000	£148,646,000
Exports to U.K.	52,115,000	83,951,000

CAPITAL.—Belgrade, population (1981) 1,455,000. Other towns are Zagreb (763,000); Skopje (503,000); Ljubljana (253,000); Sarajevo (447,000); Novi Sad (169,000); Priština (1971) (153,000); Ψ Split (152,000); Ψ Rijeka (133,000); Titograd (95,000).

FLAG.—Five-point red star outlined by narrow yellow stripe, on a ground of three horizontal bars, blue, white and red.

NATIONAL DAY.—November 29.

BRITISH EMBASSY
General Ždanova 46, Belgrade.

Ambassador Extraordinary and Plenipotentiary, His Excellency Kenneth B. A. Scott, C.M.G. (1982).
Counsellors, A. St. J. H. Figgis.
Defence and Military Attaché, Col. A. J. Smith, O.B.E.
1st Secretaries, M. J. S. Allen (*Economic*); N. D. Rampton (*Admin. and Consular*); G. M. Johnston (*Commercial*).
Attachés, D. Snape; E. Newton.
3rd Secretaries, M. J. L. Kirk (*Information*); T. C. Moore (*Chancery*); Miss C. A. Fawcett (*Admin. and Consular*).

BRITISH CONSULAR OFFICES

There are British Consular Offices at *Belgrade, Zagreb* and *Split.*

British Council Representative, O. D. Elliott, Generala Ždanova 34, (P.O. Box 248), 11001 Belgrade. British Council Reading Room, Knez Mihajlova 45, Belgrade. There are also a centre and library at Zagreb.

ZAIRE
(The Republic of Zaire)

President of the Republic and National Security, Marshal Mobutu Sésé Séko, *born* Oct. 30, 1930; *assumed office* November 25, 1965; *elected for 7-year term*, Nov. 5, 1970; *re-elected for third 7-year term*, July 28, 1984.
Premier, Kengo wa Dondo.
Vice-Premier and Administration, Mozagba Ngbuka.
Foreign Affairs, Umba di Lutete.
Justice, Bayona ba Meya.
Finance, Kiakwama Kia Kiziki.
Economy and Industry, Pay-Pay wa Sykasige.
Agriculture, Nyembo Shabani.
Mines and Energy, Umba Kyamitala.
External Trade, Lukusa Muengula.

ZAIRE EMBASSY
26 Chesham Place, SW1X 8HH
[01–235 6137]

Chargé d'Affaires, Bosolo Efeka.

The State of the Congo, founded in 1885, became a Belgian Colony on Nov. 15, 1908, and was administered by Belgium until June 30, 1960, when it became the Democratic Republic of the Congo. In October 1971 the name changed to the Republic of Zaire. Situated between long. 12°–31° E. and lat. 5° N.–13° S., the Republic of Zaire comprises an area of 905,582 sq. miles, with a population (1981 estimate) of 28,400,000.

Climate.—Apart from the coastal district in the West which is fairly dry, the rainfall averages between 60 and 80 inches. The average temperature is about 80° F., but in the South the winter temperature can fall nearly to freezing point. There has been some increase in sleeping-sickness since independence. Malaria, formerly under control in Kinshasa and Matadi, has also begun to increase.

Extensive forest covers the central districts.

Government.—On June 30, 1960, the Belgian Congo became an independent unitary state under the

Presidency of M. Kasavubu with a provisional constitution, the *Loi Fondamentale*, drawn up by the metropolitan Belgian Parliament. On July 11, M. Moise Tshombe announced the independence of the State of Katanga although he failed to obtain international recognition. Katanga did not come under the Government at Leopoldville until January 14, 1963.

The constitutional and political situation remained unsettled, the United Nations having mixed forces in the country until 1964. By the middle of 1965, the Congolese Government formed by M. Tshombe in July, 1964, had succeeded in gaining control of all the towns from the rebels and depriving them of military aid from outside the Congo.

General Joseph-Désiré Mobutu, Commander-in-Chief of the Congolese National Army, announced on November 25, 1965 that he had assumed the Presidency. After re-organizations in Dec. 1966, and Oct. 5, 1967, a new Cabinet, with the President again as Prime Minister, took office on Mar. 5, 1969.

A Presidential régime was instituted by the 1967 Constitution, subsequently amended in 1974 and totally revised in Feb. 1978. The Mouvement Populaire de la Révolution is the sole political party. The President changed his name to Mobutu Sésé Séko Kuku Ngbendu Wa Za Banga in 1972, but is usually known by the first three of these names only.

Provinces.—On December 24, 1966, the number of provinces was reduced from 21 to 8, each under a Governor and provincial administration. They have been redesignated as "regions" and are now as follows, with names of capitals in brackets: Bas-Zaire *(Matadi)*; Bandundu *(Bandundu)*; Equateur *(Mbandaka)*; Haut-Zaire *(Kisangani)*; Kivu *(Bukavu)*; Shaba, *formerly* Katanga *(Lubumbashi)*; East Kasai *(Mbuji-Mayi)*; West Kasai *(Kananga)*.

Production.—The cultivation of oil palms is widespread, palm oil being the most important agricultural cash product though it is no longer exported. Coffee, rubber, cocoa and timber are the most important agricultural exports. The production of cotton, pyrethrum and copal fell sharply on independence but is now increasing. The country is rich in minerals, particularly Shaba (*ex*-Katanga) province. Copper, widely exploited, is the country's major source of foreign exchange earnings; industrial diamonds and cobalt are also produced. Oil deposits are exploited off the Zaire estuary and reef-gold is mined in the north-east of the country.

There is a wide variety of small secondary industries, the main products being: cotton fabrics, blankets, sacks, footwear, beer, cigarettes, cement, paint, sugar, furniture, metal goods and tyres, and local assembly of motor vehicles. There are very large reserves of hydro-electric power and the huge Inga dam on the river Zaire is now supplying electricity to Matadi, Kinshasa and Shaba.

The chief exports are copper, crude oil, coffee, diamonds, rubber, cobalt, gold, cassiterite, zinc and other metals.

Communications. There are approximately 20,500 km of roads (earth-surfaced) of national importance, and 6,000 km of railways. The country has two international and 40 principal airports.

Currency.—The present unit of currency, the *Zaire*, was introduced in 1967, replacing 1,000 Old Congolese francs.

Trade with U.K.

	1982	1983
Imports from U.K.	£15,801,000	£21,128,512
Exports to U.K.	20,557,000	11,192,157

Language, Religion and Education.—The people are mainly of Bantu-Negro stock, divided into semi-autonomous tribes, each speaking a Bantu tongue. Swahili, a Bantu dialect with an admixture of Arabic, is the nearest approach to a common language in the East and South, while Lingala is the language of a large area along the river and in the north, and Kikongo of the region between Kinshasa and the sea. French is the language of administration. It is estimated there are 9,500,000 African Christians in the Republic (Roman Catholic 5,800,000, Protestant 1,600,000). The local Kimbanguist religion has over two million adherents. The National University of Zaire has campuses in Kinshasa, Kisangani and Lubumbashi, with approximately 28,000 students (1978–79).

CAPITAL.—Kinshasa (*formerly* Leopoldville), population (estimated, 1980) 2,500,000. Principal towns, Lubumbashi (*formerly* Elisabethville) (403,623); Kisangani (*formerly* Stanleyville) (310,705); Likasi (146,394); Kananga (601,239); Ψ Matadi (143,598); and Mbandaka (134,495).

FLAG.—Dark brown hand and torch with red flame in yellow roundel on green background.

NATIONAL DAY.—November 24.

BRITISH EMBASSY
B.P. 8049, Kinshasa.

Ambassador Extraordinary and Plenipotentiary, His Excellency Nicholas Peter Bayne, C.M.G. (1983).

1*st Secretary*, M. R. Crompton.

2*nd Secretary*, J. McGoran (*Commercial and Vice-Consul*).

3*rd Secretary*, J. D. Bevan.

THE UNITED NATIONS

The foundations of the Charter of the United Nations were laid at the Conference of Foreign Ministers in Moscow in 1943, and upon those foundations a structure was built at the meetings at Dumbarton Oaks, Washington, D.C., Aug. 21–Oct. 7, 1944. The design was discussed and criticized at San Francisco from April 25 to June 26, 1945, on which date representatives of 50 Allied Nations appended their signatures to the Charter.

The United Nations formally came into existence on October 24, 1945. It was later decided that its seat should be in the United States. Permanent headquarters have been erected at Manhattan, New York. October 24 has been designated "United Nations Day".

The following 158 states are members of the United Nations:—

Afghanistan, Albania, Algeria, Angola, Antigua and Barbuda, Argentina,* Australia,* Austria, Bahamas, Bahrain, Bangladesh, Barbados, Belgium, Belize,* Benin, Bhutan, Bolivia,* Botswana, Brazil,* Bulgaria, Burma, Burundi, Byelorussian Soviet Socialist Republic,* Cambodia, Cameroon, Canada,* Cape Verde, Central African Rep., Chad, Chile,* China,* Colombia,* Comoros, Congo (Pop. Repub.), Costa Rica,* Cuba,* Cyprus, Czechoslovakia,* Denmark,* Djibouti, Dominica, Dominican Republic,* Ecuador,* Egypt,* El Salvador,* Equatorial Guinea, Ethiopia,* Fiji, Finland, France,* Gabon, Gambia, Germany (East), Germany (West), Ghana, Greece,* Grenada, Guatemala,* Guinea, Guinea-Bissau, Guyana, Haiti,* Honduras,* Hungary, Iceland, India,* Indonesia, Iran,* Iraq,* Republic of Ireland, Israel, Italy, Ivory Coast, Jamaica, Japan, Jordan, Kenya, Kuwait, Laos, Lebanon,* Lesotho, Liberia,* Libya, Luxemburg,* Madagascar, Malawi, Malaysia, Maldive Islands, Mali, Malta, Mauritania, Mauritius, Mexico,* Mongolia, Morocco, Mozambique, Nepal, Netherlands,* New Zealand,* Nicaragua,* Niger, Nigeria, Norway,* Oman, Pakistan, Panama,* Papua New Guinea, Paraguay,* Peru,* Philippines,* Poland,* Portugal, Qatar, Rumania, Rwanda, St. Christopher and Nevis, St. Lucia, St. Vincent and the Grenadines, Sao Tome and Principe, Saudi Arabia,* Senegal, Seychelles, Sierra Leone, Singapore, Solomon Islands, Somalia, South Africa,* Spain, Sri Lanka, Sudan, Surinam, Swaziland, Sweden, Syria,* Tanzania, Thailand, Togo, Trinidad and Tobago, Tunisia, Turkey,* Uganda, Ukrainian Soviet Socialist Republic,* Union of Soviet Socialist Republics,* United Arab Emirates, United Kingdom,* United States of America,* Upper Volta, Uruguay, Vanuatu,* Venezuela,* Viet Nam, Western Samoa, Yemen (Arab Repub.), Yemen (P.D.R.), Yugoslavia,* Zaire, Zambia, Zimbabwe.

*Original member (i.e. from 1945). (From October 25, 1971, "China" was taken to mean the People's Republic of China.)

Brunei has applied for membership of the U.N.

The principal organs of the United Nations are:—
(1) The General Assembly; (2) The Security Council; (3) The Economic and Social Council; (4) The Trusteeship Council; (5) The International Court of Justice; (6) The Secretariat.

1. The General Assembly

The General Assembly consists of all the Members of the United Nations. Each Member is entitled to be represented at its meetings by five representatives, but has only one vote. The General Assembly meets once a year in regular session beginning on the third Tuesday in September. A new President is elected by the General Assembly at the start of every annual session. Special Sessions may also be held.

The work of the General Assembly is divided among seven Main Committees, on each of which every Member has the right to be represented:—(1) Disarmament and related security questions; (2) Economic and Financial; (3) Social, Humanitarian and Cultural; (4) Decolonization (including Non-Self Governing Territories); (5) Administrative and Budgetary; (6) Legal. There is also a Special Political Committee, to relieve the burden on the first Committee.

The Main Committees consider items referred to them by the General Assembly and recommend draft resolutions for submission to the Assembly's plenary meetings.

The Assembly has two procedural committees—a General Committee and a Credentials Committee; and three standing committees—an Advisory Committee on Administrative and Budgetary Questions, a Committee on Contributions and a Disarmament Commission.

The General Assembly appoints such *ad hoc* committees as may be required from time to time for special purposes. The Assembly is also assisted in its work by subsidiary bodies such as the Board of Auditors, the Committee on Conferences, the International Law Commission, etc. In 1964 the General Assembly set up the United Nations Conference on Trade and Development (UNCTAD) as a permanent body.

The United Nations Industrial Development Organization was set up on Jan. 1, 1967, to promote industrialization and co-ordinate United Nations activities in this field.

President of the United Nations General Assembly, Jorge E. Illueca (*Panama*) (1983).

2. The Security Council

The Security Council consists of fifteen Members, each of which has one representative and one vote. There are five *permanent Members* (China, France, U.K., U.S.A., U.S.S.R) and ten non-permanent Members elected for a two-year term.

The Security Council bears the primary responsibility for the maintenance of peace and security. Decisions on procedural questions are made by an affirmative vote of nine Members. On all other matters the affirmative vote of nine Members must include the concurring votes of the *permanent Members*, and it is this clause which makes the *Veto* possible.

The General Assembly, any member of the United Nations, or the Secretary-General, can bring to the Council's attention any matter considered to threaten international peace and security. A non-member State can bring a dispute before the Council provided it accepts in advance the U.N. Charter obligations for peaceful settlement.

The Security Council also establishes *ad hoc* committees and commissions which may be required from time to time for special purposes.

3. The Economic and Social Council

This body is responsible under the General Assembly for carrying out the functions of the United Nations with regard to international economic, social, cultural, educational, health and related matters.

It has established the following Commissions: Statistical, Human Rights, Social Development, Status of Women, Narcotic Drugs, Population, Regional Economic Commissions for Europe, Asia and the Pacific, Western Asia, Latin America and Africa.

The Council also makes recommendations for the co-ordination of the policies and activities of 15 specialized agencies and other organizations in the U.N. system.

4. Trusteeship Council

The Trusteeship Council now consists of five members: the U.S.A. (administering authority of Micronesia, the only remaining trust Territory of the original 11), and the other four permanent members of the Security Council, China, France, U.K. and U.S.S.R.

The Trusteeship Council considers reports from administering authorities; examines petitions in consultation with the administering authority; makes periodic inspection visits; and checks conditions with an annual questionnaire on the political, economic, social, and educational advancement of the inhabitants of trust territories.

5. International Court of Justice

The International Court of Justice is the principal judicial organ of the United Nations. The Statute of the court is an integral part of the Charter and all Members of the United Nations are *ipso facto* parties to it. The Court is composed of 15 judges, no two of whom may be nationals of the same State, and is based at The Hague.

If any party to a case fails to adhere to the judgment of the Court, the other party may have recourse to the Security Council.

President, Taslim Olawale Elias (*Nigeria*).

THE SECRETARIAT

Secretary-General, Javier Perez de Cuellar (*Peru*).
Director-General, Development and International Economic Co-operation, Jean Ripert (*France*).

U.N. Office and Information Centre, Ship House, 20 Buckingham Gate, S.W.1.

OTHER ORGANS

The U.N. Centre for Human Settlements (Habitat), Nairobi; U.N. Children's Fund (UNICEF), New York; U.N. Conference on Trade and Development (UNCTAD), Geneva; U.N. Development Programme (UNDP), New York; U.N. Disaster Relief Office (UNDRO), Geneva; U.N. Environment Programme (UNEP), Nairobi; U.N. Fund for Population Activities (UNFPA), New York; U.N. High Commissioner for Refugees (UNHCR), Geneva; U.N. Industrial Development Organisation (UNIDO), Vienna (N.B. UNIDO is to be upgraded to the status of a specialised agency); U.N. Institute for Training and Research (UNITAR), New York; U.N. Relief and Works Agency for Palestine Refugees in the Near East (UNRWA), Vienna; U.N. University (UNU), Tokyo; World Food Council (WFC), Rome; World Food Programme (WFP), Rome; International Research and Training Institute for the Advancement of Women (INSTRAW).

BUDGET OF THE UNITED NATIONS

The budget is now approved for periods of two years, and the appropriation for the biennium 1984–85 is U.S.$1,587,159,800 (*gross*). The scale of assessments for 1984–85 includes: Australia, 1·57 per cent.; Canada, 3·08 per cent.; China, 0·88 per cent.; France, 6·51 per cent.; India, 0·36 per cent.; Japan, 10·32 per cent.; New Zealand, 0·26 per cent.; U.K., 4·67 per cent.; U.S.S.R., 10·54 per cent.; U.S.A., 25 per cent.

U.K. MISSION TO THE UNITED NATIONS
845 Third Avenue, New York

Permanent Representative to the United Nations and Representative on the Security Council, Sir John Thomson, K.C.M.G. (1982).
Minister and Deputy Permanent Representative, (vacant).
Counsellors, Hon. D. A. Gore-Booth (*Head of Chancery*); F. D. Berman (*Legal Adviser*); J. D. I. Boyd (*Economic and Social Affairs*); A. J. Breeze.

U.K. MISSION TO THE U.N. AND OTHER INTERNATIONAL ORGANIZATIONS IN GENEVA
37–39 rue de Vermont, 1211 Geneva 20

Permanent U.K. Representative, Dame Anne Warburton, D.C.V.O., C.M.G.
Counsellor, Head of Chancery and Deputy Permanent Representative, D. J. Moss.

SPECIALISED AGENCIES

Fifteen other international organizations, having wide responsibilities in economic, social, cultural, educational and other related fields, carry out their functions in co-operation with the United Nations under agreements made with the Economic and Social Council.

International Labour Organization (ILO) Geneva (London Branch Office, 96–98 Marsham Street, S.W.1.). Established with the League of Nations in 1919 under the Treaty of Versailles, the ILO became in 1946 the first specialized agency associated with the United Nations. In May, 1983 the Organization had 150 member States. The aim of the ILO is to promote lasting peace through social justice, and to this end it works for better economic and social conditions everywhere. It was awarded the Nobel Peace Prize in 1969.

The ILO establishes international labour standards, which set guidelines for improving working conditions and protecting basic human rights; runs a world-wide programme of technical assistance to developing countries; conducts research and disseminates information on the human aspects of economic activity, with a view to improving social and economic well-being. Through its World Employment Programme, the ILO is attacking unemployment and its associated ills by aiding national and international efforts to provide productive work for the world's fast-growing population. It is also developing an international programme for the improvement of working conditions and the working environment.

The ILO is financed by contributions from its member states. A proportion of its budget is devoted to its technical assistance programme, but this is financed mainly by funds from UNDP and other sources. The total technical co-operation budget for 1982–83 amounted to about $270 million.

The International Labour Conference, composed of national delegations of two government delegates, one worker delegate and one employer delegate, meets at least once a year. It formulates international labour standards and broad policies of the Organization, provides a forum for discussion of world labour and social problems, and approves the ILO's work programme and budget, which is financed by member States.

A 56-member Governing Body, composed of 28 government members, 14 worker members and 14 employer members, acts as the Organization's executive council. Ten governments hold seats on the Governing Body because of their industrial importance.

The International Labour Office, the secretariat of the Organization, collects and distributes information, assists governments on request in drafting legislation on the basis of international labour standards, directs technical co-operation activities, and issues publications.

Director-General, Francis Blanchard (*France*).

Food and Agriculture Organization of the United Nations (FAO), Via delle Terme di Caracalla, Rome.—Established on October 16, 1945, to raise levels of nutrition and standards of living, to secure improvements in the efficiency of the production and distribution of all food and agricultural products and to better the condition of rural populations, thus contributing to the expansion of world economy and ensuring man's freedom from hunger. Among its many activities the Organization promotes the global exchange of information in the fields of agriculture, forestry and fisheries, facilitates international agreement in these fields and provides technical assistance in such subjects as nutrition and food management, soil erosion control, re-afforestation, the establishment of paper industries, irrigation engineering, control of infestation of stored foods, production of fertilizers, control of crop pests and diseases, and improvement of fishing vessels, fish distribution and marketing. Jointly with the United Nations it administers the World Food Programme, which in 1983 committed nearly $900,000,000 in cash and commodities to low-income countries. The 1983 session of the FAO governing Conference approved a budget of $421,000,000 for the two years 1983–84. In addition FAO is carrying out field programmes involving annual expenditure of about $260,000,000 under the U.N. Development Programme and other aid programmes. Through its co-operative programme with the World Bank it is helping to increase international investment in agriculture and allied fields.

The policy of the Organization is directed by a two-yearly Conference of the 156 member countries. A council (49 members) acts for the Conference between its sessions.

Director-General, Edouard Saouma (*Lebanon*).
Permanent U.K. Representative, P. S. McLean, O.B.E.

United Nations Educational, Scientific and Cultural Organization (UNESCO), 7 Place de Fontenoy, Paris 75700.—Under its constitution, the Organization makes its contribution to peace and security by promoting collaboration among its Member States in the fields of education, science, culture and communications. It aims at furthering a universal respect for justice, for the rule of law and for human rights, without distinction of race, sex, language or religion, in accordance with the Charter of the United Nations.

The Organization is composed of three organs: (i) the *General Conference*, consisting of representatives of Member States, which meets biennially to decide the programme and budget; (ii) the *Executive Board*, composed of 51 members elected by the General Conference to supervise the execution of the approved programme and (iii) the *Secretariat*, which is responsible for Unesco's day-to-day functioning and the execution of the programme. In most Member States National Commissions serve as a link with Unesco and help to carry out the programme. Member States in November 1983, 161 and three Associate Members (British Eastern Caribbean group, Netherlands Antilles and the British Virgin Islands).

Director-General, Amadou Mahtar M'Bow (*Senegal*).

Permanent U.K. Representative, Paris, J. K. Gordan.
U.K. National Commission for UNESCO, Ministry of Overseas Development, Stag Place, S.W.1.

World Health Organization (WHO), 1211 Geneva 27. Established on April 7, 1948, the aim of the World Health Organization is the attainment by all peoples of the highest possible level of health. It co-operates with its member governments in their efforts to develop health manpower, streamline health services, control communicable diseases, promote family health—including mother and child care, family planning, nutrition and health education—and strengthen environmental health. It promotes biomedical and health services research through some 500 collaborating research centres in different parts of the world. Its other services include the International Pharmacopoeia, drug evaluation and monitoring, biological standardization, epidemiological surveillance and scientific publications. Approved budget for 1984 and 1985, $520,100,000. Membership (May 1984), 164.

Organs are a *World Health Assembly* meeting annually to frame policy, an *Executive Board* (31 members), meeting at least twice a year, and a *Secretariat*.

Director-General, H. T. Mahler (*Denmark*).

International Bank for Reconstruction and Development (IBRD), Washington, D.C. 20433; European office, 66 Ave. d'Iéna, 75116, Paris, France.—Established on Dec. 27, 1945, to help raise standards of living in developing countries by the provision of financial resources through loans made for productive purposes to a government, or guaranteed by the government concerned. Loans are directed towards developing countries at more advanced stages of economic and social growth.

The Bank, which is owned by the governments of 146 countries and whose capital is subscribed by its member countries, finances its lending operations primarily from its own borrowing in the world capital markets, and derives a substantial contribution to its resources from its retained earnings and the repayment of loans. The interest rate on its loans is calculated in relation to its cost of borrowing; loans generally have a grace period of five years and are repayable over 20 years or less. The loans made by the Bank since its inception to June 30, 1983, totalled $101,565,400,000 to 106 countries. Subscribed capital, $56,010,584,000.

The *Board of Governors* consists of one Governor and one alternate appointed by each of the member countries. Twenty-one *Executive Directors* exercise all powers of the Bank except those reserved to the Board of Governors. The *President*, selected by the Executive Directors, conducts the business of the Bank, with the assistance of an international staff.

President, A. W. Clausen (*U.S.A.*).
U.K. Executive Director, N. L. Wicks, C.B.E.

International Development Association (IDA), Washington, D.C. 20433; European office, 66 Ave. d'Iéna, 75116 Paris, France.—The IDA is an affiliate of the IBRD (the two together comprising the *World Bank*) and was established in September 1960 to provide assistance for the same purposes as the IBRD but primarily in the poorer developing countries and on terms that bear less heavily on their balance of payments than IBRD loans. Assistance is concentrated on the very poor countries, i.e. those with an annual per capita GNP of less than $796 (in 1981 dollars); more than 50 countries are eligible.

Membership is open to all members of IBRD and 131 have joined to date. Funds, called credits to distinguish them from IBRD loans, come mostly in the form of subscriptions, general replenishments and special contributions by IDA's richer members, and transfers from the net earnings of the IBRD. The term of IDA credits, which are made to governments only, are ten-year grace periods, 50-year maturities, and no interest. By June 30, 1982, IDA had extended development credits totalling $33,654,000,000 in 86 countries.

Although legally and financially distinct from the IBRD, IDA is administered by the same staff, and the Board of Governors and Executive Directors are the same as those holding equivalent positions in the IBRD.

International Finance Corporation (IFC), 1818 H Street, Washington, D.C.; European representative, New Zealand House, Haymarket, S.W.1.—The IFC was established in 1956 as an affiliate of the World Bank to assist less developed member countries by promoting the growth in the private sector of their economies and helping to mobilise domestic and foreign capital for this purpose. Membership of the IBRD is a prerequisite for membership in the IFC, which has 125 members. Legally and financially the IFC and IBRD are separate entities; and the Corporation has its own operating and legal staff, but draws upon the Bank for administrative and other services. IFC's share capital was $544,238,000 at June 30, 1984, and it is also empowered to borrow up to approximately $3,100,000,000 from the World Bank for use in its lending programme. At the end of June 1984, IFC had made approvals totalling more than $6,216,000 in 84 countries.
President, A. W. Clausen (*U.S.A*).

International Monetary Fund (IMF), 700 19th Street, N.W. Washington, D.C.—Established on Dec. 27, 1945, the Fund exists to promote international monetary co-operation and the expansion of international trade; to promote exchange stability, maintain orderly exchange arrangements and avoid competitive exchange depreciations; and to assist in the establishment of a multilateral system of payments in respect of current transactions between members and in the elimination of foreign exchange restrictions which hamper world trade. 146 countries were in membership of the Fund in June, 1984.

The Fund's financial assistance takes the form of a foreign exchange transaction. The member pays to the Fund an amount of its own money equivalent to the amount of foreign currency it wishes to purchase. The member is expected to "repurchase" its own currency from the Fund, usually within three to five years, with a payment of S.D.R. or dollars or convertible currency acceptable to the Fund. These arrangements are subject to certain charges which rise in proportion to the amount of foreign exchange involved, and in some cases the length of time it is held.

Currencies drawn from the Fund may be used in a flexible way to relieve the member's payments difficulty.

Each member of the Fund is assigned a quota which determines its voting power and the amount of resources that it may draw from the Fund. The subscription of each member is equal to its quota, and is payable in the member's own currency and S.D.R.s.
Managing Director, Jacques de Larosière (*France*).
U.K. Executive Director, N. L. Wicks, C.B.E.

International Civil Aviation Organization (ICAO), International Aviation Square, 1,000 Sherbrooke Street, W., Montreal, Quebec, Canada.—In existence since April 4, 1947, to study problems of international civil aviation and the establishment of international standards and regulations for civil aviation, ICAO encourages the use of safety measures, uniform regulations or operation, and simpler procedures at international airports. It promotes the use of new technical methods and equipment. With the co-operation of members, it has evolved a pattern for meteorological services, traffic control, communications, radio beacons and ranges, search and rescue organization, and other facilities required for safe international flight. It has secured much simplification of government customs, immigration, and public health regulations as they apply to international air transport. 152 states are now members of ICAO.

An *Assembly* of delegates from member states meets at least once every three years. A *Council* of 33 members is elected by the Assembly, taking into account the countries of chief importance in air transport and the need for representation of the main geographical areas of the world. The Council is the executive body, working through subsidiary committees.
President of Council, Dr. Assad Kotaite (*Lebanon*).
Secretary-General, Yves Lambert (*France*).

Universal Postal Union (UPU), Weltpostrasse 4, 3000 Berne 15.—Established on October 9, 1874, by the postal Convention of Berne and in operation from July 1, 1875, UPU exists to form a single postal territory of all the countries, members of the Union, for the reciprocal exchange of correspondence in order to secure the organization and improvement of the various postal services and to promote in this sphere the development of international collaboration. Every member agrees to transmit the mail of all other members by the best means used for its own mail. The Union includes almost all the countries of the world. Budget, 1984, $U.S.10,757,431. A *Universal Postal Congress* meets at five-yearly intervals. The last was held in Rio de Janeiro in Sept-Oct. 1979, and the next is scheduled to take place in Hamburg in June–July 1984.
Director-General, Mohamed I. Sobhi (*Egypt*).

International Telecommunication Union (ITU), Place des Nations, Geneva.—Founded at Paris in 1865 as the International Telegraph Union. ITU became a U.N. Specialised Agency in 1947 and as from Jan. 1, 1975, is governed by the Convention adopted by the Torremolinos Conference held in 1973, amended at Nairobi in 1982. ITU exists to set up international regulations for telegraph, telephone and radio services to further their development and extend their utilization by the public, at the lowest possible rates; to promote international co-operation for the improvement and rational use of telecommunications of all kinds; the development of technical facilities and their most efficient operation. ITU allocates the radio frequency spectrum and registers radio frequency assignments. It studies, recommends, collects and publishes information on telecommunication matters, including space radio communications. The Budget for 1985 is 123,000,000 *Swiss francs.*
Secretary-General, R. E. Butler (*Australia*).

World Meteorological Organization (WMO), Geneva.—Came into existence in 1951. The present membership is 152 States and 5 Territories. WMO exists to facilitate world-wide co-operation in establishing networks of stations making observations related to meteorology and hydrology, and to promote the establishment and maintenance of centres providing meteorological and related services; to promote the establishment of systems for the rapid exchange of weather information; to promote standardization of meteorological observations and to ensure their uniform publication; to further the application of meteorology to aviation, shipping, water problems, agriculture, and other human activities; to promote activities in operational hydrology and to further close co-operation between meteorological and hydrological services; to encourage research and training in meteorology and to co-ordinate their international aspects. Budget (1984–87), $U.S.77,516,400. A *World Meteorological Congress* meets at least once every four years. An *Executive Council* (36 members), meeting at least annually, carries out the resolutions of the Congress, initiates studies and makes recommendations on matters requiring international action. Other organs are six *Regional Meteorological Associations* (Africa, Asia, S. America, N. and Central America, Europe and South-West Pacific), eight technical commissions and a Secretariat.

Secretary-General, G. O. P. Obasi (*Nigeria*).

International Maritime Organization (IMO), Albert Embankment, S.E.1. A United Nations Specialized Agency established on March 17, 1958, to provide means for co-operation and exchange of information among governments on technical matters related to international shipping, especially with regard to safety at sea and preventing marine pollution caused by ships. IMO is responsible for calling maritime conferences and drafting maritime agreements. It has produced numerous technical codes relating to the carriage of various types of cargo such as chemicals, ores, and dangerous goods and to the construction and equipment of ships, e.g., gas and chemical carriers. In June, 1984, 125 nations were in membership. Budget, 1984–85, $25,772,000. (The Organization changed its name from the Inter-Governmental Maritime Consultative Organisation (IMCO) on May 22, 1982.)

Secretary-General, C. P. Srivastava (*India*).

World International Property Organisation (WIPO), 34 chemin des Colombettes, 1211 Geneva 20, Switzerland.—Established by a 1967 convention to succeed the United International Bureau for the Protection of Intellectual Property. Became a specialised agency of the United Nations in 1974. WIPO promotes the protection of intellectual property throughout the world through co-operation among states and, where appropriate, in collaboration with other international organisations; and ensures administrative co-operation among states in the development of various international agreements on such matters as trademarks, industrial design, the classification of goods and services, the protection of appellations of origin, of literary and artistic works, of performers, producers of phonographs and broadcasting organisations.

The *Conference* and the *General Assembly* control the *International Bureau* (or secretariat). The Bureau provides the necessary documentation and other services for meetings and carries out projects for the promotion of increased international co-operation among member states.

Director-General: Arpad Bogsch (*United States*)

International Fund for Agricultural Development (IFAD), 107 Via del Serafico, 00142 Rome, Italy.—The establishment of the Fund was proposed by the 1974 World Food Conference and it began operations in December 1977. The Fund's purpose is to mobilise additional funds for agricultural and rural development in developing countries through projects and programmes directly benefiting the poorest rural population.

The Fund's operations are directed by the *Governing Council*, consisting of the entire membership. It has an 18-member Executive Board. Its governing structure provides for equal voting rights among the three groups of member countries, namely, the developed, the oil-exporting developing countries and other developing countries.

President (chief executive of IFAD and Chairman of the Executive Board): Abdelmuhsin Al-Sudeary (*Saudi Arabia*).

RELATED ORGANISATIONS

International Atomic Energy Agency, Vienna International Centre, P.O. Box 100, A–1400, Vienna. Set up on July 29, 1957, to accelerate and enlarge the contribution of atomic energy to peace, health and prosperity throughout the world and to ensure that assistance provided by it or under its supervision is not used to further any military purpose. Agreements have been reached concerning the Agency's working relationship with the United Nations and some of the specialized agencies. In June, 1984, 111 states were members.

A General Conference of all members meets in regular annual session and in such special session as may be necessary. A Board of Governors (34 members) carries out the functions of the Agency and meets usually four times a year. The Regular Budget for 1984 amounted to $100,769,000.

Director-General, Hans Blix (*Sweden*).

Permanent U.K. Representative, M. J. Wilmshurst.

General Agreement on Tariffs and Trade (GATT), Centre William Rappard, Rue de Lausanne 154, CH-1211 Geneva 21. A multilateral treaty, in operation since 1948, to which 90 countries are parties, and one acceded provisionally; a further 31 countries apply GATT *de facto*. Its rules thus govern over four-fifths of world trade. Objectives of GATT are to expand international trade and promote economic development. GATT provides a permanent forum for discussion and solution of particular international trade problems, and for multilateral negotiations to reduce tariffs and other obstacles to the expansion of international trade. Special attention is given to trade problems of developing countries. In November 1979, participating countries concluded the Tokyo Round of multilateral trade negotiations (launched in Tokyo in September 1973) with agreements covering tariff reductions, non-tariff measures, an improved framework for the conduct of international trade, bovine meat, dairy products, tropical products, civil aircraft, and a revised GATT anti-dumping code. An International Trade Centre, set up by GATT in 1964 to aid developing countries in export promotion, is now operated jointly by GATT and UNCTAD.

Director-General, A. Dunkel (*Switzerland*).

EUROPEAN COMMUNITY

The ten member states: Belgium, Denmark, France, Federal Republic of Germany, Greece, Ireland, Italy, Luxemburg, The Netherlands, the United Kingdom.

The beginnings of the European Community date from May 9, 1950, when Robert Schuman, France's Foreign Minister, proposed that France and Germany should pool their coal and steel industries under an independent ("supranational") High Authority, in a Community open to the membership of any other European country wishing to join. Not only West Germany, but also Italy, Belgium, the Netherlands, and Luxemburg accepted this invitation.

The Coal and Steel Community (E.C.S.C.), European Economic Community and Euratom share a single institutional framework: a Commission, Council of Ministers, Parliament and Court of Justice. The core of the Community policymaking process is the "dialogue" between the Commission, which initiates and implements policy, and the Council of Ministers, which takes major policy decisions. The beginnings of democratic control are exercised by the European Parliament, while the Court of Justice ensures the rule of law and is the final arbiter in all matters arising from the Community Treaties.

Since the start of the European Economic Community and Euratom in 1958, the Parliament and Court of Justice have been common to all three Communities. Up to July, 1967, each Community had its own executive body (the E.E.C. and Euratom Commissions, and the E.C.S.C. High Authority) and its own Council of Ministers.

In April, 1965, the Six signed a treaty providing for the merger of the three executive bodies in a single Commission and the three Councils in a single Council, with a view to the eventual merger of the three Communities themselves. The merger treaty came into force on July 1, 1967; the single Commission and single Council then took office. They enjoy the same powers under the three Community Treaties as did their predecessors.

On December 1 and 2, 1969, the Heads of State or Government of the Six met at the Hague and decided on the completion, strengthening, and, provided that other European countries wished to accept the Treaties of Rome, enlargement of the Community. They instructed the Commission to draw up a plan for economic and monetary union, and the Foreign Ministers to report by the end of July on possible moves towards political unification. They also resolved to intensify the co-ordination of research and development programmes.

In accordance with the Hague decisions the Council of Ministers agreed in April, 1970, that as from 1975 the Community would have its own revenue, independent of national contributions. The Foreign Ministers agreed (May, 1970) to hold formal political consultations twice a year.

In June, 1970, the Six invited Britain, the Irish Republic, Denmark and Norway to open negotiations on June 30 at Luxemburg on their applications to join the Community. Negotiations continued in 1971 and were concluded with the United Kingdom Government for all major questions by the end of June; on July 8, H.M. Government issued a White Paper on the results. On Jan. 22, 1972, the four applicant countries signed the Treaty of Accession in Brussels. Norway conducted a referendum on its Common Market entry and as a result withdrew its application. The enlarged Community of the Nine came into existence on Jan. 1, 1973.

With the advent of a Labour Government in the U.K. in 1974, there followed a period of renegotiation of the terms of Britain's entry into the Community, culminating in a referendum on June 5, 1975, as to whether or not the country should remain a member of the E.E.C. The result of the referendum showed two to one in favour of staying in. British Labour Party representatives who had hitherto boycotted the European Parliament then took up their 18 allotted seats.

In January 1976 the European Parliament approved a Report urging direct elections to the Parliament in 1978. On July 12–13, 1976, the Heads of Government or State, meeting in European Council, decided to approve a 410 member Parliament with Britain, France, West Germany and Italy allocated 81 seats each; the Netherlands 25, Belgium 24, Denmark 16, Ireland 15 and Luxemburg 6. Because some countries (including Britain) had not passed the relevant legislation in time, the date of European Elections was postponed until June 1979. When Greece joined the E.E.C. in January 1981, she was allocated 24 seats in the Parliament, bringing the total number to 434.

The "European Council", an addition to the institutionalized meetings provided under the Treaties, evolved from the "summit" conference of December 1974, when the Heads of Government decided to meet at least three times a year in order to discuss Community problems and matters requiring political co-operation.

OFFICE OF THE UNITED KINGDOM PERMANENT REPRESENTATIVE TO THE EUROPEAN COMMUNITIES
Rond-point Robert Schuman 6, 1040 Brussels

Ambassador and U.K. Permanent Representative, Sir Michael Butler, G.C.M.G.

The Commission

On July 1, 1970, the Commission was reduced from 14 members to nine, two each from Germany, France and Italy, and one each from Belgium, the Netherlands and Luxemburg. Following the 1973 enlargement, the number rose to 13, with two seats each from Britain, France, Germany, and Italy and one each for the other members. The admission of Greece in 1981, with 1 seat, brought the total to 14 Commissioners.

The members of the Commission are appointed by agreement among the ten member governments for a four-year renewable term; the president and vice-presidents are appointed from among the members for a two-year term, also renewable.

The members of the Commission are pledged to independence of the governments and of national or other particular interests. They accept joint responsibility for their decisions, which are taken by majority vote.

In addition to being the initiator of Community action and having specific powers, the Commission acts as a mediator between the member governments in Community affairs and is the guardian of the Community Treaties.

Commission of the European Communities
200 Rue de la Loi, 1049 Brussels

President, Jacques Delors (France) (from 1985).

Vice-Presidents, François-Xavier Ortoli (French), Christopher Tugendhat (British), Wilhelm Haferkamp (German); Etienne Davignon (Belgian), Lorenzo Natali (Italian). *Members,* Poul Dalsager (Danish), Edgard Pisani (French), Frans Andriessen (Dutch), Antonio Giolitti (Italian), Karl-Heinz Narjes (German), Giorgios Contogeorgis (Greek), Ivor Richard (British), Richard Burke (Irish).

The Commission maintains information offices in London (8 Storey's Gate, S.W.1.), Edinburgh (7 Alva Street), Cardiff (4 Cathedral Road), Belfast (Windsor House, 9/15 Bedford Street), Dublin (39 Molesworth Street), Washington (2100 M. Street, N.W. (Suite 707), Washington, D.C. 20037, New York (1 Dag Hammarskjöld Plaza, 245 East 47th Street, New York, N.Y. 10017), Ottawa (Inn of the Provinces, Office Tower (Suite 1110), 350 Sparks Street, Ontario, K1R 7S8), and other cities.

The new 14-member Commission was appointed by the Governments of the Ten and was sworn in on Jan. 12, 1981.

The Council of Ministers
170 Rue de la Loi, 1048 Brussels

This consists of ministers from the governments of each of the ten member states, the ministers concerned depending on the subject under discussion. A single Council exists for the three European Communities. It is the main decision-taking body within the Community legislative process. The Council acts, in almost all cases, on the basis of proposals submitted by the Commission, which is present at Council sessions to participate in the shaping of the measures taken. Before examining Commission proposals the Council normally obtains the opinions of the European Parliament and the Economic and Social Committee on them.

As prescribed by the E.E.C. treaty, under which the great majority of the Council's business falls, decisions are taken by majority vote, qualified majority vote (a system in which the members' votes are weighted) or by unanimity. The Council acts under the E.E.C. treaty by issuing (*a*) "regulations" which are binding in their entirety and directly applicable in all member states; (*b*) "directives" which are binding as to the result to be achieved but leave open to national governments the method of attaining this result; (*c*) "decisions" which bind those addressed; (*d*) "recommendations" and (*e*) "opinions", which have no binding force. The

Euratom treaty has the same system of voting and taking action; the E.C.S.C. system differs in certain respects.

The Presidency of the Council is held in rotation for periods of six months. The sessions of the Council are prepared by a Committee of Permanent Representatives of the member states. The Council and its committees are serviced by a general secretariat.

European Parliament

Secretariat: Centre Européen, Kirchberg, Luxemburg.

U.K. Information Office, 2 Queen Anne's Gate, SW1H 9AA.

The first direct elections to the European Parliament were held in mid-1979. Of 434 seats, the United Kingdom, France, Germany and Italy have 81 each, the Netherlands 25, Belgium 24, Greece 24, Denmark 16, Ireland 15 and Luxemburg 6. The Parliament meets in Strasbourg and its Committees in Brussels. The former Parliament consisted of 198 members nominated by their national Parliaments—the United Kingdom, France, Germany and Italy had 36 seats each, Belgium and the Netherlands 14 each, Denmark and Ireland 10 each and Luxemburg 6. Set up in 1952 under the European Coal and Steel Community Treaty of 1951, the Parliament's authority was extended by the 1957 Convention on Common Institutions to cover the European Economic Community and Euratom. It must be consulted on all major issues and has the right to dismiss the Commission by a vote of censure. Apart from general powers of supervision and consultation, it questions the Commission and the Council of Ministers and has a measure of control over the Community's annual budget including its final adoption. It can reject the budget as a whole and can amend items of non-obligatory expenditure (i.e. expenditure not specified in the original treaties or derived legislation—amounting to some 27 per cent. of the total budget). The Members of the Parliament serve on specialized committees and sit in political groups—Socialists, Christian Democrats, Liberals and Democrats, European Democrats, European Progressive Democrats and Communists. There are also a number of Independents in the Parliament.

President, Pierre Pflimlin (France).

European Court of Justice
L–2920 Luxemburg

The European Court superseded the Court of Justice of E.C.S.C. and is common to the three European Communities. It exists to safeguard the law in the interpretation and application of the Community treaties, to decide on the legality of decisions of the Council of Ministers or the Commission and to determine violations of the Treaties. Cases may be brought to it by the member States, the Community institutions, firms or individuals. Its decisions are directly binding in the member countries. The eleven judges and five advocates-general of the Court are appointed for renewable six-year terms by the member Governments in concert. During 1983 the court gave 181 judgements.

Judges, Hon. Lord Mackenzie Stuart (*President*); T. Koopmans (*President of 1st Chamber*); K. Bahlmann (*President of 2nd Chamber*); Y. Galmot (*President of 3rd Chamber*); P. Pescatore; A. O'Keeffe; G. Bosco; O. Due; U. Everling; R. Joliet; C. Kakouris.

Advocates-General, Sir Gordon Slynn (*1st Advocate-General*); C. O. Lenz; M. Darmon; P. VerLoren van Themaat; G. F. Mancini.

Registrar, P. E. Heim.

The European Investment Bank
100 Boulevard Konrad Adenauer,
L-2950 Luxemburg

The European Investment Bank (E.I.B.) was set up in 1958 under the terms of the Treaty of Rome with the essential function of contributing to the balanced development of the Common Market.

It grants long-term loans to enterprises, public authorities and financial institutions, to finance projects which assist the development of less advanced regions and the conversion or modernisation of older, exhausted industries. Another important role of the E.I.B. is that of helping to finance projects which serve the interests of the Community as a whole or more than one member country such as intra-Community communications and development and diversifications of the E.E.C.'s energy sources.

E.I.B. activities have also been extended outside member countries under the terms of different association or cooperation agreements which more than 70 countries have signed with the Community.

The Bank's total financing operations in 1983 amounted to 5,947·8 million E.C.U.,* of which 5,467·5 million (including 1,211·8 million from the resources of the New Community Instrument for Borrowing and Lending—'Ortoli Facility') were for investments in the E.E.C. and 480·3 million for outside the Community. Between 1973 and 1983 the E.I.B. had made available a total of 4,845·5 million E.C.U. for investment in the U.K., about 19·1 per cent of its total operations in the Community during this period (25,418·5 million E.C.U.).

The members of the European Investment Bank are the ten member countries of the Community, who have all subscribed to the Bank's capital, which the Bank's Board of Governors doubled to 14,400 million E.C.U., with effect from December 31, 1981. The funds required by the Bank to carry out its tasks are borrowed on the capital markets of the Community and non-member countries, and on the international market.

As it operates on a non-profit-making basis, the interest rates charged by the E.I.B. are therefore close to the average rates charged on the markets where it obtains its funds.

The Board of Governors of the European Investment Bank consists of Ministers nominated by the member countries, usually the Finance Minister,

who lay down general directives on the policy of the Bank and appoint members to the Board of Directors (18 nominated by the member states, 1 by the Commission of the European Communities), which takes decisions on the granting and raising of loans and the fixing of interest rates. A Management Committee, also appointed by the Board of Governors, is responsible for the day-to-day operations of the Bank.

President, Ernst-Günther Bröder.

Vice-Presidents, Alain Prate; C. Richard Ross; Arie Pais; Lucio Izzo; Noel Whelan.

(The President and Vice-Presidents also preside as Chairman and Vice-Chairmen at meetings of the Board of Directors.)

Secretary-General and Manager, General Administration Directorate, Paul Dirix.

U.K. Office: 68 Pall Mall, SW1Y 5ES.

EUROPEAN COAL AND STEEL COMMUNITY

This, the first of the European Communities, was established in 1952. Since then, for coal, iron ore and scrap, it has abolished customs duties, quantitative restrictions, the dual pricing system whereby prices charged on exported coal or steel differed from those charged to home consumers, currency restrictions and discrimination in transport rates based on the nationality of customers and the special frontier charges which made international transport of these goods within the Community dearer than transport within national frontiers. It has applied rules for fair competition and a harmonized external tariff for the whole Community.

THE TREATY OF ROME

Discussions were held at Messina, Sicily, in 1955 between the foreign ministers of the six member states of E.C.S.C. (Belgium, France, Germany, Italy, Luxemburg and The Netherlands) on proposals for further advances towards economic integration in Europe, and after intensive study of these proposals, a treaty was signed at Rome on March 25, 1957, setting up the European Economic Community.

The Treaty aimed to lay the foundations of an enduring and closer union between the European peoples by gradually removing the economic effects of their political frontiers. The Treaty provides for the elimination of customs duties and quotas in trade between member states; the establishment of a common customs tariff and a common trade policy towards third countries; the abolition of the obstacles to free movement of persons, services and capital between member states; the inauguration of common policies for agriculture and transport; the establishment of a system ensuring that competition shall not be distorted in the Common Market; the co-ordination of economic policies; the harmonization of social and economic legislation to the extent necessary in order to enable the Common Market to work; the creation of a European Social Fund in order to improve the possibilities of employment for workers

---

* The financial statements of the European Investment Bank are drawn up in E.C.U. which at May 30, 1984 equalled ± £0·59, U.S.$0·82.

and to contribute to the raising of their standard of living; the establishment of an Economic and Social Committee which must be consulted on major proposals, consisting of representatives of employers, workers, consumers and other groups; the establishment of a European Investment Bank intended to aid investment in underdeveloped areas and help to finance modernization; and the association of overseas countries and territories with the Community with a view to increasing trade and to pursuing jointly their effort towards economic and social development.

ENLARGEMENT OF THE COMMUNITY

The question of possible enlargement of the Community played an important part in its development from the autumn of 1961 when Britain, the Irish Republic, Denmark and Norway first sought membership, and Austria, Sweden, Switzerland, Spain and Cyprus sought association with the Community. The negotiations were vetoed by France in January, 1963. In May, 1967, Britain, the Irish Republic and Denmark formally submitted applications for Community membership. In July Norway followed suit and Sweden announced that it would seek to participate in the enlargement of the Community on terms compatible with its neutrality. These applications made very slow progress and appeared to come to a standstill when in December, 1967, France declared that Britain's economy would have to be strengthened before negotiations could begin. But shortly after taking office as President of France, Georges Pompidou stated in July, 1969, that there was no objection in principle to the admission of Britain to the Community. At the Hague "summit" meeting in December, 1969, the Six decided that provided that the completion of the Community was not prejudiced, and provided that the Community was strengthened to provide for enlargement, then the entry of other European countries would be desirable. After deciding on a common negotiating position, the Six invited Britain and the other applicants to begin negotiations for membership.

A single overall transitional period of five years, during which the Three were to adopt Community rules and regulations, started on January 1, 1973, giving time for the gradual integration of the economies of the Three with the Six by the end of 1977.

The first 40 per cent alignment on the Community's Common External Tariff (C.E.T.)—i.e. 40 per cent of the difference between the new members' tariffs and the C.E.T.—was made at the beginning of 1974, and three further alignments of 20 per cent each followed.

Negotiations with Greece were concluded and the Treaty of Accession signed on May 28, 1979. Greece became the tenth member of the Community on January 1, 1981. Portugal and Spain have formally applied to join the Community.

Following a plebiscite, Greenland negotiated its withdrawal from the E.E.C. (but without discontinuing relations with Denmark) and will leave in early 1985.

EUROPEAN ATOMIC ENERGY COMMUNITY (EURATOM)

A second treaty, arising from the Messina discussions between the E.C.S.C. powers on additional means of co-operation, was signed in Rome on March 25, 1957, setting up the European Atomic Energy Community. The task of *Euratom*, defined in detail in the Treaty, is to create within a short period the technical and industrial conditions necessary to utilize nuclear discoveries and especially to produce nuclear energy on a large scale. The United Kingdom, Denmark and Ireland joined Euratom on Jan. 1, 1973, and Greece on Jan. 1, 1981.

EUROPEAN PARLIAMENT SUMMARY, 1983–84

Britain's rebate (i)

There was an unexpected result to the vote at Strasbourg on Oct. 10 when M.E.P.s agreed to repay to Britain a £180 million rebate on its contributions to the E.E.C. U.K. Conservative members who were attending their party conference in Blackpool flew back to help defeat an amendment which sought to block payment but even so the motion was lost by a mere seven votes. A majority of 218 was required to pass the amendment but its supporters mustered only 211 with the U.K. Tories and Labour Euro-M.P.s gathering 79 votes. However, the Parliament voted on Oct. 27 to freeze the promised rebate of £450 million this year until permanent reform of the financing system was agreed. This time the vote was 262 in favour of an amendment to the 1984 Budget resolution which would have placed all the U.K. money plus five per cent. of proposed agriculture spending in "Chapter 100". Effectively, this meant withholding it until the Parliament agreed to its release. There were 56 votes against the amendment which were cast by U.K. members although a handful of Conservatives were reported to have voted for the freeze as the vote was not made on a roll call. But the overall 1984 Budget of about £15 billion was agreed by the Parliament, taking the E.C.C. almost to the limit of legal cash resources.

Failure of Athens Summit

There were critical speeches in Strasbourg on Dec. 13 on the failure of the Common Market summit in Athens the previous week. A bitter indictment of the 10 member Governments came from Mr. Papandreou, Prime Minister of Greece, supported by M. Gaston Thorn, president of the E.E.C. Commission. Mr. Papandreou told the European Parliament that the failure was chiefly because member countries no longer believed in Europe and measured every E.E.C. proposal by the effect it would have on their payments into, or receipts from, the E.E.C. Budget. He diagnosed the summit failure as a result of "a process of deterioration which has been going on for years, one of internal erosion and deadlock", and apportioned blame on inability to agree on financial reform of the Community on all member states although some were more conciliatory than others. M. Thorn was scornful of the manner in which the Commission's proposals for solving the financial problems had been set aside by government leaders who offered their own solutions. He also criticised member countries for taking national positions in flagrant contradiction to E.E.C. Treaty rules.

Britain's rebate (ii)

Britain's 1983 Budget rebate which was pledged at the Stuttgart E.E.C. summit in June was once more the focal point of controversy on Dec. 14 when the Budget committee of the Parliament recommended it should be frozen again until there was permanent financial reform of the Common Market. Mme Christiane Scrivener, a French spokesman, said the move was an act to put pressure on the Council of E.E.C. ministers to agree to implement the necessary reforms. Next day, Dec. 15, the Parliament indeed voted to withhold Britain's rebate and voted by 268 to 73 to place the refund into a suspense account pending agreement on comprehensive and lasting reform of the financial system. All the British Euro-M.P.s opposed the freeze and the U.K. Tory members registered their anger by subsequently voting against every amendment to the Budget resolution during the stages of its final debate, although the Budget of about £15 billion was ultimately approved.

Budget signed

The vote had no legal force until the Budget was formally signed by its President (Mr. Piet Dankert) and on Dec. 16, Mrs. Barbara Castle, leader of the British Labour group, urged the President to postpone his signature to give member governments time to put forward new proposals. Mrs. Castle said the Parliament's decision had caused intense indignation in Britain and said that a delay in bringing the Budget into law would allow time for a compromise. Another problem arose from the Budget approval by the Parliament. Parliament exceeded its legal authority on expenditure by authorising a Budget at least £60 million higher than that to which the Budget ministers of the Ten agreed; when the Foreign Ministers of the Community met in Brussels on Dec. 19 to consider their reaction to the Budget vote of approval they pointed out to Mr. Dankert that they regarded the approval as being in "disaccord" with the Budget they had themselves agreed. However, on Dec. 20, Mr. Dankert did sign the Budget thus making the Commission bound to implement it.

King Hussein of Jordan addressed the Parliament in Strasbourg on Dec. 15 and declared it should try to involve the Soviet Union in the peace process in the Middle East. The E.E.C. Middle East peace initiative, he claimed, had run out of steam in the past year or so.

On Jan. 19, the U.K. Conservative members unanimously supported a move to claim compensation from the French Government for British lorry drivers following the hi-jacking of their loads by French farmers the previous week. With the exception of some French Euro-M.P.s, the Parliament voted in favour of a resolution calling on E.E.C. Governments and the Brussels Commission to compel national authorities to indemnify the victims of such incidents. Mr. Christopher Prout, the Tory spokes-

man, said this sort of violent action could lead to reprisals which could only bring problems for everyone.

Majority voting

The Parliament approved on Feb. 14 a preliminary draft treaty which would establish the principle of majority voting by E.E.C. Ministers to be introduced over a period of 10 years. This would mean that all policy decisions taken by the E.E.C. Commission would be binding on all member countries provided they were approved by a majority of E.E.C. Ministers, but such a proposed treaty would have to be approved by member Governments first. The draft treaty also provided for a substantial increase in the powers of the European Parliament and would establish the Assembly as a joint authority with member Governments in formulating E.E.C. policy.

Wine Taxes

After opposition by several British Euro-M.P.s, a move to reduce taxes on wine in Britain and other E.E.C. countries was blocked when Sig. Giosue Ligios, an Italian member, attempted to harmonise wine taxes throughout the Community. Mr. James Provan (Con., N.E. Scotland) protested they should try to eliminate all tax anomalies and not establish special privileges for wine. Mr. Brian Hord (Con., London West) pointed out that France discriminated by taxing alcohol imports, subsidising domestic production, and dumping wine in neighbouring countries. Signor Ligios's report was sent back to committee for further consideration. Similar action was also taken on a proposal by Mr. William Hopper (Con., Greater Manchester) which, he said, would have meant that British vodka and other beverages would have been "firmly placed" on the European market. Mr. Hopper blamed the Socialists for obstructing his proposal which would have created jobs in Scotland and the North-West by making British-produced spirits cheaper on the continent with no effect on home prices.

Northern Ireland

The political affairs committee of the Parliament meeting in Paris approved on Feb. 29 a report on Ulster made by Mr. Niels Haagerup, a Danish Liberal, and adopted by 22 votes to four, with five abstentions, his draft resolution calling for increased E.E.C. financial aid to Northern Ireland. The Committee also called for the U.S.A. and other governments to take action to stop the flow of arms and funds to the Provisional I.R.A. British Tories on the committee were among those who abstained on the vote because, said Lady Ellis (Thames Valley), they still took the view that the Parliament had no right to interfere with the internal affairs of any part of the Community, including Northern Ireland as part of the U.K. On Mar. 19, the Parliament adopted Mr. Haagerup's report by 124 votes to three, with 63 abstentions, including all the U.K. Conservatives, except Lord Bethel who voted for it. Mr. John Taylor (Official Unionist, N.I.) pointed out that only 28 per cent. of the members had voted. Rev. Ian Paisley (Democratic

Unionist, N.I.) described the report as biased and riddled with falsehoods and said it was insulting and misleading. But Mr. John Hume, leader of the S.D.L.P., welcomed the report although commenting, "You cannot unite people at the point of a gun." Mr. Haagerup explained his report was not meant in a political sense and he did not want to act as a mediator.

The last week of the first five-year life of the first elected European Parliament opened in Strasbourg on May 21 when Euro-M.P.s discussed a variety of topics ranging from the level of E.E.C. spending to help for gypsies, and voted on some 70 resolutions.

President Mitterrand's address

President Mitterrand of France addressed the Parliament in Strasbourg on May 24 and electrified the Assembly by calling for a new European union which would effectively turn the Common Market into a federal state. He declared there should be an end to the practice of majority voting under which individual members could veto E.E.C. policies. Those who wanted European union, he explained, could draw up a new treaty which would not replace existing treaties but would extend their scope into areas which were now ignored. Any country could opt not to join in the new union if it did not want to be involved in "this further vision of Europe". M. Mitterrand cast much of the blame for recent problems on the principle of unanimity which allowed one member to veto action. On the following day, Parliament was dissolved to enable the elections to take place.

The new Parliament

The inaugural session of the new Parliament was held in Strasbourg on July 24 when M. Pierre Pflimlin, the French Christian Democrat, was elected President for a 2½-year term of office. The new President said the high abstention rate in last month's elections was due to "staggering ignorance" about Community affairs.

Britain's rebate (iii)

There was furious British reaction when the Parliament decided on July 27 to block once again the U.K.'s rebate from the 1983 Budget. Tory and Labour Euro-M.P.s from the U.K. joined in voting against the decision which was carried by 214 votes to 70. Supporters of the decision maintained that Britain had broken the spirit of the Fontainebleau agreements by refusing to agree to short-term financing for the Common Market in 1984. However, the British case was that all the necessary procedures had been completed through agreement of the 1983 refunds by heads of Government at the Council meeting in Stuttgart a year ago, through confirmation of that agreement by the heads of Government at Fontainebleau, and through further confirmation by the Budget committee of the Parliament. The Parliament members then dispersed for the summer recess.

OTHER INTERNATIONAL ORGANIZATIONS

ASSOCIATION OF SOUTH EAST ASIAN NATIONS (A.S.E.A.N.)

Central Secretariat: Jakarta, Indonesia

Formed in 1967, the main aims of the Association are the acceleration of economic growth, social progress and cultural development, the promotion of collaboration and mutual assistance in matters of common interest, and the continuing stability of the South East Asian region.

The Heads of Government of the member countries are the highest authority and give directions to A.S.E.A.N. as and when necessary. The main policy-making body is the annual Meeting of Foreign Ministers of the member countries. The members of the Association are Brunei, Indonesia, Malaysia, the Philippines, Singapore and Thailand.

BANK FOR INTERNATIONAL SETTLEMENTS

(1930), Centrebahnplatz 2, 4002 Basle, Switzerland.

The objectives of the Bank are to promote the co-operation of central banks; to provide facilities for international financial operations; and to act as trustee or agent in international financial settlements entrusted to it. The London agent is the Bank of England, and the Governor of the Bank of England is a member of the Board of Directors, in which administrative control is vested.

CARIBBEAN COMMUNITY AND COMMON MARKET (CARICOM)

P.O. Box 10827, Georgetown, Guyana

CARICOM was established on 1973 with three objectives: economic co-operation through the Caribbean Common Market; the co-ordination of foreign policy among the independent member states; the provision of common services and co-operation in functional matters such as health, education and culture, communications and industrial relations. The principal organs are the Conference of Heads of Government, which determines policy, and the Common Market Council of Ministers, consisting of Ministers of Government (usually Ministers of Trade) designated by each member state, which is responsible for the development and smooth running of the Common Market and for the settlement of any problems arising out of its functioning. The principal administrative arm is the Secretariat, based in Guyana.

The 13 member states are Antigua and Barbuda, The Bahamas, Barbados, Belize, Dominica, Grenada, Guyana, Jamaica, Montserrat, St. Kitts.-Nevis, St. Lucia, St. Vincent and the Grenadines and Trinidad and Tobago.

Sec. Gen., R. Rainford (*Jamaica*).

COUNCIL FOR MUTUAL ECONOMIC ASSISTANCE (C.M.E.A. OR COMECON)

56 Kalinin Avenue, Moscow G–205, U.S.S.R

Established in 1949, the Council's aim is to promote the development of the national economies of the member states and the development of socialist economic integration, through the co-operation of members in the most rational use of resources and the acceleration of economic and technical progress, industrialisation and productivity. The highest body is the Session of the Council, which consists of delegations from all member states, usually led by the heads of government. The Executive Committee consists of representatives of member states at the level of deputy heads of government, and is responsible for the implementation of the tasks set by the Session of the Council and for directing the work of the Committees, Standing Commissions, Secretariat and other bodies.

The member countries are Bulgaria, Cuba, Czechoslovakia, East Germany, Hungary, Mongolia, Poland, Romania, U.S.S.R. and Vietnam. Yugoslavia participates in the work of some C.M.E.A. bodies, and there are co-operation agreements with Finland, Iraq, Mexico and Nicaragua.

THE COUNCIL OF EUROPE

Headquarters: 67006 Strasbourg, France.
Secretary-General, M. Oreja

A European organization founded in 1949 whose aim is to achieve greater unity between its Members to safeguard their European heritage and to facilitate their economic and social progress through discussion and common action in economic, social, cultural, educational, scientific, legal and administrative matters and in the maintenance and furtherance of human rights and fundamental freedoms.

The 21 members are Austria, Belgium, Cyprus, Denmark, France, the Federal Republic of Germany, Greece, Iceland, the Republic of Ireland, Italy, Liechtenstein, Luxemburg, Malta, Netherlands, Norway, Portugal, Spain, Sweden, Switzerland, Turkey and the U.K.

The organs are the Committee of Ministers, consisting of the Foreign Ministers of member countries, who meet twice yearly, and the Parliamentary Assembly of 170 members, elected or chosen by the national parliaments of member countries in proportion to the relative strength of political parties. There is also a Joint Committee of Ministers and Representatives of the Parliamentary Assembly.

The Committee of Ministers is the executive organ of the Council. Certain of its conclusions take the form of international agreements or recommendations to governments. Decisions of the Ministers may also be embodied in partial agreements to which a limited number of member governments are party. All Ministers have appointed Deputies to act on their behalf. The Committee of Deputies meets every month to transact business and to take decisions on behalf of Ministers. Member governments accredit Permanent Representatives to the Council in Strasbourg, who are also the Ministers' Deputies.

The Committee is a forum for political discussions between member governments, supervises the work of the technical expert committees and considers recommendations received from the Parliamentary Assembly. Conferences of Ministers responsible for such areas as education, justice, the environment and public health meet at the invitation of a member government every two or three years and address their proposals for action in their respective fields to the Committee of Ministers.

The Parliamentary Assembly holds three weeklong sessions a year. It debates reports on, inter alia, political, economic, agricultural, social, educational, legal and regional planning affairs, and also reports received annually from the O.E.C.D., other European organisations and certain specialised agencies of the United Nations. Its 13 permanent committees meet, normally in private, once or twice between each public plenary session of the Assembly. The Standing Conference of Local and Regional Authorities of Europe each year brings together mayors and municipal councillors in the same numbers as the members of the Parliamentary Assembly.

One of the principal achievements of the Council of Europe is the European Convention of Human Rights (1950) under which was established the European Commission and the European Court of Human Rights. Over 110 other conventions and agreements have now been concluded. They include the European Social Charter, the European Social Security Code, and conventions on extradition, the legal status of migrant workers, the conservation of European wildlife and natural habitats, the protection of individuals with regard to the automatic processing of personal data, transfrontier co-operation and the transfer of sentenced prisoners.

Non-member states take part in certain Council of Europe activities on a regular or ad hoc basis; thus Finland and the Holy See participate in all the educational, cultural and sports activities. The European Youth Foundation funds events in both Eastern and Western European countries and in some outside Europe, while nationals of these countries attend courses and seminars at the European Youth Centre.

Permanent U.K. Representative, His Excellency Christopher Duncan Lush, C.M.G.

EUROPEAN FREE TRADE ASSOCIATION (E.F.T.A.)

Member States: Austria, Iceland, Norway, Portugal, Sweden, Switzerland. Associate Member: Finland.

Following the unsuccessful attempt to create a European Free Trade Area linking the E.E.C. with other members of the O.E.E.C., seven European States came together in 1959 to form the European Free Trade Association. The seven were Austria, Denmark, Norway, Portugal, Sweden, Switzerland and the United Kingdom. The E.F.T.A. Convention became effective on May 3, 1960, and just over a year later, on June 26, 1961, Finland became an associate member. Iceland applied for full membership in November, 1968, and acceded to the Association and to the Finland–E.F.T.A. Agreement on March 1, 1970.

In 1973 all the E.F.T.A. Member States entered into a new relationship with the E.E.C. Two—Denmark and the United Kingdom—withdrew from E.F.T.A. at the end of December 1972 to become members of the E.E.C. on January 1, 1973. Agreements establishing industrial free trade between five of the other E.F.T.A. Member States (Austria, Iceland, Portugal, Sweden and Switzerland) and the E.E.C. came into force on that same date. Similar agreements with Norway and Findland came into force on July 1, 1973, and January 1, 1974, respectively.

The Convention defines the objects of the Association as (1) to promote economic expansion in the area of the Association and in each member state; (2) to ensure that trade between member states takes place in conditions of fair competition; (3) to avoid significant disparity between member states in the condition of supply of raw materials produced within the area; and (4) to contribute to the harmonious development and expansion of world trade and to the progressive removal of barriers to it.

Since December 31, 1966 the member countries of the Association have constituted a virtually complete industrial free trade area. There is no common external tariff for the Association, each member country being free to fix the level of its tariffs against countries outside the area. The Convention includes rules governing the origin of goods manufactured in the area. It also contains provisions relating to the "rules of competition"—government subsidies, restrictive business practices, etc. There are special provisions relating to trade in agricultural and fish products.

The free trade agreements between the E.F.T.A. countries and the E.E.C. provided for the complete removal by July 1, 1977 of the tariffs on almost all industrial products traded between them. This deadline was observed, and free trade was thereby established over almost all of Western Europe. A multilateral free trade agreement between the seven E.F.T.A. countries and Spain came into force on May 1, 1980.

E.F.T.A. has done much work on the removal of non-tariff barriers to trade, especially technical barriers to trade. Seven international schemes and two international conventions to overcome obstacles to trade in specific categories of products were devised in E.F.T.A. but are independent of the Association, and now involve the participation of other countries alongside E.F.T.A. countries.

The Council of E.F.T.A. meets every two weeks at the level of officials—the heads of the permanent national delegations to E.F.T.A.—usually twice a year at the level of ministers. Each state has a single vote and recommendations must normally be unanimous. Decisions of the Council are binding on member countries.

Secretary-General, Per Kleppe (Norway) 9–11 Rue de Varembé, 1211 Geneva 20.

LEAGUE OF ARAB STATES

37 Av. Khereddine Pacha, Tunis, Tunisia

The purpose of the League of Arab States (founded 1945) is to ensure co-operation among member states and protect their independence and sovereignty, to supervise the affairs and interests of Arab countries and to control the execution of agreements concluded among the member states. The League considers itself a regional organisation and is an observer at the United Nations.

Member states are Algeria, Bahrain, Djibouti, Iraq, Jordan, Kuwait, Lebanon, Libya, Mauritania, Morocco, Oman, Palestine, Qatar, Saudi Arabia, Somalia, Sudan, Syria, Tunisia, United Arab Emirates, Arab Republic of Yemen and Democratic Republic of Yemen. (The membership of Egypt, a founder state, was suspended in 1979.)

Secretary-General, Chedli Klibi (*Tunisia*).

U.K. OFFICE.—Arab Information Centre, 52 Green Street, W.1.

NORTH ATLANTIC TREATY ORGANIZATION

Headquarters: Brussels 1110, Belgium.
Secretary General, The Lord Carrington (*United Kingdom*).

The North Atlantic Treaty was signed on April 4, 1949, by the Foreign Ministers of twelve nations. The twelve are Belgium, Canada, Denmark, France, Iceland, Italy, Luxemburg, the Netherlands, Norway, Portugal, the United Kingdom and United States. Greece and Turkey acceded to the Treaty in 1952, the Federal Republic of Germany in 1955, and Spain in 1982. The North Atlantic Council, chaired by the

Secretary General, is the highest authority of the Alliance and is composed of permanent representatives of the sixteen member countries. It meets at ministerial levels (Foreign Ministers) at least twice per year. The permanent representatives (Ambassadors) head national delegations of advisers and experts.

Defence matters are dealt with in the Defence Planning Committee (D.P.C.), composed of representatives of the member countries participating in the N.A.T.O. integrated military structure. Within the specialised field of defence, the D.P.C. has the same functions and authority as the Council. Like the Council it meets regularly at ambassador level and twice a year in ministerial sessions, when the nations are represented by their Defence Ministers.

The Council/D.P.C., as a unique forum for confidential and constant inter-governmental consultation and as the main decision-making body within the North Atlantic Alliance, is assisted by an International Staff, divided into five divisions: Political Affairs; Defence Planning and Policy; Defence Support; Infrastructure, Logistics and Council Operations; Scientific Affairs.

U.K. Permanent Representative, His Excellency Sir John Graham, K.C.M.G. (1979).

The senior military authority in N.A.T.O. is the Military Committee composed of the Chief of Defence of each member country except France and Iceland. The Military Committee, which is assisted by an international military staff, functions in permanent session with permanent military representatives and is responsible for making recommendations to the Council and Defence Planning Committee on measures considered necessary for the common defence of the N.A.T.O. area and for supplying guidance on military matters to the major N.A.T.O. Commanders.

Chairman of the Military Committee, Gen. C. de Jager (*Netherlands*).

The strategic area covered by the North Atlantic Treaty is divided among three Commands (European, Atlantic and Channel) and a Regional Planning Group (Canada and the United States).

The Major N.A.T.O Commanders are responsible for the development of defence plans for their respective areas, for the determination of force requirements and for the deployment and exercise of the forces under their command. The Major N.A.T.O. Commanders report to the Military Committee.

The three Major N.A.T.O Commanders are:

Supreme Allied Commander, Europe, Gen. Bernard W. Rogers (*U.S.*).

Supreme Allied Commander, Atlantic, Adm. Wesley L. McDonald (*U.S.*).

Commander-in-Chief, Channel, Ad. Sir William Staveley (*U.K.*).

ORGANIZATION FOR ECONOMIC CO-OPERATION AND DEVELOPMENT

Headquarters: 2, rue André-Pascal, 75116 Paris.
Secretary-General, J. C. Paye.

Formed on September 30, 1961, the O.E.C.D. replaced the Organization for European Economic Co-operation (O.E.E.C.). The O.E.C.D. is the instrument for international co-operation among industrialized member countries on economic and social policies. Its objectives are to assist its member governments in the formulation and co-ordination of policies designed to achieve high, sustained economic growth while maintaining financial stability, to contribute to world trade on a multilateral basis and to stimulate members' aid to developing countries.

The following countries belong to the O.E.C.D.: Australia, Austria, Belgium, Canada, Denmark, Federal Republic of Germany, Finland, France, Greece,

Iceland, Irish Republic, Italy, Japan, Luxemburg, the Netherlands, New Zealand, Norway, Portugal, Spain, Sweden, Switzerland, Turkey, U.K. and U.S.A. (Yugoslavia participates with a special status).

The Council is the supreme body of the Organization. Composed of one representative for each member country, it meets at Permanent Representative level under the Chairmanship of the Secretary General, or at Ministerial level (usually once a year) under the Chairmanship of a Minister elected annually. Decisions and Recommendations are adopted by mutual agreement of all members of the Council. Fourteen members of the Council are chosen annually to form an Executive Committee to assist the Council. However, most of the O.E.C.D.'s work is undertaken in over 200 specialized committees and working parties. Four autonomous or semi-autonomous bodies also belong to the Organization: the Nuclear Energy Agency, the International Energy Agency, the Development Centre, and the Centre for Educational Research and Innovation. These bodies, the committees and the Council are serviced by an international Secretariat headed by the Secretary-General of the Organization.

U.K. Permanent Representative, K. J. Uffen, C.M.G., 19 rue de Franqueville, Paris 16.

ORGANIZATION OF AFRICAN UNITY (O.A.U.)

P.O. Box 3243, Addis Ababa, Ethiopia

The Organization of African Unity was established in 1963 and has 32 members. It aims to further African unity and solidarity, to co-ordinate political, economic, social and defence policies, and to eliminate colonialism in Africa.

The chief organs are the Assembly of heads of state or government and the Council of Foreign Ministers. The main administrative body is the Secretariat, based in Addis Ababa.

ORGANIZATION OF AMERICAN STATES (O.A.S.)

17th Street and Constitution Ave. N.W., Washington D.C. 20006, U.S.A.

Originally founded in 1890 for largely commercial purposes, the O.A.S adopted its present name and charter in 1948. Its aims are to strengthen the peace and security of the continent; to prevent possible causes of difficulties and to ensure the pacific settlement of disputes that may arise among the member states; to provide for common action on the part of those states in the event of aggression; to seek the solution of political, juridicial and economic problems that may arise among them; and to promote, by co-operative action, their economic, social and cultural development. The O.A.S. is a regional organization within the United Nations.

Policy is determined by the annual General Assembly. Meetings of Ministers of Foreign Affairs consider urgent problems, and advise in cases of armed attack and threats to peace.

The 32 member states are Antigua and Barbuda, Argentina, Bahamas, Barbados, Bolivia, Brazil, Chile, Colombia, Costa Rica, Cuba, Dominica, Dominican Republic, Ecuador, El Salvador, Grenada, Guatemala, Haiti, Honduras, Jamaica, Mexico, Nicaragua, Panama, Paraguay, Peru, St. Kitts-Nevis, St. Lucia, St. Vincent and the Grenadines, Surinam, Trinidad and Tobago, U.S.A., Uruguay and Venezuela.

Secretary-General, João Clemente Baena Soares.

ORGANIZATION OF THE PETROLEUM EXPORTING COUNTRIES (O.P.E.C.)

Obere Donaustrasse 93, A-1020 Vienna, Austria

The Organization of the Petroleum Exporting Countries was created in 1960 as a permanent intergovernmental organization with the aims of unifying and co-ordinating the pertroleum policies of members and determining the best means of protecting their interests, individually and collectively.

The supreme authority is the Conference of Ministers of Oil, Mines and Energy of member countries which meets at least twice a year and formulates policy. The Board of Governors, nominated by member countries, directs the management of O.P.E.C. and implements Conference resolutions. The Secretariat, based in Vienna, carries out executive functions under the direction of the Board of Governors.

The 13 member countries are Algeria, Ecuador, Gabon, Indonesia, Iran, Iraq, Kuwait, Libya, Nigeria, Qatar, Saudi Arabia, U.A.E. and Venezuela.

THE WORLD COUNCIL OF CHURCHES

150 route de Ferney, CH–1211 Geneva 20, Switzerland

General-Secretary, Dr. Emilio Castro
(*Uruguay*).

The World Council of Churches was constituted in 1948 to promote unity between the many different Christian churches. It has a membership of 303 churches of widely varying traditions and cultural backgrounds, representing 400 million Christians in over 100 countries.

The policies of the Council are determined by delegates of the member churches meeting in Assembly, normally every seven years. More detailed decisions are taken by a 150-member Central Committee which is elected by the Assembly and meets, with the seven W.C.C. Presidents, annually. The Central Committee in turn appoints a smaller Executive Committee and also nominates commissions and working groups, and guides the various programmes. The implementation of the policies laid down by the churches and the co-ordination of the three programme units (Faith and Witness, Justice and Service, and Education and Renewal) are the responsibility of the General Secretariat.

British Council of Churches, 2 Eaton Gate, S.W.1.

CURRENCIES OF THE WORLD

Country	Monetary Unit	Denomination in Circulation	
		Notes	Coins
Afghanistan	Afghani of 100 Puls	Afghanis 1,000, 500, 100, 50, 20, 10	Afghanis 5, 2, 1; Puls 50, 25
Albania	Lek of 100 Qindarka	Leks 100, 50, 25, 10, 5, 3, 1	Lek 1: Quindarka 50, 20, 10, 5
Algeria...........	Dinar of 100 Centimes	Dinars 200, 100, 20, 10, 5	Dinars 5, 1; Centimes 50, 20, 10, 5, 2, 1
Angola	Kwanza of 100 Lweis	Kwanzas 1,000, 500, 100, 50, 20	Kwanzas 20, 10, 5, 2, 1; Lweis 50
Argentina	Peso of 100 Centavos or 100 Old Pesos	Pesos 100, 50, 10, 5, 1	Centavos 50, 10, 5, 1
Australia.........	Dollar of 100 Cents	$A 50, 20, 10, 5, 2, 1	$A200, 10; Cents 50, 20, 10, 5, 2, 1
Austria	Schilling of 100 Groschen	Schillings 1,000, 500, 100, 50, 20	Schillings 1,000, 500, 100, 50, 25, 20, 10, 5, 1; Groschen 50, 10, 5, 2, 1
Bahamas	Bahamian Dollar of 100 Cents	B.$ 100, 50, 20, 10, 5, 3, 1; Cents 50	B.$ 5, 2, 1; Cents 50, 25, 15, 10, 5, 1
Bahrain	Dinar of 1,000 Fils	Dinars 20, 10, 5, 1, ½	Fils 100, 50, 25, 10, 5
Bangladesh	Taka of 100 Poisha	Taka 500, 100, 50, 20, 10, 5, 1	Taka 1; Poisha 50, 25, 10, 5, 1
Barbados	Dollar of 100 Cents	BDS$100, 20, 10, 5, 2, 1	BDS$1; Cents 25, 10, 5, 1
Belgium	Belgian Franc of 100 Centimes	Frs. 5,000, 1,000, 500, 100, 50	Frs. 500, 250, 100, 20, 10, 5, 1; Centimes 50
Belize	Dollar of 100 Cents	$100, 20, 10, 5, 1	Cents 50, 25, 10, 5, 1
Benin	Franc C.F.A.	Frs. 10,000, 5,000, 1,000, 500, 100, 50	Frs. 100, 50, 25, 10, 5, 2, 1
Bermuda	Dollar of 100 Cents	$100, 50, 20, 10, 5, 1	Cents 50, 25, 10, 5, 1
Bolivia	Peso of 100 Centavos	Pesos 100, 50, 20, 10, 5, 1	Peso 1; Centavos 50, 25, 20, 10, 5
Botswana	Pula of 100 Thebe	Pula 20, 10, 5, 2, 1	Pula 1; Thebe 50, 25, 10, 5, 2, 1
Brazil	Cruzeiro of 100 Centavos	Cruzeiro 5,000, 1,000, 500, 200, 100, 50, 10, 5, 1	Cruzeiro 50, 20, 10, 5, 1; Centavos 50, 20, 10
Brunei	Brunei Dollar of 100 Sen	$1,000, 500, 100, 50, 10, 5, 1	Sen 50, 20, 10, 5, 1
Bulgaria	Lev of 100 Stotinki	Léva 20, 10, 5, 2, 1	Léva 2, 1; Stotinki 50, 20, 10, 5, 2, 1
Burma	Kyat of 100 Pyas	Kyats 100, 50, 25, 20, 10, 5, 1	Kyat 1; Pyas 50, 25, 10, 5, 1
Burundi	Burundi Franc	Frs. 5,000, 1,000, 500, 100, 50, 20, 10	Frs. 10, 5, 1
Cameroon (Federal Republic of)	Franc C.F.A.	Frs. 10,000, 5,000, 1,000, 500, 100	Frs. 100, 50, 25, 10, 5, 2, 1
Canada...........	Dollar of 100 Cents	$1,000, 100, 50, 20, 10, 5, 2, 1	$1; Cents 50, 25, 10, 5, 1
Cape Verde Islands	Escudo of 100 Centavos	Esc 1,000$00, 500$00, 100$00	Esc 50$00, 20$00, 10$00, 2$50, 1$00, Centavos $50, $20
Cayman Islands ...	Dollar of 100 Cents	$25, 10, 5, 1	Cents 25, 10, 5, 1
Central African Republic	Franc C.F.A.	Frs. 10,000, 5,000, 1,000, 500, 100	Frs. 100, 50, 25, 10, 5, 2,, 1
Chad	Franc C.F.A.	Frs. 10,000, 5,000, 1,000, 500, 100	Frs. 100, 50, 25, 10, 5, 2, 1
Chile.............	New Peso of 100 Centavos	Pesos 5,000, 1,000, 500, 100, 50	Pesos 50, 10, 5, 1; Centavos 50
China	Renminbi or Yuan of 10 Jiao or 100 Fen	Yuan 10, 5, 2, 1; Jiao 5, 2, 1	Fen 5, 2, 1
Colombia	Peso of 100 Centavos	Pesos 1,000, 500, 200, 100, 50, 20, 10, 5, 2, 1	Pesos 10, 5, 2, 1; Centavos 50, 25, 20, 10
Congo	Franc C.F.A.	Frs. 10,000, 5,000, 1,000, 500, 100	Frs. 100, 50, 25, 10, 5, 2, 1
Costa Rica	Colon of 100 Céntimos	Colones 1,000, 500, 100, 50, 20, 10, 5	Colones 20, 10, 5, 2, 1; Centimos 50, 25, 10, 5
Cuba	Peso of 100 Centavos	Pesos $100, 50, 20, 10, 5, 1	Centavos 40, 20, 5, 2, 1
Cyprus	Cyprus Pound of 1,000 Mils	£10, 5, 1; Mils 500, 250	£50, 1; Mils 500, 100, 50, 25, 5, 3, 1
Czechoslovakia ...	Koruna (Crown) of 100 Haléru (Heller)	Kcs 500, 100, 50, 20, 10	Kcs 5, 2, 1; Heller 50, 20, 10, 5, 1
Denmark	Krone of 100 Ore	Kroner 1,000, 500, 100, 50, 20	Kroner 10, 5, 1; Ore 25, 10, 5
Dominican Republic	Peso of 100 Centavos	RD$1,000, 500, 100, 50, 20, 10, 5, 1	Peso 1; Centavos 50, 25, 10, 5, 1
East Caribbean Territory	East Caribbean Dollar of 100 Cents	$100, 20, 5, 1	Cents 50, 25, 10, 5, 2, 1
Ecuador	Sucre of 100 Centavos	Sucres 1,000, 500, 100, 50, 20, 10, 5	Sucre 1; Centavos 50, 20, 10

Country	Monetary Unit	Denomination in Circulation	
		Notes	Coins
Egypt	*Egyptian Pound* of 100 Piastres or 1,000 Millièmes	£E100, 20, 10, 5, 1, $\frac{1}{2}$, $\frac{1}{4}$; Piastres 10, 5	Piastres 10, 5; *Millièmes* 20, 10, 5, 2, 1
El Salvador	*Colón* of 100 Centavos	Colones 100, 50, 25, 10, 5, 2, 1	Centavos 50, 25, 10, 5, 3, 2, 1
Equatorial Guinea	*Ekuele*	E. 1000, 500, 100, 50, 25	—
Ethiopia..........	*Ethiopian Birr* of 100 Cents	EB 100, 50, 10, 5, 1	Cents 50, 25, 10, 5, 1
Falkland Islands ..	*Pound* of 100 Pence	£10, 5, 1; 50p	As in U.K., except no 50p
Faröe Islands	*Krone* of 100 Øre	Kr. 1,000, 500, 100, 50, 20, 10	As in Denmark
Fiji	*Fiji Dollar* of 100 Cents	$20, 10, 5, 2, 1	Cents 50, 20, 10, 5, 2, 1
Finland	*Markka* of 100 Penniä	Mk 500, 100, 50, 10, 5, 1	Mk 5, 1; P 50, 20, 10, 5, 1
France	*Franc* of 100 Centimes	Francs 500, 200, 100, 50, 20, 10	Francs 10, 5, 2, 1, $\frac{1}{2}$; Centimes 20, 10, 5, 1
Gabon.............	*Franc C.F.A.*	Frs. 10,000, 5,000, 1,000, 500, 100	Frs. 100, 50, 25, 10, 5, 2, 1
Gambia (The)	*Dalasi* of 100 Bututs	Dalasis 25, 10, 5, 1	Dalasi 1; Bututs 50, 25, 10, 5, 1
Germany (East) ...	*Mark der Deutschen Demokratischen Republik (M.)* of 100 Pfennig	M. 100, 50, 20, 10, 5	M. 20, 10, 5, 2, 1; Pfennig 50, 20, 10, 5, 1
Germany (Federal Republic of)	*Deutsche Mark* of 100 Pfennig	D.M. 1,000, 500, 100, 50, 20, 10, 5	D.M. 10, 5, 2, 1; Pfennig 50, 10, 5, 2, 1
Ghana	*Cedi* of 100 Pesewa	Cedis 10, 5, 2, 1	Pesewas 20, 10, 5, 2$\frac{1}{2}$, 1, $\frac{1}{2}$
Gibraltar	*Pound* of 100 pence	£20, 10, 5, 1	As in U.K.
Greece	*Drachma* of 100 Lepta	Drachmae 1,000, 500, 100, 50	Drachmae 20, 10, 5, 2, 1; Lepta 50, 20, 10
Guatemala	*Quetzal* of 100 Centavos	Quetzales 100, 50, 20, 10, 5, 1; Centavos 50	Centavos 25, 10, 5, 1
Guinea...........	*Syli* of 100 Cauris	Sy 100, 50, 25, 10	Sy 5, 2, 1, $\frac{1}{2}$
Guinea-Bissau (Republic of)	*Escudos* of 100 Centavos	Esc. 1,000$00, 500$00, 100$00, 50$00	Esc. 20$00, 10$00, 5$00, 2$50, 1$00; Centavos $50, $20, $10, $05
Guyana	*Guyana Dollar* of 100 Cents	Dollars 20, 10, 5, 1	Cents 100, 50, 25, 10, 5, 1
Haiti.............	*Gourde* of 100 Centimes*	Gourdes 500, 250, 100, 50, 10, 5, 2, 1	Gourdes 1,000, 200, 100, 50, 25, 20, 10, 5; Centimes 50, 20, 10, 5
Honduras	*Lempira* of 100 Centavos	Lempiras 100, 50, 20, 10, 5, 2, 1	Centavos 50, 20, 10, 5, 2, 1
Hong Kong	*Hong Kong Dollar* of 100 Cents	Dollars 1,000, 500, 100, 50, 10; Cents 1	Dollars 5, 2, 1; Cents 50, 20, 10, 5
Hungary	*Forint* of 100 Fillér	Forints 500, 100, 50, 20, 10	Forints 100, 20, 10, 5, 2, 1; Fillér 50, 20, 10, 5, 2
Iceland	*Króna* of 100 Aurar	Kr. 500, 100, 50, 10	Kr. 5, 1; Aurar 50, 10, 5
India.............	*Rupee* of 100 Paise	Rupees 100, 50, 20, 10, 5, 2, 1	Rupees 2, 1; Paise 50, 25, 20, 10, 5
Indonesia	*Rupiah* of 100 Sen	Rupiahs 10,000, 5,000, 1,000, 500, 100; Sen 50, 25, 10, 5, 1	Rupiahs 100, 50, 25, 10, 5, 2, 1
Iran	*Rial* of 100 Dinars	Rials 10,000, 5,000, 1,000, 500, 200, 100	Rials 50, 20, 10, 5, 2, 1
Iraq..............	*Iraqi Dinar* of 1000 Fils	Dinars 25, 10, 5, 1, $\frac{1}{2}$, $\frac{1}{4}$	Fils 100, 50, 25, 10, 5, 1
Ireland (Republic of)	*Pound* of 100 Pence	£20, 10, 5, 1	New Pence 50, 10, 5, 2, 1, $\frac{1}{2}$
Israel	*Israeli Shekel* of 100 New Agora	IS 100, 50, 10, 5, 1	IS $\frac{1}{2}$; New Agora 10, 5, 1
Italy	*Lira* of 100 Centesimi	Lire 100,000, 50,000, 20,000, 10,000, 5,000, 2,000, 1,000, 500	Lire 1,000, 500, 200, 100, 50, 20, 10, 5, 2, 1
Ivory Coast (Republic of)	*Franc C.F.A.*	Frs. C.F.A. 10,000, 5,000, 1,000, 500, 100, 50	Frs. C.F.A. 100, 50, 25, 10, 5, 2, 1
Jamaica	*Jamaican Dollar* of 100 Cents	$20, 10, 5, 2, 1	$1, Cents 50, 25, 20, 10, 5, 1
Japan	*Yen*	Yen 10,000, 5,000, 1,000, 500	Yen 500, 100, 50, 10, 5, 1
Jordan (Hashemite Kingdom of)	*Jordanian Dinar* of 1,000 Fils	J. Dinars 20, 10, 5, 1; Fils 500	Fils 250, 100, 50, 25, 20, 10, 5, 1
Kenya	*Kenya Shilling* of 100 Cents	Shillings 100, 50, 20, 10, 5	Shillings 1; Cents 50, 10, 5
Korea (South)	*Won* of 100 Jeon	Won 10,000, 5,000, 1,000, 500	Won 500, 100, 50, 10, 5, 1
Korea (North)	*Won* of 100 Chon	Won 100, 50, 10, 5, 1	Jeon 50, 10, 5, 1

* U.S.A. Currency also used.

Country	Monetary Unit	Denomination in Circulation	
		Notes	Coins
Kuwait	*Kuwait Dinar* of 1,000 *Fils*	*Dinars* 10, 5, 1, ½, ¼	*Fils* 100, 50, 20, 10, 5, 1
Laos	*Kip* of 100 *Ats*	*Kips* 500, 200, 50, 20, 10	——
Lebanon	*Lebanese Pound* of 100 *Piastres*	*LL.* 250, 100, 50, 25, 10, 5, 1	*LL.* 1; *Piastres* 50, 25, 10, 5, 2½, 1
Liberia	*Liberian* $ of 100 *Cents*	$20, 10, 5, 1 (U.S. notes)	$5, 1; *Cents* 50, 25, 10, 5, 1*
Libya	*Libyan Dinar* of 1,000 *Dirhams*	*LD.* 10, 5, 1, ½, ¼	*Dirham* 100, 50, 20, 10, 5, 1
Luxembourg	*Franc* of 100 *Centimes*†	*Francs* 100, 50, 20	*Francs* 250, 100, 20, 10, 5, 1; *Centimes* 25
Macau	*Pataca* of 100 *Avos*	*Patacas* 500, 100, 50, 10	*Patacas* 5, 1; *Avos* 50, 20, 10
Malagasy Republic	*Franc Malgache (F.M.G.)*	*Frs.* 5,000, 1,000, 500, 100, 50	*Frs.* 100, 50, 20, 10, 5, 2, 1
Malawi	*Malawi Kwacha* of 100 *Tambala*	*K.* 10, 5, 1; *Tambala* 50	*Tambala* 20, 10, 5, 2, 1
Malaysia	*Malaysian Dollar (Ringgit)* of 100 *Cents*	*Dollars* 1,000, 500, 100, 50, 10, 5, 1	*Dollar* 1; *Cents* 50, 20, 10, 5, 1
Maldive Islands	*Rupee* of 100 *Laris*	*Rs* 100, 50, 10, 5, 2, 1, ½	——
Mali (Republic of)	*Franc C.F.A.*	*Frs.* 10,000, 5,000, 1,000, 500, 100	*Frs.* 100, 50, 25, 10, 5
Malta	*Maltese Pound* of 100 *cents* or 1,000 *Mils*	*£M*10, 5, 1	*Cents* 50, 25, 10, 5, 2, 1; *Mils* 5, 3, 2
Mauritania	*Ouguiya* of 5 *khoums*	*UM* 1,000, 500, 200, 100	*UM* 20, 10, 5, 1, ⅕
Mauritius	*Rupee* of 100 *Cents*	*Rs.* 50, 25, 10, 5	*R.* 1; *Cents* 50, 25, 10, 5, 2, 1
Mexico	*Peso* of 100 *Centavos*	*Pesos* 10,000, 1,000, 500, 100, 50, 20, 10, 5, 1	*Pesos* 10, 5, 1; *Centavos* 50, 20, 10
Monaco	*Franc of* 100 *Centimes*	As in France	*Francs* 50, 10, 5, 1; *Centimes* 50, 20, 10
Mongolian People's Republic	*Tugrik* of 100 *Mongo*	*Tugriks* 100, 50, 25, 10, 5, 3, 1	*Tugrik* 1; *Mongo* 50, 20, 15, 10, 5, 2, 1
Morocco	*Dirham* of 100 *Centimes*	*DH* 100, 50, 10, 5	*DH* 5, 1; *Centimes* 50, 20, 10, 5, 2, 1
Mozambique	*Metical* of 100 *Centavos*	*Meticais* 1,000, 500, 100, 50	*Meticais* 20, 10, 5, 2½, 1, ½
Nepal	*Rupee* of 100 *Paisa*	*Rupees* 1,000, 500, 100, 50, 10, 5, 2, 1	*Rupee* 1; *Paisa* 50, 25, 20, 10, 5, 2, 1
Netherlands (The)	*Florin (Guilder)* of 100 *Cents*	*Florins* 1,000, 100, 25, 10, 5, 2½, 1	*Florins* 10, 2½, 1; *Cents* 25, 10
Netherlands Antilles (The)	*N.A. Guilder* of 100 *Cents*	*Guilders* 250, 100, 50, 25, 10, 5, 2½, 1	*Guilders* 2½, 1, ¼, $\frac{1}{10}$; *Cent* 5, 2½, 1
New Zealand	*New Zealand Dollar* of 100 *Cents*	N.Z.$ 100, 20, 10, 5, 2, 1	*Cents* 50, 20, 10, 5, 2, 1
Nicaragua	*Córdoba* of 100 *Centavos*	*Córdobas* 1,000, 500, 100, 50, 20, 10, 5, 2, 1	*Cordobas* 5, 1; *Centavos* 50, 25, 10, 5
Niger (Republic of)	*Franc C.F.A.*	*Frs. C.F.A.* 10,000, 5,000, 1,000, 500, 100, 50	*Frs. C.F.A.* 100, 50, 25, 10, 5, 2, 1
Nigeria	*Naira* of 100 *Kobo*	N.20, 10, 5, 1	*k.*25, 10, 5, 1, ½
Norway	*Krone* of 100 *Ore*	*Kroner* 1,000, 500, 100, 50, 10	*Kroner* 5, 1; *Ore* 50, 25, 10, 5
Oman	*Rial Omani* of 1,000 *Baiza*	*Rial Omani* 50, 20, 10, 5, 1, ½, ¼; *Baiza* 100	*Baiza* 500, 250, 100, 50, 25, 10, 5, 2
Pakistan	*Rupee* of 100 *Paisa*	*Rupees* 100, 50, 10, 5, 2, 1	*Rupee* 1, ½, ¼; *Paisa* 50, 25, 10, 5, 2, 1
Panama	*Balboa* of 100 *Cents* (= *U.S.$*)	As in U.S.A.	*Balboa* 5, 1, ½, ¼, $\frac{1}{10}$, $\frac{1}{20}$, $\frac{1}{40}$; *Cent* 1.*
Papua New Guinea	*Kina* = 100 *Toea*	*K* 20, 10, 5, 2	*K* 1; *T* 50, 20, 10, 5, 2, 1
Paraguay	*Guarani* of 100 *Céntimos*	*Guaraníes* 10,000, 5,000, 1,000, 500, 100, 50, 10, 5, 1	——
Peru	*Gold Sol* of 100 *Centavos*	*Soles* 10,000, 5,000, 1,000, 500	*Soles* 100, 50, 10, 5, 1
Philippines	*Philippine Peso* of 100 *Centavos*	*Pesos* 100, 50, 20, 10, 5, 2	*Peso* 1; *Centavos* 50, 25, 10, 5, 1
Poland	*Zloty* of 100 *Groszy*	*Zlotys* 5,000, 2,000, 1,000, 500, 200, 100, 50, 20, 10	*Zlotys* 2,000, 1,000, 500, 200, 100, 50, 20, 10, 5, 2, 1; *Groszy* 50, 20, 10, 5, 2
Portugal	*Escudo* of 100 *Centavos*	*Escudos* 5,000$00, 1,000$00, 500$00, 100$00, 50$00	*Escudos* 25$00, 5$00, 2$50, 1$00, $50
Portuguese Timor	*Escudo* of 100 *Centavos*	*Esc.* 1,000$00, 500$00, 100$00, 50$00, 20$00	*Esc.* 10$00, 5$00, 2$50, 1$00; *Centavos* $50, $20, $10
Qatar	*Qatar Riyal* of 100 *Dirhams*	*Qatar Riyals* 500, 100, 50, 10, 5, 1	*Dirhams* 50, 25, 10, 5, 1
Rumania	*Leu* of 100 *Bani*	*Lei* 100, 50, 25, 10, 5, 3, 1	*Lei* 5, 3, 1; *Bani* 25, 15, 10, 5, 3, 1

* U.S. coins also circulate. † Belgian currency is also legal tender.

Country	Monetary Unit	Denomination in Circulation	
		Notes	Coins
Rwanda	*Rwanda Franc*	*Frs.* 5,000, 1,000, 500, 100	*Frs.* 50, 20, 10, 5, 1
St. Helena	St. Helena *Pound* of 100 *Pence*	£10, 5, 1, 50p	As in U.K.
Samoa (Western)..	*Tala* of 100 *Sene*	*Tala* 20, 10, 5, 2, 1	*Sene* 50, 20, 10, 5, 2, 1
Sao Tomé and Principé	*Dobra* of 100 *Centimos*	*Dobras* 1,000, 500, 100, 50	*Dobras* 20, 10, 5, 2, 1; *Centimos* 50
Saudi Arabia	*Riyal* of 20 *Qursh* or 100 *Halalas*	*Riyals* 100, 50, 10, 5, 1	*Qursh* 4, 2, 1; *Halala* 50, 25, 10, 5, 1
Senegal	*Franc C.F.A.*	*Frs.* 10,000, 5,000, 1,000, 500, 100, 50	*Frs.* 100, 50, 25, 10, 5, 2, 1
Seychelles	*Rupee* of 100 *Cents*	*Rs.* 100, 50, 25, 10	*Rupees* 1,500, 1,000, 100, 50, 10, 5, 1; *Cents* 50, 25, 10, 5, 1
Sierra Leone	*Leone* of 100 *Cents*	*Le.* 10, 5, 2, 1; *Cents* 50	*Cents* 50, 20, 10, 5, 1, ½
Singapore	*S. Dollar* of 100 *Cents*	*S*$10,000, 1,000, 500, 100, 50, 25, 20, 10, 5, 1	*S*$1; *Cents* 50, 20, 10, 5, 1
Solomon Islands...	*Solomon Islands Dollar* of 100 *Cents*	*SI*$20, 10, 5, 2	*SI*$1; *Cents* 20, 10, 5, 2, 1
Somali Democratic Republic	*Somali Shilling* of 100 *Cents*	*S. Shillings* 100, 20, 10, 5	*Shillings* 1, ½; *Cents* 10, 5, 1
South Africa	*Rand* of 100 *Cents*	*R* 20, 10, 5, 2, 1	*R* 1; *Cents* 50, 20, 10, 5, 2, 1, ½
Spain	*Peseta* of 100 *Céntimos*	*Pesetas* 5,000, 1,000, 500, 100	*Pesetas* 100, 50, 25, 5, 1; *Céntimos* 50
Sri Lanka	*Rupee* of 100 *Cents*	*Rupees* 1,000, 500, 100, 50, 20, 10, 5, 2	*Re.* 1; *Cents* 50, 25, 10, 5, 2, 1
Sudan............	*Sudanese Pound* of 100 *Piastres* or 1,000 *Milliemes*	£*S* 20, 10, 5, 1; *Piastres* 50, 25	*Piastres* 50, 10, 5, 2; *Milliemes* 10, 5, 2, 1
Surinam	*Guilder* of 100 *Cents*	*Guilders* 500, 100, 25, 10, 5, 2½, 1	*Guilder* 1; *Cents* 25, 10, 5, 1
Swaziland	*Lilangeni* (plural *Emalangeni*) of 100 *cents*	*E* 20, 10, 5, 2; 1	*E* 2, 1; *Cents* 50, 20, 10, 5, 2, 1
Sweden	*Krona* of 100 *Ore*	*Kronor* 10,000, 1,000, 100, 50, 10, 5	*Kronor* 200, 100, 50, 10, 5, 2, 1; *Ore* 50, 25, 10, 5
Switzerland	*Franc* of 100 *Centimes*	*Francs* 1,000, 500, 100, 50, 20, 10	*Francs* 5, 2, 1; *Centimes* 50, 20, 10, 5, 1
Syria.............	*Syrian Pound* of 100 *Piastres*	*S. Pounds* 500, 100, 50, 25, 10, 5, 1	*Pound* 1, ½; *Piastres* 50, 25, 10, 5, 2½
Taiwan	*New Taiwan Dollar* of 100 *Cents*	*NT*$ 1,000, 500, 100, 50, 10, 5, 1	*NT*$10, 5, 1; *Cents* 50, 10
Tanzania	*T. Shilling* of 100 *Cents*	*Shillings* 100, 20, 10	*Shilling* 5, 1; *Cents* 50, 20, 10, 5
Thailand	*Baht* of 100 *Stangs*	*Bahts* 500, 100, 20, 10, 5, 1; *Stangs* 50	*Baht* 5, 1; *Stangs* 50, 25, 10, 5, 1
Togo (Republic of) .	*Franc C.F.A.*	*Frs. C.F.A.* 10,000, 5,000, 1,000, 500, 100, 50	*Frs. C.F.A.* 100, 50, 25, 10, 5, 2, 1
Tonga............	*Pa'anga* (*T*$) of 100 *Seniti*	*Pa'anga* 10, 5, 2, 1, ½	*Pa'anga* 2, 1; *Seniti* 50, 20, 10, 5, 2, 1
Trinidad and Tobago	*Trinidad and Tobago Dollar* of 100 *Cents*	*Dollars* 100, 20, 10, 5, 1	*Dollar* 1; *Cents* 50, 25, 10, 5, 1
Tunisia	*Tunisian Dinar* of 1,000 *Millimes*	*Dinars* 10, 5, 1, ½	*Dinars* 5, 1, ½; *Millimes* 100, 50, 20, 10, 5, 2, 1
Turkey...........	*Turkish Lira* of 100 *Kurus*	*TL* 1,000, 500, 100, 50, 20, 10, 5	*TL* 10, 5, 2, 1; *Kurus* 50, 25, 10, 5, 1
Uganda	*U. Shilling* of 100 *Cents*	*Shillings* 100, 50, 20, 10	*Shillings* 5, 2, 1; *Cents* 50, 20, 10, 5
United Arab Emirates	*Dirham* of 100 *Fils*	*Dirhams* 1,000, 100, 50, 10, 5, 1	*Dirham* 1; *Fils* 50, 25, 10, 5, 1
United Kingdom ..	*Pound* of 100 *pence*	£50, £20, £10, £5, £1	£*1;* *Pence* 50, 20, 10, 5, 2, 1, ½; 5s. (25p)
U.S.A.............	*Dollar* of 100 *Cents*	$100, 50, 20, 10, 5, 2, 1	$1; *Cents* 50, 25, 10, 5, 1
Upper Volta (Republic of)	*Franc C.F.A.*	*Frs. C.F.A.* 10,000, 5,000, 1,000, 500, 100, 50	*Frs. C.F.A.* 100, 50, 25, 10, 5, 2, 1
Uruguay	*New Peso* of 100 *Centésimos*	*New Pesos* 10,000, 5,000, 1,000, 500, 100, 50	*New Pesos* 10, 5, 2, 1; *Cents* 50, 20, 10, 5
U.S.S.R.	*Rouble* of 100 *Copecks*	*Roubles* 100, 50, 25, 10, 5, 3, 1	*Rouble* 1; *Copecks* 50, 20, 15, 10, 5, 3, 2, 1
Venezuela	*Bolivar*	*Bolivares* 500, 100, 50, 20, 10, 5	*Bolivares* 100, 20, 10, 5, 2, 1, ¼, ⅛, ⅟₁₆, ⅟₂₀
Vietnam	*Dong* of 10 *Hào* or 100 *Xu*	*Dong* 10, 5, 2, 1; *Hào* 5, 2, 1; *Xu* 5	*Xu* 5, 2, 1

Country	Monetary Unit	Denomination in Circulation	
		Notes	Coins
Yemen (Arab Republic)	*Riyal* of 100 *Fils*	*Riyals* 100, 50, 20, 10, 5, 1	*Fils* 50, 25, 10, 5, 1
Yemen (People's Democratic Republic)	*Southern Yemen Dinar (YD)* of 1,000 *Fils*	*YD* 10, 5, 1; *Fils* 500, 250	*Fils* 50, 25, 5, 2½, 1
Yugoslavia	*Dinar* of 100 *Paras*	*Dinars* 1,000, 500, 100, 50, 20, 10, 5	*Dinar* 10, 5, 2, 1; *Paras* 50, 20, 10, 5, 2, 1
Zaire (Congolese Republic)	*Zaire* of 100 *Makuta* or 10,000 *Senghi*	*Zaires* 10, 5, 1; *Makuta* 50	*Makuta* 20, 10, 5, 1; *Sengi* 10
Zambia	*Kwacha* of 100 *Ngwee*	*Kwacha* 20, 10, 5, 2, 1	*Ngwee* 50, 20, 10, 5, 2, 1
Zimbabwe	*Dollar* of 100 cents	Z$ 20, 10, 5, 2	Z$1, *Cents* 50, 20, 10, 5, 1

WEATHER INFORMATION AND FORECASTS

Recorded weather forecasts for the areas listed below are available by telephoning the numbers shown:

Herts, Beds and		
Inland Essex	Bedford 8091	
	Bishops Stortford 8091	
	Cambridge 8091	
	London 01–246 8099	
	Luton 8091	
Northern Ireland	Belfast 8091	
West Midlands and	021–246 8091	
Warwickshire	Coventry 8091	
Avon and	Bristol 8091	
Somerset	Swindon 8091	
Glamorgan, Gwent		
and South Dyfed		
	Cardiff 8091	
	Newport 8091	
	Swansea 8091	
Devon and Cornwall	Exeter 8091	
	Plymouth 8091	
	Torquay 8091	
Dundee, Tayside		
and Fife	Dundee 8091	
Edinburgh, S. Fife		
and Borders	031–246 8091	
Glasgow area	041–246 8091	
Grampian	Aberdeen 8091	
N. Kent and	01–246 8096	
S. Essex Coast	Canterbury 8091	
	Medway 8091	
	Chelmsford 8091	
	Colchester 8091	
	Southend 8091	
N.W. England	051–246 8091	
	061–246 8091	

	Blackburn 8091	
	Blackpool 8091	
	Southport 8091	
West		
Yorkshire	Bradford 8091	
	Huddersfield 8091	
	Leeds 8091	
Greater London	01–246 8091	
	Tunbridge Wells 8091	
East Anglia	Cambridge 8092	
	Norwich 8091	
	Ipswich 8091	
	Lowestoft 8091	
North East England		
(incl. N. Yorks)		
	Peterborough 8091	
	Middlesbrough 8091	
	Newcastle upon Tyne 8091	
Lincs &		
Humberside	Grimsby 8091	
	Lincoln 8091	
Anglesey and		
N. Wales Coast	051–246 8093	
	061–246 8093	
	Chester 8091	
	Colwyn Bay 8091	
East Midlands	Nottingham 8091	
	Leicester 8091	
	Derby 8091	
	Northampton 8091	
S. Yorkshire and		
Peak District	Sheffield 8091	

	Doncaster 8091	
Dorset and Hants. Coast		
(including I.O.W.)		
	Bournemouth 8091	
	Portsmouth 8091	
	Southampton 8091	
South-West Midlands		
	Cheltenham 8091	
	Gloucester 8091	
	Hereford 8091	
Sussex and		
S. Kent Coast	01–246 8097	
	Brighton 8091	
	Hastings 8091	
	Canterbury 8092	
Oxon, Berks and		
Bucks	01–246 8090	
	High Wycombe 8091	
	Oxford 8091	
	Reading 8091	
North Downs and		
the Weald	01–246 8092	
Staffs and Shropshire		
	Stoke-on-Trent 8091	
	Shrewsbury 8091	
Lake District	Carlisle 8092	
	Kendal 8092	
	Leeds 8092	
Central Southern		
England	Southampton 8092	

RETROSPECT OF SPORT 1983–84

THE WINTER OLYMPIC GAMES 1984

The Games took place at Sarajevo, Yugoslavia from February 8 to 19. The following is a list of the gold medallists:

Alpine Skiing

Men's Giant Slalom.—M. Julen (Switzerland).
Men's Slalom.—P. Mahre (U.S.A.).
Men's Downhill.—B. Johnson (U.S.A.).
Women's Giant Slalom.—D. Armstrong (U.S.A.).
Women's Slalom.—P. Magoni (Italy).
Women's Downhill.—M. Figini (Switzerland).

Bobsledding

Two-man.—G.D.R. II.
Four-man.—G.D.R. I.

Figure Skating

Men's Singles.—S. Hamilton (U.S.A.).
Women's Singles.—K. Witt (G.D.R.).
Pairs.—E. Valova & O. Vassilyev (U.S.S.R.).
Ice Dance.—J. Torvill & C. Dean (G.B.).

Ice Hockey

Winners.—U.S.S.R.

Lugeing

Men's Singles.—P. Hildgartner (Italy).
Two-man.—F.R.G.
Women's Singles.—S. Martin (G.D.R.).

Nordic Skiing (Men)

15,000 Metres.—G. Svan (Sweden).
30,000 Metres.—N. Zimyatov (U.S.S.R.).
50,000 Metres.—T. Wassberg (Sweden).
4 × 10,000 Metres Relay.—Sweden.
Nordic Combination.—T. Sandberg (Norway).
70 Metre Ski Jump.—J. Weissflog (G.D.R.).
90 Metre Ski Jump.—M. Nykanen (Finland).
10,000 Metres Biathlon.—E. Kvalfoss (Norway).
20,000 Metres Biathlon.—P. Angerer (F.R.G.).
4 × 7,500 Metres Biathlon Relay.—U.S.S.R.

Nordic Skiing (Women)

5,000 Metres.—M.-L. Hamalainen (Finland).
10,000 Metres.—M.-L. Hamalainen (Finland).
20,000 Metres.—M.-L. Hamalainen (Finland).
4 × 5,000 Metres Relay.—Norway.

Speed Skating (Men)

500 Metres.—S. Fokichev (U.S.S.R.).
1,000 Metres.—G. Boucher (Canada).
1,500 Metres.—G. Boucher (Canada).
5,000 Metres.—T. Gustafson (Sweden).
10,000 Metres.—I. Malkov (U.S.S.R.).

Speed Skating (Women)

500 Metres.—C. Rothenburger (G.D.R.).
1,000 Metres.—K. Enke (G.D.R.).
1,500 Metres.—K. Enke (G.D.R.).
3,000 Metres.—A. Schoene (G.D.R.).

MEDAL TABLE

	Gold	Silver	Bronze
G.D.R.	9	9	6
U.S.S.R.	6	10	9
U.S.A.	4	4	—
Finland	4	3	6
Sweden	4	2	2
Norway	3	2	4
Switzerland	2	2	1
Canada	2	1	1
F.R.G.	2	1	1
Italy	2	—	—
Great Britain	1	—	—
Czechoslovakia	—	2	4
France	—	1	2
Japan	—	1	—
Yugoslavia	—	1	—
Liechtenstein	—	—	2
Austria	—	—	1
	39	39	39

THE OLYMPIC GAMES

The XXIIIrd Olympic Games took place in Los Angeles from July 28 to August 12, 1984.

Previous Games have been held as follows: I, Athens, 1896; II, Paris, 1900; III, St. Louis, 1904; IV, London, 1908; V, Stockholm, 1912; VII, Antwerp, 1920; VIII, Paris, 1924; IX, Amsterdam, 1928; X, Los Angeles, 1932; XI, Berlin, 1936; XIV, London, 1948; XV, Helsinki, 1952; XVI, Melbourne, 1956; XVII, Rome, 1960; XVIII, Tokyo, 1964; XIX, Mexico, 1968; XX, Munich, 1972; XXI, Montreal, 1976; XXII, Moscow, 1980.

The VIth Games scheduled for Berlin in 1916, the XIIth for Tokyo and then Helsinki in 1940, and the XIIIth for London in 1944 did not take place owing to World Wars.

The XXIV Games in 1988 will be held in Seoul, Korea and the Winter Olympic Games in Calgary, Canada.

OLYMPIC GOLD MEDALLISTS 1984

Archery

		points
Men	D. Pace (U.S.A.)	2,616
Women	Hyang-Soon Seo (S. Korea)	2,568

Athletics

Men:		hr. min. sec.
100 m.	C. Lewis (U.S.A.)	9·99
200 m.	C. Lewis (U.S.A.)	19·80
400 m.	A. Babers (U.S.A.)	44·27
800 m.	J. Cruz (Brazil)	1 43·00
1,500 m.	S. Coe (G.B.)	3 32·53
5,000 m.	S. Aouita (Morocco)	13 05·59
10,000 m.	A. Cova (Italy)	27 47·54
Marathon	C. Lopes (Portugal)	2 09 21
3,000 m. Steeple-chase	J. Korir (Kenya)	8 11·80
110 m. Hurdles	R. Kingdom (U.S.A.)	13·20
400 m. Hurdles	E. Moses (U.S.A.)	47·75
20,000 m. Walk	E. Canto (Mexico)	1 23 13
50,000 m. Walk	R. Gonzalez (Mexico)	3 47 26
4 × 100 m. Relay	U.S.A.	37·83
4 × 400 m. Relay	U.S.A.	2 57·91
High Jump	D. Mogenburg (F.R.G.)	2·35 m.
Pole Vault	P. Quinon (France)	5·75 m.
Long Jump	C. Lewis (U.S.A.)	8·54 m.
Triple Jump	A. Joyner (U.S.A.)	17·26 m.
Shot	A. Andrei (Italy)	21·26 m.
Discus	R. Danneberg (F.R.G.)	66·60 m.
Hammer	J. Tiainen (Finland)	78·08 m.
Javelin	A. Härkönen (Finland)	86·76 m.
Decathlon	D. Thompson (G.B.)	8,797 pts.

Women:		hr. min. sec.
100 m.	E. Ashford (U.S.A.)	10·97
200 m.	V. Brisco-Hooks (U.S.A.)	21·81
400 m.	V. Brisco-Hooks (U.S.A.)	48·83
800 m.	D. Melinte (Romania)	1 57·60
1,500 m.	G. Dorio (Italy)	4 03·25
3,000 m.	M. Puica (Romania)	8 35·96
Marathon	J. Benoit (U.S.A.)	2 24 52
100 m. Hurdles	B. Fitzgerald-Brown (U.S.A.)	12·84
400 m. Hurdles	N. El Moutawakel (Morocco)	54·61
4 × 100 m. Relay	U.S.A.	41·65
4 × 400 m. Relay	U.S.A.	3 18·29
High Jump	U. Meyfarth (F.R.G.)	2·02 m.
Long Jump	A. Stanciu (Romania)	6·96 m.
Shot	C. Losch (F.R.G.)	20·48 m.
Discus	R. Stalman (Holland)	65·36 m.
Javelin	T. Sanderson (G.B.)	69·56 m.
Heptathlon	G. Nunn (Australia)	6,390 pts.

Basketball

Men	U.S.A.
Women	U.S.A.

Boxing

Light Flyweight	P. Gonzales (U.S.A.)
Flyweight	S. McCrory (U.S.A.)
Bantamweight	M. Stecca (Italy)
Featherweight	M. Taylor (U.S.A.)
Lightweight	P. Whitaker (U.S.A.)
Light Welterweight	J. Page (U.S.A.)
Welterweight	M. Breland (U.S.A.)
Light Middleweight	F. Tate (U.S.A.)
Middleweight	Joon-Sup Shin (S. Korea)
Light Heavyweight	A. Josipovic (Yugoslavia)
Heavyweight	H. Tillman (U.S.A.)
Super Heavyweight	T. Biggs (U.S.A.)

Canoeing

Men:		min. sec.
Kayak Singles (K-1) 500 m.	I. Ferguson (N.Z.)	1 47·84
Kayak Pairs (K-2) 500 m.	New Zealand	1 34·21
Kayak Singles (K-1) 1,000 m.	A. Thompson (N.Z.)	3 45·73
Kayak Pairs (K-2) 1,000 m.	Canada	3 24·22
Kayak Fours (K-4) 1,000 m.	New Zealand	3 02·28
Canadian Singles (C-1) 500 m.	L. Cain (Canada)	1 57·01
Canadian Pairs (C-2) 500 m.	Yugoslavia	1 43·67
Canadian Singles (C-1) 1,000 m.	U. Eicke (F.R.G.)	4 06·32
Canadian Pairs (C-2) 1,000 m.	Romania	3 40·60

Women:		
Kayak Singles (K-1) 500 m.	A. Andersson (Sweden)	1 58·72
Kayak Pairs (K-2) 500 m.	Sweden	1 45·25
Kayak Fours (K-4) 500 m.	Romania	1 38·34

Cycling

Men:		hr. min. sec.
1,000 m. Time Trial	F. Schmidtke (F.R.G.)	1 06·10
1,000 m. Sprint	M. Gorski (U.S.A.)	
4,000 m. Individual Pursuit	S. Hegg (U.S.A.)	4 39·35
4,000 m. Team Pursuit	Australia	4 25·99
Individual Points Race	R. Ilegems (Belgium)	
Individual Road Race	A. Grewal (U.S.A.)	4 59 57
Road Team Time Trial	Italy	1 58 28

Women:		hr. min. sec.
Individual Road Race	C. Carpenter-Phinney (U.S.A.)	2 11 14

Equestrianism

Individual Dressage	R. Klimke (F.R.G.)	1,504 pts.
Team Dressage	F.R.G.	4,955 pts.
Individual Three-Day Event	M. Todd (N.Z.)	51·60 pts.
Team Three-Day Event	U.S.A.	186·00 pts.
Individual Jumping	J. Fargis (U.S.A.)	
Team Jumping	U.S.A.	12·00 pts.

Fencing

Men:	
Individual Foil	M. Numa (Italy)
Team Foil	Italy
Individual Epée	P. Boisse (France)
Team Epée	F.R.G.
Individual Sabre	J-F. Lamour (France)
Team Sabre	Italy

Women:	
Individual Foil	J. Luan (China)
Team Foil	F.R.G.

Football

France

Gymnastics

Men:		points
Team	U.S.A.	591·40
Individual		
All-Around	K. Gushiken (Japan)	118·700
Floor Exercise	Li Ning (China)	19·925
Pommel Horse	Li Ning (China)	19·950
	P. Vidmar (U.S.A.)	19·950
Rings	K. Gushiken (Japan)	19·850
	Li Ning (China)	19·850
Horse Vault	Lou Yun (China)	19·950
Parallel Bars	B. Conner (U.S.A.)	19·950
Horizontal Bar	S. Morisue (Japan)	20·000

Women:		
Team	Romania	392·20
Individual		
All-Round	M. L. Retton (U.S.A.)	79·175
Horse Vault	E. Szabo (Romania)	19·875
Asymmetrical	Ma Yanhong (China)	19·950
Bars	J. McNamara (U.S.A.)	19·950
Balance Beam	S. Pauca (Romania)	19·800
	E. Szabo (Romania)	19·800
Floor Exercise	E. Szabo (Romania)	19·975
Modern Rhythmic	L. Fung (Canada)	57·950

Handball

Men	Yugoslavia
Women	Yugoslavia

Hockey

Men	Pakistan
Women	Holland

Judo

Up to 60 kg.	S. Hosokawa (Japan)
Up to 65 kg.	Y. Matsuoka (Japan)
Up to 71 kg.	Byeong-Keun Ahn (S. Korea)
Up to 78 kg.	F. Wieneke (F.R.G.)
Up to 86 kg.	P. Seisenbacher (Austria)
Up to 95 kg.	Hyoung-Zou Ha (S. Korea)
Over 95 kg.	H. Saito (Japan)
Open	Y. Yamashita (Japan)

Modern Pentathlon

Individual	D. Masala (Italy)	5,469 pts.
Team	Italy	16,060 pts.

Rowing

Men:		min. sec.
Single Sculls	P. Karppinen (Finland)	7 00·24
Double Sculls	U.S.A.	6 36·87
Coxless Quadruple		
Sculls	F.R.G.	5 57·55
Coxless Pairs	Romania	6 45·39
Coxed Pairs	Italy	7 05·99
Coxless Fours	New Zealand	6 03·48
Coxed Fours	Great Britain	6 20·28
Eights	Canada	5 41·32

Women:		
Single Sculls	V. Racila (Romania)	3 40·68
Double Sculls	Romania	3 26·75
Coxless Pairs	Romania	3 32·60
Coxed Quadruple		
Sculls	Romania	3 14·11
Coxed Fours	Romania	3 19·30
Eights	U.S.A.	2 59·80

Shooting

Men:		points
Free Pistol	Xu Haifeng (China)	566
Rapid-Fire Pistol	T. Kamachi (Japan)	595
Small-Bore Rifle		
(3 pos.)	M. Cooper (G.B.)	1,173
Small-Bore Rifle		
(prone)	E. Etzel (U.S.A.)	599
Running Game		
Target	Li Yuwei (China)	587
Air Rifle	P. Heberle (France)	589

Women:		points
Sport Pistol	L. Thom (Canada)	585
Standard Rifle	Wu Xiaoxuan (China)	581
Air Rifle	P. Spurgin (U.S.A.)	393

Mixed:		
Trap	L. Giovanetti (Italy)	192
Skeet	M. Dryke (U.S.A.)	198

Swimming

Men:		min. sec.
100 m. Freestyle	A. Gaines (U.S.A.)	49·80
200 m. Freestyle	M. Gross (F.R.G.)	1 47·44
400 m. Freestyle	G. DiCarlo (U.S.A.)	3 51·23
1,500 m. Freestyle	M. O'Brien (U.S.A.)	15 05·20
100 m. Breaststroke	S. Lundquist (U.S.A.)	1 01·65
200 m. Breaststroke	V. Davis (Canada)	2 13·34
100 m. Backstroke	R. Carey (U.S.A.)	55·79
200 m. Backstroke	R. Carey (U.S.A.)	2 00·23
100 m. Butterfly	M. Gross (F.R.G.)	53·08
200 m. Butterfly	J. Sieben (Australia)	1 57·04
200 m. Medley	A. Baumann (Canada)	2 01·42
400 m. Medley	A. Baumann (Canada)	4 17·41
4 × 100 m. Freestyle	U.S.A.	3 19·03
4 × 200 m. Freestyle	U.S.A.	7 15·69
4 × 100 m. Medley	U.S.A.	3 39·30
Springboard	G. Louganis (U.S.A.)	
Diving		754·41 pts.
Platform Diving	G. Louganis (U.S.A.)	
		710·91 pts.
Water Polo	Yugoslavia	

Women:		min. sec.
100 m. Freestyle	C. Steinseifer (U.S.A.)	55·92
	N. Hogshead (U.S.A.)	55·92
200 m. Freestyle	M. Wayte (U.S.A.)	1 59·23
400 m. Freestyle	T. Cohen (U.S.A.)	4 07·10
800 m. Freestyle	T. Cohen (U.S.A.)	8 24·95
100 m. Breaststroke	P. Van Staveren (Holland)	
		1 09·88
200 m. Breaststroke	A. Ottenbrite (Canada)	2 30·38
100 m. Backstroke	T. Andrews (U.S.A.)	1 02·55
200 m. Backstroke	J. De Rover (Holland)	2 12·38
100 m. Butterfly	M. Meagher (U.S.A.)	59·26
200 m. Butterfly	M. Meagher (U.S.A.)	2 06·90
200 m. Medley	T. Caulkins (U.S.A.)	2 12·64
400 m. Medley	T. Caulkins (U.S.A.)	4 39·24
4 × 100 m. Freestyle	U.S.A.	3 43·43
4 × 100 m. Medley	U.S.A.	4 08·34
Springboard		
Diving	S. Bernier (Canada)	530·70 pts.
Platform Diving	Zhou Jihong (China)	
		435·51 pts.
Synchronized		
Swimming Solo	T. Ruiz (U.S.A.)	198·467 pts.
Synchronized		
Swimming Duet	U.S.A.	195·584 pts.

Volleyball

Men	U.S.A.
Women	China

Weightlifting

		kg.
Up to 52 kg.	Zeng Guoqiang (China)	235·0
Up to 56 kg.	Wu Shude (China)	267·5
Up to 60 kg.	Chen Weiqiang (China)	282·5
Up to 67·5 kg.	Yao Jingyuan (China)	320·0
Up to 75 kg.	K.-H. Radschinsky (F.R.G.)	340·0
Up to 82·5 kg.	P. Becheru (Romania)	355·0
Up to 90 kg.	N. Vlad (Romania)	392·5
Up to 100 kg.	R. Milser (F.R.G.)	385·0
Up to 110 kg.	N. Oberburger (Italy)	390·0
Over 110 kg.	D. Lukim (Australia)	412·5

Wrestling

Freestyle:

48 kg.	R. Weaver (U.S.A.)
52 kg.	S. Trstena (Yugoslavia)
57 kg.	H. Tomiyama (Japan)
62 kg.	R. Lewis (U.S.A.)
68 kg.	In-Tak You (S. Korea)
74 kg.	D. Schultz (U.S.A.)
82 kg.	M. Schultz (U.S.A.)
90 kg.	E. Banach (U.S.A.)
100 kg.	L. Banach (U.S.A.)
100 kg. plus	B. Baumgartner (U.S.A.)

Greco-Roman:

48 kg.	V. Maenza (Italy)
52 kg.	A. Miyahara (Japan)
57 kg.	P. Passarelli (F.R.G.)
62 kg.	Weon-Kee Kim (S. Korea)
68 kg.	V. Lisjak (Yugoslavia)
74 kg.	J. Salomaki (Finland)
82 kg.	I. Draica (Romania)
90 kg.	S. Fraser (U.S.A.)
100 kg.	V. Andrei (Romania)
100 kg. plus	J. Blatnick (U.S.A.)

Yachting

		points
Soling	U.S.A.	33·70
Star	U.S.A.	29·70
Flying Dutchman	U.S.A.	19·70
470	Spain	33·70
Finn	R. Coutts (N.Z.)	34·70
Tornado	New Zealand	14·70
Windglider		
Boardsailing	S. Van Den Berg (Holland)	27·70

MEDAL TABLE

	Gold	Silver	Bronze	Total
U.S.A.	83	61	31	175
Romania	20	16	17	53
F.R.G.	17	19	23	59
China	15	8	9	32
Italy	14	6	12	32
Canada	10	18	16	44
Japan	10	8	14	32
New Zealand	8	1	2	11
Yugoslavia	7	4	7	18
S. Korea	6	6	7	19
Great Britain	5	11	21	37
France	5	7	15	27
Holland	5	2	6	13
Australia	4	8	12	24
Finland	4	2	6	12
Sweden	2	10	6	18
Mexico	2	3	1	6
Morocco	2	—	—	2
Brazil	1	5	2	8
Spain	1	2	2	5
Belgium	1	1	2	4
Austria	1	1	1	3
Portugal	1	—	2	3
Kenya	1	—	2	3
Pakistan	1	—	—	1
Switzerland	—	5	3	8
Denmark	—	3	3	6
Jamaica	—	1	2	3
Norway	—	1	2	3
Greece	—	1	1	2
Nigeria	—	1	1	2
Puerto Rico	—	1	1	2
Colombia	—	1	—	1
Egypt	—	1	—	1
Ireland	—	1	—	1
Ivory Coast	—	1	—	1
Peru	—	1	—	1
Syria	—	1	—	1
Thailand	—	1	—	1
Turkey	—	—	3	3
Venezuela	—	—	3	3
Algeria	—	—	2	2
Cameroon	—	—	1	1
Dom. Rep.	—	—	1	1
Iceland	—	—	1	1
Taiwan	—	—	1	1
Zambia	—	—	1	1
	226	219	242	687

The following countries: Afghanistan, Albania, Angola, Bulgaria, Cuba, Czechoslovakia, Ethiopia, G.D.R., Hungary, Iran, Laos, Libya, Mongolia, North Korea, Poland, South Yemen, Upper Volta, U.S.S.R. and Vietnam did not appear at Los Angeles.

ATHLETICS
WORLD RECORDS

(All the world records given below have been accepted by the International Amateur Athletic Federation except those marked with an asterisk* which are awaiting homologation.)

Fully automatic timing to 1/100th second is mandatory up to and including 400 metres. For distances up to and including 10,000 metres records will be accepted to 1/100th second if timed automatically, and to 1/10th if hand timing is used.

MEN'S EVENTS

Running

Distances	Time hr. min. sec.			Name	Nation	Year
100 metres			9·93	C. Smith	U.S.A.	1983
200 metres (turn)			19·72	P. Mennea	Italy	1979
400 metres			43·86	L. Evans	U.S.A.	1968
800 metres		1	41·73	S. Coe	G.B.	1981
1,000 metres		2	12·18	S. Coe	G.B.	1981
1,500 metres		3	30·77	S. Ovett	G.B.	1983
1 mile		3	47·33	S. Coe	G.B.	1981
2,000 metres		4	51·4	J. Walker	N.Z.	1976
3,000 metres		7	32·1	H. Rono	Kenya	1978
5,000 metres		13	00·41	D. Moorcroft	G.B.	1982
10,000 metres		27	13·81*	F. Mamede	Portugal	1984
20,000 metres		57	24·2	J. Hermens	Netherlands	1976
20,944 metres (13 miles 24 yards 2 feet)	1	00	00·0	J. Hermens	Netherlands	1976
25,000 metres	1	13	55·8	T. Seko	Japan	1981
30,000 metres	1	29	18·8	T. Seko	Japan	1981
110 metres hurdles			12·93	R. Nehemiah	U.S.A.	1981
400 metres hurdles			47·02	E. Moses	U.S.A.	1983
3,000 metres steeplechase		8	05·4	H. Rono	Kenya	1978

Relay Racing

Distance	Time min. sec.		Nation	Year
4 × 100 metres		37·83	U.S.A.	1984
4 × 200 metres	1	20·26	Univ. of S. Calif.	1978
4 × 400 metres	2	56·16	U.S.A.	1977
4 × 800 metres	7	03·89	G.B.	1982
4 × 1,500 metres	14	38·8	Germany	1977

Jumping and Throwing

	ft.	in.	metres	Name	Nation	Year
High Jump	7	10	2·39	Zhu Jian Hua	China	1984
Pole Vault	19	6	5·94	S. Bubka	U.S.S.R.	1984
Long Jump	29	2½	8·90	R. Beamon	U.S.A.	1968
Triple Jump	58	8½	17·89	J. de Oliveira	Brazil	1975
Shot	72	10½	22·22	U. Beyer	G.D.R.	1983
Discus	235	9	71·86	Y. Dumchev	U.S.S.R.	1983
Hammer	283	3	86·34	Y. Sedykh	U.S.S.R.	1984
Javelin	343	9	104·80	U. Hohn	G.D.R.	1984
Decathlon			8,798 pts.	J. Hingsen	F.R.G.	1984

Walking (Track)

Distance	Time hr. min. sec.			Name	Nation	Year
20,000 metres	1	18	40	E. Canto	Mexico	1984
28,358 metres (17 miles 1029 yards)	2	00	00·0	R. Kowalsky	G.D.R.	1982
30,000 metres	2	06	54·0	R. Kowalsky	G.D.R.	1982
50,000 metres	3	41	39·00	R. Gonzalez	Mexico	1979

WOMEN'S EVENTS
Running

Distance	Time min. sec.		Name	Nation	Year
100 metres		10·76	E. Ashford	U.S.A.	1984
200 metres		21·71	M. Koch	G.D.R.	1979
400 metres		47·99	J. Kratochvilova	Czechoslovakia	1983
800 metres	1	53·28	J. Kratochvilova	Czechoslovakia	1983
1,500 metres	3	52·47	T. Kazankina	U.S.S.R.	1980
1 mile	4	15·8	N. Artemova	U.S.S.R.	1984
3,000 metres	8	22·82	T. Kazankina	U.S.S.R.	1984
5,000 metres	14	58·89*	I. Kristiansen	Norway	1984
10,000 metres	31	13·78	O. Bondarenko	U.S.S.R.	1984
100 metres hurdles (2 ft. 9 in.)		12·36	G. Rabsztyn	Poland	1980
400 metres hurdles		53·58	M. Ponomaryeva	U.S.S.R.	1984

Relays

Distance	Time min. sec.		Nation	Year
4 × 100 metres		41·53	G.D.R.	1983
4 × 200 metres	1	28·15	G.D.R.	1980
4 × 400 metres	3	15·92	G.D.R.	1984
4 × 800 metres	7	50·17	U.S.S.R.	1984

Women's Jumping and Throwing

	ft.	in.	metres	Name	Nation	Year
High Jump	6	9¼	2·07	L. Andonova	Bulgaria	1984
Long Jump	24	4½	7·43	A. Cusmir	Romania	1983
Shot Putt	73	8	22·45	I. Slupianek	G.D.R.	1980
Discus	244	7	74·56	Z. Silhava	Czechoslovakia	1984
Javelin	245	3	74·76	T. Lillak	Finland	1983
Heptathlon†		6,867 pts.		S. Paetz	G.D.R.	1984

† Seven events comprising 100 m hurdles, shot, high jump, 200 m, long jump, Javelin, 800 m.

UNITED KINGDOM (NATIONAL) RECORDS
(Records made anywhere by athletes eligible to represent Great Britain and Northern Ireland)

Men

100 *metres*—10·11 sec. (A. Wells 1980).
200 *metres*—20·21 sec. (A. Wells, 1980).
400 *metres*—44·93 (D. Jenkins, 1975).
800 *metres*—1 min. 41·73 (S. Coe, 1981).
1,000 *metres*—2 min. 12·18 sec. (S. Coe, 1981).
1,500 *metres*—3 min. 30·77 sec. (S. Ovett, 1983).
1 *mile*—3 min. 47·33 sec. (S. Coe, 1981).
2,000 *metres*—4 min. 57·71 sec. (S. Ovett, 1982).
3,000 *metres*—7 min. 32·79 sec. (D. Moorcroft, 1982).
5,000 *metres*—13 min. 00·41 sec. (D. Moorcroft, 1982).
10,000 *metres*—27 min. 30·3 sec. (B. Foster, 1978).
20,000 *metres*—58 min. 39·0 sec. (R. Hill, 1968).
12 *miles* 1,268 *yards*—1 hr. (R. Hill, 1968).
25,000 *metres*—1 hr. 15 min. 22·6 sec. (R. Hill, 1965).
30,000 *metres*—1 hr. 31 min. 30·4 sec. (J. Alder, 1970).
3,000 *metres Steeplechase*—8 min. 13·78 sec. (C. Reitz, 1984).
110 *metres Hurdles*—13·43 sec. (M. Holtom, 1982).
400 *metres Hurdles*—48·12 sec. (D. P. Hemery, 1968).
4 × 100 *metres Relay*—38·62 (G.B. Team, 1980)
4 × 200 *metres*—1 min. 24·1 sec. (G.B. Team, 1971).
4 × 400 *metres*—2 min. 59·13 sec. (G.B. Team, 1984).
4 × 800 *metres*—7 min. 03·89 sec. (G.B. Team, 1982).
4 × 1,500 *metres*—14 min. 56·8 sec. (G.B. Team, 1979).
High Jump—2·26 m.,7 ft. 5 in. (G. Parsons, 1984).
Pole Vault—5·65 m., 18 ft. 6¼ in. (K. Stock, 1981).
Long Jump—8·23 m., 27 ft. 0 in. (L. Davies, 1968).
Triple Jump—17·57 m., 57 ft. 7¾ in. (K. Connor, 1982).
Shot—21·68 m., 71 ft. 1½ in. (G. Capes, 1980).
Discus—64·32 m., 211 ft. 0 in. (W. Tancred, 1974).
Hammer—77·54 m., 254 ft. 5 in. (M. Girvan, 1984).
Javelin—88·26 m., 289 ft. 7 in. (R. Bradstock, 1984).
Decathlon—8,797 pts. (D. Thompson, 1984).

Walking (Track)

20,000 *metres*—1 hr. 26 min. 22 sec. (S. Barry, 1981).
2 *Hours*—16 miles 315 yds. (R. Wallwork, 1971).
30,000 *metres*—2 hr. 22 min. 55 sec. (D. Jackson, 1981).
50,000 *metres*—4 hr. 11 min. 22·0 sec. (R. Dobson, 1974).

Women

100 *metres*—11·10 sec. (K. Cook, 1981).
200 *metres*—22·10 sec. (K. Cook, 1984).
400 *metres*—49·42 sec. (K. Cook, 1984).
800 *metres*—1 min. 59·05 sec. (C. Boxer, 1979).
1,500 *metres*—4 min. 00·57 sec. (C. Boxer, 1984).
1 *mile*—4 min. 22·64 sec. (C. Boxer, 1984).
3,000 *metres*—8 min. 37·06 sec. (W. Sly, 1983).
5,000 *metres*—15 min. 14·51 sec. (P. Fudge, 1981)
10,000 *metres*—32 min. 57·17 sec. (K. Binns, 1980).
100 *metres Hurdles*—12·87 sec. (S. Strong, 1983).
400 *metres Hurdles*—56·04 sec. (S. Morley, 1983).
4 × 100 *metres Relay*—42·43 sec. (G.B. Team, 1980).
4 × 200 *metres Relay*—1 min. 31·57 sec. (G.B. Team, 1977).
4 × 400 *metres Relay*—3 min. 25·51 sec. (G.B. Team, 1984).
4 × 800 *metres Relay*—8 min. 23·8 sec. (G.B. Team, 1971).
High Jump—1·95 m., 6 ft. 4½ in. (D. Elliott, 1982).
Long Jump—6·90 m., 22 ft. 7¾ in. (B. Kinch, 1983).
Shot—18·99 m., 62 ft. 3¾ in. (M. Ritchie, 1983).
Discus—67·48 m., 221 ft. 5 in. (M. Ritchie, 1981).
Javelin—73·58 m., 241 ft. 5 in. (T. Sanderson, 1983).
Heptathlon—6,353 pts. (J. Livermore, 1983).

Oxford v. Cambridge

Cross Country, held December 3, 1983. Oxford beat Cambridge by 33 points to 45. Individual winner—John Barton (O). Women, Cambridge beat Oxford by 19 points to 26. Individual winner—H. Shaw (C).

Athletics, held at Oxford on May 19, 1984. Oxford beat Cambridge by 125 points to 87. Women, Cambridge beat Oxford, 69 points to 65.

A.A.A. and W.A.A.A. Indoor Championships

Held at Cosford, January 13/14, 1984

Men's Events

Metres	min.	sec.
60—E. Obeng (Belgrave/Ghana)		6·79
200—A. Mafe (London Irish)		21·38
400—W. McCoy (U.S.A.)		48·23
800—P. Norgate (Epsom & Ewell)	1	50·27
1,500—S. Crabb (Enfield)	3	44·47
3,000—G. Staines (Belgrave)..........	8	04·72
Steeplechase—C. Walker (Gateshead)..	5	35·38
60 Hurdles—M. Holtom (Wolverhampton)................................		7·98
		metres
High Jump—D. Biczysko (Poland)		2·25
Pole Vault—M. Klimczyk (Poland) ...		5·30
Long Jump—D. Brown (Longwood) ...		7·52
Triple Jump—A. Joyner (U.S.A.)		16·54
Shot—M. Winch (Blackheath)		18·52

Women's Events

Metres	min.	sec.
60—B. Kinch (Hounslow)		7·26
200—S. Jabobs (Reading).............		23·87
400—R. Patten (Nottingham).........		53·47
800—K. Steer (Exeter)	2	11·06
1,500—L. MacDougall (Glasgow)	4	16·89
60 Hurdles—K. Robin-Millerchip (Birchfield)		8·38
		metres
High Jump—D. Elliott (Leicester)		1·84
Long Jump—S. Hearnshaw (Hull).....		6·50
Shot—J. Oakes (Croydon)		17·67

Held at Cosford, January 7, 1984

Metres	min.	sec.
3,000—Y. Murray (Edinburgh AC)	9	22·0

United Kingdom v. German Democratic Republic

Held at Cosford, February 1, 1984

Men's Events

Metres	min.	sec.
60—T. Schröder (G.)		6·71
200—A. Mafe (U.K.)		21·3
400—J. Carlowitz (G.)		48·1
800—A. Busse (G.)	1	50·10
1,500—A. Busse (G.)	3	43·43
3,000—A. Krippschock (G.)	8	01·7
60 Hurdles—H. Pohland (G.)..........		7·78
		metres
High Jump—U. Austel (G.)		2·23
Pole Vault—A. Kramss (G.)		5·20
Long Jump—L. Dombrowski (G.)		7·66
Triple Jump—E. McCalla (U.K.)		16·69
Shot—U. Timmermann (G.)		20·66

G.D.R. beat U.K. by 81 pts. to 49.

Women's Events

Metres	min.	sec.
60—M. Göhr (G.)		7·25

200—B. Wöckel (G.)		23·5
400—U. Bremer (G.)		53·29
800—C. Wachtel (G.).................	2	04·2
1,500—C. Wartenberg (G.)............	4	11·59
3,000—G. Martins (G.)	8	57·79
60 Hurdles—C. Riefstahl (G.)		8·01
		metres
High Jump—S. Helm (G.)		1·86
Long Jump—H. Daute (G.)		6·78
Shot—I. Müller (G.)		20·39

G.D.R. beat U.K. by 71 pts. to 38.

United Kingdom v. France (Indoors)

Held at Vittel, France, February 4, 1984

Men's Events

Metres	min.	sec.
60—E. Roofe (U.K.)		6·76
200—P. Barré (F.)		21·71
400—H. Llatser (F.).................		48·87
800—P. Norgate (U.K.)	1	50·36
1,500—D. Begouin (F.)	3	46·10
3,000—P. Levisse (F.)	8	11·85
60 Hurdles—N. Walker (U.K.)		7·92
4 × 400 Relay—U.K.	3	13·17
		metres
High Jump—F. Bonnet (F.)		2·19
Pole Vault—T. Vigneron (F.)		5·73
Long Jump—D. Brown (U.K.)		7·72
Triple Jump—E. McCalla (U.K.)		16·86
Shot—L. Viudes (F.)		18·69
Pentathlon—J.-F. Raffali (F.)	3,983 pts.	

France beat U.K. by 78 pts. to 68.

Women's Events

Metres	min.	sec.
60 { J. Christian (U.K.) / M.-C. Cazier (F.) }		7·30
200—M.-C. Cazier (F.)...............		23·64
400—Y. Wray (U.K.)		55·02
800—J. Marlow (U.K.)	2	07·86
1,500—L. MacDougall (U.K.)	4	22·79
60 Hurdles—L. Elloy (F.)		8·08
4 × 400 Relay—France	3	41·4
		metres
High Jump—M. Ewanje-Epée (F.)		1·86
Long Jump—G. Bonnin (F.)		6·25
Shot—S. Creantor (F.)		16·78
Pentathlon—K. Hagger (U.K.)	4,391 pts.	

France beat U.K. by 60 pts. to 53.

National Women's Cross-Country Championships

Held at Knebworth, February 18, 1984

Senior	min.	sec.
1. J. Furniss (Sheffield)	16	35
2. C. Haigh (Holmfirth)	17	11
3. R. Smeeth (Aldershot).........	17	12
Team result		
1. Aldershot, Farnham & District AC	76 pts.	
2. Cardiff AC	137 pts.	
3. Dartford H	146 pts.	
Intermediate		
1. B. Smyth (Phoenix)	13	48
Team result		
1. Sale H	137 pts.	
Junior	min.	sec.
1. L. Reilly (Morpeth)	12	05
Team result		
1. Crawley	125 pts.	

National Cross-Country Championships

Held at Newark, March 3, 1984

Senior		min.	sec.
1.	E. Martin (Basildon)	41	50
2.	R. Hackney (Aldershot)	41	58
3.	J. Goater (Shaftesbury)........	41	59

Team result
1. Aldershot, Farnham & District
   AC...................... 227 pts.
2. Tipton H...................... 416 pts.
3. Birchfield H.................. 418 pts.

Junior		min.	sec.
1.	R. Carter (Brighton)	29	01

Team result
1. Tipton H...................... 89 pts.

Youth		min.	sec.
1.	R. Findlow (Airedale)	18	43

Team result
1. Tonbridge AC .... 62 pts.

R.W.A. 10 miles Road Walk

Held at Southend, March 24, 1984

		min.	sec.
1.	I. McCombie (Cambridge H)	67	32
2.	P. Vesty (Leicester)	68	09
3.	D. O'Connor (U.S.A.)..............	69	31

R.W.A. 20,000 metres Road Walk

Held at Redditch, May 12, 1984

		hr.	min.	sec.
1.	I. McCombie (Cambridge H)	1	25	34
2.	C. Maddocks (Dawlish)	1	26	51
3.	T. Berrett (Tonbridge)	1	30	18

Team result: Sheffield........ 48 pts.

R.W.A. 35,000 metres Road Walk

Held at Sheffield, June 16, 1984

		hr.	min.	sec.
1.	P. Blagg (Cambridge H)	3	03	54
2.	L. Morton (Sheffield)	3	06	03
3.	A. Seddon (Enfield)	3	07	33

Team result: Sheffield........ 42 pts

Women's National 5,000 metres Road Walk

Held at Redditch, May 12, 1984

		min.	sec.
1.	J. Barrett (Verlea)	23	38
2.	V. Birch (Brighton)	23	41
3.	N. Jackson (Trowbridge)	23	44

Team result: Brighton .... 22 pts.

International Cross-Country Championships

Held at Newark, New Jersey, U.S.A., March 25, 1984

Senior		min.	sec.
1.	C. Lopes (Portugal)	33	25
2.	T. Hutchings (England)	33	30
3.	S. Jones (Wales)	33	32

Team result
1. Ethiopia (8,9,16,24,31,46)....... 134 pts.
2. U.S.A. (4,6,17,28,41,65)........ 161 pts.
3. Portugal (1,23,25,26,64,84) ..... 223 pts.

Junior		min.	sec.
1.	P. Casacuberto (Spain)	21	32
2.	D. Tessemma (Ethiopia)	21	34
3.	G. Castellano (Canada)	21	37

Team result
1. Ethiopia (2,4,7,8) .... 21 pts.
2. Spain (1,5,11,17) .... 34 pts.
3. England (6,10,22,30) .... 68 pts.

Women		min.	sec.
1.	M. Puica (Romania)	15	56
2.	G. Zakharova (U.S.S.R.)	15	58
3.	G. Waitz (Norway)............	15	58

Team result
1. U.S.A. (9,10,16,17)............. 52 pts.
2. England (5,6,15,39) .... 65 pts.
3. New Zealand (14,19,27,31) ...... 91 pts.

A.A.A./London Marathon

Held in London, May 13, 1984

Men		hr.	min.	sec.
1.	C. Spedding (Gateshead) ...	2	09	57
2.	K. Forster (Gateshead)	2	11	41
3.	D. Fowles (Cardiff)........	2	12	12

Women		hr.	min.	sec.
1.	I. Kristiansen (Norway) ...	2	24	26
2.	P. Welch (Nuneaton)......	2	30	06
3.	S. Rowell (Dartford)	2	31	28

United Kingdom Championships

Held at Cwmbran, May 27–28, 1984

Men's Events

Metres	min.	sec.
100—M. McFarlane (Haringey)		10·08
200—T. Bennett (Southampton)		20·36
400—K. Akabusi (Southampton)		46·10
800—P. Elliott (Rotherham)	1	46·08
1,500—A. Salter (Birchfield)	3	43·31
5,000—E. Martin (Basildon)	13	32·11
10,000—N. Rose (Bristol)	28	00·70
Steeplechase—P. Davies-Hale		
(Cannock)...................	8	33·16
110 *Hurdles*—H. Teape (Enfield)		13·98
400 *Hurdles*—M. Briggs (Stoke).......		50·97
10,000 *Walk*—P. Vesty (Leicester)	43	53·60

	metres
High Jump—A. Kruger (Liverpool) ...	2·15
Pole Vault—K. Stock (Haringey)	5·35
Long Jump—D. Brown (Longwood) ...	7·71
Triple Jump—A. Moore (Birchfield) ...	16·80
Shot—W. Cole (Thurrock)............	17·57
Discus—P. Mardle (Wolverhampton)..	59·70
Hammer—D. Smith (Hull)............	72·34
Javelin—P. Yates (Blackheath)	82·54

Women's Events

Metres	min.	sec.
100—H. Oakes (Haringey)		11·08
200—H. Oakes (Haringey)		23·00
400—J. Parry (Stretford).............		53·46
800—C. Boxer (Aldershot)	2	01·64
1,500—Z. Budd (Aldershot)	4	04·39
3,000—C. Benning (Southampton)	8	56·79
5,000—A. Tooby (Cardiff)	15	27·56
100 *Hurdles*—P. Rollo (Pitreavie)		13·12
400 *Hurdles*—G. Taylor (Essex)		58·2
5,000 *Walk*—J. Barrett (Verlea).......	23	53·13

	metres
High Jump—D. Elliott (Leicester).....	1·90
Long Jump—S. Hearnshaw (Hull).....	7·00
Shot—J. Oakes (Croydon)	17·94
Discus—V. Head (Cardiff)............	57·44
Javelin—F. Whitbread (Thurrock)	65·44

Olympic Trials

Held at various venues May/June, 1984

Men's Events

Metres	min.	sec.
100—M. McFarlane (Haringey)		10·59
200—A. Mafe (London Irish)		20·77

	min.	sec.
400—T. Bennett (Southampton)		45·56
800—P. Elliott (Rotherham)	1	45·72
1,500—Not held		
5,000—E. Martin (Basildon)	13	23·33
10,000—N. Rose (Bristol)	28	00·70
3,000 *Steeplechase*—R. Hackney (Aldershot)	8	20·16
110 *Hurdles*—N. Walker (Cardiff)		14·17
400 *Hurdles*—M. Briggs (Stoke)		49·86

	metres
High Jump—M. Naylor (Hillingdon)	2·22
Pole Vault—K. Stock (Haringey)	5·10
Long Jump—D. Brown (Longwood)	7·66
Triple Jump—E. McCalla (Birmingham)	16·79
Shot—M. Winch (Blackheath)	18·75
Discus—A. Weir (Birchfield)	61·30
Hammer—M. Girvan (Wolverhampton)	74·34
Javelin—D. Ottley (Telford)	85·86
Decathlon—B. McStravick (Sheffield)	7,975 pts.

Women's Events

Metres	min.	sec.
100—H. Oakes (Haringey)		11·38
200—S. Whittaker (Glasgow)		23·23
400—K. Cook (Wolverhampton)		51·53
800—L. Baker (Coventry)	2	02·61
1,500—C. Boxer (Aldershot)	4	05·33
3,000—Z. Budd (Aldershot)	8	40·22
100 *Hurdles*—S. Strong (Stretford)		13·31
400 *Hurdles*—S. Morley (Hickleton Main)		57·63

	metres
High Jump—D. Elliott (Leicester)	1·89
Long Jump—S. Hearnshaw (Hull)	6·71
Shot—V. Head (Cardiff)	18·59
Discus—M. Ritchie (Edinburgh)	61·48
Javelin—T. Sanderson (Wolverhampton)	67·02
Heptathlon—K. Hagger (Essex Ladies)	6,100 pts.

W.A.A.A. Championships

Held at Crystal Palace, June 15/16, 1984

Metres	min.	sec.
100—K. Cook (Wolverhampton)		11·44
200—K. Cook (Wolverhampton)		22·77
400—T. Lawton (Enfield)		52·74
800—H. Barralet (Australia)	2	02·37
1,500—C. Benning (Southampton)	4	07·27
5,000—S. Samy (Bracknell)	16	10·10
100 *Hurdles*—S. Strong (Stretford)		12·96
400 *Hurdles*—G. Taylor (Essex Ladies)		56·78
5,000 *Walk*—J. Barrett (Verlea)	23	51·63

	metres
High Jump—D. Elliott (Leicester)	1·86
Long Jump—S. Hearnshaw (Hull)	6·79
Shot—J. Oakes (Croydon H)	18·01
Discus—L. Whiteley (Enfield)	57·32
Javelin—F. Whitbread (Thurrock)	65·76

A.A.A. Championships

Held at Crystal Place, June 23/24, 1984

Metres	min.	sec.
100—D. Reid (Shaftesbury)		10·42
200—T. Bennett (Southampton)		20·79

	min.	sec.
400—D. Clark (Australia)		45·66
800—S. Cram (Jarrow)	1	46·84
1,500—P. Elliott (Rotherham)	3	39·66
5,000—R. Flynn (Ireland)	13	19·52
10,000—S. Jones (Newport)	28	09·97
Steeplechase—D. Ramon (Spain)	8	23·12
110 *Hurdles*—N. Walker (Cardiff)		13·78
400 *Hurdles*—M. Gillingham (Shaftesbury)		50·24
3,000 *Walk*—P. Vesty (Leicester)	11	42·94

	metres
High Jump—J. Centelles (Cuba)	2·30
Pole Vault—J. Gutteridge (Windsor)	5·40
Long Jump—F. Salle (Shaftesbury)	7·59
Triple Jump—L. Betancourt (Cuba)	16·93
Shot—M. Winch (Blackheath)	18·39
Discus—R. Weir (Birchfield)	62·50
Hammer—D. Smith (Hull)	72·40
Javelin—D. Ottley (Telford)	81·34

Held at Birmingham, March 17, 1984

	min.	sec.
10,000 *Walk*—I. McCombie (Cambridge H)	41	33

Held at Hendon, July 14/15, 1984

Decathlon—K. Atkinson (Ireland)	7,451 pts.

Eight Nations Meeting

Held at Tokyo, Japan, September 14/15, 1984

Men's Events

Metres	min.	sec.
100—C. Lewis (U.S.A.)		10·13
200—K. Baptiste (U.S.A.)		20·47
400—S. Takano (Asia/Japan)		45·68
800—V. Kalinkin (U.S.S.R.)	1	46·21
1,500—S. Cram (U.K.)	3	47·12
5,000—T. Hutchings (U.K.)	13	40·20
10,000—V. Abramov (U.S.S.R.)	30	14·37
3,000 *Steeplechase*—H. Melzer (G.D.R.)	8	35·87
110 *Hurdles*—T. Campbell (U.S.A.)		13·30
400 *Hurdles*—B. Williams (U.S.A.)		49·64
4 × 100 *Relay*—U.S.S.R.		38·70
4 × 400 *Relay*—G.D.R.	3	01·95

	metres
High Jump—G. Avdeyenko (U.S.S.R.)	2·30
Pole Vault—K. Volkov (U.S.S.R.)	5·55
Long Jump—L. Dombrowski (G.D.R.)	8·20
Triple Jump—A. Yakovlev (U.S.S.R.)	17·20
Shot—V. Timmermann (G.D.R.)	20·73
Javelin—U. Hohn (G.D.R.)	92·76

Women's Events

Metres	min.	sec.
100—M. Göhr (G.D.R.)		10·97
200—M. Koch (G.D.R.)		22·22
400—O. Vladykina (U.S.S.R.)		50·22
800—I. Podyalovskaya (U.S.S.R.)	2	00·45
10,000—U. Bruns (G.D.R.)	32	46·08
100 *Hurdles*—S. Paetz (G.D.R.)		12·72
4 × 100 *Relay*—G.D.R.		42·44

	metres
High Jump—L. Butuzova (U.S.S.R.)	1·95
Long Jump—H. Drechsler (G.D.R.)	6·95
Javelin—P. Felke (G.D.R.)	72·86

Result: G.D.R. 183 pts; U.S.S.R. 171 pts; U.K. 149 pts.

THE TURF

The turf in Great Britain is under the control of The Jockey Club.

The *Jockey Club* (incorporating the National Hunt Committee, 42 Portman Square, London, W.1.). Stewards are: The Lord Manton (*Senior Steward*); Gen. Sir Cecil Blacker (*Deputy Senior Steward*); Sir John Astor; L. Freedman; The Marquess of Hartington; Capt. M. Gosling.

Leading Owners and Trainers, 1984
(Flat Season up to Sept. 11)

Winning Owners		Winning Trainers	
R. E. Sangster	£384,055	J. Dunlop	408,812
K. Abdullah	323,893	H. Cecil	397,110
Sheikh		G. Harwood	358,462
Mohammed	277,679	W. R. Hern	344,794
L. Miglitti	227,680	B. Hills	318,394
J. C. Smith	193,582	M. R. Stoute	316,217
Sir Robin		D. V. O'Brien	227,680
McAlpine	174,149	G. Wragg	206,639
Hamdan Al-		M. V. O'Brien	199,140
Maktoum	173,789	R. Sheather	198,866
E. B. Moller	170,506	C. Brittain	181,171
Capt. M. Lemos	136,237	P. Cole	159,497
H. H. Aga Khan	123,043		
S. Niarchos	112,329		
R. J. McAlpine	107,871		

Leading Breeders, 1984
(Up to Sept. 11)

	Value
E. P. Taylor	£325,530
Swettenham Stud	214,548
Capt. A. Rogers	202,750
Mrs. C. Drake	165,733
E. B. Moller and White Lodge Stud	157,095
H. H. Aga Khan	143,075
Red House Stud	124,874
Warren Hill Stud and Mimika Financiers	120,437
R. J. McAlpine	107,871
Allez France Stables Ltd.	92,338
A. R. Jones Morgan	85,713
Lord Howard de Walden	78,683
Lord Rotherwick	77,520

Winning Jockeys, 1984
(Up to Sept. 11)

	1st	2nd	3rd	Unpl.	Total Mts.
S. Cauthen	112	88	86	331	617
P. Eddery	83	64	58	258	463
L. Piggott	78	64	56	169	367
T. Ives	78	89	58	290	515
W. R. Swinburn	74	56	44	250	424
G. Duffield	66	75	59	352	552
W. Carson	65	78	66	238	447
B. Rouse	56	43	64	360	523
J. Reid	49	47	47	338	481
P. Robinson	48	57	42	303	450
T. Quinn	46	33	30	134	243
B. Raymond	45	41	51	281	418
J. Lowe	45	31	48	329	453

Winning Sires, 1984
(Up to Sept. 11)

	Horses	Races won	Value
Northern Dancer (1961), by Nearctic	8	9	£420,760
Sharpen Up (1969), by Atan	25	36	221,565
High Top (1969), by Derring-Do	11	19	210,652
Ballad Rock (1974), by Bold Lad	4	6	201,739
Youth (1973), by Ack Ack	2	4	159,068
Home Guard (USA) (1969), by Forli	9	12	142,379
Be My Guest (USA) (1974), by Northern Dancer	16	25	142,166
Habitat (1966), by Sir Gaylord	11	24	123,007
Shirley Heights (1975), by Mill Reef (USA)	15	18	118,516
Rheingold (1969), by Faberge II	4	7	108,533
Mill Reef (USA) (1968), by Never Bend	13	18	103,269
Dominion (1972), by Derring-Do	8	14	100,570

THE DERBY, 1974–1984

For particulars of the Derby from 1780–1973 see 1921–74 editions.

The *Distance* of the Derby course at Epsom is 1½ miles. Lord Egremont won Derby in 1782, 1804, 5, 7, 26 (also, 5 Oaks); Duke of Grafton, 1802, 9, 10, 15 (also, 9 Oaks); Mr. Bowes, 1835, 43, 52, 3; Sir J. Hawley, Teddington (1851), Beadsman (1858), Musjid (1859), and Blue Gown (1868), the 1st Duke of Westminster, Bend Or (1880), Shotover (1882), Ormonde (1886), and Flying Fox (1899). Lady James Douglas was the first lady to win the Derby—War Substitute at Newmarket (1918); at Epsom, Mrs. G. B. Miller (1937). First winner was Sir Charles Bunbury's Diomed in 1780. From 1940 to 1945 a substitute Derby was run at Newmarket. By winning his 5th Derby, the late Aga Khan equalled Lord Egremont's record. He also won 2 Oaks.

Year	Owner and Name of Winner	Betting	Jockey	Trainer	No. of Run'rs
1974	Mrs. N. Phillips' Snow Knight	50–1	B. Taylor	P. M. Nelson	25
1975	Dr. C. Vittadini's Grundy	5–1	P. Eddery	P. Walwyn	18
1976	Mr. N. B. Hunt's Empery (Fr.)	10–1	L. Piggott	M. Zilber	23
1977	Mr. R. Sangster's The Minstrel (Ir.)	5–1	L. Piggott	M. V. O'Brien	22
1978	Lord Halifax's Shirley Heights	8–1	G. Starkey	J. Dunlop	25
1979	Sir Michael Sobell's Troy	6–1	W. Carson	W. R. Hern	23
1980	Mrs. A. Plesch's Henbit	7–1	W. Carson	W. R. Hern	24
1981	H. H. Aga Khan's Shergar	10–11 F.	W. R. Swinburn	M. R. Stoute	18
1982	Mr. R. Sangster's Golden Fleece (Ir.)	3–1 F.	P. Eddery	M. V. O'Brien	18
1983	Mr. E. Moller's Teenoso	9–2 F.	L. Piggott	G. Wragg	21
1984	Mr. L. Miglitti's Secreto	14–1	C. Roche	D. O'Brien	17

Record times, 2 min. 34 secs. by Hyperion in 1933; Windsor Lad in 1934; 2 min. 33·8 sec. Mahmoud in 1936.

TWO THOUSAND GUINEAS. First Run, 1809. Rowley Mile. Newmarket. 9st.

Year	Owner and Name of Winner	Betting	Jockey	Trainer	No. of Run'rs
1980	Mr. K. Abdulla's Known Fact	14 to 1	W. Carson	J. Tree	14
1981	Mrs. A. Muinos's To-Agori-Mou	5 to 2 F.	G. Starkey	G. Harwood	19
1982	Mr. G. Oldham's Zino	8 to 1	F. Head	F. Boutin	26
1983	Mr. R. Sangster's Lomond	9 to 1	P. Eddery	M. V. O'Brien	16
1984	Mr. R. Sangster's El Gran Senor	15 to 8 F.	P. Eddery	M. V. O'Brien	9

ONE THOUSAND GUINEAS. 1814. Rowley Mile. Newmarket. Fillies. 9st.

Year	Owner and Name and Winner	Betting	Jockey	Trainer	No. of Run'rs
1980	Mr. O. Phipps's Quick As Lightning ...	12 to 1	B. Rouse........	J. Dunlop........	23
1981	Mr. H. Joel's Fairy Footsteps	6 to 4 F.	L. Piggott	H. Cecil	14
1982	Sir Philip Oppenheimer's On The House	33 to 1	J. Reid	H. Wragg	15
1983	Maktoum Al Maktoum's Ma Biche	5 to 2 F	F. Head	Miss C. Head	18
1984	Capt. M. Lemos's Pebbles	8 to 1	P. Robinson	C. Brittain	15

OAKS. 1779. Epsom. 1½ Mile. Fillies. 9 st.

Year	Owner and Name of Winner	Betting	Jockey	Trainer	No. of Run'rs
1980	Mr. R. Hollingsworth's Bireme	9 to 2	W. Carson	W. R. Hern	11
1981	Mrs. B. Firestone's Blue Wind	3 to 1 JF.	L. Piggott	D. Weld	12
1982	R. Barnett's Time Charter	12 to 1	W. Newnes	H. Candy	13
1983	Sir Michael Sobell's Sun Princess	6 to 1	W. Carson	W. R. Hern	15
1984	Sir Robin McAlpine's Circus Plume	4 to 1	L. Piggott	J. Dunlop........	15

ST. LEGER. 1776(8). Doncaster. 1¾ mile, 127 yards.

Year	Owner and Name of Winner	Betting	Jockey	Trainer	No. of Run'rs
1980	Mr. H. Joel's Light Cavalry...........	3 to 1	J. Mercer	H. Cecil	7
1981	Sir John Astor's Cut Above	28 to 1	J. Mercer	W. R. Hern	7
1982	Maktoum Al Maktoum's Touching Wood	7 to 1	P. Cook........	T. Jones	15
1983	Sir Michael Sobell's Sun Princess	11 to 8F	W. Carson	W. R. Hern	10
1984	Mr. I. Allan's Commanche Run	7 to 4 F	L. Piggott	L. Cumani	11

	Lincoln Handicap Doncaster—1 mile.	Free Handicap Newmarket—3yrs.—7f.	Jockey Club Stakes Newmarket—1½ miles.	Coronation Cup Epsom—1½ miles.
1981	Saher 5y 8st 12lb	Motavato 8st 13lb	Master Willie 4y 8st 12lb ...	Master Willie 4y 9st ....
1982	King's Glory 4y 8st 3lb	Match Winner 9st 4lb	Ardross 6y 8st 12lb	Easter Sun 5y 9st ....
1983	Mighty Fly 4y 8st 4lb....	Boom Town Charlie 8st 11lb	Electric 4y 8st 10lb	Be My Native 4y 9st ......
1984	Saving Mercy 4y 8st 9lb....	Cutting Wind 8st 8lb	Gay Lemur 4y 8st 7lb......	Time Charter 5y 8st 11lb ...

	Ascot Stakes 2½ miles	Gold Cup Ascot—2½ miles.	Coventry Stakes Ascot—2 yrs—6 furlongs.	Irish Sweeps Derby Curragh—3 yrs—1½ miles.
1981	Atlantic Traveller 4y 7st 12lb	Ardross 5y 9st	Red Sunset 8st 11lb........	Shergar ....
1982	Popsi's Joy 7y 8st 11lb	Ardross 6y 9st	Horage 8st 11lb	Assert ....
1983	Right Regent 5y 8st 8lb	Little Wolf 5y 9st	Chief Singer 8st 11lb	Shareef Dancer ....
1984	Kayudee 4y 8st 9lb........	Gildoran 9st	Primo Dominie 8st 11lb	El Gran Senor ....

	Chester Cup Chester—2¼m. 97 yd.	Gimcrack Stakes York—2yrs.—6 Furlongs.	Eclipse Stakes Sandown Park—1¼m.	King George VI and Queen Elizabeth Stakes Ascot—1½ miles.
1981	Donegal Prince 5y 8st 4lb....	Full Extent 9st	Master Willie 4y 9st 7lb	Shergar 3y 8st 8lb ....
1982	Dawn Johnny 5y 8st 8lb....	Horage 9st	Kalaglow 4y 9st 7lb	Kalaglow 4y 9st 7lb .....
1983	(Abandoned)	Precocious 9st...........	Solford 3y 8st 8lb	Time Charter 4y 9st 4lb .....
1984	Contester 4y 8st 2lb	Doulab 9st.............	Sadler's Wells 3y 8st 8lb....	Teenoso 4y 9st 7lb ......

	Prix de L'Arc de Triomphe Longchamp—1½ m.	Cheltenham Gold Cup	Cambridgeshire Newmarket—9f.	Middle Park Stakes Newmarket—2yrs.—6f.
1981	Gold River 4y 9st 1lb	Little Owl 7y 12st	Braughing 4y 8st 2lb	Cajun 9st ....
1982	Akiyda 3y 8st 8lb........	Silver Buck 10y 12st	Century City 3y 9st 6lb	Diesis 9st ....
1983	All Along 4y 9st 1lb	Bregawn 12st...........	Sagamore 4y 7st 8lb	Creag-an-Sgor 9st ....
1984	Sagace 4y 9st 4lb	Burrough Hill Lad 8y 12st ..	Leysh 3y 8st 7lb	Bassenthwaite 9st........

	Cesarewitch Newmarket—2¼m.	Washington Int'national Laurel Park—1½ m.	Champion Stakes Newmarket—1¼ m.	Grand National Liverpool—4m. 856 yds.
1981	Halsbury 3y 8st 4lb	Providential II	Vayrann 3y 8st 10lb........	Aldaniti 11y 10st 13lb ......
1982	Mountain Lodge 3y 7st 10lb .	April Run	Time Charter 3y 8st 7lb	Grittar 9y 11st 5lb ......
1983	Bajan Sunshine 4y 8st 8lb ...	All Along	Cormorant Wood 3y 8st 7lb ..	Corbiere 8y 11st 4lb ......
1984	Tom Sharp 4y 7st 5lb	....	Palace Music	Hallo Dandy 10y 10st 2lb ....

CRICKET

Marylebone Cricket Club (1787), Lord's, N.W.8. *Pres.*, F. G. Mann, c.b.e., d.s.o., m.c.; *Sec.*, J. A. Bailey; *Asst. Sec. Admin.*, Lt.-Col. L. G. James; *Asst. Sec. Cricket*, Lt.-Col. J. R. Stephenson, o.b.e.; *Asst. Sec. Chief Accountant*, Wg. Cdr. V. J. W. M. Lawrence; *Curator*, S. E. A. Green.

TEST MATCHES

India v. Pakistan, 1983

First Test.—(Bangalore, Sept. 14–19). Drawn. India 275 and 176 for no wkt.; Pakistan 288.
Second Test.—(Jullundur, Sept. 24–29). Drawn. Pakistan 337 and 16 for no wkt.; India 374.
Third Test.—(Nagpur, Oct. 5–10). Drawn. India 245 and 262 for 8 (dec.); Pakistan 322 and 42 for 1.

India v. W. Indies, 1983

First Test.—(Kanpur, Oct. 21–25). West Indies won by an innings and 83 runs. West Indies 454; India 207 and 164.
Second Test.—(New Delhi, Oct. 29–Nov. 3). Drawn. India 464 and 233; West Indies 384 and 120 for 2.
Third Test.—(Ahmedabad, Nov. 12–16). West Indies won by 138 runs. West Indies 281 and 201; India 241 and 103.
Fourth Test.—(Bombay, Nov. 24–29). Drawn. India 463 and 173 for 5 (dec.); West Indies 393 and 104 for 4.
Fifth Test.—(Calcutta, Dec. 10–14). West Indies won by an innings and 46 runs. India 241 and 90; West Indies 377.
Sixth Test.—(Madras, Dec. 24–29). Drawn. West Indies 313 and 64 for 1; India 451 for 8 (dec.).

Australia v. Pakistan, 1983–84

First Test.—(Perth, Nov. 11–14). Australia won by an innings and 9 runs. Australia 436 for 9 (dec.); Pakistan 129 and 298.
Second Test.—(Brisbane, Nov. 25–29). Drawn. Pakistan 156 and 82 for 3; Australia 509 for 7 (dec.).
Third Test.—(Adelaide, Dec. 9–13). Drawn. Australia 465 and 310 for 7; Pakistan 624.
Fourth Test.—(Melbourne, Dec. 26–30). Drawn. Pakistan 470 and 238 for 7; Australia 555.
Fifth Test.—(Sydney, Jan. 2–6). Australia won by ten wickets. Pakistan 278 and 210; Australia 454 for 6 (dec.) and 35 for no wkt.

New Zealand v. England, 1984

First Test.—(Wellington, Jan. 20–24). Drawn. New Zealand 219 and 537; England 463 and 69 for no wkt.
Second Test.—(Christchurch, Feb. 3–5). New Zealand won by an innings and 132 runs. New Zealand 307; England 82 and 93.
Third Test.—(Auckland, Feb. 10–15). Drawn. New Zealand 496 for 9 (dec.) and 16 for no wkt.; England 439.

Pakistan v. England, 1984

First Test.—(Karachi, Mar. 2–6). Pakistan won by three wickets. England 182 and 159; Pakistan 277 and 66 for 7.

Second Test.—(Faisalabad, Mar. 12–17). Drawn. Pakistan 449 for 8 (dec.) and 137 for 4; England 546 for 8 (dec.).
Third Test.—(Lahore, Mar. 19–24). Drawn. England 241 and 344 for 9 (dec.); Pakistan 343 and 217 for 6.

West Indies v. Australia, 1984

First Test.—(Georgetown, Mar. 2–7). Drawn. Australia 279 and 273 for 9 (dec.); West Indies 230 and 250 for no wkt.
Second Test.—(Port of Spain, Mar. 16–21). Drawn. Australia 255 and 299 for 9; West Indies 468 for 8 (dec.).
Third Test.—(Bridgetown, Mar. 30–Apr. 4). West Indies won by ten wickets. Australia 429 and 97; West Indies 509 and 21 for no wkt.
Fourth Test.—(Antigua, April 7–11). West Indies won by an innings and 36 runs. Australia 262 and 200; West Indies 498.
Fifth Test.—(Kingston, April 28–May 2). West Indies won by ten wickets. Australia 199 and 160; West Indies 305 and 55 for no wkt.

Sri Lanka v. New Zealand, 1984

First Test.—(Kandy, Mar. 9–14). New Zealand won by 165 runs. New Zealand 276 and 201 for 8 (dec.); Sri Lanka 215 and 97.
Second Test.—(Colombo, Mar. 16–21). Drawn. Sri Lanka 174 and 289 for 9 (dec.); New Zealand 198 and 123 for 4.
Third Test.—(Colombo, Mar. 24–29); New Zealand won by an innings and 61 runs. Sri Lanka 256 and 142; New Zealand 459.

England v. West Indies, 1984

First Test.—(Edgbaston, June 14–18). West Indies won by an innings and 180 runs. England 191 and 235; West Indies 606.
Second Test.—(Lord's, June 28–July 3). West Indies won by nine wickets. England 286 and 300 for 9 (dec.); West Indies 245 and 344 for 1.
Third Test.—(Headingley, July 12–16). West Indies won by eight wickets. England 270 and 159; West Indies 302 and 131 for 2.
Fourth Test.—(Old Trafford, July 26–31). West Indies won by an innings and 64 runs. West Indies 500; England 280 and 156.
Fifth Test.—(The Oval, Aug. 9–14). West Indies won by 172 runs. West Indies 190 and 346; England 162 and 202. (*See next page for Averages.*)

England v. Sri Lanka, 1984

At Lord's, Aug. 23–28. Drawn. Sri Lanka 491 for 7 (dec.) and 294 for 7 (dec.); England 370.

England v. West Indies, 1984 (Averages)

ENGLAND BATTING

Batsmen	Innings	Times not out	Runs	Highest Score	Average
A. J. Lamb	10	1	386	110	42.88
I. T. Botham	10	0	347	81	34.70
R. M. Ellison	2	1	33	20*	33.00
C. J. Tavaré	2	0	65	49	32.50
G. Fowler	10	0	260	106	26.00
B. C. Broad	8	0	195	55	24.37
P. R. Downton	10	1	210	56	23.33
R. G. D. Willis	5	3	43	22	21.50
D. I. Gower	10	1	171	57*	19.00
D. R. Pringle	6	1	81	46*	16.20
N. A. Foster	2	1	15	9*	15.00
M. W. Gatting	2	0	30	29	15.00
P. J. W. Allott	6	0	67	26	11.16
G. Miller	4	0	42	22	10.50
N. G. Cowans	2	0	14	14	7.00
J. P. Agnew	2	1	7	5	7.00
V. P. Terry	3	0	16	8	5.33
N. G. B. Cook	6	0	25	13	4.16
D. W. Randall	2	0	1	1	0.50
P. I. Pocock	4	0	0	0	0.00

Also batted: T. A. Lloyd 10*   *Not out

BOWLING

Bowlers	Overs	Maidens	Runs	Wickets	Average
R. M. Ellison	44	10	94	5	18.80
P. J. W. Allott	104.5	26	282	14	20.14
I. T. Botham	163.2	30	667	19	35.10
P. I. Pocock	53.3	17	145	4	36.25
D. R. Pringle	71.3	10	257	5	51.40
N. G. B. Cook	95	15	297	5	59.40
R. G. D. Willis	85	14	367	6	61.16

Also bowled: J. P. Agnew, 26-4-97-2; G. Miller, 28-1-142-1; N. G. Cowans, 19-2-76-0; N. A. Foster, 18-2-82-0.

WEST INDIES BATTING

Batsmen	Innings	Times not out	Runs	Highest Score	Average
C. G. Greenidge	8	1	572	223	81.71
H. A. Gomes	8	3	400	143	80.00
C. H. Lloyd	6	1	255	71	51.00
I. V. A. Richards	7	1	250	117	41.66
P. J. Dujon	6	0	210	101	35.00
E. A. E. Baptiste	6	1	174	87*	34.80
M. A. Holding	5	0	158	69	31.60
D. L. Haynes	8	0	235	125	29.37
R. Harper	6	1	96	39*	19.20
M. D. Marshall	5	0	47	29	9.40
J. Garner	6	1	29	10*	5.80

Also batted: W. W. Davis, 77; M. Small, 3*   *Not out

BOWLING

Bowlers	Overs	Maidens	Runs	Wickets	Average
M. D. Marshall	167.4	50	437	24	18.20
J. Garner	217.5	60	540	29	18.62
R. Harper	128.4	47	276	13	21.23
M. A. Holding	122.2	24	343	15	22.86
E. A. E. Baptiste	125	39	265	8	33.12

Also bowled: M. Small, 21-2-78-3; W. W. Davis, 23-3-77-2; I. V. A. Richards, 1-0-2-0.

County Championship Table, 1984

Order for 1984 in brackets	Played	Won	Lost	Drawn	Tied	Bonus Btg.	Bonus Blng.	Points
Essex (1)	24	13	3	8	0	64	83	355
Nottinghamshire(14)	24	12	3	9	0	68	81	341
Middlesex (2)	24	8	7	9	0	63	78	269
Leicestershire (4)	24	8	2	14	0	60	78	266
Kent (7)	24	8	3	11	2	45	65	254
Sussex (11)	24	7	6	10	1	54	79	249
Somerset (10)	24	6	7	11	0	60	78	234
Surrey (8)	24	6	6	12	0	62	72	230
Warwickshire (5)	24	6	7	11	0	71	60	227
Worcestershire (16)	24	5	5	14	0	66	74	220
Derbyshire (9)	24	4	6	14	0	72	66	202
Northamptonshire (6)	24	5	9	9	1	58	56	202
Glamorgan (15)	24	4	2	18	0	65	71	200
Yorkshire (17)	24	5	4	15	0	59	55	194
Hampshire (3)	24	3	13	8	0	58	62	168
Lancashire (13)	24	1	9	14	0	49	72	137
Gloucestershire (12)	24	1	10	13	0	56	61	133

(Sussex total includes 12pts for a win in a match reduced to one innings.)

Other Results, 1984

NatWest Trophy.—Middlesex beat Kent by four wickets. Kent 232 for 6; Middlesex 236 for 6.

Benson and Hedges Cup Final.—Lancashire beat Warwickshire by six wickets. Warwickshire 139; Lancashire 140 for 4.

John Player Sunday League Champions.—Essex.

Universities.—Oxford won by five wickets. Cambridge 271 for 7 (dec.) and 195; Oxford 206 for 1 (dec.) and 261 for 5.

Eton and Harrow.—Match drawn. Eton 166; Harrow 73 for 6.

County Champions since 1948

1948	Glamorgan	1956	Surrey	1966	Yorkshire	1976	Middlesex
1949	{ Middlesex / Yorkshire	1957	Surrey	1967	Yorkshire	1977	{ Kent / Middlesex
1950	{ Lancashire / Surrey	1958	Surrey	1968	Yorkshire		
		1959	Yorkshire	1969	Glamorgan	1978	Kent
1951	Warwickshire	1960	Yorkshire	1970	Kent	1979	Essex
1952	Surrey	1961	Hampshire	1971	Surrey	1980	Middlesex
1953	Surrey	1962	Yorkshire	1972	Warwickshire	1981	Nottinghamshire
1954	Surrey	1963	Yorkshire	1973	Hampshire	1982	Middlesex
1955	Surrey	1964	Worcestershire	1974	Worcestershire	1983	Essex
		1965	Worcestershire	1975	Leicestershire	1984	Essex

BATTING AND BOWLING AVERAGES

English Batting Averages, 1984
(Qualification, 8 Innings)

English Bowling Averages, 1984
(Qualification, 10 Wickets)

Batsmen	Number of Innings	Times not out	Total Runs	Highest Innings	Average	Bowlers	Overs	Maidens	Runs	Wickets	Average
M. W. Gatting	43	10	2257	258	68·39	R. J. Hadlee	772·2	245	1645	117	14·05
P. W. Denning	8	3	338	90	67·60	R. Harper	314·1	109	676	37	18·27
G. A. Gooch	45	7	2559	227	67·34	P. J. W. Allott	604·5	171	1496	79	18·93
Javed Miandad	15	2	832	212*	64·00	D. L. Underwood	676·4	250	1511	77	19·62
G. Boycott	35	10	1567	153*	62·68	T. M. Tremlett	669·5	209	1444	71	20·33
J. G. Wright	21	1	1201	177	60·05	A. Sidebottom	488·1	105	1292	63	20·50
D. L. Amiss	50	10	2239	122	55·97	G. S. le Roux	604·2	154	1647	78	21·11
M. D. Crowe	41	6	1870	190	53·42	S. T. Clarke	651·1	165	1687	78	21·62
V. J. Marks	34	10	1262	134	52·58	N. G. Cowans	493·1	76	1593	73	21·82
A. I. Kallicharran	50	6	2301	200*	52·29	J. K. Lever	874·5	195	2550	116	21·98
R. J. Hadlee	31	8	1179	210*	51·26	N. E. Briers	109	24	264	12	22·00
R. T. Robinson	47	7	2032	171	50·80	P. M. Such	386·5	122	937	42	22·30
P. Johnson	14	1	647	133	49·76	G. A. Gooch	321·1	75	850	38	22·36
T. A. Lloyd	14	2	590	110	49·16	R. M. Ellison	535·5	142	1323	59	22·42
C. E. B. Rice	39	7	1553	152*	48·53	M. Weston	123·4	29	315	14	22·50
G. W. Humpage	47	8	1891	205	48·48	T. M. Alderman	559·4	149	1725	76	22·69
V. P. Terry	28	3	1208	175*	48·32	A. M. E. Roberts	265	70	769	33	23·30
R. A. Smith	13	3	483	132	48·30	Kapil Dev	296·3	75	819	35	23·40
P. A. Neale	42	6	1706	143	47·38	E. E. Hemmings	797·5	234	2220	94	23·61
P. M. Roebuck	37	1	1702	159	47·27	C. M. Wells	497·2	146	1396	59	23·66
P. Parker	40	4	1692	181	47·00	M. Davis	500·4	108	1569	66	23·77
K. S. McEwan	44	6	1755	142*	46·18	N. A. Foster	687·1	148	2098	87	24·11
K. J. Barnett	41	3	1734	144	45·63	R. Ellcock	221·2	32	714	29	24·62
B. C. Broad	40	5	1549	108*	44·25	K. B. S. Jarvis	570·5	128	1788	72	24·83
Younis Ahmed	35	4	1369	158*	44·16	A. Jones	208·1	44	636	25	25·44
J. Derrick	15	7	351	69*	43·87	C. E. Waller	610·3	221	1349	53	25·45
D. L. Haynes	18	1	743	125	43·70	G. Monkhouse	460·5	120	1273	50	25·46
C. M. Wells	39	7	1389	203	43·40	P. B. Clift	623·1	165	1608	63	25·52
G. S. Clinton	28	6	948	192	43·09	G. Miller	897·2	257	2236	87	25·70
W. N. Slack	46	8	1631	145	42·92	P. I. Pocock	638·5	168	1621	63	25·73
Kapil Dev	19	4	640	95	42·66	D. Reeve	572·4	175	1420	55	25·81
T. Curtis	36	3	1405	129	42·57	V. J. Marks	808	226	2233	86	25·96
D. M. Smith	31	5	1093	189*	42·03	J. Simmons	619·4	177	1644	63	26·09
D. Turner	37	4	1365	153	41·36	S. Barwick	477·4	123	1314	50	26·28
D. W. Randall	40	3	1528	136	41·29	I. T. Botham	449·4	93	1562	59	26·47
T. E. Jesty	44	4	1625	248	40·62	K. Cooper	623·2	217	1364	51	26·74
J. Lloyds	30	10	812	113*	40·60	N. Phillip	275·2	48	911	34	26·79
A. J. Lamb	34	4	1209	133*	40·30	W. W. Daniel	462	86	1463	54	27·09
R. Butcher	40	7	1326	116	40·18	P. H. Edmonds	823·3	233	2096	77	27·22
P. Robinson	24	5	756	92	39·78	J. Steele	678	175	1867	68	27·45
T. Boon	37	6	1233	144	39·77	J. E. Emburey	865·3	255	1978	72	27·47
G. Cook	43	4	1539	102	39·46	D. J. Thomas	505·4	114	1654	60	27·56
R. D. V. Knight	35	3	1254	142	39·18	W. Davis	547·5	118	1725	62	27·82
K. Sharp	39	2	1445	173	39·05	D. R. Pringle	580·1	127	1784	64	27·87
R. A. Woolmer	14	3	427	153	38·81	A. M. Ferreira	772·1	156	2208	79	27·94
M. A. Lynch	41	1	1546	144	38·65	L. McFarlane	272·5	45	875	31	28·22
M. Haysman	10	4	230	102*	38·33	J. Barclay	417	117	1023	36	28·41
A. R. Butcher	41	4	1415	135*	38·24	R. Finney	584	130	1770	62	28·54
M. R. Benson	26	2	914	127	38·08	G. Small	643·4	127	2027	71	28·54
R. Bailey	45	8	1405	114	37·97	J. P. Agnew	668·1	127	2413	84	28·72
C. W. J. Athey	52	4	1812	114*	37·75	C. H. Dredge	533	125	1534	53	28·94
D. L. Bairstow	26	5	787	94	37·47	C. M. Old	496	134	1306	45	29·02
A. L. Jones	51	2	1811	132	36·95	R. C. Ontong	837·4	221	2155	74	29·12
J. C. Balderstone	36	2	1260	181*	37·05	S. Turner	285	95	617	21	29·38
J. Abrahams	39	6	1216	201*	36·84	D. A. Graveney	667·4	202	1588	54	29·40
J. Hardy	20	6	513	95	36·64	N. Gifford	812·4	238	1919	65	29·52
J. Whitaker	32	2	1097	160	36·56	A. P. Pridgeon	719·5	168	1949	66	29·53
W. Larkins	49	3	1656	183*	36·00	C. Rowe	135	41	356	12	29·66
P. Willey	45	4	1472	167	35·90	C. S. Cowdrey	271·1	57	832	28	29·71
D. I. Gower	30	2	999	117*	35·67	D. L. Acfield	577·4	174	1368	46	29·73
R. C. Ontong	45	8	1320	204*	35·67	I. Folley	374	91	1015	34	29·85
M. D. Moxon	32	3	1034	126*	35·65	C. E. B. Rice	206	53	569	19	29·94
R. G. Lumb	17	2	534	165*	35·60	P. Willey	544·1	163	1291	43	30·02
D. G. Aslett	45	3	1491	221*	35·50	S. Hughes	314·2	53	1051	35	30·02
P. Romaines	52	2	1844	141	35·46	M. D. Crowe	435	101	1353	44	30·75
J. Morris	28	1	948	135	35·11	S. Booth	409·2	117	1172	38	30·84
R. Dyer	36	2	1187	106*	34·91	I. A. Greig	648	153	1913	62	30·85

* Denotes not out.

RUGBY FOOTBALL

INTERNATIONAL UNION TABLE, 1984

Country	Played	Won	Drawn	Lost	Points Scored		Points
					For	Against	
Scotland	4	4	0	0	86	36	8
France	4	3	0	1	90	67	6
Wales	4	2	0	2	67	60	4
England	4	1	0	3	51	83	2
Ireland	4	0	0	4	39	87	0

CALCUTTA CUP
England v. Scotland

1970 Scotland 14–5
1971 Scotland 16–15
1972 Scotland 23–9
1973 England 20–13
1974 Scotland 16–14
1975 England 7–6
1976 Scotland 22–12
1977 England 26–6
1978 England 15–0
1979 Draw 7–7
1980 England 30–18
1981 England 23–17
1982 Draw 9–9
1983 Scotland 22–12
1984 Scotland 18–6

COUNTY
CHAMPIONSHIP

Staffordshire.
Surrey.
Gloucestershire.
Lancashire.
Gloucestershire.
Gloucestershire.
Gloucestershire.
Lancashire.
North Midlands.
Middlesex.
Lancashire.
Northumberland.
Lancashire.
Gloucestershire.
Gloucestershire.

INTERNATIONAL MATCHES, 1983–84

1983
Nov. 12 Edinburgh: Scotland 25 N. Zealand 25
Bucharest: Rumania 24 Wales 6
Nov. 19 Twickenham: England 15 N. Zealand 9
1984
Jan. 21 Paris: France 25 Ireland 12
Cardiff: Wales 9 Scotland 15
Feb. 4 Edinburgh: Scotland 18 England 6
Dublin: Ireland 9 Wales 18
Feb. 18 Cardiff: Wales 16 France 21
Twickenham: England 12 Ireland 9
Mar. 3 Dublin: Ireland 9 Scotland 32
Paris: France 32 England 18
Mar. 17 Edinburgh: Scotland 21 France 12
Twickenham: England 15 Wales 24
June 2 P. Elizabeth: S. Africa 33 England 15
9 Joh'burg: S. Africa 35 England 9

COUNTY CHAMPIONSHIP FINAL
Gloucestershire beat Somerset 36–18

OTHER CHIEF MATCHES, 1983–84

Universities. 1983. Cambridge beat Oxford by 20–9 at Twickenham on Dec. 6.

Services Championship.—Army beat Royal Navy 13–6; Royal Navy beat R.A.F. 10–9; R.A.F. beat Army 19–15.

John Player Special Cup Final.—Bath beat Bristol 10–9 at Twickenham on April 28.

Hospitals Cup Final.—St. Mary's beat Royal Free 22–3 (after 9–9 draw).

Middlesex Sevens.—London Welsh.

RUGBY FOOTBALL LEAGUE (Est. 1895)

Test Matches

1984
Jan. 29 Avignon: Gt. Britain 12 France 0
Feb. 17 Leeds: Gt. Britain 10 France 0

Under 24—Internationals

1983
Nov. 11 Villeneuve: Gt. Britain 28 France 23
Dec. 4 Oldham: Gt. Britain 48 France 1

Rugby League Challenge Cup.—Final. Widnes beat Wigan 19–6 pts. at Wembley on May 5, 1984.

Premiership Trophy Final.—Hull K.R. beat Castleford 18–10 pts. at Headingley on May 12, 1984.

Slalom Lager Champions.—Hull K.R.

Second Division Champions.—Barrow.

Yorkshire Cup.—Hull beat Castleford 13–2 pts.

Lancashire Cup.—Barrow beat Widnes 12–8 pts.

John Player Special Trophy.—Final. Leeds beat Widnes 18–10 pts.

HOCKEY, 1983–84

MEN'S HOCKEY

County Championship Final.—Yorkshire and Middlesex drew 1–1 (Yorks. won on penalties).

National Club Championship Final.—East Grinstead beat Blackheath 1–0.

National Indoor Club Championship Final.—Slough beat Firebrands 8–7.

Universities.—Cambridge beat Oxford 2–1.

WOMEN'S HOCKEY, 1984

LEADING MATCHES

England beat Wales 1–0; England lost to Ireland 0–1; England drew with Scotland 1–1; England lost to Netherlands 1–2 and 1–4. *European Cup*: England finished 4th.

CHESS, 1984

British Championship.—N. D. Short.
Ladies.—B. Sathe; V. Unni.
Under-21.—S. C. Brown.
Under-18.—N. Crickmore; N. McDonald.

ASSOCIATION FOOTBALL

ENGLAND v. SCOTLAND

			g. g.
1971	England	..3—1
1972	England	..1—0
1973	England	..1—0
1974	Scotland	..2—0
1975	England	..5—1
1976	Scotland	..2—1
1977	Scotland	..2—1
1978	England	..1—0
1979	England	..3—1
1980	England	..2—0
1981	Scotland	..1—0
1982	England	..1—0
1983	England	..2—0
1984	Draw	..1—1

FOOTBALL ASSOCIATION CUP

	g. g.
Arsenal *b*. Liverpool	....2—1
Leeds U. *b*. Arsenal	.....1—0
Sunderland *b*. Leeds U.	.1—0
Liverpool *b*. Newcastle .	.3—0
West Ham U. *b*. Fulham .	.2—0
Southampton *b*. Man. U.	1—0
Man.U. *b*. Liverpool	....2—1
Ipswich T. *b*. Arsenal	...1—0
Arsenal *b*. Man. U.	....3—2
West Ham U. *b*. Arsenal .	1—0
Tottenham H. *b*. Man. C.	3—2
Tottenham H. *b*.Q.P.R.	.1—0
Man. U. *b*. Brighton	....4—0
Everton *b*. Watford	.....2—0

LEAGUE COMPETITION, 1983–84

Div. I.—Liverpool, 80 pts. Runners-up: Southampton, 77 pts. Relegated: Birmingham C., 48 pts.; Notts Co., 41 pts.; Wolverhampton W., 29 pts.

Div. II.—Promoted: Chelsea, 88 pts.; Sheffield W., 88 pts.; Newcastle U., 80 pts. Relegated: Derby Co., 42 pts.; Swansea C., 29 pts.; Cambridge U., 24 pts.

Div. III.—Promoted: Oxford U., 95 pts.; Wimbledon, 87 pts.; Sheffield U., 83 pts. Relegated: Scunthorpe U., 46 pts.; Southend U., 44 pts.; Port Vale, 43 pts.; Exeter C., 33 pts.

Div. IV.—Promoted: York C., 101 pts.; Doncaster R., 85 pts.; Reading, 82 pts.; Bristol C., 82 pts.

SCOTTISH LEAGUE.—*Premier Div.*—Aberdeen, 57 pts. *Div. I.*—Morton, 54 pts. *Div. II.*—Forfar A., 63 pts.

REPRESENTATIVE MATCHES, 1983–84
HOME INTERNATIONAL CHAMPIONSHIP

1983				
Dec. 13	Belfast:	N. Ireland 2	Scotland 0
1984				
Feb. 28	Hampden Park:	Scotland 2	Wales 1
April 4	Wembley:	England 1	N. Ireland 0
May 2	Wrexham:	Wales 1	England 0
May 22	Swansea:	Wales 1	N. Ireland 1
May 26	Hampden Park:	Scotland 1	England 1

	P	W	D	L	F	A	Pts.
N. Ireland	3	1	1	1	3	2	3
Wales	3	1	1	1	3	3	3
England	3	1	1	1	2	2	3
Scotland	3	1	1	1	3	4	3

OTHER INTERNATIONALS

1984				
Feb. 29	Paris:	France 2	England 0
June 2	Wembley:	England 0	U.S.S.R. 2
June 10	Rio de Janeiro:	Brazil 0	England 2
June 13	Montevideo:	Uruquay 2	England 0
June 17	Santiago:	Chile 0	England 0

EUROPEAN CHAMPIONSHIP

1983				
Oct. 12	Budapest:	Hungary 0	England 3
Nov. 16	Luxembourg:	Luxembourg 0	England 4

EUROPEAN CHAMPIONSHIP FINALS (FRANCE)

Semi Finals: France beat Portugal 3–2 in Marseilles; Denmark and Spain drew 1–1 in Lyon—Spain won 5–4 on penalties.
FINAL.—France beat Spain 2–0 in Paris on June 27.

EUROPEAN UNDER-21 CHAMPIONSHIP, 1982–84

FINAL.—England beat Spain 3–0 on aggregate.

CUP FINALS, 1983–84

F.A. CUP.—*S.F.:* April 14 (Villa Park), Watford beat Plymouth 1–0; (Highbury), Everton beat Southampton 1–0.
Final: May 19 (Wembley Stadium), Everton beat Watford 2–0.

MILK CUP.—*Final:* March 28 (Maine Road), Liverpool beat Everton 1–0 (after 0–0 draw at Wembley).

F.A. VASE.—*Final:* Stansted beat Stamford 3–2.

F.A. TROPHY.—*Final:* Northwich Victoria beat Bangor C. 2–1 (after 1–1 draw).

F.A. YOUTH CUP.—*Winners:* Everton.

ARTHUR DUNN CUP.—*Final:* Lancing beat Carthusians 2–0.

SCOTTISH F.A. CUP.—*Final:* May 19 (Hampden Park), Aberdeen beat Celtic 2–1.

SCOTTISH LEAGUE CUP.—*Final:* Rangers beat Celtic 3–2.

EUROPEAN CUP.—*S.F.:* AS Roma beat Dundee U. 3–2 (on aggregate); Liverpool beat Dinamo Bucharest 3–1 (on aggregate).
Final: Liverpool and AS Roma drew 1–1 in Rome. Liverpool won 4–2 on penalties.

EUROPEAN CUP-WINNERS' CUP.—*Final:* Juventus beat FC Porto 2–1 in Basle.

U.E.F.A. CUP.—*Final:* Tottenham Hotspur and Anderlecht drew 2–2 (on aggregate). Tottenham won 4–3 on penalties.

Universities.—Oxford and Cambridge drew 2–2 (*100th match*).

PAST WORLD CUP WINNERS

1930 (*Played in Uruguay*)	Uruguay
1934 (*Italy*)	Italy
1938 (*France*)	Italy
1950 (*Brazil*)	Uruguay
1954 (*Switzerland*)	West Germany
1958 (*Sweden*)	Brazil
1962 (*Chile*)	Brazil
1966 (*England*)	England
1970 (*Mexico*)	Brazil
1974 (*West Germany*)	West Germany
1978 (*Argentina*)	Argentina
1982 (*Spain*)	Italy

GOLF, 1983–84

CHAMPIONSHIPS

OPEN
(Instituted 1860)

1967 R. de Vicenzo (Argentina), 278.
1968 G. Player (S. Africa), 289.
1969 A. Jacklin (G.B.), 280.
1970 J. Nicklaus (U.S.A.) beat D. Sanders (U.S.A.) after tie, 283.
1971 L. Trevino (U.S.A.), 278.
1972 L. Trevino (U.S.A.), 278.
1973 T. Weiskopf (U.S.A.), 276.
1974 G. Player (S. Africa), 282.
1975 T. Watson (U.S.A.) beat J. Newton (Australia) after tie, 279.
1976 J. Miller (U.S.A.), 279.
1977 T. Watson (U.S.A.), 268.
1978 J. Nicklaus (U.S.A.), 281.
1979 S. Ballesteros (Spain), 283.
1980 T. Watson (U.S.A.), 271.
1981 W. Rogers (U.S.A.), 276.
1982 T. Watson (U.S.A.), 284.
1983 T. Watson (U.S.A.), 275.
1984 S. Ballesteros (Spain), 276.

AMATEUR
(1885)

1967 B. Dickson (U.S.A.).
1968 M. F. Bonallack.
1969 M. F. Bonallack.

1970 M. F. Bonallack.
1971 S. N. Melnyk (U.S.A.).
1972 T. Homer.
1973 R. Siderowf (U.S.A.).
1974 T. Homer.
1975 M. Giles (U.S.A.).
1976 R. Siderowf (U.S.A.).
1977 P. McEvoy.
1978 P. McEvoy.
1979 J. Sigel (U.S.A.).
1980 D. Evans.
1981 P. Ploujoux (France).
1982 M. Thompson.
1983 P. Parkin.
1984 J.-M. Olazabal (Spain).

LADIES
(1893)

1967 Miss D. E. Chadwick.
1968 Mlle. B. Varangot (France).
1969 Mlle. C. Lacoste (France).
1970 Miss D. L. Oxley.
1971 Miss M. Walker.
1972 Miss M. Walker.
1973 Miss A. Irvin.
1974 Miss C. Semple (U.S.A.).
1975 Mrs. N. Syms (U.S.A.).
1976 Miss C. Panton.
1977 Mrs. A. Uzielli.
1978 Miss E. Kennedy (Australia).
1979 Miss M. Madill.
1980 Mrs. A. Sander (U.S.A.).
1981 Mrs. B. Robertson.
1982 Miss K. Douglas.
1983 Mrs. J. Thornhill.
1984 Miss J. Rosenthal (U.S.A.).

RYDER CUP
(Palm Beach, Florida, Oct. 1983)

U.S.A. beat Europe 14½–13½.

CURTIS CUP
(Muirfield, June 1984)

U.S.A. beat Great Britain and Ireland by 9½ to 8½.

OTHER GOLF EVENTS, 1983–84

Spanish Open.—E. Darcy (Ireland).

Sanyo Open.—D. Smyth (Ireland).

Johnnie Walker Trophy.—B. Langer (W. Germany).

Australian Open.—P. Fowler.

Halford Hewitt Cup (Final).—Charterhouse beat Malvern 3–2.

English Amateur Championship.—D. Gilford.

Brabazon Trophy.—M. Davis.

Whyte and Mackay P.G.A. Championship.—H. Clark.

Madrid Open.—H. Clark.

English Girls' Championship.—C. Swallow.

Golf Illustrated Gold Vase.—J. Marks.

Portuguese Open.—S. Torrance.

World Cup.—U.S.A.

Berkhamsted Trophy.—R. Willison.

English Women's Championship.—Miss C. Waite.

Glasgow Open.—K. Brown.

Timex Open.—M. Clayton (Australia).

P.G.A. Seniors' Championship.—E. Jones.

British Women's Amateur Strokeplay Championship.—Miss C. Waite.

U.S. Masters.—B. Crenshaw.

U.S. Open.—F. Zoeller.

U.S., P.G.A. Championship.—L. Trevino.

U.S. Tournament Players' Championship.—F. Couples.

Home International Championship.—England.

Universities.—Cambridge beat Oxford by 11½–3½.

Tunisian Open.—S. Torrance.

Car Care Plan International.—N. Faldo.

Tillman Trophy.—P. Cherry.

British Youths' Championship.—R. Morris.

Ford Women's Classic.—Miss K. Douglas.

President's Putter.—A. Edmond.

Lytham Trophy.—J. Hawksworth.

South African Open.—A. Johnstone (Zimbabwe).

French Open.—B. Langer (W. Germany).

British Girls' Championship.—C. Swallow.

Benson and Hedges International.—S. Torrance.

Lawrence Batley International.—J. Rivero (Spain).

Jersey Open.—B. Gallacher.

Tournament Players' Championship.—J. Gonzalez (Brazil).

European Open.—G. Brand, Jnr.

Carris Trophy.—J. Coe.

Italian Open.—S. Lyle.

Sunningdale Foursomes.—Miss M. McKenna and Miss M. Madill.

German Open.—W. Grady (Australia).

European Masters.—J. Anderson (Canada).

Dutch Open.—B. Langer (W. Germany).

Carrolls Irish Open.—B. Langer (W. Germany).

Scandinavian Open.—I. Woosnam.

Monte Carlo Open.—I. Mosey.

Canadian Open.—G. Norman (Australia).

Celtic International Classic.—G. Brand, Jnr.

British Boys' Championship.—L. Vannet.

LAWN TENNIS

THE DAVIS CUP CHALLENGE ROUNDS
(Founder—Dwight Filley Davis (1879–1945), First Played, 1900.)

1936 Great Britain beat Australia 3–2	1956 Australia beat U.S.A. 3–2	1970 U.S.A. beat W. Germany. . . . 5–0
1937 U.S.A. beat Great Britain. . . 4–1	1957 Australia beat U.S.A. 3–2	1971 U.S.A. beat Rumania 3–2
1938 U.S.A. beat Australia 3–2	1958 U.S.A. beat Australia 3–2	1972 U.S.A. beat Rumania 3–2
1939 Australia beat U.S.A. 3–2	1959 Australia beat U.S.A. 3–2	1973 Australia beat U.S.A. 5–0
1946 U.S.A. beat Australia 5–0	1960 Australia beat Italy 4–1	1974 S. Africa won by default.
1947 U.S.A. beat Australia 3–1	1961 Australia beat Italy 5–0	1975 Sweden beat Czechoslovakia 3–2
1948 U.S.A. beat Australia 5–0	1962 Australia beat Mexico 5–0	1976 Italy beat Chile 4–1
1949 U.S.A. beat Australia 4–1	1963 U.S.A. beat Australia 3–2	1977 Australia beat Italy 3–1
1950 Australia beat U.S.A. 4–1	1964 Australia beat U.S.A. 3–2	1978 U.S.A. beat Great Britain . . . 4–1
1951 Australia beat U.S.A. 3–1	1965 Australia beat Spain 4–1	1979 U.S.A. beat Italy 5–0
1952 Australia beat U.S.A. 4–1	1966 Australia beat India 4–1	1980 Czechoslovakia beat Italy . . . 4–1
1953 Australia beat U.S.A. 3–2	1967 Australia beat Spain 4–1	1981 U.S.A. beat Argentina 3–1
1954 U.S.A. beat Australia 3–0	1968 U.S.A. beat Australia 4–1	1982 U.S.A. beat France 4–1
1955 Australia beat U.S.A. 5–0	1969 U.S.A. beat Rumania 5–0	1983 Australia beat Sweden 3–2

THE CHAMPIONSHIPS (WIMBLEDON)
1984

Men's Singles.—J. McEnroe (U.S.A.) beat J. Connors (U.S.A.), 6–1, 6–1, 6–2.

Women's Singles.—Miss M. Navratilova (U.S.A.) beat Mrs J. Lloyd (U.S.A.), 7–6, 6–2.

Men's Doubles.— P. Fleming and J. McEnroe (U.S.A.) beat P. Cash and P. McNamee (Australia), 6–2, 5–7, 6–2, 3–6, 6–3.

Women's Doubles.—Miss M. Navratilova and Miss P. Shriver (U.S.A.) beat Miss K. Jordan and Miss A. Smith (U.S.A.), 6–3, 6–4.

Mixed Doubles.—J. Lloyd (G.B.) and Miss W. Turnbull (Australia) beat S. Denton and Miss K. Jordan (U.S.A.), 6–3, 6–3.

All England Plate:
Women's Singles.—Miss M. Brown (U.S.A.) beat Miss R. White (U.S.A.), 6–2, 7–5.

Junior International Invitation Tournament:
Boys' Singles.—M. Kratzmann (Australia) beat S. Kruger (S. Africa), 6–4, 4–6, 6–3.
Girls' Singles.—Miss A. Croft (G.B.) beat Miss E. Reinach (S. Africa), 3–6, 6–3, 6–2.
Boys' Doubles.—R. Brown and R. Weiss (U.S.A.) beat M. Kratzmann (Australia) and J. Svensson (Sweden), 1–6, 6–4, 11–9.
Girls' Doubles.—Miss C. Kuhlman and Miss S. Rehe (U.S.A.) beat Miss V. Milvidskaya and Miss L. Savchenko (U.S.S.R.), 6–3, 5–7, 6–4.

Over 35s Men's.—Singles: S. Smith (U.S.A.) beat C. Dibley (Australia), 7–6, 6–3. *Doubles:* M. Riessen and S. Stewart (U.S.A.) beat C. Dibley (Australia) and J. Fillol (Chile), 6–3, 3–6, 10–8.

WIGHTMAN CUP, 1983
(Williamsburg, Virginia, Nov.)

U.S.A. beat G.B. by 6 matches to 1.

U.S.A. Championships:
Men's Singles.—J. McEnroe (U.S.A.).
Women's Singles.—Miss M. Navratilova (U.S.A.).
Men's Doubles.—J. Fitzgerald (Australia) and T. Smid (Czechoslovakia).
Women's Doubles.—Miss M. Navratilova and Miss P. Shriver (U.S.A.).
Mixed Doubles.—Miss M. Maleeva (Bulgaria) and T. Gullikson (U.S.A.).

French Championships:
Men's Singles.—I. Lendl (Czechoslovakia).
Women's Singles.—Miss M. Navratilova (U.S.A.).
Men's Doubles.—H. Leconte and Y. Noah (France).

Women's Doubles.—Miss M. Navratilova and Miss P. Shriver (U.S.A.).
Mixed Doubles.—D. Stockton and Miss A. Smith (U.S.A.).

Federation Cup.—Czechoslovakia.

Youll Cup.—Repton.
Clark Cup.—Repton.

Prudential County Cup—Men: Middlesex; *Women:* Kent.

STELLA ARTOIS TOURNAMENT (Men only)
(Queen's Club)

Singles.—J. McEnroe (U.S.A.) beat L. Shiras (U.S.A.), 6–1, 3–6, 6–2.

Doubles.—P. Cash and P. McNamee (Australia) beat B. Mitton and B. Walts (U.S.A.), 6–4, 6–3.

REAL TENNIS, 1983–84

British Amateur Singles Championship.—A. Lovell beat M. Dean, 3–0.

British Open Singles Championship.—C. Ronaldson beat L. Deuchar, 3–0.

British Open Doubles Championship.—C. Ronaldson and M. Dean beat C. Lumley and L. Deuchar, 3–1.

British Professional Singles Championship.—C. Ronaldson beat L. Deuchar, 3–1.

Henry Leaf Cup.—Winchester beat Haileybury, 2–1.

Universities.—Cambridge beat Oxford, 4–2.

BADMINTON, 1984
ALL-ENGLAND CHAMPIONSHIPS

Men's Singles.—M. Frost (Denmark) beat Liem Swie King (Indonesia), 2–1.

Ladies' Singles.—Li Lingwei (China) beat Han Aiping (China), 2–0.

Men's Doubles.—R. Heryanto and H. Kartono (Indonesia) beat M. Dew and M. Tredgett (England), 2–0.

Ladies' Doubles.—Lin Ying and Wu Dixi (China) beat Yun Ya Kim and Sang Hee Yoo (S. Korea), 2–1.

Mixed Doubles.—M. Dew and Mrs. G. Gilks (England) beat N. Tier and G. Gowers (England), 2–0.

SQUASH RACKETS, 1983–84

World Open Championship.—J. Khan (Pakistan) beat C. Dittmar (Australia), 3–0.
British Open Championship.—J. Khan (Pakistan) beat Q. Zaman (Pakistan), 3–0.
British Women's Open Championship.—Miss S. Devoy (N.Z.) beat Miss L. Opie (G.B.), 3–1.
British Closed Championship.—P. Kenyon beat G. Briars, 3–2.
British Women's Closed Championship.—Miss L. Opie beat Miss M. Le Moignan, 3–0.
British Under-23 Open.—S. Qaiser (Pakistan) beat S. Davenport (New Zealand), 3–1.
Home International Championships.—*Men:* England; *Women:* England.
Inter-County.—Lancashire.
Drysdale Cup.—D. Lloyd beat R. Owen, 3–0.

FENCING, 1983–84

British Championships.
  Foil.—W. Gosbee (Salle Paul).
  Sabre.—P. Klenerman (Salle Ganchev).
  Epée.—R. Johnson (Salle Boston).
  Ladies' Foil.—Miss L. Martin (Salle Paul).
Sporting Record Cup.—Salle Paul.
Granville Cup.—Salle Boston.
Magrini Cup.—Salle Ganchev.
Savage Shield.—Salle Boston.
Martin Edmunds Cup.—Salle Paul.
Luke Fildes Cup.—K. Griffiths (Reading).
Millfield International.—J. Pitman (G.B.).
Challenge Martini International Epée.—P. Boisse (France).

RACKETS, 1983–84

British Professional Championship.—S. Hazell beat N. Cripps, 3–0.
British Amateur Singles Championship.—W. R. Boone beat M. Nicholls, 3–0.
British Amateur Doubles Championship.—W. R. Boone and R. S. Crawley beat J. A. N. Prenn and C. J. Hue Williams, 4–3.
British Open Singles Championship.—W. R. Boone beat R. S. Crawley, 4–0.
British Open Doubles Championship.—W. R. Boone and R. S. Crawley beat J. A. N. Prenn and J. Male, 4–0.
Swallow Trophy.—S. Hazell beat R. Ellis, 3–2.
Noel Bruce Cup.—Eton (W. R. Boone and D. M. Norman) beat Tonbridge II (G. Cowdrey and J. Spurling), 4–0.
Foster Cup.—A. Spurling (Tonbridge) beat A. Giddins (Eton), 3–0.
Public Schools Doubles Championship.—Harrow beat Wellington, 4–1.
Universities.—Cambridge beat Oxford, 2–1.

RUGBY FIVES, 1984

Amateur Singles Championship.—G. W. Enstone beat I. P. Fuller.
Amateur Doubles Championship.—D. J. Hebden and I. P. Fuller beat G. W. Enstone and S. Ashton.
Invitation World Championships.—*Singles:* G. W. Enstone beat I. P. Fuller; *Doubles:* G. W. Enstone and S. Ashton beat D. J. Hebden and I. P. Fuller.
National Schools' Championships.—*Singles:* M. G. Hajialexandrou (St. Dunstan's) beat M. Thompson (Merchant Taylors').
  Doubles: Merchant Taylors' beat St. Dunstan's.

POLO, 1984

Queen's Cup.—Foxcote beat "B.B.'s", 10–9.
Cowdray Park Gold Cup.—Southfield beat "B.B.'s", 9–2.
Royal Windsor Cup.—Windsor Park beat "B.B.'s", 5–4.
Coronation Cup.—Rest of the World beat England, 8–7.
Silver Jubilee Trophy.—Spain beat England II, 5–4.
Universities.—Cambridge beat Oxford, 6–3.
Warwickshire Cup.—Southfield beat Cowdray Park, 6–5.

TABLE TENNIS, 1984

ENGLISH CLOSED CHAMPIONSHIPS
(Bletchley)

Men's Singles: D. Douglas beat G. Sandley, 3–1.
Women's Singles: A. Gordon beat L. Bellinger, 3–1.
Men's Doubles: D. Douglas and P. Day beat C. Prean and D. Parker, 2–0.
Women's Doubles: A. Gordon and M. Sainsbury beat J. Grundy and J. Parker, 2–1.
Mixed Doubles: S. Andrew and C. Moore beat N. Eckersley and J. Grundy, 2–0.

CYCLING, 1984

Tour de France.—L. Fignon (France).
Milk Race.—O. Czougeda (U.S.S.R.).
British Professional Road Race Championship.—S. Joughin.
Sealink International.—M. Elliott.

BOWLS, 1984

English Bowling Association Championships (Worthing).
Fours.—*S.F.:* Middlesbrough (Yorks.) beat Plessey B.C. (Notts.) 19–14; Boscombe Cliff (Hants.) beat Bedford Borough (Beds.) 19–15. *F.:* Boscombe Cliff beat Middlesbrough 18–16.
Triples.—*S.F.:* Kettering Lodge (Northants.) beat Cleethorpes (Lincs.) 16–15; Clevedon (Somerset) beat Abbey (Cambs.) 22–11. *F.:* Clevedon beat Kettering Lodge 18–15.
Pairs.—*S.F.:* Marlow (Bucks.) beat Preston (Sussex) 23–19; Lenham (Kent) beat View Lane (Durham) 16–14. *F.:* Lenham beat Marlow 17–15.
Singles: *S.F.:* J. Kilyon (Loughborough, Leics.) beat B. Carter (West Moors Mem., Dorset) 21–8; W. Richards (Mid Surrey) beat D. Phillips (Edmonton, Middx.) 21–11. *F.:* Richards beat Kilyon 21–15.
Inter-County Championship (Middleton Cup).—Somerset beat Northumberland 127–103.

BRITISH SHOW JUMPING, 1984

ROYAL INTERNATIONAL HORSE SHOW, BIRMINGHAM

King George V Cup.—N. Skelton on St. James.
Queen Elizabeth II Cup.—Mrs. V. Whitaker on Jingo.
Everest Grand Prix.—N. Skelton on St. James.
Radio Rentals Puissance.—P. Darrath on Carroll's Young Diamond.
Crown Life Assurance Championship.—M. Pyrah on Towerlands Anglezarke.

ANGLING

Year	Venue	No. of teams	Individual Winner	Weight	Team Winners	Points	Division
				lb. oz.			
1982	R. Huntspill	78	A. Mayer (Stockport Fed.)	21 13	Rotherham	718	1st
	Bristol Avon	74	E. Bird (East Lincs.)	44 5½	Swindon	648	2nd
	R. Trent	76	R. Moir (Hayes and Harlington)	27 15½	Bawtry	741	3rd
	Leeds & Liverpool Canal	78	E. Townsin (Ely Beet Sports & Social)	8 13	Congleton	741	4th
1983	U. Trent	57	D. Howell (Atherstone)	42 8½	Notts. Fed.	741	1st
	Yorkshire Ouse & R. Ure	57	A. Whitehead (Winsford)	12 15½	Redditch	689	2nd
	Oxford Canal	31	W. Pearce (Lamb A.C.)	9 10	Northern Awards B.C.	724	3rd
	R. Witham	29	A. V. Curd (Rye & Dist.)	22 3½	Kirkstead A.C.	980	4th

SWIMMING

Men:
50 metres Free Style.—D. Lowe.
400 metres Free Style.—J. Davey.
100 metres Butterfly.—D. Williams.
200 metres Individual Medley.—P. Brew.
200 metres Free Style.—J. Davey.
200 metres Back Stroke.—J. Davey.
1,500 metres Free Style.—T. Day.
200 metres Butterfly.—D. Emerson.
200 metres Breast Stroke.—M. Buswell.
100 metres Back Stroke.—J. Davey.
400 metres Individual Medley.—G. Binfield.
100 metres Free Style.—D. Lowe.
100 metres Breast Stroke.—N. Ali.
400 metres Team Free Style.—Barnet Copthall.
400 metres Team Medley.—Salford.

Women:
50 metres Free Style.—N. Fibbens.
100 metres Breast Stroke.—S. Bowman.
200 metres Breast Stroke.—N. Herbert.
800 metres Free Style.—S. Hardcastle.
100 metres Back Stroke.—K. Read.
200 metres Free Style.—C. Jackson.
200 metres Butterfly.—S. Purvis.
400 metres Individual Medley.—K. Read.
100 metres Free Style.—C. Jackson.
200 metres Individual Medley.—C. Jackson.
400 metres Free Style.—S. Hardcastle.
100 metres Butterfly.—S. Purvis.
200 metres Back Stroke.—K. Read.
400 metres Team Medley.—Millfield.
400 metres Team Free Style.—City of Manchester.

Men:
100 metres Free Style.—A. Gaines (U.S.A.), 49·36 s.
200 metres Free Style.—M. Gross (F.R.G.), 1 m. 47·44 s.
400 metres Free Style.—V. Salnikov (U.S.S.R.), 3 m. 48·32 s.
800 metres Free Style.—V. Salnikov (U.S.S.R.), 7 m. 52·33 s.

1,500 metres Free Style.—V. Salnikov (U.S.S.R.), 14 m. 54·76 s.
100 metres Breast Stroke.—S. Lundquist (U.S.A.), 1 m. 01·65 s.
200 metres Breast Stroke.—V. Davis (Canada), 2 m. 13·34 s.
100 metres Butterfly.—P. Morales (U.S.A.), 53·38 s.
200 metres Butterfly.—J. Sieben (Australia), 1 m. 57·04 s.
100 metres Back Stroke.—R. Carey (U.S.A.), 55·19 s.
200 metres Back Stroke.—S. Zabolotnov (U.S.S.R.), 1 m. 58·41 s.
200 metres Medley.—A. Baumann (Canada), 2 m. 01·42 s.
400 metres Medley.—A. Baumann (Canada), 4 m. 17·41 s.
4 × 100 metres Free Style Relay.—U.S.A., 3 m. 19·03 s.
4 × 200 metres Free Style Relay.—U.S.A., 7 m. 15·89 s.
4 × 100 metres Medley Relay.—U.S.A., 3 m. 39·30 s.

Women:
100 metres Free Style.—B. Krause (G.D.R.), 54·79 s.
200 metres Free Style.—K. Otto (G.D.R.), 1 m. 57·75 s.
400 metres Free Style.—T. Wickham (Australia), 4 m. 06·28 s.
800 metres Free Style.—T. Wickham (Australia), 8 m. 24·62 s.
1,500 metres Free Style.—K. Linehan (U.S.A), 16 m. 04·49 s.
100 metres Breast Stroke.—S. Gerasch (G.D.R.), 1 m. 08·29 s.
200 metres Breast Stroke.—L. Kachushite (U.S.S.R), 2 m. 28·36 s.
100 metres Butterfly.—M. Meagher (U.S.A.), 57·93 s.
200 metres Butterfly.—M. Meagher (U.S.A), 2 m. 05·96 s.
100 metres Back Stroke.—I. Kleber (G.D.R.), 1 m. 00·59 s.
200 metres Back Stroke.—C. Sirch (G.D.R.), 2 m. 09·91 s.
200 metres Medley.—U. Geweniger (G.D.R.), 2 m. 11·73 s.
400 metres Medley.—P. Schneider (G.D.R.), 4 m. 36·10 s.
4 × 100 metres Freestyle Relay.—G.D.R., 3 m. 42·41 s.
4 × 200 metres Freestyle Relay.—G.D.R., 8 m. 02·27 s.
4 × 100 metres Medley Relay.—G.D.R., 4 m. 03·69 s.

HENLEY ROYAL REGATTA, 1984

Grand Challenge Cup.—Leander and London beat Univ. of Washington (U.S.A.) by 3 lengths, 6 m. 22 s.

Ladies Challenge Plate.—Brown Univ. (U.S.A.) beat Temple Univ. (U.S.A.) by 1 length, 6 m. 42 s.

Princess Elizabeth Cup.—St. Edward's School beat St. Joseph's Prep. School (U.S.A.) by ½ length, 6 m. 48 s.

Thames Cup.—Cantabrigian beat Leander by 2 lengths, 6 m. 30 s.

Stewards' Cup.—Notts. Co. and Tyne beat Univ. of London and Univ. of London Tyrian, by canvas, 6 m. 57 s.

Prince Philip Cup.—Marlow and Univ. of London Tyrian beat Koninklijke Students Njord (Netherlands), easily, 7 m. 1 s.

Queen Mother Cup.—Maidenhead and Bewdley beat Quintin, easily, 6 m. 56 s.

Visitors' Cup.—Shiplake College and Sir William Borlase's School beat Reading Univ. by 3½ lengths, 7 m. 27 s.

Wyfold Cup.—Notts. Co. beat Nautilus Lightweight by 1¼ lengths, 6 m. 59 s.

Britannia Challenge Cup.—Tideway Scullers School beat Neptune (Ireland) by 1½ lengths, 7 m. 22 s.

Silver Goblets.—E. Pearson and C. Riches (Cambridge Univ. and Molesey) beat J. Beattie and R. Stanhope (Thames Tradesmen), not rowed out, 7 m. 57 s.

Double Sculls.—M. Espersen and L. Kruse (Bagsvaerd and Kolding, Denmark) beat T. Crooks and H. Matheson (Notts. Co. and Kingston) by 1¼ lengths, 7 m. 25 s.

Diamond Sculls.—C. Baillieu (Leander) beat B. Eltang (Danish Students), by 4 lengths, 7 m. 57 s.

Special Schools Race.—Shrewsbury School beat Cheltenham College by ½ length, 4 m. 37 s.

THE UNIVERSITY BOAT RACE

(Putney-Mortlake, 4 m. 1 f. 180 yds.)

Year	Winner	m. s.	Won by
1978	Oxford	19	Camb. sank
1979	Oxford	20 33	3½ lengths
1980	Oxford	19 20	A canvas
1981	Oxford	18 11	8 lengths
1982	Oxford	18 21	3½ lengths
1983	Oxford	19 7	4½ lengths
1984	Oxford	16 45*	3¾ lengths

Cambridge have won 68 times, Oxford 61 and there has been 1 dead-heat.
*Record.

OTHER ROWING EVENTS

Oxford Summer Eights.—Oriel.
Oxford Torpids.—Oriel.
Cambridge Lents.—Downing.
Cambridge Mays.—Downing.
Doggett's Coat and Badge (Estab. 1715, 270th race, London Bridge-Chelsea, 4½ miles).—S. McCarthy (Blackwall & Poplar).
Wingfield Sculls.—C. Baillieu.
Head of the River.—A.R.A. National Squad.

SKATING, 1983–84

WORLD CHAMPIONSHIPS
(Ottawa)

Men's Figure.—S. Hamilton (U.S.A.).
Ladies' Figure.—Miss K. Witt (E. Germany).
Pairs.—P. Martini and B. Underhill (Canada).
Ice Dancing.—Miss J. Torvill and C. Dean (G.B.).

EUROPEAN CHAMPIONSHIPS
(Budapest)

Men's Figure.—A. Fadeev (U.S.S.R.).
Ladies' Figure.—Miss K. Witt (East Germany).
Pairs.—O. Vasiliev and E. Valova (U.S.S.R.).
Ice Dancing.—Miss J. Torvill and C. Dean (G.B.).

BRITISH CHAMPIONSHIPS (Ice)

Men's Figure.—P. Robinson.
Ladies' Figure.—Miss S. Jackson.
Pairs.—I. Jenkins and Miss S. Garland.
Dancing.—Miss J. Torvill and C. Dean.

SHOOTING–BISLEY, 115th N.R.A., 1984

Queen's Prize.—1, D. F. P. Richards, 284 pts.; 2, Capt. N. P. Blampeid, 283; 3, R. M. Roberts, 283.

Prince of Wales Prize.—P. G. Kent.

St. George's Challenge Vase.—1, M. L. Kent, 148 pts.; 2, S. Belither, 148; 3, R. E. Hind, 148.

Grand Aggregate.—1, J. C. Bullock, 594 pts.; 2, G. W. Berman, 591; 3, L. E. King, 590.

Elcho Challenge Shield.—1, England, 1,668; 2, Scotland, 1,583; 3, Ireland, 1,572.

National Match.—1, England, 2,022; 2, Wales, 1,995; 3, Scotland, 1,992; 4, Ireland, 1,957.

Kolapore.—1, Jersey, 1,153; 2, Great Britain, 1,149; 3, Canada, 1,147.

International Service Rifle Match.—1, Great Britain, 2,490; 2, Canadian Forces, 2,227; 3, Central Military Command, U.A.E., 2,141.

Chancellor's Challenge Plate.—1, CURA, 1,110; 2, Oxford University, 1,049.

Inter-Services Long Range.—1, Territorial Army, 1,093; 2, Royal Air Force, 1,091; 3, Regular Army, 1,078.

Inter-Services Short Range.—1, Canadian Cadets, 1,113; 2, Canadian Forces, 1,106; 3, Regular Army, 1,102.

United Service.—1, Regular Army, 1,386; 2, Royal Marines, 1,292; 3, Royal Navy, 1,272.

Ashburton Shield.—1, Bedford, 521; 2, Harrow, 518; 3, Wellington, 516.

CLAY PIGEON SHOOTING, 1984

International Cup (Down-the-Line).—1, England, 7,386/7,500; 2, Wales, 7,358; 3, Scotland, 7,351; 4, Ireland, 7,344.

British Open Down-the-Line Championship.—S. Williams (Wales), 300/300.

Down-the-Line High Gun Trophy.—S. Williams (Wales), 600/600.

Mackintosh Trophy.—England, 7,386/7,500.

British Open Skeet Championship.—I. Macdonald, 100/100.

British Open Sporting Championship.—A. Harvison, 93/100.

Coronation Cup.—A. Benson, 379/400.

Grand Prix of Great Britain (Olympic Trap).—K. Borley, 191/200.

Grand Prix of Great Britain (International Skeet).—P. Oldring, 197/200.

Grand Prix of Great Britain (International Sporting).—B. Simpson, 130/150.

World Championship (International Sporting).—G. Cowler (G.B.), 183/200; *Juniors:* P. Foster (G.B.), 156/200; *Ladies:* D. Eyre (G.B.), 132/200; *Team:* Great Britain, 714/800.

European Championship (International Sporting).—A. J. Smith (G.B.), 190/200; *Juniors:* P. Foster (G.B.), 172/200; *Team:* Great Britain, 724/800.

Game Fair Championship.—A. Miller, 25/25.

BOXING, 1984

A.B.A. CHAMPIONSHIPS (Winners)

Light-Flyweight.—J. Lyon; *Flyweight.*—P. Clinton; *Bantam.*—J. Hyland; *Feather.*—K. Taylor; *Light.*—A. Dickson; *Light-Welter.*—D. Griffiths; *Welter.*—M. Hughes; *Light-Middle.*—R. Douglas; *Middle.*—B. Schumacher; *Light-Heavy.*—T. Wilson; *Heavy.*—D. Young; *Super Heavy.*—R. Wells.

PROFESSIONAL BOXING
WORLD (W.B.C.) CHAMPIONS

Heavy.—P. Thomas (U.S.A.); *Cruiser.*—C. de Leon (U.S.A.); *Light-Heavy.*—M. Spinks (U.S.A.); *Middle.*—M. Hagler (U.S.A.); *Light-Middle.*—T. Hearns (U.S.A.); *Welter.*—M. McCrory (U.S.A.); *Light-Welter.*—B. Costello (U.S.A.); *Light.*—E. Rosario (U.S.A.); *Super-Feather.*—vacant; *Feather.*—W. Gomez (Puerto Rico); *Super-Bantam.*—J. Garza (U.S.A.); *Bantam.*—A. Davila (U.S.A.); *Super-Fly.*—J. Watanabe (Japan); *Fly.*—G. Bernal (Mexico); *Light-Fly.*—J. Chang (Korea).

WORLD (W.B.A.) CHAMPIONS

Heavy.—G. Coetzee (S. Africa); *Cruiser.*—O. Ocasio (Puerto Rico); *Light-Heavy.*—M. Spinks (U.S.A.); *Middle.*—M. Hagler (U.S.A.); *Light-Middle.*—vacant; *Welter.*—D. Curry (U.S.A.); *Light-Welter.*—G. Hatcher (U.S.A.); *Light.*—L. Bramble (U.S.A.); *Super-Feather.*—R. Lockridge (U.S.A.); *Feather.*—E. Pedroza (Panama); *Super-Bantam.*—V. Callejas (Puerto Rico); *Bantam.*—R. Sandoval (U.S.A.); *Super-Fly.*—vacant; *Fly.*—S. Laciar (Argentina); *Light-Fly.*—F. Quiroz (Dominica).

BRITISH CHAMPIONS

Heavy.—D. Pearce; *Cruiser.*—vacant; *Light-Heavy.*—D. Andries; *Middle.*—M. Kaylor; *Light-Middle.*—J. Cable; *Welter.*—L. Honeyghan; *Light-Welter.*—C. McKenzie; *Light.*—G. Feeney; *Feather.*—B. McGuigan; *Bantam.*—J. Feeney; *Fly.*—H. Russell.

COMMONWEALTH CHAMPIONS

Heavy.—T. Berbick (Canada); *Cruiser.*—S. Lithgo (G.B.); *Light-Heavy.*—L. Mwale (Zambia); *Middle.*—M. Kaylor (G.B.); *Light-Middle.*—K. Salisbury (Australia); *Welter.*—vacant; *Light-Welter.*—B. Famous (Nigeria); *Light.*—C. Noel (Trinidad and Tobago); *Super-Feather.*—J. Sitchula (Zambia); *Feather.*—A. Nelson (Ghana); *Bantam.*—P. Ferrarri (Australia); *Fly.*—K. Wallace (G.B.).

EUROPEAN CHAMPIONS

Heavy.—L. Rodriguez (France); *Light-Heavy.*—A. Blanchard (Holland); *Middle.*—T. Sibson (G.B.); *Light-Middle.*—G. Steinherr (Germany); *Welter.*—G. Rosi (Italy); *Light-Welter.*—P. Oliva (Italy); *Light.*—R. Weller (Germany); *Super-Feather.*—P. Cowdell (G.B.); *Feather.*—B. McGuigan (G.B.); *Bantam.*—W. Giorgetti (Italy); *Fly.*—C. Magri (G.B.).

SNOOKER AND BILLIARDS

World Professional Snooker Championship.—S. Davis beat J. White by 18–16 frames.

Benson and Hedges Masters Snooker Tournament.—J. White beat T. Griffiths by 9–5.

U.K. Professional Snooker Championship.—A. Higgins beat S. Davis by 16–15.

World Doubles Snooker Championship.—S. Davis and T. Meo beat T. Knowles and J. White by 10–2.

World Professional Billiards Championship.—M. Wildman (G.B.) beat E. Charlton (Australia) by 1,045 to 1,012.

World Amateur Billiards Championship.—M. Ferreira (India) beat S. Agrawal (India) by 3,933 to 2,744.

OXFORD AND CAMBRIDGE
PRINCIPAL EVENTS AND WINNERS, 1983–84

Event (with date of first meeting)	Summary of Results			Results 1983–84
	Ox.	Camb.	Drawn	
Cricket (1827)	46	53	41	Oxford
Boat Race (1829)	61	68	1	Oxford
Athletics (1864)	54	49	7	Oxford
Football—				
Association (1873–4)	38	42	21	Draw
Rugby (1871–2)	43	46	13	Camb.
Golf (1878)	37	51	5	Camb.
Hockey (1890)	28	38	15	Camb.

OTHER UNIVERSITY EVENTS AND WINNERS, 1983–84

Rackets .... Cambridge
Polo .... Cambridge
Real Tennis .... Cambridge

MOTOR CYCLING, 1984

Manx Grand Prix 1,000 c.c.—1, D. Pither (Honda); 2, I. Ogden (Suzuki); 3, G. King (Suzuki).

Senior 500 c.c. T.T., Isle of Man.—1, R. McElnea (Suzuki); 2, R. Marshall (Honda); 3, T. Nation (Suzuki).

Junior 250 c.c. T.T., Isle of Man.—1, G. McGregor (EMC); 2, C. Williams (Yamaha); 3, B. Reid (EMC).

British 500 c.c. Grand Prix (Silverstone).—R. Mamola (Honda).

Transatlantic Trophy.—U.S.A.

MOTOR SPORT, 1984

Grand Prix of Europe, 1983.—(*Brands Hatch*).—1, N. Piquet (Brabham); 2, A. Prost (Renault); 3, N. Mansell (Lotus–Renault).

Dallas Grand Prix.—1, K. Rosberg (Williams); 2, R. Arnoux (Ferrari); 3, E. de Angelis (Lotus).

Monaco Grand Prix.—1, A. Prost (McLaren); 2, A. Senna (Toleman Hart); 3, S. Bellof (Tyrrell–Ford).

French Grand Prix.—1, N. Lauda (McLaren); 2, P. Tambay (Renault); 3, N. Mansell (Lotus–Renault).

San Marino Grand Prix.—1, A. Prost (McLaren); 2, R. Arnoux (Ferrari); 3, E. de Angelis (Lotus).

British Grand Prix.—(*Brands Hatch*).—1, N. Lauda (McLaren); 2, D. Warwick (Renault); 3, A. Senna (Toleman–Hart).

Brazilian Grand Prix.—1, A. Prost (McLaren); 2, K. Rosberg (Williams); 3, E. de Angelis (Lotus).

Italian Grand Prix.—1, N. Lauda (McLaren); 2, M. Alboreto (Ferrari); 3, R. Patrese (Alfa Romeo).

Austrian Grand Prix.—1, N. Lauda (McLaren); 2, N. Piquet (Brabham); 3, M. Alboreto (Ferrari).

German Grand Prix.—1, A. Prost (McLaren); 2, N. Lauda (McLaren); 3, D. Warwick (Renault).

Canadian Grand Prix.—1, N. Piquet (Brabham); 2, N. Lauda (McLaren); 3, A. Prost (McLaren).

Dutch Grand Prix.—1, A. Prost (McLaren); 2, N. Lauda (McLaren); 3, N. Mansell (Lotus–Renault).

Belgian Grand Prix.—1, M. Alboreto (Ferrari); 2, D. Warwick (Renault); 3, R. Arnoux (Ferrari).

Detroit Grand Prix.—1, N. Piquet (Brabham); 2, M. Brundle (Tyrrell–Ford); 3, E. de Angelis (Lotus).

South African Grand Prix.—1, N. Lauda (McLaren); 2, A. Prost (McLaren); 3, D. Warwick (Renault).

Le Mans (24-hour).—H. Pescarole and K. Ludwig (Porsche).

Monte Carlo Rally.—W. Rohrl (Audi Quattro).

Lombard R.A.C. Rally, 1983.—S. Blomqvist (Audi Quattro).

SPORTS REPRESENTATIVE BODIES

ANGLING.—National Anglers' Council, 11 Cowgate, Peterborough PE1 1LZ. *Exec. Dir.*, P. H. Tombleson, O.B.E.

ASSOCIATION FOOTBALL.—The Football Association. *Gen. Sec.*, E. A. Croker, 16 Lancaster Gate, W.2.

ATHLETICS.—Amateur Athletic Association. *Gen. Sec.*, M. A. Farrell, Francis House, Francis Street, SW1P 1DL.

— British Amateur Athletic Board. *Gen. Sec.*, N. Cooper, Francis House, Francis Street, SW1P 1DL.

— Women's Amateur Athletic Association. *Hon. Sec.*, Miss M. Hartman, C.B.E., Francis House, Francis Street, SW1P 1DE.

BADMINTON.—Badminton Association of England. *Chief Exec.*, Air Vice-Marshal G. C. Lamb, C.B., C.B.E., A.F.C., National Badminton Centre, Loughton Lodge, Bradwell Road, Milton Keynes, Bucks.

BASKET BALL.—English Basket Ball Association. *Dir.*, K. K. Mitchell, O.B.E., Dept. of Physical Education, The University, Leeds.

BILLIARDS.—Billiards and Snooker Control Council. *Chairman*, S. Brooke, Coronet House, Queen Street, Leeds LS1 2TN.

BOBSLEIGH.—British Bobsleigh Association, 118 Eaton Square, S.W.1. *Sec.*, Camilla Fane.

BOWLS.—English Bowling Association. *Sec.*, J. F. Elms, 2a Iddesleigh Road, Bournemouth BH3 7JR.

BOXING.—Amateur Boxing Association of England, Francis House, Francis Street, SW1P 1DE.—*Sec.*, L. Mills, M.B.E.

— British Boxing Board of Control, 70 Vauxhall Bridge Road, S.W.1.—*Gen. Sec.*, R. L. Clarke, O.B.E.

CANOEING.—British Canoe Union, Flexel House, 45–47 High Street, Addlestone, Weybridge, Surrey KT15 1JV.—*Dir.*, R. W. Emes, M.B.E.

CLAY PIGEON SHOOTING.—Clay Pigeon Shooting Association. *Dir.*, A. P. Page, 107 Epping New Road, Buckhurst Hill, Essex IG9 5TQ.

CRICKET.—International Cricket Conference, Lord's Ground, N.W.8. *Chmn.*, F. G. Mann, C.B.E., D.S.O., M.C.; *Sec.*, J. A. Bailey. Cricket Council, Lord's Ground, N.W.8. *Chmn.*, C. H. Palmer, C.B.E.; *Sec.*, D. B. Carr.

CROQUET.—Croquet Association, The Hurlingham Club, Ranelagh Gardens, SW6 3PR. *Sec.*, B. C. Macmillan.

CYCLING.—British Cycling Federation, 16 Upper Woburn Place, WC1H 0QE.—*Sec.*, L. A. Unwin.

FENCING.—Amateur Fencing association. *Sec.*, Mrs. J. Pienne, 83 Perham Road, W. Kensington, W.14.

GLIDING.—British Gliding Association, Kimberley House, Vaughan Way, Leicester. *Sec.*, B. Rolfe.

GOLF.—Royal and Ancient Golf Club, St. Andrews, Fife. *Sec.*, M. F. Bonallack, O.B.E.

— English Golf Union. *Sec.*, I. R. H. M. A. Erskine, 12A Denmark Street, Wokingham, Berks.

— Ladies' Golf Union, 12, The Links, St. Andrews, Fife KY16 9JB.—*Gen. Administrator*, Miss A. McIntosh.

GYMNASTICS.—British Amateur Gymnastics Association, 2 Buckingham Avenue East, Slough, Berks SL1 3EA. *Sec.*, T. D. Rowe.

HOCKEY.—Hockey Association.—*Sec.-Gen.*, Col. D. M. R. Eagan, 16 Upper Woburn Place, WC1H 0QD.

— All England Women's Hockey Association, 3rd Flr, Argyle House, 29–31 Euston Road, N.W.1.

JUDO.—British Judo Association, 16 Upper Woburn Place, WC1H 0QH. *Gen. Sec.*, Miss G. M. Kenneally.

LACROSSE.—English Lacrosse Union. *Hon. Sec.*, R. Balls, 70 High Road, Rayleigh, Essex SS6 7AD.

— All England Women's Lacrosse Association, 16 Upper Woburn Place, WC1H 0QJ. *Organising Secretary*, Mrs. J. Cantell.

LAWN TENNIS.—Lawn Tennis Association. *Sec.*, J. C. U. James, Barons Court, W.14.

— International Tennis Federation, Church Road, Wimbledon, S.W.19.

MOTOR CYCLING.—Auto-Cycle Union, Millbuck House, Corporation Street, Rugby, Warwicks. CV21 2DN. *Sec.-Gen.*, K. E. Shierson.

MOUNTAINEERING.—British Mountaineering Council, Crawford House, Precinct Centre, Booth Street East, Manchester. *Gen. Sec.*, D. D. Gray.

NETBALL.—All England Netball Association Ltd., Francis House, Francis Street, SW1P 1DE.

ORIENTEERING.—British Orienteering Federation, 41 Dale Road, Matlock, Derbyshire DE4 3LT. *Professional Officer*, R. F. Mason.

POLO.—The Hurlingham Polo Association, Ambersham Farm, Ambersham, Midhurst, W. Sussex GU29 0BX. *Hon. Sec.*, Lt.-Col. A. F. Harper, D.S.O.

RACING.—The Jockey Club (incorporating National Hunt Committee), 42 Portman Square, W1H 0EN *Sec.*, C. Foster.

RIFLE SHOOTING.—National Rifle Association. *Sec.*, Brig. P. G. A. Prescott, M.C., Bisley Camp, Brookwood, Woking, Surrey.

— National Small-bore Rifle Association. *Sec.*, R. C. Russell, Lord Roberts House, Bisley Camp, Brookwood, Woking, Surrey.

ROWING.—Amateur Rowing Association. *Exec. Sec.*, D. Lunn-Rockliffe, 6 Lower Mall, W6 9DJ.

RUGBY FIVES.—Rugby Fives Association. *Hon. Sec.*, P. J. Reeder, 32 Dulwich Common, SE21 7EX.

RUGBY FOOTBALL.—The Rugby Football Union, Whitton Road, Twickenham, Middx. *Sec.*, Air Commodore R. H. G. Weighill, C.B.E., D.F.C.

— The Rugby Football League. *Sec.-Gen.*, D. S. Oxley, 180 Chapeltown Road, Leeds LS7 4HT.

SKATING.—National Skating Association of Great Britain. *Gen. Administrator*, E. Waughray, 117 Charterhouse Street, E.C.1.

SKI-ING.—British Ski Federation. *Sec.*, Brig. A. A. Fielder, 118 Eaton Square, SW1W 9AF.

SQUASH RACKETS.—Squash Rackets Association. *Chief Executive*, R. I. Morris, Francis House, Francis Street, SW1P 1DE.

— Women's Squash Rackets Association. *Sec.*, Miss C. Myers, 345 Upper Richmond Road West, S.W.14.

SWIMMING.—Amateur Swimming Association, Harold Fern House, Derby Square, Loughborough, Leics. LE11 0AL. *Sec.*, H. W. Hassall.

TABLE TENNIS.—English Table Tennis Association. *Gen. Sec.*, A. W. Shipley, 21 Claremont, Hastings.

TOBOGGANING.—British Racing Tobogganing Association.—*Pres.*, Dr. R. Liversedge, Oak Cottage, Flaunden, Herts.

UNDERWATER SWIMMING.—British Sub-Aqua Club, 16 Upper Woburn Place, WC1H 0QW. *General Manager*, D. D. Robertson.

VOLLEYBALL.—British Volleyball Association, 128 Melton Road, West Bridgford, Nottingham. *National Dir.*, G. Bulman.

WALKING.—Race Walking Association. *Hon. Sec.*, P. Marlow, 65 Lordship Lane, S.E.22.

WATER SKI-ING.—British Water Ski Federation, 390 City Road, E.C.1. *Sec.*, Ms. G. Hill.

WEIGHT-LIFTING.—British Amateur Weight Lifters Association. *Hon. Sec.*, W. Holland, O.B.E., 3 Iffley Turn, Iffley, Oxford.

WRESTLING.—English Olympic Wrestling Association. *Sec.*, H. I. Jacob, O.B.E., 2 Huxley Drive, Bramhall, Stockport, Cheshire SK7 2PH.

YACHTING.—Royal Yachting Association, Victoria Way, Woking, Surrey. *Sec.-Gen.*, J. Durie.

SPORTS COUNCIL.—16 Upper Woburn Place, WC1H 0QP. *Dir.-Gen.*, J. Wheatley.

DRAMA SUMMARY, 1983–84

After several years of gloom and despondency in the theatre world a few rays of light were seen in late 1983 and 1984. At one stage in 1982, almost one-quarter of London theatres were dark. In September 1983, only six of the 46 theatres in the Society of West End Theatres were shut, but most were busy again by Christmas. Attendances in 1983, with some nine million seats sold, were 6 per cent up on 1982, itself 5 per cent up on 1981.

The air of optimism prevailed, with the reopening of the splendidly restored Old Vic, to the huge investment in Lloyd Webber's *Starlight Express*, which seemed set to run and run ... Equity agreed that the musical *Snoopy* could present Sunday performances, an experiment which was reportedly very successful, although other managements have not found it so easy to reach agreements with the unions involved.

Various theatres changed hands: the Mermaid, Lord Miles's brainchild, which has never managed to settle down satisfactorily since its reopening, was sold by the Corporation of the City of London in September 1983, despite his opposition. It was bought by Gomba Holdings, who already owned the Garrick and Duchess Theatres. The Phoenix closed in July 1984, causing the premature demise of the musical *Peg*. The theatre had opened in 1930 with Coward's *Private Lives*, but may be shut for some time as it forms part of a block which may be redeveloped. The Theatre of Comedy Company, which took over the Shaftesbury Theatre in early 1983, in September acquired the Ambassadors for experimental work and unusual revivals. Anthony Quayle, for nine years an actor-manager at Stratford, founded a new touring theatre company, called Compass, which opened in Blackpool in April 1984 with the 18th century comedy *The Clandestine Marriage*. Having taken the play to eight provincial centres, the Company found a theatre in London in June when the Edgar Wallace thriller *On the Spot* (written in three days in 1929) failed to draw the crowds, and closed prematurely at the Albery.

The National Theatre had its fingers burned when its musical *Jean Seberg* closed early after a critical slating. The show had been dogged by bad luck, with cast injury causing the first night to be delayed. After 22 previews, played, apparently, to appreciative packed houses, the critics' views caused attendances to drop to half to two-thirds of capacity. Many people considered that the National Theatre should not be used for a Broadway "try-out", although if the show had been a success, some kudos and financial benefit would have accrued to the Company. The story of the unknown teenager who, with no training and little talent, was plucked from obscurity to "star" in Otto Preminger's film *Saint Joan*, became involved in militant black politics, and an F.B.I. target, was a peculiarly American Drama. However, whether or not the story was a suitable subject for a musical drama, the show had no strong songs to redeem it, and two actresses playing the tragic heroine to add to the confusion. It was ironic that one of the National's great successes, the classic musical *Guys and Dolls*, was brought back to plug the gaps in the programme.

Bad luck also beset a new musical entitled *Roza*, based on "La Vie devant Soi" by Romain Gary (Jean Seberg's husband). Having been advertised for some months, with a June opening scheduled at the Adelphi, and Hal Prince as director—his first London Show since *Evita*—it was cancelled on the very day rehearsals were due to begin, when the greatest proportion of its £1 million finance fell through in America. The musical fantasy "*Y*" at the Piccadilly, for which the theatre had been expensively con-

verted, closed with reportedly huge losses. The Cambridge Theatre was sold, and will reopen as a Theatre of Magic.

Awards

In the premier London theatre awards, the 29th Standard Drama Awards, the Sydney Edwards award for best director was given to Yuri Lyubimov, for *Crime and Punishment*. Based on Dostoevsky's classic novel, the play would have confused those unfamiliar with the book. However, the production was stunning, with the Russian Director drawing out remarkable performances from the English cast. Michael Pennington in particular excelled as Raskolnikov (and dieted three stones from his weight to play the part). Sadly, Lyubimov was fired from his post at the Taganka Theatre in Moscow while in Britain. He had criticised the bureaucrats who censored his plays in an interview in *The Times*. It was unfortunate that the production did not transfer to the West End.

The award for best actor was won by Derek Jacobi, for his four superb rôles with the Royal Shakespeare Company in *Peer Gynt, Cyrano de Bergerac, The Tempest* and *Much Ado About Nothing*. Best actress was Geraldine McEwan for her Mrs. Malaprop in *The Rivals* at the Olivier.

Christopher Hampton's *Tales from Hollywood* was adjudged best comedy. The playwright had resurrected the Hungarian writer, Odon von Horvath (who was killed in Paris in 1938 when a branch of a tree under which he was sheltering fell on him) and transported him to Los Angeles in the 1950s to observe the effects of the American way of life on other European emigrés, such as Thomas Mann, the Marx Brothers, and Brecht—at whose expense much fun was had. The play was witty and well acted, although it was notable that the American characters were not drawn as sympathetically as the emigrés, which probably accounted for the play's cool reception in the U.S.A., even though it had been commmissioned in Los Angeles.

The South African playwright Athol Fugard won the best play award for his *Master Harold and the Boys*, seen at the National's Cottesloe Theatre. This short, autobiographical piece, brilliantly acted by members of the Market Theatre Company of Johannesburg, concerned the relationship between a white boy and a black waiter, the one instructing the other in the knowledge he gained at school, whilst in turn being instructed in being a decent human being. The South African Authorities had tried, but failed to ban this very personal and moving work; it confirmed Fugard's reputation. It had also enjoyed success on Broadway.

The best musical award went to *The Little Shop of Horrors*, a lively, witty musical with Faustian undertones, based on a 1960 film by Roger Corman. Set in a florist's shop, it concerned a small cactus plant which thrived on human flesh and blood, eventually taking over the stage and threatening the audience. An off-Broadway hit, distinguished by a marvellous comic performance from Ellen Greene, the musical—and the plant, named Audrey II—flourished at the Comedy Theatre.

The most promising playwright award was given to Phil Young for *Crystal Clear* (noted last year).

Old Vic, New Ed

The Old Vic Theatre has experienced many changes in its fortunes since it was opened as the Royal

Coburg in 1818. Lilian Baylis owned it from 1914 to 1937, and it housed the National Theatre Company until their South Bank home was opened. In recent years it has been more down than up, and when it was bought for £550,000 in June 1982, few people can have anticipated what was in store for it. The purchaser was a Canadian businessman known as "Honest" Ed Mirvish—an epithet unlikely to endear him immediately to the more reserved British. However, it transpired that Mirvish had bought, restored and made a success of the Royal Alexandra Theatre in Toronto in 1962, and although he had outbid the ubiquitous Lloyd Webber, omens were propitious for the Old Vic. An expensive programme of restoration and refurbishment was undertaken, which cost some £2 million, twice the budgeted amount, when structural defects were revealed. Nevertheless, the Old Vic reopened on time, and was a splendid sight.

Whilst attitudes to the Canadian "interloper" softened, his insistence on introducing the subscription system that he operated successfully abroad was doomed to failure—so the cynics thought. (After all, the British would not book six shows, even at a discount.) However, early signs were favourable, and Mirvish began to earn respect and admiration. Furthermore, an Old Vic annexe was loaned, free of charge, to the National Theatre to use as a rehearsal studio for five years.

The Old Vic reopened, somewhat ironically, with a new work by Lloyd Webber's erstwhile partner, Tim Rice, this time in collaboration with Stephen Oliver. *Blondel*—"a musical of the '80s—the 1180s"—was a lightweight piece, based on the story of the troubadour who travelled through Europe seeking out the imprisoned monarch Richard I. Relying rather heavily on anachronistic, schoolboyish humour, *Blondel* had some enjoyable moments, and transferred successfully to the Aldwych.

Blondel was followed by David Pownall's *Master Class*, a fascinating piece about the Soviet ban on "formalist" musical composition. Set in the Kremlin, the play had Prokofiev and Shostakovich visiting Stalin and Marshall Zhdanov, and attempting to justify their works, then helping Stalin compose a cantata based on a Georgian poem. With serious points to make about the place of art in a tyrannical society, the work had some marvellous moments, and was most enjoyable, also receiving a well deserved West End transfer.

To round off a varied and interesting first season, the Old Vic also presented a successful Canadian production of *The Mikado*; the Market Theatre Company, Johannesburg, production, *Saturday Night at the Palace*; John Arden's modern classic, *Serjeant Musgrave's Dance* (which divides the critics as much now as when first produced at the Royal Court in 1959), with Albert Finney starring and directing; and Sandy Wilson's delightful 1953 pastiche of early musicals, *The Boyfriend*, which was well received.

Musicals

Peter Nichols' *Poppy*, the story of the Opium War between Britain and China from 1839–42, was rechoreographed and rewritten, and produced again by the Royal Shakespeare Company at the Adelphi. It was intended that the show should transfer to Broadway, but after difficulties raised for the British cast by American Equity, who wanted to restrict them to ten weeks only, the deal was cancelled.

Dear Anyone, an English musical set in New York, about an "agony-aunt", was, in spite of the years devoted to its creation, disappointing. *Snoopy*, based on the famous "Peanuts" cartoon strip, was billed as the canine answer to *Cats*, and was surprisingly engaging. *West Side Story* was faithfully recreated 15 years after its first British production. Its director, Tom Abbott, had been a Jet in the original 1956 Broadway production.

At the Palace, *On Your Toes* reappeared, having previously been seen there in 1937 on its London opening. George Abbott, 96-year-old co-author of the show, supervised the production, which in 1983 won Broadway Tony Awards for best revival, and for Makarova's performance as the Russian ballet star. Ron Moody recreated his marvellous Fagin in Lionel Bart's *Oliver!*, while *Hello Dolly* served as a star vehicle for female impersonator Danny la Rue, with no other justification for the reappearance of this overrated piece. Bob Fosse's tribute to American dance, called simply *Dancin'*, ran for four years on Broadway, and won a Tony Award, but although the American cast were technically adroit, and the tunes familiar, the show was slick without inspiration, and the 14 dances not sufficient to sustain it without a plot. It had been intended that the American cast would be replaced by a British troupe after six months, but the eventuality never arose: *Dancin'* closed after barely two months. *42nd Street* at the same theatre, based on the 1932 film, had fine dancing with a plot to sustain it, but the preponderance of dated American musicals in London has tended to make theatregoers more discriminating in what they actually choose to see.

Accordingly, home-grown quality products continue to flourish, with *Evita* and *Cats* still playing to full houses. It was thus apparent that a new Lloyd Webber show could hardly fail, and *Starlight Express*, with lyrics by Richard Stilgoe, choreography by Arlene Phillips, design by John Napier, and directed by Trevor Nunn had all the ingredients for success. The show did not disappoint on grounds of excitement or theatrical experience. Some 1,300 of the Apollo Victoria's 2,700 seats were removed to accommodate roller skating tracks around the theatre, on which the cast of 33 hurtled at speeds of around 40 m.p.h. £2 million was spent on the production, with £1·4 million on conversion work alone. The special effects were stunning, and as pure theatre, the show was inspired and thrilling. However, since its long-term future seems assured, it is not really churlish to state that the plot, or what there is of it, about express trains racing to discover the fastest one, becomes repetitive, if not downright silly and childish, but Lloyd Webber and his talented colleagues deserve much credit for the boost they have given to London theatre.

Drama

Alan Ayckbourn's output has shown some diminution of his powers of late. His technical brilliance is not in question, but the novelty of multiple variations in his plays has begun to wear thin. His 1982 play *Intimate Exchanges* surfaced in Greenwich in 1984, and gained a West End transfer. It required two actors to play ten characters, with combinations of 30 scenes making eight different versions, the turn of events hingeing on whether or not a headmaster's wife lit her first cigarette of the day before or after 6 o'clock. In Scarborough, his new plays include a comedy thriller, *It Could be Any One of Us*, with two possible murder victims and five suspects making up the permutations, and *A Chorus of Disapproval*, about a widower seeking companionship.

Michael Frayn's *Noises Off* has been very successful on both sides of the Atlantic. His new play, *Benefactors*, was more serious, but beautifully constructed. Set in 1968, it concerned the relationships between two couples, and the plan of one of the husbands, an architect, to replace old houses with residential tower blocks, in which he is eventually thwarted when the other leads a protest against it. Michael Frayn also translated and adapted Jean Anouilh's *Le Nombril*,—here, *Number One*—with Leo McKern playing an elderly French playwright writing a play about self-centredness. Anouilh suffered a heart attack soon after completing the play, and seems unlikely to write any more plays.

Dennis Potter, who has had a long and distinguished career writing for television, has now written his first stage play. *Sufficient Carbohydrate* followed a "soap opera" format, but the plot did not quite rise to the dialogue. Stephen Fagan's *The Hard Shoulder*, which surfaced in Hampstead in 1982, reappeared at the Aldwych a year later. This well-constructed comedy concerned a wine merchant's attempts to make his fortune in property deals, despite a threatened motorway scheme, and his subsequent plan to burn the property for the insurance money.

Charles Dyer, who wrote *Rattle of a Simple Man* in 1962, resurfaced with *Lovers Dancing*, a well-acted drama about two couples who meet each year to mark a ballroom dancing competition, after which a child had been conceived.

A group of distinguished British actors have formed a company to be known as United British Artists. Including Albert Finney, Maggie Smith, Glenda Jackson, and Richard Johnson, they were responsible for the disturbing—but factual—drama *The Biko Inquest*, an account of the inquest into the death of the Black Consciousness leader in South Africa, Steve Biko, based on transcripts of the hearing. Albert Finney, as Kentridge, counsel for Biko's family, led a distinguished cast.

Pack of Lies by Hugh Whitemore was an incisive study of the nature of betrayal, and was based on the real situation in which a suburban family found themselves, when they were used by the intelligence service to trap the Krogers and Lonsdale, who were Soviet spies.

Among the more notable revivals, *The Aspern Papers*, adapted from Henry James's story by Michael Redgrave, was produced as a tribute to her father by Vanessa Redgrave, making a welcome return to the London stage. The Women's Playhouse Trust, formed in 1980 to provide more opportunities for women in the theatre, resurrected *The Lucky Chance* at the Royal Court. Written in 1686 by Aphra Behn, one-time spy for Charles II and the first female English professional dramatist, the play was thought "too indecent" when originally performed!

NATIONAL THEATRE

The World première of *Glengarry Glen Ross*, by American playwright David Mamet, was given at the Cottesloe in September 1983. This powerful drama concerned the machinations of the world of real estate in Chicago. Equally impressive was *Strider*, a parable of 19th century Russia, told as the story of a horse, and the adaptation of Orwell's *Animal Farm* was a striking portrayal of tyranny. The revival of a traditional Victorian pantomime, *Cinderella*, at the Lyttelton, was misconceived, but Otway's 1682 drama, *Venice Preserv'd*, was an effective vehicle for McKellen and Pennington, as it had been for Gielgud and Schofield in 1953. Clifford Odets' most popular play, *Golden Boy*, was dramatically effective, even if its tale of a violinist risking his hands as a boxer was somewhat contrived. *Wild Honey* was an adaptation by Michael Frayn of Chekhov's first, untitled, play (more commonly known as *Platonov*).

At the Olivier, apart from the ill-starred *Jean Seberg*, Frances de la Tour gave an inspired perfor-mance in Shaw's *St. Joan*, while John Mortimer's *A Little Hotel on the Side*, an adaptation of Feydeau's 1894 farce—more commonly known as *Hotel Parad-iso*—showed that there are few experiences more amusing than an expertly controlled version of a well-constructed farce. An unusual revival was Machiavelli's *Mandragola*, written in 1512, but set—not wholly successfully—in modern Venice.

ROYAL SHAKESPEARE COMPANY

While the National Theatre was disappointed to receive only a 3 per cent rise in its grant from the Arts Council, the Royal Shakespeare Company fared somewhat better. Having survived an investigation into its finances commissioned by the Arts Minister, and been cleared of suggested inefficiency and extravagance, the R.S.C. was deemed to be under-funded if it was expected to continue as a flagship of the arts, and had its deficit wiped out and extra finance provided. The future of its London showcase, the Barbican, thus seemed assured; in its second season, it had played to 90 per cent of its capacity, with some notable Stratford transfers.

At Stratford, the 1983 season was completed with Adrian Noble's production of *Measure for Measure*, which moved to London in April 1984. *Henry V* opened the 1984 season, with Kenneth Branagh excellent in the title role. McDiarmid's Shylock in the *Merchant of Venice* caused much controversy: his portrayal of the Jew as a comic villain was contrasted unfavourably with the understated brilliance of Alec Guinness's interpretation in the Chichester production. In *Richard III*, Antony Sher gave a superb performance as the much-maligned monarch, hurtling about the stage on crutches which became an extension of his demonic personality.

At The Other Place, a varied programme included revivals of Calderon's classic Spanish drama, *Life's a Dream*, and Jonson's *Volpone*. However, although the R.S.C.'s Stratford base showed the Company in fine fettle, with a string of excellent productions, and successful transfers to the Barbican, the most exciting development was the announcement in September 1984 of a new Stratford theatre. It transpired that an anonymous benefactor had made the funds available to enable a project last mooted in 1978 to come to fruition. The theatre will be known as The Swan, and should open in 1986 on the site of the present rehearsal room and conference hall. It is anticipated that the theatre will be used largely for non-Shakespearian plays, from the period 1570 to 1750, and will seat 430 people (compared with The Other Place's 150 seats).

At the Barbican, apart from the Stratford transfers, which seemed to improve with age and the change of theatre, David Edgar's *Maydays* was a stimulating, original political drama on the grand scale, spanning 25 years of contemporary history. J. M. Barrie's *Peter Pan* reappeared in the much-praised Barbican production, and John Whiting's *The Devils*, last seen in London in 1961, made a welcome appearance at the Pit.

PRODUCTIONS

London productions between September 1, 1983 and August 31, 1984, included the following:

ADELPHI: Strand, W.C.2. (1983) Nov. 22. *Poppy*, book and lyrics by Peter Nichols, music by Monty Norman, with Alfred Marks, Geoffrey Hutchings, Antonia Ellis and David Firth, directed by Terry Hands, designed by Farrah, costumes by Alexander Reid (Royal Shakespeare Company production).

ALBERY: St. Martin's Lane, W.C.2. (1983) Oct. 27. *Lovers Dancing* by Charles Dyer, with Paul Eddington, Colin Blakely, Georgina Hale and Jane Carr, dir. by Donald McWhinnie, des. by Peter Rice. (1984) Jan. 31. *Sufficient Carbohydrate* by Dennis Potter (Hampstead production). May 9. *On the Spot* by Edgar Wallace, with Simon Callow, James Warwick, John Bluthal and James Faulkner, adapted and dir. by Robert Walker. June 7. *The Clandestine Marriage* by David Garrick and George Colman, with Roy Kinnear, Anthony Quayle, Joyce Redman, Belinda Lang, John Quentin and Fiona McArthur, dir. by Anthony Quayle, des. by Tanya Moiseiwitsch.

ALDWYCH: W.C.2. (1983) Oct. 3. *The Hard Shoulder* by Stephen Fagan, with Stephen Moore, Liza Goddard, Peter Blythe and Glynn Owen, dir. by Nancy Meckler, des. by Tanya McCallin. Dec. 14. *Oliver!* by Lionel Bart, with Ron Moody, Peter Bayliss, Meg Johnson, David Garlick, Anthony Pearson and Jackie Marks, dir. by Peter Coe. (1984) Jan. 20. *Blondel* by Tim Rice and Stephen Oliver (Old Vic production).

AMBASSADORS: West St., Cambridge Circus, W.C.2. (1983) Nov. 1. *Sister Mary Ignatius Explains It All for You* and *The Actor's Nightmare* by Christopher Durang, with Maria Aitken and Christopher Timothy, dir. by Richard Digby Day. Dec. 20. *Special Occasions*, written and dir. by Bernard Slade, with John Alderton and Jan Waters. (1984) March 8. *Loot* by Joe Orton, with Leonard Rossiter, Gemma Craven, Neil Pearson and Paul McGann, dir. by Jonathan Lynn. May 31. *The Importance* by John Hugh Dean, with Robert Dorning, Patrick Ryecart, Sheila Bernette and Judy Campbell, dir. by Tony Craven. Aug. 10. *Intimate Exchanges* written and dir. by Alan Ayckbourn (Greenwich production).

APOLLO: Shaftesbury Avenue, W.1. (1983) Sept. 27. *The Country Girl* by Clifford Odets, with Hannah Gordon, Martin Shaw, John Stride and Stephen Hoye, dir. by Robin Lefevre, des. by John Byrne. (1984) July 26. *Corpse!* by Gerald Moon, with Keith Baxter and Milo O'Shea, dir. by John Tillinger, des. by Alan Tagg.

APOLLO VICTORIA: S.W.1. (1984) March 27. *Starlight Express*, music by Andrew Lloyd Webber, lyrics by Richard Stilgoe, with Jeffrey Daniel, Stephanie Lawrence, Tom Jobe, Lon Satton, Jeff Shankley and Ray Shell, dir. by Trevor Nunn, des. by John Napier, lighting by David Hersey, choreography by Arlene Phillips.

ARTS: Gt. Newport St., W.C.2. (1984) Feb. 1. *Loving Women* by Pam Gems, with David Beames, Marion Bailey and Gwyneth Strong, dir. by Philip Davis. April 5. *Long Day's Journey into Night* by Eugene O'Neill, with Darlene Johnson, Trevor Martin, Michael Deacon, Sean Mathias and Wendy Miller, dir. by Ludovica Villar-Hauser.

BARBICAN: E.C.2. (1983) Oct. 14. *Maydays* by David Edgar, with John Shrapnel, Ken Bones, Tony Church, Bob Peck, Antony Sher and Alison Steadman, dir. by Ron Daniels, des. by John Gunter. Sept. 13. Shakespeare's *The Tempest*, with Derek Jacobi, Bob Peck, Christopher Benjamin, Ian Talbot, Mark Rylance and Alice Krige, dir. by Ron Daniels, des. by Maria Björnson. Dec. 17. *Peter Pan* by J. M. Barrie, with Mark Rylance, Stephen Moore, Katy Behean, Edward Petherbridge and Frances Tomelty, dir. by John Caird, des. by John Napier. (1984) April 17. Shakespeare's *Measure for Measure*, with Daniel Massey and Juliet Stevenson, dir. by Adrian Noble, des. by Bob Crowley. May 8. Shakespeare's *The Comedy of Errors*, with Richard O'Callaghan, Paul Greenwood, Peter McEnery and Zoë Wanamaker, dir. by Adrian Noble, des. by Ultz. May 29. Shakespeare's *Julius Caesar*, with Emrys James, Peter McEnery, Gemma Jones, David Schofield and Joseph O'Conor, dir. by Ron Daniels, des. by Farrah. July 24. *The Happiest Days of Your Life* by John Dighton, with Peggy Mount, Sheila Ballantine, Maria Aitken, Richard O'Callaghan, John Cater, Paul Greenwood and Griffith Jones, dir. by Clifford Williams, des. by Carl Toms. Aug. 22. Shakespeare's *Twelfth Night*, with Miles Anderson, Emrys James, Gemma Jones, Stephen Moore and Richard O'Callaghan, dir. by John Caird, des. by Robin Don.

BARBICAN PIT: (1983) Sept. 8. *Molière* by Mikhail Bulgakov, adapted by Dusty Hughes, with Antony Sher, John Carlisle and Penelope Beaumont, dir. by Bill Alexander, des. by Ralph Koltai. Oct. 19. *The Custom of the Country* by Nicholas Wright, with Sinead Cusack, Sara Kestelman, Bruce Myers, Tom Mannion, David Bradley, Christopher Guard and Josette Simon, dir. by David Jones, des. by Ralph Koltai. (1984) Jan. 2. *Softcops* by Caryl Churchill, with Ian Talbot, Malcolm Storry and Geoffrey Freshwater, dir. by Howard Davies. April 11. *Volpone* by Ben Jonson, with Richard Griffiths, Miles Anderson, Gemma Jones and Julie Peasgood, dir. by Bill Alexander, des. by Alison Chitty. May 2. *Life's a Dream* by Calderon, adapted by Adrian Mitchell and John Barton, with Miles Anderson, Barbara Kellerman, Charles Kay, Anthony O'Donnell, Lesley Duff and Christopher Neame, dir. by John Barton, des. by Christopher Morley. May 23. *The Time of Your Life* by William Saroyan, with Trevor Peacock, Daniel Massey, Zoë Wanamaker and Bruce Alexander, dir. by Howard Davies. July 25. *Red Star* by Charles Wood, with Richard Griffiths, David Schofield and Geoffrey Beevers, dir. by John Caird. Aug. 23. *The Devils* by John Whiting, with Peter McEnery, Estelle Kohler, Geoffrey Beevers and Timothy Knightley, dir. by John Barton, des. by Christopher Morley. Rooftop production: May 22. Shakespeare's *Hamlet*, with Robert Lindsay, Philip Madoc, Alison Fiske and Geraldine Alexander, dir. Braham Murray.

CAMBRIDGE: Earlham St., Cambridge Circus, W.C.2. (1983) Nov. 8. *Dear Anyone*, book by Jack Rosenthal, lyrics by Don Black, music by Geoff Stephens, with Jane Lapotaire, Stubby Kaye and Peter Blake, des. by Ralph Koltai and Nadine Baylis, dir. by David Taylor.

COMEDY: Panton St., W.C.2. (1983) Oct. 12. *Little Shop of Horrors*, book by Howard Ashman, music by Alan Menken, with Barry James, Ellen Greene and Anthony B. Asbury, dir. by Howard Ashman, des. by Edward Gianfrancesco and Tim Goodchild.

CRITERION: Piccadilly Circus, W.1. (1983) Dec. 12. *Run For Your Wife* by Ray Cooney (transferred from Shaftesbury Theatre).

DONMAR WAREHOUSE: Earlham St., Covent Garden, W.C.2. (1984) March 12. *The Jew of Malta* by Christopher Marlowe, dir. by Peter Benedict. Aug. 28. The Beckett Plays (*Catastrophe, What Where* and *Ohio Impromptu*) by Samuel Beckett, with Rand Mitchell, David Warrilow, Leigh Taylor-Young and Donald Davis, dir. by Alan Schneider.

DUCHESS: Catherine St., W.C.2. (1983) Sept. 20. *Snoopy*, music by Larry Grossman, lyrics by Hal Hackady, with Teddy Kempner, Zoë Bright, Mark Hadfield, Susie Blake, Robert Locke and Nicky Croydon, dir. by Arthur Whitelaw, des. by David Graden.

DUKE OF YORK'S: St. Martin's Lane, W.C.2. (1983) Dec. 15. *The School for Scandal* by Richard Sheridan, with Donald Sinden, Beryl Reid, Michael Denison, Dulcie Gray, Nicola Pagett, Clive Francis, Harold Innocent and Bill Fraser, dir. by John Barton, des. by Christopher Morley. (1984) April 5. *Strange Interlude* by Eugene O'Neill, with Glenda Jackson, Brian Cox, James Hazeldine and Edward Petherbridge, dir. by Keith Hack, des. by Voytek. July 24. *American Buffalo* by David Mamet, with Al Pacino, J. J. Johnston and Bruce MacVittie, dir. by Arvin Brown.

FORTUNE: Russell St., W.C.2. (1984) Aug. 15. *Butley* by Simon Gray, with John Nettles and Jeff Rawle, dir. by Philip Grout.

GREENWICH: Croom's Hill, S.E.10. (1983) Sept. 13. *A Streetcar Named Desire* by Tennessee Williams, with Sheila Gish, Paul Herzberg, Duncan Preston and Clare Higgins, dir. by Alan Strachan, des. by Bernard Culshaw. Oct. 28. *Francis* by Julian Mitchell, with Kenneth Branagh and Frederick Treves, dir. by David William. Dec. 14. *An Inspector Calls* by J. B. Priestley, with Jenny Quayle, William Lucas, David Swift, Margaret Tyzack and Peter Woodward, dir. by Alan Strachan. (1984) Feb. 2. *The White Devil* by John Webster, with Julie Legrand, Gerald Murphy, Paola Dionisotti, David William and Rupert Everett, dir. by Philip Prowse. March 14. *The Way of the World* by Congreve, with Avis Bunnage, Ann Mitchell, Rupert Frazer, Paola Dionisotti and Patrick Pearson, dir. by Giles Havergal, des. by Sue Blane. April 25. *The Seagull* by Chekhov, translated by Robert David MacDonald, with Maria Aitken, Robert Gwilym, Johanna Kirby, Ciaran Hinds and David William, dir. by Philip Prowse. June 11. *Intimate Exchanges* written and dir. by Alan Ayckbourn, with Lavinia Bertram and Robin Herford.

HAMPSTEAD: Swiss Cottage, N.W.3. (1983) Sept. 15. *Birds of Paradise* by Hanif Kureishi, with Raad Rawi, Rowena Cooper and Joe Melia, dir. by Howard Davies. Dec. 7. *Sufficient Carbohydrate* by Dennis Potter, with Dinsdale Landen, Nicky Henson, Jill Baker, Jennifer Hilary and Rupert Graves, dir. by Nancy Meckler, des. by Tanya McCallin. (1984) Feb. 22. *Boesman and Lena* by Athol Fugard, with Janet Suzman, Tommy Buson and Stuart Wilson, dir. by Clare Davidson. April 27. *Kingdom of Earth* by Tennessee Williams, with Nichola McAuliffe, Stephen Rea and David Taylor, dir. by Kenneth MacMillan. June 13. *The War at Home* by James Duff, with Timothy West, Frances Sternhagen, David Threlfall and Sylvestra Le Touzel, dir. by Michael Attenborough. July 27. *A Little Like Drowning* by Anthony Minghella, with Alfred Molina, Morag Hood and Constance Chapman, dir. by John Dove.

HER MAJESTY'S: Haymarket, S.W.1. (1984) May 16. *West Side Story*, music by Leonard Bernstein, lyrics by Stephen Sondheim, book by Arthur Laurents, with Jan Hartley, Steven Pacey, Lee Robinson, Richard A. Pettyfer and Sam Williams, dir. by Tom Abbott, des. by Martin Johns.

LYRIC: Hammersmith, W.6. (1983) Sept. 7. *Crime and Punishment* by Dostoevsky, with Michael Pennington, Paola Dionisotti, Bill Stewart, Christopher Guince, Veronica Roberts and Elizabeth Romilly, dir. by Yuri Lyubimov. Oct. 20. *The Relapse* by Vanbrugh, with Simon Callow, Nicky Henson, Oliver Cotton, Lorna Heilbron and Dona Croll, dir. by William Gaskill, des. by Sally Jacobs. Dec. 13. *Abbacadabra*, book by David Wood, lyrics by Don Black, with Elaine Page, B. A. Robertson, Sylvester McCoy and Phil Daniels, dir. by Peter James. (1984)

Feb. 7. *Rents* by Michael Wilcox, with Kenny Ireland, Stevan Rimkus and Paul Jesson, dir. by William Gaskill. March 14. *Marriage* by Gogol, with Maggie Wells, James Smith, Philip Voss and John Price, adapted and directed by Mike Alfreds with the Shared Experience Company. April. *The Complete Guide to Sex*, with Patrick Barlow, Andrea Durant and Jim Broadbent of the National Theatre of Brent. May 14. *Black Ball Game* by Don Webb, with Lee Walker, Hugh Quarshie, Michael Medwin and Carol Drinkwater, dir. by Roger Smith, des. by Roger Glossop. July 3. *The Common Pursuit* by Simon Gray, with Ian Ogilvy, Clive Francis, Simon Williams, Robert East, Nina Thomas and Nicholas Le Prevost, dir. by Harold Pinter.

LYRIC STUDIO: Hammersmith, W.6. (1983) Oct. 10. *Fly Away Home* by William Humble, with Hywell Bennett, Diana Quick, Roger Lloyd-Pack and Tim Woodward, dir. by Peter James. Nov. 8. *False Admissions* and (Nov. 15) *Successful Strategies* by Marivaux, translated by Timberlake Wertenbaker, with James Smith, Holly Wilson, Sandra Voe, Nick Dunning and Philip Voss, dir. by Mike Alfreds, des. by Paul Dart (The Shared Experience Company). (1984) Jan. 23. *Eve* by Larry Fineberg, with Constance Cummings, dir. by Ronnie Letham. March. *One for the Road* by Harold Pinter, with Alan Bates, Jenny Quayle and Roger Lloyd-Pack. Feb. 27. *The Man Who Fell in Love with His Wife* by Ted Whitehead, with Tom Bell and Lynn Farleigh, dir. by Peter James, des. by Poppy Mitchell.

LYRIC: Shaftesbury Ave., W.1. (1983) Oct. 26. *Pack of Lies* by Hugh Whitemore, with Judi Dench, Michael Williams, Richard Vernon and Barbara Leigh-Hunt, dir. by Clifford Williams, des. by Ralph Koltai.

MERMAID: Puddle Dock, Blackfriars, E.C.4. (1984) Feb. 28. *A Streetcar Named Desire* by Tennessee Williams (Greenwich Theatre production). May 31. *Kipling* by Brian Clark, with Alec McCowen, dir. by Patrick Garland, des. by Pamela Hansford.

NATIONAL THEATRE: South Bank, S.E.1. COTTESLOE: (1983) Sept. 22. *Glengarry Glen Ross* by David Mamet, with Jack Shepherd, Derek Newark, Tony Haygarth, Karl Johnson, Trevor Ray and James Grant, dir. by Bill Bryden. Oct. 26. *Antigone* by Sophocles, with Barbara Flynn, directed by John Burgess and Peter Gill (workshop production). (1984) Jan. 26. *Strider—The Story of a Horse* by Tolstoy, adapted by Mark Rozovsky, translated by Peter Tegel, with Michael Pennington and James Hayes, dir. by Michael Bogdanov, des. by Terry Mortimer. Nov. 24. *Master Harold . . . and the Boys* by Athol Fugard, with John Kani, Duart Sylwain and Ramolao Makhene. April 25. *Animal Farm* by George Orwell, adapted and directed by Peter Hall, with Kamlesh Kupta, Barrie Rutter, Windy Morgan, David Ryall and Greg Hicks, lyrics by Adrian Mitchell, written by Richard Peaslee. May 17. *Antigone* by Sophocles, translated by C. A. Trypanis, with Jane Lapotaire, Peter Sproule, John Bailey, Ron Pember and Janet Whiteside, dir. by Peter Gill and John Burgess. July 5. *Anton Chekhov* with Michael Pennington.

LYTTELTON: (1983) Dec. 15. *Cinderella* with Susan Fleetwood, Janet Dibley, Jack Shepherd, John Tam, Robert Stephens, Trevor Ray, Derek Newark and James Grant, dir. by Bill Bryden, des. by William Dudley. (1984) April 12. *Venice Preserv'd* by Thomas Otway, with Michael Pennington, Jane Lapotaire, Ian McKellen, Hugh Paddick and Stephanie Beacham, dir. by Peter Gill. May 22. *Golden Boy* by Clifford Odets, with Jeremy Flynn, Lisa Eichhorn,

Derek Newark and Jack Shepherd, dir. by Bill Bryden, des. by Hayden Griffin. June 22. *The Spanish Tragedy* by Thomas Kyd, with Michael Bryant, Miranda Foster and Stephan Brennan, dir. by Michael Bogdanov, des. by Chris Dyer. July 19. *Wild Honey* by Chekhov, translated and adapted by Michael Frayn, with Ian McKellen, Charlotte Cornwell, Elizabeth Garvie, Brewster Mason, Hugh Paddick and Heather Tobias, dir. by Christopher Morahan, des. by John Gunter.

OLIVIER: (1983) Sept. 1. *Tales from Hollywood* by Christopher Hampton, with Michael Gambon, Ian McDiarmid, Guy Rolfe, Philip Locke and Billie Whitelaw, dir. by Peter Gill. Dec. 1. *Jean Seberg*, composed by Marvin Hamlisch, lyrics by Christopher Adler, book by Julian Barry, with Joss Ackland, Elizabeth Counsell, Kelly Hunter, John Savident and Michael Bryant, dir. by Peter Hall, des. by John Bury. (1984) Feb. 16. *Saint Joan* by G. B. Shaw, with Frances de la Tour, Cyril Cusack, Philip Locke, Anton Rodgers, Michael Bryant and Timothy Spall, dir. by Ronald Eyre. June 14. *Mandragola* by Machiavelli, translated by Wallace Shawn, with Nicky Henson, John Savident, Phyllis Roome and Jim Norton, dir. by David Gilmore, des. by Roger Glossop. Aug. 10. *A Little Hotel on the Side* by Feydeau, adapted by John Mortimer, with Dina Stabb, Michael Bryant, John Savident, Graeme Garden, Deborah Norton and Benjamin Whitrow, dir. by Jonathan Lynn, des. by Saul Radonsky.

NEW END: N.W.3. (1983) Sept. 23. *Angel City* by Sam Shepard, with Nigel Le Vaillant, Tim McInnerny and Anne Sky, dir. by Adrian Jackson.

OLD VIC: The Cut, S.E.1. (1983) Nov. 9. *Blondel*, lyrics by Tim Rice, music by Stephen Oliver, with Paul Nicholas, Sharon Lee Hill, Chris Langham and David Burt, dir. by Peter James, des. by Tim Goodchild. (1984) Jan. 18. *Master Class* by David Pownall, with Timothy West, Peter Kelly, Jonathan Adams and David Bamber, dir. by Justin Greene, des. by Martin Johns, musical director John White. Feb. 29. *The Mikado* by Gilbert and Sullivan, with Marie Baron, Christine James, Karen Wood, Karen Skidmore, Avo Kitlask and Richard McMillan, dir. by Brian Macdonald (Stratford Festival, Canada, production). April 11. *Saturday Night at the Palace* by Paul Slabolepszy, with Fats Dibero, Bill Flynn and Paul Slabolepszy, dir. by Bobby Heaney (Market Theatre Company, Johannesburg, production). May 23. *Serjeant Musgrave's Dance* by John Arden, with Albert Finney, Eileen Atkins, Max Wall, Graham Crowden, Alun Armstrong, Mark Jefferis, Allan Surtees and Willoughby Goddard, dir. by Albert Finney, des. by Di Seymour. July 18. *The Boyfriend* by Sandy Wilson, with Jane Wellman, Rosemary Ashe, Anna Quayle, Derek Waring, Simon Greene, Peter Bayliss and Linda-Mae Brewe, dir. by Christopher Hewett, des. by Robin Don.

OPEN AIR: Regent's Park, W.1. (1984) June 4. Shakespeare's *Merry Wives of Windsor*, with Ronald Fraser, Dora Bryan, Kate O'Mara, James Cairncross, Malcolm James, Paul Raffield and Berwick Kaler, dir. by David Conville, des. by Sarah Jane McClelland. June 19. Shakespeare's *A Midsummer Night's Dream*, with Alexandra Mathie, Richard Rees, Berwick Kaler and Allan Corduner, dir. by Bernard Hopkins, des. by Tim Goodchild. July 31. *Bashville* by Benny Green and Denis King (adapted from G. B. Shaw), with Peter Woodward, Felicity Jane Goodson, Christopher Hancock and Richard Rees, dir. by David William.

PALACE: Shaftesbury Ave., W.1. (1984) June 12. *On Your Toes* by Rodgers and Hart, with Natalia Makarova, Honor Blackman, John Bennett, Nicholas Johnson, Tim Flavin and Siobhan McCarthy, dir. by George Abbott and Peter Walker.

PHOENIX: Charing Cross Rd., W.C.2. (1984) April 12. *Peg*, music and lyrics by David Heneker, with Siân Phillips, Edward Duke and Ann Morrison, dir. by Ian Judge.

PRINCE OF WALES: Coventry St., W.1. (1984) Jan. 3. *Hello Dolly* by Michael Stewart and Jerry Herman, with Danny la Rue, Lionel Jefferies, Lorna Dallas, Michael Sadler and Mark Haddigan, dir. by Peter Coe. May 30. *Little Me*, book by Neil Simon, music by Cy Coleman, lyrics by Carolyn Leigh, with Russ Abbot, Sheila White, Lynda Baron, Vivienne Martin, Valerie Walsh and Tudor Davies, dir. by Val May, des. by Tony Watton.

QUEEN'S: Shaftesbury Ave., W.1. (1983) Oct. 25. *Hay Fever* by Noël Coward, with Penelope Keith, Moray Watson, Donald Pickering, David Delve, Abigail McKern and Elizabeth Bradley, dir. by Kim Grant, des. by Carl Toms. (1984) April 24. *Number One* by Jean Anouilh, translated and adapted by Michael Frayn, with Leo McKern, Joe Melia, Margaret Whiting, Anthony Sharp and Peter Blythe, dir. by Robert Chetwyn. Aug. 13. *Forty Years On* by Alan Bennett (Chichester Festival production).

RIVERSIDE STUDIO: Hammersmith, W.6. (1983) Sept. 13. *Medea* by Franz Grillparzer, adapted and directed by Barney Simon, with Terence Wilton, Yvonne Bryceland and David Calder. (1984) Jan. 31. *The Biko Inquest* by Jon Blair and Norman Fenton, with Albert Finney, John Standing, Nigel Davenport, Michael Gough, Richard Johnson, Michael Aldridge and Mark Dignam, dir. by Albert Finney. July 4. *Seachange* by Stephen Lowe, with Terence Wilton and Caroline Embling, dir. by David Leveaux, des. by Brien Vahey. Aug. 28. *Playboy of the Western World* by J. M. Synge, dir. by Lindsay Anderson.

ROYAL COURT: Sloane Sq., S.W.1. (1983) Sept. 12. *The Genius* by Howard Brenton, with Trevor Eve, Clive Swift, Joanna Whalley and Hugh Fraser, dir. by Danny Boyle. Nov. 1. *The Grass Widow* by Snoo Wilson, with Ron Cook, Alan Rickman, Tracey Ullman and Leslie Udwin, dir. by Max Stafford-Clark, des. by Peter Hartwell. (1984) Feb. 8. *Tom and Viv* by Michael Hastings, with Tom Wilkinson, Margaret Tyzack, Julie Covington and David Haig, dir. by Max Stafford-Clark, des. by Anthony McDonald. April 3. *The Great Celestial Cow* by Sue Townsend, with Souad Faress, Dev Sagoo, Zohra Segal and Feroza Syal, dir. by Carole Hayman. May 5. *Cries from the Mammal House* by Terry Johnson, with Roger Rees and Leo Wringer, dir. by Phil Young. July 4. *The Lucky Chance* by Aphra Behn, with Harriet Walter, Denis Lawson, Kathryn Pogson, Jonathan Adams, Alan Rickman and Pam Ferris, dir. by Jules Wright.

SHAFTESBURY: Shaftesbury Ave., W.C.2. (1984) Feb. 14. *See How They Run* by Philip King, with Maureen Lipman, Royce Mills, Michael Denison, Derek Nimmo and Liza Goddard, dir. by Ray Cooney. May 15. *Pygmalion* by G. B. Shaw, with Peter O'Toole, John Thaw, Jack Watling, Joyce Carey, Barbara Murray, Lally Bowers and Jackie Smith-Wood, dir. by Ray Cooney, des. by Douglas Heap. July 12. *A Friend Indeed* by William Douglas Home, with Derek Nimmo, Geoffrey Palmer, Moira Lister and Colette Gleeson, dir. by Jan Butlin.

SHAW: Euston Rd., N.W.1. (1984) April 10. *Gulls* by Robert Hewett, with Jeffrey Chiswick, Carol Burns and Evie Garratt, dir. by Andy Jordan. May 16.

Ghosts by Ibsen, translated by Michael Meyer, with Lynn Farleigh, Bill Simpson, Lysette Anthony and Bob Mason, dir. by Caroline Eves. Aug. 20. *A Credit to the Force* by Chris Short, dir. by Michael Croft (National Youth Theatre). July 5. *White Game* by Peter Dawson and Mike Brearley, with David Troughton and Jim Findley.

THEATRE ROYAL: Drury Lane, W.C.2. (1983) Nov. 14. *Dancin'* by Bob Fosse, directed by Gail Benedict. (1984) Aug. 8. *42nd Street*, lyrics by Al Dubin, music by Harry Warren, book by Michael Stewart and Mark Bramble, with Clare Leach, James Laurenson, Margaret Courtenay, Georgia Brown and Michael Howe, dir. by Lucia Victor.

THEATRE ROYAL: Haymarket, S.W.1. (1983) Oct. 18. *The Cherry Orchard* by Chekhov, with Joan Plowright, Frank Finlay, Leslie Phillips, Joanna David, Bill Fraser, Frank Grimes and Bernard Miles, dir. by Lindsay Anderson. Nov. 24. *The Sleeping Prince* by Terence Rattigan, with Omar Sharif, Judy Campbell, John Moffatt and Debbie Arnold, dir. by Peter Coe, des. by Peter Rice (Chichester Festival production). (1984) March 8. *The Aspern Papers* by Henry James, adapted by Michael Redgrave, with Vanessa Redgrave, Wendy Hiller and Christopher Reeve, dir. by Frith Banbury, des. by Carl Toms. June 20. *Aren't We All* by Frederick Lonsdale, with Rex Harrison, Claudette Colbert, Nicola Pagett, Michael Gough and Francis Matthews, dir. by Clifford Williams, des. by Finlay James.

THEATRE ROYAL: Stratford East, E.15. (1983) Sept. 27. *Gas and Candles* by David Henry Wilson, with Doris Hare and Derek Francis, dir. by Philip Hedley. Oct. 31. Shakespeare's *Pericles*, with Martin Duncan, Felicity Dean, Brian Protheroe, Darlene Johnson and Gerard Murphy, dir. by David Ultz. (1984) April 9. *Breakneck* by Vince Foxall, with Mary Maddox and Robert Daws, dir. by Philip Hedley, des. by Jenny Tiramani. June 18. *A Mad World My Masters* by Barrie Keeffe, with Imelda Staunton, Trevor Martin, Janette Legge and Ian Lindsay, dir. by Jane Howell, des. by Stephanie Howard.

VAUDEVILLE: Strand, W.C.2. (1983) Nov. 3. *Dial M for Murder* by Frederick Knott, with Simon Ward, Hayley Mills and Peter Adamson, dir. by Allan Davis. (1984) April 4. *Benefactors* by Michael Frayn, with Tim Pigott-Smith, Oliver Cotton, Patricia Hodge and Brenda Blethyn, dir. by Michael Blakemore, des. by Michael Annals.

VICTORIA PALACE: S.W.1. (1983) Dec. 22. *Hi-De-Hi* by Jimmy Perry and David Croft, with Simon Cadell, Ruth Madoc, Jeffrey Holland, Paul Shane and Su Pollard.

WESTMINSTER: Palace St., S.W.1. (1984) June 21. *Morning's at Seven* by Paul Osborn, with Teresa Wright, Margaret Tyzack, Doreen Mantle, Faith Brook, Don Fellows, Peter Jones, Alan MacNaughtan, John Church and Andree Melly, dir. by Vivian Metalon.

WYNDHAM'S: Charing Cross Rd., W.C.2. (1984) Feb. 28. *Master Class* by David Pownall (Old Vic production). April 23. *Passion Play* by Peter Nichols, with Heather Wright, Leslie Phillips, Judy Parfitt, Zena Walker and Barry Foster, dir. by Mike Ockrent.

YOUNG VIC: The Cut, S.E.1. (1984) May 3. Shakespeare's *Othello*, with Rudolph Walker, David Calder, Brian Protheroe and Kate Fahy, dir. by David Thacker. Aug. 30. *A View from the Bridge* by Arthur Miller, with Annie Ross, Malcolm Tierney and Maria Brooker, dir. by Roger Smith.

Productions outside London included the following:

STRATFORD MEMORIAL THEATRE (Royal Shakespeare Company): (1983) Sept. 29. *Measure for Measure*, with Daniel Massey, Juliet Stevenson, Peggy Mount, Anthony O'Donnell and Richard O'Callaghan, dir. by Adrian Noble, des. by Bob Crowley. (1984) March. *Henry V*, with Kenneth Branagh, Sebastian Shaw, Harold Innocent, Brian Blessed, Patricia Routledge and Ian McDiarmid, dir. by Adrian Noble, des. by Bob Crowley. April. *The Merchant of Venice* with Ian McDiarmid, Sebastian Shaw, Frances Tomelty, Adam Bareham, Brian Parr, Christopher Ravenscroft and Josette Simon, dir. by John Caird, des. by Ultz. June. *Richard III* with Antony Sher, Malcolm Storry, Roger Allam, Brian Blessed, Frances Tomelty, Penny Downie, Harold Innocent and Patricia Routledge, dir. by Bill Alexander, des. by William Dudley. Aug. *Hamlet* with Roger Rees, Kenneth Branagh, Brian Blessed, Virginia McKenna and Frank Middlemass, dir. by Ron Daniels.

OTHER PLACE: (1983) Sept. 28. *Volpone* by Ben Jonson, with Richard Griffiths, Miles Anderson, Gemma Jones and Julie Peasgood, dir. by Bill Alexander, des. by Alison Chitty. Nov. 23. *Life is a Dream* by Calderon, adapted by Adrian Mitchell and John Barton, with Miles Anderson, Charles Kay, Barbara Kellerman, Anthony O'Donnell, Lesley Duff and Christopher Neame, dir. by John Barton, des. by Christopher Morley. (1984). *A Midsummer Night's Dream*, with Charles Milham, Roger Allam, Penny Downie, David Whitaker, Amanda Roots, Philip Jackson, George Raistrick, Jimmy Yuill and Frank Middlemass, dir. by Sheila Hancock, des. by Bob Crowley. April. *Camille* by Pam Gems, with Francis Barber, Nicholas Farrell and Charles Milham, dir. by Ron Daniels. April. *Romeo and Juliet*, with Amanda Root, Simon Templeman, Roger Allam, Frank Middlemass and Polly James, dir. by John Caird, des. by Bob Crowley. June. *Golden Girls* by Louise Page, with Jimmy Yuill, Polly James, Derek Crewe, George Raistrick, Josette Simon, Kenneth Branagh and Cathy Tyson, dir. by Barry Kyle, des. by Kit Surrey. Aug. *The Party* by Trevor Griffiths, with Roger Allam, Malcolm Storry, David Threlfall and Ian McDiarmid, dir. by Howard Davies and David Edgar.

CHICHESTER FESTIVAL THEATRE: (1984) May 2. *Forty Years On*, by Alan Bennett, with Paul Eddington, Annette Crosbie, Doris Hare, John Fortune and Stephen Fry, dir. by Patrick Garland. May 17. *Oh Kay!* by George Gershwin and P. G. Wodehouse, adapted by Ned Sherrin, with Jane Carr, dir. by Ian Judge. July 11. Shakespeare's *The Merchant of Venice*, with Alec Guiness, Joanna McCallum, David Yelland, Martin Chamberlain and Leslee Udwin, dir. by Patrick Garland. Aug. 1. *The Way of the World* by Congreve, with Maggie Smith, Joan Plowright, Sara Kestelman, Michael Jayston and Ian Hogg, dir. by William Gaskill, des. by Hayden Griffin.

MANCHESTER ROYAL EXCHANGE: (1983) Nov. 3. Shakespeare's *Hamlet*, with Robert Lindsay, Philip Madoc, Derek Griffiths, Derek Smith, Alison Fiske and Geraldine Alexander, dir. by Braham Murray. Dec. 23. Herman Melville's *Moby Dick*, adapted and directed by Michael Elliott, with Nigel Terry, Brian Cox, Terence Weilton and John Cording, des. by Lawrie Dennett. Sept. 18. *Dance of Death* by Strindberg, with Jill Bennett and Edward Fox, dir. by Kenneth MacMillan. March. *Jumpers* by Tom Stoppard, with Tom Courtenay and Julie Walters, dir. by Nicholas Hytner, des. by Mark Thompson.

Following the radical change brought about in the provision of television services in Britain, with the introduction of Channel 4 and S4C in November 1982, and early morning programmes on both main channels in early 1983, a period of quiet consolidation would have been welcome before the further upheavals that would occur with direct broadcasting by satellite in 1986. However, it was not to be: the BBC suffered a traumatic period, plagued by disputes, trounced in the ratings, ruminating over satellite services, morale at a low ebb, and the prospect looming of having to recommence the next round of negotiations with an unsympathetic Government for a major increase in the licence fee. The ITV companies also suffered from industrial problems, and had to withdraw from coverage of the Olympic Games. However, ITV won conclusively in the ratings battle with the BBC, and enhanced its reputation for quality programmes with the excellent series *The Jewel in the Crown*. Furthermore, it was announced in September 1984 that the long-running dispute between Equity and the Institute of Practitioners in Advertising over fees for actors appearing in commercials on Channel 4 and TV-AM had at last been resolved, although whether the extra advertising would be enough to save TV-AM from final collapse remained to be seen.

BBC Annual Report

It was noted last year that BBC coverage of the Falklands War fell outside the scope of the 1983 Annual Report and Handbook, but the Director-General nevertheless felt constrained to respond to what was perceived to be hasty and ill-informed criticism. Similarly, the Chairman stated that the 1984 Report would "deal more fully with the problems raised by Direct Broadcasting by Satellite (D.B.S.) and Cable, as well as with the introduction of Breakfast Television." He summed up the Corporation's attitude as being that "the new technologies must be the servant and not the master of programmes ... [they] must bring about a genuine expansion of choice."

In the 1984 Report, as promised, the Chairman returned to those themes. Since the Report covered the period April 1982–March 1983, its defence of the Falklands War coverage is mainly of historic interest, but it is worth citing his words, as a reminder of the BBC's well-deserved reputation for independence, and the justification for the maintenance of its status, especially during a difficult period. Lord Howard of Henderskelfe wrote: "Ultimately I believe our coverage was fair, balanced and a credit to all concerned. We succeeded because, although plainly not neutral between Britain and the aggressor, we upheld our overriding commitment to truth and to freedom of expression of all shades of opinion. We had built up a reputation over sixty years for being believed. At the end of the Falklands War that reputation was intact ... I cannot refrain from adding that the Falklands War demonstrated the folly of cutting our External Services, for the sake of miniscule savings, and that the importance of those services became abundantly clear once the conflict had started. That they were not more universally audible incontrovertibly demonstrated the importance of strategically sited and up-to-date relay transmitters of a power which enables them to be heard in an ever more competitive babel from around the world."

The Chairman then referred to the introduction of Breakfast Television "in the face of considerable scepticism". He saluted the service as "an outstanding success". It was noted last year that the BBC's expedited launch of a Breakfast Time service in direct competition with its independent rival TV-

AM had been the cause of many of the latter station's problems. However, what also became apparent was that the BBC's conscious decision to set the tone of its morning programmes deliberately down-market had the immediate effect of sabotaging TV-AM's "mission to explain". It is unlikely that TV-AM, as originally constituted, could have successfully transmitted its ideals into programmes, but when confronted by a lightweight magazine programme on the BBC, it was forced to drop its sights even lower to survive. Indicative of the BBC's approach was its inclusion of an astrologer on its Breakfast-Time service. Whether, as the outgoing Chairman concluded, "Britain should be proud of a public service broadcasting system which is the envy of the rest of the world" is debatable when the Corporation descends from its high ideals.

Lord Howard of Henderskelfe was succeeded as Chairman of the BBC in 1983 by Mr. Stuart Young, who paid tribute to his predecessor in the Report. He stated that he hoped to maintain the BBC's financial and constitutional sound footing: "In particular I want to uphold the licence fee system and the relationship it gives us with the individual licence-payer. I believe that system acts as a spur to us to deliver value for money and is, at the same time, a guarantee of our editorial independence. However we may be affected in the coming years by technological challenges, my first priorities will be the maintenance of our editorial freedom, and of the licence fee system, which together can provide a climate conducive to excellence."

In the Report, the BBC stated, *vis-à-vis* cable television and its evidence to the Hunt Committee, that its attitude was "neither fatalistic nor Luddite", but "formed by contrasting it with the potential benefits of Direct Broadcasting by Satellite. We had ... obtained permission to provide two D.B.S. services. We knew, however, that our duty to the licence payer demanded the most meticulous scrutiny of the implications before we could go ahead. This was, therefore, a year of general technical and financial education." What the new Chairman, an accountant by training, discovered in relation to D.B.S. was that the BBC was in danger of mortgaging its future to a new service which might never recoup the huge investment required to inaugurate it. The complex negotiations in regard to D.B.S. are summarised below.

The BBC was affected by several industrial disputes during the course of the year, with outside broadcasting crews causing disruption to sports coverage and drama location work in October 1983 because their expenses claims were affected by an Inland Revenue ruling. In January 1984, BBC news was hit by a dispute over computer technology, but industrial action by scenery workers in March and April, followed by the dismissal of 600 staff, and a walk-out in sympathy by other BBC employees, resulted in all programmes on BBC 1 being blacked out on April 5.

The Corporation also suffered when its new season of programmes in Autumn 1983 was comprehensively beaten in the ratings by ITV. Home-produced series, such as *By The Sword Divided*, a worthy if uninspired saga of the Civil War, fell victim to imported American "mini-series" on ITV, which had great success with *The Winds of War*, based on Herman Wouk's tale of an American family during the war years 1939–41; it reputedly cost £25 million to make, lasted some 16 hours, and featured a languid Robert Mitchum in the leading role, well supported by Victoria Tennant who re-established her career, but with Ali McGraw totally miscast the series had its longueurs. Nevertheless, it gave the ITV schedules a much-needed boost.

The BBC made more serious errors, with its

replacement of the successful *Nationwide* with *Sixty Minutes*, fronted by an ill-at-ease Desmond Wilcox, who had been head of general features from 1972–80. He eventually left the programme in January 1984, but it never achieved any sort of success, appearing to be a "supper" version of the breakfast service, and was eventually scrapped in June 1984. Its replacement, *Six O'Clock News*, appeared to be a return in the right direction to current affairs and news-oriented early evening programming. However, the general malaise was not confined to *Sixty Minutes*; another of the "new season" programmes, *Harty*, was a magazine format mish-mash of the trivial and the transitory. BBC "flagship" programmes, such as *Panorama*, also had problems; in particular, an investigation into alleged penetration by extreme right-wing political groups in the Conservative party produced a flurry of writs. However, at least *Panorama* was occupied with important matters; it was therefore disconcerting to see that its new season was delayed in Autumn 1984 by the scheduling of another American "mini-series" in its slot. When two senior BBC employees spoke out in public against this act at the Edinburgh Television Conference, they were reprimanded by their superiors for disloyalty.

Thorn in its Side

More ire was provoked by the Corporation's decision to schedule its own American import, *The Thorn Birds*, directly against the prestigious Granada production, *The Jewel in the Crown*. The BBC claimed that it was unable to screen repeats of some of its own much-acclaimed drama productions (except, in the weeks before the B.A.F.T.A. awards, when it reruns programmes which are tipped for prizes), yet it paid some £600,000 to screen an American adaptation of Colleen McCullough's novel which had cost £12 million to make, yet was ineptly acted and badly produced and directed. To attempt to entice viewers away from a series of the highest quality, which many thought the BBC should have created, to watch an imported drama about a priest and his love for a farm-girl, was felt to be an abrogation of its duties. Government Ministers criticised the Corporation, and hinted that declining standards would weaken its case for a licence fee increase (although the opposite argument could be said to apply equally). The Managing Director of BBC Television, Mr. Aubrey Singer, stated that the BBC was "completely dedicated to maintaining broadcasting standards", and the Chairman stressed the need for it to have popular appeal, while speaking to the Broadcasting Press Guild of "quality—above all". It was perhaps ironic that the BBC felt it necessary to show populist programmes such as *The Thorn Birds*, to help it compete in the ratings with ITV, which in turn felt obliged occasionally to produce quality programmes such as *The Jewel in the Crown* to compete with the BBC at its best. The BBC has the dilemma of considering itself above the so-called "ratings war", but obliged to compete because a substantial drop in its market share decreases its justification for licence increases. But further indications of its lack of control and direction were given by its disastrous *Saturday Night Affairs* (BBC 1), which purported to make interesting viewing out of minor celebrities partying (at the viewers' expense); it was cancelled after two shows.

Moves were eventually made to stop the rot: Mr. Aubrey Singer was replaced by Mr. Bill Cotton as Managing Director of BBC Television, but the unprecedented decision was taken to appoint, from outside the Corporation's ranks, to the vital position of controller of BBC 1, Mr. Michael Grade, formerly of London Weekend Television, who had been working in the U.S.A. for some years. It remains to be seen whether the Corporation will recover from a traumatic period, and in which direction it will move.

It would, of course, be wrong to give the impression that no good programmes came out of BBC Television, but having set the standards in the past, expectations are inevitably higher. Of particular note was *An Englishman Abroad* (BBC 1), directed by John Schlesinger, written by Alan Bennett, and featuring Alan Bates as the traitor Guy Burgess, and Coral Browne, playing herself, based on real incidents in 1958 when she had been in Moscow with an English theatre company performing *Hamlet*. The play was subtle, understated, yet with much to say, and the acting and directing flawless. It was a deserving award winner. BBC-2's serialisation of C. P. Snow's *Strangers and Brothers*, dramatised by Julian Bond, was a worthy attempt to transfer the 11 novels, written between 1940 and 1970, to the small screen, but even in 13 parts this celebrated journey through the ranks of the English establishment, from Bar, to Whitehall, to Westminster, obscured the message of the novels, that its protagonist Lewis Eliot was one of the new breed who struggled to the highest positions in public office despite a poor background. Shaughan Seymour was excellent in the leading role, with fine support from Sheila Ruskin and Nigel Havers in this cerebral drama.

Less satisfactory was BBC 1's adaptation (by Andrew Davies) of R. F. Delderfield's *Diana*, which, unlike the same author's *To Serve Them All My Days*, degenerated into melodrama. *Missing from Home* (BBC 1) by Roger Marshall was a thoughtful drama about the pressures that caused a husband and father to leave his family without warning, with Judy Loe excellent as the wife suddenly having to examine her life afresh. *Give Us A Break* (BBC 1) by Geoff McQueen attempted to exploit the current obsession with snooker, with Robert Lindsay effective as a street-wise manager, but it never acquired the style or charm of ITV's consistently good *Minder*, starring George Cole and Dennis Waterman. On BBC 2, Ronald Harwood attempted a history of the theatre in 13 parts in *All The World's A Stage*, while the anarchic comedy of *The Young Ones* showed that there was still a place for innovative, and often outrageous humour. The significance of the year 1984 was not lost on either Channel, with several programmes about George Orwell, in particular *Orwell on Jura* (BBC) and *The Road to 1984* (ITV).

Olympic Relief

Independent Television's industrial problems were less acute than the BBC's, except in London where Thames TV was off the air for five days in August 1984. Potentially more serious was a disagreement with the A.C.T.T.; TV-AM had to withdraw from coverage of the Olympics as it failed to agree extra payments with the Union, and considered it would not be able to raise sufficient advertising revenue to pay for the expense that would be incurred. ITV then considered various options, such as running a second commercial channel for the duration of the Games, or transferring coverage to Channel 4. However, having invested £1·5 million of a £5 million budget, agreement could not be reached with the A.C.T.T., which wanted to send one more assistant than the companies were prepared to pay for; thus, for the sake of £5,000 and a principle, ITV pulled out of coverage of the Olympics altogether. This decision was ironic, as ITV had just outbid the BBC, and made a deal for exclusive showing of major athletics events with the Amateur Athletic Association. However, the viewer benefited, as the wasteful and unnecessary duplication of major sporting events by both Channels, which has infuriated those uninterested in the sports concerned, as well as the majority who are indifferent as to which Channel shows them, was for once avoided. It is to be hoped that this precedent will not be ignored in future. ITV's main replacement programme, an imported U.S. science fiction series entitled *V*, took a good idea and stretched it so far that it snapped, but at least viewers were provided with alternative fare.

Granada's Jewel

The triumph of the year on ITV was without doubt Granada's *The Jewel in the Crown*, an adaptation in 14 parts of Paul Scott's "Raj Quartet". Granada had shown what it was capable of with its excellent adaptation of Evelyn Waugh's *Brideshead Revisited*, the only fault of which had been to stretch the novel's resources too far. *The Jewel in the Crown* was beautifully paced, excellently acted, exquisitely photographed, and showed a mastery of the medium and its subject-matter that all other programme makers should aspire to. The series cost £5·5 million to make, and took three years. Set between 1942–47 in India, it concerned the life of the English in that country, and the country's effect on them. Adapted by Ken Taylor, and directed by Christopher Morahan and Jim O'Brien, it featured Ari Malik, Susan Wooldridge, Tim Pigott-Smith, Peggy Ashcroft, Charles Dance, Geraldine James, Eric Porter and Judy Parfitt.

Channel 4 showed another Anglo-Indian spectacular, *The Far Pavilions*, based on M. M. Kaye's novel. This £9 million Goldcrest production was by no means disastrous, and gave a much-needed boost to the fledgling Channel's ratings, but compared with *Jewel*, the somewhat ponderous plot sank under the spectacle. The cast included Ben Cross, Robert Hardy, Omar Sharif, Christopher Lee, John Gielgud, Felicity Dean and Amy Irving.

Nuclear Power

The main controversy on ITV centred around an American drama about the effects of nuclear war. *The Day After* was considered insidious propaganda by some, and a courageous attempt to confront the public with the reality of nuclear weapons by others. In America it was seen by 75 million viewers, and had a powerful effect, prompting a statement from the U.S. Secretary of State. In Britain, the National Viewers' and Listeners' Association demanded that the film should not be screened. The Defence Minister, Mr. Michael Heseltine, insisted that he be interviewed alone before any discussion programme about the points raised, then the following morning cancelled an appearance on TV-AM because the General Secretary of the Campaign for Nuclear Disarmament, Monsignor Bruce Kent, was appearing the same morning, albeit in a separate programme. The Defence Minister said that the film was a powerful argument in favour of the present defence policy; he also condemned it as propaganda. The I.B.A. had considered that as the programme was "entertainment", a statement was not necessary, and some ITV companies accordingly did not carry Mr. Heseltine's interview or the panel discussion.

One of the more original programmes to appear on ITV during the year was a 13-week series set on a building site in West Germany, concerning the life and problems of Geordie labourers abroad. *Auf Wiedersehen, Pet*, written by Dick Clement and Ian La Frenais, was a well-scripted, intelligently constructed and developed series, which allowed its comedy to develop naturally without resorting to the usual clichés and stereotypes from which too much comedy is derived on television. Also of note was *Kennedy*, a British-made series which gave a dramatic and coherent account of the presidency of John F. Kennedy, well played by Martin Sheen, in the 20th anniversary of his assassination.

Satire reared its head on ITV with *Spitting Image*, a series which used puppet caricatures made by Law and Fluck to make pertinent comment on current issues and people. The scripts often failed to rise to the standard of the models, but occasionally succeeded brilliantly, bringing a welcome breath of sharp comedy to the often anodyne offerings on ITV.

Channel 4

Channel 4's output was varied, as intended, and brought a welcome new dimension to ITV's output. It screened esoteric but worthwhile programmes such as *The Oresteia at Epidaurus*, a documentary about the National Theatre's production of Aeschylus's trilogy before a Greek audience, followed by the screening of Peter Hall's production. G. F. Newman's *The Nation's Health* was a powerful documentary drama about the decline of the national health service as a metaphor for the state of the nation. Tom Stoppard's *Squaring the Circle* was a clever, stylised account of the Solidarity trade union movement in Poland, with Bernard Hill as Lech Walesa. *Jesus—The Evidence* was an intelligent examination of myth and fact in the Bible, which attracted quite undue hostility, and *Diverse Reports* was a stimulating current affairs series. An interesting innovation was *Case on Camera*, which resolved genuine disputes (where the amount in contention was less than £500) in a televised arbitration before a retired Old Bailey judge, with all costs and awards—both winners and losers—paid by the television company, Yorkshire.

The "Film on Four" Series continued the fruitful collaboration between Channel 4 and the cinema, with notable examples such as *Another Time, Another Place*, *Those Glory, Glory Days* and *Good and Bad at Games* being screened during the year. Channel 4 also screened Abel Gance's *Napoleon*, the silent cinema masterpiece restored by Kevin Brownlow.

Morning Sickness

TV-AM's problems were compounded. It managed to claw back some supremacy over the BBC in the ratings, but its programmes bore little relation to the concept that convinced the I.B.A. to award it the franchise. The I.B.A. eventually responded to criticisms by warning TV-AM in May 1984 that if it pared its costs any further it would be in danger of being closed down if programme quality suffered. However, problems continued; the editor-in-chief brought in to boost its ratings resigned in protest at the economies, his successor leaving soon after when TV-AM withdrew from coverage of the Olympic Games. In its annual report in 1984, the I.B.A. told TV-AM to improve and expand its news coverage, stating that "its impatience in wishing to see this achieved is tempered only by its knowledge of TV-AM's financial constraints". TV-AM's avowed intention to consist "primarily but not exclusively of news, information and current affairs" had begun to seem like a poor joke. Whether or not the ending of the Equity–I.P.A. dispute would give a much-needed boost to its income, with a consequent improvement in programme quality, remained to be seen.

Cable and Satellite

Following the publication of the Government White Paper on Cable Broadcasting, in which it was stated that applications would be invited for 12 pilot franchises, in November 1983 conditional licences were awarded to only 11 companies out of 37 applicants, with a bias towards the south-east. However, in December, 11 more companies were given Government approval to expand their existing cable networks. A Cable Television Authority was established, with responsibility for awarding franchises and monitoring the companies' output. Mr. Richard A. Burton was appointed chairman, and the Cable and Broadcasting Act eventually received the Royal Assent on July 26, 1984.

However, doubts began to be raised about the viability of some of the companies awarded franchises; problems were experienced in raising the necessary capital, and the Government dealt a severe blow to the scheme by its ending of capital allowances in the 1984 Finance (No. 2) Act. It was inevitable that this would delay any possible profitable return on investment, and it was felt that some companies would drop out of the scheme.

The satellite saga became even more convoluted. The United Kingdom had been allocated five D.B.S. television channels in 1977, two of which were allocated to the BBC. In September 1983, the Home Secretary announced that the Independent Television Companies would also be allocated two satellite channels. However, the BBC became seriously concerned about the financial implications of the service, which would have to be financed by borrowing. In December 1983, the BBC Governors decided that the 1986 launch date was not feasible, and that the £350 million cost could bankrupt the Corporation. It was then suggested that the BBC and I.B.A. should be involved in a joint satellite project, but it seemed unlikely that agreement could be reached. After much further discussion and conjecture, in May 1984, the Home Secretary announced, during the second reading of the Cable and Broadcasting Bill, the formation of a joint partnership between the BBC, ITV and independent parties. He also proposed that two new satellite channels would be offered three years after the main scheme started (which would in effect be providing competition before the BBC and ITV had begun making a profit on their scheme). Further, the Home Secretary announced that the satellite consortium would be allowed to decide on whether or not the service should carry advertising (which would have provided competition for the ITV companies). However, they would receive an effective eight-year extension on their franchises, which would not now be readvertised in 1989. Renewal would not be guaranteed, but the franchises would probably last until 1997 (the companies had pointed out that they could not be expected to commit themselves to costly investment in satellite if there was a chance that their contracts might be terminated before any return was realised).

In July, the Government announced that the BBC would have a 50 per cent share in the satellite project, the I.B.A. 30 per cent, with the remaining 20 per cent being split between five other companies. It was unlikely that the satellite would in fact be launched before 1988. However, in January 1984, Sky Channel, the first commercial satellite channel to be beamed over Europe and available in the U.K., became available to those in Swindon on the cable service. It was suggested that Sky Channel might be available on a French satellite over the U.K. in 1986, and that the Government of the Irish Republic would have its own satellite in service in 1987, beaming programmes into Britain. With the chances of a cable network being established over more than a small area of the country being quite remote, and insufficient receiving equipment being available in quantity in time for satellite reception, there would seem to be vast amounts of money being invested in or committed to services for which there is no proven demand.

B.A.F.T.A. Awards

In 1983, the British Academy of Film and Television Arts presented the prize for best single drama to John Schlesinger's *An Englishman Abroad* (BBC); Alan Bennett received the writer's award, and Alan Bates and Coral Browne received best actor and actress awards for the same production. *Kennedy* (ITV) was the best drama series, and *Forty Minutes* (BBC 2) best factual series. *Carrott's Lib* (BBC 1) was best light entertainment programme, and *Hi-de-Hi* (BBC 1) best comedy series. The best programme or series without a category was *Arena* (BBC 2), and the best actuality coverage was ITN's coverage of the Lebanon crisis. Best performance in a light entertainment programme was Tracey Ullman in *Three of a Kind* (BBC), and the Richard Dimbleby Award was presented to John Tusa of *Newsnight* (BBC 2).

BROADCASTING

BRITISH BROADCASTING CORPORATION
(see also entry on page 377)

Radio

BBC Radio broadcasts four national services to the United Kingdom, Isle of Man and the Channel Islands plus a fifth tier consisting of national regional services in Wales, Scotland and Northern Ireland and local radio services in England and the Channel Islands. In Wales there are two regional services based on the Welsh and English languages respectively.

The four national services are:

Radio 1: ("Pop" and "rock" network)—Monday to Sunday 6 a.m. to 12 midnight. Frequencies: MF 1053 kHz/285m and 1089 kHz/275m, plus two local fillers giving population coverage 96% (day) and 57% (night); VHF 88–91 MHz (shared with Radio 2), coverage 97%.

Radio 2: (Light music, entertainment and sport)—24 hours a day. Frequencies: MF 693 kHz/433m and 909 kHz/330m plus three local fillers giving population coverage 98% (day) and 65% (night); VHF 88–91 MHz (shared with Radio 1), coverage 97%.

Radio 3: (Serious music, drama and documentaries)—Monday to Friday 6.55 a.m. to 11.15 p.m.; Saturday and Sunday 7.55 a.m. to 11.15 p.m. Frequencies: VHF 90·2–92·5 MHz, population coverage 97%. MF (Main centres of population only), 1215 kHz/247m, plus four local fillers on 1197 kHz/251m, coverage 87% (day) and 38% (night).

Radio 4: (News, documentaries, drama and entertainment)—Monday to Friday 6 a.m. to 12 midnight, Saturday and Sunday 6.30 a.m. to 12 midnight. Frequencies: LF 200 kHz/1500m plus eight local fillers on MF giving population coverage 98% (day) and 91% (night): VHF (England, C.I. and I.O.M. plus part of South Wales, S.W. Scotland) 92–95 MHz, coverage 98%.

The national regional services are:

Radio Scotland: Frequencies: MF 810 kHz/370m plus two local fillers, coverage 95% (day) and 87% (night); VHF 92–95 MHz, coverage 94%.

Radio Ulster: Frequencies: MF 1341 kHz/224m plus one local filler, coverage 96% (day) and 80% (night); VHF 92–95 MHz, coverage 97%.

Radio Wales: Frequency: MF 882 kHz/340m plus two local fillers giving coverage 95% (day) and 63% (night).

Radio Cymru (Welsh-language): Frequencies: VHF 92–95 MHz, coverage 91%.

Local Radio: There are 30 local stations serving England and the Channel Islands (*see* below).

Television

The BBC's experiments in television broadcasting started in 1929 and in 1936 the BBC began the world's first public service of high-definition television from Alexandra Palace.

The BBC broadcasts two national television services, BBC 1 (BBC Wales in Wales) and BBC 2. These are broadcast in colour on 625-lines and UHF from a network of transmitting stations planned and built jointly with the Independent Broadcasting Authority. All stations (with a few exceptions) carry four channels including the two IBA channels.

The original service of BBC Television (latterly BBC 1) was broadcast on 405 lines in the VHF band and was finally closed down at the end of 1984. The 625-line UHF service was introduced in 1964 (BBC 2) with BBC 1 added in 1969. Colour was introduced in July 1967. Transmissions from 49 main stations and more than 650 relays are available to more than 99% of the population.

External Services

The External Services broadcast over 700 hours of programmes a week in 37 languages including English on the BBC World Service. Eighty five transmitters are used, 50 of them in the U.K. and 35 at relay stations overseas. In addition the External Services supply many recorded programmes to other radio stations.

World Service, on the air in English for 24 hours a day, directed to all parts of the world, and with additional streams of programmes specially designated for audiences in Africa and South Asia at appropriate peak listening times.

African Service, which broadcasts in Swahili, Somali and Hausa.

Arabic Service, on the air for 9 hours a day to Middle East and North Africa.

Eastern Service, which broadcasts in Bengali, Burmese, Hindi, Nepali, Pashto, Persian, Tamil and Urdu.

Far Eastern Service, in Chinese (Cantonese and Standard Chinese), Indonesian, Japanese, Malay, Thai and Vietnamese.

Latin American Service, in Spanish and Portuguese.

French Service, directed to Europe and Africa.

German Service, directed to West and East Germany and Austria.

Central European Service, in Czech and Slovak, Hungarian, Polish and Finnish.

East European Service, in Bulgarian, Romanian, Russian, Serbo-Croat and Slovene.

South European Service, in Greek, Portuguese to Europe and Africa, and Turkish.

Topical Tapes provides a variety of programmes on tape for overseas radio stations and produces the twice-weekly Calling the Falklands programme.

BBC English by Radio and Television teaches English to learners outside Britain through radio, television and a wide range of published courses.

Transcription Service produces and sells to overseas radio stations recorded programmes drawn from the whole range of BBC Radio.

Monitoring Service provides regional summaries and a teleprinted news service from the output of overseas radio stations.

BBC Local Radio Stations

BRISTOL, 3 Tyndalls Park Road, Bristol. (Tel: 0272 741111). *Wavelengths:* 194/227m, 1548/1323 kHz, 95·5 vhf.

CAMBRIDGESHIRE, Broadcasting House, Hills Road, Cambridge. (Tel: 0223 315970). *Wavelengths:* 207/292m, 1449/1026 kHz, 96·0/103·9 vhf.

CLEVELAND, PO Box 1548, Broadcasting House, Middlesbrough, Cleveland. (Tel: 0642 225211). *Wavelengths:* 194m, 1548 kHz, 96·6/95·8 vhf.

CORNWALL, Phœnix Wharf, Truro, Cornwall. (Tel: 0872 75421). *Wavelengths:* 476/457m, 630/657 kHz, 95·2/96·4/97·3 vhf.

CUMBRIA, Hilltop Heights, London Road, Carlisle, Cumbria. (Tel: 0228 31661). *Wavelengths:* 397/206/358m, 756/1458/837 kHz, 95·6/96·1 vhf.

DERBY, 56 St. Helen's Street, Derby. (Tel: 0332 361111). *Wavelengths:* 269m, 1116 kHz, 96·5/94·2 vhf.

DEVON, St. David's Hill, Exeter, Devon. (Tel: 0392 215651). *Wavelengths:* 351/303/206/375m, 855/990/1458/801 kHz, 97·5/97·0/96·2/103·9 vhf.

FURNESS (Radio Cumbria), Broadcasting House, Hartington Street, Barrow-in-Furness, Cumbria. (Tel: 0229 36767). *Wavelengths:* 358m, 837 kHz, 96·1 vhf.

HUMBERSIDE, 63 Jameson Street, Hull. (Tel: 0482 23232). *Wavelengths:* 202m, 1485 kHz, 96·9 vhf.

KENT, 30 High Street, Chatham, Kent. (Tel: 0634 46284). *Wavelengths:* 290/388m, 1035/774 kHz, 96·7 vhf.

LANCASHIRE, King Street, Blackburn, Lancs. (Tel: 0254 62411). *Wavelengths:* 351/193m, 855/1557 kHz, 96·4/103·3 vhf.

LEEDS, Broadcasting House, Woodhouse Lane, Leeds. (Tel: 0532 442131). *Wavelengths:* 388m, 774 kHz, 92·4/195·3 vhf.

LEICESTER, Epic House, Charles Street, Leicester. (Tel: 0533 27113). *Wavelengths:* 358m, 837 kHz, 95·1 vhf.

LINCOLNSHIRE, Radion Buildings, Newport, Lincoln. (Tel: 0522 40011). *Wavelengths:* 219m, 1368 kHz, 94·9 vhf.

LONDON, PO Box 4LG, 35a Marylebone High Street, London, W1. (Tel: 01-486 7611). *Wavelengths:* 206m, 1458 kHz, 94·9 vhf.

MANCHESTER, PO Box 90, New Broadcasting House, Oxford Road, Manchester. (Tel: 061-228 3434). *Wavelengths:* 206m, 1458 kHz, 95·1 vhf.

MERSEYSIDE, 55 Paradise Street, Liverpool. (Tel: 051-708 5500). *Wavelengths:* 202m, 1485 kHz, 95·8 vhf.

NEWCASTLE, Crestina House, Archbold Terrace, Newcastle upon Tyne. (Tel: 0632 814243). *Wavelengths:* 206m, 1458 kHz, 95·4/96·3 vhf.

NORFOLK, Norfolk Tower, Surrey Street, Norwich. (Tel: 0603 617411). *Wavelengths:* 351/344m, 855/873 kHz, 95·1/96·7 vhf.

NORTHAMPTON, PO Box 1107, Northampton. (Tel: 0604 20621). *Wavelengths:* 271m, 1107 kHz, 96·6/103·3 vhf.

NOTTINGHAM, York House, Mansfield Road, Nottingham. (Tel: 0602 415161). *Wavelengths:* 197/189m, 1521/1584 kHz, 95·4 vhf.

OXFORD, 242/254 Banbury Road, Oxford. (Tel: 0865 53411). *Wavelengths*: 202m, 1485 kHz, 95·2 vhf.
SHEFFIELD, Ashdell Grove, 60 Westbourne Road, Sheffield. (Tel: 0742 686185). *Wavelengths*: 290m, 1035 kHz, 97·4/88·6 vhf.
SOLENT, South Western House, Canute Road, Southampton. (Tel: 0703 31311). *Wavelengths*: 300m, 999 kHz, 96·1 vhf., 221m, 1359 kHz (in Bournemouth).
STOKE ON TENT, Conway House, Cheapside, Hanley, Stoke-on-Trent, Staffs. (Tel: 0782 24827). *Wavelengths*: 200m, 1503 kHz, 96·1/94·6 vhf.
SUSSEX, Marlborough Place, Brighton, Sussex (Tel: 0273 680231). *Wavelengths*: 202/258m, 1485/1161 kHz, 95·3/101·3 vhf.
WM (WEST MIDLANDS), PO Box 206, Birmingham. (Tel: 021-472 5141). *Wavelengths*: 206/362m, 1458/ 828 kHz, 95·6 vhf.
YORK, 20 Bootham Row, York. (Tel: 0904 641351). *Wavelengths*: 450/238m, 666/1260 kHz, 90·2/97·2 vhf.

Two Stations outside the UK :—

GUERNSEY, Commerce House, Les Banques, St. Peter Port, Guernsey. (Tel: 0481 28977). *Wavelengths*: 269m, 1116 kHz.
JERSEY, Broadcasting House, Rouge Bouillon, St. Helier, Jersey. (Tel: 0534 70000). *Wavelengths*: 292m, 1026 kHz, 88·8 vhf.

INDEPENDENT BROADCASTING AUTHORITY

(*see also* entry on pages 406–7)

Independent Television Programme Companies, etc.

ANGLIA TELEVISION (*East of England*), Anglia House, Norwich (Tel: 0603 615151).
BORDER TELEVISION (*The Borders*), Television Centre, Carlisle. (Tel: 0228 25101).
CENTRAL INDEPENDENT TELEVISION (*East and West Midlands*), Central House, Broad Street, Birmingham. (Tel: 021-643 9898).
CHANNEL TELEVISION (*Channel Islands*), The Television Centre, St. Helier, Jersey. (Tel: 0534 73999).
GRAMPIAN TELEVISION (*North Scotland*), Queen's Cross, Aberdeen. (Tel: 0224 646464).
GRANADA TELEVISION (*North-West England*), Granada TV Centre, Manchester. (Tel: 061-832 7211).
HTV (*Wales and West of England*), HTV Wales, Television Centre, Cardiff. (Tel: 0222 590590).
LONDON WEEKEND TELEVISION (*London* [*weekends*]), South Bank Television Centre, Kent House, Upper Ground, London SE1. (Tel: 01-261 3434).
SCOTTISH TELEVISION (*Central Scotland*), Cowcaddens, Glasgow. (Tel: 041-332 9999).
THAMES TELEVISION (*London* [*weekdays*]), Thames Television House, 306–316 Euston Road, London NW1. (Tel: 01-387 9494).
TSW (TELEVISION SOUTH WEST) (*South-West England*), Derry's Cross, Plymouth. (Tel: 0752 663322).
TVS (TELEVISION SOUTH) (*South and South-East England*), Television Centre, Southampton. (Tel: 0703 34211).
TYNE TEES TELEVISION (*North-East England*), The Television Centre, City Road, Newcastle upon Tyne. (Tel: 0632 610181).
ULSTER TELEVISION (*Northern Ireland*), Havelock House, Ormeau Road, Belfast. (Tel: 0232 225122).
YORKSHIRE TELEVISION (*Yorkshire*), The Television Centre, Leeds. (Tel: 0532 438283).
BREAKFAST-TIME TELEVISION, Hawley Crescent, London N.W.1. (Tel: 01-267 4300).
CHANNEL FOUR TELEVISION COMPANY LTD, 60 Charlotte Street, London W.1. (Tel: 01-631 4444).
INDEPENDENT TELEVISION COMPANIES ASSOCIATION

LTD., Knighton House, 56 Mortimer Street, London W.1. (Tel: 01-636 6866).
INDEPENDENT TELEVISION NEWS LTD, ITN House, 48 Wells Street, London W.1. (Tel: 01-637 2424).
ORACLE TELETEXT LTD., Craven House, 25–32 Marshall Street, London W.1. (Tel: 01-434 3121).

[NOTE: It has only been possible to give one address for each of the Programme Companies].

Independent Local Radio Stations

LBC (London Broadcasting Company Limited), Communications House, Gough Square, London EC4. (Tel: 01-353 1010). *Wavelengths*: 261m, 1152 kHz, 97·3 vhf.
CAPITAL RADIO LIMITED, Euston Tower, London NW1. (Tel: 01-388 1288). *Wavelengths*: 194m, 1548 kHz, 95·8 vhf.
RADIO CLYDE LIMITED, Clydebank Business Park, Clydebank, Glasgow. (Tel: 041-941 1111). *Wavelengths*: 261m, 1152 kHz, 95·1 vhf.
BRMB RADIO, (Birmingham Broadcasting Limited), PO Box 555, Radio House, Aston Road North, Aston, Birmingham. (Tel: 021-359 4481/9). *Wavelengths*: 261m, 1152 kHz, 94·8 vhf.
PICCADILLY RADIO LIMITED, 127/131 The Piazza, Piccadilly Plaza, Manchester. (Tel: 061-236 9913). *Wavelengths*: 261m, 1152 kHz, 97·0 vhf.
METRO RADIO (North East Broadcasting Company Limited), Radio House, Long Rigg, Swalwell, Newcastle upon Tyne. (Tel: 0632 883131). *Wavelengths*: 261m, 1152 kHz, 97·0 vhf.
SWANSEA SOUND LIMITED, Victoria Road, Gowerton, Swansea. (Tel: 0792 893751). *Wavelengths*: 257m, 1170 kHz, 95·1 vhf.
RADIO HALLAM LIMITED, PO Box 194, Hartshead, Sheffield. (Tel: 0742 71188). *Wavelengths*: 194m, 1548 kHz, 95·9 vhf (Rotherham), 95·2 vhf (Sheffield).
RADIO CITY (Sound of Merseyside Limited), PO Box 194, 8–10 Stanley Street, Liverpool. (Tel: 051-227 5100). *Wavelengths*: 194m, 1548 kHz, 96·7 vhf.
RADIO FORTH LIMITED, Forth House, Forth Street, Edinburgh. (Tel: 031-556 9255). *Wavelengths*: 194m, 1548 kHz, 96·8 vhf.
PLYMOUTH SOUND LIMITED, Earl's Acre, Alma Road, Plymouth. (Tel: 0752 27272). *Wavelengths*: 261m, 1152 kHz, 96·0 vhf.
RADIO TEES (Sound Broadcasting (Teesside) Limited), 74 Dovecot Street, Stockton-on-Tees, Cleveland. (Tel: 0642 615111). *Wavelengths*: 257m, 1170 kHz, 95·0 vhf.
RADIO TRENT LIMITED, 29–31 Castle Gate, Nottingham. (Tel: 0602 581731). *Wavelengths*: 301m, 999 kHz, 96·2 vhf.
PENNINE RADIO, (Bradford Community Radio Limited), PO Box 235, Pennine House, Forster Square, Bradford. (Tel: 0274 731521). *Wavelengths*: 235/ 196m, 1278/1530 kHz, 96·0 vhf.
RADIO VICTORY LIMITED, PO Box 257, 247 Fratton Road, Portsmouth. (Tel: 0705 827799). *Wavelengths*: 257m, 1170 kHz, 95·0 vhf.
RADIO ORWELL LIMITED, Electric House, Lloyds Avenue, Ipswich. (Tel: 0473 216971). *Wavelengths*: 257m, 1170 kHz, 97·1 vhf.
RADIO 210 THAMES VALLEY (Thames Valley Broadcasting Limited), PO Box 210, Reading, Berkshire. (Tel: 0734 413131). *Wavelengths*: 210m, 1431 kHz, 97·0 vhf.
DOWNTOWN RADIO (Community Radio Services Limited), PO Box 293, Kiltonga Industrial Estate, Newtownards, Northern Ireland. (Tel: 0247 815555). *Wavelengths*: 293m, 1026 kHz, 96·0 vhf.
BEACON RADIO (Beacon Broadcasting Limited), PO Box 303, 267 Tettenhall Road, Wolverhampton. (Tel: 0902 757211). *Wavelengths*: 303m, 990 kHz, 97·2 vhf.

CARDIFF BROADCASTING COMPANY LIMITED, Radio House, West Canal Wharf, Cardiff. (Tel: 0222 384041). *Wavelengths*: 221m, 1359 kHz, 96·0 vhf.

MERCIA SOUND (Midland Community Radio Limited), Hertford Place, Coventry. (Tel: 0203 28451). *Wavelengths*: 220m, 1359 kHz, 95·9 vhf.

HEREWARD RADIO LIMITED, PO Box 225. 114 Bridge Street, Peterborough. (Tel: 0733 46225). *Wavelengths*: 225m, 1332 kHz, 95·7 vhf.

TWO COUNTIES RADIO LIMITED, 5–7 Southcote Road, Bournemouth. (Tel: 0202 294881). *Wavelengths*: 362m, 828 kHz, 97·2 vhf.

RADIO TAY (Tay Sound Broadcasting Limited), PO Box 123, Dundee. (Tel: 0382 29551). *Wavelengths*: Dundee 258m, 1161 kHz, 95·8 vhf; Perth 189m, 1584 kHz, 96·4 vhf.

SEVERN SOUND (Gloucestershire Broadcasting Company Limited), PO Box 388, Old Talbot House, 67 Southgate Street, Gloucester. (Tel: 0452 423791). *Wavelengths*: 388m, 774 kHz, 95·0 vhf.

DEVONAIR RADIO LIMITED, The Studio Centre, 35–37 St. David's Hill, Exeter. (Tel: 0392 30703). *Wavelengths*: Exeter 450m, 666 kHz, 95·8 vhf; Torbay 314m, 954 kHz, 95·1 vhf.

NORTHSOUND (North of Scotland Radio Limited), 45 Kings Gate, Aberdeen. (Tel: 0224 632234). *Wavelengths*: 290m, 1035 kHz, 96·9 vhf.

RADIO AIRE (West Yorkshire Broadcasting PLC), PO Box 362, 51 Burley Road, Leeds. (Tel: 0532 452299). *Wavelengths*: 362m, 828 kHz, 94·6 vhf.

ESSEX RADIO P.L.C., Radio House, Clifftown Road, Southend-on-Sea, Essex. (Tel: 0702 333711). *Wavelengths*: Southend 210m, 1431 kHz, 95·3 vhf; Chelmsford 220m, 1359 kHz, 96·4 vhf.

CHILTERN RADIO P.L.C., Chiltern Radio, Dunstable, Bedfordshire. (Tel: 0582 666001). *Wavelengths*: Luton 362m, 828 kHz, 97·6 vhf; Bedford 378m, 792 kHz, 95·5 vhf.

WEST SOUND (Radio Ayrshire Limited), Radio House, 54 Holmston Road, Ayr. (Tel: 0292 283662). *Wavelengths*: Ayr 290m, 1035 kHz, 96·2 vhf; Girvan 97·1 vhf.

RADIO WEST (Radio Avonside Limited), PO Box 963, Watershed, Canons Road, Bristol. (Tel: 0272 279900). *Wavelengths*: 238m, 1260 kHz, 96·3 vhf.

MORAY FIRTH RADIO LIMITED, PO Box 271, Inverness. (Tel: 0463 224433). *Wavelengths*: 271m, 1107 kHz, 95·9 vhf.

RADIO WYVERN P.L.C., 5/6 Barbourne Terrace, Worcester. (Tel: 0905 612212). *Wavelengths*: Hereford 314m, 954 kHz, 95·8 vhf; Worcester 196m, 1530 kHz, 96·2 vhf.

RED ROSE RADIO P.L.C., PO Box 301, St. Paul's Square, Preston, Lancashire. (Tel: 0772 556301). *Wavelengths*: 301m, 999 kHz, 97·3 vhf.

WILTSHIRE RADIO P.L.C., Old Lime Kiln, High Street, Wootton Bassett, Swindon, Wiltshire. (Tel: 0793 853222). *Wavelengths*: Swindon 258m, 1161 kHz, 96·4 vhf; West Wiltshire 321m, 936 kHz, 97·4 vhf.

SAXON RADIO LIMITED IN ASSOCIATION WITH RADIO ORWELL LIMITED, Long Brackland, Bury St. Edmunds, Suffolk. (Tel: 0284 701511). *Wavelengths*: 240m, 1251 kHz, 96·3 vhf.

COUNTY SOUND P.L.C., The Friary, Guildford. (Tel: 0483 505566). *Wavelengths*: 203m, 1476 kHz, 96·6 vhf.

SOUTHERN SOUND P.L.C., Radio House, Franklin Road, Portslade. (Tel: 0273 422288). *Wavelengths*: 225m, 1332 kHz, 103·4 MHz.

MARCHER SOUND/SAIN-Y-GORORAU, The Studios, Mold Road, Gwersyllt, Wrexham, Clwyd. (Tel: 0978 752202). *Wavelengths*: 238m, 1260 kHz, 95·4 vhf.

GWENT BROADCASTING, 173 Chepstow Road, Maindee, Newport, Gwent. (Tel: 0633 56230). *Wavelengths*: 230m, 1305 kHz, 104 vhf.

SIGNAL RADIO, 67–73 Stoke Road, Stoke-on-Trent, Staffordshire. (Tel: 0782 417111). *Wavelengths*: 257m, 1170 kHz, 1170 vhf.

VIKING RADIO LTD., Commercial Road, Hull. (Tel: 0482 25141). *Wavelengths*: 258m, 1161 kHz, 102·7 vhf.

INVICTA SOUND P.L.C. (incorporating Northdown Radio), 15 Station Road East, Canterbury, Kent. (Tel: 0227 58761). *Wavelengths*: 242m, 1242 kHz, 103·8 vhf.

RADIO MERCURY, Broadfield House, Brighton Road, Crawley, W. Sussex. (Tel: 0293 519161). *Wavelengths*: 197m, 1521 kHz, 103·6 vhf.

INVICTA SOUND P.L.C. (incorporating Network East Kent), 15 Station Road East, Canterbury, Kent. (Tel: 0227 58761). *Wavelengths*: 497m, 603 kHz, Dover 97·0 vhf, Thanet 95·9 vhf, Canterbury 95·1 vhf, Ashford to be announced.

RADIO BROADLAND, PO Box 260, Norwich. (Tel: 0603 660926). *Wavelengths*: 260m, 1152 kHz, 97·6 MHz.

HEREWARD RADIO P.L.C., PO Box 193, 73 Abington Street, Northampton. (Tel: 0733 46225). *Wavelengths*: 193m, 1557 kHz, vhf to be announced.

FILM AND CINEMA, 1983–84

In its White Paper on Film Policy, the Government, as expected, proposed an end to the Eady Levy, the tax on cinema box office takings, which was introduced in 1957, and raised some £4·5 million a year to assist film producers. The National Film Finance Corporation's functions would be transferred to the private sector, and a new advisory body for the film industry was proposed. The National Film and Television School, currently funded by Eady, would be supported by cinema and television companies. The Government also intended that the film industry should be deregulated, with eight statutes and 25 regulations governing it being removed, including the cinema quota for showing a proportion of British films in cinemas, which had been introduced in 1927 but suspended in 1983. Of more immediate import was the Chancellor of the Exchequer's budget announcement that capital allowances would be ended. The tax régime in Britain had been particularly favourable to film-makers, especially from the U.S.A., who had been led to believe that the allowances would remain until at least 1987. The *Superman* films and *Star Wars* series had been made using British studios and expertise, but the producers declared their intention of moving elsewhere, losing the country valuable income.

Academy Awards

After the British successes of the past two years, with *Chariots of Fire* and *Gandhi* taking the honours at the Oscar ceremonies, it was reasonable to expect that the Americans would find a home-grown product to regain some prestige. Although hopes were high at the nominations stage, with four British actors and one actress in the running, and the film *The Dresser*, based on Ronald Harwood's play, nominated in five categories, it was the American film *Terms of Endearment* which scooped the major awards.

The main awards were: best film, *Terms of Endearment*; best director, James L. Brooks (*Terms of Endearment*); best actor, Robert Duvall (*Tender Mercies*); best actress, Shirley Maclaine (*Terms of Endearment*); best supporting actor, Jack Nicholson (*Terms of Endearment*); best supporting actress, Linda Hunt (*The Year of Living Dangerously*). *Terms of Endearment* also received the award for best adapted screenplay, while best screenplay went to *Tender Mercies*. Ingmar Bergman's *Fanny and Alexander* won four Oscars—best foreign language film, cinematography, art direction and costume design. *The Right Stuff* also received four awards—best original music score, film editing, sound and sound effects editing. Barbra Streisand's *Yentl* won the award for best song score.

At the British Academy of Film and Tele-vision Arts Awards, best film was *Educating Rita*; best director, Bill Forsyth (*Local Hero*); best original screenplay, Paul D. Zimmerman (*The King of Comedy*); best adapted screenplay, Ruth Prawer Jhabvala (*Heat and Dust*); best actor, Michael Caine (*Educating Rita*) and Dustin Hoffman (*Tootsie*); best actress, Julie Walters (*Educating Rita*); best supporting actor, Denholm Elliott (*Trading Places*); best supporting actress, Jamie Lee Curtis (*Trading Places*); most outstanding newcomer, Phyllis Logan (*Another Time, Another Place*); best score, Ryuichi Sakamoto (*Merry Christmas, Mr. Lawrence*); best foreign language film, *Danton*; and best short film, *Goodie Two Shoes*. Best cinematography was awarded to Sven Nykvist for *Fanny and Alexander*; best production design and art direction to Franco Zeffirelli and Gianna Quaranta (*La Traviata*); best costume design, Piero Tosi (*La Traviata*); film editing, Bud Smith and Walt Mulconery (*Flashdance*); best sound, *War Games*; best special visual effects, *Return of the Jedi*, and best make-up, *Tootsie*.

London Film Festival

The 27th London Film Festival showed 150 films, in the 50th anniversary of the British Film Institute. It was notable that of the 15 new British films at the Festival, eleven had been made by or for television companies. The main interest at the Festival was caused by the showing of five 'lost' Hitchcock films, prior to general release. The films, four of which featured James Stewart, had been withdrawn over the years due to problems over literary rights, the copyright reverting to Hitchcock. All extant prints were destroyed (apart from the odd unofficial copy which circulated), and Hitchcock retained the negatives. It has been suggested that he was keeping them as a pension for his old age, or until a satisfactory offer was made for them. Whatever the position (and a hint of mystery and suspense does not come amiss where he is concerned), the films have confirmed Hitchcock's brilliance as a director. The five were *Rear Window*, in which Stewart played a photographer confined to a wheelchair who sees a murder in a flat opposite his window. Made in 1954, it also featured Grace Kelly and Raymond Burr. *Vertigo* (1958) starred Stewart with Kim Novak and Barbara Bel Geddes, in a tale about a detective who has lost his head for heights being tricked in a complex mistaken identity case. *The Trouble with Harry* (1956) was Shirley Maclaine's first feature film, and concerned a corpse that would not stay buried. *Rope* (1948) was notable for its experimental ten-minute takes, and *The Man Who Knew Too Much* (1956) was a remake of Hitchcock's 1934 film.

The Festival opened with Truffaut's *Finally, Sunday*, a black-and-white comedy thriller dedicated to Hitchcock and 1940s' crime thrillers. It was based on Charles Williams' 1962 film *Confidentially Yours*, and featured Jean-Louis Trintignant and Fanny Ardant.

At the Venice Film Festival, Ingmar Bergman's *Fanny and Alexander* was shown in the full, five-and-a-half hour version, out of competition. The Golden Lion for best film was awarded to Jean-Luc Godard's *Prénom Carmen*, in which he himself appeared as a demented film-maker. The film also received prizes for its camerawork and soundtrack. The jury special prize was given to *Biquefarre*, directed by Georges Rouquier of France, and best actress was Darling Legitimus in Euzhan Palcy's remarkable film from Martinique, *Rue Cases Negres*. Robert Altman's skill with ensemble playing was recognized with the best actor award given to the cast of six in his film *Streamers*, which concerned American soldiers in barracks before going to fight in Vietnam.

At the Berlin Film Festival, the Golden Bear was awarded to John Cassavetes' *Love Streams*, with Albert Finney receiving the Silver Bear for his part in *The Dresser*. The best director was Ettore Scola for *Le Bal*, a French-Algerian-Italian co-production. At San Sebastian, the critics' prize went to *Coup de Foudre*, directed by Diane Kurys (France), and best director was shared between Antonio Zorrilla of Spain for *El Arreglo*, and Marc Didden of Belgium for *Brussels by Night*.

At the 37th Cannes Film Festival, the *Palme d'Or* was awarded to Wim Wenders' *Paris, Texas*, written by Sam Shepard, and featuring Harry Dean Stanton and Nastassja Kinski. Helen Mirren was best actress for *Cal*, and Bertrand Tavernier best director for *Sunday in the Country*.

Productions

Educating Rita was a deserved British success (noted last year), for which both Michael Caine and Julie Walters received Oscar nominations, which would probably have been converted into awards had not a mild backlash set in after previous successes. Also deservedly acclaimed was *The Dresser*, directed by Peter Yates and based on Ronald Harwood's stage success. Albert Finney gave a marvellous bravura performance as 'Sir', the over-the-hill actor manager attempting to perform *King Lear* in Bradford in wartime. Apart from an Oscar nomination, Finney won best actor prize in Berlin. Tom Courtenay was also nominated for his part as the theatrical dresser of the title. The principals were ably supported by Edward Fox and Eileen Atkins.

Hugh Hudson, whose directorial début in *Chariots of Fire* achieved international acclaim, took as his next project the somewhat hackneyed story of Tarzan, but with the sensible notion of remaining faithful to Edgar Rice Burroughs' original 1912 novel. *Greystoke—The Legend of Tarzan, Lord of the Apes*, was adapted by Michael Austin and P. H. Vazak, and told the story of how John Clayton, Earl of Greystoke, came to live in the jungle, following a shipwreck which killed his parents. Suckled and brought up by apes— with some excellent make-up by Rick Baker— Tarzan returns to England for his inheritance. The film's early promise is dissipated in its latter stages, as it seems that the studio's determination to keep it to a certain length has necessitated cuts which destroy the narrative thread. However, it is a worthy and enjoyable film, with fine performances from Christopher Lambert in the title role, Ralph Richardson, Ian Holm, James Fox and Ian Charleson.

John Irvin's *Champions* would have been dismissed as too far-fetched to be conceivable, were it not that the true story of Bob Champion's fight back from cancer to win the 1981 Grand National on Aldaniti was so well known. John Hurt was effective as the jockey, and the racing sequence at Aintree was expertly recreated.

Julian Mitchell's successful stage play *Another Country* was transferred to the screen, directed by Marek Kanievska. Rupert Everett recreated his role as the public schoolboy who became a traitor, with Colin Firth, Anna Massey and Carey Elwes. *Secret Places*, written and directed by Zelda Barron, was set in an English girls' school, and concerned the problems faced by a German refugee at the school in wartime. Based on Janice Elliott's novel, the film featured Jenny Agutter, Sylvia Coleridge, Simon Relph, Cassie Stuart and Marie-Theres Relin.

Also of note were two comic and well-made British films, directed by Richard Eyre. *Loose Connections*, written by Maggie Brooks, featured Stephen Rea and Lindsay Duncan on a hilarious car journey of discovery. *Laughterhouse*, written by Brian Glover, featured Ian Holm as a poultry farmer who walks his flock of geese from Norfolk to Smithfield Market in London. David Jones's *Betrayal* starred Ben Kingsley, Jeremy Irons and Patricia Hodge in Harold Pinter's adaptation of his own play.

American Films

The Oscar success, *Terms of Endearment*, an episodic account of the relationship between a mother and daughter over some 30 years, was well acted, especially by Shirley Maclaine and Jack Nicholson who won awards, and also by Debra Winger who received a nomination. However, it appeared too artful in its manipulation of the audience's emotions to distinguish it as a great film.

Woody Allen displayed further virtuosity and breadth in the remarkable *Zelig*, a brief but well-paced pastiche documentary about the life of Leonard Zelig, a human chameleon who cropped up throughout the inter-war years, for example, at Hitler's side at a Munich rally, with Charlie Chaplin, and Babe Ruth the baseball player. Real people, such as novelist Saul Bellow, appear in the film (as in Warren Beatty's *Reds*) to reminisce about the fictional Zelig, and documentary footage was brilliantly edited to incorporate the mysterious Zelig in the events depicted. Allen was ably assisted by Mia Farrow, who also appeared in his next film, *Broadway Danny Rose*, about an unsuccessful theatrical agent lumbered with unemployable clients.

Graham Greene's novel *The Honorary Consul* was adapted for the screen by Christopher Hampton and directed by John Mackenzie. It featured Michael Caine, Richard Gere, Bob Hoskins and Elpidia Carrillo. The version screened in the U.S.A. was altered by the studio, and retitled *Beyond the Limit*, as market research indicated that no one understood the original title! Martin Cruz Smith's *Gorky Park* was adapted by Dennis Potter, and directed by Michael Apted. Starring William Hurt, Lee Marvin, Joanna Pacula and Brian Dennehey, the film was made in Helsinki, which unfortunately was no substitute for the city of Moscow which dominated the novel with its brooding presence.

Barbra Streisand's one-woman show *Yentl*, which she directed, starred in, and co-wrote with Jack Rosenthal aroused mixed reactions. The author of the original story, Isaac Bashevis Singer, was quoted as saying: "Miss Streisand was exceedingly kind to herself. The result is that Miss Streisand is always present while poor Yentl is absent. The passion for learning and the passion for singing are not much related in my mind. One cannot cover up with songs the shortcomings of the direction and acting." The story about a girl who has to disguise herself as a man at the turn of the century to study religious texts such as the Talmud and the Torah, which were forbidden to women, has been softened and sentimentalized in the film. Furthermore, the songs (for which the film received its only Oscar) are almost totally superfluous, and sung only by Streisand. The film was not without merit, but historical inaccuracies also lessened its impact. While its nomination for only five Academy Awards in minor categories was seen as a snub for Streisand, she collected Hollywood Golden Globes for best musical and best direction.

The Right Stuff, written and directed by Philip Kaufman from Tom Wolfe's book, concerned the pioneering days of space exploration. The film had some marvellous moments, but its impact was undercut by the sending up of the scientists and politicians involved (with the exception of Kennedy, seen only in contemporary film-clips). It featured Sam Shepard, Scott Glen and Ed Harris.

Sidney Lumet's *Daniel* was based on E. L. Doctorow's *The Book of Daniel*, about the Rosenbergs who were executed in 1953 after being convicted of conspiring to pass atomic secrets to the Russians. The names and a few details were changed, but this story of a period of paranoia in American consciousness, and the suggestion that the couple were innocent, coupled with gruesomely realistic execution scenes, did not go down well in the U.S.A., where critical reaction was harsh. *Daniel* featured Timothy Hutton, Mandy Patinkin, Lindsay Crouse, Edward Asner and Joseph Leon.

Brian de Palma's *Scarface*, dedicated to Ben Hecht and Howard Hawks, who made the 1932 original, was a brash, violent updated gangster thriller, concerning Cuban drug dealers in Miami. Al Pacino was effective in the title role, supported by Michelle Pfeiffer.

Bob Fosse's *Star 80* was a dramatization of the life and tragic death of Dorothy Stratten, a victim of the American dream for fame and success. A *Playboy* magazine model on the verge of a successful film career, she was killed by her former mentor whose own inadequacies were exposed by her success. Mariel Hemingway played the tragic Dorothy, with Cliff Robertson, Roger Rees and Eric Roberts.

Rumble Fish by Francis Ford Coppola, heavily influenced by the German expressionists, was an interesting and partially successful study of small-town American teenagers. The title referred to Siamese fish, so fierce that they will even attack their own reflections, and to emphasize the point, the film was made in black-and-white, with only the fish in colour. Written by S. E. Hinton, the film featured Matt Dillon, Mickey Rourke and Dennis Hopper.

Mel Brooks starred with Anne Bancroft in *To Be Or Not To Be*, directed by Alan Johnson, a remake of Ernst Lubitsch's 1942 film which was felt in bad taste at the time, as it made comedy from the situation in Poland in 1939.

Come Back to the Five and Dime, Jimmy Dean, Jimmy Dean was directed by Robert Altman, based on a play by Ed Graczyk which he had originally directed on Broadway. The film made a virtue of its stagey setting, and drew excellent performances from the cast of Karen Black, Sandy Dennis and Cher.

Something Wicked This Way Comes was based on Ray Bradbury's short story "Black Ferris", which Gene Kelly had wanted to direct in 1958. It was expanded to novel-length in 1962. Produced by Walt Disney, this tale about a Satanic carnival, in which customers' deepest desires are realized before they end up as waxworks was directed by Jack Clayton, his first film since *The Great Gatsby* nine years previously. It featured Jason Robards, Jonathan Pryce and Vidal Peterson, with photography by Stephen H. Burum particularly impressive.

Steven Spielberg's *Indiana Jones and the Temple of Doom*, with Harrison Ford and Kate Capshaw, capitalized on the huge success of *Raiders of the Lost Ark*, but lacked some of that film's charm. *Reuben Reuben*, written by Julius Epstein (who wrote *Casablanca*), and directed by Robert Ellis Miller, featured Tom Conti as a drunken poet, for which role he received an Oscar nomination. In Mike Nichols' *Silkwood*, Meryl Streep was nominated for an Oscar for her superbly downbeat performance: she played a worker in a plutonium plant who died in mysterious circumstances on her way to meet a journalist to expose inadequate safety precautions at the plant. *White Dog*, directed by Sam Fuller, was a powerful parable about an animal turned into a racialist killer, with Kristy McNichol and Burl Ives. *Splash*, directed by Ron Howard, was a bright comedy about a mermaid, with Daryl Hannah as the scaly maiden.

Other productions included *Under the Volcano*, directed by John Huston, and based on Malcolm Lowry's flawed masterpiece, with Albert Finney, Anthony Andrews and Jacqueline Bisset; *The Star Chamber*, directed by Peter Hyams, with Michael Douglas, a drama about a group of vigilante judges meting out their own brand of justice to criminals acquitted on technicalities; *Under Fire*, directed by Roger Spottiswoode, was a topical drama set in Nicaragua, with Nick Nolte as a photographer becoming involved with the events he filmed. This effective moral drama also featured Gene Hackman, Joanna Cassidy and Ed Harris. *Breathless* was a remake of Jean-Luc Godard's 1960 film *À Bout de Souffle*, made as a star vehicle for Richard Gere, but lifeless in comparison with the original. National Lampoon's *Vacation*, directed by Harold Ramis, featured Chevy Chase. Lawrence Kasdan's *The Big Chill* featured William Hurt, Kevin Kline, Tom Berenger, Jo Beth Williams and Meg Tilly.

Sean Connery returned as James Bond in *Never Say Never Again*, directed by Irvin Kershner, but even though this was a rerun of the plot of *Thunderball*, Roger Moore in *Octopussy* paled in comparison. John Landis's *Trading Places* was a skilful comedy, featuring Dan Aykroyd, Eddie Murphy, Jamie Lee Curtis and Denholm Elliott, and David Cronenberg's *The Dead Zone*, with Christopher Walken and Martin Sheen was an imaginative thriller.

Foreign Productions

Notable foreign-made productions during the year included the Hungarian film *Forbidden Relations*, directed by Zsolt Kezdi-Kovacs, a sensitive study of the difficult subject of incest. *Nostalgia* by Tarkovsky, distinguished Russian director of *Solaris*, was made in Italy, and concerned a poet retracing the steps of an 18th century Russian composer. While in the West, Tarkovsky complained that Soviet bureaucracy was hampering his career, and in July 1984 he sought political asylum. From Australia came *We of the Never Never*, directed by Igor Auzin, with Angela Punch McGregor and Arthur Dignam, based on the classic book by Mrs. Aeneas Gunn, and *Monkey Grip*, directed by Ken Cameron, with Noni Hazlehurst and Colin Friels. *The Return of Martin Guerre* was an intriguing French film, based on a true medieval story, about a man who returned to his village, nine years after he left it, a changed person. Directed by Daniel Vigne, it featured Gerard Depardieu and Nathalie Baye. *Danton*, directed by Polish director Andrzej Wajda, was a powerful study of the struggle between Robespierre and Danton, with Gerard Depardieu and Wojciech Pszoniak as the protagonists, with wider implications on the effect of revolution on its participants. *Swann in Love* was an international production, which cleverly extracted one theme from Proust's *À la Recherche du Temps Perdu* to suggest the flavour of that massive work. Jeremy Irons played Swann, with Ornella Muti as the Countess, Fanny Ardant, and Alain Delon, cast against type, brilliant as Baron de Charlus.

THE ACADEMY AWARDS, 1980–83

1980 Best Picture: *Ordinary People*.
    Best Director: Robert Redford, *Ordinary People*.
    Best Actor: Robert De Niro, *Raging Bull*.
    Best Actress: Sissy Spacek, *Coalminer's Daughter*.
1981 Best Picture: *Chariots of Fire*.
    Best Director: Warren Beatty, *Reds*.
    Best Actor: Henry Fonda, *On Golden Pond*.
    Best Actress: Katharine Hepburn, *On Golden Pond*.

1982 Best Picture: *Gandhi*.
    Best Director: Sir Richard Attenborough, *Gandhi*.
    Best Actor: Ben Kingsley, *Gandhi*.
    Best Actress: Meryl Streep, *Sophie's Choice*.
1983 Best Picture: *Terms of Endearment*.
    Best Director: James L. Brooks, *Terms of Endearment*.
    Best Actor: Robert Duvall, *Tender Mercies*.
    Best Actress: Shirley Maclaine, *Terms of Endearment*.

OPERA AND DANCE 1983–84

Bowing Out

The 1983–84 season saw the retirement from the operatic stage of the Welsh baritone *Sir Geraint Evans*. Born in 1922, Sir Geraint entered the Guildhall School of Music after serving with the R.A.F. during the war. He made his debut at Covent Garden in 1948 as the Nightwatchman in *Die Meistersinger von Nürnberg*, and only a year later gave his first performance as Figaro for the House. The same year, 1949, saw his debut at Glyndebourne and he sang there regularly for over ten years, adding Guglielmo (*Così fan tutte*), Masetto and Leporello (*Don Giovanni*), Abbate (*Arlecchino*) and Falstaff to his roles, which have, thanks to the considerable range of his voice, included much of the lyric (baritone) repertoire. Among the roles which he created in London are Mr. Flint (*Billy Budd*), Mountjoy (*Gloriana*) and Antenor (*Troilus and Cressida*), but Sir Geraint's greatest successes have probably been with more comic roles, such as Falstaff, Leporello, Papageno and Beckmesser. These have given the greatest scope to his facility for lively and humane characterization, and a comic timing which is, apparently, modelled on that of Bob Hope and Jack Benny!

Sir Geraint had announced in February 1982 his intention of retiring at the end of this season and in the intervening period had made final appearances in some of the roles for which he was renowned, *Don Pasquale* and Beckmesser (*Die Meistersinger von Nürnberg*) in spring 1983 and Dulcamara, the itinerant quack medico, (*L'elisir d'amore*) in May–June 1984; illness prevented a final Balstrode (*Peter Grimes*) at the Olympic Arts Festival in Los Angeles in July 1984. Sir Geraint's final performance at the Royal Opera House was marked by presentations by the orchestra, the chorus and the Royal Opera's general director, Sir John Tooley. The performance was recorded for transmission by the Welsh Fourth T.V. Channel and shown on June 17.

L'elisir d'amore (Donizetti). *Production* by John Copley, *rehearsed* by Christopher Renshaw; *designer*, Beni Montresor; *conductor*, Gabriele Bellini. *Adina*, Sona Ghazarian; *Nemorino*, Luis Lima/Alejandro Ramirez; *Belcore*, Ingvar Wixell; *Dulcamara*, Geraint Evans; *Gianetta*, Cathryn Pope.

The Royal Opera's appearances at the Olympic Arts Festival in July 1984 also saw the retirement from the operatic stage of *Heather Harper*. The Belfast-born soprano, in Los Angeles to sing Ellen Orford, announced her retirement just before the final performance on July 19 of *Peter Grimes*. After her debut in 1954 with the Oxford University Opera Society, Miss Harper appeared at Glyndebourne (initially in the chorus), with the English Opera Group from 1956, and from

1962 at Covent Garden, where her roles have included Helena (*Midsummer Night's Dream*), Gutrune (*Götterdämmerung*), Eva (*Die Meistersinger von Nürnberg*), Antonia (*Les Contes d'Hoffman*) and *Arabella*. Although ending her operatic career, Miss Harper intends to continue giving concert performances and to increase her teaching commitments.

David Wall retired in August 1984 after 20 years as a dancer, 18 of them as a Principal. After training at White Lodge and the Royal Ballet School he graduated into the Touring Company (now Sadler's Wells Royal Ballet). At the age of 18, and two years later, he was appointed a Principal, the youngest in the history of the Company. In 1970, he joined The Royal Ballet at Covent Garden. Strong technique and a lively personality allied to a flair for dramatic characterization and subtlety, won him much praise for his interpretations of classic roles and his fine skills both as a partner and a solo performer. David Wall's many created roles include Prince Rudolf (*Mayerling*), Lescaut (*Manon*), Summer (*The Four Seasons*), Caliban (*The Tempest*), Giorgio's Father (*Valley of Shadows*), a leading role in *Adieu*, *Fleeting Figures*, the pas de deux *The Walk to the Paradise Garden*, *Villa d'Este*, *Impromptu* and *Chanson*; and he also danced in the first performances by the Royal Ballet of *Dances at a Gathering*, *Adagio Hammerklavier*, *Voluntaries*, *Troy Game* and *Napoli divertissement*. On September 1, 1984, David Wall took up the position of Associate Director with the Royal Academy of Dancing, but emerges briefly from retirement in October 1984 to give a farewell performance in *Mayerling* when it returns to the Royal Ballet's repertoire.

Obituaries

Sir Anton Dolin, who died in Paris on November 25, 1983 at the age of 79, was one of the first British dancers this century to become world-famous. Born Patrick Healey-Kay in Sussex in 1904, he made his professional debut in pantomime at the age of 16 and in his youth partnered Dame Adeline Genee, a star of the Victorian and Edwardian era, before joining the Diaghilev Ballet in 1923. Here he established an international reputation, particularly with *Le Train Bleu*, created for him by Nijinska, which showed both his classical and more acrobatic techniques.

Not only a virile soloist but also a fine partner in classical roles, Dolin formed in 1931 a twenty-year partnership with Alicia Markova, initially as stars of the then Vic-Wells Ballet and from 1935 as directors and principals of their own company, which took a wide repertoire on tour to all parts of the country. The war years were spent mostly in the U.S.A., but in 1949 a group in London formed around Markova and Dolin grew into the London Festival Ballet, of which Dolin was a Principal dancer in the 1950s and artistic director until 1960.

After the conclusion in 1952 of his partnership with Markova, Dolin pursued a varied career, as a dancer, latterly in character roles such as Dr. Coppelius (*Coppélia*) and Dr. Drosselmeyre (*The Nutcracker*), as a teacher and producer of ballet, and as artistic director to the Rome Opera House Ballet and Ballet National Canadien, Montreal. As well as the roles he created for Nijinska and Balanchine during his time with the Diaghilev Company, and later for de Valois and Massine, Dolin also created his own ballets, including *Hymn to the Sun*, *The Rose and the Nightingale*, *Rhapsody in Blue* and *Espagnol*. Although these contained little that was radical or unusually novel, they displayed the strong sense of presentation and stagecraft, and the considerable knowledge of traditional classical ballet which informed Dolin's dancing and which he brought to teaching and producing for companies throughout the world in the latter stages of his career. He was knighted in 1981.

The Italian baritone *Tito Gobbi* died in Rome on March 5, 1984 at the age of 68. He made his debut in Rome in 1938 and first appeared at La Scala in 1942. By 1950, when he first appeared in London, his reputation was established and within the next few years he had achieved international success. Tito Gobbi's first visits to London were with the La Scala company and included appearances as Belcore (*L'elisir d'amore*), Falstaff and Iago (*Otello*) at Covent Garden in 1950 and Figaro (*Il barbiere di Siviglia*) and Scarpia (*Tosca*) at the Stoll Theatre in 1952. He performed regularly at Covent Garden for nearly twenty years, rarely missing a season between 1955 and 1974, in a number of Verdi, Puccini and Mozart roles. To all of them he brought a voice of great purity and firmness used with exemplary skill and refinement. However, the quality which, even more than an excellent voice and vocal technique, set his performances apart from others was his accomplished acting. He took as great pains with the dramatic as with the vocal presentation of a role, seeking a stance, gait and gestures which established the character as a fully-rounded individual and which developed an audience's understanding of the character. This liveliness and freshness of characterization was used to memorable effect in his roles, most notably in *Rigoletto*, *Macbeth*, *Falstaff*, Iago (*Otello*) and *Simon Boccanegra*. And where his artistry as a singing-actor was matched by that of his fellow-performers, Scarpia to Callas's *Tosca*, Posa opposite Boris Christoff's King Philip (*Don Carlos*), performances have become legendary.

Singing was not Gobbi's sole contribution to opera; in 1964 he directed as well as sang the title role in Covent Garden's first production of *Simon Boccanegra* and also produced a number of operas in the U.S.A.; and after his retirement he spent considerable time teaching. For many years he gave masterclasses, both at the opera studio he had established in Asolo, Italy, and at the National Opera studio in London, and in 1983 the Tito Gobbi International Competition for Singers was established at his birthplace Bassano del Grapo, near Venice.

Professor Peter Wishart, composer and teacher of music, died on August 14, 1984 at the age of 63. His published compositions, numbering over 100, include orchestral and choral works, but his reputation as a composer is based mainly on five operas: two one-act pieces, *Two in the Bush* (1959) and *The Captive* (1960), and *The Clandestine Marriage* (1971), *Clytemnestra* (1973) and *The Lady of the Inn* (1983). In the course of his career as a teacher, Peter Wishart lectured at Birmingham, the Guildhall School of Music and Drama, the University of Bath and King's College, London, before becoming Professor and head of the Music Department of Reading University in 1977.

Novel Operas

In autumn 1983, the five-year-old Opera North presented its first world première, *Rebecca*, a new work commissioned by the Company. The three-act opera, based on Daphne du Maurier's novel of the same name, is the work of Wilfred Josephs, whose previous compositions include a children's opera, major orchestral and choral works and a wide variety of film and television scores. *Rebecca* is, however, his first full-scale opera. The opera, which has a libretto by Edward Marsh, departs from the original story in turning Rebecca's murder into suicide, but retains the concluding destruction of Manderley, after a one-day course on holography enabled the composer to overcome the technical problems of burning down the set at every performance. The work was received at its première with cheers and prolonged applause and critical approval for the composer's pacing of both music and dramatic tension, and accomplished setting of the libretto. For production details, see page 1027.

The world première by Opera North was made possible by the award of an Arts Council bursary to the composer and the financial assistance to the company of sponsorship by Schweppes. Wilfred Josephs has since been given another Arts Council award for a new opera based on *Alice in Wonderland*, commissioned by the Harrogate Festival.

January 1984 saw the British première of Glyndebourne's production of *Where The Wild Things Are*, a fantasy children's opera by Oliver Knussen to a libretto adapted by author and artist Maurice Sendak from his children's book of the same name. Sendak also designed the sets and costumes for the opera, copying and elaborating on the book illustrations. The opera was presented at the National Theatre (the Lyttelton theatre) to packed houses of "raptly attentive" children and an enthusiastic response from the Press. There were 17 performances in all, two on January 9 and three per day on January 10–14, an arduous schedule shared by two conductors, and two sopranos in the leading role; the orchestra was the London Sinfonietta. The production was recorded by B.B.C. Television and transmitted in April.

Although not presented at the 1983 Festival, *Where The Wild Things Are* was performed during the Glyndebourne Touring Company's autumn tour on a double bill with *Higglety Pigglety Pop!*, a new Knussen/Sendak collaboration commissioned for Glyndebourne by the B.B.C. This double bill will be brought into the main Glyndebourne Festival in 1985.

Where The Wild Things Are (Knussen). *Producer*, Frank Corsaro; *designer*, Maurice Sendak; *choreographer*, Jonathan Wolken; *conductors*, Oliver Knussen/Jane Glover.

Max, Karen Beardsley/Rosemary Hardy; *Mama/Tzippy*, Mary King; *Moishe/Goat*, Hugh Hetherington; *Bruno*, Jeremy Munro; *Emile*, Stephen Rhys-Williams; *Bernard*, Andrew Gallacher.

OPERA PRODUCTIONS

In the summaries of company activities shown below the dates in brackets indicate the year in which the current production of the work entered the repertoire of that company.

THE ROYAL OPERA (1946)
Royal Opera House, Covent Garden, W.C.2

Productions from the repertoire were *Lulu* (1981), *La clemenza di Tito* (1974), *Werther* (1979), *Otello* (1955), *Die Fledermaus* (1977), *Wozzeck* (1952), *La Bohème* (1974), *Peter Grimes* (restaged 1975), *Rigoletto* (1964), *Così fan tutte* (1968), *A Midsummer Night's Dream* (1961), *L'elisir d'amore* (1975), *Tosca* (1964), *Falstaff* (1982).

New productions were:
Sept 19, 1983. *The Nightingale* (Stravinsky). *Producer*, John Dexter; *designer*, David Hockney; *conductor*, David Atherton.
Fisherman, Philip Langridge (danced by Anthony Dowell); *Nightingale*, Phyllis Bryn-Julson (danced by Natalia Makarova); *Cook*, Anne Howells; *Chamberlain*, Richard Van Allan; *Bonze*, Joseph Rouleau; *Emperor of China*, David Wilson-Johnson; *Death*, Alfreda Hodgson; *Japanese Envoys*, Kim Begley, Stuart Harling, Francis Egerton.

and *L'Enfant et les sortilèges* (Ravel). *Producer*, John Dexter; *designer*, David Hockney; *conductor*, David Atherton.
Child, Ann Murray; *Mother*, Anne Collins; *Armchair*, Joseph Rouleau; *Louis XV Chair*, Meryl Drower; *Grandfather Clock/Tom Cat*, David Wilson-Johnson; *Tea Pot*, Philip Langridge; *Chinese Cup*, Alfreda Hodgson; *Fire/Nightingale*, Sandra Dugdale; *Shepherd*, Fiona Kimm; *Shepherdess*, Maria Motl; *Princess*, Joan Rodgers; *Little Old Man*, Francis Egerton; *Cat*, Della Jones; *Tree*, Richard Van Allan; *Dragonfly*, Patricia Parker; *Bat*, Suzan Bingemann; *Owl*, Elizabeth Robson; *Frog*, Kim Begley; *Squirrel*, Anne Howells.

Oct. 31, 1983. *Boris Godunov* (Mussorgsky). *Producer*, Andrei Tarkovsky; *designer*, Nicolas Dvigoubsky; *conductor*, Claudio Abbado.
Boris Godunov, Robert Lloyd; *Prince Schuisky*, Philip Langridge; *Pimen*, Gwynne Howell; *Grigory/Dimitri*, Michel Svetlov; *Misail*, Francis Egerton; *Varlaam*, Aage Haugland; *Xenia*, Joan Rodgers; *Feodor*, Fiona Kimm; *Marina*, Eva Randova; *Rangoni*, John Shirley-Quirk; *The Simpleton*, Patrick Power; *Shchelkalov*, Jonathan Summers, *Nikitich*, Paul Hudson; *Mitiukha*, John Gibbs; *Lavitsky*, William Mackie.

Nov. 28, 1983. *Esclarmonde* (Massenet). *Producer*, Lotfi Mansouri; *designer*, Beni Montresor; *conductor*, Richard Bonynge.
L'Emperor, Gwynne Howell; *Esclarmonde*, Joan Sutherland; *Parséis*, Diana Montague; *Enéas*, Ryland Davies; *Roland*, Ernesto Veronelli; *Le Roi Cléomer*, Geoffrey Moses; *L'Envoye Sarrazin*, John Dobson; *Le Héraut Byzantin*, Kim Begley; *L'Evêque de Blois*, Jonathan Summers.

Feb. 10, 1984. *Andrea Chénier* (Giordano) in association with Cologne Opera. *Producer*, Michael Hampe; *designer*, William Orlandi, after Frigerio; *conductor*, Richard Armstrong.
Andrea Chenier, José Carreras: *Madeleine*, Rosalind Plowright; *Charles Gérard*, Bernd Weikl; *Abbé*, Alexander Oliver; *Bersi*, Cynthia Buchan; *Fléville*, Gordon Sandison; *Mathieu*, Richard Van Allan; *Roucher*, Jonathan Summers; *Fouquier-Tinville*, John Gibbs; *Countess de Colgny*, Patricia Johnson; *Incredibile*, John Dobson.

March 26, 1984. *I Capuleti e i Montecchi* (Bellini). *Producer and designer*, Pier-Luigi Pizzi; *conductor*, Ricardo Muti.
Giulietta, Edita Gruberova; *Romeo*, Agnes Baltsa; *Tebaldo*, Dano Raffanti; *Capellio*, Gwynne Howell; *Lorenzo*, John Tomlinson.

June 2, 1984. *Aida* (Verdi). *Producer and designer*, Jean-Pierre Ponnelle; *conductor*, Zubin Mehta.
Aida, Katia Ricciarelli; *Ramfis*, Paata Burchuladze; *Radames*, Luciano Pavarotti; *Amneris*, Stefania Toczyska; *Amonasro*, Ingvar Wixell; *Il Re*, Sean Rea.

The Company performed *Il trovatore* (1964), *Madama Butterfly* (1950) and *La clemenza di Tito* during a two-week visit to the Palace Theatre, Manchester, in September 1983. At the Olympic Arts Festival in Los Angeles, U.S.A., in July 1984 the Company performed *Peter Grimes*, *Die Zauberflöte* (1979) and a new production of *Turandot* (premièred at Covent Garden in the 1984–85 season).

ENGLISH NATIONAL OPERA (1931)
London Coliseum, St. Martin's Lane, W.C.2

Productions from the repertoire were *Don Giovanni* (1976), *Rigoletto* (1982), *Toussaint* (1977), *Orfeo* (1981), *The Tales of Hoffmann* (1970), *Madam Butterfly* (1974), *The Adventures of Mr. Brouček* (1978), *La Traviata* (1973), *The Turn of the Screw* (1979), *Patience* (1969), *The Barber of Seville* (1978), *Gloriana* (1966), *War and Peace* (1972), *Der Rosenkavalier* (1975) and *The Magic Flute* (1975).

New productions were:
Sept. 15, 1983. *Ariadne auf Naxos* (R. Strauss). *Producer*, Graham Vick; *designer*, Russell Craig; *conductor*, Walter Weller.

Prima Donna/Ariadne, Janice Cairns; *Tenor/Bacchus*, Jan Blinkhof; *The Composer*, Sally Burgess; *Zerbinetta*, Marilyn Hill Smith; *Harlequin*, Alan Opie; *Scaramuccio*, Harry Nicoll; *Truffaldino*, William Mackie; *Brighella*, Bonaventura Bottone; *Music Master*, Norman Bailey; *Wig-maker*, Peter Kestner; *Dancing Master*, Stuart Kale; *Major-Domo*, Donald Sinden; *Naiad*, Anne Dawson; *Dryad*, Linda McLeod; *Echo*, Helen Lawson.

Sept. 29, 1983. *Rienzi* (Wagner). *Producer*, Nicholas Hytner; *designer*, David Fielding; *conductor*, Heribert Esser.

Rienzi, Kenneth Woollam; *Adriano*, Felicity Palmer; *Irene*, Kathryn Harries; *Colonna*, Dennis Wicks; *Paolo Orsini*, Malcolm Donnelly; *Cardinal Raimondi*, Sean Rea; *Baroncelli*, Alan Woodrow; *del Vecchio*, Geoffry Moses.

Oct. 22, 1983. *The Valkyrie* (Wagner). *Producer*, David Pountney; *designer*, Maria Bjornson; *conductor*, Mark Elder.

Siegmund, Alberto Remedios; *Sieglinde*, Josephine Barstow; *Hunding*, Willard White; *Wotan*, Anthony Raffell; *Fricka*, Sarah Walker; *Brünnhilde*, Marie Hayward Segal*; *Valkyries*—Angela Bostock, Suzan Bingemann, Anne-Marie Owens, Claire Livingstone, Ludmilla Andrew, Penelope Walker, Anne Mason, Joan Clarkson.

(*replacing an indisposed Linda Esther Gray).

Nov 16, 1983. *The Rape of Lucretia* (Britten). *Producer*, Graham Vick; *designer*, Russell Craig; *conductor*, Steuart Bedford.

Lucretia, Jean Rigby; *Tarquinius*, Russell Smythe; *Collatinus*, Richard Van Allan; *Junius*, Robert Dean; *Bianca*, Anne-Marie Owens; *Lucia*, Cathryn Pope; *Female Chorus*, Kathryn Harries; *Male Chorus*, Anthony Rolfe Johnson.

Dec. 1, 1983. *Mireille* (Gounod), a co-production with Grand Théâtre, Geneva. *Producer*, Antoine Bourseiller; *designer*, Bernard Daydé; *conductor*, Serge Baudo.

Mireille, Valerie Masterson; *Vincent*, Adrian Martin; *Taven*, Ann Howard; *Ourrias*; Malcolm Donnelly; *Maître Ramon*, Dennis Wicks; *Maître Ambroise/Ferryman*, Mark Richardson; *Vincenette*, Catherine Benson; *Andreloun*, Rosanne Brackenridge.

Feb. 4, 1984. *The Mastersingers of Nuremberg* (Wagner). *Producer*, Elijah Moshinsky; *designer*, Timothy O'Brien; *conductor*, Mark Elder.

Hans Sachs, Gwynne Howell; *Walther*, Kenneth Woollam; *Eva*, Janice Cairns; *David*, Graham Clark; *Magdalene*, Jean Rigby; *Beckmesser*, Alan Opie; *Pogner*, Sean Rea; *Kothner*, Malcolm Donnelly.

April 19, 1984. *The Sicilian Vespers* (Verdi), a production on loan from the Paris Opera. *Producer*, John Dexter; *designer*, Josef Svoboda; *conductor*, Mark Elder.

Elena, Rosalind Plowright; *Arrigo*, Kenneth Collins; *Guy de Montfort*, Neil Howlett; *Giovanni de Procida*, Richard Van Allan.

A Royal Gala Performance of *Gloriana* was given in the presence of T.R.H. Prince and Princess Michael of Kent on March 12, 1984, and a Charity Gala Performance of *The Magic Flute* was given on May 3, 1984.

In May and June 1984, the Company spent five weeks in the U.S.A., their first visit. Performances were given in Texas, Louisiana and at the Metropolitan Opera House, New York, of *Rigoletto*, *War and Peace*, *Gloriana*, *Patience* and *The Turn of the Screw*.

NEW SADLER'S WELLS OPERA (1982)
Sadler's Wells Theatre, Rosebery Avenue, E.C.1.

In its second season the Company performed *Countess Maritza* (1983), *The Mikado* (1983) and three new productions:

Jan. 25, 1984. *Martha* (Flotow). *Director*, Nicholas Hytner; *designers*, Stefanos Lazaridis, Johann Engels; *conductor*, Anthony Hose.

Lady Harriet, Marilyn Hill Smith; *Nancy*, Eirian James; *Lionel*, John Brecknock; *Lord Tristram*, Gordon Sandison; *Plunkett*, Roger Bryson.

Feb 9, 1984. *The Gondoliers* (Sullivan/Gilbert). *Director*, Christopher Renshaw; *designer*, Tim Goodchild; *choreographer*, Derek Deane; *conductor*, Wyn Davies.

The Duke of Plaza Toro, John Fryatt; *Luiz*, Christopher Gillett; *Don Alhambra*, Donald Adams; *Marco*, Kim Begley; *Giuseppe*, Richard Jackson; *Duchess of Plaza Toro*, Joan Davies; *Casilda*, Sandra Dugdale; *Gianetta*, Laureen Livingstone; *Tessa*, Janine Roebuck.

June 4, 1984. **H.M.S. Pinafore** (Sullivan/ Gilbert). *Director*, Christopher Renshaw; *designer*, Tim Goodchild; *conductor*, Barry Wordsworth.

Josephine, Elizabeth Ritchie; *Buttercup*, Linda Ormiston; *Ralph*, Hugh Hetherington; *Capt. Corcoran*, Gordon Sandison; *Sir Joseph Porter*, Nickolas Grace; *Dick Deadeye*, Thomas Lawlor.

WELSH NATIONAL OPERA (1946)
John Street, Cardiff.

Productions from the repertoire were *Carmen* (1983), *The Magic Flute* (1979), *The Bartered Bride* (1982), *Jenufa* (1975), *From the House of the Dead* (1982) *La Traviata*.

New productions were:
Sept. 6, 1983. **Peter Grimes** (Britten). *Producer*, John Copley; *designers*, Robert Don, Michael Stennart; *conductor*, Richard Armstrong.

Peter Grimes, John Mitchinson; *Ellen Orford*, Josephine Barstow; *Capt. Balstrode*, Terence Sharpe; *Swallow*, Peter Massocchi; *Bob Boles*, Arthur Davies; *Ned Keene*, Donald Maxwell; *Mrs. Sedley*, Helen Watt; *Auntie*, Menai Davies.

Oct. 21, 1983. **The Rhinegold** (Wagner). *Producer*, Göran Järvefelt; *designer*, Carl Friedrich Oberle; *conductor*, Richard Armstrong.

Wotan, Philip Joll; *Loge*, Nigel Douglas; *Alberich*, Nicolas Folwell; *Froh*, Richard Morton; *Donner*, Donald Maxwell; *Fafner*, Roderick Earle; *Fasolt*, John Tranter; *Erda*, Anne Collins; *Fricka*, Patricia Payne; *Freia*, Anne Williams-King; *Woglinde*, Marie-Claire O'Reirdan; *Flosshilde*, Marion McCullough; *Wellgunde*, Caroline Saxon.

Feb. 18, 1984. **The Valkyrie** (Wagner). *Producer*, Göran Järvefelt; *designer*, Carl Friedrich Oberle; *conductor*, Reginald Goodall.

Siegmund, Warren Ellsworth; *Sieglinde*, Kathryn Harries; *Hunding*, Roderick Earle; *Wotan*, Philip Joll; *Fricka*, Patricia Payne; *Brünnhilde*, Anne Evans.

Feb. 28, 1984. **The Merry Widow** (Lehár). *Producer*, Andrei Serban; *designer*, Michael Yeargan; *conductor*, György Fischer.

Hanna Glawari, Suzanne Murphy; *Danilo*, Thomas Allen; *Valencienne*, Kate Flowers; *Baron Zeta*, Thomas Helmsley; *Camille*, Robin Leggate; *Njegus*, Julian Moyle.

May 8, 1984. **La Bohème** (Puccini). *Producer*, Göran Järvefelt; *designer*, Michael Yeargan; *conductor*, Kees Bakels.

Mimi, Helen Field; *Rodolfo*, John Fowler; *Musetta*, Suzanne Murphy; *Marcello*, Donald Maxwell; *Schaunard*, Nicholas Folwell; *Colline*, Matthew Best.

All new productions were premièred at the New Theatre, Cardiff. Performances were given also at Birmingham, Bristol, Liverpool, London (Dominion), Oxford, Southampton, Swansea and Llandudno.

SCOTTISH OPERA (1962)
Theatre Royal, Hope Street, Glasgow 2.

Productions from the repertoire were *The Magic Flute* (1983), *The Golden Cockerel* (1975), *Hänsel and Gretel* (1978), *L'elisir d'amore* (1980), *La Bohème* (1967 and *L'Egisto* (1982).

New productions were:
Aug. 26, 1983. **Death In Venice** (Britten). A co-production with Grand Théâtre, Geneva, premièred at the Edinburgh Festival. *Producer*, François Rochaix; *designer*, Jean-Claude Maret; *conductor*, Roderick Brydon.

Gustav von Aschenbach, Anthony Rolfe Johnson; *Strawberry Seller/Lace Seller/Newspaper Seller/Strolling Player*, Una Buchanan; *Traveller/Fop/Gondolier/Hotel Manager/Hotel Barber/Leader of Players/Voice of Dionysus*, Barry Mora; *Guide/Priest/English Clerk*, Alan Opie; *Apollo*, Andrew Dalton; *Hotel Porter*, John Robertson; *Glass Maker/Strolling Player*, Grant Richards.

Oct. 19, 1983. **Idomeneo** (Mozart). *Producer*, John Cox; *designer*, Roger Butlin; *conductor*, György Fischer.

Ilia, Margaret Marshall; *Idamante*, Ian Caley; *Electra*, Paula Scalera; *Arbace*, Gordon Christie; *Idomeneo*, Michael Myers.

April 18, 1984. **Turandot** (Puccini). *Producer*, Tony Palmer; *designers*, Kenneth Carey and Barbara Lane; *conductor*, Alexander Gibson.

Turandot/Elvira, Ludmila Andrew; *Calaf/Puccini*, Eduardo Alvarez; *Liù/Doria*, Marie Slorach; *Timur*, Willard White; *Mandarin*, Norman White; *Altoum*, John Robertson; *The Masks*, Alan Oke, Hugh Hetherington, Gordon Christie.

The Company visited Liverpool, Newcastle and Edinburgh with the above productions, and in May–June 1984 visited Perth, Ayr, Stirling, Dundee, Dunfermline and Inverness with a double bill of early Rossini pieces. *The Silken Ladder* and *The Marriage Contract* were both produced by Graham Vick, designed by Russell Craig and conducted by Richard Honner. The lovers in both operas were sung by Meryl Drower and Harry Nicoll, with other parts taken by William McCue, Eric Roberts and Alan Watt.

OPERA NORTH (1978)
Grand Theatre, 46 New Briggate, Leeds.

Productions from the repertoire were *Così fan tutte* (1982), *The Bartered Bride* (1981), *Tosca* (1979) and *Madam Butterfly* (1982).

New productions were:
Oct. 7, 1983. **Die Fledermaus** (J. Strauss). *Producer*, Hans Hollman; *designers*, John Gunter and Sue Blane; *choreographer*, Peter Morin; *conductor*, Clive Timms.

Rosalinde, Penelope MacKay; *Adèle*, Lynda Russell; *Prince Orlofsky*, Marilyn de Blieck; *Eisenstein*, Jonny Blanc; *Alfred*, Adrian Martin; *Falke*, Stephen Roberts; *Frank*, Derek Hammond-Stroud; *Frosch*, Bill Maynard.

Oct. 15, 1983. *Rebecca* (Josephs). *Producer*, Colin Graham; *designer*, Stefanos Lazaridis; *conductor*, David Lloyd-Jones.
Second Mrs. de Winter, Gillian Sullivan; *Mrs. Van Hopper*, Nuala Willis; *Maxim de Winter*, Peter Knapp; *Mrs. Danvers*, Ann Howard; *Beatrice Lacy*, Linda Hibberd; *Giles Lacy*, Thomas Lawlor; *Frank Crawley*, Geoffry Pogson; *Jack Favell*, Malcolm Rivers; *Jane Julyan*, Eleanor Smith; *Col. Julyan*, John Gilbert.

Dec. 21, 1983. *Il trovatore* (Verdi). *Producer*, Andrei Serban; *designer*, Michael Yeargan; *conductor*, Yan Pascal Tortelier.
Leonora, Natalia Rom; *Azucena*, Cynthia Buchan; *Manrico*, Eduardo Alvares; *Luna*, James Dietsch; *Ferrando*, John Tranter.

Dec. 22, 1983. *Eugene Onegin* (Tchaikovsky). *Producer*, Graham Vick; *designs* by Roger Butlin, borrowed from Scottish Opera; *costumes*, Deidre Clancy; *choreographer*, Terry Gilbert; *conductor*, David Lloyd-Jones.
Tatyana, Eilene Hannan; *Olga*, Fiona Kimm; *Larina*, Maureen Morelle; *Filipyevna*, Elizabeth Bainbridge; *Lensky*, Robin Leggate; *Triquet*, Neil Jenkins; *Onegin*, Jonathan Summers; *Gremin*, John Tranter.

Jan. 6, 1984. *The Cunning Little Vixen* (Janáček), the Welsh National Opera/Scottish Opera production. *Conductor*, Wyn Davies.
Vixen, Helen Field; *Fox*, Gordon Christie; *Schoolmaster*, Neil Jenkins; *Forester*, Willard White; *Poacher*, William Shimell; *Parson*, Thomas Lawlor; *Solo dancers*, Seonaid MacLeod, David Turner.

March 3, 1984. *Orpheus and Eurydice* (Gluck). *Producer and designer*, Philip Prowse; *conductor*, David Lloyd-Jones.
Orpheus, Felicity Palmer; *Eurydice*, Patricia Rozario; *Amor*, Cathryn Pope.

May 25, 1984. *Salome* (R. Strauss). A major restaging by Lesley Lee of the E.N.O. production. *Conductor*, David Lloyd-Jones.
Salome, Penelope Daner; *Herodias*, Della Jones; *Herod*, Nigel Douglas; *Narraboth*, Ian Caley; *Jokanaan*, Philip Joll; *Page*, Beverley Mills.

May 29, 1984. *A Village Romeo and Juliet* (Delius). *Producer*, Robert Carsen; *designer*, Russell Craig; *conductor*, Nicholas Cleobury.
Vrenchen, Anne Williams King; *Sali*, Peter Jeffes; *Dark Fidler*, David Wilson-Johnson; *Manz*, Henry Newman; *Marti*, Philip O'Reilly.

June 28, 1984. *The Threepenny Opera*

(Weill). *Producer and designer*, Philip Prowse; *conductor*, John Pryce-Jones.
Macheath, Peter Savidge; *Polly*, Beverley Mills; *Jenny*, Eiddwen Harrhy; *Lucy*, Sally Daley; *Peachum*, Mark Lufton; *Mrs. Peachum*, Clare Moll; *Tiger Brown*, Martin Nelson; *Narrator*, Geoffrey Dolton.

The Company performed also at Birmingham, Nottingham, Manchester, Hull, Norwich, Sheffield and York.

KENT OPERA (1969)
Pembles Cross, Egerton, Ashford, Kent.

Productions from the repertoire were *Falstaff* (1980) and *Don Giovanni* (1983).
New productions were:
Oct. 6, 1983. *Robinson Crusoe* (Offenbach). *Producer*, Adrian Slack; *designer*, Dermot Hayes; *conductor*, Roger Norrington.
Robinson, Neil Jenkins; *Toby*, Christopher Gillett; *Jim Cocks*, Gordon Sandison; *Man Friday*, Eirian James; *Edwige*, Vivian Tierney; *Suzanne*, Eileen Hulse; *Deborah*, Catherine Wyn Rogers; *Mr. Crusoe*, Gerwyn Morgan; *Will Atkins*, Andrew Shore.

March 15, 1984. *The Seraglio* (Mozart). *Producer*, Norman Platt; *designer*, Roger Butlin; *conductor*, Ivan Fischer.
Belmonte, Maldwyn Davies; *Constanze*, Angela Denning; *Osmin*, Harry Coghill; *Pedrillo*, John Graham-Hall; *Blonde*, Eileen Hulse; *Pasha Selim*, Andrew Shore.

Kent Opera has no home theatre and all productions were performed on tour at Dartford, Tunbridge Wells, Cambridge, Northampton, Eastbourne, Bath, Norwich, Southsea, Plymouth and Brighton.

GLYNDEBOURNE FESTIVAL OPERA (1934)
Glyndebourne, Lewes, E. Sussex.

Glyndebourne opened on May 28th, 1934 with *Le nozze di Figaro*, and the 50th anniversary was marked by opening the 1984 season on the same date with the same opera, in the 1973 production by Peter Hall. Two other Peter Hall productions were revived, *Così fan tutte* (1978) and *A Midsummer Night's Dream* (1981), and there were two new productions.

May 29, 1984. *L'incoronazione di Poppea* (Monteverdi). *Director*, Peter Hall; *designer*, John Bury; *conductor*, Raymond Leppard.
Poppea, Maria Ewing; *Nerone*, Dennis Bailey; *Ottone*, Dale Duesing; *Ottavia*, Cynthia Clarey; *Drusilla*, Elizabeth Gale; *Seneca*, Robert Lloyd.

July 7, 1984. *Arabella* (R. Strauss). *Director*, John Cox; *designer*, Julia Trevelyan Oman; *conductor*, Bernard Haitink.
Arabella, Ashley Putnam; *Zidenka*, Gianna Rolandi; *Adelaide*, Regina Sarfaty; *Count Waldner*, Artur Korn; *Mandryka*, John Bröcheler; *Matteo*, Keith Lewis.

Her Majesty The Queen attended the performance of *Arabella* on July 31, 1984 to mark Glyndebourne's 50th anniversary season.

The Touring Company presented *Le nozze di Figaro, Così fan tutte* and the Knussen double bill *Where The Wild Things Are* and *Higglety Pigglety Pop!* at Glyndebourne, Oxford, Southampton, Plymouth, Manchester and Norwich.

DANCE PRODUCTIONS

THE ROYAL BALLET (1931)
Royal Opera House, Covent Garden, W.C.2.

Productions of full-length ballets from the repertoire were *Swan Lake* (Petipa/Ivanov, additional choreography by Ashton and Nureyev: 1979), *Manon* (MacMillan: 1974), *Cinderella* (Ashton: 1965), *The Sleeping Beauty* (Sergueyev after Petipa, additional choreography by Ashton: 1977) *La Fille mal gardée* (Ashton; 1960) and *Romeo and Juliet* (MacMillan: 1975).

Programmes also included combinations of shorter pieces, including the following, from the repertoire: *A Wedding Bouquet* (Ashton), *Voluntaries* (Tetley), *A Month in the Country* (Ashton), *The Tempest* (Nureyev), *Monotones* (Ashton), *Voices of Spring* (Ashton), *Facade* (Ashton), *Apollo* (Balanchine), *Varii Capricci* (Ashton), *Raymonda Act III* (Nureyev after Petipa), *Chanson* (Deane), *Requiem* (MacMillan), *La Bayadère* (Nureyev after Petipa), *Valley of Shadows* (MacMillan), *La Fin du jour* (MacMillan), *Afternoon of a Faun* (Robbins), *Song of the Earth* (MacMillan), *Rhapsody* (Ashton), *Enigma Variations* (Ashton), *Les Noces* (Nijinska), *Elite Syncopations* (MacMillan), *Agon* (Balanchine), *Les Biches* (Nijinska), *Shadowplay* (Tudor), *Gloria* (MacMillan), *The Firebird* (Fokine), *Scènes de ballet* (Ashton), *My Brother, My Sisters* (MacMillan).

New ballets were:
Dec. 7, 1983. *Consort Lessons,* a one act ballet *choreographed* by David Bintley; set to Stravinsky's *Concerto for Piano and Wind; designs* by Terry Bartlett. The cast of 12 dancers included Lesley Collier, Antony Dowson, Alessandra Ferri, Wayne Eagling, Julian Hosking, Stephan Jefferies, Karen Paisley and Genesia Rosato.

Midsummer, a one act ballet *choreographed* by Richard Alston; set to Tippett's *Fantasia Concertante on a theme of Corelli; designs* by John Hubbard. The cast of 12 dancers was led by Bryony Brind, Fiona Chadwick, Jonathan Cope and Ashley Page.

Feb. 24, 1984. *Different Drummer,* a one act ballet *choreographed* by Kenneth MacMillan; *music,* Webern's *Passacaglia Opus 1,* and Schoenberg's *Verklärte Nacht; designs,* Yolanda Sonnabend. The cast included Wayne Eagling (*Woyzeck*), Alessandra Ferri

(*Marie*), Guy Niblett (*Andres*), Stephen Jeffries (*Drum Major*), Jonathan Burrows (*Doctor*), David Drew (*Captain*) and Jonathan Cope.

April 11, 1984. *Fleeting Figures,* a one act ballet *choreographed* by Derek Deane; set to Suk's *Serenade for Strings; designs* by Mathilde Sandberg. The cast of 20 dancers was led by Antoinette Sibley, David Wall, Maria Almeida and Jay Jolley.

and the first performance by the Company of *Return to the Strange Land, created* 1975 by Jiři Kylián; set to *music* by Janáček; *designs* by Jiři Kylián. The cast of six comprised Bryony Brind, Alessandra Ferri, Wayne Eagling, Julian Hosking, Jay Jolley and Stephen Sheriff.

July 24, 1984. *Party Game,* a one act ballet *choreographed* by Michael Corder; *music,* Stravinsky's *Concerto in D for Strings; designs,* Patrick Caulfield. The cast of five comprised Bryony Brind, Deirdre Eyden, Ravenna Tucker, Guy Niblett and Stephen Sheriff.

Aug. 2, 1984. *A Broken Set of Rules,* a one act ballet *choreographed* by Ashley Page; *commissioned score* by Michael Nyman; *designs* by Deanna Petherbridge. The cast of six comprised Maria Almeida, Sharon McGorian, Nicola Roberts, Jonathan Cope, David Peden and Bruce Sansom.

The Company spent one week in June 1984 at the Palace Theatre, Manchester, performing *Romeo and Juliet, Les Biches, Scènes de ballet* and *A Month in the Country.* The following week was spent at the Bristol Hippodrome with a programme identical to that presented in Manchester except for the replacement of *Les Biches* by *The Firebird.*

SADLER'S WELLS ROYAL BALLET (1931)
Sadler's Wells Theatre, Rosebery Avenue,
E.C.1.

Full-length ballets from the repertoire were *La Fille mal gardée* (Ashton: 1960), *The Taming of the Shrew* (Cranko: 1980), *Giselle* (Petipa after Coralli and Perrot: 1968), *Coppélia* (after Petipa and Cecchetti: 1979), *The Swan of Tuonela* (Bintley: 1982) and *Swan Lake* (Petipa and Ivanov, with additional choreography by Wright: 1980).

Programmes included combinations of the following shorter ballets: *Night Moves* (Bintley), *The Invitation* (MacMillan), *St. Anthony Variations* (Corder), *The Winter Play* (Burrows), *Checkmate* (de Valois), *Paquita* (Petipa), *La Boutique fantasque* (Massine), *Elite Syncopations* (MacMillan), *Prodigal Son* (Balanchine), *Pineapple Poll* (Cranko), *Les Sylphides* (Fokine), *Raymonda Act III* (Nureyev after Petipa), and *Les Rendezvous* (Ashton).

New productions were:
Sept. 20, 1983. *Choros,* a one-act ballet

choreographed by David Bintley, set to a specially commissioned *score* by Aubrey Meyer, with *designs* by Terry Bartlett. The cast at the première included Marion Tait, Michael Batchelor and Roland Price.

March 8, 1984. **Petrushka,** at Congress Theatre, Eastbourne. First performance by the Company of Fokine's ballet; *designs* by Alexandre Benois; *staged* by John Auld. Cast included Alain Dubreuil (*Petrushka*), Margaret Barbieri (*Ballerina*), Desmond Kelly (*The Moor*).

April 10, 1984. **Metamorphosis,** a one act ballet *choreographed* by David Bintley; specially commissioned *score* by Peter McGowan; *designs* by Mike Becket. Cast included Margaret Barbieri (*Gregor's mother*), Leanne Benjamin (*Gregor's sister*), Desmond Kelly (*Gregor's father*), Graham Lustig (*Gregor*) and Stephen Wicks (*Lodger*).

April 13, 1984. **Common Ground,** a one-act ballet *choreographed* by Jennifer Jackson; *set to* Lennox Berkeley's *Serenade for Strings*; *designs* by Ella Huhne. Cast included Samira Asidi, Michael Batchelor, Karen Donovan, Michael O'Hare and David Yow.

In addition to performances at their home theatre, the Company also toured to Birmingham, Plymouth, Southampton, Manchester, Eastbourne, Bristol, Leeds, Newcastle and Bournemouth, and visited The Big Top in Sheffield for three weeks.

The Company also undertook a six and a half week tour to Canada in autumn 1983, visiting Kitchener, Ottawa, Toronto, Winnipeg, Regina, Saskatoon, Edmonton, Calgary and Vancouver. The works performed were *Swan Lake* and a triple bill of *The Invitation, Night Moves* and *Raymonda Act III*.

LONDON FESTIVAL BALLET (1950)
Festival Ballet House, 39 Jay Mews, S.W.7.

Productions of full-length ballets from the repertoire included *Cinderella* (Stevenson: 1973), *The Nutcracker* (Hynd: 1976), *Giselle* (Skeaping, after Perrot, Coralli, Petipa: 1971) and *Swan Lake* (Field, after Petipa and Ivanov: 1982).

Programmes also included combinations of the following one-act ballets: *Les Sylphides* (Fokine), *Three Preludes* (Stevenson), *Dances from Napoli* (Schaufuss, after Bournonville), *Britten Pas de Deux* (Stevenson), *Four Last Songs* (Stevenson), *Graduation Ball* (Lichine), *The Sanguine Fan* (Hynd), *Prince Igor* (Fokine), *The Storm* (Prokovsky), *Scheherazade* (Fokine), *The Three-Cornered Hat* (Massine) and *The Seasons* (Hynd).

New productions were:

May 22, 1984. **Onegin,** London première of the full-length ballet by John Cranko, set to *music* by Tchaikovsky, *arranged* by Kurt-Heinz Stolze, with *designs* by Jurgen Rose.

Cast included Patricia Ruanne, Ben van Cauwenbergh, Renata Calderini, Maurizio Bellezza and Frederic Jahn-Werner. The première was a Royal Gala performance in the presence of T.R.H. Prince and Princess Michael of Kent.

June 12, 1984. **Pulcinella,** a one-act ballet *choreographed* by Glen Tetley; set to *music* by Stravinsky (after Pergolesi); *designs*, Rouben Ter-Arutunian. Cast included Matz Skoog as *Pulcinella* and Elisabetta Terabust as *Pimpinella*.

These works were performed in London, at the Dominion Theatre, the Coliseum and the Royal Festival Hall, and on tour.

A group of leading artists from the Company undertook a tour of towns with smaller theatre accommodation with a specially devised programme to piano accompaniment. The programme comprised variations from *Les Sylphides, Three Preludes* and two new pieces, *Emily* and *The Aquarium*.

Emily, a one-act ballet *choreographed* by Kate Simmons, set to *music* by Pascal Sevajols, with *costumes* by Kim Baker, *settings* by Andrew Peat.

and **The Aquarium,** a one-act ballet *choreographed* by Andre Prokovsky, set to *music* by George Gershwin, with *designs* by Peter Farmer.

BALLET RAMBERT (1926)
Mercury Theatre, Ladbroke Road, W.11.

The Company's 1983–84 season opened on August 29, 1983 with its debut at the 1983 Edinburgh Festival, premièring **Murderer Hope of Women,** a short work by Glen Tetley, commissioned by the Festival with the aid of the Tennent Caledonian Award. The work is set in part to Schoenberg's *Chamber Symphony Op. 9* and is designed by Nadine Baylis. The cast was led by Lucy Burge as *The Woman* and Albert van Nierop as *The Pallid Man*. Also premièred at the Edinburgh Festival, on Sept. 1, 1983, was **Colour Moves,** a short ballet by Robert North, set to *music* by Christopher Benstead, with *settings* by Bridget Riley and *costumes* by Andrew Storer. The cast included North, Frances Carty, Mary Evelyn, Michael Ho, Ikky Maas, Paul Melis, Cathrine Price and Diane Walker.

These two works were subsequently performed on tour and given their London première at the Sadler's Wells Theatre in March 1984.

Repertoire works performed during the year were *Pribaoutki* (North), *Concertino* (Bruce), *Chicago Brass* (Alston), *Fielding Sixes* (Cunningham), *L'Apres-midi d'un Faune* (Nijinsky), *Five Brahms Waltzes in the Manner of Isadora Duncan* (Ashton), *Capriol Suite* (Ashton), *Apollo Distraught* (Alston) and *Ghost Dances* (Bruce).

Other new works were:

Feb. 9, 1984, at Royal Northern College of Music, Manchester. *Entre Dos Aguas. Choreographer*, Robert North; *score* based on flamenco and Latin American arranged by Rogers and de Lucia; *designs*, Andrew Storer.

Feb. 16, 1984, at the Repertory Theatre, Birmingham. *Intimate Pages. Choreographer*, Christopher Bruce; *score*, Janacek's *String Quartet No. 2*; *designs*, Walter Nobbe. The cast of six was led by Frances Carty and Albert van Nierop.

March 27, 1984, at Sadler's Wells Theatre, London. *Voices and Light Footsteps. Choreographer*, Richard Alston; *score*, eight madrigals by Monteverdi; *sets*, Peter Mumford; *costumes*, Candida Cook.

May 17, 1984, at the Theatre Royal, Brighton. *Wildlife. Choreographer*, Richard Alston; *score*, commissioned from Nigel Osborn; *designs*, Richard Smith. Cast included Lucy Burge, Mark Baldwin, Mary Evelyn, Ikky Maas, Bruce Michelson and Cathrine Price.

The Company's home tours took this repertoire to Newcastle, Oxford, Liverpool, Nottingham, Aberdeen, Glasgow, Leeds, Manchester, Birmingham, York, Leicester, London (Sadler's Wells Theatre), Brighton, Southampton, Plymouth, Exeter and Bristol.

The Company's overseas tours included a visit to Germany in Sept. 1983 when programmes including *Fielding Sixes, Murderer Hope of Women, Ghost Dances* and *Lonely Town, Lonely Street* were performed in Ludwigshaven, Frankfurt, Weisbaden, Leverkusen and Cologne. In April 1984, the Company visited Lisbon and Oporto with programmes which, *inter alia*, included *Intimate Pages, Entre Dos Aguas, Apollo Distraught* and *Lonely Town, Lonely Street*. The final overseas tour of the season was to Istanbul and Cyprus in June–July 1984.

LONDON CONTEMPORARY DANCE THEATRE
(1967)
The Place, 17 Dukes Road, W.C.1.

Performances from the repertoire were *The Dancing Department* (Davies), *Cell* (Cohan), *Nympheas* (Cohan), *Songs, Lamentations and Praises* (Cohan), *Chamber Dances* (Cohan), *Three Epitaphs* (Taylor), *Esplanade* (Taylor).

New productions were:

Sept. 20, 1983 at the Haymarket Theatre, Leicester. *Spinnaker,* a ballet for five dancers. *Choreography*, Jayne Lee; *music*, Eleanor Alberga; *designs*, Craig Givens.

and *Under The Same Sun,* for five dancers. *Choreography*, Darshan Bhuller; *music*, John Millar and Clem Alford; *costumes*, Celeste Dandeker.

Sept. 22, 1983 at the Haymarket Theatre, Leicester. *Run Like Thunder,* for nine dancers. *Choreography*, Tom Jobe; *music*, Barrington Pheloung; *designs*, Paul Dart.

Oct. 20, 1983 at the Arts Centre, Warwick University. *Canso Trobar. Choreography*, Christopher Bannerman; *music*, medieval Troubadour music, arranged by Martin Best; *designs*, Antony McDonald.

Dec. 6, 1983 at Sadler's Wells Theatre, London. *Carnival. Choreography*, Siobhan Davies; *music*, Saint-Saens' *Carnival of the Animals*; *designs*, David Buckland and Antony McDonald.

May 15, 1984 at Sadler's Wells Theatre, London. *New Galileo,* for eight dancers. *Choreography*, Siobhan Davies; *music*, John Adams' *Phrygian Gates*; *designs*, David Buckland and Peter Mumford.

May 22, 1984 at Sadler's Wells Theatre, London. *Agora. Choreography*, Robert Cohan; *music*, Bach's *Chaconne in D Minor* and *Brandenburg Concerto No. 6*, additional music by Barrington Pheloung; *designs*, Norberto Chiesa.

In addition to two seasons at Sadler's Wells Theatre, London, and touring to Leicester, Mold, Warwick, Bristol, Exeter and Cardiff, the Company also appeared at the Helsinki Festival in September 1983 and the Dublin Festival in Oct. 1983. In May–June 1984, performances were given in Barcelona, and June saw performances at the Bergen International Festival and the Gothenberg Festival. The 1983–84 season concluded with the Company's participation in the Olympic Arts Festival, U.S.A., with performances of *Class* (Cohan), *Forest* (Cohan), *New Galileo, Run Like Thunder, The Dancing Department* and *Stabat Mater* (Cohan), preceded by appearances at the American International Dance Festival in North Carolina with the above works and *Songs, Lamentations and Praises*.

LITERATURE OF THE YEAR

Golding Medal

The award of the 1983 Nobel Prize for Literature to William Golding aroused controversy. He has been on the fringes of the literary establishment since the publication of his first, and best known, novel *Lord of the Flies*—respected, but attracting mixed reviews—and only achieved the position his work deserved, in the mainstream of English 20th century fiction, with *Rites of Passage*, which won the 1980 Booker Prize. Golding is the first English writer since Sir Winston Churchill in 1953, and the seventh in all, to be so honoured. However, it has long been a source of disappointment to many people that, if one accepts that it is desirable and possible to select the best writers in the world, and that an English writer merits the Prize, Graham Greene should yet again have been passed over. Golding is a worthy recipient of the Prize, worth some £130,000, but such an award is somewhat tarnished when it ignores a writer such as Greene.

According to the Swedish Academy, Golding was chosen "for his novels which, with the perspicuity of realistic narrative art and the diversity and universality of myth, illuminate the human condition in the world today". His work is concerned with "the terrible disease of being human". However, in an almost unprecedented display of pique, one of the academicians publicly dissented from the choice; he dismissed Golding as "a little English phenomenon of no special interest". The author was reported to have responded, "I had been picked by the panel, and for one man to come out screaming in rage is rather subjective".

Unfortunately, the Nobel award prompted his publishers to advance the publication date of Golding's latest novel, and since it was something of a let-down after *Rites of Passage*, the notices were fairly harsh. *The Paper Men* does not sit easily with the rest of Golding's work. It appears to have had its genesis in Golding's second volume of essays, published in 1982, *A Moving Target*. In the title essay, Golding wrote, "I am the raw material of an academic light industry". He wrote of "the post-graduate students in search of a thesis", and Wilfred Barclay, the alcoholic middle-aged author narrator of the novel is similarly afflicted, by one Rick L. Tucker, a minor American academic.

The book opens with Barclay, rising in a drunken stupor, shooting what he takes to be a badger rifling through his dustbin; the badger is in fact Tucker, hunting for significant papers. The book veers uneasily between farce and tragedy, with none of the characters totally engaging the reader's sympathies. "We'll show the world what we are—paper men, you can call us. How about that for a title?" Barclay asks Tucker. The surprise ending, which is not wholly inconsistent with the rest of the book, ensures that that title is used but whether "paper men" are so insubstantial that they can be taken seriously—or, indeed, whether this novel can be—remains to be seen.

An interesting insight into the establishment of the Nobel Prizes is given in *The Legend of Alfred Nobel* by Ragnar Sohlman, Nobel's executor. First published posthumously in 1950, this translation by Elspeth Harley Schubert has been reissued to mark the 150th anniversary of Nobel's birth. The Prizes are now well established, but the difficulties involved in setting them up originally, and in fulfilling the terms of Nobel's will, make fascinating reading.

Good Companions

During the year, Golding and Samuel Beckett were appointed Companions of Literature by the Royal Society of Literature, the number of Companions being limited to ten at any one time.

Books and Booker

The Booker Prize continued to attract widespread publicity, and no little controversy. In what was considered by many to be a non-vintage year, a "hung" jury produced a compromise winner which seemed to satisfy very few people, and did not reap the reward of vast sales normally assured to the winner. The judging panel were "looking for excellence aligned to purpose, or literary merit which somehow managed to express both", and they chose J. M. Coetzee's *Life & Times of Michael K*, declaring that it was a consensus choice, "not unanimous, but certainly not a compromise book", although they convinced no-one. Coetzee's fable, set in South Africa in the near future, in a society at constant war with itself, concerned a simple-minded gardener, who takes his mother out of the city to the country in a wheelbarrow. He is described as "a pebble that, having lain around quietly minding its own business since the dawn of time, is now suddenly picked up and tossed randomly from hand to hand". This Kafka-esque tale of the triumph of the human spirit in adversity may well have been "a novel of remarkable power and simplicity; a work of great inventiveness and imagination, superbly controlled', as Fay Weldon, chairman of the judges described it, but it failed to capture the public's interest.

The panel were rumoured to have been deadlocked over Salman Rushdie's *Shame* (noted last year), but as a previous winner, and a writer who seemed to arouse equal measures of support and antipathy, his extravagant saga on the creation of modern Pakistan was rightly discounted. Of the other finalists, Graham Swift's *Waterland*, an ambitious, if occasionally overblown, allegory of fenland, was widely praised, and had the consolation of the Winifred Holtby Prize. John Fuller's brief but beautifully constructed *Flying to Nowhere* received the Whitbread Award for best first novel of the year. Set in a medieval Welsh monastery, where the abbot is engaged in dissecting drowned pilgrims to try to locate their souls, Fuller's poetic novella was a work of exceptional promise. Anita Mason's *The Illusionist*, the story of Simon Magus, 1st century sorcerer who gave his name to Simony, was a surprising choice for the final six books, as it was badly written in parts. The sixth finalist was Malcolm Bradbury's *Rates of Exchange*.

That the Booker McConnell Prize for Fiction is good for books is not in dispute: few would begrudge the winner his £10,000, to be increased to £15,000 for the 1984 award. However, it would appear that the judges are set an almost impossible task, expected to read literally dozens of novels, with no consistency in the members of the judging panel, chosen afresh each year, thus throwing up some surprising finalists, and some unexpected winners. If Booker is ever to attain the prestige attached to the Prix Goncourt in France, some rationalisation is needed in the selection and judging process.

Hard Trask

The first awards from the bequest left by romantic novelist Betty Trask were given during the year. The prize generated some initial amusement in the press, and first reports suggested the scheme might be an embarrassing flop. One month before the closing date, only two works had been submitted. However, the substantial financial inducements eventually persuaded 283 authors under the age of 35 to enter novels which complied with the requirement that they should be "a romantic novel, or other novel of a traditional rather than experimental nature". Of the entrants, 26 were published works and 257 unpublished. The judges eventually awarded a joint first prize of £6,750 each to two authors: Ronald Frame, for *Winter Journey*, and Claire Nonhebel, for *Cold Showers*. Runners-up prizes of £1,000 each were awarded to James Buchan, for *A Parish of Rich Women*, Helen Harris, for *Playing Fields in Winter*, Gareth Jones, for *The Disinherited*, and Simon Rees, for *The Devil's Looking Glass*.

The W. H. Smith Literary Award, for the most outstanding contribution to English literature in a book published the previous year, was given to Philip Larkin for his *Required Writing: Miscellaneous Pieces 1955–*

82, an enjoyable prose selection of essays, autobiography, interviews and criticism. Mr. Larkin claimed that the Muse of Poetry had deserted him, but he was widely expected to succeed the late—and much lamented—Sir John Betjeman to the Poet Laureateship.

The Whitbread Fiction Prize was won by William Trevor for *Fools of Fortune*. The Whitbread Biography Prize was awarded jointly to Victoria Glendenning's *Vita: The Life of V. Sackville-West*, and Kenneth Rose's *King George V*, which also won the Wolfson Prize. The Whitbread Children's Book of the Year was Roald Dahl's *The Witches*. Lisa St. Aubin de Teran received the John Llewellyn Rhys Memorial Prize for *The Slow Train to Milan*, and the first recipient of the Dylan Thomas Award for Poetry was Peter Reading's *Diplopic*. Anthony Powell received the prestigious American Bennett Award, worth £10,000, and awarded biennially by The Hudson Review, a New York literary and arts magazine, "in recognition of his distinguished achievement in the art of the novel". The Somerset Maugham Awards were presented to Peter Ackroyd, for *The Last Testament of Oscar Wilde*, Timothy Garton Ash, for *The Polish Revolution: Solidarity*, and Sean O'Brien, for *The Indoor Park*. Cholmondeley Awards for Poetry went to Michael Baldwin, Michael Hoffman and Carol Rumens, and the Hawthornden Prize for imaginative literature to Jonathan Keates, for *Allegro Postillions*.

Authors' Rights

During the year, a measure of justice was at last meted out to those authors whose income suffers through the lending of their works by public libraries: the first payments were made under the Public Lending Right scheme. It was reported that over £1·5 million was distributed to 6,086 authors: 46 received the maximum pay-out of £5,000 (which represented nearly half-a-million loans for each work); 81 received over £2,500; 3,878 received less than £100; and, 1,614 of those registered received no payment.

Amis and the Women

Kingsley Amis's new novel, *Stanley and the Women*, is a marvellously sustained work, a study in sanity and madness. The central figure, Stanley Duke, is a hard-drinking advertisement manager on a Fleet Street daily newspaper, divorced from his first wife, the actress Nowell, and remarried to Susan, assistant literary editor on a Sunday newspaper. Stanley's difficulties begin when his son by his first wife has a nervous breakdown, and he attempts to help him to a cure whilst various psychiatrists dispute the methods by which this might best be achieved. Meanwhile, Stanley's problems magnify, and the question is posed as to where to draw the dividing line between sanity and madness: whether those people going about their apparently normal daily lives are more sane than someone who has suffered a breakdown. The novel has caused some controversy, as it has been read as suggesting that all women are mad—and reputedly for this reason has had difficulty in finding an American publisher. However, this is far too simplistic a view: as Nash the psychiatrist says of women, "No. They're not mad. They're all too monstrously, sickeningly, *terrifyingly* sane. That's the *whole trouble*." *Stanley and the Women* is beautifully written, and shows Amis at his comic best.

David Hughes's *The Pork Butcher* is based on the story of the destruction by the Germans of the French village of Oradour-sur-Glane, and the massacre of its inhabitants. In the novel, a German soldier involved in the killings, on finding he has only a few months to live, returns to the village 40 years later in an attempt to salve his conscience. The village is preserved exactly as it was in the war, as "an act of hostile piety", and the mayor, who has escaped the carnage, has found it far easier to come to terms with the events than the soldier, whose affair with a French girl had sparked off the massacre.

D. M. Thomas continues to tease and tantalise critics and readers. His latest novel, *Swallow*, continues the literary games he began in *Ararat*: it is set in a story-telling Olympiad in Finland, and it transpires that *Ararat* was one of the improvisational stories, parts of which reappear in the latest work, along with rewritten extracts from *King Solomon's Mines*. One of the contestants is accused of plagiarism, as Thomas himself has been, but his well-worked obsessions are becoming self-indulgent, and the literary conceit is a little tiresome.

Dick Francis's thriller, *The Danger*, is a well-researched story of international kidnapping. The hero, Andrew Douglas, is a partner in an organisation called Liberty Market, which specialises in arranging ransoms and recovering victims. The opening sequence, set in Bologna, Italy, is expertly controlled, and although the later sequences are more traditional Francis, with hero and villain locked in deadly combat, Francis's style and skill confirm his status as a master in his genre.

Hi Noon

A literary curiosity emerged during the year, in the shape of a lost D. H. Lawrence novel. *Mr. Noon* was written in 1920–21, but the first part, based on a friend's experience, was thought too brief and controversial by his publishers, although it surfaced later in the collection *Phoenix 2*. However, it transpired that Lawrence had in fact expanded the piece to novel length, and, having been retained by his American publisher (although he sought its return), it eventually passed through various hands to the Humanities Research Centre, University of Texas, whence it was published. *Mr. Noon* is of interest as a thinly disguised account of the author's early relationship with his wife Frieda.

Joyce Rejoiced

Of great interest to scholars of James Joyce, and to the many readers who have been puzzled by difficulties and obscurities in the text of his great work *Ulysses*, was the news that a corrected edition has now appeared, albeit some 60 years after the original publication. Joyce, apparently, was "extremely irritated by all those printer's errors" in the first edition, but they have remained ever since, until the publication of the three-volume *A Critical and Synoptic Edition* by Garland Publishing Inc., of New York. It has been reported that the truly astonishing total of 5,000 errors has been eradicated—on average, seven per page—caused through difficulties in reading Joyce's script. The edition has been five years in preparation, and costs £163, so it is to be hoped that the new text may soon be accepted as authoritative, and that cheaper editions—much closer to the author's intended version—will become readily available.

In "The Year of *the* Book", the literary industry has been less prominent in marketing George Orwell memorabilia than the cinema and television industries. However, of interest to scholars was the publication of a facsimile edition of the extant remains of the original manuscript and typescript of *1984*. Orwell rarely retained his manuscripts, and just over half of the text of *1984* survived, from various drafts made over three years of work, giving an interesting insight into his working methods and development of the book. The BBC wartime news commentaries that Orwell broadcast weekly on the Indian Service were located by a diligent researcher during the year. The 60 scripts and various letters had apparently been misfiled 40 years ago.

Other novels published during the year included Harriet Waugh's *Kate's House*, a black comedy about a four-year-old girl whose childish fantasies concerning her doll's house are mirrored by real events elsewhere. Fay Weldon's *The Life and Loves of a She-Devil* is a bizarre tale of an American housewife who loses her husband to his mistress, sets out to take revenge, and is remodelled in the mistress's image. Philip Roth's *The Anatomy Lesson* continues the saga of Nathan Zuckerman, seen previously in *The Ghost Writer* and *Zuckerman Unbound*. Now totally incapacitated by pains that ruin his life and prevent him from writing, he tries every conceivable cure in this very funny book, eventually leaving New York for Chicago and life as a doctor, but with a worse fate to come. Thomas Berger, author of the excellent *Little Big Man*, in *The Feud* has written a farce, with serious undertones, about the battling Beelers and Bullards families in the 1930s. Thomas Keneally's *The Cut-Rate Kingdom* was published in Australia in 1980, and thus predates his brilliant Booker winner *Schindler's Ark*. Opening with the fall of Singapore in 1942, its narrator is a political journalist, Maurice "Paperboy" Tyson, who lost both legs in Gallipoli. The novel is concerned with conscription in Australia in the 1940s, and fictional characters are interwoven with real events. The kingdom in the title is Australia, its king the Labour Prime Minister, John Mulhall. Francis King's latest novel, *Voices in an Empty Room*, is a sensitively handled tale of three bereaved women who try to make contact with their dear departed through spiritualist mediums and extra-sensory perception. Nobel Laureate Saul Bellow has published a fine collection of three short stories and two novellas, entitled *Him With His Foot in His Mouth*; particularly noteworthy was the piece "What Kind of a Day Did You Have?"

Apart from the usual prizes and awards, the world of literature forced its attention on the public by means of the Book Marketing Council's "Best Novels of Our Time" campaign, which had the desired effect of making controversy out of nothing, and selling more books. Anthony Burgess, not unreasonably, was excluded from the selection, but his prompt rejoinder with a work called *99 Novels: The Best in English Since 1939—A Personal Choice*, fanned the flames wonderfully, and helped increase the royalties of any number of authors. Burgess's pamphlet showed signs of having been compiled—or reassembled—in some haste, and also excluded his own works; presumably the 100th selection, left to the reader's discretion, would be his *Earthly Powers*. Unfortunately, few people would choose Burgess's latest novel, *Enderby's Dark Lady*, in which he resurrected a hero who would better have remained interred. However, if not all of Burgess's novels reach the high standards of which he is capable, his energy and creative powers are not in dispute. It is perhaps salutary to note that one of the most popular books in the bestsellers' lists was a work by former M.P. turned novelist Jeffrey Archer. What price artistic integrity, when, for the American market, his U.S. editor was reported to have removed one of the main characters, and completely changed the ending of the book (called *First Among Equals*)?

Greek Tragedy

One of the most remarkable books to be published during the year was billed, somewhat melodramatically, on its cover as "a savage war, a mother's love, and a son's revenge". It is to be hoped that potential readers were not dissuaded from purchasing this story by those words. *Eleni* is a true story, set in the remote, primitive mountain village of Lia in northern Greece, near the Albanian border. The peasant community is brilliantly evoked; deeply religious and superstitious, scratching out an existence on the hillside. A drama gradually unfolds which transcends its time and place. Eleni Gatzoyiannis, married to a Greek who had left for America to try to make a new life for his family, became a pawn in the wars and civil wars that raged through Greece. In an attempt to save her children from the *"pedomasoma"*, the forcible abduction of children by the Communists to sympathetic neighbouring countries, she organised the escape of four of her five children from the village. Unable to leave herself, she was arrested by the guerrillas occupying her home, brutally tortured, tried in a "people's court", and shot by a firing squad in a mountain ravine.

One of the children who escaped, her only son Nikola, aged nine at the time of her death, became obsessed with finding out everything he possibly could about his mother's life and death, with the intention of avenging himself on her killers. He became a journalist in America, and later the *New York Times* correspondent in Greece, but eventually devoted himself full-time to his quest. At a memorial service held in 1969 in his birthplace of Lia, a schoolteacher had said "This woman's death was not an ordinary one ... She was executed alone, with her husband far away, because she tried to save her children. She was a victim of her fellow Greeks. She was murdered!" Piecing together the story after some 400 interviews, the son, now known as Nicholas Gage, eventually came to confront the judge he believed responsible for his mother's death. The dreaded Katis, whom he has pledged himself to kill, is located living in comfortable retirement, denying any involvement in criminal acts in the war. In scenes of almost unbearable tension, the author has his opportunity for revenge, but comes to the realisation that he would be lowering himself to the level of his mother's murderers. His revenge is the book, a tribute to the mother who died in saving him, and an expiation of his quest.

The author, although widely praised, and recipient of the Heinemann Award, has been criticised for detracting from the value of the work as a historical document by recreating conversations that were not documented. The point has some validity, but the book is far more than history, and as the author states in a brief epilogue, "following the example of Thucydides, 'I put into the mouth of each speaker the sentiments proper to the occasion, expressed as I thought he would be likely to express them.'" The technique is effective; the prose suffers from the occasional purple patch, but the overall impression is of a remarkable story, compellingly told.

Letters

The sixth and final volume of the *Lyttelton Hart-Davis Letters*, covering the years 1961–62, was published. This entertaining and erudite correspondence between an ex-Eton schoolmaster and former pupil turned publisher had its genesis when Lyttelton complained that no-one wrote to him. The following six years produced over 600 letters, closing only by reason of Lyttelton's death in 1962. The book ends touchingly, with a letter written by Rupert Hart-Davis for an old boys' dinner which would have marked his correspondent's 100th birthday.

"O Beloved Kids": Rudyard Kipling's Letters to His Children, selected and edited by Elliot L. Gilbert, cover the years 1906–15. Didactic, informative, and affectionate, with little drawings included, Kipling seems not quite to have grown up. One daughter Josephine had died of pneumonia aged seven, and the remaining two children, Elsie and John, were dearly loved. The letters end with John's death in the war in 1915, his father having arranged him a commission. It would seem that Kipling never fully recovered from this shock.

Barbara Pym achieved some success as a novelist between 1950 and 1961, and then her novels were rejected by publishers. Her career was resuscitated when the *Times Literary Supplement* produced a feature on underestimated writers, in which her name was mentioned by both Lord David Cecil and Philip Larkin. She died in 1980, but a fine tribute to her has appeared in the form of *A Very Private Eye: Barbara Pym—An Autobiography in Letters and Diaries*, edited by Hazel Holt and Hilary Pym, with much fascinating material drawn from the 82 notebooks she had assiduously filled since the age of 18.

Also published were *Selected Letters of E. M. Forster: Vol. I: 1879–1920*, edited by Mary Lago and P. N. Furbank, a selection of some 200 letters from the 15,000 in existence, and *Jean Rhys, Letters 1931–1966*, edited by Francis Wyndham and Diana Melly. A one-volume edition of *The Lisle Letters*, selected by Bridget Boland, based on Muriel St. Clare Byrne's six-volume edition, was published. There are few equals to this marvellous evocation of life at the Court of Henry VIII, where Lord Lisle, illegitimate son of Edward IV, last of the Plantagenets, eventually fell victim to the intrigues of Thomas Cromwell.

One Swallow

Arthur Ransome, best known for his 1932 children's book *Swallows and Amazons*, had a remarkable life, which is excellently recounted in Hugh Brogan's *The Life of Arthur Ransome*, issued in the centenary year of his birth. Ransome had fled to Russia to escape his first wife, who had such disconcerting habits as tipping poached eggs over her head in bed. He then reported the Russian Revolution, the *Daily News* correspondent having been taken ill, was recalled for criticising British policy, and interviewed by the Special Branch, to whom he described his politics as "fishing". He also married Trotsky's secretary, who never approved of the works by which his name is now remembered.

Sound as a Belloc

"When I am dead, I hope it may be said: 'His sins were scarlet, but his books were read'." Unfortunately, Hilaire Belloc's wish has not been fulfilled, but the man described by Anthony Powell as "odiously bad mannered . . . charmless" has found a sympathetic biographer in A. N. Wilson. Of his subject, he writes, Belloc is "out of fashion, out of print, in most cases out of mind, not because of the quality of his literary output, but, very largely, because of the nature of his political and religious beliefs". Unfortunately, he does not state his case wholly convincingly, as the unevenness of Belloc's prodigious output counts against him more than his biographer would concede. Nevertheless, it is a signal feat to have made him, if not less odious, at least more readily understandable.

Till Wells Run Dry

A literary war is raging over the remains and reputations of H. G. Wells and Dame Rebecca West. The offspring of this famous relationship, Anthony West, fired the first shots, following his mother's recent death, with the publication for the first time in Britain of his novel *Heritage*, previously published in New York in 1955, but here withheld by reason of the libel laws. In his introduction, written in 1983, he states: "The truth of how things were between my mother and myself was that from the time that I reached the age of puberty, and she came to the point of a final rupture with my father, she was minded to do me what hurt she could, and that she remained set in that determination as long as there was breath in her body to sustain her malice." The novel, written, as he says, in anger, nevertheless stands on its own as a comedy of manners, but a certain piquancy is added with knowledge of its background.

West also published a biography of his father, which he commenced in 1948, although denied access to pertinent papers. *H. G. Wells: Aspects of a Life* continues the feud, blaming his mother for damaging Wells' reputation to bolster her own. The portrait of his father is affectionate, but such bitter passions inevitably cloud objectivity.

Arthur Koestler and his wife Cynthia committed suicide in 1983. He was 77 years old, and chronically sick, while she was 55 and in perfect health. *Stranger on the Square* is the third, unfinished volume of his autobiography, written jointly with his wife and covering the years 1940 to 1956. Koestler led a remarkable life, previously chronicled in *Arrow in the Blue* and *Invisible Writing*; he was a brilliant thinker and writer, who should be remembered for such works as *Darkness at Noon*, rather than his posthumous bequest to leave his money to endow a chair in paranormal studies at a university. His friend George Mikes published a touching tribute to him in *Arthur Koestler: The Story of a Friendship*.

In *My Mind's Eye* by Michael Redgrave was a most enjoyable, and discreet, memoir by one of the finest English stage actors of this century. Now sadly stricken with illness, he dictated the book to his son Corin. Redgrave last appeared on the stage in 1979 at the National Theatre, in Simon Gray's *Close of Play*, in a part which mirrored his own situation. .

The life of one of the geniuses of 20th century cinema is engagingly recalled in *My Last Breath* by Luis Buñuel, written with Jean-Claude Carrière and translated by Abigail Israel. Buñuel's famous surrealist first film, *Un Chien Andalou*, was financed by his mother and made in two weeks. At its première, he hid behind the screen with handfuls of stones to throw at the audience if they were unappreciative! The reminiscences and thoughts of this paradoxical figure (who made the memorable remark, "Thank God I am still an atheist"), are well worth reading.

Masters of War

The death in 1984 at the age of 91 of one of the most controversial figures of the Second World War has freed for publication his official biography, written some ten years ago. *"Bomber" Harris: The Story of Marshal of the Royal Air Force Sir Arthur Harris* by Dudley Saward is a fine—if not wholly objective—account of the uncompromising leader who took over control of Bomber Command in 1942, revitalised it, and pursued a relentless policy of mass bombing of German cities. Goebbels, with characteristic overstatement, said of him, "Brutality, cold cynicism and an undiluted lust for murder are his chief characteristics". Harris himself justified his policy by saying that "Attacks on cities are strategically justified in so far as they tend to shorten the war and so preserve the lives of

Allied soldiers"; and "I do not personally regard the whole of the remaining cities of Germany as worth the bones of one British Grenadier". Whether or not, in the context of war, the destruction of Dresden was justified, and however successful his attacks on the production centres of the German war effort, it is apparent that British Bomber Command would have been far less effective without Harris, and that alone of British military leaders, he received shabby treatment at the hands of Government immediately following the cessation of war.

An interesting volume was Peter Padfield's *Dönitz—The Last Führer*, in which he made out a convincing case for his assertion that the German U-boat commander escaped lightly at Nuremburg with a ten-year sentence, as his involvement with and complicity in the activities and crimes of the Third Reich went far deeper than was hitherto suspected. Even until his recent death, Dönitz was held in some esteem, and thought of as a gentleman sailor, merely doing his military duty when appointed to succeed Hitler, whereas in fact he knew about the Holocaust, and had been responsible for the killing of defenceless survivors of merchant ships sunk by his submarines.

Monty, Master of the Battlefield 1942–44 by Nigel Hamilton is the second volume of official biography of Field Marshal Viscount Montgomery of El Alamein; unfortunately, the author draws too heavily on archive material, much of which could have been edited down, but Montgomery's military strategy is well analysed. Also published was *Montgomery in Europe 1943–45: Success or Failure?* by Richard Lamb.

War Diaries: Politics and War in the Mediterranean, January 1943–May 1945 by Harold Macmillan, while duplicating the second volume of his memoirs, *The Blast of War*, nevertheless provides a much more lively and readable account of his time as Minister Resident in the Mediterranean, based as it is on letters to his wife. Also of note was *Overlord: D-Day and the Battle for Normandy*, Max Hastings' well-researched account of a critical period in the war, which is disturbing for showing up the supremacy of German arms and forces when confronted with the Allies on equal terms.

Also published during the year were: *John Maynard Keynes: Volume 1: Hopes Betrayed, 1883–1920*, Robert Skidelsky's biography of the influential economist. *Beyond the Pale— Sir Oswald Mosley 1933–80*, was the second volume of his son Nicholas's biography, following *The Rules of the Game*. In *My Time: An Autobiography* by Lord Elwyn-Jones, former Labour Lord Chancellor, who was called to the Bar in 1935, is particularly interesting in his account of the Nuremburg Trial where, a newly-elected Labour M.P., he was briefed as a counsel for the prosecution. *Thomas Carlyle: A Biography* by Fred Kaplan is an exhaustive account of the life of the dyspeptic, self-styled genius. Allan Bullock has written a masterly account of the life of *Ernest Bevin: Foreign Secretary, 1945–51*, and *The Diary of Hugh Gaitskell, 1945–56*, edited by Philip M. Williams, is revealing on the life of one of the great Labour leaders. *Caveat: Realism, Reagan and Foreign Power* by Alexander Haig, is a fascinating and candid account by a former U.S. Secretary of State of his years in office. He is particularly revealing on the Falklands Conflict, which he tried to forestall by shuttle diplomacy. *Home and Dry* is the third volume of autobiography of the building society solicitor and poet, Roy Fuller.

Other publications include: *The Weaker Vessel: Woman's Lot in Seventeenth Century England* by Antonia Fraser; *Helliconia Summer* by Brian Aldiss; *Milady Vine: The Autobiography of Philippe de Rothschild* by Joan Littlewood; *Albert Prince Consort* by Robert Rhodes James; *Elizabeth R: A Biography* by Elizabeth Longford; *Peter Hall's Diaries: The Story of a Dramatic Battle*, edited by John Goodwin; *The Kingdom by the Sea* by Paul Theroux; *The Pride and the Fall; Iran 1974–1979* by Anthony Parsons; *F. E. Smith, First Earl of Birkenhead* by John Campbell; and *Edwina, Countess Mountbatten of Burma* by Richard Hough.

BOOKER-McCONNELL PRIZEWINNERS

1969 *Something to Answer For*—P. H. Newby (Faber).
1970 *The Elected Member*—Bernice Rubens (Eyre & Spottiswoode).
1971 *In A Free State*—V. S. Naipaul (Andre Deutsch).
1972 *G*—John Berger (Weidenfeld).
1973 *The Siege of Krishnapur*—J. G. Farrell (Weidenfeld).
1974 *The Conservationist*—Nadine Gordimer (Cape).
      Holiday—Stanley Middleton (Hutchinson).
1975 *Heat and Dust*—Ruth Prawer Jhabvala (Murray).
1976 *Saville*—David Storey (Cape).
1977 *Staying On*—Paul Scott (Heinemann).
1978 *The Sea, The Sea*—Iris Murdoch (Chatto & Windus).
1979 *Offshore*—Penelope Fitzgerald (Collins).
1980 *Rites of Passage*—William Golding (Faber).
1981 *Midnight's Children*—Salman Rushdie (Cape).
1982 *Schindler's Ark*—Thomas Keneally (Hodder & Stoughton).
1983 *Life & Times of Michael K*—J. M. Coetzee (Secker & Warburg).

The finalists for the 1984 prize are:
According to Mark—Penelope Lively (Heinemann), *Empire of the Sun*—J. G. Ballard (Gollancz), *Flaubert's Parrot*—Julian Barnes (Cape), *Hôtel du Lac*—Anita Brookner (Cape), *In Custody*—Anita Desai (Heinemann), *Small World*—David Lodge (Secker & Warburg).

1038

[1985

ARCHAEOLOGY IN 1983–84

English Heritage

The 1st of April, 1984 was a momentous day for archaeology in England, for on this date the Historic Buildings and Monuments Commission for England, constituted under the terms of the National Heritage Act 1983, was inaugurated. The new Commission, which has chosen to call itself "English Heritage", has two statutory advisory committees for ancient monuments and historic buildings. Its budget for 1984–85 is £53 million net.

The Commission has a duty to secure the preservation of ancient monuments and historic buildings, to promote the preservation and enhancement of the character and appearance of conservation areas, and to promote the public's enjoyment, and advance their knowledge, of ancient monuments and historic buildings. Further, it has responsibilities for the provision of educational services, giving advice, carrying out research and making records.

The most obvious immediate result of the changes associated with the setting up of the Commission is that the new body has taken over the management from the Department of the Environment of some 400 monuments, including such famous structures as Stonehenge, Dover Castle and parts of Hadrian's Wall. The Commission has also taken over from the Department responsibility for making grants to the owners of historic buildings and ancient monuments and also for rescue archaeology purposes. It is already clear that one of the more subtle changes is that the Commission will have greater freedom in speaking publicly on contentious matters than did the Secretary of State.

It should not be thought that all the duties, nor indeed the staff, have been transferred across to the new Commission. The matter of Royal Palaces in occupation remains a Civil Service function and the Secretary of State still retains his authority in matters relating to giving consent over private property, for example, the granting of scheduled monument consent for ancient monuments which are not in guardianship. Nevertheless there has been a radical change in responsibilities, probably the most important since the passing of the original Ancient Monuments legislation; the archaeological world will watch with great interest how the new Commission discharges its responsibilities.

Ancient Monuments Board

One of the results of the establishment of the Historic Buildings and Monuments Commission for England is that the Ancient Monuments Board for England is abolished, its work being included within the remit of the new body. Therefore, the *30th Annual Report* of the Board for 1983–84 is its final one. The Board held its first meeting on April 1,

1914 and its final one on March 30, 1984, thus completing a cycle of 70 years.

During the period January 1, 1983 until March 31, 1984, some 126 monuments were scheduled on the recommendation of the Board and approximately half this number relates to the rescheduling of Hadrian's Wall. Nine monuments were descheduled. Amongst those threatened or damaged, the Board drew attention to Bank Quay Transporter Bridge at Warrington in Cheshire, noting that "this is an example of a very unusual class of bridge. Only four were built in Britain, three of which survive." The Board welcomed the Department's intention to refuse scheduled monument consent for demolition. A totally different kind of threat was that caused to sites and monuments, especially in Cornwall, as a result of the "Golden Egg" treasure hunt competition promoted by Cadbury Schweppes Ltd. The Board reports: "The damage to some of the sites may be incalculable, both in terms of actual physical damage and, perhaps more important in the long term, in influencing the public's attitude towards preservation of archaeological sites. It is accepted that Cadbury Schweppes Ltd. never intended to encourage the disturbance of any site or monument. We were appalled to find that nevertheless by the end of March of this year, 19 scheduled sites and monuments, and two unscheduled monuments, had suffered damage." The competition was terminated by the Company at the request of Ministers.

During the period under review, of the 126 monuments scheduled on the recommendation of the Board, 36 were in Northumberland and 27 in Cumbria; the next highest County totals were for Leicestershire and Tyne and Wear with seven each, followed by Cambridgeshire with five. These 126 monuments are divided into the following categories: caves, 1; burial mounds, Megalithic monuments and ritual ceremonial sites, 3; camps and settlements, 5; Roman remains, 74; linear earthworks, 1; ecclesiastical buildings, 5; crosses, 3; castles and fortifications, 4; deserted villages, settlements and moated sites, 8; industrial monuments, 9; other secular sites, 10; and bridges, 3.

DISCOVERIES AND EXCAVATIONS

Archaeological excavations and the interpretation of the results are time-consuming activities, especially when the sites in question may take a number of years to become available for thorough investigation. Summaries therefore tend to concentrate on short-term excavations or particularly interesting chance discoveries. For more detailed accounts of work undertaken, or in progress, the reader is advised to consult the appropriate journals.

Roman Britain

A comprehensive account of current work relevant to the Roman period may be found in *Britannia*, Vol. XIV for 1983. Among the reports may be noted the discovery at Guilsfield in Powys of a scattered hoard of 4,666 Constantinian coins, which had been buried in two pottery vessels, one, it is noted, an Oxfordshire colour-coated beaker, and the other a storage jar possibly made in the Severn Valley. The coins were on the whole in good condition, ranging in date between A.D. 318 and 328, their burial taking place by 330. In Scotland, at Ochtertyre in the Central Region, part of a marching-camp was identified by aerial photography in pasture on the south bank of the River Teith, thus suggesting a possible crossing-point of the river. On Hadrian's Wall at Castle Nick part of the wall on either side of Mile Castle 39 was examined, as was the north side of the Mile Castle itself. At Carlisle, in excavations at Annetwell Street, some five phases of second century timber buildings were recognized. The structures were centred on the line of the north-south road first laid down in the Agricolan fort and in one phase there was a timber-lined pit in one building, perhaps a latrine in which were found fragments of a writing-tablet.

Moving south to Lincolnshire, at Pointon, a scattered hoard of 38 Constantinian coins, ending with issues of 330–7, was found on the surface, while at Tattershall Thorpe, a hoard of 5,074 third century coins, down to the Emperor Probus (A.D. 276–82), was found in a pot during quarrying. At Stonea Grange in Cambridgeshire, it is reported that "an Iron Age pit and post-holes dating probably to the fifth century B.C., were found in the north-east corner of the site. Another pit dated to the mid first century A.D.; this together with Stonea Camp itself and the discovery of Icenian coin hoards at Field Baulk, March and at Langwood Fenn, Chatteris, reinforces the evidence of previous coin hoards that the area was occupied by a pagus of the Iceni at the time of the Boudiccan rebellion." In Northamptonshire, at Ashton, excavations of the site of the small Roman town continued in advance of road works; among the discoveries was the fact that in the fourth century, part of the area was used as a cemetery and it is noted that "some graves had a stone lining, some had contained wooden coffins, and in some the body had rested on a bier; two burials were decapitated, with the head placed at the foot of the grave." In Hertfordshire, the excavations at Gorhambury Villa were completed after 11 seasons and the various phases were distinguished, while at Colchester in Essex, it is reported that "the first phase of work was completed with the excavation of the corners of two tribunes' houses separated by

a street five metres wide." This excavation took place in Culver Street and in the corner of the northern building was a long narrow timber-lined cess-pit, "which yielded fragments of at least ten bowls of North Italian egg-shell ware. Among other finds were crucible fragments, which laboratory examination showed had been used in the manufacture of brass, a rare discovery. There is a possibility that the tribunes' houses were not demolished before c. 55 and thus that the brass-making is colonial rather than military."

Extensive investigations continue in the City of London and amongst these may be noted work at Billingsgate lorry park in Lower Thames Street where the earliest feature was a substantial third century quay. It is reported that "the feature represents a major reclamation in front of the first century quays found north of Thames Street at Pudding Lane, Peninsular House and Miles Lane, in previous years". Also in the City, at no. 14 Garlick Hill, two phases of timber building were discovered associated with Neronian pottery, which included a group of wasters and the comment is offered that "if a kiln lies in the vicinity it would represent the earliest pottery production yet known in the City." At Beddington sewage farm in south London, the excavation of the villa and bath building was completed in advance of destruction by gravel-digging. Unfortunately much of the villa had been destroyed earlier this century but enough remained for the excavators to distinguish several phases.

At Claydon Pike in Gloucestershire, the investigation of an aisled building was completed and that of the main building begun. At this interesting site it is noted that "a few pieces of possibly military equipment, including a bronze vine-leaf medallion and a leaf-shaped harness-pendant with red and yellow enamel, together with a pair of fine trumpet-brooches and a graffito mentioning *Legio II Augusta*, hint at an official establishment in the first century, when also some buildings were given substantial masonry foundations and *opus signinum* floors." At Ilchester, Somerset, investigations were carried out at the Northover House cemetery which is thought to contain up to 1,500 inhumations. At Dover in Kent, part of the south wall of the Saxon shore fort was revealed within the Market Hall in the Market Square. It is reported that this length of wall was "still standing 4 m. high and built of flint and tufa. Behind it was a bank c. 12 m. wide, beyond which was a layer of black soil 2 m. thick containing a large number of third and fourth century coins. Beneath these deposits lay demolished clay walls and floors of second-century buildings. Large areas of fallen wall plaster were found intact and were lifted. These structures relate to the *Classis Britannica* fort and stood c. 40 m. from its east wall."

The Medieval Period

Recent investigations concerning the medieval period are noted in *Medieval Archaeology*, Vol. XXVII for 1983, and, among them may be recalled the excavations in Redcliff Street, Bristol, Avon, where much evidence for iron-working was found, including large quantities of iron slag and iron ore associated with small bowl-features and a larger rectangular one, possibly a forge. Evidence for bronze-working was also found in the vicinity. It is noted that large quantities of pottery were found, which "attest to the wealth of the area in the medieval period." The pottery included "several Saintonge polychrome jugs, Spanish and Italian wares, as well as local Ham Green and Redcliffe-wares, including a highly decorated Redcliffe-ware jug of late 14th century date." In Bedfordshire, excavations at Grove Priory in Leighton Buzzard have permitted the provisional identification of one of the buildings as one of those commissioned in 1155 for the refurbishment of the royal manor of Leighton and in extended form it may have been used as royal quarters in the late 13th and 14th centuries. In the neighbouring county of Buckinghamshire two areas of probably late 13th century pottery production were investigated during the construction of the M 40/25 interchange at Denham. On the southern site the bulk of the wares were of a reduced sandy fabric with cooking pots, unglazed jugs and bowls being the more important types although curfews were also made.

Moving northwards to Cheshire, a particularly interesting excavation was undertaken in Princess Street, Chester, where a site, it is noted, "behind the Town Hall produced some information of significance concerning the appearance of this part of Chester in the late Saxon period. It was now possible to demonstrate that, although there had been some robbing of masonry in the vicinity, a major Roman building remained standing and substantially intact (albeit in a ruinous condition and largely roofless) until at least the 10th century and very probably until the later 11th century when its walls were systematically robbed for re-use elsewhere. From beneath a patch of rubble derived from the ruination of the Roman building came, *inter alia*, a fine example of a copper-alloy open-work brooch, complete with back plate (but with its pin missing), in the Jellinge style, of c. 10th century date."

In Derbyshire, at Kniveton, rescue excavations disclosed three single and two double inhumation burials of the 6th/7th century cut into a Bronze cairn. Amongst the grave goods were knives, spears, a sword, buckles, a strike-a-light and box fittings. In the same county at Repton School excavations continue and one of a group of six mounds "has revealed a mass burial containing the disarticulated bones of more than 50 bodies." The report notes that "the mound was thrown up over the remains of a massively constructed masonry building. This contained two chambers and was sunk about 0·6 m. into the ground. It was partly decorated with stucco mouldings. The building is thought to be a royal mausoleum of one or more of the kings of Mercia, two of whom are known to have been buried at Repton. Squatters later occupied this building, leaving a litter of animal bones, iron objects and querns (some from the Eifel district of Germany) covering the floor. These squatters may have been members of the Danish Viking army who wintered at Repton in 874–75." The remains of at least 50 and possibly as many as 75 people were found in the eastern chamber of the building and it is noted that "it is already clear that the bones were not articulated, the majority were male, the ages ranging mainly between teens and forties, and there was evidence of both healed and unhealed wounds caused by sharp instruments. The bone deposit also contained iron knives, an iron axe, a few pieces of broken jewellery and coins of Alfred (871–99) and Aethelred I (866–71). It is suggested that the bones are remains collected from a battlefield after lying exposed long enough for the bodies to decay and the bones to become disjointed, but not long enough for all clothes and leather gear to have rotted." On the evidence of the coins it is proposed that the mass burial is connected with the events of 874–75 when the Viking army wintered at Repton and deposed the Mercian king. "The fact that the bones were clearly not buried at once suggests that they are the remains of a defeated Mercian army."

At Springfield Lyons in Essex excavations have continued at the site of a Saxon cemetery which overlies a late Bronze Age enclosure. So far, 14 cremations and 50 inhumations have been investigated. Because the cremations were not deeply buried, there has been much damage by ploughing, and, because of the acidity of the soil, none of the bones from the inhumations survive except for some teeth. However, about a third of the burials contained grave goods, among which were amber and glass necklaces, brooches, belt fittings, knives, spear heads, a shield boss and a brass-bound bucket. The final season of excavation took place at Six Dials, Southampton, Hampshire and it is noted that all the pre-19th century features were middle Saxon apart from two of late Iron Age date, a Romano-British ditch, a 13th–14th century field boundary and a post-medieval drain. The coin evidence suggests that the initial occupation of Six Dials should be dated to around 700 and that the site was abandoned by the late ninth century.

In the county of Hereford and Worcester investigations were made at Kilpeck Castle because part of the inner bailey has been destroyed by grave digging without any archaeological record being made and a further area is under threat from a new extension to the graveyard. Some seven periods of occupation were found and below the rampart the pre-castle ground surface was reached. The pottery which related to the earliest period consisted of medieval cooking pots and glazed jug fragments providing a date range from the 12th to the 14th or 15th centuries. Among the excavations undertaken in St. Albans, Hertfordshire, may be noted the one at Gentle's Yard, where the fill of a cellar "produced an important group of late 15th century material including three bone tuning pegs and quantities of animal and fish bones, together with a useful selection of local pottery associated with such imports as Spanish, Maiolica and Langerwehe stoneware.

In Humberside, at Barton-upon-Humber, some 40 inhumation burials have been investigated and it is reported that "most of the burials are accompanied by types of grave goods normal in an Anglian cemetery such as iron knives, spears, annular brooches and beads. One, however, had a Frankish buckle; and another, of which only the lower half survived, was accompanied at the pelvis by a Frankish pot. Another had a triangular garnet, the setting for which was missing, unless a small piece of beaded gold wire in the same grave originally formed a part of it. Grave 29 contained the only skeleton accompanied by a cruciform brooch." At St. Peter's Church in Barton-upon-Humber a further season of excavations and recording took place at this redundant church. It is reported that the excavation of the interior of the church has been completed apart from the medieval chancel and work is being undertaken in the churchyard; a further 600 graves were excavated bringing the total to 1,920. "While most of the medieval and later internments were straightforward and call for no special comment at this stage, the Saxon cemetery yielded results of exceptional importance, owing to water-logging." Burial had begun by the ninth century with the earliest burials being uncoffined with no grave furniture. It is noted that "one grave was remarkable in that it contained the skeletons of two adult males, with three children carefully placed on top of them, some of their limbs being interlocked." From a later phase there were ten cases of long slender sticks ("hazel wands") found inside coffins. This was a common ritual in Scandinavia but few cases have been reported in England. In Lincolnshire, at Fillingham, a chance discovery of human bones west of the present church led to the discovery of a charnel pit and a double grave lined with limestone. As other burials have been found in this area at the west end of the present village, it is thought that the site of an earlier church may be indicated.

Among the many significant investigations

in the City of London, the excavation at 7–10 Foster Lane may be noted, for here two medieval cesspits were discovered. One of these, dated by the pottery in it to the first half of the 14th century, contained crucible fragments, of which two had traces of silver, as well as about 50 pieces of enamelled glass beakers, of "Syro-Frankish" type, which is extremely rare although it has a distribution range from the Middle East to Scandinavia. It is not clear whether this kind of glass was made in Syria to European specifications, or in Europe using Syrian techniques. Still in the City, at 1–6 Old Bailey/42–45 Ludgate Hill much material dating to about 1300–25 was found in the back filling of the last ditch, "including a large pottery group, horse skeletons and industrial waste suggestive of Fleet Valley industries, and a well preserved wattle fence, perhaps representative of early suburban encroachment, crossing and blocking the ditch cut." Across the Thames in Southwark, 13th century and later pits were excavated at 4–26 St. Thomas Street and in one of these was found a hoard of forged coins of Henry III.

In Northumberland, at Alnamsheles, excavations continued at the site of a deserted hamlet. It was found at the first house site that the earliest stone building had dated to the late 14th to 15th centuries and consisted of three bays supported on cruck timbers; the living area was based on a hearth-slab at the head of the byre. Previous to this stone house there had been a timber building of late 13th to early 14th century date occupying the same site and access. It was found that its gable ends were supported by earth-fast posts and its wall was set in a shallow foundation trench; divided in half by a partition, its living area with a clay hearth lay to the west. A second stone house was investigated and displayed characteristics similar to the first. In the same county, further excavations took place at Edlingham Castle and it is reported that "all the domestic structures of the 14th to 16th century castle have been excavated, and the defensive sequence has been sampled in two areas. The castle now provides a typesite for the domestic, architectural, and military evolution of the many small fortified manors and castles of the late medieval north of England."

At Wenlock Priory in Shropshire the southerly of the three chapels in the north transept was excavated down to natural giving a sequence from the Roman period to the 16th century. Five Saxon burials were recovered and the skeletons are to be dated by the radio-carbon method. At Lichfield Cathedral in Staffordshire a burial which had been accidentally found was examined. It was in the south wall of the undercroft to St. Chad's Head chapel. The chapel had been built against the south side of the quire in the early 13th century with provision being made from the beginning for the inclusion of a massive sandstone coffin in the south wall of the east bay. It is reported that "the internal hollowing of the coffin includes a trefoil-headed canopy at the west end. The lid comprises a single slab, which originally supported the sill of a 13th century window above, which in turn was replaced by a late Perpendicular opening. The burial inside was that of a cleric, as evidenced by the fragmentary remains of a pewter mortuary chalice beside the right forearm; traces of vestments and leather sanctuary slippers also survived. The integration of the tomb with the construction of the chapel suggests this may be the founder's grave, probably an early 13th century dean. In the late 15th century the tomb was opened and some of the major bones removed, apparently for use as relics of which the chapel housed many. However, the disturbed bones, with the exception of the skull, were returned to the tomb, tied up in a bundle with red silk and string. The return of the relics is likely to have taken place at the onset of the Reformation, and is paralleled by similar activity at Wells Cathedral."

In York, at 16–22 Coppergate, a watching brief on a development site led to the discovery of a plank-lined pit in which was an iron spear with field-maple shaft, a perforated oak disc, and a brass-bound helmet of later eighth century manufacture. It consisted of cap, hinged cheek-pieces and mail neck-guard. It is noted that "hatched eyebrows terminated in animal heads shown in profile, fanged, with comma-shaped eyes and spiral ears." In addition to further decoration the helmet also was inscribed, making it, arguably, one of the most important finds from the excavations in York.

Recent Centuries

For more recent times, discoveries and excavations are reviewed in *Post-Medieval Archaeology*, Vol. 17, 1983. Amongst the reports it may be noted that a 16th century coffin burial of a priest was found during excavations on the south side of the chapel at Wenlock Priory in Shropshire. This is interesting because a brown-glazed ceramic vessel, usually known as a "salt", was found in the burial and it is thought that this may be a cheaper substitute for the metal mortuary chalice frequently found in priests' graves. Another ecclesiastical site investigated is that of All Saints Church at Ilkley in West Yorkshire, where 17th century bell-making was suggested by two successive casting pits and a melting furnace, the former containing pieces of moulds. One complete base was discovered which showed that the diameter of this particular bell mouth would have been 1·15 m. In the same county at Pontefract Castle excavations revealed three pits from

the time of the great siege of 1649–50; it is suggested that these pits were originally dug as listening shafts with the intention of getting information on any attempt to undermine the defences. One shaft was about half way along the curtain wall and the finds from the fill were of Civil War date and included armour. In another shaft amongst the finds were fragments of wall plaster, one of which had on it a date in the 1650s.

Moving south, at Totnes in Devon, a small excavation at 39 Fore Street revealed a late 16th century stone-lined cesspit which was later used as a rubbish pit. From this feature came two large pottery groups datable to about 1600, including much "Totnes type" local ware as well as imported pottery from Spain, Portugal, Italy, the Low Countries, France and Germany, together with Wan Li porcelain.

In the City of London excavations at 61–5 Crutched Friars/1–2 Rangoon Street revealed the great brick and stone foundation of the East India Company's tea and drugs warehouse constructed in 1796. At 21–9 Mansell Street, also in the City, excavations took place in an area which documents suggested was a non-conformist burial ground in the 18th century and over 100 burials, mostly in wooden coffins, were noted; the coffins were stacked as many as nine on top of each other in closely packed rows; some 57 adults, seven children and ten infants were identified from the bones recovered. Among the other excavations in the City may be noted that at Swan Lane/Upper Thames Street where a mid-17th century barrel well and late 17th and 19th century pits were discovered. These all produced pottery groups and the objects from the well included leaden cloth seals, together with samples tentatively identified as fuller's earth; these discoveries may relate to cloth-finishing processes undertaken in the vicinity.

At Rayleigh in Essex the discovery during renovations at the Dutch Cottage of a fireplace lined with re-used Delft tiles, prompted the study of one of the three surviving octagonal Dutch houses in the county. A trench dug from the central stack to the blocked front door demonstrated that the stack had been erected on a prepared clay base, after which a clay platform was constructed around it as a level base for the walls. It is noted that only brick fragments were obtained from the clay base and the recording of floor boards on the first floor indicates that there was an entrance by a vertical ladder against the north wall and possibly a second one between the south and east buttresses of the central stack.

In the West Country at Thornbury Castle in Avon an area of tiled pavement was found on the east side of the inner court; it had been constructed between 1511 and 1521 with the tiles being probably commissioned by Edward

Stafford, third Duke of Buckingham, and set in what was perhaps the old hall beneath the Duke of Bedford's lodgings. At Exeter, in Devon, bell-founders' workshops were excavated at 15 Paul Street. The foundry was in the rear part of a tenement set against the inner face of the City Wall and it was worked by members of the Pennington family between about 1625 and 1720. Before the Civil War it may have been that bell-casting was undertaken outside the North Gate with the Paul Street tenement site being used mainly for the casting of cauldrons and skillets.

In Shropshire, at the Blists Hill Upper Mine, work continued on the engine and associated buildings. Two shafts had been sunk, possibly in the 1780s, initially for coal and iron ore but later for tile and fire clays. A Newcomen-type engine was at work there until about 1906. The investigations so far have produced a pair of haystack boiler bases with a central chimney and associated stoke pit, which had a plateway leading into it to supply coal; steam pipes run into an engine pit with three sets of holding-down bolts and bearings for a pivot. With other excavated buildings it is intended to display the site after consolidation as it lies within the Blists Hill Open Air Museum, part of the Iron Bridge Gorge complex which is so important for understanding the industrial heritage of this country.

H.M. COASTGUARD

Founded in 1822 to guard our coasts against smuggling, H.M. Coastguard's role today is a very different one—that of complete dedication to the guarding and saving of all life at sea. Administered by the Department of Transport, it is responsible for co-ordinating all civil marine search and rescue operations around the 2,500 mile coastline of Great Britain and Northern Ireland, and 1,200 miles into the Atlantic, as well as co-operating with search and rescue organizations of neighbouring countries both in Western Europe and around the Atlantic seaboard. In addition the Service maintains a 24-hour watch on the Dover Strait, providing a Channel Navigation Information Service for all shipping in one of the busiest sea lanes in the world.

Since 1978 H.M. Coastguard has been organized into six Regions, each with a Regional Controller operating from a Maritime Rescue Co-ordination Centre. Each Region is subdivided into Districts under District Controllers, operating from Maritime Rescue Sub-Centres. In all there are 25 of these major centres. They are on 24-hour watch and are fitted with a comprehensive range of communications and rescue equipment. They are supported by some 350 smaller stations manned by Auxiliary Coastguards under the direction of Regulars, each of which keeps its parent centre fully informed of day to day casualty risk, particularly on the more remote danger spots around the coast.

Between January 1 and December 31, 1983, the 560 Regular and 9,000 Auxiliary Coastguards co-ordinated 4,967 incidents requiring search and rescue facilities, resulting in assistance being given to 8,856 persons. All distress telephone and radio calls are centralized on the 25 centres, which are particularly on the alert for people or vessels in distress, shipping hazards and oil slicks. Using their modern telecommunications equipment and the extensive facilities provided by British Telecom's Coast Radio Stations, they can alert the most appropriate rescue facilities: RNLI lifeboats, Royal Navy or RAF helicopters, fixed-wing aircraft, Naval vessels, ships in the vicinity, and Coastguard shore and cliff rescue teams.

For those who regularly sail in local waters, or make longer passages, the Coastguard Yacht and Boat Safety Scheme provides a valuable free service. Its aim is to give the Coastguard a record of the details of craft, their normal operating areas and their passage plans. Yacht and Boat Safety Scheme Cards are available from all Coastguard stations, harbourmasters' offices and most yacht clubs and marinas.

Members of the public who see an accident or a potentially dangerous incident on or around the coast should without hesitation dial '999' and ask for the Coastguard.

BRITISH ARCHITECTURE, 1983–84

THE R.I.B.A. 150TH ANNIVERSARY

During 1984 the Royal Institute of British Architects has been celebrating 150 years of corporate existence, with a number of exhibitions, presentations, conferences and sundry other events held nationwide under the general title of a "Festival of Architecture". It was on December 19, 1834 that the first meeting of the council of the Institute of Architects took place, at the Thatched House Tavern in St. James's. However, it was not until three years later, in 1837, that the Institute was granted a Royal Charter, and then not until 1866 that it was allowed by Queen Victoria to call itself Royal.

During its history the Institute has had its full share of glorious achievements and moments of vilification. Its continuing prestige in society owed much to the zealous protection and upholding of a rigid code of conduct, and it is this as much as anything that lies at the root of any claim to "professionalism". That these principles are today being gradually but steadily eroded and modified is a sure sign that the position of the architect in society and the nature of his everyday business has undergone a quantum change from those heady first days of the mid-nineteenth century. At a time when public esteem for architects is at an all time low while public awareness of, and debate about, architecture has reached new levels, albeit not very inspiring ones, it is perhaps salutary to reflect that a large part of the architectural profession's claim to some degree of integrity and open-mindedness lies in its continuing propensity for an, at times, quite destructive amount of self-criticism. If the public, quite rightly, think that architects have sometimes got it wrong, they should not be misled into thinking that the problems are not also clearly perceived by the majority of practitioners.

Architecture is a difficult field in which to practise; its complexity and degree of official regulation at once daunting and yet challenging. It is one of the few areas in which art meets science head on, and this surely is why so many people find it so fascinating a subject to study and practise and probably why so many others feel qualified to speak as so-called experts. Yet it needs to be spelled out quite clearly that the practice of architecture is determined by the express wishes of those people and institutions within our society who have the power, that is to say the money, to commission buildings. Architecture has a prime responsibility to meet their needs and must then attempt to address itself to the wider and more nebulous demands of society in general. It is therefore inescapably a mirror of the society of its time, in all its aspects, and while it is probably an oversimplification, it is not too far from the truth to say that society gets the architecture it deserves.

The aim of the "Festival" apart from celebrating a notable anniversary, has been to increase the level of public awareness of architecture, and to promote informed discussion in the press, on television and amongst ordinary people. Public interest has fortunately been growing, even without the assistance of the "Festival", and it is essential that the general level of debate improves—there is a widespread belief that as a nation we are visually illiterate. Even if this is the case, and it is a difficult thesis to refute, there is no need to assume that it is an incurable disease. It will be one of the Institute's most pressing tasks in the years that lie ahead to maintain and guide this newfound impetus in the right directions. 1984, of all years, was perhaps not the most auspicious in which to be celebrating the anniversary of a profession whom many commentators hold directly responsible for many of the least pleasing aspects of our modern environment, and cynical references to the anti-personal horrors of Orwell's vision will no doubt abound. Certainly the year has seen battle engaged on all the most persistently difficult issues that have faced architects for the last fifty years. General dissatisfaction with the architectural competition system reached new heights with the still-on-going débâcle over the National Gallery extension; the battle between modern architecture and conservation continues along its familiar entrenched lines with the public inquiry into the proposed Mansion House Square project; while, perhaps more insidiously than either, the shoddy legacy of the years devoted to cheap, quick, system building developed in response to the crude housing numbers game embarked on by the authorities of central and local government back in the 50's and 60's now threatens to consume vast amounts of the national resource as the defects of their building methods become sickeningly apparent. Ronan Point must surely rank high on the list of buildings known to feature prominently within the public consciousness.

Yet despite all this, it is possible to demonstrate that certainly within the last ten years, modern architecture has made significant progress towards a more humanistic approach to design, and coupled with this has been an increasing awareness of the economic sense of building in quality materials and conserving energy by efficient management systems. Architects must play their part in ensuring that these trends are encouraged, and it may be that with the greater freedom of activity recently permitted by relaxations of the code of conduct, the profession will be in a better position to exert some influence on the patterns of development of the future. If it is going to be denied the protection of "expert" status and guaranteed levels of remuneration in relation to an established level of service, because the policy of the current Government is firmly in favour of the open market and full competition, then it is essential that architects grasp whatever possibilities arise and display a far greater expertise in serving the very varied needs of society than has hitherto been the case.

The Institute finds itself therefore in the mid-eighties at something of a crossroads and needs to adapt itself to a changing world. There is still a strong role to be performed by the Institute if it has courage and foresight, yet, while promoting the best interests of the profession, it must still keep in mind its original objective as stated in the charter, namely "the general advancement of civil architecture."

THE BURRELL GALLERY, POLLOK PARK, GLASGOW

Architect: Barry Gasson Architects

Sir William Burrell (1861–1958) was a wealthy Glaswegian shipowner who, with his brother George, amassed a vast fortune from a shrewd yet courageous manipulation of the fluctuations of the world shipping market. Their tactic was simple, bold and very risky, yet it worked and paid off handsomely. In times of slump, the company would order ships at rock bottom prices, so that when the market revived they had a fleet of ships available for a number of years of highly profitable trading. While the boom period was still on however they would then sell their ships, for a sizeable profit, and lie dormant until the next slump, when they would repeat the process. It was after this process had been successfully repeated, following the end of the First World War, that William Burrell, with his money carefully invested, decided to devote the rest of his life to his one great passion, the amassing of a huge art collection.

Burrell had in fact been collecting (and selling) works of art since the 1890's, and was the largest single lender to the Glasgow International Exhibition of 1901, but not much is known of his collecting activities after that until, in 1911, he started keeping detailed records of all his purchases in a series of school exercise books. There are twenty eight of these covering the years 1911–1957, recording in detail the date of acquisition, description, from whom it was acquired, price and date of delivery. Following the sale of the bulk of his fleet around 1915 his spending accelerated rapidly and between 1911 and 1957 his outlay averaged some £20,000 per annum. In the 1930's, Burrell developed the idea of forming a permanent collection that he could eventually hand over to public ownership. Thus it was that in 1944, after discussions with a number of interested parties, Sir William and Lady Burrell donated the huge collection, which at that time numbered some 6,000 items, to the City of Glasgow, the city of his birth and centre of his business activities. A few years later he gave a generous sum to the Corporation for the construction of a suitable building in which to house and display the treasures—but in doing so made certain strict provisions concerning its siting, stating that it should be built in a rural setting, within four miles of Killearn in Stirlingshire and not less than sixteen miles from the Royal Exchange in Glasgow.

The search for a suitable site was still not resolved when Burrell died in 1958 at the age of 96, and it was not until 1967 that a site became available in Pollok Park, when Pollok House and its estate were presented to the City by Mrs. Anne Maxwell Macdonald. Burrell had never stopped adding to his collection, even after it had been donated to the City, and between 1944 and 1957 a further 2,000 items had been added, many of which were bought deliberately to reinforce certain specialized areas of interest and round off the collection. Among these purchases were an important series of mediaeval stone doorways, windows and niches, some superb stained glass pieces and a number of timber screens and other architectural features. Burrell stipulated that these should be incorporated into the fabric of the proposed gallery. Another interesting factor to be considered arose from Burrell's expressed wish, stated in his 1944 memorandum of agreement, that the three most important rooms of his residence, the dining room, drawing room and hall of Hutton Castle, near Berwick-on-Tweed, be reproduced in the new building exactly as they were when Sir William was living there.

The difficult problem of finding a designer for the new building was solved by the initiation in 1971 of an architectural competition, based on a very detailed and thorough brief that was not completed until the entire collection had been examined and carefully catalogued. The design was intended to provide a permanent home for the collection, enabling it to be displayed for all to enjoy and experience, but at the same time ensuring that these priceless relics of civilization could be adequately protected and conserved for future generations to come. The collection was described in the brief in terms of what it contained, together with an assessment of each section's importance and the space that was likely to be required, the understanding being that for reasons of both cost and public comprehension only a limited proportion of the collection would be on show at any one time. The use of the word "home" rather than gallery or museum made it clear that, although housing a major collection of international stature, the building should not be an institution but should present a more welcoming and sympathetic environment geared to the particular needs of the collection and responding to its parkland setting.

The two-stage competition was won by Barry Gasson, John Meunier and Brit Andreson, who submitted a modest, elegant and particularly well-sited design. The site offered was superb, a large sloping green field completely surrounded by mature trees, but while most competitors simply selected the middle or took the dominating position at the top of the slope, the winning design placed the gallery close to the trees, lower down and to one side of the field, leaving the majority of the green expanse untouched. The siting of the gallery provides an important clue to one of the guiding principles of the design, namely that this was to be a collection in a park, not a city, and it has enabled the natural setting of trees, grass and woodland plants to form a backdrop for the collection and reflect the innate relationships between art and nature that one sees reflected in the long traditions of craftsmanship as displayed by the objects on view.

The north face of the building has accordingly been placed right up to the line of trees, which is set at an acute angle to the rectangular geometry of the entrance wing and main gallery. Being thus shaded from the sun and protected from the north, the entire elevation has been treated as a glass wall, providing the most immediate connection between the gallery spaces and the woodland. This transparent boundary has been developed as part of a primary circulation route, around the perimeter of the gallery, and constitutes a "walk in the woods" through a number of varying exhibition spaces that are also linked through to other parts of the gallery.

A further important consideration was how to incorporate the various architectural elements, not only those pieces acquired for the collection, but also the three reconstructed rooms from Hutton Castle, with the many other types of object such as tapestries, carpets, paintings, sculpture and ceramics. The Hutton Rooms were essentially interiors and yet required to be lit naturally within the framework of the gallery, implying that there would necessarily be an exterior expression as well. In the event the importance of these rooms not only to the assembled contents of the collection but also for their relevance to Sir William, has led them to be sited around the central glazed courtyard which offers light and a physical "exterior" presence and allows them to be seen as they would have existed, though necessarily as discrete separated elements within the gallery as a whole. The various architectural elements have been brilliantly incorporated into the gallery fabric itself, that is actually built in on site, and the particular material of the two gateway arches from Hornby Castle in Yorkshire was a strong influence in the selection of the pink sandstone used for the walls in which they are placed. Other arches have been placed with reference to their period and context—a pair of small arched window openings have been set high up on a balcony overlooking the tapestry gallery, another is used to announce a particular section of the collection.

In setting out the basic spaces of the gallery, the architects sought to order the various sections of what is an extensive and very varied collection of artefacts in such a way as to make it easily comprehended by the visitor. The perimeter route was devised as a means of providing a continuous line of reference around which the different elements of the collection could be arranged, and also of ensuring that even a short simple visit would reveal a selection of the major pieces and give a general impression of the range of exhibits to be found elsewhere.

The route, obviously, starts from the main entrance, sited at the end of a slender wing of accommodation extending southwards from the south west corner of the main building so that it approaches the driveway and main access point from the car park. This linear extension immediately gives some directional impetus, as the visitor enters through the oak doors of the low but massive stone arched gateway set into the plain windowless sandstone faced gable end. It also establishes from the outset the pattern of associations and interrelationships between the museum artefact and its architectural setting, between present and past, that is further developed along the route. The public gateway is the first of the two acquisitions from the 16th century Hornby Castle.

Once inside, a further theme soon becomes apparent in the alternating sequences of high and light, low and dark, as the route progresses from the dark solidity of the oak doors through the transparent lightness of glass inner doors to the tall slender daylit space of the entrance hall; thence via the low ceilinged artificially lit space of the shop and inquiry desk out once again into a tall day-lit volume, this time the handsomely proportioned central courtyard with trees laid out in planters around the enormous (8¼ tons) 2nd century Warwick Vase, and a bold chequerboard flooring pattern in pink Lazonby sandstone and Portland Stone.

Here the restrained and carefully articulated range of structural elements can be seen to good effect. Tall freestanding circular concrete columns are capped with steel shoes into which are bolted the massive primary roof beams of laminated timber construction, with interconnecting steel tie rods, and timber purlins supporting timber rafters spaced to receive the mullion grid of the glazed rooflights. It is a simple and dignified arrangement, displaying the rigour of an intellectual discipline in the way the component parts are carefully set apart from each other, the various junctions being resolved in the design of the connecting steel plates.

Set into the north wall of the courtyard is the magnificent second archway from Hornby Castle, which acts as the entry point into the collection proper. As one passes from courtyard to gallery, the massive stone walls disappear and the quite stunning impression is of walking into a room in the woods, so immediate is the impact of the landscape at this the narrowest point of the expanding wedge of display space along the north side. Progressing through the freeform gallery space, the visitor is taken through several different aspects of the collection, with the long uninterrupted line of glass wall to one side and the regular stepped profile of the back wall projecting forward on the other to create an increasing number of internal display spaces behind.

At intermediate points the north and south legs of the perimeter route are connected by two partly daylit cross-routes, repeating the structural vocabulary of the courtyard, and offering the possibility of short cuts. The axial views along these routes are memorable, focussing to the north on the leafy woodland glades, while to the south the view of the park is seen through another major part of the collection, a series of beautiful, vibrantly coloured stained glass panels.

One of the cross-route galleries houses the oriental collection and there is a superb view north framed by cool glass cabinets and the massive timber roof beams in which a majestic oriental ceramic figure of a seated Lohan (disciple) is placed on axis against the magnificent forest backdrop.

At the end of the glazed north wall the route turns into the picture gallery ranged along the eastern side. Here the basic components of the structure are adjusted to provide a tall linear gallery space under a sloping timber roof, with clerestory lighting, entirely appropriate for the display of pictures, and this is linked to a series of lower more intimate rooms, an internal world focussing the attention solely on the displays. This change demonstrates another important aspect of the building which is that it has been designed to accommodate the varying needs of the constituent parts of the collection by providing on a permanent basis a variety of different environments each suited to its particular section, with differing qualities of natural and artificial light. This is more easily accomplished in the context of a known and permanent collection but is nevertheless to be preferred to the alternative of endlessly flexible but similar rooms that in the end are not ideally suited to anything in particular.

One of the few dramatic incidents in an otherwise calm and ordered building occurs at the point of departure from the picture gallery section, when one passes through a magnificent 12th century limestone portal to emerge suddenly into a brightly lit double height space along a balcony which overlooks the restaurant area, spread round the south-east corner. Here daylight floods in through the fully glazed sloping roof and the glazed walls which continue right down to the floor level, giving fine views out over the surrounding expanse of green field, with the trees in the distance. Here again the structural elements and materials are repeated; large laminated timber rafters spring from a horizontal timber plate, supported by special steel brackets from the slender cylindrical concrete columns, and rake downwards under the glass roof until with a simple mitred joint they are transformed into mullions for the glazed wall. The finished effect is bold, warmly colourful but incredibly simple—the sort of simplicity however that can only be achieved after a great deal of time and effort has been expended in the detailed design development.

The restaurant floor is a full storey below the main gallery level—thus sufficiently removed from the main route not to disrupt the different activity patterns of the gallery spaces—yet intimately connected with the overall massing and disposition of the various parts of the building. Even in the restaurant, the opportunity for display has not been relinquished, and a fine series of 16th century armorial stained glass panels have been mounted at high level between the timber mullions around the perimeter. The staircase from the restaurant joins the perimeter route along the south side, past the dimly lit carpet galleries and finally through another old stone archway, past more magnificent stained glass, and back into the central courtyard.

Since its opening in late 1983 the museum has received much critical acclaim and has unquestionably been a resounding success with the public who have poured in to admire the superb range and quality of the several thousand objects on display. That a visit to the gallery proves to be such a refreshing experience owes much to the ability of the architects, who have managed to create a unified and ordered architecture out of a diversity of spaces, views and cross vistas in which the past and present impinge on each other in fascinating ways. The building is artless and yet full of art, and as Burrell's character draws a common thread through his fabulous collection, so Barry Gasson's reticent and reductive approach to the assembly of the structural components holds together the modest yet very elaborately detailed architectural expression of this wonderfully successful gallery building.

ISMAILI CENTRE, KENSINGTON, LONDON

Architect: Casson Conder Partnership

Visitors to London's famous "Museum Row" in South Kensington will probably have noticed the emergence of an unorthodox and very striking new building which has recently been completed on an island site on the opposite side of the Cromwell Road from the Victoria and Albert Museum. It is in fact a religious, social and cultural centre for the Ismaili community, designed by the architects for the Aga Khan Foundation. Although intended to function primarily as a religious building, one floor is almost completely taken up with a prayer hall capable of accommodating 1,200 people; the centre also incorporates social meeting and sitting areas, an art gallery, reading rooms, various administrative facilities, including a committee room and council chamber, and even a roof-top courtyard garden.

The need for a larger and more permanent centre for the Ismaili community arose following the expulsion of the Asians from Idi Amin's Uganda. Many of the Shiah Imami Ismaili Muslims found their way to Britain, swelling the size of the community to over 12,000 people, far too many to be adequately served by the small centre that had previously been established in London in 1957.

As a result of difficulties encountered with planning problems on the original choice of site in Albany Street, Camden, the Aga Khan Foundation successfully bid for the Kensington site, acquiring it from the G.L.C. in 1977. Although, being an island site, design was not complicated by adjoining buildings, the architects were nevertheless faced with a considerable challenge in designing such a prominent structure within the context of a very sensitive and well known urban environment, and in resolving the often contradictory demands of Muslim culture, Western constructional methods, urban and functional planning constraints and environmental requirements.

The building adopts a low and compact form, filling the site to its boundary on three sides and reflecting the alignment of the adjoining roads with its diminishing rectangular plan shape. The squatness of the form derives from the need to preserve existing day-light angles to the houses in Thurloe Place and has the advantage of allowing the spires and domes of the Victoria and Albert Museum to dominate and be seen from surrounding streets. The effect of satisfying the light angles in Thurloe Place has generated one of the building's most distinctive features, the broad sloping solid face above the second storey, and this has been carried round all four sides, imparting to the building a feeling of mass and strength that vertical surfaces alone could never have done.

The size of the prayer hall is such that it occupies nearly a complete floor, and this, coupled with the need for an escape staircase in each corner, led to the decision to place the prayer hall on the second floor so that the ground and first floors could be laid out in the manner of a series of ante-rooms to control the flow through the building of large numbers of people and avoid large crowds suddenly spilling on to the pavement. The principal entrance is from the two sides of the acute angled corner between Cromwell Place and Thurloe Place, and is recessed deeply behind the overhanging oriel window structures of the first floor hall. An outer entrance hall, with a bank of six tall screen-like doors and a raised pool reflecting the geometrical intricacy of the patterned floor gives on to an inner hall and thence up a short flight of stairs to the main vertical circulation space. Here there are two lifts and the floors are opened up to give glimpses of the upper levels lit by a flood of light from the lantern above. At this point the main staircase turns back on itself to give access to the large multi-purpose social hall on the first floor. The feeling of a continuous and controlled progression through the building suggests almost a processional route, and is assisted by the ingenious device of splitting the floor levels slightly so that each move-

ment from space to space involves a change of level upwards but only of approximately half a floor at a time so that the spaces ahead and behind are always related to each other. A short flight from the foyer of the social hall gives access past the light well in front of the lifts to the long rectangular space of the shoe hall. Here, under a delicately moulded and intricately faceted ceiling, the worshippers leave their footwear in wooden racks, before ascending a few broad steps at the opposite end, passing through a further set of wooden screen-like doors and climbing the main staircase up to the foyer of the prayer hall on the second floor. It is a complex and interesting route, with numerous twists and turns, that takes participants through a series of varying spatial experiences across the length and breadth of the building before admitting them to the inner sanctuary of the prayer hall.

The quiet, enclosed and inward looking nature of the prayer hall creates the massive and largely windowless upper storey, further emphasized by the sloping upper surfaces, which dominates the external elevations. The ground and first floors are treated as a series of contrasting recessive openings controlled by the rhythm of the external columns.

The distinctive chamfered top in fact conceals the extra depth of the reinforced concrete slab and beam structure required by the long spans over the open spaces of the prayer hall and to support the weight of the roof garden hidden within the top storey. The mass of the resulting structure enabled the reading room, committee rooms and council chamber above to be freed from the main structural grid, with a lighter steel framed structure, and these areas have large windows opening on to the generously planted roof-top garden.

Within the two storey high arcade, around the greater part of the perimeter, are a number of intricately framed overhanging oriel windows, which far from opening up the interior to the view of passers-by, act instead like mysterious veils leaving the onlooker to ponder on exactly what events might unfold or who might look down from behind. The complex and graduated proportions of the teak window grilles are highlighted on the outside with stainless steel strips, and the chamfered panes of glass further emphasize the visual complexity by breaking up the interior-exterior view into a mass of reflections and mini-images as though seen through a faceted crystal.

The external face of the building is clad in a pale grey Sardinian granite which has been given a most interesting decorative finish with alternating polished and flame textured vertical stripes that give what might otherwise be a heavy and insensitive material an exquisite, almost "precious", quality. In fact, the jewel-like precision of the exterior arising out of a fastidious attention to detail, very superior quality materials, and superb workmanship is one of the principal characteristics of the building, serving to lighten the visual weight of its massive sculptural forms. The architects have further enhanced the jewel-like quality of the granite cladding by picking out the edge of the recessed openings of the two storey arcade and the tall vertical slot windows of the upper storey in contrasting narrow strips of blue Bahia granite.

Completed in November 1983 at a cost of £10 million, the Ismaili Centre exerts a powerful presence in an area of London already renowned for the quality of its public buildings. In creating this most unconventional masterpiece, the architects have quite clearly combined aspects of both Muslim and Western civilization with great sensitivity and flair, and have managed to identify a thoroughly modern building, designed very positively from the basis of a functional analysis of the client's requirements, with some of the traditional and symbolic aspects of a culture that reaches back over hundreds of years.

THE RIDINGS SHOPPING CENTRE, WAKEFIELD, YORKSHIRE

Architect: Chapman Taylor Partners

Wakefield, the county town of the West Riding of Yorkshire, is a regional centre with a population of some 320,000, and although never quite having attained pre-eminence as a major industrial centre, can lay claim to some historical significance as an early centre of the Yorkshire clothing trade and subsequently the coalmining industry. Being strategically well placed near the Yorkshire "motorway box" and thus able to call on a retail catchment area with well over 2 million people, it is therefore an ideal location for an important shopping centre.

In an attempt to rejuvenate the shopping patterns within the city centre and make use of underdeveloped backland areas behind the main street frontages, the City of Wakefield Metropolitan District Council organized a design competition in 1978, inviting four short-listed companies to prepare development proposals. Following this, Capital and Counties plc, with their architects Chapman Taylor Partners, were appointed to carry out the development.

A number of planning and design objectives were established, three principal ones among them being: to extend and integrate into the proposed new centre three existing major stores, to link to and refurbish an existing open air shopping precinct, which although only ten years old was not trading well and in need of new life, and thirdly, to extend the existing street pattern for city centre shoppers by providing a new pedestrian connection through the site linking Kirkgate, the main street running in front of the Cathedral Church, to lower Kirkgate, its continuation, running at right angles to it. By these means it was hoped to open up the backland site to full pedestrian use and thus raise it to prime retail value, and by so doing enhance the reputation of Wakefield as a regional shopping centre without enormous disruption in physical terms to the existing perceived fabric of the city centre. It was felt strongly by the development team that the key to success lay in achieving a scheme of the very highest standards and that this should also embody up to date, even innovative, concepts in shopping centre design.

At the heart of the design solution adopted lies a bold and successful concept for handling the pedestrian route through the scheme. What could for some have been a serious problem, the steeply sloping site, was instead welcomed as an opportunity to convert normally cautious retailers to an acceptance of multilevel trading, notwithstanding that there are many poor examples of double level shopping precincts that simply do not work. In fact the developers have achieved a three level arrangement, and this has been made to work successfully by spreading the principal pedestrian generators between all three levels.

At the highest point, the main entrance from Kirkgate gives access to the two upper levels, a gentle ramp rising to the upper mall, Cathedral Walk, while escalator and stairs lead down to the lower mall, Bishopgate. Most importantly at this point the design of the vistas and handling of levels is well controlled so that both levels are equally tempting to the shopper. At the upper level, connections are made into the rear of existing major shops fronting Kirkgate, and the broad expanse of walkway is cut away at intervals to accommodate interconnecting staircases and to allow shafts of day-light from the glazed roof above to penetrate to the lower level mall.

Vertical circulation points are positioned to emphasize changes in direction of the malls as the main route twists and turns through the site, and are treated in a light and airy, colourful, almost jazzy way to provide visual interest and complexity along the way. The seemingly rather nervous chopping and changing of axis has no doubt been developed as a deliberate ploy to create visual interest and variety in the line of shopfronts and character of spaces, although in unskilled hands one feels it could lead to a rather disturbing loss of orientation. At Wakefield this has been avoided by the consistently high quality of design and by the important use of natural daylight.

The lowest of the levels connects with the pavement in lower Kirkgate via the refurbished 1960's shopping precinct which has been renamed All Saints' Walk. This former shopping backwater has been transformed with a new entrance, incorporating in super graphics the name of the centre and its rather curious logo of curved lines, and has been roofed over, restyled and generally upgraded to match the detailing and standards of finishes in the rest of the centre, most of the existing tenants having remained in occupation and trading.

Lower and upper levels meet with a flourish at the heart of the site in a dramatic explosion of space and light through a four storey high atrium, complete with lavish planting, banks of escalators, "wall climber" scenic lift (a must for every atrium these days), and most important of all, Britain's first genuine "fast-food" court, an exciting innovation developed after a great deal of research and first hand study of successful North American examples.

The importance of cheap, convenient but good quality catering operations had been recognized right from the beginning and a good deal of time and trouble has gone into establishing the right type of environment and securing a number of quality food producers. The overall scheme contains two restaurants, two wine bars and a mall café, but the "fast-food" court known as "The Garden", with ten selected food outlets offering a very wide range of specialist menus, has received particular attention, and has quickly become a central attraction and a magnet trader in its own right. The ratio of 10 outlets to 375 seats was set at a deliberately conservative level helping to maintain intimacy and excitement and yet discourage excessive loitering by creating pressure for places to achieve a quick turnround time. A variety of fixed and movable seating has been employed, ranged around a terrace and pool, with the shop units ranged around the perimeter and set back underneath the walkways overhead. The prevailing atmosphere is very much that of the pavement café, and the inclusion of features such as a bandstand, gazebo and summerhouse reinforces the impression that this is a true public square as well as a commercial catering facility. The dramatic use of natural light enables fully grown trees to flourish as well as plants at various levels, and this creates a strong indoor/outdoor illusion, aided by the use of a planted water feature around the foot of the escalators and scenic lift, and other more subtle hints such as the pierced cast iron street gratings used to surround the trees.

The fascias of the overhanging walkways and the side panels of the "flying" banks of escalators are all mirror clad. The addition of fully glazed and chrome topped balcony handrails to this sea of reflections means that there are few visually dull areas, and views across the atrium are constantly enlivened by the reflections of plants, objects and people, producing a sense of movement, glamour and excitement of a high order. To the trained eye, however, and this seems almost inevitable given current commercial attitudes, traces of an underlying hypocrisy can be detected, though it would seem churlish to place complete responsibility for this at the architect's door. For instance, what is one to make of a central area that tries so hard to generate the ambience of an outdoor pavement café, and would probably succeed totally were it not for the patently temporary and unconvincing treatment of the water feature around the lift. One wonders why was it also felt necessary, given the razzmatazz treatment of the lift, the acres of mirror and the clean, uncomplicated, unadorned and essentially 20th century lines of the glazed roof, to try and fool people into thinking that the columns are cast-iron and Edwardian, and the mall names direct descendants of some mediaeval street system that never existed.

At Wakefield, the architects have developed their own version of a traditional 19th century industrial building, typical of the area, in which to clothe the disparate and fragmented forms of the exterior. This is far preferable to the bleak concrete manifestations of twenty years ago, and does seem to adapt well to its locality. It certainly provides plenty of visual interest with its carefully detailed brickwork corbels, pilasters, string courses and cornice, round-headed and circular windows, and generous tiled hipped roofs with ornate ridge tiles and finials. However, the pedestrian entrances to the scheme cannot be said to stamp their personality on the traditional street scene, tending to formal reticence and small scale.

Notwithstanding the rather purist criticisms, one fact cannot be denied. Since it opened on October 17, 1983, some two–three thousand shoppers a week have poured into the centre and it has therefore proved to be a huge commercial success, something which the architects must take credit for. The food court in particular has been a great success, and proves very popular with the people of Wakefield. To be truly successful against a background of increasing competition and a less than dynamic economic situation a shopping centre must be more than just a collection of the right shops in a convenient location, it has also to be an exciting place to visit and must maintain this interest on subsequent visits.

The Ridings certainly provides all the right ingredients—good parking, with 1,100 spaces on site and 3,000 more near at hand—a wide range of desirable shops, with local firms and national market leaders among the 88 units occupying some 350,000 sq. ft. of space—and a vibrant exciting atmosphere capable of maintaining its interest through repeated visits. This was fittingly recognized when it was awarded the European Council of Shopping Centres Award for 1984.

REBUILDING OF THE PARISH CHURCH OF ST. MARY, BARNES, LONDON

Architect: Edward Cullinan Architects

Until a fateful night in 1978, the Church of St. Mary in Barnes, S.W. London, could well have been cited as a classic example of that humble but much loved building type—the English Parish Church. The patchwork quilt of its fabric illustrated to perfection the historical continuity and traditions developed painstakingly over many centuries and embodied in the successive endowments of its faithful parishioners and benefactors.

The Church at Barnes certainly has a long history. Its mediaeval stone nave and chancel were completed in 1215; a brick bell tower was added at the west end in the sixteenth century; and a local family, the Hoares, in the 18th century added a Gothic family pew on the north side which was expanded by the Victorians in 1852 into a north aisle as long as the original church. Finally the Edwardians expanded yet again, adding to the north aisle to turn it into a central nave, with a further new aisle to the north,

and an apsidal vestry in the north east corner, so that by the time all these additions had been completed the original 13th century church was left to function merely as a south aisle, with its entrance porch on the south side. But, on June 8, 1978, disaster struck, and the church was gutted by fire.

Apart from the practical inconvenience to the parishioners of such a traumatic event, such as having nowhere to continue the daily worship, the more significant and long term problems facing the community are inevitably bound up with the "psychological" effects of the potential destruction of all links with the past and the resultant break in the continuity of faith and heritage. It was therefore immediately apparent that the process of reconstruction should do all it could to restore as far as possible the severed connections with the past and that this would have to be done on the basis of retaining as much as feasible of the fabric that remained.

To this extent it was fortunate that there were significant elements of the fabric that survived the fire, most importantly the brick sixteenth century bell tower, but also the porch and south wall of the mediaeval church including the chancel arch and east end, the apsidal end of the Edwardian vestry and a spiral stair turret in the north west corner. Right from the start the architect resolved to restore the former mediaeval nave, chancel and tower to something approaching their former condition, while resisting the desire of a small but vocal minority to simply rebuild a "gothic" replica in the Victorian style. The origins of the final solution lie in the basic structural and geometric principles established by the architect from the basis of the existing remains, and this developed to embrace the current ecumenical preference for a large open space in which every member of the congregation has a clear visual relationship with the altar.

Working in particular from the basis of two columns that remained where the former Victorian nave had been opened up to the mediaeval church along its north wall, and from the axial centreline of the apsidal ended Edwardian vestry, the architect has very ingeniously turned the primary axis of the new church through 90° with the projected centre-lines of the two reconstructed Victorian columns defining the body of the new "nave", now centred on the original south porch. Two secondary axes, that of the mediaeval nave and chancel, and the line of the apse projected westwards, therefore generate a double cross, or H-shape, on plan.

Where the dual north/south centrelines from the columns cross the east/west line of the vestry, a rectangular area is generated against the new north wall. Over this area is raised a three sided clerestorey lantern enabling the sun to shine down on the altar and flood the north wall with light. Thus on entering the church through the original porch this luminous focal point is the first thing to catch the attention. Thereafter the eye can begin to explore the smaller secondary spaces generated to the sides by the cross axes of the mediaeval church and the vestry wing.

The single most dominant feature of the interior is the roof, which swoops down to little more than head height in the north east and north west corners, framing the altar wall, and in the central "waist" of the H shape. The architects have developed in the constructional detailing the theme of "detachment", whereby in fact the roof, in general, never directly meets with the walls but is supported on groups of structural timber mullions that either extend down to ground level or rise out of the sill of a loggia window at first floor level that "disengages" the roof from the load bearing masonry walls. This articulation of the basic elements of the building is further emphasized by the use of a consistent structural vocabulary, highlighted by the use of colour coding, to create a hierarchy of structural components, and serves to order and lighten the complex web of steel and timber trusses supporting the great oversailing canopy of stained softwood boarding. The primary structural elements of the roof are two ridge trusses spanning from the two reconstructed columns on to the new north wall, but also cantilevered at the southern end to take the load of the reconstructed roof over the mediaeval nave. The construction of the trusses combines steel and Douglas Fir sections and the metal serves to lighten the proportions of the timber members, although both materials are used structurally. Inclined timber rafters meet the top of the trusses within triangular shaped steel plates welded to the top boom while from the bottom boom diamond shaped steel plates are used to suspend timber collars, stained dark blue, that are housed into the rafters. Beneath the flat central section a series of linked flying rafters plunge downwards through the line of the bottom collars to create a series of dramatic pointed V's leading the eye along the principal axis and focussing on the altar and the large simple timber cross suspended above it.

If the roof is the dominant visual feature of the interior, a no less important part, particularly as far as the exterior is concerned, is played by the masonry walls, some new, some restored, which envelope the building and link together its many parts. Many of the original bricks were salvaged from the burnt out ruin, together with a number of stone window mouldings from the later Victorian and Edwardian periods. These have all been lovingly and meticulously restored and occasionally remoulded, before being inserted within the newly built walls, as for instance with the nineteenth century east window of the nave, which has been incorporated in the new north wall behind the new altar position. All the new masonry walls have been built up to the level of the surviving vestry apse wall, and are treated as a series of freestanding panels separated from the next by a glazed full height timber screen. These wall panels are capped by horizontal bands of loggia type windows, which light the first floor rooms in the transepts either side of the new nave and also follow the line of the splayed ends of the apse around the east end to generate the hipped roofshape.

The spiral stair turret in the north west corner was re-roofed and now gives access to the first floor Sunday school room. The tower has been neatly drawn into the fold of the new structure by returning the new walls either side at right-angles and creating a V-shaped opening in the roof by means of small hips which form two re-entrant triangles above the entrance doorway to the Sunday school, the projecting reveals of which house sizeable toy cupboards. The potentially awkward problem of detailing a randomly placed feature within a regular gridded framework has therefore been given a practical solution but at the same time turned to maximum architectural advantage.

The north wall of the earlier chancel has been reconstructed in a way obviously designed to reflect the mass and modelling to be found in the remaining mediaeval walls and thereby re-establish a three dimensional reference to the form of the original church. This is particularly noticeable in the deep splayed window reveals, which together with the large cavity generated, have been used to advantage to house the heating plant. A similar approach has also been adopted with the new north wall where the returned faces of the walls either side of the altar have generated substantial buttresses which support the ends of the primary roof trusses.

Finally, the architect has also turned his attention to the design of the furniture and fittings and has derived much of the inspiration for these from the principles developed in the roof and mullion struc-

tures. Hence we see the principle of "detachment" exploited again, with steel and timber structural members treated as discrete elements either bolted together or jointed as if tied with invisible string, but not housed within each other as with, say, traditional halved or dovetailed joints. Lengthy discussions between the architect and the rebuilding committee eventually led to the creation of a pew front that takes the form of a pierced screen in its vertical position, demarcating the three groups of seating around the three sides of the sanctuary, but which is in fact hinged and can be brought forward to provide instant extra seating for overspill congregation or to absorb the arrival of Sunday school children during a service. The steel posts are slotted into the floor so that the whole screen can be removed for plays or concerts. Two lecterns follow the same principles, with a pierced front that can be lowered to provide a raised platform to enable children to use the lectern effectively, and the bishop's chair develops the same idea, with a carved headpiece suggestive of the bishop's mitre.

The Bishop of Southwark in fact rehallowed the church at a service of rededication on February 26, 1984 and it was immediately apparent that the architects had unquestionably succeeded in creating a fitting building for a place of worship, satisfying not only in practical terms but also in its response to deeper spiritual questions. In combining the ancient and modern with flair and sensitivity, the architect has been able not only to preserve a factual record of the church's own particular history through the restoration of its fabric but has also been instrumental in reaffirming in a more general non-specific way the continuity of faith and life that has lain at the heart of our society for many hundreds of years.

FESTIVAL HALL, LIVERPOOL

Architect: Arup Associates

The 1984 International Garden Festival, which opened in Liverpool on May 2, has provided landscape architects of many nations with a wonderful opportunity to demonstrate to the public what they can achieve in a dramatically short space of time. The 250-acre site has been transformed from a derelict condition, where there was no topsoil but tons of rubbish, in a mere twenty-four months.

The Festival Hall forms the principal focus of this man-made landscape and its design was the result of an architectural competition organized by the Merseyside Development Corporation. Initially the building was required to function as an exhibition hall and greenhouse for the six months duration of the garden festival, but the brief then stipulated that the hall would be required to change its use after the Festival to become a sports complex. In its adapted state the building will be able to house a sports hall with spectator seating, small gymnasia and projectile halls, and a swimming pool with changing facilities.

It is surely appropriate that the selected design should follow very sure-footedly in the long established English tradition of glazed garden structures, as exemplified by the glasshouses at Kew and the former Crystal Palace. The structure takes the form of a huge barrel vaulted roof 15 metres high and of a clear span of 60 metres, with a hemispherical dome at each end, giving a total length of 140 metres, thus making it one of the largest barrel vaulted structures ever built. The total area covered by the hall is some 7,500 sq. metres.

However, the engineers have risen to the challenge of enclosing this vast space with a most economical and lightweight structure of great elegance and simplicity. The barrel vaulted roof of the central section is formed with a series of shallow curved trusses springing from supports at ground level around the perimeter and connected at the apex on a three-arch principle. A further, much smaller, barrel vault runs along the ridge line above the main trusses, and this feature helps to draw off passive solar heat gains by means of banks of louvres. The curved trusses of the main roof, though they appear light and insubstantial, in fact generate great strength but require a proportionately low quantity of steel; the entire structure uses only 300 tonnes of steel. This light and airy structure itself supports a translucent cladding of 1 m. × 6 metre polycarbonate hollow sectioned profiled sheets, a material which combines strength and high impact resistance with very light weight and, because of its double skin design, also offers a high degree of thermal insulation. The translucent skin covers the entire barrel vault and thus even on an overcast day the hall is filled with a pleasing quality of light that will provide an ideal background for the sports hall activities which it will eventually accommodate.

The hemi-spherical domed ends of the structure are constructed using a much simpler radial arrangement of ribs and purlins, and these are clad with opaque corrugated aluminium sandwich construction panels. These were chosen to provide a high degree of insulation and also to counter the effects of potentially noisy activities that might be housed in the ends, such as a swimming pool or squash courts.

Seen from the surrounding landscaped areas it is clear that the elegant curvilinear form of the structure is intended to enable a huge space to be accommodated within the small scale patchwork of garden landscapes without excessively dominating them and is very successful in the way it blends into the smooth undulating contours of the garden site.

The form of the external envelope is also articulated in a very sophisticated way. The ribbed aluminium covered domed ends are not made to align on the same plane as the translucent cladding of the main barrel vault but slide gently underneath, the gap generated at the junction between them revealing glimpses of the intricate trussed structure of the principal space. This "breathing space", as it were, is taken up the curved slope to the apex until it meets the smaller ridge vault which projects beyond the end of the main roof and caps the top of the domed ends with a smaller version of the same thing. At this point the gap turns through 90° and is cleverly transformed into a clerestorey window running horizontally around the top of the aluminium dome until it again meets the gap formed by the junction of materials on the opposite side of the vault. The precision of detailing and inventiveness of form lift what could so easily have been a particularly boring exterior into a subtle and pleasing architectural composition.

Construction of the building had to meet a very tight programme and it was completed in only a year at a cost of £2·5 m. The steel trusses of the roof were prefabricated off the site and the frame took only eight weeks to erect. The short time scale also ruled out the possibility of including a solar roof, although it would be possible to install one at a later date if so desired.

Architecturally, the Festival Hall is clearly the dominant feature of the Festival and one of the more distinguished buildings of 1984, demonstrating that economy and speed do not necessarily have to conflict with quality of design. It is to be hoped that the momentum and goodwill generated by the Garden Festival will continue in the successful management of the landscaped environment and thus ensure that the people of Merseyside gain the maximum benefit from this unique investment.

DERNGATE CENTRE, NORTHAMPTON

Architect: Renton Howard Wood Levin Partnership

At a time of continuing economic constraint, the multi-purpose hall has become an increasingly popular choice for the community seeking to provide adequate facilities for the arts and entertainment and yet avoid the financial burdens of constructing expensive specialized facilities to cater for each of a number of diverse activities, particularly when in smaller communities there may not be the audience to fill say a concert/opera hall every night of the week.

Several highly successful examples have emerged in recent years, among them the Nottingham Royal Centre and Theatre Royal, Plymouth, but in all of these the multi-purpose function has involved complex and expensive machinery aimed at reducing the seating capacity or varying the acoustical performance of the auditorium to suit a limited range of activities within the general performing arts field. At the Derngate Centre, however, an interesting technical development has led the architects to devise perhaps the most truly multi-purpose hall of them all, in which whole sections of the auditorium can be moved around at will into different configurations, thus giving a range of forms adaptable to a wide range of activities.

The particular device which has been developed for use at the Derngate Centre is called an "air castor", based on an adaptation of the hovercraft principle. It enables heavy objects, such as banks of box seating, to be "floated" off the floor and moved around manually either into new positions or away into store. Thus, where earlier attempts have concentrated on minor adjustments to the stage format, ceiling profile, acoustics or lighting to accommodate a range of functions within a constant basic architectural framework, at Derngate the design provides a multi-form solution rather than a multi-function one, in which the whole stage and auditorium profile can be radically altered.

At the rear of the hall are two banks of permanent raked seating forming the gallery and upper gallery, and on either side a range of three fixed seating boxes. All other seating within the auditorium is mobile, comprising either seating towers (boxes one above the other) or seating "wagons" (extending sections of raked seating rather like bleachers). The banks of seating are each fitted with air pads attached to a compressed airline, enabling them to float and be pushed about by two or three men when the layout is to be changed. This technique does of course demand rigid adherence to tight constructional tolerances in the floor finish if air losses are not to occur through small gaps between the pads and the floor. However, the units do have one major advantage over traditional bleacher seating in that, once manoeuvred into the final position, they are much more stable for, not being on mechanical castors, they sit firmly and squarely on the floor. The design therefore allows for a heavier form of construction and much higher quality seating than with traditional lightweight structures. These contribute to the very necessary feeling of permanence required for prestige events and which was expressly requested in the brief.

The decision to steer away from the modern obsession with equality of vision from all positions throughout the audience has enabled the architects to develop a more traditional format where side walls are treated as boxes and the audience therefore placed in much closer contact with the stage. Tiers of boxes can very easily be separated into individual towers, as they do not require an excessive depth, just sufficient for two rows of seating and an access passageway at the rear. However, it was obviously important that the mobile parts of the auditorium should, when in position, be indistinguishable from the fixed parts, and this has certainly been achieved, there being a consistent treatment of decor and seating throughout. For example, the fixed boxes and ends of the gallery have been provided with the same composite double width frame, a vertical or sloping red painted edging strip, that occurs when the side walls of two mobile units are placed together.

The Derngate Centre uses varying combinations of the mobile box towers and seating wagons in conjunction with the fixed elements, to create four basic options of form, and hence function. These are categorized as "Concert", "Arena", "Lyric" and "Flat Floor" formats.

In the "Concert" layout (1,400 seats), all the mobile towers and wagons are used and the seating extends around the stage with boxes at the sides and choir galleries at the rear. This gives the effect of making the stage feel very much at the centre of events and definitely boosts the "presence" of orchestral groups, although technically the arrangement is still "end stage". One continuous rake of seats is formed in the body of the auditorium by placing one group of seating wagons on the fixed floor at the rear of the hall, and by placing the remainder on the central section of the floor which is capable of being lowered. The acoustic characteristics of the resulting auditorium are controlled by raising (for classical music) or lowering (for rock concerts) a number of acoustic banners on the side wall behind the boxes.

For the "Arena" format (1,483 seats), all the box towers are retained in their "Concert" positions, but the seating wagons are rearranged. Some of these, not being required for the layout, are stored in the spaces below the fixed portions of the hall floor, the others are disposed at either end to make two continuous rakes of seating facing into the central free area. Finally some additional tiered rostra, which are not on air castors, are positioned on the remaining two sides and three hinged ceiling elements stored vertically within the flytower are lowered and turned horizontal to close off the flytower and form a continuous level ceiling over the entire hall. The arrangement is extremely successful in focussing attention on to the central performance area, an effect which is greatly enhanced by the placing of part of the audience within the box towers wrapped around the walls.

The "Lyric" format seats slightly fewer (1,151 seats), and constitutes the proscenium arch alternative, where all the seating is confined to the front of stage area. Horizontal wall pieces and vertical fire curtains are slid into place to form the proscenium arch and the moveable ceiling panels are retracted into the flytower. Four mobile box towers are used, the remaining six being stored off stage in the scene dock. The main central bank of seats is as for the "Concert" layout with the exception of the flat section at the front which, being part of the central area, is lowered even further to form an orchestra pit. Most of the audience have a perfectly acceptable view of the stage; those in the immediate side boxes, as with traditional designs, miss out on action in the corners of the stage but more than make up for it by the extra immediacy and involvement they enjoy not only with the performers but also with the main body of the audience.

The fourth option, "Flat Floor" format, is more or less self-explanatory. Here all the mobile box towers are in place to provide an all embracing feature wall, while all the bleachers and wagons are withdrawn or stored below the hall floor to leave a large clear area of 648 square metres which can be laid out for banquets, receptions, dinner dances, exhibitions, trade shows and practically any other activity that may come along.

The permanent ceiling over the main part of the

auditorium is in reality a criss-crossing arrangement of lighting bridges. For an area which in some auditoria is a nightmarish complexity of ducts, wires, tubes, rails, trusses, ladders and other paraphernalia, the zone above the ceiling is remarkably uncluttered. This is due principally to a simple yet elegant structural solution for the main roof, which has been formed from a series of upturned U-shaped concrete box section arches that support the intermediate areas of roof slab and which also very neatly house the acoustically lined supply air ducts, feeding through nozzles projecting below the flat soffit of the roof plane. The resulting freedom of access and movement must be a dream come true for the lighting engineers.

Technically then this is a brilliantly conceived and well worked out solution to the problem of how to accommodate the widest possible range of activities in appropriate spatial arrangements without extraordinary expense or serious compromise on each option's suitability for its particular function. The design of the decor in the foyer spaces, even in the hall itself and its fittings, does not seem to have been blessed with quite the same degree of conviction and boldness. The lack of decorative complexity and very sparing use of colour has tended to produce rather bland and uninspiring areas where surely there is a heaven sent opportunity, given the three dimensional possibilities of multi-level foyers, to generate atmosphere and excitement. There is to some extent a more difficult problem with the design of the hall itself as it has to provide an acceptable background for widely differing activities. Lighting variations can play a large part in altering the general "mood" but at the end of the day the hall is bound to appear not very dissimilar regardless of what is on the programme.

That said, there is no doubt that the people of Northampton have been very well provided for by the architects, and for a figure of slightly over £6 million have acquired not only the first genuinely multi-function hall to be built in Britain but have also benefited from the inclusion within the overall development of a small existing proscenium theatre, the Royal Theatre, which now opens on to the long winding street-like foyer space and adds yet another entertainment dimension to this exciting new complex.

OFFICE DEVELOPMENT ON THE MILLBANK ESTATE, PIMLICO, LONDON

The Millbank Estate, bordering the River Thames at Vauxhall, has a history which goes back nearly three hundred years. In 1799, the Commissioners for Woods and Forests (predecessors of the Crown Estate Commissioners) purchased 53 acres of land in Spring Gardens at Vauxhall from the Marquis of Salisbury for £12,000. The original intention was to use the whole site for a prison, but when the Millbank Penitentiary was built in 1812, only a third of the area was used for this purpose. The distinctive crystal-shaped Penitentiary was first used for the convicts bound for the Antipodes and many hundreds must have walked down the stairs on to the ships that took them to Botany Bay.

In 1837, the Commissioners requested Thomas Cubitt, one of London's greatest speculative builders, to submit a plan for their Estate which was adjacent to Lord Grosvenor's Neathouse Estate (now Victoria Station) developed by Cubitt. The Commissioners accepted Cubitt's plans for their Estate in 1845, and it was completed in 1860. Over the past 120 years, however, the Estate and the surrounding neighbourhood has changed a great deal.

In 1972, when Pimlico Station opened, Chapman Taylor Partners, planning consultants to the Crown Estate, prepared a report on the continuing development of the 27-acre Millbank Estate. The main objectives were to retain the primarily residential function—upgrading accommodation for a broad range of income levels, to allow a controlled amount of new offices, and to restore Bessborough Gardens as a traffic-free public open space.

The plan was approved by Westminster City Council in 1976, and the implementation of its various proposals will be largely completed by the end of the decade with the building of three sides of the new square (Bessborough Gardens) and the new town house square to the west. One of the proposals involved the creation of a new two acre island site bounded by Bessborough Street, Rampayne Street, Vauxhall Bridge Road, and a newly created street—Drummond Gate—which takes the name of Lord Perth, a former First Crown Estate Commissioner, and this site was allocated for office development use. The recently completed office complex consists of 200,000 sq. ft. of offices in three buildings, 75,000 sq. ft. in Phase 1, which comprises a tall building and a low long block all clad in traditional brickwork, and 125,000 sq. ft. in Phase 2, a six-storey building incorporating an interior atrium. The complete development has been leased to the Metropolitan Police to house their civil staff, numbering more than 1,000, who were previously scattered throughout a number of different buildings in the city.

The Drummond Gate office complex was officially opened by the Queen on June 26, 1984. Both phases are in their own different ways very interesting architecturally and illustrate to perfection the point that, no matter how strongly one argues that the form of a building follows inevitably in response to its functional requirements, this assertion simply does not fit the evidence—buildings do not design themselves automatically—and no two architects will ever interpret the same brief in identical ways.

PHASE 1

Architect: William Whitfield & Partners

The first phase of the development occupies the northern half of the site facing Rampayne Street and was actually designed with a different companion building in mind for the southern half, which would have completed the three remaining sides of a central square intended to be open to the public. In the event, the tenants for the southern half opted for another location and so the principles of the massing and site layout were altered. In developing the concept for his new building, Whitfield has obviously been influenced by the earlier red brick housing of Lillington Gardens immediately to the north in his choice of materials and has chosen to develop this theme rather than the white painted stucco to be found in many of the surrounding streets.

The main block placed on the corner of Rampayne and Bessborough Streets is a massive polygonal brick and stone tower seven storeys high with a deep, highly modelled attic storey clad in lead. This is linked, via a curious and uncharacteristically lightweight glazed corridor, to a long low block three storeys high running parallel to Rampayne Street. The exterior treatment reflects the architect's dislike of brick cladding stuck on to concrete structures, and has taken the form of a truly self-supporting structure of tiers of massive segmental brick arches springing from stone imposts. These are extended horizontally through the blank sections of wall to form deep string courses, the pale stone colour contrasting strongly with the purple-grey bricks used for the walls and the soft orange-red stocks used for the arches. The latter were required because the arches had to be constructed from cut bricks, and the soft stocks are ideal for the purpose. The large glazed openings are

deeply recessed behind the arches and the piers have splayed jambs, emphasizing the strength and robustness of the structure. The overall effect is slightly ambiguous though with strong overtones of Victorian warehouses and ancient castle architecture.

The pattern of openings created by the tiers of arches has been carefully controlled to give the right feeling of repose and balance, particularly for the tower. The two-storey high openings around the base provide a suitably massive lower order from which the middle section of storey-high broad span arches rises, finishing with a double storey height "cornice" in which the rhythm of the openings quickens as intermediate brick mullions reduce the width of the wide arches and create three narrower arched openings for each wide one below. The visual complexity therefore increases towards the top, and reaches its climax in the powerfully modelled lead mansard roof, in which tall square projecting bay windows punch their way through the inclined plane of the roof, which is visually separated from the cornice by means of a deep eaves level recess.

The building has a rather novel system of air conditioning that is fully integrated with the fabric of the exterior and the interior lighting, and is intended to achieve considerable energy savings. The fenestration to the offices is set well back from the front of the heavy brick facade and thus benefits from some solar shading from the deep arches, but the most significant aspect is the design of the glazing itself. The windows are in fact triple glazed, with a double glazed sealed unit outside, and a single pane of internal glazing with a large cavity between, in which are located vertical louvre drape blinds so that the occupants can control locally the amount of direct sunlight, glare and overlooking. Treated air is passed down to the offices from the roof via vertical ducts set within voids where the brick cladding abuts the concrete columns around the perimeter. From these it is passed to the central core through ducts cast into the concrete coffered floor slabs and is then pumped out again through diffusers at ceiling level.

Used air is removed from the offices in two ways, firstly via special lighting luminaries fixed within the ceiling coffers, and secondly via the external windows. The air is drawn up from low level through extract slots in the upstand below the windows, and then between the inner single glazed and outer double glazed windows, and out via air extract ducts located at the head of the windows. Being, therefore, "ventilated" windows, in winter, the inner panes of glass are kept at higher temperatures because of the passage of warm air and thus reduce cold radiation and downdraughts, while in summer the same process will reduce local increases in temperature due to solar heat gain. The decrease in the total amount of heat loss has enabled the boilers to be sized with a third of the capacity they might otherwise have needed.

Finally, there was the problem of what to do with the two pieces of servicing equipment which could not be accommodated within the roof, a pair of air cooling towers. In the time honoured way of dealing with awkward problems, it was decided to "make a feature of them" and so they sit between the two buildings on a pedestal doubling as an air conditioning vent, transformed into a fantastic piece of modern industrial sculpture by the artist Eduardo Paolozzi.

PHASE 2, ONE DRUMMOND GATE

Architect: Chapman Taylor Partners

For a situation where two buildings share the same site and the same owner, and are both leased to the same tenant and form part of a single comprehensive urban design strategy, it would indeed be hard to find

---

two more diametrically opposed approaches to architectural expression than are apparent here.

By contrast to Whitfield's massive warehouse—inspired detailing of stone and brick for phase 1, phase 2 employs the crisp lines and clean looks of modern curtain walling allied to a clear articulation of each of its structural components to create an equally distinctive but very different and arguably more contemporary style. The first and abiding impression of this building is of its whiteness, clearly intended to reflect the white stucco of the surrounding terraces within a thoroughly modern idiom.

The form adopted for the building is that of a rectangular ring of offices approximately 11·5 metres deep and of four storeys high, placed over two lower floors of deep plan office space. This arrangement creates a large open central space which has been roofed over to form a dramatic atrium roughly five storeys in height, divided into two by the centrally placed lifts and spiral stair. The four corners of the building are emphasized by making them read as towers, extending up above the main parapet line to provide accommodation at roof level for servicing plant. Immediately adjacent to the corners on the long sides are the four emergency escape staircases which are expressed on the exterior with a projecting faceted bay window running full height. Around the exterior of the building, the structural frame has been projected beyond the face of the building, separating the curtain wall facade behind into a series of slightly projecting bays that set back into the building at the column positions. The columns themselves are circular and clad in a pale buff-pink granite which has been given a flame textured finish on vertical surfaces but is polished where the material is used horizontally, such as around the beam connections into the facade at each floor level and at the cornice level where the columns are tied together with a transverse beam that forms a conspicuous knuckle joint at each column position.

In order to get day-light into the basement areas, the site has been cut away extensively around all four sides to provide a large area which has been paved and landscaped. On the north side facing phase 1 this forms the central courtyard, with pool and water fountains, which is used as a social place in summer months, being accessible from the restaurant and bar areas located at basement level. The fact that the basement was opened up to the outside in this way had other advantages in that it was not classified as a basement storey for the purpose of building regulations and it was therefore possible to open

up the cafeteria area by means of sloping glazed walls to the atrium space at the centre of the building, providing dramatic visual connections between all floors of the offices.

The cutting away of the atrium floor area to achieve these effects has unfortunately made them less easy of access from the central circulation core. Some areas of planting have been introduced at each end in projecting balconies and some small trees and shrubs placed in planters on the floor, but ultimately these spaces appear somewhat as dead left-over areas whose function has not been properly clarified. Given the authorities' current reluctance to permit social or catering uses to be established in atria, it does seem that to be successful they must engage intimately with the primary circulation patterns of the building.

Perhaps the most striking feature of the atrium derives from the exploitation of the air conditioning systems. Being a symetrically planned building, the air handling units, mounted in rooftop "conservatories" around the top of the atrium, could easily be arranged to serve the office floors with alternating supply and extract systems to each successive structural bay. The circular ducts for these have been brought down the inner faces, reducing in section at each floor level, with paired connections through the curtain wall spandrel panels into the ceiling void at each floor level. Each structural bay therefore contains one supply connection and one extract connection at each floor level, and the different functions have been emphasized by the alternate colouring of the ducts in terracotta and pale blue. Spanning right across the atrium on a diagonal axis, the double glazed sawtooth section atrium rooflights are supported on simple slender tubular section steel portal frames. The atrium roof, together with the proportion of warm and cool return air thrown into the atrium rather than discarded to the outside air, results in significant energy saving benefits.

Construction started on One Drummond Gate in June 1981 and was completed at the end of November, 1983. The finished building is in the words of the architect an attempt "to produce a building which responded to the established scale and grain of Pimlico while expressing its own sense of time." The design has a strangely nautical air, with its fresh clean white lines, the suggestions of rigging in the rails at the top of the corner towers, and in the way some of the window openings are recessed behind the crisp metal cladding panels.

SCIENCE AND DISCOVERY 1983–84

Active Volcanoes on Venus?—Much of the data collected from space probes to the planet Venus suggests that volcanic activity has played a major role in shaping the surface of that planet. However, no conclusive evidence could be gleaned from the tremendous amount of data studied. Small localized areas of the surface have been photographed from probes that have successfully penetrated the hostile atmosphere and radar maps have been drawn with ever increasing resolution. But it is from continuous observations of the atmosphere that fairly positive evidence has emerged to indicate that there has been at least one major eruption during the last decade.

At a recent meeting of planetary scientists, Larry W. Esposito, of the University of Colorado, suggests that a major eruption took place on the planet in the mid-1970's. His claim is based on the fact that the ultra-violet spectrometer on board the *Pioneer Venus* orbiter, which reached the planet in 1978, registered a much higher level of sulphur dioxide than had been recorded from previous observations. In addition, there existed a prominent high altitude haze of microscopic particles, most likely consisting of sulphuric acid droplets, resulting from the breakdown of sulphur dioxide by ultra-violet light. Over the next five years, the amount of sulphur dioxide gradually dropped to about 10 per cent of the 1978 value and the intensity of the haze dropped correspondingly.

In addition, probes that have penetrated the lower atmosphere have also recorded excess sulphur dioxide in the regions. It is thought that such a presence in the lower atmosphere indicates a recent source because it is considered that the calcium in the rocks would react with and remove the gas.

It has also been noted that a similar clearing of haze took place in the late 1950's. As an indication of the size of these eruptions, it has been calculated that the amount of haze is about ten times that produced by El Chichon, the Mexican volcano which erupted in 1982.

Age of the Universe.—Of fundamental importance to the cosmologist is the determination of a reliable age for the universe. The time since the "Big Bang" is usually given as a value lying between 10 and 20 thousand million years. This wide range in values permits inclusion of all the current estimates obtained using a variety of techniques, but of late cosmologists have been tending to gravitate to a figure towards the lower end of this range.

The universe must be older than the oldest stars and so the recent discovery that stars in the globular clusters M92 and M15 have ages in the region of 18,000 million years has created quite a stir in astronomical circles. Star clusters are traditionally dated by comparing their Hertzsprung-Russell diagrams (a graph showing their brightness against their spectral type) with those calculated from stellar evolutionary theory, a method which is open to many sources of error. Allan Sandage of Mount Wilson and Las Campanas Observatories has avoided these pitfalls by determining the relative distances of several clusters by the brightnesses of their RR Lyrae

stars and then determining their absolute values by comparing the cluster's main sequence stars with those of relatively close population II stars whose distances have been determined by trigonometric parallax methods. The results obtained were then compared with new theoretical models, leading to a value towards the top end of the age range. It is fairly certain now that values towards the lower end will be rejected.

Breakthrough in Organic Synthesis.—Phenol is an exceptionally useful starting point for the preparation of many organic compounds used in polymers, drugs, antiseptics, fungicides and detergents. Until now phenol itself has been prepared from benzene but although current methods are quite efficient, they are very costly. From a chemical point of view the process is simply an oxidation process, although even the strongest oxidizing agents will not actually carry out the process directly. The commonest current process is to combine benzene with propylene to form isopropylbenzene which is then oxidized by air at 110° C to form a peroxide derivative which itself breaks down to give phenol and acetone.

Another process involves converting benzene into benzene sulphonic acid which is subsequently heated to 300° C with molten caustic soda. The sodium phenoxide is then treated with acids to give phenol. This is about 85 per cent efficient.

A new, relatively simple method was discovered by accident. Two Polish chemists noticed that some phenol was formed when a weak solution of benzene in sulphuric acid had been in contact with a piece of corroded copper. A Japanese chemist, Kuzuo Sasaki, took up this original discovery and has improved the process. He shook a mixture of benzene, dilute sulphuric acid and copper chloride so that it absorbed oxygen from the air. He found that the copper salt slowly dissolved and phenol was produced in the solution. The reaction can take place at room temperature but is only about 8 per cent efficient. The addition of hydrogen peroxide increases the yield to about a third. There have been several theories put forward to explain the reaction but the one most favoured is that in solution the copper ions combine with oxygen to form CuO_2^+ ions which react directly with benzene to give phenol.

Britain's Biggest Earthquake.—Britain is not a country in which severe earthquakes are a common feature, but occasionally quite strong tremors are reported. Such was the case at 0656 GMT on July 19, 1984 when a tremor measuring 5·5 on the Richter scale was felt over a very wide area, covering Northern Ireland, the Midlands and north and southwest England. The tremor and the aftershocks were caused by movements along the large Dinorwic fault which runs between Anglesey and the mainland of Wales. The hypocentre, the source of the earthquake, was much deeper than usual for Britain. Damage to buildings was limited to north Wales and the Liverpool area.

A spokesman at the Global Seismological Unit at Edinburgh said the event was the largest for 100 years and remarked that it was fortunate that so few injuries and no serious damage had occurred because earthquakes of similar magnitude in other countries had produced far worse results. The small degree of damage was due to the great depth of the hypocentre.

At least three severe tremors have occurred in the region in the past, the epicentres being within 10 km. of that of the recent event; they were in 1690, 1852 and 1903. On a smaller scale, tremors occurred in the region in 1969 and 1970.

The recent tremor can be compared with the two other severe earthquakes which have taken place in Britain in the last 100 years: the Dogger Bank earthquake of 1931, possibly of magnitude 5·6, which was not felt over such a wide area; and the 1884 event which hit Essex, killed four people and caused considerable damage.

The most intense global earthquakes occur at tectonic plate boundaries and are quite common. Intraplate earthquakes, those which occur well away from the edges of the plates, are relatively rare and are not so well understood. Although seismic recorders have been used since the turn of the century, it is only in the last 20 years that they have been used to study minor events. Britain is almost alone amongst north-west European countries in not having a co-ordinated national network of seismic stations, but from records of borough histories, monastic chronicles, newspapers, etc., over 1,000 events have been identified since the 7th century.

Britain's Conifer Forests under Threat.—It appears that the tree population of the British Isles is now under attack from a further source. Coming so soon after the devastation of the elms by Dutch Elm disease, it is very disheartening to find that now the conifer forests are threatened.

A small beetle about the size of a centimetre is attacking the conifers by feeding on the bark of the trees that are at least 25 years old. It throws out a coarse excrement which mixes with the resin from the tree to build up a reddish brown resin tube. The main symptoms are dead tree tops, fresh resin tubes and woodpeckers peeling off the bark. The beetle does not attack the timber but eventually the tree dies. The beetle was first discovered in a private woodland near Ludlow, Shropshire in the summer of 1982. It quickly spread over much of Wales, West Midlands, Gloucestershire and the Forest of Dean. It is thought that the beetle was blown into this country by the wind from the Continent where it has been a serious pest in the spruce forests of Denmark, Holland, Germany and France.

The spread of the disease is being monitored by the Forestry Commission and programmes of debarking, spraying and felling are being carried out to curb the infestation. Strict regulations have been brought in to control the movement of timber and the import of spruce products has been restricted. Spruce trees can only be imported from the E.E.C. if they are less than three metres. Imports from outside the E.E.C. have been stopped completely. Barked material is completely banned.

The problem of Dutch Elm disease is getting worse. The disease is getting more virulent. The populations of the fungi-strains, which are responsible for the disease, have changed from being non-aggressive to being much more aggressive. Research being carried out in the Netherlands is meeting with some success but there is a long way to go before the disease can be eradicated.

Continental Drift.—Laser techniques and very long baseline interferometry have been used to measure the drifting of continental plates to a much greater accuracy than has hitherto been possible. The first results using these techniques have recently been published by NASA.

NASA has established more than 20 stations around the world to monitor these movements. The positions of these stations are known very accurately within the plate as most of the major plates support a continent, the exception being the Pacific Plate, but here a station has been set up on Hawaii.

In the very long baseline method, the distances between two stations are measured by noting the difference in time between a signal being received from a quasar. With three radio telescopes both in America and Europe, the results have shown that these two continents are moving apart at a rate of 1·5 cm. per year, with an accuracy of less than 0·5 cm.

With laser ranging, the time is recorded for a laser beam to be reflected from a satellite. This gives a very accurate value for the distance of the satellite. Observations from stations on various plates provide very accurate values for the distances between the stations. If observations are taken over a long period of time, any change in the distance between the stations becomes apparent.

Laser stations monitoring the San Andreas fault have revealed that the motion along the fault over the last 11 years has been a steady 6 cm. per year. North America is moving away from the Pacific plate at 4 cm. per year but the Australian plate is approaching the Pacific plate at 7 cm. per year. The motion of the North American plate relative to the Australian plate is negligible. It is claimed that these values are accurate to within 1 cm.

Co-ordinated Movement in Flocks of Birds.— Most people have seen a flock of birds weaving and changing direction simultaneously. The question is how is it done and why do they do it? Some investigators have suggested that there could be thought transference or electromagnetic communication, but alternatively it was proposed that co-ordination was achieved by a selected number of birds executing preliminary movements which signalled to the rest of the flock that a turn was imminent. Recent work carried out by Wayne K. Potts of Utah State University, Logan, has shown that maybe just one bird could be responsible for a turn.

Potts filmed a flock of dunlins in slow motion whilst they were carrying out co-ordinated turns and then studied the films, frame by frame, and hence was able to determine a pattern of behaviour. He found similarities with the human chorus line. An earlier film study of a chorus line showed that rehearsed moves, started without warning, propagated along the line nearly twice as fast as the human reaction time. In the flock of dunlins, a turn began with one or two birds turning into the flock. It took about 67 milliseconds for birds in the neighbourhood to turn, but well away from the initial position the mean propagation time was about 14 milliseconds, a value considerably lower than the laboratory measured startle time reaction of 38 milliseconds. Therefore the manoeuvres travelled through the flock nearly three times faster than if flock members followed the reaction of adjacent birds. The study has shown that neighbours of the initial bird will change course relatively slowly. Further away the response will be quicker because each bird will see the manoeuvre wave and will time its response to coincide with the arrival of the wave. Hence the high speed of the movement is due to anticipation, as with chorus line manoeuvres. No initial movement which might signal the turn was found.

No follow up took place if a bird turned away from the flock. This fits in well with the behaviour of birds of prey which are known to attack individuals separated from a flock. It is thought that rapid turning of flocks started by individuals prevents indecision and allow flocks to react quickly when attacked by predators.

Decoding by Computer.—The main purpose for coding a message is to ensure that no third party can use the information being transmitted. It is fairly easy to code a message but the problem is to use a code that cannot be broken. The advent of computers has revolutionized the approach to methods of coding and the whole problem of coding and decoding now involves very advanced mathematical techniques. Nearly a decade ago, computer scientists from Stanford University proposed a new cryptographic code in which it would be very easy for a person to encode a message, but virtually impossible for anyone to decode it unless they were in full possession of the details on encoding. These so-called public key crypto-systems are ideal from a practical point of view, but unfortunately, they are not as safe as was once thought.

In one particular technique, using the discrete exponential system, in which strings of numbers in binary form are raised to a power, the encoding is relatively easy to perform. The decoding is the difficult process because it is necessary to know what original number was raised to what power. The original proposals were modified so that the coding and decoding could be done in a particular mathematical system called a Galois field with 2^n elements, the value of n determining how the code was constructed. This is called the key size. The larger the value of n, the harder it is to break the code. For technical reasons a value of 127 was thought ideal, but Donald Coppersmith of IBM's Thomas J. Watson Research Center in New York has found a very quick method of cracking the code. His method is based on techniques developed earlier by workers at the University of Waterloo. The method involves two stages. The first is called precomputation and involves building up a huge database to solve equations, a process which takes about an hour on a mainframe computer. This has to be carried out only once. The next stage is to find particular keys, a process taking just a few seconds.

Even larger key sizes have been considered. For a key size of 241, the precomputation would take about a month and the next stage a few hours. Nevertheless Coppersmith's work has shown that this particular system is nowhere near as safe as was once thought and it is now believed that methods using discrete exponentials are unsatisfactory for practical use.

Dust Rings around the Sun.—It has been known for a very long time that there exists around the Sun a ring of dust particles. This dust ring, known as the Zodiacal Light, can be seen quite easily from tropical regions and from higher latitudes at selected times of the year. This ring appears as a cone of light stretching up from the western horizon after it has become properly dark and similarly from the eastern horizon before dawn. This light is the reflection of the Sun on dust particles which orbit the Sun stretching from about the orbit of Mercury to beyond that of Mars. Recently a more distant ring has been discovered by instruments on board the infra-red satellite IRAS and is situated in the region of the asteroid belt. It is estimated that the mass of dust in this ring is equivalent to that of an asteroid about 1 km. in diameter.

A third disc has now been discovered by a team of Japanese and Indonesian astronomers during the total solar eclipse of June 11, 1983. This disc lies about two solar diameters from the Sun's limb. The total amount of material in this disc is estimated at between 1 and 10 million tons and as having a temperature of about 1,000°C. According to Syuzo Isobe of Tokyo Observatory, the dust grains consist of silicate material, as opposed to the predominantly graphite material of the ring situated in the asteroid belt.

The big question is whether these new rings are permanent or transient features. As far as the IRAS ring is concerned, if permanent, there must be a continual replenishment. This could occur if asteroids continually collide and grind themselves into dust. If it is a transient feature, it has been suggested that a dust laden comet disintegrated on collision with an asteroid. The inner ring, however, is thought to have originated in the outer regions of the solar system. The so-called Poynting-Robinson effect would cause the particles to spiral in slowly towards the Sun. When sufficiently near to the Sun, the material would vaporize and be blown back into space by solar radiation pressure. This vaporization marks the inner edge of the ring.

Earthquake prediction.—Over the last few years there have been descriptions of many phenomena which could be used for earthquake predictions. Unfortunately none seem to work every time. Nevertheless the quest for finding an efficient method is a top priority in many institutions throughout the world. At the Californian Institute of Technology, a team of investigators have been studying the variation in the amount of radon gas which is continually escaping from the Earth's interior. It is possible that this variation has no connection with seismic activity but the data collected so far seems to indicate a positive association.

Radon is an inert radioactive gas produced in the decay of uranium. The leakage from the Earth's surface is fairly small under normal conditions but if small cracks occur in the crust, this rate can increase quite markedly. Such increases in radon emission have been recorded in Japan, the Soviet Union, China and the U.S.A.

The Caltech team have installed over the last few years 11 automated radon monitors in southern California. On one occasion in June 1979 increased radon emission was recorded and a month later an earthquake of intensity 6.6 on the Richter scale occurred in Imperial Valley, about 290 km. from the nearest monitor. However, increasing radon emission in August 1981 at two sites 100 km. apart was not followed by any seismic activity. The 1979 event was also preceded by changes in crustal strain, gravity, electrical resistivity, magnetic field and background seismic activity, but most of this information was not processed until after the earthquake. No such activity was recorded in the 1981 event. It is thought that in this latter event, the increase in radon was due to falls in the water level in the bore holes where the probes were placed and this caused some of the dissolved carbon dioxide to evaporate and carry excess radon with it.

It is realised that monitoring must be carried out by a variety of instruments using techniques which are in no way related and that methods must be used which can be monitored in real time and not after the event. Fortunately radon measurement is one such method.

Earth's Temperature to Rise?—A report by the National Academy of Sciences in America confirmed an Environmental Protection Agency report of serious climatic changes in the future, causing melting ice caps, rising seas and widespread flooding. The report, published in 1983, estimated that the build-up of carbon dioxide emissions caused largely by burning fossil fuels would double the atmospheric carbon dioxide concentration by the third quarter of the next century. This would result in an increase in the average earth temperature of between two and eight degrees fahrenheit and a sea-level rise of about two feet. The American scientists believe that the "greenhouse effect" will begin in the 1990s, much sooner than generally expected and could ultimately cause climates in northern areas, such as New York, to become semi-tropical. The effect might be felt on American agriculture around the year 2,000 and in the north the growing season would become longer while in the south drier conditions would decrease crop yields. The rise in sea-levels might necessitate a gradual retreat to higher ground.

Europe's New Observatory in Canary Islands.—Britain's optical astronomers now have at their disposal a first-class instrument mounted at a first-class observing site. The Isaac Newton telescope, which originally was sited at the Royal Greenwich Observatory, Herstmonceux, and had a 98 inch pyrex-type glass mirror, could not be used to its full potential due to natural haze and light pollution from nearby towns. It has now been re-equipped with a slightly larger mirror made of Zerodur, a glass ceramic

material which does not alter its shape over normal temperature ranges. The mounting has also been improved taking advantage of modern developments in telescope control and instrumentation, and the telescope has now been mounted at the top of a 2,400 metre volcano on La Palma in the Canary Islands.

The Roque de los Muchachos Observatory is one of the best observing sites in the world and was chosen after exhaustive tests at many potential locations. The actual site is officially Spanish but the Observatory itself is truly European, it being originally a joint venture involving Spain, Sweden, Denmark and the U.K., which now also includes the Netherlands and the Republic of Ireland. Although Spain does not have its own telescope, their astronomers have been allocated one-fifth of the available time on all the instruments. The first telescopes to become operational were two Swedish instruments. One of these, a 60 cm. reflector, is designed to study the fairly bright stars through filters which allow passage of a very narrow range of wavelengths. This narrow band photometry permits very accurate estimates of the star's temperature to be made, as well as its chemical composition and the degree of polarization of its light. In addition, it will provide information on the absorption of the light by dust in interstellar space. The other telescope is a 21 metre high tower refracting telescope designed for solar investigations. Although only a 20 cm. lens has been used so far, eventually it is hoped to employ a 45 cm. lens.

Of prime importance is the instrument previously used by Danish astronomers. The Carlsberg Automatic Transit Circle, which is operated as a joint Anglo-Danish project, is an 18 cm. refractor which can only be used along a north-south axis, the declination axis, and is used exclusively for measuring the positions of stars as they cross the meridian. It runs completely automatically. A computer selects the stars to be measured from a catalogue in the right order and when the star is about to cross the meridian the computer points the star in the correct direction. A photoelectric detector watches the behaviour of the light from the star as it passes across two slits tilted towards each other in the form of a V. Another computer averages the time of passage through the slits to give the Right Ascension of the star whilst the timing of the separation of the two times permits a very accurate value for the Declination to be calculated. In actual practice, the slits are moved by small amounts to give up to 16 readings which are then averaged to give a position with an accuracy of about 0·2 arc seconds. The whole process takes less than half a minute. In one recent run of 2½ hours, the Circle recorded the positions of 200 stars. The instrument has the potential of determining the positions of about half a million stars. With such data it will be possible to measure quite accurately the manner of the rotation of our galaxy.

The main British contributions to the Observatory are two large reflectors, one of which is the modernized Isaac Newton 2·5 metre telescope. The first results from the telescope indicate that the instrument has a very great potential. The other, a 4·2 metre telescope named the William Herschel, is currently being constructed and it is hoped that it will be operational by 1987. The mirror and metalwork have been completed and the formations for the instrument have already been laid. A third instrument having a diameter of 1 metre employs a new mirror system which enables it to take wide-angled photographs up to 1·5° across. Its main use is to identify the bright sources of radiation at U/V, X- and radio wavelengths with their optical counterparts which are often quite faint. By examining the photographic plates taken by the 1 metre instruments, astronomers can locate the faint sources very accurately, because each plate will contain enough bright star images whose positions are known precisely from data supplied by the Carlsberg Transit Circle.

The future for the Observatory appears to be assured. Many more countries are planning to site instruments there. A consortium involving Sweden, Norway, Denmark and Finland are considering a 2·5 metre reflector and the Italians are currently testing the site for a 3·5 metre instrument. British astronomers are putting forward proposals for a multiple-mirror telescope which would have the same light-gathering capacity as a single 18 metre telescope.

Fluctuations in the Earth's Rotational Period.—It was not very long ago that the Earth's rotational period, i.e. the day, was considered absolutely constant and all time measurements were geared to this fact. Clocks were regularly adjusted to fall in line with the length of the day determined by timing transits of stars across the meridian. With the advent of quartz clocks, with their greater accuracy, it soon became apparent that the length of the day varied by a few milliseconds. This variation was found to be due not only to systematic periodic fluctuations at annual, semi-annual, monthly and fortnightly periods but super-imposed on these were irregular variations which could not be explained. With the development of atomic clocks, the whole concept of time measurement changed with the length of the day being discarded in favour of vibrations of the Caesium atom.

Variations in the length of the day are important in their own right, both from a scientific aspect and applications such as navigation and space travel. The variations have been investigated from three main unrelated standpoints—very long baseline interferometry, lunar laser ranging (using the Moon as a laser reflector) and satellite laser ranging. In the last of these, a satellite called *Lageos*, a 60 cm. sphere with over 400 laser reflectors launched in 1976 has been used over the last three years for detecting changes in the Earth's rotation. It has been found that changes by as much as 5 milliseconds have occurred within a few weeks. These and other changes are thought to be due to the physical interaction between the mantle and the atmosphere. These changes have also been detected by the very long baseline interferometry measurements.

Linked closely with the changes in period is the behaviour of the El Niño effect which has produced abnormal warming of huge tracts of the Pacific Ocean and also creates large changes in global weather. Further studies may give a better understanding of weather patterns and hence help weather forecasting.

Genetic Master Group Identified.—Much progress has been made over the last few years in the field of genetics, but this last year has produced possibly the most important discovery yet in this field. Two groups of workers at the University of Colorado, U.S.A. and the University of Basle, Switzerland, have identified a genetic group which appears to act as a master switch and control all stages of the growth of an organism from the egg stage to adulthood. It also seems to be common in all creatures from the fruit fly to humans.

The workers have identified these particular genes from the thousands of genes contained in the long coiled strands of the DNA molecule, which are found in the nucleus of every living cell. What is so surprising is the fact that these identical groups have been found in human beings, chickens, earthworms, frogs and flies. In addition it has been found that these groups also regulate growth and development.

At the present time the mechanism whereby this process is carried out is not understood. Of fundamental importance is the understanding of why, when a cell divides, the daughter cells know to which type they belong so that a particular component of the living cell can develop into such organs as limbs or kidneys. However, the new discovery provides fuel for the idea that there is a universal set of rules which controls all cell differentiation.

Dr. Gary Struhl of the Department of Biochemistry and Molecular Biology at Harvard University, has put forward the idea that human birth defects may be due to the breakdown of the genetic rules during the development of the embryo. This has been found to be true in the case of fruit flies, when it has been noticed that damaged genes have caused a disruption in the normal development producing abnormal features.

The importance of this discovery will no doubt stimulate further research and it can be confidently expected that quite rapid progress will be made in the reasonably near future.

Giant Fossils Unearthed.—In a quarry near Lyon, France, archaeologists have recently recovered the skeleton of one of the largest ichthyosaurus known. A cement company stopped work for one week to allow the scientists to recover 300 fragments which made up the skeleton. It is 11 metres long, much larger than any of the previously recovered specimens. About 50 complete specimens have previously been found, ranging in size from one to ten metres, but most have been less than three metres in length.

This reptile lived about 180 million years ago in the Mesozoic period and the skeleton was found encased in clay about 40 metres below ground level. The ichthyosaurus had an elongated snout, a tail and had four paddles. It was carnivorous, feeding on fish, ammonites and belemnites. These were also found in great quantities in the quarry. What is of interest is that some of these showed traces of ichthyosaurus teeth marks.

Another large fossil has been discovered recently. Although only 50 million years old, the remains of a fossilized snake about 9 metres long have been found in Eocene deposits in Mali, central Africa. 268 loose vertebrae from the backbones of several snakes were discovered, each vertebra being over 4 cm. long. The snake belongs to a completely extinct family, the palaeophidae, which lived from 70 to 37 million years ago. The nearest living relatives are boa constrictors, anacondas and pythons, all non-poisonous.

Horse Gives Birth to Zebra.—A unique experiment in implanting a zebra embryo in the womb of a horse mare proved a total success in May, 1984. The brood mare gave birth to her new foal, a 65 lb zebra, in Louisville Zoo, Kentucky. The mare, a Kentucky quarter horse, had served as a surrogate mother. Veterinary surgeons had implanted the zebra embryo, fertilized normally a year ago, in the mare's womb the previous May. They induced labour on May 17 after waiting a month past the normal 11-month gestation period for horses and zebras. Zoo officials pointed out that the experiment was important because a similar procedure could be used to increase the population of disappearing and endangered equine breeds.

Hydrogen in the Earth's Core.—It is generally accepted that the Earth's core is made of iron and many phenomena can be explained by the existence of such an iron core. One big problem arises, however, and that is the explanation of why its density is less than that of iron. Recent work seems to indicate that the discrepancy can be explained by accepting that the iron has large quantities of hydrogen dissolved in it.

The possibility that the iron contained hydrogen was first put forward in 1977, but studies then seemed to indicate that the solubility of hydrogen in iron was far too small to explain the discrepancy. However, more recent studies have indicated that the solubility is very large at high pressures.

Yuh Fukai and colleagues at Chuo University, Tokyo, have studied the reactions in detail and have shown that initially iron reacts with water to give iron oxide and hydrogen and that at the high temperatures which exist in the core the hydrogen will readily dissolve in the molten iron. Experimental data has shown that this reaction is complete at pressures greater than 4 GPa and at temperatures higher than 700 K. The pressure of 4 GPa corresponds to a depth of 110 km. below the surface, where the temperature is thought to be higher than 1,000 K. Fukai claims that sufficient hydrogen can be incorporated to explain the density discrepancy.

This iron-water reaction can be extended to explain the early evolution of the Earth. Fukai suggests that from the early stages and throughout the accretion process, the iron-water reaction proceeded continuously in the inner region of the growing Earth. Molten blobs of iron with dissolved hydrogen would sink to form the proto-core. Subsequently the surface layer, being less dense than the iron depleted proto-mantle, underwent a convection overturn. During this process the iron sank to join the core without dissolving any appreciable hydrogen whilst the water was largely degassed to form a hydrosphere. This natural explanation for the sudden formation of an atmosphere, an event indicated by argon isotope studies, may help to explain a problem troubling geologists for a long time.

Infra-red Satellite IRAS.—British, Dutch and American astronomers have combined to provide a systematic survey of the universe at infra-red wavelengths by monitoring radiation over four bands, at 12, 25, 60 and 100 μm, using the Infra-red Astronomical Satellite (IRAS). The satellite was launched by NASA on January 26, 1983 and immediately began sending back useful information. It was placed in a near-polar orbit at a height of just over 900 km., enabling it to remain over the Earth's terminator as it travelled around it. Its 56 cm. telescope scanned the sky in a direction at right angles to the Sun so that over a period of six months it was able to monitor the whole of the sky. To suppress any unwanted infra-red radiation from the satellite itself, the telescope was cooled by helium to a temperature of 2·5 K. The supply of helium was exhausted by November 21, bringing to an end the useful life of the satellite. The information collected by the detectors was relayed back to the Rutherford-Appleton Laboratory in Berkshire twice daily. Commands were also sent to the satellite twice daily giving instructions for the next 12 hours.

Preliminary results indicate that there are nearly 9,000 infra-red sources. Away from the plane of the Milky Way, over half the sources at 12 and 25 μm were found to be associated with bright stars. At longer wave-lengths a large number of the sources were identified with known galaxies but many others are considered to be more local sources within dust clouds. The situation in areas within a few degrees of the galactic plane is completely different. There is so much activity that it has been found very difficult to isolate individual sources.

IRAS hit the headlines early in May when it discovered a comet. Delay in analysing the data allowed two amateur astronomers, Genichi Araki of Japan and George Alcock of England, to report independently the presence of the comet. The comet is officially known as IRAS-Araki-Alcock, 1983 d. A few weeks later this comet passed closer to the Earth than any other since Lexell's comet in 1770. By the end of its useful life IRAS had discovered four more comets. All were picked up when they were exceedingly faint visually. The reason why IRAS was capable of detecting them was that the satellite was extremely sensitive to radiation from warm dust, a major constituent of comets.

On October 11, Simon Green of Leicester University noticed that seven consecutive scans made by IRAS showed a fast moving object near the head of Draco. Analysis of the orbit showed that it was an Apollo type asteroid, i.e. those that pass inside the Earth's orbit. Known as 1983 TB, it has been found to pass nearer to the Sun than any known asteroid. Its perihelion distance is only about one-third of the average distance of Mercury from the Sun. It was subsequently discovered that 1983 TB had identical orbital elements to those of the Geminid meteors, suggesting that it is not really an asteroid but the remains of a cometary nucleus and thereby providing a further case for the association of comets with meteor streams.

Dust seems to be a very common constituent in the Galaxy. In addition to the dust ring around the Sun, IRAS identified patches of "infra-red cirrus" in the direction of the galactic poles. The character of the radiation from these clouds suggests that they are made of graphite particles, created in the atmosphere of stars. Alternatively, the cirrus could be gravitationally bound to the Sun, say part of Oort's comet cloud. At the moment it is known that the clouds, whatever they are, are at a distance of over 1,000 astronomical units, about 25 times the distance of the planet Pluto.

Early on in its life, IRAS detected a cool cloud of solid particles surrounding the star Vega, the particles having diameters of about 1 mm. or more and having a total mass of about 1 per cent of that of the Earth. If the size distribution is the same as that for the asteroid belt, the cloud would have a mass of about 3,000 Earths, a figure comparable to the total mass of the major planets. Later on the same team of investigators discovered cool solid material orbiting another star, Fomalhaut. These two cases increase considerably the chances that other planetary systems exist and also increases the chances of life on other planets.

Possibly the most important aspect of the data gleaned by IRAS is in connection with star formation. Chamaeleon I, a dark interstellar cloud, was studied in great detail. By comparing radiation at the various wavelengths it has been found that within the cloud there are regions which have properties of stellar objects surrounded by dust grains. It is thought they are newly formed stars which have not yet reached the main sequence of stellar evolution. Studies of another cloud, Barnard 5, have also revealed stars in the process of being formed.

The Andromeda Galaxy, M31, was a prime target for IRAS and the results indicate that the infra-red radiation is very weak, suggesting that star formation within the galaxy is taking place at a very low rate.

As with the surveys of the universe at the very short wavelengths, which revealed many new types of objects, IRAS has provided a number of so far unidentified sources. Whether or not these turn out to be completely new types of object remains to be seen. At the moment a big question centres on their distances. If they turn out to be relatively near, there is a possibility that they may be distant planets outside the orbit of Pluto. Only further studies will solve these problems.

Israeli Rain Making Success.—Israel has become the leading country in the world in artificially induced rainfall. Winter rainfall in areas of the Middle East has risen by up to a fifth because of experiments in Israel which could practically benefit many of the most dry regions around the globe. Winter rainfall in Israel is now up 15 per cent and that of Jordan, Lebanon, and Syria has increased by 20 per cent, according to Prof. A. Gagin, who heads the Israeli team experimenting on the project. These scientists are making available their knowledge to governments in other arid and drought-suffering regions and schemes have already begun to bring fertility to desert areas in Egypt, Peru, and South

Africa. Prof. Gagin explains that they do not actually make rain but encourage clouds to let down more precipitation. He states: "Our success is in knowing which clouds to bombard with a fine powder of silver iodine filings. White clouds in the desert will produce rain if chemicals are used to fortify the tiny moisture particles into becoming rain drops".

Life-Expectancy Gap.—An American expert told a conference on sex differentials in ageing in February that in 50 years the average woman could be outliving the average man by about 10 years. Another research scientist from the U.S.A. propounded a series of reasons for the lengthening gap between the sexes in life expectation. She indicated that men took greater health risks, drinking and smoking more and using more illicit drugs. They also drive more. Advances in such areas as hormone research and pre-natal care have improved female longevity. Women who work outside the home—a growing proportion on both sides of the Atlantic—have lower mortality rates than housewives. Women's longevity is unaffected by widowhood but generally men who lose their wives die sooner. Urbanization, which usually carries with it better education, better nutrition and improved status of women, increases the female life span.

Light Fluctuations in Halley's Comet.—Halley's Comet is still over 1,000 million kilometres away on its journey towards the Sun which it will reach in 1986, but it is already providing very interesting information. Normally comets are not seen or monitored whilst they are so distant and therefore very little is known about their behaviour in those regions. The fact that Halley's Comet is so famous and that it has been such a regular visitor to the inner regions of the Solar System every 76 years, has provided the impetus for monitoring the Comet whilst it is still in the outer regions of the Solar System.

French astronomers from Meudon Observatory, Paris, reported that during February 1984 the Comet seemed to get brighter during the night. This evidence was supported by photographs employing electronic techniques, using the 3·6 metre Canada–France–Hawaii telescope in Hawaii. These showed there was a rapid increase in the brightness over one-hour periods regularly in a cycle of just over 24 hours. These effects were still observed in March and were recorded by Palomar Observatory in May. This is the first time that such a phenomenon has been observed.

Jean Lecacheux, leader of the Meudon team, has proposed several hypotheses for this variation in light. One suggests that there may be two light emitters of unequal brightness in the nucleus of the Comet and that the Comet's rotation produces the variation. Alternatively, the variation may be caused by the disturbance of a layer of dust on the surface of the Comet due to the start of gaseous emission as the Sun is approached. It is essential that the correct explanation is obtained fairly quickly otherwise it will be too late. Soon the gaseous emission will be too great and it will mask any variation from the surface. Due to the line of sight proximity of the Sun during the summer months, very little can be done until October.

Mankind made Redundant by Computers?— At the turn of the year, Dr. William Mclaughlin, a distinguished scientist, pronounced in an article in the British journal *Inter-Disciplinary Science Reviews* that mankind was likely to be redundant within 100 years because of decision-making computers. He explained that this might happen because computers could already process information 100 million times faster than people, a rate which would increase a thousandfold within 100 years. Dr. Mclaughlin said the human brain consisted of three layers on top of each other; two of these layers, the mammal brain and the reptile brain, inherited from our primeval ancestors, worked very slowly and inefficiently. While the top layer, the cerebral cortex, had an imagination which worked at the speed of light, the two lesser brains had their own sequential, ritualistic way of doing things which could not be hurried. Therefore computers were rapidly closing the evolutionary gap. Future advances in machine intelligence would be in the field of generating ideas. Ideas produced by machines so far had been in response to human orders to solve particular problems, but it could not be long before the machines with human encouragement began to formulate problems themselves. Said Dr. Mclaughlin: "It is likely that mathematical theorems formulated by intelligent machines will on the whole be incomprehensible to even the greatest human mathematicians". His assessment was that eventually our machine partners would become so much more efficient that they would take over completely.

Measuring Time in the Past.—Of fundamental importance to the geologist is the ability to measure as accurately as possible the time when a new species appeared and when there was a change in climatic conditions. For the period covering the last few tens of thousands of years, carbon-14 dating can be used but it is unsuitable for longer periods. Further back in time it has been possible to date radiometrically reversals in the Earth's magnetic field. Recently a group of paleoceanographers, headed by John Imbrie of Brown University, have reported that they can measure time in marine sediments and hence be able to date events which took place hundreds of thousands of years ago.

One of the major problems in dating the past has been co-ordinating the various methods to give a consistent picture. Between 20,000 and 1 million years ago only one direct radiometric and two paleomagnetic dates have been accurately located in marine sediments. With no evidence to the contrary, it had to be assumed that sedimentation took place at a constant rate. This is by no means true and so any quoted dates could be in error by as much as 30,000 years or even more. Recently it has been found that magnetic reversals are not the only indicators. Another technique involves a chain linking climate, glacial ice, ocean water and the oxygen isotope composition of skeletal remains of microscopic marine life which are found in marine deposits. The ratio of the various oxygen isotopes varies with changes in climatic conditions, these changes being due mainly to variations in the Earth's orbital parameters. Some of the variations are periodic and can be calculated precisely, but their effect on climatic conditions and their separation from random effects present a major problem.

The team have so far been able to pinpoint about 75 locations along the time curve going back some 800,000 years with an accuracy of 3,000 to 5,000 years. It is thought that with further research it may be possible to go back as far as 15 million years but the existence of an accurate time scale going back 800,000 years will be sufficient for most studies.

Methane C-H Bond Activated.—The carbon-hydrogen bond in saturated hydrocarbons is very strong and much research has been carried out in the past to study the use of transition metal complexes to activate saturated aromatic compounds. Such activation enables further reactions to take place with other hydrocarbons, thus enabling the synthesis of more complex organic compounds. This has been achieved with most types of hydrocarbons with the important exception of methane, the simplest one of all, the main reason being that the C-H bond in methane is exceptionally strong and resistant to activation.

At a recent meeting of the American Chemical Society, two groups of workers reported that they had independently achieved this activation. They were not really the first to achieve this, the first being reported the previous year but on a relatively restricted scale. William A. G. Graham and colleagues at the University of Alberta used a simple iridium complex dissolved in perfluorohexane at room temperature under a pressure of eight atmospheres of methane. Under these conditions the methane forms a very complex unstable compound which reacts with carbon tetrachloride to form a stable compound. Robert G. Bergman and co-workers at the University of California, Berkeley, used similar complex compounds but dissolved them in cyclooctane heated to 150°C under 20 atmospheres of methane. This product was also unstable but was readily converted to the more stable chlorine complex.

These are obviously the first stages in the breakthrough which could lead to methods of synthesizing many compounds, but the complexity of the processes suggests that commercial applications are a long way off.

More Evidence for Black Holes.—Using data gleaned from the International Ultra-violet Explorer satellite, a team of European astronomers is convinced that the Seyfert galaxy NGC 4151, a barred spiral galaxy in the constellation Canes Venatici, contains a condensed object in its core with a mass of about 100 million solar masses. Seyfert galaxies are now considered to be smaller versions of quasars and have exceptionally bright nuclei, the optical spectra of which are identical with those of quasars. But being much nearer, it is possible to study NGC 4151 in greater detail than has hitherto been the case.

Research has concentrated on the spectroscopic features in the ultra-violet. The team has identified emission lines of ionized carbon and magnesium, these lines being broadened by Doppler shifts. Assuming that the gas clouds are orbiting around the centre of the galaxy, it has been found possible to convert the line widths into orbital velocities. Doubly ionized carbon (carbon III) was found to have a speed of 4,000 km. per second, whilst the singly ionized magnesium (magnesium II) had a speed of 11,000 km. per second. Triply ionized carbon (carbon IV) has an even larger speed of 14,000 km. per second. Linking this information to that found in 1979, when the galaxy flared up sharply, it has been found possible to calculate the mass of the core. It took the carbon IV lines 13 days to flare up after the initial flare but the magnesium lines took 30 days. The carbon III lines have never flared. This information indicates that the carbon IV clouds are 13 light days from the centre and the magnesium clouds some 30 light days. A value of 100 million solar masses is indicated, a value supported by theoretical evidence based on thermal emission.

The broadening of the spectral lines could be due to turbulence, in which case the central mass has been overestimated. But NGC 4151 is almost face on and so the observed orbital speeds could have been underestimated and hence the mass of the core underestimated.

It has yet to be proved that this massive core is in fact a black hole but it is difficult to visualize how such a dense cluster of bodies could have been formed and exist without condensing into a black hole.

Neptune—a most peculiar planet.—The possibility that Neptune might have a ring system like the other major planets was considered most likely, but recent work has suggested that, as with several other properties associated with the planet, Neptune may be the odd one out.

In June 1983, Neptune occulted a faint star and astronomers positioned along a line stretching from Tasmania to Taiwan watched for flickering of the light from the star, indicating the passing of the star behind a ring. Although the results have yet to be finalized, preliminary information indicates that no rings exist. Even astronomers flying in the Kuiper Airborn Observatory, with exceedingly sensitive equipment, recorded nothing. It is now thought that the suspected ring reported from data collected in 1968, based on a dip in the light as the planet passed in front of another star, did not in fact exist.

The lack of a ring system presents problems. Neptune is the only one of the giant planets not to have one, although Uranus, virtually the same size, has a well documented system. Neptune has the only large inner satellite, Triton, that orbits the planet in a retrograde direction. Another satellite, Nereid, has the distinction of having the highest orbital eccentricity in the solar system. To explain these facts, astronomers have put forward the idea that some intruder, possibly a tenth planet, wandered through the Neptunian system and produced these abnormalities, including the possible ejection of one of them, which subsequently became known as the planet Pluto. There are, however, many objections to this theory but most workers think that whatever

produced the peculiar satellite orbits may have been responsible for the missing rings.

An occultation which occurred on May 24, 1981 produced a light fluctuation which has now been interpreted as a satellite about 180 km. in diameter and about 50,000 km. from the planet. This may indicate that there are other undiscovered satellites, but these and the possibility of a very faint ring system will remain unresolved until the fly-by of *Voyager 2* in 1989, or by the space telescope to be launched in a few years' time.

New Family of Sharks.—Scientists have now published full details of a most unusual type of shark that was hauled out of the sea off Hawaii in 1976. It was entangled in one of two parachutes being deployed as sea anchors by a U.S. Navy research vessel. The shark is completely unlike any other known.

It has a bulbous head with huge blubbery lips and has a gaping jaw which protrudes far more than that of any other shark. It has been given the name *Megachasma pelagios* and placed in the sub-order of shark known as lamnoid. Its common name is megamouth and is only the third known variety of shark which feeds exclusively on plankton. Megamouth, however, is completely different from the other two filter feeders. The specimen was an adult male weighing 750 kg. and was 4·46 metres long. It had very thick lips surrounding a jaw that spanned 1,025 mm. when retracted. It had 236 very small teeth which were used as a sieve and not for biting or tearing. Inside the mouth were closely packed gill rakers, finger-like tissues used to filter out plankton and a huge tongue which virtually filled the mouth when closed. An examination of the stomach revealed a large quantity of shrimp, which suggests that the shark swims between 150 and 500 metres below the surface in a region which is fairly dark. It is speculated that the shark attracts the shrimps by bioluminescence but there is not sufficient evidence to confirm this.

Megamouth has other distinguishing features, such as the pattern of the fins and that both the intestine and skeleton appear to be made of soft cartilage. It is also thought that it was a weak slow swimmer.

The length of the shark puts it in the giant category. Until further specimens are found it is difficult to estimate the normal size for this species. In sharks, it is usual for the female adult to be larger than the male.

Interest in the shark was not confined entirely to the shark specialist because inside its gut was an unknown species of tapeworm.

New Phylum Discovered.—Although predicted in 1961, and even found but not recognized by an American biologist in 1974, the credit for the discovery and identification of a new phylum, only the third this century, goes to Reinhardt Kristensen of the University of Copenhagen. Even Kristensen came across the organism in 1965 but it was destroyed during preparation for microscopic study.

In 1976, Kristensen found larval forms in shell gravel off western Greenland and later in sand deposits in the Coral Sea. However, mature forms were not discovered until 1982 when they were found in nearly clean shelly gravel from a depth of 25 to 30 metres at Roscoff, France. In the gravel, Kristensen found a complete series of life history stages of the new animals. A month later he identified mature specimens, although a different species, in western Greenland. In 1982, Kristensen went to work with Robert Higgins, the American biologist mentioned above, and they were able to confirm that the 1974 Higgins specimen was a member of the new phylum, but in larval form. Later work by both biologists has revealed mature animals near the Smithsonian Marine Biological Station at Fort Pierce, Florida.

The larval form measures less than 195 micrometres and has rotor-like appendages which allow it to swim quite effectively. The mature form, however, is sedentary and is only slightly larger than the larva. The new phylum *Loricifera* is one of many minute creatures that live in the sand and gravel at depths between 10 and 100 metres below the sea's surface. These microfauna, of which there are now five phyla identified, exist in a relatively unexplored region of the sea bed. Although having similar features to other phyla, this new organism is unique in that the mouth structure is a flexible tube which can be retracted into the animal. The combination of a free-swimming larva with a sedentary adult is most unusual, so this new discovery can be considered outstanding in more ways than one.

1,500 year-old Mayan Tomb Discovered.—One of the most important archaeological discoveries of recent years has been made at a site at Rio Azul in northern Guatemala. Prof. Richard E. W. Adams, an anthropologist from the University of Texas, leading a team of archaeologists from the U.S.A. and Guatemala, had gone to the area principally to record the mural paintings of the tombs which had been reported as having been heavily looted. On arrival the team found a painted Mayan tomb, more than 1,500 years old, untouched by looters and virtually in perfect condition.

During the excavation, Guatemalan Government guards stood by with weapons to protect the site from looters. After having dug a deep pit, the team cleared the remaining rubble away from the entrance to the tomb before entering the tomb itself. Before actually entering, the tomb was scanned by a tiny video camera. What made the tomb unusual was the fact that they are normally buried deep beneath massive pyramids.

Preliminary investigations indicate that the tomb was built for a blood relative of a ruler buried in a large pyramid nearby, this tomb having been stripped and looted in recent years. The newly discovered tomb contained, amongst other items, six covered cylindrical jars with tripod legs. The lids of the jars, highly decorated, were attached to the jars by a screw thread. Initial reports indicate that the tomb contained no immediately decipherable hieroglyphics but the team are hopeful of determining the identity of the person buried. On the floor of the tomb they found a male skeleton. It was so fragile that it appeared as though it was a drawn outline in the earth on which it lay.

This last find should provide much more information on the life-style of the Mayan people. In 1952, the most famous of all Mayan tombs revealed an elaborately carved sarcophagus of Pacal, the ruler of Palenque in the 7th century. In 1968, a royal tomb in Belize was found containing a 10 lb. jade head of a Mayan sun-god. Unfortunately most of the sites have been looted and their contents stolen.

Origin of Man.—Recent discoveries have once again stirred up the controversy about the origin of man. Early in 1983, Richard Leakey of the National Museum of Kenya and Alan Walker of Johns Hopkins University in the U.S.A. found upper and lower jaw fragments of an extinct ape, about the size of a modern chimpanzee, which lived in northern Kenya about 17 million years ago. This discovery, far from consolidating recent ideas about the origin of man, has added a new and controversial element to the problem.

It has been generally assumed that the orang-utan, which lives in Asia is, in evolutionary terms, the most specialized of the great apes and that the African chimpanzee and gorilla resemble more closely the last common ancestor between man and ape. Until recently, the divergence was thought to have taken place about 15 million years ago. Studies involving proteins and DNA have indicated that the split took place about 4 to 5 million years ago, but this new discovery could push the date back to about 10 million years.

About 17 million years ago plate movements brought together the African and Eurasian land masses, resulting, amongst other things, in the interchange of fauna. Interest has been centred on two types of ape, the small *Ramapithecus* and the much larger *Sivapithecus* and studies of facial features have suggested that these apes have much in common with the modern orang-utan and African apes. If this is true, then they evolved separately from the hominoid line. An exceptionally well preserved *Sivapithecus* face was discovered in 1982 in Pakistan and has been dated precisely at 8 million years. Other specimens in the same and other regions have indicated ages of about 13 million years. This and other data suggested that the Hominid-African ape split took place between 7 and 10 million years ago, but these views were disputed by many. A study of the fossils found recently in Kenya shows strong similarities with *Sivapithecus*. If after detailed study this view is still held, it implies that the ancestry of the orang-utan can be taken back to at least 17 million years and the Hominid-African ape split took place at least 10 million years ago. Also *Sivapithecus* possessed features which were common to the basic hominoid stock at the time. The basic question, however, is whether or not the facial features are primatial or derived. Only further studies and more fossils will solve this.

Permafrost Concern in Russia.—It was reported in August 1984 that Russian scientists had been displaying increasing concern at damage being done in Siberia to permafrost, permanently frozen soil. Certain areas of permafrost were reported to be in danger of turning to marsh and that in one region north of the Chinese border, permafrost was thawing out and destabilizing. The scientists link this to a gradual rise in temperatures caused by greater concentrations of carbon dioxide in the atmosphere. It is thought that large-scale thawing could disrupt road and rail links and render construction impossible in worst-hit areas. Also attributed to permafrost damage in the far north-east is the excessive felling of timber.

Quark Family completed?.—CERN, the European high energy physics laboratory at Geneva, has once again shown that it is in the forefront as far as sub-atomic physics is concerned. Last year, it announced the discovery of two new sub-atomic particles, the W and Z particles, which are associated with the electroweak forces. The same team, working under the leadership of Carlo Rubbia, has now announced the discovery of a third particle, the missing sixth quark called *top*. This particle has been predicted for a long time but has never been identified until now.

This discovery has put some order into the ever increasing list of sub-atomic particles. In addition to completing the list of basic components from which all chemical elements are formed, it strengthens the experimental evidence supporting the electroweak theory. Current ideas indicate that the natural world consists of three leptons—the electron, the muon and the tauon—each having its own oppositely charged antiparticle. All three leptons are associated with their own distinctive neutrinos, particles having no charge or mass. These neutrinos are involved with the leptons in weak nuclear interaction, such as the radioactive beta decay. The idea that quarks, another group of particles but associated with strong nuclear forces, exist in pairs has been suspected for a long time and much of our understanding of particle physics is dependent on this possibility. Nucleons such as protons, neutrons and other baryons are combinations of three types of quarks. For example, the proton consists of two *up* quarks, having charge 2/3, and one *down* quark, having a charge of −1/3. The *strange* quark, discovered in cosmic rays, is paired with one called *charm*. Of the third group, that called *bottom* was first identified in proton-proton collisions in 1977 and it is its pair, called *top* that has just been identified. Its discovery is a direct sequel to the discovery last year of the W and Z bosons. In fact it was identified through the decay of the W particle. *Top* has now been unambiguously identified on six occasions.

Whether further pairs of leptons and quarks exist is still an open question and whether these discoveries will help in the development of a unified field theory is still a matter for the future.

Recent Studies of Leptons.—Sub-atomic physics involves so many particles that the only way of understanding the forces involved and the manner in which all these particles fit into the structure of the atom is to try and build up a systematic and consistent picture in which all these particles are involved. At the present time, one problem involves finding the reasons why there exist heavy variations of the electron, these together with the normal electron being collectively known as leptons. The muon and tauon (or simply tau) have the same charge as the electron but have respectively masses 210 and 3,550 times that of the electron. The electron is considered to be stable but the heavier leptons decay rapidly into lighter particles via the weak nuclear force, the force responsible for the radioactivity of many atomic nuclei. Theory predicts that the three leptons differ only in their masses but until recently this had never been proved experimentally.

The muon has a lifetime of 2.2×10^{-6} seconds whilst the tau has one of only 10^{-13} seconds. In practical terms the measurement of these times involves the measurement of the path length travelled by the particle before it decays. Provided the total energy is high enough, when an electron collides with a positron, the antimatter counterpart of the electron carrying a positive charge, it will create a tau and an antitau. These travel at speeds close to that of light and so the path length before decay will be about a millimetre. West Germany's National Accelerator Laboratory, using a detector built at Imperial College, London and the Rutherford Appleton Laboratory, has devised a method of measuring this length and thus overcoming the problem of recording the decays which occur in a tube 13 cm. in diameter. In the 48 cases recorded, the experimenters have found that the path lengths agree quite closely with the predicted value and also the values obtained in similar experiments carried out in the U.S.A. The studies have shown that the decayed particles produce three pions and a neutrino, which theoretically is just one of many possible acceptable decay processes. The big problem still is to find an acceptable explanation of why there are three types of lepton if their only difference is that of mass.

65 Million Years Ago.—In 1980, it was suggested that the extinction of the dinosaurs 65 million years ago was due to meteoritic impact. The theory was based on the discovery of high concentrations of iridium and other platinum group metals in sediments deposited at the boundary between the Cretaceous and Tertiary periods. Such concentrations have been found in many localities. Geologists have argued that the iridium must have come from an impacting body because no known geological process was capable of producing such high concentrations. Crustal rocks contain very little iridium but meteorites are known to be rich in the metal. Although there is much further evidence to support the theory, it is by no means universally accepted. Recent work, however, provides more supporting evidence.

Although geochemical reactions can separate and enrich different elements, these reactions cannot separate and concentrate isotopes of a particular element. Jean-Marc Luck and Karl Turekian of Yale University investigated closely the concentrations of the isotopes of the metal osmium, osmium-186 and -187, the latter being produced by the radioactive decay of rhenium-187. Consequently the osmium-187/osmium-186 ratio varies with time and also with the rhenium-187/osmium-186 ratio. The latter has a value of about 3·2 in meteorites and the Earth's mantle and produces an Os-187/Os-186 ratio of about 1 at the present time. The Earth's continental crust, however, has an estimated rhenium-187/osmium-186 ratio of about 400, so by making due allowances for the age of the continents, a ratio of the two osmium isotopes of about 10 is expected. Marine manganese nodules give a value which does not conflict with this. Values obtained from samples taken from the Cretaceous-Tertiary boundary give an osmium isotope ratio of 1·5, which is not too different from a typical meteorite value.

One objection to the meteorite theory is that the osmium isotope tests eliminate only continental rocks as a source. It does not eliminate the possibility of volcanic activity providing material from the deep mantle. Such material, however, is relatively poor in iridium because that metal tends to be left behind in the mantle. The supporting evidence for the impact theory is becoming so strong that it is becoming very hard to explain the facts in any other way.

"Solar Max" repaired.—The continuous detailed monitoring of the Sun is of prime importance and so astronomers looked forward to several years of precise data when a special satellite, the *Solar Maximum Mission*, known simply as *Solar Max*, was launched in 1980. The satellite carried spectrometers, photometers and imaging devices to monitor the Sun in U/V, X-ray and gamma radiation. Of particular importance were the studies of solar flares which have a noticeable effect on the terrestrial environment. At first, the spacecraft worked perfectly, monitoring selected regions on the solar disc on instruction from ground-based observers. When an area brightened rapidly, the imaging x-ray detector automatically brought into action the other experiments to concentrate on that region. Unfortunately after nine and a half months in orbit the attitude control system malfunctioned and it became impossible to pinpoint the equipment accurately. Ground engineers did manage to send it into a gentle spin that kept the Sun within three of the eight instruments.

Solar Max was the first satellite designed for retrieval by the Space Shuttle. On April 6, 1984, a Shuttle was launched primarily to repair the satellite. Two days later, astronaut George Nelson headed out into open space to the slowly rotating satellite but he was not able to stabilize it. The mother ship *Challenger* was then manoeuvred very close to the satellite in a last-ditch attempt but the result was a faster tumbling satellite. There was nothing more the astronauts could do, so engineers at Goddard Space Flight Center carried out a do-or-die manoeuvre. They activated a set of electromagnets linked to the spacecraft's three main axes, but these failed to stabilize the satellite. A further program called "B-dot" was loaded into the satellite's computer but by this time the spacecraft's batteries were almost flat. By sheer luck, there was a precession of the satellite so that the Sun shone on the solar panels for 10 minutes, thus giving it sufficient energy to carry out attitude manoeuvres; within an hour the batteries were fully charged and the magnetic torquers had stopped the tumbling completely. *Challenger* homed in again and the satellite was soon in the Shuttle's cargo bay. Repairs took 45 minutes and on April 12 the rejuvenated *Solar Max* was back in orbit and its instruments being tested and calibrated for further solar studies.

Solo Polar Trek.—David Hempleman Adams, a 27-year-old British explorer, became the first man to complete a solo trek to the magnetic north pole on May 15, 1984. He had walked 250 miles across the Arctic in temperatures below freezing. Mr. Hempleman Adams hauled most of his supplies on a plastic sledge although he had one air drop of supplies. He was reported to be in good condition after his 22-day trek across the pack ice. On one occasion Mr. Hempleman Adams had to shoot dead a polar bear which attacked after appearing outside his tent and another time he fell through a patch of thin ice into the sea but managed to scramble out to safety.

Standard Metre Redefined.—The metre was originally defined as one ten millionth of the distance between the equator and the pole, but due to the impracticability of the definition, the French Academy of Sciences used a platinum bar whose length was equal to the theoretical length. Unfortunately the wrong value for the flattening of the Earth was used and the standard metre was in fact 0·22 mm. too short. Nevertheless this standard metre was used for the next 90 years. In 1889, the International Metre was redefined as the distance between two lines engraved on an alloy bar and was, within the limits of accuracy obtainable at the time, the same as the original length. Some 70 years later, with the improvement in techniques for measuring, the metre was redefined again in terms of the wavelength of krypton light. This enabled physicists to compare standard lengths to an accuracy of 4 parts in 10^9. For present day research, even this is not good enough and so in October 1983, the General Conference on Weights and Measures, meeting in Paris, redefined once again the length of a metre.

The reason for this redefining lay in the ability of physicists to compare wavelengths of laser beams to a few parts in 10^{11}, while being unable to calculate absolute values for these wavelengths. In addition, radio astronomers were not able to measure distances between their telescopes accurately enough to use the data collected by the telescopes to their full advantage. The new definition is based on the speed of light which can now be determined quite accurately. The metre is now the length of the path travelled by light in a vacuum during a time interval of 1/299 792 458 of a second. If by chance the speed of light used is found to be in error, the metre will be automatically changed to restore the defined value for the speed of light. The length of a second is known quite precisely, being defined using the caesium clock in 1967, with an accuracy of 1 part in 10^{13}, equivalent to about 1 second in 300,000 years.

Strong Gamma Ray Source in Cygnus.—The X-ray source Cygnus X-3 has been of great interest for over ten years but recent results have shown it to be far more interesting than originally thought. Gamma ray emission was first reported by Soviet astronomers in 1972 and this emission was found to have the same period as the 4·8 hour period reported from X-ray studies. Although there is much confusion over the behaviour of this source at low gamma ray energies, the picture is much clearer at higher energy radiation in the region of 10^{12} eV.

The evidence so far suggests that Cygnus X-3 is radiating possibly as much energy as 100,000 Suns just in X- and gamma radiation. In fact it radiates more gamma ray energy than the whole of the Milky Way Galaxy. Observations made last year by astronomers from West Germany and later confirmed by British workers have detected radiation at even higher energies—10^{15} to 10^{16} eV. This value is some 10,000 times greater than the highest energy yet reached by particle accelerators on Earth.

This very high energy radiation occurs in two bursts separated by 1·9 hours, each burst lasting for a maximum of 15 minutes although it could be much less, even as small as 40 seconds. The cycle is repeated every 4·8 hours in agreement with the period found earlier.

The current explanation for this strange emission is that it is thought to be a very young pulsar as a member of a binary system. The ultra high energy particles are thought to be reacting with the corona of the companion star. The bursts as seen from Earth occur only at times when the emitting regions are visible from the Earth. If the burst lasted only 40 seconds it is calculated that the pulsar must be at least 300,000 times brighter than the Sun and would be the youngest pulsar yet identified.

Even these ideas may soon be altered drastically because current reports indicate that radiation as high as 10^{17} eV has been detected in that part of the sky and if this is found to have a period of 4·8 hours, the current theories are no longer tenable.

Three Magellanic Clouds.—The Magellanic Clouds are visible from the southern hemisphere and appear like two very bright detached fragments of the Milky Way. They were first described by Ferdinand Magellan in 1521 during his voyage round the world. Since that time they have been the target of much research and are now known to be small galaxies orbiting our own Milky Way Galaxy. They are both about 160,000 light years distant. The larger of the two, the Large Magellanic Cloud (LMC) contains the largest known gaseous nebula, 30 Doradus, but it is the Small Magellanic Cloud (SMC) that has produced the surprising result that it actually consists of two clouds some 20,000 light years apart and separating at about 30 km. per second.

Astronomers from Mount Stromlo and Siding Spring Observatories in Australia used the 64-metre radio telescope at Parkes to survey the distribution of neutral hydrogen in the SMC and confirmed the existence of two Doppler shifts differing by 30 km. per second. The separation of the cloud into two distinct clouds in the same line of sight has been supported by evidence from other sources. The cloud exhibits similar dichotomies in the radial velocities of stars, ionized hydrogen regions and planetary nebulae existing within the cloud.

The SMC is now separated into two galaxies, the Small Magellanic Cloud Remnant (SMCR), nearest the Earth and the Mini Magellanic Cloud (MMC) about 20,000 light years farther out.

One theory put forward to explain the existence of the two clouds is that the SMC and the LMC nearly collided about 200,000 million years ago and this close approach split the former into the two components just identified.

Tree Rings and Volcanic Eruptions.—The spacing of tree rings has been recognised for a long time as an indicator of the growing conditions existing at the time, the wider the ring spacings the better the growing conditions. Recent studies have shown that a more detailed study of the rings can provide much more information than just a general indication of climatic conditions.

It is now possible to date quite precisely the occurrence of severe spring or autumn frosts, a weather pattern closely associated with the years immediately after major volcanic eruptions. Valmore Lamarche and Katherine Hirschboeck of the University of Arizona have produced evidence that the date of the eruption of Santorini in the Aegean Sea can be fixed at some time between 1628 and 1626 B.C.

Normally trees do not grow in winter so signs of frost damage during winter periods are rare. However, during the growth season, if the tree experiences two successive nights with temperatures as low as $-5°$C and an intervening day of about freezing point, this will be sufficient to show evidence of damage. This damage will show up as a narrow ring within the growth ring. The position of this secondary ring gives information as to when the frost occurred. By studying the long-lived pines in California and Colorado, the scientists have identified dates which coincide with eruptions such as Krakatoa in 1883. The following year showed frost damage in the rings. The existence of cold spells at that time was confirmed from normal meteorological records. The existence of a parallel situation in the 1626 B.C. tree rings points immediately to the Santorini eruption which had previously been dated by archaeologists as 1688 B.C. + /− 57 years.

More detailed study of the rings has provided further interesting information. The varying amount of radiocarbon (Carbon-14) has confirmed the reality of changes in solar activity, whilst studies of the width of the rings has provided data on climatic conditions and the frequency of droughts in the Midwest of the U.S.A. There is every indication that it may not be long before we experience droughts of the intensity of 1890 and 1930.

Unusual type of Frog.—Australia is noted for its unusual fauna and recent events have shown that many more surprises are in store for the observant naturalist and biologist. The gastric brooding frog, *Rheobatrachus silus*, was until recently quite common in a hilly rainforest area northwest of Brisbane, but suddenly in 1981 it vanished and was subsequently considered extinct. The frog was a very important type because the female incubated her eggs in her stomach. Nobody is quite sure why the frog vanished but some conservationists have blamed extensive logging in the area.

The disappearance of the frog caused much concern and the Queensland National Parks and Wildlife Service commenced searches in other areas of rainforest. Recently Keith McDonald, whilst searching the Eungella district near Mackay, found specimens of a frog which behaved in a similar manner to the gastric brooding frog but it was twice the size. One of the females started to give birth shortly after being caught and she was quickly sent to Adelaide for examination by a team of zoologists and physicians.

By studying the frog, doctors hope to learn how it is able to protect its young from the acids which exist in the stomach. They are trying to find the substance which inhibits the destructive effects of hydrochloric acid and other enzymes in the frog's digestive system.

Although the results are only preliminary, it is thought that the substance responsible is prostaglandin which is first produced in the jelly surrounding the egg and then by secretions from the tadpole's mouth and skin.

These studies are very important because they may lead to the discovery of new treatments for ulcers which occur in man. This new frog is definitely a different species from the earlier known gastric brooder and it may even be a different genus. Obviously the search for the frogs will continue and maybe more surprises will follow.

EXPECTATION OF LIFE

	England and Wales		Scotland		Northern Ireland	
	Life Table, 1978–80		Life Table, 1978–80		Life Table, 1978–80	
Age	Males	Females	Males	Females	Males	Females
0	70·4	76·5	68·4	74·6	68·4	74·8
5	66·6	72·5	64·5	70·6	64·6	71·0
10	61·7	67·5	59·7	65·7	59·8	66·1
15	56·8	62·6	54·7	60·7	54·9	61·2
20	52·0	57·7	50·0	55·8	50·2	56·3
25	47·2	52·8	45·2	51·0	45·5	51·4
30	42·4	47·9	40·5	46·1	40·9	46·6
35	37·6	43·1	35·7	41·3	36·1	41·8
40	32·9	38·3	31·1	36·5	31·5	37·0
45	28·2	33·6	26·6	31·9	26·9	32·3
50	23·8	29·0	22·3	27·5	22·7	27·7
55	19·7	24·7	18·5	23·3	18·7	23·4
60	16·0	20·6	14·9	19·4	15·2	19·4
65	12·7	16·7	11·9	15·8	12·0	15·7
70	9·8	13·1	9·2	12·5	9·2	12·2
75	7·5	9·9	7·0	9·5	6·9	9·1
80	5·6	7·2	5·2	6·9	5·0	6·4
85	4·2	5·1	3·9	4·9	3·2	4·3

ARCHITECTURAL CONSERVATION IN 1984

The year 1984 was dominated by two events, one planned, the other entirely unexpected. The first was the establishment of the Historic Buildings and Monuments Commission in April, the other the fire at York Minster in July.

The Commission takes over nearly all the functions of the Department of the Environment that relate to historic buildings, ancient monuments and archaeology. It now cares for the 400 sites in guardianship, offers grants for the repair of historic buildings in private hands and compiles the lists of protected structures (although these are confirmed and issued by the Department). It is wholly funded by Government except for the money it receives as gate receipts. In 1984–85, it has been allocated £54·4 m., of which £17·8 m. is for grants and £5·3 m. for Rescue Archaeology. Little change in outlook from the previous regime has been displayed so far but the Commission is certain to acquire a more public voice if only because it has been advising local planning authorities, from October 1st, on all applications affecting buildings listed Grade I and Grade II*.

York Minster is considered by many to be England's greatest building. The fire that claimed the roof of the south transept in the summer destroyed an outstanding example of medieval carpentry that had only recently been repaired. Controversy broke out over the cause of the blaze and on how the roof is to be rebuilt. However, the work of conservation began almost immediately.

The resurvey of the lists of statutarily protected buildings gathered considerable momentum under Mr. Heseltine and has been maintained since under the present Environment Secretary, Mr Jenkin. 21,113 buildings were added in 1983 bringing the total to 308,465. 126 sites of archaeological interest were scheduled as Ancient Monuments in the same period bringing that total to 12,786.

In 1983, permission was given to demolish 171 listed buildings. Another major building to be badly damaged by fire, in 1984, Heveningham Hall, Suffolk, where the famous library was destroyed, is to be faithfully repaired.

The Budget brought the welcome news that the National Heritage Memorial Fund was to be given an extra £5 m. to enable it to endow Calke Abbey in Derbyshire, so that it might be taken over by the National Trust. However, the Chancellor also announced that V.A.T., at the standard rate of 15 per cent, was to be imposed on all works to existing buildings whereas there would continue to be no V.A.T. on new buildings. After a considerable outcry the Chancellor relented and listed buildings, although not unlisted buildings in Conservation Areas, are now exempt from V.A.T. on works of conversion, alteration and extension. The tax will, however, continue to be imposed on works of repair and maintenance. The threatened Budget changes were particularly bad news for Building Preservation Trusts and a number of their schemes were held up while the matter was resolved. The number of such Trusts continues to grow and the total is now 68.

Historic houses open to the public for the first time in 1984 included Grimsthorpe in Lincolnshire, Canons Ashby in Northamptonshire (National Trust), Belsay House in Northumberland (Historic Buildings & Monuments Commission) and Beverley Friary in North Humberside. Belton House, Lincolnshire, was saved for the nation by the National Trust, as was Fyvie Castle, Aberdeenshire, by the National Trust for Scotland. Kedleston Hall in Derbyshire has been offered to the nation although it is not yet decided if it should be run by the National Trust or the Historic Buildings & Monuments Commission.

The Redundant Churches Fund, which looks after outstanding but disused Anglican churches, and is funded 60 per cent by the State and 40 per cent by the Church of England, has taken a number of important buildings into its care, including the 18th century Christ Church, Macclesfield.

In the course of the year, the Historic Buildings Bureau ceased the publication of its quarterly list of historic buildings for sale but its place has now been taken by the Period Property Register issued from Chobham Park House, Chobham, Surrey, GU24.

Membership of local civic societies now stands at 300,000. Places covered for the first time in 1984 include Oswestry, Polesworth and Youlgreave.

The English Tourist Board continues to publish the "Heritage Monitor" which remains a comprehensive source of information on all matters related to architectural conservation.

NEW MUSEUMS, 1983–84

Despite the cuts in public expenditure, 1983–84 has seen many exciting developments in the museum world.

In *1983* the museums opened included:

1. Bradford; the National Museum of Photography, Film & Television (*see also* p. 418), opened in June. This is housed in a building of the mid-Sixties constructed to provide a new theatre for the city but never used as such. The cost of modifications (£1,900,000) was met by Bradford Council. The Government provided £500,000 to meet the cost of fitting out and the Science Museum, of which it is an "outstation", provides the staff.

The exhibits include the earliest known photograph of a photographer at work, the 1843 Daguerreotype of Jabez Hogg, photographing William S. Johnson; the photo library of "The Daily Herald"; a reconstructed High Street studio of 1870 and a selection of one hundred historic scientific photographs. There is also a Camera Obscura Gallery from which the visitor can view the city and a 320 seat auditorium that boasts the largest cinema screen in the country, 45 feet high and 62 feet wide. The Museum includes full-scale exhibitions on film and television which, as with those on photography, both review the past and forecast the future.

2. Bristol; the National Lifeboat Museum (*see also* p. 653), formed in a disused dockside transit shed adjoining the city's Industrial Museum on Princes Wharf and *S.S. Great Britain*. The Museum, which first admitted the public to a temporary display in May 1981, is still developing but hopes to form a representative collection of ex-RNLI lifeboats. Special emphasis is being placed on the traditional wooden boats gradually being withdrawn from service.

The RNLI has welcomed and encouraged the Museum project from its inception although no RNLI funds are being diverted. A Founder Members Society has been established to enable individuals to support the Museum. It is intended that the Museum will eventually be self-supporting with any profits being donated to the RNLI.

3. Glasgow; the Burrell Gallery (*see also* p. 654 and p. 1044). Undoubtedly the most important collection

open to the public in the period under review was that of Sir William Burrell, the Scottish shipowner (it was opened by the Queen in October). Burrell, who died in 1958 at the age of 97, had left his collection of 8,000 art treasures to the City of Glasgow by a decision announced in 1944. Many of the treasures were acquired at bargain prices including architectural elements purchased cheaply from William Randolph Hearst. Burrell's trustees eventually agreed to a site for the Museum only 3 miles from the centre of Glasgow in Pollok Park, an estate itself bequeathed to the city in 1967 by Mrs. Anne Maxwell MacDonald.

The exhibits include the great Warwick Vase, stained glass from St. Denis, "The Rehearsal" by Edgar Degas, important Rembrandt etchings, "Le Chateau de Medan" by Cezanne, and spectacular architectural elements including complete rooms from Burrell's home, Hutton Castle near Berwick-on-Tweed.

4. Hendon, Greater London. In April, the Queen Mother opened the new Bomber Command wing at the R.A.F. Museum, Hendon (*see also* p. 421). The Museum which cost £2¼ million, displays famous bomber aircraft including the Lancaster, Wellington and Vulcan.

5. South Kensington, London; the Victoria & Albert Museum (*see also* pp. 418–19). In March, the Queen opened the Henry Cole Wing at the Museum. Created at a cost of £5¼ million, this is the first extension to the Museum in seventy years and is housed in the large building in the Exhibition Road built in 1867–71 as the Science School of the South Kensington Museum. The programme of works began in 1977 and has provided the V. & A. with 90,000 square feet of additional space. The wing is named after Sir Henry Cole, the Museum's first Director (1856–73) and has retained important internal features including the extraordinary Great North Staircase.

The wing provides new conservation workshops, storage and offices as well as gallery space for over a million works from the Department of Prints, Drawings and Photographs and from the collection of paintings. There is a special gallery for the National Collection of the Art of Photography which now numbers some 300,000 items and one hundred of Constable's paintings and sketches are exhibited on the top floor. There is a large new gallery devoted to British paintings of 1700–1900 and two dark rooms containing twelve extraordinary paintings on glass, lit from behind, executed by Gainsborough. There is a new Print Room and an alphabetical index of designers of the last half millenium working in fourteen fields. Perhaps the single most extraordinary item rehoused in the wing is a 55' long oil painting presenting a completely circular vista of Rome in 1824 painted by Caracciolo and the only known example of "panorama painting" in Britain.

6. Manchester; the Museum of Science and Industry (*see also* p. 655) at Castlefield was opened in September and received 80,000 visitors in the first four months. The Museum brings together the Air and Space Collection housed in the City's former Exhibition Hall and the Liverpool Road Station of 1825. The Museum won a Civic Trust Award and a Europa Nostra Award for 1983.

7. Margam, Port Talbot. The largest sculpture park in Britain, and the first in Wales, was opened in June at the Margram Country Park near Port Talbot in West Glamorgan with a display of 65 sculptures including work by Henry Moore, Barbara Hepworth and Elizabeth Frink. The Margam Estate, which also preserves a particularly beautiful early Georgian orangery, the ruins of a Cistercian monastery and

the fire-gutted remains of an early 19th century Gothic castle will be further embellished in 1985 by the opening of a maze.

8. Newhaven, Sussex. The National Coastal Defence Museum at Newhaven based on a fort constructed in the 1860's was opened in June. There are plans for a continuous display of artillery from the 16th century onwards.

9. Newmarket, Suffolk. The National Horseracing Museum (*see also* p. 655). In April the Queen opened Britain's first museum dedicated to the history of horseracing, housed in the former subscription rooms adjacent to the Jockey Club in High Street, Newmarket. The Museum, which cost £1¼ million, contains five display areas concentrating on the history of racing, "A Day at the Races", the development of the thoroughbred, the stories of individual horses and those of their owners. Exhibits at Newmarket will be interchangeable with those in the existing Museum at York Racecourse. The exhibits include the skeleton of one of the most famous of all 18th century horses "Eclipse", Frith's famous mid-19th century painting of "Derby Day" and a reconstruction of a 19th century weighing room with memorabilia associated with Fred Archer who rode 2,748 winners in the 1870's and 1880's. A considerable number of exhibits have been loaned by the Queen including an 18th century prize cup and a letter to Edward VII when Prince of Wales from his jockey Sam Chifney. The Queen Mother has loaned Sickert's study of King George V with his racing manager.

10. Windsor, Berkshire. Queen Victoria's Waiting Room in Windsor Station has been repaired and used to house a waxwork display by Madame Tussaud's. Other exhibits include Royal trains.

Perhaps the most spectacular attraction of *1984* was temporary: the International Garden Festival opened on May 2 and was staged for nearly six months on the banks of the Mersey in Liverpool. Combining theme gardens and floral displays with sculpture and architecture, the Festival hoped to attract three million people. Its approved budget was for the gross expenditure of £19·3 million to be offset to some extent by sponsorship and gate receipts. The buildings on the site include the main Festival Hall (*see also* p. 1050) and the Arena Theatre, which will survive the dismantling of the rest of the display.

Permanent museums opened in *1984* included:

1. Aldershot Military Museum, Hampshire, opened in April. Exhibits include a complete Victorian barrack room.

2. Botley, Hampshire. The Hampshire Farm Museum designed to highlight agricultural life and times in the county between 1850 and 1950 was opened on June 30. It is planned to complete the second part of the Museum by 1987.

3. Dudley, West Midlands. A working Glass Museum and visitors centre was opened at Easter in the 18th century "cone" at the Stuart Glass Factory in Stourbridge.

4. Helmshore, Lancashire. The Museum of the Lancashire Textile Industry housed in a 19th century mill adjacent to the Higher Mill Museum was opened on April 20.

5. Liverpool. Summer 1984 saw the first exhibition within Albert Dock; prior to their purchase in 1981 by the Merseyside Development Corporation, these had been the largest group of derelict Grade I listed buildings in the country. Some of the huge complex of early to mid-19th century warehouses is to be converted into offices and shops. However, there is also to be a considerable museum use and a special

preliminary display was mounted in 1984. By the time the scheme is complete in 1986 there will be permanent exhibitions on Liverpool's maritime history and the history of migration (*see also* p. 655).

6. London (Islington). A new St. John Ambulance Museum was opened in March in St. John's Gate, Clerkenwell.

7. Macclesfield, Cheshire. The Paradise Silk Mill opened as a museum on April 11. The history of the industry is presented.

8. Manchester. The first provincial Jewish Museum opened on March 25 in Cheetham Hill, Manchester.

9. Middle Wallop, Hampshire. The Museum of Army Flying was opened in the summer.

10. Newham, London Borough of. A museum specializing in the the history of the Great Eastern Railway opened late in 1984 in the former North Woolwich Station building.

11. Portsmouth. The year 1984 was certainly an exceptional year for Portsmouth. On June 3, the Queen Mother opened the City Council's £1 million D-Day Museum (*see also* p. 656) to mark the 40th anniversary of the Normandy landings. A prime exhibit is the Overlord Embroidery depicting the Allied invasion given to the nation by Lord Dulverton and consisting of 34 panels each 8 feet long and 3 feet high. The embroidery took 20 craftsmen at the Royal School of Needlework five years to complete. A month later, the Prince of Wales opened the £800,000 Museum of finds recovered from Henry VIII's flagship *Mary Rose* which has been the subject of a most concentrated exercise in marine archaeology. The Museum is housed in the early 19th century No. 5 Boathouse in the docks. The Royal Navy Submarine Museum, opened in 1982, has also been enlarged. Its exhibits include the Navy's first submarine *Holland I* built in 1901, which had sunk on the way to the breaker's yard in 1913 and was recovered off Start Point in November 1982.

12. Selkirk, Scotland. Halliwell's House Museum was opened on May 30 in what is believed to be the oldest continuously inhabited house in the town. There are special displays on the history of the town, the Battle of Flodden and the ironmonger's shop housed in the building for 200 years.

13. Westminster, London. The Cabinet War Rooms (*see also* p. 420) run by the Imperial War Museum were opened on April 6. The Rooms, situated in the basement of the Government Offices in Great George Street, were in operational use throughout the War and include the Cabinet Room, the Prime Minister's Room and the famous Map Room. The creation of the Museum which has been carried out with minimum disturbance to the rooms themselves cost £1,400,000.

14. Yeovilton, Somerset. A special exhibition on the Falkland Islands campaign was opened by Prince Andrew at the Fleet Air Arm Museum. Items on display include five captured Argentine aircraft.

15. York. The Jorvik Viking Centre, (*see also* p. 656) opened on April 14, was designed to give impressions of the Viking civilization uncovered during the exceptionally important archaeological dig in Coppergate. The Museum also incorporates the most up-to-date museum devices including "time cars" taking visitors on a thousand-year time circuit. The reality of Viking life is intensified by a complex system of sound and even smells. Visitors are encouraged to touch some of the finds. The Centre, built as part of a new shopping complex, cost £2½ million.

PRISONS

Receptions into prison: by number of previous convictions (England and Wales)

Number of previous convictions	1974	1975	1976	1977	1978	1979	1980	1981	1982
Males: total	27,138	30,667	32,914	33,906	34,832	36,412	38,016	43,388	46,779
None	1,361	1,915	2,028	2,135	1,936	1,634	1,731	1,518	1,773
1–2 sentence	1,983	2,309	2,511	2,516	2,500	2,484	2,685	3,002	3,164
3–5 sentences	4,261	4,804	5,079	5,401	5,399	5,652	6,092	7,161	7,312
6–10 sentences	7,744	8,631	8,960	9,177	9,470	9,412	9,665	11,152	11,845
11 or more sentences	8,152	9,221	10,280	10,893	11,011	11,340	11,905	13,343	14,057
Previous conviction information not recorded	3,637	3,787	4,056	3,784	4,516	5,890	5,938	7,212	8,628
Females: total	1,112	1,351	1,614	1,839	2,000	2,109	2,265	2,533	2,692
None	147	226	259	231	240	156	155	177	176
1–2 sentences	55	71	120	152	149	148	172	234	261
3–5 sentences	100	118	204	285	279	293	322	423	445
6–10 sentences	142	135	230	279	253	287	331	434	443
11 or more sentences	110	94	125	207	189	196	195	267	322
Previous conviction information not recorded	558	707	676	685	890	1,029	1,090	998	1,045

EDUCATION IN THE UNITED KINGDOM

ENGLAND AND WALES

Decline in numbers

In primary education and, to a greater extent than before, in secondary education pupil numbers again declined in 1983 in England as the effects of the drop in the birthrate in the 1960s and 70s continued to be felt.

Expenditure

For 1983–84 the Government planned to spend (provisional figure) on education and science a total of £13,356 million cash. About three-quarters was to be spent by local authorities (*see below*), mainly on schools (including meals, milk and transport) but also on institutions of higher and further education and the youth service. The rest was expenditure by central government. Of the £13,356 million, £12,766 million was for current expenditure and £590 million for capital expenditure.

These figures relate only to those areas (*see below*) which are the responsibility of the Secretary of State for Education and Science.

Department of Education and Science

The Department of Education and Science (D.E.S.) is responsible for all aspects of education in England and for government policy towards universities in England, Scotland and Wales. Responsibility in Wales for nursery, primary and secondary education, and for all non-university institutions of higher and further education, the youth and community services, and adult education lies with the Secretary of State for Wales.

The Department's main concern is the formulation of national policies for education. It is responsible for the broad allocation of resources for education, for the rate and distribution of educational building and for the supply, training and superannuation of teachers. It is concerned with basic educational standards. The Department does not run any schools or colleges or engage any teachers.

The D.E.S. is also responsible for government support for civil science.

It acts within a framework of estimates approved by Parliament. The money which the Department itself spends is a small part of the total public expenditure on education, the major part being expenditure by local authorities (*see below*). This expenditure by local authorities is financed from rates and from the rate support grant payable from the national Exchequer.

The Department commissions research, related to policy interests of the D.E.S. and the L.E.A.s, from universities and other bodies such as the National Foundation for Educational Research.

H.M. Inspectorate

Her Majesty's Inspectors inspect schools and other educational establishments apart from universities, report to the Secretary of State for Education and Science on the efficiency of the educational system (excluding universities) and offer independent professional advice based on their observation and judgement to the Secretary of State, the Department of Education and Science, the local education authorities, and teachers. There are some 400 H.M.I.s in England and 50 in Wales. Much of the work of H.M. Inspectorate relates to national surveys of primary and secondary education. In 1983 for the first time H.M. Inspectors' reports (about 230 in all) were published after school and college inspections and follow-up arrangements instituted.

Local Education Authorities

The educational service is a national service locally administered. Among its main features are:—

(*a*) its administration is decentralized, the responsibility for providing state primary, secondary and further education (but not university education) to meet the needs of their areas being that of the local education authorities (L.E.A.'s).

These local authorities appoint education committees consisting of some of their own members (a majority of the committee) and other people with experience in education and knowledge of the local education situation. The L.E.A.'s maintain schools and colleges and build new ones, employ teachers and provide equipment. Most of the public money spent on education is disbursed by the local authorities. L.E.A.'s are financed by rate support grants from the Department of the Environment and from the rates; teachers' salaries account for about half of local authority expenditure on education.

Voluntary Agencies

(*b*) Voluntary agencies play an important part in educational provision often in co-operation with the State. Some indication of its nature and extent is given below.

SCHOOLS AND PUPILS

Schooling is compulsory for all children between 5 and 16 years. Some provision is made for children under 5 and many pupils remain at school after the minimum leaving age. No fees are charged in any publicly maintained school.

There are three main categories of school: (*a*) those *maintained* by local education authorities, the authorities meeting their expenditure partly from local rates and partly from grants made by the Department of the Environment; (*b*) *direct grant* schools which have been assisted by grants from the Department of Education and Science but from 1980 have almost all been reclassified as independent schools; (*c*) *independent* schools.

County and Voluntary Schools

Maintained schools are of two types: (*i*) *county schools* (17,146 in 1982 in England) which are built, maintained and staffed by local education authorities. Their managers (primary schools) and governors (secondary schools) are appointed by the L.E.A.'s. (*ii*) *Voluntary schools* (8,102 in 1982 in England and attended in 1982 by about 22 per cent of all pupils in maintained schools) which although built by voluntary bodies (mainly religious denominations) are financially maintained by an L.E.A. Of the 1,695,478 pupils attending voluntary schools 49 per cent were at Church of England schools, 41 per cent at Roman Catholic schools, 0·5 per cent at Jewish schools and 0·3 per cent at Methodist schools. Voluntary schools are of three kinds: controlled (3,349), aided (4,652), and special agreement (101). In *controlled* schools the L.E.A. nominates two-thirds of the managers or governors (the rest are nominated by the voluntary body), bears all costs and appoints the teachers.

In *aided* schools the managers or governors (two-thirds appointed by the voluntary interest and one-third by the L.E.A.) are responsible for repairs to the outside of the school building and for improvements and alterations to it though the Department of Education and Science may reimburse part of approved capital expenditure. The L.E.A. meets all running costs. The managers or governors control the appointment of teachers. *Special agreement* schools are those where the L.E.A. may, by special agreement, pay between one-half and three-quarters of the cost of building a new, or extending an existing, voluntary school, almost always a secondary school. Two-thirds of the governors are appointed by the voluntary body and the remainder by the L.E.A. Expenditure is normally apportioned between the authority and the voluntary body.

Parental involvement in maintained schools is growing. The *Education Act 1980* gave parents and teachers the right for the first time to be on school governing bodies; and gave parents the right to express a preference for a particular school for their children which local authorities are obliged to meet whenever possible. In addition L.E.A.s have to publish information about their schools and admission arrangements. The Act relaxed the statutory obligations on L.E.A.s to provide meals and milk for pupils at maintained schools. It gave them discretion to charge for what they decide to provide, but required them to provide refreshment free of charge for children from poor families and to provide free facilities for children bringing their own food. It amended the law on the education of children under five years so that L.E.A.s have a power, not a duty, to provide education for this age group.

In a Green (consultative) Paper, *Parental Influence in Schools*, the Secretaries of State for England and Wales proposed in May 1984 to give parents the right to elect, from amongst themselves, the majority on most school governing bodies.

Public Schools

By the term *public schools* is usually meant the independent schools in the membership of the Headmasters' Conference, the Governing Bodies Association or the Governing Bodies of Girls' Schools Association. Most public schools are for one sex (about half of them for girls only) but some boys' schools admit girls to their sixth forms.

Independent schools charge fees and do not receive grants from public funds. *Preparatory schools* are mainly for boys from about 7 to 13 years who wish to enter public schools. All independent schools are open to inspection by H.M. Inspectors (*see above*) and must register with the Department of Education and Science which lays down certain minimum standards and can make schools remedy any unacceptable features of their building or instruction and exclude any unsuitable teacher or proprietor. In 1983 there were in England 2,344 independent schools. The arrangements by which independent schools could be "recognized as efficient", *i.e.* could satisfy the D.E.S. that their standards were broadly comparable with those of grant-aided schools, have been discontinued.

The Education Act 1980 empowered the Secretary of State to establish and operate a scheme for assisted places, under which some parents receive income-related help with the cost of tuition fees at selected independent schools. 5,000–6,000 *assisted places* are available each year at more than 200 independent schools in England and Wales for academically able children whose parents cannot afford the full tuition fees. In September 1983 4,147 of the new places offered for 11–13 year olds were taken up and 745 of the sixth-form places. 70 per cent of the grand total of 13,102 pupils who benefited in this third year of the scheme came from families with below average incomes and 36 per cent of them qualified for a completely free place. The cost of the scheme in the financial year 1983–84 was expected to be £16·5 million.

The State System

Nursery Education is for children under 5 years who may attend a nursery school or a nursery class attached to a primary school. The number of pupils under 5 years of age in such schools and classes was 247,800 in 1983, 12,400 more than the previous year.

In addition there were 210,400 under-fives in reception classes in maintained primary schools (9,000 more than in 1982). Of all 3- and 4-year-olds, 22 per cent were receiving maintained nursery education (mostly part-time) and 18 per cent were attending reception classes in primary schools.

Primary Stage.—This begins at 5 years and the transfer to secondary school is generally made at 11 years. Primary schools consist mainly of *infants' schools* for children aged 5 to 7, *junior schools* for those aged 7 to 11 and *junior and infant schools* for both age groups. In addition *first schools* in some areas cater for ages from 5 to 8, 9 or 10. (They are the first stage of a three-tier system: first, middle and secondary.)

Middle Schools.—Middle schools (which take children from first schools) cover varying age ranges between 8 and 14.

Secondary Stage.—Secondary schools are for children aged 11 to 16 and over. The largest have over 2,000 pupils but 83 per cent of the schools take between 400 and 1,500 pupils. In January, 1983, when there were in England 3,740,900 pupils in maintained secondary schools the main types were: (*a*) *comprehensive* schools (91 per cent of pupils), whose admission arrangements are without reference to ability or aptitude; (*b*) *secondary modern* schools (5 per cent) providing mainly a general education with a practical bias; (*c*) *secondary grammar* schools (3 per cent) providing an academic course from 11 to 16–18 years; and (*d*) *technical* schools (1 per cent) providing an integrated academic and technical course.

Tertiary Colleges are being developed in some areas. They provide normal sixth form school courses as well as a range of courses for further education students over the age of 16.

Special Education is provided for children who require it because of physical or mental disability. In January 1983 there were 119,200 pupils in special schools (of whom about 112,300 were in maintained schools) in England and, in addition, about 3,300 pupils with special educational needs were receiving education in hospital special schools. About 7,300 pupils also attended independent schools catering wholly or mainly for the handicapped and around 15,400 handicapped pupils were attending special classes in county and voluntary schools.

Primary and Secondary Schools

In 1983 there were 29,417 maintained and non-maintained schools in England, 348 fewer than in 1982. The total number of full-time and part-time pupils in them fell by 225,400 over the year to 8,276,100 in 1983. The number of maintained secondary schools (4,553 in 1983) fell slightly for the sixth successive year. Over the same period the number of primary schools has also fallen; in 1983 the total of 20,384 was 266 below the total for 1982.

Of the 8,276,100 pupils at school in January 1983 almost all were full-time. Of those in maintained schools, 49,700 were in nursery schools, 3,844,100 in primary schools, and 3,740,900 in secondary schools. In addition there were 516,500 in non-maintained schools and 124,800 in special schools (maintained and non-maintained).

The downward trend of primary school rolls continues with 162,600 fewer in 1983 than in 1982. Since 1974 the total number of pupils in primary schools has fallen by 1,066,100.

Boys and girls are taught together in almost all maintained primary schools. Most pupils in maintained secondary schools in England and Wales attend mixed schools. At secondary level most recognized independent schools are for boys only or girls only.

Staying on. The number of boys staying on in maintained secondary schools in England beyond the school-leaving age rose from 119,800 in 1974 to 166,400 in 1983 but the increase in the number of girls was greater—from 113,000 to 179,500. Of such boys, 78·2 per cent were on A-level courses and 18·7 on O-level/C.S.E. courses. For girls, the percentages were 73·6 and 21·1. In 1983 the percentage of 16-year-olds staying on at school was 28·9 (22·8 in 1974) and of 17-year-olds 17·9 (15·5 in 1974).

School leavers. In 1982–83 in England, 10·1 per cent of school leavers left maintained schools with no G.C.E. or C.S.E. qualification; 23·3 per cent had five or more higher grade O-levels/C.S.E.; and 11·3 per cent had two or more A-levels. The corresponding 1971–72 percentages were 45·8, 19·8 and 10.

Pupil-teacher ratios continue to improve. The ratio within maintained primary schools improved from 24·9 pupils per qualified teacher in 1974 to 22·3 in 1983. For maintained secondary schools the ratio was 16·5 after three years at 16·6.

Class Sizes.—The average size of class in maintained primary and secondary schools continued to fall in 1983. In primary schools the drop was from 25·4 in 1982 to 25·1 in 1983. In secondary schools, the average size of class fell from 21·3 to 21·1.

School Meals. In 1983 at maintained schools in England, 51·4 per cent of pupils present took meals: 35·5 per cent on payment (2,407,000) and 15·9 per cent free (1,075,000).

Advanced levels.—The number of boys in England taking A-level courses for the G.C.E. (*see below*) at maintained schools rose from 102,400 in 1972 to 131,000 in 1983. There was an even bigger increase for girls from 90,100 to 132,900 in the same period. For the second year in succession, the number of girls taking A-level courses exceeded the number of boys. The number of school-leavers in England with one or more A-levels was 99,560 in 1981–82 compared to 74,770 in 1973–74. Expressed as a percentage of all leavers, the increase was from 12·5 in 1973–74 to 14·1 in 1981–82.

Examinations: current and future.—Secondary school pupils (and others) can at present take the General Certificate of Education (G.C.E.) or the Certificate of Secondary Education (C.S.E.). The G.C.E. was introduced in 1951 (it replaced the School Certificate and Higher School Certificate) and the C.S.E. in 1965. The examinations for the G.C.E., which are conducted by eight examining bodies (most connected with universities) are set at two levels: Ordinary level ("O") and Advanced level ("A"). A-level is usually taken after two years in the sixth form following O-level, which is normally taken at 16 years (earlier only if the head teacher agrees). The G.C.E. is not a "grouped subject" examination and candidates at either level may take one or more subjects as they wish. At A-level passes are awarded in five grades. A-level candidates may take Special papers which are usually set on the same syllabus as the basic A-level papers but contain more searching questions.

Under the grading system for O-level, attainment in an O-level subject is indicated by a grade A, B, C, D or E of which grade A is the highest and grade E the lowest. Candidates awarded grade A, B or C have reached the standard of the former subject pass at O-level. Grades D and E indicate lower levels of attainment.

Like the G.C.E. the Certificate of Secondary Education (C.S.E.) can be taken in one or more subjects. It is open to boys and girls in any school completing five years of secondary education, and is meant for pupils of about 16 years who are around the average in terms of ability for their age groups. Five grades are awarded. The C.S.E. can be examined in a number of ways, internal and external, and is controlled largely by serving teachers sitting on the 13 regional examining boards.

It was, however, announced by the Secretary of State for Education and Science in June 1984 that the G.C.E. O-level and C.S.E. examinations are to be replaced by a new single system of examinations— the *General Certificate of Secondary Education (G.C.S.E.) examinations.* Under a tight timetable it is planned that the last O-level, C.S.E. and joint 16+ examinations will be held in summer and winter 1987, and that the first G.C.S.E. courses will start in the autumn of 1986 with the first examinations being held in summer 1988.

The purpose of the change is to improve the examination courses and to raise the standard of performance of all candidates. To achieve this, there would be: fewer examining groups; syllabuses based on national criteria; differentiated assessment (i.e. different papers or questions for different ranges of ability); and grade-related criteria (i.e. grades to be awarded on absolute rather than relative performance). The G.C.S.E. will be a single system of examinations, not a single examination.

The G.C.S.E. certificates will be awarded, it is planned, by each examining group, with a seven-point scale: A to G. Grades A to C will embody standards at least as high as the corresponding O-level grades A to C now do. Distinction certificates will be awarded to candidates achieving good grades in a broad range of subjects. Sole responsibility for setting and maintaining these standards will rest with the G.C.E. boards. The C.S.E. boards will have a similar responsibility for grades D to G. The examinations will be supervised by the Secondary Examinations Council (*see below*).

The Secretary of State said that the new examinations would: do more than O-levels to stretch the ablest pupils; do more than C.S.E. to motivate other pupils; promote more effectively worthwhile knowledge, understanding and skills; grade candidates by what they know, understand and can do; be clearer to candidates, their parents and employers than the present system; and be more cost effective.

The intention is that the present 20 examination boards will come together in five groups—four in England and one in Wales.

A-level examinations will continue but the Secretary of State announced in May 1984 proposals to introduce new *Advanced Supplementary level (AS-level) examinations.* Their purpose would be to broaden the curriculum for A-level students but without diluting academic standards. It is hoped that courses leading to AS-level can start in September 1986 and that the first examinations will be held in summer 1988.

AS-levels would be designed for full-time A-level students but others could take them too. An AS-level syllabus would cover not less than half the amount of ground covered by the corresponding A-level syllabus and would in most cases be closely related to it. An AS-level course would last two years and require not less than half the teaching time of the corresponding A-level course. It is envisaged that students hoping to go on to higher education would continue (where they do so now) to take A-level courses in the subjects they want to specialize in. AS-level courses would be intended to supplement and broaden these studies.

AS-levels would be developed by the G.C.E. boards in co-operation with the Secondary Examinations Council (*see below*) and examinations would be held at the same time as A-levels.

Higher education institutions are now considering the implications of these proposed new examinations for their entrance requirements.

At the Government's request, the Business and Technician Education Council and the City and Guilds of London Institute have established a joint board for pre-vocational education. Its purpose is to devise a curriculum and administrative structure for the introduction of a new 17+ qualification, the *Certificate of Pre-Vocational Education,* in schools and colleges in September 1985. This new national qualification is meant for those young people with modest or no successes at 16+ who wish to continue their full-time education but do not yet wish to commit themselves to a particular occupation. The one-year course will have a practical emphasis.

In 1983 two new bodies were set up to replace the Schools Council. They are the *Secondary Examinations Council* (S.E.C.) and the *School Curriculum Development Committee* (S.C.D.C.). The purpose of the S.E.C. is to co-ordinate and try to improve the school examination system and other forms of school-based assessment in England and Wales; and to advise the Government on these policy areas. The S.C.D.C.'s task is to inform itself of school curriculum development work being done by others in England and Wales; to identify any important gaps; to undertake appropriate work in such areas or to stimulate others to do so; and to promote the dissemination of curriculum development. The S.E.C. is wholly funded by Central Government but the S.C.D.C. is jointly funded by the Department of Education and Science and the local authorities.

TEACHERS
(see also p. 532)

Although it is the duty of each Local Education Authority to ensure that there is efficient education to meet the needs of the local population, what is taught in the schools is normally decided on their behalf by the head teachers of schools.

Teachers are appointed by local education authorities, school governing bodies or managers. Those in publicly maintained schools must be approved as "qualified" by the Department of Education and Science. To become a qualified teacher it is necessary to have successfully completed an initial course of teacher training. Teacher training is now largely integrated with the rest of higher education with training places concentrated in polytechnics, institutes or colleges of higher education, and universities. Non-graduates usually qualify by way of a three- or four-year course leading to a B.Ed. degree while graduates take a one-year postgraduate certificate of education.

Entry requirements are high with a reduced number of training places available. On entry to a course of initial teacher training leading to qualified teacher status (whether at undergraduate or postgraduate level) students are expected to provide evidence of, inter alia, a level of competence in English and mathematics at least equivalent to passes at a minimum of Grade C at G.C.E. "O" level or Grade 1 in C.S.E.

For entry at undergraduate level candidates must also normally have five passes in the G.C.E. (two of which should be at "A" level) or four passes (three of which should be at "A" level).

With certain exceptions, the profession now has an all-graduate entry. Teachers in further education, however, are not required to have qualified teacher status but roughly half have a teaching qualification and most have industrial, commercial or professional experience.

The Government is setting up a Council for the Accreditation of Teacher Education to ensure that in future all initial teacher training courses meet new stringent conditions.

New Intake. In recent years there has been a sharp drop in the number of places for students admitted to teacher-training courses. This is due to the drop in pupil numbers at school (*see above*) and to restrictions on public spending. Compared to a total in 1981 of nearly 18,700, in 1982 (provisional) of nearly 17,000,

and in 1983 (provisional) of 16,220, planned admissions to initial teacher training courses in England and Wales in universities and in non-university institutions are—1984: 16,750; and 1985: 17,350.

Shortage Subjects. In recent years there have been shortages of teachers in a number of secondary subjects, particularly mathematics, the physical sciences and craft, design and technology (C.D.T.). But, with a good recruitment to postgraduate courses in mathematics and physics, it now looks as if shortages are easing and it is expected that the situation will improve as the demand for secondary teachers declines with falling secondary pupil numbers. But in C.D.T. a shortage persists and as an incentive the Department of Education and Science runs a Training Award Scheme under which there are payable maintenance allowances (at a higher level than the normal student grant) for suitably qualified and experienced mature people taking certain shortened courses.

Serving Teachers. In 1984 there were 410,500 full-time and full-time equivalent teachers in maintained nursery, primary and secondary schools in England. This compares with 438,100 in 1980, 429,200 in 1981, 420,000 in 1982 and 414,600 in 1983. The percentage decrease in relation to the previous year was 1980: -2.7; 1981: -8.9; 1982: -9.2; 1983: -5.4; 1984: -4.1.

The latest breakdown available by the type of school relates to 1983. In that year, of the 414,600 teachers 1,688 were in nursery schools, 176,404 in primary schools and 235,943 in secondary schools. In addition, there were 96,800 teachers in further education, 18,300 in special schools and 1,100 providing education otherwise than at school.

Unemployed Teachers. 16 per cent of those who in 1982 successfully completed initial training courses in public sector institutions in England and Wales were unemployed in October 1982 and still seeking a teaching post.

HIGHER EDUCATION

"Higher Education" consists of the education provided in universities and in "advanced" courses in polytechnics and certain other educational establishments. In 1983–84 there were (provisional figures) in higher education in Great Britain some 560,000 full-time and sandwich students. This compares to 553,000 the previous year and 446,000 in 1970–71. Of the 560,000 students in 1983–84, 515,000 were home students. Of these home students, 50 per cent were at universities and 50 per cent in non-university institutions; 8 per cent were postgraduates and 92 per cent were taking first degree or other advanced courses. The home student total had steadily risen from 422,000 in 1970–71 to 456,000 in 1975–76, 468,000 in 1980–81, 492,000 in 1981–82, and 507,000 in 1982–83. On the other hand, there had been a steady drop in recent years in the number of overseas students (the total of 45,000 in 1983–84 compares with 50,000 in 1981–82 and 53,000 in 1980–81) although the 1983–84 total was 88 per cent up on the 1970–71 figure.

The 1983–84 figures (provisional) for England show that of a total of 719,000 students in higher education 518,000 were full-time or sandwich and 201,000 were part-time. Of the full-time and sandwich students 290,000 were in universities (Great Britain) and 228,000 in non-university institutions (England). The university full-time figures show a decline from 300,000 in 1981–82 to 290,000 in 1983–84 but the non-university figures have risen from 184,000 in 1979–80 to 228,000 in 1983–84. For overseas students full-time numbers at universities have dropped from 35,000 in 1979–80 to 31,000 in 1982–83 and 1983–84 and at non-university institutions from 19,000 in 1979–80 to 12,000 in 1983–84. Part-time numbers have risen in both universities (from 30,000 in 1979–80 to 34,000 in 1982–83 and 1983–84) and non-university institutions (from 149,000 in 1979–80 to 167,000 in 1983–84).

Outside the universities higher education covers any course—full-time, sandwich or part-time—of a standard higher than G.C.E. "A" level. It thus includes research, degree-level courses, higher diploma and higher certificate courses, and courses leading to a wide variety of professional qualifications. In that sense higher education is offered in some 400 institutions outside the universities most of them maintained by L.E.A.s within the overall provision they make for further education.

An important body with few, if any, parallels in other countries is the *Council for National Academic Awards* (C.N.A.A.) which awards degrees to students taking courses approved by it in non-university institutions. Following a recommendation of the Robbins Committee it was established by Royal Charter in 1964 as a self-governing body. More than 100 colleges in Britain conduct courses leading to its degrees: B.A., B.Ed., B.Sc., and the higher degrees of M.A. and M.Sc. (for post-graduate course work) and M.Phil. and Ph.D. (for research which may be undertaken jointly in industry and college).

The *Diploma of Higher Education* (Dip.H.E.) is a two-year diploma intended to serve as either a terminal qualification or as a stepping stone to a degree or other further study; it has a normal entry requirement of two "A" levels. The Dip. H.E. is awarded by either the Council for National Academic Awards (*see above*) or by a university. In England and Wales, courses leading to it are offered by some 50 polytechnics and colleges. The emphasis in most Dip. H.E. courses is on the humanities and social sciences but many colleges offer scientific options.

The Government has set up a *National Advisory Body for Public Sector Higher Education*. It advises the Secretary of State on a co-ordinated approach to the planning of courses, student intakes and the allocation of funds in Polytechnics and other local authority and voluntary colleges in respect of courses leading to qualifications higher than A-level.

See also "Universities" *below.*

FURTHER EDUCATION

The term "Further Education" usually means all post-school education except "higher education"(*see above*).

In 1982–83 full-time and sandwich course enrolments at maintained, assisted and grant-aided establishments in England were 573,000 (8 per cent up on 1981–82). In addition there were at those establishments 1,316,000 part-time course enrolments. If adult education centres are included the total for all further education establishments was 3,405,000 course enrolments, 2 per cent up on 1981–82. (Some students enrol on more than one course so the number of students is lower than the number of course enrolments.)

Local Education Authorities are responsible for providing full-time and part-time courses of post-secondary education (other than university education) in their areas.

Regional Advisory Councils. Responsibility for co-ordinating further education provision in different areas of England and Wales rests with 10 Regional Advisory Councils (*see* p. 532) set up by the local education authorities in each region. The councils bring together representatives of the L.E.A.s, colleges, universities, industry and commerce.

The 4,470 further education establishments in England may be grouped in the following main categories. All three are grant-aided and were in 1982–83 attended by a total of 3,334,178 students of whom 11 per cent were on advanced courses:—

1. *Polytechnics* (*see also* p. 510)—Thirty major centres in which a wide range of full-time, sandwich and part-time courses are provided for students at all levels of higher education, and entirely or almost entirely for those of 18 years or more. They have governing bodies with a large measure of autonomy and are mainly teaching institutions though provision is made for certain research where it is essential to the proper fulfilment of teaching functions and the maintenance of close links with industry. A centralized admissions system for degree courses in polytechnics is being set up. In England in 1982–83 there was a total of 220,787 students enrolled at polytechnics; of these 203,072 were on advanced courses and 17,715 on non-advanced courses; of those on advanced courses 138,916 were full-time or sandwich.

2. *Other Major Establishments* (483 in England).—Including all major establishments (maintained, assisted by L.E.A.s, direct grant from D.E.S. or voluntary), other than polytechnics, providing courses in teacher training, art, agricultural, commercial, technical and other subjects. In England there were 178,453 on advanced courses including 78,867 on full-time or sandwich; and 1,401,394 on non-advanced courses.

3. *Adult Education Centres* (3,958). Establishments maintained by local education authorities and offering a wide range of courses, many of them recreational, mainly for evening students, and often housed in premises used by day for other educational purposes. 1,533,544 students in England.

In addition there are some 100 Independent Establishments.

In 1983, of the 394,000 enrolments on advanced courses in major establishments of further education in England, 58 per cent were full-time or sandwich and 42 per cent part-time.

In 1983, the *Business and Technician Education Council* (B.T.E.C.) was set up by the Secretary of State for Education and Science to replace the Business Education Council (1974) and the Technician Education Council (1973) and to continue their work of developing a national system of non-degree vocational courses in these fields.

Adult Education (see p. 515–516).

Trade Union Education.—The Secretaries of State for Education and Science and Employment support financially approved expenditure on trade union education and training. In 1983–84 the joint grant was £1·78 million.

The *Youth Service* provides for the spare-time activities of young people. The Local Education Authorities co-operate with voluntary bodies in their areas and may maintain their own youth clubs. There are various national voluntary youth organizations. There are some 3,000 full-time youth workers in England and Wales who are employed by local education authorities and voluntary youth organizations. In addition there are many thousands of part-time paid and unpaid workers. In England and Wales there is a basic two-year training for youth and community workers, and in-service courses, both validated by the Council for Education and Training in Youth and Community Work.

Training Services.—The main responsibility for carrying out industrial and commercial training lies with individual employers, but the Manpower Services Commission (M.S.C.), which is separate from government but responsible to the Secretary of State for Employment, provides, with government support, opportunities for individuals to acquire new skills and helps to improve the effectiveness of training generally.

A major new programme, the *Youth Training Scheme* (Y.T.S.) began in September 1983 with the aim of finding places for 460,000 young people in 1983–84. It offers year-long training programmes for employed and unemployed 16-year old school-leavers and some unemployed 17-year old school-leavers. Young people who take part as employees are paid a wage. If they are unemployed they are paid a training allowance. All programmes include direct practical experience; training in a group of skills related to an area of work; at least 13 weeks off-the-job further education or training; and a certificate is given at the end to show what the young person can do.

At national level, a Youth Training Board oversees the whole scheme.

The Y.T.S., which is not compulsory, is meant not just as an alternative to unemployment but as a permanent training scheme for those young people who leave school at 16 to look for a job. It is part of an overall policy whose aim is to ensure that all young people under 18 have a better opportunity than in the past either to continue in full-time education or to enter upon a period of planned work-experience combined with work-related training and education.

Information about the Y.T.S. can be obtained from local careers offices and job centres or from the area offices of the Manpower Services Commission's Training Division.

An *Advanced Further Education Information Service* is provided each summer by the local education authorities in cooperation with the polytechnics and other colleges offering full-time degree and higher diploma courses, and the Department of Education and Science. It aims to provide up-to-date information and advice about full-time degree, higher diploma and Dip.H.E. courses in the colleges for those who find themselves, late in the summer, without a place on a course. A list of local advisory officers is available from the D.E.S.

UNIVERSITIES

Universities are self-governing institutions, usually established by Royal Charter, which are responsible for all academic matters including appointments and staffing, curriculum and student admissions. They are not subject to ministerial directive but they do depend on the State for most of their income.

There are 46 universities in the United Kingdom (*see* pp. 504–509). Of these, 35 are in England, eight in Scotland, two in Northern Ireland and one (a federal institution) in Wales.

The non-residential "*Open University*" provides courses leading to degrees by a combination of television, radio, correspondence, tutorials, short residential courses and local audio-visual centres. The Open University offers undergraduate (no qualifications needed for entry), post-experience and postgraduate courses. It is grant-aided directly by the Department of Education and Science and does not come within the University Grants Committee system. More than 7,000 students graduated in 1983 from the Open University and some 66,000 students were studying for first degrees, 750 studying for higher degrees and 43,000 students on continuing education courses.

The independent University at Buckingham provides a two-year course leading to a bachelor's degree and its tuition fees are £4,700 for 1985. It receives no capital or recurrent income from the government but its students are eligible for mandatory awards from L.E.A.'s. Its academic year consists of 4 terms of 10 weeks each.

Enrolments. In 1982–83 there were enrolled at universities in the U.K., excluding the Open University, 303,965 full-time students of whom 39% were women. 257,733 were undergraduates and 46,232 postgraduates. Of the undergraduates, 80,842 were new entrants. Between 1981–82 and 1982–83 the number of U.K.-domiciled full-time undergraduates at U.K. universities went up by 0·8% and of postgraduates went down 3·8%.

In addition there were 34,942 part-time students enrolled at universities in the U.K.

Subjects. The subjects studied by the 257,733 undergraduates fell into the following groups: administrative, business and social studies 24%; biological and physical sciences 24%; engineering and technology 15%; language, literature and area studies 13%; medicine, dentistry and health 11%; arts other than languages 9%; agriculture, forestry and veterinary science 2%; architecture and other professional/ vocational subjects 2%; and education 2%.

The four subject groups in which the largest numbers of postgraduates were studying were: biological and physical sciences 23%; administrative, business and social studies 22%; education 17%; and engineering and technology 14%.

Overseas students. Of the 257,733 full-time undergraduates, 7% had an overseas domicile, and of the 46,232 postgraduates 35%.

Degrees awarded. In 1982, 74,061 students at universities in Great Britain successfully completed courses at undergraduate level of whom 95% were awarded first degrees, an increase of 2·5% over the previous year. Between 1977 and 1982, the number of successful students rose steadily, by 19% overall. The number from overseas almost doubled in that period, accounting for 7% of the first degrees awarded in 1981. Of the successful home students, the number of women rose by 30%.

Of the 30,773 who successfully completed postgraduate courses in 1982, an 8% increase over the 1977 total, 64% gained higher degrees, 19% higher diplomas and 17% a professional teaching qualification. Since 1977 the number of higher degrees awarded has risen by 14%. About a third of higher degrees and diplomas were awarded to overseas-domiciled students.

Academic staff. In 1982–83, the number of full-time teaching and research staff in universities in Great Britain decreased by 2% to 41,994, but the number of part-time staff rose by 38% to 12,266. Of the overall 1982–83 total, 14% were women. Of the full-time staff wholly financed from general university funds, 13% were professors, 26% were readers or senior lecturers and 60% were lecturers.

Admission. Students applying for admission to a first degree course at a university do so through the Universities Central Council on Admissions (U.C.C.A.) which was set up by the universities in 1961 on the initiative of the Committee of Vice-Chancellors and Principals. All universities participate in the U.C.C.A. scheme except the Open University and the University of Buckingham, which conduct their own admissions direct. The U.C.C.A. office is in Cheltenham.

The requirements for entry to first degree courses vary somewhat from one university to another, but the universities publish co-operatively an annual Compendium which describes these requirements in detail.

Fees. Students with mandatory awards (*see* p. 512–513) do not pay tuition fees.

As part of the government's plan to restrain public expenditure, new entrants from overseas (other than from other European Community countries) to higher and further education courses in Great Britain must pay tuition fees based on the full recurrent cost of the courses. For universities in 1984–85 these were *not less than* £3,150 for arts courses, £4,150 for science courses and £7,650 for clinical medicine, dentistry and veterinary science.

The *University Grants Committee* advises the Secretary of State for Education and Science on university matters. Most of its members are academics or businessmen. The U.G.C. acts as a buffer between the Government from which it receives a block grant of money and the universities to which it allocates this grant.

Although the universities have freedom in academic matters, the government, through the U.G.C., determines the total size of the university student population, its distribution between arts, science, medicine, etc., and the part which the university sector plays in the whole higher education system.

Reshaping the university system. Unprecedented cuts to the income and home student numbers of universities in Great Britain have been implemented as another part of the government's intention to cut public spending. In 1982–83 the number of U.K.-domiciled undergraduates fell for the first time in many years and the total from overseas decreased for the third year running. The number of full-time academic staff went down by 2%. The Secretary of State for Education and Science intends to introduce legislation to limit the nature of academic tenure in *future* appointments of academic staff so that such appointments could be terminated for reasons of redundancy or financial exigency. He has also arranged for an efficiency study of management systems and methods in universities.

Finance. The universities' recurrent grant for the academic year 1984–85 is £1,265 million.

SCOTLAND

The educational system of Scotland has developed independently of that of England and has a number of distinctive features. The general supervision of the national system of education, except for the universities, is the responsibility of the Secretary of State for Scotland acting through the Scottish Education Department. The duty of providing education locally rests with the nine regional councils and three island councils. Educational facilities of various kinds are also provided by the governing bodies of grant-aided schools, "central institutions", colleges of education, and national voluntary organizations in the field of informal further education.

Schools in Scotland fall into three main categories, viz. *education authority schools* which are financed and managed by the regional and islands councils; *grant-aided schools*, conducted by voluntary managers who receive grants direct from the department; and *independent schools* which receive no direct grant, but which are subject to inspection and registration.

In 1982–83, there were 3,843 education authority and grant-aided schools and departments, of which 541 were nursery, 2,509 primary, 463 secondary and 330 special. There were also 87 registered independent schools. The total number of pupils in education authority and grant-aided schools and departments (including special) was 929,967 (474,434 boys, 455,533 girls) of which 34,862 (17,948 boys, 16,914 girls) received nursery education. There were a further 15,160 pupils in independent schools (8,750 boys, 6,410 girls).

Schooling normally starts at the age of 5, and the primary school course lasts for 7 years. Primary schools usually take both boys and girls. Pupils transfer from the primary course to secondary courses about the age of 12.

Over 99 per cent of pupils in education authority secondary schools attend schools with a comprehensive intake. Most of these schools provide a full range of courses appropriate to all levels of ability from first to sixth year.

The Scottish Certificate of Education Examination is conducted by the Scottish Examination Board. Pupils may attempt as many of a wide range of subjects as they are capable of, on either the Ordinary grade which corresponds to the Ordinary level of the General Certificate of Education, or on the Higher grade which is normally taken one year after Ordinary grade. The shorter length of course inevitably means that Higher grades are normally studied to a lesser depth than Advanced levels; on the other hand it is common for pupils to be presented for four or more Higher grades at a single diet of the examination. The Board grants a Certificate of Sixth Year Studies designed to give direction and purpose to sixth-year work by encouraging pupils who have completed their main subjects at Higher grade to study a maximum of three such subjects in depth. Pupils may also use the sixth year to gain improved or additional Higher grades or Ordinary grades.

Further Education.—Facilities for further education are provided by 14 Central Institutions (grant-aided colleges administered by independent Boards of Governors) and by 61 further education colleges managed by education authorities. The Central Institutions provide mainly advanced courses in science and technology, commerce, art, music, domestic science, and other subjects, leading to their own diplomas, to professional qualifications or to degrees validated by C.N.A.A. or universities.

The further education colleges normally provide less advanced courses which are mainly part-time covering vocational and non-vocational subjects, but a few offer courses of degree level. Courses are offered in a wide variety of subjects but to make the most economic use of resources, provision of certain courses is made on a regional or even a national basis.

Teachers.—All teachers in public or grant-aided schools in Scotland are required to be registered with the General Teaching Council for Scotland (which is independent of the Scottish Education Department) and normally to hold a teaching qualification awarded by a Scottish College of Education. There are seven of these colleges, five of which provide both one and three year courses leading to a Teaching Qualification (Primary Education), and a one year course leading to a Teaching Qualification (Secondary Education). Of the remaining two colleges, one is a residential college of physical education for women and the other provides only courses leading to a Teaching Qualification (Primary Education). All seven colleges, in conjunction with local universities or the Council for National Academic Awards, provide four year combined courses leading to the degree of B.Ed.

The basic scales of teachers' salaries are for primary and secondary levels, with additional payments for qualifications and for posts of special responsibility.

NORTHERN IRELAND

Education in Northern Ireland is administered centrally by the Department of Education and locally by five Education and Library Boards. There are two main categories of school: controlled schools which are managed by the Education and Library Boards with all costs paid from public funds; and voluntary schools which get grants towards capital costs.

Nursery education for under-fives is provided in nursery schools or nursery classes in primary schools. Primary education is for children up to 11–12 years and is free, though children educated in preparatory departments of grammar schools pay fees. Entry, at 11–12 years, to a secondary (intermediate) school or grammar school is selective in most areas but children can subsequently transfer from one to the other. Grammar schools provide an academic type of secondary education leading to O- and A-levels, while secondary (intermediate) schools follow a curriculum suited to aptitudes and abilities leading to C.S.E. and G.C.E. examinations. Northern Ireland has 26 institutions of further education (with 154 out-centres), three general colleges of education, and two universities (the Ulster Polytechnic has merged with the New University of Ulster to form the University of Ulster).

In January 1983 the total number of pupils enrolled in the 1,401 grant-aided schools was 352,840 of whom 4,413 were in nursery schools, 182,632 in primary schools, 163,197 in secondary schools and 2,598 in special schools. Between 1978 and 1983, enrolments at primary schools declined by over 21,500 while those at secondary schools went up by nearly 1,000. Pupil-teacher ratios improved from 23·9 to 23·3 in primary schools and 16·0 to 15·5 in secondary schools. Staying-on rates for 16-year olds increased from 35 per cent to 41·7 per cent.

There were 18,827 full-time equivalent teachers (1 per cent down on 1978) of whom 10,527 were in secondary schools and 7,844 in primary.

In 1982–83, there were 8,465 students on advanced courses of whom 41 per cent were part-time. In addition, there were 43,521 students on non-advanced vocational courses of further education of whom 64 per cent were part-time.

Public expenditure on education and related services in 1982–83 was: current—£485·6 million; capital £40·8 million.

DUKE OF EDINBURGH'S AWARD SCHEME

The Duke of Edinburgh's Award Scheme, which operates under a variety of titles in over forty countries around the world, provides an incentive and a challenge to young people to reach certain standards in leisure-time activities with the voluntary help of adults. Entrants must be between their 14th and 23rd birthdays, and can enter through their school, their firm, a youth organization, or on their own. Bronze, Silver and Gold Awards can be gained by those who qualify in the four sections of the Scheme: Service, Expeditions, Skills and Physical Recreation. The qualifying standards are expressed in terms of proficiency, perseverance or sustained effort, participants being assessed on the use they make of their personal abilities and aptitudes, and not in competition with others.

In 1983, there were 71,433 new entrants from the United Kingdom and 39,448 from overseas; a total of 49,304 Awards were gained world-wide. Since the Scheme began in 1956, over two million young people have taken part.

Head Office: 5 Prince of Wales Terrace, W.8. Director: R. Heron.

PRINCIPAL BOOK PUBLISHERS AND THEIR ADDRESSES

More than 9,000 firms, individuals and societies have published one or more books in recent years. The list which follows is a selective one comprising, in the main, those firms whose names are most familiar to the general public. An interleaved list containing some 2,500 names and addresses is available, price (1984 edition) £2·80 post free, from the publishers of "Whitaker".

Abelard-Schuman, Furnival House, 14–18 High Holborn, W.C.1.
Allan (Ian), Terminal House, Shepperton, Mddx.
Allen (J. A.), 1 Lower Grosvenor Pl., S.W.1.
Allen (W. H.), 44 Hill St., W.1.
Allen & Unwin, 40 Museum St., W.C.1.
Angus & Robertson, 16 Golden Square, W.1.
Architectural Press, 9 Queen Anne's Gate, S.W.1.
Argus Books, P.O. Box 35, Hemel Hempstead, Herts.
Arlington Books, 15 King St., S.W.1.
Armada Books, 8 Grafton St., W.1.
Arms & Armour Press, 2 Hampstead High St., N.W.3.
Arnold (Edward), 41 Bedford Sq., W.C.1.
Arnold (E. J.) & Son, Parkside Lane, Leeds.
Arrow Books, 17 Conway St., W.1.
Athlone Press, 44 Bedford Row, W.C.1.
Autobooks, Bradford Rd., E. Ardsley, Wakefield, Yorks.
B.B.C. Publications, 35 Marylebone High St., W.1.
Baillière, Tindall, 1 St. Anne's Rd., Eastbourne, Sx.
Baker (John), 35 Bedford Row, W.C.1.
Bantam Bks., 61 Uxbridge Rd., W.5.
Barker (Arthur), 91 Clapham High St., S.W.4.
Barrie & Jenkins, 17 Conway St., W.1.
Bartholomew & Son, 12 Duncan St., Edinburgh.
Batsford, 4 Fitzhardinge St., Portman Square, W.1.
Bell & Hyman, 37 Queen Elizabeth St., S.E.1.
Benn (Ernest), 35 Bedford Row, W.C.1.
Bingley (Clive), 7 Ridgmount St., W.C.1.
Black (A. & C.), 35 Bedford Row, W.C.1.
Blackie, Bishopbriggs, Glasgow, and Furnival House, 14–18 High Holborn, W.C.1.
Blackwell (Basil), 108 Cowley Rd., Oxford.
Blackwood Pillans & Wilson, 162 Leith Walk, Edinburgh.
Blandford Press, Link Ho., West St., Poole, Dorset.
Blond (Anthony), 55 Gt. Ormond St., W.C.1.
Bodley Head, 9 Bow St., W.C.2.
Bowes & Bowes, 9 Bow St., W.C.2.
Boyars (Marion), 18 Brewer St., W.1.
British Museum, 46 Bloomsbury St., W.C.1.
Brown, Son & Ferguson, 4 Darnley St., Glasgow.
Burke Pub. Co., 116 Golden Lane, E.C.1.
Butterworth & Co., Borough Green, Sevenoaks, Kent.
Calder (John), 18 Brewer St., W.1.
Cambridge Univ. Press, Shaftesbury Rd., Cambridge.
Cape (Jonathan), 30 Bedford Square, W.C.1.
Cassell, 1 Vincent Sq., S.W.1.
Centaur Press, Fontwell, Arundel, Sx.
Century Publishing Co., 12 Greek St., W.1.
Chambers (W. & R.), 43 Annandale St., Edinburgh.
Chapman & Hall, 11 New Fetter Lane, E.C.4.
Chapman (Geoffrey), 1 Vincent Sq., S.W.1.
Chatto & Windus, 40 William IV St., W.C.2.
Churchill Livingstone, 1–3 Baxter's Place, Leith Walk, Edinburgh.
Collier-Macmillan, Stockley Rd., W. Drayton, Mddx.
Collins (William), 8 Grafton St., W.1.
Colour Library, 86 Epsom Rd., Guildford, Sy.
Constable & Co., 10 Orange St., W.C.2.
Consumers' Assn., 14 Buckingham St., W.C.2.
Corgi Books, 61 Uxbridge Road, W.5.
Darton, Longman & Todd, 89 Lillie Rd., S.W.6.
David & Charles, Brunel House, Newton Abbot, Devon.
Davies (Peter), 10 Upper Grosvenor St., W.1.
Deans International, 52 Southwark St., S.E.1.
Dent (J. M.) & Sons, 33 Welbeck St., W.1.
Deutsch (A.), 105 Gt. Russell St., W.C.1.
Dobson Books, Brancepeth Castle, Durham.

Dorling Kindersley, 9 Henrietta St., W.C.2.
Duckworth & Co., 43 Gloucester Crescent, N.W.1.
E.P. Group, Bradford Rd., E. Ardsley, Wakefield, Yorks.
Elliot Right Way Books, Kingswood Bldg., Kingswood, Tadworth, Surrey.
Encyclopædia Britannica, 4 Winsley St., W.1.
Epworth Press, 1 Central Bldgs., S.W.1
Evans Bros., 2A Portman Mans., Chiltern St., W.1.
Eyre & Spottiswoode, North Way, Andover, Hants.
Faber & Faber, 3 Queen Square, W.C.1.
Focal Press, Borough Green, Sevenoaks, Kent.
Fontana, 8 Grafton St., W.1.
Foulis (G. T.), Sparkford, Yeovil, Som.
Foulsham & Co., Yeovil Rd., Slough, Berks.
Fountain Press, 65 Victoria St., Windsor, Berks.
French (Samuel), 52 Fitzroy St., W.1.
Futura, see Macdonald & Co.
Gall & Inglis, 62 Buckstone Terrace, Edinburgh, 10.
Gee & Co., 27 Charing Cross Rd., W.C.2.
Geographia, 17 Conway St., W.1.
Gibbons (Stanley), 399 Strand, W.C.2.
Gibson (Robert), 17 Fitzroy Place, Glasgow.
Ginn & Co., Prebendal Ho., Parson's Fee, Aylesbury, Bucks.
Glasgow (Mary), 140 Kensington Church St., W.8.
Gollancz (Victor), 14 Henrietta St., W.C.2.
Gower Press, Croft Rd., Aldershot, Hants.
Graham (Frank), 6 Queen's Terrace, Newcastle.
Granada Publishing, 8 Grafton St., W.1.
Green (W.), 2 St. Giles St., Edinburgh.
Griffin (Charles), 5A Crendon St., High Wycombe, Bucks.
Guinness Superlatives, 2 Cecil Court, London Road, Enfield.
H.M. Stationery Office, 51 Nine Elms Lane, S.W.8.
Hale (Robert), 45 Clerkenwell Green, E.C.1.
Hamilton (Hamish), 57 Long Acre, W.C.2.
Hamlyn, Astronaut Ho., Hounslow Road, Feltham, Mddx.
Harlequin, 15 Brook's Mews, W.1.
Harrap, 19 Ludgate Hill, E.C.4.
Hart-Davis, 8 Grafton St., W.1.
Harvester Press, 16 Ship St., Brighton, Sussex.
Harvill Press, 8 Grafton St., W.1.
Haynes (J. H.), Sparkford, Yeovil, Som.
Heinemann (Wm.), 10 Upper Grosvenor St., W.1.
Hodder & Stoughton, 47 Bedford Sq., W.C.1.
Hodge & Co., 34 N. Frederick St., Glasgow.
Hogarth Press, 40 William IV St., W.C.2.
Hollis & Carter, 9 Bow St., W.C.2.
Holmes-Macdougall, 137 Leith Walk, Edinburgh.
Holt-Saunders, 1 St. Anne's Rd., Eastbourne, Sx.
Hurst & Blackett, 17 Conway St., W.1.
Hutchinson, 17 Conway St., W.1.
Jackdaw Publications, 30 Bedford Sq., W.C.1.
Jane's Publishing Co., 238 City Rd., E.C.1.
Jarrold Colour, Barrack Street, Norwich.
Jarrolds, 17 Conway St., W.1.
Johnston & Bacon, P. O. Box 1, Stirling.
Jordan & Sons, 15 Pembroke Rd., Bristol.
Joseph (Michael), 44 Bedford Sq., W.C.1.
Kaye & Ward, Windmill Press, Kingswood, Tadworth, Surrey.
Kelly's Directories, East Grinstead House, East Grinstead, Sussex.
Kimber (Wm.), 100 Jermyn St., S.W.1.
Kimpton Medical, 205 Gt. Portland St., W.1.
Ladybird, Beeches Rd., Loughborough.
Lane (Allen), see Viking.
Lawrence & Wishart, 39 Museum St., W.C.1.

Lewis (H. K.), 136 Gower St., W.C.1.
Lion Publishing, Icknield Way, Tring, Herts.
Longman Group, Burnt Mill, Harlow, Essex.
Lund Humphries, 26 Litchfield St., W.C.2.
Lutterworth Press, 7 All Saints Passage, Cambridge.
Macdonald & Co., 74 Worship St., E.C.2.
Macdonald & Evans, Estover Rd., Plymouth.
McGraw-Hill, Shoppenhangers Rd., Maidenhead, Berks.
Macmillan Publishers, Little Essex St., W.C.2.
Marshall Cavendish, 58 Old Compton St., W.1.
Marshall, Morgan & Scott, 3 Beggarwood Lane, Basingstoke, Hants.
Mayflower, 8 Grafton St., W.1.
Methodist Publishing, Wellington Rd., S.W.19.
Methuen & Co., 11 New Fetter Lane, E.C.4.
Mills & Boon, 15 Brook's Mews, W.1.
Mitchell Beazley, 14 Manette St., W.1.
Mowbray, St. Thomas Ho., Becket St., Oxford.
Muller, Blond & White, 55 Gt. Ormond St., W.C.1.
Murray (John), 50 Albemarle St., W.1.
National Christian Education Council, Robert Denholm Ho., Nutfield, Redhill, Sy.
Nelson (T.), Mayfield Rd., Walton-on-Thames, Sy.
New English Library, 47 Bedford Sq., W.C.1.
Nisbet & Co., Digswell Pl., Welwyn Garden City, Herts.
Nonesuch Library, 9 Bow St., W.C.2.
Novello & Co., Borough Green, Sevenoaks, Kent.
Octopus Books, 59 Grosvenor St., W.1.
Oliphants, 3 Beggarwood Lane, Basingstoke, Hants.
Oliver & Boyd, 1–3 Baxter's Place, Leith Walk, Edinburgh.
Owen (Peter), 73 Kenway Rd., S.W.5.
Oxford Univ. Press, Walton St., Oxford.
Paladin Bks., 8 Grafton St., W.1.
Pan Books, 18 Cavaye Place, S.W.10.
Panther, 8 Grafton St., W.1.
Paul (Kegan), 14 Leicester Sq., W.C.2.
Paul (Stanley), 17 Conway St., W.1.
Pelham Books, 44 Bedford Sq., W.C.1.
Penguin Books, Harmondsworth, Mddx.
Pergamon Press, Headington Hill Hall, Oxford.
Phaidon Press, St. Ebbes St., Oxford.
Pharmaceutical Press, 1 Lambeth High St., S.E.1.
Philip (George), 12 Long Acre, W.C.2.
Piatkus Books, 40 Hanway St., W.1.
Piccadilly Press, 64 Greenfield Gdns., N.W.2.
Pickering & Inglis, 3 Beggarwood Lane, Basingstoke, Hants.
Pitkins, 11 Wyfold Rd., S.W.6.
Pitman Publishing, 128 Long Acre, W.C.2.
Purnell Books, Paulton, Bristol.
Putnam & Co., 9 Bow St., W.C.2.
Quartet Books, 27 Goodge St., W.1.
Queen Anne Press, *see* Macdonald & Co.
Quiller Press, 50 Albemarle St., W.1.
Reader's Digest, 25 Berkeley Sq., W.1.
Reinhardt (Max), 9 Bow St., W.C.2.

Religious & Moral Education Press, Hennock Rd., Exeter.
Rider & Co., 17 Conway St., W.1.
Routledge & Kegan Paul, 14 Leicester Sq., W.C.2.
S.C.M. Press, 26 Tottenham Rd., N.1.
S.P.C.K., Holy Trinity Church, Marylebone Rd., N.W.1.
St. Andrew Press, 121 George St., Edinburgh.
Scripture Union, 130 City Rd., E.C.1.
Secker & Warburg, 54 Poland St., W.1.
Severn House, 4 Brook St., W.1.
Sheed & Ward, 2 Creechurch Lane, E.C.3.
Sheldon Press, Holy Trinity Church, Marylebone Rd., N.W.1.
Sidgwick & Jackson, 1 Tavistock Chambers, W.C.1.
Smith (M. Temple), Jubilee Ho., Chapel Rd., Hounslow, Middx.
Smythe (Colin), P.O. Box 6, Gerrards Cross, Bucks.
Souvenir Press, 43 Gt. Russell St., W.C.1.
Spearman (N.), 57 Friars St., Sudbury, Suffolk.
Sphere Books, 30 Gray's Inn Rd., W.C.1.
Spon (E. & F. N.), 11 New Fetter Lane, E.C.4.
Stanford Maritime, 12–14 Long Acre, W.C.2.
Stephens (Patrick), Denington Estate, Wellingborough, Northants.
Stevens & Sons, 11 New Fetter Lane, E.C.4.
Sunshine Books, 12 Little Newport St., W.C.2.
Sweet & Maxwell, 11 New Fetter Lane, E.C.4.
Talbot Press, Ballymount Rd., Dublin, 12.
Tavistock Publications, 11 New Fetter Lane, E.C.4.
Technical Press, Freeland, Oxford.
Thames & Hudson, 30 Bloomsbury St., W.C.1.
Thorsons, Denington Estate, Wellingborough, Northants.
Times Books, 16 Golden Sq., W.1.
Turnstone Books, Denington Estate, Wellingborough, Northants.
University of Wales Press, Gwennyth St., Cardiff.
University Tutorial Press, 842 Yeovil Rd., Slough.
Vallentine Mitchell, 11 Gainsborough Rd., E.11.
Viking, 536 Kings Rd., S.W.10.
Virago Press, 41 William IV St., W.C.2.
Walker Books, 184 Drummond St., N.W.1.
Ward Lock, 82 Gower Street, W.C.1.
Ward Lock Educational Co., 47 Marylebone Lane, W.1.
Warne, 536 Kings Rd., S.W.10.
Webb & Bower, 9 Colleton Cres., Exeter.
Weidenfeld & Nicolson, 91 Clapham High St., S.W.4.
Wheaton (A.), Hennock Rd., Exeter.
"Whitaker," 12 Dyott St., W.C.1.
Wildwood House, Jubilee Ho., Chapel Rd., Hounslow, Middx.
Witherby (H. F. & G.), 32 Aylesbury St., E.C.1.
Wolfe Publishing, 3–5 Conway St., W.1.
World's Work, Kingswood, Tadworth, Surrey.
Wright (John), 823 Bath Rd., Bristol 4.
Zomba Books, 165 Willesden High Rd., N.W.10.

Most of the principal book publishers are members of The Publishers Association (*see* page 1130).

BOOK PRODUCTION AND BOOK EXPORTS

These figures for book production and exports are issued by the Department of Industry. The totals for the years 1970 to 1983 are shown below:

Year	Total value of Books produced in U.K.	Total value of Books exported from U.K.	Year	Total value of Books produced in U.K.	Total value of Books exported from U.K.
1970	153,676,000	67,842,000	1977	467,036,000	203,904,000
1971	179,099,000	77,856,000	1978	521,425,000	211,782,000
1972	205,266,000	81,207,000	1979	580,380,000	215,333,000
1973	230,106,000	95,855,000	1980	666,928,000	213,691,000
1974	281,508,000	119,359,000	1981	737,974,000	234,451,000
1975	342,408,000	138,621,000	1982	759,142,000	232,781,000
1976	£408,301,000	£175,778,000	1983 (Provisional)	831,910,000	261,106,000

BOOKS PUBLISHED IN GREAT BRITAIN IN 1983

This table, from *The Bookseller* of January 14, 1984, shows the books published in 1983 with the number of new editions, translations and limited editions. Books and pamphlets priced at less than 12½p have been omitted, as are also all Government publications except the more important issued by H.M. Stationery Office.

Classification	Total	Reprints and New Editions	Translations	Limited Editions
Aeronautics	206	36	1	—
Agriculture and Forestry	427	68	18	2
Architecture	426	62	9	—
Art	1,312	186	30	9
Astronomy	171	40	5	—
Bibliography and Library Economy	675	136	3	—
Biography	1,969	734	78	5
Chemistry and Physics	697	115	30	—
Children's Books	3,449	790	194	11
Commerce	1,377	345	3	1
Customs, Costumes, Folklore	172	37	6	—
Domestic Science	781	209	29	—
Education	1,421	245	5	—
Engineering	1,714	315	22	1
Entertainment	598	102	16	1
Fiction	5,265	2,156	204	6
General	856	97	2	—
Geography and Archaeology	437	118	5	—
Geology and Meteorology	348	40	27	—
History	1,740	361	46	1
Humour	242	43	2	—
Industry	612	109	9	1
Language	708	129	7	4
Law and Public Administration	1,787	403	8	—
Literature	2,187	1,013	79	3
Mathematics	1,011	142	22	—
Medical Science	3,165	520	27	—
Military Science	167	44	2	—
Music	489	113	22	—
Natural Sciences	1,177	169	44	3
Occultism	188	35	17	—
Philosophy	695	167	59	—
Photography	294	40	2	6
Plays	381	201	35	2
Poetry	925	222	72	31
Political Science and Economy	4,177	823	92	—
Psychology	705	127	13	—
Religion and Theology	2,257	394	189	3
School Textbooks	1,964	288	9	—
Science, General	76	16	4	—
Sociology	1,162	172	16	1
Sports and Outdoor Games	610	123	2	3
Stockbreeding	265	53	7	—
Trade	563	127	2	2
Travel and Guidebooks	956	379	24	5
Wireless and Television	267	47	1	—
Totals	51,071	12,091	1,499	101

COPYRIGHT

The Government Department dealing with Copyright is the *Industrial Property and Copyright Dept., Department of Trade*, 25 Southampton Bldgs., W.C.2.

Subject to the provisions of the Copyright Act, 1956, copyright subsists automatically in every original literary, dramatic, musical and artistic work and continues to subsist until the end of the period of fifty years from the end of the calendar year in which the author died and shall then expire. *No registration nor other formalities are required in order to obtain the protection of the Act.* Protection is conferred not only against reproduction but also against the public performance of a work without permission. Copyright may also subsist in sound recordings, cinematograph films (including video recordings) and television and sound broadcasts. Libraries entitled, under a provision still in force of the Copyright Act,

1911, to receive free copies of books published in the United Kingdom are the British Library, the Bodleian Library, Oxford, University Library, Cambridge, the National Library of Wales, the National Library of Scotland and Trinity College, Dublin.

As the U.K. is a party to both the Berne Copyright Convention and the Universal Copyright Convention, a work originating in this country is automatically protected in all the other countries which are members of these Conventions.

Voluntary Registration at Stationers' Hall.—Compulsory registration at Stationers' Hall was terminated by the Copyright Act of 1911, but in 1924 the Stationers' Company established a *new* Register in which Books and Fine Arts can be registered.

ANNUAL REFERENCE BOOKS

Advertiser's Annual.—East Grinstead House, East Grinstead, W. Sussex. £28·00.

Aeromodeller Annual.—14 St. James Rd., Watford. £3·25.

Aircraft Annual.—Terminal House, Shepperton, Middx. £4·95.

Annual Art Sales Index.—Pond Ho., Weybridge, Sy. (Nov.) 2v. £60·00.

Annual Register of World Events.—Longman Ho., Burnt Mill, Harlow, Essex. £40·00.

Antique Shops of Britain, Guide to the.—5 Church St., Woodbridge, Suffolk. £6·95.

Astronomical Ephemeris.—H.M. Stationery Office, Atlantic House, Holborn Viaduct, E.C.1. (Jan.) £13·00.

Automobile Year.—Bar Hill, Cambridge. (Feb.) £19·95.

B.B.C. Annual Report & Handbook.—144 Bermondsey St., S.E.1. £3·00.

Baily's Hunting Directory.—1 Lower Grosvenor Place, S.W.1. (Oct.) £11·95.

Banker's Almanac & Year Book.—East Grinstead House, East Grinstead, W. Sussex. (Feb.) £55·00.

Bar List of the U.K.—11, New Fetter Lane, E.C.4. (May) £10·00.

Benedictine Year Book.—Ampleforth Abbey, York. £0·60.

Benn's Hardware & Do-it-Yourself Directory.—Union Ho., Eridge Rd., Tunbridge Wells, Kent. £38·00.

Benn's Press Directory.—Union Ho., Eridge Rd., Tunbridge Wells, Kent. (Feb.) 2v. £45·00; £46·00.

Boat World.—39 East St., Epsom, Surrey. £6·00.

British Art & Antiques Year Book.—72 Broadwick St., W.1. £8·50.

British Books in Print.—12 Dyott St., W.C.1. £78·00.

British Clothing Industry Year Book.—1–5 Bath St., E.C.1. £21·50.

British Industry & Services in the Common Market.—East Grinstead House, East Grinstead, W. Sussex. £15·00.

British Music Year Book.—35 Bedford Row, W.C.1. £9·50.

British Paperbacks in Print.—12 Dyott St., W.C.1 (June) £25·00.

British Textile Register.—East Grinstead House, East Grinstead, W. Sussex. (Mar.) £10·50.

Brown's Nautical Almanack.—4–10 Darnley St., Glasgow, S.1. (Sept.) £16·00.

Building Societies Who's Who.—2–3 Burgon St., E.C.4. (July) £15·00.

Building Societies Year Book.—2–3 Burgon St., E.C.4. £21·20.

Buses Annual.—Terminal Ho., Shepperton, Middx. £4·95.

Caravan & Camp Sites In Britain.—Diary Ho., Borough Rd., S.E.1. £1·95.

Carpet Annual.—Union Ho., Eridge Rd., Tunbridge Wells, Kent. £30·00.

Catholic Directory.—18 Crosby Road North, Liverpool. £12·00.

Charities Digest.—501–5 Kingsland Rd., E.8. £6·25.

Chemical Industry Directory.—Sovereign Way, Tonbridge, Kent. (Nov.) £42·00.

Chemist & Druggist Directory.—Union Ho., Eridge Rd., Tunbridge Wells, Kent. £37·00.

Christies' Review of the Season.—Littlegate House, Oxford. (Dec.) £25·00.

Church of England Year Book.—Church House, Dean's Yard, Westminster, S.W.1. (Jan.) £11·50.

Church of Scotland Year Book.—121 George St., Edinburgh 2. (Apr.) £6·75.

City of London Directory.—Fairfax Ho., Colchester. £15·50, £13·50.

Commonwealth Universities Year Book.—36 Gordon Square, W.C.1. (Sept.) £56·00.

Computer Users' Year Book.—Evelyn House, 62 Oxford St., W.1. £52·95.

Concrete Year Book.—Swan House, Leatherhead, Surrey £30·00.

Consulting Engineers Who's Who & Year Book.—178–202 Gt. Portland St., W.1. £16·50.

"Containerization International" Year Book.—72 Broadwick St., W.1. (Mar.) £56·00.

Contractors and Public Works, Annual Directory of.—Beauchamp Clark Garden Centre, Willesborough, Ashford, Kent. £9·90.

Coventry Evening Telegraph Year Book and Who's Who.—Coventry Newspapers Ltd., Corporation St., Coventry. (Nov.) £6·75.

Current Law Year Book.—11 New Fetter La., E.C.4. £42·00.

"Daily Mail" Year Book.—Carmelite House, Fleet St., E.C.4. (Dec.) £3·00, £2·00.

Decorating Contractor Annual Directory.—2 Queensway, Redhill, Surrey. £5·50.

Decorative Art & Modern Interiors.—35 Red Lion Sq., W.C.1. £19·95.

Diplomatic Service List.—H.M.S.O., Atlantic House, Holborn Viaduct, E.C.1. (April) £16·95.

Directory of Directors.—East Grinstead House, East Grinstead, W. Sussex. (Apr.) £49·00.

Directory of Official Architecture & Planning.—Estover Rd., Estover, Plymouth. £21·00.

Directory of Opportunities for Graduates.—76 Dean St., W.1. £11·50.

Do-it-Yourself Annual.—Link House, Dingwall Ave., Croydon. (Jan.) 85p.

Dod's Parliamentary Companion.—Elm Cottage, Chilsham Lane, Herstmonceux, Sx. £28·00.

Education Authorities' Directory and Annual.—Derby House, Bletchingley Rd., Merstham, Surrey. (Jan.) £26·00.

Electrical & Electronic Trader Year Book.—40 Bowling Green Lane, E.C.1. £10·00.

Electrical & Electronics Trades Directory.—P.O. Box 26, Station House, Hitchin, Herts. (Feb.) £36·00.

Electrical Contractor's Yearbook.—34 Palace Court, W.2. £2·50.

Electricity Supply Handbook.—40 Bowling Green Lane, E.C.1. (Apr.) £7·00.

"Engineer" Buyers' Guide, 30 Calderwood St., S.E.18. £13·50.

Europa Year Book.—18 Bedford Square, W.C.1. 2 vols. (Apr.) £54·00, £50·00.

European Chemical Buyers' Guide.—40 Bowling Green Lane, E.C.1. £25·00.

European Glass Directory & Buyer's Guide.—2 Queensway, Redhill, Surrey. £21·50.

European Plastics Buyers' Guide.—40 Bowling Green Lane, E.C.1. £25·00.

Export Data: Exporter's Year Book.—Sovereign Way, Tonbridge, Kent. (Dec./Jan.) £20·00.

Fairplay International World Shipping Year Book.—52–54 Southwark St., S.E.1. £25·00.

Farm and Garden Equipment Guide.—40 Bowling Green Lane, E.C.1. £5·50.

Finishing Diary.—4 Local Board Rd., Watford. £6·00.

Finishing Handbook and Directory.—127 Stanstead Rd., S.E.23. £16·50.

Fire Protection Directory.—Sovereign Way, Tonbridge, Kent. (Nov.) £15·00.

"Flight" Directory of British Aviation.—40 Bowling Green Lane, E.C.1. £20·00.

Food Industry Directory.—48 Poland St., WIV 4PP. £18·00.

Frozen Foods Yearbook.—2 Queensway, Redhill, Surrey. £20·00.

Fruit Trades World Directory.—1–5 Bath St., E.C.1. (Jan.) £5·00.

Furnishing Trade, Directory to the.—Union Ho., Eridge Rd., Tunbridge Wells, Kent. (Jan.) £45·00.

Gas Directory.—Union Ho., Eridge Rd., Tunbridge Wells, Kent. (Jan.) £34·00.

Gibbons' Stamps of the World Catalogue.—391 Strand, W.C.2. (Oct.) 2v. each £11·50.

Girls' School Year Book.—35 Bedford Row, W.C.1. (May) £6·95.

Good Food Guide.—14 Buckingham St., W.C.2. £7·95.

Government & Municipal Contractors Register.—39 East St., Epsom, Surrey. (Jan.) £15·00.

Guinness Book of Records.—2 Cecil Court, London Rd., Enfield. (Oct.) £6·50.

Hambro Tax Guide.—8 Shepherdess Walk, N.1. £9·95.

Hi-fi Year Book.—40 Bowling Green Lane, E.C.1. £3·00.

Hollis Press and P.R. Annual.—Contact House, Lower Hampton Rd., Sunbury-on-Thames. (Oct.) £30·50.

Horse & Hound Hunter Chasers & Point to Pointers.—King's Reach Tower, Stamford St., S.E.1. £5·45.

Hospitals & Health Services Yearbook.—75 Portland Place, W.1. (Nov.) £24·30.

Hotel, Restaurant & Catering Supplies.—39 East St., Epsom, Sy. £15·00.

Hutchins' Priced Schedules.—33 Station Rd., Bexhill-on-Sea. £18·00, £17·00.

Insurance Directory & Yearbook.—The Butts, Half Acre, Brentford, Middx. £12·50.

International Art & Antiques Yearbook.—72 Broadwick St., W.1. (Jan.) £12·00.

International Film & Television Year Book.—142 Wardour St., W.1. (Jan./Feb.) £18·00.

International Shipping & Shipbuilding Directory.—Sovereign Way, Tonbridge, Kent. £29·00.

International Yearbook & Statesman's Who's Who.—East Grinstead House, East Grinstead, W. Sussex. (Apr.) £55·00.

Iron & Steel Year Book.—Atlantic House, Holborn Viaduct, E.C.1. £11·40.

Jane's All The World's Aircraft.—238 City Rd., E.C.1. (Oct.) £60·00.

Jane's Fighting Ships.—238 City Rd., E.C.1. (Aug.) £57·50.

Jane's Freight Containers.—238 City Rd., E.C.1. (Nov.) £60·00.

Jane's Infantry Weapons.—238 City Rd., E.C.1. (May) £57·50.

Jane's Major Companies of Europe.—238 City Rd., E.C.1. (May) £30·00.

Jane's Surface Skimmer Systems.—238 City Rd., E.C.1. (Dec.) £50·00.

Jane's Weapon Systems.—238 City Rd., E.C.1. (Dec.) £55·00.

Jane's World Railways.—238 City Rd., E.C.1. £57·50.

Jewish Year Book.—25 Furnival St., E.C.4. (Jan.) £8·95.

Kelly's Handbook to the Titled, Landed and Official Classes.—East Grinstead House, East Grinstead, W. Sussex. £18·00.

Kelly's Post Office London Directory.—East Grinstead House, East Grinstead, W. Sussex. (Jan.) £45·00.

Kempe's Engineers Year Book.—30 Calderwood St., S.E.18. £29·50.

Kemp's Directory.—1–5 Bath St., E.C.1. (Sept.) 3 v, £18·00.

Kemp's International Film & T.V. Directory.—1–5 Bath St., E.C.1. (May) £22·50.

Kemp's International Music & Recording Industry Year Book.—1–5 Bath St., E.C.1. £15·00.

Kime's International Law Directory.—170 Sloane St., S.W.1. (June) £12·00.

Law List, International.—Pitman Ho., Parker St., W.C.2. £21·00.

Laxton's Building Price Book.—East Grinstead House, East Grinstead, W. Sussex. £23·00.

Library Association Yearbook.—7 Ridgmount St., Store St., W.C.1. (May) £14·75.

Lloyd's Calendar.—Lime St., E.C.3. (Oct.) £4·50.

London Chamber of Commerce and Industry Directory.—2 Queensway, Redhill, Surrey. (Nov.) £28·00.

Macmillan & Silk Cut Nautical Almanack.—Little Essex St., W.C.2. £9·95.

Magistrates' Court Guide.—Borough Green, Sevenoaks, Kent. £11·75.

Manufacturers & Merchants Directory.—East Grinstead House, East Grinstead, W. Sussex. £50·00.

"Mechanical World" Electrical Year Book.—14 St. James Rd., Watford. £3·95.

"Mechanical World" Year Book.—14 St. James Rd., Watford. £4·50.

Medical Annual.—42–44 Triangle West, Bristol. (Sept.) £17·00.

Medical Directory.—1–3 Baxter's Place, Edinburgh. (Apr.) 2 v, £52·00.

Medical Register.—44 Hallam St., W.1. (Mar.) £32·00.

Middle East & North Africa.—18 Bedford Sq., W.C.1. (Oct.) £48·00.

"Mining" Annual Review.—P.O. Box 10, Edenbridge, Kent. £12·50.

Mining International Year Book.—Pinnacles, Harlow, Essex. (June) £44·00.

Modern Publicity.—35 Red Lion Sq., W.C.1. (Sept.) £19·50.

Motor Industry of Great Britain.—Forbes House, Halkin St., S.W.1. (Oct.) £32·50.

Municipal Yearbook & Public Services Directory, 178 Gt. Portland St., W.1. (Dec.) £40·00.

Music Guide, International.—136 Tooley St., S.E.1. £6·50.

National Trust Year Book.—18 Bedford Sq., W.C.1. £7·00.

Nautical Almanac.—H.M.S.O., Atlantic House, Holborn Viaduct, E.C.1. (Oct.) £9·50.

North Sea & Europe Offshore Yearbook.—Minster Ho., Arthur St., E.C.4. £25·00.

Off Licence News Directory.—5 Southwark St., S.E.1. £6·00.

Offshore Oil & Gas Year Book.—126 Pentonville Rd., N.1. £50·00.

Old Moore's Almanac.—Yeovil Rd., Slough, Bucks. (July) 35p.

Owen's Business Directory and Travel Guide.—22 Mount Pleasant, Alperton, Middx. (Mar.) £52·00.

Packaging Review Directory.—40 Bowling Green Lane, E.C.1. £28·00.

Paper Trade Directory of the World, Phillips'.—Union Ho., Eridge Rd., Tunbridge Wells, Kent. (Jan.) £50·00.

Pears Cyclopedia.—44 Bedford Square, W.C.1. £7·95.

Penrose Annual.—10–16 Elm St., W.C.1. (Apr.) £21·00.

Personnel & Training Databook.—120 Pentonville Rd. N.1. £17·95.

Photography Year Book.—14 St. James Rd., Watford. £12·95.

Polymers, Paint & Colour Year Book.—2 Queensway, Redhill, Surrey. £19·00.

Ports of the World.—Union Ho., Eridge Rd., Tunbridge Wells, Kent. £59·00.

Printing Industries Annual.—11 Bedford Row, W.C.1. £20·00.

Printing Trades Directory.—Union Ho., Eridge Rd., Tunbridge Wells, Kent. £44·00.

Public and Preparatory Schools Year Book.—35 Bedford Row, W.C.1. (May) £12·95; £9·95.

Publishing, Directory of.—35 Red Lion Square, W.C.1. (Oct.) £16·95.

R.A.C. Continental Handbook.—P.O. Box 100, RAC House, Lansdowne Rd., Croydon. (Mar.) £9·00.

R.A.C. Guide & Handbook.—P.O. Box 100, RAC House, Lansdowne Rd., Croydon. (Apr.) £4·50.

R.U.S.I. & Brassey's Defence Year Book.—Headington Hill Hall, Oxford. £25·00.

Raceform Up-to-date Form Book: Flat Racing.—2 York Rd., S.W.11. (Dec.) £10·00.

Raceform Up-to-date Form Book: National Hunt.—Thomson Ho., Withy Grove, Manchester. (Aug.) £10·00.

Railway Directory & Year Book.—40 Bowling Green Lane, E.C.1. (Dec.) £22·00.

Reed's Nautical Almanac.—36–37 Cock Lane, E.C.1. (Oct.) £10·95.

Register of Defunct & Other Companies.—East Grinstead House, East Grinstead, W. Sussex. £5·00.

RIBA Directory of Practices.—Royal Institute of British Architects, 35–37 Moreland St., E.C.1. (Oct.) £9·00.

Royal Society Year Book.—6 Carlton Ho. Terr., S.W.1. (Feb.) £9·00.

Ruff's Guide to the Turf.—67 Shoe Lane, E.C.4. (Dec.) £20·00.

Salvation Army Year Book.—117–121 Judd St., W.C.1. (Nov.) £1·50, £0·95.

Scottish Current Law Year Book.—St. Giles St., Edinburgh. £21·00.

Scottish Law Directory.—34–36 North Frederick St., Glasgow. £15·00.

Screen World.—Victoria Works, Edgware Rd., N.W.2. £12·95.

Sell's Aviation Europe.—39 East St., Epsom, Surrey. £25·00.

Sell's British Exporters.—39 East St., Epsom, Surrey. £15·00.

Sell's Building Index.—39 East St., Epsom, Surrey. £20·00.

Sell's Directory of Products and Services.—39 East St., Epsom, Surrey. (July) £24·00.

Sell's Health Service Buyers Guide.—39 East St., Epsom, Surrey. £15·00.

Sheet Metal Industries Year Book.—2 Queensway, Redhill, Surrey. £21·50.

Shipowners, Shipbuilders & Marine Engineers, Directory of.—40 Bowling Green Lane, E.C.1. £38·00.

Specification.—9–13 Queen Anne's Gate, S.W.1. (May) 5v. £45·00.

Spon's Architects' & Builders' Price Book.—11 New Fetter La., E.C.4. (Oct.) £20·00.

Spon's Mechanical & Electrical Services Prices Book.—11 New Fetter La., E.C.4. £20·00.

Statesman's Yearbook.—Little Essex St., W.C.2. (Aug.) £20·00.

Stock Exchange Official Year Book.—Houndmills Estate, Basingstoke, Hants. £70·00.

Stone's Justices' Manual.—Borough Green, Sevenoaks, Kent. 3v. (May) £72·50.

Stores, Shops, Supermarkets Retail Directory.—48 Poland St., W.1. £48·00.

T.V. & Radio: Guide to Independent Television.—247 Tottenham Court Rd., W.1. £3·90.

Tanker Register.—52 Bishopgate, E.C.2. (May) £70·00.

Theatre Directory, British.—P.O. Box 64, Eastbourne, Sx. £13·00.

Timber Trades Directory.—Sovereign Way, Tonbridge, Kent. £25·00.

Trades Register of London.—1–5 Bath St., E.C.1. (Jan.) £4·50.

Travel Trade Directory.—30 Calderwood St., S.E.18. (July) £12·50.

U.K. Kompass Register of British Industry & Commerce.—East Grinstead House, East Grinstead, W. Sussex. £90·00.

Unit Trust Year Book.—Greystoke Pl., Fetter Lane, E.C.4. (Mar.) £13·50.

United Reformed Church Year Book.—86 Tavistock Pl., W.C.1. (Sept.) £6·00.

Veterinary Annual.—42–44 Triangle West, Bristol. (Dec.) £18·00.

"Watchmaker, Jeweller & Silversmith" Directory.—40 Bowling Green Lane, E.C.1. £5·00.

Water Services Year Book.—2 Queensway, Redhill, Surrey. (Oct.) £21·50.

Which Degree?—53 Frith St., W.1. 5v. £34·75.

Whitaker's Almanack.—12 Dyott St., W.C.1. (Nov.) £18·50, £11·95, £5·95.

Whitaker's Publishers in the United Kingdom and their Addresses.—12 Dyott St., W.C.1. (Mar.) £2·80.

Who Owns Whom?—6–8 Bonhill St., E.C.2. 2v. £79·00.

Who's Who.—35 Bedford Row, W.C.1. (Apr.) £45·00.

Who's Who, International.—18 Bedford Sq., W.C.1. (Sept.) £60·00.

Willing's Press Guide.—East Grinstead House, East Grinstead, W. Sussex. (Feb.) £35·00.

Wine & Spirit Trade International Year Book.—76 Dean St., W.1. £18·50.

Wisden Cricketers' Almanack.—8 Shepherdess Walk, N.1. £11·95; £9·95.

World Hotel Directory.—Pinnacles, Harlow, Essex. £26·00.

World Insurance Year Book.—Pinnacles. Harlow, Essex. £43·00.

World of Learning.—18 Bedford Square, W.C.1. (Jan.) 2v. £72·00.

World Shipping Year Book.—Minster House, Arthur St., E.C.4. £25·00.

Writers' & Artists' Year Book.—35 Bedford Row, W.C.1. (Jan.) £4·50.

Year Book of World Affairs.—11 New Fetter Lane, E.C.4. £19·00.

THE PRESS COUNCIL
1 Salisbury Square, EC4Y 8AE
[01–353 1248]

In April, 1947, a Royal Commission was appointed to enquire into the control, management and ownership, etc., of the Press and news agencies and to make recommendations thereon. The Commission, in its report of June, 1949, recommended *inter alia* that a voluntary Press Council be formed.

A constitution ultimately set up provided for the establishment of such a council on July 1, 1953. This constitution was materially amended in 1963 by the introduction of an independent chairman and up to 20 per cent lay membership. In 1973, the Council was increased to 30 (excluding the Chairman) of whom one-third were lay members. Following a recommendation of the third Royal Commission on the Press made in 1977, the size of the Council was increased in 1978 to 36 (excluding the Chairman) of which half are press members and half non-press members. The objects of the Council are (1) to preserve the established freedom of the British Press; (2) to maintain the character of the British Press in accordance with the highest professional and commercial standards; (3) to consider complaints about the conduct of the Press or the conduct of persons and organizations towards the Press; to deal with these complaints in whatever manner might seem practical and appropriate and record resultant action; (4) to keep under review developments likely to restrict the supply of information of public interest

and importance; (5) to report publicly on developments that may tend towards greater concentration or monopoly in the Press (including changes in ownership, control and growth of Press undertakings) and to publish statistical information relating thereto; (6) to make representations on appropriate occasions to the Government, organs of the United Nations and Press organizations abroad; and (7) to publish periodical reports recording the Council's work and to review, from time to time, developments in the Press and the factors affecting them.

The constitution of the Council provides for editorial and managerial nominees of The Newspaper Publishers Association Ltd. (3), The Newspaper Society (3), The Periodical Publishers Association Ltd. (2), The Scottish Daily Newspaper Society (1), Scottish Newspaper Proprietors' Association (1), The Guild of British Newspaper Editors (2), The National Union of Journalists (4), The Institute of Journalists (2) plus (18) lay members appointed by the Press Council Appointments Commission. In addition each constituent body nominates one official as a non-voting member.

Chairman, Rt. Hon. Prof. Sir Zelman Cowen, G.C.M.G., G.C.V.O., Q.C.
Director, K. Morgan, O.B.E.

PRINCIPAL NEWSPAPERS

DAILY NEWSPAPERS

National

Daily Express, 121–128 Fleet St., E.C.4.
Daily Mail, Carmelite House, E.C.4.
Daily Mirror, 33 Holborn, E.C.1.
Daily Star, Great Ancoats Street, Manchester.
Daily Telegraph, 135 Fleet St., E.C.4.
Financial Times, 10 Cannon St., E.C.4.
The Guardian, 119 Farringdon Rd., E.C.1.
Morning Advertiser, 57 Effra Rd., S.W.2.
Morning Star, 75 Farringdon Rd., E.C.1.
Sporting Life, 9 New Fetter Lane, E.C.4.
The Sun, 30 Bouverie St., E.C.4.
The Standard, 121 Fleet St., E.C.4.
The Times, Gray's Inn Road, W.C.1.

ABERDEEN—Press and Journal and Evening Express, Lang Stracht, Mastrick.
BARROW—North-Western Evening Mail, Abbey Road.
BATH—Bath and West Evening Chronicle, 33–34 Westgate Street.
BELFAST—Belfast Telegraph, 124 Royal Avenue; Irish News, 113–117 Donegall Street.
BIRMINGHAM—Birmingham Post, Colmore Circus; Evening Mail, Colmore Circus.
BLACKBURN—Lancs. Evening Telegraph, New Telegraph House.
BLACKPOOL—W. Lancs. Ev. Gazette, Victoria Street.
BOLTON—Evening News, Mealhouse Lane.
BOURNEMOUTH—Evening Echo, Richmond Hill.
BRADFORD—Telegraph and Argus, Hall Ings.
BRIGHTON—Evening Argus, North Road.
BRISTOL—Evening Post, Temple Way, Old Market; Western Daily Press, Temple Way, Old Market.
BURNLEY—Evening Star, St. James's Street.
BURTON—Burton Daily Mail, 65–68 High Street.
CAMBRIDGE—Cambridge Evening News, 51 Newmarket Road.
CARDIFF—South Wales Echo, Thomson House; Western Mail, Thomson House.
CARLISLE—Cumberland Evening News, Newspaper House, Dalston Road.
CHELTENHAM—Gloucestershire Echo, 1 Clarence Parade.
CLEVELAND—Evening Gazette, Borough Road, Middlesbrough.
COLCHESTER—Evening Gazette, Culver Street West; Lloyd's List, Sheepen Place.
COVENTRY—Coventry Evening Telegraph, Corporation Street.
DARLINGTON—Northern Echo, Priestgate; Evening Despatch, Priestgate.
DERBY—Derby Evening Telegraph, Northcliffe House.
DONCASTER—Doncaster Evening Post, 10 North Bridge Road.
DUNDEE—Courier and Advertiser, 7 Bank Street; Evening Telegraph and Post, 7 Bank Street.
EDINBURGH—Scotsman, 20 North Bridge; Evening News, 20 North Bridge.
EXETER—Express and Echo, 160 Sidwell Street.
GLASGOW—Glasgow Herald, 195 Albion Street; Daily Record, Anderston Quay; Evening Times, 195 Albion Street.
GLOUCESTER—Citizen, St. John's Lane.

GREENOCK—Evening Telegraph, 2 Crawfurd Street.
GRIMSBY—Evening Telegraph, 80 Cleethorpes Road.
GUERNSEY—Guernsey Evening Press and Star, Braye Road, Vale.
HALIFAX—Halifax Evening Courier, P.O. Box 19, King Cross Street.
HEREFORD—Evening News, Berrow's House, Bath Street.
HUDDERSFIELD—Huddersfield Daily Examiner, Ramsden Street.
HULL—Daily Mail, Jameson Street.
IPSWICH—East Anglian Daily Times, 30 Lower Brook Street.
JERSEY—Evening Post, P.O. Box 582, Five Oaks, St. Saviour.
KETTERING—Northants Evening Telegraph, Northfield Avenue.
LEAMINGTON SPA—Leamington & District Morning News, Tachbrook Road.
LEEDS—Yorkshire Evening Post, Wellington Street; Yorkshire Post, Wellington Street.
LEICESTER—Leicester Mercury, St. George Street.
LINCOLN—Lincolnshire Echo, St. Benedict Square.
LIVERPOOL—Liverpool Daily Post, P.O. Box 48, Old Hall Street; Liverpool Echo, P.O. Box 48, Old Hall Street; Journal of Commerce, Fowler Buildings, 7 Victoria Street.
MAIDSTONE—Kent Evening Post, Messenger House, New Hythe Lane, Larkfield.
MANCHESTER—Manchester Evening News, 164 Deansgate.
NEWCASTLE—Evening Chronicle, Thomson House, Groat Market; Journal, Thomson House, Groat Market.
NEWPORT—South Wales Argus, Cardiff Road, Maesglas.
NORTHAMPTON—Chronicle and Echo (Northampton), Upper Mounts.
NORWICH—Eastern Daily Press, Prospect House, Rouen Road; Eastern Evening News, Prospect House, Rouen Road.
NOTTINGHAM—Evening Post, P.O. Box 99.
NUNEATON—Nuneaton Evening Tribune, Watling House, Whitacre Road.
OLDHAM—Oldham Evening Chronicle, Union Street.
OXFORD—Oxford Mail, Osney Mead.
PAISLEY—Paisley Daily Express, Express Buildings, 20 New Street.
PETERBOROUGH—Peterborough Evening Telegraph, Oundle Road, Woodston.
PLYMOUTH—Western Morning News, Leicester Harmsworth House, 65 New George Street; Western Evening Herald, Leicester Harmsworth House, 65 New George Street.
PORTSMOUTH—The News, The News Centre, Hilsea.
PRESTON—Lancashire Evening Post, 127 Fishergate.
READING—Evening Post, 8 Tessa Road.
SCARBOROUGH—Scarborough Evening News, Aberdeen Walk.
SCUNTHORPE—Scunthorpe Evening Telegraph, Telegraph House, Doncaster Road.
SHEFFIELD—Morning Telegraph, York Street; Star, York Street.
SOUTH SHIELDS—Shields Gazette and Shipping Telegraph, Chapter Row.
SOUTHAMPTON—Southern Evening Echo, Above Bar.
STOKE-ON-TRENT—Evening Sentinel, Northcliffe House, Hanley.
SUNDERLAND—Echo, Pennywell Industrial Estate.
SWANSEA—South Wales Evening Post, Adelaide Street.
SWINDON—Evening Advertiser, Newspaper House, 100 Victoria Road.
TELFORD—Shropshire Star, Ketley.

TORQUAY—Herald Express, Barton Hill Road.
WEYMOUTH—Dorset Evening Echo, 57 St. Thomas Street.
WOLVERHAMPTON—Express and Star, 50 Queen Street.
WORCESTER—Evening News, Berrow's House.
YORK—Yorkshire Evening Press, 15 Coney Street.

SUNDAY NEWSPAPERS

Mail on Sunday—Carmelite House, E.C.4.

News of the World—30 Bouverie St., E.C.4.

Observer—8 St. Andrews Hill, E.C.4.

Sunday Express—121–128 Fleet St., E.C.4.

Sunday Mail—Anderston Quay, Glasgow.

Sunday Mercury—Colmore Circus, Birmingham.

Sunday Mirror—33 Holborn, E.C.1.

Sunday News—51 Donegall St., Belfast.

Sunday People—33 Holborn, E.C.1.

Sunday Post—144 Port Dundas Road, Glasgow.

Sunday Sun—Groat Market, Newcastle-on-Tyne.

Sunday Telegraph—135 Fleet St., E.C.4.

Sunday Times—200 Gray's Inn Rd., W.C.1.

RELIGIOUS PAPERS

[*W.* = Weekly; *M.* = Monthly; *Q.* = Quarterly]

Baptist Times—4 Southampton Row, W.C. 1. *W.*

British Weekly and Christian Record—146 Queen Victoria St., E.C.4. *W.*

Catholic Herald—Lambs Passage, Bunhill Row, E.C.1. *W.*

Challenge, the Good News Paper—Revenue Buildings, Chapel Rd., Worthing, Sussex. *M.*

Christian Herald—27 Chapel Road, Worthing, Sussex. *W.*

Church of England Newspaper—146 Queen Victoria St., E.C.4. *W.*

Church of Ireland Gazette—48 Bachelor's Walk, Lisburn, co. Antrim. *W.*

Church Times—7 Portugal St., W.C.2. *W.*

English Churchman—P.O. Box 217, S.E.5. *Alt. W.*

Friend—Drayton House, Gordon St., W.C.1. *W.*

Inquirer—1–6 Essex St., W.C.2. *Alt. W.*

Jewish Chronicle—25 Furnival St., E.C.4. *W.*

Jewish Gazette—18 Cheetham Parade, Manchester 8. *W.*

Jewish Telegraph—11 Park Hill, Bury Old Road, Prestwich, Manchester 25. *W.*

Life and Work—121 George St., Edinburgh 2. *M.*

Methodist Recorder—176 Fleet St., E.C.4. *W.*

Tablet—48 Great Peter St., S.W.1. *W.*

Today—130 City Road, E.C.1. *M.*

Universe—33–39 Bowling Green Lane, E.C.1. *W.*

War Cry—101 Queen Victoria St., E.C.4. *W.*

PERIODICALS, MAGAZINES AND REVIEWS

[*W.* = Weekly; *M.* = Monthly; *Q.* = Quarterly]

Amateur Gardening—Westover House, West Quay Road, Poole, Dorset. *W.*

Amateur Photographer—1 Throwley Way, Sutton, Surrey. *W.*

Angler's Mail—King's Reach Tower, Stamford St., S.E.1. *W.*

Antiquaries' Journal—Ass. Sec., Society of Antiquaries, Burlington House, Piccadilly, W.1. *Twice a year.*

Antique Collector—72 Broadwick St., W.1. *M.*

Apollo—22 Davies Street, W.1. *M.*

Art and Artists—445 Brighton Road, Croydon, Surrey. *M.*

Autocar— Quadrant House, Sutton, Surrey. *W.*

Birds and Country Magazine—79 Surbiton Hill Park, Surbiton, Surrey. *Twice a year.*

Boxing News—30–34 Langham St., W.1. *W.*

Brain—Oxford U. Press, Walton Street, Oxford. *Q.*

Brides and Setting-up Home—Vogue House, Hanover Sq., W.1. *Alt. M.*

British Birds—Fountains, Park Lane, Bedford. *M.*

British Book News—The British Council, 65 Davies St., W.1. *M.*

Bunty—185 Fleet St., E.C.4. *W.*

Burlington Mag.—10–16 Elm St., W.C.1. *M.*

Buses—Terminal House, Shepperton. *M.*

Cage and Aviary Birds—1 Throwley Way, Sutton, Surrey. *W.*

Caravan—Link House, Dingwall Ave., Croydon, Surrey. *M.*

Caravanning Monthly—Link House, Dingwall Ave., Croydon, Surrey.

Classical Quarterly—Oxford U. Press, Walton St., Oxford. *Twice a Year.*

Classical Review—Oxford U. Press, Walton St., Oxford. *Twice a Year.*

Coal News—Hobart House, Grosvenor Place, S.W.1. *M.*

Coin and Medal News—Wheel House, 5 Station Road, Liphook, Hants. *M.*

Coin Monthly—Sovereign House, Brentwood, Essex.

Connoisseur—72 Broadwick St., W.1. *M.*

Contemporary Review— 61 Carey St., W.C.2. *M.*

Country Life—King's Reach Tower, Stamford St., S.E.1. *W.*

Countryman—Sheep Street, Burford, Oxford. *Q.*

Cricketer International—29 Cavendish Road, Redhill, Surrey. *M.*

Criminologist—P.O. Box 18, Bognor Regis, Sussex. *Q.*

Cycling—1 Throwley Way, Sutton, Surrey. *W.*

Dalton's Weekly—60 Windsor Ave., S.W.19. *W.*

Dancing Times—45–47 Clerkenwell Green, E.C.1. *M.*

Dog World—Clergy House., Ashford, Kent. *W.*

Do It Yourself—Link House, Dingwall Ave, Croydon. *M.*

Drama—9 Fitzroy Sq., W.1. *Q.*

Drive & Trail—Fanum House, Basingstoke, Hants. *M.*

Economic Journal—Cambridge U. Press, Shaftesbury Road, Cambridge. *Q.*

Economica—Lond. Sch. of Economics, Houghton St., W.C.2. *Q.*

Economist, The—25 St. James's St., S.W.1. *W.*

Edinburgh Gazette (*Official*)—Exchequer Office, 13A Castle Street, Edinburgh 2. *Twice a week.*

Encounter—59 St. Martin's Lane, W.C.2. *M.*

English Historical Review—Westgate House, Burnt Mill, Harlow, Essex. *Q.*

Exchange and Mart—Link House, West Street, Poole, Dorset. *W.*

Family Circle—Elm House, Elm St., W.C.1. *M.*

Field, The—Carmelite House, E.C.4. *W.*

Freethinker, The—702 Holloway Rd., N.19. *M.*

Garden News—Bushfield House, Orton Centre, Peterborough. *W.*

Gardeners' Chronicle—38–42 Hampton Rd., Teddington, Middx. *W.*

Geographical Journal—Royal Geographical Society, Kensington Gore, S.W.7. *Three times a year.*

Geographical Magazine—23–27 Tudor Street, E.C.4. *M.*

Golf Illustrated—Carmelite House, Carmelite St., E.C.4. *W.*

Golf Monthly—1 Park Circus, Glasgow.

Good Housekeeping—72 Broadwick St., W.1. *M.*

Good Motoring—352 Lewisham High Street, S.E.13. *Alt. M.*

Gramophone—177–179 Kenton Road, Harrow, Mddx. *M.*

Greece and Rome—Oxford U. Press, Walton St., Oxford. *Twice a year.*

Guiding—17–19 Buckingham Palace Rd., S.W.1. *M.*

Harper's Queen—72 Broadwick St., W.1. *M.*

Health & Strength—30 Craven Street, Strand, W.C.1. *M.*

Health Education Journal—78 New Oxford St., W.C.1. *Q.*

History—59A Kennington Park Road, S.E.11. *Three times a year.*

Homefinder—10 East Road, N.1. *M.*

Homes and Gardens—King's Reach Tower, Stamford Street, S.E.1. *M.*

Homoeopathy—27A Devonshire St., W.1. *Alt. M.*

Honey—King's Reach Tower, Stamford Street, S.E.1. *M.*

Horse and Hound—King's Reach Tower, Stamford Street, S.E.1. *W.*

House and Garden—Vogue House, Hanover Sq., W.1. *Ten times a year.*

Ideal Home—King's Reach Tower, Stamford Street, S.E.1. *M.*

Illustrated London News—Elm House, Elm Street, W.C.1. *M.*

In Britain—B.T.A., 4 Bromells Rd., S.W.4. *M.*

International Affairs—Chatham House, St. James's Square, S.W.1. *Q.*

Jazz Journal International—4 Great Queen Street, W.C.2. *M.*

Kennel Gazette—1 Clarges St., Piccadilly, W.1. *M.*

Labour Research— 78 Blackfriars Rd., S.E.1. *M.*

Lady—39–40 Bedford St., W.C.2. *W.*

Land and Liberty—177 Vauxhall Bridge Rd., S.W.1. *Alt. M.*

Liberal News—1 Whitehall Place, S.W.1. *W.*

Light (*Psychic*)—16 Queensbury Place, S.W.7. *Q.*

Listener, The—35 Marylebone High St., W.1. *W.*

Living—Elm House, Elm St., W.C.1. *M.*

Local Government Chronicle—11–12 Bury St., E.C.3. *W.*

London Gazette (*Official*)—Atlantic House, Holborn Viaduct, E.C.1. *Five times a week.*

London Magazine—30 Thurloe Place, S.W.7. *M.*

London Weekly Diary of Social Events—26 D'Arblay Street, W.1.

Mayfair—95A Chancery Lane, W.C.2. *M.*

Melody Maker—King's Reach Tower, Stamford St., S.E.1. *W.*

Meteorological Magazine—P.O. Box 569, S.E.11. *M.*

Mind—108 Cowley Rd., Oxford. *Q.*

Model Boats—Wolsey House, Hemel Hempstead, Herts. *M.*

Model Railway Constructor—Terminal House, Shepperton. *M.*

Model Railways—Wolsey House, Hemel Hempstead, Herts. *M.*

Modern Languages—24A Highbury Grove, N.5. *Q.*

Month—114 Mount St., W.1. *M.*

Monthly Digest of Statistics (*Official*)—P.O. Box 569, S.E.1.

Mother—Commonwealth House, 1–19 New Oxford St., W.C.1. *M.*

Motor Cycle News—38 High St., Kettering. *W.*

Movie Maker—Wolsey House, Hemel Hempstead, Herts. *M.*

Municipal Review—36 Old Queen St., Westminster, S.W.1. *Ten times a year.*

Museums Bulletin—34 Bloomsbury Way, W.C.1. *M.*

Music and Letters—Oxford U. Press, Walton St., Oxford. *Q.*

My Weekly—185 Fleet St., E.C.4.

Nature—4 Little Essex St., W.C.2. *W.*

Nautical Magazine—4–10 Darnley Street, Glasgow. *M.*

Navy International—Hunters Moon, Hogspudding Lane, Newdigate, Dorking, Surrey. *M.*

New Musical Express—5–7 Carnaby St., W.1. *W.*

New Scientist—1–19 New Oxford St., W.C.1. *W.*

New Society—Commonwealth House, 1–19 New Oxford Street, W.C.1. *W.*

New Statesman—14–16 Farringdon Lane, E.C.1. *W.*

19—King's Reach Tower, Stamford Street, S.E.1. *M.*

Notes and Queries—Oxford U. Press, Walton St., Oxford. *Q.*

Nursery World—Wells House, Wells Street, W.1. *W.*

Opera—6 Woodland Rise, N.10. *M.*

Our Dogs—5 Oxford Road, Station Approach, Manchester. *W.*

Oxford—8 Wellington Square, Oxford. *Twice a year.*

Parade—Gadoline Hse., Whyteleafe, Surrey. *M.*

Parliamentary Debates (Lords) (Hansard)—P.O. Box 569, S.E.1. *Daily during Session.*

Parliamentary Debates (Commons) (Hansard)—P.O. Box 569, S.E.1. *Daily during Session.*

Penthouse—2 Bramber Rd., W.14. *M.*

People's Friend—7 Bank Street, Dundee. *W.*

Philosophy—Cambridge U. Press, Shaftesbury Road, Cambridge. *Q.*

Pins and Needles—20 Soho Square, W.1. *M.*

Playhour—King's Reach Tower, Stamford Street, S.E.1. *W.*

Poetry Review—21 Earls Court Square, S.W.5. *Q.*

Political Quarterly, The—Elm House, 10–16 Elm Street, W.C.1.

Pony—104 Ash Road, Sutton, Surrey. *M.*

Popular Gardening—King's Reach Tower, Stamford Street, S.E.1. *W.*

Poultry World—1 Throwley Way, Sutton, Surrey. *W.*

Practical Boat Owner—Westover House, West Quay Rd., Poole, Dorset. *M.*

Practical Camper—38–42 Hampton Rd., Teddington, Middx. *M.*

Practical Caravan—38–42 Hampton Rd., Teddington, Middx. *M.*

Practical Gardening—Bushfield House, Orton Centre, Peterborough. *M.*

Practical Householder—Westover House, West Quay Rd., Poole, Dorset. *M.*

Progress (*Braille Type*)—338–346 Goswell Rd., E.C.1. *M.*

Punch—23–27 Tudor St., E.C.4. *W.*

Racing Calendar—Sanders Road, Wellingborough, Northants. *W.*

Radio Control Models and Electronics—Wolsey House, Hemel Hempstead, Herts. *M.*

Radio Times—35 Marylebone High St., W.1. *W.*

Railway Magazine—Quadrant House, Sutton, Surrey. *M.*

Railway World—Terminal House, Shepperton. *M.*

Readers Digest—25 Berkeley Sq., W.1. *M.*

Red Star Weekly—185 Fleet St., E.C.4.

Riding—King's Reach Tower, Stamford Street, S.E.1. *M.*

Scots Independent—51 Cowane St., Stirling. *M.*

Scottish Field—12 York St., Glasgow. *M.*

Scouting—Baden Powell House, Queen's Gate, S.W.7. *M.*

Seafarer—202 Lambeth Rd., S.E.1. *Q.*

She—72 Broadwick St., W.1. *M.*

Shoot!—King's Reach Tower, Stamford Street, S.E.1. *W.*

Shooting Times and Country Magazine—10 Sheet St., Windsor. *W.*

Sociological Review—University of Keele, Staffs. *Q.*

Spectator—56 Doughty Street, W.C.1. *W.*

Strad—7 Lower James St., W.1. *M.*

Studio International—25 Denmark St., W.C.2. *Q.*

Tatler—Vogue House, Hanover Square. W.1. *M.*

Tennis World—2–4 Wendell Rd., W.12. *Ten times a year.*

35 mm Photography—Wolsey House, Hemel Hempstead, Herts. *M.*

This England—Alma House, Rodney Road, Cheltenham, Glos. *Q.*

Time (British Isles)—Time and Life Bldg., New Bond St., W.1. *W.*

Times Educational Suppl't.—Gray's Inn Rd., W.C.1. *W.*

Times Higher Education Suppl't.—Gray's Inn Rd., W.C.1. *W.*

Times Literary Suppl't.—Gray's Inn Rd., W.C.1. *W.*

Tribune—308 Grays Inn Rd., W.C.1. *W.*

Trout and Salmon—Bretton Court, Bretton, Peterborough. *M.*

True Romances—12–18 Paul St., E.C.2. *M.*

True Story Magazine—12–18 Paul Street, E.C.2. *M.*

TV Times—247 Tottenham Court Rd., W.1. *W.*

Vacher's Parliamentary Companion—Leeder House, Erskine Road, N.W.3. *Q.*

Vogue—Vogue House, Hanover Square, W.1. *Sixteen times a year.*

Weather—James Glaisher House, Grenville Place, Bracknell, Berks. *M.*

Weekend—Carmelite House, E.C.4. *W.*

Welsh Nation—51 Cathedral Rd., Caerdydd, Cardiff. *M.*

West Africa—53 Holborn Viaduct, E.C.1. *W.*

Woman—King's Reach Tower, Stamford Street, S.E.1. *W.*

Woman and Home—King's Reach Tower, Stamford Street, S.E.1. *M.*

Woman's Journal—King's Reach Tower, Stamford Street, S.E.1. *M.*

Woman's Own—King's Reach Tower, Stamford Street, S.E.1. *W.*

Woman's Realm—King's Reach Tower, Stamford Street, S.E.1. *W.*

Woman's Weekly—King's Reach Tower, Stamford Street, S.E.1.

World Today—Chatham House, St. James's Sq., S.W.1. *M.*

Yachting Monthly—King's Reach Tower, Stamford Street, S.E.1.

Yachting World—Quadrant House, Sutton, Surrey. *M.*

Yachts and Yachting—196 Eastern Esplanade, Southend-on-Sea. *Alt. W.*

TRADE, PROFESSIONAL AND BUSINESS JOURNALS

[*W.* = Weekly; *M.* = Monthly; *Q.* = Quarterly]

Accountancy—56–66 Goswell Rd., E.C.1. *M.*

Accountant—151 Strand, W.C.2. *W.*

Accountants' Magazine—27 Queen St., Edinburgh. *M.*

Achievement—145 High St., Sevenoaks, Kent. *Eight times a year.*

Agricultural Machinery Journal—1 Throwley Way, Sutton, Surrey. *M.*

Anti-Corrosion—127 Stanstead Rd., S.E.23. *M.*

Antique Dealer and Collectors Guide—Kings Reach Tower, Stamford Street, S.E.1. *M.*

Architects' Journal—9 Queen Anne's Gate, S.W.1. *W.*

Architectural Review—9 Queen Anne's Gate, S.W.1. *M.*

Artist—102 High St., Tenterden. *M.*

Bakers' Review—886 High Rd., Finchley, N.12. *M.*

Banker—Greystoke Place, Fetter Lane, E.C.4. *M.*

Banking World—Maxwell House, 74 Worship St., E.C.2. *M.*

Bookseller—12 Dyott St., W.C.1. *W.*

Brewers' Guardian—178–202 Great Portland Street, W.1. *M.*

British Baker—Maclaren House, 19 Scarbrook Rd., Croydon. *W.*

British Business—Dept. of Industry, Millbank Tower, S.W.1. *W.*

British Clothing Manufacturer—20 Soho Sq., W.1. *Q.*

British Dental Journal—64 Wimpole St., W.1. *Twice a month.*

British Food Journal—Peterson House, Northbank, Droitwich, Worcs. *Alt. M.*

British Jeweller and Watch Buyer—27 Frederick St., Birmingham. *M.*

British Journal for the Philosophy of Science—Farmers Hall, Aberdeen. *Q.*

British Journal of Photography—28 Great James Street, W.C.1. *W.*

British Medical Journal—B.M.A. House, Tavistock Square, W.C.1. *W.*

British Printer—76 Oxford St., W.1. *M.*

British Steelmaker—5 Pond St., Hampstead, N.W.3. *Alt. M.*

British Sugar Beet Review—P.O. Box 26, Oundle Rd., Peterborough. *Q.*

British Tax Review—11 New Fetter Lane, E.C.4. *Alt. M.*

British Veterinary Journal—1 Vincent Square, S.W.1. *Alt. M.*

Brushmaking International—Penn House, Penn Place, Rickmansworth. *Alt. M.*

Builders' and Timber Merchant—Sovereign Way, Tonbridge, Kent. *M.*

Building—1–3 Pemberton Row, E.C.4. *W.*

Cabinet Maker and Retail Furnisher—Sovereign Way, Tonbridge, Kent. *W.*

Campaign—22 Lancaster Gate, W.2. *W.*

Carpet and Floorcoverings Review—Sovereign Way, Tonbridge, Kent. *Alt. W.*

Caterer and Hotelkeeper—Quadrant House, Sutton, Surrey. *W.*

Catering and Hotel Management—Link House, Dingwall Ave., Croydon. *M.*

Catering Times—Quadrant House, Sutton, Surrey. *W.*

Chemist and Druggist—Sovereign Way, Tonbridge, Kent. *W.*

Chemistry and Industry—14–15 Belgrave Sq., S.W.1. *Twice a month.*

Chemistry in Britain—Burlington House, W.1. *M.*

Child Education—Westfield Road, Southam, Warks. *M.*

Chiropodist—8 Wimpole St., W.1. *M.*

Civil Engineering and Public Works Review—Morgan Grampian House, Calderwood St., S.E.18. *M.*

Club Mirror—18 Queens Rd., Brighton. *M.*

Colliery Guardian—Queensway House, Redhill, Surrey. *M.*

Commerce International—Albany House, Hirst Street, Birmingham. *M.*

Commercial Motor—The Quadrant, Sutton, Surrey. *W.*

Computer Survey—33–35 Bowling Green Lane, E.C.1. *Alt. M.*

Concrete—Swan House, 32 Swan Court, Leatherhead, Surrey. *M.*

Containerisation International—72 Broadwick St., W.1. *M.*

Contract Journal—1 Throwley Way, Sutton, Surrey. *W.*

Control and Instrumentation—Morgan Grampian House, Calderwood St., S.E.18. *M.*

Cordage, Canvas and Jute World—177 Hagden Lane, Watford, Herts. *Yearly.*

C.S.E. News (Camping and Sports Equipment)—4 Spring St., W.2. *M.*

Dairy Farmer—Wharfedale Rd., Ipswich. *M.*

Dairy Industries International—33–35 Bowling Green Lane, E.C.1. *M.*

Design—The Design Council, 28 Haymarket, S.W.1. *M.*

Dock and Harbour Authority—19 Harcourt St., W.1. *M.*

Drapers Record—20 Soho Sq., W.1. *W.*

Education—Westgate House, Harlow, Essex. *W.*

Education Equipment—Sovereign Way, Tonbridge, Kent. *M.*

Electrical & Electronic Trader—Quadrant House, Sutton, Surrey. *W.*

Electrical and Radio Trading—Quadrant House, Sutton, Surrey. *W.*

Electrical Review—Quadrant House, Sutton, Surrey. *W.*

Electrical Times—Quadrant House, Sutton, Surrey. *W.*

Electronic Engineering—Morgan Grampian House, Calderwood St., S.E.18. *M.*

Electronics Weekly—Quadrant House, Sutton, Surrey.

Embroidery—161 Kenton Road, Kenton, Harrow. *Q.*

Engineer—Morgan Grampian House, Calderwood St., S.E.18. *W.*

Engineering—28 Haymarket, S.W.1. *M.*

Engineer's Digest—Swan House, 32 Swan Court, Leatherhead, Surrey. *M.*

Estates Gazette—151 Wardour St., W.1. *W.*

Export News—The International Export Association, Bourne, Lincs. *Q.*

Fairplay International Shipping Weekly—52–54 Southwark St., S.E.1.

Farmers Weekly—1 Throwley Way, Sutton, Surrey.

Fire (British Fire Service)—Queensway House, Redhill, Surrey. *M.*

Fire Protection—Stanley House, 9 West Street, Epsom, Surrey. *M.*

Fish Friers Review—289 Dewsbury Road, Leeds. *M.*

Fish Trader—2 Queensway, Redhill, Surrey. *W.*

Flight International—Quadrant House, Sutton, Surrey. *W.*

Food Trade Review—29 High Street, Orpington, Kent. *M.*

Forestry and British Timber—Sovereign Way, Tonbridge, Kent. *M.*

Foundry Trade Journal—Queensway House, Redhill, Surrey. *Alt. W.*

Frozen Foods—Queensway House, Redhill, Surrey. *M.*

Fuel—Westbury House, Bury St., Guildford. *M.*

Funeral Service Journal—King & Hutchings, Cricketfield Rd., Uxbridge, Middx. *M.*

Fur Weekly News—122 Lea Bridge Rd., E.5.

Gas Marketing—Sovereign Way, Tonbridge, Kent. *M.*

Gas World—Sovereign Way, Tonbridge, Kent. *M.*

Gifts International—Sovereign Way, Tonbridge, Kent. *M.*

Glass—Queensway House, Redhill, Surrey. *M.*

Grocer—5–7 Southwark St., S.E.1. *W.*

Grower—50 Doughty St., W.C.1. *W.*

Hair and Beauty—Quadrant House, Sutton, Surrey. *M.*

Hairdressers' Journal International—Quadrant House, The Quadrant, Sutton. *W.*

Handy Shipping Guide—230–234 Long Lane, S.E.1. *W.*

Hardware Trade Journal—Sovereign Way, Tonbridge, Kent. *W.*

Harper's Sports—Harling House, 47–51 Gt. Suffolk St., S.E.1. *Alt. W.*

Harper's Wine and Spirit Gazette—Harling House, 47–51 Gt. Suffolk St., S.E.1. *W.*

Health Visitor—124 Belgrave Road, S.W.1. *M.*

Heating and Ventilating Engineer—886 High Rd., Finchley, N.12. *Ten times a year.*

Hospital and Health Services Review—Westgate House, Harlow, Essex. *Alt. M.*

Ice Cream & Frozen Confectionery—90–94 Grays Inn Rd., W.C.1. *M.*

Industrial Society—Peter Runge House, 3 Carlton House Terrace, S.W.1. *Q.*

Insurance Mail—44 Fleet St., E.C.4. *M.*

Insurance Record—11 Old Bond Street, W.1. *M.*

Investors Chronicle (inc. Investor's Review)—Greystoke Place, Fetter Lane, E.C.4. *W.*

Jeweller—177 Hagden Lane, Watford, Herts. *M.*

Journal of Advertising—1 St. Anne's Road, Eastbourne, E. Sussex. *Q.*

Journal of the Chemical Society—Burlington House, W.1. *In six parts.*

Journalist—314 Gray's Inn Rd., W.C.1. *M.*

Justice of the Peace—Little London, Chichester. *W.*

Knitting and Haberdashery Review—80A South Street, Romford, Essex. *Alt. M.*

Lancet—7 Adam Street, W.C.2. *W.*

Law Quarterly Review—11 New Fetter Lane, E.C.4.

Law Reports—3 Stone Buildings, Lincoln's Inn, W.C.2. *M.*

Law Society's Gazette—113 Chancery Lane, W.C.2. *W.*

Leather—Sovereign Way, Tonbridge, Kent. *M.*

Leathergoods—Sovereign Way, Tonbridge, Kent. *M.*

Legal Executive—Ilex House, Barrhill Rd., S.W.2. *Alt. M.*

Library Review—137 Leith Walk, Edinburgh. *Q.*

Litho Week—38–42 Hampton Rd., Teddington, Middx.

Lloyd's Loading List—Sheepen Place, Colchester, Essex. *W.*

Locomotive Journal—9 Arkwright Rd., N.W.3. *M.*

London Corn Circular—52–57 Mark Lane, E.C.3. *W.*

Machinery and Production Engineering—Franks Hall, Horton, Kirby, Kent. *Twice a month.*

Machinery Market—6 Blyth Road, Bromley, Kent. *W.*

Management Accounting—63 Portland Place, W.1. *M.*

Management Decision—198–200 Keighley Rd., Bradford. *Six times a year.*

Management Today—76 Dean St., W.1. *M.*

Manufacturing Chemist—Morgan Grampian House, Calderwood St., S.E.18. *M.*

Marketing—22 Lancaster Gate, W.2. *W.*

Materials Reclamation Weekly—Maclaren House, 19 Scarbrook Rd., Croydon.

Meat Trades Journal—93–99 Goswell Rd., E.C.1. *W.*

Medico-Legal Journal—129 Long Lane, S.E.1. *Q.*

Men's Wear—20 Soho Sq., W.1. *W.*

Metal Bulletin—Park House, Park Terrace, Worcester Park, Surrey. *Twice a week.*

Metallurgia—Queensway House, Redhill, Surrey. *M.*

Milk Industry—19 Cornwall Terrace, N.W.1. *M.*

Mining Journal—15 Wilson St., Moorgate, E.C.2. *W.*

Mining Magazine—15 Wilson St., Moorgate, E.C.2. *M.*

Model Engineer—Wolsey House, Hemel Hempstead, Herts. *Twice a month.*

Modern Law Review—11 New Fetter Lane, E.C.4. *Alt. M.*

Modern Railways—Terminal House, Shepperton. *M.*

Motor—1 Throwley Way, Sutton, Surrey. *W.*

Motor Boat and Yachting—Quadrant House, Sutton, Surrey. *M.*

Motor Cycle Weekly—1 Throwley Way, Sutton, Surrey.

Motorcycle Trader—Penn House, Penn Place, Rickmansworth. *M.*

Motor Trader—Quadrant House, Sutton, Surrey. *W.*

Motor Transport—Quadrant House, Sutton, Surrey. *W.*

Musical Times—8 Lower James St., W.1. *M.*

National Builder—82 New Cavendish St., W.1. *M.*

Natural Gas—Sovereign Way, Tonbridge, Kent. *Alt. M.*

New Law Journal—Butterworths, Borough Green, Sevenoaks, Kent. *W.*

Nuclear Engineering International—Quadrant House, Sutton, Surrey. *M.*

Nurseryman & Garden Centre—Sovereign Way, Tonbridge, Kent. *W.*

Nursing Mirror—1 Throwley Way, Sutton, Surrey. *W.*

Nursing Times—4 Little Essex St., W.C.2. *W.*

Off Licence News—5–7 Southwark St., S.E.1. *W.*

Ophthalmic Optician—233–234 Blackfriars Rd., S.E.1. *Alt. M.*

Optician—Quadrant House, Sutton, Surrey. *W.*

Packaging—886 High Road, Finchley, N.12. *M.*

Packaging Review—886 High Road, Finchley, N12. *M.*

Paint & Resin—Penn House, Penn Place, Rickmansworth. *Alt. M.*

Painting and Decorating Journal—23 Low Street, Diss, Norfolk. *M.*

Paper—Sovereign Way, Tonbridge, Kent. *Alt. W.*

Personnel Management—1 Hills Place, W.1. *M.*

Pharmaceutical Journal—1 Lambeth High Street, S.E.1. *W.*

Philatelic Magazine—42 Maiden Lane, W.C.2. *M.*

Photographer, The—1 Gayford Road, W12. *M.*

Physics Bulletin—Techno House, Redcliffe Way, Bristol. *Twelve issues a year.*

Physics Education—Techno House, Redcliffe Way, Bristol. *Seven issues a Year.*

Physics in Technology—Techno House, Redcliffe Way, Bristol. *Alt. M.*

Plumbing and Heating Equipment News—Peterson House, Northbank, Droitwich, Worcs. *M.*

Police Review—14 St. Cross St., E.C.1. *W.*

Policy Holder Insurance News—1 Harlequin Ave., Brentford, Middx. *W.*

Post Magazine and Insurance Monitor—38 The Butts, Brentford, Middx. *W.*

Power Farming—1 Throwley Way, Sutton, Surrey. *M.*

Practical Wireless—Westover House, West Quay Rd., Poole, Dorset. *M.*

Practical Woodworking—Hatfield House, Stamford St., S.E.1. *M.*

Practitioner—Morgan-Grampian House, Calderwood St., S.E.18. *M.*

Printing World—Sovereign Way, Tonbridge, Kent. *W.*

Product Finishing—127 Stanstead Rd., S.E.23. *M.*

Professional Administration—16 Park Crescent, W.1. *M.*

Public Law—11 New Fetter Lane, E.C.4. *Q.*

Public Ledger—Penn House, Penn Place, Rickmansworth, Herts. *Daily.*

Public Service—1 Mabledon Place, W.C.1 *M.*

Quarry Management and Products—7 Regent St., Nottingham. *M.*

Quarterly Journal of Experimental Psychology—24–28 Oval Rd., N.W.1.

Quarterly Journal of Medicine—Oxford U. Press, Walton St., Oxford.

Railway Gazette International—Quadrant House, Sutton, Surrey. *M.*

Rating and Valuation Reporter—2 Paper Bldgs., Temple, E.C.4. *M.*

Resale Weekly—Unit 4, Sewell St., Plaistow, E.13.

Retail Jeweller—Knightway House, 20 Soho Square, W.1. *Alt. W.*

Retail Newsagent, Tobacconist & Confectioner—Onslow House, 60/66 Saffron Hill, E.C.1. *W.*

Review: Worldwide Reinsurance—33–35 Bowling Green Lane, E.C.1. *Alt. W.*

Review of English Studies—Oxford U. Press, Walton St., Oxford. *Q.*

Safety at Sea—Queensway House, Redhill, Surrey. *M.*

Scottish Farmer—39 York St., Glasgow. *W.*

Scottish Grocer—34–6 North Frederick St., Glasgow. *W.*

Service Station—178–202 Gt. Portland St., W.1. *M.*

Sheet Metal Industries—Queensway House, Redhill, Surrey. *M.*

Shipping World and Shipbuilder—42–43 Lower Marsh, S.E.1. *M.*

Shoe and Leather News—84–88 Great Eastern St., E.C.2. *W.*

Soap, Perfumery and Cosmetics—33–35 Bowling Green Lane, E.C.1. *M.*

Solicitors' Journal—21–27 Lamb's Conduit Street, W.C.1. *W.*

Sports Trader—Sovereign Way, Tonbridge, Kent. *Alt. W.*

Stage and Television Today—47 Bermondsey St., S.E.1. *W.*

Structural Engineer—11 Upper Belgrave St., S.W.1. *16 issues a year.*

Surveyor and Public Works Weekly—1 Throwley Way, Sutton, Surrey.

Tableware International—Queensway House, Redhill, Surrey. *M.*

Taxation—98 Park St., W.1. *W.*

Teacher—Hamilton House, Hastings Street, W.C.1. *W.*

Teaching History—59A Kennington Park Rd., S.E.11. *Three times a year.*

Television—Tavistock House East, Tavistock Square, W.C.1. *Alt. M.*

Textile Horizons—10 Blackfriars St., Manchester. *M.*

Textile Month—Grove House, Skerton Rd., Old Trafford, Manchester.

Timber Trades Journal and Wood Processing—Sovereign Way, Tonbridge, Kent. *W.*

Tobacco—Queensway House, Redhill, Surrey. *M.*

Tooling—127 Stanstead Rd., S.E.23. *M.*

Town and Country Planning—17 Carlton House Terrace, S.W.1. *M.*

Town Planning Review—Dept. of Civic Design, Liverpool University. *Q.*

Toy Trader—Penn House, Penn Place, Rickmansworth. *M.*

Trade Marks Journal—25 Southampton Bldgs., Chancery Lane, W.C.2. *W.*

Traffic Engineering and Control—29 Newman St., W.1. *M.*

U.K. Press Gazette—244–249 Temple Chambers, Temple Avenue, E.C.4. *W.*

Ultrasonics—P.O. Box 63, Westbury House, Bury Street, Guildford, Surrey. *Alt. M.*

Watchmaker, Jeweller and Silversmith—Quadrant House, Sutton, Surrey. *M.*

Weekly Law Reports—3 Stone Buildings, Lincoln's Inn, W.C.2.

Welding and Metal Fabrication—Quadrant House, Sutton, Surrey. *Ten times a year.*

Which?—14 Buckingham St., W.C.2. *M.*

Whitaker's Books of the Month and Books to Come—12 Dyott St., W.C.1. *M.*

Whitaker's Classified Monthly Booklist—12 Dyott St., W.C.1.

Whitaker's Cumulative Book List—12 Dyott St., W.C.1. *Q.*

Wire Industry—110–12 Station Road East, Oxted, Surrey. *M.*

Wireless World—Quadrant House, Sutton, Surrey. *M.*

Woodworker—Wolsey House, Hemel Hempstead. *M.*

Woodworking Crafts—170 High St., Lewes, E. Sussex. *M.*

Wool Record—91 Kirkgate, Bradford. *M.*

World Crops—Yew Tree House, Horne, Horley, Surrey. *Alt. M.*

World's Fair—2 Daltry St., Shaw Rd., Oldham. *W.*

NORTHERN IRISH NEWSPAPERS

London Offices

Ballymena Observer—30 Fleet St., E.C.4.

Banbridge Chronicle—30 Fleet St., E.C.4.

Belfast Telegraph—Greater London House, Hampstead Road, N.W.1.

Coleraine Chronicle—30 Fleet St., E.C.4.

Derry Journal—30 Fleet St., E.C.4.

Down Recorder—30 Fleet St., E.C.4.

Impartial Reporter (Enniskillen)—30 Fleet St., E.C.4.

Irish News—70 Hatton Garden, E.C.1.

Irish Weekly—70 Hatton Garden, E.C.1.

Mid Ulster Mail—30–32 Fleet St., E.C.4.

Northern Constitution (Coleraine)—30 Fleet St., E.C.4.

Strabane Weekly News—30 Fleet St., E.C.4.

Tyrone Constitution—30 Fleet St., E.C.4.

Ulster Gazette (Armagh)—30 Fleet St., E.C.4.

Ulster Herald (Omagh)—80 Fleet Street, E.C.4.

REPORTING AND NEWS AGENCIES IN LONDON

ASSOCIATED PRESS LTD.,
36/38 Whitefriars Street, E.C.4. 01–353 7191.

BRENARD PRESS LTD.,
Heathrow Airport, Hounslow, Middx. 01–759 1235.

CENTRAL PRESS FEATURES,
161 Fleet, Street, E.C.4. 01–353 7131.

EXCHANGE TELEGRAPH CO., LTD.,
Extel House, East Harding Street, E.C.4. 01–353 1080.

HAYTERS SPORTS REPORTING
4–5 Gough Square, E.C.4. 01–353 0971.

NATIONAL PRESS AGENCY LTD.,
Newspaper House, 8–16 Great New Street, E.C.4. 01–353 1030.

PARLIAMENTARY NEWS SERVICES,
19 Kingsdowne Road, Surbiton. 01–339 2049.

PRESS ASSOCIATION LTD.,
85 Fleet Street, E.C.4. 01–353 7440.

REUTERS LTD.,
85 Fleet Street, E.C.4. 01–250 1122.

UNITED PRESS INTERNATIONAL, LTD.,
8 Bouverie St., E.C.4. 01–353 2282.

UNIVERSAL NEWS SERVICES, LTD.,
Gough Square, Fleet St., E.C.4. 01–353 5200.

THE ZODIAC

The Zodiac is an imaginary belt in the heavens within which lie the apparent paths of the Sun, Moon and major planets. It is bounded by two parallels generally taken as lying 8° on either side of the ecliptic or path of the Sun in its annual course. The Zodiac is divided into twelve equal parts of 30° called Signs, which are not used by astronomers, but have some import in astrology, for which the division of the Zodiac was probably made originally. The Signs of the Zodiac take their names from certain of the constellations with which they once coincided. They are assumed to begin at the vernal equinox or intersection of the plane of the ecliptic with that of the equator. This point is still called the First Point of Aries, although the Sign of Aries now lies in the constellation of Pisces, some 30° to the west. This retrograding of the equinox by about 50″ a year is due to precession; the signs no longer coincide with the constellation whose names they bear.

A catalogue has been made (Grimaldi, 1905) of all, so far as is known, sculptured or incised representations on ancient monuments or tablets of the traditional constellation figures, either Zodiacal or otherwise, together with many modern pictures of the Zodiac. The first in the list is a roughly shaped upright, black stone about 2¼ feet high and 1½ feet broad in the Babylonian room of the British Museum on the front of which are lightly incised ten out of the twelve Signs and other constellation figures. This was found near Baghdad and its date is estimated to be about 1187–1175 B.C.

PRINCIPAL LONDON CLUBS

Club and Address	Secretary	Subscription		Remarks
		Entr.	Ann.	
		£	£	
Alpine (1857), 74 S. Audley St., W.1.	S. W. Town (*Hon.*)	4·00 to 20·00	18·00	Mountaineering.
American (1919), 95 Piccadilly, W.1.	D. J. Child	100·00	175·00	Americans in London.
American Women's (1899), 95 Piccadilly, W.1.	Mrs. J. Shaughnessy ...	..	..	American Women in London.
Anglo-Belgian (1955), 60 Knightsbridge, S.W.1.	Baron de Gerlache de Gomery, M.V.O. (*Hon.*)	85·00	85·00	Social.
Army and Navy (1837), 36 Pall Mall, S.W.1.	Col. D. O. O'Reilly	*Nil*	99·00 & 64·00	Commissioned officers of H.M. Forces.
Arts (1863), 40 Dover Street, W.1.	A. E. Eldon-Edington.	90·55	252·75	Arts, Literature, Science.
Arts Theatre (1927), 7 Great Newport Street, W.C.2	Miss C. Dowling	*Nil*	6·00 to 15·00	Social.
The Athenæum (1824), 107 Pall Mall, S.W.1.	Capt. D. S. Wyatt, O.B.E., R.N.	150·00	300·00	Literature and Science, Public Services, The Arts.
Authors' (1892) 40 Dover Street, W.1.	Mrs. H. Ridgway	90·55	252·75	Literary and Social.
Beefsteak (1876), 9a Irving Street, W.C.2.	E. Pool, M.C.	83·00	125·00	Dining and Social.
Boodle's (1762), 28 St. James's St., S.W.1.	R. J. Edmonds	300·00	345·00	Social: non-political.
Brooks's (1764), St. James's Street, S.W.1.	G. H. Irving	..	..	Social: non-political.
Buck's (1919), 18 Clifford Street, W.1.	A. Cowley	200·00	310·00	Social: non-political.
Caledonian (1891), 9 Halkin St., S.W.1.	Cdr. C. M. Bagguley, R.N.	150·00	190·00	Strictly Scottish.
Canning (1910), 42 Half Moon Street, W.1.	R. B. Baker	110·00	165·00	Social: S. American.
Carlton (1832), 69 St. James's St., S.W.1.	R. N. Linsley	200·00	280·00	Social: Conservative.
Cavalry and Guards (1893), 127 Piccadilly, W.1.	L. D. de Pinna	35·00	240·00	Officers of Mounted and Guards Regiments.
Challoner (1949), 59/61 Pont Street, S.W.1.	J. S. Tosh	*Nil*	Various	Roman Catholic residential.
Chelsea Arts (1891), 143 Old Church Street, S.W.3.	Hon. D. Winterbottom .	Various	65·00 to 145·00	Arts and Literature.
City Livery (1914), Sion College, Victoria Embankment, E.C.4.	B. L. Morgan, C.B.E. (*Hon.*)	..	..	Liverymen of City only.
City of London (1832), 19 Old Broad Street, E.C.2.	P. Merritt	350·00	250·00	Business Interests.
City University (1895), 50 Cornhill, E.C.3.	Mrs. B. J. Latta	..	..	Social. Primarily Oxbridge Graduates.
East India (Devonshire, Sports and Public Schools) (1849), 16 St. James's Square, S.W.1.	P. H. Wallace	172·50	250·00	Social and Residential.
Eccentric (1890), 9 Ryder Street, S.W.1.	A. H. Streeter	..	198·38	Social: non-political.
Farmers' (1842), 3 Whitehall Ct., S.W.1.	Lt.-Col. J. L. S. Andrews, O.B.E.	10·00	15·00 to 80·00	Agricultural Interests.
Flyfishers' (1884), 24a Old Burlington Street, W.1.	Cdr. N. T. Fuller, R.N. (*ret.*)	140·00	150·00	Flyfishing and Social.
Garrick (1831), 15 Garrick Street, W.C.2.	M. J. Harvey	250·00	290·00	Dramatic and Literary.
Green Room (1877), 9 Adam Street, W.C.2.	P. Corneille (*Hon.*)	10·00	75·00	Dramatic Profession.
Gresham (1843), 15 Abchurch Lane, E.C.4.	Mrs. J. S. Downing	..	Various	Social: non-political.
Hurlingham (1869), Ranelagh Gardens, S.W.6.	D. F. A. Trewby	250·00	208·00	Social: non-political.
Kempton Park (1878), Sunbury-on-Thames, Middlesex.	Miss S. Bainbridge	..	70·00	Racing.
Kennel (1873), 1 Clarges St., W.1.	M. H. Sinnatt, C.B.	80·00	40·00	For improving breed of dogs.
Lansdowne (1934), 9 Fitzmaurice Place, Berkeley Square, W.1.	M. de Lisle Bush	25·00	5·00 to 60·00	Social, Sports and Residential.

Club and Address	Secretary	Subscription		Remarks
		Entr.	Ann.	
		£	£	
London Thames Fencing (1848), 83 Perham Road, W.14.	Miss K. Smith.........	Nil	Various (up to 70·00)	Fencing.
London Rowing (1856), Embankment, Putney, S.W.15.	N. A. Smith...........	2·00	82·80	Amateur Rowing.
M.C.C. (Marylebone Cricket Club) (1787), Lord's Cricket Ground, N.W.8.	J. A. Bailey...........	60·00	60·00	Headquarters of Cricket.
Mining (1910), 3 London Wall Bldgs, E.C.2.	R. A. Higgs...........	..	..	Mining and metallurgical interests.
National (1845), c/o Carlton Club (q.v.).	E. Priefert...........	..	..	Clerical and social.
National Liberal (1882), 1 Whitehall Place, S.W.1.	M. J. Cook (Hon.)......	25·00	55·00 to 80·00	Social: political.
Naval (1946), 38 Hill Street, W.1.	Cdr. C. R. Parkes (ret.) .	40·00	Various	Officers of R.N., R.N.R., W.R.N.S., etc.
Naval and Military (1864), 94 Piccadilly, W.1.	R. B. Raworth, v.r.d.	112·00	164·50	Officers of R.N., Army, Marines, R.A.F.
Oriental (1824), Stratford House, Stratford Place, W.1.	R. N. Rapson, m.v.o. ...	175·00	25·00 to 230·00	Social.
Portland (1816), 42 Half Moon Street, W.1.	R. B. Little	100·00	100·00	Social: Non-political.
Pratt's (1841), 14 Park Place, S.W.1.	Capt. P. W. E. Parry, M.B.E.	Nil	100·00	Social.
Press (1882), International Press Centre, 76 Shoe Lane, E.C.4.	Jan Newton	23·00	11·50 to 75·00	Journalistic.
Queen's (1886), Palliser Road, W. Kensington, W.14.	J. A. S. Edwardes......	300·00	200·00	Lawn Tennis, Real Tennis, Rackets and Squash Rackets.
Railway (1899), Keen House, 4 Calshott Street, N.1.	N. C. Farebrother (Hon.)	1·00	15·00	Railway interests.
Reform (1836), 104–5 Pall Mall, S.W.1.	R. G. Tennant.........	150·00	345·00	Social.
Roehampton (1901), Roehampton Lane, S.W.15.	R. W. Varley	300·00	305·00	Golf, Lawn Tennis, Squash, Croquet, Swimming.
Royal Air Force (1918), 128 Piccadilly, W.1.	Sqn. Ldr. J. Swaffield ..	33·00*	33·00*	Officers of R.A.F., R.A.F.V.R., W.R.A.F., etc.
Royal Automobile (1897), 89–91 Pall Mall, S.W.1.	Capt. J. C. Judge, r.n. ...	200·00	210·00	And at Woodcote Park, Epsom.
Royal Commonwealth Society (1868), 18 Northumberland Avenue, W.C.2.	Sir Michael Scott, K.C.V.O., C.M.G.	..	..	Commonwealth Affairs, Social & Residential.
Royal Ocean Racing (1925), 20 St. James's Place, S.W.1.	E. A. Green	27·50	55·00	Off-shore Yacht Racing.
Royal Over-Seas League (1910), Over-Seas House, St. James's Street, S.W.1.	Capt. J. B. Rumble (Dir. Gen.)	20·00	25·00 to 75·00	Social: Non-political.
Royal Thames Yacht (1775), 60 Knightsbridge, S.W.1.	Capt. A. R. Ward, c.b.e., R.N.	Various	Various	Yachting.
St. Stephen's Constitutional (1870), 34 Queen Anne's Gate, S.W.1.	H. W. R. Ham	50·00	100·00	Conservative and Social.
Savage (1857), 9 Fitzmaurice Place, Berkeley Square, W.1.	A. Wykes (Hon.).......	57·50	50·00 to 100·00	Arts, Science, Law.
Savile (1868), 69 Brook Street, W.1.	P. Aldersley	120·00	255·00	Social: Non-political.
Ski Club of G.B. (1903), 118 Eaton Square, S.W.1.	P. R. Doyne	Nil	7·00 to 27·00	Ski-ing and Social.
Thames Rowing (1860), Embankment, Putney, S.W.15.	F. S. Beardmore (Hon.)	3·00	63·00	Men and Women.
Travellers' (1819), 106 Pall Mall, S.W.1.	G. S. Chisholm	115·00	300·00	Social: Non-political.
Turf (1868), 5 Carlton House Terrace, S.W.1.	P.A. Chandler.........	147·50	295·00	Social & Residential.
United Nursing Services (1921), 40 South Street, W.1.	W. Oakes	..	..	Social.
United Oxford & Cambridge University (1972), 71 Pall Mall, S.W.1.	D. J. McDougall	Nil	41·40 to 270·25	Oxford & Cambridge.
University Women's (1886), 2 Audley Square, W.1.	Mrs. E. Hord	57·50	25·00 to 85·00	University Graduates.

* Non-Serving Officers.

Club and Address	Secretary	Subscription		Remarks
		Entr.	Ann.	
		£	£	
V.A.D. (1920), 44 Great Cumberland Place, W.1.	G. Mayle	40·00	48·00	Social and Residential: Men and Women.
Victoria (1863), 150–162 Edgware Road, W.2.	L. A. Holland	*Nil*	36·75	Social & Sporting.
Victory Services (1907), 63–79 Seymour Street, W.2.	R. Wheeler	*Nil*	5·75	Social and residential; Serving and Ex-Service Men and Women.
White's (1693), 37–8 St. James's St., S.W.1.	W. H. West	230·00	310·00	Social: Non-political.
Wig and Pen (1908), 229–230 Strand, W.C.2.	J. Reynolds	15·00	35·00	Law and Journalism.

PRINCIPAL CLUBS OUTSIDE LONDON

Club and Address (with date of foundation)	Secretary or *Hon Sec.	Subscription	
		Entr.	Ann.
		£	£
Aldershot (Royal A~Officers) (1856), Farnborough Road.	Lt. Col. A. F. J. Channon, M.B.E.	*Nil*	47·00 to 77·00
Bath (Bath and County) (1865), Queen's Parade.	D. R. L. Brown	*Nil*	..
Birmingham—			
(Birmingham Club) (1872), Winston Churchill House, 8 Ethel Street.	*N. J. Masterton	..	..
(Chamber of Commerce) (1922), 75 Harborne Road, Edgbaston.	J. R. Dixon	*Nil*	63·00
(St. Paul's) (1859), 34 St. Paul's Square.	*J. S. Scott, T.D.	60·00	120·00
Bishop Auckland (The Club) (1868), 1 Victoria Avenue.	*A. Chapman	5·00	27·50
Bristol (Beaufort) (1885), Marsh Street.	Col. J. R. Lewes, T.D.	*Nil*	25·00
(Clifton) (1882), 22 The Mall.	*W. C. T. Worf, O.B.E. ...	*Nil*	72·00
Cambridge (Amateur Dramatic) (1855), Park Street.	*L. Argent	*Nil*	4·00
(Hawks) (1874), Jesus Lane.	*R. W. Tyler	..	..
(Union) (1815), Bridge Street.	B. Thoday (*Chief Clerk*).	*Nil*	19·50
Canterbury (Kent and Canterbury) (1868), 17 Old Dover Road.	P. L. Wood	10·00	45·00
Cardiff (Cardiff and County) (1866), 2 Westgate Street.	*A. Robinson, T.D.	300·00	47·00 to 153·00
Cheltenham (The New Club) (1874), Montpellier Parade.	*J. A. Warhurst, O.B.E. ..	25·00	115·00
Chester (Grosvenor) (1866), Vicars Lane.	* A. R. Fontes	..	..
(City) (1807), St. Peter's Church Yard.	G. R. Hargreaves	75·00	75·00
Chichester (W. Sussex County) (1872), 5 Stirling Rd.	J. S. Winny	..	..
Colchester (The Club) (1874), 3–5 Culver Street W.	N. Duncan	..	..
Devizes (Devizes & District) (1932), 27 St. John Street.	D. J. J. Cox	..	..
Durham (County) (1890), 52 Old Elvet.	Mrs. C. Arnot	..	..
Eastbourne (Devonshire) (1872), Hartington Place.	*B. S. M. Kerry	30·00	30·00
Exeter (Exeter and County) (1871), 5 Cathedral Close.	S. F. Hodge, M.B.E.	15·00	45·00
Harrogate (The Club) (1857), 36 Victoria Avenue.	*C. L. Leslie	..	..
Henley-on-Thames (Leander) (1818), Henley.	*Col. R. S. Langton	10·00	38·00
(Phyllis Court) (1906), Marlow Road.	R. I. Bulloch	..	..
Hove (The Hove Club) (1882), 28 Fourth Avenue.	G. A. Inverarity, D.F.C.	30·00	85·00
Jersey (Victoria) (1853), Beresford St., St. Helier.	J. W. E. Holmes, D.F.C., A.F.C.	60·00	60·00
Leamington (Tennis Court) (1846), 50 Bedford Street.	*O. D. R. Dixon	15·00	10·00 to 160·00
Leeds (The Leeds Club) (1850), 3 Albion Place.	*M. J. C. Reynolds (*Manager*)	..	110·00
Leicester (Leicestershire Club) (1873), 9 Welford Place.	J. A. Evans (*Manager*)...	*Nil*	18·00 to 92·00
Liverpool (Athenæum) (1797), Church Alley.	*D. R. Wetherell	*Nil*	90·00
Manchester (The Manchester Club) (1867), 50 Spring Gardens.	*Fiona Riley	25·00 to 80·00	30·00 to 180·00
(St. James's Club), St. James's House, Charlotte Street	R. M. G. Carter	200·00	200·00
Newcastle upon Tyne (Northern Constitutional) (1882), 37 Pilgrim Street.	J. L. Browne	*Nil*	138·00
Northampton (Northampton and County) (1873), George Row.	Maj. G. D. Denholm, B.E.M.	10·00 to 25·00	29·00 to 87·00

Club and Address (with date of foundation)	Secretary or *Hon Sec.	Subscription Entr.	Subscription Ann.
		£	£
Norwich (Norfolk) (1770), 17 Upper King Street.	A. J. M. Williamson	15·00	100·00
Oxford (Frewen) (1869), 98 St. Aldate's.	*W. H. Miller, B.E.M.	50·00	45·00
(Union) (1823), Frewin Court.	D. J. Burden (*Chief Clerk*)	50·50	5·00
(Vincent's) (1863), King Edward Street.	G. C. G. Light (*Steward*).	..	..
Peterborough (City and Counties) (1867), Priestgate.	Mrs. S. Rycroft	..	..
Reading (Berkshire Athenæum) (1972), 53 Blagrave Street.	*W. J. Stuck	..	..
Rye (Dormy House) (1896), Rye, Sussex.	*A. Dale	5·00	20·00 to 40·00
St. Leonards on Sea (East Sussex) (1893), 1 Warrior Square.	*E. J. Morris	..	..
Sheffield (The Club) (1843), Church Street.	Lt.-Col. J. R. Pattison. ..	30·00	110·00
Shrewsbury (The Salop) (1974), 6 The Square.	*Maj. S. Davies, T.D.	Nil	1·05 to 42·00
Teddington (Royal Canoe) (1866), Trowlock Island, Middx.	*Mrs. G. V. Barnard	4·00 to 5·00	28·00 to 38·00
Torbay (The Paignton Club) (1882), The Esplanade.	*P. Grafton	50·00	30·00
Worcester (Union and County) (1861), 40 Foregate Street.	M. G. Maton	Nil	75·00
York (Yorkshire) (1839), 17 Museum St.	*Miss I. C. Corner	50·00	105·00
(City) (1976), 4 Museum Street.	*C. H. Copeland	..	..

Scotland

Club and Address (with date of foundation)	Secretary or *Hon Sec.	Subscription Entr.	Subscription Ann.
Ayr (County) (1872), Savoy Park Hotel.	*W. W. McHarg	Nil	7·00
Edinburgh (Caledonian) (1825), 34 Abercromby Place.	P. A. S. Walker	Nil	100·00
(New) (1787), 86 Princes Street.	Cdr. G. Creedy, M.V.O., R.N.	263·00	68·00 to 210·00
Glasgow (Art) (1867), 185 Bath Street.	L. J. McIntyre	5·00	120·00
(Royal Scottish Automobile) (1899), 11 Blythswood Square.	H. Dewar	30·00 to 60.00	60·00 to 130·00
(The Western Club) (1825), 32 Royal Exchange Square.	D. H. Gifford	50·00	72·00 to 180·00

Ireland

Club and Address (with date of foundation)	Secretary or *Hon Sec.	Subscription Entr.	Subscription Ann.
Belfast (Ulster Reform) (1885), 4 Royal Avenue.	D. G. Johnston	..	..
Dublin (Stephen's Green) (1840), 9 St. Stephen's Green	J. P. Oxley	..	..
Enniskillen (Fermanagh County) (1883), 20 Church Street.	Lt.-Col. G. E. Liddle, C.B.E.	..	15·00

YACHT CLUBS

Club and Address (with date of foundation)	Secretary or *Hon Sec.	Subscription Entr.	Subscription Ann.
		£	£
Beaumaris (Royal Anglesey) (1802), 6–7 Green Edge.	*K. G. Brettell	25·00 to 30·00	25·00 to 30·00
Bembridge, I. of W. (Sailing) (1886), Embankment Road.	W. J. R. Linaker........	50·00	92·50
Birkenhead (Royal Mersey) (1844), Bedford Road East, Rock Ferry.	*H. H. Browne	20·00	60·00
Bridlington (Royal Yorks) (1847), 1 Windsor Cresent.	I. Harness	10·00	13·00 to 90·00
Burnham-on-Crouch. (Royal Corinthian) (1872), Burnham-on-Crouch.	*A. J. Marsh	Nil	105·00
Caernarvon (Royal Welsh) (1847), Porth-Yr-Aur.	*J. N. L. Thomas	10·00	17·50
Cowes (Royal Yacht Squadron) (1815), The Castle, Cowes.	Maj. R. P. Rising, R.M. (*ret.*)	Various	Various
(Royal London) (1838), The Parade.	A. J. Clarke.............	Various	Various
Dover (Royal Cinque Ports) (1872), Waterloo Crescent.	R. J. Barrett	10·00	34·50 to 63·00
Essex (1890), (Yacht), Leigh-on-Sea.	*A. Manning	..	33·93
Fishbourne, I. of W. (Royal Victoria) (1844), Fishbourne Lane.	B. Bowers	..	..
Fowey (Royal Fowey) (1881), Fowey.	*Cdr. W. P. T. Croome, R.N.	..	..

Club and Address (with date of foundation)	Secretary or *Hon Sec.	Subscription	
		Entr.	Ann.
		£	£
Harwich (Royal Harwich) (1843), Woolverstone, Ipswich.	Col. C. H. Bavin	55·00	55·00
Jersey (Royal Channel Islands) (1862), The Bulwarks, St. Aubin, Jersey.	*A. K. Jackson	30·00	25·00
Kingswear (Royal Dart) (1866), Priory Street, Kingswear, S. Devon.	*J. A. King	33·00	24·00 to 33·00
London (Cruising Association) (1908), Ivory House, St. Katharine Dock, E.1.	Lindsay Nunn (*Gen. Sec.*)	7·50	21·50
(Royal Cruising) (1880), c/o Naval and Military Club, 42 Half Moon Street, W.1.	*E. Bourne	Various	Various
Lowestoft (Royal Norfolk and Suffolk) (1859), Royal Plain.	Sqn. Ldr. F. W. Flowers, R.A.F. (*ret.*)	23·00	85·10
Lymington (Royal Lymington) (1922), Bath Road.	Gp. Capt. H. L. Lewis.	100·00	65·00
Penarth (Penarth) (1880), The Esplanade.	*W. H. Jones	18·23	50·60
Plymouth (Royal Western) (1827), 9 Grand Parade, West Hoe.	Cdr. L. R. R. Foster, R.N. (*ret.*)	Various	Various
(Royal Plymouth Corinthian) (1877), Madeira Road.	*Col. G. A. L. Davies, T.D.	2·50 to 10·00	5·00 to 40·00
Poole (East Dorset Sailing) (1875), Sandbanks Rd.	*Mrs. B. Okey	16·00	16·00
(Parkstone) (1895), Pearce Avenue, Parkstone.	Brig. H. J. Goodson, O.B.E.	50·00	74·00
(Poole Harbour) (1949), Salterns Way, Lilliput.	R. Kelly-Wiseman (*Club Manager*)	9·00 to 52·00	12·00 to 70·00
(Yacht) (1865), New Quay Road, Hamworthy.	Capt. G. E. Thornton, M.N. (*ret.*)	40·50	40·50
Ramsgate (Royal Temple) (1857), 6 Westcliff Mansions.	*B. L. Martin	30·00	45·00 to 90·00
Southampton:			
(Royal Air Force) (1932), Riverside Ho., Hamble.	Lt. Cdr. S. L. Revett, D.S.C., V.R.D.	..	..
(Royal Southampton), 10 Northlands Road.	Mrs. J. Freer...........	8·05 to 46·00	18·00 to 90·00
(Royal Southern) (1837), Hamble.	Mrs. W. J. F. Clampett	75·00	81·00
Southend (Alexandra) (1873), Clifton Terrace.	*Mrs. P. Spacey	Nil	6·74 to 33·62
Southsea (Royal Naval and Royal Albert) (1867), Pembroke Road, Portsmouth.	Cdr. T. C. C. Greaves, O.B.E., R.N.	25·00	Various
Swansea (Bristol Channel) (1875), 744 Mumbles Road, Mumbles.	*P. G. Cawker..........	34·50	50·60 to 74·75
Westcliff-on-Sea (Thames Estuary) (1895), 3 The Leas.	*G. R. Noble	Various	Various
Weymouth (Royal Dorset) (1875), 11 Custom House Quay.	*J. C. T. Plummer	Nil	47·75
Windermere (Royal Windermere) (1860), Fallbarrow Road, Bowness.	*D. McCann	50·00	50·00
Yarmouth (Royal Solent) (1878), Yarmouth, I.O.W.	Maj. F. R. Sillitoe, R.M. ..	Various	Various

Scotland

Dundee (Royal Tay) (1885), 34 Dundee Road, Broughty Ferry.	*T. Black	5·00	5·00 to 48·00
Edinburgh (Royal Forth) (1868), 1 Boswall Road, Edinburgh, 5.	R. A. Flett	Nil	75·00
Glasgow (Royal Clyde) (1856), Rhu, Dunbartonshire.	D. M. Paul, 111 Union Street, Glasgow.	..	..
(Royal Western) (1875), 48 St. Vincent Street.	*A. S. Weatherhead.	1·00	1·00
Oban (Royal Highland) (1881), Dalriada, Ardentallen.	Lt. Cdr. R. F. Heap, O.B.E., D.S.C., R.N.	10·00	5·00
Rhu (Royal Northern and Clyde) (1978), Rhu, Dunbartonshire.	*J. A. Ritchie	10·00	Various

Northern Ireland

Bangor (Royal Ulster) (1866), 101 Clifton Road, Bangor, Co. Down.	*G. D. Ralston	..	..

PRINCIPAL BRITISH AND IRISH SOCIETIES AND INSTITUTIONS

THE ROYAL ACADEMY OF ARTS (1768), Burlington House, W.1.—*President*, Sir Hugh Casson, K.C.V.O., (1976); *Keeper*, Peter Greenham, C.B.E., R.A.; *Treas.*, Roger de Grey, R.A.; *Sec.* Piers Rodgers; *Comptroller*, K. J. Tanner, M.V.O.

Royal Academicians

1972 Adams, Norman
1956*Bawden, Edward, C.B.E.
1976 Blackadder, Miss Elizabeth, O.B.E.
1981 Blake, Peter
1975 Blamey, Norman
1978 Blow, Miss Sandra
1975 Bowey, Miss Olwyn
1981 Bowyer, William
1971 Bratby, John R.
1972 Brown, Ralph
1956 Buhler, Robert
1972 Butler, James
1975 Cadbury-Brown, H. T., O.B.E.
1970 Casson, Sir Hugh, K.C.V.O.
1976 Clarke, Geoffrey
1973 Clatworthy, Robert
1972 Coker, Peter
1972 Cooke, Miss Jean
1968 Cowern, Raymond T.
1974 Cuming, Frederick
1983 Dannatt, Trevor
1969 de Grey, Roger
1976 Dickson, Miss Jennifer
1955*Dring, William
1968 Dunstan, Bernard
1953*Eurich, Richard, O.B.E.
1965 Freeth, H. Andrew
1977 Frink, Dame Elisabeth, D.B.E.
1972*Fry, E. Maxwell, C.B.E.

1975*Goldfinger, Ernö
1972 Gore, Frederick
1977 Green, Anthony
1960 Greenham, Peter, C.B.E.
1981 Harpley, Sydney
1970 Hayes, Colin
1961*Hepple, Norman
1974 Kneale, Bryan
1963 McFall, David
1956 Machin, Arnold, O.B.E.
1979 Manasseh, Leonard, O.B.E.
1973 Middleditch, Edward
1979 Moynihan, Rodrigo, C.B.E.
1979 Paolozzi, Eduardo, C.B.E.
1981 Philipson, Sir Robin
1977 Powell, Sir Philip, O.B.E.
1973 Roberts-Jones, Ivor, C.B.E.
1969 Rosoman, Leonard, O.B.E.
1983*Rothenstein, Michael
1961 Sanders, Christopher C.
1969*Soukop, Willi
1954 Spear, Ruskin, C.B.E.
1979 Swanwick, Miss Betty
1979 Tindle, David
1965 Ward, John
1965*Weight, Carel, C.B.E.
1974 Williams, Kyffin, O.B.E.

Associates

1978 Aitchison, Craigie
1982 Ayres, Gillian
1974 Camp, Jeffrey
1980 Christopher, Ann
1982 Crosby, Theo
1979 Dowson, Sir Philip, C.B.E.
1976 Eyton, Anthony
1983 Foster, Norman
1975 Fraser, Donald Hamilton
1978 Gowing, Sir Lawrence, C.B.E.
1974 Hogarth, Paul
1983 Howard, Ken
1983 Hoyland, John
1981 Jones, Allen
1976 Kenny, Michael
1977 King, Philip, C.B.E.

1984 Kitaj, R. B.
1982 Lawson, Sonia
1975 Levene, Ben
1980 Partridge, John, C.B.E.
1984 Phillips, Tom
1978 Rogers, Richard
1977 Rothenstein, M.
1982 Sandle, Michael
1977 Scott, William, C.B.E.
1975 Stephenson, Ian
1983 Stevens, Norman
1977 Sutton, Philip
1983 Symons, Patrick
1980 Whishaw, Anthony
1983 Wragg, John

* Senior ‡Honorary Retired

Former Presidents of the Royal Academy

Sir J. Reynolds, 1768	Sir F. Dicksee, 1924
Benjamin West, 1792	Sir W. Llewellyn, 1928
James Wyatt, 1805	Sir E. Lutyens, 1938
Benjamin West, 1806	Sir A. J. Munnings,
Sir T. Lawrence, 1820	1944
Sir M. A. Shee, 1830	Sir G. F. Kelly, 1949
Sir C. Eastlake, 1850	Sir A. E. Richardson,
Sir F. Grant, 1866	1954
Lord Leighton, 1878	Sir C. Wheeler, 1956
Sir J. Millais, 1896	Sir T. Monnington,
Sir E. Poynter, 1896	1966
Sir A. Webb, 1919	

THE ROYAL CAMBRIAN ACADEMY OF ART (1882), Plas Mawr, Conwy.—*Pres.*, R. Fields; *Hon. Sec.*, Audrey Hinds; *Curator and Sec.*, L. H. S. Mercer.

THE ROYAL SCOTTISH ACADEMY (1826), Princes Street, Edinburgh.—*Pres.*, H. A. Wheeler, O.B.E., R.S.A.; *Sec.*, R. J. Steedman, R.S.A.; *Treas.*, W. J. L. Baillie, R.S.A.; *Librarian*, A. Campbell, R.S.A.; *Admin. Sec.*, F. K. B. Murdoch, C.V.O., M.B.E., T.D.

Hon. Retired Academicians:
1958 Armour, Mrs. M.
1956 Kininmonth, Sir William
1964 Miller, James
1966 Johnston, Ninian
1937 Schotz, Benno
1970 Sutherland, Scott

Royal Scottish Academicians

1979 Baillie, W. J. L.
1972 Blackadder, Elizabeth
1977 Butler, Vincent
1971 Cameron, Gordon S.
1981 Campbell, Alex
1974 Collins, Peter
1974 Crosbie, William
1970 Cumming, James
1962 Donaldson, David A.
1956 Fleming, Ian
1981 Glover, J. Hardie, O.B.E.
1967 Gordon, Esmé
1972 Houston, John
1979 Knox, John
1973 Littlejohn, W.

1957 Lorimer, Hew
1971 McClure, David
1976 Malcolm, Ellen
1972 Michie, David
1963 Morocco, Alberto
1957 Patrick, J. McIntosh
1966 Peploe, Denis
1962 Philipson, Sir Robin
1976 Reeves, Philip
1977 Robertson, R. Ross
1984 Scott, Bill (*elect.*)
1979 Steedman, R. R.
1975 Wheeler, H. Anthony, O.B.E.
1977 Whiston, Peter
1982 Walker, Frances

Associates

Balmer, Barbara
Boys, John
Brotherston, William
Brown, Neil Dallas
Bryce, Gordon
Buchan, Dennis
Bushe, Frederick
Campbell, A. Buchanan
Clifford, J. G.
Cocker, Douglas
Docherty, Michael
Donald, George
Evans, David
Fairgrieve, James

Fraser, Alexander
Harvey, Jake
Howard, Ian
Johnstone, John
Law, Graham C.
McIntosh, Iain R.
Maclean, William J.
MacMillan, Andrew
Main, Kirkland
Merrylees, Andrew
Metzstein, Isi
Mooney, John
Morris, James
Morrison, James

Onwin, Glen
Pelly, Frances
Pottinger, Frank
Rae, Barbara
Reiach, Alan, O.B.E.
Renton, James S., O.B.E.
Richards, John, C.B.E.
Robertson, James D.

Ross, Alastair
Shanks, Duncan F.
Smart, Alastair
Smith, Ian McKenzie
Snowden, Michael
Squire, Geoffrey
Stiven, Fred

Hon. Retired Associates, Miss Elizabeth Dempster. *Non-Resident Associates*, Charles Pulsford; Peter Womersley, Leon Morrocco.

ROYAL IRISH ACADEMY (1786), 19 Dawson Street, Dublin 2.—*Pres.*, W. A. Watts; *Treas.*, T. D. Spearman; *Sec.*, J. O. Scanlan.

ABBEYFIELD SOCIETY, 186–192 Darkes Lane, Potters Bar, Herts.—Supportive housing for lonely elderly people.—*Gen. Sec.*, D. A. L. Charles.

ACCOUNTANTS, INSTITUTE OF CHARTERED, in England and Wales (1880), Chartered Accountants' Hall, Moorgate Place, E.C.2.—*Sec.*, E. J. D. Warne, C.B.

ACCOUNTANTS, ASSOCIATION OF CERTIFIED (1904), 29 Lincoln's Inn Fields, W.C.2.—*Sec.*, R. A. Dudman.

ACCOUNTANTS OF SCOTLAND, THE INSTITUTE OF CHARTERED (1854), 27 Queen Street, Edinburgh—*Pres.*, Prof. W. C. C. Morrison; *Sec.*, E. Tait.

ACCOUNTANTS IN IRELAND, INSTITUTE OF CHARTERED (1888), 87/89 Pembroke Road, Dublin 4.—*Dir.*, R. F. Hussey.

ACCOUNTANTS, SOCIETY OF COMPANY AND COMMERCIAL (1974), 40 Tyndalls Park Road, Bristol.—*Sec.-Gen.*, B. T. Banks.

ACTION RESEARCH FOR THE CRIPPLED CHILD (National Fund for Research into Crippling Diseases) (1952), Vincent House, North Parade, Horsham, Sussex.—*Dir.*, Col. A. N. Brearley-Smith, O.B.E.

ACTORS' BENEVOLENT FUND (1882), 6 Adam Street, W.C.2.—*Sec.*, Mrs. R. Stevens.

ACTORS' CHARITABLE TRUST (incorporating DENVILLE HALL), Bedford Chambers, Covent Garden, W.C.2.—Assists children of theatrical parentage who are in need; Home for elderly and infirm actors and actresses.—*Gen. Sec.* Miss M. M. Brisley.

ACTORS' CHURCH UNION (1899), St. Paul's Church, Bedford Street, W.C.2.—*Senior Chaplain*, Rev. M. Hurst-Bannister.

ACTUARIES IN SCOTLAND, THE FACULTY OF (1856), Hall and Library, 23 St. Andrew Square, Edinburgh.—*Sec.*, W. W. Mair.

ACTUARIES, INSTITUTE OF (1848), Staple Inn Hall, W.C.1.—*Sec.-Gen.*, C. D. Mackie.

ADDICTION (TO ALCOHOL AND OTHER DRUGS), SOCIETY FOR THE STUDY OF (1884).—*Sec.*, Prof. M. Lader, Church Close, Rectory Lane, Holcot, Northants.

ADDITIONAL CURATES SOCIETY; HOME MISSIONS OF CHURCH OF ENGLAND AND THE CHURCH IN WALES (1837), St. Mark's Church House, 264a Washwood Heath Road, Birmingham.—*Sec.*, Rev. A. J. Prescott.

ADMINISTRATIVE ACCOUNTANTS, INSTITUTE OF (1916), Burford House, 44 London Road, Sevenoaks, Kent.—*Dir.-Gen.*, D. W. Bradley.

ADMINISTRATIVE MANAGEMENT, INSTITUTE OF (1915), 40 Chatsworth Parade, Petts Wood, Kent.—*Sec.*, J. Ainsworth.

ADVERTISING BENEVOLENT SOCIETY, NATIONAL (1913), 3 Crawford Place, W.1.—*Director and Gen. Sec.*, Miss R. Bell.

ADVERTISING, INSTITUTE OF PRACTITIONERS IN, 44 Belgrave Square, S.W.1.—*Dir.*, D. Wheeler.

ADVERTISING STANDARDS AUTHORITY (1962), 2–16 Torrington Place, W.C.1.—*Director General*, P. Thomson.

AERONAUTICAL SOCIETY, ROYAL (1866) (incorporating the Institution of Aeronautical Engineers and the Helicopter Association of Great Britain), 4 Hamilton Place, W.1.—*Pres.* (1983–84), Prof. M. G. Farley; *Sec.*, N. A. M. Eastwood.

AEROSPACE COMPANIES, SOCIETY OF BRITISH (1916), 29 King Street, S.W.1.—*Dir.*, Sir John Curtiss, K.C.B., K.B.E.

AFRICAN INSTITUTE, INTERNATIONAL (1926), 38 King Street, W.C.2.—*Hon. Dir.*, Prof. I. M. Lewis.

AFRICAN MEDICAL AND RESEARCH FOUNDATION, 68 Upper Richmond Road, S.W.15.—*Administrator*, Mrs. E. Young.

AGED PILGRIMS' FRIEND SOCIETY (1807), 175 Tower Bridge Road, S.E.1.—*Sec.*, R. D. Stewart.

AGED POOR SOCIETY (1708) AND ST. JOSEPH'S HOUSE, 42 Brook Green, W.6.—*Sec.*, Flt. Lt. W. Watson (*ret'd*).

AGEING, CENTRE FOR POLICY ON, Nuffield Lodge Studio, Regent's Park, N.W.1.—*Dir.*, Dr. E. Midwinter.

AGRICULTURAL BENEVOLENT INSTITUTION, ROYAL, Shaw House, 27 West Way, Oxford.—*Chairman*, W. T. Gauntlett; *Chief Exec.*, Maj.-Gen. P. L. Spurgeon, C.B.

AGRICULTURAL BENEVOLENT INSTITUTION, ROYAL SCOTTISH (1897), Ingliston, Newbridge, Midlothian.—*Sec.*, K. M. Campbell, W.S.

AGRICULTURAL BOTANY, NATIONAL INSTITUTE OF (1919), Huntingdon Road, Cambridge.—*Director*, G. M. Milbourn, PH.D.

AGRICULTURAL SOCIETY, EAST OF ENGLAND, East of England Showground, Peterborough.—*Sec.*, R. W. Bird, M.B.E..

AGRICULTURAL SOCIETY, ROYAL ULSTER (1826), The King's Hall, Balmoral, Belfast.—*Chief Exec.*, W. H. Yarr.

AGRICULTURE, ASSOCIATION OF (1947), Victoria Chambers, 16/20 Strutton Ground, S.W.1.—*Gen. Sec.*, Miss J. H. D. Bostock, M.B.E.

AIR LEAGUE, THE (1909), 4 Hamilton Place, W.1.—*Chairman*, Dr. J. E. Henderson.

ALEXANDRA ROSE DAY FUND, 1 Castelnau, Barnes, S.W.13.—*Organiser*, Mrs. L. Weston.

ALLOTMENT AND LEISURE GARDENERS LIMITED, NATIONAL SOCIETY OF, 22 High Street, Flitwick, Beds.—*Sec.*, G. Jones.

ALMSHOUSES, NATIONAL ASSOCIATION OF, Billingbear Lodge, Wokingham, Berks.—*Dir.*, D. M. Scott.

ANAESTHETISTS OF GREAT BRITAIN AND IRELAND, ASSOCIATION OF (1932). Room 475, Tavistock House South, Tavistock Square, W.C.1.

ANCIENT BUILDINGS, SOCIETY FOR THE PROTECTION OF (1877), 37 Spital Square, E.1.—*Sec.*, P. Venning.

ANCIENT MONUMENTS SOCIETY (1924).—*Sec.*, M. J. Saunders, St. Andrew-by-the-Wardrobe, Queen Victoria Street, E.C.4.

ANGLO-ARAB ASSOCIATION (1961), The Arab British Centre, 21 Collingham Road, S.W.5.—*Exec. Dir.*, D. R. Collard, O.B.E.

ANGLO-BELGIAN SOCIETY (incorporating the Anglo-Belgian Union (1918) and the Cercle Royal Belge de Londres (1922)).—*Hon. Sec.*, Mrs. S. G. Ault, Tor House, Maybury Hill, Woking, Surrey.

ANGLO-BRAZILIAN SOCIETY (1943), 2 Belgrave Square, S.W.1.—*Sec.*, Mrs. M. J. Fyfe.

ANGLO-DANISH SOCIETY (1924), 7 St. Helen's Place, Bishopsgate, E.C.3.—*Chairman*, Sir Robert Bellinger, G.B.E.

ANGLO-NORSE SOCIETY, 25 Belgrave Square, S.W.1.—*Chairman*, Sir Peter Scott, K.B.E., C.M.G.

ANGLO-SWEDISH SOCIETY, 5 Mansfield Street, W.1.

ANGLO-THAI SOCIETY (1962).—*Hon. Sec.*, c/o 40 St. Mary Axe, E.C.3.

ANIMAL HEALTH TRUST, Lanwades Hall, Kennett, Newmarket, Suffolk.—*Dir.*, W. B. Singleton, C.B.E., F.R.C.V.S.

ANTHROPOLOGICAL INSTITUTE, ROYAL (1843), 56 Queen Anne Street, W.1.—*Dir.*, J. Benthall.

ANTHROPOSOPHICAL SOCIETY IN GREAT BRITAIN, Rudolf Steiner House, 35 Park Road, N.W.1.—*Sec.*, R. Zienko.

ANTIQUARIES, SOCIETY OF (1717), Burlington House, W.1.—*Pres.*, Prof. J. D. Evans, PH.D., F.B.A.; *Treas.*, R. M. Robbins, C.B.E.; *Dir.*, G. J. Wainwright, PH.D.; *Sec.*, R. W. Lightbown.

ANTIQUARIES OF SCOTLAND, SOCIETY OF (1780), National Museum of Antiquities of Scotland, Queen Street, Edinburgh.—*Sec.*, T. F. Watkins, PH.D.; *Treas.*, R. J. Mercer.

ANTI-SLAVERY SOCIETY FOR THE PROTECTION OF HUMAN RIGHTS (1839), 180 Brixton Road, S.W.9.—*Dir.*, R. P. H. Davies, O.B.E.

ANTI-VIVISECTION: BRITISH UNION FOR THE ABOLITION OF VIVISECTION (INC.) (1898), 16A Crane Grove, N.7.—*Office Manager*, Margaret Manzoni.

ANTI-VIVISECTION SOCIETY, THE NATIONAL (1875), 51 Harley Street, W.1.—*Gen. Sec.*, B. Gunn.

ANTI-VIVISECTION SOCIETY, SCOTTISH, 121 West Regent Street, Glasgow.—*Organising Sec.*, J. F. Robins.

APOSTLESHIP OF THE SEA (1920). For active seafarers. *National Headquarters.*—Atlantic House, Hardman Street, Liverpool.—*Dir.*, Rev. A. Stringfellow.

APOTHECARIES, SOCIETY OF (1617).—Black Friars Lane, E.C.4.—*Clerk*, Maj. J. C. O'Leary; *Registrar*, D. H. C. Barrie.

ARBITRATORS, THE CHARTERED INSTITUTE OF, 75 Cannon Street, E.C.4.—*Dir. and Sec.*, B. W. Vigrass, O.B.E., V.R.D.

ARCHÆOLOGICAL ASSOCIATION, BRITISH (1843), 61 Old Park Ridings, Winchmore Hill, N.21.—*Hon. Asst. Treas. and Sec.*, Miss I. B. McClure.

ARCHÆOLOGICAL ASSOCIATION, CAMBRIAN (1846).—*Pres.* (1983–84), H. A. Wheeler; *Gen. Sec.*, G. L. Jones, Lleifior, 60 Dan-y-Coed, Aberystwyth, Dyfed.

ARCHÆOLOGICAL INSTITUTE, ROYAL (1843).—*Hon. Sec.*, A. J. Clark, PH.D., F.S.A.; *Asst. Sec.*, Miss. W. E. Phillips, 304 Addison House, Grove End Road, N.W.8.

ARCHÆOLOGY, COUNCIL FOR BRITISH (1944), 112 Kennington Road, S.E.11.—*President*, T. G. Hassall, F.S.A.; *Sec.*, Dr. P. W. Dixon; *Dir.*, Dr. H. F. Cleere, F.S.A.

ARCHITECTS, THE ROYAL INSTITUTE OF BRITISH (1834), 66 Portland Place, W.1.—*Pres.*, M. J. Manser; *Sec.*, P. K. Harrison, C.B.E.

ARCHITECTS REGISTRATION COUNCIL OF THE UNITED KINGDOM, 73 Hallam Street, W.1.—*Chairman*, Prof. D. Hinton; *Registrar*, K. J. Forder.

ARCHITECTS AND SURVEYORS, INCORPORATED ASSOCIATION OF (1925), Jubilee House, Billing Brook Road, Weston Favell, Northampton.—*Pres.*, F. A. Hunt; *Hon. Sec.*, W. J. Clark.

ARCHITECTS AND SURVEYORS, THE FACULTY OF, LTD: (incorporating The Institute of Registered Architects Ltd), 15 St. Mary Street, Chippenham, Wiltshire—*Sec.*, A. D. G. Webb.

ARCHITECTS BENEVOLENT SOCIETY (1850), 66 Portland Place, W.1.—*Sec.*, R. P. B. Roth.

ARCHITECTS IN SCOTLAND, ROYAL INCORPORATION OF (1922), 15 Rutland Square, Edinburgh.—*Sec. and Treasurer*, C. A. McKean.

ARCHITECTURAL ASSOCIATION (INC.) (1847), 34–36 Bedford Square, W.C.1.—*Sec.*, E. Le Maistre.

ARCHIVISTS, SOCIETY OF (1947), *Hon. Sec.*, Mrs. C. M. Short, South Yorkshire County Record Office, Ellin Street, Sheffield.

ARLIS (Art Libraries Society) (1969).—*Sec.*, L. Turpin, Brighton Polytechnic, Faculty of Art and Design Library, Grand Parade, Brighton.

ARMY BENEVOLENT FUND (1944), 41 Queen's Gate, S.W.7.—*Controller*, Maj.-Gen. P. J. Bush, O.B.E.

ARMY CADET FORCE ASSOCIATION (1930), Millbank Barracks, John Islip Street, S.W.1.—*Gen. Sec.*, Brigadier D. M. Pontifex, C.B.E.

ART-COLLECTIONS FUND, NATIONAL (1903), 20 John Islip Street, S.W.1.—*Dir.*, Sir Peter Wakefield, K.B.E., C.M.G.

ART EDUCATION, NATIONAL SOCIETY FOR (1888), 7a High Street, Corsham, Wilts.—*Gen. Sec.*, J. M. Steers.

ART WORKERS GUILD (1884), 6 Queen Sq., Bloomsbury, W.C.1.—*Master*, J. Skelton, F.R.B.S.; *Sec.*, D. Pullen.

ARTHRITIS AND RHEUMATISM COUNCIL FOR RESEARCH, 41 Eagle Street, W.C.1.—*Gen. Sec.*, J. Norton.

ARTHRITIS CARE, 6 Grosvenor Crescent, S.W.1.—*Sec.*, A. M. Davey.

ARTISTS' GENERAL BENEVOLENT INSTITUTION (1814) AND ARTISTS' ORPHAN FUND (1871), Burlington House, Piccadilly, W.1.—*Sec.*, T. Miles.

ARTISTS UNITED SOCIETY OF (1921), 17 Carlton House Terrace, S.W.1.—*Pres.*, R. Hill.

ARTS COUNCIL OF GREAT BRITAIN, 105 Piccadilly W.1.—*Chairman*, Sir William Rees-Mogg; *Secretary-General*, L. Rittner.

ASLIB (1924). (The Association for Information Management), 3 Belgrave Square, S.W.1.—*Sec. and Dir.*, Dr. D. A. Lewis.

ASSISTANT MASTERS AND MISTRESSES ASSOCIATION, 7 Northumberland Street, W.C.2.

ASTHMA RESEARCH COUNCIL, St. Thomas' Hospital, Lambeth Palace Road, S.E.1.—*Chairman*, D. M. Walters, M.B.E., M.P.

ASTRONOMICAL ASSOCIATION, BRITISH.—*Office*, Burlington House, Piccadilly, W.1. Meetings at 23 Savile Row, W.1.—*President*, P. A. Moore, O.B.E.; *Sec.*, N. J. Goodman; *Asst. Sec.*, E. Watson Jones.

ASTRONOMICAL SOCIETY, ROYAL (Founded 1820), Burlington House, W.1.—*Pres.*, Prof. R. Hide, F.R.S.; *Secs.*, Prof. R. D. Davies; Dr. B. A. Hobbs; Dr. Carole Jordan.

A.T.S. and W.R.A.C. BENEVOLENT FUNDS (1964), Queen Elizabeth Park, Guildford, Surrey.—*Sec.*, Mrs. E. Laurence-Smith.

AUDIT BUREAU OF CIRCULATIONS LTD., 13 Wimpole Street, W.1.—*Dir.*, K. Derbyshire.

AUTHORS, THE SOCIETY OF, 84 Drayton Gardens, S.W.10.—*Gen. Sec.*, M. Le Fanu.

AUTOMOBILE ASSOCIATION (1905), Fanum House, Basingstoke, Hants.—*Chairman*, The Lord Erroll of Hale, P.C.; *Dir. Gen.*, O. F. Lambert, C.B.E.

AVICULTURAL SOCIETY (1894).—*Hon. Sec.*, H. J. Horswell, Windsor Forest Stud, Mill Ride, Ascot, Berks.

AYRSHIRE CATTLE SOCIETY OF GREAT BRITAIN AND IRELAND (1877), 1 Racecourse Road, Ayr.—*Gen. Sec.*, S. J. Thomson.

BALTIC AIR CHARTER ASSOCIATION, The Baltic Exchange, 28 St. Mary Axe, E.C.3.—*Chief Exec.*, R. B. Haseldine.

BALTIC EXCHANGE LTD. (1903), 14–20 St. Mary Axe, E.C.3.—*Chairman*, H. L. C. Grieg, C.V.O.; *Sec.*, D. J. Walker.

BALTIC EXCHANGE CHARITABLE SOCIETY (1978), 14–20 St. Mary Axe, E.C.3.—*Sec.*, R. T. Wheelans.

BANKERS, THE INSTITUTE OF (1879), 10 Lombard Street, E.C.3.—*Sec.-Gen.*, E. Glover.

BANKERS IN SCOTLAND, THE INSTITUTE OF (1875), 20 Rutland Square, Edinburgh.—*Sec.*, B. McKenna.

BAPTIST MISSIONARY SOCIETY (1792), 93–97 Gloucester Place, W.1.—*Gen. Sec.*, Rev. R. G. S. Harvey.

BAR ASSOCIATION FOR LOCAL GOVERNMENT AND THE PUBLIC SERVICE.—*Chairman*, E. W. Andrews, Runnymede Borough Council, Station Road, Addlestone, Weybridge, Surrey.

(DR.) BARNARDO'S (1866), *Head Offices:* Tanners Lane, Barkingside, Essex. More than 270,000 children have been helped. Over 9,000 boys and girls are helped each year in residential and non-residential settings.—*Sen. Dir. and Dir. of Child Care*, R. Singleton.

BARONETAGE, STANDING COUNCIL OF THE (1898), *Sec.*, H. Bedingfeld, The College of Arms, Queen Victoria Street, E.C.4.

BARRISTERS' BENEVOLENT ASSOCIATION (1873), 3 Raymond Buildings, Grays Inn, W.C.1.—*Hon. Treasurers*, P. Curry, Q.C.; C. H. McCall; *Sec.*, Miss K. M. Hopper.

BEIT MEMORIAL FELLOWSHIPS (for Medical Research) (1909).—*Admin. Sec.*, D. Billington, Histopathology Dept., St. Bartholomew's Hospital, E.C.1.

BERNARD SHAW SOCIETY, 125 Markyate Road, Dagenham, Essex.—*Sec.*, E. Ford.

BIBLE CHURCHMEN'S MISSIONARY SOCIETY (1922), 251 Lewisham Way, S.E.4.—*Gen. Sec.*, Rev. J. M. Ball.

BIBLE SOCIETY, BRITISH AND FOREIGN (1804), 146 Queen Victoria Street, E.C.4.—*Gen. Dir.*, Rev. N. B. Cryer.

BIBLIOGRAPHICAL SOCIETY (1892), c/o British Library, Great Russell Street, W.C.1.—*Hon. Sec.*, Dr. M. M. Foot.

BIBLIOGRAPHICAL SOCIETY, EDINBURGH (1890), c/o National Library of Scotland, Edinburgh, 1.—*Hon. Sec.*, I. C. Cunningham.

BIOCHEMICAL SOCIETY, THE (1911), 7 Warwick Court, W.C.1.—*Exec. Sec.*, G. D. Jones.

BIOLOGICAL ENGINEERING SOCIETY.—*Hon. Sec.*, Dr. M. Jordan, c/o Royal College of Surgeons, Lincoln's Inn Fields, W.C.2.

BIOLOGISTS, ASSOCIATION OF APPLIED.—*Hon. Gen. Sec.*, Dr. D. G. Jones, Dept. of Agricultural Botany, University College of Wales, Penglais, Aberystwyth, Dyfed.

BIOLOGY, INSTITUTE OF, 20 Queensberry Place, S.W.7.—*Pres.*, Prof. J. L. Harvey, C.B.E., F.R.S.; *Gen. Sec.*, P. N. O'Donoghue.

BIRD PRESERVATION, INTERNATIONAL COUNCIL FOR (BRITISH SECTION), c/o Natural History Museum, Cromwell Road, S.W.7.—*Hon. Sec.*, R. D. Chancellor.

BIRMINGHAM AND MIDLAND INSTITUTE (1854) and PRIESTLEY LIBRARY (1779), Margaret Street, Birmingham.—*Admin. and Lib.* J. Hunt.

BLIND, GREATER LONDON FUND FOR THE, 2 Wyndham Place, W.1.—*Pres.*, The Lord Mayor of London; *Gen. Sec.*, Group Capt. J. S. Goodwin, M.B.E.

BLIND, GUIDE DOGS FOR THE, ASSOCIATION, Alexandra House, 9–11 Park Street, Windsor, Berks.—*Dir.-Gen.*, Maj.-Gen. J. P. Groom, C.B., C.B.E.

BLIND, INCORPORATED ASSOCIATION FOR PROMOTING THE GENERAL WELFARE OF THE (1854), 37–55 Ashburton Grove, N.7.—*Chief Exec.*, G. P. Robinson.

BLIND, LONDON ASSOCIATION FOR THE (1857), 14–16 Verney Road, S.E.16. A national charity helping blind and partially-sighted people throughout the country.—*Dir.*, G. J. Entwistle.

BLIND, ROYAL COMMONWEALTH SOCIETY FOR THE (1950), Commonwealth House, Haywards Heath, West Sussex.—*Dir.*, A. W. Johns, O.B.E.

BLIND, ROYAL NATIONAL INSTITUTE FOR THE (1868), 224 Great Portland Street, W.1.—*Runs education advisory service for parents, nurseries and schools for blind and additionally handicapped children, a further education college for school leavers, training centres, a rehabilitation centre, homes for elderly blind and deaf-blind people, hotels for holidays and a London hostel; helps blind people find commercial and professional jobs; runs Homeworkers scheme in S.E. England; runs braille and tape libraries for students and Talking Book Library; publishes books, magazines and music in braille and Moon and information leaflets in print; sells specially designed or adapted goods; gives financial assistance to blind people in need; funds research into the prevention of blindness; helps blind sportsmen and women; trains sighted mobility instructors.*

BLIND, NATIONAL LIBRARY FOR THE (1882), Cromwell Road, Bredbury, Stockport, Cheshire.—A national charity providing free library service in embossed types for the blind and partially-sighted. Also large-print service. Over 350,000 volumes available.—*Director-General*, A. Leach, F.L.A.

BLIND, THE ROYAL LONDON SOCIETY FOR THE (1838), *Head Office and Workshops*, 105–9 Salusbury Road, Brondesbury, N.W.6; *School*, Dorton House, Seal, nr. Sevenoaks, Kent; *Home Workers' Scheme.*—*Sec.-Gen.*, R. J. Pocock.

BLIND, ROYAL NATIONAL COLLEGE (1872), College Road, Hereford.—*Principal*, L. Marshall. Further education and training for open employment for visually-handicapped.

BLIND, ROYAL SCHOOL FOR THE (1799), Leatherhead, Surrey.—*Dir.*, Rev. B. A. E. Coote.

BLIND (LONDON) SPORTS CLUB FOR THE (1932).—*Sec.*, Miss E. Wright, 27 Underhill Road, Dulwich, S.E.22.

BLOOD TRANSFUSION. See GREATER LONDON RED CROSS BLOOD TRANSFUSION SERVICE.

BLUE CROSS, THE (Incorporating Our Dumb Friends' League) (1897), Animals' Hospital, Hugh Street, Victoria, S.W.1.—*Sec.*, P. Carpmael, M.B.E.

BMMF INTERNATIONAL (formerly Bible and Medical Missionary Fellowship) (1852), 186 Kennington Park Road, S.E.11.—*Gen. Sec.*, A. M. S. Pont.

BODLEIAN, FRIENDS OF THE, Bodleian Library, Oxford.—*Sec.*, G. Groom.

BOOK-KEEPERS, INSTITUTE OF (1916), (see under Administrative Accounting, Institute of).

BOOKSELLERS ASSOCIATION OF GREAT BRITAIN AND IRELAND (1895), 154 Buckingham Palace Road, S.W.1.—*Dir.*, T. E. Godfray.

BOOK TRADE BENEVOLENT SOCIETY (1967), Dillon Lodge, The Booksellers Retreat, Kings Langley, Herts.—*Pres.*, T. Joy, M.V.O., F.R.S.A.; *Exec. Sec.*, Mrs. A. R. Brown.

BOTANICAL SOCIETY OF THE BRITISH ISLES (1836), c/o Dept. of Botany, British Museum (Natural History), Cromwell Road, S.W.7.—*Hon. Gen. Sec.*, Mrs M. Briggs, M.B.E., F.L.S.

BOTANICAL SOCIETY OF EDINBURGH, Royal Botanic Garden, Inverleith Row, Edinburgh 3.—*Hon. Gen. Sec.*, Miss J. Muscott.

BOY SCOUTS ASSOCIATION, *see* SCOUT ASSOCIATION, THE.

BOYS' BRIGADE, THE (INCORPORATED) (1883), Brigade House, Parsons Green, S.W.6. Membership worldwide: 582,000.—*Sec.*, A. A. J. Hudson, C.B.E.

BOYS' CLUBS, NATIONAL ASSOCIATION OF, 24 Highbury Grove, N.5. Incorporated 1925. Responsible for the development and co-ordination of boys' club work throughout the country, and has affiliated to it, either directly or through local organizations, 2,000 clubs—*Nat. Dir.*, D. P. C. Harris.

BOYS' CLUBS, NORTHERN IRELAND ASSOCIATION OF (1940), 28 Bedford Street, Belfast.—*Gen. Sec.*, C. E. Larmour, M.B.E.

BREWING, INSTITUTE OF (1886), 33 Clarges Street, W.1.—*Sec.*, Capt. K. A. Leppard, C.B.E., R.N.

BRIDEWELL ROYAL HOSPITAL, King Edward's School, Witley, Surrey (1553).—*Treas.*, I. Allan; *Clerk to the Governors*, Mrs. A. C. R. Mitchell.

BRITISH ACADEMY, THE (1901), 20–21 Cornwall Terrace, N.W.1.—*President*, Rev. Prof. W. O. Chadwick, O.M., K.B.E.; *Treas.*, Prof. P. Mathias; *Sec.*, P. W. H. Brown; *Foreign Sec.*, Prof. E. W. Handley, C.B.E.

BRITISH AND FOREIGN SCHOOL SOCIETY (1808). Richard Mayo Hall, Eden Street, Kingston on Thames, Surrey.—*Sec.*, S. M. A. Banister.

BRITISH ARTISTS, FEDERATION OF (1959), 17 Carlton House Terrace, S.W.1.—*Sec. Gen.*, C. de Winter.

BRITISH ASSOCIATION FOR THE ADVANCEMENT OF SCIENCE (1831), Fortress House, 23 Savile Row, W.1.—*Pres.*, Sir Hans Kornberg, F.R.S.; *Exec. Sec.*, Dr. D. Morley.

BRITISH ASSOCIATION FOR COMMERCIAL AND INDUSTRIAL EDUCATION, 16 Park Crescent, W.1.—*Dir.*, Dr. P. J. C. Perry, O.B.E.

BRITISH ASSOCIATION FOR EARLY CHILDHOOD EDUCATION, Montgomery Hall, Kennington Oval, S.E.11.—*Sec.*, Miss D. E. Hewitt.

BRITISH ASSOCIATION OF THE HARD OF HEARING.— *Sec.-Gen.*, P. Hannon, 7/11 Armstrong Road, W.3.

BRITISH ATLANTIC COMMITTEE, 30A St. James's Square, Whitehall, S.W.1—*Dir.*, Maj. Gen. C. J. Popham, C.B.

BRITISH BEE-KEEPERS' ASSOCIATION (1874).—*Gen. Sec.*, M. H. F. Coward, National Agricultural Centre, Stoneleigh, Kenilworth, Warwicks.

BRITISH BOARD OF FILM CENSORS, 3 Soho Square, W.1.—*Sec.*, J. Ferman.

BRITISH BUTTERFLY CONSERVATION SOCIETY (1968), Tudor House, Quorn, Nr. Loughborough, Leics.— *Chairman*, C. J. Tatham, M.B.E.

BRITISH COLLEGE OF OPHTHALMIC OPTICIANS (OPTOMETRISTS), 10 Knaresborough Place, S.W.5.—*Gen. Sec.*, T. H. Collingridge.

BRITISH COMMONWEALTH EX-SERVICES LEAGUE, 48 Pall Mall, S.W.1.—*Sec.-Gen.*, Col. G. Stocker, C.B.E.

BRITISH COMPUTER SOCIETY (1957), 13 Mansfield Street, W.1.—*Sec.-Gen.*, D. W. Harding.

BRITISH COTTON GROWING ASSOCIATION LTD. (1904), Ralli House, 60 Old Hall Street, Liverpool.— *Managing Director*, R. Derbyshire.

BRITISH CYCLING FEDERATION (1878), 16 Upper Woburn Place, W.C.1.—*Sec.*, L. Unwin.

BRITISH DENTAL ASSOCIATION (1880), 64 Wimpole Street, W.1.—*Sec.*, K. Johnson.

BRITISH DIABETIC ASSOCIATION (1934), 10 Queen Anne Street, W.1.—*Sec.-Gen.*, D. Armytage, C.B.E.

BRITISH DRIVING SOCIETY, 27 Dugard Place, Barford, Warwick.—*Sec.*, Mrs. J. M. Dillon.

BRITISH EDUCATIONAL MANAGEMENT AND ADMINISTRATION SOCIETY (1971).—*Sec.*, Miss M. E. Hewitt, Buxton Girls' School, Derbys.

BRITISH EQUESTRIAN FEDERATION, British Equestrian Centre, Kenilworth, Warwicks.—*Dir. Gen.*, Maj.-Gen. J. R. Reynolds, C.B., O.B.E.

BRITISH EXPORT-FINANCE ADVISORY COUNCIL (1981), 2 Deanery Street, Park Lane, W.1.—*Chairman*, C. D. Hankes-Drielsma.

BRITISH FIELD SPORTS SOCIETY (1930), 59 Kennington Road, S.E.1.—*Dir.*, Maj. Gen. J. M. Brockbank, C.B.E., M.C.

BRITISH FILM INSTITUTE (1933), 127 Charing Cross Road, W.C.2.—*Dir.*, A. Smith; *Controller, National Film Theatre*, L. Hardcastle, O.B.E.

BRITISH FOUNDRYMEN, THE INSTITUTE OF (1904), Bridge House, 121 Smallbrook Queensway, Birmingham.—*Sec.*, G. A. Schofield.

BRITISH GLIDING ASSOCIATION (1930), affiliated to Royal Aero Club. Kimberley House, Vaughan Way, Leicester.—*Gen. Sec.*, B. Rolfe.

BRITISH GOAT SOCIETY (1879), *Sec.*, Mrs. T. T. F. May, Lion House, Rougham, Bury St. Edmunds, Suffolk.

BRITISH HEART FOUNDATION (1963), 102 Gloucester Place, W.1.—*Dir. Gen.*, Brig. M. C. T. Pelham.

BRITISH HEDGEHOG PRESERVATION SOCIETY, THE (1982), *Sec.*, Maj. A. H. Coles, T.D., Knowbury House, Knowbury, Ludlow, Shropshire.

BRITISH HOMOEOPATHIC ASSOCIATION, THE (1902), 27A Devonshire Street, W.1.—*Gen. Sec.*, Mrs. M. Munday.

BRITISH HORSE SOCIETY (*incorporating* THE PONY CLUB), British Equestrian Centre, Kenilworth, Warwicks.—*Dir.*, Col. N. F. Grove-White.

BRITISH INSTITUTE IN EASTERN AFRICA, 1 Kensington Gore, S.W.7.—*London Sec.*, Mrs. J. Filson.

BRITISH INSTITUTE OF ARCHÆOLOGY AT ANKARA, c/o British Academy, 20–21 Cornwall Terrace, N.W.1.—*Hon. Sec.*, A. S. Hall, F.S.A.

BRITISH INSTITUTE OF INTERNATIONAL AND COMPARATIVE LAW, Charles Clore House, 17 Russell Square, W.C.1.—*Dir.*, Lady Fox.

BRITISH INSTITUTE OF INTERIOR DESIGN (1899), 1C Devonshire Avenue, Beeston, Nottingham.—*Sec.*, N. Parker.

BRITISH INSTITUTE OF PERSIAN STUDIES (1961), *Asst. Sec.*, Mrs. M. E. Gueritz, M.B.E., 13 Cambrian Road, Richmond, Surrey.

BRITISH INSTITUTE OF RADIOLOGY, 36 Portland Place, W.1.—*Gen. Sec.*, Mrs. S. Johnstone.

BRITISH INSURANCE BROKERS ASSOCIATION, Fountain House, 14 Bevis Marks, E.C.3.—*Dir. Gen.*, M. Morris.

BRITISH INTERPLANETARY SOCIETY (1933), 27–29 South Lambeth Road, S.W.8.—*Exec. Sec.*, L. J. Carter.

BRITISH ISRAEL WORLD FEDERATION (1919), Mount Avalon, Bove Town, Glastonbury, Somerset.—*Sec.*, R. B. H. Hall.

BRITISH LEGION, ROYAL. *Headquarters*, 48 Pall Mall, S.W.1.—*Gen. Sec.*, Maj. R. Tomlins, O.B.E.

BRITISH MEDICAL ASSOCIATION (1832), B.M.A. House, Tavistock Square, W.C.1.—*President*, Sir Douglas Black, F.R.C.P.; *Sec.*, J. D. J. Havard, M.D.

BRITISH MIGRAINE ASSOCIATION, 178A, High Road, Byfleet, Weybridge, Surrey.—*Hon. Sec.*, Mrs. J. Liddell.

BRITISH MUSIC HALL SOCIETY (1963), 1 King Henry Street, N.16.—*Chairman*, J. Seaton.

BRITISH MUSIC INFORMATION CENTRE, 10 Stratford Place, W.1.—*Manager*, R. W. Wright.

BRITISH NATURALISTS' ASSOCIATION (1905).—*Hon. Mem. Sec.*, Mrs. Y. H. Griffiths, 23 Oak Hill Close, Woodford Green, Essex.

BRITISH NUTRITION FOUNDATION (1967), 15 Belgrave Square, S.W.1.—*Dir. Gen.*, Dr. D. H. Shrimpton, PH.D.

BRITISH POULTRY BREEDERS AND HATCHERIES ASSOCIATION LTD., 52–54 High Holborn, W.C.1.—*Gen. Sec.*, I. S. Knight.

BRITISH PROPERTY FEDERATION, 35 Catherine Place, S.W.1.—*Sec.*, S. H. Bristow.

BRITISH RECORDS ASSOCIATION (1932), Master's Court, The Charterhouse, Charterhouse Square, E.C.1.—*Pres.*, Rt. Hon. Sir John Donaldson, Master of the Rolls; *Hon. Sec.*, T. R. Padfield.

BRITISH RECORD SOCIETY (1887).—*Hon. Sec.*, P. L. Dickinson, College of Arms, Queen Victoria Street, E.C.4.

BRITISH RED CROSS SOCIETY (1870).—*National Headquarters*, 9 Grosvenor Crescent, S.W.1.—*Dir. Gen.*, D. J. Piggott.

BRITISH SAILORS' SOCIETY (1818), 406/410 Eastern Avenue, Ilford, Essex.—*Gen. Sec.*, G. Chambers.

BRITISH SCHOOL AT ATHENS.—*Chairman of the Managing Committee*, Prof. R. M. Cook, F.B.A.; *Dir.*, H. W. Catling, O.B.E., D.Phil, F.S.A.; *Sec.*, Mrs. S. E. Waywell, PH.D., 31–34 Gordon Square, W.C.1.

BRITISH SCHOOL AT ROME (1901).—*Chairman of Executive Committee*, A. G. Shepherd Fidler, C.B.E.; *Director*, Dr. G. Barker; *Hon. Gen. Sec.*, C. A. H. James, 1 Lowther Gardens, Exhibition Road, S.W.7.

BRITISH SCHOOL OF ARCHÆOLOGY IN JERUSALEM (1919), The British Academy, 20 Cornwall Terrace, N.W.1.—*Pres.*, The Rev. Prof. H. Chadwick, D.D., F.B.A.; *Dir.*, Dr. R. Harper, F.S.A.

BRITISH SEAMEN'S BOYS HOME, Grenville House, Brixham.—*Supt.*, Capt. E. M. Marks, R.D., R.N.R.

BRITISH SHIP ADOPTION SOCIETY, *see* SEAFARERS EDUCATION SERVICE.

BRITISH SOCIAL BIOLOGY COUNCIL, 69 Eccleston Square, S.W.1.—*Sec.*, D. M. Jeynes.

BRITISH STANDARDS INSTITUTION, 2 Park Street, W.1.—*Dir. Gen.*, D. G. Spickernell, C.B.

BRITISH THEATRE ASSOCIATION (1919) (incorporating the British Theatre Play Library), 9 Fitzroy Square, W.1.

BRITISH TRAVEL AGENTS, THE ASSOCIATION OF (1950), 55–57 Newman Street, W.1.—*Chief Exec.*, M. Elton.

BRITISH UNITED PROVIDENT ASSOCIATION LIMITED, Provident House, 24–7 Essex Street, W.C.2.—*Chief Exec.*, R. M. Graham.

BRITISH VETERINARY ASSOCIATION (1881), 7 Mansfield Street, W.1.—*Sec.*, P. B. Turner, M.A.

BRUSH MANUFACTURERS' ASSOCIATION, BRITISH, 6A East Street, Epsom, Surrey.—*Sec.*, J. A. Snellgrove.

BUDDHIST SOCIETY, THE (1924), 58 Eccleston Square, S.W.1.—*Gen. Sec.*, J. Snelling.

BUILDING, CHARTERED INSTITUTE OF (1834), Englemere, Kings Ride, Ascot, Berks.—*Chief Exec.*, D. A. Neale, O.B.E., M.C.

BUILDING SERVICES, CHARTERED INSTITUTION OF (1897), Delta House, 222 Balham High Road, S.W.12.—*Sec.*, B. A. Hodges, O.B.E.

BUILDING SOCIETIES ASSOCIATION, 3 Savile Row, W.1.—*Sec.-Gen.*, R. S. Weir.

BUILDING SOCIETIES INSTITUTE, THE CHARTERED, Fanhams Hall, Ware, Hertfordshire.—*Sec.*, R. D. Crerar.

BULWER LYTTON CIRCLE, 125 Markyate Road, Dagenham, Essex.—*Sec.*, E. Ford.

BUS AND COACH COUNCIL (Confederation of British Road Passenger Transport) (1974), Sardinia House, 52 Lincoln's Inn Fields, W.C.2.—*Dir.-Gen.*, D. R. Quin.

BUSINESS AND PROFESSIONAL WOMEN, UNITED KINGDOM FEDERATION OF (1938), 23 Ansdell Street, W.8.

BUSINESS ARCHIVES COUNCIL, Denmark House, 15 Tooley Street, S.E.1.—*Chairman*, S. H. G. Twining, O.B.E.; *Hon. Sec.*, H. C. McMurray.

BUTCHERS' CHARITABLE INSTITUTION (1828).—*Sec.*, J. A. Fordyce, 61 West Smithfield, E.C.1.

BUYERS, THE INSTITUTION OF (1974) (see Sales Engineers).

CALOUSTE GULBENKIAN FOUNDATION, LISBON, United Kingdom Branch (1956), 98 Portland Place, W.1.—*Dir.*, L. C. Taylor.

CAMBRIDGE PRESERVATION SOCIETY (1929).—*Chairman*, Sir Desmond Lee; *Sec.*, M. R. Francis, Wandlebury Ring, Gog Magog Hills, Babraham, Cambridge.

CAMERA CLUB (1885), 8 Great Newport Street, W.C.2.—*Sec.*, J. Legate.

CAMERON FUND LTD., (1971), Tavistock House North, Tavistock Square, W.C.1.—*Sec.*, Miss H. C. Pullen.

CAMPAIGN FOR NUCLEAR DISARMAMENT (1958), 11 Goodwin Street, N.4.—*Gen. Sec.*, Mgr. Bruce Kent.

CANADA UNITED KINGDOM CHAMBER OF COMMERCE, British Columbia House, 3 Regent Street, S.W.1.—*Manager*, W. E. Ferguson.

CANCER RESEARCH CAMPAIGN, 2 Carlton House Terrace, S.W.1.—For research into the disease of cancer in all its forms.—*Sec. Gen.*, D. de Peyer.

CANCER RELIEF, NATIONAL SOCIETY FOR (1911), Michael Sobell House, 30 Dorset Square, N.W.1.—*Gen. Sec.*, S. H. Creswell.

CANCER RESEARCH FUND, IMPERIAL (1902), Lincoln's Inn Fields, W.C.2. Research into causes, prevention, treatment and cure of all forms of cancer; in own laboratories and extra-mural units.—*Sec.*, A. B. L. Clarke, O.B.E.

CANCER RESEARCH, INSTITUTE OF: ROYAL CANCER HOSPITAL, 34 Sumner Place, S.W.7.—*Sec.*, J. Defries.

CAREER TEACHERS, ASSOCIATION OF, Hillsboro., Castledine Street, Loughborough, Leics.—*Gen. Sec.*, Miss R. Yaffé.

CARNEGIE DUNFERMLINE TRUST (1903). (Social and cultural purposes in Dunfermline) Income £200,000.—*Sec.*, F. Mann, Abbey Park House, Dunfermline, Fife.

CARNEGIE HERO FUND TRUST (1908). Income £90,000. Makes grants and allowances to people injured or the dependants of people killed in saving human life within the British Isles and territorial waters.—*Sec.*, F. Mann, Abbey Park House, Dunfermline, Fife.

CARNEGIE UNITED KINGDOM TRUST (1913). Comely Park House, Dunfermline, Fife.—*Object*, The improvement of the well-being of the masses of the people of Great Britain and Ireland by means which are "charitable" in law and are to be selected by the Trustees. The Trust is particularly concerned with innovatory schemes in community services, amateur participation in the arts, particularly for the disabled, and heritage interpretation developments; grants are not made to individuals, or in response to general appeals, or for research and travel. Management—By trustees. *Sec.*, G. Lord.

CATHEDRALS ADVISORY COMMISSION FOR ENGLAND, 83 London Wall, E.C.2.—*Sec.*, P. A. T. Burman, F.S.A., F.R.S.A.

CATHOLIC MARRIAGE ADVISORY COUNCIL (National Headquarters), 15 Lansdowne Road, W.11; *Chief Exec.*, B. L. Cawley.

CATHOLIC RECORD SOCIETY (1904).—*Hon. Sec.*, Miss R. Rendel, c/o 114 Mount Street, W.1.

CATHOLIC TRUTH SOCIETY (1868), P.O. Box 422, 38–40 Eccleston Square, S.W.1.—*Gen. Sec.*, D. Murphy, M.A.

CATHOLIC UNION OF GREAT BRITAIN.—*Pres.*, The Duke of Norfolk, C.B., C.B.E., M.C.; *Sec.*, Mrs. J. Stuyt, M.B.E., 1 Bolton Gardens Mews, S.W.10.

CATTLE BREEDER'S CLUB, BRITISH, Lavenders, Isfield, nr. Uckfield, Sussex.—*Sec.*, C. R. Stains.

CECIL HOUSES (Inc.) (Housing Association Charity), 2 Priory Road, Kew, Richmond, Surrey.—*Sec.*, A. G. Wilmot.

CERAMIC SOCIETY, BRITISH (1900), Shelton House, Stoke Road, Shelton, Stoke-on-Trent, Staffs.—*Pres.*, A. J. Owen.

CERAMICS INSTITUTE OF (1955), Shelton House, Stoke Road, Stoke-on-Trent, Staffs.—*Hon. Sec.*, R. Harrison.

CHADWICK TRUST (1895) (for the promotion of health and prevention of disease).—Chadwick Professor of Civil Engineering, University College London, Gower Street, W.C.1.

CHAMBERS OF COMMERCE.—*See* COMMERCE.

CHANTREY BEQUEST (1875).—*Sec. to the Trustees*, P. Rodgers, Royal Academy of Arts, Burlington House, Piccadilly, W.1.

CHARTERED SECRETARIES AND ADMINISTRATORS, INSTITUTE OF (1891), 16 Park Crescent, W.1.—*Sec.*, B. Barker, M.B.E.

CHEMICAL ENGINEERS, INSTITUTION OF (1922), George E. Davis Building, 165–171 Railway Terrace, Rugby, Warks. *Gen. Sec.*, T. J. Evans.

CHEMICAL INDUSTRY, SOCIETY OF, 14/15 Belgrave Square, S.W.1.—*Pres.*, Dr. I. Graham-Bryce, F.R.S.C.; *Gen. Sec.*, P. P. King, F.R.S.C.

CHEMISTRY, THE ROYAL SOCIETY OF, Burlington House, Piccadilly, W.1.—*Pres.*, Prof. R. O. C. Norman, F.R.S.; *Sec.-Gen.*, R. D. Guthrie, PH.D.

(LEONARD) CHESHIRE FOUNDATION (1955), 26–29 Maunsel Street, S.W.1. Foundation presides over 75 homes in U.K. and affiliated to a further 145 world-wide.—*Dir.*, A. L. Bennett.

CHESS FEDERATION, BRITISH, 9a Grand Parade, St. Leonards-on-Sea, East Sussex.—*Gen. Sec.*, P. Buswell.

CHEST, HEART AND STROKE ASSOCIATION (1899), Tavistock House North, Tavistock Square, W.C.1.—*Dir. Gen.*, Air Marshal Sir Ernest Sidey, K.B.E., C.B., M.D.

CHILDREN'S AID & ADOPTION, MISSION OF HOPE FOR, 14 South Park Hill Road, Croydon, Surrey.—*Gen. Sec.*, Rev. R. H. Johnson.

CHILDREN'S COUNTRY HOLIDAYS FUND, 1 York Street, W.1—*Gen. Sec.*, Mrs. J. M. Meekins, M.B.E.

CHINA ASSOCIATION (1889), Regis House, 43–46 King William Street, E.C.4.—*Exec. Dir.*, Brig. B. G. Hickey, O.B.E., M.C.

CHIROPODISTS, THE SOCIETY OF, 53 Welbeck Street, W.1.—*Sec.*, G. C. Jenkins.

CHOIRS SCHOOLS ASSOCIATION (1921).—*Hon. Sec.*, R. A. Ford, King's School, Rochester, Kent.

CHRISTIAN ACTION—*Dir.*, Canon E. James, Southbank House, Black Prince Road, S.E.1.

CHRISTIAN AID (1945), P.O. Box 1, S.W.9.—*Dir.*, Rev. Dr. C. Elliott.

CHRISTIAN EDUCATION MOVEMENT (1965), 2 Chester House, Pages Lane, N.10. *Gen. Sec.*, Rev. J. M. Sutcliffe.

CHRISTIAN EVIDENCE SOCIETY (1870).—*Hon. Sec.*, Mrs. D. Hutchinson, 56 Rushmore Road, E.5.

CHRISTIAN KNOWLEDGE, SOCIETY FOR PROMOTING (1698), Holy Trinity Church, Marylebone Road, N.W.1.—*Gen. Sec.*, P. N. G. Gilbert.

CHRISTIANS AND JEWS, COUNCIL OF (1942), 48 Onslow Gardens, S.W.7.—*Gen. Sec.*, L. Goss.

CHURCH ARMY, Independents Road, Blackheath, S.E.3. *Chief Sec.*, Rev. M. Rees.

CHURCH BUILDING SOCIETY, INCORPORATED (1818), Fulham Palace, S.W.6.—*Sec.*, Maj. R. I. Radford, M.B.E.

CHURCH EDUCATION CORPORATION, Bedgebury School, Goudhurst, Kent.—*Sec.*, R. P. Gilbert.

CHURCH HOUSE, THE CORPORATION OF (1888), Dean's Yard, S.W.1.—*Sec.*, Capt. P. W. E. Parry, M.B.E.

CHURCH LADS' AND CHURCH GIRLS' BRIGADE, *National Headquarters*, 15 Etchingham Park Road, N.3.—*Gen. Sec.*, Rev. C. Grice, M.B.E.

CHURCH MISSIONARY SOCIETY (1799), 157 Waterloo Road, S.E.1. Income, 1983, £3,102,900.—*Secs.*, Rev. Canon S. Barrington-Ward (*General*); Miss E. A. E. Pointon (*Britain*); C. B. Fernihough (*Financial*).

CHURCH OF ENGLAND CHILDREN'S SOCIETY (1881) (The Children's Society), Old Town Hall, Kennington Road, S.E.11.—*Dir.*, Miss C. W. Stone.

CHURCH OF ENGLAND MEN'S SOCIETY (1899), 18 Hertford Street, Coventry.—*Gen. Sec.*, Rev. E. D. Murfet.

CHURCH OF ENGLAND PENSIONS BOARD (1926), 53 Tufton Street, S.W.1.—*Sec.*, D. Thackray.

CHURCH OF ENGLAND SOLDIERS', SAILORS' AND AIRMEN'S CLUBS (1891), and CHURCH OF ENGLAND SOLDIERS', SAILORS' AND AIRMEN'S HOUSING ASSOCIATION LTD. (1974), 1 Shakespeare Terrace, 126 High Street, Portsmouth. *Chairman*, Rear-Adm. A. G. Watson, C.B.

CHURCH OF SCOTLAND BOARD OF SOCIAL RESPONSIBILITY, 121 George Street, Edinburgh 2.—*Gen. Sec.*, Rev. F. S. Gibson.

CHURCH PASTORAL AID SOCIETY (1836), Falcon Court, 32 Fleet Street, E.C.4.—*Gen. Sec.*, Rev. D. B. Bubbers.

CHURCH UNION (1859), 7 Tufton Street, S.W.1.—*Gen. Sec.*, Rev. P. J. E. Geldard.

CHURCHES, BRITISH COUNCIL OF (1942), 2 Eaton Gate, S.W.1.—*Gen. Sec.*, Dr. P. Morgan.

CHURCHES, COUNCIL FOR CARE OF, 83 London Wall, E.C.2.—*Sec.*, P. A. T. Burman, F.S.A., F.R.S.A.

CHURCHES, FRIENDLESS, FRIENDS OF (1957), 12 Edwardes Square, W.8.—*Hon. Dir.*, I. Bulmer-Thomas; *Hon. Sec.*, L. E. Jones.

CHURCHES MAIN COMMITTEE (1941), Fielden House, Little College Street, S.W.1.—*Sec.*, B. M. Thimont, C.B.

CITIZENS ADVICE BUREAUX, NATIONAL ASSOCIATION OF (1931), Myddelton House, 115/123 Pentonville Road, N.1.—*Chief Exec. Officer*, Elizabeth Filkin.

CITY PAROCHIAL FOUNDATION (Trustees of the London Parochial Charities), 10 Fleet Street, E.C.4.—*Clerk*, B. H. Woods, M.B.E.

CIVIL DEFENCE, INSTITUTE OF (1938), P.O. Box 229, 3 Little Montague Court, E.C.1.—*Hon. Gen. Sec.*, E. C. Stanbridge.

CIVIL DEFENCE AND EMERGENCY PLANNING OFFICERS, ASSOCIATION OF, Room 147, County Hall, George Row, Northampton.—*Hon. Gen. Sec.*, A. G. Farrell.

CIVIL ENGINEERS, INSTITUTION OF (1818), Great George Street, S.W.1.—*Pres.*, J. A. Gaffney; *Sec.*, J. C. McKenzie.

CIVIL LIBERTIES, NATIONAL COUNCIL FOR (1934), 21 Tabard Street, S.E.1.—*Sec.*, L. Gostin.

CIVIL SERVICE COUNCIL FOR FURTHER EDUCATION.—*Sec.*, G. F. Burns, Old Admiralty Building, Whitehall, S.W.1.

CLASSICAL ASSOCIATION (1903).—*Hon. Treas.*, G. R. Watson, Dept. of Classical and Archæological Studies, The University, Nottingham.

CLASSICAL TEACHERS, JOINT ASSOCIATION OF (1962), 31–34 Gordon Square, W.C.1.—*Exec. Sec.*, I. D. Jenkins.

CLERGY ORPHAN CORPORATION (1749), 57B Tufton Street, Westminster, S.W.1.—*Sec.*, Miss J. Buncher.

CLERKS OF WORKS OF GREAT BRITAIN INCORPORATED, INSTITUTE OF (1882), 41 The Mall, W.5.—*Sec.*, A. P. Macnamara.

COACHING CLUB (1871), 2 Treville Street, S.W.15.—*Sec.*, D. H. Clarke.

COAL TRADE BENEVOLENT ASSOCIATION (1888), 63 Narrow Street, Limehouse, E.14.—*Sec.*, H. C. F. Squire, O.B.E.

COLLEGE OF THE SEA, *see* SEAFARERS EDUCATION SERVICE.

COMBINED CADET FORCE ASSOCIATION (1952), Millbank Barracks, John Islip Street, S.W.1.—*Sec.*, Brig. D. M. Pontifex, C.B.E.

COMMERCE, ASSOCIATION OF BRITISH CHAMBERS OF (1860).—*Pres.*, Sir David Nicolson; *Dir. Gen.*, R. G. Taylor, Sovereign House, 212A Shaftesbury Avenue, W.C.2.

COMMERCE AND INDUSTRY, LONDON CHAMBER OF (1881), 69 Cannon Street, E.C.4.—*Pres.*, Sir David Steel, D.S.O., M.C., T.D.; *Dir.*, W. F. Nicholas, O.B.E.

COMMERCE, ASSOCIATION OF SCOTTISH CHAMBERS OF, 30 George Square, Glasgow.—*Sec.*, K. E. Marwick.

COMMERCE AND MANUFACTURES, EDINBURGH CHAMBER OF (1786), 3 Randolph Crescent, Edinburgh 3.—*Chief Exec.*, D. M. Mowat.

COMMERCE AND MANUFACTURES, GLASGOW CHAMBER OF (1783), 30 George Square, Glasgow.—*Sec.*, K. E. Marwick.

COMMERCIAL TRAVELLERS' BENEVOLENT INSTITUTION

(1849), 49 Lawrie Park Avenue, S.E.26.—*Chief Exec.*, E. B. Auger.

COMMISSIONAIRES, THE CORPS OF (1859), founded by the late Captain Sir Edward Walter; for the employment of ex-Soldiers, Sailors and Airmen and ex-police, fire service and merchant navy servicemen. *Headquarters*, 3 Crane Court, Fleet Street, E.C.4. *Outquarters*, War Memorial Building, Waring St., Belfast 1.; Room 53, Guildhall Buildings, Navigation Street, Birmingham; 87 Park Street, Bristol; 99 Shandwick Place, Edinburgh; 180 W. Regent Street, Glasgow; 10–12 East Parade, Leeds; 61 Lord Street, Liverpool; 2 St. John Street, Deansgate, Manchester; 10 Bigg Market, Newcastle upon Tyne 1. Total strength, 2,700—*Commandant*, Col. R. B. Robertson; *Adjutant*, Col. A. M. Thorburn.

COMMONWEALTH ASSOCIATION OF PLANNERS (1971), 26 Portland Place, W.1.—*Hon. Sec.*, R. Shaw.

COMMONWEALTH PARLIAMENTARY ASSOCIATION.—*Sec.*, U.K. Branch, P. Cobb, Westminster Hall, S.W.1.

COMMONWEALTH PRESS UNION (1909), Studio House, 184 Fleet Street, E.C.4.—*Dir.*, Lt.-Col. T. Pierce-Goulding, M.B.E., C.D.

COMMONWEALTH SETTLEMENT, CHURCH OF ENGLAND COUNCIL FOR (1925), (see OVERSEAS SETTLEMENT, C. of E. COMMITTEE FOR).

COMMONWEALTH SOCIETY FOR THE DEAF (1959), 105, Gower Street, W.C.1.—*Admin. Sec.*, Miss E. Lubienska.

COMMONWEALTH UNIVERSITIES, ASSOCIATION OF, John Foster House, 36 Gordon Square, W.C.1.—*Sec. Gen.*, A. Christodoulou, C.B.E.

COMMUNITY MEDICINE, CENTRE FOR EXTENSION TRAINING IN (London School of Hygiene and Tropical Medicine) (1972), Keppel Street, W.C.1.—*Admin.*, P. F. V. Waters, F.R.S.A.

COMMUNITY MEDICINE, SOCIETY OF (1856), 28 Portland Place, W.1.—*Pres.*, Dr. P. A. Gardner.

COMPOSERS' GUILD OF GREAT BRITAIN, THE (1945), 10 Stratford Place, W.1.—*Gen. Sec.*, Miss E. Yeoman.

CONSERVATION OF HISTORIC AND ARTISTIC WORKS, INTERNATIONAL INSTITUTE FOR, 6 Buckingham Street, W.C.2.—*Pres.*, G. Thomson; *Sec. Gen.*, N. Brommelle.

CONSERVATION SOCIETY, LTD. (1966), 12A Guildford Street, Chertsey, Surrey.—*Dir.*, Dr. J. Davoll.

CONSERVATION VOLUNTEERS, BRITISH TRUST FOR (1970), 36 St. Mary's Street, Wallingford, Oxon.—*Dir.*, I. Branton.

CONSERVATIVE AND UNIONIST ASSOCIATIONS, NATIONAL UNION OF (1867), 32 Smith Square, S.W.1.—*Sec.*, Alan Smith.

CONSERVATIVE CLUBS, LTD., ASSOCIATION OF (1894), 56 Buckingham Gate, S.W.1.—*Sec.*, L. G. Waterman, O.B.E.

CONSTRUCTION SURVEYORS' INSTITUTE (1952), 203 Lordship Lane, S.E.22.—*Development Officer*, B. A. Hunt.

CONSULTING ENGINEERS, ASSOCIATION OF (1913), Alliance House, 12 Caxton Street, S.W.1.—*Sec.*, Maj.-Gen. P. J. M. Pellereau.

CONSULTING SCIENTISTS, ASSOCIATION OF, Owles Hall, Buntingford, Herts.—*Sec.*, Mrs. H. M. W. Gibbons.

CO-OPERATIVE SOCIETIES AND ASSOCIATIONS:—

Co-operative Party, 158 Buckingham Palace Road, S.W.1.—*Sec.*, D. Wise, O.B.E.

Co-operative Union (1869), Holyoake House, Hanover Street, Manchester.—*Chief Exec. Officer*, D. L. Wilkinson.

Co-operative Wholesale Society (C.W.S.) (1863), New Century House, Manchester 4.—*Chief Exec. Officer*, D. M. Landau; *Sec.*, G. J. Melmoth.

Co-operative Women's Guild, 342 Hoe Street, Walthamstow, E.17.—*Gen. Sec.*, (vacant).

Fisheries Organization Society, Ltd. (1914), New Fish Quay, Brixham, Devon.—*A. H. Dobbie.*

International Co-operative Alliance (1895), 35 rue des Pâquis BP 862, CH 1211, Geneva 1.—*Interim Dir.*, Ms. F. Baulier.

Plunkett Foundation for Co-operative Studies (1919), 31 St. Giles, Oxford.—*Dir.*, E. Parnell.

COPYRIGHT COUNCIL, BRITISH (1953), 29–33 Berners Street, W.1.

CORONERS' SOCIETY OF ENGLAND AND WALES (1846).— *Hon. Sec.*, J. Burton, Coroner's Court, 77 Fulham Palace Road, W.6.

CORPORATE TREASURERS, ASSOCIATION OF, 16 Park Crescent, Regents Park, W.1.—*Sec.*, Richenda Eaton.

CORPORATE TRUSTEES, ASSOCIATION OF, 2 Withdean Rise, Brighton, E. Sussex.—*Sec.*, L. C. Howes.

CORRESPONDENCE COLLEGES, ASSOCIATION OF BRITISH (1955), 6 Francis Grove, S.W.19.—*Sec.*, Mrs. M. Coren.

COUNCIL FOR SMALL INDUSTRIES IN RURAL AREAS, 141 Castle Street, Salisbury, Wilts.—*Sec.*, R. G. Searle.

COUNSEL AND CARE FOR THE ELDERLY (Elderly Invalids Fund), 131 Middlesex Street, E.1.—*Sec.*, J. H. Hobart.

COUNTRY LANDOWNERS' ASSOCIATION (1907), 16 Belgrave Square, S.W.1.—*Dir. Gen.*, J. M. Douglas.

COUNTY CHIEF EXECUTIVES, ASSOCIATION OF.—*Hon. Sec.*, R. W. Adock, County Hall, Chelmsford, Essex.

COUNTY COUNCILS, ASSOCIATION OF, Eaton House, 66A Eaton Square, S.W.1.—*Sec.*, J. Stevenson.

COUNTY EMERGENCY PLANNING OFFICERS' SOCIETY, County Hall, Spetchley Road, Worcester.—*Hon. Sec.*, P. W. Fenn, T.D.

COUNTY SECRETARIES, SOCIETY OF.—*Hon. Sec.*, T. Harrison, County Hall, Glenfield, Leicester.

COUNTY SURVEYORS' SOCIETY (1884).—*President*, J. W. M. Vallis, Warwickshire County Council, Shire Hall, Warwick; *Hon. Sec.*, M. N. T. Cottell, Kent County Council, Sandling Block, Springfield, Maidstone, Kent.

COUNTY TREASURERS, SOCIETY OF (1903), County Hall, Beverley, N. Humberside.—*Hon. Sec.*, J. A. Parkes.

CRAFTS CENTRE, BRITISH (1948), 43 Earlham Street, Covent Garden, W.C.2.—*Dir.*, Tatjana Marsden.

CRUELTY TO ANIMALS, ROYAL SOCIETY FOR THE PREVENTION OF. *See* "ROYAL."

CRUELTY TO ANIMALS, CENTRAL COUNCIL OF SOCIETIES IN SCOTLAND FOR PREVENTION OF (1950), 19 Melville Street, Edinburgh.—*Hon. Sec.*, Sir Cameron Rusby, K.C.B., M.V.O.

CRUELTY TO CHILDREN. *See* "NATIONAL" and "ROYAL SCOTTISH."

CULTURAL EXCHANGE, ASSOCIATION FOR (1958), Babraham, Cambridge.—*Sec.*, P. B. Barnes.

CURATES' AUGMENTATION FUND (1866), 27 Medway Street, S.W.1.—*Hon. Sec.*, J. M. Greany.

CYCLISTS TOURING CLUB (1878), Cotterell House, 69 Meadrow, Godalming, Surrey.—*Sec.*, A. J. Leng.

CWMNI URDD GOBAITH CYMRU, Swyddfa'r Urdd, Aberystwyth.—*Dir.*, J. E. Williams.

CYMMRODORION, THE HONOURABLE SOCIETY OF (1751).—*Hon. Sec.*, Mrs. J. Gruffydd, 30 Eastcastle Street, W.1.

DAIRY ASSOCIATION, UNITED KINGDOM (1950), Giggs Hill Green, Thames Ditton, Surrey.—*Sec.*, Miss J. E. Smith.

DAIRY TECHNOLOGY, SOCIETY OF (1943), 72 Ermine Street, Huntingdon, Cambs.—*Sec.*, P. H. F. Lee.

D-DAY AND NORMANDY FELLOWSHIP.—*Hon. Secs.*, Mr. and Mrs. L. R. Reed, 9 South Parade, Southsea, Hants.

DEAF ASSOCIATION, BRITISH (1890 *formerly* BRITISH DEAF AND DUMB ASSOCIATION), 38 Victoria Place, Carlisle.—*Gen. Sec.*, A. W. Verney.

DEAF, ROYAL NATIONAL INSTITUTE FOR THE (1911), 105 Gower Street, W.C.1.—*Dir.*, R. Sydenham.

DEAF AND DUMB, ROYAL ASSOCIATION IN AID OF, To promote the general, social and spiritual welfare of deaf and blind/deaf people in Greater London, Essex, Surrey and Kent. 27 Old Oak Road, Acton, W.3.—*Director*, Rev. I. Scott-Oldfield.

DEAF AND DUMB WOMEN, BRITISH HOME FOR, 26 Clapton Common, E.5.—*Matron and Sec.*, Miss E. McFarlane.

DEAF CHILDREN, ROYAL SCHOOL FOR (1792), Margate. *Office*, Victoria Road, Margate, Kent.—*Sec.* D. E. Downs.

DEER MANAGEMENT SOCIETIES, THE FEDERATION OF (1975), The Old Well Cottage, Beech Road, Yorkney, Lydney, Glos.—*Co-ordinator*, J. H. Absalom.

DEER SOCIETY, BRITISH.—*Dir.*, N. J. Foll, Green Lane, Ufton Nervet, Reading, Berks.

DENTAL COUNCIL, GENERAL, 37 Wimpole Street, W.1.—*Registrar*, N. T. Davies, M.B.E.

DENTAL HOSPITALS OF THE UNITED KINGDOM, ASSOCIATION OF (1942).—*Hon. Sec.*, Mrs. P. Harrington, Dental Hospital, St. Chad's Queensway, Birmingham 4.

DESIGN AND INDUSTRIES ASSOCIATION (1915), c/o 17 Lawn Crescent, Kew Gardens, Surrey.—*Hon. Dir.*, R. Plummer.

DEVON AND CORNWALL RECORD SOCIETY (1904).—c/o Devon and Exeter Institution, 7 The Close, Exeter.—*Hon. Sec.*, J. D. Brunton.

DICKENS FELLOWSHIP, Dickens House, 48 Doughty Street, W.C.1.—*Hon. Gen. Sec.*, A. S. Watts.

DIRECTORS, INSTITUTE OF, 116 Pall Mall, S.W.1.—*Dir. Gen.*, Sir John Hoskyns.

DISABILITY AND REHABILITATION, THE ROYAL ASSOCIATION FOR, 25 Mortimer Street, W.1.—*Dir.*, G. Wilson.

DISPENSING OPTICIANS, ASSOCIATION OF (1925), 22 Nottingham Place, W.1.—*Sec. Gen.*, A. P. D. Westhead.

DISTRESSED GENTLEFOLK'S AID ASSOCIATION (1897), (Headquarters and London Nursing Home), Vicarage Gate House, Vicarage Gate, Kensington, W.8.—*Gen. Sec.*, J. A. Marshall, C.B.

DISTRICT COUNCILS, ASSOCIATION OF (1974), 9 Buckingham Gate, S.W.1.—*Sec.*, G. McCartney.

DISTRICT MEDICAL OFFICERS, ASSOCIATION OF (1982). *Hon. Sec.*, Dr. P. W. Briggs, Ealing Hospital, St. Bernard's Wing, Uxbridge Road, Southall, Middx.

DISTRICT SECRETARIES ASSOCIATION OF, Smokey Acre, Broadoak Hill, Dundry, Bristol.—*Hon. Sec.*, B. J. Quoroll.

DITCHLEY FOUNDATION, Ditchley Park, Enstone, Oxford.—*Dir.*, Sir Reginald Hibbert, G.C.M.G.

DOCKLAND SETTLEMENTS, headquarters and office at Isle of Dogs, E.14. Branches at Bristol; Rotherhithe, S.E.16; Glasgow; Stratford, E.15; Hainault, Essex.

DOMESTIC SERVANTS' BENEVOLENT INSTITUTION (1846), Royal Bank of Scotland P.L.C., 7 Burlington Gardens, W.1.—*Sec.*, D. C. F. Small.

DOMINION STUDENTS' HALL TRUST (see Overseas Graduates, London House for).

DOWSERS, BRITISH SOCIETY OF.—*Sec.*, M. D. Rust, Sycamore Cottage, Hastingleigh, Nr. Ashford, Kent.

DRAINAGE AUTHORITIES, ASSOCIATION OF (1937).—*Sec.*, D. Noble, 31 Castlegate, Newark-on-Trent, Notts.

DRINKING FOUNTAIN ASSOCIATION (formerly Metropolitan Drinking Fountain and Cattle Trough Association) (1859), 105 Wansunt Road, Bexley, Kent.—*Sec.* D. R. W. Randall.

DRUG DEPENDENCE, INSTITUTE FOR THE STUDY OF, 1/4 Hatton Place, E.C.1.—*Dir.*, J. Woodcock.

DUKE OF EDINBURGH'S AWARD, 5 Prince of Wales Terrace, W.8.—*Director*, R. Heron.

DYERS AND COLOURISTS, SOCIETY OF (1884), Perkin House, P.O. Box 244, 82 Grattan Road, Bradford, W. Yorks.—*Gen. Sec.*, M. Tordoff, PH.D.

EARL HAIG'S (BRITISH LEGION) APPEAL FUND. See "BRITISH LEGION."

EARL HAIG FUND (SCOTLAND). Established for the relief of distress among ex-service personnel and their dependants in Scotland. Applications to *North, South and East Area*, New Haig House, Logie Green Road, Edinburgh.—*Gen. Sec.*, Brig. R. W. Riddle, O.B.E.; or *Glasgow and South-West Area*, 1 Fitzroy Place, Glasgow, C.3.—*Sec.*, Maj. J. B. A. Smyth.

EARLY ENGLISH TEXT SOCIETY (1864).—*Hon. Director*, Prof. J. Burrow; *Exec. Sec.*, Dr. M. Godden, Exeter College, Oxford.

ECCLESIASTICAL HISTORY SOCIETY.—*Sec.*, Dr. Judith Champ, King's College, Strand, W.C.2.

ECCLESIOLOGICAL SOCIETY.—*Hon. Sec.*, S. C. Humphrey, St. Andrew-by-the-Wardrobe, Queen Victoria Street, E.C.4.

EDUCATION OFFICERS, SOCIETY OF.—*Gen. Sec.*, R. P. Harding, C.B.E., 5 Bentinck Street, W.1.

EDUCATION OFFICERS' SOCIETY, COUNTY.—*Hon. Sec.*, R. D. Clark, Education Dept., The Castle, Winchester, Hants.

EDUCATION THROUGH ART, SOCIETY FOR, Bath Academy of Art, Corsham, Wilts.—*Chairman*, R. Clement.

EDUCATIONAL CENTRES ASSOCIATION, Chequer Centre, Chequer Street, E.C.1.—*Sec.*, D. Delahunt.

EDUCATIONAL FOUNDATION FOR VISUAL AIDS, Paxton Place, Gipsy Road, S.E.27.—*Chief Exec.*, G. C. Marchant.

EDUCATIONAL INSTITUTE OF DESIGN, CRAFT AND TECHNOLOGY.—*Gen. Sec.*, G. Day, 24 Elm Road, Kingswood, Bristol, Avon.

EDUCATIONAL INSTITUTE OF SCOTLAND (1847), 46 Moray Place, Edinburgh.—*Gen. Sec.*, J. D. Pollock.

EDUCATIONAL RESEARCH IN ENGLAND AND WALES, NATIONAL FOUNDATION FOR, The Mere, Upton Park, Slough, Berks.—*Dir.*, Dr. Clare Burstall.

EDUCATIONAL VISITS AND EXCHANGES, CENTRAL BUREAU FOR, Seymour Mews House, Seymour Mews, W.1.—*Dir.*, J. Platt.

EDWARDIAN STUDIES ASSOCIATION, 125 Markyate Road, Dagenham, Essex.—*Sec.*, E. Ford.

EGYPT EXPLORATION SOCIETY (1882), 3 Doughty Mews, W.C.1.—*Chairman*, T. G. H. James, F.B.A.; *Sec.*, Mrs S. K. Strong, PH.D.

ELECTORAL REFORM SOCIETY OF GREAT BRITAIN AND IRELAND (founded 1884 as Proportional Representation Soc.), 6 Chancel Street, S.E.1.—*Chief Exec.*, S. Burke.

ELECTRICAL ENGINEERS, INSTITUTION OF (1871), Savoy Place, W.C.2.—*Sec.*, H. H. W. Losty, F.I.E.E.

ELECTRICAL INSTALLATION CONTRACTING, NATIONAL INSPECTION COUNCIL FOR, 237 Kennington Lane, S.E.11.—*Dir. and Sec.*, J. T. Jennings, D.F.C.

ELECTRICITY CONSUMERS' COUNCIL, Brook House, 2/16 Torrington Place, W.C.1.—*Sec.*, R. E. D. Coldwell.

ELECTRONIC AND RADIO ENGINEERS, INSTITUTION OF (1925), 99 Gower Street, W.C.1.—*Sec.*, D. D. Duffett.

ELGAR FOUNDATION, Elgar's Birthplace, Lower Broadheath, Worcester.—*Hon. Sec.*, J. Bennett.

ELGAR SOCIETY (1951).—*Sec.*, A. H. A. Neill, 17 Earlsfield Road, S.W.18.

ENERGY INDUSTRIES COUNCIL, Newcombe House, 45 Notting Hill Gate, W.11.—*Dir. Gen.*, R. A. Custis.

ENERGY, INSTITUTE OF (1927), 18 Devonshire Street, Portland Place, W.1.—*Sec.*, H. M. Lodge.

ENGINEERING COUNCIL, THE, Canberra House, Maltravers Street, W.C.2.—*Sec.*, J. Carlill, O.B.E.

ENGINEERING DESIGNERS, INSTITUTION OF (1945), Courtleigh, Westbury Leigh, Westbury, Wilts.—*Gen. Sec.*, P. J. Booker.

ENGINEERING, FELLOWSHIP OF (1976), 2 Little Smith Street, S.W.1.—*Exec. Sec.*, V. J. Osola, C.B.E.

ENGINEERING INDUSTRIES ASSOCIATION, 16 Dartmouth Street, S.W.1.—*Dir.*, Col. W. T. Williams.

ENGINEERS AND SHIPBUILDERS IN SCOTLAND, INSTITUTION OF (1857), Charing Cross Tower, 10 Elmbank Gardens, Glasgow, G.2.—*Pres.*, A. M. M. Stephen.

ENGINEERS AND SHIPBUILDERS, N.E. COAST INSTITUTION OF (1884), 12 Windsor Terrace, Jesmond, Newcastle upon Tyne—*Sec.*, Mrs. A. M. Wilson.

ENGINEERS, INSTITUTION OF BRITISH (1928), Regency House, 3 Marlborough Place, Brighton.—*Sec.*, Mrs. D. Henry.

ENGINEERS, SOCIETY OF (Incorporated) (1854), 21–23 Mossop Street, S.W.3.—*Sec.*, E. C. Burton.

ENGLISH ASSOCIATION, THE (1906), 1 Priory Gardens, W.4.—*Sec.*, Dr. Ruth Fairbanks-Joseph.

ENGLISH FOLK DANCE AND SONG SOCIETY (1932), Cecil Sharp House, 2 Regent's Park Road, N.W.1.—*Dir.*, S. A. Matthews, M.B.E., T.D.

ENGLISH PLACE-NAME SOCIETY (1923).—*Hon. Director*, Prof. K. Cameron, PH.D., F.S.A., F.B.A., The University, Nottingham.

ENGLISH-SPEAKING UNION OF THE COMMONWEALTH (1918), 37 Charles Street, Berkeley Square, W.1.—*Chairman*, Sir Donald Tebbit, G.C.M.G.; *Dir. Gen.*, A. L. Williams, O.B.E.

ENTOMOLOGICAL SOCIETY OF LONDON, ROYAL (1833), 41 Queen's Gate, S.W.7.—*Registrar*, G. G. Bentley.

ENTOMOLOGY, COMMONWEALTH INSTITUTE OF (1909), 56 Queen's Gate, S.W.7.—*Director*, N. C. Pant, PH.D.

ENVIRONMENTAL CONSERVATION, COUNCIL FOR (1969), Zoological Gardens, Regent's Park, N.W.1.—*Pres.*, The Duke of Wellington, M.V.O., O.B.E., M.C.; *Chairman*, G. England; *Sec.*, E. Dawson.

ENVIRONMENTAL HEALTH OFFICERS, INSTITUTION OF, Chadwick House, Rushworth Street, S.E.1.—*Sec.*, K. J. Tyler.

EPILEPSY ASSOCIATION, BRITISH, Crowthorne House, Bigshotte, Wokingham, Berks.—*Sec.*, T. J. O'Leary.

EPILEPSY, THE NATIONAL SOCIETY FOR (1892), Chalfont Centre for Epilepsy, Chalfont St. Peter, Bucks.—*Sec.*, Col. H. V. Trewhella.

ESPERANTO ASSOCIATION OF BRITAIN (1977), 140 Holland Park Avenue, W.11.—*Hon. Sec.*, J. Brownlee.

EUGENICS SOCIETY (1907), 69 Eccleston Square, S.W.1.—*Gen. Sec.*, Miss S. E. Walters.

EUROPEAN SCHOOL (1978), Culham, Abingdon, Oxon.—*Head*, D. G. E. Hurd.

EVANGELICAL ALLIANCE (1846), 186 Kennington Park, Road, S.E.11.—*Gen. Sec.*, Rev. C. R. Calver.

EVANGELICAL LIBRARY, THE, 78A Chiltern Street, W.1.—*Librarian*, G. R. Sayer.

EXAMINERS UNDER SOLICITORS (SCOTLAND) ACT (1980), Law Society's Hall, 26–27 Drumsheugh Gardens, Edinburgh.—*Clerk*, K. W. Pritchard.

EXECUTIVES ASSOCIATION OF GREAT BRITAIN LTD., 7 Central Buildings, 24 Southwark Street, S.E.1.—*Sec.*, C. E. Nicholson.

EXPORT, INSTITUTE OF, World Trade Centre, E.1.—*Sec.*, D. N. Royce.

EX-SERVICES MENTAL WELFARE SOCIETY (for H.M. Forces and Merchant Navy men and women, suffering from psychiatric disabilities and more particularly those with active or long regular service), Broadway House, The Broadway, Wimbledon, S.W.19.—*Gen. Sec.*, J. S. Le Blanc Smith, R.N.

FABIAN SOCIETY (1884), 11 Dartmouth Street, S.W.1.—*Gen. Sec.*, I. Martin.

FAIRBRIDGE SOCIETY (1909), 119–126 Bush House (N.E.), Aldwych, W.C.2.—*Dir. and Sec.*, Mrs. C. P. MacGregor.

FAIR ISLE BIRD OBSERVATORY TRUST, 21 Regent Terrace, Edinburgh.—*Hon. Sec.*, Mrs. I. Waterston.

FAMILY CONCILIATION COUNCIL, NATIONAL (1982), c/o 155 High Street, Dorking, Surrey.—*Chairman*, B. R. Pearce.

FAMILY HISTORY SOCIETIES, FEDERATION OF (1974),—*Gen. Sec.*, Mrs. A. V. Chiswell, 96 Beaumont Street, Milehouse, Plymouth.

FAMILY PLANNING ASSOCIATION, 27–35 Mortimer Street, W.1.—*Gen. Sec.*, A. Service.

FAMILY WELFARE ASSOCIATION (Founded 1869 as CHARITY ORGANIZATION SOCIETY), 501–5 Kingsland Road, E.8.—*Dir.*, R. E. Morley.

FAUNA AND FLORA PRESERVATION SOCIETY (1903).—*Office*, c/o Zoological Society of London, Regent's Park, N.W.1.—*Hon. Sec.*, D. M. Jones.

FELLOWSHIP HOUSES TRUST (Flatlets for the elderly) (1937), Clock House, Byfleet, Surrey.—*Sec.*, L. P. Leech.

FIELD STUDIES COUNCIL (1943), 62 Wilson Street, E.C.2.—*Sec.*, R. S. Chapman.

FIRE ENGINEERS, INSTITUTION OF, 148 New Walk, Leicester.—*Gen. Sec.*, Mrs. C. E. Mackwood.

FIRE PROTECTION ASSOCIATION, Aldermary House, Queen Street, E.C.4.—*Dir.*, C. D. Woodward.

FIRE SERVICES ASSOCIATION, THE BRITISH, 86 London Road, Leicester.—*Gen. Sec.*, T. A. Plummer.

FIRE SERVICES NATIONAL BENEVOLENT FUND (1943),

Marine Court, Fitzalan Road, Littlehampton, W. Sussex.—*Hon. Sec.*, H. G. Pollock.

FOLKLORE SOCIETY, c/o University College London, Gower Street, W.C.1.—*Hon. Sec.*, A. R. Vickery.

FOOD SCIENCE AND TECHNOLOGY, INSTITUTE OF, 20 Queensberry Place, S.W.7.—*Chief Exec.*, Helen G. Wild.

FOOD FROM BRITAIN, 301–344 Market Towers, 1 Nine Elms Lane, S.W.8.—*Chairman*, N. Saphir.

FORCES HELP SOCIETY AND LORD ROBERTS WORKSHOPS (1899), 122 Brompton Road, S.W.3. *Comptroller and Sec.*, Col. A. W. Davis, M.B.E.

FOREIGN BONDHOLDERS, COUNCIL OF (1873), 35 High Street, Bromley, Kent.—*Dir.*, M. Gough.

FOREIGN PRESS ASSOCIATION IN LONDON, 11 Carlton House Terrace, S.W.1.—*Pres.*, R. Darroch.

FORENSIC SCIENCES, BRITISH ACADEMY OF (1959).—*Sec.-Gen.*, Prof. J. M. Cameron, Dept. of Forensic Medicine, The London Hospital Medical College, Turner Street, E.1.

FORESTERS, INSTITUTE OF CHARTERED (1982), 22 Walker Street, Edinburgh.—*Sec.*, Mrs. M. W. Dick.

FORESTRY ASSOCIATION, COMMONWEALTH (1921), c/o Commonwealth Forestry Institute, South Parks Road, Oxford.

FORESTRY SOCIETY OF ENGLAND, WALES AND NORTHERN IRELAND, ROYAL (1882), 102 High Street, Tring, Herts.—*Dir.*, E. H. M. Harris.

FORESTRY SOCIETY, ROYAL SCOTTISH (1854), 1 Rothesay Terrace, Edinburgh.—*Sec. and Treas.*, W. B. C. Walker.

FRANCO-BRITISH SOCIETY, 1 Old Burlington Street, W.1.—*Sec.*, Mrs. C. Stowell.

FREE CHURCH FEDERAL COUNCIL, 27 Tavistock Square, W.C.1.—*Moderator*, Rev. H. H. Williams, PH.D.; *Gen. Sec.*, Rev. R. J. Hamper.

FREEDOM ASSOCIATION (1975), Avon House, 360–366 Oxford Street, W.1.—*Executive Officer*. J. F. Fletcher.

FREEMASONS, GRAND LODGE OF SCOTLAND (1736), Freemasons' Hall, 96 George Street, Edinburgh.—*Grand Master Mason of Scotland*, J. M. Marcus Humphrey of Dinnet; *Grand Sec.*, E. S. Falconer.

FREEMASONS, UNITED GRAND LODGE OF ENGLAND, Freemasons' Hall, Great Queen Street, W.C.2.—*Grand Master*, H.R.H. the Duke of Kent, G.C.M.G., G.C.V.O., A.D.C.; *Pro Grand Master*, The Lord Cornwallis, O.B.E., D.L.; *Deputy Grand Master*, Hon. E. L. Baillieu; *Asst. Grand Master*, The Lord Fareham; *Grand Wardens*, The Viscount Gough; Rt. Hon. Sir I. Percival, Q.C., M.P.; *Grand Chaplain*, Rev. Dr. M. Morgan; *Grand Sec.*, Cdr. M. B. S. Higham, R.N.

FREEMEN OF CITY OF LONDON, GUILD OF (1908), P.O. Box 153, 40A Ludgate Hill, E.C.4.—*Master*, Sir Peter Gadsden, G.B.E.; *Clerk*, D. Reid.

FREEMEN OF ENGLAND (1966), Pradoe, Oswestry, Shropshire.—*Pres.*, Col. J. F. Kenyon, O.B.E., M.C.

FREIGHT FORWARDERS LTD., THE INSTITUTE OF, Suffield House, 9 Paradise Road, Richmond, Surrey.

FRESHWATER BIOLOGICAL ASSOCIATION (1929), The Ferry House, Far Sawrey, Ambleside, Cumbria.—*Sec. and Director of Laboratories*, Dr. R. T. Clarke.

FRIENDLY SOCIETIES, NATIONAL CONFERENCE OF—*Sec.*, P. M. Madders, Room 313, Victoria House, Vernon Place, W.C.1.

FRIENDS OF CATHEDRAL MUSIC (1956), c/o Addington Palace, Croydon.—*Hon. Gen. Sec.*, N. T. Barnes.

FRIENDS OF THE CLERGY CORP. (incorporating the Friend of the Clergy Corp. and the Poor Clergy Relief Corp.), 27 Medway Street, S.W.1.—*Sec.*, J. M. Greany.

FRIENDS OF THE NATIONAL LIBRARIES, c/o The British Library, W.C.1.—*Chairman*, The Lord Kenyon, C.B.E.; *Hon. Sec.*, J. F. Fuggles.

FRIENDS OF THE ELDERLY & GENTLEFOLK'S HELP (*formerly* FRIENDS OF THE POOR), 42 Ebury Street, S.W.1.—*Gen. Sec.*, Rev. J. Schofield.

FURNITURE HISTORY SOCIETY (1964).—*Hon. Sec.*, Mrs. H. Hayward, c/o Dept. of Furniture and Woodwork, Victoria and Albert Museum, S.W.7.

GALLIPOLI ASSOCIATION (1915).—*Hon. Sec.*, K. Tranmer, 100 Ramsgill Drive, Ilford, Essex.

GAME CONSERVANCY, THE, Fordingbridge, Hants.—*Dir.*, R. M. Van Oss.

GARDEN HISTORY SOCIETY (1965), 66 Granville Park, S.E.13.—*Hon. Membership Sec.*, Mrs. A. Richards.

GARDENERS' ASSOCIATION, THE GOOD, Arkley Manor Farm, Arkley, nr. Barnet, Herts.—*Hon. Dir.*, C. R. G. Shewell-Cooper, N.C.H.

GARDENERS' ROYAL BENEVOLENT SOCIETY (1839), Bridge House, 139 Kingston Road, Leatherhead, Surrey.—*Dir.*, R. E. Lloyd-Smith.

GAS CONSUMERS' COUNCIL, NATIONAL, 4th Floor, 162 Regent Street, W.1.—*Dir.*, J. Hosker.

GAS ENGINEERS, INSTITUTION OF (1863), 17 Grosvenor Crescent, S.W.1.—*Sec.*, D. J. Chapman.

GEMMOLOGICAL ASSOCIATION OF GREAT BRITAIN (1931), St. Dunstan's House, Carey Lane, E.C.2.—*Sec.*, C. Lenan.

GENEALOGICAL RESEARCH SOCIETY, IRISH.—*Sec.*, F. B. Payton, Glenholme, High Oakham Road, Mansfield, Notts.

GENEALOGISTS AND RECORD AGENTS, ASSOCIATION OF (1968), 31 Alexandra Grove, North Finchley, N.12.

GENEALOGISTS, SOCIETY OF (1911), 14 Charterhouse Buildings, Goswell Road, E.C.1.—*Dir.*, A. J. Camp.

GENERAL PRACTITIONERS, ROYAL COLLEGE OF (1952), 14 Princes Gate, S.W.7.—*Gen. Adminstr.*, Mrs. S. Fountain.

GENTLEPEOPLE, GUILD OF AID FOR (1904), 10 St. Christopher's Place, W.1.—*Sec.*, Mrs. G. A. Burgess.

GEOGRAPHICAL ASSOCIATION, 343 Fulwood Road, Sheffield.—*Joint Hon. Secs.*, M. T. Williams; Miss E. M. Fyfe.

GEOGRAPHICAL SOCIETY, ROYAL (1830), Kensington Gore, S.W.7.—*Pres.*, Sir George Bishop, C.B., O.B.E.; *Hon. Secs.*, Prof. E. H. Brown; Prof. A. S. Goudie; *Hon. Foreign Sec.*, Lt.-Col. S. Gilbert; *Hon. Treas.*, A. Tritton; *Director and Sec.*, Dr. J. Hemming; *Keeper of the Map Room*, Brig. G. A. Hardy; *Librarian*, D. Wileman.

GEOGRAPHICAL SOCIETY, MANCHESTER (1884), 274, The Corn Exchange Buildings, Manchester.—*Sec.*, Miss E. Whalley.

GEOGRAPHICAL SOCIETY, ROYAL SCOTTISH (1884), 10 Randolph Crescent, Edinburgh 3.—*Sec.*, D. G. Moir.

GEOLOGICAL SOCIETY (1807), Burlington House, Piccadilly, W.1.—*Pres.*, Prof. C. H. Holland; *Secs.*, Dr. R. G. Park; K. Coe, PH.D., W. J. French, PH.D.; *Foreign Sec.*, F. W. Dunning, O.B.E.; *Exec. Sec.*, R. M. Bateman.

GEOLOGISTS' ASSOCIATION.—*Hon. Gen. Sec.*, C. P. Green, D.Phil., Burlington House, Piccadilly, W.1.

GEOLOGISTS, THE INSTITUTION OF (1977), Burlington House, Piccadilly, W.1.—*Pres.*, D. C. Ion; *Secs.*, B. N. F. Hunt, Dr. P. C. Wright.

GEORGIAN GROUP (1937), 37 Spital Square, E.1.—*Sec.*, R. White.

GIFTED CHILDREN, NATIONAL ASSOCIATION FOR (1966), 1 South Audley Street, W.1.—*Dir.*, F. Sherwood.

GILBERT AND SULLIVAN SOCIETY.—*Hon. Sec.*, 273 Northfield Avenue, W.5.

GIRL GUIDES ASSOCIATION.—An organization founded by the first Lord Baden-Powell as a sister movement to the Scouts and incorporated by Royal Charter in 1922. In 1983 the total membership in the United Kingdom was 814,876. *Commonwealth Headquarters*, 17–19 Buckingham Palace Road, S.W.1.

GIRLS' BRIGADE, THE, Brigade House, Parsons Green, S.W.6.—*Brigade Sec. for Eng. & Wales*, Miss D. M. Cosser.

GIRLS' FRIENDLY SOCIETY AND TOWNSEND FELLOWSHIP (1875), 126 Queens Gate, S.W.7.—*Gen. Sec.*, Miss B. Cowderoy.

GIRLS OF THE REALM GUILD (1900).—Small educational grants towards schooling or initial training of single girls. Applications before February for ensuing academic year to: Mrs. B. Hayward, 2 Watchoak, Blackham, Tunbridge Wells, Kent.

GIRLS' SCHOOLS ASSOCIATION, GOVERNING BODIES OF (1942).—*Sec.*, Lt. Col. C. J. M. Hamilton, O.B.E., The Flat, The Lambdens, Reading, Berks.

GIRLS' VENTURE CORPS, Redhill Aerodrome, Kings Mill Lane, South Nutfield, Redhill, Surrey. A uniformed youth movement for girls between 13 and 20.—*Sec.*, Miss H. Prosper.

GLASS TECHNOLOGY, SOCIETY OF (1916), 20 Hallam Gate Road, Sheffield.—*Hon. Sec.*, T. S. Busby.

GOVERNING BODIES ASSOCIATION (Public schools) (1941).—*Sec.*, Lt. Col. C. J. M. Hamilton, O.B.E., The Flat, The Lambdens, Reading, Berks.

GRAPHIC ARTISTS, SOCIETY OF (1919), 17 Carlton House Terrace, S.W.1.—*Pres.*, Lorna B. Kell.

GREATER LONDON PLAYING FIELDS ASSOCIATION (1926), 25 Ovington Square, S.W.3.—*Sec.*, Capt. D. N. Forbes, D.S.C., R.N. (*ret.*).

GREATER LONDON RED CROSS BLOOD TRANSFUSION SERVICE (1921), 4 Collingham Gardens, S.W.5 [01-373 1056]. Hours, 9 a.m. to 10 p.m. every day.

GREEK INSTITUTE (1969) (for the promotion of modern Greek studies), 34 Bush Hill Road, N.21.—*Dir.*, Dr. Kypros Tofallis.

GROCERS ASSOCIATION, BRITISH INDEPENDENT, 17 Farnborough Street, Farnborough, Hants.—*Nat. Sec.*, I. A. McKee.

GULBENKIAN FOUNDATION, *see* CALOUSTE.

HAKLUYT SOCIETY (1846), c/o Map Library, The British Library, Ref. Div., Great Russell Street, W.C.1—*Joint Hon. Secs.*, Dr. T. E. Armstrong; Mrs. S. Tyacke.

HANSARD SOCIETY FOR PARLIAMENTARY GOVERNMENT (1944), 16 Gower Street, W.C.1.—*Sec.*, Mrs. M. Vlieland.

HARVEIAN SOCIETY OF LONDON.—*Exec. Sec.*, Maj. T. Tudor-Williams, 11 Chandos Street, Cavendish Square, W.1.

HEAD TEACHERS, NATIONAL ASSOCIATION OF.—*Gen. Sec.*, D. M. Hart, Holly House, 6 Paddockhall Road, Haywards Heath, West Sussex.

HEALTH AUTHORITIES IN ENGLAND AND WALES, THE NATIONAL ASSOCIATION (1974), Garth House, 47 Edgbaston Park Road, Birmingham.—*Dir.*, P. A. Hunt.

HEALTH EDUCATION COUNCIL, THE (1968), 78 New Oxford Street, W.C.1.—*Dir.-Gen.*, Dr. D. A. Player.

HEALTH EDUCATION, INSTITUTE OF.—*Hon. Sec.*, Dr. L. Baric, 14 High Elm Road, Hale Barns, Cheshire.

HEALTH, GUILD OF (1904), Edward Wilson House, 26 Queen Anne Street, W.1.—*Chairman*, J. Drewett.

HEALTH SERVICE ADMINISTRATORS, INSTITUTE OF (1902), 75 Portland Place, W.1.—*Sec.*, L. B. Akid.

HELLENIC STUDIES, SOCIETY FOR THE PROMOTION OF (1879), 31–34 Gordon Square, W.C.1.—*Pres.*, Prof. G. B. Kerferd; *Hon. Sec.*, Prof. J. P. Barron, F.S.A.

HENRY GEORGE FOUNDATION, 177 Vauxhall Bridge Road, S.W.1.—*Sec.*, Mrs. B. P. Sobrielo.

HERALDIC AND GENEALOGICAL STUDIES, INSTITUTE OF (1961), 80–82 Northgate, Canterbury, Kent.—*Dir.*, Dr. G. M. Swinfield.

HERALDRY SOCIETY, THE (1947), Museum Street, W.C.1.—*Sec.*, Mrs. V. Wreford Smith.

HERALDRY SOCIETY OF SCOTLAND (1977).—*Sec.*, W. R. M. Adams, Limegrove, High Street, Gifford, East Lothian.

HERPETOLOGICAL SOCIETY, BRITISH (1947), c/o Zoological Society of London, Regent's Park, N.W.1.—*Pres.*, The Earl of Cranbrook.

HIGHWAYS AND TRANSPORTATION, INSTITUTION OF (1930), 3 Lygon Place, Ebury Street, S.W.1.—*Sec.*, Miss P. A. Steel.

HISTORICAL ASSOCIATION (1906), 59A Kennington Park Road, S.E.11.—*Sec.*, Miss C. M. Povall.

HISTORICAL SOCIETY, ROYAL (1868), University College London, Gower Street, W.C.1.—*Pres.*, Prof. J. C. Holt, F.B.A.; *Exec. Sec.*, Mrs. J. Chapman.

HONG KONG ASSOCIATION (1961), Regis House, 43–46 King William Street, E.C.4.—*Exec. Dir.*, Brig. B. G. Hickey, O.B.E., M.C.

HORATIAN SOCIETY (1933).—*Hon. Sec.*, C. P. Sydenham, 4 Stone Buildings, Lincolns Inns, W.C.2.

HOROLOGICAL INSTITUTE, BRITISH (1858), Upton Hall, Upton, Newark, Notts.—*Sec.*, W. M. G. Evans.

HOROLOGICAL SOCIETY, ANTIQUARIAN (1953), New House, High Street, Ticehurst, E. Sussex.—*Sec.*, Cdr. G. Clarke.

HOSPITAL FEDERATION, INTERNATIONAL (1947), 126 Albert Street, N.W.1.—*Dir. Gen.*, M. C. Hardie.

HOSPITALS CONTRIBUTORY SCHEMES ASSOCIATION, BRITISH (1948), Royal London House, Queen Charlotte Street, Bristol.—*Sec.*, C. D. M. Kerr.

HOSPITAL SATURDAY FUND, THE (1873).—*Head Office*, 192–198 Vauxhall Bridge Road, S.W.1. *Sec.*, Miss I. Gleeson.

HOSPITAL SAVING ASSOCIATION, THE, Hambleden House, Andover, Hants.—*Gen. Sec.*, I. Forbes, M.B.E., D.F.C.

HOTEL CATERING AND INSTITUTIONAL MANAGEMENT ASSOCIATION, 191 Trinity Road, S.W.17.—*Dir.*, Miss E. Gadsby.

HOTELS, RESTAURANTS AND CATERERS ASSOCIATION, BRITISH (1907), 40 Duke Street, W.1.—*Chief Exec.*, C. Derby, O.B.E.

HOUSE OF HOSPITALITY LTD., Holy Cross Priory, Cross-in-Hand, Heathfield, Sussex. 28 homes for old people.—*Dir.*, Mother Mary Garson.

HOUSE OF ST. BARNABAS IN SOHO (House of Charity for Homeless Women in London) (1846), 1 Greek Street, Soho Square, W.1.—*Chief Exec.*, Gp. Capt. H. A. Lax.

HOUSING AID SOCIETY, CATHOLIC (1956), 189a Old Brompton Road, S.W.5.—*Dir.*, R. Kahn.

HOUSING AND TOWN PLANNING COUNCIL, NATIONAL (1900), 14–18 Old Street, E.C.1.—*Dir.*, R. Walker.

HOUSING ASSOCIATION FOR OFFICERS' FAMILIES (1916), Alban Dobson House, Green Lane, Morden, Surrey.—*Gen. Sec.*, R. Davis.

HOVERCRAFT SOCIETY, THE (1971), Forest Lodge West, Fawley Road, Hythe, Southampton, Hants.—*Sec.*, Miss J. M. Walker.

HOWARD LEAGUE, THE (1866), 322 Kennington Park Road, S.E.11. For education and research into the criminal justice system.—*Dir.*, D. E. S. Jenkins.

HUGUENOT SOCIETY OF LONDON (1885), c/o Barclays Bank, Ltd., 1 Pall Mall East, S.W.1.—*Hon. Sec.*, Miss I. Scouloudi, M.SC., F.S.A., F.R.Hist.S.

HUNTERIAN SOCIETY, The Hunterian Room, The Wellcome Building, Euston Road, N.W.1. *Secs.*, Dr. D. W. Findlay; G. Jantet.

HYDROFOIL SOCIETY, INTERNATIONAL, 51 Welbeck Street, W.1.—*Chief Exec.*, Juanita Kalerghi.

HYDROGRAPHIC SOCIETY (1972), North East London Polytechnic Dept. of Land Surveying, Dagenham, Essex.—*Hon. Sec.*, A. E. Ingham.

HYMN SOCIETY OF GREAT BRITAIN AND IRELAND, THE (1936), *Sec.*, Rev. A. Luff, 7 Little Cloister, Westminster Abbey, S.W.1.

INDEPENDENT SCHOOLS BURSURS' ASSOCIATION, *Sec.*, D. J. Bird, Woodlands, Closewood Road, Denmead, Hants.

INDEPENDENT SCHOOLS CAREERS ORGANIZATION, 12A–18A Princess Way, Camberley, Surrey.—*Dir. and Chief Exec.*, R. N. Exton, M.A.

INDEPENDENT SCHOOLS INFORMATION SERVICE (I.S.I.S.) (1972), 56 Buckingham Gate, S.W.1.—*Dir.*, T. Devlin.

INDEPENDENT SCHOOLS JOINT COUNCIL, *Sec.*, D. J. Bird, Woodlands, Closewood Road, Denmead, Hants.

INDEXERS, SOCIETY OF, 7a Parker Street, Cambridge.—*Hon. Sec.*, Mrs. C. Robertson.

INDUSTRIAL ARTISTS AND DESIGNERS, SOCIETY OF (1930), 12 Carlton House Terrace, S.W.1.—*Dir.*, M. Sadler-Forster.

INDUSTRIAL CHRISTIAN FELLOWSHIP (1877), 4 Streche Road, Swanage, Dorset.—*Dir.*, J. D. Davis.

INDUSTRIAL MANAGERS, INSTITUTION OF, Industrial Management House, Cardiff Road, Luton, Beds.

INDUSTRIAL MARKETING RESEARCH ASSOCIATION.— *Admin. Sec.*, Mrs. M. Everard, 11 Bird Street, Lichfield, Staffs.

INDUSTRIAL PARTICIPATION ASSOCIATION (1884), 85 Tooley Street, S.E.1.—*Sec.*, D. Wallace Bell.

INDUSTRIAL SOCIETY, THE (1918), 3 Carlton House Terrace, S.W.1.—*Dir.*, W. J. P. M. Garnett, C.B.E.; *Sec.*, M. R. Hyde.

INDUSTRY AND PARLIAMENT TRUST, 25 Victoria Street, S.W.1. Aims to provide practical ways of bridging the gap between industry and parliament.—*Pres.*, Rt. Hon. B. Weatherill, M.P.; *Dir.*, A. Maisner, C.B., C.B.E., A.F.C.

INFORMATION SCIENTISTS, INSTITUTE OF (1958), Harvest House, 62 London Road, Reading, Berks.— *Hon. Sec.*, Mrs. P. J. Brown.

INNER WHEEL CLUBS IN GREAT BRITAIN AND IRELAND, ASSOCIATION OF (1934), 51 Warwick Square, S.W.1.—*Gen. Sec.*, Miss J. Dobson.

INSURANCE BROKERS REGISTRATION COUNCIL, 15 St. Helen's Place, E.C.3.—*Registrar and Sec.*, J. E. Fryer, M.B.E.

INSURANCE INSTITUTE, CHARTERED (1897), 20 Aldermanbury, E.C.2.—*Sec.-Gen.*, P. V. Saxton.

INTERCONTINENTAL CHURCH SOCIETY, 175 Tower Bridge Road, S.E.1.—*Gen. Sec.*, Rev. Canon D. R. Irving.

INTERNATIONAL FRIENDSHIP LEAGUE (1931), 3 Creswick Road, Acton, W.3.—*Pres.*, The Baroness Vickers, D.B.E.

INTERNATIONAL LAW ASSOCIATION (1873), 3 Paper Buildings, Temple, E.C.4.—*Chairman*, The Rt. Hon. Lord Wilberforce, P.C., C.M.G., O.B.E.; *Hon. Sec.-Gen.*, Hon. J. B. S. Edwards; *Sec.*, M. Phillips.

INTERNATIONAL POLICE ASSOCIATION (British Section).—*National Headquarters*, 1 Fox Road, West Bridgford, Nottingham.—*Chief Exec. Officer*, K. H. Robinson.

INTERNATIONAL SHIPPING FEDERATION (1909), 30–32 St. Mary Axe, E.C.3.—*Pres.*, W. N. Menzies-Wilson; *Sec.*, C. L. A. Edgington.

INTERNATIONAL STUDENTS TRUST (1962), 229 Gt. Portland Street, W.1.—*President*, The Duke of Grafton, K.G.; *Dir.*, G. Rates.

INTERNATIONAL TIN RESEARCH INSTITUTE (1932), Fraser Road, Perivale, Greenford, Middlesex.—*Dir.*, D. A. Robins, PH.D.

INTERNATIONAL UNION FOR LAND VALUE TAXATION AND FREE TRADE, 177 Vauxhall Bridge Road, S.W.1.—*Sec.*, Mrs. B. P. Sobrielo.

INTERNATIONAL VOLUNTARY SERVICE (1920), Ceresole House, 53 Regent Road, Leicester.—*Gen. Sec.*, P. Wood.

INTER-VARSITY CLUBS, ASSOCIATION OF (1946), 3–5 The Piazza, Covent Garden, W.C.2.—*Sec.*, D. Lorking.

INVALID CHILDREN'S AID ASSOCIATION (LONDON), INCORPORATED (1888), 126 Buckingham Palace Road, S.W.1.—Information service on all aspects of handicap; family social work in parts of London and Surrey; residential special schools.—*Dir.*, J. McKinnon.

INVALIDS-AT-HOME (1966).—*Hon. Sec.*, Mrs. E. Pierce, 23 Farm Avenue, N.W.2. Helps seriously disabled people living at home.

IRAN SOCIETY (1936), 42 Devonshire Street, W.1.—*Pres.*, The Viscount Runciman of Doxford, O.B.E., A.F.C.; *Sec.*, K. Bradford.

IRISH LINEN MERCHANTS' ASSOCIATION (1872), Lambeg, Lisburn, N. Ireland.—*Sec.*, E. O. L. Seccombe, O.B.E..

IRISH SOCIETY, THE HONOURABLE THE (1613), Irish Chamber, Guildhall Yard, E.C.2.—*Sec.*, B. E. Manning; *Representative (Ireland)*, Cmdr. P. C. D. Campbell, M.V.O., D.L., R.N.

IRON AND STEEL INSTITUTE, see METALS SOCIETY.

JAPAN ASSOCIATION (1950), Regis House, 43–46 King William Street, E.C.4.—*Exec. Dir.*, Brig. B. G. Hickey, O.B.E., M.C.

JAPAN SOCIETY OF LONDON (1891), 656 Grand Buildings, Trafalgar Square, W.C.2.—*Hon. Sec.*, Mrs. E. F. Dobson, O.B.E.

JERUSALEM AND THE MIDDLE EAST CHURCH ASSOCIATION (1887), The Old Gatehouse, Castle Hill, Farnham, Surrey.—*Gen. Sec.*, The Ven. R. Lindley, C.B.E.

JEWISH WELFARE BOARD (1859).—*Exec. Dir.*, M. I. Carlowe, 221 Golders Green Road, N.W.11.

JEWISH HISTORICAL SOCIETY OF ENGLAND, Mocatta Library, University College, W.C.1.—*Hon. Sec.*, C. Drukker, 33 Seymour Place, W.1.

JEWISH YOUTH, ASSOCIATION FOR (1899), A.J.Y. House, 50 Lindley Street, E.1.—*Exec. Dir.*, A. Greenbat.

JEWS, CHURCH'S MINISTRY AMONG THE, 30c Clarence Road, St. Albans, Herts (from March 1984).—*Secs.*, Rev. W. F. Barker; Rev. D. Ryder.

JEWS AND CHRISTIANS, LONDON SOCIETY OF (1927), 28 St. John's Wood Road, N.W.8.—*Pres.*, Rev. Prof. G. Parrinder, D.D., PH.D., D.LITT.; *Joint Chairmen*, Rabbi Dr. John D. Rayner, D.D.; The Dean of Westminster; *Sec.*, Mrs. E. Nathan.

JOHN BUCHAN SOCIETY, THE (1979).—*Sec.*, R. J. Angus, 13 Bruntsfield Avenue, Edinburgh.

JOHN INNES INSTITUTE (1910), Colney Lane, Norwich.—*Director*, Prof. H. W. Woolhouse, PH.D.

JOURNALISTS, THE INSTITUTE OF, Bedford Chambers, Covent Garden, W.C.2.—*Gen. Sec.*, R. F. Farmer.

JULES VERNE CIRCLE, 125 Markyate Road, Dagenham, Essex.—*Sec.* E. Ford.

JUSTICE (British Section of the International Commission of Jurists) (1957), 95A Chancery Lane, W.C.2.—*Dir.*, Leah Levin.

JUSTICES' CLERKS' SOCIETY (1839).—*Hon. Sec.*, G. Sullivan, Magistrates' Court, P.O. Box 107, Nelson Street, Bristol.

KEEP BRITAIN TIDY GROUP, Bostel House, 37 West Street, Brighton, Sussex.—*Dir. Gen.*, D. J. Lewis.

KING EDWARD'S HOSPITAL FUND FOR LONDON (1897), 14 Palace Court, W.2.—A charity which uses its annual income to help hospitals improve the effectiveness and efficiency of their service to patients. The Fund divides its income between several major activities; making grants to hospitals and related organizations both within and outside the National Health Service but confined to those in or serving the Greater London area; providing education for health services staffs through the King's Fund College; sponsoring experiment and enquiry and providing information through its various experts and through the King's Fund Centre.—*Chairman of Management Committee*, The Hon. H. Astor; *Treasurer*, R. J. Dent; *Secretary*, R. J. Maxwell.

KING GEORGE'S FUND FOR SAILORS (1917), 1 Chesham Street, S.W.1. The central fund for all charities which support seafarers in need and their families. Distributes over £100,000 in grants annually.—*Gen. Sec.*, K. Sutherland.

KING GEORGE'S JUBILEE TRUST, 8 Buckingham Street, W.C.2.—Inaugurated in 1935 in commemoration of the Silver Jubilee of King George V. Its objects are the advancement of the physical, mental and spiritual welfare of the younger generation.—*Dir.*, H. Haywood, O.B.E., D.L.

LADIES IN REDUCED CIRCUMSTANCES, SOCIETY FOR THE ASSISTANCE OF (1886), Lancaster House, 25 Hornyold Road, Malvern, Worcs.—*Sec.*, Mrs. E. M. Klee.

LANCASTRIANS IN LONDON, ASSOCIATION OF (1892), Burnley House, 129 Kingsway, W.C.2.—*Hon. Sec.*, J. D. Dwyer.

LANDSCAPE INSTITUTE (Professional Institute for Landscape Architects, Managers and Scientists), 12 Carlton House Terrace, S.W.1.

LAND-VALUE TAXATION LEAGUE, 177 Vauxhall Bridge Road, S.W.1.—*Pres.*, V. G. Saldji.

LAW REPORTING FOR ENGLAND AND WALES, INCORPORATED COUNCIL OF (1865), 3 Stone Buildings, Lincoln's Inn, W.C.2.

LEAGUE OF THE HELPING HAND, Baileys, Church Street, Charlbury, Oxford.—*Sec.*, Mrs. D. R. Colvin.

LEAGUE OF WELLDOERS (incorporated) (1893), 119 & 133 Limekiln Lane, Liverpool, 5.—*Warden and Sec.*, K. H. Stanton.

LEATHER AND HIDE TRADES' BENEVOLENT INSTITUTION (1860), 60 Wickham Hill, Hurstpierpoint, Sussex.—*Sec.*, Mrs. G. M. Stapleton, M.B.E.

LEGAL EXECUTIVES, INSTITUTE OF, Kempston Manor, Kempston, Bedford.—*Sec.*, L. A. Evans.

LEPROSY GUILD, ST FRANCIS (1895), 21 The Boltons, S.W.10.—*Hon. Sec.*, Sr. Eileen McKee.

LEPROSY MISSION, THE (England and Wales) (1874), 50 Portland Place, W.1.—*Chairman*, Lady Richardson; *Exec. Dir.*, The Rev. R. J. Findlay.

LEUKAEMIA RESEARCH FUND (1962), 43 Great Ormond Street, W.C.1.—*Dir.*, G. J. Piller, O.B.E.

LIBRARY ASSOCIATION (1877), 7 Ridgmount Street, W.C.1.—*Chief Exec.*, G. Cunningham.

LIFEBOATS. *See* "ROYAL NATIONAL."

LIFE OFFICES' ASSOCIATION, THE (1889), Aldermary House, Queen Street, E.C.4.—*Sec. Gen.*, T. H. M. Oppé.

LINGUISTS, INSTITUTE OF (1910), 24a Highbury Grove, N.5.—*Gen. Sec.*, A. Bell.

LINNEAN SOCIETY OF LONDON (1788), Burlington House, W.1.—*Pres.*, Prof. R. J. Berry; *Treas.*, C. M. Hutt; *Secs.*, Dr. F. A. Bisby (*Botany*); Dr. Doris M. Kermack (*Zoology*); Dr. C. Patterson (*Editorial*); *Exec. Sec.*, Cdr. J. H. Fiddian-Green.

LIONS CLUBS INTERNATIONAL (British Isles & Ireland) (1949).—*Gen. Sec.*, T. L. Packer, 22 Craddock Street, Swansea, W. Glamorgan.

LIVERPOOL COTTON ASSOCIATION, 620 Cotton Exchange Buildings, Edmund Street, Liverpool, 3.—*Dir. Gen. and Sec.*, J. Wilson-Smith.

LLOYD'S, Lime Street, E.C.3.—*Chairman* (1984), P. N. Miller; *Deputy Chairmen*, W. N. M. Lawrence; F. Barber; *Chief Exec.*, I. H. Davison.

LLOYD'S PATRIOTIC FUND (1803), Lloyd's, Lime Street, E.C.3.—*Sec.*, J. Gawler.

LLOYD'S REGISTER OF SHIPPING (1760), 71 Fenchurch Street, E.C.3.—*Chairman*, H. R. MacLeod; *Deputy Chairman and Chairman of the Sub-Committees of Classification*, H. J. C. Browne, O.B.E.; *Managing Director*, B. Hildrew, C.B.E.; *Chief Ship Surveyor*, J. R. Cheshire; *Chief Engineer Surveyor*, C. Archer; *Managing Engineer Industrial Services*, R. Baldwin; *Secretary*, W. T. Leadbetter. Office of *Lloyd's Register Book, Rules for the Classification of Ships*, etc.

LOCAL AUTHORITIES, INTERNATIONAL UNION OF (1913), (*also* COUNCIL OF EUROPEAN MUNICIPALITIES (1951)), British Section, 12 Old Queen Street, S.W.1.—*Exec. Sec.*, P. N. Bongers.

LOCAL AUTHORITY CHIEF EXECUTIVES, SOCIETY OF.—*Hon. Sec.*, A. J. Greenwell, County Hall, Northampton.

LONDON APPRECIATION SOCIETY (1932), 17 Manson Mews, S.W.7. Visits to places of historic and modern interest in and around London.—*Hon. Sec.*, H. L. Bryant Peers.

LONDON BOROUGHS ASSOCIATION (1964), Westminster City Hall, Victoria Street, S.W.1.—*Hon. Sec.*, R. G. Brooke.

LONDON CITY MISSION (1835), 175 Tower Bridge Road, S.E.1.—*Gen. Sec.*, Rev. D. M. Whyte.

LONDON CORNISH ASSOCIATION (1898), *Hon. Gen. Sec.*, N. S. Bunney, 119 Warwick Road, N.11.

LONDON COURT OF INTERNATIONAL ARBITRATION (1892), 75 Cannon Street, E.C.4.—*Chairman*, A. B. Shindler. *Registrar*, B. W. Vigrass, O.B.E., V.R.D.

LONDON FLOTILLA (Association of Reserve and Retired Officers of The Royal Navy).—*Hon. Sec.*, Lt.

Cdr. P. A. G. Norman R.D., R.N.R., Marden Rise, 81 Marden Hill, Fetcham, Surrey.

LONDON LIBRARY, THE (1841), 14 St. James's Square, S.W.1.—*Librarian*, D. Matthews.

LONDON MAGISTRATES' CLERKS' ASSOCIATION (1889), *Hon. Sec.*, Miss A. F. Damazer, Deputy Chief Clerk, Thames Magistrates' Court, Aylward Street, E.1.

LONDON MISSIONARY SOCIETY, *see* CONGREGATIONAL COUNCIL.

"LONDON OVER THE BORDER" CHURCH FUND (1878), Guy Harlings, New Street, Chelmsford.—*Sec.*, D. J. Newman.

LONDON PLAYING FIELDS SOCIETY (1890), Headquarters, Boston Manor Playing Field, Boston Gardens, Brentford, Middlesex.—*Sec.*, C. J. M. Clayton.

LONDON SOCIETY, THE, Room G210, The City University, Northampton Square, E.C.1.—*Hon. Sec.*, Mrs. G. M. Gorer.

LORD MAYOR TRELOAR COLLEGE, for education and care of physically handicapped boys and girls. Administered by the Treloar Trust, Froyle, Nr. Alton, Hants.—*Sec.*, B. E. Roberts.

LORD'S DAY OBSERVANCE SOCIETY (1831), 5 Victory Avenue, Morden, Surrey.—*Gen. Sec.*, J. G. Roberts.

LORD'S TAVERNERS, THE, 1 St. James's Street, S.W.1.—*Dir.*, Capt. J. A. R. Swainson, O.B.E., R.N.

LOTTERIES COUNCIL, c/o Winkworth and Pemberton, 22 Greencoat Place, S.W.1.—*Sec.* R. A. Cummins.

MAGISTRATES' ASSOCIATION (1920), 28 Fitzroy Square, W.1.—*Pres.*, The Lord Chancellor; *Sec.*, G. Norman.

MAIL USERS' ASSOCIATION, 137 Dulwich Road, S.E.24.—*Exec. Dir.*, M. E. Corby.

MALAYSIA, SINGAPORE AND BRUNEI ASSOCIATION (1955), 90 Fenchurch Street, E.C.3.—*Sec.*, Mrs. J. Taylor.

MALAYSIAN RUBBER PRODUCERS' RESEARCH ASSOCIATION (1938), Tun Abdul Razak Laboratory, Brickendonbury, Herts.—*Dir. of Research*, Dr. D. Barnard.

MALCOLM SARGENT CANCER FUND FOR CHILDREN.—*Gen. Administrator*, Miss S. Darley, 26 Lamont Road, S.W.10.

MALONE SOCIETY (for the study of Early English Drama).—*Hon. Sec.*, Dr. Lois Potter, Dept. of English, University of Leicester.

MANAGEMENT, BRITISH INSTITUTE OF, Management House, Parker Street, W.C.2.—*Dir.-Gen.*, R. Close, C.B.E.

MANAGEMENT AND PROFESSIONAL STAFFS, ASSOCIATION OF, 175 Station Road, Swinton, Manchester.—*Exec. Sec.*, Dr. M. Gillibrand.

MANAGEMENT SERVICES, INSTITUTE OF, 1 Cecil Court, London Road, Enfield, Middx.—*Dir. and Gen. Sec.*, E. A. King.

MANORIAL SOCIETY OF GREAT BRITAIN (1906), 104 Kennington Road, S.E.11.—*Hon. Chairman*, R. Smith.

MARIE CURIE MEMORIAL FOUNDATION (for the welfare of cancer patients), 28 Belgrave Square, S.W.1.—*Sec.*, P. A. Sturgess.

MARINE ARTISTS, ROYAL SOCIETY OF (1939), 17 Carlton House Terrace, S.W.1.—*Pres.*, D. Cobb.

MARINE BIOLOGICAL ASSOCIATION OF THE U.K. (1884), The Laboratory, Citadel Hill, Plymouth.—*Sec. to Council and Director of Plymouth Laboratory*, E. J. Denton, C.B.E., SC.D., F.R.S.

MARINE ENGINEERS, INSTITUTE OF (1889), 76 Mark Lane, E.C.3.

MARINE SOCIETY, THE (1756), 202 Lambeth Road, S.E.1.—*Dir.*, R. Hope, O.B.E., D.Phil.; *Sec.*, Lt. Cdr. R. M. Frampton, R.N.

MARIO LANZA EDUCATIONAL FOUNDATION.—*Hon. Sec.*, Pauline Franklin, Flat 21, Chiswick House, 210 Bell Barn Road, Edgbaston, Birmingham.

MARKET AUTHORITIES, NATIONAL ASSOCIATION OF BRITISH.—*Sec.*, B. Ormshaw, 19 Derwent Drive, Milnrow, Rochdale, Lancs.

MARKETING, INSTITUTE OF (1911), Moor Hall, Cookham, Maidenhead, Berks.—*Sec.*, W. E. Hinder.

MARK MASTER MASONS, GRAND LODGE OF (1856), Mark Masons' Hall, 86 St. James's Street, S.W.1.— *Grand Master*, H.R.H. Prince Michael of Kent; *Grand Sec.*, W. J. Leake.

MASONIC BENEVOLENT INSTITUTION, ROYAL (1842), 20 Great Queen Street, W.C.2.—*Sec.*, N. A. Grout.

MASONIC BENEVOLENT INSTITUTIONS IN IRELAND; *Masonic Girls' Benefit Fund* (1792); *Masonic Boys' Benefit Fund* (1867); *Victoria Jubilee Masonic Annuity Fund* (1887).—*Sec.*, R. J. Clinton, 17/19 Molesworth Street, Dublin 2.

MASONIC DEGREES—ORDER OF THE TEMPLE, Mark Masons' Hall, 86 St. James's Street, S.W.1.—*Grand Master*, H. D. Still; *Great Seneschal*, Lord Swansea; *Great Vice-Chancellor*, W. J. Leake.

MASONIC INSTITUTION FOR BOYS, ROYAL (Incorporated) (1798), 26 Great Queen Street, W.C.2.—*Sec.*, A. R. Jole.

MASONIC INSTITUTION FOR GIRLS, ROYAL (1788). *Offices*, 31 Great Queen Street, W.C.2.—*Sec.*, Col. R. K. Hind.

MASTER BUILDERS, FEDERATION OF, Gordon Fisher House, 33 John Street, W.C.1.—*Nat. Dir.*, W. S. Hilton.

MASTERS OF FOXHOUNDS ASSOCIATION (1881), Parsloes Cottage, Bagendon, Cirencester, Glos.—*Sec.*, A. H. B. Hart.

MATERNAL AND CHILD WELFARE, NATIONAL ASSOCIATION FOR (1911), 1 South Audley Street, W.1.— *Gen. Sec.*, W. Rice.

MATHEMATICAL ASSOCIATION (1871), 259 London Road, Leicester.—*Pres.*, P. B. Coaker; *Hon. Secs.*, Miss M. M. Lawton; H. Neill.

MATHEMATICS AND ITS APPLICATIONS, INSTITUTE OF (1964), Maitland House, Warrior Square, Southend, Essex.—*Sec.*, N. Clarke, O.B.E.

MEASUREMENT AND CONTROL, INSTITUTE OF (1944), 20 Peel Street, W.8.—*Sec.*, A. Sensicle.

MECHANICAL ENGINEERS, INSTITUTION OF, 1 Birdcage Walk, S.W.1.—*Sec.*, A. McKay, C.B.

MEDIC-ALERT FOUNDATION, 11–13 Clifton Terrace, N.4.—*Hon. Chairman*, D. J. C. Gilchrist. For the protection, in emergencies, of those with a medical disability; to prevent mistakes.

MEDICAL COUNCIL, GENERAL, 44 Hallam Street, W.1. *Registrar*, P. L. Towers.

MEDICAL SOCIETY OF LONDON (1773), 11 Chandos Street, Cavendish Square, W.1.—*Pres.* (1984–85), I. P. Todd, M.D., F.R.C.S.; *Hon. Sec.*, Dr. A. C. Keat; *Registrar*, Maj. T. Tudor-Williams.

MEDICAL WOMEN'S FEDERATION (1917), Tavistock House North, Tavistock Square, W.C.1.—*Pres.*, Dr. Jean M. Scott; *Hon. Sec.*, Dr. Lotte T. Newman.

MEDIEVAL ARCHAEOLOGY, SOCIETY FOR (1957), University College, Gower Street, W.C.1.—*Hon. Sec.*, Dr. Helen Clarke.

MEN OF THE TREES (1922), Crawley Down, Crawley, Sussex.—*Sec.*, Mrs. E. Sandwell.

MENTAL AFTER CARE ASSOCIATION (1879), for the care and rehabilitation of those recovering from mental illness.—*Sec.*, Mrs. J. Moore, 110 Jermyn Street, S.W.1.

MENTAL HEALTH FOUNDATION (1949), 8 Hallam Street, W.1.—*Dir.*, R. B. Loudoun, C.B., O.B.E.

MERCHANT NAVY WELFARE BOARD, 19–21 Lancaster Gate, W.2.—*Sec.*, J. W. Walker.

METALLURGISTS, THE INSTITUTION OF, P.O. Box 471, 1 Carlton House Terrace, S.W.1.—*Registrar-Sec.*, B. D. Gibson, F.I.M.

METALS SOCIETY, THE (1974) (*Amalgamation of* Institute of Metals and Iron and Steel Institute), 1 Carlton House Terrace, S.W.1.—*Dir.*, Sir Geoffrey Ford.

METEOROLOGICAL SOCIETY, ROYAL (1850), James Glaisher House, Grenville Place, Bracknell, Berks.—*Pres.*, A. Gilchrist; *Hon. Secs.*, D. N. Axford, PH.D.; I. N. James, PH.D.; J. M. Walker.

METHODIST CHURCH OVERSEAS DIVISION (1786), 25 Marylebone Road, N.W.1. Income, 1981, £3,176,595.

METROPOLITAN AND CITY POLICE ORPHANS FUND (1870), 30 Hazlewell Road, Putney, S.W.15.—*Sec.*, J. Murray, M.B.E.

METROPOLITAN AUTHORITIES, ASSOCIATION OF (1974), 36 Old Queen Street, S.W.1.—*Sec.*, L. A. Plowman.

METROPOLITAN HOSPITAL-SUNDAY FUND (1872), 40 High Street, Teddington, Middx. In 1983, £44,482 was distributed to N.H.S. hospitals in the form of Samaritan Fund grants, special grants and long stay/geriatric patient holiday grants through hospital social workers. £157,450 was distributed to hospitals outside the N.H.S., and £6,600 to other medical charities.—*Sec.*, D. A. B. Lynch.

METROPOLITAN PUBLIC GARDENS ASSOCIATION (1882), 4 Carlos Place, W.1.—*Sec.*, M. Upward.

MIDDLE EAST ASSOCIATION (1961), 33 Bury Street, St. James's, S.W.1.—*Dir.-Gen.*, Sir David Roberts, K.B.E., C.M.G., C.V.O.; *Sec.*, Miss L. V. Marsh-Smith.

MIDWIVES, ROYAL COLLEGE OF (1881), 15 Mansfield Street, W.1.—*Gen. Sec.*, Miss R. M. Ashton.

MIGRAINE TRUST (1965), 45 Great Ormond Street, W.C.1.—*Dir.*, Cdr. O. Wright.

MILITARY HISTORICAL SOCIETY.—*Hon. Sec.*, J. Gaylor, National Army Museum, Royal Hospital Road, Chelsea, S.W.3.

MIND (National Association for Mental Health), 22 Harley Street, W.1.—*Dir.*, C. Heginbotham.

MINERALOGICAL SOCIETY (1876).—*Pres.*, Dr. S. O. Agrell; *Hon. Gen. Sec.*, Dr. M. G. Bown, 41 Queen's Gate, S.W.7.

MINES OF GREAT BRITAIN, FEDERATION OF SMALL, 30 King Street, Wigan, Lancs.—*Sec.*, J. Wainwright.

MINIATURE PAINTERS, SCULPTORS AND GRAVERS, ROYAL SOCIETY OF (1895), 17 Carlton House Terrace, S.W.1.—*Pres.*, Mrs. Suzanne Lucas.

MINIATURISTS, SOCIETY OF (1895), Bankside Gallery, 48 Hopton Street, Blackfriars, S.E.1.—*Sec.*, M. Spender.

MINING AND METALLURGY, INSTITUTION OF (1892), 44 Portland Place, W.1.—*Sec.* M. J. Jones.

MINING ENGINEERS, THE INSTITUTION OF (1889), 6A South Parade, Doncaster.—*Pres.* (1984–85), R. Rawlinson; *Sec.*, W. J. W. Bourne.

MINING INSTITUTE OF SCOTLAND, c/o National Coal Board, Green Park, Greenend, Edinburgh.—*Sec.*, E. R. Rodger.

MISSIONS TO SEAMEN, THE, AND ST. ANDREW'S WATERSIDE CHURCH MISSION FOR SAILORS, St. Michael Paternoster Royal, College Hill, E.C.4.—*Gen. Sec.*, Rev. W. J. D. Down.

MODERN CHURCHMEN'S UNION (1898), for the Advancement of Liberal Religious Thought—*Pres.*, The Dean of Westminster; *Hon. Gen. Sec.*, P. Croft, 4 Cathedral Close, Guildford, Surrey.

MODERN LANGUAGE ASSOCIATION (incorporating the Association of Teachers of German), 24A Highbury Grove, N.5.—*Gen. Sec.*, Miss E. Ingham.

MONUMENTAL BRASS SOCIETY (1887), *Hon. Sec.*, W. Mendelsson, 57 Leeside Crescent, N.W.11.

MORAVIAN MISSIONS, LONDON ASSOCIATION IN AID OF (1817), Moravian Church House, 5/7 Muswell Hill, N.10.—*Sec.*, Rev. F. Linyard.

MORDEN COLLEGE (1695), Blackheath, S.E.3.—*Clerk to the Trustees*, A. A. Snashall.

MOTOR INDUSTRY, THE INSTITUTE OF THE, Fanshaws, Brickendon, Hertford.—*Sec.*, R. K. Ward.

MOUNTBATTEN (EDWINA) TRUST, 1 Grosvenor Crescent, S.W.1.—*Sec.*, Miss D. M. Lee.

MOUNTBATTEN MEMORIAL TRUST (1979), Tremaynes, 26 Kimpton Road, Blackmore End, Wheathampstead, Herts.—*Dir.*, J. Biles, O.B.E., Q.P.M.

MULTIPLE SCLEROSIS SOCIETY, 286 Munster Road, Fulham, S.W.6.—*Gen. Sec.*, J. Walford.

MUNICIPAL ENGINEERS, INSTITUTION OF (1873), 25 Eccleston Square, S.W.1.—*Sec.*, J. R. Sparey, M.A.

MUSEUMS ASSOCIATION (1889), 34 Bloomsbury Way, W.C.1.—*Dir. Gen.*, J. A. Fox.

MUSICIANS BENEVOLENT FUND, 16 Ogle Street, W.1.—*Sec.*, M. B. M. Williams. *Private Hotel*, Westgate-on-Sea. *Permanent Homes*, Hereford and Bromley.

MUSICIANS, INCORPORATED SOCIETY OF (1882) 10 Stratford Place, W.1.—*Gen. Sec.*, D. Padgett-Chandler.

MUSICIANS OF GREAT BRITAIN, ROYAL SOCIETY OF (1738), 10 Stratford Place, W.1.—*Sec.*, Mrs. M. E. Gleed, M.B.E.

MUSIC SOCIETIES, NATIONAL FEDERATION OF (1935), Francis House, Francis Street, S.W.1.—*Gen. Sec.*, J. Crisp.

NATIONAL ADULT SCHOOL ORGANISATION (1899), Norfolk House, Smallbrook Queensway, Birmingham.—*Sec.*, Mrs. C. M. N. Bryant.

NATIONAL ALLIANCE OF PRIVATE TRADERS (1943), 369 Corn Exchange, Hanging Ditch, Manchester 4.

NATIONAL AND UNIVERSITY LIBRARIES, STANDING CONFERENCE OF (1950).—*Sec.*, A. J. Loveday, 102 Euston Street, N.W.1.

NATIONAL ASSOCIATION OF ESTATE AGENTS (1962), Arbon House, 21 Jury Street, Warwick.—*Sec.*, A. B. Clark.

NATIONAL ASSOCIATION OF LOCAL COUNCILS (1947), 108 Great Russell Street, W.C.1.—*Gen. Sec.*, J. Clark.

NATIONAL BENEVOLENT INSTITUTION (1812), 61 Bayswater Road, W.2.—*Sec.*, Air Cmdre, D. C. Saunders, C.B.E., A.F.C.

NATIONAL BIRTHDAY TRUST FUND (1928), 57 Lower Belgrave Street, S.W.1. For Extension of Maternity Services.—*Sec.*, Mrs. M. C. Matthews.

NATIONAL BOOK LEAGUE (1925), Book House, 45 East Hill, Wandsworth, S.W.18.—*Dir.*, M. Goff, O.B.E.

NATIONAL CATTLE BREEDERS' ASSOCIATION, 106 High Street, Tring, Herts.—*Sec.*, J. Thorley.

NATIONAL CHILDBIRTH TRUST, THE, (1956), 9 Queensborough Terrace, Bayswater, W.2.—*Nat. Sec.*, Mrs. H. Corbishley.

NATIONAL CHILDREN'S HOME (1869). *Chief Office*, 85 Highbury Park, N.5. Cares for 7,000 socially, educationally, or physically handicapped children annually in residential homes, special schools, family centres, foster homes and community projects in Great Britain and overseas.—*Principal*, Rev. G. E. Barritt, O.B.E..

NATIONAL CHRISTIAN EDUCATION COUNCIL (*incorporating* International Bible Reading Association and Denholm House Press), Robert Denholm House, Nutfield, Redhill, Surrey.—*Sec.*, Rev. S. J. Oxley.

NATIONAL COUNCIL FOR VOLUNTARY ORGANISATIONS, 26 Bedford Square, W.C.1.—*Dir.*, N. Hinton.

NATIONAL COUNCIL OF WOMEN OF GREAT BRITAIN (1895), 34 Lower Sloane Street, S.W.1.—*Sec.*, Mrs. J. D. Norman.

NATIONAL FEDERATION OF OLD AGE PENSIONS ASSOCIATIONS, (PENSIONERS' VOICE), 91 Preston New Road, Blackburn, Lancs.—*Gen. Sec.*, G. Dunn.

NATIONAL FEDERATION OF SELF EMPLOYED AND SMALL BUSINESSES LTD. (1974), 32 St. Annes Road West, Lytham St. Annes, Lancs.—*National Chairman*, Dr. B. A. Juby.

NATIONAL FEDERATION OF YOUNG FARMERS' CLUBS, Y.F.C. Centre, National Agricultural Centre, Kenilworth, Warwicks.—*Gen. Sec. and Treasurer*, F. E. Shields.

NATIONAL LIGHT HORSE BREEDING SOCIETY (H.I.S.) (1885), 96 High Street, Edenbridge, Kent.—*Sec.*, G. W. Evans.

NATIONAL MARKET TRADERS' FEDERATION (1899).—*Pres.*, J. Burton; *Gen. Sec.*, D. J. Glasby, Yorkshire Bank Chambers, Loundside Chapeltown, Sheffield.

NATIONAL MARRIAGE GUIDANCE COUNCIL, Herbert Gray College, Little Church Street, Rugby, Warwicks.—*Chief Officer*, N. J. Tyndall.

NATIONAL MONUMENTS RECORD (1941), Royal Commission on Historical Monuments (England), Fortress House, 23 Savile Row, W.1.—*Sec.*, P. J. Fowler, PH.D.

NATIONAL OPERATIC AND DRAMATIC ASSOCIATION (1899), 1 Crestfield Street, W.C.1.—*Chief Exec.*, B. Clarke.

NATIONAL PEACE COUNCIL (1908), 29 Great James Street, W.C.1.—*Gen. Sec.*, Mrs. S. Oakes.

NATIONAL PURE WATER ASSOCIATION.—*Sec.*, N. Brugge, Southern Ash, Gilberts Lane, Whixall, Whitchurch, Shropshire.

NATIONAL SECULAR SOCIETY (1866), 702 Holloway Road, N.19.—*Gen. Sec.*, T. Mullins.

NATIONAL SOCIETY FOR CLEAN AIR (1899), 136 North Street, Brighton, E. Sussex.—*Sec.-Gen.*, Air Cmdre. J. Langston, C.B.E.

NATIONAL SOCIETY (CHURCH OF ENGLAND) FOR PROMOTING RELIGIOUS EDUCATION (1811), Church House, Dean's Yard, S.W.1.—*Gen. Sec.*, C. Alves.

NATIONAL SOCIETY FOR THE PREVENTION OF CRUELTY TO CHILDREN (1884), *Headquarters*, 67 Saffron Hill, E.C.1.—*Chairman*, Lady Holland-Martin, D.B.E., D.L.; *Hon. Treas.*, M. Weinberg; *Dir.*, Dr. A. Gilmour, C.B.E.

NATIONAL TRUST for places of historic interest or natural beauty (1895), 36 Queen Anne's Gate, S.W.1.—*Dir. Gen.*, A. Stirling.

NATIONAL TRUST FOR SCOTLAND for places of historic interest or natural beauty (1931), 5 Charlotte Square, Edinburgh 2.—*Dir.*, L. Borley.

NATIONAL UNION OF STUDENTS, 3 Endsleigh Street, W.C.1.

NATIONAL VIEWERS' AND LISTENERS' ASSOCIATION.— *President*, Mrs. M. Whitehouse, C.B.E, Blachernae, Ardleigh, Colchester, Essex.

NATION'S FUND FOR NURSES, 57 Lower Belgrave Street, S.W.1.—*Administrator*, P. E. Starr.

NATURE CONSERVATION, ROYAL SOCIETY FOR (1912).— *Gen. Sec.*, Dr. F. H. Perring, The Green, Nettleham, Lincoln.

NAUTICAL RESEARCH, SOCIETY FOR (1911), c/o National Maritime Museum, Greenwich, S.E.10.— *Hon. Sec.*, J. Munday, F.S.A.

NAVAL, MILITARY AND AIR FORCE BIBLE SOCIETY (1780), Radstock House, Eccleston Street, S.W.1. Copies and portions of the Scriptures circulated to the Forces (1983), 180,679.—*Sec.*, N. Brown.

NAVAL ARCHITECTS, ROYAL INSTITUTION OF (1860), 10 Upper Belgrave Street, S.W.1.—*Sec.*, P. W. Ayling.

NAVIGATION, ROYAL INSTITUTE OF, at the Royal Geographical Society, 1 Kensington Gore, S.W.7. *Dir.*, Rear Adm. R. M. Burgoyne, C.B.

NAVY RECORDS SOCIETY, Public Record Office, Kew, Richmond, Surrey. Publishes editions of historical documents relating to the Royal Navy.—*Hon. Sec.*, N. A. M. Rodger.

NEWCOMEN SOCIETY (1920), for the Study of the History of Engineering and Technology, Science Museum, S.W.7.—*Exec. Sec.*, I. McNeil.

NEW ENGLISH ART CLUB (1886), 17 Carlton House Terrace, S.W.1.—*Sec.*, W. Bowyer, R.A.

NEWSAGENTS, NATIONAL FEDERATION OF RETAIL, 2 Bridewell Place, E.C.4.—*Gen. Sec.*, K. E. J. Peters.

NEWSPAPER EDITORS, GUILD OF BRITISH (1946), Whitefriars House, Carmelite Street, E.C.4.—*Pres.*, J. V. Addison (*Carlisle Evening News and Star*); *Sec.-Treas.*, C. Gordon Page.

NEWSPAPER PRESS FUND (1864), Dickens House, 35 Wathen Road, Dorking, Surrey.—*Gen. Sec.*, P. W. Evans.

NEWSPAPER SOCIETY (1836), Whitefriars House, Carmelite Street, E.C.4.—*Pres.*, T. Morris (*Birmingham Post and Mail*); *Dir.*, D. Nisbet-Smith.

NEWSVENDORS' BENEVOLENT INSTITUTION (1839), P.O. Box 306, Dunmow, Essex.—*Sec.*, R. A. Jones.

NEW TOWNS ASSOCIATION, Metro House, 57/58 St. James's Street, S.W.1.—*Head of Secretariat*, J. R. C. Pinccombe, M.B.E.

NOISE ABATEMENT SOCIETY, P.O. Box 8, Bromley, Kent.—*Chairman*, J. Connell.

NON-SMOKERS, NATIONAL SOCIETY OF (1926), Latimer House, 40–48 Hanson Street, W.1.—*Hon. Dir. and Sec.*, T. W. Hurst.

NORTHERN IRELAND TOURIST BOARD, River House, 48 High Street, Belfast 1.—*Chief Exec.*, S. Belford.

NORWOOD CHILD CARE (Welfare Organization for Jewish children); 315/317 Ballards Lane, N.12.— *Exec. Dir.*, P. Shaw.

NUCLEAR ENERGY SOCIETY, BRITISH (1962), 1—7, Great George Street, S.W.1.

NUFFIELD FOUNDATION (1943), Nuffield Lodge, Regent's Park, N.W.1.—*Dir.*, J. P. Cornford.

NUFFIELD PROVINCIAL HOSPITALS TRUST (1939), 3 Prince Albert Road, N.W.1.—*Gen. Sec.*, G. McLachlan, C.B.E.

NUMISMATIC SOCIETY, BRITISH.—*Hon. Sec.*, W. Slayter, 63 West Way, Edgware, Middx.

NUMISMATIC SOCIETY, ROYAL, c/o Dept. of Coins and Medals, The British Museum, W.C.1.—*Pres.*, Dr. J. P. C. Kent, PH.D., F.S.A.; *Hon. Secs.*, A. Burnett, PH.D., F.S.A.; J. E. Cribb.

NURSES', RETIRED, NATIONAL HOME, Riverside Avenue, Bournemouth.—*Chairman*, Dr. R. E. Chaplin.

NURSES, ROYAL NATIONAL PENSION FUND FOR, 15 Buckingham Street, W.C.2.—*General Manager and Actuary*, V. G. West.

NURSING, MIDWIFERY AND HEALTH VISITING, U.K. CENTRAL COUNCIL FOR, 23 Portland Place, W.1.— *Registrar and Chief Exec.*, Miss M. Storey.

England.—Victory House, 170 Tottenham Court Road, W.1.

Wales.—Pearl Assurance House, Greyfriars Road, Cardiff.

Scotland.—22 Queen Street, Edinburgh.

N.I.—RAC House, 79 Chichester Street, Belfast.

NURSING, ROYAL COLLEGE OF, 20 Cavendish Square, W.1.—*Gen. Sec.*, T. Clay.

NUTRITION SOCIETY (1941).—*Hon. Sec.*, Dr. Margaret Ashwell, Chandos House, 2 Queen Anne Street, W.1.

OBSTETRICIANS AND GYNAECOLOGISTS, ROYAL COLLEGE OF (1929), 27 Sussex Place, Regent's Park, N.W.1.—*Pres.*, Prof. M. C. Macnaughton; *Sec.*, A. G. S. Taylour.

OCCUPATIONAL SAFETY AND HEALTH, INSTITUTION OF, 222 Uppingham Road, Leicester.—*Sec.*, J. R. Barrell.

OFFICERS' ASSOCIATION, THE (1920), 48 Pall Mall, S.W.1. Affords relief to ex-officers of the Royal Navy, Army and R.A.F. and their widows and dependants in distress; assists such persons to find accommodation in homes for the elderly; helps unemployed ex-officers to find employment.—*Gen. Sec.*, Brig. P. D. Johnson.

OFFICERS' FAMILIES FUND (1899), 48 Pall Mall, S.W.1.—*Sec.*, Mrs. I. C. Riley.

OFFICERS' PENSIONS SOCIETY, LTD., 15 Buckingham Gate, S.W.1.—*Gen. Sec.*, Maj. Gen. L. W. A. Gingell, C.B., C.B.E.

OIL PAINTERS, ROYAL INSTITUTE OF (1883), 17 Carlton House Terrace, S.W.1.—*Pres.*, K. Barratt.

OILSEED, OIL AND FEEDINGSTUFFS TRADES BENEVOLENT ASSOCIATION, THE, 14–20 St. Mary Axe, E.C.3.—*Sec.*, R. T. Wheelans.

ONE PARENT FAMILIES, NATIONAL COUNCIL FOR, 255 Kentish Town Road, N.W.5.—*Dir.*, Dr. Carol Smart.

OPEN-AIR MISSION (1853), 19 John Street, W.C.1.— *Sec.*, A. J. Greenbank.

OPEN SPACES SOCIETY (COMMONS, OPEN SPACES AND FOOTPATHS PRESERVATION SOCIETY) (1865), 25A Bell Street, Henley-on-Thames, Oxon.—*Hon. Sec.*, Miss K. Ashbrook.

OPTICAL COUNCIL, GENERAL, 41 Harley Street, W.1.— *Registrar*, J. D. Devlin, O.B.E.

ORDERS AND MEDALS RESEARCH SOCIETY.—*Gen. Sec.*, N. G. Gooding, 123 Turnpike Link, Croydon.

ORIENTAL CERAMIC SOCIETY (1921), 31B Torrington Square, W.C.1.—*Sec.*, Vice-Admiral Sir John Gray, K.B.E., C.B.

ORNITHOLOGISTS' CLUB, THE SCOTTISH, 21 Regent Terrace, Edinburgh.—*Sec.*, J. C. Davies.

ORNITHOLOGISTS' UNION, BRITISH, c/o Zoological Society of London, Regent's Park, N.W.1.—*Sec.*, Dr. D. C. Houston.

ORNITHOLOGY, BRITISH TRUST FOR (1932), Beech Grove, Tring, Herts.—*Administrator*, J. C. G. Wolf.

ORNITHOLOGY, FIELD, THE EDWARD GREY INSTITUTE OF (1938), Dept. of Zoology, South Parks Road, Oxford.—*Dir.*, Dr. C. M. Perrins.

ORTHOPÆDIC ASSOCIATION, BRITISH (1918), at the Royal College of Surgeons, Lincoln's Inn Fields, W.C.2.—*Hon. Sec.*, M. Swann, F.R.C.S.

OUTWARD BOUND TRUST, 12 Upper Belgrave Street, S.W.1.—*Dir.*, I. L. Fothergill.

OVERSEAS DEVELOPMENT INSTITUTE (1960), 10–11 Percy Street, W.1.—*Dir.*, T. Killick.

OVERSEAS GRADUATES, LONDON HOUSE FOR, Mecklenburgh Square, W.C.1.

OVERSEAS SERVICE PENSIONERS' ASSOCIATION (1960), 63 Church Road, Hove, Sussex.—*Sec.*, C. D. Stenton.

OVERSEAS SETTLEMENT, CHURCH OF ENGLAND BOARD FOR SOCIAL RESPONSIBILITY (1925), Church House, Dean's Yard, S.W.1.—*Admin.-Sec.*, Miss P. J. Hallett.

OXFAM (1942), 274 Banbury Road, Oxford.—*Dir.*, A. G. Stringer.

OXFORD AND CAMBRIDGE SCHOOLS EXAMINATION BOARD (1873). *Offices*, 10 Trumpington Street, Cambridge and Elsfield Way, Oxford.—*Secs.*, K. Schoenenberger, Oxford; H. F. King, Cambridge.

OXFORD PRESERVATION TRUST (1927), 10 Turn Again Lane, St. Ebbes, Oxford.—*Sec.*, Mrs. H. Turner.

OXFORD SOCIETY (1932), 8 Wellington Square, Oxford.—*Sec.*, Mrs. D. M. Lennie.

PAINTER-ETCHERS AND ENGRAVERS, ROYAL SOCIETY OF (1880), Bankside Gallery, 48 Hopton Street, Blackfriars, S.E.1.—*Pres.*, H. N. Eccleston, O.B.E.; *Sec.*, M. Spender.

PAINTERS IN WATER COLOURS, ROYAL INSTITUTE OF (1831), 17 Carlton House Terrace, S.W.1.—*Pres.*, C. Bone; *Treas.*, Mr. Folkes.

PAINTERS IN WATER COLOURS, ROYAL SOCIETY OF (1804), Bankside Gallery, 48 Hopton Street, Blackfriars, S.E.1.—*Pres.*, M. Sheppard; *Sec.*, M. Spender.

PAINTERS, SCULPTORS AND PRINTMAKERS, NATIONAL SOCIETY OF (1930), 17 Carlton House Terrace, S.W.1.—*Pres.*, K. Barratt.

PALÆONTOGRAPHICAL SOCIETY (1847). *Sec.*, F. G. Dimes, c/o British Geological Survey, Exhibition Road, S.W.7.—*Sec.*, F. G. Dimes.

PALÆONTOLOGICAL ASSOCIATION (1957).—*Sec.*, Dr. R. Riding, Dept. of Geology, University College, Cardiff.

PALESTINE EXPLORATION FUND (1865), 2 Hinde Mews, Marylebone Lane, W.1.—*Chairman*, Brig. A. Walmesley White, C.B.E., M.A., F.R.G.S.

PARKINSON'S DISEASE SOCIETY (1969), 36 Portland Place, W.1.—*Exec. Dir.*, C. A. A. Kilmister.

PARLIAMENTARY AND SCIENTIFIC COMMITTEE.—*Sec.*, A. Butler, 30 Farringdon Street, E.C.4.

PASTEL SOCIETY (1899), 17 Carlton House Terrace, S.W.1.—*Pres.*, L. Parry.

PASTORAL PSYCHOLOGY, GUILD OF (1936).—*Hon. Sec.*, Mrs. M. Ditchfield, 37 Hogarth Hill, N.W.11.

PATENT AGENTS, CHARTERED INSTITUTE OF (1882), Staple Inn Buildings, W.C.1.—*Sec. and Registrar*, Miss M. E. Poole.

PATENTEES AND INVENTORS, INSTITUTE OF (1919), Staple Inn Buildings South, 335 High Holborn, W.C.1.—*Sec.*, E. J. Gear.

PATHOLOGISTS, ROYAL COLLEGE OF, 2 Carlton House Terrace, S.W.1.—*Sec.*, B. A. Prideaux.

PATIENTS ASSOCIATION (1963), 18 Charing Cross Road, W.C.2.—*Chairman*, Dame Elizabeth Ackroyd, D.B.E.

PEARSON'S HOLIDAY FUND, 112 Regency Street, S.W.1.—*Gen. Sec.*, G. Holloway.

PEDESTRIANS' ASSOCIATION, 1–5 Wandsworth Road, S.W.8.—*Chairman*, C. Myerscough.

P.E.N., INTERNATIONAL (1921), 38 King Street, W.C.2. World association of writers.—*International Sec.*, A. Blokh.

PENSION FUNDS, NATIONAL ASSOCIATION OF, LTD (1923).—*Dir. Gen.*, H. L. James; *Sec.*, B. W. Lofthouse, Sunley House, Bedford Park, Croydon, Surrey.

PEOPLE'S DISPENSARY FOR SICK ANIMALS (1917), PDSA House, South Street, Dorking, Surrey.—*Gen. Sec.*, M. R. Curtis, M.B.E.

PERFORMING RIGHT SOCIETY LTD. (1914), 29–33 Berners Street, W.1.—*Chief Executive*, M. J. Freegard; *Sec.*, G. M. Neighbour.

PERIODICAL PUBLISHERS ASSOCATION LTD., Imperial House, 15–19 Kingsway, W.C.2.—*Exec. Dir.*, M. J. Finley.

PESTALOZZI CHILDREN'S VILLAGE TRUST, Sedlescombe, Battle, Sussex.—*Warden*, A. G. Hatter.

PHARMACEUTICAL SOCIETY OF GREAT BRITAIN, 1 Lambeth High Street, S.E.1.—*Sec. and Registrar*, D. F. Lewis, O.B.E.

PHARMACOLOGICAL SOCIETY, BRITISH.—*Hon. Gen. Sec.*, Prof. A. T. Birmingham, Dept. of Physiology & Pharmacology, Queen's Medical Centre, Nottingham.

PHILOLOGICAL SOCIETY (1842).—*Hon. Sec.*, Prof. R. H. Robins, School of Oriental and African Studies, Malet Street, W.C.1.

PHILOSOPHY, ROYAL INSTITUTE OF, 14 Gordon Square, W.C.1.—*Director*, Prof. A. Phillips Griffiths.

PHOTOGRAMMETRIC SOCIETY (1952), Dept. of Photogrammetry & Surveying, University College London, Gower Street, W.C.1.—*Hon. Sec.*, A. S. Walker.

PHOTOGRAPHY, BRITISH INSTITUTE OF PROFESSIONAL (1901), 2 Amwell End, Ware, Herts.—*Sec.*, P. A. Large.

PHYSICAL EDUCATION ASSOCIATION OF GREAT BRITAIN AND N. IRELAND, THE, 162 King's Cross Road, W.C.1.—*Gen. Sec.*, A. J. Petherick.

PHYSICAL RECREATION, CENTRAL COUNCIL OF (1935), Francis House, Francis Street, S.W.1.—*Gen. Sec.*, P. Lawson.

PHYSICIANS, ROYAL COLLEGE OF (1518), 11 St. Andrew's Place, N.W.1.—*Pres.*, Sir Raymond Hoffenberg, K.B.E., M.D., F.R.C.P.; *Treas.*, N. D. Compston, M.D.; *Registrar*, D. A. Pyke, M.D.; *Sec.*, G. M. G. Tibbs.

PHYSICIANS AND SURGEONS, ROYAL COLLEGE OF (Glasgow) (1599), 234–242 St. Vincent Street, Glasgow.—*Pres.*, I. A. McGregor; *Hon. Sec.*, A. D. Beattie.

PHYSICIANS OF EDINBURGH, ROYAL COLLEGE OF (1681), *Hall and Library*, 9 Queen Street, Edinburgh.—*Sec.*, Dr. T. M. Chalmers.

PHYSICS, INSTITUTE OF (1874), 47 Belgrave Square, S.W.1.—*Pres.*, Sir Robert Clayton; *Sec.*, L. Cohen, PH.D.

PHYSIOLOGICAL SOCIETY (1876), Dept. of Physiology and Pharmacology, Bute Medical Buildings, St. Andrews, Fife.—*Hon. Sec.*, Prof. J. F. Lamb.

PHYSIOTHERAPY, CHARTERED SOCIETY OF (1894), 14 Bedford Row, W.C.1.—*Sec.*, G. F. Barber.

PIG BREEDERS ASSOCIATION, NATIONAL (1884), 1 Rickmansworth Road, Watford, Herts.—*Chief Exec. and Sec.*, G. E. Welsh.

PILGRIM TRUST, THE (1930), Fielden House, Little College Street, S.W.1.—*Sec.*, Hon. A. H. Millar.

PILGRIMS OF GREAT BRITAIN, THE (1902), Savoy Hotel, W.C.2.—*Pres.*, The Rt. Hon. Lord Carrington, C.H., K.C.M.G., M.C.; *Hon. Sec.*, Lt.-Col. S. W. Chant-Sempill, O.B.E., M.C.

PILGRIMS OF THE U.S., THE (1903).—*Pres.*, Hugh Bullock, G.B.E., 74 Trinity Place, New York, N.Y. 10006, U.S.A.

PLANT ENGINEERS, INSTITUTION OF, 138 Buckingham Palace Road, S.W.1.—*Sec.*, J. K. Bennett.

PLASTICS AND RUBBER INSTITUTE, THE (1921), 11 Hobart Place, S.W.1.—*Sec.-Gen.* J. N. Ratcliffe.

PLAYING CARD SOCIETY, THE INTERNATIONAL (1972), 188 Sheen Lane, East Sheen, S.W.14.—*Sec.*, A. J. Beale.

PLAYING FIELDS ASSOCIATION, NATIONAL (1925), 25 Ovington Square, S.W.3.—*Chairman*, A. C. Gilmour; *Director and Gen. Sec.*, Lt. Col. R. G. Satterthwaite, O.B.E.

P.N.E.U., WORLD-WIDE EDUCATION SERVICE OF THE (1888), Strode House, 44/50 Osnaburgh Street, N.W.1.—*Dir.*, H. Boulter.

POETRY SOCIETY (1909), 21 Earl's Court Square, S.W.5.—*Dir. and Gen. Sec.*, B. G. Mitchell.

POLICY STUDIES INSTITUTE, 1–2 Castle Lane, S.W.1.—*Dir.*, J. Pinder, O.B.E.

POLIO FELLOWSHIP, BRITISH (1939), Bell Close, West End Road, Ruislip, Middlesex.—*Gen. Sec.*, L. P. Jackson.

POLYTECHNICS, COMMITTEE OF DIRECTORS OF, 309 Regent Street, W.1.—*Chairman*, Dr. H. D. Law; *Sec.*, Dr. M. S. Lewis.

POLYTECHNIC TEACHERS, ASSOCIATION OF (1973), Throgmorton House, 27 Elphinstone Road, Southsea, Hants.—*Chief Executive*, Maureen Douglass.

PORTRAIT SCULPTORS, SOCIETY OF (1962), 17 Carlton House Terrace, S.W.1.—*Pres.*, R. Browne, F.R.B.S..

POST OFFICE USERS' NATIONAL COUNCIL (1970), 8 Bulstrode Street, W.1.—*Sec.*, J. F. Heath.

POULTRY CLUB, THE (1877) (incorporating the British Bantam Association).—*Sec.*, Mrs. S. Hawksworth, 24 Faris Barn Drive, Woodham, Weybridge, Surrey.

PRAYER BOOK SOCIETY, THE (1975), 40 Great Smith Street, S.W.1.—*Deputy Chairman*, C. A. A. Kilmister.

PRECEPTORS, COLLEGE OF, Coppice Row, Theydon Bois, Epping, Essex. Membership is admitted to practising educationalists; Fellowships are reserved for those who have made an outstanding contribution to education.—*Chief Admin. Officer*, P. R. Daniels.

PREPARATORY SCHOOLS, INCORPORATED ASSOCIATION OF, 138 Kensington Church Street, W.8.—*Sec.*, J. M. C. Coates.

PRE-SCHOOL PLAYGROUPS ASSOCIATION.—Alford House, Aveline Street, S.E.11.—*Gen. Sec.*, Miss J. Atkinson.

PRESS ASSOCIATION (1868), 85 Fleet Street, E.C.4.—*Chairman* (1984–85), D. B. Anderson (*Reed Regional Publishing Ltd.*); *General Manager*, I. H. N. Yates; *Sec.*, E. G. Rhodes.

PRINCESS LOUISE SCOTTISH HOSPITAL (Erskine Hospital) for disabled ex-servicemen and women (1916),

Bishopton, Renfrewshire.—*Treasurer*, I. W. Grimmond.

PRINTERS' CHARITABLE CORPORATION (1827), 61 Doughty Street, W.C.1. Homes for elderly printers and widows at Basildon and Bletchley, holidays and convalescence.—*Dir. & Sec.*, T. Dyball.

PRINTING HISTORICAL SOCIETY (1964), St. Bride Institute, Bride Lane, E.C.4.—*Hon. Sec.*, C. L. Hicks.

PRINTING, INSTITUTE OF (1961), 8 Lonsdale Gardens, Tunbridge Wells, Kent.—*Sec.*, M. A. Smith.

PRISON VISITORS, NATIONAL ASSOCIATION OF (1922), 46B Hartington Street, Bedford.—*Gen. Sec.*, Mrs. A. G. McKenna.

PRIVATE LIBRARIES ASSOCIATION (1957), Ravelston, South View Road, Pinner, Middlesex.—*Hon. Sec.*, F. Broomhead.

PROCURATORS IN GLASGOW, ROYAL FACULTY OF (1600).—*Treas., Clerk and Fiscal*, J. H. Sinclair, 62 St. Georges Place, Glasgow.

PRODUCTION CONTROL, INSTITUTE OF, National Westminster House, Wood Street, Stratford-upon-Avon, Warwickshire.—*Gen. Sec.*, K. Roberts.

PRODUCTION ENGINEERS, INSTITUTION OF, Rochester House, 66 Little Ealing Lane, W.5.—*Sec.*, R. J. Miskin.

PROFESSIONAL CLASSES AID COUNCIL, 10 St. Christopher's Place, W.1.—*Sec.*, Mrs. G. A. Burgess.

PROFESSIONAL ENGINEERS, U.K. ASSOCIATION OF, Hayes Court, West Common Road, Bromley, Kent.—*Sec.*, C. H. Hickling.

PROFESSIONAL FOOTBALLERS' ASSOCIATION, 124 Corn Exchange Buildings, Manchester 4.—*Sec.*, G. Taylor.

PROFESSIONS SUPPLEMENTARY TO MEDICINE, COUNCIL FOR, Park House, 184 Kennington Park Road, S.E.11.—*Registrar*, B. L. Donald, PH.D.

PROPAGATION OF THE GOSPEL, UNITED SOCIETY FOR THE (U.S.P.G.), 15 Tufton Street, S.W.1.—*Sec.*, Rev. H. V. Taylor.

PROTECTION OF LIFE FROM FIRE, SOCIETY FOR THE (1836), Aldermary House, Queen Street, E.C.4.—*Sec.*, E. H. Gledhill.

PROTESTANT ALLIANCE, THE (1845), 112 Colin Gardens, N.W.9.—*Sec.*, Rev. A. G. Ashdown.

PROVINCIAL NOTARIES SOCIETY (1907), P.O. Box 102, Amersham, Bucks.—*Sec.*, P. D. Leonard.

PSORIASIS ASSOCIATION, THE (1968), 7 Milton Street, Northampton.—*Nat. Sec.*, Mrs. L. A. Henley.

PSYCHIATRISTS, ROYAL COLLEGE OF (1971, *formerly* Royal Medico-Psychological Association founded in 1841), 17 Belgrave Square, S.W.1.—*Registrar*, Prof. R. G. Priest.

PSYCHICAL RESEARCH, SOCIETY FOR (1882), 1 Adam and Eve Mews, Kensington, W.8.—*Pres.*, Prof. D. J. West.

PSYCHOLOGICAL SOCIETY, THE BRITISH (1901), St. Andrews House, 48 Princess Road East, Leicester.—*Pres.*, Prof. C. I. Howarth; *Hon. Gen. Sec.*, Dr. P. E. Morris.

PUBLIC ADMINISTRATION, ROYAL INSTITUTE OF (1922), 3 Birdcage Walk, S.W.1.—*Dir. Gen.*, W. Plowden.

PUBLIC FINANCE AND ACCOUNTANCY, CHARTERED INSTITUTE OF (1885).—*Dir.*, N. P. Hepworth, O.B.E., 3 Robert Street, W.C.2.

PUBLIC HEALTH AND HYGIENE, THE ROYAL INSTITUTE OF (1937), 28 Portland Place, W.1.—*Sec.*, Rear-Adm. W. A. Waddell, C.B., O.B.E.

PUBLIC HEALTH ENGINEERS, INSTITUTION OF (1895), 13 Grosvenor Place, S.W.1.—*Sec.*, D. J. Dacam, O.B.E.

PUBLIC RELATIONS, INSTITUTE OF (1948), Gate House, St. John's Square, E.C.1.—*Exec. Dir.*, J. B. Lavelle.

PUBLIC TEACHERS OF LAW, SOCIETY OF (1908).—*Pres.*, Prof. D. N. MacCormick, University of Edinburgh; *Hon. Sec.*, Prof. D. B. Casson, University of Buckingham.

PURCHASING AND SUPPLY, INSTITUTE OF (1967), Easton House, Easton on the Hill, Stamford, Lincs.—*Dir.-Gen.*, I. G. S. Groundwater.

QUALITY ASSURANCE, INSTITUTE OF, 54 Princes Gate, Exhibition Road, S.W.7.—*Sec.-Gen.*, R. Knowles, C.B.E.

QUARRIER'S HOMES (1871), Bridge of Weir, Renfrewshire, Scotland.

QUARRYING, INSTITUTE OF (1917), 7 Regent Street, Nottingham.—*Sec.*, R. Oates.

QUEEN ELIZABETH'S FOUNDATION FOR THE DISABLED (1967), Leatherhead, Surrey.—*Dir.*, M. B. Clark, PH.D. Incorporating Queen Elizabeth's Training College (1934), Banstead Place Assessment and Further Education Centre for Handicapped School Leavers (1973), Dorincourt Sheltered Workshops (1958) and Lulworth Court Holiday and Convalescent Home (1959).

QUEEN VICTORIA CLERGY FUND (1897), *Central Fund*, Church House, Dean's Yard, S.W.1.—*Sec.*, Capt. P. W. E. Parry, M.B.E.

QUEEN VICTORIA SCHOOL, Dunblane, Perthshire.—*Commandant*, Brig. H. H. M. Marston, M.C. (*ret.*); *Headmaster*, J. D. Hankinson.

QUEEN'S ENGLISH SOCIETY—*Hon. Sec.*, A. I. Thompson, 2 South Side, Pulborough, Sussex.

QUEEN'S NURSING INSTITUTE (1887), 57 Lower Belgrave Street, S.W.1.—*Dir.*, P. E. Starr.

QUEKETT MICROSCOPICAL CLUB, c/o British Museum (Natural History), Cromwell Road, S.W.7.

RADIO SOCIETY OF GREAT BRITAIN (Incorporated), Alma House, Cranbourne Road, Potters Bar, Herts.—*Gen. Manager*, D. A. Evans.

RADIOLOGISTS, ROYAL COLLEGE OF (1934), 38 Portland Place, W.1.—*Sec.*, A. J. Cowles.

RAILWAY AND CANAL HISTORICAL SOCIETY, THE.—*Hon. Sec.*, R. E. Kilsby, Banestree, Jacobs Well Road, Guildford, Surrey.

RAILWAY BENEVOLENT INSTITUTION (1858), 67 Ashbourne Road, Derby. Railway Children's and Old People's Home at Derby; financial assistance given.—*Exec. Officer*, W. W. K. Humphreys.

RAINER FOUNDATION, 89a Blackheath Hill, S.E.10. A national charity helping young people in trouble.—*Dir.*, R. Kay.

RAMBLERS' ASSOCIATION (1935), 1–5 Wandsworth Road, S.W.8.—*Sec.*, A. Mattingly.

RATEPAYERS' ASSOCIATIONS, NATIONAL UNION OF, 4 Eysham Court, Station Road, New Barnet, Herts.—*Hon. Gen. Sec.*, Mrs. D. E. Pannell.

RATING AND VALUATION ASSOCIATION (1882), 115 Ebury Street, S.W.1.—*Sec.*, B. L. Hill.

RED CROSS SOCIETY, BRITISH. *See* BRITISH.

RED POLL CATTLE SOCIETY AND BRITISH DANE CATTLE SOCIETY OF GREAT BRITAIN AND IRELAND, 6 Church Street, Woodbridge, Suffolk.—*Sec.*, P. Ryder-Davies.

REEDHAM CHILDREN'S TRUST (1844), Purley, Surrey.—*Sec.*, Mrs. E. M. Johnston.

REED'S SCHOOL (1813), *Offices*, 2–4 Russia Row, Milk Street, E.C.2.—*Sec.*, D. G. Cooper.

REFRIGERATION, INSTITUTE OF (1899), Kelvin House, 76 Mill Lane, Carshalton, Surrey.—*Sec.*, M. J. Horlick.

REGIONAL STUDIES ASSOCIATION, 29 Great James Street, W.C.1.—*Exce. Sec.*, Gloria Frankel.

REGULAR FORCES EMPLOYMENT ASSOCIATION (1885), 25 Bloomsbury Square, W.C.1. Finds employment for non-commissioned ex-Regulars.—*General Manager*, Maj.-Gen. A. M. L. Hogge, C.B.

REINDEER COUNCIL OF THE UNITED KINGDOM (1949), Newton Road, Harston, Cambridge.—*Hon. Sec.*, Dr. E. J. Lindgren.

RELIGION AND MEDICINE, INSTITUTE OF (1964).—*Organising Sec.*, H. Sinclair, St. Marylebone Parish Church, Marylebone Road, N.W.1.

RENT OFFICERS, INSTITUTE OF.—*Hon. Sec.*, M. R. Webber, Paris Street Arcade, Exeter.

RESEARCH DEFENCE SOCIETY, Grosvenor Gardens House, Grosvenor Gardens, S.W.1.—*Hon. Sec.*, Prof. T. J. Biscoe.

RETAIL, BOOK, STATIONERY AND ALLIED TRADES EMPLOYEES' ASSOCIATION, 8/9 Commercial Road, Swindon, Wilts.—*Gen. Sec.*, D. A. Williamson.

RICHARD III SOCIETY.—*Sec.*, Miss E. M. Nokes, 4 Oakley Street, S.W.3.

R.N. AND R.M. CHILDREN'S TRUST, Collingwood Block, Khyber Road, Chatham, Kent.—*Sec.*, Lt.-Cdr. H. Blease, R.N. (*ret.*).

ROAD SAFETY OFFICERS, INSTITUTE OF (1971), 21 Windmill Drive, Northowram, Halifax, W. Yorks.—*Sec.*, Mrs. J. A. Thornton.

ROAD TRANSPORT ENGINEERS, INSTITUTE OF (1945), 1 Cromwell Place, S.W.7.—*Sec.*, J. A. Fletcher, M.B.E.

ROMAN AND MEDIAEVAL LONDON EXCAVATION COUNCIL.—*Hon. Sec.*, R. A. Woods, M.B.E., F.S.A., 31 Goodyers Avenue, Radlett, Herts.

ROMAN STUDIES, SOCIETY FOR PROMOTION OF, 31–34 Gordon Square, W.C.1.—*Pres.*, Prof. S. S. Frere, C.B.E., F.B.A., F.S.A.; *Sec.*, Mrs. P. Gilbert.

ROTARY INTERNATIONAL IN GREAT BRITAIN AND IRELAND (1914), Sheen Lane House, Sheen Lane, S.W.14.—*Sec.*, J. H. Jackson.

ROUND TABLES OF GREAT BRITAIN AND IRELAND, NATIONAL ASSOCIATION OF (1927), Marchesi House, 15 Park Road, N.W.1.—*Gen. Sec.*, P. W. Tipton.

ROYAL AFRICAN SOCIETY (1901), 18 Northumberland Avenue, W.C.2.—*Sec.*, Mrs. P. North.

ROYAL AGRICULTURAL SOCIETY OF ENGLAND (1838), National Agricultural Centre, Stoneleigh, Kenilworth, Warwicks.—*Chief Exec.*, J. D. M. Hearth.

ROYAL AGRICULTURAL SOCIETY OF THE COMMONWEALTH (1957).—*Hon. Sec.*, F. R. Francis, M.V.O., M.B.E., Robarts House, Rossmore Road, N.W.1.

ROYAL AIR FORCE BENEVOLENT FUND (1919), 67 Portland Place, W.1.—*Controller*, Air Chief Marshal Sir Alasdair Steedman, G.C.B., C.B.E., D.F.C.

ROYAL AIR FORCES ASSOCIATION, 43 Grove Park Road, W.4.—*Sec. Gen.*, D. Milne.

ROYAL ALEXANDRA AND ALBERT SCHOOL (1758), *Offices*, Gatton Park, Reigate, Surrey.—*Sec.*, A. R. Rainbow, M.B.E.

ROYAL ALFRED SEAFARERS' SOCIETY (1865), Weston Acres, Woodmansterne Lane, Banstead, Surrey.—*Gen. Sec.*, J. H. Moore.

ROYAL ARMOURED CORPS BENEVOLENT FUND, *Headquarters*, R.A.C. Centre, Bovington Camp, Wareham, Dorset; *Sec.*, Lt.-Col. C. H. Rayment, M.B.E.

ROYAL ARTILLERY ASSOCIATION, Artillery House, Connaught Barracks, Grand Depot Road, S.E.18.—*Gen. Sec.*, Col. R. H. Haynes, M.B.E.

ROYAL ASIATIC SOCIETY OF GREAT BRITAIN AND IRELAND (1823), 56 Queen Anne Street, W.1.—*Sec.,* Miss E. V. Gibson.

ROYAL ASSOCIATION OF BRITISH DAIRY FARMERS (1876), Robarts House, Rossmore Road, N.W.1.— *Chief Exec.,* F. R. Francis, M.V.O., M.B.E.

ROYAL BRITISH NURSES ASSOCIATION, 94 Upper Tollington Park, N.4.—*Hon. Sec.,* Mrs. H. M. Vorstermans, M.B.E.

ROYAL CALEDONIAN SCHOOLS (1815), Bushey, Herts.— *The Master,* Capt. R. E. Wilson, C.B.E., D.F.C., R.N.

ROYAL CAMBRIDGE HOME FOR SOLDIERS' WIDOWS, 82-84 Hurst Road, East Molesey, Surrey.—*Sec.,* Mrs. H. E. Gunn.

ROYAL CELTIC SOCIETY (1820), 49 Queen Street, Edinburgh.—*Sec.,* J. G. S. Cameron, W.S.

ROYAL CHORAL SOCIETY (1871), Royal Albert Hall, S.W.7.—*Gen. Man.,* M. Heyland.

ROYAL COLLEGE OF VETERINARY SURGEONS, 32 Belgrave Square, S.W.1.—*Pres.,* Prof. E. J. L. Soulsby, PH.D.; *Registrar,* A. R. W. Porter.

ROYAL COMMONWEALTH SOCIETY (1868), Northumberland Avenue, W.C.2.—(21,000 members). —*Sec.-Gen.,* Sir Michael Scott, K.C.V.O., C.M.G.

ROYAL DESIGNERS FOR INDUSTRY, FACULTY OF (1936) (Royal Society of Arts), John Adam Street, W.C.2.—*Master,* Dr. W. C. Brown, O.B.E.; *Sec.,* C. T. Lucas.

ROYAL ENGINEERS ASSOCIATION, *Headquarters,* R.S.M.E., Chatham, Kent.—*Controller,* Col. G. S. Harris.

ROYAL ENGINEERS, THE INSTITUTION OF (1875), Brompton Barracks, Chatham.—*Sec.,* Col. E. E. Peel.

ROYAL HIGHLAND AND AGRICULTURAL SOCIETY OF SCOTLAND (1784), Ingliston, Newbridge, Midlothian.—*Sec.,* J. R. Good.

ROYAL HORTICULTURAL SOCIETY (1804).—*Offices,* 80 Vincent Square, S.W.1. *Garden,* Wisley, Woking, Surrey.—*Sec.,* J. R. Cowell.

ROYAL HOSPITAL AND HOME FOR INCURABLES, PUTNEY (1854), West Hill, S.W.15.—*Chief Exec.,* Col. B. E. Blunt.

ROYAL HOSPITAL SCHOOL, Ipswich, Suffolk.—*Headmaster,* M. A. B. Kirk.

ROYAL HUMANE SOCIETY (1774).—Gives about 650 awards annually for saving and attempting to save human life.—*Offices,* Brettenham House, Lancaster Place, W.C.2.—*Sec.,* Maj. A. J. Dickinson.

ROYAL INSTITUTE OF INTERNATIONAL AFFAIRS (1920), Chatham House, 10 St. James's Square, S.W.1.— *Dir.,* Adm. Sir James Eberle, G.C.B.

ROYAL INSTITUTION OF GREAT BRITAIN (1799), 21 Albemarle Street, W.1.—*Pres.,* H.R.H. The Duke of Kent, G.C.M.G., G.C.V.O.; *Dir.,* Prof. Sir George Porter, F.R.S.; *Sec.,* Prof. E. A. Ash, C.B.E., F.R.S.

ROYAL LIFE SAVING SOCIETY, THE (1891), Mountbatten House, Studley, Warwickshire.—*Dir.,* K. H. Sach.

ROYAL LITERARY FUND (1790), 144 Temple Chambers, Temple Avenue, E.C.4. Grants to necessitous authors of some published work of approved literary merit or to their immediate dependants.— *Pres.,* A. Crook; *Sec.,* A. Mackenzie Smith, O.B.E., M.C.

ROYAL MEDICAL BENEVOLENT FUND (1836), 24 King's Road, Wimbledon, S.W.19.—*Sec.,* P. G. Gordon-Smith.

ROYAL MEDICAL SOCIETY (1737), Students Centre, Bristo Square, Edinburgh.—*Sec.,* Mrs. P. E. Strong.

ROYAL METAL TRADES BENEVOLENT SOCIETY (1843), 9 Totteridge Avenue, High Wycombe, Bucks.—*Sec.,* A. Whittle, M.B.E.

ROYAL MICROSCOPICAL SOCIETY, 37–38 St. Clements, Oxford.—*Administrator,* Lt.-Col. P. G. Fleming.

ROYAL MILITARY POLICE ASSOCIATION (1946), Regimental Headquarters, Corps of Royal Military Police, Roussillon Barracks, Chichester, Sussex.— *Sec.,* Major P. N. Ross *(ret.).*

ROYAL MUSICAL ASSOCIATION (1874), 5 Church Street, Harston, Cambridge.—*Sec.,* Rosemary Dooley.

ROYAL NATIONAL LIFEBOAT INSTITUTION, THE (1824).—*Income* (1983) £16,636,000, expenditure £15,309,000; rescued in 1983, 1,348. 257 lifeboats are maintained on the coasts of Great Britain and Ireland. *Offices,* West Quay Road, Poole, Dorset.— *Chairman,* The Duke of Atholl.

ROYAL NATIONAL MISSION TO DEEP SEA FISHERMEN (1881), 43 Nottingham Place, W.1.—*Sec.,* D. M. MacMillan, M.B.E.

ROYAL NAVAL AND ROYAL MARINES CHILDREN'S TRUST (1834), H.M.S. *Nelson,* Portsmouth.

ROYAL NAVAL ASSOCIATION (1950), 82 Chelsea Manor Street, S.W.3.—*Gen. Sec.,* Capt. D. W. Beadle, C.B.E., R.N.

ROYAL NAVAL BENEVOLENT SOCIETY (1739), 1 Fleet Street, E.C.4.—*Sec.,* Lt. Cdr. A. J. G. Newbery, O.B.E., R.N. *(ret.).*

ROYAL NAVAL BENEVOLENT TRUST (Grand Fleet and Kindred Funds) (1922), 1 High Street, Brompton, Gillingham, Kent (Local Committees at Chatham, Devonport, Portsmouth and Rosyth).—*Gen. Sec.,* Lt.-Cdr. D. C. Lawrence, R.N. *(ret.).*

ROYAL NAVY OFFICERS, ASSOCIATION OF (Trafalgar Day, 1925), 70 Porchester Terrace, W.2.—*Sec.-Treas.,* Lt.-Cdr. J. V. Watson, M.B.E., R.N.

ROYAL OVER-SEAS LEAGUE (1910), Over-Seas House, Park Place, St. James's Street, S.W.1.—*Chairman,* Sir David Scott, G.C.M.G.; *Dir. Gen.,* Capt. J. Rumble.

ROYAL PATRIOTIC FUND CORPORATION (1854), 9 Gloucester Gate, N.W.1. Administers funds for the benefit of widows, children and other dependants of deceased officers and servicemen of the Armed Forces.—*Sec.,* Brig. D. C. Blomfield-Smith, M.B.E.

ROYAL PHILHARMONIC SOCIETY (1813), 10 Stratford Place, W.1.—*Hon. Sec.,* M. Pope.

ROYAL PHOTOGRAPHIC SOCIETY (1853), R.P.S. National Centre of Photography, The Octagon, Milsom Street, Bath.—*Sec.,* K. R. Warr.

ROYAL PINNER SCHOOL FOUNDATION, 110 Old Brompton Road, S. Kensington, S.W.7. (Trustee: The Royal Commercial Travellers' School Trust Ltd.) Assists in the education of children of sales representatives where families have suffered some adversity.—*Sec.,* S. Thurtell.

"ROYAL SAILORS' RESTS" (Miss Agnes Weston's) (1876). *Head Office,* 2b South Street, Gosport, Hants. Centres for naval personnel at Devonport, St. Budeaux, Ilchester, Portland, Gosport, Portsmouth, Faslane and Rosyth.—*Sec.,* A. A. Lockwood.

ROYAL SCHOOL OF NEEDLEWORK (1872), 25 Princes Gate, S.W.7.—*Principal,* Mrs. J. Field.

ROYAL SCOTTISH COUNTRY DANCE SOCIETY (1923), 12 Coates Crescent, Edinburgh.—*Sec.,* Miss M. M. Gibson.

ROYAL SCOTTISH SOCIETY FOR PREVENTION OF CRUELTY TO CHILDREN (1884), Melville House, 41 Polwarth Terrace, Edinburgh.—*Gen. Sec.,* A. M. M. Wood.

ROYAL SEAMEN'S PENSION FUND (Incorporated) (1919), 58 High Street, Sutton, Surrey.—*Sec.*, R. F. Van Houten.

ROYAL SIGNALS INSTITUTION (1950), Cheltenham Terrace, S.W.3.—*Sec.*, Lt.-Col. E. J. Beale.

ROYAL SOCIETY, THE (1660), 6 Carlton House Terrace, S.W.1.—*Pres.*, Sir Andrew Huxley, O.M., F.R.S.; *Treas. and Vice-Pres.*, Sir John Mason, C.B., F.R.S.; *Secretaries and Vice-Presidents*, Prof. R. J. Elliott, F.R.S.; Prof. D. C. Smith, F.R.S.; *Foreign Secretary and Vice-Pres.*, Sir Arnold Burgen, F.R.S.; *Executive Sec.*, Dr. R. W. J. Keay, C.B.E.

ROYAL SOCIETY FOR ASIAN AFFAIRS (1901). 42 Devonshire Street, W.1.—*Pres.*, The Lord Denman, M.C.; *Sec.*, Miss M. FitzSimons.

ROYAL SOCIETY FOR THE ENCOURAGEMENT OF ARTS MANUFACTURES AND COMMERCE (Royal Society of Arts) (1754), 6–8 John Adam Street, Adelphi, W.C.2.—*Chairman*, M. Moss, C.B.E.; *Sec.*, C. T. Lucas.

ROYAL SOCIETY FOR THE PREVENTION OF ACCIDENTS, Cannon House, Priory Queensway, Birmingham.—*Dir. Gen.*, R. M. Warburton.

ROYAL SOCIETY FOR THE PREVENTION OF CRUELTY TO ANIMALS (1824), Causeway, Horsham, Sussex.—*Exec. Dir.*, F. D. Ward, C.B.E.

ROYAL SOCIETY FOR THE PROTECTION OF BIRDS (1889), The Lodge, Sandy, Beds.—*Dir.*, I. Prestt.

ROYAL SOCIETY OF BRITISH ARTISTS (1823), 17 Carlton House Terrace, S.W.1.—*Pres.*, P. Garrard; *Vice-President*, D. Carpanini; *Keeper*, C. de Winter.

ROYAL SOCIETY OF BRITISH SCULPTORS (1904), 108 Old Brompton Road, S.W.7.—*Pres.*, M. Rizzello, O.B.E.; *Sec.*, Miss M. O'Connor.

ROYAL SOCIETY OF EDINBURGH (1783), 22 George Street, Edinburgh 2.—*Pres.*, Sir John Atwell, C.B.E.; *Gen. Sec.*, Prof. R. M. S. Smellie, PH.D., D.SC.; *Treas.*, Dr. Ian Forbes; *Curator*, Prof. D. M. Henderson.

ROYAL SOCIETY OF HEALTH (1876), to promote the health of the people, 13 Grosvenor Place, S.W.1.—*Sec.*, G. M. T. Large.

ROYAL SOCIETY OF LITERATURE (1823), 1 Hyde Park Gardens, W.2.—*Sec.*, Mrs. P. M. Schute.

ROYAL SOCIETY OF MEDICINE (1805), 1 Wimpole Street, W.1.—*Pres.*, (1984–85), Sir John Walton, T.D., F.R.C.P.; *Exec. Dir.*, R. N. Thomson.

ROYAL SOCIETY OF PORTRAIT PAINTERS (1891), 17 Carlton House Terrace, S.W.1.—*Pres.*, D. Poole.

ROYAL SOCIETY OF ST. GEORGE (1894), 4 Upper Belgrave Street, S.W.1.—*Gen. Sec.*, Mrs. W. M. Bourne.

ROYAL STAR AND GARTER HOME FOR DISABLED SAILORS, SOLDIERS, AND AIRMEN (1916), Richmond-upon-Thames.—*Commandant*, Col. R. N. Harris, M.B.E.

ROYAL STATISTICAL SOCIETY (1834), 25 Enford Street, W.1.—*Pres.*, Dr. W. F. Bodmer, F.R.S.; *Sec.*, I. H. Blenkinsop.

ROYAL TANK REGIMENT ASSOCIATION and BENEVOLENT FUND, H.Q. R.A.C. Centre, Bovington Camp, Wareham, Dorset.—*Regimental Sec.*, Lt.-Col. C. H. Rayment, M.B.E.

ROYAL TELEVISION SOCIETY, Tavistock House East, Tavistock Square, W.C.1.—*Hon. Sec.*, A. Pilgrim.

ROYAL UNITED KINGDOM BENEFICENT ASSOCIATION (1863), 6 Avonmore Road, W.14.—*Gen. Sec.*, Rear Adm. B. C. Perowne, C.B.

ROYAL UNITED SERVICES INSTITUTE FOR DEFENCE STUDIES, Whitehall, S.W.1.—*Dir.*, Gp. Capt. D. Bolton, R.A.F. (*ret.*).

RUBBER GROWERS' ASSOCIATION LTD., 90 Fenchurch Street, E.C.3.—*Sec.*, Mrs. J. Taylor.

RURAL ENGLAND, COUNCIL FOR THE PROTECTION OF (1926), 4 Hobart Place, S.W.1.—*Dir.*, R. B. Grove-White.

RURAL SCOTLAND, ASSOCIATION FOR PROTECTION OF (1926), 14a Napier Road, Edinburgh.—*Dir. and Sec.*, R. L. Smith, O.B.E.

RURAL WALES, COUNCIL FOR THE PROTECTION OF, Ty Gwyn, 31 High Street, Welshpool, Powys.—*Dir.*, S. R. J. Meade.

SAILORS' CHILDREN'S SOCIETY, THE (1821), Newland, Hull. Cares for British seamen's children who have lost a parent and for short periods during a mother's illness if father is at sea. Provides welfare facilities for seamen in Humber area, and Homes for aged seafarers at Hull and S. Shields.—*Sec.*, C. G. R. Streatfeild-James.

ST. DEINIOL'S RESIDENTIAL LIBRARY (1902), Hawarden, Deeside, Clwyd.—*Warden and Chief Librarian*, Rev. P. J. Jagger, F.R.Hist.S.

ST. DUNSTAN'S, for men and women blinded on War Service, 12–14 Harcourt Street, W.1. In March 1984, the number of blinded men and women in the care of the organization was 1,355.—*Pres.*, Col. Sir Michael Ansell, C.B.E., D.S.O.; *Chairman*, Adm. of the Fleet Sir Henry Leach, G.C.B.; *Sec.*, W. C. Weisblatt.

ST. JOHN AMBULANCE ASSOCIATION AND BRIGADE, 1 Grosvenor Crescent, S.W.1. Voluntary unpaid body providing first-aid cover at public gatherings.—*Chief Commander*, Maj.-Gen. P. R. Leuchars, C.B.E.; *Commissioner-in-Chief*, Maj.-Gen. Sir John Younger, Bt., C.B.E. *Brigade Strengths* (U.K. 1983), Ambulance Personnel, 15,509; Nursing Personnel, 16,029; Ambulance Cadets 11,244; Nursing Cadets, 25,943.—*Chief Sec.*, Brig. P. R. Body.

SALES AND MARKETING MANAGEMENT, INSTITUTE OF.—*Chief Exec.*, J. H. Goodman, Georgian House, 31 Upper George Street, Luton, Beds.

SALMON AND TROUT ASSOCIATION (1903), Fishmongers' Hall, E.C.4.—*Dir.*, T. D. Thompson.

SALTIRE SOCIETY (1936), Saltire House, Atholl Crescent, Edinburgh.—*Hon. Sec.*, I. A. G. Kinniburgh.

SAMARITANS, THE (to help the suicidal and despairing).—*Gen. Sec.*, Rev. D. Evans, 17 Uxbridge Road, Slough, Berks.

SAMUEL PEPYS CLUB—*Sec.*, R. H. Adams, T.D., F.S.A., 14 Dale Close, Oxford.

SANITARY ENGINEERS, INSTITUTION OF. *See* PUBLIC HEALTH ENGINEERS.

SAVE THE CHILDREN FUND, THE (1919), 17 Grove Lane, Camberwell, S.E.5.—*Dir. Gen.*, J. A. Cumber, C.M.G., M.B.E., T.D.

SCHOOL LIBRARY ASSOCIATION, Victoria House, 29–31 George Street, Oxford.—*Sec.*, Miriam Curtis.

SCHOOL NATURAL SCIENCE SOCIETY, 22 Chada Avenue, Gillingham, Kent.—*Hon. Gen. Sec.*, J. Williams.

SCHOOLMASTERS, SOCIETY OF (1798) (for the relief of Necessitous Schoolmasters and of their Widows and Orphans), 1 Turk's Head Court, Eton, Berks.—*Sec.*, Mrs. M. S. Freeburn.

SCHOOLMISTRESSES AND GOVERNESSES BENEVOLENT INSTITUTION, Queen Mary House, Manor Park Road, Chislehurst, Kent. Helps schoolmistresses, matrons and women employed in an administrative capacity in independent schools, as well as governesses and self-employed women teachers; annuities, grants, a home.—*Sec.*, R. W. Hayward.

SCIENCE AND LEARNING, SOCIETY FOR THE PROTECTION OF, 20–21 Compton Terrace, N.I.—*Sec.*, Miss E. Fraser.

SCIENCE EDUCATION, ASSOCIATION FOR, College Lane, Hatfield, Herts.—*Gen. Sec.*, B. G. Atwood.

SCOTCH WHISKY ASSOCIATION, 20 Atholl Crescent, Edinburgh.—*Dir. Gen. and Sec.*, Col. H. F. O. Bewsher, O.B.E.; *Information and Development Office*, 17 Half Moon Street, W.1.

SCOTTISH GENEALOGY SOCIETY (1953).—*Hon. Sec.*, Miss J. P. S. Ferguson, 21 Howard Place, Edinburgh 3.

SCOTTISH HISTORY SOCIETY (1886).—*Hon. Sec.*, D. Stevenson, PH.D., Dept. of History, University of Aberdeen.

SCOTTISH LANDOWNERS' FEDERATION (1906).—*Dir.*, D. J. Hughes Hallett, 18 Abercromby Place, Edinburgh.

SCOTTISH LAW AGENTS SOCIETY, 61 High Street, Dunblane, Perthshire.

SCOTTISH LIFE OFFICES, ASSOCIATED (1841), 23 St. Andrew Square, Edinburgh.—*Sec.*, G. C. Train.

SCOTTISH MARINE BIOLOGICAL ASSOCIATION (1914), Dunstaffnage Marine Research Laboratory, P.O. Box 3, Oban, Argyll.—*Dir., and Sec.*, Prof. R. I. Currie, C.B.E., F.R.S.E.

SCOTTISH NATIONAL BLOOD TRANSFUSION ASSOCIATION (1940), 29 Abercromby Place, Edinburgh.—*Sec.*, P. C. Taylor.

SCOTTISH NATIONAL INSTITUTION FOR THE WAR BLINDED. Workshops at Glasgow and Linburn.—*Appeals Director*, Maj. D. F. Callander, M.C., P.O. Box 304, 38 Albany Street, Edinburgh.

SCOTTISH NATIONAL WAR MEMORIAL (1927), The Castle, Edinburgh.—*Sec.*, J. D. M. Watson, 17 Melville Street, Edinburgh; *Curator*, T. C. Barker.

SCOTTISH RECORD SOCIETY, Scottish History Dept., Univ. of Glasgow.—*Hon. Sec.*, Dr. J. Kirk.

SCOTTISH SECONDARY TEACHERS' ASSOCIATION, 15 Dundas Street, Edinburgh.—*Gen. Sec.*, A. A. Stanley.

SCOTTISH SOCIETY FOR PREVENTION OF CRUELTY TO ANIMALS (1839), 19 Melville Street, Edinburgh.—*Chief Exec.*, Sir Cameron Rusby, K.C.B., M.V.O.

SCOTTISH SOCIETY FOR THE PROTECTION OF WILD BIRDS (1927), Foremount House, Kilbarchan, Renfrewshire.—*Hon. Sec. and Treas.*, Dr. J. A. Gibson.

SCOTTISH TOURIST BOARD (1969), 23 Ravelston Terrace, Edinburgh.—*Chief Exec.*, Dr. D. A. Pattison.

SCOTTISH WILDLIFE TRUST (1964), 25 Johnston Terrace, Edinburgh.—*Chief Exec.*, B. Gilchrist, M.B.E.

SCOTTISH WOMEN'S RURAL INSTITUTES (1917), 42 Heriot Row, Edinburgh.—*Gen. Sec.*, Mrs. J. A. Noble.

SCOUT ASSOCIATION, THE, *Headquarters*, Baden-Powell House, Queen's Gate, S.W.7.—*Chief Scout*, Maj.-Gen. M. J. H. Walsh, C.B., D.S.O.; *Chief Exec.*, Comm. K. H. Stevens, C.B.E. Membership in U.K. (1983), 627,000; World Membership over 16,000,000 in over 150 countries.

SCRIBES AND ILLUMINATORS, THE SOCIETY OF.—*Hon. Sec.*, Mrs. S. Cavendish, c/o 43 Earlham Street, W.C.2.

SCRIPTURE GIFT MISSION (1888), Radstock House, 3 Eccleston Street, S.W.1. Copies and selections of the Scriptures circulated (1983), 15,700,434.—*Sec.*, N. Brown.

SCRIPTURE UNION (1867), 130 City Road, E.C.1.—*Gen. Dir.*, A. C. N. Martin.

SEA CADET ASSOCIATION, Broadway House, Broadway, Wimbledon, S.W.19.—*Pres.*, Admiral of the Fleet Sir Henry Leach, G.C.B.; *Gen. Sec.*, Cmdr. P. J. Everett, O.B.E., R.N.

SEAMEN'S CHRISTIAN FRIEND SOCIETY (1846), 26 Davyhulme Road East, Stretford, Manchester.

SECONDARY HEADS ASSOCIATION, 107 St. Paul's Road, N.1.—*Gen. Sec.*, T. P. Snape. (Association formed from amalgamation of Headmasters Association and Association of Headmistresses).

SELDEN SOCIETY (1887), Faculty of Laws, Queen Mary College, Mile End Road, E.1. To encourage the study and advance the knowledge of the History of English Law.—*Pres.*, Prof. G. R. Elton, F.B.A.; *Sec.*, V. Tunkel.

SHAFTESBURY HOMES AND *Arethusa* (1843), 3 Rectory Grove, S.W.4.—*Gen. Sec.*, Maj. R. P. A. de Berniere-Smart.

SHAFTESBURY SOCIETY, THE (1844), Shaftesbury House, 112 Regency Street, S.W.1.—Engaged in social service among the physically handicapped and the poor. Maintains Residential Schools for physically handicapped children, Hostels for Muscular Dystrophy sufferers over 16 years, Holiday centres for the disabled and Missions in Greater London.—*Sec.*, G. Holloway.

SHEEP ASSOCIATION, NATIONAL, nr. Tring, Herts.—*Sec.*, J. Thorley.

SHELLFISH ASSOCIATION OF GREAT BRITAIN, Fishmongers' Hall, London Bridge, E.C.4.—*Dir.*, Dr. E. Edwards.

SHELTER (National Campaign for the Homeless), 157 Waterloo Road, S.E.1.; *Pres.*, Cardinal Hume; *Dir.*, N. McIntosh.

SHERLOCK HOLMES SOCIETY OF LONDON (1951), The Old Crown Inn, Lopen, Somerset.—*Hon. Sec.*, Capt. W. R. Michell, R.N. (*ret.*).

SHIPBROKERS, INSTITUTE OF CHARTERED (1911), 24 St. Mary Axe, E.C.3.—*Sec.*, J. H. Parker.

SHIPWRECKED FISHERMEN AND MARINERS' ROYAL BENEVOLENT SOCIETY (1839), 1 North Pallant, Chichester, West Sussex.—*Gen. Sec.*, Miss V. G. Austin.

SHIRE HORSE SOCIETY (1878), East of England Showground, Peterborough.—*Sec.*, R. W. Bird, M.B.E.

SHRIEVALTY ASSOCIATION, c/o A. J. Wilson, The Sheriff's Office, 6 Chapel Street, Preston, Lancs.—*Sec.-Treas.*, E. A. Nickson.

SIMPLIFIED SPELLING SOCIETY (1908).—*Chairman*, C. Jolly, 12 Pembridge Mews, Notting Hill, W.11.

SIR OSWALD STOLL FOUNDATION, 446 Fulham Road, S.W.6.—*Sec.*, Rev. J. A. Garwell, R.N.

SMALLFARMERS' ASSOCIATION, THE (1979), Room L1, University of Reading, 1 Earley Gate, Reading, Berks.—*Hon. Sec.*, Mrs. R. B. Weiss.

SOCIAL RESPONSIBILITY AND EDUCATION DEPARTMENT OF THE RELIGIOUS SOCIETY OF FRIENDS, Friends House, Euston Road, N.W.1.

SOCIAL WORKERS, BRITISH ASSOCIATION OF (1970), 16 Kent Street, Birmingham.—*Gen. Sec.*, J. Cypher.

SOCIALIST PARTY OF GREAT BRITAIN (1904), 52 Clapham High Street, S.W.4.—*Gen. Sec.*, A. G. Atkinson.

SOIL ASSOCIATION LTD., Walnut Tree Manor, Haughley, Stowmarket, Suffolk.—*Hon. Gen. Sec.*, The Lady Eve Balfour.

SOLDIERS' AND AIRMEN'S SCRIPTURE READERS ASSOCIATION, THE (1838), 75–79 High Street, Aldershot, Hants.—*Gen. Sec.*, Lt.-Col. K. W. Sear (*ret.*).

SOLDIERS' DAUGHTERS' SCHOOL, ROYAL (1855), 65 Rosslyn Hill, Hampstead, N.W.3.—*Sec.*, Col. J. G. Palmer.

SOLDIERS', SAILORS' AND AIRMEN'S FAMILIES ASSOCIATION (1885), 27 Queen Anne's Gate, S.W.1.— *Chairman*, Lt.-Gen. Sir Napier Crookenden, K.C.B., D.S.O., O.B.E.; *Controller*, D. Smithers; *Sec.*, Gp. Capt. D. G. F. Palmer, O.B.E. (*ret.*).

SOLDIERS, SAILORS AND AIRMEN'S HELP SOCIETY (Incorporated) (1899), *See* FORCES HELP SOCIETY.

SOLICITORS' BENEVOLENT ASSOCIATION (1858), 30 Lonsdale Chambers, 27 Chancery Lane, W.C.2.— *Sec.*, Lt.-Col. P. B. Wakelin, M.C.

SOLICITORS IN THE SUPREME COURTS OF SCOTLAND, SOCIETY OF.—*Sec.*, A. R. Brownlie, 2 Abercromby Place, Edinburgh 3.—*Treas.*, D. A. Lamb.

S.O.S. SOCIETY, THE (1929), 14 Culford Gardens, S.W.3. Old people's homes (5), Mental Rehabilitation homes (2), Ex-offenders hostel (1), Young Men's Hostel (1).—*Chief Exec.*, Lt.-Col. P. Rew.

SOUTH AMERICAN MISSIONARY SOCIETY, Allen Gardiner House, Pembury Road, Tunbridge Wells, Kent.—*Gen. Sec.*, Rev. Canon P. D. King.

SOUTH WALES INSTITUTE OF ENGINEERS (1857), Institute Buildings, Park Place, Cardiff.—*Hon. Sec.*, R. E. Lindsay.

SPASTICS SOCIETY, THE (1952), 12 Park Crescent, W.1.—*Sec.*, A. V. M. Diamond, M.B.E.

SPEAKERS CLUBS, THE ASSOCIATION OF (1971), 16 Rowanbank, Scone.—*Sec.*, K. A. MacLeod Lewison.

SPINA BIFIDA AND HYDROCEPHALUS, ASSOCIATION FOR, 22 Upper Woburn Place, W.C.1.—*Exec. Dir.*, Miss M. P. Gilbertson.

SPORTS MEDICINE, INSTITUTE OF (1963), c/o School of Engineering & Science, Polytechnic of Central London, 115 New Cavendish Street, W.1.—*Hon. Sec.*, P. Sebastian.

SPURGEON'S HOMES (1867), Haddon House, Station Road, Birchington, Kent.—*Sec.*, P. E. Johnson.

STATISTICIANS, INSTITUTE OF (1948), 36 Churchgate Street, Bury St. Edmunds, Suffolk.—*Sec.*, P. S. Cleary.

STATUTE LAW SOCIETY (1968), 186 City Road, E.C.4.— *Hon. Sec.*, H. Hudson.

STEWART SOCIETY (1899), 48 Castle Street, Edinburgh.—*Hon. Sec.*, D. F. Stewart, W.S.

STRATEGIC STUDIES, THE INTERNATIONAL INSTITUTE FOR (1958), 23 Tavistock Street, W.C.2.—*Sec.*, Lt.-Col. P. M. B. Carthew, M.B.E.

STRUCTURAL ENGINEERS, INSTITUTION OF (1908), 11 Upper Belgrave Street, S.W.1.—*Sec.*, D. J. Clark.

STUDENT CHRISTIAN MOVEMENT OF GREAT BRITAIN (1889), Manor House, Moat Lane, Birmingham 5.— *Gen. Sec.*, Rev. T. E. McClure.

SUFFOLK HORSE SOCIETY, 6 Church Street, Woodbridge, Suffolk.—*Sec.*, P. Ryder-Davies.

SURGEONS OF ENGLAND, ROYAL COLLEGE OF (1800), Lincoln's Inn Fields, W.C.2.—*Pres.*, Prof. Sir Geoffrey Slaney, K.B.E.; *Sec.*, R. S. Johnson-Gilbert, O.B.E.

SURGEONS OF EDINBURGH, ROYAL COLLEGE OF (1505), Nicolson Street, Edinburgh.—*Sec.*, P. Edmond, C.B.E., Q.H.S., T.D.

SURGICAL TECHNOLOGISTS, BRITISH INSTITUTE OF, 103 New Oxford Street, W.C.1.—*Sec.*, I. F. Sherwood.

SURVEYORS, ROYAL INSTITUTION OF CHARTERED (incorporating the Institute of Quantity Surveyors) (1868), 12 Great George Street, S.W.1.—*Sec. Gen.*, R. Steel, C.B.E.

SUSSEX CATTLE SOCIETY (1887), Station Road, Robertsbridge, E. Sussex.—*Manager*, Mrs. D. Jowitt.

SUTTON HOUSING TRUST (1901), Sutton Court, Tring, Herts.—*Gen. Manager*, I. C. F. Butcher.

SWEDENBORG SOCIETY (1810), 20–21 Bloomsbury Way, W.C.1.—*Sec.*, Madeline G. Waters.

TALKING BOOKS FOR THE HANDICAPPED (National Listening Library), 12 Lant Street, S.E.1.—*Exec. Dir.*, R. Shead.

TAVISTOCK INSTITUTE OF HUMAN RELATIONS, Tavistock Centre, 120 Belsize Lane, N.W.3.—*Sec.*, P. M. Foster.

TAXATION, INSTITUTE OF (1930), 3 Grosvenor Crescent, S.W.1.—*Sec.*, J. F. Martin.

TAX PAYERS' SOCIETY, Room 22, Wheatsheaf House, 4 Carmelite Street, E.C.4.—*Dir.*, D. J. Bryant.

TEACHERS IN COMMERCE LTD., FACULTY OF, 141 Bedford Road, Sutton Coldfield, West Midlands.— *Sec.*, J. Snowdon.

TEACHERS OF HOME ECONOMICS LTD., NATIONAL ASSOCIATION OF, Hamilton House, Mabledon Place, W.C.1.—*Gen. Man.*, P. G. Higgins.

TEACHERS OF MATHEMATICS, ASSOCIATION OF, Kings Chambers, Queen Street, Derby.—*Hon. Sec.*, J. D. Warwick.

TEACHERS OF SPEECH AND DRAMA, SOCIETY OF, St. Bride Institute, Fleet Street, E.C.4.—*Hon. Sec.*, Marguerite Turnbull, Abbot's Lodging, Marshside, Canterbury.

TEACHERS OF THE DEAF, BRITISH ASSOCIATION OF.— Rycroft Centre, Royal Schools for the Deaf, Stanley Road, Cheadle Hulme, Cheadle, Cheshire.

TEACHERS' UNION, ULSTER (1919), 94 Malone Road, Belfast.—*Gen. Sec.*, D. Allen.

TELECOMMUNICATIONS USERS' ASSOCIATION, 34 Grand Avenue, N.10.—*Dirs.*, E. J. Donahue, M. Elwes.

TEMPERANCE SOCIETIES:—

British National Temperance League (1834), Livesey-Clegg House, 44 Union Street, Sheffield, 1.— *Office Sec.*, Mrs. P. M. Bullen.

British Women's Temperance Association, S.C.U. (1876), 8 North Bank Street, Edinburgh 1.—*Hon. Sec.*, Miss J. E. H. Gillon.

Church of England National Council for Social Aid, 38 Ebury Street, S.W.1.—*Gen. Sec.*, Rev. E. W. F. Agar.

Churches Council on Alcohol and Drugs (1915), 4 Southampton Row, W.C.1.—*Gen. Sec.*, Rev. J. K. Lawton.

Division of Social Responsibility of the Methodist Church, No. 1 Central Buildings, Westminster, S.W.1.—*Gen. Sec.*, Rev. G. M. Burt.

Independent Order of Rechabites, Salford Unity Friendly Society, London District (1870), No. 30, 18 Doughty Street, W.C.1.

International Christian Federation for the Prevention of Alcoholism and Drug Addiction, 27 Tavistock Square, W.C.1.—*Gen. Sec.*, Rev. J. K. Lawton.

Order of the Sons of Temperance, 21 Victoria Avenue, Harrogate.—*Sec.*, K. Unsworth.

Royal Naval Temperance Society (auxiliary of Royal Sailors' Rests), 2b South Street, Gosport, Hants.—*Sec.*, A. A. Lockwood.

Social Responsibility Dept., General Assembly of Unitarian and Free Christian Churches, Essex Hall, Essex Street, W.C.2.—*Sec.*, G. Cox.

Social Responsibility Committee of the Mission Board, Scottish Episcopal Church (1919).—*Gen. Sec.*, I. D. Stuart, 21 Grosvenor Crescent, Edinburgh.

United Kingdom Alliance, Alliance House, 12 Caxton Street, S.W.1.—*Gen. Sec.*, Rev. B. Kinman.

TEMPLETON FOUNDATION, 16 Kingfisher Lane, Turners Hill, Crawley, Sussex.—*Vice-Pres.*, Rev. W. Forker.

TERRITORIAL, AUXILIARY AND VOLUNTEER RESERVE ASSOCIATIONS, COUNCIL OF (1908), Centre Block, Duke of York's Headquarters, Chelsea, S.W.3.—*Sec.*, Maj.-Gen. W. Bate, C.B., O.B.E., D.L.

TEXTILE INSTITUTE (1910), 10 Blackfriars Street, Manchester.—*Gen. Sec.*, R. G. Denyer.

THEATRE RESEARCH, SOCIETY FOR (1948).—*Hon. Secs.*, Dr. K. M. Barker, D. Forbes, 77 Kinnerton Street, S.W.1.

THEATRICAL FUND ASSOCIATION, ROYAL GENERAL (1839), 11 Garrick Street, W.C.2.—*Sec.*, J. Berkeley.

THEATRICAL LADIES' GUILD OF CHARITY (1892), Bedford Chambers, King Street, Covent Garden, W.C.2.—*Admin. Sec.*, Mrs. K. Nichols.

THEOSOPHICAL SOCIETY IN ENGLAND (1875), 50 Gloucester Place, W.1.—*Gen. Sec.*, Dr. H. Gray.

THISTLE FOUNDATION, THE (1945), 27A Walker Street, Edinburgh.—*Dir.*, P. Croft.

THOMAS CORAM FOUNDATION FOR CHILDREN (1739), 40 Brunswick Square, W.C.1.—*Dir. and Sec.*, C. P. Masters.

THORACIC SOCIETY, THE BRITISH.—*Hon. Secs.*, A. E. Tattersfield, F.R.C.P., Centre Block, Southampton General Hospital, Tremone Road, Southampton; I. A. Campbell, M.R.C.P., Llandough Hospital, Cardiff.

TOC H (TALBOT HOUSE) (1915), *Headquarters*, 1 Forest Close, Wendover, Bucks.—*Gen. Sec.*, A. E. Dudman.

TOWN AND COUNTRY PLANNING ASSOCIATION, 17 Carlton House Terrace, S.W.1.—*Dir.*, D. Hall.

TOWN PLANNING INSTITUTE, ROYAL (1914), 26 Portland Place, W.1.

TOWNSWOMEN'S GUILDS, NATIONAL UNION OF (1929), 75 Harborne Road, Edgbaston, Birmingham.—*Nat. Sec.*, Mrs. R. Campbell-Tanner.

TOYNBEE HALL, THE UNIVERSITIES' SETTLEMENT IN EAST LONDON, 28 Commercial Street, Whitechapel, E.1.—*Warden*, D. P. Chesworth.

TRADE MARK AGENTS, INSTITUTE OF (1934), Suite 3, Panther House, 38 Mount Pleasant, W.C.1.—*Sec.*, E. R. Wenman.

TRADE, NATIONAL CHAMBER OF (1897), Enterprise House, Henley-on-Thames, Oxon.—*Dir. Gen.*, L. E. S. Seeney, O.B.E.

TRADING STANDARDS ADMINISTRATION, INSTITUTE OF —*Admin. Officer*, J. T. Fisher, Metropolitan House, 37 Victoria Avenue, Southend-on-Sea, Essex.

TRANSPORT ADMINISTRATION, INSTITUTE OF (1944), 32 Palmerston Road, Southampton.—*Dir.*, G. C. McCarthy.

TRANSPORT, CHARTERED INSTITUTE OF (1919), 80 Portland Place, W.1.—*Dir.-Gen.*, J. C. F. Cameron.

TRANSPORT CONSULTATIVE COMMITTEE, CENTRAL (1948), 1st Floor, Golden Cross House, Duncannon Street, W.C.2.—*Sec.*, L. A. Dumelow.

TROPICAL MEDICINE AND HYGIENE, ROYAL SOCIETY OF (1907), Manson House, 26 Portland Place, W.1.

TURNER SOCIETY, BCM Box Turner, W.C.1.— *Sec.*, Dr. S. Whittingham.

UFAW (Universities Federation for Animal Welfare) (1926), 8 Hamilton Close, South Mimms, Potters Bar, Herts.—*Sec.*, Lt. Col. T. J. Reynolds.

UNIT TRUST ASSOCIATION (1959), Park House, 16 Finsbury Circus, E.C.2.—*Sec.*, A. C. Smith.

UNITED NATIONS ASSOCIATION OF GREAT BRITAIN AND NORTHERN IRELAND (1945), 3 Whitehall Court, S.W.1.—*Dir.*, M. Harper.

UNITED REFORMED CHURCH HISTORY SOCIETY, 86 Tavistock Place, W.C.1.—*Hon. Sec.*, Rev. Dr. S. Orchard.

UNITED SOCIETY FOR CHRISTIAN LITERATURE, THE, Luke House, Farnham Road, Guildford, Surrey.— *Gen. Sec.*, Rev. A. Gilmore; *Gen. Manager*, M. E. Foxell.

UNITED SYNAGOGUE (1870).—*Pres.*, V. Lucas; *Sec.*, J. J. Julius, Woburn House, Upper Woburn Place, W.C.1.

UNIVERSITIES CENTRAL COUNCIL ON ADMISSIONS (1961), P.O. Box 28, Cheltenham, Glos.—*Gen. Sec.*, L. R. Kay.

UNIVERSITY WOMEN, BRITISH FEDERATION OF (1907), Crosby Hall, Cheyne Walk, S.W.3.—*Sec.*, Mrs. C. Ellis.

VALUERS AND AUCTIONEERS, INCORPORATED SOCIETY OF, 3 Cadogan Gate, S.W.1.—*Sec.*, M. Astbury.

VEGETARIAN SOCIETY OF THE UNITED KINGDOM LTD., Parkdale, Dunham Road, Altrincham, Cheshire.— *Gen. Sec.*, Sandra Allen.

VENEREAL DISEASES, MEDICAL SOCIETY FOR THE STUDY OF, St. Thomas's Hospital, S.E.1.—*Hon. Sec.*, Dr. M. A. Waugh, Dept. of Genito-Urinary Medicine, Leeds General Infirmary, Great George Street, Leeds.

VICE-CHANCELLORS AND PRINCIPALS OF THE UNIVERSITIES OF THE UNITED KINGDOM, COMMITTEE OF, 29 Tavistock Square, W.C.1.—*Chairman*, The Lord Flowers, F.R.S.; *Sec. Gen.*, B. H. Taylor.

VICTORIA CROSS AND GEORGE CROSS ASSOCIATION, THE, Room 04, Archway Block South, Old Admiralty Building, S.W.1.—*Chairman*, Rear-Adm. B. C. G. Place, V.C., C.B., D.S.C.

VICTORIA INSTITUTE (Philosophical Society of Great Britain).—*Pres.*, Sir Norman Anderson, O.B.E., Q.C., F.B.A.; *Asst. Sec.*, B. H. T. Weller, 29 Queen Street, E.C.4.

VICTORIA LEAGUE FOR COMMONWEALTH FRIENDSHIP (1901), 18 Northumberland Avenue, W.C.2.—*Sec.*, Mrs. S. Barnett, O.B.E.

VICTORIAN SOCIETY (1958), 1 Priory Gardens, Bedford Park, W.4.—*Sec.*, Mrs. J. Freeman.

VICTORY (SERVICES) ASSOCIATION LTD. AND CLUB, THE, 63–79 Seymour Street, W.2.—*Gen. Manager.*, D. G. Stovey.

VIKING SOCIETY FOR NORTHERN RESEARCH, University College, Gower Street, W.C.1.—*Hon. Secs.*, Mrs. U. Dronke; Prof. M. P. Barnes.

VITREOUS ENAMELLERS, INSTITUTE OF, Ripley, Derby.—*Sec.*, J. D. Gardom.

VOLUNTARY SERVICE OVERSEAS (1958), 9 Belgrave Square, S.W.1.—*Dir.*, F. Judd.

WATER ENGINEERS AND SCIENTISTS, INSTITUTION OF, 31–33 High Holborn, W.C.1.—*Pres.* (1984–85), H. Fish, C.B.E.; *Sec.*, J. P. Banbury, M.B.E.

WELDING INSTITUTE, THE, Abington Hall, Cambridge and 54 Princes Gate, S.W.7.—*Dir.-Gen.*, Dr. A. A. Wells, O.B.E., F.R.S.

WELFARE OFFICERS, INSTITUTE OF (1945), 25 Cross Street, Manchester.—*Hon. Gen. Sec.*, E. Rhodes, PH.D.

WELLCOME TRUST (1936), 1 Park Square West, N.W.1.—*Dir.*, P. O. Williams, M.B., F.R.C.P.

WELLS (H. G.) SOCIETY, Dept. of Language and Literature, Polytechnic of North London, Prince of Wales Road, N.W.5.

WELSH JOINT EDUCATION COMMITTEE (1948), 245 Western Avenue, Cardiff.—*Sec.*, G. L. Jones.

WESLEY HISTORICAL SOCIETY (1893).—*Gen. Sec.*, Mrs. E. D. Graham, 34 Spiceland Road, Birmingham.

WEST AFRICA COMMITTEE (1956), 315 Oxford Street, W.1.—*Secs.*, Group Capt. P. R. Magrath; J. A. R. Macdonald.

WEST INDIA COMMITTEE (1750), 48 Albemarle Street, W.1.—*Dir.*, D. A. Jessop.

WEST LONDON MISSION (1887), 19 Thayer Street, W.1.—*Supt.*, Rev. Dr. J. A. Newton.

WIDOWS, SOCIETY FOR THE RELIEF OF DISTRESSED (1823) (residing within seven miles of Charing Cross and applying within four months of widowhood), 175 Tower Bridge Road, S.E.1.—*Sec.*, W. N. Barr.

WILDLIFE ARTISTS, SOCIETY OF (1962), 17 Carlton House Terrace, S.W.1.—*Pres.*, K. Shackleton.

WILLIAM MORRIS SOCIETY AND KELMSCOTT FELLOWSHIP (1918).—*Hon. Sec.*, Dr. R. S. Smith, Kelmscott House, 26 Upper Mall, W.6.

WINE AND SPIRIT ASSOCIATION OF GREAT BRITAIN AND NORTHERN IRELAND (INC), Five Kings House, Kennet Wharf Lane, Upper Thames Street, E.C.4.—*Dir.*, R. H. Insoll, E.R.D.

WOMEN ARTISTS, SOCIETY OF (1855), 17 Carlton House Terrace, S.W.1.—*Pres.*, Mrs. G. Dawson.

WOMEN, NATIONAL ADVISORY CENTRE ON CAREERS FOR (formerly Women's Employment Federation) (1933), Drayton House, 30 Gordon Street, W.C.1.—*Dir.*, Miss K. M. Menon.

WOMEN PILOTS' ASSOCIATION, BRITISH (1955), 25 Foubert's Place, W.1.

WOMEN, SOCIETY FOR PROMOTING THE TRAINING OF (1859) (Women's Loan Training Fund), The Dean Cottages, Hedgerley, Bucks.—*Sec.*, Mrs. W. M. Golding.

WOMEN'S ENGINEERING SOCIETY (1920), 25 Foubert's Place, W.1.—*Sec.*, Mrs. A. Soteriou.

WOMEN'S HOLIDAY FUND (1895), 125 Wilton Road, S.W.1.—*Sec.*, Mrs. E. Hendrie.

WOMEN'S INSTITUTES, NATIONAL FEDERATION OF (1915), 39 Eccleston Street, S.W.1.—*Gen. Sec.*, Mrs. A. Ballard.

WOMEN'S INTERNATIONAL LEAGUE FOR PEACE AND FREEDOM (1915) British Section, 29 Great James Street, W.C.1.—*Hon. Sec.*, Bronwen Meredith.

WOMEN'S NATIONAL CANCER CONTROL CAMPAIGN, 1 South Audley Street, W.1.—*Chief Administrator*, Mrs. M. K. Cooper.

WOMEN'S PROTESTANT UNION (INC.), and THE SENTINELS' UNION, Sentinels Court, 130 South Coast Road, Peacehaven, Newhaven, Sussex.

WOMEN'S ROYAL NAVAL SERVICE BENEVOLENT TRUST, 1a Chesham Street, S.W.1

WOMEN'S ROYAL VOLUNTARY SERVICE (WRVS) (1938), 17 Old Park Lane, W.1.—*National Chairman*, Mrs. B. Shenfield.

WOMEN'S TRANSPORT SERVICE (FANY) (1907), Duke of York's H.Q., Chelsea, S.W.3.—*Corps Commander*, Mrs. S. Y. Parkinson, O.B.E.

WOOD PRESERVING ASSOCIATION, BRITISH, Premier House, 150 Southampton Row, W.C.1.—*Dir.*, J. Bick.

WORCESTERSHIRE ASSOCIATION (1926).—*Hon. Sec.*, D. M. Alexander, 8 Sansome Walk, Worcester.

WORKERS' EDUCATIONAL ASSOCIATION, Temple House, 9 Upper Berkeley Street, W.1.—*Gen. Sec.*, R. J. Jefferies.

WORKS AND HIGHWAYS TECHNICIAN ENGINEERS, INSTITUTION OF, Suite 21, 4th Floor, 125 High Holborn, W.C.1.—*Gen. Sec. and Registrar*, S. H. Crowle.

WORLD CONGRESS OF FAITHS (1936), 28 Powis Gardens, W.11.—*Pres.*, Very Rev. E. F. Carpenter.

WORLD EDUCATION FELLOWSHIP (1921), *International Headquarters*, 33 Kinnaird Avenue, W.4.—*Gen. Sec.*, Mrs. R. Crommelin.

WORLD ENERGY CONFERENCE (1924), *Central Office*, 34 St. James's Street, S.W.1.—*Sec.-Gen.*, *International Executive Council*, E. Ruttley.

WORLD MISSION, COUNCIL FOR (1977), Livingstone House, 11 Carteret Street, S.W.1.—Formerly the Congregational Council for World Mission, the London Missionary Society, the Commonwealth Missionary Society and the Presbyterian Church of England Overseas Mission.—*Gen. Sec.*, B. D. Scopes (*acting*).

WORLD SHIP SOCIETY (1946).—*Sec.*, S. J. F. Miller, 35 Wickham Way, Haywards Heath, W. Sussex.

WORLD SOCIETY FOR THE PROTECTION OF ANIMALS, *Headquarters*, 106 Jermyn Street, S.W.1.—*Dir. Gen.*, T. H. Scott.

WORLD WILDLIFE FUND—U.K. (1961), 11–13 Ockford Road, Godalming, Surrey.—*Dir.*, G. J. Medley.

WRITERS TO H.M. SIGNET, SOCIETY OF, Parliament Square, Edinburgh.—*Deputy Keeper of the Signet*, P. C. Millar, O.B.E.; *Sub-Keeper and Clerk*, A. M. Kerr.

YEOMANRY BENEVOLENT FUND, 206 Brompton Road, S.W.3.—*Sec.*, Mrs. C. W. Chrystie.

YORKSHIRE AGRICULTURAL SOCIETY (1837), Great Yorks Showground, Hookstone Oval, Harrogate.—*Sec.-Gen.*, Lt.-Col. M. G. A. Young.

YORKSHIRE SOCIETY, THE (1812), 18 Broom Lock, Teddington, Middx.—*Sec.*, G. G. Prince, T.D.

YOUNG MEN'S CHRISTIAN ASSOCIATION, *National Council*, 640 Forest Road, E.17.—*Nat. Sec.*, C. J. Naylor.

YOUNG WOMEN'S CHRISTIAN ASSOCIATION (1855), *National Headquarters*, 2 Weymouth Street, W.1.—*Gen. Sec.*, Miss F. E. Sharples.

YOUTH CLUBS, NATIONAL ASSOCIATION OF, 30 Peacock Lane, Leicester.—*Chief Exec.*, J. M. Butterfield.

YOUTH CLUBS, NORTHERN IRELAND ASSOCIATION OF, Hampton, Glenmachan Park, Belfast.—*Dir.*, G. Johnston.

YOUTH HOSTELS ASSOCIATION (ENGLAND AND WALES) (1930), *National Office*, Trevelyan House, 8 St. Stephens Hill, St. Albans, Herts.—*Sec.*, H. B. Livingstone.

YOUTH HOSTELS ASSOCIATION (SCOTTISH) (1931), *National Office*, 7 Glebe Crescent, Stirling.—*Gen. Sec.*, J. Martin.

YOUTH HOSTELS ASSOCIATION OF NORTHERN IRELAND LTD. (1931), Bradbury Buildings, 56 Bradbury Place, Belfast.—*Hon. Sec.*, E. R. Henderson.

ZOOLOGICAL SOCIETY OF LONDON, Regent's Park, N.W.1.—*Pres.*, Sir William Henderson, D.SC., F.R.S.E., F.R.S. Attendances (1983), Regent's Park, 1,239,000, and Whipsnade Park, 375,852.

ZOOLOGICAL SOCIETY OF SCOTLAND, ROYAL, Scottish National Zoological Park, Murrayfield, Edinburgh 12.—*Dir.*, R. J. Wheater.

THE CIVIC TRUST

17 Carlton House Terrace, S.W.1.
[01–930 0914]

Founded in 1957, the Trust is a recognized charity supported by voluntary contributions. It encourages the protection and improvement of the environment. It makes Awards for good development of all kinds. Among some particular concerns have been the initiation of co-operative street improvement schemes; the promotion of new techniques for transplanting semi-mature trees; industrial dereliction and urban wasteland; the problems of damage and disruption caused by heavy lorries. The Trust encourages the formation of local amenity societies and gives advice and support to nearly 1,000 such societies now on its register. It was closely associated with the drafting of the Civic Amenities Act 1967, which created the concept of the Conservation Area, and of the Town and Country Amenities Act 1974. It administers the Architectural Heritage Fund, which provides loan capital to local buildings preservation trusts; and on behalf of the Department of the Environment, the work of the Heritage Education Group. Associate Trusts are linked with it in the North West, the North East, Scotland and Wales. From 1973 to 1981 it administered government grant-aid to conservation projects in non-outstanding conservation areas on behalf of the Historic Buildings Council.

LOCAL HISTORY AND ARCHÆOLOGICAL SOCIETIES

England and Wales

Anglesey.—ANGLESEY ANTIQUARIAN SOCIETY. *Hon. Sec.*, S. C. G. Caffell, 7 Hendurnpike, Tregarth, Bangor, Gwynedd.

Bedfordshire.—SOUTH BEDFORDSHIRE ARCHÆOLOGICAL SOCIETY. *Hon. Sec.* D. H. Kennett, 27 Lords Lane, Bradwell, Great Yarmouth, Norfolk.

Berkshire.—BERKSHIRE ARCHÆOLOGICAL SOCIETY. *Hon. Sec.*, L. J. Over, 43 Laburnham Road, Maidenhead, Berks.

NEWBURY DISTRICT FIELD CLUB. *Hon. Sec.*, Mrs. D. E. Hawkes, 22 Westgate Road, Newbury.

Buckinghamshire.—BUCKS ARCHÆOLOGICAL SOCIETY. *Hon. Sec.*, Dr. R. P. Hagerty, County Museum, Church Street, Aylesbury, Bucks.

Cambridgeshire.—CAMBRIDGE ANTIQUARIAN SOCIETY. *Sec.*, Dr. E. Leedham-Green, University Library, West Road, Cambridge.

Cheshire.—CHESTER ARCHÆOLOGICAL SOCIETY. *Hon. Sec.*, B. E. Harris, PH.D., 2nd Floor, 24 Nicholas Street, Chester. *See also* under *Lancashire.*

Cornwall.—ROYAL INSTITUTION OF CORNWALL, County Museum and Art Gallery, Truro. *Hon. Sec.*, A. J. Lyne.

Cumberland and Westmorland.—CUMBERLAND AND WESTMORLAND ANTIQUARIAN AND ARCHÆOLOGICAL SOCIETY. *Hon. Sec.*, R. Hall, 2 High Tenterfell, Kendal, Cumbria.

Derbyshire.—DERBYSHIRE ARCHÆOLOGICAL SOCIETY, c/o Trent Valley Archæological Committee, University of Nottingham, Nottingham. *Hon. Sec.*, C. J. Drage.

Devonshire.—DEVON ARCHÆOLOGICAL SOCIETY. *Hon. Sec.*, N. Shiel, 4 St. Leonards Road, Exeter, F.S.A.

Dorset.—DORSET NATURAL HISTORY AND ARCHÆOLOGICAL SOCIETY, Dorset County Museum, Dorchester. *Curator and Sec.*, R. N. R. Peers.

Durham.—DURHAM AND NORTHUMBERLAND ARCHITECTURAL AND ARCHÆOLOGICAL SOCIETY. *Hon. Sec.*, c/o The University, Dept. of Archæology, 46 Saddler Street, Durham.

Dyfed.—CEREDIGION ANTIQUARIAN SOCIETY. *Hon. Sec.*, D. M. Jones, 24 Alban Square, Aberaeron, Dyfed.

Essex.—ESSEX ARCHÆOLOGICAL SOCIETY, Hollytrees Museum, High Street, Colchester. *Sec.*, Mrs. E. Sellars.

Gloucestershire.—BRISTOL AND GLOUCESTERSHIRE ARCHÆOLOGICAL SOCIETY, 9 Pembroke Road, Bristol 8. *Hon. Sec.*, Miss E. Ralph, F.S.A.

Hampshire.—HAMPSHIRE FIELD CLUB AND ARCHÆOLOGICAL SOCIETY. *Hon. Sec.*, Dr. M. A. Hicks, King Alfred's College, Winchester, Hants.

Herefordshire.—WOOLHOPE NATURALISTS' FIELD CLUB. *Hon. Sec.*, c/o The Hereford Library, Broad Street, Hereford.

Hertfordshire.—EAST HERTFORDSHIRE ARCHÆOLOGICAL SOCIETY. *Hon. Sec.*, C. L. Lee, 107 Queens Road, Hertford.

ST. ALBANS AND HERTFORDSHIRE ARCHITECTURAL AND ARCHÆOLOGICAL SOCIETY. *Hon. Sec.*, F. I. Kilvington, 122 Marshalswick Lane, St. Albans.

Kent.—KENT ARCHÆOLOGICAL SOCIETY. *Gen. Sec.*, A. C. Harrison, F.S.A., c/o The Museum, Maidstone.

Lancashire. HISTORIC SOCIETY OF LANCASHIRE AND CHESHIRE. *Hon. Sec.*, Miss J. E. Hollinshead, Liverpool Institute of H.E., Stand Park Road, Liverpool.

Leicestershire.—LEICESTERSHIRE ARCHÆOLOGICAL AND HISTORICAL SOCIETY, The Guildhall, Guildhall Lane, Leicester. *Hon. Sec.*, A. D. McWhirr, F.S.A.

London and Middlesex.—CITY OF LONDON ARCHÆOLOGICAL SOCIETY. *Hon. Sec.*, D. R. Lewis, 28 Rothesay Avenue, S.W.20.

LONDON AND MIDDLESEX ARCHÆOLOGICAL SOCIETY, Museum of London, London Wall, E.C.2. *Hon. Sec.*, J. Clark, F.S.A.

Norfolk.—NORFOLK AND NORWICH ARCHÆOLOGICAL SOCIETY. *Hon. Gen. Sec.*, I. Cresswell, F.S.A., The Old Rectory, Shelton, Norwich.

Northumberland and Tyne and Wear.—SOCIETY OF ANTIQUARIES OF NEWCASTLE UPON TYNE. *Sec.*, Dr. C. M. Fraser, c/o Department of Adult Education, University of Newcastle upon Tyne.

SUNDERLAND ANTIQUARIAN SOCIETY. *Hon. Sec.*, G. Patterson, 8 Humbledon View, Sunderland.

Nottinghamshire.—THOROTON SOCIETY OF NOTTINGHAMSHIRE, Bromley House, Angel Row, Nottingham. *Hon. Sec.*, J. S. Childs, F.R.S.A.

Oxfordshire. OXFORDSHIRE ARCHITECTURAL AND HISTORICAL SOCIETY. *Hon. Sec.*, Mrs. L. Armstrong, c/o Ashmolean Museum, Oxford.

Powys: Montgomery District; POWYSLAND CLUB. *Hon. Sec.*, W. G. J. Hughes, The Library, Brook Street, Welshpool, Powys.

Radnor District; RADNORSHIRE SOCIETY. *Hon. Sec.*, J. A. Stratton, 'Chaddesley,' Broadway, Llandrindod Wells, Powys.

Shropshire.—SHROPSHIRE ARCHÆOLOGICAL SOCIETY. *Hon. Sec.,* Yvette Staelens, c/o Much Wenlock Museum, High Street, Much Wenlock.

Somerset.—SOMERSET ARCHÆOLOGICAL AND NATURAL HISTORY SOCIETY, Taunton Castle, Taunton. *Hon. Sec.,* J. V. Carrington.

Staffordshire.—NORTH STAFFORDSHIRE FIELD CLUB. *Hon. Sec.,* R. A. Tribbeck, Dept. of Chemistry and Biology, North Staffordshire Polytechnic, College Road, Stoke-on-Trent.

CITY OF STOKE-ON-TRENT MUSEUM ARCHÆOLOGICAL SOCIETY, City Museum, Stoke-on-Trent. *Chairman,* C. F. Hawke-Smith.

SOUTH STAFFORDSHIRE ARCHÆOLOGICAL AND HISTORICAL SOCIETY. *Hon. Sec.,* Dr. J. G. L. Cole

Suffolk.—SUFFOLK INSTITUTE OF ARCHÆOLOGY AND HISTORY. *Hon. Sec.,* E. A. Martin, Oak Tree Farm, Finborough Road, Hitcham, Ipswich.

Surrey.—SURREY ARCHÆOLOGICAL SOCIETY, Castle Arch, Guildford. *Hon. Secs.,* J. L. and M. Gower.

Sussex.—SUSSEX ARCHÆOLOGICAL SOCIETY, Barbican House, High Street, Lewes. *Gen. Administrator,* J. Houghton.

Warwickshire.—BIRMINGHAM AND WARWICKSHIRE ARCHÆOLOGICAL SOCIETY, c/o Birmingham and Midland Institute, Margaret Street, Birmingham 3. *Hon. Sec.,* M. A. Hodder.

Wight.—ISLE OF WIGHT NATURAL HISTORY AND ARCHÆOLOGICAL SOCIETY, 66 Carisbrooke Road, Newport. *Hon. Sec.,* Mrs. T. Goodley, Ivy Cottage, New Barn Lane, Shorwell.

Wiltshire.—WILTSHIRE ARCHÆOLOGICAL AND NATURAL HISTORY SOCIETY, The Museum, 41 Long Street, Devizes. *Sec.,* M. Heath.

Worcestershire.—WORCESTERSHIRE ARCHÆOLOGICAL SOCIETY. *Hon. Sec.,* R. F. Panton, Birchdale, 4 Orchard Road, Gt. Malvern.

Yorkshire.—HUNTER ARCHÆOLOGICAL SOCIETY. *Hon. Sec.,* S. R. Penny, 37 Chesterwood Drive, Sheffield 10.

YORKSHIRE ARCHÆOLOGICAL SOCIETY. *Hon. Sec.,* P. B. Davidson, Claremont, 23 Clarendon Road, Leeds.

HALIFAX ANTIQUARIAN SOCIETY. *Hon. Sec.,* E. Webster, 28 Westborough Drive, Highroad Well, Halifax.

THORESBY SOCIETY, Claremont, 23 Clarendon Road, Leeds 2. *Hon. Sec.,* D. M. Watson.

Channel Islands

SOCIETE JERSIAISE, The Jersey Museum, Pier Road, St. Helier. *Hon. Sec.,* Rev. Canon L. Hibbs.

Scotland

AYRSHIRE ARCHÆOLOGICAL AND NATURAL HISTORY SOCIETY. *Hon. Sec.,* G. E. Sleight, 1 Portmark Avenue, Ayr.

DUMFRIESSHIRE AND GALLOWAY NATURAL HISTORY AND ANTIQUARIAN SOCIETY. *Hon. Sec.,* R. H. McEwen, Seaforth, 13 Douglas Terrace, Lockerbie, Dumfries.

GLASGOW ARCHÆOLOGICAL SOCIETY. *Hon. Secs.,* L. Keppie, Hunterian Museum, University of Glasgow; A. Gordon, Glasgow Art Gallery, Kelvingrove, Glasgow.

HAWICK ARCHÆOLOGICAL SOCIETY. *Hon. Sec.,* I. A. Landles, Orrock House, Stirches Road, Hawick, Borders.

INVERNESS FIELD CLUB, c/o Innes and MacKay, 19 Union Street, Inverness. *Hon. Sec.,* Mrs. E. H. L. MacAskill, 9 Dores Road, Inverness.

CAR PRODUCTION IN MAIN PRODUCING COUNTRIES (thousands)

	1974	1975	1976	1977	1978	1979	1980	1981	1982	1983
United Kingdom	1,534	1,268	1,333	1,328	1,223	1,070	924	955	888	1,645
France	2,699	2,546	2,980	3,092	3,111	3,220	2,939	2,612	2,777	2,961
W. Germany	2,840	2,908	3,547	3,790	3,890	3,933	3,521	3,578	3,761	3,878
Italy	1,631	1,349	1,471	1,440	1,509	1,481	1,445	1,257	1,297	1,396
Sweden	327	316	317	235	254	297	235	258	295	345
Japan	3,932	4,568	5,028	5,431	5,748	6,176	7,038	6,974	6,887	7,152
U.S.A. (Factory Sales)	7,325	6,717	8,498	9,214	9,176	8,434	6,376	6,253	5,073	6,781
Canada.............	1,165	1,045	1,137	1,162	1,143	988	847	863	808	969
Total...............	21,453	20,717	24,311	25,692	26,054	25,599	23,325	22,750	21,786	24,527
UK % of total	7	6	5	5	5	4	4	4	4	4

BRITISH MOTOR VEHICLE PRODUCTION AND EXPORTS

Year	Weeks	Passenger Cars (including taxis)			Commercial Road Vehicles		
		For Export*	Total	Weekly average	For Export*	Total	Weekly average
1977.......	...52...	573,552	1,327,820	25,535	186,048	386,420	7,431
1978.......	...52...	494,579	1,222,949	23,518	168,968	384,518	7,395
1979.......	...52...	392,637	1,070,452	20,586	162,570	408.060	7,847
1980.......	...52...	349,592	923,744	17,764	156,270	389,170	7,484
1981.......	...52...	304,678	954,650	18,359	113,862	229,555	4,416
1982.......	...52...	225,865	887,679	17,070	92,510	268,798	5,169
1983.......	...53...	237,376	1,044,597	19,709	62,801	244,514	4,613

*Export Allocation

CONFEDERATION OF BRITISH INDUSTRY
Centre Point, 103 New Oxford Street, London, W.C.1.
[01–379 7400]

The Confederation of British Industry was founded in August 1965 and is an independent non-party political body financed entirely by industry and commerce. It exists primarily to ensure that the Government understands the intentions, needs and problems of British business. It is the recognized spokesman for the business viewpoint and is consulted as such by the Government.

The C.B.I. represents, directly and indirectly, some 250,000 companies. All the nationalized industries are in membership and thereby able to work with the C.B.I. on problems that are the concern of all management.

The governing body of the C.B.I. is the 400-strong Council, which meets monthly in London under the chairmanship of the President. It is assisted by some 24 expert standing committees which advise on the main aspects of policy. There are 13 Regional Councils and offices covering the administrative regions of England, Scotland, Wales and Northern Ireland.

President, Sir James Cleminson.
Director-General, Sir Terence Beckett.
Secretary, D. E. Jackson.

NATIONAL ASSOCIATION OF INDUSTRIES FOR THE BLIND AND DISABLED INC.
Triton House, 43A High Street South,
Dunstable, Beds. LU6 3RZ
[0582–606796]

The National Association of Industries for the Blind and Disabled Inc. was established in 1929 and incorporated in 1936; it is registered as a charity.

The Association acts in the nature of a trade association providing facilities for consultation and co-operation between its 40 members who operate workshops employing blind and disabled people and it represents their interests in discussions with, and

representations to, other organisations (e.g. government departments and local authorities) concerned with sheltered employment. It does not own or operate any of the workshops, which are run by local authorities or voluntary organisations acting as their agents.
Chairman (1983–84), G. W. Mann.
Hon. Secretary, G. W. Guy.

EMPLOYERS' AND TRADE BODIES

ADVERTISING ASSOCIATION, Abford House, 15 Wilton Road, SW1V 1NJ.—*Dir. Gen.*, R. Underhill, O.B.E.

AGRICULTURAL EXPORT COUNCIL, BRITISH, 35 Belgrave Square, SW1X 8QN.—*Chief Exec.*, J. Thorneloe.

BAKERS, FEDERATION OF, 20 Bedford Square, WC1B 3HF.—*Dir.*, A. Casdagli, C.B.E.

BANKERS' ASSOCIATION, BRITISH, 10 Lombard Street, EC3V 9EL.—*Sec.-Gen.*, J. B. Atherton.

BREWERS' SOCIETY, 42 Portman Square, W1H 0BB.—*Dir. and Chief Exec.*, Maj. Gen. W. D. Mangham, C.B.

BUILDING EMPLOYERS CONFEDERATION, 82 New Cavendish Street, W1M 8AD.—*Dir. Gen.*, J. A. Newby.

BUILDING MATERIAL PRODUCERS, NATIONAL COUNCIL OF, 33 Alfred Place, WC1E 7EN.—*Dir. Gen.*, N. M. Chaldecott.

BUS AND COACH COUNCIL, Sardinia House, 52 Lincoln's Inn Fields, WC2A 3LZ.—*Dir. Gen.*, D. R. Quin.

CHEMICAL INDUSTRIES ASSOCIATION LTD., Alembic House, 93 Albert Embankment, SE1 7TU.—*Dir. Gen.*, M. E. Trowbridge.

CLOTHING INDUSTRY ASSOCIATION LTD., BRITISH, Wellington House, 6/9 Upper St. Martin's Lane, WC2H 9DL.—*Dir.* J. R. Wilson.

DAIRY TRADE FEDERATION, 19 Cornwall Terrace, NW1 4QP.—*Dir. Gen.*, M. Evans.

ENGINEERING EMPLOYERS' FEDERATION, Broadway House, Tothill Street, SW1H 9NQ.—*Dir. Gen.*, Dr. J. McFarlane.

FARMERS' UNION OF ENGLAND AND WALES, THE NATIONAL, Agriculture House, 25–31 Knightsbridge, SW1X 7NJ.—*Dir. Gen.*, R. W. Watson, C.B.E.

FARMERS' UNION OF SCOTLAND, NATIONAL, 17 Grosvenor Crescent, Edinburgh EH12 5EN.—*Dir.*, D. S. Johnston.

FARMERS' UNION, ULSTER, Dunedin, 475–477 Antrim Road, Belfast BT15 3DA.

FOOD AND DRINK FEDERATION, 6 Catherine Street, WC2B 5JJ.—*Dir. Gen.*, Maj.-Gen. Sir Jeremy Moore, K.C.B., O.B.E., M.C.

FREIGHT TRANSPORT ASSOCIATION LTD., Hermes House, 157 St. John's Road, Tunbridge Wells, Kent TN4 9UZ.—*Dir. Gen.*, G. Turvey.

INSURANCE ASSOCIATION, BRITISH, Aldermary House, Queen Street, EC4N 1TU.—*Sec. Gen.*, R. C. W. Bardell, O.B.E.

KNITTING INDUSTRIES' FEDERATION LTD., 7 Gregory Boulevard, Nottingham NG7 6NB.—*Dir.*, J. P. Harrison.

LEATHER CONFEDERATION, BRITISH, Leather Trade House, Kings Park Road, Moulton Park, Northampton NN3 1JD.—*Dir.*, Dr. R. L. Sykes.

LEATHER PRODUCERS' ASSOCIATION, Leather Trade House, Kings Park Road, Moulton Park, Northampton NN3 1JD.—*Nat. Sec.*, J. Purvis.

MAN-MADE FIBRE FEDERATION, BRITISH, 24 Buckingham Gate, SW1E 6LB.—*Dir.*, D. Anderson.

MOTOR MANUFACTURERS AND TRADERS LTD., SOCIETY OF, Forbes House, Halkin Street, S.W.1.—*Dir.*, A. W. Fraser.

NEWSPAPER PUBLISHERS ASSOCIATION LTD., 6 Bouverie Street, EC4Y 8AY.—*Dir.*, J. E. Lepage.

PAPER AND BOARD INDUSTRY FEDERATION, BRITISH, 3 Plough Place, Fetter Lane, EC4A 1AL.—*Dir. Gen.*, W. J. Bartlett.

PLASTICS FEDERATION, BRITISH, 5 Belgrave Square, SW1X 8PH.—*Dir.*, R. Lewis, O.B.E.

PORT EMPLOYERS, NATIONAL ASSOCIATION OF, Commonwealth House, 1–19 New Oxford Street, WC1A 1DZ.—*Dir.*, N. H. Finney.

PORTS ASSOCIATION, BRITISH, Commonwealth House, 1–19 New Oxford Street, WC1A 1DZ.—*Dir.* N. H. Finney.

PRINTING INDUSTRIES FEDERATION, BRITISH, 11 Bedford Row, WC1R 4DX.—*Dir. Gen.*, S. Bradley.

PUBLISHERS' ASSOCIATION, 19 Bedford Square, WC1B 3HJ.—*Chief Exec.*, C. Bradley.

RADIO CONTRACTORS LTD., ASSOCIATION OF INDEPENDENT, Regina House, 259–269 Marylebone Road, NW1 5RA.—*Dir.*, B. West.

RETAIL CONSORTIUM, THE, Commonwealth House, 1–19 New Oxford Street, WC1A 1PA.—*Chairman*, P. Firmston.

ROAD FEDERATION LTD., BRITISH, Cowdray House, 6 Portugal Street, WC2A 2HG.—*Dir.*, J. D. W. Gent.

ROAD HAULAGE ASSOCIATION LTD., Roadway House, 104 New Kings Road, SW6 4LN.—*Dir. Gen.*, F. J. Plaskett.

RUBBER MANUFACTURERS' ASSOCIATION LTD., BRITISH, 90 Tottenham Court Road, W1P 0BR.—*Chief Exec.*, G. C. Gullan.

SHIP AND BOAT BUILDERS NATIONAL FEDERATION, Boating Industry House, Weybridge, Surrey KT13 9NS.—*Dir. Gen.*, T. A. Webb.

SHIPPING, GENERAL COUNCIL OF BRITISH, 30–32 St. Mary Axe, EC3A 8ET.—*Dir. Gen.*, W. P. Shovelton, C.B., C.M.G.

SPORT AND ALLIED INDUSTRIES FEDERATION LTD., BRITISH, Prudential House (10th Floor, East Wing), Wellesley Road, Croydon, Surrey CR0 9XY.—*Chief Exec.*, E. Bainbridge.

STATIONERY AND OFFICE PRODUCTS FEDERATION, BRITISH, 6 Wimpole Street, W1M 8AS.—*Dir.*, D. F. Hall.

TELEVISION COMPANIES ASSOCIATION LTD., INDEPENDENT, 56 Mortimer Street, W1N 8AN.—*Gen Sec.*, D. Shaw.

TEXTILE CONFEDERATION, BRITISH, 24 Buckingham Gate, SW1E 6LB.—*Dir.*, I. MacArthur.

TIMBER GROWERS' UNITED KINGDOM, Agriculture House, Knightsbridge, SW1X 7NJ.—*Chief Exec.*, A. R. Williams.

TIMBER MERCHANTS' ASSOCIATION, BRITISH, Blackburn House, 1 Warwick Street, Leamington Spa, Warks. CV32 5LW.—*Exec. Sec.*, R. Whitaker.

TIMBER TRADE FEDERATION OF THE U.K., Clareville House, Whitcomb Street, WC2H 7DL.—*Chief Exec.*, L. A. Woodburn-Bamberger.

U.K. OFFSHORE OPERATORS ASSOCIATION LTD., 192 Sloane Street, SW1X 9QX.—*Dir.*, G. C. Band.

U.K. PETROLEUM INDUSTRY ASSOCIATION LTD., 9 Kingsway, WC2B 6XH.—*Dir. Gen.*, Dr. I. D. G. Berwick.

ROMAN EMPERORS

[The *First Triumvirate* (Julius Cæsar, Pompey and Crassus) 60–53 B.C.]

The Twelve Cæsars

I. Caius JULIUS CÆSAR, *born* A.U.C. 651 (102 B.C.); *Dictator* A.U.C. 705 (48 B.C.); *Assassinated* A.U.C. 709 (44 B.C.).

[The *Second Triumvirate* (Octavian, Antony and Lepidus) 44–31 B.C.]

II. Caius Julius Cæsar Octavianus AUGUSTUS, *born* 63 B.C.; *Emperor* 27 B.C.; *Died* A.D. 14.
III. Claudius Nero Cæsar TIBERIUS, *born* 24 B.C.; *Emperor* A.D. 14; *Died* A.D. 37.
IV. Caius Cæsar CALIGULA, *born* A.D. 12; *Emperor* A.D. 37; *Assassinated* A.D. 41.
V. Tiberius Drusus CLAUDIUS, *born* 10 B.C.; *Emperor* A.D. 41; *Assassinated* A.D. 54.
VI. Claudius NERO, *born* A.D. 37; *Emperor* A.D. 54; *Suicide* A.D. 68.
VII. Servius Sulpicius GALBA, *born* 3 B.C.; *Emperor* A.D. 68; *Assassinated* A.D. 69.
VIII. Marcus Salvius OTHO, *born* A.D. 32; *Emperor* A.D. 69; *Suicide* A.D. 69.
IX. AULUS VITELLIUS, *born* A.D. 15; *Emperor* A.D. 69; *Assassinated* A.D. 69.
X. Titus Flavius VESPASIAN, *born* A.D. 9; *Emperor* A.D. 69; *Died* A.D.79.
XI. Flavius Sabinus Vespasianus TITUS, *born* A.D. 48; *Emperor* A.D. 79; *Died* A.D. 81.
XII. Titus Flavius DOMITIAN, *born* A.D. 52; *Emperor* A.D. 81; *Assassinated* A.D. 96.

A TABLE OF THE NUMBER OF DAYS FROM ANY DAY IN ONE MONTH TO THE SAME IN ANY OTHER MONTH IN ORDINARY YEARS

	Jan.	Feb.	Mar.	April	May	June	July	Aug.	Sept.	Oct.	Nov.	Dec.
January.......	365	31	59	90	120	151	181	212	243	273	304	334
February......	334	365	28	59	89	120	150	181	212	242	273	303
March	306	337	365	31	61	92	122	153	184	214	245	275
April..........	275	306	334	365	30	61	91	122	153	183	214	244
May	245	276	304	335	365	31	61	92	123	153	184	214
June	214	245	273	304	334	365	30	61	92	122	153	183
July	184	215	243	274	304	335	365	31	62	92	123	153
August........	153	184	212	243	273	304	334	365	31	61	92	122
September	122	153	181	212	242	273	303	334	365	30	61	91
October	92	123	151	182	212	243	273	304	335	365	31	61
November	61	92	120	151	181	212	242	273	304	334	365	30
December	31	62	90	121	151	182	212	243	274	304	335	365

TRADES UNION CONGRESS (T.U.C.)
Congress House, 23–28 Great Russell Street, WC1B 3LS
[01–636–4030]

The Trades Union Congress, founded in 1868, is a voluntary association of Trade Unions, the representatives of which meet annually to consider matters of common concern to their members. The Congress has met annually since 1871 and in recent years has met normally on the first Monday in September, its sessions extending through the succeeding four days. Congress is constituted by delegates of the affiliated unions on the basis of one delegate for every 5,000 members, or fraction thereof, on whose behalf affiliated fees are paid. Affiliated unions (in 1984–85) totalled 98 with an aggregate membership of 10,082,144.

The main business of the annual Congress is to consider the report of its General Council dealing with the activities of the Congress year, along with motions from affiliated societies on questions of policy and organization.

The Standing Committees of the General Council are serviced by a full time staff appointed by the General Secretary, who is himself elected by Congress and who remains in office until the age of 65, subject to decision of Congress or the General Council.

Through the General Council and its committees the trade union movement maintains systematic relations with the Government and Government Departments, with the Confederation of British Industry and with a large number of other bodies. It is represented on the National Economic Development Council, the Manpower Services Commission, the Health and Safety Commission, the Council of the Advisory Conciliation and Arbitration Service and a number of other bodies.

Among powers vested in the General Council by consent of the unions in Congress is the responsibility of intervening in disputes and differences between affiliated organizations; if possible this is done through informal conciliation meetings under T.U.C. auspices but where necessary a Disputes Committee is formed consisting of one member of the General Council and two senior officials of unions not involved in the dispute. This investigates the matter concerned and issues its findings.

Unions retain full control of their own affairs and the only sanctions which Congress can apply are suspension or exclusion from membership.

Chairman (1984–85), J. F. Eccles, c.b.e. (*General, Municipal, Boilermakers and Allied Trades Union*).
General Secretary, N. D. Willis.

SCOTTISH TRADES UNION CONGRESS
16 Woodlands Terrace, Glasgow G3 6DF
[041-332 4946]

The Congress was formed in 1897 and acts as a national centre for the trade union movement in Scotland. In 1983 it consisted of 76 unions with a membership of 1,010,577 and 47 directly affiliated Trades Councils. The majority of the unions organize throughout Britain and affiliate on their membership in Scotland.

The Annual Congress in April elects a 26-member General Council on the basis of 13 industrial sections. Congress has been prominent in pressing for economic expansion and full employment in Scotland and the development of the social services, most of which are separately organized in Scotland.

Chairman (1984–85), T. Dougan.
General Secretary, J. Milne.

TRADE UNIONS AFFILIATED TO T.U.C.

A list of the Trade Unions affiliated to the Trades Union Congress in September, 1984. The number of members of each Union is shown in parenthesis.

AMALGAMATED ASSOCIATION OF BEAMERS, TWISTERS AND DRAWERS, THE (550), 27 Every Street, Nelson, Lancs. BB9 7NE—*Gen. Sec.*, R. A. Little.

AMALGAMATED SOCIETY OF TEXTILE WORKERS AND KINDRED TRADES (3,692), Foxlowe, Market Place, Leek, Staffs. ST13 6AD—*Gen. Sec.*, A. Hitchmough.

AMALGAMATED SOCIETY OF WIRE DRAWERS AND KINDRED WORKERS, THE (5,148), Prospect House, Alma Street, Sheffield S3 8SA—*Gen. Sec.*, A. M. Ardron.

AMALGAMATED TEXTILE WORKERS' UNION (15,273), 5 Caton Street, Rochdale, Lancs. OL16 1QJ—*Gen. Sec.*, J. Brown.

AMALGAMATED UNION OF ASPHALT WORKERS, THE (2,266), Jenkin House, 173a Queens Road, Peckham, SE15 2NF—*Gen. Sec.*, H. M. Wareham.

AMALGAMATED UNION OF ENGINEERING WORKERS (A.U.E.W.) (943,538), 110 Peckham Road, SE15 5EL—*Gen. Sec.*, G. H. Laird.

CONSTRUCTIONAL SECTION (20,262), Construction House, 190 Cedars Road, Clapham, SW4 0PP—*Gen. Sec.*, J. Baldwin, o.b.e.

FOUNDRY SECTION (41,287), 164 Chorlton Road, Brook's Bar, Manchester M16 7NU—*Gen. Sec.*, R. Garland, o.b.e.

TECHNICAL, ADMINISTRATIVE AND SUPERVISORY SECTION (TASS) (215,052), Onslow Hall, Little Green, Richmond, Surrey TW9 1QN—*Gen. Sec.*, K. Gill.

ASSOCIATED METALWORKERS' UNION, THE (2,010), 92 Deansgate, Manchester M3 2QG—*Gen. Sec.*, R. Marron.

ASSOCIATED SOCIETY OF LOCOMOTIVE ENGINEERS AND FIREMEN (A.S.L.E.F.) (23,589), 9 Arkwright Road, Hampstead, NW3 6AB—*Sec.*, R. W. Buckton.

ASSOCIATION OF CINEMATOGRAPH, TELEVISION AND ALLIED TECHNICIANS (22,560), 2 Soho Square, W1V 6DD—*Gen. Sec.*, A. Sapper.

ASSOCIATION OF FIRST DIVISION CIVIL SERVANTS (7,503), 17 Northumberland Avenue, WC2N 5AP—*Gen. Sec.*, C. J. Ward.

ASSOCIATION OF PATTERNMAKERS AND ALLIED CRAFTSMEN, THE (7,556), 15 Cleve Road, West Hampstead, NW6 1YA—*Gen. Sec.*, G. Eastwood.

ASSOCIATION OF PROFESSIONAL, EXECUTIVE, CLERICAL AND COMPUTER STAFF (APEX) (100,177), 22 Worple Road, SW19 4DF—*Gen. Sec.*, R. Grantham.

ASSOCIATION OF SCIENTIFIC, TECHNICAL AND MANAGERIAL STAFFS (A.S.T.M.S.) (390,000), 79 Camden Road, NW1 9ES—*Gen. Sec.*, C. Jenkins.

ASSOCIATION OF UNIVERSITY TEACHERS (32,526), United House, 1 Pembridge Road, W11 3HJ—*Gen. Sec.*, Diana Warwick.

BAKERS', FOOD AND ALLIED WORKERS' UNION (37,487), Stanborough House, Great North Road, Welwyn Garden City, Herts. AL8 7TA—*Gen. Sec.*, J. Marino.

BANKING, INSURANCE AND FINANCE UNION, THE (156,476), 17 Hillside, Wimbledon, SW19 4NL—*Gen. Sec.*, L. Mills.

BRITISH ACTORS' EQUITY ASSOCIATION (32,416), 8 Harley Street, W1N 2AB—*Gen. Sec.*, P. Plouviez.

BRITISH AIR LINE PILOTS ASSOCIATION, THE (3,750), 81 New Road, Harlington, Hayes, Middlesex UB3 5BG—*Gen. Sec.*, M. Young.

BRITISH ASSOCIATION OF COLLIERY MANAGEMENT, THE (15,584), 317 Nottingham Road, Old Basford, Nottingham NG7 7DP—*Gen. Sec.*, A. Wilson.

CARD SETTING MACHINE TENTERS' SOCIETY (106), 36 Greenton Avenue, Scholes, Cleckheaton, W. Yorks. BD19 6DT—*Sec.*, G. Priestley.

CERAMIC AND ALLIED TRADES UNION, THE (28,873), Hillcrest House, Garth Street, Hanley, Stoke-on-Trent ST1 2AB—*Gen. Sec.*, A. W. Clowes.

CIVIL AND PUBLIC SERVICES ASSOCIATION, THE (190,832), 215 Balham High Road, SW17 7BN—*Sec.*, J. A. Graham.

CIVIL SERVICE UNION (40,123), 5 Praed Street, W2 1NJ—*Sec.*, J. D. Sheldon.

CLOTH PRESSERS' SOCIETY (16), 34 Southgate, Honley, Huddersfield HD7 2MT—*Sec.*, G. Kaye.

COMMUNICATION MANAGERS' ASSOCIATION (19,450), Hughes House, Ruscombe Road, Twyford, Reading RG10 9JD—*Gen. Sec.*, R. J. Cowley.

CONFEDERATION OF HEALTH SERVICE EMPLOYEES (C.O.H.S.E.) (222,869), Glen House, High Street, Banstead, Surrey SM7 2LH—*Gen. Sec.*, D. Williams.

EDUCATIONAL INSTITUTE OF SCOTLAND, THE (45,665), 46 Moray Place, Edinburgh EH3 6BH—*Gen. Sec.*, J. D. Pollock.

ELECTRICAL, ELECTRONIC, TELECOMMUNICATION AND PLUMBING UNION (E.E.T.P.U.) (365,000), Hayes Court, West Common Road, Bromley BR2 7AU—*Sec.*, E. A. Hammond.

ENGINEERS' AND MANAGERS' ASSOCIATION (41,419), Station House, Fox Lane North, Chertsey, Surrey KT16 9HW—*Gen. Sec.*, J. Lyons.

ENTERTAINMENT TRADES' ALLIANCE (37,251), 155 Kennington Park Road, SE11 4JU—*Gen. Secs.*, D. A. Hearn (A.B.S. Section); J. L. Wilson (N.A.T.T.K.E. Section).

FILM ARTISTES' ASSOCIATION (3,578), 61 Marloes Road, W8 6LF—*Sec.*, S. Brannigan.

FIRE BRIGADES UNION, THE (43,405), 59 Fulham High Street, SW6 3JN—*Gen. Sec.*, K. Cameron.

FURNITURE, TIMBER AND ALLIED TRADES UNION (58,244), Fairfields, Roe Green, Kingsbury, NW9 0PT—*Sec.*, B. Rubner.

GENERAL, MUNICIPAL, BOILERMAKERS AND ALLIED TRADES UNION (GMW) (875,187), Thorne House, Claygate, Esher, Surrey KT10 0TL—*Gen. Sec.*, D. Basnett.

GENERAL UNION OF ASSOCIATIONS OF LOOM OVER-LOOKERS (1,325), Overlookers Institute, Jude Street, Nelson, Lancs. BB9 7NP—*Pres.*, R. Richardson.

GREATER LONDON COUNCIL STAFF ASSOCIATION (16,090), 150 Waterloo Road, SE1 8SB—*Sec.*, A. Capelin.

HEALTH VISITORS' ASSOCIATION (14,884), 36 Eccleston Square, SW1V 1PF—*Gen. Sec.*, Shirley Goodwin.

HOSPITAL CONSULTANTS AND SPECIALISTS ASSOCIATION, THE (2,873), The Old Court House, London Road, Ascot, Berks. SL5 7EN—*Chief Exec.*, R. B. Martin.

INLAND REVENUE STAFF FEDERATION (56,957), Douglas Houghton House, 231 Vauxhall Bridge Road, SW1V 1EH—*Gen. Sec.*, A. M. G. Christopher, C.B.E.

INSTITUTION OF PROFESSIONAL CIVIL SERVANTS, THE (93,090), 75–79 York Road, SE1 7AQ—*Gen. Sec.*, W. McCall.

IRON AND STEEL TRADES CONFEDERATION, THE (91,006), Swinton House, 324 Gray's Inn Road, WC1X 8DD—*Sec.*, W. Sirs.

MERCHANT NAVY AND AIRLINE OFFICERS' ASSOCIATION, THE (24,368), Oceanair House, 750/760 High Road, Leytonstone, E11 3BB—*Gen. Sec.*, E. Nevin.

MILITARY AND ORCHESTRAL MUSICAL INSTRUMENT MAKERS' TRADE SOCIETY (200), 60 Stanborough Avenue, Boreham Wood, Herts.—*Gen. Sec.*, T. H. Withers.

MUSICIANS' UNION (39,091), 60–62 Clapham Road, SW9 0JJ—*Gen. Sec.*, J. Morton.

NATIONAL AND LOCAL GOVERNMENT OFFICERS' ASSOCIATION (N.A.L.G.O.) (780,037), 1 Mabledon Place, WC1H 9AJ—*Gen. Sec.*, J. Daly.

NATIONAL ASSOCIATION OF COLLIERY OVERMEN, DEPUTIES AND SHOTFIRERS (17,079), Simpson House, 48 Netherhall Road, Doncaster, S. Yorks. DN1 2PZ—*Sec.*, P. McNestry.

NATIONAL ASSOCIATION OF CO-OPERATIVE OFFICIALS (5,053), Saxone House, 56 Market Street, Manchester M1 1PW—*Gen. Sec.*, L. W. Ewing.

NATIONAL ASSOCIATION OF LICENSED HOUSE MAN-AGERS (16,952), 9 Coombe Lane, Raynes Park, SW20 8NE—*Nat. Sec.*, L. Adams.

NATIONAL ASSOCIATION OF PROBATION OFFICERS (5,638), 3–4 Chivalry Road, SW11 1HT—*Sec.*, Ms. J. Kirkpatrick.

NATIONAL ASSOCIATION OF SCHOOLMASTERS/UNION OF WOMEN TEACHERS (N.A.S./U.W.T.) (119,668), 22 Upper Brook Street, W1Y 2HD—*Gen. Sec.*, F. A. Smithies.

NATIONAL ASSOCIATION OF TEACHERS IN FURTHER AND HIGHER EDUCATION (73,395), Hamilton House, Mabledon Place, WC1H 9BH—*Gen. Sec.*, P. Dawson.

NATIONAL GRAPHICAL ASSOCIATION (N.G.A.'82) (129,231), Graphic House, 63/67 Bromham Road, Bedford MK40 2AG—*Sec.*, A. D. Dubbins.

NATIONAL LEAGUE OF THE BLIND AND DISABLED, THE (3,115), 2 Tenterden Road, N17 8BE—*Sec.*, M. A. Barrett.

NATIONAL SOCIETY OF METAL MECHANICS (29,076), 70 Lionel Street, Birmingham B3 1JG—*Sec.*, C. P. McCarthy.

NATIONAL UNION OF BLASTFURNACEMEN, ORE MINERS, COKE WORKERS AND KINDRED TRADES, THE (5,057), 93 Borough Road West, Middlesbrough TS1 3AJ—*Gen. Sec.*, N. Leadley.

NATIONAL UNION OF DOMESTIC APPLIANCE AND GEN-ERAL METAL WORKERS, THE (4,000), First Floor, Imperial Buildings, Corporation Street, Rotherham, Yorks. S60 1PB—*Gen. Sec.*, R. D. Preston.

NATIONAL UNION OF HOSIERY AND KNITWEAR WORK-ERS, THE (53,651), 55 New Walk, Leicester LE1 7EB—*Gen. Sec.*, T. Kirk.

NATIONAL UNION OF INSURANCE WORKERS (18,480), 46 Quicks Road, Wimbledon, SW19 1EY—*Sec.*, J. P. Brown.

NATIONAL UNION OF JOURNALISTS (N.U.J.) (32,689), Acorn House, 314/320 Gray's Inn Road, WC1X 8DP—*Gen. Sec.*, K. B. Ashton.

NATIONAL UNION OF LOCK AND METAL WORKERS (5,009), Bellamy House, Wilkes Street, Willenhall, West Midlands WV13 2BS—*Sec.*, J. Martin, M.B.E.

NATIONAL UNION OF MINEWORKERS (N.U.M.) (208,051), St. James' House, Vicar Lane, Sheffield S1 2EX—*Sec.*, P. E. Heathfield.

NATIONAL UNION OF PUBLIC EMPLOYEES (N.U.P.E.) (689,046), Civic House, 20 Grand Depot Road, SE18 6SF—*Sec.*, R. K. Bickerstaffe.

NATIONAL UNION OF RAILWAYMEN (N.U.R.) (143,218), Unity House, Euston Road, NW1 2BL—*Gen. Sec.*, J. Knapp.

NATIONAL UNION OF SCALEMAKERS (1,210), 4th Floor, Herbert House, 71 Cornwall Street, Birmingham B3 2EE—*Gen. Sec.*, A. F. Smith.

NATIONAL UNION OF SEAMEN (N.U.S.) (25,000), Maritime House, Old Town, Clapham, SW4 0JP—*Gen. Sec.*, J. H. Slater, C.B.E.

NATIONAL UNION OF TAILORS AND GARMENT WORKERS (76,130), 16 Charles Square, N1 6HP—*Gen. Sec.*, A. Smith.

NATIONAL UNION OF TEACHERS (N.U.T.) (210,499), Hamilton House, Mabledon Place, WC1H 9BD—*Gen. Sec.*, F. Jarvis.

NATIONAL UNION OF THE FOOTWEAR, LEATHER AND ALLIED TRADES (41,897), The Grange, 108 Northampton Road, Earls Barton, Northampton NN6 0JH—*Sec.*, G. G. Stewart.

NORTHERN CARPET TRADES' UNION (1,010), 22 Clare Road, Halifax HX1 2HX—*Gen. Sec.*, K. Edmondson.

PATTERN WEAVERS' SOCIETY (60), New Field End, Hill Top, Cumberworth, Huddersfield HD8 8YE—*Gen. Sec.*, D. G. Hawley.

POST OFFICE ENGINEERING UNION (P.O.E.U.) (129,950), Greystoke House, 150 Brunswick Road, W5 1AW—*Sec.*, B. C. Stanley.

POWER LOOM CARPET WEAVERS' AND TEXTILE WORKERS' UNION (3,200), Callows Lane, Kidderminster, Worcs. DY10 2JG—*Gen. Sec.*, B. C. Moule.

PRISON OFFICERS' ASSOCIATION (22,820), Cronin House, 245 Church Street, Edmonton, N9 9HW—*Gen. Sec.*, D. Evans.

RADIO AND ELECTRONIC OFFICERS' UNION (2,434), 4/6 Branfill Road, Upminster, Essex RM14 2XX—*Gen. Sec.*, K. A. Murphy.

ROSSENDALE UNION OF BOOT, SHOE AND SLIPPER OPERATIVES, THE (4,191), Taylor House, 7 Tenterfield Street, Waterfoot, Rossendale, Lancs.—*Gen. Sec.*, M. Murray.

SCOTTISH PRISON OFFICERS' ASSOCIATION (2,755), 21 Calder Road, Edinburgh EH11 3PF—*Gen. Sec.*, J. B. Renton, M.B.E.

SCOTTISH UNION OF POWER-LOOM OVERLOOKERS (100), 3 Napier Terrace, Dundee, Tayside.—*Sec.*, J. Reilly.

SCREW, NUT, BOLT AND RIVET TRADE UNION (600), 368 Dudley Road, Birmingham B18 4HH—*Gen. Sec.*, E. C. Bowcott.

SHEFFIELD SAWMAKERS' PROTECTION SOCIETY (116), 94 Club Garden Road, Sheffield S11 8BW—*Sec.*, R. Parkin.

SHEFFIELD WOOL SHEAR WORKERS' UNION (26), 50 Bankfield Road, Malin Bridge, Sheffield S6 4RD—*Sec.*, R. Cutler.

SOCIETY OF CIVIL AND PUBLIC SERVANTS (93,481), 124/130 Southwark Street, SE1 0TU—*Gen. Sec.*, G. Gillman.

SOCIETY OF GRAPHICAL AND ALLIED TRADES (SOGAT '82) (213,605), Sogat House, 274/288 London Road, Hadleigh, Essex SS7 2DE—*Gen. Sec.*, W. H. Keys.

SOCIETY OF SHUTTLEMAKERS (67), 15 Hanover Gardens, Horton Hall Close, Little Horton Lane, Bradford BD5 0NG—*Pres.*, E. V. Littlewood.

SOCIETY OF TELECOM EXECUTIVES (23,005), 102/104 Sheen Road, Richmond, Surrey TW9 1UF—*Gen. Sec.*, P. W. Davies.

SPRING TRAPMAKERS' SOCIETY (90), Bellamy House, Wilkes Street, Willenhall, West Midlands WV13 2BS—*Sec.*, J. Martin.

TOBACCO MECHANICS ASSOCIATION (208), 16 Clifton Terrace, Whitley Bay, Tyne-and-Wear NE26 2JD—*Sec.*, J. Middleton.

TOBACCO WORKERS' UNION, THE (15,165), 9 Station Parade, High Street, Wanstead, E11 1QF—*Sec.*, C. D. Grieve.

TRANSPORT AND GENERAL WORKERS' UNION (T.G.W.U.) (1,547,443), Transport House, Smith Square, Westminster, SW1P 3JB—*Sec.*, A. M. Evans.

TRANSPORT SALARIED STAFFS' ASSOCIATION (53,521), Walkden House, 10 Melton Street, NW1 2EJ—*Gen. Sec.*, C. A. Lyons.

UNION OF COMMUNICATION WORKERS, THE (196,426), UCW House, Crescent Lane, SW4 9RN—*Gen. Sec.*, A. D. Tuffin.

UNION OF CONSTRUCTION, ALLIED TRADES AND TECHNICIANS (U.C.A.T.T.) (260,000), UCATT House, 177 Abbeville Road, Clapham, SW4 9RL—*Sec.*, L. Wood.

UNION OF SHOP, DISTRIBUTIVE AND ALLIED WORKERS (U.S.D.A.W.) (403,446), Oakley, 188 Wilmslow Road, Fallowfield, Manchester M14 6LJ—*Sec.*, W. H. P. Whatley.

UNITED ROAD TRANSPORT UNION (22,628), 76 High Lane, Manchester M21 1FD—*Gen. Sec.*, J. Moore, M.B.E.

WRITERS' GUILD OF GREAT BRITAIN, THE (1,349), 430 Edgware Road, W2 1EH—*Gen. Sec.*, W. J. Jeffrey.

YORKSHIRE ASSOCIATION OF POWER LOOM OVERLOOKERS (643), Textile Hall, Westgate, Bradford BD1 2RG—*Sec.*, G. Slack.

LABOUR STATISTICS

Industrial Stoppages (Thousands)

	Workers involved	Total working days lost						
		All industries and services	Coal, coke, mineral oil and natural gas	Metals, engineering and vehicles	Textiles, clothing and footwear	Construction	Transport and communication	All other industries and services
Estimated number of employees in employment at June 1982		*21,103*	*326*	*2,941*	*587*	*1,050*	*1,383*	*14,817*
1978	1,001	9,405	201	5,985	179	416	360	2,264
1979	4,583	29,474	128	20,390	109	834	1,419	6,594
1980	830	11,964	166	10,155	44	281	253	1,065
1981	1,499	4,266	237	1,731	39	86	359	1,814
1982	2,101	5,313	380	1,457	61	41	1,675	1,699
†1983	538	3,593	581	1,418	34	70	167	1,322
†1984 January	127	298	96	65	3	5	12	117
February	291	508	148	68	32	3	21	236
March	242	1,930	1,606	141	9	14	41	118
April	89	2,214	2,002	97	2	7	17	90
May	101	2,265	2,001	87	4	2	33	139

† Provisional.

INDUSTRIAL RESEARCH ASSOCIATIONS

The following are members of the C.D.R.A., The Federation of Technology Centres, Palace Chambers, Bridge Street, S.W.1.:—

ASLIB, 3 Belgrave Square, S.W.1.—*Dir.*, Dr. D. A. Lewis.

ASSOCIATED BRITISH PORTS, Hayes Road, Southall, Middlx.—*Dir.*, W. H. Jackson.

ATOMIC ENERGY AUTHORITY, U.K., Bldg. 329, A.E.R.E. Harwell, Oxon.—*Dir., Industrial Research*, Dr. R. G. Sowden.

BHRA FLUID ENGINEERING, Cranfield, Beds.—*Dir.*, G. F. W. Adler, O.B.E.

BRICK DEVELOPMENT ASSOCIATION, Woodside House, Winkfield, Windsor, Berks.—*Dir.-Gen.*, R. Lloyd-Jones.

BRITISH BOARD OF AGREEMENT, P.O. Box 195, Bucknalls Lane, Garston, Watford, Herts.—*Dir.*, T. P. R. Lant.

BRITISH BRUSH MANUFACTURERS' RESEARCH ASSOCIATION, c/o Dept. of Textile Industries, The University, Leeds.—*Dir.*, D. I. Fothergill.

BRITISH CERAMIC RESEARCH ASSOCIATION, Queen's Road, Penkhull, Stoke-on-Trent.—*Dir.*, Dr. D. W. F. James.

BRITISH GLASS INDUSTRY RESEARCH ASSOCIATION, Northumberland Road, Sheffield 10.—*Dir.*, Dr. E. A. Kellett.

BRITISH INTERNAL COMBUSTION ENGINE RESEARCH INSTITUTE, 111–12 Buckingham Avenue, Slough, Bucks.—*Dir.*, I. A. C. Brown.

BRITISH LEATHER MANUFACTURERS' Research Association, King's Park Road, Moulton Road, Northampton.—*Dir.*, Dr. R. L. Sykes.

BUILDING SERVICES RESEARCH AND INFORMATION ASSOCIATION, Old Bracknell Lane, Bracknell, Berks.—*Dir.*, Dr. D. P. Gregory.

CONSTRUCTION INDUSTRY RESEARCH AND INFORMATION ASSOCIATION, 6 Storey's Gate, S.W.1.—*Dir.*, L. S. Blake, PH.D.

CUTLERY AND ALLIED TRADES RESEARCH ASSOCIATION, Henry Street, Sheffield, 3.—*Dir.*, E. A. Oldfield.

DROP FORGING RESEARCH ASSOCIATION, Shepherd Street, Sheffield 3.—*Dir.*, S. E. Rogers, PH.D.

FABRIC CARE RESEARCH ASSOCIATION, Forest House Laboratories, Knaresborough Road, Harrogate.—*Dir.*, Dr. R. M. Neale.

FIRE INSURERS' RESEARCH AND TESTING ORGANISATION, Melrose Avenue, Borehamwood, Herts.—*Dir.*, R. W. Pickard.

FURNITURE INDUSTRY RESEARCH ASSOCIATION, Maxwell Road, Stevenage, Herts.—*Dir.*, D. M. Heughan.

LAMBEG INDUSTRIAL RESEARCH ASSOCIATION (*Linen*), Research Institute, Lambeg, Lisburn, Co. Antrim, N. Ireland.—*Dir.*, Dr. W. W. Foster.

MACHINE TOOL INDUSTRY RESEARCH ASSOCIATION, Hulley Road, Hurdsfield, Macclesfield, Cheshire.—*Dir.*, L. K. Lord.

NATIONAL COMPUTING CENTRE, Oxford Road, Manchester 1.—*Dir.*, D. R. Fairbairn.

PAINT RESEARCH ASSOCIATION, Paint Research Station, Waldegrave Road, Teddington, Middlesex.—*Dir.*, G. de W. Anderson, PH.D.

PAPER AND BOARD, PRINTING AND PACKAGING INDUS-
TRIES RESEARCH ASSOCIATION (Pira), Randalls
Road, Leatherhead, Surrey.—*Dir.*, N. K. Bridge,
Ph.D.

PROCESSORS AND GROWERS RESEARCH ORGANISATION,
The Research Station, Great North Road, Peterborough.—*Dir.*, G. P. Gent.

PRODUCTION ENGINEERING RESEARCH ASSOCIATION
OF GREAT BRITAIN, Melton Mowbray, Leics.—*Dir.-
Gen.*, (vacant).

RUBBER AND PLASTICS RESEARCH ASSOCIATION OF
GREAT BRITAIN, Shawbury, Shrewsbury, Shropshire.—*Dir.*, Dr. J. P. Berry.

SHIPOWNERS REFRIGERATED CARGO RESEARCH ASSO-
CIATION, 140 Newmarket Road, Cambridge.—*Dir.*,
G. R. Scrine.

SHOE AND ALLIED TRADES RESEARCH ASSOCIATION,
Satra House, Rockingham Road, Kettering, Northants.—*Dir.*, J. G. Butlin, O.B.E.

SPRING RESEARCH AND MANUFACTURERS' ASSOCIA-
TION, Henry Street, Sheffield 3.—*Dir.*, J. A. Bennett.

STEEL CASTINGS RESEARCH AND TRADE ASSOCIATION,
5 East Bank Road, Sheffield 2.—*Dir.*, Dr. J. A.
Reynolds.

TIMBER RESEARCH AND DEVELOPMENT ASSOCIATION,
Hughenden Valley, High Wycombe, Bucks.—*Dir.*,
J. G. Sunley.

WATER RESEARCH CENTRE, Henley Road, Medmen-
ham, Marlow, Bucks.—*Chief Exec.*, (vacant).

WOOL INDUSTRIES RESEARCH ASSOCIATION (Wira),
Wira House, West Park Ring Road, Leeds 16.—
Dir., B. E. King, Ph.D.

The following are members of the Association of
Independent Contract Research Organisations

(A.I.C.R.O.), Bridge Works, Shoreham-by-Sea, W.
Sussex.

BCIRA (*Foundry and associated industries*), Alvechurch, Birmingham.

BHRA FLUID ENGINEERING, Cranfield, Bedford.

BNF METALS (*Non-ferrous metals*), Denchworth
Road, Wantage, Oxon.

ERA TECHNOLOGY (*Electrotechnology*), Cleeve Road,
Leatherhead, Surrey.

FULMER RESEARCH INSTITUTE (*The science and technology of materials*), Stoke Poges, Slough, Berks.

HAZLETON LABORATORIES EUROPE LTD. (*Life sciences*), Otley Road, Harrogate, N. Yorks.

INTERNATIONAL RESEARCH AND DEVELOPMENT (*Engineering, materials technology, applied physics and
biotechnology*), Fossway, Newcastle-upon-Tyne.

INVERESK RESEARCH INTERNATIONAL LTD. (*Life sciences*), Inveresk Gate, Musselburgh, Midlothian.

LIFE SCIENCE RESEARCH, Eye, Suffolk.

MOTOR INDUSTRY RESEARCH ASSOCIATION, Watling
Street, Nuneaton, Warwicks.

RICARDO CONSULTING ENGINEERS, P.L.C. (*Combustion
engine technology*), Bridge Works, Shoreham-by-
Sea, Sussex.

ROBERTSON RESEARCH INTERNATIONAL (*Energy and
natural resource exploration and development*),
Ty'n-y-Coed, Llanrhos, Llandudno, Gwynedd.

SHIRLEY INSTITUTE (*Textiles*), Didsbury, Manchester.

SIRA INSTITUTE LTD. (*Instrumentation technology*),
South Hill, Chislehurst, Kent.

THE WELDING INSTITUTE, Abington Hall, Abington,
Cambs.

AGRICULTURAL RESEARCH INSTITUTES AND UNITS

The following research institutes are under the
direct control of the Agricultural and Food Research
Council (*see* Index):—

Animal Breeding Research Organisation, West
Main Road, Edinburgh 9.—*Dir.* R. B. Land, Ph.D.

Food Research Institute, Colney Lane, Norwich.—
Dir., R. F. Curtis, Ph.D., Sc.D.

Insect Chemistry and Physiology Group, University of Sussex, Falmer, Brighton.—*Head of Group*,
G. T. Brooks, Ph.D.

Institute of Animal Physiology, Babraham,
Cambs.—*Dir.*, B. A. Cross, C.B.E., Ph.D., Sc.D., F.R.S.

Institute for Research on Animal Diseases, Compton, Newbury, Berks.—*Dir.*, J. M. Payne, Ph.D.

Letcombe Laboratory, Letcombe Regis, Wantage,
Oxon.—*Dir.*, J. V. Lake, Ph.D.

Meat Research Institute, Langford, nr. Bristol.—
Dir., Prof. A. J. Bailey, Ph.D. (also Weston Laboratory, Bridge Road, Weston-super-Mare).

Poultry Research Centre, Roslin, Midlothian.—
Dir., D. W. F. Shannon, Ph.D.

Weed Research Organisation, Begbroke Hill,
Sandy Lane, Yarnton, Oxford.—*Dir.*, J. D. Fryer,
C.B.E.

**Unit of Insect Neurophysiology and Pharmacol-
ogy**, Zoology Dept., University of Cambridge,
Downing Street, Cambridge.—*Hon. Dir.*, J. E.
Treherne, Ph.D., Sc.D.

Unit of Nitrogen Fixation, University of Sussex,
Brighton.—*Dir.*, Prof. J. Postgate, F.R.S.

Unit of Statistics, University of Edinburgh, Edinburgh 8.—*Hon. Dir.*, Prof. D. J. Finney, C.B.E., Sc.D.,
F.R.S., F.R.S.E.

Statistics Group, Dept. of Applied Biology, Pembroke Street, Cambridge.—*Officer in Charge*, D. E.
Walters.

GRANT-AIDED RESEARCH INSTITUTES

In addition to the above there are other institutes which, while retaining their own individuality, are financed wholly or in the main by grants made from Government funds. Most of these Institutes have governing bodies of their own to which they are directly responsible. The maintenance grants for Institutes in England and Wales are met from funds voted by Parliament and administered by the Agricultural and Food Research Council; the Scottish Institutes are borne on the vote of the Department of Agriculture and Fisheries for Scotland.

Animal Virus Research Institute, Pirbright, Surrey.—*Dir.*, B. Mahey.

East Malling Research Station, Maidstone, Kent.—*Dir.*, I. J. Graham-Bryce, D.Phil.

Glasshouse Crops Research Institute, Worthing Road, Littlehampton, Sussex.—*Dir.*, D. Rudd-Jones, C.B.E., Ph.D.

Grassland Research Institute, Hurley, nr. Maidenhead, Berks.—*Dir.*, Prof. J. H. D. Prescott, Ph.D.

Hannah Research Institute, Ayr.—*Dir.*, M. Peaker, Ph.D.

Hill Farming Research Organisation, Bush Estate, Penicuik, Midlothian.—*Dir.*, J. Eadie.

Hop Research Department, Wye College, Ashford, Kent.—*Dir.*, R. A. Neve, O.B.E., Ph.D.

Houghton Poultry Research Station,* Houghton, Huntingdon.—*Dir.*, Prof. P. M. Biggs, Ph.D., F.R.S.

John Innes Institute, Colney Lane, Norwich.—*Dir.*, Prof. H. W. Woolhouse, Ph.D., F.R.S.C.

Long Ashton Research Station, Bristol.—*Dir.*, Prof. J. M. Hirst, D.Sc., Ph.D., F.R.S.

Macaulay Institute for Soil Research, Craigiebuckler, Aberdeen.—*Dir.*, Prof. T. West, Ph.D., F.R.S.E.

Moredun Institute, 408 Gilmerton Road, Edinburgh.—*Dir.*, W. B. Martin, Ph.D.

National Institute of Agricultural Engineering, Wrest Park, Silsoe, Bedford.—*Dir.*, (acting), S. W. R. Cox, O.B.E.

National Institute for Research in Dairying, Shinfield, nr. Reading.—*Dir.*, (acting), C. C. Balch, D.S.C.

National Vegetable Research Stn. Wellesbourne, Warwick.—*Dir.*, Prof. J. K. A. Bleasdale, Ph.D.

Plant Breeding Institute, Maris Lane, Trumpington, Cambridge.—*Dir.*, Prof. P. R. Day, Ph.D.

Rowett Research Institute, Bucksburn, Aberdeen.—*Dir.*, W. P. T. James, Ph.D.

Rothamsted Experimental Station, Harpenden, Herts.—*Dir.*, Sir Leslie Fowden, Ph.D., F.R.S.

Scottish Crop Research Institute, Invergowrie, Dundee.—*Dir.*, C. E. Taylor, C.B.E., Ph.D., F.R.S.E.

Scottish Institute of Agricultural Engineering, Bush Estate, Penicuik, Midlothian.—*Dir.*, D. P. Blight, Ph.D.

Welsh Plant Breeding Station, Plas Gogerddan, nr. Aberystwyth.—*Dir.*, Prof. R. Q. Connell, Ph.D.

*Financed jointly by the Agricultural and Food Research Council and the Animal Health Trust.

MASTERS OF THE QUEEN'S/KING'S MUSIC

	Apptd.		Apptd.
Nicholas Lanier	1626	Francois (Franz) Cramer	1834
Louis Grabu	1666	George Frederick Anderson	1848
Nicholas Staggins	1674	Sir William George Cusins	1870
John Eccles	1700	Sir Walter Parratt	1893
Maurice Greene	1735	Sir Edward Elgar	1924
William Boyce	1755 (1757)	Sir Henry Walford Davies	1934
John Stanley	1779	Sir Arnold Edward Trevor Bax	1941
Sir William Parsons	1786	Sir Arthur Bliss	1953
William Shield	1817	Malcolm Williamson	1975
Christian Kramer	1829		

POETS LAUREATE

Samuel Daniel	1599	Rev. Laurence Eusden	1718	Lord Tennyson	1850
Ben Jonson	1619	Colley Cibber	1730	Alfred Austin	1890
Sir William D'Avenant	1637	William Whitehead	1757	Robert Bridges	1913
John Dryden	1670	Rev. Thomas Warton	1785	John Masefield	1930
Thomas Shadwell	1688	Henery James Pye	1790	Cecil Day Lewis	1967
Nahum Tate	1692	Robert Southey	1813	Sir John Betjeman	1972
Nicholas Rowe	1715	William Wordsworth	1843		

PRINCIPAL CHARITABLE BEQUESTS OF THE YEAR

The alphabetical list below represents the principal charitable bequests from estates published since the last edition. As in previous lists the exact amount actually distributed to charities is not known, as other legacies, testamentary legal charges and Capital Transfer Tax are all deducted from the estates.

Two of the larger estates in the list are those of Baron Sherborne, who left the residue of his £7 million estate to the National Trust "to safeguard the continuity of the Sherborne Estate", and Jane Port, of Bexhill, who also left the residue of her £2·9 million estate to the Trust. Christobel Young, of Bournemouth, left three-quarters of her £699,797 estate to the Trust and one-quarter to the Victoria and Albert Museum, while the British Museum received the residue of the £924,916 estate of Sir John Addis, one of its Trustees.

Trinity College, Cambridge, received the residue of the £1·5 million estate of Piero Sraffa, economist and Fellow of the College. Vera Cox left £27,000 and 90 per cent. of the residue of her £174,638 estate to St. Edmund Hall, Oxford, and Dorothea Gray, a Fellow of St. Hugh's College, Oxford, left most of her £151,306 estate to the College. James Kerr, of Taunton, left the residue of his £425,085 estate to found scholarships for Scottish students to be administered by the University of Edinburgh, and Dr. Jane Thompson, of Newcastle, left the residue of her £227,561 estate to Aberdeen University, to found a Chair in the Mental Health Department. Richard Burdon-Sanderson left the residue of his £981,924 estate to Middlesex Hospital Medical School for the advancement of medical education methods, and Baron Amulree left half the residue of his £1·2 million estate to a travelling studentship fund, for grants to doctors trained at University College Hospital and studying outside the U.K. and Eire.

The other half of the residue of Baron Amulree's estate was left for the welfare of the elderly, and Hope Malins left the residue of her £1·4 million estate to endow homes for old people. Nancie Leitch left a fourth of the residue of her £920,373 estate for the needs of the elderly, destitute, sick or dying, and the residue of the £121,900 estate of Walter Lucas was left to Hastings Community Council, for old people's welfare. Mabel Higgins, who also lived at Hastings, left the whole of her £259,110 estate "for the benefit of very elderly people", and another Sussex resident, Reginald Fry, left the bulk of his £130,317 estate to benefit the handicapped, needy and deprived in his area. William Pinn, of Gravesend, left the residue of his £1·3 million estate to a trust fund to make a twice-yearly payment of at least £25 to pensioners living in the district.

London's College of Psychic Studies received the residue of the £1 million estate of Margaret Newton. Imogen Holst, the daughter of the composer, left the residue of her £245,186 estate for such charitable purposes as her Trustees decided. Alice Harding left the residue of her £168,852 estate to the Lincoln Cathedral Fabric Fund, and Ivan Lumsden left a Bluthner Grand Piano and Goble Spinet to Carlisle Cathedral, and most of his £181,585 estate to the Friends of the Cathedral, in memory of his brother, a former assistant organist there.

One of the year's largest single bequests was the entire £393,960 estate of Hiram Lewis, of Torquay, left to the Sunshine Home for Blind Children, Bristol. Edith Currie, who had already made a gift of £250,000 to the R.N.L.I. in her lifetime, left the residue of her £1·3 million estate between 10 other charities. Diplomat Ian Mackay left most of his £190,021 estate to the Foreign Office Century House Benevolent Fund, and Dennis Pollard left the residue of his

£191,573 estate to the R.A.F. Benevolent Fund "in memory of The Few in the Battle of Britain". The residue of the £131,095 estate of Olive Wiggins was left between the Royal Ulster Constabulary Benevolent Fund and the Belfast Protestant Relief Fund, and most of the £206,365 estate of Estrella Carreras was left to Amnesty International.

Sir John Mansfield Addis, K.C.M.G., of Frant, East Sussex £924,916
(The residue to the British Museum)

Mr. Arthur Leslie Allen, of Winchcombe, Gloucs. £173,026
(All his property to Dr. Barnardo's)

Mrs. Madeline Jane Allen, of Plas Newton, Chester £526,966
(The residue to Gravesend Boy Scout Association)

Basil William Sholto MacKenzie, 2nd Baron Amulree, K.B.E., of Cranbrook, Kent £1,267,932
(Half the residue for the welfare of the elderly as his Trustees choose, and half the residue to a charitable fund to be called the Amulree Travelling Studentship Fund)

Mrs. Evelyn Ethel Preston-Avery, of Godalming, Surrey £213,721
(The residue to R.U.K.B.A.)

Mrs. Ivy Primrose Backwith, of Woking, Surrey £659,545
(The residue equally between Dr. Barnardo's, London Association for the Blind and the Cancer Research Campaign)

Mr. Reginald Vernon Beal, of Tunbridge Wells, Kent £257,351
(The residue to the Cancer Research Campaign)

Mr. Philip Henry Ferris Begbey, of Lancing, West Sussex £142,673
(The residue to the Arthritis and Rheumatism Council)

Mrs. Dorothy Bigg, of Buckhurst Hill, Essex £563,476
(The residue equally between the R.A.F. Benevolent Fund and R.N.L.I.)

Annie Lydia Blaker, of Duncton, Petworth, West Sussex £554,407
(The residue equally between the Aldingbourne County Centre, Norton, Chichester, the King Edward VII Hospital, Midhurst, and the R.N.L.I.)

Miss Ethel Irene Nancy Bradshaw, of Cheltenham, Gloucs. £173,471
(The residue to the Royal College of Music, London, for scholarships)

Mrs. Letitia Mary Bretherton, of Godalming, Surrey £178,192
(The residue to the R.N.L.I.)

Miss Edith Elsie Burge, of Barton on Sea, Hants. £225,456
(The residue equally between the R.N.I.B., R.S.P.C.A., Arthritis and Rheumatism Council, R.S.P.B. and R.N.I.D.)

Estrella Carlota Ada Carreras, of Grange over Sands, Cumbria £206,365
(The residue to Amnesty International)

Mr. Allan Craig Cooper, of Peppard Common, Oxon £251,823
(The residue to the British and Foreign Bible Society)

Mrs. Vera Lucinda Cox, of Hampton Wick, Middlesex £174,638
(£27,000 and 90 per cent of the residue to St. Edmund Hall, Oxford)

Mrs. Edith Emelie Currie, of Shenfield, Essex....................................£1,367,303
(The residue equally between the Police Dependants Trust, Children's Society, Dr. Barnardo's, P.D.S.A., N.S.P.C.C., R.S.P.C.A., Imperial Cancer Research Fund, Arthritis and Rheumatism Council, the Royal Agricultural Benevolent Institution and Malcolm Sargent Cancer Fund for Children)

Mrs. Bootosh Manockjee Cursetjee, of Hook Norton, Oxon...................................£185,165
(The residue to the Royal Society of Musicians)

Dorothy May Digby, of Littlewick Green, Maidenhead, Berks. £262,058
(The residue to the Multiple Sclerosis Society)

Dr. Sullivan Bernard Eadham, of Nottingham £467,663
(The residue to the J.N.F. Charitable Trust)

Mrs. Hilda Kathleen Eldridge, of Abingdon, Oxon....................................£214,746
(£10,000 to St. Michael's Church, Abingdon, and the residue to St. Helen's Church, Abingdon)

Mr. Harry Ellard, of Shirley, Solihull, West Midlands £4,366,940
(The residue to the United Grand Lodge of England Grand Charity)

Mrs. Gladys May Ellis, of Hull, North Humberside £307,104
(The residue equally between St. Dunstan's, Dr. Barnardo's and the Imperial Cancer Research Fund)

Mr. Claude McGeorge Frost, of Bromley, Kent..................................£211,793
(The residue to Help the Aged)

Mr. Reginald Robert William Fry, of Hankham, Pevensey, East Sussex £130,317
(The residue for such charitable purposes as his Trustees select that will benefit the inhabitants of the Hankham, Hailsham, Pevensey, Westham, and Stone Cross area, particularly the handicapped, needy and deprived)

Mr. George Arthur Brassey Gottlieb, of Parkstone, Dorset £264,448
(The residue for such charitable purposes as his Trustees determine)

Miss Dorothea Helen Forbes Gray, O.B.E., of Oxford £151,306
(The residue to St. Hugh's College, Oxford)

Alice Mary Harding, of Lincoln £168,852
(The residue to Lincoln Cathedral Fabric Appeal Fund)

Mr. Eric Lyde Hargreaves, of Oxford £230,844
(The residue equally between Oriel College, Oxford, National Trust and St. Dunstan's)

Mrs. Ethel Louise Harnden, of Worthing, West Sussex £113,381
(The residue to the Cancer Research Campaign)

Mr. Cecil Wilfred Hawes, of Gloucester Place, London, N.W.1 ....£245,189
(The residue to the Charities Aid Foundation)

Gwenllian Hawtin, of St. Brides Major, Mid-Glamorgan £734,942
(The residue equally between the Salvation Army, Dr. Barnardo's and the Tenovus Cancer Research Fund, Cardiff)

Miss Marjorie Healey, of Wooburn Green, Bucks. £136,856
(The residue to the Parish Council of St. Paul, Wooburn Green, for general church purposes)

Doris Muriel Henty, of Mulberry Walk, London, S.W.3 ....£639,388
(The residue for such charitable institutions or objects in England and Wales as Lord Allen of Abbeydale thinks proper)

Mrs. Hilda Mary Hewitt, of Witney, Oxon . £448,602
(The residue equally between the Church Army and Salvation Army)

Mrs. Marthe Hicks, of Bromley, Kent......£130,524
(The residue to the United Reformed Church, Widmore Road, Bromley)

Mabel Higgins, of Hastings, East Sussex ...£259,110
(All her property "to be used for the benefit of very elderly people")

Christopher, Baron Hinton of Bankside, O.M., K.B.E., F.R.S., of Dulwich Common, London, S.E.21 ....£346,250
(£25,000 to the Fellowship of Engineering Trust Fund, £10,000 to Trinity College, Cambridge, and £1,500, effects and half the residue to the Institution of Mechanical Engineers, Bury St. Edmunds)

Miss Imogen Clare Holst, C.B.E., of Aldeburgh, Suffolk £245,186
(The residue for such charitable purposes as her Trustees think fit)

Mrs. Olive Mima Holt, of Heaton, Bradford, West Yorks. £110,135
(The residue to the P.D.S.A., Bradford Branch)

Mrs. Mary Ann Hooper, of Teddington, Middlesex £162,262
(The residue to the National Trust)

Mr. Bertram Ernest Robert Horlock, of Hoveton St. John, Norfolk £265,293
(The residue equally between the Guide Dogs for the Blind Association, National Canine Defence League and the International League for the Protection of Horses)

Mr. Edmund George Humphrey, of Patcham, Brighton, East Sussex.........................£185,632
(The residue to the Church of St. Peter and St. Paul, Rustington)

Rita Jackson, of Arlington Street, London, S.W.1 ....£297,670
(The residue equally between the R.N.L.I. and Guide Dogs for the Blind Association)

Hilda Jessie Jarrett, of Whyteleafe, Surrey £228,795
(The residue to the R.N.L.I.)

Helen Gladys Jones, of Wrexham, Clwyd ... £181,201
(The residue equally between the St. John Ambulance Brigade, Wrexham Division, and the Wrexham and East Denbighshire Memorial Hospital)

Mrs. Elizabeth Jowett, of Wollaton Park, Nottingham £282,263
(The residue equally between the British Heart Foundation, the Royal Midland Institution for the Blind, Nottingham, Leukaemia Research Fund, for use in the Nottingham area, and the P.D.S.A. for similar use)

Mrs. Hope Malins Keith, of Rusper, West Sussex..................................£1,419,256
(The residue to establish and endow a home or homes for old people according to a memorandum left by her)

Mr. James Matthew Kerr, of Taunton, Somerset £425,085
(The residue to found research or experimental scholarships for former pupils of the George Watson's Boys' and Girls' Schools and graduates of Edinburgh University, to be administered by that University)

Lottie Doreen Lamerton, of Richmond, Surrey £385,730
(The residue to the R.N.I.B.)

Evyleen Lawrence, of Worthing, West Sussex..................................£280,782
(All her property for charitable purposes as her executors select)

Mrs. Mary Ada Dorothy Leech, of Chelmsford, Essex £230,835
(The residue to the Mother Teresa Charity, Calcutta)

Mrs. Nancie Stansfield Leitch, of Alverdiscott, Bideford, Devon £920,373
(A fourth of the residue each to the Association for the Propagation of the Faith, the Mill Hill Missionaries, London, N.W.7, and the Plymouth Roman Catholic Diocesan Children's Society, and a fourth of the residue for such charities in England as her Trustees select, which cater for the needs of the elderly, destitute, sick or dying)

Dr. Louise Wilhelmine Leven, of Hindhead, Surrey £383,804
(The residue to the Association of Jewish Refugees' Charitable Trust)

Mr. Hiram George Lewis, of Torquay, Devon £393,960
(All his property to the Sunshine Home for Blind Children, Bristol)

Mrs. Millie Little, of Sunbury on Thames, Middlesex £155,364
(The residue to the British Organisation for Rehabilitation and Training)

Miss Phyllis Lomer, of Bournemouth, Dorset £198,106
(All her property equally between the Bournemouth West and Poole East committee of the Cancer Research Campaign, the R.N.I.B. and R.N.I.D.)

Mrs. Elaine May Lowry, of Haywards Heath, West Sussex £177,910
(Nine-tenths of the residue to the Gardeners' Royal Benevolent Society and one-tenth of the residue to Lady Margaret Hall, Oxford)

Mr. Walter Edwin Lucas, of. St. Leonards on Sea, East Sussex £121,900
(The residue to Hastings Community Council, for old people's welfare)

Mr. Ivan Marshall Lumsden, of Chearsley, Bucks. £181,585
(The residue to the Friends of Carlisle Cathedral, to purchase an organ and establish a fund for the maintenance of the music)

Mr. Ian Masson Mackay, of Richmond, Surrey £190,021
(The residue to the Century House Benevolent Fund of the Foreign and Commonwealth Office)

Edna Hope Mansfield, of Wimbish, Saffron Walden, Essex £191,641
(The residue equally between the R.N.I.B. and the British Heart Foundation)

Dorothy Helsby Marshall, of South Croydon, Surrey £769,209
(The residue equally between the Unitarian and Free Christian Church, Croydon, the Save the Children Fund, Children's Country Holidays Fund, R.S.P.B., National Trust, Professional Classes Aid Council, R.N.I.B., Dr. Barnardo's, Oxfam, Royal Commonwealth Society for the Blind, Girl Guides Association, N.S.P.C.C. and R.S.P.C.A.)

Ethel Alice Martin, of Eastbourne, East Sussex £104,773
(All her property to the British Kidney Patient Association, Bordon)

Margaret Frances Maud Martin, of Shaw, Melksham, Wilts. £326,051
(The residue equally between the Women's Holiday Fund and the Institute of Cancer Research)

Mr. Sydney Frederick Mills, of Swindon, Wilts. £240,948
(The residue to the Princess Margaret Hospital, Swindon, for the purchase of medical equipment)

Mr. Laurence Misener, of Maidenhead, Berks. £666,709
(The residue to the Laurence Misener Charitable Trust)

Mrs. Josceline Frances Newcombe, of Exmouth, Devon £158,496
(£5,000 to Help the Aged, and the residue to the Cheshire Foundation)

Margaret Hildred Newton, of Great Maplestead, Essex £1,014,390
(The residue to the College of Psychic Studies, London, S.W.1)

Mr. Alfred Charles Cuthbert Parker, of Sevenoaks, Kent £712,601
(The residue to benefit the Ranyard Memorial Charitable Trust)

Miss Winifred Mary Parker, of Seer Green, Beaconsfield, Bucks. £308,986
(The residue to the Imperial Cancer Research Fund)

Mr. Robert Petrie, of Tintagel, Cornwall ... £308,325
(The residue equally between the R.N.L.I., the Quarriers' Home, Bridge of Weir, Renfrewshire, the Glasgow and West of Scotland Society for the Prevention of Cruelty to Animals, Arthritis and Rheumatism Council, Chest and Heart Association, R.S.P.B., R.N.I.D., Glasgow, the Scottish National Institution for War Blinded, and Scottish Council for the Care of Spastics)

Mr. Frank William George Pickford, of Heston, Middlesex £440,689
(The residue equally between Dr. Barnardo's, the Children's Society, the Chest Heart and Stroke Association, Marie Curie Memorial Foundation, Spastics Society, Artists' General Benevolent Fund, the Cardio-Thoracic Institute, R.N.I.B. and the Save the Children Fund)

Vera Mary Julia Kemp Pine, of Crapstone, Yelverton, Devon £308,432
(The residue equally between the Cancer Research Campaign, Arthritis and Rheumatism Council, R.S.P.B., R.N.I.B., Multiple Sclerosis Society and the British Retinitis Pigmentosa Society)

Mr. William Frank Pinn, of Gravesend, Kent £1,392,543
(The residue to establish a fund, the income to be distributed as minimum payments of £25 on 1st June and 1st December each year to needy pensioners living in Gravesend and surrounding districts)

Mr. Dennis Edward Pollard of Webheath, Redditch, Worcs. £191,573
(The residue to the R.A.F. Benevolent Fund, "in memory of The Few in the Battle of Britain")

Miss Jane Port, of Bexhill on Sea, East Sussex £2,998,090
(£50,000 to the R.N.L.I., £10,000 each to the Imperial Cancer Research Fund, the National Library for the Blind and the Friends of the Poor and Gentlefolk's Help, £5,000 each to the R.S.P.C.A. and P.D.S.A., and the residue to the National Trust)

Mr. Reginald Richard Rendell, of South Wonston, Hants. £165,432
(The residue to S.S.A.F.A.)

Mrs. Sarah Robson, of Cheyne Walk, London, S.W.10 .... £121,728
(The residue to the Hadassah Hospital, Jerusalem)

Mr. Richard Lionel Burdon-Sanderson, of Constantine Bay, Cornwall £981,924
(£5,000 to the Duchy Hospital, Truro, and the residue to Middlesex Hospital General School, to establish a fund for the further advances in methods of medical education, but not where live animals are used)

Charles Dutton, 7th Baron Sherborne, of Aldsworth, Gloucs. £7,025,347
(The residue to the National Trust)

Mrs. Mary Catherine Shoveller, of Lovedean, Portsmouth, Hants £108,266
(The residue to the Sue Ryder Foundation at Bordean House, Langrish, Petersfield, for the funding of beds there)

Mr. Evan Henry Sims, late of Cimla, Neath, West Glamorgan £194,519
(The residue equally between the Neath Local Committee of the Cancer Research Campaign, and the Welsh National School of Medicine, Cardiff, for the Department of Cardiology)

Frances Wilson-Smith, of Bournemouth, Dorset £518,215
(The residue to the Poole Body Scanner Appeal, Bournemouth)

Mrs. Phyllis Maud Sprinz, of Ewell, Surrey £268,911
(The residue equally between the Guide Dogs for the Blind Association, N.S.P.C.C., R.S.P.C.A. and the National Canine Defence League)

Mr. Piero Sraffa, F.B.A., of Cambridge £1,592,188
(The residue to Trinity College, Cambridge)

Mr. Ernest Bretherton Sumner, of Leyland, Lancs. £545,103
(The residue to the Salvation Army)

Catherine Denholm Swann, of Harden, Bingley, West Yorks. £189,240
(All her property to the War on Cancer Trust, Bradford University)

Mrs. Vera Templeton, of Cerne Abbas, Dorset £216,022
(£5,000 to the P.D.S.A., and the residue to the Abbeyfield Society)

Dr. Jane Henderson Thompson, of Kenton, Newcastle upon Tyne £227,561
(£10,000 to St. Nicholas Cathedral, Newcastle, and the residue to Aberdeen University, to help to found a Professorial Chair in the Department of Mental Health)

Agnes Enid Timms, of Bexhill on Sea, East Sussex £165,196
(The residue to the Salvation Army)

Kathleen Ellen Vyall, of Lymington, Hants. £303,850
(The residue equally beteen Dr. Barnardo's, the Mission to Seamen, the R.A.F. Escaping Society, St. John's Hostels, the Indian Government Officers (Retired) Association, Help the Aged, Police Dependants Trust, Shelter, Royal National Mission to Deep Sea Fishermen, Royal British Legion, R.N.L.I., Church Army, Sea Cadet Association, British and Foreign Bible Society, S.S.A.F.A., R.U.K.B.A., King George's Fund for Sailors and the Hampshire Association for the Care of the Blind)

Mrs. Hilda May Vyvyan, of Wateringbury, Maidstone, Kent £179,784
(The residue to the R.N.L.I., for a lifeboat in the Orkneys)

Mr. Frederick Charles Whatford, of Boscombe, Dorset £198,201
(The residue to the R.N.L.I.)

Olive Myra Wiggins, of Cowfold, West Sussex £131,095
(The residue equally between the Royal Ulster Constabulary Benevolent Fund, Belfast, and the Belfast Protestant Relief Fund)

Mr. John Geoffrey McCammon Gillespie Wightman, of Bournemouth, Dorset £530,773
(£5,000 each to the Western Orchestral Society, Poole, and R.S.P.C.A., and the residue to the Methodist Missionary Society)

Mrs. Mary Alicia Lisle Williams, of Slaidburn, Clitheroe, Lancs. £295,133
(£5,000 to the Lancashire East Branch of the R.S.P.C.A., and the residue to the Multiple Sclerosis Society)

Mr. Philip Winstone, of Bournemouth, Dorset £530,373
(The residue to the British Heart Foundation)

Nellie Worwood, of Weston super Mare, Avon £250,116
(£5,000 each to the Multiple Sclerosis Society and Leukaemia Research Fund, and the residue to the Cancer Research Campaign)

Miss Christobel Young, of Talbot Woods, Bournemouth, Dorset £699,797
(£20,000 each to the R.A.F. Association, for the Richard Peck House, Lytham St. Annes, and Immanuel Church, Southbourne; £16,000 each to the Shaftesbury Society, the National Star Centre for Disabled Youth, Cheltenham, the Royal College of Surgeons of England, the Royal College of Physicians, the Salvation Army, the Retired Nurses National Home, Bournemouth, Arthritis and Rheumatism Council, R.N.L.I., Royal Hospital and Home for Incurables, Putney, and the Abbeyfield Poole Society, and three-fourths of the residue to the National Trust, and a fourth of the residue to the Victoria and Albert Museum, London.

BRASS BAND CHAMPIONS

The British Open Brass Band Championships
1984 (Sept.)

Test Piece—*Comedy* (J. Ireland).

1. Grimethorpe Colliery (G. Brand)—195 pts.
2. Black Dyke Mills (Maj. P. Parkes)—193 pts.
3. Fairey Engineering (H. Williams)—192 pts.
4. Brighouse and Rastrick (J. Watson)—191 pts.
5. Desford Colliery Dowty (H. Snell)—190 pts.
6. Foden O.T.S. (H. Snell)—189 pts.

The National Brass Band Championship of Great Britain 1984 (Oct.)

Championship.—Cory (Maj. A. H. Kenney)
Second Section.—Lockwood (P. Kitson)
Third Section.—Bedford (M. Brownbill)
Fourth Section.—Bolden Colliery (G. Rowell)
Youth Section.—West Glamorgan Youth (D. A. Small)

European Championships 1984 (May) Black Dyke Mills (Maj. P. Parkes)

LIFE ASSURANCE AND GENERAL INSURANCE

BRITISH INSURANCE COMPANIES IN 1983

There was again an unsatisfactory underwriting loss amounting to 11·2% (1982—11·3% loss) on worldwide premiums of £12·2 billion. This was partly due to adverse weather, especially in U.S.A., but severe competition against the background of over-capacity and a worldwide economic recession had a continuing adverse effect on premium rates. Taking into account income from general insurance assets, an improved trading surplus of £546 million was achieved.

Premiums increased by 10·3% over 1982, part of this growth being due to the depreciation of sterling against other currencies. This was especially significant for U.S.A. business, where the sterling:dollar exchange rate fell by around 10% over the year. The relatively modest underlying growth rate again reflects continuing competition in world markets and the increasing importance attached by many members to achieving profitability rather than premium growth.

General insurance invested assets rose by 16·3% and at the end of the year stood at £23·4 billion. Overseas investments and the interest arising therefrom were enhanced in terms of sterling by the downward movement of the pound.

RESULTS IN MAJOR TERRITORIES
United Kingdom

Fire and accident business showed an underwriting loss of 7·4% of premiums against a loss of 10·2% of premiums in 1982. The cost of weather losses in the U.K. was lower than for 1982 but household business was affected by a 24% increase in the cost of theft claims at £171 million; the cost has in two years risen by over 50%. The house buildings account was significantly affected by the cost of claims for subsidence damage which, at an estimated £85 million, was at a similar level to 1976, the previous peak year, after allowing for inflation.

The estimated cost of fire damage in 1983 was £566 million. Competition in the commercial fire account again prevented the achievement of profitable underwriting results.

Motor premiums increased by only 3%, an indication of continuing strong competition in the market. The underwriting loss was 6·4% of premiums (1982—4·5% of premiums). Claims frequency continued to rise, showing an increase of about 5% coupled with a rise in the average cost of a private motor claim of approximately 9%.

United States

Allowing for changes in the sterling:dollar exchange rate, fire and accident premiums showed a small fall compared with 1982. The underwriting loss was 21% of premiums. Motor premiums grew by about 9% after allowing for exchange rate changes, with an underwriting loss of 15·9% of premiums. Excessive competition and overcapacity continued to affect the performance of the industry, with rates clearly inadequate for most classes of commercial business. The winter weather losses and Hurricane Alicia also had a severe effect.

Rest of the World

Results varied by territory but overall the underwriting loss reduced to 7·8% of total premiums of £2·7 billion compared with the 1982 loss of 10·0%.

Overseas Earnings

Insurance companies derived 54% of general premium income from their operations overseas, enabling a substantial contribution to be made to U.K. foreign currency earnings. Insurance activities, comprising companies, Lloyd's and brokers, produced invisible earnings of £1,174 million in 1982, the latest published figure.

Long Term Insurance

Invested assets relating to long-term insurance totalled £99·3 billion at market values at 31st December 1983, from which income of £6·4 billion was received, a 9·4% increase over 1982.

NOTE: Insurance company figures refer to British Insurance Association members who transact some 95% of the worldwide business of the British insurance company market.

WORLDWIDE GENERAL PREMIUMS 1982 & 1983

	1982	1983	Increase
	£m	£m	%
Fire and Accident (non-motor)	6,605	7,355	11·4
Motor..	3,642	3,960	8·7
Marine, Aviation and Transport	806	871	8·1
TOTAL	11,053	12,186	10·3

WORLDWIDE UNDERWRITING RESULTS 1982 & 1983

	1982			1983		
	Premiums	Profit/Loss	% of Premiums	Premiums	Profit/Loss	% of Premiums
	£m	£m	%	£m	£m	%
Fire and Accident (non-motor) ...	5,778	−691·2	−12·0	6,243	−698·5	−11·2
Motor..........................	3,620	−300·5	−8·3	3,927	−344·8	−8·8
Marine, Aviation & Transport	806	−82·9	−10·3	871	−84·1	−9·7
Treaty Reinsurance & other 3 year Account business	849	−171·3	−20·2	1,145	−240·1	−21·0
TOTAL	11,053	−1,245·9	−11·3	12,186	−1,367·5	−11·2

WORLDWIDE LONG-TERM PREMIUMS 1982 & 1983

	1982	1983	Increase
	£m	£m	%
Ordinary Long-Term (U.K.)	7,020	8,829	25·8
Ordinary Long-Term (Overseas)	1,426	1,720	20·6
Industrial Long-Term (U.K.)	1,019	1,080	6·0
TOTAL	9,465	11,629	22·9

U.K. UNDERWRITING 1982 & 1983

	1982			1983		
	Premiums	Profit/Loss	% of Premiums	Premiums	Profit/Loss	% of Premiums
	£m	£m	%	£m	£m	%
Fire and Accident (non-motor)	2,771	−282·0	−10·2	3,076	−227·1	−7·4
Motor	1,729	−78·1	−4·5	1,784	−114·2	−6·4
TOTAL	4,500	−360·1	−8·0	4,860	−341·3	−7·0

U.S.A. UNDERWRITING 1982 & 1983

	1982			1983		
	Premiums	Profit/Loss	% of Premiums	Premiums	Profit/Loss	% of Premiums
	£m	£m	%	£m	£m	%
Fire and Accident (non-motor)	1,429	−221·6	−15·5	1,540	−322·9	−21·0
Motor	873	−149·3	−17·1	1,058	−167·7	−15·9
TOTAL	2,302	−370·9	−16·1	2,598	−490·6	−18·9

REST OF THE WORLD UNDERWRITING 1982 & 1983

	1982			1983		
	Premiums	Profit/Loss	% of Premiums	Premiums	Profit/Loss	% of Premiums
	£m	£m	%	£m	£m	%
Fire and Accident (non-motor)	1,578	−187·6	−11·9	1,627	−148·5	−9·1
Motor	1,018	−73·1	−7·2	1,085	−62·9	−5·8
TOTAL	2,596	−260·7	−10·0	2,712	−211·4	−7·8

LLOYD'S OF LONDON

Lloyds of London is an incorporated society of private underwriters who provide an international market for almost any type of insurance. Ships, aircraft, oil rigs, cargo of all descriptions, motor cars, civil engineering projects, fire, personal accident and third party liability are a few random examples of the everyday risks placed at Lloyd's which currently bring some £4,000 million of premiums to underwriters each year. Three-quarters of this business comes from outside Great Britain and makes a valuable contribution to the country's balance of payments.

Today, as it was three centuries ago, a policy is subscribed at Lloyd's by private individuals with unlimited liability. Now that Lloyd's members are numbered in their thousands, however, the method of underwriting is the same only in principle. The merchant of the past, signing policies as a sideline to his main business, has long since given way to the specialist underwriter who accepts risks at Lloyd's on behalf of members (often referred to as "names") grouped in a syndicate. There are currently about 400 syndicates of varying sizes, some with over two thousand names and each managed by an underwriting agent approved by the Council of Lloyd's.

Lloyd's membership today is drawn from many sources. Industry, commerce and the professions are strongly represented while many members work at Lloyd's either on the broking or the underwriting side.

Underwriting membership of Lloyd's is open to men and women of any nationality provided that they meet the stringent financial requirements of the Society, or Corporation, of Lloyd's. Assets of up to £225,000 have to be shown and a deposit lodged with the Corporation as security for underwriting liabilities. This deposit, which must be in the form of approved securities, is determined at a percentage of the member's annual premium income, ranging from 25% for an "external" member resident in the United Kingdom, to 50% for a name working in the Lloyd's market and showing nominal means.

Lloyd's is incorporated by Act of Parliament (Lloyd's Acts 1871–1982) and governed by a Council of 28 members, 16 of whom are elected from and by underwriting members working at Lloyd's and 8 from and by the external membership. Four Council members are nominated by the Council subject to confirmation by the Governor of the Bank of England.

The Council is responsible for managing the Society's affairs, for regulating the Lloyd's market, for the election of new underwriting members, and for establishing the requirements of membership and the rules governing the financial security to be provided by those doing business at Lloyd's.

The Corporation is a non-profit-making body chiefly financed by its members' subscriptions. It provides the premises, administrative staff and services enabling Lloyd's underwriting syndicates to conduct their business. It does not, however, assume corporate liability for the risks accepted by its members, who remain responsible to the full extent of their personal means for their underwriting affairs.

Lloyd's syndicates have no direct contact with the public. All business is transacted through some 270 firms of insurance brokers accredited by the Corporation of Lloyd's.

Lloyd's also provides the most comprehensive shipping intelligence service available in the world. The enormous volume of shipping and other information received from Lloyd's Agents, shipowners, news agencies and other sources throughout the world, is collated and distributed to newspapers, radio and television services, as well as to the maritime and commercial communities in general.

This information is compiled, edited and published by a subsidiary company, Lloyd's of London Press Ltd., and distributed worldwide. "Lloyd's List" is London's oldest daily newspaper and contains news of general commercial interest as well as shipping information. "Lloyd's Shipping Index" also published daily, lists some 20,000 ocean-going vessels in alphabetical order and gives the latest known report of each.

LLOYD'S THREE YEAR BUSINESS SUMMARY

	Premiums	Underwriting Profit	Investment Income and Appreciation
	£'000	£'000	£'000
Short Term Life			
1978	1,286	257	87
1979	1,766	450	194
1980	2,051	585	286
Accident & Health			
1978	77,723	13,786	5,966
1979	103,554	14,084	8,819
1980	121,390	9,082	13,163
Motor Vehicle Damage & Liability			
1978	222,362	16,968	15,256
1979	273,072	26,882	21,710
1980	325,342	38,722	34,075
Ships, Aircraft Damage & Liability & Transit			
1978	897,454	59,497	67,823
1979	1,184,438	18,324	92,839
1980	1,568,384	64,682	147,548
All other Insurance Business			
1978	964,456	20,303	80,153
1979	1,296,638	(22,607)	110,063
1980	1,636,205	(91,323)	179,355

LLOYD'S MEMBERSHIP SYNDICATES AND BROKERS 1977–1983

	1983	1982	1981	1980	1979	1978	1977
Membership	21,601	20,145	19,136	18,552	17,278	14,091	10,730
Including: Overseas	3,013	2,181	1,982	1,841	1,650	1,209	740
Syndicates	417	431	427	437	404	363	330
Lloyd's Brokers	272	266	270	265	268	269	267

LLOYD'S GLOBAL UNDERWRITING ACCOUNTS

Net Premium Income			
	1980 A/C	1981 A/C	1982 A/C
	£'000	£'000	£'000
Life	1,458	1,246	2,284
Accident & Health	89,046	97,958	73,024
Motor Vehicle Damage & Liability	237,060	265,481	246,385
Ships, Aircraft Damage & Liability and Transit	877,202	951,282	748,378
All Other Insurance Business	657,521	745,747	607,496
TOTAL	1,862,287	2,061,714	1,677,567

LIFE ASSURANCE IN 1983

Total new premiums for life assurances and annuities increased in 1983 by 37% to £5,400 million. New sums assured rose by 19% to £84,600 million and new annuities per annum by 3% to £1,720 million. The following figures include all forms of life assurance and annuities, including linked-life assurance and occupational pension and life assurance schemes in the United Kingdom.

	1983 £m	1982 £m
Total new premiums— annual and single	5,400	3,930
Benefits secured by these premiums—		
New sums assured	84,600	71,100
New annuities per annum, deferred and immediate	1,720	1,670

HOME SERVICE INSURANCE IN 1982

The following figures are based on returns from 19 "home service" insurance offices, which together transact over 99% of industrial (collected premium) life business. While they, unlike all other insurers, transact industrial life business, they also carry on a very substantial volume of ordinary life and general insurance, much of it in policyholders' homes through the field staffs.

	1982 £m	1981 £m
Industrial Life Business		
1. Premium Income	1,019·4	950·0
2. Investment Income (Gross)	645·3	556·9
3. Industrial Assurance Fund as at the end of the year (after transfers to and from investment reserves etc.)	5,790·0	5,152·8
4. New Business:		
(a) New Sums Assured	3,877·2	3,505·0
(b) New Premiums per annum	226·5	210·3
5. Payments to policyholders:		
(a) On death	160·2	143·1
(b) On maturity	309·4	264·1
(c) On surrender	267·6	209·5
TOTAL	737·2	616·7

NEW LINKED LIFE ASSURANCE BUSINESS
ANNUAL STATISTICS

	Year ended Dec. 31, 1980	Year ended Dec. 31, 1981	Year ended Dec. 31, 1982	Year ended Dec. 31, 1983
	£m	£m	£m	£m
1. *New Annual Premiums:*				
(a) Assurances & Annuities	141	180	217	302
(b) Personal Pensions (See note below)	30	54	65	73
Total new annual premiums:	171	234	282	375
2. *New Single Premiums:*				
(a) Assurances & Annuities	312	548	740	1,440
(b) Personal Pensions (See note below)	13	40	57	71
Total new single premiums:	325	588	797	1,511

NOTE: Personal pensions are contracts available to the self-employed and those not in pensionable employment.

POLICYHOLDERS PROTECTION BOARD
Aldermary House, Queen Street, London E.C.4

The Policyholders Protection Act 1975 put into effect the scheme whereby private policyholders of companies in liquidation will normally be granted 90 per cent (100 per cent for any policyholder in the case of compulsory insurance) of the benefits due under their policies at the date of winding up. The scheme will be financed mainly by a compulsory levy on insurance companies limited to a maximum of 1 per cent of their annual net premium income. The Board consists of five members, of whom three are drawn from the management of insurance companies and at least one must be qualified to represent the interests of policyholders.

INSURANCE COMPANY INVESTMENTS
Long Term Funds

	1982 £m	1982 %	1983 £m	1983 %
British Government authority securities	21,681	26·4	24,487	24·7
Foreign and Commonwealth Government, provincial and municipal stocks	2,739	3·3	3,695	3·7
Debentures, loan stocks, preference and guaranteed stocks and shares	3,734	4·6	4,589	4·6
Ordinary stocks and shares	28,065	34·2	37,620	37·9
Mortgages	5,100	6·2	5,550	5·6
Real property and ground rents	17,267	21·1	18,850	19·0
Other investments	3,461	4·2	4,506	4·5
TOTAL INVESTED FUNDS	82,047	100·0	99,297	100·0
INCOME FROM INVESTMENTS	5,886		6,441	

NOTE: The above figures are at market values.

INSURANCE COMPANY INVESTMENTS
Other Funds

	1982 £m	1982 %	1983 £m	1983 %
British Government authority securities	3,777	18·8	4,128	17·7
Foreign and Commonwealth Government, provincial and municipal stocks	3,709	18·5	4,255	18·2
Debentures, loan stocks, preference and guaranteed stocks and shares	2,957	14·7	3,232	13·8
Ordinary stocks and shares	5,100	25·4	6,690	28·6
Mortgages	742	3·7	786	3·4
Real property and ground rents	2,041	10·2	2,153	9·2
Other investments	1,757	8·7	2,117	9·1
TOTAL INVESTED FUNDS	20,083	100·0	23,361	100·0
INCOME FROM INVESTMENTS	1,734		1,913	

NOTE: The above figures are at market values.

THE LIFE ASSURANCE COMPANIES

The list on the following pages contains the names of all the more important British life offices, and of Commonwealth offices (marked C) which transact life business in this country.

Class of business. The second column shows whether the company is conducted on the mutual system whereby the whole of the divisible profit is allotted to participating policyholders (M), or whether the company has proprietors by whom part (usually a very small proportion) of such profits received (P). Life offices transacting other business are marked (O) in this column. In such cases the life funds are kept separately, and are not liable for the claims of other departments. The share capital is usually liable for the claims of all branches. Those having an industrial branch are indicated by letter (I).

Figures. These are taken from the latest annual accounts available at date of going to press and in the majority of cases refer to annual reports for the financial year ended December 31, 1983.

Life funds. The amounts of these funds, though of interest, are not in themselves a sufficient indication of the financial stability of a company, which cannot be judged unless liabilities are actually compared with assets.

Premium income. The annual premium income is in all cases stated after deduction of the amount paid to other companies for reassuring parts of the risk.

Consideration for annuities.—These are the amounts received to provide various types of annuities.

Interest.—The rate of interest earned is important for comparison with the rate assumed in valuing liabilities, since the greater the margin between these rates the greater is the surplus available from this source bonus declaration. The rate of interest given is before deduction of Income Tax except where marked (N)—net.

Valuation.—The valuation returns which are required to be made by the companies to the Department of Trade and Industry indicate liability under existing policies, after making allowance for the amounts to be paid and received. It is assumed that deaths will occur in accordance with a mortality table (various tables are used) and that interest will be earned at a certain rate. If a company assumes that it will earn a high rate of interest in the future the net liability will appear less than if it assumes a low rate, while the liability on account of mortality appears greater by some tables than by others. The position of an office is most satisfactory when a stringent basis of valuation is adopted, because the margin between the calculated and experienced liability is larger and the surplus available for bonuses is greater. The lower the rate of interest assumed the more stringent is the valuation. The foregoing remarks, however, do not apply in the case of an office which has adopted a Bonus Reserve Valuation.

Types of policy.—Although there are scores of life offices in Britain each offering their own particular products under a wide variety of labels, there are really only four basic types of contract. These are:

1. "Term" assurance (sometimes called "temporary" assurance). With this type of policy the assurer, in return for a regular premium agrees to pay the sum assured if the person assured should die within the term of years stated by the policy.

Such policies take care of the temporary need for protection of the family while the children are growing up, and the family is therefore most vulnerable. The commonest and most popular forms are to cover the mortgage on the family home or to assume a regular tax-free income for the family over so many years should the breadwinner die. This is much the cheapest form of life assurance because the majority of policies invariably do not result in claims.

2. "Whole-life" assurance is one under which the assurer undertakes to keep the assurance in force provided the premiums are paid for the whole life of the assured. They will then pay the agreed sum whenever death takes place. This costs a good deal more than term, naturally. All policies end in claims.

3. "Endowment" assurance. This contract really is one which uses a fund for saving to a particular target sum by a particular future date and at the same time secures payment of the sum assured should the saver die before that date arrives. In return for the continued payment of a regular premium over a fixed number of years, the assurer agrees to pay the sum assured at the end of that time, or earlier if the assured person should die. The bulk of an endowment assurance premium is savings; consequently the premium of such a contract is a lot higher than that for a whole life assurance.

4. "Annuities". Life assurance can be divided broadly speaking into death or survival benefits. Death benefits are paid to a policyholder's dependants if and when he dies. Survival benefits are paid to the policyholder himself either in the form of a cash sum when he reaches a certain age or in the form of a guaranteed annual income for life, which is known as an annuity. Pensions are annuities of a kind and a very large proportion of the pensions due to people are being and will be paid by funds run by life offices.

INDUSTRIAL COMPANIES

Established	Class	Name of Office	Life Funds	Life Premium Income	Rate of interest % Earned	Interest % assumed at Valuation
			£m	£,000		
1866	PO	Britannic	453·6	86,424	12·80	3·00
1862	M	City of Glasgow†	17·3	2,251	11·26	3·00
1867	MIO	Co-operative	854·2	159,500	10·20	3·00
1939	P	Irish Life†	83·8	12,337	11·70	4·00
1843	M	Liverpool Victoria	610·0	74,593	11·55	3·50
1869	PO	London and Manchester	172·0	28,489	—	3·00
1864	PO	Pearl	872·1	160,674	12·25	3·00 & 3·50
1891	M	Pioneer Mutual	33·8	3,062	8·24	3·00
1848	PO	Prudential	1,910·5	320,500	12·00	3·00 & 4·50
1911	MI	Reliance Mutual	15·6	2,357	10·50	2·50 & 3·25
1850	M	Royal Liver	266·4	45,953	11·49	3·75
1861	MO	Royal London	486·7	45,952	12·04	2·50
1908	P	United Friendly	321·1	83,468	10·80	3·00
1841	MO	Wesleyan and General	134·8	22,182	12·22	3·00

†1982 Figures.

INDUSTRIAL LIFE NEW BUSINESS 1983

Name of Office	No. of policies issued	Net sums assured	Net annual premiums
		£	£
Britannic	418,505	435,540,000	24,558,000
City of Glasgow†	9,989	8,470,000	461,906
Co-operative	449,397	522,600,000	31,600,000
Irish Life†	49,668	73,789,000	2,427,000
Liverpool Victoria	238,100	178,100,000	14,244,000
London and Manchester	148,441	106,880,000	7,234,000
Pearl	469,853	398,507,000	32,986,000
Pioneer Mutual†	2,211	2,278,117	94,121
Prudential	818,675	1,845,800,000	72,300,000
Reliance Mutual	17,404	10,725,000	747,000
Royal Liver	139,158	101,910,391	8,280,704
Royal London	116,569	160,446,000	9,261,000
United Friendly	492,902	288,668,000	88,239,000
Wesleyan and General	79,871	55,210,375	4,565,528

†1982 Figures.

PRINCIPAL LIFE ASSURANCE COMPANIES

Established	Class	Name of Office	Annual Accounts				
			Life and Annuity Funds	Life Premium Income	Consideration for Annuities	Rate of Interest % Earned	Interest % assumed at Valuation
			£m	£000	£000		
1961	P	Abbey Life*	882·6	144,289	51,502	—	Various
1921	P	American Life†	216·0	124,161	9,291	11·49	Various
1849	M	Australian Mutual Prov. (C)	123·6	11,265	80	13·25	Various
1925	PO	Avon	32·0	3,340	560	11·71	Various
1965	P	Barclays Life	326·0	51,800	—	5·75	—
1866	PIO	Britannic (Ord.)	223·7	26,288	198	12·80	3·00–6·00
1920	PO	British National	15·7	2,919	—	10·00	Various
1847	M	Canada Life	2,330·1	142,328	201,650	11·27	Various
1963	P	Cannon†	162·3	35,777	3,801	8·50	Various
1963	P	Chartered Life†	7·8	2,248		11·88	
1862	MI	City of Glasgow (Ord.)†	11·1	2,071	30,154	11·26	3·00
1824	M	Clerical, Medical Group	1,234·8	60,000	189,800	7·40	7·00
1873	M	Colonial Mutual (C)	488·0		82,000	12·00	3·50–7·00
1861	PO	Commercial Union	3,510·4	203,671	197,095	9·62	3·00
1871	M	Confederation Life	1,981·0	110,470	71,380	10·79	Various
1867	MIO	Co-operative (Ord.)	767·8	97,800	10,200	10·10	2·75
1900	M	Crown Life†	100·0	38,000	17,000	15·00	Various
1899	PO	Crusader	350·5	54,157	17,890	10·90	Various
1904	PO	Eagle Star	2,212·1	251,900	62,400	10·06	Various
1887	MO	Ecclesiastical	34·7	3,800	1,700	7·30	3·50
1901	P	Economic†	15·3	2,409	329	9·50	5·00
1762	M	Equitable Life	1,099·4		219,400	10·00	Various
1832	M	Friends' Provident	1,220·1	110,686	72,047	11·99	2·75
1899	M	FS Assurance	45·9	6,100	3,000	10·80	2·50
1848	P	Gresham Life	141·5	21,163	509	11·30	3·50 & 4·50
1821	PO	Guardian Royal Exchange	2,795·4	223,400	100,900	7·40	Various
1965	P	Hambro Life	2,234·0	255,100	196,800		Various
1960	P	Hill Samuel	381·6	44,051	14,998	9·90	Various
1932	P	Ideal†	1·1	150		18·03	3·00
1896	P	Imperial Life of Canada (C)	1,161·1		177,198	12·08	Various
1935	P	Insurance Corp. Life	124·8	68,981	5,812	9·20	4·00
1939	PI	Irish Life (Ord.)†	981·0	64,903	118,842	9·64	3·50
1836	PO	Legal and General	2,893·0	365,000	23,000	12·50	Various
1838	P	Life Assoc. of Scotland	210·6		31,682	10·40	2·50–6·50
1843	MI	Liverpool Victoria (Ord.)	130·5	16,476		11·60	3·50
1971	P	Lloyd's Life	154·8	42,168	6,015	8·40	Various
1869	PIO	London and Manchester (Ord.)	409·7		70,990	—	Various
1806	M	London Life	864·5	77,700	18,500	9·11 (N)	Various
1887	M	Manufacturers Life (C)†	3,573·0	221,600	270,400	—	Various
1961	P	M & G Assurance	208·0	29,800	—	—	—
1852	M	MGM Assurance	318·2	20,686	75,548	11·40	Various
1884	M	Medical, Sickness	47·8	5,699	1,267	11·65	Various
1890	M	Nalgo Insurance†	17·4	1,449	—	6·10	2·50
1910	MO	National Farmers Union	316·6	17,471	11,289	11·43	Various
1869	M	National Mut. Life of Australasia	174·8	10,515	134	—	Various
1830	M	National Mutual	202·7	18,904	15,259	11·04	Various
1835	M	National Provident	893·9	32,600	112,000	10·50	Various
1924	PIO	New Ireland	155·1	32,269		—	Various
1808	M	Norwich Union	3,772·1		578,100	11·16	4·00–9·00
1864	PIO	Pearl (Ord.)	967·8	111,395	16,035	12·24	Various
1782	PO	Phoenix	1,101·4	164,522	8,796	12·80	3·25 & 3·50
1891	MI	Pioneer Mutual (Ord.)	98·0	19,521	—	10·74	3·00
1877	P	Provident Life Assoc.	137·8	22,629	457	9·58	3·25–7·50
1840	M	Provident Mutual	1,074·1	43,420	94,221		Various
1848	PIO	Prudential Group (Ord.)	7,171·0	900,300	79,200	10·60	Various
1911	MI	Reliance Mutual (Ord.)	46·7	6,639	2	8·00	2·75 & 4·25
1845	PO	Royal Life	1,917·2	135,990	122,652	10·20	2·50–3·75
1850	MI	Royal Liver (Ord.)	95·3	13,625	—	11·49	3·75
1861	MIO	Royal London (Ord.)	285·6	40,211	75	10·58	3·00
1887	M	Royal Nat. Pen. Fund for Nurses	130·5	13,400	2,000	12·10	6·25
1963	P	Save & Prosper	531·9	58,633	31,272	—	Various
1965	P	Schroder	186·2	36,588	20,068	6·40	Various
1826	M	Scottish Amicable	2,070·0	454,000	—	—	Various
1831	M	Scottish Equitable	947·8	28,875	104,845	8·69	Various
1881	M	Scottish Life	511·9	59,892	12,718	10·23	4·25
1883	MO	Scottish Mutual	442·8	44,724	7,869	10·91	Various
1837	M	Scottish Provident	822·0	64,200	39,500	11·30	Various
1815	M	Scottish Widows'	2,840·4	114,784	187,345	9·20	Various
1964	P	Stalwart Assurance	18·1	128	5,488	12·30	10·00
1825	M	Standard	5,246·0		659,706	9·84	Various
1710	PO	Sun Alliance	1,356·5	245,968	6,563		Various
1810	P	Sun Life Ass. Group	2,796·0		390,026	10·71	Various
1865	M	Sun Life of Canada (C)	5,679·4	302,163	133,935	10·41	Various
1936	P	Teachers'	21·4	5,350	—	12·30	2·50
1969	P	Trident Life	245·5	106,608	8	7·50	12·00
1908	P	United Friendly (Ord.)	95·4	14,557	—	10·80	3·00
1840	M	UK Provident	920·5	116,100	87,800	5·80	Various
1841	MIO	Wesleyan & General (Ord.)	92·9	9,813	703	13·19	Various
1837	P	Yorkshire-General	602·5	52,115	42,641	13·12	3·50
1960	P	Zurich Life	59·5	26,094	375	11·70	3·75 & 4·00

† 1982 figures   * 1981 figures   (C) denotes Commonwealth Office

LIFE ASSURANCE NEW BUSINESS 1983

Name of Office	No. of policies issued	Net sums assured	Net annual premiums	Net single premiums
		£000	£000	£000
Abbey Life*	197,776	1,308,802	43,266	113,270
American Life†	206,735	3,397,047	38,957	10,983
Australian Mutual Provident (C)	9,899	103,754	2,188	58
Avon	3,213	36,251	700	123
Barclays Life	50,272	282,000	14,600	20,700
Britannic (Ord.)	43,199	242,549	7,121	359
British National	10,549	49,922	1,194	934
Canada Life	41,547	2,470,451	21,240	181,634
Cannon†	27,928	254,126	4,911	21,743
Chartered Life†	2,864	96,682	496	3,371
City of Glasgow (Ord.)†	1,542	11,250	240	1,106
Clerical, Medical Group	63,496	2,030,100	32,900	72,900
Colonial Mutual (C)	60,000	711,000	16,000	10,000
Commercial Union	178,908	4,419,121	33,173	31,107
Confederation Life	67,699	3,427,630	95,590	41,010
Co-operative (Ord.)	121,546	954,100	25,100	28
Crown Life†	35,000	346,000	9,000	7,000
Crusader	29,000	1,645,000	14,700	24,000
Eagle Star	91,030	3,277,000	53,600	98,600
Ecclesiastical	3,172	17,700	860	1,930
Economic†	4,694	60,521	254	1,423
Equitable Life	50,239	997,900	65,800	47,700
Friends' Provident	120,807	2,581,100	54,000	27,000
FS Assurance	6,127	101,900	2,800	3,200
Gresham Life	24,835	350,681	6,147	1,081
Guardian Royal Exchange	265,000	5,841,300	65,800	101,800
Hambro Life	188,000	3,550,000	79,700	161,000
Hill Samuel	44,792	563,006	7,271	29,467
Ideal†	921	5,987	92	—
Imperial Life of Canada (C)	50,923	1,428,608	38,327	56,834
Insurance Corp. Life	13,032	269,474	3,316	68,118
Irish Life (Ord.)†		1,372,945	30,329	64,197
Legal & General	265,000	2,773,000	64,000	32,000
Life Association of Scotland	13,165	277,394	6,890	5,128
Liverpool Victoria (Ord.)	24,629	111,894	4,013	—
Lloyd's Life	67,870	403,756	8,330	27,460
London & Manchester (Ord.)	60,983	443,009	14,626	33,893
London Life	26,700	494,600	15,300	42,800
Manufacturers Life (UK) (C)†	27,885	270,000	7,108	20,963
M & G Assurance	20,620	95,900	3,700	14,600
MGM Assurance	33,432	161,243	9,972	68,581
Medical, Sickness	8,110	117,433	1,543	1,290
Nalgo Insurance†	2,488	28,270	230	—
National Farmers Union	10,625	91,329	4,103	3,443
National Mut. Life of Australasia	12,842	183,855	2,980	351
National Mutual	21,795	312,827	10,882	2,515
National Provident	44,990	361,922	20,924	55,678
New Ireland	44,309		5,000	1,113
Norwich Union	339,850	5,461,835	112,053	177,989
Pearl (Ord.)	89,594	635,275	24,830	24,048
Phoenix		4,111,000	32,400	52,100
Pioneer Mutual (Ord.)	24,032	191,354	5,088	4,591
Provident Life Association	18,140	279,433	5,628	3,846
Provident Mutual	90,857	991,288	31,609	22,759
Prudential Group (Ord.)	446,820	8,058,500	191,300	210,800
Reliance Mutual (Ord.)	10,404	88,696	2,083	1,175
Royal Life	154,000	2,345,900	57,700	84,100
Royal Liver (Ord.)	17,715	71,836	2,918	8
Royal London (Ord.)	38,831	351,001	9,725	5,734
Royal Nat. Pen. Fund for Nurses	13,989	37,700	2,900	1,900
Save & Prosper	52,924	227,524	10,257	53,553
Schroder	46,654	197,769	14,401	28,920
Scottish Amicable	190,000	2,200,000	75,000	208,000
Scottish Equitable	—	564,420	22,960	44,190
Scottish Life	29,712	686,694	17,798	12,718
Scottish Mutual	33,921	784,500	14,330	7,870
Scottish Provident	109,000	690,000	15,100	31,800
Scottish Widows'	44,287	—	17,696	40,294
Stalwart Assurance	3,659	29,340	51*	5,523
Standard	214,800		88,057	190,825
Sun Alliance		2,372,112	53,834	55,554
Sun Life Assurance Group	135,476	1,276,446	31,015	81,176
Sun Life of Canada (C)	211,192	9,488,357	105,500	113,000
Teachers'	2,705	19,420	311	3,234
Trident Life	34,464	291,202	9,011	49,726
United Friendly (Ord.)	23,752	220,059	2,830	—
UK Provident	94,863	1,927,300	41,300	87,800
Wesleyan & General (Ord.)	10,893	98,727	2,763	269
Yorkshire-General	99,000	2,974,697	27,334	17,315
Zurich Life	18,737	758,462	8,161	37

† 1982 figures   * 1981 figures   (C) denotes Commonwealth Office

DIRECTORY OF INSURANCE COMPANIES

The class of Insurance undertaken is shown in the second column as follows: A—Accident (which includes Motor, Employers' Liability, etc.); F—Fire (including Burglary); L—Life; and M—Marine. A number of offices are now included in a Group—the initials of which appear after the name. The main Groups are as follows—E.S.—Eagle Star; C.U.—Commercial Union; G.R.E.—Guardian Royal Exchange; G.A.—General Accident; N.U.—Norwich Union; R—Royal; S.A.—Sun Alliance & London.

Est'd.	Nature of Business	Name of Company	Address
1961	L	Abbey Life	Holdenhurst Rd., Bournemouth.
1951	AFM	Albion	Plantation House, 31/35 Fenchurch St., E.C.3.
1824	AFM	Alliance ...S.A.	1 Bartholomew Lane, E.C.2.
1921	L	American Life	2–8 Altyre Road, Croydon.
1960	AFLM	Ansvar	St. Leonards Rd., Eastbourne.
1808	ALFM	Atlas ...G.R.E.	Royal Exchange, E.C.3.
1849	L	Australian Mutual Provident	A.M.P. Ho., Dingwall Rd., Croydon.
1925	AFL	Avon	1 Church St., Stratford-upon-Avon.
1905	AFM	Baptist	4 Southampton Row, W.C.1.
1965	L	Barclays	252 Romford Rd., E.7.
1883	AFM	Beacon ...S.A.	1 Bartholomew Lane, E.C.2.
1894	AFM	Bedford General	Zurich House, Stanhope Rd., Portsmouth.
1925	AFM	Black Sea and Baltic	65 Fenchurch St., E.C.3.
1959	AFLM	Bradford	North Park, Halifax.
1866	AFL	Britannic	Moor Green, Moseley, Birmingham.
1863	M	British & Foreign Marine ...R.	New Hall Place, Liverpool.
1878	Machinery	British Engine, &c ...R.	Longbridge House, Manchester 4.
1854	AFL	British Equitable ...G.R.E.	Royal Exchange, E.C.3.
1904	AFM	British General ...C.U.	St. Helen's, 1 Undershaft, E.C.3.
1888	AFM	British Law ...S.A.	1 Bartholomew Lane, E.C.2.
1896	L	British Life	Reliance House, Tunbridge Wells, Kent.
1920	AFL	British Nat. Life	Harlands Rd., Haywards Heath, W. Sussex.
1908	AFM	British Oak ...G.R.E.	Royal Exchange, E.C.3.
1881	A	Builders' Accident	31 & 32 Bedford St., Strand, W.C.2.
1805	AFLM	Caledonian ...G.R.E.	Royal Exchange, E.C.3.
1934	AFM	Cambrian ...G.R.E.	Royal Exchange, E.C.3.
1847	AL	Canada Life	Canada Life House, Potters Bar, Herts.
1963	L	Cannon	1 Olympic Way, Wembley.
1903	AFM	Car & General ...G.R.E.	Royal Exchange, E.C.3.
1885	AFM	Century	4–5 King William St., E.C.4.
1963	L	Chartered Life	114/116 St. Mary St., Cardiff.
1922	AFMex-motor	Chemists' Mutual	321 Chase Rd., Southgate, N.14.
1862	L	City of Glasgow Friendly	200 Bath Street, Glasgow C.2.
1824	L	Clerical, Medical & Gen.	15 St. James's Square, S.W.1.
1873	L & Pers. Acc.	Colonial Mutual	24 Ludgate Hill, E.C.4.
1919	AFM	Comrcl. Ins. Co. of Ireland	5 Donegall Square, S., Belfast.
1861	AFLM	Commercial Union	St. Helen's, 1 Undershaft, E.C.3.
1871	L	Confederation	50/52 Chancery Lane, W.C.2.
1891	AF	Congregational	21–22 Apsley Crescent, Bradford 8.
1867	AFLM	Co-operative	Miller St., Manchester.
1905	AFM	Cornhill	32 Cornhill, E.C.3.
1900	L	Crown Life	Crown Life House, Woking, Surrey.
1899	AFLM	Crusader	Woodhatch, Reigate, Surrey.
1908	AFM	Dominion	92/94 Gracechurch St., E.C.3.
1904	AFLM	Eagle Star	1 Threadneedle St., E.C.2.
1887	AFL	Ecclesiastical	Beaufort House, Brunswick Rd., Gloucester.
1901	AFLM	Economic	125/135 Fenchurch St., E.C.3.
1823	AFM	Edinburgh ...C.U.	St. Helen's, 1 Undershaft, E.C.3.
1880	AFM	Employers' Liability ...C.U.	St. Helen's, 1 Undershaft, E.C.3.
1932	Animal Ins.	Equine and Livestock	610–616 Chiswick High Rd, W.4.
1762	L	Equitable Life	4 Coleman St., E.C.2.
1844	L	Equity & Law	20 Lincoln's Inn Fields, W.C.2.
1802	AF	Essex & Suffolk ...G.R.E.	Royal Exchange, E.C.3.
1894	AFM	Excess	13 Fenchurch Avenue, E.C.3.
1925	AFL	Federation Mutual	29 Linkfield Lane, Redhill, Surrey.
1890	AF	Fine Art & General ...C.U.	St. Helen's, 1 Undershaft, E.C.3.
1832	L	Friends' Prov	Pixham End, Dorking, Surrey.
1899	L	FS Assurance	190 West George St., Glasgow.
1885	AFM	General Accident	General Buildings, Perth, Scotland.
1848	L	Gresham Life	2–6 Prince of Wales Rd., Bournemouth.
1910	AFM	Gresham Fire & Accident	11 Queen Victoria St., E.C.4.
1840	AFM	Guarantee Society ...G.A.	36–37 Old Jewry, E.C.2.
1821	ALFM	Guardian ...G.R.E.	Royal Exchange, E.C.3.

Est'd.	Nature of Business	Name of Company	Address
1965	L	Hambro	Station Rd, Swindon.
1908	AFM	Hibernian	Haddington Road, Dublin, 4.
1960	L	Hill Samuel	NLA Tower, Addiscombe Rd., Croydon.
1966	AF	Household & General ..... S.A.	1 Bartholomew Lane, E.C.2.
1932	FL	Ideal	Pitmaston, Birmingham, 13.
1896	L	Imperial Life of Canada	London Road, Guildford, Surrey.
1935	AFM	Insurance Corporation Life	Burlington Road, Dublin 4.
1939	L	Irish Life	Lr. Abbey St., Dublin 2.
1880	A	Iron Trades Employers'	Iron Trades Ho., 21–24 Grosvenor Pl., S.W.1.
1845	AF	Law Fire ..................S.A.	1 Bartholomew Lane, E.C.2.
1806	AFM	Law Union & Rock ....R.	1 North John St., Liverpool, 2.
1907	AFM	Legal ....R.	1 North John St., Liverpool, 2.
1836	AFLM	Legal and General	Temple Court, 11 Queen Victoria St., E.C.4.
1970	L	Liberty Life	Kingmaker House, Station Rd., New Barnet.
1890	AFLM	Licenses & General	14 Bonhill Street, E.C.2.
1838	L	Life Assoc. of Scotland	10 George St., Edinburgh.
1836	AFM	L'pool & London & Globe. ....R.	New Hall Place, Liverpool.
1918	AFM	Liverpool Marine & General....	4–5 King William St., E.C.4.
1843	L	Liverpool Victoria Friendly	Victoria House, Southampton Row., W.C.1.
1971	L	Lloyds Life	20 Clifton St., E.C.2
1890	AFM	Local Government Guarantee G.R.E.	Royal Exchange, E.C.3
1836	AFM	Lombard Insurance............	31–35 Fenchurch St., E.C.3.
1720	AFLM	London Assurance .........S.A.	1 Bartholomew Lane, E.C.2.
1869	AFM	London Guar. & Reinsurance ...	4 King William St., E.C.4.
1919	AFM	London & Lancashire..........	New Hall Place, Liverpool.
1806	L	London Life	80 Coleman St., London, E.C.2.
1869	AFL	London & Manchester	Winslade Park, Exeter, Devon.
1860	AFM	London & Provincial Marine G.A.	Lloyd's Building, Lime St., E.C.3.
1862	AFM	London & Scottish .... C.U.	St. Helen's, 1 Undershaft, E.C.3.
1961	L	M & G Assurance	91/99 New London Rd., Chelmsford
1887	L	Manufacturers Life	St. George's Way, Stevenage.
1836	M	Marine....................R.	34–36 Lime St., E.C.3.
1852	L	Marine & General	MGM House, Heene Rd., Worthing.
1864	M	Maritime .... N.U.	Surrey St., Norwich.
1884	L Sickness A	Med., Sickness, Ann. and Life...	7–10 Chandos St., Cavendish Sq., W.1.
1907	Reinsurance	Mercantile & General..........	Moorfields House, Moorfields, E.C.2.
1970	L	Merchant Investors	High Street, Croydon.
1871	M	Merchants' Marine .... C.U.	St. Helens, 1 Undershaft, E.C.3.
1872	AF	Methodist	Brazennose House, Brazennose St., Manchester.
1940	AFM	Minster	Minster House, Arthur St., E.C.4.
1906	AFM	Motor Union ...........G.R.E.	Royal Exchange, E.C.3.
1903	AF	Municipal Mutual	22 Old Queen St., Westminster, S.W.1.
1890	AFL	Nalgo Insurance Association ...	1 Mabledon Place, W.C.1.
1935	L	National Employers' Life.......	Milton Court, Dorking, Surrey.
1914	AFM	National Employers' Mutual ...	N.E.M. House, Mitre Sq., E.C.3.
1910	AFL	National Farmers' Union	Church St., Stratford-upon-Avon.
1863	Fidelity Guar.	Natl. Guaran. & Suretyship C.U.	St. Helen's, 1 Undershaft, E.C.3.
1894	AF	National Ins. & Guarantee Cor..	Heron House, 145 City Rd., E.C.1.
1830	L	National Mutual Life	5 Bow Churchyard (off Cheapside), E.C.4.
1869	L	National Mutual of Australasia .	N.M. House, Serpentine Rd., Poole, Dorset
1835	L	National Provident............	48 Gracechurch St., E.C.3.
1854	Plate Glass	National Provincial .....G.R.E.	Royal Exchange, E.C.3.
1864	Machinery	National Vulcan Eng. Ins. Group.................S.A.	Empire House, St. Martin's-le-Grand, E.C.1.
1921	Naval Officers risks, etc.	Navigators & General ...... E.S.	1 Threadneedle St., E.C.2.
1924	L	New Ireland	11/12 Dawson St., Dublin, 2.
1809	AFLM	North British & Mercantile C.U.	St. Helen's, 1 Undershaft, E.C.3.
1862	FM	North Pacific ...........G.R.E.	Royal Exchange, E.C.3.
1836	AFLM	Northern................. C.U.	St. Helen's, 1 Undershaft, E.C.3.
1797	AFM	Norwich Union Fire...........	Surrey Street, Norwich.
1808	L	Norwich Union Life	Surrey Street, Norwich.
1871	AFM	Ocean Accident .... C.U.	St. Helen's, 1 Undershaft, E.C.3.
1859	M	Ocean Marine .... C.U.	4 Fenchurch Ave., E.C.3.
1931	AFM	Orion	70–72 King William St., E.C.4.
1886	AF	Palatine	108 Cannon St., E.C.4.
1864	AFLM	Pearl........................	High Holborn, W.C.1.
1958	Sickness A	Permanent	7–10 Chandos Street, Cavendish Sq., W.1.
1782	AFLM	Phoenix	Phoenix House, King William St., E.C.4.

Est'd.	Nature of Business	Name of Company	Address
1891	L	Pioneer Mutual	16 Crosby Rd. N., Liverpool.
1920	AFM	Planet Assurance ..........S.A.	1 Bartholomew Lane, E.C.2.
1969	L	Property Growth..............	Leon House, High St., Croydon
1877	L	Prov. Life Assocn. of London ...	266 Bishopsgate, E.C.2.
1840	L	Provident Mutual Life	Wedgwood Way, Stevenage.
1903	AFM	Provincial	Stramongate, Kendal, Cumbria.
1848	AFLM	Prudential...................	Holborn Bars, E.C.1.
1849	AF	Railway Passengers ...... C.U.	St. Helen's, 1 Undershaft, E.C.3.
1864	AFL	Refuge	Oxford St., Manchester M60.
1911	L	Reliance Mutual	Reliance House, Tunbridge Wells, Kent.
1906	AF	Reliance Fire & Accident	Reliance House, Tunbridge Wells, Kent.
1881	AFM	Reliance Marine ........G.R.E.	Royal Exchange, E.C.3.
1823	Reversions	Reversionary Interest Society. .	4 Coleman St., E.C.2.
1918	AF	Road Transport & General G.A.	77 Upper Richmond Rd., S.W.15.
1845	AFLM	Royal Life	New Hall Place, Liverpool.
1720	AFL	Royal Exchange...............	Royal Exchange, E.C.3.
1850	L	Royal Liver Friendly	Royal Liver Building, Liverpool 3.
1861	AFL	Royal London................	Royal London House, Middleborough, Colchester.
1887	L	Royal Nat. Pensions (Nurses) ...	15 Buckingham St., W.C.2.
1909	AFM	Salvation Army...............	101 Queen Victoria St., E.C.4.
1963	L	Save and Prosper..............	4 Great St. Helens, E.C.3.
1965	L	Schroder Life	Enterprise House, Isambard Brunel Rd., Portsmouth.
1826	L	Scottish Amicable	150 St. Vincent St., Glasgow.
1881	FM	Scottish Boiler .... G.A.	250 St. Vincent St., Glasgow.
1831	L	Scottish Equitable.............	31 St. Andrew Square, Edinburgh.
1919	AFM	Scottish General .... G.A.	100 West Nile St., Glasgow, G.2.
1852	L	Scottish Legal	95 Bothwell St., Glasgow, G.2.
1881	L	Scottish Life	19 St. Andrew Square, Edinburgh, 2.
1876	AF	Scottish Metropolitan .... C.U.	St. Helen's, 1 Undershaft, E.C.3.
1883	AL	Scottish Mutual...............	109 St. Vincent Street, Glasgow, G.2.
1837	L	Scottish Provident	6 St. Andrew Square, Edinburgh.
1824	AFLM	Scottish Union & National N.U.	Surrey St., Norwich.
1815	L	Scottish Widows'.............	15 Dalkeith Rd., Edinburgh.
1875	AFM	Sea .......................S.A.	1 Bartholomew Lane, E.C.2.
1904	AFL	Sentinel.....................	2 Eyre Street Hill, E.C.1.
1964	L	Stalwart Assurance	Tuition Hse., St. George's Rd., Wimbledon.
1825	L	Standard Life	3 George Street, Edinburgh.
1891	AFM	State..................G.R.E.	Royal Exchange, E.C.3.
1710	AFM	Sun ......................S.A.	1 Bartholomew Lane, E.C.2.
*	AFLM	Sun Alliance & London	1 Bartholomew Lane, E.C.2.
1810	AFL	Sun Life Assurance Group	107 Cheapside, E.C.2.
1865	L	Sun Life of Canada	2, 3 & 4 Cockspur St., S.W.1.
1936	FL	Teacher's Assurance	12 Christchurch Rd., Bournemouth.
1969	L	Trident	London Road, Gloucester.
1869	M	Tunstall & District	Station Chambers, Tunstall, Stoke on Trent.
1867	M	Ulster Marine .... G.A.	5 Donegall Sq., S., Belfast.
1714	AFM	Union Assurance......... C.U.	St. Helen's, 1 Undershaft, E.C.3.
1835	AFM	Union Ins. Soc. of Canton G.R.E.	Royal Exchange, E.C.3.
1863	M	Union Marine	4–5, King William St., E.C.4.
1915	AFM	United British ..........G.R.E.	Royal Exchange, E.C.3.
1908	AFL	United Friendly...............	42 Southwark Bridge Road, S.E.1.
1840	L	U.K.Provident	Castle St., Salisbury, Wiltshire.
1825	L	University	4 Coleman St., E.C.2.
1974	L	Vanbrugh	41–43 Maddox St., W.1.
1919	Reinsurance	Victory Reinsurance	Castle Hill Ave., Folkestone, Kent
1875	AFM	Warden ....R.	1 North John St., Liverpool.
1911	AF	Welsh Insurance Corpn. .. C.U.	St. Helen's, 1 Undershaft, E.C.3.
1841	AFL	Wesleyan & General	Colmore Circus, Ringway, Birmingham, 4.
1886	AF	West of Scotland .... C.U.	26 George St., Edinburgh 2.
1851	AFM	Western Assurance..........R.	New Hall Place, Liverpool.
1912	AFLM	Western Australian	Swan Court, Mansel Rd., Wimbledon, S.W.19.
1717	AF	Westminster Fire .........S.A.	1 Bartholomew Lane, E.C.2.
1865	AF	White Cross .... C.U.	St. Helen's, 1 Undershaft, E.C.3.
1894	AFM	World Marine & General .. C.U.	Dunster House, Mark Lane, E.C.3.
1837	L	Yorkshire General Life ... G.A.	Rougier St., York.
1872	AF	Zurich	Stanhope Road, Portsmouth.

* Sun Alliance & London—Incorporating Funds established 1710, 1720 and 1824.

BRITISH MONETARY UNITS

COIN

GOLD COINS	NICKEL-BRASS (COPPER/
Five Pound £5	NICKEL/ZINC)
Two Pound £2	One Pound £1
Sovereign £1	
Half-Sovereign 10s.	
BRONZE COINS	CUPRO-NICKEL (SILVER)
*2 Pence 2p	Crown 5s. (25p)
*1 Penny 1p	Florin 2s. (10p)
*½ Penny ½p	Shilling 1s. (5p)
	*50 Pence 50p
	*Crown 25p
	*20 Pence 20p
	*10 Pence 10p
	*5 Pence 5p

SILVER

*Crown 25p
Maundy Money‡

Fourpence 4p	Twopence 2p
Threepence 3p	Penny 1p

*For further details of decimal coins, see next page.
‡Gifts of special money distributed by the Sovereign annually on Maundy Thursday to the number of aged poor persons corresponding to the Sovereign's own age.

Gold Coin.—Gold ceased to circulate during the First World War. An Order of April 27, 1966, made it illegal for U.K. residents to continue holding more than 4 gold coins minted after 1837, or to acquire such coins unless they had been licensed as genuine collectors by the Bank of England. This Order was revoked on April 1, 1971, by the Exchange Control (Gold Coins Exemption) Order, 1971, whereby residents of the United Kingdom, Channel Islands and the Isle of Man may freely buy and sell and hold gold coins.

The 1971 Order was revoked on April 15, 1975, by the Exchange Control (Gold Coins Exemption) Order, 1975. Under this Order Section 1 of the Exchange Control Act 1947 (which prohibits dealings in gold or foreign currency except with Treasury permission) was exempted for gold coins minted in or before 1837. The import of gold coins minted after 1837 was prohibited except by authorised dealers in gold with individual import licences from the Department of Trade, and dealing between other U.K. residents was restricted to coins already held in the U.K.

Under an amendment, dated December 16, 1977, the exemptions contained in the 1975 Order were extended to cover gold coins minted in or before 1937.

The 1975 controls over the import of and dealing in gold coins were abolished on June 13, 1979 under the Exchange Control (Gold Coins Exemption) Order 1979, and gold coins, with certain exceptions,* may now be imported and exported without restriction.

On April 1, 1982 the Government introduced VAT (currently 15 per cent) on sales of all gold coin.

Silver.—Prior to 1920 our silver coins were struck from standard silver—an alloy of which 925 parts in 1,000 were silver. In 1920 the proportion of silver was reduced to 500 parts. From January 1, 1947 all "silver" coins, except Maundy money, have been struck from cupro-nickel—an alloy of copper 75 parts and nickel 25 parts. Maundy coins since 1947 have been struck from standard silver.

Bronze, introduced in 1860 to replace copper, is an alloy of copper 97 parts, zinc 2½ parts and tin ½ part. These proportions are subject to slight variation.

*Gold coins which are more than fifty years old and valued at a sum in excess of £8,000 cannot be exported without specific authorization from the Department of Trade.

The "Remedy" is the amount of variation from standard permitted in weight and fineness of coins when first issued from the Mint.

Legal tender of coin.—Gold, dated 1838 onwards, if not below least current weight, is legal tender to any amount. The £1 coin introduced on April 21, 1983 is legal tender to any amount. 50p and 20p coins are legal tender up to £10; 10p and 5p coins are legal tender up to £5 and bronze coins are legal tender for amounts up to 20p. Farthings ceased to be legal tender on December 31, 1960, the halfpenny on August 1, 1969, the halfcrown on January 1, 1970, the threepence and penny on August 31, 1971, and the sixpence on June 30, 1980.

Since 1982 the word "new" in "new pence" displayed on decimal coins has been dropped.

BANK NOTES

Bank of England notes are currently issued in denominations of £1, £5, £10, £20 and £50 for the amount of the Fiduciary Note Issue, and are legal tender in England and Wales. Only £1 notes are legal tender in Scotland and Northern Ireland.

The old white notes for £10, £20, £50, £100, £500 and £1,000, which were issued until April 22, 1943, ceased to be legal tender in May 1945.

The old white £5 notes dated up to September 20, 1956, the £5 notes issued between 1957 and 1963, bearing a portrait of Britannia and the first series to bear a portrait of the Queen, issued between 1963 and 1971, ceased to be legal tender on March 14, 1961, June 27, 1967 and September 1, 1973 respectively. The series of £1 notes issued during the years 1928 to 1960 and the 10s. notes of the same type issued from 1928 to 1961—those without the royal portrait—ceased to be legal tender on May 29 and October 30, 1962 respectively. The £1 note first issued in March 1960 (bearing on the back a representation of Britannia) and the £10 note first issued in February 1964 (bearing a lion on the back) both bearing a portrait of the Queen on the front ceased to be legal tender on June 1, 1979. The 10s. note was replaced by the 50p coin in October 1969, and ceased to be legal tender on November 21, 1970. Bank notes which are no longer legal tender are payable when presented at the Head Office of the Bank of England in London.

The first of the current series of Bank notes was a £20 note issued on July 9, 1970. This was followed by the £5 note on November 11, 1971, £10 note on February 20, 1975, £1 note on February 9, 1978 and £50 note on March 20, 1981. The predominant identifying feature of each note is the portrayal on the back of a prominent figure from Britain's history namely, £1: Sir Isaac Newton; £5: The Duke of Wellington; £10: Florence Nightingale; £20: William Shakespeare; and £50: Sir Christopher Wren.

Note circulation is highest at the two peak spending periods of the year—around Christmas and during the summer holiday period. A peak of £12,869 million was reached immediately prior to Christmas 1983, a 5·07 per cent increase on the previous year.

The proportion of the total value of notes in circulation of £1 and £5 notes at end-February 1984 compared with the previous year, fell from 5·8 per cent and 25·9 per cent to 5·1 per cent and 22·3 per cent respectively; whereas £10 notes increased from 41·2 per cent to 42·3 per cent, £20 notes increased from 17·0 per cent to 17·3 per cent and £50 from 5·7 per cent to 7·9 per cent.

On February 29, 1984 the values of notes in circulation were; £1: £582,866,611; £5: £2,554,630,255; £10: £4,845,942,570; £20: £1,978,602,740; £50: £909,237,800.

Other Bank Notes.—Bank notes are issued by three

Scottish banks. The Royal Bank of Scotland and the Bank of Scotland issue notes for £1, £5, £10, £20 and £100. The Clydesdale Bank issues notes for £1, £5, £10, £20, £50, £100. Scottish notes are not legal tender, but in Scotland they enjoy a status equal to that of the Bank of England note.

Channel Islands and the Isle of Man.—The states of Jersey and Guernsey issue notes for £1, £5, £10 and £20. The Government of the Isle of Man issues notes for 50p, £1, £5, £10 and £20. These are legal tender only in their respective islands.

Although none of the series of notes specified above is legal tender in the United Kingdom they are generally accepted by the banks irrespective of their place of issue. At one time the banks made a commission charge for handling Scottish and Irish notes but this was abolished some years ago.

The Channel Islands and the Isle of Man also issue their own coinage. The states of Jersey and Guernsey issue coins for ½p, 1p, 2p, 5p, 10p, 20p, 50p and £1. The Isle of Man issues coins for ½p, 1p, 2p, 5p, 10p, 20p, 50p and £1.

Denomination	Metal	Standard Weight (grams)	Standard Diameter (centimetres)
Halfpenny	bronze	1·78200	1·7145
Penny	bronze	3·56400	2·0320
2 pence	bronze	7·12800	2·5910
5 pence	cupro-nickel	5·65518	2·3595
10 pence	cupro-nickel	11·31036	2·8500
20 pence	cupro-nickel	5·0	2·14
25p Crown	silver	28·27590	3·8608
25p Crown	cupro-nickel	28·27590	3·8608
50 pence	cupro-nickel	13·5	3·0
£1	copper/nickel/zinc	9·5	2·25

THE STOCK EXCHANGE IN THE UNITED KINGDOM AND IRELAND

Broker Members of The Stock Exchange buy and sell shares for members of the public. This is done for individual investors, for their advisers such as bank managers, solicitors and accountants, and for investing institutions like insurance companies, pension funds, unit trusts and merchant banks. For this the stockbroker is paid a fixed scale of commission based on the value of the securities purchased. In addition to this service, brokers advise their clients, according to their particular circumstances and needs, on how to invest their money to greatest advantage. In addition, they will undertake to review periodically the portfolios of their clients.

The Stock Exchange provides facilities for raising capital for industry. Any Broker will give advice on how a company can finance its growth by getting a listing. For companies already listed, other methods are possible—such as rights issues and debenture or loan stocks—for obtaining additional funds. Brokers' advice is also available to industrialists on matters such as mergers and acquisitions.

All listed British companies are incorporated under the Companies' Acts, which contain stringent regulations for their management and control. They are limited liability companies, which means that if you are a shareholder in such a company you cannot be called upon to pay any part of its debt or liabilities if it gets into difficulties, unless, in quite exceptional cases, you are a holder of partly-paid shares, in which event your liability is limited to the amount required to make the shares fully paid. The Stock Exchange serves investors, whether inexperienced or expert, big or small, and the authorities of The Stock Exchange insist on compliance with stringent regulations to ensure that the public are fully informed of the constitution and record of every company whose securities are admitted to the market.

In London the foundation stone of the building was laid in 1801, but the building was almost entirely reconstructed in 1854 from the designs of Thomas Allason. The Stock Exchange has now been rebuilt as a large tower block, 331 feet high with a new Trading Floor to the west of the block.

There are other Trading Floors in Liverpool, Birmingham, Glasgow, Belfast and Dublin.

The Stock Exchange provides a market for the purchase and sale of about 7,100 securities valued at over £828,566,700,000, and also securities listed on overseas Exchanges. At present, the Members of the Stock Exchange, consisting of Brokers (agents for clients) and Jobbers (dealers as principals in specific securities), number about 4,500.

The Stock Exchange

Chairman, Sir Nicholas Goodison; *Deputy Chairmen,* P. B. Mitford-Slade; G. R. Russell; *Chief Exec.,* J. R. Knight.

Administrative Units

The Stock Exchange, London, E.C.2; Stock Exchange, Margaret Street, Birmingham; Stock Exchange, Norfolk Street, Manchester; Stock Exchange, 69 St. George's Place, Glasgow; Stock Exchange, 28 Anglesea Street, Dublin 2; Stock Exchange, Northern Bank House, 10 High Street, Belfast.

COUNCIL FOR THE SECURITIES INDUSTRY, 20th Floor, The Stock Exchange Building, E.C.2.—*Dir. Gen.,* T. G. Barker.

FRIENDLY SOCIETIES—GREAT BRITAIN
Acts 1974–1981

Friendly societies are voluntary mutual organizations the main purposes of which are the provision of relief or maintenance during sickness, unemployment or retirement, and the provision of life assurance. Many of the older traditional societies complement their business activities by social activity and a general care for individual members in ways normally outside the scope of a purely commercial organization. There are three main categories of friendly societies—societies with separately registered branches, commonly called orders, centralized societies, which conduct business directly with members (having no separately registered branches), and collecting societies. Collecting societies conduct industrial assurance business and are subject to the requirements of the Industrial Assurance Acts in addition to the Friendly Societies Acts. Industrial assurance is life assurance, the premiums in respect of which are payable at intervals of less than two months and are received by means of collectors who make house to house visits for the purpose.

At the end of 1982 there were 25 orders with 3,510 branches, 392 centralized societies, and 42 collecting societies.

Long before the term "Friendly Society" came into use, the seeds of voluntary mutual insurance had been sown in the ancient religious and trade "Guilds". As is evident from the many extant parchment returns detailing their rules and possessions under a decree of Richard II, Guilds had become widespread in Britain by the 14th century. By then, the purely charitable character of the original Guilds had largely changed with the emergence of numerous small institutions adopting primitive mutual insurance methods of a regular flat rate contribution to insure relief when sick or in old age and a payment to the widow in the event of death.

The present register of Friendly Societies includes several societies which have been in existence for upwards of 200 years, the oldest, operating in Scotland, being the "Incorporation of Carters in Leith" established as long ago as 1555.

The first Act for the encouragement and protection of "Friendly Societies" in this country was not passed until 1793, but various amending Acts were put on the Statute Book during the next century as the result of the recommendations of successive Select Committees (including a Royal Commission in 1871). For example, it was not until the 1829 Act that all registered Friendly Societies were required to keep proper records of individual sickness and mortality amongst their members, which data enabled the construction of standard actuarial tables showing the expected (average) duration or sickness at successive ages, and also (with data from the Census) the corresponding mortality rates.

The rules and other documents of societies deposited with local justices passed into the custody of the Registrar following the Act of 1846 and are of considerable interest to social historians. Those relating to some societies no longer on the register have been transferred to the Public Record Office for permanent preservation.

The Friendly Societies Act 1974, which came into force in April, 1975, consolidated the nine Acts which comprised the Friendly Societies Acts 1896 to 1971 and a few other minor enactments relating to societies to which those Acts applied. The Act allows various specific classes other than "Friendly Societies" to be registered thereunder, but tax exemption (irrespective of the extent of interest income) is enjoyed only by registered "Friendly Societies". Removal of life assurance premium relief, and reductions in the limits applying to the tax-exempt business announced in the Budget in March, and a subsequent announcement as to the type of business undertaken, significantly affected friendly societies in 1984. Particularly affected were those registered in recent years to maximize the tax advantages, with what is in form a life assurance contract, but in practice a savings facility. Such societies have found it necessary to reconsider their business to accommodate substantially reduced tax-exempt limits on the one hand, and a relaxation on the other as to the type of business they may undertake, including a range of taxable business that had previously been denied to them.

In addition to friendly societies there are three other main classes of society which may be registered under the Friendly Societies Act 1974: benevolent societies, working men's clubs and specially authorized societies. Benevolent societies are established for any charitable or benevolent purpose, to provide the same type of benefits as would be permissible for a friendly society, but in contrast the benefits must be for persons who are not members instead of, or in addition to, members. Working men's clubs provide social and recreational facilities for members. Specially authorized societies are registered for any purpose authorized by the Treasury as a purpose to which some or all of the provisions of the 1974 Act ought to be extended. Examples are societies for the promotion of science, literature and the fine arts, or to enable members to pursue an interest in sports and games. At the end of 1982 there were 93 benevolent societies, 2502 working men's clubs, and 165 specially authorized societies.

The principal statistics at the end of 1981 are given in the table below.

	Friendly Societies (a)	Collecting Societies	Benevolent Societies	Working Men's Clubs	Special Authorized Societies		Other
					Loan	Others	
Number of Societies	4,069	42	97	2,507	16	153	4
Number of Members 000's	3,431	20,263 (b)	332	2,331 (c)	20	128	3
Total Benefits Paid £000's	59,792	80,377	4,234	Not applicable	Not applicable	—	41
Total Funds £000	613,817	980,971	12,113	122,912 (c)	497	10,087	298

(a) Centralized societies, orders and branches of orders
(b) Assurances

(c) 1980 figures

INDUSTRIAL AND PROVIDENT SOCIETIES—GREAT BRITAIN

Acts 1965–1978

The familiar "Co-op" societies are amongst the wide variety which are registered under the Industrial and Provident Societies Act 1965. This consolidating Act, which like the Friendly and the Building Societies Act is administered by the Chief Registrar of Friendly Societies, provides for the registration of societies and lays down the broad framework within which they must operate. Internal relations of societies are governed by their registered rules.

Registration under the Act confers upon a society corporate status by its registered name with perpetual succession and a common seal, and limited liability. A society qualifies for registration if it is carrying on an industry, business or trade, and it satisfies the Registrar that either (a) it is a bona fide co-operative society or (b) in view of the fact that its business is being, or is intended to be, conducted for the benefit of the community there are special reasons why it

should be registered under the Act rather than as a company under the Companies Act.

Registration of a new class of society under the 1965 Act was introduced in Great Britain by the Credit Unions Act 1979 which also lays down supervision requirements. A similar framework of law for credit unions has existed in Northern Ireland since 1969.

During 1982 the number of registered societies decreased by 133 to 9,603. The largest single group was the 3,480 housing societies. The largest group in terms of turnover was that consisting of the retail societies which includes those trading under the familiar "Co-op" sign, with sales (in 1981) of £3,644 million. Sales of wholesale and productive societies amounted to £2,266 million in 1981. The principal statistics at the end of 1981 are given in the table below.

	Retail	Wholesale and Productive	Agricultural	Fishing	Social and Recreational Clubs	General Service	Housing	Credit Unions	Total
Number of Societies	251	165	1,044	101	3,683	640	3,779	73	9,736
Number of Members 000's	9,426	44	412	8	2,954	533	158	12	13,547
Funds of Members 000's	585,579	313,448	154,112	2,587	145,427	1,401,042	2,235,639	1,496	4,839,330
Total Assets £000's	1,168,651	613,912	348,560	7,748	247,829	1,738,370	4,805,748	1,571	8,932,388

BUILDING SOCIETIES—GREAT BRITAIN

Act 1962

The purposes of a building society are defined in section 1 of the Building Societies Act 1962 as being the raising of a fund of money from its members (investors) to advance on the security of first mortgage of freehold or leasehold property to other members (borrowers). Societies can only undertake those activities which are permitted by the 1962 Act, which is administered by the Chief Registrar of Friendly Societies: the rules, annual returns and accounts which societies are required to send to him are open to public inspection, with other relevant documents, at the Registry.

The number of building societies declined from 227 at the end of 1982 to 206 at the end of 1983 as a result of 18 mergers, the dissolution of 4 societies, and the establishment of one new society. The number of societies has declined by more than half (241) in the last decade from the total of 447 at the end of 1973. At the end of 1960 the number was 726. Over the last decade the total assets of all building societies have increased almost five-fold from the figure of £17,545 million at the end of 1973 to £85,868 million at the

end of 1983. The largest 5 societies (Halifax, Abbey National, Nationwide, Leeds Permanent, and Woolwich) accounted for 56 per cent of the 1983 figure and the largest 20 societies accounted for 87 per cent. In contrast, the smallest 129 societies (more than 62 per cent of the total number of societies) accounted for less than 2 per cent of total assets. Mortgage demand remained strong during 1983 with a recovery in the housing market and a significant increase in housebuilding activity. Bank lending decreased markedly compared to the previous year although still accounting for some 23% of net advances. A record of £19,341 million was lent by societies to 950,000 home buyers in 1983. Building Societies investment rates were below the general level of interest rates in the first half of the year but this situation changed markedly in the second half with increased building society rates and decreases in other rates. Net receipts in the second half of the year were more than twice the level of the first half. Total net receipts for 1983 were £7,088 million. The principal statistics for the years 1973 to 1983 are set out in the table below:

BUILDING SOCIETIES, GREAT BRITAIN, 1973–1983

Year	1 Number of Societies	2 Number of Share Holders 000's	3 Number of Depositors 000's	4 Number of Borrowers 000's	5 Share Balances £m	6 Deposit Balances £m
1973	447	14,385	672	4,204	16,021	596
1974	416	15,856	641	4,250	18,021	633
1975	382	17,916	677	4,397	22,134	762
1976	364	19,991	712	4,609	25,760	848
1977	339	22,536	760	4,836	31,110	1,224
1978	316	24,999	781	5,108	36,186	1,254
1979	287	27,878	797	5,251	42,023	1,281
1980	273	30,636	915	5,383	48,915	1,742
1981	253	33,388	995	5,490	55,463	2,539
1982	227	36,609	1,094	5,643	64,977	3,447
1983	206	37,713	1,202	5,928	75,180	5,610

Year	7 Mortgage Balances £m	8 Total Assets £m	Advances during year		11 Average Mortgage Rate %	12 Average Share Rate %
			9 Number 000's	10 Amount £m		
1973	14,532	17,545	720	3,513	9·59	6·51
1974	16,030	20,094	546	2,945	11·05	7·53
1975	18,802	24,204	798	4,908	11·08	7·21
1976	22,565	28,202	913	6,183	11·06	7·02
1977	26,427	34,288	946	6,745	11·05	6·98
1978	31,598	39,538	1,184	8,808	9·55	6·46
1979	36,801	45,789	1,040	9,002	11·94	8·45
1980	42,437	53,793	936	9,503	14·92	10·34
1981	48,875	61,815	1,096	12,005	14·01	9·19
1982	56,691	73,033	1,320	14,971	13·32	8·77
1983	67,490	85,868	1,513	19,357	11·05	7·26

There were notable changes in the methods by which building societies determined the interest rates they should pay and charge in 1983. There were indications during the year that some of the larger societies were no longer willing to see other societies continually offering higher than Building Societies Association recommended rates which they could equally afford. This eventually led to the decision in October 1983 to replace the BSA's recommended rate system to one in which advised rates were given to societies.

Particulars of the recommended (and now advisory) mortgage, and corresponding share rate changes since the beginning of 1980 are as follows:—

Date of recommendation/advice	Mortgages %	Shares %
December 1980	14·00	9·25
March 1981	13·00	8·50
October 1981	15·00	9·75
March 1982	13·50	8·75
August 1982	12·00	7·75
November 1982	10·00	6·25
June 1983	11·25	7·25
March 1984	10·25	6·25
July 1984	12·50	7·75

The Building Societies (Authorization) Regulations 1981 came into effect on 1st December 1981, and represent a change in emphasis of prudential supervision of building societies. Hitherto, the powers in the Building Societies Act 1962 have essentially been to allow intervention when something is seen to be going wrong. The intention of authorization is that the onus rests with the building societies to satisfy the Chief Registrar that it is a safe recipient of investors' money if authorization is to be granted or is to continue. The system came immediately into full effect only for new societies. Other societies, which were not subject to control orders or in the course of winding up, were deemed to be authorized on 1st December, 1981. Their authorization could not be revoked on grounds of inadequate capital or absence of effective direction until 1st June 1983. The Chief Registrar now has to be satisfied that those authorized do in fact meet the requirements.

A significant development for the future of building societies generally was the issue by the Government of its Green Paper "Building Societies: A New Framework" (Cmnd 9316) in July 1984. This discussion document will form the basis of new legislation for building societies to replace the Building Societies Act 1962.

A society meeting certain basic requirements as to assets and liabilities, liquid funds, reserves and other matters may be designated by the Chief Registrar under section 1 of the House Purchase and Housing Act 1959 for the purposes of trustee status. The requirements are set out in The Building Societies (Designation for Trustee Investment) Regulations 1972, (as amended). The shares and deposits of a society so designated become authorised investments for trustees subject to the provisions of the Trustee Investments Act 1971. Designated societies are identified in the list below by a letter "D" in the first column.

SOCIETIES WITH TOTAL ASSETS EXCEEDING £1 MILLION AT END OF
FINANCIAL YEAR 1983

Year Estab- lished	* Name of Society (abbreviated) Head Office	Share Investors	Assets Total £'000
1849D	Abbey National, Abbey House, 27 Baker St., London W1	8,571,360	14,312,454
1885	Aid to Thrift, 38 Finsbury Sq., London EC2	822	2,592
1863D	Alliance, Alliance House, Hove Park, Hove, East Sussex	845,634	2,791,141
1848D	Anglia, Moulton Park, Northampton	1,740,383	3,819,885
1870D	Argyle, Argyle Ho., 105 Seven Sisters Rd., Holloway, London N7	5,241	23,321
1871	Banffshire, 186 Mid Street, Keith	762	1,716
1853D	Barnsley, Regent St., Barnsley, South Yorks	19,103	61,776
1953D	Bath Investment and Bldg. Soc., 20 Charles St., Bath	9,928	16,535
1879D	Bedford, 65 Midland Rd., Bedford	10,341	25,345
1881D	Bedford Crown, 117 Midland Rd., Bedford	2,670	7,062
1866D	Beverley, 57 Market Place, Beverley, Yorks	5,059	9,589
1914D	Bexhill-on-Sea, 2 Devonshire Sq., Bexhill-on-Sea, Sussex	3,993	8,368
1853D	Bideford, 5 The Quay, Bideford, Devon	5,665	16,005
1889D	Birmingham and Bridgwater, 42/44 Waterloo Street, Birmingham	215,111	446,147
1903D	Blackheath, Cranford Ho., 14 Long Lane, Rowley Regis, Warley, West Midlands	9,207	24,536
1864D	Bolton, 213 Baker St., London NW1	5,863	39,330
1851D	Bradford and Bingley, P.O. Box 2, Bingley, West Yorks.	1,298,623	2,686,858
1853D	Bristol Econ., St. John's Court, Broad St., Bristol	2,229	6,065
1850D	Bristol and West, Broad Quay, Bristol	608,716	1,574,022
1856D	Britannia, P.O. Box 20, Newton House, Leek, Staffs.	951,139	2,376,351
1907D	Buckinghamshire, High St., Chalfont St. Giles, Bucks.	6,354	15,499
1866D	Bury St. Edmunds, 87 Guildhall St., Bury St. Edmunds	3,371	9,989
1850D	Cambridge, 32 St. Andrew's St., Cambridge	33,404	96,842
1865D	Cardiff, 92 St. Mary St., Cardiff	4,650	20,293
1960D	Catholic, 7 Strutton Ground, London SW1	2,452	7,648
1899	Century, 21–23 Albany St., Edinburgh	1,383	5,630
1862D	Chatham, Room 704, Corn Exchange Bldg, Fenwick St., Liverpool	341	728
1898D	Chatham Reliance, Reliance House, Manor Rd., Chatham, Kent	39,085	72,148
1875D	Chelsea, Chelsea House, 255 Kensington High St., London W8	136,829	400,905
1850D	Cheltenham and Gloucester, 37–43 Clarence St., Cheltenham, Glos.	587,265	2,041,516
1845D	Chesham, 12 Market Sq., Chesham, Bucks.	8,512	20,799
1888D	Chilterns, Norfolk House, Station Rd., Chesham, Bucks.	2,790	5,724
1870D	Cheshire, Castle St., Macclesfield	198,063	304,755
1861D	Cheshunt, 100 Crossbrook St., Waltham Cross, Herts.	42,701	115,579
1859D	Chorley and Dt., 51 St. Thomas's Rd., Chorley, Lancs.	6,056	17,955
1905D	Citizens Regency, Clarence Hse., 30/31 North Street, Brighton, Sussex	38,998	104,881
1946D	City and Metropolitan, 37 Ludgate Hill, London EC4	12,215	37,462
1862D	City of London, 34 London Wall, London EC2	29,815	130,727
1931D	Civil Service, 5 Brighton Road, South Croydon, Surrey	6,857	31,187
1876	Clapham P., 3–4 Gt. Marlborough St., London W1V 2HE	101	573
1859D	Clay Cross Benefit, 42 Thanet St., Clay Cross, Chesterfield	3,569	6,732
1869D	Colchester, 42–48 North Station Road, Colchester	10,955	40,297
1977	Country, 1 Icknield Way West, Letchworth, Herts SG6 4AP	911	1,943
1884D	Coventry, P.O. Box 9, High Street, Coventry	310,564	572,137
1850D	Cumberland, 38 Fisher St., Carlisle	60,762	146,441
1946D	Darlington, Tubwell Row, Market Pl., Darlington, Co. Durham	40,231	93,793
1859D	Derbyshire, Duffield Hall, Duffield, Derby	212,948	453,922
1923D	Dillwyn P., 11 Cradock St., Swansea, Glam.	3,474	8,420
1883	Dover and Folkestone, 35 Castle St., Dover, Kent	1,239	3,546
1858D	Dudley, Dudley Hse., Stone St., Dudley, Worcs.	14,512	30,961
1869D	Dunfermline, 48–56 East Port, Dunfermline, Fife.	67,839	201,113
1927D	Ealing and Acton, 55 The Mall, Ealing, London W5	2,661	11,179
1857D	Earl Shilton, 22 The Hollow, Earl Shilton, Leicester	8,567	19,029
1903D	East Surrey, 54 Station Rd., Redhill, Surrey	10,647	33,855
1877D	Eastbourne Mut., Eastbourne Hse., 22 Gildredge Rd., Eastbourne, Sussex	52,626	155,880
1980	Ecology, 43 Main St., Cross Hills, Keighley, West Yorks BD20 8TT	474	557
1847D	Essex Eq., 5 Brooke Road, Grays, Essex	4,732	12,852
1970	Foresters, 13 College Place, London Road, Southampton SO9 1FP	570	1,383
1860D	Frome Selwood P., 3 Market Pl., Frome, Som.	11,186	21,248
1865D	Furness, 51–55 Duke Street, Barrow-in-Furness	52,821	104,025
1911D	Gainsborough, 26 Lord St., Gainsborough, Lincs.	2,809	6,914
1924D	Gateway, P.O. Box 18, Worthing, W. Sussex	431,442	1,137,932
1852D	Greenwich, 279–283 Greenwich High Rd., London SE10	30,100	70,053
1871D	Guardian, Guardian Hse., 120 High Holborn, London WC1	76,380	569,267
1853D	Halifax, P.O. Box 60, Trinity Rd., Halifax, West Yorks.	6,762,086	16,782,035
1866D	Hampshire, Anchor Hse., Kingston Crescent, Portsmouth	14,114	41,952
1854D	Hanley Econ., 42 Cheapside, Hanley, Stoke-on-Trent, Staffs.	29,153	61,529

* P. = Permanent; B. = Benefit. The words "Building Society" are the last words in every society's name.

Year Estab-lished	Name of Society (abbreviated)　　　Head Office	Share Investors	Assets Total £'000
1953D	Harpenden, 14 Station Rd., Harpenden, Herts.	5,966	15,097
1882D	Harrow, Cunningham Hse., Bessborough Rd., Harrow, Middx.	9,165	30,323
1866	Hartlepool and Dt., 5 Victoria Rd., Hartlepool, County Cleveland	1,417	3,674
1931D	Haslemere, 18 High St., Haslemere, Surrey	1,416	4,739
1890D	Haywards Heath and Dt., 33 The Broadway, Haywards Heath, West Sussex	18,193	47,721
1863D	Heart of England, 22–26 Jury St., Warwick	132,316	252,170
1884D	Hemel Hempstead, 43 Marlowes, Hemel Hempstead, Herts.	10,037	35,739
1926D	Hendon, 9 Central Circus, Hendon, London NW4	3,776	18,580
1888D	Herne Bay, 39 William St., Herne Bay	5,040	18,615
1888D	Herts. and Essex, 4 Market Sq., Bishop's Stortford, Herts.	4,274	12,957
1874D	Hibernian, 22 High St., Cardiff, Glam.	3,992	11,423
1865D	Hinckley, Upper Bond St., Hinckley, Leics.	37,130	80,127
1855D	Holmesdale B., 43 Church St., Reigate, Surrey	8,090	23,502
1875	Huntley, 10 The Square, Huntley, Aberdeenshire	436	1,120
1853D	Ilkeston P., 16 Queen St., Ilkeston, Derby	3,392	6,700
1849D	Ipswich, 44 Upper Brook St., Ipswich	26,088	53,414
1847	Kent and Canterbury P.B., 3 The Parade, Canterbury, Kent	572	2,076
1961	Kidderminster Eq., 17 Church St., Kidderminster.	889	2,672
1852D	Lambeth, 118–120 Westminster Bridge Rd., London SE1	64,291	260,224
1853D	Leamington Spa, Imperial House, Holly Walk, Leamington Spa, Warws.	98,929	343,903
1875D	Leeds and Holbeck, 105 Albion St., Leeds	177,557	417,246
1848D	Leeds P., Permanent Hse., The Headrow, Leeds	2,061,508	4,822,632
1863D	Leek United and Midlands, 50 St. Edward St., Leek, Staffs.	45,637	101,890
1875D	Leicester, Oadby, Leicester	1,042,362	2,476,899
1878D	London Grosvenor, 5 Old Brompton Rd., SW7	1,364	3,025
1848	London P., 14 Tufton St., London SW1P 3QZ	2,161	8,501
1867D	Loughborough P., 6 High St., Loughborough, Leics.	9,638	25,614
1877	Louth, Mablethorpe and Sutton P.B., 3 Eastgate, Louth, Lincs.	1,179	2,999
1922D	Manchester, 18–20 Bridge St., Manchester	5,809	25,490
1956	Manchester Unity of Odd Fellows, Odd Fellows House, 40 Fountain Street, Manchester M2 2AB	660	757
1870D	Mansfield, Regent Hse., Regent St., Mansfield, Notts.	15,126	44,164
1944	Marble Arch, 190 St. Albans Rd., Watford, Herts ED2 4AT	1,124	1,336
1870D	Market Harborough, Welland Hse., The Sq., Market Harborough, Leics.	24,028	53,258
1860D	Marsden, 6–20 Russell St., Nelson, Lancs.	31,631	83,522
1874D	Melton Mowbray, 39 Nottingham St., Melton Mowbray, Leics.	24,230	63,160
1966D	Mercantile, 75 Howard St., North Shields, Tyne and Wear	20,781	42,840
1882	Merseyside, 41 North John St., Liverpool	541	2,164
1886D	Metrogas, Katherine Hse., Katherine St., Croydon	5,006	11,201
1872D	Middleton, Sadler Street, Middleton, Manchester	36,502	76,222
1859D	Midshires, 35–49 Litchfield Street, Wolverhampton	387,273	677,144
1880D	Mid-Sussex, Mid-Sussex Hse., 66 Church Rd., Burgess Hill, Sussex	6,065	12,645
1883D	Mitcham and Metropolitan, 173 London Rd., Mitcham, Surrey	2,730	5,208
1869D	Monmouthshire, John Frost Sq., Newport, Gwent	11,948	30,334
1866D	Mornington, 158 Kentish Town Rd., London NW5	20,500	78,537
1869D	National and Provincial, Provincial Hse., Bradford	1,355,922	3,917,645
1896D	National Counties, Waterloo Hse., High St., Epsom, Surrey	39,258	187,938
1884D	Nationwide, New Oxford Hse., High Holborn, London WC1	3,163,648	7,347,840
1856D	Newbury, 17–20 Bartholomew St., Newbury, Berks.	26,745	66,473
1863D	Newcastle, Grainger Chambers, Hood Street, Newcastle upon Tyne	88,974	304,795
1876D	North East Globe, 18 Ridley Place, Newcastle upon Tyne	3,605	12,106
1866D	North Kent, North Kent Hse., Windmill St., Gravesend, Kent	23,087	54,206
1877D	North of England, 57 Fawcett St., Sunderland	53,133	99,402
1983D	North Wilts Ridgeway, 18 and 19 Commercial Rd., Swindon, Wilts.	9,991	28,630
1850D	Northern Rock, Northern Rock Hse., P.O. Box No. 2, Gosforth, Newcastle upon Tyne	456,868	1,063,628
1852D	Norwich, St. Andrew's Hse., St. Andrew St., Norwich, Norfolk	60,924	137,657
1850D	Nottingham, 5–13 Upper Parliament St., Nottingham	120,120	201,353
1935D	Nottingham Oddfellows, Imperial Bldg., 29 Bridgeford Rd., West Bridgeford, Nottingham	5,202	8,513
1879D	Paddington, 125 Westbourne Grove, London W2	9,997	32,037
1879D	Peckham Mut., Hanover Park Hse., 14/16 Hanover Park, London SE15	9,115	24,964
1877D	Penrith, 7 King St., Penrith, Cumb.	8,368	19,869
1860D	Peterborough, Manor Hse., 57 Lincoln Rd., Peterborough	65,998	155,454
1881D	Portman, 40 Portman Sq., London W1	126,458	337,558
1896D	Portsmouth, 176 London Rd., North End, Portsmouth	53,298	186,505
1860D	Principality, Principality Bldgs., Queen St., Cardiff	163,349	312,583
1941D	Property Owners, 4 Cavendish Place, London W1	44,006	235,710
1846D	Ramsbury, 25 High Street, Ramsbury, Marlborough, Wilts	70,481	143,547
1888D	Rowley Regis, 223 Halesowen Rd., Crawley Heath, Warley, Worcs	27,733	56,066
1849D	Saffron Walden and Essex, Market Place, Saffron Walden, Essex	26,741	59,703

Year Established	Name of Society (abbreviated) Head Office	Share Investors	Assets Total £'000
1937D	St. Pancras, 200 Finchley Rd., London NW3	8,595	36,875
1955	St. Stephens, 70 Chepstow Road, London W2	358	1,066
1846D	Scarborough, Prospect House, 442/444 Scalby Road, Scarborough, Yorks...	38,917	85,682
1848D	Scottish, 2 York Place, Edinburgh	11,055	29,022
1935D	Sheffield, 66 Campo Lane, Sheffield, Yorks.	3,257	10,504
1879D	Shepshed, Bull Ring, Shepshed, Loughborough, Leics.	5,980	11,990
1853D	Skipton, 59 High St., Skipton, Yorks.	140,754	367,109
1876	South Shields Sun P., 9 Beach Rd., South Shields, Co. Durham	864	2,350
1877D	Stafford Railway, 4 Market Sq., Stafford	6,874	16,962
1902D	Staffordshire, 5 Princes St., Jubilee Hse., P.O. Box 66, 84 Salop St., Wolverhampton	132,867	262,007
1875D	Standard, 64 Church Way, North Shields, Tyne and Wear	2,215	6,553
1970D	Stanley, Cromarty Hse., Front St., Stanley, Co. Durham	4,897	10,383
1850D	Stroud, 7 Russell St., Stroud, Glos.	44,400	81,009
1853D	Sunderland and Shields, 50 Fawcett St., Sunderland, Co. Durham	127,640	233,961
1870D	Sussex County, 40/42 Friars Walk, Lewes, East Sussex	77,994	203,757
1872D	Sussex Mutual, Sussex Hse., 130 Western Rd., Hove, Sussex	30,767	145,717
1868D	Swindon P., 1 Commercial Rd., Swindon, Wilts.	7,422	19,156
1966D	Teachers, Allenview Hse., Wimborne, Dorset	12,402	48,201
1886	Thrift, 3/4 Turnpike Parade, Green Lanes, London N15	3,918	8,146
1901D	Tipton and Coseley, 57–60 High St., Tipton, Staffs.	13,717	26,554
1853D	Town and Country, 215 Strand, London WC2	240,019	638,353
1866D	Tyldesley, 209–215 Elliott St., Tyldesley, Manchester	12,988	25,733
1855D	Tynemouth, 53–55 Howard St., North Shields, Tyne and Wear	4,707	12,794
1863D	Universal, 41 Pilgrim St., Newcastle upon Tyne	20,890	52,051
1924D	Vernon, 26 St. Petersgate, Stockport, Chesh.	13,766	30,828
1847D	Waltham Abbey, 6 Church St., Waltham Abbey, Essex	24,151	38,435
1877D	Walthamstow, 869 Forest Rd., Walthamstow, London E17	34,320	93,152
1949D	Wessex, 115 Old Christchurch Rd., Bournemouth, Hants.	23,850	101,555
1849D	West Bromwich, 374 High St., West Bromwich, Staffs.	257,736	364,647
1882D	West Cumbria, Cumbria Hse., Murray Rd., Workington	5,810	16,217
1862D	Western Counties, Bank End, Bideford, Devon	47,348	110,959
1847D	Woolwich Eq., Equitable Hse., London SE18	2,327,672	4,542,178
1885D	Yorkshire, Yorkshire House, Westgate, Bradford	479,322	1,214,228

PERIODS OF GESTATION AND INCUBATION

The table shows approximate periods of gestation or incubation for some common animals and birds. In some cases the periods may vary and where doubt arises professional advice should be sought.

Species	Shortest Period. Days	Usual Period. Days	Longest Period. Days	Species	Shortest Period. Days	Usual Period. Days	Longest Period. Days
Human	240	273	313	Duck	28	28	32
Mare	305	336	340	Goose	28	30	32
Ass	365	—	374	Pigeon	17	18	19
Cow	273	280	294	Canary	12	14	14
Ewe	140	147–50	160	Guinea Pig	63	—	70
Goat	147	151	155	Mouse	18	—	19
Sow	109	112	125	Rat	21	—	24
Bitch	55	63	70	Elephant		21–22 months	
Cat	53	56	63				
Rabbit	30	32	35	Camel		45 weeks	
Hen	20	21	22	Zebra		56 weeks	
Turkey	25	28	28				

BANKING IN BRITAIN

The main institutions within the British banking system are the Bank of England (the central bank, see p. 376), the clearing banks (the major retail banks), the merchant banks, the overseas banks and the discount houses.

The clearing banks are Barclays, Co-operative, Coutts, Lloyds, Midland, National Girobank, National Westminster, Williams & Glyns and the Trustee Savings Bank of England and Wales (see p. 450), and, in Scotland, the Bank of Scotland, Clydesdale, Royal Bank of Scotland and the Trustee Savings Bank of Scotland.

Under the Banking Act 1979 deposit-taking businesses require authorization from the Bank of England unless they are specifically exempted from the authorization provisions of the Act. Institutions may be authorized either as recognized banks or as licensed deposit-takers and are subject to the Bank of England's supervision. There follows a list of these recognized banks and a list of the licensed deposit-taking institutions (as at August 17, 1984):—

Recognized Banks

A P Bank Ltd.
Alexanders Discount p.l.c
Algemene Bank Nederland N.V.
Allied Arab Bank Ltd.
Allied Bank International
Allied Bank of Pakistan Ltd.
Allied Irish Banks Ltd.
Allied Irish Investment Bank Ltd.
American Express International Banking Corporation
American National Bank and Trust Company of Chicago
Amsterdam-Rotterdam Bank N.V.
Anglo-Romanian Bank Ltd.
Henry Ansbacher & Co. Ltd.
Arab Bank Ltd.
Arbuthnot Latham Bank Ltd.
Associated Japanese Bank (International) Ltd.
Atlantic International Bank Ltd.
Australia & New Zealand Banking Group Ltd.

Banca Commerciale Italiana
Banca Nazionale del Lavoro
Banco Central, S.A.
Banco de Bilbao S.A.
Banco de la Nación Argentina
Banco de Santander, S.A.
Banco de Vizcaya S.A.
Banco di Roma S.p.A.
Banco do Brasil S.A.
Banco do Estado de São Paulo S.A.
Banco Espirito Santo e Comercial de Lisboa
Banco Exterior-U.K. S.A.
Banco Mercantil de São Paulo S.A.
Banco Nacional de Mexico S.N.C.
Banco Português do Atlântico
Banco Real S.A.
Banco Totta & Açores E.P.
Banco Urquijo Hispano Americano Ltd.
Bancomer, S.N.C.
Bangkok Bank Ltd.
Bank Julius Baer & Co. Ltd.
Bank Bumiputra Malaysia Berhad
Bank für Gemeinwirtschaft A.G.
Bank Hapoalim B.M.
Bank Leumi (U.K.) p.l.c.
Bank Mellat
Bank Melli Iran
Bank of America International Ltd.
Bank of America N.T. & S.A.
Bank of Baroda
The Bank of California N.A.
Bank of Ceylon
Bank of China
Bank of Cyprus (London) Ltd.
Bank of India
The Bank of Ireland
Bank of London & South America Ltd.
Bank of Montreal
The Bank of New York
Bank of New Zealand

The Bank of Nova Scotia
Bank of Scotland
The Bank of Tokyo, Ltd.
Bank of Tokyo International Ltd.
The Bank of Tokyo Trust Company
The Bank of Yokohama Ltd.
Bank Saderat Iran
Bank Sepah
Bankers Trust Company
Banque Belge Ltd.
Banque Belgo-Zairoise S.A.
Banque Bruxelles Lambert S.A.
Banque Française du Commerce Extérieur
Banque Indosuez
Banque Nationale de Paris p.l.c.
Banque Paribas
Barclays Bank p.l.c.
Barclays Bank International Ltd.
Barclays Merchant Bank Ltd.
Baring Brothers & Co. Ltd.
Bayerische Hypotheken-und-Wechsel-Bank A.G.
Bayerische Landesbank Girozentrale
Bayerische Vereinsbank
Berliner Bank A.G.
The British Bank of the Middle East
The British Linen Bank Ltd.
Brown, Shipley & Co. Ltd.

Canadian Imperial Bank of Commerce
Carolina Bank Ltd.
Cater Allen Ltd.
Centerre Bank N.A.
Central Bank of India
Central Trustee Savings Bank Ltd.
The Chartered Bank
Charterhouse Japhet p.l.c.
Chase Bank (Ireland) Ltd.
The Chase Manhattan Bank, N.A.
Chase Manhattan Ltd.
Chemical Bank
Chemical Bank International Ltd.
The Cho-Heung Bank, Ltd.
The Chuo Trust & Banking Company Ltd.
Citibank N.A.
Citicorp International Bank Ltd.
Clive Discount Company Ltd.
Clydesdale Bank p.l.c.
Comerica Bank-Detroit
Commercial Bank of Korea Ltd.
The Commercial Bank of the Near East p.l.c.
Commercial Bank of Wales p.l.c.
Commerzbank A.G.
Commonwealth Bank of Australia
Continental Illinois National Bank and Trust Company of Chicago
Co-operative Bank p.l.c.
County Bank Ltd.
Coutts & Co.
Crédit Industriel et Commercial
Crédit Lyonnais
Credit Lyonnais Bank Nederland N.V.

Crédit Suisse
Credit Suisse First Boston Ltd.
Creditanstalt-Bankverein
Credito Italiano
Crocker National Bank
The Cyprus Popular Bank

The Dai-Ichi Kangyo Bank, Ltd.
The Daiwa Bank, Ltd.
Deutsche Bank A.G.
Discount Bank (Overseas) Ltd.
Dresdner Bank A.G.

Euro-Latinamerican Bank Ltd.
European Arab Bank Ltd.
European Banking Company Ltd.
European Brazilian Bank Ltd.

The Fidelity Bank
First City National Bank of Houston
First Interstate Bank of California
First Interstate Ltd.
The First National Bank of Boston
The First National Bank of Chicago
First National Bank of Maryland
First National Bank of Minneapolis
First Pennsylvania Bank N.A.
First Wisconsin National Bank of Milwaukee
Robert Fleming & Co. Ltd.
French Bank of Southern Africa Ltd.
The Fuji Bank, Ltd.

Gerrard & National p.l.c.
Ghana Commercial Bank
Grindlay Brandts Ltd.
Grindlays Bank p.l.c.
Guinness Mahon & Co. Ltd.
Gulf International Bank B.S.C.

Habib Bank A.G. Zurich
Habib Bank Ltd.
Hambros Bank Ltd.
Hanil Bank
Havana International Bank Ltd.
Hessische Landesbank-Girozentrale
Hill Samuel & Co. Ltd.
C. Hoare & Co.
The Hokkaido Takushoku Bank, Ltd.
The Hongkong and Shanghai Banking Corporation
Hungarian International Bank Ltd.

The Industrial Bank of Japan, Ltd.
InterFirst Bank Dallas, N.A.
International Commercial Bank p.l.c.
International Energy Bank Ltd.
International Mexican Bank Ltd.
International Westminster Bank p.l.c.
Irving Trust Company
Italian International Bank p.l.c.

Japan International Bank Ltd.
Jessel, Toynbee & Gillett p.l.c.
Johnson Matthey Bankers Ltd.
Leopold Joseph & Sons Ltd.

King & Shaxson p.l.c.
Kleinwort, Benson Ltd.
Korea Exchange Bank
Korea First Bank
The Kyowa Bank, Ltd.

Lazard Brothers & Co., Ltd.
Libra Bank Ltd.
Lloyds Bank p.l.c.
Lloyds Bank International Ltd.
Lloyds Bank International (France) Ltd.
London & Continental Bankers Ltd.
London Interstate Bank Ltd.
The Long-Term Credit Bank of Japan, Ltd.

Malayan Banking Berhad
Manufacturers Hanover Ltd.

Manufacturers Hanover Trust Company
Marine Midland Bank N.A.
Mellon Bank, N.A.
Mercantile Bank Ltd.
Merrill Lynch International Bank Ltd.
Midland Bank p.l.c.
The Mitsubishi Bank Ltd.
The Mitsubishi Trust and Banking Corporation
The Mitsui Bank Ltd.
The Mitsui Trust & Banking Company Ltd.
Samuel Montagu & Co. Ltd.
Morgan Grenfell & Co. Ltd.
Morgan Guaranty Trust Company of New York
Moscow Narodny Bank Ltd.

NCNB National Bank of North Carolina
National Bank of Abu Dhabi
National Bank of Canada
National Bank of Detroit
National Bank of Greece S.A.
The National Bank of New Zealand Ltd.
National Bank of Pakistan
National Commercial Banking Corporation of Aus-
   tralia Ltd.
National Westminster Bank p.l.c.
Nederlandsche Middenstandsbank N.V.
Nedbank Ltd.
The Nippon Credit Bank, Ltd.
Noble Grossart Ltd.
Nordic Bank p.l.c.
Northern Bank Ltd.
The Northern Trust Company

Orion Royal Bank Ltd.
Oversea-Chinese Banking Corporation Ltd.
Overseas Union Bank Ltd.

PK Christiania Bank (UK) Ltd.
Philippine National Bank
Postipankki (UK) Ltd.
Privatbanken Ltd.
Punjab National Bank

Qatar National Bank S.A.Q.
Gerald Quin, Cope & Co. Ltd.

Rafidain Bank
Rea Brothers p.l.c.
P. S. Refson & Co. Ltd.
RepublicBank Dallas, N.A.
Reserve Bank of Australia
The Riggs National Bank of Washington, D.C.
N. M. Rothschild & Sons Ltd.
The Royal Bank of Canada
The Royal Bank of Scotland p.l.c.
The Royal Trust Company of Canada

The Saitama Bank, Ltd.
The Sanwa Bank, Ltd.
Saudi International Bank (Al-Bank Al-Saudi Al-
   Alami Ltd.)
Scandinavian Bank Ltd.
J. Henry Schroder Wagg & Co. Ltd.
Seattle-First National Bank
Seccombe Marshall & Campion p.l.c.
Security Pacific National Bank
Shanghai Commercial Bank Ltd.
Singer & Friedlander Ltd.
Smith St. Aubyn & Co. Ltd.
Société de Banque Occidentale
Société Générale
Société Générale Merchant Bank Ltd.
Sonali Bank
The Standard Bank p.l.c.
Standard Chartered Bank p.l.c.
Standard Chartered Merchant Bank Ltd.
State Bank of India
The Sumitomo Bank, Ltd.
The Sumitomo Trust and Banking Company Ltd.

Swiss Bank Corporation
Syndicate Bank

The Taiyo Kobe Bank Ltd.
Texas Commerce Bank N.A.
The Thai Farmers Bank Ltd.
The Tokai Bank, Ltd.
The Toronto-Dominion Bank
The Toyo Trust & Banking Company Ltd.
Trade Development Bank

UBAF Bank Ltd.
Ulster Bank Ltd.
Ulster Investment Bank Ltd.
Union Bank of Switzerland
The Union Discount Company of London p.l.c.
United Bank Ltd.
The United Bank of Kuwait Ltd.

United Commercial Bank
United Overseas Bank Ltd.

S. G. Warburg & Co. Ltd.
Wardley London Ltd.
Wells Fargo Bank N.A.
Westdeutsche Landesbank Girozentrale
Westpac Banking Corporation
Williams & Glyn's Bank p.l.c.
Wintrust Securities Ltd.
Württembergische Kommunale Landesbank Giro-
zentrale

The Yasuda Trust and Banking Co., Ltd.
Yorkshire Bank p.l.c.

Zambia National Commercial Bank Ltd.
Zivnostenská Banka National Corporation

Licensed Deposit-taking Institutions

A1 (Investment) Ltd.
Abbey Finance Co. Ltd.
Adam & Company p.l.c.
Afghan National Credit & Finance Ltd.
African Continental Bank Ltd.
Aitken Hume Ltd.
Ak International Ltd.
Al Baraka International Ltd.
Al Saudi Banque S.A.
The Alliance Trust p.l.c.
Allied Banking Corporation
Allied Irish Finance Co. Ltd.
Altajir Ltd.
Anglo-Yugoslav (LDT) Ltd.
Arab African International Bank
Arab Bank Investment Co. Ltd.
Arab Banking Corporation B.S.C.
Armada Investments Ltd.
Armco Trust Ltd.
Assemblies of God Property Trust
Associated Credits Ltd.
Associates Capital Corporation Ltd.
Auban Finance Ltd.
Avco Trust Ltd.

B.A.I.I. p.l.c.
B.C.F. Finance Co. Ltd.
B.M.I. (Hampshire) Ltd.
Badische Kommunale Landesbank Girozentrale
Banca Nazionale dell'Agricoltura SpA
Banca Serfin S.N.C.
Banco de Jerez S.A.
Banco di Santo Spirito
Banco di Sicilia
Bank Handlowy w Warszawie S.A.
Bank Mees & Hope N.V.
Bank of Credit and Commerce International S.A.
Bank of Ireland Finance Ltd.
Bank of Ireland Finance (N.I.) Ltd.
The Bank of Nova Scotia Trust Company (United
Kingdom) Ltd.
Bank of Oman Ltd.
Bank of Seoul & Trust Co.
Bank Tejarat
Bankers Trust International Ltd.
Banque du Liban et d'Outre-Mer
Banque Internationale pour l'Afrique Occidentale
S.A.
The Baptist Union Corporation Ltd.
Barbados National Bank
Barclays Bank Trust Company Ltd.
Barclays Bank UK Ltd.
Thomas Barlow & Bro. Ltd.
Beaver Investments Ltd.
Beirut Riyad Bank S.A.L.
Beneficial Trust Ltd.
Boston Trust & Savings Ltd.

Bradford Investments
Bridgeover Ltd.
Bridgeway Finance Ltd.
British Credit Trust Ltd.
Brook Securities & Co. Ltd.
Buchanan Securities Ltd.
Bucks Land & Building Co. Ltd.
Bunge & Co. Ltd.
Burns-Anderson Trust Company Ltd.
Business Mortgages Trust p.l.c.
Byblos Bank S.A.L.

Caisse Nationale de Crédit Agricole
Calculus Finance p.l.c.
Canada Permanent Trust Co. (U.K.) Ltd.
Canara Bank
Cassa di Risparmio delle Provincie Lombarde
Castle Court Trust Ltd. (in creditors' voluntary
liquidation)
Castle Phillips Finance Co. Ltd.
Cattles Holdings Finance Ltd.
Cayzer Ltd.
Cedar Holdings Ltd.
Century Factors Ltd.
Chancery Securities p.l.c.
Charter Consolidated Financial Services Ltd.
Chartered Trust p.l.c.
Charterhouse Japhet Credit Ltd.
Chesterfield Street Trust Ltd.
CP Choularton, Sons & Partners Ltd.
Citibank Trust Ltd.
City Trust Ltd.
Close Brothers Ltd.
Clydesdale Bank Finance Corporation Ltd.
CE Coates & Co. Ltd.
Cobnar Finance Co. Ltd.
Combined Capital Ltd.
Commercial Credit Services Ltd.
Commonwealth Savings Bank of Australia
Consolidated Credits & Discounts Ltd.
Consumer Credit Investments Ltd.
The Continental Trust Ltd.
Co-operative Bank (Commercial) Ltd.
Copenhagen Handelsbank A/S
Coutts Finance Co.
Craneheath Securities Ltd.
Crédit Commercial de France
Crédit du Nord
Cross & Bevingtons (Finance) Ltd.
Cue & Co.
Cyprus Credit Bank Ltd.
Cyprus Finance Corporation (London) Ltd.

Dalbeattie Finance Co. Ltd.
Darlington Merchant Credits Ltd.
Dartington & Co. Ltd.
Den Danske Bank af 1871 Aktieselskab
Deutsche Genossenschaftsbank

The Development Bank of Singapore Ltd.
The Dorset, Somerset & Wilts Investment Society
Ltd.
Dryfield Finance Ltd.
Dunbar & Co. Ltd.
Duncan Lawrie Ltd.
Dunsterville Allen p.l.c.

E. T. Trust Ltd.
Eagil Trust Co. Ltd.
East Anglian Securities Trust Ltd.
East Midlands Finance Co. Ltd.
Eccles Savings and Loans Ltd.
The English Association Trust Ltd.
Ensign Discount Co. Ltd.
Enskilda Securities-Skandinaviska Enskilda Ltd.
Equatorial Trust Corporation Ltd.
Everett Chettle Associates
Exeter Trust Ltd.

FIBI Financial Trust Ltd.
Fairmont Trust Ltd.
Family Finance Ltd.
Farmers (WCF) Finance Ltd.
Federated Trust Corporation Ltd.
FennoScandia Ltd.
Financial and General Securities Ltd.
James Finlay Corporation Ltd.
Finova Finance Ltd.
First Bank of Nigeria Ltd.
First Commercial Bank
First Co-operative Finance Ltd.
First Indemnity Credit Ltd.
First National Boston Ltd.
First National Securities Ltd.
Fleet National Bank
Ford Financial Trust Ltd.
Ford Motor Credit Co. Ltd.
Foreign & Colonial Management Ltd.
Forward Trust Ltd.
Robert Fraser & Partners Ltd.

Gillespie Bros. & Company Ltd.
Girozentrale und Bank der österreichischen Spark-
assen A.G.
Goldman Sachs Ltd.
Goode Durrant Trust p.l.c.
Gota (UK) Ltd.
Granville Finance Ltd.
H. T. Greenwood Ltd.
Greetwell Finance Ltd.
Gresham Trust p.l.c.
Greyhound Guaranty Ltd.
Grindlays Humberclyde Ltd.
Grindlays Industrial Finance Ltd.
Grosvenor Acceptances Ltd.
Gulf Guarantee Trust Ltd.

HFC Trust & Savings Ltd.
H. & J. Finance Co. (Midlands) Ltd.
The Hardware Federation Finance Co. Ltd.
Harris Trust and Savings Bank
Harrods Trust Ltd.
Harton Securities Ltd.
The Heritable & General Trust Ltd.
Hobart Securities Ltd.
Holdenhurst Securities Ltd.
Houston Financial Services Ltd.

IBJ International Ltd.
Industrial Finance and Investment Corporation p.l.c.
Industrial Funding Trust Ltd.
The Investment Bank of Ireland Ltd.
Investment Trustees Ltd.
Investors in Industry p.l.c.
Investors in Industry Group p.l.c.
Iran Overseas Investment Corporation Ltd.
Istituto Bancario San Paolo di Torino
ItaB Group Ltd.

Jabac Finances Ltd.

Kansallis-Osake-Pankki
Keesler Federal Credit Union
Kingsnorth Trust Ltd.
Kintyre Securities Ltd.
Knowsley & Co. Ltd.

Little Lakes Finance Ltd.
Lloyds & Scottish p.l.c.
Lloyds Bank (LABCO) Ltd.
Lloyds Bowmaker Ltd.
Lodhi Finance Ltd.
Lombard Acceptances Ltd.
Lombard & Ulster Ltd.
Lombard North Central p.l.c.
Lombard Street Investment Trust Co. Ltd.
London and Arab Investments Ltd.
London Law Securities Ltd.
London Scottish Finance Corporation p.l.c.
Lordsvale Finance Ltd.

McNeill Pearson Ltd.
Mallinhall Ltd.
Manchester Exchange Trust Ltd.
W. M. Mann & Co. (Investments) Ltd.
Edward Manson & Co. Ltd.
Manufacturers Hanover Export Finance Ltd.
Manufacturers Hanover Finance Ltd.
The Mardun Investment Co. Ltd.
Matheson Trust Co. Ltd.
Medens Trust Ltd.
Meghraj & Sons Ltd.
Mercantile Credit Company Ltd.
Mercury Provident Society Ltd.
Merseyside Finance Ltd.
The Methodist Chapel Aid Association Ltd.
Middle East Bank Ltd.
Midland Bank Finance Corporation Ltd.
Midland Bank Industrial Equity Holdings Ltd.
Midland Bank Trust Company Ltd.
Milford Mutual Facilities Ltd.
Minster Trust Ltd.
Moneycare Ltd.
Moorgate Mercantile Holdings p.l.c.
Mount Credit Corporation Ltd.
Multibanco Comermex S.N.C.
Muslim Commercial Bank Ltd.
Mynshul Trust Ltd.

N.I.I.B. Group Ltd.
National Bank of Egypt
National Bank of Fort Sam Houston
The National Bank of Kuwait S.A.K.
National Bank of Nigeria Ltd.
National Commercial & Glyns Ltd.
National Guardian Finance Corporation Ltd.
New Nigeria Bank Ltd.
The North of Scotland Finance Co. Ltd.
North West Securities Ltd.
Northern Bank Development Corporation Ltd.
Northern Bank Executor & Trustee Company Ltd.
Northern Ireland Industrial Bank (I.O.M.) Ltd.
Norwich General Trust Ltd.

Omega Trust Co. Ltd.
Oppenheimer Money Management Ltd.
Oriental Credit Ltd.
Overseas Trust Bank Ltd.

PL Investments & Savings Ltd.
Park Street Securities Ltd.
The People's Trust & Savings Ltd.
Phibrobank A.G.
Philadelphia National Bank
Pointon York Ltd.
Prestwick Investment Trust p.l.c.
Punjab & Sind Bank

Ralli Investment Company Ltd.
R. Raphael & Sons p.l.c.
Rathbone Bros. & Co.
Reliance Trust Ltd.
Republic National Bank of New York
Rhone Trust Ltd.
Riyad Bank
Roxburghe Guarantee Corporation Ltd.
The Rural and Industries Bank of Western Australia

S.P. Finance Ltd.
St. Margaret's Trust Ltd.
Schroder Leasing Ltd.
Scottish Amicable Money Managers Ltd.
Security Pacific Trust Ltd.
Shawlands Securities Ltd.
The Siam Commercial Bank, Ltd.
Smith & Williamson Securities
South Notts Finance Ltd.
Southsea Mortgage & Investment Co. Ltd.
Spring Gardens Securities p.l.c.
Spry Finance Ltd.
Standard Credit Services Ltd.
Standard Property Investment p.l.c.
State Bank of New South Wales
State Bank of South Australia
State Bank of Victoria
State Street Bank and Trust Company
Sterling Trust Ltd.
Svenska International Ltd.
Swiss Bank Corporation International Ltd.

TCB Ltd.
The Teachers & General Investment Co. Ltd.

Thames Trust Ltd.
Thorncliffe Finance Ltd.
Treloan Ltd.
Trucanda Trusts Ltd.
The Trust Bank of Africa Ltd.
Tullett and Riley Money Management Ltd.
Turkish Bank Ltd.
Türkiye İş Bankasi A.Ş.
Tyndall & Co.

Ulster Bank Trust Company
Union Bank of India
Union Bank of Nigeria Ltd.
United Dominions Trust Ltd.
United Mizrahi Bank Ltd.
Unity Trust Ltd.
Universal Credit Ltd.

Barrie Vanger & Co. Ltd.
Venture Finance Ltd.
Vernons Trust Corporation
Volkskas Ltd.

Wagon Finance Ltd.
Wallace, Smith Trust Co. Ltd.
Welbeck Finance p.l.c.
Wells Fargo Ltd.
West Riding Securities Ltd.
Western Trust & Savings Ltd.
Whiteaway Laidlaw & Co. Ltd.
Wimbledon & South West Finance Co. Ltd.
N. H. Woolley & Co. Ltd.

Yorkshire Bank Finance Ltd.
H. F. Young & Co. Ltd.

London Banking Hours are 9.30 a.m. to 3.30 p.m. (Saturdays, *closed*, except Barclays, open mornings only). In addition, some branches open on one evening a week from 4.30 p.m. to 6.00 p.m. *Scotland.*—Banking hours in Scotland are: Mon.–Wed., 9.30–12.30; 1.30–3.30; Thursday, 9.30–12.30; 1.30–3.30; 4.30–6 p.m.; Fri. 9.30–3.30; Saturday, *closed*.

FINANCIAL FIGURES, ETC. FOR THE "BIG FOUR" BANKS, 1983

Bank Group	Profit before taxation £m	Profit after taxation £m	Total Assets £m	Number of U.K. branches
Barclays	557 (495)	337 (364)	64,904 (59,046)	Over 2,900
Lloyds	419 (329)	284 (249)	38,432 (34,435)	2,467
Midland	225 (251)	125 (170)	52,613 (47,999)	2,500
National Westminster	503 (439)	—	60,017 (54,487)	Over 3,200

1982 figures in parentheses.

NATIONAL GIROBANK

The National Girobank provides a broad range of corporate and personal banking facilities. It operates through more than 20,000 U.K. post offices.

OPERATING STATISTICS	1982–83	1983–84
Number of accounts at year end, thousands	1,330	1,600
Average customer balances for year, £m	722	810
Number of transactions (including social security payments), millions	333	356

CLEARING BANKS, ETC.

Committee of London Clearing Bankers
(1821), 10 Lombard Street, EC3V 9AP

The Committee consists of the Chairmen of Barclays, Coutts, Lloyds, Midland, National Westminster, and Williams & Glyn's and meets regularly to discuss matters of common interest. It is the body through which the Bank of England communicates official policy to the banks and through which the banks may present their views to the Bank of England and the Treasury.
Secretary-General, K. S. Lucas.

Bankers' Automated Clearing Services, Ltd.
3 De Havilland Road, Edgware, Middlesex

Bankers' Automated Clearing Services is wholly owned by the five largest clearing banks. Its function is to accept transactions recorded on magnetic media, check, merge and sort them and distribute them to the 14 sponsoring banks. Nearly all standing orders are interchanged through BACS, as are direct debits originated by non-banking organizations for payments of rates, insurance premiums, hire purchase payments etc, and automated credit transfers. Credits are also received on magnetic media, mainly for payment of salaries and pensions.

A direct telecommunications service, linking users direct to BACS became available in 1983.
Managing Director, D. J. Pyne.

London Bankers' Clearing House
10 Lombard Street, EC3V 9AP

The Clearing System came into being in London during the second half of the 18th century and the London Bankers' Clearing House has served as a pattern for the Clearing Houses that have been established since throughout the world.

Two Cheque Clearings are operated each business day. The Town Clearing enables cheques of £10,000 and over to be cleared the same day, provided that such cheques are paid into and drawn on one of the hundred Clearing Bank branches, designated as Town Clearing branches, situated within a half-mile radius of the Clearing House. The General Clearing handles cheques which cannot be passed through the Town Clearing. On an average day, 6,000,000 cheques with a total value of £21,800 million are exchanged and paid through these two clearings. Inter-branch clearings are dealt with separately by each Bank.

A Credit Clearing is also operated. The daily average for this clearing, including work passed through the Bankers' Automated Clearing Service, is 2,000,000 items with a total value of £635 million.

At the end of the day each bank works out the net balance resulting from its transactions in that day's Town Clearing, the previous day's General Clearing and Credit Clearing and B.A.C.S. output and such differences as need to be adjusted. This net balance is either credited to or deducted from the bank's own account at the Bank of England.
Chief Inspector, E. W. Stubbs.

British Bankers' Association
10 Lombard Street, EC3V 9EL

The Association provides a means of communication and consultation for the banking industry in this country. Membership is open to institutions accepted as recognized banks by the Bank of England—nearly 300. The Association is a member of the E.C. Banking Federation.
Secretary-General, J. B. Atherton.

Finance Houses Association
18 Upper Grosvenor Street, W1X 9PB

Director-Secretary, J. B. Damer, o.b.e.

Bank for International Settlements
(1930), Centrebahnplatz 2, 4002 Basle, Switzerland.

The objectives of the Bank are to promote the co-operation of central banks; to provide facilities for international financial operations; and to act as trustee or agent in international financial settlements entrusted to it. The London agent is the Bank of England, and the Governor of the Bank of England is a member of the Board of Directors, in which administrative control is vested.

THE NATIONAL DEBT

Net central government borrowing each year represents an addition to the National Debt. At the end of March 1983 the National Debt amounted to some £127,000 million of which £3,000 million was in currencies other than sterling. Of the £124,000 million sterling debt, £96,000 million consisted of gilt-edged stock; of this, 29 per cent had a maturity of up to five years, 38 per cent a maturity of over five years and up to 15 years and 34 per cent a maturity of over 15 years or undated. The remaining sterling debt was made up mainly of national savings (£17,000 million), certificates of tax deposits, Treasury bills, and Ways and Means advances (very short-term government borrowing).

LEGAL NOTES

IMPORTANT

The Purpose of these notes is to outline some of the more common parts of the law as they may affect the average person, and they are, of course, believed to be correct at the time of going to press. The law is constantly developing and changing, however, and it is dangerous for the layman to seek to be his own lawyer—he may not have access to completely up to date books and his case may, because of its special facts, come within an exception to the general rules set out herein.

It is always best to take expert advice, and if you have a Solicitor who has acted for you in the past you should take any legal problems you have to him. If you do not have a Solicitor a friend may be able to recommend one. Failing this your local Citizens' Advice Bureau (whose address can be obtained from the Telephone Directory or from any Post Office or Town Hall) has a list of Solicitors in your area who deal with that particular type of problem which you have. If you are not able to find a Solicitor in any of these ways you should ask for help in doing so from The Law Society, 113 Chancery Lane, London, W.C.2 or 26 Drumsheugh Gardens, Edinburgh.

The Legal Aid and Legal Advice and Assistance schemes exist to make the help of the trained lawyer available to everyone whatever their means as of right. The best policy is if in doubt go to a Solicitor without delay—timely advice will set your mind at rest but sitting on your rights can mean that you lose them.

Remember also that it is not necessary for a dispute to have arisen before you go to a Solicitor—the Legal Advice and Assistance Scheme enables him to advise you on your rights say under a tenancy agreement, the estate of a deceased person or in connection with matrimonial and consumer matters, and to write letters or take other steps on your behalf. He can also act for you where there is no question of a dispute at all, e.g. in the making of a will.

Your entitlement to take advantage of the Scheme depends on your means (see below) but a Solicitor or Citizens' Advice Bureau will be able to tell you whether you are covered by it.

BRITISH CITIZENSHIP

Types of citizenship.—There are three types of citizenship known as "British Citizenship", "Citizenship of the British Dependent Territories", and "British Overseas Citizenship".

Acquisition of citizenship on change of law.—The British Nationality Act 1981 which came into force on 1st January 1983 made substantial changes to the law of citizenship (which before that date did not distinguish between the three types of citizenship referred to above). Almost all persons who were then both citizens of the U.K. and Colonies and who had a right of abode in the U.K. became British Citizens when the Act came into force. Most U.K. and Colonies Citizens who did not have a right of abode in the U.K. became Citizens of the British Dependent Territories. This type of citizenship was, broadly speaking, conferred on citizens of the U.K. and Colonies by birth naturalization or registration in dependent territories. Dependent territories include Hong Kong, Gibraltar, the Falkland Islands, St Christopher and Nevis and St Helena and its dependencies. Any U.K. and Colonies Citizen who, on 1st Jan. 1983, did not acquire either British or British Dependent Territories' Citizenship became a British Overseas Citizen.

Later acquisition of British Citizenship.—British Citizenship is acquired automatically by those born in the U.K. (including, for this purpose, the Channel Islands and the Isle of Man) who have a parent who is a British Citizen or a parent who is settled in the U.K. Certain other categories of children born in the U.K. also acquire this type of citizenship i.e. foundlings, those whose parents subsequently settle in the U.K., those who live in the U.K. for 10 years from birth and those adopted in the U.K.

A person born outside the U.K. may acquire British Citizenship in the following ways:—

(i) if one of his parents is a British Citizen otherwise than by descent (e.g. parent was born in the U.K.).

(ii) if one of his parents is a British Citizen serving the Crown overseas.

(iii) if the Secretary of State consents to his registration while he is a minor.

(iv) if he is a Citizen of the British Dependent Territories, a British Overseas Citizen, a British Subject or a British Protected Person (these last two are residual categories of people who have not acquired one of the 3 new types of citizenship) and has been lawfully resident in the U.K. for 5 years without any time restriction.

(v) if he is a British Dependent Territories Citizen who is a national of the U.K. for the purposes of the E.E.C. (i.e. a Gibraltarian).

(vi) if he is naturalized. Naturalization may be applied for only by adults and the Secretary of State has a discretion whether to permit it. The basic requirements are five years' residence, good character, sufficient knowledge of the English or Welsh language, and an intention to reside in the U.K. permanently. The requirements are somewhat less restrictive in the case of an applicant who is married to a British Citizen.

(vii) various rights to Citizenship given under the old law are perserved for a period of five years in respect of Commonwealth Citizens settled in the U.K. before 1973, wives of Citizens of the U.K. and Colonies, persons descended from U.K. Citizens and persons who have previously renounced citizenship.

Acquisition of British Dependent Territories and British Overseas Citizenship after the Act.—These citizenships are intended for persons connected with certain Commonwealth countries other than the U.K. In the case of Dependent Territories the rules are very similar to those for acquiring British Citizenship except that the connection is with the Dependent Territory rather than with the U.K. British Overseas Citizenship may be acquired by the minor children and wives of British Overseas Citizens in certain circumstances.

Retention of nationality by persons born in or who are citizens of the Republic of Ireland.—By the Ireland Act 1949, a person who was born before December 6th, 1922, in what is now the Republic of Ireland (Eire) and was a British subject immediately before January 1st, 1949, is not deemed to have ceased to be a British subject unless either (i) he was domiciled in the Irish Free State on December 6th, 1922 or (ii) was on or after April 10th, 1935, and before January 1st, 1949, permanently resident there, or (iii) had before January 1st, 1949, been registered as a citizen of Eire under the laws of that country.

In addition by the British Nationality Act 1948, any citizen of Eire who immediately before January 1st, 1949, was also a British subject can retain that status by submitting at any time a claim to the Home Secretary on any of the following grounds:

(a) he has been in the service of the United Kingdom Government;

(b) he holds a British passport issued in the United Kingdom or in any colony, protectorate, United Kingdom mandated or trust territory;

(c) he has associations by way of descent, residence or otherwise with any such place; or on complying with similar legislation in any of the "Dominions".

The British Nationality Act 1981 provides that persons who have made a claim may continue to be British subjects. Any citizen of Eire who was a British subject before January 1st, 1949, who has not yet made a claim may do so provided:

(a) that he is or has been in Crown Service under the government of the United Kingdom; or

(b) he has associations by way of descent, residence or otherwise with the United Kingdom or any dependent territory.

Renunciation and Resumption.—A person may cease to be a British Citizen by renouncing his citizenship (with the consent of the Secretary of State in wartime). The renunciation will be required to be registered with the Secretary of State and will be revoked if no new citizenship or nationality is acquired within six months. Once renounced, citizenship may be reacquired if the renunciation was necessary to retain or acquire some other citizenship or nationality. Similar rules as to renunciation and reacquisition apply in the case of British Dependent Territories Citizenships and of renunciation (but not reacquisition) in the case of British Overseas Citizenship.

Status of Aliens.—Property may be held by an alien in the same manner as by a natural-born British subject, but he may not hold public office, exercise the franchise or own a British ship or aircraft. The Republic of Ireland Act 1949 declares that the Republic, though not part of H.M. Dominions, is not a foreign country, and any reference in an Act of Parliament to foreigners, aliens, foreign countries, etc., shall be construed accordingly.

CONSUMER LAW

1. THE SUPPLY OF GOODS AND SERVICES

(a) The Sale of Goods Act 1979 provides protection to the purchaser of goods, by implying certain terms into every contract for the Sale of Goods. These implied terms are:

(i) A condition that the seller will pass good title to the buyer (unless the seller agrees to transfer only such title as he or his principal has) and warranties that the goods will be free from undisclosed encumbrances, and that the buyer will enjoy quiet possession of the goods.

(ii) Where there is a sale of goods by description, a condition that the goods will correspond with that description, and where the sale is by sample and description, a condition that the bulk of the goods shall correspond with both sample and description.

(iii) Where the seller sells goods in the course of a business, a condition that the goods will be of merchantable quality, unless before the contract is made, the buyer has examined the goods and ought to have noticed the defect, bearing in mind the purchaser's knowledge of the goods and the extent of the examination, or the seller has specifically drawn the attention of the buyer to the defect. Merchantable quality means fit for the purpose for which goods of the kind are commonly bought, taking into account any description applied to them, the price and other relevant circumstances.

(iv) A condition that where the seller sells goods in the course of a business, the goods are reasonably fit for any purpose made known to the seller by the buyer, unless the buyer does not rely on the seller's skill and judgment, or it would be unreasonable for him to do so.

(v) Where there is a sale of goods by sample, conditions that the bulk of the goods shall correspond with the sample in quality, that the buyer will have a reasonable opportunity of comparing the bulk with the sample, and that the goods are free from any defect rendering them unmerchantable, which would not be apparent from the sample.

For these purposes, the broad difference between a condition and a warranty is that the remedy for a breach of an implied condition may enable the buyer to reject the goods and recover damages if he has suffered loss whereas the remedy for a breach of warranty will only enable the buyer to recover damages.

It is possible for a seller to exclude some of the above terms from a contract, subject to restrictions imposed by the Unfair Contract Terms Act 1977 as given below. These restrictions give more protection ... where the buyer "deals as consumer". In a contract of sale of goods, a buyer "deals as consumer" where there is ... a sale by a seller in the course of a business, the goods are of a type ordinarily bought for private use or consumption, and are sold to a person who does not buy or hold himself out as buying them in the course of a business. A buyer in a sale by auction or competitive tender never "deals as consumer".

The 1977 Act prohibits the exclusion of the implied terms given in (ii) to (v) above, where the buyer "deals as consumer". In sales where the buyer does not "deal as consumer", terms purporting to exclude these implied terms, may be relied upon only to the extent that it would be reasonable to allow reliance. The Act provides guidelines for determining whether it would be reasonable to allow reliance. The implied terms in (i) above cannot be excluded whether the buyer "deals as consumer" or not.

(b) Under the Supply of Goods and Services Act 1982, terms similar to those in the Sale of Goods Act relating to quiet possession, compliance with description, merchantable quality, fitness for purpose and correspondence with sample are implied into other types of contract under which ownership of goods passes (e.g. a contract for "work and materials" such as a supply of new parts during the servicing of a motor car) and also into contracts for the hire of goods. In the case of contracts under which ownership of goods is to pass, there is also an implied condition as to title.

The 1977 Act limits the exclusion of these implied terms in a similar manner to the implied terms in the Sale of Goods Act.

(c) The Supply of Goods and Services Act 1982 also implies into a contract for the supply of services, terms that the supplier will use reasonable care and skill, carry out the service within a reasonable time (unless the time is agreed) and charge a reasonable charge (unless the charge is agreed).

(d) The Trade Descriptions Act 1968 provides that it is a criminal offence for a trader or business-man to apply a false trade description to any goods, or to supply or offer to supply any goods to which a false trade description has been applied. A trade description includes a description as to quantity, size, method, place and date of manufacture, other history, composition, other physical characteristics, fitness for purpose, behaviour or accuracy, testing or approval. It is also an offence to give a false indication as to the price of goods. Prosecutions are brought by Inspectors of Weights and Measures.

(e) The Fair Trading Act 1973 is also designed to protect the consumer. It provides for the appointment of a Director General of Fair Trading, whose duties include keeping under review commercial activities in the U.K. relating to the supply of goods or services to consumers, and to collect information to discover practices that may adversely affect the economic interests of the consumer. He may refer certain consumer trade practices to the Consumer Protection Advisory Committee, or, of his own initiative take proceedings against firms that are trading unfairly. He may also publish information and advice to consumers. Examples of practices which have been prohibited by virtue of references made under this Act, include the use of certain void exclusion clauses in contracts for the sale of goods and hire-purchase, and advertisements by traders appearing to sell as private persons.

Scotland

The Sale of Goods Act, 1979, a consolidating Act, applies with some modification to Scotland. For example, it is not necessary in Scotland to distinguish between the words condition and warranty. The remedies of the buyer in both cases are the same, that is, he can either within a reasonable time reject the goods and treat the contract as repudiated, or retain the goods and treat the failure to perform such material part as a breach which may give rise to a claim for compensation or damages.

2. HIRE PURCHASE

England and Wales

At present, protection of the hirer against unscrupulous dealings and against delivery of shoddy goods is given by the Hire-Purchase Act 1965, which applies to hire-purchase agreements under which the hire-purchase price, *i.e.*, the total sum payable by the hirer to complete the purchase of the goods, does not exceed £7,500. The Act also provides that where the hirer is a body corporate, the Act is not to apply at all. [Note: Regulations have been made under which hire-purchase agreements entered into on or after May 19, 1985 will be regulated by the Consumer Credit Act.]

Before any agreement is made, the owner of the goods must state in writing to the hirer the cash price at which the goods can be purchased, and the agreement must be in writing signed by the hirer himself and by or on behalf of the owner and any guarantor. The agreement must contain (i) the cash price, (ii) the hire-purchase price, (iii) the amount of each instalment, (iv) when each instalment falls due, (v) a list of the goods, and (vi) a notice informing the hirer of his rights to terminate the agreement (*below*), and of the restrictions on the owner's right to recover the goods (*below*). If the agreement is complete as soon as the hirer signs it, and he signs it at trade premises, he must be given a copy there and then; in all other cases he must be given one copy when he signs and another within seven days of the completion of the agreement. There are also regulations dealing with such matters as the size of the print. In breach of any of these conditions the owner can neither recover the goods from the hirer nor enforce the agreement or any security given, although the Court can dispense with any of the conditions save that as to the signed agreement. The same results ensue (while default continues) if the owner fails without reasonable cause within four days after written request (with a tender of 12½p for expenses) to supply to the hirer a copy of the agreement and a statement of amounts paid, in arrear, and not yet payable. Before the last instalment becomes due, the hirer may by writing determine the agreement, and, although he remains liable for any instalments already due, he will be under no further obligation *under the agreement*. Under the Act, however, he must allow the owner to retake the goods and, if one-half of the hire-purchase price exceeds the total of the sums paid and due he must pay the difference to the owner unless the court considers that a lesser sum is sufficient to compensate the owner. These rights of the hirer cannot be taken away from him, but he can enforce more favourable rights (if any) under the agreement.

An important new provision in the Act gives the hirer the right to cancel the agreement and recover all sums paid if he signed it at a place other than trade premises. This right (which was designed to cover the activities of door-step salesmen) must be exercised within 4 days of receiving the second statutory copy of the agreement.

Any provision in the agreement giving the owner a right to enter any premises for the purpose of seizing the goods is invalidated by the Act. Further, even though the agreement may have been terminated because the hirer has broken it, or because the owner has exercised a right to terminate it, if one-third of the hire-purchase price has been paid or tendered, the owner cannot recover the goods otherwise than by action in a County Court, in which the Court can ensure that the hirer is fairly treated. If the owner disregards this provision, the hirer cannot recover the goods, but can recover all sums paid under the agreement.

The Trade Descriptions Act, 1968, further protects the consumer by making it a criminal offence for traders falsely to describe or advertise the quantity or price of goods or services; prosecutions are brought by Inspectors of Weights and Measures. The Act provides no civil remedies but, if there is a conviction, a consumer may be able to recover compensation under the Powers of Criminal Courts Act 1973.

An important new provision is the Unfair Contract Terms Act 1977 which provides, *inter alia*, that clauses purporting to exclude the owner from liability for defects in the goods shall be void in the case of agreements, where the hirer "deals as consumer", and in other agreements are valid only if they satisfy the requirement of reasonableness.

Consumer Credit Act 1974. This Act has received the Royal Assent, but many of its provisions are not yet in force. It is intended that the majority of such provisions will come into force on May 19, 1985. It provides a new system for the protection of the consumer, of licensing and control of all matters relating to the provision of credit, or the supply of goods on hire or hire-purchase, administered by the Director-General of Fair Trading. The Act takes the place of previous Acts of Parliament relating to moneylenders, pawnbrokers and hire-purchase traders, and the protection provided by the Trade Description Act 1968 and Unfair Contract Terms Act 1977 will be retained. The Act extends to the United Kingdom. Certain provisions of the Act have been brought into force, which are summarised below. A licence is required to carry on a consumer credit or consumer hire business, or to deal in credit brokerage, debt adjusting, counselling or collecting, for which group licences are available. Any "fit person" may apply to the Director of Fair Trading for a licence which is normally renewable after 10 years. A licence is not necessary if such types of business are only transacted "occasionally" or if exempt agreements only are involved.

For the Act's provisions to apply the agreement must be "regulated", *i.e.* be to individuals or partnerships only; must not be exempt, *e.g.* certain loans by local authorities or building societies; and the total credit must not exceed £15,000. The terms of a regulated agreement can be varied by the creditor, but only if the agreement gives him the right to do so, and the debtor receives notice in the prescribed form.

To be enforceable the agreement must be properly executed, and the specified information must be given during the antecedent negotiations for the contract. These are conducted by the creditor, credit broker or supplier (these being the creditor's agents) and begin when the parties first begin discussions.

Where there are arrangements or connections between the creditor and supplier the former is generally liable for any misrepresentation or breach of contract by the latter, and will thus be liable to indemnify the debtor.

Where the agreement requires the debtor to make grossly exorbitant payments or is contrary to the ordinary principles of fair dealing the Court can reopen it either at the debtor's request or during enforcement proceedings and (*inter alia*) alter the terms of the contract or set aside any obligations it imposes so as to do justice between the parties. Whether an agreement is such an extortionate credit bargain is decided by reference (*inter alia*) to interest rates prevailing at the date of agreement, the pressure for finance the debtor was under, etc.

If a credit reference agency was used to check the debtor's financial standing the creditor must give the agency's name to the debtor who is entitled to see the agency's file on him on payment of a fee of 25 pence.

Scotland

The Hire Purchase (Scotland) Act 1965 provides a Scots code corresponding to, but not identical with English law. The Supply of Goods (Implied Terms) Act 1973 also applies to Scotland. Parts II and III only of the Unfair Contract Terms Act 1977 apply to Scotland.

The Sale of Goods Act, 1979, applies with some modification to Scotland. The Consumer Credit Act (see above) also extends to Scotland, and goes far in assimilating the Scots law on this topic with English law.

3. RECEIPTS

The law on receipts in Scotland is governed by the Prescription and Limitations (Scotland) Act 1973, which for this purpose came into force on July 25, 1976. Now, receipts need only be kept for a period of five years and if a creditor does not make a relevant claim within that period no action can be raised.

CROWN—PROCEEDINGS AGAINST

Before 1947 proceedings against the Crown were generally possible only by a procedure known as a petition of right, which placed the litigant at a considerable disadvantage and which was not normally available at all in cases of tort (i.e., civil wrongs other than breach of contract). Thus, no proceedings would normally lie against the Government if a subject were injured by the negligent driving of a Government vehicle (although the driver could be sued) or if a Government employee were injured by the defective condition of the Crown premises on which he worked. Now however, by the Crown Proceedings Act 1947, which came into operation on Jan. 1, 1948, the Crown, in its public capacity, is largely placed in the same position as a subject, although some procedural disadvantages remain. Exceptions to the Act include the immunity of the Crown and any member of the armed forces when on duty from liability in tort in respect of death of, or personal injury to, another member of the armed forces on duty (or even if not on duty, on any land, ship or vehicle being used for the purposes of the Armed Forces of the Crown), provided that the death or injury is certified as attributable to service for purposes of pension.

Scotland.—The Act extends to Scotland and has the effect of bringing the practice of the two countries as closely together as the different legal systems will permit. While formerly actions against the Crown, when permissible, were confined to the Court of Session, proceedings may now be brought in the Sheriff Court.

The Act lays down that arrestment of money in the hands of the Crown or of a Government Department is competent in any case where arrestment in the hands of a subject would have been competent, but an exception is made in respect of National Savings Bank deposits. Section 2 (1) of the Law Reform (Miscellaneous Provisions) (Scotland) Act 1966 removes the privilege whereby the wages of Crown servants, other than serving members of the armed forces, are exempt from arrestment in execution.

DEATHS

REGISTRATION, BURIAL AND CREMATION

REGISTRATION

(For Certificates, *see* under FAMILY LAW–CERTIFICATES)

In England and Wales.—When a death takes place, personal information of it must be given to the local Registrar of Births and Deaths, and the register signed in his presence, by one of the following persons: (1) A relative of the deceased present at the death, or in attendance during the last illness. If they fail (2) some other relative of the deceased. In default of any relatives (3) a person present at the death; or, the occupier of the house in which the death happened. If all the above-named fail (4) an inmate of the house. A person (other than a relative) registering the death must be causing the disposal of the body. Relatives present or in attendance are first required to attend to the registration. The registration must be made within five days of the death, or within the same time written notice of the death sent to the Registrar. If the deceased was attended during his last illness by a registered medical practitioner, a certificate of cause of death must be sent by the doctor to the Registrar. The doctor must give to the informant of the death a written notice of the signing of the certificate, which must be delivered to the Registrar. It is essential that a certificate for disposal should be obtained from the Registrar before the funeral and delivered to the clergyman or other person in charge of the churchyard or cemetery. No fee is chargeable for this certificate. If the death is not registered within five days (or fourteen days if written notice of the occurrence of the death is sent to him) the Registrar may require any one of the above-mentioned persons to attend to register at a stated time and place. Failure to comply involves a penalty of ten pounds. The registration of a death is free of charge. After twelve months no death can be registered without the Registrar General's consent.

Whenever the death of a child is registered, particulars of the name and occupation of the mother are to be entered in the register.

A body must not be disposed of until (1) either the Registrar has given a certificate to the effect that he has registered or received notice of the death, or (2) until the Coroner has made a disposal order (*Births and Deaths Registration Act* 1926, s. 1).

A person disposing of a body must within ninety-six hours deliver to the Registrar a notification as to the date, place, and means of the disposal of the body (*ib.*, S. 3).

"Still-born" child (*see* under Births (Registration), p. 1176).

Death at Sea.—The master of a British ship must record any death on board and send particulars to the Registrar General of Shipping.

Death Abroad.—Consular Officers are authorized to register deaths of British subjects occurring abroad. Certificates are procurable at the Registrar General's Office, London. If the deceased was of *Scottish* domicile, particulars are sent to the Registrar General for Scotland.

With regard to the registration of deaths of members of the armed forces, and deaths occurring on H.M. ships and aircraft, *see* the Registration of Births, etc. Act 1957.

Deaths (Registration) in Scotland.—The Registration of Births, Deaths and Marriages (Scotland) Act 1965 supersedes provisions in former Acts.

Personal notification within 8 days must be given to the registrar of (*a*) the registration district in which the death took place or (*b*) any registration district in which the deceased was ordinarily resident immediately before his death, and (*c*) when a body is found and the place of death is not known, either the registration district in which the body was found or any other registration district appropriate by virtue of the preceding paragraph. When a person dies (in or out of Scotland) in a ship, aircraft or land vehicle during a journey and the body is conveyed therein to any place in Scotland the death shall, unless the Registrar General otherwise directs, be deemed to have occurred at that place.

The register must be signed in the presence of the registrar by one of the following: (*a*) any relative of the deceased; (*b*) any person present at the death; (*c*) the deceased's executor or other legal representative; (*d*) the occupier, at the time of the death, of the premises where the death took place; (*e*) if these fail, any other person having knowledge of the particulars to be registered. Failure to comply involves a penalty not exceeding £50.

The medical practitioner who attended the deceased during the last illness must sign a certificate of the cause of death within 7 days. If there is no such medical practitioner, any medical practitioner who is able to do so, may sign the certificate. At the time of registering the death the registrar shall, without charge, give the informant a certificate of registration, and the person to whom the certificate is given must hand it to the undertaker previous to cremation. A body may, however, be interred before the death is registered, in which case the undertaker must deliver a certificate of burial to the Registrar within three days.

There is, available from the Department of Health and Social Security, a death grant. Provided the deceased had paid enough Class I contributions and, if male, was not born before July 5, 1883 and if female, was not born before July 5, 1888, then the grant will be paid to his or her personal representatives. It normally amounts to £30 and is meant to help to pay for the deceased's funeral.

BURIAL

The duty of burial is incumbent on the deceased person's executors (if any appointed); it is also a recognized obligation of the husband of a woman, and the parent of a child, also of a householder where the body lies. Funeral expenses of a reasonable amount will be repayable out of deceased's estate in priority to any other claims. Directions as to place and mode of burial are frequently contained in the deceased's will or in some memorandum placed with private papers, or may have been communicated verbally to a relative. Consequently steps should immediately be taken to ascertain the deceased's wishes from the above sources. If the wishes are considered objectionable, they are not necessarily enforceable; legal advice should be taken. A person may legally leave directions for the anatomical examination of his body. As to the place of burial—unless closed by Order in Council—the parish churchyard is the normal burying place for parishioners, or any person dying in the Parish, but nowadays this will apply only in villages and the smaller towns. In populous districts cemeteries and crematoria have been established either by the local council, or a private company, and burials will take place there in accordance with the regulations. For an exclusive right to a burial space in the churchyard a faculty is required from the Ecclesiastical Court. Poor persons may be buried at the public expense by the local authority. As to the necessity for obtaining a registrar's certificate or authority from the Coroner for disposal, *see* above.

CREMATION

Under the Cremation Acts, 1902 and 1952, regulations are made by the Home Secretary dealing fully with the cremation of a body, disposal of ashes, etc., and containing numerous essential safeguards.

If Cremation is desired it is advisable for instructions to be left in writing to that effect. However, in Scotland, even if the deceased wished his body to be cremated or anatomically dissected, relatives can still veto his or her wishes.

To arrange for Cremation the Executor or near relative should instruct the undertaker to that effect and obtain from him the Statutory Forms required as given in the Cremation Regulations issued in 1930 (Statutory Rules and Orders, 1930, No. 1016), as amended by the Cremation Regulations 1965 (No. 1146).

INTESTACY

ENGLAND AND WALES

As regards deaths on or after March 15, 1977, the position is governed by the Administration of Estates Act, 1925, as amended by the Intestates' Estates Act, 1952, the Family Provision Act, 1966 and Orders made thereunder. The S.I. 1981/255 increased the benefits of a surviving spouse of an intestate. These notes deal with the present position, so that if the death occurred before March 1, 1981 reference must be made elsewhere. If the intestate leaves a spouse and issue, the spouse takes (i) the "personal chattels"; (ii) £40,000 with interest at 6 per cent. from death until payment; and (iii) a life interest in half of the rest of the estate. This life interest can be capitalized at the option of the spouse. "Personal chattels" are articles of household use or ornament (including motor-cars), not used for business purposes. The rest of the estate goes to the issue. If the intestate leaves a spouse and no issue, but leaves a parent or brother or sister of the whole blood or issue of such brothers and sisters the spouse takes (i) the "personal chattels"; (ii) £85,000 with interest at 6 per cent. from death until payment, and (iii) half of the rest of the estate absolutely. The other half of the rest of the estate goes to the parents, equally if more than one, or, if none, to the brothers and sisters of the whole blood or issue of such brothers and sisters. If the intestate leaves a spouse, but no issue, no parents and no brothers or sisters of the whole blood or their issue, the spouse takes the whole estate absolutely. If resident therein at the intestate's death, the surviving spouse may generally require the personal representatives to appropriate the interest of the intestate in the matrimonial home in or towards satisfaction of any absolute interest of the spouse, including the capitalized value of a life interest. In certain cases, leave of Court is required. On a partial intestacy any benefit (other than personal chattels specifically bequeathed) received by the surviving spouse under the will must be brought into account against the statutory legacy of £40,000 or £85,000, as the case may be. If there is no surviving spouse, the estate is distributed among those who survive the intestate in the following order (those entitled under earlier numbers taking to the exclusion of those entitled under later numbers):—(1) children; (2) father or mother (equally, if both alive); (3) brothers and sisters of the whole blood; (4) brothers and sisters of the half blood; (5) grandparents (equally, if more than one alive); (6) uncles and aunts of the whole blood; (7) uncles and aunts of the half blood; (8) the Crown.

In cases (1), (3), (4), (6) and (7) the persons entitled lose their interests unless they or their issue not only survive the intestate, but also attain eighteen or marry under that age, their shares going to the persons (if any) within the same group who do attain eighteen or marry. Moreover, in the same cases, succession is not *per capita*, but *per stirpes, i.e.*, by stocks or families. Thus, if the intestate leaves one child and two grandchildren, being the children of a child of the intestate, who pre-deceased the intestate, the two grandchildren represent their deceased parent and take between them one-half of the issue's share, the remaining half going to the surviving child. Similarly, nephews and nieces represent a deceased brother, and so on.

When the deceased died partially intestate (*i.e.*, leaving a will which disposed of only part of his property), the above rules apply to the intestate part.

Children must bring into account (hotchpot) any substantial advances received from the intestate during his lifetime before claiming any further share under the intestacy. Special hotchpot provisions apply to partial intestacy.

By the Family Law Reform Act, 1969, the position of an illegitimate child is equated with that of a legitimate child in respect of all deaths occurring on or after January 1, 1970. In respect of deaths after March 1976 the provisions of the Inheritance (Provision for Family and Dependants) Act 1975 may allow other persons to claim provision out of the estate. See *post* under "Wills".

For personal application for Letters of Administration—see p. 1173.

SCOTLAND

The Succession (Scotland) Act, 1964, provides that the whole estate of any person dying intestate shall devolve without distinction between heritable and moveable property. By that Act the surviving spouse of an intestate may, as a prior right (in addition to legal rights, *see* below), claim the matrimonial home to a maximum of £50,000, or a choice of one matrimonial home if more than one (or in certain circumstances the value thereof), with its furniture and plenishings not exceeding £10,000 in value, plus the sum of £15,000 if the deceased left issue or, if no issue, the sum of £25,000. These figures apply from 1st August 1981 and may be increased from time to time by order of the Secretary of State.

The Act has been modified by the Law Reform (Miscellaneous Provisions) (Scotland) Act, 1968, which provided that an illegitimate child had exactly the same rights of succession in the estate of his parents as a legitimate child. However, the position still remains that an illegitimate child has no succession rights in the estate of a grandparent even though such would have fallen to his predeceasing parent.

Legal rights, referred to above, are:—

Jus relicti (æ): the right of a surviving spouse to one half of the deceased's net moveable estate after satisfaction of prior rights if there are no surviving children, or to one third if there are any surviving children.

Legitim: right of surviving children to one-half of the net moveable estate of deceased parents if no surviving spouse, or one-third of the net moveable estate of deceased parents after satisfaction of prior rights where there is a surviving spouse.

There are no legal rights in heritage.

In general, the lines of succession are: (1) descendants; (2) collaterals; (3) ascendants and their collaterals, and so on in the ascending scale. The Crown is ultimus haeres. The right of representation, *i.e.*, the right of the issue of a person, who would have succeeded if he had survived the intestate, is open to any line of succession where previously it was limited to apply only when there were next of kin or the issue of predeceasing next of kin. The surviving mother of an intestate now has equal rights of succession with the surviving father, where formerly these were restricted. The intestate's maternal relations, who prior to the Act had no rights of succession, are now on an equal footing with his paternal relations. Where the intestate is survived only by parents, and by brothers and sisters (collaterals) half of the estate is taken by the parents and the other half by the brothers and sisters, those of the whole blood being preferred to those of the half blood; where, however, succession opens to collaterals—(which expression can include the brothers and sisters of an ancestor of the intestate)—of the half blood, they shall rank equally amongst themselves, whether related to the intestate (or his ancestor) through their father or their mother.

WILLS

IMPORTANT NOTE.—The following notes and those on Intestacy must be read subject to the provisions of the Inheritance (Provision for Family and Dependants) Act 1975 which can affect the estate of anyone dying domiciled in England and Wales after March 1976. Very broadly a spouse, former spouse who has not remarried, a child of the deceased himself or one treated by him as a child of his family, or any person maintained by him at his death may apply to the Court under the Act. If the Court thinks that the will or the law of intestacy or both do not make reasonable provision for the applicant it may order payment out of the net estate of maintenance or a lump sum. It may also order the transfer of property, vary certain trusts and the powers can affect property disposed of by the deceased in his lifetime intending to defeat the Act. It is up to the applicant to take the initiative, and the application must generally be made within six months of the grant of Probate or Letters of Administration.

In respect of earlier deaths, earlier Acts apply with a narrower class of applicants and less ample powers for the Court.

REASONS FOR MAKING A WILL.—Every person over the age of 18 should make a will. However small the estate the rules of Intestacy (see above) may not reflect a person's wishes as to his property; in any case a will can do more than just deal with property—it can in particular appoint executors, give directions as to the disposal of the body and appoint guardians to take care of children in the event of the parents' death. For the wealthier person an appropriately drawn will can operate to reduce the burden of Capital Transfer Tax.

It is considered desirable for a will to be properly drawn up by a Solicitor, and the making of a will is one of the services which he can provide under the Legal Advice and Assistance Scheme (see above).

In no circumstances should one person prepare a Will for another person where the former is to take any benefit under it—this can easily lead to a suggestion of undue influence which may cause the will to be held bad.

Assuming a lawyer is not employed, a person having resolved to make a will must remember that it is only after a person is dead, and cannot explain his meaning, that his will can be open to dispute. It is the more necessary, therefore, to express what is meant in language of the utmost clearness, avoiding the use of any word or expression that admits of another meaning than the one intended. Avoid the use of "legal terms," such as "heirs" and "issue," when the same thing may be expressed in plain language. If in writing the will a mistake be made, it is better to rewrite the whole. Before a will is executed (*see below*) an alteration *may* be made by striking through the words with a pen, but opposite to such alteration the testator and witnesses should write their names or place their initials. Never scratch out a word with a knife or other instrument, and no alteration *of any kind whatever* must be made after the will is executed. If the testator afterwards wishes to change the disposition of his estate, it is best to make a new will, revoking the old one. The use of *codicils* should be left to the lawyer. *A will should be written in ink and very legibly, on a single sheet of paper.* Although, of course, forms of wills must vary to suit different cases, the following forms may be found useful to those who, in cases of emergency, are called upon to draw up wills, either for themselves or others.

Nothing more complicated should be attempted. The forms should be studied in conjunction with the notes following.

This is the last will and testament of me [*Thomas Smith*] of [*Vine Cottage, Silver Street, Reading, Berks*] which I make this [*thirteenth*] day of [*February,* 1985] and whereby I revoke all previous wills and testamentary dispositions.

1. I hereby appoint [*John Green of —— and Richard Brown of ——*] to be the executor(s) of this my will.

2. I give all my property real and personal to [*my wife Mary or my sons Raymond and David equally* or as the case may be].

Signed by the testator in the presence of us both present at the same time who, at his request, in his presence and in the presence of each other have hereunto set our names as witnesses.
    Thomas Smith
    Signature of Testator;

William Jones (*signed*) of Green Gables, South Street, Reading, tailor.

Henry Morgan (*signed*) of 16, North Street, Reading, butcher.

Should it be desired to give legacies and/or gifts of specific property, instead of giving the whole estate to one or more persons, the form above should be used with the substitution for clause 2 of the following clauses:—

2. I give to —— of —— the sum of £—— and to —— of —— the sum of £—— and to —— of —— all my books (*or as the case may require*).

3. All the residue of my property real and personal I give to —— of ——.

TERMS.—Real property includes freehold land and houses; while personal property includes debts due, arrears of rents, money, leasehold property, house furniture, goods, assurance policies, stocks and shares in companies, and the like. The words "my money," apart from the context, will normally only include actual real money. The expression "goods and chattels" should not be used. In giving *particular* property, ordinary language is sufficient, *e.g.,* "my house, Vine Cottage, Silver Street, Reading, Berks." Such specific gifts fail if not owned by the testator at his death.

RESIDUARY LEGATEES.—It is well in all cases where legacies or specific gifts are made, to leave to some person or persons "the residue of my property," although it may be thought that the whole of the property has been disposed of in legacies, etc., already mentioned in the will. *It should be remembered that a will operates on property owned at the time it is made or acquired after it has been made.*

EXECUTION OF A WILL, AND WITNESSES.—The testator should sign his name at the foot or end of the will, in the presence of two witnesses, who will immediately afterwards sign their names in his and in each other's presence. A person who has been left any gift or share of residue in the will, or whose wife or husband has been left such a gift, should not be an attesting witness. Their attestation would be good, but they would forfeit the gift. It is better that a person named as executor should not be a witness. Husband and wife may both be witnesses, provided neither is a legatee. If a solicitor be appointed executor, it is lawful to direct that his ordinary fees and charges shall be paid; but in this case he (as an interested party) must not be a witness to the will.

It is desirable that the witnesses should be fully described, as they may possibly be wanted at some future time. If the testator should be too ill to sign, even by a mark, another person may sign the testator's name to the will for him, in his presence and by his direction, and in this case it should be shown that the testator knew the contents of the document. The attestation clause should therefore be worded: "Signed by Thomas Brown, by the direction and in the presence of the testator, Thomas Smith, in the joint presence of us, who thereupon signed our names in his presence and in the presence of each other, the will having been first read over to the testator, who appeared fully to understand the same."

Where there is any suspicion that the Testator is not, by reason of age or infirmity, fully in command of his faculties it is desirable to ask his Doctor to act as a witness (see Testamentary capacity below).

A *blind person* may make a will in Braille. If the testator be blind the will should be read aloud to him in the presence of the witnesses, and the fact mentioned in the attestation clause. A blind person cannot witness a will.

If by inadvertence the testator should have signed his will without the witnesses being present, then the attestation should be:—"The testator acknowledged his signature already made as his signature to his last will and testament, in the joint presence," etc. Any omission in the observance of these details may invalidate the will. *The stringency of the law as to signature and witnessing of a will is only relaxed in favour of soldiers, sailors and airmen in certain circumstances.*

EXECUTORS.—It is usual to appoint two executors, although one is sufficient; any number up to and including four may be appointed. The name and address of each executor should be given in full. An executor may be a legatee. Thus a child of full age or wife to whom the whole or a portion of the estate is left may be appointed sole executor, or one or two executors. The addresses of the executors are not essential; but it is desirable here as elsewhere, to avoid ambiguity or vagueness.

LAPSED LEGACIES.—If a legatee dies in the lifetime of the testator, the legacy generally lapses and falls into the residue. Where a residuary legatee predeceases the testator, his share of the residuary estate will not generally pass to the other residuary legatees, but will pass to the persons entitled on the deceased's intestacy. In all such cases it is desirable to make a new will.

An important exception to the general rule of lapse stated above is contained in the Administration of Justice Act 1982, where there is a gift to a child or remoter issue of the testator who dies before the testator leaving issue who survive the testator.

TESTAMENTARY CAPACITY.—A person under the age of 18 cannot make a will (except for soldiers, sailors and airmen and then only in exceptional circumstances).

So far as mental capacity is concerned the Testator must be able to understand and appreciate the nature and effect of making a will, the property of which he can dispose and the claims to which he ought to give effect. If a person is not mentally able to make a will provision exists (under the Mental Health Act, 1983) for the Court to do this for him.

REVOCATION.—A later will revokes an earlier will if it expressly says so, or is completely inconsistent with it. Otherwise the earlier one is only revoked insofar as it is inconsistent with the later one. A will may also be revoked by burning, tearing or otherwise *destroying* the will with the intention of revoking it. Such destruction must either be by the testator or by some other person in his presence and at his direction. *It is not sufficient to obliterate the will with a pen.* Marriage in every case acts as the revocation of a will, except that under the Administration of Justice Act 1982, there is a provision to the effect that if it appears from a will that at the time it was made the testator was expecting to be married to a particular person and that he intended that the will (or a disposition in the will) should not be revoked by the marriage to that person, the will will not be revoked by marriage to that person. The Act also provides that where after a testator has made a will the testator's marriage is terminated by a decree of divorce or nullity, any gift to a spouse shall lapse and any appointment of the spouse as executor shall be omitted from the will unless the will shows a contrary intention.

PERSONAL APPLICATION FOR PROBATE OR
LETTERS OF ADMINISTRATION

Application for probate or for letters of administration may be made *in person* at the Personal Application Dept. of the Principal Registry of the Family Division, a district probate registry or sub-registry, or a probate office by the executors or persons entitled to a grant of administration. Applicants should bring (1) the will, if any; (2) a certificate of death; (3) particulars of all property and assets left by the deceased; and (4) a list of debts and funeral expenses.

Intending applicants, before attending at a registry or probate office, should write or telephone to the nearest probate registry or sub-registry for the necessary forms. Postal or telephone applications cannot be dealt with at the local probate offices, which are part-time only.

Certain property can be disposed of on death without a grant of probate or administration, or in pursuance of a nomination made by the deceased, provided the amount involved does not exceed £5,000. *See* the Administration of Estates (Small Payments) Act, 1965.

WHERE TO FIND A PROVED WILL

A will proved since 1858 must have been proved either at the Principal Registry at Somerset House, or a District Registry. In the former case the original will itself is carefully preserved at Somerset House, the copy of which probate has been granted is in the hands of the executors who proved the will, and another copy for Parliament is bound up in a folio volume of wills made by testators of that initial and date; the indices to these volumes fill a room of considerable size at Somerset House, where the indices may be examined and a copy of any will read. In the latter case, the original will proved in the District Registry, is kept there, and may be seen or a *copy* obtained, but a copy is sent to and filed at Somerset House, where also it may be seen. A general index of grants, both probates and administrations, is prepared and printed annually in lexicographical form, and may be seen at either the Principal or a District Registry. This index is usually ready by about October of the following year.

RECENT DEATHS.—A system introduced in 1975 enables a person to discover when a grant of Probate or Letters of Administration is made which may be invaluable to a creditor of the deceased or applicant under the Inheritance (Provision for Family and Dependants) Act 1975—see above. A "standing search" may be made by sending a request in the form set out below to the Record Keeper at the Principal Registry of the Family Division with a small fee. The searcher will receive particulars of any grant made in the previous 12 months or the following 6 months, including names and addresses of the executors or administrators and the Registry in which the grant was made.

FORM OF SEARCH

In the High Court of Justice
Family Division
The Principal Registry (Probate)
I/We apply for the entry of a standing search so that there shall be sent to me/us an office copy of every grant of representation in England & Wales in the estate of:—
Full name of deceased:
Alternative or alias name
Full address
Exact date of death
Which either has issued not more than 12 months before the entry of this application or issues within 6 months hereafter
Sgd.—(full address).

SCOTS LAW OF WILLS

A domiciled Scotsman, unlike a domiciled English-man, cannot in certain circumstances dispose effec-tively of the entirety of his estate. If he leave a widow and children, the widow is entitled to a one-third share in the whole of the moveable estate (her *jus relictae*), and the children are entitled to another one-third share equally between them (their *legitim*). If he leave a widow but no children—or children but no widow—the *jus relictae* or *legitim* is increased to a one-half share of the net moveable estate. The remaining portion is known as the *dead's part*. A surviving husband and children have comparable rights (*jus relicti* and *legitim*) in the wife's estate. The *dead's part* is the only portion of which the testator can freely dispose. Legacies and bequests are payable only out of the *dead's part*. All debts are payable out of the whole estate before any division. Pupils, *i.e.* a girl up to the age of twelve or a boy up to the age of fourteen, cannot make wills. Formerly a minor could dispose only of movables but since the passing of the Succession (Scotland) Act, 1964 he has a like capacity to test on heritable property. A will must be in writing and may be typewritten or even in pencil. A will may be either (1) *holograph, i.e.* written, dated and subscribed by the testator himself, in which case no witnesses are necessary; a printed form filled up by the testator or a typewritten document is not necessarily a *holograph* but may become so if the testator writes, in hand, at the foot of the form or document the words "*adopted as holograph*" followed by his signature and the date. Words written on erasure or marginal additions or interlineations in *holograph* writings, if proved to be in the handwriting of the maker of the deed, are valid; (2) *attested,* i.e. signed in presence of two witnesses. It is not necessary that these witnesses should sign in presence of one another, or even that they should see the testator signing so long as the testator acknowledges his signature to the witnesses. The Conveyancing and Feudal Reform (Scotland) Act, 1970 whilst altering generally the rules for the subscription of deeds, specifically (s. 44 (2)) makes no change in the rules applying to wills which must still be signed by the testator on every page. If the testator cannot write, or is blind, his will may be authenticated by a law agent, notary public or justice of the peace and two witnesses. It is better that the will be not witnessed by a beneficiary thereunder, although this circumstance will not invalidate the attestation of the will or (as it would in England) the gift. A parish minister may act as a notary for the purpose of subscribing a will in his own parish. Wills may be registered in the Books of the Sheriffdom in which the deceased died domiciled, or in the Books of Council and Session, H.M. General Register House, Edinburgh. The original deed may be inspected on payment of a small fee and a certified official copy may be obtained. A Scottish will is not revoked by the subsequent marriage of the testator. The subse-quent birth of a child, no testamentary provision having been made for him, may revoke a will. A will may be revoked by a subsequent will, either expressly or by implication; but in so far as the two can be read together both wills have effect. If a subsequent will is revoked, the earlier will is revived.

"Confirmation", the Scottish equivalent of Pro-bate, is obtained in the Sheriff Court of the Sheriffdom in which the deceased was domiciled at the date of his death or, where he had no fixed domicile or died abroad, in the commissariot of Edinburgh. Executors are either "nominate" or "dative". An Executor nominate is one nominated by the deceased in his will or, where such person has predeceased the testator, by the residuary beneficiary. An Executor dative is one appointed by the Court in the case of intestacy or where the deceased had failed to name an executor in his will and there is no residuary beneficiary. In the former case the deceased's next-of-kin are all entitled to be declared executors dative. An inventory of the deceased's estate and a schedule of debts, together with an affidavit, must first be given up. In estates under £10,000 gross, confirma-tion is obtained under a simplified procedure at reduced fees.

Presumption of Survivorship.—The Succession (Scotland) Act, 1964, referred to above provides, by s. 31, that where two persons die in circumstances indicating that they died simultaneously or if it is uncertain which was the survivor, the younger will be deemed to have survived the elder unless the elder person left testamentary provision in favour of the younger, whom failing in favour of a third person, the younger person having died intestate (partially or wholly); but if the persons so dying were husband and wife, neither shall be presumed to have survived the other.

EMPLOYMENT

WAGES AND HOLIDAYS

Under the Truck Acts, it is in general forbidden for an employer to pay wages other than in current coin of the realm, and it is illegal for an employer to deduct from the employee's wages sums alleged to be due to the employer. However, the application of these Acts is confined to manual workers, and domestic servants are specifically excluded from their operation. Even in the case of payments to workmen, certain deductions, including rent and the price of food to be consumed on the employers' premises, are not forbidden where the employee's written consent is obtained. Further, under the Payment of Wages Act, 1960, it is permissible for wages to be paid otherwise than in cash at the request of the employee, *e.g.,* by cheque, money order, postal order or into a banking account.

Under the Social Security and Housing Benefits Act 1982, an employee absent from work due to illness or injury is entitled to receive Statutory Sick Pay from the employer for a maximum of eight weeks in any year. No payment is made for the first three days of any period of illness. The employer can recoup the payments from his National Insurance contributions. The Equal Pay Act 1970, which extends to Scotland, and which came into force on December 29, 1975, prevents discrimination, as regards terms and con-ditions of employment between men and women employed on like work in the same employment.

PARTICULARS OF TERMS OF EMPLOYMENT

Under the Employment Protection (Consolidation) Act 1978, an employer must give each full-time employee within 13 weeks of the beginning of the employment a written statement containing the following particulars of the contract between them:

(1) the date when the employment began (when continuous employment began if previous work counts as continuous with this job);
(2) The rate of remuneration (or how it is calcu-lated);
(3) the intervals at which wages are paid;
(4) the hours of work;
(5) the employee's entitlement to holidays (includ-ing public holidays) and holiday pay;
(6) the title of the employee's job;
(7) terms relating to sickness, injury and sick pay;
(8) details of any pension scheme;
(9) the length of notice which the employee should give and receive in order to terminate the contract.

In addition, the written particulars must specify any disciplinary rules; and also must identify the person to whom the employee can apply if he is dissatisfied with any disciplinary decision or to seek redress of any grievance and what further steps may ensue.

TERMINATION OF EMPLOYMENT

An employee may be dismissed without notice if he is guilty of gross breach of contract, such as disobedience to a lawful order or dishonesty. He is then only entitled to wages accrued due at the date of dimissal.

In other cases, the employee is entitled to reasonable notice which, under the Employment Protection (Consolidation) Act 1978, must not be less than one week if he has been continuously employed for four weeks, but less than two years; after two years it is two weeks' notice increasing by one week's notice for each further full year worked up to a maximum of 12 weeks' notice after 12 years' service.

An employer who wrongfully dismisses an employee (i.e. with less than the length of notice to which he is entitled) is generally liable to pay wages for the period of proper notice.

An employee who has a fixed term contract has no claim against his employer for wrongful dismissal if his contract is not renewed when it expires. He may, however, have a claim for a redundancy payment or compensation for unfair dismissal. If he is wrongfully dismissed before his contract expires, he is generally entitled to remuneration payable over the full period of the contract.

An employee may be entitled to a redundancy payment or to compensation for unfair dismissal if the employment has been terminated by the employer (with or without proper notice) or he has a fixed term contract which expires without being renewed or the employment has been terminated by the employee by reason of the employer's breach of contract.

Under the Employment Protection (Consolidation) Act 1978, an employee who satisfies the foregoing conditions and has been continuously employed for two years and who is dismissed by reason of redundancy may be entitled to a redundancy payment calculated by reference to his age, pay and length of service.

The Employment Protection (Consolidation) Act 1978 also enables an employee who is unfairly dismissed to complain to an Industrial Tribunal (generally within 3 months of dismissal). The onus will then be on the employer to prove that the dismissal was due to capability, conduct, redundancy, illegality or some other substantial reason justifying dismissal. The tribunal must then decide whether the employer acted reasonably in dismissing the employee. If the employer fails to prove that the dismissal was due to one or more of the above five reasons, or the tribunal decides that the employer did not act reasonably in dismissing the employee, the dismissal will be unfair, in which case the tribunal can

(a) order re-engagement or reinstatement or
(b) award compensation consisting of a basic and a compensatory award.

For an employee to bring himself within the unfair dismissal provisions, he must have been continuously employed for a period not less than one year (2 years if the employer has not more than 20 employees).

All complaints of unfair dismissal are referred to a conciliation officer or the Department of Employment and a very high proportion of complaints are disposed of in this way.

FAMILY LAW
ADOPTION OF CHILDREN

In England and Wales this is now mainly governed by the Children Act 1975 and the Adoption Act 1976 though these are not yet fully in force. A court order is necessary to legalise the adoption, which, when completed, has the effect of making the adopted child the child of the adopter as if he or she had been born to the adopter in lawful wedlock, and the original rights and duties of the natural parents are thereby cut. The adopter has full rights as to custody, education etc. and the child is treated as his for the purpose of any devolution of property on an intestacy occurring or under any disposition made after the adoption order. The application may be made to the High Court (Family Division) or to a County Court or Magistrates' Court.

Orders may be made in favour of married couples, single, widowed or divorced persons, but not of one party to a marriage alone unless the other spouse cannot be found, is physically or mentally incapable of making an application, or they are separated in circumstances likely to be permanent. A person aged under 21 cannot adopt.

The child's parents or guardians must consent unconditionally to the making of the order unless the court dispenses with the consent, which it may do if the parent cannot be found or is incapable of giving his consent, is withholding his consent unreasonably, or has neglected or ill-treated the child.

Restrictions are placed on societies which may arrange adoptions.

An adopted person aged over 18 may apply to the Registrar General for information to enable him to obtain a full certificate of his birth, but before being supplied with the information he will be informed that counselling services are available to him.

An adopter and the adopted child are within the prohibited degrees for the purposes of marriage to one another.

All Adoptions in Great Britain are registered in the Registers of Adopted Children kept by the Registrars General in London and Edinburgh respectively. Certificates from these registers including short certificates which contain no reference to adoptions, can be obtained on conditions similar to those relating to birth certificates, (See below).

Scotland.—The Adoption Act 1958 and the Children Act 1975 are the main statutes governing adoption in Scotland. The Law is consolidated in the Adoption (Scotland) Act 1978 which however is not yet in force. A petition for adoption is presented either to the Sheriff Court or the Court of Session. As in England the petitioner(s) must be 21 or over and may be a married couple or one person who, if married, is living apart permanently from his or her spouse. The consent of the child's natural parents/guardians is required unless dispensed with, or the child is already free for adoption.

The Succession (Scotland) Act 1964, gives the adopted child the same rights of succession as a child born to the adopter in wedlock but deprives him of any such rights in the estates of his natural parents. The law is consolidated in the Adoption (Scotland) Act 1978 which is not yet in force.

BIRTHS (REGISTRATION)

When a birth takes place, personal information of it must be given to the Registrar of Births and Deaths for the sub-district in which the birth occurred, and the register signed in his presence, by one of the following persons:—

1. The father or mother of the child. If they fail; 2. the occupier of the house in which the birth happened; 3. a person present at the birth; or, 4. the person having charge of the child. The duty of attending to the registration therefore rests firstly on the parents. The mother is responsible for the registration of the birth of an illegitimate child. The registration is required to be made within 42 days of the birth. Failure to do this, without reasonable cause, involves liability to a penalty of twenty pounds. The registration of a birth is free. In England or Wales, the informant, instead of attending before the registrar of the sub-district where the birth occurred, may make a declaration of the particulars required to be registered in the presence of any registrar. Under the Public Health Act 1936, notice of every birth must be given by the father, or person in attendance on the mother, to the district medical officer of health by post within 36 hours of the birth. *This is in addition to the registration already mentioned.*

A "Stillbirth" must be registered and a certificate signed by the doctor or midwife who was present at the birth or has examined the body of the child must be produced to the registrar. The certificate must, where possible, state the cause of death and the estimated duration of the pregnancy. A stillbirth may only be registered within 3 months of the birth.

The re-registration of the birth of a person legitimated by the subsequent marriage of the parents is provided for in the Births and Deaths Registration Act 1953. When the Children Act 1975 takes effect special provisions will apply to the registration and re-registration of births of abandoned children, and the re-registration of births of illegitimate children showing the father's name; the mother must be party to the latter application and if the child is under 16 must show the father's formal admission or a court's finding of paternity.

Birth at Sea: The master of a British ship must record any birth on board and send particulars to the Registrar General of Shipping.

Birth Abroad: Consular Officers are authorized to register births of British subjects occurring abroad. Certificates are procurable in due course at Registrar General's Office, London.

The registration of births occurring out of the United Kingdom among members of the armed forces, or occurring on board H.M. ships and aircraft, is provided for by the Registration of Births, Deaths and Marriages (Special Provisions) Act 1957, applicable also to Scotland.

SCOTLAND

The Registration of Births, Deaths and Marriages (Scotland) Act 1965, supersedes former Acts. Personal notification within 21 days of any birth, must be given to the registrar of (*a*) the registration district in which the birth took place, or (*b*) any registration district in which the mother of the child was ordinarily resident at the time of the birth and (*c*) in the case of a foundling child, dead or alive, when the place of birth is not known, the registration district in which the child, or the body, was found, within two months from the date on which the child was found. When a child is born (in or out of Scotland) in a ship, aircraft or land vehicle during a journey and the child is conveyed therein to any place in Scotland, the birth shall, unless the Registrar General otherwise directs, be deemed to have occurred at that place.

The register must be signed in the presence of the registrar by the father or mother of the child, and if

they fail, by one of the following: (*a*) any relative of either parent who has knowledge of the birth; (*b*) the occupier of the premises in which the child was, to the knowledge of that occupier, born; (*c*) any person present at the birth; (*d*) any person having charge of the child. Failure without reasonable cause involves a penalty not exceeding £50.

The name of the father of an illegitimate child may be entered in the register of births at the time of registration if jointly requested by the mother and father, and the latter's name may also be recorded at a later date on declaration by both parents. A free abbreviated certificate of birth will be issued to the informant at the time of registration. Provision is made for the re-registration of the birth of a person made legitimate by the subsequent marriage of the parents or whose birth entry is affected by any matter respecting status or paternity, or has been so made as to imply that he is a foundling.

A still-birth must be registered and a certificate, signed by the doctor or certified midwife present at the birth or who has examined the body of the child, must be produced.

CERTIFICATES OF BIRTHS, MARRIAGES, OR DEATHS

England and Wales.—Certificates of Births, Deaths, or Marriages can be obtained at the Office of Population Censuses and Surveys, St. Catherine's House, 10, Kingsway, W.C.2 or from the Superintendent Registrar having the legal custody of the register containing the entry of which a certificate is required. Certificates of marriage can also be obtained from the incumbent of the church in which the marriage took place; or from the Nonconformist minister (or other "authorized person") where the marriage takes place in a registered building (*see, post,* under Marriage).

It is considered desirable when a certificate is required to consult the nearest Register Office who, if told the exact or approximate date and place of registration, will be able to advise on the best way of obtaining it, and any fees payable, which vary according to the type of certificate required and other factors.

English Registers.—Records of births, deaths and marriages registered in England and Wales since 1837 are kept at the Office of Population Censuses and Surveys, St. Catherine's House, 10, Kingsway, W.C.2. *The Society of Genealogists,* 37 Harrington Gardens, S.W.7, possess many records of Baptisms, Marriages and Deaths prior to 1837, including copies, in whole or in part of about 4,000 Parish Registers.

Scottish Registers of Births, Deaths, Marriages and Divorces.—Certificates of births, deaths or marriages registered from 1855 when compulsory registration commenced in Scotland can be obtained personally at the General Register Office, New Register House, Edinburgh, or from the appropriate local Registrar, on payment of the fee of £5·00 for a full extract entry of birth, death, or marriage, and £2·50 for an abbreviated certificate of birth. An abbreviated certificate of registration of deaths is issued free of charge for National Insurance purposes in certain cases. As from May 1, 1984 a central register of divorces was set up to accommodate the new divorce procedure in the Sheriff Courts. The fee for an extract decree of divorce is £5.

There are also available at the General Register Office old parish registers of the date prior to 1855, which were formerly kept under the administration of the Established Church of Scotland. An extract of an entry in these registers may be obtained on payment of the appropriate fee. A fee of £7·50 per day is payable for a general search of all the Scottish registers.

Registration of Presumed Deaths. (Prescription of Particulars) (Scotland) Regulations 1978 as read with Presumption of Death (Scotland) Act 1977 prescribe the particulars to be notified by the Clerk of Court to the Registrar General after a decree or variation order has been granted in an action of declarator of death of a missing person.

DIVORCE, SEPARATION AND ANCILLARY MATTERS

Preliminary—Matrimonial Suits may be conveniently divided into two classes, viz. (1) those in which it is sought to annul the marriage because of some defect; and (2) those in which, the marriage being admitted, it is sought to end the marriage or the duties arising from it. By virtue of the Matrimonial Causes Act 1967, all matrimonial causes are now commenced in one of the divorce county courts designated by the Lord Chancellor or in the Divorce Registry in London. If the suit becomes defended, it must be transferred to the High Court.

(1) *Nullity of Marriage.*—This is now mainly governed as to England and Wales by the Matrimonial Causes Act 1973. A marriage is void *ab initio* if the parties were within the prohibited degrees of affinity, or were not male and female, or if it was bigamous or if one of the parties was under the age of consent, i.e. 16, or in the case of a polygamous marriage entered into outside England and Wales, that either party was at the time of the marriage domiciled in England and Wales. Where the *formalities* of the marriage were defective, the marriage is generally void if *both* parties knew of the defect (*e.g.*, where marriage took place otherwise than in an authorized building). But absence of the consent of parents or guardians (or of the Court or other authority, in lieu thereof) in the case of minors does not invalidate the marriage.

A marriage is voidable (i.e. a decree of nullity may be obtained but until such time the marriage remains valid) on the following grounds—(*a*) incapacity of either party to consummate; (*b*) respondent's wilful refusal to consummate; (*c*) that either party did not validly consent to the marriage, whether in consequence of duress, mistake, unsoundness of mind or otherwise, (*d*) that either party at the time of marriage was a mentally disordered person; (*e*) that at the time of marriage the respondent was suffering from communicable venereal disease; (*f*) that at the time of the marriage the respondent was pregnant by another man. In cases (*e*) and (*f*) the petitioner must have been ignorant of the grounds at the date of the marriage and in (*c*), (*d*), (*e*) and (*f*) proceedings must be instituted within 3 years of the marriage. In all cases the court shall not grant a decree where the petitioner has led the respondent to believe that he would not seek a decree and it would be unjust for it to be granted.

The 1973 Act provides that a decree of nullity in a voidable marriage only annuls the marriage from the date of the decree. The marriage remains valid until the decree, and any children of the marriage are legitimate. Children of a void marriage are illegitimate unless the father was domiciled in England and Wales at the child's birth (or father's death, if earlier) and at the time of conception (or marriage if later) both or either of the parents reasonably believed the marriage was valid.

A spouse's insistence upon the use of contraceptives will not constitute wilful refusal to consummate within (*b*) above, even though there has been no normal intercourse, but it may in certain circumstances constitute unreasonable behaviour for the pur-

pose of divorce (as to which *see* below). Further it has been allowed as a *defence* to a charge of desertion against the aggrieved party.

(2) *Judicial Separation and Divorce.*—The second class of suit includes a suit for judicial separation (which does not dissolve a marriage) and a suit for divorce (which, if successful, dissolves the marriage altogether and leaves the parties at liberty to marry again). Either spouse may petition for judicial separation. It is not necessary to prove that the marriage has broken down irretrievably and the five facts listed (*a*) to (*e*) under divorce (below) are grounds for judicial separation.

Divorce.—The sole ground on which a divorce is obtained by either husband or wife is the irretrievable breakdown of the marriage. However, the court is precluded from holding that a marriage has irretrievably broken down unless it is satisfied of one or more of the following facts: (a) that the respondent has committed adultery since the marriage and the petitioner finds it intolerable to live with the respondent; (b) such behaviour by the respondent that the petitioner cannot reasonably be expected to continue co-habitation; (c) desertion by the respondent for 2 years immediately before the petition; (d) 5 years separation immediately before the petition (but only 2 years where the respondent consents to the decree). Matrimonial Causes Act 1973.

The foregoing is subject to a clause prohibiting any petition for divorce (but not for judicial separation) before the lapse of three years from the date of marriage, except in the case of exceptional hardship (upon petitioner) or of exceptional depravity of respondent (either party will be entitled to petition after one year when the Matrimonial and Family Proceedings Bill comes into force).

Desertion may be defined as a voluntary withdrawal from cohabitation by one spouse without just cause and against the wishes of the other. Where one spouse is guilty of conduct of a serious nature which forces the other to leave, the party at fault is said to be guilty of constructive desertion.

Provisions designed to encourage reconciliation.—The 1973 Act requires the solicitor for the petitioner to certify whether he has or has not discussed the possibility of a reconciliation and whether or not he has given the petitioner the names and addresses of persons qualified to help effect a reconciliation.

A total period of less than six months during which the parties have resumed living together is to be disregarded in determining whether the prescribed period of desertion or separation has been continuous. Similar provision for effecting a reconciliation exists in relation to the other proofs of break-down, but a petitioner cannot claim that it is intolerable to live with the other party if they have lived together for more than six months after discovery of the respondent's adultery.

Obtaining the Decree Nisi. Where the suit is defended, *i.e.* the respondent opposes the dissolution or the fact/ground on which the petitioner seeks it—the petition will be heard by a Judge in open court, the parties giving oral evidence. Where the suit is undefended, the evidence will normally take the form of a sworn written statement made by the petitioner which will be sent to the Court and read over by the Registrar. If he is satisfied that he or she has proved the contents of the petition, he will simply fix a date for a Judge to pronounce the decree nisi, it being unnecessary for either party to attend. Only if the Registrar is not satisfied as above will he order that the petition be heard formally by the Judge.

Children.—Subject to exceptions, the decree nisi cannot be made absolute unless a Judge by order declares that he is satisfied with the proposed arrangements for the welfare of any child of the family who is under 16 or under 18 and receiving education or vocational training. If the petition is heard in open court the Judge will normally do so at that time. Otherwise if there is no dispute as to the children between the parties and the proposed arrangements for residence, education etc. are specific, an appointment will be made for the Judge to interview one or both parents informally and if satisfied he will make an order to that effect. If not the Registrar may inform the parties that it is up to them to seek a hearing before the Judge to resolve the matters in dispute.

Decree Absolute.—Every decree of divorce or nullity is in the first instance a decree nisi, and the marriage subsists until the decree is made absolute, usually six weeks after decree nisi on the petitioner's application. After the decree absolute either party is free to remarry.

Maintenance, etc.—The court has wide powers to order either party to the marriage to make financial provision (*e.g.* periodical payments, a lump sum, the transfer of property) for the other party or any child of the family, having regard to the party's means, the recipient's needs and all the important aspects of the case. These so-called 'ancillary matters' often present more difficulty than the divorce itself especially affecting the home, and may go on long after the marriage is dissolved. There is, however, nothing to stop financial matters being negotiated by the parties through their solicitors before the divorce goes through.

The court may, where the husband has wilfully neglected to provide reasonable maintenance for the wife or children, order the husband to make provision for them, *even though* no matrimonial suit is pending between the parties to the marriage, and while such an order is in force the court may also deal with custody of and access to the children.

CUSTODY OF CHILDREN ETC.

The Court may make orders in respect of access to and the custody, maintenance and education of children in connection with a suit for divorce, nullity or judicial separation (above) or with an application to the Magistrates (below) whether the suit succeeds or not. In addition, if there is no other matrimonial suit involved a parent may apply for custody under the Guardianship of Minors Acts 1971, and any person may apply to the High Court for the child to be made a ward of court.

In all cases the welfare of the child is the first and paramount consideration. The categories of child who may be covered by any particular type of proceedings differ according to the nature of those proceedings and to the nature of the particular relief sought, but it should be borne in mind that in connection with divorce, nullity and judicial separation a child which has been *treated* by the spouses as a child of the family may be included as a 'child of the family' as well as the children of the spouses themselves. This also applies to most maintenance cases in the magistrate's court—see below.

When the Children Act 1975 comes into effect a new procedure called "Custodianship" will be introduced, basically allowing long term foster parents to apply for custody of the foster child.

Any dispute relating to the above matters should be placed in the hands of a Solicitor without delay (see Legal Aid, etc. below) and in particular it should be borne in mind that where there is financial need (because of, *e.g.* continuing education or disability) maintenance may be ordered for children even beyond the age of majority.

SEPARATION BY AGREEMENT

Husband and wife may enter into an agreement to separate and live apart, but the agreement, to be valid, must be followed by an immediate separation. It is most desirable to consult a solicitor in every such case, who will often advise obtaining a court order by consent to reduce the burden of tax.

MAGISTRATES' CUSTODY AND MAINTENANCE ORDERS

For many years the law relating to domestic proceedings in magistrates' courts was out of line with the divorce law which was reformed in 1969. The Domestic Proceedings and Magistrates' Courts Act 1978 took effect in early 1981 and now contains the relevant law.

A husband or wife can apply to a magistrates' court for a matrimonial order on the grounds that the other spouse (a) has failed to pay reasonable maintenance for the applicant or (b) has failed to make a proper contribution towards the reasonable maintenance of a child of the family or (c) has deserted the applicant or (d) has behaved in such a way that the applicant cannot reasonably be expected to live with the respondent. If the case is proved the court can order (a) periodical payments for the applicant (b) periodical payments for a child of the family (c) a lump sum (not exceeding £500) for the benefit of the applicant and for any child of the family. In deciding what orders (if any) to make the magistrates must consider a number of guidelines which are similar to those governing financial orders on divorce. There are also special provisions relating to consent orders and separation by agreement. The court also has powers to make orders relating to the legal custody of a child of the family and these orders together with orders for child maintenance can be made even though the court makes no order for spouse maintenance. Legal custody can only be granted to one person but the court may order that the other party shall retain certain parental rights and exercise them jointly with the person who is awarded legal custody. Other provisions of the Act relate to access by grandparents, interim orders, and variation, discharge and revival of orders. An order may be enforceable even though the parties are living together, but in some cases it will cease to have effect if they continue to do so for six months. The hearing of matrimonial disputes is separate from ordinary court business, and the public are not admitted.

DOMESTIC VIOLENCE

The Domestic Violence and Matrimonial Proceedings Act 1976, the Domestic Proceedings and Magistrates' Courts Act 1978 (the former not being applicable to Scotland and the latter only to a limited extent; but see note below) and the Matrimonial Homes Act 1983 have made it easier for one spouse who has been subjected to violence by the other to obtain an order to restrain further violence and if need be to have the other excluded from the home. Such orders can be obtained very quickly, and a person disobeying them is liable to be imprisoned for contempt of court. There are some differences of detail between the three Acts; in particular the 1976 Act also applies to unmarried couples. Such orders may also be obtained in the issue of suits for divorce and judicial separation.

SCOTLAND
Divorce

Actions of divorce could formerly only be raised in the Court of Session, having jurisdiction to entertain such actions only if either of the parties to the marriage in question (a) is domiciled in Scotland on the date when the action is begun; or (b) was habitually resident in Scotland throughout the period of one year ending with that date. As from May 1, 1984, however, when the Divorce Jurisdiction, Court Fees and Legal Aid (Scotland) Act 1983 came into force, actions of divorce may also be raised in the Sheriff Courts provided the above conditions (a) and (b) are complied with, and provided either party to the marriage was resident in the Sheriffdom for a period of forty days ending with the date the action was begun, or was resident in the Sheriffdom for a period of not less than forty days ending not more than forty days before the date the action was begun.

The Scots Law of Divorce is now governed by the Divorce (Scotland) Act 1976, which for the purposes of divorce came into force on January 1, 1977. The sole ground of divorce is now irretrievable breakdown of the marriage. This can only be established in one of the following ways:

(a) The defending spouse has committed adultery since the date of the marriage. Here it is not necessary for the pursuing spouse to prove that the fact of adultery made it intolerable to live with the defending spouse.

(b) The defending spouse has behaved in such a way that the pursuing spouse cannot reasonably be expected to cohabit with him or her. It is immaterial whether or not the conduct founded upon is active or passive.

(c) The defending spouse has deserted the pursuing spouse for a continuous period of two years. There must be no question of the pursuing spouse having refused a genuine and reasonable offer to adhere. Nor is irretrievable breakdown established if cohabitation is resumed for a period of more than three months, after the two year period has expired.

(d) There has been no cohabitation at any time during a continuous period of two years immediately preceding the action between the parties to the action, and the defending spouse consents to the divorce being granted.

(e) There has been no cohabitation at any time during a continuous period of five years, as in (d) *supra*, except that on the expiry of the five year period, the consent of the defending spouse is not required.

The facts of desertion and separation are not interrupted by the parties cohabiting for a period or periods not exceeding six months. However such a period or periods of cohabitation would not be included in the calculation of the two-year or five-year periods.

Encouragement of Reconciliation: The burden of promoting a reconciliation between spouses in a divorce action in Scotland falls upon the Court by virtue of the 1976 Act. Where an action of divorce has been raised, it may be postponed by the Court to enable the parties to seek to effect a reconciliation, if the Court feels that there may be a reasonable prospect of such reconciliation. If the parties do cohabit during such postponement, no account shall be taken of such cohabitation if the action later proceeds.

Maintenance, etc.: The 1976 Act also provides that either party to a marriage can apply to the Court at any time prior to decree being granted for (a) an order for interim aliment for him or herself and/or for children of the marriage under 16 years of age of whom he/she has custody (b) an order for interim custody of all or some of the children of the marriage under 16 years of age (c) an order for access to all or some of the children of the marriage under 16 years of age in the custody of the other party (d) an order

for a capital sum or a variation of a marriage settlement. The Court in granting or refusing such an order, known as an *interim* award, takes into account the respective means of the parties, and also all the circumstances of the case.

Nullity of Marriage.—A declaration of nullity of marriage may be obtained on the ground of any impediment, viz., consanguinity and affinity, subsistence of a previous marriage, non-age of one of the parties, incapacity or insanity of one of the parties, or by the absence of genuine consent.

Procedure.—Appearance in Court at a Proof in an undefended Divorce Action has been rendered unnecessary since April, 1978. A full Proof is still necessary if the action is defended in any respect. In place of court appearance Affidavits (Statements sworn before a Notary Public) by the pursuer and any witnesses are lodged in the Court together with a Minute by Counsel craving Decree.

A new Simplified Procedure for "do-it-yourself divorce" was introduced in January 1983 for certain divorces. Thus, if the action is based on (d) or (e) above and will not be opposed, there are no children under 16 and no financial claims, then the applicant can write directly to the Court of Session, Divorce Section (SP), Parliament House, Edinburgh or the local Sheriff Court for the appropriate forms to enable him or her to proceed. The fee is £40 unless the applicant receives supplementary benefit, family income supplement or legal advice and assistance in which case there is no fee.

Separation

Under the Divorce (Scotland) Act 1976 *supra*, a decree of Judicial Separation can be obtained by proof of the same facts necessary to obtain decree of divorce—except that for the principle of irretrievable breakdown there is substituted that of grounds justifying separation. This type of action is competent in both the Court of Session and the Sheriff Court.

Custody of Children

In actions for divorce and separation, the Court has a discretion in awarding the custody of the children of the parties. The welfare of the children is the paramount consideration, and the mere fact that a spouse, by reason of his or her behaviour, brought about the breakdown of the marriage does not of itself preclude him or her from being awarded custody. The Children Act 1975 (*supra*) also applies to Scotland.

Domestic Violence

The Matrimonial Homes (Family Protection) (Scotland) Act 1981 introduces a provision where one spouse—whether or not he or she has title to the matrimonial home—can obtain an exclusion order suspending the other spouse's occupancy rights in the matrimonial home. The Court (either Court of Session or Sheriff Court) is empowered to make such an order if satisfied that it is necessary to protect the applicant or any child of the family from any conduct, actual or threatened or reasonably apprehended of the other spouse which would be injurious to the physical or mental health of the applicant or child. In making the order the Court may include a warrant for the summary ejection of the non-applicant spouse from the matrimonial home and for an interdict prohibiting him/her from entering it.

ILLEGITIMACY AND LEGITIMATION
ENGLAND AND WALES

A man may be summoned to petty sessions on the application of the mother of an illegitimate child, or by the Supplementary Benefits Commission where benefit has been paid for the requirements of the child, and the Justices, on his being proved to be the father of the child, may make an order requiring him to pay for its maintenance and education a sum in their discretion. The woman is not bound to give evidence in every case but if she does so it must be *corroborated* in some material particular. The mother has the custody of her illegitimate children. *Prima facie* every child born of a married woman during a marriage is legitimate; and this presumption can only be rebutted by strong evidence. However, under the Family Reform Act 1969, any presumption of law as to the legitimacy (or illegitimacy) of any person may in civil proceedings be rebutted by evidence showing that it is more probable than not that the person is illegitimate (or legitimate) and in any proceedings where paternity is in question, blood tests may be ordered. If however the husband and wife are separated under an Order of the Court, a child conceived by the wife during such separation is presumed not to be the husband's child.

LEGITIMATION.—The Legitimacy Act 1976 consolidates earlier legislation dating back to January 1, 1927. Where the parents of an illegitimate person marry, or have married, whether before or after that date, the marriage, if the father is at the date thereof domiciled in England or Wales, renders that person, if living, legitimate as from Jan. 1, 1927, or from the date of the marriage, whichever last happens. Marriage legitimates a person even though the father or mother was married to a third person at the time when the illegitimate person was born. It is the duty of the parents to supply to the Registrar-General information for re-registration of the birth of a legitimate child.

Declarations of Legitimacy.—A person claiming that he, his parents, or any remoter ancestor has become legitimated, may petition the High Court or the County Court for the necessary declaration.

Rights and Duties of Legitimated Persons.—A legitimated person, his spouse or issue may take property under an intestacy occurring after the date of legitimation, or under any disposition (*e.g.*, a will) coming into operation after such date, as if he had been legitimate.

He must maintain all persons whom he would be bound to maintain had he been born legitimate, and he is entitled to the benefit of any Act of Parliament which confers rights on legitimate persons to recover damages or compensation. The Act specially provides that nothing therein contained is to render any person capable of succeeding to or transmitting a right to any dignity or title.

Property Rights of Illegitimate Children.—By the Family Law Reform Act 1969 the rights of an illegitimate child on an intestacy are now broadly equated with those of a legitimate child. Also, in any disposition made after December 31, 1969, any reference to "children" or other relatives shall, unless the contrary intention appears, be construed as including any person who is illegitimate or who is related through another person who is illegitimate.

SCOTLAND

Illegitimate Children (Scotland) Act 1930.—The mother of an illegitimate child may raise an action of affiliation and aliment against the father, either in the Court of Session or, more usually, in the Sheriff Court. Where in any such action the Court finds that the defender is the father of the child, the Court shall, in awarding inlying expenses, or aliment, have regard to the means of the parties, and the whole circumstances of the case. The Court may, upon application by the mother or by the father of any

illegitimate child, or in any action for aliment for an illegitimate child, make such order as it may think fit regarding the custody of such child and the right of access thereto of either parent, having regard to the welfare of the child and to the conduct of the parents and to the wishes as well of the mother as of the father and may on the application of either parent recall or vary such order. The obligation of the mother and of the father of an illegitimate child to provide aliment for such child shall (without prejudice to any obligation attaching at common law) endure until the child attains the age of sixteen.

By Scots Law an illegitimate child is legitimated by and on the date of the subsequent marriage of its parents and there is no objection to there having been an impediment to the marriage of the parents at the time of the child's conception—*see* the Legitimation (Scotland) Act 1968, which came into operation on June 8, 1968, on which date thousands of existing illegitimate children were regarded as legitimated. By the Registration of Births, Deaths and Marriages (Scotland) Act 1965, a child so legitimated, who has already been registered as illegitimate, may be re-registered as legitimate. The consent of the father of an illegitimate child to its adoption is not required.

The Law Reform (Miscellaneous Provisions) (Scotland) Act 1968, gives an illegitimate child full rights of succession (including legitim) in the estate of both parents, while the father and mother share equally in the estate of their illegitimate child. Unless expressly excluded, a reference in a deed executed on or after November 25, 1968, to a relationship, *e.g.*, "issue" or "children" is presumed to include illegitimate children.

MARRIAGE
A.—MARRIAGE ACCORDING TO RITES OF THE CHURCH OF ENGLAND

1. MARRIAGE BY BANNS.—The Marriage Act 1949, prescribes audible publication according to the rubric, on three Sundays preceding the ceremony during morning service or, if there is no morning service on a Sunday on which the banns are to be published, during evening service. Where the parties reside in different parishes, the banns must be published in both. Under the Act, banns may be published and the marriage solemnized in the parish church, *which is the usual place of worship* of the persons to be married or either of them, although neither of such persons dwells in such parish; but this publication of banns is *in addition* to any other publication required by law and does not apply if the church or the residence of either party is in Wales. The Act provides specially for the case where one of the parties resides in Scotland and the other in England, the publication being then in the parish in England in which one party resides, and, according to the law and custom in Scotland, in the place where the other party resides. After the lapse of three months from the last time of publication, the banns become useless, and the parties must either obtain a licence (*see below*), or submit to the republication of banns.

2. MARRIAGE BY LICENCE.—Marriage licences are of two kinds:—

   (i) *A Common Licence*, dispensing with the necessity for banns, granted by the Archbishops and Bishops through their Surrogates, for marriages in any church or chapel duly licensed for marriages. A Common Licence can be obtained in London by application at the Faculty Office (1 The Sanctuary, Westminster, S.W.1) and (for marriages in London) at the Bishop of London's Diocesan Registry (1 The Sanctuary, S.W.1), by one of the parties about to be married. In the country they may be obtained at the offices of the Bishop's Registrars, but licences obtained at the Bishop's Diocesan Registry only enable the parties to be married in the diocese in which they are issued; those procured at the Faculty Office are available for *all* England and Wales. No instructions, either verbal or in writing, can be received, except from one of the parties. Affidavits are prepared from the personal instructions of one of the parties about to be married, and the licence is delivered to the party upon payment of fees amounting to six pounds. *No previous notice is required and the licence is available as soon as it is issued.* Before a licence can be granted one of the parties must make an affidavit that there is no legal impediment to the intended marriage; and also that one of such parties has had his or her usual place of abode for the space of fifteen days immediately preceding the issuing of the licence within the parish or ecclesiastical district of the church in which the marriage is to be solemnized, *or* the church in which the marriage is to be solemnized is the usual place of worship of the parties or one of them. In the country there may generally be found a parochial clergyman (Surrogate) before whom the affidavit may be taken, and whose office it is to deliver the licence personally to the applicant. (In some dioceses it is necessary for the Surrogate to procure the licence from the Bishop's Registry.) The licence continues in force for three months from its date.

(ii) *A Special Licence* granted by the Archbishop of Canterbury, under special circumstances, for marriage at any place with or without previous residence in the district, or at any time, etc.; but the reasons assigned must meet with his Grace's approval. Application must be made to the Faculty Office. Fees for licence, etc., £25.

3. MARRIAGE UNDER SUPERINTENDENT REGISTRAR'S CERTIFICATE.—A marriage may be performed in church on the Superintendent Registrar's Certificate (as to which see below) without banns, provided that the incumbent's consent is obtained. One of the parties must be resident within the ecclesiastical parish of the church in which the marriage is to take place unless the church is the usual place of worship of the parties or one of them.

MARRIAGE FEES.—The Church Commissioners settle tables of fees for all parishes. The usual fees are paid although a stranger-clergyman may be invited to perform the service.

B.—MARRIAGE UNDER SUPERINTENDENT REGISTRAR'S CERTIFICATE

The following marriages may be solemnized on the authority of a Superintendent Registrar's Certificate (either with or without a licence):—

(a) A marriage in a registered building (*e.g.*, a nonconformist church registered for the solemnization of marriages therein).

(b) A marriage in a register office.

(c) A marriage according to the usages of the Society of Friends (commonly called Quakers).

(d) A marriage between two persons professing the Jewish religion according to the usages of the Jews.

(e) A marriage according to the rites of the Church of England (*see* above—in this case the marriage can only be *without* licence).

NOTICE.—Notice of the intended marriage must be given as follows:—

(i) Marriage by certificate (*without* licence)—if both parties reside in the same registration district, they must both have resided there for seven days before the notice can be given. It may then be given by either party. If the parties reside in different registration districts, notice must be given by each to the Superintendent Registrar of the district in which he or she resides, and the preliminary residential qualification of seven days must be fulfilled by each before either notice can be given.

(ii) Marriage by certificate (*with* licence)—one notice only is necessary, whether the parties live in the same or in different registration districts. Either party may give the notice, which must be given to the Superintendent Registrar of any registration district in which one of the parties has resided for the period of fifteen days immediately preceding the giving of notice, but both parties must be resident in England or Wales on the day notice is given.

The notice (in either case) must be in the prescribed form and must contain particulars as to names, marital status, occupation, residence, length of residence, and the building in which the marriage is to take place. The notice must also contain or have added at the foot thereof a solemn declaration that there is no legal impediment to the marriage, and, in the case of minors, that the consent of the person whose consent to the marriage is required by law (*see below*) has been duly given, and that the residential qualifications (mentioned above) have been complied with. A person making a false declaration renders himself or herself liable to prosecution for perjury. The notice is entered in the marriage notice book.

ISSUE OF CERTIFICATE:

(i) *Without licence.*—The notice (or an exact copy thereof) is affixed in some conspicuous place in the Superintendent Registrar's office for 21 days next after the notice was entered in the marriage notice book. After the lapse of this period the Superintendent Registrar may, provided no impediment is shown, issue his certificate for the marriage which can then take place at any time within three months from the date of entry of the notice.

(ii) *With licence.*—The notice in this case is not affixed in the office of the Superintendent Registrar. After the lapse of one whole day (other than a Sunday, Christmas Day or Good Friday) from the date of entry of the notice, the Superintendent Registrar may, provided no impediment is shown, issue his certificate and licence for the marriage, which can then take place on any day within three months from the date of entry of the notice.

SOLEMNIZATION OF THE MARRIAGE:

(i) *In a Registered Building.*—The marriage must generally take place at a building within the district of residence of one of the parties, but if the usual place of worship of either is outside the district of his or her residence, it may take place in such usual place of worship. Further, if there is not within the district of residence of one of the parties a registered building within which marriages are solemnized according to the rites and ceremonies which the parties desire to adopt in solemnizing their marriage, it may take place in an appropriate registered building in the nearest district.

The presence of a Registrar of Marriages is not necessary at marriages at registered buildings which have adopted the provisions of section 43 of the Marriage Act 1949. This section provides for the appointment of an "authorized person" (a person, usually the minister or an official of the building, certified by the trustees or governing body as having been duly authorized for the purpose) who must be present and must register the marriage.

The marriage must be solemnized between the hours of 8 a.m. and 6 p.m., with open doors in the presence of two or more witnesses. The parties must at some time during the ceremony make the following declaration—"I do solemnly declare that I know not of any lawful impediment why I, A. B., may not be joined in matrimony to C. D." Also each of the parties must say to the other: "I call upon these persons here present to witness that I, A. B., do take thee, C. D., to be my lawful wedded wife [or husband]," *or*, if the marriage is solemnized in the presence of an authorized person without the presence of a Registrar, each party may say in lieu thereof: "I, A. B., do take thee, C. D., to be my wedded wife [or husband]."

(ii) *In a Register Office.*—The marriage may be solemnized in the office of the Superintendent Registrar to whom notice of the marriage has been given. The marriage must be solemnized between the hours of 8 a.m. and 6 p.m., with open doors in the presence of the Superintendent Registrar or a Registrar of the registration district of that Superintendent Registrar, and in the presence of two witnesses. The parties must make the following declaration: "I do solemnly declare that I know not of any lawful impediment why I, A. B., may not be joined in matrimony to C. D.," and each party must say to the other: "I call upon these persons here present to witness that I, A. B., do take thee, C. D., to be my lawful wedded wife [or husband]." No religious ceremony may take place in the Register Office,though the parties may, on production of their marriage certificate, go through a subsequent religious ceremony in any church or persuasion of which they are members.

(iii) *Other Cases.*—If both parties are members of the Society of Friends (Quakers), or if, not being in membership, they have been authorized by the Society of Friends to solemnize their marriage in accordance with its usages, they may be married in a Friends' meeting-house. The marriage must be registered by the registering officer of the Society appointed to act for the district in which the meeting house is situated. The presence of a Registrar of Marriages is not necessary.

If both parties are Jews they may marry according to their usages in a synagogue, which has a certified marriage secretary, or private dwelling-house at any hour; the building may be situated within or without the district of residence. The marriage must be registered by the secretary of the synagogue of which the man is a member. The presence of a Registrar of Marriages is not necessary.

C.—MARRIAGE UNDER REGISTRAR GENERAL'S LICENCE

The main purpose of the Marriage (Registrar General's Licence) Act 1970, which came into force

on January 1, 1971, is to enable non-Anglicans to be married in unregistered premises where one of the ersons to be married is seriously ill, is not expected to recover and cannot be moved to registered premises. A fee of £15 is payable to the Registrar General for the licence, though he has power to remit this in whole or in part to avoid hardship.

D.—DETAINED AND HOUSE-BOUND PERSONS

The Marriage Act 1983 (which does not extend to Scotland) enables marriages of detained persons and house-bound persons to be solemnized at their place of residence . The Act came into operation on May 1, 1984.

MISCELLANEOUS NOTES

Consanguinity and Affinity.—A marriage between persons within the prohibited degrees of consanguinity or affinity is void. Relaxations have, however, been made by various statutes which have now been replaced by the Marriage Act 1949 (see the 1st Schedule to the Act) and the Marriage (Enabling) Act 1960. It is now permitted to contract a marriage with:—

Sister, aunt or niece of a former wife (whether living or not). Former wife of brother, uncle or nephew (whether living or not).

No clergyman can be compelled to solemnize any of the foregoing marriages, but he may allow his church to be used for the purpose by another minister.

Minors.—Persons under 18 years of age are generally required to obtain the consent of certain persons (see Marriage Act 1949, section 3 and 2nd Schedule as amended by the Family Law Reform Act 1969). Where both parents are living, both must consent, where one is dead, the survivor, or, if there is a guardian appointed by the deceased parent, the guardian and the survivor. No consent is required in the case of an infant's second marriage. In certain exceptional cases consent may be dispensed with, *e.g.*, the insanity of a parent. If consent is refused the Court may, on application being made, consent to the marriage; application can be made for this purpose to the High Court, the County Court, or a Court of Summary Jurisdiction. The Act *prohibits* any marriage where either party is under 16 years of age.

E.—MARRIAGE IN ENGLAND OR WALES WHEN ONE PARTY LIVES IN SCOTLAND OR NORTHERN IRELAND

Notice for a marriage by a Superintendent Registrar's certificate in a register office or registered building may be given in the usual way by the party resident in England. As regards Scotland, the party there should give notice of intention to marry to the registrar; as regards Northern Ireland, the party there, after a residence of seven days, must give notice to the District Registrar of Marriages. Notice cannot be given for such marriages to take place by Certificate *with* licence of the Superintendent Registrar.

Marriage of such parties may take place in a church of the Church of England after the publication of banns, or by Ecclesiastical licence.

MARRIAGES IN SCOTLAND

According to the law of Scotland, marriage is a contract which is completed by the mutual consent of parties. The Marriage (Scotland) Act 1977, which came into force on January 1, 1978, states or restates the law in convenient form. References in this section are to that Act.

Impediments to Marriage: These are (a) Nonage, *i.e.*, where either party is under the age of 16. (b) Forbidden degrees of relationship (Section 2). (c) Subsisting previous marriage. (d) Incapacity to understand the nature of the contract. (e) Both parties of the same sex. (f) Non-residence, *i.e.*, if the requirements of prior residence of one or other of the parties in Scotland have not been complied with. The Act also states the grounds on which certain marriages may be declared void but this is amended by the Law Reform (Miscellaneous Provisions) (Scotland) Act 1980 which prevents a marriage being rendered void solely due to the failure to comply with certain formalities, provided the particulars of that marriage are entered in a register of marriages by or at the behest of an appropriate registrar.

Marriages may be regular or irregular, thus:—

REGULAR MARRIAGES

A regular marriage is one which is celebrated by a Minister of Religion or authorised Registrar or other celebrant specified in the Act. The parties must submit to the District Registrar a statutory notice of intention to marry the fee for which is £6·50. The Registrar will then enter the parties' names and particulars in the Marriage Notice Book which must also show the intended date of the marriage. He must then display the notice of intention to marry in a prominent public place until the intended date, and any person claiming an interest may lodge written objections thereto with the Registrar (Section 5). The Registrar, after fourteen days of receipt of the Marriage Notice and on being satisfied that there are no legal impediments to the marriage, will issue to either or both parties a Marriage Schedule. The fourteen day period may be shortened under exceptional circumstances. The Marriage Schedule must be produced to the celebrant of the marriage. The fee for the solemnization ceremony in a Registry Office is £10. After the ceremony the marriage must be registered with the Registrar General for inclusion in the Register of Births, Deaths and Marriages, within three days. Within one month of the ceremony, the fee for an extract marriage certificate is £2; thereafter it is £5.

IRREGULAR MARRIAGES

Since the Marriage (Scotland) Act 1939 the only form of irregular marriage to be recognised by law—viz., marriage by habit and repute, remains competent under the 1977 Act. If the parties live together constantly as husband and wife and are held to be such by the general repute of the neighbourhood and among their friends and relations, then there may arise a presumption from which marriage can be inferred. Before such a marriage can be registered, however, a decree of declarator of marriage must be obtained from the Deputy Principal Clerk of the Court of Session. It is the duty of the Deputy Principal Clerk to register the decree as soon as it is granted.

JURY SERVICE

Every local or parliamentary elector between the ages of eighteen and sixty-five who has resided in the United Kingdom, Channel Islands or Isle of Man for at least five years since he attained the age of thirteen will be qualified to serve on a jury unless he is "ineligible" or "disqualified".

Ineligible persons include those who have at any time been judges, magistrates and certain senior court officials, those who within the previous ten years have been concerned with the law (such as barristers and solicitors and their clerks, court officers, coroners, police, prison and probation offi-cers); priests of any religion and vowed members of religious communities; and certain sufferers from mental illness.

Disqualified persons are those who have at any time been sentenced by a Court in the United Kingdom, Channel Islands or Isle of Man, to a term of imprisonment exceeding five years, or who have in the previous ten years served any part of a sentence exceeding three months or been sentenced to Borstal.

Some others are excusable as of right. These include members and officers of the Houses of Parliament, full-time serving members of the forces (including Women's forces) and registered and practising members of the medical, dental, nursing, veterinary and pharmaceutical professions and any person who has served on a jury in the two years before he is summoned. In other cases the court may excuse a juror at its discretion (*e.g.*, where the service would be a hardship to the juror).

If a person serves on a jury knowing himself to be disqualified or ineligible he is liable to be fined up to £400 or £100 respectively.

A juror is entitled to subsistence and travelling expenses, compensation for other expenses incurred in consequence of attendance for jury service, loss of earnings and loss of national insurance benefits, but certain maximum figures (which are revised from time to time) are laid down.

A verdict of a jury must normally be unanimous but after two hours consideration (or such longer period as the Court thinks reasonable), a majority verdict is acceptable if ten jurors agree to it (or nine if the size of the jury has been reduced to ten, *e.g.*, by illness during the trial).

Jury trial is now very unusual in civil cases but a person charged with any but the least serious crimes is entitled to be tried by a jury. The defendant may object to any juror if he can show that that juror ought not to be on the jury (*e.g.*, because he is ineligible or is biased against him) and may object to three jurors without giving any reason.

The Coroners' Juries Act 1983 (which does not extend to Scotland) makes new provision in relation to qualification to serve on coroners' juries.

JURY SERVICE IN SCOTLAND

It is the duty of the sheriff principal of each sheriffdom, in respect of each sheriff court district in his sheriffdom, to maintain a book, known as the "general jury book", containing the names and designations of persons within the district who are qualified and liable to serve as jurors. The book, which is compiled from information which every householder is required to provide, is kept open for the inspection by any person, upon payment of a nominal fee, at the sheriff clerk's office for the district. Part II of the Juries Act 1949 (amended by regulations following thereon and by the Law Reform (Miscellaneous Provisions) (Scotland) Act 1980) applies only to Scotland and provides, *inter alia*, for the payment of travelling expenses and subsistence allowances to jurors and for loss of earnings.

The number of a jury in a civil cause in the Court of Session is twelve and in the Sheriff Court seven. In a criminal trial the number is fifteen.

QUALIFICATIONS

Under S.1 of the Law Reform (Miscellaneous Provisions) (Scotland) Act 1980, every man or woman between the ages of 18 and 65 who is for the time being registered as a parliamentary or local government elector and who has been ordinarily resident in the United Kingdom, the Channel Islands or the Isle of Man for any period of at least five years since attaining the age of 13 years, is qualified to serve on a jury.

Ineligible persons include those who at any time within the past ten years have been judges of the supreme courts, sheriffs and certain other senior court officials, those who at any time within the past five years have been concerned with the administration of justice (such as advocates and their clerks, solicitors, court staff, police officers, prison officers, sheriff officers, procurator fiscals, and members of parole boards and children's panels), and certain sufferers from mental illness.

The same rules for disqualified persons operate in Scotland as in England. Those excusable as of right are members and officers of the Houses of Parliament, full time serving members of H.M. naval, army and air forces, registered and practising members of the medical, dental, nursing, veterinary and pharmaceutical professions, ministers of religion and other persons in holy orders, and any person who has attended for jury service in the past five years.

If a person serves on a jury knowing himself to be disqualified or ineligible, he is liable to be fined up to £1,000 or £200 respectively. Jurors failing to attend without good cause are liable to a maximum fine of £200.

LANDLORD AND TENANT
ENGLAND AND WALES

Although basically the relationship between the parties to the lease is governed by the lease itself, the position is complicated by numerous statutory provisions. The few points dealt with may show the desirability of seeking professional assistance in these matters. Important provisions include:—

(1) As to agricultural holdings—the Agricultural Holdings Act 1948 and later statutes. Among other things, these Acts regulate the length of notice necessary to determine an agricultural tenancy, the tenant's right to remove fixtures on the land, his right to compensation for damage done by game, for improvements and for disturbance, and his right to require the consent of the Agricultural Land Tribunal to the operation of a notice to quit.

The Agriculture (Miscellaneous Provisions) Act 1976, contains provisions for succession on the death of a tenant of an agricultural holding. Subject to certain conditions and qualifications, a member of a deceased tenant's family (as defined in the Act) can within three months of the death apply to the Agricultural Land Tribunal for a direction entitling him to a tenancy of the holding. However, the Agricultural Holdings Bill 1984 provides for the abolition of statutory succession to agricultural holdings in the case of new tenancies.

(2) As to business premises—the Landlord and Tenant Acts 1927 and 1954, and the Law of Property Act 1969, Pt. I. Part II of the 1954 Act gives security of tenure to the tenant of most business premises, and in effect he can only be ousted on one or more of the seven grounds set out in the Act. In some cases, where the landlord can resume possession, the tenant is entitled to compensation.

(3) As to dwelling houses. The complicated mass of legislation is now mainly embodied in the Rent Act 1977, which does not extend to Scotland or Northern Ireland. If the house is within the Act, a tenant has a personal right to reside there, and he may only be ousted on certain grounds.

A number of amendments to the 1977 Act have been made by the Housing Act 1980.

Tenancies with full Rent Act protection are known as regulated tenancies. The maximum rent recoverable under such a tenancy is the rent agreed between the landlord and tenant, unless a fair rent has been registered, in which case that is the maximum rent recoverable. Application for the registration of a fair rent may be made by either the landlord or tenant, to the Local Rent Officer, and appeal against his decision lies to the Rent Assessment Committee.

(4) As to dwelling houses with resident landlords. The Rent Act 1974 gave tenants of dwellings let furnished the same security of tenure as those of unfurnished dwellings unless the landlord lived in part of the house. In the latter case, and in the case of a tenancy of a dwelling granted by a resident landlord after August 13, 1974, the tenancy will usually be outside full Rent Act protection, but may fall within the restricted contract provisions of the Rent Act 1977. In this event, the landlord or the tenant may apply to the Rent Tribunal for a reasonable rent to be registered, and once registered, this is the maximum rent recoverable.

(5) The Protection from Eviction Act 1977 provides that if any person with intent to cause the residential occupier of any premises to give up the occupation thereof does any act calculated to interfere with the peace or comfort of the residential occupier or members of his household, he shall be guilty of an offence. A further provision prevents a landlord enforcing a right to possession against a tenant (who is not protected by any security of tenure legislation) without a court order, and there are special rules in such cases relating to agricultural employees.

(6) A notice to quit *any* dwellinghouse must be given at least four weeks before it is to take effect, and must be in writing and in the prescribed statutory form.

(7) Part I of the Landlord and Tenant Act 1954, applies to most tenancies of houses for over twenty-one years at a ground rent. Where it applies, the contractual tenancy is continued until brought to an end in the manner prescribed by the Act, and in effect the landlord can only get possession on limited grounds.

Further, under the Leasehold Reform Act 1967, tenants of houses under leases for over twenty-one years at a rent less than two-thirds of the rateable value of the house are in most cases given a right to purchase the freehold or to take an extended lease for a term of fifty years, provided the tenant at the time when he seeks to exercise the right has been occupying the house as his residence for the last three years or for periods amounting to three years in the last ten years.

(8) Full Rent Act protection is available only if a house is let on a tenancy, so that if the occupier of a house has a mere licence to occupy, he does not have Rent Act protection. Further, even if he has a tenancy, he will not be Rent Act protected if the rent payable is less than two-thirds of the rateable value of the house. For these reasons, many occupants of houses owned by farmers and occupied by farm workers did not enjoy full security of tenure. The Rent (Agriculture) Act 1976 contains detailed provisions conferring security of tenure on certain agricultural workers housed by their employers and on their successors on death.

(9) Under the Housing Act, 1961 (which does not extend to Scotland), in a lease of a dwelling-house granted after October 24, 1961, for a term of less than 7 years, there is implied a covenant by the landlord (a) to keep in repair the structure and exterior of the house and (b) to keep in repair and proper working order the installations in the house (i) for the supply

of water, gas and electricity, and for sanitation, and (ii) for space heating or heating water.

(10) The Housing Act 1980 gives security of tenure to tenants of local authorities and certain other bodies. Further, and subject to certain conditions, such tenants may have the right to purchase their houses or to take a long lease of their flats. Certain amendments to the 1980 Act have been made by the Housing and Building Control Act, 1984.

SCOTLAND

A Lease is a Contract, the relationship of the parties being governed by the terms thereof. As is also the case in England (see the foregoing Section) legislation has played an important part in regulating that relationship. Thus, what at Common Law was an Agreement binding only the parties to the deed, becomes in virtue of the Leases Act 1449, a contract binding the landlord's successors, as purchasers or creditors, provided the following four conditions are observed; (1) the lease, if for more than one year, must be in writing, (2) there must be a rent, (3) there must be a term of expiry, and (4) the tenant must have entered into possession.

It would be impracticable in a brief section of these Notes to enter upon a general discussion of this branch of the law and, accordingly, the plan adopted in the preceding Section of quoting a few important Statutes is followed here.

The Agricultural Holdings (Scotland) Act 1949 (amended by the Agriculture Act 1958), which is a consolidating Act applicable to Scotland, contains provisions similar to those in the English Act, alluded to in the preceding Section. It cannot here be analysed in detail.

It is of interest to note that the Small Landholders Act, 1911, provided for the setting up of the Land Court which has jurisdiction over a large proportion of agricultural and pastoral land in Scotland.

In Scotland business premises are not controlled by Statute to so great an extent as in England, but the Tenancy of Shops (Scotland) Act, 1949 gives a measure of security to tenants of shops. This Act enables the tenant of a shop who is threatened with eviction to apply to the Sheriff for a renewal of the tenancy. If the landlord has offered to sell the subjects to the tenant at an agreed price the application for a renewal of the tenancy may be dismissed. Reference should be made to Section 1 (3) of the 1949 Act for particulars of other circumstances under which the Sheriff has a discretion to dismiss an application. The Act extends to premises held by the Crown or Government Departments, either as landlord or tenant.

The Housing (Scotland) Act 1969 and the Rent (Scotland) Act 1971, as amended by the Rent Act 1974, define controlled tenancies and regulated tenancies, both furnished and unfurnished, and lay down the system by which a landlord or tenant may obtain from the Rent Officer registration of a fair rent. The Acts also give to the tenants either of furnished or unfurnished lets a substantial degree of security of tenure. There are, however, certain exceptions; thus, they do not apply to tenancies where the interest belongs to the Crown or to a Government Department or to a local authority, a development corporation of a new town or a Housing Corporation. There must be a true tenancy for the Acts to apply. They do not apply to licensees such as lodgers or persons allowed to occupy houses on a grace and favour basis or to service occupiers. The Acts define the circumstances under which a landlord may apply for increased rent as a consequence of having carried out improvements to his property and

also lay down the system of phasing of such rent increases. On the death of a statutory successor to a tenancy the tenancy may pass for a second time to a member of the family or a relative who has been in residence in the house for a period of at least six months. The Acts also lay down the duties and functions of Rent Officers and Rent Assessment Committees with regard to unfurnished accommodation and of Rent Tribunals for furnished accommodation.

The Tenants Rights, Etc. (Scotland) Act 1980 contains a number of important provisions and deals mainly with the rights of public sector tenants to purchase the houses which they occupy. S. 46 converts all remaining controlled tenancies into regulated tenancies and s. 34 creates a particular type of protected tenancy known as a "short tenancy."

It also makes provisions in relation to housing rents and connected tenancies; the Act makes provision for a tenant's right to security of tenure and to a written lease. It also allows for amendment to the Housing Bill by introducing a landlord's right, in certain circumstances, to refuse to sell a house designed or adapted for occupation by the elderly to a tenant who would otherwise have the right to buy.

LEGAL AID

LEGAL AID IN CIVIL PROCEEDINGS

The Legal Aid Act 1974 (as amended) is designed to make legal aid and advice more readily available for persons of small and moderate means. The main structure of the service is contained in the Act itself and the Regulations made thereunder, administered by the Law Society.

Legal aid is available for proceedings (including matrimonial causes) in the House of Lords, Court of Appeal, High Court, County Courts, Lands Tribunal, Restrictive Practices Court, before the Commons Commissioners, and civil proceedings in Magistrates' Courts. In any event, an application for legal aid will not be approved if it appears that the applicant would gain only a trivial advantage from the proceedings. Further, proceedings wholly or partly in respect of defamation are excepted from the scheme, as are also relator actions and election petitions. It is generally not available for obtaining the decree in undefended divorce and judicial separation, although the Legal Advice and Assistance Scheme (*post*) will be, and Legal Aid is still available to deal with property, custody disputes etc., arising in the suit.

Where a person is concerned in proceedings only in a representative, fiduciary or official capacity, his personal resources are not to be taken into account in considering eligibility for legal aid. Apart from this, eligibility in civil proceedings depends upon an applicant's "disposable income" and "disposable capital". The figures change frequently; particulars can be obtained from a solicitor, the Law Society or a Citizens' Advice Bureau. Disposable income is calculated by making deductions from gross income in respect of certain matters such as dependants, interest on loans, income tax, rates, rent and other matters for which the applicant must or reasonably may provide. Disposable capital is calculated by excluding from gross capital part of the value of the house in which the applicant resides, of furniture and household possessions; allowances are made in respect of dependants. Except in cases where the spouses are living apart, or have a contrary interest, any resources of a person's wife or husband are to be treated as that person's resources. These figures will be assessed by the Department of Health and Social Security, and will be referred to a General Committee, who will determine whether reasonable grounds exist for the grant of a civil aid certificate. Appeal from refusal of a certificate lies to an Area Committee. A person resident in England or Wales desiring legal aid should apply for a certificate to the appropriate General Committee for the area in which s/he resides; if resident elsewhere application should be made to a General Committee for London. If a certificate is granted, the applicant may select his solicitor, and, if necessary, counsel from a panel. The costs of the assisted person's solicitor and counsel will be paid out of the legal aid fund. When, however, damages or property are recovered or preserved by the assisted person the legal aid fund has a charge over them in respect of these costs less any contribution towards costs recovered from the unsuccessful party. In matrimonial cases, maintenance is exempt, as is the first £2,500 of any property settlement. The court may order that the costs of a successful unassisted party shall be paid out of the legal aid fund.

In an urgent case, say of domestic violence, or to restrain the kidnapping abroad of a child, Legal Aid may be granted without the applicant's means being fully investigated beforehand. If on a full examination later he is found financially ineligible he is liable to pay all the costs incurred on his behalf, if he does not attend for an examination.

LEGAL ADVICE AND ASSISTANCE

The Scheme is governed by the Legal Aid Act 1974 (as amended).

Under this legal advice and assistance scheme a client may obtain such advice or assistance as is normally provided by a solicitor and if necessary the advice of a barrister may be obtained, but, with the exception of domestic proceedings in a magistrates' court and certain other proceedings (see below) the scheme does not extend to taking any step in any proceedings before any court or tribunal. Where legal aid is available for civil proceedings (see above) or in criminal cases (see below) the scheme covers work done in making application for such legal aid.

A person is eligible for advice or assistance under the scheme provided his disposable capital and his disposable income do not exceed limits in force from time to time or if he receives Supplementary Benefit or Family Income Supplement. For a married man or person with children or other dependants deductions will be made from gross income and capital and allowances are made in respect of income tax, National Insurance contributions, etc. It is intended that the financial limits shall approximate to those applying for legal aid in civil proceedings (see above). Except when they are separated or have conflicting interests the means of husband and wife will be aggregated for the purpose of determining financial eligibility. As in the case of Legal Aid, depending on his means, a person may be called upon to pay a contribution towards the costs of work done for him. Particulars may again be obtained from a solicitor, the Law Society or a Citizens' Advice Bureau.

Solicitor's costs and expenses, which should not together exceed £50 (V.A.T. exclusive), or £75 in the case of divorce etc. (not applicable to Scotland, where the £50 limit still applies) without leave of the Area Legal Aid Committee, will be paid out of the client's contribution and any monies recovered in respect of costs or damages from another party (although this may be waived by leave of the Area Committee in cases of hardship) and the balance will be paid by the Legal Aid Fund.

The Act also extends the scheme to cover the costs of a solicitor who is present within the precincts of a

magistrates' court or county court and is requested by the court to advise or represent a person who is in need of help.

In April 1980 the Scheme was enlarged to cover the cost of representation in domestic proceedings in a magistrates' court. It has since been extended to cover the representation of patients in case proceedings in a magistrates' court, of patients before Mental Health Review Tribunals, and certain parents of children who are the subject of care proceedings. Subject to financial eligibility limits, application is made to the area or local committee for "approval of assistance by way of representation" which will replace legal aid for such proceedings. However the £50 costs limit referred to above will not apply. An applicant who is outside the financial limits but eligible for *legal aid* will still have to apply for a legal aid certificate as before.

LEGAL AID IN CRIMINAL CASES

The Legal Aid Act 1974 Part II and Legal Aid Act 1982 provide for legal aid in criminal proceedings. A criminal court (*e.g.* magistrates' court, Crown Court) has power to order legal aid to be granted where it appears desirable to do so in the interests of justice. The court shall make an order in certain cases, *e.g.*, where a person is committed for trial on a charge of murder. However, the court may not make an order unless it appears to the court that the person's disposable income and capital are such that he requires assistance in meeting the costs of the particular proceedings in question. Application should be made to the appropriate court where proceedings are to take place.

An applicant shall be required to make a contribution towards the costs of the action if his disposable income and capital exceed certain prescribed limits. Persons in receipt of Supplementary Benefit are automatically exempt. In order to ascertain the amount of this contribution he will have to produce written evidence of his means. Investigation of means will be carried out by the court. Any person who falls into arrears with the payment of contribution is liable to have the order revoked.

Any practising barrister or solicitor may act for a legally aided person in criminal proceedings unless excluded by reason of misconduct. In general where legal aid is given it will normally include representation by both counsel and solicitor. However, in connection with magistrates' courts, representation will be by solicitor alone unless it is a serious offence.

Where any doubt arises about the grant of a legal aid order that doubt is to be resolved in favour of the applicant. The court also has power to amend or revoke a legal aid order. Legal aid may also be granted in connection with appellate proceedings, *e.g.*, on appeal to the Criminal Division of the Court of Appeal under the Criminal Appeal Act 1968.

SCOTLAND
CIVIL PROCEEDINGS

The Legal Aid (Scotland) Act 1967 and the Legal Advice and Assistance Act 1972 form the basis of a scheme to provide legal advice in most civil actions in the House of Lords on appeals from the Court of Session, in the Court of Session, the Lands Valuation Appeal Court, the Scottish Land Court, the Employment Appeal Tribunal, the Sheriff Court, the Restrictive Practices Court and Lands Tribunal for Scotland.

As to those to whom legal aid is available, the same considerations as to income and capital apply in Scotland as in England. (*See* the preceding paragraph.) The decision of the Supplementary Benefits

Commission is final as to financial eligibility. A person believing himself to be eligible may instruct any solicitor of his own choice who is on the official lists, or he may apply for a solicitor to one of the various Legal Aid Committees which are set up to administer the scheme. In a case where litigation is not immediately necessary, the client can seek advice under the Legal Advice and Assistance Act 1972 which is similar to the legal advice and assistance provisions of the Legal Aid Act 1974 (see above). In an instance where litigation is expected, application for a certificate granting legal aid is thereafter made to the appropriate Committee by the applicant's solicitor. He is required to prepare for the signature of the applicant a memorandum setting forth the grounds of the proposed action, and submit the same along with supporting documentation and relevant application forms to the Committee. Investigation into the applicant's financial means is carried out by the Supplementary Benefits Commission after the Committee has considered the memorandum and accompanying papers and, on a suitable contribution, if any, by the applicant being approved, a Certificate is granted enabling the applicant to proceed with his action. The Legal Aid (Scotland) Act 1967 provides for the payment (to a limited extent) out of the legal aid funds of expenses incurred by successful opponents of legally aided litigants.

LEGAL ADVICE

Legal advice, as distinct from legal aid in proceedings, is available to anyone in Scotland on terms similar to those stated in a preceding paragraph dealing with legal advice in England—the Scottish scheme being administered under the Legal Advice and Assistance Act 1972.

CRIMINAL PROCEEDINGS

Legal Aid in criminal cases is administered under the Legal Aid (Scotland) (Criminal Proceedings) Scheme and Regulations, 1975.

Subject to the financial eligibility of the applicant and the merits of his case, Legal Aid is available for proceedings in the High Court of Justiciary, the Sheriff Court and the District Court, as well as for appeals from those courts. Separate lists of practitioners prepared to act on behalf of assisted persons are kept, as regards counsel, by the Faculty of Advocates, and, as regards solicitors, by the Supreme Court and Local Legal Aid Committees of the Law Society of Scotland. Generally, an applicant may nominate to act on his behalf any solicitor whose name appears on the lists. The Scheme also provides for a rota of Duty Solicitors to act for persons taken into custody on homicide charges and persons who are in custody awaiting the first hearing of their case before the Sheriff or District Court.

Applications for Legal Aid must normally be made on the prescribed form to the clerk of the court in question and an applicant is required to provide therein particulars of the merits of his case and his financial circumstances. Where less than 7 days before his trial an accused lodges an application it shall be refused unless, on special cause shown, the court decides the application to be timeously made. In certain cases, i.e. where a person is in custody on a charge of serious crime, an oral application to the clerk of court will be sufficient. Applications are dealt with by the courts themselves and the results communicated to the relevant Committee of the Law Society. An award may be made subject to a contribution to the Legal Aid Fund. Where an applicant has a right to legal representation at the expense of a third party—e.g. a Trade Union—he will be refused Legal Aid, although a person with a high income may be awarded Legal Aid if the Court is satisfied that he would be unable without grave financial hardship to meet the costs of his defence.

A solicitor acting for an assisted person in a murder trial or appeal may instruct without the prior sanction of the Law Society both senior and junior counsel. In all other cases before the High Court only junior counsel may be instructed without prior sanction.

TOWN AND COUNTRY PLANNING

The Town and Country Planning Act 1971 (consolidating earlier Acts) contains very far-reaching provisions affecting the liberty of an owner of land to develop and use it as he will. A person has generally to get planning permission before carrying out any development on his land from the Local Planning Authority. Under the Development Land Tax Act 1976 a charge to development land tax may arise where a person realises development value by a disposal of an interest in land in the U.K. on or after August 1, 1976.

What is Development:—

(a) Carrying out of building, engineering, mining or other operations.

(b) Making a material change in use.

It is expressly provided that if one dwelling-house is converted into two or more dwelling-houses, this involves a material change in use.

Examples of what is not deemed Development:—

(a) Maintaining, improving or altering the interior of a building (except works for making good war damage), provided there is no material change to the exterior, with the exception that since December 5, 1968, any expansion, or works begun for the expansion, of a building below ground level constitutes development.

(b) Change of use of property within the curtilage of a dwelling-house for a purpose incidental to the use of the dwelling-house as such. (It will, however, be development if building operations are carried out.)

Application can be made to the Local Planning Authority to determine whether or not an operation or change of use constitutes development.

Planning Permission.—Application for such permission is not always necessary, as the Secretary of State may make Development Orders giving general permission for a specified type of development. Thus a General Development Order of 1977 as amended in 1981, specifies a number of types of development for which no permission is usually required, e.g., enlargement of a dwelling-house (including erection of a garage), so long as the cubic content of the original dwelling (external measurement) is not exceeded by more than 70 cubic metres or 15 per cent, whichever is greater, subject to a maximum of 115 cubic metres.

Appeal against refusal of permission lies to the Secretary of State and from his decision, in limited circumstances, to the High Court. If the result of the appeal is unsatisfactory, an applicant may in certain circumstances require the Council to purchase the land.

SCOTLAND

The Town and Country Planning (Scotland) Act 1972 consolidates the statute law relating to town and country planning in Scotland.

The Act contains provisions for an appeal to the Secretary of State against the refusal of planning permission. The decision of the Secretary of State is final.

Sections 87 and 92 of the Local Government, Planning and Land Act 1980 contain important provisions on planning applications and, unlike certain parts of this Act, extend to Scotland.

VOTERS' QUALIFICATIONS

The franchise is governed by the Representation of the People Act 1983. Those entitled to vote as electors at a parliamentary election in any constituency are all persons resident there on the qualifying date who, at that date and on the date of the poll are Commonwealth citizens or citizens of the Republic of Ireland and not subject to any legal incapacity to vote and who on the date of the poll are at least 18 years of age. However, a person is not entitled to vote at a parliamentary election in any constituency in Northern Ireland unless he was resident in Northern Ireland during the whole of the period of three months ending on the qualifying date for that election. Also, no person can use his vote unless he is on the Register of electors kept for the constituency. A person who is of voting age on the date of the poll at a parliamentary or local government election is entitled to vote, whether or not he is of voting age on the qualifying date. Accordingly, a qualified person will be entitled to be registered in a register of parliamentary electors or a register of local government electors if he will attain voting age within twelve months from the date on which the register is required to be published.

The Register is prepared by the Registration Officer in each constituency in Great Britain. It is the registration officer's duty to have a house to house or other official inquiry made as to the persons entitled to be registered and to publish preliminary electors lists showing the persons appearing to him to be entitled to be registered. Any person whose name is omitted may claim registration, and any person on the list may object to the inclusion therein of other persons' names: the registration officer determines the claims and objections.

Voters at a parliamentary or local government election must generally vote in person at the allotted polling station, except for those entitled to vote by post or at any polling station, and those for whom proxies have been appointed. Certain people can apply to be treated as absent voters at a parliamentary election and thus able to vote by post—among these are registered service voters, those unable by reason of blindness or other physical incapacity to go in person to the polling station, and those unable to go in person from their qualifying address to the polling station without making a journey by air or sea.

Unless entitled to vote by post, a person registered as a service voter may vote by proxy at a parliamentary or local government election. A proxy may also be appointed by a registered elector who is unable to go in person to the polling station by reason of the general nature of his occupation and who is likely to be at sea or out of the United Kingdom on the date of the poll, provided he applies to be treated as an absent voter. The appointment of a person to vote as proxy at parliamentary elections has effect also for the purposes of local government elections.

THE PROBATION SERVICE

The Probation Service is employed in each county by an independent committee of justices and it provides a professional social work agency in the courts, with responsibility for a wide range of duties which include: (a) a social enquiry service for the criminal courts; (b) provision of a range of non-custodial measures involving the supervision of offenders in the community; (c) supervisory aftercare for offenders released from custody, together with social work in penal establishments and help for the families of those serving sentences; (d) an enquiry, conciliation and supervision service in the divorce and domestic courts; (e) support for and promotion of preventive and containment measures in the community designed to reduce the level of crime and domestic breakdown. It is a direct grant service funded 80 per cent from the Home Office and 20 per cent from the relevant County Council.

Its national representative bodies are: (i) The Central Council of Probation Committees, 38 Belgrave Square, London SW1X 8NT—Tel: 01-245-9364 (*Secretary*, R. S. Bailey); (ii) The Association of Chief Officers of Probation, 20–30 Lawefield Lane, Wakefield WF2 8SP—Tel: 0924 364141 (*Hon. Secretary*, W. R. Weston); (iii) The National Association of Probation Officers, 3/4 Chivalry Road, Battersea, London SW11 1HT—Tel: 01-223-4887 (*Gen. Secretary*, Mrs. J. Kirkpatrick).

INCOME TAX 1984–85

INTRODUCTION

Income tax is charged on the total income of individuals for a year of assessment commencing on April 6 and ending on the following April 5. The rates of tax and the calculation of liability will frequently differ as between one year of assessment and another. The following information is confined to the year of assessment 1984–85, ending on April 5, 1985.

Liability is determined by establishing the taxable income for a year of assessment. The income may be reduced by an individual's personal allowances and other reliefs. The first slice of taxable income remaining is assessable to income tax at the basic rate of 30 per cent. The rates of tax progressively increase and eventually reach 60 per cent on the slice of income exceeding £38,100. The full rates of income tax chargeable are as follows:

£	%
1–15,400	30
15,401–18,200	40
18,201–23,100	45
23,101–30,600	50
30,601–38,100	55
over 38,100	60

In previous years, where investment income exceeded stated limits the excess incurred liability at the additional rate of 15 per cent (the investment income surcharge). This rate has no application for 1984–85. It follows that both earned and investment income now receive identical treatment when calculating liability to income tax.

The tables on the following pages show the income tax payable for 1984–85 by an individual on the amount of income specified, after deducting the personal allowance and age allowance. The taxpayer may, however, be entitled to further reliefs and allowances which reduce the tax payable below the amount shown in the tables.

Trustees administering settled property are chargeable to income tax at the basic rate of 30 per cent. Where the trustees retain discretionary powers, or income is accumulated, there will also be liability to the additional rate of 15 per cent. Companies residing in the United Kingdom are not liable to income tax but suffer corporation tax on income, profits and gains.

The charge to income tax broadly arises on all taxable income accruing from sources in the United Kingdom. Individuals who are resident in this territory may also become liable on income arising overseas. An individual is resident in the United Kingdom if he or she normally resides here. Persons not normally residing in the United Kingdom may become resident if they visit this territory for periods which average three months or more throughout a period of years. The existence of a place of abode in the United Kingdom may be sufficient to indicate residence if visits of any duration are made.

Income arising overseas will often incur liability to foreign taxation. If that income is also chargeable to United Kingdom income tax, excessive liability may well arise. The United Kingdom has concluded Double Taxation Agreements with many overseas territories which ensure that the same slice of income is not doubly assessed. In the absence of such an agreement, foreign tax suffered can usually be relieved when calculating liability to income tax.

The special rules for taxing income derived by a husband and wife are examined later.

INCOME TAXABLE

Income tax is assessed and collected under several Schedules. Each Schedule determines the extent of liability and establishes the amount to be included in taxable income. In some instances the actual income arising in a year of assessment will be charged to income tax for that year. A different basis of assessment may arise for income taxable under Cases I to V of Schedule D. Frequently, income assessable under these Cases will be that arising in a previous year or period but there are special rules where a new source is acquired or an existing source discontinued. The contents of the various Schedules are shown below:

Schedule A.—Tax is charged on annual profits from the ownership or occupation of land in the United Kingdom. This will include rents, ground rents and other income arising from land. Expenditure incurred by the landlord on maintenance, repairs, insurance and management can be subtracted from the annual profits. This Schedule does not include profits from farming, market gardening or woodlands, nor does it extend to mineral rents and royalties. Premiums arising on the grant of a lease for a period not exceeding fifty years are assessed to income tax. However, the amount of the taxable premium may be reduced by 2 per cent for each year, after the first year, of the leasing period. Income from furnished lettings is assessable under Case VI of Schedule D, unless an option is exercised for own income to be assessed under Schedule A. Where income arises from furnished holiday lettings additional expenditure may be included in calculating income chargeable to tax. Income of this nature is treated as earned income.

Schedule B.—Assessment is confined to woodlands in the United Kingdom managed on a commercial basis and with a view to the realisation of profits. The assessment will be based on one-third of the annual value. The occupier of woodlands retains the option of being assessed under Case I of Schedule D on profits arising from management.

Schedule C.—This Schedule is confined to interest or dividends on Government or public authority funds and certain payments made out of the public revenues of overseas countries.

Schedule D.—This Schedule is divided into six Cases as follows:

Cases I and II.—Profits arising from trades, professions and vocations, including farming and market gardening. Where an individual carrying on a business is absent from the United Kingdom for not less than thirty qualifying days in 1984–85 the amount of profits chargeable to tax may be reduced. Capital expenditure incurred on assets used for business purposes will often produce an entitlement to capital allowances which reduce the profits chargeable. These profits may also be reduced following the submission of claims.

Case III.—Interest on Government Stocks not taxed at source (e.g. War Loan and British Savings Bonds), bank deposit interest and discounts. Interest up to £70 on ordinary National Savings Bank deposits is exempt from income tax. The exemption applies to both husband and wife separately. Interest on National Savings Bank Special Investment Accounts is not exempt.

Cases IV and V.—Interest from overseas securities, rents, dividends and all other income accruing

(1) SINGLE PERSONS

Income	Persons under 65		Persons 65 or over	
	Income Tax	Average Rate	Income Tax	Average Rate
£	£	per cent	£	per cent
2,100	28	1·3	—	—
2,500	148	5·9	3	0·1
3,000	298	10·0	153	5·1
4,000	598	15·0	453	11·3
5,000	898	18·0	753	15·1
6,000	1,198	20·0	1,053	17·6
7,000	1,498	21·4	1,353	19·3
8,000	1,798	22·5	1,653	20·7
9,000	2,098	23·3	2,098	23·3
10,000	2,398	24·0	2,398	24·0
12,000	2,998	25·0	2,998	25·0
14,000	3,598	25·7	3,598	25·7
16,000	4,198	26·2	4,198	26·2
18,000	4,858	27·0	4,858	27·0
20,000	5,658	28·3	5,658	28·3
25,000	7,897	31·6	7,897	31·6
50,000	21,757	43·5	21,757	43·5
100,000	51,757	51·8	51,757	51·8

outside the United Kingdom. Assessment is based on the full amount arising, whether remitted to the United Kingdom or retained overseas, but individuals who are either not domiciled in the United Kingdom or who are ordinarily resident overseas may apply the remittance basis. Overseas pensions are taxable but the amount arising may be reduced by 10 per cent for assessment purposes. Profits from trades, professions or vocations carried on overseas may be reduced by 12½ per cent for 1984–85, but no similar reduction is available for future years.

Case VI.—Sundry profits and annual receipts not assessed under any other Case or Schedule. These may include insurance commissions, post-cessation receipts and numerous other receipts specifically charged under Case VI.

Schedule E.—All emoluments from an office or employment are assessable under this Schedule. There are three Cases as follows:

Case I.—This applies to all emoluments of an individual resident and ordinarily resident in the United Kingdom.

Case II.—Of application where the individual is not resident or not ordinarily resident and extends to emoluments for duties undertaken in the United Kingdom.

Case III.—Applies to other emoluments remitted to the United Kingdom.

Special rules apply to emoluments received by non-domiciled employees employed by non-resident employers. In general, where the duties are performed in the United Kingdom such earnings will be assessable subject to a percentage deduction. This deduction, which is gradually being withdrawn, applies at different rates which are governed by personal circumstances.

Although foreign earnings may be assessable under Case I where the employee is resident and ordinarily resident in the United Kingdom, a deduction of 100 per cent or 12½ per cent may be available for 1984–85. The 100 per cent deduction can be obtained where duties are performed overseas for a continuous period reaching or exceeding 365 days. A limited deduction of 12½ per cent applies where the employee is absent from the United Kingdom for 30 or more qualifying

days in the year of assessment. An alternative deduction of 12½ per cent will be granted where emoluments arise from employment with a foreign employer and all the duties are performed outside the United Kingdom. Although the 100 per cent deduction remains, the reduced deduction of 12½ per cent ceases to apply after 1984–85.

The emoluments assessable under Schedule E include all salaries, wages, director's fees and other money sums. In addition, there is a wide range of benefits which must also be added to taxable emoluments. These include the provision of living accommodation on advantageous terms and advantages arising from the use of vouchers.

Further taxable benefits accrue to directors and employees receiving emoluments of £8,500 or more in the year of assessment. These benefits include the reimbursement of expenses, the availability of motor cars for private motoring, the provision of petrol or other fuel for private motoring, the provision of interest free loans, and other benefits provided at the employer's expense.

In arriving at the amount to be assessed under Schedule E all expenses incurred wholly, exclusively and necessarily in the performance of the duties may be deducted. This includes fees and subscriptions to certain professional bodies and learned societies.

Compensation for loss of office and other sums received on the termination of an office or employment are assessable to tax. However, the first £25,000 may be excluded and only the balance remains chargeable, subject to some reduction in the amount of tax payable.

Schedule F.—This Schedule is concerned with company dividends and distributions. A United Kingdom resident company paying a dividend or distribution must account to the Inland Revenue for advance corporation tax on the amount paid. A shareholder residing in the United Kingdom receives the dividend or distribution, together with a tax credit equal to the amount of advance corporation tax. The dividend or distribution is regarded as having suffered income tax, equal to the tax credit, at the basic rate, and where the shareholder is not liable, or fully liable, at this rate a repayment can be obtained. Individuals liable at rates in excess of the

(2) Married Couples

Income	Couples under 65		Couples 65 or over	
	Income Tax	Average Rate	Income Tax	Average Rate
£	£	per cent	£	per cent
3,200	13	0·4	—	—
3,500	103	3·0	—	—
4,000	253	6·3	13	0·3
5,000	553	11·1	313	6·3
6,000	853	14·2	613	10·2
7,000	1,153	16·5	913	13·1
8,000	1,453	18·2	1,213	15·2
9,000	1,753	19·5	1,693	18·8
10,000	2,053	20·5	2,053	20·5
12,000	2,653	22·1	2,653	22·1
14,000	3,253	23·2	3,253	23·2
16,000	3,853	24·1	3,853	24·1
18,000	4,453	24·7	4,453	24·7
20,000	5,198	26·0	5,198	26·0
25,000	7,380	29·5	7,380	29·5
50,000	21,067	42·1	21,067	42·1
100,000	51,067	51·1	51,067	51·1

basic rate will incur further liability. Some payments made by an unquoted trading company to redeem or purchase its own shares will not be treated as distributions.

INCOME NOT TAXABLE

This includes interest on National Savings Certificates, most scholarship income, bounty payments to members of the armed services and annuities payable to the holders of certain awards. Building society interest received is not liable to income tax at the basic rate but may be chargeable at rates in excess of the basic rate where the individual's income is sufficiently substantial. This treatment of building society interest is being extended to most payments of bank deposit interest after April 5, 1985.

SOCIAL SECURITY BENEFITS

Many Social Security benefits are not liable to income tax. These include the maternity allowance, long term sickness benefit, child benefit, war widow's pension, death grant, mobility allowance and numerous others. Among the limited range of benefits which are taxable is the retirement pension, widow's allowance, widowed mother's allowance, and most unemployment benefit and supplementary benefit paid to the unemployed. Short-term sickness benefit payable by an employer is also chargeable to tax.

PAY AS YOU EARN

The Pay As You Earn system is not an independent form of taxation but has been designed to collect income tax by deduction from most emoluments. When paying emoluments to employees an employer is usually required to deduct income tax and account for that tax to the Inland Revenue. In many cases this deduction procedure will fully exhaust the individual's liability to income tax, unless there is other income.

PERSONAL ALLOWANCES

The following personal allowances are available to individuals and may be subtracted when calculating income chargeable to income tax:

Personal Allowance.—A single person is entitled to a personal allowance of £2,005. This is increased to £3,155 for a married man whose wife is living with or maintained by him. For the year of marriage the increased allowance will only be available if marriage occurs before May 6. The increased allowance is then reduced by one-twelfth of £1,150 (£3,155 less £2,005) for each complete month preceding the marriage date.

The increased married man's allowance may be withdrawn where a wife's earning election is made (see "Husband and Wife" below).

Age Allowance.—A single person who has attained the age of 65 years and is in receipt of income not exceeding £8,100 receives an age allowance of £2,490. This is increased to £3,955 where a married man, or his wife living with him, has reached 65. If the income exceeds £8,100 the allowance is reduced by two-thirds of the amount of the excess. This reduction continues until the age allowance is reduced to the amount of the normal personal allowance. Age allowance is in substitution for, and not in addition to, the personal allowance.

Wife's Earned Income Allowance.—An allowance equal to the wife's earned income, but limited to a maximum of £2,005, may be obtained. This allowance is not granted in the year of marriage or where a wife's earnings election is made (see "Husband and Wife" below).

Additional Personal Allowance.—An allowance of £1,150 is available to a single person who has a qualifying child resident with him or her in the year of assessment. The allowance can also be obtained by a married man whose wife is totally incapacitated by physical or mental infirmity throughout the year and a child is similarly resident.

A "qualifying child" for 1984–85 must be born during the year, be under the age of 16 years at the commencement of the year, or over the age of 16 years at the commencement of the year and either receiving full-time instruction at a university, college, school or other educational establishment or undergoing training for a trade, profession or vocation throughout a minimum period of two years. It is also necessary that the child is the claimant's own or, if not such a child, was either born during 1984–85 or under the age of 18 years at the commencement of the year and maintained by the claimant at his or her own expense during the whole of the succeeding twelve month period.

Housekeeper Allowance.—An allowance of £100 is available to a widow or widower having a relative residing to act as a housekeeper. This allowance is also available where a housekeeper is employed for a similar purpose.

Son's or Daughter's Services Allowance.—A person who, by reason of his or his wife's old age or infirmity, has to retain the services of a son or daughter is entitled to an allowance of £55.

Dependent Relative Allowance.—The maximum deduction for each dependent relative is normally £100 but an increased allowance of £145 may be claimed where the claimant is a woman (other than a married woman living with her husband). The allowance is reduced by £1 for every £1 by which the relative's own taxable income exceeds the basic Social Security Retirement Pension. The relative must be incapacitated by old age or infirmity from maintaining himself or herself, except in the case of the claimant's, or the claimant's wife's mother who may be widowed, living apart from her husband or divorced. Additionally, the relative must be maintained by the claimant. If more than one person provides support to the dependent relative the allowance must be apportioned between them.

Blind Person's Allowance.—An allowance of £360 is available to a single person if at any time during the year ending on April 5, 1985, that person was registered as blind on a register maintained by a local authority. The allowance will also be available to a married man if either he or his wife living with him is similarly registered. An increased allowance of £720 will be available if both husband and wife are registered blind persons.

Widow's Bereavement Allowance.—For the year of assessment in which a husband dies his surviving widow may obtain a widow's bereavement allowance of £1,150. It is a necessary requirement that the parties were living together immediately before death. Similar allowance will be available in the year following death, unless the widow remarried in the year of death. The special widow's bereavement allowance is available only for the year of death and the following year. It cannot be obtained in subsequent years.

Life Assurance Relief.—Life assurance deduction relief is limited to premiums paid on policies made before March 14, 1984. No relief is available for policies issued after this date. Where the terms of a policy made before March 14, 1984 are subsequently varied or extended to produce increased benefits, future premium paid may no longer qualify for relief.

In those cases where relief can be obtained for premiums paid on life assurance and other policies, this is not given through the tax system. To qualify for relief premiums must be paid on an approved policy providing life assurance or deferred annuities. Relief is confined to policies made by the payer and covering his own life or that of his or her spouse. Only policyholders residing in the United Kingdom can usually obtain relief and payments must be made to a United Kingdom company or friendly society or to a United Kingdom branch of an overseas company.

When paying premiums under a qualifying policy made before March 14, 1984 the payer will deduct and retain income tax at the rate of 15 per cent. The ability to retain deductions made in this manner is not affected by the payer's liability to income tax on taxable income. No restriction to the deduction procedure arises if aggregate premiums paid during a year of assessment do not exceed £1,500. Should premiums exceed this amount, relief will be confined to £1,500 or one-sixth of total income, whichever is the greater. Where sums deducted exceed this maximum limit, the excess must be accounted for to the Inland Revenue.

OTHER DEDUCTIONS

In addition to personal allowances,* which may reduce taxable income, other eligible deductions may be available to an individual. These include payments of interest.

In some instances interest paid by a business proprietor may be relieved when calculating profits chargeable to income tax under Case I or Case II of Schedule D. Many private individuals cannot obtain relief in this manner and must satisfy stringent requirements before relief will be forthcoming. In general terms, before interest can qualify for relief it must be annual, as opposed to short, interest or paid to a bank, stockbroker or discount house. Relief will not be available to the extent that interest exceeds a reasonable commercial rate and no relief will be forthcoming for interest on an overdraft.

For 1984–85 relief will be available on the following payments:

(i) Interest on a loan to purchase, develop or improve an interest in land owned by the individual and used as his only or main residence or similarly used by a dependent relative or a former or separated spouse, "Land" includes larger houseboats and caravans used for a similar purpose. If the loan or aggregate of several loans, exceeds £30,000 relief is restricted to interest on that amount. Relief may also be forthcoming for interest on a loan used to acquire some other property, perhaps to be used as the only or main residence on retirement, by an individual who is compelled to occupy property by reason of his or her work.

(ii) Interest on a loan to purchase or improve an interest in land which is let or available for letting at a commercial rent. This interest is only capable of being deducted from rental income.

(iii) Interest on a loan made to acquire an interest in a close company or in a partnership.

(iv) Interest on a loan to a member of a partnership to acquire machinery or plant for use in the partnership business.

(v) Interest on a loan to an employed person to acquire machinery or plant for the purposes of his employment.

(vi) Interest on a loan made for the purpose of contributing capital to an industrial co-operative.

(vii) Interest on a loan applied for investment in an employee-controlled company.

(viii) Interest on a loan made to elderly persons for the purchase of an annuity where the loan is secured on land. If the loan exceeds £30,000 relief is limited to interest on this amount.

(ix) Interest on a loan to personal representatives for the payment of capital transfer tax.

Relief for many payments of mortgage interest is obtained through a special system known as MIRAS (mortgage interest relief at source). This applies to interest paid to a building society, bank, insurance company and certain other persons. When making payments of this nature the payer will deduct and retain income tax at the basic rate. This will provide the payer with full relief at the basic rate and no other relief will be necessary, unless the payer is liable at rates in excess of the basic rate. Payments of interest outside the MIRAS system continue to produce relief by deduction for income chargeable to income tax.

Many individuals pay contributions to approved pension schemes. The amount of their contributions may be deducted when establishing emoluments assessable under Schedule E.

Self-employed individuals and those who are not in pensionable employment may pay premiums on qualifying retirement annuity policies. The amount of these premiums may usually be relieved in calculating taxable income but limitations are placed on the maximum amount available for relief.

Subject to a maximum of £40,000 in any one year the cost of subscribing for shares in an unquoted company may qualify as a deduction from taxable income under the Business Expansion Scheme. This applies to subscriptions in 1983–84 and each of the following three years. Many requirements must be satisfied before this relief can be obtained.

HUSBAND AND WIFE

It is a general rule that the income of a married woman living with her husband will be aggregated with his income for the purpose of charging income tax. Aggregation does not, however, apply for the year of assessment in which the parties marry. For that year the husband will receive the personal allowance appropriate to a married man, although the amount of this allowance may require some restriction if marriage takes place after May 5. The wife will be taxed for the year of marriage as if she were a single person and no wife's earned income allowance can be obtained by the husband.

For subsequent years of assessment the incomes of husband and wife will be aggregated and if the husband does not satisfy the total tax liability the Inland Revenue may require the wife to pay the tax appropriate to her income.

Husband and wife may, however, claim to be separately assessed. This claim does not affect the total amount of income tax payable but allocates the liability between the parties. A quite different election may be made for separate assessment of wife's earnings. The effect of such an election is that the husband will be assessed on his income and on the wife's investment income and will receive the personal allowance appropriate to a single man. The wife will be separately assessed on her earned income and receive allowances as a single person. The wife's earnings election may be of advantage where the saving in higher rates of tax on the wife's income is greater than the increased tax resulting from the loss of the married personal allowance.

CAPITAL GAINS TAX

INTRODUCTION

A person is chargeable to capital gains tax on chargeable gains which accrue to him or her during a year of assessment ending on April 5. Liability extends to persons who are either resident or ordinarily resident for the year but special rules apply where a person permanently leaves the United Kingdom or comes to this territory for the purpose of acquiring residence. Non-residents are not liable to capital gains tax unless, exceptionally, they carry on a business in the United Kingdom through a branch or agency.

Chargeable gains accruing to companies are assessable to corporation tax and not to capital gains tax.

Capital gains tax is chargeable on the total of chargeable gains which accrue to a person in a year of assessment, after subtracting allowable losses arising in the same year. Allowable losses brought forward from some earlier year may be offset against chargeable gains but in the case of individuals this must not reduce the net chargeable gains for 1984–85 to below £5,600.

RATE OF TAX

Where the net chargeable gains accruing to an individual during 1984–85 do not exceed £5,600 there will be no liability to capital gains tax. If the net gains exceed £5,600 the excess is chargeable at the flat rate of 30 per cent.

Capital gains tax for 1984–85 falls due for payment on or before December 1, 1985. If the return or other information recording chargeable gains is delayed, interest may become chargeable at the rate of 8 per cent per annum.

HUSBAND AND WIFE

In the year of marriage chargeable gains accruing to husband and wife are separately assessed. Each party may independently obtain the £5,600 exemption for 1984–85 and there is no aggregation. For subsequent years, however, chargeable gains arising to a married woman living with her husband are assessed and charged on the husband, unless an election for separate assessment is made. This election will not reduce the aggregate tax payable but merely apportions liability between the spouses on an equitable basis.

DISPOSAL OF ASSETS

Before liability to capital gains tax can arise a disposal, or deemed disposal, of an asset must take place. This occurs not only where assets are sold or exchanged but applies on the making of a gift. There is also a disposal of assets where any capital sum is derived from assets, for example, where compensation is received for loss or damage to an asset.

The date on which a disposal must be treated as having taken place will determine the year of assessment in which the chargeable gain or allowable loss falls. In those cases where a disposal is made under an unconditional contract, the time of disposal will be that when the contract was entered into and not the subsequent date of conveyance or transfer. A disposal under a conditional contract or option is treated as taking place when the contract becomes unconditional or the option is exercised. Disposals by way of gift are undertaken when the gift becomes effective.

VALUATION OF ASSETS

The amount actually received as consideration for the disposal of an asset will be the sum from which very limited outgoings must be deducted for the purpose of establishing the gain or loss. In some cases, however, the consideration passing will not accurately reflect the value of the asset and some other basis must be used. This applies, in particular, where an asset is transferred by way of gift or otherwise than by a bargain made at arm's length. Such transactions are deemed to take place for a consideration representing market value, which will determine both the disposal proceeds accruing to the transferor and the cost of acquisition to the transferee.

Market value represents the price which an asset might reasonably be expected to fetch on a sale in the open market. In the case of unquoted shares or securities it is to be assumed that the hypothetical purchaser in the open market would have available all the information which a prudent prospective purchaser of shares or securities might reasonably require if he were propsosing to purchase them from a willing vendor by private treaty and at arm's length. This is an important consideration as the amount of information deemed to be available to a hypothetical purchaser may materially affect the price "reasonably" offered in an open market situation. The market value of unquoted shares or securities will usually be established following negotiations with the Shares Valuation Division of the Capital Taxes Office.

Special rules apply to determine the market value of shares quoted on the Stock Exchange.

DEDUCTION FOR OUTGOINGS

Once the actual or notional disposal proceeds have been determined it only remains to subtract eligible outgoings for the purpose of computing the gain or loss. There is the general rule that any outgoings deducted, or which are available to be deducted, when calculating income tax liability must be ignored. Subject to this, deductions will usually be limited to—

(a) the cost of the asset, together with incidental costs wholly and exclusively incurred in connection with the acquisition;

(b) expenditure incurred wholly and exclusively on the asset in enhancing its value, being expenditure reflected in the state or nature of the asset at the time of the disposal, and any other expenditure wholly and exclusively incurred in establishing, preserving or defending title to, or a right over, the asset; and

(c) the incidental costs of making the disposal.

Where the disposal concerns a leasehold interest having less than 50 years to run, any expenditure falling under (a) and (b) must be written off throughout the duration of the lease. This recognises that a lease is a wasting asset and at the termination of the leasing period will retain no value.

INDEXATION ALLOWANCE

A special indexation allowance may be available where the disposal of an asset takes place after April 5, 1982. This allowance is based on increases in the retail prices index between March 1982, or twelve months after expenditure has been incurred (whichever is the later) and the month of disposal. The increase is applied to the items of expenditure in (a) and (b) above, to determine the indexation allowance.

The amount of this allowance is then subtracted from the gain arising on disposal. No indexation allowance is available when calculating losses, nor can the allowance convert a gain into a loss.

EXEMPTIONS

There is a general exemption from liability to capital gains tax where the net gains of an individual for 1984–85 do not exceed £5,600.

The disposal of many assets will not give rise to chargeable gains or allowable losses and these include—

(a) private motor cars;

(b) Government securities retained for a minimum period of twelve months.

(c) Loan stock and other securities (but not shares) quoted on a United Kingdom stock exchange or dealt in on the Unlisted Securities market and retained for a minimum period of twelve months;

(d) National Savings Certificates, Premium Bonds, Defence Bonds and National Development Bonds;

(e) currency of any description acquired for personal expenditure outside the United Kingdom;

(f) decorations awarded for valour;

(g) betting wins and pools, lottery or games prizes;

(h) compensation or damages for any wrong or injury suffered by an individual in his person or in his profession or vocation;

(i) life assurance and deferred annuity contracts where the person making the disposal is the original beneficial owner;

(j) dwelling-houses and land enjoyed with the residence which is an individual's only or main residence;

(k) tangible movable property, the consideration for the disposal of which does not exceed £3,000;

(l) certain tangible movable property which is a wasting asset having a life not exceeding 50 years;

(m) assets transferred to charities and other bodies;

(n) works of art, historic buildings and other assets;

(o) assets used to provide maintenance funds for historic buildings;

(p) assets transferred to trustees for the benefit of employees.

DWELLING-HOUSES

Exemption from capital gains tax will usually be available for any gain which accrues to an individual from the disposal of, or of an interest in, a dwelling-house or part of a dwelling-house which has been his only or main residence. The exemption extends to land which has been occupied and enjoyed with the residence as its garden or grounds. Some restriction may be necessary where the land exceeds one acre.

The gain will not be chargeable to capital gains tax if the dwelling-house, or part, has been the individual's only or main residence throughout the period of ownership, or throughout the entire period except for all or any part of the last two years. A proportionate part of the gain will be exempt if the dwelling-house has been the individual's only or main residence for part only of the period of ownership.

Where part of the dwelling-house has been used exclusively for business purposes, part of the gain arising on disposal will not be exempt. It will be comparatively unusual for any part to be used exclusively for such a purpose, except perhaps in the case of doctors' or dentists' surgeries.

In those cases where part of a qualifying dwelling-house has been used to provide rented accommodation this may frequently be ignored when calculating exemption from capital gains tax, unless relatively substantial sums are involved.

Dwellings occupied by dependent relatives, separated or divorced former spouses, and also by beneficiaries under trusts, may also qualify for the exemption.

ROLL-OVER RELIEF

Persons carrying on business will often undertake the disposal of an asset and use the proceeds to finance the acquisition of a replacement asset. Where this situation arises a claim for roll-over relief may be made. The broad effect of such a claim is that all or part of the gain arising on the disposal of the old assset may be disregarded. The gain or part is then subtracted from the cost of acquiring the replacement asset. As this cost is reduced, any gain arising from the future disposal of the replacement asset will be correspondingly increased, unless of course a further roll-over situation then develops.

It remains a requirement that both the old and the replacement asset must be used for the purpose of the taxpayer's business. Relief will only be available if the acquisition of the replacement asset takes place within a period commencing twelve months before, and ending three years after, the disposal of the old asset, although the Board of Inland Revenue retain a discretion to extend this period where the circumstances were such that it was impossible for the taxpayer to acquire the replacement asset before the expiration of the normal time limit.

Whilst many business assets qualify for roll-over relief there are exceptions.

GIFTS

Although the gift of an asset is deemed to be a disposal made for a consideration representing market value, a claim can frequently be made to avoid capital gains tax liability. This claim applies to the gift of all assets by one individual to a second individual, by an individual to trustees, by trustees to an individual, or between trustees, residing in the United Kingdom. The effect of the claim is similar to that arising following a claim for roll-over relief and the cost to the transferor will be reduced. Adjustments will be necessary where a transaction undertaken, otherwise than by way of bargain made at arm's length, involves some inadequate consideration.

A limited claim may also be made on the disposal of assets by an individual to some other person, perhaps a company. This claim is confined to the disposal of business assets, including shares in certain companies.

RETIREMENT RELIEF

Relief is available to an individual who has attained the age of 60 years and disposes by way of sale or gift of the whole or part of a business. It does not necessarily follow that the isolated disposal of assets will represent the disposal of the whole or part of a business. The main condition for granting this relief is that throughout a period of at least one year ending with the disposal the business has been owned either by the individual or by a trading company in which the individual retained a sufficient shareholding interest. The relief extends also to cases where an individual disposes by way of sale or gift of shares or securities of a company. It must be demonstrated that the company was a trading company, the individual retained a sufficient shareholding interest, and he was engaged as a full-time working director for a period or at least one year before the time of disposal.

The maximum retirement relief is governed by the age of the individual at the time of disposal. The relief is nil on the sixtieth birthday and progressively increases to £100,000 at the age of 65. The amount of relief will then be governed by the period throughout which the various conditions have been satisfied, subject to a maximum of ten years. Where the disposal is of shares or securities issued by a company the available retirement relief may be limited if all assets retained by the company have not been used for business purposes.

ASSETS HELD ON APRIL 6, 1965

Capital gains tax is chargeable on gains which accrue from disposals undertaken after April 6, 1965. Special rules must therefore be applied to calculate gains and losses arising from the disposal of assets acquired before this date.

This is often achieved by computing the overall gain and apportioning that gain equally throughout the period of ownership. Only that part of the gain attributable to the period commencing on April 6, 1965, and ending at the time of disposal will be chargeable to capital gains tax.

This time apportionment procedure may be withdrawn in certain circumstances. It cannot apply to the disposal of quoted shares or securities, unit trust holdings or land retaining development value which are deemed to be acquired for a consideration representing market value on April 6, 1965. Where time apportionment is otherwise available, an election can be made to treat the asset as having been acquired at market value on April 6, 1965. A comparison between this notional cost of acquisition and the eventual disposal proceeds will usually disclose the chargeable gain. Restrictions may have to be applied where the calculation produces a loss.

DEATH

No capital gains tax is chargeable on the value of assets retained at the time of death. However, the personal representatives administering the deceased's estate are deemed to acquire assets for a consideration representing market value on death. This ensures that any increase in value occurring before the date of death will not be chargeable to capital gains tax. If a legatee or other person acquires an asset under a will or intestacy no chargeable gain will accrue to the personal representatives, and the person taking the asset will also be treated as having acquired it at the time of death for its then market value.

CAPITAL TRANSFER TAX

INTRODUCTION

Liability to capital transfer tax may arise on lifetime gifts and other dispositions and also on the value of assets retained at the time of death. The tax was introduced by the Finance Act 1975 but numerous changes have been made subsequently both to the rates charged and in the calculation of liability.

An individual's domicile at the time of any gift or on death is an important matter. Domicile will generally be determined by applying normal rules but special considerations may be necessary where an individual was domiciled in the United Kingdom during 1974, or on a subsequent occasion, and eventually acquires a different domicile overseas. Where a person was domiciled in the United Kingdom at the time of a disposition, or on death, the location of assets is immaterial and full liability to capital transfer tax arises. Individuals domiciled outside the United Kingdom are, however, chargeable to capital transfer tax only on transactions affecting assets located in the United Kingdom.

The assets of husband and wife are not merged for capital transfer tax purposes. Each spouse is treated as a separate individual entitled to receive the benefit of his or her exemptions, reliefs and rates of tax. Where both husband and wife retain similar assets special "related property" provisions may require the merger of those assets for valuation purposes.

LIFETIME DISPOSITIONS

Lifetime dispositions are vulnerable to capital transfer tax liability. Liability is measured by the "value transferred", which represents the difference between the value of an individual's estate immediately before and immediately following the transfer. It will sometimes be found that the value transferred considerably exceeds the value received by a donee or transferee. This may arise where an individual transfers part of a shareholding interest in an unquoted company. The fall in value reflected by the transfer may well substantially exceed the actual value of shares transferred.

Unless the donee satisfies any capital transfer tax becoming payable, the value transferred must be increased by the amount of that tax. This "grossing up" procedure may considerably increase liability to capital transfer tax.

A disposition is not a transfer of value if it can be shown that there was no intention to confer gratuitous benefit. This requires that the transaction was concluded on terms similar to those expected from persons dealing at arm's length.

DEATH

Immediately before the time of death an individual is deemed to make a transfer of value. This transfer will comprise the value of assets forming part of the deceased's estate after subtracting most liabilities. The "grossing up" procedure does not apply to the value of assets at the time of death.

SETTLED PROPERTY

Complex rules apply to establish capital transfer tax liability on settled property. Where a person is beneficially entitled to an interest in possession, that person will be deemed to "own" the property in which the interest subsists. It follows that, where the interest comes to an end during the beneficiary's lifetime and some other person becomes entitled to the property, the beneficiary is treated as having made a transfer of value. No liability will arise, however, where the property vests into the absolute ownership of the previous beneficiary. The death of a person entitled to an interest in possession will require the value of the underlying property to be added to the value of the deceased's estate.

In the case of other settled property where there is no interest in possession (e.g. discretionary trusts), liability to tax will arise on each ten-year anniversary. There will also be liability if property ceases to be held on discretionary trusts before the first ten-year anniversary date is reached or between anniversaries. The rate of tax suffered will be governed by several considerations including previous dispositions made by the settlor, transactions concluded by the trustees, and the period throughout which property has been held in trust.

Accumulation and maintenance settlements which require assets to be distributed not later than a beneficiary's twenty-fifth birthday may be exempt from any liability to capital transfer tax.

EXEMPT TRANSFERS

A wide range of exempt transfers are excluded from any liability to capital transfer tax. These apply to lifetime dispositions and, subject to restrictions, are of application to assets retained at the time of death. The exempt transfers are listed below:

Transfers between Spouses.—Transfers between husband and wife are usually exempt. However, if one spouse is domiciled in the United Kingdom and the other is not transfers will be exempt only to the extent that the total does not exceed £55,000. Unlike the requirement used for income tax and capital gains tax purposes, it is immaterial whether husband and wife are "living together".

Annual Exemption.—The first £3,000 of gifts and other dispositions made in a year ending on April 5 is exempt. If the exemption is not used, or not wholly used, in any year the balance may be carried forward to the following year only. This exemption has no application on death.

Small Gifts.—Outright gifts of £250 or less to any person in one year ending on April 5 are exempt. The exemption is not available on death.

Normal Expenditure.—A transfer made during lifetime and comprising normal expenditure is exempt. To obtain this exemption it must be shown that—

(a) the transfer was made as part of the normal expenditure of the transferor;

(b) taking one year with another, the transfer was made out of income; and

(c) after allowing for all transfers of value forming part of normal expenditure, the transferor was left with sufficient income to maintain his or her usual standard of living.

Gifts in consideration of marriage.—These are exempt if they satisfy certain requirements. The amount allowed will be governed by the relationship between the donor and a party to the marriage. The allowable amounts comprise—

(a) gifts by a parent—£5,000

(b) gifts by a grandparent—£2,500

(c) gifts by a party to the marriage—£2,500

(d) gifts by other persons—£1,000

Gifts to Charities.—Gifts to charities are exempt from liability. Before March 15, 1983 gifts made on death, or within a period of one year preceding death were limited to £250,000 for exemption purposes but this restriction no longer applies.

Gifts to Political Parties.—Gifts to political parties which satisfy certain requirements are generally exempt. However, a limit of £100,000 is placed on gifts made on or within a period of one year before the date of death.

Gifts for National Purposes.—Gifts made to an extensive list of bodies are exempt from liability. These include, among others—

(a) The National Gallery;

(b) The British Museum;

(c) The National Trust for Places of Historic Interest or Natural Beauty;

(d) The National Art Collections Fund;

(e) The Nature Conservancy Council;

(f) The Historic Buildings and Monuments Commission for England;

(g) Any local authority;

(h) Any university or university college in the United Kingdom.

A number of other gifts made for the public benefit are also exempt.

VALUATIONS

The valuation of assets is an important matter as this will establish the value transferred for lifetime dispositions and also the value of a person's estate at the time of death. The value of property will represent the price which might reasonably be expected from a sale in the open market. This price cannot be reduced on the ground that the whole property is placed on the market simultaneously and may therefore depress values.

In some cases it may be necessary to incorporate the value of "related property". This will include property comprised in the estate of the transferor's spouse and certain property previously transferred to charities. The purpose of the related property valuation rules is not to add the value of that property to the estate of the transferor. Related property must be merged to establish the aggregate value of the respective interests and this value is then apportioned, usually on a pro rata basis, to the separate interests.

The value of shares and securities quoted on a stock exchange will be determined by extracting figures from the daily list of official prices.

Where quoted shares and securities are sold within a period of twelve months following the date of death a claim may be made to substitute the proceeds for the value on death. This claim will only be beneficial if the gross proceeds realized are lower than market value on death. A similar claim may be available for interests in land sold within a period of three years following death.

RELIEF FOR ASSETS

Special relief is made available for certain assets, notably woodlands, agricultural property and business property. The effect of this relief, which may require the submission of an election, is summarized below:

Woodlands.—Where woodlands pass on death the value will usually be included in the deceased's estate. However, an election may be made in respect of land in the United Kingdom on which trees or underwood are growing to delete the value of those assets. Relief is confined to the value of trees or underwood and does not extend to the land on which they are growing. Liability to tax will arise if and when the trees or underwood are sold on a future occasion.

Agricultural property.—Relief is available for the agricultural value of agricultural property. Such property must be occupied and used for agricultural purposes and relief is confined to the agricultural value. Where that value is increased by development potential no relief can be obtained on the excess value.

For transfers made or deaths occurring before March 10, 1981, relief was broadly confined to working farmers. The effect of this relief was to reduce the value transferred by 50 per cent.

Transfers made, or deaths occurring, on or after this date may obtain alternative percentage deductions from the value transferred. A higher deduction of 50 per cent will be available if the transferor had vacant possession or could obtain that possession within a period of twelve months following the transfer. The increased deduction of 50 per cent may also be obtained for certain agricultural property held on March 9, 1981. In other cases, notably including land let to tenants, a reduced deduction of 30 per cent (or 20 per cent for transfers made before March 15, 1983) is available.

It remains a requirement that the agricultural property was either occupied by the transferor for the purposes of agriculture throughout a two year period ending on the date of the transfer or was owned by him throughout a period of seven years ending on that date and occupied for agricultural purposes.

Business Property.—Where value transferred is attributable to relevant business property, that value may be reduced by a percentage. The reduction in value applies to—

(a) property consisting of a business or an interest in a business;

(b) shares or securities of a company which, either by themselves or together with other shares or securities owned by the transferor, gave the transferor control of the company immediately before the transfer. Control for this purpose may include that created by related property.

(c) shares in a company which do not fall within (b) and are not quoted on a recognized stock exchange;

(d) any land, building, machinery or plant which, immediately before the transfer, was used wholly or mainly for the purposes of a business carried on by a company of which the transferor had control;

(e) any land, building, machinery or plant which, immediately before the transfer, was used wholly or mainly for the purposes of a business carried on by a partnership of which the transferor was a partner; and

(f) any land, building, machinery or plant which, immediately before the transfer, was used wholly or mainly for the purposes of a business carried on by the transferor, and was then settled property in which he retained an interest in possession.

For property falling within (a) or (b) the deduction is 50 per cent. A reduced deduction of 30 per cent applies to property in (d) or (e). The deduction for property in (c) was previously 20 per cent but for transfers after March 14, 1983 this was increased to 30 per cent.

It is a general requirement that the property must have been retained for a period of two years before the transfer or death and restrictions may be necessary if the property has not been used wholly for business purposes. The same slice of property cannot obtain both the business property relief and the relief available for agricultural property.

RATES OF TAX

Once the amount of chargeable transfers has been established it will be necessary to determine the amount of capital transfer tax payable. Each chargeable transfer made during lifetime is added to earlier transfers to establish a cumulative total. On death the value of the estate must be added to lifetime transfers also to arrive at a cumulative total. However, this cumulative total will only include chargeable transfers made within a period of ten years before the current lifetime disposition or death. As capital transfer tax first applied to dispositions made on and after March 27, 1974, restrictions in the cumulative total could not be relevant until the initial ten year period expired on March 26, 1984 at the earliest.

The cumulative total which includes the current transfer or the value on death must be compared with a table to establish the rate or rates of capital transfer tax payable. There are two separate tables—

(a) one applying to lifetime dispositions, other than those made within a period of three years before the date of death; and

(b) one applying to the value of the estate at the time of death and also to lifetime dispositions made within the previous three year period.

The rates of capital transfer tax have been amended on several occasions. The first table reproduced below shows the rates of capital transfer tax for deaths occurring on or after March 13, 1984. It also applies to lifetime dispositions made within a period of three years preceding the date of death and falling after that date. The second table is of application to other lifetime dispositions made on or after March 13, 1984.

First Table
For values on death and transfers within 3 years before death

Deaths or transfers on or after March 13, 1984	
Portion of value	Rate of tax
£ £	%
0– 64,000	Nil
64,001– 85,000	30
85,001–116,000	35
116,001–148,000	40
148,001–185,000	45
185,001–232,000	50
232,001–285,000	55
285,001 and above	60

Second Table
For lifetime gifts (other than in 3 years before death)

Gifts on and after March 13, 1984	
Portion of value	Rate of tax
£ £	%
0– 64,000	Nil
64,001– 85,000	15
85,001–116,000	17½
116,001–148,000	20
148,001–185,000	22½
185,001–232,000	25
232,001–285,000	27½
285,001 and above	30

PAYMENT OF TAX

Capital transfer tax usually falls due for payment six months after the end of the month in which the chargeable transaction takes place. Where a transfer, other than that made on death, takes place after April 5 and before the following October 1, tax falls due on the following April 30, although there are some exceptions to this general rule.

Capital transfer tax attributable to the transfer of certain land, controlling shareholding interests, unquoted shares, businesses and interests in businesses, together with agricultural property, may usually be satisfied by instalments. No liability to interest arises where tax is paid on the due date. In other cases, delay in the payment of tax may involve liability to interest.

CORPORATION TAX

INTRODUCTION

Profits, gains and income accruing to companies resident in the United Kingdom incur liability to corporation tax. Non-resident companies are immune from this tax unless they carry on a trade in the United Kingdom through a permanent establishment, branch or office. Companies residing outside the United Kingdom may be liable to income tax at the basic rate on other income arising in the United Kingdom, perhaps from letting property. The following comments are confined to companies resident in the United Kingdom and have little application to those residing overseas.

Liability to corporation tax is governed by the profits, gains or income for an accounting period. This is the period for which financial accounts are made up, and in the case of companies preparing accounts to the same accounting date annually will comprise successive periods of twelve months.

RATE OF TAX

The amount of profits or income for an accounting period must be determined on normal taxation principles. The special rules which apply to individuals where a source of income is acquired or discontinued do not apply and consideration is confined to the actual profits or income for an accounting period.

The rate of corporation tax is fixed for a financial year ending on March 31. Where the accounting period of a company overlaps this date and there is a change in the rate of corporation tax, profits and income must be apportioned.

For several years the full rate of corporation tax was 52 per cent but this is being progressively reduced as follows:

Financial year	Per cent
12 months ending March 31, 1984	50
12 months ending March 31, 1985	45
12 months ending March 31, 1986	40
12 months ending March 31, 1987	35

The progressive reduction in the rate of corporation tax is being made to compensate companies for the loss of stock relief and the progressive withdrawal of certain allowances for capital expenditure which increase the amount of profits and income chargeable to that tax.

SMALL COMPANIES RATE

Where the profits of a company do not exceed stated limits corporation tax becomes payable at the small companies rate. It is the amount of profits and not the size of the company which governs the application of this rate.

The level of profits which a company may derive without losing the benefit of the small companies rate has been frequently changed. However, for financial years commencing on and after April 1, 1983, the following small companies rate applies where profits do not exceed £100,000:

Financial year	Per cent
12 months ending March 31, 1984	38
12 months ending March 31, 1985, 1986 and 1987	30

If profits do exceed £100,000 but fall below £500,000 a marginal small companies rate applies. The broad effect of marginal relief is that the first £100,000 of profits is taxed at the small companies rate of 38 or 30 per cent. Profits falling in the margin exceeding £100,000 then incur liability at the following marginal rates:

Financial year	Per cent
12 months ending March 31, 1984	55
12 months ending March 31, 1985	48·75
12 months ending March 31, 1986	42·5
12 months ending March 31, 1987	36·25

If the accounting period of a company overlaps March 31, profits must be apportioned to establish the appropriate rate for each part of those profits.

The lower limit of £100,000 and the upper limit of £500,000 applies for a period of twelve months in duration and must be proportionately reduced for shorter periods. Some restriction in the small companies rate and the marginal rate may be necessary if there are two or more "associated companies", namely companies under common control.

CAPITAL GAINS

Chargeable gains arising to a company are calculated in a manner similar to that used for individuals. However, companies cannot obtain the annual exemption of £5,600, nor are they assessed to capital gains tax. In place of this tax companies suffer liability to corporation tax on chargeable gains. Only a fraction of the chargeable gains is taxable at the full corporation tax rate. The fraction selected ensures that companies effectively suffer corporation tax at the rate of 30 per cent on the full chargeable gain.

DISTRIBUTIONS

Dividends and other qualifying distributions made by a United Kingdom resident company are not satisfied after deduction of income tax. However, when making a distribution a company is required to account to the Inland Revenue for an amount of advance corporation tax. For distributions made in the year ending April 5, 1985, the amount of advance corporation tax will represent three-sevenths of the distribution. Thus a cash dividend of £70 paid to a shareholder will also require satisfaction of advance corporation tax amounting to £30.

Advance corporation tax accounted for in this manner for distributions made in an accounting period may usually be set against a company's corporation tax liability for the same period. Some restrictions are imposed on the amount which can be offset but any surplus can be carried forward, or carried backwards, and set against corporation tax due for other accounting periods.

A United Kingdom resident shareholder receiving a qualifying distribution also obtains a tax credit, which for the year ending April 5, 1985, is equal to three-sevenths of the distribution made. Therefore the total income of the individual comprises the aggregate of the distribution and the tax credit. If the individual is not liable, or not fully liable, to income tax at the basic rate, all or part of the tax credit can be refunded by the Inland Revenue. Individuals with substantial income incur liability to income tax at the higher rates exceeding 30 per cent on the aggregate of the distribution and the tax credit.

PAYMENT OF TAX

Corporation tax, less any relief for advance corporation tax, usually falls due for payment nine months following the end of the accounting period to which the tax relates. Companies who were carrying on business before 1966 may have a later due and payable date.

INTEREST

On making many payments of interest a company is required to deduct income tax at the basic rate and account for the tax deducted to the Inland Revenue. The gross amount of interest paid will usually comprise a charge on income to be offset against profits on which corporation tax becomes payable.

GROUPS OF COMPANIES

Each company within a group is separately charged to corporation tax on profits, gains and income. However, where one group member realizes a loss, other than a capital loss, a claim may be made to offset the deficiency against profits of some other member of the same group.

Claims are also available to avoid the payment of advance corporation tax on distributions, or the deduction of income tax on the payment of interest, for transactions between members of a group of companies. The transfer of capital assets from one member of a group to a fellow member will incur no liability to tax on chargeable gains.

VALUE ADDED TAX

INTRODUCTION

Unlike income tax, capital gains tax, capital transfer tax and corporation tax, which are collected and administered by the Inland Revenue, value added tax is the responsibility of Customs and Excise. Value added tax is charged on the value of supplies made in the United Kingdom by a registered trader and extends both to the supply of goods and to the supply of services. Liability also arises on the value of goods imported into the United Kingdom.

REGISTRATION

All traders, including professional men and women, together with companies, making taxable supplies of a value exceeding stated limits are required to register for value added tax purposes. Taxable supplies represent the supply of goods and services potentially chargeable with value added tax. The limits which govern mandatory registration are amended annually but from March 14, 1984, an unregistered trader must register—

(a) at any time, if there are reasonable grounds for believing that the value of taxable supplies in the year then beginning will exceed £18,700, or

(b) at the end of any quarter, namely March 31, June 30, September 30 or December 31, if the total amount of taxable supplies has exceeded either £6,200 in the last quarter or £18,700 in the last four quarters. Registration will not be mandatory if it can be shown that the value of taxable supplies in the last quarter and the next three quarters is not expected to exceed £18,700.

Where the limits governing mandatory registration have been exceeded it is necessary for the trader concerned to notify Customs and Excise. Failure to provide prompt notification may have unfortunate results as the person concerned will be required to account for value added tax from the proper registration date. In some situations a trader whose taxable supplies do not reach the mandatory registration limits may apply for voluntary registration.

A registered trader may submit an application for de-registration if the value of taxable supplies subsequently falls. From June 4, 1984, an application for de-registration can be made if the value of taxable supplies for the year beginning on the application date is not expected to exceed £17,700. De-registration can also be achieved if the value of taxable supplies in each of the two previous years did not exceed £18,700 and is unlikely to exceed this threshold in the following twelve-month period.

INPUT TAX

A registered trader will both suffer tax (input tax) when obtaining goods or services for the purposes of his business and also become liable to account for tax (output tax) on the value of goods and services which he supplies. Relief can usually be obtained for input tax incurred, either by setting that tax against output tax due or by repayment. Most items of input tax suffered can be relieved in this manner but there are exceptions including the prohibition of relief for the cost of business entertaining. Where a registered trader makes both exempt supplies and also taxable supplies to his customers or clients there may be some restriction in the amount of input tax which can be recovered.

OUTPUT TAX

When making a taxable supply of goods or services a registered trader must account for output tax, if any, on the value of the supply. Usually the price charged by the registered trader will be increased by adding value added tax but failure to make the required addition will not remove liability to account for output tax.

EXEMPT SUPPLIES

No value added tax is chargeable on the supply of goods or services which are treated as exempt supplies. These include the provision of burial and cremation facilities, insurance, finance and education. The granting of a lease to occupy land will usually comprise an exempt supply, but there are numerous exceptions.

Exempt supplies do not enter into the value of taxable supplies which govern liability to mandatory registration. Such supplies made by a registered trader may however limit the amount of input tax which can be relieved.

RATES OF TAX

Two rates of value added tax have applied since June 18, 1979, namely:

(a) a zero, or nil, rate; and

(b) a standard rate of 15 per cent.

Although no tax is due on a zero-rated supply, this does comprise a taxable supply which must be included on the calculation governing liability to register.

ZERO-RATING

A large number of supplies are zero-rated, including the following, among others—

(a) the supply of many items of food and drink for human consumption. This does not include ice creams, chocolates, sweets, potato crisps and alcoholic drinks. Nor does it extend to supplies made in the course of catering, for example, at a wedding reception or other social function, or to items supplied for consumption in a restaurant or cafe. Previously, many take-away items of food and drink supplied for consumption outside the supplier's premises were zero-rated. Although this continues to apply to the supply of "cold" items, for example, sandwiches, the supply of "hot" food, for example, fish and chips, ceased to remain zero-rated after April 30, 1984;

(b) animal feeding stuffs;

(c) sewerage and water;

(d) books, brochures, pamphlets, leaflets, newspapers, maps and charts;

(e) talking books for the blind and handicapped and wireless sets for the blind;

(f) newspaper advertising;

(g) electricity, gas and coal;

(h) supplies made in the construction of a building. Zero-rating previously applied to the installation of double glazing, the alteration of a building, the installation of fitted cupboards and the construction of a garage or other building in the grounds of a dwelling-house. However, for supplies made after May 31, 1984, this list of items was substantially reduced and zero-rating is limited to the alteration of a listed building, the construction of a garage in conjunction with the construction of a new dwelling and the installation of working surfaces in the kitchen of a new building;

(i) the transportation of persons in a vehicle, ship or aircraft designed to carry not less than twelve persons;

(j) supplies of drugs, medicines and other aids for the handicapped;

(k) supplies of clothing and footwear for young persons;

(l) exports.

This list is not exhaustive but indicates the wide range of supplies which may be zero-rated.

COLLECTION OF TAX

Registered traders submit value added tax returns for accounting periods. Each accounting period is for three months in duration but arrangements can be made to submit returns on a monthly basis. The return will show both the output tax due for supplies made by the trader in the accounting period and also the input tax for which relief is claimed. If the output tax exceeds input tax the balance must be remitted with the value added tax return. Where input tax suffered exceeds the output tax due the registered trader may claim recovery of the excess from Customs and Excise.

This basis for collecting tax explains the structure of value added tax. Where supplies are made between registered traders the supplier will account for an amount of tax which will usually be identical to the tax recovered by the person to whom the supply is made. However, where the supply is made to a person who is not a registered trader there can be no recovery of input tax and it is on this person that the final burden of value added tax eventually falls. Tax on imports into the United Kingdom must be satisfied at the time of importation or perhaps later where special arrangements have been agreed.

BAD DEBTS

Many retailers operate special retail schemes for calculating the amount of value added tax due. These schemes are, broadly, based on the volume of consideration received in an accounting period. Should a customer fail to pay for goods or services supplied, there will be no consideration on which value added tax falls to be calculated. In other cases, where the special retailers' schemes do not apply, output tax falls due on the value of the supply and liability is not affected by failure to receive consideration. This implies that there will be no relief for the value added tax element in bad debts. However, relief for this element may be obtained where the debtor is formally declared insolvent or a debtor company is compulsorily wound up.

OTHER SPECIAL SCHEMES

In addition to the schemes for retailers, there are several special schemes applied to calculate the amount of value added tax due and which also limit the ability to recover input tax. These schemes apply to the supply of second-hand motor cars, motor cycles, caravans, boats, electronic organs, aircraft and firearms, together with works of art, antiques and collectors' pieces.

OTHER TAXES AND STAMP DUTIES

The Commissioners as a general rule allow deeds, etc., to be stamped after execution:—

WITHOUT PENALTY, ON PAYMENT OF DUTY ONLY.
Deeds and instruments not otherwise excepted, within 30 days of *first* execution.
NOTE.—Where wholly executed *abroad*, the period begins to run from the date of arrival here.

PENALTIES ENFORCEABLE ON STAMPING IN ADDITION TO DUTY:—
Instruments presented after the proper time (subject to special provisions in some cases and subject to the commissioner's power to mitigate) a penalty equal to the duty   £10

AGREEMENT for Lease, *see* LEASES.
AGREEMENT FOR SALE OF PROPERTY—charged with *ad val.* duty as if an actual conveyance on sale with certain exceptions, *e.g.* agreements for the sale of land, stocks and shares, goods, wares or merchandise, or a ship (*see* s. 59 (1), Stamp Act 1891). If *ad val.* duty is paid on an agreement in accordance with this provision, the subsequent conveyance or transfer is not chargeable with any *ad val.* duty and the Commissioners will upon application either place a denoting stamp on such conveyance or transfer or will transfer the *ad val.* duty thereto. Further, if such an agreement is rescinded, not performed, etc., the Commissioners will return the *ad val.* duty paid.
AGREEMENT under seal subject to exemptions.   50p
APPOINTMENT of a new trustee or in exercise of a power over property, not being by a will; also on retirement of trustee, although no new trustee be appointed................   50p

ASSIGNMENT:
By way of sale—*see* Conveyance.
By way of gift—*see* Voluntary Disposition.
ASSURANCE—*see* Insurance Policies.
BEARER INSTRUMENT:
Inland bearer instrument, *i.e.* share warrant, stock certificate to bearer or any other instrument to bearer by which stock can be transferred, issued by a company or body formed or established in U.K. Duty of an amount equal to three times the transfer duty (usually £3% of the market value).
Overseas bearer instrument, *i.e.*, such an instrument issued in G.B. by a company formed out of the U.K. Duty equal to twice the transfer duty (usually £2% of the market value). Even if issued out of G.B. the instrument must be stamped before transfer in G.B. The issue or transfer of a bearer instrument relating to stock expressed in the currency of a territory outside the Scheduled territories is exempt from duty.
BILL OF SALE, Absolute, *see* CONVEYANCE ON SALE.
CAPITAL DUTY.—Where a *chargeable transaction* of a *capital company* takes place after July 31, 1973, duty of £1 is payable on every £100 or fraction of £100 of the actual value of the assets contributed by the members (as opposed to the previous duty of 50p per £100 of the nominal capital), provided the place of effective management of the company is in G.B. or its registered office is in G.B. but the place of its effective management is outside the E.E.C. (Finance Act 1973).

A statement containing prescribed particulars must be delivered to the Commissioners within one month of the transaction unless there is an obligation under the Companies Act 1948 (*e.g.*, on the formation of a limited liability company) or the Limited Partnerships Act 1907 (*e.g.*, on the registration of a limited partnership) to send a statement to the registrar of companies as a result of the transaction.

Capital company includes a company incorporated with limited liability under U.K. law, a limited partnership under the Limited Partnerships Act 1907, a company incorporated according to the law of any other member of the E.E.C. and any other corporation or body of persons whose members have the right freely to dispose of their shares and whose liability for debts is limited.

Chargeable transactions includes the formation of a capital company, an increase in its capital by the contribution of assets of any kind, the transfer to G.B. of its place of effective management from a country outside the E.E.C. if its registered office is in such a country, and the transfer to G.B. of its registered office from a country outside the E.E.C. if its place of effective management is in such a country.

CAPITAL TRANSFER TAX

A new tax on the transmission of wealth, made by way of gift during a person's lifetime and on death, was introduced by the Finance Act 1975. It applies retrospectively to March 27, 1974, unless the donor died before March 13, 1975 (when Estate Duty or modified Estate Duty will apply).

Tax is charged at progressive rates on the cumulative totals of chargeable gifts made during a person's lifetime, with a final cumulation of the value of a person's estate on his death. The rates of tax for lifetime transfers are those shown in Table 1. For transfers on death, or within 3 years of death, the rates applicable are those in Table 2.

Table 1

Value transferred		Rate of tax
Lower limit £	Upper limit £	Per cent
0	64,000	*Nil*
64,000	85,000	15
85,000	116,000	17½
116,000	148,000	20
148,000	185,000	22½
185,000	232,000	25
232,000	285,000	27½
285,000	—	30

Table 2

Value transferred		Rate of tax
Lower limit £	Upper limit £	Per cent
0	64,000	*Nil*
64,000	85,000	30
85,000	116,000	35
116,000	148,000	40
148,000	185,000	45
185,000	232,000	50
232,000	285,000	55
285,000	—	60

In calculating the value transferred on lifetime gifts, the amount of tax paid by the donor on the gift must be taken into account. The value transferred on death is the value of the person's estate at the moment before his death.

Certain exemptions and reliefs are given, including:

(*a*) *For lifetime transfers only:*
(i) The first £3,000 of gifts made in each tax year (April 6 to the following April 5) are exempt. Only the balance over £3,000 is taxable. There is provision for the carry forward of this relief for one year only, in so far as it has not been used in the previous year.
(ii) Gifts not exceeding £250 to any one donee in the tax year are exempt. This cannot be used to exempt the first £250 of a larger gift.
(iii) Gifts which are normal expenditure out of income are exempt, provided the donor is left with sufficient income to maintain his standard of living.
(iv) Gifts in consideration of marriage are exempt up to £5,000 if made by a parent; £2,500 if made by a grandparent or some other lineal ancestor, or by one party to another; and £1,000 in any other case.
(v) Gifts of certain types of property, including works of art, are exempt if made to a body not established or conducted for profit.

(*b*) *For lifetime transfers and on death:*
(i) Transfers between spouses are exempt to the extent that the gift increases the value of the donee spouse's estate.
(ii) Lifetime gifts to Charities and certain Political Parties are exempt without limit. If made on death or within one year of death, gifts to charities are exempt (political parties £100,000).
(iii) Gifts to listed heritage bodies including National Gallery, British Museum, and Government Departments, are exempt.
(iv) Agricultural relief:
Provided certain conditions are satisfied, on a transfer of Agricultural land, the agricultural value is reduced by 50% if the transferor has occupied the land for the purposes of Agriculture for two years up to the time of the transfer, or by 20% if he has owned the land for the last seven years and it has been occupied by someone for the purposes of Agriculture throughout that period.
(v) There is also relief for business property in certain circumstances.

(*c*) *For transfers on death only:*
Conditional exemptions exist for works of art, timber and for death on active service. There is an exemption in respect of woodlands available on death.

Tax must be paid within 6 months of the end of the month in which the chargeable event occurs unless the event is a lifetime transfer, made between April 5 and October 1 in any year, when tax is due at the end of the next following April. In certain circumstances, tax may be payable by instalments.

Interest on unpaid tax runs from the date the tax is due.

CONTRACT, *see* AGREEMENT.

CONTRACT NOTE for the sale or purchase of any stock or marketable security; where the value of the stock or marketable security—
Does not exceed £500 for every £50 or part
thereof 50p

Exceeds £500 for every £100 or part thereof ..   £1
(Special adhesive stamps)

Option Contract Notes are chargeable with
half the above rates only, unless the option
is a double one.
Contract Note following a duly stamped
option contract note chargeable with half
the above rates only.

CONTRACT OR GRANT FOR PAYMENT OF A
SUPERANNUATION ANNUITY: for every £10
or fractional part of £10 ....   5p

CONVEYANCE OR TRANSFER ON SALE (in the
case of a Voluntary Disposition, *see* below)
of any property (*except* stock or marketable
securities for which, *see* above), where the
Conveyance or Transfer contains a certificate of value certifying that the transaction
does not form part of a larger transaction or
a series of transactions in respect of which
the aggregate amount or value of the consideration exceeds £30,000...................   nil
Exceeds £30,000 (for every £100 or fraction
of £100) £1
If the Conveyance or Transfer on Sale does
not contain the appropriate statement
duty at the full rate of £1 for every £100
or fraction of £100 will be payable whatever the amount of the consideration.
However, if the consideration does not
exceed £500, and the instrument does not
contain a certificate of value, there are
graduated duties ranging from 50p to £5.
Conveyances to charities are exempt from
duty under this head provided the instrument is stamped with a denoting stamp.

CONVEYANCE OR TRANSFER of any other kind
.... fixed duty   50p
Included under this head are Transfers for
nominal consideration within any of the
following categories:
  (*a*) Transfers vesting the property in
     trustees on the appointment of a new
     trustee of a pre-existing trust, or on
     the retirement of a trustee.
  (*b*) Transfers, where no beneficial inter-
     est in the property passes, (i) to a mere
     nominee of the transferor; (ii) from a
     mere nominee of the transferee; (iii)
     from one nominee to another nominee
     of the same beneficial owner.
  (*c*) Transfer to a residuary legatee of
     stock, etc., forming part of the residue
     divisible under a will.
  (*d*) Transfers to a beneficiary under a will
     of a specific legacy of stock, etc.
     (*Note.*—Transfers by executors in dis-
     charge, or partial discharge, of a
     pecuniary legacy (unless made under
     an express power of appropriation)
     are chargeable with *ad valorem* duty
     on the amount of the legacy so dis-
     charged.)
  (*e*) Transfers of stock, etc., forming part
     of an intestate's estate to the person
     entitled to it.
  (*f*) Transfers to a beneficiary under
     settlement on a distribution of the
     trust funds of stock, etc., forming the
     share or part of the share of those
     funds to which the beneficiary is
     entitled in accordance with the terms
     of the settlement.
  (*g*) Transfers on the occasion of a mar-
     riage to trustees of stocks, etc., to be

held on the terms of a settlement made
in consideration of marriage.
  (*h*) Transfers by the liquidator of a com-
     pany of stocks, etc., forming part of
     the assets of the company to the
     persons who were shareholders, in
     satisfaction of their rights on a wind-
     ing-up.
The evidence necessary to establish that a
transfer is liable to the fixed duty of 50p
should take the form of a certificate setting
forth the facts of the transaction. In cases
falling within (*b*) such a certificate should
be signed by (1) both transferor and
transferee or (2) a member of a Stock
Exchange or a solicitor acting for one or
other of the parties or (3) an accredited
representative of a bank; in the last case
when the bank or its official nominee is a
party to the transfer, the certificate,
instead of setting out the facts, may be to
the effect that "the transfer is excepted
from Section 74 of the Finance (1909–10)
Act 1910." A certificate in other cases
should be signed by a solicitor or other
person (*e.g.*, a bank acting as trustee or
executor) having a full knowledge of the
facts.
Registering Officers will in any case in
which a Marketing Officer's certificate
has not been given require such evidence
in order to satisfy themselves that a
transfer stamped with the 50p fixed duty
is duly stamped.

COVENANT—For original creation and sale of
any annuity, *see* CONVEYANCE.
Separate Deed of, made on occasion of sale,
but not being an instrument chargeable
with *ad valorem* duty as a Conveyance:
same duty as a Conveyance on sale, but
not to exceed 50p

DECLARATION OF TRUST, not being a Will or
Settlement 50p

DEED of any kind not charged under some
special head 50p

DEMISE, *see* LEASE

DUPLICATE OR COUNTERPART
Same duty as original, but not to exceed ...   50p

GIFT (*see* VOLUNTARY DISPOSITION).

GUARANTEE:
If under seal 50p

HIRE-PURCHASE AGREEMENTS:
Under seal 50p
    (Finance Act 1907, s. 7)
N.B.—If the agreement amounts to a "credit-
sale" the position is the same.

INSURANCE POLICIES:
Life:—
Exc. £50 and not exc. £1,000, for every £100
or part of £100 ....   5p
Exc. £1,000, for every £1,000 or any frac-
tional part of £1,000 ....   50p
Made after 1 August 1966 for period not
exceeding 2 years......................   5p

LEASES:—Lease or tack for any definite term less
than a year of any furnished dwelling-house or
apartments where the rent for such term exceeds
£500, £1; of any lands, tenements, etc., in consideration of any rent, according to the following
table:—

Annual rent not exceeding	*Term not exceeding			Term exceeding 100 years
	7 years	35 years	100 years	
£	£ p	£ p	£ p	£ p
5	Nil	0·10	0·60	1·20
10	Nil	0·20	1·20	2·40
15	Nil	0·30	1·80	3·60
20	Nil	0·40	2·40	4·80
25	Nil	0·50	3·00	6·00
50	Nil	1·00	6·00	12·00
75	Nil	1·50	9·00	18·00
100	Nil	2·00	12·00	24·00
150	Nil	3·00	18·00	36·00
200	Nil	4·00	24·00	48·00
250	Nil	5·00	30·00	60·00
300	Nil	6·00	36·00	72·00
350	Nil	7·00	42·00	84·00
400	Nil	8·00	48·00	96·00
450	Nil	9·00	54·00	108·00
500	Nil	10·00	60·00	120·00
Exceeding £500 for every £50 or fraction of £50	0·50	1·00	6·00	12·00

*If the term is indefinite the same duty is payable as if the term did not exceed 7 years.

Agreement for lease, same as actual lease.

Where a consideration other than rent is payable and duty is charged on that consideration at conveyance rates, the same rule applies where the consideration does not exceed £30,000 as under Conveyance or Transfer on Sale (except stock or marketable securities), provided that any rent payable does not exceed £300 a year.

Leases to charities are exempt from duty under this head provided the instrument is stamped with a denoting stamp.

MORTGAGES are exempt.

POWER OF ATTORNEY, etc., for receiving certain prize-money or wages 5p

For the receipt of any money, or bill, or note, not exceeding £20, or of any periodical payments not exceeding £10 annually ... 25p

For the receipt of dividends or interest of any stock, if for one payment only 5p
Ditto in any other case 25p
Power of attorney of any other kind 50p

PROCURATION, Deed, etc., of 50p

RECEIPTS FOR SALARIES, Wages and Superannuation, and other like allowances are exempt.

REVOCATION of any TRUST or Property not being a Will 50p

TRANSFER OF STOCK AND SHARES by way of gift or sale—for each £50 or part of £50 . . . . £1

UNIT TRUST INSTRUMENT—Any trust instrument of a unit trust scheme—For every £100, and also for any fractional part of £100, of the amount or value of the property subject to the trusts created or recorded by the instrument 25p

VOLUNTARY DISPOSITION *inter vivos*:—
On any instrument being a voluntary disposition (*inter vivos*) of any property (except stock or marketable securities, *see ante*, under Conveyance of Transfer) where the value of the property conveyed or transferred does not exceed £30,000 . . . . *nil*

Exceeds £30,000, for every £100 and fraction of £100 . . . . £1

The instrument must contain similar certificates of value as a Conveyance or Transfer on Sale with the substitution of the words "property conveyed or transferred" for the word "consideration."

If the value of the property does not exceed £500 the same graduated rates apply as under Conveyance of Transfer on Sale (except Stock or marketable securities).

THE COST OF LIVING

The first cost-of-living index to be calculated in Great Britain was the one which took July, 1914, as 100 and was based on the pattern of expenditure of working class families in 1904. Since 1947 the Index of Retail Prices has superseded the cost-of-living index, although the older term is still often popularly applied to it. This index is designed to reflect the month-by-month changes in the average level of retail prices of goods and services purchased by the "majority" of households in the United Kingdom, including practically all wage-earners and most small and medium salary-earners. For spending coming within the scope of the index, a representative list of items is selected and the prices actually charged for these items are collected at regular intervals. In working out the index figure, the price changes are "weighted"—that is, given different degrees of importance—in accordance with the pattern of consumption of the average family.

A more widely used guide when considering changes in the average level of prices of all consumer goods and services, particularly over a number of years, is the consumer price index, now renamed the consumers' expenditure deflator. This index, which has been calculated back to 1938, covers the expenditure of all consumers as defined for national income

purposes, and compares the price of goods and services actually purchased in a given year with the prices of the same goods and services in a base year.

During 1973 the Central Statistical Office constructed an annual index of prices of consumer goods and services over the period 1914 to 1972. This index has been constructed by linking together the pre-war cost of living index for the period 1914–1938, the consumers' expenditure deflator for the period 1938 and 1946–62* and the General Index of Retail Prices for the period 1962–1972.

In August 1979, the tax and price index (TPI) was introduced in order to provide a statistic which incorporates the effects of direct and indirect taxation, as well as prices, on taxpayers. The TPI is not directly concerned with the purchasing power of money, however, but with the purchasing power of pre-tax income. The General Index of Retail Prices thus retains its function of measuring the changes in the prices of goods and services purchased by households (from their post-tax income), and therefore as an indicator of the purchasing power of money.

In 1974 the General Index of Retail Prices was rebased taking January 1974 = 100. Using this index the following table has been constructed:

	General Index of Retail Prices (all items) Jan. 1974 = 100	Comparable Purchasing Power of £1 in 1983
	Annual averages	
1914	11·1	30·19
1915	13·7	24·46
1920	27·7	12·10
1925	19·6	17·10
1930	17·6	19·04
1935	15·9	21·07
1940	24·4	13·73
1945	29·3	11·44
1950	35·6	9·41
1955	44·1	7·60
1960	49·6	6·76
1965	58·4	5·74
1970	73·1	4·58
1971	80·0	4·19
1972	85·7	3·91
1973	93·5	3·58
1974	108·5	3·09
1975	134·8	2·49
1976	157·1	2·13
1977	182·0	1·84
1978	197·1	1·70
1979	223·5	1·50
1980	263·7	1·27
1981	295·0	1·14
1982	320·4	1·05
1983	335·1	1·00

By employing this table an annual purchasing power of the pound index may be derived by taking the inverse of the price index. So, for example, if the purchasing power of the pound is taken to be 100p in 1972, then its comparable purchasing power in 1983 would be:

$$100 \times \frac{85·7}{335·1} = 25·5p$$

It should be noted that these figures can only be approximate.
* There are no official figures for 1939–45.

CRIMINAL STATISTICS
ENGLAND AND WALES
Notifiable offences recorded by the police (thousands)

	Total	Violence against the person	Sexual offences	Burglary	Robbery	Theft and handling stolen goods	Fraud and forgery	Criminal damage	Other
1980	2,688·2	97·2	21·1	622·6	15·0	1,463·5	105·2	359·5	4·1
1981	2,963·8	100·2	19·4	723·2	20·3	1,603·2	106·7	386·7	4·1
1982	3,262·4	108·7	19·7	810·6	22·8	1,755·9	123·1	417·8	3·8
1983	3,247·0	111·3	20·4	813·4	22·1	1,705·9	121·8	443·3	8·7†
1983 1st quarter	797·2	23·6	4·5	214·5	5·3	412·7	29·7	105·3	1·6
2nd quarter	821·0	28·3	5·2	203·3	5·5	431·6	31·1	114·0	2·1
3rd quarter	784·9	30·6	6·0	183·7	5·2	421·0	30·9	105·0	2·5
4th quarter	844·4	28·9	4·7	211·9	6·2	440·6	30·1	119·0	2·6
1984 1st quarter	838·0	24·9	4·2	230·8	6·0	421·3	30·4	118·2	2·2

† Includes from the beginning of 1983 offences of 'trafficking in controlled drugs'.

SCOTLAND
Crimes and offences recorded by the police (thousands)

	Total crimes and offences (annual)	†Total crimes and offences (monthly)	Non-sexual crimes of violence against the person	Crimes involving indecency	Crimes involving dishonesty	Fire-raising, malicious and reckless conduct	Other crimes	Miscellaneous offences	Offences relating to motor vehicles
1980	724·7	729·2	11·3	5·3	281·6	60·4	8·4	124·5	237·8
1981	744·7	740·6	12·2	4·8	318·5	61·3	9·5	117·8	216·4
1982	762·5	766·1	12·3	5·0	343·2	66·4	12·0	115·8	211·5
1983	799·9	800·3	13·3	5·5	345·2	72·9	14·1	112·8	236·6
1983 1st quarter	190·9		2·9	1·4	82·4	17·5	2·9	26·2	57·6
2nd quarter	198·0		3·3	1·3	84·8	18·0	3·5	26·1	61·1
3rd quarter	203·8		3·4	1·5	87·2	17·8	3·7	31·6	58·6
4th quarter	207·6		3·6	1·3	90·8	19·7	4·0	28·9	59·3

†Components may not add to totals due to separate rounding.

NATIONAL HEALTH SERVICE
(and Local Authority Personal Social Services)

The National Health Service came into being on July 5, 1948, as a result of the *National Health Service Act* 1946. The Act placed a duty on the Secretary of State for Social Services to promote the establishment in England and Wales of a comprehensive Health Service designed to secure improvement in the mental and physical health of the people and the prevention, diagnosis and treatment of illness. The Secretary of State for Wales administers the National Health Service in Wales. There are separate Acts for Scotland and Northern Ireland, where the Health Services are run on very similar lines. The Secretaries of State are responsible to Parliament for seeing that Health Services of all kinds of the highest possible quality are available to all who need them.

The National Health Service covers a comprehensive range of hospital, specialist, family practitioner (medical, dental, ophthalmic and pharmaceutical), artificial limb and appliance, ambulance, and community health services. Everyone normally resident in this country is entitled to use any of these services, there are no contribution conditions and the charges made (except those for amenity beds) are reduced or waived in cases of hardship. In addition the Secretary of State for Social Services is responsible under the Local Authority Social Services Act 1970 for the provision by local authorities of social services for the elderly, the mentally handicapped, the physically disabled and also for families and children. The 1980 Health Services Act led to major changes in the structure of the Health Service. Under arrangements which became operational in April 1982, District Health Authorities (DHAs)— of which there are 192 in England and nine in Wales—are responsible for the operational management of health services and for planning within regional and national strategic guidelines. Each DHA is required to arrange its services into units of management at hospital and community services level, and as many decisions as possible are delegated to unit level. Arrangements for the Family Practitioner Service continued to be administered by Family Practitioner Committees (FPCs)—90 in England and eight in Wales. FPCs also contribute to the planning of health services.

The 14 Regional Health Authorities (RHAs) in England are responsible for regional planning, the allocation of resources to District Authorities, and the promotion of national policies and priorities. Performance review meetings are held annually between each DHA and its RHA, and between each RHA and Department of Health and Social Security Ministers, thereby strengthening Authorities' accountability to Parliament, whilst respecting the essentially locally-based nature of decision making. Professional advisory machinery incorporated within the structure ensures that Health Authorities and their staffs make decisions in the full knowledge of expert opinion.

The cost of the reorganized NHS is still financed mainly from taxation and met from moneys voted by Parliament. In Great Britain this amounts to more than £12 billion a year. The Department of Health and Social Security makes capital and revenue allocations to the RHAs and from these the RHAs meet the cost of their own services and make allocations to DHAs as well as funding Community Health Councils.

THE HEALTH SERVICES

Family Doctor Service

In England and Wales the Family Doctor Service (or General Medical Services) is organized by 98 Family Practitioner Committees which also organize the General Dental, Pharmaceutical and Ophthalmic Services for their areas. There is a Family Practitioner Committee for one or more District Health Authorities; members, who serve voluntarily, are appointed by local doctors, dentists, pharmacists and opticians (15), the Local Authority or Authorities (4) and the District Health Authority or Authorities jointly (11). Under the Health and Social Security Act 1984, FPCs are to become employing authorities in their own right on April 1, 1985, and all the members and the chairmen (31 in all) are to be appointed by the Secretary of State. Twenty-three of the appointments are to be made from the nominations received from local doctors (8), dentists (3), pharmacists (2), opticians (2), DHAS (4) and local authorities (4). The change is to bring DHAs and FPCs into a closer working partnership and to improve the efficiency and accountability of FPCs.

Any doctor may take part in the Family Doctor Scheme, provided the area in which he wishes to practise has not already an adequate number of doctors, and about 24,500 general practitioners do so. They may at the same time have private fee-paying patients. Family doctors are paid for their Health Service work in accordance with a scheme of remuneration which includes *inter alia* a basic practice allowance, capitation fees, reimbursement of certain practice expenses and payments for "out of hours" work.

Everyone aged 16 or over can choose his doctor (parents or guardians choose for children under 16) and the doctor is also free to accept a person or not as he chooses. A person may change his doctor if he wishes, either at once if he has changed his address or obtained permission from the doctor on whose list he is, or by informing the Family Practitioner Committee (in which case 14 days must elapse before the other doctor can accept him). When people are away from home they can still use the Family Doctor Service if they ask to be treated as "temporary residents", and in an emergency, if a person's own doctor is not available, any doctor in the service will give treatment and advice.

Patients are treated either in the Doctor's surgery or, when necessary, at home. Doctors may prescribe for their patients all drugs and medicines which are medically necessary for their treatment and also a certain number of surgical appliances (the more elaborate being provided through the hospitals).

Dental Service

Dentists, like doctors, may take part in the Service and may also have private patients. About 13,000 of the dentists available for general practice in England provide National Health Service general dental services. They are responsible to the Family Practitioner Committees in whose areas they provide services.

Patients are free to go to any dentist taking part in the Service and willing to accept them, and cannot register with any particular dentist. Dentists receive payment for items of treatment for individual patients, instead of the capitation fee received by doctors. There is no need for the patient to obtain a recommendation before seeking dental treatment. All treatment and dentures considered by the dentist to be necessary for dental fitness are available under the NHS. But for certain more expensive items such as metal dentures, bridges and gold fillings, it is necessary for the dentist to obtain the prior approval of the Dental Estimates Board.

A dentist may, with the approval of the Dental Estimates Board, charge his patients a prescribed sum for such types of treatment as crowns, inlays or metal dentures where these are not clinically necessary, if the patient wishes to have them. Where a denture supplied under the Service has to be replaced because of loss or damage the whole or part of the cost may be charged to the patient if he has been careless. From April 1, 1971, the system of charges was changed so that patients became liable for a proportion of the cost of treatment, including the supply of dentures, if required, up to a maximum charge of £10 for one course of treatment, unless they were exempt from charges or entitled to remission on income grounds. A revised system of charges was introduced on January 1, 1976, so that the patient paid the full cost of each item of treatment (excluding dentures) up to a maximum charge of £3·50 for one course of treatment. The most recent revision of charges was introduced on April 1, 1984. They are as follows:—

1. The patient pays the full cost of each item of treatment (except dentures, bridges, crowns, inlays, pinlays and gold fillings) up to a maximum charge of £14·50 for one course of treatment.

2. For a denture or a bridge—

	Synthetic resin	Metal or Porcelain
(a) 1, 2 or 3 teeth	£24	£47
(b) 4–8 teeth	£26	£49
(c) More than 8 teeth	£28	£51
Maximum for more than one denture (or bridge)	£44	£92

3. For crowns, inlays, pinlays and gold fillings—
   (a) per tooth restored — £30 or £59 depending on the percentage of gold used (these charges include any other restorations in the same tooth, apart from root fillings)
   (b) maximum if more than one tooth restored £110

No charge is made for clinical examination of a patient's mouth, arrest of bleeding, repairs to dentures, the cost of travelling if the dentist has to visit the patient at home or re-opening of the surgery in an emergency. Expectant mothers or women who have had a child during the preceding twelve months,

children under 16, or up to 19, but still in full-time attendance at school, do not pay charges. Young people over 16, not in full-time education, pay for dentures. Full remission of charges is automatically available to people in receipt of supplementary benefit or F.I.S., and those entitled to free prescriptions and milk and vitamins on income grounds. Full or partial remission may also be available to those with incomes somewhat above supplementary benefits if they claim.

Pharmaceutical Service

Patients may obtain medicines, appliances and oral contraceptives prescribed under the NHS from any pharmacy whose owner has entered into arrangements with the Family Practitioner Committee to provide this service. Almost all pharmacy owners have done so and display notices that they dispense under the NHS: the number of these pharmacies in England and Wales at the end of 1981 was about 9,500. There are also some appliance suppliers who only provide special appliances. In country areas where access to a pharmacy may be difficult patients may be able to obtain medicines etc. from their doctor.

Except for contraceptives (for which there is no charge), a charge of £1·60 is payable for each item supplied unless the patient is exempt and the declaration on the back of the prescription form is completed. Exemptions cover children under 16, men aged 65 and over and women aged 60 and over, pregnant women and mothers who have had a baby within the last 12 months, people suffering from certain medical conditions, people who receive F.I.S. or supplementary benefit, people on low income and war pensioners (for their accepted disablements). In addition prepayment certificates may be purchased by those patients not entitled to exemption who require frequent prescriptions. Further information about the exemption and prepayment arrangements is given in leaflet P.11.

General Ophthalmic Services

General Ophthalmic Services, which are administered by Family Practitioner Committees, form part of the ophthalmic services available under the National Health Service and provide for the testing of sight and supply of glasses to meet more normal needs only. Diagnosis and specialist treatment of eye conditions is available through the Hospital Eye Service as well as the provision of glasses of a special type. Testing of sight may be carried out by any ophthalmic medical practitioner or ophthalmic optician, and glasses supplied by any ophthalmic optician or dispensing optician taking part in the Services.

Sight testing is free. The charges for lenses are £4·25 to £9·45 for each single-vision lens, £10·15 to £16·50 for each bifocal lens, plus, where required, £1·50 to £3·25 each lens for prisms, £2·40 or £4·80 for each tinted lens, subject to a maximum of £16·50 for each lens.

The cost of the frame must also be paid; NHS frames cost from £2·05 to £13·05. Children up to the age of 16 or young people under 19 in full-time education may be supplied free of charge with standard lenses in children's standard frames. Additionally, school-children aged 10 years or over and young people under 19 in full-time education may be supplied with standard lenses without charge if any other type of NHS frame is used. The charge for the frame must then be paid. People on a low income may receive help with the cost of NHS glasses, and this is automatic for those who receive supplementary benefit, F.I.S., free milk or vitamins, or free prescriptions because of low income.

Primary Health Care Services

Primary health care services include the general medical, dental, ophthalmic and pharmaceutical services, health centres and clinics, family planning outside the hospital service and preventive activities in the community including vaccination, immunisation and fluoridation. The district nursing and health visiting services, much ante- and post-natal care; and chiropody are also an integral part of the primary health care service.

Community Child Health Services

Pre-school services, usually at child health clinics, provide regular surveillance of children's physical, mental and emotional health and development, and advice to parents on their children's health and welfare. The School Health Service provides for the medical and dental examination of school-children, and advises the local education authority, the school, the parents and the pupil of any health factors which may require special consideration during the pupil's school life.

Hospitals and Other Services

The Secretary of State for Social Services has a duty to provide, to such extent as he/she considers necessary to meet all reasonable requirements, hospital and other accommodation; medical, dental, nursing and ambulance services; other facilities for the care of expectant and nursing mothers and young children, facilities for the prevention of illness, and the care and after-care of persons suffering from illness and such other services as are required for the diagnosis and treatment of illness. Rehabilitation services (occupational therapy, physiotherapy and speech therapy) may also be provided for those who need it and surgical and medical appliances are supplied in appropriate cases.

Specialists and consultants who take part in the Service can engage in private practice, including the treatment of their private patients in NHS hospitals.

In a number of hospitals accommodation is available for the treatment of private in-patients who undertake to pay full hospital maintenance costs and (usually) separate medical fees to a specialist as well. The amount of the medical fees is a matter for agreement between doctor and patient.

Hospital charges for private resident patients are determined annually, on a national basis for classes of hospitals, by the Secretary of State in accordance with the National Health Service Act 1977. These charges are revised annually from April 1 each year to reflect the average cost, which it is estimated will be incurred during the current financial year in the treatment of in-patients in each class of hospital. They also include a contribution towards capital costs.

For in-patients paying specialists' fees separately, the hospital daily charges from April 1, 1984, for accommodation and services in each class of hospital are as follows:

Class A. Long stay hospitals
Single Room	*Other Accommodation*
£57·00	£52·00

Class B. Psychiatric hospitals
Single Room	*Other Accommodation*
£45·00	£41·00

Class C1. Mainly acute and other hospitals in non-teaching districts
Single Room	*Other Accommodation*
£96·00	£87·00

Class C2. Acute and other hospitals in non-teaching districts
Single Room	*Other Accommodation*
£110·00	£100·00

Class D. London teaching hospitals
Single Room	*Other Accommodation*
£140·00	£127·00

Class E. Provincial teaching hospitals
Single Room	*Other Accommodation*
£115·00	£105·00

Class F. London Postgraduate teaching hospitals managed by Boards of Governors and Special Health Authorities
Single Room	*Other Accommodation*
£167·00	£152·00

Class G. Hospitals managed by Hammersmith Special Health Authority
Single Room	*Other Accommodation*
£192·00	£175·00

For those patients who have not made separate arrangements with a specialist for private treatment the charges range from £54 in a long stay hospital to £186 in certain London Postgraduate teaching hospitals.

The following daily charges apply to services provided for overseas visitors who are in-patients.

	Single Room £	*Other Accommodation* £
Class A (Long-Stay Hospitals)	59·00	54·00
Class B (Psychiatric Hospitals)	47·00	43·00
Class C1 (Mainly acute and other hospitals in non-teaching districts)	100·00	91·00
Class C2 (Acute and other hospitals in non-teaching districts)	114·00	104·00
Class D (Hospitals in London teaching districts (other than hospitals in *Classes A* and *B*))	148·00	135·00
Class E (Hospitals in provincial teaching districts (other than hospitals in *Classes A* and *B*))	122·00	111·00
Class F (London Postgraduate Teaching Hospitals managed by Boards of Governors or Special Health Authorities except the hospitals managed by Hammersmith Special Health Authority)	177·00	161·00
Class G (Hospitals managed by Hammersmith Special Health Authority)	203·00	186·00

Certain hospitals have accommodation in single rooms or small wards which, if not required for patients who need privacy for medical reasons, may be made available to patients who desire it as an amenity. Amenity bed charges are at present £10 per day in single rooms and £5 per day in small wards. In such cases the patients are treated in every other respect as National Health patients.

There is no charge for drugs supplied to National Health hospital in-patients but out-patients pay £1 per item unless they are exempt.

With certain exceptions, hospital out-patients have to pay fixed charges for dentures, glasses and certain appliances. The charge for glasses will be related to the type of lens prescribed; and for dentures will be up to a maximum charge of £60·00.

Local Authority Personal Social Services

Local authorities are responsible for the organization, management and administration of the personal social services and each authority has a Director of Social Services and a Social Services Committee responsible for the social services functions placed upon them by the Local Authority Social Services Act 1970.

NATIONAL INSURANCE AND RELATED CASH BENEFITS

The State insurance and assistance schemes in force from July 5, 1948, comprised schemes of national insurance and industrial injuries insurance, national assistance and non-contributory old age pensions, and family allowances. The Ministry of Social Security Act, 1966, introduced a scheme of non-contributory benefits, termed supplementary allowances and pensions, in place of national assistance and non-contributory old age pensions, and provided for the establishment of a new Ministry of Social Security (now the Department of Health and Social Security), with overall responsibility for the existing insurance schemes and family allowances scheme and the new scheme of supplementary benefits, in place of the Ministry of Pensions and National Insurance and the National Assistance Board, which were abolished.

The Conservative Government's Social Security Act, 1973, which was intended to be brought into force in April, 1975, provided for the replacement of the National Insurance scheme by a basic scheme of social security, offering a range of benefits, including flat-rate basic pensions, similar to those under the existing legislation; a separate reserve pension scheme providing, in addition to the basic pension, earnings-related pensions for those employees not in recognized pensionable employment; and the assimilation of the Industrial Injuries scheme to the basic scheme. It also laid down minimum conditions for recognition of occupational pension schemes so as to exempt the employers and employees concerned from liability to contribute to the reserve pension scheme.

The new Labour Government decided that the basic pension scheme provisions of the 1973 Act should come into force on April 6, 1975, as planned, but it decided not to bring into effect the provisions of that Act relating to the reserve pension scheme or the recognition tests for occupational pension schemes seeking exemption from the reserve pension scheme (except the provisions relating to the preservation of benefits under occupational schemes). Effect was given to the Government's decisions by an order made in June 1974 under the 1973 Act, and by the Social Security (Amendment) Act, 1974, passed in December, 1974.

Three measures—the Social Security Act, 1975 (now the principal Act); the Social Security (Consequential Provisions) Act, 1975; and the Industrial Injuries and Diseases (Old Cases) Act, 1975—were enacted on March 20, 1975, for the purpose of consolidating the law relating to social security in Great Britain, and corresponding measures were passed for Northern Ireland.

The Labour Government published in September, 1974, in a White Paper, "Better Pensions fully protected against inflation", its proposals for a new State pensions scheme. The Social Security Pensions Act, 1975, based upon these proposals came into force on April 6, 1978. Retirement, widows' and invalidity pensions under the new scheme started in April, 1979 (see p. 1213).

The Pensioners' Payments and Social Security Act, 1979, provided for a £10 bonus for pensioners in 1979 and also for the payment of bonuses in succeeding years at levels then to be determined.

SOCIAL SECURITY SCHEME, 1975

From April 6, 1975, the National Insurance scheme 1948–1975 was replaced by a new scheme of social security benefits and contributions, which now operates under the Social Security Acts, 1975 to 1980, and orders and regulations made thereunder. Like the former scheme, the new scheme is financed on a pay-as-you-go basis mainly by contributions but in part out of Exchequer funds (rates of benefit and of contributions being reviewed normally annually in accordance with statutory criteria), but the new scheme contributions, to a greater extent than national insurance contributions, are earnings-related. The graduated pension scheme 1961–1975 has been wound up (existing rights being preserved); otherwise the new scheme provides a pattern of pension and other benefits similar to that of the old scheme, but supplemented from April, 1979, by additional pensions related to employees' earnings provided for by the Social Security Pensions Act, 1975, as amended (see p. 1213). The Industrial Injuries scheme continues with only minor changes, but steps have been taken to assimilate the industrial injuries legislation to the general scheme: thus the separate industrial injuries contribution and the Treasury supplement thereto under the Industrial Injuries Acts have been abolished, and the Industrial Injuries Fund has been merged with the National Insurance Fund.

CONTRIBUTIONS AND
CONTRIBUTION CONDITIONS

The funds required for paying benefits payable under the Social Security Acts out of the National Insurance Fund and not out of other public money; for the making of payments towards the cost of the National Health Service and into the Redundancy and Maternity Pay Funds; and for paying benefit under the Industrial Injuries and Diseases (Old Cases) Act, 1975, are provided by means of contributions payable by earners, employers and others (such as non-employed persons paying voluntary contributions), together with the Treasury supplement.

Contributions are of four classes:

Class 1, earnings-related:
  (a) primary Class 1 contributions from employed earners; and
  (b) secondary Class 1 contributions from employers and other persons paying earnings;

Class 2, flat-rate, payable weekly by self-employed earners;

Class 3, flat-rate, payable by earners and others voluntarily with a view to providing entitlement to benefit, or making up entitlement; and

Class 4, payable by self-employed persons in respect of the profits or gains of a trade, profession or vocation, or in respect of equivalent earnings.

Particulars of the contribution rates and earnings limits for contribution liability for the tax year which started on April 6, 1984, are given on pp. 1216–1217.

Regulations state the cases in which earners may be excepted from liability to pay contributions, and the conditions upon which contributions are credited to persons who are excepted.

The Secretary of State for Social Services is empowered by the Social Security Acts to alter certain rates of contributions by order approved by both Houses of Parliament, and is required by the same enactments to make annual reviews of the general level of earnings in order to determine whether such an order should be made. The Government Actuary has pointed out that with a system of mainly earnings-related contributions the income of the National Insurance Fund will rise automatically with increases in the general level of earnings and will broadly be sufficient to meet the cost of corresponding increases in the level of benefits, provided the earnings limits for contribution liability and the flat-rate (Classes 2 and 3) contributions are adjusted regularly. Following the decision in the summer of 1979 to make further increases in benefits in November, 1979, provision was made by orders and regulations in December, 1979, for new rates of contribution and earnings limits for the various classes of contributors to apply from the beginning of the tax year (*see* pp. 1203–4).

From April 6, 1982, the yearly Treasury supplement to the National Insurance Fund is equal to 13 per cent of all contributions (ignoring the contribution reductions in respect of the contracted-out) after deducting the National Health Service allocation and the allocation to the Redundancy, etc., Funds (*see* p. 1213).

BENEFITS

The benefits payable under the Social Security Acts are as follows:

(1) Contributory Benefits:
    Unemployment benefit.
    Sickness benefit.
    Invalidity pension and allowance.
    Maternity allowance.
    Widow's benefit, comprising widow's allowance, widowed mother's allowance and widow's pension.
    Child's special allowance.
    Retirement pensions of the following categories:
      Category A.
      Category B.
    Death grant.

(2) Non-contributory Benefits:

    Maternity grant (see p. 1211).
    Guardian's allowance (*see* p. 1215–16).
    Attendance allowance (*see* p. 1215).
    Non-contributory invalidity pension (*see* p. 1215).
    Mobility Allowance (*see* p. 1215).
    Invalid care allowance (*see* p. 1215).
    Retirement pensions of the following categories.
      Category C (*see* p. 1215).
      Category D (*see* p. 1215).

(3) Benefits for Industrial Injuries and Diseases.

Cash benefits provided under other enactments (supplementary benefits, child benefit, and family income supplement) are dealt with on pp. 1213–1215. Leaflets relating to the various benefits are obtainable from local Social Security offices.

The Social Security Acts empower the Secretary of State to increase certain rates of benefit by order approved by both Houses of Parliament, and require him to increase certain rates by such an order if an annual review shows that they have not retained their value in relation to the general level of prices obtaining in Great Britain.

An order providing for increases in benefit rates took effect from November 12, 1979. Further increases in benefits were authorized by Social Security Benefits Uprating Orders, 1980, 1981, 1982, 1983 and 1984. The new rates from the last mentioned order apply from November 26, 1984.

Entitlement to the contributory benefits provided by the Social Security Acts (except invalidity benefit) depends on contribution conditions being satisfied either by the claimant or by some other person (depending on the kind of benefit). The class or classes of contribution which for this purpose are relevant to each benefit are as follows:

Short-term benefits

Unemployment benefit	Class 1
Sickness benefit	Class 1 or 2
Maternity allowance	Class 1 or 2
Widow's allowance	Class 1, 2 or 3

Other benefits

Widowed mother's allowance	
Widow's pension	
Child's special allowance	
Category A retirement pension	Class 1, 2 or 3
Category B retirement pension	
Death grant	

With the change from a system of flat-rate national insurance and industrial injuries contributions and graduated pension contributions to a system of wholly earnings-related contributions for employed earners the contribution conditions for entitlement to benefit could no longer be based on the number of weekly contributions paid in a contribution year or throughout a working life. The Social Security Act, 1975, introduced a new system of contribution conditions related to yearly levels of earnings on which contributions have been paid. The contribution conditions for different benefits are set out in sections 13 to 33 of and Schedule 3 to the Act, and in summary form in leaflets on the benefits available at local Social Security offices. There are two contribution conditions for most of the benefits. The first condition must be satisfied to qualify for benefit at all; the second condition generally determines whether benefit is paid at the standard rate or at a reduced rate. Under the arrangements made for the transition from the old scheme to the new one, provision was made for such matters as treating old-style flat-rate contributions as new-style earnings-related contributions and vice versa, and the use of modified contribution tests for short-term benefits for an initial period following the start of the new scheme.

DETERMINATION OF CLAIMS AND QUESTIONS

The Health and Social Services and Social Security Adjudications Act 1983 introduced a unified system of adjudication for all claims for benefit under the Social Security Acts.

With a few exceptions, claims and questions relating to benefits are decided by statutory authorities who operate independently of D.H.S.S. These consist, in the first instance, of adjudication officers appointed by the Secretary of State. A claimant who is dissatisfied with an adjudication officer's decision on his claim has the right of appeal to a social security appeal tribunal. Appeal tribunals consist of a chairman nominated by the President of Social Security Appeal Tribunals and appointed by the Lord Chancellor, and two members who represent employed earners and employers, and who have knowledge or experience of conditions in the area. There is a further right of appeal to the Social Security Commissioner against the tribunal's decision. In certain cases appeal is only possible with leave. In the case of supplementary benefit and family incomes supplement, this right of appeal to the Commissioner must be on a point of law.

Provision is also made for the determination of certain questions by the Secretary of State for Social Services. 'Disablement questions' are decided by medical boards or an adjudicating medical practitioner or medical appeal tribunal or, on appeal with leave and on a point of law, by the Commissioner.

A leaflet explaining how to appeal is available from D.H.S.S. offices.

The rates of benefit stated below are, unless otherwise indicated, the standard rates having effect from dates in the week beginning November 26, 1984.

Unemployment Benefit

The standard weekly rates of flat-rate benefit payable to primary Class 1 contributors are as follows:

	£
Man or woman..........................	28·45
Increase of benefit for wife or other adult dependant where payable	17·55

(Increase of benefit for children ended November 26, 1984.)

Duration of Benefit.—Benefit is payable in a period of interruption of employment for up to 312 days (a year, excluding Sundays). Spells of unemployment and sickness not separated by more than 8 weeks (13 weeks prior to September 14, 1980) count as one period of interruption of employment.

Requalification for Benefit.—A person who has exhausted benefit requalifies when he has again worked as an employed earner for at least 16 hours a week for 13 weeks. These weeks need not be consecutive nor fall within the same year.

Disqualifications.—There are disqualifications for receiving benefit, *e.g.* for a period not exceeding six weeks if a person has lost his employment through his misconduct, or has voluntarily left his employment without just cause, or has, without good cause, refused an offer of suitable employment or training.

Sickness Benefit

Standard Rates of flat-rate Benefit payable to primary Class 1 and to Class 2 contributors while incapable of work through illness or disablement are as follows:—man or woman £27·25; increase of benefit for wife or other adult dependant where payable £16·80.

Duration of Benefit.—Sickness benefit is payable for up to 28 weeks of sickness in a period of interruption of employment and is then replaced by invalidity benefit (*see* below).

Disqualifications.—Regulations provide for disqualifying a person for receiving sickness or invalidity benefit for a period not exceeding six weeks if he has become incapable of work through his own misconduct or if he fails without good cause to attend for or submit himself to prescribed medical or other examination or treatment, or observe prescribed rules of behaviour.

Under the provisions of the Social Security and Housing Benefits Act 1982, from April 1983 the first 8 weeks of sick pay in any tax year will be paid by employers. Employers will be compensated for these payments through deductions in their National Insurance contributions. For employees who earn above the lower earnings limit for National Insurance contributions, this Statutory Sick Pay will replace Sickness Benefit, although Sickness Benefit will still be available to those not entitled to statutory sick pay.

Invalidity Benefit

Normally, after 28 weeks of sickness, sickness benefit is replaced by an *invalidity pension* of £34·25 (increased by £20·55 for a wife or other adult dependant). In addition an *invalidity allowance* is payable if incapacity for work begins more than five years before pension age. The allowance varies in amount from £2·40 to £7·50 a week, according to the age on falling sick, and if still in payment at pension age will continue as a higher rate as an addition to retirement pension. The increases of benefit for children of an invalidity pensioner are £7·65 for each child, in addition to child benefit. Since April, 1979, employees' invalidity pensions have been earnings-related under the new State pension scheme (*see* p. 1213). As to the age addition if the pensioner or

dependant is 80 or over, and non-contributory invalidity pensions, *see* p. 1215.

Maternity Benefits

Maternity Grant.—A cash grant of £25 for each confinement. Extra grants are payable, in certain circumstances, if more than one child is born. There are no contribution conditions for the grant which is payable to all mothers who can satisfy a simple "presence in Great Britain" test.

Maternity Allowance.—A woman who has been employed or self-employed and paying contributions at the full rate receives in addition a maternity allowance of £25·95 a week normally for 18 weeks beginning eleven weeks before the expected week of confinement, provided that she has no paid work during that period. The rate of allowance is increased where the woman has an adult dependent.

Widow's Benefits

Only the late husband's contributions of any class count for widow's benefit in any of its three forms.

Widow's Allowance.—A woman who at her husband's death is under 60 (or over 60, if he had not retired), receives (during the first 26 weeks of widowhood) a cash allowance usually of £50·10 a week with increases of £7·65 for each child, in addition to child benefit.

Widowed Mother's Allowance.—When the 26 weeks of widow's allowance have elapsed, a widow who is left with one or more dependent children receives a cash allowance usually of £35·80 a week with increases of £7·65 for each child, in addition to child benefit. A widowed mother's personal allowance, usually of £35·80 a week, is payable to widows who, when their widow's or widowed mother's allowance ends, have living with them a son or daughter under 19, who has left school.

Widow's Pension.—A widow receives this pension usually of £35·80 a week when widow's allowance ends, if she was over 50 at the time of her husband's death; or when her widowed mother's allowance or widowed mother's personal allowance ends, if she is then over 50 (40 if widowed before February 4, 1957).

Flat-rate widow's pensions on a graduated scale were introduced in April 1971 for women who are widowed between the ages of 40 and 50, or who cease to be entitled to a widowed mother's allowance between those ages.

Widow's benefit of any form ceases upon re-marriage.

Since April, 1979, widow's pension and widowed mother's allowance have been related to employees' earnings under the new State pension scheme (*see* p. 1213).

Child's Special Allowance

A woman whose marriage has been dissolved or annulled and who has not re-married and is not living with a man as his wife is paid a special allowance on the ex-husband's death based on his contribution record. The normal condition is that she has a child living with her to whose maintenance he was contributing, or had been liable to contribute, at least 25p a week in cash or its equivalent. The allowance is £7·65 a week for each child, in addition to child benefit.

Retirement Pension
(Categories A and B)

A *Category A pension* is payable for life to men or women on their own contributions if (a) they are over pension age (65 for a man and 60 for a woman), and (b) they have retired from regular employment. Men aged 70 or over and women aged 65 or over are not required to satisfy condition (b).

The standard flat-rate pension, when the contribution conditions are fully satisfied, is £35·80, *plus* £21·50 for a wife or other adult dependent who is not qualified for a pension, *plus* £7·65 for each child, in addition to child benefit. (As to the age addition payable at 80, *see* p. 1215.)

Where a person does not retire at 65 (60 for a woman) or later cancels retirement, and does not draw a Category A pension, the weekly rate of pension is increased, when he or she finally retires or reaches the age of 70 (65 for a woman), in respect of weeks when pension is foregone during the five years after reaching minimum pension age. For periods of deferred retirement after April 5, 1975, the rate of pension (without any increases except invalidity allowance), when it is finally awarded, will normally be increased by one-eighth of one per cent (from April 5, 1979, one-seventh of one per cent) for each week of deferment except those weeks in which other benefits (such as sickness or unemployment benefit) were drawn. A married man can also earn extra pension for his wife.

A *Category B pension* is normally payable for life to a woman on her husband's contributions when he has retired, or is over 70, and has qualified for his own Category A pension, and she has reached 60 and retired from regular work or has reached 65. It is also payable on widowhood after 60 whether or not the late husband had retired and qualified for his own pension. The weekly pension is payable at the lower rate of £21·50 while the husband is alive, and at the higher rate of £35·80 on widowhood after 60. Where a woman is widowed before she reaches 60, a Category B pension is paid to her on reaching 60 at the same weekly rate as her widow's pension if she retires. If a woman qualifies for a pension of each category she receives whichever pension is the larger. For periods of deferred retirement after April 5, 1975, a Category B pension will normally be increased by one-sixteenth of one per cent (from April 5, 1979, one-seventh of one per cent) of the husband's pension rate (apart from any increase other than invalidity allowance) for each week while both husband and wife defer retirement. If the husband dies after April 5, 1975, the extra pension which he earned for his wife up to April 6, 1979, by not drawing his pension after she reached 60 will be not be doubled. She will also receive half of any extra pension he earned for any period before she reached 60. (As to the age addition payable at 80, *see* p. 1214.)

Since April, 1979, retirement pension has been related to employees' earnings under the new State pension scheme (*see* p. 1213).

A man aged 65 to 70, or a woman aged 60 to 65, who has qualified for pension will have it reduced if he or she earns more than a certain amount. From the week beginning November 26 1984, the weekly earnings limit for retirement pensioners was increased by £5 to £70. A man's pension is not affected by his wife's earnings unless he is drawing an increase of his pension for her. If she is living with him, her earnings will affect the increase if they exceed £45·09 a week. Otherwise, no increase is payable if they exceed £21·50 a week.

Unemployment, sickness or invalidity benefit is payable to men between 65 and 70 and women between 60 and 65 who have not retired from regular work and who would have been entitled to a retirement pension if they had retired at pension age. This applies in the case of sickness and invalidity benefit if incapacity for work is the result of an industrial accident or prescribed disease. These rates of benefit for people over pension age are shown in leaflet N.I.

196. A retirement pension will be increased by the amount of any invalidity allowance the pensioner was getting within the period of 8 weeks and one day before reaching minimum pension age. As to attendance allowance and invalid care allowance, *see* p. 1215. Persons who do not qualify for a Category A or B pension may qualify for a Category C or D pension (*see* p. 1215), or for a supplementary pension (*see* p. 1215).

Graduated Pension

The graduated pension scheme under which national insurance contributions and retirement pensions were graduated within specified limits, according to earnings, was discontinued in April, 1975, under the Social Security Act, 1975. Any graduated pension which an employed person over 18 and under 70 (65 for a woman) had earned by paying graduated contributions between April 6, 1961, when the scheme started and April 5, 1975, will be paid when the contributor retires, or at 70 (65 for a woman), in addition to any retirement pension for which he or she qualifies.

Graduated pension is at the rate of 4·67p a week for each "unit" of graduated contributions paid by the employee (half a unit or more counts as a whole unit). A unit of contributions is £7·50 for men, and £9·00 for women, of graduated contributions paid.

A wife can get a graduated pension in return for her own graduated contributions, but not for her husband's. A widow gets a graduated addition to her retirement pension equal to half of any graduated additions earned by her late husband, plus any additions earned by her own graduated contributions. If a person defers retirement beyond 65 (60 for a woman), half the graduated pension he or she has forgone by deferring retirement for any period before April 6, 1979, will be treated as extra graduated contributions paid, and will count towards further graduated pension on retirement or at 70 (65 for a woman). From April 6, 1979, graduated pension will normally be increased by one-seventh of one per cent for each week of deferred retirement.

Death Grant

A death grant is payable on the death of a qualifying contributor or of his wife, child or widow or, if the contributor is a woman, of her husband, child or widower, and also in respect of the deaths of certain handicapped persons on the insurance of close relatives. The normal grant is for an adult £30, a child aged 6–17 £22·50, a child aged 3–5 £15, a child under 3 £9. For the deaths of people who on July 5, 1948, were between 55 and 65 (men) or between 50 and 60 (women) the grant is £15. No grant is payable for deaths of persons already over pension age on July 5, 1948.

The grant is paid to the deceased person's executors or administrators, if any; otherwise it is paid to the person who meets the funeral expenses or to the next of kin.

The Death Grant is under review at present. The Government issued a Consultative Document in March 1982 setting out a number of alternative proposals.

INDUSTRIAL INJURIES BENEFITS

The National Insurance (Industrial Injuries) Act, 1946, substituted for the Workmen's Compensation Acts, 1925 to 1945, a system of insurance against personal injury caused by accident arising out of and in the course of a person's employment and against prescribed diseases and injuries due to the nature of a person's employment. The scheme, which insures against personal injuries caused and prescribed diseases and injuries developed on or after July 5, 1948, now operates under the Social Security Acts, 1975 to 1980, and regulations and orders made under the Acts. The Social Security Benefits Uprating Order, 1984, provides for increases in the rates of benefit with effect from dates in the week beginning November 26, 1984. Rates of benefit are now reviewed annually.

Supplementary allowances payable in certain circumstances in cases arising before the Industrial Injuries scheme started are governed by the Industrial Injuries and Diseases (Old Cases) Act, 1975, as amended and regulations made under the Act. Statutory schemes have also been made providing for the payment of allowances supplementing workmen's compensation in certain circumstances, and for the payment of benefits in certain cases where neither workmen's compensation nor Industrial Injuries benefits are payable.

The scope of "employed earners" and their employments to which the industrial injuries scheme applies is defined in the Social Security Act, 1975, as amended and regulations made under the Act.

Separate industrial injuries contributions were discontinued in April, 1975. The Industrial Injuries Fund was at the same time merged in the National Insurance Fund, and the separate Treasury Supplement to the Industrial Injuries Fund came to an end.

BENEFITS

Disablement Benefit is normally payable 15 weeks (90 days) after the date of accident or onset of disease if the employed earner suffers from loss of physical or mental faculty such that the resulting disablement is assessed at not less than one per cent. (In cases of pneumoconiosis and byssinosis disablement benefit is paid from the start.) The amount of disablement benefit varies according to the degree of disablement (in the form of a percentage) assessed by a medical board or medical appeal tribunal. In cases of disablement of less than 20 per cent, except in pneumoconiosis or byssinosis cases, benefit normally takes the form of a *gratuity* paid according to a prescribed scale, but not exceeding £3,880. Where the degree of disablement is 20 per cent or more, or if it is due to pneumoconiosis or byssinosis, the benefit is a weekly *pension* payable either for a limited period or for life, according to the following scale:

Degree of disablement	Weekly rate £
100 per cent	58·40
90 ,, ,,	52·56
80 ,, ,,	46·72
70 ,, ,,	40·88
60 ,, ,,	35·04
50 ,, ,,	29·20
40 ,, ,,	23·36
30 ,, ,,	17·52
20 ,, ,,	11·68

These are basic rates applicable to adults and to juveniles entitled to an increase for a child or adult dependant; other juveniles receive lower rates.

Basic rates of pension are not related to the pensioner's loss of earning power, and are payable whether he is in work or not. Upon prescribed conditions, however, pension is supplemented for unemployability and in cases of special hardship. There is provision also for increases of pension during approved hospital treatment or if the pensioner requires constant attendance or if his disablement is exceptionally severe. If the beneficiary is entitled to an unemployability supplement there are increases of £7·65 for each child in addition to child benefit, and, subject to the earnings rule, £20·55 for an adult dependant. Subject to certain exceptions, a pensioner who is not in receipt of unemployability supplement can draw sickness or invalidity benefit as appropriate, in addition to disablement pension, during spells of incapacity for work.

Death Benefit, in the form of a pension, a gratuity or a weekly allowance for a limited period, available for widows and other dependants in fatal cases, depends in amount upon their relationship to the deceased and their circumstances at the time of death and not upon the deceased's earnings. A widow who was living with her husband at the time of his death receives a pension of £50·10 a week for the first 26 weeks, and thereafter a pension of £36·35 or less a week according to circumstances, *plus* £7·65 for each child, in addition to child benefit.

Regulations impose certain obligations on claimants and beneficiaries and on employers, including, in the case of claimants for injury or disablement benefit, that of submitting to medical examination and treatment.

Industrial Diseases, etc.—The scheme extends insurance to prescribed industrial diseases and prescribed personal injuries not caused by accident, which are due to the nature of an employed earner's employment and developed on or after July 5, 1948.

Determination of Questions and Claims.—Provision is made for the determination of certain questions by the Secretary of State for Social Services, and of "disablement questions" by a medical board (or a single doctor) or medical appeal tribunal or, on appeal on a point of law, by the Commissioners, subject to leave. Claims for benefit and certain questions arising in connection with a claim for or award of benefit (*e.g.* whether the accident arose out of and in the course of the employment) are determined by an adjudication officer appointed by the Secretary of State, or a Social Security Appeal Tribunal consisting of a chairman appointed by the Lord Chancellor (in Scotland, the Lord Advocate) and equal numbers of members representing employers and employed earners, or, on appeal, by the Commissioners.

FINANCE

On April 1, 1975, the National Insurance (Reserve) Fund and the Industrial Injuries Fund were wound up and their liabilities and assets transferred to the National Insurance Fund. The National Insurance Fund receives all social security contributions (less only the National Health Service and Redundancy Fund and Maternity Pay Fund allocations and the National Insurance Surcharge for taxation purposes) together with the Consolidated Fund supplement; and it bears the cost of all contributory benefits provided by the Social Security Acts and the cost of administration.

Approximate receipts and payments of the National Insurance Fund for the year ended March 31, 1983, were as follows:

Receipts	£'000
Balance, April 1, 1982	4,046,465
Contributions under the Social Security Acts	16,302,652
Consolidated Fund Supplement	2,591,000
Income from Investments	496,268
Other receipts	3,089
	23,439,474

Payments	£'000	£'000
Benefit:—		
Unemployment benefit.	1,499,648	
Sickness benefit	494,456	
Invalidity benefit	1,593,181	
Maternity benefit	153,000	
Widow's benefit	725,000	
Guardian's allowance and child's special allowance	2,100	
Retirement pension	13,548,856	
Death grant	16,935	
Industrial injuries benefits	46,469	
Disablement benefits. . . .	343,535	
Death benefit	51,000	
Other benefits	5,400	
Pensioners lump sum payments	102,000	
Payments in lieu of benefit forgone	29,189	
		18,610,769
Transfers to Northern Ireland		84,770
Administration		720,187
Other payments		287
Balance, March 31, 1983		4,023,461
		23,439,474

THE NEW STATE PENSION SCHEME

The Social Security Pensions Act, 1975, which came into force in April, 1978, embodied proposals for the future coordinated development of State and occupational pensions. Since April 6, 1979, flat-rate retirement and other State pensions have been augmented for employed earners by additional pensions related to earnings, but it will be twenty years before these additional pensions become payable at the full rate.

The aims of the Act will be, by providing better pensions, to reduce reliance upon means-tested supplementary benefit in old age, in widowhood and in chronic ill-health; to ensure that occupational pension schemes which are contracted out of part of the State scheme fulfil the conditions of a good scheme; that pensions are adequately protected against inflation; and that in both the State and occupational schemes men and women are treated equally.

Under the new State scheme retirement, invalidity and widow's pensions for employees are related to the earnings on which national insurance contributions have been paid. The lower earnings limit for Class 1 contribution liability is broadly the current level of the basic component of the personal retirement pension—in April 1984 terms £34·00 a week. Employees with earnings at or above this base level in any week pay contributions on all their earnings up to a limit of about seven times the base level—in April 1984 terms £250 a week. The standard rate of contribution set by the Act and applying for the tax year commencing April 6, 1984 (not including the National Insurance Surcharge which will be abolished on October 1, 1984) is 19·45 per cent (which includes 1·35 per cent for the National Health Service and 0·45 per cent for the Redundancy and Maternity Pay Funds), employees paying 9 per cent and employers 10·45 per cent. The rates and earnings limits are subject to annual review. Employees who are contracted out pay the full rate of contribution on earnings up to the lower limit, but on higher earnings up to the upper limit the rate set by the Act and applying for the tax year commencing April 6, 1984,

is 13·2 per cent (6·85 per cent for employees and 6·35 per cent for employers), the rate to be reviewed at intervals of not more than five years. The Treasury supplement is 13 per cent of all contributions (calculated so as to include those that would have been received if there had been no contracting out) after deducting the allocations to the National Health Service and the Redundancy and Maternity Pay Funds. Self-employed persons pay contributions towards the basic pension. The non-employed and employees with earnings below the lower limit may contribute voluntarily for basic pension. Women who marry for the first time no longer have a right to elect not to pay the full contribution rate. No primary Class 1 contributions or Class 2 or Class 4 contributions are payable by persons who work beyond pension age (65 for men, 60 for women), but the employer's liability for secondary Class 1 contributions continues if earnings are at or above the lower earnings limit. Class 4 contributions are still payable up to the end of the tax year during which pension age is reached.

The new system of State pensions for retirement, widowhood and invalidity provides for employees of either sex with a complete insurance record a category A retirement pension in two parts, a basic and an additional component. The basic pension corresponds to the old personal flat-rate national insurance pension (from November 26, 1984, £35·80), *see* pp. 1211–12. The additional component is 1¼ per cent of average earnings between the lower weekly earnings limit for contribution liability (£34·00 from April, 1984) and the upper earnings limit (£250 from April, 1984) for each year of such earnings under the scheme, and will thus build up to 25 per cent in twenty years. When the number of years exceeds twenty, pensions will be based on contributors' twenty best years of earnings between age 16 and pension age (65 for men, 60 for women). Actual earnings are to be revalued in terms of the earnings level current in the last complete tax year before pension age (or death or incapacity). Both components of pensions in payment will be uprated annually in line with the movement of prices. Graduated retirement pensions in payment and rights to such pensions earned by people who are still working will be brought into the annual review of benefits.

Widows will get the whole or part of additional pensions earned by their husbands with their widowed mother's allowances or widow's pensions; and can add to the retirement pensions earned by their own contributions any additional pensions earned by their husbands up to the maximum payable on one person's contributions. Men whose wives die when they are both over pension age can add together their own and their wives' pension rights in the same way as widows. Among the steps taken to give women equal treatment in benefit provision the State scheme permits years of home responsibilities to count towards satisfying the contribution conditions for retirement pension, widowed mother's allowance and widow's pension, and the "half-test" by which a married woman who married before age 55 could not qualify for a Category A retirement pension unless she had contributed on earnings at the basic level in at least half the years between marriage and pension age has been abolished in certain cases. The range of short-term social security benefits and industrial injury benefits under the Social Security Act, 1975, continues with only minor changes: these include the repeal of the provision which previously imposed a lower rate of sickness and unemployment benefit on married women.

Members of occupational pension schemes which meet the standards laid down by the Pensions Act can be contracted out of a part of the State retirement and widow's benefits. A contracted-out scheme will be required to provide a minimum level of pension calculated on a basis similar to that for the additional component of retirement pension under the State scheme, with a widow's pension at half this rate. The benefits payable from the State scheme will be correspondingly reduced. The State scheme will help in meeting the cost of giving pensions under contracted-out schemes the same protection against inflation as if they had not been contracted out. The Act contains provisions designed to give women the same rights as men to belong to an occupational pension scheme. The Occupational Pension Board, an independent statutory body established under the Social Security Act, 1973, is responsible for deciding whether an occupational scheme should be accepted as a contracted-out scheme, and for ensuring that a contracted-out scheme has adequate financial resources. The Secretary of State for Social Services has made regulations for employers to inform employees and their organisations and to have consultations before deciding whether or not to contract out. Leaflets relating to the new pensions and for the guidance of employers with occupational pension schemes are obtainable from local Social Security offices.

SUPPLEMENTARY BENEFITS

The Ministry of Social Security Act, 1966, introduced a scheme of non-contributory benefits termed supplementary allowances and pensions in place of national assistance and of non-contributory old age pensions. Until November 1980 a Supplementary Benefits Commission within the Department of Health and Social Security was responsible under the Supplementary Benefits Act, 1976, as amended, and Regulations made thereunder by the Secretary of State for Social Services, for operating the scheme.

Changes in the supplementary benefits scheme under the Social Security Act, 1980, which came into effect on November 24, 1980, abolished the Supplementary Benefits Commission and made a new Social Security Advisory Committee responsible for advising the Secretary of State on the supplementary benefits scheme as well as the national insurance, child benefit and family income supplement schemes. With the aim of simplifying the supplementary benefits scheme and reducing its reliance on discretionary payments, the Act enabled the Secretary of State to lay down the detailed rules governing entitlement to supplementary benefit in regulations.

Regulations made in July and August 1980 dealt inter alia with requirements, resources and single payments to meet exceptional need. Leaflets explaining in detail how the new scheme works and the changes it introduced in the calculation of income and capital resources and of each category of requirements (normal requirements, additional requirements and certain housing costs) are available from social security offices. Claimants will be sent a written notice showing how their benefit has been worked out, as is done for family income supplement.

The supplementary pension may be claimed by persons of pension age (65 for men, 60 for women) and the supplementary allowance normally by persons aged 16 or over but under pension age, who are not in full-time work. Benefit can be paid on top of retirement pension or other benefits or of earnings from part-time work. The benefit payable is the amount, assessed under the provisions of the Act and regulations made thereunder, by which the claimant's resources fall short of his requirements. The

ordinary weekly scale rates of supplementary benefit (exclusive of rent) from November 26, 1984, have been as follows:

	£
Married couple	45·55
Single householder	28·05
Other persons:	
Aged 18 or over	22·45
Aged 16–17	17·30
Aged 11–15	14·35
Aged under 11	9·60

The long-term scale rates which apply, with certain exceptions, to all beneficiaries who are aged over 60, and also to younger beneficiaries who are not required to be available for work, after they have been in receipt of supplementary allowance or another qualifying benefit continuously for at least one year, are as follows:

	£
Married couple	57·10
Single householder	35·70
Other persons:	
Aged 18 or over	28·55
Aged under 18	21·90

There is an addition of £1·25 to the standard scale rates for blind people. Claimants and dependants aged 80 or over qualify for an addition of 25p. to long-term rates. As to attendance allowance, *see* below.

OLD PERSONS' PENSIONS

The Social Security Act, 1975, as amended, provides, subject to a residence test, a non-contributory retirement pension of £21·50 a week (£12·85 for a wife or other adult dependant) for persons who were over pensionable age on July 5, 1948, and for women whose husbands are so entitled if they are over pension age and have retired from regular work, with increases for adult and child dependants (Category C pension); and for others when they reach 80 if they are not already getting a retirement pension of any category or if they are getting that pension at less than these rates (Category D pension). An *age addition* of 25p per week is payable if persons entitled to retirement pension or their dependants are aged 80 or over.

ATTENDANCE ALLOWANCE

The Act of 1975 as amended provides for the payment out of Exchequer funds of a tax-free and non-means-tested attendance allowance to the severely disabled, as determined by the Attendance Allowance Board. The full rate of £28·60 a week is paid to those in need of a great deal of attention or supervision both by day and by night. The allowance is paid at the lower rate of £19·10 a week to those whose need for attention or supervision arises either by day or by night. The allowance is treated as an additional requirement under the supplementary benefits scheme.

NON-CONTRIBUTORY INVALIDITY PENSION

The Social Security Act, 1975, provides for a non-contributory invalidity pension for persons of working age who have been continuously incapable of work for a period of at least 28 weeks but who do not qualify for a contributory invalidity pension. Married women qualify if they are also unable to perform normal household duties. The benefit is normally payable at the rate of £21·50 a week, with additions for dependants. The cost is met from the Consolidated Fund.

INVALID CARE ALLOWANCE

The Social Security Act, 1975, also provides for a non-contributory invalid care allowance for persons of working age, other than married women supported by their husbands, who are not gainfully employed because they are regularly and substantially engaged in caring for a severely disabled person who is receiving attendance allowance or Constant Attendance Allowance with either a war or services pension, industrial disablement workman's compensation, or an allowance under the Pneumoconiosis, Byssinasis and Miscellaneous Diseases Benefit Scheme. The benefit is payable at the rate of £21·50 a week, with additions for dependants. The cost is met from the Consolidated Fund.

MOBILITY ALLOWANCE

The Social Security Pensions Act, 1975, as amended, made provision for a new non-contributory cash benefit under the principal Act which, subject to certain conditions, is payable to persons who are suffering from such physical disablement that they are unable to walk or virtually unable to do so, and their handicap is likely to last for at least a year. It can be claimed by persons over the age of 5 and under 65 (for this purpose a claim may be made up to 12 months from that birthday) and may be retained to age 75. The weekly rate of the allowance was initially £5·00, but provision has been made for the rate to be reviewed in each tax year, and in November, 1984, the rate was raised to £20·00. The cost is met from the Consolidated Fund. The allowance is tax free.

GUARDIAN'S ALLOWANCE

Where the parents of a child are dead, the person who has the child in his family receives a guardian's allowance of £7·65 a week, in addition to child benefit. The allowance is a non-contributory benefit under the Social Security Act, 1975, and, in exceptional circumstances, is payable on the death of only one parent.

CHILD BENEFIT

From April 5, 1977, when the permanent provisions of the Child Benefit Act came into operation, family allowances and child interim benefit were replaced by child benefit payable for all children in a family within the age limits, including the first or only child. The rates at the outset were £1·00 for the first or only child (£1·50 in the case of certain one-parent families) and £1·50 for each child after the first. Consequential adjustments were made in dependency benefit for first or only children under the Social Security Act, 1975. The rates were increased in April and November 1978, in April and November 1979, in November 1980, 1981, 1982, 1983 and 1984. From November 1984 the standard rate was raised to £6·85 and the rate for the first child in one-parent families to £11·10.

FAMILY INCOME SUPPLEMENT

A benefit met out of Exchequer funds is payable under the Family Income Supplements Act, 1970, as amended and regulations made thereunder, to families, including one parent families, with at least one dependent child under 16 (or over 16 if still at school), whose total family income is below the "prescribed amount" if the man or woman is employed or self-employed, and normally so engaged, in remunerative full-time work (*i.e.*, 30 or more hours per week, 24 in the case of single parents). The "prescribed amount" is £90 if there is one child in the family and rises by £10 for each additional child. "Total income" includes the gross earnings of the claimant and his wife, but excludes child benefit or children's income, except for children's maintenance. The supplement is one-half of the amount by which the family's total income falls below the "prescribed amount", subject, since November 27, 1984, to a maximum payment of £23·00 for families with one child, rising by £2·00 for each additional child; odd amounts are rounded up to the next 10p above, and the minimum amount payable is 20p a week. Usually the supplement is awarded for 52 weeks and is not affected if the claimant's circumstances change during that time. Claim forms (FIS 1) can be obtained at a Social Security Office or a Post Office.

NATIONAL INSURANCE CONTRIBUTIONS

From April 6, 1975, when the National Insurance and Industrial Injuries schemes were replaced by a new scheme of social security benefits and contributions under the Social Security Act, 1975, combined weekly flat-rate Class 1 contributions ceased to be payable, and the graduated pension scheme was wound up (existing rights being preserved). Under the new scheme employees and their employers both pay wholly earnings-related contributions, based on a percentage of the employee's earnings (Class 1). Self-employed persons continue to pay flat-rate Class 2 contributions, but may also be liable to pay a contribution (Class 4) based on their profits or gains within certain limits. Class 3 contributions are voluntary, and may be paid to help qualify for certain benefits, including retirement pension. The contribution rates and earnings limits for contribution liability stated below apply for the tax year starting on April 6, 1984.

Class 1 contributions.—Primary Class 1 contributions are payable by employed earners and office-holders over age 16 with gross earnings at or above the lower earnings limit of £34·00 a week. For those with gross earnings at or above this level, contributions are payable on *all* earnings up to an upper limit of £250 a week. "Gross earnings" include overtime pay, commission, bonus, etc., without deduction of any superannuation contributions. The standard rate of primary contribution is 9 per cent of reckonable earnings (National Insurance Fund 9·00 per cent; National Health Service 0·75 per cent, Employment Protection Allocation 0·25 per cent). Married women and widows who before May 11, 1977, elected not to pay contributions at the full rate pay (while they still retain that right) a reduced rate of 3·85 per cent over the same earnings range: this covers industrial injuries benefits and a contribution of 0·75 per cent to the National Health Service. No primary contributions are payable by persons over pension age even when retirement is deferred. *Secondary* Class 1 contributions are payable by employers of employed earners, and by the appropriate authorities in the case of office-holders, except in the case of persons earning less than the lower earnings limit of £34·00 a week. The rate (excluding for taxation purposes the National Insurance Surcharge, abolished on October 1, 1984) is 10·45 per cent (National Insurance Fund 9·65 per cent; National Health Service 0·6 per cent; Redundancy etc. Funds 0·2 per cent) over the same earnings range as primary contributions (regardless of the employed earner's contribution rate). Where the employee is contracted out (*see* p. 1214) the full rate of contribution is payable on earnings up to the lower limit, but on higher earnings up to the upper limit the rate is 6·85 per cent for employees and 6·35 per cent for employers. Primary contributions are deducted from earnings by the employer, and are paid, together with the employer's contributions, to the Inland Revenue along with income tax collected under the PAYE system, so dispensing with contribution cards for employed earners.

Class 2 contributions.—These contributions are payable by self-employed earners over age 16 at a flat rate of £4·60 a week for both sexes. Those with earnings below £1,850 a year can apply for exception from liability to pay Class 2 contributions for the tax year 1984–85. Married women and widows can no longer choose not to pay Class 2 contributions when self-employed if they paid the contribution after May 10, 1977. No Class 2 contributions are payable by an earner after he attains pensionable age. There are special rules for those who are concurrently employed and self-employed. Class 2 contributions may be paid by direct debit through a bank or National Giro account or by stamping a contribution card. People who while self-employed are excepted from liability to pay contributions on the grounds of small earnings may pay either Class 2 or Class 3 contributions voluntarily. Self-employed earners (whether or not they pay Class 2 contributions) may also be liable to pay Class 4 contributions based on profits or gains within certain limits.

Class 3 contributions.—These are voluntary flat-rate contributions payable by persons over school-leaving age who would otherwise be unable to qualify for retirement pension and certain other benefits because they have an insufficient record of Class 1 or Class 2 contributions. The rate is £4·50 a week.

Payment may be made by stamping a contribution card or by direct debit through a bank or Giro account. Married women and widows who on or before May 11, 1977, elected not to pay Class 1 (full rate) or Class 2 contributions cannot pay Class 3 contributions while they retain this right.

Class 4 contributions.—These contributions are payable by self-employed earners, whether or not they pay Class 2 contributions, on annual profits or gains from a trade, profession or vocation chargeable to income tax under Schedule D. The rate of contribution is 6·3 per cent (including a contribution of 0·95 per cent to the National Health Service) of such profits or gains falling between £3,950 and £13,000 a year. The maximum Class 4 contribution, payable on profits or gains of £13,000 or more, is £570·15. The contribution is based on profits or gains subject to certain allowances and relief, which differ in some respects from those for income tax. Class 4 contributions are generally assessed and collected by the Inland Revenue along with Schedule D income tax. Self-employed persons under 16, or who at the beginning of a tax year are over pension age even where retirement is deferred, are not liable to pay Class 4 contributions. There are special rules for people who have more than one job, or who pay Class 1 contributions on earnings which are chargeable to income tax under Schedule D.

Leaflets relating to each class of contribution, and an employer's guide to national insurance contributions, are obtainable from local Social Security offices.

POST OFFICE FINANCIAL RESULTS, etc.

	1982–83 (£m.)			1983–84 (£m.)		
	Posts	National Giro-bank	£m. Total 1982–83	Posts	National Giro-bank	£m. Total 1983–84
INCOME						
Main Services	2086·6	132·3	2218·9	2219·1	144·5	2363·6
Other Services	562·4	75·0	637·4	557·5	82·6	640·1
Total................	2649·0	207·3	2856·3	2776·6	227·1	3003·7
EXPENDITURE						
Staff costs	1698·7	47·4	1746·1	1789·1	52·9	1842·0
Depreciation..............	43·6	1·5	45·1	35·9	3·6	39·5
Other operating charges ..	777·6	142·8	920·4	836·1	158·7	994·8
Extraordinary charges....	—	—	—	—	—	—
Interest payable (receivable)..............	(2·5)	2·0	(0·5)	(1·4)	2·0	0·6
Tax	—	6·7	6·7	5·6	2·3	7·9
Dividend	—	2·0	2·8	—	2·0	2·0
Total................	2517·4	202·4	2719·8	2665·3	221·5	2886·8
PROFIT RETAINED/(LOSS) ...	131·6	4·9	136·5	111·3	5·6	116·9

POSTAL AND TELECOMMUNICATIONS INFORMATION

GENERAL POSTAL REGULATIONS

Export Restrictions.—Under Department of Trade and Industry regulations the exportation of some goods by post is prohibited except under Department of Trade licence. Enquiries in the matter should be addressed to the Export Data Branch, Export Services and Promotions Division, Department of Trade and Industry, Dean Bradley House, 52 Horseferry Road, London, S.W.1.

Prohibited Articles.—Among prohibitions are offensive or dangerous things, packets likely to impede the P.O. sorters, and certain kinds of advertisement.

Certificate of Posting.—Issued free on request at the time of posting.

Recorded Delivery (inland). Charge: 21p.—This service provides for a record of posting and delivery and is available for inland letters. Advice of delivery, a further 20p at time of posting, 50p after time of posting. No compensation is payable in respect of money or jewellery sent by this service.

Unpaid Mail.—All unpaid or underpaid letters are treated as second class mail. The recipient will be charged the amount of underpayment plus 10p per item. The same rates apply to unpaid or underpaid parcels.

Undelivered Mail.—Undelivered mail is returned to the sender without charge provided the return address is indicated either on the outside of the envelope or inside. If the sender's address is not available, items not containing property are destroyed; however, if the packet contains something of intrinsic value, it is retained for up to three months pending reclaim before being disposed of. Perishable items within this category are dealt with as requisite. Exceptionally, items in the minimum weight step on which a rebate of postage has been allowed are destroyed unopened unless there is a return address shown on the outside of the cover. In addition, undeliverable second class mail in the minimum weight step, which, upon opening, is found to consist only of newspapers, magazines or commercial advertising material is also destroyed. *British packets undelivered abroad:* instructions for disposal are required if parcel is undeliverable and must be given at the time of posting. A parcel which cannot be delivered will be returned to sender at his expense.

International Reply Coupons, for the purpose of prepaying replies to letters, are exchangeable abroad for stamps representing the minimum surface mail letter rate from the country concerned to the U.K. Cost: 35p each.

Poste Restante (solely for the convenience of travellers, and for three months only in any one town).—A packet may be addressed as a rule to any Post Office except Town Sub-Offices, and should have the words "Poste Restante" or "to be called for" in the address. If addressed to initials, fictitious names, or Christian name only, it is treated as undeliverable. Applicants must furnish sufficient particulars to ensure delivery to the proper person. Redirection from a Poste Restante is undertaken for up to three months. Letters at a seaport for an expected ship are kept 2 months; otherwise letters are kept for 2 weeks—or 1 month if originating from abroad—at the end of which time they are treated as undeliverable, unless bearing a request for return at or before the end of the period.

Redirection.—(1) By agent of addressee: *Packets other than parcels, business reply and Freepost items* may be reposted free not later than the day after delivery (not counting Sundays and public holidays) if unopened and not tampered with, and if original addressee's name is unobscured. *Parcels* may be redirected free of charge within the same time limits, only if the original and the substituted address are both within the same local parcel delivery area (or within the London Postal Area). *Registered packets,* which must be taken to a Post Office, are *re-registered* free only up to day after delivery. (2) By the Post Office: Requests for redirection of *letters,* etc., should be on printed forms, obtainable from any post office, and must be signed by the person to whom the letters are to be addressed. The fees for redirection are as follows:—redirection for an initial period of up to one calendar month, £2·25; redirection for a period of up to three calendar months, commencing before the first anniversary of redirection, £5·50; redirection for a period of up to twelve calendar months, commencing before the first anniversary of redirection, £13·00; redirection for a period of up to 12 calendar months where redirection has already been in operation for 12 months or more, £45·00. A fee is payable for each different surname on the application form. Additional postage is generally due on redirected parcels (*see* above). Separate forms must be filled in for the forwarding of *telegrams.*

Registration, Inland (First Class letters only).— All packets intended for registration *must be handed to an officer of the Post Office, and a certificate of posting obtained.* The fees for registration (exclusive of first class postage) are: £1·10 covering compensation up to £600; £1·25, £1,250; £1·40, £1,750 (maximum). (No legal right to compensation exists in respect of registered letters sent to and from Irish Republic or the Channel Islands.) *Registered packets* (C.F.) parcels, fees: 27p up to £60 compensation; 37p up to £125; 55p up to £225; 70p up to £350. Advice of delivery, a further 20p at time of posting, 50p after time of posting.

Compensation in respect of money of any kind (coin, notes, orders, cheques, stamps, etc.) is only given if the money is sent by *registered letter* post in one of the special envelopes sold officially. Compensation cannot be paid for loss or damage in the case of any packet containing anything not legally transmissible by post; and for fragile articles only if they have been adequately packed. No compensation is paid for deterioration due to delay of perishable articles or for damage to exceptionally fragile articles, liquids or semi-liquids sent by letter or parcel post to or from Irish Republic, whether registered or not.

Compensation, Inland.—The ordinary mail services are not designed as compensation services, however, compensation up to a maximum limit of £18·00 may be paid where it can be shown that a letter or parcel was damaged or lost in the post. The onus of making up properly any packet sent by post and of packing adequately any article or articles enclosed therein lies on the sender, and the Post Office does not accept any responsibility for loss arising from faulty or inadequate packing. No compensation may be claimed for consequential injury or damage arising in respect of anything sent by post unless the item is registered and covered by Consequential Loss Insurance. This special insurance is arranged with certain Lloyds underwriters. Ask for details at the Post Office. The service is available only to U.K. addresses. *Recorded delivery packets:* maximum compensation £18 provided no contents inadmissible. Fee 21p.

Registration, Overseas (except for parcels and printed paper items posted in bulk), is in force to all countries with the exception of British Indian Ocean Territory or Republic of Maldives. No compensation is payable for the loss of or damage to valuable articles or other items sent in an unregistered letter. Fee £1·10. If claimed within a year compensation is paid to the sender for entire loss of registered packets while in the custody of a country in the Universal Postal Union, subject to certain conditions. Compensation is also payable for the partial or complete loss of or damage to the contents of registered items in the service with certain countries (*see* Post Office Guide for list).

Insurance, Overseas, may be effected on packets to many countries at the following rates:—£1·10 for up to £100 cover; 20p for each additional £100 up to £2·90 for £1,000. *For H.M. Ships abroad and also members of H.M. Army and Air Force overseas using closed Forces addresses* (*e.g.,* British Forces Post Office followed by a number) only parcels are insurable, up to £100. Fee £1·10. Packets containing valuable papers, (banknotes, etc.), documents (press, etc.) and, in some cases, valuable articles such as jewellery, can be insured as letters, or as parcels if the country of destination does not accept dutiable goods in the letter post.

The Post Office Guide should be consulted for details of the conditions of Insurance.

Compensation up to a maximum of £13·00 for parcels up to 5 kg. in weight, £20·00 for parcels up to 10 kg., £25·00 for parcels up to 15 kg. and £30·00 for parcels up to 20 kg may be given for loss or damage in the U.K. to *uninsured* parcels to or from most overseas countries, if certificate of posting is produced.

No compensation will be paid for any loss or damage due to the act of the Queen's Enemies.

Cash on Delivery Service, Inland (*not* to or from Irish Republic, nor to H.M. Ships).—A sum (Trade Charge) up to £350 can, under certain conditions, be collected from addresses and remitted to sender of a parcel containing an invoice. Invoice values over £50 are only collected at Post Office premises. Fee (extra to normal postage and registration charges): 65p.

Cash on Delivery, Overseas.—Applicable to parcels only, but not all countries, nor to H.M. Naval and Military Forces and R.A.F. serving overseas. A fee, starting at £2.20 per parcel, must be prepaid in addition to the postage for outward parcels. For inward parcels the delivery fee is 70p. The Trade Charge (amount to be collected) may not exceed £1,000, but to most non-European countries the limit is lower. Addressee has also to pay on delivery, besides Customs, if any, a further fee (£1 in U.K.) not prepayable. If Trade Charge cannot be collected, special rules for undeliverable C.O.D. parcels apply.

Datapost.—A guaranteed service for the delivery of important documents and packages. Datapost Sameday provides same day collection and delivery in many areas. Datapost Overnight offers next day delivery nationwide. Items may be collected or handed in at post offices. Contractual arrangements may be made for regular consignments. There are also equally reliable and secure Datapost links with a number of overseas countries. For further details contact your local Head Post Office.

Swiftair.—Express delivery of air mail letters and packets anywhere in the world. Items normally arrive at least one day in advance of normal air mail. Items should be handed in at a post office counter. Cost: normal postage plus £1·50.

Intelpost.—A public facsimile transmission service linking many towns and cities in the U.K. and also with international connections. Documents up to A4 size can be transmitted and received within minutes and the service can be used with hand delivery and collection services. Cost: from £3.

Royal Mail Special Delivery.—Offers special messenger treatment where necessary to ensure next day delivery of first class letters and packets. Special fee of £1·50 refunded if next working day delivery is not achieved provided items are posted before latest recommended posting times.

Airway Letters.—On certain internal air routes operated by the British Airways (European Division), First Class letters may be handed in at certain Airport offices for conveyance by the next available direct air service to be transferred to the post at the distant airport or town terminal or to be called for at the airport or town terminal. Fee (besides postage) £3·45 plus VAT, maximum weight 1 lb. This service is not available to the Irish Republic, Isle of Man or to any country overseas. Full information can be obtained from any office of British Airways (European Division).

Express Delivery.—This service from the office of delivery by special messenger is available to or from certain countries. In some countries the service is restricted to certain towns. Fee payable in addition to postage, £1·50.

Business Reply and Freepost (Inland, excluding Irish Republic).—These services enable a person or firm to receive replies to advertisements, letters from clients, etc. without prepayment of postage, the addressee paying the postage together with a handling charge of 0·5p per item delivered. A licence costing £20 p.a. must be obtained to use either service and these are available from Head Postmasters who will also provide any further information required.

Postage Forward Parcel Service.—This service enables a person or firm to receive parcels from clients without prepayment of postage, the addressee pays a fee of 8p on each parcel in addition to postage. A special label is used for this service. A licence costing £22 p.a., to use the service must first be obtained from the local Head Postmaster.

Articles for the Blind (Inland, including Irish Republic).—Books, papers, literature and specified articles specially adapted for the use of the blind are admissible subject to certain conditions. A packet should bear on the outside the indication "Articles for the Blind" and the name and address of the sender. Packets must be capable of easy examination in the post. Postage free up to a maximum weight of 7 kg.

Blind Literature, Overseas (in other respects treated as Printed Papers).—Papers, periodicals and books, if printed in special type (also plates for embossing blind literature, and voice recordings and special paper intended solely for the use of the blind) subject to certain conditions of posting, marked outside "Literature for the Blind (Cécogrammes)", with name and address of sender. Packets must be capable of easy examination in the post. They may be sent post free up to 7 kg by surface route to all parts and free by air mail up to 1 kg to Europe; the air mail charge to other countries is 1p per 50 g up to 7 kg.

Small Packets Post (OVERSEAS).—For the transmission of goods (including trade samples) in the same mails as Printed Papers up to 1 kg. Registration is allowed; not insurance. Available to all countries, but to some countries there is a limit of 500 g. A customs declaration is required.

Newspaper Post (INLAND).—For newspapers "registered at the P.O.".

Copies of registered newspapers may be posted by the publishers or their agents in wrappers open at both ends, in unsealed envelopes approved by the Post Office for the purpose or without covers and tied with string which can be removed without cutting. Wrappers and envelopes must be prominently marked NEWSPAPER POST in the top left-hand corner and be easily removable for the purpose of examination. No writing or additional printing is permitted, other than the words "with compliments", name and address of sender, request for return if undeliverable and a reference to a page.

Newspapers posted by the public or supplements to registered newspapers despatched apart from their ordinary publications are transmitted under the conditions governing the First or Second Class Letter Services.

STAMPS, ENVELOPES, POSTCARDS, &c.

POSTAGE STAMPS are sold in values of ½p, 1p, 2p, 3p, 4p, 5p, 10p, 13p, 16p, 17p, 18p, 20p, 22p, 24p, 26p, 28p, 31p, 34p, 50p, 75p, £1, £1·33, £2, and £5.

Books containing stamps to the value of 50p are only available at vending machines. Books are sold containing 10 at 13p (£1·30); 6 at 17p (£1·02); 4 at 13p (£1·54) and 10 at 17p (£1·70). Rolls of 13p and 17p stamps are sold: mixed value rolls are only available on special order from post offices.

REGISTERED LETTER ENVELOPES printed with a £1·27 stamp (£1·10 for registration and 17p for postage) are in three sizes: G, 156 mm × 95 mm, £1·35 each; H, 203 mm × 120 mm, £1·38 each; K, 292 mm × 152 mm, £1·46 each.

FORCES AEROGRAMMES, 13p.

ENVELOPES printed with 13p stamp: (220 mm × 110 mm) 17p each. With 17p stamp: (220 mm × 110 mm) 21p each.

POSTNOTES: Notepaper and envelope all in one, with first class postage paid up to 60g, 22p each (pack of 5, 99p).

Aerogrammes to all destinations, 26p.

Printed postage stamps cut out of envelopes, postcards, lettercards, air letter forms or newspaper-wrappers may be used as adhesive stamps in payment of postage or telegrams provided they are not imperfect, mutilated or defaced in any way.

POSTAL ORDERS

Postal Orders (British pattern) are issued and paid at nearly all post offices in the United Kingdom during the ordinary hours of business on weekdays. They are also issued and/or paid in many countries overseas. These countries are listed in the Post Office Guide which may be seen at any post office transacting postal order business. Transmission of postal orders to any other country is prohibited except to members of H.M. Forces. British postal orders are paid and issued in the Channel Islands and the Isle of Man and paid in the Irish Republic. They are printed, with a counterfoil, for denominations of 25p and then every multiple of 5p up to and including 50p, then 60p, 70p, 75p, 80p, 90p, £1, followed by £1 steps to £10. Adhesive unmarked British Postage Stamps not exceeding two in number, if affixed in the space provided, may increase the value of an order by not more than 9p. Fees: 20p on each order up to £1, then 30p. The name of the payee must be inserted. If not presented within six months of the last day of the month of issue orders must be sent to the local Head Postmaster or, in London, to the District Postmaster, to ascertain whether the order may still be paid.

TELEMESSAGE

The inland telegram service was replaced on Oct. 1, 1982 by the telemessage service. Telemessages can be sent by telephone or telex to anywhere in the UK

for 'hard copy' delivery the next working day, including Saturdays. To achieve this, a Telemessage must be telephoned/telexed before 10 p.m. Monday to Saturday (7 p.m. Sundays and Bank Holidays). Dial 100 (190 in London) and ask for the Telemessage Service or see the telex directory for dialling codes. The telephone or telex calls are free.

A Telemessage costs £3 for the first 50 words and £1·50 for each subsequent group of 50 words—the name and address are free. A sender's copy costs 75p. A wide selection of colourful cards is available for special occasions at 50p per card. All prices are subject to VAT. Telemessage has a number of services for businesses. Call Freefone 2741 for details.

Telemessage is also available to the U.S.A. For next working day delivery in America a Telemessage must be filed by 10 p.m. U.K. time Monday to Saturday (7 p.m. Sundays and Bank Holidays). U.S. addresses must include the ZIP code. Charges are £5 for the first 50 words and £2 for each subsequent group of 50 words—the name and address are free. All charges are subject to VAT.

INTERNATIONAL TELEGRAMS

Ordinary telegrams are available to all countries. Dial 100 (190 in London) for full details and tariffs.

MARITIME COMMUNICATIONS

British Telecom International Maritime Radio provides a comprehensive range of maritime communication services and facilities to all suitably equipped ships and boats, ranging from radiotelegram to data over satellite.

RADIOTELEGRAMS

The charge for radiotelegrams is 41p per word (standard rate). Radiotelegrams at the standard rate should be addressed Portishead Radio unless the sender nominates another coast station. The address should contain (1) the name or rank of the addressee, (2) the name of the ship and (3) the name of the coast station in the British Isles if the sender knows that the ship is within range of that station.

Radiotelegrams to H.M. Ships should contain in the address (1) the name of the addressee and his rank or rating, (2) the word "Warship" (or "Submarine"), (3) the name of the ship (or identifying letters and number) and (4) the word "Admiraltyradio".

In addition to the per word charges quoted a fixed charge of £2·00p per radiotelegram applies.

Radiotelegrams may also be sent to R.A.F. vessels. Such radiotelegrams should be addressed in the same way as for commercial vessels and in addition should include the words "R.A.F. Vessel" before the name of the ship.

RADIOTELEPHONE SERVICE

Radiotelephone services are available between telephone subscribers (but not from coin-box telephones or call offices unless the caller is a holder of a British Telecom telephone credit card) in Great Britain, Northern Ireland, the Channel Islands and the Isle of Man and suitably equipped ships. The service is generally available at all hours of the day and night, but the periods of communication with a particular ship vary with the ship's position and are dependent on radio conditions.

Calls are normally made through the coast stations, listed below, and callers should ask the local exchange telephone operator for SHIPS' TELEPHONE SERVICE adding, if known, the telephone number and name of the coast station through which the call should be made. If the name of the coast station is not known, the caller will be connected to Portishead Radio. When connected to the coast station operator, the caller should ask for SHIPS' RADIO TELEPHONE CALL giving the name of the ship and the name (or designation) of the person required.

Anglesey Radio	0407 83 0541
Bacton Radio (restricted short range VHF services)	0521 73447
Buchan Radio (restricted short range VHF services)	0569 62917
Cardigan Bay Radio (restricted short range VHF services)	0407 830541
Celtic Radio (restricted short range VHF services)	0271 63453
Clyde Radio (restricted short range VHF services)	0776 81 311
Collafirth Radio (restricted short range VHF services)	0955 2271
Cromarty Radio (restricted short range VHF services)	0955 2271
Cullercoats Radio	0632 531318
Forth Radio (restricted short range VHF services)	0569 62917
Grimsby Radio (restricted short range VHF services)	0521 73447
Hastings Radio (restricted short range VHF services)	0843 20592
Hebrides Radio (restricted short range VHF services)	0569 62917
Humber Radio	0521 73447
Ilfracombe Radio	0271 63453
Islay Radio (restricted short range VHF services)	0776 81 311
Land's End Radio	0736 87 363
Lewis Radio (restricted short range VHF services)	0569 62917
Morecambe Bay Radio (restricted short range VHF services)	0407 830541
Niton Radio	0983 730495
North Foreland Radio	0843 20592
Oban Radio..............	0631 62059
Orfordness Radio (restricted short range VHF services)	0843 20592
Orkney Radio (restricted short range VHF services)	0955 2271
Pendennis Radio (restricted short range VHF services)	0736 87 363
Portishead Radio..........	027 878 1111
Portpatrick Radio	0776 81 311
Scillies Radio (restricted short range VHF services)	0736 87 363
Severn Radio (restricted short range VHF services)	0271 63453
Shetland Radio (restricted short range VHF services)	0955 2271
Skye Radio (restricted short range VHF services)	0569 62917

Start Point Radio (restricted short range VHF services)	0736 87 363
Stonehaven Radio	0569 62917
Thames Radio (restricted short range VHF services)	0843 20592
Whitby Radio (restricted short range VHF services)	0632 531318
Wick Radio	0955 2271

The service is also available for calls to and from H.M. Ships, subject to the approval of the Duty Commander M.O.D. Navy, through whom all calls to H.M. Ships should be booked. The charges are the same as those for merchant ships but as H.M. Ships do not normally keep watch for private radiotelephone calls from the shore, no attempt should be made to book a call to one of H.M. Ships unless prior arrangements have been made with the person concerned on the ship. The caller must be able to give the name of the coast station through which the call is to be made, or the approximate position of the ship at the time the call is required.

The holder of a British Telecom telephone credit card issued in Great Britain, Northern Ireland, the Channel Islands or the Isle of Man may use it to make radio-telephone calls to ships at sea from any telephone in this country (including coin-box telephones and call offices).

Radioteleprinter Service.—Telex subscribers may be connected via Portishead Radio, Wick Radio, Stonehaven Radio, Cullercoats Radio, Hebrides Radio, North Foreland Radio and Land's End Radio for two-way teleprinter communication with suitably equipped ships at sea.

INLAND TELEPHONES

The quarterly rental for an exclusive business exchange line is £22·00 and £14·15 for any other exclusive exchange line. For shared service, in which two subscribers share one line but have practically the same facilities as those provided by individual lines, each customer pays £4 per annum less than for exclusive line service. A condition of telephone service is that all new and removing residential customers since January, 1948, are liable to share their lines if called upon to do so. Subscriber trunk dialling (STD) facilities are provided to most destinations at all exchanges. Local and dialled trunk calls from these exchanges are charged in 4·4p units when made from ordinary lines, in 5p units when dialled from pay on answer coin-box lines and 8p minimum charge from Press-Button payphones with 2p incremental units. All charges are subject to Value Added Tax (VAT). VAT on call charges from ordinary lines is charged as a percentage of the total on quarterly bills and VAT on calls from pay on answer coin-box lines is included in the unit fee. The length of time per unit depends on the distance of the call and time of day, from eight minutes for a local call to twelve seconds for distances over 56 kilometres.

Operator connected trunk calls from ordinary lines have a three minute minimum charge (and thereafter by the minute) which varies with distance and time of day, but those from coinbox lines are charged in 3 minute periods at the coinbox tariff. For calls that have to be passed through the operator because the caller cannot dial or because a dialled call had failed, the charge is equivalent to the dialled rate, subject normally to the three minute minimum. Generally higher charges apply to other operator connected calls including special services calls and those to the Irish Republic and the Channel Isles. All trunk calls are cheaper if made after 6 p.m. or at weekends.

Personal calls (to specified person) 44p extra from ordinary lines and 55p from coinbox lines, if the person cannot be found nothing further is charged. For fuller information *see* Preface to Telephone Directory, Dialling Instruction Booklet (where appropriate) and Post Office Guide.

TELEX SERVICE

There are now 198 countries that can be reached by Telex from the UK; 185 of them by Direct Dial.

The new generation of electronic teleprinters are now available for sale or rental from British Telecom. Direct Dialled calls to Europe and North Africa are charged in 2·75p units. The time bought by a unit varies according to country called; between five and ten secs. Direct Dialled calls to other international destinations are charged in six second steps depending upon the country called (between 5·3p and 10·6p). Calls via the operator are charged in one minute steps with a three minute minimum, plus a £1 surcharge per call.

Calls made via British Telecom's Telex Plus store and forward facility attract normal Telex charges plus a surcharge of 10p for inland delivered messages and 20p for international delivered messages. For information regarding Telex contact your local Area telephone office Telex Sales Department.

DATA COMMUNICATIONS PRODUCTS

Data communications products consist of a family of modems for data transfer at 300 to 72,000 bit/s, linedriver, auto callers, statistical multiplexers and network management systems.

The products are described briefly as follows:

Datel 300 Duplex—for duplex data transmission over 2-wire circuits, using either a private circuit or an exchange line on the public switched telephone network (PSTN), at rates up to 300 bit/s.

Datel 1200—for half duplex asynchronous transmission at rates up to 1200 bit/s using a single exchange line or 2-wire private circuit, and duplex transmission on 4-wire circuits.

Datel 1200 Duplex—provides for duplex data transmission at 1200 bit/s over a single exchange line or 2-wire private circuits. The modem will handle both synchronous and asynchronous inputs, and offers a comprehensive range of diagnostic and test facilities.

Datel 1230—this unique modem is designed for instation PSTN use, and offers automatic switching between V21 (300 bit/s duplex) and V22 (1200 bit/s duplex) operation.

Datel 2400—enables data to be transmitted synchronously in half duplex mode at 2400 bit/s, using either a single exchange line, 2-wire private circuit, or multipoint circuit.

Datel 2400 Duplex—duplex transmission at 2400 bit/s over a single exchange line or 2-wire private circuit. Automatic selection of 1200 or 2400 bit/s data rate when responding to an incoming call.

Datel 4800—service offers synchronous data transmission at 4800 bit/s, with fall-back to 2400 bit/s. Suitable for use on 2 or 4-wire point-to-point circuits including the PSTN. A range of features make it particularly suitable for multipoint use.

Datel 9600—permits transmission of duplex or half duplex synchronous data at rates of 9600, 7200 and 4800 bit/s. May be used on 2 or 4-wire private circuits with single or double dial-up standby, or on the PSTN as the main mode of operation. The modem is particularly suitable for multipoint use and offers a wide range of facility options.

Data Auto-caller 4050—when used in conjunction with a CCITT modem, allows the terminal equipment to originate a call on the PSTN automatically.

Datel 64K—for data transmission at 48K, 56K, 60K, 64K and 72K bit/s over specially engineered wideband circuits.

Datelmux 5100—4/8 channel statistical multiplexer for point-to-point applications. An enhanced version allows interworking with Datelmux 5300/5500 networking products. Other 5100 products cater for synchronous traffic and access to packet switched networks.

Datelmux 5300—Statistical multiplexer with up to 32 asynchronous channels, with onward linking facility. Synchronous options are also available.

Datelmux 5500—true networking multiplexer with user switching, comprehensive network management, automatic re-routing and port contention. Datelmux 5500, which can handle up to 240 asynchronous channels, is also suitable for local data switching in an office automation environment

Four levels of network management are currently available:

(i) *Tech Control*—at the lowest level this gives flexibility between modems and FEP ports, and allows access for test equipment. This enables the customer to monitor faults and take remedial action quickly.

(ii) *Tech/Network Control*—at the central site this gives automatic switching between modems and ports. The addition of an intelligent terminal permits displays of network status, control of local and remote diagnostics, and creation of user files. The customer can now monitor and test his network without involving remotely located staff.

(iii) *Network Control*—this package extends switching and monitoring facilities to remote sites. It also provides a fault detection and alarm monitoring capability. The user interface is a standard VDU.

(iv) *Network Management*—at the highest level this enables central staff to access, control and analyse every local and remote component in the network. When a fault occurs, it can be identified, isolated and corrected. Network information can be displayed on a VDU in graphical form.

A range of local area products provide access to PBXs or nodal switches. Products include Dateldriver (linedrivers); Datelnet (data over voice equipment); and the Datel Modem 4192, which operates at 19200 bit/s duplex over 2-wire baseband circuits.

INTERNATIONAL DATA TRANSMISSION SERVICES

(i) PUBLIC SWITCHED TELEPHONE NETWORK

BTI International Business Services offer data transmission over the public switched telephone network using International Direct Dialling (IDD). Calls are charged at the same rate as for telephone calls. Modems used must be approved for connection to the public network.

BTI does not impose limitations as regards transmission speeds or standards but recommends that where possible terminal equipment used conforms to the recommendations of the CCITT (Consultative Committee on Telephones and Telegraphs).

BTI has reached agreement with 63 countries for such use of the telephone network.

Data calls over the network are charged at the same rate as telephone calls. Quality and speed of transmission cannot be guaranteed.

For more information dial 100 and ask for Freefone International Datel.

(ii) PRIVATE CIRCUITS

International private circuits are available for data transmission and are provided in accordance with the Recommendations of the International Telephone & Telegraph Consultative Committee (CCITT). Using suitable modems, higher transmission rates than those offered by the Datel services are usually obtainable over voice bandwidth circuits.

In addition, high speed data transmission, e.g. 72K Bit/s may be achieved over wide-band leases (telephone circuits grouped together to give 48KHz bandwidth). A reduced tariff for 1200–9600 bit/s service and a 56K bit/s service is available to some countries.

(iii) INTERNATIONAL PACKET SWITCHING SERVICE (IPSS)

Packet switching is the switching and transmission of data in discrete quantities called packets, each packet or block of data carrying its own routing and control information. Packet switching technology permits intercommunication between different terminal types and transmission rates and is sufficiently flexible to support a diversity of data communications applications on dedicated data networks providing high reliability and low error rates.

IPSS provides service to and from Australia, Austria, Belgium, Brazil, Canada, Denmark, Finland, France, French Antilles, Gabon, Fed. Rep. of Germany, Greece, Guadeloupe, Hong Kong, Irish Republic, Italy, Ivory Coast, Japan, Luxembourg, Martinique, Netherlands, Norway, Portugal, Singapore, South Africa, Spain, Sweden, Switzerland and the U.S.A. Data calls can also be made to the U.K. from Bahrain, Barbados, Bermuda, Israel, New Zealand, Oman, South Korea and the United Arab Emirates.

PRESTEL

Prestel, British Telecommunications' public viewdata service, links adapted television screens to computers through ordinary telephone lines so information and two-way services can be delivered directly into offices and homes. Over 94 per cent of the U.K.

telephone population can now use Prestel at local call rates, and over 45,000 terminals are attached to the network. Information on Prestel (from over 1,200 different sources) can be updated by the minute and is available 24 hours a day.

In addition, by using "Gateways" private computers can be linked to Prestel sets via Prestel computers. This facility makes possible services such as home banking, home shopping and for travel agents confirmed reservations of airline tickets.

Because the system is two-way, all customers can send messages, make bookings or request information at the touch of a button. There are well over 300,000 frames (or "pages") of information available. Some of the specialist services Prestel offers are Homelink, CitiService, Messaging, Private Prestel and Prestel Microcomputing.

INTERNATIONAL TELEPHONES

The charges are the same for calls originating in any part of Great Britain, Northern Ireland and the Isle of Man. All U.K. customers have had access to International Direct Dialling from this country since 28 July, 1982 and can now dial direct to numbers on most exchanges in over 155 countries worldwide. The number of places abroad to which calls may be dialled direct is also increasing. Callers should consult their dialling codes booklets or International Telephone Guide for information on how to make calls.

Directly dialled calls are charged in units of time costing 4·4p. For charge bands A, B, C, D and F cheap rates apply from 8 p.m. to 8 a.m. nightly, at any time on Saturdays and Sundays and all day on selected Bank Holidays. For charge band E, the economy rate applies from 12 p.m. to 7 a.m. and 2.30 p.m. to 7.30 p.m. every day and all day at Bank Holidays and weekends adjoining Bank Holidays. For charge band C, the peak rate applies on weekdays from 3 p.m. to 5 p.m. Standard rate applies on all charge bands at all other times. Cheap rates are not available for calls in charge band G. Where I.D.D. access to a country is not yet available callers should dial the International Exchange, specifying the country required.

BRITISH TELECOM FINANCIAL RESULTS

The telecommunications income for the year 1983–84 totalled £6,876m, of which £6,646m was derived from main services and £230m from other sources (compared to main services, £6,187m and other sources, £199m, totalling £6,377m in the year 1982–83).

Total expenditure, including interest and depreciation as well as all operating and maintenance costs, was £5,886m for 1983–84, a decrease on the 1982–83 total of £6,012m. This resulted in a profit for the year 1983–84 of £990m, compared with a profit of £365m for 1982–83.

BASIC RATE OF INLAND LETTER POST

1840	1d	1975	7p
1918	1½d	Sept. 1975	8½p
1940	2½d	June 1977	9p
1957	3d	Aug. 1979	10p
1965	4d	Feb. 1980	12p
1968*	5d	Jan. 1981	14p
1971	3p	Feb. 1982	15½p
1973	3½p	April 1983	16p
1974	4½p	Sept. 1984	17p

(*Two-tier postal system introduced—subsequent figures are for 1st class letter post)

DUTY AND TAX-FREE ALLOWANCES

You are entitled to the allowances in either of the columns below (but not both) for any category of goods, as represented by the boxes (see Notes on allowances). Passengers under 17 are not, however, entitled to tobacco and drinks allowances.

Column 1
Goods obtained duty and tax free in the EEC, or duty and tax free on a ship or aircraft, or goods obtained outside the EEC.

Column 2
Goods obtained duty and tax paid in the EEC.

Column 1	Column 2
Tobacco goods 200 cigarettes **or** 100 cigarillos **or** 50 cigars **or** 250 grammes of tobacco } double if you live outside Europe	**Tobacco goods** 300 cigarettes **or** 150 cigarillos **or** 75 cigars **or** 400 grammes of tobacco
Alcoholic drinks 1 litre of alcoholic drinks over 22% vol. **or** 2 litres of alcoholic drinks not over 22% vol. **or** fortified **or** sparkling wine **plus** 2 litres of still table wine	**Alcoholic drinks** 1½ litres of alcoholic drinks over 22% vol. **or** 3 litres of alcoholic drinks not over 22% vol. **or** fortified **or** sparkling wine **plus** 4 litres of still table wine
Perfume 50 grammes (60 cc or 2 fl oz)	**Perfume** 75 grammes (90 cc or 3 fl oz)
Toilet water 250 cc (9 fl oz)	**Toilet water** 375 cc (13 fl oz)
Other goods £28 worth	**Other goods** £163 worth

N.B. A maximum of 50 litres of beer and 25 lighters may be imported duty-free, subject to the limitations of the 'Other goods' monetary allowance.

If you are visiting the United Kingdom for less than six months, you are also entitled to bring in, free of duty and tax, all personal effects (except tobacco goods, alcoholic drinks and perfume) which you intend to take with you when you leave.

NOTES ON ALLOWANCES

(1) The countries of the EEC (Common Market) are Belgium, Denmark, France, West Germany, Greece, the Irish Republic, Italy, Luxemburg, the Netherlands and the United Kingdom (but not the Channel Islands).
(2) The allowances apply only to goods carried and cleared by you at the time of your arrival.
(3) The allowances do not apply to goods brought in for sale or for other commercial purposes.
(4) Reduced allowances apply to certain persons crossing the Irish land boundary and to seamen and aircrew members.
(5) Whisky, gin, rum, brandy, vodka and most liqueurs normally exceed 22% vol. (38.8° proof) but advocaat, cassis, fraise, suze and aperitifs may be less. Fortified wines include port, sherry, vermouth and madeira. Sparkling wines include champagne, perelada, spumante and semi-sparkling wines. Still table wines include claret, Sauterne, Graves and Chianti. Burgundy, Chablis, hock and Moselle may be either sparkling or still, depending on manufacture.
(6) You may not mix goods obtained duty and tax free or outside the EEC with goods of the same category (as represented by the boxes) obtained duty and tax paid in the EEC to obtain the higher allowance. E.g. you will not get the higher allowance for Alcoholic Drinks if *any* of the items in that category were obtained duty and tax free or outside the EEC.

(7) Where there are alternative quantities within a category of goods they may be apportioned. For example, 150 cigarettes (half allowance) plus 75 cigarillos (half allowance).
(8) One litre is approximately 1¾ pints or 35 fl oz.
(9) A cigarillo is a cigar with a maximum weight of 3 grammes.

PROHIBITED AND RESTRICTED GOODS

The customs officer will be able to provide full information. This is a list of commoner and more frequently met items:
Controlled drugs, such as opium, heroin, morphine, cocaine, cannabis, amphetamines and lysergide (LSD).
Firearms (including gas pistols and similar weapons), ammunition and explosives (including fireworks).
Flick knives.
Counterfeit coins.
Horror comics. Indecent and obscene books, magazines, films and other articles.
Radio transmitters (walkie-talkies, Citizen's Band radios etc.) capable of operating on certain frequencies.
Meat and poultry (not fully cooked).
Plants, bulbs, trees, potatoes and certain other vegetables and fruit.
Most animals and birds, whether alive or dead (e.g.

stuffed); certain articles derived from rare species including furskins, ivory, reptile leather and goods made from them.

NOTE: Cats, dogs and other mammals must not be landed unless a British import licence (rabies) has previously been issued.

EXPORT CONTROL

The following are some of the goods subject to export control and should be declared to the customs officer. There are formalities to be completed in respect of these goods prior to your arrival at the port of exportation and further information is available through any local office of Customs and Excise (address in the telephone directory).

● Controlled drugs.
● Firearms and ammunition.
● Photographic material over 60 years old and valued at £200 or more.
● Portraits (including sculptures) of British Historical Personages which are over 50 years old and valued at £2,000 or more.
● Antiques, collectors' items, etc. (including paintings and other works of art) over 50 years old and valued at £8,000 or more.
● Certain archaeological material.
● Most live animals and birds, and items made from animals occurring wild in the U.K.

BRITISH PASSPORT REGULATIONS

Applications for United Kingdom passports must be made on the forms obtainable at any of the Passport Offices (addresses given below) or at any Main Post Office (except in Northern Ireland).

London.—Clive House, 70–78 Petty France, S.W.1.
Liverpool.—India Buildings, Water Street, Liverpool, 2.
Newport, Gwent.—Olympia House, Upper Dock Street.
Peterborough.—Passport Office, 55 Westfield Road, Peterborough.
Glasgow.—1st Floor, Empire House, 131 West Nile Street, Glasgow, C.1.
Belfast.—Passport Office, Hampton House, 47–53 High Street, Belfast.

Hours. The above offices are open Mon.-Fri. 9 a.m. to 4.30 p.m. The Passport Office, London, is also open for cases of special emergency (*e.g.* death or serious illness) arising outside normal office hours between 4.30 p.m. and 6.00 p.m. and on Saturdays between 10 a.m. and noon.

Completed forms of application should be sent to one of the six Passport Offices, with photographs, supporting documents and the fee of £15 (£22·50 if particulars of spouse included), in the form of a Cheque or Postal Order which should be crossed and made payable to the Passport Office.

A Passport cannot be issued or extended on behalf of *a person already abroad*; such person should apply, in a foreign country, to the nearest British Mission or Consulate, or, within the British Commonwealth outside the United Kingdom of Great Britain and N. Ireland, to the nearest British Passport issuing authority.

United Kingdom Passports are granted to:—
(i) British Citizens.
(ii) British Dependent Territories Citizens.
(iii) British Overseas Citizens.
(iv) British Subjects.
(v) British Protected Persons.

A passport granted to a child under 16 will normally be valid for an initial period of five years, after which it may be extended for a further five years with no extra charge. A passport granted to a person over 16 will normally be valid for 10 years and will not be renewable. Thereafter, or if at any time the Passport contains no further space for visas, a new Passport must be obtained.

A Passport including particulars of the *holder's* spouse is not available for his/her use when he/she is travelling alone. A spouse's particulars may *only* be added at the time of issue of a passport.

Children who have reached the age of sixteen years require separate Passports. Their applications must be signed by one of their parents.

Passport applications must be countersigned by a Member of Parliament, Justice of the Peace, Minister of Religion, Doctor, Lawyer, Bank Officer, Police Officer or any person of similar standing who has been personally acquainted with the applicant for at least two years. The applicant's birth certificate and other evidence in support of the statements made in the application must be produced.

In the case of children under the age of 16 requiring a separate passport, an application should be made by one of the parents on form (B).

If the applicant for a Passport be a British national by naturalization or registration, the Certificate of Naturalization or registration must be produced with the application.

British Passports are generally available for travel *to all countries*. The possession of a Passport does not, however, exempt the holder from compliance with any *Immigration Regulations* in force in British or foreign countries, or from the necessity of obtaining a *visa* where required.

Photographs

Duplicate unmounted photographs of applicant (and wife/husband, if to be included in the Passport) must be sent. These photographs should be printed on normal thin photographic paper. They should measure not more than 2½ in. by 2 in. (63 mm. by 50 mm.), or less than 2 in. by 1½ in. (50 mm. by 38 mm.), and should be taken full face without a hat.

Extension of Passports

Applications for the extension of United Kingdom passports must be made on Form D.

94-Page Passports

On May 1, 1973, a new type of passport became available. Intended to meet the needs of frequent travellers who fill standard passports well before the ten-year validity has expired, it contains 94 pages, is valid for ten years and costs £30 (£45 if particulars of spouse included).

British Visitors' Passports

A simplified form of travel document is available for British Citizens, British Dependent Territories Citizens or British Overseas Citizens wishing to pay short visits (not exceeding three months) to certain foreign countries, *viz.*

ANDORRA; AUSTRIA; BELGIUM; BERMUDA; CANADA; DENMARK; FINLAND; FRANCE (incl. CORSICA); GREECE (& THE GREEK ISLANDS); W. GERMANY (incl. West Berlin by air only); GIBRALTAR; ICELAND; ITALY; LIECHTENSTEIN; LUXEMBOURG; MALTA; MONACO; NETHERLANDS; NORWAY; PORTUGAL (incl. MADEIRA & AZORES); SAN MARINO; SPAIN (incl. BALEARIC

& CANARY ISLANDS); SWEDEN; SWITZERLAND; TUNISIA; TURKEY.

A fee of £7·50 (£11·25 if particulars of spouse included) is charged for the issue of a British Visitors' Passport, which is valid for 12 months, cannot be amended and is not renewable; on expiry application should be made for a new passport if required. Particulars of an applicant's spouse and/or children under 16 years can be included at *the time of issue only* at no extra cost. A child of 8 years of age and over is eligible to hold a British Visitors' Passport. Applications for, or including, a person under 18 years of age (unless married or serving in H.M. Forces) must be countersigned by the legal guardian.

British Visitors' Passports are obtainable by application on Form VP (from any Main Post Office except in Northern Ireland). Applicants in England, Scotland and Wales should take the completed form in person to any Main Post Office which will normally issue the passport without further delay; applicants in Northern Ireland to the Passport Office, Belfast from whom application forms may be obtained. *British Visitors' Passports are not obtainable from Passport Offices other than Belfast.* Two recent passport photographs will be required of the applicant and of his/her spouse, if to be included; photographs of children are not required. Size of photographs must be 2 in. × 1½ in. (50 mm. by 38 mm.) They should be unmounted and must be printed on normal thin photographic paper. No visas are required on British Visitors' Passports.

Applicants must also produce for the purpose of identification a N.H.S. Medical Card, birth certificate or retirement pension book.

VISAS

Visa regulations are liable to change and enquiries should be made either at the Passport Office or at the Consulate or Embassy concerned (addresses and telephone numbers are given in the Commonwealth and Foreign Countries sections).

For entry into the following countries a visa or permit may be required: Afghanistan; Albania; Algeria; Angola; Antigua; Argentina; Austria; Bahrain; Benin; Bermuda; Bolivia; Brazil; Brunei; Bulgaria; Burma; Burundi; Cameroon Republic; Cape Verde; Central African Republic; Chad; Chile; China; Colombia; Congo; Costa Rica; Cuba; Czechoslovakia; Dominica; Dominican Republic; Ecuador; Egypt; El Salvador; Equatorial Guinea; Ethiopia; Finland; Gabon; German Democratic Republic; Germany, Federal Republic of; Gibraltar; Grenada; Guatemala; Guinea; Guinea Bissau; Haiti; Honduras; Hong Kong; Hungary; Indonesia; Iran; Iraq; Israel; Ivory Coast; Japan; Jordan; Korea; Kuwait; Laos; Lebanon; Liberia; Libya; Madagascar; Mali; Mauritania; Mexico; Mongolia; Morocco; Mozambique; Nepal; Nicaragua; Niger; Oman; Pakistan; Panama; Paraguay; Peru; Philippines; Poland; Qatar; Romania; Rwanda; St. Lucia; St. Vincent and the Grenadines; Saudi Arabia; Senegal; Somali Democratic Republic; South Africa; Sudan; Sweden; Switzerland; Syria; Thailand; Togo; Tunisia; Turkey; United Arab Emirates; Upper Volta; Uruguay; U.S.A.; U.S.S.R.; Venezuela; Vietnam; Yemen Arab Republic; Yemen, People's Democratic Republic of; Yugoslavia; Zaire.

WORK AND BUSINESS OVERSEAS

A passport issued after December 31, 1982 showing the holder's national status as British citizen will secure for the holder the right to take employment or to establish himself in business or other self-employed activity in another member state of the European Community (except Greece). A passport bearing the endorsement "holder has the right of abode in the United Kingdom" where the holder so qualifies will also secure the same right. Employment permits are required in most other countries, even for casual labour. The nearest representative of the country concerned should be consulted. Local Employment Offices have a booklet entitled "Working abroad".

Those planning to travel abroad on export business are advised to contact the Overseas Trade Division of the Department of Trade and Industry, 1 Victoria Street, London S.W.1 or the Export Section of Regional Offices in London E.C.4, Birmingham, Bristol, Leeds, Manchester, Newcastle upon Tyne and Nottingham. For Wales: Welsh Office Industry Department, Block 2, Government Buildings, Gabalfa, Cardiff; for Scotland: Export Office for Scotland, Scottish Economic Planning Department, Alhambra House, 45 Waterloo Street, Glasgow; for Northern Ireland: Northern Ireland Department of Commerce, Chichester House, 64 Chichester Street, Belfast. These offices will send advance notification of the visit to the Commercial Section of the relevant Consulate or Embassy, and can offer advice and information about the markets to be visited.

VACCINATION

In very general terms vaccination for protection against cholera, typhoid and polio are recommended for all countries outside Europe, except North America, Australia and New Zealand. Protection, in the form of tablets, is advised for malaria similarly.

Vaccination against yellow fever is essential for entry into Benin, Cameroon, Central African Republic, Congo, French Guiana, Gambia, Ivory Coast, Mali, Mauritania, Niger, Nigeria, Sao Tome and Principe, Senegal, Uganda and Upper Volta, and is recommended for most other African and South American countries. Fuller details are set out in D.H.S.S. leaflet SA 35 "Protect your health abroad". For up-to-date information about vaccination requirements, contact one of the following health departments: *England*—International Relations Division, D.H.S.S., Alexander Fleming House, Elephant and Castle, London SE1 6BY (01-407 5522 ext. 6749); Communicable Disease Surveillance Centre, 61 Colindale Avenue, London NW9 5EQ (01-200 6868); *Wales*—Welsh Office, Cathays Park, Cardiff CF1 3NQ (0222-825111 ext. 3395); *Scotland*—Scottish Home and Health Department, St. Andrew's House, Edinburgh EH1 3DE (031-5568501 ext. 2438); *Northern Ireland*—D.H.S.S., Dundonald House, Upper Newtownards Road, Belfast BT4 3SF (0232-63939 ext. 2593).

Your doctor should be consulted six to eight weeks before departure, and will advise you and arrange vaccinations. If children will be travelling outside Europe, North America, Australia and New Zealand the doctor should be informed, especially if they have not completed their full course of childhood immunization.

Details of free or reduced cost medical treatment when visiting other European countries, Hong Kong or New Zealand are set out in leaflet SA 30 "Medical costs abroad", available from travel agents, local social security offices or the D.H.S.S. Leaflets Unit, P.O. Box 21, Stanmore, Middx.

VEHICLE LICENCES, ETC.

From October 1, 1974, registration and first licensing of vehicles has been done through local offices (known as Local Vehicle Licensing Offices) of the Department of Transport's Driver and Vehicle Licensing Centre in Swansea. The records of existing vehicles are held at Swansea. Local facilities for relicensing are available as follows:—

  (i) with a licence reminder (form V11) in person at any Post Office which deals with vehicle licensing or post it to the Head Post Office, shown on the form.
  (ii) with a vehicle licence application (form V10) either in person at any "licensing" Post Office if you have the Registration Document or post it to the Head Postmaster at one of the Head Post Offices listed on the back of the V10. If you do not have the Registration Document only, apply to a Local Vehicle Licensing Office, not to D.V.L.C.

Details of the present duties chargeable on motor vehicles are available at Post Offices and Local Vehicle Licensing Offices. The Vehicles (Excise) Act, 1971 provides *inter alia* that any vehicle kept on a public road but not used on roads is chargeable to excise duty as if it were in use.

Rates of duty for motor car and motor cycle licences are shown below. For Hackney Carriages the rates of duty are: Hackney Carriage with seating capacity not exceeding 20 persons, £45·00; additional for each person above 20 (excluding the driver) for which the vehicle has seating capacity, 90p.

Type of Vehicle	Exceeding	Not Exceeding	12 Months	6 Months
MOTOR CARS			£	£
Those first registered before January 1, 1947	—	—	60·00	33·00
Other than above	—	—	90·00	49·50
MOTOR CYCLES				
With or without sidecar	—	150 c.c.	9·00	—
With or without sidecar	150 c.c.	250 c.c.	18·00	—
With or without sidecar	250 c.c.	—	36·00	19·80
If first licensed before 1 Jan. 1933 and weighs not more than 101·6 kgs.	250 c.c.	—	17·00	—
THREE WHEELERS				
Other than pedestrian-controlled	—	150 c.c.	9·00	—
Other than pedestrian-controlled	150 c.c.	—	36·00	19·80
PEDESTRIAN-CONTROLLED VEHICLES (Other than mowing machines)				
Three wheeled	—	150 c.c.	9·00	—
Three wheeled	150 c.c.	—	18·00	—
More than three wheels	—	—	18·00	—

Driving Licences—Fees

	On or after 1.10.82		On or after 1.10.82
FULL LICENCE		(iii) Issued after 1.1.76 not being an	
First full licence	£10·00*	Exchange licence and no additional entitlement claimed ...	Free
Renewal of full licence if last full licence was:		PROVISIONAL LICENCE	
(i) Issued before 1.1.76	£10·00*	First provisional licence	£10·00*
(ii) Issued after 1.1.76 and additional entitlement claimed ...	£3.00	DUPLICATE LICENCE	£3·00
		EXCHANGE LICENCE	£3·00

* Once you have paid £10 for *either* a provisional *or* a full licence all renewals are free except where additional entitlement is required.

Driving Test–Fees

For cars	£14·40
For motor cycles, part I	£17·95*
part II	£14·40

*When conducted by the Department of Transport. Appointed motor cycle training organisations, who conduct the majority of part I tests within the framework of their own training courses, are free to set their own fee.

Driving tests for invalid carriages are free.

M.o.T. Testing

Cars, motor cycles, motor caravans, light goods and dual-purpose vehicles which are more than three years old must be covered by an effective vehicle test certificate (often called the M.o.T. certificate). Copies of the legislation governing M.o.T. testing can be obtained from any H.M.S.O. bookshop or bookshops which stock H.M.S.O. publications. The legislation comprises The Road Traffic Act 1972 (Sections 44 and 45), The Motor Vehicles (Test) Regulations 1981, The Motor Vehicles (Extension) Order 1981, and The Motor Vehicles (Production of Test Certificate) Regulations 1969.

HALLMARKS ON GOLD, SILVER AND PLATINUM WARES
London (Goldsmiths' Hall) Date Letters
From 1498

	Style	Period		Style	Period
	Black letter, small	1498–9 to 1517–8		Roman letter, small	1739–40 to 1755–6
	Lombardic	1518–9 ,, 1537–8		Old English, capitals ..	1756–7 to 1775–6
	Roman and other capitals	1538–9 ,, 1557–8		Roman letter, small ...	1776–7 ,, 1795–6
	Black letter, small	1558–9 ,, 1577–8		Roman letter, capitals .	1796–7 ,, 1815–6
	Roman letter, capitals	1578–9 ,, 1597–8		Roman letter, small ...	1816–7 ,, 1835–6
	Lombardic, external cusps	1598–9 ,, 1617–8		Old English, capitals ..	1836–7 ,, 1855–6
	Italic letter, small	1618–9 ,, 1637–8		Old English, small	1856–7 ,, 1875–6
	Court hand	1638–9 ,, 1657–8		Roman letter, capitals [A to M *square* shield N to Z as shown]	1876–7 ,, 1895–6
	Black letter, capitals ..	1658–9 ,, 1677–8		Roman letter, small ...	1896–7 ,, 1915–6
	Black letter, small	1678–9 ,, 1696–7		Black letter, small	1916–7 ,, 1935–6
	Court hand	1697 ,, 1715–6		Roman letter, capitals .	1936–7 ,, 1955–6
	Roman letter, capitals	1716–7 ,, 1735–6		Italic letter, small	1956–7 ,, 1974
	Roman letter, small ...	1736–7 ,, 1738–9		Italic letter, capitals ..	1975 ,, ...

Hallmarks are the symbols stamped on gold, silver, or platinum articles to indicate that they have been chemically tested and that they conform to one of the legal standards. With certain exceptions, all gold, silver, or platinum articles are required by law to be hallmarked before they are offered for sale. Hallmarking was instituted in 1300 under a statute of Edward I.

Normally a complete modern hallmark consists of four symbols—the maker's mark or sponsor's mark, assay office mark, standard mark and date letter.

Additional marks have been authorized from time to time.

Maker's Mark.—Instituted in 1363, the maker's mark was originally a device such as a bird or *fleur-de-lys* and now consists invariably of the initials of the Christian and surnames of the maker or sponsor, or of the firm.

Assay Office Mark.—The existing assay offices and their distinguishing marks are:—

LONDON (Goldsmiths' Hall).
A leopard's head (uncrowned from 1300 to 1478–9, when it became crowned until 1821, since when it has been uncrowned). From 1697 to 1974 a lion's head erased was used on silver of the higher (Britannia) standard.

BIRMINGHAM (Newhall Street).........An anchor
SHEFFIELD (137 Portobello Street) ....A rose
EDINBURGH (Goldsmiths' Hall, 15 Queen Street)
                                          A castle

Offices formerly existed in other towns, *e.g.* Chester, Glasgow, Newcastle, Exeter, York and Norwich, each having its own distinguishing mark.

Standard Mark.—Instituted in 1544. The current legal standards and their marks are as follows:—

                                          PLATINUM

SILVER.—Sterling silver (92·5 per cent. silver) is marked by English assay offices with a *lion passant* and by the Edinburgh Assay Office with a *lion rampant*. A full-length figure of *Britannia* was impressed on silver of a higher standard (95·84 per cent. silver) between 1697 and 1720 and this mark is still used occasionally by all British assay offices.

GOLD.—Since 1975 gold articles are marked with a crown followed by the millesimal figure for the standard, i.e. 916 for 22 carat, 750 for 18 carat, 585 for 14 carat and 375 for 9 carat.

Date Letter.—Instituted in 1478. The date letter denotes the year in which an article was assayed and hallmarked. Each alphabetical cycle has a distinctive style of lettering or shape of shield. The date letters were different at the various assay offices and the particular office must be established from the assay office mark before reference is made to tables of date letters. Specimen shields and letters used by the London Office on silver articles in each period from 1498 to date are shown on the previous page. The same letters are found on gold articles but the surrounding shield may differ.

OTHER MARKS

Duty Mark.—In 1784 an additional mark of the reigning sovereign's head was introduced to signify that the excise duty had been paid. The mark became obsolete on the abolition of the duty in 1890.

Commemorative Marks.—There are three other marks to commemorate special events, the Silver Jubilee of King George V and Queen Mary in 1935, the Coronation of Queen Elizabeth II in 1953 and her Silver Jubilee in 1977.

Foreign Wares.—Since 1842 foreign wares imported into Great Britain have been required to be hallmarked before sale. The marks consist of the importer's mark, a special assay office mark (*see below*), the figures denoting fineness and the annual date letter. The current assay office marks for foreign wares are as follows:—

LONDON.—The sign of the Constellation Leo.
BIRMINGHAM.—Equilateral triangle.
SHEFFIELD.—The sign of the Constellation Libra.
EDINBURGH.—St. Andrew's Cross.

Special marks at authorised Assay Offices of the signatory countries of the International Convention—United Kingdom, Austria, Finland, Ireland, Portugal, Norway, Sweden and Switzerland—are legally recognised in the United Kingdom as approved hallmarks. These marks consist of a Sponsor's Mark, a Common Control Mark, a Fineness Mark (arabic numerals showing the standard in parts per thousand) and an Assay Office Mark. There is no date letter.

CLOSE SEASONS AND TIMES

Hunting and Ground Game.—There is no statutory close-time for fox-hunting or rabbit-shooting, nor for hares: but by an Act passed in 1892 the *sale* of hares or leverets in Great Britain is prohibited from March 1 to July 31 inclusive under a penalty of a pound. The First of November is the recognized date for the opening of the *fox-hunting* season, which continues till the following April.

Deer.—The table below shows the statutory close seasons for deer (all dates inclusive).

Species	Sex	England and Wales	Scotland
RED	M.	1 May–31 July	21 Oct.–30 June
	F.	1 Mar.–31 Oct.	16 Feb.–20 Oct.
FALLOW	M.	1 May–31 July	1 May–31 July
	F.	1 Mar.–31 Oct.	16 Feb.–20 Oct.
SIKA	M.	1 May–31 July	21 Oct.–30 June
	F.	1 Mar.–31 Oct.	16 Feb.–20 Oct.
ROE	M.	1 Nov.–31 Mar.	21 Oct.–31 Mar.
	F.	1 Mar.–31 Oct.	1 Apr.–20 Oct.
RED/SIKA HYBRIDS	M.		21 Oct.–30 June
	F.		16 Feb.–20 Oct.

Wild Birds.—The *Wildlife and Countryside Act*, 1981, lays down a close season for wild birds (other than Game Birds) from February 1 to August 31 inclusive, each year. Exceptions to these dates are made for—
Capercaillie and (except Scotland) *Woodcock*, Feb. 1—Sept. 30.
Snipe, Feb. 1—Aug. 11.
Wild Duck and *Wild Goose* (below high water mark), Feb. 21—Aug. 31.
Birds which may be killed or taken outside the close season (except on Sundays and on Christmas Day in Scotland, and on Sundays in prescribed areas of England and Wales) are the above and coot, certain wild duck (gadwall, goldeneye, mallard, pintail, pochard, shoveler, teal, tufted duck, wigeon), certain wild geese (Canada, greylag, pink-footed, white-fronted (in England and Wales only)), moorhen, golden plover and woodcock.
Certain wild birds may be killed or taken at any time by authorized persons—crow, collared dove, gull (great and lesser black-backed or herring), jackdaw, jay, magpie, pigeon (feral or wood), rook, sparrow and starling.

Game Birds.—In each case the dates are inclusive:—
Black Game—Dec. 11 to Aug. 19 (Aug. 31 in Somerset, Devon, and New Forest).
Grouse—Dec. 11 to Aug. 11.
Partridge—Feb. 2 to Aug. 31.

Pheasant—Feb. 2 to Sept. 30.
Ptarmigan—(Scotland only) Dec. 11 to Aug. 11.

It is also unlawful (in *England* and *Wales*) to kill the game marked * on a Sunday or Christmas Day.

All other British birds are fully protected by law throughout the year.

Angling.—Close seasons (dates inclusive) are: *Coarse fishing.*—Yorkshire, last day in Feb. to May 31; South West, none; rest of country, March 15 to June 15. *Game fishing.*—Trout, Oct. 1 to last day of Feb.*; Salmon, Nov. 1 to Jan. 31*.

* The above dates are statutory close times. Particularly with salmon, migratory trout and trout, close seasons vary in accordance with water authority local by-laws. In all cases, it is best to check with the water authority concerned.

PROTECTED SPECIES:—The following are protected animals under the provision of the *Wildlife and Countryside Act*, 1981:—

Bat (all species of the horseshoe and the typical bat), rainbow leaf beetle, burbot, butterfly (chequered skipper, heath fritillary, large blue, swallowtail), cricket (field, mole), dolphin (bottle-nosed, common), Norfolk aeshna dragonfly, wart-biter grasshopper, sand lizard, moth (barberry carpet, black-veined, Essex emerald, New Forest burnet, reddish buff), great-crested newt, common otter, harbour porpoise, snail (Carthusian, glutinous, sandbowl), smooth snake, spider (fen raft, ladybird), red squirrel, natter-jack toad.

It is illegal to buy or sell the following:—adder, common frog, viviparous lizard, newt (palmate, smooth), slow-worm, grass snake, common toad.

THE COUNTRY CODE:—The following are the points of The Country Code, issued by the Countryside Commission:

(a) Enjoy the countryside and respect its life and work; (b) Guard against all risks of fire; (c) Fasten all gates; (d) Keep your dogs under close control; (e) Keep to public paths across farmland; (f) Use gates and stiles to cross fences, hedges and walls; (g) Leave livestock, crops and machinery alone; (h) Take your litter home; (i) Help to keep all water clean; (j) Protect wildlife, plants and trees; (k) Take special care on country roads; (l) Make no unnecessary noise.

INSOLVENCY

Bankruptcies, etc. (England and Wales)

	1975	1976	1977	1978	1979	1980	1981	1982
Number of bankruptcies, etc.								
Debtors adjudicated bankrupt	6,676	6,681	4,078	3,526	3,158	3,634	4,730	5,303
Compositions and schemes of arrangement	2	—	2	—	1	7	3	2
Administration orders of deceased debtors' estates	20	19	15	14	11	11	11	14
Liabilities (£ thousand)								
Debtors adjudicated bankrupt	81,553	76,692	104,674	205,809	65,805	68,580	169,608	210,615
Compositions and schemes of arrangement	13	—	11	—	18	116	46	39
Administration orders of deceased debtors' estates	2,718	1,517	774	427	532	421	573	380
Assets (£ thousand)								
Debtors adjudicated bankrupt	21,215	22,300	15,834	20,093	21,768	39,327	39,433	34,464
Compositions and schemes of arrangement	6	—	3	—	8	75	63	43
Administration orders of deceased debtors' estates	543	212	319	145	124	155	166	135

Sequestrations (Bankruptcies) in Scotland

	1975	1976	1977	1978	1979	1980	1981	1982
Number of sequestrations	89	80	76	80	66	111	117	144
Liabilities (£ thousand)	3,461	3,171	3,213	4,338	2,470	4,843	12,266	9,757
Assets (£ thousand)	1,513	1,305	1,025	648	994	2,060	4,228	3,975

WEIGHTS AND MEASURES

The Weights and Measures Act of 1963 enacts the legal measures for Great Britain, basing them upon "United Kingdom primary standards" in the custody of the Standards Department of the Dept. of Trade. The primary standards are the yard, pound, metre and kilogramme. The GALLON, the capacity standard, wet or dry, is based upon the Pound. The Act of 1963 defines the GALLON as the space occupied by 10 pounds weight of distilled water of density 0·998 859 gramme per millilitre weighed in air of density 0·001 217 gramme per millilitre against weights of density 8·136 grammes per millilitre. The METRE and the LITRE have the meanings assigned by order of the Dept. of Trade to reproduce in English the international definition of these measures in force at the time of making of the orders.

New definitions for an *international yard* and *pound* were adopted on Jan. 1, 1959, by the standards laboratories of the United Kingdom, Canada, Australia, New Zealand, South Africa and the United States: *international yard* = 0·914 4 metre.				*international pound* = 0·453 592 37 kilogramme.

The following list shows the definitions of measures set out in the Weights and Measures Act, 1963 and some useful conversions.

Measurement of Length

Imperial Units

Mile = 1,760 yards.	1 mil = 1/1000 inch.
Furlong = 220 yards.	12 inches (*in.*) = 1 foot (*ft.*).
Chain = 22 yards.	3 feet = 1 yard (*yd.*).
YARD = 0·914 4 metre.	6 feet = 1 fathom.
Foot″ = ⅓ yard.	22 yards = 1 chain = 100 links.
Inch″ = 1/36 yard.	10 chains = 1 furlong.
	8 furlongs = 1 mile = 1,760 yards.

Metric Units

Kilometre = 1,000 metres.	10 millimetres (*mm.*) = 1 centimetre (*cm.*) = 0·393 701 inch.
METRE (*see above*) = 1·094 yards.	10 centimetres = 1 decimetre (*dm.*) = 3·937 011 inches.
Decimetre = 1/10 metre.	10 decimetres = 1 METRE (*m.*) = 1·093 614 yards.
Centimetre = 1/100 metre.	10 metres = 1 dekametre (*dam.*) = 10·936 143 yards.
Millimetre = 1/1000 metre.	10 dekametres = 1 hectometre (*hm.*) = 109·361 43 yards.
	10 hectometres = 1 kilometre (*km.*) = 0·621 371 mile.

A kilometre is approximately *five-eighths* of a mile, so that 8 kilometres may be regarded as 5 miles.

Measurement of Area

Imperial Units

Square mile = 640 acres.	144 sq. inches = 1 sq. foot.
Acre = 4,840 square yards.	9 sq. feet = 1 sq. yard.
Rood = 1,210 square yards.	4 roods = 1 acre.
SQUARE YARD = a superficial area equal to that of a square each side of which measures one yard.	10 square chains = 1 acre = 4,840 sq. yards.
	640 acres = 1 square mile.
Square foot = 1/9 square yard.	
Square inch = 1/144 square foot.	

Metric Units

Hectare = 100 ares.	1 sq. centimetre = 0·155 sq. inch.
Dekare = 10 ares.	1 sq. METRE = 10·763 9 sq. feet = 1·195 99 sq. yds.
Are = 100 square metres.	1 are (*a.*) = 0·098 8 rood.
SQUARE METRE = a superficial area equal to that of a square each side of which measures one metre.	1 hectare (10,000 sq. metres) (*ha.*) = 2·471 05 acres.
	1 sq. kilometre = 0·386 102 sq. mile.
Square decimetre = 1/100 square metre.	
Square centimetre = 1/100 square decimetre.	
Square millimetre = 1/100 square centimetre.	

Measurement of Volume

Imperial Units

CUBIC YARD = a volume equal to that of a cube each edge of which measures one yard.	1,728 cubic inches = 1 cubic foot.
	27 cubic feet = 1 cubic yard.
Cubic foot = 1/27 cubic yard.	
Cubic inch = 1/1728 cubic foot.	

Metric Units

CUBIC METRE = a volume equal to that of a cube each edge of which measures one metre.	1 cubic metre (*cbm.* or *m³.*) = 35·314 7 cu. ft. = 1·307 95 cu. yds.
Cubic decimetre = 1/1000 cubic metre.	(1 stere (= 1 cu. metre) is used as a unit of measurement of timber.)
Cubic centimetre = 1/1000 cubic decimetre.	1 cubic cm. (water) = 1 gram; 1,000 cubic cm. (water) or 1 litre = 1 kilogram; 1 metric metre (1,000 litres, 1,000 kilograms) = 1 metric ton.

Measurement of Capacity

Imperial Units

GALLON (*see above*).	4 gills = 1 pint.
Quart = ¼ gallon.	2 pints = 1 quart.
Pint = ½ quart.	4 quarts = 1 GALLON.
Gill = ¼ pint.	1 gallon = 160 fluid ounces.
Fluid ounce = 1/20 pint.	= 277·274 cubic inches.

Bushel = 8 gallons.	2 gallons = 1 peck.	1 hectolitre = 2·749 69 bushels.
Peck = 2 gallons.	4 pecks = 1 bushel.	1 hectolitre per hectare = 1·11 bushels per acre.
	8 bushels = 1 quarter.	1 quintal = 3·674 3 bushels.
	A chaldron is 36 bushels = 4½ quarters.	1 quintal per hectare = 1·49 bushels per acre.

Fluid drachm = ⅛ fluid ounce.
Minim = 1/60 fluid drachm.

See Apothecaries' Weight (*below*).

Metric Units
Hectolitre = 100 litres.
LITRE = The volume occupied by the mass of 1 kilogramme of pure water at its temperature of maximum density and under a pressure of one standard atmosphere (14·696 lb. per sq. inch).
Decilitre = 1/10 litre.
Centilitre = 1/100 litre.
Millilitre = 1/1000 litre.

1 centilitre (*cl.*) = 0·070 4 gill.
1 LITRE (1/1,000 cubic metre) (*lit.*) = 1·759 8 pints = 0·88 Imp. quart = 80·22 Imp. gallon = 61·025 5 cu. inch = 0·035 315 7 cu. ft.
1 hectolitre (*hl.*) = 21·997 5 Imp. gallons = 26·417 1 U.S. gallons = 2·749 Imp. bushels = 2·837 7 U.S. bushels.

Measurement of Mass or Weight

Imperial Units
Ton = 2,240 pounds.
Hundredweight = 112 pounds.
Cental = 100 pounds.
Quarter = 28 pounds.
Stone = 14 pounds.
POUND = 0·453 592 37 kilogram.
Ounce = 1/16 pound.
Dram = 1/16 ounce.
Grain = 1/7,000 pound.

7,000 grains (*gr.*) = 1 pound (*lb.*).
16 drams (*dr.*) = 1 ounce (*oz.*).
16 ounces = 1 POUND (*lb.*).
14 pounds = 1 stone.
28 pounds = 1 quarter (of a *cwt.*).
4 quarters (112 *lb.*) = 1 hundredweight (*cwt.*).
20 hundredweight (2,240 *lb.*) = 1 ton.

20 pennyweights (*dwt.*) = 1 Troy ounce.

Ounce Troy = 480 grains
Pennyweight = 24 grains

For gold and silver the ounce, divided decimally, and *not* into grains, is the sole unit of weight. The Troy ounce is the same as the Apothecaries' ounce = 480 Avoirdupois grains (31·1035 *Grammes*) in weight. A Troy POUND (= 5,760 grains) is legalized in the United States.

Ounce apothecaries' = 480 grains.
Drachm = ⅛ ounce apothecaries.
Scruple = ⅓ drachm.

See Apothecaries' Weight (*below*)

Metric Units
Metric ton = 1,000 kilograms.
Quintal = 100 kilograms.

1 milligram (*mg.*) = 0·015 432 grains.
1 centigram (*cg.*) = 0·154 32 grains.
1 decigram (*dg.*) = 1·543 2 grains.
1 gramme (*grm.*) = 15·432 4 grains.
1 dekagram (*dag.*) = 5·643 8 drams.
1 hectogram (*hg.*) = 3·527 4 oz.
1 KILOGRAM (*kg.*) = 32·150 7 oz. Troy = 35·273 4 oz. Avoirdupois = 2·204 62 lb. Avoirdupois.
1 myriagram = 22·046 2 lb. Avoirdupois.
1 quintal (*q.*) = 100 kg. = 220·5 lb. Avoirdupois = 1·968 4 cwt.
1 tonne (*t.*) = 0·984 207 U.K. or long ton = 1·102 31 U.S. or short ton

Measurement of Electricity

Units of measurement of electricity, the AMPERE (unit of electrical current), the OHM (unit of electrical resistance), the VOLT (unit of difference of electrical potential) and the WATT (unit of electrical power) have the meanings assigned to them respectively by order of the Dept. of Trade, to reproduce in English the international definitions in force at the date of the making of the order.

Kilowatt = 1,000 watts.　　Megawatt = 1,000,000 watts.

Apothecaries' Weight

Measures of Weight.
20 grains　　= 1 scruple (℈1).
3 scruples　= 1 drachm (ʒ1).
8 drachms　= 1 ounce.

Measures of Capacity.
60 minims (*min.*)　= 1 fluid drachm.
8 fluid drachms　= 1 fluid ounce.
5 fluid ounces　= 1 gill.
4 gills　= 1 pint.
8 pints　= 1 GALLON.

The Apothecaries' grain is the Avoirdupois grain, and the Apothecaries' ounce is the Troy ounce, of 480 grains. The Apothecaries' *drachm* is not the same as the Avoirdupois *dram*, and is spelled differently. A fluid ounce of distilled water at a temperature of 62° Fahrenheit is equal in weight to the Avoirdupois ounce (437·5 grains). A fluid *drachm* (54·6875 grains) is equal in weight to TWO Avoirdupois *drams*.

Angular or Circular Measure

60 seconds (″) = 1 minute (′).
60 minutes = 1 degree (°).

90 degrees = 1 right angle or quadrant.
Diameter of circle × 3·141 6 = circumference.
Diameter squared × ·7854 = area of circle.
Diameter squared × 3·141 6 = surface of sphere.
Diameter cubed × ·523 = solidity of sphere.
One degree of circumference × 57·3 = radius.*
Diameter of cylinder × 3·141 6; product by length or height, gives the surface.
Diameter squared × ·7854; product by length or height, gives solid content.
* Or, one radian (the angle subtended at the centre of a circle by an arc of the circumference equal in length to the radius) = 57·3 degrees, nearly.
Note.—A circle of 7 yards diameter has, in practice, a circumference of 22 yards = 1 chain.

Water Measures

Cubic inch .... = 252·458 grains.
Gallon (277·274 cu. in.) .... = 10 lb. (distilled).
Cubic foot .... = 62·321 lb.
35·943 cubic ft. (224 gals.) .. = 1 ton.
Water for Ships: Tun, 210 gals., Butt 110, Puncheon 72, Barrel 36, Kilderkin 18 gals.

THERMOMETER COMPARISONS

Comparison between Scales of Fahrenheit, Réaumur and Centigrade

CENT.	FAH'T.	RMR.	CENT.	FAH'T.	RMR.
°	°	°	°	°	°
100B.	212B.	80B.	25	77	20
99	210·2	79·2	24	75·2	19·2
98	208·4	78·4	23	73·4	18·4
97	206·6	77·6	22	71·6	17·6
96	204·8	76·8	21	69·8	16·8
95	203	76	20	68	16
94	201·2	75·2	19	66·2	15·2
93	199·4	74·4	18	64·4	14·4
92	197·6	73·6	17	62·6	13·6
91	195·8	72·8	16	60·8	12·8
90	194	72	15	59	12
89	192·2	71·2	14	57·2	11·2
88	190·4	70·4	13	55·4	10·4
87	188·6	69·6	12	53·6	9·6
86	186·8	68·8	11	51·8	8·8
85	185	68	10	50	8
84	183·2	67·2	9	48·2	7·2
83	181·4	66·4	8	46·4	6·4
82	179·6	65·6	7	44·6	5·6
81	177·8	64·8	6	42·8	4·8
80	176	64	5	41	4
79	174·2	63	4	39·2	3·2
78	172·4	62·4	3	37·4	2·4
77	170·6	61·6	2	35·6	1·6
76	168·8	60·8	1	33·8	0·8
75	167	60	*zero*	32	*zero*
74	165·2	59·2	1	30·2	0·8
73	163·4	58·4	2	28·4	1·6
72	161·6	57·6	3	26·6	2·4
71	159·8	56·8	4	24·8	3·2
70	158	56	5	23	4
69	156·2	55·2	6	21·2	4·8
68	154·4	54·4	7	19·4	5·6
67	152·6	53·6	8	17·6	6·4
66	150·8	52·8	9	15·8	7·2
65	149	52	10	14	8
64	147·2	51·2	11	12·2	8·8
63	145·4	50·4	12	10·4	9·6
62	143·6	49·6	13	8·6	10·4
61	141·8	48·8	14	6·8	11·2
60	140	48	15	5	12
59	138·2	47·2	16	3·2	12·8
58	136·4	46·4	17	1·4	13·6
57	134·6	45·6	18	0·4	14·4
56	132·8	44·8	19	2·2	15·2
55	131	44	20	4	16
54	129·2	43·2	21	5·8	16·8
53	127·4	42·4	22	7·6	17·6
52	125·6	41·6	23	9·3	18·4
51	123·8	40·8	24	11·2	19·2
50	122	40	25	13	20
49	120·2	39·2	26	14·8	20·8
48	118·4	38·4	27	16·6	21·6
47	116·6	37·6	28	18·4	22·4
46	114·8	36·8	29	20·2	23·2
45	113	36	30	22	24
44	111·2	35·2	31	23·8	24·8
43	109·4	34·4	32	25·6	25·6
42	107·6	33·6	33	27·4	26·4
41	105·8	32·8	34	29·2	27·2
40	104	32	35	31	28
39	102·2	31·2	36	32·8	28·8
38	100·4	30·4	37	34·6	29·6
37	98·6	29·6	38	36·4	30·4
36	96·8	28·8	39	38·2	31·2
35	95	28	40	40	32
34	93·2	27·2	41	41·8	32·8
33	91·4	26·4	42	43·6	33·6
32	89·6	25·6	43	45·4	34·4
31	87·8	24·8	44	47·2	35·2
30	86	24	45	49	36
29	84·2	23·2	46	50·8	36·8
28	82·4	22·4	47	52·6	37·6
27	80·6	21·6	48	54·4	38·4
26	78·8	20·8	49	56·2	39·2

CONVERSION: Let F = Fahr., C = Cent., R = Réaum.

$$F = C + R + 32$$

$$*F = \frac{9C}{5} + 32 \qquad F = \frac{9R}{4} + 32$$

$$C = 5\frac{(F-32)}{9} \qquad R = \frac{4(F-32)}{9}$$

NOTE.—The *normal* temperature of the *human body* is 98·4°F., or 37° (36·9°) C., or 29·5° R. *Freezing* point = 32°F. = 0°C. = 0°R.; *Boiling* point = 212° F. = 100° C. = 80° R.

"*Absolute*" Temperature is Temperature reckoned from "*Absolute Zero*," which is at 273° C. below 0° C., 459·4° below 0° F., and 218·4° below 0° R. and is denoted by the letter "K."

* Below 32° F. *subtract* 32.

An *Inch of Rain* on the surface of an acre (43,560 sq. feet) = 3,630 cubic feet = 100·992 tons.

Cisterns: A cistern 4 feet by 2½ and 3 deep will hold brimful 186·963 gallons, weighing 16 cwt. 2 qrs. 21·6 lbs. in addition to its own weight.

Million, Billion, etc.

Value in the United Kingdom

Million	thousand × thousand (10^6)
Billion	million × million (10^{12})
Trillion	million × billion (10^{18})
Quadrillion	million × trillion (10^{24})

Value in U.S.A.

Million	thousand × thousand (10^6)
Billion	thousand × million (10^9)
Trillion	million × million (10^{12})
Quadrillion	million × billion U.S. (10^{15})

United Kingdom (and other European) usage above follows the decision of the 9th Gen. Conference on Weights and Measures, 1948.

PAPER AND BOOK MEASURES

Writing Paper	*Printing Paper*
480 sheets = 1 ream	516 sheets = 1 ream
24 sheets = 1 quire	2 reams = 1 bundle
20 quires = 1 ream	5 bundles = 1 bale

Sizes of Writing and Drawing Papers

Emperor	=	72 × 48	inches
Antiquarian	=	53 × 31	,,
Double Elephant	=	40 × 26¾	,,
Grand Eagle	=	42 × 28¾	,,
Atlas	=	34 × 26	,,
Colombier	=	34½ × 23½	,,
Imperial	=	30 × 22	,,
Elephant	=	28 × 23	,,
Cartridge	=	26 × 21	,,
Super Royal	=	27 × 19	,,
Royal	=	24 × 19	,,
Medium	=	22 × 17½	,,
Large Post	=	21 × 16½	,,
Copy or Draft	=	20 × 16	,,
Demy	=	20 × 15½	,,
Post	=	19 × 15¼	,,
Pinched Post	=	18½ × 14¾	,,
Foolscap	=	17 × 13½	,,
Sheet and ⅓ Foolscap	=	22 × 13½	,,
Sheet and ½ Foolscap	=	24½ × 13½	,,
Double Foolscap	=	26½ × 16½	,,
Double Post	=	30½ × 19	,,
Double Large Post	=	33 × 21	,,
Double Demy	=	31 × 20	,,
Brief	=	16½ × 13¼	,,
Pott	=	15 × 12½	,,

Sizes of Printing Papers

Foolscap	=	17 × 13½	inches
Double Foolscap	=	27 × 17	,,
Crown	=	20 × 15	,,
Double Crown	=	30 × 20	,,
Quad Crown	=	40 × 30	,,
Double Quad Crown	=	60 × 40	,,
Post	=	19¼ × 15½	,,
Double Post	=	31½ × 19½	,,
Double Large Post	=	33 × 21	,,
Sheet and ½ Post	=	23½ × 19½	,,
Demy	=	22½ × 17½	,,
Double Demy	=	35 × 22½	,,
Quad Demy	=	45 × 35	,,
Music Demy	=	20 × 15½	,,
Medium	=	23 × 18	,,
Royal	=	25 × 20	,,
Super Royal	=	27½ × 20½	,,
Elephant	=	28 × 23	,,
Imperial	=	30 × 22	,,

Sizes of Brown Papers

Casing	=	46 × 36	inches
Double Imperial	=	45 × 29	,,
Elephant	=	34 × 24	,,
Double Four Pound	=	31 × 21	,,
Imperial Cap	=	29 × 22	,,
Haven Cap	=	26 × 21	,,
Bag Cap	=	24 × 19½	,,
Kent Cap	=	21 × 18	,,

Sizes of Bound Books

Demy 16mo	=	5⅝ × 4⅜	inches
Demy 18mo	=	5¾ × 3¾	,,
Foolscap Octavo (8vo)	=	6¾ × 4¼	,,
Crown 8vo	=	7½ × 5	,,
Large Crown 8vo	=	8 × 5¼	,,
Demy 8vo	=	8¾ × 5⅝	,,
Medium 8vo	=	9½ × 6	,,
Royal 8vo	=	10 × 6¼	,,
Super Royal 8vo	=	10¼ × 6⅞	,,
Imperial 8vo	=	11 × 7½	,,
Foolscap Quarto (4to)	=	8½ × 6¾	,,
Crown 4to	=	10 × 7½	,,
Demy 4to	=	11¼ × 8¾	,,
Royal 4to	=	12½ × 10	,,
Imperial 4to	=	15 × 11	,,
Crown Folio	=	15 × 10	,,
Demy Folio	=	17½ × 11¼	,,
Royal Folio	=	20 × 12½	,,
Music	=	14 × 10¼	,,

NOTE.—*Folio* means a sheet folded in half, *quarto* folded into four, and so on; thus, a crown 8vo page is one-eighth the size of a crown sheet. Books are usually bound up in sheets of 16 or 32 pages. *Octavo* books are generally printed 64 pages at a time (32 pages on each side of a sheet of quad); a crown octavo book of 320 pages will therefore require 5 sheets of quad crown, or 10 reams per 1,000 copies, the odd 16 sheets in each ream being allowed as waste. Newspapers (and some books in editions of 50,000 or over) are printed on rotary presses, for which the paper is supplied in continuous reels.

INTERNATIONAL PAPER SIZES

Simplification of the large number of stock paper sizes in use in the United Kingdom has been proceeding since publication of British Standard 730 in 1937. Recommendations made by the International Organization for Standardization were accepted by the United Kingdom in 1959 and it is considered that general adoption of the international or A size will bring great economies to users of paper.

The basis of the international series of paper sizes is a rectangle having an area of one square metre, the sides of which are in the proportion of $1:\sqrt{2}$. In other words, taking one side as X and the other as Y, the basic size provides the equation—$X:Y=1:\sqrt{2}$; and $X \times Y = 1$. It may be noted that the proportions $1:\sqrt{2}$ have a geometrical relationship, the side and diagonal of any square being in this proportion. As the basic size is one square metre in area, this means that X=841 millimetres and Y=1,189 millimetres. The effect of this arrangement is that if the short side is doubled or the longer side is halved, *i.e.*, if the area of the sheet is doubled or halved, the shorter side and the longer side of the new sheet are still in the same proportion $1:\sqrt{2}$. This feature is particularly useful where photographic enlargement or reduction is used, as the proportions remain the same.

Description of the A series is by capital A followed by a figure. The basic size has the description A0 and the higher the figure following the letter, the greater is the number of sub-divisions and therefore the smaller the sheet. Half A0 is A1 and half A1 is A2. Where larger dimensions are required the A is *preceded* by a figure. Thus 2A means twice the size A0; 4A is four times the size of A0.

It is an essential feature of these series that the dimensions are of the trimmed or finished size.

'A' Series of Trimmed Sizes

Designation	SIZE	
	mm	inches
A0	841 × 1189	33·11 × 46·81
A1	594 × 841	23·39 × 33·11
A2	420 × 594	16·54 × 23·39
A3	297 × 420	11·69 × 16·54
A4	210 × 297	8·27 × 11·69
A5	148 × 210	5·83 × 8·27
A6	105 × 148	4·13 × 5·83
A7	74 × 105	2·91 × 4·13
A8	52 × 74	2·05 × 2·91
A9	37 × 52	1·46 × 2·05
A10	26 × 37	1·02 × 1·46

Subsidiary Series.—A series of B sizes has been devised for use in exceptional circumstances when sizes intermediate between any two adjacent sizes of the A series are needed.

'B' Series of Trimmed Sizes

Designation	SIZE	
	mm	inches
B0	1000 × 1414	39·37 × 55·67
B1	707 × 1000	27·83 × 39·37
B2	500 × 707	19·68 × 27·83
B3	353 × 500	13·90 × 19·68
B4	250 × 353	9·84 × 13·90
B5	176 × 250	6·93 × 9·84
B6	125 × 176	4·92 × 6·93
B7	88 × 125	3·46 × 4·92
B8	62 × 88	2·44 × 3·46
B9	44 × 62	1·73 × 2·44
B10	31 × 44	1·22 × 1·73

In addition there is a series of C sizes which is used much less. A is for magazines and books, B for posters, wall charts and other large items, C for envelopes particularly where it is necessary for an envelope (in C series) to fit into another envelope. The size recommended for business correspondence is A4.

Long Sizes.—Long sizes are obtainable by dividing any appropriate sizes from the two series above into three, four or eight equal parts parallel with the shorter side in such a manner that the proportions mentioned in paragraph 2 (above) are not maintained, the ratio between the longer and the shorter sides being greater than $\sqrt{2}:1$. In practice long sizes should be produced from the A series only.

THE NOBEL PRIZES

The Nobel Prizes are awarded each year from the income of a trust fund established by the Swedish scientist Alfred Nobel, the inventor of dynamite, who died on December 10, 1896, leaving a fortune of £1,750,000. They are awarded to those who have contributed most to the common good in the domain of (a) Physics; (b) Chemistry; (c) Physiology and Medicine; (d) Literature; (e) Peace. The first awards were made in 1901 on the fifth anniversary of Nobel's death. The awarding authorities are the Royal Swedish Academy of Sciences: (a) Physics—(b) Chemistry; the Royal Caroline Institute, Stockholm—(c) Physiology and Medicine; the Swedish Academy—(d) Literature; a committee of five persons elected by the Norwegian Storting—(e) Peace. The Trust is administered by the Board of Directors of the Nobel Foundation, Stockholm. The Board consists of five members and three deputy members. The Swedish Government appoints a chairman and a deputy chairman, the remaining members being appointed by the awarding authorities.

The nationality of prizewinners is indicated as follows: (a) Great Britain; (b) U.S.A.; (c) France; (d) Sweden; (e) Belgium; (f) U.S.S.R.; (g) Germany; (h) Netherlands; (i) Switzerland; (k) Denmark; (l) Norway; (m) Spain; (n) Poland; (o) Austria; (p) Italy; (q) India; (r) Hungary; (s) Finland; (t) Canada; (u) Chile; (v) Argentina; (w) Japan; (x) Portugal; (y) Irish Free State; (z) Republic of Ireland; (aa) South Africa; (bb) Iceland; (cc) China; (dd) Czechoslovakia; (ee) Australia; (ff) Yugoslavia; (gg) Greece; (hh) Israel; (ii) Guatemala; (kk) Egypt; (ll) Pakistan; (mm) West Indies; (nn) Bulgaria; (oo) Colombia; (pp) Mexico. The distribution by nationalities is shown at foot of table.

For prize winners for the years 1901–1976, *see* earlier editions of WHITAKER'S ALMANACK.

Year	(a) PHYSICS	(b) CHEMISTRY	(c) PHYSIOLOGY AND MEDICINE	(d) LITERATURE	(e) PEACE
1977	Prof. P. W. Anderson (b) Prof. Sir Nevill Francis Mott (a) Prof. J. H. Van Vleck (b)	Prof. I. Prigogine (e)	Rosalyn S. Yalow (b) Prof. R. Guillemin (b) Prof. A. V. Schally (b)	V. Aleixandre (m)	Amnesty International
1978	Prof. P. L. Kapitsa (f) A. A. Penzias (b) R. W. Wilson (b)	P. Mitchell (a)	Prof. W. Arber (i) D. Nathans (b) H. Smith (b)	I. B. Singer (b)	A. Sadat (kk) M. Begin (hh)
1979	Prof. S. L. Glashow (b) Prof. A. Salam (ll) Prof. S. Weinberg (b)	Prof. H. C. Brown (b) Prof. G. Wittig (g)	Prof. A. M. Cormack (b) G. N. Hounsfield (a)	O. Alepoudellis (gg)	Mother Teresa (ff)
1980	Prof. J. Cronin (b) Prof. V. Fitch (b)	Prof. P. Berg (b) Prof. W. Gilbert (b) Prof. F. Sanger (a)	G. Snell (b) J. Dausset (c) B. Benacerraf (b)	Prof. C. Milosz (n)	A. P. Esquivel (v)
1981	Prof. K. Siegbahn (d) Prof. N. Bloembergen (b) Prof. A. Schawlow (b)	Prof. K. Fukui (w) Prof. R. Hoffmann (n)	Prof. R. Sperry (b) Prof. D. Hubel (b) Prof. T. Wiesel (d)	E. Canetti (nn)	Office of the U.N. High Commission for Refugees
1982	Prof. K. G. Wilson (b)	Dr. A. Klug (a)	Prof. S. K. Bergstrom (d) Prof. B. I. Samuelson (d) Dr. J. R. Vane (a)	G. Garcia Marquez (oo)	A. Garcia Robles (pp) Mrs. A. Myrdal (d)
1983	Prof. S. Chandrasekhar (b) Prof. W. Fowler (b)	Prof. H. Taube (b)	Dr. B. McClintock (b)	W. Golding (a)	L. Walesa (n)

The awards have been distributed as follows: PHYSICS.—*U.S.A.*, 47; *Gt. Britain*, 20; *Germany*, 14; *France*, 9; *U.S.S.R.*, 7; *Netherlands*, 5; *Austria*, 3; *Denmark*, 3; *Japan*, 3; *Sweden*, 4; *China*, 2; *Italy*, 2; *India*, 1; *Ireland*, 1; *Pakistan*, 1.

CHEMISTRY.—*U.S.A.*, 26; *Germany*, 24; *Gt. Britain*, 22; *France*, 6; *Sweden*, 4; *Switzerland*, 4; *Netherlands*, 2; *Australia*, 1; *Austria*, 1; *Czechoslovakia*, 1; *Finland*, 1; *Hungary*, 1; *Italy*, 1; *Norway*, 1; *U.S.S.R.*, 1; *Argentina*, 1; *Canada*, 1; *Belgium*, 1; *Japan*, 1; *Poland*, 1.

PHYSIOLOGY AND MEDICINE.—*U.S.A.*, 56; *Gt. Britain*, 19; *Germany*, 10; *France*, 7; *Austria*, 5; *Belgium*, 4; *Denmark*, 4; *Sweden*, 6; *Switzerland*, 5; *Netherlands*, 3; *Australia*, 2; *Canada*, 2; *Hungary*, 2; *Italy*, 2; *U.S.S.R.*, 2; *Argentina*, 1; *Portugal*, 1; *South Africa*, 1; *Spain*, 1.

LITERATURE.—*France*, 11; *U.S.A.*, 8; *Germany*, 7; *Gt. Britain*, 7; *Sweden*, 6; *Italy*, 5; *U.S.S.R.*, 4; *Denmark*, 3; *Norway*, 3; *Spain*, 4; *Chile*, 2; *Greece*, 2; *Ireland*, 2; *Poland*, 3; *Switzerland*, 2; *Australia*, 1; *Belgium*, 1; *Finland*, 1; *Guatemala*, 1; *Iceland*, 1; *India*, 1; *Israel*, 1; *Japan*, 1; *Yugoslavia*, 1; *Bulgaria*, 1; *Colombia*, 1.

PEACE.—*U.S.A.*, 16; *Institutions*, 12; *France*, 9; *Gt. Britain*, 8; *Germany*, 4; *Sweden*, 5; *Belgium*, 3; *Switzerland*, 3; *Austria*, 2; *Norway*, 2; *Argentina*, 2; *Canada*, 1; *Denmark*, 1; *Ireland*, 1; *Italy*, 1; *Japan*, 1; *Netherlands*, 1; *South Africa*, 1; *U.S.S.R.*, 1; *Egypt*, 1; *Israel*, 1; *Yugoslavia*, 1; *Mexico*, 1; *Poland*, 1.

In 1969 a Nobel Prize for Economic Sciences was instituted, to be awarded by the Royal Swedish Academy of Sciences. Prize-winners have been: 1969, J. Tintergen (h) and R. Frisch (l); 1970, P. A. Samuelson (b); 1971, S. Kuznets (b); 1972, Sir John Hicks (a) and K. J. Arrow (b); 1973, W. Leontief (b); 1974, F. von Hayek (a) and G. Myrdal (d); 1975, Prof. L. V. Kantorovich (f) and Prof. T. C. Koopmans (b); 1976, Prof. M. Friedman (b); 1977, Prof. J. E. Meade (a) and Prof. B. Ohlin (d); 1978, Prof. H. A. Simon (b); 1979, Prof. T. W. Shultz (b) and Prof. Sir Arthur Lewis (mm); 1980, Prof. L. Klein (b); 1981, Prof. J. Tobin (b); 1982, Prof. G. Stigler (b); 1983, Prof. G. Debreu (b).

DIARY OF EVENTS IN 1985

This diary is based on information (available at the time of going to press) supplied by the British Tourist Authority. The horse-racing fixtures are the copyright of The Jockey Club.

SHOWS, PAGEANTS AND EXHIBITIONS

Jan. 3–13	London International Boat Show	Earls Court, London
Feb. 8–10	Cruft's Dog Show	Earls Court, London
Mar. 6–31	*Daily Mail* Ideal Home Exhibition	Earls Court, London
April 10–13	The London Book Fair	Barbican Centre, London
May 9–12	Royal Windsor Horse Show	Home Park, Windsor
*May 21–24	Chelsea Flower Show	Royal Hospital, Chelsea, London
June 15	Trooping the Colour	Horse Guards Parade, London
July 1–4	Royal International Agricultural Show	Stoneleigh, Warwicks.
July 10–27	Royal Tournament	Earls Court, London
Aug. 8	Battle of Flowers	Jersey
Aug. 9–31	Edinburgh Military Tattoo	Edinburgh Castle
Sept. 7	Royal Highland Gathering	Braemar, Grampian
Sept. 13–21	Southampton International Boat Show	Mayflower Park, Southampton
Oct. 21–26	International Business Show	National Exhibition Centre, Birmingham
Nov. 9	Lord Mayor's Procession and Show	City of London
*Dec. 2–5	Royal Smithfield Show and Agricultural Machinery Exhibition	Earls Court, London

MUSIC AND DRAMA FESTIVALS

May 24–June 9	Bath Festival	Bath, Avon
May–Aug.	Glyndebourne Festival Opera Season	Glyndebourne, nr. Lewes
May–Sept.	Chichester Festival Theatre Season	Chichester, W. Sussex
June 7–23	Aldeburgh Festival	Aldeburgh, Suffolk
July 25–28	Southern Cathedrals' Festival	Winchester, Hants.
July 31–Aug. 14	Harrogate International Festival	Harrogate
Aug. 3–10	Royal National Eisteddfod of Wales	Lampeter, Dyfed
Aug. 11–31	Edinburgh International Festival	Edinburgh
Aug. 18–23	Three Choirs Festival	Worcester

HORSE RACING

March 14	Cheltenham Gold Cup	Cheltenham
March 23	Lincoln Handicap	Doncaster
March 30	Grand National	Liverpool
May 2	One Thousand Guineas	Newmarket
May 4	Two Thousand Guineas	Newmarket
June 5	The Derby	Epsom
June 6	Coronation Cup	Epsom
June 8	The Oaks	Epsom
June 18–21	Royal Ascot	Ascot
July 27	King George VI and Queen Elizabeth Diamond Stakes	Ascot
Sept. 14	St. Leger	Doncaster
Oct. 5	Cambridgeshire	Newmarket
Oct. 19	Cesarewitch	Newmarket

OTHER SPORTS

Feb. 16	Rugby Union: Wales v. England	Cardiff Arms Park
March 16	Rugby Union: England v. Scotland	Twickenham, London
April 18–21	Badminton Horse Trials	Badminton, Avon
May 18	Football: F.A. Cup Final	Wembley Stadium, London
June 3–8	Golf: British Amateur Championship	Royal Dornoch, Highland
June 24–July 7	Lawn Tennis Championships	Wimbledon, London
July 4–7	Henley Royal Regatta	Henley-on-Thames
July 18–21	Golf: Open Championship	Royal St. George's, Sandwich
Oct. 7–12	Horse of the Year Show	Wembley Arena, London

* Provisional dates only.